Statistics Sources

ISSN 0585-198X

Statistics Sources

Nineteenth Edition

1996

A Subject Guide to Data on Industrial, Business, Social, Educational, Financial, and Other Topics for the United States and Internationally

Volume 1
A-I

Jacqueline Wasserman O'Brien
and **Steven R. Wasserman**
Editors

Gale Research Inc.
An International Thomson Publishing Company

I(T)P

NEW YORK • LONDON • BONN • BOSTON • DETROIT • MADRID
MELBOURNE • MEXICO CITY • PARIS • SINGAPORE • TOKYO
TORONTO • WASHINGTON • ALBANY NY • BELMONT CA • CINCINNATI OH

Jacqueline Wasserman O'Brien and Steven R. Wasserman, *Editors*
Richard Rose, *Word Processing Consultant*

Gale Research Inc. Staff

Donna Wood, *Senior Editor and Project Coordinator*

Mary Beth Trimper, *Production Manager*
Shanna Heilveil, *Production Assistant*

Cynthia D. Baldwin,, *Product Design Manager*
Barbara J. Yarrow, *Graphic Services Supervisor*
Sherrell Hobbs, *Macintosh Artist*

Library of Congress Catalog Card Number: 84-82356
ISBN 0-8103-9091-4 (set)
ISBN 0-8103-9092-2 (Volume 1)
ISBN 0-8103-9093-0 (Volume 2)
ISSN 0585-198X

Printed in the United States of America

I(T)P™ Gale Research Inc., an International Thomson Publishing Company.
ITP logo is a trademark under license.

CONTENTS

Volume 1

Selected Bibliography of Key Statistical Sources

Federal Statistical Telephone Contacts

Federal Statistical Data Bases

Volume 2

PREFACE

As *Statistics Sources* approaches its twentieth edition (the present volume is the nineteenth edition), the constant and painstaking effort to continue to bolster and add value to its content in the interest of its users continues unabated. The work continues to be an easy-to-use alphabetically arranged dictionary and guide to current sources of factual quantitative information on well over 20,000 specific subjects, incorporating almost 100,000 citations and more than 2,000 sources readily leading users to the widest possible range of print and non-print, published and unpublished, and electronic and other forms of U.S. and international statistical sources for economic, business, financial, industrial, cultural, social, educational, and other topics.

Revisions and Additions for the Nineteenth Edition

In an effort to consolidate and merge redundant material, countless entries have been fully revised. The nineteenth edition also marks the addition of innumerably more sources than ever before in order to further strengthen access to the widest possible range of pertinent approaches to locating data. While the number of pages in this edition is a small reduction from the previous edition, a far more extensive range of new sources is being included for the first time. For the user this means that many more citations are provided without sacrificing access to narrow specific topics. The result is to make the work easier to use and at the same time more comprehensive. The following examples illustrate this point: ITALY - Cocoa (Beans) Production - See ITALY - Crops; FRANCE - Tungsten Production and Consumption - See FRANCE - Mining and Mineral Products; INDIA - Egg Production - See INDIA - Dairy Products. The merging of naturally related topics permits the user to find sources under narrow and specific subjects. The exhaustive use of cross references refers the user to the broader term where an expanded range of sources is identified.

Preparation of This Edition

This nineteenth edition of *Statistics Sources* fully and thoroughly updates, revises, and extends the scope and content of the eighteenth edition. Complete revisions incorporate a wider range of current data sources from the "Selected Bibliography of Key Statistical Sources," "Federal Statistical Telephone Contacts," and "Federal Statistical Data Bases" sections, through the main body of the work, and throughout the two appendixes.

During the preparation of this edition, as in each earlier edition, the editors thoroughly analyzed and indexed hundreds of American information sources, several years of *Statistical Abstract of the United States*, numerous basic statistical publications from many organizations, and special statistical issues of professional, technical, and trade journals. Additional sources of international statistics are cited in this edition, increasing the range of access points within a user's reference shelves.

Arrangement and Content

The familiar and convenient arrangement of the basic work continues as a straight alphabetic list of subjects. Sources of statistical information are arranged alphabetically by issuing organization within each subject category. In addition to both print and machine-readable sources, a considerable number of organizations, government agencies, trade and professional groups, and international bodies are cited because they are important sources of statistical data, even if they do not ordinarily publish all of the statistics they compile. In such instances, specific inquiries may be addressed to the organization mentioned. As in earlier editions, the street address of the publisher of any work cited has been provided wherever possible, followed by the telephone number of the source.

Interfiled within the subject categories are geographic headings for states and individual countries. Listings for state data center agencies that make census information and data available to the public are included with the citations of sources for each state. These listings appear under the heading "State Data Center Agencies," which immediately follows the citation for "Primary Statistics Source" under each state subheading.

Individual citations for each country are subarranged by an alphabetic list of specific subjects, enabling the user to pinpoint sources of statistics on subjects such as agriculture, education, energy, imports, population, and consumer prices. Two types of key statistical sources are cited in listings for countries (as applicable and available) and precede the alphabetical listing of specific subjects for the country. The first citation is to the National Statistical Office, if the country has such an office. This is followed by a reference to the major printed sources for the country, termed the Primary Statistics Source or Sources. These sources should be consulted by users seeking more in-depth data, particularly for technical and commercial activities in countries other than the U. S. and Canada.

Introductory Materials Pinpoint Key Sources and Individuals

The "Selected Bibliography of Key Statistical Sources," "Federal Statistical Telephone Contacts," and the "Federal Statistical Data Bases" sections precede the main section of *Statistics Sources*. The "Selected Bibliography" provides an annotated guide to a selected group of major, general statistical compendia and related works, and includes dictionaries of terms, almanacs, census publications, periodical sources, and guides to machine-readable and online data sources. Both governmental and non-governmental sources are cited. A source's availability in machine-readable form or as an online database is noted wherever possible. The "Telephone Contacts" section provides the names and telephone numbers of individuals and agencies within the U. S. federal government with expertise in identifying the most current sources of statistical data. "Federal Statistical Data Bases" identifies the most significant U. S. federal government statistical files available in machine-readable form, including magnetic tape, diskette, and, in some instances, CD-

ROM. This section, arranged by broad subject category, identifies the issuing agency of each file and provides details on how to obtain the file.

Appendixes Identify Published and Nonpublished Sources

Two appendixes identify the sources of information used to compile this directory. The "Source Publications" appendix provides an alphabetic listing of the specific publication titles of every printed source mentioned in *Statistics Sources*, along with the issuing or publishing bodies, their addresses and phone numbers. The "Sources of Nonpublished Statistical Data" appendix identifies the agencies, institutions, and other organizations which are cited as sources of nonpublished statistical information in this edition.

The Status of Eastern European Countries

Efforts have continued to revise and reorganize the arrangement of statistical data on and about the countries which comprised the former Eastern European Bloc. But even while some of the new jurisdictional entities have been in existence for some months, this has not translated itself into more than a limited and spotty selection of new statistical tools and sources reflecting the recently formed nations. Thus, the majority of statistical resources still arrange the data along the lines of the former nation states such as the Soviet Union, Yugoslavia, and Czechoslovakia, since so much data is still presented in many essential statistical tools issued by international governmental and non-governmental bodies. But we also include the names of the recently constituted nations and provide, where they have come into being, details of statistical sources covering the new states that have just appeared. We also link the two possibilities together through the use of "see also" references so that the user continues to have recourse to all the current options.

Editors' Note

Statistics Sources may best be described as a finding guide to statistics. It does not purport to cite sources of in depth statistics on technical and commercial activities in specific foreign countries. For such purposes, the reader is referred to the Primary Statistics Source, or the National Statistical Office mentioned at the head of the geographic listings, as well as to the particular works cited in the selected bibliography which forms the first component of the work.

The painstaking task of accurately inputting the manuscript for this edition has been the contribution of Carla Rose and Peggy Barrett. Particular thanks is due to Carla Rose for the composing and printing of the entire manuscript.

Jacqueline Wasserman O'Brien
and Steven R. Wasserman
Editors

Selected Bibliography of Key Statistical Sources

This section describes a selected group of major, general statistical compendia and related works in the English language. Both governmental and non-governmental sources are included. For ease of reference, these sources are presented according to the following categories.

Many of the sources are available in machine-readable form, as online databases, or in CD-ROM form, and this has been noted wherever possible in the individual source citations.

ENCYCLOPEDIAS, DICTIONARIES OF TERMS, AND OTHER GENERAL SOURCES

Howard Berlin. *Handbook of Financial Market Indexes, Averages, and Indicators.* Burr Ridge, Illinois, Irwin Professional Publishing, ((708) 789-4000), 1990.

An overview of the various measures of market activity. Simple and uncomplicated description of the elements used in the construction of more than 200 financial market averages covering 24 countries. Particularly useful for foreign stock market and bond indexes.

Crispell, Diane, ed. *The Insider's Guide to Demographic Know-How: Everything Marketers Need to Know About How to Find, Analyze and Use Information About Their Customers*, 3rd ed. Ithaca, New York, American Demographics Press, ((607) 273-6343), 1993.

An introductory guide to the subject and a ready reference tool for locating demographic data. One part offers articles explaining the value, uses and methods of demographic analysis. The second part outlines tips on finding data with chapters covering various type of sources of data.

Melvyn N. Freed and Virgil P. Diodata. *Business Information Desk Reference: Where to Find Answers to Business Questions.* New York, Macmillan, ((800) 858-7674), 1992.

Directs users to appropriate business sources in a question-answer format. Section A offers "Guidelines for Finding and Evaluating Business Information," especially asking the right question. Section B, "Linking the Research Question to the Business Information Source," is a mini-guide listing types of questions and linking them to types of appropriate sources. Sections describe and characterize both print and online sources.

Alfred Garwood and Louise Hornor. *Dictionary of U.S. Government Statistical Terms.* Palo Alto, California, Information Publications, ((415) 965-4449), 1991.

Provides U.S. government statistical terms with the government agency name appearing in each entry along with abbreviations where appropriate. An introduction, list of abbreviations, and bibliography round out the volume.

Philip M. Hauser. *Social Statistics In Use.* New York, Russell Sage Foundation, ((212) 750-6000), 1975.

This work describes how statistics are compiled, where they are available, and how they can be used by government, labor, educators, and the general public.

Maurice G. Kendall and A.E. Doig. *Bibliography of Statistical Literature.* 3 vols. Edinburgh and London, Oliver and Boyd.

With a total of over 26,000 entries, this work covers the literature of statistics from the sixteenth century to 1958; vol. 1, 1950-1958; vol. 2, 1940-1949; and vol. 3, pre-1940. The material cited is that which the compilers believe will be most useful to historians and researchers. Arranged by author, this bibliography covers periodicals, international conferences, and national meetings. Twelve statistical journals are indexed almost completely and forty-three others analyzed for relevant articles. Coverage is worldwide, but the bulk of the citations are from American, British, and Russian publications.

Samuel Kotz and Norman L. Johnson, eds. *Encyclopedia of Statistical Sciences.* New York, John Wiley & Sons, ((800) 225-5945), 1982-1988.

A nine-volume guide to statistical methods, and techniques and their applications to nearly all aspects of human endeavor.

William H. Kruskal and Judith M. Tanur, eds. *International Encyclopedia of Statistics.* New York, Macmillan Publishing Company, ((800) 858-7674), 1978.

In two volumes, the development of modern statistical methods and the operations, interpretations, and applications of the various statistical techniques are described. Much of the content is an updated version of statistical material originally appearing in the *International Encyclopedia of the Social Sciences.*

Michael R. Lavin. *Business Information: How to Find It, How to Use It.* 2nd ed. Phoenix, Oryx Press, ((800) 279-ORYX), 1992.

A research guide to both published and unpublished sources of business information. Sources covered include: publications, databases, directories, financial data, registered trademarks, statistical and industry-wide information, and business law.

M. G. Mulhall. *The Dictionary of Statistics.* 4th ed. Detroit, Gale Research Inc., ((800) 877-GALE), 1974.

Originally published in 1899, this reference book is useful for locating historical statistical information not available in other standard sources. Comparative tables on a wide variety of subjects from the time of the Emperor Diocletian to 1899. Supplemented by *The New Dictionary of Statistics*, covering the period 1899-1909.

Robert Sicignano and Doris Prichard, compilers. *Special Issues Index.* Westport, Connecticut, Greenwood Publishing Group, ((203) 226-3571), 1982.

Includes more than 1,300 North American business, industrial and consumer journals, identifying which issue annually offers a special statistical number, buyer's guide or directory. Entries include journal title, address, frequency, subscription rate, individual issue price and presence of classified or product/service ads. This is supplemented by an index.

Jean Slemmons Stratford and Juri Stratford, eds. *Major U.S. Statistical Series: Definitions, Publications, Limitations.* Chicago, ALA Books, ((800) 545-2433), 1992.

The text provides the reader (both information specialist and patron) with a framework for understanding statistical data and locating the series which report such data on a regular basis. It describes the construction and publications of a number of basic statistical measures and provides an introduction to data producing agencies and their publication series.

Charles L. Taylor and David Jodice, eds. *World Handbook of Political and Social Indicators.* 3rd ed. New Haven, Yale University Press, ((203) 432-0940), 1983.

Offers comparative indicators useful in reviewing the countries of the world in terms of their political and social characteristics and is designed to serve as a research tool in cross-cultural study. Broad topics treated include government and politics, communications, wealth, health, education, social relations, distribution of income, religion, natural resources, and foreign affairs.

ALMANACS

Canadian Almanac and Directory. Toronto, Copp Clark Longman, Canadian Almanac & Directory Publishing Company ((416) 972-6645), 1847-. (Annual).

In addition to directory and almanac information, this volume covers current and historical Canadian statistics.

Information Please Almanac. Boston, Houghton Mifflin, ((800) 352-5455), 1947-. (Annual).

An almanac of miscellaneous information, with a general arrangement and a subject index. Offers statistical details covering many types of phenomena.

Sumner K. Levine, ed. *The Irwin Business and Investment Almanac.* Burr Ridge, Illinois, Irwin Professional Publishing, ((708) 789-4000), 1977-. (Annual).

Covers such topics as: Largest Corporations, Stock and Commodities Market, Price Data and World Population, and Gross National Product by Country. Prefixed by a day-to-day accounting of the Business Year in Review.

1990 - 1991 Almanac of Consumer Markets: A Guide to Today's More Complex and Harder-to-Find Customers. Ithaca, New York, American Demographics Press, ((607) 273-6343), 1990. (1990).

Offers recent demographic data and forecasts by age group, with comparable data for each group on population, households, marital status, fertility, education, wealth and health. Sources are provided for each table and explanatory notes are furnished.

Whitaker's Almanac. London, J. Whitaker and Sons, 1868-. (Annual). (Distributed in the U.S. by Gale Research Inc., ((800) 877-GALE).

Similar to American almanacs except for emphasis on Britain and the Commonwealth.

World Almanac and Book of Facts. Mahwah, New Jersey, Funk & Wagnalls, ((201) 529-6900). 1868-. (Annual).

The most comprehensive and frequently useful of the American almanacs of miscellaneous information. Contains statistics on social, industrial, political, financial, religious, educational and other subjects, political organizations, societies, historical lists of famous events, etc.; up-to-date and in general, reliable; sources for many of the statistics are given. Issues dating back to the first in 1868 are available on microform from the Bell and Howell Company.

U.S. STATISTICS
Non-Government U.S. Publications

American Statistics Index: A Comprehensive Guide and Index to the Statistical Publications of the United States Government. Bethesda, Maryland, Congressional Information Service, ((800) 638-8380), 1973-.

Covers more than 500 active federal statistics-producers including major statistical agencies, analytic and research agencies, and administrative and regulatory agencies. Indexed by subjects and names, by categories (such as geographic, economic and demographic breakdown), by titles and by agency report number. The annual supplement includes a guide to selected standard classifications used by the various federal agencies to arrange and present data. The 1974 edition is the base edition. Monthly issues are cumulated into annual supplements. A retrospective edition covering from the early 1960's to 1974 is also available. American Statistics Index is accessible online (from Dialog Information Services, Inc.) and documents indexed are available on microfiche. ASI is also available on CD-ROM on *Statistical Masterfile* from Congressional Information Service.

The American Tally: Statistics and Ranking for 3,165 U.S. Cities and Towns: Covering All U.S. Cities and Towns With Populations Over 10,000. Milpitas, California, Toucan Valley Publications ((415) 956-9492), 1993.

Presents comparative raw data (as collected for the 1990 federal census) or percentages for 27 variables for cities and towns with populations greater than 10,000. There are sections for ethnic and age distribution, educational attendance and achievement, language and nativity, income and employment, and housing.

America's Top Rated Cities. Boca Raton, Florida, Universal Reference Publications, ((800) 377-7551), 1995.

This handbook includes statistical information and other data with tables and charts on the U.S. cities which have been cited in various magazine surveys as being the best places for business and living opportunities. There is a special section with comparative statistics.

M. Balachandran. *A Guide to Statistical Sources in Money, Banking, and Finance.* Phoenix, Oryx Press, ((800) 279-ORYX), 1988.

A guide to detailed monetary data and state, local and foreign banking statistics, both current and historical. Divided into local, state, U.S., and foreign sources and textual and numeric databases. Sources cited deal with capital and credit markets, interest rates, consumer finance and credit cards, money supply, treasury operations, bank deposits, assets, liabilities, and foreign exchange markets.

M. Balachandran and Sarojini Balachandran. *State and Local Statistics Sources.* Detroit, Gale Research Inc., ((800) 877-GALE), 1993.

Covers citations to almost 40,000 sources of data in publications from state, local and national agencies, universities, research centers and commercial agencies.

Linda Holman Bentley and Jennifer J. Kiesl. *Investment Statistics Locator, Revised and Expanded.* Phoenix, Oryx Press, ((800) 279-ORYX), 1994.

A guide to data on investment and economic statistical sources. Contains 53 source listings, including several new investment publications not available at the time of the first edition. Building on Chapman's original guide this edition has more periodicals and electronic sources, in addition to selected government documents. A wider variety of subjects is covered, including mutual funds and variable annuity/life accounts, overseas investment data, and worldwide economic statistics.

Book of the States. Lexington, Kentucky, Council of State Governments, ((606) 231-1939), 1935-. (Biennial).

Statistical coverage for state activities is grouped under major headings such as intergovernmental relations, legislatures, finances, services, etc.

Donald J. Bogue. *The Population of the United States.* New York, Macmillan, ((800) 858-7674), 1985.

A statistical abstract of recent population trends in the United States and their interpretation. Bibliography at the end of each chapter cites additional statistical and interpretive sources.

Margaret Werner Cahalan, ed. *Historical Corrections Statistics in the United States, 1850-1984.* Rockville, Maryland, Westat, 1986. (Available from the National Criminal Justice Reference Service, Box 6000, Rockville, MD 20850 (800) 851-3420).

Provides statistical tables taken from a variety of published U.S. government reports as well as commentary on the tables and an historical overview. Data are given in such areas as jails, capital punishment, state and federal prisons, and parole and probation.

Stephen J. Carroll et al. *City Data: A Catalog of Data Sources for Small Cities.* Santa Monica, RAND, ((310) 393-0411), 1980.

An annotated listing of 272 sources dealing with the quality of life in small cities. Data sources are arranged into categories ranging from population and economy to recreational services. Includes an alphabetical list of data sets and a source index.

Census Plus. Washington, D.C., Slater Hall Information Products, ((202) 682-1350) on CD-ROM.

The series consists of several CD-ROMs, each containing 1990 census data plus key statistics from other data sources. *Ship County-City Plus* and *Ship County and City Compendium* are the first two *Census Plus* products. *Ship County-City Plus* is an update of the Census Bureau's County and City Databook. The *Ship County and City Compendium* disk provides more detailed data.

Bruce A. Chadwick and Tim B. Heaton, eds. *Children in American A Statistical Handbook.* Phoenix, Oryx Press, ((800) 279-ORYX), 1995.

Tables, charts, and graphs cover the family, health, child care, education, quality of life, extended and second families, working children, recreation, and much more. An extensive statistical report on children in America.

Bruce A. Chadwick and Tim Heaton, eds. *Statistical Handbook on the American Family.* Phoenix, Oryx Press, ((800) 279-ORYX), 1992.

Offers some 400 tables, charts and tabulations collected from federal and state agencies, polls, periodicals and other research sources. Topics treated include education, health, politics, employment, economic expenditures, social characteristics and other demographic and historical data.

CIS Statistical Periodicals. Bethesda, Maryland, Congressional Information Service, ((800) 638-8380), 1975-.

Complete text of more than 200 U.S. federal statistical periodicals including both depository and non-depository items. Covers the period 1975 - present.

Edwin J. Coleman and Ronald A. Morse. *Data: Where It Is and How To Get It.* Arnold, Maryland, Coleman/Morse Associates Ltd., 1993.

This book is a directory of business, environment, and energy data sources. It contains the names and areas of specialization of over 2,500 individuals in local, state, and federal governments as well as in private firms.

Commercial Atlas and Marketing Guide. Skokie, Illinois, Rand McNally, ((800) 333-0136), 1911-. (Annual).

Detailed listings and statistical material on more than 128,000 cities, towns, communities, and other locations in the United States, and indexes many additional thousands of foreign cities. In 1980 the 111th edition appeared (earlier editions were published more frequently than the current annual cycle). Most of the index and tabular material is available from the publisher on microfiche, computer tape, or online.

Commodity Yearbook. Chicago, Illinois, Commodity Research Bureau, Knight-Ridder Financial Publishing, ((800) 621-5271), 1939-. (Annual).

A reference volume covering the major raw and semifinished products, arranged alphabetically by commodity. For each material listed there is complete statistical data, for the latest year and for earlier years, of production, distribution, sales, etc. This Yearbook is supplemented by the *Commodity Yearbook Statistical Abstract Service* which provides current information four times yearly, and the weekly *Commodity Chart Service.* In addition, this is now available from the same source, *CRB INFOTECH Commodity Data.* This CD-ROM service provides 50 years of data on some 100 commodities as well as historical prices on over 300 cash, future and option markets.

Consumer Market Guide. New York, The Conference Board ((212) 339-0344), continuously updated.

A basic statistical profile of consumers and the consumer market, presented in tabular form. Statistics are organized into 12 chapters - population, marriages and births, households and families, education, labor force and occupation, employment and earnings, income, expenditures, housing, retailing and advertising, prices and production, and miscellaneous. The Conference Board's Consumer Research Center maintains and updated file of these statistics, and Guide users can secure such information by contacting Lynn Franco.

Arsen J. Darnay and Helen S. Fisher, eds. *American Cost of Living Survey: A Compilation of Price Data for Nearly 600 Goods and Services in 443 U.S. Cities from More Than 70 Sources.* Detroit, Gale Research, Inc., ((800) 877-4253), 1994.

Provides comparative prices in 443 cities for products and services. Subjects covered include housing, transportation, food, clothing and other consumer goods, utilities, insurance, entertainment, taxes, education, and more.

Arsen J. Darnay, ed. *Economic Indicators Handbook.* 2nd ed. Detroit, Gale Research Inc., ((800) 877-4253), 1994.

Offers a unique source of aggregate national statistics on approximately 175 U.S. economic indicators including those covering economics and general business; government and personal finance; prices; and personal income, expenditures, and savings. ECONOMIC INDICATORS HANDBOOK provides both historical and current perspectives on the U.S. economy by presenting original values for all statistics since their inception as well as recalculated and rebased figures reflecting current values. In addition, each statistical series includes methods of calculation, inclusions and exclusions, an historical overview, and changes in definition over time.

Arsen J. Darney, ed. *Statistical Record of Native North Americans.* 2nd ed. Detroit, Gale Research Inc., ((800) 877-4253), 1995.

This is the first reference to present current and historical statistical data on Native Americans in a highly accessible, graphic format. This work pulls together nearly 1,000 charts, graphs and tables and quantifies the experience of indigenous peoples of North America from the centuries before Columbus to the social, political and economic situations of the present day. It charts the experiences of approximately 200 Native American tribes, including extinct tribes and those native to what is now Canada.

Arsen J. Darnay, ed. *Statistical Record of Older Americans.* 1st ed. Detroit, Gale Research Inc., ((800) 877-4253), 1994.

Drawing together information once only found in scattered 1990 census data and government reports, journals, newspapers, associations and other sources this work presents clearly, highly informative charts, graphs and tables of data on typical issues concerning the elderly. Provides comprehensive statistical analyses of issues at the forefront of concern to older Americans, including: pensions and pension funds; crime and safety; health; income; homelessness; loneliness; life expectancy; political influence of older Americans; and more.

Demographic Information Service. New York, The Conference Board ((212) 339-0344), Four times each year.

A series of statistical reports showing distribution of households and income by major demographic characteristics based on special Census Bureau data developed for the Consumer Research Center. Characteristics include age, household, type, household size, children, earners, income, education, occupation, home ownership, and race.

Donald B. Dodd, ed. *Historical Statistics of the States of the United States: Two Centuries of the Census, 1790-1990.* Westport, Connecticut, Greenwood Publishing Group, ((203) 226-3571), 1993.

A state-by-state presentation of 18 population items, 1790-1990, 27 agriculture items, 1850-1990, six manufacturing items 1850-1990, and 12 manufacturing items, 1899-1989. There are also population figures, 1790-1990, for the 200 cities that had 100,000 inhabitants or more in 1990. Many footnotes to the tables define the data items, and the data sources are cited in endnotes. A glossary explains historical variations in the definitions, noting the effects of such changes on the comparability of the figures.

Henry J. Dubester, ed. *Catalog of United States Census Publications, 1790-1945.* U.S. Library of Congress. New York, Greenwood Publishing Group, ((203) 226-3571), 1969.

This book lists all materials issued by the Bureau of the Census and its predecessor organizations starting with the first decennial census report of 1790 and ending with publications released to the close of 1945. The CATALOG is divided into two general sections: the first covers publications issued in concert with the successive decennial censuses, and the second includes Bureau of the Census publications released as a result of its other surveys. Its primary importance now is historical statistics. From 1946 to the present, refer to the Bureau of the Census *Catalog and Guide* or see Greenwood Press's *Catalog of United States Census Publications: 1946-72.*

Joseph W. Duncan and Andrew C. Gross, eds. *Statistics for the 21st Century.* New York, Dun & Bradstreet Corporation, ((800) 526-0651), 1993.

The authors describe and analyze current practices and problems in governmental programs in collecting and disseminating statistics and recommend changes in order to improve and update the process. The work includes a valuable bibliographical essay feature which describes and assesses the major studies and analyses which have been prepared in recent years concerning the statistical efforts, treating economics, environment, health, international trade and social and demographic data.

Editor and Publisher Market Guide. New York, Editor and Publisher Company, Inc., ((212) 675-4380), 1901-. (Annual).

Organized by states and territories of the United States and Canada, with separate city entries listed thereunder. Each city entry includes such data as location, market area, economic features, transportation, population, housing, banks, auto registration, numbers of electric and gas meters and telephones of principal industries with number of wage earners and average weekly pay, colleges and universities, climate, water, agriculture, mining, retailing, with location of shopping centers, names of chief stores, and other data, retail sales figures, names of newspapers with circulations. Also available on CD-ROM.

William R. Evinger, ed. *Federal Statistical Source: Where to Find Agency Experts and Personnel.* Phoenix, Oryx Press, ((800) 279-ORYX), 1991.

Provides details of agencies, key contact names with titles and areas of expertise, phone numbers and fax numbers. In all some 4,000 statistical personnel within the federal government are identified.

Facts and Figures on Government Finance. Washington, D.C., Citizens for a Sound Economy, ((202) 783-3870), 1974-. (Annual).

Citizens for a Sound Economy is a nonprofit research organization with the purpose of investigating and publishing facts on the fiscal and management aspects of government at all levels. This handbook of statistics on government income and expenditures is its best known publication. Tables are grouped according to the level of government: federal, state and local.

Catherine Friedman, ed. *Commodity Prices.* 2nd ed. Detroit, Gale Research Inc., ((800) 877-4253), 1991.

Identifies in which source over 10,400 commodities' prices can be located. Arrangement is alphabetical by commodity and 198 source publications are indexed.

Norman Frumkin. *Guide to Economic Indicators.* 2nd ed. Armonk, New York, M. E. Sharpe, ((800) 541-6563), 1994.

Offers information about the main characteristics and sources of 50 key economic indicators, primarily developed by governmental agencies.

Gale State Rankings Reporter, 1st ed. Detroit, Gale Research, Inc., ((800) 877-GALE), 1994.

More than 3,000 ranked lists of states under 35 subject headings such as housing, education, income levels, the environment, arts and leisure, and more. Rankings are derived from diverse sources, like newspapers and popular magazines, books, journals and research institution publications, as well as federal and state government publications. For city and metro rankings on more than 1,500 U.S. cities and metropolitan statistical areas (MSA's), consult *Gale City and Metro Rankings Reporter*, 1st edition, 1994.

Susan B. Gall and Timothy L. Gall, eds. *Statistical Record of Asian Americans.* 1st ed. Detroit, Gale Research Inc., ((800) 877-4253), 1993.

This unique graphic reference is the only source of its kind to provide up-to-date U.S. and Canadian government census data as well as information culled from organization reports and journals and other widely scattered published and unpublished sources. More than 850 charts, graphs and tables give insight into the current and historical status of 19 Asian nationality groups in the U.S. and Canada.

John V. Ganly, ed. *Data Sources for Business and Market Analysis.* 4th ed. Metuchen, New Jersey, Scarecrow Press, ((908) 548-8600), 1994.

A guide to public and private sources of information available both in print and as computerized databases. Emphasis on data, both domestic and international, relating to economic conditions, business trends, and consumer and industrial markets.

Guide to U.S. Government Statistics. Manassas, Virginia, Documents Index, ((800) 899-4988), 1964-. (Annual).

All publications containing statistical data are fully listed under department and issuing bureau, with a description of the publication, type of statistics, and frequency of publication. Independent agencies, the judiciary, executive and legislative branches are also included. An effectively organized and logically arranged approach to data available from the U.S. Government, particularly valuable for use in library acquisitions.

Mary Hashman and C. Edward Wall. *A Matter of Fact.* Ann Arbor, Michigan, Pierian Press, ((800) 678-2435), 1985-.

Contains abstracts which include statistics on current social, economic, environmental, and political issues. This publication comes out twice each year and covers policy issues such as health care, environment, technological growth and other issues with political implications. It is available online through OCLC EPIC and OCLC First Search Catalog. It is also available on CD-ROM from Silver Platter Information, Inc.

Hispanic Databook of U.S. Cities and Counties. Milpitas, California, Toucan Valley Publications ((415) 956-9492), 1994.

Provides comprehensive data on the Hispanic population of the United States. The book consists of selected data derived from the 1990 Census of Population and Housing Summary Tape Files 3B and 3C.

Arline Alchian Hoel, et al. *Economics Sourcebook of Government Statistics.* New York, The Free Press, ((800) 223-2336), 1983.

Provides descriptions of about 50 key U.S. statistical measures such as the prime rate, housing starts, and the consumer price index. Limitations and biases of each indicator are explained, and publications where the indicators regularly appear are noted.

Edith Hornor, ed. *Almanac of the 50 States: Basic Data Profiles With Comparative Tables.* Palo Alto, California, Information Publications, ((415) 965-4449), Annual.

Main body of this volume is devoted to statistical profiles of each state with data organized topically under such headings as geography and environment, demographics, vital statistics and health, and government finance. Also contains more than fifty comparative tables covering such subjects as unemployment rate, lawyers per 1,000 persons, per capita energy consumption, and birth rates.

Louise Hornor, ed. *Black Americans: A Statistical Sourcebook.* Information Publications, Palo Alto, California ((415) 965-4449). (Annual).

This volume is a compilation of statistical information about the black American population of the United States. Tables included have been taken from previously published standard statistical sources produced by the government. Topics covered include: demographics and characteristics of the population; vital statistics and health; education; government; elections and public opinion; crime; law enforcement and corrections; labor force, employment and unemployment; earnings, income, poverty and wealth; and a section of special topics. A companion volume, *Hispanic Americans: A Statistical Sourcebook* is also available.

Hospital Statistics: Data From the AHA Annual Survey. Chicago, American Hospital Association, ((800) 242-2626), 1971-. (Annual).

Aggregate trend data at the state and national level are presented for a 15-year period. Tables present aggregate utilization, personnel, and financial data by census divisions, individual states, territories, SMSAs, and the 100 largest central cities. Data for individual hospitals can be found in a companion volume, the *AHA Guide to the Health Care Field,* which is also available on diskette.

Index to Health Information. Bethesda, Maryland, Congressional Information Service, ((800) 638-8380). (Quarterly with annual cumulations).

A guide to statistical and congressional publications on public health. Sources indexed include trade and professional associations, business organizations, commercial publishers, the U.S. Congress, federal agencies, international governmental organizations, private research organizations, state government agencies, and universities. Topic coverage is wide - ranging -from health care service to vital statistics. In microfiche with annual clothbound cumulations.

George Kurian, ed. *Datapedia of the United States, 1790-2000 American Year by Year.* Lanham, Maryland. Bernan Press, ((800) 274-4447), 1994.

An updated version of the classic two-volume *Historical Statistics of the United States, Colonial Times to 1970, Datapedia of the U.S.* provides revisions through 1991 and presents extended forecasts through the year 2000 and beyond.. Through the use of data tables and text DATAPEDIA examines the nation's growth-revealing historical patterns and principal changes that have occurred in such key areas as: agriculture, crime, education, health, business, employment, economics, housing, communications, international trade, the environment, and population.

Mark. T. Mattson, ed. *Atlas of the 1990 Census.* New York, Macmillan Publishing Company, ((800) 858-7674), 1992.

The Atlas carves information from the 1990 census into easily accessible components. Provides color-coded maps on population, households, housing, race, economy, and education. Each chapter starts with a page of text, followed by maps, charts, and figures. The Atlas ends with a "Metro Fact Finder," which provides quick information on close to 1,000 localities, arranged by population.

Gordon Melton, ed. *Statistical Record of Religion in America.* 2nd ed. Detroit, Gale Research, Inc., ((800) 877-GALE), 1995.

Covers all religions and religious groups currently active in the U.S. Provides comprehensive information on such topics as: number of churches or other places of worship, numbers/sizes of affiliated institutions, church membership, church attendance, charitable activities, attitudes and opinions on religious issues, and more.

Municipal Yearbook. Washington, D.C., ICMA-The Professional Local Government Management Association, ((202) 289-ICMA), 1934-. (Annual).

Information on population and economic data is supplied on American cities. A number of statistical charts portray municipal activities, finances, and other areas. Government data in municipalities 25,000 and under is also available from ICMA.

Judith M. Nixon. *The Hotel and Restaurant Industries: An Information Sourcebook.* Phoenix, Oryx Press, ((800) 279-ORYX), 1989.

Describes more than 1,000 recent information sources on the hospitality industry. Of particular interest to statistics users is the section devoted to industry handbooks, directories, indexes, and statistics.

Frederick M. O'Hara, Jr. and Robert Scignand, eds. *Handbook of United States Economic and Financial Indicators.* Westport, Connecticut, Greenwood Publishing Group, ((203) 226-3571), 1985.

An alphabetical index of profiles of hundreds of key economic indicators. Each profile describes the indicator, gives its derivation, intended used, source, frequency, and contact for further information.

James E. Person, Jr., ed. *Statistical Forecasts of the United States.* 2nd ed. Detroit, Gale Research Inc., ((800) 877-4253), 1995.

Population, employment, labor, crime, education, health care -- all the key areas of American life are covered. Goes beyond standard demographic data and it is presented in hundreds of charts, graphs, tables and other statistical illustrations portraying both long and short-term forecasts of future developments in the U.S.

Phyllis Pierce, ed. *The Dow Jones Averages 1885-1990.* Burr Ridge, Illinois, Irwin Professional Publishing, ((708) 789-4000), 1991.

105 years of the monthly averages for industrials, transportations, and utilities are presented.

Charles J. Popovich and M. Rita Costello, eds. *Directory of Business and Financial Information Services.* 9th ed. Washington, D.C., Special Libraries Association, ((202) 234-4700), 1994.

A selective list of newsletters, bulletins, reports, and other published services covering business, economics, and finance. Both U.S. and international services are described.

Marlita A. Reddy, ed. *Statistical Record of Hispanic Americans.* 2nd ed. Detroit, Gale Research Inc., ((800) 877-4253), 1995.

This reference quantifies the current state of Hispanic American culture through a series of highly accessible charts, graphs and tables based on a wide variety of reliable published information. Offers wide-ranging facts that bear on political, economic and social aspects of Americans with ancestry or origins in Mexico, Puerto Rico, Cuba, Spanish-speaking Central and South America and Spain.

Frank L. Schick and Renee Schick, eds. *Statistical Handbook on U.S. Hispanics.* Phoenix, Oryx Press, ((800) 279-ORYX), 1991.

Provides access to over 300 statistical charts, graphs, and tables. Contains recent data on U.S. Hispanics, including demographics, immigration and naturalization, social characterization, education, health, politics, labor force, and economic conditions.

Renee Schick, ed. *Statistical Handbook on Aging Americans.* 2nd ed. Phoenix, Oryx Press, ((800) 279-ORYX), 1994.

Contains recent statistical data about older Americans, including information about the economic, social, health, employment, and financial status of the elderly. Contains more than 300 statistical tables and illustrative charts, accompanied by explanatory text. Also includes a bibliographic guide to statistical sources.

Linda Schmittroth, ed. *Statistical Record of Children.* 1st ed. Detroit, Gale Research, Inc., ((800) 877-GALE), 1994.

Provides statistics to educators, scholars, libraries, and governments about a diverse range of topics focusing on children. Subjects include children's health, education, welfare, minority affairs, poverty, child abuse, and much more. Statistics cover pre-teen children living in the U.S., with selected international coverage on major topics.

Suzanne Schulze. *Population Information in Twentieth Century Census Volumes: 1950-1980.* Phoenix, Oryx Press, ((800) 279-ORYX), 1988.

For each decennial census lists volumes containing population data and an abstract on the history, publication, scope, and format of data for that census. Companion volumes are also available: *Population Information in the Twentieth Century Census Volumes: 1900-1940*; and *Population Information in Nineteenth Century Census Volumes.*

Jean L. Sears and Marilyn K. Moody. *Using Government Information Sources: Print and Electronic.* 2nd ed. Phoenix, Oryx Press, ((800) 279-ORYX), 1994.

Explains the uses and accessibility of government information sources within the context of actual research. Coverage has been expanded to include the wealth of information now available through electronic sources. Each section provides a checklist for quick identification of sources, suggests a series of steps for using the listed sources, and supplies a narrative analysis of each source. Also included are descriptions of related references to consult for additional information.

Secondary Information Service Statistics. Philadelphia, NFAIS (National Federation of Abstracting and Indexing Services), ((215) 893-1561), 1989.

Changes in revenue patterns, connect hours and hits, pricing hours and hits, pricing methods, print erosion, number of records generated annually, throughout time and other data related to access to information systems and services.

Robert Skapura, ed. *Charts, Graphs and Stats Index 1988-1991: An Index to the Most Current Statistics Behind Today's Most Important Stories.* Fort Atkinson, Wisconsin, Highsmith Press ((414) 563-9571), 1992.

This volume provides indexing to hundreds of statistics from organizations, publications, and independent research cited in magazine articles. Covers nine general interest periodicals. Annual updates.

Courtenay M. Slater and George E. Hall, eds. *1994 County and City Extra*. Lanham, Maryland. Bernan Press, ((800) 274-4447). (Annual).

This comprehensive source augments the information found in the U.S. Census Bureau's *County and City Data Book*. Unlike the *County and City Data Book*, the *County and City Extra* is updated annually. Includes comprehensive statistics on every county, state, city, and metropolitan area within the U.S. gathered from government and private agencies. This is also available on CD-ROM under the title *County and City Plus*. A companion volume, *Places, Towns and Townships*, is also available.

Jessie Carney Smith and Robert L. Johns, eds. *Statistical Record of Black America*. 3rd ed. Detroit, Gale Research Inc., ((800) 877-GALE), 1995.

Offers nearly 1,000 statistical graphs and tables arranged in 19 broad subject chapters covering such topics as population, vital statistics, family, labor, employment, educators, etc. Includes a comprehensive index and draws its data from published and non-published, private, commercial and governmental sources.

Sourcebook of ZIP Code Demographics. Arlington, Virginia, CACI, 1993 (Available from Gale Research Inc. (800) 877-GALE)).

For every zip code in the USA, over 75 demographic and socioeconomic characteristics are given, from median household income to number of households. Business as well as household statistics are given. Additional features include forecasts for the next two five year periods, new purchasing potential indexes, and national and state rankings for key variables. A companion volume provides the same type of data at the county level. The same consumer and business data is also available in a separate volume for each county in the *Sourcebook of County Demographics*. Both titles are also available on CD-ROM.

Standard and Poor's Corporation, Trade and Securities: Statistics. New York, Standard and Poor's Corporation, ((212) 208-8000).

This service brings together a great volume of statistical data. Most of the leading indexes are reproduced in addition to many original compilations of indexes of security prices and yields. While the heaviest emphasis is on financial data, there is a large amount of statistical material on general business conditions, cost of living, and prices. Published in three parts: the annual *Basic Statistics* section covering the preceding twelve months; a monthly update, *Current Statistics*; and a biennial, *Security Price Index Record*.

Marilyn McAnally Stark. *Mining and Mineral Industries, An Information Sourcebook*. Phoenix, Oryx Press, ((800) 279-ORYX), 1988.

A comprehensive sourcebook covering such information sources as recent reference volumes, periodicals, journals, and specialized non-print materials.

Stat Fact. Quarterly or Annual Subscription, New Canaan, Connecticut, Newsbank ((800) 762-8182). On CD ROM.

A collection of more than a half million facts and statistics on each of the 50 states. Data covers such areas as labor, education, government and elections, and business. Can be used to search individual state data or comparative data.

Statistical Handbook of Working America. 1st ed. Detroit, Gale Research, Inc., ((800) 877-GALE), 1995.

Contains a unique compilation of statistics, rankings, and forecasts on a variety of occupations, careers and the working environment. Entries offer statistical pictures of about 600 occupations, and include: demographic profile, industry statistics, educational enrollment within the field, employment patterns, accidents and injuries on the job, receipt of pensions and other benefits, legal and ethical issues, skills training and education, industrial relations, production and technology, and more.

Statistical Record of Health and Medicine. 1st ed. Detroit, Gale Research, Inc., ((800) 877-GALE), 1994.

More than 900 statistical tables, graphs and charts combine hard-to-locate research in a single volume. Twelve convenient chapters provide comprehensive insight into virtually every aspect of health and medicine including lifestyles and health, politics, opinion and law, medical professions, and more.

Statistical Record of the Environment. 2nd ed. Detroit, Gale Research, Inc., ((800) 877-GALE), 1994.

Provides approximately 851 graphs, charts and tables reporting information and analysis on today's hottest environmental topics. Information is presented in 10 subject chapters covering pollutants, costs, solutions, industry and government data, laws and regulations, politics, and opinions.

Statistical Reference Index. Bethesda, Maryland, Congressional Information Service, ((800) 638-8380), 1980-.

This publication is a selective guide to American statistic sources from sources other than the United States government. Covers information on business, industry, finance, economic and social conditions, government and politics, the environment, population, and other subjects. Although the sources are American, coverage includes data on foreign countries. Indexed by subjects, names and categories. Published in monthly index and monthly abstract issues with an annual accumulation. Most cited publications are available in microfiche from the publisher. SRI is also available on CD-ROM on *Statistical Masterfile* from Congressional Information Service.

Statmaster. Phoenix, Oryx Press, ((800) 279-ORYX), 1992. On diskette.

A collection of over 1.2 million statistics on 14,000 locations. This software product contains U.S. census data from the *1990 Census of Population and Housing, County and City Data Book*, and *State and Metropolitan Area Data Book*.

Paul Stewart. *Nations Within a Nation*. Westport, Connecticut, Greenwood Publishing Group, ((203) 226-3571), 1987.

This historical abstract on native Americans draws on a variety of mostly federal government sources published during the past 100 years. Statistics are organized in chapters covering a wide range of topics such as population, health, employment, and economic development.

Juri Stratford and Jean Slemmons Stratford. *Guide to Statistical Materials Published by Governments and Associations in the United States.* Alexandria, Virginia, Chadwyck-Healey, ((800) 752-0515), 1987.

A guide to more than 700 statistical publications issued by U.S. federal and state governments as well as by major associations. Includes citations to U.S. statistics only, and emphasis is given to recurrent publications that can be relied on to provide updated data on at least a biennial basis.

Survey of Buying Power Issue. New York, Bill Communications, Incorporated, ((212) 592-6200), 1918-. (Annual).

Published each year in two parts, the first in the July issue of *Sales and Marketing Management*, the second in the October issue. This publication contains much market data and information: consumer trends, effective buying income, and farm income by sections, states, counties, and cities.

Cynthia Taeuber, ed. *Statistical Handbook on Women in America.* Phoenix, Oryx Press, ((800) 279-ORYX), 1991.

This compendium features over 400 tables and charts for specific and detailed reference. The contents present statistics covering population, births, marriage and divorce, voting and political involvement, labor force issues, economic issues, alcoholism and drug abuse, and many more topics.

Upclose 1990 Census Sourcebook. El Granada, California, Upclose Publishing, ((800) 352-5673), 1990.

A digest of the very latest census data. More than two million statistics, organized by region into five volumes: Northeast, South, Midwest, West, and a National edition. Includes demographics, housing and employment data. Also available on diskette.

Vital Statistics in Corrections. Laurel, Maryland, American Correctional Association, ((800) 825-2665), 1994.

This statistical compendium provides current information on correctional departments in the U.S. Covers information on jails and detention centers, inmate populations, state corrections budgets and operating expenditures, educational requirements, salaries, and unions.

J. Thomas Vogel and Barbara Lowry. *The Textile Industry: An Information Sourcebook.* Phoenix, Oryx Press, ((800) 279-ORYX), 1989.

1,300 entries cover a wide range of subjects such as associations, patents and trademarks, and statistics. Priority is given to U.S. and English-language materials although selective international coverage is provided also.

Who Knows What: A Guide to Experts. Washington, D.C., Washington Researchers, ((202) 333-3499), Annual.

United States government experts for a wide variety of topics are listed by subject area and department. More than 14,500 experts and 12,000 topics are covered. Useful as a supplement to printed sources of statistics.

James Woy, ed. *Encyclopedia of Business Information Sources*, 10th ed. Detroit, Gale Research Inc., ((800) 877-GALE), 1994.

A topical guide to information sources on 1,000 subjects ranging from air freight to the tuna fish industry. Each subject is divided into subsections on abstract services and indexes, directories, online data bases, periodicals and newsletters, research centers and institutes, statistics sources, trade associations, and other categories. A supplement is issued between editions. The same type of business information is also provided in an internationally oriented companion guide, *Encyclopedia of Business Information Sources: Europe.*

Publications of the U.S. Bureau of the Census

The U.S. Bureau of the Census is a prolific publisher of statistical data in print, computerized and more recently, CD-ROM formats. The data are, for the most part, based on the following periodic censuses:

1990 Census of Housing
1990 Census of Population
1992 Census of Agriculture
1992 Census of Business
1992 Census of Construction Industries
1992 Census of Governments
1992 Census of Manufactures
1992 Census of Mineral Industries
1992 Census of Retail Trade
1992 Census of Service Industries
1992 Census of Transportation
1992 Census of Wholesale Trade

Complete information on publications, data tapes, and CD-ROM's appear in the annual *Census Catalog and Guide.* The *Monthly Product Announcement* provides current information.

Many current and historical Bureau of the Census publications are available in microfiche from Congressional Information Service, 4520 East-West Highway, Bethesda, Maryland 20814. Current titles include: *1980 Decennial Census*, *1970 Decennial Census*, and *Non-Decennial Census Publications.*

CENDATA, an on-line service providing census information, is available through DIALOG Information Services and CompuServe Business Information Service. The Census Bureau also has an International Data Base of demographic and socio-economic statistics on every country in the world which is available on diskette.

The Census Bureau has recently embarked on a CD-ROM program with a view toward releasing data from its Censuses in this format. Another innovation is the use of "electronic bulletin boards" which permit on line access to news, software, and data. The Census Bureau offers several such bulletin boards. For more information, contact the Census Microcomputer Information Center at the address shown below.

For more information on Census Bureau products and programs, contact: Customer Services, Bureau of Census, Washington, D.C. 20233, telephone (301) 763-4100.

Descriptions of the Bureau's best known publication, the *Statistical Abstract of the United States*, and of other important Bureau publications follow.

Annual Survey of Manufactures. Washington, D.C., U.S. Bureau of the Census, ((301) 763-4100), 1949-. (Annual).

Provides data on manufacturing activity for industry groups; important individual industries; and for geographic divisions, States, large standard metropolitan district areas, and large industrial counties. Items include value added by manufacture; value of shipments; cost of materials, fuels, electric energy consumed, employment, man-hours, payrolls, and capital expenditures.

Bureau of the Census Catalog of Publications, 1790-1972. Washington, D.C., U.S. Bureau of the Census, ((301) 763-4100).

Contains details on all census publications from the very first U.S. Census to 1972. Annual, non-cumulative Census Bureau catalogs were issued during the balance of the 1970's. They are out of print but available on microfiche from Customer Services, Bureau of the Census, Washington, D.C. 20233, telephone (301) 763-4100.

Census and You. Washington, D.C., U.S. Bureau of the Census, ((301) 763-4100), 1966-. (Monthly).

Formerly titled *Data Users News*. This monthly newsletter provides information on Census Bureau products, services, and activities as well as news about data and services from federal, state, and local agencies and other organizations. New economic reports and data tapes are also announced. This report is available online through CENDATA.

Census Catalog and Guide. Washington, D.C., U.S. Bureau of the Census, ((301) 763-4100). (Annual).

The comprehensive bibliography and descriptive listing of all the publications, files, data services, resources, and avenues of access to the programs of this major governmental statistical agency. An invaluable resource for keeping abreast and gaining clear and timely information on what's available, in what forms and how to acquire all the products and services from Census.

Census Daily List. Washington, D.C., U.S. Bureau of the Census, ((301) 763-4100), 1989-. (Daily).

A subscription publication which lists in one or two pages everything just published or released by the Census Bureau on computer tape or CD-Rom. Issued only if more than one or two new items are released, but frequency is close to daily issuance. This report is also available online from CENDATA.

Congressional District Atlas, Districts of the 99th Congress. Washington, D.C., U.S. Bureau of the Census, ((301) 763-4100), 1985.

Presents maps showing boundaries of the congressional districts for the 99th Congress and includes maps for the District of Columbia, Puerto Rico, and the outlying areas.

Congressional Districts of the 98th Congress. Washington, D.C., Bureau of the Census, ((301) 763-4100), 1983-.

Based on 1980 date, this series of 51 state (and District of Columbia) reports, presents selected statistics for congressional districts of the 98th Congress. Each report includes district boundary maps. Data are also available on microfiche and computer tape.

County and City Data Book, 1988. (A Statistical Abstract Supplement). Washington, D.C., U.S. Bureau of the Census, ((301) 763-4100), 1988.

Covers U.S. regions, divisions, states, counties, incorporated cities of 25,000 or more, and places of 2,500 or more. Brings together a variety of social and economic data from Census Bureau and other sources. Subject coverage is broadest for the largest areas. The publications presents 203 data items for counties and larger areas, 134 items for cities of 2,500 or more, and 4 items for places of 25,000 or more. Available also on diskettes, magnetic tapes, and CD-ROM.

County Business Patterns. Washington, D.C., U.S. Bureau of the Census, ((301) 763-4100), 1946-. (Annual).

Data are presented on employment, number and employment size of reporting units, and taxable payrolls by industry groups for private non-farm activities. Annual edition includes a separate paperbound report for each state, District of Columbia, and Puerto Rico and Outlying Areas. Also available on diskette, computer tape, CD-ROM, and CENDATA.

Data Developments. Washington, D.C., U.S. Bureau of the Census, ((301) 763-4100), 1992-. (Periodically).

Describes, in individual issues, a data file recently released by the Census Bureau. It provides information on the file's subject matter, geographic coverage, reference materials, and availability.

Directory of Federal Statistics for Local Areas: A Guide to Sources. Washington, D.C., U.S. Bureau of the Census, ((301) 763-4100), 1978.

This directory is a comprehensive reference guide to statistics for local areas (that is, areas smaller than States) presented in publications of federal agencies. The directory contains no figures; rather, it describes the detailed information provided in federal publications and specifies the kind of area (SMSA's, counties, cities, rural areas, city blocks, special districts, etc.) for which the information is provided, the frequency of the data, and the publication in which the data appear. Includes a useful section on guides to federal and municipal statistics. *Urban Update 1977-1978* was issued in 1979.

Factfinder for the Nation. Washington, D.C., U.S. Bureau of the Census, ((301) 763-4100), 1976-. (Irregular).

Originally published as a single volume, this publication now appears on an irregular basis as a series of brief, topical brochures which are sometimes revised and updated. Some of the subjects included in the series are statistics on minorities, agriculture, foreign trade, manufactures, and transportation. (Other brochures cover topics such as the history and organization of the Census Bureau). Computer tape availability is generally noted. For statistics users, one of the most important issues is the periodic *Reference Sources*, last published in 1988. It lists guides, directories, catalogs, and indexes to Census Bureau and related statistics. Selected reprints of the *Factfinders* are included as an appendix to the *Census Catalog and Guide*.

Guide to Foreign Trade Statistics. Washington, D.C., U.S. Bureau of the Census, ((301) 763-4100), 1991.

This is a guide to the published and unpublished sources of foreign trade statistics prepared by the Bureau of the Census; it describes the content and arrangement of the data and tells where the statistics can be found. It lists the titles of the published reports and illustrates the tables included in them. Unpublished tabulations are also listed and the statistics in these are illustrated. The book also describes the coverage of the import and export statistics program, and discusses the methodology of the data, such as the procedure for estimating low-valued shipments. Special services available from the Census Bureau for those wishing to obtain additional statistics are also described.

Guide to Industrial Statistics. Washington, D.C., U.S. Bureau of the Census, ((301) 763-4100), 1978.

A comprehensive description of the programs of the Census Bureau relating to industry. Sections cover: industrial statistics program, contents of manufactures reports, location guide to published data, types of data presented, publications of major censuses, reference lists and other sources of statistics. A related but much briefer guide is the *Industrial Statistics Data Finder* (1982).

Guide to Service Industry Statistics and Related Data. Washington, D.C., U.S. Bureau of the Census, ((301) 763-4100), 1984.

Contains references to specialized data in economic, demographic, governmental, and agricultural censuses, and in foreign trade and other related statistical programs and surveys.

Guide to the 1987 Census of Agriculture and Related Statistics. Washington, D.C., U.S. Bureau of the Census, ((301) 763-4100), 1988.

Provides general information about the uses, scope, content, coverage, and geographic detail for the census and its related surveys. Describes each of the reports and offers cross-references to related Census Bureau programs. Suggests reference sources, lists information contacts, and tells where and how to order products.

Guide to the 1982 Census of Governments. Washington, D.C., U.S. Bureau of the Census, ((301) 763-4100), 1985.

Contains a display of table samples from reports in the *Census of Governments Report* series. Also included are sections presenting the contents, pages, and table formats for each volume.

Guide to the 1987 Economic Censuses and Related Statistics. Washington, D.C., U.S. Bureau of the Census, ((301) 763-4100), 1990.

Describes the economic censuses and surveys, as well as sources of related data. Following general explanations, the guide discusses individual programs. For each program, it defines the scope and summarizes the report series and other products. Appendixes include a list of standard industrial classification (SIC) short titles and of metropolitan statistical areas (MSA's), publication schedule dates, regional offices, state data centers, and economic subject specialists.

Historical Statistics of the United States, Colonial Times to 1970. Washington, D.C., U.S. Bureau of the Census, ((301) 763-4100), 1976. (Also available as *The Statistical History of the United States.* New York, Basic Books, 1976).

This periodically-revised supplement to the *Statistical Abstract of THE United States*, includes more than 12,500 statistical time series, largely annual, on American social and economic development covering the period 1610 to 1970. Definitions of terms and descriptive text are provided, as well as source notes guiding the reader to original published sources for further reference and additional data. Indexed by subject.

Long Term Economic Growth: 1860-1970. 2nd ed. Washington, D.C., U.S. Bureau of the Census, ((301) 763-4100), 1973.

This report provides a comprehensive, long-range view of the United States economy, bringing together under one cover the complete statistical basis for a study of long-term economic trends. Divided into five parts: Aggregate Output, Input and Productivity; Processes Related to Economic Growth; Regional and Industry Trends; International Comparisons; and Growth Rate Triangles. Three appendices - Growth Rate Conversion and Compound Interest Rate Tables; Series Descriptions and Sources; and Basic Data are included. A computer tape file of the time series included in the report is available for purchase.

Monthly Product Announcement. Washington, D.C., U.S. Bureau of the Census, ((301) 763-4100), Monthly.

A free listing of all Census Bureau products becoming available each month with ordering information and descriptive details for data files, microfiche, printed maps, publications, and selected abstracts. Supplements the annual *Census Catalog and Guide.* Also available online through CENDATA.

Quarterly Financial Report for Manufacturing, Mining and Trade Corporations. Washington, D.C., U.S. Bureau of the Census, ((301) 763-4100), 1947-. (Quarterly).

The purpose of this publication is to present aggregate statistics on the financial results and position of United States corporations classified by both industry and asset size. Data are presented in financial statement and balance sheet form. Also available on diskette and available online through CENDATA.

Social Indicators III. Washington, D.C., U.S. Bureau of the Census, ((301) 763-4100), 1980.

This publication includes statistics on the major social trends in population, health, public safety, education, employment, income, housing, leisure, and social mobility. Data are presented in both chart and tabular forms.

State and Metropolitan Area Data Book. (A Statistical Abstract Supplement). 4th ed. Washington, D.C., U.S. Bureau of the Census, ((301) 763-4100), 1991.

Similar in presentation to the *County and City Data Book*, this volume covers the states, SMSA's and their component counties with both current and historical data. Also available online through CENDATA.

Statistical Abstract of the United States. Washington, D.C., U.S. Bureau of the Census, ((301) 763-4100), 1878-. (Annual).

Presents the most important statistical information gathered by all branches of the federal government, covering vital statistics, political data, economic life, and many cultural subjects. Most of the data are presented in tabular form and are well organized for reference. An annual supplement, *USA Statistics in Brief*, is also available. Available online through CENDATA and CD-ROM.

Statistical Brief. Washington, D.C., U.S. Bureau of the Census, ((301) 763-4100), 1992.

Includes succinct reports issued occasionally and providing timely data on specific issues of public policy. Presented in narrative style with graphs, the reports summarize data from demographic surveys of the U.S. population. This report is available online through CENDATA.

U.S. Merchandise Trade: Selected Highlights. Washington, D.C., U.S. Bureau of the Census, ((301) 763-4100), Monthly.

Presents data on domestic and foreign exports, general imports, and imports for consumption. The report also includes data on U.S. customs districts and method of transportation, and world area by country of origin and country of destination. Some of the tables were previously published in *Highlights of U.S. Export and Import Trade* last published in December 1988.

USA Counties on CD-ROM. Washington, D.C., U.S. Bureau of the Census, ((301) 763-4100), 1992.

Presents 2,080 data items on a variety of demographic, economic, and governmental subjects from 1969-1990. The files include all of the data published for counties in the last three editions of the *State and Metropolitan Databook* and the last two editions of the *County and City Databook*, as well as a number of data items not previously published. Emphasis is placed on extending time series, in contrast to many other statistical files that feature data for the most recent period.

World Population Profile. Washington, D.C., U.S. Bureau of the Census, ((301) 763-4100), 1991.

Presents general demographic statistics for all countries and territories of the world with a population of at least 5,000 in 1991. The report shows population estimates and projections, annual population growth rate, birth and death rates, life expectancy, and infant mortality. Also available online through CENDATA.

Publications and Other Materials from U.S. Government Agencies and Departments

Note: Approximately 200 Federal statistical publications are available on microfiche from: Congressional Information Service, 4520 East-West Highway, Bethesda, Maryland 20814 (800) 638-8380.

Agricultural Outlook. Washington, D.C., U.S. Department of Agriculture, Economic Research Service, (202) 219-0515. (Monthly).

Contains data and analysis on U.S. food and fiber economy. Includes information on commodity supply and demand, prices and marketing, farm income, and world agriculture and trade.

Agricultural Statistics. Washington, D.C., U.S. Department of Agriculture, National Agricultural Statistics Service, ((202) 219-0504), 1936-. (Annual).

Brings together the more important series of statistics compiled in this department and others whose work concerns agriculture. Prior to 1936, statistical data appeared in the Statistical Section of the *Yearbook of Agriculture*.

Annual Energy Review. Washington, D.C., U.S. Energy Information Administration, ((202) 586-8800), 1984-. (Annual).

Provides statistics on U.S. energy supply, production, disposition, and consumption. Ten sections cover energy overview; energy indicators; energy exploration, resources, development and reserves; petroleum; natural gas; wood, waste, solar and geothermal energy; and international energy.

BLS News Releases On Line. Washington, D.C., U.S. Bureau of Labor Statistics, ((202) 606-7828).

Economic Indicators from BLS are available at the time of their release. The information is available through a commercial contractor by paying only for actual computer time used. The data includes more then 100 releases a year on all the fields in which BLS collects information regularly.

Balance Sheet of the Farming Sector. Washington, D.C., U.S. Department of Agriculture, Economic Research Service, ((202) 219-0515), 1945-. (Annual).

This publication views agriculture as though it were one large enterprise. The annual changes shown provide a means of appraising the effects of the financial structure of agricultural development in both the farm and non-farm sectors of the economy.

Budget of the United States Government. Washington, D.C., Office of Management and Budget, ((202) 395-7332), 1923-. (Annual).

Comprehensive details, contained in summary tables, on receipts, expenditures, etc. of the federal government. Accompanying the Budget Message is a detailed account by departments and agencies of proposed budget items, giving previous year's actual figures, present year's estimated, and coming year's proposed amounts.

Business Cycle Indicators. Washington, D.C., U.S. Bureau of Economic Analysis, ((202) 606-9900), Monthly.

Contains monthly indicators to track business cycles that appear in the C-pages of the *Survey of Current Business.* The system features the composite indexes of leading, coincident, and lagging indicators. Also available on diskette and online through Electronic Bulletin Board.

Business Statistics. Washington, D.C., U.S. Bureau of Economic Analysis, ((202) 606-9900), 1963-1991. (Biennial).

Contains monthly or quarterly data for series that appear in the S-pages of the *Survey of Current Business*. These series include business sales, inventories, and orders, prices; employment and unemployment; construction; banking and finance; transportation; and many other industries and commodities

Center for Electronic Records' Title List: A Partial and Preliminary List of The Datasets in the Custody of the National Archives. Washington, D.C., National Archives and Records Administration, Center for Electronic Records, ((202) 501-5400), continuously revised.

References to computer-readable data files in the custody of the Center for Electronic Records. Ultimately, the list is expected to incorporate information on all the electronic datasets that have been accessioned by the National Archives. The files are drawn from federal agencies and departments which have transferred their records to the National Archives.

Construction Review. Washington, D.C., U.S. Department of Commerce, International Trade Administration, ((202) 482-2185). (Bimonthly).

Contains all of the government's current statistics related to construction.

CPI Detailed Report. Washington, D.C., U.S. Bureau of Labor Statistics, (202) 606-7828), 1974-. (Monthly).

Covers the Consumer Price Index for All Urban Consumers (CPI-U) and the Consumer Price Index for Wage Earners and Clerical Workers (CPI-W). Data presented in both textual and tabular format with technical notes. Data is also available in *Consumer Price Index Mailgram* available from NTIS with delivery by mailgram through Western Union. Data also appear in the *Consumer and Producer Price Indexes* database available from The WEFA Group, Reuters Information Services, Canada Ltd., and the Human Resource Information Network.

Digest of Education Statistics. Washington, D.C., National Center for Education Statistics, ((800) 424-1616), 1962-. (Annual).

Provides an abstract of statistical information covering the entire field of American education from kindergarten through graduate school. Listed are figures pertaining to such topics as schools, enrollments, teachers, graduates, attainment, and expenditures. A companion volume published annually, *Projections of Education Statistics*, shows trends for the past 10 years and projects data for the next 10 years. A related publication, *The Condition of Education*, provides an overview of trends and current issues.

Economic Indicators. Washington, D.C., U.S. President's Council of Economic Advisors, ((202) 395-5084), 1948-. (Monthly).

A publication presenting basic statistical series produced by federal agencies on prices, employment and wages, production and business activity, purchasing power, credit, money and federal finance, and the total output of the economy. Its chief value is as a summary review of the major yardsticks of national business conditions.

Economic Indicators of the Farm Sector. Washington, D.C. U.S. Department of Agriculture, Economic Research Service, ((202) 219-0515). (6 times per year).

Comprises six reports published annually that updates economic trends in U.S. agriculture. Each issue explores a different aspect of income and expenses, national and state financial summaries, production and efficiency statistics, costs of production, and an annual overview.

Economic Report of the President. Washington, D.C., Executive Office of the President, ((202) 395-3080), 1947-. (Annual).

This publication includes the economic report of the President to Congress, the annual report of the Council of Economic Advisors and a series of statistical tables pertaining to national income, employment, productivity, government finances, international trade and finance, agriculture, and prices. Statistics are both current and retrospective.

EIA Publications Directory. Washington, D.C., Energy Information Administration, ((202) 586-8800), 1980-. (Annual).

This volume is a guide to the data contained in publications of the Energy Information Administration of the U.S. Department of Energy. EIA publishes statistical information on actual and projected energy resource reserves, production, consumption, supply and demand, prices, and related economic information. In addition, EIA publishes *EIA News Releases* bimonthly which contains the latest available publications and upcoming reports.

Electronic News Service. Washington, D.C., U.S. Bureau of Labor Statistics, ((202) 606-7828).

Major BLS news releases are available electronically at the time of release. Ask for specific information from the Office of Publications, Bureau of Labor Statistics, 2 Massachusetts Avenue, NE, Washington, D.C. 20212 (202) 606-7828.

Employment and Earnings Statistics for States and Areas. Washington, D.C., U.S. Bureau of Labor Statistics, ((202) 606-7828), 1939-. (Annual).

Designates for all States and 202 major areas annual averages for more than 7,500 series on payroll employment by industry and 3,300 series on hours and earnings of production workers by industry from the earliest date of availability. Also contains summary and analytical tables comparing employment and earnings trends by region, State, and major area. Contains industry detail currently published by each State agency cooperating with the Bureau of Labor Statistics. Annual averages from the earliest date through 1974 are shown on employment hours and earnings for the fifty States and 230 major areas. Also available online from GE Information Services (GEIS) and The WEFA Group.

Employment and Earnings Statistics for the United States. Washington, D.C., U.S. Bureau of Labor Statistics, ((202) 606-7828), 1909-. (Annual).

National data from the earliest date of availability are provided for over 400 industries. Includes monthly and annual averages for employment, hours and earnings, and labor turnover; seasonally adjusted data, indexes of weekly hours and weekly payrolls, net spendable earnings, hourly earnings excluding overtime, summary and analytical items. Two monthly publications, *Employment and Earnings*, and *Monthly Report on the Labor Force* are also available. Also available from GE Information Services (GEIS) and The WEFA Group.

EPUB. Washington, D.C., Energy Information Administration, (202) 586-8800.

EPUB is an electronic publishing system maintained by the Energy Information Administration of the U.S. Department of Energy. EPUB allows the general public to electronically access selected energy data from many of EIA's statistical reports. The system is a menu-driven, bulletin-board-type system with extensive online help capabilities.

Fact Book of U.S. Agriculture. Washington, D.C., U.S. Department of Agriculture, ((202) 720-USDA), 1979-. (Annual).

Describes major trends in U.S. agriculture. Includes information on production, operation, marketing, agricultural services, and rural social environment.

Federal Reserve Bulletin. Washington, D.C., Board of Governors of the Federal Reserve System, ((202) 452-3000), 1915-. (Monthly).

Articles on economic topics and news about the Federal Reserve System are included along with both national and international financial and business statistics.

Foreign Agricultural Trade of the United States. Washington, D.C., U.S. Department of Agriculture, Economic Research Service, ((202) 219-0515), 1962-. (Eight issues per year).

Contains tables showing value and quantity of agricultural commodities imported and exported, with annual supplements on trade by commodities and trade by countries.

Foreign Direct Investment in the United States. Washington, D.C., U.S. Department of Commerce, Bureau of Economic Analysis, ((202) 606-9900), 1980-. (Annual).

Includes financial and operating data, and direct investment positions and balance of payment data for U.S. businesses which are owned 10 percent or more by a foreign entity.

A Guide to Selected National Environmental Statistics in The U.S. Government. Washington, D.C., Environmental Protection Agency, ((202) 260-2080), 1993.

This guide contains information on selected sources of environmental statistics from U.S. government agencies. Provides national-level, time-series environmental statistics that are compiled and distributed by the U.S. government on a regular basis. The programs are arranged by government department and agency, and each entry contains information about a separate statistical program (e.g., program purpose, data coverage and collection methods, geographic coverage, agency contacts, pertinent publications, and database access options). Also available on diskette.

Handbook of Agricultural Charts. Washington, D.C., U.S. Department of Agriculture, ((202) 720-USDA), 1984.

Charts and graphs illustrating farm population, consumer economic indicators, food and nutrition, commodity trends, and U.S. trade and world production.

Handbook of Labor Statistics. Washington, D.C., U.S. Bureau of Labor Statistics, ((202) 606-7828), 1924/26-. (Annual).

All the major statistical series compiled by the Bureau are included. Sections include prices and cost of living, earnings, hours, and wage rates, etc. Both current and historical data are presented covering the earliest reliable data.

Health United States. Hyattsville, Maryland, U.S. National Center for Health Statistics, ((301) 436-8500), 1976-. (Annual).

Presents statistics concerning recent trends in the health care sector and detailed discussions of selected current health issues. Covers such topics as population, fertility, mortality, determinants and measures of health, manpower, and health care expenditures.

Local Area Personal Income. Washington, D.C., U.S. Bureau of Economic Analysis, ((202) 606-9900), 19-. (Annual).

Personal income by type, major industries, population, and per capita income for states, counties, BEA areas and SMSA's is presented in one summary volume and eight regional volumes.

Major Programs of the Bureau of Labor Statistics. Washington, D.C., U.S. Bureau of Labor Statistics, ((202) 606-7828), 1991.

In highly condensed form, this publication presents the scope of the Bureau's major statistical programs, the data available, the form of publication, some of the uses of the data, and selected publications, data tapes, and diskettes.

The Medicare and Medicaid Data Book. Washington, D.C., U.S. Health Care Financing Administration, ((410) 597-5063), 1982-. (Annual).

Includes a description of the Medicare and Medicaid programs, detailed data on the Medicaid program, and explains how the programs evolved.

Minerals Yearbook. Washington, D.C., U.S. Bureau of Mines, ((202) 501-9757), 1932-. (Annual).

Comprehensive summary of details governing mining and minerals activity in this country and a factual record of economic and technological developments and trends. Volume I covers metals and minerals. Volume II covers domestic area reports. Volume III covers international area reports.

Monthly Energy Review. Washington, D.C., U.S. Energy Information Administration, ((202) 586-8800), 1975-. (Monthly).

Current data for production, consumption, stocks, imports, exports, and prices for the major energy commodities in the U.S. Annual data is published in the *Annual Energy Review.* Data from *Monthly Energy Review* can also be obtained from EPUB.

Monthly Labor Review. Washington, D.C., U.S. Bureau of Labor Statistics, ((202) 606-7828), 1915-. (Monthly).

Important statistical information on fluctuations in the cost of living, wage rates, hours of labor, industrial relations, output per man-hours, wholesale and retail prices, etc. Includes research summaries and foreign labor developments. Other BLS periodicals include: *Current Wage Developments; Employment and Earnings; Occupational Outlook Quarterly.* BLS makes its current news releases available through the on-line "BLS Electronic News Release Service." Some data available online in *Employment and Earnings* database from GE Information Systems (GEIS).

National Transportation Statistics. Washington, D.C., U.S. Department of Transportation, ((202) 366-4000), 1969-. (Annual).

Selected transportation statistics from government and private sources. Includes cost, inventory, and performance data for cargo and passenger operations for major transportation modes.

NCJRS Electronic Bulletin Board. Rockville, Maryland, National Criminal Justice Reference Service, Access by modem on (301) 738-8895.

This bulletin board provides quick and easy access to a variety of Bureau of Justice Statistics (BJS) publications and information sources. Once online, the user can select from seven menu options: BJS press releases, latest BJS findings, Justice Statistics Clearinghouse information, BJS conference activity, news from the Drugs and Crime Data Center and Clearinghouse, National Archive of Criminal Justice data, and news from State Statistical Analysis centers.

OERI Electronic Bulletin Boards. Washington, D.C., U.S. Department of Education, Office of Educational Research and Improvement, (202) 708-5366.

Contains three files of information for education professionals including OERI data tapes, OERI publications, and OERI reports.

Producer Price Indexes. Washington, D.C., U.S. Bureau of Labor Statistics, ((202) 606-7828), 1978-. (Monthly).

Covers producer price movements in both textual and tabular format with technical notes. Annual supplement contains monthly data for the calendar year, annual averages, and information on weights and changes in the sample. Available on computer tape. Also available online from Reuters Information Services, Canada, Ltd., and The WEFA Group.

Science Indicators. Arlington, Virginia, National Science Board, National Science Foundation, ((703) 306-1234), 1972-. (Biennial).

Data are presented on international research and development, resources for research and development, resources for basic research, industrial research and development and innovation, science and engineering personnel, and public attitudes toward science and technology. A combination of text, tables, and graphs is used.

Social Security Bulletin. Washington, D.C., U.S. Social Security Administration, ((202) 282-7138), 1938-. (Monthly).

Provides current data on social security program operations. Also contains data on recipients and payments under public assistance programs; unemployment insurance; and railroad, civil service, and veterans programs. An annual statistical supplement is also published.

Sourcebook of Criminal Justice Statistics. Rockville, Maryland, National Criminal Justice Reference Service, ((800) 732-3277), 1973-. (Annual).

This work compiles statistical information from all levels of government, public and private agencies, academic institutions, research organizations, and public opinion polling firms. It is divided into six sections: characteristics of the criminal justice system, public attitudes toward crime, nature and distribution of known offenses, characteristics and distribution of persons arrested, judicial processing of defendants, and persons under correctional supervision. Information is generally provided at the national or state level, with some information for large cities. Sources are listed at the end of each table, and an annotated list of references is also provided. Indexed.

Statistics of Income. Washington, D.C., U.S. Internal Revenue Service, ((202) 874-0410), 1916-. (Quarterly).

Gives summary tabulations on financial information obtained from the various tax returns. Individual reports have been issued for each type of return beginning with data from 1954. For 1953 and prior years, the information was released in two parts: Part 1 for individuals, and Part 2 for Corporations, with special studies for selected years included in Part 1.

Statistics of the Communications Industry in the U.S. Washington, D.C., Federal Communications Commission, ((202) 632-7000), 1939-. (Annual).

Lists financial and operating data on telephone, wire-telegraph, ocean-cable, and radiotelegraph carriers and controlling companies; employment and compensation; and number of telephones in home, by States and by principal cities.

Survey of Current Business. Washington, D.C., U.S. Bureau of Economic Analysis, ((202) 606-9900), 1921-. (Monthly).

The major reporting publication for business statistics, including indexes for income payments, industrial production, commodity prices, statistics on construction and real estate, domestic trade, employment conditions and wages, finance, foreign trade, transportation and communication, products by kind, etc. Some reports on the business situation and conditions in specific industries are included. BEA also publishes *User's Guide to BEA Information* which lists the most frequently requested products and services from BEA. Note: Some current data may be accessed online from BEA'S Economic Bulletin Board.

Treasury Bulletin. Washington, D.C., U.S. Department of the Treasury, ((202) 622-2000), 1939-. (Monthly).

This official organ of the Treasury Department consists entirely of statistical tables and charts on all phases of public finance. Major categories of tables and charts include: federal fiscal operations; federal obligations; account of the U.S. Treasury; monetary statistics; federal debt; public debt operations; U.S. Savings Bonds; U.S. Savings Notes; ownership of federal securities; Treasury survey of ownership; market quotations on federal securities; average yields of long term bonds; exchange stabilization fund; international financial statistics; capital movements; financial operations of government agencies and funds.

Uniform Crime Reports for the United States. Washington, D.C., Federal Bureau of Investigation, ((202) 324-3691), 1930-. (Annual).

Data for this publication are received by the FBI from over 15,000 law enforcement agencies that participate in the Uniform Crime Reporting Program. Information is provided for eight offenses: murder and nonnegligent manslaughter, aggravated assault, forcible rape, robbery, burglary, larceny-theft, motor vehicle theft, and arson. National, state, county, metropolitan area, and selected city data are provided. Not indexed.

U.S. Industrial Outlook. Washington, D.C., U.S. Department of Commerce, International Trade Administration, ((202) 482-2185), 1955-. (Annual).

This reference includes industry-by-industry analyses, historical data, current trends, forecasts, and industry statistical profiles.

Vital Statistics of the United States. Hyattsville, Maryland, U.S. National Center for Health Statistics, ((301) 436-8500), 1937-. (Annual).

Covers matters of life, health and welfare. Reports on birth and death registrations, causes of death, incidence of specified diseases; marriage and divorce, etc. In three volumes: Volume 1, Natality; Volume 2, Mortality; Volume 3, Marriage and Divorce. Supplemented by the *Monthly Vital Statistics Report*.

Guides to Machine-Readable U.S. Government Data Sources

In addition to the print sources described below, statistics users may want to contact the Federal Computer Products Center at the National Technical Information Service (NTIS) in Springfield, VA (703) 487-4807. The Center currently sells more than 4,500 software packages and data files from over 100 Federal agencies.

BLS Data Diskettes. Washington, D.C., Bureau of Labor Statistics, ((202) 606-7828).

A listing of all the diskettes available from the Bureau of Labor Statistics. Selected BLS Series are available on diskettes for use with IBM-compatible microcomputers.

BLS Data Files on Tape. Washington, D.C., Bureau of Labor Statistics, ((202) 606-7828).

Provides a listing of all the major data series which are available on magnetic tape and cartridge tape from the Bureau of Labor Statistics. The standard format is 9-track, 6250 BPI.

Catalog of Electronic Data Products from National Center for Health Statistics. Hyattsville, Maryland, National Center for Health Statistics, ((301) 436-8500), 1990.

Lists data available on computer tapes concerning health facilities, health resources utilization, and vital statistics. The catalog also describes how the data was collected and the programs for which the data was assembled.

Ching-Chih Chen and Peter Hernon, eds. *Numeric Databases*. Norwood, New Jersey, Ablex Publishing Corporation, ((201) 767-8450), 1984.

Information on federally produced statistical data. Also describes the use of non-bibliographic databases in libraries.

Directory of U.S. Government Data Files for Mainframes and Microcomputers. Springfield, Virginia, National Technical Information Service, ((703) 487-4600), 1994.

Describes more than 1,600 data files for unique federal numeric and textual data. Divided into 25 subject areas to facilitate scanning, each entry lists full bibliographic information, summaries, and ordering information. Includes subject, hardware and agencies indexes. Updated irregularly.

Economic Research Service-Finders Advisory System, Washington, D.C., U.S. Department of Agriculture, Economic Research Service, ((202) 219-0515), 1990.

FINDERS is an advisory ("expert") system developed to provide enhanced user access to ERS information and data resources dealing primarily with agribusiness. Through a series of menus, one is lead to information on reports, contacts and data products. The system offers advice on obtaining these resources and provides order forms for data products and publications.

Matthew Lesko. *The Federal Database Finder: A Directory of Free and Fee-Based Data Bases and Files Available from the Federal Government*. Kensington, Maryland, Information USA Inc., ((800) 955-POWER), 1995.

A directory on thousands of data files available from the federal government. Especially useful for identifying files not commercially available although most of the more familiar government online databases are covered as well.

National Archive of Criminal Justice Data. Washington, D.C., Sponsored by the Bureau of Justice Statistics, U.S. Department of Justice and operated by the Inter-University Consortium for Political and Social Research, ((800) 999-0960), Spring 1994.

Catalog includes descriptions of the data collections carried out on criminal justice, organized by topic, with details on the content and records included.

OERI Directory of Computer Data Files. Washington, D.C., U.S. Office of Educational Research and Improvement, ((800) 424-1616), 1991, with 1992 supplement available.

A catalog of available data tape files governing information available on elementary and secondary education, higher, vocational and adult education; libraries and special studies. The data is drawn from the Center for Education Statistics which has been collecting such statistics for more than 20 years.

User's Guide to BEA Information. Washington, D.C., U.S. Bureau of Economic Analysis, ((202) 606-9900). (Annual).

This catalog lists print sources, computer tapes, diskettes, and CD-ROMS, along with the necessary ordering information and prices. Further information may be obtained from the Information Services

Division, Bureau of Economic Analysis, U.S. Department of Commerce, Washington, D.C. 20230.

INTERNATIONAL SOURCES

General International Publications

A.M. Abdul Huq, Compiler. *The Global Economy: An Information Sourcebook.* Phoenix, Oryx Press, ((800) 279-ORYX), 1988.

Lists and describes more than 500 books, databases, periodicals and reference publications pertaining to the complex economic conditions throughout the world. A major portion of the volume focuses on UN publications although coverage also includes data distributed by information producers in international economies and other specialized agencies that cover regional and world economic conditions.

Africa South of the Sahara. London, Europa Publications, (Available from Gale Research Inc., (800) 877-GALE), 1971-. (Annual).

Covers approximately 50 countries with an individual chapter for each. Chapters include a statistical survey, as well as articles on such topics as geography, religion, and economy. Some statistical data are presented in the general survey section.

African Development Indicators. Washington, D.C., World Bank Publications, ((202) 473-1155), 1994.

This collection provides the most detailed data available on Africa in one volume. Includes statistics on education, health, demographics, the environment and natural resources, and labor markets. It also includes the economic and financial indicators in the original volume, updated to include data for 1988-1990. Data are arranged in separate tables for over 275 indicators. Economic and financial data are grouped in 12 sections: national accounts, prices and exchange rates, money and banking, the external sector, debt and related flows, government finance, agriculture, industry, public enterprises, labor force, employment and unemployment, and aid flows. Social data include indicators on demographics, health and education. Environmental data include indicators on land use, forests, water and energy. 52 bank member countries in Africa are included. Also available on diskette.

Agriculture: Statistical Yearbook. Washington, D.C., European Community Information Service, (Annual). (Available from UNIPUB (800) 274-4888).

Gives the most recent statistical data on agriculture, forestry and fisheries in the European communities. Values noted are converted into European Currency Units for easy comparisons between countries.

Annual Abstract of Statistics. London, Central Statistical Office, 1976-. (Annual).

This key statistics publication covers a wide range of topics for the whole United Kingdom. Among these are climate, social conditions, labor, production, balance of payments, etc. An index of sources and a subject index are included. A companion volume, *Regional Trends* is also available. Current data are published monthly in *Economic Trends*, *Monthly Digest of Statistics*, and *Financial Statistics*. Data from the Central Statistical Office are available online from CISI - Wharton U.K. (23 Lower Belgrave Street, London SW1) and from I.P. Sharp Associates.

Annual Bulletin of General Energy Statistics for Europe. Geneva, Economic Commission for Europe, (Available in the U.S. from UNIPUB (800) 274-4888), 1968-.

Data on the overall energy situation are provided for European countries, Canada, and the United States. Coverage includes the most recent two-year period.

Annual Reports of the World's Central Banks. Alexandria, Virginia, Chadwyck-Healey Inc., ((800) 752-0515).

From the comprehensive collection in the Joint Library of the International Monetary Fund and the World Bank, financial, economic and statistical profiles of 128 countries available as a complete collection, by region and by country. Available on microfiche with MARC cataloguing and annual updates. Each report contains detailed statistical tables and graphs.

Annual Statistical Bulletin. Vienna, Organization of the Petroleum Exporting Countries (OPEC), Vienna, Austria, 1966-.

Oil statistics for the thirteen member countries are provided. Statistics are up to three to four years old by the time they appear in the *Annual.*

Balance of Payments Statistics Yearbook. Washington, D.C., International Monetary Fund, ((202) 623-7000), 1949-. (Annual).

Balance of payment statistics for over 140 countries are presented. Each edition covers the eight or nine most recent periods available. Analytical tables and commentaries on significant developments are included. Annual issue contains data for standard components and their aggregates. Monthly booklets are published to update the aggregated statements, and a supplement presenting series topically, rather than by country is also available. Available on magnetic tape. Data also available online from The WEFA Group.

R. Bar-On, ed. *Travel and Tourism Data: A Comprehensive Research Handbook on World Travel.* Phoenix, Oryx Press, ((800) 279-ORYX), 1989.

Provides both a comprehensive review of the differing methods of measuring and analyzing travel data used throughout the world as well as guide to international sources of travel trade statistics.

Basic Statistics of the European Community. Washington, D.C., European Community Information Service, (Annual). (Available from UNIPUB (800) 274-4888).

Provides general statistical data on the European Communities for the recent year. Has information on a broad range of topics such as agriculture, employment, regional and international market prices, education, population, and much more.

Alexander Besher, ed. *The Pacific Rim Almanac.* New York, Harper Collins ((212) 207-7000), 1991.

A resource guide which includes facts, statistics, trends, products, and technologies of the Asia-Pacific region.

Bibliography of Selected Statistical Sources of the American Nations. A Guide to the Principal Statistical Materials of the 22 American Nations Including Data Analyses, Methodology and Laws and Organization of Statistical Agencies. Washington, D.C., Inter-American Statistical Institute, Pan American Union, 1947. (Reprinted by Blaine Ethridge Books, Detroit, 1974).

An annotated guide to major South and Central American statistical sources. Description of entries are in English and the language of the original publication. Background information on compilation of statistical publication is included. In addition to the detailed alphabetical and classified indexes, thorough information is offered about statistical publications of each country, including censuses yearbooks and sources in particular fields of activity. Supplemented by *Estadistica: Journal of the Inter-American Statistical Institute, 1948-.*

Bibliography on Income and Wealth. New York, International Association for Research in Income and Wealth, ((212) 924-4386), (Vol. 1--, 1937/47).

The eighth volume of this annotated bibliography covers the four-year period 1957 to 1960 inclusive. This volume, like its predecessors, is the cooperative effort of national income scholars, from nearly forty countries and from numerous international organizations. The general subject covered is the measurement of income and wealth of nations, including distribution of income, labor force, and economic analysis related to income or wealth. This is an excellent source for locating data, both factual and theoretical, on countries outside of the United States. Still a useful source work. The Association's quarterly publication, *The Review of Income and Wealth*, provides a current treatment of the subject.

Judith Blake and Jerry J. Donovan. *Western European Censuses, 1960, An English Language Guide.* University of California, Institute of International Studies, Berkeley, 1971. (Reprinted by Greenwood Press, Westport, Connecticut, 1976).

An annotated guide to Western European Censuses of Population. Entries are both in English and in the language of original publication for the most widely spoken language of publication. Includes detailed annotations, glossaries of technical terms, comparative analyses of concepts common to more than one country, and descriptive titles for statistical tables in census reports.

Bulletin of International Statistical Institute. Voorburg, The Netherlands, International Statistical Institute. (Biennial).

Statistics on economics, housing, building, public utilities, population, and transportation, as well as cultural, sports, and vital statistics are reported from major European cities. Non-European cities in Africa, India, Korea, Japan, Israel, Canada and South America are also represented.

Canadian Markets, 1990. Financial Post Information Service.

Data on urban and rural Canada including taxation, price indexes, manufacturing, demographic and other forms of information. Statistics are distilled from major sources on the nation, provinces, census divisions, and municipalities.

Catalogue of Statistical Materials of Developing Countries. Tokyo, Institute of Developing Economics, 1974-. (Annual).

Statistical sources for Asia, the Middle East, Africa and Latin America are arranged by regions, countries, and subjects. Coverage includes population, agriculture, mining, transport, external trade, wages, prices, enterprises, banking, and social statistics. An appendix gives addresses of organizations.

China Urban Statistics 1988. Greenwood Publishing Group, Westport, Connecticut, ((203) 226-3571), 1990.

Provides both general information and statistics about Chinese cities, ports, and special economic zones. Includes a statistical survey of more than 150 cities covering such social and economic indicators as demography, agriculture, industry, transport, telecommunications, urban development, trade and commerce, education and culture, public health, labor, and public finance.

Commodity Trade and Price Trends. Washington, D.C., The World Bank, ((202) 473-1155), 1993.

Historical data on the trends of developing countries. Includes market price quotations for important commodities in international trade. Tables and graphs indicate commodity price movements relative to the international price level. French and Spanish translations provided alongside the English.

Consumer Asia. 2nd edition. London, Euromonitor, ((312) 541-8024), 1995.

This title presents statistical and analytical surveys of diverse Asian consumer markets, concentrating on Hong Kong, Taiwan, Singapore, South Korea, Indonesia, and Malaysia, with assessments and overviews of the region as a whole.

Consumer China. London, Euromonitor, ((312) 541-8024), 1994.

Provides comprehensive statistical coverage of China's consumer markets, together with a wealth of background data on business, economic and social conditions.

Consumer Eastern Europe. 2nd edition. London, Euromonitor, ((312) 541-8024), 1994.

This reference provides valuable data on the market for consumer goods and services in Eastern European countries. Subject chapters include, demography, economic indicators, standard of living, household characteristics, advertising and media access, regional distribution, consumer expenditure, market demand, service industries, consumer markets, and more.

Consumer Europe. London, Euromonitor, ((312) 541-8024), 1994.

This handbook covers over 230 consumer goods markets across 17 European countries. Topics covered for each country include, among others, productive capacity, import and export levels, annual consumption, brand share and manufacturers. General data are provided for basic market indicators.

Consumer International. London, Euromonitor, ((312) 541-8024), 1994.

Covers a wide range of consumer markets in Argentina, Australia, Brazil, Canada, Chile, China, Colombia, Ecuador, Hong Kong, India, Indonesia, Japan, Malaysia, Mexico, Pakistan, Peru, Philippines, Singapore, South Africa, South Korea, Taiwan, Thailand, United States, and Venezuela.

Consumer Japan. 2nd ed. London, Euromonitor, ((312) 541-8024), 1993.

Sources of statistics for the Japanese consumer market, including market data on over 150 consumer products sold in Japan. Includes 80 statistical tables revealing market details such as gross domestic product growth, trends in hobby participation, employment by sector, advertising expenditures, and more.

Consumer Latin America. London, Euromonitor, ((312) 541-8024), 1993.

Presents a statistical and analytical survey of the diverse Latin American countries.

Consumer South America. 1st ed. London, Euromonitor, ((312) 541-8024), 1993.

Provides detailed data on trends in the changing markets of South American countries and details market factors for the region in four distinct chapters: general market profile of the region; comparative statistical profiles of the markets of each country; market sizes for specific consumer products; and country-by-country surveys.

Consumer Southern Europe. 1st ed. London, Euromonitor, ((312) 541-8024), 1993.

Presents a complete dossier of up-to-the minute data on the range of durable and non-durable consumer products from Greece, Turkey, and Portugal. Includes an overview of the region, statistics and more.

Country Reports. New York, Economist Intelligence Unit, ((800) 938-4685), Quarterly.

Analyses of economic and political trends every quarter. *Country Reports* are periodic updates of the situation in 180 countries around the world. Information is gathered from a worldwide network of economists and specialist correspondents, and 25-40 page reports are produced on the investment environment of each country. Included in each is an in-depth analysis of a country's current political and economic climate as well as short-term economic projections. In addition to the four country reports, a subscription to any country chapter includes an annual *Country Profile*. The *Country Profile* is an overview of the country, giving an historical perspective to its current politics, economy and industries. It includes statistical tables that cover 6 years of main macroeconomic indicators.

Current National Statistical Compendiums. Bethesda, Maryland, Congressional Information Service, ((800) 638-8380), 1970-. (Annual).

A microfiche collection of national statistical compendiums from more than 100 countries. Coverage begins in 1970 and is updated annually. Generally published in English or another western language, each compendium presents a wide range of social, economic, and demographic data.

Countries of the World and Their Leaders Yearbook. Detroit, Gale Research Inc., ((800) 877-GALE), 19-. (Annual).

Compiled from information gathered from the Central Intelligence Agency and the U.S. State Department, this handbook covers 170 countries and provides information ranging from climate to business services to embassy personnel. Of particular interest to statistics users is basic social, political, and economic data for each country.

Arsen Darnay, ed. *Statistical Record of the Environment*. 2nd ed. Detroit, Gale Research Inc., ((800) 877-GALE), 1994.

Covering such topics as hazardous waste, nuclear energy, acid rain, pesticides, radon in the home, offshore pollution levels, and loss of wetlands. The data is drawn from U.S. government sources, United Nations Environment Program material, and local and regional sources. The work includes some 1,000 graphs, charts, and tables. There are subject and keyword indexes to the content. Also available on diskette and magnetic tape.

Direction of Trade Statistics. Washington, D.C., International Monetary Fund, ((202) 623-7000), 1958/62-. (Monthly with Annual Supplement).

This publication presents statistics for value of trade (separated into exports and imports) between member countries and other countries. Monthly issues contain data only for the corresponding period of the preceding year. The annual issue, the *Yearbook*, provides full year data for a number of years, and summary tables for various areas of the world and world aggregates. Also available on magnetic tape. For more information, contact Publications Section, IMF, Washington, D.C. 20431. Online database available from DRI/McGraw Hill, Reuters Information Services (Canada), Ltd. and The WEFA Group.

Kathleen Droste and Jennifer Dye, eds. *Gale Book of Averages*. Gale Research Inc., ((800) 877-4253), 1994.

Compilation of statistical, tabular, and textual data, international in scope, culled from a wide variety of sources, including government publications, books, newspapers, and magazines. Approximately 1,100 entries are arranged by broad subject categories (e.g., pollution and recycling, consumption, vital statistics, weather and nature) and include thousands of specific average values.

John Dunning and John Cantwell, eds. *IRM Directory of Statistics of International Investment and Production*. London, MacMillan Publishers, Ltd., ((800) 428-5331 in U.S.), 1987.

Brings together data on the international direct investment position of approximately 80 countries. Presented in two sections; County Tables and Comparative Tables - Tables organize data from a variety of perspectives such as sectoral, geographical and industrial distribution of foreign direct capital stock.

Eastern Europe and the Commonwealth of Independent States. London, Europa Publications. (Available from Gale Research Inc., (800) 877-GALE), 1994.

Leading experts examine the social, political, and economic background of the region consisting of Albania, Bulgaria, Czechoslovakia, Hungary, Poland, Romania and the former Yugoslavia and the USSR. Separate chapters examine individual countries and include a geographical profile, a chronology, essays on recent history and the economy, statistical surveys, directory material and more.

The Economist Book of Vital World Statistics. London, Times Books, (Available in U.S. (212) 751-2600), 1990.

Data is presented on 110 topics. Information is drawn from the Economist Intelligence Unit and treats some 146 countries on such subjects as population, land use, trade, labor force, consumer goods, and demographic information.

Energy Statistical Yearbook. Washington, D.C., European Community Information Service, (Annual). (Available from UNIPUB (800) 274-4888).

Offers an overview of the European Economic Community's energy status for the recent year. Has explanatory notes for defining this survey's terms, industry branch breakdowns, and abbreviations. Tables feature international energy comparisons, economic indicators, structures of net production and characteristics of the year specifically under study.

Peter M. Enggass. *Tourism and the Travel Industry: An Information Sourcebook.* Phoenix, Oryx Press, ((800) 279-ORYX), 1988.

A guide to current business sources including books, handbooks, yearbooks, U.S. government publications, trade publications, magazines, and newsletters.

The Environmental Data Book: A Guide to Statistics on the Environment and Development. Washington, D.C., International Bank for Reconstruction and Development/World Bank, ((202) 473-1155), 1993.

Environment and economic development are interrelated, each factor capable of both enhancing and hindering the other. For countries of more than one million people, maps and statistical tables reflect water, land, air, and atmosphere indicators of environmental quality and other economic and social indicators.

The Europa World Year Book. London, Europa Publications Ltd. (Available from Gale Research Inc. (800) 877-GALE), 1926-. (Annual).

This reference work on the political and economic life of countries throughout the world includes a statistical survey for each country. Published in two volumes. Topics covered include: area and population, agriculture, forestry, mining industry, finance, external trade, tourism, transport, communications media, and education.

European Advertising, Marketing, and Media Data Statistics. 2nd ed. London, Euromonitor, ((312) 541-8024), 1992.

A comprehensive and detailed look at European marketing statistics covering 16 major Western European markets. Arranged by country, each section provides details and statistics on market geography, demographic parameters, economic indicators, consumer spending, market penetration levels, retail sales and distribution, advertising expenditure, media access and availability, leading advertisers, leading advertising agencies, and media operators.

European Directory of Non-Official Statistical Sources, 1993. London, Euromonitor, ((312) 541-8024).

Lists more than 2000 non-official sources of time-series statistics from Western European Countries, with special attention to UK, France, Italy, and Germany. Sources cited include statistics on particular markets, industries, products, and sectors. Also covered are opinion surveys, market research and salary surveys.

European Marketing Data and Statistics. London, Euromonitor, ((312) 541-8024), 1964-. (Annual).

Comprehensive statistical data on 33 countries of Europe. More than 240 statistical tables comparing essential market data, arranged in four economic groups. Also available on CD-ROM with *International Marketing Data and Statistics.*

Victoria K. Evalds, ed. *Union List of African Censuses, Development Plans and Statistical Abstracts.* New Jersey, K.G. Saur, ((908) 665-3576), 1985.

Provides a comprehensive listing of the combined holdings of 12 major U.S. research collections of government documents concerned with African development plans, censuses, and statistical abstracts for the period 1945-1983.

Far East and Australasia. London, Europa Publications. (Available from Gale Research Inc. (800) 877-GALE), 1969-. (Annual).

Similar to other area publications by Europa, this volume reports on 30 countries and territories with an individual chapter devoted to each. Chapters include a statistical survey, as well as articles on such topics as geography, religion and economy. Some statistical data are also presented in the general survey section.

Gale Country and World Rankings Reporter, 1st ed. Detroit, Gale Research, Inc., ((800) 877-4253), 1995.

More than 180 countries are represented and approximately 3,000 statistical charts and tables from a diverse range of sources, including the United Nations and national government publications. Users can easily compare the world's physical, social, business, cultural, economic, demographic, governmental, leisure, and other statistics.

Government Finance Statistics Yearbook. Washington, D.C., International Monetary Fund, ((202) 623-7000), 1977-.

Data on revenues, grants, expenditures, leadings minus repayments, and financing are presented for more than 100 countries. For each country, statistical tables, institutional tables, and information sources are presented. World tables are also included. Also available in machine-readable form. from Publications Section, IMF, Washington, D.C. 20431; available online from The WEFA Group.

Guide to Official Statistics. No. 6. London, Central Statistical Office, 1989.

This guide identifies and describes some 2,500 sources of official United Kingdom statistics published during the last ten years. Coverage not only includes regular publications, but also special reports, articles, etc. Sources are arranged by subject, and an alphabetical index, bibliography, and list of government contacts are provided. *Government Statistics: A Brief Guide to Sources* is published annually and may be obtained from: Central Statistical Office, Great George Street, London SW1P 3AQ, England. *Statistical News*, available from the same office, is published quarterly.

Guide to Petroleum Statistical Information. New York, American Petroleum Institute, ((212) 366-4040).

Lists and describes recurring statistical features in such publications as *Bulletin De L'Industrie Petroliere, Oil and Gas Journal*, and *Platt's Oilgram News.* A subject guide is included as well as examples of each of the tables.

Handbook of International Economic Statistics. Washington, D.C., Central Intelligence Agency, ((703) 351-2053), 1945-. (Annual).

Provides basic statistics for comparing worldwide economic performance. Topics include environmental issues, labor force and labor costs, energy, agriculture, minerals and metals, chemicals and manufactured goods, and foreign trade and aid. A subject index and conversion factors are provided.

Historically Planned Economies: A Guide to the Data. Washington, D.C., World Bank Publications, ((202) 473-1155), 1993.

A guide to the socioeconomic data on centrally planned economies, as well as economies in transition to a market system. Detailed data are presented for 17 Historically Planned Economies, and data for 35 other economies are included in the Global Tables for comparison. Data in the country tables are presented as annual time series covering 1970-1990. Most data in the Global Tables are presented for 1970, 1980, and 1990.

Joan M. Harvey. *Statistics Europe: Sources for Economic, Social, and Market Research.* 5th ed. Beckenham, Kent, England, CBD Research Ltd. (Available from Gale Research Inc. (800) 877-GALE), 1987.

Sources of statistics for European countries including Turkey and the U.S.S.R. listed in this publication include national government agencies, international organizations, trade associations, and research institutes. Statistical sources pertaining to agricultural production, industrial production, external and internal trade, internal distribution, population, and standard of living are included. Descriptions include frequency of publication, pagination, time lag, language, and subject coverage.

Index to International Statistics. Bethesda, Maryland, Congressional Information Service, ((800) 638-8380), 1983-.

A guide to statistics from more than 90 international governmental organizations (IGOs) including various United Nations bodies. Abstracts describe publications and data, and entries are extensively indexed. Published monthly with an annual cumulation. Most publications and data are available on microfiche from the publisher. Also available on CD-ROM on *Statistical Masterfile* from Congressional Information Service.

Indicators of Market Size for 117 Countries. New York, Economist Intelligence Unit, ((800) 938-4685), 1981-. (Annual).

This volume provides basic and analytical market data on 131 of the world's national markets. For each country, data are provided in six categories: Key Indicators of Market Size; GDP by Activity; Demographic and Labor Force Data; Wages and Prices; Foreign Trade; and Miscellaneous Production and Consumption Data.

International Directory of Non-Official Statistical Sources. 1st ed. London, Euromonitor, ((312) 541-8024), 1990.

Information sources from countries throughout the world are profiled. Brief descriptions of more than 1,000 key business periodicals, trade association publications, economic research journals, university newspaper, statistical database newsletters, company magazines, and other nongovernment publications.

International Energy Annual. Washington, D.C., U.S. Energy Information Administration, ((202) 586-8800), 1980-. (Annual).

Statistics for over 190 countries on production, consumption, stocks, imports and exports for primary energy commodities. Prices of crude petroleum and petroleum products in selected countries is also provided.

International Financial Statistics. Washington, D.C., International Monetary Fund, ((202) 623-7000), 1948-. (Monthly).

A journal which provides a continuing statistical record of the financial status of member nations. All indicators are listed in terms on the value of the United States dollar. Tables covering such factors as exchange rates, gold prices and production, world trade, and price levels are regularly featured. The *International Financial Statistics Yearbook*, with annual data covering a thirty-year period, is issued as a supplement. In addition, *International Financial Statistics; Supplement on Countries of the Former Soviet Union* is also available. This supplement was issued in 1993. Subscription is available on tape from Publications Section, IMF, Washington, D.C. 20431; also available online from DRI/McGraw Hill, Reuters Information (Canada) Ltd., GE Information Services (GEIS), GSI-ECO, and The WEFA Group.

International Marketing Data and Statistics. London. Euromonitor, ((312) 541-8024), 1975-. (Annual).

A marketing handbook covering 153 countries in the Americas, Africa, Asia, and Australasia, and the Middle East. Deals with such topics as population, employment, labor costs, energy, ownership and consumption, tourism, and mass media. Includes an index and notes on sources. Also available on CD-ROM with *European Marketing Data and Statistics.*

Iron and Steel Statistical Yearbook. Washington, D.C., European Community Information Service. (Annual). (Available from UNIPUB (800) 274-4888).

A comprehensive outline of the yearly statistics on the Community's iron and steel industry. Includes data on employment, size of enterprises, iron and scrap balances, production of iron ore, consumption of raw materials, deliveries and receipts, external trade of scrap and ECSC products, indirect foreign trade, steel consumption, investments of the iron and steel industry, and more. Multilingual with detailed tables and charts.

George Kurian. *The New Book of World Rankings*. New York, Facts on File, ((800) 322-8755), 1991.

Provides charts with rankings of more than 200 countries. It spans over 250 categories, ranging from military expenditures to fuel prices, from crop production to birth control, from climate to crime. For each category, a standardized chart ranks each country's standing relative to others and provides the relevant data that determine the rankings.

George Kurlan, ed. *GEO-DATA: The World Geographical Encyclopedia*. Detroit, Gale Research Inc. ((800) 877-GALE), 1990.

Provides geographic and demographic data for the United States and countries of the world. For the U.S., state, county, city, and town level data are given. For other countries, country, city, and administrative division level data are provided.

Thelma Leisner. *One Hundred Years of Economic Statistics*. New York, Facts on File, ((800) 322-8755), 1990.

A presentation of comparative statistics for nine countries: United Kingdom, United States, France, Germany, Italy, Japan, Australia, Canada, and Sweden. Comparable data series are given for each country; analytical tables and charts compare the individual country data. Statistics cover such categories as national output and expenditure, personal income and profits, trade, balance of payments, finance, prices, and population.

Middle East and North Africa. London, Europa Publications. (Available from Gale Research Inc. (800) 877-GALE), 1948-. (Annual).

Countries are covered individually in chapters that include a statistical survey, as well as articles on such topics as geography, religion, and economy. Some statistical data are also presented in the general survey section.

B.R. Mitchell, ed. *International Historical Statistics Europe 1750-1988*. New York, Stockton Press, ((800) 221-2123), 1992.

This volume provides data, in easy-to-use tables, for all principal economic and social activity for European countries. The user will find statistics relating to agriculture, industry, trade, finance, labor, transportation, communication and education. *Volume Two: The Americas 1750-1988* and *Volume Three: Africa, Asia & Oceana 1750-1988* are also available.

David Mort and Leona Siddall, eds. *Sources of Unofficial UK Statistics*. Farnborough, England, Gower Publishing Company, ((802) 276-3162) in U.S., 1990.

A descriptive guide to more than 1,000 UK statistics sources including trade associations, local authorities, banks, trade unions, and many others. Includes an extensive subject index. Also available is *UK Statistics: A Guide for Business Users*.

Muller, Georg P. *Comparative World Data: A Statistical Handbook for Social Science*. Baltimore, Johns Hopkins University Press, ((800) 537-5487), 1989.

Each county has its own table for each of the 45 socioeconomic and political variables covered. To make comparisons feasible the data are presented in comparable units. A chapter outlines ways to use the data and another provides international summary data. Data is also available on diskettes.

Ruth A. Pagell and Michael Halprin, eds. *International Business Information, How To Find It, How To Use It*. Phoenix, Oryx Press, ((800) 279-ORYX), 1994.

All major business environments outside the U.S. are covered in this comprehensive resource, including special coverage of the most recent sources on Eastern Europe, the former Soviet Union, and Asia. A wealth of electronic and print sources for information about companies, industries, markets, and finance.

B.P. Pockney, ed. *Soviet Statistics Since 1950*. New York, Saint Martin's Press, ((800) 817-2525), 1991.

Provides statistics on social and economic indicators in the Soviet Union. Statistical tables are organized into five main chapters: population and labor, industry, energy, agriculture, and foreign trade.

Population Index. Princeton, New Jersey, Office of Population Research, Princeton University and the Population Association of America, ((609) 258-4873), 1935-. (Quarterly).

This publication is an annotated bibliography of book and periodical literature on all phases of population problems. Arranged by class with annual cumulated indexes by author and country. Includes special articles and current items. Arrangement is by authors and geographic areas. Also available online from John Hopkins University, Center for Communication Programs (800) 638-8480, on POPLINE.

Marlita Reddy, ed. *Statistical Abstract of the World*, 1st ed. Detroit, Gale Research Inc., ((800) 877-GALE), 1994.

Provides statistical facts on a wide array of subjects from nearly 200 countries. Subjects include labor, employment and occupations, income, expenditure and wealth, population, health and medical care, education, law enforcement, environment, energy, geography, politics and government, and more.

Retail Trade International. London, Euromonitor, ((312) 541-8024), 1994.

Statistical data on retail distribution for 50 countries are provided. For each country, introductory profiles, retail sales figures, leading retailers, and other related statistics are given.

John L. Scherer, ed. *USSR Facts & Figures Annual*. Gulf Breeze, Florida, Academic International Press, 1977-. (Annual).

Presents an extensive range of social and economic data on topics such as government, party, armed forces, economy, foreign trade, and transportation. Contains both narrative and tabular information.

Linda Schmittroth, ed. *Statistical Record of Women Worldwide*, 2nd ed. Detroit, Gale Research Inc., ((800) 877-GALE), 1993.

Offers some 814 tables treating broad and then narrower topics. About half the data deals with the U.S., often covering the period from 1970 on. Can be used effectively along with the United

Nation's publication, *The World's Women 1970-1990* which analyzes data and presents it as indicators that show the status of women in different countries.

Paul S. Shoup. *The East European and Soviet Data Handbook: Political, Social, and Developmental Indicators, 1945-1975.* New York, Columbia University Press, ((212) 316-7100), 1981.

Presents basic social science data on both Eastern Europe and the Soviet Union. Covers such topics as population, party membership, national and religious affiliations, educational attainment, and occupations.

Victor Showers. *World Facts and Figures.* 3rd ed. New York, John Wiley & Sons, ((800) 225-5945), 1989.

Updated and expanded edition of work last issued in 1979. Tables with data on countries and cities take up the first part of the book. The country-comparisons section offers data on 50 countries in rank order, while the tables with comparative data on geographic features occupy the latter part of the volume. A 12 page bibliography lists 258 sources the compiler considers most useful.

Sources of European Economic and Business. Farnborough, England, Gower Publishing Company, ((802) 276-3162 in U.S.), 1993.

A guide to sources of economic and business data for Western European countries. More than 2,000 entries for statistical bulletins, yearbooks, general publications, directories, special supplements and reports. A title list, subject index, and addresses and telephone numbers of publishing bodies are included.

South America, Central America, and the Caribbean. London, Europa Publications. (Available from Gale Research Inc.). (Annual).

Similar to other Europa regional guides, this volume provides detailed statistics and directories for major countries of the region.

Statesman's Yearbook. London, Macmillan, ((800) 221-7945 in U.S.), 1864-. (Annual).

A primary statistical summary of the countries of the world. Separate sections for the international organizations, British Commonwealth, and the United States of America; other countries arranged alphabetically, with constitution and government (including national flag and anthem), area, population, religion, education, justice, social welfare, finance, defense, agriculture, post and telegraph, planning, transportation, industry, commerce, communications, money, diplomatic representatives, and valuable bibliography for each country (statistical, official, and unofficial publications).

Statistical Bulletin of the OAS. Washington, D.C., Organization of American States, ((202) 458-3533), 1979-. (Semi-annual).

Includes a synthesis of economic performance in Latin America for the period, regional tables on topics ranging from demographic trends to public finances, and country tables.

Statistics Canada Catalogue. Ottawa, Statistics Canada, ((800) 267-6677). (Annual).

This publication lists and in many cases annotates current statistical documents available from the Canadian government. Publications are presented in broad subject categories with a title, subject, and commodity index following. The *Historical Catalogue of Statistics Canada Publications 1918-1980*, is also available. The catalogue notes the availability of data tapes and other non-print products. An online database of data from Statistics Canada programs, CANSIM, is available from DRI/McGraw Hill, Reuters Information Services, Canada, Ltd., or The WEFA Group.

Statistics Canada Index. Toronto, Micromedia Limited, ((416) 362-5211). Annual.

A reference volume containing indexes and abstracts of statistical publications from across Canada. CD ROM products include: *STATCAN: Selected Data Disc* and *STATCAN: Reference Disc.* Full details on these services as well as microfiche copies of any *Statistics Canada* publication from 1850 to date is available from Micromedia Limited, 20 Victoria Street, Toronto, Ontario, M5C 2N8, Canada.

John M. Stopford, et al. *World Directory of Multinational Enterprises.* 2nd ed. London, Macmillan, ((800) 858-7674 in U.S.), 1982-83.

Contains detailed information on 550 multinational corporations. In addition to corporate profiles, five year financial summaries provide data on sales, profits, operating statistics and many other related topics. Comparative statistical tables rank multinationals by sales, diversification, and other measures.

Hsueh Tien-tung, Li Qiang, and Liu Shuchens, eds. *China's Provincial Statistics, 1949-1989.* Boulder, Colorado, Westview Press, ((303) 444-3541), 1993.

This publication provides economic and social statistics. Data is gathered into 15 categories: income, investment, consumption, finance, labor, population, agriculture, industry, transport, domestic and foreign trade, prices, education, environment, and social factors. These categories are further divided by approximately 100 economic and social variables, and sources are given for each tabulation.

Tourism: Annual Statistics. Washington, D.C., European Community Information Service. (Annual). (Available from UNIPUB (800) 274-4888).

Contains statistical data on tourism in the European Community including figures on tourist accommodation by category and capacity, arrivals and overnight stays of resident and non-resident visitors, specific data on employment activities and tourist costs, as well as pertinent information on the balance of payment headings for travel and passenger transport.

Transport Annual Statistics. Washington, D.C., European Community Information Service. (Annual). (Available from UNIPUB (800) 274-4888).

Contains the most important figures on transport statistics for the EEC and its member states in time-series. It includes data for infrastructure, mobile equipment, the distances covered by various modes of transport, and selected data for traffic accidents and post telecommunications.

United Kingdom Statistical Sources. 4th Ed. London, The Library Association, 1985.

This selection guide for libraries provides an excellent overview of United Kingdom Statistical Sources. Recommendations are given for a basic minimum collection of UK sources (primarily those published by the Central Statistical Office) as well as for an extended list of more specialized sources in over a dozen subject areas ranging from agriculture to public finance.

USA/USSR: Facts and Figures. Washington, D.C., U.S. Bureau of the Census and Information-Publication Center, State Committee on Statistics of the U.S.S.R. ((301) 763-4100), 1991.

This volume includes information on population, social statistics, labor force and employment, industry, energy, agriculture, transportation, and consumer goods. Differences in comparability of the data are explained in introductory and table notes. *Supplement to USA/USSR: Facts and Figures: Selected Materials on the Regions of the Soviet Union*, published in October 1991, provides a selection of Soviet regional data compiled by the U.S. Bureau of the Census. The supplement was published in recognition of the upheaval and changes occurring in the Soviet Union at that time.

Vienna Institute for Comparative Economic Studies, ed. *COMECON Data.* Westport, Connecticut, Greenwood Publishing Group, ((203) 226-3571), 1990.

Provides a variety of economic data on Eastern European countries. Data are derived from more than 50 statistical yearbooks and similar publications.

Western Europe. London, Europa Publications. (Available from Gale Research Inc., (800) 877-GALE), 1993.

This reference work provides analytical surveys of the Western European countries and territories. Includes important statistics, socio-economic trends, industry and energy policies, and integration.

Gloria Westfall, ed. *Guide to Official Publications of Foreign Countries.* Bethesda, Maryland, Congressional Information Service, ((800) 638-8380), 1990.

Identifies publications of most foreign countries along with a brief abstract of the publication. Each entry contains the name and address of the distributing agency or vendor and includes information on acquiring publications in microform

James W. Wilkie, and Stephen Haber, eds. *Statistical Abstract of Latin America.* Los Angeles, U.C.L.A. Latin America Center Publications, ((310) 825-6634), 1955-. (Annual).

Statistics are presented primarily in tabular form covering the following topic areas: Main indicators; geographical, social, socioeconomic, and economic data; international statistics; and political data. A subject index and list of sources are provided.

World Agricultural Supply and Demand Estimates. Washington, D.C., U.S. Department of Agriculture, Economic Research Service, ((202) 219-0515). (Monthly).

Provides the most current USDA information on global supply use balances of the major grains, soybeans and products, cotton and U.S. supply and use of livestock products.

World Bank Atlas. Washington, D.C., World Bank, ((202) 473-1155), 1966-. (Annual).

Provides estimates of population, GNP, and average annual growth rates for 184 countries, and territories by continent. Material is presented by a combination of tables and maps.

World Debt Tables: External Debt of Developing Countries. Washington, D.C., World Bank, ((202) 473-1155), 1973-. (Annual with periodic supplements).

Provides data on the external debt of more than 100 developing countries augmented by information, where available, on major economic aggregates plus indicators used to analyze debt and credit worthiness. Shows statistical tables by country, including figures for external public debt outstanding, commitments, disbursements, service payments, and net borrowings. Published in two volumes: *Analysis and Summary Tables* and *Country Tables.* A briefer version is available entitled *Coping With External Debt in the 1980's: Current Trends and Prospects.* The main volumes are also available on computer tape and diskette. Online access is available from Reuters Information Services, Canada, Ltd., and The WEFA Group.

World Development Report. New York, Oxford University Press (published for the International Bank for Reconstruction and Development, and the World Bank), ((202) 473-1155), 1978-. (Annual).

Narrative, graphic, and tabular presentations are used to provide a review of world development trends and issues for 126 countries. Beginning with the 1984 edition, a new *Population Data Supplement* is included covering age composition, density and capacity, fertility, status of women, and policy indicators. A statistical annex to the *Report, World Development Indicators*, is also available on diskette. The annex also includes population projections by age and sex for over 150 countries.

World Economic Data. 3rd ed. Santa Barbara, California, ABC-Clio, ((800) 422-2546), 1991.

Drawn from ABC-Clio's *Kaleidoscope: Current World Data* database, the information comes from major statistical compilations. Organized alphabetically by country. Complementary works from the same source are: *World Communication and Transportation Data*, *World Quality of Life Indicators*, and *World Defense Forces.*

World Economic Factbook. London, Euromonitor, ((312) 541-8024), 1994/95.

Provides international statistics on over 200 countries. Covers economic and demographic indicators including area, location, political structure, head of state, governing party, political risk, territorial disputes, currency, principal industries, energy requirements, balance of trade, economic situation, inflation, exchange rate, GDP, exports, imports, consumer expenditure, population, households, and tourism.

The World Factbook. Washington, D.C., Central Intelligence Agency, ((703) 351-2053), 1972-. (Annual).

Brief description oi each country of the world. Includes statistics on the land, nationality, religion, language, literacy, political parties, economy, exports and imports. Available on tape and diskette. Available commercially from Gale Research Inc. under the title *Handbook of the Nations*.

The World in Figures. 5th ed. Boston, G. K. Hall, ((617) 423-3990), 1987.

A guide to the economies of more than 200 countries, complied by *The Economist*. The first section covers world information: standard of living, population, national income, world trade, and production. Section two presents information on each country including land, climate, currency, economic, and political information. Tables, maps, and diagrams.

The World Market Atlas. 2nd ed. New York, Economist Intelligence Unit, ((800) 938-4685), 1992.

Provides over 1,700 charts, graphs and maps containing vital business and economic data on 153 countries. In two parts, Part I provides comparative statistics, and Part II offers country profiles. EIU also offers other territories of the world. They include *CIS Market Atlas (1992)*; *China Market Atlas (1992)*; *Asia Investment Flows (1992)*; *The New Latin America Market Atlas (1991)*; *Asian Market Atlas (1991)*; and *Hong Kong Market Atlas (1990)*.

World Military Expenditures and Arms Transfers. Washington, D.C., U.S. Arms Control and Disarmament Agency, ((202) 647-8677), 1994.

Projections of world military expenditures, gross national product, central government expenditures, arms transfers, imports and exports. Also includes population by region, organization, and country.

World Tables. Washington, D.C., World Bank, ((202) 473-1155), 1992. (Annual with supplement).

Data are presented for 137 bank members and Switzerland in two ways. The first are tables arranged by countries which include 21-year time series absolute values on such topics as current GNP per capita, population, domestic prices, and balance of payments. The second set of data provide ratios or growth rates grouped by topic on topics such as agriculture, industry, gross domestic product and value of merchandise exports and imports. Data are presented as annual time series covering 1969-91. Also available on computer tape and diskette.

Yearbook of Tourism Statistics. Madrid, World Tourism Organization, 19-. (Annual).

Presents data on a variety of travel topics including: international tourist arrivals; international tourism receipts and expenditures; international fare payments and receipts. Tabular data on domestic tourism is presented for major countries.

Publications of the Organisation for Economic Cooperation and Development (OECD)

OECD was established in 1961 and now has 24 member countries including European nations, Turkey, Australia, New Zealand, Japan, and the United States. It is a prolific publisher of statistics as well as research and policy studies. Many OECD statistical publications are available in more than one medium (print, fiche, and machine-readable). Several OECD databases are also available online from commercial database vendors (these are noted in the citations). For complete details on OECD statistical publications, consult OECD's annual catalog titled, *OECD Publications Catalogue*. OECD's main office is located at: 2, rue Andre-Pascal, 75775 Paris Cedex 16, France. In the U.S., contact the OECD Publications and Information Center, 2001 L Street, N.W., Suite 700, Washington, D.C. 20036-4095 (202) 785-6323. A selection of some of the more important OECD statistical resources follows.

Balances of Payments of OECD Countries: 1963-1982. Paris, Organisation for Economic Cooperation and Development, ((202) 785-6323), 1986.

Brings together the main series of individual OECD countries' balances of payments for the period and gives totals for the OECD area. Details on current invisible transactions (non-factor services, factor income and transfer payments) and on capital movements are also presented. In addition, the principal analytical concepts are explained and national sources are indicated.

Coal Information. Paris, Organisation for Economic Cooperation and Development ((202) 785-6323), 1983-. (Annual).

Provides historical data on coal supply and demand, information on coal resources and reserves, and forecasts for supply, trade, and demand. Also includes analysis of trends in coal prices, demand, trade, production, and transportation. Information on coal port facilities and coal-fired power stations is also provided. Also available on magnetic tape and diskette.

Education in OECD Countries: A Compendium of Statistical Information. Paris, Organisation for Economic Cooperation and Development, ((202) 785-6323), 1991. (Annually).

This compendium contains comparative statistics on education systems in all OECD countries. Organization charts for each country show how each country's system is structured.

Energy Statistics of OECD Countries. Paris, Organisation for Economic Cooperation and Development, ((202) 785-6323), 1961-. (Annual).

Provides a wide range of energy statistics for OECD countries. Data are provided for the most recent year. Available on diskette and magnetic tape.

Indicators of Industrial Activity. Paris, Organisation for Economic Cooperation and Development, (202) 785-6323), 1979-. (Quarterly).

Overview of short-term economic developments for all OECD countries. Includes indices of output, new orders, unfilled orders, prices and employment. Qualitative data from business tendency surveys also included. Available online from The WEFA Group, GSI-ECO, DRI-McGraw Hill, and Reuters Information Services, Canada,

Ltd. Also available on magnetic tape and diskette.

International Direct Investment Statistics Yearbook. Paris, Organisation for Economic Development, ((202) 785-6323), 1993.

Contains the first complete series of foreign direct investment statistics in a standardized format combining sectoral and geographical breakdowns for flow and stock data for all OECD countries.

Labour Force Statistics. Paris, Organisation for Economic Cooperation and Development, (202) 785-6323), 1961-. (Annual).

Contains historical time series on the evolution of the population and labor force for the OECD's twenty-four member countries. A section of general tables is provided in addition to sections for each country. Time series cover a ten-year period. Data available on magnetic tape. Quarterly supplement, *Quarterly Labour Force Statistics,* is now available, beginning with 1978. The latter is also available online from Reuters Information Services (Canada) Ltd.

Main Economic Indicators. Paris. Organisation for Economic Cooperation and Development, ((202) 785-6323), 1965-. (Monthly).

Designed to provide a picture of the most recent changes in the economics of member countries. Indicators covered include national accounts, industrial production, deliveries, stocks and orders, construction, retail sales, labor, wages, prices, home finance, interest rates, foreign finance, and balance of payments. A special section is devoted to a graphical presentation of cyclical indicators in manufacturing industries. Also available on diskette and magnetic tape. DRI/McGraw Hill, GSI-ECO, Reuters Information Services, Canada, Ltd., and FAME Software Corporation offer *Main Economic Indicators* online.

National Accounts of OECD Countries. Paris, Organisation for Economic Cooperation and Development, ((202) 785-6323), 1966-. (Annual).

A two-volume compendium of statistics on such areas as production, income, and capital transactions for OECD member countries. Data cover a twelve to twenty-year period. In English and French. Supplemented by the *Quarterly National Accounts.* Available on magnetic tape and diskette from OECD. Also available online from The WEFA Group, DRI/McGraw Hill, and Reuters Information Services (Canada) Ltd.

OECD Economic Outlook. Paris, Organisation for Economic Cooperation and Development, ((202) 785-6323), 1970-. (Biannual).

Historical and forecast data on the GNP, government accounts, fiscal and monetary indicators, labor markets, wages and prices, foreign trade and international monetary developments of the 24 member countries of the OECD. Also provides forecasts for Eastern Europe and developing countries. *OECD Economic Outlook Historical Statistics* provides historical background to the analyses and forecasts posted above. *Economic Outlook* available on diskettes from OECD and online from Reuters Information Services (Canada) Ltd. provides a wide selection of basic economic data on an annual basis for each OECD country covering the period 1975 to date and forecast data where available. A reference diskette provides similar data for the period of 1960-1975.

OECD Economic Surveys. Paris, Organisation for Economic Cooperation and Development, ((202) 785-6323), 1953-. (Annual).

Separate annual surveys of economic developments in each of the 24 OECD countries and Yugoslavia. Coverage includes demand, production, employment, prices and wages, conditions in the money and capital markets, and balance of payments.

OECD Financial Statistics. Paris, Organisation for Economic Development and Cooperation, ((202) 785-6323), 1967-. (Annual).

Beginning in 1981, this publication has a new format with the following components: (1) Monthly Financial Statistics (24 issues per year); (2) Financial Accounts (2 issues per year); (3) Non-Financial Enterprises Financial Statements (annual); and (4) Methodological Supplement (annual).

OECD Health Systems: Facts and Trends. Paris, Organisation for Economic Cooperation and Development, ((202) 785-6323), 1993.

Provides comparative health systems data for member OECD countries. On diskette OECD offers *OECD Health Data: Comparative Analysis of the Health Systems.* The database covers the period 1960 to present and includes information on demographic and health status indicators, health spending and health care financing, current medical practices, and much more.

OECD Import-Export Microtables. Paris, Organisation for Economic Cooperation and Development, ((202) 785-6323), 1980-.

Sets of computer microfiche for each country provide the most current and detailed form of foreign trade statistics available from OECD. Data are broken down by SITC number and trading partner. Published in two series: *Annual Foreign Trade Statistics by Country,* and *Trade Statistics by Commodity.* (For Series A, see *Statistics of Foreign Trade.*) Available on microfiche from OECD.

OECD Main Science and Technology Indicators. Paris, Organisation for Economic Cooperation and Development, ((202) 785-6323), 1984-. (Irregular).

Contains data on the scientific and technological performance of member countries, including final and provisional results and forecasts for governments. Topics covered include resources devoted to R&D in government, industry, education and defense; patents; technological balance of payments; and international trade and high-technology products. Available by subscription in print or on diskette.

Quarterly Oil Statistics and Energy Balances. Paris, Organisation for Economic Cooperation and Development, ((202) 785-6323), 1976-.

Provides detailed data on production of crude oil, natural gas, liquids and refinery feedstocks, crude oil and product trades, refinery data, consumption and stock levels. Annual data can be found in *Oil and Gas Information.* Available on diskette and magnetic tape. Available online from Reuters Information Services (Canada), Ltd.

Revenue Statistics of OECD Member Countries. Paris, Organisation for Economic Cooperation and Development, ((202) 785-6323), 1965-. (Annual).

Contains information on national, state, local, and social security tax revenues. Also includes analysis of tax levels and structures. Available on magnetic tape from OECD. Available online from DRI/McGraw Hill, GSI-ECO, Reuters Information Services, Canada, Ltd., The WEFA Group, and IBM Information Network Services - Europe.

The State of the Environment 1985. Paris, Organisation for Economic Cooperation and Development, ((202) 785-6323), 1985.

Analysis on the environmental resources and problems in the 24 OECD countries. Discusses government, industry, and public response to these environmental issues. Companion volume, the *OECD Environmental Data Compendium 1991* contains data on changes in the environment in the OECD Countries and governmental response to these changes.

Statistics of Foreign Trade. Paris, Organisation for Economic Cooperation and Development, ((202) 785-6323), 1959-.

Series A is *Monthly Statistics of Foreign Trade.* This presents an overall picture of trade of OECD countries including analyses by flows with countries and country groupings of origin and destination; seasonally adjusted foreign trade indicators and summary monthly tables. Subscriptions available in print or diskette. *Series C* is *Foreign Trade By Commodities.* Summary information on the value of trade flows of member countries by commodity. Five volumes are being issued annually, each with import and export data for five countries, and each having a six-year time series. The discontinued *Series B* is now available as part of the *OECD Import-Export Microtables.* Statistics are available on magnetic tape from OECD. Reuters Information Services (Canada), Ltd. offers Series A online, and series A is also available on diskette.

Publications of the United Nations and Affiliated Organizations

The United Nations publishes scores of yearbooks, specialized studies, bulletins, and other compilations of interest to statistics users. The annual *Catalogue of United Nations Publications* (United Nations Publications, Room DC2-0853, New York, NY 10017) provides a comprehensive guide to U.N. publications in print. Microfiche users should consult *United Nations Documentation in Microfiche. UNDOC: Current Index (United Nations Documentation Index)* provides monthly bibliographic coverage of U.N. documentation.

Many of the international statistics published by the United Nations are available in machine readable format. Databases are currently available for the following areas: demographics, energy, external trade, maritime transport, industry, national accounts, and women and youth. Tapes or diskettes of these data files are produced by the United Nations Statistical Office. For more information on the format and prices of these databases please write to: United Nations Publications, Sales Section, Room DC2-853, New York, New York 10017, USA or call (800) 253-9646.

Some U.N. databases are also available online from commercial vendors as noted in the individual citations below. For further information on 872 databases, consult the *Directory of United Nations Databases and Information Systems 1994.*

The following section covers many of the more important U.N. statistical publications.

African Statistical Yearbook. New York, United Nations, Economic Commission for Africa, ((800) 253-9646). (Biennial).

Published in different volumes and parts covering the following regions: Central Africa and other African countries, East and Southern Africa, North Africa, and West Africa. Data are arranged on a country basis for 52 countries and cover statistics on population and employment, national accounts, agriculture, forestry and fishing, industry, transport and communications, foreign trade, prices, finance, and social statistics.

Agricultural Review for Europe. New York, United Nations, 1958-. (Annual). (Available from UNIPUB (800) 274-4888).

Provides all types of data on European dairy, meat, grain, and produce industries. Formerly titled *Review of the Agricultural Situation in Europe.*

Annual Bulletin of General Energy Statistics for Europe. Geneva, Economic Commission for Europe, 1968-. (Annual). (Available from UNIPUB (800) 274-4888).

Provides basic data on the energy situation as a whole as well as details on the production of energy by form, overall energy balance sheets, deliveries of petroleum products for inland consumption, liquid fuel and nuclear, hydro and geo-thermal energy. Not only covers European countries but also Canada and the United States since there is no separate regional economic commission for North America.

Annual Bulletin of Steel Statistics for Europe. New York, United Nations, (Annual). (Available from UNIPUB (800) 274-4888).

Presents pertinent data on the development of steel production and trade, consumption and trade of raw materials, movements of scrap, consumption of energy in the steel industry and steel deliveries to consuming industries in the European countries, the United States, and Japan. Data on iron ore, crude steel, pig-iron, and metallurgical coke is provided as well.

Annual Bulletin of Transport Statistics for Europe. New York, United Nations, ((800) 253-9646).

Statistics and brief studies on transport plus tables on energy consumption for transport are included. Data covers Europe, Canada, and the U.S.

Civil Aviation Statistics of the World. Montreal, International Civil Aviation Organization, ((514) 285-8219), 1975-.

Summary data on civil aviation are reported. More detailed data can be found in ICAO's *Digest of Statistics.*

Commodity Balance Statistics Database. Vienna, Austria, United Nations Industrial Development Organization (UNIDO).

Available on tape or diskette this database contains more than 404,000 record lines. Each record line includes data for one country, year, and four variables (production, imports, exports, apparent consumption) according to the International Standard Industrial Classification (ISIC) code.

Commodity Trade Statistics. New York, United Nations, Department for Economic and Social Information and Policy Analysis, ((800) 253-9646), 1951-. (Annual).

Issued in parts, each of which provides import and export statistics for particular countries on a worldwide basis. Available online from Reuters Information Services, Canada, Ltd.

Compendium of Human Settlement Statistics. New York, United Nations, ((800) 253-9646), 1974-. (Irregular).

Based on national housing censuses and other surveys, data are presented for more than 150 countries or areas. Categories include population, dwelling construction, costs of housing and building, land use and environmental pollution.

Compendium of Social Statistics and Indicators. New York, United Nations, ((800) 253-9646), 1991-. (Irregular).

Comprises basic statistical indicators required for describing the major aspects of the social situation in the world and the regions, as well as changes and trends in the levels of living. Sections include: Population and Vital Statistics, Health Conditions, Food Consumption and Nutrition, Housing, Education and Cultural Activities, Labour Force and Conditions of Employment, Income and Expenditure, and Consumer Prices.

Construction Statistics Yearbook. New York, United Nations, ((800) 253-9646), 1974-1985.

A variety of dwelling construction statistics are provided for 135 countries. Data provided for a ten-year period cover such topics as general indicators, permits authorized, and construction projects completed.

Country Tables - Basic Data on the Agriculture Sector. Rome, United Nations Food and Agriculture Organization, (Available from UNIPUP (800) 274-4888). (Annual).

Provides food and agricultural commodity data for FAO countries.

Demographic Yearbook. New York, United Nations, 1949-. (Annual). (Available from UNIPUB (800) 274-4888).

A central source for demographic data from approximately 220 countries. Topics center around population changes throughout the world: rate of increase, birth and death rates, population by sex, urban population, international migration, marriage and divorce. Divided into two sections: an annual World Summary: and Special Topic Tables (in the most recent edition these included abortions, infant and fetal deaths, and life expectancy). A separate 30th Anniversary issue provides historical time series for the first 30 years of the *Yearbook's* publication. An online database, *U.N. Demographics*, is available from The WEFA Group and GE Information Services (GEIS).

Directory of United Nations Databases and Information Services, 5th ed. New York, United Nations, ((800) 253-9646), 1994.

Provides detailed description of selected services, including statistical programs offering computerized, numeric, and factual databases.

Disability Statistics Compendium. New York, United Nations, ((800) 253-9646), 1990.

Based on national statistics available in DISTAT, United Nations Disability Statistics Data Base, this first international compendium of disability statistics provides detailed national data from 55 countries. The 12 major topics covering disabled persons include age, sex, residence, educational attainment, economic activity, marital status, household characteristics, causes of impairment, and special aids used.

Economic Survey of Europe. New York, United Nations. (Annual). (Available from UNIPUB (800) 274-4888).

An internationally recognized economic report covering a wide range of research, recording the changing patterns of trade and output in Europe, Canada and the United States.

Energy Statistics Yearbook. New York, United Nations, 1952-. (Annual). (Available from UNIPUB (800) 274-4888).

The first five tables of this volume present an historical view of world and regional production and consumption of commercial energy in coal, oil, and joule equivalents, in index number form and as a percentage of total consumption for the years 1955-1979. The next five tables provide a similar ten-year series for individual countries. Additional tables cover data for the most recent ten-year period for individual commodities for world regions and countries. Updated production figures are included in the *Monthly Bulletin of Statistics.*

Foreign Trade Statistics for Africa. New York, United Nations, ((800) 253-9646). (Annual).

Statistical data providing details for overall trade, trade between nations, regional trade and specific product information.

Foreign Trade Statistics of Asia and the Pacific. New York, United Nations, ((800) 253-9646). 1987.

Contains statistics on import-export trade in the Asian-Oceanic region for 1983-1987. Tables give data for overall trade, trade between countries, intraregional trade and major specific products.

Handbook of Industrial Statistics. Vienna, UNIDO (Biennial). (Available from Edward Elgar Publishing Company (800) 535-9544).

Presents internationally comparable statistics for over 120 countries, 28 industries and more than 100 manufactured commodities. The data appearing in the Handbook have been collected from both national and international sources and supplemented through field work by UNIDO statisticians.

Handbook of International Trade and Development Statistics. New York, United Nations Conference on Trade and Development (UNCTAD) ((800) 253-9646), 1969-. (Irregular).

Handbook editions and supplements provide a complete basic collection of statistical data relevant to the analysis of world trade and development.

Industrial Property Statistics. Geneva, Switzerland, World Intellectual Property Organization (WIPO), 1989.

Industrial property statistics based on information supplied by the industrial property offices of the world. Issued in two volumes. Part one consists of patents and similar industrial property rights. Part two consists of trademarks and service marks, utility models, industrial designs, varieties of plants, and microorganisms.

Industrial Statistics Yearbook. New York, United Nations, 1950-. (Annual). (Available from UNIPUB (800) 274-4888).

Volume 1, *General Industrial Statistics*, provides basic country data, as well as indicators showing the global and regional trends in industrial activity. Volume 2, *Commodity Production Data*, gives statistics for more than 500 industrial commodities and 200 countries. For both volumes, data usually cover a ten-year period. Available online from General Electric Information Services Co. (GEISCO).

International Sea-Borne Trade Statistics Yearbook. New York, United Nations, ((800) 253-9646), 1950-1986.

Gives data on international sea trade statistics so as to yield aggregates that are useful to those who seek to assess the pattern of goods which flow on important world-wide sea lanes.

International Trade Statistics Yearbook. New York, United Nations, 1950-. (Annual). (Available from UNIPUB (800) 274-4888).

Statistical tables show for each country of the world the quantity and value of exports and imports of various commodities over the past several years. Other tables show for each country the value of its total exports and imports with every other country over the past five years. Broken into two volumes: Volume 1, *Trade by Country*, and Volume 2, *Trade by Commodity, Commodity Matrix Tables*.

Monthly Bulletin of Statistics. New York, United Nations, ((800) 253-9646), 1947-. (Monthly).

World economic statistics by country. Covers population, manpower, forestry, industrial production, mining, transportation, internal and external trade, wages and prices, national income, and finance. Provides current economic and social data for many of the tables published in the *United Nations Statistical Yearbook*.

Monthly Commodity Price Bulletin. Geneva, United Nations, ((800) 253-9646), 1969-. (Monthly).

Contains tables and graphs with monthly and average annual prices for all types of commodities including agricultural commodities, minerals, and metals.

National Accounts Statistics. New York, United Nations, 1957-. (Annual). (Available from UNIPUB (800) 274-4888).

Country estimates are shown for 159 countries for expenditure of gross national product, industrial origin of gross domestic product, distribution of the national income, finance of gross domestic capital formation, private consumption data, and government revenue and expenditures. Published in two volumes: Volume 1, *Main Aggregates and Detailed Tables*; and Volume 2, *Analysis of Main Aggregates*. The *United Nations National Account Database* is available online from General Electric Information Services Co. (GEISCO).

Population and Vital Statistics Report. New York, United Nations, ((800) 253-9646), 1949-. (Quarterly).

Population and vital statistics for over 200 countries and areas of the world are covered. Provides latest census data plus worldwide demographic statistics on birth and mortality.

Production Yearbook. Rome, United Nations Food and Agriculture Organization, 1947-. (Annual). (Available from UNIPUB (800) 274-4888).

This publication contains about 225 tables which contain annual data on all important aspects of food and agriculture, including population, index numbers of agricultural and of food production, food supplies, means of production, prices, freight rates, and wages throughout the world. Where no official or semi-official figures are available from countries, estimates are made by FAO on area and production of major crops, livestock and products. Tables are in English, French, or Spanish. Data are also available on computer tape. For more information write to the Computer Systems Branch, Management Services Division, FAO, Via delle Terme di Caracalla, 00100 Rome, Italy.

STATBASE Locator on Disk: UNSTAT'S Guide to International Computerized Statistical Databases: World Statistics in Brief-Special Issue. New York, United Nations, ((800) 253-9646), 1994.

Available in diskette format, this locator provides the means to finding international computerized statistical databases that offer access to statistical information. It offers a description of the database, information on access available, access keys, subject areas, classification system used, span of data, update frequency and annual increase in size of the database. The databases covered are maintained by the United Nations, United Nations Agencies, and affiliated or other international organizations.

The State of Food and Agriculture. Rome, United Nations Food and Agriculture Organization, 1947-. (Annual). (Available from UNIPUB (800) 274-4888).

A narrative and statistical review of the year in food, agriculture and related areas such as forestry and fisheries. Emphasis is on developing countries.

Statistical Indicators of Short-Term Economic Changes in ECE Countries. New York, United Nations, ((800) 253-9646), 1959-. (Monthly).

Provides an up-to-date overall picture of short-term economic trends in Europe, Canada, and the United States.

Statistical Yearbook for Asia and the Pacific. Bangkok, United Nations, Economic and Social Commission for Asia and the Pacific (ESCAP), ((800) 253-9646), 1973-. (Annual).

Provides current and retrospective statistical data on economic, demographic, agricultural, and social conditions in countries of the Near and Far Eastern Asian regions. Data are in both English and French. Supplemented by *Quarterly Bulletin of Statistics for Asia and the Pacific*, and *Statistical Indicators for Asia and the Pacific* (issued several times each year).

Statistical Yearbook for Latin America and the Caribbean. New York, United Nations, ((800) 253-9646), 1975-. (Annual).

Provides statistical series for the overall region as well as subregions in the area. In addition, statistical series are presented for each country covering population, national accounts, agriculture, industry, transport, external trade, prices, balance of payments, and social statistics.

Statistical Indicators for Asia and the Pacific. New York, United Nations, ((800) 253-9646). (Annual).

Published in several parts and volumes each year. The data afford the statistical evidence for assessing demographic and economic trends in the region.

Statistics and Indicators on Women in Africa. New York, United Nations, ((800) 253-9646), 1989.

Offers data for 52 countries or areas in Africa with tables on population, households and families, education and literacy, health and health services, housing conditions, criminal justice and other types of data relating to women and women's concerns.

Trade Yearbook. Rome, United Nations Food and Agriculture Organization, 1947-. (Annual). (Available from UNIPUB (800) 274-4888).

This publication contains a large number of tables which show both quantities and values of trade for different agricultural commodities and agricultural requisites throughout the world. Beginning with the 1976 issue, fishery products and forestry import/export values have been included. Data are also available on computer tape. For further information, contact the Computer Systems Branch, Management Services Division, FAO, Via delle Terme di Caracalla, 00100 Rome, Italy. Where meaningful summation of quantities is possible, summary tables are also shown. In an effort to make coverage as complete as possible, official trade data have sometimes been supplemented.

UNCTAD Commodity Yearbook. New York, United Nations Conference on Trade and Development (UNCTAD), ((800) 253-9646), 1984-. (Annual).

Provides statistical data at the regional and country levels for trade in selected commodities including: agricultural primary commodities, minerals, ores, and metals. An online database, *United Nations Commodity Trade Statistics*, is available from Reuters Information Systems (Canada), Ltd.

UNCTAD Statistical Pocket Book. Geneva, United Nations Commission on Trade and Development, ((800) 253-9646), 1984.

Provides a variety of data on trade and development including basic development indicators for developing countries.

UNESCO Statistical Yearbook. Paris, United Nations Educational, Scientific and Cultural Organization, 1963-. (Annual). (Available from UNIPUB (800) 274-4888).

This work contains tables grouped according to various subjects: population, education, science and technology, libraries and museums, book production, newspapers and other periodicals, paper consumption, film and cinema, radio broadcasting, television and cultural expenditure. The information it contains has been supplied by over 200 countries or territories in reply to UNESCO questionnaires, as well as from official reports and publications. In English, French and Spanish. A briefer publication, the *Statistical Digest*, is also available (1981-).

United Nations Statistical Yearbook. New York, United Nations, ((800) 253-9646), 1949-. (Annual).

This publication has a worldwide coverage of statistics in categories such as population, manpower, agriculture, forestry, fishing, industrial production, mining and quarrying, manufacturing, construction, energy, internal trade, external trade, transport, communications, consumption, balance of payments, wages and prices, national accounts, finance, public finance, development assistance, housing, health, education, science and technology, and culture. Conversion coefficients and factors, country nomenclature, and a county index are provided. Also available on CD-ROM. Beginning in 1976, *World Statistics in Brief* is also available.

United Nations Women's Indicators and Statistics Database On Microcomputer Diskettes (WISTAT): Version 2: (Machine Readable Datafiles), 1991. New York, United Nations, ((800) 253-9646).

Provides access to a variety of women's issues including population composition and distribution; learning and educational services; economic activity; households, marital status and fertility; housing conditions and human settlements; health and health services; public affairs and political participation; crime and criminal justice; and national product and expenditure.

World Economic Survey. New York, United Nations, 1948-. (Annual). (Available from UNIPUB (800) 274-4888).

A comprehensive annual review and analysis of world economic conditions and trends. Basic data are taken chiefly from published governmental or intergovernmental sources, or as officially reported to the United Nations. Includes separate studies on developing economies, developed market economies, and centrally planned economies.

World Health Statistics Annual. Geneva, World Health Organization, 1969-.

This publication is a continuation of a series of publications, the *Annual Epidemiological and Vital Statistics*, published since 1939. It is a result of a joint effort by national health and statistical administrations of various countries, the Statistical Office of the United Nations and the World Health Organization. It consists of three parts: Volume I, *Vital Statistics and Causes of Death*; Volume II, *Infectious Diseases*: *Cases and Deaths*; and Volume III, *Health Personnel and Hospital Establishments*. Supplemented on a quarterly basis by *World Health Statistics Quarterly.*

World Statistics in Brief: United Nations Statistical Pocketbook. New York, United Nations, ((800) 253-9646). (Biennial).

Intended as a convenient ready source of statistical data. Covers demography, labor force, national accounts, agriculture and industry, trade, finance, tourism, transport and communication, education, health and nutrition. Data is given for 159 countries, by regions and for the world as a whole, for the last decade.

Yearbook of Fishery Statistics. Rome, United Nations Food and Agriculture Organization, 1947-. (Annual). (Available from UNIPUB (800) 274-4888).

Data on catches and landings are shown by countries and by species items according to major inland and marine fishing areas.

Yearbook of Forest Products. Rome, United Nations Food and Agriculture Organization, 1947-. (Annual). (Available from UNIPUB (800) 274-4888).

Arranged in three sections. Part 1 provides data on volume of production and volume and value of trade. Part 2 deals with the direction of trade. Part 3 shows unit value in trade for selected commodities. Data are shown for up to an eleven-year period. Available on computer tape from Computer Systems Branch, Management Services Division, FAO, Via delle Terme di Caracalla, 00100 Rome, Italy.

Yearbook of Labour Statistics. Geneva, International Labour Office, 1950-. (Annual). (Available from UNIPUB (800) 274-4888).

Statistical data from more than 180 countries and territories are provided on such subjects as population, employment, hours of work, wages, consumer prices, household budgets, industrial accidents, industrial disputes and exchange rates. An index of countries, territories, and areas is provided. The *Yearbook* is supplemented by the *Bulletin of Labour Statistics*, published quarterly with eight supplements. A technical guide, *Statistical Sources and Methods*, is also available. All information is given in English, French and Spanish.

STATISTICAL DATABASES ONLINE

There are literally hundreds of commercially available online databases of interest to statistics users. These are described, along with thousands of other databases, in the sources listed below under "Guides to Online Databases". Because excellent coverage of online databases is readily available in these guides, we have limited our specific database coverage in "Selected Online Statistical Databases" to capsule descriptions of a small, representative sampling of key statistical files featuring either U.S. or international statistics. However, because the list of currently available online databases is constantly changing, it is perhaps even more important to be aware of the major commercial vendors of online statistical databases. These are described in the "Selected Vendors of Online Statistical Databases" part of this section.

Note: There seems to be no consensus (at least in common usage) as to whether the term "database" should be written as one word or two. We have chosen to use the single-word form but have preserved the alternate form when used in the names/titles of the sources described in this section.

Guides to Online Data Bases

Data Base Directory. White Plains, New York, Knowledge Industry Publications, ((914) 328-9157), 1984-. (Biannual).

Provides information on more than 2,600 online data bases generated by producers worldwide. Available in both print and electronic form. Supplemented by the monthly *Data Base Alert*. Available online from BRS Information Technologies, Inc. under title "KIPD."

Kathleen Young Maraccio, ed. *Gale Directory of Databases*. Detroit, Gale Research Inc., ((800) 877-GALE), 1994.

Profiles nearly 9,075 databases available in a variety of electronic formats. Published in two volumes each January and July. Volume One describes over 5,300 online databases; Volume Two covers over 3,765 CD-ROM, diskette, magnetic tape, batch access and hand-held print products. In addition, this title is available on diskette, magnetic tape, online, or CD-ROM.

Annette Novallo, ed. *Information Industry Directory*. 15th ed. Detroit, Gale Research Inc., ((800) 877-GALE), 1995.

This guide includes many organizations that provide computerized statistical services. Citations describe each system and service and provide information on scope-subject, input sources, holdings and storage media, publications, and computer-based products and services. Published in two volumes: Descriptive Listings and Indexes. This title is also available on diskettes or magnetic tape.

Selected Online Statistical Databases

American Statistics Index (ASI)

ASI provides abstracts of U.S. Federal Government statistical publications dating back to 1970. Abstracts contain some time series and statistical data as well as descriptions of source publications. ASI corresponds to the printed publication as well as CD-ROM of the same name, produced by Congressional Information Service. Available from Dialog Information Services, Inc.

CANSIM

A computerized information system for socioeconomic time series and multidimensional data acquired from Statistics Canada and other governmental and private sources. Produced by Statistics Canada and available from The WEFA Group, Analyste-Conseil Systeme Informatique Ltd., DRI/McGraw Hill, Reuters Information Services (Canada) Ltd., as well as Statistics Canada.

CENDATA

CENDATA offers current U.S. economic and demographic data as well as historical time series dating back to 1970. *CENDATA* is produced by the U.S. Bureau of the Census and is derived from a variety of Bureau publications. Available from Dialog Information Services, Inc. and CompuServe Information Service.

CITIBASE

CITIBASE provides broad coverage of U.S. economic statistics dating back to 1947. The file includes finance, prices, industrial production, labor statistics, and other economic categories. Related databases are *CITIBASE-Weekly* and *CITIBASE Daily*. Citibase is produced by FAME Software Corporation and is available from GE Information Services, Reuters Information Services (Canada) Ltd., FAME Software Corporation, NEEDS, CompuServe Information Service, and The Conference Board of Canada. Also available on diskette and magnetic tape.

CLUSTERPLUS

A demographic retrieval and report generation system that contains data from the 1980 and 1990 Census of Population and Housing and current-year estimates. Produced by Strategic Mapping, Inc. and available through the SMI CONQUEST Consumer Marketing System. Also available on CD-ROM.

COMEXT

Contains statistical data on the European Communities external trade as well as between EEC member countries. Produced by the Statistical Office of the European Communities (EUROSTAT) and Commission of the European Communities (CES), and available from The WEFA Group. Also available on diskette and magnetic tape.

COMPUSTAT

Contains financial and statistical information on more than 7,000 major New York Stock Exchange, American Stock Exchange, and over-the-counter companies. Produced by Standard & Poor's Compustat Services, Inc. and available online by a number of hosts, including ADP Network Services, Inc., CompuServe Information Service, Interactive Data Corporation, and Vestek Systems, Inc.

Consumer and Producer Price Indexes (CPI/PPI)

Produced by the U.S. Bureau of Labor Statistics, *CPI* contains time series on average changes in prices over time of a fixed market basket of goods and services. *CPI* provides breakdowns by geographic location and broad population categories as well as indexes on specific product and service groups. Available from ADP Network Services Inc., The WEFA Group, Reuters Information Services (Canada) Ltd., and Human Resource Information Network (HRIN). Corresponds to data published in various BLS news releases and publications.

CRONOS

Provides comprehensive coverage of European macroeconomic statistics. Chronological series are presented according to standard Eurostat subject categories. Produced by the Commission of European Communities and the Statistical Office of the European Communities, and available from The WEFA Group and GSI-ECO. Also available on diskette and magnetic tape.

DRI U.S. Central

Contains U.S. economic, financial, and demographic statistics. Available from DRI/McGraw Hill.

DRI World Forecast

Contains economic, financial, and special forecasts for 46 countries covering approximately 100 concepts. Available from DRI/McGraw Hill.

Dun's Financial Records Plus

DFR provides up to three years of financial statements for more than 750,000 private and public companies. Data include information derived from balance sheets and income statements, standard business ratios, and company identification data such as SIC codes. Related D & B files include *Dun's Market Identifiers (DMI)*, *European Dun's Market Identifiers (EDMI)*, and the *Million Dollar Directory (MDD)*. Available from Dialog Information Services, Inc., Dow Jones News/Retrieval, and Information America.

ECONBASE: Time Series & Forecasts

Produced by The WEFA Group, this file provides a wide range of econometric time series as well as forecast data in such areas as demographics, finance, and manufacturing. Coverage is both domestic and international. Available from Dialog Information Services, Inc. Also available on diskette and magnetic tape.

Economist's Statistics

Produced by James R. LymBurner & Sons, Ltd. A database system that contains a wide range of economic and financial data including international commodities, currency exchange rates, international economics, and international securities. Available from LymBurner & Sons, Ltd., P. O. Box 289, Station A, Toronto, Ontario, Canada M5W 1B2 (416) 964-0789.

General Industrial Statistics

Contains approximately 17,500 annual time series for more than 100 countries on manufacturing, mining, quarrying, and public utilities. Covers labor force and employment, wages and salaries, investment, electricity consumption, output, and value added, along with industrial production indexes. Produced by the United Nations Statistical Office and available from GE Information Services (GEIS). Also available on diskette and magnetic tape.

International Financial Statistics (IFS)

Produced by the International Monetary Fund (IMF) and corresponding to the print publication of the same name, *IFS* is a basic source of economic and financial statistics on more than 150 countries. Data are provided on such topics as exchange rates, banking, production, and prices. Coverage dates back as far as 1948. Available from The WEFA Group, FAME Software Corporation, GE Information Services (GEIS), DRI/McGraw Hill, GSI-ECO, and Reuters Information Services (Canada) Ltd. Also available on CD-ROM and magnetic tape.

INTLINE

Historical macroeconomic data for more than 40 countries including the United States and Canada. Key data types include national accounts; government finance; industrial production, producer price indices; wholesale and retail sales; construction, housing starts; population; labor, wages and unemployment rates; money and banking; foreign trade, exports, imports and balance; balance of payments; and official reserves. Available from The WEFA Group. Also available on diskette and magnetic tape.

LABSTAT

This computer readable system comprises more than 200,000 data series gathered by the U.S. Bureau of Labor Statistics. Its range of coverage treats every aspect of labor including employment, unemployment, economic growth, prices, occupational safety and health. Available from the Bureau of Labor Statistics, 2 Massachusetts Avenue, NE, Washington, D.C. 20212 (202) 606-7828.

Latin America Forecast

Contains macroeconomic forecasts for Argentina, Brazil, Chile, Colombia, Ecuador, Mexico, Peru, Uruguay, and Venezuela. Covers employment indicators; exchange rates and inflation; balance of payments; exports, imports, and trade balances; industrial production; commodity prices and exports; and financial indicators. Produced by and available from WEFA Group. Also available on diskette and magnetic tape.

OECD Main Economic Indicators

Contains approximately 7,200 monthly, quarterly, and annual economic time series for the 25 OECD member countries and selected totals for North America, the European Community, OECD-Europe, and all OECD countries. Includes national income and product accounts; industrial production; stock, deliveries, and orders; labor force and employment; construction; domestic and foreign trade; interest rates; prices and wages; and balance of payments and international liquidity. Most series are available both seasonally adjusted and unadjusted. Corresponds to data in MAIN ECONOMIC INDICATORS. Produced by Organisation for Economic Cooperation and Development (OECD), Electronic Publications Service and available online from The WEFA Group, DRI/McGraw Hill, Reuters Information Services (Canada) Ltd., GSI-ECO, and FAME Software Corporation.

Predicasts Forecasts (U.S. and International)

Produced by Information Access Company, this file covers published forecasts (with historical data) for all countries of the world. Derived from more than 1,000 government, trade association and international agency sources as well as newspapers, trade journals, etc. The files correspond to *Predicasts Forecasts* and *Worldcasts*. Available from Dialog Information Services, Inc., NEXIS, and Data-Star.

SUPERSITE

Demographic data for defined areas of the United States based on the 1980 and 1990 Census of Population and Housing. Produced by CACI Marketing Systems and is available from CompuServe Information Service and DRI/McGraw Hill. Also available on diskette and magnetic tape.

SMI Demographics

Contains demographic data, current-year estimates, and 5-year projections based on the 1980 and 1990 U.S. Census of Population and Housing Data for cities, counties, states, ZIP codes, Metropolitan Statistical Areas (MSA's), Arbitron Areas of Dominant Influence (ADI's), A.C. Nielsen Designated Marketing Areas (DMA's), and the entire U.S. Produced by Strategic Mapping Inc.

TRADSTAT

Collects the official import and export figures on over 60,000 products from 23 countries for all their trading partners worldwide. Data is derived from a variety of government information sources. Produced by Data-Star and is available online from Data-Star.

U.N. Demographics

Provides historical and projected demographic data for most countries as well as regional aggregates. Demographic indicators include growth rates, birth and death rates, life expectancy, and many others. Data are given at five-year intervals for the period 1950-2025. Corresponds to the *U.N. Demographic Yearbook*. Produced by the U.N. Population Division, this database is available from The WEFA Group, and GE Information Services (GEIS).

UNIDO Industrial Statistics Database

Provides industrial data on 150 countries. The main emphasis in on employment, wages and salaries, value added, gross output and index numbers of industrial production. UNIDO is produced and made available by the United Nations Industrial Development Organization, (800) 253-9646. Also available on magnetic tape or diskette.

United Nations Commodity Trade Statistics

Provides data on trade between more than 31 reporting countries and 270 countries and groups of countries. 3,000 commodities, defined according to the Standard International Trade Classification (SITC), are covered. Derived in part from the printed source of the same name. Produced by United Nations Statistical Office, and available from Reuters Information Services Canada, Ltd.

United Nations National Accounts (UNNIA)

Detailed historical national income and product accounts for approximately 158 countries as reported by the United Nations in the *National Account Statistics: Main Aggregates and Detailed Tables*. Produced by the United Nations Statistical Office and available online from The WEFA Group and GE Information Services (GEIS).

U.S. Central Data Bank

Provides broad coverage of U.S. economic, financial, and demographic data derived from a variety of U.S. Federal Government publications. National accounts, retail trade, labor force, housing starts, and consumer credit are just a few of the many areas covered. Data ranges from 1947 to the present. Produced by, and available from, DRI/McGraw-Hill.

U.S. Economic Statistics

Contains approximately 5,800 time series on the U.S. economy. Covers the major components of gross national product, consumer and producer price indexes, import and export price indexes, housing starts, value of new construction in place, selected interest rates, plant and equipment expenditures, industrial production, capacity utilization, manufacturer's shipments, inventories and orders, and money supply. Produced by Haver Analytics and available from GE Information Services (GEIS).

U.S. Time Series

Compressed of two subfiles, *Predicasts Composites* and *Predicasts Basebook*, this database provides time series in a wide variety of subject areas. Period covered varies by time series with 1957 being the earliest beginning date. Coverage includes industrial and market activity, government, and demographics. Produced by Information Access Company and available from Dialog Information Services, Inc., NEXIS, and Data-Star.

World Debt Tables

Provides historical public and publicly guaranteed debt data for 138 developing countries and 6 regions sorted by type of creditor as reported in the World Bank Publication, *World Debt Tables*. Available from The WEFA Group, GE Information Services (GEIS), and GSI-ECO. Also available on diskette and magnetic tape.

Selected Vendors of Online Statistical Databases

ADP Network Services, Inc.
175 Jackson Plaza
Ann Arbor, MI 48106
313-769-6800
800-521-3166

ADP offers a number of U.S. and international statistical databases including: *COMPUSTAT*; *Consumer Price Index*; and *Producer Price Indexes*.

CompuServe Information Service
5000 Arlington Centre Blvd.
Columbus, OH 43220
614-457-8600
800-848-8199

CompuServe offers several databases of interest to statistics users, including: *CENDATA*; *CITIBASE*; *SUPERSITE*; and *COMPUSTAT*.

Control Data Corporation (CDC)
Business Information Services
500 W. Putnam Avenue
Greenwich, CT 06836
203-622-2000

CDC offers more than a dozen U.S. and international statistical databases, including: *EURABANK* and *Financial Institution Data Base*.

Data-Star
Haymarket House
28 Haymarket
London SW1Y 4ER England
071-930-5503

Data-Star is the European equivalent of U.S. online services such as Dialog Information Services. It offers more than 175 databases, a mixture of bibliographic, textual, and--to a lesser extent--numeric data files. Representative databases include: *TRADSTAT*; *Financial Times Abstracts Database*; *Industry Data Sources*; and *Predicasts Forecasts*.

Dialog Information Services, Inc.
3460 Hillview Avenue
Palo Alto, California 94304
415-858-3785
800-334-2564
800-387-2689 (in Canada)

Although Dialog primarily offers bibliographic and textual databases, it does make available several important statistical files including: *American Statistics Index*; *CENDATA*; *DUN's Financial Records Plus*; *ECONBASE*; and *U.S. Times Series*.

Dow Jones and Company, Inc.
P.O. Box 300
Princeton, NJ 08543-0300
609-520-4000

Dow Jones offers a variety of textual and statistical files, primarily in economics and finance. Representative databases of interest to statistics users include: *Dow Jones Futures and Index Quotes*; *Media General Financial Services*; *MMS Weekly Market Analysis*.

DRI/McGraw-Hill
24 Hartwell Avenue
Lexington, Massachusetts 02173
(617) 863-5100

Approximately 100 statistical databases are available from DRI/McGraw-Hill. Economic and financial data are emphasized with some industry-specific files available. Coverage of U.S., Canadian, and European statistics is strong, and a number of broadly international files are also available. Representative databases include: *DRI Commodities*; *DRI U.S. Central*; *Direction of Trade Statistics*; and, *OECD Main Economic Indicators*.

FAME Software Corporation
77 Water Street, 7th Floor
New York, NY 10043
212-898-7200

Offers several U.S. and international statistical databases of interest to statistics users, many produced by FAME Software Corporation. Representative databases include: *CITIBASE*; *CITIBASE Weekly*; and, *International Interest and Exchange Rate Database (FXBASE)*.

GE Information Services
401 N. Washington Street
Rockville, MD 20850
301-340-4000
800-638-9636

Offers more than twenty online statistical databases, a number of them of broad general interest. Coverage includes both U.S. and international data. Representative databases include: *CITIBASE*; *International Financial Statistics*; *World Debt Tables*; *National Accounts Statistics*; *Producer Price Indexes*; and *U.N. Demographics*.

GSI-ECO
45, rue de la Procession
F-75015 Paris, France
01 45667889

Offers a number of statistical databases including *CRONOS*; *Industrial Statistics*; *International Financial Statistics*; *OECD Indicators of Industrial Activity*; *OECD Main Economic Indicators*; *OECD Revenue Statistics*; and *World Debt Tables*.

Haver Analytics
60 East 42nd Street, Suite 620
New York, New York 10165
212-986-9300
Fax (212) 986-5857

Specializes in databases and software products for economic analysis and business decision making. Approximately 50 statistical databases are available from Haver Analytics. Representative databases of interest to statistics users include *United Nations National Accounts*; *U.S. Economic Statistics*; *U.S. Population*; and *Gross State Product*.

Reuters Information Services Canada Ltd.
Exchange Tower, Suite 1900
2 First Canadian Place
Toronto, Ontario M5X 1E3, Canada
800-387-1588
416-364-5361

Reuters Information Services Canada Ltd. is the vendor of well over 180 online statistical databases. Coverage is strongest in Australian, Canadian, U.S., and OECD statistics. Representative databases include: *Australian Export Statistics-Harmonized*; *International Financial Statistics*; *OECD Economic Outlook*; *U.S. International Air Travel Statistics*; *United Nations's Commodity Trade Statistics*; and *CITIBASE*. Economic and financial data predominate, but demographic and industrial data are also available in some databases.

The WEFA Group
401 City Line Avenue, Suite 300
Bala Cynwyd, PA 19004
215-667-6000

The WEFA Group offers more than 125 databases, most providing economic, financial, and industrial sector data. U.S., foreign country, and worldwide statistics are all covered. Representative databases include: *Annual Survey of Manufactures*; *Consumer Spending Forecast*; *Latin America Forecast*; *Middle East and Africa Forecast*; *ASIA Forecast*; *CANSIM*; and *INTLINE*.

Federal Statistical Telephone Contacts

The federal government is the most important collector, disseminator, and repository of statistical information available, covering virtually every subject on today's society. Its highly-informed cadre of subject specialists is of great potential assistance to information-seekers. In a time when those seekers are becoming more inclined to go beyond traditional published sources in their search for the most current data, federal government specialists represent a unique, but often untapped, source of information.

An inventory of the federal government's statistical information sources is listed below. First arranged under broader subject categories, the inventory is then broken down further to name precise government units or individual specialists who can be called upon for help in a specific topic area. The specialists are experienced at answering questions, and do not charge for their time or assistance. When they cannot provide the specific data sought, the specialists can often make referrals to other expert contacts with the most current statistical information available.

AGRICULTURE

The National Agricultural Statistics Service collects data on crops, livestock, poultry, dairy, chemical use, prices, and labor. Its 45 field offices can provide information about agricultural production, stocks, prices and other data on individual county, and/or state bases. The agricultural experts are listed below.

Crops, Dairy, Livestock, and Poultry

AQUACULTURE
- Robert Little (202) 720-6147
- Joel Moore (202) 720-3244
- Dave Harvey (202) 219-0085

COFFEE & TEA
- Fred Gray (202) 219-0888

COLD STORAGE
- John Lange (202) 720-0585

COTTON
- Roger Latham (202) 720-5944
- Robert Skinner (202) 219-0841
- Leslie Meyer (202) 219-0840

DAIRY PRODUCTS-Milk, Ice Cream, etc.
- Dan Buckner (202) 720-4448
- Jim Miller (202) 219-0770
- Sara Short (202) 219-0769

DRY EDIBLE BEANS
- Arvin Budge (202) 720-4285
- Gary Lucier (202) 219-0884
- Charles Plummer (202) 219-0886

FEED GRAINS-Corn, Sorghum, Barley, Oats
- Charles Van Lahr (202) 720-7369
- Thomas Tice (202) 219-0840
- Peter Riley--World (202) 219-0824
- James Cole (202) 219-0840

FLORICULTURE
- Jim Brewster (202) 720-7688
- Doyle Johnson (202) 219-0884

FOOD GRAINS-Wheat, Rice
- Vaughn Siegenthaler--Wheat (202) 720-8068
- Ed Allen--Wheat (202) 219-0841
- Dan Keretes--Rice (202) 720-9526
- Janet Livezey--Rice (202) 219-0840
- Sara Schwartz--World Wheat (202) 219-0824
- Randall Schnepf--World Rice (202) 219-0824

FRUITS & TREE NUTS
- Jim Brewster (202) 720-7688
- Kevin Hintzman (202) 720-5412
- Doyle Johnson--Tree Nuts (202) 219-0884
- Dennis Shields (202) 219-0884
- Diane Bertelsen (202) 219-0884
- Boyd Buxton (202) 219-0884

HAY
- Herb Eldridge (202) 720-7621
- Thomas Tice (202) 219-0840

Allen Baker	(202) 219-0840

HONEY

Tom Kruchten--Prod.	(202) 690-4870
Debra Kenerson--Prices	(202) 690-0270
Fred Hoff	(202) 219-0883

LIVESTOCK

Glenda Shepler--Cattle	(202) 720-3040
Ron Gustafson--Cattle & Sheep	(202) 219-1286
Tom Kurtz--Hogs	(202) 720-3106
Leland Southard--Hogs	(202) 219-0767
Linda Simpson--Sheep	(202) 720-3578
Steve Reed--Sheep & Cattle	(202) 219-1285
Linda Bailey--World	(202) 219-1286
Shayle Shagam--World	(202) 219-0767

MINK

Tom Kruchten	(202) 690-4870

OILSEEDS-Soybeans, Sunflowers

Dan Kerestes	(202) 720-9526
Mark Ash	(202) 219-0840
George Douvelis	(202) 219-0840
Nancy Morgan--World	(202) 219-0826
Jaime Castaneda--World	(202) 219-0862

PEANUTS

Kirby Cavett	(202) 720-8843
Scott Stanford	(202) 219-0840
George Douvelis--World	(202) 219-0840

POTATOES

Arvin Budge	(202) 720-4285
Gary Lucier	(202) 219-0884
Charles Plummer	(202) 219-0883

POULTRY-Broilers, Turkeys, Eggs

Joel Moore	(202) 720-3244
Tom Kruchten	(202) 690-4870
Robert Little	(202) 720-6147
Lee Christensen	(202) 219-0714
Larry Witucki--World	(202) 219-0766
Milton Madison	(202) 219-0714

SUGAR & SWEETENERS

Herb Eldridge	(202) 720-7621
Ronald Lord	(202) 219-0888
Peter Buzzanell	(202) 219-0888
Annette Clauson	(202) 219-0880

TOBACCO

Herb Eldridge	(202) 720-7621
Verner Grise	(202) 219-0890
Tom Capehart	(202) 219-0890
Annette Clauson	(202) 219-0880

VEGETABLES

Dave Mueller--Fresh & Proc.	(202) 720-2157
Arvin Budge	(202) 720-4285
Kevin Hintzman	(202) 720-5412
Gary Lucier	(202) 219-0884
John Love	(202) 219-0886
Shannon Hamm	(202) 219-0886

WOOL & MOHAIR

John Lawler	(202) 219-0840
Robert Skinner	(202) 219-0841
Linda Simpson	(202) 720-3578

U.S. Trade & International Agriculture

AFRICA & MIDDLE EAST

Gene Mathia	(202) 219-0630

North Africa & Middle East

Mike Kurtzig	(202) 219-0630

Sub-Saharan Africa

Shahla Shapouri	(202) 219-0630

ASIA

William Coyle	(202) 219-0610

China

Francis Tuan	(202) 219-0610

East Asia & Oceania

John Dyck	(202) 219-0610

Japan

Larry Deaton	(202) 219-0610

South and Southeast Asia

Terri Raney	(202) 219-0610

EUROPE

Robert Koopman	(202) 219-0620

Central & Eastern Europe

Robert Koopman	(202) 219-0620

Western Europe

Michael Herlihy	(202) 219-0620

EXPORTS & IMPORTS--U.S.

Thomas Warden	(202) 219-0822
Steve MacDonald--Exports	(202) 219-0822
Karen Ackerman--Programs	(202) 219-0821

FOOD AID

Margaret Misiaen	(202) 219-0630

FOREIGN AGRICULTURAL RESOURCES

Francis Urban	(202) 219-0680

FOREIGN AGRICULTURAL SUBSIDIES

Donna Roberts	(202) 219-0680
Fred Nelson	(202) 219-0689

FOREIGN ECONOMIC CONDITIONS

Ralph Monaco	(202) 219-0680

FOREIGN FOOD DEMAND & EXPENDITURES

Larry Traub	(202) 219-0705

FOREIGN FOOD POLICIES & SUBSIDIES

Donna Roberts	(202) 219-0680

FORMER USSR

Christian Foster	(202) 219-0620

INTERNATIONAL MARKETS & COMPETITION

Mathew Shane	(202) 219-0705

TRADE & DEVELOPMENT POLICIES
Barry Krissoff (202) 219-0680

TRADE & ENVIRONMENT
Margot Anderson (202) 219-0448
Suchada Langley (202) 219-0687
John Sullivan (202) 219-0680
Steve Haley (202) 219-0680

WESTERN HEMISPHERE
Harry Baumes (202) 219-0687

Central America
John Link (202) 219-0690

South America
David Peacock (202) 219-0690

Canada
Mark Simone (202) 219-0690

Caribbean
Richard Brown (202) 219-0687

WORLD FARM INPUTS & PRODUCTIVITY
Francis Urban (202) 219-0680

Agricultural Finances

CASH RECEIPTS
Robert Williams (202) 219-0804
Connie Dixon (202) 219-0804

COSTS & RETURNS
Mitch Morehart (202) 219-0801

CREDIT & FINANCIAL MARKETS
Jerry Stam (202) 219-0892
Pat Sullivan (202) 219-0719

FARM SECTOR FINANCES
Mitch Morehart (202) 219-0801
Duane Hacklander (202) 219-0798
Jim Ryan (202) 219-0798

FUTURES MARKETS
Richard Heifner (202) 219-0868
Linwood Hoffman--Crops (202) 219-0840

INCOME
Bob McElroy--Farm Forecast (202) 219-0800
Roger Strickland--Farm, Annual (202) 219-0804
Janet Perry--Farm Household (202) 219-0807

PRICES, PARITY, & INDEXES
Herb Vanderberry--Received (202) 720-5446
Doug Kleweno--Paid (202) 720-4214
Bob Milton (202) 720-3570

PRODUCTION COSTS
Doug Kleweno (202) 720-4214
Mitch Morehart--Dairy & Livestock (202) 219-0801
John Jinkins (202) 219-0789
Ronald Lord--Sweeteners (202) 219-0888
Annette Clauson--Tob./Sweeteners (202) 219-0890

TAXES
Ron Durst (202) 219-0897
Peter DeBraal--Farm Real Estate (202) 219-0425

WAGES AND LABOR
Doug Kleweno (202) 720-4214
Jack Runyan (202) 219-0932
Victor Oliveira (202) 219-0932

Farms & Land

CORPORATE & FAMILY FARMS
Leslie Whitener (202) 219-0932

FARM NUMBERS
Dan Ledbury (202) 720-1790

FARM REAL ESTATE
Roger Hexem (202) 219-0419
Mark Denbaly (202) 219-0428

FOREIGN LAND OWNERSHIP
Peter DeBraal (202) 219-0425

LAND OWNERSHIP & TENURE
Gene Wunderlich (202) 219-0425

LAND USE
Arthur Daugherty (202) 219-0424

Food

FOOD POLICY
Dave Smallwood (202) 219-0864
Bill Levedahl (202) 219-0864

FOOD ASSISTANCE & NUTRITION
Dave Smallwood (202) 219-0864
Masao Matsumoto (202) 219-0864

FOOD AWAY FROM HOME
Charlene Price (202) 219-0866

FOOD CONSUMPTION
Judy Putnam (202) 219-0870

FOOD DEMAND & EXPENDITURES
James Blaylock (202) 219-0862
Richard Haidacher (202) 219-0870

FOOD MANUFACTURING & RETAILING
Charles Handy (202) 219-0866
Tony Gallo--Manufacturing (202) 219-0866
Phil Kaufman--Retailing (202) 219-0866

FOOD PRICES & CONSUMER PRICE INDEX
Ralph Parlett (202) 219-0870
Denis Dunham (202) 219-0870

FOOD SAFETY & QUALITY
Tanya Roberts (202) 219-0864
Bina-Hwah Lin (202) 219-0459

Laurian Unnevehr	(202) 219-0469

FOOD WHOLESALING

Walter Epps	(202) 219-0866

MARKETING MARGINS & STATISTICS

Richard Haidacher	(202) 219-0870
Denis Dunham	(202) 219-0870
Howard Elitzak	(202) 219-0870
Charles Handy	(202) 219-0866

PRICE SPREADS

Larry Duewer--Meat	(202) 219-0712

Rural Development

AGRICULTURE & COMMUNITY LINKAGES

Fred Hines	(202) 219-0525

BUSINESS & INDUSTRY

Andrew Bernat	(202) 219-0540

COMMUNITY DEVELOPMENT

David Sears	(202) 219-0544

CREDIT & FINANCIAL MARKETS

Pat Sullivan	(202) 219-0719

EMPLOYMENT

Paul Swaim	(202) 219-0552
Tim Parker	(202) 219-0541

LOCAL GOVERNMENT FINANCE

Richard Reeder	(202) 219-0542
Anicca Jansen	(202) 219-0542

RURAL DEVELOPMENT

Sara Mazie	(202) 219-0530
David McGranahan	(202) 219-0532

STATE RURAL DEVELOPMENT COUNCIL

Tom Rowley	(202) 219-0546

Special Topics

AGRICULTURAL HISTORY

Douglas Bowers	(202) 219-0787

ALTERNATIVE CROPS

Lewrene Glaser	(202) 219-0085

BIOTECHNOLOGY

John Reilly	(202) 219-0450
Richard Fallert--Dairy	(202) 219-0712

COMMODITY PROGRAMS & PRICES

Joy Harwood--Crops	(202) 219-0840
Paul Westcott--Crops	(202) 219-0313
Sam Evans--Crops	(202) 219-0840
Richard Fallert--Dairy	(202) 219-0712
Mark Smith--Exports	(202) 219-0821
Ron Lord--Sugar	(202) 219-0888
Verner Grise--Tobacco	(202) 219-0890
Fred Hoff--Honey	(202) 219-0883

ECONOMIC LINKAGES TO AGRICULTURE

William Edmondson	(202) 219-0785

ENERGY

Mohinder Gill	(202) 219-0464
James Hrubovcak	(202) 219-0405

FARM LABOR LAWS

Jack Runyan--Laws	(202) 219-0932
Leslie Whitener--Market	(202) 219-0932

FARM MACHINERY

Marlow Vesterby	(202) 219-0422

FARM STRUCTURE

Leslie Whitener	(202) 219-0932

FERTILIZER

Harold Taylor	(202) 219-0464
Sam Rives	(202) 720-7092

GEOGRAPHIC INFORMATION SYSTEMS

Ralph Heimlich	(202) 219-0431

GLOBAL CLIMATE CHANGE

John Reilly	(202) 219-0450
George Frisvold	(202) 219-0423

MACROECONOMIC CONDITIONS

John Kitchen	(202) 219-0782
Tim Baxter--World	(202) 219-0706

NATURAL RESOURCE POLICY

Tim Osborn	(202) 219-0401
Marc Ribaudo	(202) 219-0444

PESTICIDES

Merritt Padgitt	(202) 219-0433
Ann Vandeman	(202) 219-0433
Herman Delvo	(202) 219-0456
John Love	(202) 219-0886
Sam Rives	(202) 720-3896

POPULATION

Calvin Beale	(202) 219-0535
Linda Swanson	(202) 219-0535

SEEDS

Mohinder Gill	(202) 219-0464

SOIL CONSERVATION

Tim Osborn	(202) 219-0405
Richard Magleby	(202) 219-0435

SUSTAINABLE AGRICULTURE

Greg Gajewski	(202) 219-0085
Ann Vandeman	(202) 219-0433
Linda Calvin	(202) 219-0085
Doug Beach	(202) 219-0085

TRANSPORTATION

T. Q. Hutchinson	(202) 219-0840

WATER & IRRIGATION

Noel Gollehon	(202) 219-0410
John Hostetler	(202) 219-0410

WATER QUALITY
Marc Ribaudo (202) 219-0444
Steve Crutchfield (202) 219-0444
Sam Rives (202) 720-3896

WEATHER
Dave Mueller (202) 720-2157

State Statisticians In Charge Of The National Agricultural Statistics Service

The following people can provide information about agricultural production, stocks, prices and other data for individual States and, in many cases for counties in those States.

ALABAMA - Montgomery
Dave Kleweno (205) 279-3555

ALASKA - Palmer
Delon Brown (907) 745-4272

ARIZONA - Phoenix
Will N. Sherman (602) 280-8850

ARKANSAS - Little Rock
Benjamin Klugh (501) 378-5145

CALIFORNIA - Sacramento
H. James Tippett (916) 551-1533

COLORADO - Lakewood
Charles Hudson (303) 236-2300

DELAWARE - Dover
Thomas Feurer (302) 736-4811

FLORIDA - Orlando
Robert Freie (407) 648-6013

GEORGIA - Athens
Larry Snipes (404) 546-2236

HAWAII - Honolulu
Homer Rowley (808) 973-9588

IDAHO - Boise
Donald Gerhardt (208) 334-1507

ILLINOIS - Springfield
Jerry Clampet (217) 492-4295

INDIANA - West Lafayette
Ralph Gann (317) 494-8371

IOWA - Des Moines
Duane Skow (515) 284-4340

KANSAS - Topeka
Thomas Byram (913) 233-2230

KENTUCKY - Louisville
David Williamson (502) 582-5293

LOUISIANA - Baton Rouge
Albert Frank (504) 922-1362

MARYLAND - Annapolis
Melvin West (410) 841-5740

MICHIGAN - Lansing
Donald Fedewa (517) 377-1831

MINNESOTA - St. Paul
Carroll Rock (612) 296-2230

MISSISSIPPI - Jackson
Thomas Gregory (601) 965-4575

MISSOURI - Columbia
Robert Bellinghausen (314) 876-0950

MONTANA - Helena
James Sands (406) 449-5303

NEBRASKA - Lincoln
William Dobbs (402) 437-5541

NEVADA - Reno
Clemence Lies (702) 784-5584

NEW ENGLAND - Concord, N.H. (Maine, New Hampshire, Vermont, Connecticut, Massachusetts, Rhode Island)
Aubrey Davis (603) 224-9639

NEW JERSEY - Trenton
Robert Battaglia (609) 292-6385

NEW MEXICO - Las Cruces
Charles Gore (505) 522-6023

NEW YORK - Albany
Robert Schooley (518) 457-5570

NORTH CAROLINA - Raleigh
Robert Murphy (919) 856-4394

NORTH DAKOTA - Fargo
Steve Wiyatt (701) 239-5306

OHIO - Columbus
James Ramey (614) 469-5590

OKLAHOMA - Oklahoma City
Barry Bloyd (405) 525-9226

OREGON - Portland
Paul Williamson (503) 326-2131

PENNSYLVANIA - Harrisburg
Wally Evans (717) 787-3904

SOUTH CAROLINA - Columbia
Henry Power (803) 765-5333

SOUTH DAKOTA - Sioux Falls
John Ranek (605) 330-4235

TENNESSEE - Nashville
Burgess Guinn (Acting) (615) 781-5300

TEXAS - Austin
Dennis Findley (512) 482-5581

UTAH - Salt Lake City
Delroy Gneiting (801) 524-5003

VIRGINIA - Richmond
Robert Bass (804) 786-3500

WASHINGTON - Tumwater
Douglas Hasslen (206) 902-1940

WEST VIRGINIA - Charleston
David Loos (304) 558-2217

WISCONSIN - Madison
Lyle Pratt (608) 264-5317

WYOMING - Cheyenne
Richard Coulter (307) 772-2181

BANKING AND FINANCIAL DATA

The Federal Reserve System, the central bank of the U.S., is charged with administering and making policy for the nation's credit and monetary affairs. Listed below are information specialists available to answer questions on a broad range of banking and financial matters.

Affiliates, Domestic	Molly Wassom	(202) 452-2305
Affiliates, Foreign	Michael Martinson	(202) 452-3640
Aggregate Reserves	Leigh Ribble	(202) 452-2385
Agricultural Credit	Nicholas Walraven	(202) 452-2655
Agriculture	John Rosine	(202) 452-2971
Automobile Credit, Analysis	Charles Luckett	(202) 452-2925
Automobile Credit, Data	Millie Middleton	(202) 452-2924
Automobile Loans	Charles Luckett	(202) 452-2925
Balance of Payments, U.S.	Kathryn Morisse	(202) 452-3773
	William Helkie	(202) 452-3836
Balance Sheets for the U.S. Economy	Elizabeth Fogler	(202) 452-3491
Balance Sheets for Federal Reserve Banks	Paul Bettge	(202) 452-3174
Bank for International Settlements (BIS)	Charles Siegman	(202) 452-3308
Bank Loans	Dennis Farley	(202) 452-3021
Bank Rates on Business Loans	Dennis Farley	(202) 452-3021
Bank Service Corporations	Thomas Corsi	(202) 452-3275
	Sidney Sussan	(202) 452-2638
Bank Report Form Projects	Kathleen Conley	(202) 452-2389
Banking, International	Allen Frankel	(202) 452-3578
	William Ryback	(202) 452-2722
	Larry Promisel	(202) 452-3533
Banking Markets	Stephen Rhoades	(202) 452-3906
Banking Structure	Dean Amel	(202) 452-2911
	Donald Savage	(202) 452-2613
Bills of Exchange	Patrick McDivitt	(202) 452-3818
Bond Markets	John Rea	(202) 452-3631
Corporate	Leland Crabbe	(202) 452-3022
Municipal, Tax-exempt	Chris Turner	(202) 452-2983
Broker Loans	Laura Homer	(202) 452-2781
	Scott Holz	(202) 452-2781
Business Finance	John Rea	(202) 452-3744
Business Fixed Investments	Stephen Oliner	(202) 452-3134
	Kevin Hassett	(202) 452-2669
C&CA Computation of Reserve Requirement	Martha Bethea	(202) 452-3181
Call Reports	Suzanne Mitchell	(202) 452-3684
	Thomas Boemio	(202) 452-2982
Capacity Utilization	Richard Raddock	(202) 452-3197
Capital Adequacy Guidelines	Roger Cole	(202) 452-2618
	Roger Pugh	(202) 728-5883
	Norah Barger	(202) 452-2402
Capital Flows, International	Lois Stekler	(202) 452-3716
Capital Markets	John Rea	(202) 452-3631
Certificates of Deposit	Brian Reid	(202) 452-3589
Chart Book Figures	Ellen Dykes	(202) 452-3952
Commercial Paper		
Interest Hotline	Deborah McMillian	(202) 452-3400
	Leonard Culbreth	(202) 452-3400
Outstandings	Mitchell Post	(202) 452-2720
Competitive Analysis of Mergers and Acquisitions	James Burke	(202) 452-2612
	Stephen Rhoades	(202) 452-3906
Conditions Reports	Douglas Carpenter	(202) 452-2740
Consumer Credit, Data	Millie Middleton	(202) 452-2924
Consumer Credit, Analysis	Charles Luckett	(202) 452-2925
	James August	(202) 452-3741
Consumer Leasing	Cecilia Hurt	(202) 452-2412
	W. Kurt Schumacher	(202) 452-2412
Counterfeit Notes	Jon Cameron	(202) 452-2220
Country Exposure Reports U.S. Banks, Foreign Banks	Sarah Adams	(202) 452-2634
Credit Cards, Data	Millie Middleton	(202) 452-2924

Credit Cards, Analysis	Charles Luckett	(202) 452-2925
Criminal Violations	Herbert Biern	(202) 452-2920
	Richard Small	(202) 452-5235
Debt		
Domestic Non-Financial	Sarah Holden	(202) 452-3483
	Susan McIntosh	(202) 452-3484
Discount Rate at FR Banks	Joseph Coyne	(202) 452-3204
	Bob Moore	(202) 452-3215
Earnings, FR Banks	Paul Bettge	(202) 452-3174
Electric Power Statistics	Cora Moyers	(202) 452-2476
Electronic Fund Transfer System	Gayle Brett	(202) 452-2934
Employment Figures	William Wascher	(202) 452-2812
	David Lebow	(202) 452-3057
	Maria Otto	(202) 452-2236
Energy	Mark French	(202) 452-2348
Energy, International	William Melick	(202) 452-2296
Establishing a Bank	Richard Fabrizio	(202) 452-3423
Eurobond Market	Lois Stekler	(202) 452-3716
Eurocurrency Market	Allen Frankel	(202) 452-3578
Examinations of Bank Holding Companies	Howard Amer	(202) 452-2958
	Jack Jennings	(202) 452-3053
Securities Affiliates, Section 20 Subsidiaries	Michael Schoenfeld	(202) 452-2781
Examination of Foreign Banks	Michael Martinson	(202) 452-3640
Excess Reserves	Leigh Ribble	(202) 452-2385
	Jack Walton	(202) 452-2660
Exchange Rates	Ralph Smith	(202) 452-3712
Exchange Rates, Data	Patrick Decker	(202) 452-3314
Export-Import Bank	Thomas Connors	(202) 452-3672
Export-Trading Companies	William Ryback	(202) 452-2722
	Deborah Burand	(202) 452-3427
	John Rogers	(202) 452-2798
	N. Peter Knoll	(202) 452-5237
Federal Budget Receipts and Outlays	Wolfhard Ramm	(202) 452-2381
	Glen Follette	(202) 452-2448
	Randall Mariger	(202) 452-3703
Federal Reserve Bulletin		
Articles	Ellen Dykes	(202) 452-3952
Tables	Gwenavere White-Dubose	(202) 452-3567
Financial Assets & Liabilities in U.S.	Albert Teplin	(202) 452-3482
	Elizabeth Fogler	(202) 452-3491
Financial Markets International	Ralph Smith	(202) 452-3712
Financial Reports	Mary McLaughlin	(202) 452-3829
Flow of Funds and Savings	Albert Teplin	(202) 452-3482
Foreign Banking Holding Companies in U.S.	William Ryback	(202) 452-2722
	Kathleen O'Day	(202) 452-3786
	Deborah Burand	(202) 452-3427
Inspections of	Michael Martinson	(202) 452-3640
	Sandra Richardson	(202) 452-6404
Foreign Banking	Allen Frankel	(202) 452-3578
	William Ryback	(202) 452-2722
Foreign Banks, In U.S.	Kathleen O'Day	(202) 452-3786
	Sandra Richardson	(202) 452-6404
	Deborah Burand	(202) 452-3427
	Donna Nordenberg	(202) 452-3281
Economic Analysis	Barbara Key	(202) 452-3522
Examination of	Elizabeth Roberts	(202) 452-3846
Foreign Branches	Michael Martinson	(202) 452-3640
	Kathleen O'Day	(202) 452-3786
Foreign Economies		
Developing Countries (Africa, Asia, Latin America)	Thomas Connors	(202) 452-3639
Industrial Countries (Canada, Europe, Japan)	Karen Johnson	(202) 452-2345
Restructuring Economies (Europe, Former USSR)	Lewis Alexander	(202) 452-3067
	Valarie Chang	(202) 452-2375
Foreign Exchange Markets	Ralph Smith	(202) 452-3712
	Richard Freeman	(202) 452-2344
Foreign Exchange Rates	Patrick Decker	(202) 452-3314
	Priscilla Harvison	(202) 452-2361
Foreign Margin Stock List	Margaret Wolffrum	(202) 452-2781
Foreign Official Reserves	Ralph Smith	(202) 452-3712
Foreign Securities Margin Requirements	Scott Holz	(202) 452-2781
Foreign Trade, U.S.	Kathryn Morisse	(202) 452-3773
Foreign Trust Activities	Donald Vinnedge	(202) 452-2717
Form Control	Lois Lawrence	(202) 452-2984
Freedom of Information Office	Susanne Mitchell	(202) 452-3684
Futures Trading	Robert Plotkin	(202) 452-2782
	Laura Homer	(202) 452-2781
Gold	Donald Adams	(202) 452-2364
Government Finance	Timothy Simon	(202) 452-2383
Household Balance Sheets & Net Worth	Elizabeth Fogler	(202) 452-3491

Housing Starts and Residential Construction		
Data	Frederick Whetzel	(202) 452-3094
Analysis	James Fergus	(202) 452-2868
Industrial Output	Carol Corrado	(202) 452-3521
Industrial Production Index	Gerald Storch	(202) 452-2932
Information System FR Bank Operations	Rick May	(202) 452-3995
Interest Bearing Notes	Alyssa Montecalvo	(202) 452-3471
Interest on Deposits	Hoyt Stewart	(202) 452-3513
	Patrick McDivitt	(202) 452-3818
Interest on Federal Reserve Notes	Paul Bettge	(202) 452-3174
	Florence Printis	(202) 452-3916
Interest on Savings Accounts	Brian Reid	(202) 452-3589
	Lawranne Stewart	(202) 452-3513
	Patrick McDivitt	(202) 452-3818
Interest Rate Hotline	Bonnie Garrett	(202) 452-3400
Domestic	Deborah McMillian	(202) 452-2851
	Leonard Culbreth	(202) 452-2852
Foreign	Patrick Decker	(202) 452-3314
International Banking	Allen Frankel	(202) 452-3578
	William Ryback	(202) 452-2722
	Kathleen O'Day	(202) 452-3786
International Banking Facilities (IBFs)	Sidney Key	(202) 452-3522
	Michael Martinson	(202) 452-3640
International Capital Transactions	Lois Stekler	(202) 452-3716
International Development	Thomas Connors	(202) 452-3639
International Information Center	Cynthia Sutton	(202) 452-3411
International Monetary Fund (IMF)	Thomas Connors	(202) 452-3639
International Taxation	Allen Frankel	(202) 452-3578
International Trade		
Foreign	Richard Freeman	(202) 452-2344
	Deborah Lindner	(202) 452-2363
U.S.	Kathleen Morisse	(202) 452-3773
International Trade Policy, U.S.	Catherine Mann	(202) 452-2374
	Virginia Carper	(202) 452-3661
International Transactions, U.S.	William Helkie	(202) 452-3836
	Peter Hooper	(202) 452-3426
Interstate Banking	Donald Savage	(202) 452-2613
Labor Markets and Wages	David Lebow	(202) 452-3057
	Maria Otoo	(202) 452-2236
	William Wascher	(202) 452-2812

Manufacturing Capacity	Charles Gilbert	(202) 452-3197
Member Bank Reserves	Lawranne Stewart	(202) 452-3513
	Oliver Ireland	(202) 452-3625
	Patrick McDivitt	(202) 452-3818
Member Banks, Trust Activities	Donald Vinnedge	(202) 452-2717
Mergers (Bank & BHC)	Sidney Sussan	(202) 452-2638
Minority Banks	Jacqueline McDaniel	(202) 452-3132
	Anna Monteiro	(202) 452-2948
Money Supply Deposits and Reserves, U.S.	Leigh Ribble	(202) 452-2385
	Jack Walton	(202) 452-2660
Mortgage Market		
Data	Frederick Whetzel	(202) 452-3094
Analysis	Stephen Lumpkin	(202) 452-2378
	John Goodman	(202) 452-2872
Multi-Country Model (MCM)	Ralph Tryon	(202) 452-2368
Municipal Securities Dealer Banks	Michael Schoenfeld	(202) 452-2781
	Susan Meyers	(202) 452-2781
National Debt	Wolfhard Ramm	(202) 452-2381
	Glenn Follette	(202) 452-2448
National Income	Sandy Struckmeyer	(202) 452-3090
National Information Center	Maureen Hannan	(202) 452-3618
	Jacqueline McDaniel	(202) 452-3132
	Alison Waldron	(202) 452-2538
Negotiable Orders of Withdrawal (NOW)	Leigh Ribble	(202) 452-2385
	Jack Walton	(202) 452-2660
Nonbank Acquisitions	Sidney Sussan	(202) 452-2638
	Molly Wassom	(202) 452-2305
NOW Accounts (Negotiable Orders of Withdrawal)	Leigh Ribble	(202) 452-2385
Open Market Operations	Timothy Simon	(202) 452-2383
	Bonnie Garrett	(202) 452-2869
Organization for Economic Cooperation & Development (OECD)	Larry Promisel	(202) 452-3533
	Karen Johnson	(202) 452-2345
OTC (Over-The-Counter Margin Stock List)	Margaret Wolffrum	(202) 452-2781
Price and Inflation Developments	Sandy Struckmeyer	(202) 452-3090
	Daniel Sichel	(202) 452-3896
Private Pension Funds	Joel Lander	(202) 452-2227
Quarterly Econometric Model	Flint Brayton	(202) 452-2670
Research Library	Susan Vincent	(202) 452-3398
	Judy Back	(202) 452-3332

Reserves		
Aggregates	Leigh Ribble	(202) 452-2385
Computation of	Martha Bethea	(202) 452-3181
Foreign	Ralph Smith	(202) 452-3712
Requirements	Oliver Ireland	(202) 452-3625
	Patrick McDivitt	(202) 452-3818
	Lawranne Stewart	(202) 452-3513
Reserves of Depository Institutions	Oliver Ireland	(202) 452-3625
	Patrick McDivitt	(202) 452-3818
	Lawranne Stewart	(202) 452-3513
Resolution Trust Corporation Oversight Board	Frederick Struble	(202) 452-3794
Savings Bonds	Donna DeCorleto	(202) 452-3956
	Michael Bermudez	(202) 452-2216
Savings Deposits	Brian Reid	(202) 452-3589
Savings Flow in U.S. Economy	Elizabeth Fogler	(202) 452-3491
Savings and Loan Associations	Wayne Passmore	(202) 452-6432
Savings Statistics	Elizabeth Fogler	(202) 452-3491
Seasonal Adjustments	David Pierce	(202) 452-3895
Securities Credit Regulation	Laura Homer	(202) 452-2781
	Scott Holz	(202) 452-2781
	Susan Meyers	(202) 452-2781
Securities Exchange Act	Robert Plotkin	(202) 452-2782
	Laura Homer	(202) 452-2781
Securities Exchange Compliance	Laura Homer	(202) 452-2781
	Robert Plotkin	(202) 452-2782
Special Studies, Monetary Policy Stabilization	P. A. Tinsley	(202) 452-2438
State and Local Sector Fiscal Data	Laura Rubin	(202) 452-3130
Survey of Consumer Finances	Gerhard Fries	(202) 452-2578
	Arthur Kennickell	(202) 452-2247
	Janice Shack-Marquez	(202) 452-2653
Swap Network	Ralph Smith	(202) 452-3712
Technical Information on T. Bills, Notes, Bonds	Donna Decorleto	(202) 452-3956
	Michael Bermudez	(202) 452-2216
Thrift Acquisitions	Terence Browne	(202) 452-3707
	Timothy Byrne	(202) 452-3565
	Sidney Sussan	(202) 452-2638
Trade and Financial Studies	Ralph Tryon	(202) 452-2368
Transfer of Funds	Gayle Brett	(202) 452-2934
Treasury Securities		
Interest Rate Hotline	Deborah McMillian	(202) 452-3400
	Leonard Culbreth	(202) 452-3400
Interest Rate & Yield Analysis	Bonnie Garrett	(202) 452-2869
Unemployment Figures	David Lebow	(202) 452-3057
	Maria Otoo	(202) 452-2236
	William Wascher	(202) 452-2812
U.S. International Transactions	William Helkie	(202) 452-3836
	Peter Hooper	(202) 452-3426
Wage Figures	David Lebow	(202) 452-3057
	Maria Otoo	(202) 452-2236
	William Wascher	(202) 452-2812
World Payments and Economic Activity	Richard Freeman	(202) 452-2344

CENSUS DATA

These specialists can tell precisely what statistical data is available in their subject areas. The information is arranged by program and subject area.

Agriculture

Crop Statistics
Donald Jahnke (AGR) (202) 763-8567

Data Requirements and Outreach
Douglas Miller (AGR) (202) 763-8561

Farm Economics
James Liefer (AGR) (202) 763-8514

General Information
Tom Manning (AGR) (800) 523-3215

Irrigation and Horticulture Statistics
John Blackledge (AGR) (202) 763-8559

Livestock Statistics
Linda Hutton (AGR) (202) 763-8569

Puerto Rico, Virgin Islands, Guam, Northern Marianas, and American Samoa
Kent Hoover (AGR) (202) 763-8564

Special Surveys
John Blackledge (AGR) (202) 763-8559

Communications and Utilities

Census
Dennis Shoemaker (BUS) (202) 763-2662

Current Programs
Tom Zabelsky (BUS) (202) 763-5528

Construction

Building Permits
Linda Hoyle (CSD) (202) 763-7244

Census
Bill Visnansky (CSD) (202) 763-7546

Construction in MSA's
Joseph Gilvary (CSD) (202) 763-7842

Housing Starts and Completions
David Fondelier (CSD) (202) 763-5731

Residential Characteristics, Price Index, Sales
Steve Berman (CSD) (202) 763-7842

Residential Improvements and Repairs
Joe Huesman (CSD) (202) 763-5705

Value of New Construction
George Roff (CSD) (202) 763-5717

Finance, Insurance, and Real Estate

Census
Sidney Marcus (BUS) (202) 763-1386

Foreign Trade

Data Services
Richard Preuss (FTD) (202) 763-5140/7754

Shippers' Declaration
Hal Blyweiss (FTD) (202) 763-5310

Manufacturing

Exports from Manufacturing Establishments
Philippe Morris (IND) (202) 763-7066

Fuels and Electric Energy Consumed
Frank Roy (IND) (202) 763-7066

Industries
Electrical and Transportation Equipment, Instruments, and Miscellaneous
Bruce Goldhirsch (IND) (202) 763-2518

Food, Textiles, and Apparel
Judy Dodds (IND) (202) 763-5911

Metals and Industrial Machinery
Kenneth Hansen (IND) (202) 763-7304

Wood, Furniture, Paper, Printing, Chemicals, Petroleum Products, Rubber and Plastics
Michael Zampogna (IND) (202) 763-2510

Monthly Shipments, Inventories, Orders
Steve Andrews (IND) (202) 763-2512

Technology, Innovation, Research and Development, Capacity, and Pollution Abatement
Thomas Flood (IND) (202) 763-5616

Retail Trade

Advance Monthly
Ronald Piencykosky (BUS) (202) 763-5294

Census
Ann Russell (BUS) (202) 763-7035

Monthly Report
Irving True (BUS) (202) 763-7128

Service

Census
Jack Moody (BUS) (202) 763-7039

Current Reports
Thomas Zabelsky (BUS) (202) 763-5528

Transportation

Census
Dennis Shoemaker (BUS) (202) 763-2662

Commodity Flow Survey
John Fowler (BUS) (202) 763-6087

Truck Inventory and Use
Bill Bostic (BUS) (202) 763-2735

Warehousing and Trucking
Tom Zabelsky (BUS) (202) 763-5528

Wholesale Trade

Census
John Trimble (BUS) (202) 763-5281

Current Sales and Inventories
Nancy Piesto (BUS) (202) 763-3916

Special Topics

Business Investment
Elinor Champion (IND) (202) 763-7161

Census Products
Robert Marske/Paul Zeisset (ECSD) (202) 763-1792

County Business Patterns
Zigmund Decker (ECSD) (202) 763-5430

Enterprise Statistics
Eddie Salyers (ECSD) (202) 763-5470

Industry and Commodity Classification
James Kristoff (ECSD) (202) 763-1935

Mineral Industries
Patricia Horning (IND) (202) 763-5116

Minority- and Women-Owned Businesses
Valerie Strang (ECSD) (202) 763-5779

Quarterly Financial Report
Paul Zarrett (ESD) (202) 763-2718

Puerto Rico and Outlying Areas
Kent Hoover (AGR) (202) 763-8559/8564

Demographics and Population

Aging Population, U.S.
Staff (POP) (202) 763-7883

Ancestry
Staff (POP) (202) 763-7955

Apportionment
Staff (POP) (202) 763-7962

Child Care
Martin O'Connell/Lynne Casper (POP) (202) 763-5303

Children
Donald Hernandez (POP) (202) 763-7987

Citizenship
Staff (POP) (202) 763-7955

Commuting, Means of Transportation, and Place of Work
Phil Salopek/Celia Boertlein (POP) (202) 763-3850

Crime
Gail Hoff (DSD) (202) 763-1735

Current Population Survey:

General Information (DUSD) (202) 763-4100

Questionnaire Content
Ronald Tucker (DSD) (202) 763-2773

Sampling Methods
Preston Waite (DSMC) (202) 763-2672

Demographic Surveys (General Information) (202) 763-2776

Disability
Jack McNeil/Bob Bennefield (HHES) (202) 763-8300/8578

Education (POP) (202) 763-1154

Education Surveys
Lawrence McGinn (DSD) (202) 763-2850

Equal Employment Opportunity Data
Tom Scopp (HHES) (202) 763-8199

Fertility and Births
Martin O'Connell/Amara Bachu (POP) (202) 763-5303/4547

Foreign Born
Staff (POP) (202) 763-7955

Group Quarters Population
Denise Smith (POP) (202) 763-2784

Health Surveys
Robert Mangold (DSD) (202) 763-5684

Hispanic and Ethnic Statistics (POP) (202) 763-7955

Homeless
Annetta Clark (POP) (202) 763-2784

Household Estimates (POP) (202) 763-5002

Households and Families
Steve Rawlings (POP) (202) 763-7987

Immigration (Legal/Undocumented) and Emigration
Edward Fernandez (POP) (202) 763-5590

Journey to Work
Phil Salopek/Gloria Swieczkowski (POP) (202) 763-3850

Language (POP) (202) 763-1154

Longitudinal Surveys
Sarah Higgins (DSD) (202) 763-2767

Marital Status and Living Arrangements
Arlene Saluter (POP) (202) 763-7987

Metropolitan Areas (MA's):

Population (POP) (202) 763-5002

Standards
James Fitzsimmons (POP) (202) 763-5158

Migration
Kristen Hansen/Diana DeAre (POP) (202) 763-3850

National Estimates and Projections (POP) (202) 763-5002

Outlying Areas
Michael Levin (POP) (202) 763-5134

Place of Birth
Kristen Hansen (POP) (202) 763-3850

Population Information (202) 763-5002
(202) 763-5020 TTY

Prisoner Surveys
Gail Hoff (DSD) (202) 763-1735

Puerto Rico
Lourdes Flaim (DSD) (202) 763-2903

Race Statistics (POP) (202) 763-2607/7572

Reapportionment and Redistricting
Marshall Turner, Jr. (DUSD) (202) 763-5820

Sampling Methods, Decennial Census
Henry Woltman (DSSD) (202) 763-5987

School District Data
Jane Ingold (POP) (202) 763-5476

Special Demographic Surveys
Sarah Higgins (DSD) (202) 763-2767

Special Population Censuses
Elaine Csellar (ISPC) (202) 763-5604

Special Tabulations
Rose Cowan (POP) (202) 763-5476

State and County Estimates (POP) (202) 763-5002

State Projections (POP) (202) 763-5002

Undercount, Demographic Analysis
Gregg Robinson (POP) (202) 763-5590

Veterans Status
Thomas Palumbo/Selwyn Jones (HHES) (202) 763-8574

Women
Denise Smith (POP) (202) 763-2784

Geographic Concepts

Annexations, Boundary Changes
Nancy Goodman (GEO) (202) 763-3827

Area Measurement
Staff (GEO) (202) 763-3827

Census Geographic Concepts (GEO) (202) 763-3827

State Boundary Certification
Louis Stewart (GEO) (202) 763-3827

Census Tracts
Cathy Miller (GEO) (202) 763-3827

Centers of Population
Lourdes Ramirez (GEO) (202) 763-4710

Congressional Districts:

Address Allocations (POP) (202) 763-5692

Boundaries, Component Areas
Cathy McCully (GEO) (202) 763-3827

Fee-Paid Block Splits
Joel Miller (GEO) (202) 763-3827

FIPS Codes
Virgeline Davis (GEO) (202) 763-3827

Internal Points
Tony Costanzo (GEO) (202) 763-4710

Maps:

Computer Mapping
Fred Broome (GEO) (202) 763-3973

School Districts
Dave Aultman (GEO) (202) 763-3827

1980 Census Map Orders
Ann Devore (DPD) (812) 288-3192

1990 Census Maps (DUSD) (202) 763-4100

Metropolitan Areas
James Fitzsimmons (POP) (202) 763-5158

Outlying Areas
Virgeline Davis (GEO) (202) 763-3827

TIGER System:

Applications and Product Information
Larry Carbaugh (DUSD) (202) 763-1384

Future Plans and Products (GEO) (202) 763-4664

Update
Jim Avore (GEO) (202) 763-4664

Urban/Rural Residence
Staff (POP) (202) 763-7962

Urbanized Areas and Urban/Rural Concepts
Nancy Torrieri (GEO) (202) 763-3827

User-Defined Areas Program (Neighborhood Statistics)
Carol Briggs (DMD) (202) 763-4282

Voting Districts
Cathy McCully (GEO) (202) 763-3827

ZIP Codes:

Demographic Data (DUSD) (202) 763-4100

Economic Data
Anne Russell (BUS) (202) 763-7038

Geographic Relationships
Rose Quarato (GEO) (202) 763-4667

Governments

Criminal Justice
Alan Stevens (GOVS) (202) 763-7789

Employment
Larry MacDonald (GOVS) (202) 763-5086

Federal Expenditure Data
Robert McArthur (GOVS) (202) 763-5276

Finance
Gerard Keffer (GOVS) (202) 763-5356

Governmental Organization
Alan Stevens (GOVS) (202) 763-7789

Survey Operations
Russell Price (GOVS) (202) 763-7783

Taxation
Gerard Keffer (GOVS) (202) 763-5356

Housing

American Housing Survey
Edward Montfort (HHES) (202) 763-8551
John Cannon (DSD) (202) 763-5468

Census
Robert Bonnette (HHES) (202) 763-8553

Components of Inventory Change Survey
Barbara Williams (HHES) (202) 763-8551

Housing Affordability
Peter Fronczek/Howard Savage (HHES) (202) 763-8165

Market Absorption/Residential Finance
Anne Smoler (HHES) (202) 763-8165
Peter Fronczek (HHES) (202) 763-8165

New York City Housing and Vacancy Survey
Margaret Harper (HHES) (202) 763-8171

Vacancy Data
Wallace Fraser (HHES) (202) 763-8165
Robert Callis (HHES) (202) 763-8165

Income, Poverty, and Wealth

Consumer Expenditure Survey
Ron Dopkowski (DSD) (202) 763-2063

Household Wealth
T.J. Eller (HHES) (202) 763-8578

Income Statistics (HHES) (202) 763-8576

Poverty Statistics (HHES) (202) 763-8578

Survey of Income and Program Participation (SIPP)
Enrique Lamas/Judy Eargle (HHES) (202) 763-8375

General Information
Don Fischer (DSD) (202) 763-2764

Microdata Files
Carmen Campbell (DUSD) (202) 763-2005

Statistical Methods
Vicki Huggins (DSMD) (202) 763-7944

International Statistics

Africa, Asia, Latin America, North America, and Oceania
Frank Hobbs/Patricia Rowe (CIR) (202) 763-4221

Aging Population
Kevin Kinsella (CIR) (202) 763-4884

China, People's Republic
Loraine West/Christina Harbaugh (CIR) (202) 763-4012

Europe
Victoria Velkoff (CIR) (202) 763-4012

Former Soviet Union
Marc Rubin/Stephen Rapawy (CIR) (202) 763-4020

Health
Karen Stanecki (CIR) (202) 763-4086

International Data Base
Peter Johnson (CIR) (202) 763-4811

International Visitors Program
Nina Pane Pinto/Gene Vandrovec (ISPC) (202) 763-2839

Women in Development
Patricia Rowe (CIR) (202) 763-4221

Labor Force

Commuting, Means of Transportation and Place of Work
Phil Salopek (POP) (202) 763-3850
Celia Boertlein (POP) (202) 763-3850

Employment and Unemployment
Thomas Palumbo (HHES) (202) 763-8574
Selwyn Jones (HHES) (202) 763-8574

Journey to Work
Phil Salopek (POP) (202) 763-3850
Gloria Swieczkowski (POP) (202) 763-3850

Occupation and Industry Statistics (HHES) (202) 763-8574

State and Local Data Centers

Business and Industry Data Centers (DUSD) (202) 763-1580

Clearinghouse for Census Data Services
Larry Carbaugh (DUSD) (202) 763-1384

National Census Information Centers
Barbara Harris (DUSD) (202) 763-1580

State Data Center Program (DUSD) (202) 763-1580

Regional Assistance

ATLANTA
Census Awareness & Products (404) 730-3833

BOSTON
Census Awareness & Products (617) 565-7078

CHARLOTTE
Census Awareness & Products (704) 344-6144

CHICAGO
Census Awareness & Products (312) 353-0980

DALLAS
Census Awareness & Products (214) 767-7105

DENVER
Census Awareness & Products (303) 969-7750

DETROIT
Census Awareness & Products (313) 259-0056

KANSAS CITY
Census Awareness & Products (913) 236-3711

LOS ANGELES
Census Awareness & Products (818) 904-6339

NEW YORK
Census Awareness & Products (212) 264-4730

PHILADELPHIA
Census Awareness & Products (215) 597-8313

SEATTLE
Census Awareness & Products (206) 728-5314

CRIME

The Justice Department's National Criminal Justice Reference Service of the U.S. Justice Department operates a valuable fact finding service and can be a highly useful source of data on crime statistics in the United States. Toll-free telephone numbers are provided below for information-seekers dealing with either of the two following major categories:

Justice Statistics Clearinghouse (800) 732-3277
Juvenile Justice Clearinghouse (800) 638-8736

Subject specialists are as follows:

ADJUDICATION
Carol Kaplan (Federal) (202) 616-0759
Patrick Langan (202) 616-3490

BAIL
Carol Kaplan (Federal) (202) 307-0759
Brian Reaves (202) 616-3287
Paul White (202) 307-0771

CAPITAL PUNISHMENT
Lawrence Greenfeld (202) 616-3281
James Stephan (202) 616-3285

CAREER CRIMINALS
Patrick Langan (202) 616-3490
Allen Beck (202) 616-3277

COMPUTER CRIME
(see CRIME TYPES, COMPUTER)

COMPUTER SYSTEMS
Donald A. Manson (202) 616-3491

CONFIDENTIALITY OF CRIMINAL JUSTICE DATA
Carol Kaplan (202) 307-0759

CORRECTIONS
Robyn Cohen (202) 616-3278
Tracy Snell (202) 616-3284
Allen Beck (202) 616-3288
James Stephan (202) 616-3289
Caroline Wolf Harlow (202) 307-0757
Craig Perkins (202) 307-0758
Carol Kaplan (Federal) (202) 307-0759
Darrell Gilliard (202) 616-3280

COST OF CRIME
--to Government
Sue Lindgren (202) 307-0760

--to Victims
Patsy Klaus (202) 307-0776

COURTS: GENERAL, APPEALS, CASELOADS, CASE PROCESSING TIME, ORGANIZATION
Carol Kaplan (Federal) (202) 307-0759
Patrick Langan (202) 616-3490

CRIME INCIDENCE, RATES, AND TRENDS
Patsy Klaus (202) 307-0776
Michael Rand (202) 616-3494
Bruce Taylor (202) 616-3498
Lisa Bastian (202) 616-3276

CRIME, LOCATION OF
Patsy Klaus (202) 307-0776
Michael Rand (202) 616-3494

CRIME MEASUREMENT METHODS
Bruce Taylor (202) 616-3498

CRIMINAL DEFENDANTS
Carol Kaplan (Federal) (202) 307-0759
Patrick Langan (202) 616-3490

CRIMINAL HISTORY RECORDS
Carol Kaplan (202) 307-0759

CRIMINAL JUSTICE AGENCIES
Sue Lindgren (202) 307-0760

CROWDING (see JAIL and PRISON)

DATA TAPES, GENERAL
Bruce Taylor (202) 616-3498

--Adjudication
Carol Kaplan (Federal) (202) 307-0759
Patrick Langan (202) 616-3490

--Agency Characteristics
Sue Lindgren (202) 307-0760

--Corrections
Darrell Gilliard (202) 616-3280
James Stephan (202) 616-3289

--Expenditure and Employment
Sue Lindgren (202) 307-0760

--Law Enforcement Statistics
Brian Reaves (202) 616-3287

--National Crime Victimization Survey
Marshall DeBerry (202) 307-0775
Michael Rand (202) 616-3494
Bruce Taylor (202) 616-3498

--Pretrial Release
Brian Reaves (202) 616-3287

--State Offender-Based Transactions
Donald Manson (202) 616-3491

DOMESTIC VIOLENCE
Patsy Klaus (202) 307-0776
Michael Rand (202) 616-3494
Patrick Langan (202) 616-3490
Ronet Bachman (202) 616-3625

DRUGS
- Drugs and Crime Data Center & Clearinghouse (800) 666-3332
- Marianne Zawitz (202) 616-3499

DRUNK DRIVING
- Lawrence Greenfeld (202) 307-0765
- Robyn Cohen (202) 616-3278

ELDERLY
- Ronet Bachman (202) 616-3625

FAMILY VIOLENCE (see DOMESTIC VIOLENCE)

FEDERAL JUSTICE
- Carol Kaplan (202) 307-0759

FINGERPRINT IDENTIFICATION SYSTEMS
- Bernard Shipley (202) 307-0773
- Carol Kaplan (202) 307-0759

INCAPACITATION (see CORRECTIONS, COURTS)

INDIGENT DEFENSE (see COURTS)

INTERNATIONAL CRIME & JUSTICE STATISTICS*
- Carol Kalish (202) 307-0235

JAILS, INMATES, AND CROWDING
- James Stephan (202) 616-3289
- Lawrence Greenfeld (202) 616-3281
- Caroline Wolf Harlow (202) 307-0757
- Darrell Gilliard (202) 616-3280

JUDICIARY AND JUDGES
- Carol Kaplan (202) 307-0759
- Patrick Langan (202) 616-3490

JUSTICE EXPENDITURE AND EMPLOYMENT
- Sue Lindgren (202) 307-0760

JUVENILES
- Allen Beck (202) 616-3277
- James Stephen (202) 616-3289

LAW ENFORCEMENT STATISTICS
- Brian Reaves (202) 616-3287
- Paul White (202) 307-0771

NATIONAL CRIME VICTIMIZATION SURVEY, GENERAL
- Patsy Klaus (202) 307-0776
- Michael Rand (202) 616-3494
- Bruce Taylor (202) 616-3287
- Marshall DeBerry (202) 616-3276
- Ronet Bachman (202) 616-3625

--Data Tapes
- Marshall DeBerry (202) 307-0775
- Michael Rand (202) 616-3494
- Bruce Taylor (202) 616-3498

--Household Crime
- Michael Rand (202) 616-3494

--Redesign
- Bruce Taylor (202) 616-3498
- Charles Kindermann (202) 616-3489

--Reporting Crime to Police
- Patsy Klaus (202) 307-0776

--Supplemental Questionnaires
- Charles Kindermann (202) 616-3489

NATIONAL INCIDENT-BASED REPORTING SYSTEM

--Analysis
- Brian Reaves (202) 616-3287
- Pheny Smith (202) 616-3488

--Implementation
- Paul White (202) 307-0771
- Donald Manson (202) 616-3491

OFFENDER-BASED TRANSACTION STATISTICS*
- Donald Manson (202) 616-3491
- Jacob Perez (202) 616-3286

OFFENDERS (see CORRECTIONS)

PAROLE AND PAROLEES
- Robyn Cohen (202) 616-3278
- Craig Perkins (202) 307-0758

PRETRIAL RELEASE
- Paul White (202) 307-0771
- Brian Reaves (202) 616-3287
- Carol Kaplan (Federal) (202) 307-0759

PRISONS, PRISONERS, AND CROWDING
- Darrell Gilliard (202) 616-3280
- Lawrence Greenfeld (202) 616-3281
- James Stephan (202) 616-3289

--Women in Prison
- Caroline Wolf Harlow (202) 307-0757
- Tracy Snell (202) 616-3288

PRIVACY AND SECURITY OF CRIMINAL JUSTICE DATA
- Carol Kaplan (202) 307-0759

PROBATION AND PROBATIONERS
- Patrick Langan (202) 616-3490
- Robyn Cohen (202) 616-3278
- Allen Beck (202) 616-3277
- Tom Bonczar (202) 616-3615

PROSECUTION
- Carol Kaplan (Federal) (202) 307-0759
- Patrick Langan (202) 616-3490
- Steven Smith (202) 616-3485

PUBLIC DEFENDERS (see COURTS)

PUBLIC SERIES, GENERAL
- Marilyn Marbrook (202) 307-1043

--Bulletins and Special Reports
- Thomas Hester (202) 616-3283

--Compendium of Federal Justice Statistics
- Carol Kaplan (202) 307-0759

--Criminal Justice Information Policy
- Carol Kaplan (202) 307-0759

--Directory of Automated Criminal Justice Information Systems
- Paul White (202) 307-0771

--Report to the Nation on Crime and Justice
- Marianne Zawitz (202) 616-3499

--Sourcebook of Criminal Justice Statistics
Sue Lindgren (202) 307-0760

PUBLIC OPINION ON CRIME
Sue Lindgren (202) 307-0760

RECIDIVISM
Allen Beck (202) 616-3277
Patrick Langan (202) 616-3490

SELF-PROTECTION AGAINST CRIME (see VICTIMS OF CRIME)

SENTENCING
Carol Kaplan (Federal) (202) 307-0759
Patrick Langan (202) 616-3490
Craig Perkins (202) 307-0758

STATE STATISTICAL ANALYSIS CENTERS
Linda Ruder (202) 514-9056
Donald Manson (202) 616-3491
Paul White (202) 307-0771

STRANGER-TO-STRANGER CRIME (see VICTIMS OF CRIME)

TIME SERVED IN PRISON
Craig Perkins (202) 307-0758
Carol Kaplan (Federal) (202) 307-0759

UNIFORM CRIME REPORTING DATA (see NATIONAL INCIDENT-BASED REPORTING)

URBAN AND RURAL CRIME
Ronet Bachman (202) 616-3625

VARIABLE PASSTHROUGH DATA FOR ANTI-DRUG ABUSE ACT FORMULA GRANTS (see JUSTICE EXPENDITURE AND EMPLOYMENT)

VICTIMS OF CRIME
Michael Rand (202) 616-3494
Patsy Klaus (202) 307-0776
Bruce Taylor (202) 616-3498
Ronet Bachman (202) 616-3625
Lisa Bastian (202) 616-3276
Marshall DeBerry (202) 307-0775

WEAPONS AND CRIME
Michael Rand (202) 616-3494
Bruce Taylor (202) 616-3498
Allen Beck (202) 616-3277

STATE ANALYSIS CENTERS

The Bureau of Justice Statistics has sponsored the development of statistical analysis centers in 47 states, 3 territories, and the District of Columbia. Users desiring data specific to single States should call or write the persons listed below. Users unable to contact a particular State center should contact Linda Ruder at (202) 514-9056 or the Justice Research and Statistics Association at (202) 624-8560.

ALABAMA
Larry Wright, Director
Alabama Criminal Justice Information Center
770 Washington Avenue, Suite 350
Montgomery, Alabama 36130
(205) 242-4900, Fax 242-0577

ALASKA
Allan R. Barnes, Director
Statistic Analysis Center
University of Alaska
3211 Providence Drive
Anchorage, Alaska 99508
(907) 786-1810, Fax 786-7777

ARIZONA
Roy Holt, Director
Statistical Analysis Center
Arizona Criminal Justice Commission
1501 West Washington Street, Suite 207
Phoenix, Arizona 85007
(602) 542-1928, Fax 542-4852

ARKANSAS
Larry B. Cockrell, Manager
Special Services Section
Arkansas Crime Information Center
One Capitol Mall
Little Rock, Arkansas 72201
(501) 682-2222, Fax 682-7444

CALIFORNIA
Quint Hegner, Program Manager
Statistical Analysis Center
Post Office Box 903427
Sacramento, California 94203-4270
(916) 227-3531, Fax 227-3880

COLORADO
Kim English, Director
Division of Criminal Justice
Statistical Analysis Center
700 Kipling Street, Suite 3000
Denver, Colorado 80215
(303) 239-4453, Fax 239-4491

CONNECTICUT
Dolly Reed, Chief of Research
Policy Development and Planning Division
Office of Policy and Management
80 Washington Street
Hartford, Connecticut 06106
(203) 566-3522, Fax 566-1589

DELAWARE
John P. O'Connell, Director
Statistical Analysis Center
60 The Plaza
Dover, Delaware 19901
(302) 739-4846, Fax 739-4630

DISTRICT OF COLUMBIA
Claire Johnson, Director
Criminal Justice Research Center
2000 14th Street, N.W., 8th Floor
Washington, D.C. 20009
(202) 727-6161

FLORIDA
Diane L. Zahm, Chief
Statistical Analysis Center
Florida Department of Law Enforcement
Post Office Box 1489
Tallahassee, Florida 32302
(904) 487-4808, Fax 487-4812

GEORGIA
Robert Friedman, Director
Georgia Criminal Justice
Georgia State University
Post Office Box 4018
Atlanta, Georgia 30302-4018
(404) 651-3515, Fax 651-3658

HAWAII
Thomas Green, Administrator
Crime Prevention Division
Department of the Attorney General
810 Richards Street, Suite 701
Honolulu, Hawaii 96813
(808) 548-6714, Fax 586-1424

IDAHO
Dawn Burns, Director
Support Services Bureau
Department of Law Enforcement
6111 Clinton Street
Boise, Idaho 83704
(208) 327-7170, Fax 327-7176

ILLINOIS
Alice Jones, Director
Information Resource Center
Criminal Justice Information Authority
120 South Riverside Plaza, 10th Floor
Chicago, Illinois 60606
(312) 793-8550, Fax 793-8422

INDIANA
Catherine O'Connor, Director
Statistical Analysis Center
Indiana Criminal Justice Institute
302 West Washington, Room E209
Indianapolis, Indiana 46204
(317) 232-1233, Fax 232-4979

IOWA
Richard G. Moore, Administrator
Division of Criminal Justice and Juvenile Planning
Lucas State Office Building
Des Moines, Iowa 50319
(515) 242-5816, Fax 242-6119

KANSAS
Michael E. Boyer, Supervisor
Statistical Analysis Center
Kansas Bureau of Investigation
1620 Tyler Street
Topeka, Kansas 66612
(913) 232-6000, Fax 296-6781

KENTUCKY
Jack Ellis, Director
Statistical Analysis Center
Office of the Attorney General
209 St. Clair Street
Frankfort, Kentucky 40601
(502) 564-5193, Fax 564-8317

LOUISIANA
Carle L. Jackson
State Criminal Justice Policy Advisor
Louisiana Commission on Law Enforcement
1885 Wooddale Boulevard, Suite 708
Baton Rouge, Louisiana 70806
(504) 925-4440, Fax 925-1998

COMMONWEALTH OF THE NORTHERN MARIANA ISLANDS
Joaquin Ogumoro, Executive Director
Criminal Justice Planning Agency
Commonwealth of the Northern Mariana Islands
Post Office Box 1133
Saipan, MP 96950
(670) 322-9350, Fax 322-6311

MAINE
Robert E. Pendleton, Director
Maine Criminal Justice Data Center
Department of Corrections
State House, Station 111
Augusta, Maine 04333
(207) 287-4343, Fax 287-4370

MARYLAND
Charles F. Wellford, Director Justice
Analysis Center
Institute of Criminal Justice and Criminology
University of Maryland
College Park, Maryland 20742
(301) 405-4699, Fax 405-4733

MASSACHUSETTS
William M. Holmes, Director
Statistical Analysis Center
Massachusetts Committee on Criminal Justice
100 Cambridge Street, Room 2100
Boston, Massachusetts 02202
(617) 727-0237, Fax 727-5356

MICHIGAN
John Kost, Director
Department of Management and Budget
Post Office Box 30026
Lansing, Michigan 48909
(517) 373-6510, Fax 335-1575

MINNESOTA
Daniel Storkamp, Director
Criminal Justice Statistical Analysis Center
State Planning Agency
658 Cedar Street
St. Paul, Minnesota 55155
(612) 296-7819, Fax 296-3698

MISSISSIPPI
Herbert Terry, Director
Statistical Analysis Center
Department of Criminal Justice Planning
301 West Pearl Street
Jackson, Mississippi 39203
(601) 949-2225, Fax 960-4263

MISSOURI
Martin P. Carso, Jr., Director
Statistical Analysis Center
Department of Public Safety
1510 East Elm Street
Jefferson City, Missouri 65101
(314) 751-4026, Fax 751-9382

MONTANA
Edwin Hall, Executive Director
Montana Department of Justice
Board of Crime Control
303 North Roberts Street
Helena, Montana 59620
(406) 444-3604, Fax (406) 444-4722

NEBRASKA
Michael Overton, Director
Statistical Analysis Center
Commission on Law Enforcement and Criminal Justice
Post Office Box 94946
Lincoln, Nebraska 68509
(402) 471-2194, Fax (402) 471-2837

NEVADA
Dennis De Bacco
Crime Information Services Bureau
Nevada Highway Patrol
555 Wright Way
Carson City, Nevada 89701
(702) 687-5713, Fax 687-3168

NEW HAMPSHIRE
Mark C. Thompson, Director
Statistical Analysis Center
Office of the Attorney General
State House Annex
Concord, New Hampshire 03301
(603) 271-3658, Fax (603) 271-2110

NEW JERSEY
Christine Boyle, Chief
Research and Evaluation
Department of Law and Public Safety
Hughes Justice Complex CN-085
Trenton, New Jersey 08625
(609) 984-2737, Fax (609) 984-4496

NEW MEXICO
Gary D. LaFree. Director
Statistical Analysis Center
Institute for Criminal Justice Studies
Onate Hall, University of New Mexico
Albuquerque, New Mexico 87131
(505) 277-4257, Fax (505) 277-4215

NEW YORK
Henry Brownstein, Chief
Bureau of Statistical Services
Division of Criminal Justice Services
Executive Park Tower, Stuyvesant Plaza
Albany, New York 12203
(518) 457-8381, Fax (518) 457-3089

NORTH CAROLINA
David E. Jones, Director
Criminal Justice Analysis Center
Governor's Crime Commission
3824 Barrett Drive, Suite 100
Raleigh, North Carolina 27609-7220
(919) 571-4736, Fax (919) 571-4745

NORTH DAKOTA
Robert J. Helten, Director
Information Services Section
Bureau of Criminal Investigation
4205 State Street
Bismarck, North Dakota 58502
(701) 221-5514, Fax (701) 221-5510

OHIO
Jeffrey J. Knowles, Chief
Office of Criminal Justice Services
Ohio Department of Development
400 East Town Street, Suite 120
Columbus, Ohio 43215
(614) 466-0310, Fax 466-0308

OKLAHOMA
Les D. Crabtree, Administrator
Oklahoma Criminal Justice Resource Center
621 North Robinson, Suite 445
Oklahoma City, Oklahoma 73102
(405) 232-3328, Fax (405) 235-4977

OREGON
Stephen Willhite, Director
Criminal Justice Council
Statistical Analysis Center
155 Cottage Street, Northeast
Salem, Oregon 97310
(503) 378-4123, Fax 378-8666

PENNSYLVANIA
Phillip J. Renninger, Director
Bureau of Statistics and Policy Research
Pennsylvania Commission on Crime and Delinquency
Box 1167
Harrisburg, Pennsylvania 17108
(717) 787-5152, Fax (717) 783-7713

PUERTO RICO
Julio L. Rosa Santiago, Director
Statistical Analysis Center
Office of the Attorney General
Post Office Box 192
San Juan, Puerto Rico, 00902
(809) 729-2445 or (809) 729-2261

RHODE ISLAND
Norman Dakake, Director
Statistical Analysis Center
Governor's Commission on Justice
222 Quaker Lane, Suite 100
West Warwick, Rhode Island 02893
(401) 277-2620, Fax 277-1294

SOUTH CAROLINA
Ernest C. Euler, Assistant Deputy Director
Office of Criminal Justice Programs
Office of the Governor
1205 Pendleton Street
Columbia, South Carolina 29201
(803) 734-0423, Fax (803) 734-0486

SOUTH DAKOTA
Don Brekke, Director
State Statistical Center
Office of the Attorney General
500 East Capitol Street
Pierre, South Dakota 57501
(605) 773-3215, Fax (605) 773-4629

TENNESSEE
Jacqueline Vandercook, Director
Information Systems
Tennessee Bureau of Investigation
Post Office Box 100940
Nashville, Tennessee 37244-0940
(615) 726-7970, Fax 741-4789

TEXAS
Antonio Fabelo, Director of Research
Criminal Justice Policy Council
Post Office Box 13332, Capitol Station
Austin, Texas 78711-3332
(512) 463-1810, Fax 4475-4843

U.S. VIRGIN ISLANDS
Gaylord Sprauve, Director
Law Enforcement Planning Commission
8172 Subbase, Suite 3
St. Thomas, U.S. Virgin Islands 00802-5803
(809) 774-6400, Fax 774-6400

UTAH
Richard J. Oldroyd, Director of Research
Commission on Criminal and Juvenile Justice
Room 101, Utah State Capitol
Salt Lake City, Utah 84114
(801) 538-1059

VERMONT
Max Schlueter, Director
Center for Justice Research
33 College Street
Northfield, Vermont 05602
(802) 828-8511, Fax 828-8855

VIRGINIA
Martin B. Mait, Deputy Director
Department of Criminal Justice
805 East Broad Street
Richmond, Virginia 23219
(804) 786-4000, Fax 371-8981

WASHINGTON
Glenn Olson, Director
Statistical Analysis Center
Office of Financial Management
Post Office Box 43113
Olympia, Washington 98504
(206) 586-2501, Fax (206) 586-8941

WEST VIRGINIA
Girmay Berhie, Special Projects Coordinator
Office of Research and Economic Development
Marshall University
1050 Fourth Street
Huntington, West Virginia 25701
(304) 696-2718, Fax 696-6277

WISCONSIN
Stephen W. Grohmann, Director
Office of Justice Assistance
222 State Street, 2nd Floor
Madison, Wisconsin 53702
(608) 266-7185, Fax (608) 266-6676

WYOMING
Sandy Mays, Deputy Director
Division of Criminal Investigation
Office of the Attorney General
316 West 22nd Street
Cheyenne, Wyoming 82002
(307) 777-7523, Fax 777-7252

DRUGS

The Drug Enforcement Administration of the U.S. Justice Department is a source of data on facts, figures and trends of illicit use of drugs. The information includes statistics on drug-related deaths and hospital admission due to drug abuse.

Telephone inquiries can be made to the Drug Enforcement Administration (202) 307-7977.

ECONOMICS

A list of the experts within the Bureau of Economic Analysis follows:

International Economics

Balance of Payments:	Christopher L. Bach	(202) 606-9545
Current Account Analysis	Anthony J. DiLullo	(202) 606-9558
Current Account Estimates	Howard Murad	(202) 606-9577
Capital Expenditures of Majority-Owned Foreign Affiliates of U.S. Companies	Mahnaz Fahim-Nader	(202) 606-9828
Foreign Direct Investment in the U.S.:		
Benchmark & Annual Surveys David H. Galler		(202) 606-5577
Analysis	William J. Zeile	(202) 606-9893
Quarterly & Annual Balance of Payments Data	Gregory G. Fouch	(202) 606-5577

Analysis	Sylvia E. Bargas	(202) 606-9804
New Investment Survey Analysis	Joseph F. Cherry	(202) 606-5577
	Mahnza Fahim-Nader	(202) 523-9828
Establishment-Level (Linked)	Ned G. Howenstine	(202) 606-9845
Foreign Military Sales	William O. McCormick	(202) 606-9574
Government Transactions	Christopher L. Bach	(202) 606-9545
International Transportation	Patricia Watts	(202) 606-9589
International Travel	Joan E. Bolyard	(202) 606-9550
Merchandise Trade	Kwok Lee	(202) 606-3384
U.S. Multinational Corporations, Analysis of Activities	Raymond J. Mataloni	(202) 606-9867
Private Capital Transactions	Russell B. Scholl	(202) 606-9579
Services: U.S. Transactions with Unaffiliated Foreigners:		
Benchmark Survey & Annual Selected Services Survey	Shirley J. Davis	(202) 606-5588
Other Annual Surveys, except International Transportation and Travel	Rafael I. Font	(202) 606-5588
Analysis	Anthony J. DiLullo	(202) 606-9558
	Obie G. Whichard	(202) 606-9890
U.S. Direct Investment Abroad:		
Benchmark & Annual Surveys	Patricia G. Walker	(202) 606-5566
Quarterly and Annual Balance of Payments Data	Mark W. New	(202) 606-5566
Analysis	Raymond J. Mataloni	(202) 606-9867

National Economics

Auto Output	Clint McCully	(202) 606-9735
Capital Consumption	Shelby Herman	(202) 606-9721
Capital Expenditures	Carol Moylan	(202) 606-9711
Capital Stock	Shelby Herman	(202) 606-9721
Computer Price Index	David W. Wasshausen	(202) 606-9752
Construction	Brooks B. Robinson	(202) 606-9742
Corporate Profits and Taxes	Kenneth A. Petrick	(202) 606-9738
Cyclically-Adjusted Budget	Michael Webb	(202) 606-5590
Depreciation	Shelby Herman	(202) 606-9721
Disposable Personal Income	Pauline M. Cypert	(202) 606-5301
Dividends	Kenneth A. Petrick	(202) 606-9738
Employee Benefit Plans	Paul Lally	(202) 606-9743
Employee Compensation	Paul Lally	(202) 606-9743
Environmental Studies	Gary L. Rutledge	(202) 606-5350
Farm Output, Product, and Income	George Smith	(202) 606-9746
Government, Federal:	Pamela A. Kelly	(202) 606-5591
National Defense Purchases	Karl D. Galbraith	(202) 606-5592
Nondefense Purchases	Raymen G. Labella	(202) 606-5593
Contributions and Transfers	Benyam Tsehaye	(202) 606-5591
Government, State and Local:	David F. Sullivan	(202) 606-5594
Purchases	Donald L. Peters	(202) 606-5594
Contributions and Transfers	David F. Sullivan	(202) 606-5594
Gross Domestic Product (Gross National Product):		
Computer Tapes, Diskettes, and Printouts	Phyllistine M. Barnes	(202) 606-9700
Current Estimates	Virginia H. Mannering	(202) 606-9732
Gross Domestic Product by Industry	Robert Yuskavage	(202) 606-5307
Gross Private Domestic Investment	Carol Moylan	(202) 606-9711
Input-Output Tables:		
Benchmark Tables	Mark A. Planting	(202) 606-5586
Goods-Producing Industries	Belinda Bonds	(202) 606-5586
Services-Producing Industries	Ann M. Lawson (Acting)	(202) 606-5586
Annual Tables	Karen J. Horowitz	(202) 606-5587
Computer Tapes, Diskettes and Printouts	Esther M. Carter	(202) 606-5585
Interest Income and Payments	Teresa L. Weadock	(202) 606-9753
Inventories	David B. Wasshausen	(202) 606-9752
Inventory/Sales Ratios	David B. Wasshausen	(202) 606-9752

National Income	Leon W. Taub	(202) 606-9722
Net Exports	Corrine Krincek	(202) 606-9729
Output Measures	Christian Ehemann	(202) 606-9717
Personal Consumption Expenditures	Clint McCully	(202) 606-9735
Autos	Everette P. Johnson	(202) 606-9725
Other Goods	Greg Key	(202) 606-9727
Prices	Clint McCully	(202) 606-9735
Services	Craig Yokum Myung Han	(202) 606-9705 (202) 606-9719
Personal Income	Pauline M. Cypert	(202) 606-5301
Plant and Equipment Expenditures	Jeffrey W. Crawford	(202) 606-9713
Pollution Abatement and Control Spending	Gary L. Rutledge	(202) 606-5350
Price Measures (Fixed Weighted)	Christian Ehemann	(202) 606-9717
Producers' Durable Equipment	Jeffrey W. Crawford	(202) 606-9713
Proprietors' Income, Nonfarm	Willie J. Abney	(202) 606-9701
Rental Income	Denise A. McBride	(202) 606-9733
Residential Construction	Brooks B. Robinson	(202) 606-9742
Saving	Gerald F. Donahoe	(202) 606-9715
Structures	Brooks B. Robinson	(202) 606-9742
United Nations and OECD System of National Accounts	Eugene P. Seskin	(202) 606-9744
Wages and Salaries	Paul Lally	(202) 606-9743
Wealth Estimates	Shelby Herman	(202) 606-9721

Regional Economics

BEA Long-Term Projections	Staff	(202) 606-5341
BEA Mid-Term Projections	Staff	(202) 606-5342
RIMS II, Regional Multipliers	Staff	(202) 606-5343
READ, Press Releases and Current Economic Analysis	Staff	(202) 606-5344
Gross State Product Estimates	Staff	(202) 606-5340

Personal Income and Employment -- States, Metropolitan Areas, and Counties		(202) 606-4500
Requests for Personal Income and Employment Data	Regional Economic Information Systems Staff	(202) 606-5360
Disposable Personal Income	Robert Brown	(202) 606-4500
Dividends, Interest, and Rental Income	Charles A. Jolley	(202) 606-4500
Farm Proprietors' Income and Employment	James M. Zavrel	(202) 606-4500
Methodology	Wallace K. Bailey	(202) 606-4500
Nonfarm Proprietors' Income and Employment	Bruce Levine	(202) 606-4500
Residence Adjustment	Daniel Zabronsky	(202) 606-4500
State Quarterly Personal Income	Isabelle P. Whiston	(202) 606-4500
Transfer Payments	Bruce Levine	(202) 606-4500
Wage and Salary Income and Employment	Sharon Carnevale	(202) 606-4500

EDUCATION

The U.S. Department of Education's National Library of Education collects and disseminates information on topics such as enrollment, teaching staff, retention rates, educational finances, educational performance, financial assistance. Information covers all educational levels from elementary to vocational education, and includes data on libraries and public television.

For information call the Statistical Information Office (800) 424-1616.

ENERGY

The National Energy Information Center of the U.S. Department of Energy provides statistical and analytical energy data, and information, referral assistance to the government and private sectors, academia, and the general public.

For questions of a general nature about energy data call (202) 586-8800. For specific topics, call the above number and speak to the following individuals:

COAL

Dorothy Karsteter Karen Vassallo	(202) 586-8800

DISTRIBUTION OF MACHINE-READABLE DATA

Sandra Wilkins	(202) 586-8800

ELECTRIC AND NUCLEAR POWER
Tom Welch (202) 586-8800

NATURAL GAS
Paula Altman (202) 586-8800

PETROLEUM
Leola Withrow (202) 586-8800

RENEWABLE ENERGY RESOURCES/CONSERVATION
Marion King (202) 586-8800
Karen Freedman

FOREIGN COUNTRIES STATISTICS OR INTERNATIONAL STATISTICS ON SPECIFIC COUNTRIES

The Census Bureau's Center for International Research maintains an electronic data base offering computerized statistical tables on social, demographic and economic information on most of the countries in the world. To make inquiries on how to access this data call Peter Johnson (301) 457-1403.

HEALTH

The National Center for Health Statistics of the U.S. Department of Health and Human Services collects and disseminates data on every aspect of health and health care in the United States. To identify specific agency programs which provide inquiry assistance, callers may contact (301) 436-7085.

HOUSING

The U.S. Department of Housing and Urban Development is the principal federal agency responsible for programs concerned with the Nation's housing needs, fair housing opportunities, and improvement and development of the Nation's communities. Inquiries on housing statistics can be made to (202) 708-1600.

INTERNATIONAL TRADE

Listing of Country Desk Officers

Afghanistan	Timothy Gilman	(202) 482-2954
Albania	Jeremy Keller	(202) 482-4915
Algeria	Christopher Cerone	(202) 482-1860
	Claude Clement	(202) 482-5545
Angola	Finn Holm-Olsen	(202) 482-4228
Anguilla	Michelle Brooks	(202) 482-2527
Antigua/Barbuda	Michelle Brooks	(202) 482-2527
Argentina	Randolph Mye	(202) 482-1548
Armenia	Lynn Fabrizio	(202) 482-0988
Aruba	Michelle Brooks	(202) 482-2527
ASEAN	George Paine	(202) 482-3877
Australia	Gary Bouck	(202) 482-2471
	William Golike	(202) 482-2471
Austria	Philip Combs	(202) 482-2920
Azerbaijan	Lynn Fabrizio	(202) 482-0988
Bahamas	Mark Siegelman	(202) 482-5680
Bahrain	Claude Clement	(202) 482-5545
	Chris Cerone	(202) 482-1860
Balkin States	Jeremy Keller	(202) 482-4915
Bangladesh	John Simmons	(202) 482-2954
Barbados	Michelle Brooks	(202) 482-2527
Belarus	Christine Lucyk	(202) 482-1104
Belgium	Simon Bensimon	(202) 482-5041
Belize	Michelle Brooks	(202) 482-2527
Benin	Debra Henke	(202) 482-5149
Bermuda	Michelle Brooks	(202) 482-2527
Bhutan	Timothy Gilman	(202) 482-2954
Bolivia	Rebecca Hunt	(202) 482-2521
Botswana	Finn Holm-Olsen	(202) 482-4228
Brazil	Larry Farris	(202) 482-3871
	Horace Jennings	(202) 482-3872
Brunei	Raphael Cung	(202) 482-3877
Bulgaria	Jeremy Keller	(202) 482-4915
Burkina Faso	Phillip Michelini	(202) 482-4388
Burma (Myanmar)	George Paine	(202) 482-3877
Burundi	Phillip Michelini	(202) 482-4388
Cambodia	Hong-Phong B. Pho	(202) 482-3877
Cameroon	Debra Henke	(202) 482-5149
Canada	Jonathan Don	(202) 482-3103
Cape Verde	Phillip Michelini	(202) 482-4388
Caribbean Basin	Jay Dowling	(202) 482-1648
Cayman Islands	Michelle Brooks	(202) 482-2527
Central African Republic	Phillip Michelini	(202) 482-4388
Chad	Phillip Michelini	(202) 482-4388
Chile	Roger Turner	(202) 482-1495
Colombia	Paul Moore	(202) 482-1659
Comoros	Chandra Watkins	(202) 482-4564
Congo	Debra Henke	(202) 482-5149
Costa Rica	Mark Siegelman	(202) 482-5880
Cote d'Ivoire	Philip Michelini	(202) 482-4388
Cuba	Mark Siegelman	(202) 482-5880
Cyprus	Ann Corro	(202) 482-3945
Czech Republic	Mark Mowrey	(202) 482-4915
Denmark	Maryanne Kendall	(202) 482-3254
D'Jibouti	Chandra Watkins	(202) 482-4564
Dominica	Michelle Brooks	(202) 482-2527
Dominican Republic	Mark Siegelman	(202) 482-5880
East Caribbean	Michelle Brooks	(202) 482-2527
Ecuador	Paul Moore	(202) 482-1659
Egypt	Thomas Sams	(202) 482-1860
	Corey Wright	(202) 482-5508
El Salvador	Helen Lee	(202) 482-2528
Equatorial Guinea	Philip Michelini	(202) 482-4388
Eritrea	Chandra Watkins	(202) 482-4564
Estonia	Pam Green	(202) 482-4915
Ethiopia	Chandra Watkins	(202) 482-4564
European Community	Charles Ludolph	(202) 482-5276
Finland	Maryanne Kendall	(202) 482-3254
France	Elena Mikalis	(202) 482-6008
Gabon	Debra Henke	(202) 482-5149
Gambia	Phillip Michelini	(202) 482-4388
Georgia	Lynn Fabrizio	(202) 482-0988
Germany	Brenda Fisher	(202) 482-2435
	John Larsen	(202) 482-2434
Ghana	Debra Henke	(202) 482-5149
Greece	Ann Corro	(202) 482-3945

Grenada	Michelle Brooks	(202) 482-2527
Guadeloupe	Michelle Brooks	(202) 482-2527
Guatemala	Helen Lee	(202) 482-2528
Guinea	Phillip Michelini	(202) 482-4388
Guinea-Bissau	Phillip Michelini	(202) 482-4388
Guyana	Michelle Brooks	(202) 482-2527
Haiti	Mark Siegelman	(202) 482-5680
Honduras	Helen Lee	(202) 482-2528
Hong Kong	Sheila Baker	(202) 482-3932
Hungary	Brian Toohey	(202) 482-4915
Iceland	Maryanne Kendall	(202) 482-3254
India	John Simmons	(202) 482-2954
	John Crown	
	Tim Gilman	
Indonesia	Karen Goddin	(202) 482-3877
Iran	Paul Thanos	(202) 482-1860
Iraq	Thomas Sams	(202) 482-1860
	Corey Wright	(202) 482-5506
Ireland	Boyce Fitzpatrick	(202) 482-2177
Israel	Paul Thanos	(202) 482-1860
Italy	Boyce Fitzpatrick	(202) 482-2177
Ivory Coast	Phillip Michelini	(202) 482-4388
Jamaica	Mark Siegelman	(202) 482-5680
Japan	Edward A. Leslie	(202) 482-2425
	Eric Kennedy	
	Cynthia Campbell	
	Allan Christian	
Jordan	Corey Wright	(202) 482-5508
	Thomas Sams	(202) 482-1860
Kazakhstan	Pam Feodoroff	(202) 482-0360
Kenya	Chandra Watkins	(202) 482-4564
Korea	Dan Duvall	(202) 482-4390
	Jeffrey Donius	
Kuwait	Corey Wright	(202) 482-5506
	Thomas Sams	(202) 482-1860
Kyrgsztan	Pam Feodoroff	(202) 482-0360
Laos	Hong-Phong B. Pho	(202) 482-3877
Latria	Pam Green	(202) 482-4915
Lebanon	Corey Wright	(202) 482-5506
	Thomas Sams	(202) 482-1860
Lesotho	Finn Holm-Olsen	(202) 482-4228
Liberia	Phillip Michelini	(202) 482-4388
Libya	Claude Clement	(202) 482-5545
	Christopher Cerone	(202) 482-1860
Lithuania	Pam Green	(202) 482-4915
Luxembourg	Simon Bensimon	(202) 482-5401
Macau	Shelia Baker	(202) 482-3932
Madagascar	Chandra Watkins	(202) 482-4564
Malawi	Finn Holm-Olsen	(202) 482-4228
Malaysia	Raphael Cung	(202) 482-3877
Maldives	John Simmons	(202) 482-2954
Mali	Phillip Michelini	(202) 482-4388
Malta	Robert McLaughlin	(202) 482-3748
Martinique	Michelle Brooks	(202) 482-2527
Mauritania	Phillip Michelini	(202) 482-4388
Mauritius	Chandra Watkins	(202) 482-4564
Mexico	Shawn Ricks	(202) 482-0300
Moldora	Lynn Fabrizio	(202) 482-0988
Mongolia	Shelia Baker	(202) 482-3932
Montserrat	Michelle Brooks	(202) 482-2527
Morocco	Claude Clement	(202) 482-5545
	Christopher Cerone	(202) 482-1860
Mozambique	Finn Holm-Olsen	(202) 482-4228
Namibia	Finn Holm-Olsen	(202) 482-4228
Nepal	Timothy Gilman	(202) 482-2954
Netherlands	Simon Bensimon	(202) 482-5401
Netherlands Antilles	Michelle Brooks	(202) 482-2527
New Zealand	Gary Bouck	(202) 482-3647
	William Golike	
Nicaragua	Jay Dowling	(202) 482-1648
Niger	Phillip Michelini	(202) 482-4388
Nigeria	Debra Henke	(202) 482-5149
Norway	James Devlin	(202) 482-4414
Oman	Paul Thanos	(202) 482-1860
Pacific Islands	Gary Bouck	(202) 482-2471
	William Golike	
Pakistan	Timothy Gilman	(202) 482-2954
Panama	Helen Lee	(202) 482-2528
Paraguay	Randolph Mye	(202) 482-1548
People's Rep. of China	Cheryl McQueen	(202) 482-3932
	Laura McCall	(202) 482-3583
Peru	Rebecca Hunt	(202) 482-2521
Philippines	George Paine	(202) 482-3877
Poland	Audrey Zuck	(202) 482-4915
Portugal	Mary Beth Double	(202) 482-4508
Puerto Rico	Mark Siegelman	(202) 482-5680
Qatar	Paul Thanos	(202) 482-1870
Romania	Pam Green	(202) 482-4915
Russia	Lyn Fabrizio	(202) 482-0988
Rwanda	Phillip Michelini	(202) 482-4388
Sao Tome & Principe	Phillip Michelini	(202) 482-4388
Saudi Arabia	Christopher Cerone	(202) 482-1860
	Claude Clement	(202) 482-5545
Senegal	Phillip Michelini	(202) 482-4388
Seychelles	Chandra Watkins	(202) 482-4564
Sierra Leone	Phillip Michelini	(202) 482-4388
Singapore	Raphael Cung	(202) 482-3877
Slovak Republic	Mark Mowrey	(202) 482-4915
Somalia	Chandra Watkins	(202) 482-4564
South Africa	Emily Solomon	(202) 482-5148
Spain	Mary Beth Double	(202) 482-4508
Sri Lanka	John Simmons	(202) 482-2954
St. Batholemey	Michelle Brooks	(202) 482-2527
St. Kitts-Nevis	Michelle Brooks	(202) 482-2527
St. Lucia	Michelle Brooks	(202) 482-2527
St. Martin	Michelle Brooks	(202) 482-2527
St. Vincent-Grenadines	Michelle Brooks	(202) 482-2527
Sudan	Chandra Watkins	(202) 482-4564
Suriname	Michelle Brooks	(202) 482-2527
Swaziland	Finn Holm-Olsen	(202) 482-4228
Sweden	James Devlin	(202) 482-4414
Switzerland	Philip Combs	(202) 482-2920
Syria	Corey Wright	(202) 482-5506
	Thomas Sams	(202) 482-1860
Taiwan	Robert Chu	(202) 482-4390
	Dan Duvall	
Tajikistan	Pam Feodoroff	(202) 482-0360
Tanzania	Finn Holm-Olsen	(202) 482-4228
Thailand	Jean Kelly	(202) 482-3877
Togo	Debra Henke	(202) 482-3317
Trinidad & Tobago	Michelle Brooks	(202) 482-2527
Tunisia	Corey Wright	(202) 482-5506
	Thomas Sams	(202) 482-1860
Turkey	Ann Corro	(202) 482-3945
Turkmemistan	Pam Feodoroff	(202) 482-0360
Turks & Caicos Islands	Mark Siegelman	(202) 482-5680
Uganda	Chandra Watkins	(202) 482-4564
Ukraine	Chris Lucyk	(202) 482-1104
United Arab Emirates	Claude Clement	(202) 482-5545
	Chris Cerone	(202) 482-1860
United Kingdom	Robert McLaughlin	(202) 482-3748
Uruguay	Roger Turner	(202) 482-1495
Uzbekistan	Pam Feodoroff	(202) 482-0360
Venezuela	Laura Zeiger-Hatfield	(202) 482-4303
Vietnam	Hong-Phong B. Pho	(202) 482-3877
Virgin Islands (UK)	Michelle Brooks	(202) 482-2527
Virgin Islands (US)	Mark Siegelman	(202) 482-5680
Yemen, Republic of	Paul Thanos	(202) 482-1860

Yugoslavia Republics (former)	Jeremy Keller	(202) 482-4915
Zaire	Phillip Michelini	(202) 482-4388
Zambia	Finn Holm-Olsen	(202) 482-4228
Zimbabwe	Finn Holm-Olsen	(202) 482-4228

Listing of ITA Industry Desks

Abrasive Products	Graylin Presbury	(202) 482-5158
Accounting	J. Marc Chittum	(202) 482-0345
Adhesives/Sealants	Raimundo Prat	(202) 482-0128
Advanced Materials	George Driscoll	(202) 482-4431
Advertising	Frederick Elliott	(202) 482-1134
Aerospace Financing Issues	Jeff Jackson	(202) 482-4222
Aerospace Industry Analysis	Juliet Bender	(202) 482-4222
Aerospace Industry Data	Eric McDonald	(202) 482-4222
Aerospace Information and Analysis	Eric McDonald	(202) 482-4222
Aerospace Market Development	Tony Largay	(202) 482-2835
Aerospace Market Promo	Tony Largay	(202) 482-2835
Aerospace-Space Market Support	Clay Mowry	(202) 482-4222
Aerospace Marketing Support	Heather Pederson	(202) 482-2835
Aerospace, Office of	Sally H. Beth	(202) 482-1229
Aerospace-Space Programs	Clay Mowry	(202) 482-4222
Aerospace Trade Policy Issues	Juliet Bender	(202) 482-4222
Aerospace (Trade Promo)	Tony Largay	(202) 482-2835
Agribusiness (Major Project)	Richard Bell	(202) 482-2460
Agricultural Chemicals	Francis P. Maxey	(202) 482-0128
Agricultural Machinery	Mary Weining	(202) 482-4708
Air Conditioning Equipment	Richard Bell	(202) 482-5126
Air Couriers	Frederick Elliot	(202) 482-5126
Air, Gas Compressors	Edward McDonald	(202) 482-0680
Air, Gas Compressors (Trade Promo)	George Zanetakos	(202) 482-0552
Air Pollution Control Equipment	Loretta Jonkers	(202) 482-0564
Aircraft and Aircraft Engines (Market Support)	Heather Pederson	(202) 482-2835
Aircraft Auxiliary Equipment (Market Support)	Heather Pederson	(202) 482-2835
Aircraft Parts (Market Support)	Audrey Smerkanich	(202) 482-1228
Airlines	Eugene Alford	(202) 482-5071
Airport Equipment	Audrey Smerkanich	(202) 482-1228
Airports (Major Projects)	Jay L. Smith	(202) 482-4642
Air Traffic Control Equipment	Audrey Smerkanich	(202) 482-1228
Air Transport Services	Eugene Alford	(202) 482-5071
Alcoholic Beverages	Cornelius Kenney	(202) 482-2428
Aluminum	David Cammarota	(202) 482-5157
Aluminum Oxide	Graylin Presbury	(202) 482-5158
Analytical Instrument	Marquarite Nealon	(202) 482-3411
Analytical & Scientific Instruments (Trade Promo)	Franc Manzolillo	(202) 482-2991
Apparel	William J. Dulka	(202) 482-4058
Apparel (Trade Promo)	Ferenc Molnar	(202) 482-2043
Artificial Intelligence	Shelagh Montgomery	(202) 482-0397
Asbestos/Cement Product	Charles Pitcher	(202) 482-0132
Audio Visual Services	John Siegmund	(202) 482-4781
Auto Industry Affairs	Stuart Keitz	(202) 482-0554
Auto Industry (Trade Promo)	John C. White	(202) 482-0671
Auto Parts & Supplies	Robert O. Reck	(202) 482-1418
Aviation Services	Eugene Alford	(202) 482-5071
Avionics Marketing	Heather Pederson	(202) 482-2835
Bakery Products	William V. Janis	(202) 482-2250
Ball Bearings	Richard Reise	(202) 482-3489
Banking Services	John Shuman	(202) 482-3050
Basic Paper & Board Mfg	Gary Stanley	(202) 482-0375
Bauxite, Alumina	David Cammarota	(202) 482-5157
Beer	Cornelius Kenney	(202) 482-2428
Belting and Hose	Raimundo Prat	(202) 482-0128
Beryllium	Barbara Males	(202) 482-0606
Beverages	Cornelius Kenney	(202) 482-2428
Bicycles	John Vanderwolf	(202) 482-0348
Biomass Energy Equip.	Les Garden	(202) 482-0556
Biotechnology	Emily Arakaki	(202) 482-0128
Boats	John Vanderwolf	(202) 482-0348
Books	William S. Lofquist	(202) 482-0379
Books (Export Promo)	Edward Kimmel	(202) 482-3640
Breakfast Cereal	William V. Janis	(202) 482-2250
Bridges (Major Proj)	Jay L. Smith	(202) 482-4642
Broadcasting Equipment	Theresa Rettig	(202) 482-4466
Brooms and Brushes	John M. Harris	(202) 482-1178
Building Materials & Const.	Charles B. Pitcher	(202) 482-0132
Business Forms	Rose Marie Bratland	(202) 482-0380
CAD/CAM/CAE Software	Vera A. Swann	(202) 482-0396
Canned Food Products	William V. Janis	(202) 482-2250
Carbon Black	Raimundo Prat	(202) 482-0128
Cellular Radio Telephone Equipment	S. McCullough	(202) 482-4466
Cement	Charles B. Pitcher	(202) 482-0132
Cements Plants (Major Proj)	Jay Brandes	(202) 482-3352
Chemical Industrial Mach.	Eugene Shaw	(202) 482-3494
Chemical Plants (Major Proj)	Jay Brandes	(202) 482-3352
Chemical and Allied Products	Michael Kelly	(202) 482-0128
Chinaware	Rose Marie Bratland	(202) 482-0380
Chromium	Graylin Presbury	(202) 482-5158
Civil Aircraft Agreement	Juliet Bender	(202) 482-4222
Civil Aviation Policy	Eugene Alford	(202) 482-5071
Coal Exports	John Rasmussen	(202) 482-1466
Cobalt	Graylin Presbury	(202) 482-5158
Columbium	Graylin Presbury	(202) 482-5158
Commercial Aircraft (Trade Policy)	Juliet Bender	(202) 482-4222
Commercial Lighting Fixtures	John Bodson	(202) 482-0681
Commercial/Industrial Refrigeration Equipment	Richard Bell	(202) 482-5126
Commercial Printing	William S. Lofquist	(202) 482-0379
Commercialization of Space (Market)	Clay Mowry	(202) 482-4222
Computer Consulting	Robert Atkins	(202) 482-4781
Computer and DP Services	Robert Atkins	(202) 482-4781
	Mary C. Inoussa	(202) 482-5820
Computer Software	Heidi Hijikata	(202) 482-0569
Computer Systems	Timothy O. Miles	(202) 482-2990
Computers, Large Scale	Jonathan Streeter	(202) 482-0480
Computer, Personal	R. Clay Woods	(202) 482-3013
Computer, Portable	Heidi M. Hoffman	(202) 482-0569

Computers, Trade Promo	Judy A. Fogg	(202) 482-4936
Computers, Workstations	Heidi Hoffman	(202) 482-2053
Confectionery Products	Cornelius Kenney	(202) 482-2428
Construction	Patrick MacAuley	(202) 482-0132
Construction Machinery Large, Off Road	L. Heimowitz	(202) 482-0558
Consumer Electronics	Howard Fleming	(202) 482-5163
Consumer Goods	Harry Bodansky	(202) 482-5783
Containers & Packaging	Patrick Cosslett	(202) 482-5125
Copper	Barbara Males	(202) 482-0606
Cosmetics (Export Promo)	Edward K. Kimmel	(202) 482-3640
Countertrade Services	Paula Michell	(202) 482-4471
	Pompiliu Verzariu	(202) 482-4434
Cutlery	Rose Marie Bratland	(202) 482-0380
Dairy Products	William V. Janis	(202) 482-2250
Data Base Services	Mary C. Inoussa	(202) 482-5820
Data Processing Services	Robert C. Atkins	(202) 482-4781
Dental Equipment	Patricia Eyring	(202) 482-2846
Dental Equipment (Trade Promo)	George Keen	(202) 482-2010
Desalination/Water Reuse	Frederica Wheeler	(202) 482-3509
Desalination (Major Proj)	William Holroyd	(202) 482-6168
Diamond, Industrial	Graylin Presbury	(202) 482-5158
Direct Marketing	Fred Elliott	(202) 482-1134
Disk Storage	Daniel Valverde	(202) 482-0573
Distilled Spirits	Cornelius Kenney	(202) 482-2428
Dolls	Donald Hodgen	(202) 482-3346
Drugs	William Hurt	(202) 482-0128
Durable Consumer Goods	Kevin M. Ellis	(202) 482-1176
Earthenware	Rose Marie Bratland	(202) 482-0380
Education Facilities (Major Project)	Barbara White	(202) 482-4160
Educational/Training	A. Chandersekaran	(202) 482-1316
Electric Industrial Apparatus Nec	John Bodson	(202) 482-0681
Electric/Power Plants (Major Proj)	Robert Dollison	(202) 482-2733
Elec, Power Gen, Trans. & Dist. Eqmt (Trade Promo)	Anthony Kostalas	(202) 482-2390
Electrical Test & Measuring, Instruments	Erin Finn	(202) 482-2795
Electricity	William Sugg	(202) 482-1466
Electronic Components	Judee Mussehl-Aziz	(202) 482-0429
Electronic Components/ Production & Test Equip (Trade Promo)	Marlene Ruffin	(202) 482-0570
Electronic Database Services	Mary C. Inoussa	(202) 482-5820
ElectroOptical Instruments (Trade Promo)	Franc Manzollilo	(202) 482-2991
ElectroOptical Instruments	Marguerite Nealon	(202) 482-3411
Elevators, Moving Stairways	Mary Weining	(202) 482-4708
Energy (Commodities)	Joseph J. Yancik	(202) 482-1466
Energy, Renewable	Les Garden	(202) 482-0556
Energy Services	Helen Burroughs	(202) 482-1542
Entertainment Industries	John Siegmund	(202) 482-4781
Environment Trade Promo	Loretta Jonkers	(202) 482-0564
	Mildred Mack	(202) 482-0616
	Catherine P. Vial	(202) 482-0617
	Frederica Wheeler	(202) 482-3509
Explosives	Francis P. Maxey	(202) 482-0128
Export Trading Companies Don Stow		(202) 482-5131
Fabricated Metal Construction Materials	Franklin Williams	(202) 482-0132
Factoring	Mary Ann Ring	(202) 482-4472
Farm Machinery	Mary Weining	(202) 482-4708
Fasteners (Industrial)	Richard Reise	(202) 482-3489
Fats and Oils	William V. Janis	(202) 482-2250
Fencing (Metal)	Patrick MacAuley	(202) 482-0132
Ferroalloys Products	Graylin Presbury	(202) 482-5158
Ferrous Scrap	Charles Bell	(202) 482-0608
Fertilizers	Francis P. Maxey	(202) 482-0128
Fertilizer Plants Major Projects	Jay Brandes	(202) 482-3352
Fiber Optics	Anthony Mocenigo	(202) 482-4466
Filters/Purifying Eqmt	Frederica Wheeler	(202) 482-3509
Flat Panel Displays	Heidi M. Hoffman	(202) 482-2053
Flexible Manufacturing Systems	Megan Pilaroscia	(202) 482-0609
Floor Covering, Hard Surf	Patrick MacAuley	(202) 482-0132
Flour	William V. Janis	(202) 482-2250
Fluid Power	Edward McDonald	(202) 482-0680
Food Products Machinery	Eugene Shaw	(202) 482-3494
Food Retailing	Cornelius Kenney	(202) 482-2428
Footwear	James E. Byron	(202) 482-4034
Foreign Sales Corporations	Helen Burroughs	(202) 482-1542
Forest Products	Gary Stanley	(202) 482-0375
Forfaiting	Mary Ann Ring	(202) 482-4472
Forgings Semifinished Steel	Charles Bell	(202) 482-0608
Fossil Fuel Power Gen. (Major Project)	Robert Dollison	(202) 482-2733
Foundry Industry	Charles Bell	(202) 482-0608
Frozen Foods Producsts	William V. Janis	(202) 482-2250
Fruits	William V. Janis	(202) 482-2250
Fur Goods	James E. Bryon	(202) 482-4034
Furniture	Donald Hodgen	(202) 482-3346
Gallium	David Cammarota	(202) 482-5157
Games and Children's Vehicles	Donald Hodgen	(202) 482-3346
Gaskets/Gasketing Materials	Richard Reise	(202) 482-3489
General Aviation Aircraft	Ron Green	(202) 482-4222
Geothernal Energy Eqmt	Les Garden	(202) 482-0556
Germanium	David Cammarota	(202) 482-5157
Giftware (Trade Promo)	Reginald Beckham	(202) 482-5478
Glass, Flat	Franklin Williams	(202) 482-0132
Glassware	Rose Marie Bratland	(202) 482-0380
Gloves (Work & Dress)	James E. Byron	(202) 482-4034
Gold	Graylin Presbury	(202) 482-5158
Grain Mill Products	William V. Janis	(202) 482-2250
Greeting Cards	Rose Marie Bratland	(202) 482-0380
Grocery Retailing	Cornelius Kenney	(202) 482-2428
Ground Water Exploration and Development	Frederica Wheeler	(202) 482-3509
Guns and Ammunition	John Vanderwolf	(202) 482-0348
Hand Saws, Saw Blades	Edward Abrahams	(202) 482-0312
Hand/Edge Tools Ex Mach TI/Saws	Edward Abrahams	(202) 482-0312
Handbags	James E. Byron	(202) 482-4034
Hardware (Export Promo)	Reginald Beckham	(202) 482-5478
Health Care Services	Simon Francis	(202) 482-2697
Helicopters	Ron Green	(202) 482-4222
Helicopters (Market Sup)	George Driscoll	(202) 482-2835
High Tech Trade, U.S. Competitiveness	Victoria L. Hatter	(202) 482-3895
Highways (Major Proj)	Jay L. Smith	(202) 482-4642
Hoists, Overhead Cranes	Mary Weining	(202) 482-4708

Hose and Belting	Raimundo Prat	(202) 482-0128
Hospitals (Major Proj)	Wallace Haraguchi	(202) 482-4877
Hotel and Restaurants Equip (Export Promo)	Edward K. Kimmel	(202) 482-3640
Household Appliances	John M. Harris	(202) 482-1178
Household Appliances (Export Promo)	Reginald Beckham	(202) 482-5478
Household Furniture	Donald Hodgen	(202) 482-3346
Housewares (Export Promo)	Reginald Beckham	(202) 482-5478
Housing Construction, Domestic	Patrick McAuley	(202) 482-0132
Housing Construction, International	Patrick Cosslett	(202) 482-5125
Hydroelectric Power, Major Projects	Robert Dollison	(202) 482-2733
Industrial Controls	John Bodson	(202) 482-0681
Industrial Drives/Gears	Richard Reise	(202) 482-3489
Industrial Organic Chemicals	William Hurt	(202) 482-0128
Industrial Robots	Megan Pilaroscia	(202) 482-0609
Industrial Trucks	Mary Wiening	(202) 482-4608
Information Services	Mary C. Inoussa	(202) 482-5820
Insulation	Patrick McAuley	(202) 482-0132
Insurance	Bruce McAdam	(202) 482-0346
	S. Cassin Muir	(202) 482-0349
Iridium	Graylin Presbury	(202) 482-5158
Irrigation Equipment	Mary Wiening	(202) 482-4608
Jams and Jellies	William V. Janis	(202) 482-2250
Jewelry	John Harris	(202) 482-1178
Jewelry (Trade Promo)	Reginald Beckham	(202) 482-5478
Jute Products	Maria D'Andrea	(202) 482-4058
Kitchen Cabinets	Barbara Wise	(202) 482-0375
LNG Plants, Major Proj	Jay Brandes	(202) 482-3352
Laboratory Instruments	Marguerite Nealon	(202) 482-3411
Laboratory Instruments (Trade Promo)	Franc Manzollilo	(202) 482-2991
Lasers	Marguerite Nealon	(202) 482-3411
Lasers (Trade Promo)	Franc Manzollilo	(202) 482-2991
Lawn and Garden Equip	Donald Hodgen	(202) 482-3346
Lead Products	David Larrabee	(202) 482-0607
Leasing Equipment	Elmora Uzzelle	(202) 482-4854
Leather Products	James E. Byron	(202) 482-4034
Leather Tanning	James E. Byron	(202) 482-4034
Legal Services	J. Marc Chittum	(202) 482-0345
Local Area Networks	Mary Davin	(202) 482-0568
Logs, Wood	Barbara Wise	(202) 482-0375
Luggage	James E. Byron	(202) 482-4034
Lumber	Barbara Wise	(202) 482-0375
Machine Tool Accessories	Edward Abrahams	(202) 482-0312
Magazines	Rose Marie Bratland	(202) 482-0380
Magnesium	David Cammarota	(202) 482-5157
Management Consulting	J. Marc Chittum	(202) 482-0345
Manganese	Graylin Presbury	(202) 482-5158
Manifold Business Forms	Rose Marie Bratland	(202) 482-0380
Manmade Fiber	William Dulka	(202) 482-4058
Margarine	William V. Janis	(202) 482-2250
Marine Insurance	C. William Johnson	(202) 482-5012
Marine Recreational Equip (Export Promo)	Reginald Beckham	(202) 482-5478
Maritime Shipping	C. William Johnson	(202) 482-5012
Mass Transit (Major Proj)	Jay L. Smith	(202) 482-4642
Mattresses & Bedding	Donald Hodgen	(202) 482-3346
Meat Products	William V. Janis	(202) 482-2250
Mechanical Power Transmission Equipment	Richard Reise	(202) 482-3489
Medical/Dental Eqmt, Special Projects	Gregory Rathmell	(202) 482-2798
Medical Equipment	Matthew Edwards	(202) 482-0550
	Victoria Kader	(202) 482-4073
Medical Facilities (Major Project)	Wallace Haraguchi	(202) 482-4877
Medical Instruments (Trade Promo)	George B. Keen	(202) 482-2010
Metal Building Products	Franklin Williams	(202) 482-0132
Metal Cookware	Rose Marie Bratland	(202) 482-0380
Metal Cutting Machine Tools	Megan Pilaroscia	(202) 482-0609
Metal Forming Machine Tools	Megan Pilaroscia	(202) 482-0609
Metal Powders	Barbara Males	(202) 482-0606
Metals, Secondary	David Cammarota	(202) 482-5157
Metalworking	Megan Pilaroscia	(202) 482-0609
Mica	Graylin Presbury	(202) 482-5158
Microelectronics	Margaret Donnelly	(202) 482-5466
Microwave Communications	Carrie Neff	(202) 482-4466
Millwork	Franklin Williams	(202) 482-0132
Mineral Based Construction Materials (Clay/Concrete/Gypsum)	Charles B. Pitcher	(202) 482-0132
Mining Machinery	Edward McDonald	(202) 482-0680
Mining Machinery (Trade Promo)	George Zanetakos	(202) 482-0552
Mining (Major Promo)	Jay Brandes	(202) 482-3352
Miscellaneous Publishing	William S. Lofquist	(202) 482-0379
Mobile Homes	Patrick Cosslett	(202) 482-5125
Mobile Radios	Carrie Neff	(202) 482-4466
Molybdenum	Graylin Presbury	(202) 482-5158
Monorails, Industrial	Mary Weining	(202) 482-4708
Motion Pictures	John Siegmund	(202) 482-4781
Motor Vehicles	Albert T. Warner	(202) 482-0669
Motorcycles	John Vanderwolf	(202) 482-0348
Motors, Electric	John Bodson	(202) 482-0681
Music	John Siegmund	(202) 482-4781
Musical Instruments	John Harris	(202) 482-1178
Mutual Funds	S. Cassin Muir	(202) 482-0349
NATO	Alexis Kemper	(202) 482-4466
Natural Gas	Tom Gillett	(202) 482-1466
Natural, Synthetic Rubber	Raimundo Prat	(202) 482-0128
Newspapers	Rose Marie Bratland	(202) 482-0380
Nickel Products	Graylin Presbury	(202) 482-5158
Niobium	Graylin Presbury	(202) 482-5158
Nonalcoholic Beverages	Cornelius Kenney	(202) 482-2428
Noncurrent Carrying Wiring Devices	John Bodson	(202) 482-0681
Nondurable Consumer Goods	Leslie B. Simon	(202) 482-0341
Nonferrous Metals	David Cammarota	(202) 482-5157
Nonresidential Construction	Patrick MacAuley	(202) 482-0132
Nuclear Power Plants (Major Project)	Robert Dollison	(202) 482-2733
Numerical Controls for Machinery Tools	Megan Pilaroscia	(202) 482-0609
Nuts, Bolts, Washers	Richard Reise	(202) 482-3489
Ocean Shipping	C. William Johnson	(202) 482-5012
Office Buildings, Major Proj	Wallace Haraguchi	(202) 482-4877
Office Furniture	Donald Hodgen	(202) 482-3346

Oil and Gas Development & Refining (Major Proj)	Jay Brandes	(202) 482-3352
Oil and Gas (Fuels Only)	Tom Gillett	(202) 482-1466
Oil/ Gas Field Machinery	Edward McDonald	(202) 482-0680
Oil/Gas Field Machinery (Trade Promo)	Max Miles	(202) 482-0679
Operations & Maintenance	James Walsh	(202) 482-5131
Osmium	Graylin Presbury	(202) 482-5158
Outdoor Lighting Fixtures	John Bodson	(202) 482-0681
Outdoor Power Equipment	Donald Hodgen	(202) 482-3346
Packaging and Containers	Patrick Cosslett	(202) 482-5125
Packaging Machinery	Eugene Shaw	(202) 482-3494
Paints/Coatings	Raimundo Prat	(202) 482-0128
Palladium	Graylin Presbury	(202) 482-5158
Paper	Gary Stanley	(202) 482-0375
Paper and Board Packaging	Gary Stanley	(202) 482-0375
Paper Industries Machinery	Edward Abrahams	(202) 482-0312
Pasta	William V. Janis	(202) 482-2250
Paving Materials (Asphalt) Patrick MacAuley		(202) 482-0132
Paving Materials (Concrete)	Charles Pitcher	(202) 482-0132
Pens/Pencils, etc.	John Vanderwolf	(202) 482-0348
Periodicals	Rose Marie Bratland	(202) 482-0380
Personal Communications	Linda Gossack	(202) 482-4466
Pet Food	William V. Janis	(202) 482-2250
Pet Products (Trade Promo)	Edward K. Kimmel	(202) 482-3640
Petrochemicals	Michael Kelly	(202) 482-0128
Petrochemicals Plants (Major Projects)	Jay Brandes	(202) 482-3352
Petroleum, Crude & Refined Products	Tom Gillett	(202) 482-1466
Petroleum Refining Mach	Eugene Shaw	(202) 482-3494
Pharmaceuticals	William Hurt	(202) 482-0128
Photographic Equipment and Supplies	Joyce Watson	(202) 482-0574
Pipelines (Major Proj)	Jay Brandes	(202) 482-3352
Plastic Construction Products (Most)	Franklin Williams	(202) 482-0132
Plastic Materials	Raimundo Prat	(202) 482-0128
Plastic Products Machinery	Robert M. Shaw	(202) 482-5124
Platemaking Services	William S. Lofquist	(202) 482-0379
Platinum	Graylin Presbury	(202) 482-5158
Plumbing Fixtures and Fittings	Robert Shaw	(202) 482-5124
Plywood Panel Products	Kathy McNamara	(202) 482-0375
Point-of-Use Water Treatment	Frederica Wheeler	(202) 482-3509
Pollution Control Equipment	Loretta Jonkers	(202) 482-0564
Porcelain Electrical Supplies	John Bodson	(202) 482-0681
Ports, Harbors, Major Proj	Jay L. Smith	(202) 482-4642
Potato Chips	William V. Janis	(202) 482-2250
Pottery	Rose Maria Bratland	(202) 482-0380
Poultry Products	William V. Janis	(202) 482-2250
Power Distribution & Transmission (Major Proj)	Robert Dollison	(202) 482-2733
Power Generation & Dist. Equip. (Trade Promo)	Anthony Kostalas	(202) 482-2390
Power Hand Tools	Edward Abrahams	(202) 482-0312
Precious Metal Jewelry	John M. Harris	(202) 482-1178
Prefabricated Buildings (Metal)	Franklin Williams	(202) 482-0132
Prefabricated Buildings (Wood)	Patrick Cosslett	(202) 482-5125
Prepared Meats	William V. Janis	(202) 482-2250
Pretzels	William V. Janis	(202) 482-2250
Printing and Publishing	William S. Lofquist	(202) 482-0379
Printing Trade Services	William S. Lofquist	(202) 482-0379
Printing Trades Machinery/ Equipment	Robert M. Shaw	(202) 482-5124
Process Control Instruments	Marguerite Nealon	(202) 482-3411
Process Control Instruments (Trade Promo)	Frank Marcolillo	(202) 482-2991
Project Finance	Michael Hinds	(202) 482-5131
Pulp and Paper Mills (Major Project)	Jay Brandes	(202) 482-3352
Pulpmills	Gary Stanley	(202) 482-0375
Pumps, Pumping Equipment	Edward McDonald	(202) 482-0680
Pumps, Compressors	George Zanetakos	(202) 482-0552
Radio and TV Broadcasting	John Siegmund	(202) 482-4781
Radio Communications Eqmt	Linda Gossack	(202) 482-4466
Railroad Services	J. Richard Sousane	(202) 482-4581
Railroads	Jay L. Smith	(202) 482-4642
Recorded Music	John Siegmund	(202) 482-4781
Recreational Equipment (Trade Promo)	Reginald Beckham	(202) 482-5478
Recycling Waste Management	Kimberly Copperhite	(202) 482-0560
Refrigeration Equipment	Richard Bell	(202) 482-5126
Renewable Energy Equipment	Les Garden	(202) 482-0556
Residential Lighting Fixtures	John Bodson	(202) 482-0681
Retail Trade	James Walsh	(202) 482-5086
Rhodium	Graylin Presbury	(202) 482-5158
Rice Milling	William V. Janis	(202) 482-2250
Roads (Major Projects)	Jay L. Smith	(202) 482-4642
Robots	Megan Pilaroscia	(202) 482-0609
Roofing, Asphalt	Franklin Williams	(202) 482-0132
Roller Bearings	Richard Reise	(202) 482-3489
Rubber & Rubber Products	Raimundo Prat	(202) 482-0128
Saddlery & Harness Products	James E. Byron	(202) 482-4304
Safety and Security Equipment (Trade Promo)	Dwight Umstead	(202) 482-2410
Satellite Communication Equipment	Patricia Cooper	(202) 482-4466
Satellite Communication Services	Patricia Cooper	(202) 482-4466
Satellites & Space Vehicles Marketing	Clay Mowry	(202) 482-4222
Science & Electronics (Trade Promo)	Jake Moose	(202) 482-4125
Science Policy	Edwin B. Shykind	(202) 482-4694
Scientific Instruments (Trade Promo)	Frank Manzolillo	(202) 482-2991
Scientific Measurement/ Control Equipment	Marguerite Nealon	(202) 482-3411
Screw Machine Products	Richard Reise	(202) 482-3489
Screws, Washers	Richard Reise	(202) 482-3489
Search & Navigation Eqmt.	Alexis Kemper	(202) 482-4466
Securities	S. Cassin Muir	(202) 482-0349

Semiconductor Product Eqmt	Erin Finn	(202) 482-2795
Semiconductor Materials	Dorothea Blouin	(202) 482-1333
Semiconductors (except Japan)	Robin Roark	(202) 482-3090
Semiconductors (Japan)	Robert Scott	(202) 482-3360
Services Data Base Dev.	Robert G. Atkins	(202) 482-4781
Services, Telecom	Robert G. Atkins	(202) 482-4781
	Daniel Edwards	(202) 482-4466
Shingles (Wood)	Barbara Wise	(202) 482-0375
Shipping, Maritime	C. William Johnson	(202) 482-5012
Shoes	James E. Byron	(202) 482-4034
Silicon/Silicon Carbide	Graylin Presbury	(202) 482-5158
Silver	Graylin Presbury	(202) 482-5158
Silverware	John Harris	(202) 482-1178
Small Arms, Ammunition	John Vanderwolf	(202) 482-0348
Small Business Trade Policy	Sylvia L. Prosak	(202) 482-4792
Snackfood	William V. Janis	(202) 482-2250
Soaps, Detergents, Cleaners	William Hurt	(202) 482-0128
Software	Heidi C. Hijikata	(202) 482-0569
Software, Packaged	Mary Smolenski	(202) 482-0551
Software (Trade Promo)	Judy Fogg	(202) 482-4936
Solar Cells/Photovoltaic Devices	Les Garden	(202) 482-0556
Solar Equipment	Les Garden	(202) 482-0556
Soy Products	William V. Janis	(202) 482-2250
Space Commercialization Equipment	Clay Mowry	(202) 482-4222
Space Policy Development	Clay Mowry	(202) 482-4222
Space Vehicles Marketing	Clay Mowry	(202) 482-4222
Speed Changers	Richard Reise	(202) 482-3489
Sporting and Athletic Goods	John Vanderwolf	(202) 482-0348
Sporting Goods (Trade Promo)	Reginald Beckham	(202) 482-5478
Steel Industry Products	Charles Bell	(202) 482-0608
Steel Mill Products	Charles Bell	(202) 482-0608
Steel Mills (Major Proj)	Jay Brandes	(202) 482-3352
Storage Batteries	David Larrabee	(202) 482-0607
Supercomputers	Jonathan P. Streeter	(202) 482-0480
Superconductors	Roger Chiarado	(202) 482-0402
Switchgear and Switchboard Apparatus	John Bodson	(202) 482-0681
Tantalum	Graylin Presbury	(202) 482-5158
Technology Affairs	Edwin B. Shykind	(202) 482-4694
Telecommunications Customer Premises Eqmt	William Bien	(202) 482-4466
Telecommunications Major Projects	Richard Paddock	(202) 482-4466
Telecommunications Military Comm. Eqmt	Alexis Kemper	(202) 482-4466
Telecommunications Network Eqmt	John Henry	(202) 482-4466
Telecommunictions Services	Robert G. Atkins	(202) 482-4781
	Daniel Edwards	(202) 482-4466
Telecommunications Trade Promo	Theresa Rettig	(202) 482-2952
Telecommunications, Wireless/Radio Eqmt Services	Linda Gossack	(202) 482-4466
Teletext Services	Mary C. Inoussa	(202) 482-5820
Textile Prod. Machinery	Edward McDonald	(202) 482-0680
Textile Prod. Machinery Trade Promo	Max Milo	(202) 482-0679
Textiles	William J. Dulka	(202) 482-4058
Textiles (Trade Promo)	Ferenc Molnar	(202) 482-2043
Timber Products, Tropical	Kathy McNamara	(202) 482-0375
Tin	Graylin Presbury	(202) 482-5158
Tires	Raimundo Prat	(202) 482-0128
Titanium	Graylin Presbury	(202) 482-5158
Tools/Dies/Jigs/Fixtures	Megan Pilaroscia	(202) 482-0609
Toys		
Donald Hodgen		(202) 482-3346
Toys and Games (Export Promo)	Reginald Beckham	(202) 482-5478
Trade Finance	John Shuman	(202) 482-3050
Transborder Data Flows	Mary C. Inoussa	(202) 482-5820
Transformers	John Bodson	(202) 482-0681
Transportation Industries	C. William Johnson	(202) 482-5012
Trucking Services	J. Richard Sousane	(202) 482-4581
Trucks, Trailers, Buses Trade Promo	John White	(202) 482-0671
Tungsten Products	David Cammarota	(202) 482-5157
Tunnels, Major Projects	Jay L. Smith	(202) 482-4642
Typesetting	William S. Lofquist	(202) 482-0379
Uranium	William Sugg	(202) 482-1466
Used Reconditioned Eqmt	John Bodson	(202) 482-0681
Value Added Telecommunications Svcs	Robert G. Atkins	(202) 482-4781
	Richard Reise	(202) 482-3489
Valves, Pipe Fittings Except Brass	Richard Reise	(202) 482-3489
Vanadium	Graylin Presbury	(202) 482-5158
Vegetables	William V. Janis	(202) 482-2250
Venture Capital	Michael Hinds	(202) 482-5086
Videotex Services	Mary C. Inoussa	(202) 482-5820
Wallets, Billfolds, Flatgoods	James E. Byron	(202) 482-4034
Warm Air Heating Eqmt	Vacant	(202) 482-3509
Wastepaper	Gary Stanley	(202) 482-0375
Watches	John Harris	(202) 482-1178
Water and Sewerage Treatment Plants (Major Proj)	William Holroyd	(202) 482-6168
Water Resource Equipment	Frederica Wheeler	(202) 482-3509
Water Supply & Dist.	Frederica Wheeler	(202) 482-3509
Welding/Cutting Apparatus	Edward Abrahams	(202) 482-0312
Wholesale Trade	James Walsh	(202) 482-5086
Wind Energy Systems	Les Garden	(202) 482-0556
Wine	Cornelius Kenney	(202) 482-2428
Wire and Wire Products	Les Garden	(202) 482-0556
Wire Cloth	Patrick MacAuley	(202) 482-0132
Wire Cloth, Industrial	Richard Reise	(202) 482-3489
Wood Products	Barbara Wise	(202) 482-0375
Wood Working Machinery	Richard Bell	(202) 482-5126
Writing Instruments	John Vanderwolf	(202) 482-0348
Yarn	William J. Dulka	(202) 482-4058
Zinc	David Larrabee	(202) 482-0607

LABOR

The following experts are drawn from the Department of Labor Statistics.

Employment and Unemployment Statistics

Absences from work	Staff	(202) 606-6378
Business establishment list	Michael Searson	(202) 606-6469
Discouraged workers	Harvey Hamel	(202) 606-6378
Displaced workers	Jennifer Gardner	(202) 606-6378
Educational attainment	Staff	(202) 606-6378
Employment and Earnings Periodical	Gloria P. Green	(202) 606-6373
Employment and wages (ES 202)	Staff	(202) 606-6567
Data diskettes and tapes	Staff	(202) 606-6567
Employment Situation:		
News release	Staff	(202) 606-6378 or (606) 606-6373
Recorded messages	24-hour hotline	(202) 606-7828
Establishment survey employment, hours, earnings:		
National data	Staff	(202) 606-6555
Benchmarks	Patricia Getz	(202) 606-6521
Data Diskettes	David Hiles	(202) 606-6551
States and area data	Kenneth Shipp	(202) 606-6559
Data diskettes	Guy Podgornik	(202) 606-6559
Flextime and shift work	Earl Mellor	(202) 606-6378
Foreign direct investment data	Staff	(202) 606-6568
Home-based worked	William Deming	(202) 606-6378
Job tenure	Lawrence Leith	(202) 606-6378
Job vacancy statistics	Richard Devens	(202) 606-6402
Labor force data:		
Concepts and definitions	Staff	(202) 606-6373
Employment and unemployment trends	Staff	(202) 606-6378
Machine-readable data and diskettes	Gloria P. Green	(202) 606-6373
Microdata tapes	Rowena Lipscomb	(202) 606-6345
Longitudinal data/ gross flows	Francis Horvath	(202) 606-6345
Marital and family characteristics	Howard Hayghe	(202) 606-6378
Mass layoff statistics	Lewis Siegel	(202) 606-6404
Minimum wage data	Steve N. Haugen	(202) 606-6378
Minority workers	Peter Cattan	(202) 606-6378
Multiple jobholders	John Stinson	(202) 606-6373
Occupational data:		
Current Population Survey	Staff	(202) 606-6378
Occupational Employment Statistics Survey	Lawrence Johnson	(202) 606-6569
Occupational Mobility	Lawrence Leith	(202) 606-6378
Older workers	Diane Herz	(202) 606-6378
Part-time workers	Thomas Nardone	(202) 606-6378
Real earnings-news release	David Hiles	(202) 606-6547
Seasonal adjustment methodology	Robert McIntire	(202) 606-6345
Standard Industrial Classification System	Mary Anne Phillips	(202) 606-6473
Standard Occupational Classification System	Michael McElroy	(202) 606-6516
State and area labor force data:		
Demographic characteristics	Edna Biederman	(202) 606-6392
Data diskettes and tapes	Jessie Marcus	(202) 606-6392
Unemployment insurance claims	Yvonne Terwilliger	(202) 606-6392
Veterans	Sharon Cohany	(202) 606-6378
Weekly and annual earnings-Current Population Survey	Staff	(202) 606-6378
Women in the labor force	Howard Hayghe	(202) 606-6378
Work experience	Staff	(202) 606-6378
Working poor	Jennifer Gardner	(202) 606-6378
Youth, students and dropouts	Abraham Mosisa	(202) 606-6378

Employment Projections

Data tapes and diskettes:		
Industry-occupation matrix	David Frank	(202) 606-5708
Input-output and employment requirements	Art Andreassen	(202) 606-5689
Economic growth and industry projections	Charles Bowman	(202) 606-5702
Economic projections	Norman Saunders	(202) 606-5723
Employment projections industry	James Franklin	(202) 606-5709
Final demand projections	Betty Su	(202) 606-5729
Industry-occupation matrix	Delores Turner	(202) 606-5730
Intermediate demand projections	Art Andreassen	(202) 606-5689
Labor force projections	Howard Fullerton	(202) 606-5711
Occupational Outlook Handbook	Michael Pilot	(202) 606-5703
Occupational Outlook Quarterly	Neale Baxter	(202) 606-5691
Occupational projections	Neal Rosenthal	(202) 606-5701

Prices and Living Conditions

Consumer expenditure survey	Staff	(202) 606-6900
Survey data and tapes	William Passero	(202) 606-6900
Survey operations	Richard Dietz	(202) 606-6872
Consumer price indexes	Staff	(202) 606-7000
Analysis and data	Patrick Jackman	(202) 606-6952
Average retail food prices-monthly	William Cook	(202) 606-6988
Average retail prices and indexes-motor fuels only	Joseph Chelena	(202) 606-6982
Average retail prices and indexes of fuels and utilities-monthly	Robert Adkins	(202) 606-6985
Data diskettes	Sharon Gibson	(202) 606-6968
Department store inventory indexes (LIFO)	Sharon Gibson	(202) 606-6968
Recorded CPI summary	24-hour quickline	(202) 606-6994
Recorded CPI detail	24-hour hotline	(202) 606-7828
International price indexes	Katrina Reut	(202) 606-7100

Current analysis of U.S. import and export price indexes	Michelle Vachris	(202) 606-7155
Energy and services	Ilene Fischer	(202) 606-7102
Food, raw materials, and apparel	Rob Frumkin	(202) 606-7106
Machinery	Brian Costello	(202) 606-7107
Methodology	William Alterman	(202) 606-7108
Revision	Katrina Reut	(202) 606-7100
Price and index number research	Staff	(202) 606-6573
Producer price indexes	Thomas Tibbetts	(202) 606-7700
Analysis and data	Craig Howell	(202) 606-7705
Data diskettes	Elliott Rosenberg	(202) 606-7728
Electric machinery	John Murphy	(202) 606-7740
Energy, textiles and leather	Maria Caswell	(202) 606-7713
Food and chemicals	Rodger Hippen	(202) 606-7723
Forestry and construction	Wanda Davies	(202) 606-7714
Metals	Edward Kazanowski	(202) 606-7735
Methodology	Elliot Rosenberg	(202) 606-7728
Non-electric machinery and transportation equipment	Bryandt Dickerson	(202) 606-7744
Recorded PPI detail	24-hour Hotline	(202) 606-7828
Services	Irwin Gerduk	(202) 606-7748
Statistical methods	Brian Hedges	(202) 606-6897

Productivity and Technology

Data diskettes	Lawrence J. Fulco	(202) 606-5604
Data tapes	Bertram Kriebel	(202) 606-5606
Foreign countries-hourly compensation costs	Patricia Capdevielle	(202) 606-5654
Foreign countries-labor force and unemployment	Constance Sorrentino	(202) 606-5654
Foreign countries-prices	Todd Godbout	(202) 606-5654
Foreign countries-productivity unit labor costs, and other economic indicators	Arthur Neef	(202) 606-5654
Multifactor productivity, labor composition, and hours worked survey	Larry Rosenblum	(202) 606-5606
Productivity and costs-news release	Lawrence J. Fulco	(202) 606-5604
Productivity in government	Darlene J. Forte	(202) 606-5621
Productivity research, capital measurement	Michael Harper	(202) 606-5603
Productivity trends in selected industries and federal government	Charles W. Ardolini	(202) 606-5618
Technological trends in major industries	Richard Riche	(202) 606-5626

Compensation and Working Conditions

Agreements - collective bargaining-public file	Michael Cimini	(202) 606-6275
Annual survey of occupational injuries	Ethel Jackson	(202) 606-6179
Data Diskettes	Staff	(202) 606-6179
Data Tapes	Staff	(202) 606-6179
Census of Fatal Occupational Injuries	Guy Toscano	(202) 606-6165
Child care/parental leave/ family benefits	Staff	(202) 606-6222
Collective bargaining Agreements analysis	Michael Cimini	(202) 606-6275
Settlements, private industry	Janice M. Devine	(202) 606-6267
State and local governments	Michael Cimini	(202) 606-6275
Compensation and working conditions periodical	Michael Cimini	(202) 606-6275
Employee benefits	Staff	(202) 606-6222
Employment cost index	Wayne Shelly	(202) 606-6199
Data diskettes	Brenda Rogers	(202) 606-6199
Employer costs for employee compensation	Brenda Rogers	(202) 606-6199
Recorded messages	24-hour hotline	(202) 606-7828
Health and life insurance	Staff	(202) 606-6222
Health studies and special projects	William Webber	(202) 606-6162
Industry injuries and illnesses		
Estimates and incidence rates	Staff	(202) 606-6180
Injuries and illnesses characteristics	Elyce Biddle	(202) 606-6170
Occupational compensation surveys:		
Area data	Staff	(202) 606-6220
Data diskettes	Dolphene Williams	(202) 606-6253
Industry data	Staff	(202) 606-6220
National data	Staff	(202) 606-6220
Paid leave and disability benefits	Staff	(202) 606-6222
Retirement and capital accumulation benefits	Staff	(202) 606-6222
Supplementary data system-worker's compensation statitics	Elyce Biddle	(202) 606-6170
Unions, employee associations, and their membership	Michael Cimini	(202) 606-6275
Work injury reports surveys	Ethel Jackson	(202) 606-6180
Work stoppages	Michael Cimini	(202) 606-6275

MEDICAID

Data on Medicaid and the hospitals, nursing homes, doctors, and recipients, is amassed and is available from the Department of Health and Human Services, Health Care Financing Administration, Medicaid Bureau. Inquiries can be made to (410) 966-3870.

MINES AND MINERALS

Abrasives, manmade/ natural	Gordon Austin	(202) 501-9388
Aluminum	Patricia A. Plunkert	(202) 501-9419
Antimony	Thomas O. Llewellyn	(202) 501-9395

Arsenic	J. Roger Loebenstein	(202) 501-9416
Asbestos	Robert L. Vitra	(202) 501-9384
Asphalt natural	Cheryl Solomon	(202) 501-9393
Barite	James Searls	(202) 501-9407
Bauxite	Errol Sehnke	(202) 501-9421
Beryllium	Deborah Kramer	(202) 501-9394
Bismuth	Stephen M. Jasinski	(202) 501-9418
Boron	Phyllis Lyday	(202) 501-9405
Bromine	Phyllis Lyday	(202) 501-9405
Cadmium	Peter Kuck	(202) 501-9436
Calcium	Michael Miller	(202) 501-9409
Calcium carbonate	Valentin Tepordei	(202) 501-9392
Cement	Cheryl Solomon	(202) 501-9393
Cesium	Robert Reese, Jr.	(202) 501-9413
Chromium	John Papp	(202) 501-9438
Clays	Robert Virta	(202) 501-9384
Cobalt	Kim Shedd	(202) 501-9420
Columbium	Larry Cunningham	(202) 501-9443
Copper	Daniel Edelstein	(202) 501-9415
Corundum-emery	Gordon Austin	(202) 501-9388
Diamond	Gordon Austin	(202) 501-9388
Diatomite	Lawrence L. Davis	(202) 501-9386
Explosives	Raymond Cantrell	(202) 501-9581
Feldspar	Michael Potter	(202) 501-9387
Fluorspar	Michael Miller	(202) 501-9409
Fused Alumina	Gordon Austin	(202) 501-9388
Gallium	Deborah Kramer	(202) 501-9394
Garnet	Gordon Austin	(202) 501-9388
Gem Stones	Gordon Austin	(202) 501-9388
Germanium	Errol Sehnke	(202) 501-9421
Gold	John Lucas	(202) 501-9417
Graphite	Harold Taylor	(202) 501-9754
Greensand	James Searls	(202) 501-9407
Gypsum	Lawrence Davis	(202) 501-9386
Hafnium	David Templeton	(202) 501-9391
Helium	William D. Leachman	(806) 376-2604
Indium	Stephen M. Jasinski	(202) 501-9418
Iodine	Phyllis Lyday	(202) 501-9405
Iron ore	William Kirk	(202) 501-9430
Iron and steel	Gerald Houck	(202) 501-9439
Iron and steel scrap	Raymond E. Brown	(202) 501-9427
Iron and steel slag	Cheryl Solomon	(202) 501-9393
Kyanite-mullite	Michael Potter	(202) 501-9387
Lead	James Carlin	(202) 501-9426
Lime	Michael Miller	(202) 501-9409
Lithium	Joyce Ober	(202) 501-9406
Magnesium & Mg Comps	Deborah Kramer	(202) 501-9394
Manganese	Thomas Jones	(202) 501-9428
Mercury	Stephen Jasinski	(202) 501-9418
Mica	Lawrence Davis	(202) 501-9386
Molybdenum	John W. Blossom	(202) 501-9435
Nepheline syenite	Michael Potter	(202) 501-9387
Nickel	Peter Kuck	(202) 501-9436
Nitrogen	Raymond Cantrell	(202) 501-9581
Peat	Raymond Cantrell	(202) 501-9581
Perlite	Wallace Bolen	(202) 501-9389
Phosphate rock	William Stowasser	(202) 501-9408
Platinum group metals	J. Roger Loebenstein	(202) 501-9416
Potash	James Searls	(202) 501-9407
Pumice	Wallace Bolen	(202) 501-9389
Quartz crystal	Joyce Ober	(202) 501-9406
Rare earths	James Hedrick	(202) 501-9412
Rhenium	John Blossom	(202) 501-9435
Rubidium	Robert Reese, Jr.	(202) 501-9413
Salt	Dennis Kostick	(202) 501-9410
Sand & gravel, construction	Valentin Tepordei	(202) 501-9392
Sand & gravel, industrial	Wallace P. Bolen	(202) 501-9389
Scandium	James B. Hedrick	(202) 501-9412
Selenium	Stephen Jasinski	(202) 501-9418
Silicon	Larry Cunningham	(202) 501-9443
Silicon Carbide (Abrasive)	Gordon Austin	(202) 501-9388
Silver	Robert G. Reese, Jr.	(202) 501-9413
Sodium Compounds	Dennis S. Kostick	(202) 501-9410
Staurolite	Gordon Austin	(202) 501-9388
Stone, crushed	Valentin V. Tepordei	(202) 501-9392
Stone, dimension	Harold A. Taylor	(202) 501-9754
Strontium	Joyce A. Ober	(202) 501-9406
Sulfur	Joyce A. Ober	(202) 501-9406
Talc	Robert Virta	(202) 501-9384
Tantalum	Larry D. Cunningham	(202) 501-9443
Tellurium	Stephen Jasinski	(202) 501-9418
Thallium	Errol Sehnke	(202) 501-9421
Thorium	James B. Hedrick	(202) 501-9412
Tin	James F. Carlin, Jr.	(202) 501-9426
Titanium	Joseph Gambogi	(202) 501-9390
Tripoli	Gordon Austin	(202) 501-9388
Tungsten	Gerald R. Smith	(202) 501-9431
Uranium statistics	Henry E. Hilliard	(202) 501-9429
Vanadium	Henry E. Hilliard	(202) 501-9429
Vermiculite	Michael J. Potter	(202) 501-9387
Wollastonite	Michael J. Potter	(202) 501-9387
Yttrium	James B. Hedrick	(202) 501-9412
Zeolites	Robert Virta	(202) 501-9384
Zinc	Errol Sehnke	(202) 501-9421
Zirconium	David A. Templeton	(202) 501-9391
Afghanistan	Chin Kuo	(202) 501-9693
Albania	Walter Steblez	(202) 501-9672
Algeria	Bernadette Michalski	(202) 501-9699
Angola	Philip Mobbs	(202) 501-9679
Antarctica	David Doan	(202) 501-9678
Antigua & Barbuda	George Rabchevsky	(202) 501-9670
Argentina	Pablo Velasco	(202) 501-9677
Armenia	Richard Levine	(202) 501-9682
Aruba	George Rabchevsky	(202) 501-9670
Australia	Travis Lyday	(202) 501-9695
Austria	Jozef Plachy	(202) 501-9673
Azerbaijan	Richard Levine	(202) 501-9682
Bahamas	George Rabchevsky	(202) 501-9670
Bahrain	Bernadette Michalski	(202) 501-9699
Bangladesh	Chin Kuo	(202) 501-9693
Barbados	George Rabshevsky	(202) 501-9670
Belgium	William Zajac	(202) 501-9671
Belize	Pablo Velasco	(202) 501-9677
Belarus	Richard Levine	(202) 501-9682
Benin	Philip Mobbs	(202) 501-9679
Bermuda	George Rabchevsky	(202) 501-9670
Bhutan	John Wu	(202) 501-9697
Bolivia	Pablo Velasco	(202) 501-9677
Bosnia & Hercegovina	Walter Steblez	(202) 501-9672
Botswana	Lloyd Antonides	(202) 501-9686
Brazil	Alfredo Gurmendi	(202) 501-9681
Brunei	John Wu	(202) 501-9697
Bulgaria	Walter Steblez	(202) 501-9672
Burkina Faso	Philip Mobbs	(202) 501-9679
Burma	John Wu	(202) 501-9697
Burundi	Lloyd Antonides	(202) 501-9686
Cambodia	Travis Lyday	(202) 501-9695
Cameroon	Thomas Dolley	(202) 501-9690
Canada	Michael Heydari	(202) 501-9688
Cape Verde Islands	Philip Mobbs	(202) 501-9679
Central African Republic	Thomas Dolley	(202) 501-9690
Chad	Thomas Dolley	(202) 501-9690
Chile	Pablo Velasco	(202) 501-9677
China	Pui-Kwan Tse	(202) 501-9696
Christmas Island	Travis Lyday	(202) 501-9695

Colombia	George Rabchevsky	(202) 501-9670
Comoros	Lloyd Antonides	(202) 501-9686
Congo	Thomas Dolley	(202) 501-9690
Costa Rica	George Rabchevsky	(202) 501-9670
Cote D'Ivoire	Thomas Dolley	(202) 501-9690
Croatia	Walter Steblez	(202) 501-9672
Cuba	George Rabchevsky	(202) 501-9670
Cyprus	Philip Mobbs	(202) 501-9679
Czechoslovakia	Walter Steblez	(202) 501-9672
Denmark	Walter Zajac	(202) 501-9671
Djibouti	Lloyd Antonides	(202) 501-9686
Dominica	George Rabchevsky	(202) 501-9670
Dominican Republic	David Doan	(202) 501-9678
Ecuador	Pablo Velasco	(202) 501-9677
Egypt	Thomas Dolley	(202) 501-9690
El Salvador	Pablo Velasco	(202) 501-9677
Equatorial Guinea	Thomas Dolley	(202) 501-9690
Estonia	Richard Levine	(202) 501-9682
Ethiopia	Lloyd Antonides	(202) 501-9686
Fiji	Travis Lyday	(202) 501-9695
Finland	Jozef Plachy	(202) 501-9673
France	Harold R. Newman	(202) 501-9669
French Guinea	Alfredo Gurmendi	(202) 501-9681
Gabon	Philip Mobbs	(202) 501-9679
Gambia	Thomas Dolley	(202) 501-9690
Georgia	Richard Levine	(202) 501-9682
Germany	William Zajac	(202) 501-9671
Ghana	Hendrik van Oss	(202) 501-9687
Greece	William Zajac	(202) 501-9671
Greenland	William Zajac	(202) 501-9671
Grenada	George Rabchevsky	(202) 501-9670
Guadaloupe	George Rabchevsky	(202) 501-9670
Guatemala	Pablo Velasco	(202) 501-9677
Guinea	David Izon	(202) 501-9692
Guinea-Bissau	Thomas Dolley	(202) 501-9690
Guyana	David Doan	(202) 501-9678
Haiti	George Rabchevsky	(202) 501-9670
Honduras	George Rabchevsky	(202) 501-9670
Hong Kong	Pui-Kwan Tse	(202) 501-9696
Hungary	Walter Steblez	(202) 501-9672
Iceland	Jozef Plachy	(202) 501-9673
India	Edmond Chin	(202) 501-9698
Indonesia	Chin Kuo	(202) 501-9693
Iran	Michael Heydari	(202) 501-9688
Iraq	Lloyd Antonides	(202) 501-9686
Ireland	Harold R. Newman	(202) 501-9669
Israel	David Izon	(202) 501-9674
Italy	Harold Newman	(202) 501-9669
Jamaica	David Doan	(202) 501-9678
Japan	John Wu	(202) 501-9697
Jordan	Thomas Dolley	(202) 501-9690
Kazakhstan	Richard Levine	(202) 501-9682
Kenya	David Izon	(202) 501-9692
Kiribati (Gilbert Islands)	Travis Lyday	(202) 501-9695
Korea, North	Chin Kuo	(202) 501-9693
Korea, Republic of	Chin Kuo	(202) 501-9693
Kuwait	Bernadette Michalski	(202) 501-9699
Kyrgyzstan	Richard Levine	(202) 501-9682
Laos	Travis Lyday	(202) 501-9695
Latvia	Richard Levine	(202) 501-9682
Lebanon	Bernadette Michalski	(202) 501-9699
Lesotho	Philip Mobbs	(202) 501-9679
Liberia	David Izon	(202) 501-9674
Libya	Thomas Dolley	(202) 501-9690
Lithuania	Richard Levine	(202) 501-9682
Luxembourg	William Zajac	(202) 501-9671
Macedonia	Walter Steblez	(202) 501-9672
Madagascar	Thomas Dolley	(202) 501-9690
Malawi	Philip Mobbs	(202) 501-9679
Malaysia	John Wu	(202) 501-9697
Mali	Hendrik Van Oss	(202) 501-9687
Malta	Jozef Plachy	(202) 501-9673
Martinique	George Rabchevsky	(202) 501-9670
Mauritania	Bernadette Michalski	(202) 501-9699
Mauritius	Lloyd Antonides	(202) 501-9686
Mexico	Michael Heydari	(202) 501-9688
Minerals in the World Economy	Charles Kimball	(202) 501-9659
Moldova	Richard Levine	(202) 501-9682
Mongolia	John Wu	(202) 501-9697
Monserrat	George Rabchevsky	(202) 501-9670
Morocco	Thomas Dolley	(202) 501-9690
Mozambique	Hendrik Van Oss	(202) 501-9687
Namibia	Michael Heydari	(202) 501-9688
Nauru	Travis Lyday	(202) 501-9695
Nepal	John Wu	(202) 501-9697
Netherlands	William Zajac	(202) 501-9671
Netherlands Antilles	George Rabchevsky	(202) 501-9670
New Caledonia	Travis Lyday	(202) 501-9695
New Zealand	Travis Lyday	(202) 501-9695
Nicaragua	George Rabchevsky	(202) 501-9670
Niger	David Izon	(202) 501-9692
Nigeria	David Izon	(202) 501-9692
Norway	Jozef Plachy	(202) 501-9673
Oman	Bernadette Michalski	(202) 501-9699
Pakistan	Chin Kuo	(202) 501-9693
Panama	George Rabchevsky	(202) 501-9670
Papua New Guinea	Travis Lyday	(202) 501-9695
Paraguay	Alfredo Gurmendi	(202) 501-9681
Peru	Alfredo Gurmendi	(202) 501-9678
Philippines	Travis Lyday	(202) 501-9695
Poland	Walter Steblez	(202) 501-9672
Portugal	Harold Newman	(202) 501-9669
Qatar	David Izon	(202) 501-9692
Reunion	Lloyd Antonides	(202) 501-9686
Romania	Walter Steblez	(202) 501-9672
Russia	Richard Levine	(202) 501-9682
Rwanda	Lloyd Antonides	(202) 501-9686
Sao Tome and Principe	Thomas Dolley	(202) 501-9690
Saudi Arabia	Bernadette Michalski	(202) 501-9699
Senegal	Thomas Dolley	(202) 501-9690
Serbia and Montenegro	Walter Steblez	(202) 501-9672
Seychelles	Lloyd Antonides	(202) 501-9686
Sierra Leone	Bernadette Michalski	(202) 501-9699
Singapore	Pui-Kwan Tse	(202) 501-9696
Slovakia	Walter Steblez	(202) 501-9672
Slovenia	Walter Steblez	(202) 501-9672
Solomon Islands	Travis Lyday	(202) 501-9695
Somalia	Lloyd Antonides	(202) 501-9686
South Africa, Republic of	Hendrik Van Oss	(202) 501-9687
Spain	Harold R. Newman	(202) 501-9669
Sri Lanka	Chin Kuo	(202) 501-9693
St. Kitts and Nevis	George Rabchevsky	(202) 501-9670
St. Lucia	George Rabchevsky	(202) 501-9670
St. Vincent and Grenadines	George Rabchevsky	(202) 501-9670
Sudan	Lloyd Antonides	(202) 501-9686
Suriname	Alfredo Gurmendi	(202) 501-9681
Swaziland	Hendrik Van Oss	(202) 501-9687
Sweden	Jozef Plachy	(202) 501-9673
Switzerland	Jozef Plachy	(202) 501-9673
Syria	Bernadette Michalski	(202) 501-9699
Taiwan	Pui-Kwan Tse	(202) 501-9696
Tajikistan	Richard Levine	(202) 501-9682
Tanzania	David Izon	(202) 501-9692

Thailand	Pui-Kwan Tse	(202) 501-9696
Togo	Philip Mobbs	(202) 501-9679
Tonga	Travis Lyday	(202) 501-9695
Trinidad and Tobago	David Doan	(202) 501-9678
Tunisia	Thomas Dolley	(202) 501-9690
Turkey	Hendrik Van Oss	(202) 501-9687
Turkmenistan	Richard Levine	(202) 501-9682
Uganda	David Izon	(202) 501-9692
Ukraine	Richard Levine	(202) 501-9682
United Arab Emirates	Philip Mobbs	(202) 501-9679
United Kingdom	Harold Newman	(202) 501-9669
Uruguay	Alfredo Gurmendi	(202) 501-9681
Uzbekistan	Richard Levine	(202) 501-9682
Vanuatu	Travis Lyday	(202) 501-9695
Venezuela	David Doan	(202) 501-9678
Vietnam	Travis Lyday	(202) 501-9695
Western Sahara	Thomas Dolley	(202) 501-9690
Yemen, Republic of	Bernadette Michalski	(202) 501-9699
Zaire	Philip Mobbs	(202) 501-9679
Zambia	Lloyd Antonides	(202) 501-9686
Zimbabwe	Philip Mobbs	(202) 501-9679

RURAL ELECTRIFICATION

The Rural Electrification Administration is a major source of information on the electric and telephone utilities industries. It collects data by making loans to rural electric and rural telephone systems for facilities improvement.

For information on statistical data call:

Iris B. Adams (202) 720-8959

SOCIAL SECURITY

The Social Security Administration collects a great deal of data on the composition of the population in relation to demographic information such as age and income levels, and the years of population concentration. The statistics deal with historic, current and projected trends. The main office can direct callers to staff specialists who are knowledgeable on specific subjects; the general information number is (800) 772-1213.

TRANSPORTATION

The U.S. Department of Transportation establishes the nation's overall transportation policy. There are ten separate administrations within the Department of Transportation whose main offices can direct callers to specialists who are knowledgeable on specific subjects: Federal Aviation Administration (202) 366-4000, Federal Highway Administration (202) 366-0660; Federal Railroad Administration (202) 366-4000; Maritime Administration (202) 366-5807; National Highway Traffic Safety Administration (202) 366-9550; Research and Special Programs Administration (202) 366-4433; Saint Lawrence Seaway Development Corporation (202) 366-0091; U.S. Coast Guard (202) 267-1587; Federal Transit Administration (202) 366-4043, and the Bureau of Transportation Statistics may be reached by calling (202) 366-DATA.

Federal Statistical Data Bases

Because users of government data typically require access to the most current statistical information in whatever form the data may be available, this section identifies the major data files available from government agencies in electronic form from 1985 to date. File formats include magnetic tapes, diskettes, and CD-ROMs.

The information is arranged under broad subject categories, with details identifying specific files and how each file may be acquired. The information provided after each file's listing includes an order number (when available) and the name of the agency from which the file can be purchased. Rather than repeat ordering details in each entry, the eleven agencies that make the files available are listed below. Users should refer to this list to determine where to write or call when ordering a particular file.

The National Technical Information Service is a major provider of federal data files. Through its Federal Computer Products Center, it offers access to many of the computer files produced by major U.S. agencies.

The Center seeks to improve public access to computer products produced by the U.S. Government. Using extensive contacts with various federal agencies, the Center maintains a steady flow of new and updated data files and software. A wide variety of computer products pertinent to business and scientific interests are thereby made available for sale. The principal files available from NTIS are included in the following listings.

The Center for Electronic Records of the Archives and Records Administration maintains earlier data files, which might also be of value to some users for historical purposes. For information regarding the availability of such historic data files, the user can call the Center at (202) 501-5579 and request the assistance of an archives specialist.

Users of statistical data from the Census Bureau can get many current statistics, announcements of new products, and other information on the Census Bureau's online data system, CENDATA. CompuServe and DIALOG, information service companies, are offering CENDATA to their customers. For more information about CENDATA content and online services, contact CompuServe (800) 848-8199 or DIALOG Information Services (800) 334-2564. Or, for content information only: Data Access and Use Staff, Data User Services Division, Bureau of the Census, Washington, DC 20233 (301) 763-2074.

Guide to Availability

BLS Data Diskettes
U.S. Department of Labor
BLS Data Diskettes
2 Massachusetts Avenue, NE
Washington, DC 20212
(202) 606-7789

BLS, Division of Planning and Financial Management
U.S. Department of Labor
Bureau of Labor Statistics
Division of Planning and Financial Management
2 Massachusetts Avenue, NE
Washington, DC 20212
(202) 606-7789

Bureau of the Census, Data User Services Division
U.S. Department of Commerce
Bureau of the Census
Customer Services
Washington, DC 20233-8300
(301) 763-4100
Fax (301) 763-4794

Division of Health Interview Statistics
U.S. Department of Health and Human Services
National Center for Health Statistics
Division of Health Interview Statistics
Presidential Building, Room 850
6525 Belcrest Road
Hyattsville, Maryland 20782
(301) 436-7087

Economic and Statistical Analysis/BEA
U.S. Department of Commerce
Bureau of Economic Analysis
Public Information Office
Order Desk, BE-53
Washington, DC 20230
(202) 606-9900

ERS-NASS Electronic Data Products
U.S. Department of Agriculture
ERS-NASS
341 Victory Drive
Herndon, Virginia 22070
(800) 999-6779
(703) 834-0125

FEC Data Systems Development Division
Federal Election Commission
Data Systems Development Division
Washington, DC 20463
(800) 424-9530

National Archive of Criminal Justice Data
U.S. Department of Justice
Bureau of Justice Statistics
Inter-university Consortium for Political & Social Research
National Archive of Criminal Justice Data
P.O. Box 1248
Ann Arbor, Michigan 48106-1248
(800) 999-0960

NODC User Services Branch
U.S. Department of Commerce
National Oceanic and Atmospheric Administration
National Oceanic Data Center
User Services Branch
NOAA/NESDIS E/OC21
1825 Connecticut Avenue, NW
Washington, DC 20235
(202) 606-4549
Fax (202) 606-4586

NTIS
U.S. Department of Commerce
National Technical Information Service
5285 Port Royal Road
Springfield, Virginia 22161
(703) 487-4650
Fax (703) 321-8547

U.S. Department of Education
U.S. Department of Education
Information Technology Branch
555 New Jersey Avenue, NW
Washington, DC 20208-5725
(202) 219-1522
(800) 424-1616

* * * * * * * * * * *

* * * * * * * * * * *

Agriculture

Acid Rain.
Order #92017
Availability: ERS-NASS Electronic Data Products

Advance (State and County) File: 1987.
(Computer Tape and Diskette)
Availability: Bureau of the Census, Data User Services Division

Africa Grain Supply and Utilization, 1966 - 85.
Order #86002
Availability: ERS-NASS Electronic Data Products

Agricultural Chemical Use: 1993 Field Crop Summary
Order #94171
Availability: ERS-NASS Electronic Data Products

Agricultural Chemical Usage, 1992 Vegetables Summary.
Order #93172
Availability: ERS-NASS Electronic Data Products

Agricultural Chemical Usage, 1993 Fruits Summary.
Order #94172
Availability: ERS-NASS Electronic Data Products

Agricultural Commodity Output.
Order #91008
Availability: ERS-NASS Electronic Data Products

Agricultural Economics and Land Ownership Survey: 1988 (Diskette).
Availability: Bureau of the Census, Data User Services Division

Agricultural Outlook Yearbook, 1960 - 91.
Order #87011
Availability: ERS-NASS Electronic Data Products

Agricultural Statistics for the Former Soviet Republics and the Baltic
Republics, 1980 - 91.
Order #93009A-93009F
Availability: ERS-NASS Electronic Data Products

Agricultural Statistics of Eastern Europe and the Soviet Union, 1965 - 85.
Order #89020
Availability: ERS-NASS Electronic Data Products

Agricultural Statistics of the European Community, 1960 - 85.
Order #89010
Availability: ERS-NASS Electronic Data Products

Agricultural Water Use, 1979 - 86.
Order #90001
Availability: ERS-NASS Electronic Data Products

Agriculture and Trade: Europe.
Order #94001
Availability: ERS-NASS Electronic Data Products

Agriculture Specialty Publications and 1987 Public Use Files on CD-ROM.
Availability: Bureau of the Census, Data User Services Division

Americans and Food.
Order #91002A
Availability: ERS-NASS Electronic Data Products

Asia/Near East Agricultural Trade, 1962 - 86.
Order #89012
Availability: ERS-NASS Electronic Data Products

Bank Operating Statistics, 1980 - 91.
Order #94014
Availability: ERS-NASS Electronic Data Products

Beef Packer Cost Analyzer.
Order #91012
Availability: ERS-NASS Electronic Data Products

Caribbean Fruits and Vegetables, 1975 - 87.
Order #88015A and #88015B
Availability: ERS-NASS Electronic Data Products

Cash Receipts, 1960 - 91.
Order #89014
Availability: ERS-NASS Electronic Data Products

Cash Rents for U.S. Farmland, 1960 - 94.
Order #90025
Availability: ERS-NASS Electronic Data Products

Catfish Processing, 1970 - 92
Order #93140
Availability: ERS-NASS Electronic Data Products

CCC Crop Loans, 1985 - 91.
Order #93003
Availability: ERS-NASS Electronic Data Products

Census of Agriculture, 1987 on CD-ROM.
Availability: ERS-NASS Electronic Data Products

Census of Agriculture, Geographic Area Series: 1987 (CD-ROM).
Availability: Bureau of the Census, Data User Services Division

Census of Agriculture, 1987, Advance State and County File. (Computer Tape).
Availability: Bureau of the Census, Data User Services Division

Census of Agriculture, 1987, Advance State and County File. (Diskette).
Availability: Bureau of the Census, Data User Services Division

Census of Agriculture, 1987, Final County File. (Computer Tape).
Availability: Bureau of the Census, Data User Services Division

Census of Agriculture, 1987, Final State File. (Computer Tape).
Availability: Bureau of the Census, Data User Services Division

Census of Agriculture, 1987, Volume 1, Geographic Area Series, State and County Data Files.
Availability: Bureau of the Census, Data User Services Division

Census of Horticultural Specialties: 1988 (Diskette).
Availability: Bureau of the Census, Data User Services Division.

Changes in Food Consumption and Expenditures.
Order #93004
Availability: ERS-NASS Electronic Data Products

China, Agricultural Inputs and Infrastructure, 1980 - 91.
Order #90015
Availability: ERS-NASS Electronic Data Products

China, Agricultural Prices, 1986 - 91.
Order #90016
Availability: ERS-NASS Electronic Data Products

China: Basic Social and Economic Indicators, 1979 - 91.
Order #90010
Availability: ERS-NASS Electronic Data Products

China, Cost of Agricultural Production, 1984 - 90.
Order # 90017
Availability: ERS-NASS Electronic Data Products

China, Fibers and Oilseeds Statistics, 1979 - 91.
Order #90012
Availability: ERS-NASS Electronic Data Products

China, Grain Statistics, 1979 - 91.
Order #90011
Availability: ERS-NASS Electronic Data Products

China: Income, Consumption, and Expenditure Statistics, 1980 - 91.
Order #90021
Availability: ERS-NASS Electronic Data Products

China: International Agricultural Trade, 1950 - 91.
Order #90019
Availability: ERS-NASS Electronic Data Products

China, Livestock Statistics.
Order #90014
Availability: ERS-NASS Electronic Data Products

China, Miscellaneous Crop Statistics, 1979 - 91.
Order #90013
Availability: ERS-NASS Electronic Data Products

Conservation Reserve Program Statistics, 1986 - 89.
Order #89031
Availability: ERS-NASS Electronic Data Products

Costs of Production, 1982 - 92.
Order #94010
Availability: ERS-NASS Electronic Data Products

Cotton and Wool Yearbook, 1960 - 93.
Order #89004
Availability: ERS-NASS Electronic Data Products

Crop Progress and Condition, 1985 - 92.
Order #93115
Availability: ERS-NASS Electronic Data Products

Cropping Practices, 1990 - 92
Order #93018A, 93018B & 93018C
Availability: ERS-NASS Electronic Data Products

Crops by State, 1988 - 91.
Order #92111
Availability: ERS-NASS Electronic Data Products

Crops County Data, 1972 - 92.
Order #93100A, 93100B & 93100C
Availability: ERS-NASS Electronic Data Products

Dairy Yearbook, 1965 - 90.
Order #89032
Availability: ERS-NASS Electronic Data Products

Dry Beans and Peas, 1970 - 91.
Order #86003
Availability: ERS-NASS Electronic Data Products

DWOPSIM.
Order #93001
Availability: ERS-NASS Electronic Data Products

East European Agriculture, 1971 - 87.
Order #89009
Availability: ERS-NASS Electronic Data Products

ERS Electronic Data Products CD-ROM (Combines files from 118 ERS electronic data products)
Order #93050
Availability: ERS-NASS Electronic Data Products

ERS Publications, 1985 - 92.
Order #93017
Availability: ERS-NASS Electronic Data Products

Exchange Rates, 1960 - 90.
Order #88021
Availability: ERS-NASS Electronic Data Products

Farm and Ranch Irrigation, 1984.
Order #87014
Availability: ERS-NASS Electronic Data Products

Farm and Ranch Irrigation Survey: 1988 (Diskette).
Availability: Bureau of the Census, Data User Services Division

Farm Business Balance Sheet, 1960 - 91.
Order #93013
Availability: ERS-NASS Electronic Data Products

Farm Credit System Operating Statistics, 1986 - 91.
Order #94011
Availability: ERS-NASS Electronic Data Products

Farm Employment and Wage Rates, 1974 - 90.
Order #91005Z
Availability: ERS-NASS Electronic Data Products

Farm Machinery Statistics, 1944 - 90.
Order #86016
Availability: ERS-NASS Electronic Data Products

Farm Operating and Financial Characteristics, 1990.
Order #93016
Availability: ERS-NASS Electronic Data Products

Farm Real Estate Taxes, 1909 - 1991.
Order #92002
Availability: ERS-NASS Electronic Data Products

Farm Real Estate Values, 1950 - 94.
Order #86010
Availability: ERS-NASS Electronic Data Products

Farm Sector Balance Sheet, 1960 - 89.
Order #91013
Availability: ERS-NASS Electronic Data Products

Farm Sector Balance Sheet by Sales Class, 1960 - 89.
Order #92003
Availability: ERS-NASS Electronic Data Products

Farm Sector Financial Ratios, 1960 - 91.
Order #93012
Availability: ERS-NASS Electronic Data Products

Feed Grain Data by States, 1949 - 86.
Order #87013
Availability: ERS-NASS Electronic Data Products

Feed Grain Yearbook, 1950 - 90.
Order #88007A and #88007B
Availability: ERS-NASS Electronic Data Products

Feed Manufacturing, 1984.
Order #89005
Availability: ERS-NASS Electronic Data Products

Fertilizer Use and Price Statistics, 1964 - 90.
Order #86012
Availability: ERS-NASS Electronic Data Products

Field Crop County Estimates, 1989 and 1990.
Order #92101
Availability: ERS-NASS Electronic Data Products

Field Crop State Estimates, 1975 - 91.
Order #92111
Availability: ERS-NASS Electronic Data Products

Final County File: 1987. (Computer Tape).
Availability: Bureau of the Census, Data User Services Division

Final State File: 1987. (Computer Tape).
Availability: Bureau of the Census, Data User Services Division

Financial Characteristics of Horticultural Farms, 1987 - 91.
Order #93019
Availability: ERS-NASS Electronic Data Products

Food, Beverages, and Tobacco Expenditures, 1970 - 88.
Order #86014A and #86014B
Availability: ERS-NASS Electronic Data Products

Food Consumption, 1966 - 91.
Order #89015B and #92PK01
Availability: ERS-NASS Electronic Data Products

Food Spending in American Households, 1980 - 88.
Order #90005A and #90005B
Availability: ERS-NASS Electronic Data Products

Foreign-owned Agricultural Land.
Order #87015
Availability: ERS-NASS Electronic Data Products

Foreign Production, Supply and Distribution of Agricultural Commodities.
PB85-115616
Availability: NTIS

Foreign Production, Supply and Distribution of Agricultural Commodities, 1986/87.
PB87-171971
Availability: NTIS

Fresh Fruit Prices and Marketing Spreads, 1985 - 91.
Order #88002
Availability: ERS-NASS Electronic Data Products

Fresh Vegetable Prices and Marketing Spreads, 1985 - 91.
Order #88009
Availability: ERS-NASS Electronic Data Products

Fruit and Nut Yearbook, 1970 - 91.
Order #89022
Availability: ERS-NASS Electronic Data Products

Geographic Area Series: 1987 (CD-ROM).
Availability: Bureau of the Census, Data User Services Division

Geographic Distribution of Federal Funds, 1985.
Order #88022
Availability: ERS-NASS Electronic Data Products

Global Competitive Advantages, 1985 - 89.
Order #93005
Availability: ERS-NASS Electronic Data Products

Government Payments and Market Value of Agricultural Products Sold (Diskette).
Availability: Bureau of the Census, Data User Services Division

Greenhouse and Nursery Statistics, 1960 - 88.
Order #90024A and #90024B
Availability: ERS-NASS Electronic Data Products

High-Value Export Indexes, 1961 - 86.
Order #91018
Availability: ERS-NASS Electronic Data Products

Historical State Farm Income Accounts, 1949 - 91.
Order #93007
Availability: ERS-NASS Electronic Data Products

Interstate Movement of Animals, State Regulations Data.
PB86-121639
Availability: NTIS

Irrigation Production Data System.
Order #89023
Availability: ERS-NASS Electronic Data Products

JARE Title/Abstract Database.
Order #91D01
Availability: ERS-NASS Electronic Data Products

Livestock and Dairy Costs of Production, 1972 - 90.
Order #90002
Availability: ERS-NASS Electronic Data Products

Livestock and Poultry Inventories.
Order #92131
Availability: ERS-NASS Electronic Data Products

Livestock County Data, 1991 - 93.
Order #93105B
Availability: ERS-NASS Electronic Data Products

Livestock Slaughter, 1974 - 93.
Order #94145
Availability: ERS-NASS Electronic Data Products

Major Land Uses, 1945 - 87.
Order #89003
Availability: ERS-NASS Electronic Data Products

Middle East Grain Supply and Utilization, 1966 - 85.
Order #86017
Availability: ERS-NASS Electronic Data Products

Monthly Cash Receipts, 1960 - 91.
Order #93008
Availability: ERS-NASS Electronic Data Products

National Financial Summary, 1950 - 91.
Order #88010A and #88010B
Availability: ERS-NASS Electronic Data Products

Oil Crops Yearbook, 1965 - 92.
Order #89002
Availability: ERS-NASS Electronic Data Products

Onion Statistics, 1960 - 93.
Order #94013
Availability: ERS-NASS Electronic Data Products

Ozone, 1987.
Order #92018
Availability: ERS-NASS Electronic Data Products

PL480 and Other Concessional U.S. Exports, 1985 - 89.
Order #86013
Availability: ERS-NASS Electronic Data Products

Plant Protection and Quarantine, 1983 - 88 & 1991 - 92.
Order #92019
Availability: ERS-NASS Electronic Data Products

Policy Impact Codes.
Order #86005A and #86005B
Availability: ERS-NASS Electronic Data Products

Potato Statistics, 1949 - 92.
Order #91011
Availability: ERS-NASS Electronic Data Products

Poultry and Egg Statistics, 1960 - 90.
Order #89007B
Availability: ERS-NASS Electronic Data Products

Price Spreads for Beef and Pork, 1970 - 91.
Order #90006
Availability: ERS-NASS Electronic Data Products

Prices Received by Farmers Historic Prices and Indexes, 1981 - 91.
Order #92152
Availability: ERS-NASS Electronic Data Products

Prices Received by Farmers for Field Crops, 1984 - 92.
Order #92151
Availability: ERS-NASS Electronic Data Products

Processed Food Trade, 1988 - 91.
Order #92016
Availability: ERS-NASS Electronic Data Products

Producer and Consumer Subsidy Equivalents, 1982 - 87.
Order #90009
Availability: ERS-NASS Electronic Data Products

Production and Efficiency Statistics, 1947 - 89.
Order #89026
Availability: ERS-NASS Electronic Data Products

PS&D View '93 (USDA Production, Supply, and Distribution database).
Order #93002A (Annual), 93002Q (Quarterly), 93002M (Monthly)
Availability: ERS-NASS Electronic Data Products

Rankings, 1993.
Order #93180
Availability: ERS-NASS Electronic Data Products

Red Meat Statistics, 1970 - 92.
Order #94006
Availability: ERS-NASS Electronic Data Products

Referendum CVM Programs.
Order #93010
Availability: ERS-NASS Electronic Data Products

Rice Yearbook, 1970 - 90.
Order #89001
Availability: ERS-NASS Electronic Data Products

Rural Development.
Order #88013A and #88013B
Availability: ERS-NASS Electronic Data Products

Rural Public Water Systems.
Order #89013
Availability: ERS-NASS Electronic Data Products

Rural - Urban Continuum Codes.
Order #89021
Availability: ERS-NASS Electronic Data Products

Soil Depletion Estimates Model.
Order #90004
Availability: ERS-NASS Electronic Data Products

State Financial Summary, 1985 - 90.
Order #88012A and #88012B
Availability: ERS-NASS Electronic Data Products

State - Level Costs of Production, 1987 - 89.
Order #92013
Availability: ERS-NASS Electronic Data Products

State - Level Wheat Statistics, 1948 - 88.
Order #89016
Availability: ERS-NASS Electronic Data Products

Sugar and Sweetener Yearbook, 1980 - 93.
Order #89019
Availability: ERS-NASS Electronic Data Products

Sugar Statistical Compendium, 1950 - 90.
Order #91006
Availability: ERS-NASS Electronic Data Products

SWOPSIM '92. (Studies of Agricultural Trade Liberalization)
Order #92012
Availability: ERS-NASS Electronic Data Products

Tobacco Industry, 1950 - 87.
Order #89018
Availability: ERS-NASS Electronic Data Products

Tobacco Statistics, 1935 - 92.
Order #94012
Availability: ERS-NASS Electronic Data Products

Tobacco Yearbook, 1950 - 91.
Order #92015
Availability: ERS-NASS Electronic Data Products

Tomato Statistics, 1960 - 90.
Order #92010
Availability: ERS-NASS Electronic Data Products

Trade Liberalization, 1984 and 1986.
Order #89017
Availability: ERS-NASS Electronic Data Products

U.S. Agricultural Trade, 1988 - 90.
Order #91010
Availability: ERS-NASS Electronic Data Products

U.S. and State Agricultural Profiles.
Order #87017
Availability: ERS-NASS Electronic Data Products

U.S. Broiler Industry, 1965 - 87.
Order #89006
Availability: ERS-NASS Electronic Data Products

U.S. Corn and Soybean Weather/Production Models.
Order #92001
Availability: ERS-NASS Electronic Data Products

U.S. Farm Income, 1910 - 89.
Order #90022
Availability: ERS-NASS Electronic Data Products

U.S. Food Expenditures, 1969 - 89.
Order #91003
Availability: ERS-NASS Electronic Data Products

U.S. Fresh-Market Fruit Exports, 1978 - 91.
Order #93006
Availability: ERS-NASS Electronic Data Products

U.S. Fruit, Nut, and Berry Farms.
Order #92005
Availability: ERS-NASS Electronic Data Products

U.S. Fruit, Nut, and Berry Production - Berries.
Order #91015E
Availability: ERS-NASS Electronic Data Products

U.S. Fruit, Nut, and Berry Production - Citrus Fruits.
Order #91015C
Availability: ERS-NASS Electronic Data Products

U.S. Fruit, Nut, and Berry Production - Subtropical Fruits.
Order #91015B
Availability: ERS-NASS Electronic Data Products

U.S. Fruit, Nut, and Berry Production - Tree Fruits.
Order #91015A
Availability: ERS-NASS Electronic Data Products

U.S. Fruit, Nut, and Berry Production - Tree Nuts.
Order #91015D
Availability: ERS-NASS Electronic Data Products

U.S. Greenhouse and Nursery Farms.
Order #92006
Availability: ERS-NASS Electronic Data Products

U.S. Greenhouse and Nursery Production.
Order #91016
Availability: ERS-NASS Electronic Data Products

U.S. Live Cattle Imports, 1970 - 90.
Order #91007
Availability: ERS-NASS Electronic Data Products

U.S. Monthly Cash Receipts, 1960 - 90.
Order # 90008
Availability: ERS-NASS Electronic Data Products

U.S./Pacific Rim Agricultural Trade, 1968 - 90.
Order #90007
Availability: ERS-NASS Electronic Data Products

U.S. Trade, 1978 - 87.
Order #89030
Availability: ERS-NASS Electronic Data Products

US - USSR Bilateral Trade, 1970 - 90.
Order #88019
Availability: ERS-NASS Electronic Data Products

U.S. Vegetable and Melon Farms.
Order #92004
Availability: ERS-NASS Electronic Data Products

U.S. Vegetable and Melon Production - Dry Beans and Peas.
Order #91014F
Availability: ERS-NASS Electronic Data Products

U.S. Vegetable and Melon Production - Leafy Green Vegetables.
Order #91014B
Availability: ERS-NASS Electronic Data Products

U.S. Vegetable and Melon Production - Melons.
Order #91014E
Availability: ERS-NASS Electronic Data Products

U.S. Vegetable and Melon Production - Potatoes and Root Vegetables.
Order #91014C
Availability: ERS-NASS Electronic Data Products

U.S. Vegetable and Melon Production - Sweet Corn, Snap Beans, Broccoli, etc.
Order #91014A
Availability: ERS-NASS Electronic Data Products

U.S. Vegetable and Melon Production - Tomatoes, Peppers, and Cucumbers.
Order #91014D
Availability: ERS-NASS Electronic Data Products

U.S. Watermelon Industry.
Order #89029
Availability: ERS-NASS Electronic Data Products

USDA Outlays, 1963 - 95.
Order #89D01
Availability: ERS-NASS Electronic Data Products

USSR Agricultural Trade, 1986 - 89.
Order #88016A, #88016B and 88016C
Availability: ERS-NASS Electronic Data Products

USSR Grain Harvesting Progress (Selected Years 1971 - 89).
Order #88003
Availability: ERS-NASS Electronic Data Products

USSR Grain Production, 1955 - 87.
Order #88020
Availability: ERS-NASS Electronic Data Products

USSR Grain Seeding Progress (Selected Years 1971 - 90).
Order #88004
Availability: ERS-NASS Electronic Data Products

USSR Oilseeds, 1955/56 - 1990/91.
Order #90003
Availability: ERS-NASS Electronic Data Products

USSR Production and Procurement, 1985 - 87.
Order #89027
Availability: ERS-NASS Electronic Data Products

USSR Trade Compendium, 1955 - 89.
Order #88023
Availability: ERS-NASS Electronic Data Products

Value of Land and Buildings Per Acre, 1950 - 87.
Order #87012
Availability: ERS-NASS Electronic Data Products

Vegetable Yearbook, 1970 - 92.
Order #89011A and #89011B
Availability: ERS-NASS Electronic Data Products

WASDE Crop Estimates, 1973 - 92.
Order #93501
Availability: ERS-NASS Electronic Data Products

WATI/TS - VIEW, 1961 - 89.
Order #91017
Availability: ERS-NASS Electronic Data Products

Weather in U.S. Agriculture, 1950 - 90
Order #92008A and #92008B
Availability: ERS-NASS Electronic Data Products

Wheat Yearbook, 1950 - 92.
Order #88008A and #88008B
Availability: ERS-NASS Electronic Data Products

World Agricultural Trade Flows - Feed Grains, 1962 - 90.
Order #91001B
Availability: ERS-NASS Electronic Data Products

World Agricultural Trade Flows - Food Grains, 1962 - 90.
Order #91001A
Availability: ERS-NASS Electronic Data Products

World Agricultural Trade Flows - Nonfood Oilseed Products, 1962 - 90.
Order #91001F
Availability: ERS-NASS Electronic Data Products

World Agricultural Trade Flows - Peanut, Maize, and Olive Oil, 1962 - 90.
Order #91001G
Availability: ERS-NASS Electronic Data Products

World Agricultural Trade Flows - Soybean Products and Other Oilseed Meal, 1962 - 90.
Order #91001C
Availability: ERS-NASS Electronic Data Products

World Agricultural Trade Flows - Rape and Sunflower Seed and Oil, 1962 - 90.
Order #91001D
Availability: ERS-NASS Electronic Data Products

World Agricultural Trade Flows, Tropical Oils, 1962 - 90.
Order #91001E
Availability: ERS-NASS Electronic Data Products

World Agricultural Trends and Indicators - Australia and New Zealand, 1961 - 89.
Order #89024L
Availability: ERS-NASS Electronic Data Products

World Agricultural Trends and Indicators - The Caribbean, 1961 - 89.
Order #89024C
Availability: ERS-NASS Electronic Data Products

World Agricultural Trends and Indicators - Central America, 1961 - 89.
Order #89024B
Availability: ERS-NASS Electronic Data Products

World Agricultural Trends and Indicators - East Asia and People's Republic of China, 1961 - 89.
Order #89024K
Availability: ERS-NASS Electronic Data Products

World Agricultural Trends and Indicators - Eastern Europe and USSR, 1961 - 89.
Order #89024F
Availability: ERS-NASS Electronic Data Products

World Agricultural Trends and Indicators - EC - 12, 1961 - 89.
Order #89024M
Availability: ERS-NASS Electronic Data Products

World Agricultural Trends and Indicators - North Africa and Middle East, 1961 - 89.
Order #89024H
Availability: ERS-NASS Electronic Data Products

World Agricultural Trends and Indicators - North America, 1961 - 89.
Order #89024A
Availability: ERS-NASS Electronic Data Products

World Agricultural Trends and Indicators - South America, 1961 - 89.
Order #89024D
Availability: ERS-NASS Electronic Data Products

World Agricultural Trends and Indicators - South Asia, 1961 - 89.
Order #89024I
Availability: ERS-NASS Electronic Data Products

World Agricultural Trends and Indicators - Southeast Asia, and Pacific Islands, 1961 - 89.
Order #89024J
Availability: ERS-NASS Electronic Data Products

World Agricultural Trends and Indicators - Sub-Saharan Africa, 1961 - 89.
Order #89024G
Availability: ERS-NASS Electronic Data Products

World Agricultural Trends and Indicators - Western Europe, 1961 - 89.
Order #89024E
Availability: ERS-NASS Electronic Data Products

World Agricultural Trends and Indicators - World and Regional Data Series, 1961 - 89.
Order #89024N
Availability: ERS-NASS Electronic Data Products

World Red Meat and Poultry Consumption, 1975 - 91.
Order #91004
Availability: ERS-NASS Electronic Data Products

ZIP Code Tabulations of Selected Items: 1987 (Diskette and CD-ROM)
Availability: Bureau of the Census, Data User Services Division

ZIPFIP.
Order #93014 and #93015C&D
Availability: ERS-NASS Electronic Data Products

Banking

Bank/Branch Structure File Tape.
PB87-903700
Availability: NTIS

Bank Credit Tape, January 1973 - December 1988.
PB89-186001
Availability: NTIS

Bank Holding Company Annual Tape (Y-6), December 1984.
PB86-143195
Availability: NTIS

Bank Holding Company Quarterly Tape (Y-9), March 1990.
PB90-590050
Availability: NTIS

Bank Holding Company Quarterly Tape (Y-9), June 1990.
PB90-590-060
Availability: NTIS

Bank Holding Company Subscription Tape (Y9), June 1992.
PB92-590060
Availability: NTIS

Banking Reserves Tape, 1959-1992 (Diskette).
PB92-5030135
Availability: NTIS

Branch Office Deposit Report for FSLIC - Insured Thrift Institutions, June 1991.
PB92-501030
Availability: NTIS

Capacity Utilization Tape (Monthly Cumulative from 1948 to Current).
PB85-246403
Availability: NTIS

Changes to Bank Structure, September 1991 (Diskette).
PB91-591830
Availability: NTIS

Consumer Installment Credit 1980-1987 (Diskette).
PB88-180732
Availability: NTIS

Consumer Installment Credit Data Tape (January 1975-January 1986).
PB86-179470
Availability: NTIS

Credit Union Financial and Statistical Data File, June 1992.
PB92-592020
Availability: NTIS

Flow of Funds.
PB91-591-580
Availability: NTIS

Industrial Production Index Tape (Monthly Cumulative January 1919 to Current).
PB85-217602
Availability: NTIS

Money Stock Diskette, 1959-1991 (Diskette).
PB92-501550
Availability: NTIS

Report of Condition and Income for Commercial Banks and Selected Other Financial Institutions. Call and Income Report Data Dictionary.
PB88-934500
Availability: NTIS

Report of Condition and Income for Commercial Banks and Selected Other Financial Institutions. Call and Income Report Microdata Reference Manual.
PB86-105624
Availability: NTIS

Report of Condition and Income for Commercial Banks and Selected Other Financial Institutions, December 31, 1990. Call and Income Report.
PB90-590120
Availability: NTIS

Report of Condition and Income for Commercial Banks and Selected Other Financial Institutions, June 30, 1991. Call and Income Report.
PB91-590100
Availability: NTIS

Report of Condition and Income for Commercial Banks and Selected Other Financial Institutions, March 31, 1991. Call and Income Report.
PB91-590090
Availability: NTIS

Report of Condition and Income for Commercial Banks and Selected Other Financial Institutions, September 30, 1991. Call and Income Report.
PB91-590110
Availability: NTIS

Selected Interest Rates (H-15), Quarterly (Diskette).
PB91-592120
Availability: NTIS

Selected Interest Rates (H-15) Tape, Quarterly Cumulative 1919 to Date.
PB91-591540
Availability: NTIS

Summary of Deposits for Each FDIC-Insured Bank and Branch in the U.S., June 30, 1991.
PB91-504216
Availability: NTIS

Survey of Currency and Transaction Account Data, 1984 - 1986.
PB90-501636
Availability: NTIS

Thrift Financial Report, Quarterly, March 1991.
PB91-590010
Availability: NTIS

Thrift Financial Report, Quarterly, June 1991.
PB91-590020
Availability: NTIS

Thrift Financial Report, Quarterly, September 1991.
PB91-590030
Availability: NTIS

Thrift Financial Report, Quarterly, December 1991.
PB91-590040
Availability: NTIS

U.S. Balance Sheet Data (Flow of Funds), Balance Sheets for the U.S. Economy (1945 - 1990).
PB91-592080
Availability: NTIS

Budgeting

Budget and Budget Title Files, FY 93 (United States Government).
PB92-502152
Availability: NTIS

Standard Industrial Classification Manual, 1987.
PB87-100020
Availability: NTIS

Standard Industrial Classification Manual, 1987 (for IBM PC/AT Microcomputers).
PB87-199576
Availability: NTIS

Standard Industrial Classification Manual, 1987 (for IBM PC Microcomputers).
PB87-199568
Availability: NTIS

Standard Industrial Classification Manual, 1987 (for MacIntosh Microcomputers).
PB87-199584
Availability: NTIS

Business - Trade and Services

Census of Retail Trade, 1987, Geographic Area Series File (Computer Tape).
Availability: Bureau of the Census, Data User Services Division

Census of Service Industries: 1987, Establishment and Firm Size File (Computer Tape).
Availability: Bureau of the Census, Data User Services Division

Census of Wholesale Trade, 1987: Establishment and Firm Size (Computer Tape).
Availability: Bureau of the Census, Data User Services Division

Census of Wholesale Trade, 1987, Geographic Area Series File.
Availability: Bureau of the Census, Data User Services Division

County Business Patterns: 1981-1990 Diskette Extract Files.
Availability: Bureau of the Census, Data User Services Division

County Business Patterns: 1986, 1987, 1988, 1989 & 1990 (Computer Tape and CD-ROM).
Availability: Bureau of the Census, Data User Services Division

Economic Censuses, Release 2A, Volume 2, 1987. ZIP Code Statistics (CD-ROM).
Availability: Bureau of the Census, Data User Services Division

Establishment and Firm Size File (RC87-S-1(T)) (Computer Tape and CD-ROM).
Availability: Bureau of the Census, Data User Services Division

Geographic Area Series (RC87-A(T)) (Computer Tape and CD-ROM).
Availability: Bureau of the Census, Data User Services Division

Geographic Area Series (SC87-A(T)) (Computer Tape and CD-ROM).
Availability: Bureau of the Census, Data User Services Division

Geographic Area Series (WC87-A(T)) (Computer Tape and CD-ROM).
Availability: Bureau of the Census, Data User Services Division

Merchandise Line Sales File (RC87-S-3(T)) (Computer Tape and CD-ROM).
Availability: Bureau of the Census, Data User Services Division

Monthly Retail: Sales and Inventories on Diskette.
Availability: Bureau of the Census, Data User Services Division

Nonemployer Statistics File (RC87-N(T)) (Computer Tape and CD-ROM).
Availability: Bureau of the Census, Data User Services Division

Research and Development in Industry, 1958-1983.
Availability: Bureau of the Census, Data User Services Division

Unpublished Monthly Retail Sales Estimates (Diskette).
Availability: Bureau of the Census, Data User Services Division

ZIP Code Statistics File (RC87-Z(T)), 1987 (Computer Tape and CD-ROM).
Availability: Bureau of the Census, Data User Services Division

ZIP Code Statistics File (SC87-Z(T), 1987 (Computer Tape).
Availability: Bureau of the Census, Data User Services Division

Communications

Aeronautical Frequency Lists and Geographic Location of Radio Stations Operating Near Frequencies Commonly Used by Cable Television Systems.
PB90-502386
Availability: NTIS

Amateur Radio Service Master File Updates.
PB90-591350
Availability: NTIS

Broadcast AM Data Base (AM Engineering Data Base).
PB90-591370
Availability: NTIS

Broadcast TV Data Base.
PB90-591360
Availability: NTIS

Cable Television Community Unit System, 1987.
PB89-196091
Availability: NTIS

Common Carrier Land Mobile Data Base, Pending.
PB90-591420
Availability: NTIS

Common Carrier Land Mobile Stations, Granted.
PB90-591410
Availability: NTIS

Common Carrier Microwave Database.
PB90-591440
Availability: NTIS

Common Carrier Overseas Telecommunications Traffic Data, 1986 (for Microcomputers).
PB88-221924
Availability: NTIS

Directional Antenna Data Base.
PB90-591450
Availability: NTIS

Directional Antenna Data Base (for Microcomputers).
PB86-151610
Availability: NTIS

FCC Broadcast FM Data Base.
PB90-591380
Availability: NTIS

FCC (Federal Communications Commission) Decision File, Volume 92, Number 1.
PB84-145275
Availability: NTIS

FCC (Federal Communications Commission) Decision File, Volume 92, Number 2.
PB84-145267
Availability: NTIS

FCC (Federal Communications Commission) Decision File, Volume 92, Number 3.
PB84-145259
Availability: NTIS

FCC (Federal Communications Commission) Decision File, Volume 92, Number 4.
PB84-145242
Availability: NTIS

FCC (Federal Communications Commission) Decision File, Volume 92, Number 5.
PB84-145234
Availability: NTIS

FCC M3 Map Data File (for Microcomputers).
PB87-222253
Availability: NTIS

Fourier Coefficients Representing the 1 MHz Worldwide Distribution of Atmospheric Radio Noise.
PB86-100021
Availability: NTIS

Marine Data Base.
PB90-591460
Availability: NTIS

Master Frequency File - Complete.
PB85-215473
Availability: NTIS

Master Frequency File Subset 1 - Broadcast Services.
PB85-215481
Availability: NTIS

Master Frequency File Subset 2 - Common Carrier Services (Except Land Mobile and Microwave).
PB85-215556
Availability: NTIS

Master Frequency File Subset 3 - Common Carrier Services: Land Mobile.
PB85-215564
Availability: NTIS

Master Frequency File Subset 4 - Experimental Services (Office of Science and Technology).
PB85-215572
Availability: NTIS

Master Frequency File Subset 5 - Microwave Services: Private, Cable and Common Carrier.
PB85-215531
Availability: NTIS

Master Frequency File Subset 6 - Private Radio Services: Land Mobile.
PB85-215523
Availability: NTIS

Master Frequency File Subset 7 - Private Radio Services: Industrial Services (Except Industrial Business).
PB85-215515
Availability: NTIS

Master Frequency File Subset 8 - Private Radio Services: Public Safety and Land Transportation.
PB85-215549
Availability: NTIS

Master Frequency File Subset 9 - Private Radio Services: Industrial Business.
PB85-215499
Availability: NTIS

Master Frequency File Subset 10 - Private Radio Services: Specialized Mobile Radio.
PB85-215598
Availability: NTIS

Master Frequency File Subset 11 - Aviation Ground and Marine Radio Services.
PB85-215507
Availability: NTIS

NTIMIT Telephone Network
Acoustic-Phonetic Continuous Speech Corpus (on CD-ROM).
PB92-502087
Availability: NTIS

Overseas Traffic Data File, January-December 1984 (FCC Part 43.61).
PB86-121647
Availability: NTIS

Overseas Traffic Data File, July-December 1983 (FCC Part 43.61). PB85-194298
Availability: NTIS

Construction

Building Permits Summary File: January - December 1990 (Cumulative) (Computer Tape).
Availability: Bureau of the Census, Data User Services Division

Building Permits Survey (Monthly and Annual), (Year) (Computer Tape).
Availability: Bureau of the Census, Data User Services Division

Characteristics of New Housing - Microdata Sample (Computer Tape).
Availability: Bureau of the Census, Data User Services Division

Construction Statistics, Microdata from the Survey of Housing Starts, Sales and Completions File (Computer Tape).
Availability: Bureau of the Census, Data User Services Division

Current Month and Historical Building Permits Data by State, Metropolitan Area, and Individual Permit-Issuing Places.
Availability: Bureau of the Census, Data User Services Division

1987 Census of Construction Industries, Geographic Area Series (CC87-A-1 to 10) (CD-ROM).
Availability: Bureau of the Census, Data User Services Division

1987 Census of Construction Industries, Industry Series (CC87-I-1 to 28) (CD-ROM).
Availability: Bureau of the Census, Data User Services Division

Value of New Construction Put in Place: 1964-1985 Diskette File.
Availability: Bureau of the Census, Data User Services Division

Criminal Justice

ABC News "Nightline" Drugs and Alcohol Poll, August 1988.
Availability: National Archive of Criminal Justice Data

ABC News Supreme Court Nomination Poll, July 1991.
Availability: National Archive of Criminal Justice Data

ABC News/Washington Post Clarence Thomas Vote Delay Polls, October 1991.
Availability: National Archive of Criminal Justice Data

ABC News/Washington Post Poll, January 1990.
Availability: National Archive of Criminal Justice Data

ABC News/Washington Post Poll, February 1990.
Availability: National Archive of Criminal Justice Data

ABC New/Washington Post Souter Nomination Poll, July 1990.
Availability: National Archive of Criminal Justice Data

Access to Justice in Ontario, 1985 - 1988.
Availability: National Archive of Criminal Justice Data

Age-by-Race Specific Crime Rates, 1965 - 1985: (United States).
Availability: National Archive of Criminal Justice Data

American's Use of Time, 1985.
Availability: National Archive of Criminal Justice Data

Analyzing Trial Time in California, Colorado, and New Jersey, 1986.
Availability: National Archive of Criminal Justice Data

Anticipating Community Drug Problems in Washington, D.C. and Portland, Oregon, 1984 - 1990.
Availability: National Archive of Criminal Justice Data

Augmented Federal Probation, Sentencing, and Supervision Information System, 1985.
Availability: National Archive of Criminal Justice Data

Automated Reporting System Pilot Project in Los Angeles, 1990.
Availability: National Archive of Criminal Justice Data

British Crime Survey, 1988.
Availability: National Archive of Criminal Justice Data

Calls for Service to Police as a Means of Evaluating Crime Trends in Oklahoma City, 1986 - 1988.
Availability: National Archive of Criminal Justice Data

Capital Punishment in the United States, 1973 - 1990.
Availability: National Archive of Criminal Justice Data

CBS News "48 Hours" Gun Poll, March 1989.
Availability: National Archive of Criminal Justice Data

CBS News/New York Times Abortion Poll, July 1989.
Availability: National Archive of Criminal Justice Data

CBS News/New York Times Abortion Polls, September - October 1989.
Availability: National Archive of Criminal Justice Data

CBS News/New York Times Drug Poll, September 1989.
Availability: National Archive of Criminal Justice Data

CBS News/New York Times Monthly Poll, March - April 1990.
Availability: National Archive of Criminal Justice Data

Census of Public and Private Juvenile Detention, Correctional, and Shelter Facilities, 1990 - 1991: (United States).
Availability: National Archive of Criminal Justice Data

Census of State and Federal Adult Correctional Facilities, 1990.
Availability: National Archive of Criminal Justice Data

Census of State Felony Courts, 1985: (United States).
Availability: National Archive of Criminal Justice Data

Center for Research on Social Reality (Spain) Survey, December 1993: Attitudes and Behavior Regarding Alcohol, Tobacco, and Drugs.
Availability: National Archive of Criminal Justice Data

Changing Patterns of Drug Abuse and Criminality Among Crack Cocaine Users in New York City, 1988 - 1989.
Availability: National Archive of Criminal Justice Data

Charlotte (North Carolina) Spouse Assault Replication Project, 1987 - 1989.
Availability: National Archive of Criminal Justice Data

Child Abuse, Neglect, and Violent Criminal Behavior in a Midwest Metropolitan Area of the United States, 1967 - 1988.
Availability: National Archive of Criminal Justice Data

City Police Expenditures, 1946 - 1985: (United States).
Availability: National Archive of Criminal Justice Data

Community Policing in Baltimore, 1986 - 1987.
Availability: National Archive of Criminal Justice Data

Comparison of Drug Control Strategies in San Diego, 1989.
Availability: National Archive of Criminal Justice Data

Concerns of Police Survivors, 1986: (United States).
Availability: National Archive of Criminal Justice Data

Crime Commission Rates Among Incarcerated Felons in Nebraska, 1986 - 1990.
Availability: National Archive of Criminal Justice Data

Criminal Justice Outcomes of Male Offenders in 14 Jurisdictions in the United States, 1985 - 1988.
Availability: National Archive of Criminal Justice Data

Criminal Victimization Among Women in Cleveland, Ohio: Impact on Health Status and Medical Service Usage, 1986.
Availability: National Archive of Criminal Justice Data

Criminal Violence and Incapacitation in California, 1962 - 1988.
Availability: National Archive of Criminal Justice Data

Dangerous Sex Offenders: Classifying, Predicting, and Evaluating Outcomes of Clinical Treatment in Bridgewater, Massachusetts, 1982 - 1985.
Availability: National Archive of Criminal Justice Data

Deinstitutionalization of Status Offenders: A Study of Intervention Practices for Youth In Seven Cities in the United States, 1987 - 1991.
Availability: National Archive of Criminal Justice Data

Delinquency in a Birth Cohort II: Philadelphia, 1958 - 1986.
Availability: National Archive of Criminal Justice Data

Deterring Drug Use With Intensive Probation in New Jersey, 1989 - 1990.
Availability: National Archive of Criminal Justice Data

Directory of Law Enforcement Agencies, 1986: (United States).
Availability: National Archive of Criminal Justice Data

Disturbed Violent Offenders in New York, 1985.
Availability: National Archive of Criminal Justice Data

Domestic Violence Experience in Omaha, Nebraska, 1986 - 1987.
Availability: National Archive of Criminal Justice Data

Drinking and Driving: A Survey of Licensed Drivers in the United States, 1986.
Availability: National Archive of Criminal Justice Data

Drug Testing of Juvenile Detainees to Identify High-Risk Youth in Florida, 1986 - 1987.
Availability: National Archive of Criminal Justice Data

Drug Use Forecasting in 24 Cities in the United States, 1987 - 1992.
Availability: National Archive of Criminal Justice Data

Drugs, Alcohol, and Student Crime in the United States, April - May 1989.
Availability: National Archive of Criminal Justice Data

Effects of Cognitive Interviewing, Practice, and Interview Style on Children's Recall Performance in California, 1989 - 1990.
Availability: National Archive of Criminal Justice Data

Effects of Drug Testing on Defendant Risk in Dade County, Florida, 1987.
Availability: National Archive of Criminal Justice Data

Effects of Foot Patrol Policing in Boston, 1977 - 1985.
Availability: National Archive of Criminal Justice Data

Effects of "U.S. v. Leon" on Police Search Warrant Practices, 1984 - 1985.
Availability: National Archive of Criminal Justice Data

Electronic Monitoring of Nonviolent Convicted Felons: An Experiment in Home Detention in Marion County, Indiana 1986 - 1988.
Availability: National Archive of Criminal Justice Data

Euro-Barometer 32: The Single European Market, Drugs, Alcohol, and Cancer, November 1989.
Availability: National Archive of Criminal Justice Data

Evaluating Alternative Police Responses to Spouse Assault in Colorado Springs: An Enhanced Replication of the Minneapolis Experiment, 1987 - 1989.
Availability: National Archive of Criminal Justice Data

Evaluating Network Sampling in Victimization Surveys in Peoria, Illinois, 1986.
Availability: National Archive of Criminal Justice Data

Evaluation of a Repeat Offender Unit in Phoenix, Arizona, 1987 - 1989.
Availability: National Archive of Criminal Justice Data

Evaluation of Adult Urine Testing/Drug Use Surveillance Project in Washington, D.C., 1984 - 1986.
Availability: National Archive of Criminal Justice Data

Evaluation of Arizona Pretrial Services Drug Testing Programs, 1987 - 1989.
Availability: National Archive of Criminal Justice Data

Evaluation of the Impact of Innovative Policing Programs on Social Disorder in Seven Cities in the United States, 1983 - 1990.
Availability: National Archive of Criminal Justice Data

Evaluation of the Maricopa County (Arizona) Demand Reduction Program, 1989 - 1991.
Availability: National Archive of Criminal Justice Data

Executions in the United States, 1608 - 1991: The Espy File.
Availability: National Archive of Criminal Justice Data

Expenditure and Employment Data for the Criminal Justice System: Individual Units File and Estimates File, 1985-1988.
Availability: National Archive of Criminal Justice Data

Expenditure and Employment Data for the Criminal Justice System (United States): Extract files, 1985, 1986, 1987, 1988, 1989, 1990, and 1991.
Availability: National Archive of Criminal Justice Data

Exploring the House Burglar's Perspective: Observing and Interviewing Offenders in St. Louis, 1989 - 1990.
Availability: National Archive of Criminal Justice Data

Factors Influencing the Quality and Utility of Government-Sponsored Criminal Justice Research in the United States, 1975 - 1986.
Availability: National Archive of Criminal Justice Data

Federal Court Cases 1970 - 1989: Integrated Data Base.
Availability: National Archive of Criminal Justice Data

Federal District Court Civil Decisions, 1981 - 1987: Detroit, Houston, and Kansas City.
Availability: National Archive of Criminal Justice Data

Federal Justice Statistics Program Data, 1978 - 1986: (United States).
Availability: National Archive of Criminal Justice Data

Fines as a Criminal Sanction: Practices and Attitudes of Trial Court Judges in the United States, 1985.
Availability: National Archive of Criminal Justice Data

Fraud Victimization Survey, 1990: (United States).
Availability: National Archive of Criminal Justice Data

Gang Involvement in "Rock" Cocaine Trafficking in Los Angeles, 1984 - 1985.
Availability: National Archive of Criminal Justice Data

Gender of Prisoners Admitted to State and Federal Institutions in the United States, 1926 - 1987.
Availability: National Archive of Criminal Justice Data

General Social Surveys, 1972 - 1993: (Cumulative file).
Availability: National Archive of Criminal Justice Data

Historical Statistics on Prisoners in State and Federal Institutions, Year-end 1925 - 1986: (United States).
Availability: National Archive of Criminal Justice Data

Illegal Immigration and Crime in San Diego and El Paso Counties, 1985 - 1986.
Availability: National Archive of Criminal Justice Data

Impact of Legislation to Prohibit "Happy Hours" in Indiana, 1983 - 1986.
Availability: National Archive of Criminal Justice Data

Impact of Sentencing Guidelines on the Use of Incarceration in Federal Criminal Courts in the United States, 1984 - 1990.
Availability: National Archive of Criminal Justice Data

Impact of Sentencing Reforms and Speedy Trial Laws in the United States, 1969 - 1989.
Availability: National Archive of Criminal Justice Data

Impact on the Court Process on Sexually Abused Children in North Carolina, 1983 - 1986.
Availability: National Archive of Criminal Justice Data

Implementation of Quantitative Decision Aids in the Oklahoma Probation and Parole System, 1989 - 1990.
Availability: National Archive of Criminal Justice Data

Improving Evidence Collection Through Police - Prosecutor Coordination in Baltimore, 1984 - 1985.
Availability: National Archive of Criminal Justice Data

Improving Prison Classification Procedures in Vermont: Applying an Interaction Model, 1983 - 1985.
Availability: National Archive of Criminal Justice Data

Improving the Investigation of Homicide and the Apprehension Rate of Murderers in Washington State, 1981 - 1986.
Availability: National Archive of Criminal Justice Data

Intensive Supervision Program in New Jersey, 1983 - 1986.
Availability: National Archive of Criminal Justice Data

International Victimization Survey, 1988.
Availability: National Archive of Criminal Justice Data

Intra- and Intergenerational Aspects of Serious Domestic Violence and Alcohol and Drug Abuse in Buffalo, 1987.
Availability: National Archive of Criminal Justice Data

Justice Assistance Data for the United States: Individual Units and Estimates, 1988.
Availability: National Archive of Criminal Justice Data

Juvenile Court Statistics, 1988 and 1989: (United States).
Availability: National Archive of Criminal Justice Data

Juvenile Court Statistics, 1986: Reported Cases in Calendar Year Data Base.
Availability: National Archive of Criminal Justice Data

Juvenile Detention and Correctional Facility, Census, 1984 - 1985.
Availability: National Archive of Criminal Justice Data

Juvenile Detention and Correctional Facility, Census, 1986 - 1987: Public Facilities.
Availability: National Archive of Criminal Justice Data

Juvenile Detention and Correctional Facility, Census, 1988 - 1989: Public Facilities.
Availability: National Archive of Criminal Justice Data

Law Enforcement Management and Administrative Statistics (LEMAS), 1987 and 1990.
Availability: National Archive of Criminal Justice Data

Management of Death Row Inmates, 1986 - 1987: (United States).
Availability: National Archive of Criminal Justice Data

Mandatory Drug Offender Processing Data, 1986: Alaska, California, Iowa, Minnesota, Nebraska, New York, North Carolina, and Virginia.
Availability: National Archive of Criminal Justice Data

Mandatory Drug Offender Processing Data, 1987: New York.
Availability: National Archive of Criminal Justice Data

Mental Disorder and Violent Crime: A 20-Year Cohort Study in New York State, 1968 - 1988.
Availability: National Archive of Criminal Justice Data

Mentally Disordered Offenders in Pursuit of Celebrities and Politicians.
Availability: National Archive of Criminal Justice Data

Minimum Legal Drinking Age and Crime in the United States, 1980 - 1987.
Availability: National Archive of Criminal Justice Data

Minneapolis Intervention Project, 1986 - 1987.
Availability: National Archive of Criminal Justice Data

Minnesota Juvenile Court Records, 1984 - 1987.
Availability: National Archive of Criminal Justice Data

Missouri Juvenile Court Records, 1984 - 1987.
Availability: National Archive of Criminal Justice Data

Modern Policing and the Control of Illegal Drugs: Testing New Strategies in Oakland, California, and Birmingham, Alabama, 1987 - 1989.
Availability: National Archive of Criminal Justice Data

Monitoring of Federal Criminal Sentences, 1987 - 1992.
Availability: National Archive of Criminal Justice Data

Monitoring the Future: A Continuing Study of the Lifestyles and Values of Youth, 1976 - 1992: Concatenated Core File.
Availability: National Archive of Criminal Justice Data

Monitoring the Future: A Continuing Study of the Lifestyles and Values of Youth, 1985, 1986, 1987, 1988, 1989, 1990, 1991 and 1992.
Availability: National Archive of Criminal Justice Data

Murder Cases in 33 Large Urban Counties in the United States, 1988.
Availability: National Archive of Criminal Justice Data

National Assessment Program Survey of Criminal Justice Personnel in the United States, 1986.
Availability: National Archive of Criminal Justice Data

National Corrections Reporting Program, 1989, 1990: (United States).
Availability: National Archive of Criminal Justice Data

National Crime Surveys: Crime School Supplement, 1989.
Availability: National Archive of Criminal Justice Data

National Crime Surveys Longitudinal File, 1988 - 1989: (Selected Variables).
Availability: National Archive of Criminal Justice Data

National Crime Surveys: National Sample, 1979 - 1987 (Revised Questionnaire).
Availability: National Archive of Criminal Justice Data

National Crime Surveys: National Sample, 1986 - 1992 (Near-Term Data).
Availability: National Archive of Criminal Justice Data

National Household Survey on Drug Abuse, 1988, 1990, and 1991.
Availability: National Archive of Criminal Justice Data

National Incidence Studies of Missing, Abducted, Runaway, and Thrown Away Children (NISMART), 1988.
Availability: National Archive of Criminal Justice Data

National Jail Census, 1988.
Availability: National Archive of Criminal Justice Data

National Judicial Reporting Program, 1988 and 1990: (United States).
Availability: National Archive of Criminal Justice Data

National Justice Agency List, 1985, 1986, 1987, and 1992.
Availability: National Archive of Criminal Justice Data

National Pretrial Reporting Program, 1990 - 1991.
Availability: National Archive of Criminal Justice Data

National Prosecutors Survey, 1990 and 1992.
Availability: National Archive of Criminal Justice Data

National Survey of Children: Wave III, 1987.
Availability: National Archive of Criminal Justice Data

National Survey of Field Training Programs for Police Officers, 1985 - 1986.
Availability: National Archive of Criminal Justice Data

National Survey of Jails: Jurisdiction-Level and Jail-Level Data, 1985 and 1986.
Availability: National Archive of Criminal Justice Data

National Survey of Jails: Jurisdiction-Level Data, 1987, 1989, 1990.
Availability: National Archive of Criminal Justice Data

National Survey of Judges and Court Practitioners, 1991.
Availability: National Archive of Criminal Justice Data

National Survey of Law Enforcement Agencies, 1987.
Availability: National Archive of Criminal Justice Data

National Youth Gang Intervention and Suppression Survey, 1980 - 1987.
Availability: National Archive of Criminal Justice Data

Nebraska Juvenile Court Records, 1975 - 1987.
Availability: National Archive of Criminal Justice Data

New Orleans Offender Study, 1973 - 1986.
Availability: National Archive of Criminal Justice Data

New York City and Suburban Poll, November 1991.
Availability: National Archive of Criminal Justice Data

New York Times Race Relations Survey, March 1987: New York City.
Availability: National Archive of Criminal Justice Data

Offender Based Transaction Statistics (OBTS), 1985: Alaska, California, Delaware, Georgia, Minnesota, Missouri, Nebraska, New York, Ohio, Pennsylvania, and Virginia.
Availability: National Archive of Criminal Justice Data

Offender Based Transaction Statistics (OBTS), 1986: Alabama, Alaska, California, Delaware, Georgia, Minnesota, Missouri, Nebraska, New York, Ohio, Pennsylvania, and Virginia.
Availability: National Archive of Criminal Justice Data

Offender Based Transaction Statistics (OBTS), 1987: Alaska, California, Delaware, Minnesota, Missouri, Nebraska, New Jersey, Pennsylvania, and Vermont.
Availability: National Archive of Criminal Justice Data

Offender Based Transaction Statistics (OBTS), 1988: Alabama, Alaska, California, Delaware, Idaho, Kentucky, Minnesota, Missouri, Nebraska, New Jersey, New York, Oregon, Pennsylvania, Utah, Vermont, and Virginia.
Availability: National Archive of Criminal Justice Data

Offender Based Transaction Statistics (OBTS), 1989: Alabama, Alaska, California, Idaho, Kentucky, Minnesota, Missouri, Nebraska, New Jersey, New York, Pennsylvania, Vermont, and Virginia.
Availability: National Archive of Criminal Justice Data

Offender Based Transaction Statistics (OBTS), 1990: Alabama, Alaska, California, Idaho, Minnesota, Missouri, Nebraska, New Jersey, New York, Pennsylvania, Vermont, and Virginia.
Availability: National Archive of Criminal Justice Data

Organizations Convicted in Federal Criminal Courts, 1988 - 1990: (United States).
Availability: National Archive of Criminal Justice Data

Organized Crime Business Activities and Their Implications for Law Enforcement, 1986 - 1987.
Availability: National Archive of Criminal Justice Data

Patterns of Drug Use and Their Relation to Improving Prediction of Patterns of Delinquency and Crime in Racine, Wisconsin, 1961 - 1988.
Availability: National Archive of Criminal Justice Data

Perceptual Deterrence and Desistance From Crime: A Study of Repetitive Serious Property Offenders in Tennessee, 1987 - 1988.
Availability: National Archive of Criminal Justice Data

Physical Violence in American Families, 1985.
Availability: National Archive of Criminal Justice Data

Police Documentation of Drunk Driving Arrests, 1984 - 1987: Los Angeles, Denver, and Boston.
Availability: National Archive of Criminal Justice Data

Police Response to Street Gang Violence in California: Improving the Investigative Process, 1985.
Availability: National Archive of Criminal Justice Data

Prejudice and Violence in the American Workplace, 1988 - 1991: Survey of an Eastern Corporation.
Availability: National Archive of Criminal Justice Data

Pretrial Home Detention With Electronic Monitoring: An Evaluation in Marion County, Indiana, 1988 - 1989.
Availability: National Archive of Criminal Justice Data

Prosecution of Felony Arrests, 1986: Indianapolis, Los Angeles, New Orleans, Portland, St. Louis, and Washington, DC.
Availability: National Archive of Criminal Justice Data

Prosecutorial Discretion and Plea Bargaining in Federal Criminal Courts in the United States, 1983 - 1990.
Availability: National Archive of Criminal Justice Data

Providing Help to Victims: A Study of Psychological and Material Outcomes in New York City, 1984 - 1985.
Availability: National Archive of Criminal Justice Data

Race of Prisoners Admitted to State and Federal Institutions in the United States, 1926 - 1986.
Availability: National Archive of Criminal Justice Data

Recidivism of Felons on Probation, 1986 - 1989: (United States).
Availability: National Archive of Criminal Justice Data

Reducing Prison Violence by More Effective Inmate Management: An Experiment Field Test of the Prisoner Management Classification (PMC) System in Washington State, 1987 - 1988.
Availability: National Archive of Criminal Justice Data

Reexamining the Minneapolis Repeat Complaint Address Policing (RECAP) Experiment, 1986 - 1987.
Availability: National Archive of Criminal Justice Data

Repeat Complaint Address Policing: Two Field Experiments in Minneapolis, 1985 - 1987.
Availability: National Archive of Criminal Justice Data

Reporting of Drug Related Crimes: Resident and Police Perspectives in the United States, 1988 - 1990.
Availability: National Archive of Criminal Justice Data

Retail-Level Heroin Enforcement and Property Crime in 30 Cities in Massachusetts, 1980 - 1986.
Availability: National Archive of Criminal Justice Data

Sandhills (North Carolina) Vocational Delivery System Evaluation Project, 1983 - 1987.
Availability: National Archive of Criminal Justice Data

Screening of Youth at Risk for Delinquency in Oregon, 1980 - 1985.
Availability: National Archive of Criminal Justice Data

Selecting Career Criminal for Priority Prosecution, 1984 - 1986: Los Angeles County, California and Middlesex County, Massachusetts.
Availability: National Archive of Criminal Justice Data

Sentencing Outcomes in 28 Felony Courts, 1985 (United States).
Availability: National Archive of Criminal Justice Data

Shock Incarceration in Louisiana, 1987 - 1989.
Availability: National Archive of Criminal Justice Data

Socioeconomic and Demographic Characteristics of Synthetic Drug Users in San Diego and Washington, D.C., 1990.
Availability: National Archive of Criminal Justice Data

State Court Statistics, 1987: (United States).
Availability: National Archive of Criminal Justice Data

State Strategic Planning Under the Drug Control and System Improvement Formula Grant Program in the United States, 1990.
Availability: National Archive of Criminal Justice Data

Strategic Lawsuits Against Public Participation (SLAPPs), 1987 - 1990: (United States).
Availability: National Archive of Criminal Justice Data

Study of Tribal and Alaska Native Juvenile Justice Systems in the United States, 1990.
Availability: National Archive of Criminal Justice Data

Survey of Expenditures for Criminal Justice Agencies (United States): Full File and Extract File, 1985.
Availability: National Archive of Criminal Justice Data

Survey of Facilities for Runaway and Homeless Youth, 1983 - 1988.
Availability: National Archive of Criminal Justice Data

Survey of Inmates of Federal Correctional Facilities, 1991.
Availability: National Archive of Criminal Justice Data

Survey of Inmates of Local Jails, 1989: (United States).
Availability: National Archive of Criminal Justice Data

Survey of Inmates of State Correctional Facilities, 1991: (United States).
Availability: National Archive of Criminal Justice Data

Survey of Lawyers in the Metropolitan New York Media Market, 1989.
Availability: National Archive of Criminal Justice Data

Survey of Parents and Children, 1990: (United States).
Availability: National Archive of Criminal Justice Data

Survey of Tort Litigants in Three State Courts, 1989 - 1990: (United States).
Availability: National Archive of Criminal Justice Data

Survey of Youths in Custody, 1987: (United States).
Availability: National Archive of Criminal Justice Data

Teenage Attitudes and Practices Survey, 1989: (United States).
Availability: National Archive of Criminal Justice Data

Uniform Crime Reporting Program Data: (United States).
Availability: National Archive of Criminal Justice Data

Uniform Crime Reporting Program Data (United States): County Level Detailed Arrest and Offense Data, 1988, 1989, 1990.
Availability: National Archive of Criminal Justice Data

Uniform Crime Reporting Program Data (United States): Detailed Arrest and Offense Data for 321 Counties, 1988.
Availability: National Archive of Criminal Justice Data

Uniform Crime Reporting Program Data (United States): Offenses Known and Clearances by Arrest in All Cities With Populations Over 250,000, 1987 - 1988 and 1989.
Availability: National Archive of Criminal Justice Data

Uniform Crime Reports: Arrest Data for 121 Counties in the United States, 1986.
Availability: National Archive of Criminal Justice Data

Uniform Crime Reports: Arrest Data for the 75 Most Populous Counties in the United States, 1986.
Availability: National Archive of Criminal Justice Data

United States Federal Mandatory Minimum Statutes Study, 1989 - 1990.
Availability: National Archive of Criminal Justice Data

United States Supreme Court Judicial Database, 1953 - 1992 Terms.
Availability: National Archive of Criminal Justice Data

Use and Effectiveness of Hypnosis and the Cognitive Interview for Enhancing Eyewitness Recall: Philadelphia, 1988 - 1989.
Availability: National Archive of Criminal Justice Data

Use of Adjuncts to Supplement Judicial Resources in Six Jurisdictions, 1983 - 1986: (United States).
Availability: National Archive of Criminal Justice Data

Validating Prison Security Classification Instruments in Hawaii, 1984 - 1985.
Availability: National Archive of Criminal Justice Data

Validation of the Rand Selective Incapacitation Survey and the Iowa Risk Assessment Scale in Colorado, 1986.
Availability: National Archive of Criminal Justice Data

Victim Impact Statements: Their Effect on Court Outcomes and Victim Satisfaction in New York, 1988 - 1990.
Availability: National Archive of Criminal Justice Data

Victims' Needs and Victim Services, 1988 - 1989: Evanston, Rochester, Pima County, and Fayette County.
Availability: National Archive of Criminal Justice Data

Violence Against Police: Baltimore County, Maryland, 1984 - 1986.
Availability: National Archive of Criminal Justice Data

WABC-TV/New York Daily News Race Relations Poll, January 1988.
Availability: National Archive of Criminal Justice Data

Washington Post Mayor Barry Poll, January 1990.
Availability: National Archive of Criminal Justice Data

Washington Post Mayor Barry Verdict Poll, August 1990.
Availability: National Archive of Criminal Justice Data

WCBS-TV News/New York Times Race Relations Poll, June 1988.
Availability: National Archive of Criminal Justice Data

WCBS-TV News/New York Times Race Relations Poll, June 1990.
Availability: National Archive of Criminal Justice Data

Economics

Annual 85 - Industry Input - Output Tables Based on the 1977 Benchmark Input - Output Study: 1980 (Revised) Summary Input-Output Tables (Computer Tape).
Order #51-87-00-002
Availability: Economic and Statistical Analysis/BEA

Annual 85 - Industry Input - Output Tables Based on the 1977 Benchmark Input-Output Study: 1980 (Revised) Summary Input - Output Tables (Diskette).
Order #51-87-40-406
Availability: Economic and Statistical Analysis/BEA

Annual 85 - Industry Input - Output Tables Based on the 1977 Benchmark Input - Output Study: 1981 Summary Input - Output Tables (Computer Tape).
Order #51-87-00-003
Availability: Economic and Statistical Analysis/BEA

Annual 85 - Industry Input - Output Tables Based on the 1977 Benchmark Input - Output Study: 1981 Summary Input - Output Tables (Diskette).
Order #51-87-40-401
Availability: Economic and Statistical Analysis/BEA

Annual 85 - Industry Input - Output Tables Based on the 1977 Benchmark Input - Output Study: 1982 Summary Input - Output Tables (Computer Tape).
Order #51-88-00-001
Availability: Economic and Statistical Analysis/BEA

Annual 85 - Industry Input - Output Tables Based on the 1977 Benchmark Input - Output Study: 1982 Summary Input - Output Tables (Diskette).
Order #51-88-40-401
Availability: Economic and Statistical Analysis/BEA

Annual 85 - Industry Input - Output Tables Based on the 1977 Benchmark Input - Output Study: 1983 Summary Input - Output Tables (Computer Tape).
Order #51-89-00-001
Availability: Economic and Statistical Analysis/BEA

Annual 85 - Industry Input - Output Tables Based on the 1977 Benchmark Input - Output Study: 1983 Summary Input - Output Tables (Diskette).
Order #51-89-40-401
Availability: Economic and Statistical Analysis/BEA

Annual 85 - Industry Input - Output Tables Based on the 1977 Benchmark Input - Output Study: 1984 Summary Input-Output Tables (Computer Tape).
Order #51-89-00-002
Availability: Economic and Statistical Analysis/BEA

Annual 85 - Industry Input - Output Tables Based on the 1977 Benchmark Input - Output Study: 1984 Summary Input-Output Tables (Diskette).
Order #51-89-40-402
Availability: Economic and Statistical Analysis/BEA

Annual 85 - Industry Input - Output Tables Based on the 1977 Benchmark Input - Output Study: 1985 Summary Input-Output Tables (Computer Tape).
Order #51-90-00-001
Availability: Economic and Statistical Analysis/BEA

Annual 85 - Industry Input - Output Tables Based on the 1977 Benchmark Input - Output Study: 1985 Summary Input-Output Tables (Diskette).
Order #51-90-40-401
Availability: Economic and Statistical Analysis/BEA

Annual 85 - Industry Input - Output Tables Based on the 1977 Benchmark Input - Output Study: 1986 Summary Input-Output Tables (Computer Tape).
Order #51-91-00-001
Availability: Economic and Statistical Analysis/BEA

Annual 85 - Industry Input - Output Tables Based on the 1977 Benchmark Input - Output Study: 1986 Summary Input - Output Tables (Diskette).
Order #51-91-40-401
Availability: Economic and Statistical Analysis/BEA

BEA Regional Projections to 2040, Volume 1: States (Diskette).
Order #61-90-40-201
Availability: Economic and Statistical Analysis/BEA.

BEA Regional Projections to 2040, Volume 1: States (CD-ROM).
Availability: Economic and Statistical Analysis/BEA

BEA Regional Projections to 2040, Volume 2: Metropolitan Statistical Areas (Diskette).
Order #61-90-40-202
Availability: Economic and Statistical Analysis/BEA.

BEA Regional Projections to 2040, Volume 2: Metropolitan Statistical Areas (CD-ROM).
Availability: Economic and Statistical Analysis/BEA

BEA Regional Projections to 2040, Volume 3: BEA Economic Areas (Diskette).
Order #61-90-40-203
Availability: Economic and Statistical Analysis/BEA.

BEA Regional Projections to 2040, Volume 3: BEA Economic Areas (CD-ROM).
Availability: Economic and Statistical Analysis/BEA

BEARFACTS, 1991 - 92 or 1982 - 92 (Diskette).
Availability: Economic and Statistical Analysis/BEA

Business Cycle Indicators Current Data, (Diskette).
Order #52-86-41-401
Availability: Economic and Statistical Analysis/BEA

Business Cycle Indicators Historical Data, (Diskette).
Order #52-86-40-402
Availability: Economic and Statistical Analysis/BEA

Business Cycle Indicators Historical Data for User-Selected Series, (Diskette).
Availability: Economic and Statistical Analysis/BEA

Business Statistical Historical Data for User - Selected Series, (Diskette).
Availability: Economic and Statistical Analysis/BEA

County Projections to 2040, (Diskette).
Order #61-92-40-352

Current Business Statistics (Diskette).
Order #52-92-41-411
Availability: Economic and Statistical Analysis/BEA.

Current and Historical Data for U.S. International Transactions (Diskette).
Order #s 53-94-41-001
53-94-40-001
53-94-40-002
Availability: Economic and Statistical Analysis/BEA.

Detailed Investment by Industry (Computer Tape).
Order #54-89-00-002
Availability: Economic and Statistical Analysis/BEA

Detailed Investment by Industry (Diskette).
Order #54-89-40-005
Availability: Economic and Statistical Analysis/BEA

Detailed Wealth by Industry (Computer Tape).
Order #54-89-00-003
Availability: Economic and Statistical Analysis/BEA

Detailed Wealth by Industry (Diskette).
Order #54-89-40-006
Availability: Economic and Statistical Analysis/BEA

Disposable Personal Income, Per Capita Disposable Personal Income, and Total Population, 1948 - 93 (Diskette).
Availability: Economic and Statistical Analysis/BEA

Economic Development Administration Industrial Location Planning System (ILPS) - Summary Data Tape.
COM-74-11095/8
Availability: NTIS

Farm Income and Expenses, 1969 - 92 (Computer Tape and Diskette).
Availability: Economic and Statistical Analysis/BEA

Foreign Direct Investment in the United States, 1987 Benchmark Survey, Final Results (Diskette).
Order #50-90-40-401
Availability: Economic and Statistical Analysis/BEA

Foreign Direct Investment in the United States: Direct Investment Position and Related Capital and Income Flows, 1987 - 92, (Diskette).
Order #50-93-40-606
Availability: Economic and Statistical Analysis/BEA

Foreign Direct Investment in the United States: Establishment Data for Manufacturing, 1991, (Diskette).
Order #50-93-40-791
Availability: Economic and Statistical Analysis/BEA.

Foreign Direct Investment in the United States: Operations of U.S. Affiliates of Foreign Companies, Preliminary 1991 Estimates, (1993), (Diskette).
Order #50-93-40-402
Availability: Economic and Statistical Analysis/BEA

Foreign Direct Investment in the United States: Operations of U.S. Affiliates of Foreign Companies, Revised 1990 Estimates, (1993), (Diskette).
Order #50-93-40-401
Availability: Economic and Statistical Analysis/BEA

Full-Time and Part-Time Employment by Industry, 1969 - 92 (Computer Tape and Diskette).
Availability: Economic and Statistical Analysis/BEA

Full-Time and Part-Time Employment by Major Industry, 1969 - 92 (Computer Tape and Diskette).
Availability: Economic and Statistical Analysis/BEA

Full-Time and Part-Time Wage and Salary Employment by Industry, 1969 - 92 (Computer Tape and Diskette).
Availability: Economic and Statistical Analysis/BEA

Gross Output by Detailed Industry. (Computer Tape).
Order #54-91-00-010
Availability: Economic and Statistical Analysis/BEA.

Gross Output by Detailed Industry. (Diskette).
Order #54-91-40-410
Availability: Economic and Statistical Analysis/BEA.

Gross Product by Industry. (Computer Tape).
Order #54-91-00-006
Availability: Economic and Statistical Analysis/BEA.

Gross Product by Industry. (Diskette).
Order #54-91-40-406
Availability: Economic and Statistical Analysis/BEA.

Gross State Product, Annual Estimates, 1963 - 86. (Computer Tape).
Order #BEA REA 88-401
Availability: Economic and Statistical Analysis/BEA

Gross State Product, Annual Estimates, 1963 - 86, Far West (Plus Alaska and Hawaii), (Diskette).
Order #BEA REA 88-410
Availability: Economic and Statistical Analysis/BEA

Gross State Product, Annual Estimates, 1963 - 86, Great Lakes (Diskette).
Order #BEA REA 88-404
Availability: Economic and Statistical Analysis/BEA

Gross State Product, Annual Estimates, 1963 - 86, Mideast (Diskette).
Order #BEA REA 88-403
Availability: Economic and Statistical Analysis/BEA

Gross State Product, Annual Estimates, 1963 - 86, New England (Diskette).
Order #BEA REA 88-402
Availability: Economic and Statistical Analysis/BEA

Gross State Product, Annual Estimates, 1963 - 86, Plains (Diskette).
Order #BEA REA 88-405
Availability: Economic and Statistical Analysis/BEA

Gross State Product, Annual Estimates, 1963 - 86, Rocky Mountain, (Diskette).
Order #BEA REA 88-409
Availability: Economic and Statistical Analysis/BEA

Gross State Product, Annual Estimates, 1963 - 86, Southeast (Alabama - Louisiana), (Diskette).
Order #BEA REA 88-406
Availability: Economic and Statistical Analysis/BEA

Gross State Product, Annual Estimates, 1963 - 86, Southeast (Mississippi - West Virginia), (Diskette).
Order #BEA REA 88-407
Availability: Economic and Statistical Analysis/BEA

Gross State Product, Annual Estimates, 1963 - 86, Southwest, (Diskette).
Order #BEA REA 88-408
Availability: Economic and Statistical Analysis/BEA

Journey-to-Work, 1990. (Computer Tape and Diskette).
Availability: Economic and Statistical Analysis/BEA.

Manufacturing Establishment Shipments. (Computer Tape).
Order #54-91-00-007
Availability: Economic and Statistical Analysis/BEA.

Manufacturing Establishment Shipments. (Diskette).
Order #54-91-40-407
Availability: Economic and Statistical Analysis/BEA.

Manufacturing Product Shipments. (Computer Tape).
Order #54-91-00-008
Availability: Economic and Statistical Analysis/BEA.

Manufacturing Product Shipments. (Diskette).
Order #54-91-40-408
Availability: Economic and Statistical Analysis/BEA.

Monthly Advance National Income and Product Accounts Tables, (Diskette).
Order #54-85-41-401
Availability: Economic and Statistical Analysis/BEA

National Economic, Social, and Environmental Data Bank (CD-ROM).
Availability: Economic and Statistical Analysis/BEA

National Income and Product Accounts (Computer Tape).
Order #54-83-01-001
Availability: Economic and Statistical Analysis/BEA

National Income and Product Accounts (Diskette).
Order #54-89-41-401
Availability: Economic and Statistical Analysis/BEA

National Trade Data Bank (CD-ROM).
Availability: Economic and Statistical Analysis/BEA

1977 (Revised) 85 - Industry Input - Output Tables (Computer Tape).
Order #BEA IED 87-001
Availability: Economic and Statistical Analysis/BEA

1977 (Revised) 85 - Industry Input - Output Tables (Diskette).
Order #BEA IED 87-403
Availability: Economic and Statistical Analysis/BEA

1982 Benchmark 85 - Industry Input-Output Tables. (Computer Tape).
Order #51-91-00-004
Availability: Economic and Statistical Analysis/BEA

1982 Benchmark 85 - Industry Input-Output Tables. (Diskette).
Order #51-91-40-008
Availability: Economic and Statistical Analysis/BEA

1987 Annual Tables Based on the 1982 Benchmark Input-Output Study. (Diskette).
Order #51-92-40-401
Availability: Economic and Statistical Analysis/BEA

1987 Economic Censuses (CD-ROM): Volume (Number) - Release (Number).
Availability: Bureau of the Census, Data User Services Division

1987 Economic Censuses (CD-ROM): Volume 1 - 10. Retail Trade, Wholesale Trade, Service Industries, Transportation, Manufactures, Mineral Industries, and Construction Industries File.
Availability: Bureau of the Census, Data User Services Division

Personal Income by Major Source and Earnings by Industry, 1929 - 92 (Computer Tape and Diskette).
Availability: Economic and Statistical Analysis/BEA

Personal Income by Major Source and Earnings by Major Industry, 1969 - 92 (Computer Tape and Diskette).
Availability: Economic and Statistical Analysis/BEA

Personal Income, Per Capita Personal Income, and Total Population, 1969 - 93 (Computer Tape and Diskette).
Availability: Economic and Statistical Analysis/BEA

Personal Tax and Nontax Payments, 1948 - 92 (Computer Tape and Diskette).
Availability: Economic and Statistical Analysis/BEA

Quarterly Personal Income by Major Source and Earnings by Industry, 1969 - 93 (Diskette and Computer Tape).
Availability: Economic and Statistical Analysis/BEA

Quarterly Wages and Salaries by Major Source and Major Industry, 1969 - 93 (Diskette and Computer Tape).
Availability: Economic and Statistical Analysis/BEA

Regional Economic Information System (REIS) CD-ROM, 1969 - 92 (CD-ROM).
Order #55-92-30-599
Availability: Economic and Statistical Analysis/BEA

Regional Economic Profile, 1969 - 92 (Computer Tape).
Availability: Economic and Statistical Analysis/BEA

Research and Development Satellite Account Data. (Diskette).
Order #53-94-40-001
Availability: Economic and Statistical Analysis/BEA

Revised Gross State Product, Annual Estimates, 1977 - 90 (CD-ROM).
Availability: Economic and Statistical Analysis/BEA

Revised Gross State Product, Annual Estimates, 1977 - 90 (Diskette).
Order #61-93-40-421
Availability: Economic and Statistical Analysis/BEA

Total Commuters' Income Flows, 1969 - 92 (Computer Tape and Diskette).
Availability: Economic and Statistical Analysis/BEA

Total Wages and Salaries, Total Wage and Salary Employment, and Average Wage Per Job, 1969 - 92 (Computer Tape and Diskette).
Availability: Economic and Statistical Analysis/BEA

Transfer Payments, 1969 - 92 (Computer Tape and Diskette).
Availability: Economic and Statistical Analysis/BEA

U.S. Business Enterprises Acquired or Established by Foreign Direct Investors, Supplementary Tables, 1980 - 86 (Diskette).
Order #50-89-40-406
Availability: Economic and Statistical Analysis/BEA

U.S. Business Enterprises Acquired or Established by Foreign Direct Investors, Supplementary Tables, 1987 - 93 (Diskette).
Order #50-94-40-405
Availability: Economic and Statistical Analysis/BEA

U.S. Direct Investment Abroad, Country by Industry Estimates, 1950 - 92, (Computer Tape).
Order #50-93-00-667
Availability: Economic and Statistical Analysis/BEA

U.S. Direct Investment Abroad: 1989 Benchmark Survey, Final Results (Diskette).
Order #50-92-40-403
Availability: Economic and Statistical Analysis/BEA

U.S. Direct Investment Abroad: Operations of U.S. Parent Companies and Their Foreign Affiliates, Preliminary 1991 Estimates, (1993), (Diskette).
Order #50-93-40-404
Availability: Economic and Statistical Analysis/BEA

U.S. Direct Investment Abroad: Operations of U.S. Parent Companies and their Foreign Affiliates, Revised 1990 Estimates, (1993), (Diskette).
Order #50-93-40-403
Availability: Economic and Statistical Analysis/BEA

U.S. Merchandise Trade Data, Monthly, (Diskette).
Order #58-86-41-401
Availability: Economic and Statistical Analysis/BEA

U.S. Merchandise Trade Data, Quarterly, (Diskette).
Order #58-86-41-402
Availability: Economic and Statistical Analysis/BEA

U.S. Merchandise Trade: Exports and Imports by End-Use Category, U.S. Merchandise Exports, Annually, (Computer Tape).
Order #58-86-01-005
Availability: Economic and Statistical Analysis/BEA

U.S. Merchandise Trade: Exports and Imports by End-Use Category, U.S. Merchandise Exports, Monthly, (Computer Tape).
Order #58-86-01-001
Availability: Economic and Statistical Analysis/BEA

U.S. Merchandise Trade: Exports and Imports by End-Use Category, U.S. Merchandise Exports, Quarterly, (Computer Tape).
Order #58-86-01-003
Availability: Economic and Statistical Analysis/BEA

U.S. Merchandise Trade: Exports and Imports by End-Use Category, U.S. Merchandise Imports, Annually, (Computer Tape).
Order #58-86-01-006
Availability: Economic and Statistical Analysis/BEA

U.S. Merchandise Trade: Exports and Imports by End-Use Category, U.S. Merchandise Imports, Monthly, (Computer Tape).
Order #58-86-01-002
Availability: Economic and Statistical Analysis/BEA

U.S. Merchandise Trade: Exports and Imports by End-Use Category, U.S. Merchandise Imports, Quarterly, (Computer Tape).
Order #58-86-01-004
Availability: Economic and Statistical Analysis/BEA

Wage and Salary Disbursements by Industry, 1929 - 92 (Computer Tape and Diskette).
Availability: Economic and Statistical Analysis/BEA

Wealth (Computer Tape).
Order #54-89-00-001
Availability: Economic and Statistical Analysis/BEA

Wealth (Diskette).
Order #54-89-40-004
Availability: Economic and Statistical Analysis/BEA

Education

Classification System for Postsecondary Education Courses, 1986.
Availability: U.S. Department of Education

College and University Libraries. 1988 - 89.
Availability: U.S. Department of Education

Consolidated (CN) Survey Form. 1990.
Availability: U.S. Department of Education

Directory of Postsecondary Institutions, 1993 - 94.
Availability: U.S. Department of Education

Earned Degrees (Completions), 1991 - 92.
Availability: U.S. Department of Education

Faculty Salaries, 1992 - 93.
Availability: U.S. Department of Education

Fall Enrollment in Occupationally Specific Programs, Fall 1987 and 1990 - 91.
Availability: U.S. Department of Education

Fall Staff, 1991 - 92.
Availability: U.S. Department of Education

Financial Statistics, 1992 - 92.
Availability: U.S. Department of Education

High School Transcript File (NAEP), 1987.
Availability: U.S. Department of Education

Institutional Characteristics, 1991 - 92.
Availability: U.S. Department of Education

Library Networks, 1985 - 86.
Availability: U.S. Department of Education

Longitudinal Study of Immersion Strategy, Early-Exit and Late-Exit Transitional Bilingual Education for Language - Minority Children.
PB91-509943
Availability: NTIS

National Education Longitudinal Study Files - NELS: 88 Dropout Data, 1992.
Availability: U.S. Department of Education

National Education Longitudinal Study Files - NELS: 88 Parent Data, 1992.
Availability: U.S. Department of Education

National Education Longitudinal Study Files - NELS: 88 School Data, 1992.
Availability: U.S. Department of Education

National Education Longitudinal Study Files - NELS: 88 Student Data, 1992.
Availability: U.S. Department of Education

National Education Longitudinal Study Files - NELS: 88 Teacher Data, 1992.
Availability: U.S. Department of Education

National Household Education Survey of 1991 (Adult Education (AE) Component), 1991.
Availability: U.S. Department of Education

National Household Education Survey of 1991 (Early Childhood Education (ECE) Component), 1991.
Availability: U.S. Department of Education

National Longitudinal Study File - NLS - 72 Fifth Followup, 1986.
Availability: U.S. Department of Education

National Longitudinal Study File - NLS - 72 Fifth Followup (Teaching Supplement), 1986.
Availability: U.S. Department of Education

National Longitudinal Study File - NLS - 72 Military Personnel Records, 1984 - 86.
Availability: U.S. Department of Education

National Longitudinal Study File - NLS - 72 Postsecondary Institution FICE Code File, 1972 - 1986.
Availability: U.S. Department of Education

National Postsecondary Student Aid Study (Parent Survey Supplement Data File), 1986 - 1987.
Availability: U.S. Department of Education

National Postsecondary Student Aid Study (Student Loan Recipient Survey), 1987.
Availability: U.S. Department of Education

National Postsecondary Student Aid Study (Student Loan Recipient Transcript Survey), 1987.
Availability: U.S. Department of Education

National Postsecondary Student Aid Study (Student Survey Data File),
1986 - 1987.
Availability: U.S. Department of Education

National Survey of Postsecondary Faculty (Departmental Chairs Data File), 1987 - 88.
Availability: U.S. Department of Education

National Survey of Postsecondary Faculty (Institutional Survey Data File), 1987 - 88.
Availability: U.S. Department of Education

Opening Fall Enrollment, 1992 - 93.
Availability: U.S. Department of Education

Postsecondary Student Aid Field Test, 1985 - 86.
Availability: U.S. Department of Education

Private Schools and Teachers Survey, 1985 - 86.
Availability: U.S. Department of Education

Public and Private School Libraries and Media Centers, 1985 - 86.
Availability: U.S. Department of Education

Public Libraries. 1990.
Availability: U.S. Department of Education

Public Library Data, FY 1988.
Availability: U.S. Department of Education

Public School Districts, 1992 - 93.
Availability: U.S. Department of Education

Public School Universe, 1992 - 93.
Availability: U.S. Department of Education

Public Schools and Teachers Survey, 1985 - 86.
Availability: U.S. Department of Education

Recent College Graduates, 1991 - 92.
Availability: U.S. Department of Education

Recent College Graduates (Combined File), 1991 - 92.
Availability: U.S. Department of Education

Recent College Graduates (Transcript File), 1991 - 92.
Availability: U.S. Department of Education

State Summary of Non-Fiscal Data, 1991 - 92.
Availability: U.S. Department of Education

State Summary of School District Finance, 1982 - 90.
Availability: U.S. Department of Education

Total Institutional Activity, 1987 - 88.
Availability: U.S. Department of Education

Elections

Freedom of Information Act (FOIA) - Candidate Master.
Availability: FEC Data Systems Development Division

Freedom of Information Act (FOIA) - Detailed Report Tape.
Availability: FEC Data Systems Development Division

Freedom of Information Act (FOIA) - Committee Master.
Availability: FEC Data Systems Development Division

Freedom of Information Act (FOIA) - Composite.
Availability: FEC Data Systems Development Division

Freedom of Information Act (FOIA) - Individual Contributor.
Availability: FEC Data Systems Development Division

Freedom of Information Act (FOIA) - Mailing List.
Availability: FEC Data Systems Development Division

Freedom of Information Act (FOIA) - Miscellaneous Transactions.
Availability: FEC Data Systems Development Division

Freedom of Information Act (FOIA) - PAC Contributions.
Availability: FEC Data Systems Development Division

Freedom of Information Act (FOIA) - Receipts and Disbursements.
Availability: FEC Data Systems Development Division

Reports on Financial Activity (RFA) - House/Senate, 1993 - 1994.
Availability: FEC Data Systems Development Division

Reports on Financial Activity (RFA) - Longitudinal Non-Party Tape, 1993 - 1994.
Availability: FEC Data Systems Development Division

Reports on Financial Activity (RFA) - Non-Party, 1993 - 1994.
Availability: FEC Data Systems Development Division

Reports on Financial Activity (RFA) - Party, 1993 - 1994.
Availability: FEC Data Systems Development Division

Reports on Financial Activity (RFA) - Presidential, 1987 - 1988.
Availability: FEC Data Systems Development Division

Energy

Alternative Fuel Demand Due to Natural Gas Deficiencies (E1A-50), April 1, 1984-March 31, 1985.
PB86-131018
Availability: NTIS

Annual Electric Generator Report, 1991.
PB93-502979
Availability: NTIS

Annual Electric Utility Report, 1989.
PB92-500404
Availability: NTIS

Annual Energy Review, 1991 (Diskette)
PB92-503143
Availability: NTIS

Annual Report of Major Electric Utilities: Licensees and Others, 1990.
PB92-501188
Availability: NTIS

Annual Report of Public Electric Utilities, 1990.
PB92-501469
Availability: NTIS

Annual Survey of Domestic Oil and Gas Reserves, Extracted Data from Form E1A-23: Operator/Address, (1982, 1984), Field Operator Data (1984).
PB86-130176
Availability: NTIS

Coal Distribution Data, 1988 (EIA Form 6).
PB90-500497
Availability: NTIS

Coal Supply and Transportation Model Stand Alone, 1991.
PB91-508036
Availability: NTIS

Commercial Buildings Energy Consumption Survey, 1989.
PB92-504235
Availability: NTIS

Cost and Quality of Fuels for Electric Utility Plants, 1984 - 1991.
PB92-504182
Availability: NTIS

Electric Plant Cost and Power Production Expenses, 1979 - 1990.
PB92-504240
Availability: NTIS

Electric Power Use by Industries (Monthly Cumulative from 1972 to Current).
PB85-246395
Availability: NTIS

Electric Utilities Sales and Revenue Monthly Report, 1989 (EIA-826).
PB91-507616
Availability: NTIS

Electric Utility Company Monthly Statement, 1986 (E1A-826).
PB88-110598
Availability: NTIS

Field Size Distributions for U.S. Oil and Gas Provinces, 1989.
PB92-503416
Availability: NTIS

Fuel Oil and Kerosene Sales, 1993
Availability: NTIS

Gas Analysis Modeling System, 1991
PB91-506980
Availability: NTIS

Gas Analysis Modeling System Additional Computer Runs, 1991.
PB92-501352
Availability: NTIS

Gas Reservoir/Wellbore Orientation Screening Study: Survey of Horizontal Gas Wells (for Microcomputers).
PB92-503267
Availability: NTIS

Generating Unit Reference File (GURF), 1900-1984.
PB86-172376
Availability: NTIS

Historical Monthly Energy Review Data Base, 1973 - 1992 (Diskette).
PB92-500511
Availability: NTIS

Historical Plant Cost and Annual Production Expense, 1985.
PB88-100417
Availability: NTIS

Intermediate Future Forecasting System (High Macro), 1992.
PB92-504190
Availability: NTIS

Intermediate Future Forecasting System (High Oil), 1992.
PB92-503606
Availability: NTIS

Intermediate Future Forecasting System (Low Macro), 1992.
PB92-504208
Availability: NTIS

Intermediate Future Forecasting System (Low Oil), 1992.
PB92-503614
Availability: NTIS

Intermediate Future Forecasting System (Reference), 1992.
PB92-501196
Availability: NTIS

International Coal Statistics Database (ICSD), 1991 (Diskette).
PB92-500610
Availability: NTIS

International Coal Trade Model, 1990.
PB92-500073
Availability: NTIS

International Nuclear Model - PC1NM, 1993.
Availability: NTIS

International Nuclear Model, 1992.
PB93-503019
Availability: NTIS

International Nuclear Model - PC Version, 1992.
PB92-503001
Availability: NTIS

Interstate Pipeline's Annual Report of Gas Supply, 1989.
PB91-507483
Availability: NTIS

Levelized Nuclear Fuel Cycle Costs, 1990 (Diskette).
PB91-507285
Availability: NTIS

Low-Income Household Energy Assistance Program, 1992.
PB93-503027
Availability: NTIS

Major Electric Utilities, Licensees and Others, Annual Report, 1990 (Form 1).
PB92-501188
Availability: NTIS

Market Penetration Model, 1992 (Diskette).
PB92-502417
Availability: NTIS

Monthly Electric Utility Sales and Revenue Report, Jan. 1994 - July 1994.
PB93-592460
Availability: NTIS

Monthly Energy Review Data Base, Oct. 1994.
PB91-591650
Availability: NTIS

Monthly Imports Report, Jan. 1991 - Oct. 1992.
PB90-591210
Availability: NTIS

Monthly Power Plant Report, Jan. 1994 - July 1994.
PB93-592450
Availability: NTIS

National Coal Model, Version 8 (Reference Scenario), 1992.
PB92-504455
Availability: NTIS

National Coal Model (High Economic Growth Case), 1992.
PB92-504539
Availability: NTIS

National Labor Surplus Area (LSA) Zip Code File, 1987.
PB87-193017
Availability: NTIS

Natural Gas Annual, 1990.
PB92-503134.
Availability: NTIS

Natural Gas Pipeline Co. Monthly Statement (January 1983-September 1984). FERC-11.
PB85-182061
Availability: NTIS

Natural Gas Policy Act - Notices of Determination, 1978 - 1992.
PB91-591220
Availability: NTIS

Nonresidential Buildings Energy Consumption Survey: 1989.
PB92-504232
Availability: NTIS

Nonresidential Energy Consumption Survey: and Characteristics, Annual Consumption and Expenditures, October 1979 through January 1980 - 1985 Updated Version.
PB85-194348
Availability: NTIS

Nonutility Generation Supply Model, 1992.
PB92-502020
Availability: NTIS

Oak Ridge Uranium Market Model, 1991.
PB92-502012
Availability: NTIS

Oil and Gas Field Code Master List, 1994.
Availability: NTIS

Oil Market Simulation Model, 1992.
PB93-500338
Availability: NTIS

Petroleum Marketing Monthly, January - December 1993.
PB91-591230
Availability: NTIS

Petroleum Supply Annual, 1983 - 1990.
PB92-501618
Availability: NTIS

Petroleum Supply Monthly, January 1991 - October 1991.
PB90-591240
Availability: NTIS

Power Plant Report (Form EIA-759), 1984 - 1990.
PB92-501485
Availability: NTIS

Privately Owned Electric Utilities, 1985 (Form 1).
PB87-194221
Availability: NTIS

Production of Onshore Lower 48 Oil and Gas Supply, 1991.
PB92-500909
Availability: NTIS

Public Use Energy Statistical Data Base 1949-1987.
PB87-186474
Availability: NTIS

Publicly Owned Electric Utilities, Annual Report, 1990 (EIA-412).
PB92-501469
Availability: NTIS

Publicly Owned Electric Utilities in the United States, 1987 (EIA 412).
PB89-158687
Availability: NTIS

Quarterly Coal Report (QCB), 1988.
PB90-500505
Availability: NTIS

Report of Oil Imports into the United States and Puerto Rico, 1990 (Form EIA-814) Historic.
PB91-509786
Availability: NTIS

Report of Oil Imports into the United States and Puerto Rico, Monthly Cumulative 1991 (Form EIA/814).
PB91-591210
Availability: NTIS

Residential Energy Consumption Survey, 1987, and Residential Transportation Energy Consumption Survey, 1988: Public Use Tape.
PB90-501461
Availability: NTIS

Resources Allocation and Mine Cost Model, 1992.
PB92-500941
Availability: NTIS

Short-Term Coal Analysis System, (SCOAL91B), 1991 (2Q).
PB92-504-364
Availability: NTIS

Short-Term Coal Analysis System, (SCOAL91C), 1991 (3Q).
PB92-504-372
Availability: NTIS

Short-Term Coal Analysis System, (SCOAL91D), 1991 (4Q).
PB92-504-380
Availability: NTIS

Short-Term Coal Analysis System, (SCOAL92A), 1992 (1Q).
PB92-504-398
Availability: NTIS

Short-Term Integrated Forecasting System, 1994 (3Q)
Availability: NTIS

State Energy Data System, Region 1, 1960 - 90.
PB92-502277
Availability: NTIS

State Energy Data System, Region 2, 1960 - 1990.
PB92-502285
Availability: NTIS

State Energy Data System, Region 3, 1960 - 1990.
PB92-502293
Availability: NTIS

State Energy Data System, Region 4, 1960 - 1990.
PB92-502301
Availability: NTIS

State Energy Data System U.S. + 4 Regions, 1960 - 1990.
PB92-502269
Availability: NTIS

State Energy Price and Expenditure Data System 1970 - 1992 (Diskettes).
Availability: NTIS

Statistics of Interstate Natural Gas Pipeline Companies, 1988-1990.
PB92-502061
Availability: NTIS

Statistics of Major Interstate Natural Gas Companies, 1988 - 1990 (FERC-2).
PB92-502061
Availability: NTIS

Steam-Electric Plant Operation and Design Report, 1984 (Form EIA-767).
PB88-172317
Availability: NTIS

Typical Net Monthly (Electric) Bills (EIA-213), 1989.
PB90-502840
Availability: NTIS

Uranium Market Model - UMM, 1993.
Availability: NTIS

U.S. Coal Production and Related Data, 1986-1988.
PB90-502378
Availability: NTIS

U.S. Crude Oil, Natural Gas, and Natural Gas Liquids Reserves, 1977 - 1993, (for Microcomputers).
Availability: NTIS

U.S. Crude Oil & Natural Gas Reserves, 1977 - 1989.
PB91-507046
Availability: NTIS

Wellhead Gas Productive Capacity Model (GASCAP), 1990.
PB92-500875
Availability: NTIS

World Energy Projection System, 1994.
Availability: NTIS

World Integrated Nuclear Evaluation System, 1991.
PB92-501311
Availability: NTIS

Environmental Protection

Annual NAPAP Emissions Inventory (Version 2): U.S. Annual Point Sources, 1985.
PB91-505859
Availability: NTIS

AQUIRE: Aquatic Toxicity Information Retrieval Data Base.
PB92-500453
Availability: NTIS

Enforcement Document Retrieval System (EDRS) Update File (November 1991 to April 1992).
PB92-592390
Availability: NTIS

Environmental Fate Data Base (ENVIROFATE): Chemical Identification Information File (CHEM-FATE), September 1989.
PB90-501263
Availability: NTIS

Environmental Fate Data Base (ENVIROFATE): Chemical Name File CASLST), September 1989.
PB90-501297
Availability: NTIS

Environmental Fate Data Base (ENVIROFATE): Data Pointer File (DATALOG), September 1989.
PB90-501289
Availability: NTIS

Environmental Fate Data Base (ENVIROFATE): Journal Citations (XREF), April 1990.
PB90-502071
Availability: NTIS

Environmental Fate Data Base (ENVIROFATE): Microbial Degradation/Toxicity Data (BIOLOG), September 1989.
PB90-501271
Availability: NTIS

Environmental Fate Data Base (ENVIROFATE): Value Biodegradation (BIODEG), October 1989.
PB90-501305
Availability: NTIS

Fish and Chemistry Data for the Upper Peninsula of Michigan Report (for Microcomputers).
PB92-503085
Availability: NTIS

Hazardous Waste Collection Database (for Microcomputers).
PB87-945000
Availability: NTIS

Industrial Audiometric Data.
PB88-117916
Availability: NTIS

Industrial Exposure and Control Technologies for OSHA Regulated Hazardous Substances.
PB90-501909
Availability: NTIS

National Sewage Sludge Survey (NSSS) (SAS Transport Version).
PB90-501834
Availability: NTIS

Needs Survey Report to Congress, 1988: Assessment of Needed Publicly Owned Wastewater Treatment Facilities in the United States.
PB89-215412
Availability: NTIS

Outdoor Chamber Study to Test Multi-Day Effects: Computer-Readable Environmental Chamber Data.
PB85-161636
Availability: NTIS

Registry of Toxic Effects of Chemical Substances (RTECS), 1990 Computer Tape.
PB90-591630
Availability: NTIS

Resource Conservation and Recovery Act (RCRA) Notification Extract File
PB88-913801
Availability: NTIS

Resource Conservation and Recovery Information System (RCRIS) Extract Tape.
PB92-592290
Availability: NTIS

RTECS (Registry of Toxic Effects of Chemical Substances) Regulatory Subfile. Regulations, Recommendations and Assessments (for Microcomputers).
PB87-197133
Availability: NTIS

Terrestrial Toxicity Data Base (TERRE-TOX), 1970-1985.
PB86-178043
Availability: NTIS

Toxic Release Inventory (TRI), 1990.
PB92-501816
Availability: NTIS

Toxic Release Inventory (TRI), 1987 - 1990. (CD-ROM)
PB93-500742
Availability: NTIS

Toxic Substances Control Act (TSCA) Chemical Substances Inventory: Reissued Inventory Plantsite Information, May 1986.
PB86-220795
Availability: NTIS

Toxic Substances Control Act (TSCA) Chemical Substances Inventory: Reissued Inventory Preferred Name File, May 1986.
PB86-220878
Availability: NTIS

Toxic Substances Control Act (TSCA) Chemical Substances Inventory: Reissued Inventory - Production Information File, May 1986.
PB86-220803
Availability: NTIS

Toxic Substances Control Act (TSCA) Chemical Substances Inventory: Reissued Inventory Synonym File, May 1986.
PB86-220860
Availability: NTIS

Toxic Substances Control Act (TSCA) Test Submissions Data Base (TSCATS). Comprehensive Update for Tape.
PB90-591290
Availability: NTIS

Fire Protection

National Fire Incident Reporting System (NFIRS) Data Base. (1990 Equipment/Casualty File).
PB92-502178
Availability: NTIS

National Fire Incident Reporting System (NFIRS) Data Base. (1990 Incident File).
PB92-502160
Availability: NTIS

National Fire Incident Reporting System (NFIRS) Data Base (1990 Master File).
PB92-502129
Availability: NTIS

Foreign Trade

Geographic Concordance Master Tape.
Availability: Bureau of the Census, Data User Services Division

Harmonized Commodity Concordance Master Tape
Availability: Bureau of the Census, Data User Services Division

Import Concordance Master Tape
Availability: Bureau of the Census, Data User Services Division

Listing of Vessel Clearances (TM-785) (Computer Tape).
Availability: Bureau of the Census, Data User Services Division

Listing of Vessel Entrances (TM-385) (Computer Tape).
Availability: Bureau of the Census, Data User Services Division

Monthly Vessel Clearances (TM-785) (Computer Tape).
Availability: Bureau of the Census, Data User Services Division

Monthly Vessel Entrances (TM-385) (Computer Tape).
Availability: Bureau of the Census, Data User Services Division

National Trade Data Base (NTDB) (CD-ROM).
PB91-591960
Availability: NTIS

Shipments of Merchandise Between the United States and Puerto Rico and From the United States to the Virgin Islands (EM-595) (Computer Tape).
Availability: Bureau of the Census, Data User Services Division

Shipments of Merchandise Between the United States and Puerto Rico and Shipments From the United States to the Virgin Islands (EA-695) (Computer Tape).
Availability: Bureau of the Census, Data User Services Division

Shipments of Merchandise From the United States to Puerto Rico and U.S. Virgin Islands, and Shipments From Puerto Rico to the United States (EA-695) (Computer Tape).
Availability: Bureau of the Census, Data User Services Division

Shipments of Merchandise From the United States to Puerto Rico and U.S. Virgin Islands, and Shipments From Puerto Rico to the United States (EM-595) (Computer Tape).
Availability: Bureau of the Census, Data User Services Division

Shipping Master Tape
Availability: Bureau of the Census, Data User Services Division

U.S. Exports by State/Region of Origin (Computer Tape).
Availability: Bureau of the Census, Data User Services Division

U.S. Exports Commodity Classification International Harmonized System (HS-Based Schedule B).
Availability: Bureau of the Census, Data User Services Division

U.S. Exports - International Harmonized System Commodity Classification (HS - Based Schedule B) Country (Puerto Rico, U.S. Virgin Islands) and Customs District (EM-595) (Computer Tape).
Availability: Bureau of the Census, Data User Services Division

U.S. Exports - International Harmonized System Commodity Classification (HS - Based Schedule B) Country (Puerto Rico, U.S. Virgin Islands) and Customs District (EA-695) (Computer Tape).
Availability: Bureau of the Census, Data User Services Division

U.S. Exports of Domestic and Foreign Merchandise (EM-545) (Computer Tape).
Availability: Bureau of the Census, Data User Services Division

U.S. Exports of Domestic and Foreign Merchandise by State/Region/Port (EQ-912, EQ-932, EQ-952) (Computer Tapes).
Availability: Bureau of the Census, Data User Services Division

U.S. Exports of Merchandise and Outbound In-Transit Cargo (TA-780/780-IT) (Computer Tape).
Availability: Bureau of the Census, Data User Services Division

U.S. Exports of Merchandise and Outbound In-Transit Cargo (TM-780/780-IT) (Computer Tape).
Availability: Bureau of the Census, Data User Services Division

U.S. Exports of Merchandise - International Harmonized System Commodity Classification (HS-Based Schedule B) by Country, Country by Customs District (F.A.S. Value) (EM-545) (Computer Tape).
Availability: Bureau of the Census, Data User Services Division

U.S. Exports of Merchandise on CD Rom.
Availability: Bureau of the Census, Data User Services Division

U.S. General Imports and Imports for Consumption: Annual. (Computer Tape).
Availability: Bureau of the Census, Data User Services Division

U.S. General Imports from the U.S. Virgin Islands, Guam, American Samoa, and the Northern Mariana Islands (IM-160) (Computer Tape)
Availability: Bureau of the Census, Data User Services Division

U.S. General Imports of Merchandise and Imports of Merchandise for Consumption (IM-145) (Computer Tape).
Availability: Bureau of the Census, Data User Services Division

U.S. General Imports of Merchandise and Imports of Merchandise for Consumption (IA-245) (Computer Tape).
Availability: Bureau of the Census, Data User Services Division

U.S. General Imports of Merchandise and Inbound In-Transit Cargo (TA-380/380-IT) (Computer Tape).
Availability: Bureau of the Census, Data User Services Division

U.S. General Imports of Merchandise and Inbound In-Transit Cargo (TM-380/380-IT) (Computer Tape).
Availability: Bureau of the Census, Data User Services Division

U.S. Imports for Consumption and General Imports (IA-245 and IA-245A) (Computer Tapes).
Availability: Bureau of the Census, Data User Services Division

U.S. Imports for Consumption and General Imports (IM-145 and IM-145A) (Computer Tapes)
Availability: Bureau of the Census, Data User Services Division

U.S. Imports for Consumption - HTSUSA Commodity by Country: Annual (FT247).
Availability: Bureau of the Census, Data User Services Division

U.S. Imports of Merchandise on CD Rom.
Availability: Bureau of the Census, Data User Services Division

U.S. Waterborne Exports and Outbound In-Transit Shipments (TA-380/380-IT) (Computer Tape).
Availability: Bureau of the Census, Data User Services Division

U.S. Waterborne Exports and Outbound In-Transit Shipments (TA-780/780-IT) (Computer Tapes).
Availability: Bureau of the Census, Data User Services Division

U.S. Waterborne Exports and Outbound In-Transit Shipments (TM-780/780-IT) (Computer Tapes).
Availability: Bureau of the Census, Data User Services Division

U.S. Waterborne General Imports and Inbound In-Transit Shipments (TM-380 and TA-380) (Computer Tapes).
Availability: Bureau of the Census, Data User Services Division

Geography

City Reference File, 1987 (Computer Tape).
Availability: Bureau of the Census, Data User Services Division

Codes for Named Populated Places, Primary County Divisions, and Other Locational Entities of the United States (FIPS PUB 55), 9th Update.
PB87-142436
Availability: NTIS

Contiguous County File
Availability: Bureau of the Census, Data User Services Division

Countries, Dependencies, and Areas of Special Sovereignty.
PB-267 936/3
Availability: NTIS

Countries, Dependencies, and Areas of Special Sovereignty, and Their Principal Administrative Divisions (FIPS PUB 10-3).
PB85-222859
Availability: NTIS

County and City Data Book, 1988, Diskette File
Availability: Bureau of the Census, Data User Services Division

County and City Data Book, 1988 Tape File
Availability: Bureau of the Census, Data User Services Division

County and City Data Book: 1988 Files on CD-ROM.
Availability: Bureau of the Census, Data User Services Division

County Statistics Tape File 4. (CO-STAT 4).
Availability: Bureau of the Census, Data User Services Division

Decennial Geocoding Software Source Code Programs (COBOL) (Computer Tape).
Availability: Bureau of the Census, Data User Services Division

Geographic Concordance Master Tape.
Availability: Bureau of the Census, Data User Services Division

Geographic Reference File - Names, 1990 (Precensus Version) (Computer Tape).
Availability: Bureau of the Census, Data User Services Division

Implementation of ANSI (American National Standards Institute) Codes for the Representation of Names of Countries, Dependencies, and Areas of Special Sovereignty for Information Interchange (FIPS PUB 104).
PB85-226918
Availability: NTIS

Map Sheet Corner Point Coordinate File (Computer Tape).
Availability: Bureau of the Census, Data User Services Division

Metropolitan Statistical Areas, 1990: Lists I - IV. Diskette.
PB91-507590
Availability: NTIS

1991 National Survey of Fishing, Hunting, and Wildlife-Associated Recreation (CD-ROM).
Availability: Bureau of the Census, Data User Services Division

Standard Abbreviations and Codes for States and Outlying Areas of the U.S. (FIPS PUB 5-1) and Counties and County Equivalents of the States of the United States and the District of Columbia (FIPS PUB 6-3).
PB85-152288
Availability: NTIS

State and Metropolitan Area Data Book: 1991 Files on Diskette.
Availability: Bureau of the Census, Data User Services Division

Statistical Abstract of the United States (CD-ROM).
Availability: Bureau of the Census, Data User Services Division

TIGER/Census Tract Comparability File (Computer Tape).
Availability: Bureau of the Census, Data User Services Division

TIGER/Census Tract Street Index (Computer Tape).
Availability: Bureau of the Census, Data User Services Division

TIGER/GICS Census File (Computer Tape).
Availability: Bureau of the Census, Data User Services Division

TIGER/GRF-N 1990 (Computer Tape).
Availability: Bureau of the Census, Data User Services Division

TIGER/Line Files, 1992 (Computer Tape and CD-ROM).
Availability: Bureau of the Census, Data User Services Division

TIGER/Line Mapping Software (Computer Tape).
Availability: Bureau of the Census, Data User Services Division

TIGER/Line 1990 Census File (Computer Tape and CD-ROM).
Availability: Bureau of the Census, Data User Services Division

TIGER/103rd Congressional District Boundary File (Computer Tape).
Availability: Bureau of the Census, Data User Services Division

TIGER/103rd Congressional District Geographic Entity File (Computer Tape).
Availability: Bureau of the Census, Data User Services Division

TIGER/Line Prototype Diskette File: Boone County, Missouri 1988
Availability: Bureau of the Census, Data User Services Division

TIGER/Line Prototype File: Boone County, Missouri: 1988
Availability: Bureau of the Census, Data User Services Division

TIGER/Map Sheet Corner Point Coordinate File (Computer Tape).
Availability: Bureau of the Census, Data User Services Division

TIGER/UA Limit File (Computer Tape).
Availability: Bureau of the Census, Data User Services Division

USA Counties on CD-ROM.
Availability: Bureau of the Census, Data User Services Division

World Data Bank 1 (WDBI) (for Microcomputers).
PB86-167574
Availability: NTIS

World Data Bank II (WDBII).
PB87-184768
Availability: NTIS

World Data Bank II (WDBII). Volume 1. North America.
PB87-184776
Availability: NTIS

World Data Bank 2. Volume 1. North America (for Microcomputers).
PB85-209930
Availability: NTIS

World Data Bank II (WDBII). Volume 2. South America.
PB87-184784
Availability: NTIS

World Data Bank II (WDBII). Volume 3. Europe/Africa.
PB87-184792
Availability: NTIS

World Data Bank II (WDBII). Volume 4. Asia.
PB87-184800
Availability: NTIS

Zip Code, Latitude, Longitude. (Zip Lat Long).
AD-A023 226/4
Availability: NTIS

Governments

Census of Governments: 1987 (Computer Tape).
Availability: Bureau of the Census, Data User Services Division

Consolidated Federal Funds Report (CFFR), Fiscal Year 1992 (Computer Tape).
Availability: Bureau of the Census, Data User Services Division

County Statistics Tape 4 (CO-STAT4), 1960 - 1988.
Availability: Bureau of the Census, Data User Services Division

Directory of Governments File (Computer Tape).
Availability: Bureau of the Census, Data User Services Division

Directory of Governments, (1988): Name and Address File (Computer Tape).
Availability: Bureau of the Census, Data User Services Division

Employee-Retirement Systems - File E, 1986-1987 (Computer Tape).
Availability: Bureau of the Census, Data User Services Division

Employment Statistics File, 1987 (Computer Tape).
Availability: Bureau of the Census, Data User Services Division

Federal Assistance Award Data System (FAADS) File (Computer Tape).
Availability: Bureau of the Census, Data User Services Division

Finance Statistics File (Computer Tape).
Availability: Bureau of the Census, Data User Services Division

Finances of Public School Systems - File D (Computer Tape).
Availability: Bureau of the Census, Data User Services Division

Government Finances on Diskette Series: 1989.
Availability: Bureau of the Census, Data User Services Division

Government Organization File (Computer Tape).
Availability: Bureau of the Census, Data User Services Division

Survey of Governments, 1988: Employee-Retirement Systems (Files D and E) Computer Tape.
Availability: Bureau of the Census, Data User Services Division

Survey of Governments, 1989: Education Finance (89SCH - File C) (Computer Tape).
Availability: Bureau of the Census, Data User Services Division

Survey of Governments, 1990: Annual Finance Statistics (Computer Tape).
Availability: Bureau of the Census, Data User Services Division

Survey of Governments, 1990: Education Finance (90SCH - File C) (Computer Tape).
Availability: Bureau of the Census, Data User Services Division

Survey of Governments, 1991: Annual Employment Statistics File (Computer Tape).
Availability: Bureau of the Census, Data User Services Division

Health

Adult Use of Tobacco Survey, 1986.
PB90-501321
Availability: NTIS

Bureau of Health Professions Area Resource File (ARF) Documentation Tape, 1991.
PB91-507525
Availability: NTIS

Bureau of Health Professions Area Resource File (ARF) Tape, September 1987.
PB88-122320
Availability: NTIS

Bureau of Health Professions Area Resource File (ARF) (for Microcomputers): Complete Set.
PB87-135349
Availability: NTIS

Bureau of Health Professions Area Resource File (ARF) (for Microcomputers): Complete Set Micro Data Series User Documentation and Technical Documentation.
PB87-208252.
Availability: NTIS

Bureau of Health Professions Area Resource File (ARF) (for Microcomputers): Demographic Micro Data Series User Documentation and Technical Documentation.
PB87-208260.
Availability: NTIS

Bureau of Health Professions Area Resource File (ARF) (for Microcomputers): Demographic State by County.
PB88-906300.
Availability: NTIS

Bureau of Health Professions Area Resource File (ARF) (for Microcomputers): Demographic State by County -- Alabama.
PB88-906301
Availability: NTIS

Bureau of Health Professions Area Resource File (ARF) (for Microcomputers): Demographic State by County -- Alaska, Idaho, Oregon.
PB88-906302
Availability: NTIS

Bureau of Health Professions Area Resource File (ARF) (for Microcomputers): Demographic State by County-Arizona, California, Hawaii, Nevada.
PB88-906303
Availability: NTIS

Bureau of Health Professions Area Resource File (ARF) (for Microcomputers): Demographic State by County--Arkansas.
PB88-906304
Availability: NTIS

Bureau of Health Professions Area Resource File (ARF) (for Microcomputers): Demographic State by County--Colorado, Utah.
PB88-906305
Availability: NTIS

Bureau of Health Professions Area Resource File (ARF) (for Microcomputers): Demographic State by County--Connecticut, New Jersey, New York, Rhode Island.
PB88-906306
Availability: NTIS

Bureau of Health Professions Area Resource File (ARF) (for Microcomputers): Demographic State by County-Delaware, District of Columbia, Maryland, Pennsylvania.
PB88-906307
Availability: NTIS

Bureau of Health Professions Area Resource File (ARF) (for Microcomputers): Demographic State by County--Florida.
PB88-906308
Availability: NTIS

Bureau of Health Professions Area Resource File (ARF) (for Microcomputers): Demographic State by County--Georgia (East), South Carolina.
PB88-906310
Availability: NTIS

Bureau of Health Professions Area Resource File (ARF) (for Microcomputers): Demographic State by County--Georgia (West).
PB88-906309
Availability: NTIS

Bureau of Health Professions Area Resource File (ARF) (for Microcomputers): Demographic State by County--Illinois.
PB88-906311
Availability: NTIS

Bureau of Health Professions Area Resource File (ARF) (for Microcomputers): Demographic State by County--Indiana.
PB88-906312.
Availability: NTIS

Bureau of Health Professions Area Resource File (ARF) (for Microcomputers): Demographic State by County--Iowa.
PB88-906313.
Availability: NTIS

Bureau of Health Professions Area Resource File (ARF) (for Microcomputers): Demographic State by County--Kansas
PB88-906314
Availability: NTIS

Bureau of Health Professions Area Resource File (ARF) (for Microcomputers): Demographic State by County--Kentucky (East), West Virginia.
PB88-906316
Availability: NTIS

Bureau of Health Professions Area Resource File (ARF) (for Microcomputers): Demographic State by County--Kentucky (West).
PB88-906315
Availability: NTIS

Bureau of Health Professions Area Resource File (ARF) (for Microcomputers): Demographic State by County--Louisiana.
PB88-906317.
Availability: NTIS

Bureau of Health Professions Area Resource File (ARF) (for Microcomputers): Demographic State by County--Maine, Massachusetts, New Hampshire, Vermont.
PB88-906318.
Availability: NTIS

Bureau of Health Professions Area Resource File (ARF) (for Microcomputers): Demographic State by County--Michigan.
PB88-906319.
Availability: NTIS

Bureau of Health Professions Area Resource File (ARF) (for Microcomputers): Demographic State by County--Minnesota.
PB88-906320.
Availability: NTIS

Bureau of Health Professions Area Resource File (ARF) (for Microcomputers): Demographic State by County--Mississippi.
PB88-906321.
Availability: NTIS

Bureau of Health Professions Area Resource File (ARF) (for Microcomputers): Demographic State by County--Missouri.
PB88-906322.
Availability: NTIS

Bureau of Health Professions Area Resource File (ARF) (for Microcomputers): Demographic State by County--Montana, North Dakota.
PB88-906323
Availability: NTIS

Bureau of Health Professions Area Resource File (ARF) (for Microcomputers): Demographic State by County--Nebraska.
PB88-906324
Availability: NTIS

Bureau of Health Professions Area Resource File (ARF) (for Microcomputers): Demographic State by County--New Mexico, Texas (West).
PB88-906330
Availability: NTIS

Bureau of Health Professions Area Resource File (ARF) (for Microcomputers): Demographic State by County--North Carolina.
PB88-906325
Availability: NTIS

Bureau of Health Professions Area Resource File (ARF) (for Microcomputers): Demographic State by County--Ohio.
PB88-906326
Availability: NTIS

Bureau of Health Professions Area Resource File (ARF) (for Microcomputers): Demographic State by County--Oklahoma.
PB88-906327
Availability: NTIS

Bureau of Health Professions Area Resource File (ARF) (for Microcomputers): Demographic State by County--Set.
PB87-135356
Availability: NTIS

Bureau of Health Professions Area Resource File (ARF) (for Microcomputers): Demographic State by County--South Dakota, Wyoming.
PB88-906328.
Availability: NTIS

Bureau of Health Professions Area Resource File (ARF) (for Microcomputers): Demographic State by County--Tennessee.
PB88-906329.
Availability: NTIS

Bureau of Health Professions Area Resource File (ARF) (for Microcomputers): Demographic State by County--Texas (East).
PB88-906332
Availability: NTIS

Bureau of Health Professions Area Resource File (ARF) (for Microcomputers): Demographic State by County--Texas (Mid).
PB88-906331
Availability: NTIS

Bureau of Health Professions Area Resource File (ARF) (for Microcomputers): Demographic State by County--Virginia.
PB88-906333
Availability: NTIS

Bureau of Health Professions Area Resource File (ARF) (for Microcomputers): Demographic State by County--Washington.
PB88-906334
Availability: NTIS

Bureau of Health Professions Area Resource File (ARF) (for Microcomputers): Demographic State by County--Wisconsin.
PB88-906335
Availability: NTIS

Bureau of Health Professions Area Resource File (ARF) (for Microcomputers): Demographic U.S. by State.
PB88-906336
Availability: NTIS

Bureau of Health Professions Area Resource File (ARF) (for Microcomputers): Health Facilities, Health Professions, and Demographics Micro Data Series Updates, June 1987--Alabama.
PB88-906601.
Availability: NTIS

Bureau of Health Professions Area Resource File (ARF) (for Microcomputers): Health Facilities, Health Professions, and Demographics Micro Data Series Updates, June 1987--Alaska, Idaho, Oregon.
PB88-906602.
Availability: NTIS

Bureau of Health Professions Area Resource File (ARF) (for Microcomputers): Health Facilities, Health Professions, and Demographics Micro Data Series Updates, June 1987--Arkansas.
PB88-906604.
Availability: NTIS

Bureau of Health Professions Area Resource File (ARF) (for Microcomputers): Health Facilities, Health Professions, and Demographics Micro Data Series Updates, June 1987-California, Hawaii, Nevada, Arizona.
PB88-906603.
Availability: NTIS

Bureau of Health Professions Area Resource File (ARF) (for Microcomputers): Health Facilities, Health Professions, and Demographics Micro Data Series Updates, June 1987--Utah, Colorado.
PB88-906605.
Availability: NTIS

Bureau of Health Professions Area Resource File (ARF) (for Microcomputers): Health Facilities, Health Professions, and Demographics Micro Data Series Updates, June 1987--Connecticut, New Jersey, New York, Rhode Island.
PB88-906606.
Availability: NTIS

Bureau of Health Professions Area Resource File (ARF) (for Microcomputers): Health Facilities, Health Professions, and Demographics Micro Data Series Updates, June 1987--Delaware, District of Columbia, Maryland, Pennsylvania.
PB88-906607.
Availability: NTIS

Bureau of Health Professions Area Resource File (ARF) (for Microcomputers): Health Facilities, Health Professions, and Demographics Micro Data Series Updates, June 1987--Florida.
PB88-906608.
Availability: NTIS

Bureau of Health Professions Area Resource File (ARF) (for Microcomputers): Health Facilities, Health Professions, and Demographics Micro Data Series Updates, June 1987--Georgia (East), South Carolina.
PB88-906610.
Availability: NTIS

Bureau of Health Professions Area Resource File (ARF) (for Microcomputers): Health Facilities, Health Professions, and Demographics Micro Data Series Updates, June 1987--Georgia (West).
PB88-906609.
Availability: NTIS

Bureau of Health Professions Area Resource File (ARF) (for Microcomputers): Health Facilities, Health Professions, and Demographics Micro Data Series Updates, June 1987--Illinois.
PB88-906611.
Availability: NTIS

Bureau of Health Professions Area Resource File (ARF) (for Microcomputers): Health Facilities, Health Professions, and Demographics Micro Data Series Updates, June 1987--Indiana.
PB88-906612.
Availability: NTIS

Bureau of Health Professions Area Resource File (ARF) (for Microcomputers): Health Facilities, Health Professions, and Demographics Micro Data Series Updates, June 1987--Iowa.
PB88-906613.
Availability: NTIS

Bureau of Health Professions Area Resource File (ARF) (for Microcomputers): Health Facilities, Health Professions, and Demographics Micro Data Series Updates, June 1987--Kansas.
PB88-906614.
Availability: NTIS

Bureau of Health Professions Area Resource File (ARF) (for Microcomputers): Health Facilities, Health Professions, and Demographics Micro Data Series Updates, June 1987--Kentucky (East), West Virginia.
PB88-906616.
Availability: NTIS

Bureau of Health Professions Area Resource File (ARF) (for Microcomputers): Health Facilities, Health Professions, and Demographics Micro Data Series Updates, June 1987--Kentucky (West).
PB88-906615.
Availability: NTIS

Bureau of Health Professions Area Resource File (ARF) (for Microcomputers): Health Facilities, Health Professions, and Demographics Micro Data Series Updates, June 1987--Louisiana.
PB88-906617.
Availability: NTIS

Bureau of Health Professions Area Resource File (ARF) (for Microcomputers): Health Facilities, Health Professions, and Demographics Micro Data Series Updates, June 1987--Maine, Massachusetts, New Hampshire, Vermont.
PB88-906618.
Availability: NTIS

Bureau of Health Professions Area Resource File (ARF) (for Microcomputers): Health Facilities, Health Professions, and Demographics Micro Data Series Updates, June 1987--Michigan.
PB88-906619.
Availability: NTIS

Bureau of Health Professions Area Resource File (ARF) (for Microcomputers): Health Facilities, Health Professions, and Demographics Micro Data Series Updates, June 1987--Minnesota.
PB88-906620.
Availability: NTIS

Bureau of Health Professions Area Resource File (ARF) (for Microcomputers): Health Facilities, Health Professions, and Demographics Micro Data Series Updates, June 1987--Mississippi.
PB88-906621.
Availability: NTIS

Bureau of Health Professions Area Resource File (ARF) (for Microcomputers): Health Facilities, Health Professions, and Demographics Micro Data Series Updates, June 1987--Missouri.
PB88-906622.
Availability: NTIS

Bureau of Health Professions Area Resource File (ARF) (for Microcomputers): Health Facilities, Health Professions, and Demographics Micro Data Series Updates, June 1987--Montana, North Dakota.
PB88-906623.
Availability: NTIS

Bureau of Health Professions Area Resource File (ARF) (for Microcomputers): Health Facilities, Health Professions, and Demographics Micro Data Series Updates, June 1987--Nebraska.
PB88-906624.
Availability: NTIS

Bureau of Health Professions Area Resource File (ARF) (for Microcomputers): Health Facilities, Health Professions, and Demographics Micro Data Series Updates, June 1987--New Mexico, Texas (West).
PB88-906630.
Availability: NTIS

Bureau of Health Professions Area Resource File (ARF) (for Microcomputers): Health Facilities, Health Professions, and Demographics Micro Data Series Updates, June 1987--North Carolina.
PB88-906625.
Availability: NTIS

Bureau of Health Professions Area Resource File (ARF) (for Microcomputers): Health Facilities, Health Professions, and Demographics Micro Data Series Updates, June 1987--Ohio.
PB88-906626.
Availability: NTIS

Bureau of Health Professions Area Resource File (ARF) (for Microcomputers): Health Facilities, Health Professions, and Demographics Micro Data Series Updates, June 1987--Oklahoma.
PB88-906627.
Availability: NTIS

Bureau of Health Professions Area Resource File (ARF) (for Microcomputers): Health Facilities, Health Professions, and Demographics Micro Data Series Updates, June 1987--South Dakota, Wyoming.
PB88-906628.
Availability: NTIS

Bureau of Health Professions Area Resource File (ARF) (for Microcomputers): Health Facilities, Health Professions, and Demographics Micro Data Series Updates, June 1987--State by County.
PB88-906600.
Availability: NTIS

Bureau of Health Professions Area Resource File (ARF) (for Microcomputers): Health Facilities, Health Professions, and Demographics Micro Data Series Updates, June 1987--State/National.
PB88-906636.
Availability: NTIS

Bureau of Health Professions Area Resource File (ARF) (for Microcomputers): Health Facilities, Health Professions, and Demographics Micro Data Series Update, June 1987--Tennessee.
PB88-906629
Availability: NTIS

Bureau of Health Professions Area Resource File (ARF) (for Microcomputers): Health Facilities, Health Professions, and Demographics Micro Data Series Update, June 1987--Texas (East).
PB88-906632
Availability: NTIS

Bureau of Health Professions Area Resource File (ARF) (for Microcomputers): Health Facilities, Health Professions, and Demographics Micro Data Series Update, June 1987--Texas (Mid).
PB88-906631
Availability: NTIS

Bureau of Health Professions Area Resource File (ARF) (for Microcomputers): Health Facilities, Health Professions, and Demographics Micro Data Series Update, June 1987--Utah, Colorado.
PB88-906605
Availability: NTIS

Bureau of Health Professions Area Resource File (ARF) (for Microcomputers): Health Facilities, Health Professions, and Demographics Micro Data Series Update, June 1987--Virginia.
PB88-906633
Availability: NTIS

Bureau of Health Professions Area Resource File (ARF) (for Microcomputers): Health Facilities, Health Professions, and Demographics Micro Data Series Update, June 1987--Washington.
PB88-906634
Availability: NTIS

Bureau of Health Professions Area Resource File (ARF) (for Microcomputers): Health Facilities, Health Professions, and Demographics Micro Data Series Update, June 1987--Wisconsin.
PB88-906635
Availability: NTIS

Bureau of Health Professions Area Resource File (ARF) (for Microcomputers): Health Facilities, Health Professions, and Demographics Micro Data Series Update, June 1987--State by County.
PB88-906600
Availability: NTIS

Bureau of Health Professions Area Resource File (ARF) (for Microcomputers): Health Facilities Micro Data Series User Documentation and Technical Documentation.
PB87-208278
Availability: NTIS

Bureau of Health Professions Area Resource File (ARF) (for Microcomputers): Health Facilities State by County.
PB88-906500
Availability: NTIS

Bureau of Health Professions Area Resource File (ARF) (for Microcomputers): Health Facilities State by County--Alabama.
PB88-906501
Availability: NTIS

Bureau of Health Professions Area Resource File (ARF) (for Microcomputers): Health Facilities State by County--Alaska, Idaho, Oregon.
PB88-906502
Availability: NTIS

Bureau of Health Professions Area Resource File (ARF) (for Microcomputers): Health Facilities State by County--Arizona, Nevada.
PB88-906503
Availability: NTIS

Bureau of Health Professions Area Resource File (ARF) (for Microcomputers): Health Facilities State by County--Arkansas.
PB88-906504
Availability: NTIS

Bureau of Health Professions Area Resource File (ARF) (for Microcomputers): Health Facilities State by County--California, Hawaii.
PB87-135760
Availability: NTIS

Bureau of Health Professions Area Resource File (ARF) (for Microcomputers): Health Facilities State by County--Colorado, Utah.
PB88-906506
Availability: NTIS

Bureau of Health Professions Area Resource File (ARF) (for Microcomputers): Health Facilities State by County--Connecticut, New Jersey, Rhode Island.
PB88-906507
Availability: NTIS

Bureau of Health Professions Area Resource File (ARF) (for Microcomputers): Health Facilities State by County--Delaware, District of Columbia, Maryland.
PB88-906508
Availability: NTIS

Bureau of Health Professions Area Resource File (ARF) (for Microcomputers): Health Facilities State by County--Florida.
PB88-906509
Availability: NTIS

Bureau of Health Professions Area Resource File (ARF) (for Microcomputers): Health Facilities State by County--Georgia (East).
PB88-906511
Availability: NTIS

Bureau of Health Professions Area Resource File (ARF) (for Microcomputers): Health Facilities State by County--Georgia (West).
PB88-906510
Availability: NTIS

Bureau of Health Professions Area Resource File (ARF) (for Microcomputers): Health Facilities State by County--Illinois (North), Wisconsin.
PB88-906513
Availability: NTIS

Bureau of Health Professions Area Resource File (ARF) (for Microcomputers): Health Facilities State by County--Illinois (South).
PB88-906512
Availability: NTIS

Bureau of Health Professions Area Resource File (ARF) (for Microcomputers): Health Facilities State by County--Indiana.
PB88-906514
Availability: NTIS

Bureau of Health Professions Area Resource File (ARF) (for Microcomputers): Health Facilities State by County--Iowa.
PB88-906515
Availability: NTIS

Bureau of Health Professions Area Resource File (ARF) (for Microcomputers): Health Facilities State by County--Kansas (East), Missouri (West).
PB88-906517
Availability: NTIS

Bureau of Health Professions Area Resource File (ARF) (for Microcomputers): Health Facilities State by County--Kansas (West).
PB88-906516
Availability: NTIS

Bureau of Health Professions Area Resource File (ARF) (for Microcomputers): Health Facilities State by County--Kentucky (East), Virginia (far West), West Virginia.
PB88-906520
Availability: NTIS

Bureau of Health Professions Area Resource File (ARF) (for Microcomputers): Health Facilities State by County--Kentucky (West).
PB88-906519
Availability: NTIS

Bureau of Health Professions Area Resource File (ARF) (for Microcomputers): Health Facilities State by County--Louisiana.
PB88-906522
Availability: NTIS

Bureau of Health Professions Area Resource File (ARF) (for Microcomputers): Health Facilities State by County--Maine, Massachusetts, New Hampshire, Vermont.
PB88-906523
Availability: NTIS

Bureau of Health Professions Area Resource File (ARF) (for Microcomputers): Health Facilities State by County--Michigan.
PB88-906524
Availability: NTIS

Bureau of Health Professions Area Resource File (ARF) (for Microcomputers): Health Facilities State by County--Minnesota.
PB88-906525
Availability: NTIS

Bureau of Health Professions Area Resource File (ARF) (for Microcomputers): Health Facilities State by County--Mississippi.
PB88-906526
Availability: NTIS

Bureau of Health Professions Area Resource File (ARF) (for Microcomputers): Health Facilities State by County--Missouri (East).
PB88-906518
Availability: NTIS

Bureau of Health Professions Area Resource File (ARF) (for Microcomputers): Health Facilities State by County--Montana.
PB88-906527
Availability: NTIS

Bureau of Health Professions Area Resource File (ARF) (for Microcomputers): Health Facilities State by County--Nebraska.
PB88-906528
Availability: NTIS

Bureau of Health Professions Area Resource File (ARF) (for Microcomputers): Health Facilities State by County--New York.
PB88-906529
Availability: NTIS

Bureau of Health Professions Area Resource File (ARF) (for Microcomputers): Health Facilities State by County--North Carolina.
PB88-906530
Availability: NTIS

Bureau of Health Professions Area Resource File (ARF) (for Microcomputers): Health Facilities State by County--North Dakota.
PB88-906531
Availability: NTIS

Bureau of Health Professions Area Resource File (ARF) (for Microcomputers): Health Facilities State by County--Ohio.
PB88-906532
Availability: NTIS

Bureau of Health Professions Area Resource File (ARF) (for Microcomputers): Health Facilities State by County--Oklahoma.
PB88-906533
Availability: NTIS

Bureau of Health Professions Area Resource File (ARF) (for Microcomputers): Health Facilities State by County--Pennsylvania.
PB88-906534
Availability: NTIS

Bureau of Health Professions Area Resource File (ARF) (for Microcomputers): Health Facilities State by County--Set.
PB87-135711
Availability: NTIS

Bureau of Health Professions Area Resource File (ARF) (for Microcomputers): Health Facilities State by County--South Carolina.
PB88-906535
Availability: NTIS

Bureau of Health Professions Area Resource File (ARF) (for Microcomputers): Health Facilities State by County--South Dakota, Wyoming.
PB88-906536
Availability: NTIS

Bureau of Health Professions Area Resource File (ARF) (for Microcomputers): Health Facilities State by County--Tennessee.
PB88-906540
Availability: NTIS

Bureau of Health Professions Area Resource File (ARF) (for Microcomputers): Health Facilities State by County--Texas (East).
PB88-906539
Availability: NTIS

Bureau of Health Professions Area Resource File (ARF) (for Microcomputers): Health Facilities State by County--Texas (Mid).
PB88-906538
Availability: NTIS

Bureau of Health Professions Area Resource File (ARF) (for Microcomputers): Health Facilities State by County--Texas (West), New Mexico.
PB88-906537
Availability: NTIS

Bureau of Health Professions Area Resource File (ARF) (for Microcomputers): Health Facilities State by County--U.S. by State.
PB88-906542
Availability: NTIS

Bureau of Health Professions Area Resource File (ARF) (for Microcomputers): Health Facilities State by County--Virginia (East).
PB88-906521
Availability: NTIS

Bureau of Health Professions Area Resource File (ARF) (for Microcomputers): Health Facilities State by County--Washington.
PB88-906541
Availability: NTIS

Bureau of Health Professions Area Resource File (ARF) (for Microcomputers): Health Facilities U.S. by State.
PB87-141586
Availability: NTIS

Bureau of Health Professions Area Resource File (ARF) (for Microcomputers): Health Professions Micro Data Series User Documentation and Technical Documentation.
PB87-208286
Availability: NTIS

Bureau of Health Professions Area Resource File (ARF) (for Microcomputers): Health Professions State by County.
PB88-906400
Availability: NTIS

Bureau of Health Professions Area Resource File (ARF) (for Microcomputers): Health Professions State by County--Alabama.
PB88-906401
Availability: NTIS

Bureau of Health Professions Area Resource File (ARF) (for Microcomputers): Health Professions State by County--Alaska, Idaho, Oregon.
PB88-906402
Availability: NTIS

Bureau of Health Professions Area Resource File (ARF) (for Microcomputers): Health Professions State by County--Arizona, California, Hawaii, Nevada.
PB88-906403
Availability: NTIS

Bureau of Health Professions Area Resource File (ARF) (for Microcomputers): Health Professions State by County--Arkansas.
PB88-906404
Availability: NTIS

Bureau of Health Professions Area Resource File (ARF) (for Microcomputers): Health Professions State by County--Colorado, Utah.
PB88-906405
Availability: NTIS

Bureau of Health Professions Area Resource File (ARF) (for Microcomputers): Health Professions State by County--Connecticut, New Jersey, New York, Rhode Island.
PB88-906406
Availability: NTIS

Bureau of Health Professions Area Resource File (ARF) (for Microcomputers): Health Professions State by County--Delaware, District of Columbia, Maryland, Pennsylvania.
PB88-906407
Availability: NTIS

Bureau of Health Professions Area Resource File (ARF) (for Microcomputers): Health Professions State by County--Florida.
PB88-906408
Availability: NTIS

Bureau of Health Professions Area Resource File (ARF) (for Microcomputers): Health Professions State by County--Georgia (East), South Carolina.
PB88-906410
Availability: NTIS

Bureau of Health Professions Area Resource File (ARF) (for Microcomputers): Health Professions State by County--Georgia (West).
PB88-906409
Availability: NTIS

Bureau of Health Professions Area Resource File (ARF) (for Microcomputers): Health Professions State by County--Illinois.
PB88-906411
Availability: NTIS

Bureau of Health Professions Area Resource File (ARF) (for Microcomputers): Health Professions State by County--Indiana.
PB88-906412
Availability: NTIS

Bureau of Health Professions Area Resource File (ARF) (for Microcomputers): Health Professions State by County--Iowa.
PB88-906413
Availability: NTIS

Bureau of Health Professions Area Resource File (ARF) (for Microcomputers): Health Professions State by County--Kansas.
PB88-906414
Availability: NTIS

Bureau of Health Professions Area Resource File (ARF) (for Microcomputers): Health Professions State by County--Kentucky (East), West Virginia.
PB88-906416
Availability: NTIS

Bureau of Health Professions Area Resource File (ARF) (for Microcomputers): Health Professions State by County--Kentucky (West).
PB88-906415
Availability: NTIS

Bureau of Health Professions Area Resource File (ARF) (for Microcomputers): Health Professions State by County--Louisiana.
PB88-906417
Availability: NTIS

Bureau of Health Professions Area Resource File (ARF) (for Microcomputers): Health Professions State by County--Maine, Massachusetts, New Hampshire, Vermont.
PB88-906418
Availability: NTIS

Bureau of Health Professions Area Resource File (ARF) (for Microcomputers): Health Professions State by County--Michigan.
PB88-906419
Availability: NTIS

Bureau of Health Professions Area Resource File (ARF) (for Microcomputers): Health Professions State by County--Minnesota.
PB88-906420
Availability: NTIS

Bureau of Health Professions Area Resource File (ARF) (for Microcomputers): Health Professions State by County--Mississippi.
PB88-906421
Availability: NTIS

Bureau of Health Professions Area Resource File (ARF) (for Microcomputers): Health Professions State by County--Missouri.
PB88-906422
Availability: NTIS

Bureau of Health Professions Area Resource File (ARF) (for Microcomputers): Health Professions State by County--Montana, North Dakota.
PB88-906423
Availability: NTIS

Bureau of Health Professions Area Resource File (ARF) (for Microcomputers): Health Professions State by County--Nebraska.
PB88-906424
Availability: NTIS

Bureau of Health Professions Area Resource File (ARF) (for Microcomputers): Health Professions State by County--New Mexico, Texas (West).
PB88-906430
Availability: NTIS

Bureau of Health Professions Area Resource File (ARF) (for Microcomputers): Health Professions State by County--North Carolina.
PB88-906425
Availability: NTIS

Bureau of Health Professions Area Resource File (ARF) (for Microcomputers): Health Professions State by County--Ohio.
PB88-906426
Availability: NTIS

Bureau of Health Professions Area Resource File (ARF) (for Microcomputers): Health Professions State by County--Oklahoma.
PB88-906427
Availability: NTIS

Bureau of Health Professions Area Resource File (ARF) (for Microcomputers): Health Professions State by County--South Dakota, Wyoming.
PB88-906428
Availability: NTIS

Bureau of Health Professions Area Resource File (ARF) (for Microcomputers): Health Professions State by County--Tennessee.
PB88-906429
Availability: NTIS

Bureau of Health Professions Area Resource File (ARF) (for Microcomputers): Health Professions State by County--Texas East).
PB88-906432
Availability: NTIS

Bureau of Health Professions Area Resource File (ARF) (for Microcomputers): Health Professions State by County--Texas (Mid).
PB88-906431
Availability: NTIS

Bureau of Health Professions Area Resource File (ARF) (for Microcomputers): Health Professions State by County--U.S. by State.
PB88-906436
Availability: NTIS

Bureau of Health Professions Area Resource File (ARF) (for Microcomputers): Health Professions State by County--Virginia.
PB88-906433
Availability: NTIS

Bureau of Health Professions Area Resource File (ARF) (for Microcomputers): Health Professions State by County--Washington.
PB88-906434
Availability: NTIS

Bureau of Health Professions Area Resource File (ARF) (for Microcomputers): Health Professions State by County--Wisconsin.
PB88-906435
Availability: NTIS

Bureau of Health Professions Area Resource File (ARF) (for Microcomputers): Health Professions U.S. by State.
PB87-141594
Availability: NTIS

Bureau of Health Professions Area Resource File (ARF) Tape, September 1987.
PB88-122320
Availability: NTIS

Chemical Carcinogenesis Research Information System (CCRIS) Data Bank, 1981-June 1986, (1988 Version).
PB88-173588
Availability: NTIS

Compressed Mortality File, 1968 - 85.
PB88-246566
Availability: NTIS

End-Stage Renal Disease (ESRD) Facility Survey, 1989.
PB90-502824
Availability: NTIS

Epidemiologic Catchment Area Study, Public Use Data Tape, Export Version, for Use on AOS/VS, PRIMOS, VMS, UNIX, and OS/2 Operating Systems.
PB92-503499
Availability: NTIS

Epidemiologic Catchment Area Study, Public Use Data Tape, Export Version, for Use on CMS, MVS, and VSE Operating Systems.
PB92-503481
Availability: NTIS

Fetal Death Data, 1988.
PB92-501378
Availability: NTIS

HCFA (Health Care Financing Administration) Common Procedure Coding System (HCPCS), 1987.
PB87-172474
Availability: NTIS

HCRIS-180 Extract - Data from the Hospital Cost Report Information System.
PB86-207693
Availability: NTIS

Health Care Delivery Concept Lists - Alphabetized, Rockville, Md.
PB-207 77910
Availability: NTIS

Health Care Delivery Concept Lists - Categorized Version.
PB-207 77812
Availability: NTIS

Health Care Delivery Concept Lists - Hierarchal List and Program Tape. Magnetic Tape Record.
PB-207 78018
Availability: NTIS

Health, United States, 1990 (CD-ROM and Diskettes).
Availability: NTIS

Inventory of Long-Term Care Places Survey, 1986.
PB88-110606
Availability: NTIS

Linked Birth/Infant Death Data Set, 1987, Birth Cohort.
PB92-504604
Availability: NTIS

Longitudinal Study of Aging, Version 4 (1984 - 1990).
PB92-500099
Availability: NTIS

Mortality Followback Survey, 1986.
PB90-501800
Availability: NTIS

National Ambulatory Medical Care Survey, 1990.
PB92-501683
Availability: NTIS

National Ambulatory Medical Care Survey, Drug Mentions, 1990.
PB92-501840
Availability: NTIS

National Drug Code Directory.
PB92-501881
Availability: NTIS

National Health Interview Survey, 1987.
PB89-140651
Availability: NTIS

National Health Interview Survey, 1987 (CD-ROM).
PB91-505073
Availability: NTIS

National Health Interview Survey, 1988.
PB90-501180
Availability: NTIS

National Health Interview Survey, 1989.
PB91-506279
Availability: NTIS

National Health Interview Survey, 1990.
PB92-501170
Availability: NTIS

National Health Interview Survey (NHIS) - Access to Care, 1993.
Availability: Division of Health Interview Statistics

National Health Interview Survey (NHIS) - Adoption, 1987.
Availability: Division of Health Interview Statistics

National Health Interview Survey (NHIS) - AIDS Knowledge and Attitudes, 1987, 1988, 1989, 1990, 1991, 1992, and 1993.
Availability: Division of Health Interview Statistics

National Health Interview Survey (NHIS) - Alcohol, 1988.
Availability: Division of Health Interview Statistics

National Health Interview Survey (NHIS) - Cancer Control and Epidemiology, 1992.
Availability: Division of Health Interview Statistics

National Health Interview Survey (NHIS) - Child Health Supplement, 1991.
Availability: Division of Health Interview Statistics

National Health Interview Survey (NHIS) - Dental Care, 1989.
Availability: Division of Health Interview Statistics

National Health Interview Survey (NHIS) - Dental Health, 1986.
Availability: Division of Health Interview Statistics

National Health Interview Survey (NHIS) - Digestive Disorders, 1989.
Availability: Division of Health Interview Statistics

National Health Interview Survey (NHIS) - Environmental Health, 1991.
Availability: Division of Health Interview Statistics

National Health Interview Survey (NHIS) - Epidemiology Study File, 1987.
Availability: Division of Health Interview Statistics

National Health Interview Survey (NHIS) - Functional Limitations, 1986.
Availability: Division of Health Interview Statistics

National Health Interview Survey (NHIS) - Health Insurance, 1986, 1989, 1992, and 1993.
Availability: Division of Health Interview Statistics

National Health Interview Survey (NHIS) - Health Promotion and Disease Prevention, 1985, 1990 and 1991.
Availability: Division of Health Interview Statistics

National Health Interview Survey (NHIS) - Hearing, 1990 and 1991.
Availability: Division of Health Interview Statistics

National Health Interview Survey (NHIS) - Immunization, 1989, 1992 and 1993.
Availability: Division of Health Interview Statistics

National Health Interview Survey (NHIS) - Injury Control and Child Safety and Health, 1990.
Availability: Division of Health Interview Statistics

National Health Interview Survey (NHIS) - Longest Held Job, 1986.
Availability: Division of Health Interview Statistics

National Health Interview Survey (NHIS) - Longitudinal Study of Aging (LSOA) 1986, Version 2, 1988; Version 3, 1989; and Version 4, 1991.
Availability: Division of Health Interview Statistics

National Health Interview Study (NHIS) - Medical Device Implants (MDI) - Device and Extended Person Files Combined, 1988.
Availability: Division of Health Interview Statistics

National Health Interview Study (NHIS) - Medical Device Implants (MDI) - MDI Device File, 1988.
Availability: Division of Health Interview Statistics

National Health Interview Study (NHIS) - Medical Device Implants (MDI) - MDI Extended Person file, 1988.
Availability: Division of Health Interview Statistics

National Health Interview Survey (NHIS) - Mental Health, 1989.
Availability: Division of Health Interview Statistics.

National Health Interview Survey (NHIS) - Occupational Health, 1988.
Availability: Division of Health Interview Statistics

National Health Interview Survey (NHIS) - Orofacial Pain, 1989.
Availability: Division of Health Interview Statistics

National Health Interview Survey (NHIS) - Podiatry, 1990.
Availability: Division of Health Interview Statistics.

National Health Interview Survey (NHIS) - Poliomyelitis, 1987.
Availability: Division of Health Interview Statistics

National Health Interview Survey (NHIS) - Pregnancy and Smoking, 1990 and 1991.
Availability: Division of Health Interview Statistics

National Health Interview Survey (NHIS) - Sample Person Tape, 1985.
Availability: Division of Health Interview Statistics

National Health Interview Survey (NHIS) - Smoking History During Pregnancy, 1985.
Availability: Division of Health Interview Statistics

National Health Interview Survey (NHIS) - Teenage Attitudes and Practices II, 1993.
Availability: Division of Health Interview Statistics

National Health Interview Survey (NHIS) - Unintentional Injuries, 1991.
Availability: Division of Health Interview Statistics

National Health Interview Survey (NHIS) - Vitamin and Mineral Supplement Intake, 1986.
Availability: Division of Health Interview Statistics

National Health Interview Survey (NHIS) - Year 2000 Objectives, 1993.
Availability: Division of Health Interview Statistics

National Health Interview Survey (NHIS) - Youth Risk Behavior Survey, 1992.
Availability: Division of Health Interview Statistics

National Hospital Discharge Survey, 1990.
PB92-500818
Availability: NTIS

National Hospital Discharge Survey, 1990 (CD-ROM and Diskettes).
Availability: NTIS

National Hospital Discharge Survey, Data Access System, 1990, Data Diskettes.
PB92-501071
Availability: NTIS

National Hospital Discharge Survey, All-Listed Diagnoses, 1989, Data Diskettes.
PB91-507079
Availability: NTIS

National Hospital Discharge Survey, Multi-Year Data Access Systems, 1988, Data Diskettes.
PB90-502287
Availability: NTIS

National Maternal and Infant Health Survey, Mother's Segment, 1988.
PB92-500081
Availability: NTIS

National Nursing Home Survey, 1985.
PB89-159503
Availability: NTIS

National Nursing Home Survey: Next of Kin Component and Followup, 1986.
Availability: NTIS

National Sample Survey of Registered Nurses, 1988.
PB89-231492
Availability: NTIS

National Survey of Family Growth, 1988.
PB90-501248
Availability: NTIS

National Survey of Personal Health Practices and Consequences, Wave 1 and 2 (for Microcomputers).
PB86-167533
Availability: NTIS

NHANES 1 (National Health and Nutrition Examination Survey), Epidemiologic Followup Study, Health Care Facility Stay, 1987.
PB92-501147
Availability: NTIS

NHANES 1 (National Health and Nutrition Examination Survey), Epidemiologic Followup Study, Interview, 1987.
PB92-501154
Availability: NTIS

NHANES 1 (National Health and Nutrition Examination Survey), Epidemiologic Followup Study, Mortality, 1987.
PB92-501063
Availability: NTIS

NHANES 1 (National Health and Nutrition Examination Survey), Epidemiologic Followup Study, Vital and Tracing Status, 1987.
PB92-501162
Availability: NTIS

NIMH Treatment of Depression Collaborative Research Program Public Use Data File.
PB92-501758
Availability: NTIS

Physician's Practice Costs and Income Survey 1988.
PB92-504224
Availability: NTIS

Stroke Data Bank, 1983 - 1986.
PB92-500313
Availability: NTIS

Third Wave Prevalence Findings from the Massachusetts Health Care Panel Study.
PB85-116168
Availability: NTIS

Traumatic Coma Data Bank, (January 1984 - June 1988).
PB91-509893
Availability: NTIS

U.S. Renal Data System (USRDS), 1990. Diskettes.
PB90-502949
Availability: NTIS

Vaccine Adverse Event Reporting System (VAERS), 1990 (November) to Present (for Microcomputers).
PB92-592280
Availability: NTIS

Vital Statistics Divorce Data, Detail, 1988.
PB91-507731
Availability: NTIS

Vital Statistics Marriage Data, Detail, 1987.
PB90-501842
Availability: NTIS

Vital Statistics Mortality Data, Cause of Death Summary, 1988.
PB91-506634
Availability: NTIS

Vital Statistics Mortality Data, Detail, 1989.
PB92-504554
Availability: NTIS

Vital Statistics Mortality Data, Local Area Summary, 1988.
PB91-506642
Availability: NTIS

Vital Statistics Mortality Data, Multiple Cause of Death, Detail, 1989.
PB92-504596
Availability: NTIS

Vital Statistics Natality Data, Detail, 1988.
PB90-504168
Availability: NTIS

Vital Statistics Natality Data, Local Area Summary, 1988.
PB90-504150
Availability: NTIS

Vital Statistics Natality Data, State Summary, 1988.
PB90-504176
Availability: NTIS

Labor

Area Wage Surveys.
Availability: BLS, Division of Planning and Financial Management

Consumer Expenditure Survey: 1984 - 1990, Integrated Data.
Availability: BLS Data Diskettes

Consumer Expenditure Survey: 1989 - 90, Integrated Data by Age-Income Cross-Tabulation.
Availability: BLS Data Diskettes

Consumer Expenditure Survey: 1989 - 90, Integrated Data by CU Size-Income Cross-Tabulation.
Availability: BLS Data Diskettes

Consumer Expenditure Survey: 1989 - 90, Integrated Data by Region-Income Cross-Tabulation
Availability: BLS Data Diskettes

Consumer Expenditure Survey: 1989 - 90, Integrated Data Four Diskette Package.
Availability: BLS Data Diskettes

Consumer Expenditure Survey: 1986 - 87, Integrated Data by Age-Income Cross-Tabulation.
Availability: BLS Data Diskettes

Consumer Expenditure Survey: 1989 - 90, Integrated Data, High Density Diskette.
Availability: BLS Data Diskettes

Consumer Expenditure Survey: 1985 Integrated Data.
Availability: BLS Data Diskettes

Consumer Expenditure Survey: High Density Diskette of the Three 1986 -87 Cross-Tabulations.
Availability: BLS Data Diskettes

Consumer Expenditure Survey: Three Diskette Package of 1986 - 87 Cross-Tabulations.
Availability: BLS Data Diskettes

Consumer Expenditure Survey: Three Diskette Package of 1986 - 87 Metropolitan Statistical Areas.
Availability: BLS Data Diskettes

Consumer Expenditures, 1984, 1985, 1986, 1987, 1988: Diary Survey.
Availability: BLS, Division of Planning and Financial Management

Consumer Expenditures, 1984, 1985, 1986, 1987, 1988: Interview Survey.
Availability: BLS, Division of Planning and Financial Management

Consumer Price Index.
Availability: BLS Data Diskettes

Consumer Price Index.
Availability: BLS, Division of Planning and Financial Management

Dictionary of Occupational Titles, 4th Edition, and 1986 DOT Supplement.
PB87-194528/XDD
Availability: NTIS

Economic Growth (Historical).
Availability: BLS Data Diskettes

Economic Growth (Projections).
Availability: BLS Data Diskettes

Employee Benefits in Medium and Large Firms, 1981 - 86: Complete Annual Survey.
Availability: BLS, Division of Planning and Financial Management

Employee Benefits in Medium and Large Firms, 1981 - 86: One Benefit Area.
Availability: BLS, Division of Planning and Financial Management

Employment Cost Index.
Availability: BLS Data Diskettes

Employment Cost Index.
Availability: BLS, Division of Planning and Financial Management

Employment, Hours, and Earnings: National.
Availability: BLS Data Diskettes

Employment, Hours, and Earnings: National - 5 Months for 500 Industries -Employment, Hours and Earnings.
Availability: BLS Data Diskettes

Employment, Hours, and Earnings: National - 5 Years for 58 Industries - Employment, Hours and Earnings.
Availability: BLS Data Diskettes

Employment Projections and Their Historical Background: Historical Industry Employment.
Availability: BLS Data Diskettes

Employment Projections and Their Historical Background: Historical Industry Output.
Availability: BLS Data Diskettes

Employment Projections and Their Historical Background: Projections.
Availability: BLS Data Diskettes

Employment Projections and Their Historical Background: Labor Force Projections.
Availability: BLS, Division of Planning and Financial Management

Employment Projections and Their Historical Background: 228 - Order Input - Output Tables.
Availability: BLS Data Diskettes

Export - Import Price Indexes.
Availability: BLS, Division of Planning and Financial Management

Food and Fuel, Average Prices.
Availability: BLS, Division of Planning and Financial Management

Foreign Labor Force Statistics.
Availability: BLS Data Diskettes

Imports - By Tariff Commodity Class: 1968 to Date (Updated Quarterly).
PB82-948800/XDD
Availability: NTIS

Imports: Industrial Commodity Classes.
Availability: BLS, Division of Planning and Financial Management

Imports: Tariff Commodity Classes
Availability: BLS, Division of Planning and Financial Management

Industry and Federal Government Productivity.
Availability: BLS Data Diskettes

Industry Employment, Hours, and Earnings: National.
Availability: BLS, Division of Planning and Financial Management

Industry Employment, Hours and Earnings: States and Areas.
Availability: BLS, Division of Planning and Financial Management

Industry - Occupational Matrix, 1988 and 2000.
Availability: BLS, Division of Planning and Financial Management

Industry Price Indexes
Availability: BLS, Division of Planning and Financial Management

Input - Output Matrix
Availability: BLS, Division of Planning and Financial Management

International Labor and Price Trend Comparisons.
Availability: BLS, Division of Planning and Financial Management

Labor Force: National.
Availability: BLS Data Diskettes

Labor Force.
Availability: BLS, Division of Planning and Financial Management

Local Area Unemployment Statistics.
Availability: BLS Data Diskettes

Local Area Unemployment Statistics (LAUS).
Availability: BLS, Division of Planning and Financial Management

National Labor Surplus Area ZIP Code File, 1992.
PB92-500867
Availability: NTIS

National Labor Surplus Area (LSA) ZIP Code File, 1992 (Diskette).
PB92-501022
Availability: NTIS

1989 - 90 Cross-Tabulations Three-Diskette Package.
Availability: BLS Data Diskettes

1989 - 90 Metropolitan Statistical Areas.
Availability: BLS Data Diskettes

1989 - 90 Metropolitan Statistical Areas - Single Persons by Sex and Age, Cross-Tabulations.
Availability: BLS Data Diskettes

1989 - 90 Metropolitan Statistical Areas - Single Persons by Sex and Income, Cross-Tabulations.
Availability: BLS Data Diskettes

Occupational Employment Statistics.
Availability: BLS, Division of Planning and Financial Management

Occupational Injury and Illness Incidence Rates.
Availability: BLS Data Diskettes

Occupational Injury and Illness Incidence Rates.
Availability: BLS, Division of Planning and Financial Management

Producer Price Index.
Availability: BLS Data Diskettes

Producer Price Index - Industries and Products.
Availability: BLS, Division of Planning and Financial Management

Producer Price Index - Stage of Processing and Commodities.
Availability: BLS, Division of Planning and Financial Management

Productivity and Cost Indexes.
Availability: BLS, Division of Planning and Financial Management

Productivity - Federal Government.
Availability: BLS, Division of Planning and Financial Management

Productivity: Foreign Productivity and Labor Cost Statistics.
Availability: BLS Data Diskettes

Productivity - Industry.
Availability: BLS, Division of Planning and Financial Management

Productivity: Industry Labor and Multifactor Productivity and Federal, State, and Local Government Productivity.
Availability: BLS Data Diskettes

Productivity: Major Sector Labor and Multifactor Productivity.
Availability: BLS Data Diskettes

State and Local Governments, 1987: Complete Annual Survey.
Availability: BLS, Division of Planning and Financial Management

State and Local Governments, 1987: One Benefit Area.
Availability: BLS, Division of Planning and Financial Management

Supplementary Data System, Microdata File Disability Database (File A), 14 States, 1988.
PB90-502832
Availability: NTIS

Table Producing Language System (TPL)
Availability: BLS, Division of Planning and Financial Management

U.S. Export and Import Price Indexes.
Availability: BLS Data Diskettes

Manufacturing

Fuels and Electric Energy Consumed (MC82-S-4(T).
Availability: Bureau of the Census, Data User Services Division

Geographic Area and Industry File (MC82-A and -I (T).
Availability: Bureau of the Census, Data User Services Division

Industry Series (MC87-I) (CD-ROM).
Availability: Bureau of the Census, Data User Services Division

Location of Manufacturing Plants (MC82-LM(T).
Availability: Bureau of the Census, Data User Services Division.

Manufacturers' Shipments, Inventories, and Orders, Published and Unpublished Data: 1958-1993 (Computer Tape).
Availability: Bureau of the Census, Data User Services Division.

Plant and Equipment Expenditures: Unpublished Data (Diskette).
Availability: Bureau of the Census, Data User Services Division

Preliminary Industry Series (MC87-I-(P)) (CD-ROM).
Availability: Bureau of the Census, Data User Services Division

Product and Materials File (MC82-I(T).
Availability: Bureau of the Census, Data User Services Division.

Quarterly Financial Report for Manufacturing, Mining, and Trade Corporations File (Diskette).
Availability: Bureau of the Census, Data User Services Division

Statistics for Industry Groups and Industries (Including Capital Expenditures; Inventories; and Supplemental Labor, Fuel, and Electric Energy Costs) (M91 (AS)-1) (CD-ROM).
Availability: Bureau of the Census, Data User Services Division

Mineral Industries

Aeromagnetic Data for Western Central Sierra Nevada, California, January, 1986.
PB86-197415
Availability: NTIS

Analyses of Natural Gases, January 1, 1917-December 1991.
PB92-501337
Availability: NTIS

Analytical Results for Rock and B-Horizon Soil Samples Collected from the Ely Greenstone Belt, Northeastern Minnesota.
PB88-103668
Availability: NTIS

Analytical Results for Rocks, Soils, Stream-Sediments, and Heavy-Mineral Concentrate Samples Collected from the Butte 1 X 2 degree Quadrangle, Montana.
PB86-119484
Availability: NTIS

Analytical Results for Stream-Sediment and Nonmagnetic Heavy-Mineral-Concentrate Samples Collected from the Sherbrooke and Lewiston 1 X 2 degree Quadrangles and the White Mountain Wilderness Study Areas, Maine, New Hampshire and Vermont.
PB85-195493
Availability: NTIS

Analytical Results of Stream-Sediment and Non-Magnetic Heavy-Mineral-Concentrate Samples from Portions of the Challis 1 x 2 Quadrangle, Idaho.
PB85-103109
Availability: NTIS

Description of Magnetic Tape and "Read-Only" Retrieval Program of Geochemical Data, Coeur d'Alene District, Idaho.
PB-209 567/7
Availability: NTIS

Digital Magnetic Tapes of Single Channel Seismic Reflection Profiles on the Continental Shelf and Slope between Bering Strait and Barrow, Alaska, and MacKenzie Bay, Canada.
PB-232 345-SET
Availability: NTIS

Federally Owned Minerals for Exploration and Development in Western States: New Mexico, 1988 (for Microcomputers).
PB89-228860
Availability: NTIS

Ferrous Metals, Nonferrous Metals, and Industrial Minerals Supply/Demand Data, 1974-1984 (for Microcomputers).
PB86-217361
Availability: NTIS

Ferrous Metals Supply/Demand Data, 1974-1984 (for Microcomputers).
PB86-217338
Availability: NTIS

Gravity Data for the State of Washington.
PB85-163301
Availability: NTIS

Hydrologic Data for Soldier Creek Basin, Kansas.
PB-292 892/7
Availability: NTIS

Industrial Minerals Supply/Demand Data, 1974-1984 (for Microcomputers).
PB86-217353
Availability: NTIS

Input/Output Data for a Digital Computer Model of the Basin-Fill Aquifer in Smith Creek Valley, Lander County, Nevada.
PB87-142907
Availability: NTIS

Magnetic Data for a Gridded Format for Conterminous U.S. and Adjacent Marine Areas.
PB87-126017
Availability: NTIS

Master Environmental Control and Mine System Design Simulator for Underground Coal Mining-Test Data File.
PB-264 777/4
Availability: NTIS

Principal Facts for Gravity Stations in and Adjacent to the Dillion 1 deg and 2 deg Quandrangle, Montana and Idaho, 1977-1985.
PB86-197407
Availability: NTIS

Spectra of Minerals: Mid-Infrared (2.1-25.0 μm).
PB89-178453
Availability: NTIS

Spectrographic and Chemical Analyses of Geochemical Samples from the Washakie Wilderness and Nearby Roadless Areas, Park County, Wyoming.
PB85-161594
Availability: NTIS

Nutrition

Chinese Food Composition Tables
PB92-500644
Availability: NTIS

Continuing Survey of Food Intakes by Individuals (CSFII): One Day's Food Intake Data for Low Income Women and Their Children 1-5 Years of Age, 1986.
PB89-124382
Availability: NTIS

Continuing Survey of Food Intakes by Individuals (CSFII): One Day's Food Intake Data for Men 19-50 Years of Age, 1985-1986.
PB87-197141
Availability: NTIS

Continuing Survey of Food Intakes by Individuals (CSFII): Six Waves of Food Intake Data for Women and Their Children 1-5 Years of Age, 1986.
PB89-205546
Availability: NTIS

Continuing Survey of Food Intakes by Individuals (CSFII): Women 19-50 Years and Their Children 1-5 Years, 1 Day, 1986.
PB88-117767
Availability: NTIS

Continuing Survey of Food Intakes by Individuals: One Day's Food Intake Data for Women and Their Children 1-5 Years of Age, 1986.
PB89-154355
Availability: NTIS

Federal Survey of PCBs (Polychlorinated Biphenyls) in Atlantic Coast Bluefish, 1984-1986 (for Microcomputers).
PB87-142881
Availability: NTIS

Food Consumption Files Used in the Tolerance Assessment System (TAS).
PB87-142352
Availability: NTIS

Human Nutrition Research and Information Management (HNRIM) System: Database of Federally Supported Human Nutrition Research Projects (FY82-FY89).
PB92-503275
Availability: NTIS

National Evaluation of the Special Supplemental Food Program for Women, Infants and Children (WIC), 1982-85: Historical Study of Pregnancy Outcome, and SAS Analytic Files.
PB86-192911
Availability: NTIS

National Evaluation of the Special Supplemental Food Program for Women, Infants and Children (WIC), 1982-85: Historical Study of Pregnancy Outcome; Women's Longitudinal Study; Infant and Children Study; Food Expenditure Study; and SAS Analytic Files.
PB86-202348
Availability: NTIS

National Evaluation of the Special Supplemental Food Program for Women, Infants and Children (WIC), 1982-85: Women's Longitudinal Study; Infant and Children Study; Food Expenditure Study, and SAS Analytic Files.
PB86-202355
Availability: NTIS

Nationwide Food Consumption Survey, 1987-1988, Individual Intake.
PB90-504044
Availability: NTIS

Nutritive Values of Foods as in Home and Garden Bulletin No. 72 Revised 1990.
PB91-506956
Availability: NTIS

Total Water and Tap Water Intake in the United States: Population-Based Estimates of Quantities and Sources.
PB92-503168
Availability: NTIS

USDA (United States Department of Agriculture) Nutrient Data Base for Standard Reference, Abbreviated Version, Release 9.
PB90-502568
Availability: NTIS

USDA (United States Department of Agriculture) Nutrient Data Base for Standard Reference, Abbreviated Version, Release 9 (for Microcomputers).
PB90-502535
Availability: NTIS

USDA (United States Department of Agriculture) Nutrient Data Base for Standard Reference, Full Version, Release 9.
PB90-502717
Availability: NTIS

USDA (United States Department of Agriculture) Nutrient Data Base for Standard Reference, Full Version, Release 9 (for Microcomputers).
PB90-502584
Availability: NTIS

Oceanography

Bathythermograph (BT) Data - Expendable Bathythermograph Data (XBT), 1965 - 1989.
Availability: NODC, User Services Branch

Bathythermograph (BT) Data - Mechanical Bathythermograph Data (MBT), 1941 - 1988.
Availability: NODC, User Services Branch

Bathythermograph (BT) Data - Radio Message Bathythermograph Data (IBT), 1972 - 1989.
Availability: NODC, User Services Branch

Bathythermograph (BT) Data - Selected Level Bathythermograph Data (SBT), 1955 - 1989.
Availability: NODC, User Services Branch

Chesapeake Bay Land Classification Data Set, 1988 - 89.
Availability: NODC, User Services Branch

Current Meter Data (Components) (F015), 1962 - 1988.
Availability: NODC, User Services Branch

Current Meter Data (Resultants) (F005), 1973 - 1985.
Availability: NODC, User Services Branch

Drifting Buoy Data (F156), 1975 - present.
Availability: NODC, User Services Branch

GEOSAT Altimeter Data (T2GDR's) from the Exact Repeat Mission (CD-ROM).
Availability: NODC, User Services Branch

GEOSAT Crossover Difference Data from the Geodetic Mission (CD-ROM).
Availability: NODC, User Services Branch

GEOSAT Geodetic Mission Data for the Southern Ocean (CD-ROM).
Availability: NODC, User Services Branch

GEOSAT Geophysical Data Records from the Exact Repeat Mission, 1986 - 1990, (CD-ROM).
Availability: NODC, User Services Branch

GEOSAT Satellite Altimetry Data.
Availability: NODC, User Services Branch

GEOSAT Wind/Wave Data from the Geodetic Mission.
Availability: NODC, User Services Branch

Global Ocean Temperature and Salinity Profiles (CD-ROM).
Availability: NODC, User Services Branch

High-resolution CTD/STD Data (F022), 1969 - present.
Availability: NODC, User Services Branch

Low-resolution CTD/STD Data (C022), 1967 - 1989.
Availability: NODC, User Services Branch.

Marine Toxic Substances and Pollutants (F144), 1970 - 1987.
Availability: NODC, User Services Branch

Meteorology, Oceanography and Wave Spectra from Buoys (F291), 1970 - present.
Availability: NODC, User Services Branch

NODC Taxonomic Code.
Availability: NODC, User Services Branch

Oceanic Station Data (SD2), 1900 - 1988.
Availability: NODC, User Services Branch

Pacific and Indian Ocean Sea Level Data Set (Tape and Diskette).
Availability: NODC, User Services Branch

Pacific Ocean Temperature and Salinity Profiles NODC-01, 1900 - 1988. (CD-ROM).
Availability: NODC, User Services Branch

Pressure Gauge Data (F017), 1975 - 1987.
Availability: NODC, User Services Branch

SEQUAL/FOCAL Data Sets.
Availability: NODC, User Services Branch

Southern Ocean Atlas Data.
Availability: NODC, User Services Branch

Water Physics and Chemistry (F004), 1951 - 1985.
Availability: NODC, User Services Branch

Wind Measurements from Buoys (F101), 1975 - 1985.
Availability: NODC, User Services Branch

Worldwide Ocean Water Color/Water Transparency Data.
Availability: NODC, User Services Branch

Population and Housing

American Housing Survey: 1985, 1986, 1987, 1988, 1989, 1990, and 1991 Metropolitan Statistical Area File (Computer Tape and CD-ROM).
Availability: Bureau of the Census, Data User Services Division

American Housing Survey: 1985, 1987, 1989, 1990, and 1991 National Core and Supplemental File (Computer Tape and CD-ROM).
Availability: Bureau of the Census, Data User Services Division

Characteristics of New Housing - Microdata Sample (Computer Tape).
Availability: Bureau of the Census, Data User Services Division

Computer Programs for Demographic Analysis.
Availability: Bureau of the Census, Data User Services Division

County Household Estimates: Provisional Estimates of Households for Counties: July 1, 1985.
Availability: Bureau of the Census, Data User Services Division

County Population Estimates (Experimental) by Age, Sex, And Race: 1980 - 1985 (Computer Tape).
Availability: Bureau of the Census, Data User Services Division

Current Population Survey, January-December 1968 to 1992 (Computer Tape and CD-ROM).
Availability: Bureau of the Census, Data User Services Division

Current Population Survey, March 1986: After-Tax Money Income Estimates (Computer Tape).
Availability: Bureau of the Census, Data User Services Division

Current Population Survey, March 1986: Estimates of Noncash Benefit Values (Computer Tape).
Availability: Bureau of the Census, Data User Services Division

Current Population Survey, May 1988: Survey of Employee Benefits File.
Availability: Bureau of the Census, Data User Services Division

Current Population Survey, June 1988: Fertility, Birth Expectations, and Immigration Survey File.
Availability: Bureau of the Census, Data User Services Division

Current Population Survey, August 1988: Retiree Health Insurance File. Availability: Bureau of the Census, Data User Services Division

Current Population Survey, October 1988: School Enrollment File.
Availability: Bureau of the Census, Data User Services Division

Current Population Survey, November 1988: Voting and Registration File. Availability: Bureau of the Census, Data User Services Division

Current Population Survey, September 1991: Veterans Supplement (Computer Tape).
Availability: Bureau of the Census, Data User Services Division

Current Population Survey, March 1992: Annual Demographic File (Computer Tape and CD-ROM).
Availability: Bureau of the Census, Data User Services Division

Current Population Survey, July 1992: Telephone Availability File (Computer Tape).
Availability: Bureau of the Census, Data User Services Division

Estimates of the Population of States by Age, Sex, and Race, Hispanic Origin: 1981-1989 (Diskette).
Availability: Bureau of the Census, Data User Services Division

Immigrants Admitted into the United States as Legal Permanent Residents, FY88-FY90.
PB92-501980
Availability: NTIS

International Data Base, Machine Readable File: 1988 and 1990 (Computer Tapes).
Availability: Bureau of the Census, Data User Services Division

Legalization Population Survey, 1989.
PB92-501915
Availability: NTIS

1980 - 1990 Components of Change File (Diskette).
Availability: Bureau of the Census, Data User Services Division

1988 Dress Rehearsal Census of St. Louis City, East Central Missouri, and Eastern Washington P.L. 94-171 Data 1988 (Computer Tape).
Availability: Bureau of the Census, Data User Services Division

1988 Dress Rehearsal Census of St. Louis City, East Central Missouri, and Eastern Washington Summary Tape File 1A (Computer Tape).
Availability: Bureau of the Census, Data User Services Division

1990 Census of Population and Housing: Equal Employment Opportunity (EEO) File (CD-ROM and Computer Tape).
Availability: Bureau of the Census, Data User Services Division

1990 Census of Population and Housing, Modified Age/Race, Sex and Hispanic Origin (MARS) File (1990 STF-S-2A, 2B, 3 and 4) (Computer Tapes.
Availability: Bureau of the Census, Data User Services Division

1990 Census of Population and Housing, Population and Housing Unit Counts (STF-S-1) (Computer Tape).
Availability: Bureau of the Census, Data User Services Division

1990 Census of Population and Housing: Public Use Microdata Samples: 1 Percent and 5 Percent (Computer Tape).
Availability: Bureau of the Census, Data User Services Division

1990 Census of Population and Housing, Selected Population and Housing Data Paper Listing (1990 CPH-L) (Diskette).
Availability: Bureau of the Census, Data User Services Division

1990 Census of Population and Housing, Summary Tape File 1A, 1B, 1C, 1D, 2A, 2B, 2C, 3A, 3B, 3C, 3D, 4A, and 4B (Computer Tape).
Availability: Bureau of the Census, Data User Services Division

1990 Census of Population and Housing, Summary Tape File 3A Record Sequence Example File (Computer Tape).
Availability: Bureau of the Census, Data User Services Division

1990 Census of Population and Housing, Summary Tape File (STF) 1A, 1B, 1C, & 3A (CD-ROM).
Availability: Bureau of the Census, Data User Services Division

1990 Census of Population and Housing, Summary Tape File (STF) 2A, 2B and 3 - Puerto Rico (Computer Tapes).
Availability: Bureau of the Census, Data User Services Division

1990 Census of Population and Housing, Summary Tape File (STF) 1 & 3 - Pacific Outlying Areas (Computer Tape).
Availability: Bureau of the Census, Data User Services Division

1991 New York City Housing and Vacancy Survey (Longitudinal Microdata File) (Computer Tape).
Availability: Bureau of the Census, Data User Services Division

1991 New York City Housing and Vacancy Survey: Single Room Occupancy (SRO) (Microdata File).
Availability: Bureau of the Census, Data User Services Division

Population (1986) and Per Capita Income (1985) Estimates: Governmental Units Diskette File.
Availability: Bureau of the Census, Data User Services Division

Population (1988) and Per Capita Income (1987) Estimates: Governmental Units 1979 - 1988 (Computer Tape).
Availability: Bureau of the Census, Data User Services Division

Population Estimates for States and Counties with Components of Change: 1981 - 87 (Computer Tape).
Availability: Bureau of the Census, Data User Services Division

Population Projections of the United States by Age, Sex, Race, and Hispanic Origin: 1992 - 2050 (Computer Tape).
Availability: Bureau of the Census, Data User Services Division

Population Projections of the United States by Age, Six, Race, and Hispanic Origin: 1992 - 2050 - Middle Series (Diskette).
Availability: Bureau of the Census, Data User Services Division

Projections of the Population of the United States by Age, Sex, and Race: 1988 to 2080 (Computer Tape).
Availability: Bureau of the Census, Data User Services Division

Projections of the Population of States by Age, Sex, and Race: 1988 to 2010 (Computer Tape).
Availability: Bureau of the Census, Data User Services Division.

Projections of the Spanish Origin Population of the United States: 1988 to 2080 (Computer Tape).
Availability: Bureau of the Census, Data User Services Division

Public Law (P.L.) 94-171 Data 1990 (Computer Tape, CD-ROM and Diskette).
Availability: Bureau of the Census, Data User Services Division

Puerto Rico Redistricting Data (CD-ROM and Computer Tape).
Availability: Bureau of the Census, Data User Services Division

Revised Estimates of the Population of Counties by Age, Sex, and Race: 1980 - 1989 (Computer Tape).
Availability: Bureau of the Census, Data User Services Division

Survey of Income and Program Participation (SIPP) 1983-1991 (Computer Tapes.)
Availability: Bureau of the Census, Data User Services Division

Survey of Natural and Social Scientists and Engineers (SSE): 1989 (Computer Tape).
Availability: Bureau of the Census, Data User Services Division

Women in Development IV.
Availability: Bureau of the Census, Data User Services Division

Social Services

Aid to Families with Dependent Children, Characteristics, 1990.
PB92-502343
Availability: NTIS

Transportation

Census of Transportation: 1987 (Computer Tape).
Availability: Bureau of the Census, Data User Services Division

Geographic Area Series (Computer Tape and CD-ROM).
Availability: Bureau of the Census, Data User Services Division

Merchant Vessels of the United States, 1991.
PB92-501766
Availability: NTIS

Truck Inventory and Use Survey (Computer Tape).
Availability: Bureau of the Census, Data User Services Division

STATISTICS SOURCES
A–I

A

ABORTIONS

Alan Guttmacher Institute, 111 Fifth Avenue, New York, New York 10003 (212) 254-5656; *Abortion Factbook, Abortion Services in the United States, Family Planning Perspectives, 1992 Edition: Readings, Trends, and State and Local Data to 1988,* and unpublished data.

U.S. Department of Health and Human Services, National Center for Health Statistics, 3700 East-West Highway, Hyattsville, Maryland 20782 (301) 436-8500; *Monthly Vital Statistics Report.*

ABRASIVES - STONE

U.S. Department of the Interior, Bureau of Mines, 810 Seventh Street, NW, Washington, D.C. 20241 (202) 501-9649; *Minerals Yearbook, Annual Reports,* and *Mineral Commodity Summaries.*

ACCIDENTS AND FATALITIES

Association of American Railroads, American Railroads Building, 50 F Street, NW, Washington, D.C. 20001 (202) 639-2333; *Railroad Facts, Statistics of Railroads of Class I,* and *Analysis of Class I Railroads.*

National Safety Council, 1121 Spring Lake Drive, Itasca, Illinois 60143-3201 (708) 285-1121; *Accident Facts.*

U.S. Department of Health and Human Services, National Center for Health Statistics, 3700 East-West Highway, Hyattsville, Maryland 20782 (301) 436-8500; *Vital and Health Statistics,* and unpublished data.

U.S. Department of Labor, Mine Safety and Health Administration, 4015 Wilson Boulevard, Arlington, Virginia 22203 (703) 235-1452; unpublished data.

U.S. Department of Transportation, Bureau of Transportation Statistics, 400 Seventh Street, SW, Washington, D.C. 20590 (202) 366-DATA; *National Transportation Statistics Annual, Historical Compendium Information Report.*

U.S. Department of Transportation, Federal Highway Administration, 400 Seventh Street, SW, Washington, D.C. 20590 (202) 366-0660; *Fatal and Injury Accident Rates on Public Roads in the U.S.* and *Selected Highway Statistics and Charts.*

U. S. Department of Transportation, Federal Railroad Administration, 400 Seventh Street, SW, Washington, D.C. 20590 (202) 366-0881; *Accident Bulletin.*

U.S. Department of Transportation, National Highway Traffic Safety Administration, 400 Seventh Street, SW, Washington, D.C. 20590 (202) 366-9550; *General Estimates System.*

ACCIDENTS AND FATALITIES - AIRCRAFT

International Civil Aviation Organization, 1000 Sherbrooke Street, West Montreal, Quebec H3A 2R2 Canada (514) 285-8219; *Civil Aviation Statistics of the World.*

U.S. Department of Health and Human Services, National Center for Health Statistics, 3700 East-West Highway, Hyattsville, Maryland 20782 (301) 436-8500; *Vital Statistics of the United States,* and unpublished data.

U.S. Department of Transportation, Bureau of Transportation Statistics, 400 Seventh Street, SW, Washington, D.C. 20590 (202) 366-DATA; *National Transportation Statistics Annual, Historical Compendium Information Report.*

U.S. Department of Transportation, Federal Aviation Administration, 800 Independence Avenue, SW, Washington, D.C. 20591 (202) 366-4000; *FAA Statistical Handbook of Aviation,* and unpublished data.

ACCIDENTS AND FATALITIES - COSTS

National Safety Council, 1121 Spring Lake Drive, Itasca, Illinois 60143-3201 (708) 285-1121; *Accident Facts.*

ACCIDENTS AND FATALITIES - DEATHS AND DEATH RATES

National Safety Council, 1121 Spring Lake Drive, Itasca, Illinois 60143-3201 (708) 285-1121; *Accident Facts.*

U.S. Department of Health and Human Services, National Center for Health Statistics, 3700 East-West Highway, Hyattsville, Maryland 20782 (301) 436-8500; *Monthly Vital Statistics Report, Vital Statistics of the United States,* and unpublished data.

U.S. Department of Transportation, Federal Highway Administration, 400 Seventh Street, SW, Washington, D.C. 20590 (202) 366-0660; *Fatal and Injury Accident Rates on Public Roads in the U.S.,* and *Fatal Accident Reporting System.*

U.S. Department of Transportation, Federal Railroad Administration, 400 Seventh Street, SW, Washington, D.C. 20590 (202) 366-0881; *Accident Bulletin.*

U.S. Department of Transportation, National Highway Traffic Safety Administration, 400 Seventh Street, SW, Washington, D.C. 20590 (202) 366-9550; *Lives Saved by Child Restraints.*

ACCIDENTS AND FATALITIES - DEATHS AND DEATH RATES - FOREIGN COUNTRIES

World Health Organization, Avenue Appia, Office of Publications, CH-1211 Geneva, 27, Switzerland (Telephone Number in U.S. (518) 436-9686); *World Health Statistics Annual.*

ACCIDENTS AND FATALITIES - DEATHS AND DEATH RATES - INFANTS

U.S. Department of Health and Human Services, National Center for Health Statistics, 3700 East-West Highway, Hyattsville, Maryland 20782 (301) 436-8500; *Monthly Vital Statistics Report,* and *Vital Statistics of the United States.*

ACCIDENTS AND FATALITIES - DROWNINGS

U.S. Department of Health and Human Services, National Center for Health Statistics, 3700 East-West Highway, Hyattsville, Maryland 20782 (301) 436-8500; *Vital Statistics of the United States,* and unpublished data.

ACCIDENTS AND FATALITIES - FALLS

U.S. Department of Health and Human Services, National Center for Health Statistics, 3700 East-West Highway, Hyattsville, Maryland 20782 (301) 436-8500; *Vital Statistics of the United States,* and unpublished data.

ACCIDENTS AND FATALITIES - FIRES

National Fire Protection Association, One Batterymarch Park, Post Office Box 9101, Quincy, Massachusetts 02269-9101 (617) 770-3000; *NFPA Reports on U.S. Fire Loss* in *Fire Journal.*

ACCIDENTS AND FATALITIES - INDUSTRIAL

National Safety Council, 1121 Spring Lake Drive, Itasca, Illinois 60143-3201 (708) 285-1121; *Accident Facts.*

U.S. Department of Labor, Bureau of Labor Statistics, Two Massachusetts Avenue, NE, Washington, D.C. 20212 (202) 606-7828; *Occupational Injuries and Illnesses in the United States by Industry.*

U.S. Department of Labor, Mine Safety and Health Administration, 4015 Wilson Boulevard, Arlington, Virginia 22203 (703) 235-1452; unpublished data.

ACCIDENTS AND FATALITIES - MOTOR VEHICLES

American Automobile Manufacturers Association, 1401 H Street, NW, Suite 900, Washington, D.C. 20005 (202) 326-5500; *Motor Vehicle Facts and Figures.*

National Safety Council, 1121 Spring Lake Drive, Itasca, Illinois 60143-3201 (708) 285-1121; *Accident Facts.*

U.S. Department of Health and Human Services, National Center for Health Statistics, 3700 East-West Highway, Hyattsville, Maryland 20782 (301) 436-8500; *Monthly Vital Statistics Report, Vital Statistics of the United States,* and unpublished data.

U.S. Department of Transportation, Federal Highway Administration, 400 Seventh Street, SW, Washington, D.C. 20590 (202) 366-0660; *Fatal and Injury Accident Rates on Public Roads in the U.S.,* and *Selected Highway Statistics and Charts.*

U.S. Department of Transportation, National Highway Traffic Safety Administration, 400 Seventh Street, SW, Washington, D.C. 20590 (202) 366-9550; *Fatal Accident Reporting System.*

ACCIDENTS AND FATALITIES - MOTORCYCLE

Insurance Information Institute, 110 William Street, New York, New York 10038 (212) 669-9200; *Insurance Facts.*

National Safety Council, 1121 Spring Lake Drive, Itasca, Illinois 60143-3201 (708) 285-1121; *Accident Facts.*

U.S. Department of Transportation, Federal Highway Administration, 400 Seventh Street, SW, Washington, D.C. 20590 (202) 366-9550; *General Estimates System.*

U.S. Department of Transportation, National Highway Traffic Safety Administration, 400 Seventh Street, SW, Washington, D.C. 20590 (202) 366-9550; *Fatal Accident Reporting System.*

ACCIDENTS AND FATALITIES - POLICE OFFICERS ASSAULTED - KILLED

U.S. Department of Justice, Federal Bureau of Investigation, Ninth Street and Pennsylvania Avenue, NW, Washington, D.C. 20535 (202) 324-3000; *Law Enforcement Officers Killed and Assaulted.*

ACCIDENTS AND FATALITIES - PRIVATE EXPENDITURES FOR SOCIAL WELFARE

U.S. Department of Health and Human Services, Social Security Administration, 6401 Security Boulevard, Baltimore, Maryland 21235 (410) 965-1234; *Annual Statistical Supplement to the Social Security Bulletin.*

ACCIDENTS AND FATALITIES - RAILROAD

Association of American Railroads, American Railroads Building, 50 F Street, NW, Washington, D.C. 20001 (212) 639-2333; *Analysis of Class I Railroads,* and *Railroad Facts, Statistics of Railroads of Class I.*

U.S. Department of Transportation, Federal Railroad Administration, 400 Seventh Street, SW, Washington, D.C. 20590 (202) 366-0881; *Accident Bulletin.*

ACCIDENTS AND FATALITIES - TANKER CASUALTIES

Tanker Advisory Center, Ten East End Avenue, New York, New York 10028 (212) 628-7686; *Worldwide Tanker Casualty Returns.*

ACCIDENTS AND FATALITIES - TRANSPORTATION

U.S. Department of Health and Human Services, National Center for Health Statistics, 3700 East-West Highway, Hyattsville, Maryland 20782 (301) 436-8500; *Vital Statistics of the United States.*

U.S. Department of Transportation, Bureau of Transportation Statistics, 400 Seventh Street, SW, Washington, D.C. 20590 (202) 366-DATA; *National Transportation Statistics Annual, Historical Compendium Information Report.*

U.S. Department of Transportation, Transportation Systems Center, Kendall Square, Cambridge, Massachusetts 02142 (617) 494-2224; *Transportation Safety Information Report.*

ACCIDENTS AND FATALITIES - WORK TIME LOST

National Safety Council, 1121 Spring Lake Drive, Itasca, Illinois 60143-3201 (708) 285-1121; *Accident Facts.*

ACCOUNTANTS AND AUDITORS

U.S. Department of Labor, Bureau of Labor Statistics, Two Massachusetts Avenue, NE, Washington, D.C. 20212 (202) 606-7828; *Employment and Earnings.*

ACCOUNTING, AUDITING AND BOOKKEEPING - EARNINGS

U.S. Department of Commerce, Bureau of the Census, Suitland, Maryland 20233 (301) 763-4040; *Census of Service Industries,* and *County Business Patterns.*

International Franchise Association, 1350 New York Avenue, Suite 900, Washington, D.C. 20005 (202) 628-8000; *Franchising in the Economy.*

ACCOUNTING, AUDITING, AND BOOKKEEPING - EMPLOYEES

U.S. Department of Commerce, Bureau of the Census, Suitland, Maryland 20233 (301) 763-4040; *County Business Patterns,* and *Census of Service Industries.*

ACCOUNTING, AUDITING, AND BOOKKEEPING - ESTABLISHMENTS

International Franchise Association, 1350 New York Avenue, Suite 900, Washington, D.C. 20005 (202) 628-8000; *Franchising in the Economy.*

U.S. Department of Commerce, Bureau of the Census, Suitland, Maryland 20233 (301) 763-4040; *County Business Patterns,* and *Census of Service Industries.*

ACCOUNTING, AUDITING, AND BOOKKEEPING - RECEIPTS

U.S. Department of Commerce, Bureau of the Census, Suitland, Maryland 20233 (301) 763-4040; *Census of Service Industries, Current Business Reports,* and *Service Annual Survey.*

ACQUIRED IMMUNODEFICIENCY SYNDROME (AIDS)

American Hospital Association, 840 North Lake Shore Drive, Chicago, Illinois 60611 (312) 280-6000; *Hospital Statistics,* and *Annual Survey of Hospitals.*

Intergovernmental Health Policy Project, George Washington University, 2021 K Street, NW, Suite 800, Washington, D.C. 20006 (202) 872-1445; *Intergovernmental AIDS Reports.*

U.S. Department of Health and Human Services, Center for Disease Control, 1600 Clifton Road, NE, Atlanta, Georgia 30333 (404) 639-3311; *Summary of Notifiable Diseases, United States, Morbidity and Mortality Weekly Report, Surveillance Report,* and unpublished data.

U.S. Department of Health and Human Services, National Center for Health Statistics, 3700 East-West Highway, Hyattsville, Maryland 20782 (301) 436-8500; *Health, United States, Monthly Vital Statistics Report, Vital Statistics of the United States,* and unpublished data.

ACQUISITION OF TERRITORY BY THE UNITED STATES

U.S. Department of Commerce, Bureau of the Census, Suitland, Maryland 20233 (301) 763-4040; unpublished data.

U.S. Department of the Interior, C Street between Eighteenth and Nineteenth Streets, NW, Washington, D.C. 20240 (202) 208-3171; *Areas of Acquisitions to the Territory of the United States.*

U.S. General Services Administration, General Services Building, Eighteenth and F Streets, NW, Washington, D.C. 20405 (202) 708-5082; *Inventory Report on Real Property Owned by the United States Throughout the World.*

ACTORS

U.S. Department of Labor, Bureau of Labor Statistics, Two Massachusetts Avenue, NE, Washington, D.C. 20212 (202) 606-7828; *Employment and Earnings.*

ADMISSION TO STATEHOOD

U.S. Department of Commerce, Bureau of the Census, Suitland, Maryland 20233 (301) 763-4040; *Census of Population and Housing,* and unpublished data.

ADOPTIVE FAMILIES

U.S. Department of Commerce, Bureau of the Census, Suitland, Maryland 20233 (301) 763-4040; *Current Population Reports.*

ADULT EDUCATION

U.S. Department of Education, National Center for Education Statistics, 400 Maryland Avenue, SW, Washington, D.C. 20202 (202) 708-5366; *Adult Education Profile.*

ADVERTISING - EARNINGS

U.S. Department of Commerce, Bureau of the Census, Suitland, Maryland 20233 (301) 763-4040; *County Business Patterns,* and *Census of Service Industries.*

U.S. Department of Labor, Bureau of Labor Statistics, Two Massachusetts Avenue, NE, Washington, D.C. 20212 (202) 606-7828; *Employment and Earnings,* and Bulletins 2370 and 2429.

ADVERTISING - EMPLOYEES

U.S. Department of Commerce, Bureau of the Census, Suitland, Maryland 20233 (301) 763-4040; *County Business Patterns,* and *Census of Service Industries.*

U.S. Department of Labor, Bureau of Labor Statistics, Two Massachusetts Avenue, NE, Washington, D.C. 20212 (202) 606-7828; *Employment and Earnings,* and Bulletins 2370 and 2429.

ADVERTISING - ESTABLISHMENTS

U.S. Department of Commerce, Bureau of the Census, Suitland, Maryland 20233 (301) 763-4040; *County Business Patterns,* and *Census of Service Industries.*

ADVERTISING - RECEIPTS

U.S. Department of Commerce, Bureau of the Census, Suitland, Maryland 20233 (301) 763-4040; *Current Business Reports, Census of Service Industries,* and *Service Annual Survey.*

AEROBICS

National Sporting Goods Association, Lake Center Plaza Building, 1699 Wall Street, Mount Prospect, Illinois 60056 (708) 439-4000; *Sports Participation in 1992: Series I,* and *The Sporting Goods Market in 1993.*

AERONAUTICS, CIVIL - See AIR TRANSPORTATION

AEROSPACE INDUSTRY - CAPITAL

U.S. Department of Commerce, International Trade Administration, Fourteenth Street between Constitution Avenue and E Street, NW, Washington, D.C. 20230 (202) 482-3809; *U.S. Industrial Outlook.*

AEROSPACE INDUSTRY - EARNINGS

U.S. Department of Commerce, International Trade Administration, Fourteenth Street between Constitution Avenue and E Street, NW, Washington, D.C. 20230 (202) 482-3809; *U.S. Industrial Outlook.*

U.S. Department of Labor, Bureau of Labor Statistics, Two Massachusetts Avenue, NE, Washington, D.C. 20212 (202) 606-7828; *Employment and Earnings,* and Bulletins 2370 and 2429.

AEROSPACE INDUSTRY - EMPLOYEES

U.S. Department of Commerce, International Trade Administration, Fourteenth Street between Constitution Avenue and E Street, NW, Washington, D.C. 20230 (202) 482-3809; *U.S. Industrial Outlook.*

U.S. Department of Transportation, Federal Aviation Administration, 800 Independence Avenue, SW, Washington, D.C. 20591 (202) 366-0881; *FAA Statistical Handbook of Aviation,* and unpublished data.

AEROSPACE INDUSTRY - FOREIGN TRADE

U.S. Department of Commerce, Bureau of the Census, Suitland, Maryland 20233 (301) 763-4040; *U.S. Merchandise Trade.*

U.S. Department of Commerce, International Trade Administration, Fourteenth Street between Constitution Avenue and E Street, NW, Washington, D.C. 20230 (202) 482-3809; *U.S. Industrial Outlook.*

AEROSPACE INDUSTRY - NEW ORDERS - BACKLOG

U.S. Department of Commerce, Bureau of the Census, Suitland, Maryland 20233 (301) 763-4040; *Current Industrial Reports.*

AEROSPACE INDUSTRY - SALES

Aerospace Industries Association of America, 1250 I Street, NW, Washington, D.C. 20005 (202) 371-8400; *Year-end Review and Forecast.*

Time Warner, 1675 Broadway, Rockefeller Center, New York, New York 10019 (212) 522-1212; *The Fortune Directories.*

U.S. Department of Commerce, Bureau of the Census, Suitland, Maryland 20233 (301) 763-4040; *Current Industrial Reports.*

AEROSPACE INDUSTRY - SHIPMENTS

U.S. Department of Commerce, International Trade Administration, Fourteenth Street between Constitution Avenue and E Street, NW, Washington, D.C. 20230 (202) 482-3809; *U.S. Industrial Outlook.*

Afghanistan - National Statistical Office

Central Statistics Office, Co-ordination Department, Post Office Box 2002, Kabul, Afghanistan.

Afghanistan - Primary Statistics Sources

Central Statistics Office, Co-ordination Department, Post Office Box 2002, Kabul, Afghanistan; *Statistical Yearbook,* and *Survey of Progress.*

AFGHANISTAN - AGRICULTURE

Asian Development Bank, P.O. Box 789, 1099 Manila, Philippines; *Key Indicators of Developing Asian and Pacific Countries.*

Central Statistics Office, Kabul, Afghanistan; *Afghan Agriculture In Figures.*

Euromonitor Publications Limited, 87-88 Turnmill Street, London EC1M 5QU, England; *International Marketing Data and Statistics.*

Facts on File, 460 Park Avenue South, New York, New York 10016 (800) 443-8323; *The New Book of World Rankings.*

Federal Statistical Office, Gustav - Stresemann - Ring 11, D-6200 Wiesbaden, Germany; *Afghanistan.*

Food and Agricultural Organization of the United Nations (FAO), Via delle Terme di Caracalla, 00100 Rome, Italy (Telephone Number in U.S. (202) 653-2400); *Production Yearbook, The State of Food and Agriculture,* and *Trade Yearbook.*

G.K. Hall and Company, 70 Lincoln Street, Boston, Massachusetts 02111 (617) 423-3990; *The World in Figures.*

Statistical Office of the United Nations, Publishing Service, New York, New York 10017 (800) 253-9646; *Statistical Yearbook,* and *Statistical Yearbook for Asia and the Pacific.*

Times Books, 201 East 50th Street, New York, New York 10022 (212) 751-2600; *The Economist Book of Vital World Statistics.*

AFGHANISTAN - AIRLINE SERVICE

The Economist Intelligence Unit (Asia) Limited, 10th Floor, Luk Kwok Centre, 72 Gloucester Road, Wanchai, Hong Kong (Phone Number in U.S. (800) 938-4685); *Asian Market Atlas.*

Facts on File, 460 Park Avenue South, New York, New York 10016 (800) 443-8323; *The New Book of World Rankings.*

G.K. Hall and Company, 70 Lincoln Street, Boston, Massachusetts 02111 (617) 423-3990; *The World in Figures.*

International Civil Aviation Organization, 1000 Sherbrooke Street West, Suite 400, Montreal, Quebec, Canada H3A 2R2; *Civil Aviation Statistics of the World.*

Statistical Office of the United Nations, Publishing Service, New York, New York 10017 (800) 253-9646; *Statistical Yearbook.*

Times Books, 201 East 50th Street, New York, New York 10022 (212) 751-2600; *The Economist Book of Vital World Statistics.*

AFGHANISTAN - ALUMINUM PRODUCTION AND CONSUMPTION - See AFGHANISTAN - MINING AND MINERAL PRODUCTS

AFGHANISTAN - ANIMAL HEALTH

Food and Agricultural Organization of the United Nations (FAO), Via delle Terme di Caracalla, 00100 Rome, Italy (Telephone Number in U.S. (202) 653-2400); *Animal Health Yearbook.*

AFGHANISTAN - AREA AND DENSITY OF POPULATION

Euromonitor Publications Limited, 87-88 Turnmill Street, London EC1M 5QU, England; *International Marketing Data and Statistics.*

Facts on File, 460 Park Avenue South, New York, New York 10016 (800) 443-8323; *The New Book of World Rankings.*

Federal Statistical Office, Gustav - Stresemann - Ring 11, D-6200 Wiesbaden, Germany; *Afghanistan.*

Food and Agricultural Organization of the United Nations (FAO) Via Delle Terme di Caracalla, 00100 Rome, Italy (Telephone Number in U.S. (202) 653-2400); *The State of Food and Agriculture.*

G.K. Hall and Company, 70 Lincoln Street, Boston, Massachusetts 02111 (617) 423-3990; *The World in Figures.*

Statistical Office of the United Nations, Publishing Service, New York, New York 10017 (800) 253-9646; *Statistical Yearbook.*

Times Books, 201 East 50th Street, New York, New York 10022 (212) 751-2600; *The Economist Book of Vital World Statistics.*

AFGHANISTAN - ARMS EXPORTS AND IMPORTS

U.S. Arms Control and Disarmament Agency, 320 Twenty-first Street, NW, Washington, D.C. 20451 (202) 647-8677; *World Military Expenditures and Arms Transfers.*

AFGHANISTAN - BALANCE OF PAYMENTS

The Economist Intelligence Unit, 111 West 57th Street, New York, New York 10019 (800) 938-4685; *The World Market Atlas.*

Federal Statistical Office, Gustav - Stresemann - Ring 11, D-6200 Wiesbaden, Germany; *Afghanistan.*

G.K. Hall and Company, 70 Lincoln Street, Boston, Massachusetts 02111 (617) 423-3990; *The World in Figures.*

International Monetary Fund, 700 Nineteenth Street, NW, Washington, D.C. 20431 (202) 623-7000; *International Financial Statistics.*

Times Books, 201 East 50th Street, New York, New York 10022 (212) 751-2600; *The Economist Book of Vital World Statistics.*

AFGHANISTAN - BANKING

Asian Development Bank, P.O. Box 789, 1099 Manila, Philippines; *Key Indicators of Developing Asian and Pacific Countries.*

Facts on File, 460 Park Avenue South, New York, New York 10016 (800) 443-8323; *The New Book of World Rankings.*

G.K. Hall and Company, 70 Lincoln Street, Boston, Massachusetts 02111 (617) 423-3990; *The World in Figures.*

International Monetary Fund, 700 Nineteenth Street, NW, Washington, D.C. 20431 (202) 623-7000; *International Financial Statistics.*

AFGHANISTAN - BARLEY PRODUCTION - See AFGHANISTAN - CROPS

AFGHANISTAN - BEER PRODUCTION

Facts on File, 460 Park Avenue South, New York, New York 10016 (800) 443-8323; *The New Book of World Rankings.*

AFGHANISTAN - BIRTH RATES

The Economist Intelligence Unit (Asia) Limited, 10th Floor, Luk Kwok Centre, 72 Gloucester Road, Wanchai, Hong Kong (Phone Number in U.S. (800) 938-4685); *Asian Market Atlas.*

Facts on File, 460 Park Avenue South, New York, New York 10016 (800) 443-8323; *The New Book of World Rankings.*

Statistical Office of the United Nations, Publishing Service, New York, New York 10017 (800) 253-9646; *Demographic Yearbook.*

Times Books, 201 East 50th Street, New York, New York 10022 (212) 751-2600; *The Economist Book of Vital World Statistics.*

AFGHANISTAN - BONDS

G.K. Hall and Company, 70 Lincoln Street, Boston, Massachusetts 02111 (617) 423-3990; *The World in Figures.*

AFGHANISTAN - BOOK PRODUCTION

G.K. Hall and Company, 70 Lincoln Street, Boston, Massachusetts 02111 (617) 423-3990; *The World in Figures.*

United Nations Educational, Scientific and Cultural Organization (UNESCO), 7 Place de Fontenoy, F-75700 Paris, France (Telephone Number in U.S. (212) 963-5981); *Statistical Yearbook.*

AFGHANISTAN - BROADCASTING

Billboard Limited, P.O. Box 9027, 1006 AA Amsterdam, The Netherlands (Telephone Number in U.S. (212) 764-7300); *World Radio TV Handbook.*

The Economist Intelligence Unit (Asia) Limited, 10th Floor, Luk Kwok Centre, 72 Gloucester Road, Wanchai, Hong Kong (Phone Number in U.S. (800) 938-4685); *Asian Market Atlas.*

G.K. Hall and Company, 70 Lincoln Street, Boston, Massachusetts 02111 (617) 423-3990; *The World in Figures.*

Times Books, 201 East 50th Street, New York, New York 10022 (212) 751-2600; *The Economist Book of Vital World Statistics.*

United Nations Educational, Scientific and Cultural Organization (UNESCO), 7 Place de Fontenoy, F-75700 Paris, France (Telephone Number in U.S. (212) 963-5981); *Statistical Yearbook.*

AFGHANISTAN - BUSINESS

G.K. Hall and Company, 70 Lincoln Street, Boston, Massachusetts 02111 (617) 423-3990; *The World in Figures.*

AFGHANISTAN - BUTTER PRODUCTION - See AFGHANISTAN - DAIRY PRODUCTS

AFGHANISTAN - CALORIE SUPPLY

Asian Development Bank, P.O. Box 789, 1099 Manila, Philippines; *Key Indicators of Developing Asian and Pacific Countries.*

Food and Agricultural Organization of the United Nations (FAO) Via Delle Terme di Caracalla, 00100 Rome, Italy (Telephone Number in U.S. (202) 653-2400); *The State of Food and Agriculture.*

AFGHANISTAN - CAPITAL INVESTMENT

Asian Development Bank, P.O. Box 789, 1099 Manila, Philippines; *Key Indicators of Developing Asian and Pacific Countries.*

AFGHANISTAN - CAPITAL REVENUE

Asian Development Bank, P.O. Box 789, 1099 Manila, Philippines; *Key Indicators of Developing Asian and Pacific Countries.*

AFGHANISTAN - CARPET EXPORTS

International Monetary Fund, 700 Nineteenth Street, NW, Washington, D.C. 20431 (202) 623-7000; *International Financial Statistics.*

AFGHANISTAN - CATTLE - See AFGHANISTAN - LIVESTOCK AND POULTRY

AFGHANISTAN - CEMENT PRODUCTION - See AFGHANISTAN - MINING AND MINERAL PRODUCTS

AFGHANISTAN - CHEESE PRODUCTION - See AFGHANISTAN - DAIRY PRODUCTS

AFGHANISTAN - CHEMICAL (ORGANIC) PRODUCTION - See AFGHANISTAN - MINING AND MINERAL PRODUCTS

AFGHANISTAN - CHICKENS - See AFGHANISTAN - LIVESTOCK AND POULTRY

AFGHANISTAN - CIGARETTE PRODUCTION - See AFGHANISTAN - TOBACCO PRODUCTION

AFGHANISTAN - CLASS STRUCTURE

G.K. Hall and Company, 70 Lincoln Street, Boston, Massachusetts 02111 (617) 423-3990; *The World in Figures.*

AFGHANISTAN - CLIMATE

Facts on File, 460 Park Avenue South, New York, New York 10016 (800) 443-8323; *The New Book of World Rankings.*

G.K. Hall and Company, 70 Lincoln Street, Boston, Massachusetts 02111 (617) 423-3990; *The World in Figures.*

AFGHANISTAN - COAL PRODUCTION - See AFGHANISTAN - MINING AND MINERAL PRODUCTS

AFGHANISTAN - COFFEE PRODUCTION - See AFGHANISTAN - CROPS

AFGHANISTAN - COMMUNICATIONS

Federal Statistical Office, Gustav - Stresemann - Ring 11, D-6200 Wiesbaden, Germany; *Afghanistan.*

G.K. Hall and Company, 70 Lincoln Street, Boston, Massachusetts 02111 (617) 423-3990; *The World in Figures.*

Statistical Office of the United Nations, Publishing Service, New York, New York 10017 (800) 253-9646; *Statistical Yearbook for Asia and the Pacific.*

AFGHANISTAN - CONSTRUCTION INDUSTRY

Facts on File, 460 Park Avenue South, New York, New York 10016 (800) 443-8323; *The New Book of World Rankings.*

Statistical Office of the United Nations, Publishing Service, New York, New York 10017 (800) 253-9646; *Construction Statistics Yearbook.*

AFGHANISTAN - CONSUMER PRICE INDEX

Asian Development Bank, P.O. Box 789, 1099 Manila, Philippines; *Key Indicators of Developing Asian and Pacific Countries.*
Federal Statistical Office, Gustav - Stresemann - Ring 11, D-6200 Wiesbaden, Germany; *Afghanistan.*

G.K. Hall and Company, 70 Lincoln Street, Boston, Massachusetts 02111 (617) 423-3990; *The World in Figures.*

Statistical Office of the United Nations, Publishing Service, New York, New York 10017 (800) 253-9646; *Statistical Yearbook.*

AFGHANISTAN - CONSUMER PRICES

Federal Statistical Office, Gustav - Stresemann - Ring 11, D-6200 Wiesbaden, Germany; *Afghanistan.*

International Labour Office, I.L.O. Publications, CH-1211, Geneva 22, Switzerland; *Yearbook of Labour Statistics.*

Times Books, 201 East 50th Street, New York, New York 10022 (212) 751-2600; *The Economist Book of Vital World Statistics.*

AFGHANISTAN - CONSUMPTION

G.K. Hall and Company, 70 Lincoln Street, Boston, Massachusetts 02111 (617) 423-3990; *The World in Figures.*

AFGHANISTAN - COPPER PRODUCTION -See AFGHANISTAN - MINING AND MINERAL PRODUCTS

AFGHANISTAN - CORN PRODUCTION - See AFGHANISTAN - CROPS

AFGHANISTAN - CORPORATE TAXES - See AFGHANISTAN - TAXATION

AFGHANISTAN - COTTON - See AFGHANISTAN - CROPS

AFGHANISTAN - CROPS

Asian Development Bank, P.O. Box 789, 1099 Manila, Philippines; *Key Indicators of Developing Asian and Pacific Countries.*

Facts on File, 460 Park Avenue South, New York, New York 10016 (800) 443-8323; *The New Book of World Rankings.*

Food and Agricultural Organization of the United Nations (FAO) Via Delle Terme di Caracalla, 00100 Rome, Italy (Telephone Number in U.S. (202) 653-2400); *The State of Food and Agriculture.*

G.K. Hall and Company, 70 Lincoln Street, Boston, Massachusetts 02111 (617) 423-3990; *The World in Figures.*

International Monetary Fund, 700 Nineteenth Street, NW, Washington, D.C. 20431 (202) 623-7000; *International Financial Statistics.*

Statistical Office of the United Nations, Publishing Service, New York, New York 10017 (800) 253-9646; *Statistical Yearbook.*

AFGHANISTAN - CUSTOMS DUTIES

G.K. Hall and Company, 70 Lincoln Street, Boston, Massachusetts 02111 (617) 423-3990; *The World in Figures.*

AFGHANISTAN - DAIRY PRODUCTS

Facts on File, 460 Park Avenue South, New York, New York 10016 (800) 443-8323; *The New Book of World Rankings.*

Food and Agricultural Organization of the United Nations (FAO) Via Delle Terme di Caracalla, 00100 Rome, Italy (Telephone Number in U.S. (202) 653-2400); *The State of Food and Agriculture.*

Statistical Office of the United Nations, Publishing Service, New York, New York 10017 (800) 253-9646; *Statistical Yearbook.*

AFGHANISTAN - DEATH RATES

The Economist Intelligence Unit (Asia) Limited, 10th Floor, Luk Kwok Centre, 72 Gloucester Road, Wanchai, Hong Kong (Phone Number in U.S. (800) 938-4685); *Asian Market Atlas.*

G.K. Hall and Company, 70 Lincoln Street, Boston, Massachusetts 02111 (617) 423-3990; *The World in Figures.*

Times Books, 201 East 50th Street, New York, New York 10022 (212) 751-2600; *The Economist Book of Vital World Statistics.*

World Health Organization, Office of Publications, Avenue Appia, CH-1211 Geneva 27, Switzerland (Telephone Number in U.S. (518) 436-9686); *World Health Statistics Annual.*

AFGHANISTAN - DEFENSE EXPENDITURES

G.K. Hall and Company, 70 Lincoln Street, Boston, Massachusetts 02111 (617) 423-3990; *The World in Figures.*

U.S. Arms Control and Disarmament Agency, 320 Twenty-first Street, NW, Washington, D.C. 20451 (202) 647-8677; *World Military Expenditures and Arms Transfers.*

AFGHANISTAN - DEMOGRAPHY

The Economist Intelligence Unit (Asia) Limited, 10th Floor, Luk Kwok Centre, 72 Gloucester Road, Wanchai, Hong Kong (Phone Number in U.S. (800) 938-4685); *Asian Market Atlas.*

The Economist Intelligence Unit, 111 West 57th Street, New York, New York 10019 (800) 938-4685; *The World Market Atlas.*

Facts on File, 460 Park Avenue South, New York, New York 10016 (800) 443-8323; *The New Book of World Rankings.*

Federal Statistical Office, Gustav - Stresemann - Ring 11, D-6200 Wiesbaden, Germany; *Afghanistan.*

G.K. Hall and Company, 70 Lincoln Street, Boston, Massachusetts 02111 (617) 423-3990; *The World in Figures.*

AFGHANISTAN - DEVELOPMENT ASSISTANCE

Asian Development Bank, P.O. Box 789, 1099 Manila, Philippines; *Key Indicators of Developing Asian and Pacific Countries.*

G.K. Hall and Company, 70 Lincoln Street, Boston, Massachusetts 02111 (617) 423-3990; *The World in Figures.*

Statistical Office of the United Nations, Publishing Service, New York, New York 10017 (800) 253-9646; *Statistical Yearbook.*

AFGHANISTAN - DIAMOND PRODUCTION - See AFGHANISTAN - MINING AND MINERAL PRODUCTS

AFGHANISTAN - DISEASES

Economist Publications Limited, 25 St. James's Street, London SW1A 1HG England; *The World in Figures.*

G.K. Hall and Company, 70 Lincoln Street, Boston, Massachusetts 02111 (617) 423-3990; *The World in Figures.*

World Health Organization, Office of Publications, Avenue Appia, CH-1211 Geneva 27, Switzerland (Telephone Number in U.S. (518) 436-9686); *World Health Statistics Annual.*

AFGHANISTAN - DIVORCE

Facts on File, 460 Park Avenue South, New York, New York 10016 (800) 443-8323; *The New Book of World Rankings.*

Statistical Office of the United Nations, Publishing Service, New York, New York 10017 (800) 253-9646; *Demographic Yearbook.*

AFGHANISTAN - DOMESTIC PRODUCT

G.K. Hall and Company, 70 Lincoln Street, Boston, Massachusetts 02111 (617) 423-3990; *The World in Figures.*

AFGHANISTAN - ECONOMY

Asian Development Bank, P.O. Box 789, 1099 Manila, Philippines; *Key Indicators of Developing Asian and Pacific Countries.*

Euromonitor Publications Limited, 87-88 Turnmill Street, London EC1M 5QU, England; *International Marketing Data and Statistics.*

Facts on File, 460 Park Avenue South, New York, New York 10016 (800) 443-8323; *The New Book of World Rankings.*

Federal Statistical Office, Gustav - Stresemann - Ring 11, D-6200 Wiesbaden, Germany; *Afghanistan.*

G.K. Hall and Company, 70 Lincoln Street, Boston, Massachusetts 02111 (617) 423-3990; *The World in Figures.*

AFGHANISTAN - EDUCATION

The Economist Intelligence Unit (Asia) Limited, 10th Floor, Luk Kwok Centre, 72 Gloucester Road, Wanchai, Hong Kong (Phone Number in U.S. (800) 938-4685); *Asian Market Atlas.*

The Economist Intelligence Unit, 111 West 57th Street, New York, New York 10019 (800) 938-4685; *The World Market Atlas.*

Facts on File, 460 Park Avenue South, New York, New York 10016 (800) 443-8323; *The New Book of World Rankings.*

Federal Statistical Office, Gustav - Stresemann - Ring 11, D-6200 Wiesbaden, Germany; *Afghanistan.*

G.K. Hall and Company, 70 Lincoln Street, Boston, Massachusetts 02111 (617) 423-3990; *The World in Figures.*

Statistical Office of the United Nations, Publishing Service, New York, New York 10017 (800) 253-9646; *Statistical Yearbook for Asia and the Pacific.*

Times Books, 201 East 50th Street, New York, New York 10022 (212) 751-2600; *The Economist Book of Vital World Statistics.*

United Nations Educational, Scientific and Cultural Organization (UNESCO), 7 Place de Fontenoy, F-75700 Paris, France (Telephone Number in U.S. (212) 963-5981); *Statistical Yearbook.*

AFGHANISTAN - EGG PRODUCTION - See AFGHANISTAN - DAIRY PRODUCTS

AFGHANISTAN - ELECTRICITY

Asian Development Bank, P.O. Box 789, 1099 Manila, Philippines; *Key Indicators of Developing Asian and Pacific Countries.*

Facts on File, 460 Park Avenue South, New York, New York 10016 (800) 443-8323; *The New Book of World Rankings.*

Statistical Office of the United Nations, Publishing Service, New York, New York 10017 (800) 253-9646; *Electric Power in Asia and the Pacific,* and *Statistical Yearbook.*

Times Books, 201 East 50th Street, New York, New York 10022 (212) 751-2600; *The Economist Book of Vital World Statistics.*

AFGHANISTAN - EMPLOYMENT

Euromonitor Publications Limited, 87-88 Turnmill Street, London EC1M 5QU, England; *International Marketing Data and Statistics.*

Facts on File, 460 Park Avenue South, New York, New York 10016 (800) 443-8323; *The New Book of World Rankings.*

Federal Statistical Office, Gustav - Stresemann - Ring 11, D-6200 Wiesbaden, Germany; *Afghanistan.*

International Labour Office, I.L.O. Publications, CH-1211, Geneva 22, Switzerland; *Yearbook of Labour Statistics.*

AFGHANISTAN - ENERGY

Facts on File, 460 Park Avenue South, New York, New York 10016 (800) 443-8323; *The New Book of World Rankings.*

Food and Agricultural Organization of the United Nations (FAO) Via Delle Terme di Caracalla, 00100 Rome, Italy (Telephone Number in U.S. (202) 653-2400); *The State of Food and Agriculture.*

G.K. Hall and Company, 70 Lincoln Street, Boston, Massachusetts 02111 (617) 423-3990; *The World in Figures.*

Statistical Office of the United Nations, Publishing Service, New York, New York 10017 (800) 253-9646; *Energy Statistics Yearbook,* and *Statistical Yearbook.*

Times Books, 201 East 50th Street, New York, New York 10022 (212) 751-2600; *The Economist Book of Vital World Statistics.*

AFGHANISTAN - EXCHANGE RATES

Asian Development Bank, P.O. Box 789, 1099 Manila, Philippines; *Key Indicators of Developing Asian and Pacific Countries.*

The Economist Intelligence Unit, 111 West 57th Street, New York, New York 10019 (800) 938-4685; *The Asian Market Atlas.*

Euromonitor Publications Limited, 87-88 Turnmill Street, London EC1M 5QU, England; *International Marketing Data and Statistics.*

International Civil Aviation Organization, 1000 Sherbrooke Street West, Suite 400, Montreal, Quebec, Canada H3A 2R2; *Civil Aviation Statistics of the World.*

International Monetary Fund, 700 Nineteenth Street, NW, Washington, D.C. 20431 (202) 623-7000; *International Financial Statistics.*

Statistical Office of the United Nations, Publishing Service, New York, New York 10017 (800) 253-9646; *Statistical Yearbook.*

AFGHANISTAN - EXPORTS

Asian Development Bank, P.O. Box 789, 1099 Manila, Philippines; *Key Indicators of Developing Asian and Pacific Countries.*

The Economist Intelligence Unit (Asia) Limited, 10th Floor, Luk Kwok Centre, 72 Gloucester Road, Wanchai, Hong Kong (Phone Number in U.S. (800) 938-4685); *Asian Market Atlas.*

The Economist Intelligence Unit, 111 West 57th Street, New York, New York 10019 (800) 938-4685; *The World Market Atlas.*

Euromonitor Publications Limited, 87-88 Turnmill Street, London EC1M 5QU, England; *International Marketing Data and Statistics.*

Food and Agricultural Organization of the United Nations (FAO) Via Delle Terme di Caracalla, 00100 Rome, Italy (Telephone Number in U.S. (202) 653-2400); *The State of Food and Agriculture.*

G.K. Hall and Company, 70 Lincoln Street, Boston, Massachusetts 02111 (617) 423-3990; *The World in Figures.*

International Monetary Fund, 700 Nineteenth Street, NW, Washington, D.C. 20431 (202) 623-7000; *Direction of Trade Statistics,* and *International Financial Statistics.*

Statistical Office of the United Nations, Publishing Service, New York, New York 10017 (800) 253-9646; *Statistical Yearbook.*

Times Books, 201 East 50th Street, New York, New York 10022 (212) 751-2600; *The Economist Book of Vital World Statistics.*

AFGHANISTAN - EXTERNAL FINANCING

Asian Development Bank, P.O. Box 789, 1099 Manila, Philippines; *Key Indicators of Developing Asian and Pacific Countries.*

AFGHANISTAN - EXTERNAL INDEBTEDNESS

Asian Development Bank, P.O. Box 789, 1099 Manila, Philippines; *Key Indicators of Developing Asian and Pacific Countries.*

AFGHANISTAN - EXTERNAL TRADE

Asian Development Bank, P.O. Box 789, 1099 Manila, Philippines; *Key Indicators of Developing Asian and Pacific Countries.*

Central Statistics Office, Kabul, Afghanistan; *Exports of Merchandise from Afghanistan.*

Food and Agricultural Organization of the United Nations (FAO) Via Delle Terme di Caracalla, 00100 Rome, Italy (Telephone Number in U.S. (202) 653-2400); *The State of Food and Agriculture,* and *Trade Yearbook.*

G.K. Hall and Company, 70 Lincoln Street, Boston, Massachusetts 02111 (617) 423-3990; *The World in Figures.*

Statistical Office of the United Nations, Publishing Service, New York, New York 10017 (800) 253-9646; *Statistical Yearbook*, and *Statistical Yearbook for Asia and the Pacific*.

AFGHANISTAN - FABRIC PRODUCTION - See AFGHANISTAN - TEXTILE INDUSTRY

AFGHANISTAN - FARM CROPS - See AFGHANISTAN - CROPS

AFGHANISTAN - FEMALE WORKING POPULATION - See AFGHANISTAN - EMPLOYMENT

AFGHANISTAN - FERTILITY RATES

The Economist Intelligence Unit (Asia) Limited, 10th Floor, Luk Kwok Centre, 72 Gloucester Road, Wanchai, Hong Kong (Phone Number in U.S. (800) 938-4685); *Asian Market Atlas*.

Facts on File, 460 Park Avenue South, New York, New York 10016 (800) 443-8323; *The New Book of World Rankings*.

Times Books, 201 East 50th Street, New York, New York 10022 (212) 751-2600; *The Economist Book of Vital World Statistics*.

AFGHANISTAN - FERTILIZER PRODUCTION AND CONSUMPTION

Food and Agricultural Organization of the United Nations (FAO), Via delle Terme di Caracalla, 00100 Rome, Italy (Telephone Number in U.S. (202) 653-2400); *Fertilizer Yearbook*, and *The State of Food and Agriculture*.

Statistical Office of the United Nations, Publishing Service, New York, New York 10017 (800) 253-9646; *Statistical Yearbook*.

AFGHANISTAN - FETAL MORTALITY

Statistical Office of the United Nations, Publishing Service, New York, New York 10017 (800) 253-9646; *Demographic Yearbook*.

AFGHANISTAN - FILM - See AFGHANISTAN - MOTION PICTURES

AFGHANISTAN - FINANCE

Asian Development Bank, P.O. Box 789, 1099 Manila, Philippines; *Key Indicators of Developing Asian and Pacific Countries*.

Facts on File, 460 Park Avenue South, New York, New York 10016 (800) 443-8323; *The New Book of World Rankings*.

Federal Statistical Office, Gustav - Stresemann - Ring 11, D-6200 Wiesbaden, Germany; *Afghanistan*.

G.K. Hall and Company, 70 Lincoln Street, Boston, Massachusetts 02111 (617) 423-3990; *The World in Figures*.

International Monetary Fund, 700 Nineteenth Street, NW, Washington, D.C. 20431 (202) 623-7000; *International Financial Statistics*.

Statistical Office of the United Nations, Publishing Service, New York, New York 10017 (800) 253-9646; *Statistical Yearbook for Asia and the Pacific*.

AFGHANISTAN - FISHERIES

Facts on File, 460 Park Avenue South, New York, New York 10016 (800) 443-8323; *The New Book of World Rankings*.

Federal Statistical Office, Gustav - Stresemann - Ring 11, D-6200 Wiesbaden, Germany; *Afghanistan*.

Food and Agricultural Organization of the United Nations (FAO) Via Delle Terme di Caracalla, 00100 Rome, Italy (Telephone Number in U.S. (202) 653-2400); *The State of Food and Agriculture*, and *Yearbook of Fishery Statistics*.

Statistical Office of the United Nations, Publishing Service, New York, New York 10017 (800) 253-9646; *Statistical Yearbook*.

AFGHANISTAN - FOOD

Food and Agricultural Organization of the United Nations (FAO) Via Delle Terme di Caracalla, 00100 Rome, Italy (Telephone Number in U.S. (202) 653-2400); *Production Yearbook*, and *The State of Food and Agriculture*.

G.K. Hall and Company, 70 Lincoln Street, Boston, Massachusetts 02111 (617) 423-3990; *The World in Figures*.

Statistical Office of the United Nations, Publishing Service, New York, New York 10017 (800) 253-9646; *Statistical Yearbook for Asia and the Pacific*.

AFGHANISTAN - FOREIGN AID

G.K. Hall and Company, 70 Lincoln Street, Boston, Massachusetts 02111 (617) 423-3990; *The World in Figures*.

AFGHANISTAN - FOREIGN TRADE

Asian Development Bank, P.O. Box 789, 1099 Manila, Philippines; *Key Indicators of Developing Asian and Pacific Countries*.

The Economist Intelligence Unit (Asia) Limited, 10th Floor, Luk Kwok Centre, 72 Gloucester Road, Wanchai, Hong Kong (Phone Number in U.S. (800) 938-4685); *Asian Market Atlas*.

Euromonitor Publications Limited, 87-88 Turnmill Street, London EC1M 5QU, England; *International Marketing Data and Statistics*.

Facts on File, 460 Park Avenue South, New York, New York 10016 (800) 443-8323; *The New Book of World Rankings*.

Federal Statistical Office, Gustav - Stresemann - Ring 11, D-6200 Wiesbaden, Germany; *Afghanistan*.

G.K. Hall and Company, 70 Lincoln Street, Boston, Massachusetts 02111 (617) 423-3990; *The World in Figures*.

Organisation for Economic Co-operation and Development (OECD), 2 rue Andre-Pascal, 75 Paris 16, France (Telephone Number in U.S. (202) 785-6323); *Trade by Commodities*.

Statistical Office of the United Nations, Publishing Service, New York, New York 10017 (800) 253-9646; *International Trade Statistics Yearbook*, and *Statistical Yearbook*, and *Trade in Manufactures of Developing Countries*.

AFGHANISTAN - FORESTRY AND FOREST PRODUCTS

The Economist Intelligence Unit (Asia) Limited, 10th Floor, Luk Kwok Centre, 72 Gloucester Road, Wanchai, Hong Kong (Phone Number in U.S. (800) 938-4685); *Asian Market Atlas*.

Facts on File, 460 Park Avenue South, New York, New York 10016 (800) 443-8323; *The New Book of World Rankings*.

Federal Statistical Office, Gustav - Stresemann - Ring 11, D-6200 Wiesbaden, Germany; *Afghanistan.*

Food and Agricultural Organization of the United Nations (FAO) Via Delle Terme di Caracalla, 00100 Rome, Italy (Telephone Number in U.S. (202) 653-2400); *The State of Food and Agriculture,* and *Yearbook of Forest Products.*

G.K. Hall and Company, 70 Lincoln Street, Boston, Massachusetts 02111 (617) 423-3990; *The World in Figures.*

Statistical Office of the United Nations, Publishing Service, New York, New York 10017 (800) 253-9646; *Statistical Yearbook.*

United Nations Educational, Scientific and Cultural Organization (UNESCO), 7 Place de Fontenoy, F-75700 Paris, France (Telephone Number in U.S. (212) 963-5981); *Statistical Yearbook.*

AFGHANISTAN - FRUIT EXPORTS - See AFGHANISTAN - CROPS

AFGHANISTAN - GAS - See AFGHANISTAN - MINING AND MINERAL PRODUCTS

AFGHANISTAN - GENERAL INDUSTRIAL STATISTICS

Federal Statistical Office, Gustav - Stresemann - Ring 11, D-6200 Wiesbaden, Germany; *Afghanistan.*

Statistical Office of the United Nations, Publishing Service, New York, New York 10017 (800) 253-9646; *Industrial Statistics Yearbook.*

AFGHANISTAN - GENERAL MORTALITY

Statistical Office of the United Nations, Publishing Service, New York, New York 10017 (800) 253-9646; *Demographic Yearbook.*

AFGHANISTAN - GEOGRAPHIC DATA

Facts on File, 460 Park Avenue South, New York, New York 10016 (800) 443-8323; *The New Book of World Rankings.*

Federal Statistical Office, Gustav - Stresemann - Ring 11, D-6200 Wiesbaden, Germany; *Afghanistan.*

AFGHANISTAN - GOATS - See AFGHANISTAN - LIVESTOCK AND POULTRY

AFGHANISTAN - GOLD HOLDINGS

International Monetary Fund, 700 Nineteenth Street, NW, Washington, D.C. 20431 (202) 623-7000; *International Financial Statistics.*

Statistical Office of the United Nations, Publishing Service, New York, New York 10017 (800) 253-9646; *Statistical Yearbook.*

AFGHANISTAN - GOLD PRODUCTION AND CONSUMPTION - See AFGHANISTAN - MINING AND MINERAL PRODUCTS

AFGHANISTAN - GOVERNMENT

Asian Development Bank, P.O. Box 789, 1099 Manila, Philippines; *Key Indicators of Developing Asian and Pacific Countries.*

G.K. Hall and Company, 70 Lincoln Street, Boston, Massachusetts 02111 (617) 423-3990; *The World in Figures.*

AFGHANISTAN - GRAIN PRODUCTION - See AFGHANISTAN - CROPS

AFGHANISTAN - GROSS DOMESTIC PRODUCT

Asian Development Bank, P.O. Box 789, 1099 Manila, Philippines; *Key Indicators of Developing Asian and Pacific Countries.*

The Economist Intelligence Unit (Asia) Limited, 10th Floor, Luk Kwok Centre, 72 Gloucester Road, Wanchai, Hong Kong (Phone Number in U.S. (800) 938-4685); *Asian Market Atlas.*

The Economist Intelligence Unit, 111 West 57th Street, New York, New York 10019 (800) 938-4685; *The World Market Atlas.*

Euromonitor Publications Limited, 87-88 Turnmill Street, London EC1M 5QU, England; *International Marketing Data and Statistics.*

Facts on File, 460 Park Avenue South, New York, New York 10016 (800) 443-8323; *The New Book of World Rankings.*

G.K. Hall and Company, 70 Lincoln Street, Boston, Massachusetts 02111 (617) 423-3990; *The World in Figures.*

Statistical Office of the United Nations, Publishing Service, New York, New York 10017 (800) 253-9646; *Statistical Yearbook.*

Times Books, 201 East 50th Street, New York, New York 10022 (212) 751-2600; *The Economist Book of Vital World Statistics.*

AFGHANISTAN - GROSS NATIONAL PRODUCT

Asian Development Bank, P.O. Box 789, 1099 Manila, Philippines; *Key Indicators of Developing Asian and Pacific Countries.*

Euromonitor Publications Limited, 87-88 Turnmill Street, London EC1M 5QU, England; *International Marketing Data and Statistics.*

U.S. Arms Control and Disarmament Agency, 320 Twenty-first Street, NW, Washington, D.C. 20451 (202) 647-8677; *World Military Expenditures and Arms Transfers.*

AFGHANISTAN - HEALTH

The Economist Intelligence Unit (Asia) Limited, 10th Floor, Luk Kwok Centre, 72 Gloucester Road, Wanchai, Hong Kong (Phone Number in U.S. (800) 938-4685); *Asian Market Atlas.*

Facts on File, 460 Park Avenue South, New York, New York 10016 (800) 443-8323; *The New Book of World Rankings.*

Federal Statistical Office, Gustav - Stresemann - Ring 11, D-6200 Wiesbaden, Germany; *Afghanistan.*

G.K. Hall and Company, 70 Lincoln Street, Boston, Massachusetts 02111 (617) 423-3990; *The World in Figures.*

Statistical Office of the United Nations, Publishing Service, New York, New York 10017 (800) 253-9646; *Statistical Yearbook.*

Times Books, 201 East 50th Street, New York, New York 10022 (212) 751-2600; *The Economist Book of Vital World Statistics.*

World Health Organization, Office of Publications, Avenue Appia, CH-1211 Geneva 27, Switzerland (Telephone Number in U.S. (518) 436-9686); *World Health Statistics Annual.*

AFGHANISTAN - HIDE PRODUCTION

Food and Agricultural Organization of the United Nations (FAO), Via delle Terme di Caracalla, 00100 Rome, Italy (Telephone Number in U.S. (202) 653-2400); *Production Yearbook.*

AFGHANISTAN - HIGHWAYS

The Economist Intelligence Unit (Asia) Limited, 10th Floor, Luk Kwok Centre, 72 Gloucester Road, Wanchai, Hong Kong (Phone Number in U.S. (800) 938-4685); *Asian Market Atlas.*

G.K. Hall and Company, 70 Lincoln Street, Boston, Massachusetts 02111 (617) 423-3990; *The World in Figures.*

International Road Federation, 525 School Street, SW, Washington, D.C. 20024 (202) 554-2106; *World Road Statistics.*

AFGHANISTAN - HORSES - See AFGHANISTAN - LIVESTOCK AND POULTRY

AFGHANISTAN - HOURS OF WORK - See AFGHANISTAN - EMPLOYMENT

AFGHANISTAN - HOUSING

Facts on File, 460 Park Avenue South, New York, New York 10016 (800) 443-8323; *The New Book of World Rankings.*

AFGHANISTAN - ILLITERATE POPULATION

The Economist Intelligence Unit, 111 West 57th Street, New York, New York 10019 (800) 938-4685; *The World Market Atlas.*

G.K. Hall and Company, 70 Lincoln Street, Boston, Massachusetts 02111 (617) 423-3990; *The World in Figures.*

United Nations Educational, Scientific and Cultural Organization (UNESCO), 7 Place de Fontenoy, F-75700 Paris, France (Telephone Number in U.S. (212) 963-5981); *Statistical Yearbook.*

AFGHANISTAN - IMPORTS

Asian Development Bank, P.O. Box 789, 1099 Manila, Philippines; *Key Indicators of Developing Asian and Pacific Countries.*

The Economist Intelligence Unit (Asia) Limited, 10th Floor, Luk Kwok Centre, 72 Gloucester Road, Wanchai, Hong Kong (Phone Number in U.S. (800) 938-4685); *Asian Market Atlas.*

The Economist Intelligence Unit, 111 West 57th Street, New York, New York 10019 (800) 938-4685; *The World Market Atlas.*

Euromonitor Publications Limited, 87-88 Turnmill Street, London EC1M 5QU, England; *International Marketing Data and Statistics.*

Food and Agricultural Organization of the United Nations (FAO) Via Delle Terme di Caracalla, 00100 Rome, Italy (Telephone Number in U.S. (202) 653-2400); *The State of Food and Agriculture.*

G.K. Hall and Company, 70 Lincoln Street, Boston, Massachusetts 02111 (617) 423-3990; *The World in Figures.*

International Monetary Fund, 700 Nineteenth Street, NW, Washington, D.C. 20431 (202) 623-7000; *Direction of Trade Statistics,* and *International Financial Statistics.*

Statistical Office of the United Nations, Publishing Service, New York, New York 10017 (800) 253-9646; *Trade in Manufactures of Developing Countries.*

AFGHANISTAN - INDUSTRY

Euromonitor Publications Limited, 87-88 Turnmill Street, London EC1M 5QU, England; *International Marketing Data and Statistics.*

Facts on File, 460 Park Avenue South, New York, New York 10016 (800) 443-8323; *The New Book of World Rankings.*

Federal Statistical Office, Gustav - Stresemann - Ring 11, D-6200 Wiesbaden, Germany; *Afghanistan.*

G.K. Hall and Company, 70 Lincoln Street, Boston, Massachusetts 02111 (617) 423-3990; *The World in Figures.*

International Labour Office, I.L.O. Publications, CH-1211, Geneva 22, Switzerland; *Yearbook of Labour Statistics.*

Statistical Office of the United Nations, Publishing Service, New York, New York 10017 (800) 253-9646; *Statistical Yearbook for Asia and the Pacific.*

Times Books, 201 East 50th Street, New York, New York 10022 (212) 751-2600; *The Economist Book of Vital World Statistics.*

AFGHANISTAN - INFANT AND MATERNAL MORTALITY

The Economist Intelligence Unit (Asia) Limited, 10th Floor, Luk Kwok Centre, 72 Gloucester Road, Wanchai, Hong Kong (Phone Number in U.S. (800) 938-4685); *Asian Market Atlas.*

Statistical Office of the United Nations, Publishing Service, New York, New York 10017 (800) 253-9646; *Demographic Yearbook.*

Times Books, 201 East 50th Street, New York, New York 10022 (212) 751-2600; *The Economist Book of Vital World Statistics.*

AFGHANISTAN - INTERNAL TRADE

Statistical Office of the United Nations, Publishing Service, New York, New York 10017 (800) 253-9646; *Statistical Yearbook for Asia and the Pacific.*

AFGHANISTAN - INTERNATIONAL LIQUIDITY

International Monetary Fund, 700 Nineteenth Street, NW, Washington, D.C. 20431 (202) 623-7000; *International Financial Statistics.*

AFGHANISTAN - INTERNATIONAL RESERVES EXCLUDING GOLD

Asian Development Bank, P.O. Box 789, 1099 Manila, Philippines; *Key Indicators of Developing Asian and Pacific Countries.*

AFGHANISTAN - INTERNATIONAL STATISTICS

Asian Development Bank, P.O. Box 789, 1099 Manila, Philippines; *Key Indicators of Developing Asian and Pacific Countries.*

AFGHANISTAN - INVESTMENTS

International Monetary Fund, 700 Nineteenth Street, NW, Washington, D.C. 20431 (202) 623-7000; *International Financial Statistics.*

AFGHANISTAN - IRON ORE PRODUCTION AND CONSUMPTION - See AFGHANISTAN - MINING AND MINERAL PRODUCTS

AFGHANISTAN - IRRIGATION

Euromonitor Publications Limited, 87-88 Turnmill Street, London EC1M 5QU, England; *International Marketing Data and Statistics.*

AFGHANISTAN - LABOR FORCE

The Economist Intelligence Unit (Asia) Limited, 10th Floor, Luk Kwok Centre, 72 Gloucester Road, Wanchai, Hong Kong (Phone Number in U.S. (800) 938-4685); *Asian Market Atlas.*

Euromonitor Publications Limited, 87-88 Turnmill Street, London EC1M 5QU, England; *International Marketing Data and Statistics.*

Facts on File, 460 Park Avenue South, New York, New York 10016 (800) 443-8323; *The New Book of World Rankings.*

Food and Agricultural Organization of the United Nations (FAO) Via Delle Terme di Caracalla, 00100 Rome, Italy (Telephone Number in U.S. (202) 653-2400); *The State of Food and Agriculture.*

G.K. Hall and Company, 70 Lincoln Street, Boston, Massachusetts 02111 (617) 423-3990; *The World in Figures.*

AFGHANISTAN - LABOR PRODUCTIVITY

International Labour Office, I.L.O. Publications, CH-1211, Geneva 22, Switzerland; *Yearbook of Labour Statistics.*

AFGHANISTAN - LAND USE

Euromonitor Publications Limited, 87-88 Turnmill Street, London EC1M 5QU, England; *International Marketing Data and Statistics.*

Food and Agricultural Organization of the United Nations (FAO), Via delle Terme di Caracalla, 00100 Rome, Italy (Telephone Number in U.S. (202) 653-2400); *Production Yearbook.*

G.K. Hall and Company, 70 Lincoln Street, Boston, Massachusetts 02111 (617) 423-3990; *The World in Figures.*

AFGHANISTAN - LIBRARIES

Facts on File, 460 Park Avenue South, New York, New York 10016 (800) 443-8323; *The New Book of World Rankings.*

AFGHANISTAN - LIFE EXPECTANCY

The Economist Intelligence Unit (Asia) Limited, 10th Floor, Luk Kwok Centre, 72 Gloucester Road, Wanchai, Hong Kong (Phone Number in U.S. (800) 938-4685); *Asian Market Atlas.*

AFGHANISTAN - LIVESTOCK AND POULTRY

Euromonitor Publications Limited, 87-88 Turnmill Street, London EC1M 5QU, England; *International Marketing Data and Statistics.*

Facts on File, 460 Park Avenue South, New York, New York 10016 (800) 443-8323; *The New Book of World Rankings.*

Food and Agricultural Organization of the United Nations (FAO), Via delle Terme di Caracalla, 00100 Rome, Italy (Telephone Number in U.S. (202) 653-2400); *Production Yearbook,* and *The State of Food and Agriculture.*

G.K. Hall and Company, 70 Lincoln Street, Boston, Massachusetts 02111 (617) 423-3990; *The World in Figures.*

Statistical Office of the United Nations, Publishing Service, New York, New York 10017 (800) 253-9646; *Statistical Yearbook.*

AFGHANISTAN - LIVING LEVELS

G.K. Hall and Company, 70 Lincoln Street, Boston, Massachusetts 02111 (617) 423-3990; *The World in Figures.*

Times Books, 201 East 50th Street, New York, New York 10022 (212) 751-2600; *The Economist Book of Vital World Statistics.*

AFGHANISTAN - MAIL - NUMBER OF PIECES SENT OR RECEIVED

Statistical Office of the United Nations, Publishing Service, New York, New York 10017 (800) 253-9646; *Statistical Yearbook.*

AFGHANISTAN - MANPOWER

Statistical Office of the United Nations, Publishing Service, New York, New York 10017 (800) 253-9646; *Statistical Yearbook for Asia and the Pacific.*

AFGHANISTAN - MANUFACTURING

Asian Development Bank, P.O. Box 789, 1099 Manila, Philippines; *Key Indicators of Developing Asian and Pacific Countries.*

Facts on File, 460 Park Avenue South, New York, New York 10016 (800) 443-8323; *The New Book of World Rankings.*

G.K. Hall and Company, 70 Lincoln Street, Boston, Massachusetts 02111 (617) 423-3990; *The World in Figures.*

Statistical Office of the United Nations, Publishing Service, New York, New York 10017 (800) 253-9646; *Statistical Yearbook.*

AFGHANISTAN - MARRIAGE RATES

Facts on File, 460 Park Avenue South, New York, New York 10016 (800) 443-8323; *The New Book of World Rankings.*

Statistical Office of the United Nations, Publishing Service, New York, New York 10017 (800) 253-9646; *Demographic Yearbook.*

AFGHANISTAN - MEAT PRODUCTION - See AFGHANISTAN - LIVESTOCK AND POULTRY

AFGHANISTAN - MERCHANT SHIPPING

G.K. Hall and Company, 70 Lincoln Street, Boston, Massachusetts 02111 (617) 423-3990; *The World in Figures.*

AFGHANISTAN - MILITARY

The Economist Intelligence Unit (Asia) Limited, 10th Floor, Luk Kwok Centre, 72 Gloucester Road, Wanchai, Hong Kong (Phone Number in U.S. (800) 938-4685); *Asian Market Atlas.*

G.K. Hall and Company, 70 Lincoln Street, Boston, Massachusetts 02111 (617) 423-3990; *The World in Figures.*

The International Institute for Strategic Studies, 23 Tavistock Street, London WC2E 7NQ, England; *The Military Balance.*

U.S. Arms Control and Disarmament Agency, 320 Twenty-first Street, NW, Washington, D.C. 20451 (202) 647-8677; *World Military Expenditures and Arms Transfers.*

AFGHANISTAN - MILK PRODUCTION - See AFGHANISTAN - DAIRY PRODUCTS

AFGHANISTAN - MILLET PRODUCTION - See AFGHANISTAN - CROPS

AFGHANISTAN - MINING AND MINERAL PRODUCTS

Asian Development Bank, P.O. Box 789, 1099 Manila, Philippines; *Key Indicators of Developing Asian and Pacific Countries.*

Facts on File, 460 Park Avenue South, New York, New York 10016 (800) 443-8323; *The New Book of World Rankings.*

G.K. Hall and Company, 70 Lincoln Street, Boston, Massachusetts 02111 (617) 423-3990; *The World in Figures.*

International Monetary Fund, 700 Nineteenth Street, NW, Washington, D.C. 20431 (202) 623-7000; *International Financial Statistics.*

Statistical Office of the United Nations, Publishing Service, New York, New York 10017 (800) 253-9646; *Statistical Yearbook.*

AFGHANISTAN - MONEY EXCHANGE RATE

Euromonitor Publications Limited, 87-88 Turnmill Street, London EC1M 5QU, England; *International Marketing Data and Statistics.*

International Monetary Fund, 700 Nineteenth Street, NW, Washington, D.C. 20431 (202) 623-7000; *International Financial Statistics.*

Statistical Office of the United Nations, Publishing Service, New York, New York 10017 (800) 253-9646; *Statistical Yearbook.*

AFGHANISTAN - MONEY RESERVES

Euromonitor Publications Limited, 87-88 Turnmill Street, London EC1M 5QU, England; *International Marketing Data and Statistics.*

AFGHANISTAN - MONEY SUPPLY

Asian Development Bank, P.O. Box 789, 1099 Manila, Philippines; *Key Indicators of Developing Asian and Pacific Countries.*

Euromonitor Publications Limited, 87-88 Turnmill Street, London EC1M 5QU, England; *International Marketing Data and Statistics.*

Federal Statistical Office, Gustav - Stresemann - Ring 11, D-6200 Wiesbaden, Germany; *Afghanistan.*

G.K. Hall and Company, 70 Lincoln Street, Boston, Massachusetts 02111 (617) 423-3990; *The World in Figures.*

International Monetary Fund, 700 Nineteenth Street, NW, Washington, D.C. 20431 (202) 623-7000; *International Marketing Data and Statistics.*

Statistical Office of the United Nations, Publishing Service, New York, New York 10017 (800) 253-9646; *Statistical Yearbook.*

AFGHANISTAN - MOTION PICTURES

Statistical Office of the United Nations, Publishing Service, New York, New York 10017 (800) 253-9646; *Statistical Yearbook.*

United Nations Educational, Scientific and Cultural Organization (UNESCO), 7 Place de Fontenoy, F-75700 Paris, France (Telephone Number in U.S. (212) 963-5981); *Statistical Yearbook.*

AFGHANISTAN - MOTOR VEHICLES IN USE

G.K. Hall and Company, 70 Lincoln Street, Boston, Massachusetts 02111 (617) 423-3990; *The World in Figures.*

International Road Federation, 525 School Street, SW, Washington, D.C. 20024 (202) 554-2106; *World Road Statistics.*

Statistical Office of the United Nations, Publishing Service, New York, New York 10017 (800) 253-9646; *Statistical Yearbook.*

Times Books, 201 East 50th Street, New York, New York 10022 (212) 751-2600; *The Economist Book of Vital World Statistics.*

AFGHANISTAN - MULES - See AFGHANISTAN - LIVESTOCK AND POULTRY

AFGHANISTAN - MUSEUMS

Facts on File, 460 Park Avenue South, New York, New York 10016 (800) 443-8323; *The New Book of World Rankings.*

United Nations Educational, Scientific and Cultural Organization (UNESCO), 7 Place de Fontenoy, F-75700 Paris, France (Telephone Number in U.S. (212) 963-5981); *Statistical Yearbook.*

AFGHANISTAN - NATALITY

Statistical Office of the United Nations, Publishing Service, New York, New York 10017 (800) 253-9646; *Demographic Yearbook.*

AFGHANISTAN - NATIONAL ACCOUNTS

Federal Statistical Office, Gustav - Stresemann - Ring 11, D-6200 Wiesbaden, Germany; *Afghanistan.*

International Monetary Fund, 700 Nineteenth Street, NW, Washington, D.C. 20431 (202) 623-7000; *International Financial Statistics.*

Statistical Office of the United Nations, Publishing Service, New York, New York 10017 (800) 253-9646; *National Accounts Statistics,* and *Statistical Yearbook,* and *Statistical Yearbook for Asia and the Pacific.*

AFGHANISTAN - NATIONAL INCOME

Facts on File, 460 Park Avenue South, New York, New York 10016 (800) 443-8323; *The New Book of World Rankings.*

G.K. Hall and Company, 70 Lincoln Street, Boston, Massachusetts 02111 (617) 423-3990; *The World in Figures.*

Statistical Office of the United Nations, Publishing Service, New York, New York 10017 (800) 253-9646; *Statistical Yearbook.*

AFGHANISTAN - NATIONAL PRODUCT

Facts on File, 460 Park Avenue South, New York, New York 10016 (800) 443-8323; *The New Book of World Rankings.*

Statistical Office of the United Nations, Publishing Service, New York, New York 10017 (800) 253-9646; *Statistical Yearbook.*

AFGHANISTAN - NATURAL GAS - See AFGHANISTAN - MINING AND MINERAL PRODUCTS

AFGHANISTAN - NET MATERIAL PRODUCT

Statistical Office of the United Nations, Publishing Service, New York, New York 10017 (800) 253-9646; *Statistical Yearbook.*

AFGHANISTAN - NEWSPAPER - See AFGHANISTAN - FORESTRY AND FOREST PRODUCTS

AFGHANISTAN - NEWSPRINT - See AFGHANISTAN - FORESTRY AND FOREST PRODUCTS

AFGHANISTAN - NUPTIALITY - See AFGHANISTAN - MARRIAGE RATES

AFGHANISTAN - NUTS EXPORTS - See AFGHANISTAN - CROPS

AFGHANISTAN - OCCUPATIONS - See AFGHANISTAN - LABOR FORCE

AFGHANISTAN - PAPER - See AFGHANISTAN - FORESTRY AND FOREST PRODUCTS

AFGHANISTAN - PEANUT PRODUCTION - See AFGHANISTAN - CROPS

AFGHANISTAN - PERIODICALS

United Nations Educational, Scientific and Cultural Organization (UNESCO), 7 Place de Fontenoy, F-75700 Paris, France (Telephone Number in U.S. (212) 963-5981); *Statistical Yearbook.*

AFGHANISTAN - PESTICIDE USE

Food and Agricultural Organization of the United Nations (FAO) Via Delle Terme di Caracalla, 00100 Rome, Italy (Telephone Number in U.S. (202) 653-2400); *The State of Food and Agriculture.*

AFGHANISTAN - PETROLEUM INDUSTRY

Asian Development Bank, P.O. Box 789, 1099 Manila, Philippines; *Key Indicators of Developing Asian and Pacific Countries.*

Facts on File, 460 Park Avenue South, New York, New York 10016 (800) 443-8323; *The New Book of World Rankings*, and *The State of Food and Agriculture.*

G.K. Hall and Company, 70 Lincoln Street, Boston, Massachusetts 02111 (617) 423-3990; *The World in Figures.*

AFGHANISTAN - PIGS - See AFGHANISTAN - LIVESTOCK AND POULTRY

AFGHANISTAN - POPULATION

Asian Development Bank, P.O. Box 789, 1099 Manila, Philippines; *Key Indicators of Developing Asian and Pacific Countries.*

The Economist Intelligence Unit (Asia) Limited, 10th Floor, Luk Kwok Centre, 72 Gloucester Road, Wanchai, Hong Kong (Phone Number in U.S. (800) 938-4685); *Asian Market Atlas.*

The Economist Intelligence Unit, 111 West 57th Street, New York, New York 10019 (800) 938-4685; *The World Market Atlas.*

Euromonitor Publications Limited, 87-88 Turnmill Street, London EC1M 5QU, England; *International Marketing Data and Statistics.*

Federal Statistical Office, Gustav - Stresemann - Ring 11, D-6200 Wiesbaden, Germany; *Afghanistan.*

Facts on File, 460 Park Avenue South, New York, New York 10016 (800) 443-8323; *The New Book of World Rankings.*

Food and Agricultural Organization of the United Nations (FAO), Via delle Terme di Caracalla, 00100 Rome, Italy (Telephone Number in U.S. (202) 653-2400); *Production Yearbook.*

G.K. Hall and Company, 70 Lincoln Street, Boston, Massachusetts 02111 (617) 423-3990; *The World in Figures.*

International Labour Office, I.L.O. Publications, CH-1211, Geneva 22, Switzerland; *Yearbook of Labour Statistics.*

Statistical Office of the United Nations, Publishing Service, New York, New York 10017 (800) 253-9646; *Demographic Yearbook, Statistical Yearbook*, and *Statistical Yearbook for Asia and the Pacific.*

Times Books, 201 East 50th Street, New York, New York 10022 (212) 751-2600; *The Economist Book of Vital World Statistics.*

U.S. Arms Control and Disarmament Agency, 320 Twenty-first Street, NW, Washington, D.C. 20451 (202) 647-8677; *World Military Expenditures and Arms Transfers.*

World Health Organization, Office of Publications, Avenue Appia, CH-1211 Geneva 27, Switzerland; *World Health Statistics Annual.*

AFGHANISTAN - POST OFFICES

Facts on File, 460 Park Avenue South, New York, New York 10016 (800) 443-8323; *The New Book of World Rankings.*

AFGHANISTAN - POTATO PRODUCTION - See AFGHANISTAN - CROPS

AFGHANISTAN - POWER PRODUCTION INDUSTRY

Statistical Office of the United Nations, Publishing Service, New York, New York 10017 (800) 253-9646; *Electric Power in Asia and the Pacific.*

AFGHANISTAN - PRICES

Asian Development Bank, P.O. Box 789, 1099 Manila, Philippines; *Key Indicators of Developing Asian and Pacific Countries.*

Facts on File, 460 Park Avenue South, New York, New York 10016 (800) 443-8323; *The New Book of World Rankings.*

Federal Statistical Office, Gustav - Stresemann - Ring 11, D-6200 Wiesbaden, Germany; *Afghanistan.*

Food and Agricultural Organization of the United Nations (FAO), Via delle Terme di Caracalla, 00100 Rome, Italy (Telephone Number in U.S. (202) 653-2400); *Production Yearbook*, and *The State of Food and Agriculture.*

G.K. Hall and Company, 70 Lincoln Street, Boston, Massachusetts 02111 (617) 423-3990; *The World in Figures.*

International Labour Office, I.L.O. Publications, CH-1211, Geneva 22, Switzerland; *Yearbook of Labour Statistics.*

AFGHANISTAN - PRINTING AND WRITING PAPER - See AFGHANISTAN - FORESTRY AND FOREST PRODUCTS

AFGHANISTAN - PRODUCTION

Facts on File, 460 Park Avenue South, New York, New York 10016 (800) 443-8323; *The New Book of World Rankings.*

G.K. Hall and Company, 70 Lincoln Street, Boston, Massachusetts 02111 (617) 423-3990; *The World in Figures.*

AFGHANISTAN - PRODUCTIVITY

Euromonitor Publications Limited, 87-88 Turnmill Street, London EC1M 5QU, England; *International Marketing Data and Statistics.*

AFGHANISTAN - PUBLIC FINANCE

Facts on File, 460 Park Avenue South, New York, New York 10016 (800) 443-8323; *The New Book of World Rankings.*

Federal Statistical Office, Gustav - Stresemann - Ring 11, D-6200 Wiesbaden, Germany; *Afghanistan.*

AFGHANISTAN - RADIO BROADCASTING - See AFGHANISTAN - BROADCASTING

AFGHANISTAN - RAILWAYS

G.K. Hall and Company, 70 Lincoln Street, Boston, Massachusetts 02111 (617) 423-3990; *The World in Figures.*

Jane's Information Group, Sentinel House, 163 Brighton Road, Coulsdon, Surrey CR5 2NH, England (Telephone Number in U.S. (703) 683-3700); *Jane's World Railways.*

AFGHANISTAN - RELIGION

Facts on File, 460 Park Avenue South, New York, New York 10016 (800) 443-8323; *The New Book of World Rankings.*

AFGHANISTAN - RENT PRICES

International Labour Office, I.L.O. Publications, CH-1211, Geneva 22, Switzerland; *Yearbook of Labour Statistics.*

AFGHANISTAN - RETAIL TRADE

G.K. Hall and Company, 70 Lincoln Street, Boston, Massachusetts 02111 (617) 423-3990; *The World in Figures.*

AFGHANISTAN - RICE PRODUCTION - See AFGHANISTAN - CROPS

AFGHANISTAN - ROOT AND TUBER PRODUCTION - See AFGHANISTAN - CROPS

AFGHANISTAN - ROUNDWOOD PRODUCTION - See AFGHANISTAN - FORESTRY AND FOREST PRODUCTS

AFGHANISTAN - RUBBER PRODUCTION

Facts on File, 460 Park Avenue South, New York, New York 10016 (800) 443-8323; *The New Book of World Rankings.*

AFGHANISTAN - SALT PRODUCTION - See AFGHANISTAN - MINING AND MINERAL PRODUCTS

AFGHANISTAN - SAWNWOOD PRODUCTION - See AFGHANISTAN - FORESTRY AND FOREST PRODUCTS

AFGHANISTAN - SENIOR CITIZENS

Facts on File, 460 Park Avenue South, New York, New York 10016 (800) 443-8323; *The New Book of World Rankings.*

AFGHANISTAN - SESAME SEED PRODUCTION - See AFGHANISTAN - CROPS

AFGHANISTAN - SHEEP - See AFGHANISTAN - LIVESTOCK AND POULTRY

AFGHANISTAN - SILVER PRODUCTION AND CONSUMPTION - See AFGHANISTAN - MINING AND MINERAL PRODUCTS

AFGHANISTAN - SKINS EXPORTS

International Monetary Fund, 700 Nineteenth Street, NW, Washington, D.C. 20431 (202) 623-7000; *International Financial Statistics.*

AFGHANISTAN - SOCIAL DATA

Asian Development Bank, P.O. Box 789, 1099 Manila, Philippines; *Key Indicators of Developing Asian and Pacific Countries.*

Facts on File, 460 Park Avenue South, New York, New York 10016 (800) 443-8323; *The New Book of World Rankings.*

G.K. Hall and Company, 70 Lincoln Street, Boston, Massachusetts 02111 (617) 423-3990; *The World in Figures.*

AFGHANISTAN - STATE BUDGET REVENUE AND EXPENDITURES

Euromonitor Publications Limited, 87-88 Turnmill Street, London EC1M 5QU, England; *International Marketing Data and Statistics.*

AFGHANISTAN - STEEL - See AFGHANISTAN - MINING AND MINERAL PRODUCTS

AFGHANISTAN - STOCKS - COMMODITY - MARKET PRICE -INDEX

Food and Agricultural Organization of the United Nations (FAO) Via Delle Terme di Caracalla, 00100 Rome, Italy (Telephone Number in U.S. (202) 653-2400); *The State of Food and Agriculture.*

AFGHANISTAN - SUGAR PRODUCTION - See AFGHANISTAN - CROPS

AFGHANISTAN - TAXATION

G.K. Hall and Company, 70 Lincoln Street, Boston, Massachusetts 02111 (617) 423-3990; *The World in Figures.*

International Road Federation, 525 School Street, SW, Washington, D.C. 20024 (202) 554-2106; *World Road Statistics.*

AFGHANISTAN - TEA - See AFGHANISTAN - CROPS

AFGHANISTAN - TELEGRAPH SERVICE

Statistical Office of the United Nations, Publishing Service, New York, New York 10017 (800) 253-9646; *Statistical Yearbook.*

AFGHANISTAN - TELEPHONES IN USE

American Telephone and Telegraph Company, 26 Parsippany Road, Whippany, New Jersey 07981 (800) 338-4038; *The World's Telephones.*

The Economist Intelligence Unit (Asia) Limited, 10th Floor, Luk Kwok Centre, 72 Gloucester Road, Wanchai, Hong Kong (Phone Number in U.S. (800) 938-4685); *Asian Market Atlas.*

G.K. Hall and Company, 70 Lincoln Street, Boston, Massachusetts 02111 (617) 423-3990; *The World in Figures.*

Statistical Office of the United Nations, Publishing Service, New York, New York 10017 (800) 253-9646; *Statistical Yearbook.*

AFGHANISTAN - TELEVISION BROADCASTING - See AFGHANISTAN - BROADCASTING

AFGHANISTAN - TEXTILE INDUSTRY

G.K. Hall and Company, 70 Lincoln Street, Boston, Massachusetts 02111 (617) 423-3990; *The World in Figures.*

Statistical Office of the United Nations, Publishing Service, New York, New York 10017 (800) 253-9646; *Statistical Yearbook,* and *Trade in Manufactures of Developing Countries.*

AFGHANISTAN - TOBACCO PRODUCTION

Facts on File, 460 Park Avenue South, New York, New York 10016 (800) 443-8323; *The New Book of World Rankings.*

AFGHANISTAN - TOURISM

Civil Aviation and Tourism Authority, Afghan Tourist Organization, Kabul, Afghanistan; *Tourism Statistics: Annual Report.*

Facts on File, 460 Park Avenue South, New York, New York 10016 (800) 443-8323; *The New Book of World Rankings.*

Federal Statistical Office, Gustav - Stresemann - Ring 11, D-6200 Wiesbaden, Germany; *Afghanistan.*

G.K. Hall and Company, 70 Lincoln Street, Boston, Massachusetts 02111 (617) 423-3990; *The World in Figures.*

Statistical Office of the United Nations, Publishing Service, New York, New York 10017 (800) 253-9646; *Statistical Yearbook.*

Times Books, 201 East 50th Street, New York, New York 10022 (212) 751-2600; *The Economist Book of Vital World Statistics.*

AFGHANISTAN - TRADE - See AFGHANISTAN - FOREIGN TRADE

AFGHANISTAN - TRANSPORTATION AND COMMUNICATIONS

The Economist Intelligence Unit (Asia) Limited, 10th Floor, Luk Kwok Centre, 72 Gloucester Road, Wanchai, Hong Kong (Phone Number in U.S. (800) 938-4685); *Asian Market Atlas.*

Facts on File, 460 Park Avenue South, New York, New York 10016 (800) 443-8323; *The New Book of World Rankings.*

Federal Statistical Office, Gustav - Stresemann - Ring 11, D-6200 Wiesbaden, Germany; *Afghanistan.*

G.K. Hall and Company, 70 Lincoln Street, Boston, Massachusetts 02111 (617) 423-3990; *The World in Figures.*

Statistical Office of the United Nations, Publishing Service, New York, New York 10017 (800) 253-9646; *Statistical Yearbook for Asia and the Pacific.*

AFGHANISTAN - UNEMPLOYMENT

Euromonitor Publications Limited, 87-88 Turnmill Street, London EC1M 5QU, England; *International Marketing Data and Statistics.*

International Labour Office, I.L.O. Publications, CH-1211, Geneva 22, Switzerland; *Yearbook of Labour Statistics.*

AFGHANISTAN - UTILITIES

Statistical Office of the United Nations, Publishing Service, New York, New York 10017 (800) 253-9646; *Electric Power in Asia and the Pacific.*

AFGHANISTAN - VITAL STATISTICS

Euromonitor Publications Limited, 87-88 Turnmill Street, London EC1M 5QU, England; *International Marketing Data and Statistics.*

G.K. Hall and Company, 70 Lincoln Street, Boston, Massachusetts 02111 (617) 423-3990; *The World in Figures.*

World Health Organization, Office of Publications, Avenue Appia, CH-1211 Geneva 27, Switzerland (Telephone Number in U.S. (518) 436-9686); *World Health Statistics Annual.*

AFGHANISTAN - WAGES

Federal Statistical Office, Gustav - Stresemann - Ring 11, D-6200 Wiesbaden, Germany; *Afghanistan.*

G.K. Hall and Company, 70 Lincoln Street, Boston, Massachusetts 02111 (617) 423-3990; *The World in Figures.*

International Labour Office, I.L.O. Publications, CH-1211, Geneva 22, Switzerland; *Yearbook of Labour Statistics.*

Statistical Office of the United Nations, Publishing Service, New York, New York 10017 (800) 253-9646; *Statistical Yearbook,* and *Statistical Yearbook for Asia and the Pacific.*

AFGHANISTAN - WATERMELON PRODUCTION - See AFGHANISTAN - CROPS

AFGHANISTAN - WEATHER

Facts on File, 460 Park Avenue South, New York, New York 10016 (800) 443-8323; *The New Book of World Rankings.*

G.K. Hall and Company, 70 Lincoln Street, Boston, Massachusetts 02111 (617) 423-3990; *The World in Figures.*

AFGHANISTAN - WHEAT PRODUCTION - See AFGHANISTAN - CROPS

AFGHANISTAN - WHOLESALE PRICES

Asian Development Bank, P.O. Box 789, 1099 Manila, Philippines; *Key Indicators of Developing Asian and Pacific Countries.*

AFGHANISTAN - WINE PRODUCTION

Facts on File, 460 Park Avenue South, New York, New York 10016 (800) 443-8323; *The New Book of World Rankings.*

AFGHANISTAN - WOOL EXPORTS

International Monetary Fund, 700 Nineteenth Street, NW, Washington, D.C. 20431 (202) 623-7000; *International Financial*

Statistics.

AFGHANISTAN - WOOL PRODUCTION

Facts on File, 460 Park Avenue South, New York, New York 10016 (800) 443-8323; *The New Book of World Rankings.*

AFGHANISTAN - YARN PRODUCTION

Statistical Office of the United Nations, Publishing Service, New York, New York 10017 (800) 253-9646; *Statistical Yearbook.*

AFL - CIO

American Federation of Labor and Congress of Industrial Organizations, 815 16th Street, NW, Washington, D.C. 20433 (202) 637-5000; *Report of the AFL-CIO Executive Council.*

AGE OF POPULATION - See POPULATION

AGGRAVATED ASSAULT

U.S. Department of Justice, Bureau of Justice Statistics, 633 Indiana Avenue, NW, Washington, D.C. 20531 (800) 732-3277; *Criminal Victimization in the United States.*

U.S. Department of Justice, Federal Bureau of Investigation, Ninth Street and Pennsylvania Avenue, NW, Washington, D.C. 20535 (202) 324-3000; *Crime in the United States.*

AGRICULTURAL IMPLEMENTS AND MACHINERY INDUSTRY

U.S. Department of Commerce, Bureau of the Census, Suitland, Maryland 20233 (301) 763-4040; *Census of Manufactures,* and *Annual Survey of Manufactures.*

AGRICULTURAL LOANS - See FARM MORTGAGE LOANS

AGRICULTURAL NONPROFIT ASSOCIATIONS

Gale Research Incorporated, 835 Penobscot Building, Detroit, Michigan 48226 (800) 877-4253; compiled from *Encyclopedia of Associations.*

AGRICULTURAL PRODUCTS - See FARMS and Individual Products

AGRICULTURAL SCIENCES - DEGREES CONFERRED

National Science Foundation, 1800 G Street, NW, Washington, D.C. 20550 (202) 357-5000; *Survey of Earned Doctorates.*

U.S. Department of Education, National Center for Education Statistics, 400 Maryland Avenue, SW, Washington, D.C. 20202 (202) 708-5366; *Digest of Education Statistics.*

AGRICULTURAL SERVICES - EMPLOYEES

U.S. Department of Commerce, Bureau of the Census, Suitland, Maryland 20233 (301) 763-4040; *County Business Patterns.*

U.S. Department of Labor, Bureau of Labor Statistics, Two Massachusetts Avenue, NE, Washington, D.C. 20212 (202) 606-7828; *Employment and Earnings,* and *Monthly Labor Review.*

AGRICULTURAL SERVICES - ESTABLISHMENTS

U.S. Department of Commerce, Bureau of the Census, Suitland, Maryland 20233 (301) 763-4040; *County Business Patterns.*

AGRICULTURE - See also FARMS AND FARMERS AND FARMWORKERS

AGRICULTURE - ADVERTISING EXPENDITURES

Television Bureau of Advertising, Incorporated, 850 Third Avenue, New York, New York 10022 (212) 486-1111; data compiled by Competitive Media Reporting, 11 West 42nd Street, New York, New York 10036 (212) 789-1400.

AGRICULTURE - EMPLOYEES

U.S. Department of Labor, Bureau of Labor Statistics, Two Massachusetts Avenue, NE, Washington, D.C. 20212 (202) 606-7828; *Employment and Earnings.*

AGRICULTURE - EMPLOYMENT PROJECTIONS

U.S. Department of Labor, Bureau of Labor Statistics, Two Massachusetts Avenue, NE, Washington, D.C. 20212 (202) 606-7828; *Monthly Labor Review.*

AGRICULTURE - FEDERAL AID TO STATE AND LOCAL GOVERNMENTS

Executive Office of the President, Office of Management and Budget, Executive Office Building, Washington, D.C. 20503 (202) 395-3080; *Historical Tables, Budget of the United States Government.*

AGRICULTURE - FOREIGN TRADE

U.S. Department of Agriculture, Economic Research Service, Fourteenth Street and Independence Avenue, SW, Washington, D.C. 20250 (202) 219-1504; *Foreign Agricultural Trade of the United States,* and *Agricultural Statistics.*

AGRICULTURE - OUTLYING AREAS OF UNITED STATES

U.S. Department of Commerce, Bureau of the Census, Suitland, Maryland 20233 (301) 763-4040; *Census of Agriculture.*

AGRICULTURE, FORESTRY, AND FISHING INDUSTRY - EARNINGS

U.S. Department of Commerce, Bureau of Economic Analysis, Fourteenth Street between Constitution Avenue and E Street, NW, Washington, D.C. 20230 (202) 606-9900; *The National Income and Product Accounts of the United States,* and *Survey of Current Business.*

AGRICULTURE, FORESTRY, AND FISHING INDUSTRY - EMPLOYEES

U.S. Department of Agriculture, Economic Research Service, Fourteenth Street and Independence Avenue, SW, Washington, D.C. 20250 (202) 219-1504; unpublished data.

U.S. Department of Commerce, Bureau of Census, Suitland, Maryland 20233 (301) 763-4040; *Annual Survey of Manufactures, Census of Manufactures,* and *County Business Patterns.*

U.S. Department of Labor, Bureau of Labor Statistics, Two Massachusetts Avenue, NE, Washington, D.C. 20212 (202) 606-7828; *Employment and Earnings,* and *Monthly Labor Review.*

AGRICULTURE, FORESTRY, AND FISHING INDUSTRY - FAILURES

Dun and Bradstreet Corporation, 299 Park Avenue, 24th Floor, New York, New York 10171 (212) 593-6800; *Business Failure Record.*

AGRICULTURE, FORESTRY, AND FISHING INDUSTRY - FINANCES

U.S. Department of the Treasury, Internal Revenue Service, 1111 Constitution Avenue, NW, Washington, D.C. 20224 (202) 566-5000; *Statistics of Income*, various publications and unpublished data.

AGRICULTURE, FORESTRY, AND FISHING INDUSTRY - MERGERS AND ACQUISITIONS

Securities Data Company, 1180 Raymond Boulevard, Newark, New Jersey 07102 (201) 622-3100; *Merger and Corporate Transactions Database.*

AGRICULTURE, FORESTRY, AND FISHING INDUSTRY - OCCUPATIONAL SAFETY

National Safety Council, 1121 Spring Lake Drive, Itasca, Illinois 60143-3201 (708) 285-1121; *Accident Facts.*

U.S. Department of Labor, Bureau of Labor Statistics, Two Massachusetts Avenue, NE, Washington, D.C. 20212 (202) 606-7828; *Occupational Injuries and Illnesses in the U.S. by Industry.*

AGRICULTURE, FORESTRY, AND FISHING INDUSTRY - PROFITS

U.S. Department of Commerce, Bureau of Economic Analysis, Fourteenth Street between Constitution Avenue and E Street, NW, Washington, D.C. 20230 (202) 606-9900; *Survey of Current Business*, and *The National Income and Product Accounts of the United States.*

U.S. Department of the Treasury, Internal Revenue Service, 1111 Constitution Avenue, NW, Washington, D.C. 20224 (202) 566-5000; *Statistics of Income*, various publications.

AGRICULTURE, FORESTRY, AND FISHING INDUSTRY - RECEIPTS

U.S. Department of the Treasury, Internal Revenue Service, 1111 Constitution Avenue, NW, Washington, D.C. 20224 (202) 566-5000; *Statistics of Income*, various publications and unpublished data.

AGRICULTURE, FORESTRY, AND FISHING INDUSTRY - SALES, SHIPMENTS, RECEIPTS

U.S. Department of Commerce, Bureau of Economic Analysis, Fourteenth Street between Constitution Avenue and E Street, NW, Washington, D.C. 20230 (202) 606-9900; *Survey of Current Business*, and *The National Income and Product Accounts of the United States.*

U.S. Department of the Treasury, Internal Revenue Service, 1111 Constitution Avenue, NW, Washington, D.C. 20224 (202) 566-5000; *Statistics of Income*, various publications.

AGRICULTURE, FORESTRY, AND FISHING INDUSTRY - VALUE ADDED

U.S. Department of Agriculture, Economic Research Service, Fourteenth Street and Independence Avenue, SW, Washington, D.C. 20250 (202) 219-1504; unpublished data.

AID TO FAMILIES WITH DEPENDENT CHILDREN

U.S. Department of Health and Human Services, Administration for Children and Families, 370 L'Enfant Promenade, SW, Washington, D.C. 20447 (202) 401-9200; *Quarterly Public Assistance Statistics.*

U.S. Department of Health and Human Services, Office of Child Support Enforcement, 370 L'Enfant Promenade, SW, Washington, D.C. 20447 (202) 401-9373; *Annual Report to Congress.*

U.S. Department of Health and Human Services, Social Security Administration, 6401 Security Boulevard, Baltimore, Maryland 21235 (410) 965-1234; *Social Security Bulletin*, and *Annual Statistical Supplement to the Social Security Bulletin.*

U.S. Library of Congress, Congressional Research Service, 10 First Street, SE, Washington, D.C. 20540 (202) 707-5000; *Cash and Noncash Benefits for Persons With Limited Income: Eligibility Rules, Recipient and Expenditure Data.*

AIDS (ACQUIRED IMMUNO-DEFICIENCY SYNDROME)

American Hospital Association, 840 North Lake Shore Drive, Chicago, Illinois 60611 (312) 280-6000; *Hospital Statistics*, and *Annual Survey of Hospitals.*

Intergovernmental Health Policy Project, George Washington University, 2021 K Street, NW, Suite 800, Washington, D.C. 20006 (202) 872-1445; *Intergovernmental AIDS Reports.*

U.S. Department of Health and Human Services, Center for Disease Control, 1600 Clifton Road, NE, Atlanta, Georgia 30333 (404) 639-3311; *Summary of Notifiable Diseases, United States, Morbidity and Mortality Weekly Report, Surveillance Report*, and unpublished data.

U.S. Department of Health and Human Services, National Center for Health Statistics, 3700 East-West Highway, Hyattsville, Maryland 20782 (301) 436-8500; *Vital and Health Statistics, Monthly Vital Statistics Report, Vital Statistics of the United States, Health, United States*, and unpublished data.

AIR CONDITIONING - HOMES WITH

U.S. Department of Commerce, Bureau of the Census, Suitland, Maryland 20233 (301) 763-4040; *Current Housing Reports*, and *American Housing Survey.*

U.S. Department of Energy, Energy Information Administration, Washington, D.C. 20585 (202) 586-8800; *Housing Characteristics.*

AIR CONDITIONING - SHIPMENTS

U.S. Department of Commerce, Bureau of the Census, Suitland, Maryland 20233 (301) 763-4040; *Current Industrial Reports.*

AIR FORCE - DEPARTMENT OF - PERSONNEL

U.S. Department of Defense, Office of the Secretary, The Pentagon, Washington, D.C. 20301 (703) 545-6700; *Selected Manpower Statistics.*

AIR POLLUTION

U.S. Department of Commerce, Bureau of the Census, Suitland, Maryland 20233 (301) 763-4040; *Current Industrial Reports.*

U.S. Environmental Protection Agency, 401 M Street, NW, Washington, D.C. 20460 (202) 382-2090; *National Air Pollutant Emission Trends, National Air Quality and Emissions Trends Report, Air Quality Update*, and *Toxics Release Inventory Public Data Release.*

AIR POLLUTION - EXPENDITURES FOR ABATEMENT

U.S. Department of Commerce, Bureau of the Census, Suitland, Maryland 20233 (301) 763-4040; *Current Industrial Reports.*

U.S. Department of Commerce, Bureau of Economic Analysis, Fourteenth Street between Constitution Avenue and E Street, NW, Washington, D.C. 20230 (202) 606-9900; *Survey of Current Business.*

AIR POLLUTION GREENHOUSE GASES

U.S. Department of Energy, Energy Information Administration, 1000 Independence Avenue, SW, Washington, D.C. 20585 (202) 586-8800; *Emissions of Greenhouse Gases in the U.S.*

AIR TRAFFIC CONTROL SPECIALISTS

U.S. Department of Transportation, Federal Aviation Administration, 800 Independence Avenue, SW, Washington, D.C. 20591 (202) 366-0881; *FAA Statistical Handbook of Aviation*, and unpublished data.

AIR TRANSPORTATION - ACCIDENTS AND DEATHS

International Civil Aviation Organization, 1000 Sherbrooke Street, West, Montreal, Quebec H3A 2R2 Canada (514) 285-8219; *Civil Aviation Statistics of the World.*

U.S. Department of Health and Human Services, National Center for Health Statistics, 3700 East-West Highway, Hyattsville, Maryland 20782 (301) 436-8500; *Vital Statistics of the United States.*

U.S. Department of Transportation, Bureau of Transportation Statistics, 400 Seventh Street, SW, Washington, D.C. 20590 (202) 366-DATA; *National Transportation Statistics Annual, Historical Compendium Information Report.*

U.S. Department of Transportation, Federal Aviation Administration, 800 Independence Avenue, SW, Washington, D.C. 20591 (202) 366-0881; *FAA Statistical Handbook of Aviation*, and unpublished data.

U.S. Department of Transportation, Transportation Systems Center, Kendall Square, Cambridge, Massachusetts 02142 (617) 494-2224; *Transportation Safety Information Report.*

AIR TRANSPORTATION - AIRLINE MARKETS

Air Transport Association of America, 1301 Pennsylvania Avenue, NW, Washington, D.C. 20004 (202) 626-4000; *Air Transport.*

AIR TRANSPORTATION - AIRPORT SUMMARY

U.S. Department of Transportation, Federal Aviation Administration, 800 Independence Avenue, SW, Washington, D.C. 20591 (202) 366-0881; *Airport Activity Statistics.*

U.S. Department of Transportation, Office of Consumer Affairs, 400 Seventh Street, SW, Washington, D.C. 20590 (202) 366-4000; *Air Travel Consumer Report.*

AIR TRANSPORTATION - AIRPORT SUMMARY - FLIGHT ON-TIME PERFORMANCE

U.S. Department of Transportation, Office of Consumer Affairs, 400 Seventh Street, SW, Washington, D.C. 20590 (202) 366-4000; *Air Travel Consumer Report.*

AIR TRANSPORTATION - BOMB THREATS

U.S. Department of Transportation, Federal Aviation Administration, 800 Independence Avenue, SW, Washington, D.C. 20591 (202) 366-4000; *FAA Statistical Handbook on Aviation*, and unpublished data.

AIR TRANSPORTATION - CIVIL AVIATION

U.S. Department of Transportation, Federal Aviation Administration, 800 Independence Avenue, SW, Washington, D.C. 20591 (202) 366-4000; *FAA Statistical Handbook of Aviation*, and unpublished data.

AIR TRANSPORTATION - CONSUMER COMPLAINTS

U.S. Department of Transportation, Office of Consumer Affairs, 400 Seventh Street, SW, Washington, D.C. 20590 (202) 366-4000; *Air Travel Consumer Report.*

AIR TRANSPORTATION - COST INDEXES

Air Transport Association of America, 1301 Pennsylvania Avenue, NW, Washington, D.C. 20004-7017 (202) 626-4000; *Air Transport*, and unpublished data.

AIR TRANSPORTATION - EMPLOYED

Air Transport Association of America, 1301 Pennsylvania Avenue, NW, Washington, D.C. 20004 (202) 626-4000; *Air Transport*, and *Air Transport, Facts and Figures.*

AIR TRANSPORTATION - FEDERAL OUTLAYS

Executive Office of the President, Office of Management and Budget, Executive Office Building, Washington, D.C. 20503 (202) 395-3080; *The Budget of the United States Government.*

AIR TRANSPORTATION - FINANCES

Air Transport Association of America, 1301 Pennsylvania Avenue, NW, Washington, D.C. 20004 (202) 626-4000; *Air Transport*, and *Air Transport, Facts and Figures.*

AIR TRANSPORTATION - HIJACKING INCIDENTS

U.S. Department of Transportation, Federal Aviation Administration, 800 Independence Avenue, SW, Washington, D.C. 20591 (202) 366-4000; *FAA Statistical Handbook of Aviation*, and unpublished data.

AIR TRANSPORTATION - PASSENGER OUTLAYS

ENO Transportation Foundation, 44211 Statestone Court, Lansdowne, Virginia 22075 (703) 729-7200; *Transportation in America.*

AIR TRANSPORTATION - PASSENGER SCREENING

U.S. Department of Transportation, Federal Aviation Administration, 800 Independence Avenue, SW, Washington, D.C. 20591 (202) 366-4000; *Annual Report to Congress on Civil Aviation Security.*

AIR TRANSPORTATION - PRICE INDEXES

U.S. Department of Labor, Bureau of Labor Statistics, Two Massachusetts Avenue, NE, Washington, D.C. 20212 (202) 606-7828; *Monthly Labor Review*, and *CPI Detailed Report.*

AIR TRANSPORTATION - REGIONAL AIRLINES

Regional Airline Association, 1101 Connecticut Avenue, NW, Suite 700, Washington, D.C. 20036 (202) 857-1170; *Annual Report of the Regional Airline Industry.*

AIR TRANSPORTATION - TRAFFIC CARRIED

Air Transport Association of America, 1301 Pennsylvania Avenue, NW, Washington, D.C. 20004 (202) 626-4000; *Air Transport*, and *Air Transport Facts and Figures.*

ENO Transportation Foundation, 44211 Statestone Court, Lansdowne, Virginia 22075 (703) 729-7200; *Transportation in America.*

Regional Airline Association, 1101 Connecticut Avenue, NW, Washington, D.C. 20036 (202) 857-1170; *Annual Report of the Regional Airline Industry.*

U.S. Department of Transportation, Federal Aviation Administration, 800 Independence Avenue, SW, Washington, D.C. 20591 (202) 366-4000; *Air Carrier Traffic Statistics*, and *Air Carrier Financial Statistics.*

AIR TRANSPORTATION INDUSTRY - EARNINGS

U.S. Department of Labor, Bureau of Labor Statistics, Two Massachusetts Avenue, NE, Washington, D.C. 20212 (202) 606-7828; *Employment and Earnings*, and Bulletins 2370 and 2429.

AIR TRANSPORTATION INDUSTRY - EMPLOYEES

Air Transport Association of America, 1301 Pennsylvania Avenue, NW, Washington, D.C. 20004 (202) 626-4000; *Air Transport*, and *Air Transport, Facts and Figures.*

U.S. Department of Labor, Bureau of Labor Statistics, Two Massachusetts Avenue, NE, Washington, D.C. 20212 (202) 606-7828; *Employment and Earnings*, and Bulletins 2370 and 2429.

AIR TRANSPORTATION INDUSTRY - FINANCES

Air Transport Association of America, 1301 Pennsylvania, NW, Washington, D.C. 20004-7017 (202) 626-4000; *Air Transport*, and *Air Transport, Facts and Figures.*

U.S. Department of Transportation, Federal Aviation Administration, 800 Independence Avenue, SW, Washington, D.C. 20591 (202) 366-4000; *Air Carrier Financial Statistics.*

U.S. Department of Labor, Bureau of Labor Statistics, Two Massachusetts Avenue, NE, Washington, D.C. 20212 (202) 606-7828; *Employment and Earnings*, and Bulletins 2370 and 2429.

United States Travel Data Center, Two Lafayette Center, 1133 21st Street, NW, Washington, D.C. 20036 (202) 293-1040; *Economic Review of Travel in America.*

AIR TRANSPORTATION INDUSTRY - FOREIGN TRADE

U.S. Department of Commerce, Bureau of the Census, Suitland, Maryland 20233 (301) 763-4040; *U.S. Merchandise Trade: Selected Highlights.*

AIR TRANSPORTATION INDUSTRY - OCCUPATIONAL SAFETY

U.S. Department of Labor, Bureau of Labor Statistics, Two Massachusetts Avenue, NE, Washington, D.C. 20212 (202) 606-7828; *Occupational Injuries and Illnesses in the U.S. by Industry.*

AIR TRANSPORTATION INDUSTRY - PRODUCTIVITY

U.S. Department of Labor, Bureau of Labor Statistics, Two Massachusetts Avenue, NE, Washington, D.C. 20212 (202) 606-7828; *Productivity Measures for Selected Industries and Government Services*, and Bulletin 2440.

AIR TRANSPORTATION INDUSTRY - PROFITS

Air Transport Association of America, 1301 Pennsylvania Avenue, NW, Washington, D.C. 20004-7017 (202) 626-4000; *Air Transport*, and *Air Transport Facts and Figures.*

Forbes Incorporated, 60 Fifth Avenue, New York, New York 10011 (212) 620-2200; *Forbes Annual Report on American Industry.*

AIR TRANSPORTATION INDUSTRY - SALES

Forbes Incorporated, 60 Fifth Avenue, New York, New York 10011 (212) 620-2200; *Forbes Annual Report on American Industry.*

AIRCRAFT AND PARTS INDUSTRY - MANUFACTURING - EARNINGS

U.S. Department of Commerce, Bureau of the Census, Suitland, Maryland 20233 (301) 763-4040; *Census of Manufactures*, and *Annual Survey of Manufactures.*

U.S. Department of Labor, Bureau of Labor Statistics, Two Massachusetts Avenue, NE, Washington, D.C. 20212 (202) 606-7828; *Employment and Earnings*, and Bulletins 2370 and 2429.

AIRCRAFT AND PARTS INDUSTRY - MANUFACTURING - EMPLOYEES

U.S. Department of Commerce, Bureau of the Census, Suitland, Maryland 20233 (301) 763-4040; *Census of Manufactures*, and *Annual Survey of Manufactures.*

U.S. Department of Labor, Bureau of Labor Statistics, Two Massachusetts Avenue, NE, Washington, D.C. 20212 (202) 606-7828; *Employment and Earnings*, and Bulletins 2370 and 2429.

AIRCRAFT AND PARTS INDUSTRY - MANUFACTURING - ESTABLISHMENTS

U.S. Department of Commerce, Bureau of the Census, Suitland, Maryland 20233 (301) 763-4040; *Census of Manufactures*, and *Annual Survey of Manufactures.*

AIRCRAFT AND PARTS INDUSTRY - MANUFACTURING - FOREIGN TRADE

U.S. Department of Commerce, International Trade Administration, Fourteenth Street between Constitution Avenue and E Street, NW, Washington, D.C. 20230 (202) 482-5487; *U.S. Industrial Outlook.*

AIRCRAFT AND PARTS INDUSTRY - MANUFACTURING - INVENTORIES

U.S. Department of Commerce, Bureau of the Census, Suitland, Maryland 20233 (301) 763-4040; *Current Industrial Reports, Manufactures' Shipments, Inventories, and Orders.*

AIRCRAFT AND PARTS INDUSTRY - MANUFACTURING - RESEARCH AND DEVELOPMENT

U.S. National Science Foundation, 1800 G Street, NW, Washington, D.C. 20550 (202) 357-5000; *Research and Development in Industry.*

AIRCRAFT AND PARTS INDUSTRY - MANUFACTURING - SHIPMENTS

U.S. Department of Commerce, Bureau of the Census, Suitland, Maryland 20233 (301) 763-4040; *Census of Manufactures, Current*

Industrial Reports Manufactures' Shipments, Inventories and Orders, Annual Survey of Manufacturers, and *Current Industrial Reports.*

AIRCRAFT AND PARTS INDUSTRY - MANUFACTURING - VALUE ADDED

U.S. Department of Commerce, Bureau of the Census, Suitland, Maryland 20233 (301) 763-4040; *Census of Manufactures,* and *Annual Survey of Manufactures.*

AIRLINE OPERATIONS - See AIR TRANSPORTATION

AIRMAIL SERVICE

U.S. Postal Service, 475 L'Enfant Plaza, SW, Washington, D.C. 20260 (202) 268-2000; *Annual Report of the Postmaster General.*

AIRPORTS OR AIRFIELDS

U.S. Department of Transportation, Federal Aviation Administration, 800 Independence Avenue, SW, Washington, D.C. 20591 (202) 366-4000; *FAA Statistical Handbook of Aviation,* and unpublished data.

AIRPORTS OR AIRFIELDS - AIRPORT AND AIRWAY TRUST FUND

Executive Office of the President, Office of Management and Budget, Executive Office Building, Washington, D.C. 20503 (202) 395-3080; *Budget of the United States Government.*

AIRPORTS OR AIRFIELDS - CITY EXPENDITURES

U.S. Department of Commerce, Bureau of the Census, Suitland, Maryland 20233 (301) 763-4040; *City Government Finances.*

AIRPORTS OR AIRFIELDS - FEDERAL AID TO STATE AND LOCAL GOVERNMENT

Executive Office of the President, Office of Management and Budget, Executive Office Building, Washington, D.C. 20503 (202) 395-3080; *Historical Tables, Budget of the United States Government.*

AIRPORTS OR AIRFIELDS - SERVING REGIONAL AIRLINES

Regional Airline Association, 1101 Connecticut Avenue, NW, Washington, D.C. 20036 (202) 857-1170; *Annual Report of the Regional Airline Industry.*

AIRPORTS OR AIRFIELDS - TRAFFIC

U.S. Department of Transportation, Federal Aviation Administration, 800 Independence Avenue, SW, Washington, D.C. 20591 (202) 366-4000; *Airport Activity Statistics.*

U.S. Department of Transportation, Office of Consumer Affairs, 400 Seventh Street, SW, Washington, D.C. 20590 (202) 366-4000; *Air Travel Consumer Report.*

AIRPORTS OR AIRFIELDS - TRAFFIC - FLIGHT ON-TIME PERFORMANCE

U.S. Department of Transportation, Office of Consumer Affairs, 400 Seventh Street, SW, Washington, D.C. 20590 (202) 366-4000; *Air Travel Consumer Report.*

ALABAMA - See also STATE DATA (FOR INDIVIDUAL STATES)

Alabama - Primary Statistics Source

Center for Business and Economic Research, University of Alabama, Post Office Box 870221, Tuscaloosa, Alabama 35487 (205) 348-6191; *Economic Abstract of Alabama.*

Alabama - State Data Centers

Center for Business and Economic Research, University of Alabama, Post Office Box 870221, Tuscaloosa, Alabama 35487-0221, Ms. Annette Watters (205) 348-6191.

Alabama Department of Economic and Community Affairs, Office of State Planning, Post Office Box 5690, 3465 Norman Bridge Road, Montgomery, Alabama 36103-5690, Mr. Parker Collins (205) 242-5493.

Alabama Public Library Service, 6030 Monticello Drive, Montgomery, Alabama 36130, Mr. Vince Thacker (205) 277-7330.

ALASKA - See also STATE DATA (FOR INDIVIDUAL STATES)

Alaska - Primary Statistics Source

Department of Commerce and Economic Development, Division of Economic Development, Post Office Box 110804, Juneau, Alaska 99811 (907) 465-2017; *The Alaska Economy Performance Report.*

Alaska - State Data Centers

Alaska State Data Center, Research and Analysis, Department of Labor, Post Office Box 25504, Juneau, Alaska 99802-5504, Ms. Kathryn Lizik (907) 465-6026.

Office of Management and Budget, Division of Policy, Pouch AD, Juneau, Alaska 99811, Mr. Jack Kreinheder (907) 465-3640.

Department of Education, Division of Libraries and Museums, Alaska State Library, Pouch G, Juneau, Alaska 99811, Ms. Patience Fredrickson (907) 465-2927.

Department of Community and Regional Affairs, Division of Municipal and Regional Assistance, Post Office Box BH, Juneau, Alaska 99811, Ms. Laura Walters (907) 465-4750.

Institute for Social and Economic Research, University of Alaska, 3211 Providence Drive, Anchorage, Alaska 99508, Mr. Jim Kerr (907) 786-7710.

ALASKA PURCHASE

U.S. Department of Commerce, Bureau of the Census, Suitland, Maryland 20233 (301) 763-4040; unpublished data.

U.S. Department of the Interior, C Street between Eighteenth and Nineteenth Streets, NW, Washington, D.C. 20240 (202) 208-3171; estimated area, Bureau of Land Management; all other data, Office of the Secretary, *Areas of Acquisitions to the Territory of the United States, 1922.*

Albania - National Statistical Office

Drejtoria e Statistikes, Ministria e Ekonomise, Tirane, Albania.

Albania - Primary Statistics Source

Drejtoria e Statistikes, Tirane, Albania; *Statistical Yearbook of Albania.*

ALBANIA - AGRICULTURE

Facts on File, 460 Park Avenue South, New York, New York 10016 (800) 443-8323; *The New Book of World Rankings.*

Federal Statistical Office, Gustav - Stresemann - Ring 11, D-6200 Wiesbaden, Federal Republic of Germany; *Albanien.*

Food and Agricultural Organization of the United Nations (FAO), Via delle Terme di Caracalla, 00100 Rome, Italy (Telephone Number in U.S. (202) 653-2400); *Production Yearbook, The State of Food and Agriculture,* and *Trade Yearbook.*

G.K. Hall and Company, 70 Lincoln Street, Boston, Massachusetts 02111 (617) 423-3990; *The World in Figures.*

Statistical Office of the United Nations, Publishing Service, New York, New York 10017 (800) 253-9646; *Statistical Yearbook.*

Times Books, 201 East 50th Street, New York, New York 10022 (212) 751-2600; *The Economist Book of Vital World Statistics.*

ALBANIA - AIRLINE SERVICE

Facts on File, 460 Park Avenue South, New York, New York 10016 (800) 443-8323; *The New Book of World Rankings.*

G.K. Hall and Company, 70 Lincoln Street, Boston, Massachusetts 02111 (617) 423-3990; *The World in Figures.*

ALBANIA - ALUMINUM PRODUCTION AND CONSUMPTION - See ALBANIA - MINING AND MINERAL PRODUCTS

ALBANIA - ANIMAL HEALTH

Food and Agricultural Organization of the United Nations (FAO), Via delle Terme di Caracalla, 00100 Rome, Italy (Telephone Number in U.S. (202) 653-2400); *Animal Health Yearbook.*

ALBANIA - AREA AND DENSITY OF POPULATION

Facts on File, 460 Park Avenue South, New York, New York 10016 (800) 443-8323; *The New Book of World Rankings.*

Federal Statistical Office, Gustav - Stresemann - Ring 11, D-6200 Wiesbaden, Germany; *Albanien.*

Food and Agricultural Organization of the United Nations (FAO) Via Delle Terme di Caracalla, 00100 Rome, Italy (Telephone Number in U.S. (202) 653-2400); *The State of Food and Agriculture.*

G.K. Hall and Company, 70 Lincoln Street, Boston, Massachusetts 02111 (617) 423-3990; *The World in Figures.*

Statistical Office of the United Nations, Publishing Service, New York, New York 10017 (800) 253-9646; *Statistical Yearbook.*

Times Books, 201 East 50th Street, New York, New York 10022 (212) 751-2600; *The Economist Book of Vital World Statistics.*

ALBANIA - ARMS EXPORTS AND IMPORTS

U.S. Arms Control and Disarmament Agency, 320 Twenty-first Street, NW, Washington, D.C. 20451 (202) 647-8677; *World Military Expenditures and Arms Transfers.*

ALBANIA - BALANCE OF PAYMENTS

The Economist Intelligence Unit, 111 West 57th Street, New York, New York 10019 (800) 938-4685; *The World Market Atlas.*

Federal Statistical Office, Gustav - Stresemann - Ring 11, D-6200 Wiesbaden, Germany; *Albanien.*

G.K. Hall and Company, 70 Lincoln Street, Boston, Massachusetts 02111 (617) 423-3990; *The World in Figures.*

Times Books, 201 East 50th Street, New York, New York 10022 (212) 751-2600; *The Economist Book of Vital World Statistics.*

ALBANIA - BANKING

Facts on File, 460 Park Avenue South, New York, New York 10016 (800) 443-8323; *The New Book of World Rankings.*

G.K. Hall and Company, 70 Lincoln Street, Boston, Massachusetts 02111 (617) 423-3990; *The World in Figures.*

ALBANIA - BARLEY PRODUCTION - See ALBANIA - CROPS

ALBANIA - BEER PRODUCTION

Facts on File, 460 Park Avenue South, New York, New York 10016 (800) 443-8323; *The New Book of World Rankings.*

Statistical Office of the United Nations, Publishing Service, New York, New York 10017 (800) 253-9646; *Statistical Yearbook.*

ALBANIA - BIRTH RATES

Facts on File, 460 Park Avenue South, New York, New York 10016 (800) 443-8323; *The New Book of World Rankings.*

Statistical Office of the United Nations, Publishing Service, New York, New York 10017 (800) 253-9646; *Demographic Yearbook,* and *Statistical Yearbook.*

Times Books, 201 East 50th Street, New York, New York 10022 (212) 751-2600; *The Economist Book of Vital World Statistics.*

ALBANIA - BONDS

G.K. Hall and Company, 70 Lincoln Street, Boston, Massachusetts 02111 (617) 423-3990; *The World in Figures.*

ALBANIA - BOOK PRODUCTION

Euromonitor Publications Limited, 87-88 Turnmill Street, London EC1M 5QU, England; *European Marketing Data and Statistics.*

G.K. Hall and Company, 70 Lincoln Street, Boston, Massachusetts 02111 (617) 423-3990; *The World in Figures.*

ALBANIA - BROADCASTING

Billboard Limited, P.O. Box 9027, 1006 AA Amsterdam, The Netherlands (Telephone Number in U.S. (212) 764-7300); *World Radio TV Handbook.*

Facts on File, 460 Park Avenue South, New York, New York 10016 (800) 443-8323; *The New Book of World Rankings.*

G.K. Hall and Company, 70 Lincoln Street, Boston, Massachusetts 02111 (617) 423-3990; *The World in Figures.*

Times Books, 201 East 50th Street, New York, New York 10022 (212) 751-2600; *The Economist Book of Vital World Statistics.*

ALBANIA - BUSINESS

G.K. Hall and Company, 70 Lincoln Street, Boston, Massachusetts 02111 (617) 423-3990; *The World in Figures.*

ALBANIA - BUTTER PRODUCTION - See ALBANIA - DAIRY PRODUCTS

ALBANIA - CALORIE SUPPLY

Food and Agricultural Organization of the United Nations (FAO) Via Delle Terme di Caracalla, 00100 Rome, Italy (Telephone Number in U.S. (202) 653-2400); *The State of Food and Agriculture.*

ALBANIA - CATTLE - See ALBANIA - LIVESTOCK AND POULTRY

ALBANIA - CEMENT PRODUCTION - See ALBANIA - MINING AND MINERAL PRODUCTS

ALBANIA - CEREALS PRODUCTION - See ALBANIA - CROPS

ALBANIA - CHEESE PRODUCTION - See ALBANIA - DAIRY PRODUCTS

ALBANIA - CHEMICAL (ORGANIC) PRODUCTION - See ALBANIA - MINING AND MINERAL PRODUCTS

ALBANIA - CHROMITE PRODUCTION AND CONSUMPTION -See ALBANIA - MINING AND MINERAL PRODUCTS

ALBANIA - CHROMIUM ORE PRODUCTION AND CONSUMPTION - See ALBANIA - MINING AND MINERAL PRODUCTS

ALBANIA - CIGARETTE PRODUCTION - See ALBANIA - TOBACCO PRODUCTION

ALBANIA - CLASS STRUCTURE

Columbia University Press, 562 West 113th Street, New York, New York 10014 (212) 316-7100; *East European and Soviet Data Book.*

G.K. Hall and Company, 70 Lincoln Street, Boston, Massachusetts 02111 (617) 423-3990; *The World in Figures.*

ALBANIA - CLIMATE

Facts on File, 460 Park Avenue South, New York, New York 10016 (800) 443-8323; *The New Book of World Rankings.*

G.K. Hall and Company, 70 Lincoln Street, Boston, Massachusetts 02111 (617) 423-3990; *The World in Figures.*

ALBANIA - COAL PRODUCTION - See ALBANIA - MINING AND MINERAL PRODUCTS

ALBANIA - COFFEE PRODUCTION - See ALBANIA - CROPS

ALBANIA - COKE OVEN COKE PRODUCTION - See ALBANIA - MINING AND MINERAL PRODUCTS

ALBANIA - COMMUNICATIONS

Federal Statistical Office, Gustav - Stresemann - Ring 11, D-6200 Wiesbaden, Germany; *Albanien.*

G.K. Hall and Company, 70 Lincoln Street, Boston, Massachusetts 02111 (617) 423-3990; *The World in Figures.*

ALBANIA - CONSTRUCTION INDUSTRY

Facts on File, 460 Park Avenue South, New York, New York 10016 (800) 443-8323; *The New Book of World Rankings.*

ALBANIA - CONSUMER PRICE INDEX

Federal Statistical Office, Gustav - Stresemann - Ring 11, D-6200 Wiesbaden, Germany; *Albanien.*

G.K. Hall and Company, 70 Lincoln Street, Boston, Massachusetts 02111 (617) 423-3990; *The World in Figures.*

ALBANIA - CONSUMER PRICES

Euromonitor Publications Limited, 87-88 Turnmill Street, London EC1M 5QU, England; *European Marketing Data and Statistics.*

Federal Statistical Office, Gustav - Stresemann - Ring 11, D-6200 Wiesbaden, Germany; *Albanien.*

ALBANIA - CONSUMPTION

G.K. Hall and Company, 70 Lincoln Street, Boston, Massachusetts 02111 (617) 423-3990; *The World in Figures.*

ALBANIA - COPPER AND COPPER ORE - See ALBANIA - MINING AND MINERAL PRODUCTS

ALBANIA - CORN PRODUCTION - See ALBANIA - CROPS

ALBANIA - CORPORATE TAXES - See ALBANIA - TAXATION

ALBANIA - COTTON - See ALBANIA - CROPS

ALBANIA - CROPS

Euromonitor Publications Limited, 87-88 Turnmill Street, London EC1M 5QU, England; *European Marketing Data and Statistics.*

Facts on File, 460 Park Avenue South, New York, New York 10016 (800) 443-8323; *The New Book of World Rankings.*

Food and Agricultural Organization of the United Nations (FAO) Via Delle Terme di Caracalla, 00100 Rome, Italy (Telephone Number in U.S. (202) 653-2400); *Production Yearbook,* and *The State of Food and Agriculture.*

G.K. Hall and Company, 70 Lincoln Street, Boston, Massachusetts 02111 (617) 423-3990; *The World in Figures.*

Statistical Office of the United Nations, Publishing Service, New York, New York 10017 (800) 253-9646; *Statistical Yearbook.*

ALBANIA - CUSTOMS DUTIES

G.K. Hall and Company, 70 Lincoln Street, Boston, Massachusetts 02111 (617) 423-3990; *The World in Figures.*

ALBANIA - DAIRY PRODUCTS

Facts on File, 460 Park Avenue South, New York, New York 10016 (800) 443-8323; *The New Book of World Rankings.*

Food and Agricultural Organization of the United Nations (FAO) Via Delle Terme di Caracalla, 00100 Rome, Italy (Telephone Number in U.S. (202) 653-2400); *The State of Food and Agriculture.*

Statistical Office of the United Nations, Publishing Service, New York, New York 10017 (800) 253-9646; *Statistical Yearbook.*

ALBANIA - DEATH RATE

G.K. Hall and Company, 70 Lincoln Street, Boston, Massachusetts 02111 (617) 423-3990; *The World in Figures.*

Statistical Office of the United Nations, Publishing Service, New York, New York 10017 (800) 253-9646; *Statistical Yearbook.*

Times Books, 201 East 50th Street, New York, New York 10022 (212) 751-2600; *The Economist Book of Vital World Statistics.*

ALBANIA - DEFENSE EXPENDITURES

G.K. Hall and Company, 70 Lincoln Street, Boston, Massachusetts 02111 (617) 423-3990; *The World in Figures.*

U.S. Arms Control and Disarmament Agency, 320 Twenty-first Street, NW, Washington, D.C. 20451 (202) 647-8677; *World Military Expenditures and Arms Transfers.*

ALBANIA - DEMOGRAPHY

The Economist Intelligence Unit, 111 West 57th Street, New York, New York 10019 (800) 938-4685; *The World Market Atlas.*

Facts on File, 460 Park Avenue South, New York, New York 10016 (800) 443-8323; *The New Book of World Rankings.*

Federal Statistical Office, Gustav - Stresemann - Ring 11, D-6200 Wiesbaden, Germany; *Albanien.*

G.K. Hall and Company, 70 Lincoln Street, Boston, Massachusetts 02111 (617) 423-3990; *The World in Figures.*

ALBANIA - DEVELOPMENT ASSISTANCE

G.K. Hall and Company, 70 Lincoln Street, Boston, Massachusetts 02111 (617) 423-3990; *The World in Figures.*

ALBANIA - DIAMOND PRODUCTION - See ALBANIA - MINING AND MINERAL PRODUCTS

ALBANIA - DISEASE

G.K. Hall and Company, 70 Lincoln Street, Boston, Massachusetts 02111 (617) 423-3990; *The World in Figures.*

ALBANIA - DIVORCE RATES

Facts on File, 460 Park Avenue South, New York, New York 10016 (800) 443-8323; *The New Book of World Rankings.*

Statistical Office of the United Nations, Publishing Service, New York, New York 10017 (800) 253-9646; *Demographic Yearbook,* and *Statistical Yearbook.*

ALBANIA - DOMESTIC PRODUCT

G.K. Hall and Company, 70 Lincoln Street, Boston, Massachusetts 02111 (617) 423-3990; *The World in Figures.*

ALBANIA - ECONOMY

Euromonitor Publications Limited, 87-88 Turnmill Street, London EC1M 5QU, England; *European Marketing Data and Statistics.*

Facts on File, 460 Park Avenue South, New York, New York 10016 (800) 443-8323; *The New Book of World Rankings.*

Federal Statistical Office, Gustav - Stresemann - Ring 11, D-6200 Wiesbaden, Germany; *Albanien.*

G.K. Hall and Company, 70 Lincoln Street, Boston, Massachusetts 02111 (617) 423-3990; *The World in Figures.*

ALBANIA - EDUCATION

The Economist Intelligence Unit, 111 West 57th Street, New York, New York 10019 (800) 938-4685; *The World Market Atlas.*

Euromonitor Publications Limited, 87-88 Turnmill Street, London EC1M 5QU, England; *European Marketing Data and Statistics.*

Facts on File, 460 Park Avenue South, New York, New York 10016 (800) 443-8323; *The New Book of World Rankings.*

Federal Statistical Office, Gustav - Stresemann - Ring 11, D-6200 Wiesbaden, Germany; *Albanien.*

G.K. Hall and Company, 70 Lincoln Street, Boston, Massachusetts 02111 (617) 423-3990; *The World in Figures.*

United Nations Educational, Scientific and Cultural Organization (UNESCO), 7 Place de Fontenoy, F-75700 Paris, France (Telephone Number in U.S. (212) 963-5981); *Statistical Yearbook.*

Times Books, 201 East 50th Street, New York, New York 10022 (212) 751-2600; *The Economist Book of Vital World Statistics.*

ALBANIA - EGG PRODUCTION - See ALBANIA - DAIRY PRODUCTS

ALBANIA - ELECTRICITY

Facts on File, 460 Park Avenue South, New York, New York 10016 (800) 443-8323; *The New Book of World Rankings.*

Penn Well Publishing Company, 1421 South Sheridan Road, P.O. Box 1260, Tulsa, Oklahoma 74101 (800) 752-9764; *International Energy Statistics Sourcebook.*

Statistical Office of the United Nations, Publishing Service, New York, New York 10017 (800) 253-9646; *Statistical Yearbook.*

Times Books, 201 East 50th Street, New York, New York 10022 (212) 751-2600; *The Economist Book of Vital World Statistics.*

ALBANIA - EMPLOYMENT

Euromonitor Publications Limited, 87-88 Turnmill Street, London EC1M 5QU, England; *European Marketing Data and Statistics.*

Facts on File, 460 Park Avenue South, New York, New York 10016 (800) 443-8323; *The New Book of World Rankings.*

Federal Statistical Office, Gustav - Stresemann - Ring 11, D-6200 Wiesbaden, Germany; *Albanien.*

ALBANIA - ENERGY

Euromonitor Publications Limited, 87-88 Turnmill Street, London EC1M 5QU, England; *European Marketing Data and Statistics.*

Facts on File, 460 Park Avenue South, New York, New York 10016 (800) 443-8323; *The New Book of World Rankings.*

Food and Agricultural Organization of the United Nations (FAO) Via Delle Terme di Caracalla, 00100 Rome, Italy (Telephone Number in U.S. (202) 653-2400); *The State of Food and Agriculture.*

G.K. Hall and Company, 70 Lincoln Street, Boston, Massachusetts 02111 (617) 423-3990; *The World in Figures.*

Penn Well Publishing Company, 1421 South Sheridan Road, P.O. Box 1260, Tulsa, Oklahoma 74101 (800) 752-9764; *International Energy Statistics Sourcebook.*

Statistical Office of the United Nations, Publishing Service, New York, New York 10017 (800) 253-9646; *Energy Statistics Yearbook, Statistical Yearbook,* and *World Energy Supplies.*

Times Books, 201 East 50th Street, New York, New York 10022 (212) 751-2600; *The Economist Book of Vital World Statistics.*

ALBANIA - EXCHANGE RATES

Statistical Office of the United Nations, Publishing Service, New York, New York 10017 (800) 253-9646; *Statistical Yearbook.*

ALBANIA - EXPORTS

The Economist Intelligence Unit, 111 West 57th Street, New York, New York 10019 (800) 938-4685; *The World Market Atlas.*

Food and Agricultural Organization of the United Nations (FAO) Via Delle Terme di Caracalla, 00100 Rome, Italy (Telephone Number in U.S. (202) 653-2400); *The State of Food and Agriculture.*

G.K. Hall and Company, 70 Lincoln Street, Boston, Massachusetts 02111 (617) 423-3990; *The World in Figures.*

International Monetary Fund, 700 Nineteenth Street, NW, Washington, D.C. 20431 (202) 623-7000; *Direction of Trade Statistics.*

Times Books, 201 East 50th Street, New York, New York 10022 (212) 751-2600; *The Economist Book of Vital World Statistics.*

ALBANIA - EXTERNAL TRADE

Food and Agricultural Organization of the United Nations (FAO) Via Delle Terme di Caracalla, 00100 Rome, Italy (Telephone Number in U.S. (202) 653-2400); *The State of Food and Agriculture,* and *Trade Yearbook.*

G.K. Hall and Company, 70 Lincoln Street, Boston, Massachusetts 02111 (617) 423-3990; *The World in Figures.*

ALBANIA - FARM CROPS - See ALBANIA - CROPS

ALBANIA - FERTILITY RATES

Facts on File, 460 Park Avenue South, New York, New York 10016 (800) 443-8323; *The New Book of World Rankings.*

Times Books, 201 East 50th Street, New York, New York 10022 (212) 751-2600; *The Economist Book of Vital World Statistics.*

ALBANIA - FERTILIZER

Food and Agricultural Organization of the United Nations (FAO), Via delle Terme di Caracalla, 00100 Rome, Italy (Telephone Number in U.S. (202) 653-2400); *Fertilizer Yearbook,* and *The State of Food and Agriculture.*

Statistical Office of the United Nations, Publishing Service, New York, New York 10017 (800) 253-9646; *Statistical Yearbook.*

ALBANIA - FETAL MORTALITY

Statistical Office of the United Nations, Publishing Service, New York, New York 10017 (800) 253-9646; *Demographic Yearbook.*

ALBANIA - FINANCE

Facts on File, 460 Park Avenue South, New York, New York 10016 (800) 443-8323; *The New Book of World Rankings.*

Federal Statistical Office, Gustav - Stresemann - Ring 11, D-6200 Wiesbaden, Germany; *Albanien.*

G.K. Hall and Company, 70 Lincoln Street, Boston, Massachusetts 02111 (617) 423-3990; *The World in Figures.*

International Monetary Fund, 700 Nineteenth Street, NW, Washington, D.C. 20431 (202) 623-7000; *International Financial Statistics.*

ALBANIA - FISHERIES

Euromonitor Publications Limited, 87-88 Turnmill Street, London EC1M 5QU, England; *European Marketing Data and Statistics.*

Facts on File, 460 Park Avenue South, New York, New York 10016 (800) 443-8323; *The New Book of World Rankings.*

Federal Statistical Office, Gustav - Stresemann - Ring 11, D-6200 Wiesbaden, Germany; *Albanien.*

Food and Agricultural Organization of the United Nations (FAO) Via Delle Terme di Caracalla, 00100 Rome, Italy (Telephone Number in U.S. (202) 653-2400); *The State of Food and Agriculture,* and *Yearbook of Fishery Statistics.*

Statistical Office of the United Nations, Publishing Service, New York, New York 10017 (800) 253-9646; *Statistical Yearbook.*

ALBANIA - FOOD

Food and Agricultural Organization of the United Nations (FAO) Via Delle Terme di Caracalla, 00100 Rome, Italy (Telephone Number in U.S. (202) 653-2400); *Production Yearbook,* and *The State of Food and Agriculture.*

G.K. Hall and Company, 70 Lincoln Street, Boston, Massachusetts 02111 (617) 423-3990; *The World in Figures.*

ALBANIA - FOREIGN AID

G.K. Hall and Company, 70 Lincoln Street, Boston, Massachusetts 02111 (617) 423-3990; *The World in Figures.*

ALBANIA - FOREIGN TRADE

Euromonitor Publications Limited, 87-88 Turnmill Street, London EC1M 5QU, England; *European Marketing Data and Statistics.*

Facts on File, 460 Park Avenue South, New York, New York 10016 (800) 443-8323; *The New Book of World Rankings.*

Federal Statistical Office, Gustav - Stresemann - Ring 11, D-6200 Wiesbaden, Germany; *Albanien.*

G.K. Hall and Company, 70 Lincoln Street, Boston, Massachusetts 02111 (617) 423-3990; *The World in Figures.*

Organisation for Economic Co-operation and Development (OECD), 2 rue Andre-Pascal, 75 Paris 16, France (Telephone Number in U.S. (202) 785-6323); *Trade by Commodities.*

Statistical Office of the United Nations, Publishing Service, New York, New York 10017 (800) 253-9646; *Statistical Yearbook.*

ALBANIA - FORESTRY AND FOREST PRODUCTS

Euromonitor Publications Limited, 87-88 Turnmill Street, London EC1M 5QU, England; *European Marketing Data and Statistics.*

Facts on File, 460 Park Avenue South, New York, New York 10016 (800) 443-8323; *The New Book of World Rankings.*

Federal Statistical Office, Gustav - Stresemann - Ring 11, D-6200 Wiesbaden, Germany; *Albanien.*

Food and Agricultural Organization of the United Nations (FAO) Via Delle Terme di Caracalla, 00100 Rome, Italy (Telephone Number in U.S. (202) 653-2400); *The State of Food and Agriculture,* and *Yearbook of Forest Products.*

G.K. Hall and Company, 70 Lincoln Street, Boston, Massachusetts 02111 (617) 423-3990; *The World in Figures.*

Statistical Office of the United Nations, Publishing Service, New York, New York 10017 (800) 253-9646; *Statistical Yearbook.*

United Nations Educational, Scientific and Cultural Organization (UNESCO), 7 Place de Fontenoy, F-75700 Paris, France (Telephone Number in U.S. (212) 963-5981); *Statistical Yearbook.*

ALBANIA - GAS PRODUCTION - See ALBANIA - MINING AND MINERAL PRODUCTS

ALBANIA - GENERAL INDUSTRIAL STATISTICS

Federal Statistical Office, Gustav - Stresemann - Ring 11, D-6200 Wiesbaden, Germany; *Albanien.*

ALBANIA - GENERAL MORTALITY

Statistical Office of the United Nations, Publishing Service, New York, New York 10017 (800) 253-9646; *Demographic Yearbook.*

ALBANIA - GEOGRAPHIC DATA

Facts on File, 460 Park Avenue South, New York, New York 10016 (800) 443-8323; *The New Book of World Rankings.*

Federal Statistical Office, Gustav - Stresemann - Ring 11, D-6200 Wiesbaden, Germany; *Albanien.*

ALBANIA - GOLD PRODUCTION AND CONSUMPTION - See ALBANIA - MINING AND MINERAL PRODUCTS

ALBANIA - GOVERNMENT

G.K. Hall and Company, 70 Lincoln Street, Boston, Massachusetts 02111 (617) 423-3990; *The World in Figures.*

ALBANIA - GRAIN PRODUCTION - See ALBANIA - CROPS

ALBANIA - GROSS DOMESTIC PRODUCT

The Economist Intelligence Unit, 111 West 57th Street, New York, New York 10019 (800) 938-4685; *The World Market Atlas.*

Facts on File, 460 Park Avenue South, New York, New York 10016 (800) 443-8323; *The New Book of World Rankings.*

G.K. Hall and Company, 70 Lincoln Street, Boston, Massachusetts 02111 (617) 423-3990; *The World in Figures.*

Times Books, 201 East 50th Street, New York, New York 10022 (212) 751-2600; *The Economist Book of Vital World Statistics.*

ALBANIA - GROSS NATIONAL PRODUCT

U.S. Arms Control and Disarmament Agency, 320 Twenty-first Street, NW, Washington, D.C. 20451 (202) 647-8677; *World Military Expenditures and Arms Transfers.*

ALBANIA - HEALTH

Facts on File, 460 Park Avenue South, New York, New York 10016 (800) 443-8323; *The New Book of World Rankings.*

Federal Statistical Office, Gustav - Stresemann - Ring 11, D-6200 Wiesbaden, Germany; *Albanien.*

G.K. Hall and Company, 70 Lincoln Street, Boston, Massachusetts 02111 (617) 423-3990; *The World in Figures.*

Statistical Office of the United Nations, Publishing Service, New York, New York 10017 (800) 253-9646; *Statistical Yearbook.*

Times Books, 201 East 50th Street, New York, New York 10022 (212) 751-2600; *The Economist Book of Vital World Statistics.*

ALBANIA - HIDE PRODUCTION

Food and Agricultural Organization of the United Nations (FAO), Via delle Terme di Caracalla, 00100 Rome, Italy (Telephone Number in U.S. (202) 653-2400); *Production Yearbook.*

ALBANIA - HIGHWAYS

G.K. Hall and Company, 70 Lincoln Street, Boston, Massachusetts 02111 (617) 423-3990; *The World in Figures.*

ALBANIA - HORSES - See ALBANIA - LIVESTOCK AND POULTRY

ALBANIA - HOUSING AND HOUSING UNITS

Facts on File, 460 Park Avenue South, New York, New York 10016 (800) 443-8323; *The New Book of World Rankings.*

ALBANIA - ILLITERATE POPULATION

Columbia University Press, 562 West 113th Street, New York, New York 10014 (212) 316-7100; *East European and Soviet Data Book.*

The Economist Intelligence Unit, 111 West 57th Street, New York, New York 10019 (800) 938-4685; *The World Market Atlas.*

G.K. Hall and Company, 70 Lincoln Street, Boston, Massachusetts 02111 (617) 423-3990; *The World in Figures.*

United Nations Educational, Scientific and Cultural Organization (UNESCO), 7 Place de Fontenoy, F-75700 Paris, France (Telephone Number in U.S. (212) 963-5981); *Statistical Yearbook.*

ALBANIA - IMPORTS

The Economist Intelligence Unit, 111 West 57th Street, New York, New York 10019 (800) 938-4685; *The World Market Atlas.*

Food and Agricultural Organization of the United Nations (FAO) Via Delle Terme di Caracalla, 00100 Rome, Italy (Telephone Number in U.S. (202) 653-2400); *The State of Food and Agriculture.*

G.K. Hall and Company, 70 Lincoln Street, Boston, Massachusetts 02111 (617) 423-3990; *The World in Figures.*

International Monetary Fund, 700 Nineteenth Street, NW, Washington, D.C. 20431 (202) 623-7000; *Direction of Trade Statistics.*

ALBANIA - INDUSTRY

Facts on File, 460 Park Avenue South, New York, New York 10016 (800) 443-8323; *The New Book of World Rankings.*

Federal Statistical Office, Gustav - Stresemann - Ring 11, D-6200 Wiesbaden, Germany; *Albanien.*

G.K. Hall and Company, 70 Lincoln Street, Boston, Massachusetts 02111 (617) 423-3990; *The World in Figures.*

Times Books, 201 East 50th Street, New York, New York 10022 (212) 751-2600; *The Economist Book of Vital World Statistics.*

ALBANIA - INFANT AND MATERNAL MORTALITY

Statistical Office of the United Nations, Publishing Service, New York, New York 10017 (800) 253-9646; *Demographic Yearbook,* and *Statistical Yearbook.*

Times Books, 201 East 50th Street, New York, New York 10022 (212) 751-2600; *The Economist Book of Vital World Statistics.*

ALBANIA - IRON ORE PRODUCTION AND CONSUMPTION - See ALBANIA - MINING AND MINERAL PRODUCTS

ALBANIA - LABOR FORCE

Facts on File, 460 Park Avenue South, New York, New York 10016 (800) 443-8323; *The New Book of World Rankings.*

Food and Agricultural Organization of the United Nations (FAO) Via Delle Terme di Caracalla, 00100 Rome, Italy (Telephone Number in U.S. (202) 653-2400); *The State of Food and Agriculture.*

G.K. Hall and Company, 70 Lincoln Street, Boston, Massachusetts 02111 (617) 423-3990; *The World in Figures.*

ALBANIA - LAND USE

Euromonitor Publications Limited, 87-88 Turnmill Street, London EC1M 5QU, England; *European Marketing Data and Statistics.*

Food and Agricultural Organization of the United Nations (FAO), Via delle Terme di Caracalla, 00100 Rome, Italy (Telephone Number in U.S. (202) 653-2400); *Production Yearbook.*

G.K. Hall and Company, 70 Lincoln Street, Boston, Massachusetts 02111 (617) 423-3990; *The World in Figures.*

ALBANIA - LIBRARIES

Euromonitor Publications Limited, 87-88 Turnmill Street, London EC1M 5QU, England; *European Marketing Data and Statistics.*

Facts on File, 460 Park Avenue South, New York, New York 10016 (800) 443-8323; *The New Book of World Rankings.*

ALBANIA - LIGNITE PRODUCTION - See ALBANIA - MINING AND MINERAL PRODUCTS

ALBANIA - LIVESTOCK AND POULTRY

Euromonitor Publications Limited, 87-88 Turnmill Street, London EC1M 5QU, England; *European Marketing Data and Statistics.*

Facts on File, 460 Park Avenue South, New York, New York 10016 (800) 443-8323; *The New Book of World Rankings.*

Food and Agricultural Organization of the United Nations (FAO), Via delle Terme di Caracalla, 00100 Rome, Italy (Telephone Number in U.S. (202) 653-2400); *Production Yearbook,* and *The State of Food and Agriculture.*

G.K. Hall and Company, 70 Lincoln Street, Boston, Massachusetts 02111 (617) 423-3990; *The World in Figures.*

Statistical Office of the United Nations, Publishing Service, New York, New York 10017 (800) 253-9646; *Statistical Yearbook.*

ALBANIA - LIVING LEVELS

G.K. Hall and Company, 70 Lincoln Street, Boston, Massachusetts 02111 (617) 423-3990; *The World in Figures.*

Times Books, 201 East 50th Street, New York, New York 10022 (212) 751-2600; *The Economist Book of Vital World Statistics.*

ALBANIA - MANUFACTURING

Facts on File, 460 Park Avenue South, New York, New York 10016 (800) 443-8323; *The New Book of World Rankings.*

G.K. Hall and Company, 70 Lincoln Street, Boston, Massachusetts 02111 (617) 423-3990; *The World in Figures.*

Times Books, 201 East 50th Street, New York, New York 10022 (212) 751-2600; *The Economist Book of Vital World Statistics.*

ALBANIA - MARRIAGE RATES

Facts on File, 460 Park Avenue South, New York, New York 10016 (800) 443-8323; *The New Book of World Rankings.*

Statistical Office of the United Nations, Publishing Service, New York, New York 10017 (800) 253-9646; *Demographic Yearbook,* and *Statistical Yearbook.*

ALBANIA - MEAT PRODUCTION - See ALBANIA - LIVESTOCK AND POULTRY

ALBANIA - MERCHANT FLEET CHARACTERISTICS - See ALBANIA - MERCHANT SHIPPING

ALBANIA - MERCHANT SHIPPING

G.K. Hall and Company, 70 Lincoln Street, Boston, Massachusetts 02111 (617) 423-3990; *The World in Figures.*

Statistical Office of the United Nations, Publishing Service, New York, New York 10017 (800) 253-9646; *Statistical Yearbook.*

Times Books, 201 East 50th Street, New York, New York 10022 (212) 751-2600; *The Economist Book of Vital World Statistics.*

U.S. Department of Commerce, Maritime Administration, Washington, D.C. 20230; *A Statistical Analysis of the World's Merchant Fleets.*

ALBANIA - MILITARY

G.K. Hall and Company, 70 Lincoln Street, Boston, Massachusetts 02111 (617) 423-3990; *The World in Figures.*

The International Institute for Strategic Studies, 23 Tavistock Street, London WC2E 7NQ, England; *The Military Balance.*

U.S. Arms Control and Disarmament Agency, 320 Twenty-first Street, NW, Washington, D.C. 20451 (202) 647-8677; *World Military Expenditures and Arms Transfers.*

ALBANIA - MILK PRODUCTION - See ALBANIA - DAIRY PRODUCTS

ALBANIA - MINING AND MINERAL PRODUCTS

Asian Development Bank, P.O. Box 789, 1099 Manila, Philippines; *Key Indicators of Developing Asian and Pacific Countries.*

Commodity Research Bureau, Incorporated, 75 Wall Street, New York, New York 10005 (212) 504-7754; *Commodity Year Book.*

Facts on File, 460 Park Avenue South, New York, New York 10016 (800) 443-8323; *The New Book of World Rankings.*

G.K. Hall and Company, 70 Lincoln Street, Boston, Massachusetts 02111 (617) 423-3990; *The World in Figures.*

Penn Well Publishing Company, 1421 South Sheridan Road, P.O. Box 1260, Tulsa, Oklahoma 74101 (800) 752-9764; *International Energy Statistics Sourcebook.*

Statistical Office of the United Nations, Publishing Service, New York, New York 10017 (800) 253-9646; *Statistical Yearbook.*

ALBANIA - MONEY EXCHANGE RATES

Statistical Office of the United Nations, Publishing Service, New York, New York 10017 (800) 253-9646; *Statistical Yearbook.*

ALBANIA - MONEY SUPPLY

Federal Statistical Office, Gustav - Stresemann - Ring 11, D-6200 Wiesbaden, Germany; *Albanien.*

G.K. Hall and Company, 70 Lincoln Street, Boston, Massachusetts 02111 (617) 423-3990; *The World in Figures.*

ALBANIA - MOTOR VEHICLES IN USE

G.K. Hall and Company, 70 Lincoln Street, Boston, Massachusetts 02111 (617) 423-3990; *The World in Figures.*

ALBANIA - MULES - See ALBANIA - LIVESTOCK AND POULTRY

ALBANIA - MUSEUMS

Euromonitor Publications Limited, 87-88 Turnmill Street, London EC1M 5QU, England; *European Marketing Data and Statistics.*

Facts on File, 460 Park Avenue South, New York, New York 10016 (800) 443-8323; *The New Book of World Rankings.*

ALBANIA - NATALITY

Statistical Office of the United Nations, Publishing Service, New York, New York 10017 (800) 253-9646; *Demographic Yearbook.*

ALBANIA - NATIONAL ACCOUNTS

Federal Statistical Office, Gustav - Stresemann - Ring 11, D-6200 Wiesbaden, Germany; *Albanien.*

Statistical Office of the United Nations, Publishing Service, New York, New York 10017 (800) 253-9646; *Statistical Yearbook.*

ALBANIA - NATIONAL INCOME

G.K. Hall and Company, 70 Lincoln Street, Boston, Massachusetts 02111 (617) 423-3990; *The World in Figures.*

Facts on File, 460 Park Avenue South, New York, New York 10016 (800) 443-8323; *The New Book of World Rankings.*

ALBANIA - NATIONAL PRODUCT

Facts on File, 460 Park Avenue South, New York, New York 10016 (800) 443-8323; *The New Book of World Rankings.*

Statistical Office of the United Nations, Publishing Service, New York, New York 10017 (800) 253-9646; *Statistical Yearbook.*

ALBANIA - NATURAL GAS PRODUCTION - See ALBANIA - MINING AND MINERAL PRODUCTS

ALBANIA - NEWSPAPER PRODUCTION - See ALBANIA - FORESTRY AND FOREST PRODUCTS

ALBANIA - NICKEL ORE PRODUCTION AND CONSUMPTION - See ALBANIA - MINING AND MINERAL PRODUCTS

ALBANIA - NUPTIALITY - See ALBANIA - MARRIAGE RATES

ALBANIA - OATS PRODUCTION - See ALBANIA - CROPS

ALBANIA - OCCUPATIONS - See ALBANIA - LABOR FORCE

ALBANIA - PARTY LEADERS

Columbia University Press, 562 West 113th Street, New York, New York 10014 (212) 316-7100; *East European and Soviet Data Book.*

ALBANIA - PARTY MEMBERSHIP

Columbia University Press, 562 West 113th Street, New York, New York 10014 (212) 316-7100; *East European and Soviet Data Book.*

ALBANIA - PEANUT PRODUCTION - See ALBANIA - CROPS

ALBANIA - PESTICIDE USE

Food and Agricultural Organization of the United Nations (FAO) Via Delle Terme di Caracalla, 00100 Rome, Italy (Telephone Number in U.S. (202) 653-2400); *The State of Food and Agriculture.*

ALBANIA - PETROLEUM INDUSTRY

Euromonitor Publications Limited, 87-88 Turnmill Street, London EC1M 5QU, England; *European Marketing Data and Statistics.*

Facts on File, 460 Park Avenue South, New York, New York 10016 (800) 443-8323; *The New Book of World Rankings.*

Food and Agricultural Organization of the United Nations (FAO) Via Delle Terme di Caracalla, 00100 Rome, Italy (Telephone Number in U.S. (202) 653-2400); *The State of Food and Agriculture.*

G.K. Hall and Company, 70 Lincoln Street, Boston, Massachusetts 02111 (617) 423-3990; *The World in Figures.*

Penn Well Publishing Company, 1421 South Sheridan Road, P.O. Box 1260, Tulsa, Oklahoma 74101 (800) 752-9764; *International Energy Statistics Sourcebook.*

Statistical Office of the United Nations, Publishing Service, New York, New York 10017 (800) 253-9646; *Statistical Yearbook.*

ALBANIA - PIGS - See ALBANIA - LIVESTOCK AND POULTRY

ALBANIA - POPULATION

Columbia University Press, 562 West 113th Street, New York, New York 10014 (212) 316-7100; *East European and Soviet Data Book.*

The Economist Intelligence Unit, 111 West 57th Street, New York, New York 10019 (800) 938-4685; *The World Market Atlas.*

Euromonitor Publications Limited, 87-88 Turnmill Street, London EC1M 5QU, England; *European Marketing Data and Statistics.*

Facts on File, 460 Park Avenue South, New York, New York 10016 (800) 443-8323; *The New Book of World Rankings.*

Federal Statistical Office, Gustav - Stresemann - Ring 11, D-6200 Wiesbaden, Germany; *Albanien.*

Food and Agricultural Organization of the United Nations (FAO), Via delle Terme di Caracalla, 00100 Rome, Italy (Telephone Number in U.S. (202) 653-2400); *Production Yearbook.*

G.K. Hall and Company, 70 Lincoln Street, Boston, Massachusetts 02111 (617) 423-3990; *The World in Figures.*

Statistical Office of the United Nations, Publishing Service, New York, New York 10017 (800) 253-9646; *Demographic Yearbook,* and *Statistical Yearbook.*

Times Books, 201 East 50th Street, New York, New York 10022 (212) 751-2600; *The Economist Book of Vital World Statistics.*

U.S. Arms Control and Disarmament Agency, 320 Twenty-first Street, NW, Washington, D.C. 20451 (202) 647-8677; *World Military Expenditures and Arms Transfers.*

World Health Organization, Office of Publications, Avenue Appia, CH-1211 Geneva 27, Switzerland (Telephone Number in U.S. (518) 436-9686); *World Health Statistics Annual.*

ALBANIA - POST OFFICES

Facts on File, 460 Park Avenue South, New York, New York 10016 (800) 443-8323; *The New Book of World Rankings.*

ALBANIA - POTATO PRODUCTION - See ALBANIA - CROPS

ALBANIA - POULTRY - See ALBANIA - LIVESTOCK AND POULTRY

ALBANIA - PRICES

Facts on File, 460 Park Avenue South, New York, New York 10016 (800) 443-8323; *The New Book of World Rankings.*

Federal Statistical Office, Gustav - Stresemann - Ring 11, D-6200 Wiesbaden, Germany; *Albanien.*

Food and Agricultural Organization of the United Nations (FAO), Via delle Terme di Caracalla, 00100 Rome, Italy (Telephone Number in U.S. (202) 653-2400); *Production Yearbook,* and *The State of Food and Agriculture.*

G.K. Hall and Company, 70 Lincoln Street, Boston, Massachusetts 02111 (617) 423-3990; *The World in Figures.*

ALBANIA - PRODUCTION

Facts on File, 460 Park Avenue South, New York, New York 10016 (800) 443-8323; *The New Book of World Rankings.*

G.K. Hall and Company, 70 Lincoln Street, Boston, Massachusetts 02111 (617) 423-3990; *The World in Figures.*

ALBANIA - PUBLIC FINANCE

Facts on File, 460 Park Avenue South, New York, New York 10016 (800) 443-8323; *The New Book of World Rankings.*

Federal Statistical Office, Gustav - Stresemann - Ring 11, D-6200 Wiesbaden, Germany; *Albanien.*

ALBANIA - RADIO BROADCASTING - See ALBANIA - BROADCASTING

ALBANIA - RAILWAYS

Euromonitor Publications Limited, 87-88 Turnmill Street, London EC1M 5QU, England; *European Marketing Data and Statistics.*

G.K. Hall and Company, 70 Lincoln Street, Boston, Massachusetts 02111 (617) 423-3990; *The World in Figures.*

Jane's Information Group, Sentinel House, 163 Brighton Road, Coulsdon, Surrey CR5 2NH, England (Telephone Number in U.S. (703) 683-3700); *Jane's World Railways.*

ALBANIA - RELIGION

Facts on File, 460 Park Avenue South, New York, New York 10016 (800) 443-8323; *The New Book of World Rankings.*

ALBANIA - RETAIL TRADE

G.K. Hall and Company, 70 Lincoln Street, Boston, Massachusetts 02111 (617) 423-3990; *The World in Figures.*

ALBANIA - RICE PRODUCTION - See ALBANIA - CROPS

ALBANIA - ROOT AND TUBER PRODUCTION - See ALBANIA - CROPS

ALBANIA - ROUNDWOOD PRODUCTION - See ALBANIA - FORESTRY AND FOREST PRODUCTS

ALBANIA - RUBBER PRODUCTION

Facts on File, 460 Park Avenue South, New York, New York 10016 (800) 443-8323; *The New Book of World Rankings.*

ALBANIA - SAWNWOOD PRODUCTION - See ALBANIA - FORESTRY AND FOREST PRODUCTS

ALBANIA - SENIOR CITIZENS

Facts on File, 460 Park Avenue South, New York, New York 10016 (800) 443-8323; *The New Book of World Rankings.*

ALBANIA - SHEEP - See ALBANIA - LIVESTOCK AND POULTRY

ALBANIA - SILVER PRODUCTION AND CONSUMPTION - See ALBANIA - MINING AND MINERAL PRODUCTS

ALBANIA - SOCIAL DATA

Facts on File, 460 Park Avenue South, New York, New York 10016 (800) 443-8323; *The New Book of World Rankings.*

G.K. Hall and Company, 70 Lincoln Street, Boston, Massachusetts 02111 (617) 423-3990; *The World in Figures.*

ALBANIA - STEEL - See ALBANIA - MINING AND MINERAL PRODUCTS

ALBANIA - STOCKS - COMMODITY - MARKET PRICE - INDEX

Food and Agricultural Organization of the United Nations (FAO) Via Delle Terme di Caracalla, 00100 Rome, Italy (Telephone Number in U.S. (202) 653-2400); *The State of Food and Agriculture.*

ALBANIA - SUGAR PRODUCTION - See ALBANIA - CROPS

ALBANIA - TELEPHONES IN USE

American Telephone and Telegraph Company, 26 Parsippany Road, Whippany, New Jersey 07981 (800) 338-4038; *The World's Telephones.*

G.K. Hall and Company, 70 Lincoln Street, Boston, Massachusetts 02111 (617) 423-3990; *The World in Figures.*

ALBANIA - TELEVISION BROADCASTING - See ALBANIA - BROADCASTING

ALBANIA - TEXTILE PRODUCTION

G.K. Hall and Company, 70 Lincoln Street, Boston, Massachusetts 02111 (617) 423-3990; *The World in Figures.*

ALBANIA - TOBACCO PRODUCTION

Euromonitor Publications Limited, 87-88 Turnmill Street, London EC1M 5QU, England; *European Marketing Data and Statistics.*

Facts on File, 460 Park Avenue South, New York, New York 10016 (800) 443-8323; *The New Book of World Rankings.*

Statistical Office of the United Nations, Publishing Service, New York, New York 10017 (800) 253-9646; *Statistical Yearbook.*

ALBANIA - TOURISM

Euromonitor Publications Limited, 87-88 Turnmill Street, London EC1M 5QU, England; *European Marketing Data and Statistics.*

Facts on File, 460 Park Avenue South, New York, New York 10016 (800) 443-8323; *The New Book of World Rankings.*

Federal Statistical Office, Gustav - Stresemann - Ring 11, D-6200 Wiesbaden, Germany; *Albanien.*

G.K. Hall and Company, 70 Lincoln Street, Boston, Massachusetts 02111 (617) 423-3990; *The World in Figures.*

ALBANIA - TRADE - See ALBANIA - FOREIGN TRADE

ALBANIA - TRANSPORTATION AND COMMUNICATIONS

Facts on File, 460 Park Avenue, New York, New York 10016 (800) 443-8323; *The New Book of World Rankings.*

Federal Statistical Office, Gustav - Stresemann - Ring 11, D-6200 Wiesbaden, Germany; *Albanien.*

G.K. Hall and Company, 70 Lincoln Street, Boston, Massachusetts 02111 (617) 423-3990; *The World in Figures.*

ALBANIA - UNEMPLOYMENT

Euromonitor Publications Limited, 87-88 Turnmill Street, London EC1M 5QU, England; *European Marketing Data and Statistics.*

ALBANIA - VITAL STATISTICS

G.K. Hall and Company, 70 Lincoln Street, Boston, Massachusetts 02111 (617) 423-3990; *The World in Figures.*

Statistical Office of the United Nations, Publishing Service, New York, New York 10017 (800) 253-9646; *Statistical Yearbook.*

World Health Organization, Office of Publications, Avenue Appia, CH-1211 Geneva 27, Switzerland (Telephone Number in U.S. (518) 436-9686); *World Health Statistics Annual.*

ALBANIA - WAGES

Euromonitor Publications Limited, 87-88 Turnmill Street, London EC1M 5QU, England; *European Marketing Data and Statistics.*

Federal Statistical Office, Gustav - Stresemann - Ring 11, D-6200 Wiesbaden, Germany; *Albanien.*

G.K. Hall and Company, 70 Lincoln Street, Boston, Massachusetts 02111 (617) 423-3990; *The World in Figures.*

ALBANIA - WEATHER

Facts on File, 460 Park Avenue South, New York, New York 10016 (800) 443-8323; *The New Book of World Rankings.*

G.K. Hall and Company, 70 Lincoln Street, Boston, Massachusetts 02111 (617) 423-3990; *The World in Figures.*

ALBANIA - WHEAT - See ALBANIA - CROPS

ALBANIA - WINE PRODUCTION

Facts on File, 460 Park Avenue South, New York, New York 10016 (800) 443-8323; *The New Book of World Rankings.*

Statistical Office of the United Nations, Publishing Service, New York, New York 10017 (800) 253-9646; *Statistical Yearbook.*

ALBANIA - WOOL PRODUCTION

Facts on File, 460 Park Avenue South, New York, New York 10016 (800) 443-8323; *The New Book of World Rankings.*

ALCOHOLIC BEVERAGES - See also LIQUORS AND BEVERAGES

ALCOHOLIC BEVERAGES - ALCOHOLISM TREATMENT

U.S. Department of Health and Human Services, Substance Abuse and Mental Health Administration, 5600 Fisher's Lane, Rockville, Maryland 20857 (301) 443-4797; and U.S. Department of Health and Human Services, National Institute on Alcohol Abuse and Alcoholism, 5600 Fisher's Lane, Rockville, Maryland 20857 (301) 443-4373; *National Drug and Alcoholism Treatment Unit Survey, and Selected Trends.*

U.S. Department of Labor, Bureau of Labor Statistics, Two Massachusetts Avenue, NE, Washington, D.C. 20212 (202) 606-7828; *Employee Benefits in State and Local Governments, Employee Benefits in Medium and Large Private Establishments,* and *Employee Benefits in Small Private Establishments.*

ALCOHOLIC BEVERAGES - CONSUMER EXPENDITURES

U.S. Department of Labor, Bureau of Labor Statistics, Two Massachusetts Avenue, NE, Washington, D.C. 20212 (202) 606-7828; *Consumer Expenditures in 1992,* and unpublished data.

ALCOHOLIC BEVERAGES - CONSUMPTION

U.S. Department of Agriculture, Economic Research Service, Fourteenth Street and Independence Avenue, SW, Washington, D.C. 20005-4789 (202) 219-1504; *Food Consumption, Prices, and Expenditures,* and unpublished data.

U.S. Department of Health and Human Services, Substance Abuse and Mental Health Administration, 5600 Fishers Lane, Rockville, Maryland 20857 (301) 443-4797; *National Household Survey on Drug Abuse.*

U.S. Department of the Treasury, Bureau of Alcohol, Tobacco and Firearms, 650 Massachusetts Avenue, NW, Washington, D.C. 20226 (202) 927-8500; *Alcohol and Tobacco Summary Statistics.*

ALCOHOLIC BEVERAGES - LEGISLATION

National Safety Council, 1121 Spring Lake Drive, Itasca, Illinois 60143 (708) 285-1121; *Accident Facts.*

ALCOHOLIC BEVERAGES - PRICE INDEXES

U.S. Department of Labor, Bureau of Labor Statistics, Two Massachusetts Avenue, NE, Washington, D.C. 20212 (202) 606-7828; *Monthly Labor Review,* and *CPI Detailed Report.*

ALCOHOLIC BEVERAGES - PRODUCTION

U.S. Department of the Treasury, Bureau of Alcohol, Tobacco and Firearms, 650 Massachusetts Avenue, NW, Washington, D.C. 20226 (202) 927-8500; *Alcohol and Tobacco Summary Statistics.*

ALEUT POPULATION

U.S. Department of Commerce, Bureau of the Census, Suitland, Maryland 20233 (301) 763-4040; *Census of Agriculture, Census of Population,* and *Current Population Reports.*

Algeria - National Statistical Office

Office National de la Statistique, 8/10 Rue des Moussebiline, B.P. 55 Alger-Gare, Alger, Algeria.

Algeria - Primary Statistics Sources

Office National de la Statistique, 8/10 Rue des Moussebiline, B.P. 55 Alger-Gare, Alger, Algeria; *Statistiques: revue de l'Office National des Statistiques.*

Sous - Direction des Statistiques, Direction des Statistiques et de la Comptabilite Nationale, BP 478, Alger, Algeria; *Annuaire Statistique de l'Algerie* (Statistical Yearbook).

ALGERIA - AGRICULTURE

Agricultural Organization of the United Nations (FAO) Via Delle Terme di Caracalla, 00100 Rome, Italy (Telephone Number in U.S. (202) 653-2400); *The State of Food and Agriculture.*

Euromonitor Publications Limited, 87-88 Turnmill Street, London EC1M 5QU, England; *International Marketing Data and Statistics, Middle East Economic Handbook,* and *Third World Economic Handbook.*

Facts on File, 460 Park Avenue South, New York, New York 10016 (800) 443-8323; *The New Book of World Rankings.*

Federal Statistical Office, Gustav - Stresemann - Ring 11, D-6200 Wiesbaden, Germany; *Algerien.*

Food and Agricultural Organization of the United Nations (FAO), Via delle Terme di Caracalla, 00100 Rome, Italy (Telephone Number in U.S. (202) 653-2400); *Production Yearbook, The State of Food and Agriculture,* and *Trade Yearbook.*

G.K. Hall and Company, 70 Lincoln Street, Boston, Massachusetts 02111 (617) 423-3990; *The World in Figures.*

Statistical Office of the United Nations, Publishing Service, New York, New York 10017 (800) 253-9646; *Statistical Yearbook,* and *Survey of Economic and Social Conditions in Africa.*

Times Books, 201 East 50th Street, New York, New York 10022 (212) 751-2600; *The Economist Book of Vital World Statistics.*

United Nations Economic Commission for Africa, Africa Hall, P.O. Box 3001, Addis Ababa, Ethiopia (Telephone Number in U.S. (800) 253-9646); *African Statistical Yearbook.*

The World Bank, 1818 H Street, NW, Washington, D.C. 20433 (202) 477-1234; *World Tables.*

ALGERIA - AIRLINE SERVICE

Facts on File, 460 Park Avenue South, New York, New York 10016 (800) 443-8323; *The New Book of World Rankings.*

G.K. Hall and Company, 70 Lincoln Street, Boston, Massachusetts 02111 (617) 423-3990; *The World in Figures.*

International Civil Aviation Organization, 1000 Sherbrooke Street West, Suite 400, Montreal, Quebec, Canada H3A 2R2; *Civil Aviation Statistics of the World.*

Statistical Office of the United Nations, Publishing Service, New York, New York 10017 (800) 253-9646; *Statistical Yearbook.*

Times Books, 201 East 50th Street, New York, New York 10022 (212) 751-2600; *The Economist Book of Vital World Statistics.*

United Nations Economic Commission for Africa, Africa Hall, P.O. Box 3001, Addis Ababa, Ethiopia (Telephone Number in U.S. (800) 253-9646); *African Statistical Yearbook.*

ALGERIA - ALMOND PRODUCTION - See ALGERIA - CROPS

ALGERIA - ALUMINUM PRODUCTION AND CONSUMPTION - See ALGERIA - MINING AND MINERAL PRODUCTS

ALGERIA - ANIMAL HEALTH

Food and Agricultural Organization of the United Nations (FAO), Via delle Terme di Caracalla, 00100 Rome, Italy (Telephone Number in U.S. (202) 653-2400); *Animal Health Yearbook.*

ALGERIA - AREA AND DENSITY OF POPULATION

African Development Bank, 01 BP 1387, Abidjan 01, Cote D'Ivoire; *Selected Statistics on Regional Member Countries.*

Direction des Statistiques et de la Comptabilite Nationale, BP 478, Alger, Algeria; *Statistical Yearbook of Algeria.*

Euromonitor Publications Limited, 87-88 Turnmill Street, London EC1M 5QU, England; *International Marketing Data and Statistics,* and *Middle East Economic Handbook.*

Facts on File, 460 Park Avenue South, New York, New York 10016 (800) 443-8323; *The New Book of World Rankings.*

Federal Statistical Office, Gustav - Stresemann - Ring 11, D-6200 Wiesbaden, Germany; *Algerien.*

Food and Agricultural Organization of the United Nations (FAO) Via Delle Terme di Caracalla, 00100 Rome, Italy (Telephone Number in U.S. (202) 653-2400); *The State of Food and Agriculture.*

G.K. Hall and Company, 70 Lincoln Street, Boston, Massachusetts 02111 (617) 423-3990; *The World in Figures.*

Statistical Office of the United Nations, Publishing Service, New York, New York 10017 (800) 253-9646; *Statistical Yearbook,* and *Survey of Economic and Social Conditions in Africa.*

Times Books, 201 East 50th Street, New York, New York 10022 (212) 751-2600; *The Economist Book of Vital World Statistics.*

ALGERIA - ARMS EXPORTS AND IMPORTS

U.S. Arms Control and Disarmament Agency, 320 Twenty-first Street, NW, Washington, D.C. 20451 (202) 647-8677; *World Military Expenditures and Arms Transfers.*

ALGERIA - ARTICHOKE PRODUCTION - See ALGERIA - CROPS

ALGERIA - BALANCE OF PAYMENTS

African Development Bank, 01 BP 1387, Abidjan 01, Cote D'Ivoire; *Selected Statistics on Regional Member Countries.*

The Economist Intelligence Unit, 111 West 57th Street, New York, New York 10019 (800) 938-4685; *The World Market Atlas.*

Euromonitor Publications Limited, 87-88 Turnmill Street, London EC1M 5QU, England; *Third World Economic Handbook.*

Federal Statistical Office, Gustav - Stresemann - Ring 11, D-6200 Wiesbaden, Germany; *Algerien.*

G.K. Hall and Company, 70 Lincoln Street, Boston, Massachusetts 02111 (617) 423-3990; *The World in Figures.*

International Monetary Fund, 700 Nineteenth Street, NW, Washington, D.C. 20431 (202) 623-7000; *Balance of Payments Yearbook,* and *International Financial Statistics.*

Times Books, 201 East 50th Street, New York, New York 10022 (212) 751-2600; *The Economist Book of Vital World Statistics.*

United Nations Economic Commission for Africa, Africa Hall, P.O. Box 3001, Addis Ababa, Ethiopia (Telephone Number in U.S. (800) 253-9646); *African Statistical Yearbook.*

The World Bank, 1818 H Street, NW, Washington, D.C. 20433 (202) 477-1234; *World Tables.*

ALGERIA - BANKING

Facts on File, 460 Park Avenue South, New York, New York 10016 (800) 443-8323; *The New Book of World Rankings.*

G.K. Hall and Company, 70 Lincoln Street, Boston, Massachusetts 02111 (617) 423-3990; *The World in Figures.*

International Monetary Fund, 700 Nineteenth Street, NW, Washington, D.C. 20431 (202) 623-7000; *International Financial Statistics.*

United Nations Economic Commission for Africa, Africa Hall, P.O. Box 3001, Addis Ababa, Ethiopia (Telephone Number in U.S. (800) 253-9646); *African Statistical Yearbook.*

ALGERIA - BARLEY PRODUCTION - See ALGERIA - CROPS

ALGERIA - BEER PRODUCTION

Facts on File, 460 Park Avenue South, New York, New York 10016 (800) 443-8323; *The New Book of World Rankings.*

Statistical Office of the United Nations, Publishing Service, New York, New York 10017 (800) 253-9646; *Statistical Yearbook.*

ALGERIA - BIRTH RATES

Euromonitor Publications Limited, 87-88 Turnmill Street, London EC1M 5QU, England; *Middle East Economic Handbook,* and *Third World Economic Handbook,*

Facts on File, 460 Park Avenue South, New York, New York 10016 (800) 443-8323; *The New Book of World Rankings.*

Statistical Office of the United Nations, Publishing Service, New York, New York 10017 (800) 253-9646; *Demographic Yearbook,* and *Survey of Economic and Social Conditions in Africa.*

Times Books, 201 East 50th Street, New York, New York 10022 (212) 751-2600; *The Economist Book of Vital World Statistics.*

The World Bank, 1818 H Street, NW, Washington, D.C. 20433 (202) 477-1234; *World Tables.*

ALGERIA - BONDS

G.K. Hall and Company, 70 Lincoln Street, Boston, Massachusetts 02111 (617) 423-3990; *The World in Figures.*

ALGERIA - BOOK PRODUCTION

G.K. Hall and Company, 70 Lincoln Street, Boston, Massachusetts 02111 (617) 423-3990; *The World in Figures.*

ALGERIA - BROADCASTING

Billboard Limited, P.O. Box 9027, 1006 AA Amsterdam, The Netherlands (Telephone Number in U.S. (212) 764-7300); *World Radio TV Handbook.*

Facts on File, 460 Park Avenue South, New York, New York 10016 (800) 443-8323; *The New Book of World Rankings.*

G.K. Hall and Company, 70 Lincoln Street, Boston, Massachusetts 02111 (617) 423-3990; *The World in Figures.*

Times Books, 201 East 50th Street, New York, New York 10022 (212) 751-2600; *The Economist Book of Vital World Statistics.*

ALGERIA - BUSINESS

G.K. Hall and Company, 70 Lincoln Street, Boston, Massachusetts 02111 (617) 423-3990; *The World in Figures.*

ALGERIA - CALORIE SUPPLY

African Development Bank, 01 BP 1387, Abidjan 01, Cote D'Ivoire; *Selected Statistics on Regional Member Countries.*

Food and Agricultural Organization of the United Nations (FAO) Via Delle Terme di Caracalla, 00100 Rome, Italy (Telephone Number in U.S. (202) 653-2400); *The State of Food and Agriculture.*

ALGERIA - CATTLE - See ALGERIA - LIVESTOCK AND POULTRY

ALGERIA - CAUSTIC SODA PRODUCTION

Statistical Office of the United Nations, Publishing Service, New York, New York 10017 (800) 253-9646; *Statistical Yearbook.*

ALGERIA - CEMENT PRODUCTION - See ALGERIA - MINING AND MINERAL PRODUCTS

ALGERIA - CHEMICALS (ORGANIC) PRODUCTION - See ALGERIA - MINING AND MINERAL PRODUCTS

ALGERIA - CHICK PEA PRODUCTION - See ALGERIA - CROPS

ALGERIA - CHICKENS - See ALGERIA - LIVESTOCK AND POULTRY

ALGERIA - CIGAR PRODUCTION - See ALGERIA - TOBACCO PRODUCTION

ALGERIA - CIGARETTE PRODUCTION - See ALGERIA - TOBACCO PRODUCTION

ALGERIA - CLASS STRUCTURE

G.K. Hall and Company, 70 Lincoln Street, Boston, Massachusetts 02111 (617) 423-3990; *The World in Figures.*

ALGERIA - CLIMATE

Direction des Statistiques et de la Comptabilite Nationale, BP 478, Alger, Algeria; *Statistical Yearbook of Algeria.*

Facts on File, 460 Park Avenue South, New York, New York 10016 (800) 443-8323; *The New Book of World Rankings.*

G.K. Hall and Company, 70 Lincoln Street, Boston, Massachusetts 02111 (617) 423-3990; *The World in Figures.*

ALGERIA - CLOTHING EXPORTS AND IMPORTS - See ALGERIA - TEXTILE INDUSTRY

ALGERIA - COAL PRODUCTION - See ALGERIA - MINING AND MINERAL PRODUCTS

ALGERIA - COFFEE PRODUCTION - See ALGERIA - CROPS

ALGERIA - COMMUNICATIONS

Euromonitor Publications Limited, 87-88 Turnmill Street, London EC1M 5QU, England; *Third World Economic Handbook.*

Federal Statistical Office, Gustav - Stresemann - Ring 11, D-6200 Wiesbaden, Germany; *Algerien.*

G.K. Hall and Company, 70 Lincoln Street, Boston, Massachusetts 02111 (617) 423-3990; *The World in Figures.*

United Nations Economic Commission for Africa, Africa Hall, P.O. Box 3001, Addis Ababa, Ethiopia (Telephone Number in U.S. (800) 253-9646); *African Statistical Yearbook.*

ALGERIA - CONSTRUCTION INDUSTRY

Facts on File, 460 Park Avenue South, New York, New York 10016 (800) 443-8323; *The New Book of World Rankings.*

Statistical Office of the United Nations, Publishing Service, New York, New York 10017 (800) 253-9646; *Construction Statistics Yearbook,* and *Statistical Yearbook.*

United Nations Economic Commission for Africa, Africa Hall, P.O. Box 3001, Addis Ababa, Ethiopia (Telephone Number in U.S. (800) 253-9646); *African Statistical Yearbook.*

ALGERIA - CONSUMER PRICE INDEX

African Development Bank, 01 BP 1387, Abidjan 01, Cote D'Ivoire; *Selected Statistics on Regional Member Countries.*

Federal Statistical Office, Gustav - Stresemann - Ring 11, D-6200 Wiesbaden, Germany; *Algerien.*

G.K. Hall and Company, 70 Lincoln Street, Boston, Massachusetts 02111 (617) 423-3990; *The World in Figures.*

Statistical Office of the United Nations, Publishing Service, New York, New York 10017 (800) 253-9646; *Statistical Yearbook,* and *Survey of Economic and Social Conditions in Africa.*

United Nations Economic Commission for Africa, Africa Hall, P.O. Box 3001, Addis Ababa, Ethiopia (Telephone Number in U.S. (800)

253-9646); *African Statistical Yearbook.*

ALGERIA - CONSUMER PRICES

Federal Statistical Office, Gustav - Stresemann - Ring 11, D-6200 Wiesbaden, Germany; *Algerien.*

International Labour Office, I.L.O. Publications, CH-1211, Geneva 22, Switzerland; *Yearbook of Labour Statistics.*

International Monetary Fund, 700 Nineteenth Street, NW, Washington, D.C. 20431 (202) 623-7000; *International Financial Statistics.*

Times Books, 201 East 50th Street, New York, New York 10022 (212) 751-2600; *The Economist Book of Vital World Statistics.*

ALGERIA - CONSUMPTION

African Development Bank, 01 BP 1387, Abidjan 01, Cote D'Ivoire; *Selected Statistics on Regional Member Countries.*

Euromonitor Publications Limited, 87-88 Turnmill Street, London EC1M 5QU, England; *Middle East Economic Handbook.*

G.K. Hall and Company, 70 Lincoln Street, Boston, Massachusetts 02111 (617) 423-3990; *The World in Figures.*

International Lead and Zinc Study Group, Metro House, 58 St. James's Street, London SW1A 1LD, England; *Lead and Zinc Statistics.*

Statistical Office of the United Nations, Publishing Service, New York, New York 10017 (800) 253-9646; *Survey of Economic and Social Conditions in Africa.*

ALGERIA - COPPER - See ALGERIA - MINING AND MINERAL PRODUCTS

ALGERIA - CORN PRODUCTION - See ALGERIA - CROPS

ALGERIA - CORPORATE TAXES - See ALGERIA - TAXATION

ALGERIA - COTTON - See ALGERIA - CROPS

ALGERIA - CROPS

Commodity Research Bureau, Incorporated, 75 Wall Street, New York, New York 10005 (212) 504-7754; *Commodity Year Book.*

Facts on File, 460 Park Avenue South, New York, New York 10016 (800) 443-8323; *The New Book of World Rankings.*

Food and Agricultural Organization of the United Nations (FAO) Via Delle Terme di Caracalla, 00100 Rome, Italy (Telephone Number in U.S. (202) 653-2400); *Production Yearbook,* and *The State of Food and Agriculture.*

G.K. Hall and Company, 70 Lincoln Street, Boston, Massachusetts 02111 (617) 423-3990; *The World in Figures.*

Statistical Office of the United Nations, Publishing Service, New York, New York 10017 (800) 253-9646; *Statistical Yearbook.*

United Nations Economic Commission for Africa, Africa Hall, P.O. Box 3001, Addis Ababa, Ethiopia (Telephone Number in U.S. (800) 253-9646); *African Statistical Yearbook.*

ALGERIA - CUSTOMS DUTIES

G.K. Hall and Company, 70 Lincoln Street, Boston, Massachusetts 02111 (617) 423-3990; *The World in Figures.*

ALGERIA - DAIRY PRODUCTS

Facts on File, 460 Park Avenue South, New York, New York 10016 (800) 443-8323; *The New Book of World Rankings.*

Food and Agricultural Organization of the United Nations (FAO) Via Delle Terme di Caracalla, 00100 Rome, Italy (Telephone Number in U.S. (202) 653-2400); *The State of Food and Agriculture.*

Statistical Office of the United Nations, Publishing Service, New York, New York 10017 (800) 253-9646; *Statistical Yearbook.*

ALGERIA - DEATH RATES

Euromonitor Publications Limited, 87-88 Turnmill Street, London EC1M 5QU, England; *Middle East Economic Handbook,* and *Third World Economic Handbook.*

G.K. Hall and Company, 70 Lincoln Street, Boston, Massachusetts 02111 (617) 423-3990; *The World in Figures.*

Statistical Office of the United Nations, Publishing Service, New York, New York 10017 (800) 253-9646; *Statistical Yearbook,* and *Survey of Economic and Social Conditions in Africa.*

Times Books, 201 East 50th Street, New York, New York 10022 (212) 751-2600; *The Economist Book of Vital World Statistics.*

World Health Organization, Office of Publications, Avenue Appia, CH-1211 Geneva 27, Switzerland (Telephone Number in U.S. (518) 436-9686); *World Health Statistics Annual.*

ALGERIA - DEFENSE EXPENDITURES

G.K. Hall and Company, 70 Lincoln Street, Boston, Massachusetts 02111 (617) 423-3990; *The World in Figures.*

U.S. Arms Control and Disarmament Agency, 320 Twenty-first Street, NW, Washington, D.C. 20451 (202) 647-8677; *World Military Expenditures and Arms Transfers.*

ALGERIA - DEMOGRAPHY

The Economist Intelligence Unit, 111 West 57th Street, New York, New York 10019 (800) 938-4685; *The World Market Atlas.*

Facts on File, 460 Park Avenue South, New York, New York 10016 (800) 443-8323; *The New Book of World Rankings.*

Federal Statistical Office, Gustav - Stresemann - Ring 11, D-6200 Wiesbaden, Germany; *Algerien.*

G.K. Hall and Company, 70 Lincoln Street, Boston, Massachusetts 02111 (617) 423-3990; *The World in Figures.*

Statistical Office of the United Nations, Publishing Service, New York, New York 10017 (800) 253-9646; *Survey of Economic and Social Conditions in Africa.*

ALGERIA - DEVELOPMENT ASSISTANCE

G.K. Hall and Company, 70 Lincoln Street, Boston, Massachusetts 02111 (617) 423-3990; *The World in Figures.*

Statistical Office of the United Nations, Publishing Service, New York, New York 10017 (800) 253-9646; *Statistical Yearbook.*

ALGERIA - DIAMOND PRODUCTION - See ALGERIA - MINING AND MINERAL PRODUCTS

ALGERIA - DISEASES

G.K. Hall and Company, 70 Lincoln Street, Boston, Massachusetts 02111 (617) 423-3990; *The World in Figures.*

World Health Organization, Office of Publications, Avenue Appia, CH-1211 Geneva 27, Switzerland (Telephone Number in U.S. (518) 436-9686); *World Health Statistics Annual.*

ALGERIA - DIVORCE RATES

Facts on File, 460 Park Avenue South, New York, New York 10016 (800) 443-8323; *The New Book of World Rankings.*

Statistical Office of the United Nations, Publishing Service, New York, New York 10017 (800) 253-9646; *Demographic Yearbook,* and *Statistical Yearbook.*

ALGERIA - DOMESTIC PRODUCT

G.K. Hall and Company, 70 Lincoln Street, Boston, Massachusetts 02111 (617) 423-3990; *The World in Figures.*

ALGERIA - DUCKS - See ALGERIA - LIVESTOCK AND POULTRY

ALGERIA - ECONOMY

African Development Bank, 01 BP 1387, Abidjan 01, Cote D'Ivoire; *Selected Statistics on Regional Member Countries.*

Euromonitor Publications Limited, 87-88 Turnmill Street, London EC1M 5QU, England; *International Marketing Data and Statistics,* and *Third World Economic Handbook.*

Facts on File, 460 Park Avenue South, New York, New York 10016 (800) 443-8323; *The New Book of World Rankings.*

Federal Statistical Office, Gustav - Stresemann - Ring 11, D-6200 Wiesbaden, Germany; *Algerien.*

G.K. Hall and Company, 70 Lincoln Street, Boston, Massachusetts 02111 (617) 423-3990; *The World in Figures.*

Statistical Office of the United Nations, Publishing Service, New York, New York 10017 (800) 253-9646; *Foreign Trade Statistics for Africa.*

ALGERIA - EDUCATION

African Development Bank, 01 BP 1387, Abidjan 01, Cote D'Ivoire; *Selected Statistics on Regional Member Countries.*

Direction des Statistiques et de la Comptabilite Nationale, BP 478, Alger, Algeria; *Statistical Yearbook of Algeria.*

The Economist Intelligence Unit, 111 West 57th Street, New York, New York 10019 (800) 938-4685; *The World Market Atlas.*

Euromonitor Publications Limited, 87-88 Turnmill Street, London EC1M 5QU, England; *Middle East Economic Handbook.*

Facts on File, 460 Park Avenue South, New York, New York 10016 (800) 443-8323; *The New Book of World Rankings.*

Federal Statistical Office, Gustav - Stresemann - Ring 11, D-6200 Wiesbaden, Germany; *Algerien.*

G.K. Hall and Company, 70 Lincoln Street, Boston, Massachusetts 02111 (617) 423-3990; *The World in Figures.*

Statistical Office of the United Nations, Publishing Service, New York, New York 10017 (800) 253-9646; *Survey of Economic and Social Conditions in Africa.*

Times Books, 201 East 50th Street, New York, New York 10022 (212) 751-2600; *The Economist Book of Vital World Statistics.*

United Nations Economic Commission for Africa, Africa Hall, P.O. Box 3001, Addis Ababa, Ethiopia (Telephone Number in U.S. (800) 253-9646); *African Statistical Yearbook.*

United Nations Educational, Scientific and Cultural Organization (UNESCO), 7 Place de Fontenoy, F-75700 Paris, France (Telephone Number in U.S. (212) 963-5981); *Statistical Yearbook.*

The World Bank, 1818 H Street, NW, Washington, D.C. 20433 (202) 477-1234; *World Tables.*

ALGERIA - EGG PRODUCTION - See ALGERIA - DAIRY PRODUCTS

ALGERIA - ELECTRICITY

Facts on File, 460 Park Avenue South, New York, New York 10016 (800) 443-8323; *The New Book of World Rankings.*

Penn Well Publishing Company, 1421 South Sheridan Road, P.O. Box 1260, Tulsa, Oklahoma 74101 (800) 752-9764; *International Energy Statistics Sourcebook.*

Statistical Office of the United Nations, Publishing Service, New York, New York 10017 (800) 253-9646; *Statistical Yearbook,* and *Survey of Economic and Social Conditions in Africa.*

Times Books, 201 East 50th Street, New York, New York 10022 (212) 751-2600; *The Economist Book of Vital World Statistics.*

United Nations Economic Commission for Africa, Africa Hall, P.O. Box 3001, Addis Ababa, Ethiopia (Telephone Number in U.S. (800) 253-9646); *African Statistical Yearbook.*

ALGERIA - EMPLOYMENT

Direction des Statistiques et de la Comptabilite Nationale, BP 478, Alger, Algeria; *Statistical Yearbook of Algeria.*

Euromonitor Publications Limited, 87-88 Turnmill Street, London EC1M 5QU, England; *International Marketing Data and Statistics,* and *Middle East Economic Handbook.*

Facts on File, 460 Park Avenue South, New York, New York 10016 (800) 443-8323; *The New Book of World Rankings.*

Federal Statistical Office, Gustav - Stresemann - Ring 11, D-6200 Wiesbaden, Germany; *Algerien.*

International Labour Office, I.L.O. Publications, CH-1211, Geneva 22, Switzerland; *Yearbook of Labour Statistics.*

Statistical Office of the United Nations, Publishing Service, New York, New York 10017 (800) 253-9646; *Survey of Economic and Social Conditions in Africa.*

United Nations Economic Commission for Africa, Africa Hall, P.O. Box 3001, Addis Ababa, Ethiopia (Telephone Number in U.S. (800) 253-9646); *African Statistical Yearbook.*

ALGERIA - EMPLOYMENT INDEX - MANUFACTURING

Statistical Office of the United Nations, Publishing Service, New York, New York 10017 (800) 253-9646; *Statistical Yearbook.*

ALGERIA - ENERGY

Euromonitor Publications Limited, 87-88 Turnmill Street, London EC1M 5QU, England; *Middle East Economic Handbook.*

Facts on File, 460 Park Avenue South, New York, New York 10016 (800) 443-8323; *The New Book of World Rankings.*

Food and Agricultural Organization of the United Nations (FAO) Via Delle Terme di Caracalla, 00100 Rome, Italy (Telephone Number in U.S. (202) 653-2400); *The State of Food and Agriculture.*

G.K. Hall and Company, 70 Lincoln Street, Boston, Massachusetts 02111 (617) 423-3990; *The World in Figures.*

Penn Well Publishing Company, 1421 South Sheridan Road, P.O. Box 1260, Tulsa, Oklahoma 74101 (800) 752-9764; *International Energy Statistics Sourcebook.*

Statistical Office of the United Nations, Publishing Service, New York, New York 10017 (800) 253-9646; *Energy Statistics Yearbook,* and *Statistical Yearbook.*

Times Books, 201 East 50th Street, New York, New York 10022 (212) 751-2600; *The Economist Book of Vital World Statistics.*

United Nations Economic Commission for Africa, Africa Hall, P.O. Box 3001, Addis Ababa, Ethiopia (Telephone Number in U.S. (800) 253-9646); *African Statistical Yearbook.*

ALGERIA - EXCHANGE RATES

African Development Bank, 01 BP 1387, Abidjan 01, Cote D'Ivoire; *Selected Statistics on Regional Member Countries.*

Euromonitor Publications Limited, 87-88 Turnmill Street, London EC1M 5QU, England; *International Marketing Data and Statistics,* and *Middle East Economic Handbook.*

International Civil Aviation Organization, 1000 Sherbrooke Street West, Suite 400, Montreal, Quebec, Canada H3A 2R2; *Civil Aviation Statistics of the World.*

International Monetary Fund, 700 Nineteenth Street, NW, Washington, D.C. 20431 (202) 623-7000; *International Financial Statistics.*

Organization of Petroleum Exporting Countries, Obere Donaustrasse 93, 1020 Vienna 2, Austria; *OPEC Annual Statistical Bulletin.*

Statistical Office of the United Nations, Publishing Service, New York, New York 10017 (800) 253-9646; *Foreign Trade Statistics for Africa.*

Statistical Office of the United Nations, Publishing Service, New York, New York 10017 (800) 253-9646; *Statistical Yearbook.*

ALGERIA - EXPORTS

African Development Bank, 01 BP 1387, Abidjan 01, Cote D'Ivoire; *Selected Statistics on Regional Member Countries.*

The Economist Intelligence Unit, 111 West 57th Street, New York, New York 10019 (800) 938-4685; *The World Market Atlas.*

Euromonitor Publications Limited, 87-88 Turnmill Street, London EC1M 5QU, England; *International Marketing Data and Statistics, Middle East Economic Handbook,* and *Third World Economic Handbook.*

Food and Agricultural Organization of the United Nations (FAO) Via Delle Terme di Caracalla, 00100 Rome, Italy (Telephone Number in U.S. (202) 653-2400); *The State of Food and Agriculture.*

G.K. Hall and Company, 70 Lincoln Street, Boston, Massachusetts 02111 (617) 423-3990; *The World in Figures.*

International Lead and Zinc Study Group, Metro House, 58 St. James's Street, London SW1A 1LD, England; *Lead and Zinc Statistics.*

International Monetary Fund, 700 Nineteenth Street, NW, Washington, D.C. 20431 (202) 623-7000; *Direction of Trade Statistics,* and *International Financial Statistics.*

Organization of Petroleum Exporting Countries, Obere Donaustrasse 93, 1020 Vienna 2, Austria; *OPEC Annual Statistical Bulletin.*

Statistical Office of the United Nations, Publishing Service, New York, New York 10017 (800) 253-9646; *Foreign Trade Statistics for Africa, Statistical Yearbook, Survey of Economic and Social Conditions in Africa,* and *Trade in Manufactures of Developing Countries.*

Times Books, 201 East 50th Street, New York, New York 10022 (212) 751-2600; *The Economist Book of Vital World Statistics.*

United Nations Economic Commission for Africa, Africa Hall, P.O. Box 3001, Addis Ababa, Ethiopia (Telephone Number in U.S. (800) 253-9646); *African Statistical Yearbook.*

The World Bank, 1818 H Street, NW, Washington, D.C. 20433 (202) 477-1234; *World Tables.*

ALGERIA - EXTERNAL INDEBTEDNESS

African Development Bank, 01 BP 1387, Abidjan 01, Cote D'Ivoire; *Selected Statistics on Regional Member Countries.*

Euromonitor Publications Limited, 87-88 Turnmill Street, London EC1M 5QU, England; *Third World Economic Handbook.*

Statistical Office of the United Nations, Publishing Service, New York, New York 10017 (800) 253-9646; *Survey of Economic and Social Conditions in Africa.*

The World Bank, 1818 H Street, NW, Washington, D.C. 20433 (202) 477-1234; *World Tables.*

ALGERIA - EXTERNAL TRADE

African Development Bank, 01 BP 1387, Abidjan 01, Cote D'Ivoire; *Selected Statistics on Regional Member Countries.*

Food and Agricultural Organization of the United Nations (FAO) Via Delle Terme di Caracalla, 00100 Rome, Italy (Telephone Number in

U.S. (202) 653-2400); *The State of Food and Agriculture*, and *Trade Yearbook*.

G.K. Hall and Company, 70 Lincoln Street, Boston, Massachusetts 02111 (617) 423-3990; *The World in Figures*.

Statistical Office of the United Nations, Publishing Service, New York, New York 10017 (800) 253-9646; *Statistical Yearbook*.

ALGERIA - FARM CROPS - See ALGERIA - CROPS

ALGERIA - FEMALE WORKING POPULATION - See ALGERIA - EMPLOYMENT

ALGERIA - FERTILITY RATES

Facts on File, 460 Park Avenue South, New York, New York 10016 (800) 443-8323; *The New Book of World Rankings*.

Statistical Office of the United Nations, Publishing Service, New York, New York 10017 (800) 253-9646; *Survey of Economic and Social Conditions in Africa*.

Times Books, 201 East 50th Street, New York, New York 10022 (212) 751-2600; *The Economist Book of Vital World Statistics*.

The World Bank, 1818 H Street, NW, Washington, D.C. 20433 (202) 477-1234; *World Tables*.

ALGERIA - FERTILIZER

Food and Agricultural Organization of the United Nations (FAO), Via delle Terme di Caracalla, 00100 Rome, Italy (Telephone Number in U.S. (202) 653-2400); *Fertilizer Yearbook*, and *The State of Food and Agriculture*.

Statistical Office of the United Nations, Publishing Service, New York, New York 10017 (800) 253-9646; *Statistical Yearbook*.

ALGERIA - FETAL MORTALITY

Statistical Office of the United Nations, Publishing Service, New York, New York 10017 (800) 253-9646; *Demographic Yearbook*.

World Health Organization, Office of Publications, Avenue Appia, CH-1211 Geneva 27, Switzerland (Telephone Number in U.S. (518) 436-9686); *World Health Statistics Annual*.

ALGERIA - FILM - See ALGERIA - MOTION PICTURES

ALGERIA - FINANCE

African Development Bank, 01 BP 1387, Abidjan 01, Cote D'Ivoire; *Selected Statistics on Regional Member Countries*.

Euromonitor Publications Limited, 87-88 Turnmill Street, London EC1M 5QU, England; *Middle East Economic Handbook*.

Facts on File, 460 Park Avenue South, New York, New York 10016 (800) 443-8323; *The New Book of World Rankings*.

Federal Statistical Office, Gustav - Stresemann - Ring 11, D-6200 Wiesbaden, Germany; *Algerien*.

G.K. Hall and Company, 70 Lincoln Street, Boston, Massachusetts 02111 (617) 423-3990; *The World in Figures*.

International Monetary Fund, 700 Nineteenth Street, NW, Washington, D.C. 20431 (202) 623-7000; *International Financial Statistics*.

United Nations Economic Commission for Africa, Africa Hall, P.O. Box 3001, Addis Ababa, Ethiopia (Telephone Number in U.S. (800) 253-9646); *African Statistical Yearbook*.

ALGERIA - FISHERIES

Direction des Statistiques et de la Comptabilite Nationale, BP 478, Alger, Algeria; *Statistical Yearbook of Algeria*.

Facts on File, 460 Park Avenue South, New York, New York 10016 (800) 443-8323; *The New Book of World Rankings*.

Federal Statistical Office, Gustav - Stresemann - Ring 11, D-6200 Wiesbaden, Germany; *Algerien*.

Food and Agricultural Organization of the United Nations (FAO) Via Delle Terme di Caracalla, 00100 Rome, Italy (Telephone Number in U.S. (202) 653-2400); *The State of Food and Agriculture*, and *Yearbook of Fishery Statistics*.

Statistical Office of the United Nations, Publishing Service, New York, New York 10017 (800) 253-9646; *Statistical Yearbook*, and *Survey of Economic and Social Conditions in Africa*.

United Nations Economic Commission for Africa, Africa Hall, P.O. Box 3001, Addis Ababa, Ethiopia (Telephone Number in U.S. (800) 253-9646); *African Statistical Yearbook*.

ALGERIA - FLOUR PRODUCTION

Statistical Office of the United Nations, Publishing Service, New York, New York 10017 (800) 253-9646; *Statistical Yearbook*.

ALGERIA - FOOD

African Development Bank, 01 BP 1387, Abidjan 01, Cote D'Ivoire; *Selected Statistics on Regional Member Countries*.

Food and Agricultural Organization of the United Nations (FAO) Via Delle Terme di Caracalla, 00100 Rome, Italy (Telephone Number in U.S. (202) 653-2400); *Production Yearbook*, and *The State of Food and Agriculture*.

G.K. Hall and Company, 70 Lincoln Street, Boston, Massachusetts 02111 (617) 423-3990; *The World in Figures*.

ALGERIA - FOREIGN AID

G.K. Hall and Company, 70 Lincoln Street, Boston, Massachusetts 02111 (617) 423-3990; *The World in Figures*.

ALGERIA - FOREIGN ASSISTANCE

Statistical Office of the United Nations, Publishing Service, New York, New York 10017 (800) 253-9646; *Statistical Yearbook*.

ALGERIA - FOREIGN INDEBTEDNESS

Euromonitor Publications Limited, 87-88 Turnmill Street, London EC1M 5QU, England; *Middle East Economic Handbook*.

ALGERIA - FOREIGN TRADE

Direction des Statistiques et de la Comptabilite Nationale, BP 478, Alger, Algeria; *Statistical Yearbook of Algeria*.

Euromonitor Publications Limited, 87-88 Turnmill Street, London EC1M 5QU, England; *International Marketing Data and Statistics,* and *Third World Economic Handbook.*

Facts on File, 460 Park Avenue South, New York, New York 10016 (800) 443-8323; *The New Book of World Rankings.*

Federal Statistical Office, Gustav - Stresemann - Ring 11, D-6200 Wiesbaden, Germany; *Algerien.*

Food and Agricultural Organization of the United Nations (FAO) Via Delle Terme di Caracalla, 00100 Rome, Italy (Telephone Number in U.S. (202) 653-2400); *The State of Food and Agriculture.*

G.K. Hall and Company, 70 Lincoln Street, Boston, Massachusetts 02111 (617) 423-3990; *The World in Figures.*

Organisation for Economic Co-operation and Development (OECD), 2 rue Andre-Pascal, 75 Paris 16, France (Telephone Number in U.S. (212) 963-5981); *Trade by Commodities.*

Statistical Office of the United Nations, Publishing Service, New York, New York 10017 (800) 253-9646; *Foreign Trade Statistics for Africa, International Trade Statistics Yearbook,* and *Statistical Yearbook.*

United Nations Economic Commission for Africa, Africa Hall, P.O. Box 3001, Addis Ababa, Ethiopia (Telephone Number in U.S. (800) 253-9646); *African Statistical Yearbook.*

The World Bank, 1818 H Street, NW, Washington, D.C. 20433 (202) 477-1234; *World Tables.*

ALGERIA - FORESTRY AND FOREST PRODUCTS

Direction des Statistiques et de la Comptabilite Nationale, BP 478, Alger, Algeria; *Statistical Yearbook of Algeria.*

Euromonitor Publications Limited, 87-88 Turnmill Street, London EC1M 5QU, England; *Third World Economic Handbook.*

Facts on File, 460 Park Avenue South, New York, New York 10016 (800) 443-8323; *The New Book of World Rankings.*

Federal Statistical Office, Gustav - Stresemann - Ring 11, D-6200 Wiesbaden, Germany; *Algerien.*

Food and Agricultural Organization of the United Nations (FAO) Via Delle Terme di Caracalla, 00100 Rome, Italy (Telephone Number in U.S. (202) 653-2400); *The State of Food and Agriculture,* and *Yearbook of Forest Products.*

G.K. Hall and Company, 70 Lincoln Street, Boston, Massachusetts 02111 (617) 423-3990; *The World in Figures.*

Statistical Office of the United Nations, Publishing Service, New York, New York 10017 (800) 253-9646; *Statistical Yearbook.*

United Nations Economic Commission for Africa, Africa Hall, P.O. Box 3001, Addis Ababa, Ethiopia (Telephone Number in U.S. (800) 253-9646); *African Statistical Yearbook.*

United Nations Educational, Scientific and Cultural Organization (UNESCO), 7 Place de Fontenoy, F-75700 Paris, France (Telephone Number in U.S. (212) 963-5981); *Statistical Yearbook.*

ALGERIA - GAS - See ALGERIA - MINING AND MINERAL PRODUCTS

ALGERIA - GENERAL INDUSTRIAL STATISTICS

Federal Statistical Office, Gustav - Stresemann - Ring 11, D-6200 Wiesbaden, Germany; *Algerien.*

ALGERIA - GENERAL MORTALITY

Statistical Office of the United Nations, Publishing Service, New York, New York 10017 (800) 253-9646; *Demographic Yearbook.*

World Health Organization, Office of Publications, Avenue Appia, CH-1211 Geneva 27, Switzerland (Telephone Number in U.S. (518) 436-9686); *World Health Statistics Annual.*

ALGERIA - GEOGRAPHIC DATA

Facts on File, 460 Park Avenue South, New York, New York 10016 (800) 443-8323; *The New Book of World Rankings.*

Federal Statistical Office, Gustav - Stresemann - Ring 11, D-6200 Wiesbaden, Germany; *Algerien.*

ALGERIA - GOATS - See ALGERIA - LIVESTOCK AND POULTRY

ALGERIA - GOLD - See ALGERIA - MINING AND MINERAL PRODUCTS

ALGERIA - GOVERNMENT

G.K. Hall and Company, 70 Lincoln Street, Boston, Massachusetts 02111 (617) 423-3990; *The World in Figures.*

ALGERIA - GOVERNMENT CONSUMPTION

International Monetary Fund, 700 Nineteenth Street, NW, Washington, D.C. 20431 (202) 623-7000; *International Financial Statistics.*

ALGERIA - GOVERNMENT EXPENDITURE

Euromonitor Publications Limited, 87-88 Turnmill Street, London EC1M 5QU, England; *Third World Economic Handbook.*

The World Bank, 1818 H Street, NW, Washington, D.C. 20433 (202) 477-1234; *World Tables.*

ALGERIA - GOVERNMENT REVENUE

Statistical Office of the United Nations, Publishing Service, New York, New York 10017 (800) 253-9646; *Survey of Economic and Social Conditions in Africa.*

The World Bank, 1818 H Street, NW, Washington, D.C. 20433 (202) 477-1234; *World Tables.*

ALGERIA - GRAIN PRODUCTION - See ALGERIA - CROPS

ALGERIA - GROSS DOMESTIC PRODUCT

African Development Bank, 01 BP 1387, Abidjan 01, Cote D'Ivoire; *Selected Statistics on Regional Member Countries.*

The Economist Intelligence Unit, 111 West 57th Street, New York, New York 10019 (800) 938-4685; *The World Market Atlas.*

Euromonitor Publications Limited, 87-88 Turnmill Street, London EC1M 5QU, England; *International Marketing Data and Statistics, Middle East Economic Handbook,* and *Third World Economic Handbook.*

Facts on File, 460 Park Avenue South, New York, New York 10016 (800) 443-8323; *The New Book of World Rankings*.

G.K. Hall and Company, 70 Lincoln Street, Boston, Massachusetts 02111 (617) 423-3990; *The World in Figures*.

International Monetary Fund, 700 Nineteenth Street, NW, Washington, D.C. 20431 (202) 623-7000; *International Financial Statistics*.

Statistical Office of the United Nations, Publishing Service, New York, New York 10017 (800) 253-9646; *Statistical Yearbook*, and *Survey of Economic and Social Conditions in Africa*.

Times Books, 201 East 50th Street, New York, New York 10022 (212) 751-2600; *The Economist Book of Vital World Statistics*.

United Nations Economic Commission for Africa, Africa Hall, P.O. Box 3001, Addis Ababa, Ethiopia (Telephone Number in U.S. (800) 253-9646); *African Statistical Yearbook*.

The World Bank, 1818 H Street, NW, Washington, D.C. 20433 (202) 477-1234; *World Tables*.

ALGERIA - GROSS INDUSTRIAL PRODUCT

Euromonitor Publications Limited, 87-88 Turnmill Street, London EC1M 5QU, England; *Third World Economic Handbook*.

ALGERIA - GROSS NATIONAL PRODUCT

Euromonitor Publications Limited, 87-88 Turnmill Street, London EC1M 5QU, England; *International Marketing Data and Statistics*, and *Third World Economic Handbook*.

Organization of Petroleum Exporting Countries, Obere Donaustrasse 93, 1020 Vienna 2, Austria; *OPEC Annual Statistical Bulletin*.

U.S. Arms Control and Disarmament Agency, 320 Twenty-first Street, NW, Washington, D.C. 20451 (202) 647-8677; *World Military Expenditures and Arms Transfers*.

The World Bank, 1818 H Street, NW, Washington, D.C. 20433 (202) 477-1234; *World Tables*.

ALGERIA - HEALTH

African Development Bank, 01 BP 1387, Abidjan 01, Cote D'Ivoire; *Selected Statistics on Regional Member Countries*.

Euromonitor Publications Limited, 87-88 Turnmill Street, London EC1M 5QU, England; *Middle East Economic Handbook*.

Facts on File, 460 Park Avenue South, New York, New York 10016 (800) 443-8323; *The New Book of World Rankings*.

Federal Statistical Office, Gustav - Stresemann - Ring 11, D-6200 Wiesbaden, Germany; *Algerien*.

G.K. Hall and Company, 70 Lincoln Street, Boston, Massachusetts 02111 (617) 423-3990; *The World in Figures*.

Statistical Office of the United Nations, Publishing Service, New York, New York 10017 (800) 253-9646; *Statistical Yearbook*.

Times Books, 201 East 50th Street, New York, New York 10022 (212) 751-2600; *The Economist Book of Vital World Statistics*.

United Nations Economic Commission for Africa, Africa Hall, P.O. Box 3001, Addis Ababa, Ethiopia (Telephone Number in U.S. (800) 253-9646); *African Statistical Yearbook*.

World Health Organization, Office of Publications, Avenue Appia, CH-1211 Geneva 27, Switzerland (Telephone Number in U.S. (518) 436-9686); *World Health Statistics Annual*.

ALGERIA - HIDE PRODUCTION

Food and Agricultural Organization of the United Nations (FAO), Via delle Terme di Caracalla, 00100 Rome, Italy (Telephone Number in U.S. (202) 653-2400); *Production Yearbook*.

ALGERIA - HIGHWAYS

G.K. Hall and Company, 70 Lincoln Street, Boston, Massachusetts 02111 (617) 423-3990; *The World in Figures*.

International Road Federation, 525 School Street, SW, Washington, D.C. 20024 (202) 554-2106; *World Road Statistics*.

Statistical Office of the United Nations, Publishing Service, New York, New York 10017 (800) 253-9646; *Survey of Economic and Social Conditions in Africa*.

United Nations Economic Commission for Africa, Africa Hall, P.O. Box 3001, Addis Ababa, Ethiopia (Telephone Number in U.S. (800) 253-9646); *African Statistical Yearbook*.

ALGERIA - HORSES - See ALGERIA - LIVESTOCK AND POULTRY

ALGERIA - HOURS OF WORK - See ALGERIA - EMPLOYMENT

ALGERIA - HOUSING AND HOUSING UNITS

Direction des Statistiques et de la Comptabilite Nationale, BP 478, Alger, Algeria; *Statistical Yearbook of Algeria*.

Euromonitor Publications Limited, 87-88 Turnmill Street, London EC1M 5QU, England; *Third World Economic Handbook*.

Facts on File, 460 Park Avenue South, New York, New York 10016 (800) 443-8323; *The New Book of World Rankings*.

ALGERIA - ILLITERATE POPULATION

The Economist Intelligence Unit, 111 West 57th Street, New York, New York 10019 (800) 938-4685; *The World Market Atlas*.

G.K. Hall and Company, 70 Lincoln Street, Boston, Massachusetts 02111 (617) 423-3990; *The World in Figures*.

United Nations Educational, Scientific and Cultural Organization (UNESCO), 7 Place de Fontenoy, F-75700 Paris, France (Telephone Number in U.S. (212) 963-5981); *Statistical Yearbook*.

ALGERIA - IMPORTS

African Development Bank, 01 BP 1387, Abidjan 01, Cote D'Ivoire; *Selected Statistics on Regional Member Countries*.

The Economist Intelligence Unit, 111 West 57th Street, New York, New York 10019 (800) 938-4685; *The World Market Atlas*.

Euromonitor Publications Limited, 87-88 Turnmill Street, London EC1M 5QU, England; *International Marketing Data and Statistics*, *Middle East Economic Handbook*, and *Third World Economic Handbook*.

Food and Agricultural Organization of the United Nations (FAO) Via Delle Terme di Caracalla, 00100 Rome, Italy (Telephone Number in U.S. (202) 653-2400); *The State of Food and Agriculture.*

G.K. Hall and Company, 70 Lincoln Street, Boston, Massachusetts 02111 (617) 423-3990; *The World in Figures.*

International Lead and Zinc Study Group, Metro House, 58 St. James's Street, London SW1A 1LD, England; *Lead and Zinc Statistics.*

International Monetary Fund, 700 Nineteenth Street, NW, Washington, D.C. 20431 (202) 623-7000; *Direction of Trade Statistics,* and *International Financial Statistics.*

Statistical Office of the United Nations, Publishing Service, New York, New York 10017 (800) 253-9646; *Foreign Trade Statistics for Africa,* and *Statistical Yearbook,* and *Survey of Economic and Social Conditions in Africa.*

United Nations Economic Commission for Africa, Africa Hall, P.O. Box 3001, Addis Ababa, Ethiopia (Telephone Number in U.S. (800) 253-9646); *African Statistical Yearbook.*

The World Bank, 1818 H Street, NW, Washington, D.C. 20433 (202) 477-1234; *World Tables.*

ALGERIA - INDUSTRY

Euromonitor Publications Limited, 87-88 Turnmill Street, London EC1M 5QU, England; *International Marketing Data and Statistics.*

Facts on File, 460 Park Avenue South, New York, New York 10016 (800) 443-8323; *The New Book of World Rankings.*

Federal Statistical Office, Gustav - Stresemann - Ring 11, D-6200 Wiesbaden, Germany; *Algerien.*

International Labour Office, I.L.O. Publications, CH-1211, Geneva 22, Switzerland; *Yearbook of Labour Statistics.*

Statistical Office of the United Nations, Publishing Service, New York, New York 10017 (800) 253-9646; *Statistical Yearbook.*

Times Books, 201 East 50th Street, New York, New York 10022 (212) 751-2600; *The Economist Book of Vital World Statistics.*

United Nations Economic Commission for Africa, Africa Hall, P.O. Box 3001, Addis Ababa, Ethiopia (Telephone Number in U.S. (800) 253-9646); *African Statistical Yearbook.*

The World Bank, 1818 H Street, NW, Washington, D.C. 20433 (202) 477-1234; *World Tables.*

World Intellectual Property Organization, 34 Chemin des Colombettes, CH-1211 Geneva 20. Switzerland; *Industrial Property Statistics.*

ALGERIA - INFANT AND MATERNAL MORTALITY

Statistical Office of the United Nations, Publishing Service, New York, New York 10017 (800) 253-9646; *Demographic Yearbook,* and *Statistical Yearbook,* and *Survey of Economic and Social Conditions in Africa.*

Times Books, 201 East 50th Street, New York, New York 10022 (212) 751-2600; *The Economist Book of Vital World Statistics.*

The World Bank, 1818 H Street, NW, Washington, D.C. 20433 (202) 477-1234; *World Tables.*

World Health Organization, Office of Publications, Avenue Appia, CH-1211 Geneva 27, Switzerland (Telephone Number in U.S. (518) 436-9686); *World Health Statistics Annual.*

ALGERIA - INTERNATIONAL LIQUIDITY

International Monetary Fund, 700 Nineteenth Street, NW, Washington, D.C. 20431 (202) 623-7000; *International Financial Statistics.*

ALGERIA - INTERNATIONAL RESERVES EXCLUDING GOLD

African Development Bank, 01 BP 1387, Abidjan 01, Cote D'Ivoire; *Selected Statistics on Regional Member Countries.*

The World Bank, 1818 H Street, NW, Washington, D.C. 20433 (202) 477-1234; *World Tables.*

ALGERIA - INVESTMENTS

International Monetary Fund, 700 Nineteenth Street, NW, Washington, D.C. 20431 (202) 623-7000; *International Financial Statistics.*

ALGERIA - IRON ORE PRODUCTION AND CONSUMPTION - See ALGERIA - MINING AND MINERAL PRODUCTS

ALGERIA - IRRIGATION

Euromonitor Publications Limited, 87-88 Turnmill Street, London EC1M 5QU, England; *International Marketing Data and Statistics.*

ALGERIA - LABOR FORCE

African Development Bank, 01 BP 1387, Abidjan 01, Cote D'Ivoire; *Selected Statistics on Regional Member Countries.*

Euromonitor Publications Limited, 87-88 Turnmill Street, London EC1M 5QU, England; *International Marketing Data and Statistics,* and *Middle East Economic Handbook.*

Facts on File, 460 Park Avenue South, New York, New York 10016 (800) 443-8323; *The New Book of World Rankings.*

Food and Agricultural Organization of the United Nations (FAO) Via Delle Terme di Caracalla, 00100 Rome, Italy (Telephone Number in U.S. (202) 653-2400); *The State of Food and Agriculture.*

G.K. Hall and Company, 70 Lincoln Street, Boston, Massachusetts 02111 (617) 423-3990; *The World in Figures.*

Times Books, 201 East 50th Street, New York, New York 10022 (212) 751-2600; *The Economist Book of Vital World Statistics.*

The World Bank, 1818 H Street, NW, Washington, D.C. 20433 (202) 477-1234; *World Tables.*

ALGERIA - LABOR PRODUCTIVITY

International Labour Office, I.L.O. Publications, CH-1211, Geneva 22, Switzerland; *Yearbook of Labour Statistics.*

ALGERIA - LAND USE

Euromonitor Publications Limited, 87-88 Turnmill Street, London EC1M 5QU, England; *International Marketing Data and Statistics.*

Food and Agricultural Organization of the United Nations (FAO), Via delle Terme di Caracalla, 00100 Rome, Italy (Telephone Number in U.S. (202) 653-2400); *Production Yearbook.*

G.K. Hall and Company, 70 Lincoln Street, Boston, Massachusetts 02111 (617) 423-3990; *The World in Figures.*

ALGERIA - LEAD - See ALGERIA - MINING AND MINERAL PRODUCTS

ALGERIA - LIBRARIES

Facts on File, 460 Park Avenue South, New York, New York 10016 (800) 443-8323; *The New Book of World Rankings.*

United Nations Educational, Scientific and Cultural Organization (UNESCO), 7 Place de Fontenoy, F-75700 Paris, France (Telephone Number in U.S. (212) 963-5981); *Statistical Yearbook.*

ALGERIA - LIFE EXPECTANCY

African Development Bank, 01 BP 1387, Abidjan 01, Cote D'Ivoire; *Selected Statistics on Regional Member Countries.*

ALGERIA - LITERACY RATE

Statistical Office of the United Nations, Publishing Service, New York, New York 10017 (800) 253-9646; *Survey of Economic and Social Conditions in Africa.*

ALGERIA - LIVESTOCK AND POULTRY

Euromonitor Publications Limited, 87-88 Turnmill Street, London EC1M 5QU, England; *International Marketing Data and Statistics.*

Facts on File, 460 Park Avenue South, New York, New York 10016 (800) 443-8323; *The New Book of World Rankings.*

Food and Agricultural Organization of the United Nations (FAO), Via delle Terme di Caracalla, 00100 Rome, Italy (Telephone Number in U.S. (202) 653-2400); *Production Yearbook,* and *The State of Food and Agriculture.*

G.K. Hall and Company, 70 Lincoln Street, Boston, Massachusetts 02111 (617) 423-3990; *The World in Figures.*

Statistical Office of the United Nations, Publishing Service, New York, New York 10017 (800) 253-9646; *Statistical Yearbook,* and *Survey of Economic and Social Conditions in Africa.*

United Nations Economic Commission for Africa, Africa Hall, P.O. Box 3001, Addis Ababa, Ethiopia (Telephone Number in U.S. (800) 253-9646); *African Statistical Yearbook.*

ALGERIA - LIVING LEVELS

G.K. Hall and Company, 70 Lincoln Street, Boston, Massachusetts 02111 (617) 423-3990; *The World in Figures.*

Times Books, 201 East 50th Street, New York, New York 10022 (212) 751-2600; *The Economist Book of Vital World Statistics.*

ALGERIA - MAIL - NUMBER OF PIECES SENT OR RECEIVED

Statistical Office of the United Nations, Publishing Service, New York, New York 10017 (800) 253-9646; *Statistical Yearbook.*

ALGERIA - MANUFACTURING

Euromonitor Publications Limited, 87-88 Turnmill Street, London EC1M 5QU, England; *Third World Economic Handbook.*

Facts on File, 460 Park Avenue South, New York, New York 10016 (800) 443-8323; *The New Book of World Rankings.*

G.K. Hall and Company, 70 Lincoln Street, Boston, Massachusetts 02111 (617) 423-3990; *The World in Figures.*

Statistical Office of the United Nations, Publishing Service, New York, New York 10017 (800) 253-9646; *Statistical Yearbook, and Survey of Economic and Social Conditions in Africa.*

Times Books, 201 East 50th Street, New York, New York 10022 (212) 751-2600; *The Economist Book of Vital World Statistics.*

United Nations Economic Commission for Africa, Africa Hall, P.O. Box 3001, Addis Ababa, Ethiopia (Telephone Number in U.S. (800) 253-9646); *African Statistical Yearbook.*

The World Bank, 1818 H Street, NW, Washington, D.C. 20433 (202) 477-1234; *World Tables.*

ALGERIA - MARRIAGE RATES

Facts on File, 460 Park Avenue South, New York, New York 10016 (800) 443-8323; *The New Book of World Rankings.*

Statistical Office of the United Nations, Publishing Service, New York, New York 10017 (800) 253-9646; *Demographic Yearbook,* and *Statistical Yearbook.*

ALGERIA - MEAT PRODUCTION - See ALGERIA - LIVESTOCK AND POULTRY

ALGERIA - MERCHANT FLEET CHARACTERISTICS - See ALGERIA - MERCHANT SHIPPING

ALGERIA - MERCHANT SHIPPING

G.K. Hall and Company, 70 Lincoln Street, Boston, Massachusetts 02111 (617) 423-3990; *The World in Figures.*

Organization of Petroleum Exporting Countries, Obere Donaustrasse 93, 1020 Vienna 2, Austria; *OPEC Annual Statistical Bulletin.*

Statistical Office of the United Nations, Publishing Service, New York, New York 10017 (800) 253-9646; *Statistical Yearbook.*

Times Books, 201 East 50th Street, New York, New York 10022 (212) 751-2600; *The Economist Book of Vital World Statistics.*

United Nations Economic Commission for Africa, Africa Hall, P.O. Box 3001, Addis Ababa, Ethiopia (Telephone Number in U.S. (800) 253-9646); *African Statistical Yearbook.*

U.S. Department of Commerce, Maritime Administration, Washington, D.C. 20230; *A Statistical Analysis of the World's Merchant Fleets.*

ALGERIA - MERCHANT VESSELS - TONNAGE LAUNCHED - See ALGERIA - MERCHANT SHIPPING

ALGERIA - MERCURY PRODUCTION AND CONSUMPTION - See ALGERIA - MINING AND MINERAL PRODUCTS

ALGERIA - MILITARY

G.K. Hall and Company, 70 Lincoln Street, Boston, Massachusetts 02111 (617) 423-3990; *The World in Figures.*

The International Institute for Strategic Studies, 23 Tavistock Street, London WC2E 7NQ, England; *The Military Balance.*

U.S. Arms Control and Disarmament Agency, 320 Twenty-first Street, NW, Washington, D.C. 20451 (202) 647-8677; *World Military Expenditures and Arms Transfers.*

ALGERIA - MILK PRODUCTION - See ALGERIA - DAIRY PRODUCTS

ALGERIA - MINING AND MINERAL PRODUCTS

Commodity Research Bureau, Incorporated, 75 Wall Street, New York, New York 10005 (212) 504-7754; *Commodity Year Book.*

Euromonitor Publications Limited, 87-88 Turnmill Street, London EC1M 5QU, England; *Third World Economic Handbook.*

G.K. Hall and Company, 70 Lincoln Street, Boston, Massachusetts 02111 (617) 423-3990; *The World in Figures.*

International Lead and Zinc Study Group, Metro House, 58 St. James's Street, London SW1A 1LD, England; *Lead and Zinc Statistics.*

International Monetary Fund, 700 Nineteenth Street, NW, Washington, D.C. 20431 (202) 623-7000; *International Financial Statistics.*

Organization of Petroleum Exporting Countries, Obere Donaustrasse 93, 1020 Vienna 2, Austria; *OPEC Annual Statistical Bulletin.*

Penn Well Publishing Company, 1421 South Sheridan Road, P.O. Box 1260, Tulsa, Oklahoma 74101 (800) 752-9764; *International Energy Statistics Sourcebook.*

Statistical Office of the United Nations, Publishing Service, New York, New York 10017 (800) 253-9646; *Statistical Yearbook.*

United Nations Economic Commission for Africa, Africa Hall, P.O. Box 3001, Addis Ababa, Ethiopia (Telephone Number in U.S. (800) 253-9646); *African Statistical Yearbook.*

The World Bank, 1818 H Street, NW, Washington, D.C. 20433 (202) 477-1234; *World Tables.*

ALGERIA - MONEY EXCHANGE RATES

Euromonitor Publications Limited, 87-88 Turnmill Street, London EC1M 5QU, England; *International Marketing Data and Statistics.*

International Monetary Fund, 700 Nineteenth Street, NW, Washington, D.C. 20431 (202) 623-7000; *International Financial Statistics.*

Statistical Office of the United Nations, Publishing Service, New York, New York 10017 (800) 253-9646; *Statistical Yearbook.*

ALGERIA - MONEY SUPPLY

African Development Bank, 01 BP 1387, Abidjan 01, Cote D'Ivoire; *Selected Statistics on Regional Member Countries.*

Euromonitor Publications Limited, 87-88 Turnmill Street, London EC1M 5QU, England; *International Marketing Data and Statistics.*

Federal Statistical Office, Gustav - Stresemann - Ring 11, D-6200 Wiesbaden, Germany; *Algerien.*

G.K. Hall and Company, 70 Lincoln Street, Boston, Massachusetts 02111 (617) 423-3990; *The World in Figures.*

International Monetary Fund, 700 Nineteenth Street, NW, Washington, D.C. 20431 (202) 623-7000; *International Financial Statistics.*

Statistical Office of the United Nations, Publishing Service, New York, New York 10017 (800) 253-9646; *Statistical Yearbook.*

The World Bank, 1818 H Street, NW, Washington, D.C. 20433 (202) 477-1234; *World Tables.*

ALGERIA - MOTION PICTURES

Statistical Office of the United Nations, Publishing Service, New York, New York 10017 (800) 253-9646; *Statistical Yearbook.*

United Nations Educational, Scientific and Cultural Organization (UNESCO), 7 Place de Fontenoy, F-75700 Paris, France (Telephone Number in U.S. (212) 963-5981); *Statistical Yearbook.*

ALGERIA - MOTOR VEHICLE PRODUCTION AND ASSEMBLY

Statistical Office of the United Nations, Publishing Service, New York, New York 10017 (800) 253-9646; *Statistical Yearbook.*

ALGERIA - MOTOR VEHICLES IN USE

G.K. Hall and Company, 70 Lincoln Street, Boston, Massachusetts 02111 (617) 423-3990; *The World in Figures.*

International Road Federation, 525 School Street, SW, Washington, D.C. 20024 (202) 554-2106; *World Road Statistics.*

Statistical Office of the United Nations, Publishing Service, New York, New York 10017 (800) 253-9646; *Statistical Yearbook,* and *Survey of Economic and Social Conditions in Africa.*

Times Books, 201 East 50th Street, New York, New York 10022 (212) 751-2600; *The Economist Book of Vital World Statistics.*

ALGERIA - MULES - See ALGERIA - LIVESTOCK AND POULTRY

ALGERIA - MUSEUMS

Facts on File, 460 Park Avenue South, New York, New York 10016 (800) 443-8323; *The New Book of World Rankings.*

United Nations Educational, Scientific and Cultural Organization (UNESCO), 7 Place de Fontenoy, F-75700 Paris, France (Telephone Number in U.S. (212) 963-5981); *Statistical Yearbook.*

ALGERIA - NATALITY

Statistical Office of the United Nations, Publishing Service, New York, New York 10017 (800) 253-9646; *Demographic Yearbook.*

World Health Organization, Office of Publications, Avenue Appia, CH-1211 Geneva 27, Switzerland (Telephone Number in U.S. (518) 436-9686); *World Health Statistics Annual.*

ALGERIA - NATIONAL ACCOUNTS

African Development Bank, 01 BP 1387, Abidjan 01, Cote D'Ivoire; *Selected Statistics on Regional Member Countries.*

Federal Statistical Office, Gustav - Stresemann - Ring 11, D-6200 Wiesbaden, Germany; *Algerien.*

International Monetary Fund, 700 Nineteenth Street, NW, Washington, D.C. 20431 (202) 623-7000; *International Financial Statistics.*

Statistical Office of the United Nations, Publishing Service, New York, New York 10017 (800) 253-9646; *National Accounts Statistics.*

United Nations Economic Commission for Africa, Africa Hall, P.O. Box 3001, Addis Ababa, Ethiopia (Telephone Number in U.S. (800) 253-9646); *African Statistical Yearbook.*

ALGERIA - NATIONAL INCOME

Facts on File, 460 Park Avenue South, New York, New York 10016 (800) 443-8323; *The New Book of World Rankings.*

G.K. Hall and Company, 70 Lincoln Street, Boston, Massachusetts 02111 (617) 423-3990; *The World in Figures.*

Statistical Office of the United Nations, Publishing Service, New York, New York 10017 (800) 253-9646; *Statistical Yearbook.*

ALGERIA - NATIONAL PRODUCT

Facts on File, 460 Park Avenue South, New York, New York 10016 (800) 443-8323; *The New Book of World Rankings.*

ALGERIA - NATURAL GAS - PRODUCTION - See ALGERIA - MINING AND MINERAL PRODUCTS

ALGERIA - NET MATERIAL PRODUCT

Statistical Office of the United Nations, Publishing Service, New York, New York 10017 (800) 253-9646; *Statistical Yearbook.*

ALGERIA - NEWSPAPER PRODUCTION - See ALGERIA - FORESTRY AND FOREST PRODUCTS

ALGERIA - NEWSPRINT - See ALGERIA - FORESTRY AND FOREST PRODUCTS

ALGERIA - NITRIC ACID PRODUCTION - See ALGERIA - MINING AND MINERAL PRODUCTS

ALGERIA - NUPTIALITY - See ALGERIA - MARRIAGE RATES

ALGERIA - OATS PRODUCTION - See ALGERIA - CROPS

ALGERIA - OCCUPATIONS - See ALGERIA - LABOR FORCE

ALGERIA - ORANGE PRODUCTION - See ALGERIA - CROPS

ALGERIA - PAPER - See ALGERIA - FORESTRY AND FOREST PRODUCTS

ALGERIA - PATENTS

Statistical Office of the United Nations, Publishing Service, New York, New York 10017 (800) 253-9646; *Statistical Yearbook.*

World Intellectual Property Organization, 34 Chemin des Colombettes, CH-1211 Geneva 20. Switzerland; *Industrial Property Statistics.*

ALGERIA - PEANUT PRODUCTION - See ALGERIA - CROPS

ALGERIA - PERIODICALS

United Nations Educational, Scientific and Cultural Organization (UNESCO), 7 Place de Fontenoy, F-75700 Paris, France (Telephone Number in U.S. (212) 963-5981); *Statistical Yearbook.*

ALGERIA - PESTICIDE USE

Food and Agricultural Organization of the United Nations (FAO) Via Delle Terme di Caracalla, 00100 Rome, Italy (Telephone Number in U.S. (202) 653-2400); *The State of Food and Agriculture.*

ALGERIA - PETROLEUM INDUSTRY

Euromonitor Publications Limited, 87-88 Turnmill Street, London EC1M 5QU, England; *Middle East Economic Handbook.*

Facts on File, 460 Park Avenue South, New York, New York 10016 (800) 443-8323; *The New Book of World Rankings.*

Food and Agricultural Organization of the United Nations (FAO) Via Delle Terme di Caracalla, 00100 Rome, Italy (Telephone Number in U.S. (202) 653-2400); *The State of Food and Agriculture.*

G.K. Hall and Company, 70 Lincoln Street, Boston, Massachusetts 02111 (617) 423-3990; *The World in Figures.*

International Monetary Fund, 700 Nineteenth Street, NW, Washington, D.C. 20431 (202) 623-7000; *International Financial Statistics.*

Organization of Petroleum Exporting Countries, Obere Donaustrasse 93, 1020 Vienna 2, Austria; *OPEC Annual Statistical Bulletin.*

Penn Well Publishing Company, 1421 South Sheridan Road, P.O. Box 1260, Tulsa, Oklahoma 74101 (800) 752-9764; *International Energy Statistics Sourcebook.*

Statistical Office of the United Nations, Publishing Service, New York, New York 10017 (800) 253-9646; *Statistical Yearbook.*

ALGERIA - PHOSPHATE ROCK PRODUCTION - See ALGERIA - MINING AND MINERAL PRODUCTS

ALGERIA - PIG-IRON AND FERRO-ALLOYS PRODUCTION - See ALGERIA - MINING AND MINERAL PRODUCTS

ALGERIA - PIGS - See ALGERIA - LIVESTOCK AND POULTRY

ALGERIA - PIPELINES FOR OIL AND PETROLEUM PRODUCTS

Organization of Petroleum Exporting Countries, Obere Donaustrasse 93, 1020 Vienna 2, Austria; *OPEC Annual Statistical Bulletin.*

ALGERIA - PLASTIC AND RESIN PRODUCTION

Euromonitor Publications Limited, 87-88 Turnmill Street, London EC1M 5QU, England; *Third World Economic Handbook.*

ALGERIA - POPULATION

African Development Bank, 01 BP 1387, Abidjan 01, Cote d'Ivoire; *Selected Statistics on Regional Member Countries.*

Direction des Statisques et de la Comptabilite Nationale, BP 478, Alger, Algeria; *Statistical Yearbook of Algeria.*

The Economist Intelligence Unit, 111 West 57th Street, New York, New York 10019 (800) 938-4685; *The World Market Atlas.*

Euromonitor Publications Limited, 87-88 Turnmill Street, London EC1M 5QU, England; *International Marketing Data and Statistics, Middle East Economic Handbook,* and *Third World Economic Handbook.*

Facts on File, 460 Park Avenue South, New York, New York 10016 (800) 443-8323; *The New Book of World Rankings.*

Federal Statistical Office, Gustav - Stresemann - Ring 11, D-6200 Wiesbaden, Germany; *Algerien.*

Food and Agricultural Organization of the United Nations (FAO), Via delle Terme di Caracalla, 00100 Rome, Italy (Telephone Number in U.S. (202) 653-2400); *Production Yearbook.*

G.K. Hall and Company, 70 Lincoln Street, Boston, Massachusetts 02111 (617) 423-3990; *The World in Figures.*

International Labour Office, I.L.O. Publications, CH-1211, Geneva 22, Switzerland; *Yearbook of Labour Statistics.*

Statistical Office of the United Nations, Publishing Service, New York, New York 10017 (800) 253-9646; *Demographic Yearbook,* and *Statistical Yearbook,* and *Survey of Economic and Social Conditions in Africa.*

Times Books, 201 East 50th Street, New York, New York 10022 (212) 751-2600; *The Economist Book of Vital World Statistics.*

U.S. Arms Control and Disarmament Agency, 320 Twenty-first Street, NW, Washington, D.C. 20451 (202) 647-8677; *World Military Expenditures and Arms Transfers.*

World Health Organization, Office of Publications, Avenue Appia, CH-1211 Geneva 27, Switzerland (Telephone Number in U.S. (518) 436-9686); *World Health Statistics Annual.*

ALGERIA - POST OFFICES

Facts on File, 460 Park Avenue South, New York, New York 10016 (800) 443-8323; *The New Book of World Rankings.*

ALGERIA - POTATO PRODUCTION - See ALGERIA - CROPS

ALGERIA - POULTRY - See ALGERIA - LIVESTOCK AND POULTRY

ALGERIA - PRICES

Facts on File, 460 Park Avenue South, New York, New York 10016 (800) 443-8323; *The New Book of World Rankings.*

Federal Statistical Office, Gustav - Stresemann - Ring 11, D-6200 Wiesbaden, Germany; *Algerien.*

Food and Agricultural Organization of the United Nations (FAO), Via delle Terme di Caracalla, 00100 Rome, Italy (Telephone Number in U.S. (202) 653-2400); *Production Yearbook,* and *The State of Food and Agriculture.*

G.K. Hall and Company, 70 Lincoln Street, Boston, Massachusetts 02111 (617) 423-3990; *The World in Figures.*

International Labour Office, I.L.O. Publications, CH-1211, Geneva 22, Switzerland; *Yearbook of Labour Statistics.*

International Lead and Zinc Study Group, Metro House, 58 St. James's Street, London SW1A 1LD, England; *Lead and Zinc Statistics.*

International Monetary Fund, 700 Nineteenth Street, NW, Washington, D.C. 20431 (202) 623-7000; *International Financial Statistics.*

United Nations Economic Commission for Africa, Africa Hall, P.O. Box 3001, Addis Ababa, Ethiopia (Telephone Number in U.S. (800) 253-9646); *African Statistical Yearbook.*

ALGERIA - PRINTING AND WRITING PAPER - See ALGERIA - FORESTRY AND FOREST PRODUCTS

ALGERIA - PRODUCTION

Euromonitor Publications Limited, 87-88 Turnmill Street, London EC1M 5QU, England; *Third World Economic Handbook.*

Facts on File, 460 Park Avenue South, New York, New York 10016 (800) 443-8323; *The New Book of World Rankings.*

G.K. Hall and Company, 70 Lincoln Street, Boston, Massachusetts 02111 (617) 423-3990; *The World in Figures.*

International Lead and Zinc Study Group, Metro House, 58 St. James's Street, London SW1A 1LD, England; *Lead and Zinc Statistics.*

ALGERIA - PRODUCTIVITY

Euromonitor Publications Limited, 87-88 Turnmill Street, London EC1M 5QU, England; *International Marketing Data and Statistics.*

ALGERIA - PUBLIC FINANCE

Direction des Statisques et de la Comptabilite Nationale, BP 478, Alger, Algeria; *Statistical Yearbook of Algeria.*

Facts on File, 460 Park Avenue South, New York, New York 10016 (800) 443-8323; *The New Book of World Rankings.*

Federal Statistical Office, Gustav - Stresemann - Ring 11, D-6200 Wiesbaden, Germany; *Algerien.*

ALGERIA - PUBLIC HEALTH

Direction des Statisques et de la Comptabilite Nationale, BP 478, Alger, Algeria; *Statistical Yearbook of Algeria.*

ALGERIA - RADIO BROADCASTING - See ALGERIA - BROADCASTING

ALGERIA - RADIO RECEIVER PRODUCTION

Statistical Office of the United Nations, Publishing Service, New York, New York 10017 (800) 253-9646; *Statistical Yearbook.*

ALGERIA - RAILWAYS

G.K. Hall and Company, 70 Lincoln Street, Boston, Massachusetts 02111 (617) 423-3990; *The World in Figures.*

Jane's Information Group, Sentinel House, 163 Brighton Road, Coulsdon, Surrey CR5 2NH, England (Telephone Number in U.S.

(703) 683-3700); *Jane's World Railways.*

Statistical Office of the United Nations, Publishing Service, New York, New York 10017 (800) 253-9646; *Statistical Yearbook*, and *Survey of Economic and Social Conditions in Africa.*

United Nations Economic Commission for Africa, Africa Hall, P.O. Box 3001, Addis Ababa, Ethiopia (Telephone Number in U.S. (800) 253-9646); *African Statistical Yearbook.*

ALGERIA - RELIGION

Facts on File, 460 Park Avenue South, New York, New York 10016 (800) 443-8323; *The New Book of World Rankings.*

ALGERIA - RENT PRICES

International Labour Office, I.L.O. Publications, CH-1211, Geneva 22, Switzerland; *Yearbook of Labour Statistics.*

ALGERIA - RETAIL TRADE

Euromonitor Publications Limited, 87-88 Turnmill Street, London EC1M 5QU, England; *Third World Economic Handbook.*

G.K. Hall and Company, 70 Lincoln Street, Boston, Massachusetts 02111 (617) 423-3990; *The World in Figures.*

ALGERIA - RICE PRODUCTION - See ALGERIA - CROPS

ALGERIA - ROOT AND TUBER PRODUCTION - See ALGERIA - CROPS

ALGERIA - ROUNDWOOD PRODUCTION - See ALGERIA - FORESTRY AND FOREST PRODUCTS

ALGERIA - RUBBER PRODUCTION

Euromonitor Publications Limited, 87-88 Turnmill Street, London EC1M 5QU, England; *Third World Economic Handbook.*

Facts on File, 460 Park Avenue South, New York, New York 10016 (800) 443-8323; *The New Book of World Rankings.*

ALGERIA - SALT PRODUCTION - See ALGERIA - MINING AND MINERAL PRODUCTS

ALGERIA - SAWNWOOD PRODUCTION - See ALGERIA - FORESTRY AND FOREST PRODUCTS

ALGERIA - SCIENCE AND TECHNOLOGY - EXPENDITURE FOR RESEARCH

Statistical Office of the United Nations, Publishing Service, New York, New York 10017 (800) 253-9646; *Statistical Yearbook.*

ALGERIA - SCIENTISTS AND ENGINEERS

Statistical Office of the United Nations, Publishing Service, New York, New York 10017 (800) 253-9646; *Statistical Yearbook.*

United Nations Educational, Scientific and Cultural Organization (UNESCO), 7 Place de Fontenoy, F-75700 Paris, France (Telephone Number in U.S. (212) 963-5981); *Statistical Yearbook.*

ALGERIA - SENIOR CITIZENS

Facts on File, 460 Park Avenue South, New York, New York 10016 (800) 443-8323; *The New Book of World Rankings.*

ALGERIA - SHEEP - See ALGERIA - LIVESTOCK AND POULTRY

ALGERIA - SILVER PRODUCTION AND CONSUMPTION - See ALGERIA - MINING AND MINERAL PRODUCTS

ALGERIA - SOCIAL DATA

African Development Bank, 01 BP 1387, Abidjan 01, Cote d'Ivoire; *Selected Statistics on Regional Member Countries.*

Facts on File, 460 Park Avenue South, New York, New York 10016 (800) 443-8323; *The New Book of World Rankings.*

G.K. Hall and Company, 70 Lincoln Street, Boston, Massachusetts 02111 (617) 423-3990; *The World in Figures.*

ALGERIA - STATE BUDGET REVENUE AND EXPENDITURES

Euromonitor Publications Limited, 87-88 Turnmill Street, London EC1M 5QU, England; *International Marketing Data and Statistics.*

ALGERIA - STEEL - See ALGERIA - MINING AND MINERAL PRODUCTS

ALGERIA - STOCKS - COMMODITY - MARKET PRICE - INDEX

Food and Agricultural Organization of the United Nations (FAO) Via Delle Terme di Caracalla, 00100 Rome, Italy (Telephone Number in U.S. (202) 653-2400); *The State of Food and Agriculture.*

International Lead and Zinc Study Group, Metro House, 58 St. James's Street, London SW1A 1LD, England; *Lead and Zinc Statistics.*

ALGERIA - SUGAR PRODUCTION AND CONSUMPTION - See ALGERIA - CROPS

ALGERIA - SULPHURIC ACID PRODUCTION - See ALGERIA - MINING AND MINERAL PRODUCTS

ALGERIA - TAX REVENUE - See ALGERIA - TAXATION

ALGERIA - TAXATION

G.K. Hall and Company, 70 Lincoln Street, Boston, Massachusetts 02111 (617) 423-3990; *The World in Figures.*

International Road Federation, 525 School Street, SW, Washington, D.C. 20024 (202) 554-2106; *World Road Statistics.*

The World Bank, 1818 H Street, NW, Washington, D.C. 20433 (202) 477-1234; *World Tables.*ALGERIA - TEA - See ALGERIA - CROPS

ALGERIA - TELEGRAPH SERVICE

Statistical Office of the United Nations, Publishing Service, New York, New York 10017 (800) 253-9646; *Statistical Yearbook.*

ALGERIA - TELEPHONES IN USE

American Telephone and Telegraph Company, 26 Parsippany Road, Whippany, New Jersey 07981 (800) 338-4038; *The World's Telephones.*

Euromonitor Publications Limited, 87-88 Turnmill Street, London EC1M 5QU, England; *Middle East Economic Handbook*, and *Third World Economic Handbook.*

G.K. Hall and Company, 70 Lincoln Street, Boston, Massachusetts 02111 (617) 423-3990; *The World in Figures.*

Statistical Office of the United Nations, Publishing Service, New York, New York 10017 (800) 253-9646; *Statistical Yearbook.*

ALGERIA - TELEVISION BROADCASTING - See ALGERIA - BROADCASTING

ALGERIA - TELEVISION RECEIVER PRODUCTION

Statistical Office of the United Nations, Publishing Service, New York, New York 10017 (800) 253-9646; *Statistical Yearbook.*

ALGERIA - TEXTILE INDUSTRY

Euromonitor Publications Limited, 87-88 Turnmill Street, London EC1M 5QU, England; *Third World Economic Handbook.*

G.K. Hall and Company, 70 Lincoln Street, Boston, Massachusetts 02111 (617) 423-3990; *The World in Figures.*

ALGERIA - TIRE (MOTOR VEHICLE) PRODUCTION

Statistical Office of the United Nations, Publishing Service, New York, New York 10017 (800) 253-9646; *Statistical Yearbook.*

ALGERIA - TOBACCO PRODUCTION

Euromonitor Publications Limited, 87-88 Turnmill Street, London EC1M 5QU, England; *Third World Economic Handbook.*

Facts on File, 460 Park Avenue South, New York, New York 10016 (800) 443-8323; *The New Book of World Rankings.*

Statistical Office of the United Nations, Publishing Service, New York, New York 10017 (800) 253-9646; *Statistical Yearbook.*

ALGERIA - TOURISM

Direction des Statisques et de la Comptabilite Nationale, BP 478, Alger, Algeria; *Statistical Yearbook of Algeria.*

Euromonitor Publications Limited, 87-88 Turnmill Street, London EC1M 5QU, England; *Middle East Economic Handbook,* and *Third World Economic Handbook.*

Facts on File, 460 Park Avenue South, New York, New York 10016 (800) 443-8323; *The New Book of World Rankings.*

Federal Statistical Office, Gustav - Stresemann - Ring 11, D-6200 Wiesbaden, Germany; *Algerien.*

G.K. Hall and Company, 70 Lincoln Street, Boston, Massachusetts 02111 (617) 423-3990; *The World in Figures.*

Times Books, 201 East 50th Street, New York, New York 10022 (212) 751-2600; *The Economist Book of Vital World Statistics.*

United Nations Economic Commission for Africa, Africa Hall, P.O. Box 3001, Addis Ababa, Ethiopia (Telephone Number in U.S. (800) 253-9646); *African Statistical Yearbook.*

ALGERIA - TRADE - See ALGERIA - FOREIGN TRADE

ALGERIA - TRADEMARKS AND SERVICE MARKS

Statistical Office of the United Nations, Publishing Service, New York, New York 10017 (800) 253-9646; *Statistical Yearbook.*

World Intellectual Property Organization, 34 Chemin des Colombettes, CH-1211 Geneva 20. Switzerland; *Industrial Property Statistics.*

ALGERIA - TRANSPORTATION AND COMMUNICATIONS

Direction des Statisques et de la Comptabilite Nationale, BP 478, Alger, Algeria; *Statistical Yearbook of Algeria.*

Euromonitor Publications Limited, 87-88 Turnmill Street, London EC1M 5QU, England; *Middle East Economic Handbook,* and *Third World Economic Handbook.*

Facts on File, 460 Park Avenue South, New York, New York 10016 (800) 443-8323; *The New Book of World Rankings.*

Federal Statistical Office, Gustav - Stresemann - Ring 11, D-6200 Wiesbaden, Germany; *Algerien.*

G.K. Hall and Company, 70 Lincoln Street, Boston, Massachusetts 02111 (617) 423-3990; *The World in Figures.*

United Nations Economic Commission for Africa, Africa Hall, P.O. Box 3001, Addis Ababa, Ethiopia (Telephone Number in U.S. (800) 253-9646); *African Statistical Yearbook.*

ALGERIA - TURKEYS - See ALGERIA - LIVESTOCK AND POULTRY

ALGERIA - UNEMPLOYMENT

Euromonitor Publications Limited, 87-88 Turnmill Street, London EC1M 5QU, England; *International Marketing Data and Statistics,* and *Middle East Economic Handbook.*

International Labour Office, I.L.O. Publications, CH-1211, Geneva 22, Switzerland; *Yearbook of Labour Statistics.*

ALGERIA - URANIUM PRODUCTION AND CONSUMPTION - See ALGERIA - MINING AND MINERAL PRODUCTS

ALGERIA - VITAL STATISTICS

Euromonitor Publications Limited, 87-88 Turnmill Street, London EC1M 5QU, England; *International Marketing Data and Statistics, Middle East Economic Handbook,* and *Third World Economic Handbook.*

G.K. Hall and Company, 70 Lincoln Street, Boston, Massachusetts 02111 (617) 423-3990; *The World in Figures.*

Statistical Office of the United Nations, Publishing Service, New York, New York 10017 (800) 253-9646; *Statistical Yearbook.*

World Health Organization, Office of Publications, Avenue Appia, CH-1211 Geneva 27, Switzerland (Telephone Number in U.S (518) 436-9686); *World Health Statistics Annual.*

ALGERIA - WAGES

Federal Statistical Office, Gustav - Stresemann - Ring 11, D-6200 Wiesbaden, Germany; *Algerien.*

G.K. Hall and Company, 70 Lincoln Street, Boston, Massachusetts 02111 (617) 423-3990; *The World in Figures.*

International Labour Office, I.L.O. Publications, CH-1211, Geneva 22, Switzerland; *Yearbook of Labour Statistics.*

Statistical Office of the United Nations, Publishing Service, New York, New York 10017 (800) 253-9646; *Statistical Yearbook.*

ALGERIA - WATERMELON PRODUCTION - See ALGERIA - CROPS

ALGERIA - WEATHER

Facts on File, 460 Park Avenue South, New York, New York 10016 (800) 443-8323; *The New Book of World Rankings.*

G.K. Hall and Company, 70 Lincoln Street, Boston, Massachusetts 02111 (617) 423-3990; *The World in Figures.*

ALGERIA - WHEAT - See ALGERIA - CROPS

ALGERIA - WHOLESALE TRADE

Euromonitor Publications Limited, 87-88 Turnmill Street, London EC1M 5QU, England; *Third World Economic Handbook.*

ALGERIA - WINE PRODUCTION

Facts on File, 460 Park Avenue South, New York, New York 10016 (800) 443-8323; *The New Book of World Rankings.*

Statistical Office of the United Nations, Publishing Service, New York, New York 10017 (800) 253-9646; *Statistical Yearbook.*

ALGERIA - WOOD PULP PRODUCTION - See ALGERIA - FORESTRY AND FOREST PRODUCTS

ALGERIA - WOOL PRODUCTION

Facts on File, 460 Park Avenue South, New York, New York 10016 (800) 443-8323; *The New Book of World Rankings.*

ALGERIA - YARN PRODUCTION

Statistical Office of the United Nations, Publishing Service, New York, New York 10017 (800) 253-9646; *Statistical Yearbook.*

ALGERIA - ZINC AND ZINC ORE - See ALGERIA - MINING AND MINERAL PRODUCTS

ALIENS

U.S. Department of Justice, Immigration and Naturalization Service, 425 Eye Street, NW, Washington, D.C. 20536 (202) 514-4316; *Statistical Yearbook,* and unpublished data.

ALIENS - BORDER PATROL ACTIVITIES

U.S. Department of Justice, Immigration and Naturalization Service, 425 Eye Street, NW, Washington, D.C. 20536 (202) 514-4316; *Statistical Yearbook,* and unpublished data.

ALIENS - CRIMINAL VIOLATIONS

U.S. Department of Justice, Immigration and Naturalization Service, 425 Eye Street, NW, Washington, D.C. 20536 (202) 514-4316; *Statistical Yearbook,* and unpublished data.

ALIENS - DEPORTED

U.S. Department of Justice, Immigration and Naturalization Service, 425 Eye Street, NW, Washington, D.C. 20536 (202) 514-4316; *Statistical Yearbook,* and unpublished data.

ALIENS - VIOLATIONS AND PROSECUTIONS

U.S. Department of Justice, Immigration and Naturalization Service, 425 Eye Street, NW, Washington, D.C. 20536 (202) 514-4316; *Statistical Yearbook,* and unpublished data.

ALMONDS

U.S. Department of Agriculture, National Agricultural Statistics Service, Fourteenth and Independence Avenue, SW, Washington, D.C. 20250 (202) 219-1504; *Noncitrus Fruits and Nuts,* and *Economic Indicators of the Farm Sector: National Financial Summary.*

ALTITUDES - GEOGRAPHICAL

U.S. Department of the Interior, Geological Survey, National Center, 12201 Sunrise Valley Drive, Reston, Virginia 22092 (703) 648-4460; *Elevations and Distances in the United States.*

ALUMINUM - CONSUMPTION

U.S. Department of the Interior, Bureau of Mines, 810 Seventh Street, NW, Washington, D.C. 20241 (202) 501-9649; *Mineral Commodity Summaries.*

ALUMINUM - EMPLOYMENT

U.S. Department of the Interior, Bureau of Mines, 810 Seventh Street, NW, Washington, D.C. 20241 (202) 501-9649; *Mineral Commodity Summaries.*

ALUMINUM - FOREIGN TRADE

U.S. Department of Commerce, Bureau of the Census, Suitland, Maryland 20233 (301) 763-4040; *U.S. Merchandise Trade.*

U.S. Department of the Interior, Bureau of Mines, 810 Seventh Street, NW, Washington, D.C. 20241 (202) 501-9649; *Minerals Yearbook, Mineral Commodity Summaries,* and *Annual Reports.*

ALUMINUM - PRICES

U.S. Department of the Interior, Bureau of Mines, 810 Seventh Street, NW, Washington, D.C. 20241 (202) 501-9649; *Minerals Yearbook,* and *Mineral Commodity Summaries.*

ALUMINUM - RECYCLING

Franklin Associates Limited, 4121 West 83rd Street, Suite 108, Prairie Village, Kansas 66208 (913) 649-2225; *Characterization of Municipal Solid Waste in the United States.*

ALUMINUM - WORLD PRODUCTION

U.S. Department of the Interior, Bureau of Mines, 810 Seventh Street, NW, Washington, D.C. 20241 (202) 501-9649; *Minerals Yearbook, Mineral Commodity Summaries,* and *Annual Reports.*

AMERICAN COLLEGE TESTING (ACT) PROGRAM

The American College Testing Program, Box 168, Iowa City, Iowa 52243 (319) 337-1000; *High School Profile Report.*

AMERICAN FEDERATION OF LABOR (AFL)

American Federation of Labor and Congress of Industrial Organizations, 815 16th Street, NW, Washington, D.C. 20006 (202) 637-5000; *Report of the AFL-CIO Executive Council.*

AMERICAN INDIAN, ESKIMO, ALEUT POPULATION

U.S. Department of Commerce, Bureau of the Census, Suitland, Maryland 20233 (301) 763-4040; *Census of Population, Current Population Reports,* and *Census of Agriculture.*

U.S. Department of Education, National Center for Education Statistics, 400 Maryland Avenue, SW, Washington, D.C. 20202 (202) 708-5366; *Digest of Education Statistics.*

AMERICAN REVOLUTION - COST

U.S. Congress, Joint Economic Committee, The Capitol, Washington, D.C. 20510 (202) 224-3121; *The Military Budget and National Economic Priorities;* subsequently revised and updated by James L. Clayton, University of Utah, Salt Lake City, Utah.

American Samoa - National Statistical Office

Economic Development and Planning Office, Pago Pago, American Samoa 96799 (684) 633-5155.

American Samoa - Primary Statistics Source

Economic Development and Planning Office, Pago Pago, American Samoa; *American Samoa Statistical Digest.*

AMERICAN SAMOA - AGRICULTURE

Food and Agricultural Organization of the United Nations (FAO), Via delle Terme di Caracalla, 00100 Rome, Italy (Telephone Number in U.S. (202) 653-2400); *Production Yearbook, The State of Food and Agriculture, Trade Production,* and *Trade Yearbook.*

G.K. Hall and Company, 70 Lincoln Street, Boston, Massachusetts 02111 (617) 423-3990; *The World in Figures.*

Statistical Office of the United Nations, Publishing Service, New York, New York 10017 (800) 253-9646; *Statistical Yearbook.*

AMERICAN SAMOA - AIRLINE SERVICE

G.K. Hall and Company, 70 Lincoln Street, Boston, Massachusetts 02111 (617) 423-3990; *The World in Figures.*

AMERICAN SAMOA - ANIMAL HEALTH

Food and Agricultural Organization of the United Nations (FAO), Via delle Terme di Caracalla, 00100 Rome, Italy (Telephone Number in U.S. (202) 653-2400); *Animal Health Yearbook.*

AMERICAN SAMOA - AREA AND DENSITY OF POPULATION

Food and Agricultural Organization of the United Nations (FAO) Via Delle Terme di Caracalla, 00100 Rome, Italy (Telephone Number in U.S. (202) 653-2400); *The State of Food and Agriculture.*

G.K. Hall and Company, 70 Lincoln Street, Boston, Massachusetts 02111 (617) 423-3990; *The World in Figures.*

Statistical Office of the United Nations, Publishing Service, New York, New York 10017 (800) 253-9646; *Statistical Yearbook.*

AMERICAN SAMOA - BALANCE OF PAYMENTS

G.K. Hall and Company, 70 Lincoln Street, Boston, Massachusetts 02111 (617) 423-3990; *The World in Figures.*

AMERICAN SAMOA - BANKING

G.K. Hall and Company, 70 Lincoln Street, Boston, Massachusetts 02111 (617) 423-3990; *The World in Figures.*

AMERICAN SAMOA - BIRTH RATE

Statistical Office of the United Nations, Publishing Service, New York, New York 10017 (800) 253-9646; *Demographic Yearbook.*

World Health Organization, Office of Publications, Avenue Appia, CH-1211 Geneva 27, Switzerland (Telephone Number in U.S. (518) 436-9686); *World Health Statistics Annual.*

AMERICAN SAMOA - BONDS

G.K. Hall and Company, 70 Lincoln Street, Boston, Massachusetts 02111 (617) 423-3990; *The World in Figures.*

AMERICAN SAMOA - BOOK PRODUCTION

G.K. Hall and Company, 70 Lincoln Street, Boston, Massachusetts 02111 (617) 423-3990; *The World in Figures.*

United Nations Educational, Scientific and Cultural Organization (UNESCO), 7 Place de Fontenoy, (Telephone Number in U.S. (212) 963-5981) F-75700 Paris, France; *Statistical Yearbook.*

AMERICAN SAMOA - BROADCASTING

Billboard Limited, P.O. Box 9027, 1006 AA Amsterdam, The Netherlands (Telephone Number in U.S. (212) 764-7300); *World Radio TV Handbook.*

G.K. Hall and Company, 70 Lincoln Street, Boston, Massachusetts 02111 (617) 423-3990; *The World in Figures.*

AMERICAN SAMOA - BUSINESS

G.K. Hall and Company, 70 Lincoln Street, Boston, Massachusetts 02111 (617) 423-3990; *The World in Figures.*

AMERICAN SAMOA - CALORIE SUPPLY

Food and Agricultural Organization of the United Nations (FAO) Via Delle Terme di Caracalla, 00100 Rome, Italy (Telephone Number in U.S. (202) 653-2400); *The State of Food and Agriculture.*

AMERICAN SAMOA - CHEMICAL (ORGANIC) PRODUCTION - See AMERICAN SAMOA - MINING AND MINERAL PRODUCTS

AMERICAN SAMOA - CLASS STRUCTURE

G.K. Hall and Company, 70 Lincoln Street, Boston, Massachusetts 02111 (617) 423-3990; *The World in Figures.*

AMERICAN SAMOA - CLIMATE

G.K. Hall and Company, 70 Lincoln Street, Boston, Massachusetts 02111 (617) 423-3990; *The World in Figures.*

AMERICAN SAMOA - CLOTHING EXPORTS AND IMPORTS

South Pacific Commission, Post Box D5, Noumea Cedex, New Caledonia; *Statistical Bulletin of the South Pacific: Retail Price Indexes.*

AMERICAN SAMOA - COAL PRODUCTION - See AMERICAN SAMOA - MINING AND MINERAL PRODUCTS

AMERICAN SAMOA - COMMUNICATIONS

G.K. Hall and Company, 70 Lincoln Street, Boston, Massachusetts 02111 (617) 423-3990; *The World in Figures.*

AMERICAN SAMOA - CONSTRUCTION INDUSTRY

Statistical Office of the United Nations, Publishing Service, New York, New York 10017 (800) 253-9646; *Statistical Yearbook.*

AMERICAN SAMOA - CONSUMER PRICE INDEX

G.K. Hall and Company, 70 Lincoln Street, Boston, Massachusetts 02111 (617) 423-3990; *The World in Figures.*

AMERICAN SAMOA - CONSUMER PRICES

International Labour Office, I.L.O. Publications, CH-1211, Geneva 22, Switzerland; *Yearbook of Labour Statistics.*

AMERICAN SAMOA - CONSUMPTION

G.K. Hall and Company, 70 Lincoln Street, Boston, Massachusetts 02111 (617) 423-3990; *The World in Figures.*

South Pacific Commission, Post Box D5, Noumea Cedex, New Caledonia; *Statistical Bulletin of the South Pacific: Retail Price Indexes.*

AMERICAN SAMOA - CORN PRODUCTION - See AMERICAN SAMOA - CROPS

AMERICAN SAMOA - CORPORATE TAXES - See AMERICAN SAMOA - TAXATION

AMERICAN SAMOA - CROPS

Food and Agricultural Organization of the United Nations (FAO) Via Delle Terme di Caracalla, 00100 Rome, Italy (Telephone Number in U.S. (202) 653-2400); *The State of Food and Agriculture.*

G.K. Hall and Company, 70 Lincoln Street, Boston, Massachusetts 02111 (617) 423-3990; *The World in Figures.*

AMERICAN SAMOA - CUSTOMS DUTIES

G.K. Hall and Company, 70 Lincoln Street, Boston, Massachusetts 02111 (617) 423-3990; *The World in Figures.*

AMERICAN SAMOA - DAIRY PRODUCTS

Food and Agricultural Organization of the United Nations (FAO) Via Delle Terme di Caracalla, 00100 Rome, Italy (Telephone Number in U.S. (202) 653-2400); *The State of Food and Agriculture.*

AMERICAN SAMOA - DEATH RATE

G.K. Hall and Company, 70 Lincoln Street, Boston, Massachusetts 02111 (617) 423-3990; *The World in Figures.*

Statistical Office of the United Nations, Publishing Service, New York, New York 10017 (800) 253-9646; *Statistical Yearbook.*

World Health Organization, Office of Publications, Avenue Appia, CH-1211 Geneva 27, Switzerland (Telephone Number in U.S. (518) 436-9686); *World Health Statistics Annual.*

AMERICAN SAMOA - DEFENSE EXPENDITURES

G.K. Hall and Company, 70 Lincoln Street, Boston, Massachusetts 02111 (617) 423-3990; *The World in Figures.*

AMERICAN SAMOA - DEMOGRAPHY

G.K. Hall and Company, 70 Lincoln Street, Boston, Massachusetts 02111 (617) 423-3990; *The World in Figures.*

AMERICAN SAMOA - DEVELOPMENT ASSISTANCE

G.K. Hall and Company, 70 Lincoln Street, Boston, Massachusetts 02111 (617) 423-3990; *The World in Figures.*

AMERICAN SAMOA - DISEASES

G.K. Hall and Company, 70 Lincoln Street, Boston, Massachusetts 02111 (617) 423-3990; *The World in Figures.*

World Health Organization, Office of Publications, Avenue Appia, CH-1211 Geneva 27, Switzerland (Telephone Number in U.S. (518) 436-9686); *World Health Statistics Annual.*

AMERICAN SAMOA - DIVORCE RATES

Statistical Office of the United Nations, Publishing Service, New York, New York 10017 (800) 253-9646; *Demographic Yearbook,* and *Statistical Yearbook.*

AMERICAN SAMOA - DOMESTIC PRODUCT

G.K. Hall and Company, 70 Lincoln Street, Boston, Massachusetts 02111 (617) 423-3990; *The World in Figures.*

AMERICAN SAMOA - ECONOMY

G.K. Hall and Company, 70 Lincoln Street, Boston, Massachusetts 02111 (617) 423-3990; *The World in Figures.*

AMERICAN SAMOA - EDUCATION

G.K. Hall and Company, 70 Lincoln Street, Boston, Massachusetts 02111 (617) 423-3990; *The World in Figures.*

United Nations Educational, Scientific and Cultural Organization (UNESCO), 7 Place de Fontenoy, F-75700 Paris, France (Telephone Number in U.S. (212) 963-5981); *Statistical Yearbook.*

AMERICAN SAMOA - EGG PRODUCTION - See AMERICAN SAMOA - DAIRY PRODUCTS

AMERICAN SAMOA - ELECTRICITY

Statistical Office of the United Nations, Publishing Service, New York, New York 10017 (800) 253-9646; *Statistical Yearbook.*

AMERICAN SAMOA - EMPLOYMENT

International Labour Office, I.L.O. Publications, CH-1211, Geneva 22, Switzerland; *Yearbook of Labour Statistics.*

AMERICAN SAMOA - ENERGY

G.K. Hall and Company, 70 Lincoln Street, Boston, Massachusetts 02111 (617) 423-3990; *The World in Figures.*

Food and Agricultural Organization of the United Nations (FAO) Via Delle Terme di Caracalla, 00100 Rome, Italy (Telephone Number in

U.S. (202) 653-2400); *The State of Food and Agriculture.*

Statistical Office of the United Nations, Publishing Service, New York, New York 10017 (800) 253-9646; *Energy Statistics Yearbook,* and *Statistical Yearbook.*

AMERICAN SAMOA - EXPORTS

Food and Agricultural Organization of the United Nations (FAO) Via Delle Terme di Caracalla, 00100 Rome, Italy (Telephone Number in U.S. (202) 653-2400); *The State of Food and Agriculture.*

G.K. Hall and Company, 70 Lincoln Street, Boston, Massachusetts 02111 (617) 423-3990; *The World in Figures.*

South Pacific Commission, Post Box D5, Noumea Cedex, New Caledonia; *Statistical Bulletin of the South Pacific: Overseas Trade.*

AMERICAN SAMOA - EXTERNAL TRADE

Food and Agricultural Organization of the United Nations (FAO) Via Delle Terme di Caracalla, 00100 Rome, Italy (Telephone Number in U.S. (202) 653-2400); *The State of Food and Agriculture,* and *Trade Yearbook.*

G.K. Hall and Company, 70 Lincoln Street, Boston, Massachusetts 02111 (617) 423-3990; *The World in Figures.*

AMERICAN SAMOA - FARM CROPS - See AMERICAN SAMOA - CROPS

AMERICAN SAMOA - FERTILIZER

Food and Agricultural Organization of the United Nations (FAO) Via Delle Terme di Caracalla, 00100 Rome, Italy (Telephone Number in U.S. (202) 653-2400); *The State of Food and Agriculture.*

Organisation for Economic Co-operation and Development (OECD), 2 rue Andre-Pascal, 75 Paris 16, France (Telephone Number in U.S. (212) 963-5981); *Indicators of Industrial Activity.*

AMERICAN SAMOA - FETAL MORTALITY

Statistical Office of the United Nations, Publishing Service, New York, New York 10017 (800) 253-9646; *Demographic Yearbook.*

World Health Organization, Office of Publications, Avenue Appia, CH-1211 Geneva 27, Switzerland (Telephone Number in U.S. (518) 436-9686); *World Health Statistics Annual.*

AMERICAN SAMOA - FINANCE

G.K. Hall and Company, 70 Lincoln Street, Boston, Massachusetts 02111 (617) 423-3990; *The World in Figures.*

International Monetary Fund, 700 Nineteenth Street, NW, Washington, D.C. 20431 (202) 623-7000; *International Financial Statistics.*

AMERICAN SAMOA - FISHERIES

Food and Agricultural Organization of the United Nations (FAO) Via Delle Terme di Caracalla, 00100 Rome, Italy (Telephone Number in U.S. (202) 653-2400); *The State of Food and Agriculture,* and *Yearbook of Fishery Statistics.*

AMERICAN SAMOA - FOOD

Food and Agricultural Organization of the United Nations (FAO) Via Delle Terme di Caracalla, 00100 Rome, Italy (Telephone Number in U.S. (202) 653-2400); *Production Yearbook,* and *The State of Food and Agriculture.*

G.K. Hall and Company, 70 Lincoln Street, Boston, Massachusetts 02111 (617) 423-3990; *The World in Figures.*

South Pacific Commission, Post Box D5, Noumea Cedex, New Caledonia; *Statistical Bulletin of the South Pacific: Retail Price Indexes.*

AMERICAN SAMOA - FOREIGN AID

G.K. Hall and Company, 70 Lincoln Street, Boston, Massachusetts 02111 (617) 423-3990; *The World in Figures.*

AMERICAN SAMOA - FOREIGN TRADE

Food and Agricultural Organization of the United Nations (FAO) Via Delle Terme di Caracalla, 00100 Rome, Italy (Telephone Number in U.S. (202) 653-2400); *The State of Food and Agriculture.*

G.K. Hall and Company, 70 Lincoln Street, Boston, Massachusetts 02111 (617) 423-3990; *The World in Figures.*

Organisation for Economic Co-operation and Development (OECD), 2 rue Andre-Pascal, 75 Paris 16, France (Telephone Number in U.S. (212) 963-5981); *Trade by Commodities.*

South Pacific Commission, Post Box D5, Noumea Cedex, New Caledonia; *Statistical Bulletin of the South Pacific: Overseas Trade.*

Statistical Office of the United Nations, Publishing Service, New York, New York 10017 (800) 253-9646; *Statistical Yearbook.*

AMERICAN SAMOA - FORESTRY AND FOREST PRODUCTS

Food and Agricultural Organization of the United Nations (FAO) Via Delle Terme di Caracalla, 00100 Rome, Italy (Telephone Number in U.S. (202) 653-2400); *The State of Food and Agriculture.*

G.K. Hall and Company, 70 Lincoln Street, Boston, Massachusetts 02111 (617) 423-3990; *The World in Figures.*

Statistical Office of the United Nations, Publishing Service, New York, New York 10017 (800) 253-9646; *Statistical Yearbook.*

United Nations Educational, Scientific and Cultural Organization (UNESCO), 7 Place de Fontenoy, F-75700 Paris, France (Telephone Number in U.S. (212) 963-5981); *Statistical Yearbook.*

AMERICAN SAMOA - GENERAL MORTALITY

Statistical Office of the United Nations, Publishing Service, New York, New York 10017 (800) 253-9646; *Demographic Yearbook.*

World Health Organization, Office of Publications, Avenue Appia, CH-1211 Geneva 27, Switzerland (Telephone Number in U.S. (518) 436-9686); *World Health Statistics Annual.*

AMERICAN SAMOA - GOVERNMENT

G.K. Hall and Company, 70 Lincoln Street, Boston, Massachusetts 02111 (617) 423-3990; *The World in Figures.*

AMERICAN SAMOA - GRAIN PRODUCTION - See AMERICAN SAMOA - CROPS

AMERICAN SAMOA - GROSS DOMESTIC PRODUCT

G.K. Hall and Company, 70 Lincoln Street, Boston, Massachusetts 02111 (617) 423-3990; *The World in Figures.*

AMERICAN SAMOA - HEALTH

G.K. Hall and Company, 70 Lincoln Street, Boston, Massachusetts 02111 (617) 423-3990; *The World in Figures.*

South Pacific Commission, Post Box D5, Noumea Cedex, New Caledonia; *Statistical Bulletin of the South Pacific: Retail Price Indexes.*

Statistical Office of the United Nations, Publishing Service, New York, New York 10017 (800) 253-9646; *Statistical Yearbook.*

World Health Organization, Office of Publications, Avenue Appia, CH-1211 Geneva 27, Switzerland (Telephone Number in U.S. (518) 436-9686); *World Health Statistics Annual.*

AMERICAN SAMOA - HIDE PRODUCTION

Food and Agricultural Organization of the United Nations (FAO), Via delle Terme di Caracalla, 00100 Rome, Italy (Telephone Number in U.S. (202) 653-2400); *Production Yearbook.*

AMERICAN SAMOA - HIGHWAYS

G.K. Hall and Company, 70 Lincoln Street, Boston, Massachusetts 02111 (617) 423-3990; *The World in Figures.*

AMERICAN SAMOA - HOURS OF WORK - See AMERICAN SAMOA - EMPLOYMENT

AMERICAN SAMOA - HOUSING AND HOUSING UNITS

South Pacific Commission, Post Box D5, Noumea Cedex, New Caledonia; *Statistical Bulletin of the South Pacific: Retail Price Indexes.*

AMERICAN SAMOA - HOUSING EXPENDITURES

South Pacific Commission, Post Box D5, Noumea Cedex, New Caledonia; *Statistical Bulletin of the South Pacific: Retail Price Indexes.*

AMERICAN SAMOA - ILLITERATE POPULATION

G.K. Hall and Company, 70 Lincoln Street, Boston, Massachusetts 02111 (617) 423-3990; *The World in Figures.*

AMERICAN SAMOA - IMPORTS

Food and Agricultural Organization of the United Nations (FAO) Via Delle Terme di Caracalla, 00100 Rome, Italy (Telephone Number in U.S. (202) 653-2400); *The State of Food and Agriculture.*

G.K. Hall and Company, 70 Lincoln Street, Boston, Massachusetts 02111 (617) 423-3990; *The World in Figures.*

South Pacific Commission, Post Box D5, Noumea Cedex, New Caledonia; *Statistical Bulletin of the South Pacific: Overseas Trade.*

AMERICAN SAMOA - INDUSTRY

G.K. Hall and Company, 70 Lincoln Street, Boston, Massachusetts 02111 (617) 423-3990; *The World in Figures.*

International Labour Office, I.L.O. Publications, CH-1211, Geneva 22, Switzerland; *Yearbook of Labour Statistics.*

AMERICAN SAMOA - INFANT AND MATERNAL MORTALITY

Statistical Office of the United Nations, Publishing Service, New York, New York 10017 (800) 253-9646; *Demographic Yearbook,* and *Statistical Yearbook.*

World Health Organization, Office of Publications, Avenue Appia, CH-1211 Geneva 27, Switzerland (Telephone Number in U.S. (518) 436-9686); *World Health Statistics Annual.*

AMERICAN SAMOA - LABOR FORCE

Food and Agricultural Organization of the United Nations (FAO) Via Delle Terme di Caracalla, 00100 Rome, Italy (Telephone Number in U.S. (202) 653-2400); *The State of Food and Agriculture.*

G.K. Hall and Company, 70 Lincoln Street, Boston, Massachusetts 02111 (617) 423-3990; *The World in Figures.*

AMERICAN SAMOA - LABOR PRODUCTIVITY

International Labour Office, I.L.O. Publications, CH-1211, Geneva 22, Switzerland; *Yearbook of Labour Statistics.*

AMERICAN SAMOA - LAND USE

Food and Agricultural Organization of the United Nations (FAO), Via delle Terme di Caracalla, 00100 Rome, Italy (Telephone Number in U.S. (202) 653-2400); *Production Yearbook.*

G.K. Hall and Company, 70 Lincoln Street, Boston, Massachusetts 02111 (617) 423-3990; *The World in Figures.*

AMERICAN SAMOA - LIBRARIES

United Nations Educational, Scientific and Cultural Organization (UNESCO), 7 Place de Fontenoy, F-75700 Paris, France (Telephone Number in U.S. (212) 963-5981); *Statistical Yearbook.*

AMERICAN SAMOA - LIVESTOCK AND POULTRY

Food and Agricultural Organization of the United Nations (FAO), Via delle Terme di Caracalla, 00100 Rome, Italy (Telephone Number in U.S. (202) 653-2400); *Production Yearbook,* and *The State of Food and Agriculture.*

G.K. Hall and Company, 70 Lincoln Street, Boston, Massachusetts 02111 (617) 423-3990; *The World in Figures.*

AMERICAN SAMOA - LIVING LEVELS

G.K. Hall and Company, 70 Lincoln Street, Boston, Massachusetts 02111 (617) 423-3990; *The World in Figures.*

AMERICAN SAMOA - MANUFACTURING

G.K. Hall and Company, 70 Lincoln Street, Boston, Massachusetts 02111 (617) 423-3990; *The World in Figures.*

AMERICAN SAMOA - MARRIAGE RATES

Statistical Office of the United Nations, Publishing Service, New York, New York 10017 (800) 253-9646; *Demographic Yearbook*, and *Statistical Yearbook*.

AMERICAN SAMOA - MEAT PRODUCTION - See AMERICAN SAMOA - LIVESTOCK AND POULTRY

AMERICAN SAMOA - MERCHANT SHIPPING

G.K. Hall and Company, 70 Lincoln Street, Boston, Massachusetts 02111 (617) 423-3990; *The World in Figures*.

Statistical Office of the United Nations, Publishing Service, New York, New York 10017 (800) 253-9646; *Statistical Yearbook*.

AMERICAN SAMOA - MILITARY

G.K. Hall and Company, 70 Lincoln Street, Boston, Massachusetts 02111 (617) 423-3990; *The World in Figures*.

AMERICAN SAMOA - MINING AND MINERAL PRODUCTS

G.K. Hall and Company, 70 Lincoln Street, Boston, Massachusetts 02111 (617) 423-3990; *The World in Figures*.

AMERICAN SAMOA - MONEY SUPPLY

G.K. Hall and Company, 70 Lincoln Street, Boston, Massachusetts 02111 (617) 423-3990; *The World in Figures*.

AMERICAN SAMOA - MOTION PICTURES

Statistical Office of the United Nations, Publishing Service, New York, New York 10017 (800) 253-9646; *Statistical Yearbook*.

AMERICAN SAMOA - MOTOR VEHICLES IN USE

G.K. Hall and Company, 70 Lincoln Street, Boston, Massachusetts 02111 (617) 423-3990; *The World in Figures*.

Statistical Office of the United Nations, Publishing Service, New York, New York 10017 (800) 253-9646; *Statistical Yearbook*.

AMERICAN SAMOA - MUSEUMS

United Nations Educational, Scientific and Cultural Organization (UNESCO), 7 Place de Fontenoy, F-75700 Paris, France (Telephone Number in U.S. (212) 963-5981); *Statistical Yearbook*.

AMERICAN SAMOA - NATALITY - See AMERICAN SAMOA - BIRTH RATE

AMERICAN SAMOA - NATIONAL INCOME

G.K. Hall and Company, 70 Lincoln Street, Boston, Massachusetts 02111 (617) 423-3990; *The World in Figures*.

AMERICAN SAMOA - NEWSPAPER PRODUCTION - See AMERICAN SAMOA - FORESTRY AND FOREST PRODUCTS

AMERICAN SAMOA - OCCUPATIONS - See AMERICAN SAMOA - LABOR FORCE

AMERICAN SAMOA - PERIODICALS

United Nations Educational, Scientific and Cultural Organization (UNESCO), 7 Place de Fontenoy, F-75700 Paris, France (Telephone Number in U.S. (212) 963-5981); *Statistical Yearbook*.

AMERICAN SAMOA - PESTICIDE USE

Food and Agricultural Organization of the United Nations (FAO) Via Delle Terme di Caracalla, 00100 Rome, Italy (Telephone Number in U.S. (202) 653-2400); *The State of Food and Agriculture*.

AMERICAN SAMOA - PETROLEUM INDUSTRY

Food and Agricultural Organization of the United Nations (FAO) Via Delle Terme di Caracalla, 00100 Rome, Italy (Telephone Number in U.S. (202) 653-2400); *The State of Food and Agriculture*.

G.K. Hall and Company, 70 Lincoln Street, Boston, Massachusetts 02111 (617) 423-3990; *The World in Figures*.

AMERICAN SAMOA - POPULATION

Food and Agricultural Organization of the United Nations (FAO), Via delle Terme di Caracalla, 00100 Rome, Italy (Telephone Number in U.S. (202) 653-2400); *Production Yearbook*.

G.K. Hall and Company, 70 Lincoln Street, Boston, Massachusetts 02111 (617) 423-3990; *The World in Figures*.

International Labour Office, I.L.O. Publications, CH-1211, Geneva 22, Switzerland; *Yearbook of Labour Statistics*.

Statistical Office of the United Nations, Publishing Service, New York, New York 10017 (800) 253-9646; *Demographic Yearbook*, and *Statistical Yearbook*.

World Health Organization, Office of Publications, Avenue Appia, CH-1211 Geneva 27, Switzerland (Telephone Number in U.S. (518) 436-9686); *World Health Statistics Annual*.

AMERICAN SAMOA - PRICES

Food and Agricultural Organization of the United Nations (FAO), Via delle Terme di Caracalla, 00100 Rome, Italy (Telephone Number in U.S. (202) 653-2400); *Production Yearbook*, and *The State of Food and Agriculture*.

G.K. Hall and Company, 70 Lincoln Street, Boston, Massachusetts 02111 (617) 423-3990; *The World in Figures*.

International Labour Office, I.L.O. Publications, CH-1211, Geneva 22, Switzerland; *Yearbook of Labour Statistics*.

South Pacific Commission, Post Box D5, Noumea Cedex, New Caledonia; *Statistical Bulletin of the South Pacific: Overseas Trade*, and *Statistical Bulletin of the South Pacific: Retail Price Indexes*.

AMERICAN SAMOA - PRODUCTION

G.K. Hall and Company, 70 Lincoln Street, Boston, Massachusetts 02111 (617) 423-3990; *The World in Figures*.

AMERICAN SAMOA - RAILWAYS

G.K. Hall and Company, 70 Lincoln Street, Boston, Massachusetts 02111 (617) 423-3990; *The World in Figures*.

AMERICAN SAMOA - RENT PRICES

International Labour Office, I.L.O. Publications, CH-1211, Geneva 22, Switzerland; *Yearbook of Labour Statistics*.

AMERICAN SAMOA - RETAIL TRADE

G.K. Hall and Company, 70 Lincoln Street, Boston, Massachusetts 02111 (617) 423-3990; *The World in Figures.*

AMERICAN SAMOA - SCIENCE AND TECHNOLOGY - EXPENDITURE FOR RESEARCH

Statistical Office of the United Nations, Publishing Service, New York, New York 10017 (800) 253-9646; *Statistical Yearbook.*

AMERICAN SAMOA - SCIENTISTS AND TECHNICIANS

Statistical Office of the United Nations, Publishing Service, New York, New York 10017 (800) 253-9646; *Statistical Yearbook.*

AMERICAN SAMOA - SOCIAL DATA

G.K. Hall and Company, 70 Lincoln Street, Boston, Massachusetts 02111 (617) 423-3990; *The World in Figures.*

AMERICAN SAMOA - STOCKS - COMMODITY - MARKET PRICE - INDEX

Food and Agricultural Organization of the United Nations (FAO) Via Delle Terme di Caracalla, 00100 Rome, Italy (Telephone Number in U.S. (202) 653-2400); *The State of Food and Agriculture.*

AMERICAN SAMOA - TAXATION

G.K. Hall and Company, 70 Lincoln Street, Boston, Massachusetts 02111 (617) 423-3990; *The World in Figures.*

AMERICAN SAMOA - TELEPHONES IN USE

American Telephone and Telegraph Company, 26 Parsippany Road, Whippany, New Jersey 07981 (800) 338-4038; *The World's Telephones.*

G.K. Hall and Company, 70 Lincoln Street, Boston, Massachusetts 02111 (617) 423-3990; *The World in Figures.*

Statistical Office of the United Nations, Publishing Service, New York, New York 10017 (800) 253-9646; *Statistical Yearbook.*

AMERICAN SAMOA - TEXTILE INDUSTRY

G.K. Hall and Company, 70 Lincoln Street, Boston, Massachusetts 02111 (617) 423-3990; *The World in Figures.*

AMERICAN SAMOA - TOBACCO PRODUCTION

South Pacific Commission, Post Box D5, Noumea Cedex, New Caledonia; *Statistical Bulletin of the South Pacific: Retail Price Indexes.*

AMERICAN SAMOA - TOURISM

G.K. Hall and Company, 70 Lincoln Street, Boston, Massachusetts 02111 (617) 423-3990; *The World in Figures.*

World Tourism Organization, Calle Capitan Haya 42, E-28020 Madrid, Spain; *Yearbook of Tourism Statistics.*

AMERICAN SAMOA - TRADE - See AMERICAN SAMOA - FOREIGN TRADE

AMERICAN SAMOA - TRANSPORTATION AND COMMUNICATIONS

G.K. Hall and Company, 70 Lincoln Street, Boston, Massachusetts 02111 (617) 423-3990; *The World in Figures.*

South Pacific Commission, Post Box D5, Noumea Cedex, New Caledonia; *Statistical Bulletin of the South Pacific: Retail Price Indexes.*

AMERICAN SAMOA - UNEMPLOYMENT

International Labour Office, I.L.O. Publications, CH-1211, Geneva 22, Switzerland; *Yearbook of Labour Statistics.*

Statistical Office of the United Nations, Publishing Service, New York, New York 10017 (800) 253-9646; *Statistical Yearbook.*

AMERICAN SAMOA - VITAL STATISTICS

G.K. Hall and Company, 70 Lincoln Street, Boston, Massachusetts 02111 (617) 423-3990; *The World in Figures.*

Statistical Office of the United Nations, Publishing Service, New York, New York 10017 (800) 253-9646; *Statistical Yearbook.*

World Health Organization, Office of Publications, Avenue Appia, CH-1211 Geneva 27, Switzerland (Telephone Number in U.S. (518) 436-9686); *World Health Statistics Annual.*

AMERICAN SAMOA - WAGES

G.K. Hall and Company, 70 Lincoln Street, Boston, Massachusetts 02111 (617) 423-3990; *The World in Figures.*

International Labour Office, I.L.O. Publications, CH-1211, Geneva 22, Switzerland; *Yearbook of Labour Statistics.*

AMERICAN SAMOA - WEATHER

G.K. Hall and Company, 70 Lincoln Street, Boston, Massachusetts 02111 (617) 423-3990; *The World in Figures.*

AMERICAN STOCK EXCHANGE

Securities and Exchange Commission, 450 Fifth Street, NW, Washington, D.C. 20549 (202) 272-3100; unpublished data.

AMERICAN WARS - COST

U.S. Congress, Joint Economic Committee, The Capitol, Washington, D.C. 20510 (202) 224-3121; *The Military Budget and National Economic Priorities;* subsequently revised and updated by James L. Clayton, University of Utah, Salt Lake City, Utah.

AMTRAK

Association of American Railroads, American Railroads Building, 50 F Street, NW, Washington, D.C. 20001 (212) 639-2333; *Railroad Facts, Statistics of Railroads of Class I,* and *Analysis of Class I Railroads.*

AMUSEMENTS AND RECREATIONAL SERVICES - ADVERTISING EXPENDITURES

Television Bureau of Advertising, Incorporated, 850 Third Avenue, New York, New York 10022 (212) 486-1111; Data compiled by Competitive Media Reporting, 11 West 42nd Street, New York, New York 10036 (212) 789-1400.

AMUSEMENTS AND RECREATIONAL SERVICES - EARNINGS

U.S. Department of Commerce, Bureau of Census, Suitland, Maryland 20233 (301) 763-4040; *County Business Patterns*, and *Census of Service Industries*.

AMUSEMENTS AND RECREATIONAL SERVICES - EMPLOYEES

U.S. Department of Commerce, Bureau of Economic Analysis, Fourteenth Street between Constitution Avenue and E Street, NW, Washington, D.C. 20230 (202) 606-9900; *The National Income and Product Accounts of the United States*, and *Survey of Current Business*.

U.S. Department of Commerce, Bureau of the Census, Suitland, Maryland 20233 (301) 763-4040; *County Business Patterns*, and *Census of Service Industries*.

U.S. Travel Data Center, Two Lafayette Center, 1133 21st Street, NW, Washington, D.C. 20036 (202) 293-1040; *Economic Review of Travel in America*.

AMUSEMENTS AND RECREATIONAL SERVICES - ESTABLISHMENTS

U.S. Department of Commerce, Bureau of the Census, Suitland, Maryland 20233 (301) 763-4040; *County Business Patterns*, and *Census of Service Industries*.

International Franchise Association, 1350 New York Avenue, Suite 900, Washington, D.C. 20005 (202) 628-8000; *Franchising in the Economy*.

AMUSEMENTS AND RECREATIONAL SERVICES - FINANCES

U.S. Department of Commerce, Bureau of the Census, Suitland, Maryland 20233 (301) 763-4040; *Current Business Reports, Service Annual Survey*, and *Census of Service Industries*.

AMUSEMENTS AND RECREATIONAL SERVICES - GROSS NATIONAL PRODUCT

U.S. Department of Commerce, Bureau of Economic Analysis, 14th Street between Constitution Avenue and E Street, NW, Washington, D.C. 20230 (202) 606-9900; *The National Income and Product Accounts of the United States* and *Survey of Current Business*.

AMUSEMENTS AND RECREATIONAL SERVICES - OCCUPATIONAL SAFETY

U.S. Department of Labor, Bureau of Labor Statistics,Two Massachusetts Avenue, NE, Washington, D.C. 20212 (202) 606-7828; *Occupational Injuries and Illnesses in the United States by Industry*.

AMUSEMENTS AND RECREATIONAL SERVICES - RECEIPTS

U.S. Department of Commerce, Bureau of the Census, Suitland, Maryland 20233 (301) 763-4040; *Current Business Reports, Service Annual Survey, Census of Service Industries*, and *Census of Wholesale Trade*.

International Franchise Association, 1350 New York Avenue, Suite 900, Washington, D.C. 20005 (202) 628-8000; *Franchising in the Economy*.

U.S. Travel Data Center, Two Lafayette Center, 1133 21st Street, NW, Washington, D.C. 20036 (202) 293-1040; *Economic Review of Travel in America*.

ANCESTRY

U.S. Department of Commerce, Bureau of the Census, Suitland, Maryland 20233 (301) 763-4040; *Census of Population, Supplementary Report*, and *Census of Population and Housing Data Paper Listing*, and *Detailed Ancestry Groups for States*.

ANCHOVIES

U.S. Department of Commerce, National Oceanic and Atmospheric Administration, National Marine Fisheries Service, 1335 East-West Highway, Silver Spring, Maryland 20910 (301) 427-2239; *Fishery Statistics of the United States*, and *Fisheries of the United States*.

Andorra - National Statistical Office

Centro Nacional de Informatica de Andorra, Avda Meritxell 86B, Andorra La Vella, Andorra.

ANDORRA - AGRICULTURE

Food and Agricultural Organization of the United Nations (FAO), Via delle Terme di Caracalla, 00100 Rome, Italy (Telephone Number in U.S. (202) 653-2400); *Production Yearbook, The State of Food and Agriculture*, and *Trade Yearbook*.

G.K. Hall and Company, 70 Lincoln Street, Boston, Massachusetts 02111 (617) 423-3990; *The World in Figures*.

ANDORRA - AIRLINE SERVICE

G.K. Hall and Company, 70 Lincoln Street, Boston, Massachusetts 02111 (617) 423-3990; *The World in Figures*.

ANDORRA - AREA AND DENSITY OF POPULATION

Food and Agricultural Organization of the United Nations (FAO) Via Delle Terme di Caracalla, 00100 Rome, Italy (Telephone Number in U.S. (202) 653-2400); *The State of Food and Agriculture*.

G.K. Hall and Company, 70 Lincoln Street, Boston, Massachusetts 02111 (617) 423-3990; *The World in Figures*.

Statistical Office of the United Nations, Publishing Service, New York, New York 10017 (800) 253-9646; *Statistical Yearbook*.

ANDORRA - BALANCE OF PAYMENTS

G.K. Hall and Company, 70 Lincoln Street, Boston, Massachusetts 02111 (617) 423-3990; *The World in Figures*.

ANDORRA - BANKING

G.K. Hall and Company, 70 Lincoln Street, Boston, Massachusetts 02111 (617) 423-3990; *The World in Figures*.

ANDORRA - BIRTH RATES

Statistical Office of the United Nations, Publishing Service, New York, New York 10017 (800) 253-9646; *Demographic Yearbook*.

World Health Organization, Office of Publications, Avenue Appia, CH-1211 Geneva 27, Switzerland (Telephone Number in U.S. (518) 436-9686); *World Health Statistics Annual*.

ANDORRA - BONDS

G.K. Hall and Company, 70 Lincoln Street, Boston, Massachusetts 02111 (617) 423-3990; *The World in Figures.*

ANDORRA - BOOK PRODUCTION

G.K. Hall and Company, 70 Lincoln Street, Boston, Massachusetts 02111 (617) 423-3990; *The World in Figures.*

ANDORRA - BROADCASTING

Billboard Limited, P.O. Box 9027, 1006 AA Amsterdam, The Netherlands (Telephone Number in U.S. (212) 764-7300); *World Radio TV Handbook.*

G.K. Hall and Company, 70 Lincoln Street, Boston, Massachusetts 02111 (617) 423-3990; *The World in Figures.*

ANDORRA - BUSINESS

G.K. Hall and Company, 70 Lincoln Street, Boston, Massachusetts 02111 (617) 423-3990; *The World in Figures.*

ANDORRA - CALORIE SUPPLY

Food and Agricultural Organization of the United Nations (FAO) Via Delle Terme di Caracalla, 00100 Rome, Italy (Telephone Number in U.S. (202) 653-2400); *The State of Food and Agriculture.*

ANDORRA - CHEMICAL (ORGANIC) PRODUCTION - See ANDORRA - MINING AND MINERAL PRODUCTS

ANDORRA - CLASS STRUCTURE

G.K. Hall and Company, 70 Lincoln Street, Boston, Massachusetts 02111 (617) 423-3990; *The World in Figures.*

ANDORRA - CLIMATE

G.K. Hall and Company, 70 Lincoln Street, Boston, Massachusetts 02111 (617) 423-3990; *The World in Figures.*

ANDORRA - COAL PRODUCTION - See ANDORRA - MINING AND MINERAL PRODUCTS

ANDORRA - CORN PRODUCTION - See ANDORRA - CROPS

ANDORRA - COMMUNICATIONS

G.K. Hall and Company, 70 Lincoln Street, Boston, Massachusetts 02111 (617) 423-3990; *The World in Figures.*

ANDORRA - CONSUMER PRICE INDEX

G.K. Hall and Company, 70 Lincoln Street, Boston, Massachusetts 02111 (617) 423-3990; *The World in Figures.*

ANDORRA - CONSUMPTION

G.K. Hall and Company, 70 Lincoln Street, Boston, Massachusetts 02111 (617) 423-3990; *The World in Figures.*

ANDORRA - CORPORATE TAXES - See ANDORRA - TAXATION

ANDORRA - CROPS

Food and Agricultural Organization of the United Nations (FAO) Via Delle Terme di Caracalla, 00100 Rome, Italy (Telephone Number in U.S. (202) 653-2400); *The State of Food and Agriculture.*

G.K. Hall and Company, 70 Lincoln Street, Boston, Massachusetts 02111 (617) 423-3990; *The World in Figures.*

ANDORRA - CUSTOMS DUTIES

G.K. Hall and Company, 70 Lincoln Street, Boston, Massachusetts 02111 (617) 423-3990; *The World in Figures.*

ANDORRA - DEATH RATES

G.K. Hall and Company, 70 Lincoln Street, Boston, Massachusetts 02111 (617) 423-3990; *The World in Figures.*

ANDORRA - DEFENSE EXPENDITURES

G.K. Hall and Company, 70 Lincoln Street, Boston, Massachusetts 02111 (617) 423-3990; *The World in Figures.*

ANDORRA - DEMOGRAPHY

G.K. Hall and Company, 70 Lincoln Street, Boston, Massachusetts 02111 (617) 423-3990; *The World in Figures.*

ANDORRA - DEVELOPMENT ASSISTANCE

G.K. Hall and Company, 70 Lincoln Street, Boston, Massachusetts 02111 (617) 423-3990; *The World in Figures.*

ANDORRA - DISEASE

G.K. Hall and Company, 70 Lincoln Street, Boston, Massachusetts 02111 (617) 423-3990; *The World in Figures.*

ANDORRA - DIVORCE RATES

Statistical Office of the United Nations, Publishing Service, New York, New York 10017 (800) 253-9646; *Demographic Yearbook.*

ANDORRA - DOMESTIC PRODUCT

G.K. Hall and Company, 70 Lincoln Street, Boston, Massachusetts 02111 (617) 423-3990; *The World in Figures.*

ANDORRA - ECONOMY

G.K. Hall and Company, 70 Lincoln Street, Boston, Massachusetts 02111 (617) 423-3990; *The World in Figures.*

ANDORRA - EDUCATION

G.K. Hall and Company, 70 Lincoln Street, Boston, Massachusetts 02111 (617) 423-3990; *The World in Figures.*

ANDORRA - EGG PRODUCTION

Food and Agricultural Organization of the United Nations (FAO) Via Delle Terme di Caracalla, 00100 Rome, Italy (Telephone Number in U.S. (202) 653-2400); *The State of Food and Agriculture.*

ANDORRA - ENERGY

Food and Agricultural Organization of the United Nations (FAO) Via Delle Terme di Caracalla, 00100 Rome, Italy (Telephone Number in U.S. (202) 653-2400); *The State of Food and Agriculture.*

G.K. Hall and Company, 70 Lincoln Street, Boston, Massachusetts 02111 (617) 423-3990; *The World in Figures.*

ANDORRA - EXPORTS

Food and Agricultural Organization of the United Nations (FAO) Via Delle Terme di Caracalla, 00100 Rome, Italy (Telephone Number in U.S. (202) 653-2400); *The State of Food and Agriculture.*

G.K. Hall and Company, 70 Lincoln Street, Boston, Massachusetts 02111 (617) 423-3990; *The World in Figures.*

ANDORRA - EXTERNAL TRADE

Food and Agricultural Organization of the United Nations (FAO) Via Delle Terme di Caracalla, 00100 Rome, Italy (Telephone Number in U.S. (202) 653-2400); *The State of Food and Agriculture,* and *Trade Yearbook.*

G.K. Hall and Company, 70 Lincoln Street, Boston, Massachusetts 02111 (617) 423-3990; *The World in Figures.*

ANDORRA - FARM CROPS - See ANDORRA - CROPS

ANDORRA - FETAL MORTALITY

Statistical Office of the United Nations, Publishing Service, New York, New York 10017 (800) 253-9646; *Demographic Yearbook.*

ANDORRA - FERTILIZER

Food and Agricultural Organization of the United Nations (FAO) Via Delle Terme di Caracalla, 00100 Rome, Italy (Telephone Number in U.S. (202) 653-2400); *The State of Food and Agriculture.*

ANDORRA - FINANCE

G.K. Hall and Company, 70 Lincoln Street, Boston, Massachusetts 02111 (617) 423-3990; *The World in Figures.*

ANDORRA - FISHERIES

Food and Agricultural Organization of the United Nations (FAO) Via Delle Terme di Caracalla, 00100 Rome, Italy (Telephone Number in U.S. (202) 653-2400); *The State of Food and Agriculture,* and *Yearbook of Fishery Statistics.*

ANDORRA - FOOD

Food and Agricultural Organization of the United Nations (FAO), Via delle Terme di Caracalla, 00100 Rome, Italy (Telephone Number in U.S. (202) 653-2400); *Production Yearbook,* and *The State of Food and Agriculture.*

G.K. Hall and Company, 70 Lincoln Street, Boston, Massachusetts 02111 (617) 423-3990; *The World in Figures.*

ANDORRA - FOREIGN AID

G.K. Hall and Company, 70 Lincoln Street, Boston, Massachusetts 02111 (617) 423-3990; *The World in Figures.*

ANDORRA - FOREIGN TRADE

Food and Agricultural Organization of the United Nations (FAO) Via Delle Terme di Caracalla, 00100 Rome, Italy (Telephone Number in U.S. (202) 653-2400); *The State of Food and Agriculture.*

G.K. Hall and Company, 70 Lincoln Street, Boston, Massachusetts 02111 (617) 423-3990; *The World in Figures.*

ANDORRA - FORESTRY AND FOREST PRODUCTS

Food and Agricultural Organization of the United Nations (FAO) Via Delle Terme di Caracalla, 00100 Rome, Italy (Telephone Number in U.S. (202) 653-2400); *The State of Food and Agriculture.*

G.K. Hall and Company, 70 Lincoln Street, Boston, Massachusetts 02111 (617) 423-3990; *The World in Figures.*

United Nations Educational, Scientific and Cultural Organization (UNESCO), 7 Place de Fontenoy, F-75700 Paris, France (Telephone Number in U.S. (212) 963-5981); *Statistical Yearbook.*

ANDORRA - GENERAL MORTALITY

Statistical Office of the United Nations, Publishing Service, New York, New York 10017 (800) 253-9646; *Demographic Yearbook.*

World Health Organization, Office of Publications, Avenue Appia, CH-1211 Geneva 27, Switzerland (Telephone Number in U.S. (518) 436-9686); *World Health Statistics Annual.*

ANDORRA - GOVERNMENT

G.K. Hall and Company, 70 Lincoln Street, Boston, Massachusetts 02111 (617) 423-3990; *The World in Figures.*

ANDORRA - GRAIN PRODUCTION - See ANDORRA - CROPS

ANDORRA - GROSS DOMESTIC PRODUCT

G.K. Hall and Company, 70 Lincoln Street, Boston, Massachusetts 02111 (617) 423-3990; *The World in Figures.*

ANDORRA - HEALTH

G.K. Hall and Company, 70 Lincoln Street, Boston, Massachusetts 02111 (617) 423-3990; *The World in Figures.*

ANDORRA - HIGHWAYS

G.K. Hall and Company, 70 Lincoln Street, Boston, Massachusetts 02111 (617) 423-3990; *The World in Figures.*

ANDORRA - ILLITERATE POPULATION

G.K. Hall and Company, 70 Lincoln Street, Boston, Massachusetts 02111 (617) 423-3990; *The World in Figures.*

ANDORRA - IMPORTS

Food and Agricultural Organization of the United Nations (FAO) Via Delle Terme di Caracalla, 00100 Rome, Italy (Telephone Number in U.S. (202) 653-2400); *The State of Food and Agriculture.*

G.K. Hall and Company, 70 Lincoln Street, Boston, Massachusetts 02111 (617) 423-3990; *The World in Figures.*

ANDORRA - INDUSTRY

G.K. Hall and Company, 70 Lincoln Street, Boston, Massachusetts 02111 (617) 423-3990; *The World in Figures.*

ANDORRA - INFANT AND MATERNAL MORTALITY

Statistical Office of the United Nations, Publishing Service, New York, New York 10017 (800) 253-9646; *Demographic Yearbook.*

ANDORRA - LABOR FORCE

Food and Agricultural Organization of the United Nations (FAO) Via Delle Terme di Caracalla, 00100 Rome, Italy (Telephone Number in U.S. (202) 653-2400); *The State of Food and Agriculture*.

G.K. Hall and Company, 70 Lincoln Street, Boston, Massachusetts 02111 (617) 423-3990; *The World in Figures*.

ANDORRA - LAND USE

Food and Agricultural Organization of the United Nations (FAO), Via delle Terme di Caracalla, 00100 Rome, Italy (Telephone Number in U.S. (202) 653-2400); *Production Yearbook*.

G.K. Hall and Company, 70 Lincoln Street, Boston, Massachusetts 02111 (617) 423-3990; *The World in Figures*.

ANDORRA - LIVESTOCK AND POULTRY

Food and Agricultural Organization of the United Nations (FAO), Via delle Terme di Caracalla, 00100 Rome, Italy (Telephone Number in U.S. (202) 653-2400); *Production Yearbook*, and *The State of Food and Agriculture*.

G.K. Hall and Company, 70 Lincoln Street, Boston, Massachusetts 02111 (617) 423-3990; *The World in Figures*.

ANDORRA - LIVING LEVELS

G.K. Hall and Company, 70 Lincoln Street, Boston, Massachusetts 02111 (617) 423-3990; *The World in Figures*.

ANDORRA - MANUFACTURING

G.K. Hall and Company, 70 Lincoln Street, Boston, Massachusetts 02111 (617) 423-3990; *The World in Figures*.

ANDORRA - MARRIAGE RATES

Statistical Office of the United Nations, Publishing Service, New York, New York 10017 (800) 253-9646; *Demographic Yearbook*.

ANDORRA - MEAT PRODUCTION - See ANDORRA - LIVESTOCK AND POULTRY

ANDORRA - MERCHANT SHIPPING

G.K. Hall and Company, 70 Lincoln Street, Boston, Massachusetts 02111 (617) 423-3990; *The World in Figures*.

ANDORRA - MILITARY

G.K. Hall and Company, 70 Lincoln Street, Boston, Massachusetts 02111 (617) 423-3990; *The World in Figures*.

ANDORRA - MINING AND MINERAL PRODUCTS

G.K. Hall and Company, 70 Lincoln Street, Boston, Massachusetts 02111 (617) 423-3990; *The World in Figures*.

ANDORRA - MONEY SUPPLY

G.K. Hall and Company, 70 Lincoln Street, Boston, Massachusetts 02111 (617) 423-3990; *The World in Figures*.

ANDORRA - MOTOR VEHICLES IN USE

G.K. Hall and Company, 70 Lincoln Street, Boston, Massachusetts 02111 (617) 423-3990; *The World in Figures*.

ANDORRA - MUSEUMS

United Nations Educational, Scientific and Cultural Organization (UNESCO), 7 Place de Fontenoy, F-75700 Paris, France (Telephone Number in U.S. (212) 963-5981); *Statistical Yearbook*.

ANDORRA - NATALITY - See ANDORRA - BIRTH RATES

ANDORRA - NATIONAL INCOME

G.K. Hall and Company, 70 Lincoln Street, Boston, Massachusetts 02111 (617) 423-3990; *The World in Figures*.

ANDORRA - NEWSPAPER PRODUCTION - See ANDORRA - FORESTRY AND FOREST PRODUCTS

ANDORRA - OCCUPATIONS - See ANDORRA - LABOR FORCE

ANDORRA - PESTICIDE USE

Food and Agricultural Organization of the United Nations (FAO) Via Delle Terme di Caracalla, 00100 Rome, Italy (Telephone Number in U.S. (202) 653-2400); *The State of Food and Agriculture*.

ANDORRA - PETROLEUM INDUSTRY

Food and Agricultural Organization of the United Nations (FAO) Via Delle Terme di Caracalla, 00100 Rome, Italy (Telephone Number in U.S. (202) 653-2400); *The State of Food and Agriculture*.

G.K. Hall and Company, 70 Lincoln Street, Boston, Massachusetts 02111 (617) 423-3990; *The World in Figures*.

ANDORRA - POPULATION

Food and Agricultural Organization of the United Nations (FAO), Via delle Terme di Caracalla, 00100 Rome, Italy (Telephone Number in U.S. (202) 653-2400); *Production Yearbook*.

G.K. Hall and Company, 70 Lincoln Street, Boston, Massachusetts 02111 (617) 423-3990; *The World in Figures*.

Statistical Office of the United Nations, Publishing Service, New York, New York 10017 (800) 253-9646; *Demographic Yearbook*, and *Statistical Yearbook*.

World Health Organization, Office of Publications, Avenue Appia, CH-1211 Geneva 27, Switzerland (Telephone Number in U.S. (518) 436-9686); *World Health Statistics Annual*.

ANDORRA - PRICES

Food and Agricultural Organization of the United Nations (FAO), Via delle Terme di Caracalla, 00100 Rome, Italy (Telephone Number in U.S. (202) 653-2400); *Production Yearbook*, and *The State of Food and Agriculture*.

G.K. Hall and Company, 70 Lincoln Street, Boston, Massachusetts 02111 (617) 423-3990; *The World in Figures*.

ANDORRA - PRODUCTION

G.K. Hall and Company, 70 Lincoln Street, Boston, Massachusetts 02111 (617) 423-3990; *The World in Figures*.

ANDORRA - RAILWAY USE

G.K. Hall and Company, 70 Lincoln Street, Boston, Massachusetts 02111 (617) 423-3990; *The World in Figures.*

ANDORRA - RETAIL TRADE

G.K. Hall and Company, 70 Lincoln Street, Boston, Massachusetts 02111 (617) 423-3990; *The World in Figures.*

ANDORRA - SOCIAL DATA

G.K. Hall and Company, 70 Lincoln Street, Boston, Massachusetts 02111 (617) 423-3990; *The World in Figures.*

ANDORRA - STOCKS - COMMODITY - MARKET PRICE - INDEX

Food and Agricultural Organization of the United Nations (FAO) Via Delle Terme di Caracalla, 00100 Rome, Italy (Telephone Number in U.S. (202) 653-2400); *The State of Food and Agriculture.*

ANDORRA - TAXATION

G.K. Hall and Company, 70 Lincoln Street, Boston, Massachusetts 02111 (617) 423-3990; *The World in Figures.*

ANDORRA - TELEPHONES IN USE

American Telephone and Telegraph Company, 26 Parsippany Road, Whippany, New Jersey 07981 (800) 338-4038; *The World's Telephones.*

G.K. Hall and Company, 70 Lincoln Street, Boston, Massachusetts 02111 (617) 423-3990; *The World in Figures.*

ANDORRA - TEXTILE INDUSTRY

G.K. Hall and Company, 70 Lincoln Street, Boston, Massachusetts 02111 (617) 423-3990; *The World in Figures.*

ANDORRA - THEATRE

United Nations Educational, Scientific and Cultural Organization (UNESCO), 7 Place de Fontenoy, F-75700 Paris, France (Telephone Number in U.S. (212) 963-5981); *Statistical Yearbook.*

ANDORRA - TOURISM

G.K. Hall and Company, 70 Lincoln Street, Boston, Massachusetts 02111 (617) 423-3990; *The World in Figures.*

ANDORRA - TRADE - See ANDORRA - FOREIGN TRADE

ANDORRA - TRANSPORTATION AND COMMUNICATIONS

G.K. Hall and Company, 70 Lincoln Street, Boston, Massachusetts 02111 (617) 423-3990; *The World in Figures.*

ANDORRA - VITAL STATISTICS

G.K. Hall and Company, 70 Lincoln Street, Boston, Massachusetts 02111 (617) 423-3990; *The World in Figures.*

Statistical Office of the United Nations, Publishing Service, New York, New York 10017 (800) 253-9646; *Statistical Yearbook.*

World Health Organization, Office of Publications, Avenue Appia, CH-1211 Geneva 27, Switzerland (Telephone Number in U.S. (518) 436-9686); *World Health Statistics Annual.*

ANDORRA - WAGES

G.K. Hall and Company, 70 Lincoln Street, Boston, Massachusetts 02111 (617) 423-3990; *The World in Figures.*

ANDORRA - WEATHER

G.K. Hall and Company, 70 Lincoln Street, Boston, Massachusetts 02111 (617) 423-3990; *The World in Figures.*

ANEMIAS - DEATHS

U.S. Department of Health and Human Services, National Center for Health Statistics, 3700 East-West Highway, Hyattsville, Maryland 20782 (301) 436-8500; *Vital Statistics of the United States, Monthly Vital Statistics Report,* and unpublished data.

ANESTHESIOLOGISTS

American Medical Association, 515 North State Street, Chicago, Illinois 60610 (312) 464-4818; *Physician Characteristics and Distribution in the United States.*

Angola - National Statistical Office

Instituto Nacional de Estatistica, Caixa Postal 1215, Luanda, Angola.

Angola - Primary Statistics Sources

Direccao dos Servicos de Estatistica (Department of Statistical Services), Caixa Postal 1215, Luanda, Angola; *Anuario estatistico - Annuaire statistique* (Statistical Yearbook); and *Boletim mensal* (Monthly Bulletin).

ANGOLA - AGRICULTURE

Euromonitor Publications Limited, 87-88 Turnmill Street, London EC1M 5QU, England; *International Marketing Data and Statistics.*

Facts on File, 460 Park Avenue South, New York, New York 10016 (800) 443-8323; *The New Book of World Rankings.*

Federal Statistical Office, Gustav - Stresemann - Ring 11, D-6200 Wiesbaden, Germany; *Angola.*

Food and Agricultural Organization of the United Nations (FAO), Via delle Terme di Caracalla, 00100 Rome, Italy (Telephone Number in U.S. (202) 653-2400); *Production Yearbook, The State of Food and Agriculture, Trade Production,* and *Trade Yearbook.*

G.K. Hall and Company, 70 Lincoln Street, Boston, Massachusetts 02111 (617) 423-3990; *The World in Figures.*

Statistical Office of the United Nations, Publishing Service, New York, New York 10017 (800) 253-9646; *Statistical Yearbook,* and *Survey of Economic and Social Conditions in Africa.*

Times Books, 201 East 50th Street, New York, New York 10022 (212) 751-2600; *The Economist Book of Vital World Statistics.*

United Nations Economic Commission for Africa, Africa Hall, P.O. Box 3001, Addis Ababa, Ethiopia (Telephone Number in U.S. (800) 253-9646); *African Statistical Yearbook.*

ANGOLA - AIRLINE SERVICE

Facts on File, 460 Park Avenue South, New York, New York 10016 (800) 443-8323; *The New Book of World Rankings.*

G.K. Hall and Company, 70 Lincoln Street, Boston, Massachusetts 02111 (617) 423-3990; *The World in Figures.*

Times Books, 201 East 50th Street, New York, New York 10022 (212) 751-2600; *The Economist Book of Vital World Statistics.*

United Nations Economic Commission for Africa, Africa Hall, P.O. Box 3001, Addis Ababa, Ethiopia (Telephone Number in U.S. (800) 253-9646); *African Statistical Yearbook.*

ANGOLA - ALUMINUM PRODUCTION - See ANGOLA - MINING AND MINERAL PRODUCTS

ANGOLA - ANIMAL FEEDINGSTUFFS

Statistical Office of the United Nations, Publishing Service, New York, New York 10017 (800) 253-9646; *Statistical Yearbook.*

ANGOLA - ANIMAL HEALTH

Food and Agricultural Organization of the United Nations (FAO), Via delle Terme di Caracalla, 00100 Rome, Italy (Telephone Number in U.S. (202) 653-2400); *Animal Health Yearbook.*

ANGOLA - AREA AND DENSITY OF POPULATION

African Development Bank, 01 BP 1387, Abidjan 01, Cote D'Ivoire; *Selected Statistics on Regional Member Countries.*

Direccao dos Servicos de Estatistica, CP 1215, Luanda, Angola; *Statistical Yearbook.*

Euromonitor Publications Limited, 87-88 Turnmill Street, London EC1M 5QU, England; *International Marketing Data and Statistics.*

Facts on File, 460 Park Avenue South, New York, New York 10016 (800) 443-8323; *The New Book of World Rankings.*

Federal Statistical Office, Gustav - Stresemann - Ring 11, D-6200 Wiesbaden, Germany; *Angola.*

Food and Agricultural Organization of the United Nations (FAO) Via Delle Terme di Caracalla, 00100 Rome, Italy (Telephone Number in U.S. (202) 653-2400); *The State of Food and Agriculture.*

G.K. Hall and Company, 70 Lincoln Street, Boston, Massachusetts 02111 (617) 423-3990; *The World in Figures.*

Statistical Office of the United Nations, Publishing Service, New York, New York 10017 (800) 253-9646; *Survey of Economic and Social Conditions in Africa.*

Times Books, 201 East 50th Street, New York, New York 10022 (212) 751-2600; *The Economist Book of Vital World Statistics.*

ANGOLA - ARMS EXPORTS AND IMPORTS

U.S. Arms Control and Disarmament Agency, 320 Twenty-first Street, NW, Washington, D.C. 20451 (202) 647-8677; *World Military Expenditures and Arms Transfers.*

ANGOLA - BALANCE OF PAYMENTS

African Development Bank, 01 BP 1387, Abidjan 01, Cote D'Ivoire; *Selected Statistics on Regional Member Countries.*

The Economist Intelligence Unit, 111 West 57th Street, New York, New York 10019 (800) 938-4685; *The World Market Atlas.*

Federal Statistical Office, Gustav - Stresemann - Ring 11, D-6200 Wiesbaden, Germany; *Angola.*

G.K. Hall and Company, 70 Lincoln Street, Boston, Massachusetts 02111 (617) 423-3990; *The World in Figures.*

ANGOLA - BANKING

Facts on File, 460 Park Avenue South, New York, New York 10016 (800) 443-8323; *The New Book of World Rankings.*

G.K. Hall and Company, 70 Lincoln Street, Boston, Massachusetts 02111 (617) 423-3990; *The World in Figures.*

ANGOLA - BARLEY PRODUCTION - See ANGOLA - CROPS

ANGOLA - BEER PRODUCTION

Facts on File, 460 Park Avenue South, New York, New York 10016 (800) 443-8323; *The New Book of World Rankings.*

Statistical Office of the United Nations, Publishing Service, New York, New York 10017 (800) 253-9646; *Statistical Yearbook.*

ANGOLA - BIRTH RATE

Facts on File, 460 Park Avenue South, New York, New York 10016 (800) 443-8323; *The New Book of World Rankings.*

Statistical Office of the United Nations, Publishing Service, New York, New York 10017 (800) 253-9646; *Demographic Yearbook, Statistical Yearbook,* and *Survey of Economic and Social Conditions in Africa.*

Times Books, 201 East 50th Street, New York, New York 10022 (212) 751-2600; *The Economist Book of Vital World Statistics.*

ANGOLA - BONDS

G.K. Hall and Company, 70 Lincoln Street, Boston, Massachusetts 02111 (617) 423-3990; *The World in Figures.*

ANGOLA - BOOK PRODUCTION

G.K. Hall and Company, 70 Lincoln Street, Boston, Massachusetts 02111 (617) 423-3990; *The World in Figures.*

United Nations Educational, Scientific and Cultural Organization (UNESCO), 7 Place de Fontenoy, F-75700 Paris, France (Telephone Number in U.S. (212) 963-5981); *Statistical Yearbook.*

ANGOLA - BROADCASTING

Billboard Limited, P.O. Box 9027, 1006 AA Amsterdam, The Netherlands (Telephone Number in U.S. (212) 764-7300); *World Radio TV Handbook.*

Facts on File, 460 Park Avenue South, New York, New York 10016 (800) 443-8323; *The New Book of World Rankings.*

G.K. Hall and Company, 70 Lincoln Street, Boston, Massachusetts 02111 (617) 423-3990; *The World in Figures.*

Times Books, 201 East 50th Street, New York, New York 10022 (212) 751-2600; *The Economist Book of Vital World Statistics.*

ANGOLA - BUSINESS

G.K. Hall and Company, 70 Lincoln Street, Boston, Massachusetts 02111 (617) 423-3990; *The World in Figures*.

ANGOLA - CALORIE SUPPLY

African Development Bank, 01 BP 1387, Abidjan 01, Cote D'Ivoire; *Selected Statistics on Regional Member Countries*.

Food and Agricultural Organization of the United Nations (FAO) Via Delle Terme di Caracalla, 00100 Rome, Italy (Telephone Number in U.S. (202) 653-2400); *The State of Food and Agriculture*.

ANGOLA - CASHEW NUT PRODUCTION - See ANGOLA - CROPS

ANGOLA - CASTOR BEAN PRODUCTION - See ANGOLA - CROPS

ANGOLA - CATTLE - See ANGOLA - LIVESTOCK AND POULTRY

ANGOLA - CEMENT PRODUCTION - See ANGOLA - MINING AND MINERAL PRODUCTS

ANGOLA - CHEESE PRODUCTION - See ANGOLA - DAIRY PRODUCTS

ANGOLA - CHEMICALS (ORGANIC) PRODUCTION - See ANGOLA - MINING AND MINERAL PRODUCTS

ANGOLA - CHICKENS - See ANGOLA - LIVESTOCK AND POULTRY

ANGOLA - CIGARETTE PRODUCTION - See ANGOLA - TOBACCO PRODUCTION

ANGOLA - CLASS STRUCTURE

G.K. Hall and Company, 70 Lincoln Street, Boston, Massachusetts 02111 (617) 423-3990; *The World in Figures*.

ANGOLA - CLIMATE

Direccao dos Servicos de Estatistica, CP 1215, Luanda, Angola; *Statistical Yearbook*.

Facts on File, 460 Park Avenue South, New York, New York 10016 (800) 443-8323; *The New Book of World Rankings*.

G.K. Hall and Company, 70 Lincoln Street, Boston, Massachusetts 02111 (617) 423-3990; *The World in Figures*.

ANGOLA - COAL PRODUCTION - See ANGOLA - MINING AND MINERAL PRODUCTS

ANGOLA - COCOA (BEANS) PRODUCTION - See ANGOLA - CROPS

ANGOLA - COFFEE PRODUCTION - See ANGOLA - CROPS

ANGOLA - COMMUNICATIONS

Direccao dos Servicos de Estatistica, CP 1215, Luanda, Angola; *Statistical Yearbook*.

Federal Statistical Office, Gustav - Stresemann - Ring 11, D-6200 Wiesbaden, Germany; *Angola*.

G.K. Hall and Company, 70 Lincoln Street, Boston, Massachusetts 02111 (617) 423-3990; *The World in Figures*.

United Nations Economic Commission for Africa, Africa Hall, P.O. Box 3001, Addis Ababa, Ethiopia (Telephone Number in U.S. (800) 253-9646); *African Statistical Yearbook*.

ANGOLA - CONSTRUCTION INDUSTRY

Facts on File, 460 Park Avenue South, New York, New York 10016 (800) 443-8323; *The New Book of World Rankings*.

Statistical Office of the United Nations, Publishing Service, New York, New York 10017 (800) 253-9646; *Construction Statistics Yearbook*, and *Statistical Yearbook*.

United Nations Economic Commission for Africa, Africa Hall, P.O. Box 3001, Addis Ababa, Ethiopia (Telephone Number in U.S. (800) 253-9646); *African Statistical Yearbook*.

ANGOLA - CONSUMER PRICE INDEX

African Development Bank, 01 BP 1387, Abidjan 01, Cote D'Ivoire; *Selected Statistics on Regional Member Countries*.

Federal Statistical Office, Gustav - Stresemann - Ring 11, D-6200 Wiesbaden, Germany; *Angola*.

G.K. Hall and Company, 70 Lincoln Street, Boston, Massachusetts 02111 (617) 423-3990; *The World in Figures*.

Statistical Office of the United Nations, Publishing Service, New York, New York 10017 (800) 253-9646; *Survey of Economic and Social Conditions in Africa*.

ANGOLA - CONSUMER PRICES

Federal Statistical Office, Gustav - Stresemann - Ring 11, D-6200 Wiesbaden, Germany; *Angola*.

ANGOLA - CONSUMPTION

African Development Bank, 01 BP 1387, Abidjan 01, Cote D'Ivoire; *Selected Statistics on Regional Member Countries*.

G.K. Hall and Company, 70 Lincoln Street, Boston, Massachusetts 02111 (617) 423-3990; *The World in Figures*.

Statistical Office of the United Nations, Publishing Service, New York, New York 10017 (800) 253-9646; *Survey of Economic and Social Conditions in Africa*.

ANGOLA - COPPER AND COPPER ORE - See ANGOLA - MINING AND MINERAL PRODUCTS

ANGOLA - CORN PRODUCTION - See ANGOLA - CROPS

ANGOLA - CORPORATE TAXES - See ANGOLA - TAXATION

ANGOLA - COTTON - See ANGOLA - CROPS

ANGOLA - CROPS

Commodity Research Bureau, Incorporated, 75 Wall Street, New York, New York 10005 (212) 504-7754; *Commodity Year Book*.

Facts on File, 460 Park Avenue South, New York, New York 10016 (800) 443-8323; *The New Book of World Rankings*.

Food and Agricultural Organization of the United Nations (FAO) Via Delle Terme di Caracalla, 00100 Rome, Italy (Telephone Number in U.S. (202) 653-2400); *Production Yearbook*, and *The State of Food*

and Agriculture.

Statistical Office of the United Nations, Publishing Service, New York, New York 10017 (800) 253-9646; *Statistical Yearbook.*

United Nations Economic Commission for Africa, Africa Hall, P.O. Box 3001, Addis Ababa, Ethiopia (Telephone Number in U.S. (800) 253-9646); *African Statistical Yearbook.*

ANGOLA - CUSTOMS DUTIES

G.K. Hall and Company, 70 Lincoln Street, Boston, Massachusetts 02111 (617) 423-3990; *The World in Figures.*

ANGOLA - DAIRY PRODUCTS

Facts on File, 460 Park Avenue South, New York, New York 10016 (800) 443-8323; *The New Book of World Rankings.*

Food and Agricultural Organization of the United Nations (FAO) Via Delle Terme di Caracalla, 00100 Rome, Italy (Telephone Number in U.S. (202) 653-2400); *The State of Food and Agriculture.*

Statistical Office of the United Nations, Publishing Service, New York, New York 10017 (800) 253-9646; *Statistical Yearbook.*

ANGOLA - DEATH RATE

G.K. Hall and Company, 70 Lincoln Street, Boston, Massachusetts 02111 (617) 423-3990; *The World in Figures.*

Statistical Office of the United Nations, Publishing Service, New York, New York 10017 (800) 253-9646; *Statistical Yearbook,* and *Survey of Economic and Social Conditions in Africa.*

Times Books, 201 East 50th Street, New York, New York 10022 (212) 751-2600; *The Economist Book of Vital World Statistics.*

ANGOLA - DEFENSE EXPENDITURES

G.K. Hall and Company, 70 Lincoln Street, Boston, Massachusetts 02111 (617) 423-3990; *The World in Figures.*

U.S. Arms Control and Disarmament Agency, 320 Twenty-first Street, NW, Washington, D.C. 20451 (202) 647-8677; *World Military Expenditures and Arms Transfers.*

ANGOLA - DEMOGRAPHY

The Economist Intelligence Unit, 111 West 57th Street, New York, New York 10019 (800) 938-4685; *The World Market Atlas.*

Facts on File, 460 Park Avenue South, New York, New York 10016 (800) 443-8323; *The New Book of World Rankings.*

Federal Statistical Office, Gustav - Stresemann - Ring 11, D-6200 Wiesbaden, Germany; *Angola.*

G.K. Hall and Company, 70 Lincoln Street, Boston, Massachusetts 02111 (617) 423-3990; *The World in Figures.*

Statistical Office of the United Nations, Publishing Service, New York, New York 10017 (800) 253-9646; *Survey of Economic and Social Conditions in Africa.*

ANGOLA - DEVELOPMENT ASSISTANCE

G.K. Hall and Company, 70 Lincoln Street, Boston, Massachusetts 02111 (617) 423-3990; *The World in Figures.*

Statistical Office of the United Nations, Publishing Service, New York, New York 10017 (800) 253-9646; *Statistical Yearbook.*

ANGOLA - DIAMOND PRODUCTION - See ANGOLA - MINING AND MINERAL PRODUCTS

ANGOLA - DISEASE

G.K. Hall and Company, 70 Lincoln Street, Boston, Massachusetts 02111 (617) 423-3990; *The World in Figures.*

ANGOLA - DIVORCE RATES

Facts on File, 460 Park Avenue South, New York, New York 10016 (800) 443-8323; *The New Book of World Rankings.*

Statistical Office of the United Nations, Publishing Service, New York, New York 10017 (800) 253-9646; *Demographic Yearbook,* and *Statistical Yearbook.*

ANGOLA - DOMESTIC PRODUCT

G.K. Hall and Company, 70 Lincoln Street, Boston, Massachusetts 02111 (617) 423-3990; *The World in Figures.*

ANGOLA - ECONOMY

African Development Bank, 01 BP 1387, Abidjan 01, Cote D'Ivoire; *Selected Statistics on Regional Member Countries.*

Euromonitor Publications Limited, 87-88 Turnmill Street, London EC1M 5QU, England; *International Marketing Data and Statistics.*

Facts on File, 460 Park Avenue South, New York, New York 10016 (800) 443-8323; *The New Book of World Rankings.*

Federal Statistical Office, Gustav - Stresemann - Ring 11, D-6200 Wiesbaden, Germany; *Angola.*

G.K. Hall and Company, 70 Lincoln Street, Boston, Massachusetts 02111 (617) 423-3990; *The World in Figures.*

Statistical Office of the United Nations, Publishing Service, New York, New York 10017 (800) 253-9646; *Foreign Trade Statistics for Africa.*

ANGOLA - EDUCATION

African Development Bank, 01 BP 1387, Abidjan 01, Cote D'Ivoire; *Selected Statistics on Regional Member Countries.*

Direccao dos Servicos de Estatistica, CP 1215, Luanda, Angola; *Statistical Yearbook*

The Economist Intelligence Unit, 111 West 57th Street, New York, New York 10019 (800) 938-4685; *The World Market Atlas.*

Facts on File, 460 Park Avenue South, New York, New York 10016 (800) 443-8323; *The New Book of World Rankings.*

Federal Statistical Office, Gustav - Stresemann - Ring 11, D-6200 Wiesbaden, Germany; *Angola.*

G.K. Hall and Company, 70 Lincoln Street, Boston, Massachusetts 02111 (617) 423-3990; *The World in Figures.*

Statistical Office of the United Nations, Publishing Service, New York, New York 10017 (800) 253-9646; *Survey of Economic and Social Conditions in Africa.*

Times Books, 201 East 50th Street, New York, New York 10022 (212) 751-2600; *The Economist Book of Vital World Statistics.*

United Nations Economic Commission for Africa, Africa Hall, P.O. Box 3001, Addis Ababa, Ethiopia (Telephone Number in U.S. (800) 253-9646); *African Statistical Yearbook.*

United Nations Educational, Scientific and Cultural Organization (UNESCO), 7 Place de Fontenoy, F-75700 Paris, France (Telephone Number in U.S. (212) 963-5981); *Statistical Yearbook.*

ANGOLA - EGG PRODUCTION - See ANGOLA - DAIRY PRODUCTS

ANGOLA - ELECTRICITY

Facts on File, 460 Park Avenue South, New York, New York 10016 (800) 443-8323; *The New Book of World Rankings.*

Penn Well Publishing Company, 1421 South Sheridan Road, P.O. Box 1260, Tulsa, Oklahoma 74101 (800) 752-9764; *International Energy Statistics Sourcebook.*

Statistical Office of the United Nations, Publishing Service, New York, New York 10017 (800) 253-9646; *Statistical Yearbook,* and *Survey of Economic and Social Conditions in Africa.*

Times Books, 201 East 50th Street, New York, New York 10022 (212) 751-2600; *The Economist Book of Vital World Statistics.*

United Nations Economic Commission for Africa, Africa Hall, P.O. Box 3001, Addis Ababa, Ethiopia (Telephone Number in U.S. (800) 253-9646); *African Statistical Yearbook.*

ANGOLA - EMPLOYMENT

Euromonitor Publications Limited, 87-88 Turnmill Street, London EC1M 5QU, England; *International Marketing Data and Statistics.*

Facts on File, 460 Park Avenue South, New York, New York 10016 (800) 443-8323; *The New Book of World Rankings.*

Federal Statistical Office, Gustav - Stresemann - Ring 11, D-6200 Wiesbaden, Germany; *Angola.*

Statistical Office of the United Nations, Publishing Service, New York, New York 10017 (800) 253-9646; *Statistical Yearbook,* and *Survey of Economic and Social Conditions in Africa.*

United Nations Economic Commission for Africa, Africa Hall, P.O. Box 3001, Addis Ababa, Ethiopia (Telephone Number in U.S. (800) 253-9646); *African Statistical Yearbook.*

ANGOLA - ENERGY

Facts on File, 460 Park Avenue South, New York, New York 10016 (800) 443-8323; *The New Book of World Rankings.*

Food and Agricultural Organization of the United Nations (FAO) Via Delle Terme di Caracalla, 00100 Rome, Italy (Telephone Number in U.S. (202) 653-2400); *The State of Food and Agriculture.*

G.K. Hall and Company, 70 Lincoln Street, Boston, Massachusetts 02111 (617) 423-3990; *The World in Figures.*

Penn Well Publishing Company, 1421 South Sheridan Road, P.O. Box 1260, Tulsa, Oklahoma 74101 (800) 752-9764; *International Energy Statistics Sourcebook.*

Statistical Office of the United Nations, Publishing Service, New York, New York 10017 (800) 253-9646; *Energy Statistics Yearbook,* and *Statistical Yearbook,* and *World Energy Supplies.*

Times Books, 201 East 50th Street, New York, New York 10022 (212) 751-2600; *The Economist Book of Vital World Statistics.*

United Nations Economic Commission for Africa, Africa Hall, P.O. Box 3001, Addis Ababa, Ethiopia (Telephone Number in U.S. (800) 253-9646); *African Statistical Yearbook.*

ANGOLA - EXCHANGE RATES

African Development Bank, 01 BP 1387, Abidjan 01, Cote D'Ivoire; *Selected Statistics on Regional Member Countries.*

Euromonitor Publications Limited, 87-88 Turnmill Street, London EC1M 5QU, England; *International Marketing Data and Statistics.*

International Civil Aviation Organization, 1000 Sherbrooke Street West, Suite 400, Montreal, Quebec, Canada H3A 2R2 (514) 285-8219; *Civil Aviation Statistics of the World.*

Statistical Office of the United Nations, Publishing Service, New York, New York 10017 (800) 253-9646; *Foreign Trade Statistics for Africa.*

ANGOLA - EXPORTS

African Development Bank, 01 BP 1387, Abidjan 01, Cote D'Ivoire; *Selected Statistics on Regional Member Countries.*

The Economist Intelligence Unit, 111 West 57th Street, New York, New York 10019 (800) 938-4685; *The World Market Atlas.*

G.K. Hall and Company, 70 Lincoln Street, Boston, Massachusetts 02111 (617) 423-3990; *The World in Figures.*

Food and Agricultural Organization of the United Nations (FAO) Via Delle Terme di Caracalla, 00100 Rome, Italy (Telephone Number in U.S. (202) 653-2400); *The State of Food and Agriculture.*

International Monetary Fund, 700 Nineteenth Street, NW, Washington, D.C. 20431 (202) 623-7000; *Direction of Trade Statistics.*

South Pacific Commission, Post Box D5, Noumea Cedex, New Caledonia; *Statistical Bulletin of the South Pacific: Overseas Trade.*

Statistical Office of the United Nations, Publishing Service, New York, New York 10017 (800) 253-9646; *Foreign Trade Statistics for Africa,* and *Survey of Economic and Social Conditions in Africa.*

Times Books, 201 East 50th Street, New York, New York 10022 (212) 751-2600; *The Economist Book of Vital World Statistics.*

United Nations Economic Commission for Africa, Africa Hall, P.O. Box 3001, Addis Ababa, Ethiopia (Telephone Number in U.S. (800) 253-9646); *African Statistical Yearbook.*

ANGOLA - EXTERNAL INDEBTEDNESS

African Development Bank, 01 BP 1387, Abidjan 01, Cote D'Ivoire; *Selected Statistics on Regional Member Countries.*

Statistical Office of the United Nations, Publishing Service, New York, New York 10017 (800) 253-9646; *Survey of Economic and Social Conditions in Africa.*

ANGOLA - EXTERNAL TRADE

African Development Bank, 01 BP 1387, Abidjan 01, Cote D'Ivoire; *Selected Statistics on Regional Member Countries.*

Food and Agricultural Organization of the United Nations (FAO) Via Delle Terme di Caracalla, 00100 Rome, Italy (Telephone Number in U.S. (202) 653-2400); *The State of Food and Agriculture,* and *Trade Yearbook.*

G.K. Hall and Company, 70 Lincoln Street, Boston, Massachusetts 02111 (617) 423-3990; *The World in Figures.*

Statistical Office of the United Nations, Publishing Service, New York, New York 10017 (800) 253-9646; *Statistical Yearbook.*

ANGOLA - FABRIC PRODUCTION - See ANGOLA - TEXTILE INDUSTRY

ANGOLA - FARM CROPS - See ANGOLA - CROPS

ANGOLA - FEMALE WORKING POPULATION - See ANGOLA - EMPLOYMENT

ANGOLA - FERTILITY RATES

Facts on File, 460 Park Avenue South, New York, New York 10016 (800) 443-8323; *The New Book of World Rankings.*

Statistical Office of the United Nations, Publishing Service, New York, New York 10017 (800) 253-9646; *Survey of Economic and Social Conditions in Africa.*

Times Books, 201 East 50th Street, New York, New York 10022 (212) 751-2600; *The Economist Book of Vital World Statistics.*

ANGOLA - FERTILIZER

Food and Agricultural Organization of the United Nations (FAO) Via Delle Terme di Caracalla, 00100 Rome, Italy (Telephone Number in U.S. (202) 653-2400); *Fertilizer Yearbook,* and *The State of Food and Agriculture.*

Statistical Office of the United Nations, Publishing Service, New York, New York 10017 (800) 253-9646; *Statistical Yearbook.*

ANGOLA - FETAL MORTALITY

Statistical Office of the United Nations, Publishing Service, New York, New York 10017 (800) 253-9646; *Demographic Yearbook.*

ANGOLA - FINANCE

African Development Bank, 01 BP 1387, Abidjan 01, Cote D'Ivoire; *Selected Statistics on Regional Member Countries.*

Facts on File, 460 Park Avenue South, New York, New York 10016 (800) 443-8323; *The New Book of World Rankings.*

Federal Statistical Office, Gustav - Stresemann - Ring 11, D-6200 Wiesbaden, Germany; *Angola.*

G.K. Hall and Company, 70 Lincoln Street, Boston, Massachusetts 02111 (617) 423-3990; *The World in Figures.*

International Monetary Fund, 700 Nineteenth Street, NW, Washington, D.C. 20431; *International Financial Statistics.*

ANGOLA - FISHERIES

Facts on File, 460 Park Avenue South, New York, New York 10016 (800) 443-8323; *The New Book of World Rankings.*

Federal Statistical Office, Gustav - Stresemann - Ring 11, D-6200 Wiesbaden, Germany; *Angola.*

Food and Agricultural Organization of the United Nations (FAO) Via Delle Terme di Caracalla, 00100 Rome, Italy (Telephone Number in U.S. (202) 653-2400); *The State of Food and Agriculture,* and *Yearbook of Fishery Statistics.*

Statistical Office of the United Nations, Publishing Service, New York, New York 10017 (800) 253-9646; *Statistical Yearbook,* and *Survey of Economic and Social Conditions in Africa.*

United Nations Economic Commission for Africa, Africa Hall, P.O. Box 3001, Addis Ababa, Ethiopia (Telephone Number in U.S. (800) 253-9646); *African Statistical Yearbook.*

ANGOLA - FLOUR PRODUCTION

Statistical Office of the United Nations, Publishing Service, New York, New York 10017 (800) 253-9646; *Statistical Yearbook.*

ANGOLA - FOOD

African Development Bank, 01 BP 1387, Abidjan 01, Cote D'Ivoire; *Selected Statistics on Regional Member Countries.*

Food and Agricultural Organization of the United Nations (FAO) Via Delle Terme di Caracalla, 00100 Rome, Italy (Telephone Number in U.S. (202) 653-2400); *Production Yearbook,* and *The State of Food and Agriculture.*

G.K. Hall and Company, 70 Lincoln Street, Boston, Massachusetts 02111 (617) 423-3990; *The World in Figures.*

ANGOLA - FOREIGN AID

G.K. Hall and Company, 70 Lincoln Street, Boston, Massachusetts 02111 (617) 423-3990; *The World in Figures.*

ANGOLA - FOREIGN TRADE

Direccao dos Servicos de Estatistica, CP 1215, Luanda, Angola; *Statistical Yearbook.*

Euromonitor Publications Limited, 87-88 Turnmill Street, London EC1M 5QU, England; *International Marketing Data and Statistics.*

Facts on File, 460 Park Avenue South, New York, New York 10016 (800) 443-8323; *The New Book of World Rankings.*

Federal Statistical Office, Gustav - Stresemann - Ring 11, D-6200 Wiesbaden, Germany; *Angola.*

Food and Agricultural Organization of the United Nations (FAO) Via Delle Terme di Caracalla, 00100 Rome, Italy (Telephone Number in U.S. (202) 653-2400); *The State of Food and Agriculture.*

G.K. Hall and Company, 70 Lincoln Street, Boston, Massachusetts 02111 (617) 423-3990; *The World in Figures.*

Organisation for Economic Co-operation and Development (OECD), 2 rue Andre-Pascal, 75 Paris 16, France (Telephone Number in U.S. (212) 963-5981); *Trade by Commodities.*

Statistical Office of the United Nations, Publishing Service, New York, New York 10017 (800) 253-9646; *Foreign Trade Statistics for Africa, International Trade Statistics Yearbook,* and *Statistical Yearbook.*

United Nations Economic Commission for Africa, Africa Hall, P.O. Box 3001, Addis Ababa, Ethiopia (Telephone Number in U.S. (800) 253-9646); *African Statistical Yearbook.*

ANGOLA - FORESTRY AND FOREST PRODUCTS

Facts on File, 460 Park Avenue South, New York, New York 10016 (800) 443-8323; *The New Book of World Rankings.*

Federal Statistical Office, Gustav - Stresemann - Ring 11, D-6200 Wiesbaden, Germany; *Angola.*

Food and Agricultural Organization of the United Nations (FAO), Via delle Terme di Caracalla, 00100 Rome, Italy (Telephone Number in U.S. (202) 653-2400); *Yearbook of Forest Products,* and *The State of Food and Agriculture.*

G.K. Hall and Company, 70 Lincoln Street, Boston, Massachusetts 02111 (617) 423-3990; *The World in Figures.*

Statistical Office of the United Nations, Publishing Service, New York, New York 10017 (800) 253-9646; *Statistical Yearbook.*

United Nations Economic Commission for Africa, Africa Hall, P.O. Box 3001, Addis Ababa, Ethiopia (Telephone Number in U.S. (800) 253-9646); *African Statistical Yearbook.*

United Nations Educational, Scientific and Cultural Organization (UNESCO), 7 Place de Fontenoy, F-75700 Paris, France (Telephone Number in U.S. (212) 963-5981); *Statistical Yearbook.*

ANGOLA - GAS PRODUCTION - See ANGOLA - MINING AND MINERAL PRODUCTS

ANGOLA - GENERAL INDUSTRIAL STATISTICS

Federal Statistical Office, Gustav - Stresemann - Ring 11, D-6200 Wiesbaden, Germany; *Angola.*

Statistical Office of the United Nations, Publishing Service, New York, New York 10017 (800) 253-9646; *Industrial Statistics Yearbook.*

ANGOLA - GENERAL MORTALITY

Statistical Office of the United Nations, Publishing Service, New York, New York 10017 (800) 253-9646; *Demographic Yearbook.*

ANGOLA - GEOGRAPHIC DATA

Facts on File, 460 Park Avenue South, New York, New York 10016 (800) 443-8323; *The New Book of World Rankings.*

Federal Statistical Office, Gustav - Stresemann - Ring 11, D-6200 Wiesbaden, Germany; *Angola.*

ANGOLA - GOATS - See ANGOLA - LIVESTOCK AND POULTRY

ANGOLA - GOLD - See ANGOLA - MINING AND MINERAL PRODUCTS

ANGOLA - GOVERNMENT

G.K. Hall and Company, 70 Lincoln Street, Boston, Massachusetts 02111 (617) 423-3990; *The World in Figures.*

ANGOLA - GOVERNMENT REVENUE

Statistical Office of the United Nations, Publishing Service, New York, New York 10017 (800) 253-9646; *Survey of Economic and Social Conditions in Africa.*

ANGOLA - GRAIN PRODUCTION - See ANGOLA - CROPS

ANGOLA - GROSS DOMESTIC PRODUCT

African Development Bank, 01 BP 1387, Abidjan 01, Cote D'Ivoire; *Selected Statistics on Regional Member Countries.*

The Economist Intelligence Unit, 111 West 57th Street, New York, New York 10019 (800) 938-4685; *The World Market Atlas.*

Euromonitor Publications Limited, 87-88 Turnmill Street, London EC1M 5QU, England; *International Marketing Data and Statistics.*

Facts on File, 460 Park Avenue South, New York, New York 10016 (800) 443-8323; *The New Book of World Rankings.*

G.K. Hall and Company, 70 Lincoln Street, Boston, Massachusetts 02111 (617) 423-3990; *The World in Figures.*

Statistical Office of the United Nations, Publishing Service, New York, New York 10017 (800) 253-9646; *Statistical Yearbook,* and *Survey of Economic and Social Conditions in Africa.*

Times Books, 201 East 50th Street, New York, New York 10022 (212) 751-2600; *The Economist Book of Vital World Statistics.*

United Nations Economic Commission for Africa, Africa Hall, P.O. Box 3001, Addis Ababa, Ethiopia (Telephone Number in U.S. (800) 253-9646); *African Statistical Yearbook.*

ANGOLA - GROSS NATIONAL PRODUCT

Euromonitor Publications Limited, 87-88 Turnmill Street, London EC1M 5QU, England; *International Marketing Data and Statistics.*

U.S. Arms Control and Disarmament Agency, 320 Twenty-first Street, NW, Washington, D.C. 20451 (202) 647-8677; *World Military Expenditures and Arms Transfers.*

ANGOLA - GROUNDNUTS PRODUCTION - See ANGOLA - CROPS

ANGOLA - HEALTH

African Development Bank, 01 BP 1387, Abidjan 01, Cote D'Ivoire; *Selected Statistics on Regional Member Countries.*

Facts on File, 460 Park Avenue South, New York, New York 10016 (800) 443-8323; *The New Book of World Rankings.*

Federal Statistical Office, Gustav - Stresemann - Ring 11, D-6200 Wiesbaden, Germany; *Angola.*

G.K. Hall and Company, 70 Lincoln Street, Boston, Massachusetts 02111 (617) 423-3990; *The World in Figures.*

Statistical Office of the United Nations, Publishing Service, New York, New York 10017 (800) 253-9646; *Statistical Yearbook.*

Times Books, 201 East 50th Street, New York, New York 10022 (212) 751-2600; *The Economist Book of Vital World Statistics.*

United Nations Economic Commission for Africa, Africa Hall, P.O. Box 3001, Addis Ababa, Ethiopia (Telephone Number in U.S. (800) 253-9646); *African Statistical Yearbook.*

ANGOLA - HIDE PRODUCTION

Food and Agricultural Organization of the United Nations (FAO), Via delle Terme di Caracalla, 00100 Rome, Italy (Telephone Number in U.S. (202) 653-2400); *Production Yearbook.*

ANGOLA - HIGHWAYS

G.K. Hall and Company, 70 Lincoln Street, Boston, Massachusetts 02111 (617) 423-3990; *The World in Figures.*

International Road Federation, 525 School Street, SW, Washington, D.C. 20024 (202) 554-2106; *World Road Statistics.*

Statistical Office of the United Nations, Publishing Service, New York, New York 10017 (800) 253-9646; *Survey of Economic and Social Conditions in Africa.*

United Nations Economic Commission for Africa, Africa Hall, P.O. Box 3001, Addis Ababa, Ethiopia (Telephone Number in U.S. (800) 253-9646); *African Statistical Yearbook.*

ANGOLA - HORSES - See ANGOLA - LIVESTOCK AND POULTRY

ANGOLA - HOURS OF WORK - See ANGOLA - EMPLOYMENT

ANGOLA - HOUSING AND HOUSING UNITS

Facts on File, 460 Park Avenue South, New York, New York 10016 (800) 443-8323; *The New Book of World Rankings.*

ANGOLA - ILLITERATE POPULATION

The Economist Intelligence Unit, 111 West 57th Street, New York, New York 10019 (800) 938-4685; *The World Market Atlas.*

G.K. Hall and Company, 70 Lincoln Street, Boston, Massachusetts 02111 (617) 423-3990; *The World in Figures.*

United Nations Educational, Scientific and Cultural Organization (UNESCO), 7 Place de Fontenoy, F-75700 Paris, France (Telephone Number in U.S. (212) 963-5981); *Statistical Yearbook.*

ANGOLA - IMPORTS

African Development Bank, 01 BP 1387, Abidjan 01, Cote D'Ivoire; *Selected Statistics on Regional Member Countries.*

The Economist Intelligence Unit, 111 West 57th Street, New York, New York 10019 (800) 938-4685; *The World Market Atlas.*

Euromonitor Publications Limited, 87-88 Turnmill Street, London EC1M 5QU, England; *International Marketing Data and Statistics.*

Food and Agricultural Organization of the United Nations (FAO) Via Delle Terme di Caracalla, 00100 Rome, Italy (Telephone Number in U.S. (202) 653-2400); *The State of Food and Agriculture.*

G.K. Hall and Company, 70 Lincoln Street, Boston, Massachusetts 02111 (617) 423-3990; *The World in Figures.*

International Monetary Fund, 700 Nineteenth Street, NW, Washington, D.C. 20431 (202) 623-7000; *Direction of Trade Statistics.*

Statistical Office of the United Nations, Publishing Service, New York, New York 10017 (800) 253-9646; *Foreign Trade Statistics for Africa,* and *Survey of Economic and Social Conditions in Africa.*

United Nations Economic Commission for Africa, Africa Hall, P.O. Box 3001, Addis Ababa, Ethiopia (Telephone Number in U.S. (800) 253-9646); *African Statistical Yearbook.*

ANGOLA - INDUSTRIAL METALS PRODUCTION - See ANGOLA - MINING AND MINERAL PRODUCTS

ANGOLA - INDUSTRY

Euromonitor Publications Limited, 87-88 Turnmill Street, London EC1M 5QU, England; *International Marketing Data and Statistics.*

Facts on File, 460 Park Avenue South, New York, New York 10016 (800) 443-8323; *The New Book of World Rankings.*

Federal Statistical Office, Gustav - Stresemann - Ring 11, D-6200 Wiesbaden, Germany; *Angola.*

G.K. Hall and Company, 70 Lincoln Street, Boston, Massachusetts 02111 (617) 423-3990; *The World in Figures.*

Statistical Office of the United Nations, Publishing Service, New York, New York 10017 (800) 253-9646; *Survey of Economic and Social Conditions in Africa.*

Times Books, 201 East 50th Street, New York, New York 10022 (212) 751-2600; *The Economist Book of Vital World Statistics.*

United Nations Economic Commission for Africa, Africa Hall, P.O. Box 3001, Addis Ababa, Ethiopia (Telephone Number in U.S. (800) 253-9646); *African Statistical Yearbook.*

ANGOLA - INFANT AND MATERNAL MORTALITY

Statistical Office of the United Nations, Publishing Service, New York, New York 10017 (800) 253-9646; *Demographic Yearbook, Statistical Yearbook,* and *Survey of Economic and Social Conditions in Africa.*

Times Books, 201 East 50th Street, New York, New York 10022 (212) 751-2600; *The Economist Book of Vital World Statistics.*

ANGOLA - INTERNATIONAL RESERVES EXCLUDING GOLD

African Development Bank, 01 BP 1387, Abidjan 01, Cote D'Ivoire; *Selected Statistics on Regional Member Countries.*

ANGOLA - IRON ORE PRODUCTION AND CONSUMPTION - See ANGOLA - MINING AND MINERAL PRODUCTS

ANGOLA - IRRIGATION

Euromonitor Publications Limited, 87-88 Turnmill Street, London EC1M 5QU, England; *International Marketing Data and Statistics.*

ANGOLA - JUTE PRODUCTION - See ANGOLA - CROPS

ANGOLA - LABOR FORCE

African Development Bank, 01 BP 1387, Abidjan 01, Cote D'Ivoire; *Selected Statistics on Regional Member Countries.*

Direccao dos Servicos de Estatistica, CP 1215, Luanda, Angola; *Statistical Yearbook.*

Euromonitor Publications Limited, 87-88 Turnmill Street, London EC1M 5QU, England; *International Marketing Data and Statistics.*

Facts on File, 460 Park Avenue South, New York, New York 10016 (800) 443-8323; *The New Book of World Rankings.*

Food and Agricultural Organization of the United Nations (FAO) Via Delle Terme di Caracalla, 00100 Rome, Italy (Telephone Number in U.S. (202) 653-2400); *The State of Food and Agriculture.*

G.K. Hall and Company, 70 Lincoln Street, Boston, Massachusetts 02111 (617) 423-3990; *The World in Figures.*

ANGOLA - LAND USE

Euromonitor Publications Limited, 87-88 Turnmill Street, London EC1M 5QU, England; *International Marketing Data and Statistics.*

Food and Agricultural Organization of the United Nations (FAO), Via delle Terme di Caracalla, 00100 Rome, Italy (Telephone Number in U.S. (202) 653-2400); *Production Yearbook.*

G.K. Hall and Company, 70 Lincoln Street, Boston, Massachusetts 02111 (617) 423-3990; *The World in Figures.*

ANGOLA - LIBRARIES

Facts on File, 460 Park Avenue South, New York, New York 10016 (800) 443-8323; *The New Book of World Rankings.*

ANGOLA - LIFE EXPECTANCY

African Development Bank, 01 BP 1387, Abidjan 01, Cote D'Ivoire; *Selected Statistics on Regional Member Countries.*

ANGOLA - LITERACY RATE

Statistical Office of the United Nations, Publishing Service, New York, New York 10017 (800) 253-9646; *Survey of Economic and Social Conditions in Africa.*

ANGOLA - LIVESTOCK AND POULTRY

Euromonitor Publications Limited, 87-88 Turnmill Street, London EC1M 5QU, England; *International Marketing Data and Statistics.*

Facts on File, 460 Park Avenue South, New York, New York 10016 (800) 443-8323; *The New Book of World Rankings.*

Food and Agricultural Organization of the United Nations (FAO), Via delle Terme di Caracalla, 00100 Rome, Italy (Telephone Number in U.S. (202) 653-2400); *Production Yearbook,* and *The State of Food and Agriculture.*

G.K. Hall and Company, 70 Lincoln Street, Boston, Massachusetts 02111 (617) 423-3990; *The World in Figures.*

Statistical Office of the United Nations, Publishing Service, New York, New York 10017 (800) 253-9646; *Statistical Yearbook,* and *Survey of Economic and Social Conditions in Africa.*

United Nations Economic Commission for Africa, Africa Hall, P.O. Box 3001, Addis Ababa, Ethiopia (Telephone Number in U.S. (800) 253-9646); *African Statistical Yearbook.*

ANGOLA - LIVING LEVELS

G.K. Hall and Company, 70 Lincoln Street, Boston, Massachusetts 02111 (617) 423-3990; *The World in Figures.*

Times Books, 201 East 50th Street, New York, New York 10022 (212) 751-2600; *The Economist Book of Vital World Statistics.*

ANGOLA - MAIL - NUMBER OF PIECES SENT OR RECEIVED

Statistical Office of the United Nations, Publishing Service, New York, New York 10017 (800) 253-9646; *Statistical Yearbook.*

ANGOLA - MANGANESE ORE PRODUCTION - See ANGOLA - MINING AND MINERAL PRODUCTS

ANGOLA - MANUFACTURING

Facts on File, 460 Park Avenue South, New York, New York 10016 (800) 443-8323; *The New Book of World Rankings.*

G.K. Hall and Company, 70 Lincoln Street, Boston, Massachusetts 02111 (617) 423-3990; *The World in Figures.*

Statistical Office of the United Nations, Publishing Service, New York, New York 10017 (800) 253-9646; *Statistical Yearbook,* and *Survey of Economic and Social Conditions in Africa.*

United Nations Economic Commission for Africa, Africa Hall, P.O. Box 3001, Addis Ababa, Ethiopia (Telephone Number in U.S. (800) 253-9646); *African Statistical Yearbook.*

ANGOLA - MARRIAGE RATES

Facts on File, 460 Park Avenue South, New York, New York 10016 (800) 443-8323; *The New Book of World Rankings.*

Statistical Office of the United Nations, Publishing Service, New York, New York 10017 (800) 253-9646; *Demographic Yearbook,* and *Statistical Yearbook.*

ANGOLA - MEAT PRODUCTION - See ANGOLA - LIVESTOCK AND POULTRY

ANGOLA - MERCHANT FLEET CHARACTERISTICS - See ANGOLA - MERCHANT SHIPPING

ANGOLA - MERCHANT SHIPPING

G.K. Hall and Company, 70 Lincoln Street, Boston, Massachusetts 02111 (617) 423-3990; *The World in Figures.*

Lloyd's Register of Shipping, 17 Battery Place, New York, New York 10004 (212) 425-8050; *Register of Ships.*

Statistical Office of the United Nations, Publishing Service, New York, New York 10017 (800) 253-9646; *Statistical Yearbook.*

Times Books, 201 East 50th Street, New York, New York 10022 (212) 751-2600; *The Economist Book of Vital World Statistics.*

United Nations Economic Commission for Africa, Africa Hall, P.O. Box 3001, Addis Ababa, Ethiopia (Telephone Number in U.S. (800) 253-9646); *African Statistical Yearbook.*

U.S. Department of Commerce, Maritime Administration, Washington, D.C. 20230; *A Statistical Analysis of the World's Merchant Fleets.*

ANGOLA - MILITARY

G.K. Hall and Company, 70 Lincoln Street, Boston, Massachusetts 02111 (617) 423-3990; *The World in Figures.*

The International Institute for Strategic Studies, 23 Tavistock Street, London WC2E 7NQ, England; *The Military Balance.*

U.S. Arms Control and Disarmament Agency, 320 Twenty-first Street, NW, Washington, D.C. 20451 (202) 647-8677; *World Military Expenditures and Arms Transfers.*

ANGOLA - MILK PRODUCTION - See ANGOLA - DAIRY PRODUCTS

ANGOLA - MILLET PRODUCTION - See ANGOLA - CROPS

ANGOLA - MINING AND MINERAL PRODUCTS

Facts on File, 460 Park Avenue South, New York, New York 10016 (800) 443-8323; *The New Book of World Rankings.*

G.K. Hall and Company, 70 Lincoln Street, Boston, Massachusetts 02111 (617) 423-3990; *The World in Figures.*

Penn Well Publishing Company, 1421 South Sheridan Road, P.O. Box 1260, Tulsa, Oklahoma 74101 (800) 752-9764; *International Energy Statistics Sourcebook.*

Statistical Office of the United Nations, Publishing Service, New York, New York 10017 (800) 253-9646; *Statistical Yearbook.*

United Nations Economic Commission for Africa, Africa Hall, P.O. Box 3001, Addis Ababa, Ethiopia (Telephone Number in U.S. (800) 253-9646); *African Statistical Yearbook.*

ANGOLA - MONEY EXCHANGE RATE

Euromonitor Publications Limited, 87-88 Turnmill Street, London EC1M 5QU, England; *International Marketing Data and Statistics.*

ANGOLA - MONEY RESERVES

Euromonitor Publications Limited, 87-88 Turnmill Street, London EC1M 5QU, England; *International Marketing Data and Statistics.*

ANGOLA - MONEY SUPPLY

African Development Bank, 01 BP 1387, Abidjan 01, Cote D'Ivoire; *Selected Statistics on Regional Member Countries.*

Euromonitor Publications Limited, 87-88 Turnmill Street, London EC1M 5QU, England; *International Marketing Data and Statistics.*

Federal Statistical Office, Gustav - Stresemann - Ring 11, D-6200 Wiesbaden, Germany; *Angola.*

G.K. Hall and Company, 70 Lincoln Street, Boston, Massachusetts 02111 (617) 423-3990; *The World in Figures.*

ANGOLA - MOTION PICTURES

Statistical Office of the United Nations, Publishing Service, New York, New York 10017 (800) 253-9646; *Statistical Yearbook.*

ANGOLA - MOTOR VEHICLE PRODUCTION AND ASSEMBLY

Statistical Office of the United Nations, Publishing Service, New York, New York 10017 (800) 253-9646; *Statistical Yearbook.*

ANGOLA - MOTOR VEHICLES IN USE

G.K. Hall and Company, 70 Lincoln Street, Boston, Massachusetts 02111 (617) 423-3990; *The World in Figures.*

International Road Federation, 525 School Street, SW, Washington, D.C. 20024 (202) 554-2106; *World Road Statistics.*

Statistical Office of the United Nations, Publishing Service, New York, New York 10017 (800) 253-9646; *Statistical Yearbook,* and *Survey of Economic and Social Conditions in Africa.*

Times Books, 201 East 50th Street, New York, New York 10022 (212) 751-2600; *The Economist Book of Vital World Statistics.*

ANGOLA - MUSEUMS

Facts on File, 460 Park Avenue South, New York, New York 10016 (800) 443-8323; *The New Book of World Rankings.*

ANGOLA - NATALITY - See ANGOLA - BIRTH RATES

ANGOLA - NATIONAL ACCOUNTS

African Development Bank, 01 BP 1387, Abidjan 01, Cote D'Ivoire; *Selected Statistics on Regional Member Countries.*

Federal Statistical Office, Gustav - Stresemann - Ring 11, D-6200 Wiesbaden, Germany; *Angola.*

United Nations Economic Commission for Africa, Africa Hall, P.O. Box 3001, Addis Ababa, Ethiopia (Telephone Number in U.S. (800) 253-9646); *African Statistical Yearbook.*

ANGOLA - NATIONAL INCOME

Facts on File, 460 Park Avenue South, New York, New York 10016 (800) 443-8323; *The New Book of World Rankings.*

G.K. Hall and Company, 70 Lincoln Street, Boston, Massachusetts 02111 (617) 423-3990; *The World in Figures.*

Statistical Office of the United Nations, Publishing Service, New York, New York 10017 (800) 253-9646; *Statistical Yearbook.*

ANGOLA - NATIONAL PRODUCT

Facts on File, 460 Park Avenue South, New York, New York 10016 (800) 443-8323; *The New Book of World Rankings.*

ANGOLA - NATURAL GAS - See ANGOLA - MINING AND MINERAL PRODUCTS

ANGOLA - NEWSPRINT - See ANGOLA - FORESTRY AND FOREST PRODUCTS

ANGOLA - OCCUPATIONS - See ANGOLA - LABOR FORCE

ANGOLA - PAPER - See ANGOLA - FORESTRY AND FOREST PRODUCTS

ANGOLA - PEANUT PRODUCTION - See ANGOLA - CROPS

ANGOLA - PESTICIDE USE

Food and Agricultural Organization of the United Nations (FAO) Via Delle Terme di Caracalla, 00100 Rome, Italy (Telephone Number in U.S. (202) 653-2400); *The State of Food and Agriculture.*

ANGOLA - PETROLEUM INDUSTRY

Facts on File, 460 Park Avenue South, New York, New York 10016 (800) 443-8323; *The New Book of World Rankings.*

Food and Agricultural Organization of the United Nations (FAO) Via Delle Terme di Caracalla, 00100 Rome, Italy (Telephone Number in U.S. (202) 653-2400); *The State of Food and Agriculture.*

G.K. Hall and Company, 70 Lincoln Street, Boston, Massachusetts 02111 (617) 423-3990; *The World in Figures.*

Penn Well Publishing Company, 1421 South Sheridan Road, P.O. Box 1260, Tulsa, Oklahoma 74101 (800) 752-9764; *International Energy Statistics Sourcebook.*

Statistical Office of the United Nations, Publishing Service, New York, New York 10017 (800) 253-9646; *Statistical Yearbook.*

ANGOLA - PIGS - See ANGOLA - LIVESTOCK AND POULTRY

ANGOLA - POPULATION

African Development Bank, 01 BP 1387, Abidjan 01, Cote D'Ivoire; *Selected Statistics on Regional Member Countries.*

The Economist Intelligence Unit, 111 West 57th Street, New York, New York 10019 (800) 938-4685; *The World Market Atlas.*

Euromonitor Publications Limited, 87-88 Turnmill Street, London EC1M 5QU, England; *International Marketing Data and Statistics.*

Facts on File, 460 Park Avenue South, New York, New York 10016 (800) 443-8323; *The New Book of World Rankings.*

Federal Statistical Office, Gustav - Stresemann - Ring 11, D-6200 Wiesbaden, Germany; *Angola.*

Food and Agricultural Organization of the United Nations (FAO), Via delle Terme di Caracalla, 00100 Rome, Italy (Telephone Number in U.S. (202) 653-2400); *Production Yearbook.*

G.K. Hall and Company, 70 Lincoln Street, Boston, Massachusetts 02111 (617) 423-3990; *The World in Figures.*

Statistical Office of the United Nations, Publishing Service, New York, New York 10017 (800) 253-9646; *Demographic Yearbook, Statistical Yearbook,* and *Survey of Economic and Social Conditions in Africa.*

Times Books, 201 East 50th Street, New York, New York 10022 (212) 751-2600; *The Economist Book of Vital World Statistics.*

U.S. Arms Control and Disarmament Agency, 320 Twenty-first Street, NW, Washington, D.C. 20451 (202) 647-8677; *World Military Expenditures and Arms Transfers.*

World Health Organization, Office of Publications, Avenue Appia, CH-1211 Geneva 27, Switzerland (Telephone Number in U.S. (518) 436-9686); *World Health Statistics Annual.*

ANGOLA - POST OFFICES

Facts on File, 460 Park Avenue South, New York, New York 10016 (800) 443-8323; *The New Book of World Rankings.*

ANGOLA - POTATO PRODUCTION - See ANGOLA - CROPS

ANGOLA - POULTRY - See ANGOLA - LIVESTOCK AND POULTRY

ANGOLA - PRICES

Facts on File, 460 Park Avenue South, New York, New York 10016 (800) 443-8323; *The New Book of World Rankings.*

Federal Statistical Office, Gustav - Stresemann - Ring 11, D-6200 Wiesbaden, Germany; *Angola.*

Food and Agricultural Organization of the United Nations (FAO), Via delle Terme di Caracalla, 00100 Rome, Italy (Telephone Number in U.S. (202) 653-2400); *Production Yearbook,* and *The State of Food and Agriculture.*

G.K. Hall and Company, 70 Lincoln Street, Boston, Massachusetts 02111 (617) 423-3990; *The World in Figures.*

ANGOLA - PRINTING AND WRITING PAPER - See ANGOLA - FORESTRY AND FOREST PRODUCTS

ANGOLA - PRODUCTION

Facts on File, 460 Park Avenue South, New York, New York 10016 (800) 443-8323; *The New Book of World Rankings.*

G.K. Hall and Company, 70 Lincoln Street, Boston, Massachusetts 02111 (617) 423-3990; *The World in Figures.*

ANGOLA - PRODUCTIVITY

Euromonitor Publications Limited, 87-88 Turnmill Street, London EC1M 5QU, England; *International Marketing Data and Statistics.*

ANGOLA - PUBLIC FINANCE

Direccao dos Servicos de Estatistica, CP 1215, Luanda, Angola; *Statistical Yearbook.*

Facts on File, 460 Park Avenue South, New York, New York 10016 (800) 443-8323; *The New Book of World Rankings.*

Federal Statistical Office, Gustav - Stresemann - Ring 11, D-6200 Wiesbaden, Germany; *Angola.*

ANGOLA - RADIO BROADCASTING - See ANGOLA - BROADCASTING

ANGOLA - RADIO RECEIVER PRODUCTION

Statistical Office of the United Nations, Publishing Service, New York, New York 10017 (800) 253-9646; *Statistical Yearbook.*

ANGOLA - RAILWAYS

G.K. Hall and Company, 70 Lincoln Street, Boston, Massachusetts 02111 (617) 423-3990; *The World in Figures.*

Jane's Information Group, Sentinel House, 163 Brighton Road, Coulsdon, Surrey CR5 2NH, England (Telephone Number in U.S. (703) 683-3700); *Jane's World Railways.*

Statistical Office of the United Nations, Publishing Service, New York, New York 10017 (800) 253-9646; *Statistical Yearbook,* and *Survey of Economic and Social Conditions in Africa.*

United Nations Economic Commission for Africa, Africa Hall, P.O. Box 3001, Addis Ababa, Ethiopia (Telephone Number in U.S. (800) 253-9646); *African Statistical Yearbook.*

ANGOLA - RELIGION

Facts on File, 460 Park Avenue South, New York, New York 10016 (800) 443-8323; *The New Book of World Rankings.*

ANGOLA - RETAIL TRADE

Direccao dos Servicos de Estatistica, CP 1215, Luanda, Angola; *Statistical Yearbook.*

G.K. Hall and Company, 70 Lincoln Street, Boston, Massachusetts 02111 (617) 423-3990; *The World in Figures.*

ANGOLA - RICE PRODUCTION - See ANGOLA - CROPS

ANGOLA - ROOT AND TUBER PRODUCTION - See ANGOLA - CROPS

ANGOLA - ROUNDWOOD PRODUCTION - See ANGOLA - FORESTRY AND FOREST PRODUCTS

ANGOLA - RUBBER PRODUCTION

Facts on File, 460 Park Avenue South, New York, New York 10016 (800) 443-8323; *The New Book of World Rankings.*

ANGOLA - SALT PRODUCTION - See ANGOLA - MINING AND MINERAL PRODUCTS

ANGOLA - SAWNWOOD PRODUCTION - See ANGOLA - FORESTRY AND FOREST PRODUCTS

ANGOLA - SENIOR CITIZENS

Facts on File, 460 Park Avenue South, New York, New York 10016 (800) 443-8323; *The New Book of World Rankings.*

ANGOLA - SESAME SEED PRODUCTION - See ANGOLA - CROPS

ANGOLA - SHEEP - See ANGOLA - LIVESTOCK AND POULTRY

ANGOLA - SILVER PRODUCTION AND CONSUMPTION - See ANGOLA - MINING AND MINERAL PRODUCTS

ANGOLA - SISAL PRODUCTION - See ANGOLA - CROPS

ANGOLA - SOCIAL DATA

African Development Bank, 01 BP 1387, Abidjan 01, Cote D'Ivoire; *Selected Statistics on Regional Member Countries.*

Facts on File, 460 Park Avenue South, New York, New York 10016 (800) 443-8323; *The New Book of World Rankings.*

G.K. Hall and Company, 70 Lincoln Street, Boston, Massachusetts 02111 (617) 423-3990; *The World in Figures.*

ANGOLA - STATE BUDGET REVENUE AND EXPENDITURES

Euromonitor Publications Limited, 87-88 Turnmill Street, London EC1M 5QU, England; *International Marketing Data and Statistics.*

ANGOLA - STEEL - See ANGOLA - MINING AND MINERAL PRODUCTS

ANGOLA - STOCKS - COMMODITY - MARKET PRICE - INDEX

Food and Agricultural Organization of the United Nations (FAO) Via Delle Terme di Caracalla, 00100 Rome, Italy (Telephone Number in U.S. (202) 653-2400); *The State of Food and Agriculture.*

ANGOLA - SUGAR PRODUCTION - See ANGOLA - CROPS

ANGOLA - TAXATION

G.K. Hall and Company, 70 Lincoln Street, Boston, Massachusetts 02111 (617) 423-3990; *The World in Figures.*

International Road Federation, 525 School Street, SW, Washington, D.C. 20024 (202) 554-2106; *World Road Statistics.*

ANGOLA - TELEGRAPH SERVICE

Statistical Office of the United Nations, Publishing Service, New York, New York 10017 (800) 253-9646; *Statistical Yearbook.*

ANGOLA - TELEPHONES IN USE

American Telephone and Telegraph Company, 26 Parsippany Road, Whippany, New Jersey 07981 (800) 338-4038; *The World's Telephones.*

G.K. Hall and Company, 70 Lincoln Street, Boston, Massachusetts 02111 (617) 423-3990; *The World in Figures.*

Statistical Office of the United Nations, Publishing Service, New York, New York 10017 (800) 253-9646; *Statistical Yearbook.*

ANGOLA - TELEVISION BROADCASTING - See ANGOLA - BROADCASTING

ANGOLA - TEXTILE INDUSTRY

G.K. Hall and Company, 70 Lincoln Street, Boston, Massachusetts 02111 (617) 423-3990; *The World in Figures.*

Statistical Office of the United Nations, Publishing Service, New York, New York 10017 (800) 253-9646; *Statistical Yearbook.*

ANGOLA - TIRE (MOTOR VEHICLE) PRODUCTION

Statistical Office of the United Nations, Publishing Service, New York, New York 10017 (800) 253-9646; *Statistical Yearbook.*

ANGOLA - TOBACCO PRODUCTION

Facts on File, 460 Park Avenue South, New York, New York 10016 (800) 443-8323; *The New Book of World Rankings.*

Statistical Office of the United Nations, Publishing Service, New York, New York 10017 (800) 253-9646; *Statistical Yearbook.*

ANGOLA - TOURISM

Facts on File, 460 Park Avenue South, New York, New York 10016 (800) 443-8323; *The New Book of World Rankings.*

Federal Statistical Office, Gustav - Stresemann - Ring 11, D-6200 Wiesbaden, Germany; *Angola.*

G.K. Hall and Company, 70 Lincoln Street, Boston, Massachusetts 02111 (617) 423-3990; *The World in Figures.*

United Nations Economic Commission for Africa, Africa Hall, P.O. Box 3001, Addis Ababa, Ethiopia (Telephone Number in U.S. (800) 253-9646); *African Statistical Yearbook.*

ANGOLA - TRADE - See ANGOLA - FOREIGN TRADE

ANGOLA - TRANSPORTATION AND COMMUNICATIONS

Direccao dos Servicos de Estatistica, CP 1215, Luanda, Angola; *Statistical Yearbook.*

Facts on File, 460 Park Avenue South, New York, New York 10016 (800) 443-8323; *The New Book of World Rankings.*

Federal Statistical Office, Gustav - Stresemann - Ring 11, D-6200 Wiesbaden, Germany; *Angola.*

G.K. Hall and Company, 70 Lincoln Street, Boston, Massachusetts 02111 (617) 423-3990; *The World in Figures.*

United Nations Economic Commission for Africa, Africa Hall, P.O. Box 3001, Addis Ababa, Ethiopia (Telephone Number in U.S. (800) 253-9646); *African Statistical Yearbook.*

ANGOLA - UNEMPLOYMENT

Euromonitor Publications Limited, 87-88 Turnmill Street, London EC1M 5QU, England; *International Marketing Data and Statistics.*

ANGOLA - VITAL STATISTICS

Euromonitor Publications Limited, 87-88 Turnmill Street, London EC1M 5QU, England; *International Marketing Data and Statistics.*

G.K. Hall and Company, 70 Lincoln Street, Boston, Massachusetts 02111 (617) 423-3990; *The World in Figures.*

Statistical Office of the United Nations, Publishing Service, New York, New York 10017 (800) 253-9646; *Statistical Yearbook.*

World Health Organization, Office of Publications, Avenue Appia, CH-1211 Geneva 27, Switzerland (Telephone Number in U.S. (518) 436-9686); *World Health Statistics Annual.*

ANGOLA - WAGES

Federal Statistical Office, Gustav - Stresemann - Ring 11, D-6200 Wiesbaden, Germany; *Angola.*

G.K. Hall and Company, 70 Lincoln Street, Boston, Massachusetts 02111 (617) 423-3990; *The World in Figures.*

ANGOLA - WEATHER

Facts on File, 460 Park Avenue South, New York, New York 10016 (800) 443-8323; *The New Book of World Rankings.*

G.K. Hall and Company, 70 Lincoln Street, Boston, Massachusetts 02111 (617) 423-3990; *The World in Figures.*

ANGOLA - WHEAT - See ANGOLA - CROPS

ANGOLA - WINE PRODUCTION

Facts on File, 460 Park Avenue South, New York, New York 10016 (800) 443-8323; *The New Book of World Rankings.*

ANGOLA - WOOD PULP PRODUCTION - See ANGOLA - FORESTRY AND FOREST PRODUCTS

ANGOLA - WOOL PRODUCTION

Facts on File, 460 Park Avenue South, New York, New York 10016 (800) 443-8323; *The New Book of World Rankings.*

ANGOLA - YARN PRODUCTION

Statistical Office of the United Nations, Publishing Service, New York, New York 10017 (800) 253-9646; *Statistical Yearbook.*

Anguilla - National Statistical Office

Statistical Department, The Treasury, The Valley, Anguilla.

ANGUILLA - BROADCASTING

Billboard Limited, P.O. Box 9027, 1006 AA Amsterdam, The Netherlands (Telephone Number in U.S. (212) 764-7300); *World Radio TV Handbook.*

ANGUILLA - TOURISM

World Tourism Organization, Calle Capitan Haya 42, E-28020 Madrid, Spain; *Yearbook of Tourism Statistics.*

ANIMAL OILS AND FATS - See OILS, ANIMAL

ANIMALS, DOMESTIC - See also Individual Classes

ANIMALS, DOMESTIC - GRAZING - NATIONAL FORESTS

U.S. Department of Agriculture, Forest Service, Fourteenth Street and Independence Avenue, SW, Washington, D.C. 20250 (202) 720-3760; *Agricultural Statistics,* and unpublished data.

ANIMALS, DOMESTIC - INVENTORY AND PRODUCTION

U.S. Department of Agriculture, National Agricultural Statistics Service, Fourteenth Street and Independence Avenue, SW, Washington, D.C. 20250 (202) 219-1504; *Meat Animals - Production, Disposition, and Income, Agricultural Statistics,* and *Livestock and Meat Statistics.*

ANIMALS, DOMESTIC - WORK ANIMALS - HORSEPOWER OF

John A. Waring, 1320 South George Mason Drive, Arlington, Virginia 22204 (703) 521-1499; unpublished estimates.

ANNUITIES - See PENSIONS AND RETIREMENT BENEFITS

Antigua and Barbuda - National Statistical Office

Statistics Division, Ministry of Finance, Redcliffe Street, Saint John's, Antigua and Barbuda.

Antigua and Barbuda - Primary Statistics Source

Statistics Division, Ministry of Finance, Redcliffe Street, St. John's, Antigua and Barbuda; *Statistical Yearbook.*

ANTIGUA AND BARBUDA - AGRICULTURE

Food and Agricultural Organization of the United Nations (FAO), Via delle Terme di Caracalla, 00100 Rome, Italy (Telephone Number in U.S. (202) 653-2400); *Production Yearbook, The State of Food and*

Agriculture, and *Trade Yearbook*.

G.K. Hall and Company, 70 Lincoln Street, Boston, Massachusetts 02111 (617) 423-3990; *The World in Figures*.

Statistical Office of the United Nations, Publishing Service, New York, New York 10017 (800) 253-9646; *Statistical Yearbook*.

The World Bank, 1818 H Street, NW, Washington, D.C. 20433 (202) 477-1234; *World Tables*.

ANTIGUA AND BARBUDA - AIRLINE SERVICE

G.K. Hall and Company, 70 Lincoln Street, Boston, Massachusetts 02111 (617) 423-3990; *The World in Figures*.

International Civil Aviation Organization, 1000 Sherbrooke Street West, Suite 400, Montreal, Quebec, Canada H3A 2R2; *Civil Aviation Statistics of the World*.

ANTIGUA AND BARBUDA - ANIMAL HEALTH

Food and Agricultural Organization of the United Nations (FAO), Via delle Terme di Caracalla, 00100 Rome, Italy (Telephone Number in U.S. (202) 653-2400); *Animal Health Yearbook*.

ANTIGUA AND BARBUDA - AREA AND DENSITY OF POPULATION

Food and Agricultural Organization of the United Nations (FAO) Via Delle Terme di Caracalla, 00100 Rome, Italy (Telephone Number in U.S. (202) 653-2400); *The State of Food and Agriculture*.

G.K. Hall and Company, 70 Lincoln Street, Boston, Massachusetts 02111 (617) 423-3990; *The World in Figures*.

Statistical Office of the United Nations, Publishing Service, New York, New York 10017 (800) 253-9646; *Statistical Yearbook*.

ANTIGUA AND BARBUDA - BALANCE OF PAYMENTS

G.K. Hall and Company, 70 Lincoln Street, Boston, Massachusetts 02111 (617) 423-3990; *The World in Figures*.

International Monetary Fund, 700 Nineteenth Street, NW, Washington, D.C. 20431 (202) 623-7000; *Balance of Payments Yearbook*.

Statistical Office of the United Nations, Publishing Service, New York, New York 10017 (800) 253-9646; *Economic Survey of Latin America and the Caribbean*.

The World Bank, 1818 H Street, NW, Washington, D.C. 20433 (202) 477-1234; *World Tables*.

ANTIGUA AND BARBUDA - BANKING

G.K. Hall and Company, 70 Lincoln Street, Boston, Massachusetts 02111 (617) 423-3990; *The World in Figures*.

ANTIGUA AND BARBUDA - BIRTH RATE

Statistical Office of the United Nations, Publishing Service, New York, New York 10017 (800) 253-9646; *Demographic Yearbook*, and *Statistical Yearbook*.

World Health Organization, Office of Publications, Avenue Appia, CH-1211 Geneva 27, Switzerland (Telephone Number in U.S. (518) 436-9686); *World Health Statistics Annual*.

ANTIGUA AND BARBUDA - BONDS

G.K. Hall and Company, 70 Lincoln Street, Boston, Massachusetts 02111 (617) 423-3990; *The World in Figures*.

ANTIGUA AND BARBUDA - BOOK PRODUCTION

G.K. Hall and Company, 70 Lincoln Street, Boston, Massachusetts 02111 (617) 423-3990; *The World in Figures*.

ANTIGUA AND BARBUDA - BROADCASTING

Billboard Limited, P.O. Box 9027, 1006 AA Amsterdam, The Netherlands (Telephone Number in U.S. (212) 764-7300); *World Radio TV Handbook*.

G.K. Hall and Company, 70 Lincoln Street, Boston, Massachusetts 02111 (617) 423-3990; *The World in Figures*.

ANTIGUA AND BARBUDA - BUSINESS

G.K. Hall and Company, 70 Lincoln Street, Boston, Massachusetts 02111 (617) 423-3990; *The World in Figures*.

ANTIGUA AND BARBUDA - CALORIE SUPPLY

Food and Agricultural Organization of the United Nations (FAO) Via Delle Terme di Caracalla, 00100 Rome, Italy (Telephone Number in U.S. (202) 653-2400); *The State of Food and Agriculture*.

ANTIGUA AND BARBUDA - CATTLE - See ANTIGUA AND BARBUDA - LIVESTOCK AND POULTRY

ANTIGUA AND BARBUDA - CHEMICAL (ORGANIC) PRODUCTION - See ANTIGUA AND BARBUDA - MINING AND MINERAL PRODUCTS

ANTIGUA AND BARBUDA - CLASS STRUCTURE

G.K. Hall and Company, 70 Lincoln Street, Boston, Massachusetts 02111 (617) 423-3990; *The World in Figures*.

ANTIGUA AND BARBUDA - CLIMATE

G.K. Hall and Company, 70 Lincoln Street, Boston, Massachusetts 02111 (617) 423-3990; *The World in Figures*.

ANTIGUA AND BARBUDA - COAL PRODUCTION - See ANTIGUA AND BARBUDA - MINING AND MINERAL PRODUCTS

ANTIGUA AND BARBUDA - COMMUNICATIONS

G.K. Hall and Company, 70 Lincoln Street, Boston, Massachusetts 02111 (617) 423-3990; *The World in Figures*.

ANTIGUA AND BARBUDA - CONSUMER PRICE INDEX

G.K. Hall and Company, 70 Lincoln Street, Boston, Massachusetts 02111 (617) 423-3990; *The World in Figures*.

Statistical Office of the United Nations, Publishing Service, New York, New York 10017 (800) 253-9646; *Statistical Yearbook*.

ANTIGUA AND BARBUDA - CONSUMER PRICES

International Labour Office, I.L.O. Publications, CH-1211, Geneva 22, Switzerland; *Yearbook of Labour Statistics*.

ANTIGUA AND BARBUDA - CONSUMPTION

G.K. Hall and Company, 70 Lincoln Street, Boston, Massachusetts 02111 (617) 423-3990; *The World in Figures.*

ANTIGUA AND BARBUDA - CORN PRODUCTION - See ANTIGUA AND BARBUDA - CROPS

ANTIGUA AND BARBUDA - CORPORATE TAXES - See ANTIGUA AND BARBUDA - TAXATION

ANTIGUA AND BARBUDA - CROPS

Food and Agricultural Organization of the United Nations (FAO) Via Delle Terme di Caracalla, 00100 Rome, Italy (Telephone Number in U.S. (202) 653-2400); *The State of Food and Agriculture.*

G.K. Hall and Company, 70 Lincoln Street, Boston, Massachusetts 02111 (617) 423-3990; *The World in Figures.*

ANTIGUA AND BARBUDA - CUSTOMS DUTIES

G.K. Hall and Company, 70 Lincoln Street, Boston, Massachusetts 02111 (617) 423-3990; *The World in Figures.*

ANTIGUA AND BARBUDA - DAIRY PRODUCTS

Food and Agricultural Organization of the United Nations (FAO) Via Delle Terme di Caracalla, 00100 Rome, Italy (Telephone Number in U.S. (202) 653-2400); *The State of Food and Agriculture.*

ANTIGUA AND BARBUDA - DEATH RATE

G.K. Hall and Company, 70 Lincoln Street, Boston, Massachusetts 02111 (617) 423-3990; *The World in Figures.*

Statistical Office of the United Nations, Publishing Service, New York, New York 10017 (800) 253-9646; *Statistical Yearbook.*

World Health Organization, Office of Publications, Avenue Appia, CH-1211 Geneva 27, Switzerland (Telephone Number in U.S. (518) 436-9686); *World Health Statistics Annual.*

ANTIGUA AND BARBUDA - DEFENSE EXPENDITURES

G.K. Hall and Company, 70 Lincoln Street, Boston, Massachusetts 02111 (617) 423-3990; *The World in Figures.*

ANTIGUA AND BARBUDA - DEMOGRAPHY

G.K. Hall and Company, 70 Lincoln Street, Boston, Massachusetts 02111 (617) 423-3990; *The World in Figures.*

ANTIGUA AND BARBUDA - DEVELOPMENT ASSISTANCE

G.K. Hall and Company, 70 Lincoln Street, Boston, Massachusetts 02111 (617) 423-3990; *The World in Figures.*

ANTIGUA AND BARBUDA - DISEASES

G.K. Hall and Company, 70 Lincoln Street, Boston, Massachusetts 02111 (617) 423-3990; *The World in Figures.*

World Health Organization, Office of Publications, Avenue Appia, CH-1211 Geneva 27, Switzerland (Telephone Number in U.S. (518) 436-9686); *World Health Statistics Annual.*

ANTIGUA AND BARBUDA - DIVORCE RATES

Statistical Office of the United Nations, Publishing Service, New York, New York 10017 (800) 253-9646; *Demographic Yearbook,* and *Statistical Yearbook.*

ANTIGUA AND BARBUDA - DOMESTIC PRODUCT

G.K. Hall and Company, 70 Lincoln Street, Boston, Massachusetts 02111 (617) 423-3990; *The World in Figures.*

ANTIGUA AND BARBUDA - ECONOMY

G.K. Hall and Company, 70 Lincoln Street, Boston, Massachusetts 02111 (617) 423-3990; *The World in Figures.*

Statistical Office of the United Nations, Publishing Service, New York, New York 10017 (800) 253-9646; *Economic Survey of Latin America and the Caribbean.*

ANTIGUA AND BARBUDA - EDUCATION

G.K. Hall and Company, 70 Lincoln Street, Boston, Massachusetts 02111 (617) 423-3990; *The World in Figures.*

United Nations Educational, Scientific and Cultural Organization (UNESCO), 7 Place de Fontenoy, F-75700 Paris, France (Telephone Number in U.S. (212) 963-5981); *Statistical Yearbook.*

The World Bank, 1818 H Street, NW, Washington, D.C. 20433 (202) 447-1234; *World Tables.*

ANTIGUA AND BARBUDA - EGG PRODUCTION - See ANTIGUA AND BARBUDA - DAIRY PRODUCTS

ANTIGUA AND BARBUDA - ELECTRICITY

Statistical Office of the United Nations, Publishing Service, New York, New York 10017 (800) 253-9646; *Statistical Yearbook.*

ANTIGUA AND BARBUDA - EMPLOYMENT

International Labour Office, I.L.O. Publications, CH-1211, Geneva 22, Switzerland; *Yearbook of Labour Statistics.*

ANTIGUA AND BARBUDA - ENERGY

Food and Agricultural Organization of the United Nations (FAO) Via Delle Terme di Caracalla, 00100 Rome, Italy (Telephone Number in U.S. (202) 653-2400); *The State of Food and Agriculture.*

G.K. Hall and Company, 70 Lincoln Street, Boston, Massachusetts 02111 (617) 423-3990; *The World in Figures.*

Statistical Office of the United Nations, Publishing Service, New York, New York 10017 (800) 253-9646; *Energy Statistics Yearbook,* and *Statistical Yearbook,* and *World Energy Supplies.*

ANTIGUA AND BARBUDA - EXCHANGE RATES

International Civil Aviation Organization, 1000 Sherbrooke Street West, Suite 400, Montreal, Quebec, Canada H3A 2R2; *Civil Aviation Statistics of the World.*

ANTIGUA AND BARBUDA - EXPORTS

Food and Agricultural Organization of the United Nations (FAO) Via Delle Terme di Caracalla, 00100 Rome, Italy (Telephone Number in U.S. (202) 653-2400); *The State of Food and Agriculture.*

G.K. Hall and Company, 70 Lincoln Street, Boston, Massachusetts 02111 (617) 423-3990; *The World in Figures*.

The World Bank, 1818 H Street, NW, Washington, D.C. 20433 (202) 447-1234; *World Tables*.

ANTIGUA AND BARBUDA - EXTERNAL INDEBTEDNESS

The World Bank, 1818 H Street, NW, Washington, D.C. 20433 (202) 447-1234; *World Tables*.

ANTIGUA AND BARBUDA - EXTERNAL TRADE

G.K. Hall and Company, 70 Lincoln Street, Boston, Massachusetts 02111 (617) 423-3990; *The World in Figures*.

Food and Agricultural Organization of the United Nations (FAO), Via delle Terme di Caracalla, 00100 Rome, Italy (Telephone Number in U.S. (202) 653-2400); *Production Yearbook*, and *The State of Food and Agriculture*.

ANTIGUA AND BARBUDA - FARM CROPS - See ANTIGUA AND BARBUDA - CROPS

ANTIGUA AND BARBUDA - FETAL MORTALITY

Statistical Office of the United Nations, Publishing Service, New York, New York 10017 (800) 253-9646; *Demographic Yearbook*.

World Health Organization, Office of Publications, Avenue Appia, CH-1211 Geneva 27, Switzerland (Telephone Number in U.S. (518) 436-9686); *World Health Statistics Annual*.

ANTIGUA AND BARBUDA - FERTILITY RATES

The World Bank, 1818 H Street, NW, Washington, D.C. 20433 (202) 447-1234; *World Tables*.

ANTIGUA AND BARBUDA - FERTILIZER

Food and Agricultural Organization of the United Nations (FAO) Via Delle Terme di Caracalla, 00100 Rome, Italy (Telephone Number in U.S. (202) 653-2400); *The State of Food and Agriculture*.

ANTIGUA AND BARBUDA - FINANCE

G.K. Hall and Company, 70 Lincoln Street, Boston, Massachusetts 02111 (617) 423-3990; *The World in Figures*.

International Monetary Fund, 700 Nineteenth Street, NW, Washington, D.C. 20431; *International Financial Statistics*.

ANTIGUA AND BARBUDA - FISHERIES

Food and Agricultural Organization of the United Nations (FAO) Via Delle Terme di Caracalla, 00100 Rome, Italy (Telephone Number in U.S. (202) 653-2400); *The State of Food and Agriculture*, and *Yearbook of Fishery Statistics*.

ANTIGUA AND BARBUDA - FOOD

G.K. Hall and Company, 70 Lincoln Street, Boston, Massachusetts 02111 (617) 423-3990; *The World in Figures*.

Food and Agricultural Organization of the United Nations (FAO) Via Delle Terme di Caracalla, 00100 Rome, Italy (Telephone Number in U.S. (202) 653-2400); *Production Yearbook*, and *The State of Food and Agriculture*.

ANTIGUA AND BARBUDA - FOREIGN AID

G.K. Hall and Company, 70 Lincoln Street, Boston, Massachusetts 02111 (617) 423-3990; *The World in Figures*.

ANTIGUA AND BARBUDA - FOREIGN INDEBTEDNESS

Statistical Office of the United Nations, Publishing Service, New York, New York 10017 (800) 253-9646; *Economic Survey of Latin America and the Caribbean*.

ANTIGUA AND BARBUDA - FOREIGN TRADE

Food and Agricultural Organization of the United Nations (FAO) Via Delle Terme di Caracalla, 00100 Rome, Italy (Telephone Number in U.S. (202) 653-2400); *The State of Food and Agriculture*.

G.K. Hall and Company, 70 Lincoln Street, Boston, Massachusetts 02111 (617) 423-3990; *The World in Figures*.

Organisation for Economic Co-operation and Development (OECD), 2 rue Andre-Pascal, 75 Paris 16, France (Telephone Number in U.S. (212) 963-5981); *Trade by Commodities*.

Statistical Office of the United Nations, Publishing Service, New York, New York 10017 (800) 253-9646; *Economic Survey of Latin America and the Caribbean*, and *International Trade Statistics Yearbook*.

The World Bank, 1818 H Street, NW, Washington, D.C. 20433 (202) 447-1234; *World Tables*.

ANTIGUA AND BARBUDA - FORESTRY AND FOREST PRODUCTS

Food and Agricultural Organization of the United Nations (FAO) Via Delle Terme di Caracalla, 00100 Rome, Italy (Telephone Number in U.S. (202) 653-2400); *The State of Food and Agriculture*.

G.K. Hall and Company, 70 Lincoln Street, Boston, Massachusetts 02111 (617) 423-3990; *The World in Figures*.

Statistical Office of the United Nations, Publishing Service, New York, New York 10017 (800) 253-9646; *Statistical Yearbook*.

United Nations Educational, Scientific and Cultural Organization (UNESCO), 7 Place de Fontenoy, F-75700 Paris, France (Telephone Number in U.S. (212) 963-5981); *Statistical Yearbook*.

ANTIGUA AND BARBUDA - GENERAL MORTALITY

Statistical Office of the United Nations, Publishing Service, New York, New York 10017 (800) 253-9646; *Demographic Yearbook*.

World Health Organization, Office of Publications, Avenue Appia, CH-1211 Geneva 27, Switzerland (Telephone Number in U.S. (518) 436-9686); *World Health Statistics Annual*.

ANTIGUA AND BARBUDA - GOLD HOLDINGS

The World Bank, 1818 H Street, NW, Washington, D.C. 20433 (202) 447-1234; *World Tables*.

ANTIGUA AND BARBUDA - GOVERNMENT

G.K. Hall and Company, 70 Lincoln Street, Boston, Massachusetts 02111 (617) 423-3990; *The World in Figures*.

ANTIGUA AND BARBUDA - GOVERNMENT EXPENDITURE

The World Bank, 1818 H Street, NW, Washington, D.C. 20433 (202) 447-1234; *World Tables.*

ANTIGUA AND BARBUDA - GOVERNMENT REVENUE

The World Bank, 1818 H Street, NW, Washington, D.C. 20433 (202) 447-1234; *World Tables.*

ANTIGUA AND BARBUDA - GRAIN PRODUCTION - See ANTIGUA AND BARBUDA - CROPS

ANTIGUA AND BARBUDA - GROSS DOMESTIC PRODUCT

G.K. Hall and Company, 70 Lincoln Street, Boston, Massachusetts 02111 (617) 423-3990; *The World in Figures.*

Statistical Office of the United Nations, Publishing Service, New York, New York 10017 (800) 253-9646; *Statistical Yearbook.*

The World Bank, 1818 H Street, NW, Washington, D.C. 20433 (202) 447-1234; *World Tables.*

ANTIGUA AND BARBUDA - GROSS NATIONAL PRODUCT

The World Bank, 1818 H Street, NW, Washington, D.C. 20433 (202) 447-1234; *World Tables.*

ANTIGUA AND BARBUDA - HEALTH

G.K. Hall and Company, 70 Lincoln Street, Boston, Massachusetts 02111 (617) 423-3990; *The World in Figures.*

Statistical Office of the United Nations, Publishing Service, New York, New York 10017 (800) 253-9646; *Statistical Yearbook.*

World Health Organization, Office of Publications, Avenue Appia, CH-1211 Geneva 27, Switzerland (Telephone Number in U.S. (518) 436-9686); *World Health Statistics Annual.*

ANTIGUA AND BARBUDA - HIDE PRODUCTION

Food and Agricultural Organization of the United Nations (FAO), Via delle Terme di Caracalla, 00100 Rome, Italy (Telephone Number in U.S. (202) 653-2400); *Production Yearbook.*

ANTIGUA AND BARBUDA - HIGHWAYS

G.K. Hall and Company, 70 Lincoln Street, Boston, Massachusetts 02111 (617) 423-3990; *The World in Figures.*

ANTIGUA AND BARBUDA - HORSES - See ANTIGUA AND BARBUDA - LIVESTOCK AND POULTRY

ANTIGUA AND BARBUDA - HOURS OF WORK - See ANTIGUA AND BARBUDA - EMPLOYMENT

ANTIGUA AND BARBUDA - ILLITERATE POPULATION

G.K. Hall and Company, 70 Lincoln Street, Boston, Massachusetts 02111 (617) 423-3990; *The World in Figures.*

United Nations Educational, Scientific and Cultural Organization (UNESCO), 7 Place de Fontenoy, F-75700 Paris, France (Telephone Number in U.S. (212) 963-5981); *Statistical Yearbook.*

ANTIGUA AND BARBUDA - IMPORTS

Food and Agricultural Organization of the United Nations (FAO) Via Delle Terme di Caracalla, 00100 Rome, Italy (Telephone Number in U.S. (202) 653-2400); *The State of Food and Agriculture.*

G.K. Hall and Company, 70 Lincoln Street, Boston, Massachusetts 02111 (617) 423-3990; *The World in Figures.*

The World Bank, 1818 H Street, NW, Washington, D.C. 20433 (202) 447-1234; *World Tables.*

ANTIGUA AND BARBUDA - INDUSTRY

G.K. Hall and Company, 70 Lincoln Street, Boston, Massachusetts 02111 (617) 423-3990; *The World in Figures.*

International Labour Office, I.L.O. Publications, CH-1211, Geneva 22, Switzerland; *Yearbook of Labour Statistics.*

Statistical Office of the United Nations, Publishing Service, New York, New York 10017 (800) 253-9646; *Economic Survey of Latin America and the Caribbean.*

The World Bank, 1818 H Street, NW, Washington, D.C. 20433 (202) 447-1234; *World Tables.*

ANTIGUA AND BARBUDA - INFANT AND MATERNAL MORTALITY

Statistical Office of the United Nations, Publishing Service, New York, New York 10017 (800) 253-9646; *Demographic Yearbook,* and *Statistical Yearbook.*

The World Bank, 1818 H Street, NW, Washington, D.C. 20433 (202) 447-1234; *World Tables.*

World Health Organization, Office of Publications, Avenue Appia, CH-1211 Geneva 27, Switzerland (Telephone Number in U.S. (518) 436-9686); *World Health Statistics Annual.*

ANTIGUA AND BARBUDA - INFLATIONARY FACTORS

Statistical Office of the United Nations, Publishing Service, New York, New York 10017 (800) 253-9646; *Economic Survey of Latin America and the Caribbean.*

ANTIGUA AND BARBUDA - INTERNATIONAL RESERVES EXCLUDING GOLD

The World Bank, 1818 H Street, NW, Washington, D.C. 20433 (202) 447-1234; *World Tables.*

ANTIGUA AND BARBUDA - LABOR FORCE

Food and Agricultural Organization of the United Nations (FAO) Via Delle Terme di Caracalla, 00100 Rome, Italy (Telephone Number in U.S. (202) 653-2400); *The State of Food and Agriculture.*

G.K. Hall and Company, 70 Lincoln Street, Boston, Massachusetts 02111 (617) 423-3990; *The World in Figures.*

The World Bank, 1818 H Street, NW, Washington, D.C. 20433 (202) 447-1234; *World Tables.*

ANTIGUA AND BARBUDA - LABOR PRODUCTIVITY

International Labour Office, I.L.O. Publications, CH-1211, Geneva 22, Switzerland; *Yearbook of Labour Statistics.*

ANTIGUA AND BARBUDA - LAND USE

Food and Agricultural Organization of the United Nations (FAO), Via delle Terme di Caracalla, 00100 Rome, Italy (Telephone Number in U.S. (202) 653-2400); *Production Yearbook.*

G.K. Hall and Company, 70 Lincoln Street, Boston, Massachusetts 02111 (617) 423-3990; *The World in Figures.*

ANTIGUA AND BARBUDA - LIVESTOCK AND POULTRY

Food and Agricultural Organization of the United Nations (FAO), Via delle Terme di Caracalla, 00100 Rome, Italy (Telephone Number in U.S. (202) 653-2400); *Production Yearbook,* and *The State of Food and Agriculture.*

G.K. Hall and Company, 70 Lincoln Street, Boston, Massachusetts 02111 (617) 423-3990; *The World in Figures.*

Statistical Office of the United Nations, Publishing Service, New York, New York 10017 (800) 253-9646; *Statistical Yearbook.*

ANTIGUA AND BARBUDA - LIVING LEVELS

G.K. Hall and Company, 70 Lincoln Street, Boston, Massachusetts 02111 (617) 423-3990; *The World in Figures.*

ANTIGUA AND BARBUDA - MAIL - NUMBER OF PIECES SENT OR RECEIVED

Statistical Office of the United Nations, Publishing Service, New York, New York 10017 (800) 253-9646; *Statistical Yearbook.*

ANTIGUA AND BARBUDA - MANUFACTURING

G.K. Hall and Company, 70 Lincoln Street, Boston, Massachusetts 02111 (617) 423-3990; *The World in Figures.*

The World Bank, 1818 H Street, NW, Washington, D.C. 20433 (202) 447-1234; *World Tables.*

ANTIGUA AND BARBUDA - MARRIAGE RATES

Statistical Office of the United Nations, Publishing Service, New York, New York 10017 (800) 253-9646; *Demographic Yearbook,* and *Statistical Yearbook.*

ANTIGUA AND BARBUDA - MEAT PRODUCTION - See ANTIGUA AND BARBUDA - LIVESTOCK AND POULTRY

ANTIGUA AND BARBUDA - MERCHANT SHIPPING

G.K. Hall and Company, 70 Lincoln Street, Boston, Massachusetts 02111 (617) 423-3990; *The World in Figures.*

Statistical Office of the United Nations, Publishing Service, New York, New York 10017 (800) 253-9646; *Statistical Yearbook.*

ANTIGUA AND BARBUDA - MILITARY

G.K. Hall and Company, 70 Lincoln Street, Boston, Massachusetts 02111 (617) 423-3990; *The World in Figures.*

ANTIGUA AND BARBUDA - MINING AND MINERAL PRODUCTS

G.K. Hall and Company, 70 Lincoln Street, Boston, Massachusetts 02111 (617) 423-3990; *The World in Figures.*

ANTIGUA AND BARBUDA - MONEY SUPPLY

G.K. Hall and Company, 70 Lincoln Street, Boston, Massachusetts 02111 (617) 423-3990; *The World in Figures.*

The World Bank, 1818 H Street, NW, Washington, D.C. 20433 (202) 447-1234; *World Tables.*

ANTIGUA AND BARBUDA - MOTOR VEHICLES IN USE

G.K. Hall and Company, 70 Lincoln Street, Boston, Massachusetts 02111 (617) 423-3990; *The World in Figures.*

ANTIGUA AND BARBUDA - MUSEUMS

United Nations Educational, Scientific and Cultural Organization (UNESCO), 7 Place de Fontenoy, F-75700 Paris, France (Telephone Number in U.S. (212) 963-5981); *Statistical Yearbook.*

ANTIGUA AND BARBUDA - NATALITY - See ANTIGUA AND BARBUDA - BIRTH RATES

ANTIGUA AND BARBUDA - NATIONAL ACCOUNTS

Statistical Office of the United Nations, Publishing Service, New York, New York 10017 (800) 253-9646; *National Accounts Statistics.*

ANTIGUA AND BARBUDA - NATIONAL INCOME

G.K. Hall and Company, 70 Lincoln Street, Boston, Massachusetts 02111 (617) 423-3990; *The World in Figures.*

Statistical Office of the United Nations, Publishing Service, New York, New York 10017 (800) 253-9646; *Statistical Yearbook.*

ANTIGUA AND BARBUDA - NEWSPAPER PRODUCTION - See ANTIGUA AND BARBUDA - FORESTRY AND FOREST PRODUCTS

ANTIGUA AND BARBUDA - OCCUPATIONS - See ANTIGUA AND BARBUDA - LABOR FORCE

ANTIGUA AND BARBUDA - PESTICIDE USE

Food and Agricultural Organization of the United Nations (FAO) Via Delle Terme di Caracalla, 00100 Rome, Italy (Telephone Number in U.S. (202) 653-2400); *The State of Food and Agriculture.*

ANTIGUA AND BARBUDA - PETROLEUM INDUSTRY

Food and Agricultural Organization of the United Nations (FAO) Via Delle Terme di Caracalla, 00100 Rome, Italy (Telephone Number in U.S. (202) 653-2400); *The State of Food and Agriculture.*

G.K. Hall and Company, 70 Lincoln Street, Boston, Massachusetts 02111 (617) 423-3990; *The World in Figures.*

Statistical Office of the United Nations, Publishing Service, New York, New York 10017 (800) 253-9646; *Statistical Yearbook.*

ANTIGUA AND BARBUDA - PIGS - See ANTIGUA AND BARBUDA - LIVESTOCK AND POULTRY

ANTIGUA AND BARBUDA - POPULATION

Food and Agricultural Organization of the United Nations (FAO), Via delle Terme di Caracalla, 00100 Rome, Italy (Telephone Number in U.S. (202) 653-2400); *Production Yearbook.*

G.K. Hall and Company, 70 Lincoln Street, Boston, Massachusetts 02111 (617) 423-3990; *The World in Figures.*

International Labour Office, I.L.O. Publications, CH-1211, Geneva 22, Switzerland; *Yearbook of Labour Statistics.*

Statistical Office of the United Nations, Publishing Service, New York, New York 10017 (800) 253-9646; *Demographic Yearbook,* and *Statistical Yearbook.*

World Health Organization, Office of Publications, Avenue Appia, CH-1211 Geneva 27, Switzerland (Telephone Number in U.S. (518) 436-9686); *World Health Statistics Annual.*

ANTIGUA AND BARBUDA - PRICES

Food and Agricultural Organization of the United Nations (FAO), Via delle Terme di Caracalla, 00100 Rome, Italy (Telephone Number in U.S. (202) 653-2400); *Production Yearbook,* and *The State of Food and Agriculture.*

G.K. Hall and Company, 70 Lincoln Street, Boston, Massachusetts 02111 (617) 423-3990; *The World in Figures.*

International Labour Office, I.L.O. Publications, CH-1211, Geneva 22, Switzerland; *Yearbook of Labour Statistics.*

Statistical Office of the United Nations, Publishing Service, New York, New York 10017 (800) 253-9646; *Economic Survey of Latin America and the Caribbean.*

ANTIGUA AND BARBUDA - PRODUCTION

G.K. Hall and Company, 70 Lincoln Street, Boston, Massachusetts 02111 (617) 423-3990; *The World in Figures.*

ANTIGUA AND BARBUDA - RAILWAYS

G.K. Hall and Company, 70 Lincoln Street, Boston, Massachusetts 02111 (617) 423-3990; *The World in Figures.*

ANTIGUA AND BARBUDA - RENT PRICES

International Labour Office, I.L.O. Publications, CH-1211, Geneva 22, Switzerland; *Yearbook of Labour Statistics.*

ANTIGUA AND BARBUDA - RETAIL TRADE

G.K. Hall and Company, 70 Lincoln Street, Boston, Massachusetts 02111 (617) 423-3990; *The World in Figures.*

ANTIGUA AND BARBUDA - SCIENTISTS AND ENGINEERS

Statistical Office of the United Nations, Publishing Service, New York, New York 10017 (800) 253-9646; *Statistical Yearbook.*

ANTIGUA AND BARBUDA - SHEEP - See ANTIGUA AND BARBUDA - LIVESTOCK AND POULTRY

ANTIGUA AND BARBUDA - SOCIAL DATA

G.K. Hall and Company, 70 Lincoln Street, Boston, Massachusetts 02111 (617) 423-3990; *The World in Figures.*

ANTIGUA AND BARBUDA - STOCKS - COMMODITY - MARKET PRICE - INDEX

Food and Agricultural Organization of the United Nations (FAO) Via Delle Terme di Caracalla, 00100 Rome, Italy (Telephone Number in U.S. (202) 653-2400); *The State of Food and Agriculture.*

ANTIGUA AND BARBUDA - SUGAR PRODUCTION

Statistical Office of the United Nations, Publishing Service, New York, New York 10017 (800) 253-9646; *Statistical Yearbook.*

ANTIGUA AND BARBUDA - TAXATION

G.K. Hall and Company, 70 Lincoln Street, Boston, Massachusetts 02111 (617) 423-3990; *The World in Figures.*

The World Bank, 1818 H Street, NW, Washington, D.C. 20433 (202) 447-1234; *World Tables.*

ANTIGUA AND BARBUDA - TELEPHONES IN USE

American Telephone and Telegraph Company, 26 Parsippany Road, Whippany, New Jersey 07981 (800) 338-4038; *The World's Telephones.*

G.K. Hall and Company, 70 Lincoln Street, Boston, Massachusetts 02111 (617) 423-3990; *The World in Figures.*

Statistical Office of the United Nations, Publishing Service, New York, New York 10017 (800) 253-9646; *Statistical Yearbook.*

ANTIGUA AND BARBUDA - TEXTILE INDUSTRY

G.K. Hall and Company, 70 Lincoln Street, Boston, Massachusetts 02111 (617) 423-3990; *The World in Figures.*

ANTIGUA AND BARBUDA - TOURISM

G.K. Hall and Company, 70 Lincoln Street, Boston, Massachusetts 02111 (617) 423-3990; *The World in Figures.*

World Tourism Organization, Calle Capitan Haya 42, E-28020 Madrid, Spain; *Yearbook of Tourism Statistics.*

ANTIGUA AND BARBUDA - TRADE - See ANTIGUA AND BARBUDA - FOREIGN TRADE

ANTIGUA AND BARBUDA - TRANSPORTATION AND COMMUNICATIONS

G.K. Hall and Company, 70 Lincoln Street, Boston, Massachusetts 02111 (617) 423-3990; *The World in Figures.*

ANTIGUA AND BARBUDA - UNEMPLOYMENT

International Labour Office, I.L.O. Publications, CH-1211, Geneva 22, Switzerland; *Yearbook of Labour Statistics.*

Statistical Office of the United Nations, Publishing Service, New York, New York 10017 (800) 253-9646; *Statistical Yearbook.*

ANTIGUA AND BARBUDA - VITAL STATISTICS

G.K. Hall and Company, 70 Lincoln Street, Boston, Massachusetts 02111 (617) 423-3990; *The World in Figures.*

Statistical Office of the United Nations, Publishing Service, New York, New York 10017 (800) 253-9646; *Statistical Yearbook.*

World Health Organization, Office of Publications, Avenue Appia, CH-1211 Geneva 27, Switzerland (Telephone Number in U.S. (518) 436-9686); *World Health Statistics Annual.*

ANTIGUA AND BARBUDA - WAGES

G.K. Hall and Company, 70 Lincoln Street, Boston, Massachusetts 02111 (617) 423-3990; *The World in Figures.*

International Labour Office, I.L.O. Publications, CH-1211, Geneva 22, Switzerland; *Yearbook of Labour Statistics.*

ANTIGUA AND BARBUDA - WEATHER

G.K. Hall and Company, 70 Lincoln Street, Boston, Massachusetts 02111 (617) 423-3990; *The World in Figures.*

ANTIMONY

U.S. Department of the Interior, Bureau of Mines, 810 Seventh Street, NW, Washington, D.C. 20241 (202) 501-9649; *Mineral Commodity Summaries.*

APPAREL AND ACCESSORY STORES - RETAIL - EARNINGS

U.S. Department of Commerce, Bureau of Census, Suitland, Maryland 20233 (301) 763-4040; *Census of Retail Trade,* and *County Business Patterns.*

U.S. Department of Labor, Bureau of Labor Statistics, Two Massachusetts Avenue, NE, Washington, D.C. 20212 (202) 606-7828; *Employment and Earnings,* and Bulletins 2370 and 2429.

APPAREL AND ACCESSORY STORES - RETAIL - EMPLOYEES

U.S. Department of Commerce, Bureau of Census, Suitland, Maryland 20233 (301) 763-4040; *Census of Retail Trade,* and *County Business Patterns.*

U.S. Department of Labor, Bureau of Labor Statistics, Two Massachusetts Avenue, NE, Washington, D.C. 20212 (202) 606-7828; *Employment and Earnings,* and Bulletins 2370 and 2429.

APPAREL AND ACCESSORY STORES - RETAIL - ESTABLISHMENTS

U.S. Department of Commerce, Bureau of Census, Suitland, Maryland 20233 (301) 763-4040; *Census of Retail Trade,* and *County Business Patterns.*

APPAREL AND ACCESSORY STORES - RETAIL - INVENTORIES

U.S. Department of Commerce, Bureau of Census, Suitland, Maryland 20233 (301) 763-4040; *Current Business Reports, Combined Annual and Revised Monthly Retail Trade.*

APPAREL AND ACCESSORY STORES - RETAIL - SALES

Market Statistics, 633 Third Avenue, New York, New York 10017 (212) 986-4000; *The Survey of Buying Power Data Service.*

U.S. Department of Commerce, Bureau of Census, Suitland, Maryland 20233 (301) 763-4040; *Census of Retail Trade, Current Business Reports, Combined Annual and Revised Monthly Retail Trade,* and unpublished data.

APPAREL AND OTHER TEXTILE PRODUCTS INDUSTRY - MANUFACTURING - EARNINGS

U.S. Department of Commerce, Bureau of Census, Suitland, Maryland 20233 (301) 763-4040; *County Business Patterns.*

U.S. Department of Labor, Bureau of Labor Statistics, Two Massachusetts Avenue, NE, Washington, D.C. 20212 (202) 606-7828; *Employment and Earnings,* and Bulletins 2370 and 2429.

APPAREL AND OTHER TEXTILE PRODUCTS INDUSTRY - MANUFACTURING - EMPLOYEES

U.S. Department of Commerce, Bureau of Census, Suitland, Maryland 20233 (301) 763-4040; *County Business Patterns.*

U.S. Department of Commerce, International Trade Administration, Fourteenth Street between Constitution Avenue and E Street, NW, Washington, D.C. 20230 (202) 482-5487; *Employment and Earnings, Monthly Labor Review,* and Bulletins 2370 and 2429.

APPAREL AND OTHER TEXTILE PRODUCTS INDUSTRY - MANUFACTURING - GROSS NATIONAL PRODUCT

U.S. Department of Commerce, Bureau of Economic Analysis, Fourteenth Street between Constitution Avenue and E Street, NW, Washington, D.C. 20230 (202) 606-9900; *The National Income and Product Accounts of the United States,* and *Survey of Current Business.*

APPAREL AND OTHER TEXTILE PRODUCTS INDUSTRY - MANUFACTURING - MERGERS AND ACQUISITIONS

Securities Data Company, 1180 Raymond Boulevard, Newark, New Jersey 07102 (201) 622-3100; *Merger and Corporate Transactions Database.*

APPAREL AND OTHER TEXTILE PRODUCTS INDUSTRY - MANUFACTURING - OCCUPATIONAL SAFETY

U.S. Department of Labor, Bureau of Labor Statistics, Two Massachusetts Avenue, NE, Washington, D.C. 20212 (202) 606-7828; *Occupational Injuries and Illnesses in the United States by Industry.*

APPAREL AND OTHER TEXTILE PRODUCTS INDUSTRY - MANUFACTURING - PROFITS

Forbes, Inc., 60 Fifth Avenue, New York, New York 10011 (212) 620-2200; *Forbes Annual Report on American Industry.*

APPAREL AND OTHER TEXTILE PRODUCTS INDUSTRY - MANUFACTURING - SHIPMENTS

Forbes, Inc., 60 Fifth Avenue, New York, New York 10011 (212) 620-2200; *Forbes Annual Report on American Industry.*

APPAREL GOODS - ADVERTISING

Publishers Information Bureau, 575 Lexington Avenue, New York, New York 10022 (212) 752-0055.

Television Bureau of Advertising, Inc., 850 Third Avenue, New York, New York 10022 (212) 486-1111; data compiled by Competitive Media Reporting, 11 West 42nd Street, New York, New York 10019 (212) 789-1400.

APPAREL GOODS - CONSUMER EXPENDITURES

U.S. Department of Labor, Bureau of Labor Statistics, Two Massachusetts Avenue, NE, Washington, D.C. 20212 (202) 606-7828; *Consumer Expenditures in 1992.*APPAREL GOODS - FOREIGN TRADE

U.S. Department of Commerce, Bureau of Census, Suitland, Maryland 20233 (301) 763-4040; *U.S. Merchandise Trade: Exports,*

General Imports, and Imports for Consumption.

APPAREL GOODS - PRICES

U.S. Department of Labor, Bureau of Labor Statistics, Two Massachusetts Avenue, NE, Washington, D.C. 20212 (202) 606-7828; *Handbook of Labor Statistics, Monthly Labor Review,* and *CPI Detailed Report.*

APPEALS, UNITED STATES COURTS OF - CASES

Administrative Office of the United States Courts, United States Supreme Court Building, One First Street, NE, Washington, D.C. 20544 (202) 633-6094; *Annual Report of the Director.*

APPLES

U.S. Department of Agriculture, Economic Research Service, Fourteenth Street and Constitution Avenue, SW, Washington, D.C. 20250 (202) 219-1504; *Food Consumption Prices, and Expenditures, Economic Indicators of the Farm Sector: National Financial Summary, Agricultural Outlook,* and unpublished data.

U.S. Department of Agriculture, National Agricultural Statistics Service, Fourteenth Street and Independence Avenue, SW, Washington, D.C. 20250; (202) 219-1504; *Noncitrus Fruits and Nuts.*

APPLIANCES, HOUSEHOLD - HOMES WITH

U.S. Department of Energy, Energy Information Administration, 1000 Independence Avenue, SW, Washington, D.C. 20585 (202) 586-8800; *Housing Characteristics.*

APPLIANCES (HOUSEHOLD) INDUSTRY - MANUFACTURING - EARNINGS

U.S. Department of Commerce, Bureau of Census, Suitland, Maryland 20233 (301) 763-4040; *Annual Survey of Manufactures,* and *Census of Manufactures.*

U.S. Department of Labor, Bureau of Labor Statistics, Two Massachusetts Avenue, NE, Washington, D.C. 20212 (202) 606-7828; *Employment and Earnings,* and Bulletins 2370 and 2429.

APPLIANCES (HOUSEHOLD) INDUSTRY - MANUFACTURING - EMPLOYEES

U.S. Department of Commerce, Bureau of Census, Suitland, Maryland 20233 (301) 763-4040; *Annual Survey of Manufactures,* and *Census of Manufactures.*

U.S. Department of Labor, Bureau of Labor Statistics, Two Massachusetts Avenue, NE, Washington, D.C. 20212 (202) 606-7828; *Employment and Earnings,* and Bulletins 2370 and 2429.

APPLIANCES (HOUSEHOLD) INDUSTRY - MANUFACTURING - ESTABLISHMENTS

U.S. Department of Commerce, Bureau of Census, Suitland, Maryland 20233 (301) 763-4040; *Census of Manufactures,* and *Annual Survey of Manufactures.*

APPLIANCES (HOUSEHOLD) INDUSTRY - MANUFACTURING - INVENTORIES

U.S. Department of Commerce, Bureau of Census, Suitland, Maryland 20233 (301) 763-4040; *Current Industrial Reports, Manufactures' Shipments, Inventories, and Orders.*

APPLIANCES (HOUSEHOLD) INDUSTRY - MANUFACTURING - PRODUCTIVITY

U.S. Department of Labor, Bureau of Labor Statistics, Two Massachusetts Avenue, NE, Washington, D.C. 20212 (202) 606-7828; *Productivity Measures for Selected Industries and Government Services,* and Bulletin 2440.

APPLIANCES (HOUSEHOLD) INDUSTRY - MANUFACTURING - SHIPMENTS

U.S. Department of Commerce, Bureau of Census, Suitland, Maryland 20233 (301) 763-4040; *Annual Survey of Manufactures, Census of Manufactures,* and *Current Industrial Reports, Manufactures' Shipments, Inventories, and Orders.*

APPLIANCES (HOUSEHOLD) INDUSTRY - MANUFACTURING - VALUE ADDED

U.S. Department of Commerce, Bureau of Census, Suitland, Maryland 20233 (301) 763-4040; *Annual Survey of Manufactures,* and *Census of Manufactures.*

APRICOTS

U.S. Department of Agriculture, National Agricultural Statistics Service, Fourteenth Street and Independence Avenue, SW, Washington, D.C. 20250 (202) 219-1504; *Noncitrus Fruits and Nuts,* and unpublished data.

AQUACULTURE

U.S. Department of Agriculture, Economic Research Service, Fourteenth and Independence Avenue, SW, Washington, D.C. 20005-4789 (202) 219-1504; *Economic Indicators of the Farm Sector: National Financial Summary,* and *USDA.*

ARCHERY

National Sporting Goods Association, Lake Center Plaza Building, 1699 Wall Street, Mount Prospect, Illinois 60056 (708) 439-4000; *The Sporting Goods Market in 1993.*

ARCHITECTURAL SERVICES - See ENGINEERING AND ARCHITECTURAL SERVICES

AREA OF - FOREIGN COUNTRIES

Statistical Office of the United Nations, New York, New York 10017 (800) 253-9646; *Demographic Yearbook.*

U.S. Department of Commerce, Bureau of the Census, Suitland, Maryland 20233 (301) 763-4040; *International Data Base,* and *World Population Profile.*

AREA OF - FOREST LAND

U.S. Department of Agriculture, Forest Service, Fourteenth Street and Independence Avenue, SW, Washington, D.C. 20250 (202) 720-3760; *Forest Resources of the U.S., Land Areas of the National Forest System,* and unpublished data.

AREA OF - OUTLYING AREAS OF UNITED STATES

U.S. Department of Commerce, Bureau of the Census, Suitland, Maryland 20233 (301) 763-4040; *Census of Population and Housing,* and unpublished data.

AREA OF - PARKS

National Association of State Park Directors, 126 Mill Branch Road, Tallahassee, Florida 32312 (904) 893-4959; *Annual Information Exchange*.

U.S. Department of the Interior, National Park Service, C Street between Eighteenth and Nineteenth Streets, NW, Washington, D.C. 20240 (202) 208-6843; *National Park Statistical Abstract*, and unpublished data.

AREA OF - UNITED STATES

U.S. Department of Commerce, Bureau of the Census, Suitland, Maryland 20233 (301) 763-4040; *Census of Population and Housing, Current Population Reports, International Data Base*, and *World Population Profile*.

AREA OF - UNITED STATES - CITIES

U.S. Department of Commerce, Bureau of the Census, Suitland, Maryland 20233 (301) 763-4040; *Census of Population and Housing*, and unpublished data.

AREA OF - UNITED STATES - PUBLIC DOMAIN

U.S. Department of the Interior, 1849 C Street, NW, Washington, D.C. 20240 (202) 208-3171; estimated area, Bureau of Land Management; all other data, Office of the Secretary, *Areas of Acquisition to the Territory of the United States*.

AREA OF - UNITED STATES - TERRITORIAL EXPANSION

U.S. Department of Commerce, Bureau of the Census, Suitland, Maryland 20233 (301) 763-4040; *Census of Population and Housing*.

AREA OF - UNITED STATES - WATER

U.S. Department of Commerce, Bureau of the Census, Suitland, Maryland 20233 (301) 763-4040; *Current Population Reports, Census of Population and Housing, Areas of the United States*, and unpublished data.

AREA OF - WORLD

Statistical Office of the United Nations, New York, New York 10017 (800) 253-9646; *Demographic Yearbook*.

U.S. Department of Commerce, Bureau of the Census, Suitland, Maryland 20233 (301) 763-4040; *International Data Base*, and *World Population Profile*.

Argentina - National Statistical Office

Instituto Nacional de Estadistica y Censos, Hipolito Yrigoyen 250, Piso 12, Of 1210, Buenos Aires, Argentina.

Argentina - Primary Statistics Sources

Direccion General de Estadistica y Censos, Instituto Nacional de Estadistica y Censos, Hipolita Yrigoyen 250, Buenos Aires, Argentina; *Anuario estadistico*. (Statistical Yearbook), and *Boletin estadistico Trimestral* (Quarterly Statistical Bulletin.)

ARGENTINA - AGRICULTURE

The Economist Intelligence Unit, 111 West 57th Street, New York, New York 10019 (800) 938-4685; *The New Latin America Market Atlas*.

Euromonitor Publications Limited, 87-88 Turnmill Street, London EC1M 5QU, England; *International Marketing Data and Statistics*, and *Third World Economic Handbook*.

Facts on File, 460 Park Avenue South, New York, New York 10016 (800) 443-8323; *The New Book of World Rankings*. -

Federal Statistical Office, Gustav - Stresemann - Ring 11, D-6200 Wiesbaden, Germany; *Argentina*.

Food and Agricultural Organization of the United Nations (FAO), Via delle Terme di Caracalla, 00100 Rome, Italy (Telephone Number in U.S. (202) 653-2400); *Production Yearbook, The State of Food and Agriculture*, and *Trade Yearbook*.

Gale Research Incorporated, 835 Penobscot Building, Detroit, Michigan 48226 (800) 877-4253; *International Historical Statistics The Americas and Australasia*.

G.K. Hall and Company, 70 Lincoln Street, Boston, Massachusetts 02111 (617) 423-3990; *The World in Figures*.

Inter-American Development Bank, 1300 New York Avenue, NW, Washington, D.C. 20577 (202) 623-1753; *Economic and Social Progress in Latin America*.

Statistical Office of the United Nations, Publishing Service, New York, New York 10017 (800) 253-9646; *Statistical Yearbook*, and *Statistical Yearbook for Latin America and the Caribbean*.

Times Books, 201 East 50th Street, New York, New York 10022 (212) 751-2600; *The Economist Book of Vital World Statistics*.

U.C.L.A. Latin American Center Publications, University of California, Los Angeles, California 90024 (310) 825-6634; *Statistical Abstract of Latin America*.

The World Bank, 1818 H Street, NW, Washington, D.C. 20433 (202) 477-1234; *World Tables*.

ARGENTINA - AIRLINE SERVICE

The Economist Intelligence Unit, 111 West 57th Street, New York, New York 10019 (800) 938-4685; *The New Latin America Market Atlas*.

Facts on File, 460 Park Avenue South, New York, New York 10016 (800) 443-8323; *The New Book of World Rankings*.

G.K. Hall and Company, 70 Lincoln Street, Boston, Massachusetts 02111 (617) 423-3990; *The World in Figures*.

International Civil Aviation Organization, 1000 Sherbrooke Street West, Suite 400, Montreal, Quebec, Canada H3A 2R2 (514) 285-8219; *Civil Aviation Statistics of the World*.

Statistical Office of the United Nations, Publishing Service, New York, New York 10017 (800) 253-9646; *Statistical Yearbook*.

Times Books, 201 East 50th Street, New York, New York 10022 (212) 751-2600; *The Economist Book of Vital World Statistics*.

ARGENTINA - ALMOND PRODUCTION - See ARGENTINA - CROPS

ARGENTINA - ALUMINUM PRODUCTION - See ARGENTINA - MINING AND MINERAL PRODUCTS

ARGENTINA - ANIMAL HEALTH

Food and Agricultural Organization of the United Nations (FAO), Via delle Terme di Caracalla, 00100 Rome, Italy (Telephone Number in U.S. (202) 653-2400); *Animal Health Yearbook.*

ARGENTINA - APPLE PRODUCTION - See ARGENTINA - CROPS

ARGENTINA - AREA AND DENSITY OF POPULATION

Euromonitor Publications Limited, 87-88 Turnmill Street, London EC1M 5QU, England; *International Marketing Data and Statistics.*

Facts on File, 460 Park Avenue South, New York, New York 10016 (800) 443-8323; *The New Book of World Rankings.*

Federal Statistical Office, Gustav - Stresemann - Ring 11, D-6200 Wiesbaden, Germany; *Argentina.*

Food and Agricultural Organization of the United Nations (FAO) Via Delle Terme di Caracalla, 00100 Rome, Italy (Telephone Number in U.S. (202) 653-2400); *The State of Food and Agriculture.*

G.K. Hall and Company, 70 Lincoln Street, Boston, Massachusetts 02111 (617) 423-3990; *The World in Figures.*

Inter-American Development Bank, 1300 New York Avenue, NW, Washington, D.C. 20577 (202) 623-1753; *Economic and Social Progress in Latin America.*

Statistical Office of the United Nations, Publishing Service, New York, New York 10017 (800) 253-9646; *Statistical Yearbook.*

Times Books, 201 East 50th Street, New York, New York 10022 (212) 751-2600; *The Economist Book of Vital World Statistics.*

ARGENTINA - ARMS EXPORTS AND IMPORTS

U.S. Arms Control and Disarmament Agency, 320 Twenty-first Street, NW, Washington, D.C. 20451 (202) 647-8677; *World Military Expenditures and Arms Transfers.*

ARGENTINA - ARTICHOKE PRODUCTION - See ARGENTINA - CROPS

ARGENTINA - BALANCE OF PAYMENTS

The Economist Intelligence Unit, 111 West 57th Street, New York, New York 10019 (800) 938-4685; *The New Latin America Market Atlas,* and *The World Market Atlas.*

Euromonitor Publications Limited, 87-88 Turnmill Street, London EC1M 5QU, England; *Third World Economic Handbook.*

Federal Statistical Office, Gustav - Stresemann - Ring 11, D-6200 Wiesbaden, Germany; *Argentina.*

G.K. Hall and Company, 70 Lincoln Street, Boston, Massachusetts 02111 (617) 423-3990; *The World in Figures.*

Inter-American Development Bank, 1300 New York Avenue, NW, Washington, D.C. 20577 (202) 623-1753; *Economic and Social Progress in Latin America.*

International Monetary Fund, 700 Nineteenth Street, NW, Washington, D.C. 20431 (202) 623-7000; *Balance of Payments Yearbook,* and *International Financial Statistics.*

Organization of American States (OAS), General Secretariat, Washington, D.C. 20006 (202) 458-3533; *Statistical Bulletin of the OAS.*

Statistical Office of the United Nations, Publishing Service, New York, New York 10017 (800) 253-9646; *Economic Survey of Latin America and the Caribbean,* and *Statistical Yearbook for Latin America and the Caribbean.*

Times Books, 201 East 50th Street, New York, New York 10022 (212) 751-2600; *The Economist Book of Vital World Statistics.*

U.C.L.A. Latin American Center Publications, University of California, Los Angeles, California 90024 (310) 825-6634; *Statistical Yearbook for Latin America and the Caribbean.*

The World Bank, 1818 H Street, NW, Washington, D.C. 20433 (202) 477-1234; *World Tables.*

ARGENTINA - BANKING

Facts on File, 460 Park Avenue South, New York, New York 10016 (800) 443-8323; *The New Book of World Rankings.*

G.K. Hall and Company, 70 Lincoln Street, Boston, Massachusetts 02111 (617) 423-3990; *The World in Figures.*

Inter-American Development Bank, 1300 New York Avenue, NW, Washington, D.C. 20577 (202) 623-1753; *Economic and Social Progress in Latin America.*

International Monetary Fund, 700 Nineteenth Street, NW, Washington, D.C. 20431 (202) 623-7000; *Government Finance Statistics Yearbook,* and *International Financial Statistics.*

Statistical Office of the United Nations, Publishing Service, New York, New York 10017 (800) 253-9646; *Statistical Yearbook for Latin America and the Caribbean.*

ARGENTINA - BARLEY PRODUCTION - See ARGENTINA - CROPS

ARGENTINA - BEER PRODUCTION

Facts on File, 460 Park Avenue South, New York, New York 10016 (800) 443-8323; *The New Book of World Rankings.*

Statistical Office of the United Nations, Publishing Service, New York, New York 10017 (800) 253-9646; *Statistical Yearbook.*

ARGENTINA - BIRTH RATE

Euromonitor Publications Limited, 87-88 Turnmill Street, London EC1M 5QU, England; *Third World Economic Handbook.*

Facts on File, 460 Park Avenue South, New York, New York 10016 (800) 443-8323; *The New Book of World Rankings.*

Statistical Office of the United Nations, Publishing Service, New York, New York 10017 (800) 253-9646; *Demographic Yearbook, Statistical Yearbook,* and *Statistical Yearbook for Latin America and the Caribbean.*

The World Bank, 1818 H Street, NW, Washington, D.C. 20433 (202) 477-1234; *World Tables.*

World Health Organization, Office of Publications, Avenue Appia, CH-1211 Geneva 27, Switzerland (Telephone Number in U.S. (518) 436-9686); *World Health Statistics Annual.*

ARGENTINA - BONDS

G.K. Hall and Company, 70 Lincoln Street, Boston, Massachusetts 02111 (617) 423-3990; *The World in Figures.*

Inter-American Development Bank, 1300 New York Avenue, NW, Washington, D.C. 20577 (202) 623-1753; *Economic and Social Progress in Latin America.*

International Monetary Fund, 700 Nineteenth Street, NW, Washington, D.C. 20431 (202) 623-7000; *Government Finance Statistics Yearbook.*

ARGENTINA - BOOK PRODUCTION

G.K. Hall and Company, 70 Lincoln Street, Boston, Massachusetts 02111 (617) 423-3990; *The World in Figures.*

United Nations Educational, Scientific and Cultural Organization (UNESCO), 7 Place de Fontenoy, F-75700 Paris, France (Telephone Number in U.S. (212) 963-5981); *Statistical Yearbook.*

ARGENTINA - BROADCASTING

Billboard Limited, P.O. Box 9027, 1006 AA Amsterdam, The Netherlands (Telephone Number in U.S. (212) 764-7300); *World Radio TV Handbook.*

Facts on File, 460 Park Avenue South, New York, New York 10016 (800) 443-8323; *The New Book of World Rankings.*

G.K. Hall and Company, 70 Lincoln Street, Boston, Massachusetts 02111 (617) 423-3990; *The World in Figures.*

Times Books, 201 East 50th Street, New York, New York 10022 (212) 751-2600; *The Economist Book of Vital World Statistics.*

ARGENTINA - BUILDING CONSTRUCTION - See ARGENTINA - CONSTRUCTION INDUSTRY

ARGENTINA - BUSINESS

G.K. Hall and Company, 70 Lincoln Street, Boston, Massachusetts 02111 (617) 423-3990; *The World in Figures.*

Inter-American Development Bank, 1300 New York Avenue, NW, Washington, D.C. 20577 (202) 623-1753; *Economic and Social Progress in Latin America.*

ARGENTINA - BUSINESS AND PROFESSIONAL LICENSES

International Monetary Fund, 700 Nineteenth Street, NW, Washington, D.C. 20431 (202) 623-7000; *Government Finance Statistics Yearbook.*

ARGENTINA - BUTTER PRODUCTION - See DAIRY PRODUCTS

ARGENTINA - CALORIE SUPPLY

Food and Agricultural Organization of the United Nations (FAO) Via Delle Terme di Caracalla, 00100 Rome, Italy (Telephone Number in U.S. (202) 653-2400); *The State of Food and Agriculture.*

Statistical Office of the United Nations, Publishing Service, New York, New York 10017 (800) 253-9646; *Statistical Yearbook for Latin America and the Caribbean.*

ARGENTINA - CAPITAL INVESTMENT

Inter-American Development Bank, 1300 New York Avenue, NW, Washington, D.C. 20577 (202) 623-1753; *Economic and Social Progress in Latin America.*

ARGENTINA - CAPITAL REVENUE

Inter-American Development Bank, 1300 New York Avenue, NW, Washington, D.C. 20577 (202) 623-1753; *Economic and Social Progress in Latin America.*

International Monetary Fund, 700 Nineteenth Street, NW, Washington, D.C. 20431 (202) 623-7000; *Government Finance Statistics Yearbook.*

ARGENTINA - CASTOR BEAN PRODUCTION - See ARGENTINA - CROPS

ARGENTINA - CATTLE - See ARGENTINA - LIVESTOCK AND POULTRY

ARGENTINA - CAUSTIC SODA PRODUCTION

Statistical Office of the United Nations, Publishing Service, New York, New York 10017 (800) 253-9646; *Statistical Yearbook.*

ARGENTINA - CEMENT PRODUCTION - See ARGENTINA - MINING AND MINERAL PRODUCTS

ARGENTINA - CHEESE PRODUCTION - See ARGENTINA - DAIRY PRODUCTS

ARGENTINA - CHEMICALS (ORGANIC) PRODUCTION - See ARGENTINA - MINING AND MINERAL PRODUCTS

ARGENTINA - CHICK PEA PRODUCTION - See ARGENTINA - CROPS

ARGENTINA - CHICKENS - See ARGENTINA - LIVESTOCK AND POULTRY

ARGENTINA - CIGARETTE PRODUCTION - See ARGENTINA - TOBACCO PRODUCTION

ARGENTINA - CLASS STRUCTURE

G.K. Hall and Company, 70 Lincoln Street, Boston, Massachusetts 02111 (617) 423-3990; *The World in Figures.*

ARGENTINA - CLIMATE

Facts on File, 460 Park Avenue South, New York, New York 10016 (800) 443-8323; *The New Book of World Rankings.*

G.K. Hall and Company, 70 Lincoln Street, Boston, Massachusetts 02111 (617) 423-3990; *The World in Figures.*

ARGENTINA - CLOTHING EXPORTS AND IMPORTS

Euromonitor Publications Limited, 87-88 Turnmill Street, London EC1M 5QU, England; *Third World Economic Handbook.*

Statistical Office of the United Nations, Publishing Service, New York, New York 10017 (800) 253-9646; *Trade in Manufactures of Developing Countries.*

ARGENTINA - COAL PRODUCTION - See ARGENTINA - MINING AND MINERAL PRODUCTS

ARGENTINA - COFFEE PRODUCTION - See ARGENTINA - CROPS

ARGENTINA - COKE OVEN COKE PRODUCTION - See ARGENTINA - MINING AND MINERAL PRODUCTS

ARGENTINA - COMMUNICATIONS

Euromonitor Publications Limited, 87-88 Turnmill Street, London EC1M 5QU, England; *Third World Economic Handbook.*

Federal Statistical Office, Gustav - Stresemann - Ring 11, D-6200 Wiesbaden, Germany; *Argentina.*

G.K. Hall and Company, 70 Lincoln Street, Boston, Massachusetts 02111 (617) 423-3990; *The World in Figures.*

Inter-American Development Bank, 1300 New York Avenue, NW, Washington, D.C. 20577 (202) 623-1753; *Economic and Social Progress in Latin America.*

U.C.L.A. Latin American Center Publications, University of California, Los Angeles, California 90024 (310) 825-6634; *Statistical Abstract of Latin America.*

ARGENTINA - CONSTRUCTION INDUSTRY

The Economist Intelligence Unit, 111 West 57th Street, New York, New York 10019 (800) 938-4685; *The New Latin America Market Atlas.*

Facts on File, 460 Park Avenue South, New York, New York 10016 (800) 443-8323; *The New Book of World Rankings.*

Inter-American Development Bank, 1300 New York Avenue, NW, Washington, D.C. 20577 (202) 623-1753; *Economic and Social Progress in Latin America.*

Statistical Office of the United Nations, Publishing Service, New York, New York 10017 (800) 253-9646; *Construction Statistics Yearbook,* and *Statistical Yearbook.*

U.C.L.A. Latin American Center Publications, University of California, Los Angeles, California 90024 (310) 825-6634; *Statistical Abstract of Latin America.*

ARGENTINA - CONSUMER PRICE INDEX

G.K. Hall and Company, 70 Lincoln Street, Boston, Massachusetts 02111 (617) 423-3990; *The World in Figures.*

Statistical Office of the United Nations, Publishing Service, New York, New York 10017 (800) 253-9646; *Statistical Yearbook.*

U.C.L.A. Latin American Center Publications, University of California, Los Angeles, California 90024 (310) 825-6634; *Statistical Abstract of Latin America.*

ARGENTINA - CONSUMER PRICES

The Economist Intelligence Unit, 111 West 57th Street, New York, New York 10019 (800) 938-4685; *The New Latin America Market Atlas.*

International Labour Office, I.L.O. Publications, CH-1211, Geneva 22, Switzerland; *Yearbook of Labour Statistics.*

International Monetary Fund, 700 Nineteenth Street, NW, Washington, D.C. 20431 (202) 623-7000; *International Financial Statistics.*

Organization of American States (OAS), General Secretariat, Washington, D.C. 20006 (202) 458-3533; *Statistical Bulletin of the OAS.*

Times Books, 201 East 50th Street, New York, New York 10022 (212) 751-2600; *The Economist Book of Vital World Statistics.*

ARGENTINA - CONSUMPTION

The Economist Intelligence Unit, 111 West 57th Street, New York, New York 10019 (800) 938-4685; *The New Latin America Market Atlas.*

G.K. Hall and Company, 70 Lincoln Street, Boston, Massachusetts 02111 (617) 423-3990; *The World in Figures.*

Inter-American Development Bank, 1300 New York Avenue, NW, Washington, D.C. 20577 (202) 623-1753; *Economic and Social Progress in Latin America.*

International Lead and Zinc Study Group, Metro House, 58 St. James's Street, London SW1A 1LD, England; *Lead and Zinc Statistics.*

Statistical Office of the United Nations, Publishing Service, New York, New York 10017 (800) 253-9646; *Statistical Yearbook for Latin America and the Caribbean.*

ARGENTINA - COOPERATIVES

U.C.L.A. Latin American Center Publications, University of California, Los Angeles, California 90024 (310) 825-6634; *Statistical Abstract of Latin America.*

ARGENTINA - COPPER PRODUCTION - See ARGENTINA - MINING AND MINERAL PRODUCTS

ARGENTINA - CORN - See ARGENTINA - CROPS

ARGENTINA - CORPORATE INCOME TAXES - See ARGENTINA - TAXATION

ARGENTINA - CORPORATE TAXES - See ARGENTINA - TAXATION

ARGENTINA - COTTON - See ARGENTINA - CROPS

ARGENTINA - CRIME

Yale University Press, Yale Station, New Haven, Connecticut 06520 (203) 543-0940; *Violence and Crime in Cross-National Perspective.*

ARGENTINA - CROPS

Commodity Research Bureau, Incorporated, 75 Wall Street, New York, New York 10005 (212) 504-7754; *Commodity Year Book.*

The Economist Intelligence Unit, 111 West 57th Street, New York, New York 10019 (800) 938-4685; *The New Latin America Market Atlas.*

Facts on File, 460 Park Avenue South, New York, New York 10016 (800) 443-8323; *The New Book of World Rankings.*

Food and Agricultural Organization of the United Nations (FAO), Via delle Terme di Caracalla, 00100 Rome, Italy (Telephone Number in U.S. (202) 653-2400); *Production Yearbook,* and *State of Food and Agriculture.*

G.K. Hall and Company, 70 Lincoln Street, Boston, Massachusetts 02111 (617) 423-3990; *The World in Figures.*

International Monetary Fund, 700 Nineteenth Street, NW, Washington, D.C. 20431 (202) 623-7000; *International Financial Statistics.*

Statistical Office of the United Nations, Publishing Service, New York, New York 10017 (800) 253-9646; *Statistical Yearbook.*

ARGENTINA - CUSTOMS DUTIES

G.K. Hall and Company, 70 Lincoln Street, Boston, Massachusetts 02111 (617) 423-3990; *The World in Figures.*

Inter-American Development Bank, 1300 New York Avenue, NW, Washington, D.C. 20577 (202) 623-1753; *Economic and Social Progress in Latin America.*

International Monetary Fund, 700 Nineteenth Street, NW, Washington, D.C. 20431 (202) 623-7000; *Government Finance Statistics Yearbook.*

ARGENTINA - DAIRY PRODUCTS

Commodity Research Bureau, Incorporated, 75 Wall Street, New York, New York 10005 (212) 504-7754; *Commodity Year Book.*

Facts on File, 460 Park Avenue South, New York, New York 10016 (800) 443-8323; *The New Book of World Rankings.*

Food and Agricultural Organization of the United Nations (FAO) Via Delle Terme di Caracalla, 00100 Rome, Italy (Telephone Number in U.S. (202) 653-2400); *The State of Food and Agriculture.*

Statistical Office of the United Nations, Publishing Service, New York, New York 10017 (800) 253-9646; *Statistical Yearbook.*

ARGENTINA - DEATH RATE

Euromonitor Publications Limited, 87-88 Turnmill Street, London EC1M 5QU, England; *Third World Economic Handbook.*

G.K. Hall and Company, 70 Lincoln Street, Boston, Massachusetts 02111 (617) 423-3990; *The World in Figures.*

Statistical Office of the United Nations, Publishing Service, New York, New York 10017 (800) 253-9646; *Statistical Yearbook,* and *Statistical Yearbook for Latin America and the Caribbean.*

Times Books, 201 East 50th Street, New York, New York 10022 (212) 751-2600; *The Economist Book of Vital World Statistics.*

World Health Organization, Office of Publications, Avenue Appia, CH-1211 Geneva 27, Switzerland (Telephone Number in U.S. (518) 436-9686); *World Health Statistics Annual.*

ARGENTINA - DEBT

The Economist Intelligence Unit, 111 West 57th Street, New York, New York 10019 (800) 938-4685; *The New Latin America Market Atlas.*

ARGENTINA - DEFENSE

The Economist Intelligence Unit, 111 West 57th Street, New York, New York 10019 (800) 938-4685; *The New Latin America Market Atlas.*

ARGENTINA - DEFENSE EXPENDITURES

G.K. Hall and Company, 70 Lincoln Street, Boston, Massachusetts 02111 (617) 423-3990; *The World in Figures.*

International Monetary Fund, 700 Nineteenth Street, NW, Washington, D.C. 20431 (202) 623-7000; *Government Finance Statistics Yearbook.*

U.S. Arms Control and Disarmament Agency, 320 Twenty-first Street, NW, Washington, D.C. 20451 (202) 647-8677; *World Military Expenditures and Arms Transfers.*

ARGENTINA - DEMOGRAPHY

The Economist Intelligence Unit, 111 West 57th Street, New York, New York 10019 (800) 938-4685; *The World Market Atlas.*

Facts on File, 460 Park Avenue South, New York, New York 10016 (800) 443-8323; *The New Book of World Rankings.*

G.K. Hall and Company, 70 Lincoln Street, Boston, Massachusetts 02111 (617) 423-3990; *The World in Figures.*

U.C.L.A. Latin American Center Publications, University of California, Los Angeles, California 90024 (310) 825-6634; *Statistical Abstract of Latin America.*

ARGENTINA - DEVELOPMENT ASSISTANCE

G.K. Hall and Company, 70 Lincoln Street, Boston, Massachusetts 02111 (617) 423-3990; *The World in Figures.*

Inter-American Development Bank, 1300 New York Avenue, NW, Washington, D.C. 20577 (202) 623-1753; *Economic and Social Progress in Latin America.*

Statistical Office of the United Nations, Publishing Service, New York, New York 10017 (800) 253-9646; *Statistical Yearbook.*

ARGENTINA - DIAMOND PRODUCTION - See ARGENTINA - MINING AND MINERAL PRODUCTS

ARGENTINA - DISCOUNT RATES

Inter-American Development Bank, 1300 New York Avenue, NW, Washington, D.C. 20577 (202) 623-1753; *Economic and Social Progress in Latin America.*

ARGENTINA - DISEASES

G.K. Hall and Company, 70 Lincoln Street, Boston, Massachusetts 02111 (617) 423-3990; *The World in Figures.*

World Health Organization, Office of Publications, Avenue Appia, CH-1211 Geneva 27, Switzerland (Telephone Number in U.S. (518) 436-9686); *World Health Statistics Annual.*

ARGENTINA - DIVORCE RATES

Facts on File, 460 Park Avenue South, New York, New York 10016 (800) 443-8323; *The New Book of World Rankings.*

Statistical Office of the United Nations, Publishing Service, New York, New York 10017 (800) 253-9646; *Demographic Yearbook.*

ARGENTINA - DOMESTIC PRODUCT

G.K. Hall and Company, 70 Lincoln Street, Boston, Massachusetts 02111 (617) 423-3990; *The World in Figures.*

ARGENTINA - DUCKS - See ARGENTINA - LIVESTOCK AND POULTRY

ARGENTINA - ECONOMY

Euromonitor Publications Limited, 87-88 Turnmill Street, London EC1M 5QU, England; *International Marketing Data and Statistics,* and *Third World Economic Handbook.*

Facts on File, 460 Park Avenue South, New York, New York 10016 (800) 443-8323; *The New Book of World Rankings.*

G.K. Hall and Company, 70 Lincoln Street, Boston, Massachusetts 02111 (617) 423-3990; *The World in Figures.*

Inter-American Development Bank, 1300 New York Avenue, NW, Washington, D.C. 20577 (202) 623-1753; *Economic and Social Progress in Latin America.*

Statistical Office of the United Nations, Publishing Service, New York, New York 10017 (800) 253-9646; *Economic Survey of Latin America and the Caribbean.*

U.C.L.A. Latin American Center Publications, University of California, Los Angeles, California 90024 (310) 825-6634; *Statistical Abstract of Latin America.*

ARGENTINA - EDUCATION

The Economist Intelligence Unit, 111 West 57th Street, New York, New York 10019 (800) 938-4685; *The New Latin America Market Atlas,* and *The World Market Atlas.*

Facts on File, 460 Park Avenue South, New York, New York 10016 (800) 443-8323; *The New Book of World Rankings.*

Federal Statistical Office, Gustav - Stresemann - Ring 11, D-6200 Wiesbaden, Germany; *Argentina.*

Gale Research Incorporated, 835 Penobscot Building, Detroit, Michigan 48226 (800) 877-4253; *International Historical Statistics the Americas and Australasia.*

G.K. Hall and Company, 70 Lincoln Street, Boston, Massachusetts 02111 (617) 423-3990; *The World in Figures.*

International Monetary Fund, 700 Nineteenth Street, NW, Washington, D.C. 20431 (202) 623-7000; *Government Finance Statistics Yearbook.*

Statistical Office of the United Nations, Publishing Service, New York, New York 10017 (800) 253-9646; *Statistical Yearbook for Latin America and the Caribbean.*

Times Books, 201 East 50th Street, New York, New York 10022 (212) 751-2600; *The Economist Book of Vital World Statistics.*

U.C.L.A. Latin American Center Publications, University of California, Los Angeles, California 90024 (310) 825-6634; *Statistical Abstract of Latin America.*

United Nations Educational, Scientific and Cultural Organization (UNESCO), 7 Place de Fontenoy, F-75700 Paris, France (Telephone Number in U.S. (212) 963-5981); *Statistical Yearbook.*

The World Bank, 1818 H Street, NW, Washington, D.C. 20433 (202) 477-1234; *World Tables.*

ARGENTINA - EGG PRODUCTION - See ARGENTINA - DAIRY PRODUCTS

ARGENTINA - ELECTRICITY

The Economist Intelligence Unit, 111 West 57th Street, New York, New York 10019 (800) 938-4685; *The New Latin America Market Atlas.*

Facts on File, 460 Park Avenue South, New York, New York 10016 (800) 443-8323; *The New Book of World Rankings.*

Inter-American Development Bank, 1300 New York Avenue, NW, Washington, D.C. 20577 (202) 623-1753; *Economic and Social Progress in Latin America.*

Penn Well Publishing Company, 1421 South Sheridan Road, P.O. Box 1260, Tulsa, Oklahoma 74101 (800) 752-9764; *International Energy Statistics Sourcebook.*

Statistical Office of the United Nations, Publishing Service, New York, New York 10017 (800) 253-9646; *Statistical Yearbook.*

Times Books, 201 East 50th Street, New York, New York 10022 (212) 751-2600; *The Economist Book of Vital World Statistics.*

ARGENTINA - EMPLOYMENT

Euromonitor Publications Limited, 87-88 Turnmill Street, London EC1M 5QU, England; *International Marketing Data and Statistics.*

Facts on File, 460 Park Avenue South, New York, New York 10016 (800) 443-8323; *The New Book of World Rankings.*

Federal Statistical Office, Gustav - Stresemann - Ring 11, D-6200 Wiesbaden, Germany; *Argentina.*

International Labour Office, I.L.O. Publications, CH-1211, Geneva 22, Switzerland; *Yearbook of Labour Statistics.*

Statistical Office of the United Nations, Publishing Service, New York, New York 10017 (800) 253-9646; *Statistical Yearbook for Latin America and the Caribbean.*

U.C.L.A. Latin American Center Publications, University of California, Los Angeles, California 90024 (310) 825-6634; *Statistical Abstract of Latin America.*

ARGENTINA - ENERGY

The Economist Intelligence Unit, 111 West 57th Street, New York, New York 10019 (800) 938-4685; *The New Latin America Market Atlas.*

Facts on File, 460 Park Avenue South, New York, New York 10016 (800) 443-8323; *The New Book of World Rankings.*

Food and Agricultural Organization of the United Nations (FAO) Via Delle Terme di Caracalla, 00100 Rome, Italy (Telephone Number in U.S. (202) 653-2400); *The State of Food and Agriculture.*

G.K. Hall and Company, 70 Lincoln Street, Boston, Massachusetts 02111 (617) 423-3990; *The World in Figures.*

Penn Well Publishing Company, 1421 South Sheridan Road, P.O. Box 1260, Tulsa, Oklahoma 74101 (800) 752-9764; *International Energy*

Statistics Sourcebook.

Statistical Office of the United Nations, Publishing Service, New York, New York 10017 (800) 253-9646; *Energy Statistics Yearbook, Statistical Yearbook,* and *Statistical Yearbook for Latin America and the Caribbean.*

Times Books, 201 East 50th Street, New York, New York 10022 (212) 751-2600; *The Economist Book of Vital World Statistics.*

U.C.L.A. Latin American Center Publications, University of California, Los Angeles, California 90024 (310) 825-6634; *Statistical Abstract of Latin America.*

ARGENTINA - ENGINEERING AND METAL PRODUCTS EXPORTS TO DEVELOPED COUNTRIES

Statistical Office of the United Nations, Publishing Service, New York, New York 10017 (800) 253-9646; *Trade in Manufactures of Developing Countries.*

ARGENTINA - EXCHANGE RATES

Euromonitor Publications Limited, 87-88 Turnmill Street, London EC1M 5QU, England; *International Marketing Data and Statistics.*

Inter-American Development Bank, 1300 New York Avenue, NW, Washington, D.C. 20577 (202) 623-1753; *Economic and Social Progress in Latin America.*

International Civil Aviation Organization, 1000 Sherbrooke Street West, Suite 400, Montreal, Quebec, Canada H3A 2R2 (514) 285-8219; *Civil Aviation Statistics of the World.*

International Monetary Fund, 700 Nineteenth Street, NW, Washington, D.C. 20431 (202) 623-7000; *International Financial Statistics.*

U.C.L.A. Latin American Center Publications, University of California, Los Angeles, California 90024 (310) 825-6634; *Statistical Abstract of Latin America.*

ARGENTINA - EXCHANGE TAXES

International Monetary Fund, 700 Nineteenth Street, NW, Washington, D.C. 20431 (202) 623-7000; *Government Finance Statistics Yearbook.*

Organization of American States (OAS), General Secretariat, Washington, D.C. 20006 (202) 458-3533; *Statistical Bulletin of the OAS.*

ARGENTINA - EXCISE TAXES - See ARGENTINA - TAXATION

ARGENTINA - EXPORTS

American Automobile Manufacturers Association, 1401 H Street, NW, Suite 900, Washington, D.C. 20005 (202) 326-5500; *World Motor Vehicle Data.*

The Economist Intelligence Unit, 111 West 57th Street, New York, New York 10019 (800) 938-4685; *The New Latin America Market Atlas,* and *The World Market Atlas.*

Euromonitor Publications Limited, 87-88 Turnmill Street, London EC1M 5QU, England; *International Marketing Data and Statistics,* and *Third World Economic Handbook.*

Food and Agricultural Organization of the United Nations (FAO) Via Delle Terme di Caracalla, 00100 Rome, Italy (Telephone Number in U.S. (202) 653-2400); *The State of Food and Agriculture.*

G.K. Hall and Company, 70 Lincoln Street, Boston, Massachusetts 02111 (617) 423-3990; *The World in Figures.*

Inter-American Development Bank, 1300 New York Avenue, NW, Washington, D.C. 20577 (202) 623-1753; *Economic and Social Progress in Latin America.*

International Lead and Zinc Study Group, Metro House, 58 St. James's Street, London SW1A 1LD, England; *Lead and Zinc Statistics.*

International Monetary Fund, 700 Nineteenth Street, NW, Washington, D.C. 20431 (202) 623-7000; *Direction of Trade Statistics, Government Finance Statistics Yearbook,* and *International Financial Statistics.*

Organization of American States (OAS), General Secretariat, Washington, D.C. 20006 (202) 458-3533; *Statistical Bulletin of the OAS.*

Statistical Office of the United Nations, Publishing Service, New York, New York 10017 (800) 253-9646; *Statistical Yearbook for Latin America and the Caribbean,* and *Trade in Manufactures of Developing Countries.*

Times Books, 201 East 50th Street, New York, New York 10022 (212) 751-2600; *The Economist Book of Vital World Statistics.*

The World Bank, 1818 H Street, NW, Washington, D.C. 20433 (202) 477-1234; *World Tables.*

ARGENTINA - EXTERNAL FINANCING

Inter-American Development Bank, 1300 New York Avenue, NW, Washington, D.C. 20577 (202) 623-1753; *Economic and Social Progress in Latin America.*

Statistical Office of the United Nations, Publishing Service, New York, New York 10017 (800) 253-9646; *Statistical Yearbook for Latin America and the Caribbean.*

ARGENTINA - EXTERNAL INDEBTEDNESS

Euromonitor Publications Limited, 87-88 Turnmill Street, London EC1M 5QU, England; *Third World Economic Handbook.*

Inter-American Development Bank, 1300 New York Avenue, NW, Washington, D.C. 20577 (202) 623-1753; *Economic and Social Progress in Latin America.*

Statistical Office of the United Nations, Publishing Service, New York, New York 10017 (800) 253-9646; *Statistical Yearbook for Latin America and the Caribbean.*

The World Bank, 1818 H Street, NW, Washington, D.C. 20433 (202) 477-1234; *World Tables.*

ARGENTINA - EXTERNAL TRADE

Food and Agricultural Organization of the United Nations (FAO) Via Delle Terme di Caracalla, 00100 Rome, Italy (Telephone Number in U.S. (202) 653-2400); *The State of Food and Agriculture,* and *Trade Yearbook.*

Gale Research Incorporated, 835 Penobscot Building, Detroit, Michigan 48226 (800) 877-4253; *International Historical Statistics the Americas and Australasia.*

G.K. Hall and Company, 70 Lincoln Street, Boston, Massachusetts 02111 (617) 423-3990; *The World in Figures.*

Inter-American Development Bank, 1300 New York Avenue, NW, Washington, D.C. 20577 (202) 623-1753; *Economic and Social Progress in Latin America.*

Statistical Office of the United Nations, Publishing Service, New York, New York 10017 (800) 253-9646; *Statistical Yearbook for Latin America and the Caribbean.*

ARGENTINA - FAMILY PLANNING

U.C.L.A. Latin American Center Publications, University of California, Los Angeles, California 90024 (310) 825-6634; *Statistical Abstract of Latin America.*

ARGENTINA - FARM CROPS - See ARGENTINA - CROPS

ARGENTINA - FEMALE WORKING POPULATION - See ARGENTINA - EMPLOYMENT

ARGENTINA - FERTILITY RATES

Facts on File, 460 Park Avenue South, New York, New York 10016 (800) 443-8323; *The New Book of World Rankings.*

Times Books, 201 East 50th Street, New York, New York 10022 (212) 751-2600; *The Economist Book of Vital World Statistics.*

The World Bank, 1818 H Street, NW, Washington, D.C. 20433 (202) 477-1234; *World Tables.*

ARGENTINA - FERTILIZER

The Economist Intelligence Unit, 111 West 57th Street, New York, New York 10019 (800) 938-4685; *The New Latin America Market Atlas.*

Food and Agricultural Organization of the United Nations (FAO), Via delle Terme di Caracalla, 00100 Rome, Italy (Telephone Number in U.S. (202) 653-2400); *Fertilizer Yearbook,* and *The State of Food and Agriculture.*

Statistical Office of the United Nations, Publishing Service, New York, New York 10017 (800) 253-9646; *Statistical Yearbook.*

ARGENTINA - FETAL MORTALITY

Statistical Office of the United Nations, Publishing Service, New York, New York 10017 (800) 253-9646; *Demographic Yearbook.*

ARGENTINA - FIBRE PRODUCTION - See ARGENTINA - TEXTILE INDUSTRY

ARGENTINA - FILM - See ARGENTINA - MOTION PICTURES

ARGENTINA - FINANCE

Facts on File, 460 Park Avenue South, New York, New York 10016 (800) 443-8323; *The New Book of World Rankings.*

Federal Statistical Office, Gustav - Stresemann - Ring 11, D-6200 Wiesbaden, Germany; *Argentina.*

Gale Research Incorporated, 835 Penobscot Building, Detroit, Michigan 48226 (800) 877-4253; *International Historical Statistics the Americas and Australasia.*

G.K. Hall and Company, 70 Lincoln Street, Boston, Massachusetts 02111 (617) 423-3990; *The World in Figures.*

Inter-American Development Bank, 1300 New York Avenue, NW, Washington, D.C. 20577 (202) 623-1753; *Economic and Social Progress in Latin America.*

International Monetary Fund, 700 Nineteenth Street, NW, Washington, D.C. 20431 (202) 623-7000; *Government Finance Statistics Yearbook,* and *International Financial Statistics.*

Organization of American States (OAS), General Secretariat, Washington, D.C. 20006 (202) 458-3533; *Statistical Bulletin of the OAS.*

U.C.L.A. Latin American Center Publications, University of California, Los Angeles, California 90024 (310) 825-6634; *Statistical Abstract of Latin America.*

ARGENTINA - FISHERIES

Facts on File, 460 Park Avenue South, New York, New York 10016 (800) 443-8323; *The New Book of World Rankings.*

Federal Statistical Office, Gustav - Stresemann - Ring 11, D-6200 Wiesbaden, Germany; *Argentina.*

Food and Agricultural Organization of the United Nations (FAO) Via Delle Terme di Caracalla, 00100 Rome, Italy (Telephone Number in U.S. (202) 653-2400); *The State of Food and Agriculture,* and *Yearbook of Fishery Statistics.*

Inter-American Development Bank, 1300 New York Avenue, NW, Washington, D.C. 20577 (202) 623-1753; *Economic and Social Progress in Latin America.*

Statistical Office of the United Nations, Publishing Service, New York, New York 10017 (800) 253-9646; *Statistical Yearbook.*

U.C.L.A. Latin American Center Publications, University of California, Los Angeles, California 90024 (310) 825-6634; *Statistical Abstract of Latin America.*

ARGENTINA - FLAX FIBRE PRODUCTION - See ARGENTINA - TEXTILE INDUSTRY

ARGENTINA - FLOUR PRODUCTION

Commodity Research Bureau, Incorporated, 75 Wall Street, New York, New York 10005 (212) 504-7754; *Commodity Year Book.*

Statistical Office of the United Nations, Publishing Service, New York, New York 10017 (800) 253-9646; *Statistical Yearbook.*

ARGENTINA - FOOD

Food and Agricultural Organization of the United Nations (FAO) Via Delle Terme di Caracalla, 00100 Rome, Italy (Telephone Number in U.S. (202) 653-2400); *Production Yearbook,* and *The State of Food and Agriculture.*

G.K. Hall and Company, 70 Lincoln Street, Boston, Massachusetts 02111 (617) 423-3990; *The World in Figures.*

Statistical Office of the United Nations, Publishing Service, New York, New York 10017 (800) 253-9646; *Trade in Manufactures of Developing Countries.*

ARGENTINA - FOREIGN AID

G.K. Hall and Company, 70 Lincoln Street, Boston, Massachusetts 02111 (617) 423-3990; *The World in Figures.*

Inter-American Development Bank, 1300 New York Avenue, NW, Washington, D.C. 20577 (202) 623-1753; *Economic and Social Progress in Latin America.*

ARGENTINA - FOREIGN DEBT

The Economist Intelligence Unit, 111 West 57th Street, New York, New York 10019 (800) 938-4685; *The New Latin America Market Atlas.*

Inter-American Development Bank, 1300 New York Avenue, NW, Washington, D.C. 20577 (202) 623-1753; *Economic and Social Progress in Latin America.*

International Monetary Fund, 700 Nineteenth Street, NW, Washington, D.C. 20431 (202) 623-7000; *Government Finance Statistics Yearbook.*

ARGENTINA - FOREIGN FINANCE

Inter-American Development Bank, 1300 New York Avenue, NW, Washington, D.C. 20577 (202) 623-1753; *Economic and Social Progress in Latin America.*

ARGENTINA - FOREIGN INDEBTEDNESS

Inter-American Development Bank, 1300 New York Avenue, NW, Washington, D.C. 20577 (202) 623-1753; *Economic and Social Progress in Latin America.*

Statistical Office of the United Nations, Publishing Service, New York, New York 10017 (800) 253-9646; *Economic Survey of Latin America and the Caribbean.*

ARGENTINA - FOREIGN INVESTMENT

The Economist Intelligence Unit, 111 West 57th Street, New York, New York 10019 (800) 938-4685; *The New Latin America Market Atlas.*

ARGENTINA - FOREIGN TRADE

The Economist Intelligence Unit, 111 West 57th Street, New York, New York 10019 (800) 938-4685; *The New Latin America Market Atlas.*

Facts on File, 460 Park Avenue South, New York, New York 10016 (800) 443-8323; *The New Book of World Rankings.*

Federal Statistical Office, Gustav - Stresemann - Ring 11, D-6200 Wiesbaden, Germany; *Argentina.*

G.K. Hall and Company, 70 Lincoln Street, Boston, Massachusetts 02111 (617) 423-3990; *The World in Figures.*

Inter-American Development Bank, 1300 New York Avenue, NW, Washington, D.C. 20577 (202) 623-1753; *Economic and Social Progress in Latin America.*

Organisation for Economic Co-operation and Development (OECD), 2 rue Andre-Pascal, 75 Paris 16, France (Telephone Number in U.S. (212) 963-5981); *Trade by Commodities.*

Statistical Office of the United Nations, Publishing Service, New York, New York 10017 (800) 253-9646; *Economic Survey of Latin America and the Caribbean, International Trade Statistics Yearbook,* and *Statistical Yearbook.*

U.C.L.A. Latin American Center Publications, University of California, Los Angeles, California 90024 (310) 825-6634; *Statistical Abstract of Latin America.*

The World Bank, 1818 H Street, NW, Washington, D.C. 20433 (202) 477-1234; *World Tables.*

ARGENTINA - FORESTRY AND FOREST PRODUCTS

The Economist Intelligence Unit, 111 West 57th Street, New York, New York 10019 (800) 938-4685; *The New Latin America Market Atlas.*

Euromonitor Publications Limited, 87-88 Turnmill Street, London EC1M 5QU, England; *Third World Economic Handbook.*

Facts on File, 460 Park Avenue South, New York, New York 10016 (800) 443-8323; *The New Book of World Rankings.*

Food and Agricultural Organization of the United Nations (FAO) Via Delle Terme di Caracalla, 00100 Rome, Italy (Telephone Number in U.S. (202) 653-2400); *The State of Food and Agriculture,* and *Yearbook of Forest Products.*

Forest and Paper Association, 1250 Connecticut Avenue, NW, Washington, D.C. 20036 (202) 463-2455; *Wood Pulp and Fiber Statistics.*

G.K. Hall and Company, 70 Lincoln Street, Boston, Massachusetts 02111 (617) 423-3990; *The World in Figures.*

Inter-American Development Bank, 1300 New York Avenue, NW, Washington, D.C. 20577 (202) 623-1753; *Economic and Social Progress in Latin America.*

Statistical Office of the United Nations, Publishing Service, New York, New York 10017 (800) 253-9646; *Statistical Yearbook.*

U.C.L.A. Latin American Center Publications, University of California, Los Angeles, California 90024 (310) 825-6634; *Statistical Abstract of Latin America.*

United Nations Educational, Scientific and Cultural Organization (UNESCO), 7 Place de Fontenoy, F-75700 Paris, France (Telephone Number in U.S. (212) 963-5981); *Statistical Yearbook.*

ARGENTINA - GARLIC PRODUCTION - See ARGENTINA - CROPS

ARGENTINA - GAS PRODUCTION - See ARGENTINA - MINING AND MINERAL PRODUCTS

ARGENTINA - GENERAL INDUSTRIAL STATISTICS

Statistical Office of the United Nations, Publishing Service, New York, New York 10017 (800) 253-9646; *Industrial Statistics Yearbook.*

ARGENTINA - GENERAL MORTALITY

Statistical Office of the United Nations, Publishing Service, New York, New York 10017 (800) 253-9646; *Demographic Yearbook.*

World Health Organization, Office of Publications, Avenue Appia, CH-1211 Geneva 27, Switzerland (Telephone Number in U.S. (518) 436-9686); *World Health Statistics Annual.*

ARGENTINA - GEOGRAPHIC DATA

Facts on File, 460 Park Avenue South, New York, New York 10016 (800) 443-8323; *The New Book of World Rankings.*

U.C.L.A. Latin American Center Publications, University of California, Los Angeles, California 90024 (310) 825-6634; *Statistical Abstract of Latin America.*

ARGENTINA - GOATS - See ARGENTINA - LIVESTOCK AND POULTRY

ARGENTINA - GOLD HOLDINGS

International Monetary Fund, 700 Nineteenth Street, NW, Washington, D.C. 20431 (202) 623-7000; *International Financial Statistics.*

Statistical Office of the United Nations, Publishing Service, New York, New York 10017 (800) 253-9646; *Statistical Yearbook.*

The World Bank, 1818 H Street, NW, Washington, D.C. 20433 (202) 477-1234; *World Tables.*

ARGENTINA - GOLD - See ARGENTINA - MINING AND MINERAL PRODUCTS

ARGENTINA - GOLD RESERVES

The Economist Intelligence Unit, 111 West 57th Street, New York, New York 10019 (800) 938-4685; *The New Latin America Market Atlas.*

ARGENTINA - GOVERNMENT

G.K. Hall and Company, 70 Lincoln Street, Boston, Massachusetts 02111 (617) 423-3990; *The World in Figures.*

Inter-American Development Bank, 1300 New York Avenue, NW, Washington, D.C. 20577 (202) 623-1753; *Economic and Social Progress in Latin America.*

ARGENTINA - GOVERNMENT - PRIVATE

International Monetary Fund, 700 Nineteenth Street, NW, Washington, D.C. 20431 (202) 623-7000; *International Financial Statistics.*

ARGENTINA - GOVERNMENT BONDS - See ARGENTINA - BONDS

ARGENTINA - GOVERNMENT CONSUMPTION

Inter-American Development Bank, 1300 New York Avenue, NW, Washington, D.C. 20577 (202) 623-1753; *Economic and Social Progress in Latin America.*

International Monetary Fund, 700 Nineteenth Street, NW, Washington, D.C. 20431 (202) 623-7000; *International Financial Statistics.*

ARGENTINA - GOVERNMENT DEBT

International Monetary Fund, 700 Nineteenth Street, NW, Washington, D.C. 20431 (202) 623-7000; *Government Finance Statistics Yearbook.*

ARGENTINA - GOVERNMENT EXPENDITURE

Euromonitor Publications Limited, 87-88 Turnmill Street, London EC1M 5QU, England; *Third World Economic Handbook.*

Inter-American Development Bank, 1300 New York Avenue, NW, Washington, D.C. 20577 (202) 623-1753; *Economic and Social Progress in Latin America.*

Times Books, 201 East 50th Street, New York, New York 10022 (212) 751-2600; *The Economist Book of Vital World Statistics.*

The World Bank, 1818 H Street, NW, Washington, D.C. 20433 (202) 477-1234; *World Tables.*

ARGENTINA - GOVERNMENT FINANCE

Inter-American Development Bank, 1300 New York Avenue, NW, Washington, D.C. 20577 (202) 623-1753; *Economic and Social Progress in Latin America.*

International Monetary Fund, 700 Nineteenth Street, NW, Washington, D.C. 20431 (202) 623-7000; *International Financial Statistics.*

ARGENTINA - GOVERNMENT REVENUES

Inter-American Development Bank, 1300 New York Avenue, NW, Washington, D.C. 20577 (202) 623-1753; *Economic and Social Progress in Latin America.*

International Monetary Fund, 700 Nineteenth Street, NW, Washington, D.C. 20431 (202) 623-7000; *Government Finance Statistics Yearbook.*

U.C.L.A. Latin American Center Publications, University of California, Los Angeles, California 90024 (310) 825-6634; *Statistical Abstract of Latin America.*

Times Books, 201 East 50th Street, New York, New York 10022 (212) 751-2600; *The Economist Book of Vital World Statistics.*

The World Bank, 1818 H Street, NW, Washington, D.C. 20433 (202) 477-1234; *World Tables.*

ARGENTINA - GRAIN PRODUCTION - See ARGENTINA - CROPS

ARGENTINA - GRANTS

International Monetary Fund, 700 Nineteenth Street, NW, Washington, D.C. 20431 (202) 623-7000; *Government Finance Statistics Yearbook.*

ARGENTINA - GREEN PEPPER AND CHILIE PRODUCTION - See ARGENTINA - CROPS

ARGENTINA - GROSS DOMESTIC PRODUCT

The Economist Intelligence Unit, 111 West 57th Street, New York, New York 10019 (800) 938-4685; *The New Latin America Market Atlas,* and *The World Market Atlas.*

Euromonitor Publications Limited, 87-88 Turnmill Street, London EC1M 5QU, England; *International Marketing Data and Statistics*, and *Third World Economic Handbook*.

Facts on File, 460 Park Avenue South, New York, New York 10016 (800) 443-8323; *The New Book of World Rankings*.

G.K. Hall and Company, 70 Lincoln Street, Boston, Massachusetts 02111 (617) 423-3990; *The World in Figures*.

Inter-American Development Bank, 1300 New York Avenue, NW, Washington, D.C. 20577 (202) 623-1753; *Economic and Social Progress in Latin America*.

International Monetary Fund, 700 Nineteenth Street, NW, Washington, D.C. 20431 (202) 623-7000; *International Financial Statistics*.

Organization of American States (OAS), General Secretariat, Washington, D.C. 20006 (202) 458-3533; *Statistical Bulletin of the OAS*.

Statistical Office of the United Nations, Publishing Service, New York, New York 10017 (800) 253-9646; *Statistical Yearbook*, and *Statistical Yearbook for Latin America and the Caribbean*.

U.C.L.A. Latin American Center Publications, University of California, Los Angeles, California 90024 (310) 825-6634; *Statistical Abstract of Latin America*.

Times Books, 201 East 50th Street, New York, New York 10022 (212) 751-2600; *The Economist Book of Vital World Statistics*.

The World Bank, 1818 H Street, NW, Washington, D.C. 20433 (202) 477-1234; *World Tables*.

ARGENTINA - GROSS INDUSTRIAL PRODUCT

Euromonitor Publications Limited, 87-88 Turnmill Street, London EC1M 5QU, England; *Third World Economic Handbook*.

ARGENTINA - GROSS NATIONAL PRODUCT

Euromonitor Publications Limited, 87-88 Turnmill Street, London EC1M 5QU, England; *International Marketing Data and Statistics*, and *Third World Economic Handbook*.

Inter-American Development Bank, 1300 New York Avenue, NW, Washington, D.C. 20577 (202) 623-1753; *Economic and Social Progress in Latin America*.

U.S. Arms Control and Disarmament Agency, 320 Twenty-first Street, NW, Washington, D.C. 20451 (202) 647-8677; *World Military Expenditures and Arms Transfers*.

The World Bank, 1818 H Street, NW, Washington, D.C. 20433 (202) 477-1234; *World Tables*.

ARGENTINA - GROUNDNUTS PRODUCTION - See ARGENTINA - CROPS

ARGENTINA - HEALTH

The Economist Intelligence Unit, 111 West 57th Street, New York, New York 10019 (800) 938-4685; *The New Latin America Market Atlas*.

Facts on File, 460 Park Avenue South, New York, New York 10016 (800) 443-8323; *The New Book of World Rankings*.

Federal Statistical Office, Gustav - Stresemann - Ring 11, D-6200 Wiesbaden, Germany; *Argentina*.

G.K. Hall and Company, 70 Lincoln Street, Boston, Massachusetts 02111 (617) 423-3990; *The World in Figures*.

Statistical Office of the United Nations, Publishing Service, New York, New York 10017 (800) 253-9646; *Statistical Yearbook*.

Times Books, 201 East 50th Street, New York, New York 10022 (212) 751-2600; *The Economist Book of Vital World Statistics*.

U.C.L.A. Latin American Center Publications, University of California, Los Angeles, California 90024 (310) 825-6634; *Statistical Abstract of Latin America*.

World Health Organization, Office of Publications, Avenue Appia, CH-1211 Geneva 27, Switzerland (Telephone Number in U.S. (518) 436-9686); *World Health Statistics Annual*.

ARGENTINA - HEALTH EXPENDITURES

International Monetary Fund, 700 Nineteenth Street, NW, Washington, D.C. 20431 (202) 623-7000; *Government Finance Statistics Yearbook*.

Statistical Office of the United Nations, Publishing Service, New York, New York 10017 (800) 253-9646; *Statistical Yearbook for Latin America and the Caribbean*.

ARGENTINA - HIDE PRODUCTION

Food and Agricultural Organization of the United Nations (FAO), Via delle Terme di Caracalla, 00100 Rome, Italy (Telephone Number in U.S. (202) 653-2400); *Production Yearbook*.

ARGENTINA - HIGHWAYS

The Economist Intelligence Unit, 111 West 57th Street, New York, New York 10019 (800) 938-4685; *The New Latin America Market Atlas*.

G.K. Hall and Company, 70 Lincoln Street, Boston, Massachusetts 02111 (617) 423-3990; *The World in Figures*.

International Road Federation, 525 School Street, SW, Washington, D.C. 20024 (202) 554-2106; *World Road Statistics*.

ARGENTINA - HONEY PRODUCTION

Commodity Research Bureau, Incorporated, 75 Wall Street, New York, New York 10005 (212) 504-7754; *Commodity Year Book*.

ARGENTINA - HORSES - See ARGENTINA - LIVESTOCK AND POULTRY

ARGENTINA - HOURS OF WORK - See ARGENTINA - EMPLOYMENT

ARGENTINA - HOUSING AND HOUSING UNITS

Euromonitor Publications Limited, 87-88 Turnmill Street, London EC1M 5QU, England; *Third World Economic Handbook*.

Facts on File, 460 Park Avenue South, New York, New York 10016 (800) 443-8323; *The New Book of World Rankings*.

Statistical Office of the United Nations, Publishing Service, New York, New York 10017 (800) 253-9646; *Statistical Yearbook for Latin America and the Caribbean*.

U.C.L.A. Latin American Center Publications, University of California, Los Angeles, California 90024 (310) 825-6634; *Statistical Abstract of Latin America.*

ARGENTINA - HOUSING EXPENDITURES

International Monetary Fund, 700 Nineteenth Street, NW, Washington, D.C. 20431 (202) 623-7000; *Government Finance Statistics Yearbook.*

ARGENTINA - ILLITERACY RATES

The Economist Intelligence Unit, 111 West 57th Street, New York, New York 10019 (800) 938-4685; *The New Latin America Market Atlas.*

ARGENTINA - ILLITERATE POPULATION

The Economist Intelligence Unit, 111 West 57th Street, New York, New York 10019 (800) 938-4685; *The World Market Atlas.*

G.K. Hall and Company, 70 Lincoln Street, Boston, Massachusetts 02111 (617) 423-3990; *The World in Figures.*

Statistical Office of the United Nations, Publishing Service, New York, New York 10017 (800) 253-9646; *Statistical Yearbook for Latin America and the Caribbean.*

United Nations Educational, Scientific and Cultural Organization (UNESCO), 7 Place de Fontenoy, F-75700 Paris, France (Telephone Number in U.S. (212) 963-5981); *Statistical Yearbook.*

ARGENTINA - IMMIGRATION

U.C.L.A. Latin American Center Publications, University of California, Los Angeles, California 90024 (310) 825-6634; *Statistical Abstract of Latin America.*

ARGENTINA - IMPORTS

American Automobile Manufacturers Association, 1401 H Street, NW, Suite 900, Washington, D.C. 20005 (202) 326-5500; *World Motor Vehicle Data.*

The Economist Intelligence Unit, 111 West 57th Street, New York, New York 10019 (800) 938-4685; *The New Latin America Market Atlas,* and *The World Market Atlas.*

Euromonitor Publications Limited, 87-88 Turnmill Street, London EC1M 5QU, England; *International Marketing Data and Statistics,* and *Third World Economic Handbook.*

Food and Agricultural Organization of the United Nations (FAO) Via Delle Terme di Caracalla, 00100 Rome, Italy (Telephone Number in U.S. (202) 653-2400); *The State of Food and Agriculture.*

G.K. Hall and Company, 70 Lincoln Street, Boston, Massachusetts 02111 (617) 423-3990; *The World in Figures.*

Inter-American Development Bank, 1300 New York Avenue, NW, Washington, D.C. 20577 (202) 623-1753; *Economic and Social Progress in Latin America.*

International Lead and Zinc Study Group, Metro House, 58 St. James's Street, London SW1A 1LD, England; *Lead and Zinc Statistics.*

International Monetary Fund, 700 Nineteenth Street, NW, Washington, D.C. 20431 (202) 623-7000; *Direction of Trade Statistics, Government Finance Statistics Yearbook,* and *International Financial Statistics.*

Organization of American States (OAS), General Secretariat, Washington, D.C. 20006 (202) 458-3533; *Statistical Bulletin of the OAS.*

Statistical Office of the United Nations, Publishing Service, New York, New York 10017 (800) 253-9646; *Statistical Yearbook for Latin America and the Caribbean,* and *Trade in Manufactures of Developing Countries.*

The World Bank, 1818 H Street, NW, Washington, D.C. 20433 (202) 477-1234; *World Tables.*

ARGENTINA - INCOME DISTRIBUTION

Statistical Office of the United Nations, Publishing Service, New York, New York 10017 (800) 253-9646; *Statistical Yearbook for Latin America and the Caribbean.*

U.C.L.A. Latin American Center Publications, University of California, Los Angeles, California 90024 (310) 825-6634; *Statistical Abstract of Latin America.*

ARGENTINA - INCOME TAXES - See ARGENTINA - TAXATION

ARGENTINA - INDUSTRY

Euromonitor Publications Limited, 87-88 Turnmill Street, London EC1M 5QU, England; *International Marketing Data and Statistics,* and *Third World Economic Handbook.*

Facts on File, 460 Park Avenue South, New York, New York 10016 (800) 443-8323; *The New Book of World Rankings.*

Federal Statistical Office, Gustav - Stresemann - Ring 11, D-6200 Wiesbaden, Germany; *Argentina.*

Gale Research Incorporated, 835 Penobscot Building, Detroit, Michigan 48226 (800 877-4253; *International Historical Statistics the Americas and Australasia.*

International Labour Office, I.L.O. Publications, CH-1211, Geneva 22, Switzerland; *Yearbook of Labour Statistics.*

Statistical Office of the United Nations, Publishing Service, New York, New York 10017 (800) 253-9646; *Economic Survey of Latin America and the Caribbean,* and *Statistical Yearbook.*

Times Books, 201 East 50th Street, New York, New York 10022 (212) 751-2600; *The Economist Book of Vital World Statistics.*

U.C.L.A. Latin American Center Publications, University of California, Los Angeles, California 90024 (310) 825-6634; *Statistical Abstract of Latin America.*

The World Bank, 1818 H Street, NW, Washington, D.C. 20433 (202) 477-1234; *World Tables.*

ARGENTINA - INDUSTRIAL METALS PRODUCTION - See ARGENTINA - MINING AND MINERAL PRODUCTS

ARGENTINA - INFANT AND MATERNAL MORTALITY

The Economist Intelligence Unit, 111 West 57th Street, New York, New York 10019 (800) 938-4685; *The New Latin America Market Atlas.*

Statistical Office of the United Nations, Publishing Service, New York, New York 10017 (800) 253-9646; *Demographic Yearbook*, and *Statistical Yearbook*.

Times Books, 201 East 50th Street, New York, New York 10022 (212) 751-2600; *The Economist Book of Vital World Statistics*.

The World Bank, 1818 H Street, NW, Washington, D.C. 20433 (202) 477-1234; *World Tables*.

ARGENTINA - INFLATIONARY FACTORS

Statistical Office of the United Nations, Publishing Service, New York, New York 10017 (800) 253-9646; *Economic Survey of Latin America and the Caribbean*.

ARGENTINA - INTEREST RATES

Inter-American Development Bank, 1300 New York Avenue, NW, Washington, D.C. 20577 (202) 623-1753; *Economic and Social Progress in Latin America*.

ARGENTINA - INTERNATIONAL FINANCE

Inter-American Development Bank, 1300 New York Avenue, NW, Washington, D.C. 20577 (202) 623-1753; *Economic and Social Progress in Latin America*.

U.C.L.A. Latin American Center Publications, University of California, Los Angeles, California 90024 (310) 825-6634; *Statistical Abstract of Latin America*.

ARGENTINA - INTERNATIONAL LIQUIDITY

Inter-American Development Bank, 1300 New York Avenue, NW, Washington, D.C. 20577 (202) 623-1753; *Economic and Social Progress in Latin America*.

International Monetary Fund, 700 Nineteenth Street, NW, Washington, D.C. 20431 (202) 623-7000; *International Financial Statistics*.

ARGENTINA - INTERNATIONAL RESERVES

Organization of American States (OAS), General Secretariat, Washington, D.C. 20006 (202) 458-3533; *Statistical Bulletin of the OAS*.

ARGENTINA - INTERNATIONAL RESERVES EXCLUDING GOLD

Inter-American Development Bank, 1300 New York Avenue, NW, Washington, D.C. 20577 (202) 623-1753; *Economic and Social Progress in Latin America*.

The World Bank, 1818 H Street, NW, Washington, D.C. 20433 (202) 477-1234; *World Tables*.

ARGENTINA - INTERNATIONAL STATISTICS

Inter-American Development Bank, 1300 New York Avenue, NW, Washington, D.C. 20577 (202) 623-1753; *Economic and Social Progress in Latin America*.

U.C.L.A. Latin American Center Publications, University of California, Los Angeles, California 90024 (310) 825-6634; *Statistical Abstract of Latin America*.

ARGENTINA - INVESTMENTS

Inter-American Development Bank, 1300 New York Avenue, NW, Washington, D.C. 20577 (202) 623-1753; *Economic and Social Progress in Latin America*.

International Monetary Fund, 700 Nineteenth Street, NW, Washington, D.C. 20431 (202) 623-7000; *International Financial Statistics*.

Statistical Office of the United Nations, Publishing Service, New York, New York 10017 (800) 253-9646; *Statistical Yearbook for Latin America and the Caribbean*.

ARGENTINA - IRON ORE PRODUCTION AND CONSUMPTION - See ARGENTINA - MINING AND MINERAL PRODUCTS

ARGENTINA - IRRIGATION

Euromonitor Publications Limited, 87-88 Turnmill Street, London EC1M 5QU, England; *International Marketing Data and Statistics*.

Inter-American Development Bank, 1300 New York Avenue, NW, Washington, D.C. 20577 (202) 623-1753; *Economic and Social Progress in Latin America*.

ARGENTINA - LABOR FORCE

The Economist Intelligence Unit, 111 West 57th Street, New York, New York 10019 (800) 938-4685; *The New Latin America Market Atlas*.

Euromonitor Publications Limited, 87-88 Turnmill Street, London EC1M 5QU, England; *International Marketing Data and Statistics*.

Facts on File, 460 Park Avenue South, New York, New York 10016 (800) 443-8323; *The New Book of World Rankings*.

Food and Agricultural Organization of the United Nations (FAO) Via Delle Terme di Caracalla, 00100 Rome, Italy (Telephone Number in U.S. (202) 653-2400); *The State of Food and Agriculture*.

Gale Research Incorporated, 835 Penobscot Building, Detroit, Michigan 48226 (800) 877-4253; *International Historical Statistics the Americas and Australasia*.

G.K. Hall and Company, 70 Lincoln Street, Boston, Massachusetts 02111 (617) 423-3990; *The World in Figures*.

Times Books, 201 East 50th Street, New York, New York 10022 (212) 751-2600; *The Economist Book of Vital World Statistics*.

The World Bank, 1818 H Street, NW, Washington, D.C. 20433 (202) 477-1234; *World Tables*.

ARGENTINA - LABOR PRODUCTIVITY

International Labour Office, I.L.O. Publications, CH-1211, Geneva 22, Switzerland; *Yearbook of Labour Statistics*.

ARGENTINA - LAND AREA

The Economist Intelligence Unit, 111 West 57th Street, New York, New York 10019 (800) 938-4685; *The New Latin America Market Atlas*.

ARGENTINA - LAND USE

Euromonitor Publications Limited, 87-88 Turnmill Street, London EC1M 5QU, England; *International Marketing Data and Statistics.*

Food and Agricultural Organization of the United Nations (FAO), Via delle Terme di Caracalla, 00100 Rome, Italy (Telephone Number in U.S. (202) 653-2400); *Production Yearbook.*

G.K. Hall and Company, 70 Lincoln Street, Boston, Massachusetts 02111 (617) 423-3990; *The World in Figures.*

Inter-American Development Bank, 1300 New York Avenue, NW, Washington, D.C. 20577 (202) 623-1753; *Economic and Social Progress in Latin America.*

ARGENTINA - LEAD AND LEAD ORE - See ARGENTINA - MINING AND MINERAL PRODUCTS

ARGENTINA - LEATHER AND FOOTWEAR - EXPORTS AND IMPORTS

Statistical Office of the United Nations, Publishing Service, New York, New York 10017 (800) 253-9646; *Trade in Manufactures of Developing Countries.*

ARGENTINA - LIBRARIES

Facts on File, 460 Park Avenue South, New York, New York 10016 (800) 443-8323; *The New Book of World Rankings.*

United Nations Educational, Scientific and Cultural Organization (UNESCO), 7 Place de Fontenoy, F-75700 Paris, France (Telephone Number in U.S. (212) 963-5981); *Statistical Yearbook.*

ARGENTINA - LIFE EXPECTANCY RATE

The Economist Intelligence Unit, 111 West 57th Street, New York, New York 10019 (800) 938-4685; *The New Latin America Market Atlas.*

ARGENTINA - LIVESTOCK AND POULTRY

Commodity Research Bureau, Incorporated, 75 Wall Street, New York, New York 10005 (212) 504-7754; *Commodity Year Book.*

Euromonitor Publications Limited, 87-88 Turnmill Street, London EC1M 5QU, England; *International Marketing Data and Statistics.*

Facts on File, 460 Park Avenue South, New York, New York 10016 (800) 443-8323; *The New Book of World Rankings.*

Food and Agricultural Organization of the United Nations (FAO), Via delle Terme di Caracalla, 00100 Rome, Italy (Telephone Number in U.S. (202) 653-2400); *Production Yearbook,* and *The State of Food and Agriculture.*

G.K. Hall and Company, 70 Lincoln Street, Boston, Massachusetts 02111 (617) 423-3990; *The World in Figures.*

Statistical Office of the United Nations, Publishing Service, New York, New York 10017 (800) 253-9646; *Statistical Yearbook.*

ARGENTINA - LIVING LEVELS

G.K. Hall and Company, 70 Lincoln Street, Boston, Massachusetts 02111 (617) 423-3990; *The World in Figures.*

Statistical Office of the United Nations, Publishing Service, New York, New York 10017 (800) 253-9646; *Statistical Yearbook for Latin America and the Caribbean.*

Times Books, 201 East 50th Street, New York, New York 10022 (212) 751-2600; *The Economist Book of Vital World Statistics.*

ARGENTINA - MAIL - NUMBER OF PIECES SENT OR RECEIVED

Statistical Office of the United Nations, Publishing Service, New York, New York 10017 (800) 253-9646; *Statistical Yearbook.*

ARGENTINA - MAIN ECONOMIC INDICATORS - See ARGENTINA - ECONOMY

ARGENTINA - MANGANESE ORE PRODUCTION AND CONSUMPTION - See ARGENTINA - MINING AND MINERAL PRODUCTS

ARGENTINA - MANUFACTURING

American Automobile Manufacturers Association, 1401 H Street, NW, Suite 900, Washington, D.C. 20005 (202) 326-5500; *World Motor Vehicle Data.*

The Economist Intelligence Unit, 111 West 57th Street, New York, New York 10019 (800) 938-4685; *The New Latin America Market Atlas.*

Facts on File, 460 Park Avenue South, New York, New York 10016 (800) 443-8323; *The New Book of World Rankings.*

G.K. Hall and Company, 70 Lincoln Street, Boston, Massachusetts 02111 (617) 423-3990; *The World in Figures.*

Inter-American Development Bank, 1300 New York Avenue, NW, Washington, D.C. 20577 (202) 623-1753; *Economic and Social Progress in Latin America.*

International Monetary Fund, 700 Nineteenth Street, NW, Washington, D.C. 20431 (202) 623-7000; *International Financial Statistics.*

Organization of American States (OAS), General Secretariat, Washington, D.C. 20006 (202) 458-3533; *Statistical Bulletin of the OAS.*

Statistical Office of the United Nations, Publishing Service, New York, New York 10017 (800) 253-9646; *Statistical Yearbook,* and *Statistical Yearbook for Latin America and the Caribbean.*

Times Books, 201 East 50th Street, New York, New York 10022 (212) 751-2600; *The Economist Book of Vital World Statistics.*

The World Bank, 1818 H Street, NW, Washington, D.C. 20433 (202) 477-1234; *World Tables.*

ARGENTINA - MARRIAGE RATES

Facts on File, 460 Park Avenue South, New York, New York 10016 (800) 443-8323; *The New Book of World Rankings.*

Statistical Office of the United Nations, Publishing Service, New York, New York 10017 (800) 253-9646; *Demographic Yearbook,* and *Statistical Yearbook.*

ARGENTINA - MEAT EXPORTS

International Monetary Fund, 700 Nineteenth Street, NW, Washington, D.C. 20431 (202) 623-7000; *International Financial Statistics.*

Organization of American States (OAS), General Secretariat, Washington, D.C. 20006 (202) 458-3533; *Statistical Bulletin of the OAS.*

ARGENTINA - MEAT PRODUCTION - See ARGENTINA - LIVESTOCK AND POULTRY

ARGENTINA - MEDICAL PERSONNEL

U.C.L.A. Latin American Center Publications, University of California, Los Angeles, California 90024 (310) 825-6634; *Statistical Abstract of Latin America.*

ARGENTINA - MERCHANT FLEET CHARACTERISTICS - See ARGENTINA - MERCHANT SHIPPING

ARGENTINA - MERCHANT SHIPPING

G.K. Hall and Company, 70 Lincoln Street, Boston, Massachusetts 02111 (617) 423-3990; *The World in Figures.*

Inter-American Development Bank, 1300 New York Avenue, NW, Washington, D.C. 20577 (202) 623-1753; *Economic and Social Progress in Latin America.*

Lloyd's Register of Shipping, 17 Battery Place, New York, New York 10004 (212) 425-8050; *Register of Ships.*

Statistical Office of the United Nations, Publishing Service, New York, New York 10017 (800) 253-9646; *Statistical Yearbook.*

Times Books, 201 East 50th Street, New York, New York 10022 (212) 751-2600; *The Economist Book of Vital World Statistics.*

U.S. Department of Commerce, Maritime Administration, Washington, D.C. 20230; *A Statistical Analysis of the World's Merchant Fleets.*

ARGENTINA - MERCHANT VESSELS - TONNAGE LAUNCHED - See ARGENTINA - MERCHANT SHIPPING

ARGENTINA - MILITARY

The Economist Intelligence Unit, 111 West 57th Street, New York, New York 10019 (800) 938-4685; *The New Latin America Market Atlas.*

G.K. Hall and Company, 70 Lincoln Street, Boston, Massachusetts 02111 (617) 423-3990; *The World in Figures.*

The International Institute for Strategic Studies, 23 Tavistock Street, London WC2E 7NQ, England; *The Military Balance.*

U.C.L.A. Latin American Center Publications, University of California, Los Angeles, California 90024 (310) 825-6634; *Statistical Abstract of Latin America.*

U.S. Arms Control and Disarmament Agency, 320 Twenty-first Street, NW, Washington, D.C. 20451 (202) 647-8677; *World Military Expenditures and Arms Transfers.*

ARGENTINA - MILK PRODUCTION - See ARGENTINA - DAIRY PRODUCTS

ARGENTINA - MILLET PRODUCTION - See ARGENTINA - CROPS

ARGENTINA - MINING AND MINERAL PRODUCTS

Commodity Research Bureau, Incorporated, 75 Wall Street, New York, New York 10005 (212) 504-7754; *Commodity Year Book.*

The Economist Intelligence Unit, 111 West 57th Street, New York, New York 10019 (800) 938-4685; *The New Latin America Market Atlas.*

Euromonitor Publications Limited, 87-88 Turnmill Street, London EC1M 5QU, England; *Third World Economic Handbook.*

Facts on File, 460 Park Avenue South, New York, New York 10016 (800) 443-8323; *The New Book of World Rankings.*

G.K. Hall and Company, 70 Lincoln Street, Boston, Massachusetts 02111 (617) 423-3990; *The World in Figures.*

Inter-American Development Bank, 1300 New York Avenue, NW, Washington, D.C. 20577 (202) 623-1753; *Economic and Social Progress in Latin America.*

International Lead and Zinc Study Group, Metro House, 58 St. James's Street, London SW1A 1LD, England; *Lead and Zinc Statistics.*

Penn Well Publishing Company, 1421 South Sheridan Road, P.O. Box 1260, Tulsa, Oklahoma 74101 (800) 752-9764; *International Energy Statistics Sourcebook.*

Statistical Office of the United Nations, Publishing Service, New York, New York 10017 (800) 253-9646; *Statistical Yearbook,* and *Statistical Yearbook for Latin America and the Caribbean.*

U.C.L.A. Latin American Center Publications, University of California, Los Angeles, California 90024 (310) 825-6634; *Statistical Abstract of Latin America.*

ARGENTINA - MOLASSES PRODUCTION - See ARGENTINA - CROPS

ARGENTINA - MONEY EXCHANGE RATE

Euromonitor Publications Limited, 87-88 Turnmill Street, London EC1M 5QU, England; *International Marketing Data and Statistics.*

Inter-American Development Bank, 1300 New York Avenue, NW, Washington, D.C. 20577 (202) 623-1753; *Economic and Social Progress in Latin America.*

International Monetary Fund, 700 Nineteenth Street, NW, Washington, D.C. 20431 (202) 623-7000; *International Financial Statistics.*

Statistical Office of the United Nations, Publishing Service, New York, New York 10017 (800) 253-9646; *Statistical Yearbook.*

ARGENTINA - MONEY RATES - MARKET

Inter-American Development Bank, 1300 New York Avenue, NW, Washington, D.C. 20577 (202) 623-1753; *Economic and Social Progress in Latin America.*

ARGENTINA - MONEY RESERVES

Euromonitor Publications Limited, 87-88 Turnmill Street, London EC1M 5QU, England; *International Marketing Data and Statistics.*

Inter-American Development Bank, 1300 New York Avenue, NW, Washington, D.C. 20577 (202) 623-1753; *Economic and Social Progress in Latin America.*

ARGENTINA - MONEY SUPPLY

Euromonitor Publications Limited, 87-88 Turnmill Street, London EC1M 5QU, England; *International Marketing Data and Statistics.*

G.K. Hall and Company, 70 Lincoln Street, Boston, Massachusetts 02111 (617) 423-3990; *The World in Figures.*

Inter-American Development Bank, 1300 New York Avenue, NW, Washington, D.C. 20577 (202) 623-1753; *Economic and Social Progress in Latin America.*

International Monetary Fund, 700 Nineteenth Street, NW, Washington, D.C. 20431 (202) 623-7000; *International Financial Statistics.*

Statistical Office of the United Nations, Publishing Service, New York, New York 10017 (800) 253-9646; *Statistical Yearbook.*

U.C.L.A. Latin American Center Publications, University of California, Los Angeles, California 90024 (310) 825-6634; *Statistical Abstract of Latin America.*

The World Bank, 1818 H Street, NW, Washington, D.C. 20433 (202) 477-1234; *World Tables.*

ARGENTINA - MOTION PICTURES

Statistical Office of the United Nations, Publishing Service, New York, New York 10017 (800) 253-9646; *Statistical Yearbook.*

United Nations Educational, Scientific and Cultural Organization (UNESCO), 7 Place de Fontenoy, F-75700 Paris, France (Telephone Number in U.S. (212) 963-5981); *Statistical Yearbook.*

ARGENTINA - MOTOR VEHICLE PRODUCTION

American Automobile Manufacturers Association, 1401 H Street, NW, Suite 900, Washington, D.C. 20005 (202) 326-5500; *World Motor Vehicle Data.*

Statistical Office of the United Nations, Publishing Service, New York, New York 10017 (800) 253-9646; *Statistical Yearbook.*

ARGENTINA - MOTOR VEHICLE TAXES - See ARGENTINA - TAXATION

ARGENTINA - MOTOR VEHICLES IN USE

American Automobile Manufacturers Association, 1401 H Street, NW, Suite 900, Washington, D.C. 20005 (202) 326-5500; *World Motor Vehicle Data.*

The Economist Intelligence Unit, 111 West 57th Street, New York, New York 10019 (800) 938-4685; *The New Latin America Market Atlas.*

G.K. Hall and Company, 70 Lincoln Street, Boston, Massachusetts 02111 (617) 423-3990; *The World in Figures.*

International Road Federation, 525 School Street, SW, Washington, D.C. 20024 (202) 554-2106; *World Road Statistics.*

Statistical Office of the United Nations, Publishing Service, New York, New York 10017 (800) 253-9646; *Statistical Yearbook.*

Times Books, 201 East 50th Street, New York, New York 10022 (212) 751-2600; *The Economist Book of Vital World Statistics.*

ARGENTINA - MULES - See ARGENTINA - LIVESTOCK AND POULTRY

ARGENTINA - MUSEUMS

Facts on File, 460 Park Avenue South, New York, New York 10016 (800) 443-8323; *The New Book of World Rankings.*

United Nations Educational, Scientific and Cultural Organization (UNESCO), 7 Place de Fontenoy, F-75700 Paris, France (Telephone Number in U.S. (212) 963-5981); *Statistical Yearbook.*

ARGENTINA - NATALITY - See ARGENTINA - BIRTH RATE

ARGENTINA - NATIONAL ACCOUNTS

Federal Statistical Office, Gustav - Stresemann - Ring 11, D-6200 Wiesbaden, Germany; *Argentina.*

Gale Research Incorporated, 835 Penobscot Building, Detroit, Michigan 48226 (800) 877-4253; *International Historical Statistics the Americas and Australasia.*

Inter-American Development Bank, 1300 New York Avenue, NW, Washington, D.C. 20577 (202) 623-1753; *Economic and Social Progress in Latin America.*

International Monetary Fund, 700 Nineteenth Street, NW, Washington, D.C. 20431 (202) 623-7000; *International Financial Statistics.*

Organization of American States (OAS), General Secretariat, Washington, D.C. 20006 (202) 458-3533; *Statistical Bulletin of the OAS.*

Statistical Office of the United Nations, Publishing Service, New York, New York 10017 (800) 253-9646; *National Accounts Statistics.*

U.C.L.A. Latin American Center Publications, University of California, Los Angeles, California 90024 (310) 825-6634; *Statistical Abstract of Latin America.*

ARGENTINA - NATIONAL INCOME

Facts on File, 460 Park Avenue South, New York, New York 10016 (800) 443-8323; *The New Book of World Rankings.*

G.K. Hall and Company, 70 Lincoln Street, Boston, Massachusetts 02111 (617) 423-3990; *The World in Figures.*

Inter-American Development Bank, 1300 New York Avenue, NW, Washington, D.C. 20577 (202) 623-1753; *Economic and Social Progress in Latin America.*

Statistical Office of the United Nations, Publishing Service, New York, New York 10017 (800) 253-9646; *Statistical Yearbook,* and *Statistical Yearbook for Latin America and the Caribbean.*

ARGENTINA - NATIONAL PRODUCT

Facts on File, 460 Park Avenue South, New York, New York 10016 (800) 443-8323; *The New Book of World Rankings.*

Statistical Office of the United Nations, Publishing Service, New York, New York 10017 (800) 253-9646; *Statistical Yearbook.*

ARGENTINA - NATURAL GAS PRODUCTION - See ARGENTINA - MINING AND MINERAL PRODUCTS

ARGENTINA - NEWSPAPER PRODUCTION - See ARGENTINA - FORESTRY AND FOREST PRODUCTS

ARGENTINA - NEWSPRINT - See ARGENTINA - FORESTRY AND FOREST PRODUCTS

ARGENTINA - NUTRITION

Statistical Office of the United Nations, Publishing Service, New York, New York 10017 (800) 253-9646; *Statistical Yearbook for Latin America and the Caribbean.*

ARGENTINA - OATS PRODUCTION - See ARGENTINA - CROPS

ARGENTINA - OCCUPATIONS - See ARGENTINA - LABOR FORCE

ARGENTINA - ORANGE PRODUCTION - See ARGENTINA - CROPS

ARGENTINA - PAPER - See ARGENTINA - FORESTRY AND FOREST PRODUCTS

ARGENTINA - PATENTS

Statistical Office of the United Nations, Publishing Service, New York, New York 10017 (800) 253-9646; *Statistical Yearbook.*

ARGENTINA - PEANUT PRODUCTION - See ARGENTINA - CROPS

ARGENTINA - PESTICIDE USE

Food and Agricultural Organization of the United Nations (FAO) Via Delle Terme di Caracalla, 00100 Rome, Italy (Telephone Number in U.S. (202) 653-2400); *The State of Food and Agriculture.*

ARGENTINA - PETROLEUM INDUSTRY

Commodity Research Bureau, Incorporated, 75 Wall Street, New York, New York 10005 (212) 504-7754; *Commodity Year Book.*

The Economist Intelligence Unit, 111 West 57th Street, New York, New York 10019 (800) 938-4685; *The New Latin America Market Atlas.*

Facts on File, 460 Park Avenue South, New York, New York 10016 (800) 443-8323; *The New Book of World Rankings.*

Food and Agricultural Organization of the United Nations (FAO) Via Delle Terme di Caracalla, 00100 Rome, Italy (Telephone Number in U.S. (202) 653-2400); *The State of Food and Agriculture.*

G.K. Hall and Company, 70 Lincoln Street, Boston, Massachusetts 02111 (617) 423-3990; *The World in Figures.*

Inter-American Development Bank, 1300 New York Avenue, NW, Washington, D.C. 20577 (202) 623-1753; *Economic and Social Progress in Latin America.*

International Monetary Fund, 700 Nineteenth Street, NW, Washington, D.C. 20431 (202) 623-7000; *International Financial Statistics.*

Organization of American States (OAS), General Secretariat, Washington, D.C. 20006 (202) 458-3533; *Statistical Bulletin of the OAS.*

Penn Well Publishing Company, 1421 South Sheridan Road, P.O. Box 1260, Tulsa, Oklahoma 74101 (800) 752-9764; *International Energy Statistics Sourcebook.*

Statistical Office of the United Nations, Publishing Service, New York, New York 10017 (800) 253-9646; *Statistical Yearbook.*

ARGENTINA - PIG-IRON AND FERRO-ALLOYS PRODUCTION - See ARGENTINA - MINING AND MINERAL PRODUCTS

ARGENTINA - PIGS - See ARGENTINA - LIVESTOCK AND POULTRY

ARGENTINA - PLASTIC AND RESIN PRODUCTION

Euromonitor Publications Limited, 87-88 Turnmill Street, London EC1M 5QU, England; *Third World Economic Handbook.*

Statistical Office of the United Nations, Publishing Service, New York, New York 10017 (800) 253-9646; *Statistical Yearbook.*

ARGENTINA - POLITICAL DATA

U.C.L.A. Latin American Center Publications, University of California, Los Angeles, California 90024 (310) 825-6634; *Statistical Abstract of Latin America.*

ARGENTINA - POPULATION

The Economist Intelligence Unit, 111 West 57th Street, New York, New York 10019 (800) 938-4685; *The New Latin America Market Atlas,* and *The World Market Atlas.*

Euromonitor Publications Limited, 87-88 Turnmill Street, London EC1M 5QU, England; *International Marketing Data and Statistics,* and *Third World Economic Handbook.*

Facts on File, 460 Park Avenue South, New York, New York 10016 (800) 443-8323; *The New Book of World Rankings.*

Federal Statistical Office, Gustav - Stresemann - Ring 11, D-6200 Wiesbaden, Germany; *Argentina.*

Food and Agricultural Organization of the United Nations (FAO), Via delle Terme di Caracalla, 00100 Rome, Italy (Telephone Number in U.S. (202) 653-2400); *Production Yearbook.*

Gale Research Incorporated, 835 Penobscot Building, Detroit, Michigan 48226 (800) 877-4253; *International Historical Statistics the Americas and Australasia.*

G.K. Hall and Company, 70 Lincoln Street, Boston, Massachusetts 02111 (617) 423-3990; *The World in Figures.*

Inter-American Development Bank, 1300 New York Avenue, NW, Washington, D.C. 20577 (202) 623-1753; *Economic and Social Progress in Latin America.*

International Labour Office, I.L.O. Publications, CH-1211, Geneva 22, Switzerland; *Yearbook of Labour Statistics.*

Organization of American States (OAS), General Secretariat, Washington, D.C. 20006 (202) 458-3533; *Statistical Bulletin of the OAS.*

Statistical Office of the United Nations, Publishing Service, New York, New York 10017 (800) 253-9646; *Demographic Yearbook, Statistical Yearbook,* and *Statistical Yearbook for Latin America and the Caribbean.*

Times Books, 201 East 50th Street, New York, New York 10022 (212) 751-2600; *The Economist Book of Vital World Statistics.*

U.C.L.A. Latin American Center Publications, University of California, Los Angeles, California 90024 (310) 825-6634; *Statistical Abstract of Latin America.*

U.S. Arms Control and Disarmament Agency, 320 Twenty-first Street, NW, Washington, D.C. 20451 (202) 647-8677; *World Military Expenditures and Arms Transfers.*

World Health Organization, Office of Publications, Avenue Appia, CH-1211 Geneva 27, Switzerland (Telephone Number in U.S. (518) 436-9686); *World Health Statistics Annual.*

ARGENTINA - POST OFFICES

Facts on File, 460 Park Avenue South, New York, New York 10016 (800) 443-8323; *The New Book of World Rankings.*

ARGENTINA - POTATO PRODUCTION - See ARGENTINA - CROPS

ARGENTINA - PRICES

Facts on File, 460 Park Avenue South, New York, New York 10016 (800) 443-8323; *The New Book of World Rankings.*

Federal Statistical Office, Gustav - Stresemann - Ring 11, D-6200 Wiesbaden, Germany; *Argentina.*

Food and Agricultural Organization of the United Nations (FAO), Via delle Terme di Caracalla, 00100 Rome, Italy (Telephone Number in U.S. (202) 653-2400); *Production Yearbook,* and *The State of Food and Agriculture.*

Gale Research Incorporated, 835 Penobscot Building, Detroit, Michigan 48226 (800) 877-4253; *International Historical Statistics the Americas and Australasia.*

G.K. Hall and Company, 70 Lincoln Street, Boston, Massachusetts 02111 (617) 423-3990; *The World in Figures.*

International Labour Office, I.L.O. Publications, CH-1211, Geneva 22, Switzerland; *Yearbook of Labour Statistics.*

International Lead and Zinc Study Group, Metro House, 58 St. James's Street, London SW1A 1LD, England; *Lead and Zinc Statistics.*

International Monetary Fund, 700 Nineteenth Street, NW, Washington, D.C. 20431 (202) 623-7000; *International Financial Statistics.*

Statistical Office of the United Nations, Publishing Service, New York, New York 10017 (800) 253-9646; *Statistical Yearbook for Latin America and the Caribbean.*

ARGENTINA - PRINTING AND WRITING PAPER - See ARGENTINA - FORESTRY AND FOREST PRODUCTS

ARGENTINA - PRODUCTION

American Automobile Manufacturers Association, 1401 H Street, NW, Suite 900, Washington, D.C. 20005 (202) 326-5500; *World Motor Vehicle Data.*

Euromonitor Publications Limited, 87-88 Turnmill Street, London EC1M 5QU, England; *Third World Economic Handbook.*

Facts on File, 460 Park Avenue South, New York, New York 10016 (800) 443-8323; *The New Book of World Rankings.*

G.K. Hall and Company, 70 Lincoln Street, Boston, Massachusetts 02111 (617) 423-3990; *The World in Figures.*

International Lead and Zinc Study Group, Metro House, 58 St. James's Street, London SW1A 1LD, England; *Lead and Zinc Statistics.*

ARGENTINA - PRODUCTIVITY

Euromonitor Publications Limited, 87-88 Turnmill Street, London EC1M 5QU, England; *International Marketing Data and Statistics.*

ARGENTINA - PROPERTY TAXES - See ARGENTINA - TAXATION

ARGENTINA - PUBLIC CONSUMPTION FUND

Inter-American Development Bank, 1300 New York Avenue, NW, Washington, D.C. 20577 (202) 623-1753; *Economic and Social Progress in Latin America.*

ARGENTINA - PUBLIC EXPENDITURE

Inter-American Development Bank, 1300 New York Avenue, NW, Washington, D.C. 20577 (202) 623-1753; *Economic and Social Progress in Latin America.*

Organization of American States (OAS), General Secretariat, Washington, D.C. 20006 (202) 458-3533; *Statistical Bulletin of the OAS.*

Statistical Office of the United Nations, Publishing Service, New York, New York 10017 (800) 253-9646; *Statistical Yearbook for Latin America and the Caribbean.*

ARGENTINA - PUBLIC FINANCE

Facts on File, 460 Park Avenue South, New York, New York 10016 (800) 443-8323; *The New Book of World Rankings.*

Inter-American Development Bank, 1300 New York Avenue, NW, Washington, D.C. 20577 (202) 623-1753; *Economic and Social Progress in Latin America.*

ARGENTINA - PUBLIC REVENUES

Inter-American Development Bank, 1300 New York Avenue, NW, Washington, D.C. 20577 (202) 623-1753; *Economic and Social Progress in Latin America.*

Organization of American States (OAS), General Secretariat, Washington, D.C. 20006 (202) 458-3533; *Statistical Bulletin of the OAS.*

ARGENTINA - RADIO BROADCASTING - See ARGENTINA - BROADCASTING

ARGENTINA - RAILWAYS

The Economist Intelligence Unit, 111 West 57th Street, New York, New York 10019 (800) 938-4685; *The New Latin America Market Atlas.*

G.K. Hall and Company, 70 Lincoln Street, Boston, Massachusetts 02111 (617) 423-3990; *The World in Figures.*

Jane's Information Group, Sentinel House, 163 Brighton Road, Coulsdon, Surrey CR5 2NH, England (Telephone Number in U.S. (703) 683-3700); *Jane's World Railways.*

Statistical Office of the United Nations, Publishing Service, New York, New York 10017 (800) 253-9646; *Statistical Yearbook.*

ARGENTINA - RANCHING - See ARGENTINA - AGRICULTURE

ARGENTINA - RAPESEED PRODUCTION - See ARGENTINA - CROPS

ARGENTINA - RELIGION

Facts on File, 460 Park Avenue South, New York, New York 10016 (800) 443-8323; *The New Book of World Rankings.*

U.C.L.A. Latin American Center Publications, University of California, Los Angeles, California 90024 (310) 825-6634; *Statistical Abstract of Latin America.*

ARGENTINA - RENT PRICES

International Labour Office, I.L.O. Publications, CH-1211, Geneva 22, Switzerland; *Yearbook of Labour Statistics.*

ARGENTINA - RESERVES EXCLUDING GOLD

The Economist Intelligence Unit, 111 West 57th Street, New York, New York 10019 (800) 938-4685; *The New Latin America Market Atlas.*

ARGENTINA - RETAIL TRADE

Euromonitor Publications Limited, 87-88 Turnmill Street, London EC1M 5QU, England; *Third World Economic Handbook.*

G.K. Hall and Company, 70 Lincoln Street, Boston, Massachusetts 02111 (617) 423-3990; *The World in Figures.*

Inter-American Development Bank, 1300 New York Avenue, NW, Washington, D.C. 20577 (202) 623-1753; *Economic and Social Progress in Latin America.*

ARGENTINA - RICE PRODUCTION - See ARGENTINA - CROPS

ARGENTINA - ROOT AND TUBER PRODUCTION - See ARGENTINA - CROPS

ARGENTINA - ROUNDWOOD PRODUCTION - See ARGENTINA - FORESTRY AND FOREST PRODUCTS

ARGENTINA - RUBBER PRODUCTION AND CONSUMPTION

Euromonitor Publications Limited, 87-88 Turnmill Street, London EC1M 5QU, England; *Third World Economic Handbook.*

Facts on File, 460 Park Avenue South, New York, New York 10016 (800) 443-8323; *The New Book of World Rankings.*

Statistical Office of the United Nations, Publishing Service, New York, New York 10017 (800) 253-9646; *Statistical Yearbook.*

ARGENTINA - RYE PRODUCTION - See ARGENTINA - CROPS

ARGENTINA - SAFFLOWER SEED PRODUCTION - See ARGENTINA - CROPS

ARGENTINA - SALT PRODUCTION - See ARGENTINA - MINING AND MINERAL PRODUCTS

ARGENTINA - SAWNWOOD PRODUCTION - See ARGENTINA - FORESTRY AND FOREST PRODUCTS

ARGENTINA - SCIENCE AND TECHNOLOGY

U.C.L.A. Latin American Center Publications, University of California, Los Angeles, California 90024 (310) 825-6634; *Statistical Abstract of Latin America.*

Statistical Office of the United Nations, Publishing Service, New York, New York 10017 (800) 253-9646; *Statistical Yearbook.*

ARGENTINA - SCIENTISTS AND ENGINEERS

Statistical Office of the United Nations, Publishing Service, New York, New York 10017 (800) 253-9646; *Statistical Yearbook.*

ARGENTINA - SENIOR CITIZENS

Facts on File, 460 Park Avenue South, New York, New York 10016 (800) 443-8323; *The New Book of World Rankings.*

ARGENTINA - SHEEP - See ARGENTINA - LIVESTOCK AND POULTRY

ARGENTINA - SILVER PRODUCTION AND CONSUMPTION - See ARGENTINA - MINING AND MINERAL PRODUCTS

ARGENTINA - SKINS AND HIDES EXPORTS

International Monetary Fund, 700 Nineteenth Street, NW, Washington, D.C. 20431 (202) 623-7000; *International Financial Statistics.*

ARGENTINA - SOCIAL DATA

Facts on File, 460 Park Avenue South, New York, New York 10016 (800) 443-8323; *The New Book of World Rankings.*

G.K. Hall and Company, 70 Lincoln Street, Boston, Massachusetts 02111 (617) 423-3990; *The World in Figures.*

U.C.L.A. Latin American Center Publications, University of California, Los Angeles, California 90024 (310) 825-6634; *Statistical Abstract of Latin America.*

ARGENTINA - SOCIAL SECURITY

International Monetary Fund, 700 Nineteenth Street, NW, Washington, D.C. 20431 (202) 623-7000; *Government Finance Statistics Yearbook.*

Inter-American Development Bank, 1300 New York Avenue, NW, Washington, D.C. 20577 (202) 623-1753; *Economic and Social Progress in Latin America.*

ARGENTINA - SOCIOECONOMIC DATA

Inter-American Development Bank, 1300 New York Avenue, NW, Washington, D.C. 20577 (202) 623-1753; *Economic and Social Progress in Latin America.*

U.C.L.A. Latin American Center Publications, University of California, Los Angeles, California 90024 (310) 825-6634; *Statistical Abstract of Latin America.*

ARGENTINA - SOYBEAN PRODUCTION - See ARGENTINA - CROPS

ARGENTINA - STAMP TAXES AND DUTIES - See ARGENTINA - TAXATION

ARGENTINA - STATE BUDGET REVENUE AND EXPENDITURES

Euromonitor Publications Limited, 87-88 Turnmill Street, London EC1M 5QU, England; *International Marketing Data and Statistics.*

Inter-American Development Bank, 1300 New York Avenue, NW, Washington, D.C. 20577 (202) 623-1753; *Economic and Social Progress in Latin America.*

ARGENTINA - STEEL - See ARGENTINA - MINING AND MINERAL PRODUCTS

ARGENTINA - STEEL PRODUCTION - See ARGENTINA - MINING AND MINERAL PRODUCTS

ARGENTINA - STOCKS - COMMODITY - MARKET PRICE - INDEX

Food and Agricultural Organization of the United Nations (FAO) Via Delle Terme di Caracalla, 00100 Rome, Italy (Telephone Number in U.S. (202) 653-2400); *The State of Food and Agriculture.*

International Lead and Zinc Study Group, Metro House, 58 St. James's Street, London SW1A 1LD, England; *Lead and Zinc Statistics.*

ARGENTINA - SUGAR PRODUCTION AND CONSUMPTION - See ARGENTINA - CROPS

ARGENTINA - SULPHUR AND SULPHURIC ACID - See ARGENTINA - MINING AND MINERAL PRODUCTS

ARGENTINA - TAX REVENUE - See ARGENTINA - TAXATION

ARGENTINA - TAXATION

Inter-American Development Bank, 1300 New York Avenue, NW, Washington, D.C. 20577 (202) 623-1753; *Economic and Social Progress in Latin America.*

International Monetary Fund, 700 Nineteenth Street, NW, Washington, D.C. 20431 (202) 623-7000; *Government Finance Statistics Yearbook.*

Statistical Office of the United Nations, Publishing Service, New York, New York 10017 (800) 253-9646; *Statistical Yearbook for Latin America and the Caribbean.*

The World Bank, 1818 H Street, NW, Washington, D.C. 20433 (202) 477-1234; *World Tables.*

ARGENTINA - TEA - See ARGENTINA - CROPS

ARGENTINA - TELEGRAPH SERVICE

Statistical Office of the United Nations, Publishing Service, New York, New York 10017 (800) 253-9646; *Statistical Yearbook.*

ARGENTINA - TELEPHONES IN USE

American Telephone and Telegraph Company, Customer Information Center, 26 Parsippany Road, Whippany, New Jersey 07981 (800) 338-4038; *The World's Telephones.*

The Economist Intelligence Unit, 111 West 57th Street, New York, New York 10019 (800) 938-4685; *The New Latin America Market Atlas.*

Euromonitor Publications Limited, 87-88 Turnmill Street, London EC1M 5QU, England; *Third World Economic Handbook.*

G.K. Hall and Company, 70 Lincoln Street, Boston, Massachusetts 02111 (617) 423-3990; *The World in Figures.*

Statistical Office of the United Nations, Publishing Service, New York, New York 10017 (800) 253-9646; *Statistical Yearbook.*

ARGENTINA - TELEVISION BROADCASTING - See ARGENTINA - BROADCASTING

ARGENTINA - TELEVISION RECEIVER PRODUCTION

Statistical Office of the United Nations, Publishing Service, New York, New York 10017 (800) 253-9646; *Statistical Yearbook.*

ARGENTINA - TEXTILE INDUSTRY

Euromonitor Publications Limited, 87-88 Turnmill Street, London EC1M 5QU, England; *Third World Economic Handbook.*

Forest and Paper Association, 1250 Connecticut Avenue, NW, Washington, D.C. 20036 (202) 463-2455; *Pulp and Fiber Statistics.*

G.K. Hall and Company, 70 Lincoln Street, Boston, Massachusetts 02111 (617) 423-3990; *The World in Figures.*

Statistical Office of the United Nations, Publishing Service, New York, New York 10017 (800) 253-9646; *Statistical Yearbook.*

ARGENTINA - THEATERS - See ARGENTINA - MOTION PICTURES

ARGENTINA - TIN - See ARGENTINA - MINING AND MINERAL PRODUCTS

ARGENTINA - TIRE (MOTOR VEHICLE) PRODUCTION

Statistical Office of the United Nations, Publishing Service, New York, New York 10017 (800) 253-9646; *Statistical Yearbook.*

ARGENTINA - TOBACCO PRODUCTION

Euromonitor Publications Limited, 87-88 Turnmill Street, London EC1M 5QU, England; *Third World Economic Handbook.*

Facts on File, 460 Park Avenue South, New York, New York 10016 (800) 443-8323; *The New Book of World Rankings.*

Statistical Office of the United Nations, Publishing Service, New York, New York 10017 (800) 253-9646; *Statistical Yearbook.*

ARGENTINA - TOURISM

The Economist Intelligence Unit, 111 West 57th Street, New York, New York 10019 (800) 938-4685; *The New Latin America Market Atlas.*

Facts on File, 460 Park Avenue South, New York, New York 10016 (800) 443-8323; *The New Book of World Rankings.*

Federal Statistical Office, Gustav - Stresemann - Ring 11, D-6200 Wiesbaden, Germany; *Argentina.*

G.K. Hall and Company, 70 Lincoln Street, Boston, Massachusetts 02111 (617) 423-3990; *The World in Figures.*

Statistical Office of the United Nations, Publishing Service, New York, New York 10017 (800) 253-9646; *Statistical Yearbook,* and

Statistical Yearbook for Latin America and the Caribbean.

Times Books, 201 East 50th Street, New York, New York 10022 (212) 751-2600; *The Economist Book of Vital World Statistics.*

U.C.L.A. Latin American Center Publications, University of California, Los Angeles, California 90024 (310) 825-6634; *Statistical Abstract of Latin America.*

World Tourism Organization, Calle Capitan Haya 42, E-28020 Madrid, Spain; *Yearbook of Tourism Statistics.*

ARGENTINA - TRACTORS IN USE

The Economist Intelligence Unit, 111 West 57th Street, New York, New York 10019 (800) 938-4685; *The New Latin America Market Atlas.*

ARGENTINA - TRADE - See ARGENTINA - FOREIGN TRADE

ARGENTINA - TRADEMARKS AND SERVICE MARKS

Statistical Office of the United Nations, Publishing Service, New York, New York 10017 (800) 253-9646; *Statistical Yearbook.*

ARGENTINA - TRANSPORTATION AND COMMUNICATIONS

The Economist Intelligence Unit, 111 West 57th Street, New York, New York 10019 (800) 938-4685; *The New Latin America Market Atlas.*

Euromonitor Publications Limited, 87-88 Turnmill Street, London EC1M 5QU, England; *Third World Economic Handbook.*

Federal Statistical Office, Gustav - Stresemann - Ring 11, D-6200 Wiesbaden, Germany; *Argentina.*

Facts on File, 460 Park Avenue South, New York, New York 10016 (800) 443-8323; *The New Book of World Rankings.*

Gale Research Incorporated, 835 Penobscot Building, Detroit, Michigan 48226 (800) 877-4253; *International Historical Statistics the Americas and Australasia.*

G.K. Hall and Company, 70 Lincoln Street, Boston, Massachusetts 02111 (617) 423-3990; *The World in Figures.*

Inter-American Development Bank, 1300 New York Avenue, NW, Washington, D.C. 20577 (202) 623-1753; *Economic and Social Progress in Latin America.*

Statistical Office of the United Nations, Publishing Service, New York, New York 10017 (800) 253-9646; *Statistical Yearbook for Latin America and the Caribbean.*

U.C.L.A. Latin American Center Publications, University of California, Los Angeles, California 90024 (310) 825-6634; *Statistical Abstract of Latin America.*

ARGENTINA - TRAVEL FARES ABROAD

International Monetary Fund, 700 Nineteenth Street, NW, Washington, D.C. 20431 (202) 623-7000; *Government Finance Statistics Yearbook.*

ARGENTINA - TUNGSTEN PRODUCTION AND CONSUMPTION - See ARGENTINA - MINING AND MINERAL PRODUCTS

ARGENTINA - TURKEYS - See ARGENTINA - LIVESTOCK AND POULTRY

ARGENTINA - UNEMPLOYMENT

The Economist Intelligence Unit, 111 West 57th Street, New York, New York 10019 (800) 938-4685; *The New Latin America Market Atlas.*

Euromonitor Publications Limited, 87-88 Turnmill Street, London EC1M 5QU, England; *International Marketing Data and Statistics.*

International Labour Office, I.L.O. Publications, CH-1211, Geneva 22, Switzerland; *Yearbook of Labour Statistics.*

Organization of American States (OAS), General Secretariat, Washington, D.C. 20006 ((202) 458-3533; *Statistical Bulletin of the OAS.*

Statistical Office of the United Nations, Publishing Service, New York, New York 10017 (800) 253-9646; *Statistical Yearbook.*

U.C.L.A. Latin American Center Publications, University of California, Los Angeles, California 90024 (310) 825-6634; *Statistical Abstract of Latin America.*

ARGENTINA - URANIUM PRODUCTION AND CONSUMPTION - See ARGENTINA - MINING AND MINERAL PRODUCTS

ARGENTINA - UTILITIES

U.C.L.A. Latin American Center Publications, University of California, Los Angeles, California 90024 (310) 825-6634; *Statistical Abstract of Latin America.*

ARGENTINA - VITAL STATISTICS

Euromonitor Publications Limited, 87-88 Turnmill Street, London EC1M 5QU, England; *International Marketing Data and Statistics,* and *Third World Economic Handbook.*

Gale Research Incorporated, 835 Penobscot Building, Detroit, Michigan 48226 (800) 877-4253; *International Historical Statistics the Americas and Australasia.*

G.K. Hall and Company, 70 Lincoln Street, Boston, Massachusetts 02111 (617) 423-3990; *The World in Figures.*

Statistical Office of the United Nations, Publishing Service, New York, New York 10017 (800) 253-9646; *Statistical Yearbook.*

World Health Organization, Office of Publications, Avenue Appia, CH-1211 Geneva 27, Switzerland (Telephone Number in U.S. (518) 436-9686; *World Health Statistics Annual.*

ARGENTINA - WAGES

Federal Statistical Office, Gustav - Stresemann - Ring 11, D-6200 Wiesbaden, Germany; *Argentina.*

G.K. Hall and Company, 70 Lincoln Street, Boston, Massachusetts 02111 (617) 423-3990; *The World in Figures.*

International Labour Office, I.L.O. Publications, CH-1211, Geneva 22, Switzerland; *Yearbook of Labour Statistics.*

Statistical Office of the United Nations, Publishing Service, New York, New York 10017 (800) 253-9646; *Statistical Yearbook.*

U.C.L.A. Latin American Center Publications, University of California, Los Angeles, California 90024 (310) 825-6634; *Statistical Abstract of Latin America*.

ARGENTINA - WALNUT PRODUCTION - See ARGENTINA - CROPS

ARGENTINA - WATERMELON PRODUCTION - See ARGENTINA - CROPS

ARGENTINA - WEATHER

Facts on File, 460 Park Avenue South, New York, New York 10016 (800) 443-8323; *The New Book of World Rankings*. -

G.K. Hall and Company, 70 Lincoln Street, Boston, Massachusetts 02111 (617) 423-3990; *The World in Figures*.

ARGENTINA - WELFARE

Inter-American Development Bank, 1300 New York Avenue, NW, Washington, D.C. 20577 (202) 623-1753; *Economic and Social Progress in Latin America*.

International Monetary Fund, 700 Nineteenth Street, NW, Washington, D.C. 20431 (202) 623-7000; *Government Finance Statistics Yearbook*.

ARGENTINA - WHEAT - See ARGENTINA - CROPS

ARGENTINA - WHOLESALE PRICES

Inter-American Development Bank, 1300 New York Avenue, NW, Washington, D.C. 20577 (202) 623-1753; *Economic and Social Progress in Latin America*.

International Monetary Fund, 700 Nineteenth Street, NW, Washington, D.C. 20431 (202) 623-7000; *International Financial Statistics*.

Organization of American States (OAS), General Secretariat, Washington, D.C. 20006 ((202) 458-3533; *Statistical Bulletin of the OAS*.

ARGENTINA - WHOLESALE TRADE

Euromonitor Publications Limited, 87-88 Turnmill Street, London EC1M 5QU, England; *Third World Economic Handbook*.

Inter-American Development Bank, 1300 New York Avenue, NW, Washington, D.C. 20577 (202) 623-1753; *Economic and Social Progress in Latin America*.

Statistical Office of the United Nations, Publishing Service, New York, New York 10017 (800) 253-9646; *Statistical Yearbook*.

ARGENTINA - WINE PRODUCTION

Facts on File, 460 Park Avenue South, New York, New York 10016 (800) 443-8323; *The New Book of World Rankings*.

Statistical Office of the United Nations, Publishing Service, New York, New York 10017 (800) 253-9646; *Statistical Yearbook*.

ARGENTINA - WOOD AND WOOD PULP - See ARGENTINA - FORESTRY AND FOREST PRODUCTS

ARGENTINA - WOOL - INDUSTRIAL CONSUMPTION

Statistical Office of the United Nations, Publishing Service, New York, New York 10017 (800) 253-9646; *Statistical Yearbook*.

ARGENTINA - WOOL EXPORTS

International Monetary Fund, 700 Nineteenth Street, NW, Washington, D.C. 20431 (202) 623-7000; *International Financial Statistics*.

ARGENTINA - WOOL PRODUCTION

Commodity Research Bureau, Incorporated, 75 Wall Street, New York, New York 10005 (212) 504-7754; *Commodity Year Book*.

Facts on File, 460 Park Avenue South, New York, New York 10016 (800) 443-8323; *The New Book of World Rankings*.

Statistical Office of the United Nations, Publishing Service, New York, New York 10017 (800) 253-9646; *Statistical Yearbook*.

ARGENTINA - YARN PRODUCTION

Statistical Office of the United Nations, Publishing Service, New York, New York 10017 (800) 253-9646; *Statistical Yearbook*.

ARGENTINA - ZINC AND ZINC ORE - See ARGENTINA - MINING AND MINERAL PRODUCTS

ARGENTINA - ZOOS AND BOTANICAL GARDENS

United Nations Educational, Scientific and Cultural Organization (UNESCO), 7 Place de Fontenoy, F-75700 Paris, France (Telephone Number in U.S. (212) 963-5981; *Statistical Yearbook*.

ARIZONA - See also STATE DATA (FOR INDIVIDUAL STATES)

Arizona - Primary Statistics Sources

University of Arizona, Division of Economic and Business Research, College of Business and Public Administration, Tucson, Arizona 85721 (602) 621-2155; *Arizona Economic Indicators, Arizona Statistical Abstract: A Data Handbook*, and *Arizona's Economy*.

Arizona - State Data Centers

Arizona Department of Security, Mail Code DES, 1789 West Jefferson Street, Phoenix, Arizona 85007, Ms. Betty Jeffries, (602) 542-5984.

Center for Business Research, College of Business Administration, Arizona State University, Tempe, Arizona 85287, Mr. Tom Rex, (602) 965-3961.

College of Business Administration, Northern Arizona University, Box 15066, Flagstaff, Arizona 86011, Ms. Linda Stratton, (602) 523-7313.

Division of Economic and Business Research, College of Business and Public Administration, University of Arizona, Tucson, Arizona 85721, Ms. Pia Montoya, (602) 621-2155.

Research Library, Department of Library, Archives, and Public Records, 1700 West Washington, 2nd Floor, Phoenix, Arizona 85007, Ms. Janet Fisher, (602) 542-3701.

ARKANSAS - See also STATE DATA (FOR INDIVIDUAL STATES)

Arkansas - Primary Statistics Sources

University of Arkansas, Little Rock, Regional Economic Analysis Library 512, Little Rock, Arkansas 72204; *Arkansas State and County Economic Data.*

University of Arkansas at Little Rock, State Data Center, Library 508, Little Rock, Arkansas 72204 (501) 569-8530; *Arkansas Statistical Abstract.*

Arkansas - State Data Centers

State Data Center, University of Arkansas at Little Rock, 2801 South University Avenue, Little Rock, Arkansas 72204, Ms. Sarah Breshears (501) 569-8530.

Arkansas State Library, 1 Capitol Mall, Little Rock Arkansas 72201, Ms. Mary Honeycutt (501) 682-2864.

Research and Analysis Section, Arkansas Employment Security Division, Post Office Box 2981, Little Rock, Arizona 72203, Mr. Coy Cozart, (501) 682-3159.

ARMED FORCES

Presidents' Commission on Veterans' Pensions, The White House Office, 1600 Pennsylvania Avenue, NW, Washington, D.C. 20500; *Veterans' Benefits in the United States.*

U.S. Department of Defense, Office of the Secretary, The Pentagon, Washington, D.C. 20301 (703) 545-6700; *Selected Manpower Statistics*, and unpublished data.

U.S. Department of Transportation, Maritime Administration, 400 Seventh Street, SW, Washington, D.C. 20590 (202) 366-5807; *Annual Report of the Secretary of Transportation.*

U.S. National Guard Bureau, The Pentagon, Washington, D.C. 20301 (202) 433-5100; *Annual Review of the Chief, National Guard Bureau.*

ARMED FORCES - FOREIGN COUNTRIES

U.S. Arms Control and Disarmament Agency, 320 Twenty-First Street, NW, Washington, D.C. 20451 (202) 647-8677; *World Military Expenditures and Arms Transfers.*

ARMENIA - See also UNION OF SOVIET SOCIALIST REPUBLICS

ARMENIA - AGRICULTURE

Business International Moscow, 23 Profseyuznaya Ulitsa 117859, Moscow (Telephone Number in U.S. (800) 938-4685); *The CIS Market Atlas.*

Encyclopedia Britannica, Incorporated, 310 South Michigan Avenue, Chicago, Illinois 60604 (312) 347-7000; *Britannica World Data.*

The World Bank, 1818 H Street, NW, Washington, D.C. 20433 (202) 477-1234; *Statistical Handbook: States of the Former USSR.*

ARMENIA - AIRLINE SERVICE

Business International Moscow, 23 Profseyuznaya Ulitsa 117859, Moscow (Telephone Number in U.S. (800) 938-4685); *The CIS Market Atlas.*

Encyclopedia Britannica, Incorporated, 310 South Michigan Avenue, Chicago, Illinois 60604 (312) 347-7000; *Britannica World Data.*

ARMENIA - AREA AND DENSITY OF POPULATION

Business International Moscow, 23 Profseyuznaya Ulitsa 117859, Moscow (Telephone Number in U.S. (800) 938-4685); *The CIS Market Atlas.*

ARMENIA - BANKING

Business International Moscow, 23 Profseyuznaya Ulitsa 117859, Moscow (Telephone Number in U.S. (800) 938-4685); *The CIS Market Atlas.*

ARMENIA - BIRTH RATES

Business International Moscow, 23 Profseyuznaya Ulitsa 117859, Moscow (Telephone Number in U.S. (800) 938-4685); *The CIS Market Atlas.*

Encyclopedia Britannica, Incorporated, 310 South Michigan Avenue, Chicago, Illinois 60604 (312) 347-7000; *Britannica World Data.*

ARMENIA - BUDGET

Business International Moscow, 23 Profseyuznaya Ulitsa 117859, Moscow (Telephone Number in U.S. (800) 938-4685); *The CIS Market Atlas.*

ARMENIA - CATTLE - See ARMENIA - LIVESTOCK AND POULTRY

ARMENIA - CHEMICALS

Business International Moscow, 23 Profseyuznaya Ulitsa 117859, Moscow (Telephone Number in U.S. (800) 938-4685); *The CIS Market Atlas.*

ARMENIA - COAL PRODUCTION AND CONSUMPTION - See ARMENIA - MINING AND MINERAL PRODUCTION

ARMENIA - COMMUNICATIONS

Business International Moscow, 23 Profseyuznaya Ulitsa 117859, Moscow (Telephone Number in U.S. (800) 938-4685); *The CIS Market Atlas.*

ARMENIA - CONSTRUCTION INDUSTRY

Business International Moscow, 23 Profseyuznaya Ulitsa 117859, Moscow (Telephone Number in U.S. (800) 938-4685); *The CIS Market Atlas.*

Encyclopedia Britannica, Incorporated, 310 South Michigan Avenue, Chicago, Illinois 60604 (312) 347-7000; *Britannica World Data.*

ARMENIA - CONSUMER PRODUCTS

Business International Moscow, 23 Profseyuznaya Ulitsa 117859, Moscow (Telephone Number in U.S. (800) 938-4685); *The CIS Market Atlas.*

ARMENIA - CONSUMPTION

Business International Moscow, 23 Profseyuznaya Ulitsa 117859, Moscow (Telephone Number in U.S. (800) 938-4685); *The CIS Market Atlas.*

ARMENIA - COTTON PRODUCTION AND CONSUMPTION - See ARMENIA - CROPS

ARMENIA - CROPS

Business International Moscow, 23 Profseyuznaya Ulitsa 117859, Moscow (Telephone Number in U.S. (800) 938-4685); *The CIS Market Atlas.*

ARMENIA - DEATH RATES

Business International Moscow, 23 Profseyuznaya Ulitsa 117859, Moscow (Telephone Number in U.S. (800) 938-4685); *The CIS Market Atlas.*

ARMENIA - DEMOGRAPHY

Business International Moscow, 23 Profseyuznaya Ulitsa 117859, Moscow (Telephone Number in U.S. (800) 938-4685); *The CIS Market Atlas.*

Encyclopedia Britannica, Incorporated, 310 South Michigan Avenue, Chicago, Illinois 60604 (312) 347-7000; *Britannica World Data.*

ARMENIA - DISEASES

Business International Moscow, 23 Profseyuznaya Ulitsa 117859, Moscow (Telephone Number in U.S. (800) 938-4685); *The CIS Market Atlas.*

ARMENIA - DIVORCE RATES

Encyclopedia Britannica, Incorporated, 310 South Michigan Avenue, Chicago, Illinois 60604 (312) 347-7000; *Britannica World Data.*

ARMENIA - DOMESTIC INVESTMENT

Business International Moscow, 23 Profseyuznaya Ulitsa 117859, Moscow (Telephone Number in U.S. (800) 938-4685); *The CIS Market Atlas.*

ARMENIA - ECONOMY

Business International Moscow, 23 Profseyuznaya Ulitsa 117859, Moscow (Telephone Number in U.S. (800) 938-4685); *The CIS Market Atlas.*

Encyclopedia Britannica, Incorporated, 310 South Michigan Avenue, Chicago, Illinois 60604 (312) 347-7000; *Britannica World Data.*

ARMENIA - EDUCATION

Business International Moscow, 23 Profseyuznaya Ulitsa 117859, Moscow (Telephone Number in U.S. (800) 938-4685); *The CIS Market Atlas.*

Encyclopedia Britannica, Incorporated, 310 South Michigan Avenue, Chicago, Illinois 60604 (312) 347-7000; *Britannica World Data.*

ARMENIA - ELECTRICITY PRODUCTION

Business International Moscow, 23 Profseyuznaya Ulitsa 117859, Moscow (Telephone Number in U.S. (800) 938-4685); *The CIS Market Atlas.*

ARMENIA - ENERGY

Business International Moscow, 23 Profsoyuznaya Ulitsa, 117859, Moscow (Telephone Number in U.S. (800) 938-4685); *The CIS Market Atlas.*

Encyclopedia Britannica, Incorporated, 310 South Michigan Avenue, Chicago, Illinois 60604 (312) 347-7000; *Britannica World Data.*

ARMENIA - ENVIRONMENT

Business International Moscow, 23 Profseyuznaya Ulitsa 117859, Moscow (Telephone Number in U.S. (800) 938-4685); *The CIS Market Atlas.*

ARMENIA - EXPORTS

Business International Moscow, 23 Profseyuznaya Ulitsa 117859, Moscow (Telephone Number in U.S. (800) 938-4685); *The CIS Market Atlas.*

Encyclopedia Britannica, Incorporated, 310 South Michigan Avenue, Chicago, Illinois 60604 (312) 347-7000; *Britannica World Data.*

ARMENIA - FABRIC PRODUCTION AND CONSUMPTION - See ARMENIA - TEXTILE INDUSTRY

ARMENIA - FERTILITY RATES

Encyclopedia Britannica, Incorporated, 310 South Michigan Avenue, Chicago, Illinois 60604 (312) 347-7000; *Britannica World Data.*

ARMENIA - FISHERIES

Encyclopedia Britannica, Incorporated, 310 South Michigan Avenue, Chicago, Illinois 60604 (312) 347-7000; *Britannica World Data.*

ARMENIA - FOOTWEAR PRODUCTION AND CONSUMPTION - See ARMENIA - TEXTILE INDUSTRY

ARMENIA - FOREIGN INVESTMENT

Business International Moscow, 23 Profseyuznaya Ulitsa 117859, Moscow (Telephone Number in U.S. (800) 938-4685); *The CIS Market Atlas.*

ARMENIA - FOREIGN TRADE

Business International Moscow, 23 Profseyuznaya Ulitsa 117859, Moscow (Telephone Number in U.S. (800) 938-4685); *The CIS Market Atlas.*

Encyclopedia Britannica, Incorporated, 310 South Michigan Avenue, Chicago, Illinois 60604 (312) 347-7000; *Britannica World Data.*

ARMENIA - FORESTRY AND FOREST PRODUCTS

Business International Moscow, 23 Profseyuznaya Ulitsa 117859, Moscow (Telephone Number in U.S. (800) 938-4685); *The CIS Market Atlas.*

Encyclopedia Britannica, Incorporated, 310 South Michigan Avenue, Chicago, Illinois 60604 (312) 347-7000; *Britannica World Data.*

ARMENIA - GOATS - See ARMENIA - LIVESTOCK AND POULTRY

ARMENIA - HEALTH

Business International Moscow, 23 Profseyuznaya Ulitsa 117859, Moscow (Telephone Number in U.S. (800) 938-4685); *The CIS Market Atlas.*

Encyclopedia Britannica, Incorporated, 310 South Michigan Avenue, Chicago, Illinois 60604 (312) 347-7000; *Britannica World Data.*

ARMENIA - HIGHWAYS

Business International Moscow, 23 Profseyuznaya Ulitsa 117859, Moscow (Telephone Number in U.S. (800) 938-4685); *The CIS Market Atlas.*

Encyclopedia Britannica, Incorporated, 310 South Michigan Avenue, Chicago, Illinois 60604 (312) 347-7000; *Britannica World Data.*

ARMENIA - HOUSING AND HOUSING UNITS

Business International Moscow, 23 Profseyuznaya Ulitsa 117859, Moscow (Telephone Number in U.S. (800) 938-4685); *The CIS Market Atlas.*

ARMENIA - IMPORTS

Business International Moscow, 23 Profseyuznaya Ulitsa 117859, Moscow (Telephone Number in U.S. (800) 938-4685); *The CIS Market Atlas.*

Encyclopedia Britannica, Incorporated, 310 South Michigan Avenue, Chicago, Illinois 60604 (312) 347-7000; *Britannica World Data.*

ARMENIA - INDUSTRY

Business International Moscow, 23 Profseyuznaya Ulitsa 117859, Moscow (Telephone Number in U.S. (800) 938-4685); *The CIS Market Atlas.*

ARMENIA - INFANT MORTALITY RATES

Business International Moscow, 23 Profseyuznaya Ulitsa 117859, Moscow (Telephone Number in U.S. (800) 938-4685); *The CIS Market Atlas.*

ARMENIA - LABOR

Business International Moscow, 23 Profseyuznaya Ulitsa 117859, Moscow (Telephone Number in U.S. (800) 938-4685); *The CIS Market Atlas.*

ARMENIA - LAND USE

Encyclopedia Britannica, Incorporated, 310 South Michigan Avenue, Chicago, Illinois 60604 (312) 347-7000; *Britannica World Data.*

ARMENIA - LIFE EXPECTANCY

Business International Moscow, 23 Profseyuznaya Ulitsa 117859, Moscow (Telephone Number in U.S. (800) 938-4685); *The CIS Market Atlas.*

ARMENIA - LIVESTOCK AND POULTRY

Business International Moscow, 23 Profseyuznaya Ulitsa 117859, Moscow (Telephone Number in U.S. (800) 938-4685); *The CIS Market Atlas.*

Encyclopedia Britannica, Incorporated, 310 South Michigan Avenue, Chicago, Illinois 60604 (312) 347-7000; *Britannica World Data.*

ARMENIA - MANUFACTURING

Encyclopedia Britannica, Incorporated, 310 South Michigan Avenue, Chicago, Illinois 60604 (312) 347-7000; *Britannica World Data.*

ARMENIA - MARRIAGE RATES

Encyclopedia Britannica, Incorporated, 310 South Michigan Avenue, Chicago, Illinois 60604 (312) 347-7000; *Britannica World Data.*

ARMENIA - MEAT PRODUCTION - See ARMENIA - LIVESTOCK AND POULTRY

ARMENIA - MILITARY

The International Institute for Strategic Studies, 23 Tavistock Street, London WC2E 7NQ, England; *The Military Balance.*

ARMENIA - MINING AND MINERAL PRODUCTS

Business International Moscow, 23 Profseyuznaya Ulitsa 117859, Moscow (Telephone Number in U.S. (800) 938-4685); *The CIS Market Atlas.*

Encyclopedia Britannica, Incorporated, 310 South Michigan Avenue, Chicago, Illinois 60604 (312) 347-7000; *Britannica World Data.*

ARMENIA - MOTOR VEHICLES

Business International Moscow, 23 Profseyuznaya Ulitsa 117859, Moscow (Telephone Number in U.S. (800) 938-4685); *The CIS Market Atlas.*

ARMENIA - NATIONAL INCOME

Business International Moscow, 23 Profseyuznaya Ulitsa 117859, Moscow (Telephone Number in U.S. (800) 938-4685); *The CIS Market Atlas.*

ARMENIA - PIGS - See ARMENIA - LIVESTOCK AND POULTRY

ARMENIA - POPULATION

Business International Moscow, 23 Profseyuznaya Ulitsa 117859, Moscow (Telephone Number in U.S. (800) 938-4685); *The CIS Market Atlas.*

Encyclopedia Britannica, Incorporated, 310 South Michigan Avenue, Chicago, Illinois 60604 (312) 347-7000; *Britannica World Data.*

ARMENIA - POULTRY - See ARMENIA - LIVESTOCK AND POULTRY

ARMENIA - RADIO RECEIVERS

Encyclopedia Britannica, Incorporated, 310 South Michigan Avenue, Chicago, Illinois 60604 (312) 347-7000; *Britannica World Data.*

ARMENIA - RAILWAYS

Business International Moscow, 23 Profseyuznaya Ulitsa 117859, Moscow (Telephone Number in U.S. (800) 938-4685); *The CIS Market Atlas.*

Encyclopedia Britannica, Incorporated, 310 South Michigan Avenue, Chicago, Illinois 60604 (312) 347-7000; *Britannica World Data.*

ARMENIA - RETAIL TRADE

Business International Moscow, 23 Profseyuznaya Ulitsa 117859, Moscow (Telephone Number in U.S. (800) 938-4685); *The CIS Market Atlas.*

ARMENIA - ROADS - See ARMENIA - HIGHWAYS

ARMENIA - ROUNDWOOD PRODUCTION AND CONSUMPTION - See ARMENIA - FORESTRY AND FOREST PRODUCTS

ARMENIA - SHEEP - See ARMENIA - LIVESTOCK AND POULTRY

ARMENIA - STEEL PRODUCTION AND CONSUMPTION - See ARMENIA - MINING AND MINERAL PRODUCTION

ARMENIA - TELEPHONES IN USE

Encyclopedia Britannica, Incorporated, 310 South Michigan Avenue, Chicago, Illinois 60604 (312) 347-7000; *Britannica World Data.*

ARMENIA - TELEVISION RECEIVERS

Encyclopedia Britannica, Incorporated, 310 South Michigan Avenue, Chicago, Illinois 60604 (312) 347-7000; *Britannica World Data.*

ARMENIA - TEXTILE INDUSTRY

Business International Moscow, 23 Profseyuznaya Ulitsa 117859, Moscow (Telephone Number in U.S. (800) 938-4685); *The CIS Market Atlas.*

ARMENIA - TOURISM

Business International Moscow, 23 Profseyuznaya Ulitsa 117859, Moscow (Telephone Number in U.S. (800) 938-4685); *The CIS Market Atlas.*

ARMENIA - TRANSPORTATION AND COMMUNICATION

Business International Moscow, 23 Profseyuznaya Ulitsa 117859, Moscow (Telephone Number in U.S. (800) 938-4685); *The CIS Market Atlas.*

Encyclopedia Britannica, Incorporated, 310 South Michigan Avenue, Chicago, Illinois 60604 (312) 347-7000; *Britannica World Data.*

ARMENIA - VITAL STATISTICS

Encyclopedia Britannica, Incorporated, 310 South Michigan Avenue, Chicago, Illinois 60604 (312) 347-7000; *Britannica World Data.*

ARMENIA - WAGES

Business International Moscow, 23 Profseyuznaya Ulitsa 117859, Moscow (Telephone Number in U.S. (800) 938-4685); *The CIS Market Atlas.*

ARMENIA - WOOL PRODUCTION AND CONSUMPTION - See ARMENIA - TEXTILE INDUSTRY

ARMS EXPORTS AND IMPORTS

U.S. Arms Control and Disarmament Agency, 320 Twenty-first Street, NW, Washington, D.C. 20451 (202) 647-8677; *World Military Expenditures and Arms Transfers.*

ARMY - PERSONNEL

Executive Office of the President, Office of Management and Budget, Executive Office Building, Washington, D.C. 20503 (202) 395-3080; *Budget of the U.S. Government.*

U.S. Department of Defense, Office of the Secretary, The Pentagon, Washington, D.C. 20301 (703) 545-6700; *Selected Manpower Statistics.*

ARRESTS - See also LAW ENFORCEMENT

U.S. Department of Justice, Federal Bureau of Investigation, Ninth Street and Pennsylvania Avenue, NW, Washington, D.C. 20535 (202) 324-3000; *Crime in the United States.*

ARSENIC

U.S. Department of the Interior, Bureau of Mines, 810 Seventh Street, NW, Washington, D.C. 20241 (202) 501-9649; *Mineral Commodity Summaries.*

ARSON

National Fire Protection Association, One Batterymarch Park, Quincy, Massachusetts 02169 (617) 770-3000; *NFPA Reports on Fire Loss,* in Fire Journal.

U.S. Department of Justice, Federal Bureau of Investigation, Ninth Street and Pennsylvania Avenue, NW, Washington, D.C. 20535 (202) 324-3000; *Crime in the United States.*

ARTERIOSCLEROSIS - DEATHS

U.S. Department of Health and Human Services, National Center for Health Statistics, 3700 East-West Highway, Hyattsville, Maryland 20782 (301) 436-8500; *Vital Statistics of the United States, Monthly Vital Statistics Report,* and unpublished data.

ARTHRITIS AND RHEUMATISM

U.S. Department of Health and Human Services, National Center for Health Statistics, 3700 East-West Highway, Hyattsville, Maryland 20782 (301) 436-8500; *Vital and Health Statistics,* unpublished data.

ARTS AND HUMANITIES - AID TO

U.S. National Endowment for the Arts, 1100 Pennsylvania Avenue, NW, Washington, D.C. 20506 (202) 682-5400; *Annual Report.*

U.S. National Endowment for the Humanities, 1100 Pennsylvania Avenue, NW, Washington, D.C. 20506 (202) 606-8438; *Annual Report.*

ARTS AND HUMANITIES - ATTENDANCE

American Symphony Orchestra League, 777 Fourteenth Street, NW, Washington, D.C. 20005 (202) 628-0099.

Opera America, 777 14th Street, NW, Suite 520, Washington, D.C. (202) 347-9262; *Opera America-Profile.*

Theatre Communications Group, 355 Lexington Avenue, New York, New York 10017 (212) 697-5230.

Variety, 249 West 17th Street, New York, New York 10011 (212) 779-1100; various June issues.

ARTS AND HUMANITIES - CHARITABLE CONTRIBUTIONS

Gallup Organization, Incorporated, 100 Palmer Square, Princeton, New Jersey 08542 (609) 924-9600; *Giving and Volunteering in the United States.* Published by Independent Sector, 1828 L Street, NW, Washington, D.C. 20036 (202) 223-8100.

ARTS AND HUMANITIES - FEDERAL AID

U.S. National Endowment for the Arts, 1100 Pennsylvania Avenue, NW, Washington, D.C. 20506 (202) 682-5400; *Annual Report.*

U.S. National Endowment for the Humanities, 1100 Pennsylvania Avenue, NW, Washington, D.C. 20506 (202) 606-8438; *Annual Report.*

ARTS AND HUMANITIES - GRANTS, FOUNDATIONS

Foundation Center, 79 Fifth Avenue, New York, New York 10003 (212) 620-4230; *Foundation Grants Index.*

ARTS AND HUMANITIES - PHILANTHROPY

American Association of Fund Raising Counsel, 25 West 43rd Street, New York, Suite 820, New York 10036 (212) 354-5799; *Giving USA.*

ARUBA - BROADCASTING

Billboard Limited, P.O. Box 9027, 1006 AA Amsterdam, The Netherlands (Telephone Number in U.S. (212) 764-7300); *World Radio TV Handbook.*

ARUBA - TOURISM

World Tourism Organization, Calle Capitan Haya 42, E-28020 Madrid, Spain; *Yearbook of Tourism Statistics.*

ASBESTOS

Environmental Business International, 4452 Park Boulevard, Suite 306, San Diego, California 92116 (619) 295-7685; *Environmental Business Journal.*

U.S. Department of the Interior, Bureau of Mines, 810 Seventh Street, NW, Washington, D.C. 20241 (202) 501-9649; *Minerals Yearbook, Mineral Commodity Summaries,* and *Annual Reports.*

ASIA - See FOREIGN COUNTRIES

ASIAN AND PACIFIC ISLANDER POPULATION

U.S. Department of Commerce, Bureau of Census, Suitland, Maryland 20233 (301) 763-4040; *Census of Agriculture, Census of Population,* and *Current Population Reports.*

U.S. Department of Education, National Center for Education Statistics, 400 Maryland Avenue, SW, Washington, D.C. 20202 (202) 708-5366; *Digest of Education Statistics.*

ASIAN POPULATION

National Science Foundation, 1800 G Street, NW, Washington, D.C. 20550 (202) 357-5000; *Survey of Earned Doctorates.*

U.S. Department of Commerce, Bureau of the Census, Suitland, Maryland 20233 (301) 763-4040; *Census of Population,* and *Census of Agriculture.*

U.S. Department of Health and Human Services, National Center for Health Statistics, 3700 East-West Highway, Hyattsville, Maryland 20782 (301) 436-8500; *Vital Statistics of the United States, Monthly Vital Statistics Report,* and unpublished data.

ASIAN INDIAN POPULATION

U.S. Department of Commerce, Bureau of Census, Suitland, Maryland 20233 (301) 763-4040; *Census of Population.*

ASPARAGUS

U.S. Department of Agriculture, Economic Research Service, Fourteenth Street and Independence Avenue, SW, Washington, D.C. 20250 (202) 219-1504; *Food Consumption, Prices, and Expenditures,* and unpublished data.

U.S. Department of Agriculture, National Agricultural Statistics Service, Fourteenth Street and Independence Avenue, SW, Washington, D.C. 20250 (202) 219-1504; *Vegetables,* and *Agricultural Statistics.*

ASPHALT

U.S. Department of Labor, Bureau of Labor Statistics, Two Massachusetts Avenue, NE, Washington, D.C. 20212 (202) 606-7828; *Producer Price Indexes.*

U.S. Department of the Interior, Bureau of Mines, 810 Seventh Street, NW, Washington, D.C. 20241 (202) 501-9649; *Minerals Yearbook.*

ASSAULT

U.S. Department of Justice, Bureau of Justice Statistics, 633 Indiana Avenue, NW, Washington, D.C. 20531 (800) 732-3277; *Criminal Victimization in the United States,* and *Crime and the Elderly.*

U.S. Department of Justice, Federal Bureau of Investigation, Ninth Street and Pennsylvania Avenue, NW, Washington, D.C. 20535 (202) 324-3000; *Crime in the United States.*

ASSETS - PERSONAL

Board of Governors of the Federal Reserve System, Twentieth Street and Constitution Avenue, NW, Washington, D.C. 20551 (202) 452-3000; *Federal Reserve Bulletin.*

U.S. Department of Commerce, Bureau of the Census, Suitland, Maryland 20212 (301) 763-4040; *Current Population Reports.*

U.S. Department of the Treasury, Internal Revenue Service, 1111 Constitution Avenue, NW, Washington, D.C. 20224 (202) 566-5000; *Statistics of Income Bulletin.*

ASSOCIATIONS - NATIONAL - NONPROFIT

Gale Research Incorporated, 835 Penobscot Building, Detroit, Michigan 48226 (800) 877-4253; *Encyclopedia of Associations.*

ASTHMA

U.S. Department of Health and Human Services, National Center for Health Statistics, 3700 East-West Highway, Hyattsville, Maryland 20782 (301) 436-8500; *Health, United States, Monthly Vital Statistics Report, Vital Statistics of the United States,* and unpublished data.

ATHEROSCLEROSIS - DEATHS

U.S. Department of Health and Human Services, National Center for Health Statistics, 3700 East-West Highway, Hyattsville, Maryland 20782 (301) 436-8500; *Monthly Vital Statistics Report, Vital Statistics of the United States,* and unpublished data.

ATHLETIC ASSOCIATIONS

Gale Research Incorporated, 835 Penobscot Building, Detroit, Michigan 48226 (800) 877-4253; *Encyclopedia of Associations.*

ATHLETIC GOODS - See SPORTING AND ATHLETIC GOODS

ATHLETES

U.S. Department of Labor, Bureau of Labor Statistics, Two Massachusetts Avenue, NE, Washington, D.C. 20212 (202) 606-7828; *Employment and Earnings.*

ATM'S (AUTOMATED TELLER MACHINES)

Faulkner and Gray, 118 South Clinton Street, Chicago, Illinois 60661 (312) 648-0261; *Bank Network News.*

ATOMIC ENERGY DEFENSE ACTIVITIES - EXPENDITURES

Executive Office of the President, Office of Management and Budget, Executive Office Building, Washington, D.C. 20503 (202) 395-3080; *Budget of the United States Government.*

AUDITING - See ACCOUNTING, AUDITING, AND BOOKKEEPING

Australia - National Statistical Office

Australian Bureau of Statistics, Post Office Box 10, Belconnen, ACT 2616, Australia.

Australia - Primary Statistics Sources

Australian Bureau of Statistics, Post Office Box 10, Belconnen, ACT 2616, Australia; *Year Book Australia, Pocket Year Book Australia,* and *Monthly Summary of Statistics.*

Australia - Databases

AUSSTATS
Australian Bureau of Statistics
Post Office Box 10
Belconnen, ACT 2616, Australia.

Subject coverage: Balance of payments, consumer price index, labor market, national accounts, production figures, and demographic figures.

Australian Commercial Enterprise Statistics
Australian Customs Clearance Statistics
Australian Export Statistics-Harmonized
Australian Harmonized Export Trade Statistics
Australian Harmonized Import Trade Statistics
Australian Import Statistics
Australian Import Statistics-Harmonized
Australian Major Energy Statistics
Australian National Economic Statistics

All of the above databases available online from Reuters Information Services (Canada) Ltd., Data Services Division, 2 First Tower, Suite 2000, Toronto, Ontario, Canada M5X 1E3, (416) 364-5361.

AUSTRALIA - ABORTIONS

Statistical Office of the United Nations, Publishing Service, New York, New York 10017 (800) 253-9646; *Demographic Yearbook.*

AUSTRALIA - AGRICULTURE

Australian Bureau of Statistics, Canberra, Australia; *Year Book Australia.*

Euromonitor Publications Limited, 87-88 Turnmill Street, London EC1M 5QU, England; *The Pacific Basin: An Economic Handbook,* and *International Marketing Data and Statistics.*

Facts on File, 460 Park Avenue South, New York, New York 10016 (800) 443-8323; *The New Book of World Rankings.*

Federal Statistical Office, Gustav - Stresemann - Ring 11, D-6200 Wiesbaden, Germany; *Australien.*

Food and Agricultural Organization of the United Nations (FAO), Via delle Terme di Caracalla, 00100 Rome, Italy (Telephone Number in U.S. (202) 653-2400; *Production Yearbook, The State of Food and Agriculture,* and *Trade Yearbook.*

Gale Research Incorporated, 835 Penobscot Building, Detroit, Michigan 48226 (800) 877-4253; *International Historical Statistics the Americas and Australasia.*

G.K. Hall and Company, 70 Lincoln Street, Boston, Massachusetts 02111 (617) 423-3990; *The World in Figures.*

Organisation for Economic Co-operation and Development (OECD), 2 rue Andre-Pascal, 75 Paris 16, France (Telephone Number in U.S. (202) 785-6323); *Economic Accounts for Agriculture, Indicators of Industrial Activity, Industrial Structure Statistics,* and *OECD Economic Surveys: Australia.*

Statistical Office of the United Nations, Publishing Service, New York, New York 10017 (800) 253-9646; *Statistical Yearbook,* and *Statistical Yearbook for Asia and the Pacific.*

Times Books, 201 East 50th Street, New York, New York 10022 (212) 751-2600; *The Economist Book of Vital World Statistics.*

The World Bank, 1818 H Street, NW, Washington, D.C. 20433 (202) 477-1234; *World Tables.*

AUSTRALIA - AIRLINE SERVICE

The Economist Intelligence Unit (Asia) Limited, 10th Floor, Luk Kwok Centre, 72 Gloucester Road, Wanchai, Hong Kong (Phone Number in U.S. (800) 938-4685); *Asian Market Atlas.*

Facts on File, 460 Park Avenue South, New York, New York 10016 (800) 443-8323; *The New Book of World Rankings.*

G.K. Hall and Company, 70 Lincoln Street, Boston, Massachusetts 02111 (617) 423-3990; *The World in Figures.*

International Civil Aviation Organization, 1000 Sherbrooke Street West, Suite 400, Montreal, Quebec, Canada H3A 2R2 (514) 285-8219; *Civil Aviation Statistics of the World.*

Organisation for Economic Co-operation and Development (OECD), 2 rue Andre-Pascal, 75 Paris 16, France (Telephone Number in U.S. (202) 785-6323); *Tourism Policy and International Tourism in OECD Member Countries.*

Statistical Office of the United Nations, Publishing Service, New York, New York 10017 (800) 253-9646; *Statistical Yearbook.*

Times Books, 201 East 50th Street, New York, New York 10022 (212) 751-2600; *The Economist Book of Vital World Statistics.*

AUSTRALIA - ALMOND PRODUCTION - See AUSTRALIA - CROPS

AUSTRALIA - ALUMINUM PRODUCTION AND CONSUMPTION - See AUSTRALIA - MINING AND MINERAL PRODUCTS

AUSTRALIA - ANIMAL FEEDINGSTUFFS

Organisation for Economic Co-operation and Development (OECD), 2 rue Andre-Pascal, 75 Paris 16, France (Telephone Number in U.S. (202) 785-6323); *Foreign Trade by Commodities.*

Statistical Office of the United Nations, Publishing Service, New York, New York 10017 (800) 253-9646; *Statistical Yearbook.*

AUSTRALIA - ANIMAL HEALTH

Food and Agricultural Organization of the United Nations (FAO), Via delle Terme di Caracalla, 00100 Rome, Italy (Telephone Number in U.S. (202) 653-2400; *Animal Health Yearbook.*

AUSTRALIA - ANTIMONY AND ANTIMONY ORE - See AUSTRALIA-MINING AND MINERAL PRODUCTS

AUSTRALIA - APPLE PRODUCTION - See AUSTRALIA - CROPS

AUSTRALIA - AREA AND DENSITY OF POPULATION

Euromonitor Publications Limited, 87-88 Turnmill Street, London EC1M 5QU, England; *International Marketing Data and Statistics,* and *The Pacific Basin: An Economic Handbook.*

Facts on File, 460 Park Avenue South, New York, New York 10016 (800) 443-8323; *The New Book of World Rankings.*

Federal Statistical Office, Gustav - Stresemann - Ring 11, D-6200 Wiesbaden, Germany; *Australien.*

Food and Agricultural Organization of the United Nations (FAO) Via Delle Terme di Caracalla, 00100 Rome, Italy (Telephone Number in U.S. (202) 653-2400; *The State of Food and Agriculture.*

G.K. Hall and Company, 70 Lincoln Street, Boston, Massachusetts 02111 (617) 423-3990; *The World in Figures.*

Statistical Office of the United Nations, Publishing Service, New York, New York 10017 (800) 253-9646; *Statistical Yearbook.*

Times Books, 201 East 50th Street, New York, New York 10022 (212) 751-2600; *The Economist Book of Vital World Statistics.*

AUSTRALIA - ARMS EXPORTS AND IMPORTS

U.S. Arms Control and Disarmament Agency, 320 Twenty-first Street, NW, Washington, D.C. 20451 (202) 647-8677; *World Military Expenditures and Arms Transfers.*

AUSTRALIA - ARSENIC PRODUCTION AND CONSUMPTION - See AUSTRALIA - MINING AND MINERAL PRODUCTS

AUSTRALIA - BALANCE OF PAYMENTS

The Economist Intelligence Unit, 111 West 57th Street, New York, New York 10019 (800) 938-4685; *The World Market Atlas.*

Federal Statistical Office, Gustav - Stresemann - Ring 11, D-6200 Wiesbaden, Germany; *Australien.*

G.K. Hall and Company, 70 Lincoln Street, Boston, Massachusetts 02111 (617) 423-3990; *The World in Figures.*

International Monetary Fund, 700 Nineteenth Street, NW, Washington, D.C. 20431 (202) 623-7000; *Balance of Payments Yearbook,* and *International Financial Statistics.*

Organisation for Economic Co-operation and Development (OECD), 2 rue Andre-Pascal, 75 Paris 16, France (Telephone Number in U.S. (202) 785-6323); *Economic Outlook, Geographical Distribution of Financial Flows to Developing Countries, Main Economic Indicators - Historical Statistics,* and *OECD Economic Surveys: Australia.*

Times Books, 201 East 50th Street, New York, New York 10022 (212) 751-2600; *The Economist Book of Vital World Statistics.*

The World Bank, 1818 H Street, NW, Washington, D.C. 20433 (202) 477-1234; *World Tables.*

AUSTRALIA - BANKING

Facts on File, 460 Park Avenue South, New York, New York 10016 (800) 443-8323; *The New Book of World Rankings.*

G.K. Hall and Company, 70 Lincoln Street, Boston, Massachusetts 02111 (617) 423-3990; *The World in Figures.*

International Monetary Fund, 700 Nineteenth Street, NW, Washington, D.C. 20431 (202) 623-7000; *Government Finance Statistics Yearbook,* and *International Financial Statistics.*

Organisation for Economic Co-operation and Development (OECD), 2 rue Andre-Pascal, 75 Paris 16, France (Telephone Number in U.S. (202) 785-6323); *Economic Outlook, Financial Market Trends,* and *OECD Economic Surveys: Australia.*

AUSTRALIA - BARLEY PRODUCTION - See AUSTRALIA - CROPS

AUSTRALIA - BAUXITE PRODUCTION AND CONSUMPTION - See AUSTRALIA - MINING AND MINERAL PRODUCTS

AUSTRALIA - BEEF EXPORTS

International Monetary Fund, 700 Nineteenth Street, NW, Washington, D.C. 20431 (202) 623-7000; *International Financial Statistics.*

AUSTRALIA - BEER PRODUCTION

Facts on File, 460 Park Avenue South, New York, New York 10016 (800) 443-8323; *The New Book of World Rankings.*

Statistical Office of the United Nations, Publishing Service, New York, New York 10017 (800) 253-9646; *Statistical Yearbook.*

AUSTRALIA - BEVERAGES - PRODUCTION INDEX

Organisation for Economic Co-operation and Development (OECD), 2 rue Andre-Pascal, 75 Paris 16, France (Telephone Number in U.S. (202) 785-6323); *Indicators of Industrial Activity.*

AUSTRALIA - BIRTH RATE

The Economist Intelligence Unit (Asia) Limited, 10th Floor, Luk Kwok Centre, 72 Gloucester Road, Wanchai, Hong Kong (Phone Number in U.S. (800) 938-4685); *Asian Market Atlas.*

Euromonitor Publications Limited, 87-88 Turnmill Street, London EC1M 5QU, England; *The Pacific Basin: An Economic Handbook.*

Facts on File, 460 Park Avenue South, New York, New York 10016 (800) 443-8323; *The New Book of World Rankings.*

Organisation for Economic Co-operation and Development (OECD), 2 rue Andre-Pascal, 75 Paris 16, France; *Labour Force Statistics.*

Statistical Office of the United Nations, Publishing Service, New York, New York 10017 (800) 253-9646; *Demographic Yearbook*, and *Statistical Yearbook*.

Times Books, 201 East 50th Street, New York, New York 10022 (212) 751-2600; *The Economist Book of Vital World Statistics*.

The World Bank, 1818 H Street, NW, Washington, D.C. 20433 (202) 477-1234; *World Tables*.

World Health Organization, Office of Publications, Geneva, Switzerland (Telephone Number in U.S. (518) 436-9686); *World Health Statistics: Vital Statistics and Causes of Death*.

AUSTRALIA - BISMUTH PRODUCTION AND CONSUMPTION - See AUSTRALIA - MINING AND MINERAL PRODUCTS

AUSTRALIA - BONDS

G.K. Hall and Company, 70 Lincoln Street, Boston, Massachusetts 02111 (617) 423-3990; *The World in Figures*.

International Monetary Fund, 700 Nineteenth Street, NW, Washington, D.C. 20431 (202) 623-7000; *Government Finance Statistics*.

Organisation for Economic Co-operation and Development (OECD), 2 rue Andre-Pascal, 75 Paris 16, France (Telephone Number in U.S. (202) 785-6323); *Financial Market Trends*.

Statistical Office of the United Nations, Publishing Service, New York, New York 10017 (800) 253-9646; *Statistical Yearbook*.

AUSTRALIA - BOOK PRODUCTION

G.K. Hall and Company, 70 Lincoln Street, Boston, Massachusetts 02111 (617) 423-3990; *The World in Figures*.

Organisation for Economic Co-operation and Development (OECD), 2 rue Andre-Pascal, 75 Paris 16, France (Telephone Number in U.S. (202) 785-6323); *Indicators of Industrial Activity*.

United Nations Educational, Scientific and Cultural Organization (UNESCO), 7 Place de Fontenoy, F-75700 Paris, France (Telephone Number in U.S. (212) 963-5981; *Statistical Yearbook*.

AUSTRALIA - BROADCASTING

Billboard Limited, P.O. Box 9027, 1006 AA Amsterdam, The Netherlands (Telephone Number in U.S. (212) 764-7300); *World Radio TV Handbook*.

The Economist Intelligence Unit (Asia) Limited, 10th Floor, Luk Kwok Centre, 72 Gloucester Road, Wanchai, Hong Kong (Phone Number in U.S. (800) 938-4685); *Asian Market Atlas*.

Facts on File, 460 Park Avenue South, New York, New York 10016 (800) 443-8323; *The New Book of World Rankings*.

G.K. Hall and Company, 70 Lincoln Street, Boston, Massachusetts 02111 (617) 423-3990; *The World in Figures*.

Times Books, 201 East 50th Street, New York, New York 10022 (212) 751-2600; *The Economist Book of Vital World Statistics*.

United Nations Educational, Scientific and Cultural Organization (UNESCO), 7 Place de Fontenoy, F-75700 Paris, France (Telephone Number in U.S. (212) 963-5981; *Statistical Yearbook*.

AUSTRALIA - BUILDING CONSTRUCTION - See AUSTRALIA - CONSTRUCTION INDUSTRY

AUSTRALIA - BUSINESS

G.K. Hall and Company, 70 Lincoln Street, Boston, Massachusetts 02111 (617) 423-3990; *The World in Figures*.

Organisation for Economic Co-operation and Development (OECD), 2 rue Andre-Pascal, 75 Paris 16, France (Telephone Number in U.S. (202) 785-6323); *Main Economic Indicators - Historical Statistics*.

AUSTRALIA - BUSINESS AND PROFESSIONAL LICENSES

International Monetary Fund, 700 Nineteenth Street, NW, Washington, D.C. 20431 (202) 623-7000; *Government Finance Statistics Yearbook*.

AUSTRALIA - BUTTER - See AUSTRALIA - DAIRY PRODUCTS

AUSTRALIA - CABBAGE PRODUCTION - See AUSTRALIA - CROPS

AUSTRALIA - CADMIUM PRODUCTION AND CONSUMPTION - See AUSTRALIA - MINING AND MINERAL PRODUCTS

AUSTRALIA - CALORIE SUPPLY

Food and Agricultural Organization of the United Nations (FAO) Via Delle Terme di Caracalla, 00100 Rome, Italy (Telephone Number in U.S. (202) 653-2400; *The State of Food and Agriculture*.

AUSTRALIA - CAPITAL INVESTMENT

Organisation for Economic Co-operation and Development (OECD), 2 rue Andre-Pascal, 75 Paris 16, France (Telephone Number in U.S. (202) 785-6323); *Economic Outlook*, and *Financial Market Trends*.

AUSTRALIA - CAPITAL REVENUE

International Monetary Fund, 700 Nineteenth Street, NW, Washington, D.C. 20431 (202) 623-7000; *Government Finance Statistics Yearbook*.

Organisation for Economic Co-operation and Development (OECD), 2 rue Andre-Pascal, 75 Paris 16, France (Telephone Number in U.S. (202) 785-6323); *Economic Outlook*, and *Financial Market Trends*.

AUSTRALIA - CATTLE - See AUSTRALIA - LIVESTOCK AND POULTRY

AUSTRALIA - CAULIFLOWER PRODUCTION - See AUSTRALIA - CROPS

AUSTRALIA - CAUSTIC SODA PRODUCTION

Organisation for Economic Co-operation and Development (OECD), 2 rue Andre-Pascal, 75 Paris 16, France (Telephone Number in U.S. (202) 785-6323); *Indicators of Industrial Activity*.

Statistical Office of the United Nations, Publishing Service, New York, New York 10017 (800) 253-9646; *Statistical Yearbook*.

AUSTRALIA - CEMENT PRODUCTION - See AUSTRALIA - MINING AND MINERAL PRODUCTS

AUSTRALIA - CEREAL PRODUCTION - See AUSTRALIA - CROPS

AUSTRALIA - CHEESE - See AUSTRALIA - DAIRY PRODUCTS

AUSTRALIA - CHEMICAL (ORGANIC) PRODUCTION - See AUSTRALIA - MINING AND MINERAL PRODUCTS

AUSTRALIA - CHROMITE PRODUCTION AND CONSUMPTION - See AUSTRALIA - MINING AND MINERAL PRODUCTS

AUSTRALIA - CHROMIUM ORE PRODUCTION AND CONSUMPTION - See AUSTRALIA - MINING AND MINERAL PRODUCTS

AUSTRALIA - CIGARETTE PRODUCTION - See AUSTRALIA - TOBACCO PRODUCTION

AUSTRALIA - CLASS STRUCTURE

G.K. Hall and Company, 70 Lincoln Street, Boston, Massachusetts 02111 (617) 423-3990; *The World in Figures.*

AUSTRALIA - CLIMATE

Australian Bureau of Statistics, Canberra, Australia; *Year Book Australia.*

Facts on File, 460 Park Avenue South, New York, New York 10016 (800) 443-8323; *The New Book of World Rankings.*

G.K. Hall and Company, 70 Lincoln Street, Boston, Massachusetts 02111 (617) 423-3990; *The World in Figures.*

AUSTRALIA - CLOTHING EXPORTS AND IMPORTS

Organisation for Economic Co-operation and Development (OECD), 2 rue Andre-Pascal, 75 Paris 16, France (Telephone Number in U.S. (202) 785-6323); *Textile Industry in OECD Countries.*

Statistical Office of the United Nations, Publishing Service, New York, New York 10017 (800) 253-9646; *Trade in Manufactures of Developing Countries.*

AUSTRALIA - CLOTHING - PRODUCTION INDEX

Organisation for Economic Co-operation and Development (OECD), 2 rue Andre-Pascal, 75 Paris 16, France (Telephone Number in U.S. (202) 785-6323); *Indicators of Industrial Activity.*

AUSTRALIA - COAL - See AUSTRALIA - MINING AND MINERAL PRODUCTS

AUSTRALIA - COBALT PRODUCTION AND CONSUMPTION - See AUSTRALIA - MINING AND MINERAL PRODUCTS

AUSTRALIA - COFFEE PRODUCTION AND CONSUMPTION - See AUSTRALIA - CROPS

AUSTRALIA - COKE OVEN COKE PRODUCTION - See AUSTRALIA - MINING AND MINERAL PRODUCTS

AUSTRALIA - COKE OVEN ORE PRODUCTION AND CONSUMPTION - See AUSTRALIA - MINING AND MINERAL PRODUCTS

AUSTRALIA - COKE PRODUCTION AND CONSUMPTION - See AUSTRALIA - MINING AND MINERAL PRODUCTS

AUSTRALIA - COMMUNICATION

Australian Bureau of Statistics, Canberra, Australia; *Year Book Australia.*

Federal Statistical Office, Gustav - Stresemann - Ring 11, D-6200 Wiesbaden, Germany; *Australien.*

G.K. Hall and Company, 70 Lincoln Street, Boston, Massachusetts 02111 (617) 423-3990; *The World in Figures.*

Statistical Office of the United Nations, Publishing Service, New York, New York 10017 (800) 253-9646; *Statistical Yearbook for Asia and the Pacific.*

AUSTRALIA - CONSTRUCTION INDUSTRY

Australian Bureau of Statistics, Canberra, Australia; *Year Book Australia.*

Facts on File, 460 Park Avenue South, New York, New York 10016 (800) 443-8323; *The New Book of World Rankings.*

Organisation for Economic Co-operation and Development (OECD), 2 rue Andre-Pascal, 75 Paris 16, France (Telephone Number in U.S. (202) 785-6323); *Industrial Structure Statistics, The Iron and Steel Industry, Main Economic Indicators - Historical Statistics,* and *OECD Economic Surveys: Australia.*

Statistical Office of the United Nations, Publishing Service, New York, New York 10017 (800) 253-9646; *Construction Statistics Yearbook,* and *Statistical Yearbook.*

AUSTRALIA - CONSUMER PRICE INDEX

Federal Statistical Office, Gustav - Stresemann - Ring 11, D-6200 Wiesbaden, Germany; *Australien.*

G.K. Hall and Company, 70 Lincoln Street, Boston, Massachusetts 02111 (617) 423-3990; *The World in Figures.*

Organisation for Economic Co-operation and Development (OECD), 2 rue Andre-Pascal, 75 Paris 16, France (Telephone Number in U.S. (202) 785-6323); *Economic Outlook.*

Statistical Office of the United Nations, Publishing Service, New York, New York 10017 (800) 253-9646; *Statistical Yearbook.*

AUSTRALIA - CONSUMER PRICES

Federal Statistical Office, Gustav - Stresemann - Ring 11, D-6200 Wiesbaden, Germany; *Australien.*

International Labour Office, I.L.O. Publications, CH-1211, Geneva 22, Switzerland; *Yearbook of Labour Statistics.*

International Monetary Fund, 700 Nineteenth Street, NW, Washington, D.C. 20431 (202) 623-7000; *International Financial Statistics.*

Organisation for Economic Co-operation and Development (OECD), 2 rue Andre-Pascal, 75 Paris 16, France (Telephone Number in U.S. (202) 785-6323); *Economic Outlook.*

Times Books, 201 East 50th Street, New York, New York 10022 (212) 751-2600; *The Economist Book of Vital World Statistics.*

AUSTRALIA - CONSUMPTION

Euromonitor Publications Limited, 87-88 Turnmill Street, London EC1M 5QU, England; *The Pacific Basin: An Economic Handbook.*

G.K. Hall and Company, 70 Lincoln Street, Boston, Massachusetts 02111 (617) 423-3990; *The World in Figures.*

International Iron and Steel Institute, 120, rue Colonel Bourg, B-1140, Brussels, Belgium; *Steel Statistical Yearbook.*

International Lead and Zinc Study Group, Metro House, 58 St. James's Street, London SW1A 1LD, England; *Lead and Zinc Statistics.*

International Monetary Fund, 700 Nineteenth Street, NW, Washington, D.C. 20431 (202) 623-7000; *International Financial Statistics.*

International Rubber Study Group, York House, 8th Floor, Empire Way, Wembley, London HA9 0PA, England; *Rubber Statistical Bulletin.*

Organisation for Economic Co-operation and Development (OECD), 2 rue Andre-Pascal, 75 Paris 16, France (Telephone Number in U.S. (202) 785-6323); *The Footwear, Raw Hides and Skins, and Leather Industry in OECD Countries, The Iron and Steel Industry, Meat Balances in OECD Member Countries, The Non-Ferrous Metals Industry, The Pulp and Paper Industry,* and *Textile Industry in OECD Countries.*

AUSTRALIA - COPPER AND COPPER ORE - See AUSTRALIA - MINING AND MINERAL PRODUCTS

AUSTRALIA - CORN PRODUCTION - See AUSTRALIA - CROPS

AUSTRALIA - CORPORATE INCOME TAXES - See AUSTRALIA - TAXATION

AUSTRALIA - CORPORATE TAXES - See AUSTRALIA - TAXATION

AUSTRALIA - COTTON - See AUSTRALIA - CROPS

AUSTRALIA - CRIME

International Criminal Police Organization (INTERPOL), 26 rue Armengaud, 92210 Saint Cloud, France; *International Crime Statistics.*

Yale University Press, Yale Station, New Haven, Connecticut 06520; (203) 543-0940; *Violence and Crime in Cross-National Perspective.*

AUSTRALIA - CROPS

Commodity Research Bureau, Incorporated, 75 Wall Street, New York, New York 10005 (212) 504-7754; *Commodity Year Book.*

Facts on File, 460 Park Avenue South, New York, New York 10016 (800) 443-8323; *The New Book of World Rankings.*

Food and Agricultural Organization of the United Nations (FAO), Via delle Terme di Caracalla, 00100 Rome, Italy (Telephone Number in U.S. (202) 653-2400; *Production Yearbook,* and *The State of Food and Agriculture.*

G.K. Hall and Company, 70 Lincoln Street, Boston, Massachusetts 02111 (617) 423-3990; *The World in Figures.*

International Monetary Fund, 700 Nineteenth Street, NW, Washington, D.C. 20431 (202) 623-7000; *International Financial Statistics.*

Organisation for Economic Co-operation and Development (OECD), 2 rue Andre-Pascal, 75 Paris 16, France (Telephone Number in U.S. (202) 785-6323); *Economic Accounts for Agriculture, Foreign Trade by Commodities,* and *Textile Industry in OECD Countries.*

Statistical Office of the United Nations, Publishing Service, New York, New York 10017 (800) 253-9646; *Statistical Yearbook.*

AUSTRALIA - CULTURE

Australian Bureau of Statistics, Canberra, Australia; *Year Book Australia.*

AUSTRALIA - CUSTOMS DUTIES

G.K. Hall and Company, 70 Lincoln Street, Boston, Massachusetts 02111 (617) 423-3990; *The World in Figures.*

International Monetary Fund, 700 Nineteenth Street, NW, Washington, D.C. 20431 (202) 623-7000; *Government Finance Statistics Yearbook.*

Organisation for Economic Co-operation and Development (OECD), 2 rue Andre-Pascal, 75 Paris 16, France (Telephone Number in U.S. (202) 785-6323); *The Non-Ferrous Metals Industry.*

AUSTRALIA - DAIRY PRODUCTS

Commodity Research Bureau, Incorporated, 75 Wall Street, New York, New York 10005 (212) 504-7754; *Commodity Year Book.*

Facts on File, 460 Park Avenue South, New York, New York 10016 (800) 443-8323; *The New Book of World Rankings.*

Food and Agricultural Organization of the United Nations (FAO), Via delle Terme di Caracalla, 00100 Rome, Italy (Telephone Number in U.S. (202) 653-2400; *Production Yearbook.*

Organisation for Economic Co-operation and Development (OECD), 2 rue Andre-Pascal, 75 Paris 16, France (Telephone Number in U.S. (202) 785-6323); *Economic Accounts for Agriculture, Milk, Milk Products, and Egg Balances in OECD Member Countries, Production Yearbook,* and *The State of Food and Agriculture.*

Statistical Office of the United Nations, Publishing Service, New York, New York 10017 (800) 253-9646; *Statistical Yearbook.*

AUSTRALIA - DEATH RATE

The Economist Intelligence Unit (Asia) Limited, 10th Floor, Luk Kwok Centre, 72 Gloucester Road, Wanchai, Hong Kong (Phone Number in U.S. (800) 938-4685); *Asian Market Atlas.*

Euromonitor Publications Limited, 87-88 Turnmill Street, London EC1M 5QU, England; *The Pacific Basin: An Economic Handbook.*

G.K. Hall and Company, 70 Lincoln Street, Boston, Massachusetts 02111 (617) 423-3990; *The World in Figures.*

Statistical Office of the United Nations, Publishing Service, New York, New York 10017 (800) 253-9646; *Statistical Yearbook.*

Times Books, 201 East 50th Street, New York, New York 10022 (212) 751-2600; *The Economist Book of Vital World Statistics.*

World Health Organization, Office of Publications, Geneva, Switzerland (Telephone Number in U.S. (518) 436-9686); *World Health Statistics: Infectious Diseases - Cases.*

AUSTRALIA - DEFENSE EXPENDITURES

Australian Bureau of Statistics, Canberra, Australia; *Year Book Australia.*

G.K. Hall and Company, 70 Lincoln Street, Boston, Massachusetts 02111 (617) 423-3990; *The World in Figures.*

International Monetary Fund, 700 Nineteenth Street, NW, Washington, D.C. 20431 (202) 623-7000; *Government Finance Statistics Yearbook.*

U.S. Arms Control and Disarmament Agency, 320 Twenty-first Street, NW, Washington, D.C. 20451 (202) 647-8677; *World Military Expenditures and Arms Transfers.*

AUSTRALIA - DEMOGRAPHY

Australian Bureau of Statistics, Canberra, Australia; *Year Book Australia.*

The Economist Intelligence Unit, 111 West 57th Street, New York, New York 10019 (800) 938-4685; *The World Market Atlas.*

The Economist Intelligence Unit (Asia) Limited, 10th Floor, Luk Kwok Centre, 72 Gloucester Road, Wanchai, Hong Kong (Phone Number in U.S. (800) 938-4685); *Asian Market Atlas.*

Facts on File, 460 Park Avenue South, New York, New York 10016 (800) 443-8323; *The New Book of World Rankings.*

Federal Statistical Office, Gustav - Stresemann - Ring 11, D-6200 Wiesbaden, Germany; *Australien.*

G.K. Hall and Company, 70 Lincoln Street, Boston, Massachusetts 02111 (617) 423-3990; *The World in Figures.*

AUSTRALIA - DEVELOPMENT ASSISTANCE

G.K. Hall and Company, 70 Lincoln Street, Boston, Massachusetts 02111 (617) 423-3990; *The World in Figures.*

Organisation for Economic Co-operation and Development (OECD), 2 rue Andre-Pascal, 75 Paris 16, France (Telephone Number in U.S. (202) 785-6323); *Geographical Distribution of Financial Flows to Developing Countries.*

Statistical Office of the United Nations, Publishing Service, New York, New York 10017 (800) 253-9646; *Statistical Yearbook.*

AUSTRALIA - DIAMOND PRODUCTION - See AUSTRALIA - MINING AND MINERAL PRODUCTS

AUSTRALIA - DISCOUNT RATES

Organisation for Economic Co-operation and Development (OECD), 2 rue Andre-Pascal, 75 Paris 16, France (Telephone Number in U.S. (202) 785-6323); *Financial Market Trends.*

AUSTRALIA - DISEASES

G.K. Hall and Company, 70 Lincoln Street, Boston, Massachusetts 02111 (617) 423-3990; *The World in Figures.*

World Health Organization, Office of Publications, Geneva, Switzerland (Telephone Number in U.S. (518) 436-9686); *World Health Statistics: Infectious Diseases - Cases.*

AUSTRALIA - DIVORCE RATES

Facts on File, 460 Park Avenue South, New York, New York 10016 (800) 443-8323; *The New Book of World Rankings.*

Statistical Office of the United Nations, Publishing Service, New York, New York 10017 (800) 253-9646; *Demographic Yearbook,* and *Statistical Yearbook.*

AUSTRALIA - DOMESTIC PRODUCT

G.K. Hall and Company, 70 Lincoln Street, Boston, Massachusetts 02111 (617) 423-3990; *The World in Figures.*

AUSTRALIA - DUCKS - See AUSTRALIA - LIVESTOCK AND POULTRY

AUSTRALIA - ECONOMY

Euromonitor Publications Limited, 87-88 Turnmill Street, London EC1M 5QU, England; *International Marketing Data and Statistics.*

Facts on File, 460 Park Avenue South, New York, New York 10016 (800) 443-8323; *The New Book of World Rankings.*

Federal Statistical Office, Gustav - Stresemann - Ring 11, D-6200 Wiesbaden, Germany; *Australien.*

G.K. Hall and Company, 70 Lincoln Street, Boston, Massachusetts 02111 (617) 423-3990; *The World in Figures.*

Organisation for Economic Co-operation and Development (OECD), 2 rue Andre-Pascal, 75 Paris 16, France (Telephone Number in U.S. (202) 785-6323); *Economic Outlook, Geographical Distribution of Financial Flows to Developing Countries, Main Economic Indicators-Historical Statistics, OECD Economic Surveys: Australia,* and *OECD Employment Outlook.*

AUSTRALIA - EDUCATION

Australian Bureau of Statistics, Canberra, Australia; *Year Book Australia.*

The Economist Intelligence Unit, 111 West 57th Street, New York, New York 10019 (800) 938-4685; *The World Market Atlas.*

The Economist Intelligence Unit (Asia) Limited, 10th Floor, Luk Kwok Centre, 72 Gloucester Road, Wanchai, Hong Kong (Phone Number in U.S. (800) 938-4685); *Asian Market Atlas.*

Euromonitor Publications Limited, 87-88 Turnmill Street, London EC1M 5QU, England; *The Pacific Basin: An Economic Handbook.*

Facts on File, 460 Park Avenue South, New York, New York 10016 (800) 443-8323; *The New Book of World Rankings.*

Federal Statistical Office, Gustav - Stresemann - Ring 11, D-6200 Wiesbaden, Germany; *Australien.*

Gale Research Incorporated, 835 Penobscot Building, Detroit, Michigan 48226 (800) 877-4253; *International Historical Statistics the Americas and Australasia.*

G.K. Hall and Company, 70 Lincoln Street, Boston, Massachusetts 02111 (617) 423-3990; *The World in Figures.*

International Monetary Fund, 700 Nineteenth Street, NW, Washington, D.C. 20431 (202) 623-7000; *Government Finance Statistics Yearbook.*

Organisation for Economic Co-operation and Development (OECD), 2 rue Andre-Pascal, 75 Paris 16, France (Telephone Number in U.S. (202) 785-6323); *Education in OECD Countries.*

Statistical Office of the United Nations, Publishing Service, New York, New York 10017; *Statistical Yearbook for Asia and the Pacific.*

Times Books, 201 East 50th Street, New York, New York 10022 (212) 751-2600; *The Economist Book of Vital World Statistics.*

United Nations Educational, Scientific and Cultural Organization (UNESCO), 7 Place de Fontenoy, F-75700 Paris, France (Telephone Number in U.S. (212) 963-5981; *Statistical Yearbook.*

The World Bank, 1818 H Street, NW, Washington, D.C. 20433 (202) 477-1234; *World Tables.*

AUSTRALIA - EGG PRODUCTION AND CONSUMPTION - See AUSTRALIA - DAIRY PRODUCTION

AUSTRALIA - ELECTRICITY

Commodity Research Bureau, Incorporated, 75 Wall Street, New York, New York 10005 (212) 504-7754; *Commodity Year Book.*

Facts on File, 460 Park Avenue South, New York, New York 10016 (800) 443-8323; *The New Book of World Rankings.*

Organisation for Economic Co-operation and Development (OECD), 2 rue Andre-Pascal, 75 Paris 16, France (Telephone Number in U.S. (202) 785-6323); *Coal Information, Energy Statistics of OECD Countries, Indicators of Industrial Activity,* and *Industrial Structure Statistics.*

Penn Well Publishing Company, 1421 South Sheridan Road, P.O. Box 1260, Tulsa, Oklahoma 74101 (800) 752-9764; *International Energy Statistics Sourcebook.*

Statistical Office of the United Nations, Publishing Service, New York, New York 10017; *Electric Power in Asia and the Pacific,* and *Statistical Yearbook.*

Times Books, 201 East 50th Street, New York, New York 10022 (212) 751-2600; *The Economist Book of Vital World Statistics.*

AUSTRALIA - EMPLOYMENT

Euromonitor Publications Limited, 87-88 Turnmill Street, London EC1M 5QU, England; *International Marketing Data and Statistics,* and *The Pacific Basin: An Economic Handbook.*

Facts on File, 460 Park Avenue South, New York, New York 10016 (800) 443-8323; *The New Book of World Rankings.*

Federal Statistical Office, Gustav - Stresemann - Ring 11, D-6200 Wiesbaden, Germany; *Australien.*

International Labour Office, I.L.O. Publications, CH-1211, Geneva 22, Switzerland; *Yearbook of Labour Statistics.*

Organisation for Economic Co-operation and Development (OECD), 2 rue Andre-Pascal, 75 Paris 16, France (Telephone Number in U.S. (202) 785-6323); *Economic Outlook, The Iron and Steel Industry, Labour Force Statistics, OECD Economic Surveys: Australia,* and *OECD Employment Outlook,* and *Textile Industry in OECD Countries.*

Statistical Office of the United Nations, Publishing Service, New York, New York 10017 (800) 253-9646; *Statistical Yearbook.*

AUSTRALIA - ENERGY

Australian Bureau of Statistics, Canberra, Australia; *Year Book Australia.*

Facts on File, 460 Park Avenue South, New York, New York 10016 (800) 443-8323; *The New Book of World Rankings.*

G.K. Hall and Company, 70 Lincoln Street, Boston, Massachusetts 02111 (617) 423-3990; *The World in Figures.*

Organisation for Economic Co-operation and Development (OECD), 2 rue Andre-Pascal, 75 Paris 16, France (Telephone Number in U.S. (202) 785-6323); *Coal Information, Energy Statistics of OECD Countries, OECD Environmental Data,* and *Oil and Gas Information.*

Penn Well Publishing Company, 1421 South Sheridan Road, P.O. Box 1260, Tulsa, Oklahoma 74101 (800) 752-9764; *International Energy Statistics Sourcebook.*

Statistical Office of the United Nations, Publishing Service, New York, New York 10017 (800) 253-9646; *Energy Statistics Yearbook, Statistical Yearbook, Statistical Yearbook for Asia and the Pacific,* and *World Energy Supplies.*

Times Books, 201 East 50th Street, New York, New York 10022 (212) 751-2600; *The Economist Book of Vital World Statistics.*

AUSTRALIA - ENGINEERING AND METAL PRODUCTS - EXPORTS AND IMPORTS

Statistical Office of the United Nations, Publishing Service, New York, New York 10017 (800) 253-9646; *Trade in Manufactures of Developing Countries.*

AUSTRALIA - ENVIRONMENT

Organization for Economic Co-operation and Development (OECD), 2 rue Andre-Pascal, 75 Paris 16, France (Telephone Number in U.S. (202) 785-6323); *OECD Environmental Data.*

AUSTRALIA - EXCHANGE RATES

The Economist Intelligence Unit (Asia) Limited, 10th Floor, Luk Kwok Centre, 72 Gloucester Road, Wanchai, Hong Kong (Phone Number in U.S. (800) 938-4685); *Asian Market Atlas.*

Euromonitor Publications Limited, 87-88 Turnmill Street, London EC1M 5QU, England; *International Marketing Data and Statistics,* and *The Pacific Basin: An Economic Handbook.*

International Civil Aviation Organization, 1000 Sherbrooke Street West, Suite 400, Montreal, Quebec, Canada H3A 2R2 (514) 285-8219; *Civil Aviation Statistics of the World.*

International Monetary Fund, 700 Nineteenth Street, NW, Washington, D.C. 20431 (202) 623-7000; *International Financial Statistics.*

Organisation for Economic Co-operation and Development (OECD), 2 rue Andre-Pascal, 75 Paris 16, France (Telephone Number in U.S. (202) 785-6323); *Economic Outlook, Financial Market Trends, Revenue Statistics of OECD Member Countries,* and *Tourism Policy and International Tourism in OECD Member Countries.*

AUSTRALIA - EXCISE TAXES - See AUSTRALIA - TAXATION

AUSTRALIA - EXPORTS

American Automobile Manufacturers Association, 1401 H Street, NW, Suite 900, Washington, D.C. 20005 (202) 326-5500; *World Motor Vehicle Data.*

The Economist Intelligence Unit, 111 West 57th Street, New York, New York 10019 (800) 938-4685; *The World Market Atlas.*

The Economist Intelligence Unit (Asia) Limited, 10th Floor, Luk Kwok Centre, 72 Gloucester Road, Wanchai, Hong Kong (Phone Number in U.S. (800) 938-4685); *Asian Market Atlas,*

Euromonitor Publications Limited, 87-88 Turnmill Street, London EC1M 5QU, England; *International Marketing Data and Statistics,* and *The Pacific Basin: An Economic Handbook.*

Food and Agricultural Organization of the United Nations (FAO) Via Delle Terme di Caracalla, 00100 Rome, Italy (Telephone Number in U.S. (202) 653-2400; *The State of Food and Agriculture.*

G.K. Hall and Company, 70 Lincoln Street, Boston, Massachusetts 02111 (617) 423-3990; *The World in Figures.*

International Iron and Steel Institute, 120, rue Colonel Bourg, B-1140 Brussels, Belgium; *Steel Statistical Yearbook.*

International Lead and Zinc Study Group, Metro House, 58 St. James's Street, London SW1A 1LD, England; *Lead and Zinc Statistics.*

International Monetary Fund, 700 Nineteenth Street, NW, Washington, D.C. 20431; *Direction of Trade Statistics, Government Finance Statistics Yearbook,* and *International Financial Statistics.*

International Rubber Study Group, York House, 8th Floor, Empire Way, Wembley, London HA9 0PA, England; *World Rubber Statistics Handbook.*

Organisation for Economic Co-operation and Development (OECD), 2 rue Andre-Pascal, 75 Paris 16, France (Telephone Number in U.S. (202) 785-6323); *Economic Outlook, The Footwear, Raw Hides and Skins, and Leather Industry in OECD Countries, Foreign Trade by Commodities, Geographical Distribution of Financial Flows to Developing Countries, Industrial Structure Statistics, The Iron and Steel Industry, Milk, Milk Products, and Egg Balances in OECD Member Countries, OECD Economic Surveys: Australia, The Pulp and Paper Industry,* and *Review of Fisheries in OECD Member Countries.*

Statistical Office of the United Nations, Publishing Service, New York, New York 10017 (800) 253-9646; *Foreign Trade Statistics of Asia and the Pacific.*

Times Books, 201 East 50th Street, New York, New York 10022 (212) 751-2600; *The Economist Book of Vital World Statistics.*

The World Bank, 1818 H Street, NW, Washington, D.C. 20433 (202) 477-1234; *World Tables.*

AUSTRALIA - EXTERNAL FINANCING

Organisation for Economic Co-operation and Development (OECD), 2 rue Andre-Pascal, 75 Paris 16, France (Telephone Number in U.S. (202) 785-6323); *Economic Outlook,* and *Financial Market Trends.*

AUSTRALIA - EXTERNAL INDEBTEDNESS

Organisation for Economic Co-operation and Development (OECD), 2 rue Andre-Pascal, 75 Paris 16, France (Telephone Number in U.S. (202) 785-6323); *Financial Market Trends,* and *Geographical Distribution of Financial Flows to Developing Countries.*

The World Bank, 1818 H Street, NW, Washington, D.C. 20433 (202) 477-1234; *World Tables.*

AUSTRALIA - EXTERNAL TRADE

Food and Agricultural Organization of the United Nations (FAO), Via delle Terme di Caracalla, 00100 Rome, Italy (Telephone Number in U.S. (202) 653-2400; *Production Yearbook, The State of Food and Agriculture,* and *Trade Yearbook.*

Gale Research Incorporated, 835 Penobscot Building, Detroit, Michigan 48226 (800) 877-4253; *International Historical Statistics the Americas and Australasia.*

G.K. Hall and Company, 70 Lincoln Street, Boston, Massachusetts 02111 (617) 423-3990; *The World in Figures.*

Statistical Office of the United Nations, Publishing Service, New York, New York 10017 (800) 253-9646; *Statistical Yearbook,* and *Statistical Yearbook for Asia and the Pacific.*

AUSTRALIA - FABRIC PRODUCTION - See AUSTRALIA - TEXTILE INDUSTRY

AUSTRALIA - FARM CROPS - See AUSTRALIA - CROPS

AUSTRALIA - FEMALE WORKING POPULATION - See AUSTRALIA - EMPLOYMENT

AUSTRALIA - FERTILITY RATES

The Economist Intelligence Unit (Asia) Limited, 10th Floor, Luk Kwok Centre, 72 Gloucester Road, Wanchai, Hong Kong (Phone Number in U.S. (800) 938-4685); *Asian Market Atlas.*

Facts on File, 460 Park Avenue South, New York, New York 10016 (800) 443-8323; *The New Book of World Rankings.*

Times Books, 201 East 50th Street, New York, New York 10022 (212) 751-2600; *The Economist Book of Vital World Statistics.*

The World Bank, 1818 H Street, NW, Washington, D.C. 20433 (202) 477-1234; *World Tables.*

AUSTRALIA - FERTILIZER

Food and Agricultural Organization of the United Nations (FAO), Via delle Terme di Caracalla, 00100 Rome, Italy (Telephone Number in U.S. (202) 653-2400; *Fertilizer Yearbook,* and *The State of Food and Agriculture.*

Organisation for Economic Co-operation and Development (OECD), 2 rue Andre-Pascal, 75 Paris 16, France (Telephone Number in U.S. (202) 785-6323); *Economic Accounts for Agriculture, Foreign Trade by Commodities.*

Statistical Office of the United Nations, Publishing Service, New York, New York 10017 (800) 253-9646; *Statistical Yearbook.*

AUSTRALIA - FETAL MORTALITY

Statistical Office of the United Nations, Publishing Service, New York, New York 10017 (800) 253-9646; *Demographic Yearbook.*

World Health Organization, Office of Publications, Geneva, Switzerland (Telephone Number in U.S. (518) 436-9686); *World Health Statistics: Vital Statistics and Causes of Death.*

AUSTRALIA - FIBRE PRODUCTION - See AUSTRALIA - TEXTILE INDUSTRY

AUSTRALIA - FILAMENT PRODUCTION - See AUSTRALIA - TEXTILE INDUSTRY

AUSTRALIA - FILM - See AUSTRALIA - MOTION PICTURES

AUSTRALIA - FINANCE

Australian Bureau of Statistics, Canberra, Australia; *Year Book Australia.*

Euromonitor Publications Limited, 87-88 Turnmill Street, London EC1M 5QU, England; *The Pacific Basin: An Economic Handbook.*

Facts on File, 460 Park Avenue South, New York, New York 10016 (800) 443-8323; *The New Book of World Rankings.*

Federal Statistical Office, Gustav - Stresemann - Ring 11, D-6200 Wiesbaden, Germany; *Australien.*

Gale Research Incorporated, 835 Penobscot Building, Detroit, Michigan 48226 (800) 877-4253; *International Historical Statistics the Americas and Australasia.*

G.K. Hall and Company, 70 Lincoln Street, Boston, Massachusetts 02111 (617) 423-3990; *The World in Figures.*

International Monetary Fund, 700 Nineteenth Street, NW, Washington, D.C. 20431 (202) 623-7000; *Government Finance Statistics Yearbook,* and *International Financial Statistics.*

Organisation for Economic Co-operation and Development (OECD), 2 rue Andre-Pascal, 75 Paris 16, France (Telephone Number in U.S. (202) 785-6323); *Economic Outlook, Financial Market Trends, Geographical Distribution of Financial Flows to Developing Countries, Main Economic Indicators - Historical Statistics,* and *OECD Financial Statistics.*

Statistical Office of the United Nations, Publishing Service, New York, New York 10017 (800) 253-9646; *Statistical Yearbook for Asia and the Pacific.*

AUSTRALIA - FISHERIES

Australian Bureau of Statistics, Canberra, Australia; *Year Book Australia.*

Facts on File, 460 Park Avenue South, New York, New York 10016 (800) 443-8323; *The New Book of World Rankings.*

Federal Statistical Office, Gustav - Stresemann - Ring 11, D-6200 Wiesbaden, Germany; *Australien.*

Food and Agricultural Organization of the United Nations (FAO) Via Delle Terme di Caracalla, 00100 Rome, Italy (Telephone Number in U.S. (202) 653-2400; *The State of Food and Agriculture.*

Organisation for Economic Co-operation and Development (OECD), 2 rue Andre-Pascal, 75 Paris 16, France (Telephone Number in U.S. (202) 785-6323); *Foreign Trade by Commodities, Industrial Structure Statistics,* and *Review of Fisheries in OECD Member Countries.*

Statistical Office of the United Nations, Publishing Service, New York, New York 10017 (800) 253-9646; *Statistical Yearbook.*

AUSTRALIA - FLOUR PRODUCTION

Commodity Research Bureau, Incorporated, 75 Wall Street, New York, New York 10005 (212) 504-7754; *Commodity Year Book.*

Statistical Office of the United Nations, Publishing Service, New York, New York 10017 (800) 253-9646; *Statistical Yearbook.*

AUSTRALIA - FOOD

Food and Agricultural Organization of the United Nations (FAO) Via Delle Terme di Caracalla, 00100 Rome, Italy (Telephone Number in U.S. (202) 653-2400; *Production Yearbook,* and *The State of Food and Agriculture.*

G.K. Hall and Company, 70 Lincoln Street, Boston, Massachusetts 02111 (617) 423-3990; *The World in Figures.*

Organisation for Economic Co-operation and Development (OECD), 2 rue Andre-Pascal, 75 Paris 16, France (Telephone Number in U.S. (202) 785-6323); *Food Consumption Statistics,* and *Foreign Trade by Commodities.*

Statistical Office of the United Nations, Publishing Service, New York, New York 10017 (800) 253-9646; *Statistical Yearbook for Asia and the Pacific.*

AUSTRALIA - FOOTWEAR - PRODUCTION INDEX

Organisation for Economic Co-operation and Development (OECD), 2 rue Andre-Pascal, 75 Paris 16, France (Telephone Number in U.S. (202) 785-6323); *Indicators of Industrial Activity.*

AUSTRALIA - FOREIGN AID

G.K. Hall and Company, 70 Lincoln Street, Boston, Massachusetts 02111 (617) 423-3990; *The World in Figures.*

AUSTRALIA - FOREIGN DEBT

International Monetary Fund, 700 Nineteenth Street, NW, Washington, D.C. 20431 (202) 623-7000; *Government Finance Statistics Yearbook.*

Organisation for Economic Co-operation and Development (OECD), 2 rue Andre-Pascal, 75 Paris 16, France (Telephone Number in U.S. (202) 785-6323); *Economic Outlook.*

AUSTRALIA - FOREIGN INDEBTEDNESS

Euromonitor Publications Limited, 87-88 Turnmill Street, London EC1M 5QU, England; *The Pacific Basin: An Economic Handbook.*

Organisation for Economic Co-operation and Development (OECD), 2 rue Andre-Pascal, 75 Paris 16, France (Telephone Number in U.S. (202) 785-6323); *Economic Outlook,* and *Financial Market Trends.*

AUSTRALIA - FOREIGN TRADE

The Economist Intelligence Unit (Asia) Limited, 10th Floor, Luk Kwok Centre, 72 Gloucester Road, Wanchai, Hong Kong (Phone Number in U.S. (800) 938-4685); *Asian Market Atlas.*

Euromonitor Publications Limited, 87-88 Turnmill Street, London EC1M 5QU, England; *International Marketing Data and Statistics,* and *The Pacific Basin: An Economic Handbook.*

Facts on File, 460 Park Avenue South, New York, New York 10016 (800) 443-8323; *The New Book of World Rankings.*

Federal Statistical Office, Gustav - Stresemann - Ring 11, D-6200 Wiesbaden, Germany; *Australien.*

Food and Agricultural Organization of the United Nations (FAO) Via Delle Terme di Caracalla, 00100 Rome, Italy (Telephone Number in U.S. (202) 653-2400; *The State of Food and Agriculture.*

G.K. Hall and Company, 70 Lincoln Street, Boston, Massachusetts 02111 (617) 423-3990; *The World in Figures.*

International Iron and Steel Institute, 120, rue Colonel Bourg, B-1140 Brussels, Belgium; *Steel Statistical Yearbook.*

Organisation for Economic Co-operation and Development (OECD), 2 rue Andre-Pascal, 75 Paris 16, France (Telephone Number in U.S. (202) 785-6323); *Economic Outlook, The Footwear, Raw Hides and Skins, and Leather Industry in OECD Countries, Foreign Trade by Commodities, Main Economic Indicators - Historical Statistics, Maritime Transportation, Meat Balances in OECD Member Countries, OECD Economic Surveys: Australia,* and *Trade by Commodities.*

Statistical Office of the United Nations, Publishing Service, New York, New York 10017 (800) 253-9646; *International Trade Statistics Yearbook, Statistical Yearbook,* and *Trade in Manufactures of Developing Countries.*

The World Bank, 1818 H Street, NW, Washington, D.C. 20433 (202) 477-1234; *World Tables.*

AUSTRALIA - FORESTRY AND FOREST PRODUCTS

Australian Bureau of Statistics, Canberra, Australia; *Year Book Australia.*

Facts on File, 460 Park Avenue South, New York, New York 10016 (800) 443-8323; *The New Book of World Rankings.*

Federal Statistical Office, Gustav - Stresemann - Ring 11, D-6200 Wiesbaden, Germany; *Australien.*

Food and Agricultural Organization of the United Nations (FAO) Via Delle Terme di Caracalla, 00100 Rome, Italy (Telephone Number in U.S. (202) 653-2400; *The State of Food and Agriculture,* and *Yearbook of Forest Products.*

Forest and Paper Association, 1250 Connecticut Avenue, NW, Washington, D.C. 20036 (202) 463-2455; *Wood Pulp and Fiber Statistics.*

G.K. Hall and Company, 70 Lincoln Street, Boston, Massachusetts 02111 (617) 423-3990; *The World in Figures.*

Organisation for Economic Co-operation and Development (OECD), 2 rue Andre-Pascal, 75 Paris 16, France (Telephone Number in U.S. (202) 785-6323); *Foreign Trade by Commodities, Indicators of Industrial Activity, Industrial Structure Statistics,* and *The Pulp and Paper Industry.*

Statistical Office of the United Nations, Publishing Service, New York, New York 10017 (800) 253-9646; *Statistical Yearbook.*

United Nations Educational, Scientific and Cultural Organization (UNESCO), 7 Place de Fontenoy, F-75700 Paris, France (Telephone Number in U.S. (212) 963-5981; *Statistical Yearbook.*

AUSTRALIA - FRUIT PRODUCTION - See AUSTRALIA - CROPS

AUSTRALIA - FURNITURE AND WOOD PRODUCTS

Statistical Office of the United Nations, Publishing Service, New York, New York 10017 (800) 253-9646; *Trade in Manufactures of Developing Countries.*

AUSTRALIA - FURNITURE AND WOOD PRODUCTS - EXPORTS AND IMPORTS

Organisation for Economic Co-operation and Development (OECD), 2 rue Andre-Pascal, 75 Paris 16, France (Telephone Number in U.S. (202) 785-6323); *Foreign Trade by Commodities,* and *Industrial Structure Statistics.*

AUSTRALIA - GAS AND GAS LIQUIDS - See AUSTRALIA - MINING AND MINERAL PRODUCTS

AUSTRALIA - GENERAL INDUSTRIAL STATISTICS

Federal Statistical Office, Gustav - Stresemann - Ring 11, D-6200 Wiesbaden, Germany; *Australien.*

Statistical Office of the United Nations, Publishing Service, New York, New York 10017 (800) 253-9646; *Industrial Statistics Yearbook.*

AUSTRALIA - GENERAL MORTALITY

Statistical Office of the United Nations, Publishing Service, New York, New York 10017 (800) 253-9646; *Demographic Yearbook.*

World Health Organization, Office of Publications, Geneva, Switzerland (Telephone Number in U.S. (518) 436-9686); *World Health Statistics: Vital Statistics and Causes of Death.*

AUSTRALIA - GEOGRAPHIC DATA

Facts on File, 460 Park Avenue South, New York, New York 10016 (800) 443-8323; *The New Book of World Rankings.*

Federal Statistical Office, Gustav - Stresemann - Ring 11, D-6200 Wiesbaden, Germany; *Australien.*

AUSTRALIA - GLASS AND GLASS PRODUCTS - PRODUCTION INDEX - See AUSTRALIA - MINING AND MINERAL PRODUCTS

AUSTRALIA - GOATS - See AUSTRALIA - LIVESTOCK AND POULTRY

AUSTRALIA - GOLD PRODUCTION AND CONSUMPTION - See AUSTRALIA - MINING AND MINERAL PRODUCTS

AUSTRALIA - GOVERNMENT

Australian Bureau of Statistics, Canberra, Australia; *Year Book Australia.*

G.K. Hall and Company, 70 Lincoln Street, Boston, Massachusetts 02111 (617) 423-3990; *The World in Figures.*

AUSTRALIA - GOVERNMENT BONDS - See AUSTRALIA - BONDS

AUSTRALIA - GOVERNMENT CONSUMPTION

International Monetary Fund, 700 Nineteenth Street, NW, Washington, D.C. 20431 (202) 623-7000; *International Financial Statistics.*

AUSTRALIA - GOVERNMENT EXPENDITURES

International Monetary Fund, 700 Nineteenth Street, NW, Washington, D.C. 20431 (202) 623-7000; *Government Finance Statistics Yearbook.*

Organisation for Economic Co-operation and Development (OECD), 2 rue Andre-Pascal, 75 Paris 16, France (Telephone Number in U.S. (202) 785-6323); *Economic Outlook.*

Times Books, 201 East 50th Street, New York, New York 10022 (212) 751-2600; *The Economist Book of Vital World Statistics.*

The World Bank, 1818 H Street, NW, Washington, D.C. 20433 (202) 477-1234; *World Tables.*

AUSTRALIA - GOVERNMENT FINANCES

International Monetary Fund, 700 Nineteenth Street, NW, Washington, D.C. 20431 (202) 623-7000; *International Financial Statistics.*

Organisation for Economic Co-operation and Development (OECD), 2 rue Andre-Pascal, 75 Paris 16, France (Telephone Number in U.S. (202) 785-6323); *Economic Outlook.*

AUSTRALIA - GOVERNMENT REVENUE

International Monetary Fund, 700 Nineteenth Street, NW, Washington, D.C. 20431 (202) 623-7000; *Government Finance Statistics Yearbook.*

Organisation for Economic Co-operation and Development (OECD), 2 rue Andre-Pascal, 75 Paris 16, France (Telephone Number in U.S. (202) 785-6323); *Economic Outlook,* and *Revenue Statistics of OECD Member Countries.*

Times Books, 201 East 50th Street, New York, New York 10022 (212) 751-2600; *The Economist Book of Vital World Statistics.*

The World Bank, 1818 H Street, NW, Washington, D.C. 20433 (202) 477-1234; *World Tables.*

AUSTRALIA - GRAIN PRODUCTION - See AUSTRALIA - CROPS

AUSTRALIA - GRANTS

International Monetary Fund, 700 Nineteenth Street, NW, Washington, D.C. 20431 (202) 623-7000; *Government Finance Statistics Yearbook.*

Organisation for Economic Co-operation and Development (OECD), 2 rue Andre-Pascal, 75 Paris 16, France (Telephone Number in U.S. (202) 785-6323); *Geographical Distribution of Financial Flows to Developing Countries.*

AUSTRALIA - GROSS DOMESTIC PRODUCT

The Economist Intelligence Unit, 111 West 57th Street, New York, New York 10019 (800) 938-4685; *The World Market Atlas.*

The Economist Intelligence Unit (Asia) Limited, 10th Floor, Luk Kwok Centre, 72 Gloucester Road, Wanchai, Hong Kong (Phone Number in U.S. (800) 938-4685); *Asian Market Atlas.*

Euromonitor Publications Limited, 87-88 Turnmill Street, London EC1M 5QU, England; *International Marketing Data and Statistics,* and *The Pacific Basin: An Economic Handbook.*

Facts on File, 460 Park Avenue South, New York, New York 10016 (800) 443-8323; *The New Book of World Rankings.*

G.K. Hall and Company, 70 Lincoln Street, Boston, Massachusetts 02111 (617) 423-3990; *The World in Figures.*

International Monetary Fund, 700 Nineteenth Street, NW, Washington, D.C. 20431 (202) 623-7000; *International Financial Statistics.*

Organisation for Economic Co-operation and Development (OECD), 2 rue Andre-Pascal, 75 Paris 16, France (Telephone Number in U.S. (202) 785-6323); *Economic Outlook, Geographical Distribution of Financial Flows to Developing Countries,* and *Revenue Statistics of OECD Member Countries.*

Statistical Office of the United Nations, Publishing Service, New York, New York 10017 (800) 253-9646; *Statistical Yearbook.*

Times Books, 201 East 50th Street, New York, New York 10022 (212) 751-2600; *The Economist Book of Vital World Statistics.*

The World Bank, 1818 H Street, NW, Washington, D.C. 20433 (202) 477-1234; *World Tables.*

AUSTRALIA - GROSS NATIONAL PRODUCT

Euromonitor Publications Limited, 87-88 Turnmill Street, London EC1M 5QU, England; *International Marketing Data and Statistics.*

Organisation for Economic Co-operation and Development (OECD), 2 rue Andre-Pascal, 75 Paris 16, France (Telephone Number in U.S. (202) 785-6323); *Economic Outlook,* and *Geographical Distribution of Financial Flows to Developing Countries.*

U.S. Arms Control and Disarmament Agency, 320 Twenty-first Street, NW, Washington, D.C. 20451 (202) 647-8677; *World Military Expenditures and Arms Transfers.*

The World Bank, 1818 H Street, NW, Washington, D.C. 20433 (202) 477-1234; *World Tables.*

AUSTRALIA - GROUNDNUTS PRODUCTION - See AUSTRALIA - CROPS

AUSTRALIA - HEALTH

Australian Bureau of Statistics, Canberra, Australia; *Year Book Australia.*

The Economist Intelligence Unit (Asia) Limited, 10th Floor, Luk Kwok Centre, 72 Gloucester Road, Wanchai, Hong Kong (Phone Number in U.S. (800) 938-4685); *Asian Market Atlas.*

Euromonitor Publications Limited, 87-88 Turnmill Street, London EC1M 5QU, England; *The Pacific Basin: An Economic Handbook.*

Facts on File, 460 Park Avenue South, New York, New York 10016 (800) 443-8323; *The New Book of World Rankings.*

Federal Statistical Office, Gustav - Stresemann - Ring 11, D-6200 Wiesbaden, Germany; *Australien.*

G.K. Hall and Company, 70 Lincoln Street, Boston, Massachusetts 02111 (617) 423-3990; *The World in Figures.*

Organisation for Economic Co-operation and Development (OECD), 2 rue Andre-Pascal, 75 Paris 16, France (Telephone Number in U.S. (202) 785-6323); *OECD Health Systems: Facts and Trends.*

Statistical Office of the United Nations, Publishing Service, New York, New York 10017 (800) 253-9646; *Statistical Yearbook.*

Times Books, 201 East 50th Street, New York, New York 10022 (212) 751-2600; *The Economist Book of Vital World Statistics.*

World Health Organization, Office of Publications, Geneva, Switzerland (Telephone Number in U.S. (518) 436-9686); *World Health Statistics Annual.*

AUSTRALIA - HEALTH EXPENDITURES

International Monetary Fund, 700 Nineteenth Street, NW, Washington, D.C. 20431 (202) 623-7000; *Government Finance Statistics Yearbook.*

AUSTRALIA - HIDE PRODUCTION

Food and Agricultural Organization of the United Nations (FAO), Via delle Terme di Caracalla, 00100 Rome, Italy (Telephone Number in U.S. (202) 653-2400; *Production Yearbook.*

Organisation for Economic Co-operation and Development (OECD), 2 rue Andre-Pascal, 75 Paris 16, France (Telephone Number in U.S. (202) 785-6323); *The Footwear, Raw Hides and Skins, and Leather Industry in OECD Countries, Foreign Trade by Commodities,* and *Indicators of Industrial Activity.*

AUSTRALIA - HIGHWAYS

The Economist Intelligence Unit (Asia) Limited, 10th Floor, Luk Kwok Centre, 72 Gloucester Road, Wanchai, Hong Kong (Phone Number in U.S. (800) 938-4685); *Asian Market Atlas.*

G.K. Hall and Company, 70 Lincoln Street, Boston, Massachusetts 02111 (617) 423-3990; *The World in Figures.*

International Road Federation, 525 School Street, SW, Washington, D.C. 20024 (202) 554-2106; *World Road Statistics.*

AUSTRALIA - HOME FINANCE

Organisation for Economic Co-operation and Development (OECD), 2 rue Andre-Pascal, 75 Paris 16, France (Telephone Number in U.S. (202) 785-6323; *Main Economic Indicators - Historical Statistics.*

AUSTRALIA - HONEY PRODUCTION

Commodity Research Bureau, Incorporated, 75 Wall Street, New York, New York 10005 (212) 504-7754; *Commodity Year Book.*

AUSTRALIA - HOPS PRODUCTION - See AUSTRALIA - CROPS

AUSTRALIA - HORSES - See AUSTRALIA - LIVESTOCK AND POULTRY

AUSTRALIA - HOURS OF WORK - See AUSTRALIA - EMPLOYMENT

AUSTRALIA - HOUSING AND HOUSING UNITS

Australian Bureau of Statistics, Canberra, Australia; *Year Book Australia.*

Facts on File, 460 Park Avenue South, New York, New York 10016 (800) 443-8323; *The New Book of World Rankings.*

AUSTRALIA - HOUSING CONSTRUCTION - See AUSTRALIA - CONSTRUCTION INDUSTRY

AUSTRALIA - HOUSING EXPENDITURES

International Monetary Fund, 700 Nineteenth Street, NW, Washington, D.C. 20431 (202) 623-7000; *Government Finance Statistics Yearbook.*

AUSTRALIA - HYDROCHLORIC ACID PRODUCTION

Statistical Office of the United Nations, Publishing Service, New York, New York 10017 (800) 253-9646; *Statistical Yearbook.*

AUSTRALIA - ILLITERATE POPULATION

The Economist Intelligence Unit, 111 West 57th Street, New York, New York 10019 (800) 938-4685; *The World Market Atlas.*

G.K. Hall and Company, 70 Lincoln Street, Boston, Massachusetts 02111 (617) 423-3990; *The World in Figures.*

AUSTRALIA - IMPORTS

American Automobile Manufacturers Association, 1401 H Street, NW, Suite 900, Washington, D.C. 20005 (202) 326-5500; *World Motor Vehicle Data.*

The Economist Intelligence Unit, 111 West 57th Street, New York, New York 10019 (800) 938-4685; *The World Market Atlas.*

The Economist Intelligence Unit (Asia) Limited, 10th Floor, Luk Kwok Centre, 72 Gloucester Road, Wanchai, Hong Kong (Phone Number in U.S. (800) 938-4685); *Asian Market Atlas.*

Euromonitor Publications Limited, 87-88 Turnmill Street, London EC1M 5QU, England; *International Marketing Data and Statistics,* and *The Pacific Basin: An Economic Handbook.*

Food and Agricultural Organization of the United Nations (FAO) Via Delle Terme di Caracalla, 00100 Rome, Italy (Telephone Number in U.S. (202) 653-2400; *The State of Food and Agriculture.*

G.K. Hall and Company, 70 Lincoln Street, Boston, Massachusetts 02111 (617) 423-3990; *The World in Figures.*

International Iron and Steel Institute, 120, rue Colonel Bourg, B-1140, Brussels, Belgium; *Steel Statistical Yearbook.*

International Lead and Zinc Study Group, Metro House, 58 St. James's Street, London SW1A 1LD, England; *Lead and Zinc Statistics.*

International Monetary Fund, 700 Nineteenth Street, NW, Washington, D.C. 20431 (202) 623-7000; *Direction of Trade Statistics,* and *Government Finance Statistics Yearbook.*

International Rubber Study Group, York House, 8th Floor, Empire Way, Wembley, London HA9 0PA, England; *World Rubber Statistics Handbook.*

Organisation for Economic Co-operation and Development (OECD), 2 rue Andre-Pascal, 75 Paris 16, France (Telephone Number in U.S. (202) 785-6323); *Economic Outlook, The Footwear, Raw Hides and Skins, and Leather Industry in OECD Countries, Industrial Structure Statistics, The Iron and Steel Industry, Milk, Milk Products, and Egg Balances in OECD Member Countries, OECD Economic Surveys: Australia, The Pulp and Paper Industry,* and *Review of Fisheries in OECD Member Countries.*

Statistical Office of the United Nations, Publishing Service, New York, New York 10017 (800) 253-9646; *Foreign Trade Statistics of Asia and the Pacific.*

Times Books, 201 East 50th Street, New York, New York 10022 (212) 751-2600; *The Economist Book of Vital World Statistics.*

The World Bank, 1818 H Street, NW, Washington, D.C. 20433 (202) 477-1234; *World Tables.*

AUSTRALIA - INCOME TAXES - See AUSTRALIA - TAXATION

AUSTRALIA - INDUSTRIAL METALS PRODUCTION - See AUSTRALIA - MINING AND MINERAL PRODUCTS

AUSTRALIA - INDUSTRY

Euromonitor Publications Limited, 87-88 Turnmill Street, London EC1M 5QU, England; *International Marketing Data and Statistics.*

Facts on File, 460 Park Avenue South, New York, New York 10016 (800) 443-8323; *The New Book of World Rankings.*

Federal Statistical Office, Gustav - Stresemann - Ring 11, D-6200 Wiesbaden, Germany; *Australien.*

Gale Research Incorporated, 835 Penobscot Building, Detroit, Michigan 48226 (800) 877-4253; *International Historical Statistics the Americas and Australasia.*

G.K. Hall and Company, 70 Lincoln Street, Boston, Massachusetts 02111 (617) 423-3990; *The World in Figures.*

International Labour Office, I.L.O. Publications, CH-1211, Geneva 22, Switzerland; *Yearbook of Labour Statistics.*

Organisation for Economic Co-operation and Development (OECD), 2 rue Andre-Pascal, 75 Paris 16, France (Telephone Number in U.S. (202) 785-6323); *Economic Outlook, Industrial Production Historical Statistics, Industrial Structure Statistics, Main Economic Indicators - Historical Statistics,* and *OECD Environmental Data.*

Statistical Office of the United Nations, Publishing Service, New York, New York 10017 (800) 253-9646; *Statistical Yearbook,* and *Statistical Yearbook for Asia and the Pacific.*

Times Books, 201 East 50th Street, New York, New York 10022 (212) 751-2600; *The Economist Book of Vital World Statistics.*

The World Bank, 1818 H Street, NW, Washington, D.C. 20433 (202) 477-1234; *World Tables.*

World Intellectual Property Organization, 34 Chemin des Colombettes, CH-1211 Geneva 20. Switzerland; *Industrial Property Statistics.*

AUSTRALIA - INFANT AND MATERNAL MORTALITY

The Economist Intelligence Unit (Asia) Limited, 10th Floor, Luk Kwok Centre, 72 Gloucester Road, Wanchai, Hong Kong (Phone Number in U.S. (800) 938-4685); *Asian Market Atlas.*

Statistical Office of the United Nations, Publishing Service, New York, New York 10017 (800) 253-9646; *Demographic Yearbook,* and *Statistical Yearbook.*

Times Books, 201 East 50th Street, New York, New York 10022 (212) 751-2600; *The Economist Book of Vital World Statistics.*

The World Bank, 1818 H Street, NW, Washington, D.C. 20433 (202) 477-1234; *World Tables.*

World Health Organization, Office of Publications, Geneva, Switzerland (Telephone Number in U.S. (518) 436-9686); *World Health Statistics: Vital Statistics and Causes of Death.*

AUSTRALIA - INTEREST RATES

Euromonitor Publications Limited, 87-88 Turnmill Street, London EC1M 5QU, England (Telephone Number in U.S. (518) 436-9686); *The Pacific Basin: An Economic Handbook.*

Organisation for Economic Co-operation and Development (OECD), 2 rue Andre-Pascal, 75 Paris 16, France (Telephone Number in U.S. (202) 785-6323); *Economic Outlook, Financial Market Trends,* and *Main Economic Indicators - Historical Statistics,* and *OECD Financial Statistics.*

AUSTRALIA - INTERNAL TRADE

Australian Bureau of Statistics, Canberra, Australia; *Year Book Australia.*

Organisation for Economic Co-operation and Development (OECD), 2 rue Andre-Pascal, 75 Paris 16, France (Telephone Number in U.S. (202) 785-6323); *Main Economic Indicators - Historical Statistics.*

Statistical Office of the United Nations, Publishing Service, New York, New York 10017 (800) 253-9646; *Statistical Yearbook for Asia and the Pacific.*

AUSTRALIA - INTERNATIONAL FINANCE

Organisation for Economic Co-operation and Development (OECD), 2 rue Andre-Pascal, 75 Paris 16, France (Telephone Number in U.S. (202) 785-6323); *Economic Outlook,* and *Financial Market Trends.*

AUSTRALIA - INTERNATIONAL LIQUIDITY

International Monetary Fund, 700 Nineteenth Street, NW, Washington, D.C. 20431 (202) 623-7000; *International Financial Statistics.*

Organisation for Economic Co-operation and Development (OECD), 2 rue Andre-Pascal, 75 Paris 16, France (Telephone Number in U.S. (202) 785-6323); *Economic Outlook,* and *Financial Market Trends.*

AUSTRALIA - INTERNATIONAL RESERVES EXCLUDING GOLD

The World Bank, 1818 H Street, NW, Washington, D.C. 20433 (202) 477-1234; *World Tables.*

AUSTRALIA - INTERNATIONAL STATISTICS

Organisation for Economic Co-operation and Development (OECD), 2 rue Andre-Pascal, 75 Paris 16, France (Telephone Number in U.S. (202) 785-6323); *Financial Market Trends,* and *Tourism Policy and International Tourism in OECD Member Countries.*

AUSTRALIA - INVESTMENTS

International Monetary Fund, 700 Nineteenth Street, NW, Washington, D.C. 20431 (202) 623-7000; *International Financial Statistics.*

Organisation for Economic Co-operation and Development (OECD), 2 rue Andre-Pascal, 75 Paris 16, France (Telephone Number in U.S. (202) 785-6323); *Economic Outlook, Financial Market Trends, Industrial Structure Statistics, The Iron and Steel Industry,* and *Textile Industry in OECD Countries.*

AUSTRALIA - IRON AND IRON ORE - See AUSTRALIA - MINING AND MINERAL PRODUCTS

AUSTRALIA - IRRIGATION

Euromonitor Publications Limited, 87-88 Turnmill Street, London EC1M 5QU, England; *International Marketing Data and Statistics.*

AUSTRALIA - LABOR FORCE

The Economist Intelligence Unit (Asia) Limited, 10th Floor, Luk Kwok Centre, 72 Gloucester Road, Wanchai, Hong Kong (Phone Number in U.S. (800) 938-4685); *Asian Market Atlas.*

Euromonitor Publications Limited, 87-88 Turnmill Street, London EC1M 5QU, England; *International Marketing Data and Statistics,* and *The Pacific Basin: An Economic Handbook.*

Facts on File, 460 Park Avenue South, New York, New York 10016 (800) 443-8323; *The New Book of World Rankings.*

Food and Agricultural Organization of the United Nations (FAO) Via Delle Terme di Caracalla, 00100 Rome, Italy (Telephone Number in U.S. (202) 653-2400; *The State of Food and Agriculture.*

Gale Research Incorporated, 835 Penobscot Building, Detroit, Michigan 48226 (800) 877-4253; *International Historical Statistics the Americas and Australasia.*

G.K. Hall and Company, 70 Lincoln Street, Boston, Massachusetts 02111 (617) 423-3990; *The World in Figures.*

Organisation for Economic Co-operation and Development (OECD), 2 rue Andre-Pascal, 75 Paris 16, France (Telephone Number in U.S. (202) 785-6323); *Economic Outlook, The Iron and Steel Industry, Labour Force Statistics, Main Economic Indicators - Historical Statistics, Maritime Transport, OECD Economic Surveys: Australia, OECD Employment Outlook,* and *Textile Industry in OECD Countries.*

Times Books, 201 East 50th Street, New York, New York 10022 (212) 751-2600; *The Economist Book of Vital World Statistics.*

The World Bank, 1818 H Street, NW, Washington, D.C. 20433 (202) 477-1234; *World Tables.*

AUSTRALIA - LABOR PRODUCTIVITY

International Labour Office, I.L.O. Publications, CH-1211, Geneva 22, Switzerland; *Yearbook of Labour Statistics.*

Organisation for Economic Co-operation and Development (OECD), 2 rue Andre-Pascal, 75 Paris 16, France (Telephone Number in U.S. (202) 785-6323); *Economic Outlook,* and *OECD Employment Outlook.*

AUSTRALIA - LAND USE

Euromonitor Publications Limited, 87-88 Turnmill Street, London EC1M 5QU, England; *International Marketing Data and Statistics.*

Food and Agricultural Organization of the United Nations (FAO), Via delle Terme di Caracalla, 00100 Rome, Italy (Telephone Number in U.S. (202) 653-2400; *Production Yearbook.*

G.K. Hall and Company, 70 Lincoln Street, Boston, Massachusetts 02111 (617) 423-3990; *The World in Figures.*

AUSTRALIA - LEAD AND LEAD ORE - See AUSTRALIA - MINING AND MINERAL PRODUCTS

AUSTRALIA - LEATHER - PRODUCTION INDEX

Organisation for Economic Co-operation and Development (OECD), 2 rue Andre-Pascal, 75 Paris 16, France (Telephone Number in U.S. (202) 785-6323); *Indicators of Industrial Activity.*

AUSTRALIA - LEATHER AND FOOTWEAR - EXPORTS AND IMPORTS

Organisation for Economic Co-operation and Development (OECD), 2 rue Andre-Pascal, 75 Paris 16, France (Telephone Number in U.S. (202) 785-6323); *The Footwear, Raw Hides and Skins, and Leather Industry in OECD Countries.*

AUSTRALIA - LIBRARIES

Facts on File, 460 Park Avenue South, New York, New York 10016 (800) 443-8323; *The New Book of World Rankings.*

United Nations Educational, Scientific and Cultural Organization (UNESCO), 7 Place de Fontenoy, F-75700 Paris, France (Telephone Number in U.S. (212) 963-5981; *Statistical Yearbook.*

AUSTRALIA - LIFE EXPECTANCY

The Economist Intelligence Unit (Asia) Limited, 10th Floor, Luk Kwok Centre, 72 Gloucester Road, Wanchai, Hong Kong (Phone Number in U.S. (800) 938-4685); *Asian Market Atlas.*

AUSTRALIA - LIGNITE PRODUCTION - See AUSTRALIA - MINING AND MINERAL PRODUCTS

AUSTRALIA - LIVESTOCK AND POULTRY

Business International Moscow, 23 Profseyuznaya Ulitsa 117859, Moscow (Telephone Number in U.S. (800) 938-4685); *The CIS Market Atlas.*

Commodity Research Bureau, Incorporated, 75 Wall Street, New York, New York 10005 (212) 504-7754; *Commodity Year Book.*

Facts on File, 460 Park Avenue South, New York, New York 10016 (800) 443-8323; *The New Book of World Rankings.*

Food and Agricultural Organization of the United Nations (FAO), Via delle Terme di Caracalla, 00100 Rome, Italy (Telephone Number in U.S. (202) 653-2400; *Production Yearbook,* and *The State of Food and Agriculture.*

G.K. Hall and Company, 70 Lincoln Street, Boston, Massachusetts 02111 (617) 423-3990; *The World in Figures.*

Organisation for Economic Co-operation and Development (OECD), 2 rue Andre-Pascal, 75 Paris 16, France (Telephone Number in U.S. (202) 785-6323); *Economic Accounts for Agriculture,* and *Meat Balances in OECD Member Countries.*

Statistical Office of the United Nations, Publishing Service, New York, New York 10017 (800) 253-9646; *Statistical Yearbook.*

AUSTRALIA - LIVING LEVELS

G.K. Hall and Company, 70 Lincoln Street, Boston, Massachusetts 02111 (617) 423-3990; *The World in Figures.*

Organisation for Economic Co-operation and Development (OECD), 2 rue Andre-Pascal, 75 Paris 16, France (Telephone Number in U.S. (202) 785-6323); *Economic Outlook.*

Times Books, 201 East 50th Street, New York, New York 10022 (212) 751-2600; *The Economist Book of Vital World Statistics.*

AUSTRALIA - MACHINERY - PRODUCTION INDEX

Organisation for Economic Co-operation and Development (OECD), 2 rue Andre-Pascal, 75 Paris 16, France (Telephone Number in U.S. (202) 785-6323); *Indicators of Industrial Activity.*

AUSTRALIA - MAGNESIUM PRODUCTION AND CONSUMPTION - See AUSTRALIA - MINING AND MINERAL PRODUCTS

AUSTRALIA - MAIL - NUMBER OF PIECES SENT OR RECEIVED

Statistical Office of the United Nations, Publishing Service, New York, New York 10017 (800) 253-9646; *Statistical Yearbook.*

AUSTRALIA - MANGANESE AND MANGANESE ORE - See AUSTRALIA - MINING AND MINERAL PRODUCTS

AUSTRALIA- MANPOWER

Australian Bureau of Statistics, Canberra, Australia; *Year Book Australia.*

Statistical Office of the United Nations, Publishing Service, New York, New York 10017 (800) 253-9646; *Statistical Yearbook for Asia and the Pacific.*

AUSTRALIA - MANUFACTURING

American Automobile Manufacturers Association, 1401 H Street, NW, Suite 900, Washington, D.C. 20005 (202) 326-5500; *World Motor Vehicle Data.*

Australian Bureau of Statistics, Canberra, Australia; *Year Book Australia.*

Facts on File, 460 Park Avenue South, New York, New York 10016 (800) 443-8323; *The New Book of World Rankings.*

G.K. Hall and Company, 70 Lincoln Street, Boston, Massachusetts 02111 (617) 423-3990; *The World in Figures.*

International Monetary Fund, 700 Nineteenth Street, NW, Washington, D.C. 20431 (202) 623-7000; *International Financial Statistics.*

Organisation for Economic Co-operation and Development (OECD), 2 rue Andre-Pascal, 75 Paris 16, France (Telephone Number in U.S. (202) 785-6323); *Foreign Trade by Commodities, Indicators of Industrial Activity,* and *OECD Economic Surveys: Australia.*

Statistical Office of the United Nations, Publishing Service, New York, New York 10017 (800) 253-9646; *Statistical Yearbook.*

Times Books, 201 East 50th Street, New York, New York 10022 (212) 751-2600; *The Economist Book of Vital World Statistics.*

The World Bank, 1818 H Street, NW, Washington, D.C. 20433 (202) 477-1234; *World Tables.*

AUSTRALIA - MANUFACTURING STOCKS

Organisation for Economic Co-operation and Development (OECD), 2 rue Andre-Pascal, 75 Paris 16, France (202) 785-6323; *Main Economic Indicators - Historical Statistics.*

AUSTRALIA - MARRIAGE RATES

Facts on File, 460 Park Avenue South, New York, New York 10016 (800) 443-8323; *The New Book of World Rankings.*

Statistical Office of the United Nations, Publishing Service, New York, New York 10017 (800) 253-9646; *Demographic Yearbook,* and *Statistical Yearbook.*

AUSTRALIA - MEAT PRODUCTION - See AUSTRALIA - LIVESTOCK AND POULTRY

AUSTRALIA - MERCHANT SHIPPING

G.K. Hall and Company, 70 Lincoln Street, Boston, Massachusetts 02111 (617) 423-3990; *The World in Figures.*

Lloyd's Register of Shipping, 17 Battery Place, New York, New York 10004 (212) 425-8050; *Register of Ships.*

Organisation for Economic Co-operation and Development (OECD), 2 rue Andre-Pascal, 75 Paris 16, France (Telephone Number in U.S. (202) 785-6323); *Maritime Transport.*

Statistical Office of the United Nations, Publishing Service, New York, New York 10017 (800) 253-9646; *Statistical Yearbook.*

Times Books, 201 East 50th Street, New York, New York 10022 (212) 751-2600; *The Economist Book of Vital World Statistics.*

U.S. Department of Transportation, Maritime Administration, Washington, D.C. 20590 (202) 366-5807; *A Statistical Analysis of the World's Merchant Fleets.*

AUSTRALIA - MERCURY PRODUCTION AND CONSUMPTION - See AUSTRALIA - MINING AND MINERAL PRODUCTS

AUSTRALIA - MILITARY

The Economist Intelligence Unit (Asia) Limited, 10th Floor, Luk Kwok Centre, 72 Gloucester Road, Wanchai, Hong Kong (Phone Number in U.S. (800) 938-4685); *Asian Market Atlas.*

G.K. Hall and Company, 70 Lincoln Street, Boston, Massachusetts 02111 (617) 423-3990; *The World in Figures.*

The International Institute for Strategic Studies, 23 Tavistock Street, London WC2E 7NQ, England; *The Military Balance.*

U.S. Arms Control and Disarmament Agency, 320 Twenty-first Street, NW, Washington, D.C. 20451 (202) 647-8677; *World Military Expenditures and Arms Transfers.*

AUSTRALIA - MILK PRODUCTION - See AUSTRALIA - DAIRY PRODUCTS

AUSTRALIA - MILLET PRODUCTION - See AUSTRALIA - CROPS

AUSTRALIA - MINING AND MINERAL PRODUCTS

Australian Bureau of Statistics, Canberra, Australia; *Year Book Australia.*

Commodity Research Bureau, Incorporated, 75 Wall Street, New York, New York 10005 (212) 504-7754; *Commodity Year Book.*

Facts on File, 460 Park Avenue South, New York, New York 10016 (800) 443-8323; *The New Book of World Rankings.*

G.K. Hall and Company, 70 Lincoln Street, Boston, Massachusetts 02111 (617) 423-3990; *The World in Figures.*

International Iron and Steel Institute, 120, rue Colonel Bourg, B-1140, Brussels, Belgium; *Steel Statistical Yearbook.*

International Lead and Zinc Study Group, Metro House, 58 St. James's Street, London SW1A 1LD, England; *Lead and Zinc Statistics.*

International Monetary Fund, 700 Nineteenth Street, NW, Washington, D.C. 20431 (202) 623-7000; *International Financial Statistics.*

Organisation for Economic Co-operation and Development (OECD), 2 rue Andre-Pascal, 75 Paris 16, France (Telephone Number in U.S. (202) 785-6323); *Coal Information, Energy Statistics of OECD Countries, Foreign Trade by Commodities, Indicators of Industrial Activity, Industrial Structure Statistics, The Iron and Steel Industry, The Non-Ferrous Metals Industry,* and *OECD Economic Surveys: Australia.*

Penn Well Publishing Company, 1421 South Sheridan Road, P.O. Box 1260, Tulsa, Oklahoma 74101 (800) 752-9764; *International Energy Statistics Sourcebook.*

Statistical Office of the United Nations, Publishing Service, New York, New York 10017 (800) 253-9646; *Statistical Yearbook.*

The World Bank, 1818 H Street, NW, Washington, D.C. 20433 (202) 477-1234; *World Tables.*

World Bureau of Metal Statistics, 27-A High Street, Ware, Herts SG12 9BA, England; *World Metal Statistics.*

AUSTRALIA - MOLASSES - See AUSTRALIA - CROPS

AUSTRALIA - MOLYBDENUM AND MOLYBDENUM ORE - See AUSTRALIA - MINING AND MINERAL PRODUCTS

AUSTRALIA - MONEY AND CREDIT

Organization for Economic Co-operation and Development (OECD), 2 rue Andre-Pascal, 75 Paris 16, France (Telephone Number in U.S. (202) 785-6323); *OECD Economic Surveys: Australia.*

AUSTRALIA - MONEY EXCHANGE RATE

Euromonitor Publications Limited, 87-88 Turnmill Street, London EC1M 5QU, England; *International Marketing Data and Statistics.*

International Monetary Fund, 700 Nineteenth Street, NW, Washington, D.C. 20431 (202) 623-7000; *International Financial Statistics.*

Organisation for Economic Co-operation and Development (OECD), 2 rue Andre-Pascal, 75 Paris 16, France (Telephone Number in U.S. (202) 785-6323); *Economic Outlook, Financial Market Trends,* and *Tourism Policy and International Tourism in OECD Member Countries.*

Statistical Office of the United Nations, Publishing Service, New York, New York 10017 (800) 253-9646; *Statistical Yearbook.*

AUSTRALIA - MONEY RATES - MARKET

Organisation for Economic Co-operation and Development (OECD), 2 rue Andre-Pascal, 75 Paris 16, France (Telephone Number in U.S. (202) 785-6323); *Economic Outlook,* and *Financial Market Trends.*

AUSTRALIA - MONEY RESERVES

Euromonitor Publications Limited, 87-88 Turnmill Street, London EC1M 5QU, England; *International Marketing Data and Statistics.*

Organisation for Economic Co-operation and Development (OECD), 2 rue Andre-Pascal, 75 Paris 16, France (Telephone Number in U.S. (202) 785-6323); *Economic Outlook,* and *Financial Market Trends.*

AUSTRALIA - MONEY SUPPLY

Euromonitor Publications Limited, 87-88 Turnmill Street, London EC1M 5QU, England; *International Marketing Data and Statistics.*

Federal Statistical Office, Gustav - Stresemann - Ring 11, D-6200 Wiesbaden, Germany; *Australien.*

G.K. Hall and Company, 70 Lincoln Street, Boston, Massachusetts 02111 (617) 423-3990; *The World in Figures.*

International Monetary Fund, 700 Nineteenth Street, NW, Washington, D.C. 20431 (202) 623-7000; *International Financial Statistics.*

Organisation for Economic Co-operation and Development (OECD), 2 rue Andre-Pascal, 75 Paris 16, France (Telephone Number in U.S. (202) 785-6323); *Economic Outlook.*

Statistical Office of the United Nations, Publishing Service, New York, New York 10017 (800) 253-9646; *Statistical Yearbook.*

The World Bank, 1818 H Street, NW, Washington, D.C. 20433 (202) 477-1234; *World Tables.*

AUSTRALIA - MOTION PICTURES

Statistical Office of the United Nations, Publishing Service, New York, New York 10017 (800) 253-9646; *Statistical Yearbook.*

United Nations Educational, Scientific and Cultural Organization (UNESCO), 7 Place de Fontenoy, F-75700 Paris, France (Telephone Number in U.S. (212) 963-5981; *Statistical Yearbook.*

AUSTRALIA - MOTOR VEHICLE PRODUCTION

American Automobile Manufacturers Association, 1401 H Street, NW, Suite 900, Washington, D.C. 20005 (202) 326-5500; *World Motor Vehicle Data.*

Organisation for Economic Co-operation and Development (OECD), 2 rue Andre-Pascal, 75 Paris 16, France (Telephone Number in U.S. (202) 785-6323); *Foreign Trade by Commodities,* and *Indicators of Industrial Activity.*

Statistical Office of the United Nations, Publishing Service, New York, New York 10017 (800) 253-9646; *Statistical Yearbook.*

AUSTRALIA - MOTOR VEHICLE TAXES - See AUSTRALIA - TAXATION

AUSTRALIA - MOTOR VEHICLES IN USE

American Automobile Manufacturers Association, 1401 H Street, NW, Suite 900, Washington, D.C. 20005 (202) 326-5500; *World Motor Vehicle Data.*

G.K. Hall and Company, 70 Lincoln Street, Boston, Massachusetts 02111 (617) 423-3990; *The World in Figures.*

International Road Federation, 525 School Street, SW, Washington, D.C. 20024 (202) 554-2106; *World Road Statistics*.

Statistical Office of the United Nations, Publishing Service, New York, New York 10017 (800) 253-9646; *Statistical Yearbook*.

Times Books, 201 East 50th Street, New York, New York 10022 (212) 751-2600; *The Economist Book of Vital World Statistics*.

AUSTRALIA - MUSEUMS

Facts on File, 460 Park Avenue South, New York, New York 10016 (800) 443-8323; *The New Book of World Rankings*.

United Nations Educational, Scientific and Cultural Organization (UNESCO), 7 Place de Fontenoy, F-75700 Paris, France (Telephone Number in U.S. (212) 963-5981; *Statistical Yearbook*.

AUSTRALIA - NATALITY - See AUSTRALIA - BIRTH RATE

AUSTRALIA - NATIONAL ACCOUNTS

Australian Bureau of Statistics, Canberra, Australia; *Year Book Australia*.

Federal Statistical Office, Gustav - Stresemann - Ring 11, D-6200 Wiesbaden, Germany; *Australien*.

Gale Research Incorporated, 835 Penobscot Building, Detroit, Michigan 48226 (800) 877-4253; *International Historical Statistics the Americas and Australasia*.

International Monetary Fund, 700 Nineteenth Street, NW, Washington, D.C. 20431 (202) 623-7000; *International Financial Statistics*.

Organisation for Economic Co-operation and Development (OECD), 2 rue Andre-Pascal, 75 Paris 16, France (Telephone Number in U.S. (202) 785-6323); *Economic Outlook*.

Statistical Office of the United Nations, Publishing Service, New York, New York 10017 (800) 253-9646; *National Accounts Statistics*, and *Statistical Yearbook for Asia and the Pacific*.

AUSTRALIA - NATIONAL INCOME

Facts on File, 460 Park Avenue South, New York, New York 10016 (800) 443-8323; *The New Book of World Rankings*.

G.K. Hall and Company, 70 Lincoln Street, Boston, Massachusetts 02111 (617) 423-3990; *The World in Figures*.

Organisation for Economic Co-operation and Development (OECD), 2 rue Andre-Pascal, 75 Paris 16, France (Telephone Number in U.S. (202) 785-6323); *Economic Outlook*.

Statistical Office of the United Nations, Publishing Service, New York, New York 10017 (800) 253-9646; *Statistical Yearbook*.

AUSTRALIA - NATIONAL PRODUCT

Facts on File, 460 Park Avenue South, New York, New York 10016 (800) 443-8323; *The New Book of World Rankings*.

Organisation for Economic Co-operation and Development (OECD), 2 rue Andre-Pascal, 75 Paris 16, France (Telephone Number in U.S. (202) 785-6323); *Economic Outlook*, and *Main Economic Indicators - Historical Statistics*.

Statistical Office of the United Nations, Publishing Service, New York, New York 10017 (800) 253-9646; *Statistical Yearbook*.

AUSTRALIA - NATURAL GAS PRODUCTION - See AUSTRALIA - MINING AND MINERAL PRODUCTS

AUSTRALIA - NATURAL RUBBER PRODUCTION

International Rubber Study Group, York House, 8th Floor, Empire Way, Wembley, London HA9 0PA, England; *World Rubber Statistics Handbook*.

AUSTRALIA - NET MATERIAL PRODUCT

Statistical Office of the United Nations, Publishing Service, New York, New York 10017 (800) 253-9646; *Statistical Yearbook*.

AUSTRALIA - NEWSPAPER PRODUCTION - See AUSTRALIA - FORESTRY AND FOREST PRODUCTS

AUSTRALIA - NEWSPRINT CONSUMPTION - See AUSTRALIA - FORESTRY AND FOREST PRODUCTS

AUSTRALIA - NICKEL AND NICKEL ORE - See AUSTRALIA - MINING AND MINERAL PRODUCTS

AUSTRALIA - NITRIC ACID PRODUCTION - See AUSTRALIA - MINING AND MINERAL PRODUCTS

AUSTRALIA - OATS PRODUCTION - See AUSTRALIA - CROPS

AUSTRALIA - OCCUPATIONS - See AUSTRALIA - LABOR FORCE

AUSTRALIA - OIL PRODUCING CROPS

Organisation for Economic Co-operation and Development (OECD), 2 rue Andre-Pascal, 75 Paris 16, France (Telephone Number in U.S. (202) 785-6323); *Foreign Trade By Commodities*.

AUSTRALIA - ORANGE PRODUCTION - See AUSTRALIA - CROPS

AUSTRALIA - PAPER - See AUSTRALIA - FORESTRY AND FOREST PRODUCTS

AUSTRALIA - PATENTS

Statistical Office of the United Nations, Publishing Service, New York, New York 10017 (800) 253-9646; *Statistical Yearbook*.

World Intellectual Property Organization, 34 Chemin des Colombettes, CH-1211 Geneva 20. Switzerland; *Industrial Property Statistics*.

AUSTRALIA - PEANUT PRODUCTION - See AUSTRALIA - CROPS

AUSTRALIA - PERIODICALS

United Nations Educational, Scientific and Cultural Organization (UNESCO), 7 Place de Fontenoy, F-75700 Paris, France (Telephone Number in U.S. (212) 963-5981; *Statistical Yearbook*.

AUSTRALIA - PESTICIDE USE

Food and Agricultural Organization of the United Nations (FAO) Via Delle Terme di Caracalla, 00100 Rome, Italy (Telephone Number in U.S. (202) 653-2400; *The State of Food and Agriculture*.

AUSTRALIA - PETROLEUM INDUSTRY

Facts on File, 460 Park Avenue South, New York, New York 10016 (800) 443-8323; *The New Book of World Rankings*.

Food and Agricultural Organization of the United Nations (FAO) Via Delle Terme di Caracalla, 00100 Rome, Italy (Telephone Number in U.S. (202) 653-2400; *The State of Food and Agriculture*.

G.K. Hall and Company, 70 Lincoln Street, Boston, Massachusetts 02111 (617) 423-3990; *The World in Figures*.

Organisation for Economic Co-operation and Development (OECD), 2 rue Andre-Pascal, 75 Paris 16, France (Telephone Number in U.S. (202) 785-6323); *Energy Statistics of OECD Countries, Foreign Trade by Commodities, Indicators of Industrial Activity*, and *Oil and Gas Information*.

Penn Well Publishing Company, 1421 South Sheridan Road, P.O. Box 1260, Tulsa, Oklahoma 74101 (800) 752-9764; *International Energy Statistics Sourcebook*.

Statistical Office of the United Nations, Publishing Service, New York, New York 10017 (800) 253-9646; *Statistical Yearbook*.

AUSTRALIA - PHOSPHATE PRODUCTION - See AUSTRALIA - MINING AND MINERAL PRODUCTS

AUSTRALIA - PHOSPHATE ROCK PRODUCTION - See AUSTRALIA - MINING AND MINERAL PRODUCTS

AUSTRALIA - PIG-IRON AND FERRO-ALLOYS PRODUCTION - See AUSTRALIA - MINING AND MINERAL PRODUCTS

AUSTRALIA - PIGS - See AUSTRALIA - LIVESTOCK AND POULTRY

AUSTRALIA - PLASTIC AND RESIN PRODUCTION

Commodity Research Bureau, Incorporated, 75 Wall Street, New York, New York 10005 (212) 504-7754; *Commodity Year Book*.

Organisation for Economic Co-operation and Development (OECD), 2 rue Andre-Pascal, 75 Paris 16, France (Telephone Number in U.S. (202) 785-6323); *Foreign Trade by Commodities*.

Statistical Office of the United Nations, Publishing Service, New York, New York 10017 (800) 253-9646; *Statistical Yearbook*.

AUSTRALIA - PLATINUM PRODUCTION - See AUSTRALIA - MINING AND MINERAL PRODUCTS

AUSTRALIA - POPULATION

The Economist Intelligence Unit, 111 West 57th Street, New York, New York 10019 (800) 938-4685; *The World Market Atlas*.

The Economist Intelligence Unit (Asia) Limited, 10th Floor, Luk Kwok Centre, 72 Gloucester Road, Wanchai, Hong Kong (Phone Number in U.S. (800) 938-4685); *Asian Market Atlas*.

Euromonitor Publications Limited, 87-88 Turnmill Street, London EC1M 5QU, England; *International Marketing Data and Statistics*, and *The Pacific Basin: An Economic Handbook*.

Facts on File, 460 Park Avenue South, New York, New York 10016 (800) 443-8323; *The New Book of World Rankings*.

Federal Statistical Office, Gustav - Stresemann - Ring 11, D-6200 Wiesbaden, Germany; *Australien*.

Food and Agricultural Organization of the United Nations (FAO), Via delle Terme di Caracalla, 00100 Rome, Italy (Telephone Number in U.S. (202) 653-2400; *Production Yearbook*.

Gale Research Incorporated, 835 Penobscot Building, Detroit, Michigan 48226 (800) 877-4253; *International Historical Statistics the Americas and Australasia*.

G.K. Hall and Company, 70 Lincoln Street, Boston, Massachusetts 02111 (617) 423-3990; *The World in Figures*.

International Labour Office, I.L.O. Publications, CH-1211, Geneva 22, Switzerland; *Yearbook of Labour Statistics*.

Statistical Office of the United Nations, Publishing Service, New York, New York 10017 (800) 253-9646; *Demographic Yearbook, Statistical Yearbook*, and *Statistical Yearbook for Asia and the Pacific*.

Times Books, 201 East 50th Street, New York, New York 10022 (212) 751-2600; *The Economist Book of Vital World Statistics*.

U.S. Arms Control and Disarmament Agency, 320 Twenty-first Street, NW, Washington, D.C. 20451 (202) 647-8677; *World Military Expenditures and Arms Transfers*.

World Health Organization, Office of Publications, Geneva, Switzerland (Telephone Number in U.S. (518) 436-9686); *World Health Statistics: Vital Statistics and Causes of Death*.

AUSTRALIA - POST OFFICES

Facts on File, 460 Park Avenue South, New York, New York 10016 (800) 443-8323; *The New Book of World Rankings*.

AUSTRALIA - POTATO PRODUCTION - See AUSTRALIA - CROPS

AUSTRALIA - POULTRY - See AUSTRALIA - LIVESTOCK AND POULTRY

AUSTRALIA - POWER PRODUCTION INDUSTRY

Statistical Office of the United Nations, Publishing Service, New York, New York 10017 (800) 253-9646; *Electric Power in Asia and the Pacific*, and *Statistical Yearbook*.

AUSTRALIA - PRICES

Australian Bureau of Statistics, Canberra, Australia; *Year Book Australia*.

Facts on File, 460 Park Avenue South, New York, New York 10016 (800) 443-8323; *The New Book of World Rankings*.

Federal Statistical Office, Gustav - Stresemann - Ring 11, D-6200 Wiesbaden, Germany; *Australien*.

Food and Agricultural Organization of the United Nations (FAO), Via delle Terme di Caracalla, 00100 Rome, Italy (Telephone Number in U.S. (202) 653-2400; *Production Yearbook*, and *The State of Food and Agriculture*.

Gale Research Incorporated, 835 Penobscot Building, Detroit, Michigan 48226 (800) 877-4253; *International Historical Statistics the Americas and Australasia*.

G.K. Hall and Company, 70 Lincoln Street, Boston, Massachusetts 02111 (617) 423-3990; *The World in Figures*.

International Labour Office, I.L.O. Publications, CH-1211, Geneva 22, Switzerland; *Yearbook of Labour Statistics.*

International Lead and Zinc Study Group, Metro House, 58 St. James's Street, London SW1A 1LD, England; *Lead and Zinc Statistics.*

International Monetary Fund, 700 Nineteenth Street, NW, Washington, D.C. 20431 (202) 623-7000; *International Financial Statistics.*

International Rubber Study Group, York House, 8th Floor, Empire Way, Wembley, London HA9 0PA, England; *World Rubber Statistics Handbook.*

Organisation for Economic Co-operation and Development (OECD), 2 rue Andre-Pascal, 75 Paris 16, France (Telephone Number in U.S. (202) 785-6323); *Economic Outlook, The Footwear, Raw Hides and Skins, and Leather Industry in OECD Countries, Indicators of Industrial Activity, The Iron and Steel Industry, Main Economic Indicators - Historical Statistics,* and *The Pulp and Paper Industry.*

World Bureau of Metal Statistics, 27-A High Street, Ware, Herts SG12 9BA, England; *World Metal Statistics.*

AUSTRALIA - PRINTING AND WRITING PAPER PRODUCTION - See AUSTRALIA - FORESTRY AND FOREST PRODUCTS

AUSTRALIA - PRODUCTION

American Automobile Manufacturers Association, 1401 H Street, NW, Suite 900, Washington, D.C. 20005 (202) 326-5500; *World Motor Vehicle Data.*

Facts on File, 460 Park Avenue South, New York, New York 10016 (800) 443-8323; *The New Book of World Rankings.*

G.K. Hall and Company, 70 Lincoln Street, Boston, Massachusetts 02111 (617) 423-3990; *The World in Figures.*

International Iron and Steel Institute, 120, rue Colonel Bourg, B-1140 Brussels, Belgium; *Steel Statistical Yearbook.*

International Lead and Zinc Study Group, Metro House, 58 St. James's Street, London SW1A 1LD, England; *Lead and Zinc Statistics.*

International Rubber Study Group, York House, 8th Floor, Empire Way, Wembley, London HA9 0PA, England; *World Rubber Statistics Handbook.*

Organisation for Economic Co-operation and Development (OECD), 2 rue Andre-Pascal, 75 Paris 16, France (Telephone Number in U.S. (202) 785-6323); *Economic Outlook, The Footwear, Raw Hides and Skins, and Leather Industry in OECD Countries, Indicators of Industrial Activity, Industrial Structure Statistics, The Iron and Steel Industry, Meat Balances in OECD Member Countries, Milk, Milk Products, and Egg Balances in OECD Member Countries, The Non-Ferrous Metals Industry, The Pulp and Paper Industry,* and *Textile Industry in OECD Countries.*

AUSTRALIA - PRODUCTIVITY

Euromonitor Publications Limited, 87-88 Turnmill Street, London EC1M 5QU, England; *International Marketing Data and Statistics.*

Organisation for Economic Co-operation and Development (OECD), 2 rue Andre-Pascal, 75 Paris 16, France (Telephone Number in U.S. (202) 785-6323); *Economic Outlook.*

AUSTRALIA - PROPERTY TAXES - See AUSTRALIA - TAXATION

AUSTRALIA - PUBLIC CONSUMPTION FUND

Organisation for Economic Co-operation and Development (OECD), 2 rue Andre-Pascal, 75 Paris 16, France (Telephone Number in U.S. (202) 785-6323); *Revenue Statistics of OECD Member Countries.*

AUSTRALIA - PUBLIC EXPENDITURES

Organisation for Economic Co-operation and Development (OECD), 2 rue Andre-Pascal, 75 Paris 16, France (Telephone Number in U.S. (202) 785-6323); *Revenue Statistics of OECD Member Countries.*

AUSTRALIA - PUBLIC FINANCE

Facts on File, 460 Park Avenue South, New York, New York 10016 (800) 443-8323; *The New Book of World Rankings.*

Federal Statistical Office, Gustav - Stresemann - Ring 11, D-6200 Wiesbaden, Germany; *Australien.*

Organisation for Economic Co-operation and Development (OECD), 2 rue Andre-Pascal, 75 Paris 16, France (Telephone Number in U.S. (202) 785-6323); *Revenue Statistics of OECD Member Countries.*

AUSTRALIA - PUBLIC REVENUES

Organisation for Economic Co-operation and Development (OECD), 2 rue Andre-Pascal, 75 Paris 16, France (Telephone Number in U.S. (202) 785-6323); *Revenue Statistics of OECD Member Countries.*

AUSTRALIA - RADIO BROADCASTING - See AUSTRALIA - BROADCASTING

AUSTRALIA - RADIO RECEIVER PRODUCTION

Statistical Office of the United Nations, Publishing Service, New York, New York 10017 (800) 253-9646; *Statistical Yearbook.*

AUSTRALIA - RAILWAYS

G.K. Hall and Company, 70 Lincoln Street, Boston, Massachusetts 02111 (617) 423-3990; *The World in Figures.*

Jane's Information Group, Sentinel House, 163 Brighton Road, Coulsdon, Surrey CR5 2NH, England (Telephone Number in U.S. (703) 683-3700); *Jane's World Railways.*

Statistical Office of the United Nations, Publishing Service, New York, New York 10017 (800) 253-9646; *Statistical Yearbook.*

AUSTRALIA - RAPESEED PRODUCTION - See AUSTRALIA - CROPS

AUSTRALIA - RECREATIONAL ACTIVITIES

Australian Bureau of Statistics, Canberra, Australia; *Year Book Australia.*

AUSTRALIA - RELIGION

Facts on File, 460 Park Avenue South, New York, New York 10016 (800) 443-8323; *The New Book of World Rankings.*

AUSTRALIA - RENT PRICES

International Labour Office, I.L.O. Publications, CH-1211, Geneva 22, Switzerland; *Yearbook of Labour Statistics.*

AUSTRALIA - RETAIL TRADE

G.K. Hall and Company, 70 Lincoln Street, Boston, Massachusetts 02111 (617) 423-3990; *The World in Figures.*

Statistical Office of the United Nations, Publishing Service, New York, New York 10017 (800) 253-9646; *Statistical Yearbook.*

AUSTRALIA - RICE PRODUCTION - See AUSTRALIA - CROPS

AUSTRALIA - ROOT AND TUBER PRODUCTION - See AUSTRALIA - CROPS

AUSTRALIA - ROUNDWOOD PRODUCTION - See AUSTRALIA - FORESTRY AND FOREST PRODUCTS

AUSTRALIA - RUBBER PRODUCTION AND CONSUMPTION

Facts on File, 460 Park Avenue South, New York, New York 10016 (800) 443-8323; *The New Book of World Rankings.*

International Rubber Study Group, York House, 8th Floor, Empire Way, Wembley, London HA9 0PA, England; *World Rubber Statistics Handbook.*

Organisation for Economic Co-operation and Development (OECD), 2 rue Andre-Pascal, 75 Paris 16, France (Telephone Number in U.S. (202) 785-6323); *Foreign Trade by Commodities.*

Statistical Office of the United Nations, Publishing Service, New York, New York 10017 (800) 253-9646; *Statistical Yearbook.*

AUSTRALIA - SAFFLOWER SEED PRODUCTION - See AUSTRALIA - CROPS

AUSTRALIA - SALT PRODUCTION - See AUSTRALIA - MINING AND MINERAL PRODUCTS

AUSTRALIA - SAWNWOOD PRODUCTION - See AUSTRALIA - FORESTRY AND FOREST PRODUCTS

AUSTRALIA - SCIENCE AND TECHNOLOGY - EXPENDITURE FOR RESEARCH

Statistical Office of the United Nations, Publishing Service, New York, New York 10017 (800) 253-9646; *Statistical Yearbook.*

AUSTRALIA - SCIENTISTS AND TECHNICIANS

Statistical Office of the United Nations, Publishing Service, New York, New York 10017 (800) 253-9646; *Statistical Yearbook.*

AUSTRALIA - SENIOR CITIZENS

Facts on File, 460 Park Avenue South, New York, New York 10016 (800) 443-8323; *The New Book of World Rankings.*

AUSTRALIA - SHEEP - See AUSTRALIA - LIVESTOCK AND POULTRY

AUSTRALIA - SHIPBUILDING - PRODUCTION INDEX

Organisation for Economic Co-operation and Development (OECD), 2 rue Andre-Pascal, 75 Paris 16, France (Telephone Number in U.S. (202) 785-6323); *Indicators of Industrial Activity.*

AUSTRALIA - SILVER PRODUCTION AND CONSUMPTION - See AUSTRALIA - MINING AND MINERAL PRODUCTS

AUSTRALIA - SOCIAL DATA

Facts on File, 460 Park Avenue South, New York, New York 10016 (800) 443-8323; *The New Book of World Rankings.*

G.K. Hall and Company, 70 Lincoln Street, Boston, Massachusetts 02111 (617) 423-3990; *The World in Figures.*

AUSTRALIA - SOCIAL SECURITY

Australian Bureau of Statistics, Canberra, Australia; *Year Book Australia.*

International Monetary Fund, 700 Nineteenth Street, NW, Washington, D.C. 20431 (202) 623-7000; *Government Finance Statistics Yearbook.*

Organisation for Economic Co-operation and Development (OECD), 2 rue Andre-Pascal, 75 Paris 16, France (Telephone Number in U.S. (202) 785-6323); *Revenue Statistics of OECD Member Countries.*

AUSTRALIA - SOCIOECONOMIC DATA

Organisation for Economic Co-operation and Development (OECD), 2 rue Andre-Pascal, 75 Paris 16, France (Telephone Number in U.S. (202) 785-6323); *Economic Outlook.*

AUSTRALIA - SOYBEAN PRODUCTION - See AUSTRALIA - CROPS

AUSTRALIA - STATE BUDGET REVENUE AND EXPENDITURES

Euromonitor Publications Limited, 87-88 Turnmill Street, London EC1M 5QU, England; *International Marketing Data and Statistics.*

AUSTRALIA - STEEL - See AUSTRALIA - MINING AND MINERAL PRODUCTS

AUSTRALIA - STOCKS - COMMODITY - MARKET PRICE - INDEXES

Food and Agricultural Organization of the United Nations (FAO) Via Delle Terme di Caracalla, 00100 Rome, Italy (Telephone Number in U.S. (202) 653-2400; *The State of Food and Agriculture.*

International Lead and Zinc Study Group, Metro House, 58 St. James's Street, London SW1A 1LD, England; *Lead and Zinc Statistics.*

Statistical Office of the United Nations, Publishing Service, New York, New York 10017 (800) 253-9646; *Statistical Yearbook.*

World Bureau of Metal Statistics, 27-A High Street, Ware, Herts SG12 9BA, England (Telephone Number in U.S. (518) 436-9686); *World Metal Statistics.*

AUSTRALIA - SUGAR - See AUSTRALIA - CROPS

AUSTRALIA - SULPHUR AND SULPHURIC ACID - See AUSTRALIA - MINING AND MINERAL PRODUCTS

AUSTRALIA - TAXATION

International Monetary Fund, 700 Nineteenth Street, NW, Washington, D.C. 20431 (202) 623-7000; *Government Finance Statistics Yearbook.*

International Road Federation, 525 School Street, SW, Washington, D.C. 20024 (202) 554-2106; *World Road Statistics.*

Organisation for Economic Co-operation and Development (OECD), 2 rue Andre-Pascal, 75 Paris 16, France (Telephone Number in U.S. (202) 785-6323); *Revenue Statistics of OECD Member Countries.*

The World Bank, 1818 H Street, NW, Washington, D.C. 20433 (202) 477-1234; *World Tables.*

AUSTRALIA - TEA - See AUSTRALIA - CROPS

AUSTRALIA - TELEGRAPH SERVICE

Statistical Office of the United Nations, Publishing Service, New York, New York 10017 (800) 253-9646; *Statistical Yearbook.*

AUSTRALIA - TELEPHONES IN USE

American Telephone and Telegraph Company, 26 Parsippany Road, Whippany, New Jersey 07981 (800) 338-4038; *The World's Telephones.*

The Economist Intelligence Unit (Asia) Limited, 10th Floor, Luk Kwok Centre, 72 Gloucester Road, Wanchai, Hong Kong (Phone Number in U.S. (800) 938-4685); *Asian Market Atlas.*

Euromonitor Publications Limited, 87-88 Turnmill Street, London EC1M 5QU, England; *The Pacific Basin: An Economic Handbook.*

G.K. Hall and Company, 70 Lincoln Street, Boston, Massachusetts 02111 (617) 423-3990; *The World in Figures.*

Statistical Office of the United Nations, Publishing Service, New York, New York 10017 (800) 253-9646; *Statistical Yearbook.*

AUSTRALIA - TELEVISION BROADCASTING - See AUSTRALIA - BROADCASTING

AUSTRALIA - TELEVISION RECEIVER PRODUCTION

Statistical Office of the United Nations, Publishing Service, New York, New York 10017 (800) 253-9646; *Statistical Yearbook.*

AUSTRALIA - TEXTILE INDUSTRY

Forest and Paper Association, 1250 Connecticut Avenue, NW, Washington, D.C. 20036 (202) 463-2455; *Wood Pulp and Fiber Statistics.*

G.K. Hall and Company, 70 Lincoln Street, Boston, Massachusetts 02111 (617) 423-3990; *The World in Figures.*

Organisation for Economic Co-operation and Development (OECD), 2 rue Andre-Pascal, 75 Paris 16, France (Telephone Number in U.S. (202) 785-6323); *Foreign Trade by Commodities, Indicators of Industrial Activity, Industrial Structure Statistics,* and *Textile Industry in OECD Countries.*

Statistical Office of the United Nations, Publishing Service, New York, New York 10017 (800) 253-9646; *Statistical Yearbook,* and *Trade in Manufactures of Developing Countries.*

AUSTRALIA - TIN - See AUSTRALIA - MINING AND MINERAL PRODUCTS

AUSTRALIA - TIRE (MOTOR VEHICLE) PRODUCTION

International Rubber Study Group, York House, 8th Floor, Empire Way, Wembley, London HA9 0PA, England; *World Rubber Statistics Handbook.*

Statistical Office of the United Nations, Publishing Service, New York, New York 10017 (800) 253-9646; *Statistical Yearbook.*

AUSTRALIA - TOBACCO PRODUCTION

Facts on File, 460 Park Avenue South, New York, New York 10016 (800) 443-8323; *The New Book of World Rankings.*

Organisation for Economic Co-operation and Development (OECD), 2 rue Andre-Pascal, 75 Paris 16, France (Telephone Number in U.S. (202) 785-6323); *Foreign Trade by Commodities, Indicators of Industrial Activity,* and *Industrial Structure Statistics.*

Statistical Office of the United Nations, Publishing Service, New York, New York 10017 (800) 253-9646; *Statistical Yearbook.*

AUSTRALIA - TOURISM

Facts on File, 460 Park Avenue South, New York, New York 10016 (800) 443-8323; *The New Book of World Rankings.*

G.K. Hall and Company, 70 Lincoln Street, Boston, Massachusetts 02111 (617) 423-3990; *The World in Figures.*

Organisation for Economic Co-operation and Development (OECD), 2 rue Andre-Pascal, 75 Paris 16, France (Telephone Number in U.S. (202) 785-6323); *Tourism Policy and International Tourism in OECD Member Countries.*

Statistical Office of the United Nations, Publishing Service, New York, New York 10017 (800) 253-9646; *Statistical Yearbook.*

Times Books, 201 East 50th Street, New York, New York 10022 (212) 751-2600; *The Economist Book of Vital World Statistics.*

World Tourism Organization, Calle Capitan Haya 42, E-28020 Madrid, Spain; *Yearbook of Tourism Statistics.*

AUSTRALIA - TRADE - See AUSTRALIA - FOREIGN TRADE

AUSTRALIA - TRADEMARKS AND SERVICE MARKS

Statistical Office of the United Nations, Publishing Service, New York, New York 10017 (800) 253-9646; *Statistical Yearbook.*

World Intellectual Property Organization, 34 Chemin des Colombettes, CH-1211 Geneva 20. Switzerland; *Industrial Property Statistics.*

AUSTRALIA - TRANSPORTATION AND COMMUNICATIONS

Australian Bureau of Statistics, Canberra, Australia; *Year Book Australia.*

The Economist Intelligence Unit (Asia) Limited, 10th Floor, Luk Kwok Centre, 72 Gloucester Road, Wanchai, Hong Kong (Phone Number in U.S. (800) 938-4685); *Asian Market Atlas.*

Euromonitor Publications Limited, 87-88 Turnmill Street, London EC1M 5QU, England; *The Pacific Basin: An Economic Handbook.*

Facts on File, 460 Park Avenue South, New York, New York 10016 (800) 443-8323; *The New Book of World Rankings.*

Federal Statistical Office, Gustav - Stresemann - Ring 11, D-6200 Wiesbaden, Germany; *Australien.*

Gale Research Incorporated, 835 Penobscot Building, Detroit, Michigan 48226 (800) 877-4253; *International Historical Statistics*

the Americas and Australasia.

G.K. Hall and Company, 70 Lincoln Street, Boston, Massachusetts 02111 (617) 423-3990; *The World in Figures.*

Statistical Office of the United Nations, Publishing Service, New York, New York 10017 (800) 253-9646; *Statistical Yearbook for Asia and the Pacific.*

AUSTRALIA - TRAVEL

Australian Bureau of Statistics, Canberra, Australia; *Year Book Australia.*

AUSTRALIA - TUNGSTEN PRODUCTION AND CONSUMPTION - See AUSTRALIA - MINING AND MINERAL PRODUCTS

AUSTRALIA - TURKEYS - See AUSTRALIA - LIVESTOCK AND POULTRY

AUSTRALIA - UNEMPLOYMENT

Euromonitor Publications Limited, 87-88 Turnmill Street, London EC1M 5QU, England; *International Marketing Data and Statistics,* and *The Pacific Basin: An Economic Handbook.*

International Labour Office, I.L.O. Publications, CH-1211, Geneva 22, Switzerland; *Yearbook of Labour Statistics.*

Organisation for Economic Co-operation and Development (OECD), 2 rue Andre-Pascal, 75 Paris 16, France (Telephone Number in U.S. (202) 785-6323); *Economic Outlook, Labour Force Statistics, OECD Economic Surveys: Australia,* and *OECD Employment Outlook.*

Statistical Office of the United Nations, Publishing Service, New York, New York 10017 (800) 253-9646; *Statistical Yearbook.*

AUSTRALIA - URANIUM PRODUCTION AND CONSUMPTION - See AUSTRALIA - MINING AND MINERAL PRODUCTS

AUSTRALIA - UTILITIES

Statistical Office of the United Nations, Publishing Service, New York, New York 10017 (800) 253-9646; *Electric Power in Asia and the Pacific.*

AUSTRALIA - VANADIUM AND VANADIUM ORE - See AUSTRALIA - MINING AND MINERAL PRODUCTS

AUSTRALIA - VITAL STATISTICS

Euromonitor Publications Limited, 87-88 Turnmill Street, London EC1M 5QU, England; *International Marketing Data and Statistics,* and *The Pacific Basin: An Economic Handbook.*

Gale Research Incorporated, 835 Penobscot Building, Detroit, Michigan 48226 (800) 877-4253; *International Historical Statistics the Americas and Australasia.*

G.K. Hall and Company, 70 Lincoln Street, Boston, Massachusetts 02111 (617) 423-3990; *The World in Figures.*

Statistical Office of the United Nations, Publishing Service, New York, New York 10017 (800) 253-9646; *Statistical Yearbook.*

World Health Organization, Office of Publications, Geneva, Switzerland (Telephone Number in U.S. (518) 436-9686); *World Health Statistics: Vital Statistics and Causes of Death.*

AUSTRALIA - WAGES

Federal Statistical Office, Gustav - Stresemann - Ring 11, D-6200 Wiesbaden, Germany; *Australien.*

G.K. Hall and Company, 70 Lincoln Street, Boston, Massachusetts 02111 (617) 423-3990; *The World in Figures.*

International Labour Office, I.L.O. Publications, CH-1211, Geneva 22, Switzerland; *Yearbook of Labour Statistics.*

Organisation for Economic Co-operation and Development (OECD), 2 rue Andre-Pascal, 75 Paris 16, France (Telephone Number in U.S. (202) 785-6323); *Economic Outlook, Industrial Structure Statistics,* and *Main Economic Indicators - Historical Statistics.*

AUSTRALIA - WAGES AND PRICES

Statistical Office of the United Nations, Publishing Service, New York, New York 10017 (800) 253-9646; *Statistical Yearbook for Asia and the Pacific.*

AUSTRALIA - WAGES IN INDUSTRY

Organisation for Economic Co-operation and Development (OECD), 2 rue Andre-Pascal, 75 Paris 16, France (Telephone Number in U.S. (202) 785-6323); *Industrial Structure Statistics.*

AUSTRALIA - WAGES IN MANUFACTURING

Organisation for Economic Co-operation and Development (OECD), 2 rue Andre-Pascal, 75 Paris 16, France (Telephone Number in U.S. (202) 785-6323); *Economic Outlook.*

Statistical Office of the United Nations, Publishing Service, New York, New York 10017 (800) 253-9646; *Statistical Yearbook.*

AUSTRALIA - WALNUT PRODUCTION - See AUSTRALIA - CROPS

AUSTRALIA - WATER RESOURCES

Australian Bureau of Statistics, Canberra, Australia; *Year Book Australia.*

AUSTRALIA - WATERMELON PRODUCTION - See AUSTRALIA - CROPS

AUSTRALIA - WATERWAYS IN USE - See AUSTRALIA - MERCHANT SHIPPING

AUSTRALIA - WEATHER

Facts on File, 460 Park Avenue South, New York, New York 10016 (800) 443-8323; *The New Book of World Rankings.*

G.K. Hall and Company, 70 Lincoln Street, Boston, Massachusetts 02111 (617) 423-3990; *The World in Figures.*

AUSTRALIA - WELFARE

Australian Bureau of Statistics, Canberra, Australia; *Year Book Australia.*

International Monetary Fund, 700 Nineteenth Street, NW, Washington, D.C. 20431 (202) 623-7000; *Government Finance Statistics Yearbook.*

AUSTRALIA - WHALES - See AUSTRALIA - FISHERIES

AUSTRALIA - WHEAT - See AUSTRALIA - CROPS

AUSTRALIA - WHOLESALE PRICES

International Monetary Fund, 700 Nineteenth Street, NW, Washington, D.C. 20431 (202) 623-7000; *International Financial Statistics.*

AUSTRALIA - WHOLESALE TRADE

Statistical Office of the United Nations, Publishing Service, New York, New York 10017 (800) 253-9646; *Statistical Yearbook.*

AUSTRALIA - WINE PRODUCTION

Facts on File, 460 Park Avenue South, New York, New York 10016 (800) 443-8323; *The New Book of World Rankings.*

Statistical Office of the United Nations, Publishing Service, New York, New York 10017 (800) 253-9646; *Statistical Yearbook.*

AUSTRALIA - WOOD - See AUSTRALIA - FORESTRY AND FOREST PRODUCTS

AUSTRALIA - WOOL - INDUSTRIAL CONSUMPTION

Organisation for Economic Co-operation and Development (OECD), 2 rue Andre-Pascal, 75 Paris 16, France (Telephone Number in U.S. (202) 785-6323); *Textile Industry in OECD Countries.*

Statistical Office of the United Nations, Publishing Service, New York, New York 10017 (800) 253-9646; *Statistical Yearbook.*

AUSTRALIA - WOOL EXPORTS

International Monetary Fund, 700 Nineteenth Street, NW, Washington, D.C. 20431 (202) 623-7000; *International Financial Statistics.*

AUSTRALIA - WOOL PRODUCTION

Commodity Research Bureau, Incorporated, 75 Wall Street, New York, New York 10005 (212) 504-7754; *Commodity Year Book.*

Facts on File, 460 Park Avenue South, New York, New York 10016 (800) 443-8323; *The New Book of World Rankings.*

Organisation for Economic Co-operation and Development (OECD), 2 rue Andre-Pascal, 75 Paris 16, France (Telephone Number in U.S. (202) 785-6323); *Economic Accounts for Agriculture,* and *Textile Industry in OECD Countries.*

Statistical Office of the United Nations, Publishing Service, New York, New York 10017 (800) 253-9646; *Statistical Yearbook.*

AUSTRALIA - YARN PRODUCTION

Organisation for Economic Co-operation and Development (OECD), 2 rue Andre-Pascal, 75 Paris 16, France (Telephone Number in U.S. (202) 785-6323); *Foreign Trade by Commodities,* and *Textile Industry in OECD Countries.*

Statistical Office of the United Nations, Publishing Service, New York, New York 10017 (800) 253-9646; *Statistical Yearbook.*

AUSTRALIA - ZINC AND ZINC ORE - See AUSTRALIA - MINING AND MINERAL PRODUCTS

Austria - National Statistical Office

Osterreichisches Statistisches Zentralamt, Hintere Zollamtsstrasse 2b, 1033 Wien, Postfach 3000 Austria.

Austria - Primary Statistics Source

Osterreichisches Statistiches Zentralamt (Central Statistical Office), Neve Hofburg, Heldenplatz, 1014 Wien, Austria; *Statistiches Jahrbuch fur die Republik Osterreich* (Statistical Yearbook of the Austrian Republic).

Austria - Databases

Integrated Statistical Information System, Austria Central Statistical Office, Systems and Methods Division, Hintere Zollamtsstr. 2B, A-1033 Vienna, Austria. Subject coverage: Demography, social statistics, education, health, economy, taxes, and national accounts.

AUSTRIA - AGRICULTURE

Facts on File, 460 Park Avenue South, New York, New York 10016 (800) 443-8323; *The New Book of World Rankings.*

Federal Statistical Office, Gustav - Stresemann - Ring 11, D-6200 Wiesbaden, Germany; *Osterreich.*

Food and Agricultural Organization of the United Nations (FAO) Via Delle Terme di Caracalla, 00100 Rome, Italy (Telephone Number in U.S. (202) 653-2400); *The State of Food and Agriculture, Production Yearbook,* and *Trade Yearbook.*

G.K. Hall and Company, 70 Lincoln Street, Boston, Massachusetts 02111 (617) 423-3990; *The World in Figures.*

Organisation for Economic Co-operation and Development (OECD), 2 rue Andre-Pascal, 75 Paris 16, France (Telephone Number in U.S. (202) 785-6323); *Economic Accounts for Agriculture, Indicators of Industrial Activity, Industrial Structure Statistics,* and *OECD Economic Surveys: Austria.*

Statistical Office of the United Nations, Publishing Service, New York, New York 10017 (800) 253-9646; *Statistical Yearbook.*

Times Books, 201 East 50th Street, New York, New York 10022 (212) 751-2600; *The Economist Book of Vital World Statistics.*

The World Bank, 1818 H Street, NW, Washington, D.C. 20433 (202) 477-1234; *World Tables.*

AUSTRIA - AIRLINE SERVICE

Facts on File, 460 Park Avenue South, New York, New York 10016 (800) 443-8323; *The New Book of World Rankings.*

G.K. Hall and Company, 70 Lincoln Street, Boston, Massachusetts 02111 (617) 423-3990; *The World in Figures.*

International Civil Aviation Organization, 1000 Sherbrooke Street West, Suite 400, Montreal, Quebec, Canada H3A 2R2 (514) 285-8219; *Civil Aviation Statistics of the World.*

Organisation for Economic Co-operation and Development (OECD), 2 rue Andre-Pascal, 75 Paris 16, France (Telephone Number in U.S. (202) 785-6323); *Tourism Policy and International Tourism in OECD Member Countries.*

Statistical Office of the United Nations, Publishing Service, New York, New York 10017 (800) 253-9646; *Statistical Yearbook.*

Times Books, 201 East 50th Street, New York, New York 10022 (212) 751-2600; *The Economist Book of Vital World Statistics.*

AUSTRIA - ALUMINUM PRODUCTION AND CONSUMPTION - See AUSTRIA - MINING AND MINERAL PRODUCTS

AUSTRIA - ANIMAL FEEDINGSTUFFS

Organisation for Economic Co-operation and Development (OECD), 2 rue Andre-Pascal, 75 Paris 16, France (Telephone Number in U.S. (202) 785-6323); *Foreign Trade by Commodities.*

AUSTRIA - ANIMAL HEALTH

Food and Agricultural Organization of the United Nations (FAO), Via delle Terme di Caracalla, 00100 Rome, Italy (Telephone Number in U.S. (202) 653-2400); *Animal Health Yearbook.*

AUSTRIA - ANTIMONY AND ANTIMONY ORE - See AUSTRIA - MINING AND MINERAL PRODUCTS

AUSTRIA - AREA AND DENSITY OF POPULATION

Federal Statistical Office, Gustav - Stresemann - Ring 11, D-6200 Wiesbaden, Germany; *Osterreich.*

Facts on File, 460 Park Avenue South, New York, New York 10016 (800) 443-8323; *The New Book of World Rankings.*

Food and Agricultural Organization of the United Nations (FAO) Via Delle Terme di Caracalla, 00100 Rome, Italy (Telephone Number in U.S. (202) 653-2400); *The State of Food and Agriculture.*

G.K. Hall and Company, 70 Lincoln Street, Boston, Massachusetts 02111 (617) 423-3990; *The World in Figures.*

Statistical Office of the United Nations, Publishing Service, New York, New York 10017 (800) 253-9646; *Statistical Yearbook.*

Times Books, 201 East 50th Street, New York, New York 10022 (212) 751-2600; *The Economist Book of Vital World Statistics.*

AUSTRIA - ARMS EXPORTS AND IMPORTS

U.S. Arms Control and Disarmament Agency, 320 Twenty-first Street, NW, Washington, D.C. 20451 (202) 647-8677; *World Military Expenditures and Arms Transfers.*

AUSTRIA - ARSENIC PRODUCTION AND CONSUMPTION - See AUSTRIA - MINING AND MINERAL PRODUCTS

AUSTRIA - BALANCE OF PAYMENTS

The Economist Intelligence Unit, 111 West 57th Street, New York, New York 10019 (800) 938-4685; *The World Market Atlas.*

Federal Statistical Office, Gustav - Stresemann - Ring 11, D-6200 Wiesbaden, Germany; *Osterreich.*

G.K. Hall and Company, 70 Lincoln Street, Boston, Massachusetts 02111 (617) 423-3990; *The World in Figures.*

International Monetary Fund, 700 Nineteenth Street, NW, Washington, D.C. 20431 (202) 623-7000; *Balance of Payments Yearbook,* and *International Financial Statistics.*

Organisation for Economic Co-operation and Development (OECD), 2 rue Andre-Pascal, 75 Paris 16, France (Telephone Number in U.S. (202) 785-6323); *Economic Outlook, Geographical Distribution of Financial Flows to Developing Countries, Main Economic Indicators - Historical Statistics,* and *OECD Economic Surveys: Austria.*

Times Books, 201 East 50th Street, New York, New York 10022 (212) 751-2600; *The Economist Book of Vital World Statistics.*

The World Bank, 1818 H Street, NW, Washington, D.C. 20433 (202) 477-1234; *World Tables.*

AUSTRIA - BANKING

Facts on File, 460 Park Avenue South, New York, New York 10016 (800) 443-8323; *The New Book of World Rankings.*

G.K. Hall and Company, 70 Lincoln Street, Boston, Massachusetts 02111 (617) 423-3990; *The World in Figures.*

International Monetary Fund, 700 Nineteenth Street, NW, Washington, D.C. 20431; *Government Finance Statistics Yearbook,* and *International Financial Statistics.*

Organisation for Economic Co-operation and Development (OECD), 2 rue Andre-Pascal, 75 Paris 16, France (Telephone Number in U.S. (202) 785-6323); *Economic Outlook, Financial Market Trends,* and *OECD Economic Surveys: Austria.*

AUSTRIA - BARLEY PRODUCTION - See AUSTRIA - CROPS

AUSTRIA - BAUXITE PRODUCTION AND CONSUMPTION - See AUSTRIA - MINING AND MINERAL PRODUCTS

AUSTRIA - BEER PRODUCTION

Facts on File, 460 Park Avenue South, New York, New York 10016 (800) 443-8323; *The New Book of World Rankings.*

Statistical Office of the United Nations, Publishing Service, New York, New York 10017 (800) 253-9646; *Statistical Yearbook.*

AUSTRIA - BEVERAGES - PRODUCTION INDEX

Organisation for Economic Co-operation and Development (OECD), 2 rue Andre-Pascal, 75 Paris 16, France (Telephone Number in U.S. (202) 785-6323); *Indicators of Industrial Activity.*

AUSTRIA - BIRTH RATE

Facts on File, 460 Park Avenue South, New York, New York 10016 (800) 443-8323; *The New Book of World Rankings.*

Organisation for Economic Co-operation and Development (OECD), 2 rue Andre-Pascal, 75 Paris 16, France; *Labor Force Statistics.*

Statistical Office of the United Nations, Publishing Service, New York, New York 10017 (800) 253-9646; *Demographic Yearbook,* and *Statistical Yearbook.*

Times Books, 201 East 50th Street, New York, New York 10022 (212) 751-2600; *The Economist Book of Vital World Statistics.*

The World Bank, 1818 H Street, NW, Washington, D.C. 20433 (202) 477-1234; *World Tables.*

World Health Organization, Office of Publications, Avenue Appia, CH-1211 Geneva 27, Switzerland (Telephone Number in U.S. (518) 436-9686); *World Health Statistics Annual.*

AUSTRIA - BISMUTH PRODUCTION AND CONSUMPTION - See AUSTRIA - MINING AND MINERAL PRODUCTS

AUSTRIA - BONDS

G.K. Hall and Company, 70 Lincoln Street, Boston, Massachusetts 02111 (617) 423-3990; *The World in Figures.*

International Monetary Fund, 700 Nineteenth Street, NW, Washington, D.C. 20431 (202) 623-7000; *Government Finance Statistics Yearbook.*

Organisation for Economic Co-operation and Development (OECD), 2 rue Andre-Pascal, 75 Paris 16, France (Telephone Number in U.S. (202) 785-6323); *Financial Market Trends.*

Statistical Office of the United Nations, Publishing Service, New York, New York 10017 (800) 253-9646; *Statistical Yearbook.*

AUSTRIA - BOOK PRODUCTION

Euromonitor Publications Limited, 87-88 Turnmill Street, London EC1M 5QU, England; *European Marketing Data and Statistics.*

G.K. Hall and Company, 70 Lincoln Street, Boston, Massachusetts 02111 (617) 423-3990; *The World in Figures.*

Organisation for Economic Co-operation and Development (OECD), 2 rue Andre-Pascal, 75 Paris 16, France (Telephone Number in U.S. (202) 785-6323); *Indicators of Industrial Activity.*

United Nations Educational, Scientific and Cultural Organization (UNESCO), 7 Place de Fontenoy, F-75700 Paris, France; *Statistical Yearbook.*

AUSTRIA - BROADCASTING

Billboard Limited, P.O. Box 9027, 1006 AA Amsterdam, The Netherlands (Telephone Number in U.S. (212) 764-7300); *World Radio TV Handbook.*

Facts on File, 460 Park Avenue South, New York, New York 10016 (800) 443-8323; *The New Book of World Rankings.*

G.K. Hall and Company, 70 Lincoln Street, Boston, Massachusetts 02111 (617) 423-3990; *The World in Figures.*

Times Books, 201 East 50th Street, New York, New York 10022 (212) 751-2600; *The Economist Book of Vital World Statistics.*

United Nations Educational, Scientific and Cultural Organization (UNESCO), 7 Place de Fontenoy, F-75700 Paris, France; *Statistical Yearbook.*

AUSTRIA - BUILDING CONSTRUCTION - See AUSTRIA - CONSTRUCTION INDUSTRY

AUSTRIA - BUSINESS

G.K. Hall and Company, 70 Lincoln Street, Boston, Massachusetts 02111 (617) 423-3990; *The World in Figures.*

Organisation for Economic Co-operation and Development (OECD), 2 rue Andre-Pascal, 75 Paris 16, France; *Main Economic Indicators - Historical Statistics.*

AUSTRIA - BUTTER - See AUSTRIA - DAIRY PRODUCTS

AUSTRIA - CABBAGE PRODUCTION - See AUSTRIA - CROPS

AUSTRIA - CADMIUM PRODUCTION AND CONSUMPTION - See AUSTRIA - MINING AND MINERAL PRODUCTS

AUSTRIA - CALORIE SUPPLY

Food and Agricultural Organization of the United Nations (FAO) Via Delle Terme di Caracalla, 00100 Rome, Italy (Telephone Number in U.S. (202) 653-2400); *The State of Food and Agriculture.*

AUSTRIA - CAPITAL INVESTMENT

Organisation for Economic Co-operation and Development (OECD), 2 rue Andre-Pascal, 75 Paris 16, France (Telephone Number in U.S. (202) 785-6323); *Economic Outlook,* and *Financial Market Trends.*

AUSTRIA - CAPITAL REVENUE

International Monetary Fund, 700 Nineteenth Street, NW, Washington, D.C. 20431 (202) 623-7000; *Government Finance Statistics Yearbook.*

Organisation for Economic Co-operation and Development (OECD), 2 rue Andre-Pascal, 75 Paris 16, France (Telephone Number in U.S. (202) 785-6323); *Economic Outlook,* and *Financial Market Trends.*

AUSTRIA - CATTLE - See AUSTRIA - LIVESTOCK AND POULTRY

AUSTRIA - CAUSTIC SODA PRODUCTION

Organisation for Economic Co-operation and Development (OECD), 2 rue Andre-Pascal, 75 Paris 16, France (Telephone Number in U.S. (202) 785-6323); *Indicators of Industrial Activity.*

AUSTRIA - CEMENT PRODUCTION - See AUSTRIA - MINING AND MINERAL PRODUCTS

AUSTRIA - CEREAL PRODUCTION - See AUSTRIA - CROPS

AUSTRIA - CHEESE - See AUSTRIA - DAIRY PRODUCTS

AUSTRIA - CHEMICAL (ORGANIC) PRODUCTION - See AUSTRIA - MINING AND MINERAL PRODUCTS

AUSTRIA - CHROMIUM ORE PRODUCTION AND CONSUMPTION - See AUSTRIA - MINING AND MINERAL PRODUCTS

AUSTRIA - CHROMITE PRODUCTION AND CONSUMPTION - See AUSTRIA - MINING AND MINERAL PRODUCTS

AUSTRIA - CIGAR PRODUCTION - See AUSTRIA - TOBACCO PRODUCTION

AUSTRIA - CIGARETTE PRODUCTION - See AUSTRIA - TOBACCO PRODUCTION

AUSTRIA - CLASS STRUCTURE

G.K. Hall and Company, 70 Lincoln Street, Boston, Massachusetts 02111 (617) 423-3990; *The World in Figures.*

AUSTRIA - CLIMATE

Facts on File, 460 Park Avenue South, New York, New York 10016 (800) 443-8323; *The New Book of World Rankings.*

G.K. Hall and Company, 70 Lincoln Street, Boston, Massachusetts 02111 (617) 423-3990; *The World in Figures.*

AUSTRIA - CLOTHING

Organisation for Economic Co-operation and Development (OECD), 2 rue Andre-Pascal, 75 Paris 16, France (Telephone Number in U.S. (202) 785-6323); *Indicators of Industrial Activity*, and *Textile Industry in OECD Countries*.

Statistical Office of the United Nations, Publishing Service, New York, New York 10017 (800) 253-9646; *Trade in Manufactures of Developing Countries*.

AUSTRIA - COAL PRODUCTION - See AUSTRIA - MINING AND MINERAL PRODUCTS

AUSTRIA - COBALT PRODUCTION AND CONSUMPTION - See AUSTRIA - MINING AND MINERAL PRODUCTS

AUSTRIA - COFFEE PRODUCTION AND CONSUMPTION - See AUSTRIA - CROPS

AUSTRIA - COKE OVEN COKE PRODUCTION - See AUSTRIA - MINING AND MINERAL PRODUCTS

AUSTRIA - COKE OVEN ORE PRODUCTION AND CONSUMPTION - See AUSTRIA - MINING AND MINERAL PRODUCTS

AUSTRIA - COKE PRODUCTION AND CONSUMPTION - See AUSTRIA - MINING AND MINERAL PRODUCTS

AUSTRIA - COMMUNICATIONS

Federal Statistical Office, Gustav - Stresemann - Ring 11, D-6200 Wiesbaden, Germany; *Osterreich*.

G.K. Hall and Company, 70 Lincoln Street, Boston, Massachusetts 02111 (617) 423-3990; *The World in Figures*.

AUSTRIA - CONSTRUCTION INDUSTRY

Facts on File, 460 Park Avenue South, New York, New York 10016 (800) 443-8323; *The New Book of World Rankings*.

Organisation for Economic Co-operation and Development (OECD), 2 rue Andre-Pascal, 75 Paris 16, France (Telephone Number in U.S. (202) 785-6323); *Industrial Structure Statistics*, *The Iron and Steel Industry*, *Main Economic Indicators - Historical Statistics*, and *OECD Economic Surveys: Austria*.

Statistical Office of the United Nations, Publishing Service, New York, New York 10017; *Construction Statistics Yearbook*, and *Statistical Yearbook*.

AUSTRIA - CONSUMER PRICE INDEX

Federal Statistical Office, Gustav - Stresemann - Ring 11, D-6200 Wiesbaden, Germany; *Osterreich*.

G.K. Hall and Company, 70 Lincoln Street, Boston, Massachusetts 02111 (617) 423-3990; *The World in Figures*.

Organisation for Economic Co-operation and Development (OECD), 2 rue Andre-Pascal, 75 Paris 16, France (Telephone Number in U.S. (202) 785-6323); *Economic Outlook*.

Statistical Office of the United Nations, Publishing Service, New York, New York 10017 (800) 253-9646; *Statistical Yearbook*.

AUSTRIA - CONSUMER PRICES

Euromonitor Publications Limited, 87-88 Turnmill Street, London EC1M 5QU, England; *European Marketing Data and Statistics*.

Federal Statistical Office, Gustav - Stresemann - Ring 11, D-6200 Wiesbaden, Germany; *Osterreich*.

International Labour Office, I.L.O. Publications, CH-1211, Geneva 22, Switzerland; *Yearbook of Labour Statistics*.

International Monetary Fund, 700 Nineteenth Street, NW, Washington, D.C. 20431 (202) 623-7000; *International Financial Statistics*.

Organisation for Economic Co-operation and Development (OECD), 2 rue Andre-Pascal, 75 Paris 16, France (Telephone Number in U.S. (202) 785-6323); *Economic Outlook*.

AUSTRIA - CONSUMPTION

G.K. Hall and Company, 70 Lincoln Street, Boston, Massachusetts 02111 (617) 423-3990; *The World in Figures*.

International Iron and Steel Institute, 120, rue Colonel Bourg, B-1140, Brussels, Belgium; *Steel Statistical Yearbook*.

International Lead and Zinc Study Group, Metro House, 58 St. James's Street, London SW1A 1LD, England; *Lead and Zinc Statistics*.

International Monetary Fund, 700 Nineteenth Street, NW, Washington, D.C. 20431 (202) 623-7000; *International Financial Statistics*.

International Rubber Study Group, York House, 8th Floor, Empire Way, Wembley, London HA9 0PA, England; *Rubber Statistical Bulletin*.

Organisation for Economic Co-operation and Development (OECD), 2 rue Andre-Pascal, 75 Paris 16, France (Telephone Number in U.S. (202) 785-6323); *The Footwear, Raw Hides and Skins, and Leather Industry in OECD Countries*, *The Iron and Steel Industry*, *Meat Balances in OECD Member Countries*, *The Non-Ferrous Metals Industry*, *The Pulp and Paper Industry*, and *Textile Industry in OECD Countries*.

AUSTRIA - COPPER AND COPPER ORE - See AUSTRIA - MINING AND MINERAL PRODUCTS

AUSTRIA - CORN PRODUCTION - See AUSTRIA - CROPS

AUSTRIA - CORPORATE INCOME TAXES - See AUSTRIA - TAXATION

AUSTRIA - CORPORATE TAXES - See AUSTRIA - TAXATION

AUSTRIA - COTTON - See AUSTRIA - CROPS

AUSTRIA - CRIME

International Criminal Police Organization (INTERPOL), 26 rue Armengaud, 92210 Saint Cloud, France; *International Crime Statistics*.

Yale University Press, Yale Station, New Haven, Connecticut 06520; *Violence and Crime in Cross-National Perspective*.

AUSTRIA - CROPS

Commodity Research Bureau, Incorporated, 75 Wall Street, New York, New York 10005 (212) 504-7754; *Commodity Year Book.*

Euromonitor Publications Limited, 87-88 Turnmill Street, London EC1M 5QU, England; *European Marketing Data and Statistics.*

Facts on File, 460 Park Avenue South, New York, New York 10016 (800) 443-8323; *The New Book of World Rankings.*

Food and Agricultural Organization of the United Nations (FAO) Via Delle Terme di Caracalla, 00100 Rome, Italy (Telephone Number in U.S. (202) 653-2400); *Production Yearbook,* and *The State of Food and Agriculture.*

G.K. Hall and Company, 70 Lincoln Street, Boston, Massachusetts 02111 (617) 423-3990; *The World in Figures.*

Organisation for Economic Co-operation and Development (OECD), 2 rue Andre-Pascal, 75 Paris 16, France (Telephone Number in U.S. (202) 785-6323); *Economic Accounts for Agriculture,* and *Foreign Trade by Commodities,* and *Textile Industry in OECD Countries.*

Statistical Office of the United Nations, Publishing Service, New York, New York 10017 (800) 253-9646; *Statistical Yearbook.*

AUSTRIA - CUSTOMS DUTIES

G.K. Hall and Company, 70 Lincoln Street, Boston, Massachusetts 02111 (617) 423-3990; *The World in Figures.*

International Monetary Fund, 700 Nineteenth Street, NW, Washington, D.C. 20431 (202) 623-7000; *Government Finance Statistics Yearbook.*

Organisation for Economic Co-operation and Development (OECD), 2 rue Andre-Pascal, 75 Paris 16, France (Telephone Number in U.S. (202) 785-6323); *The Non-Ferrous Metals Industry.*

AUSTRIA - DAIRY PRODUCTS

Food and Agricultural Organization of the United Nations (FAO) Via Delle Terme di Caracalla, 00100 Rome, Italy (Telephone Number in U.S. (202) 653-2400); *Production Yearbook,* and *The State of Food and Agriculture.*

Organisation for Economic Co-operation and Development (OECD), 2 rue Andre-Pascal, 75 Paris 16, France (Telephone Number in U.S. (202) 785-6323); *Economic Accounts for Agriculture,* and *Milk, Milk Products, and Egg Balances in OECD Member Countries.*

Statistical Office of the United Nations, Publishing Service, New York, New York 10017 (800) 253-9646; *Statistical Yearbook.*

AUSTRIA - DEATH RATE

G.K. Hall and Company, 70 Lincoln Street, Boston, Massachusetts 02111 (617) 423-3990; *The World in Figures.*

Statistical Office of the United Nations, Publishing Service, New York, New York 10017 (800) 253-9646; *Statistical Yearbook.*

Times Books, 201 East 50th Street, New York, New York 10022 (212) 751-2600; *The Economist Book of Vital World Statistics.*

World Health Organization, Office of Publications, Avenue Appia, CH-1211 Geneva 27, Switzerland (Telephone Number in U.S. (518) 436-9686); *World Health Statistics Annual.*

AUSTRIA - DEFENSE EXPENDITURES

G.K. Hall and Company, 70 Lincoln Street, Boston, Massachusetts 02111 (617) 423-3990; *The World in Figures.*

International Monetary Fund, 700 Nineteenth Street, NW, Washington, D.C. 20431 (202) 623-7000; *Government Finance Statistics Yearbook.*

U.S. Arms Control and Disarmament Agency, 320 Twenty-first Street, NW, Washington, D.C. 20451 (202) 647-8677; *World Military Expenditures and Arms Transfers.*

AUSTRIA - DEMOGRAPHY

The Economist Intelligence Unit, 111 West 57th Street, New York, New York 10019 (800) 938-4685; *The World Market Atlas.*

Facts on File, 460 Park Avenue South, New York, New York 10016 (800) 443-8323; *The New Book of World Rankings.*

Federal Statistical Office, Gustav - Stresemann - Ring 11, D-6200 Wiesbaden, Germany; *Osterreich.*

G.K. Hall and Company, 70 Lincoln Street, Boston, Massachusetts 02111 (617) 423-3990; *The World in Figures.*

AUSTRIA - DEVELOPMENT ASSISTANCE

G.K. Hall and Company, 70 Lincoln Street, Boston, Massachusetts 02111 (617) 423-3990; *The World in Figures.*

Organisation for Economic Co-operation and Development (OECD), 2 rue Andre-Pascal, 75 Paris 16, France (Telephone Number in U.S. (202) 785-6323); *Geographical Distribution of Financial Flows to Developing Countries.*

Statistical Office of the United Nations, Publishing Service, New York, New York 10017 (800) 253-9646; *Statistical Yearbook.*

AUSTRIA - DIAMOND PRODUCTION - See AUSTRIA - MINING AND MINERAL PRODUCTS

AUSTRIA - DISCOUNT RATES

Organisation for Economic Co-operation and Development (OECD), 2 rue Andre-Pascal, 75 Paris 16, France (Telephone Number in U.S. (202) 785-6323); *Financial Market Trends,* and *Main Economic Indicators - Historical Statistics.*

Statistical Office of the United Nations, Publishing Service, New York, New York 10017 (800) 253-9646; *Statistical Yearbook.*

AUSTRIA - DISEASES

G.K. Hall and Company, 70 Lincoln Street, Boston, Massachusetts 02111 (617) 423-3990; *The World in Figures.*

World Health Organization, Office of Publications, Avenue Appia, CH-1211 Geneva 27, Switzerland (Telephone Number in U.S. (518) 436-9686); *World Health Statistics Annual.*

AUSTRIA - DIVORCE RATES

Facts on File, 460 Park Avenue South, New York, New York 10016 (800) 443-8323; *The New Book of World Rankings.*

Statistical Office of the United Nations, Publishing Service, New York, New York 10017 (800) 253-9646; *Demographic Yearbook,* and

Statistical Yearbook.

AUSTRIA - DOMESTIC PRODUCT

G.K. Hall and Company, 70 Lincoln Street, Boston, Massachusetts 02111 (617) 423-3990; *The World in Figures.*

AUSTRIA - DUCKS - See AUSTRIA - LIVESTOCK AND POULTRY

AUSTRIA - ECONOMY

Euromonitor Publications Limited, 87-88 Turnmill Street, London EC1M 5QU, England; *European Marketing Data and Statistics.*

Facts on File, 460 Park Avenue South, New York, New York 10016 (800) 443-8323; *The New Book of World Rankings.*

Federal Statistical Office, Gustav - Stresemann - Ring 11, D-6200 Wiesbaden, Germany; *Osterreich.*

G.K. Hall and Company, 70 Lincoln Street, Boston, Massachusetts 02111 (617) 423-3990; *The World in Figures.*

Organisation for Economic Co-operation and Development (OECD), 2 rue Andre-Pascal, 75 Paris 16, France (Telephone Number in U.S. (202) 785-6323); *Economic Outlook, Geographical Distribution of Financial Flows to Developing Countries, Main Economic Indicators - Historical Statistics, OECD Economic Surveys: Austria,* and *OECD Employment Outlook.*

AUSTRIA - EDUCATION

The Economist Intelligence Unit, 111 West 57th Street, New York, New York 10019 (800) 938-4685; *The World Market Atlas.*

Euromonitor Publications Limited, 87-88 Turnmill Street, London EC1M 5QU, England; *European Marketing Data and Statistics.*

Facts on File, 460 Park Avenue South, New York, New York 10016 (800) 443-8323; *The New Book of World Rankings.*

Federal Statistical Office, Gustav - Stresemann - Ring 11, D-6200 Wiesbaden, Germany; *Osterreich.*

G.K. Hall and Company, 70 Lincoln Street, Boston, Massachusetts 02111 (617) 423-3990; *The World in Figures.*

International Monetary Fund, 700 Nineteenth Street, NW, Washington, D.C. 20431 (202) 623-7000; *Government Finance Statistics Yearbook.*

Organisation for Economic Co-operation and Development (OECD), 2 rue Andre-Pascal, 75 Paris 16, France (Telephone Number in U.S. (202) 785-6323); *Education in OECD Countries.*

Times Books, 201 East 50th Street, New York, New York 10022 (212) 751-2600; *The Economist Book of Vital World Statistics.*

United Nations Educational, Scientific and Cultural Organization (UNESCO), 7 Place de Fontenoy, F-75700 Paris, France; *Statistical Yearbook.*

The World Bank, 1818 H Street, NW, Washington, D.C. 20433 (202) 477-1234; *World Tables.*

AUSTRIA - EGG - See AUSTRIA - DAIRY PRODUCTS

AUSTRIA - ELECTRICITY

Facts on File, 460 Park Avenue South, New York, New York 10016 (800) 443-8323; *The New Book of World Rankings.*

Organisation for Economic Co-operation and Development (OECD), 2 rue Andre-Pascal, 75 Paris 16, France (Telephone Number in U.S. (202) 785-6323); *Coal Information, Energy Statistics of OECD Countries, Indicators of Industrial Activity,* and *Industrial Structure Statistics.*

Penn Well Publishing Company, 1421 South Sheridan Road, P.O. Box 1260, Tulsa, Oklahoma 74101 (800) 752-9764; *International Energy Statistics Sourcebook.*

Statistical Office of the United Nations, Publishing Service, New York, New York 10017 (800) 253-9646; *Statistical Yearbook.*

Times Books, 201 East 50th Street, New York, New York 10022 (212) 751-2600; *The Economist Book of Vital World Statistics.*

AUSTRIA - EMPLOYMENT

Euromonitor Publications Limited, 87-88 Turnmill Street, London EC1M 5QU, England; *European Marketing Data and Statistics.*

Facts on File, 460 Park Avenue South, New York, New York 10016 (800) 443-8323; *The New Book of World Rankings.*

Federal Statistical Office, Gustav - Stresemann - Ring 11, D-6200 Wiesbaden, Germany; *Osterreich.*

International Labour Office, I.L.O. Publications, CH-1211, Geneva 22, Switzerland; *Yearbook of Labour Statistics.*

Organisation for Economic Co-operation and Development (OECD), 2 rue Andre-Pascal, 75 Paris 16, France (Telephone Number in U.S. (202) 785-6323); *Economic Outlook, The Iron and Steel Industry, OECD Economic Surveys: Austria, OECD Employment Outlook,* and *Textile Industries in OECD Countries.*

Statistical Office of the United Nations, Publishing Service, New York, New York 10017 (800) 253-9646; *Statistical Yearbook.*

AUSTRIA - ENERGY

Euromonitor Publications Limited, 87-88 Turnmill Street, London EC1M 5QU, England; *European Marketing Data and Statistics.*

Facts on File, 460 Park Avenue South, New York, New York 10016 (800) 443-8323; *The New Book of World Rankings.*

Food and Agricultural Organization of the United Nations (FAO) Via Delle Terme di Caracalla, 00100 Rome, Italy (Telephone Number in U.S. (202) 653-2400); *The State of Food and Agriculture.*

G.K. Hall and Company, 70 Lincoln Street, Boston, Massachusetts 02111 (617) 423-3990; *The World in Figures.*

Organisation for Economic Co-operation and Development (OECD), 2 rue Andre-Pascal, 75 Paris 16, France (Telephone Number in U.S. (202) 785-6323); *Coal Information, Energy Statistics of OECD Countries, OECD Environmental Data,* and *Oil and Gas Information.*

Penn Well Publishing Company, 1421 South Sheridan Road, P.O. Box 1260, Tulsa, Oklahoma 74101 (800) 752-9764; *International Energy Statistics Sourcebook.*

Statistical Office of the United Nations, Publishing Service, New York, New York 10017 (800) 253-9646; *Energy Statistics Yearbook,* and *World Energy Supplies.*

Times Books, 201 East 50th Street, New York, New York 10022 (212) 751-2600; *The Economist Book of Vital World Statistics.*

AUSTRIA - EXCHANGE RATES

International Civil Aviation Organization, 1000 Sherbrooke Street West, Suite 400, Montreal, Quebec, Canada H3A 2R2 (514) 285-8219; *Civil Aviation Statistics of the World.*

International Monetary Fund, 700 Nineteenth Street, NW, Washington, D.C. 20431 (202) 623-7000; *International Financial Statistics.*

Organisation for Economic Co-operation and Development (OECD), 2 rue Andre-Pascal, 75 Paris 16, France (Telephone Number in U.S. (202) 785-6323); *Economic Outlook, Financial Market Trends, Revenue Statistics of OECD Member Countries,* and *Tourism Policy and International Tourism in OECD Member Countries.*

AUSTRIA - EXCISE TAXES - See AUSTRIA - TAXATION

AUSTRIA - EXPORTS

American Automobile Manufacturers Association, 1401 H Street, NW, Washington, D.C. 20005 (202) 326-5500; *World Motor Vehicle Data.*

The Economist Intelligence Unit, 111 West 57th Street, New York, New York 10019 (800) 938-4685; *The World Market Atlas.*

Food and Agricultural Organization of the United Nations (FAO) Via Delle Terme di Caracalla, 00100 Rome, Italy (Telephone Number in U.S. (202) 653-2400); *The State of Food and Agriculture.*

G.K. Hall and Company, 70 Lincoln Street, Boston, Massachusetts 02111 (617) 423-3990; *The World in Figures.*

International Iron and Steel Institute, 120, rue Colonel Bourg, B-1140, Brussels, Belgium; *Steel Statistical Yearbook.*

International Lead and Zinc Study Group, Metro House, 58 St. James's Street, London SW1A 1LD, England; *Lead and Zinc Statistics.*

International Monetary Fund, 700 Nineteenth Street, NW, Washington, D.C. 20431 (202) 623-7000; *Direction of Trade Statistics,* and *International Financial Statistics.*

International Rubber Study Group, York House, 8th Floor, Empire Way, Wembley, London HA9 0PA, England; *Rubber Statistical Bulletin.*

Organisation for Economic Co-operation and Development (OECD), 2 rue Andre-Pascal, 75 Paris 16, France (Telephone Number in U.S. (202) 785-6323); *Economic Outlook, The Footwear, Raw Hides and Skins, and Leather Industry in OECD Countries, Foreign Trade by Commodities, Geographical Distribution of Financial Flows to Developing Countries, Industrial Structure Statistics, The Iron and Steel Industry, Milk, Milk Products, and Egg Balances in OECD Member Countries, OECD Economic Surveys: Austria,* and *The Pulp and Paper Industry.*

Times Books, 201 East 50th Street, New York, New York 10022 (212) 751-2600; *The Economist Book of Vital World Statistics.*

The World Bank, 1818 H Street, NW, Washington, D.C. 20433 (202) 477-1234; *World Tables.*

AUSTRIA - EXTERNAL FINANCING

Organisation for Economic Co-operation and Development (OECD), 2 rue Andre-Pascal, 75 Paris 16, France (Telephone Number in U.S. (202) 785-6323); *Economic Outlook,* and *Financial Market Trends.*

AUSTRIA - EXTERNAL INDEBTEDNESS

Organisation for Economic Co-operation and Development (OECD), 2 rue Andre-Pascal, 75 Paris 16, France (Telephone Number in U.S. (202) 785-6323); *Financial Market Trends,* and *Geographical Distribution of Financial Flows to Developing Countries.*

The World Bank, 1818 H Street, NW, Washington, D.C. 20433 (202) 477-1234; *World Tables.*

AUSTRIA - EXTERNAL TRADE

Food and Agricultural Organization of the United Nations (FAO) Via Delle Terme di Caracalla, 00100 Rome, Italy (Telephone Number in U.S. (202) 653-2400); *The State of Food and Agriculture,* and *Trade Yearbook.*

G.K. Hall and Company, 70 Lincoln Street, Boston, Massachusetts 02111 (617) 423-3990; *The World in Figures.*

Statistical Office of the United Nations, Publishing Service, New York, New York 10017 (800) 253-9646; *Statistical Yearbook.*

AUSTRIA - FABRIC PRODUCTION - See AUSTRIA - TEXTILE INDUSTRY

AUSTRIA - FARM CROPS - See AUSTRIA - CROPS

AUSTRIA - FERTILITY RATES

Facts on File, 460 Park Avenue South, New York, New York 10016 (800) 443-8323; *The New Book of World Rankings.*

Times Books, 201 East 50th Street, New York, New York 10022 (212) 751-2600; *The Economist Book of Vital World Statistics.*

The World Bank, 1818 H Street, NW, Washington, D.C. 20433 (202) 477-1234; *World Tables.*

AUSTRIA - FERTILIZER

Food and Agricultural Organization of the United Nations (FAO), Via delle Terme di Caracalla, 00100 Rome, Italy (Telephone Number in U.S. (202) 653-2400); *Fertilizer Yearbook,* and *The State of Food and Agriculture.*

Organisation for Economic Co-operation and Development (OECD), 2 rue Andre-Pascal, 75 Paris 16, France (Telephone Number in U.S. (202) 785-6323); *Economic Accounts for Agriculture,* and *Foreign Trade by Commodities.*

Statistical Office of the United Nations, Publishing Service, New York, New York 10017 (800) 253-9646; *Statistical Yearbook.*

AUSTRIA - FETAL MORTALITY

Statistical Office of the United Nations, Publishing Service, New York, New York 10017 (800) 253-9646; *Demographic Yearbook.*

World Health Organization, Office of Publications, Avenue Appia, CH-1211 Geneva 27, Switzerland (Telephone Number in U.S. (518) 436-9686); *World Health Statistics Annual.*

AUSTRIA - FIBRE PRODUCTION - See AUSTRIA - TEXTILE INDUSTRY

AUSTRIA - FILAMENT PRODUCTION - See AUSTRIA - TEXTILE INDUSTRY

AUSTRIA - FILM - See AUSTRIA - MOTION PICTURES

AUSTRIA - FINANCE

Facts on File, 460 Park Avenue South, New York, New York 10016 (800) 443-8323; *The New Book of World Rankings.*

Federal Statistical Office, Gustav - Stresemann - Ring 11, D-6200 Wiesbaden, Germany; *Osterreich.*

G.K. Hall and Company, 70 Lincoln Street, Boston, Massachusetts 02111 (617) 423-3990; *The World in Figures.*

International Monetary Fund, 700 Nineteenth Street, NW, Washington, D.C. 20431 (202) 623-7000; *International Financial Statistics,* and *Government Finance Statistics Yearbook.*

Organisation for Economic Co-operation and Development (OECD), 2 rue Andre-Pascal, 75 Paris 16, France (Telephone Number in U.S. (202) 785-6323); *Economic Outlook, Financial Market Trends, Geographical Distribution of Financial Flows to Developing Countries,* and *OECD Financial Statistics.*

AUSTRIA - FISHERIES

Euromonitor Publications Limited, 87-88 Turnmill Street, London EC1M 5QU, England; *European Marketing Data and Statistics.*

Facts on File, 460 Park Avenue South, New York, New York 10016 (800) 443-8323; *The New Book of World Rankings.*

Federal Statistical Office, Gustav - Stresemann - Ring 11, D-6200 Wiesbaden, Germany; *Osterreich.*

Food and Agricultural Organization of the United Nations (FAO) Via Delle Terme di Caracalla, 00100 Rome, Italy (Telephone Number in U.S. (202) 653-2400); *The State of Food and Agriculture,* and *Yearbook of Fishery Statistics.*

Organisation for Economic Co-operation and Development (OECD), 2 rue Andre-Pascal, 75 Paris 16, France (Telephone Number in U.S. (202) 785-6323); *Foreign Trade by Commodities,* and *Industrial Structure Statistics.*

Statistical Office of the United Nations, Publishing Service, New York, New York 10017 (800) 253-9646; *Statistical Yearbook.*

AUSTRIA - FLOUR PRODUCTION

Statistical Office of the United Nations, Publishing Service, New York, New York 10017 (800) 253-9646; *Statistical Yearbook.*

AUSTRIA - FOOD

Food and Agricultural Organization of the United Nations (FAO) Via Delle Terme di Caracalla, 00100 Rome, Italy (Telephone Number in U.S. (202) 653-2400); *Production Yearbook,* and *The State of Food and Agriculture.*

G.K. Hall and Company, 70 Lincoln Street, Boston, Massachusetts 02111 (617) 423-3990; *The World in Figures.*

Organisation for Economic Co-operation and Development (OECD), 2 rue Andre-Pascal, 75 Paris 16, France; *Food Consumption Statistics,* and *Foreign Trade by Commodities.*

AUSTRIA - FOOTWEAR - PRODUCTION INDEX

Organisation for Economic Co-operation and Development (OECD), 2 rue Andre-Pascal, 75 Paris 16, France (Telephone Number in U.S. (202) 785-6323); *Indicators of Industrial Activity.*

AUSTRIA - FOREIGN AID

G.K. Hall and Company, 70 Lincoln Street, Boston, Massachusetts 02111 (617) 423-3990; *The World in Figures.*

AUSTRIA - FOREIGN DEBT

International Monetary Fund, 700 Nineteenth Street, NW, Washington, D.C. 20431 (202) 623-7000; *Government Finance Statistics Yearbook.*

Organisation for Economic Co-operation and Development (OECD), 2 rue Andre-Pascal, 75 Paris 16, France (Telephone Number in U.S. (202) 785-6323); *Economic Outlook.*

AUSTRIA - FOREIGN FINANCE

Organisation for Economic Co-operation and Development (OECD), 2 rue Andre-Pascal, 75 Paris 16, France (Telephone Number in U.S. (202) 785-6323); *Economic Outlook, Financial Market Trends,* and *Main Economic Indicators - Historical Statistics.*

AUSTRIA - FOREIGN INDEBTEDNESS

Organisation for Economic Co-operation and Development (OECD), 2 rue Andre-Pascal, 75 Paris 16, France (Telephone Number in U.S. (202) 785-6323); *Economic Outlook,* and *Financial Market Trends.*

AUSTRIA - FOREIGN TRADE

Euromonitor Publications Limited, 87-88 Turnmill Street, London EC1M 5QU, England; *European Marketing Data and Statistics.*

Facts on File, 460 Park Avenue South, New York, New York 10016 (800) 443-8323; *The New Book of World Rankings.*

Federal Statistical Office, Gustav - Stresemann - Ring 11, D-6200 Wiesbaden, Germany; *Osterreich.*

Food and Agricultural Organization of the United Nations (FAO) Via Delle Terme di Caracalla, 00100 Rome, Italy (Telephone Number in U.S. (202) 653-2400); *The State of Food and Agriculture.*

G.K. Hall and Company, 70 Lincoln Street, Boston, Massachusetts 02111 (617) 423-3990; *The World in Figures.*

International Iron and Steel Institute, 120, rue Colonel Bourg, B-1140, Brussels, Belgium; *Steel Statistical Yearbook.*

Organisation for Economic Co-operation and Development (OECD), 2 rue Andre-Pascal, 75 Paris 16, France (Telephone Number in U.S. (202) 785-6323); *Economic Outlook, The Footwear, Raw Hides and Skins, and Leather Industry in OECD Countries, Foreign Trade by Commodities, Main Economic Indicators - Historical Statistics, Maritime Transport, Meat Balances in OECD Member Countries, OECD Economic Surveys: Austria,* and *Trade by Commodities.*

Statistical Office of the United Nations, Publishing Service, New York, New York 10017 (800) 253-9646; *International Trade Statistics Yearbook, Statistical Yearbook,* and *Trade in Manufactures of Developing Countries.*

The World Bank, 1818 H Street, NW, Washington, D.C. 20433 (202) 477-1234; *World Tables.*

AUSTRIA - FORESTRY AND FOREST PRODUCTS

Euromonitor Publications Limited, 87-88 Turnmill Street, London EC1M 5QU, England; *European Marketing Data and Statistics.*

Facts on File, 460 Park Avenue South, New York, New York 10016; *The New Book of World Rankings.*

Federal Statistical Office, Gustav - Stresemann - Ring 11, D-6200 Wiesbaden, Germany; *Osterreich.*

Food and Agricultural Organization of the United Nations (FAO) Via Delle Terme di Caracalla, 00100 Rome, Italy (Telephone Number in U.S. (202) 653-2400); *The State of Food and Agriculture,* and *Yearbook of Forest Products.*

Forest and Paper Association, 1250 Connecticut Avenue, NW, Washington, D.C. 20036 (202) 463-2455; *Wood Pulp and Fiber Statistics.*

G.K. Hall and Company, 70 Lincoln Street, Boston, Massachusetts 02111 (617) 423-3990; *The World in Figures.*

Organisation for Economic Co-operation and Development (OECD), 2 rue Andre-Pascal, 75 Paris 16, France (Telephone Number in U.S. (202) 785-6323); *Foreign Trade by Commodities, Indicators of Industrial Activity, Industrial Structure Statistics, The Pulp and Paper Industry,* and *Textile Industry in OECD Countries.*

Statistical Office of the United Nations, Publishing Service, New York, New York 10017 (800) 253-9646; *Statistical Yearbook.*

United Nations Educational, Scientific and Cultural Organization (UNESCO), 7 Place de Fontenoy, F-75700 Paris, France; *Statistical Yearbook.*

AUSTRIA - FRUIT PRODUCTION - See AUSTRIA - CROPS

AUSTRIA - FURNITURE AND WOOD PRODUCTS - EXPORTS AND IMPORTS

Organisation for Economic Co-operation and Development (OECD), 2 rue Andre-Pascal, 75 Paris 16, France (Telephone Number in U.S. (202) 785-6323); *Foreign Trade by Commodities,* and *Industrial Structure Statistics.*

AUSTRIA - GAS AND GAS LIQUIDS - See AUSTRIA - MINING AND MINERAL PRODUCTS

AUSTRIA - GENERAL INDUSTRIAL STATISTICS

Federal Statistical Office, Gustav - Stresemann - Ring 11, D-6200 Wiesbaden, Germany; *Osterreich.*

Statistical Office of the United Nations, Publishing Service, New York, New York 10017 (800) 253-9646; *Industrial Statistics Yearbook.*

AUSTRIA - GENERAL MORTALITY

Statistical Office of the United Nations, Publishing Service, New York, New York 10017 (800) 253-9646; *Demographic Yearbook.*

World Health Organization, Office of Publications, Avenue Appia, CH-1211 Geneva 27, Switzerland (Telephone Number in U.S. (518) 436-9686); *World Health Statistics Annual.*

AUSTRIA - GEOGRAPHIC DATA

Facts on File, 460 Park Avenue South, New York, New York 10016 (800) 443-8323; *The New Book of World Rankings.*

Federal Statistical Office, Gustav - Stresemann - Ring 11, D-6200 Wiesbaden, Germany; *Osterreich.*

AUSTRIA - GLASS AND GLASS PRODUCTS - PRODUCTION INDEX See AUSTRIA - MINING AND MINERAL PRODUCTS

AUSTRIA - GOATS - See AUSTRIA - LIVESTOCK AND POULTRY

AUSTRIA - GOLD HOLDINGS

International Monetary Fund, 700 Nineteenth Street, NW, Washington, D.C. 20431 (202) 623-7000; *International Financial Statistics.*

Statistical Office of the United Nations, Publishing Service, New York, New York 10017 (800) 253-9646; *Statistical Yearbook.*

The World Bank, 1818 H Street, NW, Washington, D.C. 20433 (202) 477-1234; *World Tables.*

AUSTRIA - GOLD - See AUSTRIA - MINING AND MINERAL PRODUCTS

AUSTRIA - GOVERNMENT

G.K. Hall and Company, 70 Lincoln Street, Boston, Massachusetts 02111 (617) 423-3990; *The World in Figures.*

AUSTRIA - GOVERNMENT BONDS - See AUSTRIA - BONDS

AUSTRIA - GOVERNMENT CONSUMPTION

International Monetary Fund, 700 Nineteenth Street, NW, Washington, D.C. 20431 (202) 623-7000; *International Financial Statistics.*

AUSTRIA - GOVERNMENT EXPENDITURES

International Monetary Fund, 700 Nineteenth Street, NW, Washington, D.C. 20431 (202) 623-7000; *Government Finance Statistics Yearbook.*

Organisation for Economic Co-operation and Development (OECD), 2 rue Andre-Pascal, 75 Paris 16, France (Telephone Number in U.S. (202) 785-6323); *Economic Outlook.*

Times Books, 201 East 50th Street, New York, New York 10022 (212) 751-2600; *The Economist Book of Vital World Statistics.*

The World Bank, 1818 H Street, NW, Washington, D.C. 20433 (202) 477-1234; *World Tables.*

AUSTRIA - GOVERNMENT FINANCES

International Monetary Fund, 700 Nineteenth Street, NW, Washington, D.C. 20431 (202) 623-7000; *International Financial Statistics.*

Organisation for Economic Co-operation and Development (OECD), 2 rue Andre-Pascal, 75 Paris 16, France (Telephone Number in U.S. (202) 785-6323); *Economic Outlook.*

AUSTRIA - GOVERNMENT REVENUES

International Monetary Fund, 700 Nineteenth Street, NW, Washington, D.C. 20431 (202) 623-7000; *Government Finance Statistics Yearbook.*

Organisation for Economic Co-operation and Development (OECD), 2 rue Andre-Pascal, 75 Paris 16, France (Telephone Number in U.S. (202) 785-6323); *Economic Outlook,* and *Revenue Statistics of OECD Member Countries.*

Times Books, 201 East 50th Street, New York, New York 10022 (212) 751-2600; *The Economist Book of Vital World Statistics.*

The World Bank, 1818 H Street, NW, Washington, D.C. 20433 (202) 477-1234; *World Tables.*

AUSTRIA - GRAIN PRODUCTION - See AUSTRIA - CROPS

AUSTRIA - GRANTS

International Monetary Fund, 700 Nineteenth Street, NW, Washington, D.C. 20431 (202) 623-7000; *Government Finance Statistics Yearbook.*

Organisation for Economic Co-operation and Development (OECD), 2 rue Andre-Pascal, 75 Paris 16, France (Telephone Number in U.S. (202) 785-6323); *Geographical Distribution of Financial Flows to Developing Countries.*

AUSTRIA - GREEN PEPPER AND CHILIE PRODUCTION - See AUSTRIA - CROPS

AUSTRIA - GROSS DOMESTIC PRODUCT

The Economist Intelligence Unit, 111 West 57th Street, New York, New York 10019 (800) 938-4685; *The World Market Atlas.*

Facts on File, 460 Park Avenue South, New York, New York 10016 (800) 443-8323; *The New Book of World Rankings.*

G.K. Hall and Company, 70 Lincoln Street, Boston, Massachusetts 02111 (617) 423-3990; *The World in Figures.*

International Monetary Fund, 700 Nineteenth Street, NW, Washington, D.C. 20431 (202) 623-7000; *International Financial Statistics.*

Organisation for Economic Co-operation and Development (OECD), 2 rue Andre-Pascal, 75 Paris 16, France (Telephone Number in U.S. (202) 785-6323); *Economic Outlook, Geographical Distribution of Financial Flows to Developing Countries,* and *Revenue Statistics of OECD Member Countries.*

Statistical Office of the United Nations, Publishing Service, New York, New York 10017 (800) 253-9646; *Statistical Yearbook.*

Times Books, 201 East 50th Street, New York, New York 10022 (212) 751-2600; *The Economist Book of Vital World Statistics.*

The World Bank, 1818 H Street, NW, Washington, D.C. 20433 (202) 477-1234; *World Tables.*

AUSTRIA - GROSS NATIONAL PRODUCT

Organisation for Economic Co-operation and Development (OECD), 2 rue Andre-Pascal, 75 Paris 16, France (Telephone Number in U.S. (202) 785-6323); *Economic Outlook,* and *Geographical Distribution of Financial Flows to Developing Countries.*

United Nations Economic Commission for Africa, Africa Hall, P.O. Box 3001, Addis Ababa, Ethiopia (Telephone Number in U.S. (800) 253-9646); *African Statistical Yearbook.*

The World Bank, 1818 H Street, NW, Washington, D.C. 20433 (202) 477-1234; *World Tables.*

AUSTRIA - HEALTH

Facts on File, 460 Park Avenue South, New York, New York 10016 (800) 443-8323; *The New Book of World Rankings.*

Federal Statistical Office, Gustav - Stresemann - Ring 11, D-6200 Wiesbaden, Germany; *Osterreich.*

G.K. Hall and Company, 70 Lincoln Street, Boston, Massachusetts 02111 (617) 423-3990; *The World in Figures.*

Organisation for Economic Co-operation and Development (OECD), 2 rue Andre-Pascal, 75 Paris 16, France (Telephone Number in U.S. (202) 785-6323); *OECD Health Systems: Facts and Trends.*

Statistical Office of the United Nations, Publishing Service, New York, New York 10017 (800) 253-9646; *Statistical Yearbook.*

Times Books, 201 East 50th Street, New York, New York 10022 (212) 751-2600; *The Economist Book of Vital World Statistics.*

World Health Organization, Office of Publications, Avenue Appia, CH-1211 Geneva 27, Switzerland (Telephone Number in U.S. (518) 436-9686); *World Health Statistics Annual.*

AUSTRIA - HIDE PRODUCTION

Food and Agricultural Organization of the United Nations (FAO), Via delle Terme di Caracalla, 00100 Rome, Italy (Telephone Number in U.S. (202) 653-2400); *Production Yearbook.*

Organisation for Economic Co-operation and Development (OECD), 2 rue Andre-Pascal, 75 Paris 16, France (Telephone Number in U.S. (202) 785-6323); *The Footwear, Raw Hides and Skins, and Leather Industry in OECD Countries, Foreign Trade by Commodities,* and *Indicators of Industrial Activity.*

AUSTRIA - HIGHWAYS

G.K. Hall and Company, 70 Lincoln Street, Boston, Massachusetts 02111 (617) 423-3990; *The World in Figures.*

International Road Federation, 525 School Street, SW, Washington, D.C. 20024 (202) 554-2106; *World Road Statistics.*

Statistical Office of the United Nations, Publishing Service, New York, New York 10017 (800) 253-9646; *Annual Bulletin of Transport Statistics for Europe.*

AUSTRIA - HOME FINANCE

Organisation for Economic Co-operation and Development (OECD), 2 rue Andre-Pascal, 75 Paris 16, France; *Main Economic Indicators - Historical Statistics.*

AUSTRIA - HORSES - See AUSTRIA - LIVESTOCK AND POULTRY

AUSTRIA - HOURS OF WORK - See AUSTRIA - EMPLOYMENT

AUSTRIA - HOUSING AND HOUSING UNITS

Facts on File, 460 Park Avenue South, New York, New York 10016 (800) 443-8323; *The New Book of World Rankings.*

AUSTRIA - HOUSING CONSTRUCTION - See AUSTRIA - CONSTRUCTION INDUSTRY

AUSTRIA - HOUSING EXPENDITURES

International Monetary Fund, 700 Nineteenth Street, NW, Washington, D.C. 20431 (202) 623-7000; *Government Finance Statistics Yearbook.*

AUSTRIA - ILLITERATE POPULATION

The Economist Intelligence Unit, 111 West 57th Street, New York, New York 10019 (800) 938-4685; *The World Market Atlas.*

G.K. Hall and Company, 70 Lincoln Street, Boston, Massachusetts 02111 (617) 423-3990; *The World in Figures.*

AUSTRIA - IMPORTS

American Automobile Manufacturers Association, 1401 H Street, NW, Washington, D.C. 20005 (202) 326-5500; *World Motor Vehicle Data.*

The Economist Intelligence Unit, 111 West 57th Street, New York, New York 10019 (800) 938-4685; *The World Market Atlas.*

Food and Agricultural Organization of the United Nations (FAO) Via Delle Terme di Caracalla, 00100 Rome, Italy (Telephone Number in U.S. (202) 653-2400); *The State of Food and Agriculture.*

G.K. Hall and Company, 70 Lincoln Street, Boston, Massachusetts 02111 (617) 423-3990; *The World in Figures.*

International Iron and Steel Institute, 120, rue Colonel Bourg, B-1140, Brussels, Belgium; *Steel Statistical Yearbook.*

International Lead and Zinc Study Group, Metro House, 58 St. James's Street, London SW1A 1LD, England; *Lead and Zinc Statistics.*

International Monetary Fund, 700 Nineteenth Street, NW, Washington, D.C. 20431 (202) 623-7000; *Direction of Trade Statistics,* and *International Financial Statistics.*

International Rubber Study Group, York House, 8th Floor, Empire Way, Wembley, London HA9 0PA, England; *Rubber Statistical Yearbook.*

Organisation for Economic Co-operation and Development (OECD), 2 rue Andre-Pascal, 75 Paris 16, France (Telephone Number in U.S. (202) 785-6323); *Economic Outlook, The Footwear, Raw Hides and Skins, and Leather Industry in OECD Countries, Industrial Structure Statistics, The Iron and Steel Industry, Milk, Milk Products, and Egg Balances in OECD Member Countries, OECD Economic Surveys: Austria,* and *The Pulp and Paper Industry.*

Times Books, 201 East 50th Street, New York, New York 10022 (212) 751-2600; *The Economist Book of Vital World Statistics.*

The World Bank, 1818 H Street, NW, Washington, D.C. 20433 (202) 477-1234; *World Tables.*

AUSTRIA - INCOME TAXES - See AUSTRIA - TAXATION

AUSTRIA - INDUSTRIAL METALS PRODUCTION - See AUSTRIA - MINING AND MINERAL PRODUCTS

AUSTRIA - INDUSTRY

Facts on File, 460 Park Avenue South, New York, New York 10016 (800) 443-8323; *The New Book of World Rankings.*

Federal Statistical Office, Gustav - Stresemann - Ring 11, D-6200 Wiesbaden, Germany; *Osterreich.*

G.K. Hall and Company, 70 Lincoln Street, Boston, Massachusetts 02111 (617) 423-3990; *The World in Figures.*

International Labour Office, I.L.O. Publications, CH-1211, Geneva 22, Switzerland; *Yearbook of Labour Statistics.*

Penn Well Publishing Company, 1421 South Sheridan Road, P.O. Box 1260, Tulsa, Oklahoma 74101 (800) 752-9764; *International Energy Statistics Sourcebook.*

Statistical Office of the United Nations, Publishing Service, New York, New York 10017 (800) 253-9646; *Statistical Yearbook.*

The World Bank, 1818 H Street, NW, Washington, D.C. 20433 (202) 477-1234; *World Tables.*

AUSTRIA - INFANT AND MATERNAL MORTALITY

Statistical Office of the United Nations, Publishing Service, New York, New York 10017 (800) 253-9646; *Demographic Yearbook,* and *Statistical Yearbook.*

Times Books, 201 East 50th Street, New York, New York 10022 (212) 751-2600; *The Economist Book of Vital World Statistics.*

The World Bank, 1818 H Street, NW, Washington, D.C. 20433 (202) 477-1234; *World Tables.*

World Health Organization, Office of Publications, Avenue Appia, CH-1211 Geneva 27, Switzerland (Telephone Number in U.S. (518) 436-9686); *World Health Statistics Annual.*

AUSTRIA - INTEREST RATES

Organisation for Economic Co-operation and Development (OECD), 2 rue Andre-Pascal, 75 Paris 16, France (Telephone Number in U.S. (202) 785-6323); *Economic Outlook, Financial Market Trends,* and *OECD Financial Statistics.*

AUSTRIA - INTERNAL TRADE

Organisation for Economic Co-operation and Development (OECD), 2 rue Andre-Pascal, 75 Paris 16, France; *Main Economic Indicators - Historical Statistics.*

AUSTRIA - INTERNATIONAL FINANCE

Organisation for Economic Co-operation and Development (OECD), 2 rue Andre-Pascal, 75 Paris 16, France (Telephone Number in U.S. (202) 785-6323); *Economic Outlook*, and *Financial Market Trends*.

AUSTRIA - INTERNATIONAL LIQUIDITY

International Monetary Fund, 700 Nineteenth Street, NW, Washington, D.C. 20431 (202) 623-7000; *International Financial Statistics*.

Organisation for Economic Co-operation and Development (OECD), 2 rue Andre-Pascal, 75 Paris 16, France (Telephone Number in U.S. (202) 785-6323); *Economic Outlook*, and *Financial Market Trends*.

AUSTRIA - INTERNATIONAL RESERVES EXCLUDING GOLD

The World Bank, 1818 H Street, NW, Washington, D.C. 20433 (202) 477-1234; *World Tables*.

AUSTRIA - INTERNATIONAL STATISTICS

Organisation for Economic Co-operation and Development (OECD), 2 rue Andre-Pascal, 75 Paris 16, France (Telephone Number in U.S. (202) 785-6323); *Financial Market Trends*, and *Tourism Policy and International Tourism in OECD Member Countries*.

AUSTRIA - INVESTMENTS

International Monetary Fund, 700 Nineteenth Street, NW, Washington, D.C. 20431 (202) 623-7000; *International Financial Statistics*.

Organisation for Economic Co-operation and Development (OECD), 2 rue Andre-Pascal, 75 Paris 16, France (Telephone Number in U.S. (202) 785-6323); *Economic Outlook*, *Financial Market Trends*, *Industrial Structure Statistics*, *The Iron and Steel Industry*, and *Textile Industry in OECD Countries*.

AUSTRIA - IRON ORE - See AUSTRIA - MINING AND MINERAL PRODUCTS

AUSTRIA - LABOR FORCE

Facts on File, 460 Park Avenue South, New York, New York 10016 (800) 443-8323; *The New Book of World Rankings*.

Food and Agricultural Organization of the United Nations (FAO) Via Delle Terme di Caracalla, 00100 Rome, Italy (Telephone Number in U.S. (202) 653-2400); *The State of Food and Agriculture*.

G.K. Hall and Company, 70 Lincoln Street, Boston, Massachusetts 02111 (617) 423-3990; *The World in Figures*.

Organisation for Economic Co-operation and Development (OECD), 2 rue Andre-Pascal, 75 Paris 16, France (Telephone Number in U.S. (202) 785-6323); *Economic Outlook*, *The Iron and Steel Industry*, *Main Economic Indicators - Historical Statistics*, *Maritime Transport*, *OECD Economic Surveys: Austria*, *OECD Economic Surveys: Austria*, *OECD Employment Outlook*, and *Textile Industry in OECD Countries*.

Times Books, 201 East 50th Street, New York, New York 10022 (212) 751-2600; *The Economist Book of Vital World Statistics*.

The World Bank, 1818 H Street, NW, Washington, D.C. 20433 (202) 477-1234; *World Tables*.

AUSTRIA - LABOR PRODUCTIVITY

International Labour Office, I.L.O. Publications, CH-1211, Geneva 22, Switzerland; *Yearbook of Labour Statistics*.

Organisation for Economic Co-operation and Development (OECD), 2 rue Andre-Pascal, 75 Paris 16, France (Telephone Number in U.S. (202) 785-6323); *Economic Outlook*, and *OECD Employment Outlook*.

AUSTRIA - LAND USE

Euromonitor Publications Limited, 87-88 Turnmill Street, London EC1M 5QU, England; *European Marketing Data and Statistics*.

Food and Agricultural Organization of the United Nations (FAO), Via delle Terme di Caracalla, 00100 Rome, Italy (Telephone Number in U.S. (202) 653-2400); *Production Yearbook*.

G.K. Hall and Company, 70 Lincoln Street, Boston, Massachusetts 02111 (617) 423-3990; *The World in Figures*.

AUSTRIA - LEAD ORE PRODUCTION AND CONSUMPTION - See AUSTRIA - MINING AND MINERAL PRODUCTS

AUSTRIA - LEATHER - PRODUCTION INDEX

Organisation for Economic Co-operation and Development (OECD), 2 rue Andre-Pascal, 75 Paris 16, France (Telephone Number in U.S. (202) 785-6323); *Indicators of Industrial Activity*.

AUSTRIA - LEATHER AND FOOTWEAR - EXPORTS AND IMPORTS

Organisation for Economic Co-operation and Development (OECD), 2 rue Andre-Pascal, 75 Paris 16, France (Telephone Number in U.S. (202) 785-6323); *The Footwear, Raw Hides and Skins, and Leather Industry in OECD Countries*.

AUSTRIA - LIBRARIES

Euromonitor Publications Limited, 87-88 Turnmill Street, London EC1M 5QU, England; *European Marketing Data and Statistics*.

Facts on File, 460 Park Avenue South, New York, New York 10016 (800) 443-8323; *The New Book of World Rankings*.

United Nations Educational, Scientific and Cultural Organization (UNESCO), 7 Place de Fontenoy, F-75700 Paris, France; *Statistical Yearbook*.

AUSTRIA - LIGNITE PRODUCTION - See AUSTRIA - MINING AND MINERAL PRODUCTS

AUSTRIA - LIVESTOCK AND POULTRY

Euromonitor Publications Limited, 87-88 Turnmill Street, London EC1M 5QU, England; *European Marketing Data and Statistics*.

Facts on File, 460 Park Avenue South, New York, New York 10016 (800) 443-8323; *The New Book of World Rankings*.

Food and Agricultural Organization of the United Nations (FAO), Via delle Terme di Caracalla, 00100 Rome, Italy (Telephone Number in U.S. (202) 653-2400); *Production Yearbook*, and *The State of Food and Agriculture*.

G.K. Hall and Company, 70 Lincoln Street, Boston, Massachusetts 02111 (617) 423-3990; *The World in Figures*.

Organisation for Economic Co-operation and Development (OECD), 2 rue Andre-Pascal, 75 Paris 16, France (Telephone Number in U.S. (202) 785-6323); *Economic Accounts for Agriculture,* and *Meat Balances in OECD Member Countries.*

Statistical Office of the United Nations, Publishing Service, New York, New York 10017 (800) 253-9646; *Statistical Yearbook.*

AUSTRIA - LIVING LEVELS

G.K. Hall and Company, 70 Lincoln Street, Boston, Massachusetts 02111 (617) 423-3990; *The World in Figures.*

Organisation for Economic Co-operation and Development (OECD), 2 rue Andre-Pascal, 75 Paris 16, France (Telephone Number in U.S. (202) 785-6323); *Economic Outlook.*

Times Books, 201 East 50th Street, New York, New York 10022 (212) 751-2600; *The Economist Book of Vital World Statistics.*

AUSTRIA - MACHINERY - PRODUCTION INDEX

Organisation for Economic Co-operation and Development (OECD), 2 rue Andre-Pascal, 75 Paris 16, France (Telephone Number in U.S. (202) 785-6323); *Indicators of Industrial Activity.*

AUSTRIA - MAGNESIUM PRODUCTION AND CONSUMPTION - See AUSTRIA - MINING AND MINERAL PRODUCTS

AUSTRIA - MAIL - NUMBER OF PIECES SENT OR RECEIVED

Statistical Office of the United Nations, Publishing Service, New York, New York 10017 (800) 253-9646; *Statistical Yearbook.*

AUSTRIA - MANGANESE PRODUCTION AND CONSUMPTION - See AUSTRIA - MINING AND MINERAL PRODUCTS

AUSTRIA - MANUFACTURING

American Automobile Manufacturers Association, 1401 H Street, NW, Washington, D.C. 20005 (202) 326-5500; *World Motor Vehicle Data.*

Facts on File, 460 Park Avenue South, New York, New York 10016 (800) 443-8323; *The New Book of World Rankings.*

G.K. Hall and Company, 70 Lincoln Street, Boston, Massachusetts 02111 (617) 423-3990; *The World in Figures.*

Organisation for Economic Co-operation and Development (OECD), 2 rue Andre-Pascal, 75 Paris 16, France (Telephone Number in U.S. (202) 785-6323); *Foreign Trade by Commodities, Indicators of Industrial Activity, Industrial Structure Statistics, Main Economic Indicators - Historical Statistics,* and *OECD Economic Surveys: Austria.*

Statistical Office of the United Nations, Publishing Service, New York, New York 10017 (800) 253-9646; *Statistical Yearbook.*

Times Books, 201 East 50th Street, New York, New York 10022 (212) 751-2600; *The Economist Book of Vital World Statistics.*

The World Bank, 1818 H Street, NW, Washington, D.C. 20433 (202) 477-1234; *World Tables.*

AUSTRIA - MARRIAGE RATES

Facts on File, 460 Park Avenue South, New York, New York 10016 (800) 443-8323; *The New Book of World Rankings.*

Statistical Office of the United Nations, Publishing Service, New York, New York 10017 (800) 253-9646; *Demographic Yearbook,* and *Statistical Yearbook.*

AUSTRIA - MEAT PRODUCTION - See AUSTRIA - LIVESTOCK AND POULTRY

AUSTRIA - MERCHANT SHIPPING

G.K. Hall and Company, 70 Lincoln Street, Boston, Massachusetts 02111 (617) 423-3990; *The World in Figures.*

Organisation for Economic Co-operation and Development (OECD), 2 rue Andre-Pascal, 75 Paris 16, France (Telephone Number in U.S. (202) 785-6323); *Annual Bulletin of Transport Statistics for Europe,* and *Maritime Transport.*

Times Books, 201 East 50th Street, New York, New York 10022 (212) 751-2600; *The Economist Book of Vital World Statistics.*

U.S. Department of Commerce, Maritime Administration, Washington, D.C. 20230; *A Statistical Analysis of the World's Merchant Fleets.*

AUSTRIA - MERCURY PRODUCTION AND CONSUMPTION - See AUSTRIA - MINING AND MINERAL PRODUCTS

AUSTRIA - MILITARY

G.K. Hall and Company, 70 Lincoln Street, Boston, Massachusetts 02111 (617) 423-3990; *The World in Figures.*

The International Institute for Strategic Studies, 23 Tavistock Street, London WC2E 7NQ, England; *The Military Balance.*

U.S. Arms Control and Disarmament Agency, 320 Twenty-first Street, NW, Washington, D.C. 20451 (202) 647-8677; *World Military Expenditures and Arms Transfers.*

AUSTRIA - MILK PRODUCTION - See AUSTRIA - DAIRY PRODUCTS

AUSTRIA - MILLET PRODUCTION - See AUSTRIA - CROPS

AUSTRIA - MINING AND MINERAL PRODUCTS

Commodity Research Bureau, Incorporated, 75 Wall Street, New York, New York 10005 (212) 504-7754; *Commodity Year Book.*

Facts on File, 460 Park Avenue South, New York, New York 10016 (800) 443-8323; *The New Book of World Rankings.*

Federal Statistical Office, Gustav - Stresemann - Ring 11, D-6200 Wiesbaden, Germany; *Osterreich.*

G.K. Hall and Company, 70 Lincoln Street, Boston, Massachusetts 02111 (617) 423-3990; *The World in Figures.*

International Iron and Steel Institute, 120, rue Colonel Bourg, B-1140, Brussels, Belgium; *Steel Statistical Yearbook.*

International Lead and Zinc Study Group, Metro House, 58 St. James's Street, London SW1A 1LD, England; *Lead and Zinc Statistics.*

Organisation for Economic Co-operation and Development (OECD), 2 rue Andre-Pascal, 75 Paris 16, France (Telephone Number in U.S. (202) 785-6323); *Coal Information, Energy Statistics of OECD Countries, Foreign Trade by Commodities, Indicators of Industrial Activity, Industrial Structure Statistics, The Iron and Steel Industry, Main Economic Indicators - Historical Statistics, The Non-Ferrous Metals Industry, OECD Economic Surveys*, and *OECD Employment Outlook.*

Penn Well Publishing Company, 1421 South Sheridan Road, P.O. Box 1260, Tulsa, Oklahoma 74101 (800) 752-9764; *International Energy Statistics Sourcebook.*

Statistical Office of the United Nations, Publishing Service, New York, New York 10017 (800) 253-9646; *Statistical Yearbook.*

World Bureau of Metal Statistics, 27-A High Street, Ware Hert SG12 9BA, England; *World Metal Statistics.*

AUSTRIA - MOLYBDENUM AND MOLYBDENUM ORE - See AUSTRIA - MINING AND MINERAL PRODUCTS

AUSTRIA - MONEY AND CREDIT

Organisation for Economic Cooperation and Development (OECD), 2 rue Andre-Pascal, 75 Paris 16, France (Telephone Number in U.S. (202) 785-6323); *OECD Economic Surveys: Austria.*

AUSTRIA - MONEY EXCHANGE RATES

International Monetary Fund, 700 Nineteenth Street, NW, Washington, D.C. 20431 (202) 623-7000; *International Financial Statistics.*

Organisation for Economic Co-operation and Development (OECD), 2 rue Andre-Pascal, 75 Paris 16, France (Telephone Number in U.S. (202) 785-6323); *Economic Outlook, Financial Market Trends*, and *Tourism Policy and International Tourism in OECD Member Countries.*

Statistical Office of the United Nations, Publishing Service, New York, New York 10017 (800) 253-9646; *Statistical Yearbook.*

AUSTRIA - MONEY RATES - MARKET

Organisation for Economic Co-operation and Development (OECD), 2 rue Andre-Pascal, 75 Paris 16, France (Telephone Number in U.S. (202) 785-6323); *Economic Outlook*, and *Financial Market Trends.*

AUSTRIA - MONEY RESERVES

Organisation for Economic Co-operation and Development (OECD), 2 rue Andre-Pascal, 75 Paris 16, France (Telephone Number in U.S. (202) 785-6323); *Economic Outlook*, and *Financial Market Trends.*

AUSTRIA - MONEY SUPPLY

Federal Statistical Office, Gustav - Stresemann - Ring 11, D-6200 Wiesbaden, Germany; *Osterreich.*

G.K. Hall and Company, 70 Lincoln Street, Boston, Massachusetts 02111 (617) 423-3990; *The World in Figures.*

International Monetary Fund, 700 Nineteenth Street, NW, Washington, D.C. 20431 (202) 623-7000; *International Financial Statistics.*

Organisation for Economic Co-operation and Development (OECD), 2 rue Andre-Pascal, 75 Paris 16, France (Telephone Number in U.S. (202) 785-6323); *Economic Outlook.*

Statistical Office of the United Nations, Publishing Service, New York, New York 10017 (800) 253-9646; *Statistical Yearbook.*

The World Bank, 1818 H Street, NW, Washington, D.C. 20433 (202) 477-1234; *World Tables.*

AUSTRIA - MOTION PICTURES

Statistical Office of the United Nations, Publishing Service, New York, New York 10017 (800) 253-9646; *Statistical Yearbook.*

United Nations Educational, Scientific and Cultural Organization (UNESCO), 7 Place de Fontenoy, F-75700 Paris, France; *Statistical Yearbook.*

AUSTRIA - MOTOR VEHICLE PRODUCTION

American Automobile Manufacturers Association, 1401 H Street, NW, Washington, D.C. 20005 (202) 326-5500; *World Motor Vehicle Data.*

Organisation for Economic Co-operation and Development (OECD), 2 rue Andre-Pascal, 75 Paris 16, France (Telephone Number in U.S. (202) 785-6323); *Foreign Trade by Commodities*, and *Indicators of Industrial Activity.*

Statistical Office of the United Nations, Publishing Service, New York, New York 10017 (800) 253-9646; *Statistical Yearbook.*

AUSTRIA - MOTOR VEHICLE TAXES - See AUSTRIA - TAXATION

AUSTRIA - MOTOR VEHICLES IN USE

American Automobile Manufacturers Association, 1401 H Street, NW, Washington, D.C. 20005 (202) 326-5500; *World Motor Vehicle Data.*

G.K. Hall and Company, 70 Lincoln Street, Boston, Massachusetts 02111 (617) 423-3990; *The World in Figures.*

International Road Federation, 525 School Street, SW, Washington, D.C. 20024 (202) 554-2106; *World Road Statistics.*

Statistical Office of the United Nations, Publishing Service, New York, New York 10017 (800) 253-9646; *Statistical Yearbook.*

Times Books, 201 East 50th Street, New York, New York 10022 (212) 751-2600; *The Economist Book of Vital World Statistics.*

AUSTRIA - MUSEUMS

Euromonitor Publications Limited, 87-88 Turnmill Street, London EC1M 5QU, England; *European Marketing Data and Statistics.*

Facts on File, 460 Park Avenue South, New York, New York 10016 (800) 443-8323; *The New Book of World Rankings.*

United Nations Educational, Scientific and Cultural Organization (UNESCO), 7 Place de Fontenoy, F-75700 Paris, France; *Statistical Yearbook.*

AUSTRIA - NATALITY - See AUSTRIA - BIRTH RATE

AUSTRIA - NATIONAL ACCOUNTS

Federal Statistical Office, Gustav - Stresemann - Ring 11, D-6200 Wiesbaden, Germany; *Osterreich.*

International Monetary Fund, 700 Nineteenth Street, NW, Washington, D.C. 20431 (202) 623-7000; *International Financial Statistics.*

Organisation for Economic Co-operation and Development (OECD), 2 rue Andre-Pascal, 75 Paris 16, France (Telephone Number in U.S. (202) 785-6323); *Economic Outlook.*

Statistical Office of the United Nations, Publishing Service, New York, New York 10017 (800) 253-9646; *National Accounts Statistics.*

AUSTRIA - NATIONAL INCOME

Facts on File, 460 Park Avenue South, New York, New York 10016 (800) 443-8323; *The New Book of World Rankings.*

G.K. Hall and Company, 70 Lincoln Street, Boston, Massachusetts 02111 (617) 423-3990; *The World in Figures.*

Organisation for Economic Co-operation and Development (OECD), 2 rue Andre-Pascal, 75 Paris 16, France (Telephone Number in U.S. (202) 785-6323); *Economic Outlook,* and *National Accounts of OECD Countries.*

Statistical Office of the United Nations, Publishing Service, New York, New York 10017 (800) 253-9646; *Statistical Yearbook.*

AUSTRIA - NATIONAL PRODUCT

Facts on File, 460 Park Avenue South, New York, New York 10016 (800) 443-8323; *The New Book of World Rankings.*

Organisation for Economic Co-operation and Development (OECD), 2 rue Andre-Pascal, 75 Paris 16, France (Telephone Number in U.S. (202) 785-6323); *Economic Outlook.*

Statistical Office of the United Nations, Publishing Service, New York, New York 10017 (800) 253-9646; *Statistical Yearbook.*

AUSTRIA - NATURAL GAS - See AUSTRIA - MINING AND MINERAL PRODUCTS

AUSTRIA - NATURAL RUBBER PRODUCTION

International Rubber Study Group, York House, 8th Floor, Empire Way, Wembley, London HA9 0PA, England; *Rubber Statistical Yearbook.*

AUSTRIA - NET MATERIAL PRODUCT

Statistical Office of the United Nations, Publishing Service, New York, New York 10017 (800) 253-9646; *Statistical Yearbook.*

AUSTRIA - NEWSPAPER - See AUSTRIA - FORESTRY AND FOREST PRODUCTS

AUSTRIA - NEWSPRINT - See AUSTRIA - FORESTRY AND FOREST PRODUCTS

AUSTRIA - NICKEL AND NICKEL ORE - See AUSTRIA - MINING AND MINERAL PRODUCTS

AUSTRIA - NITRIC ACID PRODUCTION - See AUSTRIA - MINING AND MINERAL PRODUCTS

AUSTRIA - OATS PRODUCTION - See AUSTRIA - CROPS

AUSTRIA - OCCUPATIONS - See AUSTRIA - LABOR FORCE

AUSTRIA - OIL PRODUCING CROPS

Organisation for Economic Co-operation and Development (OECD), 2 rue Andre-Pascal, 75 Paris 16, France (Telephone Number in U.S. (202) 785-6323); *Foreign Trade by Commodities.*

AUSTRIA - PAPER - See AUSTRIA - FORESTRY AND FOREST PRODUCTS

AUSTRIA - PATENTS

Penn Well Publishing Company, 1421 South Sheridan Road, P.O. Box 1260, Tulsa, Oklahoma 74101 (800) 752-9764; *International Energy Statistics Sourcebook.*

Statistical Office of the United Nations, Publishing Service, New York, New York 10017 (800) 253-9646; *Statistical Yearbook.*

AUSTRIA - PEANUT PRODUCTION - See AUSTRIA - CROPS

AUSTRIA - PERIODICALS

United Nations Educational, Scientific and Cultural Organization (UNESCO), 7 Place de Fontenoy, F-75700 Paris, France; *Statistical Yearbook.*

AUSTRIA - PESTICIDE USE

Food and Agricultural Organization of the United Nations (FAO) Via Delle Terme di Caracalla, 00100 Rome, Italy (Telephone Number in U.S. (202) 653-2400); *The State of Food and Agriculture.*

AUSTRIA - PETROLEUM INDUSTRY

Euromonitor Publications Limited, 87-88 Turnmill Street, London EC1M 5QU, England; *European Marketing Data and Statistics.*

Facts on File, 460 Park Avenue South, New York, New York 10016 (800) 443-8323; *The New Book of World Rankings.*

Food and Agricultural Organization of the United Nations (FAO) Via Delle Terme di Caracalla, 00100 Rome, Italy (Telephone Number in U.S. (202) 653-2400); *The State of Food and Agriculture.*

G.K. Hall and Company, 70 Lincoln Street, Boston, Massachusetts 02111 (617) 423-3990; *The World in Figures.*

Organisation for Economic Cooperation and Development (OECD), 2 rue Andre-Pascal, 75 Paris 16, France (Telephone Number in U.S. (202) 785-6323); *Energy Statistics of OECD Countries, Foreign Trade by Commodities, Indicators of Industrial Activity,* and *Oil and Gas Information.*

Penn Well Publishing Company, 1421 South Sheridan Road, P.O. Box 1260, Tulsa, Oklahoma 74101 (800) 752-9764; *International Energy Statistics Sourcebook.*

Statistical Office of the United Nations, Publishing Service, New York, New York 10017 (800) 253-9646; *Statistical Yearbook.*

AUSTRIA - PHOSPHATE ROCK PRODUCTION - See AUSTRIA - MINING AND MINERAL PRODUCTS

AUSTRIA - PHOSPHATES PRODUCTION - See AUSTRIA - MINING AND MINERAL PRODUCTS

AUSTRIA - PIG-IRON AND FERRO-ALLOYS PRODUCTION - See AUSTRIA - MINING AND MINERAL PRODUCTS

AUSTRIA - PIGS - See AUSTRIA - LIVESTOCK AND POULTRY

AUSTRIA - PIPELINES FOR OIL AND PETROLEUM PRODUCTS

Statistical Office of the United Nations, Publishing Service, New York, New York 10017 (800) 253-9646; *Annual Bulletin of Transport Statistics for Europe*.

AUSTRIA - PLASTIC AND RESIN PRODUCTION

Commodity Research Bureau, Incorporated, 75 Wall Street, New York, New York 10005 (212) 504-7754; *Commodity Year Book*.

Organisation for Economic Co-operation and Development (OECD), 2 rue Andre-Pascal, 75 Paris 16, France (Telephone Number in U.S. (202) 785-6323); *Foreign Trade by Commodities*.

Statistical Office of the United Nations, Publishing Service, New York, New York 10017 (800) 253-9646; *Statistical Yearbook*.

AUSTRIA - PLATINUM PRODUCTION - See AUSTRIA - MINING AND MINERAL PRODUCTS

AUSTRIA - POPULATION

The Economist Intelligence Unit, 111 West 57th Street, New York, New York 10019 (800) 938-4685; *The World Market Atlas*.

Euromonitor Publications Limited, 87-88 Turnmill Street, London EC1M 5QU, England; *European Marketing Data and Statistics*.

Facts on File, 460 Park Avenue South, New York, New York 10016 (800) 443-8323; *The New Book of World Rankings*.

Federal Statistical Office, Gustav - Stresemann - Ring 11, D-6200 Wiesbaden, Germany; *Osterreich*.

Food and Agricultural Organization of the United Nations (FAO), Via delle Terme di Caracalla, 00100 Rome, Italy (Telephone Number in U.S. (202) 653-2400); *Production Yearbook*.

G.K. Hall and Company, 70 Lincoln Street, Boston, Massachusetts 02111 (617) 423-3990; *The World in Figures*.

International Labour Office, I.L.O. Publications, CH-1211, Geneva 22, Switzerland; *Yearbook of Labour Statistics*.

Statistical Office of the United Nations, Publishing Service, New York, New York 10017 (800) 253-9646; *Demographic Yearbook*, and *Statistical Yearbook*.

Times Books, 201 East 50th Street, New York, New York 10022 (212) 751-2600; *The Economist Book of Vital World Statistics*.

U.S. Arms Control and Disarmament Agency, 320 Twenty-first Street, NW, Washington, D.C. 20451 (202) 647-8677; *World Military Expenditures and Arms Transfers*.

World Health Organization, Office of Publications, Avenue Appia, CH-1211 Geneva 27, Switzerland (Telephone Number in U.S. (518) 436-9686); *World Health Statistics Annual*.

AUSTRIA - POST OFFICES

Facts on File, 460 Park Avenue South, New York, New York 10016 (800) 443-8323; *The New Book of World Rankings*.

AUSTRIA - POTATO PRODUCTION - See AUSTRIA - CROPS

AUSTRIA - POULTRY - See AUSTRIA - LIVESTOCK AND POULTRY

AUSTRIA - PRICES

Facts on File, 460 Park Avenue South, New York, New York 10016 (800) 443-8323; *The New Book of World Rankings*.

Federal Statistical Office, Gustav - Stresemann - Ring 11, D-6200 Wiesbaden, Germany; *Osterreich*.

Food and Agricultural Organization of the United Nations (FAO), Via delle Terme di Caracalla, 00100 Rome, Italy (Telephone Number in U.S. (202) 653-2400); *Production Yearbook*, and *The State of Food and Agriculture*.

G.K. Hall and Company, 70 Lincoln Street, Boston, Massachusetts 02111 (617) 423-3990; *The World in Figures*.

International Labour Office, I.L.O. Publications, CH-1211, Geneva 22, Switzerland; *Yearbook of Labour Statistics*.

International Lead and Zinc Study Group, Metro House, 58 St. James's Street, London SW1A 1LD, England; *Lead and Zinc Statistics*.

International Monetary Fund, 700 Nineteenth Street, NW, Washington, D.C. 20431 (202) 623-7000; *International Financial Statistics*.

International Rubber Study Group, York House, 8th Floor, Empire Way, Wembley, London HA9 0PA, England; *Rubber Statistical Yearbook*.

Organisation for Economic Co-operation and Development (OECD), 2 rue Andre-Pascal, 75 Paris 16, France (Telephone Number in U.S. (202) 785-6323); *Economic Outlook*, *Indicators of Industrial Activity*, *The Iron and Steel Industry*, *Main Economic Indicators - Historical Statistics*, *The Footwear, Raw Hides and Skins, and Leather Industry in OECD Countries*, and *The Pulp and Paper Industry*.

World Bureau of Metal Statistics, 27-A High Street, Ware Hert SG12 9BA, England; *World Metal Statistics*.

AUSTRIA - PRINTING AND WRITING PAPER - See AUSTRIA - FORESTRY AND FOREST PRODUCTS

AUSTRIA - PRODUCTION

American Automobile Manufacturers Association, 1401 H Street, NW, Washington, D.C. 20005 (202) 326-5500; *World Motor Vehicle Data*.

Facts on File, 460 Park Avenue South, New York, New York 10016 (800) 443-8323; *The New Book of World Rankings*.

G.K. Hall and Company, 70 Lincoln Street, Boston, Massachusetts 02111 (617) 423-3990; *The World in Figures*.

International Iron and Steel Institute, 120, rue Colonel Bourg, B-1140, Brussels, Belgium; *Steel Statistical Yearbook*.

International Lead and Zinc Study Group, Metro House, 58 St. James's Street, London SW1A 1LD, England; *Lead and Zinc Statistics*.

International Rubber Study Group, York House, 8th Floor, Empire Way, Wembley, London HA9 0PA, England; *Rubber Statistical Yearbook*.

Organisation for Economic Co-operation and Development (OECD), 2 rue Andre-Pascal, 75 Paris 16, France (Telephone Number in U.S. (202) 785-6323); *Economic Outlook, The Footwear, Raw Hides and Skins, and Leather Industry in OECD Countries, Indicators of Industrial Activity, Industrial Structure Statistics, The Iron and Steel Industry, Meat Balances in OECD Member Countries, Milk, Milk Products, and Egg Balances in OECD Member Countries, The Non-Ferrous Metals Industry, The Pulp and Paper Industry,* and *Textile Industry in OECD Countries.*

AUSTRIA - PRODUCTIVITY

Organisation for Economic Co-operation and Development (OECD), 2 rue Andre-Pascal, 75 Paris 16, France (Telephone Number in U.S. (202) 785-6323); *Economic Outlook.*

AUSTRIA - PROPERTY TAXES - See AUSTRIA - TAXATION

AUSTRIA - PUBLIC CONSUMPTION FUND

Organisation for Economic Co-operation and Development (OECD), 2 rue Andre-Pascal, 75 Paris 16, France (Telephone Number in U.S. (202) 785-6323); *Revenue Statistics of OECD Member Countries.*

AUSTRIA - PUBLIC EXPENDITURES

Organisation for Economic Co-operation and Development (OECD), 2 rue Andre-Pascal, 75 Paris 16, France (Telephone Number in U.S. (202) 785-6323); *Revenue Statistics of OECD Member Countries.*

AUSTRIA - PUBLIC FINANCE

Facts on File, 460 Park Avenue South, New York, New York 10016 (800) 443-8323; *The New Book of World Rankings.*

Federal Statistical Office, Gustav - Stresemann - Ring 11, D-6200 Wiesbaden, Germany; *Osterreich.*

Organisation for Economic Co-operation and Development (OECD), 2 rue Andre-Pascal, 75 Paris 16, France (Telephone Number in U.S. (202) 785-6323); *Revenue Statistics of OECD Member Countries.*

AUSTRIA - PUBLIC REVENUES

Organisation for Economic Co-operation and Development (OECD), 2 rue Andre-Pascal, 75 Paris 16, France (Telephone Number in U.S. (202) 785-6323); *Revenue Statistics of OECD Member Countries.*

AUSTRIA - RADIO BROADCASTING - See AUSTRIA - BROADCASTING

AUSTRIA - RADIO RECEIVER PRODUCTION

Statistical Office of the United Nations, Publishing Service, New York, New York 10017 (800) 253-9646; *Statistical Yearbook.*

AUSTRIA - RAILWAYS

Euromonitor Publications Limited, 87-88 Turnmill Street, London EC1M 5QU, England; *European Marketing Data and Statistics.*

G.K. Hall and Company, 70 Lincoln Street, Boston, Massachusetts 02111 (617) 423-3990; *The World in Figures.*

Jane's Information Group, Sentinel House, 163 Brighton Road, Coulsdon, Surrey CR5 2NH, England (Telephone Number in U.S. (703) 683-3700); *Jane's World Railways.*

Statistical Office of the United Nations, Publishing Service, New York, New York 10017 (800) 253-9646; *Annual Bulletin of Transport Statistics for Europe,* and *Statistical Yearbook.*

AUSTRIA - RAPESEED PRODUCTION - See AUSTRIA - CROPS

AUSTRIA - RELIGION

Facts on File, 460 Park Avenue South, New York, New York 10016 (800) 443-8323; *The New Book of World Rankings.*

AUSTRIA - RENT PRICES

International Labour Office, I.L.O. Publications, CH-1211, Geneva 22, Switzerland; *Yearbook of Labour Statistics.*

AUSTRIA - RETAIL TRADE

G.K. Hall and Company, 70 Lincoln Street, Boston, Massachusetts 02111 (617) 423-3990; *The World in Figures.*

Statistical Office of the United Nations, Publishing Service, New York, New York 10017 (800) 253-9646; *Statistical Yearbook.*

AUSTRIA - RICE PRODUCTION - See AUSTRIA - CROPS

AUSTRIA - ROOT AND TUBER PRODUCTION - See AUSTRIA - CROPS

AUSTRIA - ROUNDWOOD PRODUCTION - See AUSTRIA - FORESTRY AND FOREST PRODUCTS

AUSTRIA - RUBBER PRODUCTION AND CONSUMPTION

Facts on File, 460 Park Avenue South, New York, New York 10016 (800) 443-8323; *The New Book of World Rankings.*

International Rubber Study Group, York House, 8th Floor, Empire Way, Wembley, London HA9 0PA, England; *Rubber Statistical Yearbook.*

Organisation for Economic Co-operation and Development (OECD), 2 rue Andre-Pascal, 75 Paris 16, France (Telephone Number in U.S. (202) 785-6323); *Foreign Trade by Commodities.*

AUSTRIA - RYE PRODUCTION - See AUSTRIA - CROPS

AUSTRIA - SALT PRODUCTION - See AUSTRIA - MINING AND MINERAL PRODUCTS

AUSTRIA - SAWNWOOD PRODUCTION - See AUSTRIA - FORESTRY AND FOREST PRODUCTS

AUSTRIA - SCIENCE AND TECHNOLOGY - EXPENDITURE FOR RESEARCH

Statistical Office of the United Nations, Publishing Service, New York, New York 10017 (800) 253-9646; *Statistical Yearbook.*

AUSTRIA - SCIENTISTS AND TECHNICIANS

Statistical Office of the United Nations, Publishing Service, New York, New York 10017 (800) 253-9646; *Statistical Yearbook.*

AUSTRIA - SENIOR CITIZENS

Facts on File, 460 Park Avenue South, New York, New York 10016 (800) 443-8323; *The New Book of World Rankings.*

AUSTRIA - SHEEP - See AUSTRIA - LIVESTOCK AND POULTRY

AUSTRIA - SHIPBUILDING - PRODUCTION INDEX

Organisation for Economic Co-operation and Development (OECD), 2 rue Andre-Pascal, 75 Paris 16, France (Telephone Number in U.S. (202) 785-6323); *Indicators of Industrial Activity.*

AUSTRIA - SILVER PRODUCTION AND CONSUMPTION - See AUSTRIA - MINING AND MINERAL PRODUCTS

AUSTRIA - SOCIAL DATA

Facts on File, 460 Park Avenue South, New York, New York 10016 (800) 443-8323; *The New Book of World Rankings.*

G.K. Hall and Company, 70 Lincoln Street, Boston, Massachusetts 02111 (617) 423-3990; *The World in Figures.*

AUSTRIA - SOCIAL SECURITY

International Monetary Fund, 700 Nineteenth Street, NW, Washington, D.C. 20431 (202) 623-7000; *Government Finance Statistics Yearbook.*

Organisation for Economic Co-operation and Development (OECD), 2 rue Andre-Pascal, 75 Paris 16, France (Telephone Number in U.S. (202) 785-6323); *Revenue Statistics of OECD Member Countries.*

AUSTRIA - SOCIOECONOMIC DATA

Organisation for Economic Co-operation and Development (OECD), 2 rue Andre-Pascal, 75 Paris 16, France (Telephone Number in U.S. (202) 785-6323); *Economic Outlook.*

AUSTRIA - STAMP TAXES AND DUTIES - See AUSTRIA - TAXATION

AUSTRIA - STEEL - See AUSTRIA - MINING AND MINERAL PRODUCTS

AUSTRIA - STOCKS - COMMODITY - MARKET PRICE - INDEXES

Food and Agricultural Organization of the United Nations (FAO) Via Delle Terme di Caracalla, 00100 Rome, Italy (Telephone Number in U.S. (202) 653-2400); *The State of Food and Agriculture.*

International Lead and Zinc Study Group, Metro House, 58 St. James's Street, London SW1A 1LD, England; *Lead and Zinc Statistics.*

Statistical Office of the United Nations, Publishing Service, New York, New York 10017 (800) 253-9646; *Statistical Yearbook.*

World Bureau of Metal Statistics, 27-A High Street, Ware Hert SG12 9BA, England; *World Metal Statistics.*

AUSTRIA - SUGAR - See AUSTRIA - CROPS

AUSTRIA - SULPHUR AND SULPHURIC ACID - See AUSTRIA - MINING AND MINERAL PRODUCTS

AUSTRIA - TAXATION

G.K. Hall and Company, 70 Lincoln Street, Boston, Massachusetts 02111 (617) 423-3990; *The World in Figures.*

International Monetary Fund, 700 Nineteenth Street, NW, Washington, D.C. 20431 (202) 623-7000; *Government Finance Statistics Yearbook.*

International Road Federation, 525 School Street, SW, Washington, D.C. 20024 (202) 554-2106; *World Road Statistics.*

Organisation for Economic Co-operation and Development (OECD), 2 rue Andre-Pascal, 75 Paris 16, France (Telephone Number in U.S. (202) 785-6323); *Revenue Statistics of OECD Member Countries.*

The World Bank, 1818 H Street, NW, Washington, D.C. 20433 (202) 477-1234; *World Tables.*

AUSTRIA - TELEGRAPH SERVICE

Statistical Office of the United Nations, Publishing Service, New York, New York 10017 (800) 253-9646; *Statistical Yearbook.*

AUSTRIA - TELEPHONES IN USE

American Telephone and Telegraph Communications, Customer Information Center, Post Office Box 19901, Indianapolis, Indiana 46219 (800) 338-4038; *The World's Telephones.*

G.K. Hall and Company, 70 Lincoln Street, Boston, Massachusetts 02111 (617) 423-3990; *The World in Figures.*

Statistical Office of the United Nations, Publishing Service, New York, New York 10017 (800) 253-9646; *Statistical Yearbook.*

AUSTRIA - TELEVISION BROADCASTING - See AUSTRIA - BROADCASTING

AUSTRIA - TELEVISION RECEIVER PRODUCTION

Statistical Office of the United Nations, Publishing Service, New York, New York 10017 (800) 253-9646; *Statistical Yearbook.*

AUSTRIA - TEXTILE INDUSTRY

Forest and Paper Association, 1250 Connecticut Avenue, NW, Washington, D.C. 20036 (202) 463-2455; *Wood Pulp and Fiber Statistics.*

G.K. Hall and Company, 70 Lincoln Street, Boston, Massachusetts 02111 (617) 423-3990; *The World in Figures.*

Organisation for Economic Co-operation and Development (OECD), 2 rue Andre-Pascal, 75 Paris 16, France (Telephone Number in U.S. (202) 785-6323); *Foreign Trade by Commodities, Indicators of Industrial Activity, Industrial Structure Statistics,* and *Textile Industry in OECD Countries.*

Statistical Office of the United Nations, Publishing Service, New York, New York 10017 (800) 253-9646; *Statistical Yearbook.*

AUSTRIA - TIN - See AUSTRIA - MINING AND MINERAL PRODUCTS

AUSTRIA - TIRE (MOTOR VEHICLE) PRODUCTION

International Rubber Study Group, York House, 8th Floor, Empire Way, Wembley, London HA9 0PA, England; *Rubber Statistical Yearbook.*

AUSTRIA - TOBACCO PRODUCTION

Euromonitor Publications Limited, 87-88 Turnmill Street, London EC1M 5QU, England; *European Marketing Data and Statistics.*

Facts on File, 460 Park Avenue South, New York, New York 10016 (800) 443-8323; *The New Book of World Rankings.*

Organisation for Economic Co-operation and Development (OECD), 2 rue Andre-Pascal, 75 Paris 16, France (Telephone Number in U.S. (202) 785-6323); *Foreign Trade by Commodities, Indicators of Industrial Activity,* and *Industrial Structure Statistics.*

Statistical Office of the United Nations, Publishing Service, New York, New York 10017 (800) 253-9646; *Statistical Yearbook.*

AUSTRIA - TOURISM

Euromonitor Publications Limited, 87-88 Turnmill Street, London EC1M 5QU, England; *European Marketing Data and Statistics.*

Facts on File, 460 Park Avenue South, New York, New York 10016 (800) 443-8323; *The New Book of World Rankings.*

Federal Statistical Office, Gustav - Stresemann - Ring 11, D-6200 Wiesbaden, Germany; *Osterreich.*

G.K. Hall and Company, 70 Lincoln Street, Boston, Massachusetts 02111 (617) 423-3990; *The World in Figures.*

Organisation for Economic Co-operation and Development (OECD), 2 rue Andre-Pascal, 75 Paris 16, France (Telephone Number in U.S. (202) 785-6323); *Tourism Policy and International Tourism in OECD Member Countries.*

Statistical Office of the United Nations, Publishing Service, New York, New York 10017 (800) 253-9646; *Statistical Yearbook.*

Times Books, 201 East 50th Street, New York, New York 10022 (212) 751-2600; *The Economist Book of Vital World Statistics.*

World Tourism Organization, Calle Capitan Haya 42, E-28020 Madrid, Spain; *Yearbook of Tourism Statistics.*

AUSTRIA - TRADE - See AUSTRIA - FOREIGN TRADE

AUSTRIA - TRADEMARKS AND SERVICE MARKS

Penn Well Publishing Company, 1421 South Sheridan Road, P.O. Box 1260, Tulsa, Oklahoma 74101 (800) 752-9764; *International Energy Statistics Sourcebook.*

Statistical Office of the United Nations, Publishing Service, New York, New York 10017 (800) 253-9646; *Statistical Yearbook.*

AUSTRIA - TRANSPORTATION AND COMMUNICATIONS

Facts on File, 460 Park Avenue South, New York, New York 10016 (800) 443-8323; *The New Book of World Rankings.*

Federal Statistical Office, Gustav - Stresemann - Ring 11, D-6200 Wiesbaden, Germany; *Osterreich.*

G.K. Hall and Company, 70 Lincoln Street, Boston, Massachusetts 02111 (617) 423-3990; *The World in Figures.*

AUSTRIA - TUNGSTEN PRODUCTION AND CONSUMPTION - See AUSTRIA - MINING AND MINERAL PRODUCTS

AUSTRIA - TURKEYS - See AUSTRIA - LIVESTOCK AND POULTRY

AUSTRIA - UNEMPLOYMENT

Euromonitor Publications Limited, 87-88 Turnmill Street, London EC1M 5QU, England; *European Marketing Data and Statistics.*

International Labour Office, I.L.O. Publications, CH-1211, Geneva 22, Switzerland; *Yearbook of Labour Statistics.*

Organisation for Economic Co-operation and Development (OECD), 2 rue Andre-Pascal, 75 Paris 16, France (Telephone Number in U.S. (202) 785-6323); *Economic Outlook, Labour Force Statistics, OECD Economic Surveys: Austria,* and *OECD Employment Outlook.*

Statistical Office of the United Nations, Publishing Service, New York, New York 10017 (800) 253-9646; *Statistical Yearbook.*

AUSTRIA - URANIUM PRODUCTION AND CONSUMPTION - See AUSTRIA - MINING AND MINERAL PRODUCTS

AUSTRIA - VANADIUM AND VANADIUM ORE - See AUSTRIA - MINING AND MINERAL PRODUCTS

AUSTRIA - VITAL STATISTICS

G.K. Hall and Company, 70 Lincoln Street, Boston, Massachusetts 02111 (617) 423-3990; *The World in Figures.*

Statistical Office of the United Nations, Publishing Service, New York, New York 10017 (800) 253-9646; *Statistical Yearbook.*

World Health Organization, Office of Publications, Avenue Appia, CH-1211 Geneva 27, Switzerland (Telephone Number in U.S. (518) 436-9686); *World Health Statistics Annual.*

AUSTRIA - WAGES

Euromonitor Publications Limited, 87-88 Turnmill Street, London EC1M 5QU, England; *European Marketing Data and Statistics.*

Federal Statistical Office, Gustav - Stresemann - Ring 11, D-6200 Wiesbaden, Germany; *Osterreich.*

G.K. Hall and Company, 70 Lincoln Street, Boston, Massachusetts 02111 (617) 423-3990; *The World in Figures.*

International Labour Office, I.L.O. Publications, CH-1211, Geneva 22, Switzerland; *Yearbook of Labour Statistics.*

Organisation for Economic Co-operation and Development (OECD), 2 rue Andre-Pascal, 75 Paris 16, France (Telephone Number in U.S. (202) 785-6323); *Economic Outlook, Industrial Structure Statistics,* and *Main Economic Indicators - Historical Statistics.*

Statistical Office of the United Nations, Publishing Service, New York, New York 10017 (800) 253-9646; *Statistical Yearbook.*

AUSTRIA - WALNUT PRODUCTION - See AUSTRIA - CROPS

AUSTRIA - WATERWAYS IN USE - See AUSTRIA - MERCHANT SHIPPING

AUSTRIA - WEATHER

Facts on File, 460 Park Avenue South, New York, New York 10016 (800) 443-8323; *The New Book of World Rankings.*

G.K. Hall and Company, 70 Lincoln Street, Boston, Massachusetts 02111 (617) 423-3990; *The World in Figures.*

AUSTRIA - WELFARE

International Monetary Fund, 700 Nineteenth Street, NW, Washington, D.C. 20431 (202) 623-7000; *Government Finance Statistics Yearbook.*

AUSTRIA - WHEAT PRODUCTION AND PRICES - See AUSTRIA - CROPS

AUSTRIA - WHOLESALE PRICES

International Monetary Fund, 700 Nineteenth Street, NW, Washington, D.C. 20431 (202) 623-7000; *International Financial Statistics*.

AUSTRIA - WHOLESALE TRADE

Statistical Office of the United Nations, Publishing Service, New York, New York 10017 (800) 253-9646; *Statistical Yearbook*.

AUSTRIA - WINE PRODUCTION

Facts on File, 460 Park Avenue South, New York, New York 10016 (800) 443-8323; *The New Book of World Rankings*.

Statistical Office of the United Nations, Publishing Service, New York, New York 10017 (800) 253-9646; *Statistical Yearbook*.

AUSTRIA - WOOD EXPORTS - See AUSTRIA - FORESTRY AND FOREST PRODUCTS

AUSTRIA - WOOL - INDUSTRIAL CONSUMPTION

Organisation for Economic Co-operation and Development (OECD), 2 rue Andre-Pascal, 75 Paris 16, France (Telephone Number in U.S. (202) 785-6323); *Textile Industry in OECD Countries*.

Statistical Office of the United Nations, Publishing Service, New York, New York 10017 (800) 253-9646; *Statistical Yearbook*.

AUSTRIA - WOOL PRODUCTION

Facts on File, 460 Park Avenue South, New York, New York 10016 (800) 443-8323; *The New Book of World Rankings*.

Organisation for Economic Co-operation and Development (OECD), 2 rue Andre-Pascal, 75 Paris 16, France (Telephone Number in U.S. (202) 785-6323); *Economic Accounts for Agriculture*, and *Textile Industry in OECD Countries*.

AUSTRIA - YARN PRODUCTION

Organisation for Economic Co-operation and Development (OECD), 2 rue Andre-Pascal, 75 Paris 16, France (Telephone Number in U.S. (202) 785-6323); *Foreign Trade by Commodities*, and *Textile Industry in OECD Countries*.

Statistical Office of the United Nations, Publishing Service, New York, New York 10017 (800) 253-9646; *Statistical Yearbook*.

AUSTRIA - ZINC AND ZINC ORE - See AUSTRIA -MINING AND MINERAL PRODUCTS

AUSTRIA - ZOOS AND BOTANICAL GARDENS

United Nations Educational, Scientific and Cultural Organization (UNESCO), 7 Place de Fontenoy, F-75700 Paris, France; *Statistical Yearbook*.

AUTHORS

U.S. Department of Labor, Bureau of Labor Statistics, Two Massachusetts Avenue, NE, Washington, D.C. 20212 (202) 606-7828; *Employment and Earnings*.

AUTOMOBILE LOANS

American Bankers Association, 1120 Connecticut Avenue, NW, Washington, D.C. 20036 (202) 663-5000; *Consumer Credit Delinquency Bulletin*.

Board of Governors of the Federal Reserve System, Twentieth Street and Constitution Avenue, NW, Washington, D.C. 20551 (202) 452-3000; *Federal Reserve Bulletin*, *Annual Statistical Digest*, and unpublished data.

AUTOMOBILE RENTALS AND LEASING - See AUTOMOTIVE REPAIR, SERVICES, AND PARKING

AUTOMOBILES - See also MOTOR VEHICLES

AUTOMOBILES - COST OF OWNERSHIP

American Automobile Manufacturers Association, 1401 H Street, NW, Washington, D.C. 20005 (202) 326-5500; *Motor Vehicle Facts and Figures*.

AUTOMOTIVE DEALERS AND SERVICE STATIONS - EARNINGS

U.S. Department of Commerce, Bureau of Census, Suitland, Maryland 20233 (301) 763-4040; *Census of Retail Trade*, and *County Business Patterns*.

AUTOMOTIVE DEALERS AND SERVICE STATIONS - EMPLOYEES

U.S. Department of Commerce, Bureau of Census, Suitland, Maryland 20233 (301) 763-4040; *Census of Retail Trade*, and *County Business Patterns*

AUTOMOTIVE DEALERS AND SERVICE STATIONS - ESTABLISHMENTS

U.S. Department of Commerce, Bureau of Census, Suitland, Maryland 20233 (301) 763-4040; *Census of Retail Trade*, and *County Business Patterns*.

International Franchise Association, 1350 New York Avenue, Suite 900, Washington, D.C. 20005 (202) 628-8000; *Franchising in the Economy*.

AUTOMOTIVE DEALERS AND SERVICE STATIONS - INVENTORIES

U.S. Department of Commerce, Bureau of Census, Suitland, Maryland 20233 (301) 763-4040; *Annual Retail Trade Reports*, *Current Business Reports*, and *Monthly Retail Trade Reports*.

AUTOMOTIVE DEALERS AND SERVICE STATIONS - SALES

U.S. Department of Commerce, Bureau of Census, Suitland, Maryland 20233 (301) 763-4040; *Current Business Reports*, *Combined Annual and Revised Monthly Retail Trade*.

International Franchise Association, 1350 New York Avenue, Suite 900, Washington, D.C. 20005 (202) 628-8000; *Franchising in the Economy*.

AUTOMOTIVE PRODUCTS - See MOTOR VEHICLES AND EQUIPMENT

AUTOMOTIVE REPAIR, SERVICES, AND PARKING - EARNINGS

U.S. Department of Commerce, Bureau of Census, Suitland, Maryland 20233 (301) 763-4040; *Census of Service Industries*, and *County Business Patterns*.

U.S. Department of Labor, Bureau of Labor Statistics, Two Massachusetts Avenue, NE, Washington, D.C. 20212 (202) 606-7828; *Employment and Earnings*, and Bulletins 2370 and 2429.

AUTOMOTIVE REPAIR, SERVICES, AND PARKING - EMPLOYEES

U.S. Department of Commerce, Bureau of Census, Suitland, Maryland 20233 (301) 763-4040; *Census of Service Industries*, and *County Business Patterns*.

U.S. Department of Commerce, Bureau of Economic Analysis, Fourteenth Street between Constitution Avenue and E Street, NW, Washington, D.C. 20230 (202) 606-9900; *The National Income and Product Accounts of the United States*, and *Survey of Current Business*.

U.S. Department of Labor, Bureau of Labor Statistics, Two Massachusetts Avenue, NE, Washington, D.C. 20212 (202) 606-7828; *Employment and Earnings*, and Bulletins 2370 and 2429.

AUTOMOTIVE REPAIR, SERVICES, AND PARKING - ESTABLISHMENTS

U.S. Department of Commerce, Bureau of Census, Suitland, Maryland 20233 (301) 763-4040; *Census of Service Industries*, and *County Business Patterns*.

International Franchise Association, 1350 New York Avenue, Suite 900, Washington, D.C. 20005 (202) 628-8000; *Franchising in the Economy*.

AUTOMOTIVE REPAIR, SERVICES, AND PARKING - GROSS DOMESTIC PRODUCT

U.S. Department of Commerce, Bureau of Economic Analysis, Fourteenth Street between Constitution Avenue and E Street, NW, Washington, D.C. 20230 (202) 606-9900; *Survey of Current Business*.

AUTOMOTIVE REPAIR, SERVICES, AND PARKING - PRODUCTIVITY

U.S. Department of Labor, Bureau of Labor Statistics, Two Massachusetts Avenue, NE, Washington, D.C. 20212 (202) 606-7828; *Productivity Measures for Selected Industries and Government Services*, and Bulletin 2440.

AUTOMOTIVE REPAIR, SERVICES, AND PARKING - RECEIPTS

U.S. Department of Commerce, Bureau of Census, Suitland, Maryland 20233 (301) 763-4040; *Census of Service Industries*, *Current Business Reports*, and *Service Annual Survey*.

International Franchise Association, 1350 New York Avenue, Suite 900, Washington, D.C. 20005 (202) 628-8000; *Franchising in the Economy*.

AVIATION COMMUNICATION - PRIVATE RADIO STATIONS

U.S. Federal Communications Commission, 1919 M Street, NW, Washington, D.C. 20554 (202) 632-7000; *Annual Report*, and unpublished data.

AVOCADOS

U.S. Department of Agriculture, National Agricultural Statistics Service, Fourteenth Street and Independence Avenue, SW,Washington, D.C. 20250 (202) 219-1504; *Noncitrus Fruits and Nuts*, and *Economic Indicators of the Farm Sector: National Financial Summary*.

AZERBAIJAN - See also UNION OF SOVIET SOCIALIST REPUBLICS

Azerbaijan - National Statistical Office

State Committee of Azerbaijan on Statistics, 10 Chapaena Street, Baku 370008, Azerbaijan.

AZERBAIJAN - AGRICULTURE

Business International Moscow, 23 Profseyuznaya Ulitsa 117859, Moscow (Telephone Number in U.S. (800) 938-4685); *The CIS Market Atlas*.

Encyclopedia Britannica, Incorporated, 310 South Michigan Avenue, Chicago, Illinois 60604 (312) 347-7000; *Britannica World Data*.

The World Bank, 1818 H Street, NW, Washington, D.C. 20433 (202) 477-1234; *Statistical Handbook: States of the Former USSR*.

AZERBAIJAN - AIRLINE SERVICE

Business International Moscow, 23 Profseyuznaya Ulitsa 117859, Moscow (Telephone Number in U.S. (800) 938-4685); *The CIS Market Atlas*.

Encyclopedia Britannica, Incorporated, 310 South Michigan Avenue, Chicago, Illinois 60604 (312) 347-7000; *Britannica World Data*.

AZERBAIJAN - AREA AND DENSITY OF POPULATION

Business International Moscow, 23 Profseyuznaya Ulitsa 117859, Moscow (Telephone Number in U.S. (800) 938-4685); *The CIS Market Atlas*.

AZERBAIJAN - BANKING

Business International Moscow, 23 Profseyuznaya Ulitsa 117859, Moscow (Telephone Number in U.S. (800) 938-4685); *The CIS Market Atlas*.

AZERBAIJAN - BIRTH RATES

Business International Moscow, 23 Profseyuznaya Ulitsa 117859, Moscow (Telephone Number in U.S. (800) 938-4685); *The CIS Market Atlas*.

Encyclopedia Britannica, Incorporated, 310 South Michigan Avenue, Chicago, Illinois 60604 (312) 347-7000; *Britannica World Data*.

AZERBAIJAN - BUDGET

Business International Moscow, 23 Profseyuznaya Ulitsa 117859, Moscow (Telephone Number in U.S. (800) 938-4685); *The CIS Market Atlas*.

AZERBAIJAN - CAPITAL INVESTMENT

The World Bank, 1818 H Street, NW, Washington, D.C. 20433 (202) 477-1234; *Statistical Handbook: States of the Former USSR*.

AZERBAIJAN - CATTLE - See AZERBAIJAN - LIVESTOCK AND POULTRY

AZERBAIJAN - CHEMICALS

Business International Moscow, 23 Profseyuznaya Ulitsa 117859, Moscow (Telephone Number in U.S. (800) 938-4685); *The CIS Market Atlas*.

AZERBAIJAN - COAL PRODUCTION AND CONSUMPTION - See AZERBAIJAN - MINING AND MINERAL PRODUCTS

AZERBAIJAN - COMMUNICATIONS

Business International Moscow, 23 Profseyuznaya Ulitsa 117859, Moscow (Telephone Number in U.S. (800) 938-4685); *The CIS Market Atlas.*

AZERBAIJAN - CONSTRUCTION

Business International Moscow, 23 Profseyuznaya Ulitsa 117859, Moscow (Telephone Number in U.S. (800) 938-4685); *The CIS Market Atlas.*

Encyclopedia Britannica, Incorporated, 310 South Michigan Avenue, Chicago, Illinois 60604 (312) 347-7000; *Britannica World Data.*

AZERBAIJAN - CONSUMER PRODUCTS

Business International Moscow, 23 Profseyuznaya Ulitsa 117859, Moscow (Telephone Number in U.S. (800) 938-4685); *The CIS Market Atlas.*

AZERBAIJAN - CONSUMPTION

Business International Moscow, 23 Profseyuznaya Ulitsa 117859, Moscow (Telephone Number in U.S. (800) 938-4685); *The CIS Market Atlas.*

The World Bank, 1818 H Street, NW, Washington, D.C. 20433 (202) 477-1234; *Statistical Handbook: States of the Former USSR.*

AZERBAIJAN - COTTON - See AZERBAIJAN - CROPS

AZERBAIJAN - CROPS

Business International Moscow, 23 Profseyuznaya Ulitsa 117859, Moscow (Telephone Number in U.S. (800) 938-4685); *The CIS Market Atlas.*

The World Bank, 1818 H Street, NW, Washington, D.C. 20433 (202) 477-1234; *Statistical Handbook: States of the Former USSR.*

AZERBAIJAN - DEATH RATES

Business International Moscow, 23 Profseyuznaya Ulitsa 117859, Moscow (Telephone Number in U.S. (800) 938-4685); *The CIS Market Atlas.*

AZERBAIJAN - DEMOGRAPHY

The Economist Intelligence Unit, 111 West 57th Street, New York, New York 10019 (800) 938-4685; *The World Market Atlas.*

Encyclopedia Britannica, Incorporated, 310 South Michigan Avenue, Chicago, Illinois 60604 (312) 347-7000; *Britannica World Data.*

The World Bank, 1818 H Street, NW, Washington, D.C. 20433 (202) 477-1234; *Statistical Handbook: States of the Former USSR.*

AZERBAIJAN - DISEASES

The Economist Intelligence Unit, 111 West 57th Street, New York, New York 10019 (800) 938-4685; *The World Market Atlas.*

AZERBAIJAN - DIVORCE RATES

Encyclopedia Britannica, Incorporated, 310 South Michigan Avenue, Chicago, Illinois 60604 (312) 347-7000; *Britannica World Data.*

AZERBAIJAN - DOMESTIC INVESTMENT

Business International Moscow, 23 Profseyuznaya Ulitsa 117859, Moscow (Telephone Number in U.S. (800) 938-4685); *The CIS Market Atlas.*

AZERBAIJAN - ECONOMY

Business International Moscow, 23 Profseyuznaya Ulitsa 117859, Moscow (Telephone Number in U.S. (800) 938-4685); *The CIS Market Atlas.*

Encyclopedia Britannica, Incorporated, 310 South Michigan Avenue, Chicago, Illinois 60604 (312) 347-7000; *Britannica World Data.*

AZERBAIJAN - EDUCATION

Business International Moscow, 23 Profsoyuznaya Ulitsa, 117859, Moscow (Telephone Number in U.S. (800) 938-4685); *The CIS Market Atlas.*

The Economist Intelligence Unit, 111 West 57th Street, New York, New York 10019 (800) 938-4685; *The World Market Atlas.*

Encyclopedia Britannica, Incorporated, 310 South Michigan Avenue, Chicago, Illinois 60604 (312) 347-7000; *Britannica World Data.*

AZERBAIJAN - ELECTRICITY PRODUCTION

Business International Moscow, 23 Profseyuznaya Ulitsa 117859, Moscow (Telephone Number in U.S. (800) 938-4685); *The CIS Market Atlas.*

The World Bank, 1818 H Street, NW, Washington, D.C. 20433 (202) 477-1234; *Statistical Handbook: States of the Former USSR.*

AZERBAIJAN - EMPLOYMENT

The World Bank, 1818 H Street, NW, Washington, D.C. 20433 (202) 477-1234; *Statistical Handbook: States of the Former USSR.*

AZERBAIJAN - ENERGY

Business International Moscow, 23 Profseyuznaya Ulitsa 117859, Moscow (Telephone Number in U.S. (800) 938-4685); *The CIS Market Atlas.*

Encyclopedia Britannica, Incorporated, 310 South Michigan Avenue, Chicago, Illinois 60604 (312) 347-7000; *Britannica World Data.*

The World Bank, 1818 H Street, NW, Washington, D.C. 20433 (202) 477-1234; *Statistical Handbook: States of the Former USSR.*

AZERBAIJAN - ENVIRONMENT

Business International Moscow, 23 Profseyuznaya Ulitsa 117859, Moscow (Telephone Number in U.S. (800) 938-4685); *The CIS Market Atlas.*

AZERBAIJAN - EXPORTS

Business International Moscow, 23 Profseyuznaya Ulitsa 117859, Moscow (Telephone Number in U.S. (800) 938-4685); *The CIS Market Atlas.*

Encyclopedia Britannica, Incorporated, 310 South Michigan Avenue, Chicago, Illinois 60604 (312) 347-7000; *Britannica World Data.*

The World Bank, 1818 H Street, NW, Washington, D.C. 20433 (202) 477-1234; *Statistical Handbook: States of the Former USSR.*

AZERBAIJAN - EXTERNAL TRADE

The World Bank, 1818 H Street, NW, Washington, D.C. 20433 (202) 477-1234; *Statistical Handbook: States of the Former USSR.*

AZERBAIJAN - FABRIC PRODUCTION AND CONSUMPTION - See AZERBAIJAN - TEXTILE INDUSTRY

AZERBAIJAN - FERTILITY RATES

Encyclopedia Britannica, Incorporated, 310 South Michigan Avenue, Chicago, Illinois 60604 (312) 347-7000; *Britannica World Data.*

The World Bank, 1818 H Street, NW, Washington, D.C. 20433 (202) 477-1234; *Statistical Handbook: States of the Former USSR.*

AZERBAIJAN - FISHERIES

Encyclopedia Britannica, Incorporated, 310 South Michigan Avenue, Chicago, Illinois 60604 (312) 347-7000; *Britannica World Data.*

AZERBAIJAN - FOOTWEAR PRODUCTION AND CONSUMPTION - See AZERBAIJAN - TEXTILE INDUSTRY

AZERBAIJAN - FOREIGN INVESTMENT

Business International Moscow, 23 Profseyuznaya Ulitsa 117859, Moscow (Telephone Number in U.S. (800) 938-4685); *The CIS Market Atlas.*

AZERBAIJAN - FOREIGN TRADE

Business International Moscow, 23 Profseyuznaya Ulitsa 117859, Moscow (Telephone Number in U.S. (800) 938-4685); *The CIS Market Atlas.*

Encyclopedia Britannica, Incorporated, 310 South Michigan Avenue, Chicago, Illinois 60604 (312) 347-7000; *Britannica World Data.*

The World Bank, 1818 H Street, NW, Washington, D.C. 20433 (202) 477-1234; *Statistical Handbook: States of the Former USSR.*

AZERBAIJAN - FORESTRY AND FOREST PRODUCTS

Business International Moscow, 23 Profseyuznaya Ulitsa 117859, Moscow (Telephone Number in U.S. (800) 938-4685); *The CIS Market Atlas.*

Encyclopedia Britannica, Incorporated, 310 South Michigan Avenue, Chicago, Illinois 60604 (312) 347-7000; *Britannica World Data.*

AZERBAIJAN - GOATS - See AZERBAIJAN - LIVESTOCK AND POULTRY

AZERBAIJAN - GOVERNMENT EXPENDITURE

The World Bank, 1818 H Street, NW, Washington, D.C. 20433 (202) 477-1234; *Statistical Handbook: States of the Former USSR.*

AZERBAIJAN - GOVERNMENT REVENUE

The World Bank, 1818 H Street, NW, Washington, D.C. 20433 (202) 477-1234; *Statistical Handbook: States of the Former USSR.*

AZERBAIJAN - GROSS DOMESTIC PRODUCT

The World Bank, 1818 H Street, NW, Washington, D.C. 20433 (202) 477-1234; *Statistical Handbook: States of the Former USSR.*

AZERBAIJAN - HEALTH

Business International Moscow, 23 Profseyuznaya Ulitsa 117859, Moscow (Telephone Number in U.S. (800) 938-4685); *The CIS Market Atlas.*

Encyclopedia Britannica, Incorporated, 310 South Michigan Avenue, Chicago, Illinois 60604 (312) 347-7000; *Britannica World Data.*

AZERBAIJAN - HIGHWAYS

Business International Moscow, 23 Profseyuznaya Ulitsa 117859, Moscow (Telephone Number in U.S. (800) 938-4685); *The CIS Market Atlas.*

Encyclopedia Britannica, Incorporated, 310 South Michigan Avenue, Chicago, Illinois 60604 (312) 347-7000; *Britannica World Data.*

AZERBAIJAN - HOUSING AND HOUSING UNITS

Business International Moscow, 23 Profseyuznaya Ulitsa 117859, Moscow (Telephone Number in U.S. (800) 938-4685); *The CIS Market Atlas.*

AZERBAIJAN - IMPORTS

Business International Moscow, 23 Profseyuznaya Ulitsa 117859, Moscow (Telephone Number in U.S. (800) 938-4685); *The CIS Market Atlas.*

Encyclopedia Britannica, Incorporated, 310 South Michigan Avenue, Chicago, Illinois 60604 (312) 347-7000; *Britannica World Data.*

The World Bank, 1818 H Street, NW, Washington, D.C. 20433 (202) 477-1234; *Statistical Handbook: States of the Former USSR.*

AZERBAIJAN - INDUSTRY

Business International Moscow, 23 Profseyuznaya Ulitsa 117859, Moscow (Telephone Number in U.S. (800) 938-4685); *The CIS Market Atlas.*

The World Bank, 1818 H Street, NW, Washington, D.C. 20433 (202) 477-1234; *Statistical Handbook: States of the Former USSR.*

AZERBAIJAN - INFANT MORTALITY RATES

Business International Moscow, 23 Profseyuznaya Ulitsa 117859, Moscow (Telephone Number in U.S. (800) 938-4685); *The CIS Market Atlas.*

AZERBAIJAN - LABOR

Business International Moscow, 23 Profseyuznaya Ulitsa 117859, Moscow (Telephone Number in U.S. (800) 938-4685); *The CIS Market Atlas.*

The World Bank, 1818 H Street, NW, Washington, D.C. 20433 (202) 477-1234; *Statistical Handbook: States of the Former USSR.*

AZERBAIJAN - LAND USE

Encyclopedia Britannica, Incorporated, 310 South Michigan Avenue, Chicago, Illinois 60604 (312) 347-7000; *Britannica World Data.*

AZERBAIJAN - LIFE EXPECTANCY

Business International Moscow, 23 Profseyuznaya Ulitsa 117859, Moscow (Telephone Number in U.S. (800) 938-4685); *The CIS Market Atlas.*

AZERBAIJAN - LIVESTOCK AND POULTRY

Business International Moscow, 23 Profseyuznaya Ulitsa 117859, Moscow (Telephone Number in U.S. (800) 938-4685); *The CIS Market Atlas.*

Encyclopedia Britannica, Incorporated, 310 South Michigan Avenue, Chicago, Illinois 60604 (312) 347-7000; *Britannica World Data.*

AZERBAIJAN - MANUFACTURING

Encyclopedia Britannica, Incorporated, 310 South Michigan Avenue, Chicago, Illinois 60604 (312) 347-7000; *Britannica World Data.*

AZERBAIJAN - MARRIAGE RATES

Encyclopedia Britannica, Incorporated, 310 South Michigan Avenue, Chicago, Illinois 60604 (312) 347-7000; *Britannica World Data.*

AZERBAIJAN - MEAT PRODUCTION - See AZERBAIJAN - LIVESTOCK AND POULTRY

AZERBAIJAN - MILITARY

The International Institute for Strategic Studies, 23 Tavistock Street, London WC2E 7NQ, England; *The Military Balance.*

AZERBAIJAN - MINING AND MINERAL PRODUCTS

Business International Moscow, 23 Profsoyuznaya Ulitsa, 117859, Moscow (Telephone Number in U.S. (800) 938-4685); *The CIS Market Atlas.*

Encyclopedia Britannica, Incorporated, 310 South Michigan Avenue, Chicago, Illinois 60604 (312) 347-7000; *Britannica World Data.*

AZERBAIJAN - MOTOR VEHICLES

Business International Moscow, 23 Profseyuznaya Ulitsa 117859, Moscow (Telephone Number in U.S. (800) 938-4685); *The CIS Market Atlas.*

AZERBAIJAN - NATIONAL ACCOUNTS

The World Bank, 1818 H Street, NW, Washington, D.C. 20433 (202) 477-1234; *Statistical Handbook: States of the Former USSR.*

AZERBAIJAN - NATIONAL INCOME

Business International Moscow, 23 Profseyuznaya Ulitsa 117859, Moscow (Telephone Number in U.S. (800) 938-4685); *The CIS Market Atlas.*

AZERBAIJAN - PIGS - See AZERBAIJAN - LIVESTOCK AND POULTRY

AZERBAIJAN - POPULATION

Business International Moscow, 23 Profseyuznaya Ulitsa 117859, Moscow (Telephone Number in U.S. (800) 938-4685); *The CIS Market Atlas.*

Encyclopedia Britannica, Incorporated, 310 South Michigan Avenue, Chicago, Illinois 60604 (312) 347-7000; *Britannica World Data.*

The World Bank, 1818 H Street, NW, Washington, D.C. 20433 (202) 477-1234; *Statistical Handbook: States of the Former USSR.*

AZERBAIJAN - POULTRY - See AZERBAIJAN - LIVESTOCK AND POULTRY

AZERBAIJAN - PRICES

The World Bank, 1818 H Street, NW, Washington, D.C. 20433 (202) 477-1234; *Statistical Handbook: States of the Former USSR.*

AZERBAIJAN - PRODUCTION

The World Bank, 1818 H Street, NW, Washington, D.C. 20433 (202) 477-1234; *Statistical Handbook: States of the Former USSR.*

AZERBAIJAN - PUBLIC FINANCE

The World Bank, 1818 H Street, NW, Washington, D.C. 20433 (202) 477-1234; *Statistical Handbook: States of the Former USSR.*

AZERBAIJAN - RADIO RECEIVERS

Encyclopedia Britannica, Incorporated, 310 South Michigan Avenue, Chicago, Illinois 60604 (312) 347-7000; *Britannica World Data.*

AZERBAIJAN - RAILWAYS

Business International Moscow, 23 Profsoyuznaya Ulitsa, 117859, Moscow (Telephone Number in U.S. (800) 938-4685); *The CIS Market Atlas.*

The Economist Intelligence Unit, 111 West 57th Street, New York, New York 10019 (800) 938-4685; *The World Market Atlas.*

Encyclopedia Britannica, Incorporated, 310 South Michigan Avenue, Chicago, Illinois 60604 (312) 347-7000; *Britannica World Data.*

AZERBAIJAN - RETAIL TRADE

Business International Moscow, 23 Profseyuznaya Ulitsa 117859, Moscow (Telephone Number in U.S. (800) 938-4685); *The CIS Market Atlas.*

AZERBAIJAN - ROADS - See AZERBAIJAN - HIGHWAYS

AZERBAIJAN - ROUNDWOOD PRODUCTION AND CONSUMPTION - See AZERBAIJAN - FORESTRY AND FOREST PRODUCTS

AZERBAIJAN - SHEEP - See AZERBAIJAN - LIVESTOCK AND POULTRY

AZERBAIJAN - STEEL - See AZERBAIJAN - MINING AND MINERAL PRODUCTION

AZERBAIJAN - TELEPHONES IN USE

Encyclopedia Britannica, Incorporated, 310 South Michigan Avenue, Chicago, Illinois 60604 (312) 347-7000; *Britannica World Data.*

AZERBAIJAN - TELEVISION RECEIVERS

Encyclopedia Britannica, Incorporated, 310 South Michigan Avenue, Chicago, Illinois 60604 (312) 347-7000; *Britannica World Data.*

AZERBAIJAN - TEXTILE INDUSTRY

Business International Moscow, 23 Profseyuznaya Ulitsa 117859, Moscow (Telephone Number in U.S. (800) 938-4685); *The CIS*

Market Atlas.

AZERBAIJAN - TOURISM

Business International Moscow, 23 Profsoyuznaya Ulitsa, 117859, Moscow (Telephone Number in U.S. (800) 938-4685); *The CIS Market Atlas.*

AZERBAIJAN - TRANSPORTATION AND COMMUNICATION

Business International Moscow, 23 Profseyuznaya Ulitsa 117859, Moscow (Telephone Number in U.S. (800) 938-4685); *The CIS Market Atlas.*

Encyclopedia Britannica, Incorporated, 310 South Michigan Avenue, Chicago, Illinois 60604 (312) 347-7000; *Britannica World Data.*

AZERBAIJAN - VITAL STATISTICS

Encyclopedia Britannica, Incorporated, 310 South Michigan Avenue, Chicago, Illinois 60604 (312) 347-7000; *Britannica World Data.*

AZERBAIJAN - WAGES

Business International Moscow, 23 Profseyuznaya Ulitsa 117859, Moscow (Telephone Number in U.S. (800) 938-4685); *The CIS Market Atlas.*

The World Bank, 1818 H Street, NW, Washington, D.C. 20433 (202) 477-1234; *Statistical Handbook: States of the Former USSR.*

AZERBAIJAN - WOOL PRODUCTION AND CONSUMPTION - See AZERBAIJAN - TEXTILE INDUSTRY

B

BACON

U.S. Department of Labor, Bureau of Labor Statistics, Two Massachusetts Avenue, NE, Washington, D.C. 20212 (202) 606-7828; *Monthly Labor Review*, and *CPI Detailed Report*.

Bahamas - National Statistical Office

Director of Statistics, Bahamas Government, Department of Statistics, Post Office Box N3904, Nassau, Bahamas.

Bahamas - Primary Statistics Sources

Department of Statistics, Cabinet Office, Post Office Box N3904, Nassau, Bahamas; *Commonwealth of the Bahamas Statistical Abstract*, and *Quarterly Statistical Summary*.

BAHAMAS - AGRICULTURE

Facts on File, 460 Park Avenue South, New York, New York 10016 (800) 443-8323; *The New Book of World Rankings*.

Federal Statistical Office, Gustav - Stresemann - Ring 11, D-6200 Wiesbaden, Germany; *Bahamas*.

Food and Agricultural Organization of the United Nations (FAO), Via delle Terme di Caracalla, 00100 Rome, Italy (Telephone Number in U.S. (202) 653-2400); *Production Yearbook, The State of Food and Agriculture*, and *Trade Yearbook*.

G.K. Hall and Company, 70 Lincoln Street, Boston, Massachusetts 02111 (617) 423-3990; *The World in Figures*.

Inter-American Development Bank, 1300 New York Avenue, NW, Washington, D.C. 20577 (202) 623-1753; *Economic and Social Progress in Latin America*.

Statistical Office of the United Nations, Publishing Service, New York, New York 10017 (800) 253-9646; *Statistical Yearbook*.

Times Books, 201 East 50th Street, New York, New York 10022 (212) 751-2600; *The Economist Book of Vital World Statistics*.

The World Bank, 1818 H Street, N.W., Washington, D.C. 20433 (202) 477-1234; *World Tables*.

BAHAMAS - AIRLINE SERVICE

Facts on File, 460 Park Avenue South, New York, New York 10016 (800) 443-8323; *The New Book of World Rankings*.

G.K. Hall and Company, 70 Lincoln Street, Boston, Massachusetts 02111 (617) 423-3990; *The World in Figures*.

Times Books, 201 East 50th Street, New York, New York 10022 (212) 751-2600; *The Economist Book of Vital World Statistics*.

BAHAMAS - ALUMINUM PRODUCTION AND CONSUMPTION - See BAHAMAS - MINING AND MINERAL PRODUCTS

BAHAMAS - ANIMAL HEALTH

Food and Agricultural Organization of the United Nations (FAO), Via delle Terme di Caracalla, 00100 Rome, Italy (Telephone Number in U.S. (202) 653-2400); *Animal Health Yearbook*.

BAHAMAS - AREA AND DENSITY OF POPULATION

Facts on File, 460 Park Avenue South, New York, New York 10016 (800) 443-8323; *The New Book of World Rankings*.

Federal Statistical Office, Gustav - Stresemann - Ring 11, D-6200 Wiesbaden, Germany; *Bahamas*.

Food and Agricultural Organization of the United Nations (FAO) Via delle Terme di Caracalla, 00100 Rome, Italy (Telephone Number in U.S. (202) 653-2400); *The State of Food and Agriculture*.

G.K. Hall and Company, 70 Lincoln Street, Boston, Massachusetts 02111 (617) 423-3990; *The World in Figures*.

Inter-American Development Bank, 1300 New York Avenue, NW, Washington, D.C. 20577 (202) 623-1753; *Economic and Social Progress in Latin America*.

Statistical Office of the United Nations, Publishing Service, New York, New York 10017 (800) 253-9646; *Statistical Yearbook*.

Times Books, 201 East 50th Street, New York, New York 10022 (212) 751-2600; *The Economist Book of Vital World Statistics*.

BAHAMAS - BALANCE OF PAYMENTS

The Economist Intelligence Unit, 111 West 57th Street, New York, New York 10019 (800) 938-4685; *The World Market Atlas*.

Federal Statistical Office, Gustav - Stresemann - Ring 11, D-6200 Wiesbaden, Germany; *Bahamas*.

G.K. Hall and Company, 70 Lincoln Street, Boston, Massachusetts 02111 (617) 423-3990; *The World in Figures*.

Inter-American Development Bank, 1300 New York Avenue, NW, Washington, D.C. 20577 (202) 623-1753; *Economic and Social Progress in Latin America.*

International Monetary Fund, 700 Nineteenth Street, NW, Washington, D.C. 20431 (202) 623-7000; *Balance of Payments Yearbook.*

Statistical Office of the United Nations, Publishing Service, New York, New York 10017 (800) 253-9646; *Economic Survey of Latin America and the Caribbean.*

Times Books, 201 East 50th Street, New York, New York 10022 (212) 751-2600; *The Economist Book of Vital World Statistics.*

The World Bank, 1818 H Street, N.W., Washington, D.C. 20433 (202) 477-1234; *World Tables.*

BAHAMAS - BANKING

Facts on File, 460 Park Avenue South, New York, New York 10016 (800) 443-8323; *The New Book of World Rankings.*

G.K. Hall and Company, 70 Lincoln Street, Boston, Massachusetts 02111 (617) 423-3990; *The World in Figures.*

Inter-American Development Bank, 1300 New York Avenue, NW, Washington, D.C. 20577 (202) 623-1753; *Economic and Social Progress in Latin America.*

International Monetary Fund, 700 Nineteenth Street, NW, Washington, D.C. 20431 (202) 623-7000; *Government Finance Statistics Yearbook,* and *International Financial Statistics.*

BAHAMAS - BARLEY PRODUCTION - See BAHAMAS - CROPS

BAHAMAS - BEER PRODUCTION

Facts on File, 460 Park Avenue South, New York, New York 10016 (800) 443-8323; *The New Book of World Rankings.*

BAHAMAS - BIRTH RATE

Facts on File, 460 Park Avenue South, New York, New York 10016 (800) 443-8323; *The New Book of World Rankings.*

Statistical Office of the United Nations, Publishing Service, New York, New York 10017 (800) 253-9646; *Demographic Yearbook,* and *Statistical Yearbook.*

The World Bank, 1818 H Street, N.W., Washington, D.C. 20433 (202) 477-1234; *World Tables.*

World Health Organization, Office of Publications, Avenue Appia, CH-1211 Geneva 27, Switzerland (Telephone Number in U.S. (518) 436-9686); *World Health Statistics Annual.*

BAHAMAS - BONDS

G.K. Hall and Company, 70 Lincoln Street, Boston, Massachusetts 02111 (617) 423-3990; *The World in Figures.*

Inter-American Development Bank, 1300 New York Avenue, NW, Washington, D.C. 20577 (202) 623-1753; *Economic and Social Progress in Latin America.*

International Monetary Fund, 700 Nineteenth Street, NW, Washington, D.C. 20431 (202) 623-7000; *Government Finance Statistics Yearbook.*

BAHAMAS - BOOK PRODUCTION

G.K. Hall and Company, 70 Lincoln Street, Boston, Massachusetts 02111 (617) 423-3990; *The World in Figures.*

BAHAMAS - BROADCASTING

Billboard Limited, P.O. Box 9027, 1006 AA Amsterdam, The Netherlands (Telephone Number in U.S. (212) 764-7300); *World Radio TV Handbook.*

Facts on File, 460 Park Avenue South, New York, New York 10016 (800) 443-8323; *The New Book of World Rankings.*

G.K. Hall and Company, 70 Lincoln Street, Boston, Massachusetts 02111 (617) 423-3990; *The World in Figures.*

Times Books, 201 East 50th Street, New York, New York 10022 (212) 751-2600; *The Economist Book of Vital World Statistics.*

BAHAMAS - BUILDING CONSTRUCTION - See BAHAMAS - CONSTRUCTION INDUSTRY

BAHAMAS - BUSINESS

G.K. Hall and Company, 70 Lincoln Street, Boston, Massachusetts 02111 (617) 423-3990; *The World in Figures.*

Inter-American Development Bank, 1300 New York Avenue, NW, Washington, D.C. 20577 (202) 623-1753; *Economic and Social Progress in Latin America.*

BAHAMAS - BUSINESS AND PROFESSIONAL LICENSES

International Monetary Fund, 700 Nineteenth Street, NW, Washington, D.C. 20431 (202) 623-7000; *Government Finance Statistics Yearbook.*

BAHAMAS - CALORIE SUPPLY

Food and Agricultural Organization of the United Nations (FAO) Via delle Terme di Caracalla, 00100 Rome, Italy (Telephone Number in U.S. (202) 653-2400); *The State of Food and Agriculture.*

BAHAMAS - CAPITAL INVESTMENT

Inter-American Development Bank, 1300 New York Avenue, NW, Washington, D.C. 20577 (202) 623-1753; *Economic and Social Progress in Latin America.*

BAHAMAS - CAPITAL REVENUE

Inter-American Development Bank, 1300 New York Avenue, NW, Washington, D.C. 20577 (202) 623-1753; *Economic and Social Progress in Latin America.*

International Monetary Fund, 700 Nineteenth Street, NW, Washington, D.C. 20431 (202) 623-7000; *Government Finance Statistics Yearbook.*

BAHAMAS - CATTLE - See BAHAMAS - LIVESTOCK AND POULTRY

BAHAMAS - CEMENT PRODUCTION - See BAHAMAS - MINING AND MINERAL PRODUCTS

BAHAMAS - CHEMICAL (ORGANIC) PRODUCTION - See BAHAMAS - MINING AND MINERAL PRODUCTS

BAHAMAS - CIGARETTE PRODUCTION - See BAHAMAS - TOBACCO PRODUCTION

BAHAMAS - CLASS STRUCTURE

G.K. Hall and Company, 70 Lincoln Street, Boston, Massachusetts 02111 (617) 423-3990; *The World in Figures.*

BAHAMAS - CLIMATE

Facts on File, 460 Park Avenue South, New York, New York 10016 (800) 443-8323; *The New Book of World Rankings.*

G.K. Hall and Company, 70 Lincoln Street, Boston, Massachusetts 02111 (617) 423-3990; *The World in Figures.*

BAHAMAS - COAL PRODUCTION - See BAHAMAS - MINING AND MINERAL PRODUCTS

BAHAMAS - COFFEE PRODUCTION - See BAHAMAS - CROPS

BAHAMAS - COMMUNICATIONS

Federal Statistical Office, Gustav - Stresemann - Ring 11, D-6200 Wiesbaden, Germany; *Bahamas.*

G.K. Hall and Company, 70 Lincoln Street, Boston, Massachusetts 02111 (617) 423-3990; *The World in Figures.*

Inter-American Development Bank, 1300 New York Avenue, NW, Washington, D.C. 20577 (202) 623-1753; *Economic and Social Progress in Latin America.*

BAHAMAS - CONSTRUCTION INDUSTRY

Facts on File, 460 Park Avenue South, New York, New York 10016 (800) 443-8323; *The New Book of World Rankings.*

G.K. Hall and Company, 70 Lincoln Street, Boston, Massachusetts 02111 (617) 423-3990; *The World in Figures.*

Inter-American Development Bank, 1300 New York Avenue, NW, Washington, D.C. 20577 (202) 623-1753; *Economic and Social Progress in Latin America.*

Statistical Office of the United Nations, Publishing Service, New York, New York 10017 (800) 253-9646; *Construction Statistics Yearbook,* and *Statistical Yearbook.*

BAHAMAS - CONSUMER PRICE INDEX

Federal Statistical Office, Gustav - Stresemann - Ring 11, D-6200 Wiesbaden, Germany; *Bahamas.*

G.K. Hall and Company, 70 Lincoln Street, Boston, Massachusetts 02111 (617) 423-3990; *The World in Figures.*

Statistical Office of the United Nations, Publishing Service, New York, New York 10017 (800) 253-9646; *Statistical Yearbook.*

BAHAMAS - CONSUMER PRICES

Federal Statistical Office, Gustav - Stresemann - Ring 11, D-6200 Wiesbaden, Germany; *Bahamas.*

International Labour Office, I.L.O. Publications, CH-1211, Geneva 22, Switzerland; *Yearbook of Labour Statistics.*

International Monetary Fund, 700 Nineteenth Street, NW, Washington, D.C. 20431 (202) 623-7000; *International Financial Statistics.*

Times Books, 201 East 50th Street, New York, New York 10022 (212) 751-2600; *The Economist Book of Vital World Statistics.*

BAHAMAS - CONSUMPTION

G.K. Hall and Company, 70 Lincoln Street, Boston, Massachusetts 02111 (617) 423-3990; *The World in Figures.*

Inter-American Development Bank, 1300 New York Avenue, NW, Washington, D.C. 20577 (202) 623-1753; *Economic and Social Progress in Latin America.*

BAHAMAS - COPPER PRODUCTION - See BAHAMAS - MINING AND MINERAL PRODUCTS

BAHAMAS - CORN PRODUCTION - See BAHAMAS - CROPS

BAHAMAS - CORPORATE TAXES - See BAHAMAS - TAXATION

BAHAMAS - COTTON - See BAHAMAS - CROPS

BAHAMAS - CRIME

International Criminal Police Organization (INTERPOL), 26 rue Armengaud, 92210 Saint Cloud, France; *International Crime Statistics.*

BAHAMAS - CROPS

Facts on File, 460 Park Avenue South, New York, New York 10016 (800) 443-8323; *The New Book of World Rankings.*

Food and Agricultural Organization of the United Nations (FAO) Via delle Terme di Caracalla, 00100 Rome, Italy (Telephone Number in U.S. (202) 653-2400); *The State of Food and Agriculture.*

G.K. Hall and Company, 70 Lincoln Street, Boston, Massachusetts 02111 (617) 423-3990; *The World in Figures.*

BAHAMAS - CUSTOMS DUTIES

G.K. Hall and Company, 70 Lincoln Street, Boston, Massachusetts 02111 (617) 423-3990; *The World in Figures.*

Inter-American Development Bank, 1300 New York Avenue, NW, Washington, D.C. 20577 (202) 623-1753; *Economic and Social Progress in Latin America.*

International Monetary Fund, 700 Nineteenth Street, NW, Washington, D.C. 20431 (202) 623-7000; *Government Finance Statistics Yearbook.*

BAHAMAS - DAIRY PRODUCTS

Facts on File, 460 Park Avenue South, New York, New York 10016 (800) 443-8323; *The New Book of World Rankings.*

Food and Agricultural Organization of the United Nations (FAO) Via delle Terme di Caracalla, 00100 Rome, Italy (Telephone Number in U.S. (202) 653-2400); *Production Yearbook,* and *The State of Food and Agriculture.*

BAHAMAS - DEATH RATES

G.K. Hall and Company, 70 Lincoln Street, Boston, Massachusetts 02111 (617) 423-3990; *The World in Figures.*

Statistical Office of the United Nations, Publishing Service, New York, New York 10017 (800) 253-9646; *Statistical Yearbook.*

World Health Organization, Office of Publications, Avenue Appia, CH-1211 Geneva 27, Switzerland (Telephone Number in U.S. (518) 436-9686); *World Health Statistics Annual.*

BAHAMAS - DEFENSE EXPENDITURES

G.K. Hall and Company, 70 Lincoln Street, Boston, Massachusetts 02111 (617) 423-3990; *The World in Figures.*

International Monetary Fund, 700 Nineteenth Street, NW, Washington, D.C. 20431 (202) 623-7000; *Government Finance Statistics Yearbook.*

BAHAMAS - DEMOGRAPHY

The Economist Intelligence Unit, 111 West 57th Street, New York, New York 10019 (800) 938-4685; *The World Market Atlas.*

Facts on File, 460 Park Avenue South, New York, New York 10016 (800) 443-8323; *The New Book of World Rankings.*

Federal Statistical Office, Gustav - Stresemann - Ring 11, D-6200 Wiesbaden, Germany; *Bahamas.*

G.K. Hall and Company, 70 Lincoln Street, Boston, Massachusetts 02111 (617) 423-3990; *The World in Figures.*

BAHAMAS - DEVELOPMENT ASSISTANCE

G.K. Hall and Company, 70 Lincoln Street, Boston, Massachusetts 02111 (617) 423-3990; *The World in Figures.*

Inter-American Development Bank, 1300 New York Avenue, NW, Washington, D.C. 20577 (202) 623-1753; *Economic and Social Progress in Latin America.*

Statistical Office of the United Nations, Publishing Service, New York, New York 10017 (800) 253-9646; *Statistical Yearbook.*

BAHAMAS - DIAMOND PRODUCTION - See BAHAMAS - MINING AND MINERAL PRODUCTS

BAHAMAS - DISCOUNT RATES

Inter-American Development Bank, 1300 New York Avenue, NW, Washington, D.C. 20577 (202) 623-1753; *Economic and Social Progress in Latin America.*

BAHAMAS - DISEASES

G.K. Hall and Company, 70 Lincoln Street, Boston, Massachusetts 02111 (617) 423-3990; *The World in Figures.*

World Health Organization, Office of Publications, Avenue Appia, CH-1211 Geneva 27, Switzerland (Telephone Number in U.S. (518) 436-9686); *World Health Statistics Annual.*

BAHAMAS - DIVORCE RATES

Facts on File, 460 Park Avenue South, New York, New York 10016 (800) 443-8323; *The New Book of World Rankings.*

Statistical Office of the United Nations, Publishing Service, New York, New York 10017 (800) 253-9646; *Demographic Yearbook,* and *Statistical Yearbook.*

BAHAMAS - DOMESTIC PRODUCT

G.K. Hall and Company, 70 Lincoln Street, Boston, Massachusetts 02111 (617) 423-3990; *The World in Figures.*

BAHAMAS - ECONOMY

Facts on File, 460 Park Avenue South, New York, New York 10016 (800) 443-8323; *The New Book of World Rankings.*

Federal Statistical Office, Gustav - Stresemann - Ring 11, D-6200 Wiesbaden, Germany; *Bahamas.*

G.K. Hall and Company, 70 Lincoln Street, Boston, Massachusetts 02111 (617) 423-3990; *The World in Figures.*

Inter-American Development Bank, 1300 New York Avenue, NW, Washington, D.C. 20577 (202) 623-1753; *Economic and Social Progress in Latin America.*

Statistical Office of the United Nations, Publishing Service, New York, New York 10017 (800) 253-9646; *Economic Survey of Latin America and the Caribbean.*

BAHAMAS - EDUCATION

The Economist Intelligence Unit, 111 West 57th Street, New York, New York 10019 (800) 938-4685; *The World Market Atlas.*

Facts on File, 460 Park Avenue South, New York, New York 10016 (800) 443-8323; *The New Book of World Rankings.*

Federal Statistical Office, Gustav - Stresemann - Ring 11,D-6200 Wiesbaden, Germany; *Bahamas.*

G.K. Hall and Company, 70 Lincoln Street, Boston, Massachusetts 02111 (617) 423-3990; *The World in Figures.*

International Monetary Fund, 700 Nineteenth Street, NW, Washington, D.C. 20431 (202) 623-7000; *Government Finance Statistics Yearbook.*

Times Books, 201 East 50th Street, New York, New York 10022 (212) 751-2600; *The Economist Book of Vital World Statistics.*

United Nations Educational, Scientific and Cultural Organization (UNESCO), 7 Place de Fontenoy, F-75700 Paris, France (Telephone Number in U.S. (212) 963-5981); *Statistical Yearbook.*

The World Bank, 1818 H Street, N.W., Washington, D.C. 20433 (202) 477-1234; *World Tables.*

BAHAMAS - EGG PRODUCTION - See BAHAMAS - DAIRY PRODUCTS

BAHAMAS - ELECTRICITY

Facts on File, 460 Park Avenue South, New York, New York 10016 (800) 443-8323; *The New Book of World Rankings.*

Inter-American Development Bank, 1300 New York Avenue, NW, Washington, D.C. 20577 (202) 623-1753; *Economic and Social Progress in Latin America.*

Statistical Office of the United Nations, Publishing Service, New York, New York 10017 (800) 253-9646; *Statistical Yearbook.*

Times Books, 201 East 50th Street, New York, New York 10022 (212) 751-2600; *The Economist Book of Vital World Statistics.*

BAHAMAS - EMPLOYMENT

Facts on File, 460 Park Avenue South, New York, New York 10016 (800) 443-8323; *The New Book of World Rankings.*

Federal Statistical Office, Gustav - Stresemann - Ring 11,D-6200 Wiesbaden, Germany; *Bahamas.*

International Labour Office, I.L.O. Publications, CH-1211, Geneva 22, Switzerland; *Yearbook of Labour Statistics.*

BAHAMAS - ENERGY

Facts on File, 460 Park Avenue South, New York, New York 10016 (800) 443-8323;7X*TheNew Book of World Rankings.*

Food and Agricultural Organization of the United Nations (FAO) Via delle Terme di Caracalla, 00100 Rome, Italy (Telephone Number in U.S. (202) 653-2400); *The State of Food and Agriculture.*

G.K. Hall and Company, 70 Lincoln Street, Boston, Massachusetts 02111 (617) 423-3990; *The World in Figures.*

Statistical Office of the United Nations, Publishing Service, New York, New York 10017 (800) 253-9646; *Energy Statistics Yearbook,* and *Statistical Yearbook.*

BAHAMAS - EXCHANGE RATES

Inter-American Development Bank, 1300 New York Avenue, NW, Washington, D.C. 20577 (202) 623-1753; *Economic and Social Progress in Latin America.*

BAHAMAS - EXCHANGE TAXES

International Monetary Fund, 700 Nineteenth Street, NW, Washington, D.C. 20431 (202) 623-7000; *Government Finance Statistics Yearbook,* and *International Financial Statistics.*

BAHAMAS - EXCISE TAXES - See BAHAMAS - TAXATION

BAHAMAS - EXPORTS

The Economist Intelligence Unit, 111 West 57th Street, New York, New York 10019 (800) 938-4685; *The World Market Atlas.*

Food and Agricultural Organization of the United Nations (FAO) Via delle Terme di Caracalla, 00100 Rome, Italy (Telephone Number in U.S. (202) 653-2400); *The State of Food and Agriculture.*

G.K. Hall and Company, 70 Lincoln Street, Boston, Massachusetts 02111 (617) 423-3990; *The World in Figures.*

Inter-American Development Bank, 1300 New York Avenue, NW, Washington, D.C. 20577 (202) 623-1753; *Economic and Social Progress in Latin America.*

International Monetary Fund, 700 Nineteenth Street, NW, Washington, D.C. 20431 (202) 623-7000; *Direction of Trade Statistics, Government Finance Statistics Yearbook,* and *International Financial Statistics.*

Statistical Office of the United Nations, Publishing Service, New York, New York 10017 (800) 253-9646; *Trade in Manufactures of Developing Countries.*

Times Books, 201 East 50th Street, New York, New York 10022 (212) 751-2600; *The Economist Book of Vital World Statistics.*

The World Bank, 1818 H Street, N.W., Washington, D.C. 20433 (202) 477-1234; *World Tables.*

BAHAMAS - EXTERNAL FINANCING

Inter-American Development Bank, 1300 New York Avenue, NW, Washington, D.C. 20577 (202) 623-1753; *Economic and Social Progress in Latin America.*

BAHAMAS - EXTERNAL INDEBTEDNESS

Inter-American Development Bank, 1300 New York Avenue, NW, Washington, D.C. 20577 (202) 623-1753; *Economic and Social Progress in Latin America.*

The World Bank, 1818 H Street, N.W., Washington, D.C. 20433 (202) 477-1234; *World Tables.*

BAHAMAS - EXTERNAL TRADE

Food and Agricultural Organization of the United Nations (FAO) Via delle Terme di Caracalla, 00100 Rome, Italy (Telephone Number in U.S. (202) 653-2400); *The State of Food and Agriculture,* and *Trade Yearbook.*

G.K. Hall and Company, 70 Lincoln Street, Boston, Massachusetts 02111 (617) 423-3990; *The World in Figures.*

Inter-American Development Bank, 1300 New York Avenue, NW, Washington, D.C. 20577 (202) 623-1753; *Economic and Social Progress in Latin America.*

Statistical Office of the United Nations, Publishing Service, New York, New York 10017 (800) 253-9646; *Statistical Yearbook.*

BAHAMAS - FARM CROPS - See BAHRAIN - CROPS

BAHAMAS - FERTILITY RATES

Facts on File, 460 Park Avenue South, New York, New York 10016 (800) 443-8323; *The New Book of World Rankings.*

The World Bank, 1818 H Street, N.W., Washington, D.C. 20433 (202) 477-1234; *World Tables.*

BAHAMAS - FERTILIZER

Food and Agricultural Organization of the United Nations (FAO) Via delle Terme di Caracalla, 00100 Rome, Italy (Telephone Number in U.S. (202) 653-2400); *The State of Food and Agriculture.*

BAHAMAS - FETAL MORTALITY

Statistical Office of the United Nations, Publishing Service, New York, New York 10017 (800) 253-9646; *Demographic Yearbook.*

World Health Organization, Office of Publications, Avenue Appia, CH-1211 Geneva 27, Switzerland (Telephone Number in U.S. (518) 436-9686); *World Health Statistics Annual.*

BAHAMAS - FINANCE

Facts on File, 460 Park Avenue South, New York, New York 10016 (800) 443-8323; *The New Book of World Rankings.*

Federal Statistical Office, Gustav - Stresemann - Ring 11, D-6200 Wiesbaden, Germany; *Bahamas.*

G.K. Hall and Company, 70 Lincoln Street, Boston, Massachusetts 02111 (617) 423-3990; *The World in Figures.*

Inter-American Development Bank, 1300 New York Avenue, NW, Washington, D.C. 20577 (202) 623-1753; *Economic and Social Progress in Latin America.*

International Monetary Fund, 700 Nineteenth Street, NW, Washington, D.C. 20431 (202) 623-7000; *Government Finance Statistics Yearbook.*

BAHAMAS - FISHERIES

Facts on File, 460 Park Avenue South, New York, New York 10016 (800) 443-8323; *The New Book of World Rankings.*

Federal Statistical Office, Gustav - Stresemann - Ring 11, D-6200 Wiesbaden, Germany; *Bahamas.*

Food and Agricultural Organization of the United Nations (FAO) Via delle Terme di Caracalla, 00100 Rome, Italy (Telephone Number in U.S. (202) 653-2400); *The State of Food and Agriculture,* and *Yearbook of Fishery Statistics.*

Inter-American Development Bank, 1300 New York Avenue, NW, Washington, D.C. 20577 (202) 623-1753; *Economic and Social Progress in Latin America.*

Statistical Office of the United Nations, Publishing Service, New York, New York 10017 (800) 253-9646; *Statistical Yearbook.*

BAHAMAS - FOOD

Food and Agricultural Organization of the United Nations (FAO) Via delle Terme di Caracalla, 00100 Rome, Italy (Telephone Number in U.S. (202) 653-2400); *Production Yearbook,* and *The State of Food and Agriculture.*

G.K. Hall and Company, 70 Lincoln Street, Boston, Massachusetts 02111 (617) 423-3990; *The World in Figures.*

BAHAMAS - FOREIGN AID

G.K. Hall and Company, 70 Lincoln Street, Boston, Massachusetts 02111 (617) 423-3990; *The World in Figures.*

Inter-American Development Bank, 1300 New York Avenue, NW, Washington, D.C. 20577 (202) 623-1753; *Economic and Social Progress in Latin America.*

BAHAMAS - FOREIGN DEBT

Inter-American Development Bank, 1300 New York Avenue, NW, Washington, D.C. 20577 (202) 623-1753; *Economic and Social Progress in Latin America.*

International Monetary Fund, 700 Nineteenth Street, NW, Washington, D.C. 20431 (202) 623-7000; *Government Finance Statistics Yearbook.*

BAHAMAS - FOREIGN FINANCE

Inter-American Development Bank, 1300 New York Avenue, NW, Washington, D.C. 20577 (202) 623-1753; *Economic and Social Progress in Latin America.*

BAHAMAS - FOREIGN INDEBTEDNESS

Inter-American Development Bank, 1300 New York Avenue, NW, Washington, D.C. 20577 (202) 623-1753; *Economic and Social Progress in Latin America.*

Statistical Office of the United Nations, Publishing Service, New York, New York 10017 (800) 253-9646; *Economic Survey of Latin America and the Caribbean.*

BAHAMAS - FOREIGN TRADE

Facts on File, 460 Park Avenue South, New York, New York 10016 (800) 443-8323; *The New Book of World Rankings.*

Federal Statistical Office, Gustav - Stresemann - Ring 11, D-6200 Wiesbaden, Germany; *Bahamas.*

Food and Agricultural Organization of the United Nations (FAO) Via delle Terme di Caracalla, 00100 Rome, Italy (Telephone Number in U.S. (202) 653-2400); *The State of Food and Agriculture.*

G.K. Hall and Company, 70 Lincoln Street, Boston, Massachusetts 02111 (617) 423-3990; *The World in Figures.*

Inter-American Development Bank, 1300 New York Avenue, NW, Washington, D.C. 20577 (202) 623-1753; *Economic and Social Progress in Latin America.*

Organisation for Economic Co-operation and Development (OECD), 2 rue Andre-Pascal, 75 Paris 16, France (Telephone Number in U.S. (212) 963-5981); *Trade by Commodities.*

Statistical Office of the United Nations, Publishing Service, New York, New York 10017 (800) 253-9646; *Economic Survey of Latin America and the Caribbean, International Trade Statistics Yearbook,* and *Statistical Yearbook.*

The World Bank, 1818 H Street, N.W., Washington, D.C. 20433 (202) 477-1234; *World Tables.*

BAHAMAS - FORESTRY AND FOREST PRODUCTS

Facts on File, 460 Park Avenue South, New York, New York 10016 (800) 443-8323; *The New Book of World Rankings.*

Federal Statistical Office, Gustav - Stresemann - Ring 11, D-6200 Wiesbaden, Germany; *Bahamas.*

Food and Agricultural Organization of the United Nations (FAO) Via delle Terme di Caracalla, 00100 Rome, Italy (Telephone Number in U.S. (202) 653-2400); *The State of Food and Agriculture,* and *Yearbook of Forest Products.*

G.K. Hall and Company, 70 Lincoln Street, Boston, Massachusetts 02111 (617) 423-3990; *The World in Figures.*

Inter-American Development Bank, 1300 New York Avenue, NW, Washington, D.C. 20577 (202) 623-1753; *Economic and Social Progress in Latin America.*

Statistical Office of the United Nations, Publishing Service, New York, New York 10017 (800) 253-9646; *Statistical Yearbook.*

United Nations Educational, Scientific and Cultural Organization (UNESCO), 7 Place de Fontenoy, F-75700 Paris, France (Telephone Number in U.S. (212) 963-5981); *Statistical Yearbook.*

BAHAMAS - GAS PRODUCTION - See BAHAMAS - MINING AND MINERAL PRODUCTS

BAHAMAS - GENERAL INDUSTRIAL STATISTICS

Federal Statistical Office, Gustav - Stresemann - Ring 11, D-6200 Wiesbaden, Germany; *Bahamas*.

BAHAMAS - GENERAL MORTALITY

Statistical Office of the United Nations, Publishing Service, New York, New York 10017 (800) 253-9646; *Demographic Yearbook*.

World Health Organization, Office of Publications, Avenue Appia, CH-1211 Geneva 27, Switzerland (Telephone Number in U.S. (518) 436-9686); *World Health Statistics Annual*.

BAHAMAS - GEOGRAPHIC DATA

Facts on File, 460 Park Avenue South, New York, New York 10016 (800) 443-8323; *The New Book of World Rankings*.

Federal Statistical Office, Gustav - Stresemann - Ring 11, D-6200 Wiesbaden, Germany; *Bahamas*.

BAHAMAS - GOLD HOLDINGS

International Monetary Fund, 700 Nineteenth Street, NW, Washington, D.C. 20431 (202) 623-7000; *International Financial Statistics*.

Statistical Office of the United Nations, Publishing Service, New York, New York 10017 (800) 253-9646; *Statistical Yearbook*.

The World Bank, 1818 H Street, N.W., Washington, D.C. 20433 (202) 477-1234; *World Tables*.

BAHAMAS - GOLD PRODUCTION AND CONSUMPTION - See BAHAMAS - MINING AND MINERAL PRODUCTS

BAHAMAS - GOVERNMENT

G.K. Hall and Company, 70 Lincoln Street, Boston, Massachusetts 02111 (617) 423-3990; *The World in Figures*.

Inter-American Development Bank, 1300 New York Avenue, NW, Washington, D.C. 20577 (202) 623-1753; *Economic and Social Progress in Latin America*.

BAHAMAS - GOVERNMENT BONDS - See BAHAMAS - BONDS

BAHAMAS - GOVERNMENT CONSUMPTION

Inter-American Development Bank, 1300 New York Avenue, NW, Washington, D.C. 20577 (202) 623-1753; *Economic and Social Progress in Latin America*.

BAHAMAS - GOVERNMENT EXPENDITURES

Inter-American Development Bank, 1300 New York Avenue, NW, Washington, D.C. 20577 (202) 623-1753; *Economic and Social Progress in Latin America*.

International Monetary Fund, 700 Nineteenth Street, NW, Washington, D.C. 20431 (202) 623-7000; *Government Finance Statistics Yearbook*.

Times Books, 201 East 50th Street, New York, New York 10022 (212) 751-2600; *The Economist Book of Vital World Statistics*.

The World Bank, 1818 H Street, N.W., Washington, D.C. 20433 (202) 477-1234; *World Tables*.

BAHAMAS - GOVERNMENT FINANCE

Inter-American Development Bank, 1300 New York Avenue, NW, Washington, D.C. 20577 (202) 623-1753; *Economic and Social Progress in Latin America*.

International Monetary Fund, 700 Nineteenth Street, NW, Washington, D.C. 20431 (202) 623-7000; *International Financial Statistics*.

BAHAMAS - GOVERNMENT REVENUE

Inter-American Development Bank, 1300 New York Avenue, NW, Washington, D.C. 20577 (202) 623-1753; *Economic and Social Progress in Latin America*.

International Monetary Fund, 700 Nineteenth Street, NW, Washington, D.C. 20431 (202) 623-7000; *Government Finance Statistics Yearbook*.

Times Books, 201 East 50th Street, New York, New York 10022 (212) 751-2600; *The Economist Book of Vital World Statistics*.

The World Bank, 1818 H Street, N.W., Washington, D.C. 20433 (202) 477-1234; *World Tables*.

BAHAMAS - GRAIN PRODUCTION - See BAHAMAS - CROPS

BAHAMAS - GRANTS

International Monetary Fund, 700 Nineteenth Street, NW, Washington, D.C. 20431 (202) 623-7000; *Government Finance Statistics Yearbook*.

BAHAMAS - GROSS DOMESTIC PRODUCT

The Economist Intelligence Unit, 111 West 57th Street, New York, New York 10019 (800) 938-4685; *The World Market Atlas*.

Facts on File, 460 Park Avenue South, New York, New York 10016 (800) 443-8323; *The New Book of World Rankings*.

G.K. Hall and Company, 70 Lincoln Street, Boston, Massachusetts 02111 (617) 423-3990; *The World in Figures*.

Inter-American Development Bank, 1300 New York Avenue, NW, Washington, D.C. 20577 (202) 623-1753; *Economic and Social Progress in Latin America*.

Times Books, 201 East 50th Street, New York, New York 10022 (212) 751-2600; *The Economist Book of Vital World Statistics*.

The World Bank, 1818 H Street, N.W., Washington, D.C. 20433 (202) 477-1234; *World Tables*.

BAHAMAS - GROSS NATIONAL PRODUCT

Inter-American Development Bank, 1300 New York Avenue, NW, Washington, D.C. 20577 (202) 623-1753; *Economic and Social Progress in Latin America*.

The World Bank, 1818 H Street, N.W., Washington, D.C. 20433 (202) 477-1234; *World Tables*.

BAHAMAS - HEALTH

Facts on File, 460 Park Avenue South, New York, New York 10016 (800) 443-8323; *The New Book of World Rankings.*

Federal Statistical Office, Gustav - Stresemann - Ring 11, D-6200 Wiesbaden, Germany; *Bahamas.*

G.K. Hall and Company, 70 Lincoln Street, Boston, Massachusetts 02111 (617) 423-3990; *The World in Figures.*

Statistical Office of the United Nations, Publishing Service, New York, New York 10017 (800) 253-9646; *Statistical Yearbook.*

Times Books, 201 East 50th Street, New York, New York 10022 (212) 751-2600; *The Economist Book of Vital World Statistics.*

World Health Organization, Office of Publications, Avenue Appia, CH-1211 Geneva 27, Switzerland (Telephone Number in U.S. (518) 436-9686); *World Health Statistics Annual.*

BAHAMAS - HEALTH EXPENDITURES

International Monetary Fund, 700 Nineteenth Street, NW, Washington, D.C. 20431 (202) 623-7000; *Government Finance Statistics Yearbook.*

BAHAMAS - HIDE PRODUCTION

Food and Agricultural Organization of the United Nations (FAO), Via delle Terme di Caracalla, 00100 Rome, Italy (Telephone Number in U.S. (202) 653-2400); *Production Yearbook.*

BAHAMAS - HIGHWAYS

G.K. Hall and Company, 70 Lincoln Street, Boston, Massachusetts 02111 (617) 423-3990; *The World in Figures.*

BAHAMAS - HORSES - See BAHAMAS - LIVESTOCK AND POULTRY

BAHAMAS - HOURS OF WORK - See BAHAMAS - EMPLOYMENT

BAHAMAS - HOUSING EXPENDITURES

Facts on File, 460 Park Avenue South, New York, New York 10016 (800) 443-8323; *The New Book of World Rankings.*

International Monetary Fund, 700 Nineteenth Street, NW, Washington, D.C. 20431 (202) 623-7000; *Government Finance Statistics Yearbook.*

BAHAMAS - ILLITERATE POPULATION

The Economist Intelligence Unit, 111 West 57th Street, New York, New York 10019 (800) 938-4685; *The World Market Atlas.*

G.K. Hall and Company, 70 Lincoln Street, Boston, Massachusetts 02111 (617) 423-3990; *The World in Figures.*

United Nations Educational, Scientific and Cultural Organization (UNESCO), 7 Place de Fontenoy, F-75700 Paris, France (Telephone Number in U.S. (212) 963-5981); *Statistical Yearbook.*

BAHAMAS - IMPORTS

The Economist Intelligence Unit, 111 West 57th Street, New York, New York 10019 (800) 938-4685; *The World Market Atlas.*

Food and Agricultural Organization of the United Nations (FAO) Via delle Terme di Caracalla, 00100 Rome, Italy (Telephone Number in U.S. (202) 653-2400); *The State of Food and Agriculture.*

G.K. Hall and Company, 70 Lincoln Street, Boston, Massachusetts 02111 (617) 423-3990; *The World in Figures.*

Inter-American Development Bank, 1300 New York Avenue, NW, Washington, D.C. 20577 (202) 623-1753; *Economic and Social Progress in Latin America.*

International Monetary Fund, 700 Nineteenth Street, NW, Washington, D.C. 20431 (202) 623-7000; *Direction of Trade Statistics,* and *International Financial Statistics.*

Times Books, 201 East 50th Street, New York, New York 10022 (212) 751-2600; *The Economist Book of Vital World Statistics.*

The World Bank, 1818 H Street, N.W., Washington, D.C. 20433 (202) 477-1234; *World Tables.*

BAHAMAS - INCOME TAXES - See BAHAMAS - TAXATION

BAHAMAS - INDUSTRY

Facts on File, 460 Park Avenue South, New York, New York 10016 (800) 443-8323; *The New Book of World Rankings.*

Federal Statistical Office, Gustav - Stresemann - Ring 11 D-6200 Wiesbaden, Germany; *Bahamas.*

G.K. Hall and Company, 70 Lincoln Street, Boston, Massachusetts 02111 (617) 423-3990; *The World in Figures.*

International Labour Office, I.L.O. Publications, CH-1211, Geneva 22, Switzerland; *Yearbook of Labour Statistics.*

Statistical Office of the United Nations, Publishing Service, New York, New York 10017 (800) 253-9646; *Economic Survey of Latin America and the Caribbean.*

The World Bank, 1818 H Street, N.W., Washington, D.C. 20433 (202) 477-1234; *World Tables.*

BAHAMAS - INFANT AND MATERNAL MORTALITY

Statistical Office of the United Nations, Publishing Service, New York, New York 10017 (800) 253-9646; *Demographic Yearbook,* and *Statistical Yearbook.*

The World Bank, 1818 H Street, N.W., Washington, D.C. 20433 (202) 477-1234; *World Tables.*

World Health Organization, Office of Publications, Avenue Appia, CH-1211 Geneva 27, Switzerland (Telephone Number in U.S. (518) 436-9686); *World Health Statistics Annual.*

BAHAMAS - INFLATIONARY FACTORS

Statistical Office of the United Nations, Publishing Service, New York, New York 10017 (800) 253-9646; *Economic Survey of Latin America and the Caribbean.*

BAHAMAS - INTEREST RATES

Inter-American Development Bank, 1300 New York Avenue, NW, Washington, D.C. 20577 (202) 623-1753; *Economic and Social Progress in Latin America.*

BAHAMAS - INTERNATIONAL FINANCE

Inter-American Development Bank, 1300 New York Avenue, NW, Washington, D.C. 20577 (202) 623-1753; *Economic and Social Progress in Latin America.*

BAHAMAS - INTERNATIONAL LIQUIDITY

Inter-American Development Bank, 1300 New York Avenue, NW, Washington, D.C. 20577 (202) 623-1753; *Economic and Social Progress in Latin America.*

International Monetary Fund, 700 Nineteenth Street, NW, Washington, D.C. 20431 (202) 623-7000; *International Financial Statistics.*

BAHAMAS - INTERNATIONAL RESERVES EXCLUDING GOLD

Inter-American Development Bank, 1300 New York Avenue, NW, Washington, D.C. 20577 (202) 623-1753; *Economic and Social Progress in Latin America.*

The World Bank, 1818 H Street, N.W., Washington, D.C. 20433 (202) 477-1234; *World Tables.*

BAHAMAS - INTERNATIONAL STATISTICS

Inter-American Development Bank, 1300 New York Avenue, NW, Washington, D.C. 20577 (202) 623-1753; *Economic and Social Progress in Latin America.*

BAHAMAS - INVESTMENTS

Inter-American Development Bank, 1300 New York Avenue, NW, Washington, D.C. 20577 (202) 623-1753; *Economic and Social Progress in Latin America.*

BAHAMAS - IRRIGATION

Inter-American Development Bank, 1300 New York Avenue, NW, Washington, D.C. 20577 (202) 623-1753; *Economic and Social Progress in Latin America.*

BAHAMAS - IRON ORE PRODUCTION AND CONSUMPTION - See BAHAMAS - MINING AND MINERAL PRODUCTS

BAHAMAS - LABOR FORCE

Facts on File, 460 Park Avenue South, New York, New York 10016 (800) 443-8323; *The New Book of World Rankings.*

Food and Agricultural Organization of the United Nations (FAO) Via delle Terme di Caracalla, 00100 Rome, Italy (Telephone Number in U.S. (202) 653-2400); *The State of Food and Agriculture.*

G.K. Hall and Company, 70 Lincoln Street, Boston, Massachusetts 02111 (617) 423-3990; *The World in Figures.*

Times Books, 201 East 50th Street, New York, New York 10022 (212) 751-2600; *The Economist Book of Vital World Statistics.*

The World Bank, 1818 H Street, N.W., Washington, D.C. 20433 (202) 477-1234; *World Tables.*

BAHAMAS - LABOR PRODUCTIVITY

International Labour Office, I.L.O. Publications, CH-1211, Geneva 22, Switzerland; *Yearbook of Labour Statistics.*

BAHAMAS - LAND USE

Food and Agricultural Organization of the United Nations (FAO), Via delle Terme di Caracalla, 00100 Rome, Italy (Telephone Number in U.S. (202) 653-2400); *Production Yearbook.*

G.K. Hall and Company, 70 Lincoln Street, Boston, Massachusetts 02111 (617) 423-3990; *The World in Figures.*

Inter-American Development Bank, 1300 New York Avenue, NW, Washington, D.C. 20577 (202) 623-1753; *Economic and Social Progress in Latin America.*

BAHAMAS - LIBRARIES

Facts on File, 460 Park Avenue South, New York, New York 10016 (800) 443-8323; *The New Book of World Rankings.*

United Nations Educational, Scientific and Cultural Organization (UNESCO), 7 Place de Fontenoy, F-75700 Paris, France (Telephone Number in U.S. (212) 963-5981); *Statistical Yearbook.*

BAHAMAS - LIVESTOCK AND POULTRY

Facts on File, 460 Park Avenue South, New York, New York 10016 (800) 443-8323; *The New Book of World Rankings.*

Food and Agricultural Organization of the United Nations (FAO), Via delle Terme di Caracalla, 00100 Rome, Italy (Telephone Number in U.S. (202) 653-2400); *Production Yearbook,* and *The State of Food and Agriculture.*

G.K. Hall and Company, 70 Lincoln Street, Boston, Massachusetts 02111 (617) 423-3990; *The World in Figures.*

Statistical Office of the United Nations, Publishing Service, New York, New York 10017 (800) 253-9646; *Statistical Yearbook.*

BAHAMAS - LIVING LEVELS

G.K. Hall and Company, 70 Lincoln Street, Boston, Massachusetts 02111 (617) 423-3990; *The World in Figures.*

BAHAMAS - MAIL - NUMBER OF PIECES SENT OR RECEIVED

Statistical Office of the United Nations, Publishing Service, New York, New York 10017 (800) 253-9646; *Statistical Yearbook.*

BAHAMAS - MAIN ECONOMIC INDICATORS - See BAHAMAS - ECONOMY

BAHAMAS - MANUFACTURING

Facts on File, 460 Park Avenue South, New York, New York 10016 (800) 443-8323; *The New Book of World Rankings.*

G.K. Hall and Company, 70 Lincoln Street, Boston, Massachusetts 02111 (617) 423-3990; *The World in Figures.*

Inter-American Development Bank, 1300 New York Avenue, NW, Washington, D.C. 20577 (202) 623-1753; *Economic and Social Progress in Latin America.*

Statistical Office of the United Nations, Publishing Service, New York, New York 10017 (800) 253-9646; *Statistical Yearbook.*

Times Books, 201 East 50th Street, New York, New York 10022 (212) 751-2600; *The Economist Book of Vital World Statistics.*

The World Bank, 1818 H Street, N.W., Washington, D.C. 20433 (202) 477-1234; *World Tables.*

BAHAMAS - MARRIAGE RATES

Facts on File, 460 Park Avenue South, New York, New York 10016 (800) 443-8323; *The New Book of World Rankings.*

Statistical Office of the United Nations, Publishing Service, New York, New York 10017 (800) 253-9646; *Demographic Yearbook,* and *Statistical Yearbook.*

BAHAMAS - MEAT PRODUCTION - See BAHAMAS - LIVESTOCK AND POULTRY

BAHAMAS - MERCHANT SHIPPING

G.K. Hall and Company, 70 Lincoln Street, Boston, Massachusetts 02111 (617) 423-3990; *The World in Figures.*

Lloyd's Register of Shipping, 17 Battery Place, New York, New York 10004 (212) 425-8050; *Register of Ships.*

Statistical Office of the United Nations, Publishing Service, New York, New York 10017 (800) 253-9646; *Statistical Yearbook.*

Times Books, 201 East 50th Street, New York, New York 10022 (212) 751-2600; *The Economist Book of Vital World Statistics.*

BAHAMAS - MILITARY

G.K. Hall and Company, 70 Lincoln Street, Boston, Massachusetts 02111 (617) 423-3990; *The World in Figures.*

The International Institute for Strategic Studies, 23 Tavistock Street, London WC2E 7NQ, England; *The Military Balance.*

BAHAMAS - MILK PRODUCTION - See BAHAMAS - DAIRY PRODUCTS

BAHAMAS - MINING AND MINERAL PRODUCTS

Facts on File, 460 Park Avenue South, New York, New York 10016 (800) 443-8323; *The New Book of World Rankings.*

G.K. Hall and Company, 70 Lincoln Street, Boston, Massachusetts 02111 (617) 423-3990; *The World in Figures.*

Inter-American Development Bank, 1300 New York Avenue, NW, Washington, D.C. 20577 (202) 623-1753; *Economic and Social Progress in Latin America.*

Statistical Office of the United Nations, Publishing Service, New York, New York 10017 (800) 253-9646; *Statistical Yearbook.*

BAHAMAS - MONEY EXCHANGE RATE

Inter-American Development Bank, 1300 New York Avenue, NW, Washington, D.C. 20577 (202) 623-1753; *Economic and Social Progress in Latin America.*

International Monetary Fund, 700 Nineteenth Street, NW, Washington, D.C. 20431 (202) 623-7000; *International Financial Statistics.*

Statistical Office of the United Nations, Publishing Service, New York, New York 10017 (800) 253-9646; *Statistical Yearbook.*

BAHAMAS - MONEY MARKET RATES

Inter-American Development Bank, 1300 New York Avenue, NW, Washington, D.C. 20577 (202) 623-1753; *Economic and Social Progress in Latin America.*

Statistical Office of the United Nations, Publishing Service, New York, New York 10017 (800) 253-9646; *Statistical Yearbook.*

BAHAMAS - MONEY RESERVES

Inter-American Development Bank, 1300 New York Avenue, NW, Washington, D.C. 20577 (202) 623-1753; *Economic and Social Progress in Latin America.*

BAHAMAS - MONEY SUPPLY

Federal Statistical Office, Gustav - Stresemann - Ring 11, D-6200 Wiesbaden, Germany; *Bahamas.*

G.K. Hall and Company, 70 Lincoln Street, Boston, Massachusetts 02111 (617) 423-3990; *The World in Figures.*

Inter-American Development Bank, 1300 New York Avenue, NW, Washington, D.C. 20577 (202) 623-1753; *Economic and Social Progress in Latin America.*

International Monetary Fund, 700 Nineteenth Street, NW, Washington, D.C. 20431 (202) 623-7000; *International Financial Statistics.*

Statistical Office of the United Nations, Publishing Service, New York, New York 10017 (800) 253-9646; *Statistical Yearbook.*

The World Bank, 1818 H Street, N.W., Washington, D.C. 20433 (202) 477-1234; *World Tables.*

BAHAMAS - MOTOR VEHICLE TAXES - See BAHAMAS - TAXATION

BAHAMAS - MOTOR VEHICLES IN USE

G.K. Hall and Company, 70 Lincoln Street, Boston, Massachusetts 02111 (617) 423-3990; *The World in Figures.*

Statistical Office of the United Nations, Publishing Service, New York, New York 10017 (800) 253-9646; *Statistical Yearbook.*

Times Books, 201 East 50th Street, New York, New York 10022 (212) 751-2600; *The Economist Book of Vital World Statistics.*

BAHAMAS - MUSEUMS

Facts on File, 460 Park Avenue South, New York, New York 10016 (800) 443-8323; *The New Book of World Rankings.*

United Nations Educational, Scientific and Cultural Organization (UNESCO), 7 Place de Fontenoy, F-75700 Paris, France (Telephone Number in U.S. (212) 963-5981); *Statistical Yearbook.*

BAHAMAS - NATALITY - See BAHAMAS - BIRTH RATE

BAHAMAS - NATIONAL ACCOUNTS

Federal Statistical Office, Gustav - Stresemann - Ring 11, D-6200 Wiesbaden, Germany; *Bahamas.*

Inter-American Development Bank, 1300 New York Avenue, NW, Washington, D.C. 20577 (202) 623-1753; *Economic and Social Progress in Latin America.*

BAHAMAS - NATIONAL DISPOSABLE INCOME

Inter-American Development Bank, 1300 New York Avenue, NW, Washington, D.C. 20577 (202) 623-1753; *Economic and Social Progress in Latin America.*

BAHAMAS - NATIONAL INCOME

Facts on File, 460 Park Avenue South, New York, New York 10016 (800) 443-8323; *The New Book of World Rankings.*

G.K. Hall and Company, 70 Lincoln Street, Boston, Massachusetts 02111 (617) 423-3990; *The World in Figures.*

Inter-American Development Bank, 1300 New York Avenue, NW, Washington, D.C. 20577 (202) 623-1753; *Economic and Social Progress in Latin America.*

BAHAMAS - NATIONAL PRODUCT

Facts on File, 460 Park Avenue South, New York, New York 10016 (800) 443-8323; *The New Book of World Rankings.*

BAHAMAS - NATURAL GAS PRODUCTION - See BAHAMAS - MINING AND MINERAL PRODUCTS

BAHAMAS - NEWSPAPER PRODUCTION - See BAHAMAS - FORESTRY AND FOREST PRODUCTS

BAHAMAS - NEWSPRINT - See BAHAMAS - FORESTRY AND FOREST PRODUCTS

BAHAMAS - OCCUPATIONS - See BAHAMAS - LABOR FORCE

BAHAMAS - PAPER - See BAHAMAS - FORESTRY AND FOREST PRODUCTS

BAHAMAS - PATENTS

Statistical Office of the United Nations, Publishing Service, New York, New York 10017 (800) 253-9646; *Statistical Yearbook.*

BAHAMAS - PEANUT PRODUCTION - See BAHAMAS - CROPS

BAHAMAS - PESTICIDE USE

Food and Agricultural Organization of the United Nations (FAO) Via delle Terme di Caracalla, 00100 Rome, Italy (Telephone Number in U.S. (202) 653-2400); *The State of Food and Agriculture.*

BAHAMAS - PETROLEUM INDUSTRY

Facts on File, 460 Park Avenue South, New York, New York 10016 (800) 443-8323; *The New Book of World Rankings.*

Food and Agricultural Organization of the United Nations (FAO) Via delle Terme di Caracalla, 00100 Rome, Italy (Telephone Number in U.S. (202) 653-2400); *The State of Food and Agriculture.*

G.K. Hall and Company, 70 Lincoln Street, Boston, Massachusetts 02111 (617) 423-3990; *The World in Figures.*

Inter-American Development Bank, 1300 New York Avenue, NW, Washington, D.C. 20577 (202) 623-1753; *Economic and Social Progress in Latin America.*

Statistical Office of the United Nations, Publishing Service, New York, New York 10017 (800) 253-9646; *Statistical Yearbook.*

BAHAMAS - PIGS - See BAHAMAS - LIVESTOCK AND POULTRY

BAHAMAS - POPULATION

The Economist Intelligence Unit, 111 West 57th Street, New York, New York 10019 (800) 938-4685; *The World Market Atlas.*

Facts on File, 460 Park Avenue South, New York, New York 10016 (800) 443-8323; *The New Book of World Rankings.*

Federal Statistical Office, Gustav - Stresemann - Ring 11, D-6200 Wiesbaden, Germany; *Bahamas.*

Food and Agricultural Organization of the United Nations (FAO), Via delle Terme di Caracalla, 00100 Rome, Italy (Telephone Number in U.S. (202) 653-2400); *Production Yearbook.*

G.K. Hall and Company, 70 Lincoln Street, Boston, Massachusetts 02111 (617) 423-3990; *The World in Figures.*

Inter-American Development Bank, 1300 New York Avenue, NW, Washington, D.C. 20577 (202) 623-1753; *Economic and Social Progress in Latin America.*

International Labour Office, I.L.O. Publications, CH-1211, Geneva 22, Switzerland; *Yearbook of Labour Statistics.*

Statistical Office of the United Nations, Publishing Service, New York, New York 10017 (800) 253-9646; *Demographic Yearbook,* and *Statistical Yearbook.*

Times Books, 201 East 50th Street, New York, New York 10022 (212) 751-2600; *The Economist Book of Vital World Statistics.*

United Nations Educational, Scientific and Cultural Organization (UNESCO), 7 Place de Fontenoy, F-75700 Paris, France (Telephone Number in U.S. (212) 963-5981); *Statistical Yearbook.*

World Health Organization, Office of Publications, Avenue Appia, CH-1211 Geneva 27, Switzerland (Telephone Number in U.S. (518) 436-9686); *World Health Statistics Annual.*

BAHAMAS - POST OFFICES

Facts on File, 460 Park Avenue South, New York, New York 10016 (800) 443-8323; *The New Book of World Rankings.*

BAHAMAS - POTATO PRODUCTION - See BAHAMAS - CROPS

BAHAMAS - PRICES

Facts on File, 460 Park Avenue South, New York, New York 10016 (800) 443-8323; *The New Book of World Rankings.*

Federal Statistical Office, Gustav - Stresemann - Ring 11, D-6200 Wiesbaden, Germany; *Bahamas.*

Food and Agricultural Organization of the United Nations (FAO), Via delle Terme di Caracalla, 00100 Rome, Italy (Telephone Number in U.S. (202) 653-2400); *Production Yearbook,* and *The State of Food and Agriculture.*

G.K. Hall and Company, 70 Lincoln Street, Boston, Massachusetts 02111 (617) 423-3990; *The World in Figures.*

International Labour Office, I.L.O. Publications, CH-1211, Geneva 22, Switzerland; *Yearbook of Labour Statistics.*

International Monetary Fund, 700 Nineteenth Street, NW, Washington, D.C. 20431 (202) 623-7000; *International Financial Statistics.*

Statistical Office of the United Nations, Publishing Service, New York, New York 10017 (800) 253-9646; *Economic Survey of Latin America and the Caribbean.*

BAHAMAS - PRINTING AND WRITING PAPER - See BAHAMAS - FORESTRY AND FOREST PRODUCTS

BAHAMAS - PRODUCTION

Facts on File, 460 Park Avenue South, New York, New York 10016 (800) 443-8323; *The New Book of World Rankings.*

G.K. Hall and Company, 70 Lincoln Street, Boston, Massachusetts 02111 (617) 423-3990; *The World in Figures.*

BAHAMAS - PROPERTY TAXES - See BAHAMAS - TAXATION

BAHAMAS - PUBLIC CONSUMPTION FUND

Inter-American Development Bank, 1300 New York Avenue, NW, Washington, D.C. 20577 (202) 623-1753; *Economic and Social Progress in Latin America.*

BAHAMAS - PUBLIC EXPENDITURES

Inter-American Development Bank, 1300 New York Avenue, NW, Washington, D.C. 20577 (202) 623-1753; *Economic and Social Progress in Latin America.*

BAHAMAS - PUBLIC FINANCE

Facts on File, 460 Park Avenue South, New York, New York 10016 (800) 443-8323; *The New Book of World Rankings.*

Federal Statistical Office, Gustav - Stresemann - Ring 11, D-6200 Wiesbaden, Germany; *Bahamas.*

Inter-American Development Bank, 1300 New York Avenue, NW, Washington, D.C. 20577 (202) 623-1753; *Economic and Social Progress in Latin America.*

BAHAMAS - PUBLIC REVENUES

Inter-American Development Bank, 1300 New York Avenue, NW, Washington, D.C. 20577 (202) 623-1753; *Economic and Social Progress in Latin America.*

BAHAMAS - RADIO BROADCASTING - See BAHAMAS - BROADCASTING

BAHAMAS - RAILWAYS

G.K. Hall and Company, 70 Lincoln Street, Boston, Massachusetts 02111 (617) 423-3990; *The World in Figures.*

BAHAMAS - RELIGION

Facts on File, 460 Park Avenue South, New York, New York 10016 (800) 443-8323; *The New Book of World Rankings.*

BAHAMAS - RENT PRICES

International Labour Office, I.L.O. Publications, CH-1211, Geneva 22, Switzerland; *Yearbook of Labour Statistics.*

BAHAMAS - RETAIL TRADE

G.K. Hall and Company, 70 Lincoln Street, Boston, Massachusetts 02111 (617) 423-3990; *The World in Figures.*

Inter-American Development Bank, 1300 New York Avenue, NW, Washington, D.C. 20577 (202) 623-1753; *Economic and Social Progress in Latin America.*

BAHAMAS - RICE PRODUCTION - See BAHAMAS - CROPS

BAHAMAS - ROUNDWOOD PRODUCTION - See BAHAMAS - FORESTRY AND FOREST PRODUCTS

BAHAMAS - RUBBER PRODUCTION

Facts on File, 460 Park Avenue South, New York, New York 10016 (800) 443-8323; *The New Book of World Rankings.*

BAHAMAS - SALT PRODUCTION - See BAHAMAS - MINING AND MINERAL PRODUCTS

BAHAMAS - SAWNWOOD PRODUCTION - See BAHAMAS - FORESTRY AND FOREST PRODUCTS

BAHAMAS - SCIENCE AND TECHNOLOGY - EXPENDITURE FOR RESEARCH

Statistical Office of the United Nations, Publishing Service, New York, New York 10017 (800) 253-9646; *Statistical Yearbook.*

BAHAMAS - SCIENTISTS AND TECHNICIANS

Statistical Office of the United Nations, Publishing Service, New York, New York 10017 (800) 253-9646; *Statistical Yearbook.*

United Nations Educational, Scientific and Cultural Organization (UNESCO), 7 Place de Fontenoy, F-75700 Paris, France (Telephone Number in U.S. (212) 963-5981); *Statistical Yearbook.*

BAHAMAS - SENIOR CITIZENS

Facts on File, 460 Park Avenue South, New York, New York 10016 (800) 443-8323; *The New Book of World Rankings.*

BAHAMAS - SHEEP - See BAHAMAS - LIVESTOCK AND POULTRY

BAHAMAS - SILVER PRODUCTION AND CONSUMPTION - See BAHAMAS - MINING AND MINERAL PRODUCTS

BAHAMAS - SOCIAL DATA

Facts on File, 460 Park Avenue South, New York, New York 10016 (800) 443-8323; *The New Book of World Rankings.*

G.K. Hall and Company, 70 Lincoln Street, Boston, Massachusetts 02111 (617) 423-3990; *The World in Figures.*

BAHAMAS - SOCIAL SECURITY

Inter-American Development Bank, 1300 New York Avenue, NW, Washington, D.C. 20577 (202) 623-1753; *Economic and Social Progress in Latin America.*

International Monetary Fund, 700 Nineteenth Street, NW, Washington, D.C. 20431 (202) 623-7000; *Government Finance Statistics Yearbook.*

BAHAMAS - SOCIOECONOMIC DATA

Inter-American Development Bank, 1300 New York Avenue, NW, Washington, D.C. 20577 (202) 623-1753; *Economic and Social Progress in Latin America.*

BAHAMAS - STAMP TAXES AND DUTIES - See BAHAMAS - TAXATION

BAHAMAS - STATE BUDGET REVENUE AND EXPENDITURES

Inter-American Development Bank, 1300 New York Avenue, NW, Washington, D.C. 20577 (202) 623-1753; *Economic and Social Progress in Latin America.*

BAHAMAS - STEEL PRODUCTION AND CONSUMPTION - See BAHAMAS - MINING AND MINERAL PRODUCTS

BAHAMAS - STOCKS - COMMODITY - MARKET PRICE - INDEX

Food and Agricultural Organization of the United Nations (FAO) Via delle Terme di Caracalla, 00100 Rome, Italy (Telephone Number in U.S. (202) 653-2400); *The State of Food and Agriculture.*

BAHAMAS - SUGAR PRODUCTION - See BAHAMAS - CROPS

BAHAMAS - TAXATION

G.K. Hall and Company, 70 Lincoln Street, Boston, Massachusetts 02111 (617) 423-3990; *The World in Figures.*

Inter-American Development Bank, 1300 New York Avenue, NW, Washington, D.C. 20577 (202) 623-1753; *Economic and Social Progress in Latin America.*

International Monetary Fund, 700 Nineteenth Street, NW, Washington, D.C. 20431 (202) 623-7000; *Government Finance Statistics Yearbook.*

The World Bank, 1818 H Street, N.W., Washington, D.C. 20433 (202) 477-1234; *World Tables.*

BAHAMAS - TELEPHONES IN USE

American Telephone and Telegraph Company, 26 Parsippany Road, Whippany, New Jersey 07981 (800) 338-4038; *The World's Telephones.*

G.K. Hall and Company, 70 Lincoln Street, Boston, Massachusetts 02111 (617) 423-3990; *The World in Figures.*

Statistical Office of the United Nations, Publishing Service, New York, New York 10017 (800) 253-9646; *Statistical Yearbook.*

BAHAMAS - TELEVISION BROADCASTING - See BAHAMAS - BROADCASTING

BAHAMAS - TEXTILE INDUSTRY

G.K. Hall and Company, 70 Lincoln Street, Boston, Massachusetts 02111 (617) 423-3990; *The World in Figures.*

BAHAMAS - TOBACCO PRODUCTION

Facts on File, 460 Park Avenue South, New York, New York 10016 (800) 443-8323; *The New Book of World Rankings.*

BAHAMAS - TOURISM

Facts on File, 460 Park Avenue South, New York, New York 10016 (800) 443-8323; *The New Book of World Rankings.*

Federal Statistical Office, Gustav - Stresemann - Ring 11, D-6200 Wiesbaden, Germany; *Bahamas.*

G.K. Hall and Company, 70 Lincoln Street, Boston, Massachusetts 02111 (617) 423-3990; *The World in Figures.*

Statistical Office of the United Nations, Publishing Service, New York, New York 10017 (800) 253-9646; *Statistical Yearbook.*

Times Books, 201 East 50th Street, New York, New York 10022 (212) 751-2600; *The Economist Book of Vital World Statistics.*

World Tourism Organization, Calle Capitan Haya 42, E-28020 Madrid, Spain; *Yearbook of Tourism Statistics.*

BAHAMAS - TRADE - See BAHAMAS - FOREIGN TRADE

BAHAMAS - TRADEMARKS AND SERVICE MARKS

Statistical Office of the United Nations, Publishing Service, New York, New York 10017 (800) 253-9646; *Statistical Yearbook.*

BAHAMAS - TRANSPORTATION AND COMMUNICATIONS

Facts on File, 460 Park Avenue South, New York, New York 10016 (800) 443-8323; *The New Book of World Rankings.*

Federal Statistical Office, Gustav - Stresemann - Ring 11, D-6200 Wiesbaden, Germany; *Bahamas.*

G.K. Hall and Company, 70 Lincoln Street, Boston, Massachusetts 02111 (617) 423-3990; *The World in Figures.*

Inter-American Development Bank, 1300 New York Avenue, NW, Washington, D.C. 20577 (202) 623-1753; *Economic and Social Progress in Latin America.*

BAHAMAS - TRAVEL FARES ABROAD

International Monetary Fund, 700 Nineteenth Street, NW, Washington, D.C. 20431 (202) 623-7000; *Government Finance Statistics Yearbook.*

BAHAMAS - UNEMPLOYMENT

International Labour Office, I.L.O. Publications, CH-1211, Geneva 22, Switzerland; *Yearbook of Labour Statistics.*

BAHAMAS - VITAL STATISTICS

G.K. Hall and Company, 70 Lincoln Street, Boston, Massachusetts 02111 (617) 423-3990; *The World in Figures.*

Statistical Office of the United Nations, Publishing Service, New York, New York 10017 (800) 253-9646; *Statistical Yearbook.*

World Health Organization, Office of Publications, Avenue Appia, CH-1211 Geneva 27, Switzerland (Telephone Number in U.S. (518) 436-9686); *World Health Statistics Annual.*

BAHAMAS - WAGES

Federal Statistical Office, Gustav - Stresemann - Ring 11, D-6200 Wiesbaden, Germany; *Bahamas.*

G.K. Hall and Company, 70 Lincoln Street, Boston, Massachusetts 02111 (617) 423-3990; *The World in Figures.*

International Labour Office, I.L.O. Publications, CH-1211, Geneva 22, Switzerland; *Yearbook of Labour Statistics.*

BAHAMAS - WEATHER

Facts on File, 460 Park Avenue South, New York, New York 10016 (800) 443-8323; *The New Book of World Rankings.*

G.K. Hall and Company, 70 Lincoln Street, Boston, Massachusetts 02111 (617) 423-3990; *The World in Figures.*

BAHAMAS - WELFARE

Inter-American Development Bank, 1300 New York Avenue, NW, Washington, D.C. 20577 (202) 623-1753; *Economic and Social Progress in Latin America.*

International Monetary Fund, 700 Nineteenth Street, NW, Washington, D.C. 20431 (202) 623-7000; *Government Finance Statistics Yearbook.*

BAHAMAS - WHALES - See BAHAMAS - FISHERIES

BAHAMAS - WHEAT PRODUCTION - See BAHAMAS - CROPS

BAHAMAS - WHOLESALE PRICES

Inter-American Development Bank, 1300 New York Avenue, NW, Washington, D.C. 20577 (202) 623-1753; *Economic and Social Progress in Latin America.*

BAHAMAS - WHOLESALE TRADE

Inter-American Development Bank, 1300 New York Avenue, NW, Washington, D.C. 20577 (202) 623-1753; *Economic and Social Progress in Latin America.*

BAHAMAS - WINE PRODUCTION

Facts on File, 460 Park Avenue South, New York, New York 10016 (800) 443-8323; *The New Book of World Rankings.*

BAHAMAS - WOOL PRODUCTION

Facts on File, 460 Park Avenue South, New York, New York 10016 (800) 443-8323; *The New Book of World Rankings.*

Bahrain - National Statistical Office

Directorate of Statistics, Cabinet Affairs, Post Office Box 5835, Manama, Bahrain.

Bahrain - Primary Statistics Source

Directorate of Statistics, Cabinet Affairs, Post Office Box 5835, Manama, Bahrain; *Statistical Abstract.*

BAHRAIN - AGRICULTURE

Economic Commission for Western Asia, Post Office Box 27, Baghdad, Iraq; *Statistical Abstract of Western Asia.*

Euromonitor Publications Limited, 87-88 Turnmill Street, London EC1M 5QU, England; *International Marketing Data and Statistics,* and *Middle East Economic Handbook.*

Facts on File, 460 Park Avenue South, New York, New York 10016 (800) 443-8323; *The New Book of World Rankings.*

Federal Statistical Office, Gustav - Stresemann - Ring 11, D-6200 Wiesbaden, Germany; *Bahrain.*

Food and Agricultural Organization of the United Nations (FAO) Via delle Terme di Caracalla, 00100 Rome, Italy (Telephone Number in U.S. (202) 653-2400); *Production Yearbook, The State of Food and Agriculture,* and *Trade Yearbook.*

G.K. Hall and Company, 70 Lincoln Street, Boston, Massachusetts 02111 (617) 423-3990; *The World in Figures.*

Times Books, 201 East 50th Street, New York, New York 10022 (212) 751-2600; *The Economist Book of Vital World Statistics.*

The World Bank, 1818 H Street, N.W., Washington, D.C. 20433 (202) 477-1234; *World Tables.*

BAHRAIN - AIRLINE SERVICE

Economic Commission for Western Asia, Post Office Box 27, Baghdad, Iraq; *Statistical Abstract of Western Asia.*

Facts on File, 460 Park Avenue South, New York, New York 10016 (800) 443-8323; *The New Book of World Rankings.*

G.K. Hall and Company, 70 Lincoln Street, Boston, Massachusetts 02111 (617) 423-3990; *The World in Figures.*

Times Books, 201 East 50th Street, New York, New York 10022 (212) 751-2600; *The Economist Book of Vital World Statistics.*

BAHRAIN - ALUMINUM - See BAHRAIN - MINING AND MINERAL PRODUCTS

BAHRAIN - ANIMAL HEALTH

Food and Agricultural Organization of the United Nations (FAO), Via delle Terme di Caracalla, 00100 Rome, Italy (Telephone Number in U.S. (202) 653-2400); *Animal Health Yearbook.*

BAHRAIN - AREA AND DENSITY OF POPULATION

Economic Commission for Western Asia, Post Office Box 27, Baghdad, Iraq; *Statistical Abstract of Western Asia.*

Euromonitor Publications Limited, 87-88 Turnmill Street, London EC1M 5QU, England; *International Marketing Data and Statistics,* and *Middle East Economic Handbook.*

Facts on File, 460 Park Avenue South, New York, New York 10016 (800) 443-8323; *The New Book of World Rankings.*

Federal Statistical Office, Gustav - Stresemann - Ring 11, D-6200 Wiesbaden, Germany; *Bahrain.*

Food and Agricultural Organization of the United Nations (FAO) Via delle Terme di Caracalla, 00100 Rome, Italy (Telephone Number in U.S. (202) 653-2400); *The State of Food and Agriculture.*

G.K. Hall and Company, 70 Lincoln Street, Boston, Massachusetts 02111 (617) 423-3990; *The World in Figures.*

Times Books, 201 East 50th Street, New York, New York 10022 (212) 751-2600; *The Economist Book of Vital World Statistics.*

BAHRAIN - ARMS EXPORTS AND IMPORTS

U.S. Arms Control and Disarmament Agency, 320 Twenty-first Street, NW, Washington, D.C. 20451 (202) 647-8677; *World Military Expenditures and Arms Transfers.*

BAHRAIN - BALANCE OF PAYMENTS

Economist Publications Limited, 25 St. James's Street, London SW1A 1HG England; *The World in Figures.*

The Economist Intelligence Unit, 111 West 57th Street, New York, New York 10019 (800) 938-4685; *The World Market Atlas.*

Federal Statistical Office, Gustav - Stresemann - Ring 11, D-6200 Wiesbaden, Germany; *Bahrain.*

G.K. Hall and Company, 70 Lincoln Street, Boston, Massachusetts 02111 (617) 423-3990; *The World in Figures.*

International Monetary Fund, 700 Nineteenth Street, NW, Washington, D.C. 20431 (202) 623-7000; *Balance of Payments Yearbook.*

Times Books, 201 East 50th Street, New York, New York 10022 (212) 751-2600; *The Economist Book of Vital World Statistics.*

The World Bank, 1818 H Street, N.W., Washington, D.C. 20433 (202) 477-1234; *World Tables.*

BAHRAIN - BALANCE OF TRADE

Economic Commission for Western Asia, Post Office Box 27, Baghdad, Iraq; *Statistical Abstract of Western Asia.*

BAHRAIN - BANKING

Economic Commission for Western Asia, Post Office Box 27, Baghdad, Iraq; *Statistical Abstract of Western Asia.*

Facts on File, 460 Park Avenue South, New York, New York 10016 (800) 443-8323; *The New Book of World Rankings.*

G.K. Hall and Company, 70 Lincoln Street, Boston, Massachusetts 02111 (617) 423-3990; *The World in Figures.*

International Monetary Fund, 700 Nineteenth Street, NW, Washington, D.C. 20431 (202) 623-7000; *Government Finance Statistics Yearbook,* and *International Financial Statistics.*

BAHRAIN - BARLEY PRODUCTION - See BAHRAIN - CROPS

BAHRAIN - BEER PRODUCTION

Facts on File, 460 Park Avenue South, New York, New York 10016 (800) 443-8323; *The New Book of World Rankings.*

BAHRAIN - BIRTH RATES

Euromonitor Publications Limited, 87-88 Turnmill Street, London EC1M 5QU, England; *Middle East Economic Handbook.*

Facts on File, 460 Park Avenue South, New York, New York 10016 (800) 443-8323; *The New Book of World Rankings.*

Statistical Office of the United Nations, Publishing Service, New York, New York 10017 (800) 253-9646; *Demographic Yearbook.*

Times Books, 201 East 50th Street, New York, New York 10022 (212) 751-2600; *The Economist Book of Vital World Statistics.*

The World Bank, 1818 H Street, N.W., Washington, D.C. 20433 (202) 477-1234; *World Tables.*

World Health Organization, Office of Publications, Avenue Appia, CH-1211 Geneva 27, Switzerland (Telephone Number in U.S. (518) 436-9686); *World Health Statistics Annual.*

BAHRAIN - BONDS

G.K. Hall and Company, 70 Lincoln Street, Boston, Massachusetts 02111 (617) 423-3990; *The World in Figures.*

BAHRAIN - BOOK PRODUCTION

G.K. Hall and Company, 70 Lincoln Street, Boston, Massachusetts 02111 (617) 423-3990; *The World in Figures.*

BAHRAIN - BROADCASTING

Billboard Limited, P.O. Box 9027, 1006 AA Amsterdam, The Netherlands (Telephone Number in U.S. (212) 764-7300); *World Radio TV Handbook.*

Facts on File, 460 Park Avenue South, New York, New York 10016 (800) 443-8323; *The New Book of World Rankings.*

G.K. Hall and Company, 70 Lincoln Street, Boston, Massachusetts 02111 (617) 423-3990; *The World in Figures.*

Times Books, 201 East 50th Street, New York, New York 10022 (212) 751-2600; *The Economist Book of Vital World Statistics.*

United Nations Educational, Scientific and Cultural Organization (UNESCO), 7 Place de Fontenoy, F-75700 Paris, France (Telephone Number in U.S. (212) 963-5981); *Statistical Yearbook.*

BAHRAIN - BUSINESS

G.K. Hall and Company, 70 Lincoln Street, Boston, Massachusetts 02111 (617) 423-3990; *The World in Figures.*

BAHRAIN - BUSINESS AND PROFESSIONAL LICENSES

International Monetary Fund, 700 Nineteenth Street, NW, Washington, D.C. 20431 (202) 623-7000; *Government Finance Statistics Yearbook.*

BAHRAIN - CALORIE SUPPLY

Food and Agricultural Organization of the United Nations (FAO) Via delle Terme di Caracalla, 00100 Rome, Italy (Telephone Number in U.S. (202) 653-2400); *The State of Food and Agriculture.*

BAHRAIN - CAPITAL REVENUE

International Monetary Fund, 700 Nineteenth Street, NW, Washington, D.C. 20431 (202) 623-7000; *Government Finance Statistics Yearbook.*

BAHRAIN - CATTLE - See BAHRAIN - LIVESTOCK AND POULTRY

BAHRAIN - CEMENT PRODUCTION - See BAHRAIN - MINING AND MINERAL PRODUCTS

BAHRAIN - CHEMICAL (ORGANIC) PRODUCTION - See BAHRAIN - MINING AND MINERAL PRODUCTS

BAHRAIN - CIGARETTE PRODUCTION - See BAHRAIN - TOBACCO PRODUCTION

BAHRAIN - CLASS STRUCTURE

G.K. Hall and Company, 70 Lincoln Street, Boston, Massachusetts 02111 (617) 423-3990; *The World in Figures.*

BAHRAIN - CLIMATE

Facts on File, 460 Park Avenue South, New York, New York 10016 (800) 443-8323; *The New Book of World Rankings.*

G.K. Hall and Company, 70 Lincoln Street, Boston, Massachusetts 02111 (617) 423-3990; *The World in Figures.*

BAHRAIN - COAL PRODUCTION - See BAHRAIN - MINING AND MINERAL PRODUCTS

BAHRAIN - COFFEE PRODUCTION - See BAHRAIN - CROPS

BAHRAIN - COMMUNICATIONS

Economic Commission for Western Asia, Post Office Box 27, Baghdad, Iraq; *Statistical Abstract of Western Asia.*

Federal Statistical Office, Gustav - Stresemann - Ring 11, D-6200 Wiesbaden, Germany; *Bahrain.*

G.K. Hall and Company, 70 Lincoln Street, Boston, Massachusetts 02111 (617) 423-3990; *The World in Figures.*

BAHRAIN - CONSTRUCTION INDUSTRY

Facts on File, 460 Park Avenue South, New York, New York 10016 (800) 443-8323; *The New Book of World Rankings.*

BAHRAIN - CONSUMER PRICE INDEX

Federal Statistical Office, Gustav - Stresemann - Ring 11, D-6200 Wiesbaden, Germany; *Bahrain.*

G.K. Hall and Company, 70 Lincoln Street, Boston, Massachusetts 02111 (617) 423-3990; *The World in Figures.*

BAHRAIN - CONSUMER PRICES

Federal Statistical Office, Gustav - Stresemann - Ring 11, D-6200 Wiesbaden, Germany; *Bahrain.*

International Labour Office, I.L.O. Publications, CH-1211, Geneva 22, Switzerland; *Yearbook of Labour Statistics.*

International Monetary Fund, 700 Nineteenth Street, NW, Washington, D.C. 20431 (202) 623-7000; *International Financial Statistics.*

Times Books, 201 East 50th Street, New York, New York 10022 (212) 751-2600; *The Economist Book of Vital World Statistics.*

BAHRAIN - CONSUMPTION

Euromonitor Publications Limited, 87-88 Turnmill Street, London EC1M 5QU, England; *Middle East Economic Handbook.*

G.K. Hall and Company, 70 Lincoln Street, Boston, Massachusetts 02111 (617) 423-3990; *The World in Figures.*

BAHRAIN - COPPER PRODUCTION - See BAHRAIN - MINING AND MINERAL PRODUCTS

BAHRAIN - CORN PRODUCTION - See BAHRAIN - CROPS

BAHRAIN - CORPORATE TAXES - See BAHRAIN - TAXATION

BAHRAIN - COTTON - See BAHRAIN - CROPS

BAHRAIN - CRIME

Yale University Press, Yale Station, New Haven, Connecticut 06520 (203) 432-0940; *Violence and Crime in Cross-National Perspective.*

BAHRAIN - CROPS

Facts on File, 460 Park Avenue South, New York, New York 10016 (800) 443-8323; *The New Book of World Rankings.*

Food and Agricultural Organization of the United Nations (FAO) Via delle Terme di Caracalla, 00100 Rome, Italy (Telephone Number in U.S. (202) 653-2400); *The State of Food and Agriculture.*

G.K. Hall and Company, 70 Lincoln Street, Boston, Massachusetts 02111 (617) 423-3990; *The World in Figures.*

BAHRAIN - CUSTOMS DUTIES

G.K. Hall and Company, 70 Lincoln Street, Boston, Massachusetts 02111 (617) 423-3990; *The World in Figures.*

BAHRAIN - DAIRY PRODUCTS

Economic Commission for Western Asia, Post Office Box 27, Baghdad, Iraq; *Statistical Abstract of Western Asia.*

Facts on File, 460 Park Avenue South, New York, New York 10016 (800) 443-8323; *The New Book of World Rankings.*

Food and Agricultural Organization of the United Nations (FAO) Via delle Terme di Caracalla, 00100 Rome, Italy (Telephone Number in U.S. (202) 653-2400); *The State of Food and Agriculture.*

BAHRAIN - DEATH RATES

Euromonitor Publications Limited, 87-88 Turnmill Street, London EC1M 5QU, England; *Middle East Economic Handbook.*

G.K. Hall and Company, 70 Lincoln Street, Boston, Massachusetts 02111 (617) 423-3990; *The World in Figures.*

Times Books, 201 East 50th Street, New York, New York 10022 (212) 751-2600; *The Economist Book of Vital World Statistics.*

World Health Organization, Office of Publications, Avenue Appia, CH-1211 Geneva 27, Switzerland (Telephone Number in U.S. (518) 436-9686); *World Health Statistics Annual.*

BAHRAIN - DEFENSE EXPENDITURE

G.K. Hall and Company, 70 Lincoln Street, Boston, Massachusetts 02111 (617) 423-3990; *The World in Figures.*

International Monetary Fund, 700 Nineteenth Street, NW, Washington, D.C. 20431 (202) 623-7000; *Government Finance Statistics Yearbook.*

U.S. Arms Control and Disarmament Agency, 320 Twenty-first Street, NW, Washington, D.C. 20451 (202) 647-8677; *World Military*

Expenditures and Arms Transfers.

BAHRAIN - DEMOGRAPHY

The Economist Intelligence Unit, 111 West 57th Street, New York, New York 10019 (800) 938-4685; *The World Market Atlas.*

Facts on File, 460 Park Avenue South, New York, New York 10016 (800) 443-8323; *The New Book of World Rankings.*

Federal Statistical Office, Gustav - Stresemann - Ring 11, D-6200 Wiesbaden, Germany; *Bahrain.*

G.K. Hall and Company, 70 Lincoln Street, Boston, Massachusetts 02111 (617) 423-3990; *The World in Figures.*

BAHRAIN - DEVELOPMENT ASSISTANCE

G.K. Hall and Company, 70 Lincoln Street, Boston, Massachusetts 02111 (617) 423-3990; *The World in Figures.*

Statistical Office of the United Nations, Publishing Service, New York, New York 10017 (800) 253-9646; *Statistical Yearbook.*

BAHRAIN - DIAMOND PRODUCTION - See BAHRAIN - MINING AND MINERAL PRODUCTS

BAHRAIN - DISEASES

G.K. Hall and Company, 70 Lincoln Street, Boston, Massachusetts 02111 (617) 423-3990; *The World in Figures.*

World Health Organization, Office of Publications, Avenue Appia, CH-1211 Geneva 27, Switzerland (Telephone Number in U.S. (518) 436-9686); *World Health Statistics Annual.*

BAHRAIN - DIVORCE RATES

Facts on File, 460 Park Avenue South, New York, New York 10016 (800) 443-8323; *The New Book of World Rankings.*

Statistical Office of the United Nations, Publishing Service, New York, New York 10017 (800) 253-9646; *Demographic Yearbook.*

BAHRAIN - DOMESTIC PRODUCT

G.K. Hall and Company, 70 Lincoln Street, Boston, Massachusetts 02111 (617) 423-3990; *The World in Figures.*

BAHRAIN - ECONOMY

Euromonitor Publications Limited, 87-88 Turnmill Street, London EC1M 5QU, England; *International Marketing Data and Statistics.*

Facts on File, 460 Park Avenue South, New York, New York 10016 (800) 443-8323; *The New Book of World Rankings.*

Federal Statistical Office, Gustav - Stresemann - Ring 11, D-6200 Wiesbaden, Germany; *Bahrain.*

G.K. Hall and Company, 70 Lincoln Street, Boston, Massachusetts 02111 (617) 423-3990; *The World in Figures.*

BAHRAIN - EDUCATION

Economic Commission for Western Asia, Post Office Box 27, Baghdad, Iraq; *Statistical Abstract of Western Asia.*

The Economist Intelligence Unit, 111 West 57th Street, New York, New York 10019 (800) 938-4685; *The World Market Atlas.*

Euromonitor Publications Limited, 87-88 Turnmill Street, London EC1M 5QU, England; *Middle East Economic Handbook.*

Facts on File, 460 Park Avenue South, New York, New York 10016 (800) 443-8323; *The New Book of World Rankings.*

Federal Statistical Office, Gustav - Stresemann - Ring 11, D-6200 Wiesbaden, Germany; *Bahrain.*

G.K. Hall and Company, 70 Lincoln Street, Boston, Massachusetts 02111 (617) 423-3990; *The World in Figures.*

International Monetary Fund, 700 Nineteenth Street, NW, Washington, D.C. 20431 (202) 623-7000; *Government Finance Statistics Yearbook.*

Times Books, 201 East 50th Street, New York, New York 10022 (212) 751-2600; *The Economist Book of Vital World Statistics.*

United Nations Educational, Scientific and Cultural Organization (UNESCO), 7 Place de Fontenoy, F-75700 Paris, France (Telephone Number in U.S. (212) 963-5981); *Statistical Yearbook.*

The World Bank, 1818 H Street, N.W., Washington, D.C. 20433 (202) 477-1234; *World Tables.*

BAHRAIN - EGG PRODUCTION - See BAHRAIN - DAIRY PRODUCTS

BAHRAIN - ELECTRICITY

Facts on File, 460 Park Avenue South, New York, New York 10016 (800) 443-8323; *The New Book of World Rankings.*

Penn Well Publishing Company, 1421 South Sheridan Road, P.O. Box 1260, Tulsa, Oklahoma 74101 (800) 752-9764; *International Energy Statistics Sourcebook.*

Statistical Office of the United Nations, Publishing Service, New York, New York 10017 (800) 253-9646; *Statistical Yearbook.*

Times Books, 201 East 50th Street, New York, New York 10022 (212) 751-2600; *The Economist Book of Vital World Statistics.*

BAHRAIN - EMPLOYMENT

Economic Commission for Western Asia, Post Office Box 27, Baghdad, Iraq; *Statistical Abstract of Western Asia.*

Euromonitor Publications Limited, 87-88 Turnmill Street, London EC1M 5QU, England; *International Marketing Data and Statistics,* and *Middle East Economic Handbook.*

Facts on File, 460 Park Avenue South, New York, New York 10016 (800) 443-8323; *The New Book of World Rankings.*

Federal Statistical Office, Gustav - Stresemann - Ring 11, D-6200 Wiesbaden, Germany; *Bahrain.*

International Labour Office, I.L.O. Publications, CH-1211, Geneva 22, Switzerland; *Yearbook of Labour Statistics.*

Euromonitor Publications Limited, 87-88 Turnmill Street, London EC1M 5QU, England; *International Marketing Data and Statistics.*

BAHRAIN - ENERGY

Economic Commission for Western Asia, Post Office Box 27, Baghdad, Iraq; *Statistical Abstract of Western Asia.*

Euromonitor Publications Limited, 87-88 Turnmill Street, London EC1M 5QU, England; *Middle East Economic Handbook.*

Facts on File, 460 Park Avenue South, New York, New York 10016 (800) 443-8323; *The New Book of World Rankings.*

Food and Agricultural Organization of the United Nations (FAO) Via delle Terme di Caracalla, 00100 Rome, Italy (Telephone Number in U.S. (202) 653-2400); *The State of Food and Agriculture.*

G.K. Hall and Company, 70 Lincoln Street, Boston, Massachusetts 02111 (617) 423-3990; *The World in Figures.*

Penn Well Publishing Company, 1421 South Sheridan Road, P.O. Box 1260, Tulsa, Oklahoma 74101 (800) 752-9764; *International Energy Statistics Sourcebook.*

Statistical Office of the United Nations, Publishing Service, New York, New York 10017 (800) 253-9646; *Energy Statistics Yearbook,* and *Statistical Yearbook.*

Times Books, 201 East 50th Street, New York, New York 10022 (212) 751-2600; *The Economist Book of Vital World Statistics.*

BAHRAIN - EXCHANGE RATES

Euromonitor Publications Limited, 87-88 Turnmill Street, London EC1M 5QU, England; *International Marketing Data and Statistics,* and *Middle East Economic Handbook.*

International Monetary Fund, 700 Nineteenth Street, NW, Washington, D.C. 20431 (202) 623-7000; *International Financial Statistics.*

BAHRAIN - EXCISE TAXES - See BAHRAIN - TAXATION

BAHRAIN - EXPORTS

Economic Commission for Western Asia, Post Office Box 27, Baghdad, Iraq; *Statistical Abstract of Western Asia.*

The Economist Intelligence Unit, 111 West 57th Street, New York, New York 10019 (800) 938-4685; *The World Market Atlas.*

Euromonitor Publications Limited, 87-88 Turnmill Street, London EC1M 5QU, England; *International Marketing Data and Statistics,* and *Middle East Economic Handbook.*

Food and Agricultural Organization of the United Nations (FAO) Via delle Terme di Caracalla, 00100 Rome, Italy (Telephone Number in U.S. (202) 653-2400); *The State of Food and Agriculture.*

G.K. Hall and Company, 70 Lincoln Street, Boston, Massachusetts 02111 (617) 423-3990; *The World in Figures.*

International Monetary Fund, 700 Nineteenth Street, NW, Washington, D.C. 20431 (202) 623-7000; *Direction of Trade Statistics,* and *International Financial Statistics.*

Statistical Office of the United Nations, Publishing Service, New York, New York 10017 (800) 253-9646; *Trade in Manufactures of Developing Countries.*

Times Books, 201 East 50th Street, New York, New York 10022 (212) 751-2600; *The Economist Book of Vital World Statistics.*

The World Bank, 1818 H Street, N.W., Washington, D.C. 20433 (202) 477-1234; *World Tables.*

BAHRAIN - EXTERNAL INDEBTEDNESS

The World Bank, 1818 H Street, N.W., Washington, D.C. 20433 (202) 477-1234; *World Tables.*

BAHRAIN - EXTERNAL TRADE

Food and Agricultural Organization of the United Nations (FAO) Via delle Terme di Caracalla, 00100 Rome, Italy (Telephone Number in U.S. (202) 653-2400); *The State of Food and Agriculture,* and *Trade Yearbook.*

G.K. Hall and Company, 70 Lincoln Street, Boston, Massachusetts 02111 (617) 423-3990; *The World in Figures.*

Statistical Office of the United Nations, Publishing Service, New York, New York 10017 (800) 253-9646; *Statistical Yearbook.*

BAHRAIN - FARM CROPS - See BAHRAIN - CROPS

BAHRAIN - FEMALE WORKING POPULATION - See BAHRAIN - EMPLOYMENT

BAHRAIN - FERTILITY RATES

Facts on File, 460 Park Avenue South, New York, New York 10016 (800) 443-8323; *The New Book of World Rankings.*

Times Books, 201 East 50th Street, New York, New York 10022 (212) 751-2600; *The Economist Book of Vital World Statistics.*

The World Bank, 1818 H Street, N.W., Washington, D.C. 20433 (202) 477-1234; *World Tables.*

BAHRAIN - FERTILIZER

Food and Agricultural Organization of the United Nations (FAO) Via delle Terme di Caracalla, 00100 Rome, Italy (Telephone Number in U.S. (202) 653-2400); *The State of Food and Agriculture.*

BAHRAIN - FETAL MORTALITY

Statistical Office of the United Nations, Publishing Service, New York, New York 10017 (800) 253-9646; *Demographic Yearbook.*

BAHRAIN - FINANCE

Economic Commission for Western Asia, Post Office Box 27, Baghdad, Iraq; *Statistical Abstract of Western Asia.*

Euromonitor Publications Limited, 87-88 Turnmill Street, London EC1M 5QU, England; *Middle East Economic Handbook.*

Facts on File, 460 Park Avenue South, New York, New York 10016 (800) 443-8323; *The New Book of World Rankings.*

Federal Statistical Office, Gustav - Stresemann - Ring 11, D-6200 Wiesbaden, Germany; *Bahrain.*

G.K. Hall and Company, 70 Lincoln Street, Boston, Massachusetts 02111 (617) 423-3990; *The World in Figures.*

International Monetary Fund, 700 Nineteenth Street, NW, Washington, D.C. 20431 (202) 623-7000; *Government Finance Statistics Yearbook.*

BAHRAIN - FISHERIES

Economic Commission for Western Asia, Post Office Box 27, Baghdad, Iraq; *Statistical Abstract of Western Asia.*

Facts on File, 460 Park Avenue South, New York, New York 10016 (800) 443-8323; *The New Book of World Rankings.*

Federal Statistical Office, Gustav - Stresemann - Ring 11, D-6200 Wiesbaden, Germany; *Bahrain.*

Food and Agricultural Organization of the United Nations (FAO) Via delle Terme di Caracalla, 00100 Rome, Italy (Telephone Number in U.S. (202) 653-2400); *The State of Food and Agriculture,* and *Yearbook of Fishery Statistics.*

Statistical Office of the United Nations, Publishing Service, New York, New York 10017 (800) 253-9646; *Statistical Yearbook.*

BAHRAIN - FOOD

Food and Agricultural Organization of the United Nations (FAO) Via delle Terme di Caracalla, 00100 Rome, Italy (Telephone Number in U.S. (202) 653-2400); *Production Yearbook,* and *The State of Food and Agriculture.*

G.K. Hall and Company, 70 Lincoln Street, Boston, Massachusetts 02111 (617) 423-3990; *The World in Figures.*

BAHRAIN - FOREIGN AID

G.K. Hall and Company, 70 Lincoln Street, Boston, Massachusetts 02111 (617) 423-3990; *The World in Figures.*

BAHRAIN - FOREIGN DEBT

International Monetary Fund, 700 Nineteenth Street, NW, Washington, D.C. 20431 (202) 623-7000; *Government Finance Statistics Yearbook.*

BAHRAIN - FOREIGN INDEBTEDNESS

Euromonitor Publications Limited, 87-88 Turnmill Street, London EC1M 5QU, England; *Middle East Economic Handbook.*

BAHRAIN - FOREIGN TRADE

Economic Commission for Western Asia, Post Office Box 27, Baghdad, Iraq; *Statistical Abstract of Western Asia.*

Euromonitor Publications Limited, 87-88 Turnmill Street, London EC1M 5QU, England; *International Marketing Data and Statistics. Middle East Economic Handbook.*

Facts on File, 460 Park Avenue South, New York, New York 10016 (800) 443-8323; *The New Book of World Rankings.*

Federal Statistical Office, Gustav - Stresemann - Ring 11, D-6200 Wiesbaden, Germany; *Bahrain.*

Food and Agricultural Organization of the United Nations (FAO) Via delle Terme di Caracalla, 00100 Rome, Italy (Telephone Number in U.S. (202) 653-2400); *The State of Food and Agriculture.*

G.K. Hall and Company, 70 Lincoln Street, Boston, Massachusetts 02111 (617) 423-3990; *The World in Figures.*

Statistical Office of the United Nations, Publishing Service, New York, New York 10017 (800) 253-9646; *International Trade Statistics Yearbook,* and *Statistical Yearbook.*

The World Bank, 1818 H Street, N.W., Washington, D.C. 20433 (202) 477-1234; *World Tables.*

BAHRAIN - FORESTRY AND FOREST PRODUCTS

Facts on File, 460 Park Avenue South, New York, New York 10016 (800) 443-8323; *The New Book of World Rankings.*

Federal Statistical Office, Gustav - Stresemann - Ring 11, D-6200 Wiesbaden, Germany; *Bahrain.*

Food and Agricultural Organization of the United Nations (FAO), Via delle Terme di Caracalla, 00100 Rome, Italy (Telephone Number in U.S. (202) 653-2400); *FAO Yearbook of Forest Products,* and *The State of Food and Agriculture.*

G.K. Hall and Company, 70 Lincoln Street, Boston, Massachusetts 02111 (617) 423-3990; *The World in Figures.*

Statistical Office of the United Nations, Publishing Service, New York, New York 10017 (800) 253-9646; *Statistical Yearbook.*

United Nations Educational, Scientific and Cultural Organization (UNESCO), 7 Place de Fontenoy, F-75700 Paris, France (Telephone Number in U.S. (212) 963-5981); *Statistical Yearbook.*

BAHRAIN - GAS PRODUCTION - See BAHRAIN - MINING AND MINERAL PRODUCTS

BAHRAIN - GENERAL INDUSTRIAL STATISTICS

Federal Statistical Office, Gustav - Stresemann - Ring 11, D-6200 Wiesbaden, Germany; *Bahrain.*

BAHRAIN - GENERAL MORTALITY

Statistical Office of the United Nations, Publishing Service, New York, New York 10017 (800) 253-9646; *Demographic Yearbook.*

World Health Organization, Office of Publications, Avenue Appia, CH-1211 Geneva 27, Switzerland (Telephone Number in U.S. (518) 436-9686); *World Health Statistics Annual.*

BAHRAIN - GEOGRAPHIC DATA

Facts on File, 460 Park Avenue South, New York, New York 10016 (800) 443-8323; *The New Book of World Rankings.*

Federal Statistical Office, Gustav - Stresemann - Ring 11, D-6200 Wiesbaden, Germany; *Bahrain.*

BAHRAIN - GOLD HOLDINGS

International Monetary Fund, 700 Nineteenth Street, NW, Washington, D.C. 20431 (202) 623-7000; *International Financial Statistics.*

Statistical Office of the United Nations, Publishing Service, New York, New York 10017 (800) 253-9646; *Statistical Yearbook.*

The World Bank, 1818 H Street, N.W., Washington, D.C. 20433 (202) 477-1234; *World Tables.*

BAHRAIN - GOLD PRODUCTION AND CONSUMPTION - See BAHRAIN - MINING AND MINERAL PRODUCTS

BAHRAIN - GOVERNMENT

G.K. Hall and Company, 70 Lincoln Street, Boston, Massachusetts 02111 (617) 423-3990; *The World in Figures.*

BAHRAIN - GOVERNMENT EXPENDITURES

Economic Commission for Western Asia, Post Office Box 27, Baghdad, Iraq; *Statistical Abstract of Western Asia.*

International Monetary Fund, 700 Nineteenth Street, NW, Washington, D.C. 20431 (202) 623-7000; *Government Finance Statistics Yearbook.*

Times Books, 201 East 50th Street, New York, New York 10022 (212) 751-2600; *The Economist Book of Vital World Statistics.*

The World Bank, 1818 H Street, N.W., Washington, D.C. 20433 (202) 477-1234; *World Tables.*

BAHRAIN - GOVERNMENT FINANCE

International Monetary Fund, 700 Nineteenth Street, NW, Washington, D.C. 20431 (202) 623-7000; *International Financial Statistics.*

BAHRAIN - GOVERNMENT REVENUES

Economic Commission for Western Asia, Post Office Box 27, Baghdad, Iraq; *Statistical Abstract of Western Asia.*

International Monetary Fund, 700 Nineteenth Street, NW, Washington, D.C. 20431 (202) 623-7000; *Government Finance Statistics Yearbook.*

Times Books, 201 East 50th Street, New York, New York 10022 (212) 751-2600; *The Economist Book of Vital World Statistics.*

The World Bank, 1818 H Street, N.W., Washington, D.C. 20433 (202) 477-1234; *World Tables.*

BAHRAIN - GRAIN PRODUCTION - See BAHRAIN - CROPS

BAHRAIN - GRANTS

International Monetary Fund, 700 Nineteenth Street, NW, Washington, D.C. 20431 (202) 623-7000; *Government Finance Statistics Yearbook.*

BAHRAIN - GROSS DOMESTIC PRODUCT

Economic Commission for Western Asia, Post Office Box 27, Baghdad, Iraq; *Statistical Abstract of Western Asia.*

The Economist Intelligence Unit, 111 West 57th Street, New York, New York 10019 (800) 938-4685; *The World Market Atlas.*

Euromonitor Publications Limited, 87-88 Turnmill Street, London EC1M 5QU, England; *International Marketing Data and Statistics,* and *Middle East Economic Handbook.*

Facts on File, 460 Park Avenue South, New York, New York 10016 (800) 443-8323; *The New Book of World Rankings.*

G.K. Hall and Company, 70 Lincoln Street, Boston, Massachusetts 02111 (617) 423-3990; *The World in Figures.*

Statistical Office of the United Nations, Publishing Service, New York, New York 10017 (800) 253-9646; *Statistical Yearbook.*

Times Books, 201 East 50th Street, New York, New York 10022 (212) 751-2600; *The Economist Book of Vital World Statistics.*

The World Bank, 1818 H Street, N.W., Washington, D.C. 20433 (202) 477-1234; *World Tables.*

BAHRAIN - GROSS NATIONAL PRODUCT

Euromonitor Publications Limited, 87-88 Turnmill Street, London EC1M 5QU, England; *International Marketing Data and Statistics.*

U.S. Arms Control and Disarmament Agency, 320 Twenty-first Street, NW, Washington, D.C. 20451 (202) 647-8677; *World Military Expenditures and Arms Transfers.*

The World Bank, 1818 H Street, N.W., Washington, D.C. 20433 (202) 477-1234; *World Tables.*

BAHRAIN - HEALTH

Economic Commission for Western Asia, Post Office Box 27, Baghdad, Iraq; *Statistical Abstract of Western Asia.*

Euromonitor Publications Limited, 87-88 Turnmill Street, London EC1M 5QU, England; *Middle East Economic Handbook.*

Facts on File, 460 Park Avenue South, New York, New York 10016 (800) 443-8323; *The New Book of World Rankings.*

Federal Statistical Office, Gustav - Stresemann - Ring 11, D-6200 Wiesbaden, Germany; *Bahrain.*

G.K. Hall and Company, 70 Lincoln Street, Boston, Massachusetts 02111 (617) 423-3990; *The World in Figures.*

Statistical Office of the United Nations, Publishing Service, New York, New York 10017 (800) 253-9646; *Statistical Yearbook.*

Times Books, 201 East 50th Street, New York, New York 10022 (212) 751-2600; *The Economist Book of Vital World Statistics.*

World Health Organization, Office of Publications, Avenue Appia, CH-1211 Geneva 27, Switzerland (Telephone Number in U.S. (518) 436-9686); *World Health Statistics Annual.*

BAHRAIN - HEALTH EXPENDITURES

International Monetary Fund, 700 Nineteenth Street, NW, Washington, D.C. 20431 (202) 623-7000; *Government Finance Statistics Yearbook.*

BAHRAIN - HIDE PRODUCTION

Food and Agricultural Organization of the United Nations (FAO), Via delle Terme di Caracalla, 00100 Rome, Italy (Telephone Number in U.S. (202) 653-2400); *Production Yearbook.*

BAHRAIN - HIGHWAYS

Economic Commission for Western Asia, Post Office Box 27, Baghdad, Iraq; *Statistical Abstract of Western Asia.*

G.K. Hall and Company, 70 Lincoln Street, Boston, Massachusetts 02111 (617) 423-3990; *The World in Figures.*

BAHRAIN - HORSES - See BAHRAIN - LIVESTOCK AND POULTRY

BAHRAIN - HOURS OF WORK - See BAHRAIN - EMPLOYMENT

BAHRAIN - HOUSING AND HOUSING UNITS

Facts on File, 460 Park Avenue South, New York, New York 10016 (800) 443-8323; *The New Book of World Rankings.*

Statistical Office of the United Nations, Publishing Service, New York, New York 10017 (800) 253-9646; *Statistical Yearbook.*

BAHRAIN - HOUSING EXPENDITURES

International Monetary Fund, 700 Nineteenth Street, NW, Washington, D.C. 20431 (202) 623-7000; *Government Finance Statistics Yearbook.*

BAHRAIN - ILLITERATE POPULATION

The Economist Intelligence Unit, 111 West 57th Street, New York, New York 10019 (800) 938-4685; *The World Market Atlas.*

G.K. Hall and Company, 70 Lincoln Street, Boston, Massachusetts 02111 (617) 423-3990; *The World in Figures.*

United Nations Educational, Scientific and Cultural Organization (UNESCO), 7 Place de Fontenoy, F-75700 Paris, France (Telephone Number in U.S. (212) 963-5981); *Statistical Yearbook.*

BAHRAIN - IMPORTS

Economic Commission for Western Asia, Post Office Box 27, Baghdad, Iraq; *Statistical Abstract of Western Asia.*

The Economist Intelligence Unit, 111 West 57th Street, New York, New York 10019 (800) 938-4685; *The World Market Atlas.*

Euromonitor Publications Limited, 87-88 Turnmill Street, London EC1M 5QU, England; *International Marketing Data and Statistics,* and *Middle East Economic Handbook.*

Food and Agricultural Organization of the United Nations (FAO) Via delle Terme di Caracalla, 00100 Rome, Italy (Telephone Number in U.S. (202) 653-2400); *The State of Food and Agriculture.*

G.K. Hall and Company, 70 Lincoln Street, Boston, Massachusetts 02111 (617) 423-3990; *The World in Figures.*

International Monetary Fund, 700 Nineteenth Street, NW, Washington, D.C. 20431 (202) 623-7000; *Direction of Trade Statistics, Government Finance Statistics Yearbook,* and *International Financial Statistics.*

Statistical Office of the United Nations, Publishing Service, New York, New York 10017 (800) 253-9646; *Trade in Manufactures of Developing Countries.*

Times Books, 201 East 50th Street, New York, New York 10022 (212) 751-2600; *The Economist Book of Vital World Statistics.*

The World Bank, 1818 H Street, N.W., Washington, D.C. 20433 (202) 477-1234; *World Tables.*

BAHRAIN - INCOME TAXES - See BAHRAIN - TAXATION

BAHRAIN - INDUSTRY

Euromonitor Publications Limited, 87-88 Turnmill Street, London EC1M 5QU, England; *International Marketing Data and Statistics.*

Facts on File, 460 Park Avenue South, New York, New York 10016 (800) 443-8323; *The New Book of World Rankings.*

Federal Statistical Office, Gustav - Stresemann - Ring 11, D-6200 Wiesbaden, Germany; *Bahrain.*

G.K. Hall and Company, 70 Lincoln Street, Boston, Massachusetts 02111 (617) 423-3990; *The World in Figures.*

International Labour Office, I.L.O. Publications, CH-1211, Geneva 22, Switzerland; *Yearbook of Labour Statistics.*

Times Books, 201 East 50th Street, New York, New York 10022 (212) 751-2600; *The Economist Book of Vital World Statistics.*

The World Bank, 1818 H Street, N.W., Washington, D.C. 20433 (202) 477-1234; *World Tables.*

World Intellectual Property Organization, 34 Chemin des Colombettes, CH-1211 Geneva 20. Switzerland; *Industrial Property Statistics.*

BAHRAIN - INFANT AND MATERNAL MORTALITY

Statistical Office of the United Nations, Publishing Service, New York, New York 10017 (800) 253-9646; *Demographic Yearbook.*

Times Books, 201 East 50th Street, New York, New York 10022 (212) 751-2600; *The Economist Book of Vital World Statistics.*

The World Bank, 1818 H Street, N.W., Washington, D.C. 20433 (202) 477-1234; *World Tables.*

BAHRAIN - INTERNATIONAL LIQUIDITY

International Monetary Fund, 700 Nineteenth Street, NW, Washington, D.C. 20431 (202) 623-7000; *International Financial Statistics.*

BAHRAIN - INTERNATIONAL RESERVES EXCLUDING GOLD

The World Bank, 1818 H Street, N.W., Washington, D.C. 20433 (202) 477-1234; *World Tables.*

BAHRAIN - IRON ORE PRODUCTION AND CONSUMPTION - See BAHRAIN - MINING AND MINERAL PRODUCTS

BAHRAIN - IRRIGATION

Euromonitor Publications Limited, 87-88 Turnmill Street, London EC1M 5QU, England; *International Marketing Data and Statistics.*

BAHRAIN - LABOR FORCE

Economic Commission for Western Asia, Post Office Box 27, Baghdad, Iraq; *Statistical Abstract of Western Asia.*

Euromonitor Publications Limited, 87-88 Turnmill Street, London EC1M 5QU, England; *International Marketing Data and Statistics,* and *Middle East Economic Handbook.*

Facts on File, 460 Park Avenue South, New York, New York 10016 (800) 443-8323; *The New Book of World Rankings.*

Food and Agricultural Organization of the United Nations (FAO) Via delle Terme di Caracalla, 00100 Rome, Italy (Telephone Number in U.S. (202) 653-2400); *The State of Food and Agriculture.*

G.K. Hall and Company, 70 Lincoln Street, Boston, Massachusetts 02111 (617) 423-3990; *The World in Figures.*

Times Books, 201 East 50th Street, New York, New York 10022 (212) 751-2600; *The Economist Book of Vital World Statistics.*

The World Bank, 1818 H Street, N.W., Washington, D.C. 20433 (202) 477-1234; *World Tables.*

BAHRAIN - LABOR PRODUCTIVITY

International Labour Office, I.L.O. Publications, CH-1211, Geneva 22, Switzerland; *Yearbook of Labour Statistics.*

BAHRAIN - LAND USE

Economic Commission for Western Asia, Post Office Box 27, Baghdad, Iraq; *Statistical Abstract of Western Asia.*

Euromonitor Publications Limited, 87-88 Turnmill Street, London EC1M 5QU, England; *International Marketing Data and Statistics.*

Facts on File, 460 Park Avenue South, New York, New York 10016 (800) 443-8323; *The New Book of World Rankings.*

Food and Agricultural Organization of the United Nations (FAO), Via delle Terme di Caracalla, 00100 Rome, Italy (Telephone Number in U.S. (202) 653-2400); *Production Yearbook.*

G.K. Hall and Company, 70 Lincoln Street, Boston, Massachusetts 02111 (617) 423-3990; *The World in Figures.*

BAHRAIN - LIBRARIES

Facts on File, 460 Park Avenue South, New York, New York 10016 (800) 443-8323; *The New Book of World Rankings.*

United Nations Educational, Scientific and Cultural Organization (UNESCO), 7 Place de Fontenoy, F-75700 Paris, France (Telephone Number in U.S. (212) 963-5981); *Statistical Yearbook.*

BAHRAIN - LIVESTOCK AND POULTRY

Economic Commission for Western Asia, Post Office Box 27, Baghdad, Iraq; *Statistical Abstract of Western Asia.*

Facts on File, 460 Park Avenue South, New York, New York 10016 (800) 443-8323; *The New Book of World Rankings.*

Food and Agricultural Organization of the United Nations (FAO), Via delle Terme di Caracalla, 00100 Rome, Italy (Telephone Number in U.S. (202) 653-2400); *Production Yearbook,* and *The State of Food and Agriculture.*

G.K. Hall and Company, 70 Lincoln Street, Boston, Massachusetts 02111 (617) 423-3990; *The World in Figures.*

Statistical Office of the United Nations, Publishing Service, New York, New York 10017 (800) 253-9646; *Statistical Yearbook.*

BAHRAIN - LIVING LEVELS

G.K. Hall and Company, 70 Lincoln Street, Boston, Massachusetts 02111 (617) 423-3990; *The World in Figures.*

Times Books, 201 East 50th Street, New York, New York 10022 (212) 751-2600; *The Economist Book of Vital World Statistics.*

BAHRAIN - MAIL - NUMBER OF PIECES SENT OR RECEIVED

Statistical Office of the United Nations, Publishing Service, New York, New York 10017 (800) 253-9646; *Statistical Yearbook.*

BAHRAIN - MANUFACTURING

Facts on File, 460 Park Avenue South, New York, New York 10016 (800) 443-8323; *The New Book of World Rankings.*

G.K. Hall and Company, 70 Lincoln Street, Boston, Massachusetts 02111 (617) 423-3990; *The World in Figures.*

The World Bank, 1818 H Street, N.W., Washington, D.C. 20433 (202) 477-1234; *World Tables.*

BAHRAIN - MARRIAGE RATES

Facts on File, 460 Park Avenue South, New York, New York 10016 (800) 443-8323; *The New Book of World Rankings.*

Statistical Office of the United Nations, Publishing Service, New York, New York 10017 (800) 253-9646; *Demographic Yearbook.*

BAHRAIN - MEAT PRODUCTION - See BAHRAIN - LIVESTOCK AND POULTRY

BAHRAIN - MERCHANT SHIPPING

Economic Commission for Western Asia, Post Office Box 27, Baghdad, Iraq; *Statistical Abstract of Western Asia.*

G.K. Hall and Company, 70 Lincoln Street, Boston, Massachusetts 02111 (617) 423-3990; *The World in Figures.*

Statistical Office of the United Nations, Publishing Service, New York, New York 10017 (800) 253-9646; *Statistical Yearbook.*

Times Books, 201 East 50th Street, New York, New York 10022 (212) 751-2600; *The Economist Book of Vital World Statistics.*

BAHRAIN - MILITARY

G.K. Hall and Company, 70 Lincoln Street, Boston, Massachusetts 02111 (617) 423-3990; *The World in Figures.*

The International Institute for Strategic Studies, 23 Tavistock Street, London WC2E 7NQ, England; *The Military Balance.*

U.S. Arms Control and Disarmament Agency, 320 Twenty-first Street, NW, Washington, D.C. 20451 (202) 647-8677; *World Military Expenditures and Arms Transfers.*

BAHRAIN - MILK PRODUCTION - See BAHRAIN - DAIRY PRODUCTS

BAHRAIN - MINING AND MINERAL PRODUCTS

Economic Commission for Western Asia, Post Office Box 27, Baghdad, Iraq; *Statistical Abstract of Western Asia.*

Facts on File, 460 Park Avenue South, New York, New York 10016 (800) 443-8323; *The New Book of World Rankings.*

G.K. Hall and Company, 70 Lincoln Street, Boston, Massachusetts 02111 (617) 423-3990; *The World in Figures.*

International Monetary Fund, 700 Nineteenth Street, NW, Washington, D.C. 20431 (202) 623-7000; *International Financial Statistics.*

Penn Well Publishing Company, 1421 South Sheridan Road, P.O. Box 1260, Tulsa, Oklahoma 74101 (800) 752-9764; *International Energy Statistics Sourcebook.*

Statistical Office of the United Nations, Publishing Service, New York, New York 10017 (800) 253-9646; *Statistical Yearbook.*

BAHRAIN - MONEY EXCHANGE RATE

Euromonitor Publications Limited, 87-88 Turnmill Street, London EC1M 5QU, England; *International Marketing Data and Statistics.*

International Monetary Fund, 700 Nineteenth Street, NW, Washington, D.C. 20431 (202) 623-7000; *International Financial Statistics.*

Statistical Office of the United Nations, Publishing Service, New York, New York 10017 (800) 253-9646; *Statistical Yearbook.*

BAHRAIN - MONEY RESERVES

Euromonitor Publications Limited, 87-88 Turnmill Street, London EC1M 5QU, England; *International Marketing Data and Statistics.*

BAHRAIN - MONEY SUPPLY

Economic Commission for Western Asia, Post Office Box 27, Baghdad, Iraq; *Statistical Abstract of Western Asia.*

Euromonitor Publications Limited, 87-88 Turnmill Street, London EC1M 5QU, England; *International Marketing Data and Statistics.*

Federal Statistical Office, Gustav - Stresemann - Ring 11, D-6200 Wiesbaden, Germany; *Bahrain.*

G.K. Hall and Company, 70 Lincoln Street, Boston, Massachusetts 02111 (617) 423-3990; *The World in Figures.*

International Monetary Fund, 700 Nineteenth Street, NW, Washington, D.C. 20431 (202) 623-7000; *International Financial Statistics.*

Statistical Office of the United Nations, Publishing Service, New York, New York 10017 (800) 253-9646; *Statistical Yearbook.*

The World Bank, 1818 H Street, N.W., Washington, D.C. 20433 (202) 477-1234; *World Tables.*

BAHRAIN - MOTION PICTURES

Statistical Office of the United Nations, Publishing Service, New York, New York 10017 (800) 253-9646; *Statistical Yearbook.*

BAHRAIN - MOTOR VEHICLE TAXES - See BAHRAIN - TAXATION

BAHRAIN - MOTOR VEHICLES

Economic Commission for Western Asia, Post Office Box 27, Baghdad, Iraq; *Statistical Abstract of Western Asia.*

G.K. Hall and Company, 70 Lincoln Street, Boston, Massachusetts 02111 (617) 423-3990; *The World in Figures.*

Statistical Office of the United Nations, Publishing Service, New York, New York 10017 (800) 253-9646; *Statistical Yearbook.*

Times Books, 201 East 50th Street, New York, New York 10022 (212) 751-2600; *The Economist Book of Vital World Statistics.*

BAHRAIN - MUSEUMS

Facts on File, 460 Park Avenue South, New York, New York 10016 (800) 443-8323; *The New Book of World Rankings.*

United Nations Educational, Scientific and Cultural Organization (UNESCO), 7 Place de Fontenoy, F-75700 Paris, France (Telephone Number in U.S. (212) 963-5981); *Statistical Yearbook.*

BAHRAIN - NATALITY - See BAHRAIN - BIRTH RATES

BAHRAIN - NATIONAL ACCOUNTS

Economic Commission for Western Asia, Post Office Box 27, Baghdad, Iraq; *Statistical Abstract of Western Asia.*

Economist Publications Limited, 25 St. James's Street, London SW1A 1HG England; *The World in Figures.*

Federal Statistical Office, Gustav - Stresemann - Ring 11, D-6200 Wiesbaden, Germany; *Bahrain.*

Statistical Office of the United Nations, Publishing Service, New York, New York 10017 (800) 253-9646; *National Accounts Statistics,* and *Statistical Yearbook.*

BAHRAIN - NATIONAL INCOME

Facts on File, 460 Park Avenue South, New York, New York 10016 (800) 443-8323; *The New Book of World Rankings.*

G.K. Hall and Company, 70 Lincoln Street, Boston, Massachusetts 02111 (617) 423-3990; *The World in Figures.*

Statistical Office of the United Nations, Publishing Service, New York, New York 10017 (800) 253-9646; *Statistical Yearbook.*

BAHRAIN - NATIONAL PRODUCT

Facts on File, 460 Park Avenue South, New York, New York 10016 (800) 443-8323; *The New Book of World Rankings.*

BAHRAIN - NATURAL GAS PRODUCTION - See BAHRAIN - MINING AND MINERAL PRODUCTS

BAHRAIN - NET MATERIAL PRODUCT

Statistical Office of the United Nations, Publishing Service, New York, New York 10017 (800) 253-9646; *Statistical Yearbook.*

BAHRAIN - NEWSPAPER PRODUCTION - See BAHRAIN - FORESTRY AND FOREST PRODUCTS

BAHRAIN - OCCUPATIONS - See BAHRAIN - LABOR FORCE

BAHRAIN - PAPER - See BAHRAIN - FORESTRY AND FOREST PRODUCTS

BAHRAIN - PATENTS

Statistical Office of the United Nations, Publishing Service, New York, New York 10017 (800) 253-9646; *Statistical Yearbook.*

World Intellectual Property Organization, 34 Chemin des Colombettes, CH-1211 Geneva 20. Switzerland; *Industrial Property Statistics.*

BAHRAIN - PEANUT PRODUCTION - See BAHRAIN - CROPS

BAHRAIN - PESTICIDE USE

Food and Agricultural Organization of the United Nations (FAO) Via delle Terme di Caracalla, 00100 Rome, Italy (Telephone Number in U.S. (202) 653-2400); *The State of Food and Agriculture.*

BAHRAIN - PETROLEUM INDUSTRY

Euromonitor Publications Limited, 87-88 Turnmill Street, London EC1M 5QU, England; *Middle East Economic Handbook.*

Facts on File, 460 Park Avenue South, New York, New York 10016 (800) 443-8323; *The New Book of World Rankings.*

Food and Agricultural Organization of the United Nations (FAO) Via delle Terme di Caracalla, 00100 Rome, Italy (Telephone Number in U.S. (202) 653-2400); *The State of Food and Agriculture.*

G.K. Hall and Company, 70 Lincoln Street, Boston, Massachusetts 02111 (617) 423-3990; *The World in Figures.*

International Monetary Fund, 700 Nineteenth Street, NW, Washington, D.C. 20431 (202) 623-7000; *International Financial Statistics.*

Penn Well Publishing Company, 1421 South Sheridan Road, P.O. Box 1260, Tulsa, Oklahoma 74101 (800) 752-9764; *International Energy Statistics Sourcebook.*

Statistical Office of the United Nations, Publishing Service, New York, New York 10017 (800) 253-9646; *Statistical Yearbook.*

BAHRAIN - PIGS - See BAHRAIN - LIVESTOCK AND POULTRY

BAHRAIN - POPULATION

Economic Commission for Western Asia, Post Office Box 27, Baghdad, Iraq; *Statistical Abstract of Western Asia.*

The Economist Intelligence Unit, 111 West 57th Street, New York, New York 10019 (800) 938-4685; *The World Market Atlas.*

Euromonitor Publications Limited, 87-88 Turnmill Street, London EC1M 5QU, England; *International Marketing Data and Statistics,* and *Middle East Economic Handbook.*

Facts on File, 460 Park Avenue South, New York, New York 10016 (800) 443-8323; *The New Book of World Rankings.*

Federal Statistical Office, Gustav - Stresemann - Ring 11, D-6200 Wiesbaden, Germany; *Bahrain.*

Food and Agricultural Organization of the United Nations (FAO), Via delle Terme di Caracalla, 00100 Rome, Italy (Telephone Number in U.S. (202) 653-2400); *Production Yearbook.*

G.K. Hall and Company, 70 Lincoln Street, Boston, Massachusetts 02111 (617) 423-3990; *The World in Figures.*

International Labour Office, I.L.O. Publications, CH-1211, Geneva 22, Switzerland; *Yearbook of Labour Statistics.*

Statistical Office of the United Nations, Publishing Service, New York, New York 10017 (800) 253-9646; *Demographic Yearbook,* and *Statistical Yearbook.*

Times Books, 201 East 50th Street, New York, New York 10022 (212) 751-2600; *The Economist Book of Vital World Statistics.*

U.S. Arms Control and Disarmament Agency, 320 Twenty-first Street, NW, Washington, D.C. 20451 (202) 647-8677; *World Military Expenditures and Arms Transfers.*

World Health Organization, Office of Publications, Avenue Appia, CH-1211 Geneva 27, Switzerland (Telephone Number in U.S. (518) 436-9686); *World Health Statistics Annual.*

BAHRAIN - POST OFFICES

Facts on File, 460 Park Avenue South, New York, New York 10016 (800) 443-8323; *The New Book of World Rankings.*

BAHRAIN - POTATO PRODUCTION - See BAHRAIN - CROPS

BAHRAIN - PRICES

Economic Commission for Western Asia, Post Office Box 27, Baghdad, Iraq; *Statistical Abstract of Western Asia.*

Facts on File, 460 Park Avenue South, New York, New York 10016 (800) 443-8323; *The New Book of World Rankings.*

Federal Statistical Office, Gustav - Stresemann - Ring 11, D-6200 Wiesbaden, Germany; *Bahrain.*

Food and Agricultural Organization of the United Nations (FAO), Via delle Terme di Caracalla, 00100 Rome, Italy (Telephone Number in U.S. (202) 653-2400); *Production Yearbook,* and *The State of Food and Agriculture.*

G.K. Hall and Company, 70 Lincoln Street, Boston, Massachusetts 02111 (617) 423-3990; *The World in Figures.*

International Labour Office, I.L.O. Publications, CH-1211, Geneva 22, Switzerland; *Yearbook of Labour Statistics.*

International Monetary Fund, 700 Nineteenth Street, NW, Washington, D.C. 20431 (202) 623-7000; *International Financial Statistics.*

BAHRAIN - PRINTING AND WRITING PAPER - See BAHRAIN - FORESTRY AND FOREST PRODUCTS

BAHRAIN - PRODUCTION

Facts on File, 460 Park Avenue South, New York, New York 10016 (800) 443-8323; *The New Book of World Rankings.*

G.K. Hall and Company, 70 Lincoln Street, Boston, Massachusetts 02111 (617) 423-3990; *The World in Figures.*

BAHRAIN - PRODUCTIVITY

Euromonitor Publications Limited, 87-88 Turnmill Street, London EC1M 5QU, England; *International Marketing Data and Statistics.*

BAHRAIN - PROPERTY TAXES

International Monetary Fund, 700 Nineteenth Street, NW, Washington, D.C. 20431 (202) 623-7000; *Government Finance Statistics Yearbook.*

BAHRAIN - PUBLIC FINANCE

Facts on File, 460 Park Avenue South, New York, New York 10016 (800) 443-8323; *The New Book of World Rankings*.

Federal Statistical Office, Gustav - Stresemann - Ring 11, D-6200 Wiesbaden, Germany; *Bahrain*.

BAHRAIN - RADIO BROADCASTING - See BAHRAIN - BROADCASTING

BAHRAIN - RAILWAYS

G.K. Hall and Company, 70 Lincoln Street, Boston, Massachusetts 02111 (617) 423-3990; *The World in Figures*.

BAHRAIN - RELIGION

Facts on File, 460 Park Avenue South, New York, New York 10016 (800) 443-8323; *The New Book of World Rankings*.

BAHRAIN - RENT PRICES

International Labour Office, I.L.O. Publications, CH-1211, Geneva 22, Switzerland; *Yearbook of Labour Statistics*.

BAHRAIN - RETAIL TRADE

G.K. Hall and Company, 70 Lincoln Street, Boston, Massachusetts 02111 (617) 423-3990; *The World in Figures*.

BAHRAIN - RICE PRODUCTION - See BAHRAIN - CROPS

BAHRAIN - ROUNDWOOD PRODUCTION - See BAHRAIN - FORESTRY AND FOREST PRODUCTS

BAHRAIN - RUBBER PRODUCTION

Facts on File, 460 Park Avenue South, New York, New York 10016 (800) 443-8323; *The New Book of World Rankings*.

BAHRAIN - SAWNWOOD PRODUCTION - See BAHRAIN - FORESTRY AND FOREST PRODUCTS

BAHRAIN - SCIENTISTS AND TECHNICIANS

United Nations Educational, Scientific and Cultural Organization (UNESCO), 7 Place de Fontenoy, F-75700 Paris, France (Telephone Number in U.S. (212) 963-5981); *Statistical Yearbook*.

BAHRAIN - SENIOR CITIZENS

Facts on File, 460 Park Avenue South, New York, New York 10016 (800) 443-8323; *The New Book of World Rankings*.

BAHRAIN - SHEEP - See BAHRAIN - LIVESTOCK AND POULTRY

BAHRAIN - SILVER PRODUCTION AND CONSUMPTION - See BAHRAIN - MINING AND MINERAL PRODUCTS

BAHRAIN - SOCIAL DATA

Facts on File, 460 Park Avenue South, New York, New York 10016 (800) 443-8323; *The New Book of World Rankings*.

G.K. Hall and Company, 70 Lincoln Street, Boston, Massachusetts 02111 (617) 423-3990; *The World in Figures*.

BAHRAIN - SOCIAL SECURITY

International Monetary Fund, 700 Nineteenth Street, NW, Washington, D.C. 20431 (202) 623-7000; *Government Finance Statistics Yearbook*.

BAHRAIN - STATE BUDGET REVENUE AND EXPENDITURES

Euromonitor Publications Limited, 87-88 Turnmill Street, London EC1M 5QU, England; *International Marketing Data and Statistics*.

BAHRAIN - STEEL - See BAHRAIN - MINING AND MINERAL PRODUCTS

BAHRAIN - STOCKS - COMMODITY - MARKET PRICE - INDEX

Food and Agricultural Organization of the United Nations (FAO) Via delle Terme di Caracalla, 00100 Rome, Italy (Telephone Number in U.S. (202) 653-2400); *The State of Food and Agriculture*.

BAHRAIN - SUGAR PRODUCTION - See BAHRAIN - CROPS

BAHRAIN - TAX REVENUE - See BAHRAIN - TAXATION

BAHRAIN - TAXATION

G.K. Hall and Company, 70 Lincoln Street, Boston, Massachusetts 02111 (617) 423-3990; *The World in Figures*.

International Monetary Fund, 700 Nineteenth Street, NW, Washington, D.C. 20431 (202) 623-7000; *Government Finance Statistics Yearbook*.

The World Bank, 1818 H Street, N.W., Washington, D.C. 20433 (202) 477-1234; *World Tables*.

BAHRAIN - TELEPHONES IN USE

American Telephone and Telegraph Company, 26 Parsippany Road, Whippany, New Jersey 07981 (800) 338-4038; *The World's Telephones*.

Euromonitor Publications Limited, 87-88 Turnmill Street, London EC1M 5QU, England; *Middle East Economic Handbook*.

G.K. Hall and Company, 70 Lincoln Street, Boston, Massachusetts 02111 (617) 423-3990; *The World in Figures*.

Statistical Office of the United Nations, Publishing Service, New York, New York 10017 (800) 253-9646; *Statistical Yearbook*.

BAHRAIN - TELEVISION BROADCASTING

Facts on File, 460 Park Avenue South, New York, New York 10016 (800) 443-8323; *The New Book of World Rankings*.

Times Books, 201 East 50th Street, New York, New York 10022 (212) 751-2600; *The Economist Book of Vital World Statistics*.

United Nations Educational, Scientific and Cultural Organization (UNESCO), 7 Place de Fontenoy, F-75700 Paris, France (Telephone Number in U.S. (212) 963-5981); *Statistical Yearbook*.

BAHRAIN - TEXTILE INDUSTRY

G.K. Hall and Company, 70 Lincoln Street, Boston, Massachusetts 02111 (617) 423-3990; *The World in Figures*.

BAHRAIN - TOBACCO PRODUCTION

Facts on File, 460 Park Avenue South, New York, New York 10016 (800) 443-8323; *The New Book of World Rankings.*

BAHRAIN - TOURISM

Economic Commission for Western Asia, Post Office Box 27, Baghdad, Iraq; *Statistical Abstract of Western Asia.*

Euromonitor Publications Limited, 87-88 Turnmill Street, London EC1M 5QU, England; *Middle East Economic Handbook.*

Facts on File, 460 Park Avenue South, New York, New York 10016 (800) 443-8323; *The New Book of World Rankings.*

Federal Statistical Office, Gustav - Stresemann - Ring 11, D-6200 Wiesbaden, Germany; *Bahrain.*

G.K. Hall and Company, 70 Lincoln Street, Boston, Massachusetts 02111 (617) 423-3990; *The World in Figures.*

Times Books, 201 East 50th Street, New York, New York 10022 (212) 751-2600; *The Economist Book of Vital World Statistics.*

BAHRAIN - TRADE - See BAHRAIN - FOREIGN TRADE

BAHRAIN - TRADEMARKS AND SERVICE MARKS

Statistical Office of the United Nations, Publishing Service, New York, New York 10017 (800) 253-9646; *Statistical Yearbook.*

World Tourism Organization, Calle Capitan Haya 42, E-28020 Madrid, Spain; *Yearbook of Tourism Statistics.*

BAHRAIN - TRANSPORTATION AND COMMUNICATIONS

Economic Commission for Western Asia, Post Office Box 27, Baghdad, Iraq; *Statistical Abstract of Western Asia.*

Euromonitor Publications Limited, 87-88 Turnmill Street, London EC1M 5QU, England; *Middle East Economic Handbook.*

Facts on File, 460 Park Avenue South, New York, New York 10016 (800) 443-8323; *The New Book of World Rankings.*

Federal Statistical Office, Gustav - Stresemann - Ring 11, D-6200 Wiesbaden, Germany; *Bahrain.*

G.K. Hall and Company, 70 Lincoln Street, Boston, Massachusetts 02111 (617) 423-3990; *The World in Figures.*

BAHRAIN - UNEMPLOYMENT

Euromonitor Publications Limited, 87-88 Turnmill Street, London EC1M 5QU, England; *International Marketing Data and Statistics,* and *Middle East Economic Handbook.*

International Labour Office, I.L.O. Publications, CH-1211, Geneva 22, Switzerland; *Yearbook of Labour Statistics.*

BAHRAIN - VITAL STATISTICS

Euromonitor Publications Limited, 87-88 Turnmill Street, London EC1M 5QU, England; *International Marketing Data and Statistics,* and *Middle East Economic Handbook.*

G.K. Hall and Company, 70 Lincoln Street, Boston, Massachusetts 02111 (617) 423-3990; *The World in Figures.*

World Health Organization, Office of Publications, Avenue Appia, CH-1211 Geneva 27, Switzerland (Telephone Number in U.S. (518) 436-9686); *World Health Statistics Annual.*

BAHRAIN - WAGES

Federal Statistical Office, Gustav - Stresemann - Ring 11, D-6200 Wiesbaden, Germany; *Bahrain.*

G.K. Hall and Company, 70 Lincoln Street, Boston, Massachusetts 02111 (617) 423-3990; *The World in Figures.*

International Labour Office, I.L.O. Publications, CH-1211, Geneva 22, Switzerland; *Yearbook of Labour Statistics.*

BAHRAIN - WEATHER

Facts on File, 460 Park Avenue South, New York, New York 10016 (800) 443-8323; *The New Book of World Rankings.*

G.K. Hall and Company, 70 Lincoln Street, Boston, Massachusetts 02111 (617) 423-3990; *The World in Figures.*

BAHRAIN - WELFARE

International Monetary Fund, 700 Nineteenth Street, NW, Washington, D.C. 20431 (202) 623-7000; *Government Finance Statistics Yearbook.*

BAHRAIN - WHEAT PRODUCTION - See BAHRAIN - CROPS

BAHRAIN - WINE PRODUCTION

Facts on File, 460 Park Avenue South, New York, New York 10016 (800) 443-8323; *The New Book of World Rankings.*

BAHRAIN - WOOL PRODUCTION

Facts on File, 460 Park Avenue South, New York, New York 10016 (800) 443-8323; *The New Book of World Rankings.*

BAKERIES - RETAIL

U.S. Department of Commerce, Bureau of the Census, Suitland, Maryland 20233; *County Business Patterns,* and *Census of Retail Trade.*

BALANCE SHEET - See also: Individual Industries

BALANCE SHEET - CORPORATE BUSINESS

Board of Governors of the Federal Reserve System, Twentieth Street and Constitution Avenue, NW, Washington, D.C. 20551 (202) 452-3000; *Balance Sheets for United States Economy.*

U.S. Department of the Treasury, Internal Revenue Service, 1111 Constitution Avenue, NW, Washington, D.C. 20224 (202) 566-5000; *Statistics of Income, Corporation Income Tax Returns.*

BALLET

U.S. National Endowment for the Arts, 1100 Pennsylvania Avenue, NW, Washington, D.C. 20506 (202) 682-5400; *Annual Report.*

U.S. National Endowment for the Humanities, 1100 Pennsylvania Avenue, NW, Washington, D.C. 20506 (202) 606-8438; *Annual Report.*

BANANAS

U.S. Department of Agriculture, Economic Research Service, Fourteenth Street and Independence Avenue, SW, Washington, D.C. 20005-4789 (202) 219-1504; *Agricultural Outlook, Food Consumption, Prices, and Expenditures, Foreign Agricultural Trade of the United States*, and unpublished data.

U.S. Department of Agriculture, National Agricultural Statistics Service, Fourteenth Street and Independence Avenue, SW, Washington, D.C. 20250 (202) 219-1504; *Noncitrus Fruits and Nuts*.

U.S. Department of Labor, Bureau of Labor Statistics, Two Massachusetts Avenue, NE, Washington, D.C. 20212 (202) 606-7828; *Monthly Labor Review*, and *CPI Detailed Report*.

Bangladesh - National Statistical Office

Bangladesh Bureau of Statistics, Ministry of Planning, Secretariat, Dhaka 2, Bangladesh.

Bangladesh - Primary Statistics Sources

Bureau of Statistics, Ministry of Planning, Secretariat, Dhaka 2, Bangladesh; *Statistical Yearbook of Bangladesh*, and *Monthly Statistical Bulletin of Bangladesh*.

BANGLADESH - AGRICULTURE

Asian Development Bank, P.O. Box 789, 1099 Manila, Philippines; *Key Indicators of Developing Asian and Pacific Countries*.

Bangladesh Bureau of Statistics, Statistics Division, Ministry of Planning, Government of the People's Republic of Bangladesh, Dhaka, Bangladesh; *Statistical Yearbook of Bangladesh*.

Euromonitor Publications Limited, 87-88 Turnmill Street, London EC1M 5QU, England; *International Marketing Data and Statistics*.

Facts on File, 460 Park Avenue South, New York, New York 10016 (800) 443-8323; *The New Book of World Rankings*.

Federal Statistical Office, Gustav - Stresemann - Ring 11, D-6200 Wiesbaden, Germany; *Bangladesh*.

Food and Agricultural Organization of the United Nations (FAO), Via delle Terme di Caracalla, 00100 Rome, Italy (Telephone Number in U.S. (202) 653-2400); *Production Yearbook, The State of Food and Agriculture*, and *Trade Yearbook*.

G.K. Hall and Company, 70 Lincoln Street, Boston, Massachusetts 02111 (617) 423-3990; *The World in Figures*.

Statistical Office of the United Nations, Publishing Service, New York, New York 10017 (800) 253-9646; *Statistical Yearbook*, and *Statistical Yearbook for Asia and the Pacific*.

Times Books, 201 East 50th Street, New York, New York 10022 (212) 751-2600; *The Economist Book of Vital World Statistics*.

The World Bank, 1818 H Street, N.W., Washington, D.C. 20433 (202) 477-1234; *World Tables*.

BANGLADESH - AIRLINE SERVICE

The Economist Intelligence Unit (Asia) Limited, 10th Floor, Luk Kwok Centre, 72 Gloucester Road, Wanchai, Hong Kong (Phone Number in U.S. (800) 938-4685); *Asian Market Atlas*.

Facts on File, 460 Park Avenue South, New York, New York 10016 (800) 443-8323; *The New Book of World Rankings*.

G.K. Hall and Company, 70 Lincoln Street, Boston, Massachusetts 02111 (617) 423-3990; *The World in Figures*.

International Civil Aviation Organization, 1000 Sherbrooke Street West, Suite 400, Montreal, Quebec, Canada H3A 2R2 (514) 285-8219; *Civil Aviation Statistics of the World*.

Times Books, 201 East 50th Street, New York, New York 10022 (212) 751-2600; *The Economist Book of Vital World Statistics*.

BANGLADESH - ALUMINUM PRODUCTION AND CONSUMPTION - See BANGLADESH - MINING AND MINERAL PRODUCTS

BANGLADESH - ANIMAL HEALTH

Food and Agricultural Organization of the United Nations (FAO), Via delle Terme di Caracalla, 00100 Rome, Italy (Telephone Number in U.S. (202) 653-2400); *Animal Health Yearbook*.

BANGLADESH - AREA AND DENSITY OF POPULATION

Bangladesh Bureau of Statistics, Statistics Division, Ministry of Planning, Government of the People's Republic of Bangladesh, Dhaka, Bangladesh; *Statistical Yearbook of Bangladesh*.

Euromonitor Publications Limited, 87-88 Turnmill Street, London EC1M 5QU, England; *International Marketing Data and Statistics*.

Facts on File, 460 Park Avenue South, New York, New York 10016 (800) 443-8323; *The New Book of World Rankings*.

Federal Statistical Office, Gustav - Stresemann - Ring 11, D-6200 Wiesbaden, Germany; *Bangladesch*.

Food and Agricultural Organization of the United Nations (FAO) Via delle Terme di Caracalla, 00100 Rome, Italy (Telephone Number in U.S. (202) 653-2400); *The State of Food and Agriculture*.

G.K. Hall and Company, 70 Lincoln Street, Boston, Massachusetts 02111 (617) 423-3990; *The World in Figures*.

Statistical Office of the United Nations, Publishing Service, New York, New York 10017 (800) 253-9646; *Statistical Yearbook*.

Times Books, 201 East 50th Street, New York, New York 10022 (212) 751-2600; *The Economist Book of Vital World Statistics*.

BANGLADESH - ARMS EXPORTS AND IMPORTS

U.S. Arms Control and Disarmament Agency, 320 Twenty-first Street, NW, Washington, D.C. 20451 (202) 647-8677; *World Military Expenditures and Arms Transfers*.

BANGLADESH - BALANCE OF PAYMENTS

The Economist Intelligence Unit, 111 West 57th Street, New York, New York 10019 (800) 938-4685; *The World Market Atlas*.

Federal Statistical Office, Gustav - Stresemann - Ring 11, D-6200 Wiesbaden, Germany; *Bangladesch*.

G.K. Hall and Company, 70 Lincoln Street, Boston, Massachusetts 02111 (617) 423-3990; *The World in Figures*.

Times Books, 201 East 50th Street, New York, New York 10022 (212) 751-2600; *The Economist Book of Vital World Statistics*.

The World Bank, 1818 H Street, N.W., Washington, D.C. 20433 (202) 477-1234; *World Tables.*

BANGLADESH - BANKING

Asian Development Bank, P.O. Box 789, 1099 Manila, Philippines; *Key Indicators of Developing Asian and Pacific Countries.*

Bangladesh Bureau of Statistics, Statistics Division, Ministry of Planning, Government of the People's Republic of Bangladesh, Dhaka, Bangladesh; *Statistical Yearbook of Bangladesh.*

Facts on File, 460 Park Avenue South, New York, New York 10016 (800) 443-8323; *The New Book of World Rankings.*

G.K. Hall and Company, 70 Lincoln Street, Boston, Massachusetts 02111 (617) 423-3990; *The World in Figures.*

International Monetary Fund, 700 Nineteenth Street, NW, Washington, D.C. 20431 (202) 623-7000; *Government Finance Statistics Yearbook,* and *International Financial Statistics.*

BANGLADESH - BARLEY PRODUCTION - See BANGLADESH - CROPS

BANGLADESH - BEER PRODUCTION

Facts on File, 460 Park Avenue South, New York, New York 10016 (800) 443-8323; *The New Book of World Rankings.*

BANGLADESH - BIRTH RATES

The Economist Intelligence Unit (Asia) Limited, 10th Floor, Luk Kwok Centre, 72 Gloucester Road, Wanchai, Hong Kong (Phone Number in U.S. (800) 938-4685); *Asian Market Atlas.*

Facts on File, 460 Park Avenue South, New York, New York 10016 (800) 443-8323; *The New Book of World Rankings.*

Statistical Office of the United Nations, Publishing Service, New York, New York 10017 (800) 253-9646; *Demographic Yearbook,* and *Statistical Yearbook.*

Times Books, 201 East 50th Street, New York, New York 10022 (212) 751-2600; *The Economist Book of Vital World Statistics.*

The World Bank, 1818 H Street, N.W., Washington, D.C. 20433 (202) 477-1234; *World Tables.*

BANGLADESH - BONDS

Asian Development Bank, P.O. Box 789, 1099 Manila, Philippines; *Key Indicators of Developing Asian and Pacific Countries.*

G.K. Hall and Company, 70 Lincoln Street, Boston, Massachusetts 02111 (617) 423-3990; *The World in Figures.*

International Monetary Fund, 700 Nineteenth Street, NW, Washington, D.C. 20431 (202) 623-7000; *Government Finance Statistics Yearbook.*

BANGLADESH - BOOK PRODUCTION

G.K. Hall and Company, 70 Lincoln Street, Boston, Massachusetts 02111 (617) 423-3990; *The World in Figures.*

BANGLADESH - BROADCASTING

Billboard Limited, P.O. Box 9027, 1006 AA Amsterdam, The Netherlands (Telephone Number in U.S. (212) 764-7300); *World Radio TV Handbook.*

The Economist Intelligence Unit (Asia) Limited, 10th Floor, Luk Kwok Centre, 72 Gloucester Road, Wanchai, Hong Kong (Phone Number in U.S. (800) 938-4685); *Asian Market Atlas.*

Facts on File, 460 Park Avenue South, New York, New York 10016 (800) 443-8323; *The New Book of World Rankings.*

G.K. Hall and Company, 70 Lincoln Street, Boston, Massachusetts 02111 (617) 423-3990; *The World in Figures.*

Times Books, 201 East 50th Street, New York, New York 10022 (212) 751-2600; *The Economist Book of Vital World Statistics.*

United Nations Educational, Scientific and Cultural Organization (UNESCO), 7 Place de Fontenoy, F-75700 Paris, France (Telephone Number in U.S. (212) 963-5981); *Statistical Yearbook.*

BANGLADESH - BUSINESS

G.K. Hall and Company, 70 Lincoln Street, Boston, Massachusetts 02111 (617) 423-3990; *The World in Figures.*

BANGLADESH - BUSINESS AND PROFESSIONAL LICENSES

International Monetary Fund, 700 Nineteenth Street, NW, Washington, D.C. 20431 (202) 623-7000; *Government Finance Statistics Yearbook.*

BANGLADESH - BUTTER PRODUCTION - See BANGLADESH - DAIRY PRODUCTS

BANGLADESH - CABBAGE PRODUCTION - See BANGLADESH - CROPS

BANGLADESH - CALORIE SUPPLY

Asian Development Bank, P.O. Box 789, 1099 Manila, Philippines; *Key Indicators of Developing Asian and Pacific Countries.*

Food and Agricultural Organization of the United Nations (FAO) Via delle Terme di Caracalla, 00100 Rome, Italy (Telephone Number in U.S. (202) 653-2400); *The State of Food and Agriculture.*

BANGLADESH - CAPITAL INVESTMENT

Asian Development Bank, P.O. Box 789, 1099 Manila, Philippines; *Key Indicators of Developing Asian and Pacific Countries.*

BANGLADESH - CAPITAL REVENUE

Asian Development Bank, P.O. Box 789, 1099 Manila, Philippines; *Key Indicators of Developing Asian and Pacific Countries.*

International Monetary Fund, 700 Nineteenth Street, NW, Washington, D.C. 20431 (202) 623-7000; *Government Finance Statistics Yearbook.*

BANGLADESH - CATTLE - See BANGLADESH - LIVESTOCK AND POULTRY

BANGLADESH - CAULIFLOWER PRODUCTION - See BANGLADESH - CROPS

BANGLADESH - CAUSTIC SODA PRODUCTION

Statistical Office of the United Nations, Publishing Service, New York, New York 10017 (800) 253-9646; *Statistical Yearbook.*

BANGLADESH - CEMENT PRODUCTION - See BANGLADESH - MINING AND MINERAL PRODUCTS

BANGLADESH - CHEESE PRODUCTION - See BANGLADESH - DAIRY PRODUCTS

BANGLADESH - CHEMICAL (ORGANIC) PRODUCTION - See BANGLADESH - MINING AND MINERAL PRODUCTS

BANGLADESH - CHICK PEA PRODUCTION - See BANGLADESH - CROPS

BANGLADESH - CIGARETTE PRODUCTION - See BANGLADESH - TOBACCO PRODUCTION

BANGLADESH - CLASS STRUCTURE

G.K. Hall and Company, 70 Lincoln Street, Boston, Massachusetts 02111 (617) 423-3990; *The World in Figures.*

BANGLADESH - CLIMATE

Facts on File, 460 Park Avenue South, New York, New York 10016 (800) 443-8323; *The New Book of World Rankings.*

G.K. Hall and Company, 70 Lincoln Street, Boston, Massachusetts 02111 (617) 423-3990; *The World in Figures.*

BANGLADESH - COAL PRODUCTION - See BANGLADESH - MINING AND MINERAL PRODUCTS

BANGLADESH - COFFEE PRODUCTION - See BANGLADESH - CROPS

BANGLADESH - COMMUNICATIONS

Bangladesh Bureau of Statistics, Statistics Division, Ministry of Planning, Government of the People's Republic of Bangladesh, Dhaka, Bangladesh; *Statistical Yearbook of Bangladesh.*

Federal Statistical Office, Gustav - Stresemann - Ring 11, D-6200 Wiesbaden, Germany; *Bangladesch.*

G.K. Hall and Company, 70 Lincoln Street, Boston, Massachusetts 02111 (617) 423-3990; *The World in Figures.*

Statistical Office of the United Nations, Publishing Service, New York, New York 10017 (800) 253-9646; *Statistical Yearbook for Asia and the Pacific.*

BANGLADESH - CONSTRUCTION INDUSTRY

Facts on File, 460 Park Avenue South, New York, New York 10016 (800) 443-8323; *The New Book of World Rankings.*

Statistical Office of the United Nations, Publishing Service, New York, New York 10017 (800) 253-9646; *Statistical Yearbook.*

BANGLADESH - CONSUMER PRICE INDEX

Asian Development Bank, P.O. Box 789, 1099 Manila, Philippines; *Key Indicators of Developing Asian and Pacific Countries.*

Federal Statistical Office, Gustav - Stresemann - Ring 11, D-6200 Wiesbaden, Germany; *Bangladesch.*

G.K. Hall and Company, 70 Lincoln Street, Boston, Massachusetts 02111 (617) 423-3990; *The World in Figures.*

Statistical Office of the United Nations, Publishing Service, New York, New York 10017 (800) 253-9646; *Statistical Yearbook.*

BANGLADESH - CONSUMER PRICES

Federal Statistical Office, Gustav - Stresemann - Ring 11, D-6200 Wiesbaden, Germany; *Bangladesch.*

International Labour Office, I.L.O. Publications, CH-1211, Geneva 22, Switzerland; *Yearbook of Labour Statistics.*

International Monetary Fund, 700 Nineteenth Street, NW, Washington, D.C. 20431 (202) 623-7000; *International Financial Statistics.*

Times Books, 201 East 50th Street, New York, New York 10022 (212) 751-2600; *The Economist Book of Vital World Statistics.*

BANGLADESH - CONSUMPTION

G.K. Hall and Company, 70 Lincoln Street, Boston, Massachusetts 02111 (617) 423-3990; *The World in Figures.*

BANGLADESH - COPPER PRODUCTION - See BANGLADESH - MINING AND MINERAL PRODUCTS

BANGLADESH - CORN PRODUCTION - See BANGLADESH - CROPS

BANGLADESH - CORPORATE TAXES - See BANGLADESH - TAXATION

BANGLADESH - COTTON - See BANGLADESH - CROPS

BANGLADESH - CROPS

Asian Development Bank, P.O. Box 789, 1099 Manila, Philippines; *Key Indicators of Developing Asian and Pacific Countries.*

Commodity Research Bureau, Incorporated, 75 Wall Street, New York, New York 10005 (212) 504-7754; *Commodity Year Book.*

Facts on File, 460 Park Avenue South, New York, New York 10016 (800) 443-8323; *The New Book of World Rankings.*

Food and Agricultural Organization of the United Nations (FAO) Via delle Terme di Caracalla, 00100 Rome, Italy (Telephone Number in U.S. (202) 653-2400); *The State of Food and Agriculture.*

G.K. Hall and Company, 70 Lincoln Street, Boston, Massachusetts 02111 (617) 423-3990; *The World in Figures.*

International Monetary Fund, 700 Nineteenth Street, NW, Washington, D.C. 20431 (202) 623-7000; *International Financial Statistics.*

Statistical Office of the United Nations, Publishing Service, New York, New York 10017 (800) 253-9646; *Statistical Yearbook.*

BANGLADESH - CUSTOMS DUTIES

G.K. Hall and Company, 70 Lincoln Street, Boston, Massachusetts 02111 (617) 423-3990; *The World in Figures.*

International Monetary Fund, 700 Nineteenth Street, NW, Washington, D.C. 20431 (202) 623-7000; *Government Finance Statistics Yearbook.*

BANGLADESH - DAIRY PRODUCTS

Facts on File, 460 Park Avenue South, New York, New York 10016 (800) 443-8323; *The New Book of World Rankings.*

Food and Agricultural Organization of the United Nations (FAO), Via delle Terme di Caracalla, 00100 Rome, Italy (Telephone Number in U.S. (202) 653-2400); *Production Yearbook,* and *The State of Food and Agriculture.*

Statistical Office of the United Nations, Publishing Service, New York, New York 10017 (800) 253-9646; *Statistical Yearbook.*

BANGLADESH - DEATH RATE

The Economist Intelligence Unit (Asia) Limited, 10th Floor, Luk Kwok Centre, 72 Gloucester Road, Wanchai, Hong Kong (Phone Number in U.S. (800) 938-4685); *Asian Market Atlas.*

G.K. Hall and Company, 70 Lincoln Street, Boston, Massachusetts 02111 (617) 423-3990; *The World in Figures.*

Statistical Office of the United Nations, Publishing Service, New York, New York 10017 (800) 253-9646; *Statistical Yearbook.*

Times Books, 201 East 50th Street, New York, New York 10022 (212) 751-2600; *The Economist Book of Vital World Statistics.*

World Health Organization, Office of Publications, Avenue Appia, CH-1211 Geneva 27, Switzerland (Telephone Number in U.S. (518) 436-9686); *World Health Statistics Annual.*

BANGLADESH - DEFENSE EXPENDITURES

G.K. Hall and Company, 70 Lincoln Street, Boston, Massachusetts 02111 (617) 423-3990; *The World in Figures.*

International Monetary Fund, 700 Nineteenth Street, NW, Washington, D.C. 20431 (202) 623-7000; *Government Finance Statistics Yearbook.*

U.S. Arms Control and Disarmament Agency, 320 Twenty-first Street, NW, Washington, D.C. 20451 (202) 647-8677; *World Military Expenditures and Arms Transfers.*

BANGLADESH - DEMOGRAPHY

The Economist Intelligence Unit, 111 West 57th Street, New York, New York 10019 (800) 938-4685; *The World Market Atlas.*

The Economist Intelligence Unit (Asia) Limited, 10th Floor, Luk Kwok Centre, 72 Gloucester Road, Wanchai, Hong Kong (Phone Number in U.S. (800) 938-4685); *Asian Market Atlas.*

Facts on File, 460 Park Avenue South, New York, New York 10016 (800) 443-8323; *The New Book of World Rankings.*

Federal Statistical Office, Gustav - Stresemann - Ring 11, D-6200 Wiesbaden, Germany; *Bangladesch.*

G.K. Hall and Company, 70 Lincoln Street, Boston, Massachusetts 02111 (617) 423-3990; *The World in Figures.*

BANGLADESH - DEVELOPMENT ASSISTANCE

Asian Development Bank, P.O. Box 789, 1099 Manila, Philippines; *Key Indicators of Developing Asian and Pacific Countries.*

G.K. Hall and Company, 70 Lincoln Street, Boston, Massachusetts 02111 (617) 423-3990; *The World in Figures.*

Statistical Office of the United Nations, Publishing Service, New York, New York 10017 (800) 253-9646; *Statistical Yearbook.*

BANGLADESH - DIAMOND PRODUCTION - See BANGLADESH - MINING AND MINERAL PRODUCTS

BANGLADESH - DISEASES

G.K. Hall and Company, 70 Lincoln Street, Boston, Massachusetts 02111 (617) 423-3990; *The World in Figures.*

World Health Organization, Office of Publications, Avenue Appia, CH-1211 Geneva 27, Switzerland (Telephone Number in U.S. (518) 436-9686); *World Health Statistics Annual.*

BANGLADESH - DIVORCE

Facts on File, 460 Park Avenue South, New York, New York 10016 (800) 443-8323; *The New Book of World Rankings.*

Statistical Office of the United Nations, Publishing Service, New York, New York 10017 (800) 253-9646; *Demographic Yearbook.*

BANGLADESH - DOMESTIC PRODUCT

G.K. Hall and Company, 70 Lincoln Street, Boston, Massachusetts 02111 (617) 423-3990; *The World in Figures.*

BANGLADESH - DUCKS - See BANGLADESH - LIVESTOCK AND POULTRY

BANGLADESH - ECONOMY

Asian Development Bank, P.O. Box 789, 1099 Manila, Philippines; *Key Indicators of Developing Asian and Pacific Countries.*

Euromonitor Publications Limited, 87-88 Turnmill Street, London EC1M 5QU, England; *International Marketing Data and Statistics.*

Facts on File, 460 Park Avenue South, New York, New York 10016 (800) 443-8323; *The New Book of World Rankings.*

Federal Statistical Office, Gustav - Stresemann - Ring 11, D-6200 Wiesbaden, Germany; *Bangladesch.*

G.K. Hall and Company, 70 Lincoln Street, Boston, Massachusetts 02111 (617) 423-3990; *The World in Figures.*

BANGLADESH - EDUCATION

Bangladesh Bureau of Statistics, Statistics Division, Ministry of Planning, Government of the People's Republic of Bangladesh, Dhaka, Bangladesh; *Statistical Yearbook of Bangladesh.*

The Economist Intelligence Unit, 111 West 57th Street, New York, New York 10019 (800) 938-4685; *The World Market Atlas.*

The Economist Intelligence Unit (Asia) Limited, 10th Floor, Luk Kwok Centre, 72 Gloucester Road, Wanchai, Hong Kong (Phone Number in U.S. (800) 938-4685); *Asian Market Atlas.*

Facts on File, 460 Park Avenue South, New York, New York 10016 (800) 443-8323; *The New Book of World Rankings.*

Federal Statistical Office, Gustav - Stresemann - Ring 11, D-6200 Wiesbaden, Germany; *Bangladesch.*

G.K. Hall and Company, 70 Lincoln Street, Boston, Massachusetts 02111 (617) 423-3990; *The World in Figures.*

International Monetary Fund, 700 Nineteenth Street, NW, Washington, D.C. 20431 (202) 623-7000; *Government Finance Statistics Yearbook.*

Statistical Office of the United Nations, Publishing Service, New York, New York 10017 (800) 253-9646; *Statistical Yearbook for Asia and the Pacific.*

Times Books, 201 East 50th Street, New York, New York 10022 (212) 751-2600; *The Economist Book of Vital World Statistics.*

United Nations Educational, Scientific and Cultural Organization (UNESCO), 7 Place de Fontenoy, F-75700 Paris, France (Telephone Number in U.S. (212) 963-5981); *Statistical Yearbook.*

The World Bank, 1818 H Street, N.W., Washington, D.C. 20433 (202) 477-1234; *World Tables.*

BANGLADESH - EGG PRODUCTION - See BANGLADESH - DAIRY PRODUCTS

BANGLADESH - ELECTRICITY

Asian Development Bank, P.O. Box 789, 1099 Manila, Philippines; *Key Indicators of Developing Asian and Pacific Countries.*

Facts on File, 460 Park Avenue South, New York, New York 10016 (800) 443-8323; *The New Book of World Rankings.*

Penn Well Publishing Company, 1421 South Sheridan Road, P.O. Box 1260, Tulsa, Oklahoma 74101 (800) 752-9764; *International Energy Statistics Sourcebook.*

Statistical Office of the United Nations, Publishing Service, New York, New York 10017 (800) 253-9646; *Electric Power in Asia and the Pacific.*

Times Books, 201 East 50th Street, New York, New York 10022 (212) 751-2600; *The Economist Book of Vital World Statistics.*

BANGLADESH - EMPLOYMENT

Euromonitor Publications Limited, 87-88 Turnmill Street, London EC1M 5QU, England; *International Marketing Data and Statistics.*

Facts on File, 460 Park Avenue South, New York, New York 10016 (800) 443-8323; *The New Book of World Rankings.*

Federal Statistical Office, Gustav - Stresemann - Ring 11, D-6200 Wiesbaden, Germany; *Bangladesch.*

International Labour Office, I.L.O. Publications, CH-1211, Geneva 22, Switzerland; *Yearbook of Labour Statistics.*

Statistical Office of the United Nations, Publishing Service, New York, New York 10017 (800) 253-9646; *Statistical Yearbook.*

BANGLADESH - ENERGY

Bangladesh Bureau of Statistics, Statistics Division, Ministry of Planning, Government of the People's Republic of Bangladesh, Dhaka, Bangladesh; *Statistical Yearbook of Bangladesh.*

Facts on File, 460 Park Avenue South, New York, New York 10016 (800) 443-8323; *The New Book of World Rankings.*

Food and Agricultural Organization of the United Nations (FAO) Via delle Terme di Caracalla, 00100 Rome, Italy (Telephone Number in U.S. (202) 653-2400); *The State of Food and Agriculture.*

G.K. Hall and Company, 70 Lincoln Street, Boston, Massachusetts 02111 (617) 423-3990; *The World in Figures.*

Penn Well Publishing Company, 1421 South Sheridan Road, P.O. Box 1260, Tulsa, Oklahoma 74101 (800) 752-9764; *International Energy Statistics Sourcebook.*

Statistical Office of the United Nations, Publishing Service, New York, New York 10017 (800) 253-9646; *Statistical Yearbook, Statistical Yearbook for Asia and the Pacific,* and *World Energy Supplies.*

Times Books, 201 East 50th Street, New York, New York 10022 (212) 751-2600; *The Economist Book of Vital World Statistics.*

BANGLADESH - ENVIRONMENT

Bangladesh Bureau of Statistics, Statistics Division, Ministry of Planning, Government of the People's Republic of Bangladesh, Dhaka, Bangladesh; *Statistical Yearbook of Bangladesh.*

BANGLADESH - EXCHANGE RATES

Asian Development Bank, P.O. Box 789, 1099 Manila, Philippines; *Key Indicators of Developing Asian and Pacific Countries.*

The Economist Intelligence Unit (Asia) Limited, 10th Floor, Luk Kwok Centre, 72 Gloucester Road, Wanchai, Hong Kong (Phone Number in U.S. (800) 938-4685); *Asian Market Atlas.*

Euromonitor Publications Limited, 87-88 Turnmill Street, London EC1M 5QU, England; *International Marketing Data and Statistics.*

International Civil Aviation Organization, 1000 Sherbrooke Street West, Suite 400, Montreal, Quebec, Canada H3A 2R2 (514) 285-8219; *Civil Aviation Statistics of the World.*

International Monetary Fund, 700 Nineteenth Street, NW, Washington, D.C. 20431 (202) 623-7000; *International Financial Statistics.*

BANGLADESH - EXCHANGE TAXES

International Monetary Fund, 700 Nineteenth Street, NW, Washington, D.C. 20431 (202) 623-7000; *Government Finance Statistics Yearbook.*

BANGLADESH - EXCISE TAXES - See BANGLADESH - TAXATION

BANGLADESH - EXPORTS

Asian Development Bank, P.O. Box 789, 1099 Manila, Philippines; *Key Indicators of Developing Asian and Pacific Countries.*

The Economist Intelligence Unit, 111 West 57th Street, New York, New York 10019 (800) 938-4685; *The World Market Atlas.*

The Economist Intelligence Unit (Asia) Limited, 10th Floor, Luk Kwok Centre, 72 Gloucester Road, Wanchai, Hong Kong (Phone Number in U.S. (800) 938-4685); *Asian Market Atlas.*

Euromonitor Publications Limited, 87-88 Turnmill Street, London EC1M 5QU, England; *International Marketing Data and Statistics.*

Food and Agricultural Organization of the United Nations (FAO) Via delle Terme di Caracalla, 00100 Rome, Italy (Telephone Number in U.S. (202) 653-2400); *The State of Food and Agriculture.*

G.K. Hall and Company, 70 Lincoln Street, Boston, Massachusetts 02111 (617) 423-3990; *The World in Figures.*

International Monetary Fund, 700 Nineteenth Street, NW, Washington, D.C. 20431 (202) 623-7000; *Direction of Trade Statistics, Government Finance Statistics Yearbook,* and *International Financial Statistics.*

Statistical Office of the United Nations, Publishing Service, New York, New York 10017 (800) 253-9646; *Foreign Trade Statistics of Asia and the Pacific,* and *Trade in Manufactures of Developing Countries.*

Times Books, 201 East 50th Street, New York, New York 10022 (212) 751-2600; *The Economist Book of Vital World Statistics.*

The World Bank, 1818 H Street, N.W., Washington, D.C. 20433 (202) 477-1234; *World Tables.*

BANGLADESH - EXTERNAL FINANCING

Asian Development Bank, P.O. Box 789, 1099 Manila, Philippines; *Key Indicators of Developing Asian and Pacific Countries.*

BANGLADESH - EXTERNAL INDEBTEDNESS

Asian Development Bank, P.O. Box 789, 1099 Manila, Philippines; *Key Indicators of Developing Asian and Pacific Countries.*

The World Bank, 1818 H Street, N.W., Washington, D.C. 20433 (202) 477-1234; *World Tables.*

BANGLADESH - EXTERNAL TRADE

Asian Development Bank, P.O. Box 789, 1099 Manila, Philippines; *Key Indicators of Developing Asian and Pacific Countries.*

Food and Agricultural Organization of the United Nations (FAO) Via delle Terme di Caracalla, 00100 Rome, Italy (Telephone Number in U.S. (202) 653-2400); *The State of Food and Agriculture,* and *Trade Yearbook.*

G.K. Hall and Company, 70 Lincoln Street, Boston, Massachusetts 02111 (617) 423-3990; *The World in Figures.*

Statistical Office of the United Nations, Publishing Service, New York, New York 10017 (800) 253-9646; *Statistical Yearbook,* and *Statistical Yearbook for Asia and the Pacific.*

BANGLADESH - FABRIC PRODUCTION - See BANGLADESH TEXTILE INDUSTRY

BANGLADESH - FARM CROPS - See BANGLADESH - CROPS

BANGLADESH - FEMALE WORKING POPULATION - See BANGLADESH - EMPLOYMENT

BANGLADESH - FERTILITY RATES

The Economist Intelligence Unit (Asia) Limited, 10th Floor, Luk Kwok Centre, 72 Gloucester Road, Wanchai, Hong Kong (Phone Number in U.S. (800) 938-4685); *Asian Market Atlas.*

Facts on File, 460 Park Avenue South, New York, New York 10016 (800) 443-8323; *The New Book of World Rankings.*

Times Books, 201 East 50th Street, New York, New York 10022 (212) 751-2600; *The Economist Book of Vital World Statistics.*

The World Bank, 1818 H Street, N.W., Washington, D.C. 20433 (202) 477-1234; *World Tables.*

BANGLADESH - FERTILIZER

Food and Agricultural Organization of the United Nations (FAO), Via delle Terme di Caracalla, 00100 Rome, Italy (Telephone Number in U.S. (202) 653-2400); *Fertilizer Yearbook,* and *The State of Food and Agriculture.*

Statistical Office of the United Nations, Publishing Service, New York, New York 10017 (800) 253-9646; *Statistical Yearbook.*

BANGLADESH - FETAL MORTALITY

Statistical Office of the United Nations, Publishing Service, New York, New York 10017 (800) 253-9646; *Demographic Yearbook.*

BANGLADESH - FILAMENT PRODUCTION - See BANGLADESH - TEXTILE INDUSTRY

BANGLADESH - FINANCE

Asian Development Bank, P.O. Box 789, 1099 Manila, Philippines; *Key Indicators of Developing Asian and Pacific Countries.*

Bangladesh Bureau of Statistics, Statistics Division, Ministry of Planning, Government of the People's Republic of Bangladesh, Dhaka, Bangladesh; *Statistical Yearbook of Bangladesh.*

Facts on File, 460 Park Avenue South, New York, New York 10016 (800) 443-8323; *The New Book of World Rankings.*

Federal Statistical Office, Gustav - Stresemann - Ring 11, D-6200 Wiesbaden, Germany; *Bangladesch.*

G.K. Hall and Company, 70 Lincoln Street, Boston, Massachusetts 02111 (617) 423-3990; *The World in Figures.*

International Monetary Fund, 700 Nineteenth Street, NW, Washington, D.C. 20431 (202) 623-7000; *Government Finance Statistics Yearbook,* and *International Financial Statistics.*

Statistical Office of the United Nations, Publishing Service, New York, New York 10017 (800) 253-9646; *Statistical Yearbook for Asia and the Pacific.*

BANGLADESH - FISHERIES

Bangladesh Bureau of Statistics, Statistics Division, Ministry of Planning, Government of the People's Republic of Bangladesh, Dhaka, Bangladesh; *Statistical Yearbook of Bangladesh.*

Facts on File, 460 Park Avenue South, New York, New York 10016 (800) 443-8323; *The New Book of World Rankings.*

Federal Statistical Office, Gustav - Stresemann - Ring 11, D-6200 Wiesbaden, Germany; *Bangladesch.*

Food and Agricultural Organization of the United Nations (FAO) Via delle Terme di Caracalla, 00100 Rome, Italy (Telephone Number in U.S. (202) 653-2400); *The State of Food and Agriculture,* and *Yearbook of Fishery Statistics.*

Statistical Office of the United Nations, Publishing Service, New York, New York 10017 (800) 253-9646; *Statistical Yearbook.*

BANGLADESH - FOOD

Food and Agricultural Organization of the United Nations (FAO) Via delle Terme di Caracalla, 00100 Rome, Italy (Telephone Number in U.S. (202) 653-2400); *The State of Food and Agriculture.*

G.K. Hall and Company, 70 Lincoln Street, Boston, Massachusetts 02111 (617) 423-3990; *The World in Figures.*

Statistical Office of the United Nations, Publishing Service, New York, New York 10017 (800) 253-9646; *Production Yearbook,* and *Statistical Yearbook for Asia and the Pacific.*

BANGLADESH - FOREIGN AID

G.K. Hall and Company, 70 Lincoln Street, Boston, Massachusetts 02111 (617) 423-3990; *The World in Figures.*

Statistical Office of the United Nations, Publishing Service, New York, New York 10017 (800) 253-9646; *Statistical Yearbook.*

BANGLADESH - FOREIGN DEBT

International Monetary Fund, 700 Nineteenth Street, NW, Washington, D.C. 20431 (202) 623-7000; *Government Finance Statistics Yearbook.*

BANGLADESH - FOREIGN TRADE

Asian Development Bank, P.O. Box 789, 1099 Manila, Philippines; *Key Indicators of Developing Asian and Pacific Countries.*

Bangladesh Bureau of Statistics, Statistics Division, Ministry of Planning, Government of the People's Republic of Bangladesh, Dhaka, Bangladesh; *Statistical Yearbook of Bangladesh.*

The Economist Intelligence Unit (Asia) Limited, 10th Floor, Luk Kwok Centre, 72 Gloucester Road, Wanchai, Hong Kong (Phone Number in U.S. (800) 938-4685); *Asian Market Atlas.*

Euromonitor Publications Limited, 87-88 Turnmill Street, London EC1M 5QU, England; *International Marketing Data and Statistics.*

Facts on File, 460 Park Avenue South, New York, New York 10016 (800) 443-8323; *The New Book of World Rankings.*

Federal Statistical Office, Gustav - Stresemann - Ring 11, D-6200 Wiesbaden, Germany; *Bangladesch.*

Food and Agricultural Organization of the United Nations (FAO) Via delle Terme di Caracalla, 00100 Rome, Italy (Telephone Number in U.S. (202) 653-2400); *The State of Food and Agriculture.*

G.K. Hall and Company, 70 Lincoln Street, Boston, Massachusetts 02111 (617) 423-3990; *The World in Figures.*

Organisation for Economic Co-operation and Development (OECD), 2 rue Andre-Pascal, 75 Paris 16, France (Telephone Number in U.S. (212) 963-5981); *Trade by Commodities.*

Statistical Office of the United Nations, Publishing Service, New York, New York 10017 (800) 253-9646; *International Trade Statistics Yearbook, Statistical Yearbook,* and *Trade in Manufactures of Developing Countries.*

The World Bank, 1818 H Street, N.W., Washington, D.C. 20433 (202) 477-1234; *World Tables.*

BANGLADESH - FORESTRY AND FOREST PRODUCTS

Bangladesh Bureau of Statistics, Statistics Division, Ministry of Planning, Government of the People's Republic of Bangladesh, Dhaka, Bangladesh; *Statistical Yearbook of Bangladesh.*

The Economist Intelligence Unit (Asia) Limited, 10th Floor, Luk Kwok Centre, 72 Gloucester Road, Wanchai, Hong Kong (Phone Number in U.S. (800) 938-4685); *Asian Market Atlas.*

Facts on File, 460 Park Avenue South, New York, New York 10016 (800) 443-8323; *The New Book of World Rankings.*

Federal Statistical Office, Gustav - Stresemann - Ring 11, D-6200 Wiesbaden, Germany; *Bangladesch.*

Food and Agricultural Organization of the United Nations (FAO) Via delle Terme di Caracalla, 00100 Rome, Italy (Telephone Number in U.S. (202) 653-2400); *The State of Food and Agriculture,* and *Yearbook of Forest Products.*

G.K. Hall and Company, 70 Lincoln Street, Boston, Massachusetts 02111 (617) 423-3990; *The World in Figures.*

Statistical Office of the United Nations, Publishing Service, New York, New York 10017 (800) 253-9646; *Statistical Yearbook.*

United Nations Educational, Scientific and Cultural Organization (UNESCO), 7 Place de Fontenoy, F-75700 Paris, France (Telephone Number in U.S. (212) 963-5981); *Statistical Yearbook.*

BANGLADESH - GARLIC PRODUCTION - See BANGLADESH - CROPS

BANGLADESH - GAS PRODUCTION - See BANGLADESH - MINING AND MINERAL PRODUCTS

BANGLADESH - GENERAL INDUSTRIAL STATISTICS

Federal Statistical Office, Gustav - Stresemann - Ring 11, D-6200 Wiesbaden, Germany; *Bangladesch.*

Statistical Office of the United Nations, Publishing Service, New York, New York 10017 (800) 253-9646; *Industrial Statistics Yearbook.*

BANGLADESH - GENERAL MORTALITY

Statistical Office of the United Nations, Publishing Service, New York, New York 10017 (800) 253-9646; *Demographic Yearbook.*

BANGLADESH - GEOGRAPHIC DATA

Facts on File, 460 Park Avenue South, New York, New York 10016 (800) 443-8323; *The New Book of World Rankings.*

Federal Statistical Office, Gustav - Stresemann - Ring 11, D-6200 Wiesbaden, Germany; *Bangladesch.*

BANGLADESH - GOLD HOLDINGS

International Monetary Fund, 700 Nineteenth Street, NW, Washington, D.C. 20431 (202) 623-7000; *International Financial Statistics.*

Statistical Office of the United Nations, Publishing Service, New York, New York 10017 (800) 253-9646; *Statistical Yearbook.*

The World Bank, 1818 H Street, N.W., Washington, D.C. 20433 (202) 477-1234; *World Tables.*

BANGLADESH - GOLD PRODUCTION AND CONSUMPTION - See BANGLADESH - MINING AND MINERAL PRODUCTS

BANGLADESH - GOVERNMENT

Asian Development Bank, P.O. Box 789, 1099 Manila, Philippines; *Key Indicators of Developing Asian and Pacific Countries.*

G.K. Hall and Company, 70 Lincoln Street, Boston, Massachusetts 02111 (617) 423-3990; *The World in Figures.*

BANGLADESH - GOVERNMENT BONDS - See BANGLADESH - BONDS

BANGLADESH - GOVERNMENT EXPENDITURES

Asian Development Bank, P.O. Box 789, 1099 Manila, Philippines; *Key Indicators of Developing Asian and Pacific Countries.*

International Monetary Fund, 700 Nineteenth Street, NW, Washington, D.C. 20431 (202) 623-7000; *Government Finance Statistics Yearbook.*

Times Books, 201 East 50th Street, New York, New York 10022 (212) 751-2600; *The Economist Book of Vital World Statistics.*

The World Bank, 1818 H Street, N.W., Washington, D.C. 20433 (202) 477-1234; *World Tables.*

BANGLADESH - GOVERNMENT FINANCES

Asian Development Bank, P.O. Box 789, 1099 Manila, Philippines; *Key Indicators of Developing Asian and Pacific Countries.*

International Monetary Fund, 700 Nineteenth Street, NW, Washington, D.C. 20431 (202) 623-7000; *International Financial Statistics.*

BANGLADESH - GOVERNMENT REVENUE

Asian Development Bank, P.O. Box 789, 1099 Manila, Philippines; *Key Indicators of Developing Asian and Pacific Countries.*

International Monetary Fund, 700 Nineteenth Street, NW, Washington, D.C. 20431 (202) 623-7000; *Government Finance Statistics Yearbook.*

Times Books, 201 East 50th Street, New York, New York 10022 (212) 751-2600; *The Economist Book of Vital World Statistics.*

The World Bank, 1818 H Street, N.W., Washington, D.C. 20433 (202) 477-1234; *World Tables.*

BANGLADESH - GRAIN PRODUCTION - See BANGLADESH - CROPS

BANGLADESH - GRANTS

International Monetary Fund, 700 Nineteenth Street, NW, Washington, D.C. 20431 (202) 623-7000; *Government Finance Statistics Yearbook.*

BANGLADESH - GROSS DOMESTIC PRODUCT

Asian Development Bank, P.O. Box 789, 1099 Manila, Philippines; *Key Indicators of Developing Asian and Pacific Countries.*

The Economist Intelligence Unit, 111 West 57th Street, New York, New York 10019 (800) 938-4685; *The World Market Atlas.*

The Economist Intelligence Unit (Asia) Limited, 10th Floor, Luk Kwok Centre, 72 Gloucester Road, Wanchai, Hong Kong (Phone Number in U.S. (800) 938-4685); *Asian Market Atlas.*

Euromonitor Publications Limited, 87-88 Turnmill Street, London EC1M 5QU, England; *International Marketing Data and Statistics.*

Facts on File, 460 Park Avenue South, New York, New York 10016 (800) 443-8323; *The New Book of World Rankings.*

G.K. Hall and Company, 70 Lincoln Street, Boston, Massachusetts 02111 (617) 423-3990; *The World in Figures.*

Statistical Office of the United Nations, Publishing Service, New York, New York 10017 (800) 253-9646; *Statistical Yearbook.*

Times Books, 201 East 50th Street, New York, New York 10022 (212) 751-2600; *The Economist Book of Vital World Statistics.*

The World Bank, 1818 H Street, N.W., Washington, D.C. 20433 (202) 477-1234; *World Tables.*

BANGLADESH - GROSS NATIONAL PRODUCT

Asian Development Bank, P.O. Box 789, 1099 Manila, Philippines; *Key Indicators of Developing Asian and Pacific Countries.*

Euromonitor Publications Limited, 87-88 Turnmill Street, London EC1M 5QU, England; *International Marketing Data and Statistics.*

U.S. Arms Control and Disarmament Agency, 320 Twenty-first Street, NW, Washington, D.C. 20451 (202) 647-8677; *World Military Expenditures and Arms Transfers.*

The World Bank, 1818 H Street, N.W., Washington, D.C. 20433 (202) 477-1234; *World Tables.*

BANGLADESH - GROUNDNUTS PRODUCTION - See BANGLADESH - CROPS

BANGLADESH - HEALTH

Bangladesh Bureau of Statistics, Statistics Division, Ministry of Planning, Government of the People's Republic of Bangladesh, Dhaka, Bangladesh; *Statistical Yearbook of Bangladesh.*

The Economist Intelligence Unit (Asia) Limited, 10th Floor, Luk Kwok Centre, 72 Gloucester Road, Wanchai, Hong Kong (Phone Number in U.S. (800) 938-4685); *Asian Market Atlas.*

Facts on File, 460 Park Avenue South, New York, New York 10016 (800) 443-8323; *The New Book of World Rankings.*

Federal Statistical Office, Gustav - Stresemann - Ring 11, D-6200 Wiesbaden, Germany; *Bangladesch.*

G.K. Hall and Company, 70 Lincoln Street, Boston, Massachusetts 02111 (617) 423-3990; *The World in Figures.*

Statistical Office of the United Nations, Publishing Service, New York, New York 10017 (800) 253-9646; *Statistical Yearbook.*

Times Books, 201 East 50th Street, New York, New York 10022 (212) 751-2600; *The Economist Book of Vital World Statistics.*

World Health Organization, Office of Publications, Avenue Appia, CH-1211 Geneva 27, Switzerland (Telephone Number in U.S. (518) 436-9686); *World Health Statistics Annual.*

BANGLADESH - HEALTH EXPENDITURES

International Monetary Fund, 700 Nineteenth Street, NW, Washington, D.C. 20431 (202) 623-7000; *Government Finance Statistics Yearbook.*

BANGLADESH - HEMP FIBRE PRODUCTION - See BANGLADESH - TEXTILE INDUSTRY

BANGLADESH - HIDE PRODUCTION

Food and Agricultural Organization of the United Nations (FAO), Via delle Terme di Caracalla, 00100 Rome, Italy (Telephone Number in U.S. (202) 653-2400); *Production Yearbook.*

BANGLADESH - HIGHWAYS

The Economist Intelligence Unit (Asia) Limited, 10th Floor, Luk Kwok Centre, 72 Gloucester Road, Wanchai, Hong Kong (Phone Number in U.S. (800) 938-4685); *Asian Market Atlas.*

G.K. Hall and Company, 70 Lincoln Street, Boston, Massachusetts 02111 (617) 423-3990; *The World in Figures.*

BANGLADESH - HORSES - See BANGLADESH - LIVESTOCK AND POULTRY

BANGLADESH - HOURS OF WORK - See BANGLADESH - EMPLOYMENT

BANGLADESH - HOUSING AND HOUSING UNITS

Bangladesh Bureau of Statistics, Statistics Division, Ministry of Planning, Government of the People's Republic of Bangladesh, Dhaka, Bangladesh; *Statistical Yearbook of Bangladesh.*

Facts on File, 460 Park Avenue South, New York, New York 10016 (800) 443-8323; *The New Book of World Rankings.*

BANGLADESH - HOUSING EXPENDITURES

International Monetary Fund, 700 Nineteenth Street, NW, Washington, D.C. 20431 (202) 623-7000; *Government Finance Statistics Yearbook.*

BANGLADESH - HYDROCHLORIC ACID PRODUCTION

Statistical Office of the United Nations, Publishing Service, New York, New York 10017 (800) 253-9646; *Statistical Yearbook.*

BANGLADESH - ILLITERATE POPULATION

The Economist Intelligence Unit, 111 West 57th Street, New York, New York 10019 (800) 938-4685; *The World Market Atlas.*

G.K. Hall and Company, 70 Lincoln Street, Boston, Massachusetts 02111 (617) 423-3990; *The World in Figures.*

United Nations Educational, Scientific and Cultural Organization (UNESCO), 7 Place de Fontenoy, F-75700 Paris, France (Telephone Number in U.S. (212) 963-5981); *Statistical Yearbook.*

BANGLADESH - IMPORTS

Asian Development Bank, P.O. Box 789, 1099 Manila, Philippines; *Key Indicators of Developing Asian and Pacific Countries.*

The Economist Intelligence Unit, 111 West 57th Street, New York, New York 10019 (800) 938-4685; *The World Market Atlas.*

The Economist Intelligence Unit (Asia) Limited, 10th Floor, Luk Kwok Centre, 72 Gloucester Road, Wanchai, Hong Kong (Phone Number in U.S. (800) 938-4685); *Asian Market Atlas.*

Euromonitor Publications Limited, 87-88 Turnmill Street, London EC1M 5QU, England; *International Marketing Data and Statistics.*

Food and Agricultural Organization of the United Nations (FAO) Via delle Terme di Caracalla, 00100 Rome, Italy (Telephone Number in U.S. (202) 653-2400); *The State of Food and Agriculture.*

G.K. Hall and Company, 70 Lincoln Street, Boston, Massachusetts 02111 (617) 423-3990; *The World in Figures.*

International Monetary Fund, 700 Nineteenth Street, NW, Washington, D.C. 20431 (202) 623-7000; *Direction of Trade Statistics, Government Finance Statistics Yearbook,* and *International Financial Statistics.*

Statistical Office of the United Nations, Publishing Service, New York, New York 10017 (800) 253-9646; *Foreign Trade Statistics of Asia and the Pacific.*

Times Books, 201 East 50th Street, New York, New York 10022 (212) 751-2600; *The Economist Book of Vital World Statistics.*

The World Bank, 1818 H Street, N.W., Washington, D.C. 20433 (202) 477-1234; *World Tables.*

BANGLADESH - INCOME TAXES - See BANGLADESH - TAXATION

BANGLADESH - INDUSTRY

Bangladesh Bureau of Statistics, Statistics Division, Ministry of Planning, Government of the People's Republic of Bangladesh, Dhaka, Bangladesh; *Statistical Yearbook of Bangladesh.*

Euromonitor Publications Limited, 87-88 Turnmill Street, London EC1M 5QU, England; *International Marketing Data and Statistics.*

Facts on File, 460 Park Avenue South, New York, New York 10016 (800) 443-8323; *The New Book of World Rankings.*

Federal Statistical Office, Gustav - Stresemann - Ring 11, D-6200 Wiesbaden, Germany; *Bangladesch.*

G.K. Hall and Company, 70 Lincoln Street, Boston, Massachusetts 02111 (617) 423-3990; *The World in Figures.*

International Labour Office, I.L.O. Publications, CH-1211, Geneva 22, Switzerland; *Yearbook of Labour Statistics.*

Statistical Office of the United Nations, Publishing Service, New York, New York 10017 (800) 253-9646; *Statistical Yearbook for Asia and the Pacific.*

Times Books, 201 East 50th Street, New York, New York 10022 (212) 751-2600; *The Economist Book of Vital World Statistics.*

The World Bank, 1818 H Street, N.W., Washington, D.C. 20433 (202) 477-1234; *World Tables.*

BANGLADESH - INFANT AND MATERNAL MORTALITY

The Economist Intelligence Unit (Asia) Limited, 10th Floor, Luk Kwok Centre, 72 Gloucester Road, Wanchai, Hong Kong (Phone Number in U.S. (800) 938-4685); *Asian Market Atlas.*

Statistical Office of the United Nations, Publishing Service, New York, New York 10017 (800) 253-9646; *Demographic Yearbook.*

Times Books, 201 East 50th Street, New York, New York 10022 (212) 751-2600; *The Economist Book of Vital World Statistics.*

The World Bank, 1818 H Street, N.W., Washington, D.C. 20433 (202) 477-1234; *World Tables.*

BANGLADESH - INTERNAL TRADE

Statistical Office of the United Nations, Publishing Service, New York, New York 10017 (800) 253-9646; *Statistical Yearbook for Asia and the Pacific.*

BANGLADESH - INTERNATIONAL LIQUIDITY

International Monetary Fund, 700 Nineteenth Street, NW, Washington, D.C. 20431 (202) 623-7000; *International Financial Statistics.*

BANGLADESH - INTERNATIONAL RESERVES EXCLUDING GOLD

Asian Development Bank, P.O. Box 789, 1099 Manila, Philippines; *Key Indicators of Developing Asian and Pacific Countries.*

The World Bank, 1818 H Street, N.W., Washington, D.C. 20433 (202) 477-1234; *World Tables.*

BANGLADESH - INTERNATIONAL STATISTICS

Asian Development Bank, P.O. Box 789, 1099 Manila, Philippines; *Key Indicators of Developing Asian and Pacific Countries.*

BANGLADESH - IRON ORE PRODUCTION AND CONSUMPTION - See BANGLADESH - MINING AND MINERAL PRODUCTS

BANGLADESH - IRRIGATION

Euromonitor Publications Limited, 87-88 Turnmill Street, London EC1M 5QU, England; *International Marketing Data and Statistics.*

BANGLADESH - JUTE - See BANGLADESH - CROPS

BANGLADESH - LABOR FORCE

Bangladesh Bureau of Statistics, Statistics Division, Ministry of Planning, Government of the People's Republic of Bangladesh, Dhaka, Bangladesh; *Statistical Yearbook of Bangladesh.*

The Economist Intelligence Unit (Asia) Limited, 10th Floor, Luk Kwok Centre, 72 Gloucester Road, Wanchai, Hong Kong (Phone Number in U.S. (800) 938-4685); *Asian Market Atlas.*

Euromonitor Publications Limited, 87-88 Turnmill Street, London EC1M 5QU, England; *International Marketing Data and Statistics.*

Facts on File, 460 Park Avenue South, New York, New York 10016 (800) 443-8323; *The New Book of World Rankings.*

Food and Agricultural Organization of the United Nations (FAO) Via delle Terme di Caracalla, 00100 Rome, Italy (Telephone Number in U.S. (202) 653-2400); *The State of Food and Agriculture.*

G.K. Hall and Company, 70 Lincoln Street, Boston, Massachusetts 02111 (617) 423-3990; *The World in Figures.*

Times Books, 201 East 50th Street, New York, New York 10022 (212) 751-2600; *The Economist Book of Vital World Statistics.*

The World Bank, 1818 H Street, N.W., Washington, D.C. 20433 (202) 477-1234; *World Tables.*

BANGLADESH - LABOR PRODUCTIVITY

International Labour Office, I.L.O. Publications, CH-1211, Geneva 22, Switzerland; *Yearbook of Labour Statistics.*

BANGLADESH - LAND USE

Euromonitor Publications Limited, 87-88 Turnmill Street, London EC1M 5QU, England; *International Marketing Data and Statistics.*

Food and Agricultural Organization of the United Nations (FAO), Via delle Terme di Caracalla, 00100 Rome, Italy (Telephone Number in U.S. (202) 653-2400); *Production Yearbook.*

G.K. Hall and Company, 70 Lincoln Street, Boston, Massachusetts 02111 (617) 423-3990; *The World in Figures.*

BANGLADESH - LEATHER AND FOOTWEAR - EXPORTS AND IMPORTS

Statistical Office of the United Nations, Publishing Service, New York, New York 10017 (800) 253-9646; *Trade in Manufactures of Developing Countries.*

BANGLADESH - LIBRARIES

Facts on File, 460 Park Avenue South, New York, New York 10016 (800) 443-8323; *The New Book of World Rankings.*

BANGLADESH - LIFE EXPECTANCY

The Economist Intelligence Unit (Asia) Limited, 10th Floor, Luk Kwok Centre, 72 Gloucester Road, Wanchai, Hong Kong (Phone Number in U.S. (800) 938-4685); *Asian Market Atlas.*

BANGLADESH - LIVESTOCK AND POULTRY

Bangladesh Bureau of Statistics, Statistics Division, Ministry of Planning, Government of the People's Republic of Bangladesh, Dhaka, Bangladesh; *Statistical Yearbook of Bangladesh.*

Facts on File, 460 Park Avenue South, New York, New York 10016 (800) 443-8323; *The New Book of World Rankings.*

Food and Agricultural Organization of the United Nations (FAO), Via delle Terme di Caracalla, 00100 Rome, Italy (Telephone Number in U.S. (202) 653-2400); *Production Yearbook,* and *The State of Food and Agriculture.*

G.K. Hall and Company, 70 Lincoln Street, Boston, Massachusetts 02111 (617) 423-3990; *The World in Figures.*

Statistical Office of the United Nations, Publishing Service, New York, New York 10017 (800) 253-9646; *Statistical Yearbook.*

BANGLADESH - LIVING LEVELS

G.K. Hall and Company, 70 Lincoln Street, Boston, Massachusetts 02111 (617) 423-3990; *The World in Figures.*

Times Books, 201 East 50th Street, New York, New York 10022 (212) 751-2600; *The Economist Book of Vital World Statistics.*

BANGLADESH - MAIL - NUMBER OF PIECES SENT OR RECEIVED

Statistical Office of the United Nations, Publishing Service, New York, New York 10017 (800) 253-9646; *Statistical Yearbook.*

BANGLADESH - MANPOWER

Bangladesh Bureau of Statistics, Statistics Division, Ministry of Planning, Government of the People's Republic of Bangladesh, Dhaka, Bangladesh; *Statistical Yearbook of Bangladesh.*

Statistical Office of the United Nations, Publishing Service, New York, New York 10017 (800) 253-9646; *Statistical Yearbook for Asia and the Pacific.*

BANGLADESH - MANUFACTURING

Asian Development Bank, P.O. Box 789, 1099 Manila, Philippines; *Key Indicators of Developing Asian and Pacific Countries.*

Facts on File, 460 Park Avenue South, New York, New York 10016 (800) 443-8323; *The New Book of World Rankings.*

G.K. Hall and Company, 70 Lincoln Street, Boston, Massachusetts 02111 (617) 423-3990; *The World in Figures.*

Statistical Office of the United Nations, Publishing Service, New York, New York 10017 (800) 253-9646; *Statistical Yearbook.*

Times Books, 201 East 50th Street, New York, New York 10022 (212) 751-2600; *The Economist Book of Vital World Statistics.*

The World Bank, 1818 H Street, N.W., Washington, D.C. 20433 (202) 477-1234; *World Tables.*

BANGLADESH - MARRIAGE RATES

Facts on File, 460 Park Avenue South, New York, New York 10016 (800) 443-8323; *The New Book of World Rankings.*

Statistical Office of the United Nations, Publishing Service, New York, New York 10017 (800) 253-9646; *Demographic Yearbook.*

BANGLADESH - MEAT PRODUCTION - See BANGLADESH - LIVESTOCK AND POULTRY

BANGLADESH - MERCHANT SHIPPING

G.K. Hall and Company, 70 Lincoln Street, Boston, Massachusetts 02111 (617) 423-3990; *The World in Figures.*

Lloyd's Register of Shipping, 17 Battery Place, New York, New York 10004 (212) 425-8050; *Register of Ships.*

Statistical Office of the United Nations, Publishing Service, New York, New York 10017 (800) 253-9646; *Statistical Yearbook.*

Times Books, 201 East 50th Street, New York, New York 10022 (212) 751-2600; *The Economist Book of Vital World Statistics.*

U.S. Department of Transportation, Maritime Administration, 400 Seventh Street, NW, Washington, D.C. 20590 (202) 366-5807; *A Statistical Analysis of the World's Merchant Fleet.*

BANGLADESH - MILITARY

The Economist Intelligence Unit (Asia) Limited, 10th Floor, Luk Kwok Centre, 72 Gloucester Road, Wanchai, Hong Kong (Phone Number in U.S. (800) 938-4685); *Asian Market Atlas.*

G.K. Hall and Company, 70 Lincoln Street, Boston, Massachusetts 02111 (617) 423-3990; *The World in Figures.*

The International Institute for Strategic Studies, 23 Tavistock Street, London WC2E 7NQ, England; *The Military Balance.*

U.S. Arms Control and Disarmament Agency, 320 Twenty-first Street, NW, Washington, D.C. 20451 (202) 647-8677; *World Military Expenditures and Arms Transfers.*

BANGLADESH - MILK PRODUCTION - See BANGLADESH - DAIRY PRODUCTS

BANGLADESH - MINING AND MINERAL PRODUCTS

Asian Development Bank, P.O. Box 789, 1099 Manila, Philippines; *Key Indicators of Developing Asian and Pacific Countries.*

Facts on File, 460 Park Avenue South, New York, New York 10016 (800) 443-8323; *The New Book of World Rankings.*

G.K. Hall and Company, 70 Lincoln Street, Boston, Massachusetts 02111 (617) 423-3990; *The World in Figures.*

Penn Well Publishing Company, 1421 South Sheridan Road, P.O. Box 1260, Tulsa, Oklahoma 74101 (800) 752-9764; *International Energy Statistics Sourcebook.*

Statistical Office of the United Nations, Publishing Service, New York, New York 10017 (800) 253-9646; *Statistical Yearbook.*

BANGLADESH - MONEY EXCHANGE RATES

Euromonitor Publications Limited, 87-88 Turnmill Street, London EC1M 5QU, England; *International Marketing Data and Statistics.*

International Monetary Fund, 700 Nineteenth Street, NW, Washington, D.C. 20431 (202) 623-7000; *International Financial Statistics.*

Statistical Office of the United Nations, Publishing Service, New York, New York 10017 (800) 253-9646; *Statistical Yearbook.*

BANGLADESH - MONEY RESERVES

Euromonitor Publications Limited, 87-88 Turnmill Street, London EC1M 5QU, England; *International Marketing Data and Statistics.*

BANGLADESH - MONEY SUPPLY

Asian Development Bank, P.O. Box 789, 1099 Manila, Philippines; *Key Indicators of Developing Asian and Pacific Countries.*

Euromonitor Publications Limited, 87-88 Turnmill Street, London EC1M 5QU, England; *International Marketing Data and Statistics.*

Federal Statistical Office, Gustav - Stresemann - Ring 11, D-6200 Wiesbaden, Germany; *Bangladesch.*

G.K. Hall and Company, 70 Lincoln Street, Boston, Massachusetts 02111 (617) 423-3990; *The World in Figures.*

International Monetary Fund, 700 Nineteenth Street, NW, Washington, D.C. 20431 (202) 623-7000; *International Financial Statistics.*

Statistical Office of the United Nations, Publishing Service, New York, New York 10017 (800) 253-9646; *Statistical Yearbook.*

The World Bank, 1818 H Street, N.W., Washington, D.C. 20433 (202) 477-1234; *World Tables.*

BANGLADESH - MOTOR VEHICLE TAXES - See BANGLADESH - TAXATION

BANGLADESH - MOTOR VEHICLES IN USE

G.K. Hall and Company, 70 Lincoln Street, Boston, Massachusetts 02111 (617) 423-3990; *The World in Figures.*

Statistical Office of the United Nations, Publishing Service, New York, New York 10017 (800) 253-9646; *Statistical Yearbook.*

Times Books, 201 East 50th Street, New York, New York 10022 (212) 751-2600; *The Economist Book of Vital World Statistics.*

BANGLADESH - MUSEUMS

Facts on File, 460 Park Avenue South, New York, New York 10016 (800) 443-8323; *The New Book of World Rankings.*

United Nations Educational, Scientific and Cultural Organization (UNESCO), 7 Place de Fontenoy, F-75700 Paris, France (Telephone Number in U.S. (212) 963-5981); *Statistical Yearbook.*

BANGLADESH - NATALITY - See BANGLADESH - BIRTH RATE

BANGLADESH - NATIONAL ACCOUNTS

Federal Statistical Office, Gustav - Stresemann - Ring 11, D-6200 Wiesbaden, Germany; *Bangladesch.*

Statistical Office of the United Nations, Publishing Service, New York, New York 10017 (800) 253-9646; *National Accounts Statistics, Statistical Yearbook,* and *Statistical Yearbook for Asia and the Pacific.*

BANGLADESH - NATIONAL INCOME

Bangladesh Bureau of Statistics, Statistics Division, Ministry of Planning, Government of the People's Republic of Bangladesh, Dhaka, Bangladesh; *Statistical Yearbook of Bangladesh.*

Facts on File, 460 Park Avenue South, New York, New York 10016 (800) 443-8323; *The New Book of World Rankings.*

G.K. Hall and Company, 70 Lincoln Street, Boston, Massachusetts 02111 (617) 423-3990; *The World in Figures.*

Statistical Office of the United Nations, Publishing Service, New York, New York 10017 (800) 253-9646; *Statistical Yearbook.*

BANGLADESH - NATIONAL PRODUCT

Facts on File, 460 Park Avenue South, New York, New York 10016 (800) 443-8323; *The New Book of World Rankings.*

Statistical Office of the United Nations, Publishing Service, New York, New York 10017 (800) 253-9646; *Statistical Yearbook.*

BANGLADESH - NATURAL GAS PRODUCTION - See BANGLADESH - MINING AND MINERAL PRODUCTS

BANGLADESH - NET MATERIAL PRODUCT

Statistical Office of the United Nations, Publishing Service, New York, New York 10017 (800) 253-9646; *Statistical Yearbook.*

BANGLADESH - NEWSPAPER PRODUCTION - See BANGLADESH - FORESTRY AND FOREST PRODUCTS

BANGLADESH - NEWSPRINT - See BANGLADESH - FORESTRY AND FOREST PRODUCTS

BANGLADESH - OCCUPATIONS - See BANGLADESH - LABOR FORCE

BANGLADESH - PAPER - See BANGLADESH - FORESTRY AND FOREST PRODUCTS

BANGLADESH - PATENTS

Statistical Office of the United Nations, Publishing Service, New York, New York 10017 (800) 253-9646; *Statistical Yearbook.*

BANGLADESH - PEANUT PRODUCTION - See BANGLADESH - CROPS

BANGLADESH - PESTICIDE USE

Food and Agricultural Organization of the United Nations (FAO) Via delle Terme di Caracalla, 00100 Rome, Italy (Telephone Number in U.S. (202) 653-2400); *The State of Food and Agriculture.*

BANGLADESH - PETROLEUM INDUSTRY

Asian Development Bank, P.O. Box 789, 1099 Manila, Philippines; *Key Indicators of Developing Asian and Pacific Countries.*

Facts on File, 460 Park Avenue South, New York, New York 10016 (800) 443-8323; *The New Book of World Rankings.*

Food and Agricultural Organization of the United Nations (FAO) Via delle Terme di Caracalla, 00100 Rome, Italy (Telephone Number in U.S. (202) 653-2400); *The State of Food and Agriculture.*

G.K. Hall and Company, 70 Lincoln Street, Boston, Massachusetts 02111 (617) 423-3990; *The World in Figures.*

Penn Well Publishing Company, 1421 South Sheridan Road, P.O. Box 1260, Tulsa, Oklahoma 74101 (800) 752-9764; *International Energy Statistics Sourcebook.*

Statistical Office of the United Nations, Publishing Service, New York, New York 10017 (800) 253-9646; *Statistical Yearbook.*

BANGLADESH - PIGS - See BANGLADESH - LIVESTOCK AND POULTRY

BANGLADESH - POPULATION

Asian Development Bank, P.O. Box 789, 1099 Manila, Philippines; *Key Indicators of Developing Asian and Pacific Countries.*

Bangladesh Bureau of Statistics, Statistics Division, Ministry of Planning, Government of the People's Republic of Bangladesh, Dhaka, Bangladesh; *Statistical Yearbook of Bangladesh.*

The Economist Intelligence Unit, 111 West 57th Street, New York, New York 10019 (800) 938-4685; *The World Market Atlas.*

The Economist Intelligence Unit (Asia) Limited, 10th Floor, Luk Kwok Centre, 72 Gloucester Road, Wanchai, Hong Kong (Phone Number in U.S. (800) 938-4685); *Asian Market Atlas.*

Euromonitor Publications Limited, 87-88 Turnmill Street, London EC1M 5QU, England; *International Marketing Data and Statistics.*

Facts on File, 460 Park Avenue South, New York, New York 10016 (800) 443-8323; *The New Book of World Rankings.*

Federal Statistical Office, Gustav - Stresemann - Ring 11, D-6200 Wiesbaden, Germany; *Bangladesch.*

Food and Agricultural Organization of the United Nations (FAO), Via delle Terme di Caracalla, 00100 Rome, Italy (Telephone Number in U.S. (202) 653-2400); *Production Yearbook.*

G.K. Hall and Company, 70 Lincoln Street, Boston, Massachusetts 02111 (617) 423-3990; *The World in Figures.*

International Labour Office, I.L.O. Publications, CH-1211, Geneva 22, Switzerland; *Yearbook of Labour Statistics.*

Statistical Office of the United Nations, Publishing Service, New York, New York 10017 (800) 253-9646; *Demographic Yearbook,* and *Statistical Yearbook.*

Times Books, 201 East 50th Street, New York, New York 10022 (212) 751-2600; *The Economist Book of Vital World Statistics.*

U.S. Arms Control and Disarmament Agency, 320 Twenty-first Street, NW, Washington, D.C. 20451 (202) 647-8677; *World Military Expenditures and Arms Transfers.*

World Health Organization, Office of Publications, Avenue Appia, CH-1211 Geneva 27, Switzerland (Telephone Number in U.S. (518) 436-9686); *World Health Statistics Annual.*

BANGLADESH - POST OFFICES

Facts on File, 460 Park Avenue South, New York, New York 10016 (800) 443-8323; *The New Book of World Rankings.*

BANGLADESH - POTATO PRODUCTION - See BANGLADESH - CROPS

BANGLADESH - POWER PRODUCTION INDUSTRY

Statistical Office of the United Nations, Publishing Service, New York, New York 10017 (800) 253-9646; *Electric Power in Asia and the Pacific.*

BANGLADESH - PRICES

Asian Development Bank, P.O. Box 789, 1099 Manila, Philippines; *Key Indicators of Developing Asian and Pacific Countries.*

Bangladesh Bureau of Statistics, Statistics Division, Ministry of Planning, Government of the People's Republic of Bangladesh, Dhaka, Bangladesh; *Statistical Yearbook of Bangladesh.*

Facts on File, 460 Park Avenue South, New York, New York 10016 (800) 443-8323; *The New Book of World Rankings.*

Federal Statistical Office, Gustav - Stresemann - Ring 11, D-6200 Wiesbaden, Germany; *Bangladesch.*

Food and Agricultural Organization of the United Nations (FAO), Via delle Terme di Caracalla, 00100 Rome, Italy (Telephone Number in U.S. (202) 653-2400); *Production Yearbook,* and *The State of Food and Agriculture.*

G.K. Hall and Company, 70 Lincoln Street, Boston, Massachusetts 02111 (617) 423-3990; *The World in Figures.*

International Labour Office, I.L.O. Publications, CH-1211, Geneva 22, Switzerland; *Yearbook of Labour Statistics.*

International Monetary Fund, Nineteen and H Streets, NW, Washington, D.C. 20431; *International Financial Statistics.*

BANGLADESH - PRINTING AND WRITING PAPER - See BANGLADESH - FORESTRY AND FOREST PRODUCTS

BANGLADESH - PRODUCTION

Facts on File, 460 Park Avenue South, New York, New York 10016 (800) 443-8323; *The New Book of World Rankings.*

G.K. Hall and Company, 70 Lincoln Street, Boston, Massachusetts 02111 (617) 423-3990; *The World in Figures.*

BANGLADESH - PRODUCTIVITY

Euromonitor Publications Limited, 87-88 Turnmill Street, London EC1M 5QU, England; *International Marketing Data and Statistics.*

BANGLADESH - PROPERTY TAXES - See BANGLADESH - TAXATION

BANGLADESH - PUBLIC FINANCE

Facts on File, 460 Park Avenue South, New York, New York 10016 (800) 443-8323; *The New Book of World Rankings.*

Federal Statistical Office, Gustav - Stresemann - Ring 11, D-6200 Wiesbaden, Germany; *Bangladesch.*

BANGLADESH - RADIO BROADCASTING - See BANGLADESH - BROADCASTING

BANGLADESH - RAILWAYS

G.K. Hall and Company, 70 Lincoln Street, Boston, Massachusetts 02111 (617) 423-3990; *The World in Figures.*

Jane's Information Group, Sentinel House, 163 Brighton Road, Coulsdon, Surrey CR5 2NH, England (Telephone Number in U.S. (703) 683-3700); *Jane's World Railways.*

Statistical Office of the United Nations, Publishing Service, New York, New York 10017 (800) 253-9646; *Statistical Yearbook.*

BANGLADESH - RAPESEED PRODUCTION - See BANGLADESH - CROPS

BANGLADESH - RELIGION

Facts on File, 460 Park Avenue South, New York, New York 10016 (800) 443-8323; *The New Book of World Rankings.*

BANGLADESH - RENT PRICES

International Labour Office, I.L.O. Publications, CH-1211, Geneva 22, Switzerland; *Yearbook of Labour Statistics.*

BANGLADESH - RETAIL TRADE

G.K. Hall and Company, 70 Lincoln Street, Boston, Massachusetts 02111 (617) 423-3990; *The World in Figures.*

BANGLADESH - RICE PRODUCTION - See BANGLADESH - CROPS

BANGLADESH - ROOT AND TUBER PRODUCTION - See BANGLADESH - CROPS

BANGLADESH - ROUNDWOOD PRODUCTION - See BANGLADESH - FORESTRY AND FOREST PRODUCTS

BANGLADESH - RUBBER PRODUCTION

Facts on File, 460 Park Avenue South, New York, New York 10016 (800) 443-8323; *The New Book of World Rankings.*

BANGLADESH - SALT PRODUCTION - See BANGLADESH - MINING AND MINERAL PRODUCTS

BANGLADESH - SAWNWOOD PRODUCTION - See BANGLADESH - FORESTRY AND FOREST PRODUCTS

BANGLADESH - SCIENCE AND TECHNOLOGY - EXPENDITURE FOR RESEARCH

Statistical Office of the United Nations, Publishing Service, New York, New York 10017 (800) 253-9646; *Statistical Yearbook.*

BANGLADESH - SCIENTISTS AND TECHNICIANS

Statistical Office of the United Nations, Publishing Service, New York, New York 10017 (800) 253-9646; *Statistical Yearbook.*

BANGLADESH - SENIOR CITIZENS

Facts on File, 460 Park Avenue South, New York, New York 10016 (800) 443-8323; *The New Book of World Rankings.*

BANGLADESH - SESAME SEED PRODUCTION - See BANGLADESH - CROPS

BANGLADESH - SHEEP

Facts on File, 460 Park Avenue South, New York, New York 10016 (800) 443-8323; *The New Book of World Rankings.*

Statistical Office of the United Nations, Publishing Service, New York, New York 10017 (800) 253-9646; *Statistical Yearbook.*

BANGLADESH - SILVER PRODUCTION AND CONSUMPTION - See BANGLADESH - MINING AND MINERAL PRODUCTS

BANGLADESH - SOCIAL DATA

Asian Development Bank, P.O. Box 789, 1099 Manila, Philippines; *Key Indicators of Developing Asian and Pacific Countries.*

Bangladesh Bureau of Statistics, Statistics Division, Ministry of Planning, Government of the People's Republic of Bangladesh, Dhaka, Bangladesh; *Statistical Yearbook of Bangladesh.*

Facts on File, 460 Park Avenue South, New York, New York 10016 (800) 443-8323; *The New Book of World Rankings.*

G.K. Hall and Company, 70 Lincoln Street, Boston, Massachusetts 02111 (617) 423-3990; *The World in Figures.*

BANGLADESH - SOCIAL SECURITY

International Monetary Fund, 700 Nineteenth Street, NW, Washington, D.C. 20431 (202) 623-7000; *Government Finance Statistics Yearbook.*

BANGLADESH - STAMP TAXES AND DUTIES - See BANGLADESH - TAXATION

BANGLADESH - STATE BUDGET REVENUE AND EXPENDITURES

Euromonitor Publications Limited, 87-88 Turnmill Street, London EC1M 5QU, England; *International Marketing Data and Statistics.*

BANGLADESH - STEEL - See BANGLADESH - MINING AND MINERAL PRODUCTS

BANGLADESH - STOCKS - COMMODITY - MARKET PRICE - INDEX

Food and Agricultural Organization of the United Nations (FAO) Via delle Terme di Caracalla, 00100 Rome, Italy (Telephone Number in U.S. (202) 653-2400); *The State of Food and Agriculture.*

BANGLADESH - SUGAR - See BANGLADESH - CROPS

BANGLADESH - SULPHURIC ACID PRODUCTION - See BANGLADESH - MINING AND MINERAL PRODUCTS

BANGLADESH - TAXATION

G.K. Hall and Company, 70 Lincoln Street, Boston, Massachusetts 02111 (617) 423-3990; *The World in Figures.*

International Monetary Fund, 700 Nineteenth Street, NW, Washington, D.C. 20431 (202) 623-7000; *Government Finance Statistics Yearbook.*

The World Bank, 1818 H Street, N.W., Washington, D.C. 20433 (202) 477-1234; *World Tables.*

BANGLADESH - TEA PRODUCTION - See BANGLADESH - CROPS

BANGLADESH - TELEGRAPH SERVICE

Statistical Office of the United Nations, Publishing Service, New York, New York 10017 (800) 253-9646; *Statistical Yearbook.*

BANGLADESH - TELEPHONES IN USE

American Telephone and Telegraph Company, 26 Parsippany Road, Whippany, New Jersey 07981 (800) 338-4038; *The World's Telephones.*

The Economist Intelligence Unit (Asia) Limited, 10th Floor, Luk Kwok Centre, 72 Gloucester Road, Wanchai, Hong Kong (Phone Number in U.S. (800) 938-4685); *Asian Market Atlas.*

G.K. Hall and Company, 70 Lincoln Street, Boston, Massachusetts 02111 (617) 423-3990; *The World in Figures.*

Statistical Office of the United Nations, Publishing Service, New York, New York 10017 (800) 253-9646; *Statistical Yearbook.*

BANGLADESH - TELEVISION BROADCASTING - See BANGLADESH - BROADCASTING

BANGLADESH - TEXTILE INDUSTRY

Food and Agricultural Organization of the United Nations (FAO), Via delle Terme di Caracalla, 00100 Rome, Italy (Telephone Number in U.S. (202) 653-2400); *Production Yearbook.*

G.K. Hall and Company, 70 Lincoln Street, Boston, Massachusetts 02111 (617) 423-3990; *The World in Figures.*

Statistical Office of the United Nations, Publishing Service, New York, New York 10017 (800) 253-9646; *Statistical Yearbook,* and *Trade in Manufactures of Developing Countries.*

BANGLADESH - TOBACCO PRODUCTION

Facts on File, 460 Park Avenue South, New York, New York 10016 (800) 443-8323; *The New Book of World Rankings.*

Statistical Office of the United Nations, Publishing Service, New York, New York 10017 (800) 253-9646; *Statistical Yearbook.*

BANGLADESH - TOURISM

Facts on File, 460 Park Avenue South, New York, New York 10016 (800) 443-8323; *The New Book of World Rankings.*

Federal Statistical Office, Gustav - Stresemann - Ring 11, D-6200 Wiesbaden, Germany; *Bangladesch.*

G.K. Hall and Company, 70 Lincoln Street, Boston, Massachusetts 02111 (617) 423-3990; *The World in Figures.*

Statistical Office of the United Nations, Publishing Service, New York, New York 10017 (800) 253-9646; *Statistical Yearbook.*

Times Books, 201 East 50th Street, New York, New York 10022 (212) 751-2600; *The Economist Book of Vital World Statistics.*

World Tourism Organization, Calle Capitan Haya 42, E-28020 Madrid, Spain; *Yearbook of Tourism Statistics.*

BANGLADESH - TRADE - See BANGLADESH - FOREIGN TRADE

BANGLADESH - TRADEMARKS AND SERVICE MARKS

Statistical Office of the United Nations, Publishing Service, New York, New York 10017 (800) 253-9646; *Statistical Yearbook.*

BANGLADESH - TRANSPORTATION AND COMMUNICATIONS

Bangladesh Bureau of Statistics, Statistics Division, Ministry of Planning, Government of the People's Republic of Bangladesh, Dhaka, Bangladesh; *Statistical Yearbook of Bangladesh.*

The Economist Intelligence Unit (Asia) Limited, 10th Floor, Luk Kwok Centre, 72 Gloucester Road, Wanchai, Hong Kong (Phone Number in U.S. (800) 938-4685); *Asian Market Atlas.*

Facts on File, 460 Park Avenue South, New York, New York 10016 (800) 443-8323; *The New Book of World Rankings.*

Federal Statistical Office, Gustav - Stresemann - Ring 11, D-6200 Wiesbaden, Germany; *Bangladesch.*

G.K. Hall and Company, 70 Lincoln Street, Boston, Massachusetts 02111 (617) 423-3990; *The World in Figures.*

Statistical Office of the United Nations, Publishing Service, New York, New York 10017 (800) 253-9646; *Statistical Yearbook for Asia and the Pacific.*

BANGLADESH - TRAVEL FARES ABROAD

International Monetary Fund, 700 Nineteenth Street, NW, Washington, D.C. 20431 (202) 623-7000; *Government Finance Statistics Yearbook.*

BANGLADESH - UNEMPLOYMENT

Euromonitor Publications Limited, 87-88 Turnmill Street, London EC1M 5QU, England; *International Marketing Data and Statistics.*

International Labour Office, I.L.O. Publications, CH-1211, Geneva 22, Switzerland; *Yearbook of Labour Statistics.*

BANGLADESH - UTILITIES

Statistical Office of the United Nations, Publishing Service, New York, New York 10017 (800) 253-9646; *Electric Power in Asia and the Pacific.*

BANGLADESH - VITAL STATISTICS

Euromonitor Publications Limited, 87-88 Turnmill Street, London EC1M 5QU, England; *International Marketing Data and Statistics.*

G.K. Hall and Company, 70 Lincoln Street, Boston, Massachusetts 02111 (617) 423-3990; *The World in Figures.*

Statistical Office of the United Nations, Publishing Service, New York, New York 10017 (800) 253-9646; *Statistical Yearbook.*

World Health Organization, Office of Publications, Avenue Appia, CH-1211 Geneva 27, Switzerland (Telephone Number in U.S. (518) 436-9686); *World Health Statistics Annual.*

BANGLADESH - WAGES

Bangladesh Bureau of Statistics, Statistics Division, Ministry of Planning, Government of the People's Republic of Bangladesh, Dhaka, Bangladesh; *Statistical Yearbook of Bangladesh.*

Federal Statistical Office, Gustav - Stresemann - Ring 11, D-6200 Wiesbaden, Germany; *Bangladesch.*

G.K. Hall and Company, 70 Lincoln Street, Boston, Massachusetts 02111 (617) 423-3990; *The World in Figures.*

International Labour Office, I.L.O. Publications, CH-1211, Geneva 22, Switzerland; *Yearbook of Labour Statistics.*

Statistical Office of the United Nations, Publishing Service, New York, New York 10017 (800) 253-9646; *Statistical Yearbook,* and *Statistical Yearbook for Asia and the Pacific.*

BANGLADESH - WEATHER

Facts on File, 460 Park Avenue South, New York, New York 10016 (800) 443-8323; *The New Book of World Rankings.*

G.K. Hall and Company, 70 Lincoln Street, Boston, Massachusetts 02111 (617) 423-3990; *The World in Figures.*

BANGLADESH - WELFARE

International Monetary Fund, 700 Nineteenth Street, NW, Washington, D.C. 20431 (202) 623-7000; *Government Finance Statistics Yearbook.*

BANGLADESH - WHEAT PRODUCTION AND PRICES - See BANGLADESH - CROPS

BANGLADESH - WHOLESALE PRICES

Asian Development Bank, P.O. Box 789, 1099 Manila, Philippines; *Key Indicators of Developing Asian and Pacific Countries.*

BANGLADESH - WINE PRODUCTION

Facts on File, 460 Park Avenue South, New York, New York 10016 (800) 443-8323; *The New Book of World Rankings.*

BANGLADESH - WOOL PRODUCTION

Facts on File, 460 Park Avenue South, New York, New York 10016 (800) 443-8323; *The New Book of World Rankings.*

BANGLADESH - YARN PRODUCTION

Statistical Office of the United Nations, Publishing Service, New York, New York 10017 (800) 253-9646; *Statistical Yearbook.*

BANKRUPTCIES

Administrative Office of the United States Courts, United States Supreme Court Building, 1 First Street, NE, Washington, D.C. 20544 (202) 633-6094; *Annual Report of the Director,* and unpublished data.

BANKS, COMMERCIAL - CLOSED BANKS, FINANCIAL DIFFICULTIES

Federal Deposit Insurance Corporation, 550 Seventeenth Street, NW, Washington, D.C. 20429 (202) 393-8400; *Annual Report, The FDIC Quarterly Banking Profile, Statistics on Banking,* and *Failed Bank Cost Analysis Report.*

BANKS, COMMERCIAL - CREDIT CARDS

HSN Consultants, Inc., 300 Esplanade Drive, Oxnard, California 93030 (310) 392-8478; *The Nilson Report.*

BANKS, COMMERCIAL - DELINQUENCY RATES, REPOSSESSIONS, LOANS

American Bankers Association, 1120 Connecticut Avenue, NW, Washington, D.C. 20036 (202) 663-5000; *Consumer Credit Delinquency Bulletin.*

BANKS, COMMERCIAL - DEPOSITS

American Banker-Bond Buyer, One State Street Plaza, New York, New York 10004 (212) 943-8200; *American Banker Ranking the Banks.*

Board of Governors of the Federal Reserve System, Twentieth Street and Constitution Avenue, NW, Washington, D.C. 20551 (202) 452-3000; *Annual Statistical Digest, Federal Reserve Bulletin,* and unpublished data.

Federal Deposit Insurance Corporation, 550 Seventh Street, NW, Washington, D.C. 20429 (202) 393-8400; *The FDIC Quarterly Banking Profile, Annual Report, Statistics on Banking,* and unpublished data.

BANKS, COMMERCIAL - EARNINGS

U.S. Department of Commerce, Bureau of the Census, Suitland, Maryland 20233 (301) 763-4040; *County Business Patterns.*

U.S. Department of Labor, Bureau of Labor Statistics, Two Massachusetts Avenue, NE, Washington, D.C. 20212 (202) 606-7828; *Employment and Earnings,* and Bulletins 2370 and 2429.

BANKS, COMMERCIAL - EMPLOYEES

U.S. Department of Commerce, Bureau of Economic Analysis, Fourteenth Street between Constitution Avenue and E Street, NW, Washington, D.C. 20230 (202) 606-9900; *The National Income and Product Accounts of the United States,* and *Survey of Current Business.*

U.S. Department of Commerce, Bureau of the Census, Suitland, Maryland 20233 (301) 763-4040; *County Business Patterns.*

U.S. Department of Labor, Bureau of Labor Statistics, Two Massachusetts Avenue, NE, Washington, D.C. 20212 (202) 606-7828; *Employment and Earnings,* and Bulletins 2370 and 2429.

BANKS, COMMERCIAL - ESTABLISHMENTS

American Banker-Bond Buyer, One State Street Plaza, New York, New York 10004 (212) 943-8200; *American Banker Ranking the Banks.*

Board of Governors of the Federal Reserve System, Twentieth Street and Constitution Avenue, NW, Washington, D.C. 20551 (202) 452-3000; *Banking and Monetary Statistics, Annual Statistical Digest,* and unpublished data.

Federal Deposit Insurance Corporation, 550 Seventeenth Street, NW, Washington, D.C. 20429 (202) 393-8400; *The FDIC Quarterly Profile, Annual Report, Data Book Operating Banks and Branches, Statistics on Banking,* and unpublished data.

U.S. Department of Commerce, Bureau of the Census, Suitland, Maryland 20233 (301) 763-4040; *County Business Patterns.*

BANKS, COMMERCIAL - FEDERAL RESERVE BANKS

Federal Deposit Insurance Corporation, 550 Seventeenth Street, NW, Washington, D.C. 20429 (202) 393-8400; *Statistics on Banking.*

BANKS, COMMERCIAL - FINANCES

Board of Governors of the Federal Reserve System, Twentieth Street and Constitution Avenue, NW, Washington, D.C. 20551 (202) 452-3000; *Annual Statistical Digest, Federal Reserve Bulletin,* and *Money Stock, Liquid Assets and Debt Measures, Federal Reserve Statistical Release.*

Federal Deposit Insurance Corporation, 550 Seventeenth Street, NW, Washington, D.C. 20429 (202) 393-8400; *Annual Report, The FDIC Quarterly Banking Profile, Data Book Operating Banks and Branches,* and *Statistics on Banking.*

U.S. Department of Housing and Urban Development, 451 Seventh Street, SW, Washington, D.C. 20410 (202) 708-1422; *The Supply of Mortgage Credit,* and quarterly press releases based on *Survey of Mortgage Lending Activity.*

U.S. Department of the Treasury, Fifteenth Street and Pennsylvania Avenue, NW, Washington, D.C. 20220 (202) 566-2000; *Treasury Bulletin.*

BANKS, COMMERCIAL - FLOW OF FUNDS

Board of Governors of the Federal Reserve System, Twentieth Street and Constitution Avenue, NW, Washington, D.C. 20551 (202) 452-3000; *Annual Statistical Digest.*

BANKS, COMMERCIAL - FOREIGN BANKING OFFICES IN THE UNITED STATES

Board of Governors of the Federal Reserve System, Twentieth Street and Constitution Avenue, NW, Washington, D.C. 20551 (202) 452-3000; unpublished data.

BANKS, COMMERCIAL - FOREIGN LENDING

Board of Governors of the Federal Reserve System, Twentieth Street and Constitution Avenue, NW, Washington, D.C. 20551 (202) 452-3000; statistical release.

BANKS, COMMERCIAL - GROSS DOMESTIC PRODUCT

U.S. Department of Commerce, Bureau of Economic Analysis, Fourteenth Street between Constitution Avenue and E Street, NW, Washington, D.C. 20230 (202) 606-9900; *Survey of Current Business.*

BANKS, COMMERCIAL - HOME EQUITY LOANS

Board of Governors of the Federal Reserve System, Twentieth Street and Constitution Avenue, NW, Washington, D.C. 20551 (202) 452-3000; *Domestic Offices, Commercial Bank Assets and Liabilities, Consolidated Report of Condition.*

BANKS, COMMERCIAL - INDIVIDUAL RETIREMENT ACCOUNTS

Access Research, Inc., 8 Griffen Road, North, Windsor, Connecticut 06095 (203) 688-8821; *Marketplace Update.*

Investment Company Institute, 1600 M Street, NW, Suite 600, Washington, D.C. 20036 (202) 293-7700; *Mutual Fund Fact Book.*

BANKS, COMMERCIAL - INSURED BANKS

Board of Governors of the Federal Reserve System, Twentieth Street and Constitution Avenue, NW, Washington, D.C. 20551 (202) 452-3000; *Money Stock, Liquid Assets, and Debt Measures, Federal Reserve Statistical Release.*

Federal Deposit Insurance Corporation, 550 Seventeenth Street, NW, Washington, D.C. 20429 (202) 393-8400; *Statistics on Banking,* and unpublished data.

BANKS, COMMERCIAL - INTEREST RATES

Board of Governors of the Federal Reserve System, Twentieth Street and Constitution Avenue, NW, Washington, D.C. 20551 (202) 452-3000; *Annual Statistical Digest, Federal Reserve Bulletin,* and *Money Stock, Liquid Assets, and Debt Measures, Federal Reserve Statistical Release.*

BANKS, COMMERCIAL - OCCUPATIONAL SAFETY

U.S. Department of Labor, Bureau of Labor Statistics, Two Massachusetts Avenue, NE, Washington, D.C. 20212 (202) 606-7828; *Occupational Injuries and Illnesses in the United States by Industry.*

BANKS, COMMERCIAL - PROFITS

Federal Deposit Insurance Corporation, 550 Seventeenth Street, NW, Washington, D.C. 20429 (202) 393-8400; *Annual Report, The FDIC Quarterly Banking Profile, Statistics on Banking,* and unpublished data.

BANKS, COMMERCIAL - ROBBERY

U.S. Department of Justice, Federal Bureau of Investigation, Ninth Street and Pennsylvania Avenue, NW, Washington, D.C. 20535 (202) 324-3000; *Population-at-Risk Rates and Selected Crime Indicators.*

BANKS, COMMERCIAL - STOCK AND BOND PRICES AND YIELDS

Board of Governors of the Federal Reserve System, Twentieth Street and Constitution Avenue, NW, Washington, D.C. 20551 (202) 452-3000; *Federal Reserve Bulletin.*

BANKS, COMMERCIAL - TIME (OR SAVINGS) DEPOSITS

Board of Governors of the Federal Reserve System, Twentieth Street and Constitution Avenue, NW, Washington, D.C. 20551 (202) 452-3000; *Money Stock, Liquid Assets, and Debt Measures, Federal Reserve Statistical Release.*

Barbados - National Statistical Office

Barbados Statistical Service, Third Floor, National Insurance Building, Fairchild Street, Bridgetown, Barbados.

Barbados - Primary Statistics Sources

Barbados Statistical Service, Third Floor, National Insurance Building, Fairchild Street, Bridgetown, Barbados; *Monthly Digest of Statistics,* and *Barbados Economic Report.*

BARBADOS - AGRICULTURE

Federal Statistical Office, Gustav - Stresemann - Ring 11, D-6200 Wiesbaden, Germany; *Barbados.*

Facts on File, 460 Park Avenue South, New York, New York 10016 (800) 443-8323; *The New Book of World Rankings.*

Food and Agricultural Organization of the United Nations (FAO) Via delle Terme di Caracalla, 00100 Rome, Italy (Telephone Number in U.S. (202) 653-2400); *Production Yearbook, The State of Food and Agriculture,* and *Trade Yearbook.*

Gale Research Incorporated, 835 Penobscot Building, Detroit, Michigan 48226 (800) 877-4253; *International Historical Statistics The Americas and Australasia.*

G.K. Hall and Company, 70 Lincoln Street, Boston, Massachusetts 02111 (617) 423-3990; *The World in Figures.*

Inter-American Development Bank, 1300 New York Avenue, NW, Washington, D.C. 20577 (202) 623-1753; *Economic and Social Progress in Latin America.*

Statistical Office of the United Nations, Publishing Service, New York, New York 10017 (800) 253-9646; *Statistical Yearbook,* and *Statistical Yearbook for Latin America and the Caribbean.*

Times Books, 201 East 50th Street, New York, New York 10022 (212) 751-2600; *The Economist Book of Vital World Statistics.*

The World Bank, 1818 H Street, NW, Washington, D.C. 20433 (202) 477-1234; *World Tables.*

BARBADOS - AIRLINE SERVICE

Facts on File, 460 Park Avenue South, New York, New York 10016 (800) 443-8323; *The New Book of World Rankings.*

G.K. Hall and Company, 70 Lincoln Street, Boston, Massachusetts 02111 (617) 423-3990; *The World in Figures.*

International Civil Aviation Organization, 1000 Sherbrooke Street West, Suite 400, Montreal, Quebec, Canada H3A 2R2 (514) 285-8219;

Civil Aviation Statistics of the World.

Times Books, 201 East 50th Street, New York, New York 10022 (212) 751-2600; *The Economist Book of Vital World Statistics.*

BARBADOS - ALUMINUM PRODUCTION AND CONSUMPTION - See BARBADOS - MINING AND MINERAL PRODUCTS

BARBADOS - ANIMAL HEALTH

Food and Agricultural Organization of the United Nations (FAO), Via delle Terme di Caracalla, 00100 Rome, Italy (Telephone Number in U.S. (202) 653-2400); *Animal Health Yearbook.*

BARBADOS - AREA AND DENSITY OF POPULATION

Facts on File, 460 Park Avenue South, New York, New York 10016 (800) 443-8323; *The New Book of World Rankings.*

Federal Statistical Office, Gustav - Stresemann - Ring 11, D-6200 Wiesbaden, Germany; *Barbados.*

Food and Agricultural Organization of the United Nations (FAO) Via delle Terme di Caracalla, 00100 Rome, Italy (Telephone Number in U.S. (202) 653-2400); *The State of Food and Agriculture.*

G.K. Hall and Company, 70 Lincoln Street, Boston, Massachusetts 02111 (617) 423-3990; *The World in Figures.*

Inter-American Development Bank, 1300 New York Avenue, NW, Washington, D.C. 20577 (202) 623-1753; *Economic and Social Progress in Latin America.*

Statistical Office of the United Nations, Publishing Service, New York, New York 10017 (800) 253-9646; *Statistical Yearbook.*

Times Books, 201 East 50th Street, New York, New York 10022 (212) 751-2600; *The Economist Book of Vital World Statistics.*

BARBADOS - ARMS EXPORTS AND IMPORTS

U.S. Arms Control and Disarmament Agency, 320 Twenty-first Street, NW, Washington, D.C. 20451 (202) 647-8677; *World Military Expenditures and Arms Transfers.*

BARBADOS - BALANCE OF PAYMENTS

The Economist Intelligence Unit, 111 West 57th Street, New York, New York 10019 (800) 938-4685; *The World Market Atlas.*

Federal Statistical Office, Gustav - Stresemann - Ring 11, D-6200 Wiesbaden, Germany; *Barbados.*

G.K. Hall and Company, 70 Lincoln Street, Boston, Massachusetts 02111 (617) 423-3990; *The World in Figures.*

Inter-American Development Bank, 1300 New York Avenue, NW, Washington, D.C. 20577 (202) 623-1753; *Economic and Social Progress in Latin America.*

International Monetary Fund, 700 Nineteenth Street, NW, Washington, D.C. 20431 (202) 623-7000; *Balance of Payments Yearbook.*

Organization of American States (OAS), General Secretariat, Washington, D.C. 20006 (202) 458-3533; *Statistical Bulletin of the OAS.*

Statistical Office of the United Nations, Publishing Service, New York, New York 10017 (800) 253-9646; *Economic Survey of Latin America and the Caribbean,* and *Statistical Yearbook for Latin America and the Caribbean.*

Times Books, 201 East 50th Street, New York, New York 10022 (212) 751-2600; *The Economist Book of Vital World Statistics.*

The World Bank, 1818 H Street, NW, Washington, D.C. 20433 (202) 477-1234; *World Tables.*

BARBADOS - BANKING

Facts on File, 460 Park Avenue South, New York, New York 10016 (800) 443-8323; *The New Book of World Rankings.*

G.K. Hall and Company, 70 Lincoln Street, Boston, Massachusetts 02111 (617) 423-3990; *The World in Figures.*

Inter-American Development Bank, 1300 New York Avenue, NW, Washington, D.C. 20577 (202) 623-1753; *Economic and Social Progress in Latin America.*

International Monetary Fund, 700 Nineteenth Street, NW, Washington, D.C. 20431 (202) 623-7000; *Government Finance Statistics Yearbook,* and *International Financial Statistics.*

Statistical Office of the United Nations, Publishing Service, New York, New York 10017 (800) 253-9646; *Statistical Yearbook for Latin America and the Caribbean.*

BARBADOS - BARLEY PRODUCTION - See BARBADOS - CROPS

BARBADOS - BEER PRODUCTION

Facts on File, 460 Park Avenue South, New York, New York 10016 (800) 443-8323; *The New Book of World Rankings.*

Statistical Office of the United Nations, Publishing Service, New York, New York 10017 (800) 253-9646; *Statistical Yearbook.*

BARBADOS - BIRTH RATES

Facts on File, 460 Park Avenue South, New York, New York 10016 (800) 443-8323; *The New Book of World Rankings.*

Statistical Office of the United Nations, Publishing Service, New York, New York 10017 (800) 253-9646; *Demographic Yearbook,* and *Statistical Yearbook for Latin America and the Caribbean.*

Times Books, 201 East 50th Street, New York, New York 10022 (212) 751-2600; *The Economist Book of Vital World Statistics.*

The World Bank, 1818 H Street, NW, Washington, D.C. 20433 (202) 477-1234; *World Tables.*

BARBADOS - BONDS

G.K. Hall and Company, 70 Lincoln Street, Boston, Massachusetts 02111 (617) 423-3990; *The World in Figures.*

Inter-American Development Bank, 1300 New York Avenue, NW, Washington, D.C. 20577 (202) 623-1753; *Economic and Social Progress in Latin America.*

International Monetary Fund, 700 Nineteenth Street, NW, Washington, D.C. 20431 (202) 623-7000; *Government Finance Statistics Yearbook.*

BARBADOS - BOOK PRODUCTION

G.K. Hall and Company, 70 Lincoln Street, Boston, Massachusetts 02111 (617) 423-3990; *The World in Figures.*

United Nations Educational, Scientific and Cultural Organization (UNESCO), 7 Place de Fontenoy, F-75700 Paris, France; *Statistical Yearbook.*

BARBADOS - BROADCASTING

Billboard Limited, P.O. Box 9027, 1006 AA Amsterdam, The Netherlands (Telephone Number in U.S. (212) 764-7300); *World Radio TV Handbook.*

Facts on File, 460 Park Avenue South, New York, New York 10016 (800) 443-8323; *The New Book of World Rankings.*

G.K. Hall and Company, 70 Lincoln Street, Boston, Massachusetts 02111 (617) 423-3990; *The World in Figures.*

Times Books, 201 East 50th Street, New York, New York 10022 (212) 751-2600; *The Economist Book of Vital World Statistics.*

United Nations Educational, Scientific and Cultural Organization (UNESCO), 7 Place de Fontenoy, F-75700 Paris, France; *Statistical Yearbook.*

BARBADOS - BUILDING CONSTRUCTION - See BARBADOS - CONSTRUCTION INDUSTRY

BARBADOS - BUSINESS

G.K. Hall and Company, 70 Lincoln Street, Boston, Massachusetts 02111 (617) 423-3990; *The World in Figures.*

Inter-American Development Bank, 1300 New York Avenue, NW, Washington, D.C. 20577 (202) 623-1753; *Economic and Social Progress in Latin America.*

BARBADOS - BUSINESSES AND PROFESSIONAL LICENSES

International Monetary Fund, 700 Nineteenth Street, NW, Washington, D.C. 20431 (202) 623-7000; *Government Finance Statistics Yearbook.*

BARBADOS - CALORIE SUPPLY

Food and Agricultural Organization of the United Nations (FAO) Via delle Terme di Caracalla, 00100 Rome, Italy (Telephone Number in U.S. (202) 653-2400); *The State of Food and Agriculture.*

BARBADOS - CAPITAL INVESTMENT

Inter-American Development Bank, 1300 New York Avenue, NW, Washington, D.C. 20577 (202) 623-1753; *Economic and Social Progress in Latin America.*

BARBADOS - CAPITAL REVENUE

Inter-American Development Bank, 1300 New York Avenue, NW, Washington, D.C. 20577 (202) 623-1753; *Economic and Social Progress in Latin America.*

International Monetary Fund, 700 Nineteenth Street, NW, Washington, D.C. 20431 (202) 623-7000; *Government Finance Statistics Yearbook.*

BARBADOS - CATTLE - See BARBADOS - LIVESTOCK AND POULTRY

BARBADOS - CEMENT PRODUCTION - See BARBADOS - MINING AND MINERAL PRODUCTS

BARBADOS - CHEMICAL (ORGANIC) PRODUCTION - See BARBADOS - MINING AND MINERAL PRODUCTS

BARBADOS - CIGARETTE PRODUCTION - See BARBADOS - TOBACCO PRODUCTION

BARBADOS - CLASS STRUCTURE

G.K. Hall and Company, 70 Lincoln Street, Boston, Massachusetts 02111 (617) 423-3990; *The World in Figures.*

BARBADOS - CLIMATE

Facts on File, 460 Park Avenue South, New York, New York 10016 (800) 443-8323; *The New Book of World Rankings.*

G.K. Hall and Company, 70 Lincoln Street, Boston, Massachusetts 02111 (617) 423-3990; *The World in Figures.*

BARBADOS - COAL PRODUCTION - See BARBADOS - MINING AND MINERAL PRODUCTS

BARBADOS - COFFEE PRODUCTION - See BARBADOS - CROPS

BARBADOS - COMMUNICATIONS

Federal Statistical Office, Gustav - Stresemann - Ring 11, D-6200 Wiesbaden, Germany; *Barbados.*

G.K. Hall and Company, 70 Lincoln Street, Boston, Massachusetts 02111 (617) 423-3990; *The World in Figures.*

Inter-American Development Bank, 1300 New York Avenue, NW, Washington, D.C. 20577 (202) 623-1753; *Economic and Social Progress in Latin America.*

BARBADOS - CONSTRUCTION INDUSTRY

Facts on File, 460 Park Avenue South, New York, New York 10016 (800) 443-8323; *The New Book of World Rankings.*

Inter-American Development Bank, 1300 New York Avenue, NW, Washington, D.C. 20577 (202) 623-1753; *Economic and Social Progress in Latin America.*

Statistical Office of the United Nations, Publishing Service, New York, New York 10017 (800) 253-9646; *Construction Statistics Yearbook,* and *Statistical Yearbook.*

BARBADOS - CONSUMER PRICE INDEX

Federal Statistical Office, Gustav - Stresemann - Ring 11, D-6200 Wiesbaden, Germany; *Barbados.*

G.K. Hall and Company, 70 Lincoln Street, Boston, Massachusetts 02111 (617) 423-3990; *The World in Figures.*

Statistical Office of the United Nations, Publishing Service, New York, New York 10017 (800) 253-9646; *Statistical Yearbook.*

BARBADOS - CONSUMER PRICES

Federal Statistical Office, Gustav - Stresemann - Ring 11, D-6200 Wiesbaden, Germany; *Barbados.*

International Labour Office, I.L.O. Publications, CH-1211, Geneva 22, Switzerland; *Yearbook of Labour Statistics.*

International Monetary Fund, 700 Nineteenth Street, NW, Washington, D.C. 20431 (202) 623-7000; *International Financial Statistics.*

Organization of American States (OAS), General Secretariat, Washington, D.C. 20006 (202) 458-3533; *Statistical Bulletin of the OAS.*

Times Books, 201 East 50th Street, New York, New York 10022 (212) 751-2600; *The Economist Book of Vital World Statistics.*

BARBADOS - CONSUMPTION

G.K. Hall and Company, 70 Lincoln Street, Boston, Massachusetts 02111 (617) 423-3990; *The World in Figures.*

Inter-American Development Bank, 1300 New York Avenue, NW, Washington, D.C. 20577 (202) 623-1753; *Economic and Social Progress in Latin America.*

Statistical Office of the United Nations, Publishing Service, New York, New York 10017 (800) 253-9646; *Statistical Yearbook for Latin America and the Caribbean.*

BARBADOS - COPPER PRODUCTION - See BARBADOS - MINING AND MINERAL PRODUCTS

BARBADOS - CORN PRODUCTION - See BARBADOS - CROPS

BARBADOS - CORPORATE INCOME TAXES - See BARBADOS - TAXATION

BARBADOS - CORPORATE TAXES - See BARBADOS - TAXATION

BARBADOS - COTTON - See BARBADOS - CROPS

BARBADOS - CRIME

International Criminal Police Organization (INTERPOL), 26 rue Armengaud, 92210 Saint Cloud, France; *International Crime Statistics.*

BARBADOS - CROPS

Facts on File, 460 Park Avenue South, New York, New York 10016 (800) 443-8323; *The New Book of World Rankings.*

Food and Agricultural Organization of the United Nations (FAO) Via delle Terme di Caracalla, 00100 Rome, Italy (Telephone Number in U.S. (202) 653-2400); *Production Yearbook,* and *The State of Food and Agriculture.*

G.K. Hall and Company, 70 Lincoln Street, Boston, Massachusetts 02111 (617) 423-3990; *The World in Figures.*

International Monetary Fund, 700 Nineteenth Street, NW, Washington, D.C. 20431 (202) 623-7000; *International Financial Statistics.*

Organization of American States (OAS), General Secretariat, Washington, D.C. 20006 (202) 458-3533; *Statistical Bulletin of the OAS.*

BARBADOS - CUSTOMS DUTIES

G.K. Hall and Company, 70 Lincoln Street, Boston, Massachusetts 02111 (617) 423-3990; *The World in Figures.*

Inter-American Development Bank, 1300 New York Avenue, NW, Washington, D.C. 20577 (202) 623-1753; *Economic and Social Progress in Latin America.*

International Monetary Fund, 700 Nineteenth Street, NW, Washington, D.C. 20431 (202) 623-7000; *Government Finance Statistics Yearbook.*

BARBADOS - DAIRY PRODUCTS

Facts on File, 460 Park Avenue South, New York, New York 10016 (800) 443-8323; *The New Book of World Rankings.*

Food and Agricultural Organization of the United Nations (FAO) Via delle Terme di Caracalla, 00100 Rome, Italy (Telephone Number in U.S. (202) 653-2400); *The State of Food and Agriculture.*

BARBADOS - DEATH RATE

G.K. Hall and Company, 70 Lincoln Street, Boston, Massachusetts 02111 (617) 423-3990; *The World in Figures.*

Statistical Office of the United Nations, Publishing Service, New York, New York 10017 (800) 253-9646; *Statistical Yearbook,* and *Statistical Yearbook for Latin America and the Caribbean.*

Times Books, 201 East 50th Street, New York, New York 10022 (212) 751-2600; *The Economist Book of Vital World Statistics.*

World Health Organization, Office of Publications, Avenue Appia, CH-1211 Geneva 27, Switzerland (Telephone Number in U.S. (518) 436-9686); *World Health Statistics Annual.*

BARBADOS - DEFENSE EXPENDITURES

G.K. Hall and Company, 70 Lincoln Street, Boston, Massachusetts 02111 (617) 423-3990; *The World in Figures.*

International Monetary Fund, 700 Nineteenth Street, NW, Washington, D.C. 20431 (202) 623-7000; *Government Finance Statistics Yearbook.*

U.S. Arms Control and Disarmament Agency, 320 Twenty-first Street, NW, Washington, D.C. 20451 (202) 647-8677; *World Military Expenditures and Arms Transfers.*

BARBADOS - DEMOGRAPHY

The Economist Intelligence Unit, 111 West 57th Street, New York, New York 10019 (800) 938-4685; *The World Market Atlas.*

Facts on File, 460 Park Avenue South, New York, New York 10016 (800) 443-8323; *The New Book of World Rankings.*

Federal Statistical Office, Gustav - Stresemann - Ring 11, D-6200 Wiesbaden, Germany; *Barbados.*

G.K. Hall and Company, 70 Lincoln Street, Boston, Massachusetts 02111 (617) 423-3990; *The World in Figures.*

U.C.L.A. Latin American Center Publications, University of California, Los Angeles, California 90024; *Statistical Abstract of Latin America.*

BARBADOS - DEVELOPMENT ASSISTANCE

G.K. Hall and Company, 70 Lincoln Street, Boston, Massachusetts 02111 (617) 423-3990; *The World in Figures.*

Inter-American Development Bank, 1300 New York Avenue, NW, Washington, D.C. 20577 (202) 623-1753; *Economic and Social Progress in Latin America.*

Statistical Office of the United Nations, Publishing Service, New York, New York 10017 (800) 253-9646; *Statistical Yearbook.*

BARBADOS - DIAMOND PRODUCTION - See BARBADOS - MINING AND MINERAL PRODUCTS

BARBADOS - DISCOUNT RATES

Inter-American Development Bank, 1300 New York Avenue, NW, Washington, D.C. 20577 (202) 623-1753; *Economic and Social Progress in Latin America.*

BARBADOS - DISEASES

G.K. Hall and Company, 70 Lincoln Street, Boston, Massachusetts 02111 (617) 423-3990; *The World in Figures.*

World Health Organization, Office of Publications, Avenue Appia, CH-1211 Geneva 27, Switzerland (Telephone Number in U.S. (518) 436-9686; *World Health Statistics Annual.*

BARBADOS - DIVORCE RATES

Facts on File, 460 Park Avenue South, New York, New York 10016 (800) 443-8323; *The New Book of World Rankings.*

Statistical Office of the United Nations, Publishing Service, New York, New York 10017 (800) 253-9646; *Demographic Yearbook,* and *Statistical Yearbook.*

BARBADOS - DOMESTIC PRODUCT

G.K. Hall and Company, 70 Lincoln Street, Boston, Massachusetts 02111 (617) 423-3990; *The World in Figures.*

BARBADOS - ECONOMY

Facts on File, 460 Park Avenue South, New York, New York 10016 (800) 443-8323; *The New Book of World Rankings.*

Federal Statistical Office, Gustav - Stresemann - Ring 11, D-6200 Wiesbaden, Germany; *Barbados.*

G.K. Hall and Company, 70 Lincoln Street, Boston, Massachusetts 02111 (617) 423-3990; *The World in Figures.*

Inter-American Development Bank, 1300 New York Avenue, NW, Washington, D.C. 20577 (202) 623-1753; *Economic and Social Progress in Latin America.*

Organization of American States (OAS), General Secretariat, Washington, D.C. 20006 (202) 458-3533; *Statistical Bulletin of the OAS.*

Statistical Office of the United Nations, Publishing Service, New York, New York 10017 (800) 253-9646; *Economic Survey of Latin America and the Caribbean.*

BARBADOS - EDUCATION

The Economist Intelligence Unit, 111 West 57th Street, New York, New York 10019 (800) 938-4685; *The World Market Atlas.*

Facts on File, 460 Park Avenue South, New York, New York 10016 (800) 443-8323; *The New Book of World Rankings.*

Federal Statistical Office, Gustav - Stresemann - Ring 11, D-6200 Wiesbaden, Germany; *Barbados.*

Gale Research Incorporated, 835 Penobscot Building, Detroit, Michigan 48226 (800) 877-4253; *International Historical Statistics The Americas and Australasia.*

G.K. Hall and Company, 70 Lincoln Street, Boston, Massachusetts 02111 (617) 423-3990; *The World in Figures.*

International Monetary Fund, 700 Nineteenth Street, NW, Washington, D.C. 20431 (202) 623-7000; *Government Finance Statistics Yearbook.*

Statistical Office of the United Nations, Publishing Service, New York, New York 10017 (800) 253-9646; *Statistical Yearbook for Latin America and the Caribbean.*

Times Books, 201 East 50th Street, New York, New York 10022 (212) 751-2600; *The Economist Book of Vital World Statistics.*

United Nations Educational, Scientific and Cultural Organization (UNESCO), 7 Place de Fontenoy, F-75700 Paris, France (Telephone Number in U.S. (212) 963-5981); *Statistical Yearbook.*

The World Bank, 1818 H Street, NW, Washington, D.C. 20433 (202) 477-1234; *World Tables.*

BARBADOS - EGG PRODUCTION - See BARBADOS - DAIRY PRODUCTS

BARBADOS - ELECTRICITY

Facts on File, 460 Park Avenue South, New York, New York 10016 (800) 443-8323; *The New Book of World Rankings.*

Inter-American Development Bank, 1300 New York Avenue, NW, Washington, D.C. 20577 (202) 623-1753; *Economic and Social Progress in Latin America.*

Organization of American States (OAS), General Secretariat, Washington, D.C. 20006 (202) 458-3533; *Statistical Bulletin of the OAS.*

Penn Well Publishing Company, 1421 South Sheridan Road, P.O. Box 1260, Tulsa, Oklahoma 74101 (800) 752-9764; *International Energy Statistics Sourcebook.*

Statistical Office of the United Nations, Publishing Service, New York, New York 10017 (800) 253-9646; *Statistical Yearbook.*

Times Books, 201 East 50th Street, New York, New York 10022 (212) 751-2600; *The Economist Book of Vital World Statistics.*

BARBADOS - EMPLOYMENT

Facts on File, 460 Park Avenue South, New York, New York 10016 (800) 443-8323; *The New Book of World Rankings.*

Federal Statistical Office, Gustav - Stresemann - Ring 11, D-6200 Wiesbaden, Germany; *Barbados.*

International Labour Office, I.L.O. Publications, CH-1211, Geneva 22, Switzerland; *Yearbook of Labour Statistics*.

Organization of American States (OAS), General Secretariat, Washington, D.C. 20006 (202) 458-3533; *Statistical Bulletin of the OAS*.

Statistical Office of the United Nations, Publishing Service, New York, New York 10017 (800) 253-9646; *Statistical Yearbook*, and *Statistical Yearbook for Latin America and the Caribbean*.

BARBADOS - ENERGY

Facts on File, 460 Park Avenue South, New York, New York 10016 (800) 443-8323; *The New Book of World Rankings*.

Food and Agricultural Organization of the United Nations (FAO) Via delle Terme di Caracalla, 00100 Rome, Italy (Telephone Number in U.S. (202) 653-2400); *The State of Food and Agriculture*.

G.K. Hall and Company, 70 Lincoln Street, Boston, Massachusetts 02111 (617) 423-3990; *The World in Figures*.

Penn Well Publishing Company, 1421 South Sheridan Road, P.O. Box 1260, Tulsa, Oklahoma 74101 (800) 752-9764; *International Energy Statistics Sourcebook*.

Statistical Office of the United Nations, Publishing Service, New York, New York 10017 (800) 253-9646; *Energy Statistics Yearbook*, *Statistical Yearbook*, and *Statistical Yearbook for Latin America and the Caribbean*.

Times Books, 201 East 50th Street, New York, New York 10022 (212) 751-2600; *The Economist Book of Vital World Statistics*.

BARBADOS - EXCHANGE RATES

Inter-American Development Bank, 1300 New York Avenue, NW, Washington, D.C. 20577 (202) 623-1753; *Economic and Social Progress in Latin America*.

International Civil Aviation Organization, 1000 Sherbrooke Street West, Suite 400, Montreal, Quebec, Canada H3A 2R2 (514) 285-8219; *Civil Aviation Statistics of the World*.

International Monetary Fund, 700 Nineteenth Street, NW, Washington, D.C. 20431 (202) 623-7000; *International Financial Statistics*.

Organization of American States (OAS), General Secretariat, Washington, D.C. 20006 (202) 458-3533; *Statistical Bulletin of the OAS*.

BARBADOS - EXCISE TAXES - See BARBADOS - TAXATION

BARBADOS - EXPORT DUTIES

Inter-American Development Bank, 1300 New York Avenue, NW, Washington, D.C. 20577 (202) 623-1753; *Economic and Social Progress in Latin America*.

International Monetary Fund, 700 Nineteenth Street, NW, Washington, D.C. 20431 (202) 623-7000; *Government Finance Statistics Yearbook*.

BARBADOS - EXPORTS

The Economist Intelligence Unit, 111 West 57th Street, New York, New York 10019 (800) 938-4685; *The World Market Atlas*.

Food and Agricultural Organization of the United Nations (FAO) Via delle Terme di Caracalla, 00100 Rome, Italy (Telephone Number in U.S. (202) 653-2400); *The State of Food and Agriculture*.

G.K. Hall and Company, 70 Lincoln Street, Boston, Massachusetts 02111 (617) 423-3990; *The World in Figures*.

Inter-American Development Bank, 1300 New York Avenue, NW, Washington, D.C. 20577 (202) 623-1753; *Economic and Social Progress in Latin America*.

International Monetary Fund, 700 Nineteenth Street, NW, Washington, D.C. 20431 (202) 623-7000; *Direction of Trade Statistics*, and *International Financial Statistics*.

Organization of American States (OAS), General Secretariat, Washington, D.C. 20006 (202) 458-3533; *Statistical Bulletin of the OAS*.

Statistical Office of the United Nations, Publishing Service, New York, New York 10017 (800) 253-9646; *Statistical Yearbook for Latin America and the Caribbean*.

Times Books, 201 East 50th Street, New York, New York 10022 (212) 751-2600; *The Economist Book of Vital World Statistics*.

The World Bank, 1818 H Street, NW, Washington, D.C. 20433 (202) 477-1234; *World Tables*.

BARBADOS - EXTERNAL FINANCING

Inter-American Development Bank, 1300 New York Avenue, NW, Washington, D.C. 20577 (202) 623-1753; *Economic and Social Progress in Latin America*.

Statistical Office of the United Nations, Publishing Service, New York, New York 10017 (800) 253-9646; *Statistical Yearbook for Latin America and the Caribbean*.

BARBADOS - EXTERNAL INDEBTEDNESS

Inter-American Development Bank, 1300 New York Avenue, NW, Washington, D.C. 20577 (202) 623-1753; *Economic and Social Progress in Latin America*.

Statistical Office of the United Nations, Publishing Service, New York, New York 10017 (800) 253-9646; *Statistical Yearbook for Latin America and the Caribbean*.

The World Bank, 1818 H Street, NW, Washington, D.C. 20433 (202) 477-1234; *World Tables*.

BARBADOS - EXTERNAL TRADE

Food and Agricultural Organization of the United Nations (FAO) Via delle Terme di Caracalla, 00100 Rome, Italy (Telephone Number in U.S. (202) 653-2400); *The State of Food and Agriculture*.

Gale Research Incorporated, 835 Penobscot Building, Detroit, Michigan 48226 (800) 877-4253; *International Historical Statistics The Americas and Australasia*.

G.K. Hall and Company, 70 Lincoln Street, Boston, Massachusetts 02111 (617) 423-3990; *The World in Figures*.

Inter-American Development Bank, 1300 New York Avenue, NW, Washington, D.C. 20577 (202) 623-1753; *Economic and Social Progress in Latin America*.

Statistical Office of the United Nations, Publishing Service, New York, New York 10017 (800) 253-9646; *Statistical Yearbook*, and *Statistical Yearbook for Latin America and the Caribbean*.

BARBADOS - FARM CROPS - See BARBADOS - CROPS

BARBADOS - FERTILITY RATES

Times Books, 201 East 50th Street, New York, New York 10022 (212) 751-2600; *The Economist Book of Vital World Statistics*.

The World Bank, 1818 H Street, NW, Washington, D.C. 20433 (202) 477-1234; *World Tables*.

BARBADOS - FERTILIZER

Facts on File, 460 Park Avenue South, New York, New York 10016 (800) 443-8323; *The New Book of World Rankings*.

Food and Agricultural Organization of the United Nations (FAO), Via delle Terme di Caracalla, 00100 Rome, Italy (Telephone Number in U.S. (202) 653-2400); *Fertilizer Yearbook*, and *The State of Food and Agriculture*.

Statistical Office of the United Nations, Publishing Service, New York, New York 10017 (800) 253-9646; *Statistical Yearbook*.

The World Bank, 1818 H Street, N.W., Washington, D.C. 20433 (202) 477-1234; *World Tables*.

BARBADOS - FETAL MORTALITY

Statistical Office of the United Nations, Publishing Service, New York, New York 10017 (800) 253-9646; *Demographic Yearbook*.

World Health Organization, Office of Publications, Avenue Appia, CH-1211 Geneva 27, Switzerland (Telephone Number in U.S. (518) 436-9686; *World Health Statistics Annual*.

BARBADOS - FINANCE

Facts on File, 460 Park Avenue South, New York, New York 10016 (800) 443-8323; *The New Book of World Rankings*.

Federal Statistical Office, Gustav - Stresemann - Ring 11, D-6200 Wiesbaden, Germany; *Barbados*.

Gale Research Incorporated, 835 Penobscot Building, Detroit, Michigan 48226 (800) 877-4253; *International Historical Statistics The Americas and Australasia*.

G.K. Hall and Company, 70 Lincoln Street, Boston, Massachusetts 02111 (617) 423-3990; *The World in Figures*.

Inter-American Development Bank, 1300 New York Avenue, NW, Washington, D.C. 20577 (202) 623-1753; *Economic and Social Progress in Latin America*.

International Monetary Fund, 700 Nineteenth Street, NW, Washington, D.C. 20431 (202) 623-7000; *Government Finance Statistics Yearbook*, and *International Financial Statistics*.

Organization of American States (OAS), General Secretariat, Washington, D.C. 20006 (202) 458-3533; *Statistical Bulletin of the OAS*.

BARBADOS - FISHERIES

Facts on File, 460 Park Avenue South, New York, New York 10016 (800) 443-8323; *The New Book of World Rankings*.

Federal Statistical Office, Gustav - Stresemann - Ring 11, D-6200 Wiesbaden, Germany; *Barbados*.

Food and Agricultural Organization of the United Nations (FAO) Via delle Terme di Caracalla, 00100 Rome, Italy (Telephone Number in U.S. (202) 653-2400); *The State of Food and Agriculture*, and *Yearbook of Fishery Statistics*.

Inter-American Development Bank, 1300 New York Avenue, NW, Washington, D.C. 20577 (202) 623-1753; *Economic and Social Progress in Latin America*.

Statistical Office of the United Nations, Publishing Service, New York, New York 10017 (800) 253-9646; *Statistical Yearbook*.

BARBADOS - FOOD

Food and Agricultural Organization of the United Nations (FAO) Via delle Terme di Caracalla, 00100 Rome, Italy (Telephone Number in U.S. (202) 653-2400); *Production Yearbook*, and *The State of Food and Agriculture*.

G.K. Hall and Company, 70 Lincoln Street, Boston, Massachusetts 02111 (617) 423-3990; *The World in Figures*.

BARBADOS - FOREIGN AID

G.K. Hall and Company, 70 Lincoln Street, Boston, Massachusetts 02111 (617) 423-3990; *The World in Figures*.

Inter-American Development Bank, 1300 New York Avenue, NW, Washington, D.C. 20577 (202) 623-1753; *Economic and Social Progress in Latin America*.

BARBADOS - FOREIGN DEBT

Inter-American Development Bank, 1300 New York Avenue, NW, Washington, D.C. 20577 (202) 623-1753; *Economic and Social Progress in Latin America*.

International Monetary Fund, 700 Nineteenth Street, NW, Washington, D.C. 20431 (202) 623-7000; *Government Finance Statistics Yearbook*.

BARBADOS - FOREIGN FINANCE

Inter-American Development Bank, 1300 New York Avenue, NW, Washington, D.C. 20577 (202) 623-1753; *Economic and Social Progress in Latin America*.

BARBADOS - FOREIGN INDEBTEDNESS

Inter-American Development Bank, 1300 New York Avenue, NW, Washington, D.C. 20577 (202) 623-1753; *Economic and Social Progress in Latin America*.

Statistical Office of the United Nations, Publishing Service, New York, New York 10017 (800) 253-9646; *Economic Survey of Latin America and the Caribbean*.

BARBADOS - FOREIGN TRADE

Facts on File, 460 Park Avenue South, New York, New York 10016 (800) 443-8323; *The New Book of World Rankings*.

Federal Statistical Office, Gustav - Stresemann - Ring 11, D-6200 Wiesbaden, Germany; *Barbados.*

G.K. Hall and Company, 70 Lincoln Street, Boston, Massachusetts 02111 (617) 423-3990; *The World in Figures.*

Inter-American Development Bank, 1300 New York Avenue, NW, Washington, D.C. 20577 (202) 623-1753; *Economic and Social Progress in Latin America.*

Organisation for Economic Co-operation and Development (OECD), 2 rue Andre-Pascal, 75 Paris 16, France (Telephone Number in U.S. (202) 785-6323); *Trade by Commodities.*

Statistical Office of the United Nations, Publishing Service, New York, New York 10017 (800) 253-9646; *Economic Survey of Latin America and the Caribbean, International Trade Statistics Yearbook,* and *Statistical Yearbook.*

The World Bank, 1818 H Street, N.W., Washington, D.C. 20433 (202) 477-1234; *World Tables.*

BARBADOS - FORESTRY AND FOREST PRODUCTS

Facts on File, 460 Park Avenue South, New York, New York 10016 (800) 443-8323; *The New Book of World Rankings.*

Federal Statistical Office, Gustav - Stresemann - Ring 11, D-6200 Wiesbaden, Germany; *Barbados.*

Food and Agricultural Organization of the United Nations (FAO) Via delle Terme di Caracalla, 00100 Rome, Italy (Telephone Number in U.S. (202) 653-2400); *The State of Food and Agriculture,* and *Yearbook of Forest Products.*

G.K. Hall and Company, 70 Lincoln Street, Boston, Massachusetts 02111 (617) 423-3990; *The World in Figures.*

Inter-American Development Bank, 1300 New York Avenue, NW, Washington, D.C. 20577 (202) 623-1753; *Economic and Social Progress in Latin America.*

Statistical Office of the United Nations, Publishing Service, New York, New York 10017 (800) 253-9646; *Statistical Yearbook.*

United Nations Educational, Scientific and Cultural Organization (UNESCO), 7 Place de Fontenoy, F-75700 Paris, France (Telephone Number in U.S. (212) 963-5981); *Statistical Yearbook.*

BARBADOS - GAS PRODUCTION - See BARBADOS - MINING AND MINERAL PRODUCTS

BARBADOS - GENERAL INDUSTRIAL STATISTICS

Federal Statistical Office, Gustav - Stresemann - Ring 11, D-6200 Wiesbaden, Germany; *Barbados.*

Statistical Office of the United Nations, Publishing Service, New York, New York 10017 (800) 253-9646; *Industrial Statistics Yearbook.*

BARBADOS - GENERAL MORTALITY

Statistical Office of the United Nations, Publishing Service, New York, New York 10017 (800) 253-9646; *Demographic Yearbook.*

World Health Organization, Office of Publications, Avenue Appia, CH-1211 Geneva 27, Switzerland (Telephone Number in U.S. (518) 436-9686; *World Health Statistics Annual.*

BARBADOS - GEOGRAPHIC DATA

Facts on File, 460 Park Avenue South, New York, New York 10016 (800) 443-8323; *The New Book of World Rankings.*

Federal Statistical Office, Gustav - Stresemann - Ring 11, D-6200 Wiesbaden, Germany; *Barbados.*

BARBADOS - GOLD HOLDINGS

International Monetary Fund, 700 Nineteenth Street, NW, Washington, D.C. 20431 (202) 623-7000; *International Financial Statistics.*

Statistical Office of the United Nations, Publishing Service, New York, New York 10017 (800) 253-9646; *Statistical Yearbook.*

The World Bank, 1818 H Street, N.W., Washington, D.C. 20433 (202) 477-1234; *World Tables.*

BARBADOS - GOLD PRODUCTION - See BARBADOS - MINING AND MINERAL PRODUCTS

BARBADOS - GOVERNMENT

Inter-American Development Bank, 1300 New York Avenue, NW, Washington, D.C. 20577 (202) 623-1753; *Economic and Social Progress in Latin America.*

G.K. Hall and Company, 70 Lincoln Street, Boston, Massachusetts 02111 (617) 423-3990; *The World in Figures.*

BARBADOS - GOVERNMENT BONDS - See BARBADOS - BONDS

BARBADOS - GOVERNMENT CONSUMPTION

Inter-American Development Bank, 1300 New York Avenue, NW, Washington, D.C. 20577 (202) 623-1753; *Economic and Social Progress in Latin America.*

BARBADOS - GOVERNMENT EXPENDITURES

Inter-American Development Bank, 1300 New York Avenue, NW, Washington, D.C. 20577 (202) 623-1753; *Economic and Social Progress in Latin America.*

International Monetary Fund, 700 Nineteenth Street, NW, Washington, D.C. 20431 (202) 623-7000; *Government Finance Statistics Yearbook.*

Times Books, 201 East 50th Street, New York, New York 10022 (212) 751-2600; *The Economist Book of Vital World Statistics.*

The World Bank, 1818 H Street, N.W., Washington, D.C. 20433 (202) 477-1234; *World Tables.*

BARBADOS - GOVERNMENT FINANCE

Inter-American Development Bank, 1300 New York Avenue, NW, Washington, D.C. 20577 (202) 623-1753; *Economic and Social Progress in Latin America.*

International Monetary Fund, 700 Nineteenth Street, NW, Washington, D.C. 20431 (202) 623-7000; *International Financial Statistics.*

BARBADOS - GOVERNMENT REVENUE

Inter-American Development Bank, 1300 New York Avenue, NW, Washington, D.C. 20577 (202) 623-1753; *Economic and Social Progress in Latin America.*

International Monetary Fund, 700 Nineteenth Street, NW, Washington, D.C. 20431 (202) 623-7000; *Government Finance Statistics Yearbook.*

Times Books, 201 East 50th Street, New York, New York 10022 (212) 751-2600; *The Economist Book of Vital World Statistics.*

The World Bank, 1818 H Street, N.W., Washington, D.C. 20433 (202) 477-1234; *World Tables.*

BARBADOS - GRAIN PRODUCTION - See BARBADOS - CROPS

BARBADOS - GRANTS

International Monetary Fund, 700 Nineteenth Street, NW, Washington, D.C. 20431 (202) 623-7000; *Government Finance Statistics Yearbook.*

BARBADOS - GROSS DOMESTIC PRODUCT

The Economist Intelligence Unit, 111 West 57th Street, New York, New York 10019 (800) 938-4685; *The World Market Atlas.*

Facts on File, 460 Park Avenue South, New York, New York 10016 (800) 443-8323; *The New Book of World Rankings.*

G.K. Hall and Company, 70 Lincoln Street, Boston, Massachusetts 02111 (617) 423-3990; *The World in Figures.*

Inter-American Development Bank, 1300 New York Avenue, NW, Washington, D.C. 20577 (202) 623-1753; *Economic and Social Progress in Latin America.*

Organization of American States (OAS), General Secretariat, Washington, D.C. 20006 (202) 458-3533; *Statistical Bulletin of the OAS.*

Statistical Office of the United Nations, Publishing Service, New York, New York 10017 (800) 253-9646; *Statistical Yearbook,* and *Statistical Yearbook for Latin America and the Caribbean.*

Times Books, 201 East 50th Street, New York, New York 10022 (212) 751-2600; *The Economist Book of Vital World Statistics.*

The World Bank, 1818 H Street, N.W., Washington, D.C. 20433 (202) 477-1234; *World Tables.*

BARBADOS - GROSS NATIONAL PRODUCT

Inter-American Development Bank, 1300 New York Avenue, NW, Washington, D.C. 20577 (202) 623-1753; *Economic and Social Progress in Latin America.*

U.S. Arms Control and Disarmament Agency, 320 Twenty-first Street, NW, Washington, D.C. 20451 (202) 647-8677; *World Military Expenditures and Arms Transfers.*

The World Bank, 1818 H Street, N.W., Washington, D.C. 20433 (202) 477-1234; *World Tables.*

BARBADOS - HEALTH

Facts on File, 460 Park Avenue South, New York, New York 10016 (800) 443-8323; *The New Book of World Rankings.*

Federal Statistical Office, Gustav - Stresemann - Ring 11, D-6200 Wiesbaden, Germany; *Barbados.*

G.K. Hall and Company, 70 Lincoln Street, Boston, Massachusetts 02111 (617) 423-3990; *The World in Figures.*

Statistical Office of the United Nations, Publishing Service, New York, New York 10017 (800) 253-9646; *Statistical Yearbook.*

Times Books, 201 East 50th Street, New York, New York 10022 (212) 751-2600; *The Economist Book of Vital World Statistics.*

World Health Organization, Office of Publications, Avenue Appia, CH-1211 Geneva 27, Switzerland (Telephone Number in U.S. (518) 436-9686; *World Health Statistics Annual.*

BARBADOS - HEALTH EXPENDITURES

International Monetary Fund, 700 Nineteenth Street, NW, Washington, D.C. 20431 (202) 623-7000; *Government Finance Statistics Yearbook.*

Statistical Office of the United Nations, Publishing Service, New York, New York 10017 (800) 253-9646; *Statistical Yearbook for Latin America and the Caribbean.*

BARBADOS - HIDE PRODUCTION

Food and Agricultural Organization of the United Nations (FAO), Via delle Terme di Caracalla, 00100 Rome, Italy (Telephone Number in U.S. (202) 653-2400); *Production Yearbook.*

BARBADOS - HIGHWAYS

G.K. Hall and Company, 70 Lincoln Street, Boston, Massachusetts 02111 (617) 423-3990; *The World in Figures.*

BARBADOS - HORSES - See BARBADOS - LIVESTOCK AND POULTRY

BARBADOS - HOURS OF WORK - See BARBADOS - EMPLOYMENT

BARBADOS - HOUSING AND HOUSING UNITS

Facts on File, 460 Park Avenue South, New York, New York 10016 (800) 443-8323; *The New Book of World Rankings.*

Statistical Office of the United Nations, Publishing Service, New York, New York 10017 (800) 253-9646; *Statistical Yearbook for Latin America and the Caribbean.*

BARBADOS - HOUSING EXPENDITURES

International Monetary Fund, 700 Nineteenth Street, NW, Washington, D.C. 20431 (202) 623-7000; *Government Finance Statistics Yearbook.*

BARBADOS - ILLITERATE POPULATION

The Economist Intelligence Unit, 111 West 57th Street, New York, New York 10019 (800) 938-4685; *The World Market Atlas.*

G.K. Hall and Company, 70 Lincoln Street, Boston, Massachusetts 02111 (617) 423-3990; *The World in Figures.*

Statistical Office of the United Nations, Publishing Service, New York, New York 10017 (800) 253-9646; *Statistical Yearbook for Latin America and the Caribbean.*

United Nations Educational, Scientific and Cultural Organization (UNESCO), 7 Place de Fontenoy, F-75700 Paris, France (Telephone Number in U.S. (212) 963-5981); *Statistical Yearbook.*

BARBADOS - IMPORTS

The Economist Intelligence Unit, 111 West 57th Street, New York, New York 10019 (800) 938-4685; *The World Market Atlas.*

Food and Agricultural Organization of the United Nations (FAO) Via delle Terme di Caracalla, 00100 Rome, Italy (Telephone Number in U.S. (202) 653-2400); *The State of Food and Agriculture.*

G.K. Hall and Company, 70 Lincoln Street, Boston, Massachusetts 02111 (617) 423-3990; *The World in Figures.*

Inter-American Development Bank, 1300 New York Avenue, NW, Washington, D.C. 20577 (202) 623-1753; *Economic and Social Progress in Latin America.*

International Monetary Fund, 700 Nineteenth Street, NW, Washington, D.C. 20431 (202) 623-7000; *Direction of Trade Statistics,* and *International Financial Statistics.*

Organization of American States (OAS), General Secretariat, Washington, D.C. 20006 (202) 458-3533; *Statistical Bulletin of the OAS.*

Statistical Office of the United Nations, Publishing Service, New York, New York 10017 (800) 253-9646; *Statistical Yearbook for Latin America and the Caribbean.*

Times Books, 201 East 50th Street, New York, New York 10022 (212) 751-2600; *The Economist Book of Vital World Statistics.*

The World Bank, 1818 H Street, N.W., Washington, D.C. 20433 (202) 477-1234; *World Tables.*

BARBADOS - INCOME DISTRIBUTION

Statistical Office of the United Nations, Publishing Service, New York, New York 10017 (800) 253-9646; *Statistical Yearbook for Latin America and the Caribbean.*

BARBADOS - INCOME TAXES - See BARBADOS - TAXATION

BARBADOS - INDUSTRY

Facts on File, 460 Park Avenue South, New York, New York 10016 (800) 443-8323; *The New Book of World Rankings.*

Federal Statistical Office, Gustav - Stresemann - Ring 11, D-6200 Wiesbaden, Germany; *Barbados.*

Gale Research Incorporated, 835 Penobscot Building, Detroit, Michigan 48226 (800) 877-4253; *International Historical Statistics The Americas and Australasia.*

G.K. Hall and Company, 70 Lincoln Street, Boston, Massachusetts 02111 (617) 423-3990; *The World in Figures.*

International Labour Office, I.L.O. Publications, CH-1211, Geneva 22, Switzerland; *Yearbook of Labour Statistics.*

Statistical Office of the United Nations, Publishing Service, New York, New York 10017 (800) 253-9646; *Economic Survey of Latin America and the Caribbean.*

Times Books, 201 East 50th Street, New York, New York 10022 (212) 751-2600; *The Economist Book of Vital World Statistics.*

The World Bank, 1818 H Street, N.W., Washington, D.C. 20433 (202) 477-1234; *World Tables.*

BARBADOS - INFANT AND MATERNAL MORTALITY

Statistical Office of the United Nations, Publishing Service, New York, New York 10017 (800) 253-9646; *Demographic Yearbook,* and *Statistical Yearbook.*

Times Books, 201 East 50th Street, New York, New York 10022 (212) 751-2600; *The Economist Book of Vital World Statistics.*

The World Bank, 1818 H Street, N.W., Washington, D.C. 20433 (202) 477-1234; *World Tables.*

World Health Organization, Office of Publications, Avenue Appia, CH-1211 Geneva 27, Switzerland (Telephone Number in U.S. (518) 436-9686; *World Health Statistics Annual.*

BARBADOS - INFLATIONARY FACTORS

Statistical Office of the United Nations, Publishing Service, New York, New York 10017 (800) 253-9646; *Economic Survey of Latin America and the Caribbean.*

BARBADOS - INTEREST RATES

Inter-American Development Bank, 1300 New York Avenue, NW, Washington, D.C. 20577 (202) 623-1753; *Economic and Social Progress in Latin America.*

Organization of American States (OAS), General Secretariat, Washington, D.C. 20006 (202) 458-3533; *Statistical Bulletin of the OAS.*

BARBADOS - INTERNATIONAL FINANCE

Inter-American Development Bank, 1300 New York Avenue, NW, Washington, D.C. 20577 (202) 623-1753; *Economic and Social Progress in Latin America.*

BARBADOS - INTERNATIONAL LIQUIDITY

Inter-American Development Bank, 1300 New York Avenue, NW, Washington, D.C. 20577 (202) 623-1753; *Economic and Social Progress in Latin America.*

International Monetary Fund, 700 Nineteenth Street, NW, Washington, D.C. 20431 (202) 623-7000; *International Financial Statistics.*

BARBADOS - INTERNATIONAL RESERVES

Organization of American States (OAS), General Secretariat, Washington, D.C. 20006 (202) 458-3533; *Statistical Bulletin of the OAS.*

BARBADOS - INTERNATIONAL RESERVES EXCLUDING GOLD

Inter-American Development Bank, 1300 New York Avenue, NW, Washington, D.C. 20577 (202) 623-1753; *Economic and Social*

Progress in Latin America.

The World Bank, 1818 H Street, N.W., Washington, D.C. 20433 (202) 477-1234; *World Tables.*

BARBADOS - INTERNATIONAL STATISTICS

Inter-American Development Bank, 1300 New York Avenue, NW, Washington, D.C. 20577 (202) 623-1753; *Economic and Social Progress in Latin America.*

BARBADOS - INVESTMENT

Inter-American Development Bank, 1300 New York Avenue, NW, Washington, D.C. 20577 (202) 623-1753; *Economic and Social Progress in Latin America.*

Statistical Office of the United Nations, Publishing Service, New York, New York 10017 (800) 253-9646; *Statistical Yearbook for Latin America and the Caribbean.*

BARBADOS - IRON ORE PRODUCTION AND CONSUMPTION - See BARBADOS - MINING AND MINERAL PRODUCTS

BARBADOS - IRRIGATION

Inter-American Development Bank, 1300 New York Avenue, NW, Washington, D.C. 20577 (202) 623-1753; *Economic and Social Progress in Latin America.*

BARBADOS - LABOR FORCE

Facts on File, 460 Park Avenue South, New York, New York 10016 (800) 443-8323; *The New Book of World Rankings.*

Food and Agricultural Organization of the United Nations (FAO) Via delle Terme di Caracalla, 00100 Rome, Italy (Telephone Number in U.S. (202) 653-2400); *The State of Food and Agriculture.*

Gale Research Incorporated, 835 Penobscot Building, Detroit, Michigan 48226 (800) 877-4253; *International Historical Statistics The Americas and Australasia.*

G.K. Hall and Company, 70 Lincoln Street, Boston, Massachusetts 02111 (617) 423-3990; *The World in Figures.*

Times Books, 201 East 50th Street, New York, New York 10022 (212) 751-2600; *The Economist Book of Vital World Statistics.*

The World Bank, 1818 H Street, N.W., Washington, D.C. 20433 (202) 477-1234; *World Tables.*

BARBADOS - LABOR PRODUCTIVITY

International Labour Office, I.L.O. Publications, CH-1211, Geneva 22, Switzerland; *Yearbook of Labour Statistics.*

BARBADOS - LAND USE

Food and Agricultural Organization of the United Nations (FAO), Via delle Terme di Caracalla, 00100 Rome, Italy (Telephone Number in U.S. (202) 653-2400); *Production Yearbook.*

G.K. Hall and Company, 70 Lincoln Street, Boston, Massachusetts 02111 (617) 423-3990; *The World in Figures.*

Inter-American Development Bank, 1300 New York Avenue, NW, Washington, D.C. 20577 (202) 623-1753; *Economic and Social Progress in Latin America.*

BARBADOS - LIBRARIES

Facts on File, 460 Park Avenue South, New York, New York 10016 (800) 443-8323; *The New Book of World Rankings.*

United Nations Educational, Scientific and Cultural Organization (UNESCO), 7 Place de Fontenoy, F-75700 Paris, France (Telephone Number in U.S. (212) 963-5981); *Statistical Yearbook.*

BARBADOS - LIVESTOCK AND POULTRY

Facts on File, 460 Park Avenue South, New York, New York 10016 (800) 443-8323; *The New Book of World Rankings.*

Food and Agricultural Organization of the United Nations (FAO), Via delle Terme di Caracalla, 00100 Rome, Italy (Telephone Number in U.S. (202) 653-2400); *Production Yearbook,* and *The State of Food and Agriculture.*

G.K. Hall and Company, 70 Lincoln Street, Boston, Massachusetts 02111 (617) 423-3990; *The World in Figures.*

Statistical Office of the United Nations, Publishing Service, New York, New York 10017 (800) 253-9646; *Statistical Yearbook.*

BARBADOS - LIVING LEVELS

G.K. Hall and Company, 70 Lincoln Street, Boston, Massachusetts 02111 (617) 423-3990; *The World in Figures.*

Statistical Office of the United Nations, Publishing Service, New York, New York 10017 (800) 253-9646; *Statistical Yearbook for Latin America and the Caribbean.*

Times Books, 201 East 50th Street, New York, New York 10022 (212) 751-2600; *The Economist Book of Vital World Statistics.*

BARBADOS - MAIL - NUMBER OF PIECES SENT OR RECEIVED

Statistical Office of the United Nations, Publishing Service, New York, New York 10017 (800) 253-9646; *Statistical Yearbook.*

BARBADOS - MAIN ECONOMIC INDICATORS - See BARBADOS - ECONOMY

BARBADOS - MANUFACTURING

Facts on File, 460 Park Avenue South, New York, New York 10016 (800) 443-8323; *The New Book of World Rankings.*

G.K. Hall and Company, 70 Lincoln Street, Boston, Massachusetts 02111 (617) 423-3990; *The World in Figures.*

Inter-American Development Bank, 1300 New York Avenue, NW, Washington, D.C. 20577 (202) 623-1753; *Economic and Social Progress in Latin America.*

Organization of American States (OAS), General Secretariat, Washington, D.C. 20006 (202) 458-3533; *Statistical Bulletin of the OAS.*

Statistical Office of the United Nations, Publishing Service, New York, New York 10017 (800) 253-9646; *Statistical Yearbook,* and *Statistical Yearbook for Latin America and the Caribbean.*

The World Bank, 1818 H Street, N.W., Washington, D.C. 20433 (202) 477-1234; *World Tables.*

BARBADOS - MARRIAGE RATES

Facts on File, 460 Park Avenue South, New York, New York 10016 (800) 443-8323; *The New Book of World Rankings.*

Statistical Office of the United Nations, Publishing Service, New York, New York 10017 (800) 253-9646; *Demographic Yearbook,* and *Statistical Yearbook.*

BARBADOS - MEAT PRODUCTION - See BARBADOS - LIVESTOCK AND POULTRY

BARBADOS - MERCHANT SHIPPING

G.K. Hall and Company, 70 Lincoln Street, Boston, Massachusetts 02111 (617) 423-3990; *The World in Figures.*

Statistical Office of the United Nations, Publishing Service, New York, New York 10017 (800) 253-9646; *Statistical Yearbook.*

Times Books, 201 East 50th Street, New York, New York 10022 (212) 751-2600; *The Economist Book of Vital World Statistics.*

BARBADOS - MILITARY

G.K. Hall and Company, 70 Lincoln Street, Boston, Massachusetts 02111 (617) 423-3990; *The World in Figures.*

U.S. Arms Control and Disarmament Agency, 320 Twenty-first Street, NW, Washington, D.C. 20451 (202) 647-8677; *World Military Expenditures and Arms Transfers.*

BARBADOS - MILK PRODUCTION - See BARBADOS - DAIRY PRODUCTS

BARBADOS - MINING AND MINERAL PRODUCTS

Facts on File, 460 Park Avenue South, New York, New York 10016 (800) 443-8323; *The New Book of World Rankings.*

G.K. Hall and Company, 70 Lincoln Street, Boston, Massachusetts 02111 (617) 423-3990; *The World in Figures.*

Inter-American Development Bank, 1300 New York Avenue, NW, Washington, D.C. 20577 (202) 623-1753; *Economic and Social Progress in Latin America.*

Organization of American States (OAS), General Secretariat, Washington, D.C. 20006 (202) 458-3533; *Statistical Bulletin of the OAS.*

Penn Well Publishing Company, 1421 South Sheridan Road, P.O. Box 1260, Tulsa, Oklahoma 74101 (800) 752-9764; *International Energy Statistics Sourcebook.*

Statistical Office of the United Nations, Publishing Service, New York, New York 10017 (800) 253-9646; *Statistical Yearbook,* and *Statistical Yearbook for Latin America and the Caribbean.*

BARBADOS - MONEY EXCHANGE RATES

Inter-American Development Bank, 1300 New York Avenue, NW, Washington, D.C. 20577 (202) 623-1753; *Economic and Social Progress in Latin America.*

International Monetary Fund, 700 Nineteenth Street, NW, Washington, D.C. 20431 (202) 623-7000; *International Financial Statistics.*

Statistical Office of the United Nations, Publishing Service, New York, New York 10017 (800) 253-9646; *Statistical Yearbook.*

BARBADOS - MONEY MARKET RATES

Inter-American Development Bank, 1300 New York Avenue, NW, Washington, D.C. 20577 (202) 623-1753; *Economic and Social Progress in Latin America.*

Statistical Office of the United Nations, Publishing Service, New York, New York 10017 (800) 253-9646; *Statistical Yearbook.*

BARBADOS - MONEY RESERVES

Inter-American Development Bank, 1300 New York Avenue, NW, Washington, D.C. 20577 (202) 623-1753; *Economic and Social Progress in Latin America.*

BARBADOS - MONEY SUPPLY

Federal Statistical Office, Gustav - Stresemann - Ring 11, D-6200 Wiesbaden, Germany; *Barbados.*

G.K. Hall and Company, 70 Lincoln Street, Boston, Massachusetts 02111 (617) 423-3990; *The World in Figures.*

Inter-American Development Bank, 1300 New York Avenue, NW, Washington, D.C. 20577 (202) 623-1753; *Economic and Social Progress in Latin America.*

International Monetary Fund, 700 Nineteenth Street, NW, Washington, D.C. 20431 (202) 623-7000; *International Financial Statistics.*

Statistical Office of the United Nations, Publishing Service, New York, New York 10017 (800) 253-9646; *Statistical Yearbook.*

The World Bank, 1818 H Street, N.W., Washington, D.C. 20433 (202) 477-1234; *World Tables.*

BARBADOS - MOTOR VEHICLE TAXES - See BARBADOS - TAXATION

BARBADOS - MOTOR VEHICLES IN USE

G.K. Hall and Company, 70 Lincoln Street, Boston, Massachusetts 02111 (617) 423-3990; *The World in Figures.*

Statistical Office of the United Nations, Publishing Service, New York, New York 10017 (800) 253-9646; *Statistical Yearbook.*

Times Books, 201 East 50th Street, New York, New York 10022 (212) 751-2600; *The Economist Book of Vital World Statistics.*

BARBADOS - MULES - See BARBADOS - LIVESTOCK AND POULTRY

BARBADOS - MUSEUMS

Facts on File, 460 Park Avenue South, New York, New York 10016 (800) 443-8323; *The New Book of World Rankings.*

United Nations Educational, Scientific and Cultural Organization (UNESCO), 7 Place de Fontenoy, F-75700 Paris, France (Telephone Number in U.S. (212) 963-5981); *Statistical Yearbook.*

BARBADOS - NATALITY - See BARBADOS - BIRTH RATES

BARBADOS - NATIONAL ACCOUNTS

Federal Statistical Office, Gustav - Stresemann - Ring 11, D-6200 Wiesbaden, Germany; *Barbados.*

Gale Research Incorporated, 835 Penobscot Building, Detroit, Michigan 48226 (800) 877-4253; *International Historical Statistics The Americas and Australasia.*

Inter-American Development Bank, 1300 New York Avenue, NW, Washington, D.C. 20577 (202) 623-1753; *Economic and Social Progress in Latin America.*

Organization of American States (OAS), General Secretariat, Washington, D.C. 20006 (202) 458-3533; *Statistical Bulletin of the OAS.*

Statistical Office of the United Nations, Publishing Service, New York, New York 10017 (800) 253-9646; *National Accounts Statistics,* and *Statistical Yearbook.*

BARBADOS - NATIONAL INCOME

Facts on File, 460 Park Avenue South, New York, New York 10016 (800) 443-8323; *The New Book of World Rankings.*

G.K. Hall and Company, 70 Lincoln Street, Boston, Massachusetts 02111 (617) 423-3990; *The World in Figures.*

Inter-American Development Bank, 1300 New York Avenue, NW, Washington, D.C. 20577 (202) 623-1753; *Economic and Social Progress in Latin America.*

Statistical Office of the United Nations, Publishing Service, New York, New York 10017 (800) 253-9646; *Statistical Yearbook.*

BARBADOS - NATIONAL PRODUCT

Facts on File, 460 Park Avenue South, New York, New York 10016 (800) 443-8323; *The New Book of World Rankings.*

Statistical Office of the United Nations, Publishing Service, New York, New York 10017 (800) 253-9646; *Statistical Yearbook.*

BARBADOS - NATURAL GAS PRODUCTION - See BARBADOS - MINING AND MINERAL PRODUCTS

BARBADOS - NET MATERIAL PRODUCT

Statistical Office of the United Nations, Publishing Service, New York, New York 10017 (800) 253-9646; *Statistical Yearbook.*

BARBADOS - NEWSPAPER PRODUCTION - See BARBADOS - FORESTRY AND FOREST PRODUCTS

BARBADOS - NEWSPRINT - See BARBADOS - FORESTRY AND FOREST PRODUCTS

BARBADOS - NUTRITION

Statistical Office of the United Nations, Publishing Service, New York, New York 10017 (800) 253-9646; *Statistical Yearbook for Latin America and the Caribbean.*

BARBADOS - OCCUPATIONS - See BARBADOS - LABOR FORCE

BARBADOS - PAPER - See BARBADOS - FORESTRY AND FOREST PRODUCTS

BARBADOS - PATENTS

Statistical Office of the United Nations, Publishing Service, New York, New York 10017 (800) 253-9646; *Statistical Yearbook.*

BARBADOS - PEANUT PRODUCTION - See BARBADOS - CROPS

BARBADOS - PERIODICALS

United Nations Educational, Scientific and Cultural Organization (UNESCO), 7 Place de Fontenoy, F-75700 Paris, France (Telephone Number in U.S. (212) 963-5981); *Statistical Yearbook.*

BARBADOS - PESTICIDE USE

Food and Agricultural Organization of the United Nations (FAO) Via delle Terme di Caracalla, 00100 Rome, Italy (Telephone Number in U.S. (202) 653-2400); *The State of Food and Agriculture.*

BARBADOS - PETROLEUM INDUSTRY

Facts on File, 460 Park Avenue South, New York, New York 10016 (800) 443-8323; *The New Book of World Rankings.*

Food and Agricultural Organization of the United Nations (FAO) Via delle Terme di Caracalla, 00100 Rome, Italy (Telephone Number in U.S. (202) 653-2400); *The State of Food and Agriculture.*

G.K. Hall and Company, 70 Lincoln Street, Boston, Massachusetts 02111 (617) 423-3990; *The World in Figures.*

Inter-American Development Bank, 1300 New York Avenue, NW, Washington, D.C. 20577 (202) 623-1753; *Economic and Social Progress in Latin America.*

Penn Well Publishing Company, 1421 South Sheridan Road, P.O. Box 1260, Tulsa, Oklahoma 74101 (800) 752-9764; *International Energy Statistics Sourcebook.*

Statistical Office of the United Nations, Publishing Service, New York, New York 10017 (800) 253-9646; *Statistical Yearbook.*

BARBADOS - PIGS - See BARBADOS - LIVESTOCK AND POULTRY

BARBADOS - POPULATION

The Economist Intelligence Unit, 111 West 57th Street, New York, New York 10019 (800) 938-4685; *The World Market Atlas.*

Facts on File, 460 Park Avenue South, New York, New York 10016 (800) 443-8323; *The New Book of World Rankings.*

Federal Statistical Office, Gustav - Stresemann - Ring 11, D-6200 Wiesbaden, Germany; *Barbados.*

Food and Agricultural Organization of the United Nations (FAO), Via delle Terme di Caracalla, 00100 Rome, Italy (Telephone Number in U.S. (202) 653-2400); *Production Yearbook.*

Gale Research Incorporated, 835 Penobscot Building, Detroit, Michigan 48226 (800) 877-4253; *International Historical Statistics The Americas and Australasia.*

G.K. Hall and Company, 70 Lincoln Street, Boston, Massachusetts 02111 (617) 423-3990; *The World in Figures.*

Inter-American Development Bank, 1300 New York Avenue, NW, Washington, D.C. 20577 (202) 623-1753; *Economic and Social Progress in Latin America.*

International Labour Office, I.L.O. Publications, CH-1211, Geneva 22, Switzerland; *Yearbook of Labour Statistics.*

Organization of American States (OAS), General Secretariat, Washington, D.C. 20006 (202) 458-3533; *Statistical Bulletin of the OAS.*

Statistical Office of the United Nations, Publishing Service, New York, New York 10017 (800) 253-9646; *Demographic Yearbook, Statistical Yearbook,* and *Statistical Yearbook for Latin America and the Caribbean.*

U.S. Arms Control and Disarmament Agency, 320 Twenty-first Street, NW, Washington, D.C. 20451 (202) 647-8677; *World Military Expenditures and Arms Transfers.*

Times Books, 201 East 50th Street, New York, New York 10022 (212) 751-2600; *The Economist Book of Vital World Statistics.*

World Health Organization, Office of Publications, Avenue Appia, CH-1211 Geneva 27, Switzerland (Telephone Number in U.S. (518) 436-9686; *World Health Statistics Annual.*

BARBADOS - POST OFFICES

Facts on File, 460 Park Avenue South, New York, New York 10016 (800) 443-8323; *The New Book of World Rankings.*

BARBADOS - POTATO PRODUCTION - See BARBADOS - CROPS

BARBADOS - POWER PRODUCTION INDUSTRY

Statistical Office of the United Nations, Publishing Service, New York, New York 10017 (800) 253-9646; *Statistical Yearbook.*

BARBADOS - PRICES

Facts on File, 460 Park Avenue South, New York, New York 10016 (800) 443-8323; *The New Book of World Rankings.*

Federal Statistical Office, Gustav - Stresemann - Ring 11, D-6200 Wiesbaden, Germany; *Barbados.*

Food and Agricultural Organization of the United Nations (FAO), Via delle Terme di Caracalla, 00100 Rome, Italy (Telephone Number in U.S. (202) 653-2400); *Production Yearbook,* and *The State of Food and Agriculture.*

Gale Research Incorporated, 835 Penobscot Building, Detroit, Michigan 48226 (800) 877-4253; *International Historical Statistics The Americas and Australasia.*

G.K. Hall and Company, 70 Lincoln Street, Boston, Massachusetts 02111 (617) 423-3990; *The World in Figures.*

International Labour Office, I.L.O. Publications, CH-1211, Geneva 22, Switzerland; *Yearbook of Labour Statistics.*

International Monetary Fund, 700 Nineteenth Street, NW, Washington, D.C. 20431 (202) 623-7000; *International Financial Statistics.*

Statistical Office of the United Nations, Publishing Service, New York, New York 10017 (800) 253-9646; *Statistical Yearbook for Latin America and the Caribbean.*

BARBADOS - PRINTING AND WRITING PAPER - See BARBADOS - FORESTRY AND FOREST PRODUCTS

BARBADOS - PRODUCTION

Facts on File, 460 Park Avenue South, New York, New York 10016 (800) 443-8323; *The New Book of World Rankings.*

G.K. Hall and Company, 70 Lincoln Street, Boston, Massachusetts 02111 (617) 423-3990; *The World in Figures.*

BARBADOS - PROPERTY TAXES - See BARBADOS - TAXATION

BARBADOS - PUBLIC CONSUMPTION FUND

Inter-American Development Bank, 1300 New York Avenue, NW, Washington, D.C. 20577 (202) 623-1753; *Economic and Social Progress in Latin America.*

BARBADOS - PUBLIC EXPENDITURE

Inter-American Development Bank, 1300 New York Avenue, NW, Washington, D.C. 20577 (202) 623-1753; *Economic and Social Progress in Latin America.*

Organization of American States (OAS), General Secretariat, Washington, D.C. 20006 (202) 458-3533; *Statistical Bulletin of the OAS.*

Statistical Office of the United Nations, Publishing Service, New York, New York 10017 (800) 253-9646; *Statistical Yearbook for Latin America and the Caribbean.*

BARBADOS - PUBLIC FINANCES

Facts on File, 460 Park Avenue South, New York, New York 10016 (800) 443-8323; *The New Book of World Rankings.*

Federal Statistical Office, Gustav - Stresemann - Ring 11, D-6200 Wiesbaden, Germany; *Barbados.*

Inter-American Development Bank, 1300 New York Avenue, NW, Washington, D.C. 20577 (202) 623-1753; *Economic and Social Progress in Latin America.*

Organization of American States (OAS), General Secretariat, Washington, D.C. 20006 (202) 458-3533; *Statistical Bulletin of the OAS.*

BARBADOS - PUBLIC REVENUES

Inter-American Development Bank, 1300 New York Avenue, NW, Washington, D.C. 20577 (202) 623-1753; *Economic and Social Progress in Latin America.*

Organization of American States (OAS), General Secretariat, Washington, D.C. 20006 (202) 458-3533; *Statistical Bulletin of the OAS.*

BARBADOS - RADIO BROADCASTING - See BARBADOS - BROADCASTING

BARBADOS - RAILWAYS

G.K. Hall and Company, 70 Lincoln Street, Boston, Massachusetts 02111 (617) 423-3990; *The World in Figures.*

BARBADOS - RELIGION

Facts on File, 460 Park Avenue South, New York, New York 10016 (800) 443-8323; *The New Book of World Rankings.*

BARBADOS - RENT PRICES

International Labour Office, I.L.O. Publications, CH-1211, Geneva 22, Switzerland; *Yearbook of Labour Statistics.*

BARBADOS - RETAIL TRADE

G.K. Hall and Company, 70 Lincoln Street, Boston, Massachusetts 02111 (617) 423-3990; *The World in Figures.*

Inter-American Development Bank, 1300 New York Avenue, NW, Washington, D.C. 20577 (202) 623-1753; *Economic and Social Progress in Latin America.*

BARBADOS - RICE PRODUCTION - See BARBADOS - CROPS

BARBADOS - ROOT AND TUBER PRODUCTION - See BARBADOS - CROPS

BARBADOS - ROUNDWOOD - See BARBADOS - FORESTRY AND FOREST PRODUCTS

BARBADOS - RUBBER PRODUCTION

Facts on File, 460 Park Avenue South, New York, New York 10016 (800) 443-8323; *The New Book of World Rankings.*

BARBADOS - SAWNWOOD - See BARBADOS - FORESTRY AND FOREST PRODUCTS

BARBADOS - SENIOR CITIZENS

Facts on File, 460 Park Avenue South, New York, New York 10016 (800) 443-8323; *The New Book of World Rankings.*

BARBADOS - SHEEP - See BARBADOS - LIVESTOCK AND POULTRY

BARBADOS - SILVER PRODUCTION AND CONSUMPTION - See BARBADOS - MINING AND MINERAL PRODUCTS

BARBADOS - SOCIAL DATA

Facts on File, 460 Park Avenue South, New York, New York 10016 (800) 443-8323; *The New Book of World Rankings.*

G.K. Hall and Company, 70 Lincoln Street, Boston, Massachusetts 02111 (617) 423-3990; *The World in Figures.*

BARBADOS - SOCIAL SECURITY

Inter-American Development Bank, 1300 New York Avenue, NW, Washington, D.C. 20577 (202) 623-1753; *Economic and Social Progress in Latin America.*

International Monetary Fund, 700 Nineteenth Street, NW, Washington, D.C. 20431 (202) 623-7000; *Government Finance Statistics Yearbook.*

BARBADOS - SOCIOECONOMIC DATA

Inter-American Development Bank, 1300 New York Avenue, NW, Washington, D.C. 20577 (202) 623-1753; *Economic and Social Progress in Latin America.*

BARBADOS - STAMP TAXES AND DUTIES - See BARBADOS - TAXATION

BARBADOS - STATE BUDGET REVENUE AND EXPENDITURES

Inter-American Development Bank, 1300 New York Avenue, NW, Washington, D.C. 20577 (202) 623-1753; *Economic and Social Progress in Latin America.*

BARBADOS - STEEL PRODUCTION - See BARBADOS - MINING AND MINERAL PRODUCTS

BARBADOS - STOCKS - COMMODITY - MARKET PRICE - INDEX

Food and Agricultural Organization of the United Nations (FAO) Via delle Terme di Caracalla, 00100 Rome, Italy (Telephone Number in U.S. (202) 653-2400); *The State of Food and Agriculture.*

BARBADOS - SUGAR - See BARBADOS - CROPS

BARBADOS - TAX REVENUE - See BARBADOS - TAXATION

BARBADOS - TAXATION

G.K. Hall and Company, 70 Lincoln Street, Boston, Massachusetts 02111 (617) 423-3990; *The World in Figures.*

Inter-American Development Bank, 1300 New York Avenue, NW, Washington, D.C. 20577 (202) 623-1753; *Economic and Social Progress in Latin America.*

International Monetary Fund, 700 Nineteenth Street, NW, Washington, D.C. 20431 (202) 623-7000; *Government Finance Statistics Yearbook.*

Statistical Office of the United Nations, Publishing Service, New York, New York 10017 (800) 253-9646; *Statistical Yearbook for Latin America and the Caribbean.*

The World Bank, 1818 H Street, N.W., Washington, D.C. 20433 (202) 477-1234; *World Tables.*

BARBADOS - TELEPHONES IN USE

American Telephone and Telegraph Company, 26 Parsippany Road, Whippany, New Jersey 07981; *The World's Telephones.*

G.K. Hall and Company, 70 Lincoln Street, Boston, Massachusetts 02111 (617) 423-3990; *The World in Figures.*

Statistical Office of the United Nations, Publishing Service, New York, New York 10017 (800) 253-9646; *Statistical Yearbook.*

BARBADOS - TELEVISION BROADCASTING - See BARBADOS - BROADCASTING

BARBADOS - TEXTILE INDUSTRY

G.K. Hall and Company, 70 Lincoln Street, Boston, Massachusetts 02111 (617) 423-3990; *The World in Figures.*

BARBADOS - THEATRE

United Nations Educational, Scientific and Cultural Organization (UNESCO), 7 Place de Fontenoy, F-75700 Paris, France (Telephone Number in U.S. (212) 963-5981); *Statistical Yearbook.*

BARBADOS - TOBACCO PRODUCTION

Facts on File, 460 Park Avenue South, New York, New York 10016 (800) 443-8323; *The New Book of World Rankings.*

BARBADOS - TOBACCO PRODUCTS

Statistical Office of the United Nations, Publishing Service, New York, New York 10017 (800) 253-9646; *Statistical Yearbook.*

BARBADOS - TOURISM

Facts on File, 460 Park Avenue South, New York, New York 10016 (800) 443-8323; *The New Book of World Rankings.*

Federal Statistical Office, Gustav - Stresemann - Ring 11, D-6200 Wiesbaden, Germany; *Barbados.*

G.K. Hall and Company, 70 Lincoln Street, Boston, Massachusetts 02111 (617) 423-3990; *The World in Figures.*

Organization of American States (OAS), General Secretariat, Washington, D.C. 20006 (202) 458-3533; *Statistical Bulletin of the OAS.*

Statistical Office of the United Nations, Publishing Service, New York, New York 10017 (800) 253-9646; *Statistical Yearbook,* and *Statistical Yearbook for Latin America and the Caribbean.*

Times Books, 201 East 50th Street, New York, New York 10022 (212) 751-2600; *The Economist Book of Vital World Statistics.*

World Tourism Organization, Calle Capitan Haya 42, E-28020 Madrid, Spain; *Yearbook of Tourism Statistics.*

BARBADOS - TRADE - See BARBADOS - FOREIGN TRADE

BARBADOS - TRADEMARKS AND SERVICE MARKS

Statistical Office of the United Nations, Publishing Service, New York, New York 10017 (800) 253-9646; *Statistical Yearbook.*

BARBADOS - TRANSPORTATION AND COMMUNICATIONS

Facts on File, 460 Park Avenue South, New York, New York 10016 (800) 443-8323; *The New Book of World Rankings.*

Federal Statistical Office, Gustav - Stresemann - Ring 11, D-6200 Wiesbaden, Germany; *Barbados.*

Gale Research Incorporated, 835 Penobscot Building, Detroit, Michigan 48226 (800) 877-4253; *International Historical Statistics The Americas and Australasia.*

G.K. Hall and Company, 70 Lincoln Street, Boston, Massachusetts 02111 (617) 423-3990; *The World in Figures.*

Inter-American Development Bank, 1300 New York Avenue, NW, Washington, D.C. 20577 (202) 623-1753; *Economic and Social Progress in Latin America.*

Statistical Office of the United Nations, Publishing Service, New York, New York 10017 (800) 253-9646; *Statistical Yearbook for Latin America and the Caribbean.*

BARBADOS - TRAVEL FARES ABROAD

International Monetary Fund, 700 Nineteenth Street, NW, Washington, D.C. 20431 (202) 623-7000; *Government Finance Statistics Yearbook.*

BARBADOS - UNEMPLOYMENT

International Labour Office, I.L.O. Publications, CH-1211, Geneva 22, Switzerland; *Yearbook of Labour Statistics.*

Organization of American States (OAS), General Secretariat, Washington, D.C. 20006 (202) 458-3533; *Statistical Bulletin of the OAS.*

Statistical Office of the United Nations, Publishing Service, New York, New York 10017 (800) 253-9646; *Statistical Yearbook.*

BARBADOS - VITAL STATISTICS

Gale Research Incorporated, 835 Penobscot Building, Detroit, Michigan 48226 (800) 877-4253; *International Historical Statistics The Americas and Australasia.*

G.K. Hall and Company, 70 Lincoln Street, Boston, Massachusetts 02111 (617) 423-3990; *The World in Figures.*

Statistical Office of the United Nations, Publishing Service, New York, New York 10017 (800) 253-9646; *Statistical Yearbook.*

BARBADOS - WAGES

Federal Statistical Office, Gustav - Stresemann - Ring 11, D-6200 Wiesbaden, Germany; *Barbados.*

G.K. Hall and Company, 70 Lincoln Street, Boston, Massachusetts 02111 (617) 423-3990; *The World in Figures.*

International Labour Office, I.L.O. Publications, CH-1211, Geneva 22, Switzerland; *Yearbook of Labour Statistics.*

Statistical Office of the United Nations, Publishing Service, New York, New York 10017 (800) 253-9646; *Statistical Yearbook.*

BARBADOS - WEATHER

Facts on File, 460 Park Avenue South, New York, New York 10016 (800) 443-8323; *The New Book of World Rankings.*

G.K. Hall and Company, 70 Lincoln Street, Boston, Massachusetts 02111 (617) 423-3990; *The World in Figures.*

BARBADOS - WELFARE

Inter-American Development Bank, 1300 New York Avenue, NW, Washington, D.C. 20577 (202) 623-1753; *Economic and Social Progress in Latin America.*

International Monetary Fund, 700 Nineteenth Street, NW, Washington, D.C. 20431 (202) 623-7000; *Government Finance Statistics Yearbook.*

BARBADOS - WHEAT PRODUCTION - See BARBADOS - CROPS

BARBADOS - WHOLESALE PRICES

Inter-American Development Bank, 1300 New York Avenue, NW, Washington, D.C. 20577 (202) 623-1753; *Economic and Social Progress in Latin America.*

BARBADOS - WHOLESALE TRADE

Inter-American Development Bank, 1300 New York Avenue, NW, Washington, D.C. 20577 (202) 623-1753; *Economic and Social Progress in Latin America.*

BARBADOS - WINE PRODUCTION

Facts on File, 460 Park Avenue South, New York, New York 10016 (800) 443-8323; *The New Book of World Rankings.*

BARBADOS - WOOL PRODUCTION

Facts on File, 460 Park Avenue South, New York, New York 10016 (800) 443-8323; *The New Book of World Rankings.*

BARBER SHOPS

U.S. Department of Commerce, Bureau of the Census, Suitland, Maryland 20233 (301) 763-4040; *Census of Service Industries.*

U.S. Department of Labor, Bureau of Labor Statistics, Two Massachusetts Avenue, NE, Washington, D.C. 20212 (202) 606-7828; *Productivity Measures for Selected Industries and Government Services,* and Bulletin 2440.

BARITE

U.S. Department of the Interior, Bureau of Mines, 810 Seventh Street, NW, Washington, D.C. 20241 (202) 501-9649; *Mineral Commodity Summaries, Minerals Yearbook,* and *Annual Reports.*

BARIUM

U.S. Department of the Interior, Bureau of Mines, 810 Seventh Street, NW, Washington, D.C. 20241 (202) 501-9649; *Minerals Commodity Summaries.*

BARLEY

Statistical Office of the United Nations, Publishing Service, New York, New York 10017; *Statistical Yearbook,* and *Monthly Bulletin of Statistics.*

U.S. Department of Agriculture, Economic Research Service, Fourteenth Street and Independence Avenue, SW, Washington, D.C. 20005-4789 (202) 219-1504; *Agricultural Supply and Demand Estimates, Agricultural Statistics, Agricultural Outlook, Economic Indicators of the Farm Sector: National Financial Summary, Wheat Situation,* and *World Agriculture - Trends and Indicators.*

U.S. Department of Agriculture, National Agricultural Statistics Service, Fourteenth Street and Independence Avenue, SW, Washington, D.C. 20250 (202) 219-1504; *Crop Production, Crop Values,* and *Field Crops.*

BARS - See EATING AND DRINKING PLACES

BASEBALL

The American League of Professional Baseball Clubs, 350 Park Avenue, New York, New York 10022 (212) 339-7600; *American League Red Book,* and *National League Green Book.*

Major League Baseball Players Association, 805 Third Avenue, 26th Floor, New York, New York 10022 (212) 826-0808.

National Sporting Goods Association, 1699 Wall Street, Mount Prospect, Illinois 60056 (708) 439-4000; *The Sporting Goods Market in 1993,* and *Sports Participation in 1992.*

BASKETBALL

National Basketball Association, 645 Fifth Avenue, New York, New York 10022 (212) 826-7000.

National Collegiate Athletic Association, 6201 College Boulevard, Overland Park, Kansas 66211 (913) 339-1906.

National Sporting Goods Association, 1699 Wall Street, Mount Prospect, Illinois 60056 (708) 439-4000; *Sports Participation in 1992,* and *The Sporting Goods Market in 1993.*

BAUXITE

U.S. Department of the Interior, Bureau of Mines, 810 Seventh Street, NW, Washington, D.C. 20241 (202) 501-9649; *Minerals Yearbook, Annual Reports,* and *Mineral Commodity Summaries.*

BAUXITE - CONSUMPTION

U.S. Department of the Interior, Bureau of Mines, 810 Seventh Street, NW, Washington, D.C. 20241 (202) 501-9649; *Mineral Commodity Summaries, Minerals Yearbook, Annual Reports,* and *Mineral Commodity Summaries.*

BAUXITE - EMPLOYMENT

U.S. Department of the Interior, Bureau of Mines, 810 Seventh Street, NW, Washington, D.C. 20241 (202) 501-9649; *Mineral Commodity Summaries.*

BAUXITE - FOREIGN TRADE

U.S. Department of the Interior, Bureau of Mines, 810 Seventh Street, NW, Washington, D.C. 20241 (202) 501-9649; *Minerals Yearbook,* and *Mineral Commodity Summaries.*

BAUXITE - PRICES

U.S. Department of the Interior, Bureau of Mines, 810 Seventh Street, NW, Washington, D.C. 20241 (202) 501-9649; *Mineral Commodity Summaries.*

BAUXITE - PRODUCTION

U.S. Department of the Interior, Bureau of Mines, 810 Seventh Street, NW, Washington, D.C. 20241 (202) 501-9649; *Minerals Yearbook.*

BAUXITE - STRATEGIC AND CRITICAL MATERIALS INVENTORY

U.S. Department of Defense, Defense Logistics Agency, The Pentagon, Washington, D.C. 20301 (703) 274-6000; *Statistical Supplement, Stockpile Report to the Congress.*

BAUXITE - WORLD PRODUCTION

U.S. Department of the Interior, Bureau of Mines, 810 Seventh Street, NW, Washington, D.C. 20241 (202) 501-9649; *Minerals Yearbook, Annual Reports,* and *Mineral Commodity Summaries.*

BEANS

U.S. Department of Agriculture, National Agricultural Statistics Service, Fourteenth Street and Independence Avenue, SW, Washington, D.C. 20250 (202) 219-1504; *Agricultural Statistics; Vegetables; Food Consumption, Prices, and Expenditures; Economic Indicators of the Farm Sector: National Financial Summary;* and unpublished data.

BEAUTY SHOPS

U.S. Department of Commerce, Bureau of the Census, Suitland, Maryland 20233 (301) 763-4040; *Census of the Service Industries,* and *County Business Patterns.*

U.S. Department of Labor, Bureau of Labor Statistics, Two Massachusetts Avenue, NE, Washington, D.C. 20212 (202) 606-7828; *Productivity Measures for Selected Industries and Government Services*, and Bulletin 2440.

BEEF - See also MEAT AND MEAT PRODUCTS

BEEF - CONSUMER EXPENDITURES

U.S. Department of Labor, Bureau of Labor Statistics, Two Massachusetts Avenue, NE, Washington, D.C. 20212 (202) 606-7828; *Consumer Expenditures in 1992.*

BEEF - CONSUMPTION

U.S. Department of Agriculture, Economic Research Service, Fourteenth Street and Independence Avenue, SW, Washington, D.C. 20250 (202) 219-1504; *Agricultural Outlook, Food Consumption, Prices, and Expenditures, Livestock and Meat Statistics*, and unpublished data.

U.S. Department of Agriculture, Foreign Agricultural Service, Fourteenth Street and Independence Avenue, SW, Washington, D.C. 20250 (202) 720-3448; *World Livestock Situation.*

BEEF - CONSUMPTION - FOREIGN COUNTRIES

U.S. Department of Agriculture, Foreign Agricultural Service, Fourteenth Street and Independence Avenue, SW, Washington, D.C. 20250 (202) 720-3448; *World Livestock Situation.*

BEEF - FOREIGN TRADE

U.S. Department of Agriculture, National Agricultural Statistics Service, Fourteenth Street and Independence Avenue, SW, Washington, D.C. 20250 (202) 219-1504; *Livestock and Meat Statistics, Agricultural Outlook*, and *Foreign Agricultural Trade of the U.S.*

BEEF - PRICE INDEXES

U.S. Department of Labor, Bureau of Labor Statistics, Two Massachusetts Avenue, NE, Washington, D.C. 20212 (202) 606-7828; *Monthly Labor Review*, and *CPI Detailed Report.*

BEEF - PRODUCTION

U.S. Department of Agriculture, National Agricultural Statistics Service, Fourteenth Street and Independence Avenue, SW, Washington, D.C. 20250 (202) 219-1504; *Livestock and Meat Statistics*, and *Agricultural Outlook.*

BEEF - SUPPLY

U.S. Department of Agriculture, Economic Research Service, Fourteenth Street and Independence Avenue, SW, Washington, D.C. 20005-4789 (202) 219-1504; *Livestock and Meat Statistics*, and *Agricultural Outlook.*

BEER - See MALT BEVERAGES

BELARUS - See also UNION OF SOVIET SOCIALIST REPUBLIC

Belarus - National Statistical Office

Ministry of Foreign Affairs, 8 Lenin Street Minsk, Belarus.

Belarus - Primary Statistics Source

State Committee of the Republic of Belarus on Statistics and Analysis, Minsk, Belarus; *National Economy of the Republic of Belarus.*

BELARUS - ABORTIONS

Statistical Office of the United Nations, Publishing Service, New York, New York 10017 (800) 253-9646; *Demographic Yearbook.*

BELARUS - AGRICULTURE

Business International Moscow, 23 Profseyuznaya Ulitsa 117859, Moscow (Telephone Number in U.S. (800) 938-4685); *The CIS Market Atlas.*

Encyclopedia Britannica, Incorporated, 310 South Michigan Avenue, Chicago, Illinois 60604 (312) 347-7000; *Britannica World Data.*

The World Bank, 1818 H Street, NW, Washington, D.C. 20433 (202) 477-1234; *Statistical Handbook: States of the Former USSR.*

BELARUS - AIRLINE SERVICE

Business International Moscow, 23 Profseyuznaya Ulitsa 117859, Moscow (Telephone Number in U.S. (800) 938-4685); *The CIS Market Atlas.*

Encyclopedia Britannica, Incorporated, 310 South Michigan Avenue, Chicago, Illinois 60604 (312) 347-7000; *Britannica World Data.*

BELARUS - AREA AND POPULATION DENSITY

Business International Moscow, 23 Profseyuznaya Ulitsa 117859, Moscow (Telephone Number in U.S. (800) 938-4685); *The CIS Market Atlas.*

Statistical Office of the United Nations, Publishing Service, New York, New York 10017 (800) 253-9646; *Statistical Yearbook.*

BELARUS - BANKING

Business International Moscow, 23 Profseyuznaya Ulitsa 117859, Moscow (Telephone Number in U.S. (800) 938-4685); *The CIS Market Atlas.*

BELARUS - BEER PRODUCTION

Statistical Office of the United Nations, Publishing Service, New York, New York 10017 (800) 253-9646; *Statistical Yearbook.*

BELARUS - BIRTH RATE

Business International Moscow, 23 Profseyuznaya Ulitsa 117859, Moscow (Telephone Number in U.S. (800) 938-4685); *The CIS Market Atlas.*

Encyclopedia Britannica, Incorporated, 310 South Michigan Avenue, Chicago, Illinois 60604 (312) 347-7000; *Britannica World Data.*

Statistical Office of the United Nations, Publishing Service, New York, New York 10017 (800) 253-9646; *Demographic Yearbook*, and *Statistical Yearbook.*

World Health Organization, Office of Publications, Avenue Appia, CH-1211 Geneva 27, Switzerland (Telephone Number in U.S. (518) 436-9686; *World Health Statistics Annual.*

BELARUS - BOOK PRODUCTION

United Nations Educational, Scientific and Cultural Organization (UNESCO), 7 Place de Fontenoy, F-75700 Paris, France (Telephone Number in U.S. (212) 963-5981; *Statistical Yearbook.*

BELARUS - BUDGET

Business International Moscow, 23 Profseyuznaya Ulitsa 117859, Moscow (Telephone Number in U.S. (800) 938-4685); *The CIS Market Atlas.*

BELARUS - BUILDING CONSTRUCTION - See BELARUS - CONSTRUCTION INDUSTRY

BELARUS - BUTTER PRODUCTION - See BELARUS - DAIRY PRODUCTS

BELARUS - CAPITAL INVESTMENT

The World Bank, 1818 H Street, NW, Washington, D.C. 20433 (202) 477-1234; *Statistical Handbook: States of the Former USSR.*

BELARUS - CATTLE - See BELARUS - LIVESTOCK AND POULTRY

BELARUS - CEMENT PRODUCTION - See BELARUS - MINING AND MINERAL PRODUCTS

BELARUS - CHEMICAL (ORGANIC) PRODUCTION - See BELARUS - MINING AND MINERAL PRODUCTS

BELARUS - CHEMICALS

Business International Moscow, 23 Profseyuznaya Ulitsa 117859, Moscow (Telephone Number in U.S. (800) 938-4685); *The CIS Market Atlas.*

BELARUS - CIGARETTE PRODUCTION - See BELARUS - TOBACCO PRODUCTION

BELARUS - COAL PRODUCTION AND CONSUMPTION - See BELARUS - MINING AND MINERAL PRODUCTS

BELARUS - COMMUNICATIONS

Business International Moscow, 23 Profseyuznaya Ulitsa 117859, Moscow (Telephone Number in U.S. (800) 938-4685); *The CIS Market Atlas.*

BELARUS - CONSTRUCTION INDUSTRY

Business International Moscow, 23 Profseyuznaya Ulitsa 117859, Moscow (Telephone Number in U.S. (800) 938-4685); *The CIS Market Atlas.*

Encyclopedia Britannica, Incorporated, 310 South Michigan Avenue, Chicago, Illinois 60604 (312) 347-7000; *Britannica World Data.*

Statistical Office of the United Nations, Publishing Service, New York, New York 10017 (800) 253-9646; *Construction Statistics Yearbook,* and *Statistical Yearbook.*

BELARUS - CONSUMER PRICE INDEX

Statistical Office of the United Nations, Publishing Service, New York, New York 10017 (800) 253-9646; *Statistical Yearbook.*

BELARUS - CONSUMER PRICES

International Labour Office, I.L.O. Publications, CH-1211, Geneva 22, Switzerland; *Yearbook of Labour Statistics.*

BELARUS - CONSUMER PRODUCTS

Business International Moscow, 23 Profseyuznaya Ulitsa 117859, Moscow (Telephone Number in U.S. (800) 938-4685); *The CIS Market Atlas.*

BELARUS - CONSUMPTION

Business International Moscow, 23 Profseyuznaya Ulitsa 117859, Moscow (Telephone Number in U.S. (800) 938-4685); *The CIS Market Atlas.*

The World Bank, 1818 H Street, NW, Washington, D.C. 20433 (202) 477-1234; *Statistical Handbook: States of the Former USSR.*

BELARUS - COTTON - See BELARUS - CROPS

BELARUS - CROPS

Business International Moscow, 23 Profseyuznaya Ulitsa 117859, Moscow (Telephone Number in U.S. (800) 938-4685); *The CIS Market Atlas.*

Statistical Office of the United Nations, Publishing Service, New York, New York 10017 (800) 253-9646; *Statistical Yearbook.*

The World Bank, 1818 H Street, NW, Washington, D.C. 20433 (202) 477-1234; *Statistical Handbook: States of the Former USSR.*

BELARUS - DAIRY PRODUCTS

Statistical Office of the United Nations, Publishing Service, New York, New York 10017 (800) 253-9646; *Statistical Yearbook.*

BELARUS - DEATH RATES

Business International Moscow, 23 Profseyuznaya Ulitsa 117859, Moscow (Telephone Number in U.S. (800) 938-4685); *The CIS Market Atlas.*

Statistical Office of the United Nations, Publishing Service, New York, New York 10017 (800) 253-9646; *Statistical Yearbook.*

BELARUS - DEMOGRAPHY

Business International Moscow, 23 Profseyuznaya Ulitsa 117859, Moscow (Telephone Number in U.S. (800) 938-4685); *The CIS Market Atlas.*

Encyclopedia Britannica, Incorporated, 310 South Michigan Avenue, Chicago, Illinois 60604 (312) 347-7000; *Britannica World Data.*

The World Bank, 1818 H Street, NW, Washington, D.C. 20433 (202) 477-1234; *Statistical Handbook: States of the Former USSR.*

BELARUS - DISEASES

Business International Moscow, 23 Profseyuznaya Ulitsa 117859, Moscow (Telephone Number in U.S. (800) 938-4685); *The CIS Market Atlas.*

BELARUS - DIVORCE RATES

Encyclopedia Britannica, Incorporated, 310 South Michigan Avenue, Chicago, Illinois 60604 (312) 347-7000; *Britannica World Data.*

Statistical Office of the United Nations, Publishing Service, New York, New York 10017 (800) 253-9646; *Demographic Yearbook,* and *Statistical Yearbook.*

BELARUS - DOMESTIC INVESTMENT

Business International Moscow, 23 Profseyuznaya Ulitsa 117859, Moscow (Telephone Number in U.S. (800) 938-4685); *The CIS Market Atlas.*

BELARUS - ECONOMY

Business International Moscow, 23 Profseyuznaya Ulitsa 117859, Moscow (Telephone Number in U.S. (800) 938-4685); *The CIS Market Atlas.*

Encyclopedia Britannica, Incorporated, 310 South Michigan Avenue, Chicago, Illinois 60604 (312) 347-7000; *Britannica World Data.*

BELARUS - EDUCATION

Business International Moscow, 23 Profseyuznaya Ulitsa 117859, Moscow (Telephone Number in U.S. (800) 938-4685); *The CIS Market Atlas.*

Encyclopedia Britannica, Incorporated, 310 South Michigan Avenue, Chicago, Illinois 60604 (312) 347-7000; *Britannica World Data.*

United Nations Educational, Scientific and Cultural Organization (UNESCO), 7 Place de Fontenoy, F-75700 Paris, France (Telephone Number in U.S. (212) 963-5981; *Statistical Yearbook.*

BELARUS - ELECTRICITY PRODUCTION

Business International Moscow, 23 Profseyuznaya Ulitsa 117859, Moscow (Telephone Number in U.S. (800) 938-4685); *The CIS Market Atlas.*

The World Bank, 1818 H Street, NW, Washington, D.C. 20433 (202) 477-1234; *Statistical Handbook: States of the Former USSR.*

BELARUS - EMPLOYMENT

International Labour Office, I.L.O. Publications, CH-1211, Geneva 22, Switzerland; *Yearbook of Labour Statistics.*

Statistical Office of the United Nations, Publishing Service, New York, New York 10017 (800) 253-9646; *Statistical Yearbook.*

The World Bank, 1818 H Street, NW, Washington, D.C. 20433 (202) 477-1234; *Statistical Handbook: States of the Former USSR.*

BELARUS - ENERGY PRODUCTION

Business International Moscow, 23 Profseyuznaya Ulitsa 117859, Moscow (Telephone Number in U.S. (800) 938-4685); *The CIS Market Atlas.*

Encyclopedia Britannica, Incorporated, 310 South Michigan Avenue, Chicago, Illinois 60604 (312) 347-7000; *Britannica World Data.*

The World Bank, 1818 H Street, NW, Washington, D.C. 20433 (202) 477-1234; *Statistical Handbook: States of the Former USSR.*

BELARUS - ENVIRONMENT

Business International Moscow, 23 Profseyuznaya Ulitsa 117859, Moscow (Telephone Number in U.S. (800) 938-4685); *The CIS Market Atlas.*

BELARUS - EXPORTS

Business International Moscow, 23 Profseyuznaya Ulitsa 117859, Moscow (Telephone Number in U.S. (800) 938-4685); *The CIS Market Atlas.*

Encyclopedia Britannica, Incorporated, 310 South Michigan Avenue, Chicago, Illinois 60604 (312) 347-7000; *Britannica World Data.*

The World Bank, 1818 H Street, NW, Washington, D.C. 20433 (202) 477-1234; *Statistical Handbook: States of the Former USSR.*

BELARUS - EXTERNAL TRADE

The World Bank, 1818 H Street, NW, Washington, D.C. 20433 (202) 477-1234; *Statistical Handbook: States of the Former USSR.*

BELARUS - FABRIC PRODUCTION - See BELARUS - TEXTILE INDUSTRY

BELARUS - FERTILITY RATES

Encyclopedia Britannica, Incorporated, 310 South Michigan Avenue, Chicago, Illinois 60604 (312) 347-7000; *Britannica World Data.*

The World Bank, 1818 H Street, NW, Washington, D.C. 20433 (202) 477-1234; *Statistical Handbook: States of the Former USSR.*

BELARUS - FETAL MORTALITY

Statistical Office of the United Nations, Publishing Service, New York, New York 10017 (800) 253-9646; *Demographic Yearbook.*

World Health Organization, Avenue Appia, Office of Publications, CH-1211 Geneva 27, Switzerland (Telephone Number in U.S. (518) 436-9686); *World Health Statistics: Vital Statistics and Causes of Death.*

BELARUS - FILM - See BELARUS - MOTION PICTURES

BELARUS - FISHERIES

Encyclopedia Britannica, Incorporated, 310 South Michigan Avenue, Chicago, Illinois 60604 (312) 347-7000; *Britannica World Data.*

BELARUS - FLOUR PRODUCTION - See BELARUS - CROPS

BELARUS - FOOTWEAR PRODUCTION AND CONSUMPTION - See BELARUS - TEXTILE INDUSTRY

BELARUS - FOREIGN INVESTMENT

Business International Moscow, 23 Profseyuznaya Ulitsa 117859, Moscow (Telephone Number in U.S. (800) 938-4685); *The CIS Market Atlas.*

BELARUS - FOREIGN TRADE

Business International Moscow, 23 Profseyuznaya Ulitsa 117859, Moscow (Telephone Number in U.S. (800) 938-4685); *The CIS Market Atlas.*

Encyclopedia Britannica, Incorporated, 310 South Michigan Avenue, Chicago, Illinois 60604 (312) 347-7000; *Britannica World Data.*

The World Bank, 1818 H Street, NW, Washington, D.C. 20433 (202) 477-1234; *Statistical Handbook: States of the Former USSR.*

BELARUS - FORESTRY AND FOREST PRODUCTS

Business International Moscow, 23 Profseyuznaya Ulitsa 117859, Moscow (Telephone Number in U.S. (800) 938-4685); *The CIS Market Atlas.*

Statistical Office of the United Nations, Publishing Service, New York, New York 10017 (800) 253-9646; *Statistical Yearbook.*

United Nations Educational, Scientific and Cultural Organization (UNESCO), 7 Place de Fontenoy, F-75700 Paris, France (Telephone Number in U.S. (212) 963-5981; *Statistical Yearbook.*

BELARUS - GAS PRODUCTION See BELARUS - MINING AND MINERAL PRODUCTS

BELARUS - GENERAL MORTALITY

Statistical Office of the United Nations, Publishing Service, New York, New York 10017 (800) 253-9646; *Demographic Yearbook.*

World Health Organization, Avenue Appia, Office of Publications, CH-1211 Geneva 27, Switzerland (Telephone Number in U.S. (518) 436-9686; *World Health Statistics: Vital Statistics and Causes of Death.*

BELARUS - GOATS - See BELARUS - LIVESTOCK AND POULTRY

BELARUS - GOVERNMENT EXPENDITURE

The World Bank, 1818 H Street, NW, Washington, D.C. 20433 (202) 477-1234; *Statistical Handbook: States of the Former USSR.*

BELARUS - GOVERNMENT REVENUE

The World Bank, 1818 H Street, NW, Washington, D.C. 20433 (202) 477-1234; *Statistical Handbook: States of the Former USSR.*

BELARUS - GROSS DOMESTIC PRODUCT

Statistical Office of the United Nations, Publishing Service, New York, New York 10017 (800) 253-9646; *Statistical Yearbook.*

The World Bank, 1818 H Street, NW, Washington, D.C. 20433 (202) 477-1234; *Statistical Handbook: States of the Former USSR.*

BELARUS - HEALTH

Business International Moscow, 23 Profseyuznaya Ulitsa 117859, Moscow (Telephone Number in U.S. (800) 938-4685); *The CIS Market Atlas.*

Encyclopedia Britannica, Incorporated, 310 South Michigan Avenue, Chicago, Illinois 60604 (312) 347-7000; *Britannica World Data.*

BELARUS - HIGHWAYS

Business International Moscow, 23 Profseyuznaya Ulitsa 117859, Moscow (Telephone Number in U.S. (800) 938-4685); *The CIS Market Atlas.*

Encyclopedia Britannica, Incorporated, 310 South Michigan Avenue, Chicago, Illinois 60604 (312) 347-7000; *Britannica World Data.*

BELARUS - HOURS OF WORK - See BELARUS - EMPLOYMENT

BELARUS - HOUSING AND HOUSING UNITS

Business International Moscow, 23 Profseyuznaya Ulitsa 117859, Moscow (Telephone Number in U.S. (800) 938-4685); *The CIS Market Atlas.*

BELARUS - IMPORTS

Business International Moscow, 23 Profseyuznaya Ulitsa 117859, Moscow (Telephone Number in U.S. (800) 938-4685); *The CIS Market Atlas.*

Encyclopedia Britannica, Incorporated, 310 South Michigan Avenue, Chicago, Illinois 60604 (312) 347-7000; *Britannica World Data.*

The World Bank, 1818 H Street, NW, Washington, D.C. 20433 (202) 477-1234; *Statistical Handbook: States of the Former USSR.*

BELARUS - INDUSTRY

Business International Moscow, 23 Profseyuznaya Ulitsa 117859, Moscow (Telephone Number in U.S. (800) 938-4685); *The CIS Market Atlas.*

International Labour Office, I.L.O. Publications, CH-1211, Geneva 22, Switzerland; *Yearbook of Labour Statistics.*

Statistical Office of the United Nations, Publishing Service, New York, New York 10017 (800) 253-9646; *Statistical Yearbook.*

The World Bank, 1818 H Street, NW, Washington, D.C. 20433 (202) 477-1234; *Statistical Handbook: States of the Former USSR.*

BELARUS - INFANT AND MATERNAL MORTALITY

Business International Moscow, 23 Profseyuznaya Ulitsa 117859, Moscow (Telephone Number in U.S. (800) 938-4685); *The CIS Market Atlas.*

Statistical Office of the United Nations, Publishing Service, New York, New York 10017; *Demographic Yearbook,* and *Statistical Yearbook.*

BELARUS - INTERNAL TRADE

Statistical Office of the United Nations, Publishing Service, New York, New York 10017 (800) 253-9646; *Statistical Yearbook.*

BELARUS - LABOR

Business International Moscow, 23 Profseyuznaya Ulitsa 117859, Moscow (Telephone Number in U.S. (800) 938-4685); *The CIS Market Atlas.*

The World Bank, 1818 H Street, NW, Washington, D.C. 20433 (202) 477-1234; *Statistical Handbook: States of the Former USSR.*

BELARUS - LABOR PRODUCTIVITY

International Labour Office, I.L.O. Publications, CH-1211, Geneva 22, Switzerland; *Yearbook of Labour Statistics.*

BELARUS - LAND USE

Encyclopedia Britannica, Incorporated, 310 South Michigan Avenue, Chicago, Illinois 60604 (312) 347-7000; *Britannica World Data.*

BELARUS - LIBRARIES

United Nations Educational, Scientific and Cultural Organization (UNESCO), 7 Place de Fontenoy, F-75700 Paris, France (Telephone Number in U.S. (212) 963-5981; *Statistical Yearbook.*

BELARUS - LIFE EXPECTANCY

Business International Moscow, 23 Profseyuznaya Ulitsa 117859, Moscow (Telephone Number in U.S. (800) 938-4685); *The CIS Market Atlas.*

BELARUS - LIVESTOCK AND POULTRY

Business International Moscow, 23 Profseyuznaya Ulitsa 117859, Moscow (Telephone Number in U.S. (800) 938-4685); *The CIS Market Atlas.*

Encyclopedia Britannica, Incorporated, 310 South Michigan Avenue, Chicago, Illinois 60604 (312) 347-7000; *Britannica World Data.*

BELARUS - MAIL TRAFFIC - NUMBER OF ITEMS

Statistical Office of the United Nations, Publishing Service, New York, New York 10017 (800) 253-9646; *Statistical Yearbook.*

BELARUS - MANUFACTURING

Encyclopedia Britannica, Incorporated, 310 South Michigan Avenue, Chicago, Illinois 60604 (312) 347-7000; *Britannica World Data.*

Statistical Office of the United Nations, Publishing Service, New York, New York 10017 (800) 253-9646; *Statistical Yearbook.*

BELARUS - MARRIAGE RATES

Encyclopedia Britannica, Incorporated, 310 South Michigan Avenue, Chicago, Illinois 60604 (312) 347-7000; *Britannica World Data.*

Statistical Office of the United Nations, Publishing Service, New York, New York 10017 (800) 453-9646; *Demographic Yearbook,* and *Statistical Yearbook.*

BELARUS - MEAT PRODUCTION - See BELARUS - LIVESTOCK AND POULTRY

BELARUS - MERCHANT SHIPPING

Statistical Office of the United Nations, Publishing Service, New York, New York 10017 (800) 253-9646; *Annual Bulletin of Transport Statistics for Europe.*

BELARUS - MILK PRODUCTION - See BELARUS - DAIRY PRODUCTS

BELARUS - MINING AND MINERAL PRODUCTS

Business International Moscow, 23 Profseyuznaya Ulitsa 117859, Moscow (Telephone Number in U.S. (800) 938-4685); *The CIS Market Atlas.*

Encyclopedia Britannica, Incorporated, 310 South Michigan Avenue, Chicago, Illinois 60604 (312) 347-7000; *Britannica World Data.*

Statistical Office of the United Nations, Publishing Service, New York, New York 10017 (800) 253-9646; *Statistical Yearbook.*

BELARUS - MOTION PICTURES

Statistical Office of the United Nations, Publishing Service, New York, New York 10017 (800) 253-9646; *Statistical Yearbook.*

United Nations Educational, Scientific and Cultural Organization (UNESCO), 7 Place de Fontenoy, F-75700 Paris, France (Telephone Number in U.S. (212) 963-5981; *Statistical Yearbook.*

BELARUS - MOTOR VEHICLE PRODUCTION

Business International Moscow, 23 Profseyuznaya Ulitsa 117859, Moscow (Telephone Number in U.S. (800) 938-4685); *The CIS Market Atlas.*

Statistical Office of the United Nations, Publishing Service, New York, New York 10017 (800) 253-9646; *Statistical Yearbook.*

BELARUS - MUSEUMS

United Nations Educational, Scientific and Cultural Organization (UNESCO), 7 Place de Fontenoy, F-75700 Paris, France (Telephone Number in U.S. (212) 963-5981; *Statistical Yearbook.*

BELARUS - NATALITY

Statistical Office of the United Nations, Publishing Service, New York, New York 10017 (800) 253-9646; *Demographic Yearbook.*

World Health Organization, Avenue Appia, Office of Publications, CH-1211 Geneva 27, Switzerland (Telephone Number in U.S. (518) 436-9686; *World Health Statistics: Vital Statistics and Causes of Death.*

BELARUS - NATIONAL ACCOUNTS

Statistical Office of the United Nations, Publishing Service, New York, New York 10017 (800) 253-9646; *National Accounts Statistics,* and *Statistical Yearbook.*

The World Bank, 1818 H Street, NW, Washington, D.C. 20433 (202) 477-1234; *Statistical Handbook: States of the Former USSR.*

BELARUS - NATIONAL INCOME

Business International Moscow, 23 Profseyuznaya Ulitsa 117859, Moscow (Telephone Number in U.S. (800) 938-4685); *The CIS Market Atlas.*

BELARUS - NATIONAL PRODUCT

Statistical Office of the United Nations, Publishing Service, New York, New York 10017 (800) 253-9646; *Statistical Yearbook.*

BELARUS - NATURAL GAS PRODUCTION - See BELARUS - MINING AND MINERAL PRODUCTS

BELARUS - NET MATERIAL PRODUCT

Statistical Office of the United Nations, Publishing Service, New York, New York 10017 (800) 253-9646; *Statistical Yearbook.*

BELARUS - NEWSPAPER PRODUCTION - See BELARUS - FORESTRY AND FOREST PRODUCTS

BELARUS - PAPER - See BELARUS - FORESTRY AND FOREST PRODUCTS

BELARUS - PERIODICALS

United Nations Educational, Scientific and Cultural Organization (UNESCO), 7 Place de Fontenoy, F-75700 Paris, France (Telephone Number in U.S. (212) 963-5981; *Statistical Yearbook.*

BELARUS - PETROLEUM INDUSTRY

Statistical Office of the United Nations, Publishing Service, New York, New York 10017 (800) 253-9646; *Statistical Yearbook.*

BELARUS - PIGS - See BELARUS - LIVESTOCK AND POULTRY

BELARUS - PIPELINES FOR OIL AND PETROLEUM PRODUCTS

Statistical Office of the United Nations, Publishing Service, New York, New York 10017 (800) 253-9646; *Annual Bulletin of Transport Statistics for Europe.*

BELARUS - POPULATION

Business International Moscow, 23 Profseyuznaya Ulitsa 117859, Moscow (Telephone Number in U.S. (800) 938-4685); *The CIS Market Atlas.*

Encyclopedia Britannica, Incorporated, 310 South Michigan Avenue, Chicago, Illinois 60604 (312) 347-7000; *Britannica World Data.*

International Labour Office, I.L.O. Publications, CH-1211, Geneva 22, Switzerland; *Yearbook of Labour Statistics.*

Statistical Office of the United Nations, Publishing Service, New York, New York 10017 (800) 253-9646; *Demographic Yearbook,* and *Statistical Yearbook.*

The World Bank, 1818 H Street, NW, Washington, D.C. 20433 (202) 477-1234; *Statistical Handbook: States of the Former USSR.*

World Health Organization, Avenue Appia, Office of Publications, CH-1211 Geneva 27, Switzerland (Telephone Number in U.S. (518) 436-9686); *World Health Statistics Annual.*

BELARUS - POTATO PRODUCTION - See BELARUS - CROPS

BELARUS - POULTRY - See BELARUS - LIVESTOCK AND POULTRY

BELARUS - PRICES

International Labour Office, I.L.O. Publications, CH-1211, Geneva 22, Switzerland; *Yearbook of Labour Statistics.*

The World Bank, 1818 H Street, NW, Washington, D.C. 20433 (202) 477-1234; *Statistical Handbook: States of the Former USSR.*

BELARUS - PRODUCTION

The World Bank, 1818 H Street, NW, Washington, D.C. 20433 (202) 477-1234; *Statistical Handbook: States of the Former USSR.*

BELARUS - PUBLIC FINANCE

The World Bank, 1818 H Street, NW, Washington, D.C. 20433 (202) 477-1234; *Statistical Handbook: States of the Former USSR.*

BELARUS - RADIO RECEIVER PRODUCTION

Encyclopedia Britannica, Incorporated, 310 South Michigan Avenue, Chicago, Illinois 60604 (312) 347-7000; *Britannica World Data.*

Statistical Office of the United Nations, Publishing Service, New York, New York 10017 (800) 253-9646; *Statistical Yearbook.*

BELARUS - RAILWAYS

Business International Moscow, 23 Profseyuznaya Ulitsa 117859, Moscow (Telephone Number in U.S. (800) 938-4685); *The CIS Market Atlas.*

Encyclopedia Britannica, Incorporated, 310 South Michigan Avenue, Chicago, Illinois 60604 (312) 347-7000; *Britannica World Data.*

Statistical Office of the United Nations, Publishing Service, New York, New York 10017 (800) 253-9646; *Annual Bulletin of Transport Statistics for Europe,* and *Statistical Yearbook.*

BELARUS - RETAIL TRADE

Business International Moscow, 23 Profseyuznaya Ulitsa 117859, Moscow (Telephone Number in U.S. (800) 938-4685); *The CIS Market Atlas.*

Statistical Office of the United Nations, Publishing Service, New York, New York 10017 (800) 253-9646; *Statistical Yearbook.*

BELARUS - ROADS - See BELARUS - HIGHWAYS

BELARUS - ROUNDWOOD PRODUCTION AND CONSUMPTION - See BELARUS - FORESTRY AND FOREST PRODUCTS

BELARUS - RUBBER PRODUCTION

Statistical Office of the United Nations, Publishing Service, New York, New York 10017 (800) 253-9646; *Statistical Yearbook.*

BELARUS - SCIENTISTS AND TECHNOLOGISTS

Statistical Office of the United Nations, Publishing Service, New York, New York 10017 (800) 253-9646; *Statistical Yearbook.*

BELARUS - SHEEP - See BELARUS - LIVESTOCK AND POULTRY

BELARUS - STEEL - See BELARUS - MINING AND MINERAL PRODUCTS

BELARUS - SUGAR PRODUCTION - See BELARUS - CROPS

BELARUS - SULPHURIC ACID PRODUCTION - See BELARUS - MINING AND MINERAL PRODUCTS

BELARUS - TELEGRAPH SERVICE

Statistical Office of the United Nations, Publishing Service, New York, New York 10017 (800) 253-9646; *Statistical Yearbook.*

BELARUS - TELEPHONES IN USE

Encyclopedia Britannica, Incorporated, 310 South Michigan Avenue, Chicago, Illinois 60604 (312) 347-7000; *Britannica World Data.*

BELARUS - TELEVISION RECEIVER PRODUCTION

Encyclopedia Britannica, Incorporated, 310 South Michigan Avenue, Chicago, Illinois 60604 (312) 347-7000; *Britannica World Data.*

Statistical Office of the United Nations, Publishing Service, New York, New York 10017 (800) 253-9646; *Statistical Yearbook.*

BELARUS - TEXTILE INDUSTRY

Business International Moscow, 23 Profseyuznaya Ulitsa 117859, Moscow (Telephone Number in U.S. (800) 938-4685); *The CIS Market Atlas.*

Statistical Office of the United Nations, Publishing Service, New York, New York 10017 (800) 253-9646; *Statistical Yearbook.*

BELARUS - THEATRE

United Nations Educational, Scientific and Cultural Organization (UNESCO), 7 Place de Fontenoy, F-75700 Paris, France (Telephone Number in U.S. (212) 963-5981; *Statistical Yearbook.*

BELARUS - TOBACCO PRODUCTION

Statistical Office of the United Nations, Publishing Service, New York, New York 10017 (800) 253-9646; *Statistical Yearbook.*

BELARUS - TOURISM

Business International Moscow, 23 Profseyuznaya Ulitsa 117859, Moscow (Telephone Number in U.S. (800) 938-4685); *The CIS Market Atlas.*

BELARUS - TRANSPORTATION AND COMMUNICATIONS

Business International Moscow, 23 Profseyuznaya Ulitsa 117859, Moscow (Telephone Number in U.S. (800) 938-4685); *The CIS Market Atlas.*

Encyclopedia Britannica, Incorporated, 310 South Michigan Avenue, Chicago, Illinois 60604 (312) 347-7000; *Britannica World Data.*

BELARUS - UNEMPLOYMENT

International Labour Office, I.L.O. Publications, CH-1211, Geneva 22, Switzerland; *Yearbook of Labour Statistics.*

BELARUS - VITAL STATISTICS

Encyclopedia Britannica, Incorporated, 310 South Michigan Avenue, Chicago, Illinois 60604 (312) 347-7000; *Britannica World Data.*

Statistical Office of the United Nations, Publishing Service, New York, New York 10017 (800) 253-9646; *Statistical Yearbook.*

BELARUS - WAGES

Business International Moscow, 23 Profseyuznaya Ulitsa 117859, Moscow (Telephone Number in U.S. (800) 938-4685); *The CIS Market Atlas.*

International Labour Office, I.L.O. Publications, CH-1211, Geneva 22, Switzerland; *Yearbook of Labour Statistics.*

Statistical Office of the United Nations, Publishing Service, New York, New York 10017 (800) 253-9646; *Statistical Yearbook.*

The World Bank, 1818 H Street, NW, Washington, D.C. 20433 (202) 477-1234; *Statistical Handbook: States of the Former USSR.*

BELARUS - WATERWAYS IN USE

Statistical Office of the United Nations, Publishing Service, New York, New York 10017 (800) 253-9646; *Annual Bulletin of Transport Statistics for Europe.*

BELARUS - WHEAT PRODUCTION - See BELARUS - CROPS

BELARUS - WHOLESALE TRADE

Statistical Office of the United Nations, Publishing Service, New York, New York 10017 (800) 253-9646; *Statistical Yearbook.*

BELARUS - WINE PRODUCTION

Statistical Office of the United Nations, Publishing Service, New York, New York 10017 (800) 253-9646; *Statistical Yearbook.*

BELARUS - WOOL PRODUCTION AND CONSUMPTION - See BELARUS - TEXTILE INDUSTRY

BELARUS - YARN PRODUCTION

Statistical Office of the United Nations, Publishing Service, New York, New York 10017 (800) 253-9646; *Statistical Yearbook.*

Belgium - National Statistical Office

Institut National de Statistique, rue de Louvain 44, 1000 Brussels, Belgium.

Belgium - Primary Statistics Sources

Institut National de Statistique, National Institute of Statistics, rue de Louvain 44, 1000 Brussels, Belgium; *Bulletin de Statistique,* (Statistical Bulletin), *Annuaire Statistique de Belgique* (Statistical Yearbook of Belgium), and *Annuaire Statistique de Poche* (Statistical Pocketbook).

Belgium - Databases

Fonds Quetelet, Belgium Ministry of Economic Affairs, 6, rue de l'Industrie, B-1040 Brussels, Belgium. Subject coverage: Economics, social sciences, and statistics.

Institut National de Statistique, Belgium Ministry of Economic Affairs, 44, rue de Louvain, B-1000 Brussels, Belgium. Subject coverage: The National and Statistical Institute collects, processes, and publishes Belgian statistical information.

BELGIUM - ABORTIONS

European Community Information Service, 2100 M Street, NW, Washington, D.C. 20037 (202) 862-9500; *Demographic Statistics.*

BELGIUM - AGRICULTURAL CONSUMPTION

European Community Information Service, 2100 M Street, NW, Washington, D.C. 20037 (202) 862-9500; *Basic Statistics of the Community.*

BELGIUM - AGRICULTURE

European Community Information Service, 2100 M Street, NW, Washington, D.C. 20037 (202) 862-9500; *Agriculture: Statistical Yearbook, Basic Statistics of the Community, Eurostatistics: Data for Short-Term Economic Analysis, Labor Force Sample Survey,* and *Regions: Statistical Yearbook.*

Facts on File, 460 Park Avenue South, New York, New York 10016 (800) 443-8323; *The New Book of World Rankings.*

Federal Statistical Office, Gustav - Stresemann - Ring 11, D-6200 Wiesbaden, Germany; *Belgien.*

Food and Agricultural Organization of the United Nations (FAO), Via delle Terme di Caracalla, 00100 Rome, Italy (Telephone Number in U.S. (202) 653-2400); *Production Yearbook, The State of Food and Agriculture*, and *Trade Yearbook.*

G.K. Hall and Company, 70 Lincoln Street, Boston, Massachusetts 02111 (617) 423-3990; *The World in Figures.*

Organisation for Economic Co-operation and Development (OECD), 2 rue Andre-Pascal, 75 Paris 16, France (Telephone Number in U.S. (202) 785-6323); *Economic Accounts for Agriculture, Indicators of Industrial Activity, Industrial Structure Statistics*, and *OECD Economic Surveys: Belgium-Luxembourg.*

Statistical Office of the United Nations, Publishing Service, New York, New York 10017 (800) 253-9646; *Statistical Yearbook.*

Times Books, 201 East 50th Street, New York, New York 10022 (212) 751-2600; *The Economist Book of Vital World Statistics.*

The World Bank, 1818 H Street, NW, Washington, D.C. 20433 (202) 477-1234; *World Tables.*

BELGIUM - AIRLINE SERVICE

European Community Information Service, 2100 M Street, NW, Washington, D.C. 20037 (202) 862-9500; *Basic Statistics of the Community, Regions: Statistical Yearbook*, and *Transport Annual Statistics.*

Facts on File, 460 Park Avenue South, New York, New York 10016 (800) 443-8323; *The New Book of World Rankings.*

G.K. Hall and Company, 70 Lincoln Street, Boston, Massachusetts 02111 (617) 423-3990; *The World in Figures.*

International Civil Aviation Organization, 1000 Sherbrooke Street West, Suite 400, Montreal, Quebec, Canada H3A 2R2 (514) 285-8219; *Civil Aviation Statistics of the World.*

Organisation for Economic Co-operation and Development (OECD), 2 rue Andre-Pascal, 75 Paris 16, France (Telephone Number in U.S. (202) 785-6323); *Tourism Policy and International Tourism in OECD Member Countries.*

Statistical Office of the United Nations, Publishing Service, New York, New York 10017 (800) 253-9646; *Statistical Yearbook.*

Times Books, 201 East 50th Street, New York, New York 10022 (212) 751-2600; *The Economist Book of Vital World Statistics.*

BELGIUM - ALMOND PRODUCTION - See BELGIUM - CROPS

BELGIUM - ALUMINUM PRODUCTION AND CONSUMPTION - See BELGIUM - MINING AND MINERAL PRODUCTS

BELGIUM - ANIMAL FEEDINGSTUFFS

Organisation for Economic Co-operation and Development (OECD), 2 rue Andre-Pascal, 75 Paris 16, France (Telephone Number in U.S. (202) 785-6323); *Foreign Trade by Commodities.*

Statistical Office of the United Nations, Publishing Service, New York, New York 10017 (800) 253-9646; *Statistical Yearbook.*

BELGIUM - ANIMAL HEALTH

Food and Agricultural Organization of the United Nations (FAO), Via delle Terme di Caracalla, 00100 Rome, Italy (Telephone Number in U.S. (202) 653-2400); *Animal Health Yearbook.*

BELGIUM - ANTIMONY AND ANTIMONY ORE - See BELGIUM - MINING AND MINERAL PRODUCTS

BELGIUM - APPLE PRODUCTION - See BELGIUM - CROPS

BELGIUM - AREA AND DENSITY OF POPULATION

European Community Information Service, 2100 M Street, NW, Washington, D.C. 20037 (202) 862-9500; *Basic Statistics of the Community*, and *Demographic Statistics.*

Facts on File, 460 Park Avenue South, New York, New York 10016 (800) 443-8323; *The New Book of World Rankings.*

Federal Statistical Office, Gustav - Stresemann - Ring 11, D-6200 Wiesbaden, Germany; *Belgien.*

Food and Agricultural Organization of the United Nations (FAO) Via delle Terme di Caracalla, 00100 Rome, Italy (Telephone Number in U.S. (202) 653-2400); *The State of Food and Agriculture.*

G.K. Hall and Company, 70 Lincoln Street, Boston, Massachusetts 02111 (617) 423-3990; *The World in Figures.*

Statistical Office of the United Nations, Publishing Service, New York, New York 10017 (800) 253-9646; *Statistical Yearbook.*

Times Books, 201 East 50th Street, New York, New York 10022 (212) 751-2600; *The Economist Book of Vital World Statistics.*

BELGIUM - ARMS EXPORTS AND IMPORTS

U.S. Arms Control and Disarmament Agency, 320 Twenty-first Street, NW, Washington, D.C. 20451 (202) 647-8677; *World Military Expenditures and Arms Transfers.*

BELGIUM - ARSENIC PRODUCTION AND CONSUMPTION - See BELGIUM - MINING AND MINERAL PRODUCTS

BELGIUM - BALANCE OF PAYMENTS

The Economist Intelligence Unit, 111 West 57th Street, New York, New York 10019 (800) 938-4685; *The World Market Atlas.*

European Community Information Service, 2100 M Street, NW, Washington, D.C. 20037 (202) 862-9500; *ACP: Basic Statistics, Basic Statistics of the Community, Energy Statistics Yearbook*, and *Eurostatistics: Data for Short-Term Economic Analysis.*

Federal Statistical Office, Gustav - Stresemann - Ring 11, D-6200 Wiesbaden, Germany; *Belgien.*

G.K. Hall and Company, 70 Lincoln Street, Boston, Massachusetts 02111 (617) 423-3990; *The World in Figures.*

International Monetary Fund, 700 Nineteenth Street, NW, Washington, D.C. 20431 (202) 623-7000; *Balance of Payments Yearbook*, and *International Financial Statistics.*

Organisation for Economic Co-operation and Development (OECD), 2 rue Andre-Pascal, 75 Paris 16, France (Telephone Number in U.S. (202) 785-6323); *Economic Outlook, Geographical Distribution of Financial Flows to Developing Countries*, and *OECD Economic Surveys: Belgium - Luxembourg.*

Times Books, 201 East 50th Street, New York, New York 10022 (212) 751-2600; *The Economist Book of Vital World Statistics.*

The World Bank, 1818 H Street, NW, Washington, D.C. 20433 (202) 477-1234; *World Tables.*

BELGIUM - BANANA PRODUCTION - See BELGIUM - CROPS

BELGIUM - BANKING

European Community Information Service, 2100 M Street, NW, Washington, D.C. 20037 (202) 862-9500; *ACP: Basic Statistics.*

Facts on File, 460 Park Avenue South, New York, New York 10016 (800) 443-8323; *The New Book of World Rankings.*

G.K. Hall and Company, 70 Lincoln Street, Boston, Massachusetts 02111 (617) 423-3990; *The World in Figures.*

International Monetary Fund, 700 Nineteenth Street, NW, Washington, D.C. 20431 (202) 623-7000; *Government Finance Statistics Yearbook,* and *International Financial Statistics.*

Organisation for Economic Co-operation and Development (OECD), 2 rue Andre-Pascal, 75 Paris 16, France (Telephone Number in U.S. (202) 785-6323); *Economic Outlook, Financial Market Trends,* and *OECD Economic Surveys: Belgium - Luxembourg.*

Statistical Office of the United Nations, Publishing Service, New York, New York 10017 (800) 253-9646; *Statistical Yearbook.*

BELGIUM - BARLEY PRODUCTION - See BELGIUM - CROPS

BELGIUM - BAUXITE PRODUCTION AND CONSUMPTION - See BELGIUM - MINING AND MINERAL PRODUCTS

BELGIUM - BEER PRODUCTION

Facts on File, 460 Park Avenue South, New York, New York 10016 (800) 443-8323; *The New Book of World Rankings.*

Statistical Office of the United Nations, Publishing Service, New York, New York 10017 (800) 253-9646; *Statistical Yearbook.*

BELGIUM - BEVERAGES - PRODUCTION INDEX

Organisation for Economic Co-operation and Development (OECD), 2 rue Andre-Pascal, 75 Paris 16, France (Telephone Number in U.S. (202) 785-6323); *Indicators of Industrial Activity.*

BELGIUM - BIRTH RATE

European Community Information Service, 2100 M Street, NW, Washington, D.C. 20037 (202) 862-9500; *Basic Statistics of the Community,* and *Demographic Statistics,*

Facts on File, 460 Park Avenue South, New York, New York 10016 (800) 443-8323; *The New Book of World Rankings.*

Organisation for Economic Co-operation and Development (OECD), 2 rue Andre-Pascal, 75 Paris 16, France (Telephone Number in U.S. (202) 785-6323); *Labour Force Statistics.*

Statistical Office of the United Nations, Publishing Service, New York, New York 10017 (800) 253-9646; *Demographic Yearbook,* and *Statistical Yearbook.*

Times Books, 201 East 50th Street, New York, New York 10022 (212) 751-2600; *The Economist Book of Vital World Statistics.*

The World Bank, 1818 H Street, NW, Washington, D.C. 20433 (202) 477-1234; *World Tables.*

World Health Organization, Office of Publications, Avenue Appia, CH-1211 Geneva 27, Switzerland (Telephone Number in U.S. (518) 436-9686); *World Health Statistics Annual.*

BELGIUM - BISMUTH PRODUCTION AND CONSUMPTION - See BELGIUM - MINING AND MINERAL PRODUCTS

BELGIUM - BONDS

European Community Information Service, 2100 M Street, NW, Washington, D.C. 20037 (202) 862-9500; *Basic Statistics of the Community.*

G.K. Hall and Company, 70 Lincoln Street, Boston, Massachusetts 02111 (617) 423-3990; *The World in Figures.*

International Monetary Fund, 700 Nineteenth Street, NW, Washington, D.C. 20431 (202) 623-7000; *Government Finance Statistics Yearbook.*

Organisation for Economic Co-operation and Development (OECD), 2 rue Andre-Pascal, 75 Paris 16, France (Telephone Number in U.S. (202) 785-6323); *Financial Market Trends.*

Statistical Office of the United Nations, Publishing Service, New York, New York 10017 (800) 253-9646; *Statistical Yearbook.*

BELGIUM - BOOK PRODUCTION

Euromonitor Publications Limited, 87-88 Turnmill Street, London EC1M 5QU, England; *European Marketing Data and Statistics.*

G.K. Hall and Company, 70 Lincoln Street, Boston, Massachusetts 02111 (617) 423-3990; *The World in Figures.*

Organisation for Economic Co-operation and Development (OECD), 2 rue Andre-Pascal, 75 Paris 16, France (Telephone Number in U.S. (202) 785-6323); *Indicators of Industrial Activity.*

United Nations Educational, Scientific and Cultural Organization (UNESCO), 7 Place de Fontenoy, F-75700 Paris, France (Telephone Number in U.S. (212) 963-5981); *Statistical Yearbook.*

BELGIUM - BROADCASTING

Billboard Limited, P.O. Box 9027, 1006 AA Amsterdam, The Netherlands (Telephone Number in U.S. (212) 764-7300); *World Radio TV Handbook.*

European Community Information Service, 2100 M Street, NW, Washington, D.C. 20037 (202) 862-9500; *Basic Statistics of the Community.*

Facts on File, 460 Park Avenue South, New York, New York 10016 (800) 443-8323; *The New Book of World Rankings.*

G.K. Hall and Company, 70 Lincoln Street, Boston, Massachusetts 02111 (617) 423-3990; *The World in Figures.*

Times Books, 201 East 50th Street, New York, New York 10022 (212) 751-2600; *The Economist Book of Vital World Statistics.*

United Nations Educational, Scientific and Cultural Organization (UNESCO), 7 Place de Fontenoy, F-75700 Paris, France (Telephone Number in U.S. (212) 963-5981); *Statistical Yearbook.*

BELGIUM - BUILDING CONSTRUCTION - See BELGIUM - CONSTRUCTION INDUSTRY

BELGIUM - BUSINESS

European Community Information Service, 2100 M Street, NW, Washington, D.C. 20037 (202) 862-9500; *Basic Statistics of the Community.*

G.K. Hall and Company, 70 Lincoln Street, Boston, Massachusetts 02111 (617) 423-3990; *The World in Figures.*

BELGIUM - BUSINESS AND PROFESSIONAL LICENSES

International Monetary Fund, 700 Nineteenth Street, NW, Washington, D.C. 20431 (202) 623-7000; *Government Finance Statistics Yearbook.*

BELGIUM - BUTTER - See BELGIUM - DAIRY PRODUCTS

BELGIUM - CABBAGE PRODUCTION - See BELGIUM - CROPS

BELGIUM - CADMIUM PRODUCTION AND CONSUMPTION - See BELGIUM - MINING AND MINERAL PRODUCTS

BELGIUM - CALORIE SUPPLY

Food and Agricultural Organization of the United Nations (FAO) Via delle Terme di Caracalla, 00100 Rome, Italy (Telephone Number in U.S. (202) 653-2400); *The State of Food and Agriculture.*

BELGIUM - CAPITAL INVESTMENT

Organisation for Economic Co-operation and Development (OECD), 2 rue Andre-Pascal, 75 Paris 16, France (Telephone Number in U.S. (202) 785-6323); *Economic Outlook,* and *Financial Market Trends.*

BELGIUM - CAPITAL REVENUE

International Monetary Fund, 700 Nineteenth Street, NW, Washington, D.C. 20431 (202) 623-7000; *Government Finance Statistics Yearbook.*

Organisation for Economic Co-operation and Development (OECD), 2 rue Andre-Pascal, 75 Paris 16, France (Telephone Number in U.S. (202) 785-6323); *Economic Outlook,* and *Financial Market Trends.*

BELGIUM - CASHEW NUT PRODUCTION - See BELGIUM - CROPS

BELGIUM - CASTOR BEAN PRODUCTION - See BELGIUM - CROPS

BELGIUM - CATTLE - See BELGIUM - LIVESTOCK AND POULTRY

BELGIUM - CAULIFLOWER PRODUCTION - See BELGIUM - CROPS

BELGIUM - CAUSTIC SODA PRODUCTION

European Community Information Service, 2100 M Street, NW, Washington, D.C. 20037 (202) 862-9500; *Basic Statistics of the Community.*

Organisation for Economic Co-operation and Development (OECD), 2 rue Andre-Pascal, 75 Paris 16, France (Telephone Number in U.S. (202) 785-6323); *Indicators of Industrial Activity.*

Statistical Office of the United Nations, Publishing Service, New York, New York 10017 (800) 253-9646; *Statistical Yearbook.*

BELGIUM - CEMENT PRODUCTION - See BELGIUM - MINING AND MINERAL PRODUCTS

BELGIUM - CEREAL PRODUCTION - See BELGIUM - CROPS

BELGIUM - CHEESE - See BELGIUM - DAIRY PRODUCTS

BELGIUM - CHEMICAL INDUSTRY

European Community Information Service, 2100 M Street, NW, Washington, D.C. 20037 (202) 862-9500; *Industrial Production: Quarterly Statistics.*

BELGIUM - CHEMICAL (ORGANIC) PRODUCTION - See BELGIUM - MINING AND MINERAL PRODUCTS

BELGIUM - CHESTNUT PRODUCTION

European Community Information Service, 2100 M Street, NW, Washington, D.C. 20037 (202) 862-9500; *Basic Statistics of the Community.*

BELGIUM - CHICKENS - See BELGIUM - LIVESTOCK AND POULTRY

BELGIUM - CHROMIUM ORE PRODUCTION AND CONSUMPTION - See BELGIUM - MINING AND MINERAL PRODUCTS

BELGIUM - CHROMITE PRODUCTION AND CONSUMPTION - See BELGIUM - MINING AND MINERAL PRODUCTS

BELGIUM - CIGAR PRODUCTION - See BELGIUM - TOBACCO PRODUCTION

BELGIUM - CIGARETTE PRODUCTION - See BELGIUM - TOBACCO PRODUCTION

BELGIUM - CLASS STRUCTURE

European Community Information Service, 2100 M Street, NW, Washington, D.C. 20037 (202) 862-9500; *Basic Statistics of the Community,* and *Labor Force Sample Survey.*

G.K. Hall and Company, 70 Lincoln Street, Boston, Massachusetts 02111 (617) 423-3990; *The World in Figures.*

BELGIUM - CLIMATE

Facts on File, 460 Park Avenue South, New York, New York 10016 (800) 443-8323; *The New Book of World Rankings.*

G.K. Hall and Company, 70 Lincoln Street, Boston, Massachusetts 02111 (617) 423-3990; *The World in Figures.*

BELGIUM - CLOTHING - PRODUCTION INDEX

Organisation for Economic Co-operation and Development (OECD), 2 rue Andre-Pascal, 75 Paris 16, France (Telephone Number in U.S. (202) 785-6323); *Indicators of Industrial Activity.*

BELGIUM - CLOTHING - EXPORTS AND IMPORTS

European Community Information Service, 2100 M Street, NW, Washington, D.C. 20037 (202) 862-9500; *Basic Statistics of the Community.*

Organisation for Economic Co-operation and Development (OECD), 2 rue Andre-Pascal, 75 Paris 16, France (Telephone Number in U.S. (202) 785-6323); *Textile Industry in OECD Countries.*

Statistical Office of the United Nations, Publishing Service, New York, New York 10017 (800) 253-9646; *Trade in Manufactures of Developing Countries.*

BELGIUM - COAL PRODUCTION - See BELGIUM - MINING AND MINERAL PRODUCTS

BELGIUM - COBALT PRODUCTION AND CONSUMPTION - See BELGIUM - MINING AND MINERAL PRODUCTS

BELGIUM - COCOA (BEANS) PRODUCTION - See BELGIUM - CROPS

BELGIUM - COFFEE - See BELGIUM - CROPS

BELGIUM - COKE OVEN COKE PRODUCTION - See BELGIUM - MINING AND MINERAL PRODUCTS

BELGIUM - COKE OVEN ORE PRODUCTION AND CONSUMPTION - See BELGIUM - MINING AND MINERAL PRODUCTS

BELGIUM - COKE PRODUCTION AND CONSUMPTION - See BELGIUM - MINING AND MINERAL PRODUCTS

BELGIUM - COMMUNICATIONS

European Community Information Service, 2100 M Street, NW, Washington, D.C. 20037 (202) 862-9500; *Basic Statistics of the Community*, and *Transport Annual Statistics*.

Federal Statistical Office, Gustav - Stresemann - Ring 11, D-6200 Wiesbaden, Germany; *Belgien*.

G.K. Hall and Company, 70 Lincoln Street, Boston, Massachusetts 02111 (617) 423-3990; *The World in Figures*.

BELGIUM - CONSTRUCTION INDUSTRY

European Community Information Service, 2100 M Street, NW, Washington, D.C. 20037 (202) 862-9500; *Basic Statistics of the Community*, and *Labor Force Sample Survey*.

Facts on File, 460 Park Avenue South, New York, New York 10016 (800) 443-8323; *The New Book of World Rankings*.

Organisation for Economic Cooperation and Development (OECD), 2 rue Andre-Pascal, 75 Paris 16, France (Telephone Number in U.S. (202) 785-6323); *The Iron and Steel Industry*, and *OECD Economic Surveys: Belgium - Luxembourg*.

Statistical Office of the United Nations, Publishing Service, New York, New York 10017; *Construction Statistics Yearbook*, and *Statistical Yearbook*.

BELGIUM - CONSUMER PRICE INDEX

European Community Information Service, 2100 M Street, NW, Washington, D.C. 20037 (202) 862-9500; *Basic Statistics of the Community*.

Federal Statistical Office, Gustav - Stresemann - Ring 11, D-6200 Wiesbaden, Germany; *Belgien*.

G.K. Hall and Company, 70 Lincoln Street, Boston, Massachusetts 02111 (617) 423-3990; *The World in Figures*.

Organisation for Economic Co-operation and Development (OECD), 2 rue Andre-Pascal, 75 Paris 16, France (Telephone Number in U.S. (202) 785-6323); *Economic Outlook*.

Statistical Office of the United Nations, Publishing Service, New York, New York 10017 (800) 253-9646; *Statistical Yearbook*.

BELGIUM - CONSUMER PRICES

Euromonitor Publications Limited, 87-88 Turnmill Street, London EC1M 5QU, England; *European Marketing Data and Statistics*, and *Basic Statistics of the Community*.

European Community Information Service, 2100 M Street, NW, Washington, D.C. 20037 (202) 862-9500; *Eurostatistics: Data for Short-Term Economic Analysis*, and *Money and Finance*.

Federal Statistical Office, Gustav - Stresemann - Ring 11, D-6200 Wiesbaden, Germany; *Belgien*.

International Labour Office, I.L.O. Publications, CH-1211, Geneva 22, Switzerland; *Yearbook of Labour Statistics*, and *International Financial Statistics*.

Organisation for Economic Co-operation and Development (OECD), 2 rue Andre-Pascal, 75 Paris 16, France (Telephone Number in U.S. (202) 785-6323); *Economic Outlook*.

Times Books, 201 East 50th Street, New York, New York 10022 (212) 751-2600; *The Economist Book of Vital World Statistics*.

BELGIUM - CONSUMPTION

European Community Information Service, 2100 M Street, NW, Washington, D.C. 20037 (202) 862-9500; *Basic Statistics of the Community*.

G.K. Hall and Company, 70 Lincoln Street, Boston, Massachusetts 02111 (617) 423-3990; *The World in Figures*.

International Iron and Steel Institute, 120, rue Colonel Bourg, B-1140, Brussels, Belgium; *Steel Statistical Yearbook*.

Organisation for Economic Co-operation and Development (OECD), 2 rue Andre-Pascal, 75 Paris 16, France (Telephone Number in U.S. (202) 785-6323); *The Footwear, Raw Hides and Skins, and Leather Industry in OECD Countries*, *The Iron and Steel Industry*, *Meat Balances in OECD Member Countries*, *The Non-Ferrous Metals Industry*, *The Pulp and Paper Industry*, and *Textile Industry in OECD Countries*.

BELGIUM - COPPER AND COPPER ORE - See BELGIUM - MINING AND MINERAL PRODUCTS

BELGIUM - CORN PRODUCTION - See BELGIUM - CROPS

BELGIUM - CORPORATE TAXES - See BELGIUM - TAXATION

BELGIUM - COTTON - See BELGIUM - CROPS

BELGIUM - CRIME

International Criminal Police Organization (INTERPOL), 26 rue Armengaud, 92210 Saint Cloud, France; *International Crime Statistics*.

Yale University Press, Yale Station, New Haven, Connecticut 06520 (203) 432-0940; *Violence and Crime in Cross-National Perspective*.

BELGIUM - CROPS

Commodity Research Bureau, Incorporated, 75 Wall Street, New York, New York 10005 (212) 504-7754; *Commodity Year Book*.

Euromonitor Publications Limited, 87-88 Turnmill Street, London EC1M 5QU, England; *European Marketing Data and Statistics*.

European Community Information Service, 2100 M Street, NW, Washington, D.C. 20037 (202) 862-9500; *ACP: Basic Statistics,Agriculture: Statistical Yearbook, Basic Statistics of the Community, Crop Production: Quarterly Statistics, Economic Accounts for Agriculture, Eurostatistics: Data for Short-Term Economic Analysis,* and *Regions: Statistical Yearbook.*

Facts on File, 460 Park Avenue South, New York, New York 10016 (800) 443-8323; *The New Book of World Rankings.*

Food and Agricultural Organization of the United Nations (FAO), Via delle Terme di Caracalla, 00100 Rome, Italy (Telephone Number in U.S. (202) 653-2400); *Production Yearbook,* and *The Statistics of Food and Agriculture.*

G.K. Hall and Company, 70 Lincoln Street, Boston, Massachusetts 02111 (617) 423-3990; *The World in Figures.*

Organisation for Economic Co-operation and Development (OECD), 2 rue Andre-Pascal, 75 Paris 16, France (Telephone Number in U.S. (202) 785-6323); *Economic Accounts for Agriculture, Foreign Trade by Commodities,* and *Textile Industry in OECD Countries.*

Statistical Office of the United Nations, Publishing Service, New York, New York 10017 (800) 253-9646; *Statistical Yearbook.*

BELGIUM - CUSTOMS DUTIES

European Community Information Service, 2100 M Street, NW, Washington, D.C. 20037 (202) 862-9500; *Basic Statistics of the Community.*

G.K. Hall and Company, 70 Lincoln Street, Boston, Massachusetts 02111 (617) 423-3990; *The World in Figures.*

International Monetary Fund, 700 Nineteenth Street, NW, Washington, D.C. 20431 (202) 623-7000; *Government Finance Statistics Yearbook.*

Organisation for Economic Co-operation and Development (OECD), 2 rue Andre-Pascal, 75 Paris 16, France (Telephone Number in U.S. (202) 785-6323); *The Non-Ferrous Metals Industry.*

BELGIUM - DAIRY PRODUCTS

Commodity Research Bureau, Incorporated, 75 Wall Street, New York, New York 10005 (212) 504-7754; *Commodity Year Book.*

European Community Information Service, 2100 M Street, NW, Washington, D.C. 20037 (202) 862-9500; *Basic Statistics of the Community,* and *Eurostatistics: Data for Short-Term Economic Analysis.*

Facts on File, 460 Park Avenue South, New York, New York 10016 (800) 443-8323; *The New Book of World Rankings.*

Food and Agricultural Organization of the United Nations (FAO) Via delle Terme di Caracalla, 00100 Rome, Italy (Telephone Number in U.S. (202) 653-2400); *Production Yearbook,* and *The State of Food and Agriculture.*

Organisation for Economic Co-operation and Development (OECD), 2 rue Andre-Pascal, 75 Paris 16, France (Telephone Number in U.S. (202) 785-6323); *Economic Accounts for Agriculture,* and *Milk, Milk Products, and Egg Balances in OECD Member Countries.*

Statistical Office of the United Nations, Publishing Service, New York, New York 10017 (800) 253-9646; *Statistical Yearbook.*

BELGIUM - DEATH RATE

European Community Information Service, 2100 M Street, NW, Washington, D.C. 20037 (202) 862-9500; *Basic Statistics of the Community,* and *Demographic Statistics.*

G.K. Hall and Company, 70 Lincoln Street, Boston, Massachusetts 02111 (617) 423-3990; *The World in Figures.*

Statistical Office of the United Nations, Publishing Service, New York, New York 10017 (800) 253-9646; *Statistical Yearbook.*

Times Books, 201 East 50th Street, New York, New York 10022 (212) 751-2600; *The Economist Book of Vital World Statistics.*

World Health Organization, Office of Publications, Avenue Appia, CH-1211 Geneva 27, Switzerland (Telephone Number in U.S. (518) 436-9686; *World Health Statistics Annual.*

BELGIUM - DEFENSE EXPENDITURES

European Community Information Service, 2100 M Street, NW, Washington, D.C. 20037 (202) 862-9500; *Government Financing of Research and Development.*

G.K. Hall and Company, 70 Lincoln Street, Boston, Massachusetts 02111 (617) 423-3990; *The World in Figures.*

International Monetary Fund, 700 Nineteenth Street, NW, Washington, D.C. 20431 (202) 623-7000; *Government Finance Statistics Yearbook.*

U.S. Arms Control and Disarmament Agency, 320 Twenty-first Street, NW, Washington, D.C. 20451 (202) 647-8677; *World Military Expenditures and Arms Transfers.*

BELGIUM - DEMOGRAPHY

The Economist Intelligence Unit, 111 West 57th Street, New York, New York 10019 (800) 938-4685; *The World Market Atlas.*

European Community Information Service, 2100 M Street, NW, Washington, D.C. 20037 (202) 862-9500; *Basic Statistics of the Community, Demographic Statistics, Employment and Unemployment,* and *Regions: Statistical Yearbook.*

Facts on File, 460 Park Avenue South, New York, New York 10016 (800) 443-8323; *The New Book of World Rankings.*

Federal Statistical Office, Gustav - Stresemann - Ring 11, D-6200 Wiesbaden, Germany; *Belgien.*

G.K. Hall and Company, 70 Lincoln Street, Boston, Massachusetts 02111 (617) 423-3990; *The World in Figures.*

BELGIUM - DEVELOPMENT ASSISTANCE

European Community Information Service, 2100 M Street, NW, Washington, D.C. 20037 (202) 862-9500; *ACP: Basic Statistics, Basic Statistics of the Community,* and *Government Financing of Research and Development.*

G.K. Hall and Company, 70 Lincoln Street, Boston, Massachusetts 02111 (617) 423-3990; *The World in Figures.*

Organisation for Economic Co-operation and Development (OECD), 2 rue Andre-Pascal, 75 Paris 16, France (Telephone Number in U.S. (202) 785-6323); *Geographical Distribution of Financial Flows to Developing Countries.*

Statistical Office of the United Nations, Publishing Service, New York, New York 10017 (800) 253-9646; *Statistical Yearbook.*

BELGIUM - DIAMOND - See BELGIUM - MINING AND MINERAL PRODUCTS

BELGIUM - DISCOUNT RATES

Organisation for Economic Co-operation and Development (OECD), 2 rue Andre-Pascal, 75 Paris 16, France (Telephone Number in U.S. (202) 785-6323); *Financial Market Trends.*

Statistical Office of the United Nations, Publishing Service, New York, New York 10017 (800) 253-9646; *Statistical Yearbook.*

BELGIUM - DISEASES

G.K. Hall and Company, 70 Lincoln Street, Boston, Massachusetts 02111 (617) 423-3990; *The World in Figures.*

World Health Organization, Office of Publications, Avenue Appia, CH-1211 Geneva 27, Switzerland (Telephone Number in U.S. (518) 436-9686; *World Health Statistics Annual.*

BELGIUM - DIVORCE RATES

European Community Information Service, 2100 M Street, NW, Washington, D.C. 20037 (202) 862-9500; *Demographic Statistics.*

Facts on File, 460 Park Avenue South, New York, New York 10016 (800) 443-8323; *The New Book of World Rankings.*

Statistical Office of the United Nations, Publishing Service, New York, New York 10017 (800) 253-9646; *Demographic Yearbook,* and *Statistical Yearbook.*

BELGIUM - DOMESTIC PRODUCT

European Community Information Service, 2100 M Street, NW, Washington, D.C. 20037 (202) 862-9500; *Basic Statistics of the Community.*

G.K. Hall and Company, 70 Lincoln Street, Boston, Massachusetts 02111 (617) 423-3990; *The World in Figures.*

BELGIUM - DUCKS - See BELGIUM - LIVESTOCK AND POULTRY

BELGIUM - ECONOMY

Euromonitor Publications Limited, 87-88 Turnmill Street, London EC1M 5QU, England; *European Marketing Data and Statistics.*

European Community Information Service, 2100 M Street, NW, Washington, D.C. 20037 (202) 862-9500; *ACP: Basic Statistics, Basic Statistics of the Community, Energy Statistics Yearbook, Labor Force Sample Survey,* and *Money and Finance.*

Facts on File, 460 Park Avenue South, New York, New York 10016 (800) 443-8323; *The New Book of World Rankings.*

Federal Statistical Office, Gustav - Stresemann - Ring 11, D-6200 Wiesbaden, Germany; *Belgien.*

G.K. Hall and Company, 70 Lincoln Street, Boston, Massachusetts 02111 (617) 423-3990; *The World in Figures.*

Organisation for Economic Co-operation and Development (OECD), 2 rue Andre-Pascal, 75 Paris 16, France (Telephone Number in U.S. (202) 785-6323); *Economic Outlook, Geographical Distribution of Financial Flows to Developing Countries, OECD Economic Surveys: Belgium - Luxembourg,* and *OECD Employment Outlook.*

BELGIUM - EDUCATION

The Economist Intelligence Unit, 111 West 57th Street, New York, New York 10019 (800) 938-4685; *The World Market Atlas.*

Euromonitor Publications Limited, 87-88 Turnmill Street, London EC1M 5QU, England; *European Marketing Data and Statistics,* and *Basic Statistics of the Community.*

European Community Information Service, 2100 M Street, NW, Washington, D.C. 20037 (202) 862-9500; *Regions: Statistical Yearbook.*

Facts on File, 460 Park Avenue South, New York, New York 10016 (800) 443-8323; *The New Book of World Rankings.*

Federal Statistical Office, Gustav - Stresemann - Ring 11, D-6200 Wiesbaden, Germany; *Belgien.*

G.K. Hall and Company, 70 Lincoln Street, Boston, Massachusetts 02111 (617) 423-3990; *The World in Figures.*

International Monetary Fund, 700 Nineteenth Street, NW, Washington, D.C. 20431 (202) 623-7000; *Government Finance Statistics Yearbook.*

Organisation for Economic Co-operation and Development (OECD), 2 rue Andre-Pascal, 75 Paris 16, France (Telephone Number in U.S. (202) 785-6323); *Education in OECD Countries.*

Times Books, 201 East 50th Street, New York, New York 10022 (212) 751-2600; *The Economist Book of Vital World Statistics.*

United Nations Educational, Scientific and Cultural Organization (UNESCO), 7 Place de Fontenoy, F-75700 Paris, France (Telephone Number in U.S. (212) 963-5981); *Statistical Yearbook.*

The World Bank, 1818 H Street, NW, Washington, D.C. 20433 (202) 477-1234; *World Tables.*

BELGIUM - EGG PRODUCTION AND CONSUMPTION - See BELGIUM - DAIRY PRODUCTS

BELGIUM - ELECTRICITY

European Community Information Service, 2100 M Street, NW, Washington, D.C. 20037 (202) 862-9500; *Basic Statistics of the Community, Energy Monthly Statistics, Energy Statistics Yearbook, Eurostatistics: Data for Short-Term Economic Analysis,* and *Regions: Statistical Yearbook.*

Facts on File, 460 Park Avenue South, New York, New York 10016 (800) 443-8323; *The New Book of World Rankings.*

Organisation for Economic Co-operation and Development (OECD), 2 rue Andre-Pascal, 75 Paris 16, France (Telephone Number in U.S. (202) 785-6323); *Coal Information, Energy Statistics of OECD Countries, Indicators of Industrial Activity,* and *Industrial Structure Statistics.*

Statistical Office of the United Nations, Publishing Service, New York, New York 10017 (800) 253-9646; *Statistical Yearbook.*

Times Books, 201 East 50th Street, New York, New York 10022 (212) 751-2600; *The Economist Book of Vital World Statistics.*

BELGIUM - EMPLOYMENT

Euromonitor Publications Limited, 87-88 Turnmill Street, London EC1M 5QU, England; *European Marketing Data and Statistics.*

European Community Information Service, 2100 M Street, NW, Washington, D.C. 20037 (202) 862-9500; *Basic Statistics of the Community, Earnings in Agriculture, Employment and Unemployment, Eurostatistics: Data for Short-Term Economic Analysis, Iron and Steel: Statistical Yearbook,* and *Labor Force Sample Survey.*

Facts on File, 460 Park Avenue South, New York, New York 10016 (800) 443-8323; *The New Book of World Rankings.*

Federal Statistical Office, Gustav - Stresemann - Ring 11, D-6200 Wiesbaden, Germany; *Belgien.*

International Labour Office, I.L.O. Publications, CH-1211, Geneva 22, Switzerland; *Yearbook of Labour Statistics.*

Organisation for Economic Co-operation and Development (OECD), 2 rue Andre-Pascal, 75 Paris 16, France (Telephone Number in U.S. (202) 785-6323); *Coal Information, Economic Outlook, The Iron and Steel Industry, OECD Economic Surveys: Belgium - Luxembourg,* and *OECD Employment Outlook.*

Statistical Office of the United Nations, Publishing Service, New York, New York 10017 (800) 253-9646; *Statistical Yearbook.*

BELGIUM - ENERGY

Euromonitor Publications Limited, 87-88 Turnmill Street, London EC1M 5QU, England; *European Marketing Data and Statistics.*

European Community Information Service, 2100 M Street, NW, Washington, D.C. 20037 (202) 862-9500; *Basic Statistics of the Community, Energy Monthly Statistics, Energy Statistics Yearbook, Regions: Statistical Yearbook,* and *Transport Annual Statistics.*

Facts on File, 460 Park Avenue South, New York, New York 10016 (800) 443-8323; *The New Book of World Rankings.*

Food and Agricultural Organization of the United Nations (FAO) Via delle Terme di Caracalla, 00100 Rome, Italy (Telephone Number in U.S. (202) 653-2400); *The State of Food and Agriculture.*

G.K. Hall and Company, 70 Lincoln Street, Boston, Massachusetts 02111 (617) 423-3990; *The World in Figures.*

Organisation for Economic Co-operation and Development (OECD), 2 rue Andre-Pascal, 75 Paris 16, France (Telephone Number in U.S. (202) 785-6323); *Coal Information, Energy Statistics of OECD Countries, OECD Environmental Data,* and *Oil and Gas Information.*

Statistical Office of the United Nations, Publishing Service, New York, New York 10017 (800) 253-9646; *Energy Statistics Yearbook,* and *Statistical Yearbook.*

Times Books, 201 East 50th Street, New York, New York 10022 (212) 751-2600; *The Economist Book of Vital World Statistics.*

BELGIUM - ENGINEERING AND METAL PRODUCTS - EXPORTS AND IMPORTS

European Community Information Service, 2100 M Street, NW, Washington, D.C. 20037 (202) 862-9500; *Basic Statistics of the Community,* and *Industrial Production: Quarterly Statistics.*

Statistical Office of the United Nations, Publishing Service, New York, New York 10017 (800) 253-9646; *Trade in Manufactures of Developing Countries.*

BELGIUM - ENVIRONMENT

Organization for Economic Co-operation and Development (OECD), 2 rue Andre-Pascal, 75 Paris 16, France (Telephone Number in U.S. (202) 785-6323); *OECD Environmental Data.*

BELGIUM - EXCHANGE RATES

European Community Information Service, 2100 M Street, NW, Washington, D.C. 20037 (202) 862-9500; *Eurostatistics: Data for Short-Term Economic Analysis,* and *Money and Finance.*

International Civil Aviation Organization, 1000 Sherbrooke Street West, Suite 400, Montreal, Quebec, Canada H3A 2R2 (514) 285-8219; *Civil Aviation Statistics of the World,* and *International Financial Statistics.*

Organisation for Economic Co-operation and Development (OECD), 2 rue Andre-Pascal, 75 Paris 16, France (Telephone Number in U.S. (202) 785-6323); *Economic Outlook, Financial Market Trends, Revenue Statistics of OECD Member Countries,* and *Tourism Policy and International Tourism in OECD Member Countries.*

Statistical Office of the United Nations, Publishing Service, New York, New York 10017 (800) 253-9646; *Statistical Yearbook.*

BELGIUM - EXCISE TAXES - See BELGIUM - TAXATION

BELGIUM - EXPORTS

American Automobile Manufacturers Association, 1401 H Street, NW, Suite 900, Washington, D.C. 20005 (202) 326-5500; *World Motor Vehicle Data.*

The Economist Intelligence Unit, 111 West 57th Street, New York, New York 10019 (800) 938-4685; *The World Market Atlas.*

European Community Information Service, 2100 M Street, NW, Washington, D.C. 20037 (202) 862-9500; *Basic Statistics of the Community, Energy Monthly Statistics, Energy Statistics Yearbook, Eurostatistics: Data for Short-Term Economic Analysis, External Trade: Monthly Statistics, External Trade: Statistical Yearbook,* and *Fisheries: Yearly Statistics.*

Food and Agricultural Organization of the United Nations (FAO) Via delle Terme di Caracalla, 00100 Rome, Italy (Telephone Number in U.S. (202) 653-2400); *The State of Food and Agriculture.*

G.K. Hall and Company, 70 Lincoln Street, Boston, Massachusetts 02111 (617) 423-3990; *The World in Figures.*

International Iron and Steel Institute, B120, rue Colonel Bourg, B-1140, Brussels, Belgium; *Steel Statistical Yearbook.*

International Lead and Zinc Study Group, Metro House, 58 St. James's Street, London SW1A 1LD, England; *Lead and Zinc Statistics.*

International Monetary Fund, 700 Nineteenth Street, NW, Washington, D.C. 20431 (202) 623-7000; *Direction of Trade Statistics,* and *International Financial Statistics.*

International Rubber Study Group, York House, 8th Floor, Empire Way, Wembley, London HA9 0PA, England; *Rubber Statistical Bulletin.*

Organisation for Economic Co-operation and Development (OECD), 2 rue Andre-Pascal, 75 Paris 16, France (Telephone Number in U.S. (202) 785-6323); *Economic Outlook, The Footwear, Raw Hides and Skins, and Leather Industry in OECD Countries, Foreign Trade by Commodities, Geographical Distribution of Financial Flows to Developing Countries, The Iron and Steel Industry, Industrial Structure Statistics, Milk, Milk Products, and Egg Balances in OECD Member Countries, OECD Economic Surveys: Belgium - Luxembourg, The Pulp and Paper Industry,* and *Review of Fisheries in OECD Member Countries.*

Times Books, 201 East 50th Street, New York, New York 10022 (212) 751-2600; *The Economist Book of Vital World Statistics.*

The World Bank, 1818 H Street, NW, Washington, D.C. 20433 (202) 477-1234; *World Tables.*

BELGIUM - EXTERNAL FINANCING

Inter-American Development Bank, 1300 New York Avenue, NW, Washington, D.C. 20577 (202) 623-1753; *Economic and Social Progress in Latin America.*

Organisation for Economic Co-operation and Development (OECD), 2 rue Andre-Pascal, 75 Paris 16, France (Telephone Number in U.S. (202) 785-6323); *Economic Outlook,* and *Financial Market Trends.*

BELGIUM - EXTERNAL INDEBTEDNESS

Organisation for Economic Co-operation and Development (OECD), 2 rue Andre-Pascal, 75 Paris 16, France (Telephone Number in U.S. (202) 785-6323); *Financial Market Trends,* and *Geographical Distribution of Financial Flows to Developing Countries.*

The World Bank, 1818 H Street, NW, Washington, D.C. 20433 (202) 477-1234; *World Tables.*

BELGIUM - EXTERNAL TRADE

European Community Information Service, 2100 M Street, NW, Washington, D.C. 20037 (202) 862-9500; *ACP: Basic Statistics, Basic Statistics of the Community, Eurostatistics: Data for Short-Term Economic Analysis, External Trade: Monthly Statistics,* and *External Trade: Statistical Yearbook.*

Food and Agricultural Organization of the United Nations (FAO) Via delle Terme di Caracalla, 00100 Rome, Italy (Telephone Number in U.S. (202) 653-2400); *The State of Food and Agriculture,* and *Trade Yearbook.*

G.K. Hall and Company, 70 Lincoln Street, Boston, Massachusetts 02111 (617) 423-3990; *The World in Figures.*

Statistical Office of the United Nations, Publishing Service, New York, New York 10017 (800) 253-9646; *Statistical Yearbook.*

BELGIUM - FABRIC PRODUCTION - See BELGIUM - TEXTILE INDUSTRY

BELGIUM - FARM CROPS - See BELGIUM - CROPS

BELGIUM - FEMALE WORKING POPULATION - See BELGIUM - EMPLOYMENT

BELGIUM - FERTILITY RATES

European Community Information Service, 2100 M Street, NW, Washington, D.C. 20037 (202) 862-9500; *Demographic Statistics.*

Facts on File, 460 Park Avenue South, New York, New York 10016 (800) 443-8323; *The New Book of World Rankings.*

Times Books, 201 East 50th Street, New York, New York 10022 (212) 751-2600; *The Economist Book of Vital World Statistics.*

The World Bank, 1818 H Street, NW, Washington, D.C. 20433 (202) 477-1234; *World Tables.*

BELGIUM - FERTILIZER

European Community Information Service, 2100 M Street, NW, Washington, D.C. 20037 (202) 862-9500; *Basic Statistics of the Community.*

Food and Agricultural Organization of the United Nations (FAO), Via delle Terme di Caracalla, 00100 Rome, Italy (Telephone Number in U.S. (202) 653-2400); *Fertilizer Yearbook,* and *The State of Food and Agriculture.*

Organisation for Economic Co-operation and Development (OECD), 2 rue Andre-Pascal, 75 Paris 16, France (Telephone Number in U.S. (202) 785-6323); *Economic Accounts for Agriculture,* and *Foreign Trade by Commodities.*

Statistical Office of the United Nations, Publishing Service, New York, New York 10017 (800) 253-9646; *Statistical Yearbook.*

BELGIUM - FETAL MORTALITY

European Community Information Service, 2100 M Street, NW, Washington, D.C. 20037 (202) 862-9500; *Basic Statistics of the Community, Demographic Statistics.*

Statistical Office of the United Nations, Publishing Service, New York, New York 10017 (800) 253-9646; *Demographic Yearbook.*

World Health Organization, Office of Publications, Avenue Appia, CH-1211 Geneva 27, Switzerland (Telephone Number in U.S. (518) 436-9686; *World Health Statistics Annual.*

BELGIUM - FIBRE PRODUCTION - See BELGIUM - TEXTILE INDUSTRY

BELGIUM - FILAMENT PRODUCTION - See BELGIUM - TEXTILE INDUSTRY

BELGIUM - FILM - See BELGIUM - MOTION PICTURES

BELGIUM - FINANCE

European Community Information Service, 2100 M Street, NW, Washington, D.C. 20037 (202) 862-9500; *ACP: Basic Statistics, Basic Statistics of the Community, Eurostatistics: Data for Short-Term Economic Analysis,* and *Money and Finance.*

Facts on File, 460 Park Avenue South, New York, New York 10016 (800) 443-8323; *The New Book of World Rankings.*

Federal Statistical Office, Gustav - Stresemann - Ring 11, D-6200 Wiesbaden, Germany; *Belgien.*

G.K. Hall and Company, 70 Lincoln Street, Boston, Massachusetts 02111 (617) 423-3990; *The World in Figures.*

International Monetary Fund, 700 Nineteenth Street, NW, Washington, D.C. 20431 (202) 623-7000; *Government Finance Statistics Yearbook,* and *International Financial Statistics.*

Organisation for Economic Co-operation and Development (OECD), 2 rue Andre-Pascal, 75 Paris 16, France (Telephone Number in U.S. (202) 785-6323); *Economic Outlook, Financial Market Trends, Geographical Distribution of Financial Flows to Developing Countries,* and *OECD Financial Statistics.*

BELGIUM - FISHERIES

Euromonitor Publications Limited, 87-88 Turnmill Street, London EC1M 5QU, England; *European Marketing Data and Statistics.*

European Community Information Service, 2100 M Street, NW, Washington, D.C. 20037 (202) 862-9500; *Agriculture: Statistical Yearbook, Basic Statistics of the Community,* and *Fisheries: Yearly Statistics.*

Facts on File, 460 Park Avenue South, New York, New York 10016 (800) 443-8323; *The New Book of World Rankings.*

Federal Statistical Office, Gustav - Stresemann - Ring 11, D-6200 Wiesbaden, Germany; *Belgien.*

Food and Agricultural Organization of the United Nations (FAO) Via delle Terme di Caracalla, 00100 Rome, Italy (Telephone Number in U.S. (202) 653-2400); *The State of Food and Agriculture,* and *Yearbook of Fishery Statistics.*

Organisation for Economic Co-operation and Development (OECD), 2 rue Andre-Pascal, 75 Paris 16, France (Telephone Number in U.S. (202) 785-6323); *Foreign Trade by Commodities, Industrial Structure Statistics,* and *Review of Fisheries in OECD Member Countries.*

Statistical Office of the United Nations, Publishing Service, New York, New York 10017 (800) 253-9646; *Statistical Yearbook.*

BELGIUM - FLAX FIBRE PRODUCTION - See BELGIUM - TEXTILE INDUSTRY

BELGIUM - FLAX PRODUCTION - See BELGIUM - TEXTILE INDUSTRY

BELGIUM - FLOUR PRODUCTION

European Community Information Service, 2100 M Street, NW, Washington, D.C. 20037 (202) 862-9500; *Basic Statistics of the Community.*

Statistical Office of the United Nations, Publishing Service, New York, New York 10017 (800) 253-9646; *Statistical Yearbook.*

BELGIUM - FOOD

European Community Information Service, 2100 M Street, NW, Washington, D.C. 20037 (202) 862-9500; *Basic Statistics of the Community.*

Food and Agricultural Organization of the United Nations (FAO) Via delle Terme di Caracalla, 00100 Rome, Italy (Telephone Number in U.S. (202) 653-2400); *Production Yearbook,* and *The State of Food and Agriculture.*

G.K. Hall and Company, 70 Lincoln Street, Boston, Massachusetts 02111 (617) 423-3990; *The World in Figures.*

Organisation for Economic Co-operation and Development (OECD), 2 rue Andre-Pascal, 75 Paris 16, France (Telephone Number in U.S. (202) 785-6323); *Food Consumption Statistics, Foreign Trade by Commodities,* and *Trade by Commodities.*

BELGIUM - FOOTWEAR - PRODUCTION INDEX

Organisation for Economic Co-operation and Development (OECD), 2 rue Andre-Pascal, 75 Paris 16, France (Telephone Number in U.S. (202) 785-6323); *Indicators of Industrial Activity.*

BELGIUM - FOREIGN AID

G.K. Hall and Company, 70 Lincoln Street, Boston, Massachusetts 02111 (617) 423-3990; *The World in Figures.*

BELGIUM - FOREIGN DEBT

International Monetary Fund, 700 Nineteenth Street, NW, Washington, D.C. 20431 (202) 623-7000; *Government Finance Statistics Yearbook.*

Organisation for Economic Co-operation and Development (OECD), 2 rue Andre-Pascal, 75 Paris 16, France (Telephone Number in U.S. (202) 785-6323); *Economic Outlook.*

BELGIUM - FOREIGN FINANCE

Organisation for Economic Co-operation and Development (OECD), 2 rue Andre-Pascal, 75 Paris 16, France (Telephone Number in U.S. (202) 785-6323); *Economic Outlook, Financial Market Trends,* and *Main Economic Indicators - Historical Statistics.*

BELGIUM - FOREIGN INDEBTEDNESS

Organisation for Economic Co-operation and Development (OECD), 2 rue Andre-Pascal, 75 Paris 16, France (Telephone Number in U.S. (202) 785-6323); *Economic Outlook,* and *Financial Market Trends.*

BELGIUM - FOREIGN OFFICIAL RESERVES

European Community Information Service, 2100 M Street, NW, Washington, D.C. 20037 (202) 862-9500; *Money and Finance.*

BELGIUM - FOREIGN TRADE

Euromonitor Publications Limited, 87-88 Turnmill Street, London EC1M 5QU, England; *European Marketing Data and Statistics.*

European Community Information Service, 2100 M Street, NW, Washington, D.C. 20037 (202) 862-9500; *Basic Statistics of the Community,* and *Iron and Steel: Statistical Yearbook.*

Facts on File, 460 Park Avenue South, New York, New York 10016 (800) 443-8323; *The New Book of World Rankings.*

Federal Statistical Office, Gustav - Stresemann - Ring 11, D-6200 Wiesbaden, Germany; *Belgien.*

Food and Agricultural Organization of the United Nations (FAO) Via delle Terme di Caracalla, 00100 Rome, Italy (Telephone Number in U.S. (202) 606-7828); *The State of Food and Agriculture.*

G.K. Hall and Company, 70 Lincoln Street, Boston, Massachusetts 02111 (617) 423-3990; *The World in Figures.*

International Iron and Steel Institute, 120, rue Colonel Bourg, B-1140, Brussels, Belgium; *Steel Statistical Yearbook.*

Organisation for Economic Co-operation and Development (OECD), 2 rue Andre-Pascal, 75 Paris 16, France (Telephone Number in U.S. (202) 785-6323); *Economic Outlook, The Footwear, Raw Hides and Skins, and Leather Industry in OECD Countries, Foreign Trade by Commodities, Main Economic Indicators - Historical Statistics,*

Maritime Transport, Meat Balances in OECD Member Countries, OECD Economic Surveys: Belgium - Luxembourg, and *Trade by Commodities.*

Statistical Office of the United Nations, Publishing Service, New York, New York 10017 (800) 253-9646; *International Trade Statistics Yearbook, Statistical Yearbook,* and *Trade in Manufactures of Developing Countries.*

The World Bank, 1818 H Street, NW, Washington, D.C. 20433 (202) 477-1234; *World Tables.*

World Bureau of Metal Statistics, 27-A High Street, Ware Hert SG12 9BA, England; *World Metal Statistics.*

BELGIUM - FORESTRY AND FOREST PRODUCTS

Euromonitor Publications Limited, 87-88 Turnmill Street, London EC1M 5QU, England; *European Marketing Data and Statistics.*

European Community Information Service, 2100 M Street, NW, Washington, D.C. 20037 (202) 862-9500; *Agriculture: Statistical Yearbook, Basic Statistics of the Community, Industrial Production: Quarterly Statistics.*

Facts on File, 460 Park Avenue South, New York, New York 10016 (800) 443-8323; *The New Book of World Rankings.*

Federal Statistical Office, Gustav - Stresemann - Ring 11, D-6200 Wiesbaden, Germany; *Belgien.*

Food and Agricultural Organization of the United Nations (FAO) Via delle Terme di Caracalla, 00100 Rome, Italy (Telephone Number in U.S. (202) 653-2400); *The State of Food and Agriculture,* and *Yearbook of Forest Products.*

Forest and Paper Association, 1250 Connecticut Avenue, NW, Washington, D.C. 20036 (202) 463-2455; *Wood Pulp and Fiber Statistics.*

G.K. Hall and Company, 70 Lincoln Street, Boston, Massachusetts 02111 (617) 423-3990; *The World in Figures.*

Organisation for Economic Co-operation and Development (OECD), 2 rue Andre-Pascal, 75 Paris 16, France (Telephone Number in U.S. (202) 785-6323); *Indicators of Industrial Activity, Industrial Structure Statistics,* and *The Pulp and Paper Industry.*

United Nations Educational, Scientific and Cultural Organization (UNESCO), 7 Place de Fontenoy, F-75700 Paris, France (Telephone Number in U.S. (212) 963-5981); *Statistical Yearbook.*

BELGIUM - FRUIT PRODUCTION - See BELGIUM - CROPS

BELGIUM - FURNITURE AND WOOD PRODUCTS - EXPORTS AND IMPORTS

European Community Information Service, 2100 M Street, NW, Washington, D.C. 20037 (202) 862-9500; *Basic Statistics of the Community.*

Organisation for Economic Co-operation and Development (OECD), 2 rue Andre-Pascal, 75 Paris 16, France (Telephone Number in U.S. (202) 785-6323); *Foreign Trade by Commodities, Industrial Structure Statistics,* and *OECD Economic Surveys: Belgium - Luxembourg.*

Statistical Office of the United Nations, Publishing Service, New York, New York 10017 (800) 253-9646; *Trade in Manufactures of Developing Countries.*

BELGIUM - GARLIC PRODUCTION - See BELGIUM - CROPS

BELGIUM - GAS - See BELGIUM - MINING AND MINERAL PRODUCTS

BELGIUM - GENERAL INDUSTRIAL STATISTICS

European Community Information Service, 2100 M Street, NW, Washington, D.C. 20037 (202) 862-9500; *Basic Statistics of the Community.*

Federal Statistical Office, Gustav - Stresemann - Ring 11, D-6200 Wiesbaden, Germany; *Belgien.*

Statistical Office of the United Nations, Publishing Service, New York, New York 10017 (800) 253-9646; *Industrial Statistics Yearbook.*

BELGIUM - GENERAL MORTALITY

European Community Information Service, 2100 M Street, NW, Washington, D.C. 20037 (202) 862-9500; *Basic Statistics of the Community,* and *Demographic Statistics.*

Statistical Office of the United Nations, Publishing Service, New York, New York 10017 (800) 253-9646; *Demographic Yearbook.*

World Health Organization, Office of Publications, Avenue Appia, CH-1211 Geneva 27, Switzerland (Telephone Number in U.S. (518) 436-9686; *World Health Statistics Annual.*

BELGIUM - GEOGRAPHIC DATA

European Community Information Service, 2100 M Street, NW, Washington, D.C. 20037 (202) 862-9500; *Basic Statistics of the Community.*

Facts on File, 460 Park Avenue South, New York, New York 10016 (800) 443-8323; *The New Book of World Rankings.*

Federal Statistical Office, Gustav - Stresemann - Ring 11, D-6200 Wiesbaden, Germany; *Belgien.*

BELGIUM - GLASS AND GLASS PRODUCTS - PRODUCTION INDEX - See BELGIUM - MINING AND MINERAL PRODUCTS

BELGIUM - GOATS - See BELGIUM - LIVESTOCK AND POULTRY

BELGIUM - GOLD HOLDINGS

International Monetary Fund, 700 Nineteenth Street, NW, Washington, D.C. 20431 (202) 623-7000; *International Financial Statistics.*

Statistical Office of the United Nations, Publishing Service, New York, New York 10017 (800) 253-9646; *Statistical Yearbook.*

The World Bank, 1818 H Street, NW, Washington, D.C. 20433 (202) 477-1234; *World Tables.*

BELGIUM - GOLD PRODUCTION AND CONSUMPTION - See BELGIUM - MINING AND MINERAL PRODUCTS

BELGIUM - GOVERNMENT

European Community Information Service, 2100 M Street, NW, Washington, D.C. 20037 (202) 862-9500; *Basic Statistics of the Community.*

G.K. Hall and Company, 70 Lincoln Street, Boston, Massachusetts 02111 (617) 423-3990; *The World in Figures*.

BELGIUM - GOVERNMENT BONDS - See BELGIUM - BONDS

BELGIUM - GOVERNMENT CONSUMPTION

European Community Information Service, 2100 M Street, NW, Washington, D.C. 20037 (202) 862-9500; *Basic Statistics of the Community*.

BELGIUM - GOVERNMENT EXPENDITURES

European Community Information Service, 2100 M Street, NW, Washington, D.C. 20037 (202) 862-9500; *Basic Statistics of the Community*, and *Government Financing of Research and Development*.

International Monetary Fund, 700 Nineteenth Street, NW, Washington, D.C. 20431 (202) 623-7000; *Government Finance Statistics Yearbook*.

Organisation for Economic Co-operation and Development (OECD), 2 rue Andre-Pascal, 75 Paris 16, France (Telephone Number in U.S. (202) 785-6323); *Economic Outlook*.

Times Books, 201 East 50th Street, New York, New York 10022 (212) 751-2600; *The Economist Book of Vital World Statistics*.

The World Bank, 1818 H Street, NW, Washington, D.C. 20433 (202) 477-1234; *World Tables*.

BELGIUM - GOVERNMENT FINANCES

European Community Information Service, 2100 M Street, NW, Washington, D.C. 20037 (202) 862-9500; *Basic Statistics of the Community, Government Financing of Research and Development*, and *Money and Finances*.

International Monetary Fund, 700 Nineteenth Street, NW, Washington, D.C. 20431 (202) 623-7000; *International Financial Statistics*.

Organisation for Economic Co-operation and Development (OECD), 2 rue Andre-Pascal, 75 Paris 16, France (Telephone Number in U.S. (202) 785-6323); *Economic Outlook*.

Statistical Office of the United Nations, Publishing Service, New York, New York 10017 (800) 253-9646; *Statistical Yearbook*.

BELGIUM - GOVERNMENT REVENUES

European Community Information Service, 2100 M Street, NW, Washington, D.C. 20037 (202) 862-9500; *Basic Statistics of the Community*, and *Government Financing of Research and Development*.

International Monetary Fund, 700 Nineteenth Street, NW, Washington, D.C. 20431 (202) 623-7000; *Government Finance Statistics Yearbook*.

Organisation for Economic Co-operation and Development (OECD), 2 rue Andre-Pascal, 75 Paris 16, France (Telephone Number in U.S. (202) 785-6323); *Economic Outlook*, and *Revenue Statistics of OECD Member Countries*.

Times Books, 201 East 50th Street, New York, New York 10022 (212) 751-2600; *The Economist Book of Vital World Statistics*.

The World Bank, 1818 H Street, NW, Washington, D.C. 20433 (202) 477-1234; *World Tables*.

BELGIUM - GRAIN PRODUCTION - See BELGIUM - CROPS

BELGIUM - GRANTS

International Monetary Fund, 700 Nineteenth Street, NW, Washington, D.C. 20431 (202) 623-7000; *Government Finance Statistics Yearbook*.

Organisation for Economic Co-operation and Development (OECD), 2 rue Andre-Pascal, 75 Paris 16, France (Telephone Number in U.S. (202) 785-6323); *Geographical Distribution of Financial Flows to Developing Countries*.

BELGIUM - GREEN PEPPER AND CHILIE PRODUCTION - See BELGIUM - CROPS

BELGIUM - GROSS DOMESTIC PRODUCT

The Economist Intelligence Unit, 111 West 57th Street, New York, New York 10019 (800) 938-4685; *The World Market Atlas*.

European Community Information Service, 2100 M Street, NW, Washington, D.C. 20037 (202) 862-9500; *Basic Statistics of the Community, Eurostatistics: Data for Short-Term Economic Analysis, Government Financing of Research and Development, Iron and Steel: Statistical Yearbook*, and *Money and Finance*.

Facts on File, 460 Park Avenue South, New York, New York 10016 (800) 443-8323; *The New Book of World Rankings*.

G.K. Hall and Company, 70 Lincoln Street, Boston, Massachusetts 02111 (617) 423-3990; *The World in Figures*.

Organisation for Economic Co-operation and Development (OECD), 2 rue Andre-Pascal, 75 Paris 16, France (Telephone Number in U.S. (202) 785-6323); *Economic Outlook, Geographical Distribution of Financial Flows to Developing Countries*, and *Revenue Statistics of OECD Member Countries*.

Statistical Office of the United Nations, Publishing Service, New York, New York 10017 (800) 253-9646; *Statistical Yearbook*.

Times Books, 201 East 50th Street, New York, New York 10022 (212) 751-2600; *The Economist Book of Vital World Statistics*.

The World Bank, 1818 H Street, NW, Washington, D.C. 20433 (202) 477-1234; *World Tables*.

BELGIUM - GROSS INDUSTRIAL PRODUCT

European Community Information Service, 2100 M Street, NW, Washington, D.C. 20037 (202) 862-9500; *Government Financing of Research and Development*.

BELGIUM - GROSS NATIONAL PRODUCT

European Community Information Service, 2100 M Street, NW, Washington, D.C. 20037 (202) 862-9500; *ACP: Basic Statistics*, and *Basic Statistics of the Community*.

Organisation for Economic Co-operation and Development (OECD), 2 rue Andre-Pascal, 75 Paris 16, France (Telephone Number in U.S. (202) 785-6323); *Economic Outlook*, and *Geographical Distribution of Financial Flows to Developing Countries*.

U.S. Arms Control and Disarmament Agency, 320 Twenty-first Street, NW, Washington, D.C. 20451 (202) 647-8677; *World Military Expenditures and Arms Transfers.*

The World Bank, 1818 H Street, NW, Washington, D.C. 20433 (202) 477-1234; *World Tables.*

BELGIUM - GROUNDNUT PRODUCTION - See BELGIUM - CROPS

BELGIUM - HAY PRODUCTION - See BELGIUM - CROPS

BELGIUM - HAZELNUT PRODUCTION - See BELGIUM - CROPS

BELGIUM - HEALTH

European Community Information Service, 2100 M Street, NW, Washington, D.C. 20037 (202) 862-9500; *Basic Statistics of the Community,* and *Regions: Statistical Yearbook.*

Facts on File, 460 Park Avenue South, New York, New York 10016 (800) 443-8323; *The New Book of World Rankings.*

Federal Statistical Office, Gustav - Stresemann - Ring 11, D-6200 Wiesbaden, Germany; *Belgien.*

G.K. Hall and Company, 70 Lincoln Street, Boston, Massachusetts 02111 (617) 423-3990; *The World in Figures.*

Organisation for Economic Co-operation and Development (OECD), 2 rue Andre-Pascal, 75 Paris 16, France (Telephone Number in U.S. (202) 785-6323); *OECD Health Systems: Facts and Trends.*

Statistical Office of the United Nations, Publishing Service, New York, New York 10017; *Statistical Yearbook.*

Times Books, 201 East 50th Street, New York, New York 10022 (212) 751-2600; *The Economist Book of Vital World Statistics.*

World Health Organization, Office of Publications, Avenue Appia, CH-1211 Geneva 27, Switzerland (Telephone Number in U.S. (518) 436-9686; *World Health Statistics Annual.*

BELGIUM - HEALTH EXPENDITURES

International Monetary Fund, 700 Nineteenth Street, NW, Washington, D.C. 20431 (202) 623-7000; *Government Finance Statistics Yearbook.*

BELGIUM - HEMP FIBRE PRODUCTION - See BELGIUM - TEXTILE INDUSTRY

BELGIUM - HIDE PRODUCTION

Food and Agricultural Organization of the United Nations (FAO), Via delle Terme di Caracalla, 00100 Rome, Italy (Telephone Number in U.S. (202) 653-2400); *Production Yearbook.*

Organisation for Economic Co-operation and Development (OECD), 2 rue Andre-Pascal, 75 Paris 16, France (Telephone Number in U.S. (202) 785-6323); *The Footwear, Raw Hides and Skins, and Leather Industry in OECD Countries, Foreign Trade by Commodities,* and *Indicators of Industrial Activity.*

BELGIUM - HIGHWAYS

European Community Information Service, 2100 M Street, NW, Washington, D.C. 20037 (202) 862-9500; *Basic Statistics of the Community,* and *Transport Annual Statistics.*

G.K. Hall and Company, 70 Lincoln Street, Boston, Massachusetts 02111 (617) 423-3990; *The World in Figures.*

International Road Federation, 525 School Street, SW, Washington, D.C. 20024 (202) 554-2106; *World Road Statistics.*

Statistical Office of the United Nations, Publishing Service, New York, New York 10017 (800) 253-9646; *Annual Bulletin of Transport Statistics for Europe.*

BELGIUM - HOME FINANCE

Organisation for Economic Co-operation and Development (OECD), 2 rue Andre-Pascal, 75 Paris 16, France (Telephone Number in U.S. (202) 785-6323); *Main Economic Indicators - Historical Statistics.*

BELGIUM - HOPS PRODUCTION - See BELGIUM - CROPS

BELGIUM - HORSES - See BELGIUM - LIVESTOCK AND POULTRY

BELGIUM - HOURS OF WORK - See BELGIUM - EMPLOYMENT

BELGIUM - HOUSING AND HOUSING UNITS

European Community Information Service, 2100 M Street, NW, Washington, D.C. 20037 (202) 862-9500; *Basic Statistics of the Community, Labor Force Sample Survey,* and *Regions: Statistical Yearbook.*

Facts on File, 460 Park Avenue South, New York, New York 10016 (800) 443-8323; *The New Book of World Rankings.*

BELGIUM - HOUSING CONSTRUCTION - See BELGIUM - CONSTRUCTION INDUSTRY

BELGIUM - HOUSING EXPENDITURES

European Community Information Service, 2100 M Street, NW, Washington, D.C. 20037 (202) 862-9500; *Basic Statistics of the Community.*

International Monetary Fund, 700 Nineteenth Street, NW, Washington, D.C. 20431 (202) 623-7000; *Government Finance Statistics Yearbook.*

BELGIUM - HYDROCHLORIC ACID PRODUCTION

European Community Information Service, 2100 M Street, NW, Washington, D.C. 20037 (202) 862-9500; *Basic Statistics of the Community.*

BELGIUM - ILLITERATE POPULATION

The Economist Intelligence Unit, 111 West 57th Street, New York, New York 10019 (800) 938-4685; *The World Market Atlas.*

G.K. Hall and Company, 70 Lincoln Street, Boston, Massachusetts 02111 (617) 423-3990; *The World in Figures.*

United Nations Educational, Scientific and Cultural Organization (UNESCO), 7 Place de Fontenoy, F-75700 Paris, France (Telephone Number in U.S. (212) 963-5981); *Statistical Yearbook.*

BELGIUM - IMPORTS

American Automobile Manufacturers Association, 1401 H Street, NW, Suite 900, Washington, D.C. 20005 (202) 326-5500; *World Motor Vehicle Data.*

The Economist Intelligence Unit, 111 West 57th Street, New York, New York 10019 (800) 938-4685; *The World Market Atlas.*

European Community Information Service, 2100 M Street, NW, Washington, D.C. 20037 (202) 862-9500; *Basic Statistics of the Community, Energy Statistics Yearbook, Eurostatistics: Data for Short-Term Economic Analysis, External Trade: Monthly Statistics, External Trade: Statistical Yearbook,* and *Fisheries: Yearly Statistics.*

Food and Agricultural Organization of the United Nations (FAO) Via delle Terme di Caracalla, 00100 Rome, Italy (Telephone Number in U.S. (202) 653-2400); *The State of Food and Agriculture.*

G.K. Hall and Company, 70 Lincoln Street, Boston, Massachusetts 02111 (617) 423-3990; *The World in Figures.*

International Iron and Steel Institute, 120, rue Colonel Bourg, B-1140, Brussels, Belgium; *Steel Statistical Yearbook.*

International Lead and Zinc Study Group, Metro House, 58 St. James's Street, London SW1A 1LD, England; *Lead and Zinc Statistics.*

International Monetary Fund, 700 Nineteenth Street, NW, Washington, D.C. 20431 (202) 623-7000; *Direction of Trade Statistics,* and *Government Finance Statistics Yearbook.*

International Rubber Study Group, York House, 8th Floor, Empire Way, Wembley, London HA9 0PA, England; *Rubber Statistical Bulletin.*

Organisation for Economic Co-operation and Development (OECD), 2 rue Andre-Pascal, 75 Paris 16, France (Telephone Number in U.S. (202) 785-6323); *Economic Outlook, The Footwear, Raw Hides and Skins, and Leather Industry in OECD Countries, The Iron and Steel Industry, Industrial Structure Statistics, Milk, Milk Products, and Egg Balances in OECD Member Countries, The Pulp and Paper Industry,* and *Review of Fisheries in OECD Member Countries.*

Times Books, 201 East 50th Street, New York, New York 10022 (212) 751-2600; *The Economist Book of Vital World Statistics.*

The World Bank, 1818 H Street, NW, Washington, D.C. 20433 (202) 477-1234; *World Tables.*

BELGIUM - INCOME TAXES - See BELGIUM - TAXATION

BELGIUM - INDUSTRIAL METALS PRODUCTION - See BELGIUM - MINING AND MINERAL PRODUCTS

BELGIUM - INDUSTRY

European Community Information Service, 2100 M Street, NW, Washington, D.C. 20037 (202) 862-9500; *Basic Statistics of the Community, Employment and Unemployment, Eurostatistics: Data for Short-Term Economic Analysis,* and *Labor Force Sample Survey.*

Facts on File, 460 Park Avenue South, New York, New York 10016 (800) 443-8323; *The New Book of World Rankings.*

Federal Statistical Office, Gustav - Stresemann - Ring 11, D-6200 Wiesbaden, Germany; *Belgien.*

G.K. Hall and Company, 70 Lincoln Street, Boston, Massachusetts 02111 (617) 423-3990; *The World in Figures.*

International Labour Office, I.L.O. Publications, CH-1211, Geneva 22, Switzerland; *Yearbook of Labour Statistics.*

Organisation for Economic Co-operation and Development (OECD), 2 rue Andre-Pascal, 75 Paris 16, France (Telephone Number in U.S. (202) 785-6323); *Economic Outlook, Indicators of Industrial Activity, Industrial Structure Statistics, Main Economic Indicators - Historical Statistics,* and *OECD Environmental Data.*

Statistical Office of the United Nations, Publishing Service, New York, New York 10017 (800) 253-9646; *Statistical Yearbook.*

Times Books, 201 East 50th Street, New York, New York 10022 (212) 751-2600; *The Economist Book of Vital World Statistics.*

The World Bank, 1818 H Street, NW, Washington, D.C. 20433 (202) 477-1234; *World Tables.*

BELGIUM - INFANT AND MATERNAL MORTALITY

European Community Information Service, 2100 M Street, NW, Washington, D.C. 20037 (202) 862-9500; *Basic Statistics of the Community, Demographic Statistics.*

Statistical Office of the United Nations, Publishing Service, New York, New York 10017 (800) 253-9646; *Demographic Yearbook,* and *Statistical Yearbook.*

Times Books, 201 East 50th Street, New York, New York 10022 (212) 751-2600; *The Economist Book of Vital World Statistics.*

The World Bank, 1818 H Street, NW, Washington, D.C. 20433 (202) 477-1234; *World Tables.*

World Health Organization, Office of Publications, Avenue Appia, CH-1211 Geneva 27, Switzerland (Telephone Number in U.S. (518) 436-9686; *World Health Statistics Annual.*

BELGIUM - INTEREST RATES

European Community Information Service, 2100 M Street, NW, Washington, D.C. 20037 (202) 862-9500; *Money and Finance.*

Organisation for Economic Co-operation and Development (OECD), 2 rue Andre-Pascal, 75 Paris 16, France (Telephone Number in U.S. (202) 785-6323); *Economic Outlook, Financial Market Trends, Main Economic Indicators - Historical Statistics,* and *OECD Financial Statistics.*

BELGIUM - INTERNAL TRADE

European Community Information Service, 2100 M Street, NW, Washington, D.C. 20037 (202) 862-9500; *Basic Statistics of the Community.*

Organisation for Economic Co-operation and Development (OECD), 2 rue Andre-Pascal, 75 Paris 16, France (Telephone Number in U.S. (202) 785-6323); *Main Economic Indicators - Historical Statistics.*

BELGIUM - INTERNATIONAL FINANCE

European Community Information Service, 2100 M Street, NW, Washington, D.C. 20037 (202) 862-9500; *Basic Statistics of the Community.*

Organisation for Economic Co-operation and Development (OECD), 2 rue Andre-Pascal, 75 Paris 16, France (Telephone Number in U.S. (202) 785-6323); *Economic Outlook,* and *Financial Market Trends.*

BELGIUM - INTERNATIONAL LIQUIDITY

International Monetary Fund, 700 Nineteenth Street, NW, Washington, D.C. 20431 (202) 623-7000; *International Financial Statistics.*

Organisation for Economic Co-operation and Development (OECD), 2 rue Andre-Pascal, 75 Paris 16, France (Telephone Number in U.S. (202) 785-6323); *Economic Outlook,* and *Financial Market Trends.*

BELGIUM - INTERNATIONAL RESERVES EXCLUDING GOLD

The World Bank, 1818 H Street, NW, Washington, D.C. 20433 (202) 477-1234; *World Tables.*

BELGIUM - INTERNATIONAL STATISTICS

Organisation for Economic Co-operation and Development (OECD), 2 rue Andre-Pascal, 75 Paris 16, France (Telephone Number in U.S. (202) 785-6323); *Financial Market Trends,* and *Tourism Policy and International Tourism in OECD Member Countries.*

BELGIUM - INVESTMENT

International Monetary Fund, 700 Nineteenth Street, NW, Washington, D.C. 20431 (202) 623-7000; *International Financial Statistics.*

Organisation for Economic Co-operation and Development (OECD), 2 rue Andre-Pascal, 75 Paris 16, France (Telephone Number in U.S. (202) 785-6323); *Economic Outlook, Financial Market Trends, The Iron and Steel Industry, Industrial Structure Statistics,* and *Textile Industry in OECD Countries.*

BELGIUM - IRON ORE - See BELGIUM - MINING AND MINERAL PRODUCTS

BELGIUM - JUTE PRODUCTION - See BELGIUM - CROPS

BELGIUM - LABOR FORCE

European Community Information Service, 2100 M Street, NW, Washington, D.C. 20037 (202) 862-9500; *Basic Statistics of the Community, Labor Force Sample Survey,* and *Regions: Statistical Yearbook.*

Facts on File, 460 Park Avenue South, New York, New York 10016 (800) 443-8323; *The New Book of World Rankings.*

Food and Agricultural Organization of the United Nations (FAO) Via delle Terme di Caracalla, 00100 Rome, Italy (Telephone Number in U.S. (202) 653-2400); *The State of Food and Agriculture.*

G.K. Hall and Company, 70 Lincoln Street, Boston, Massachusetts 02111 (617) 423-3990; *The World in Figures.*

Organisation for Economic Co-operation and Development (OECD), 2 rue Andre-Pascal, 75 Paris 16, France (Telephone Number in U.S. (202) 785-6323); *Economic Outlook, The Iron and Steel Industry, Main Economic Indicators - Historical Statistics, Maritime Transport, OECD Economic Surveys: Belgium - Luxembourg,* and *OECD Employment Outlook.*

Times Books, 201 East 50th Street, New York, New York 10022 (212) 751-2600; *The Economist Book of Vital World Statistics.*

The World Bank, 1818 H Street, NW, Washington, D.C. 20433 (202) 477-1234; *World Tables.*

BELGIUM - LABOR PRODUCTIVITY

International Labour Office, I.L.O. Publications, CH-1211, Geneva 22, Switzerland; *Yearbook of Labour Statistics.*

Organisation for Economic Co-operation and Development (OECD), 2 rue Andre-Pascal, 75 Paris 16, France (Telephone Number in U.S. (202) 785-6323); *Economic Outlook,* and *OECD Employment Outlook.*

BELGIUM - LAND USE

Euromonitor Publications Limited, 87-88 Turnmill Street, London EC1M 5QU, England; *European Marketing Data and Statistics.*
European Community Information Service, 2100 M Street, NW, Washington, D.C. 20037 (202) 862-9500; *Basic Statistics of the Community.*

Food and Agricultural Organization of the United Nations (FAO), Via delle Terme di Caracalla, 00100 Rome, Italy (Telephone Number in U.S. (202) 606-7828); *Production Yearbook.*

G.K. Hall and Company, 70 Lincoln Street, Boston, Massachusetts 02111 (617) 423-3990; *The World in Figures.*

BELGIUM - LAND USE

European Community Information Service, 2100 M Street, NW, Washington, D.C. 20037 (202) 862-9500; *Agriculture: Statistical Yearbook, Crop Production: Quarterly Statistics,* and *Regions: Statistical Yearbook.*

BELGIUM - LEAD AND LEAD ORE - See BELGIUM - MINING AND MINERAL PRODUCTS

BELGIUM - LEATHER - PRODUCTION INDEX

Organisation for Economic Co-operation and Development (OECD), 2 rue Andre-Pascal, 75 Paris 16, France (Telephone Number in U.S. (202) 785-6323); *Indicators of Industrial Activity.*

BELGIUM - LEATHER AND FOOTWEAR - EXPORTS AND IMPORTS

European Community Information Service, 2100 M Street, NW, Washington, D.C. 20037 (202) 862-9500; *Basic Statistics of the Community.*

Organisation for Economic Co-operation and Development (OECD), 2 rue Andre-Pascal, 75 Paris 16, France (Telephone Number in U.S. (202) 785-6323); *The Footwear, Raw Hides and Skins, and Leather Industry in OECD Countries.*

BELGIUM - LIBRARIES

Euromonitor Publications Limited, 87-88 Turnmill Street, London EC1M 5QU, England; *European Marketing Data and Statistics.*

Facts on File, 460 Park Avenue South, New York, New York 10016 (800) 443-8323; *The New Book of World Rankings.*

United Nations Educational, Scientific and Cultural Organization (UNESCO), 7 Place de Fontenoy, F-75700 Paris, France (Telephone Number in U.S. (212) 963-5981); *Statistical Yearbook.*

BELGIUM - LIGNITE PRODUCTION - See BELGIUM - MINING AND MINERAL PRODUCTS

BELGIUM - LIVESTOCK AND POULTRY

Commodity Research Bureau, Inc., 75 Wall Street, New York, New York 10005 (212) 504-7754; *Commodity Yearbook.*

Euromonitor Publications Limited, 87-88 Turnmill Street, London EC1M 5QU, England; *European Marketing Data and Statistics.*

European Community Information Service, 2100 M Street, NW, Washington, D.C. 20037 (202) 862-9500; *Agriculture: Statistical Yearbook, Basic Statistics of the Community, Eurostatistics: Data for Short-Term Economic Analysis,* and *Regions: Statistical Yearbook.*

Facts on File, 460 Park Avenue South, New York, New York 10016 (800) 443-8323; *The New Book of World Rankings.*

Food and Agricultural Organization of the United Nations (FAO), Via delle Terme di Caracalla, 00100 Rome, Italy (Telephone Number in U.S. (202) 606-7828); *Production Yearbook,* and *The State of Food and Agriculture.*

G.K. Hall and Company, 70 Lincoln Street, Boston, Massachusetts 02111 (617) 423-3990; *The World in Figures.*

Organisation for Economic Co-operation and Development (OECD), 2 rue Andre-Pascal, 75 Paris 16, France (Telephone Number in U.S. (202) 785-6323); *Economic Accounts for Agriculture,* and *Meat Balances in OECD Member Countries.*

Statistical Office of the United Nations, Publishing Service, New York, New York 10017 (800) 253-9646; *Statistical Yearbook.*

BELGIUM - LIVING LEVELS

G.K. Hall and Company, 70 Lincoln Street, Boston, Massachusetts 02111 (617) 423-3990; *The World in Figures.*

Organisation for Economic Co-operation and Development (OECD), 2 rue Andre-Pascal, 75 Paris 16, France (Telephone Number in U.S. (202) 785-6323); *Economic Outlook.*

Times Books, 201 East 50th Street, New York, New York 10022 (212) 751-2600; *The Economist Book of Vital World Statistics.*

BELGIUM - MACHINERY - PRODUCTION INDEX

Organisation for Economic Co-operation and Development (OECD), 2 rue Andre-Pascal, 75 Paris 16, France (Telephone Number in U.S. (202) 785-6323); *Indicators of Industrial Activity.*

BELGIUM - MAGNESIUM PRODUCTION AND CONSUMPTION - See BELGIUM - MINING AND MINERAL PRODUCTS

BELGIUM - MAIL - NUMBER OF PIECES SENT OR RECEIVED

European Community Information Service, 2100 M Street, NW, Washington, D.C. 20037 (202) 862-9500; *Transport Annual Statistics.*

Statistical Office of the United Nations, Publishing Service, New York, New York 10017 (800) 253-9646; *Statistical Yearbook.*

BELGIUM - MAIN ECONOMIC INDICATORS - See BELGIUM - ECONOMY

BELGIUM - MANGANESE PRODUCTION AND CONSUMPTION - See BELGIUM - MINING AND MINERAL PRODUCTS

BELGIUM - MANUFACTURING

American Automobile Manufacturers Association, 1401 H Street, NW, Suite 900, Washington, D.C. 20005 (202) 326-5500; *World Motor Vehicle Data.*

European Community Information Service, 2100 M Street, NW, Washington, D.C. 20037 (202) 862-9500; *Basic Statistics of the Community, Eurostatistics: Data for Short-Term Economic Analysis,* and *Industrial Production: Quarterly Statistics.*

Facts on File, 460 Park Avenue South, New York, New York 10016 (800) 443-8323; *The New Book of World Rankings.*

G.K. Hall and Company, 70 Lincoln Street, Boston, Massachusetts 02111 (617) 423-3990; *The World in Figures.*

Organisation for Economic Co-operation and Development (OECD), 2 rue Andre-Pascal, 75 Paris 16, France (Telephone Number in U.S. (202) 785-6323); *Foreign Trade by Commodities,* and *Indicators of Industrial Activity, Industrial Structure Statistics,* and *OECD Economic Surveys: Belgium - Luxembourg.*

Statistical Office of the United Nations, Publishing Service, New York, New York 10017 (800) 253-9646; *Statistical Yearbook.*

Times Books, 201 East 50th Street, New York, New York 10022 (212) 751-2600; *The Economist Book of Vital World Statistics.*

The World Bank, 1818 H Street, NW, Washington, D.C. 20433 (202) 477-1234; *World Tables.*

BELGIUM - MARRIAGE RATES

European Community Information Service, 2100 M Street, NW, Washington, D.C. 20037 (202) 862-9500; *Basic Statistics of the Community.*

Facts on File, 460 Park Avenue South, New York, New York 10016 (800) 443-8323; *The New Book of World Rankings.*

Statistical Office of the United Nations, Publishing Service, New York, New York 10017 (800) 253-9646; *Demographic Yearbook,* and *Statistical Yearbook.*

BELGIUM - MEAT PRODUCTION - See BELGIUM - LIVESTOCK AND POULTRY

BELGIUM - MERCHANT SHIPPING

European Community Information Service, 2100 M Street, NW, Washington, D.C. 20037 (202) 862-9500; *Basic Statistics of the Community, Fisheries: Yearly Statistics, Regions: Statistical Yearbook,* and *Transport Annual Statistics.*

G.K. Hall and Company, 70 Lincoln Street, Boston, Massachusetts 02111 (617) 423-3990; *The World in Figures.*

Lloyd's Register of Shipping, 17 Battery Place, New York, New York 10004 (212) 425-8050; *Register of Ships.*

Organisation for Economic Co-operation and Development (OECD), 2 rue Andre-Pascal, 75 Paris 16, France (Telephone Number in U.S. (202) 785-6323); *Maritime Transport.*

Statistical Office of the United Nations, Publishing Service, New York, New York 10017 (800) 253-9646; *Annual Bulletin of Transport Statistics for Europe,* and *Statistical Yearbook.*

Times Books, 201 East 50th Street, New York, New York 10022 (212) 751-2600; *The Economist Book of Vital World Statistics.*

BELGIUM - MERCURY PRODUCTION AND CONSUMPTION - See BELGIUM - MINING AND MINERAL PRODUCTS

BELGIUM - METAL PRODUCTS - See BELGIUM - MINING AND MINERAL PRODUCTS

BELGIUM - MILITARY

G.K. Hall and Company, 70 Lincoln Street, Boston, Massachusetts 02111 (617) 423-3990; *The World in Figures.*

The International Institute for Strategic Studies, 23 Tavistock Street, London WC2E 7NQ, England; *The Military Balance.*

U.S. Arms Control and Disarmament Agency, 320 Twenty-first Street, NW, Washington, D.C. 20451 (202) 647-8677; *World Military Expenditures and Arms Transfers.*

BELGIUM - MILK PRODUCTION - See BELGIUM - DAIRY PRODUCTS

BELGIUM - MILLET PRODUCTION - See BELGIUM - CROPS

BELGIUM - MINING AND MINERAL PRODUCTS

Commodity Research Bureau, Incorporated, 75 Wall Street, New York, New York 10005 (212) 504-7754; *Commodity Year Book.*

European Community Information Service, 2100 M Street, NW, Washington, D.C. 20037 (202) 862-9500; *ACP: Basic Statistics, Basic Statistics of the Community, Energy: Monthly Statistics, Energy Statistics Yearbook, Eurostatistics: Data for Short-Term Economic Analysis, Industrial Production: Quarterly Statistics, Iron and Steel: Statistical Yearbook,* and *Regions: Statistical Yearbook.*

Facts on File, 460 Park Avenue South, New York, New York 10016 (800) 443-8323; *The New Book of World Rankings.*

G.K. Hall and Company, 70 Lincoln Street, Boston, Massachusetts 02111 (617) 423-3990; *The World in Figures.*

International Iron and Steel Institute, 120, rue Colonel Bourg, B-1140, Brussels, Belgium; *Steel Statistical Yearbook.*

International Lead and Zinc Study Group, Metro House, 58 St. James's Street, London SW1A 1LD, England; *Lead and Zinc Statistics.*

Organisation for Economic Co-operation and Development (OECD), 2 rue Andre-Pascal, 75 Paris 16, France (Telephone Number in U.S. (202) 785-6323); *Coal Information, Energy Statistics of OECD Countries, Foreign Trade by Commodities, Indicators of Industrial Activity, Industrial Structure Statistics, The Iron and Steel Industry, Main Economic Indicators - Historical Statistics, The Non-Ferrous Metals Industry,* and *OECD Economic Surveys: Belgium - Luxembourg.*

Statistical Office of the United Nations, Publishing Service, New York, New York 10017 (800) 253-9646; *Statistical Yearbook.*

Times Books, 201 East 50th Street, New York, New York 10022 (212) 751-2600; *The Economist Book of Vital World Statistics.*

World Bureau of Metal Statistics, 27-A High Street, Ware Herts SG12 9BA, England; *World Metal Statistics.*

BELGIUM - MOLYBDENUM AND MOLYBDENUM ORE - See BELGIUM - MINING AND MINERAL PRODUCTS

BELGIUM - MONEY AND CREDIT

Organisation for Economic Cooperation and Development (OECD), 2 rue Andre-Pascal, 75 Paris 16, France (Telephone Number in U.S. (202) 785-6323); *OECD Economic Surveys: Belgium - Luxembourg.*

BELGIUM - MONEY EXCHANGE RATES

European Community Information Service, 2100 M Street, NW, Washington, D.C. 20037 (202) 862-9500; *Basic Statistics of the Community.*

International Monetary Fund, 700 Nineteenth Street, NW, Washington, D.C. 20431 (202) 623-7000; *International Financial Statistics.*

Organisation for Economic Co-operation and Development (OECD), 2 rue Andre-Pascal, 75 Paris 16, France (Telephone Number in U.S. (202) 785-6323); *Economic Outlook, Financial Market Trends,* and *Tourism Policy and International Tourism in OECD Member Countries.*

Statistical Office of the United Nations, Publishing Service, New York, New York 10017 (800) 253-9646; *Statistical Yearbook.*

BELGIUM - MONEY MARKET RATES

European Community Information Service, 2100 M Street, NW, Washington, D.C. 20037 (202) 862-9500; *Basic Statistics of the Community.*

Organisation for Economic Co-operation and Development (OECD), 2 rue Andre-Pascal, 75 Paris 16, France (Telephone Number in U.S. (202) 785-6323); *Economic Outlook,* and *Financial Market Trends.*

Statistical Office of the United Nations, Publishing Service, New York, New York 10017 (800) 253-9646; *Statistical Yearbook.*

BELGIUM - MONEY RESERVES

European Community Information Service, 2100 M Street, NW, Washington, D.C. 20037 (202) 862-9500; *Basic Statistics of the Community.*

Organisation for Economic Co-operation and Development (OECD), 2 rue Andre-Pascal, 75 Paris 16, France (Telephone Number in U.S. (202) 785-6323); *Economic Outlook,* and *Financial Market Trends.*

BELGIUM - MONEY SUPPLY

European Community Information Service, 2100 M Street, NW, Washington, D.C. 20037 (202) 862-9500; *Basic Statistics of the Community, Eurostatistics: Data for Short-Term Economic Analysis,* and *Money Supply.*

Federal Statistical Office, Gustav - Stresemann - Ring 11, D-6200 Wiesbaden, Germany; *Belgien.*

G.K. Hall and Company, 70 Lincoln Street, Boston, Massachusetts 02111 (617) 423-3990; *The World in Figures.*

International Monetary Fund, 700 Nineteenth Street, NW, Washington, D.C. 20431 (202) 623-7000; *International Financial Statistics.*

Organisation for Economic Co-operation and Development (OECD), 2 rue Andre-Pascal, 75 Paris 16, France (Telephone Number in U.S. (202) 785-6323); *Economic Outlook.*

Statistical Office of the United Nations, Publishing Service, New York, New York 10017 (800) 253-9646; *Statistical Yearbook.*

The World Bank, 1818 H Street, NW, Washington, D.C. 20433 (202) 477-1234; *World Tables.*

BELGIUM - MOTION PICTURES

Statistical Office of the United Nations, Publishing Service, New York, New York 10017 (800) 253-9646; *Statistical Yearbook.*

United Nations Educational, Scientific and Cultural Organization (UNESCO), 7 Place de Fontenoy, F-75700 Paris, France (Telephone Number in U.S. (212) 963-5981); *Statistical Yearbook.*

BELGIUM - MOTOR VEHICLE PRODUCTION

American Automobile Manufacturers Association, 1401 H Street, NW, Suite 900, Washington, D.C. 20005 (202) 326-5500; *World Motor Vehicle Data.*

European Community Information Service, 2100 M Street, NW, Washington, D.C. 20037 (202) 862-9500; *Basic Statistics of the Community,* and *Eurostatistics: Data for Short-Term Economic Analysis.*

Organisation for Economic Co-operation and Development (OECD), 2 rue Andre-Pascal, 75 Paris 16, France (Telephone Number in U.S. (202) 785-6323); *Foreign Trade by Commodities,* and *Indicators of Industrial Activity.*

Statistical Office of the United Nations, Publishing Service, New York, New York 10017 (800) 253-9646; *Statistical Yearbook.*

BELGIUM - MOTOR VEHICLE TAXES - See BELGIUM - TAXATION

BELGIUM - MOTOR VEHICLES IN USE

American Automobile Manufacturers Association, 1401 H Street, NW, Suite 900, Washington, D.C. 20005 (202) 326-5500; *World Motor Vehicle Data.*

European Community Information Service, 2100 M Street, NW, Washington, D.C. 20037 (202) 862-9500; *Transport Annual Statistics.*

G.K. Hall and Company, 70 Lincoln Street, Boston, Massachusetts 02111 (617) 423-3990; *The World in Figures.*

International Road Federation, 525 School Street, SW, Washington, D.C. 20024 (202) 554-2106; *World Road Statistics.*

Statistical Office of the United Nations, Publishing Service, New York, New York 10017 (800) 253-9646; *Statistical Yearbook.*

Times Books, 201 East 50th Street, New York, New York 10022 (212) 751-2600; *The Economist Book of Vital World Statistics.*

BELGIUM - MULES - See BELGIUM - LIVESTOCK AND POULTRY

BELGIUM - MUSEUMS

Euromonitor Publications Limited, 87-88 Turnmill Street, London EC1M 5QU, England; *European Marketing Data and Statistics.*

Facts on File, 460 Park Avenue South, New York, New York 10016 (800) 443-8323; *The New Book of World Rankings.*

United Nations Educational, Scientific and Cultural Organization (UNESCO), 7 Place de Fontenoy, F-75700 Paris, France (Telephone Number in U.S. (212) 963-5981); *Statistical Yearbook.*

BELGIUM - NATALITY - See BELGIUM - BIRTH RATE

BELGIUM - NATIONAL ACCOUNTS

European Community Information Service, 2100 M Street, NW, Washington, D.C. 20037 (202) 862-9500; *Basic Statistics of the Community,* and *Eurostatistics: Data for Short-Term Economic Analysis.*

Federal Statistical Office, Gustav - Stresemann - Ring 11, D-6200 Wiesbaden, Germany; *Belgien.*

International Monetary Fund, 700 Nineteenth Street, NW, Washington, D.C. 20431 (202) 623-7000; *International Financial Statistics.*

Organisation for Economic Co-operation and Development (OECD), 2 rue Andre-Pascal, 75 Paris 16, France (Telephone Number in U.S. (202) 785-6323); *Economic Outlook.*

Statistical Office of the United Nations, Publishing Service, New York, New York 10017 (800) 253-9646; *National Accounts Statistics,* and *Statistical Yearbook.*

BELGIUM - NATIONAL INCOME

Facts on File, 460 Park Avenue South, New York, New York 10016 (800) 443-8323; *The New Book of World Rankings.*

G.K. Hall and Company, 70 Lincoln Street, Boston, Massachusetts 02111 (617) 423-3990; *The World in Figures.*

Organisation for Economic Co-operation and Development (OECD), 2 rue Andre-Pascal, 75 Paris 16, France (Telephone Number in U.S. (202) 785-6323); *Economic Outlook.*

Statistical Office of the United Nations, Publishing Service, New York, New York 10017 (800) 253-9646; *Statistical Yearbook.*

BELGIUM - NATIONAL PRODUCT

European Community Information Service, 2100 M Street, NW, Washington, D.C. 20037 (202) 862-9500; *Basic Statistics of the Community.*

Facts on File, 460 Park Avenue South, New York, New York 10016 (800) 443-8323; *The New Book of World Rankings.*

Organisation for Economic Co-operation and Development (OECD), 2 rue Andre-Pascal, 75 Paris 16, France (Telephone Number in U.S. (202) 785-6323); *Economic Outlook.*

Statistical Office of the United Nations, Publishing Service, New York, New York 10017 (800) 253-9646; *Statistical Yearbook.*

BELGIUM - NATURAL GAS PRODUCTION - See BELGIUM - MINING AND MINERAL PRODUCTS

BELGIUM - NATURAL RUBBER PRODUCTION

European Community Information Service, 2100 M Street, NW, Washington, D.C. 20037 (202) 862-9500; *Basic Statistics of the*

Community.

International Rubber Study Group, York House, 8th Floor, Empire Way, Wembley, London HA9 0PA, England; *Rubber Statistical Bulletin.*

BELGIUM - NET MATERIAL PRODUCT

Statistical Office of the United Nations, Publishing Service, New York, New York 10017 (800) 253-9646; *Statistical Yearbook.*

BELGIUM - NEWSPAPER PRODUCTION - See BELGIUM - FORESTRY AND FOREST PRODUCTS

BELGIUM - NEWSPRINT - See BELGIUM - FORESTRY AND FOREST PRODUCTS

BELGIUM - NICKEL AND NICKEL ORE - See BELGIUM - MINING AND MINERAL PRODUCTS

BELGIUM - NITRIC ACID - See BELGIUM - MINING AND MINERAL PRODUCTS

BELGIUM - OATS PRODUCTION - See BELGIUM - CROPS

BELGIUM - OCCUPATIONS - See BELGIUM - LABOR FORCE

BELGIUM - OIL PRODUCING CROPS

European Community Information Service, 2100 M Street, NW, Washington, D.C. 20037 (202) 862-9500; *Basic Statistics of the Community.*

Organisation for Economic Co-operation and Development (OECD), 2 rue Andre-Pascal, 75 Paris 16, France (Telephone Number in U.S. (202) 785-6323); *Foreign Trade by Commodities.*

BELGIUM - ONION PRODUCTION - See BELGIUM - CROPS

BELGIUM - PALM KERNEL PRODUCTION - See BELGIUM - CROPS

BELGIUM - PAPER - See BELGIUM - FORESTRY AND FOREST PRODUCTS

BELGIUM - PATENTS

Statistical Office of the United Nations, Publishing Service, New York, New York 10017 (800) 253-9646; *Statistical Yearbook.*

BELGIUM - PEANUT PRODUCTION - See BELGIUM - CROPS

BELGIUM - PEPPER PRODUCTION - See BELGIUM - CROPS

BELGIUM - PERIODICALS

United Nations Educational, Scientific and Cultural Organization (UNESCO), 7 Place de Fontenoy, F-75700 Paris, France (Telephone Number in U.S. (212) 963-5981); *Statistical Yearbook.*

BELGIUM - PESTICIDE USE

Food and Agricultural Organization of the United Nations (FAO) Via delle Terme di Caracalla, 00100 Rome, Italy (Telephone Number in U.S. (202) 606-7828); *The State of Food and Agriculture.*

BELGIUM - PETROLEUM INDUSTRY

Euromonitor Publications Limited, 87-88 Turnmill Street, London EC1M 5QU, England; *European Marketing Data and Statistics.*

European Community Information Service, 2100 M Street, NW, Washington, D.C. 20037 (202) 862-9500; *ACP: Basic Statistics, Basic Statistics of the Community, Basic Statistics of the Community,* and *Energy Statistics Yearbook.*

Facts on File, 460 Park Avenue South, New York, New York 10016 (800) 443-8323; *The New Book of World Rankings.*

Food and Agricultural Organization of the United Nations (FAO) Via delle Terme di Caracalla, 00100 Rome, Italy (Telephone Number in U.S. (202) 606-7828); *The State of Food and Agriculture.*

G.K. Hall and Company, 70 Lincoln Street, Boston, Massachusetts 02111 (617) 423-3990; *The World in Figures.*

Organisation for Economic Co-operation and Development (OECD), 2 rue Andre-Pascal, 75 Paris 16, France (Telephone Number in U.S. (202) 785-6323); *Energy Statistics of OECD Countries, Foreign Trade by Commodities, Indicators of Industrial Activity,* and *Oil and Gas Information.*

Statistical Office of the United Nations, Publishing Service, New York, New York 10017 (800) 253-9646; *Statistical Yearbook.*

BELGIUM - PHOSPHATE ROCK PRODUCTION - See BELGIUM - MINING AND MINERAL PRODUCTS

BELGIUM - PHOSPHATES PRODUCTION - See BELGIUM - MINING AND MINERAL PRODUCTS

BELGIUM - PIG-IRON AND FERRO-ALLOYS - See BELGIUM - MINING AND MINERAL PRODUCTS

BELGIUM - PIGS - See BELGIUM - LIVESTOCK AND POULTRY

BELGIUM - PIPELINES FOR OIL AND PETROLEUM PRODUCTS

European Community Information Service, 2100 M Street, NW, Washington, D.C. 20037 (202) 862-9500; *Transport Annual Statistics.*

Statistical Office of the United Nations, Publishing Service, New York, New York 10017 (800) 253-9646; *Annual Bulletin of Transport Statistics of Europe.*

BELGIUM - PLASTIC AND RESIN PRODUCTION

Commodity Research Bureau, Incorporated, 75 Wall Street, New York, New York 10005 (212) 504-7754; *Commodity Year Book.*

European Community Information Service, 2100 M Street, NW, Washington, D.C. 20037 (202) 862-9500; *Basic Statistics of the Community.*

Organisation for Economic Co-operation and Development (OECD), 2 rue Andre-Pascal, 75 Paris 16, France (Telephone Number in U.S. (202) 785-6323); *Foreign Trade by Commodities.*

Statistical Office of the United Nations, Publishing Service, New York, New York 10017 (800) 253-9646; *Statistical Yearbook.*

BELGIUM - PLATINUM PRODUCTION - See BELGIUM - MINING AND MINERAL PRODUCTS

BELGIUM - POPULATION

The Economist Intelligence Unit, 111 West 57th Street, New York, New York 10019 (800) 938-4685; *The World Market Atlas.*

Euromonitor Publications Limited, 87-88 Turnmill Street, London EC1M 5QU, England; *European Marketing Data and Statistics.*

European Community Information Service, 2100 M Street, NW, Washington, D.C. 20037 (202) 862-9500; *ACP: Basic Statistics, Basic Statistics of the Community, Demographic Statistics, Employment and Unemployment, Fisheries: Yearly Statistics, Iron and Steel: Statistical Yearbook, Labor Force Sample Survey,* and *Regions: Statistical Yearbook.*

Facts on File, 460 Park Avenue South, New York, New York 10016 (800) 443-8323; *The New Book of World Rankings.*

Federal Statistical Office, Gustav - Stresemann - Ring 11, D-6200 Wiesbaden, Germany; *Belgien.*

Food and Agricultural Organization of the United Nations (FAO), Via delle Terme di Caracalla, 00100 Rome, Italy (Telephone Number in U.S. (202) 606-7828); *Production Yearbook.*

G.K. Hall and Company, 70 Lincoln Street, Boston, Massachusetts 02111 (617) 423-3990; *The World in Figures.*

International Labour Office, I.L.O. Publications, CH-1211, Geneva 22, Switzerland; *Yearbook of Labour Statistics.*

Statistical Office of the United Nations, Publishing Service, New York, New York 10017 (800) 253-9646; *Demographic Yearbook,* and *Statistical Yearbook.*

Times Books, 201 East 50th Street, New York, New York 10022 (212) 751-2600; *The Economist Book of Vital World Statistics.*

United National Educational, Scientific and Cultural Organization (UNESCO), 7 Place de Fontenoy, F-75700 Paris, France (Telephone Number in U.S. (212) 963-5981); *Statistical Yearbook.*

U.S. Arms Control and Disarmament Agency, 320 Twenty-first Street, NW, Washington, D.C. 20451 (202) 647-8677; *World Military Expenditures and Arms Transfers.*

World Health Organization, Office of Publications, Avenue Appia, CH-1211 Geneva 27, Switzerland (Telephone Number in U.S. (518) 436-9686); *World Health Statistics Annual.*

BELGIUM - POST OFFICES

Facts on File, 460 Park Avenue South, New York, New York 10016 (800) 443-8323; *The New Book of World Rankings.*

BELGIUM - POTATO PRODUCTION - See BELGIUM - CROPS

BELGIUM - POULTRY - See BELGIUM - LIVESTOCK AND POULTRY

BELGIUM - POWER PRODUCTION INDUSTRY

European Community Information Service, 2100 M Street, NW, Washington, D.C. 20037 (202) 862-9500; *Basic Statistics of the Community.*

Statistical Office of the United Nations, Publishing Service, New York, New York 10017 (800) 253-9646; *Statistical Yearbook.*

BELGIUM - PRICES

European Community Information Service, 2100 M Street, NW, Washington, D.C. 20037 (202) 862-9500; *Basic Statistics of the Community,* and *Eurostatistics: Data for Short-Term Economic Analysis.*

Facts on File, 460 Park Avenue South, New York, New York 10016 (800) 443-8323; *The New Book of World Rankings.*

Federal Statistical Office, Gustav - Stresemann - Ring 11, D-6200 Wiesbaden, Germany; *Belgien.*

Food and Agricultural Organization of the United Nations (FAO), Via delle Terme di Caracalla, 00100 Rome, Italy (Telephone Number in U.S. (202) 606-7828); *Production Yearbook,* and *The State of Food and Agriculture.*

G.K. Hall and Company, 70 Lincoln Street, Boston, Massachusetts 02111 (617) 423-3990; *The World in Figures.*

International Labour Office, I.L.O. Publications, CH-1211, Geneva 22, Switzerland; *Yearbook of Labour Statistics,* and *International Financial Statistics.*

International Lead and Zinc Study Group, Metro House, 58 St. James's Street, London SW1A 1LD, England; *Lead and Zinc Statistics.*

Organisation for Economic Co-operation and Development (OECD), 2 rue Andre-Pascal, 75 Paris 16, France (Telephone Number in U.S. (202) 785-6323); *Economic Outlook, The Footwear, Raw Hides and Skins, and Leather Industry in OECD Countries, The Iron and Steel Industry, Main Economic Indicators - Historical Statistics, Indicators of Industrial Activity,* and *The Pulp and Paper Industry.*

World Bureau of Metal Statistics, 27-A High Street, Ware Herts SG12 9BA, England; *World Metal Statistics.*

BELGIUM - PRINTING AND WRITING PAPER - See BELGIUM - FORESTRY AND FOREST PRODUCTS

BELGIUM - PRODUCTION

American Automobile Manufacturers Association, 1401 H Street, NW, Suite 900, Washington, D.C. 20005 (202) 326-5500; *World Motor Vehicle Data.*

European Community Information Service, 2100 M Street, NW, Washington, D.C. 20037 (202) 862-9500; *Basic Statistics of the Community, Eurostatistics: Data for Short-Term Economic Analysis,* and *Fisheries: Yearly Statistics.*

Facts on File, 460 Park Avenue South, New York, New York 10016 (800) 443-8323; *The New Book of World Rankings.*

G.K. Hall and Company, 70 Lincoln Street, Boston, Massachusetts 02111 (617) 423-3990; *The World in Figures.*

International Iron and Steel Institute, 120, rue Colonel Bourg, B-1140, Brussels, Belgium; *Steel Statistical Yearbook.*

Organisation for Economic Co-operation and Development (OECD), 2 rue Andre-Pascal, 75 Paris 16, France (Telephone Number in U.S. (202) 785-6323); *Economic Outlook, The Footwear, Raw Hides and Skins, and Leather Industry in OECD Countries, Indicators of Industrial Activity, Industrial Structure Statistics, The Iron and Steel Industry, Meat Balances in OECD Member Countries, Milk, Milk Products, and Egg Balances in OECD Member Countries, The Non-Ferrous Metals Industry, The Pulp and Paper Industry,* and *Textile Industry in OECD Countries.*

BELGIUM - PRODUCTIVITY

European Community Information Service, 2100 M Street, NW, Washington, D.C. 20037 (202) 862-9500; *Basic Statistics of the*

Community.

Organisation for Economic Co-operation and Development (OECD), 2 rue Andre-Pascal, 75 Paris 16, France (Telephone Number in U.S. (202) 785-6323); *Economic Outlook.*

BELGIUM - PROPERTY TAXES - See BELGIUM - TAXATION

BELGIUM - PUBLIC CONSUMPTION FUND

European Community Information Service, 2100 M Street, NW, Washington, D.C. 20037 (202) 862-9500; *Basic Statistics of the Community.*

Organisation for Economic Co-operation and Development (OECD), 2 rue Andre-Pascal, 75 Paris 16, France (Telephone Number in U.S. (202) 785-6323); *Revenue Statistics of OECD Member Countries.*

BELGIUM - PUBLIC EXPENDITURES

European Community Information Service, 2100 M Street, NW, Washington, D.C. 20037 (202) 862-9500; *Basic Statistics of the Community.*

Organisation for Economic Co-operation and Development (OECD), 2 rue Andre-Pascal, 75 Paris 16, France (Telephone Number in U.S. (202) 785-6323); *Revenue Statistics of OECD Member Countries.*

BELGIUM - PUBLIC FINANCES

Facts on File, 460 Park Avenue South, New York, New York 10016 (800) 443-8323; *The New Book of World Rankings.*

Federal Statistical Office, Gustav - Stresemann - Ring 11, D-6200 Wiesbaden, Germany; *Belgien.*

Organisation for Economic Co-operation and Development (OECD), 2 rue Andre-Pascal, 75 Paris 16, France (Telephone Number in U.S. (202) 785-6323); *Revenue Statistics of OECD Member Countries.*

BELGIUM - PUBLIC HEALTH

European Community Information Service, 2100 M Street, NW, Washington, D.C. 20037 (202) 862-9500; *Basic Statistics of the Community.*

BELGIUM - PUBLIC REVENUES

Organisation for Economic Co-operation and Development (OECD), 2 rue Andre-Pascal, 75 Paris 16, France (Telephone Number in U.S. (202) 785-6323); *Revenue Statistics of OECD Member Countries.*

BELGIUM - RADIO BROADCASTING - See BELGIUM - BROADCASTING

BELGIUM - RADIO RECEIVER PRODUCTION

Statistical Office of the United Nations, Publishing Service, New York, New York 10017 (800) 253-9646; *Statistical Yearbook.*

BELGIUM - RAILWAYS

Euromonitor Publications Limited, 87-88 Turnmill Street, London EC1M 5QU, England; *European Marketing Data and Statistics.*

European Community Information Service, 2100 M Street, NW, Washington, D.C. 20037 (202) 862-9500; *Basic Statistics of the Community, Regions: Statistical Yearbook,* and *Transport Annual Statistics.*

G.K. Hall and Company, 70 Lincoln Street, Boston, Massachusetts 02111 (617) 423-3990; *The World in Figures.*

Jane's Information Group, Sentinel House, 163 Brighton Road, Coulsdon, Surrey CR5 2NH, England (Telephone Number in U.S. (703) 683-3700); *Jane's World Railways.*

Statistical Office of the United Nations, Publishing Service, New York, New York 10017; *Annual Bulletin of Transport Statistics for Europe,* and *Statistical Yearbook.*

BELGIUM - RANCHING

European Community Information Service, 2100 M Street, NW, Washington, D.C. 20037 (202) 862-9500; *Basic Statistics of the Community.*

BELGIUM - RAPESEED PRODUCTION - See BELGIUM - CROPS

BELGIUM - RELIGION

Facts on File, 460 Park Avenue South, New York, New York 10016 (800) 443-8323; *The New Book of World Rankings.*

BELGIUM - RENT PRICES

International Labour Office, I.L.O. Publications, CH-1211, Geneva 22, Switzerland; *Yearbook of Labour Statistics.*

BELGIUM - RETAIL TRADE

European Community Information Service, 2100 M Street, NW, Washington, D.C. 20037 (202) 862-9500; *Basic Statistics of the Community,* and *Eurostatistics: Data for Short-Term Economic Analysis.*

G.K. Hall and Company, 70 Lincoln Street, Boston, Massachusetts 02111 (617) 423-3990; *The World in Figures.*

Statistical Office of the United Nations, Publishing Service, New York, New York 10017 (800) 253-9646; *Statistical Yearbook.*

BELGIUM - RICE PRODUCTION - See BELGIUM - CROPS

BELGIUM - ROOT AND TUBER PRODUCTION - See BELGIUM - CROPS

BELGIUM - ROUNDWOOD PRODUCTION - See BELGIUM - FORESTRY AND FOREST PRODUCTS

BELGIUM - RUBBER PRODUCTION AND CONSUMPTION

European Community Information Service, 2100 M Street, NW, Washington, D.C. 20037 (202) 862-9500; *Basic Statistics of the Community.*

Facts on File, 460 Park Avenue South, New York, New York 10016 (800) 443-8323; *The New Book of World Rankings.*

International Rubber Study Group, York House, 8th Floor, Empire Way, Wembley, London HA9 0PA, England; *Rubber Statistical Bulletin.*

Organisation for Economic Co-operation and Development (OECD), 2 rue Andre-Pascal, 75 Paris 16, France (Telephone Number in U.S. (202) 785-6323); *Foreign Trade by Commodities.*

Statistical Office of the United Nations, Publishing Service, New York, New York 10017 (800) 253-9646; *Statistical Yearbook.*

BELGIUM - RYE PRODUCTION - See BELGIUM - CROPS

BELGIUM - SAFFLOWER SEED PRODUCTION - SEe BELGIUM - CROPS

BELGIUM - SALT PRODUCTION - See BELGIUM - MINING AND MINERAL PRODUCTS

BELGIUM - SAVING

Organisation for Economic Co-operation and Development (OECD), 2 rue Andre-Pascal, 75 Paris 16, France (Telephone Number in U.S. (202) 785-6323); *Economic Outlook.*

BELGIUM - SAVINGS ACCOUNT DEPOSITS

European Community Information Service, 2100 M Street, NW, Washington, D.C. 20037 (202) 862-9500; *Eurostatistics: Data for Short-Term Economic Analysis.*

International Monetary Fund, 700 Nineteenth Street, NW, Washington, D.C. 20431 (202) 623-7000; *International Financial Statistics.*

BELGIUM - SAWNWOOD PRODUCTION - See BELGIUM - FORESTRY AND FOREST PRODUCTS

BELGIUM - SCIENCE AND TECHNOLOGY - EXPENDITURE FOR RESEARCH

European Community Information Service, 2100 M Street, NW, Washington, D.C. 20037 (202) 862-9500; *Basic Statistics of the Community.*

Statistical Office of the United Nations, Publishing Service, New York, New York 10017 (800) 253-9646; *Statistical Yearbook.*

BELGIUM - SCIENTISTS AND ENGINEERS

European Community Information Service, 2100 M Street, NW, Washington, D.C. 20037 (202) 862-9500; *Basic Statistics of the Community.*

BELGIUM - SCIENTISTS AND TECHNICIANS

European Community Information Service, 2100 M Street, NW, Washington, D.C. 20037 (202) 862-9500; *Basic Statistics of the Community.*

Statistical Office of the United Nations, Publishing Service, New York, New York 10017 (800) 253-9646; *Statistical Yearbook.*

United Nations Educational, Scientific and Cultural Organization (UNESCO), 7 Place de Fontenoy, F-75700 Paris, France (Telephone Number in U.S. (212) 963-5981); *Statistical Yearbook.*

BELGIUM - SENIOR CITIZENS

Facts on File, 460 Park Avenue South, New York, New York 10016 (800) 443-8323; *The New Book of World Rankings.*

BELGIUM - SESAME SEED PRODUCTION - See BELGIUM - CROPS

BELGIUM - SHEEP - See BELGIUM - LIVESTOCK AND POULTRY

BELGIUM - SHIPBUILDING - PRODUCTION INDEX

Organisation for Economic Co-operation and Development (OECD), 2 rue Andre-Pascal, 75 Paris 16, France (Telephone Number in U.S. (202) 785-6323); *Indicators of Industrial Activity.*

BELGIUM - SILVER PRODUCTION AND CONSUMPTION - See BELGIUM - MINING AND MINERAL PRODUCTS

BELGIUM - SISAL PRODUCTION - See BELGIUM - CROPS

BELGIUM - SOCIAL DATA

European Community Information Service, 2100 M Street, NW, Washington, D.C. 20037 (202) 862-9500; *ACP: Basic Statistics, Basic Statistics of the Community.*

Facts on File, 460 Park Avenue South, New York, New York 10016 (800) 443-8323; *The New Book of World Rankings.*

G.K. Hall and Company, 70 Lincoln Street, Boston, Massachusetts 02111 (617) 423-3990; *The World in Figures.*

BELGIUM - SOCIAL SECURITY

European Community Information Service, 2100 M Street, NW, Washington, D.C. 20037 (202) 862-9500; *Basic Statistics of the Community.*

International Monetary Fund, 700 Nineteenth Street, NW, Washington, D.C. 20431 (202) 623-7000; *Government Finance Statistics Yearbook.*

Organisation for Economic Co-operation and Development (OECD), 2 rue Andre-Pascal, 75 Paris 16, France (Telephone Number in U.S. (202) 785-6323); *Revenue Statistics of OECD Member Countries.*

BELGIUM - SOCIOECONOMIC DATA

European Community Information Service, 2100 M Street, NW, Washington, D.C. 20037 (202) 862-9500; *Basic Statistics of the Community.*

Organisation for Economic Co-operation and Development (OECD), 2 rue Andre-Pascal, 75 Paris 16, France (Telephone Number in U.S. (202) 785-6323); *Economic Outlook.*

BELGIUM - SOYBEAN PRODUCTION - See BELGIUM - CROPS

BELGIUM - STAMP TAXES AND DUTIES - See BELGIUM - TAXATION

BELGIUM - STEEL - See BELGIUM - MINING AND MINERAL PRODUCTS

BELGIUM - STOCKS - COMMODITY - MARKET PRICE - INDEXES

Food and Agricultural Organization of the United Nations (FAO) Via delle Terme di Caracalla, 00100 Rome, Italy (Telephone Number in U.S. (202) 606-7828); *The State of Food and Agriculture.*

International Lead and Zinc Study Group, Metro House, 58 St. James's Street, London SW1A 1LD, England; *Lead and Zinc Statistics.*

Statistical Office of the United Nations, Publishing Service, New York, New York 10017 (800) 253-9646; *Statistical Yearbook.*

World Bureau of Metal Statistics, 27-A High Street, Ware Hert SG12 9BA, England; *World Metal Statistics.*

BELGIUM - STRAW PRODUCTION - See BELGIUM - CROPS

BELGIUM - SUGAR - See BELGIUM - CROPS

BELGIUM - SUGARBEET PRODUCTION - See BELGIUM - CROPS

BELGIUM - SULPHUR AND SULPHURIC ACID - See BELGIUM - MINING AND MINERAL PRODUCTS

BELGIUM - SUNFLOWER PRODUCTION - See BELGIUM - CROPS

BELGIUM - TAXATION

European Community Information Service, 2100 M Street, NW, Washington, D.C. 20037 (202) 862-9500; *Basic Statistics of the Community.*

G.K. Hall and Company, 70 Lincoln Street, Boston, Massachusetts 02111 (617) 423-3990; *The World in Figures.*

International Monetary Fund, 700 Nineteenth Street, NW, Washington, D.C. 20431 (202) 623-7000; *Government Finance Statistics Yearbook.*

International Road Federation, 525 School Street, SW, Washington, D.C. 20024 (202) 554-2106; *World Road Statistics.*

Organisation for Economic Co-operation and Development (OECD), 2 rue Andre-Pascal, 75 Paris 16, France (Telephone Number in U.S. (202) 785-6323); *Revenue Statistics of OECD Member Countries.*

The World Bank, 1818 H Street, NW, Washington, D.C. 20433 (202) 477-1234; *World Tables.*

BELGIUM - TEA PRODUCTION - See BELGIUM - CROPS

BELGIUM - TELEGRAPH SERVICE

European Community Information Service, 2100 M Street, NW, Washington, D.C. 20037 (202) 862-9500; *Transport Annual Statistics.*

Statistical Office of the United Nations, Publishing Service, New York, New York 10017 (800) 253-9646; *Statistical Yearbook.*

BELGIUM - TELEPHONES IN USE

American Telephone and Telegraph Company, Customer Information Center, Post Office Box 19901, Whippany, New Jersey 07981 (800) 338-4038; *The World's Telephones.*

European Community Information Service, 2100 M Street, NW, Washington, D.C. 20037 (202) 862-9500; *Basic Statistics of the Community,* and *Transport Annual Statistics.*

G.K. Hall and Company, 70 Lincoln Street, Boston, Massachusetts 02111 (617) 423-3990; *The World in Figures.*

Statistical Office of the United Nations, Publishing Service, New York, New York 10017 (800) 253-9646; *Statistical Yearbook.*

BELGIUM - TELEVISION BROADCASTING - See BELGIUM - BROADCASTING

BELGIUM - TELEVISION RECEIVER PRODUCTION

European Community Information Service, 2100 M Street, NW, Washington, D.C. 20037 (202) 862-9500; *Basic Statistics of the Community.*

Statistical Office of the United Nations, Publishing Service, New York, New York 10017 (800) 253-9646; *Statistical Yearbook.*

BELGIUM - TEXTILE INDUSTRY

European Community Information Service, 2100 M Street, NW, Washington, D.C. 20037 (202) 862-9500; *Basic Statistics of the Community, Eurostatistics: Data for Short-Term Economic Analysis,* and *Industrial Production: Quarterly Statistics.*

Food and Agricultural Organization of the United Nations (FAO) Via delle Terme di Caracalla, 00100 Rome, Italy (Telephone Number in U.S. (202) 606-7828); *The State of Food and Agriculture.*

Forest and Paper Association, 1250 Connecticut Avenue, NW, Washington, D.C. 20036 (202) 463-2455; *Wood Pulp and Fiber Statistics.*

G.K. Hall and Company, 70 Lincoln Street, Boston, Massachusetts 02111 (617) 423-3990; *The World in Figures.*

Organisation for Economic Co-operation and Development (OECD), 2 rue Andre-Pascal, 75 Paris 16, France (Telephone Number in U.S. (202) 785-6323); *Foreign Trade by Commodities, Indicators of Industrial Activity, Industrial Structure Statistics,* and *Textile Industry in OECD Countries.*

Statistical Office of the United Nations, Publishing Service, New York, New York 10017 (800) 253-9646; *Trade in Manufactures of Developing Countries,* and *Statistical Yearbook.*

BELGIUM - TIMBER - See BELGIUM - FORESTRY AND FOREST PRODUCTS

BELGIUM - TIN - See BELGIUM - MINING AND MINERAL PRODUCTS

BELGIUM - TIRE (MOTOR VEHICLE) PRODUCTION

International Rubber Study Group, York House, 8th Floor, Empire Way, Wembley, London HA9 0PA, England; *Rubber Statistical Bulletin.*

Statistical Office of the United Nations, Publishing Service, New York, New York 10017 (800) 253-9646; *Statistical Yearbook.*

BELGIUM - TOBACCO PRODUCTION

Euromonitor Publications Limited, 87-88 Turnmill Street, London EC1M 5QU, England; *European Marketing Data and Statistics.*

European Community Information Service, 2100 M Street, NW, Washington, D.C. 20037 (202) 862-9500; *Basic Statistics of the Community,* and *Industrial Production: Quarterly Statistics.*

Facts on File, 460 Park Avenue South, New York, New York 10016 (800) 443-8323; *The New Book of World Rankings.*

Organisation for Economic Co-operation and Development (OECD), 2 rue Andre-Pascal, 75 Paris 16, France (Telephone Number in U.S. (202) 785-6323); *Foreign Trade by Commodities, Indicators of Industrial Activity,* and *Industrial Structure Statistics.*

Statistical Office of the United Nations, Publishing Service, New York, New York 10017 (800) 253-9646; *Statistical Yearbook.*

BELGIUM - TOURISM

Euromonitor Publications Limited, 87-88 Turnmill Street, London EC1M 5QU, England; *European Marketing Data and Statistics.*

European Community Information Service, 2100 M Street, NW, Washington, D.C. 20037 (202) 862-9500; *Transport Annual*

Statistics.

Facts on File, 460 Park Avenue South, New York, New York 10016 (800) 443-8323; *The New Book of World Rankings.*

Federal Statistical Office, Gustav - Stresemann - Ring 11, D-6200 Wiesbaden, Germany; *Belgien.*

G.K. Hall and Company, 70 Lincoln Street, Boston, Massachusetts 02111 (617) 423-3990; *The World in Figures.*

Organisation for Economic Co-operation and Development (OECD), 2 rue Andre-Pascal, 75 Paris 16, France (Telephone Number in U.S. (202) 785-6323); *Tourism Policy and International Tourism in OECD Member Countries.*

Statistical Office of the United Nations, Publishing Service, New York, New York 10017 (800) 253-9646; *Statistical Yearbook.*

Times Books, 201 East 50th Street, New York, New York 10022 (212) 751-2600; *The Economist Book of Vital World Statistics.*

World Tourism Organization, Calle Capitan Haya 42, E-28020 Madrid, Spain; *Yearbook of Tourism Statistics.*

BELGIUM - TRACTORS IN USE

European Community Information Service, 2100 M Street, NW, Washington, D.C. 20037 (202) 862-9500; *Transport Annual Statistics.*

BELGIUM - TRADE - See BELGIUM - FOREIGN TRADE

BELGIUM - TRADEMARKS AND SERVICE MARKS

Statistical Office of the United Nations, Publishing Service, New York, New York 10017 (800) 253-9646; *Statistical Yearbook.*

BELGIUM - TRANSPORTATION AND COMMUNICATIONS

European Community Information Service, 2100 M Street, NW, Washington, D.C. 20037 (202) 862-9500; *Basic Statistics of the Community, Energy Statistics Yearbook, Regions: Statistical Yearbook,* and *Transport Annual Statistics.*

Facts on File, 460 Park Avenue South, New York, New York 10016 (800) 443-8323; *The New Book of World Rankings.*

Federal Statistical Office, Gustav - Stresemann - Ring 11, D-6200 Wiesbaden, Germany; *Belgien.*

G.K. Hall and Company, 70 Lincoln Street, Boston, Massachusetts 02111 (617) 423-3990; *The World in Figures.*

BELGIUM - TUNGSTEN PRODUCTION AND CONSUMPTION - See BELGIUM - MINING AND MINERAL PRODUCTS

BELGIUM - TURKEYS - See BELGIUM - LIVESTOCK AND POULTRY

BELGIUM - UNEMPLOYMENT

Euromonitor Publications Limited, 87-88 Turnmill Street, London EC1M 5QU, England; *European Marketing Data and Statistics.*

European Community Information Service, 2100 M Street, NW, Washington, D.C. 20037 (202) 862-9500; *Basic Statistics of the Community, Employment and Unemployment, Eurostatistics: Data for Short-Term Economic Analysis, Labor Force Sample Survey,* and *Regions: Statistical Yearbook.*

International Labour Office, I.L.O. Publications, CH-1211, Geneva 22, Switzerland; *Yearbook of Labour Statistics.*

Organisation for Economic Co-operation and Development (OECD), 2 rue Andre-Pascal, 75 Paris 16, France (Telephone Number in U.S. (202) 785-6323); *Economic Outlook, Labour Statistics, OECD Economic Surveys: Belgium - Luxembourg,* and *OECD Employment Outlook.*

Statistical Office of the United Nations, Publishing Service, New York, New York 10017 (800) 253-9646; *Statistical Yearbook.*

BELGIUM - URANIUM PRODUCTION AND CONSUMPTION - See BELGIUM - MINING AND MINERAL PRODUCTS

BELGIUM - UTILITIES

European Community Information Service, 2100 M Street, NW, Washington, D.C. 20037 (202) 862-9500; *Basic Statistics of the Community.*

BELGIUM - VANADIUM AND VANADIUM ORE - See BELGIUM - MINING AND MINERAL PRODUCTS

BELGIUM - VITAL STATISTICS

European Community Information Service, 2100 M Street, NW, Washington, D.C. 20037 (202) 862-9500; *Basic Statistics of the Community.*

G.K. Hall and Company, 70 Lincoln Street, Boston, Massachusetts 02111 (617) 423-3990; *The World in Figures.*

Statistical Office of the United Nations, Publishing Service, New York, New York 10017 (800) 253-9646; *Statistical Yearbook.*

BELGIUM - WAGES

Euromonitor Publications Limited, 87-88 Turnmill Street, London EC1M 5QU, England; *European Marketing Data and Statistics.*

European Community Information Service, 2100 M Street, NW, Washington, D.C. 20037 (202) 862-9500; *Basic Statistics of the Community, Earnings in Agriculture,* and *Eurostatistics: Data for Short-Term Economic Analysis.*

Federal Statistical Office, Gustav - Stresemann - Ring 11, D-6200 Wiesbaden, Germany; *Belgien.*

G.K. Hall and Company, 70 Lincoln Street, Boston, Massachusetts 02111 (617) 423-3990; *The World in Figures.*

International Labour Office, I.L.O. Publications, CH-1211, Geneva 22, Switzerland; *Yearbook of Labour Statistics.*

Organisation for Economic Co-operation and Development (OECD), 2 rue Andre-Pascal, 75 Paris 16, France (Telephone Number in U.S. (202) 785-6323); *Economic Outlook, Industrial Structure Statistics,* and *Main Economic Indicators - Historical Statistics.*

Statistical Office of the United Nations, Publishing Service, New York, New York 10017 (800) 253-9646; *Statistical Yearbook.*

BELGIUM - WALNUT PRODUCTION - See BELGIUM - CROPS

BELGIUM - WATERWAYS IN USE - See BELGIUM - MERCHANT SHIPPING

BELGIUM - WEATHER

Facts on File, 460 Park Avenue South, New York, New York 10016 (800) 443-8323; *The New Book of World Rankings.*

G.K. Hall and Company, 70 Lincoln Street, Boston, Massachusetts 02111 (617) 423-3990; *The World in Figures.*

BELGIUM - WELFARE

European Community Information Service, 2100 M Street, NW, Washington, D.C. 20037 (202) 862-9500; *Basic Statistics of the Community.*

International Monetary Fund, 700 Nineteenth Street, NW, Washington, D.C. 20431 (202) 623-7000; *Government Finance Statistics Yearbook.*

BELGIUM - WHEAT - See BELGIUM - CROPS

BELGIUM - WHOLESALE PRICES

European Community Information Service, 2100 M Street, NW, Washington, D.C. 20037 (202) 862-9500; *Basic Statistics of the Community.*

International Monetary Fund, 700 Nineteenth Street, NW, Washington, D.C. 20431 (202) 623-7000; *International Financial Statistics.*

Statistical Office of the United Nations, Publishing Service, New York, New York 10017 (800) 253-9646; *Statistical Yearbook.*

BELGIUM - WHOLESALE TRADE

European Community Information Service, 2100 M Street, NW, Washington, D.C. 20037 (202) 862-9500; *Basic Statistics of the Community.*

Statistical Office of the United Nations, Publishing Service, New York, New York 10017 (800) 253-9646; *Statistical Yearbook.*

BELGIUM - WINE PRODUCTION

European Community Information Service, 2100 M Street, NW, Washington, D.C. 20037 (202) 862-9500; *Basic Statistics of the Community.*

Facts on File, 460 Park Avenue South, New York, New York 10016 (800) 443-8323; *The New Book of World Rankings.*

Statistical Office of the United Nations, Publishing Service, New York, New York 10017 (800) 253-9646; *Statistical Yearbook.*

BELGIUM - WOOD - See BELGIUM - FORESTRY AND FOREST PRODUCTS

BELGIUM - WOOL - INDUSTRIAL CONSUMPTION

Organisation for Economic Co-operation and Development (OECD), 2 rue Andre-Pascal, 75 Paris 16, France (Telephone Number in U.S. (202) 785-6323); *Textile Industry in OECD Countries.*

Statistical Office of the United Nations, Publishing Service, New York, New York 10017 (800) 253-9646; *Statistical Yearbook.*

BELGIUM - WOOL PRODUCTION

European Community Information Service, 2100 M Street, NW, Washington, D.C. 20037 (202) 862-9500; *Basic Statistics of the Community,* and *Economic Accounts for Agriculture.*

Facts on File, 460 Park Avenue South, New York, New York 10016 (800) 443-8323; *The New Book of World Rankings.*

Organisation for Economic Co-operation and Development (OECD), 2 rue Andre-Pascal, 75 Paris 16, France (Telephone Number in U.S. (202) 785-6323); *Textile Industry in OECD Countries.*

BELGIUM - YARN PRODUCTION

European Community Information Service, 2100 M Street, NW, Washington, D.C. 20037 (202) 862-9500; *Basic Statistics of the Community.*

Organisation for Economic Co-operation and Development (OECD), 2 rue Andre-Pascal, 75 Paris 16, France (Telephone Number in U.S. (202) 785-6323); *Foreign Trade by Commodities,* and *Textile Industry in OECD Countries.*

Statistical Office of the United Nations, Publishing Service, New York, New York 10017 (800) 253-9646; *Statistical Yearbook.*

BELGIUM - ZINC AND ZINC ORE - See BELGIUM - MINING AND MINERAL PRODUCTS

BELGIUM - ZOOS AND BOTANICAL GARDENS

United Nations Educational, Scientific and Cultural Organization (UNESCO), 7 Place de Fontenoy, F-75700 Paris, France (Telephone Number in U.S. (212) 963-5981); *Statistical Yearbook.*

Belize - Central Statistical Office

Chief Statistician, Central Statistical Office, Belmopan, Belize.

Belize - Primary Statistics Source

Ministry of Finance, Central Statistical Office, Belmopan, Belize; *Annual Abstract of Statistics.*

BELIZE - AGRICULTURE

Federal Statistical Office, Gustav - Stresemann - Ring 11, D-6200 Wiesbaden, Germany; *Belize.*

Food and Agricultural Organization of the United Nations (FAO), Via delle Terme di Caracalla, 00100 Rome, Italy (Telephone Number in U.S. (202) 606-7828); *Production Yearbook, The State of Food and Agriculture,* and *Trade Yearbook.*

G.K. Hall and Company, 70 Lincoln Street, Boston, Massachusetts 02111 (617) 423-3990; *The World in Figures.*

Statistical Office of the United Nations, Publishing Service, New York, New York 10017 (800) 253-9646; *Statistical Yearbook.*

The World Bank, 1818 H Street, NW, Washington, D.C. 20433 (202) 477-1234; *World Tables.*

BELIZE - AIRLINE SERVICE

G.K. Hall and Company, 70 Lincoln Street, Boston, Massachusetts 02111 (617) 423-3990; *The World in Figures.*

BELIZE - ANIMAL HEALTH

Food and Agricultural Organization of the United Nations (FAO), Via delle Terme di Caracalla, 00100 Rome, Italy (Telephone Number in U.S. (202) 606-7828); *Animal Health Yearbook.*

BELIZE - AREA AND DENSITY OF POPULATION

Federal Statistical Office, Gustav - Stresemann - Ring 11, D-6200 Wiesbaden, Germany; *Belize.*

Food and Agricultural Organization of the United Nations (FAO) Via delle Terme di Caracalla, 00100 Rome, Italy (Telephone Number in U.S. (202) 606-7828); *The State of Food and Agriculture.*

G.K. Hall and Company, 70 Lincoln Street, Boston, Massachusetts 02111 (617) 423-3990; *The World in Figures.*

Statistical Office of the United Nations, Publishing Service, New York, New York 10017 (800) 253-9646; *Statistical Yearbook.*

BELIZE - BALANCE OF PAYMENTS

The Economist Intelligence Unit, 111 West 57th Street, New York, New York 10019 (800) 938-4685; *The World Market Atlas.*

Federal Statistical Office, Gustav - Stresemann - Ring 11, D-6200 Wiesbaden, Germany; *Belize.*

G.K. Hall and Company, 70 Lincoln Street, Boston, Massachusetts 02111 (617) 423-3990; *The World in Figures.*

Statistical Office of the United Nations, Publishing Service, New York, New York 10017; *Economic Survey of Latin America and the Caribbean.*

The World Bank, 1818 H Street, NW, Washington, D.C. 20433 (202) 477-1234; *World Tables.*

BELIZE - BANKING

G.K. Hall and Company, 70 Lincoln Street, Boston, Massachusetts 02111 (617) 423-3990; *The World in Figures.*

BELIZE - BIRTH RATE

Statistical Office of the United Nations, Publishing Service, New York, New York 10017 (800) 253-9646; *Demographic Yearbook,* and *Statistical Yearbook.*

The World Bank, 1818 H Street, NW, Washington, D.C. 20433 (202) 477-1234; *World Tables.*

World Health Organization, Office of Publications, Avenue Appia, CH-1211 Geneva 27, Switzerland (Telephone Number in U.S. (518) 436-9686); *World Health Statistics Annual.*

BELIZE - BONDS

G.K. Hall and Company, 70 Lincoln Street, Boston, Massachusetts 02111 (617) 423-3990; *The World in Figures.*

BELIZE - BOOK PRODUCTION

G.K. Hall and Company, 70 Lincoln Street, Boston, Massachusetts 02111 (617) 423-3990; *The World in Figures.*

BELIZE - BROADCASTING

Billboard Limited, P.O. Box 9027, 1006 AA Amsterdam, The Netherlands (Telephone Number in U.S. (212) 764-7300); *World Radio TV Handbook.*

G.K. Hall and Company, 70 Lincoln Street, Boston, Massachusetts 02111 (617) 423-3990; *The World in Figures.*

BELIZE - BUSINESS

G.K. Hall and Company, 70 Lincoln Street, Boston, Massachusetts 02111 (617) 423-3990; *The World in Figures.*

BELIZE - CALORIE SUPPLY

Food and Agricultural Organization of the United Nations (FAO) Via delle Terme di Caracalla, 00100 Rome, Italy (Telephone Number in U.S. (202) 606-7828); *The State of Food and Agriculture.*

BELIZE - CATTLE - See BELIZE - LIVESTOCK AND POULTRY

BELIZE - CHEMICAL (ORGANIC) PRODUCTION - See BELIZE - MINING AND MINERAL PRODUCTS

BELIZE - CLASS STRUCTURE

G.K. Hall and Company, 70 Lincoln Street, Boston, Massachusetts 02111 (617) 423-3990; *The World in Figures.*

BELIZE - CLIMATE

G.K. Hall and Company, 70 Lincoln Street, Boston, Massachusetts 02111 (617) 423-3990; *The World in Figures.*

BELIZE - COAL PRODUCTION - See BELIZE - MINING AND MINERAL PRODUCTS

BELIZE - COMMUNICATIONS

Federal Statistical Office, Gustav - Stresemann - Ring 11, D-6200 Wiesbaden, Germany; *Belize.*

G.K. Hall and Company, 70 Lincoln Street, Boston, Massachusetts 02111 (617) 423-3990; *The World in Figures.*

BELIZE - CONSTRUCTION INDUSTRY

Statistical Office of the United Nations, Publishing Service, New York, New York 10017 (800) 253-9646; *Statistical Yearbook.*

BELIZE - CONSUMER PRICE INDEX

Federal Statistical Office, Gustav - Stresemann - Ring 11, D-6200 Wiesbaden, Germany; *Belize.*

G.K. Hall and Company, 70 Lincoln Street, Boston, Massachusetts 02111 (617) 423-3990; *The World in Figures.*

Statistical Office of the United Nations, Publishing Service, New York, New York 10017 (800) 253-9646; *Statistical Yearbook.*

BELIZE - CONSUMER PRICES

Federal Statistical Office, Gustav - Stresemann - Ring 11, D-6200 Wiesbaden, Germany; *Belize.*

BELIZE - CONSUMPTION

G.K. Hall and Company, 70 Lincoln Street, Boston, Massachusetts 02111 (617) 423-3990; *The World in Figures.*

BELIZE - CORN PRODUCTION - See BELIZE - CROPS

BELIZE - CORPORATE TAXES - See BELIZE - TAXATION

BELIZE - CROPS

Food and Agricultural Organization of the United Nations (FAO) Via delle Terme di Caracalla, 00100 Rome, Italy (Telephone Number in U.S. (202) 606-7828); *The State of Food and Agriculture.*

G.K. Hall and Company, 70 Lincoln Street, Boston, Massachusetts 02111 (617) 423-3990; *The World in Figures.*

Statistical Office of the United Nations, Publishing Service, New York, New York 10017 (800) 253-9646; *Statistical Yearbook.*

BELIZE - CUSTOMS DUTIES

G.K. Hall and Company, 70 Lincoln Street, Boston, Massachusetts 02111 (617) 423-3990; *The World in Figures.*

BELIZE - DAIRY PRODUCTS

Food and Agricultural Organization of the United Nations (FAO) Via delle Terme di Caracalla, 00100 Rome, Italy (Telephone Number in U.S. (202) 606-7828); *The State of Food and Agriculture.*

BELIZE - DEATH RATES

G.K. Hall and Company, 70 Lincoln Street, Boston, Massachusetts 02111 (617) 423-3990; *The World in Figures.*

Statistical Office of the United Nations, Publishing Service, New York, New York 10017 (800) 253-9646; *Statistical Yearbook.*

BELIZE - DEFENSE EXPENDITURES

G.K. Hall and Company, 70 Lincoln Street, Boston, Massachusetts 02111 (617) 423-3990; *The World in Figures.*

BELIZE - DEMOGRAPHY

The Economist Intelligence Unit, 111 West 57th Street, New York, New York 10019 (800) 938-4685; *The World Market Atlas.*

Federal Statistical Office, Gustav - Stresemann - Ring 11, D-6200 Wiesbaden, Germany; *Belize.*

G.K. Hall and Company, 70 Lincoln Street, Boston, Massachusetts 02111 (617) 423-3990; *The World in Figures.*

BELIZE - DEVELOPMENT ASSISTANCE

G.K. Hall and Company, 70 Lincoln Street, Boston, Massachusetts 02111 (617) 423-3990; *The World in Figures.*

Statistical Office of the United Nations, Publishing Service, New York, New York 10017 (800) 253-9646; *Statistical Yearbook.*

BELIZE - DISEASES

G.K. Hall and Company, 70 Lincoln Street, Boston, Massachusetts 02111 (617) 423-3990; *The World in Figures.*

World Health Organization, Office of Publications, Avenue Appia, CH-1211 Geneva 27, Switzerland (Telephone Number in U.S. (518) 436-9686); *World Health Statistics Annual.*

BELIZE - DIVORCE RATES

Statistical Office of the United Nations, Publishing Service, New York, New York 10017 (800) 253-9646; *Demographic Yearbook,* and *Statistical Yearbook.*

BELIZE - DOMESTIC PRODUCT

G.K. Hall and Company, 70 Lincoln Street, Boston, Massachusetts 02111 (617) 423-3990; *The World in Figures.*

BELIZE - DUCKS - See BELIZE - LIVESTOCK AND POULTRY

BELIZE - ECONOMY

Federal Statistical Office, Gustav - Stresemann - Ring 11, D-6200 Wiesbaden, Germany; *Belize.*

G.K. Hall and Company, 70 Lincoln Street, Boston, Massachusetts 02111 (617) 423-3990; *The World in Figures.*

Statistical Office of the United Nations, Publishing Service, New York, New York 10017 (800) 253-9646; *Economic Survey of Latin America and the Caribbean.*

BELIZE - EDUCATION

The Economist Intelligence Unit, 111 West 57th Street, New York, New York 10019 (800) 938-4685; *The World Market Atlas.*

Federal Statistical Office, Gustav - Stresemann - Ring 11, D-6200 Wiesbaden, Germany; *Belize.*

G.K. Hall and Company, 70 Lincoln Street, Boston, Massachusetts 02111 (617) 423-3990; *The World in Figures.*

Organisation for Economic Co-operation and Development (OECD), 2 rue Andre-Pascal, 75 Paris 16, France (Telephone Number in U.S. (202) 785-6323); *Education in OECD Countries.*

United Nations Educational, Scientific and Cultural Organization (UNESCO), 7 Place de Fontenoy, F-75700 Paris, France (Telephone Number in U.S. (212) 963-5981); *Statistical Yearbook.*

The World Bank, 1818 H Street, NW, Washington, D.C. 20433 (202) 477-1234; *World Tables.*

BELIZE - EGG PRODUCTION - See BELIZE - DAIRY PRODUCTS

BELIZE - ELECTRICITY

Statistical Office of the United Nations, Publishing Service, New York, New York 10017 (800) 253-9646; *Statistical Yearbook.*

BELIZE - EMPLOYMENT

Federal Statistical Office, Gustav - Stresemann - Ring 11, D-6200 Wiesbaden, Germany; *Belize.*

Statistical Office of the United Nations, Publishing Service, New York, New York 10017 (800) 253-9646; *Statistical Yearbook.*

BELIZE - ENERGY

Food and Agricultural Organization of the United Nations (FAO) Via delle Terme di Caracalla, 00100 Rome, Italy (Telephone Number in U.S. (202) 606-7828); *The State of Food and Agriculture.*

G.K. Hall and Company, 70 Lincoln Street, Boston, Massachusetts 02111 (617) 423-3990; *The World in Figures.*

Statistical Office of the United Nations, Publishing Service, New York, New York 10017 (800) 253-9646; *Energy Statistics Yearbook,* and *Statistical Yearbook.*

BELIZE - EXPORTS

The Economist Intelligence Unit, 111 West 57th Street, New York, New York 10019 (800) 938-4685; *The World Market Atlas.*

Food and Agricultural Organization of the United Nations (FAO) Via delle Terme di Caracalla, 00100 Rome, Italy (Telephone Number in U.S. (202) 606-7828); *The State of Food and Agriculture.*

G.K. Hall and Company, 70 Lincoln Street, Boston, Massachusetts 02111 (617) 423-3990; *The World in Figures.*

The World Bank, 1818 H Street, NW, Washington, D.C. 20433 (202) 477-1234; *World Tables.*

BELIZE - EXTERNAL INDEBTEDNESS

The World Bank, 1818 H Street, NW, Washington, D.C. 20433 (202) 477-1234; *World Tables.*

BELIZE - EXTERNAL TRADE

Food and Agricultural Organization of the United Nations (FAO) Via delle Terme di Caracalla, 00100 Rome, Italy (Telephone Number in U.S. (202) 606-7828); *The State of Food and Agriculture,* and *Trade Yearbook.*

G.K. Hall and Company, 70 Lincoln Street, Boston, Massachusetts 02111 (617) 423-3990; *The World in Figures.*

Statistical Office of the United Nations, Publishing Service, New York, New York 10017 (800) 253-9646; *Statistical Yearbook.*

BELIZE - FARM CROPS - See BELIZE - CROPS

BELIZE - FERTILITY RATES

The World Bank, 1818 H Street, NW, Washington, D.C. 20433 (202) 477-1234; *World Tables.*

BELIZE - FERTILIZER

Food and Agricultural Organization of the United Nations (FAO), Via delle Terme di Caracalla, 00100 Rome, Italy (Telephone Number in U.S. (202) 606-7828); *Fertilizer Yearbook,* and *The State of Food and Agriculture.*

Statistical Office of the United Nations, Publishing Service, New York, New York 10017 (800) 253-9646; *Statistical Yearbook.*

BELIZE - FETAL MORTALITY

Statistical Office of the United Nations, Publishing Service, New York, New York 10017 (800) 253-9646; *Demographic Yearbook.*

World Health Organization, Office of Publications, Avenue Appia, CH-1211 Geneva 27, Switzerland (Telephone Number in U.S. (518) 436-9686); *World Health Statistics Annual.*

BELIZE - FINANCE

Federal Statistical Office, Gustav - Stresemann - Ring 11, D-6200 Wiesbaden, Germany; *Belize.*

G.K. Hall and Company, 70 Lincoln Street, Boston, Massachusetts 02111 (617) 423-3990; *The World in Figures.*

BELIZE - FISHERIES

Federal Statistical Office, Gustav - Stresemann - Ring 11, D-6200 Wiesbaden, Germany; *Belize.*

Food and Agricultural Organization of the United Nations (FAO) Via delle Terme di Caracalla, 00100 Rome, Italy (Telephone Number in U.S. (202) 606-7828); *The State of Food and Agriculture,* and *Yearbook of Fishery Statistics.*

Statistical Office of the United Nations, Publishing Service, New York, New York 10017 (800) 253-9646; *Statistical Yearbook.*

BELIZE - FOOD

Food and Agricultural Organization of the United Nations (FAO) Via delle Terme di Caracalla, 00100 Rome, Italy (Telephone Number in U.S. (202) 606-7828); *Production Yearbook,* and *The State of Food and Agriculture.*

G.K. Hall and Company, 70 Lincoln Street, Boston, Massachusetts 02111 (617) 423-3990; *The World in Figures.*

BELIZE - FOREIGN AID

G.K. Hall and Company, 70 Lincoln Street, Boston, Massachusetts 02111 (617) 423-3990; *The World in Figures.*

BELIZE - FOREIGN INDEBTEDNESS

Statistical Office of the United Nations, Publishing Service, New York, New York 10017 (800) 253-9646; *Economic Survey of Latin America and the Caribbean.*

BELIZE - FOREIGN TRADE

Food and Agricultural Organization of the United Nations (FAO) Via delle Terme di Caracalla, 00100 Rome, Italy (Telephone Number in U.S. (202) 606-7828); *The State of Food and Agriculture.*

Federal Statistical Office, Gustav - Stresemann - Ring 11, D-6200 Wiesbaden, Germany; *Belize.*

G.K. Hall and Company, 70 Lincoln Street, Boston, Massachusetts 02111 (617) 423-3990; *The World in Figures.*

Statistical Office of the United Nations, Publishing Service, New York, New York 10017 (800) 253-9646; *Economic Survey of Latin America and the Caribbean, International Trade Statistics Yearbook,* and *Statistical Yearbook.*

The World Bank, 1818 H Street, NW, Washington, D.C. 20433 (202) 477-1234; *World Tables.*

BELIZE - FORESTRY AND FOREST PRODUCTS

Federal Statistical Office, Gustav - Stresemann - Ring 11, D-6200 Wiesbaden, Germany; *Belize.*

Food and Agricultural Organization of the United Nations (FAO) Via delle Terme di Caracalla, 00100 Rome, Italy (Telephone Number in U.S. (202) 606-7828); *The State of Food and Agriculture,* and *Yearbook of Forest Products.*

G.K. Hall and Company, 70 Lincoln Street, Boston, Massachusetts 02111 (617) 423-3990; *The World in Figures.*

Statistical Office of the United Nations, Publishing Service, New York, New York 10017 (800) 253-9646; *Statistical Yearbook.*

United Nations Educational, Scientific and Cultural Organization (UNESCO), 7 Place de Fontenoy, F-75700 Paris, France (Telephone Number in U.S. (212) 963-5981); *Statistical Yearbook.*

BELIZE - GENERAL INDUSTRIAL STATISTICS

Federal Statistical Office, Gustav - Stresemann - Ring 11, D-6200 Wiesbaden, Germany; *Belize.*

BELIZE - GENERAL MORTALITY

Statistical Office of the United Nations, Publishing Service, New York, New York 10017 (800) 253-9646; *Demographic Yearbook.*

World Health Organization, Office of Publications, Avenue Appia, CH-1211 Geneva 27, Switzerland (Telephone Number in U.S. (518) 436-9686); *World Health Statistics Annual.*

BELIZE - GEOGRAPHIC DATA

Federal Statistical Office, Gustav - Stresemann - Ring 11, D-6200 Wiesbaden, Germany; *Belize.*

BELIZE - GOLD HOLDINGS

The World Bank, 1818 H Street, NW, Washington, D.C. 20433 (202) 477-1234; *World Tables.*

BELIZE - GOVERNMENT

G.K. Hall and Company, 70 Lincoln Street, Boston, Massachusetts 02111 (617) 423-3990; *The World in Figures.*

BELIZE - GOVERNMENT EXPENDITURE

The World Bank, 1818 H Street, NW, Washington, D.C. 20433 (202) 477-1234; *World Tables.*

BELIZE - GOVERNMENT REVENUE

The World Bank, 1818 H Street, NW, Washington, D.C. 20433 (202) 477-1234; *World Tables.*

BELIZE - GRAIN PRODUCTION - See BELIZE - CROPS

BELIZE - GROSS DOMESTIC PRODUCT

The Economist Intelligence Unit, 111 West 57th Street, New York, New York 10019 (800) 938-4685; *The World Market Atlas.*

G.K. Hall and Company, 70 Lincoln Street, Boston, Massachusetts 02111 (617) 423-3990; *The World in Figures.*

Statistical Office of the United Nations, Publishing Service, New York, New York 10017 (800) 253-9646; *Statistical Yearbook.*

The World Bank, 1818 H Street, NW, Washington, D.C. 20433 (202) 477-1234; *World Tables.*

BELIZE - GROSS NATIONAL PRODUCT

The World Bank, 1818 H Street, NW, Washington, D.C. 20433 (202) 477-1234; *World Tables.*

BELIZE - HEALTH

Federal Statistical Office, Gustav - Stresemann - Ring 11, D-6200 Wiesbaden, Germany; *Belize.*

G.K. Hall and Company, 70 Lincoln Street, Boston, Massachusetts 02111 (617) 423-3990; *The World in Figures.*

Statistical Office of the United Nations, Publishing Service, New York, New York 10017 (800) 253-9646; *Statistical Yearbook.*

World Health Organization, Avenue Appia, Office of Publications, CH-1211 Geneva, 27, Switzerland (Telephone Number in U.S. (518) 436-9686); *World Health Statistics: Vital Statistics and Causes of Death.*

BELIZE - HIDE PRODUCTION

Food and Agricultural Organization of the United Nations (FAO), Via delle Terme di Caracalla, 00100 Rome, Italy (Telephone Number in U.S. (202) 606-7828); *Production Yearbook.*

BELIZE - HIGHWAYS

G.K. Hall and Company, 70 Lincoln Street, Boston, Massachusetts 02111 (617) 423-3990; *The World in Figures.*

BELIZE - HORSES - See BELIZE - LIVESTOCK AND POULTRY

BELIZE - ILLITERATE POPULATION

The Economist Intelligence Unit, 111 West 57th Street, New York, New York 10019 (800) 938-4685; *The World Market Atlas.*

G.K. Hall and Company, 70 Lincoln Street, Boston, Massachusetts 02111 (617) 423-3990; *The World in Figures.*

United Nations Educational, Scientific and Cultural Organization (UNESCO), 7 Place de Fontenoy, F-75700 Paris, France (Telephone Number in U.S. (212) 963-5981); *Statistical Yearbook.*

BELIZE - IMPORTS

The Economist Intelligence Unit, 111 West 57th Street, New York, New York 10019 (800) 938-4685; *The World Market Atlas.*

Food and Agricultural Organization of the United Nations (FAO) Via delle Terme di Caracalla, 00100 Rome, Italy (Telephone Number in U.S. (202) 606-7828); *The State of Food and Agriculture.*

G.K. Hall and Company, 70 Lincoln Street, Boston, Massachusetts 02111 (617) 423-3990; *The World in Figures.*

International Monetary Fund, 700 Nineteenth Street, NW, Washington, D.C. 20431 (202) 623-7000; *Direction of Trade Statistics.*

The World Bank, 1818 H Street, NW, Washington, D.C. 20433 (202) 477-1234; *World Tables*.

BELIZE - INDUSTRY

Federal Statistical Office, Gustav - Stresemann - Ring 11, D-6200 Wiesbaden, Germany; *Belize*.

G.K. Hall and Company, 70 Lincoln Street, Boston, Massachusetts 02111 (617) 423-3990; *The World in Figures*.

Statistical Office of the United Nations, Publishing Service, New York, New York 10017 (800) 253-9646; *Economic Survey of Latin America and the Caribbean*.

The World Bank, 1818 H Street, NW, Washington, D.C. 20433 (202) 477-1234; *World Tables*.

BELIZE - INFANT AND MATERNAL MORTALITY

Statistical Office of the United Nations, Publishing Service, New York, New York 10017 (800) 253-9646; *Demographic Yearbook*, and *Statistical Yearbook*.

The World Bank, 1818 H Street, NW, Washington, D.C. 20433 (202) 477-1234; *World Tables*.

World Health Organization, Office of Publications, Geneva, Switzerland; (Telephone Number in U.S. (518) 436-9686); *World Health Statistics: Vital Statistics and Causes of Death*.

BELIZE - INFLATIONARY FACTORS

Statistical Office of the United Nations, Publishing Service, New York, New York 10017 (800) 253-9646; *Economic Survey of Latin America and the Caribbean*.

BELIZE - INTERNATIONAL RESERVES EXCLUDING GOLD

The World Bank, 1818 H Street, NW, Washington, D.C. 20433 (202) 477-1234; *World Tables*.

BELIZE - LABOR FORCE

Food and Agricultural Organization of the United Nations (FAO) Via delle Terme di Caracalla, 00100 Rome, Italy (Telephone Number in U.S. (202) 606-7828); *The State of Food and Agriculture*.

G.K. Hall and Company, 70 Lincoln Street, Boston, Massachusetts 02111 (617) 423-3990; *The World in Figures*.

The World Bank, 1818 H Street, NW, Washington, D.C. 20433 (202) 477-1234; *World Tables*.

BELIZE - LAND USE

Food and Agricultural Organization of the United Nations (FAO), Via delle Terme di Caracalla, 00100 Rome, Italy (Telephone Number in U.S. (202) 606-7828); *Production Yearbook*.

G.K. Hall and Company, 70 Lincoln Street, Boston, Massachusetts 02111 (617) 423-3990; *The World in Figures*.

BELIZE - LIBRARIES

United Nations Educational, Scientific and Cultural Organization (UNESCO), 7 Place de Fontenoy, F-75700 Paris, France (Telephone Number in U.S. (212) 963-5981); *Statistical Yearbook*.

BELIZE - LIVESTOCK AND POULTRY

Food and Agricultural Organization of the United Nations (FAO), Via delle Terme di Caracalla, 00100 Rome, Italy (Telephone Number in U.S. (202) 606-7828); *Production Yearbook*, and *The State of Food and Agriculture*.

G.K. Hall and Company, 70 Lincoln Street, Boston, Massachusetts 02111 (617) 423-3990; *The World in Figures*.

Statistical Office of the United Nations, Publishing Service, New York, New York 10017 (800) 253-9646; *Statistical Yearbook*.

BELIZE - LIVING LEVELS

G.K. Hall and Company, 70 Lincoln Street, Boston, Massachusetts 02111 (617) 423-3990; *The World in Figures*.

BELIZE - MAIL TRAFFIC

Statistical Office of the United Nations, Publishing Service, New York, New York 10017 (800) 253-9646; *Statistical Yearbook*.

BELIZE - MANUFACTURING

G.K. Hall and Company, 70 Lincoln Street, Boston, Massachusetts 02111 (617) 423-3990; *The World in Figures*.

The World Bank, 1818 H Street, NW, Washington, D.C. 20433 (202) 477-1234; *World Tables*.

BELIZE - MARRIAGE RATES

Statistical Office of the United Nations, Publishing Service, New York, New York 10017 (800) 253-9646; *Demographic Yearbook*, and *Statistical Yearbook*.

BELIZE - MEAT PRODUCTION - See BELIZE - LIVESTOCK AND POULTRY

BELIZE - MERCHANT SHIPPING

G.K. Hall and Company, 70 Lincoln Street, Boston, Massachusetts 02111 (617) 423-3990; *The World in Figures*.

Statistical Office of the United Nations, Publishing Service, New York, New York 10017 (800) 253-9646; *Statistical Yearbook*.

BELIZE - MILITARY

G.K. Hall and Company, 70 Lincoln Street, Boston, Massachusetts 02111 (617) 423-3990; *The World in Figures*.

The International Institute for Strategic Studies, 23 Tavistock Street, London WC2E 7NQ, England; *The Military Balance*.

BELIZE - MINING AND MINERAL PRODUCTS

G.K. Hall and Company, 70 Lincoln Street, Boston, Massachusetts 02111 (617) 423-3990; *The World in Figures*.

BELIZE - MONEY SUPPLY

Federal Statistical Office, Gustav - Stresemann - Ring 11, D-6200 Wiesbaden, Germany; *Belize*.

G.K. Hall and Company, 70 Lincoln Street, Boston, Massachusetts 02111 (617) 423-3990; *The World in Figures*.

The World Bank, 1818 H Street, NW, Washington, D.C. 20433 (202) 477-1234; *World Tables.*

BELIZE - MONUMENTS AND HISTORICAL SITES

United Nations Educational, Scientific and Cultural Organization (UNESCO), 7 Place de Fontenoy, F-75700 Paris, France (Telephone Number in U.S. (212) 963-5981); *Statistical Yearbook.*

BELIZE - MOTION PICTURES

Statistical Office of the United Nations, Publishing Service, New York, New York 10017 (800) 253-9646; *Statistical Yearbook.*

BELIZE - MOTOR VEHICLES IN USE

G.K. Hall and Company, 70 Lincoln Street, Boston, Massachusetts 02111 (617) 423-3990; *The World in Figures.*

Statistical Office of the United Nations, Publishing Service, New York, New York 10017 (800) 253-9646; *Statistical Yearbook.*

BELIZE - MULES - See BELIZE - LIVESTOCK AND POULTRY

BELIZE - MUSEUMS

United Nations Educational, Scientific and Cultural Organization (UNESCO), 7 Place de Fontenoy, F-75700 Paris, France (Telephone Number in U.S. (212) 963-5981); *Statistical Yearbook.*

BELIZE - NATALITY - See BELIZE - BIRTH RATE

BELIZE - NATIONAL ACCOUNTS

Federal Statistical Office, Gustav - Stresemann - Ring 11, D-6200 Wiesbaden, Germany; *Belize.*

Statistical Office of the United Nations, Publishing Service, New York, New York 10017 (800) 253-9646; *National Accounts Statistics,* and *Statistical Yearbook.*

BELIZE - NATIONAL INCOME

G.K. Hall and Company, 70 Lincoln Street, Boston, Massachusetts 02111 (617) 423-3990; *The World in Figures.*

Statistical Office of the United Nations, Publishing Service, New York, New York 10017 (800) 253-9646; *Statistical Yearbook.*

BELIZE - NATIONAL PRODUCTION

Statistical Office of the United Nations, Publishing Service, New York, New York 10017 (800) 253-9646; *Statistical Yearbook.*

BELIZE - NET MATERIAL PRODUCT

Statistical Office of the United Nations, Publishing Service, New York, New York 10017 (800) 253-9646; *Statistical Yearbook.*

BELIZE - NEWSPAPER PRODUCTION - See BELIZE - FORESTRY AND FOREST PRODUCTS

BELIZE - NEWSPRINT - See BELIZE - FORESTRY AND FOREST PRODUCTS

BELIZE - OCCUPATIONS - See BELIZE - LABOR FORCE

BELIZE - PAPER - See BELIZE - FORESTRY AND FOREST PRODUCTS

BELIZE - PERIODICALS

United Nations Educational, Scientific and Cultural Organization (UNESCO), 7 Place de Fontenoy, F-75700 Paris, France (Telephone Number in U.S. (212) 963-5981); *Statistical Yearbook.*

BELIZE - PESTICIDE USE

Food and Agricultural Organization of the United Nations (FAO) Via delle Terme di Caracalla, 00100 Rome, Italy (Telephone Number in U.S. (202) 606-7828); *The State of Food and Agriculture.*

BELIZE - PETROLEUM INDUSTRY

Food and Agricultural Organization of the United Nations (FAO) Via delle Terme di Caracalla, 00100 Rome, Italy (Telephone Number in U.S. (202) 606-7828); *The State of Food and Agriculture.*

G.K. Hall and Company, 70 Lincoln Street, Boston, Massachusetts 02111 (617) 423-3990; *The World in Figures.*

BELIZE - PIGS - See BELIZE - LIVESTOCK AND POULTRY

BELIZE - POPULATION

The Economist Intelligence Unit, 111 West 57th Street, New York, New York 10019 (800) 938-4685; *The World Market Atlas.*

Federal Statistical Office, Gustav - Stresemann - Ring 11, D-6200 Wiesbaden, Germany; *Belize.*

Food and Agricultural Organization of the United Nations (FAO), Via delle Terme di Caracalla, 00100 Rome, Italy (Telephone Number in U.S. (202) 606-7828); *Production Yearbook.*

G.K. Hall and Company, 70 Lincoln Street, Boston, Massachusetts 02111 (617) 423-3990; *The World in Figures.*

Statistical Office of the United Nations, Publishing Service, New York, New York 10017 (800) 253-9646; *Demographic Yearbook,* and *Statistical Yearbook.*

United Nations Educational, Scientific and Cultural Organization (UNESCO), 7 Place de Fontenoy, F-75700 Paris, France (Telephone Number in U.S. (212) 963-5981); *Statistical Yearbook.*

World Health Organization, Office of Publications, Avenue Appia, CH-1211 Geneva 27, Switzerland (Telephone Number in U.S. (518) 436-9686); *World Health Statistics Annual.*

BELIZE - PRICES

Federal Statistical Office, Gustav - Stresemann - Ring 11, D-6200 Wiesbaden, Germany; *Belize.*

Food and Agricultural Organization of the United Nations (FAO), Via delle Terme di Caracalla, 00100 Rome, Italy (Telephone Number in U.S. (202) 606-7828); *Production Yearbook,* and *The State of Food and Agriculture.*

G.K. Hall and Company, 70 Lincoln Street, Boston, Massachusetts 02111 (617) 423-3990; *The World in Figures.*

Statistical Office of the United Nations, Publishing Service, New York, New York 10017 (800) 253-9646; *Economic Survey of Latin America and the Caribbean.*

BELIZE - PRINTING AND WRITING PAPER - See BELIZE - FORESTRY AND FOREST PRODUCTS

BELIZE - PRODUCTION

G.K. Hall and Company, 70 Lincoln Street, Boston, Massachusetts 02111 (617) 423-3990; *The World in Figures.*

BELIZE - PUBLIC FINANCE

Federal Statistical Office, Gustav - Stresemann - Ring 11, D-6200 Wiesbaden, Germany; *Belize.*

BELIZE - RAILWAYS

G.K. Hall and Company, 70 Lincoln Street, Boston, Massachusetts 02111 (617) 423-3990; *The World in Figures.*

BELIZE - RETAIL TRADE

G.K. Hall and Company, 70 Lincoln Street, Boston, Massachusetts 02111 (617) 423-3990; *The World in Figures.*

BELIZE - RICE PRODUCTION - See BELIZE - CROPS

BELIZE - ROOT AND TUBER PRODUCTION - See BELIZE - CROPS

BELIZE - SAWNWOOD PRODUCTION - See BELIZE - FORESTRY AND FOREST PRODUCTS

BELIZE - SCIENCE AND TECHNOLOGY - EXPENDITURE FOR RESEARCH

Statistical Office of the United Nations, Publishing Service, New York, New York 10017 (800) 253-9646; *Statistical Yearbook.*

BELIZE - SCIENTISTS AND TECHNICIANS

Statistical Office of the United Nations, Publishing Service, New York, New York 10017 (800) 253-9646; *Statistical Yearbook.*

United Nations Educational, Scientific and Cultural Organization (UNESCO), 7 Place de Fontenoy, F-75700 Paris, France (Telephone Number in U.S. (212) 963-5981); *Statistical Yearbook.*

BELIZE - SHEEP - See BELIZE - LIVESTOCK AND POULTRY

BELIZE - SOCIAL DATA

G.K. Hall and Company, 70 Lincoln Street, Boston, Massachusetts 02111 (617) 423-3990; *The World in Figures.*

BELIZE - STOCKS - COMMODITY - MARKET PRICE - INDEX

Food and Agricultural Organization of the United Nations (FAO) Via delle Terme di Caracalla, 00100 Rome, Italy (Telephone Number in U.S. (202) 606-7828); *The State of Food and Agriculture.*

BELIZE - SUGAR PRODUCTION - See BELIZE - CROPS

BELIZE - TAXATION

G.K. Hall and Company, 70 Lincoln Street, Boston, Massachusetts 02111 (617) 423-3990; *The World in Figures.*

The World Bank, 1818 H Street, NW, Washington, D.C. 20433 (202) 477-1234; *World Tables.*

BELIZE - TELEPHONES IN USE

American Telephone and Telegraph Company, Customer Information Center, Post Office Box 19901, Whippany, New Jersey 07981 (800) 338-4038; *The World's Telephones.*

G.K. Hall and Company, 70 Lincoln Street, Boston, Massachusetts 02111 (617) 423-3990; *The World in Figures.*

Statistical Office of the United Nations, Publishing Service, New York, New York 10017 (800) 253-9646; *Statistical Yearbook.*

BELIZE - TEXTILE INDUSTRY

G.K. Hall and Company, 70 Lincoln Street, Boston, Massachusetts 02111 (617) 423-3990; *The World in Figures.*

BELIZE - TOBACCO PRODUCTION

Statistical Office of the United Nations, Publishing Service, New York, New York 10017 (800) 253-9646; *Statistical Yearbook.*

BELIZE - TOURISM

Federal Statistical Office, Gustav - Stresemann - Ring 11, D-6200 Wiesbaden, Germany; *Belize.*

G.K. Hall and Company, 70 Lincoln Street, Boston, Massachusetts 02111 (617) 423-3990; *The World in Figures.*

The International Institute for Strategic Studies, 23 Tavistock Street, London WC2E 7NQ, England; *The Military Balance.*

World Tourism Organization, Calle Capitan Haya 42, E-28020 Madrid, Spain; *Yearbook of Tourism Statistics.*

BELIZE - TRACTORS IN USE

Statistical Office of the United Nations, Publishing Service, New York, New York 10017 (800) 253-9646; *Statistical Yearbook.*

BELIZE - TRADE - See BELIZE - FOREIGN TRADE

BELIZE - TRANSPORTATION AND COMMUNICATIONS

Federal Statistical Office, Gustav - Stresemann - Ring 11, D-6200 Wiesbaden, Germany; *Belize.*

G.K. Hall and Company, 70 Lincoln Street, Boston, Massachusetts 02111 (617) 423-3990; *The World in Figures.*

BELIZE - TURKEYS - See BELIZE - LIVESTOCK AND POULTRY

BELIZE - VITAL STATISTICS

G.K. Hall and Company, 70 Lincoln Street, Boston, Massachusetts 02111 (617) 423-3990; *The World in Figures.*

Statistical Office of the United Nations, Publishing Service, New York, New York 10017 (800) 253-9646; *Statistical Yearbook.*

World Health Organization, Office of Publications, Avenue Appia, CH-1211 Geneva 27, Switzerland (Telephone Number in U.S. (518) 436-9686); *World Health Statistics Annual.*

BELIZE - WAGES

Federal Statistical Office, Gustav - Stresemann - Ring 11, D-6200 Wiesbaden, Germany; *Belize.*

G.K. Hall and Company, 70 Lincoln Street, Boston, Massachusetts 02111 (617) 423-3990; *The World in Figures.*

BELIZE - WEATHER

G.K. Hall and Company, 70 Lincoln Street, Boston, Massachusetts 02111 (617) 423-3990; *The World in Figures.*

Benin - National Statistical Office

Institut National de la Statistique et de l'Analyse Economique, BP 323, Cotonou, Benin.

Benin - Primary Statistics Sources

Institut National de la Statistique et de l'Analyse Economique, BP 323, Cotonou, Benin, *Annuaire Statistique,* (Statistical Yearbook); and *Bulletin de Statistique,* (Bulletin of Statistics).

BENIN - AGRICULTURE

Euromonitor Publications Limited, 87-88 Turnmill Street, London EC1M 5QU, England; *International Marketing Data and Statistics.*

Facts on File, 460 Park Avenue South, New York, New York 10016 (800) 443-8323; *The New Book of World Rankings.*

Federal Statistical Office, Gustav - Stresemann - Ring 11, D-6200 Wiesbaden, Germany; *Benin.*

Food and Agricultural Organization of the United Nations (FAO) Via delle Terme di Caracalla, 00100 Rome, Italy (Telephone Number in U.S. (202) 606-7828); *Production Yearbook, The State of Food and Agriculture,* and *Trade Yearbook.*

G.K. Hall and Company, 70 Lincoln Street, Boston, Massachusetts 02111 (617) 423-3990; *The World in Figures.*

Statistical Office of the United Nations, Publishing Service, New York, New York 10017 (800) 253-9646; *Statistical Yearbook,* and *Survey of Economic and Social Conditions in Africa.*

United Nations Economic Commission for Africa, Africa Hall, P.O. Box 3001, Addis Ababa, Ethiopia (Telephone Number in U.S. (800) 253-9646); *African Statistical Yearbook.*

Times Books, 201 East 50th Street, New York, New York 10022 (212) 751-2600; *The Economist Book of Vital World Statistics.*

The World Bank, 1818 H Street, NW, Washington, D.C. 20433 (202) 477-1234; *World Tables.*

BENIN - AIRLINE SERVICE

Facts on File, 460 Park Avenue South, New York, New York 10016 (800) 443-8323; *The New Book of World Rankings.*

G.K. Hall and Company, 70 Lincoln Street, Boston, Massachusetts 02111 (617) 423-3990; *The World in Figures.*

Statistical Office of the United Nations, Publishing Service, New York, New York 10017 (800) 253-9646; *Statistical Yearbook.*

Times Books, 201 East 50th Street, New York, New York 10022 (212) 751-2600; *The Economist Book of Vital World Statistics.*

United Nations Economic Commission for Africa, Africa Hall, P.O. Box 3001, Addis Ababa, Ethiopia (Telephone Number in U.S. (800) 253-9646); *African Statistical Yearbook.*

BENIN - ALUMINUM PRODUCTION AND CONSUMPTION - See BENIN - MINING AND MINERAL PRODUCTS

BENIN - ANIMAL HEALTH

Food and Agricultural Organization of the United Nations (FAO), Via delle Terme di Caracalla, 00100 Rome, Italy (Telephone Number in U.S. (202) 606-7828); *Animal Health Yearbook.*

BENIN - AREA AND DENSITY OF POPULATION

African Development Bank, 01 BP 1387, Abidjan 01, Cote D'Ivoire; *Selected Statistics on Regional Member Countries.*

Euromonitor Publications Limited, 87-88 Turnmill Street, London EC1M 5QU, England; *International Marketing Data and Statistics.*

Facts on File, 460 Park Avenue South, New York, New York 10016 (800) 443-8323; *The New Book of World Rankings.*

Federal Statistical Office, Gustav - Stresemann - Ring 11, D-6200 Wiesbaden, Germany; *Benin.*

Food and Agricultural Organization of the United Nations (FAO) Via delle Terme di Caracalla, 00100 Rome, Italy (Telephone Number in U.S. (202) 606-7828); *The State of Food and Agriculture.*

G.K. Hall and Company, 70 Lincoln Street, Boston, Massachusetts 02111 (617) 423-3990; *The World in Figures.*

Statistical Office of the United Nations, Publishing Service, New York, New York 10017 (800) 253-9646; *Statistical Yearbook,* and *Survey of Economic and Social Conditions in Africa.*

Times Books, 201 East 50th Street, New York, New York 10022 (212) 751-2600; *The Economist Book of Vital World Statistics.*

United Nations Educational, Scientific and Cultural Organization (UNESCO), 7 Place de Fontenoy, F-75700 Paris, France (Telephone Number in U.S. (212) 963-5981); *Statistical Yearbook.*

BENIN - ARMS EXPORTS AND IMPORTS

U.S. Arms Control and Disarmament Agency, 320 Twenty-first Street, NW, Washington, D.C. 20451 (202) 647-8677; *World Military Expenditures and Arms Transfers.*

BENIN - BALANCE OF PAYMENTS

African Development Bank, 01 BP 1387, Abidjan 01, Cote D'Ivoire; *Selected Statistics on Regional Member Countries.*

The Economist Intelligence Unit, 111 West 57th Street, New York, New York 10019 (800) 938-4685; *The World Market Atlas.*

Facts on File, 460 Park Avenue South, New York, New York 10016 (800) 443-8323; *The New Book of World Rankings.*

Federal Statistical Office, Gustav - Stresemann - Ring 11, D-6200 Wiesbaden, Germany; *Benin.*

G.K. Hall and Company, 70 Lincoln Street, Boston, Massachusetts 02111 (617) 423-3990; *The World in Figures.*

International Monetary Fund, 700 Nineteenth Street, NW, Washington, D.C. 20431 (202) 623-7000; *Balance of Payments Yearbook,* and *International Financial Statistics.*

Times Books, 201 East 50th Street, New York, New York 10022 (212) 751-2600; *The Economist Book of Vital World Statistics.*

United Nations Economic Commission for Africa, Africa Hall, P.O. Box 3001, Addis Ababa, Ethiopia (Telephone Number in U.S. (800) 253-9646); *African Statistical Yearbook.*

The World Bank, 1818 H Street, NW, Washington, D.C. 20433 (202) 477-1234; *World Tables.*

BENIN - BANKING

Facts on File, 460 Park Avenue South, New York, New York 10016 (800) 443-8323; *The New Book of World Rankings.*

G.K. Hall and Company, 70 Lincoln Street, Boston, Massachusetts 02111 (617) 423-3990; *The World in Figures.*

International Monetary Fund, 700 Nineteenth Street, NW, Washington, D.C. 20431 (202) 623-7000; *International Financial Statistics.*

Statistical Office of the United Nations, Publishing Service, New York, New York 10017 (800) 253-9646; *Statistical Yearbook.*

BENIN - BARLEY PRODUCTION - See BENIN - CROPS

BENIN - BEER PRODUCTION

Facts on File, 460 Park Avenue South, New York, New York 10016 (800) 443-8323; *The New Book of World Rankings.*

Statistical Office of the United Nations, Publishing Service, New York, New York 10017 (800) 253-9646; *Statistical Yearbook.*

BENIN - BIRTH RATES

Facts on File, 460 Park Avenue South, New York, New York 10016 (800) 443-8323; *The New Book of World Rankings.*

Statistical Office of the United Nations, Publishing Service, New York, New York 10017 (800) 253-9646; *Demographic Yearbook, Statistical Yearbook,* and *Survey of Economic and Social Conditions in Africa.*

Times Books, 201 East 50th Street, New York, New York 10022 (212) 751-2600; *The Economist Book of Vital World Statistics.*

The World Bank, 1818 H Street, NW, Washington, D.C. 20433 (202) 477-1234; *World Tables.*

BENIN - BONDS

G.K. Hall and Company, 70 Lincoln Street, Boston, Massachusetts 02111 (617) 423-3990; *The World in Figures.*

BENIN - BOOK PRODUCTION

G.K. Hall and Company, 70 Lincoln Street, Boston, Massachusetts 02111 (617) 423-3990; *The World in Figures.*

United Nations Educational, Scientific and Cultural Organization (UNESCO), 7 Place de Fontenoy, F-75700 Paris, France (Telephone Number in U.S. (212) 963-5981); *Statistical Yearbook.*

BENIN - BROADCASTING

Billboard Limited, P.O. Box 9027, 1006 AA Amsterdam, The Netherlands (Telephone Number in U.S. (212) 764-7300); *World Radio TV Handbook.*

Facts on File, 460 Park Avenue South, New York, New York 10016 (800) 443-8323; *The New Book of World Rankings.*

G.K. Hall and Company, 70 Lincoln Street, Boston, Massachusetts 02111 (617) 423-3990; *The World in Figures.*

Times Books, 201 East 50th Street, New York, New York 10022 (212) 751-2600; *The Economist Book of Vital World Statistics.*

BENIN - BUSINESS

G.K. Hall and Company, 70 Lincoln Street, Boston, Massachusetts 02111 (617) 423-3990; *The World in Figures.*

BENIN - BUSINESS AND PROFESSIONAL LICENSES

International Monetary Fund, 700 Nineteenth Street, NW, Washington, D.C. 20431 (202) 623-7000; *Government Finance Statistics Yearbook.*

BENIN - CALORIE SUPPLY

African Development Bank, 01 BP 1387, Abidjan 01, Cote D'Ivoire; *Selected Statistics on Regional Member Countries.*

Food and Agricultural Organization of the United Nations (FAO) Via delle Terme di Caracalla, 00100 Rome, Italy (Telephone Number in U.S. (202) 606-7828); *The State of Food and Agriculture.*

BENIN - CAPITAL REVENUE

International Monetary Fund, 700 Nineteenth Street, NW, Washington, D.C. 20431 (202) 623-7000; *Government Finance Statistics Yearbook.*

BENIN - CASTOR BEAN PRODUCTION - See BENIN - CROPS

BENIN - CATTLE - See BENIN - LIVESTOCK AND POULTRY

BENIN - CEMENT PRODUCTION - See BENIN - MINING AND MINERAL PRODUCTS

BENIN - CENTRAL BANKS

G.K. Hall and Company, 70 Lincoln Street, Boston, Massachusetts 02111 (617) 423-3990; *The World in Figures.*

BENIN - CHEMICAL (ORGANIC) PRODUCTION - See BENIN - MINING AND MINERAL PRODUCTS

BENIN - CHICKENS - See BENIN - LIVESTOCK AND POULTRY

BENIN - CIGARETTE PRODUCTION - See BENIN - TOBACCO PRODUCTION

BENIN - CLASS STRUCTURE

G.K. Hall and Company, 70 Lincoln Street, Boston, Massachusetts 02111 (617) 423-3990; *The World in Figures.*

BENIN - CLIMATE

Facts on File, 460 Park Avenue South, New York, New York 10016 (800) 443-8323; *The New Book of World Rankings.*

G.K. Hall and Company, 70 Lincoln Street, Boston, Massachusetts 02111 (617) 423-3990; *The World in Figures.*

BENIN - COAL PRODUCTION - See BENIN - MINING AND MINERAL PRODUCTS

BENIN - COFFEE PRODUCTION - See BENIN - CROPS

BENIN - COMMUNICATIONS

Federal Statistical Office, Gustav - Stresemann - Ring 11, D-6200 Wiesbaden, Germany; *Benin.*

G.K. Hall and Company, 70 Lincoln Street, Boston, Massachusetts 02111 (617) 423-3990; *The World in Figures.*

United Nations Economic Commission for Africa, Africa Hall, P.O. Box 3001, Addis Ababa, Ethiopia (Telephone Number in U.S. (800) 253-9646); *African Statistical Yearbook.*

BENIN - CONSTRUCTION INDUSTRY

Facts on File, 460 Park Avenue South, New York, New York 10016 (800) 443-8323; *The New Book of World Rankings.*

United Nations Economic Commission for Africa, Africa Hall, P.O. Box 3001, Addis Ababa, Ethiopia (Telephone Number in U.S. (800) 253-9646); *African Statistical Yearbook.*

BENIN - CONSUMER PRICE INDEX

African Development Bank, 01 BP 1387, Abidjan 01, Cote D'Ivoire; *Selected Statistics on Regional Member Countries.*

Federal Statistical Office, Gustav - Stresemann - Ring 11, D-6200 Wiesbaden, Germany; *Benin.*

G.K. Hall and Company, 70 Lincoln Street, Boston, Massachusetts 02111 (617) 423-3990; *The World in Figures.*

Statistical Office of the United Nations, Publishing Service, New York, New York 10017 (800) 253-9646; *Survey of Economic and Social Conditions in Africa.*

BENIN - CONSUMER PRICES

Federal Statistical Office, Gustav - Stresemann - Ring 11, D-6200 Wiesbaden, Germany; *Benin.*

International Labour Office, I.L.O. Publications, CH-1211, Geneva 22, Switzerland; *Yearbook of Labour Statistics.*

Times Books, 201 East 50th Street, New York, New York 10022 (212) 751-2600; *The Economist Book of Vital World Statistics.*

BENIN - CONSUMPTION

African Development Bank, 01 BP 1387, Abidjan 01, Cote D'Ivoire; *Selected Statistics on Regional Member Countries.*

G.K. Hall and Company, 70 Lincoln Street, Boston, Massachusetts 02111 (617) 423-3990; *The World in Figures.*

Statistical Office of the United Nations, Publishing Service, New York, New York 10017 (800) 253-9646; *Survey of Economic and Social Conditions in Africa.*

BENIN - COPPER PRODUCTION - See BENIN - MINING AND MINERAL PRODUCTS

BENIN - CORN PRODUCTION - See BENIN - CROPS

BENIN - CORPORATE TAXES - See BENIN - TAXATION

BENIN - COTTON PRODUCTION - See BENIN - CROPS

BENIN - CROPS

Facts on File, 460 Park Avenue South, New York, New York 10016 (800) 443-8323; *The New Book of World Rankings.*

Food and Agricultural Organization of the United Nations (FAO) Via delle Terme di Caracalla, 00100 Rome, Italy (Telephone Number in U.S. (202) 606-7828); *Production Yearbook,* and *The State of Food and Agriculture.*

G.K. Hall and Company, 70 Lincoln Street, Boston, Massachusetts 02111 (617) 423-3990; *The World in Figures.*

Statistical Office of the United Nations, Publishing Service, New York, New York 10017 (800) 253-9646; *Statistical Yearbook.*

United Nations Economic Commission for Africa, Africa Hall, P.O. Box 3001, Addis Ababa, Ethiopia (Telephone Number in U.S. (800) 253-9646); *African Statistical Yearbook.*

BENIN - CUSTOMS DUTIES

G.K. Hall and Company, 70 Lincoln Street, Boston, Massachusetts 02111 (617) 423-3990; *The World in Figures.*

International Monetary Fund, 700 Nineteenth Street, NW, Washington, D.C. 20431 (202) 623-7000; *Government Finance Statistics Yearbook.*

BENIN - DAIRY PRODUCTS

Facts on File, 460 Park Avenue South, New York, New York 10016 (800) 443-8323; *The New Book of World Rankings.*

Food and Agricultural Organization of the United Nations (FAO) Via delle Terme di Caracalla, 00100 Rome, Italy (Telephone Number in U.S. (202) 606-7828); *Production Yearbook,* and *The State of Food and Agriculture.*

Statistical Office of the United Nations, Publishing Service, New York, New York 10017 (800) 253-9646; *Statistical Yearbook.*

BENIN - DEATH RATES

G.K. Hall and Company, 70 Lincoln Street, Boston, Massachusetts 02111 (617) 423-3990; *The World in Figures.*

Statistical Office of the United Nations, Publishing Service, New York, New York 10017 (800) 253-9646; *Statistical Yearbook,* and *Survey of Economic and Social Conditions in Africa.*

Times Books, 201 East 50th Street, New York, New York 10022 (212) 751-2600; *The Economist Book of Vital World Statistics.*

World Health Organization, Office of Publications, Avenue Appia, CH-1211 Geneva 27, Switzerland (Telephone Number in U.S. (518) 436-9686); *World Health Statistics Annual.*

BENIN - DEFENSE EXPENDITURES

G.K. Hall and Company, 70 Lincoln Street, Boston, Massachusetts 02111 (617) 423-3990; *The World in Figures.*

U.S. Arms Control and Disarmament Agency, 320 Twenty-first Street, NW, Washington, D.C. 20451 (202) 647-8677; *World Military*

Expenditures and Arms Transfers.

BENIN - DEMOGRAPHY

The Economist Intelligence Unit, 111 West 57th Street, New York, New York 10019 (800) 938-4685; *The World Market Atlas.*

Facts on File, 460 Park Avenue South, New York, New York 10016 (800) 443-8323; *The New Book of World Rankings.*

Federal Statistical Office, Gustav - Stresemann - Ring 11, D-6200 Wiesbaden, Germany; *Benin.*

G.K. Hall and Company, 70 Lincoln Street, Boston, Massachusetts 02111 (617) 423-3990; *The World in Figures.*

Statistical Office of the United Nations, Publishing Service, New York, New York 10017 (800) 253-9646; *Survey of Economic and Social Conditions in Africa.*

BENIN - DEVELOPMENT ASSISTANCE

G.K. Hall and Company, 70 Lincoln Street, Boston, Massachusetts 02111 (617) 423-3990; *The World in Figures.*

Statistical Office of the United Nations, Publishing Service, New York, New York 10017 (800) 253-9646; *Statistical Yearbook.*

BENIN - DIAMOND PRODUCTION - See BENIN - MINING AND MINERAL PRODUCTS

BENIN - DISCOUNT RATES

Statistical Office of the United Nations, Publishing Service, New York, New York 10017 (800) 253-9646; *Statistical Yearbook.*

BENIN - DISEASE

G.K. Hall and Company, 70 Lincoln Street, Boston, Massachusetts 02111 (617) 423-3990; *The World in Figures.*

World Health Organization, Office of Publications, Avenue Appia, CH-1211 Geneva 27, Switzerland (Telephone Number in U.S. (518) 436-9686); *World Health Statistics Annual.*

BENIN - DIVORCE RATES

Facts on File, 460 Park Avenue South, New York, New York 10016 (800) 443-8323; *The New Book of World Rankings.*

BENIN - DOMESTIC PRODUCT

G.K. Hall and Company, 70 Lincoln Street, Boston, Massachusetts 02111 (617) 423-3990; *The World in Figures.*

BENIN - ECONOMY

African Development Bank, 01 BP 1387, Abidjan 01, Cote D'Ivoire; *Selected Statistics on Regional Member Countries.*

Euromonitor Publications Limited, 87-88 Turnmill Street, London EC1M 5QU, England; *International Marketing Data and Statistics.*

Facts on File, 460 Park Avenue South, New York, New York 10016 (800) 443-8323; *The New Book of World Rankings.*

Federal Statistical Office, Gustav - Stresemann - Ring 11, D-6200 Wiesbaden, Germany; *Benin.*

G.K. Hall and Company, 70 Lincoln Street, Boston, Massachusetts 02111 (617) 423-3990; *The World in Figures.*

Statistical Office of the United Nations, Publishing Service, New York, New York 10017 (800) 253-9646; *Foreign Trade Statistics for Africa.*

BENIN - EDUCATION

African Development Bank, 01 BP 1387, Abidjan 01, Cote D'Ivoire; *Selected Statistics on Regional Member Countries.*

The Economist Intelligence Unit, 111 West 57th Street, New York, New York 10019 (800) 938-4685; *The World Market Atlas.*

Facts on File, 460 Park Avenue South, New York, New York 10016 (800) 443-8323; *The New Book of World Rankings.*

Federal Statistical Office, Gustav - Stresemann - Ring 11, D-6200 Wiesbaden, Germany; *Benin.*

G.K. Hall and Company, 70 Lincoln Street, Boston, Massachusetts 02111 (617) 423-3990; *The World in Figures.*

Statistical Office of the United Nations, Publishing Service, New York, New York 10017 (800) 253-9646; *Survey of Economic and Social Conditions in Africa.*

Times Books, 201 East 50th Street, New York, New York 10022 (212) 751-2600; *The Economist Book of Vital World Statistics.*

United Nations Economic Commission for Africa, Africa Hall, P.O. Box 3001, Addis Ababa, Ethiopia (Telephone Number in U.S. (800) 253-9646); *African Statistical Yearbook.*

United Nations Educational, Scientific and Cultural Organization (UNESCO), 7 Place de Fontenoy, F-75700 Paris, France (Telephone Number in U.S. (212) 963-5981); *Statistical Yearbook.*

The World Bank, 1818 H Street, NW, Washington, D.C. 20433 (202) 477-1234; *World Tables.*

BENIN - EGG PRODUCTION - See BENIN - DAIRY PRODUCTS

BENIN - ELECTRICITY

Facts on File, 460 Park Avenue South, New York, New York 10016 (800) 443-8323; *The New Book of World Rankings.*

Penn Well Publishing Company, 1421 South Sheridan Road, P.O. Box 1260, Tulsa, Oklahoma 74101 (800) 752-9764; *International Energy Statistics Sourcebook.*

Statistical Office of the United Nations, Publishing Service, New York, New York 10017 (800) 253-9646; *Statistical Yearbook,* and *Survey of Economic and Social Conditions in Africa.*

Times Books, 201 East 50th Street, New York, New York 10022 (212) 751-2600; *The Economist Book of Vital World Statistics.*

United Nations Economic Commission for Africa, Africa Hall, P.O. Box 3001, Addis Ababa, Ethiopia (Telephone Number in U.S. (800) 253-9646); *African Statistical Yearbook.*

BENIN - EMPLOYMENT

Euromonitor Publications Limited, 87-88 Turnmill Street, London EC1M 5QU, England; *International Marketing Data and Statistics.*

Facts on File, 460 Park Avenue South, New York, New York 10016 (800) 443-8323; *The New Book of World Rankings.*

Federal Statistical Office, Gustav - Stresemann - Ring 11, D-6200 Wiesbaden, Germany; *Benin.*

International Labour Office, I.L.O. Publications, CH-1211, Geneva 22, Switzerland; *Yearbook of Labour Statistics.*

Statistical Office of the United Nations, Publishing Service, New York, New York 10017 (800) 253-9646; *Survey of Economic and Social Conditions in Africa.*

United Nations Economic Commission for Africa, Africa Hall, P.O. Box 3001, Addis Ababa, Ethiopia (Telephone Number in U.S. (800) 253-9646); *African Statistical Yearbook.*

BENIN - ENERGY

Facts on File, 460 Park Avenue South, New York, New York 10016 (800) 443-8323; *The New Book of World Rankings.*

Food and Agricultural Organization of the United Nations (FAO) Via delle Terme di Caracalla, 00100 Rome, Italy (Telephone Number in U.S. (202) 606-7828); *The State of Food and Agriculture.*

G.K. Hall and Company, 70 Lincoln Street, Boston, Massachusetts 02111 (617) 423-3990; *The World in Figures.*

Penn Well Publishing Company, 1421 South Sheridan Road, P.O. Box 1260, Tulsa, Oklahoma 74101 (800) 752-9764; *International Energy Statistics Sourcebook.*

Statistical Office of the United Nations, Publishing Service, New York, New York 10017 (800) 253-9646; *World Energy Supplies.*

Times Books, 201 East 50th Street, New York, New York 10022 (212) 751-2600; *The Economist Book of Vital World Statistics.*

United Nations Economic Commission for Africa, Africa Hall, P.O. Box 3001, Addis Ababa, Ethiopia (Telephone Number in U.S. (800) 253-9646); *African Statistical Yearbook.*

BENIN - EXCHANGE RATES

African Development Bank, 01 BP 1387, Abidjan 01, Cote D'Ivoire; *Selected Statistics on Regional Member Countries.*

Euromonitor Publications Limited, 87-88 Turnmill Street, London EC1M 5QU, England; *International Marketing Data and Statistics.*

International Monetary Fund, 700 Nineteenth Street, NW, Washington, D.C. 20431 (202) 623-7000; *International Financial Statistics.*

Statistical Office of the United Nations, Publishing Service, New York, New York 10017 (800) 253-9646; *Foreign Trade Statistics for Africa.*

BENIN - EXCISE TAXES - See BENIN - TAXATION

BENIN - EXPORTS

African Development Bank, 01 BP 1387, Abidjan 01, Cote D'Ivoire; *Selected Statistics on Regional Member Countries.*

The Economist Intelligence Unit, 111 West 57th Street, New York, New York 10019 (800) 938-4685; *The World Market Atlas.*

Euromonitor Publications Limited, 87-88 Turnmill Street, London EC1M 5QU, England; *International Marketing Data and Statistics.*

Food and Agricultural Organization of the United Nations (FAO) Via delle Terme di Caracalla, 00100 Rome, Italy (Telephone Number in U.S. (202) 606-7828); *The State of Food and Agriculture.*

G.K. Hall and Company, 70 Lincoln Street, Boston, Massachusetts 02111 (617) 423-3990; *The World in Figures.*

International Monetary Fund, 700 Nineteenth Street, NW, Washington, D.C. 20431 (202) 623-7000; *Direction of Trade Statistics.*

Statistical Office of the United Nations, Publishing Service, New York, New York 10017 (800) 253-9646; *Foreign Trade Statistics for Africa,* and *Survey of Economic and Social Conditions in Africa.*

Times Books, 201 East 50th Street, New York, New York 10022 (212) 751-2600; *The Economist Book of Vital World Statistics.*

United Nations Economic Commission for Africa, Africa Hall, P.O. Box 3001, Addis Ababa, Ethiopia (Telephone Number in U.S. (800) 253-9646); *African Statistical Yearbook.*

The World Bank, 1818 H Street, NW, Washington, D.C. 20433 (202) 477-1234; *World Tables.*

BENIN - EXTERNAL INDEBTEDNESS

African Development Bank, 01 BP 1387, Abidjan 01, Cote D'Ivoire; *Selected Statistics on Regional Member Countries.*

Statistical Office of the United Nations, Publishing Service, New York, New York 10017 (800) 253-9646; *Survey of Economic and Social Conditions in Africa.*

The World Bank, 1818 H Street, NW, Washington, D.C. 20433 (202) 477-1234; *World Tables.*

BENIN - EXTERNAL TRADE

African Development Bank, 01 BP 1387, Abidjan 01, Cote D'Ivoire; *Selected Statistics on Regional Member Countries.*

Food and Agricultural Organization of the United Nations (FAO) Via delle Terme di Caracalla, 00100 Rome, Italy (Telephone Number in U.S. (202) 606-7828); *The State of Food and Agriculture.*

Food and Agricultural Organization of the United Nations (FAO), Via delle Terme di Caracalla, 00100 Rome, Italy (Telephone Number in U.S. (202) 606-7828); *Trade Yearbook.*

G.K. Hall and Company, 70 Lincoln Street, Boston, Massachusetts 02111 (617) 423-3990; *The World in Figures.*

Statistical Office of the United Nations, Publishing Service, New York, New York 10017 (800) 253-9646; *International Trade Statistics Yearbook,* and *Statistical Yearbook.*

BENIN - FARM CROPS - See BENIN - CROPS Figures.

BENIN - FEMALE WORKING POPULATION - See BENIN - EMPLOYMENT

BENIN - FERTILITY RATES

Facts on File, 460 Park Avenue South, New York, New York 10016 (800) 443-8323; *The New Book of World Rankings.*

Statistical Office of the United Nations, Publishing Service, New York, New York 10017 (800) 253-9646; *Survey of Economic and Social Conditions in Africa.*

Times Books, 201 East 50th Street, New York, New York 10022 (212) 751-2600; *The Economist Book of Vital World Statistics.*

The World Bank, 1818 H Street, NW, Washington, D.C. 20433 (202) 477-1234; *World Tables.*

BENIN - FERTILIZER

Food and Agricultural Organization of the United Nations (FAO), Via delle Terme di Caracalla, 00100 Rome, Italy (Telephone Number in U.S. (202) 606-7828); *Fertilizer Yearbook,* and *The State of Food and Agriculture.*

Statistical Office of the United Nations, Publishing Service, New York, New York 10017 (800) 253-9646; *Statistical Yearbook.*

BENIN - FINANCE

African Development Bank, 01 BP 1387, Abidjan 01, Cote D'Ivoire; *Selected Statistics on Regional Member Countries.*

Facts on File, 460 Park Avenue South, New York, New York 10016 (800) 443-8323; *The New Book of World Rankings.*

Federal Statistical Office, Gustav - Stresemann - Ring 11, D-6200 Wiesbaden, Germany; *Benin.*

G.K. Hall and Company, 70 Lincoln Street, Boston, Massachusetts 02111 (617) 423-3990; *The World in Figures.*

United Nations Economic Commission for Africa, Africa Hall, P.O. Box 3001, Addis Ababa, Ethiopia (Telephone Number in U.S. (800) 253-9646); *African Statistical Yearbook.*

BENIN - FISHERIES

Facts on File, 460 Park Avenue South, New York, New York 10016 (800) 443-8323; *The New Book of World Rankings.*

Federal Statistical Office, Gustav - Stresemann - Ring 11, D-6200 Wiesbaden, Germany; *Benin.*

Food and Agricultural Organization of the United Nations (FAO) Via delle Terme di Caracalla, 00100 Rome, Italy (Telephone Number in U.S. (202) 606-7828); *The State of Food and Agriculture,* and *Yearbook of Fishery Statistics.*

Statistical Office of the United Nations, Publishing Service, New York, New York 10017 (800) 253-9646; *Statistical Yearbook,* and *Survey of Economic and Social Conditions in Africa.*

United Nations Economic Commission for Africa, Africa Hall, P.O. Box 3001, Addis Ababa, Ethiopia (Telephone Number in U.S. (800) 253-9646); *African Statistical Yearbook.*

BENIN - FOOD

African Development Bank, 01 BP 1387, Abidjan 01, Cote D'Ivoire; *Selected Statistics on Regional Member Countries.*

Food and Agricultural Organization of the United Nations (FAO) Via delle Terme di Caracalla, 00100 Rome, Italy (Telephone Number in U.S. (202) 606-7828); *Production Yearbook,* and *The State of Food and Agriculture.*

G.K. Hall and Company, 70 Lincoln Street, Boston, Massachusetts 02111 (617) 423-3990; *The World in Figures.*

BENIN - FOREIGN AID

G.K. Hall and Company, 70 Lincoln Street, Boston, Massachusetts 02111 (617) 423-3990; *The World in Figures.*

BENIN - FOREIGN TRADE

Euromonitor Publications Limited, 87-88 Turnmill Street, London EC1M 5QU, England; *International Marketing Data and Statistics.*

Facts on File, 460 Park Avenue South, New York, New York 10016 (800) 443-8323; *The New Book of World Rankings.*

Federal Statistical Office, Gustav - Stresemann - Ring 11, D-6200 Wiesbaden, Germany; *Benin.*

Food and Agricultural Organization of the United Nations (FAO) Via delle Terme di Caracalla, 00100 Rome, Italy (Telephone Number in U.S. (202) 653-2400); *The State of Food and Agriculture.*

G.K. Hall and Company, 70 Lincoln Street, Boston, Massachusetts 02111 (617) 423-3990; *The World in Figures.*

Organisation for Economic Co-operation and Development (OECD), 2 rue Andre-Pascal, 75 Paris 16, France, *Trade by Commodities.*

Statistical Office of the United Nations, Publishing Service, New York, New York 10017 (800) 253-9646; *Foreign Trade Statistics for Africa, Statistical Yearbook,* and *Trade in Manufactures of Developing Countries.*

United Nations Economic Commission for Africa, Africa Hall, P.O. Box 3001, Addis Ababa, Ethiopia (Telephone Number in U.S. (800) 253-9646); *African Statistical Yearbook.*

The World Bank, 1818 H Street, NW, Washington, D.C. 20433 (202) 477-1234; *World Tables.*

BENIN - FORESTRY AND FOREST PRODUCTS

Facts on File, 460 Park Avenue South, New York, New York 10016 (800) 443-8323; *The New Book of World Rankings.*

Federal Statistical Office, Gustav - Stresemann - Ring 11, D-6200 Wiesbaden, Germany; *Benin.*

Food and Agricultural Organization of the United Nations (FAO) Via delle Terme di Caracalla, 00100 Rome, Italy (Telephone Number in U.S. (202) 606-7828); *The State of Food and Agriculture,* and *Yearbook of Forest Products.*

G.K. Hall and Company, 70 Lincoln Street, Boston, Massachusetts 02111 (617) 423-3990; *The World in Figures.*

Statistical Office of the United Nations, Publishing Service, New York, New York 10017 (800) 253-9646; *Statistical Yearbook.*

United Nations Economic Commission for Africa, Africa Hall, P.O. Box 3001, Addis Ababa, Ethiopia (Telephone Number in U.S. (800) 253-9646); *African Statistical Yearbook.*

United Nations Educational, Scientific and Cultural Organization (UNESCO), 7 Place de Fontenoy, F-75700 Paris, France (Telephone Number in U.S. (212) 963-5981); *Statistical Yearbook.*

BENIN - GAS PRODUCTION - See BENIN - MINING AND MINERAL PRODUCTS

BENIN - GENERAL INDUSTRIAL STATISTICS

Federal Statistical Office, Gustav - Stresemann - Ring 11, D-6200 Wiesbaden, Germany; *Benin.*

BENIN - GENERAL MORTALITY

Statistical Office of the United Nations, Publishing Service, New York, New York 10017 (800) 253-9646; *Demographic Yearbook.*

BENIN - GEOGRAPHIC DATA

Facts on File, 460 Park Avenue South, New York, New York 10016 (800) 443-8323; *The New Book of World Rankings.*

Federal Statistical Office, Gustav - Stresemann - Ring 11, D-6200 Wiesbaden, Germany; *Benin.*

BENIN - GOATS - See BENIN - LIVESTOCK AND POULTRY

BENIN - GOLD HOLDINGS

International Monetary Fund, 700 Nineteenth Street, NW, Washington, D.C. 20431 (202) 623-7000; *International Financial Statistics.*

Statistical Office of the United Nations, Publishing Service, New York, New York 10017 (800) 253-9646; *Statistical Yearbook.*

The World Bank, 1818 H Street, NW, Washington, D.C. 20433 (202) 477-1234; *World Tables.*

BENIN - GOLD PRODUCTION AND CONSUMPTION - See BENIN - MINING AND MINERAL PRODUCTS

BENIN - GOVERNMENT

G.K. Hall and Company, 70 Lincoln Street, Boston, Massachusetts 02111 (617) 423-3990; *The World in Figures.*

BENIN - GOVERNMENT EXPENDITURES

The World Bank, 1818 H Street, NW, Washington, D.C. 20433 (202) 477-1234; *World Tables.*

BENIN - GOVERNMENT REVENUES

International Monetary Fund, 700 Nineteenth Street, NW, Washington, D.C. 20431 (202) 623-7000; *Government Finance Statistics Yearbook.*

Statistical Office of the United Nations, Publishing Service, New York, New York 10017 (800) 253-9646; *Survey of Economic and Social Conditions in Africa.*

The World Bank, 1818 H Street, NW, Washington, D.C. 20433 (202) 477-1234; *World Tables.*

BENIN - GRAIN PRODUCTION - See BENIN - CROPS

BENIN - GRANTS

International Monetary Fund, 700 Nineteenth Street, NW, Washington, D.C. 20431 (202) 623-7000; *Government Finance Statistics Yearbook.*

BENIN - GROSS DOMESTIC PRODUCT

African Development Bank, 01 BP 1387, Abidjan 01, Cote D'Ivoire; *Selected Statistics on Regional Member Countries.*

The Economist Intelligence Unit, 111 West 57th Street, New York, New York 10019 (800) 938-4685; *The World Market Atlas.*

Euromonitor Publications Limited, 87-88 Turnmill Street, London EC1M 5QU, England; *International Marketing Data and Statistics.*

Facts on File, 460 Park Avenue South, New York, New York 10016 (800) 443-8323; *The New Book of World Rankings.*

G.K. Hall and Company, 70 Lincoln Street, Boston, Massachusetts 02111 (617) 423-3990; *The World in Figures.*

Statistical Office of the United Nations, Publishing Service, New York, New York 10017 (800) 253-9646; *Statistical Yearbook,* and *Survey of Economic and Social Conditions in Africa.*

Times Books, 201 East 50th Street, New York, New York 10022 (212) 751-2600; *The Economist Book of Vital World Statistics.*

United Nations Economic Commission for Africa, Africa Hall, P.O. Box 3001, Addis Ababa, Ethiopia (Telephone Number in U.S. (800) 253-9646); *African Statistical Yearbook.*

The World Bank, 1818 H Street, NW, Washington, D.C. 20433 (202) 477-1234; *World Tables.*

BENIN - GROSS NATIONAL PRODUCT

Euromonitor Publications Limited, 87-88 Turnmill Street, London EC1M 5QU, England; *International Marketing Data and Statistics.*

The World Bank, 1818 H Street, NW, Washington, D.C. 20433 (202) 477-1234; *World Tables.*

U.S. Arms Control and Disarmament Agency, 320 Twenty-first Street, NW, Washington, D.C. 20451 (202) 647-8677; *World Military Expenditures and Arms Transfers.*

BENIN - GROUNDNUTS PRODUCTION - See BENIN - CROPS

BENIN - HEALTH

African Development Bank, 01 BP 1387, Abidjan 01, Cote D'Ivoire; *Selected Statistics on Regional Member Countries.*

Facts on File, 460 Park Avenue South, New York, New York 10016 (800) 443-8323; *The New Book of World Rankings.*

Federal Statistical Office, Gustav - Stresemann - Ring 11, D-6200 Wiesbaden, Germany; *Benin.*

G.K. Hall and Company, 70 Lincoln Street, Boston, Massachusetts 02111 (617) 423-3990; *The World in Figures.*

Statistical Office of the United Nations, Publishing Service, New York, New York 10017 (800) 253-9646; *Statistical Yearbook.*

Times Books, 201 East 50th Street, New York, New York 10022 (212) 751-2600; *The Economist Book of Vital World Statistics.*

United Nations Economic Commission for Africa, Africa Hall, P.O. Box 3001, Addis Ababa, Ethiopia (Telephone Number in U.S. (800) 253-9646); *African Statistical Yearbook.*

World Health Organization, Office of Publications, Avenue Appia, CH-1211 Geneva 27, Switzerland (Telephone Number in U.S. (518) 436-9686); *World Health Statistics Annual.*

BENIN - HIDE PRODUCTION

Food and Agricultural Organization of the United Nations (FAO), Via delle Terme di Caracalla, 00100 Rome, Italy (Telephone Number in U.S. (202) 606-7828); *Production Yearbook.*

BENIN - HIGHWAYS

G.K. Hall and Company, 70 Lincoln Street, Boston, Massachusetts 02111 (617) 423-3990; *The World in Figures.*

International Road Federation, 525 School Street, SW, Washington, D.C. 20024 (202) 554-2106; *World Road Statistics.*

Statistical Office of the United Nations, Publishing Service, New York, New York 10017 (800) 253-9646; *Survey of Economic and Social Conditions in Africa.*

United Nations Economic Commission for Africa, Africa Hall, P.O. Box 3001, Addis Ababa, Ethiopia (Telephone Number in U.S. (800) 253-9646); *African Statistical Yearbook.*

BENIN - HORSES - See BENIN - LIVESTOCK AND POULTRY

BENIN - HOURS OF WORK - See BENIN - EMPLOYMENT

BENIN - HOUSING AND HOUSING UNITS

Facts on File, 460 Park Avenue South, New York, New York 10016 (800) 443-8323; *The New Book of World Rankings.*

BENIN - ILLITERATE POPULATION

The Economist Intelligence Unit, 111 West 57th Street, New York, New York 10019 (800) 938-4685; *The World Market Atlas.*

G.K. Hall and Company, 70 Lincoln Street, Boston, Massachusetts 02111 (617) 423-3990; *The World in Figures.*

United Nations Educational, Scientific and Cultural Organization (UNESCO), 7 Place de Fontenoy, F-75700 Paris, France (Telephone Number in U.S. (212) 963-5981); *Statistical Yearbook.*

BENIN - IMPORTS

African Development Bank, 01 BP 1387, Abidjan 01, Cote D'Ivoire; *Selected Statistics on Regional Member Countries.*

The Economist Intelligence Unit, 111 West 57th Street, New York, New York 10019 (800) 938-4685; *The World Market Atlas.*

Euromonitor Publications Limited, 87-88 Turnmill Street, London EC1M 5QU, England; *International Marketing Data and Statistics.*

Food and Agricultural Organization of the United Nations (FAO) Via delle Terme di Caracalla, 00100 Rome, Italy (Telephone Number in U.S. (202) 606-7828); *The State of Food and Agriculture.*

G.K. Hall and Company, 70 Lincoln Street, Boston, Massachusetts 02111 (617) 423-3990; *The World in Figures.*

International Monetary Fund, 700 Nineteenth Street, NW, Washington, D.C. 20431 (202) 623-7000; *Direction of Trade Statistics,* and *Government Finance Statistics Yearbook.*

Statistical Office of the United Nations, Publishing Service, New York, New York 10017 (800) 253-9646; *Foreign Trade Statistics for Africa,* and *Survey of Economic and Social Conditions in Africa.*

United Nations Economic Commission for Africa, Africa Hall, P.O. Box 3001, Addis Ababa, Ethiopia (Telephone Number in U.S. (800) 253-9646); *African Statistical Yearbook.*

Times Books, 201 East 50th Street, New York, New York 10022 (212) 751-2600; *The Economist Book of Vital World Statistics.*

The World Bank, 1818 H Street, NW, Washington, D.C. 20433 (202) 477-1234; *World Tables.*

BENIN - INCOME TAXES - See BENIN - TAXATION

BENIN - INDUSTRY

Euromonitor Publications Limited, 87-88 Turnmill Street, London EC1M 5QU, England; *International Marketing Data and Statistics.*

Facts on File, 460 Park Avenue South, New York, New York 10016 (800) 443-8323; *The New Book of World Rankings.*

Federal Statistical Office, Gustav - Stresemann - Ring 11, D-6200 Wiesbaden, Germany; *Benin.*

G.K. Hall and Company, 70 Lincoln Street, Boston, Massachusetts 02111 (617) 423-3990; *The World in Figures.*

International Labour Office, I.L.O. Publications, CH-1211, Geneva 22, Switzerland; *Yearbook of Labour Statistics.*

Statistical Office of the United Nations, Publishing Service, New York, New York 10017 (800) 253-9646; *Survey of Economic and Social Conditions in Africa.*

Times Books, 201 East 50th Street, New York, New York 10022 (212) 751-2600; *The Economist Book of Vital World Statistics.*

United Nations Economic Commission for Africa, Africa Hall, P.O. Box 3001, Addis Ababa, Ethiopia (Telephone Number in U.S. (800) 253-9646); *African Statistical Yearbook.*

The World Bank, 1818 H Street, NW, Washington, D.C. 20433 (202) 477-1234; *World Tables.*

BENIN - INFANT AND MATERNAL MORTALITY

Statistical Office of the United Nations, Publishing Service, New York, New York 10017 (800) 253-9646; *Demographic Yearbook,* and *Survey of Economic and Social Conditions in Africa.*

Times Books, 201 East 50th Street, New York, New York 10022 (212) 751-2600; *The Economist Book of Vital World Statistics.*

The World Bank, 1818 H Street, NW, Washington, D.C. 20433 (202) 477-1234; *World Tables.*

BENIN - INTERNATIONAL RESERVES EXCLUDING GOLD

African Development Bank, 01 BP 1387, Abidjan 01, Cote D'Ivoire; *Selected Statistics on Regional Member Countries.*

The World Bank, 1818 H Street, NW, Washington, D.C. 20433 (202) 477-1234; *World Tables.*

BENIN - IRON ORE PRODUCTION AND CONSUMPTION - See BENIN - MINING AND MINERAL PRODUCTS

BENIN - IRRIGATION

Euromonitor Publications Limited, 87-88 Turnmill Street, London EC1M 5QU, England; *International Marketing Data and Statistics.*

BENIN - LABOR FORCE

African Development Bank, 01 BP 1387, Abidjan 01, Cote D'Ivoire; *Selected Statistics on Regional Member Countries.*

Euromonitor Publications Limited, 87-88 Turnmill Street, London EC1M 5QU, England; *International Marketing Data and Statistics.*

Facts on File, 460 Park Avenue South, New York, New York 10016 (800) 443-8323; *The New Book of World Rankings.*

Food and Agricultural Organization of the United Nations (FAO) Via delle Terme di Caracalla, 00100 Rome, Italy (Telephone Number in U.S. (202) 606-7828); *The State of Food and Agriculture.*

G.K. Hall and Company, 70 Lincoln Street, Boston, Massachusetts 02111 (617) 423-3990; *The World in Figures.*

Times Books, 201 East 50th Street, New York, New York 10022 (212) 751-2600; *The Economist Book of Vital World Statistics.*

The World Bank, 1818 H Street, NW, Washington, D.C. 20433 (202) 477-1234; *World Tables.*

BENIN - LABOR PRODUCTIVITY

International Labour Office, I.L.O. Publications, CH-1211, Geneva 22, Switzerland; *Yearbook of Labour Statistics.*

BENIN - LAND USE

Euromonitor Publications Limited, 87-88 Turnmill Street, London EC1M 5QU, England; *International Marketing Data and Statistics.*

Food and Agricultural Organization of the United Nations (FAO), Via delle Terme di Caracalla, 00100 Rome, Italy (Telephone Number in U.S. (202) 606-7828); *Production Yearbook.*

G.K. Hall and Company, 70 Lincoln Street, Boston, Massachusetts 02111 (617) 423-3990; *The World in Figures.*

BENIN - LIBRARIES

Facts on File, 460 Park Avenue South, New York, New York 10016 (800) 443-8323; *The New Book of World Rankings.*

United Nations Educational, Scientific and Cultural Organization (UNESCO), 7 Place de Fontenoy, F-75700 Paris, France (Telephone Number in U.S. (212) 963-5981); *Statistical Yearbook.*

BENIN - LIFE EXPECTANCY

African Development Bank, 01 BP 1387, Abidjan 01, Cote D'Ivoire; *Selected Statistics on Regional Member Countries.*

BENIN - LITERACY RATE

Statistical Office of the United Nations, Publishing Service, New York, New York 10017 (800) 253-9646; *Survey of Economic and Social Conditions in Africa.*

BENIN - LIVESTOCK AND POULTRY

Euromonitor Publications Limited, 87-88 Turnmill Street, London EC1M 5QU, England; *International Marketing Data and Statistics.*

Facts on File, 460 Park Avenue South, New York, New York 10016 (800) 443-8323; *The New Book of World Rankings.*

Food and Agricultural Organization of the United Nations (FAO), Via delle Terme di Caracalla, 00100 Rome, Italy (Telephone Number in U.S. (202) 606-7828); *Production Yearbook,* and *The State of Food and Agriculture.*

G.K. Hall and Company, 70 Lincoln Street, Boston, Massachusetts 02111 (617) 423-3990; *The World in Figures.*

Statistical Office of the United Nations, Publishing Service, New York, New York 10017 (800) 253-9646; *Statistical Yearbook,* and *Survey of Economic and Social Conditions in Africa.*

United Nations Economic Commission for Africa, Africa Hall, P.O. Box 3001, Addis Ababa, Ethiopia (Telephone Number in U.S. (800) 253-9646); *African Statistical Yearbook.*

BENIN - LIVING LEVELS

G.K. Hall and Company, 70 Lincoln Street, Boston, Massachusetts 02111 (617) 423-3990; *The World in Figures.*

Times Books, 201 East 50th Street, New York, New York 10022 (212) 751-2600; *The Economist Book of Vital World Statistics.*

BENIN - MAIL - NUMBER OF ITEMS SENT OR RECEIVED

Statistical Office of the United Nations, Publishing Service, New York, New York 10017 (800) 253-9646; *Statistical Yearbook.*

BENIN - MANUFACTURING

Facts on File, 460 Park Avenue South, New York, New York 10016 (800) 443-8323; *The New Book of World Rankings.*

G.K. Hall and Company, 70 Lincoln Street, Boston, Massachusetts 02111 (617) 423-3990; *The World in Figures.*

Times Books, 201 East 50th Street, New York, New York 10022 (212) 751-2600; *The Economist Book of Vital World Statistics.*

Statistical Office of the United Nations, Publishing Service, New York, New York 10017 (800) 253-9646; *Survey of Economic and Social Conditions in Africa.*

United Nations Economic Commission for Africa, Africa Hall, P.O. Box 3001, Addis Ababa, Ethiopia (Telephone Number in U.S. (800) 253-9646); *African Statistical Yearbook.*

The World Bank, 1818 H Street, NW, Washington, D.C. 20433 (202) 477-1234; *World Tables.*

BENIN - MARRIAGE RATES

Facts on File, 460 Park Avenue South, New York, New York 10016 (800) 443-8323; *The New Book of World Rankings.*

BENIN - MEAT PRODUCTION - See BENIN - LIVESTOCK AND POULTRY

BENIN - MERCHANT SHIPPING

G.K. Hall and Company, 70 Lincoln Street, Boston, Massachusetts 02111 (617) 423-3990; *The World in Figures.*

Statistical Office of the United Nations, Publishing Service, New York, New York 10017 (800) 253-9646; *Statistical Yearbook.*

Times Books, 201 East 50th Street, New York, New York 10022 (212) 751-2600; *The Economist Book of Vital World Statistics.*

United Nations Economic Commission for Africa, Africa Hall, P.O. Box 3001, Addis Ababa, Ethiopia (Telephone Number in U.S. (800) 253-9646); *African Statistical Yearbook.*

BENIN - MILITARY

G.K. Hall and Company, 70 Lincoln Street, Boston, Massachusetts 02111 (617) 423-3990; *The World in Figures.*

The International Institute for Strategic Studies, 23 Tavistock Street, London WC2E 7NQ, England; *The Military Balance.*

U.S. Arms Control and Disarmament Agency, 320 Twenty-first Street, NW, Washington, D.C. 20451 (202) 647-8677; *World Military Expenditures and Arms Transfers.*

BENIN - MILK PRODUCTION - See BENIN - DAIRY PRODUCTS

BENIN - MILLET PRODUCTION - See BENIN - CROPS

BENIN - MINING AND MINERAL PRODUCTS

Facts on File, 460 Park Avenue South, New York, New York 10016 (800) 443-8323; *The New Book of World Rankings.*

G.K. Hall and Company, 70 Lincoln Street, Boston, Massachusetts 02111 (617) 423-3990; *The World in Figures.*

Penn Well Publishing Company, 1421 South Sheridan Road, P.O. Box 1260, Tulsa, Oklahoma 74101 (800) 752-9764; *International Energy Statistics Sourcebook.*

Statistical Office of the United Nations, Publishing Service, New York, New York 10017 (800) 253-9646; *Statistical Yearbook.*

United Nations Economic Commission for Africa, Africa Hall, P.O. Box 3001, Addis Ababa, Ethiopia (Telephone Number in U.S. (800) 253-9646); *African Statistical Yearbook.*

BENIN - MONEY EXCHANGE RATE

Euromonitor Publications Limited, 87-88 Turnmill Street, London EC1M 5QU, England; *International Marketing Data and Statistics.*

International Monetary Fund, 700 Nineteenth Street, NW, Washington, D.C. 20431 (202) 623-7000; *International Financial Statistics.*

Statistical Office of the United Nations, Publishing Service, New York, New York 10017 (800) 253-9646; *Statistical Yearbook.*

BENIN - MONEY RESERVES

Euromonitor Publications Limited, 87-88 Turnmill Street, London EC1M 5QU, England; *International Marketing Data and Statistics.*

BENIN - MONEY SUPPLY

African Development Bank, 01 BP 1387, Abidjan 01, Cote D'Ivoire; *Selected Statistics on Regional Member Countries.*

Euromonitor Publications Limited, 87-88 Turnmill Street, London EC1M 5QU, England; *International Marketing Data and Statistics.*

Federal Statistical Office, Gustav - Stresemann - Ring 11, D-6200 Wiesbaden, Germany; *Benin.*

G.K. Hall and Company, 70 Lincoln Street, Boston, Massachusetts 02111 (617) 423-3990; *The World in Figures.*

International Monetary Fund, 700 Nineteenth Street, NW, Washington, D.C. 20431 (202) 623-7000; *International Financial Statistics.*

Statistical Office of the United Nations, Publishing Service, New York, New York 10017 (800) 253-9646; *Statistical Yearbook.*

The World Bank, 1818 H Street, NW, Washington, D.C. 20433 (202) 477-1234; *World Tables.*

BENIN - MOTION PICTURES

Statistical Office of the United Nations, Publishing Service, New York, New York 10017 (800) 253-9646; *Statistical Yearbook.*

BENIN - MOTOR VEHICLE TAXES - See BENIN - TAXATION

BENIN - MOTOR VEHICLES IN USE

G.K. Hall and Company, 70 Lincoln Street, Boston, Massachusetts 02111 (617) 423-3990; *The World in Figures.*

International Road Federation, 525 School Street, SW, Washington, D.C. 20024 (202) 554-2106; *World Road Statistics.*

Statistical Office of the United Nations, Publishing Service, New York, New York 10017 (800) 253-9646; *Statistical Yearbook,* and *Survey of Economic and Social Conditions in Africa.*

Times Books, 201 East 50th Street, New York, New York 10022 (212) 751-2600; *The Economist Book of Vital World Statistics.*

BENIN - MUSEUMS

Facts on File, 460 Park Avenue South, New York, New York 10016 (800) 443-8323; *The New Book of World Rankings.*

United Nations Educational, Scientific and Cultural Organization (UNESCO), 7 Place de Fontenoy, F-75700 Paris, France (Telephone Number in U.S. (212) 963-5981); *Statistical Yearbook.*

BENIN - NATALITY - See BENIN - BIRTH RATE

BENIN - NATIONAL ACCOUNTS

African Development Bank, 01 BP 1387, Abidjan 01, Cote D'Ivoire; *Selected Statistics on Regional Member Countries.*

Federal Statistical Office, Gustav - Stresemann - Ring 11, D-6200 Wiesbaden, Germany; *Benin.*

Statistical Office of the United Nations, Publishing Service, New York, New York 10017 (800) 253-9646; *National Accounts Statistics,* and *Statistical Yearbook.*

United Nations Economic Commission for Africa, Africa Hall, P.O. Box 3001, Addis Ababa, Ethiopia (Telephone Number in U.S. (800) 253-9646); *African Statistical Yearbook.*

BENIN - NATIONAL INCOME

Facts on File, 460 Park Avenue South, New York, New York 10016 (800) 443-8323; *The New Book of World Rankings.*

G.K. Hall and Company, 70 Lincoln Street, Boston, Massachusetts 02111 (617) 423-3990; *The World in Figures.*

Statistical Office of the United Nations, Publishing Service, New York, New York 10017 (800) 253-9646; *Statistical Yearbook.*

BENIN - NATIONAL PRODUCT

Facts on File, 460 Park Avenue South, New York, New York 10016 (800) 443-8323; *The New Book of World Rankings.*

Statistical Office of the United Nations, Publishing Service, New York, New York 10017 (800) 253-9646; *Statistical Yearbook.*

BENIN - NATURAL GAS PRODUCTION - See BENIN - MINING AND MINERAL PRODUCTS

BENIN - NET MATERIAL PRODUCT

Statistical Office of the United Nations, Publishing Service, New York, New York 10017 (800) 253-9646; *Statistical Yearbook.*

BENIN - NEWSPAPER PRODUCTION - See BENIN - FORESTRY AND FOREST PRODUCTS

BENIN - NEWSPRINT CONSUMPTION - See BENIN - FORESTRY AND FOREST PRODUCTS

BENIN - OCCUPATIONS - See BENIN - LABOR FORCE

BENIN - PAPER CONSUMPTION - See BENIN - FORESTRY AND FOREST PRODUCTS

BENIN - PEANUT PRODUCTION - See BENIN - CROPS

BENIN - PERIODICALS

United Nations Educational, Scientific and Cultural Organization (UNESCO), 7 Place de Fontenoy, F-75700 Paris, France (Telephone Number in U.S. (212) 963-5981); *Statistical Yearbook.*

BENIN - PESTICIDE USE

Food and Agricultural Organization of the United Nations (FAO) Via delle Terme di Caracalla, 00100 Rome, Italy (Telephone Number in U.S. (202) 606-7828); *The State of Food and Agriculture.*

BENIN - PETROLEUM INDUSTRY

Facts on File, 460 Park Avenue South, New York, New York 10016 (800) 443-8323; *The New Book of World Rankings.*

Food and Agricultural Organization of the United Nations (FAO) Via delle Terme di Caracalla, 00100 Rome, Italy (Telephone Number in U.S. (202) 606-7828); *The State of Food and Agriculture.*

G.K. Hall and Company, 70 Lincoln Street, Boston, Massachusetts 02111 (617) 423-3990; *The World in Figures.*

Penn Well Publishing Company, 1421 South Sheridan Road, P.O. Box 1260, Tulsa, Oklahoma 74101 (800) 752-9764; *International Energy Statistics Sourcebook.*

BENIN - PIGS - See BENIN - LIVESTOCK AND POULTRY

BENIN - POPULATION

African Development Bank, 01 BP 1387, Abidjan 01, Cote D'Ivoire; *Selected Statistics on Regional Member Countries.*

The Economist Intelligence Unit, 111 West 57th Street, New York, New York 10019 (800) 938-4685; *The World Market Atlas.*

Euromonitor Publications Limited, 87-88 Turnmill Street, London EC1M 5QU, England; *International Marketing Data and Statistics.*

Facts on File, 460 Park Avenue South, New York, New York 10016 (800) 443-8323; *The New Book of World Rankings.*

Federal Statistical Office, Gustav - Stresemann - Ring 11, D-6200 Wiesbaden, Germany; *Benin.*

Food and Agricultural Organization of the United Nations (FAO), Via delle Terme di Caracalla, 00100 Rome, Italy (Telephone Number in U.S. (202) 606-7828); *Production Yearbook.*

G.K. Hall and Company, 70 Lincoln Street, Boston, Massachusetts 02111 (617) 423-3990; *The World in Figures.*

International Labour Office, I.L.O. Publications, CH-1211, Geneva 22, Switzerland; *Yearbook of Labour Statistics.*

Statistical Office of the United Nations, Publishing Service, New York, New York 10017 (800) 253-9646; *Demographic Yearbook,* and *Statistical Yearbook,* and *Survey of Economic and Social Conditions in Africa.*

Times Books, 201 East 50th Street, New York, New York 10022 (212) 751-2600; *The Economist Book of Vital World Statistics.*

United Nations Educational, Scientific and Cultural Organization (UNESCO), 7 Place de Fontenoy, F-75700 Paris, France (Telephone Number in U.S. (212) 963-5981); *Statistical Yearbook.*

U.S. Arms Control and Disarmament Agency, 320 Twenty-first Street, NW, Washington, D.C. 20451 (202) 647-8677; *World Military Expenditures and Arms Transfers.*

World Health Organization, Office of Publications, Avenue Appia, CH-1211 Geneva 27, Switzerland (Telephone Number in U.S. (518) 436-9686); *World Health Statistics Annual.*

BENIN - POST OFFICES

Facts on File, 460 Park Avenue South, New York, New York 10016 (800) 443-8323; *The New Book of World Rankings.*

BENIN - POTATO PRODUCTION - See BENIN - CROPS

BENIN - PRICES

Facts on File, 460 Park Avenue South, New York, New York 10016 (800) 443-8323; *The New Book of World Rankings.*

Federal Statistical Office, Gustav - Stresemann - Ring 11, D-6200 Wiesbaden, Germany; *Benin.*

Food and Agricultural Organization of the United Nations (FAO), Via delle Terme di Caracalla, 00100 Rome, Italy (Telephone Number in U.S. (202) 606-7828); *Production Yearbook,* and *The State of Food and Agriculture.*

G.K. Hall and Company, 70 Lincoln Street, Boston, Massachusetts 02111 (617) 423-3990; *The World in Figures.*

International Labour Office, I.L.O. Publications, CH-1211, Geneva 22, Switzerland; *Yearbook of Labour Statistics.*

BENIN - PRINTING AND WRITING PAPER CONSUMPTION - See BENIN - FORESTRY AND FOREST PRODUCTS

BENIN - PRODUCTION

Facts on File, 460 Park Avenue South, New York, New York 10016 (800) 443-8323; *The New Book of World Rankings.*

G.K. Hall and Company, 70 Lincoln Street, Boston, Massachusetts 02111 (617) 423-3990; *The World in Figures.*

BENIN - PRODUCTIVITY

Euromonitor Publications Limited, 87-88 Turnmill Street, London EC1M 5QU, England; *International Marketing Data and Statistics.*

BENIN - PROPERTY TAXES

International Monetary Fund, 700 Nineteenth Street, NW, Washington, D.C. 20431 (202) 623-7000; *Government Finance Statistics Yearbook.*

BENIN - PUBLIC FINANCE

Facts on File, 460 Park Avenue South, New York, New York 10016 (800) 443-8323; *The New Book of World Rankings.*

Federal Statistical Office, Gustav - Stresemann - Ring 11, D-6200 Wiesbaden, Germany; *Benin.*

BENIN - RADIO BROADCASTING - See BENIN - BROADCASTING

BENIN - RAILWAYS

G.K. Hall and Company, 70 Lincoln Street, Boston, Massachusetts 02111 (617) 423-3990; *The World in Figures.*

Jane's Information Group, Sentinel House, 163 Brighton Road, Coulsdon, Surrey CR5 2NH, England (Telephone Number in U.S. (703) 683-3700); *Jane's World Railways.*

Statistical Office of the United Nations, Publishing Service, New York, New York 10017 (800) 253-9646; *Statistical Yearbook,* and *Survey of Economic and Social Conditions in Africa.*

United Nations Economic Commission for Africa, Africa Hall, P.O. Box 3001, Addis Ababa, Ethiopia (Telephone Number in U.S. (800) 253-9646); *African Statistical Yearbook.*

BENIN - RELIGION

Facts on File, 460 Park Avenue South, New York, New York 10016 (800) 443-8323; *The New Book of World Rankings.*

BENIN - RENT PRICES

International Labour Office, I.L.O. Publications, CH-1211, Geneva 22, Switzerland; *Yearbook of Labour Statistics.*

BENIN - RETAIL TRADE

Economist Publications Limited, 25 St. James's Street, London SW1A 1HG England; *The World in Figures.*

G.K. Hall and Company, 70 Lincoln Street, Boston, Massachusetts 02111 (617) 423-3990; *The World in Figures.*

BENIN - RICE PRODUCTION - See BENIN - CROPS

BENIN - ROOT AND TUBER PRODUCTION - See BENIN - CROPS

BENIN - ROUNDWOOD PRODUCTION - See BENIN - FORESTRY AND FOREST PRODUCTS

BENIN - RUBBER PRODUCTION

Facts on File, 460 Park Avenue South, New York, New York 10016 (800) 443-8323; *The New Book of World Rankings.*

BENIN - SAVINGS ACCOUNT DEPOSITS

International Monetary Fund, 700 Nineteenth Street, NW, Washington, D.C. 20431 (202) 623-7000; *International Financial Statistics.*

BENIN - SAWNWOOD PRODUCTION - See BENIN - FORESTRY AND FOREST PRODUCTS

BENIN - SENIOR CITIZENS

Facts on File, 460 Park Avenue South, New York, New York 10016 (800) 443-8323; *The New Book of World Rankings.*

BENIN - SESAME SEED PRODUCTION - See BENIN - CROPS

BENIN - SHEEP - See BENIN - LIVESTOCK AND POULTRY

BENIN - SILVER PRODUCTION AND CONSUMPTION - See BENIN - MINING AND MINERAL PRODUCTS

BENIN - SOCIAL DATA

African Development Bank, 01 BP 1387, Abidjan 01, Cote D'Ivoire; *Selected Statistics on Regional Member Countries.*

Facts on File, 460 Park Avenue South, New York, New York 10016 (800) 443-8323; *The New Book of World Rankings.*

G.K. Hall and Company, 70 Lincoln Street, Boston, Massachusetts 02111 (617) 423-3990; *The World in Figures.*

BENIN - STAMP TAXES AND DUTIES - See BENIN - TAXATION

BENIN - STATE BUDGET REVENUE AND EXPENDITURES

Euromonitor Publications Limited, 87-88 Turnmill Street, London EC1M 5QU, England; *International Marketing Data and Statistics.*

BENIN - STEEL PRODUCTION - See BENIN - MINING AND MINERAL PRODUCTS

BENIN - STOCKS - COMMODITY - MARKET PRICE - INDEX

Food and Agricultural Organization of the United Nations (FAO) Via delle Terme di Caracalla, 00100 Rome, Italy (Telephone Number in U.S. (202) 653-2400); *The State of Food and Agriculture.*

BENIN - SUGAR PRODUCTION - See BENIN - CROPS

BENIN - TAXATION

G.K. Hall and Company, 70 Lincoln Street, Boston, Massachusetts 02111 (617) 423-3990; *The World in Figures.*

International Monetary Fund, 700 Nineteenth Street, NW, Washington, D.C. 20431 (202) 623-7000; *Government Finance Statistics Yearbook.*

International Road Federation, 525 School Street, SW, Washington, D.C. 20024 (202) 554-2105; *World Road Statistics.*

The World Bank, 1818 H Street, NW, Washington, D.C. 20433 (202) 477-1234; *World Tables.*

BENIN - TELEGRAPH SERVICE

Statistical Office of the United Nations, Publishing Service, New York, New York 10017 (800) 253-9646; *Statistical Yearbook.*

BENIN - TELEPHONES IN USE

American Telephone and Telegraph Company, 26 Parsippany Road, Whippany, New Jersey 07981 (800) 338-4038; *The World's Telephones.*

G.K. Hall and Company, 70 Lincoln Street, Boston, Massachusetts 02111 (617) 423-3990; *The World in Figures.*

Statistical Office of the United Nations, Publishing Service, New York, New York 10017 (800) 253-9646; *Statistical Yearbook.*

BENIN - TELEVISION BROADCASTING - See BENIN - BROADCASTING

BENIN - TEXTILE INDUSTRY

G.K. Hall and Company, 70 Lincoln Street, Boston, Massachusetts 02111 (617) 423-3990; *The World in Figures.*

BENIN - TOBACCO PRODUCTION

Facts on File, 460 Park Avenue South, New York, New York 10016 (800) 443-8323; *The New Book of World Rankings.*

Statistical Office of the United Nations, Publishing Service, New York, New York 10017 (800) 253-9646; *Statistical Yearbook.*

BENIN - TOURISM

Facts on File, 460 Park Avenue South, New York, New York 10016 (800) 443-8323; *The New Book of World Rankings.*

Federal Statistical Office, Gustav - Stresemann - Ring 11, D-6200 Wiesbaden, Germany; *Benin.*

G.K. Hall and Company, 70 Lincoln Street, Boston, Massachusetts 02111 (617) 423-3990; *The World in Figures.*

Statistical Office of the United Nations, Publishing Service, New York, New York 10017 (800) 253-9646; *Statistical Yearbook.*

Times Books, 201 East 50th Street, New York, New York 10022 (212) 751-2600; *The Economist Book of Vital World Statistics.*

United Nations Economic Commission for Africa, Africa Hall, P.O. Box 3001, Addis Ababa, Ethiopia (Telephone Number in U.S. (800) 253-9646); *African Statistical Yearbook.*

BENIN - TRACTORS IN USE

Statistical Office of the United Nations, Publishing Service, New York, New York 10017 (800) 253-9646; *Statistical Yearbook.*

BENIN - TRADE - See BENIN - FOREIGN TRADE

BENIN - TRANSPORTATION AND COMMUNICATIONS

Facts on File, 460 Park Avenue South, New York, New York 10016 (800) 443-8323; *The New Book of World Rankings.*

Federal Statistical Office, Gustav - Stresemann - Ring 11, D-6200 Wiesbaden, Germany; *Benin.*

G.K. Hall and Company, 70 Lincoln Street, Boston, Massachusetts 02111 (617) 423-3990; *The World in Figures.*

United Nations Economic Commission for Africa, Africa Hall, P.O. Box 3001, Addis Ababa, Ethiopia (Telephone Number in U.S. (800) 253-9646); *African Statistical Yearbook.*

BENIN - TRAVEL FARES ABROAD

International Monetary Fund, 700 Nineteenth Street, NW, Washington, D.C. 20431 (202) 623-7000; *Government Finance Statistics Yearbook.*

BENIN - UNEMPLOYMENT

Euromonitor Publications Limited, 87-88 Turnmill Street, London EC1M 5QU, England; *International Marketing Data and Statistics.*

International Labour Office, I.L.O. Publications, CH-1211, Geneva 22, Switzerland; *Yearbook of Labour Statistics.*

BENIN - VITAL STATISTICS

Euromonitor Publications Limited, 87-88 Turnmill Street, London EC1M 5QU, England; *International Marketing Data and Statistics.*

G.K. Hall and Company, 70 Lincoln Street, Boston, Massachusetts 02111 (617) 423-3990; *The World in Figures.*

Statistical Office of the United Nations, Publishing Service, New York, New York 10017 (800) 253-9646; *Statistical Yearbook.*

World Health Organization, Office of Publications, Avenue Appia, CH-1211 Geneva 27, Switzerland (Telephone Number in U.S. (518) 436 9686); *World Health Statistics Annual.*

BENIN - WAGES

Federal Statistical Office, Gustav - Stresemann - Ring 11, D-6200 Wiesbaden, Germany; *Benin.*

G.K. Hall and Company, 70 Lincoln Street, Boston, Massachusetts 02111 (617) 423-3990; *The World in Figures.*

International Labour Office, I.L.O. Publications, CH-1211, Geneva 22, Switzerland; *Yearbook of Labour Statistics.*

BENIN - WEATHER

Facts on File, 460 Park Avenue South, New York, New York 10016 (800) 443-8323; *The New Book of World Rankings.*

G.K. Hall and Company, 70 Lincoln Street, Boston, Massachusetts 02111 (617) 423-3990; *The World in Figures.*

BENIN - WHEAT PRODUCTION - See BENIN - CROPS

BENIN - WINE PRODUCTION

Facts on File, 460 Park Avenue South, New York, New York 10016 (800) 443-8323; *The New Book of World Rankings.*

BENIN - WOOL PRODUCTION

Facts on File, 460 Park Avenue South, New York, New York 10016 (800) 443-8323; *The New Book of World Rankings.*

Bermuda - National Statistical Office

Statistical Department, Post Office Box 177, Hamilton, 5, Bermuda.

Bermuda - Primary Statistics Source

Statistical Department, Post Office Box 177, Hamilton, 5, Bermuda; *Bermuda Digest of Statistics.*

BERMUDA - AGRICULTURE

Facts on File, 460 Park Avenue South, New York, New York 10016 (800) 443-8323; *The New Book of World Rankings.*

Food and Agricultural Organization of the United Nations (FAO) Via delle Terme di Caracalla, 00100 Rome, Italy (Telephone Number in U.S. (202) 653-2400); *Production Yearbook, The State of Food and Agriculture,* and *Trade Yearbook.*

G.K. Hall and Company, 70 Lincoln Street, Boston, Massachusetts 02111 (617) 423-3990; *The World in Figures.*

Statistical Office of the United Nations, Publishing Service, New York, New York 10017 (800) 253-9646; *Statistical Yearbook.*

Times Books, 201 East 50th Street, New York, New York 10022 (212) 751-2600; *The Economist Book of Vital World Statistics.*

BERMUDA - AIRLINE SERVICE

Facts on File, 460 Park Avenue South, New York, New York 10016 (800) 443-8323; *The New Book of World Rankings.*

G.K. Hall and Company, 70 Lincoln Street, Boston, Massachusetts 02111 (617) 423-3990; *The World in Figures.*

BERMUDA - ALUMINUM PRODUCTION AND CONSUMPTION - See BERMUDA - MINING AND MINERAL PRODUCTS

BERMUDA - ANIMAL HEALTH

Food and Agricultural Organization of the United Nations (FAO), Via delle Terme di Caracalla, 00100 Rome, Italy (Telephone Number in U.S. (202) 653-2400); *Animal Health Yearbook.*

BERMUDA - AREA AND DENSITY OF POPULATION

Facts on File, 460 Park Avenue South, New York, New York 10016 (800) 443-8323; *The New Book of World Rankings.*

Food and Agricultural Organization of the United Nations (FAO) Via delle Terme di Caracalla, 00100 Rome, Italy (Telephone Number in U.S. (202) 653-2400); *The State of Food and Agriculture.*

G.K. Hall and Company, 70 Lincoln Street, Boston, Massachusetts 02111 (617) 423-3990; *The World in Figures.*

Statistical Office of the United Nations, Publishing Service, New York, New York 10017 (800) 253-9646; *Statistical Yearbook.*

BERMUDA - BALANCE OF PAYMENTS

The Economist Intelligence Unit, 111 West 57th Street, New York, New York 10019 (800) 938-4685; *The World Market Atlas.*

G.K. Hall and Company, 70 Lincoln Street, Boston, Massachusetts 02111 (617) 423-3990; *The World in Figures.*

BERMUDA - BANKING

Facts on File, 460 Park Avenue South, New York, New York 10016 (800) 443-8323; *The New Book of World Rankings.*

G.K. Hall and Company, 70 Lincoln Street, Boston, Massachusetts 02111 (617) 423-3990; *The World in Figures.*

BERMUDA - BARLEY PRODUCTION - See BERMUDA - CROPS

BERMUDA - BEER PRODUCTION

Facts on File, 460 Park Avenue South, New York, New York 10016 (800) 443-8323; *The New Book of World Rankings.*

BERMUDA - BIRTH RATES

Facts on File, 460 Park Avenue South, New York, New York 10016 (800) 443-8323; *The New Book of World Rankings.*

Statistical Office of the United Nations, Publishing Service, New York, New York 10017 (800) 253-9646; *Demographic Yearbook,* and *Statistical Yearbook.*

World Health Organization, Office of Publications, Avenue Appia, CH-1211 Geneva 27, Switzerland (Telephone Number in U.S. (518) 436-9686); *World Health Statistics Annual.*

BERMUDA - BONDS

G.K. Hall and Company, 70 Lincoln Street, Boston, Massachusetts 02111 (617) 423-3990; *The World in Figures.*

BERMUDA - BOOK PRODUCTION

G.K. Hall and Company, 70 Lincoln Street, Boston, Massachusetts 02111 (617) 423-3990; *The World in Figures.*

BERMUDA - BROADCASTING

Billboard Limited, P.O. Box 9027, 1006 AA Amsterdam, The Netherlands (Telephone Number in U.S. (212) 764-7300); *World Radio TV Handbook.*

Facts on File, 460 Park Avenue South, New York, New York 10016 (800) 443-8323; *The New Book of World Rankings.*

G.K. Hall and Company, 70 Lincoln Street, Boston, Massachusetts 02111 (617) 423-3990; *The World in Figures.*

Times Books, 201 East 50th Street, New York, New York 10022 (212) 751-2600; *The Economist Book of Vital World Statistics.*

BERMUDA - BUILDING CONSTRUCTION - See BERMUDA - CONSTRUCTION INDUSTRY

BERMUDA - BUSINESS

G.K. Hall and Company, 70 Lincoln Street, Boston, Massachusetts 02111 (617) 423-3990; *The World in Figures*.

BERMUDA - CALORIE SUPPLY

Food and Agricultural Organization of the United Nations (FAO) Via delle Terme di Caracalla, 00100 Rome, Italy (Telephone Number in U.S. (202) 653-2400); *The State of Food and Agriculture*.

BERMUDA - CATTLE - See BERMUDA - LIVESTOCK AND POULTRY

BERMUDA - CEMENT PRODUCTION - See BERMUDA - MINING AND MINERAL PRODUCTS

BERMUDA - CHEMICAL (ORGANIC) PRODUCTION - See BERMUDA - MINING AND MINERAL PRODUCTS

BERMUDA - CIGARETTE PRODUCTION - See BERMUDA - TOBACCO PRODUCTION

BERMUDA - CLASS STRUCTURE

G.K. Hall and Company, 70 Lincoln Street, Boston, Massachusetts 02111 (617) 423-3990; *The World in Figures*.

BERMUDA - CLIMATE

Facts on File, 460 Park Avenue South, New York, New York 10016 (800) 443-8323; *The New Book of World Rankings*.

G.K. Hall and Company, 70 Lincoln Street, Boston, Massachusetts 02111 (617) 423-3990; *The World in Figures*.

BERMUDA - COAL PRODUCTION - See BERMUDA - MINING AND MINERAL PRODUCTS

BERMUDA - COFFEE PRODUCTION - See BERMUDA - CROPS

BERMUDA - COMMUNICATIONS

G.K. Hall and Company, 70 Lincoln Street, Boston, Massachusetts 02111 (617) 423-3990; *The World in Figures*.

BERMUDA - CONSTRUCTION INDUSTRY

Facts on File, 460 Park Avenue South, New York, New York 10016 (800) 443-8323; *The New Book of World Rankings*.

Statistical Office of the United Nations, Publishing Service, New York, New York 10017 (800) 253-9646; *Construction Statistics Yearbook*, and *Statistical Yearbook*.

BERMUDA - CONSUMER PRICE INDEX

G.K. Hall and Company, 70 Lincoln Street, Boston, Massachusetts 02111 (617) 423-3990; *The World in Figures*.

Statistical Office of the United Nations, Publishing Service, New York, New York 10017 (800) 253-9646; *Statistical Yearbook*.

BERMUDA - CONSUMER PRICES

International Labour Office, I.L.O. Publications, CH-1211, Geneva 22, Switzerland; *Yearbook of Labour Statistics*.

BERMUDA - CONSUMPTION

G.K. Hall and Company, 70 Lincoln Street, Boston, Massachusetts 02111 (617) 423-3990; *The World in Figures*.

BERMUDA - COPPER PRODUCTION - See BERMUDA - MINING AND MINERAL PRODUCTS

BERMUDA - CORN PRODUCTION - See BERMUDA - CROPS

BERMUDA - CORPORATE TAXES - See BERMUDA - TAXATION

BERMUDA - COTTON PRODUCTION - See BERMUDA - CROPS

BERMUDA - CRIME

Yale University Press, Yale Station, New Haven, Connecticut 06520 (203) 432-0940; *Violence and Crime in Cross-National Perspective*.

BERMUDA - CROPS

Facts on File, 460 Park Avenue South, New York, New York 10016 (800) 443-8323; *The New Book of World Rankings*.

Food and Agricultural Organization of the United Nations (FAO) Via delle Terme di Caracalla, 00100 Rome, Italy (Telephone Number in U.S. (202) 653-2400); *The State of Food and Agriculture*.

G.K. Hall and Company, 70 Lincoln Street, Boston, Massachusetts 02111 (617) 423-3990; *The World in Figures*.

BERMUDA - CUSTOMS DUTIES

G.K. Hall and Company, 70 Lincoln Street, Boston, Massachusetts 02111 (617) 423-3990; *The World in Figures*.

BERMUDA - DAIRY PRODUCTS

Facts on File, 460 Park Avenue South, New York, New York 10016 (800) 443-8323; *The New Book of World Rankings*.

Food and Agricultural Organization of the United Nations (FAO) Via delle Terme di Caracalla, 00100 Rome, Italy (Telephone Number in U.S. (202) 653-2400); *The State of Food and Agriculture*.

BERMUDA - DEATH RATES

G.K. Hall and Company, 70 Lincoln Street, Boston, Massachusetts 02111 (617) 423-3990; *The World in Figures*.

Statistical Office of the United Nations, Publishing Service, New York, New York 10017 (800) 253-9646; *Statistical Yearbook*.

World Health Organization, Office of Publications, Avenue Appia, CH-1211 Geneva 27, Switzerland (Telephone Number in U.S. (518) 436-9686; *World Health Statistics Annual*.

BERMUDA - DEFENSE EXPENDITURES

G.K. Hall and Company, 70 Lincoln Street, Boston, Massachusetts 02111 (617) 423-3990; *The World in Figures*.

BERMUDA - DEMOGRAPHY

The Economist Intelligence Unit, 111 West 57th Street, New York, New York 10019 (800) 938-4685; *The World Market Atlas*.

Facts on File, 460 Park Avenue South, New York, New York 10016 (800) 443-8323; *The New Book of World Rankings*.

G.K. Hall and Company, 70 Lincoln Street, Boston, Massachusetts 02111 (617) 423-3990; *The World in Figures.*

BERMUDA - DEVELOPMENT ASSISTANCE

G.K. Hall and Company, 70 Lincoln Street, Boston, Massachusetts 02111 (617) 423-3990; *The World in Figures.*

Statistical Office of the United Nations, Publishing Service, New York, New York 10017 (800) 253-9646; *Statistical Yearbook.*

BERMUDA - DIAMOND PRODUCTION - See BERMUDA - MINING AND MINERAL PRODUCTS

BERMUDA - DISEASES

G.K. Hall and Company, 70 Lincoln Street, Boston, Massachusetts 02111 (617) 423-3990; *The World in Figures.*

World Health Organization, Office of Publications, Avenue Appia, CH-1211 Geneva 27, Switzerland (Telephone Number in U.S. (518) 436-9686); *World Health Statistics Annual.*

BERMUDA - DIVORCE RATES

Facts on File, 460 Park Avenue South, New York, New York 10016 (800) 443-8323; *The New Book of World Rankings.*

Statistical Office of the United Nations, Publishing Service, New York, New York 10017 (800) 253-9646; *Demographic Yearbook,* and *Statistical Yearbook.*

BERMUDA - DOMESTIC PRODUCT

G.K. Hall and Company, 70 Lincoln Street, Boston, Massachusetts 02111 (617) 423-3990; *The World in Figures.*

BERMUDA - DUCKS - See BERMUDA - LIVESTOCK AND POULTRY

BERMUDA - ECONOMY

Facts on File, 460 Park Avenue South, New York, New York 10016 (800) 443-8323; *The New Book of World Rankings.*

G.K. Hall and Company, 70 Lincoln Street, Boston, Massachusetts 02111 (617) 423-3990; *The World in Figures.*

BERMUDA - EDUCATION

The Economist Intelligence Unit, 111 West 57th Street, New York, New York 10019 (800) 938-4685; *The World Market Atlas.*

Facts on File, 460 Park Avenue South, New York, New York 10016 (800) 443-8323; *The New Book of World Rankings.*

G.K. Hall and Company, 70 Lincoln Street, Boston, Massachusetts 02111 (617) 423-3990; *The World in Figures.*

Times Books, 201 East 50th Street, New York, New York 10022 (212) 751-2600; *The Economist Book of Vital World Statistics.*

United Nations Educational, Scientific and Cultural Organization (UNESCO), 7 Place de Fontenoy, F-75700 Paris, France (Telephone Number in U.S. (212) 963-5981; *Statistical Yearbook.*

BERMUDA - EGG PRODUCTION - See BERMUDA - DAIRY PRODUCTS

BERMUDA - ELECTRICITY

Facts on File, 460 Park Avenue South, New York, New York 10016 (800) 443-8323; *The New Book of World Rankings.*

Statistical Office of the United Nations, Publishing Service, New York, New York 10017 (800) 253-9646; *Statistical Yearbook.*

Times Books, 201 East 50th Street, New York, New York 10022 (212) 751-2600; *The Economist Book of Vital World Statistics.*

BERMUDA - EMPLOYMENT

Facts on File, 460 Park Avenue South, New York, New York 10016 (800) 443-8323; *The New Book of World Rankings.*

International Labour Office, I.L.O. Publications, CH-1211, Geneva 22, Switzerland; *Yearbook of Labour Statistics.*

BERMUDA - ENERGY

Facts on File, 460 Park Avenue South, New York, New York 10016 (800) 443-8323; *The New Book of World Rankings.*

Food and Agricultural Organization of the United Nations (FAO) Via delle Terme di Caracalla, 00100 Rome, Italy (Telephone Number in U.S. (202) 653-2400); *The State of Food and Agriculture.*

G.K. Hall and Company, 70 Lincoln Street, Boston, Massachusetts 02111 (617) 423-3990; *The World in Figures.*

Statistical Office of the United Nations, Publishing Service, New York, New York 10017 (800) 253-9646; *Energy Statistics Yearbook.*

Times Books, 201 East 50th Street, New York, New York 10022 (212) 751-2600; *The Economist Book of Vital World Statistics.*

BERMUDA - EXPORTS

The Economist Intelligence Unit, 111 West 57th Street, New York, New York 10019 (800) 938-4685; *The World Market Atlas.*

Food and Agricultural Organization of the United Nations (FAO) Via delle Terme di Caracalla, 00100 Rome, Italy (Telephone Number in U.S. (202) 653-2400); *The State of Food and Agriculture.*

G.K. Hall and Company, 70 Lincoln Street, Boston, Massachusetts 02111 (617) 423-3990; *The World in Figures.*

International Monetary Fund, 700 Nineteenth Street, NW, Washington, D.C. 20431 (202) 623-7000; *Direction of Trade Statistics.*

Times Books, 201 East 50th Street, New York, New York 10022 (212) 751-2600; *The Economist Book of Vital World Statistics.*

BERMUDA - EXTERNAL TRADE

Food and Agricultural Organization of the United Nations (FAO) Via delle Terme di Caracalla, 00100 Rome, Italy (Telephone Number in U.S. (202) 653-2400); *The State of Food and Agriculture,* and *Trade Yearbook.*

G.K. Hall and Company, 70 Lincoln Street, Boston, Massachusetts 02111 (617) 423-3990; *The World in Figures.*

Statistical Office of the United Nations, Publishing Service, New York, New York 10017 (800) 253-9646; *Statistical Yearbook.*

BERMUDA - FARM CROPS - See BERMUDA - CROPS

BERMUDA - FERTILITY RATES

Facts on File, 460 Park Avenue South, New York, New York 10016 (800) 443-8323; *The New Book of World Rankings.*

BERMUDA - FETAL MORTALITY

Statistical Office of the United Nations, Publishing Service, New York, New York 10017 (800) 253-9646; *Demographic Yearbook.*

World Health Organization, Office of Publications, Avenue Appia, CH-1211 Geneva 27, Switzerland (Telephone Number in U.S. (518) 436-9686); *World Health Statistics Annual.*

BERMUDA - FERTILIZER

Food and Agricultural Organization of the United Nations (FAO) Via delle Terme di Caracalla, 00100 Rome, Italy (Telephone Number in U.S. (202) 653-2400); *The State of Food and Agriculture.*

Organisation for Economic Cooperation and Development (OECD), 2 rue Andre-Pascal, 75 Paris 16, France (Telephone Number in U.S. (202) 785-6323); *Indicators of Industrial Activity.*

BERMUDA - FINANCE

Facts on File, 460 Park Avenue South, New York, New York 10016 (800) 443-8323; *The New Book of World Rankings.*

G.K. Hall and Company, 70 Lincoln Street, Boston, Massachusetts 02111 (617) 423-3990; *The World in Figures.*

BERMUDA - FISHERIES

Facts on File, 460 Park Avenue South, New York, New York 10016 (800) 443-8323; *The New Book of World Rankings.*

Food and Agricultural Organization of the United Nations (FAO) Via delle Terme di Caracalla, 00100 Rome, Italy (Telephone Number in U.S. (202) 653-2400); *The State of Food and Agriculture,* and *Yearbook of Fishery Statistics.*

Statistical Office of the United Nations, Publishing Service, New York, New York 10017 (800) 253-9646; *Statistical Yearbook.*

BERMUDA - FOOD

Food and Agricultural Organization of the United Nations (FAO) Via delle Terme di Caracalla, 00100 Rome, Italy (Telephone Number in U.S. (202) 653-2400); *Production Yearbook,* and *The State of Food and Agriculture.*

G.K. Hall and Company, 70 Lincoln Street, Boston, Massachusetts 02111 (617) 423-3990; *The World in Figures.*

BERMUDA - FOREIGN AID

G.K. Hall and Company, 70 Lincoln Street, Boston, Massachusetts 02111 (617) 423-3990; *The World in Figures.*

BERMUDA - FOREIGN TRADE

Facts on File, 460 Park Avenue South, New York, New York 10016 (800) 443-8323; *The New Book of World Rankings.*

Food and Agricultural Organization of the United Nations (FAO) Via delle Terme di Caracalla, 00100 Rome, Italy (Telephone Number in U.S. (202) 653-2400); *The State of Food and Agriculture.*

G.K. Hall and Company, 70 Lincoln Street, Boston, Massachusetts 02111 (617) 423-3990; *The World in Figures.*

Organisation for Economic Cooperation and Development (OECD), 2 rue Andre-Pascal, 75 Paris 16, France (Telephone Number in U.S. (202) 785-6323); *Trade by Commodities.*

Statistical Office of the United Nations, Publishing Service, New York, New York 10017 (800) 253-9646; *International Trade Statistics Yearbook,* and *Statistical Yearbook.*

BERMUDA - FORESTRY AND FOREST PRODUCTS

Facts on File, 460 Park Avenue South, New York, New York 10016 (800) 443-8323; *The New Book of World Rankings.*

Food and Agricultural Organization of the United Nations (FAO) Via delle Terme di Caracalla, 00100 Rome, Italy (Telephone Number in U.S. (202) 653-2400); *The State of Food and Agriculture.*

G.K. Hall and Company, 70 Lincoln Street, Boston, Massachusetts 02111 (617) 423-3990; *The World in Figures.*

United Nations Educational, Scientific and Cultural Organization (UNESCO), 7 Place de Fontenoy, F-75700 Paris, France (Telephone Number in U.S. (212) 963-5981); *Statistical Yearbook.*

BERMUDA - GAS PRODUCTION - See BERMUDA - MINING AND MINERAL PRODUCTS

BERMUDA - GENERAL MORTALITY

Statistical Office of the United Nations, Publishing Service, New York, New York 10017 (800) 253-9646; *Demographic Yearbook.*

World Health Organization, Office of Publications, Avenue Appia, CH-1211 Geneva 27, Switzerland (Telephone Number in U.S. (518) 436-9686); *World Health Statistics Annual.*

BERMUDA - GEOGRAPHIC DATA

Facts on File, 460 Park Avenue South, New York, New York 10016 (800) 443-8323; *The New Book of World Rankings.*

BERMUDA - GOLD PRODUCTION AND CONSUMPTION - See BERMUDA - MINING AND MINERAL PRODUCTS

BERMUDA - GOVERNMENT

G.K. Hall and Company, 70 Lincoln Street, Boston, Massachusetts 02111 (617) 423-3990; *The World in Figures.*

BERMUDA - GRAIN PRODUCTION - See BERMUDA - CROPS

BERMUDA - GROSS DOMESTIC PRODUCT

The Economist Intelligence Unit, 111 West 57th Street, New York, New York 10019 (800) 938-4685; *The World Market Atlas.*

Facts on File, 460 Park Avenue South, New York, New York 10016 (800) 443-8323; *The New Book of World Rankings.*

G.K. Hall and Company, 70 Lincoln Street, Boston, Massachusetts 02111 (617) 423-3990; *The World in Figures.*

BERMUDA - HEALTH

Facts on File, 460 Park Avenue South, New York, New York 10016 (800) 443-8323; *The New Book of World Rankings.*

G.K. Hall and Company, 70 Lincoln Street, Boston, Massachusetts 02111 (617) 423-3990; *The World in Figures.*

Statistical Office of the United Nations, Publishing Service, New York, New York 10017 (800) 253-9646; *Statistical Yearbook.*

Times Books, 201 East 50th Street, New York, New York 10022 (212) 751-2600; *The Economist Book of Vital World Statistics.*

World Health Organization, Office of Publications, Avenue Appia, CH-1211 Geneva 27, Switzerland (Telephone Number in U.S. (518) 436-9686); *World Health Statistics Annual.*

BERMUDA - HIDE PRODUCTION

Food and Agricultural Organization of the United Nations (FAO), Via delle Terme di Caracalla, 00100 Rome, Italy (Telephone Number in U.S. (202) 653-2400); *Production Yearbook.*

BERMUDA - HIGHWAYS

G.K. Hall and Company, 70 Lincoln Street, Boston, Massachusetts 02111 (617) 423-3990; *The World in Figures.*

BERMUDA - HORSES - See BERMUDA - LIVESTOCK AND POULTRY

BERMUDA - HOURS OF WORK - See BERMUDA - EMPLOYMENT

BERMUDA - HOUSING AND HOUSING UNITS

Facts on File, 460 Park Avenue South, New York, New York 10016 (800) 443-8323; *The New Book of World Rankings.*

BERMUDA - ILLITERATE POPULATION

The Economist Intelligence Unit, 111 West 57th Street, New York, New York 10019 (800) 938-4685; *The World Market Atlas.*

G.K. Hall and Company, 70 Lincoln Street, Boston, Massachusetts 02111 (617) 423-3990; *The World in Figures.*

United Nations Educational, Scientific and Cultural Organization (UNESCO), 7 Place de Fontenoy, F-75700 Paris, France (Telephone Number in U.S. (212) 963-5981); *Statistical Yearbook.*

BERMUDA - IMPORTS

The Economist Intelligence Unit, 111 West 57th Street, New York, New York 10019 (800) 938-4685; *The World Market Atlas.*

Food and Agricultural Organization of the United Nations (FAO) Via delle Terme di Caracalla, 00100 Rome, Italy (Telephone Number in U.S. (202) 653-2400); *The State of Food and Agriculture.*

G.K. Hall and Company, 70 Lincoln Street, Boston, Massachusetts 02111 (617) 423-3990; *The World in Figures.*

International Monetary Fund, 700 Nineteenth Street, NW, Washington, D.C. 20431 (202) 623-7000; *Direction of Trade Statistics.*

Statistical Office of the United Nations, Publishing Service, New York, New York 10017 (800) 253-9646; *Trade in Manufactures of Developing Countries.*

Times Books, 201 East 50th Street, New York, New York 10022 (212) 751-2600; *The Economist Book of Vital World Statistics.*

BERMUDA - INDUSTRY

Facts on File, 460 Park Avenue South, New York, New York 10016 (800) 443-8323; *The New Book of World Rankings.*

G.K. Hall and Company, 70 Lincoln Street, Boston, Massachusetts 02111 (617) 423-3990; *The World in Figures.*

International Labour Office, I.L.O. Publications, CH-1211, Geneva 22, Switzerland; *Yearbook of Labour Statistics.*

Times Books, 201 East 50th Street, New York, New York 10022 (212) 751-2600; *The Economist Book of Vital World Statistics.*

BERMUDA - INFANT AND MATERNAL MORTALITY

Statistical Office of the United Nations, Publishing Service, New York, New York 10017 (800) 253-9646; *Demographic Yearbook,* and *Statistical Yearbook.*

World Health Organization, Office of Publications, Avenue Appia, CH-1211 Geneva 27, Switzerland (Telephone Number in U.S. (518) 436-9686); *World Health Statistics Annual.*

BERMUDA - IRON ORE PRODUCTION AND CONSUMPTION - See BERMUDA - MINING AND MINERAL PRODUCTS

BERMUDA - LABOR FORCE

Facts on File, 460 Park Avenue South, New York, New York 10016 (800) 443-8323; *The New Book of World Rankings.*

Food and Agricultural Organization of the United Nations (FAO) Via delle Terme di Caracalla, 00100 Rome, Italy (Telephone Number in U.S. (202) 653-2400); *The State of Food and Agriculture.*

G.K. Hall and Company, 70 Lincoln Street, Boston, Massachusetts 02111 (617) 423-3990; *The World in Figures.*

Times Books, 201 East 50th Street, New York, New York 10022 (212) 751-2600; *The Economist Book of Vital World Statistics.*

BERMUDA - LABOR PRODUCTIVITY

International Labour Office, I.L.O. Publications, CH-1211, Geneva 22, Switzerland; *Yearbook of Labour Statistics.*

BERMUDA - LAND USE

Food and Agricultural Organization of the United Nations (FAO), Via delle Terme di Caracalla, 00100 Rome, Italy (Telephone Number in U.S. (202) 653-2400); *Production Yearbook.*

G.K. Hall and Company, 70 Lincoln Street, Boston, Massachusetts 02111 (617) 423-3990; *The World in Figures.*

BERMUDA - LIBRARIES

Facts on File, 460 Park Avenue South, New York, New York 10016 (800) 443-8323; *The New Book of World Rankings.*

United Nations Educational, Scientific and Cultural Organization (UNESCO), 7 Place de Fontenoy, F-75700 Paris, France (Telephone Number in U.S. (212) 963-5981); *Statistical Yearbook.*

BERMUDA - LIVESTOCK AND POULTRY

Facts on File, 460 Park Avenue South, New York, New York 10016 (800) 443-8323; *The New Book of World Rankings*.

Food and Agricultural Organization of the United Nations (FAO), Via delle Terme di Caracalla, 00100 Rome, Italy (Telephone Number in U.S. (202) 653-2400); *Production Yearbook*, and *The State of Food and Agriculture*.

G.K. Hall and Company, 70 Lincoln Street, Boston, Massachusetts 02111 (617) 423-3990; *The World in Figures*.

Statistical Office of the United Nations, Publishing Service, New York, New York 10017 (800) 253-9646; *Statistical Yearbook*.

BERMUDA - LIVING LEVELS

G.K. Hall and Company, 70 Lincoln Street, Boston, Massachusetts 02111 (617) 423-3990; *The World in Figures*.

BERMUDA - MAIL - NUMBER OF PIECES SENT OR RECEIVED

Statistical Office of the United Nations, Publishing Service, New York, New York 10017 (800) 253-9646; *Statistical Yearbook*.

BERMUDA - MANUFACTURING

Facts on File, 460 Park Avenue South, New York, New York 10016 (800) 443-8323; *The New Book of World Rankings*.

G.K. Hall and Company, 70 Lincoln Street, Boston, Massachusetts 02111 (617) 423-3990; *The World in Figures*.

Times Books, 201 East 50th Street, New York, New York 10022 (212) 751-2600; *The Economist Book of Vital World Statistics*.

BERMUDA - MARRIAGE RATES

Facts on File, 460 Park Avenue South, New York, New York 10016 (800) 443-8323; *The New Book of World Rankings*.

Statistical Office of the United Nations, Publishing Service, New York, New York 10017 (800) 253-9646; *Demographic Yearbook*, and *Statistical Yearbook*.

BERMUDA - MEAT PRODUCTION - See BERMUDA - LIVESTOCK AND POULTRY

BERMUDA - MERCHANT SHIPPING

G.K. Hall and Company, 70 Lincoln Street, Boston, Massachusetts 02111 (617) 423-3990; *The World in Figures*.

Statistical Office of the United Nations, Publishing Service, New York, New York 10017 (800) 253-9646; *Statistical Yearbook*.

Times Books, 201 East 50th Street, New York, New York 10022 (212) 751-2600; *The Economist Book of Vital World Statistics*.

BERMUDA - MILITARY

G.K. Hall and Company, 70 Lincoln Street, Boston, Massachusetts 02111 (617) 423-3990; *The World in Figures*.

BERMUDA - MILK PRODUCTION - See BERMUDA - DAIRY PRODUCTS

BERMUDA - MINING AND MINERAL PRODUCTS

G.K. Hall and Company, 70 Lincoln Street, Boston, Massachusetts 02111 (617) 423-3990; *The World in Figures*.

Facts on File, 460 Park Avenue South, New York, New York 10016 (800) 443-8323; *The New Book of World Rankings*.

BERMUDA - MONEY SUPPLY

G.K. Hall and Company, 70 Lincoln Street, Boston, Massachusetts 02111 (617) 423-3990; *The World in Figures*.

BERMUDA - MOTION PICTURES

Statistical Office of the United Nations, Publishing Service, New York, New York 10017 (800) 253-9646; *Statistical Yearbook*.

BERMUDA - MOTOR VEHICLES IN USE

G.K. Hall and Company, 70 Lincoln Street, Boston, Massachusetts 02111 (617) 423-3990; *The World in Figures*.

Statistical Office of the United Nations, Publishing Service, New York, New York 10017 (800) 253-9646; *Statistical Yearbook*.

Times Books, 201 East 50th Street, New York, New York 10022 (212) 751-2600; *The Economist Book of Vital World Statistics*.

BERMUDA - MUSEUMS

Facts on File, 460 Park Avenue South, New York, New York 10016 (800) 443-8323; *The New Book of World Rankings*.

United Nations Educational, Scientific and Cultural Organization (UNESCO), 7 Place de Fontenoy, F-75700 Paris, France (Telephone Number in U.S. (212) 963-5981); *Statistical Yearbook*.

BERMUDA - NATALITY - See BERMUDA - BIRTH RATE

BERMUDA - NATIONAL INCOME

Facts on File, 460 Park Avenue South, New York, New York 10016 (800) 443-8323; *The New Book of World Rankings*.

G.K. Hall and Company, 70 Lincoln Street, Boston, Massachusetts 02111 (617) 423-3990; *The World in Figures*.

BERMUDA - NATIONAL PRODUCT

Facts on File, 460 Park Avenue South, New York, New York 10016 (800) 443-8323; *The New Book of World Rankings*.

BERMUDA - NATURAL GAS PRODUCTION - See BERMUDA - MINING AND MINERAL PRODUCTS

BERMUDA - NEWSPAPER PRODUCTION - See BERMUDA - FORESTRY AND FOREST PRODUCTS

BERMUDA - OCCUPATIONS - See BERMUDA - LABOR FORCE

BERMUDA - PEANUT PRODUCTION - See BERMUDA - CROPS

BERMUDA - PESTICIDE USE

Food and Agricultural Organization of the United Nations (FAO) Via delle Terme di Caracalla, 00100 Rome, Italy (Telephone Number in U.S. (202) 653-2400); *The State of Food and Agriculture*.

BERMUDA - PETROLEUM INDUSTRY

Facts on File, 460 Park Avenue South, New York, New York 10016 (800) 443-8323; *The New Book of World Rankings.*

Food and Agricultural Organization of the United Nations (FAO) Via delle Terme di Caracalla, 00100 Rome, Italy (Telephone Number in U.S. (202) 653-2400); *The State of Food and Agriculture.*

G.K. Hall and Company, 70 Lincoln Street, Boston, Massachusetts 02111 (617) 423-3990; *The World in Figures.*

BERMUDA - PIGS

Facts on File, 460 Park Avenue South, New York, New York 10016 (800) 443-8323; *The New Book of World Rankings.*

Statistical Office of the United Nations, Publishing Service, New York, New York 10017 (800) 253-9646; *Statistical Yearbook.*

BERMUDA - POPULATION

The Economist Intelligence Unit, 111 West 57th Street, New York, New York 10019 (800) 938-4685; *The World Market Atlas.*

Facts on File, 460 Park Avenue South, New York, New York 10016 (800) 443-8323; *The New Book of World Rankings.*

Food and Agricultural Organization of the United Nations (FAO), Via delle Terme di Caracalla, 00100 Rome, Italy (Telephone Number in U.S. (202) 653-2400); *Production Yearbook.*

G.K. Hall and Company, 70 Lincoln Street, Boston, Massachusetts 02111 (617) 423-3990; *The World in Figures.*

International Labour Office, I.L.O. Publications, CH-1211, Geneva 22, Switzerland; *Yearbook of Labour Statistics.*

Statistical Office of the United Nations, Publishing Service, New York, New York 10017 (800) 253-9646; *Demographic Yearbook,* and *Statistical Yearbook.*

Times Books, 201 East 50th Street, New York, New York 10022 (212) 751-2600; *The Economist Book of Vital World Statistics.*

World Health Organization, Office of Publications, Avenue Appia, CH-1211 Geneva 27, Switzerland (Telephone Number in U.S. (518) 436-9686); *World Health Statistics Annual.*

BERMUDA - POST OFFICES

Facts on File, 460 Park Avenue South, New York, New York 10016 (800) 443-8323; *The New Book of World Rankings.*

BERMUDA - POTATO PRODUCTION - See BERMUDA - CROPS

BERMUDA - PRICES

Facts on File, 460 Park Avenue South, New York, New York 10016 (800) 443-8323; *The New Book of World Rankings.*

Food and Agricultural Organization of the United Nations (FAO), Via delle Terme di Caracalla, 00100 Rome, Italy (Telephone Number in U.S. (202) 653-2400); *Production Yearbook,* and *The State of Food and Agriculture.*

G.K. Hall and Company, 70 Lincoln Street, Boston, Massachusetts 02111 (617) 423-3990; *The World in Figures.*

International Labour Office, I.L.O. Publications, CH-1211, Geneva 22, Switzerland; *Yearbook of Labour Statistics.*

BERMUDA - PRODUCTION

Facts on File, 460 Park Avenue South, New York, New York 10016 (800) 443-8323; *The New Book of World Rankings.*

G.K. Hall and Company, 70 Lincoln Street, Boston, Massachusetts 02111 (617) 423-3990; *The World in Figures.*

BERMUDA - PUBLIC FINANCE

Facts on File, 460 Park Avenue South, New York, New York 10016 (800) 443-8323; *The New Book of World Rankings.*

BERMUDA - RADIO BROADCASTING - See BERMUDA - BROADCASTING

BERMUDA - RAILWAYS

G.K. Hall and Company, 70 Lincoln Street, Boston, Massachusetts 02111 (617) 423-3990; *The World in Figures.*

BERMUDA - RELIGION

Facts on File, 460 Park Avenue South, New York, New York 10016 (800) 443-8323; *The New Book of World Rankings.*

BERMUDA - RENT PRICES

International Labour Office, I.L.O. Publications, CH-1211, Geneva 22, Switzerland; *Yearbook of Labour Statistics.*

BERMUDA - RETAIL TRADE

G.K. Hall and Company, 70 Lincoln Street, Boston, Massachusetts 02111 (617) 423-3990; *The World in Figures.*

BERMUDA - RICE PRODUCTION - See BERMUDA - CROPS

BERMUDA - RUBBER PRODUCTION

Facts on File, 460 Park Avenue South, New York, New York 10016 (800) 443-8323; *The New Book of World Rankings.*

BERMUDA - SCIENCE AND TECHNOLOGY - EXPENDITURE FOR RESEARCH

Statistical Office of the United Nations, Publishing Service, New York, New York 10017 (800) 253-9646; *Statistical Yearbook.*

BERMUDA - SENIOR CITIZENS

Facts on File, 460 Park Avenue South, New York, New York 10016 (800) 443-8323; *The New Book of World Rankings.*

BERMUDA - SHEEP - See BERMUDA - LIVESTOCK AND POULTRY

BERMUDA - SILVER PRODUCTION AND CONSUMPTION - See BERMUDA - MINING AND MINERAL PRODUCTS

BERMUDA - SOCIAL DATA

Facts on File, 460 Park Avenue South, New York, New York 10016 (800) 443-8323; *The New Book of World Rankings.*

G.K. Hall and Company, 70 Lincoln Street, Boston, Massachusetts 02111 (617) 423-3990; *The World in Figures.*

BERMUDA - STEEL PRODUCTION - See BERMUDA - MINING AND MINERAL PRODUCTS

BERMUDA - STOCKS - COMMODITY - MARKET PRICE - INDEX

Food and Agricultural Organization of the United Nations (FAO) Via delle Terme di Caracalla, 00100 Rome, Italy (Telephone Number in U.S. (202) 653-2400); *The State of Food and Agriculture.*

BERMUDA - SUGAR PRODUCTION - See BERMUDA - CROPS

BERMUDA - TAXATION

G.K. Hall and Company, 70 Lincoln Street, Boston, Massachusetts 02111 (617) 423-3990; *The World in Figures.*

BERMUDA - TELEPHONES IN USE

American Telephone and Telegraph Company, 26 Parsippany Road, Whippany, New Jersey 07981 (800) 338-4038; *The World's Telephones.*

G.K. Hall and Company, 70 Lincoln Street, Boston, Massachusetts 02111 (617) 423-3990; *The World in Figures.*

Statistical Office of the United Nations, Publishing Service, New York, New York 10017 (800) 253-9646; *Statistical Yearbook.*

BERMUDA - TELEVISION BROADCASTING - See BERMUDA - BROADCASTING

BERMUDA - TEXTILE INDUSTRY

G.K. Hall and Company, 70 Lincoln Street, Boston, Massachusetts 02111 (617) 423-3990; *The World in Figures.*

BERMUDA - THEATRE

United Nations Educational, Scientific and Cultural Organization (UNESCO), 7 Place de Fontenoy, F-75700 Paris, France (Telephone Number in U.S. (212) 963-5981); *Statistical Yearbook.*

BERMUDA - TOBACCO PRODUCTION

Facts on File, 460 Park Avenue South, New York, New York 10016 (800) 443-8323; *The New Book of World Rankings.*

BERMUDA - TOURISM

Facts on File, 460 Park Avenue South, New York, New York 10016 (800) 443-8323; *The New Book of World Rankings.*

G.K. Hall and Company, 70 Lincoln Street, Boston, Massachusetts 02111 (617) 423-3990; *The World in Figures.*

Statistical Office of the United Nations, Publishing Service, New York, New York 10017 (800) 253-9646; *Statistical Yearbook.*

Times Books, 201 East 50th Street, New York, New York 10022 (212) 751-2600; *The Economist Book of Vital World Statistics.*

World Tourism Organization, Calle Capitan Haya 42, E-28020 Madrid, Spain; *Yearbook of Tourism Statistics.*

BERMUDA - TRACTORS IN USE

Statistical Office of the United Nations, Publishing Service, New York, New York 10017 (800) 253-9646; *Statistical Yearbook.*

BERMUDA - TRADE - See BERMUDA - FOREIGN TRADE

BERMUDA - TRANSPORTATION AND COMMUNICATIONS

Facts on File, 460 Park Avenue South, New York, New York 10016 (800) 443-8323; *The New Book of World Rankings.*

G.K. Hall and Company, 70 Lincoln Street, Boston, Massachusetts 02111 (617) 423-3990; *The World in Figures.*

BERMUDA - UNEMPLOYMENT

International Labour Office, I.L.O. Publications, CH-1211, Geneva 22, Switzerland; *Yearbook of Labour Statistics.*

BERMUDA - VITAL STATISTICS

G.K. Hall and Company, 70 Lincoln Street, Boston, Massachusetts 02111 (617) 423-3990; *The World in Figures.*

Statistical Office of the United Nations, Publishing Service, New York, New York 10017 (800) 253-9646; *Statistical Yearbook.*

World Health Organization, Office of Publications, Avenue Appia, CH-1211 Geneva 27, Switzerland (Telephone Number in U.S. (518) 436-9686); *World Health Statistics Annual.*

BERMUDA - WAGES

G.K. Hall and Company, 70 Lincoln Street, Boston, Massachusetts 02111 (617) 423-3990; *The World in Figures.*

International Labour Office, I.L.O. Publications, CH-1211, Geneva 22, Switzerland; *Yearbook of Labour Statistics.*

BERMUDA - WEATHER

Facts on File, 460 Park Avenue South, New York, New York 10016 (800) 443-8323; *The New Book of World Rankings.*

G.K. Hall and Company, 70 Lincoln Street, Boston, Massachusetts 02111 (617) 423-3990; *The World in Figures.*

BERMUDA - WHEAT PRODUCTION - See BERMUDA - CROPS

BERMUDA - WINE PRODUCTION

Facts on File, 460 Park Avenue South, New York, New York 10016 (800) 443-8323; *The New Book of World Rankings.*

BERMUDA - WOOL PRODUCTION

Facts on File, 460 Park Avenue South, New York, New York 10016 (800) 443-8323; *The New Book of World Rankings.*

BERYLLIUM

U.S. Department of the Interior, Bureau of Mines, 810 Seventh Street, NW, Washington, D.C. 20241 (202) 501-9649; *Mineral Commodity Summaries.*

BEVERAGES - See also: ALCOHOLIC BEVERAGES

BEVERAGES - ADVERTISING EXPENDITURES

Television Bureau of Advertising, Incorporated, 850 Third Avenue, New York, New York 10022 (212) 486-1111; from data compiled by Competitive Media Reporting, 11 West 42nd Street, New York, New York 10036 (212) 789-1400.

BEVERAGES - BEER

U.S. Department of the Treasury, Bureau of Alcohol, Tobacco and Firearms, 650 Massachusetts Avenue, NW, Washington, D.C. 20226 (202) 927-8500; *Alcohol and Tobacco Summary Statistics.*

BEVERAGES - CONSUMPTION

U.S. Department of Agriculture, Economic Research Service, Fourteenth Street and Independence Avenue, SW, Washington, D.C. 20005-4789 (202) 219-1504; *Food Consumption, Prices, and Expenditures,* and unpublished data.

U.S. Department of the Treasury, Bureau of Alcohol, Tobacco and Firearms, 650 Massachusetts Avenue, NW, Washington, D.C. 20226 (202) 927-8500; *Alcohol and Tobacco Summary Statistics.*

BEVERAGES - EXPENDITURES

U.S. Department of Agriculture, Economic Research Service, Fourteenth Street and Independence Avenue, SW, Washington, D.C. 20005-4789 (202) 219-1504; based on data from The United Nations, New York, New York 10017 (800) 253-9646; *National Accounts Statistics.*

BEVERAGES - FOREIGN TRADE

U.S. Department of the Treasury, Bureau of Alcohol, Tobacco and Firearms, 650 Massachusetts Avenue, NW, Washington, D.C. 20226 (202) 927-8500; *Alcohol and Tobacco Summary Statistics.*

BEVERAGES - PRICE INDEXES

U.S. Department of Labor, Bureau of Labor Statistics, Two Massachusetts Avenue, NE, Washington, D.C. 20212 (202) 606-7828; *Monthly Labor Review,* and *CPI Detailed Report.*

BEVERAGES - PRODUCTION

U.S. Department of the Treasury, Bureau of Alcohol, Tobacco and Firearms, 650 Massachusetts Avenue, NW, Washington, D.C. 20226 (202) 927-8500; *Alcohol and Tobacco Summary Statistics.*

BEVERAGES - WHISKEY

U.S. Department of Labor, Bureau of Labor Statistics, Two Massachusetts Avenue, NE, Washington, D.C. 20212 (202) 606-7828; *Monthly Labor Review,* and *CPI Detailed Report.*

U.S. Department of the Treasury, Bureau of Alcohol, Tobacco and Firearms, 650 Massachusetts Avenue, NW, Washington, D.C. 20226 (202) 927-8500; *Alcohol and Tobacco Summary Statistics.*

BEVERAGES - WINE

U.S. Department of Labor, Bureau of Labor Statistics, Two Massachusetts Avenue, NE, Washington, D.C. 20212 (202) 606-7828; *Monthly Labor Review,* and *CPI Detailed Report.*

U.S. Department of the Treasury, Bureau of Alcohol, Tobacco and Firearms, 650 Massachusetts Avenue, NW, Washington, D.C. 20226 (202) 927-8500; *Alcohol and Tobacco Summary Statistics.*

BEVERAGES, INDUSTRY - EARNINGS

U.S. Department of Commerce, Bureau of the Census, Suitland, Maryland 20233 (301) 763-4040; *Annual Survey of Manufactures,* and *Census of Manufactures.*

U.S. Department of Labor, Bureau of Labor Statistics, Two Massachusetts Avenue, NE, Washington, D.C. 20212 (202) 606-7828; *Employment and Earnings,* and Bulletins 2370 and 2429.

BEVERAGES, INDUSTRY - EMPLOYEES

U.S. Department of Commerce, Bureau of the Census, Suitland, Maryland 20233 (301) 763-4040; *Annual Survey of Manufactures,* and *Census of Manufactures.*

U.S. Department of Labor, Bureau of Labor Statistics, Two Massachusetts Avenue, NE, Washington, D.C. 20212 (202) 606-7828; *Employment and Earnings,* and Bulletins 2370 and 2429.

BEVERAGES, INDUSTRY - ESTABLISHMENTS

U.S. Department of Commerce, Bureau of the Census, Suitland, Maryland 20233 (301) 763-4040; *Annual Survey of Manufacturers,* and *Census of Manufactures.*

BEVERAGES, INDUSTRY - FOREIGN TRADE

U.S. Department of the Treasury, Bureau of Alcohol, Tobacco, and Firearms, 650 Massachusetts Avenue, NW, Washington, D.C. 20226 (202) 927-8500; *Alcohol and Tobacco Summary Statistics.*

BEVERAGES, INDUSTRY - SHIPMENTS

U.S. Department of Commerce, Bureau of the Census, Suitland, Maryland 20233 (301) 763-4040; *Annual Survey of Manufactures,* and *Census of Manufactures.*

BEVERAGES, INDUSTRY - VALUE ADDED

U.S. Department of Commerce, Bureau of the Census, Suitland, Maryland 20233 (301) 763-4040; *Annual Survey of Manufactures,* and *Census of Manufactures.*

Bhutan - Central Statistical Office

Central Statistical Office, Planning Commission, Post Box Number 338, Thimphu, Bhutan.

Bhutan - Primary Statistics Sources

Central Statistical Office, Planning Commission, Post Box Number 338, Thimphu, Bhutan; *Statistical Yearbook of Bhutan,* and *Statistics at a Glace: Bhutan.*

BHUTAN - AGRICULTURE

Asian Development Bank, P.O. Box 789, 1099 Manila, Philippines; *Key Indicators of Developing Asian and Pacific Countries.*

Euromonitor Publications Limited, 87-88 Turnmill Street, London EC1M 5QU, England; *International Marketing Data and Statistics.*

Facts on File, 460 Park Avenue South, New York, New York 10016 (800) 443-8323; *The New Book of World Rankings.*

Food and Agricultural Organization of the United Nations (FAO) Via delle Terme di Caracalla, 00100 Rome, Italy (Telephone Number in U.S. (202) 653-2400); *Production Yearbook, The State of Food and Agriculture,* and *Trade Yearbook.*

G.K. Hall and Company, 70 Lincoln Street, Boston, Massachusetts 02111 (617) 423-3990; *The World in Figures.*

Times Books, 201 East 50th Street, New York, New York 10022 (212) 751-2600; *The Economist Book of Vital World Statistics.*

Statistical Office of the United Nations, Publishing Service, New York, New York 10017 (800) 253-9646; *Statistical Yearbook of Asia and the Pacific.*

The World Bank, 1818 H Street, NW, Washington, D.C. 20433 (202) 477-1234; *World Tables.*

BHUTAN - AIRLINE SERVICE

The Economist Intelligence Unit (Asia) Limited, 10th Floor, Luk Kwok Centre, 72 Gloucester Road, Wanchai, Hong Kong (Phone Number in U.S. (800) 938-4685); *Asian Market Atlas.*

Facts on File, 460 Park Avenue South, New York, New York 10016 (800) 443-8323; *The New Book of World Rankings.*

G.K. Hall and Company, 70 Lincoln Street, Boston, Massachusetts 02111 (617) 423-3990; *The World in Figures.*

BHUTAN - ALUMINUM PRODUCTION AND CONSUMPTION - See BHUTAN - MINING AND MINERAL PRODUCTS

BHUTAN - ANIMAL HEALTH

Food and Agricultural Organization of the United Nations (FAO), Via delle Terme di Caracalla, 00100 Rome, Italy (Telephone Number in U.S. (202) 653-2400); *Animal Health Yearbook.*

BHUTAN - AREA AND POPULATION DENSITY

Euromonitor Publications Limited, 87-88 Turnmill Street, London EC1M 5QU, England; *International Marketing Data and Statistics.*

Facts on File, 460 Park Avenue South, New York, New York 10016 (800) 443-8323; *The New Book of World Rankings.*

Food and Agricultural Organization of the United Nations (FAO) Via delle Terme di Caracalla, 00100 Rome, Italy (Telephone Number in U.S. (202) 653-2400); *The State of Food and Agriculture.*

G.K. Hall and Company, 70 Lincoln Street, Boston, Massachusetts 02111 (617) 423-3990; *The World in Figures.*

Statistical Office of the United Nations, Publishing Service, New York, New York 10017 (800) 253-9646; *Statistical Yearbook.*

Times Books, 201 East 50th Street, New York, New York 10022 (212) 751-2600; *The Economist Book of Vital World Statistics.*

BHUTAN - BALANCE OF PAYMENTS

The Economist Intelligence Unit, 111 West 57th Street, New York, New York 10019 (800) 938-4685; *The World Market Atlas.*

G.K. Hall and Company, 70 Lincoln Street, Boston, Massachusetts 02111 (617) 423-3990; *The World in Figures.*

The World Bank, 1818 H Street, NW, Washington, D.C. 20433 (202) 477-1234; *World Tables.*

BHUTAN - BANKING

Asian Development Bank, P.O. Box 789, 1099 Manila, Philippines; *Key Indicators of Developing Asian and Pacific Countries.*

Facts on File, 460 Park Avenue South, New York, New York 10016 (800) 443-8323; *The New Book of World Rankings.*

G.K. Hall and Company, 70 Lincoln Street, Boston, Massachusetts 02111 (617) 423-3990; *The World in Figures.*

BHUTAN - BARLEY PRODUCTION - See BHUTAN - CROPS

BHUTAN - BEER PRODUCTION

Facts on File, 460 Park Avenue South, New York, New York 10016 (800) 443-8323; *The New Book of World Rankings.*

BHUTAN - BIRTH RATES

The Economist Intelligence Unit (Asia) Limited, 10th Floor, Luk Kwok Centre, 72 Gloucester Road, Wanchai, Hong Kong (Phone Number in U.S. (800) 938-4685); *Asian Market Atlas.*

Facts on File, 460 Park Avenue South, New York, New York 10016 (800) 443-8323; *The New Book of World Rankings.*

Statistical Office of the United Nations, Publishing Service, New York, New York 10017 (800) 253-9646; *Demographic Yearbook,* and *Statistical Yearbook.*

Times Books, 201 East 50th Street, New York, New York 10022 (212) 751-2600; *The Economist Book of Vital World Statistics.*

The World Bank, 1818 H Street, NW, Washington, D.C. 20433 (202) 477-1234; *World Tables.*

BHUTAN - BONDS

Asian Development Bank, P.O. Box 789, 1099 Manila, Philippines; *Key Indicators of Developing Asian and Pacific Countries.*

G.K. Hall and Company, 70 Lincoln Street, Boston, Massachusetts 02111 (617) 423-3990; *The World in Figures.*

BHUTAN - BOOK PRODUCTION

G.K. Hall and Company, 70 Lincoln Street, Boston, Massachusetts 02111 (617) 423-3990; *The World in Figures.*

BHUTAN - BROADCASTING

Billboard Limited, P.O. Box 9027, 1006 AA Amsterdam, The Netherlands (Telephone Number in U.S. (212) 764-7300); *World Radio TV Handbook.*

The Economist Intelligence Unit (Asia) Limited, 10th Floor, Luk Kwok Centre, 72 Gloucester Road, Wanchai, Hong Kong (Phone Number in U.S. (800) 938-4685); *Asian Market Atlas.*

Facts on File, 460 Park Avenue South, New York, New York 10016 (800) 443-8323; *The New Book of World Rankings.*

G.K. Hall and Company, 70 Lincoln Street, Boston, Massachusetts 02111 (617) 423-3990; *The World in Figures.*

Times Books, 201 East 50th Street, New York, New York 10022 (212) 751-2600; *The Economist Book of Vital World Statistics.*

BHUTAN - BUSINESS

G.K. Hall and Company, 70 Lincoln Street, Boston, Massachusetts 02111 (617) 423-3990; *The World in Figures.*

BHUTAN - CALORIE SUPPLY

Asian Development Bank, P.O. Box 789, 1099 Manila, Philippines; *Key Indicators of Developing Asian and Pacific Countries.*

Food and Agricultural Organization of the United Nations (FAO) Via delle Terme di Caracalla, 00100 Rome, Italy (Telephone Number in U.S. (202) 653-2400); *The State of Food and Agriculture.*

BHUTAN - CAPITAL INVESTMENT

Asian Development Bank, P.O. Box 789, 1099 Manila, Philippines; *Key Indicators of Developing Asian and Pacific Countries.*

BHUTAN - CAPITAL REVENUE

Asian Development Bank, P.O. Box 789, 1099 Manila, Philippines; *Key Indicators of Developing Asian and Pacific Countries.*

BHUTAN - CATTLE - See BHUTAN - LIVESTOCK AND POULTRY

BHUTAN - CEMENT PRODUCTION - See BHUTAN - MINING AND MINERAL PRODUCTS

BHUTAN - CHEMICAL (ORGANIC) PRODUCTION - See BHUTAN - MINING AND MINERAL PRODUCTS

BHUTAN - CHICKENS - See BHUTAN - LIVESTOCK AND POULTRY

BHUTAN - CIGARETTE PRODUCTION - See BHUTAN - TOBACCO PRODUCTION

BHUTAN - CLASS STRUCTURE

G.K. Hall and Company, 70 Lincoln Street, Boston, Massachusetts 02111 (617) 423-3990; *The World in Figures.*

BHUTAN - CLIMATE

Facts on File, 460 Park Avenue South, New York, New York 10016 (800) 443-8323; *The New Book of World Rankings.*

G.K. Hall and Company, 70 Lincoln Street, Boston, Massachusetts 02111 (617) 423-3990; *The World in Figures.*

BHUTAN - COAL PRODUCTION - See BHUTAN - MINING AND MINERAL PRODUCTS

BHUTAN - COFFEE PRODUCTION - See BHUTAN - CROPS

BHUTAN - COMMUNICATIONS

G.K. Hall and Company, 70 Lincoln Street, Boston, Massachusetts 02111 (617) 423-3990; *The World in Figures.*

Statistical Office of the United Nations, Publishing Service, New York, New York 10017 (800) 253-9646; *Statistical Yearbook of Asia and the Pacific.*

BHUTAN - CONSTRUCTION INDUSTRY

Facts on File, 460 Park Avenue South, New York, New York 10016 (800) 443-8323; *The New Book of World Rankings.*

BHUTAN - CONSUMER PRICE INDEX

Asian Development Bank, P.O. Box 789, 1099 Manila, Philippines; *Key Indicators of Developing Asian and Pacific Countries.*

G.K. Hall and Company, 70 Lincoln Street, Boston, Massachusetts 02111 (617) 423-3990; *The World in Figures.*

BHUTAN - CONSUMPTION

G.K. Hall and Company, 70 Lincoln Street, Boston, Massachusetts 02111 (617) 423-3990; *The World in Figures.*

BHUTAN - COPPER PRODUCTION - See BHUTAN - MINING AND MINERAL PRODUCTS

BHUTAN - CORN PRODUCTION - See BHUTAN - CROPS

BHUTAN - CORPORATE TAXES - See BHUTAN - TAXATION

BHUTAN - COTTON - See BHUTAN - CROPS

BHUTAN - CROPS

Asian Development Bank, P.O. Box 789, 1099 Manila, Philippines; *Key Indicators of Developing Asian and Pacific Countries.*

Facts on File, 460 Park Avenue South, New York, New York 10016 (800) 443-8323; *The New Book of World Rankings.*

Food and Agricultural Organization of the United Nations (FAO) Via delle Terme di Caracalla, 00100 Rome, Italy (Telephone Number in U.S. (202) 653-2400); *The State of Food and Agriculture.*

Statistical Office of the United Nations, Publishing Service, New York, New York 10017 (800) 253-9646; *Statistical Yearbook.*

BHUTAN - CUSTOMS DUTIES

G.K. Hall and Company, 70 Lincoln Street, Boston, Massachusetts 02111 (617) 423-3990; *The World in Figures.*

BHUTAN - DAIRY PRODUCTS

Facts on File, 460 Park Avenue South, New York, New York 10016 (800) 443-8323; *The New Book of World Rankings.*

Food and Agricultural Organization of the United Nations (FAO) Via delle Terme di Caracalla, 00100 Rome, Italy (Telephone Number in U.S. (202) 653-2400); *Production Yearbook,* and *The State of Food and Agriculture.*

BHUTAN - DEATH RATE

The Economist Intelligence Unit (Asia) Limited, 10th Floor, Luk Kwok Centre, 72 Gloucester Road, Wanchai, Hong Kong (Phone Number in U.S. (800) 938-4685); *Asian Market Atlas.*

G.K. Hall and Company, 70 Lincoln Street, Boston, Massachusetts 02111 (617) 423-3990; *The World in Figures.*

Statistical Office of the United Nations, Publishing Service, New York, New York 10017 (800) 253-9646; *Statistical Yearbook.*

Times Books, 201 East 50th Street, New York, New York 10022 (212) 751-2600; *The Economist Book of Vital World Statistics.*

BHUTAN - DEFENSE EXPENDITURES

G.K. Hall and Company, 70 Lincoln Street, Boston, Massachusetts 02111 (617) 423-3990; *The World in Figures.*

BHUTAN - DEMOGRAPHY

The Economist Intelligence Unit, 111 West 57th Street, New York, New York 10019 (800) 938-4685; *The World Market Atlas.*

The Economist Intelligence Unit (Asia) Limited, 10th Floor, Luk Kwok Centre, 72 Gloucester Road, Wanchai, Hong Kong (Phone Number in U.S. (800) 938-4685); *Asian Market Atlas.*

Facts on File, 460 Park Avenue South, New York, New York 10016 (800) 443-8323; *The New Book of World Rankings.*

G.K. Hall and Company, 70 Lincoln Street, Boston, Massachusetts 02111 (617) 423-3990; *The World in Figures.*

BHUTAN - DEVELOPMENT ASSISTANCE

Asian Development Bank, P.O. Box 789, 1099 Manila, Philippines; *Key Indicators of Developing Asian and Pacific Countries.*

G.K. Hall and Company, 70 Lincoln Street, Boston, Massachusetts 02111 (617) 423-3990; *The World in Figures.*

Statistical Office of the United Nations, Publishing Service, New York, New York 10017 (800) 253-9646; *Statistical Yearbook.*

BHUTAN - DIAMOND PRODUCTION - See BHUTAN - MINING AND MINERAL PRODUCTS

BHUTAN - DISEASE

G.K. Hall and Company, 70 Lincoln Street, Boston, Massachusetts 02111 (617) 423-3990; *The World in Figures.*

BHUTAN - DIVORCE RATES

Facts on File, 460 Park Avenue South, New York, New York 10016 (800) 443-8323; *The New Book of World Rankings.*

Statistical Office of the United Nations, Publishing Service, New York, New York 10017 (800) 253-9646; *Demographic Yearbook.*

BHUTAN - DOMESTIC PRODUCT

G.K. Hall and Company, 70 Lincoln Street, Boston, Massachusetts 02111 (617) 423-3990; *The World in Figures.*

BHUTAN - ECONOMY

Asian Development Bank, P.O. Box 789, 1099 Manila, Philippines; *Key Indicators of Developing Asian and Pacific Countries.*

Euromonitor Publications Limited, 87-88 Turnmill Street, London EC1M 5QU, England; *International Marketing Data and Statistics.*

Facts on File, 460 Park Avenue South, New York, New York 10016 (800) 443-8323; *The New Book of World Rankings.*

G.K. Hall and Company, 70 Lincoln Street, Boston, Massachusetts 02111 (617) 423-3990; *The World in Figures.*

BHUTAN - EDUCATION

The Economist Intelligence Unit, 111 West 57th Street, New York, New York 10019 (800) 938-4685; *The World Market Atlas.*

The Economist Intelligence Unit (Asia) Limited, 10th Floor, Luk Kwok Centre, 72 Gloucester Road, Wanchai, Hong Kong (Phone Number in U.S. (800) 938-4685); *Asian Market Atlas.*

Facts on File, 460 Park Avenue South, New York, New York 10016 (800) 443-8323; *The New Book of World Rankings.*

G.K. Hall and Company, 70 Lincoln Street, Boston, Massachusetts 02111 (617) 423-3990; *The World in Figures.*

Statistical Office of the United Nations, Publishing Service, New York, New York 10017 (800) 253-9646; *Statistical Yearbook for Asia and the Pacific.*

Times Books, 201 East 50th Street, New York, New York 10022 (212) 751-2600; *The Economist Book of Vital World Statistics.*

United Nations Educational, Scientific and Cultural Organization (UNESCO), 7 Place de Fontenoy, F-75700 Paris, France (Telephone Number in U.S. (212) 963-5981); *Statistical Yearbook.*

The World Bank, 1818 H Street, NW, Washington, D.C. 20433 (202) 477-1234; *World Tables.*

BHUTAN - EGG PRODUCTION - See BHUTAN - DAIRY PRODUCTS

BHUTAN - ELECTRICITY

Asian Development Bank, P.O. Box 789, 1099 Manila, Philippines; *Key Indicators of Developing Asian and Pacific Countries.*

Facts on File, 460 Park Avenue South, New York, New York 10016 (800) 443-8323; *The New Book of World Rankings.*

Times Books, 201 East 50th Street, New York, New York 10022 (212) 751-2600; *The Economist Book of Vital World Statistics.*

BHUTAN - EMPLOYMENT

Euromonitor Publications Limited, 87-88 Turnmill Street, London EC1M 5QU, England; *International Marketing Data and Statistics.*

Facts on File, 460 Park Avenue South, New York, New York 10016 (800) 443-8323; *The New Book of World Rankings.*

BHUTAN - ENERGY

Facts on File, 460 Park Avenue South, New York, New York 10016 (800) 443-8323; *The New Book of World Rankings.*

Food and Agricultural Organization of the United Nations (FAO) Via delle Terme di Caracalla, 00100 Rome, Italy (Telephone Number in U.S. (202) 653-2400); *The State of Food and Agriculture.*

G.K. Hall and Company, 70 Lincoln Street, Boston, Massachusetts 02111 (617) 423-3990; *The World in Figures.*

Times Books, 201 East 50th Street, New York, New York 10022 (212) 751-2600; *The Economist Book of Vital World Statistics.*

Statistical Office of the United Nations, Publishing Service, New York, New York 10017 (800) 253-9646; *Statistical Yearbook of Asia and the Pacific.*

BHUTAN - EXCHANGE RATES

Asian Development Bank, P.O. Box 789, 1099 Manila, Philippines; *Key Indicators of Developing Asian and Pacific Countries.*

The Economist Intelligence Unit (Asia) Limited, 10th Floor, Luk Kwok Centre, 72 Gloucester Road, Wanchai, Hong Kong (Phone Number in U.S. (800) 938-4685); *Asian Market Atlas.*

Euromonitor Publications Limited, 87-88 Turnmill Street, London EC1M 5QU, England; *International Marketing Data and Statistics.*

BHUTAN - EXPORTS

Asian Development Bank, P.O. Box 789, 1099 Manila, Philippines; *Key Indicators of Developing Asian and Pacific Countries.*

The Economist Intelligence Unit, 111 West 57th Street, New York, New York 10019 (800) 938-4685; *The World Market Atlas.*

The Economist Intelligence Unit (Asia) Limited, 10th Floor, Luk Kwok Centre, 72 Gloucester Road, Wanchai, Hong Kong (Phone Number in U.S. (800) 938-4685); *Asian Market Atlas.*

Euromonitor Publications Limited, 87-88 Turnmill Street, London EC1M 5QU, England; *International Marketing Data and Statistics.*

Food and Agricultural Organization of the United Nations (FAO) Via delle Terme di Caracalla, 00100 Rome, Italy (Telephone Number in U.S. (202) 653-2400); *The State of Food and Agriculture.*

G.K. Hall and Company, 70 Lincoln Street, Boston, Massachusetts 02111 (617) 423-3990; *The World in Figures.*

The World Bank, 1818 H Street, NW, Washington, D.C. 20433 (202) 477-1234; *World Tables.*

BHUTAN - EXTERNAL FINANCING

Asian Development Bank, P.O. Box 789, 1099 Manila, Philippines; *Key Indicators of Developing Asian and Pacific Countries.*

BHUTAN - EXTERNAL INDEBTEDNESS

Asian Development Bank, P.O. Box 789, 1099 Manila, Philippines; *Key Indicators of Developing Asian and Pacific Countries.*

The World Bank, 1818 H Street, NW, Washington, D.C. 20433 (202) 477-1234; *World Tables.*

BHUTAN - EXTERNAL TRADE

Asian Development Bank, P.O. Box 789, 1099 Manila, Philippines; *Key Indicators of Developing Asian and Pacific Countries.*

Food and Agricultural Organization of the United Nations (FAO) Via delle Terme di Caracalla, 00100 Rome, Italy (Telephone Number in U.S. (202) 653-2400); *The State of Food and Agriculture,* and *Trade Yearbook.*

G.K. Hall and Company, 70 Lincoln Street, Boston, Massachusetts 02111 (617) 423-3990; *The World in Figures.*

Statistical Office of the United Nations, Publishing Service, New York, New York 10017 (800) 253-9646; *Statistical Yearbook of Asia and the Pacific.*

BHUTAN - FARM CROPS - See BHUTAN - CROPS

BHUTAN - FEMALE WORKING POPULATION - See BHUTAN - EMPLOYMENT

BHUTAN - FERTILITY RATES

The Economist Intelligence Unit (Asia) Limited, 10th Floor, Luk Kwok Centre, 72 Gloucester Road, Wanchai, Hong Kong (Phone Number in U.S. (800) 938-4685); *Asian Market Atlas.*

Facts on File, 460 Park Avenue South, New York, New York 10016 (800) 443-8323; *The New Book of World Rankings.*

Times Books, 201 East 50th Street, New York, New York 10022 (212) 751-2600; *The Economist Book of Vital World Statistics.*

The World Bank, 1818 H Street, NW, Washington, D.C. 20433 (202) 477-1234; *World Tables.*

BHUTAN - FERTILIZER

Food and Agricultural Organization of the United Nations (FAO) Via delle Terme di Caracalla, 00100 Rome, Italy (Telephone Number in U.S. (202) 653-2400); *The State of Food and Agriculture.*

BHUTAN - FETAL MORTALITY

Statistical Office of the United Nations, Publishing Service, New York, New York 10017 (800) 253-9646; *Demographic Yearbook.*

BHUTAN - FINANCE

Asian Development Bank, P.O. Box 789, 1099 Manila, Philippines; *Key Indicators of Developing Asian and Pacific Countries.*

Facts on File, 460 Park Avenue South, New York, New York 10016 (800) 443-8323; *The New Book of World Rankings.*

G.K. Hall and Company, 70 Lincoln Street, Boston, Massachusetts 02111 (617) 423-3990; *The World in Figures.*

Statistical Office of the United Nations, Publishing Service, New York, New York 10017 (800) 253-9646; *Statistical Yearbook of Asia and the Pacific.*

BHUTAN - FISHERIES

Facts on File, 460 Park Avenue South, New York, New York 10016 (800) 443-8323; *The New Book of World Rankings.*

Food and Agricultural Organization of the United Nations (FAO) Via delle Terme di Caracalla, 00100 Rome, Italy (Telephone Number in U.S. (202) 653-2400); *The State of Food and Agriculture,* and *Yearbook of Fishery Statistics.*

Statistical Office of the United Nations, Publishing Service, New York, New York 10017 (800) 253-9646; *Statistical Yearbook.*

BHUTAN - FOOD

Food and Agricultural Organization of the United Nations (FAO) Via delle Terme di Caracalla, 00100 Rome, Italy (Telephone Number in U.S. (202) 653-2400); *Production Yearbook,* and *The State of Food and Agriculture.*

G.K. Hall and Company, 70 Lincoln Street, Boston, Massachusetts 02111 (617) 423-3990; *The World in Figures.*

Statistical Office of the United Nations, Publishing Service, New York, New York 10017 (800) 253-9646; *Statistical Yearbook of Asia and the Pacific.*

BHUTAN - FOREIGN AID

G.K. Hall and Company, 70 Lincoln Street, Boston, Massachusetts 02111 (617) 423-3990; *The World in Figures.*

BHUTAN - FOREIGN TRADE

Asian Development Bank, P.O. Box 789, 1099 Manila, Philippines; *Key Indicators of Developing Asian and Pacific Countries.*

The Economist Intelligence Unit (Asia) Limited, 10th Floor, Luk Kwok Centre, 72 Gloucester Road, Wanchai, Hong Kong (Phone Number in U.S. (800) 938-4685); *Asian Market Atlas.*

Euromonitor Publications Limited, 87-88 Turnmill Street, London EC1M 5QU, England; *International Marketing Data and Statistics.*

Facts on File, 460 Park Avenue South, New York, New York 10016 (800) 443-8323; *The New Book of World Rankings.*

Food and Agricultural Organization of the United Nations (FAO) Via delle Terme di Caracalla, 00100 Rome, Italy (Telephone Number in U.S. (202) 653-2400); *The State of Food and Agriculture.*

G.K. Hall and Company, 70 Lincoln Street, Boston, Massachusetts 02111 (617) 423-3990; *The World in Figures.*

Organisation for Economic Cooperation and Development (OECD), 2 rue Andre-Pascal, 75 Paris 16, France; *Trade by Commodities.*

The World Bank, 1818 H Street, NW, Washington, D.C. 20433 (202) 477-1234; *World Tables.*

BHUTAN - FORESTRY AND FOREST PRODUCTS

The Economist Intelligence Unit (Asia) Limited, 10th Floor, Luk Kwok Centre, 72 Gloucester Road, Wanchai, Hong Kong (Phone Number in U.S. (800) 938-4685); *Asian Market Atlas.*

Facts on File, 460 Park Avenue South, New York, New York 10016 (800) 443-8323; *The New Book of World Rankings.*

Food and Agricultural Organization of the United Nations (FAO) Via delle Terme di Caracalla, 00100 Rome, Italy (Telephone Number in U.S. (202) 653-2400); *The State of Food and Agriculture.*

G.K. Hall and Company, 70 Lincoln Street, Boston, Massachusetts 02111 (617) 423-3990; *The World in Figures.*

BHUTAN - GAS PRODUCTION - See BHUTAN - MINING AND MINERAL PRODUCTS

BHUTAN - GENERAL MORTALITY

Statistical Office of the United Nations, Publishing Service, New York, New York 10017 (800) 253-9646; *Demographic Yearbook.*

BHUTAN - GEOGRAPHIC DATA

Facts on File, 460 Park Avenue South, New York, New York 10016 (800) 443-8323; *The New Book of World Rankings.*

BHUTAN - GOATS - See BHUTAN - LIVESTOCK AND POULTRY

BHUTAN - GOLD HOLDINGS

The World Bank, 1818 H Street, NW, Washington, D.C. 20433 (202) 477-1234; *World Tables.*

BHUTAN - GOLD PRODUCTION AND CONSUMPTION - See BHUTAN - MINING AND MINERAL PRODUCTS

BHUTAN - GOVERNMENT

Asian Development Bank, P.O. Box 789, 1099 Manila, Philippines; *Key Indicators of Developing Asian and Pacific Countries.*

G.K. Hall and Company, 70 Lincoln Street, Boston, Massachusetts 02111 (617) 423-3990; *The World in Figures.*

BHUTAN - GOVERNMENT BONDS - See BHUTAN - BONDS

BHUTAN - GOVERNMENT EXPENDITURE

Asian Development Bank, P.O. Box 789, 1099 Manila, Philippines; *Key Indicators of Developing Asian and Pacific Countries.*

Times Books, 201 East 50th Street, New York, New York 10022 (212) 751-2600; *The Economist Book of Vital World Statistics.*

The World Bank, 1818 H Street, NW, Washington, D.C. 20433 (202) 477-1234; *World Tables.*

BHUTAN - GOVERNMENT FINANCES

Asian Development Bank, P.O. Box 789, 1099 Manila, Philippines; *Key Indicators of Developing Asian and Pacific Countries.*

BHUTAN - GOVERNMENT REVENUE

Asian Development Bank, P.O. Box 789, 1099 Manila, Philippines; *Key Indicators of Developing Asian and Pacific Countries.*

Times Books, 201 East 50th Street, New York, New York 10022 (212) 751-2600; *The Economist Book of Vital World Statistics.*

The World Bank, 1818 H Street, NW, Washington, D.C. 20433 (202) 477-1234; *World Tables.*

BHUTAN - GRAIN PRODUCTION - See BHUTAN - CROPS

BHUTAN - GROSS DOMESTIC PRODUCT

Asian Development Bank, P.O. Box 789, 1099 Manila, Philippines; *Key Indicators of Developing Asian and Pacific Countries.*

The Economist Intelligence Unit, 111 West 57th Street, New York, New York 10019 (800) 938-4685; *The World Market Atlas.*

The Economist Intelligence Unit (Asia) Limited, 10th Floor, Luk Kwok Centre, 72 Gloucester Road, Wanchai, Hong Kong (Phone Number in U.S. (800) 938-4685); *Asian Market Atlas.*

Euromonitor Publications Limited, 87-88 Turnmill Street, London EC1M 5QU, England; *International Marketing Data and Statistics.*

Facts on File, 460 Park Avenue South, New York, New York 10016 (800) 443-8323; *The New Book of World Rankings.*

G.K. Hall and Company, 70 Lincoln Street, Boston, Massachusetts 02111 (617) 423-3990; *The World in Figures.*

Statistical Office of the United Nations, Publishing Service, New York, New York 10017 (800) 253-9646; *Statistical Yearbook.*

Times Books, 201 East 50th Street, New York, New York 10022 (212) 751-2600; *The Economist Book of Vital World Statistics.*

The World Bank, 1818 H Street, NW, Washington, D.C. 20433 (202) 477-1234; *World Tables.*

BHUTAN - GROSS NATIONAL PRODUCT

Asian Development Bank, P.O. Box 789, 1099 Manila, Philippines; *Key Indicators of Developing Asian and Pacific Countries.*

Euromonitor Publications Limited, 87-88 Turnmill Street, London EC1M 5QU, England; *International Marketing Data and Statistics.*

The World Bank, 1818 H Street, NW, Washington, D.C. 20433 (202) 477-1234; *World Tables.*

BHUTAN - HEALTH

The Economist Intelligence Unit (Asia) Limited, 10th Floor, Luk Kwok Centre, 72 Gloucester Road, Wanchai, Hong Kong (Phone Number in U.S. (800) 938-4685); *Asian Market Atlas.*

Facts on File, 460 Park Avenue South, New York, New York 10016 (800) 443-8323; *The New Book of World Rankings.*

G.K. Hall and Company, 70 Lincoln Street, Boston, Massachusetts 02111 (617) 423-3990; *The World in Figures.*

Times Books, 201 East 50th Street, New York, New York 10022 (212) 751-2600; *The Economist Book of Vital World Statistics.*

BHUTAN - HIDE PRODUCTION

Food and Agricultural Organization of the United Nations (FAO), Via delle Terme di Caracalla, 00100 Rome, Italy (Telephone Number in U.S. (202) 653-2400); *Production Yearbook.*

BHUTAN - HIGHWAYS

The Economist Intelligence Unit (Asia) Limited, 10th Floor, Luk Kwok Centre, 72 Gloucester Road, Wanchai, Hong Kong (Phone Number in U.S. (800) 938-4685); *Asian Market Atlas.*

G.K. Hall and Company, 70 Lincoln Street, Boston, Massachusetts 02111 (617) 423-3990; *The World in Figures.*

BHUTAN - HORSES - See BHUTAN - LIVESTOCK AND POULTRY

BHUTAN - HOURS OF WORK - See BHUTAN - EMPLOYMENT

BHUTAN - HOUSING AND HOUSING UNITS

Facts on File, 460 Park Avenue South, New York, New York 10016 (800) 443-8323; *The New Book of World Rankings.*

BHUTAN - ILLITERATE POPULATION

The Economist Intelligence Unit, 111 West 57th Street, New York, New York 10019 (800) 938-4685; *The World Market Atlas.*

G.K. Hall and Company, 70 Lincoln Street, Boston, Massachusetts 02111 (617) 423-3990; *The World in Figures.*

BHUTAN - IMPORTS

Asian Development Bank, P.O. Box 789, 1099 Manila, Philippines; *Key Indicators of Developing Asian and Pacific Countries.*

The Economist Intelligence Unit, 111 West 57th Street, New York, New York 10019 (800) 938-4685; *The World Market Atlas.*

The Economist Intelligence Unit (Asia) Limited, 10th Floor, Luk Kwok Centre, 72 Gloucester Road, Wanchai, Hong Kong (Phone Number in U.S. (800) 938-4685); *Asian Market Atlas.*

Euromonitor Publications Limited, 87-88 Turnmill Street, London EC1M 5QU, England; *International Marketing Data and Statistics.*

Food and Agricultural Organization of the United Nations (FAO) Via delle Terme di Caracalla, 00100 Rome, Italy (Telephone Number in U.S. (202) 653-2400); *The State of Food and Agriculture.*

G.K. Hall and Company, 70 Lincoln Street, Boston, Massachusetts 02111 (617) 423-3990; *The World in Figures.*

The World Bank, 1818 H Street, NW, Washington, D.C. 20433 (202) 477-1234; *World Tables.*

BHUTAN - INDUSTRY

Euromonitor Publications Limited, 87-88 Turnmill Street, London EC1M 5QU, England; *International Marketing Data and Statistics.*

Facts on File, 460 Park Avenue South, New York, New York 10016 (800) 443-8323; *The New Book of World Rankings.*

G.K. Hall and Company, 70 Lincoln Street, Boston, Massachusetts 02111 (617) 423-3990; *The World in Figures.*

Statistical Office of the United Nations, Publishing Service, New York, New York 10017 (800) 253-9646; *Statistical Yearbook of Asia and the Pacific.*

Times Books, 201 East 50th Street, New York, New York 10022 (212) 751-2600; *The Economist Book of Vital World Statistics.*

The World Bank, 1818 H Street, NW, Washington, D.C. 20433 (202) 477-1234; *World Tables.*

BHUTAN - INFANT AND MATERNAL MORTALITY

The Economist Intelligence Unit (Asia) Limited, 10th Floor, Luk Kwok Centre, 72 Gloucester Road, Wanchai, Hong Kong (Phone Number in U.S. (800) 938-4685); *Asian Market Atlas.*

Statistical Office of the United Nations, Publishing Service, New York, New York 10017 (800) 253-9646; *Demographic Yearbook.*

Times Books, 201 East 50th Street, New York, New York 10022 (212) 751-2600; *The Economist Book of Vital World Statistics.*

The World Bank, 1818 H Street, NW, Washington, D.C. 20433 (202) 477-1234; *World Tables.*

BHUTAN - INTERNAL TRADE

Statistical Office of the United Nations, Publishing Service, New York, New York 10017 (800) 253-9646; *Statistical Yearbook of Asia and the Pacific.*

BHUTAN - INTERNATIONAL RESERVES EXCLUDING GOLD

Asian Development Bank, P.O. Box 789, 1099 Manila, Philippines; *Key Indicators of Developing Asian and Pacific Countries.*

The World Bank, 1818 H Street, NW, Washington, D.C. 20433 (202) 477-1234; *World Tables.*

BHUTAN - INTERNATIONAL STATISTICS

Asian Development Bank, P.O. Box 789, 1099 Manila, Philippines; *Key Indicators of Developing Asian and Pacific Countries.*

BHUTAN - IRON PRODUCTION - See BHUTAN - MINING AND MINERAL PRODUCTS

BHUTAN - IRRIGATION

Euromonitor Publications Limited, 87-88 Turnmill Street, London EC1M 5QU, England; *International Marketing Data and Statistics.*

BHUTAN - JUTE PRODUCTION - See BHUTAN - CROPS

BHUTAN - LABOR FORCE

The Economist Intelligence Unit (Asia) Limited, 10th Floor, Luk Kwok Centre, 72 Gloucester Road, Wanchai, Hong Kong (Phone Number in U.S. (800) 938-4685); *Asian Market Atlas.*

Euromonitor Publications Limited, 87-88 Turnmill Street, London EC1M 5QU, England; *International Marketing Data and Statistics.*

Facts on File, 460 Park Avenue South, New York, New York 10016 (800) 443-8323; *The New Book of World Rankings.*

Food and Agricultural Organization of the United Nations (FAO) Via delle Terme di Caracalla, 00100 Rome, Italy (Telephone Number in U.S. (202) 653-2400); *The State of Food and Agriculture.*

G.K. Hall and Company, 70 Lincoln Street, Boston, Massachusetts 02111 (617) 423-3990; *The World in Figures.*

The World Bank, 1818 H Street, NW, Washington, D.C. 20433 (202) 477-1234; *World Tables.*

BHUTAN - LAND USE

Euromonitor Publications Limited, 87-88 Turnmill Street, London EC1M 5QU, England; *International Marketing Data and Statistics.*

Food and Agricultural Organization of the United Nations (FAO), Via delle Terme di Caracalla, 00100 Rome, Italy (Telephone Number in U.S. (202) 653-2400); *Production Yearbook.*

G.K. Hall and Company, 70 Lincoln Street, Boston, Massachusetts 02111 (617) 423-3990; *The World in Figures.*

BHUTAN - LIBRARIES

Facts on File, 460 Park Avenue South, New York, New York 10016 (800) 443-8323; *The New Book of World Rankings.*

BHUTAN - LIFE EXPECTANCY

The Economist Intelligence Unit (Asia) Limited, 10th Floor, Luk Kwok Centre, 72 Gloucester Road, Wanchai, Hong Kong (Phone Number in U.S. (800) 938-4685); *Asian Market Atlas.*

BHUTAN - LIVESTOCK AND POULTRY

Euromonitor Publications Limited, 87-88 Turnmill Street, London EC1M 5QU, England; *International Marketing Data and Statistics.*

Facts on File, 460 Park Avenue South, New York, New York 10016 (800) 443-8323; *The New Book of World Rankings.*

Food and Agricultural Organization of the United Nations (FAO), Via delle Terme di Caracalla, 00100 Rome, Italy (Telephone Number in U.S. (202) 653-2400); *Production Yearbook,* and *The State of Food and Agriculture.*

G.K. Hall and Company, 70 Lincoln Street, Boston, Massachusetts 02111 (617) 423-3990; *The World in Figures.*

Statistical Office of the United Nations, Publishing Service, New York, New York 10017 (800) 253-9646; *Statistical Yearbook.*

BHUTAN - LIVING LEVELS

G.K. Hall and Company, 70 Lincoln Street, Boston, Massachusetts 02111 (617) 423-3990; *The World in Figures.*

Times Books, 201 East 50th Street, New York, New York 10022 (212) 751-2600; *The Economist Book of Vital World Statistics.*

BHUTAN - MAIL - NUMBER OF PIECES SENT OR RECEIVED

Statistical Office of the United Nations, Publishing Service, New York, New York 10017 (800) 253-9646; *Statistical Yearbook.*

BHUTAN - MANPOWER

Statistical Office of the United Nations, Publishing Service, New York, New York 10017 (800) 253-9646; *Statistical Yearbook of Asia and the Pacific.*

BHUTAN - MANUFACTURING

Asian Development Bank, P.O. Box 789, 1099 Manila, Philippines; *Key Indicators of Developing Asian and Pacific Countries.*

Facts on File, 460 Park Avenue South, New York, New York 10016 (800) 443-8323; *The New Book of World Rankings.*

G.K. Hall and Company, 70 Lincoln Street, Boston, Massachusetts 02111 (617) 423-3990; *The World in Figures.*

The World Bank, 1818 H Street, NW, Washington, D.C. 20433 (202) 477-1234; *World Tables.*

BHUTAN - MARRIAGE RATES

Facts on File, 460 Park Avenue South, New York, New York 10016 (800) 443-8323; *The New Book of World Rankings.*

Statistical Office of the United Nations, Publishing Service, New York, New York 10017 (800) 253-9646; *Demographic Yearbook.*

BHUTAN - MEAT PRODUCTION - See BHUTAN - LIVESTOCK AND POULTRY

BHUTAN - MERCHANT SHIPPING

G.K. Hall and Company, 70 Lincoln Street, Boston, Massachusetts 02111 (617) 423-3990; *The World in Figures.*

BHUTAN - MILITARY

The Economist Intelligence Unit (Asia) Limited, 10th Floor, Luk Kwok Centre, 72 Gloucester Road, Wanchai, Hong Kong (Phone Number in U.S. (800) 938-4685); *Asian Market Atlas.*

G.K. Hall and Company, 70 Lincoln Street, Boston, Massachusetts 02111 (617) 423-3990; *The World in Figures.*

BHUTAN - MILK PRODUCTION - See BHUTAN - DAIRY PRODUCTS

BHUTAN - MILLET PRODUCTION - See BHUTAN - CROPS

BHUTAN - MINING AND MINERAL PRODUCTS

Asian Development Bank, P.O. Box 789, 1099 Manila, Philippines; *Key Indicators of Developing Asian and Pacific Countries.*

Facts on File, 460 Park Avenue South, New York, New York 10016 (800) 443-8323; *The New Book of World Rankings.*

G.K. Hall and Company, 70 Lincoln Street, Boston, Massachusetts 02111 (617) 423-3990; *The World in Figures.*

BHUTAN - MONEY EXCHANGE RATES

Euromonitor Publications Limited, 87-88 Turnmill Street, London EC1M 5QU, England; *International Marketing Data and Statistics.*

BHUTAN - MONEY RESERVES

Euromonitor Publications Limited, 87-88 Turnmill Street, London EC1M 5QU, England; *International Marketing Data and Statistics.*

BHUTAN - MONEY SUPPLY

Asian Development Bank, P.O. Box 789, 1099 Manila, Philippines; *Key Indicators of Developing Asian and Pacific Countries.*

Euromonitor Publications Limited, 87-88 Turnmill Street, London EC1M 5QU, England; *International Marketing Data and Statistics.*

G.K. Hall and Company, 70 Lincoln Street, Boston, Massachusetts 02111 (617) 423-3990; *The World in Figures.*

The World Bank, 1818 H Street, NW, Washington, D.C. 20433 (202) 477-1234; *World Tables.*

BHUTAN - MOTOR VEHICLES IN USE

G.K. Hall and Company, 70 Lincoln Street, Boston, Massachusetts 02111 (617) 423-3990; *The World in Figures.*

BHUTAN - MULES - See BHUTAN - LIVESTOCK AND POULTRY

BHUTAN - MUSEUMS

Facts on File, 460 Park Avenue South, New York, New York 10016 (800) 443-8323; *The New Book of World Rankings.*

United Nations Educational, Scientific and Cultural Organization (UNESCO), 7 Place de Fontenoy, F-75700 Paris, France (Telephone Number in U.S. (212) 963-5981); *Statistical Yearbook.*

BHUTAN - NATALITY - See BHUTAN - BIRTH RATE

BHUTAN - NATIONAL ACCOUNTS

Statistical Office of the United Nations, Publishing Service, New York, New York 10017 (800) 253-9646; *Statistical Yearbook of Asia and the Pacific.*

BHUTAN - NATIONAL INCOME

Facts on File, 460 Park Avenue South, New York, New York 10016 (800) 443-8323; *The New Book of World Rankings.*

G.K. Hall and Company, 70 Lincoln Street, Boston, Massachusetts 02111 (617) 423-3990; *The World in Figures.*

Statistical Office of the United Nations, Publishing Service, New York, New York 10017 (800) 253-9646; *Statistical Yearbook.*

BHUTAN - NATIONAL PRODUCT

Facts on File, 460 Park Avenue South, New York, New York 10016 (800) 443-8323; *The New Book of World Rankings.*

BHUTAN - NATURAL GAS PRODUCTION - See BHUTAN - MINING AND MINERAL PRODUCTS

BHUTAN - NEWSPAPER PRODUCTION - See BHUTAN - FORESTRY AND FOREST PRODUCTS

BHUTAN - OCCUPATIONS - See BHUTAN - LABOR FORCE

BHUTAN - PEANUT PRODUCTION - See BHUTAN - CROPS

BHUTAN - PESTICIDE USE

Food and Agricultural Organization of the United Nations (FAO) Via delle Terme di Caracalla, 00100 Rome, Italy (Telephone Number in U.S. (202) 653-2400); *The State of Food and Agriculture.*

BHUTAN - PETROLEUM INDUSTRY

Asian Development Bank, P.O. Box 789, 1099 Manila, Philippines; *Key Indicators of Developing Asian and Pacific Countries.*

Facts on File, 460 Park Avenue South, New York, New York 10016 (800) 443-8323; *The New Book of World Rankings.*

Food and Agricultural Organization of the United Nations (FAO) Via delle Terme di Caracalla, 00100 Rome, Italy (Telephone Number in U.S. (202) 653-2400); *The State of Food and Agriculture.*

G.K. Hall and Company, 70 Lincoln Street, Boston, Massachusetts 02111 (617) 423-3990; *The World in Figures.*

BHUTAN - PIGS - See BHUTAN - LIVESTOCK AND POULTRY

BHUTAN - POPULATION

Asian Development Bank, P.O. Box 789, 1099 Manila, Philippines; *Key Indicators of Developing Asian and Pacific Countries.*

The Economist Intelligence Unit, 111 West 57th Street, New York, New York 10019 (800) 938-4685; *The World Market Atlas.*

The Economist Intelligence Unit (Asia) Limited, 10th Floor, Luk Kwok Centre, 72 Gloucester Road, Wanchai, Hong Kong (Phone Number in U.S. (800) 938-4685); *Asian Market Atlas.*

Euromonitor Publications Limited, 87-88 Turnmill Street, London EC1M 5QU, England; *International Marketing Data and Statistics.*

Facts on File, 460 Park Avenue South, New York, New York 10016 (800) 443-8323; *The New Book of World Rankings.*

Food and Agricultural Organization of the United Nations (FAO), Via delle Terme di Caracalla, 00100 Rome, Italy (Telephone Number in U.S. (202) 653-2400); *Production Yearbook.*

G.K. Hall and Company, 70 Lincoln Street, Boston, Massachusetts 02111 (617) 423-3990; *The World in Figures.*

Statistical Office of the United Nations, Publishing Service, New York, New York 10017 (800) 253-9646; *Demographic Yearbook, Statistical Yearbook,* and *Statistical Yearbook of Asia and the Pacific.*

World Health Organization, Office of Publications, Avenue Appia, CH-1211 Geneva 27, Switzerland (Telephone Number in U.S. (518) 436-9686); *World Health Statistics Annual.*

BHUTAN - POST OFFICES

Facts on File, 460 Park Avenue South, New York, New York 10016 (800) 443-8323; *The New Book of World Rankings.*

BHUTAN - POTATO PRODUCTION - See BHUTAN - CROPS

BHUTAN - PRICES

Asian Development Bank, P.O. Box 789, 1099 Manila, Philippines; *Key Indicators of Developing Asian and Pacific Countries.*

Facts on File, 460 Park Avenue South, New York, New York 10016 (800) 443-8323; *The New Book of World Rankings.*

Food and Agricultural Organization of the United Nations (FAO), Via delle Terme di Caracalla, 00100 Rome, Italy (Telephone Number in U.S. (202) 653-2400); *Production Yearbook,* and *The State of Food and Agriculture.*

G.K. Hall and Company, 70 Lincoln Street, Boston, Massachusetts 02111 (617) 423-3990; *The World in Figures.*

BHUTAN - PRODUCTION

Facts on File, 460 Park Avenue South, New York, New York 10016 (800) 443-8323; *The New Book of World Rankings.*

G.K. Hall and Company, 70 Lincoln Street, Boston, Massachusetts 02111 (617) 423-3990; *The World in Figures.*

BHUTAN - PRODUCTIVITY

Euromonitor Publications Limited, 87-88 Turnmill Street, London EC1M 5QU, England; *International Marketing Data and Statistics.*

BHUTAN - PUBLIC FINANCE

Facts on File, 460 Park Avenue South, New York, New York 10016 (800) 443-8323; *The New Book of World Rankings.*

BHUTAN - RADIO BROADCASTING - See BHUTAN - BROADCASTING

BHUTAN - RAILWAYS

G.K. Hall and Company, 70 Lincoln Street, Boston, Massachusetts 02111 (617) 423-3990; *The World in Figures.*

BHUTAN - RELIGION

Facts on File, 460 Park Avenue South, New York, New York 10016 (800) 443-8323; *The New Book of World Rankings.*

BHUTAN - RETAIL TRADE

G.K. Hall and Company, 70 Lincoln Street, Boston, Massachusetts 02111 (617) 423-3990; *The World in Figures.*

BHUTAN - RICE PRODUCTION - See BHUTAN - CROPS

BHUTAN - ROOT AND TUBER PRODUCTION - See BHUTAN - CROPS

BHUTAN - RUBBER PRODUCTION

Facts on File, 460 Park Avenue South, New York, New York 10016 (800) 443-8323; *The New Book of World Rankings.*

BHUTAN - SENIOR CITIZENS

Facts on File, 460 Park Avenue South, New York, New York 10016 (800) 443-8323; *The New Book of World Rankings.*

BHUTAN - SHEEP - See BHUTAN - LIVESTOCK AND POULTRY

BHUTAN - SILVER PRODUCTION AND CONSUMPTION - See BHUTAN - MINING AND MINERAL PRODUCTS

BHUTAN - SOCIAL DATA

Asian Development Bank, P.O. Box 789, 1099 Manila, Philippines; *Key Indicators of Developing Asian and Pacific Countries.*

Facts on File, 460 Park Avenue South, New York, New York 10016 (800) 443-8323; *The New Book of World Rankings.*

G.K. Hall and Company, 70 Lincoln Street, Boston, Massachusetts 02111 (617) 423-3990; *The World in Figures.*

BHUTAN - STATE BUDGET REVENUE AND EXPENDITURES

Euromonitor Publications Limited, 87-88 Turnmill Street, London EC1M 5QU, England; *International Marketing Data and Statistics.*

BHUTAN - STEEL PRODUCTION - See BHUTAN - MINING AND MINERAL PRODUCTS

BHUTAN - STOCKS - COMMODITY - MARKET PRICE - INDEX

Food and Agricultural Organization of the United Nations (FAO) Via delle Terme di Caracalla, 00100 Rome, Italy (Telephone Number in U.S. (202) 653-2400); *The State of Food and Agriculture.*

BHUTAN - SUGAR PRODUCTION - See BHUTAN - CROPS

BHUTAN - TAX REVENUE - See BHUTAN - TAXATION

BHUTAN - TAXATION

G.K. Hall and Company, 70 Lincoln Street, Boston, Massachusetts 02111 (617) 423-3990; *The World in Figures.*

The World Bank, 1818 H Street, NW, Washington, D.C. 20433 (202) 477-1234; *World Tables.*

BHUTAN - TELEPHONES IN USE

American Telephone and Telegraph Company, 26 Parsippany Road, Whippany, New Jersey 07981 (800) 338-4038; *The World's Telephones.*

The Economist Intelligence Unit (Asia) Limited, 10th Floor, Luk Kwok Centre, 72 Gloucester Road, Wanchai, Hong Kong (Phone Number in U.S. (800) 938-4685); *Asian Market Atlas.*

G.K. Hall and Company, 70 Lincoln Street, Boston, Massachusetts 02111 (617) 423-3990; *The World in Figures.*

BHUTAN - TELEVISION BROADCASTING - See BHUTAN - BROADCASTING

BHUTAN - TEXTILE INDUSTRY

G.K. Hall and Company, 70 Lincoln Street, Boston, Massachusetts 02111 (617) 423-3990; *The World in Figures.*

BHUTAN - TOBACCO PRODUCTION

Facts on File, 460 Park Avenue South, New York, New York 10016 (800) 443-8323; *The New Book of World Rankings.*

Statistical Office of the United Nations, Publishing Service, New York, New York 10017 (800) 253-9646; *Statistical Yearbook.*

BHUTAN - TOURISM

Facts on File, 460 Park Avenue South, New York, New York 10016 (800) 443-8323; *The New Book of World Rankings.*

G.K. Hall and Company, 70 Lincoln Street, Boston, Massachusetts 02111 (617) 423-3990; *The World in Figures.*

Times Books, 201 East 50th Street, New York, New York 10022 (212) 751-2600; *The Economist Book of Vital World Statistics.*

World Tourism Organization, Calle Capitan Haya 42, E-28020 Madrid, Spain; *Yearbook of Tourism Statistics.*

BHUTAN - TRADE - See BHUTAN - FOREIGN TRADE

BHUTAN - TRANSPORTATION AND COMMUNICATIONS

The Economist Intelligence Unit (Asia) Limited, 10th Floor, Luk Kwok Centre, 72 Gloucester Road, Wanchai, Hong Kong (Phone Number in U.S. (800) 938-4685); *Asian Market Atlas.*

Facts on File, 460 Park Avenue South, New York, New York 10016 (800) 443-8323; *The New Book of World Rankings.*

G.K. Hall and Company, 70 Lincoln Street, Boston, Massachusetts 02111 (617) 423-3990; *The World in Figures.*

Statistical Office of the United Nations, Publishing Service, New York, New York 10017 (800) 253-9646; *Statistical Yearbook of Asia and the Pacific.*

BHUTAN - UNEMPLOYMENT

Euromonitor Publications Limited, 87-88 Turnmill Street, London EC1M 5QU, England; *International Marketing Data and Statistics.*

BHUTAN - VITAL STATISTICS

Euromonitor Publications Limited, 87-88 Turnmill Street, London EC1M 5QU, England; *International Marketing Data and Statistics.*

G.K. Hall and Company, 70 Lincoln Street, Boston, Massachusetts 02111 (617) 423-3990; *The World in Figures.*

World Health Organization, Office of Publications, Avenue Appia, CH-1211 Geneva 27, Switzerland (Telephone Number in U.S. (518) 436-9686); *World Health Statistics Annual.*

BHUTAN - WAGES

G.K. Hall and Company, 70 Lincoln Street, Boston, Massachusetts 02111 (617) 423-3990; *The World in Figures.*

Statistical Office of the United Nations, Publishing Service, New York, New York 10017 (800) 253-9646; *Statistical Yearbook of Asia and the Pacific.*

BHUTAN - WEATHER

Facts on File, 460 Park Avenue South, New York, New York 10016 (800) 443-8323; *The New Book of World Rankings.*

G.K. Hall and Company, 70 Lincoln Street, Boston, Massachusetts 02111 (617) 423-3990; *The World in Figures.*

BHUTAN - WHEAT PRODUCTION - See BHUTAN - CROPS

BHUTAN - WHOLESALE PRICES

Asian Development Bank, P.O. Box 789, 1099 Manila, Philippines; *Key Indicators of Developing Asian and Pacific Countries.*

BHUTAN - WINE PRODUCTION

Facts on File, 460 Park Avenue South, New York, New York 10016 (800) 443-8323; *The New Book of World Rankings.*

BHUTAN- WOOL PRODUCTION

Facts on File, 460 Park Avenue South, New York, New York 10016 (800) 443-8323; *The New Book of World Rankings.*

BICYCLES

National Sporting Goods Association, 1699 Wall Street, Mount Prospect, Illinois 60056 (708) 439-4000; *The Sporting Goods Market in 1993,* and *Sports Participation in 1992.*

BICYCLES - THEFT

U.S. Department of Justice, Federal Bureau of Investigation, Ninth Street and Pennsylvania Avenue, NW, Washington, D.C. 20535 (202) 324-3000; *Population-at-Risk Rates and Selected Crime Indicators.*

BIOLOGICAL SCIENCES - DEGREES CONFERRED

U.S. National Science Foundation, Division of Science Resources Studies, 4201 Wilson Boulevard, Arlington, Virginia 22230 (703) 306-1234; *Survey of Earned Doctorates.*

BIOLOGICAL SCIENCES - EMPLOYMENT

U.S. Department of Labor, Bureau of Labor Statistics, Two Massachusetts Avenue, NE, Washington, D.C. 20212 (202) 606-7828; *Employment and Earnings,* and *Monthly Labor Review.*

BIRD OWNERSHIP

American Veterinary Medical Association, 930 North Meacham Road, Schaumburg, Illinois 60196 (708) 605-8070; *U.S. Pet Ownership and Demographics Sourcebook.*

BIRTH WEIGHTS

U.S. Department of Health and Human Services, National Center for Health Statistics, 3700 East-West Highway, Hyattsville, Maryland 20782 (301) 436-8500; *Monthly Vital Statistics Report, Vital Statistics of the United States,* and unpublished data.

BIRTHS AND BIRTH RATES

U.S. Department of Commerce, Bureau of the Census, Suitland, Maryland 20233 (301) 763-4040; *Current Population Reports,* and unpublished data.

U.S. Department of Health and Human Services, National Center for Health Statistics, 3700 East-West Highway, Hyattsville, Maryland 20782 (301) 436-8500; *Monthly Vital Statistics Report, Vital Statistics of the United States*, and unpublished data.

BIRTHS AND BIRTH RATES - AMERICAN INDIAN, ESKIMO, AND ALEUT POPULATION

U.S. Department of Health and Human Services, National Center for Health Statistics, 3700 East-West Highway, Hyattsville, Maryland 20782 (301) 436-8500; *Monthly Vital Statistics Report, Vital Statistics of the United States*, and unpublished data.

BIRTHS AND BIRTH RATES - ASIAN AND PACIFIC ISLANDER POPULATION

U.S. Department of Health and Human Services, National Center for Health Statistics, 3700 East-West Highway, Hyattsville, Maryland 20782 (301) 436-8500; *Monthly Vital Statistics Report, Vital Statistics of the United States*, and unpublished data.

BIRTHS AND BIRTH RATES - BIRTHS TO SINGLE OR UNMARRIED WOMEN

U.S. Department of Commerce, Bureau of the Census, Suitland, Maryland 20233 (301) 763-4040; *Current Population Reports*.

U.S. Department of Health and Human Services, National Center for Health Statistics, 3700 East-West Highway, Hyattsville, Maryland 20782 (301) 436-8500; *Vital Statistics of the United States*, and unpublished data.

U.S. Department of Labor, Bureau of Labor Statistics, Two Massachusetts Avenue, NE, Washington, D.C. 20212 (202) 606-7828; *Monthly Labor Review*, and unpublished data.

BIRTHS AND BIRTH RATES - BIRTH WEIGHT

U.S. Department of Health and Human Services, National Center for Health Statistics, 3700 East-West Highway, Hyattsville, Maryland 20782 (301) 436-8500; *Monthly Vital Statistics Report, Vital Statistics of the United States*, and unpublished data.

BIRTHS AND BIRTH RATES - BLACK POPULATION

U.S. Department of Commerce, Bureau of the Census, Suitland, Maryland 20233 (301) 763-4040; *Current Population Reports*.

U.S. Department of Health and Human Services, National Center for Health Statistics, 3700 East-West Highway, Hyattsville, Maryland 20782 (301) 436-8500; *Monthly Vital Statistics Report, Vital Statistics of the United States*, and unpublished data.

BIRTHS AND BIRTH RATES - CESAREAN SECTION DELIVERIES

U.S. Department of Health and Human Services, National Center for Health Statistics, 3700 East-West Highway, Hyattsville, Maryland 20782 (301) 436-8500; *Vital and Health Statistics*, and unpublished data.

BIRTHS AND BIRTH RATES - CHARACTERISTICS OF MOTHER

U.S. Department of Commerce, Bureau of the Census, Suitland, Maryland 20233 (301) 763-4040; *Current Population Reports*.

U.S. Department of Health and Human Services, National Center for Health Statistics, 3700 East-West Highway, Hyattsville, Maryland 20782 (301) 436-8500; *Vital Statistics of the United States*, and unpublished data.

BIRTHS AND BIRTH RATES - DELIVERY PROCEDURES

U.S. Department of Health and Human Services, National Center for Health Statistics, 3700 East-West Highway, Hyattsville, Maryland 20782 (301) 436-8500; *Vital and Health Statistics*, and unpublished data.

BIRTHS AND BIRTH RATES - EXPECTATIONS

U.S. Department of Commerce, Bureau of the Census, Suitland, Maryland 20233 (301) 763-4040; *Current Population Reports*.

BIRTHS AND BIRTH RATES - FIRST BIRTHS

U.S. Department of Commerce, Bureau of the Census, Suitland, Maryland 20233 (301) 763-4040; *Current Population Reports*.

BIRTHS AND BIRTH RATES - HISPANIC POPULATION

U.S. Department of Health and Human Services, National Center for Health Statistics, 3700 East-West Highway, Hyattsville, Maryland 20782 (301) 436-8500; *Monthly Vital Statistics Report, Vital Statistics of the United States*, and unpublished data.

BIRTHS AND BIRTH RATES - METROPOLITAN AREAS

U.S. Department of Health and Human Services, National Center for Health Statistics, 3700 East-West Highway, Hyattsville, Maryland 20782 (301) 436-8500; *Vital Statistics of the United States*.

BIRTHS AND BIRTH RATES - OUTLYING AREAS OF THE UNITED STATES

U.S. Department of Commerce, Bureau of the Census, Suitland, Maryland 20233 (301) 763-4040; *Current Population Reports*.

U.S. Department of Health and Human Services, National Center for Health Statistics, 3700 East-West Highway, Hyattsville, Maryland 20782 (301) 436-8500; *Vital Statistics of the United States*.

BIRTHS AND BIRTH RATES - PRENATAL CARE

U.S. Department of Health and Human Services, National Center for Health Statistics, 3700 East-West Highway, Hyattsville, Maryland 20782 (301) 436-8500; *Vital Statistics of the United States*, and unpublished data.

BIRTHS AND BIRTH RATES - PROJECTIONS

U.S. Department of Commerce, Bureau of the Census, Suitland, Maryland 20233 (301) 763-4040; *Current Population Reports*.

BIRTHS AND BIRTH RATES - RACE

U.S. Department of Commerce, Bureau of the Census, Suitland, Maryland 20233 (301) 763-4040; *Current Population Reports*.

U.S. Department of Health and Human Services, National Center for Health Statistics, 3700 East-West Highway, Hyattsville, Maryland 20782 (301) 436-8500; *Vital Statistics of the United States*, and unpublished data.

BISMUTH

U.S. Department of the Interior, Bureau of Mines, 810 Seventh Street, NW, Washington, D.C. 20241 (202) 501-9649; *Mineral Commodity*

Summaries.

BLACK LUNG BENEFIT PROGRAM

U.S. Department of Health and Human Services, Social Security Administration, 6401 Security Boulevard, Baltimore, Maryland 21235 (410) 965-1234; *Social Security Bulletin, Annual Statistical Supplement to the Social Security Bulletin,* and unpublished data.

U.S. Department of Labor, Employment Standards Administration, 200 Constitution Avenue, NW, Washington, D.C. 20210 (202) 219-8743; *Black Lung Benefits Act, Annual Report.*

BLACK POPULATION

U.S. Department of Commerce, Bureau of the Census, Suitland, Maryland 20233 (301) 763-4040; *Census of Population, Current Population Reports,* and unpublished data.

BLACK POPULATION - ABORTIONS

Alan Guttmacher Institute, 111 Fifth Avenue South, New York, New York 10003 (212) 254-5656; *Abortion Factbook, Abortion Services in the U.S., Family Perspectives,* and unpublished data.

BLACK POPULATION - AGE AND/OR SEX

U.S. Department of Commerce, Bureau of the Census, Suitland, Maryland 20233 (301) 763-4040; *Census of Population, Current Population Reports,* and unpublished data.

BLACK POPULATION - AIDS

U.S. Department of Health and Human Services, Center for Disease Control, 1600 Clifton Road, Atlanta, Georgia 30333 (404) 639-3311; *Surveillance Report,* and unpublished data.

BLACK POPULATION - ALCOHOL USE

U.S. Department of Health and Human Services, National Center for Health Statistics, 3700 East West Highway, Hyattsville, Maryland 20782 (301) 436-8500; *Health Promotion and Disease Prevention, United States, Vital and Health Statistics,* and unpublished data.

BLACK POPULATION - BIRTHS AND BIRTH RATES

U.S. Department of Commerce, Bureau of the Census, Suitland, Maryland 20233 (301) 763-4040; *Current Population Reports,* and unpublished data.

U.S. Department of Health and Human Services, National Center for Health Statistics, 3700 East-West Highway, Hyattsville, Maryland 20782 (301) 436-8500; *Monthly Vital Statistics Report, Vital Statistics of the United States,* and unpublished data.

BLACK POPULATION - BIRTHS AND BIRTH RATES - BIRTHS TO UNMARRIED WOMEN

U.S. Department of Commerce, Bureau of the Census, Suitland, Maryland 20233 (301) 763-4040; *Current Population Reports.*

U.S. Department of Health and Human Services, National Center for Health Statistics, 3700 East-West Highway, Hyattsville, Maryland 20782 (301) 436-8500; *Monthly Vital Statistics Report, Vital Statistics of the United States,* and unpublished data.

BLACK POPULATION - BIRTHS AND BIRTH RATES - EXPECTATIONS

U.S. Department of Commerce, Bureau of the Census, Suitland, Maryland 20233 (301) 763-4040; *Current Population Reports.*

BLACK POPULATION - CANCER

U.S. Department of Health and Human Services, National Center for Health Statistics, 3700 East-West Highway, Hyattsville, Maryland 20782 (301) 436-8500; *Monthly Vital Statistics Report, Vital Statistics of the United States,* and *Vital and Health Statistics.*

U.S. Department of Health and Human Services, National Institutes of Health, National Cancer Institute, 9000 Rockville Pike, Bethesda, Maryland 20892 (301) 496-5737; *Cancer Statistics Review.*

BLACK POPULATION - CHILD CARE

U.S. Department of Commerce, Bureau of the Census, Suitland, Maryland 20233 (301) 763-4040; *Current Population Reports.*

BLACK POPULATION - CHILDREN UNDER EIGHTEEN

National Center for Children in Poverty, Columbia University, 154 Haven Avenue, Manhattan, New York 10032 (212) 927-8793; unpublished data.

U.S. Department of Commerce, Bureau of the Census, Suitland, Maryland 20233 (301) 763-4040; *Current Population Reports.*

BLACK POPULATION - CHILDREN UNDER EIGHTEEN - POVERTY

National Center for Children in Poverty, Columbia University, 154 Haven Avenue, Manhattan, New York 10032 (212) 927-8793; unpublished data.

U.S. Department of Commerce, Bureau of the Census, Suitland, Maryland 20233 (301) 763-4040; *Current Population Reports,* and unpublished data.

BLACK POPULATION - CIGARETTE SMOKING

U.S. Department of Health and Human Services, National Center for Health Statistics, 3700 East West Highway, Hyattsville, Maryland 20782 (301) 436-8500; *Health Promotion and Disease Prevention, United States, Health, United States, Vital and Health Statistics,* and unpublished data.

BLACK POPULATION - CONGRESS, MEMBERS OF

Joint Center for Political and Economic Studies, 1090 Vermont Avenue, NW, Suite 1100, Washington, D.C. 20005 (202) 789-3500; *Black Elected Officials: A National Roster.*

U.S. Department of Commerce, Bureau of the Census, Suitland, Maryland 20233 (301) 763-4040; *Congressional Directory.*

BLACK POPULATION - CONTRACEPTIVE USE

U.S. Department of Health and Human Services, National Center for Health Statistics, 3700 East-West Highway, Hyattsville, Maryland 20782 (301) 436-8500; *Advance Data from Vital and Health Statistics.*

BLACK POPULATION - CRIMINAL VICTIMIZATIONS

U.S. Department of Justice, Bureau of Justice Statistics, 633 Indiana Avenue, NW, Washington, D.C. 20531 (800) 732-3277; *Crime and the Nation's Households.*

BLACK POPULATION - DEATHS AND DEATH RATES

U.S. Department of Commerce, Bureau of the Census, Suitland, Maryland 20233 (301) 763-4040; *Current Population Reports,* and unpublished data.

U.S. Department of Health and Human Services, Centers for Disease Control, 1600 Clifton Road, NE, Atlanta, Georgia 30333 (404) 639-3311; *Surveillance Report.*

U.S. Department of Health and Human Services, National Center for Health Statistics, 3700 East-West Highway, Hyattsville, Maryland 20782 (301) 436-8500; *Advance Data from Vital and Health Statistics, Monthly Vital Statistics Report, Vital Statistics of the United States,* and unpublished data.

BLACK POPULATION - DISABILITY DAYS

U.S. Department of Health and Human Services, National Center for Health Statistics, 3700 East-West Highway, Hyattsville, Maryland 20782 (301) 436-8500; *Vital and Health Statistics,* and unpublished data.

BLACK POPULATION - DISABLED PERSONS

U.S. Department of Commerce, Bureau of the Census, Suitland, Maryland 20233 (301) 763-4040; *Current Population Report.*

BLACK POPULATION - ELDERLY

U.S. Department of Commerce, Bureau of the Census, Suitland, Maryland 20233 (301) 763-4040; *Current Population Reports,* and unpublished data.

BLACK POPULATION - ELECTED OFFICIALS

Joint Center for Political and Economic Studies, 1090 Vermont Avenue, NW, Suite 1100, Washington, D.C. 20004 (202) 789-3500; *Black Elected Officials: A National Roster.*

U.S. Department of Commerce, Bureau of the Census, Suitland, Maryland 20233 (301) 763-4040; *Congressional Directory.*

BLACK POPULATION - ELECTIONS, VOTER REGISTRATION AND TURNOUT

U.S. Department of Commerce, Bureau of the Census, Suitland, Maryland 20233 (301) 763-4040; *Current Population Reports.*

BLACK POPULATION - FAMILIES - CHARACTERISTICS

U.S. Department of Commerce, Bureau of the Census, Suitland, Maryland 20233 (301) 763-4040; *Current Population Reports,* and *United States Census of Population.*

BLACK POPULATION - FARM OPERATORS

U.S. Department of Commerce, Bureau of the Census, Suitland, Maryland 20233 (301) 763-4040; *Census of Agriculture.*

BLACK POPULATION - FARM WORKERS

U.S. Department of Agriculture, Economic Research Service, Fourteenth Street and Independence Avenue, SW, Washington, D.C. 20005-4789 (202) 219-1504; unpublished data.

BLACK POPULATION - FERTILITY - FERTILITY RATE

U.S. Department of Commerce, Bureau of the Census, Suitland, Maryland 20233 (301) 763-4040; *Current Population Reports.*

U.S. Department of Health and Human Services, National Center for Health Statistics, 3700 East-West Highway, Hyattsville, Maryland 20782 (301) 436-8500; *Vital Statistics of the United States,* and unpublished data.

BLACK POPULATION - HEALTH INSURANCE COVERAGE

U.S. Department of Commerce, Bureau of the Census, Suitland, Maryland 20233 (301) 763-4040; *Current Population Reports,* and unpublished data.

BLACK POPULATION - HIGH SCHOOL GRADUATES AND DROPOUTS

U.S. Department of Commerce, Bureau of the Census, Suitland, Maryland 20233 (301) 763-4040; *Current Population Reports.*

BLACK POPULATION - HOME HEALTH AND HOSPICE CARE

U.S. Department of Health and Human Services, National Center for Health Statistics, 3700 East-West Highway, Hyattsville, Maryland 20782 (301) 436-8500; *Vital and Health Statistics, Advance Data.*

BLACK POPULATION - HOMICIDES

U.S. Department of Health and Human Services, National Center for Health Statistics, 3700 East-West Highway, Hyattsville, Maryland 20782 (301) 436-8500; *Advance Data from Vital and Health Statistics, Vital Statistics of the United States,* and *Monthly Vital Statistics Report.*

BLACK POPULATION - HOUSEHOLDS, CHARACTERISTICS

U.S. Department of Commerce, Bureau of the Census, Suitland, Maryland 20233 (301) 763-4040; *Current Population Reports, U.S. Census of Population,* and unpublished data.

BLACK POPULATION - HOUSING

U.S. Department of Commerce, Bureau of the Census, Suitland, Maryland 20233 (301) 763-4040; *Current Housing Reports,* and *United States Census of Housing, General Housing Characteristics.*

BLACK POPULATION - HOSPITAL USE

U.S. Department of Health and Human Services, National Center for Health Statistics, 3700 East-West Highway, Hyattsville, Maryland 20782 (301) 436-8500; unpublished data.

BLACK POPULATION - ILLNESS

U.S. Department of Health and Human Services, National Center for Health Statistics, 3700 East-West Highway, Hyattsville, Maryland 20782 (301) 436-8500; *Vital and Health Statistics,* and unpublished data.

BLACK POPULATION - INCOME

U.S. Department of Commerce, Bureau of the Census, Suitland, Maryland 20233 (301) 763-4040; *Current Population Reports,* and unpublished data.

BLACK POPULATION - INFANT DEATHS

U.S. Department of Health and Human Services, National Center for Health Statistics, 3700 East-West Highway, Hyattsville, Maryland 20782 (301) 436-8500; *Monthly Vital Statistics Report, Vital Statistics of the United States,* and unpublished data.

BLACK POPULATION - JAIL INMATES

U.S. Department of Justice, Bureau of Justice Statistics, 633 Indiana Avenue, NW, Washington, D.C. 20531 (800) 732-3277; *Jail Inmates,* and *Census of Local Jails.*

BLACK POPULATION - LABOR FORCE

U.S. Department of Labor, Bureau of Labor Statistics, Two Massachusetts Avenue, NE, Washington, D.C. 20212 (202) 606-7828; *Employment and Earnings, Monthly Labor Review,* and Bulletin 2307.

BLACK POPULATION - LABOR FORCE - EARNINGS

U.S. Department of Labor, Bureau of Labor Statistics, Two Massachusetts Avenue, NE, Washington, D.C. 20212 (202) 606-7828; *Bulletin 2307, Employment and Earnings,* and unpublished data.

BLACK POPULATION - LABOR FORCE - EMPLOYED

U.S. Department of Labor, Bureau of Labor Statistics, Two Massachusetts Avenue, NE, Washington, D.C. 20212 (202) 606-7828; *Employment and Earnings, Monthly Labor Review, News,* and Bulletin 2307.

BLACK POPULATION - LABOR FORCE - EMPLOYMENT STATUS

U.S. Department of Labor, Bureau of Labor Statistics, Two Massachusetts Avenue, NE, Washington, D.C. 20212 (202) 606-7828; *Employment and Earnings,* and Bulletin 2307.

BLACK POPULATION - LABOR FORCE - EMPLOYMENT STATUS - AGE

U.S. Department of Labor, Bureau of Labor Statistics, Two Massachusetts Avenue, NE, Washington, D.C. 20212 (202) 606-7828; *Employment and Earnings.*

BLACK POPULATION - LABOR FORCE - EMPLOYMENT STATUS - EDUCATIONAL ATTAINMENT

U.S. Department of Labor, Bureau of Labor Statistics, Two Massachusetts Avenue, NE, Washington, D.C. 20212 (202) 606-7828; Bulletin 2307 and unpublished data.

BLACK POPULATION - LABOR FORCE - EMPLOYMENT STATUS - GOVERNMENT EMPLOYEES AND SALARIES

Equal Employment Opportunity Commission, 1801 L Street, NW, Washington, D.C. 20507 (800) USA-EEOC; *State and Local Government Information Report.*

BLACK POPULATION - LABOR FORCE - EMPLOYMENT STATUS - HIGH SCHOOL GRADUATES AND DROPOUTS, EMPLOYMENT STATUS

U.S. Department of Labor, Bureau of Labor Statistics, Two Massachusetts Avenue, NE, Washington, D.C. 20212 (202) 606-7828; *News,* Bulletin 2307 and unpublished data.

BLACK POPULATION - LABOR FORCE - EMPLOYMENT STATUS - SCHOOL ENROLLMENT - PERSONS FIFTEEN TO TWENTY-FOUR YEARS OLD

U.S. Department of Labor, Bureau of Labor Statistics, Two Massachusetts Avenue, NE, Washington, D.C. 20212 (202) 606-7828; Bulletin 2307, *News,* and unpublished data.

BLACK POPULATION - LABOR FORCE - EMPLOYMENT STATUS - UNEMPLOYED

U.S. Department of Labor, Bureau of Labor Statistics, Two Massachusetts Avenue, NE, Washington, D.C. 20212 (202) 606-7828; *Employment and Earnings,* Bulletin 2307 and unpublished data.

BLACK POPULATION - LABOR FORCE - STATE AND LOCAL GOVERNMENT EMPLOYEES AND SALARIES

U.S. Equal Employment Opportunity Commission, 2401 E Street, NW, Washington, D.C. 20507 (800) USA-EEOC; *State and Local Government Information Report.*

BLACK POPULATION - LIFE EXPECTANCY

U.S. Department of Health and Human Services, National Center for Health Statistics, 3700 East-West Highway, Hyattsville, Maryland 20782 (301) 436-8500; *Monthly Vital Statistics Reports, Vital Statistics of the United States, United States Life Tables and Actuarial Tables,* and unpublished data.

BLACK POPULATION - MARITAL STATUS

U.S. Department of Commerce, Bureau of the Census, Suitland, Maryland 20233 (301) 763-4040; *Current Population Reports,* and *Census of Population.*

BLACK POPULATION - METROPOLITAN AREAS

U.S. Department of Commerce, Bureau of the Census, Suitland, Maryland 20233 (301) 763-4040; *Census of Population and Housing, Supplementary Reports, Metropolitan Areas as Defined by the Office of Management and Budget.*

BLACK POPULATION - MINIMUM WAGE WORKERS

U.S. Department of Labor, Bureau of Labor Statistics, Two Massachusetts Avenue, NE, Washington, D.C. 20212 (202) 606-7828; unpublished data.

BLACK POPULATION - MULTIMEDIA USERS

Mediamark Research, Incorporated, 708 Third Avenue, New York, New York 10017 (212) 599-0444; *Multimedia Audiences.*

BLACK POPULATION - OVERWEIGHT

U.S. Department of Health and Human Services, National Center for Health Statistics, 3700 East-West Highway, Hyattsville, Maryland 20782 (301) 436-8500; *Health Promotion and Disease Prevention: United States,* and *Vital and Health Statistics.*

BLACK POPULATION - PENSION PLAN COVERAGE

U.S. Department of Commerce, Bureau of the Census, Suitland, Maryland 20233 (301) 763-4040; unpublished data.

BLACK POPULATION - POVERTY

National Center for Children in Poverty, Columbia University, 154 Haven Avenue, Manhattan, New York 10032 (212) 927-8793; unpublished data.

U.S. Department of Commerce, Bureau of the Census, Suitland, Maryland 20233 (301) 763-4040; *Current Population Reports*, and unpublished data.

BLACK POPULATION - PRISONERS

U.S. Department of Justice, Bureau of Justice Statistics, 633 Indiana Avenue, NW, Washington, D.C. 20531 (800) 732-3277; *Prisoners in State and Federal Institutions on December 31st*, *Correctional Populations in the United States*, *Profile of State Prison Inmates*, and *Survey of State Prison Inmates*.

BLACK POPULATION - SCHOOL DROPOUTS - HIGH SCHOOL

U.S. Department of Commerce, Bureau of the Census, Suitland, Maryland 20233 (301) 763-4040; *Current Population Reports*.

U.S. Department of Labor, Bureau of Labor Statistics, Two Massachusetts Avenue, NE, Washington, D.C. 20212 (202) 606-7828; *News*, Bulletin 2307, and unpublished data.

BLACK POPULATION - SCHOOLS AND EDUCATION - AMERICAN COLLEGE TESTING PROGRAM

The American College Testing Program, Box 168, Iowa City, Iowa 52243 (319) 337-1000; *High School Profile Report*.

BLACK POPULATION - SCHOOLS AND EDUCATION - ATTAINMENT

U.S. Department of Commerce, Bureau of the Census, Suitland, Maryland 20233 (301) 763-4040; *Current Population Reports*, *United States Census of Population*, and unpublished data.

U.S. Department of Education, National Center for Education Statistics, 400 Maryland Avenue, SW, Washington, D.C. 20202 (202) 708-5366; *Digest of Education Statistics*.

BLACK POPULATION - SCHOOLS AND EDUCATION - COLLEGE ENROLLMENT

U.S. Department of Commerce, Bureau of the Census, Suitland, Maryland 20233 (301) 763-4040; *Current Population Reports*, and unpublished data.

BLACK POPULATION - SCHOOLS AND EDUCATION - ENROLLMENT

U.S. Department of Commerce, Bureau of the Census, Suitland, Maryland 20233 (301) 763-4040; *Current Population Reports*, and unpublished data.

BLACK POPULATION - SCHOOLS AND EDUCATION - HIGH SCHOOL DROPOUTS

U.S. Department of Commerce, Bureau of the Census, Suitland, Maryland 20233 (301) 763-4040; *Current Population Reports*, and unpublished data.

U.S. Department of Labor, Bureau of Labor Statistics, Two Massachusetts Avenue, NE, Washington, D.C. 20212 (202) 606-7828; *Bulletin 2307*, and unpublished data.

BLACK POPULATION - SCHOOLS AND EDUCATION - HIGH SCHOOL GRADUATES

U.S. Department of Commerce, Bureau of the Census, Suitland, Maryland 20233 (301) 763-4040; *Current Population Reports*, *Characteristics of the Population*, and unpublished data.

U.S. Department of Education, 400 Maryland Avenue, SW, Washington, D.C. 20202 (202) 708-5366; *Digest of Education Statistics*.

BLACK POPULATION - SCHOOLS AND EDUCATION - HIGHER EDUCATION INSTITUTIONS - DEGREES CONFERRED

U.S. National Science Foundation, Division of Science Resources Studies, 4201 Wilson Boulevard, Arlington, Virginia 22230 (703) 306-1234; *Survey of Earned Doctorates*.

BLACK POPULATION - SCHOOLS AND EDUCATION - HIGHER EDUCATION INSTITUTIONS - ENROLLMENT

U.S. Department of Commerce, Bureau of the Census, Suitland, Maryland 20233 (301) 763-4040; *Current Population Reports*, and unpublished data.

BLACK POPULATION - SCHOOLS AND EDUCATION- PREPRIMARY ENROLLMENT

U.S. Department of Commerce, Bureau of the Census, Suitland, Maryland 20233 (301) 763-4040; *Current Population Reports*, and unpublished data.

BLACK POPULATION - SCHOOLS AND EDUCATION - SCHOLASTIC APTITUDE TEST

College Entrance Examination Board, 45 Columbus Avenue, New York, New York 10023 (212) 713-8000; *National College-Bound Senior*.

BLACK POPULATION - SCHOOLS AND EDUCATION - TEACHERS

U.S. Department of Education, National Center for Education Statistics, 400 Maryland Avenue, SW, Washington, D.C. 20202 (202) 708-5366; *Digest of Education Statistics*.

BLACK POPULATION - STATES

U.S. Department of Commerce, Bureau of the Census, Suitland, Maryland 20233 (301) 763-4040; *Current Population Reports*.

BLACK POPULATION - SUICIDES

U.S. Department of Health and Human Services, National Center for Health Statistics, 3700 East-West Highway, Hyattsville, Maryland 20782 (301) 436-8500; *Advance Data from Vital and Health Statistics*, *Vital Statistics of the United States*, *Monthly Vital Statistics Report*, and unpublished data.

BLACK POPULATION - UNION MEMBERSHIP

U.S. Department of Labor, Bureau of Labor Statistics, Two Massachusetts Avenue, NE, Washington, D.C. 20212 (202) 606-7828; *Employment and Earnings*.

BLACK POPULATION - VOTER REGISTRATION AND TURNOUT

U.S. Department of Commerce, Bureau of the Census, Suitland, Maryland 20233 (301) 763-4040; *Current Population Reports*.

BLACK POPULATION - VOLUNTEERS

Independent Sector, 1828 L Street, NW, Suite 1200, Washington, D.C. 20036 (202) 223-8100; *Giving and Volunteering in the United States.*

BLACK POPULATION - WEALTH

U.S. Department of Commerce, Bureau of the Census, Suitland, Maryland 20233 (301) 763-4040; *Current Population Reports.*

BLAST FURNACES - See IRON AND STEEL PRODUCTS

BLIND PERSONS

U.S. Department of Health and Human Services, Administration for Children and Families, 370 L'Enfant Promenade, SW, Washington, D.C 20447 (202) 401-9200; *Quarterly Public Assistance Statistics.*

U.S. Department of Health and Human Services, Social Security Administration, 6401 Security Boulevard, Baltimore, Maryland 21235 (410) 965-1234; *Social Security Bulletin* and *Annual Statistical Supplement to the Social Security Bulletin.*

BLIND PERSONS - MEDICAID PAYMENTS AND RECIPIENTS

U.S. Department of Health and Human Services, Health Care Financing Administration, 200 Independence Avenue, SW, Washington, D.C. 20201 (202) 245-6113; *Health Care Financing Review.*

BLOOD BANKS

American Hospital Association, 840 North Lake Shore Drive, Chicago, Illinois 60611 (312) 280-6000; *Hospital Statistics,* and *Annual Survey of Hospitals.*

BLUE-COLLAR WORKERS

U.S. Office of Personnel Management, 1900 E Street, NW, Washington, D.C. 20415 (202) 606-1800; *Federal Civilian Workforce Statistics, Employment and Trends,* and unpublished data.

BLUE-COLLAR WORKERS - EMPLOYMENT COST INDEX

U.S. Department of Labor, Bureau of Labor Statistics, Two Massachusetts Avenue, NE, Washington, D.C. 20212 (202) 606-7828; *News, Employment Cost Index.*

BLUEFISH

U.S. Department of Commerce, National Oceanic and Atmospheric Administration, National Marine Fisheries Service, 1335 East-West Highway, Silver Spring, Maryland 20910 (301) 427-2239; *Fisheries of the United States.*

BOATING, CANOEING, ETC.

National Marine Manufacturers Association, 401 North Michigan Avenue, Chicago, Illinois 60611 (312) 836-4747.

National Sporting Goods Association, Lake Center Plaza Building, 1699 Wall Street, Mount Prospect, Illinois 60056 (708) 439-4000; *The Sporting Goods Market in 1993.*

BOATING, CANOEING, ETC. - ACCIDENTS

U.S. Department of Transportation, Bureau of Transportation Statistics, 400 Seventh Street, SW, Washington, D.C. 20590 (202) 366-DATA; *National Transportation Statistics Annual, Historical Compendium Information Report.*

Bolivia - National Statistical Office

Instituto Nacional de Estadistica, Casilla 6129, La Paz, Bolivia.

Bolivia - Primary Statistics Sources

Instituto Nacional de Estadistica, Casilla No. 6129, La Paz, Bolivia; *Boletin estadistico* (Statistical Bulletin); *Resumen estadistco* (Statistical summary), and *Bolivia en cifras* (Bolivia in figures).

BOLIVIA - AGRICULTURE

The Economist Intelligence Unit, 111 West 57th Street, New York, New York 10019 (800) 933-4685; *The New Latin America Market Atlas.*

Euromonitor Publications Limited, 87-88 Turnmill Street, London EC1M 5QU, England; *International Marketing Data and Statistics.*

Facts on File, 460 Park Avenue South, New York, New York 10016 (800) 443-8323; *The New Book of World Rankings.*

Federal Statistical Office, Gustav - Stresemann - Ring 11, D-6200 Wiesbaden, Germany; *Bolivia.*

Food and Agricultural Organization of the United Nations (FAO) Via delle Terme di Caracalla, 00100 Rome, Italy (Telephone Number in U.S. (202) 653-2400); *Production Yearbook, The State of Food and Agriculture,* and *Trade Yearbook.*

Gale Research Incorporated, 835 Penobscot Building, Detroit, Michigan 48226 (800) 877-4253; *International Historical Statistics The Americas and Australasia.*

G. K. Hall and Company, 70 Lincoln Street, Boston, Massachusetts 02111 (617) 423-3990; *The World In Figures.*

Inter-American Development Bank, 1300 New York Avenue, NW, Washington, D.C. 20577 (202) 623-1753; *Economic and Social Progress in Latin America.*

Statistical Office of the United Nations, Publishing Service, New York, New York 10017 (800) 253-9646; *Statistical Yearbook,* and *Statistical Yearbook for Latin America and the Caribbean.*

Times Books, 201 East 50th Street, New York, New York 10022 (212) 751-2600; *The Economist Book of Vital World Statistics.*

U.C.L.A. Latin American Center Publications, University of California, Los Angeles, California 90024 (310) 825-6634; *Statistical Abstract of Latin America.*

The World Bank, 1818 H Street, NW, Washington, D.C. 20433 (202) 477-1234; *World Tables.*

BOLIVIA - AIRLINE SERVICE

The Economist Intelligence Unit, 111 West 57th Street, New York, New York 10019 (800) 933-4685; *The New Latin America Market Atlas.*

Facts on File, 460 Park Avenue South, New York, New York 10016 (800) 443-8323; *The New Book of World Rankings.*

G. K. Hall and Company, 70 Lincoln Street, Boston, Massachusetts 02111 (617) 423-3990; *The World in Figures.*

International Civil Aviation Organization, 1000 Sherbrooke Street West, Suite 400, Montreal, Quebec, Canada H3A 2R2 (514) 285-8219; *Civil Aviation Statistics of the World.*

Statistical Office of the United Nations, Publishing Service, New York, New York 10017 (800) 253-9646; *Statistical Yearbook.*

Times Books, 201 East 50th Street, New York, New York 10022 (212) 751-2600; *The Economist Book of Vital World Statistics.*

BOLIVIA - ALUMINUM PRODUCTION AND CONSUMPTION - See BOLIVIA - MINING AND MINERAL PRODUCTS

BOLIVIA - ANIMAL HEALTH

Food and Agricultural Organization of the United Nations (FAO), Via delle Terme di Caracalla, 00100 Rome, Italy (Telephone Number in U.S. (202) 653-2400); *Animal Health Yearbook.*

BOLIVIA - ANTIMONY AND ANTIMONY ORE - See BOLIVIA - MINING AND MINERAL PRODUCTS

BOLIVIA - AREA AND DENSITY OF POPULATION

Euromonitor Publications Limited, 87-88 Turnmill Street, London EC1M 5QU, England; *International Marketing Data and Statistics.*

Facts on File, 460 Park Avenue South, New York, New York 10016 (800) 443-8323; *The New Book of World Rankings.*

Federal Statistical Office, Gustav - Stresemann - Ring 11, D-6200 Wiesbaden, Germany; *Bolivia.*

Food and Agricultural Organization of the United Nations (FAO) Via delle Terme di Caracalla, 00100 Rome, Italy (Telephone Number in U.S. (202) 653-2400); *The State of Food and Agriculture.*

G. K. Hall and Company, 70 Lincoln Street, Boston, Massachusetts 02111 (617) 423-3990; *The World in Figures.*

Inter-American Development Bank, 1300 New York Avenue, NW, Washington, D.C. 20577 (202) 623-1753; *Economic and Social Progress in Latin America.*

Statistical Office of the United Nations, Publishing Service, New York, New York 10017 (800) 253-9646; *Statistical Yearbook.*

Times Books, 201 East 50th Street, New York, New York 10022 (212) 751-2600; *The Economist Book of Vital World Statistics.*

BOLIVIA - ARMS EXPORTS AND IMPORTS

U.S. Arms Control and Disarmament Agency, 320 Twenty-first Street, NW, Washington, D.C. 20451 (202) 647-8677; *World Military Expenditures and Arms Transfers.*

BOLIVIA - BALANCE OF PAYMENTS

The Economist Intelligence Unit, 111 West 57th Street, New York, New York 10019 (800) 933-4685; *The New Latin America Market Atlas,* and *The World Market Atlas.*

Federal Statistical Office, Gustav - Stresemann - Ring 11, D-6200 Wiesbaden, Germany; *Bolivia.*

G. K. Hall and Company, 70 Lincoln Street, Boston, Massachusetts 02111 (617) 423-3990; *The World in Figures.*

Inter-American Development Bank, 1300 New York Avenue, NW, Washington, D.C. 20577 (202) 623-1753; *Economic and Social Progress in Latin America.*

International Monetary Fund, 700 Nineteenth Street, NW, Washington, D.C. 20431 (202) 623-7000; *Balance of Payments Handbook,* and *International Financial Statistics.*

Organization of American States (OAS), General Secretariat, Washington, D.C. 20006 (202) 458-3533; *Statistical Bulletin of the OAS.*

Statistical Office of the United Nations, Publishing Service, New York, New York 10017 (800) 253-9646; *Economic Survey of Latin America and the Caribbean,* and *Statistical Yearbook for Latin America and the Caribbean.*

Times Books, 201 East 50th Street, New York, New York 10022 (212) 751-2600; *The Economist Book of Vital World Statistics.*

U.C.L.A. Latin American Center Publications, University of California, Los Angeles, California 90024 (310) 825-6634; *Statistical Abstract of Latin America.*

The World Bank, 1818 H Street, NW, Washington, D.C. 20433 (202) 477-1234; *World Tables.*

BOLIVIA - BANKING

Facts on File, 460 Park Avenue South, New York, New York 10016 (800) 443-8323; *The New Book of World Rankings.*

G. K. Hall and Company, 70 Lincoln Street, Boston, Massachusetts 02111 (617) 423-3990; *The World in Figures.*

Inter-American Development Bank, 1300 New York Avenue, NW, Washington, D.C. 20577 (202) 623-1753; *Economic and Social Progress in Latin America.*

International Monetary Fund, 700 Nineteenth Street, NW, Washington, D.C. 20431 (202) 623-7000; *Government Finance Statistics Yearbook,* and *International Financial Statistics.*

Statistical Office of the United Nations, Publishing Service, New York, New York 10017 (800) 253-9646; *Statistical Yearbook for Latin America and the Caribbean.*

BOLIVIA - BARLEY PRODUCTION - See BOLIVIA - CROPS

BOLIVIA - BEER PRODUCTION

Facts on File, 460 Park Avenue South, New York, New York 10016 (800) 443-8323; *The New Book of World Rankings.*

Statistical Office of the United Nations, Publishing Service, New York, New York 10017 (800) 253-9646; *Statistical Yearbook.*

BOLIVIA - BIRTH RATE

Facts on File, 460 Park Avenue South, New York, New York 10016 (800) 443-8323; *The New Book of World Rankings.*

Statistical Office of the United Nations, Publishing Service, New York, New York 10017 (800) 253-9646; *Demographic Yearbook, Statistical Yearbook,* and *Statistical Yearbook for Latin America and the Caribbean.*

Times Books, 201 East 50th Street, New York, New York 10022 (212) 751-2600; *The Economist Book of Vital World Statistics*.

The World Bank, 1818 H Street, NW, Washington, D.C. 20433 (202) 477-1234; *World Tables*.

World Health Organization, Office of Publications, Avenue Appia, CH-1211 Geneva 27, Switzerland (Telephone Number in U.S. (518) 436-9686); *World Health Statistics Annual*.

BOLIVIA - BISMUTH PRODUCTION AND CONSUMPTION - See BOLIVIA - MINING AND MINERAL PRODUCTS

BOLIVIA - BONDS

G. K. Hall and Company, 70 Lincoln Street, Boston, Massachusetts 02111 (617) 423-3990; *The World in Figures*.

Inter-American Development Bank, 1300 New York Avenue, NW, Washington, D.C. 20577 (202) 623-1753; *Economic and Social Progress in Latin America*.

International Monetary Fund, 700 Nineteenth Street, NW, Washington, D.C. 20431 (202) 623-7000; *Government Finance Statistics Yearbook*.

BOLIVIA - BOOK PRODUCTION

G. K. Hall and Company, 70 Lincoln Street, Boston, Massachusetts 02111 (617) 423-3990; *The World in Figures*.

BOLIVIA - BROADCASTING

Billboard Limited, P.O. Box 9027, 1006 AA Amsterdam, The Netherlands (Telephone Number in U.S. (212) 764-7300); *World Radio TV Handbook*.

Facts on File, 460 Park Avenue South, New York, New York 10016 (800) 443-8323; *The New Book of World Rankings*.

G. K. Hall and Company, 70 Lincoln Street, Boston, Massachusetts 02111 (617) 423-3990; *The World in Figures*.

Times Books, 201 East 50th Street, New York, New York 10022 (212) 751-2600; *The Economist Book of Vital World Statistics*.

BOLIVIA - BUSINESS

G. K. Hall and Company, 70 Lincoln Street, Boston, Massachusetts 02111 (617) 423-3990; *The World in Figures*.

Inter-American Development Bank, 1300 New York Avenue, NW, Washington, D.C. 20577 (202) 623-1753; *Economic and Social Progress in Latin America*.

BOLIVIA - BUSINESS AND PROFESSIONAL LICENSES

International Monetary Fund, 700 Nineteenth Street, NW, Washington, D.C. 20431 (202) 623-7000; *Government Finance Statistics Yearbook*.

BOLIVIA - CABBAGE PRODUCTION - See BOLIVIA - CROPS

BOLIVIA - CALORIE SUPPLY

Food and Agricultural Organization of the United Nations (FAO) Via delle Terme di Caracalla, 00100 Rome, Italy (Telephone Number in U.S. (202) 653-2400); *The State of Food and Agriculture*.

Statistical Office of the United Nations, Publishing Service, New York, New York 10017 (800) 253-9646; *Statistical Yearbook for Latin America and the Caribbean*.

BOLIVIA - CAPITAL INVESTMENT

Inter-American Development Bank, 1300 New York Avenue, NW, Washington, D.C. 20577 (202) 623-1753; *Economic and Social Progress in Latin America*.

BOLIVIA - CAPITAL REVENUE

Inter-American Development Bank, 1300 New York Avenue, NW, Washington, D.C. 20577 (202) 623-1753; *Economic and Social Progress in Latin America*.

International Monetary Fund, 700 Nineteenth Street, NW, Washington, D.C. 20431 (202) 623-7000; *Government Finance Statistics Yearbook*.

BOLIVIA - CATTLE - See BOLIVIA - LIVESTOCK AND POULTRY

BOLIVIA - CEMENT PRODUCTION - See BOLIVIA - MINING AND MINERAL PRODUCTS

BOLIVIA - CHEESE PRODUCTION - See BOLIVIA - DAIRY PRODUCTS

BOLIVIA - CHEMICAL (ORGANIC) PRODUCTION - See BOLIVIA - MINING AND MINERAL PRODUCTS

BOLIVIA - CHESTNUT PRODUCTION - See BOLIVIA - CROPS

BOLIVIA - CHICK PEA PRODUCTION - See BOLIVIA - CROPS

BOLIVIA - CHICKENS - See BOLIVIA - LIVESTOCK AND POULTRY

BOLIVIA - CIGARETTE PRODUCTION - See BOLIVIA - TOBACCO PRODUCTION

BOLIVIA - CLASS STRUCTURE

G. K. Hall and Company, 70 Lincoln Street, Boston, Massachusetts 02111 (617) 423-3990; *The World in Figures*.

BOLIVIA - CLIMATE

Facts on File, 460 Park Avenue South, New York, New York 10016 (800) 443-8323; *The New Book of World Rankings*.

G. K. Hall and Company, 70 Lincoln Street, Boston, Massachusetts 02111 (617) 423-3990; *The World in Figures*.

BOLIVIA - COAL PRODUCTION - See BOLIVIA - MINING AND MINERAL PRODUCTS

BOLIVIA - COCOA (BEANS) PRODUCTION - See BOLIVIA - CROPS

BOLIVIA - COFFEE PRODUCTION - See BOLIVIA - CROPS

BOLIVIA - COMMUNICATIONS

Federal Statistical Office, Gustav - Stresemann - Ring 11, D-6200 Wiesbaden, Germany; *Bolivia*.

G. K. Hall and Company, 70 Lincoln Street, Boston, Massachusetts 02111 (617) 423-3990; *The World in Figures*.

Inter-American Development Bank, 1300 New York Avenue, NW, Washington, D.C. 20577 (202) 623-1753; *Economic and Social*

Progress in Latin America.

U.C.L.A. Latin American Center Publications, University of California, Los Angeles, California 90024 (310) 825-6634; *Statistical Abstract of Latin America.*

BOLIVIA - CONSTRUCTION INDUSTRY

The Economist Intelligence Unit, 111 West 57th Street, New York, New York 10019 (800) 933-4685; *The New Latin America Market Atlas.*

Facts on File, 460 Park Avenue South, New York, New York 10016 (800) 443-8323; *The New Book of World Rankings.*

Inter-American Development Bank, 1300 New York Avenue, NW, Washington, D.C. 20577 (202) 623-1753; *Economic and Social Progress in Latin America.*

U.C.L.A. Latin American Center Publications, University of California, Los Angeles, California 90024 (310) 825-6634; *Statistical Abstract of Latin America.*

Statistical Office of the United Nations, Publishing Service, New York, New York 10017 (800) 253-9646; *Construction Statistics Yearbook,* and *Statistical Yearbook.*

BOLIVIA - CONSUMER PRICE INDEX

G. K. Hall and Company, 70 Lincoln Street, Boston, Massachusetts 02111 (617) 423-3990; *The World in Figures.*

Statistical Office of the United Nations, Publishing Service, New York, New York 10017 (800) 253-9646; *Statistical Yearbook.*

BOLIVIA - CONSUMER PRICES

The Economist Intelligence Unit, 111 West 57th Street, New York, New York 10019 (800) 933-4685; *The New Latin America Market Atlas.*

International Labour Office, I.L.O. Publications, CH-1211, Geneva 22, Switzerland; *Yearbook of Labour Statistics.*

International Monetary Fund, 700 Nineteenth Street, NW, Washington, D.C. 20431 (202) 623-7000; *International Financial Statistics.*

Organization of American States (OAS), General Secretariat, Washington, D.C. 20006 (202) 458-3533; *Statistical Bulletin of the OAS.*

Times Books, 201 East 50th Street, New York, New York 10022 (212) 751-2600; *The Economist Book of Vital World Statistics.*

BOLIVIA - CONSUMPTION

The Economist Intelligence Unit, 111 West 57th Street, New York, New York 10019 (800) 933-4685; *The New Latin America Market Atlas.*

G. K. Hall and Company, 70 Lincoln Street, Boston, Massachusetts 02111 (617) 423-3990; *The World in Figures.*

Inter-American Development Bank, 1300 New York Avenue, NW, Washington, D.C. 20577 (202) 623-1753; *Economic and Social Progress in Latin America.*

Statistical Office of the United Nations, Publishing Service, New York, New York 10017 (800) 253-9646; *Statistical Yearbook for Latin America and the Caribbean.*

BOLIVIA - COOPERATIVES

U.C.L.A. Latin American Center Publications, University of California, Los Angeles, California 90024 (310) 825-6634; *Statistical Abstract of Latin America.*

BOLIVIA - COPPER AND COPPER ORE - See BOLIVIA - MINING AND MINERAL PRODUCTS

BOLIVIA - CORN PRODUCTION - See BOLIVIA - CROPS

BOLIVIA - CORPORATE TAXES - See BOLIVIA - TAXATION

BOLIVIA - COTTON - See BOLIVIA - CROPS

BOLIVIA - CRIME

Yale University Press, Yale Station, New Haven, Connecticut 06520 (203) 432-0940; *Violence and Crime in Cross-National Perspective.*

BOLIVIA - CROPS

The Economist Intelligence Unit, 111 West 57th Street, New York, New York 10019 (800) 933-4685; *The New Latin America Market Atlas.*

Facts on File, 460 Park Avenue South, New York, New York 10016 (800) 443-8323; *The New Book of World Rankings.*

Food and Agricultural Organization of the United Nations (FAO) Via delle Terme di Caracalla, 00100 Rome, Italy (Telephone Number in U.S. (202) 653-2400); *The State of Food and Agriculture.*

Inter-American Development Bank, 1300 New York Avenue, NW, Washington, D.C. 20577 (202) 623-1753; *Economic and Social Progress in Latin America.*

Statistical Office of the United Nations, Publishing Service, New York, New York 10017 (800) 253-9646; *Statistical Yearbook.*

BOLIVIA - CUSTOMS DUTIES

G. K. Hall and Company, 70 Lincoln Street, Boston, Massachusetts 02111 (617) 423-3990; *The World in Figures.*

Inter-American Development Bank, 1300 New York Avenue, NW, Washington, D.C. 20577 (202) 623-1753; *Economic and Social Progress in Latin America.*

International Monetary Fund, 700 Nineteenth Street, NW, Washington, D.C. 20431 (202) 623-7000; *Government Finance Statistics Yearbook.*

BOLIVIA - DAIRY PRODUCTS

Facts on File, 460 Park Avenue South, New York, New York 10016 (800) 443-8323; *The New Book of World Rankings.*

Food and Agricultural Organization of the United Nations (FAO) Via delle Terme di Caracalla, 00100 Rome, Italy (Telephone Number in U.S. (202) 653-2400); *Production Yearbook,* and *The State of Food and Agriculture.*

Statistical Office of the United Nations, Publishing Service, New York, New York 10017 (800) 253-9646; *Statistical Yearbook.*

BOLIVIA - DEATH RATES

G. K. Hall and Company, 70 Lincoln Street, Boston, Massachusetts 02111 (617) 423-3990; *The World in Figures.*

Statistical Office of the United Nations, Publishing Service, New York, New York 10017 (800) 253-9646; *Statistical Yearbook,* and *Statistical Yearbook for Latin America and the Caribbean.*

Times Books, 201 East 50th Street, New York, New York 10022 (212) 751-2600; *The Economist Book of Vital World Statistics.*

World Health Organization, Office of Publications, Avenue Appia, CH-1211 Geneva 27, Switzerland (Telephone Number in U.S. (518) 436-9686); *World Health Statistics Annual.*

BOLIVIA - DEBT

The Economist Intelligence Unit, 111 West 57th Street, New York, New York 10019 (800) 933-4685; *The New Latin America Market Atlas.*

BOLIVIA - DEFENSE EXPENDITURES

The Economist Intelligence Unit, 111 West 57th Street, New York, New York 10019 (800) 933-4685; *The New Latin America Market Atlas.*

G. K. Hall and Company, 70 Lincoln Street, Boston, Massachusetts 02111 (617) 423-3990; *The World in Figures.*

International Monetary Fund, 700 Nineteenth Street, NW, Washington, D.C. 20431 (202) 623-7000; *Government Finance Statistics Yearbook.*

U.S. Arms Control and Disarmament Agency, 320 Twenty-first Street, NW, Washington, D.C. 20451 (202) 647-8677; *World Military Expenditures and Arms Transfers.*

BOLIVIA - DEMOGRAPHY

The Economist Intelligence Unit, 111 West 57th Street, New York, New York 10019 (800) 938-4685; *The World Market Atlas.*

Facts on File, 460 Park Avenue South, New York, New York 10016 (800) 443-8323; *The New Book of World Rankings.*

G. K. Hall and Company, 70 Lincoln Street, Boston, Massachusetts 02111 (617) 423-3990; *The World in Figures.*

BOLIVIA - DEVELOPMENT ASSISTANCE

G. K. Hall and Company, 70 Lincoln Street, Boston, Massachusetts 02111 (617) 423-3990; *The World in Figures.*

Inter-American Development Bank, 1300 New York Avenue, NW, Washington, D.C. 20577 (202) 623-1753; *Economic and Social Progress in Latin America.*

Statistical Office of the United Nations, Publishing Service, New York, New York 10017 (800) 253-9646; *Statistical Yearbook.*

BOLIVIA - DIAMOND PRODUCTION - See BOLIVIA - MINING AND MINERAL PRODUCTS

BOLIVIA - DISCOUNT RATES

Inter-American Development Bank, 1300 New York Avenue, NW, Washington, D.C. 20577 (202) 623-1753; *Economic and Social Progress in Latin America.*

BOLIVIA - DISEASES

G. K. Hall and Company, 70 Lincoln Street, Boston, Massachusetts 02111 (617) 423-3990; *The World in Figures.*

World Health Organization, Office of Publications, Avenue Appia, CH-1211 Geneva 27, Switzerland (Telephone Number in U.S. (518) 436-9686); *World Health Statistics Annual.*

BOLIVIA - DIVORCE RATES

Facts on File, 460 Park Avenue South, New York, New York 10016 (800) 443-8323; *The New Book of World Rankings.*

Statistical Office of the United Nations, Publishing Service, New York, New York 10017 (800) 253-9646; *Demographic Yearbook.*

BOLIVIA - DOMESTIC PRODUCT

G. K. Hall and Company, 70 Lincoln Street, Boston, Massachusetts 02111 (617) 423-3990; *The World in Figures.*

BOLIVIA - DUCKS - See BOLIVIA - LIVESTOCK AND POULTRY

BOLIVIA - ECONOMY

Euromonitor Publications Limited, 87-88 Turnmill Street, London EC1M 5QU, England; *International Marketing Data and Statistics.*

Facts on File, 460 Park Avenue South, New York, New York 10016 (800) 443-8323; *The New Book of World Rankings.*

G. K. Hall and Company, 70 Lincoln Street, Boston, Massachusetts 02111 (617) 423-3990; *The World in Figures.*

Inter-American Development Bank, 1300 New York Avenue, NW, Washington, D.C. 20577 (202) 623-1753; *Economic and Social Progress in Latin America.*

Organization of American States (OAS), General Secretariat, Washington, D.C. 20006 (202) 458-3533; *Statistical Bulletin of the OAS.*

Statistical Office of the United Nations, Publishing Service, New York, New York 10017 (800) 253-9646; *Economic Survey of Latin America and the Caribbean.*

U.C.L.A. Latin American Center Publications, University of California, Los Angeles, California 90024 (310) 825-6634; *Statistical Abstract of Latin America.*

BOLIVIA - EDUCATION

The Economist Intelligence Unit, 111 West 57th Street, New York, New York 10019 (800) 938-4685; *The New Latin America Market Atlas,* and *The World Market Atlas.*

Facts on File, 460 Park Avenue South, New York, New York 10016 (800) 443-8323; *The New Book of World Rankings.*

Federal Statistical Office, Gustav - Stresemann - Ring 11, D-6200 Wiesbaden, Germany; *Bolivia.*

Gale Research Incorporated, 835 Penobscot Building, Detroit, Michigan 48226 (800) 877-4253; *International Historical Statistics The Americas and Australasia.*

G.K. Hall and Company, 70 Lincoln Street, Boston, Massachusetts 02111 (617) 423-3990; *The World in Figures.*

International Monetary Fund, 700 Nineteenth Street, NW, Washington, D.C. 20431 (202) 623-7000; *Government Finance Statistics Yearbook.*

Statistical Office of the United Nations, Publishing Service, New York, New York 10017 (800) 253-9646; *Statistical Yearbook for Latin America and the Caribbean.*

Times Books, 201 East 50th Street, New York, New York 10022 (212) 751-2600; *The Economist Book of Vital World Statistics.*

U.C.L.A. Latin American Center Publications, University of California, Los Angeles, California 90024 (310) 825-6634; *Statistical Abstract of Latin America.*

United Nations Educational, Scientific and Cultural Organization (UNESCO), 7 Place de Fontenoy, F-75700 Paris, France (Telephone Number in U.S. (212) 963-5981); *Statistical Yearbook.*

The World Bank, 1818 H Street, NW, Washington, D.C. 20433 (202) 477-1234; *World Tables.*

BOLIVIA - EGG PRODUCTION - See BOLIVIA - DAIRY PRODUCTS

BOLIVIA - ELECTRICITY

The Economist Intelligence Unit, 111 West 57th Street, New York, New York 10019 (800) 933-4685; *The New Latin America Market Atlas.*

Facts on File, 460 Park Avenue South, New York, New York 10016 (800) 443-8323; *The New Book of World Rankings.*

Inter-American Development Bank, 1300 New York Avenue, NW, Washington, D.C. 20577 (202) 623-1753; *Economic and Social Progress in Latin America.*

Penn Well Publishing Company, 1421 South Sheridan Road, P.O. Box 1260, Tulsa, Oklahoma 74101 (800) 752-9764; *International Energy Statistics Sourcebook.*

Statistical Office of the United Nations, Publishing Service, New York, New York 10017 (800) 253-9646; *Statistical Yearbook.*

Times Books, 201 East 50th Street, New York, New York 10022 (212) 751-2600; *The Economist Book of Vital World Statistics.*

BOLIVIA - EMPLOYMENT

Euromonitor Publications Limited, 87-88 Turnmill Street, London EC1M 5QU, England; *International Marketing Data and Statistics.*

Facts on File, 460 Park Avenue South, New York, New York 10016 (800) 443-8323; *The New Book of World Rankings.*

Federal Statistical Office, Gustav - Stresemann - Ring 11, D-6200 Wiesbaden, Germany; *Bolivia.*

International Labour Office, I.L.O. Publications, CH-1211, Geneva 22, Switzerland; *Yearbook of Labour Statistics.*

Statistical Office of the United Nations, Publishing Service, New York, New York 10017 (800) 253-9646; *Statistical Yearbook,* and *Statistical Yearbook for Latin America and the Caribbean.*

U.C.L.A. Latin American Center Publications, University of California, Los Angeles, California 90024 (310) 825-6634; *Statistical Abstract of Latin America.*

BOLIVIA - ENERGY

The Economist Intelligence Unit, 111 West 57th Street, New York, New York 10019 (800) 933-4685; *The New Latin America Market Atlas.*

Facts on File, 460 Park Avenue South, New York, New York 10016 (800) 443-8323; *The New Book of World Rankings.*

G. K. Hall and Company, 70 Lincoln Street, Boston, Massachusetts 02111 (617) 423-3990; *The World in Figures.*

Penn Well Publishing Company, 1421 South Sheridan Road, P.O. Box 1260, Tulsa, Oklahoma 74101 (800) 752-9764; *International Energy Statistics Sourcebook.*

Statistical Office of the United Nations, Publishing Service, New York, New York 10017 (800) 253-9646; *Energy Statistics Yearbook,* and *Statistical Yearbook for Latin America and the Caribbean.*

Times Books, 201 East 50th Street, New York, New York 10022 (212) 751-2600; *The Economist Book of Vital World Statistics.*

U.C.L.A. Latin American Center Publications, University of California, Los Angeles, California 90024 (310) 825-6634; *Statistical Abstract of Latin America.*

BOLIVIA - EXCHANGE RATES

Euromonitor Publications Limited, 87-88 Turnmill Street, London EC1M 5QU, England; *International Marketing Data and Statistics.*

Inter-American Development Bank, 1300 New York Avenue, NW, Washington, D.C. 20577 (202) 623-1753; *Economic and Social Progress in Latin America.*

International Civil Aviation Organization, 1000 Sherbrooke Street West, Suite 400, Montreal, Quebec, Canada H3A 2R2 (514) 285-8219; *Civil Aviation Statistics of the World.*

International Monetary Fund, 700 Nineteenth Street, NW, Washington, D.C. 20431 (202) 623-7000; *International Financial Statistics.*

Organization of American States (OAS), General Secretariat, Washington, D.C. 20006 (202) 458-3533; *Statistical Bulletin of the OAS.*

U.C.L.A. Latin American Center Publications, University of California, Los Angeles, California 90024 (310) 825-6634; *Statistical Abstract of Latin America.*

BOLIVIA - EXCHANGE TAXES - See BOLIVIA - TAXATION

BOLIVIA - EXCISE TAXES - See BOLIVIA - TAXATION

BOLIVIA - EXPORTS

The Economist Intelligence Unit, 111 West 57th Street, New York, New York 10019 (800) 938-4685; *The New Latin America Market Atlas,* and *The World Market Atlas.*

Euromonitor Publications Limited, 87-88 Turnmill Street, London EC1M 5QU, England; *International Marketing Data and Statistics.*

Food and Agricultural Organization of the United Nations (FAO) Via delle Terme di Caracalla, 00100 Rome, Italy (Telephone Number in U.S. (202) 653-2400); *The State of Food and Agriculture.*

G.K. Hall and Company, 70 Lincoln Street, Boston, Massachusetts 02111 (617) 423-3990; *The World in Figures.*

Inter-American Development Bank, 1300 New York Avenue, NW, Washington, D.C. 20577 (202) 623-1753; *Economic and Social Progress in Latin America.*

International Monetary Fund, 700 Nineteenth Street, NW, Washington, D.C. 20431 (202) 623-7000; *Direction of Trade Statistics,* and *International Financial Statistics.*

Organization of American States (OAS), General Secretariat, Washington, D.C. 20006 (202) 458-3533; *Statistical Bulletin of the OAS.*

Statistical Office of the United Nations, Publishing Service, New York, New York 10017 (800) 253-9646; *Statistical Yearbook for Latin America and the Caribbean.*

Times Books, 201 East 50th Street, New York, New York 10022 (212) 751-2600; *The Economist Book of Vital World Statistics.*

The World Bank, 1818 H Street, NW, Washington, D.C. 20433 (202) 477-1234; *World Tables.*

BOLIVIA - EXTERNAL FINANCING

Inter-American Development Bank, 1300 New York Avenue, NW, Washington, D.C. 20577 (202) 623-1753; *Economic and Social Progress in Latin America.*

Statistical Office of the United Nations, Publishing Service, New York, New York 10017 (800) 253-9646; *Statistical Yearbook for Latin America and the Caribbean.*

BOLIVIA - EXTERNAL INDEBTEDNESS

Inter-American Development Bank, 1300 New York Avenue, NW, Washington, D.C. 20577 (202) 623-1753; *Economic and Social Progress in Latin America.*

Statistical Office of the United Nations, Publishing Service, New York, New York 10017 (800) 253-9646; *Statistical Yearbook for Latin America and the Caribbean.*

The World Bank, 1818 H Street, NW, Washington, D.C. 20433 (202) 477-1234; *World Tables.*

BOLIVIA - EXTERNAL TRADE

Food and Agricultural Organization of the United Nations (FAO) Via delle Terme di Caracalla, 00100 Rome, Italy (Telephone Number in U.S. (202) 653-2400); *The State of Food and Agriculture,* and *Trade Yearbook.*

Gale Research Incorporated, 835 Penobscot Building, Detroit, Michigan 48226 (800) 877-4253; *International Historical Statistics The Americas and Australasia.*

G.K. Hall and Company, 70 Lincoln Street, Boston, Massachusetts 02111 (617) 423-3990; *The World in Figures.*

Inter-American Development Bank, 1300 New York Avenue, NW, Washington, D.C. 20577 (202) 623-1753; *Economic and Social Progress in Latin America.*

Statistical Office of the United Nations, Publishing Service, New York, New York 10017 (800) 253-9646; *Statistical Yearbook,* and *Statistical Yearbook for Latin America and the Caribbean.*

BOLIVIA - FABRIC PRODUCTION - See BOLIVIA - TEXTILE INDUSTRY

BOLIVIA - FAMILY PLANNING

U.C.L.A. Latin American Center Publications, University of California, Los Angeles, California 90024 (310) 825-6634; *Statistical Abstract of Latin America.*

BOLIVIA - FARM CROPS - See BOLIVIA - CROPS

BOLIVIA - FEMALE WORKING POPULATION - See BOLIVIA - EMPLOYMENT

BOLIVIA - FERTILITY RATES

Facts on File, 460 Park Avenue South, New York, New York 10016 (800) 443-8323; *The New Book of World Rankings.*

Times Books, 201 East 50th Street, New York, New York 10022 (212) 751-2600; *The Economist Book of Vital World Statistics.*

The World Bank, 1818 H Street, NW, Washington, D.C. 20433 (202) 477-1234; *World Tables.*

BOLIVIA - FERTILIZER

The Economist Intelligence Unit, 111 West 57th Street, New York, New York 10019 (800) 933-4685; *The New Latin America Market Atlas.*

Food and Agricultural Organization of the United Nations (FAO), Via delle Terme di Caracalla, 00100 Rome, Italy (Telephone Number in U.S. (202) 653-2400); *Fertilizer Yearbook,* and *The State of Food and Agriculture.*

Statistical Office of the United Nations, Publishing Service, New York, New York 10017 (800) 253-9646; *Statistical Yearbook.*

BOLIVIA - FETAL MORTALITY

Statistical Office of the United Nations, Publishing Service, New York, New York 10017 (800) 253-9646; *Demographic Yearbook.*

BOLIVIA - FILM - See BOLIVIA - MOTION PICTURES

BOLIVIA - FINANCE

Facts on File, 460 Park Avenue South, New York, New York 10016 (800) 443-8323; *The New Book of World Rankings.*

Federal Statistical Office, Gustav - Stresemann - Ring 11, D-6200 Wiesbaden, Germany; *Bolivia.*

Gale Research Incorporated, 835 Penobscot Building, Detroit, Michigan 48226 (800) 877-4253; *International Historical Statistics The Americas and Australasia.*

G.K. Hall and Company, 70 Lincoln Street, Boston, Massachusetts 02111 (617) 423-3990; *The World in Figures.*

Inter-American Development Bank, 1300 New York Avenue, NW, Washington, D.C. 20577 (202) 623-1753; *Economic and Social Progress in Latin America.*

International Monetary Fund, 700 Nineteenth Street, NW, Washington, D.C. 20431 (202) 623-7000; *Government Finance Statistics Yearbook*, and *International Financial Statistics*.

Organization of American States (OAS), General Secretariat, Washington, D.C. 20006 (202) 458-3533; *Statistical Bulletin of the OAS*.

U.C.L.A. Latin American Center Publications, University of California, Los Angeles, California (310) 825-6634; *Statistical Abstract of Latin America*.

BOLIVIA - FISHERIES

Facts on File, 460 Park Avenue South, New York, New York 10016 (800) 443-8323; *The New Book of World Rankings*.

Federal Statistical Office, Gustav - Stresemann - Ring 11, D-6200 Wiesbaden, Germany; *Bolivia*.

Food and Agricultural Organization of the United Nations (FAO) Via delle Terme di Caracalla, 00100 Rome, Italy (Telephone Number in U.S. (202) 653-2400); *The State of Food and Agriculture*, and *Yearbook of Fishery Statistics*.

Inter-American Development Bank, 1300 New York Avenue, NW, Washington, D.C. 20577 (202) 623-1753; *Economic and Social Progress in Latin America*.

Statistical Office of the United Nations, Publishing Service, New York, New York 10017 (800) 253-9646; *Statistical Yearbook*.

U.C.L.A. Latin American Center Publications, University of California, Los Angeles, California (310) 825-6634; *Statistical Abstract of Latin America*.

BOLIVIA - FLOUR PRODUCTION

Statistical Office of the United Nations, Publishing Service, New York, New York 10017 (800) 253-9646; *Statistical Yearbook*.

BOLIVIA - FOOD

Food and Agricultural Organization of the United Nations (FAO) Via delle Terme di Caracalla, 00100 Rome, Italy (Telephone Number in U.S. (202) 653-2400); *Production Yearbook*, and *The State of Food and Agriculture*.

G.K. Hall and Company, 70 Lincoln Street, Boston, Massachusetts 02111 (617) 423-3990; *The World in Figures*.

BOLIVIA - FOREIGN AID

G.K. Hall and Company, 70 Lincoln Street, Boston, Massachusetts 02111 (617) 423-3990; *The World in Figures*.

Inter-American Development Bank, 1300 New York Avenue, NW, Washington, D.C. 20577 (202) 623-1753; *Economic and Social Progress in Latin America*.

BOLIVIA - FOREIGN DEBT

The Economist Intelligence Unit, 111 West 57th Street, New York, New York 10019 (800) 933-4685; *The New Latin America Market Atlas*.

Inter-American Development Bank, 1300 New York Avenue, NW, Washington, D.C. 20577 (202) 623-1753; *Economic and Social Progress in Latin America*.

International Monetary Fund, 700 Nineteenth Street, NW, Washington, D.C. 20431 (202) 623-7000; *Government Finance Statistics Yearbook*.

BOLIVIA - FOREIGN FINANCE

Inter-American Development Bank, 1300 New York Avenue, NW, Washington, D.C. 20577 (202) 623-1753; *Economic and Social Progress in Latin America*.

BOLIVIA - FOREIGN INDEBTEDNESS

Inter-American Development Bank, 1300 New York Avenue, NW, Washington, D.C. 20577 (202) 623-1753; *Economic and Social Progress in Latin America*.

Statistical Office of the United Nations, Publishing Service, New York, New York 10017 (800) 253-9646; *Economic Survey of Latin America and the Caribbean*.

BOLIVIA - FOREIGN INVESTMENT

The Economist Intelligence Unit, 111 West 57th Street, New York, New York 10019 (800) 933-4685; *The New Latin America Market Atlas*.

BOLIVIA - FOREIGN TRADE

The Economist Intelligence Unit, 111 West 57th Street, New York, New York 10019 (800) 933-4685; *The New Latin America Market Atlas*.

Euromonitor Publications Limited, 87-88 Turnmill Street, London EC1M 5QU, England; *International Marketing Data and Statistics*.

Facts on File, 460 Park Avenue South, New York, New York 10016 (800) 443-8323; *The New Book of World Rankings*.

Federal Statistical Office, Gustav - Stresemann - Ring 11, D-6200 Wiesbaden, Germany; *Bolivia*.

Food and Agricultural Organization of the United Nations (FAO) Via delle Terme di Caracalla, 00100 Rome, Italy (Telephone Number in U.S. (202) 653-2400); *The State of Food and Agriculture*.

G.K. Hall and Company, 70 Lincoln Street, Boston, Massachusetts 02111 (617) 423-3990; *The World in Figures*.

Inter-American Development Bank, 1300 New York Avenue, NW, Washington, D.C. 20577 (202) 623-1753; *Economic and Social Progress in Latin America*.

Organisation for Economic Cooperation and Development (OECD), 2 rue Andre-Pascal, 75 Paris 16, France (Telephone Number in U.S. (202) 785-6323); *Trade by Commodities*.

Statistical Office of the United Nations, Publishing Service, New York, New York 10017 (800) 253-9646; *Economic Survey of Latin America and the Caribbean*, *International Trade Statistics Yearbook*, and *Statistical Yearbook*.

U.C.L.A. Latin American Center Publications, University of California, Los Angeles, California (310) 825-6634; *Statistical Abstract of Latin America*.

The World Bank, 1818 H Street, NW, Washington, D.C. 20433 (202) 477-1234; *World Tables*.

BOLIVIA - FORESTRY AND FOREST PRODUCTS

The Economist Intelligence Unit, 111 West 57th Street, New York, New York 10019 (800) 933-4685; *The New Latin America Market Atlas.*

Facts on File, 460 Park Avenue South, New York, New York 10016 (800) 443-8323; *The New Book of World Rankings.*

Food and Agricultural Organization of the United Nations (FAO) Via delle Terme di Caracalla, 00100 Rome, Italy (Telephone Number in U.S. (202) 653-2400); *The State of Food and Agriculture,* and *Yearbook of Forest Products.*

G.K. Hall and Company, 70 Lincoln Street, Boston, Massachusetts 02111 (617) 423-3990; *The World in Figures.*

Inter-American Development Bank, 1300 New York Avenue, NW, Washington, D.C. 20577 (202) 623-1753; *Economic and Social Progress in Latin America.*

Statistical Office of the United Nations, Publishing Service, New York, New York 10017 (800) 253-9646; *Statistical Yearbook.*

U.C.L.A. Latin American Center Publications, University of California, Los Angeles, California (310) 825-6634; *Statistical Abstract of Latin America.*

BOLIVIA - GARLIC PRODUCTION - See BOLIVIA - CROPS

BOLIVIA - GAS - See BOLIVIA - MINING AND MINERAL PRODUCTS

BOLIVIA - GENERAL INDUSTRIAL STATISTICS

Statistical Office of the United Nations, Publishing Service, New York, New York 10017 (800) 253-9646; *Industrial Statistics Yearbook.*

BOLIVIA - GENERAL MORTALITY

Statistical Office of the United Nations, Publishing Service, New York, New York 10017 (800) 253-9646; *Demographic Yearbook.*

World Health Organization, Office of Publications, Avenue Appia, CH-1211 Geneva 27, Switzerland (Telephone Number in U.S. (518) 436-9686); *World Health Statistics Annual.*

BOLIVIA - GEOGRAPHIC DATA

Facts on File, 460 Park Avenue South, New York, New York 10016 (800) 443-8323; *The New Book of World Rankings.*

U.C.L.A. Latin American Center Publications, University of California, Los Angeles, California 90024 (310) 825-6634; *Statistical Abstract of Latin America.*

BOLIVIA - GOATS - See BOLIVIA - LIVESTOCK AND POULTRY

BOLIVIA - GOLD HOLDINGS

International Monetary Fund, 700 Nineteenth Street, NW, Washington, D.C. 20431 (202) 623-7000; *International Financial Statistics.*

Statistical Office of the United Nations, Publishing Service, New York, New York 10017 (800) 253-9646; *Statistical Yearbook.*

The World Bank, 1818 H Street, NW, Washington, D.C. 20433 (202) 477-1234; *World Tables.*

BOLIVIA - GOLD PRODUCTION AND CONSUMPTION - See BOLIVIA - MINING AND MINERAL PRODUCTS

BOLIVIA - GOLD RESERVES

The Economist Intelligence Unit, 111 West 57th Street, New York, New York 10019 (800) 933-4685; *The New Latin America Market Atlas.*

BOLIVIA - GOVERNMENT

G.K. Hall and Company, 70 Lincoln Street, Boston, Massachusetts 02111 (617) 423-3990; *The World in Figures.*

Inter-American Development Bank, 1300 New York Avenue, NW, Washington, D.C. 20577 (202) 623-1753; *Economic and Social Progress in Latin America.*

BOLIVIA - GOVERNMENT BONDS - See BOLIVIA - BONDS

BOLIVIA - GOVERNMENT CONSUMPTION

Inter-American Development Bank, 1300 New York Avenue, NW, Washington, D.C. 20577 (202) 623-1753; *Economic and Social Progress in Latin America.*

BOLIVIA - GOVERNMENT EXPENDITURES

Inter-American Development Bank, 1300 New York Avenue, NW, Washington, D.C. 20577 (202) 623-1753; *Economic and Social Progress in Latin America.*

International Monetary Fund, 700 Nineteenth Street, NW, Washington, D.C. 20431 (202) 623-7000; *Government Finance Statistics Yearbook.*

Times Books, 201 East 50th Street, New York, New York 10022 (212) 751-2600; *The Economist Book of Vital World Statistics.*

The World Bank, 1818 H Street, NW, Washington, D.C. 20433 (202) 477-1234; *World Tables.*

BOLIVIA - GOVERNMENT FINANCES

Inter-American Development Bank, 1300 New York Avenue, NW, Washington, D.C. 20577 (202) 623-1753; *Economic and Social Progress in Latin America.*

International Monetary Fund, 700 Nineteenth Street, NW, Washington, D.C. 20431 (202) 623-7000; *International Financial Statistics.*

Statistical Office of the United Nations, Publishing Service, New York, New York 10017 (800) 253-9646; *Statistical Yearbook.*

BOLIVIA - GOVERNMENT REVENUE

Inter-American Development Bank, 1300 New York Avenue, NW, Washington, D.C. 20577 (202) 623-1753; *Economic and Social Progress in Latin America.*

International Monetary Fund, 700 Nineteenth Street, NW, Washington, D.C. 20431 (202) 623-7000; *Government Finance Statistics Yearbook.*

Times Books, 201 East 50th Street, New York, New York 10022 (212) 751-2600; *The Economist Book of Vital World Statistics.*

U.C.L.A. Latin American Center Publications, University of California, Los Angeles, California 90024 (310) 825-6634; *Statistical Abstract of Latin America.*

The World Bank, 1818 H Street, NW, Washington, D.C. 20433 (202) 477-1234; *World Tables.*

BOLIVIA - GRAIN PRODUCTION - See BOLIVIA - CROPS

BOLIVIA - GRANTS

International Monetary Fund, 700 Nineteenth Street, NW, Washington, D.C. 20431 (202) 623-7000; *Government Finance Statistics Yearbook.*

BOLIVIA - GREEN PEPPER AND CHILIE PRODUCTION - See BOLIVIA - CROPS

BOLIVIA - GROSS DOMESTIC PRODUCT

The Economist Intelligence Unit, 111 West 57th Street, New York, New York 10019 (800) 938-4685; *The New Latin America Market Atlas,* and *The World Market Atlas.*

Euromonitor Publications Limited, 87-88 Turnmill Street, London EC1M 5QU, England; *International Marketing Data and Statistics.*

Facts on File, 460 Park Avenue South, New York, New York 10016 (800) 443-8323; *The New Book of World Rankings.*

G.K. Hall and Company, 70 Lincoln Street, Boston, Massachusetts 02111 (617) 423-3990; *The World in Figures.*

Inter-American Development Bank, 1300 New York Avenue, NW, Washington, D.C. 20577 (202) 623-1753; *Economic and Social Progress in Latin America.*

Organization of American States (OAS), General Secretariat, Washington, D.C. 20006 (202) 458-3533; *Statistical Bulletin of the OAS.*

Statistical Office of the United Nations, Publishing Service, New York, New York 10017 (800) 253-9646; *Statistical Yearbook,* and *Statistical Yearbook for Latin America and the Caribbean.*

Times Books, 201 East 50th Street, New York, New York 10022 (212) 751-2600; *The Economist Book of Vital World Statistics.*

U.C.L.A. Latin American Center Publications, University of California, Los Angeles, California 90024 (310) 825-6634; *Statistical Abstract of Latin America.*

The World Bank, 1818 H Street, NW, Washington, D.C. 20433 (202) 477-1234; *World Tables.*

BOLIVIA - GROSS NATIONAL PRODUCT

Euromonitor Publications Limited, 87-88 Turnmill Street, London EC1M 5QU, England; *International Marketing Data and Statistics.*

Inter-American Development Bank, 1300 New York Avenue, NW, Washington, D.C. 20577 (202) 623-1753; *Economic and Social Progress in Latin America.*

U.S. Arms Control and Disarmament Agency, 320 Twenty-first Street, NW, Washington, D.C. 20451 (202) 647-8677; *World Military Expenditures and Arms Transfers.*

The World Bank, 1818 H Street, NW, Washington, D.C. 20433 (202) 477-1234; *World Tables.*

BOLIVIA - GROUNDNUTS PRODUCTION - See BOLIVIA - CROPS

BOLIVIA - HEALTH

The Economist Intelligence Unit, 111 West 57th Street, New York, New York 10019 (800) 933-4685; *The New Latin America Market Atlas.*

Facts on File, 460 Park Avenue South, New York, New York 10016 (800) 443-8323; *The New Book of World Rankings.*

Federal Statistical Office, Gustav - Stresemann - Ring 11, D-6200 Wiesbaden, Germany; *Bolivia.*

G.K. Hall and Company, 70 Lincoln Street, Boston, Massachusetts 02111 (617) 423-3990; *The World in Figures.*

Statistical Office of the United Nations, Publishing Service, New York, New York 10017 (800) 253-9646; *Statistical Yearbook.*

Times Books, 201 East 50th Street, New York, New York 10022 (212) 751-2600; *The Economist Book of Vital World Statistics.*

World Health Organization, Office of Publications, Avenue Appia, CH-1211 Geneva 27, Switzerland (Telephone Number in U.S. (518) 436-9686); *World Health Statistics Annual.*

BOLIVIA - HEALTH EXPENDITURES

International Monetary Fund, 700 Nineteenth Street, NW, Washington, D.C. 20431 (202) 623-7000; *Government Finance Statistics Yearbook.*

Statistical Office of the United Nations, Publishing Service, New York, New York 10017 (800) 253-9646; *Statistical Yearbook for Latin America and the Caribbean.*

BOLIVIA - HIDE PRODUCTION

Food and Agricultural Organization of the United Nations (FAO), Via delle Terme di Caracalla, 00100 Rome, Italy (Telephone Number in U.S. (202) 653-2400); *Production Yearbook.*

BOLIVIA - HIGHWAYS

The Economist Intelligence Unit, 111 West 57th Street, New York, New York 10019 (800) 933-4685; *The New Latin America Market Atlas.*

G.K. Hall and Company, 70 Lincoln Street, Boston, Massachusetts 02111 (617) 423-3990; *The World in Figures.*

International Road Federation, 525 School Street, SW, Washington, D.C. 20024 (202) 554-2105; *World Road Statistics.*

BOLIVIA - HOLDINGS

Statistical Office of the United Nations, Publishing Service, New York, New York 10017 (800) 253-9646; *Statistical Yearbook for Latin America and the Caribbean.*

U.C.L.A. Latin American Center Publications, University of California, Los Angeles, California (310) 825-6634; *Statistical Abstract of Latin America.*

BOLIVIA - HORSES - See BOLIVIA - LIVESTOCK AND POULTRY

BOLIVIA - HOURS OF WORK - See BOLIVIA - EMPLOYMENT

BOLIVIA - HOUSING AND HOUSING UNITS

Facts on File, 460 Park Avenue South, New York, New York 10016 (800) 443-8323; *The New Book of World Rankings.*

BOLIVIA - HOUSING EXPENDITURES

International Monetary Fund, 700 Nineteenth Street, NW, Washington, D.C. 20431 (202) 623-7000; *Government Finance Statistics Yearbook.*

BOLIVIA - HYDROCHLORIC ACID PRODUCTION

Statistical Office of the United Nations, Publishing Service, New York, New York 10017 (800) 253-9646; *Statistical Yearbook.*

BOLIVIA - ILLITERACY RATE

The Economist Intelligence Unit, 111 West 57th Street, New York, New York 10019 (800) 933-4685; *The New Latin America Market Atlas.*

BOLIVIA - ILLITERATE POPULATION

The Economist Intelligence Unit, 111 West 57th Street, New York, New York 10019 (800) 938-4685; *The World Market Atlas.*

G.K. Hall and Company, 70 Lincoln Street, Boston, Massachusetts 02111 (617) 423-3990; *The World in Figures.*

Statistical Office of the United Nations, Publishing Service, New York, New York 10017 (800) 253-9646; *Statistical Yearbook for Latin America and the Caribbean.*

United Nations Educational, Scientific and Cultural Organization (UNESCO), 7 Place de Fontenoy, F-75700 Paris, France (Telephone Number in U.S. (212) 963-5981); *Statistical Yearbook.*

BOLIVIA - IMMIGRATION

U.C.L.A. Latin American Center Publications, University of California, Los Angeles, California 90024 (310) 825-6634; *Statistical Abstract of Latin America.*

BOLIVIA - IMPORTS

The Economist Intelligence Unit, 111 West 57th Street, New York, New York 10019 (800) 938-4685; *The New Latin America Market Atlas,* and *The World Market Atlas.*

Euromonitor Publications Limited, 87-88 Turnmill Street, London EC1M 5QU, England; *International Marketing Data and Statistics.*

Food and Agricultural Organization of the United Nations (FAO) Via delle Terme di Caracalla, 00100 Rome, Italy (Telephone Number in U.S. (202) 653-2400); *The State of Food and Agriculture.*

G.K. Hall and Company, 70 Lincoln Street, Boston, Massachusetts 02111 (617) 423-3990; *The World in Figures.*

Inter-American Development Bank, 1300 New York Avenue, NW, Washington, D.C. 20577 (202) 623-1753; *Economic and Social Progress in Latin America.*

International Monetary Fund, 700 Nineteenth Street, NW, Washington, D.C. 20431 (202) 623-7000; *Direction of Trade Statistics, Government Finance Statistics Yearbook,* and *International Financial Statistics.*

Organization of American States (OAS), General Secretariat, Washington, D.C. 20006 (202) 458-3533; *Statistical Bulletin of the OAS.*

Statistical Office of the United Nations, Publishing Service, New York, New York 10017 (800) 253-9646; *Statistical Yearbook for Latin America and the Caribbean.*

Times Books, 201 East 50th Street, New York, New York 10022 (212) 751-2600; *The Economist Book of Vital World Statistics.*

The World Bank, 1818 H Street, NW, Washington, D.C. 20433 (202) 477-1234; *World Tables.*

BOLIVIA - INCOME DISTRIBUTION

Statistical Office of the United Nations, Publishing Service, New York, New York 10017 (800) 253-9646; *Statistical Yearbook for Latin America and the Caribbean.*

U.C.L.A. Latin American Center Publications, University of California, Los Angeles, California 90024 (310) 825-6634; *Statistical Abstract of Latin America.*

BOLIVIA - INCOME TAXES - See BOLIVIA - TAXATION

BOLIVIA - INDUSTRY

Euromonitor Publications Limited, 87-88 Turnmill Street, London EC1M 5QU, England; *International Marketing Data and Statistics.*

Facts on File, 460 Park Avenue South, New York, New York 10016 (800) 443-8323; *The New Book of World Rankings.*

Federal Statistical Office, Gustav - Stresemann - Ring 11, D-6200 Wiesbaden, Germany; *Bolivia.*

Gale Research Incorporated, 835 Penobscot Building, Detroit, Michigan 48226 (800) 877-4253; *International Historical Statistics The Americas and Australasia.*

G.K. Hall and Company, 70 Lincoln Street, Boston, Massachusetts 02111 (617) 423-3990; *The World in Figures.*

International Labour Office, I.L.O. Publications, CH-1211, Geneva 22, Switzerland; *Yearbook of Labour Statistics.*

Statistical Office of the United Nations, Publishing Service, New York, New York 10017 (800) 253-9646; *Economic Survey of Latin America and the Caribbean.*

Times Books, 201 East 50th Street, New York, New York 10022 (212) 751-2600; *The Economist Book of Vital World Statistics.*

U.C.L.A. Latin American Center Publications, University of California, Los Angeles, California 90024 (310) 825-6634; *Statistical Abstract of Latin America.*

The World Bank, 1818 H Street, NW, Washington, D.C. 20433 (202) 477-1234; *World Tables.*

BOLIVIA - INFANT AND MATERNAL MORTALITY

The Economist Intelligence Unit, 111 West 57th Street, New York, New York 10019 (800) 933-4685; *The New Latin America Market Atlas.*

Statistical Office of the United Nations, Publishing Service, New York, New York 10017 (800) 253-9646; *Demographic Yearbook,* and *Statistical Yearbook.*

Times Books, 201 East 50th Street, New York, New York 10022 (212) 751-2600; *The Economist Book of Vital World Statistics.*

The World Bank, 1818 H Street, NW, Washington, D.C. 20433 (202) 477-1234; *World Tables.*

BOLIVIA - INFLATIONARY FACTORS

Statistical Office of the United Nations, Publishing Service, New York, New York 10017 (800) 253-9646; *Economic Survey of Latin America and the Caribbean.*

BOLIVIA - INTEREST RATES

Inter-American Development Bank, 1300 New York Avenue, NW, Washington, D.C. 20577 (202) 623-1753; *Economic and Social Progress in Latin America.*

BOLIVIA - INTERNATIONAL FINANCE

Inter-American Development Bank, 1300 New York Avenue, NW, Washington, D.C. 20577 (202) 623-1753; *Economic and Social Progress in Latin America.*

U.C.L.A. Latin American Center Publications, University of California, Los Angeles, California 90024 (310) 825-6634; *Statistical Abstract of Latin America.*

BOLIVIA - INTERNATIONAL LIQUIDITY

Inter-American Development Bank, 1300 New York Avenue, NW, Washington, D.C. 20577 (202) 623-1753; *Economic and Social Progress in Latin America.*

International Monetary Fund, 700 Nineteenth Street, NW, Washington, D.C. 20431 (202) 623-7000; *International Financial Statistics.*

BOLIVIA - INTERNATIONAL RESERVES

Organization of American States (OAS), General Secretariat, Washington, D.C. 20006 (202) 458-3533; *Statistical Bulletin of the OAS.*

BOLIVIA - INTERNATIONAL RESERVES EXCLUDING GOLD

Inter-American Development Bank, 1300 New York Avenue, NW, Washington, D.C. 20577 (202) 623-1753; *Economic and Social Progress in Latin America.*

The World Bank, 1818 H Street, NW, Washington, D.C. 20433 (202) 477-1234; *World Tables.*

BOLIVIA - INTERNATIONAL STATISTICS

Inter-American Development Bank, 1300 New York Avenue, NW, Washington, D.C. 20577 (202) 623-1753; *Economic and Social Progress in Latin America.*

U.C.L.A. Latin American Center Publications, University of California, Los Angeles, California 90024 (310) 825-6634; *Statistical Abstract of Latin America.*

BOLIVIA - INVESTMENTS

Inter-American Development Bank, 1300 New York Avenue, NW, Washington, D.C. 20577 (202) 623-1753; *Economic and Social Progress in Latin America.*

International Monetary Fund, 700 Nineteenth Street, NW, Washington, D.C. 20431 (202) 623-7000; *International Financial Statistics.*

Statistical Office of the United Nations, Publishing Service, New York, New York 10017 (800) 253-9646; *Statistical Yearbook for Latin America and the Caribbean.*

BOLIVIA - IRON ORE PRODUCTION AND CONSUMPTION - See BOLIVIA - MINING AND MINERAL PRODUCTS

BOLIVIA - IRRIGATION

Euromonitor Publications Limited, 87-88 Turnmill Street, London EC1M 5QU, England; *International Marketing Data and Statistics.*

Inter-American Development Bank, 1300 New York Avenue, NW, Washington, D.C. 20577 (202) 623-1753; *Economic and Social Progress in Latin America.*

BOLIVIA - LABOR FORCE

The Economist Intelligence Unit, 111 West 57th Street, New York, New York 10019 (800) 933-4685; *The New Latin America Market Atlas.*

Euromonitor Publications Limited, 87-88 Turnmill Street, London EC1M 5QU, England; *International Marketing Data and Statistics.*

Facts on File, 460 Park Avenue South, New York, New York 10016 (800) 443-8323; *The New Book of World Rankings.*

Food and Agricultural Organization of the United Nations (FAO) Via delle Terme di Caracalla, 00100 Rome, Italy (Telephone Number in U.S. (202) 653-2400); *The State of Food and Agriculture.*

Gale Research Incorporated, 835 Penobscot Building, Detroit, Michigan 48226 (800) 877-4253; *International Historical Statistics The Americas and Australasia.*

G.K. Hall and Company, 70 Lincoln Street, Boston, Massachusetts 02111 (617) 423-3990; *The World in Figures.*

Times Books, 201 East 50th Street, New York, New York 10022 (212) 751-2600; *The Economist Book of Vital World Statistics.*

The World Bank, 1818 H Street, NW, Washington, D.C. 20433 (202) 477-1234; *World Tables.*

BOLIVIA - LABOR PRODUCTIVITY

International Labour Office, I.L.O. Publications, CH-1211, Geneva 22, Switzerland; *Yearbook of Labour Statistics.*

BOLIVIA - LAND AREA

The Economist Intelligence Unit, 111 West 57th Street, New York, New York 10019 (800) 933-4685; *The New Latin America Market Atlas.*

BOLIVIA - LAND USE

Euromonitor Publications Limited, 87-88 Turnmill Street, London EC1M 5QU, England; *International Marketing Data and Statistics.*

Food and Agricultural Organization of the United Nations (FAO), Via delle Terme di Caracalla, 00100 Rome, Italy (Telephone Number in U.S. (202) 653-2400); *Production Yearbook.*

G.K. Hall and Company, 70 Lincoln Street, Boston, Massachusetts 02111 (617) 423-3990; *The World in Figures.*

Inter-American Development Bank, 1300 New York Avenue, NW, Washington, D.C. 20577 (202) 623-1753; *Economic and Social Progress in Latin America.*

BOLIVIA - LEAD AND LEAD ORE - See BOLIVIA - MINING AND MINERAL PRODUCTS

BOLIVIA - LIBRARIES

Facts on File, 460 Park Avenue South, New York, New York 10016 (800) 443-8323; *The New Book of World Rankings.*

BOLIVIA - LIFE EXPECTANCY RATE

The Economist Intelligence Unit, 111 West 57th Street, New York, New York 10019 (800) 933-4685; *The New Latin America Market Atlas.*

BOLIVIA - LIVESTOCK AND POULTRY

Euromonitor Publications Limited, 87-88 Turnmill Street, London EC1M 5QU, England; *International Marketing Data and Statistics.*

Facts on File, 460 Park Avenue South, New York, New York 10016 (800) 443-8323; *The New Book of World Rankings.*

Food and Agricultural Organization of the United Nations (FAO), Via delle Terme di Caracalla, 00100 Rome, Italy (Telephone Number in U.S. (202) 653-2400); *Production Yearbook,* and *The State of Food and Agriculture.*

G.K. Hall and Company, 70 Lincoln Street, Boston, Massachusetts 02111 (617) 423-3990; *The World in Figures.*

Statistical Office of the United Nations, Publishing Service, New York, New York 10017 (800) 253-9646; *Statistical Yearbook.*

BOLIVIA - LIVING LEVELS

G.K. Hall and Company, 70 Lincoln Street, Boston, Massachusetts 02111 (617) 423-3990; *The World in Figures.*

Statistical Office of the United Nations, Publishing Service, New York, New York 10017 (800) 253-9646; *Statistical Yearbook for Latin America and the Caribbean.*

Times Books, 201 East 50th Street, New York, New York 10022 (212) 751-2600; *The Economist Book of Vital World Statistics.*

BOLIVIA - MAIL - NUMBER OF ITEMS SENT AND RECEIVED

Statistical Office of the United Nations, Publishing Service, New York, New York 10017 (800) 253-9646; *Statistical Yearbook.*

BOLIVIA - MAIN ECONOMIC INDICATORS - See BOLIVIA - ECONOMY

BOLIVIA - MANUFACTURING

The Economist Intelligence Unit, 111 West 57th Street, New York, New York 10019 (800) 933-4685; *The New Latin America Market Atlas.*

Facts on File, 460 Park Avenue South, New York, New York 10016 (800) 443-8323; *The New Book of World Rankings.*

G.K. Hall and Company, 70 Lincoln Street, Boston, Massachusetts 02111 (617) 423-3990; *The World in Figures.*

Inter-American Development Bank, 1300 New York Avenue, NW, Washington, D.C. 20577 (202) 623-1753; *Economic and Social Progress in Latin America.*

Statistical Office of the United Nations, Publishing Service, New York, New York 10017 (800) 253-9646; *Statistical Yearbook,* and *Statistical Yearbook for Latin America and the Caribbean.*

Times Books, 201 East 50th Street, New York, New York 10022 (212) 751-2600; *The Economist Book of Vital World Statistics.*

The World Bank, 1818 H Street, NW, Washington, D.C. 20433 (202) 477-1234; *World Tables.*

BOLIVIA - MARRIAGE RATES

Facts on File, 460 Park Avenue South, New York, New York 10016 (800) 443-8323; *The New Book of World Rankings.*

Statistical Office of the United Nations, Publishing Service, New York, New York 10017 (800) 253-9646; *Demographic Yearbook,* and *Statistical Yearbook.*

BOLIVIA - MEAT PRODUCTION - See BOLIVIA - LIVESTOCK AND POULTRY

BOLIVIA - MEDICAL PERSONNEL

U.C.L.A. Latin American Center Publications, University of California, Los Angeles, California 90024 (310) 825-6634; *Statistical Abstract of Latin America.*

BOLIVIA - MERCHANT SHIPPING

G.K. Hall and Company, 70 Lincoln Street, Boston, Massachusetts 02111 (617) 423-3990; *The World in Figures.*

Times Books, 201 East 50th Street, New York, New York 10022 (212) 751-2600; *The Economist Book of Vital World Statistics.*

BOLIVIA - MERCURY PRODUCTION AND CONSUMPTION - See BOLIVIA - MINING AND MINERAL PRODUCTS

BOLIVIA - MILITARY

The Economist Intelligence Unit, 111 West 57th Street, New York, New York 10019 (800) 933-4685; *The New Latin America Market Atlas.*

G.K. Hall and Company, 70 Lincoln Street, Boston, Massachusetts 02111 (617) 423-3990; *The World in Figures.*

The International Institute for Strategic Studies, 23 Tavistock Street, London WC2E 7NQ, England; *The Military Balance.*

U.C.L.A. Latin American Center Publications, University of California, Los Angeles, California 90024 (310) 825-6634; *Statistical*

Abstract of Latin America.

U.S. Arms Control and Disarmament Agency, 320 Twenty-first Street, NW, Washington, D.C. 20451 (202) 647-8677; *World Military Expenditures and Arms Transfers.*

BOLIVIA - MILK PRODUCTION - See BOLIVIA - DAIRY PRODUCTS

BOLIVIA - MINING AND MINERAL PRODUCTS

Commodity Research Bureau, Incorporated, 75 Wall Street, New York, New York 10005 (212) 504-7754; *Commodity Year Book.*

The Economist Intelligence Unit, 111 West 57th Street, New York, New York 10019 (800) 933-4685; *The New Latin America Market Atlas.*

Facts on File, 460 Park Avenue South, New York, New York 10016 (800) 443-8323; *The New Book of World Rankings.*

G.K. Hall and Company, 70 Lincoln Street, Boston, Massachusetts 02111 (617) 423-3990; *The World in Figures.*

Inter-American Development Bank, 1300 New York Avenue, NW, Washington, D.C. 20577 (202) 623-1753; *Economic and Social Progress in Latin America.*

International Monetary Fund, 700 Nineteenth Street, NW, Washington, D.C. 20431 (202) 623-7000; *International Financial Statistics.*

Penn Well Publishing Company, 1421 South Sheridan Road, P.O. Box 1260, Tulsa, Oklahoma 74101 (800) 752-9764; *International Energy Statistics Sourcebook.*

Statistical Office of the United Nations, Publishing Service, New York, New York 10017 (800) 253-9646; *Statistical Yearbook*, and *Statistical Yearbook for Latin America and the Caribbean.*

U.C.L.A. Latin American Center Publications, University of California, Los Angeles, California 90024 (310) 825-6634; *Statistical Abstract of Latin America.*

BOLIVIA - MONEY EXCHANGE RATE

Euromonitor Publications Limited, 87-88 Turnmill Street, London EC1M 5QU, England; *International Marketing Data and Statistics.*

Inter-American Development Bank, 1300 New York Avenue, NW, Washington, D.C. 20577 (202) 623-1753; *Economic and Social Progress in Latin America.*

International Monetary Fund, 700 Nineteenth Street, NW, Washington, D.C. 20431 (202) 623-7000; *International Financial Statistics.*

Statistical Office of the United Nations, Publishing Service, New York, New York 10017 (800) 253-9646; *Statistical Yearbook.*

BOLIVIA - MONEY RATES - MARKET

Inter-American Development Bank, 1300 New York Avenue, NW, Washington, D.C. 20577 (202) 623-1753; *Economic and Social Progress in Latin America.*

BOLIVIA - MONEY RESERVES

Euromonitor Publications Limited, 87-88 Turnmill Street, London EC1M 5QU, England; *International Marketing Data and Statistics.*

Inter-American Development Bank, 1300 New York Avenue, NW, Washington, D.C. 20577 (202) 623-1753; *Economic and Social Progress in Latin America.*

BOLIVIA - MONEY SUPPLY

Euromonitor Publications Limited, 87-88 Turnmill Street, London EC1M 5QU, England; *International Marketing Data and Statistics.*

G.K. Hall and Company, 70 Lincoln Street, Boston, Massachusetts 02111 (617) 423-3990; *The World in Figures.*

Inter-American Development Bank, 1300 New York Avenue, NW, Washington, D.C. 20577 (202) 623-1753; *Economic and Social Progress in Latin America.*

International Monetary Fund, 700 Nineteenth Street, NW, Washington, D.C. 20431 (202) 623-7000; *International Financial Statistics.*

Statistical Office of the United Nations, Publishing Service, New York, New York 10017 (800) 253-9646; *Statistical Yearbook.*

U.C.L.A. Latin American Center Publications, University of California, Los Angeles, California 90024 (310) 825-6634; *Statistical Abstract of Latin America.*

The World Bank, 1818 H Street, NW, Washington, D.C. 20433 (202) 477-1234; *World Tables.*

BOLIVIA - MOTION PICTURES

United Nations Educational, Scientific and Cultural Organization (UNESCO), 7 Place de Fontenoy, F-75700 Paris, France (Telephone Number in U.S. (212) 963-5981); *Statistical Yearbook.*

BOLIVIA - MOTOR VEHICLE TAXES - See BOLIVIA - TAXATION

BOLIVIA - MOTOR VEHICLES IN USE

The Economist Intelligence Unit, 111 West 57th Street, New York, New York 10019 (800) 933-4685; *The New Latin America Market Atlas.*

G.K. Hall and Company, 70 Lincoln Street, Boston, Massachusetts 02111 (617) 423-3990; *The World in Figures.*

International Road Federation, 525 School Street, SW, Washington, D.C. 20024 (202) 554-2105; *World Road Statistics.*

Statistical Office of the United Nations, Publishing Service, New York, New York 10017 (800) 253-9646; *Statistical Yearbook.*

Times Books, 201 East 50th Street, New York, New York 10022 (212) 751-2600; *The Economist Book of Vital World Statistics.*

BOLIVIA - MULES - See BOLIVIA - LIVESTOCK AND POULTRY

BOLIVIA - MUSEUMS

Facts on File, 460 Park Avenue South, New York, New York 10016 (800) 443-8323; *The New Book of World Rankings.*

BOLIVIA - NATALITY - See BOLIVIA - BIRTH RATE

BOLIVIA - NATIONAL ACCOUNTS

Federal Statistical Office, Gustav - Stresemann - Ring 11, D-6200 Wiesbaden, Germany; *Bolivia.*

Gale Research Incorporated, 835 Penobscot Building, Detroit, Michigan 48226 (800) 877-4253; *International Historical Statistics The Americas and Australasia.*

Inter-American Development Bank, 1300 New York Avenue, NW, Washington, D.C. 20577 (202) 623-1753; *Economic and Social Progress in Latin America.*

Organization of American States (OAS), General Secretariat, Washington, D.C. 20006 (202) 458-3533; *Statistical Bulletin of the OAS.*

Statistical Office of the United Nations, Publishing Service, New York, New York 10017 (800) 253-9646; *National Accounts Statistics.*

U.C.L.A. Latin American Center Publications, University of California, Los Angeles, California 90024 (310) 825-6634; *Statistical Abstract of Latin America.*

BOLIVIA - NATIONAL INCOME

Facts on File, 460 Park Avenue South, New York, New York 10016 (800) 443-8323; *The New Book of World Rankings.*

G.K. Hall and Company, 70 Lincoln Street, Boston, Massachusetts 02111 (617) 423-3990; *The World in Figures.*

Inter-American Development Bank, 1300 New York Avenue, NW, Washington, D.C. 20577 (202) 623-1753; *Economic and Social Progress in Latin America.*

Statistical Office of the United Nations, Publishing Service, New York, New York 10017 (800) 253-9646; *Statistical Yearbook,* and *Statistical Yearbook for Latin America and the Caribbean.*

BOLIVIA - NATIONAL PRODUCT

Facts on File, 460 Park Avenue South, New York, New York 10016 (800) 443-8323; *The New Book of World Rankings.*

Statistical Office of the United Nations, Publishing Service, New York, New York 10017 (800) 253-9646; *Statistical Yearbook.*

BOLIVIA - NATURAL GAS PRODUCTION - See BOLIVIA - MINING AND MINERAL PRODUCTS

BOLIVIA - NET MATERIAL PRODUCT

Statistical Office of the United Nations, Publishing Service, New York, New York 10017 (800) 253-9646; *Statistical Yearbook.*

BOLIVIA - NEWSPAPER PRODUCTION - See FORESTRY AND FOREST PRODUCTS

BOLIVIA - NEWSPRINT - See FORESTRY AND FOREST PRODUCTS

BOLIVIA - NUTRITION

Statistical Office of the United Nations, Publishing Service, New York, New York 10017 (800) 253-9646; *Statistical Yearbook for Latin America and the Caribbean.*

BOLIVIA - OATS PRODUCTION - See BOLIVIA - CROPS

BOLIVIA - OCCUPATIONS - See BOLIVIA - LABOR FORCE

BOLIVIA - PAPER - See BOLIVIA - FORESTRY AND FOREST PRODUCTS

BOLIVIA - PATENTS

Statistical Office of the United Nations, Publishing Service, New York, New York 10017 (800) 253-9646; *Statistical Yearbook.*

BOLIVIA - PEANUT PRODUCTION - See BOLIVIA - CROPS

BOLIVIA - PESTICIDE USE

Food and Agricultural Organization of the United Nations (FAO) Via delle Terme di Caracalla, 00100 Rome, Italy (Telephone Number in U.S. (202) 653-2400); *The State of Food and Agriculture.*

BOLIVIA - PETROLEUM INDUSTRY

The Economist Intelligence Unit, 111 West 57th Street, New York, New York 10019 (800) 933-4685; *The New Latin America Market Atlas.*

Facts on File, 460 Park Avenue South, New York, New York 10016 (800) 443-8323; *The New Book of World Rankings.*

G.K. Hall and Company, 70 Lincoln Street, Boston, Massachusetts 02111 (617) 423-3990; *The World in Figures.*

Inter-American Development Bank, 1300 New York Avenue, NW, Washington, D.C. 20577 (202) 623-1753; *Economic and Social Progress in Latin America.*

International Monetary Fund, 700 Nineteenth Street, NW, Washington, D.C. 20431 (202) 623-7000; *International Financial Statistics.*

Organization of American States (OAS), General Secretariat, Washington, D.C. 20006 (202) 458-3533; *Statistical Bulletin of the OAS.*

Penn Well Publishing Company, 1421 South Sheridan Road, P.O. Box 1260, Tulsa, Oklahoma 74101 (800) 752-9764; *International Energy Statistics Sourcebook.*

Statistical Office of the United Nations, Publishing Service, New York, New York 10017 (800) 253-9646; *Statistical Yearbook.*

BOLIVIA - PIGS - See BOLIVIA - LIVESTOCK AND POULTRY

BOLIVIA - POLITICAL DATA

U.C.L.A. Latin American Center Publications, University of California, Los Angeles, California 90024 (310) 825-6634; *Statistical Abstract of Latin America.*

BOLIVIA - POPULATION

The Economist Intelligence Unit, 111 West 57th Street, New York, New York 10019 (800) 938-4685; *The New Latin America Market Atlas,* and *The World Market Atlas.*

Euromonitor Publications Limited, 87-88 Turnmill Street, London EC1M 5QU, England; *International Marketing Data and Statistics.*

Facts on File, 460 Park Avenue South, New York, New York 10016 (800) 443-8323; *The New Book of World Rankings.*

Federal Statistical Office, Gustav - Stresemann - Ring 11, D-6200 Wiesbaden, Germany; *Bolivia.*

Food and Agricultural Organization of the United Nations (FAO), Via delle Terme di Caracalla, 00100 Rome, Italy (Telephone Number in

U.S. (202) 653-2400); *Production Yearbook.*

Gale Research Incorporated, 835 Penobscot Building, Detroit, Michigan 48226 (800) 877-4253; *International Historical Statistics The Americas and Australasia.*

G.K. Hall and Company, 70 Lincoln Street, Boston, Massachusetts 02111 (617) 423-3990; *The World in Figures.*

Inter-American Development Bank, 1300 New York Avenue, NW, Washington, D.C. 20577 (202) 623-1753; *Economic and Social Progress in Latin America.*

International Labour Office, I.L.O. Publications, CH-1211, Geneva 22, Switzerland; *Yearbook of Labour Statistics.*

Organization of American States (OAS), General Secretariat, Washington, D.C. 20006 (202) 458-3533; *Statistical Bulletin of the OAS.*

Statistical Office of the United Nations, Publishing Service, New York, New York 10017 (800) 253-9646; *Demographic Yearbook,* and *Statistical Yearbook.*

Times Books, 201 East 50th Street, New York, New York 10022 (212) 751-2600; *The Economist Book of Vital World Statistics.*

U.C.L.A. Latin American Center Publications, University of California, Los Angeles, California 90024 (310) 825-6634; *Statistical Abstract of Latin America.*

United Nations Educational, Scientific and Cultural Organization (UNESCO), 7 Place de Fontenoy, F-75700 Paris, France (Telephone Number in U.S. (212) 963-5981); *Statistical Yearbook.*

U.S. Arms Control and Disarmament Agency, 320 Twenty-first Street, NW, Washington, D.C. 20451 (202) 647-8677; *World Military Expenditures and Arms Transfers.*

World Health Organization, Office of Publications, Avenue Appia, CH-1211 Geneva 27, Switzerland (Telephone Number in U.S. (518) 436-9686); *World Health Statistics Annual.*

BOLIVIA - POST OFFICES

Facts on File, 460 Park Avenue South, New York, New York 10016 (800) 443-8323; *The New Book of World Rankings.*

BOLIVIA - POTATO PRODUCTION - See BOLIVIA - CROPS

BOLIVIA - POWER PRODUCTION INDUSTRY

Statistical Office of the United Nations, Publishing Service, New York, New York 10017 (800) 253-9646; *Statistical Yearbook.*

BOLIVIA - PRICES

Facts on File, 460 Park Avenue South, New York, New York 10016 (800) 443-8323; *The New Book of World Rankings.*

Federal Statistical Office, Gustav - Stresemann - Ring 11, D-6200 Wiesbaden, Germany; *Bolivia.*

Food and Agricultural Organization of the United Nations (FAO), Via delle Terme di Caracalla, 00100 Rome, Italy (Telephone Number in U.S. (202) 653-2400); *Production Yearbook,* and *The State of Food and Agriculture.*

Gale Research Incorporated, 835 Penobscot Building, Detroit, Michigan 48226 (800) 877-4253; *International Historical Statistics The Americas and Australasia.*

G.K. Hall and Company, 70 Lincoln Street, Boston, Massachusetts 02111 (617) 423-3990; *The World in Figures.*

International Labour Office, I.L.O. Publications, CH-1211, Geneva 22, Switzerland; *Yearbook of Labour Statistics.*

International Monetary Fund, 700 Nineteenth Street, NW, Washington, D.C. 20431 (202) 623-7000; *International Financial Statistics.*

Statistical Office of the United Nations, Publishing Service, New York, New York 10017 (800) 253-9646; *Statistical Yearbook for Latin America and the Caribbean.*

BOLIVIA - PRINTING AND WRITING PAPER - See BOLIVIA - FORESTRY AND FOREST PRODUCTS

BOLIVIA - PRODUCTION

Facts on File, 460 Park Avenue South, New York, New York 10016 (800) 443-8323; *The New Book of World Rankings.*

G.K. Hall and Company, 70 Lincoln Street, Boston, Massachusetts 02111 (617) 423-3990; *The World in Figures.*

BOLIVIA - PRODUCTIVITY

Euromonitor Publications Limited, 87-88 Turnmill Street, London EC1M 5QU, England; *International Marketing Data and Statistics.*

BOLIVIA - PROPERTY TAXES - See BOLIVIA - TAXATION

BOLIVIA - PUBLIC CONSUMPTION FUND

Inter-American Development Bank, 1300 New York Avenue, NW, Washington, D.C. 20577 (202) 623-1753; *Economic and Social Progress in Latin America.*

BOLIVIA - PUBLIC EXPENDITURES

Inter-American Development Bank, 1300 New York Avenue, NW, Washington, D.C. 20577 (202) 623-1753; *Economic and Social Progress in Latin America.*

Organization of American States (OAS), General Secretariat, Washington, D.C. 20006 (202) 458-3533; *Statistical Bulletin of the OAS.*

Statistical Office of the United Nations, Publishing Service, New York, New York 10017 (800) 253-9646; *Statistical Yearbook for Latin America and the Caribbean.*

BOLIVIA - PUBLIC FINANCE

Facts on File, 460 Park Avenue South, New York, New York 10016 (800) 443-8323; *The New Book of World Rankings.*

Inter-American Development Bank, 1300 New York Avenue, NW, Washington, D.C. 20577 (202) 623-1753; *Economic and Social Progress in Latin America.*

Organization of American States (OAS), General Secretariat, Washington, D.C. 20006 (202) 458-3533; *Statistical Bulletin of the OAS.*

BOLIVIA - PUBLIC REVENUES

Inter-American Development Bank, 1300 New York Avenue, NW, Washington, D.C. 20577 (202) 623-1753; *Economic and Social Progress in Latin America.*

Organization of American States (OAS), General Secretariat, Washington, D.C. 20006 (202) 458-3533; *Statistical Bulletin of the OAS.*

BOLIVIA - RADIO BROADCASTING - See BOLIVIA - BROADCASTING

BOLIVIA - RAILWAYS

The Economist Intelligence Unit, 111 West 57th Street, New York, New York 10019 (800) 933-4685; *The New Latin America Market Atlas.*

G.K. Hall and Company, 70 Lincoln Street, Boston, Massachusetts 02111 (617) 423-3990; *The World in Figures.*

Jane's Information Group, Sentinel House, 163 Brighton Road, Coulsdon, Surrey CR5 2NH, England (Telephone Number in U.S. (703) 683-3700); *Jane's World Railways.*

Statistical Office of the United Nations, Publishing Service, New York, New York 10017 (800) 253-9646; *Statistical Yearbook.*

BOLIVIA - RANCHING PRODUCTION

U.C.L.A. Latin American Center Publications, University of California, Los Angeles, California 90024 (310) 825-6634; *Statistical Abstract of Latin America.*

BOLIVIA - RELIGION

Facts on File, 460 Park Avenue South, New York, New York 10016 (800) 443-8323; *The New Book of World Rankings.*

U.C.L.A. Latin American Center Publications, University of California, Los Angeles, California 90024 (310) 825-6634; *Statistical Abstract of Latin America.*

BOLIVIA - RENT PRICES

International Labour Office, I.L.O. Publications, CH-1211, Geneva 22, Switzerland; *Yearbook of Labour Statistics.*

BOLIVIA - RESERVES EXCLUDING GOLD

The Economist Intelligence Unit, 111 West 57th Street, New York, New York 10019 (800) 933-4685; *The New Latin America Market Atlas.*

BOLIVIA - RETAIL TRADE

G.K. Hall and Company, 70 Lincoln Street, Boston, Massachusetts 02111 (617) 423-3990; *The World in Figures.*

Inter-American Development Bank, 1300 New York Avenue, NW, Washington, D.C. 20577 (202) 623-1753; *Economic and Social Progress in Latin America.*

BOLIVIA - RICE PRODUCTION - See BOLIVIA - CROPS

BOLIVIA - ROOT AND TUBER PRODUCTION - See BOLIVIA - CROPS

BOLIVIA - ROUNDWOOD PRODUCTION - See BOLIVIA - FORESTRY AND FOREST PRODUCTS

BOLIVIA - RUBBER PRODUCTION

Facts on File, 460 Park Avenue South, New York, New York 10016 (800) 443-8323; *The New Book of World Rankings.*

BOLIVIA - SAWNWOOD PRODUCTION - See BOLIVIA - FORESTRY AND FOREST PRODUCTS

BOLIVIA - SCIENCE AND TECHNOLOGY

Statistical Office of the United Nations, Publishing Service, New York, New York 10017 (800) 253-9646; *Statistical Yearbook for Latin America and the Caribbean.*

BOLIVIA - SCIENTISTS AND TECHNICIANS

Statistical Office of the United Nations, Publishing Service, New York, New York 10017 (800) 253-9646; *Statistical Yearbook.*

United Nations Educational, Scientific and Cultural Organization (UNESCO), 7 Place de Fontenoy, F-75700 Paris, France (Telephone Number in U.S. (212) 963-5981); *Statistical Yearbook.*

BOLIVIA - SENIOR CITIZENS

Facts on File, 460 Park Avenue South, New York, New York 10016 (800) 443-8323; *The New Book of World Rankings.*

BOLIVIA - SHEEP - See BOLIVIA - LIVESTOCK AND POULTRY

BOLIVIA - SILVER - See BOLIVIA - MINING AND MINERAL PRODUCTS

BOLIVIA - SOCIAL DATA

Facts on File, 460 Park Avenue South, New York, New York 10016 (800) 443-8323; *The New Book of World Rankings.*

G.K. Hall and Company, 70 Lincoln Street, Boston, Massachusetts 02111 (617) 423-3990; *The World in Figures.*

U.C.L.A. Latin American Center Publications, University of California, Los Angeles, California 90024 (310) 825-6634; *Statistical Abstract of Latin America.*

BOLIVIA - SOCIAL SECURITY

Inter-American Development Bank, 1300 New York Avenue, NW, Washington, D.C. 20577 (202) 623-1753; *Economic and Social Progress in Latin America.*

International Monetary Fund, 700 Nineteenth Street, NW, Washington, D.C. 20431 (202) 623-7000; *Government Finance Statistics Yearbook.*

BOLIVIA - SOCIOECONOMIC DATA

Inter-American Development Bank, 1300 New York Avenue, NW, Washington, D.C. 20577 (202) 623-1753; *Economic and Social Progress in Latin America.*

U.C.L.A. Latin American Center Publications, University of California, Los Angeles, California 90024 (310) 825-6634; *Statistical Abstract of Latin America.*

BOLIVIA - SOYBEAN PRODUCTION - See BOLIVIA - CROPS

BOLIVIA - STAMP TAXES AND DUTIES - See BOLIVIA - TAXATION

BOLIVIA - STATE BUDGET REVENUE AND EXPENDITURES

Euromonitor Publications Limited, 87-88 Turnmill Street, London EC1M 5QU, England; *International Marketing Data and Statistics.*

Inter-American Development Bank, 1300 New York Avenue, NW, Washington, D.C. 20577 (202) 623-1753; *Economic and Social Progress in Latin America.*

BOLIVIA - STEEL - See BOLIVIA - MINING AND MINERAL PRODUCTS

BOLIVIA - STOCKS - COMMODITY - MARKET PRICE - INDEX

Food and Agricultural Organization of the United Nations (FAO) Via delle Terme di Caracalla, 00100 Rome, Italy (Telephone Number in U.S. (202) 653-2400); *The State of Food and Agriculture.*

BOLIVIA - SUGAR - See BOLIVIA - CROPS

BOLIVIA - SULPHURIC ACID PRODUCTION - See - MINING AND MINERAL PRODUCTS

BOLIVIA - TAXATION

Inter-American Development Bank, 1300 New York Avenue, NW, Washington, D.C. 20577 (202) 623-1753; *Economic and Social Progress in Latin America.*

International Monetary Fund, 700 Nineteenth Street, NW, Washington, D.C. 20431 (202) 623-7000; *Government Finance Statistics Yearbook.*

International Road Federation, 525 School Street, SW, Washington, D.C. 20024 (202) 554-2105; *World Road Statistics.*

Statistical Office of the United Nations, Publishing Service, New York, New York 10017 (800) 253-9646; *Statistical Yearbook for Latin America and the Caribbean.*

The World Bank, 1818 H Street, NW, Washington, D.C. 20433 (202) 477-1234; *World Tables.*

BOLIVIA - TELEPHONES IN USE

American Telephone and Telegraph Company, 26 Parsippany Road, Whippany, New Jersey 07981 (800) 338-4038; *The World's Telephones.*

The Economist Intelligence Unit, 111 West 57th Street, New York, New York 10019 (800) 933-4685; *The New Latin America Market Atlas.*

G.K. Hall and Company, 70 Lincoln Street, Boston, Massachusetts 02111 (617) 423-3990; *The World in Figures.*

BOLIVIA - TELEVISION BROADCASTING - See BOLIVIA - BROADCASTING

BOLIVIA - TEXTILE INDUSTRY

G.K. Hall and Company, 70 Lincoln Street, Boston, Massachusetts 02111 (617) 423-3990; *The World in Figures.*

Statistical Office of the United Nations, Publishing Service, New York, New York 10017 (800) 253-9646; *Statistical Yearbook.*

BOLIVIA - TIN - See BOLIVIA - MINING AND MINERAL PRODUCTS

BOLIVIA - TOBACCO PRODUCTION

Facts on File, 460 Park Avenue South, New York, New York 10016 (800) 443-8323; *The New Book of World Rankings.*

Statistical Office of the United Nations, Publishing Service, New York, New York 10017 (800) 253-9646; *Statistical Yearbook.*

BOLIVIA - TOURISM

The Economist Intelligence Unit, 111 West 57th Street, New York, New York 10019 (800) 933-4685; *The New Latin America Market Atlas.*

Facts on File, 460 Park Avenue South, New York, New York 10016 (800) 443-8323; *The New Book of World Rankings.*

Federal Statistical Office, Gustav - Stresemann - Ring 11, D-6200 Wiesbaden, Germany; *Bolivia.*

G.K. Hall and Company, 70 Lincoln Street, Boston, Massachusetts 02111 (617) 423-3990; *The World in Figures.*

Statistical Office of the United Nations, Publishing Service, New York, New York 10017 (800) 253-9646; *Statistical Yearbook,* and *Statistical Yearbook for Latin America and the Caribbean.*

Times Books, 201 East 50th Street, New York, New York 10022 (212) 751-2600; *The Economist Book of Vital World Statistics.*

U.C.L.A. Latin American Center Publications, University of California, Los Angeles, California 90024 (310) 825-6634; *Statistical Abstract of Latin America.*

World Tourism Organization, Calle Capitan Haya 42, E-28020 Madrid, Spain; *Yearbook of Tourism Statistics.*

BOLIVIA - TRACTORS IN USE

The Economist Intelligence Unit, 111 West 57th Street, New York, New York 10019 (800) 933-4685; *The New Latin America Market Atlas.*

Statistical Office of the United Nations, Publishing Service, New York, New York 10017 (800) 253-9646; *Statistical Yearbook.*

BOLIVIA - TRADE - See BOLIVIA - FOREIGN TRADE

BOLIVIA - TRADEMARKS AND SERVICE MARKS

Statistical Office of the United Nations, Publishing Service, New York, New York 10017 (800) 253-9646; *Statistical Yearbook.*

BOLIVIA - TRANSPORTATION AND COMMUNICATIONS

The Economist Intelligence Unit, 111 West 57th Street, New York, New York 10019 (800) 933-4685; *The New Latin America Market Atlas.*

Facts on File, 460 Park Avenue South, New York, New York 10016 (800) 443-8323; *The New Book of World Rankings.*

Federal Statistical Office, Gustav - Stresemann - Ring 11, D-6200 Wiesbaden, Germany; *Bolivia.*

Gale Research Incorporated, 835 Penobscot Building, Detroit, Michigan 48226 (800) 877-4253; *International Historical Statistics The Americas and Australasia.*

G.K. Hall and Company, 70 Lincoln Street, Boston, Massachusetts 02111 (617) 423-3990; *The World in Figures.*

Inter-American Development Bank, 1300 New York Avenue, NW, Washington, D.C. 20577 (202) 623-1753; *Economic and Social Progress in Latin America.*

Statistical Office of the United Nations, Publishing Service, New York, New York 10017 (800) 253-9646; *Statistical Yearbook for Latin America and the Caribbean.*

U.C.L.A. Latin American Center Publications, University of California, Los Angeles, California 90024 (310) 825-6634; *Statistical Abstract of Latin America.*

BOLIVIA - TRAVEL FARES ABROAD

International Monetary Fund, 700 Nineteenth Street, NW, Washington, D.C. 20431 (202) 623-7000; *Government Finance Statistics Yearbook.*

BOLIVIA - TUNGSTEN PRODUCTION AND CONSUMPTION - See BOLIVIA - MINING AND MINERAL PRODUCTS

BOLIVIA - TURKEYS - See BOLIVIA - LIVESTOCK AND POULTRY

BOLIVIA - UNEMPLOYMENT

The Economist Intelligence Unit, 111 West 57th Street, New York, New York 10019 (800) 933-4685; *The New Latin America Market Atlas.*

Euromonitor Publications Limited, 87-88 Turnmill Street, London EC1M 5QU, England; *International Marketing Data and Statistics.*

International Labour Office, I.L.O. Publications, CH-1211, Geneva 22, Switzerland; *Yearbook of Labour Statistics.*

Statistical Office of the United Nations, Publishing Service, New York, New York 10017 (800) 253-9646; *Statistical Yearbook.*

U.C.L.A. Latin American Center Publications, University of California, Los Angeles, California 90024 (310) 825-6634; *Statistical Abstract of Latin America.*

BOLIVIA - UTILITIES

U.C.L.A. Latin American Center Publications, University of California, Los Angeles, California 90024 (310) 825-6634; *Statistical Abstract of Latin America.*

BOLIVIA - VITAL STATISTICS

Euromonitor Publications Limited, 87-88 Turnmill Street, London EC1M 5QU, England; *International Marketing Data and Statistics.*

Gale Research Incorporated, 835 Penobscot Building, Detroit, Michigan 48226 (800) 877-4253; *International Historical Statistics The Americas and Australasia.*

G.K. Hall and Company, 70 Lincoln Street, Boston, Massachusetts 02111 (617) 423-3990; *The World in Figures.*

World Health Organization, Office of Publications, Avenue Appia, CH-1211 Geneva 27, Switzerland (Telephone Number in U.S. (518) 436-9686); *World Health Statistics Annual.*

BOLIVIA - WAGES

Gale Research Incorporated, 835 Penobscot Building, Detroit, Michigan 48226 (800) 877-4253; *International Historical Statistics The Americas and Australasia.*

G.K. Hall and Company, 70 Lincoln Street, Boston, Massachusetts 02111 (617) 423-3990; *The World in Figures.*

International Labour Office, I.L.O. Publications, CH-1211, Geneva 22, Switzerland; *Yearbook of Labour Statistics.*

Statistical Office of the United Nations, Publishing Service, New York, New York 10017 (800) 253-9646; *Statistical Yearbook.*

U.C.L.A. Latin American Center Publications, University of California, Los Angeles, California 90024 (310) 825-6634; *Statistical Abstract of Latin America.*

BOLIVIA - WEATHER

Facts on File, 460 Park Avenue South, New York, New York 10016 (800) 443-8323; *The New Book of World Rankings.*

G.K. Hall and Company, 70 Lincoln Street, Boston, Massachusetts 02111 (617) 423-3990; *The World in Figures.*

BOLIVIA - WELFARE

Inter-American Development Bank, 1300 New York Avenue, NW, Washington, D.C. 20577 (202) 623-1753; *Economic and Social Progress in Latin America.*

International Monetary Fund, 700 Nineteenth Street, NW, Washington, D.C. 20431 (202) 623-7000; *Government Finance Statistics Yearbook.*

BOLIVIA - WHEAT - See BOLIVIA - CROPS

BOLIVIA - WHOLESALE PRICES

Inter-American Development Bank, 1300 New York Avenue, NW, Washington, D.C. 20577 (202) 623-1753; *Economic and Social Progress in Latin America.*

BOLIVIA - WHOLESALE TRADE

Inter-American Development Bank, 1300 New York Avenue, NW, Washington, D.C. 20577 (202) 623-1753; *Economic and Social Progress in Latin America.*

BOLIVIA - WINE PRODUCTION

Facts on File, 460 Park Avenue South, New York, New York 10016 (800) 443-8323; *The New Book of World Rankings.*

Statistical Office of the United Nations, Publishing Service, New York, New York 10017 (800) 253-9646; *Statistical Yearbook.*

BOLIVIA - WOOL PRODUCTION

Facts on File, 460 Park Avenue South, New York, New York 10016 (800) 443-8323; *The New Book of World Rankings.*

BOLIVIA - YARN PRODUCTION

Statistical Office of the United Nations, Publishing Service, New York, New York 10017 (800) 253-9646; *Statistical Yearbook.*

BOLIVIA - ZINC AND ZINC ORE - See BOLIVIA - MINING AND MINERAL PRODUCTS

BOLTS, NUTS, ETC. - See IRON AND STEEL PRODUCTS

BOMBERS

Executive Office of the President, Office of Management and Budget, Executive Office Building, Washington, D.C. 20503 (202) 395-3080; *Budget of the U.S. Government.*

BONDS - FOREIGN - UNITED STATES PURCHASES AND SALES OF

U.S. Department of the Treasury, Fifteenth Street and Pennsylvania Avenue, N.W., Washington, D.C. 20220 (202) 566-5000; *Treasury Bulletin.*

BONDS - HOLDINGS BY SECTOR

Board of Governors of the Federal Reserve System, Twentieth Street and Constitution Avenue, NW, Washington, D.C. 20551 (202) 452-3000; *Annual Statistical Digest.*

BONDS - LIFE INSURANCE COMPANIES

American Council of Life Insurance, 1001 Pennsylvania Avenue, NW, Washington, D.C. 20004 (202) 624-2000; *Life Insurance Fact Book,* and unpublished data.

Board of Governors of the Federal Reserve System, Twentieth Street and Constitution Avenue, NW, Washington, D.C. 20551 (202) 452-3000; *Annual Statistical Digest.*

BONDS - NEW ISSUES

Board of Governors of the Federal Reserve System, Twentieth Street and Constitution Avenue, NW, Washington, D.C. 20551 (202) 452-3000; *Annual Statistical Digest,* and *Federal Reserve Bulletin.*

BONDS - PRICES, YIELDS, SALES, AND ISSUES

Board of Governors of the Federal Reserve System, Twentieth Street and Constitution Avenue, NW, Washington, D.C. 20551 (202) 452-3000; *Federal Reserve Bulletin.*

Dow Jones and Company, Incorporated, 200 Liberty Street, New York, New York 10006 (212) 416-2000.

Moody's Investors Service, 99 Church Street, New York, New York 10007 (212) 553-0300.

New York Stock Exchange, 11 Wall Street, New York, New York 10005 (212) 656-3000; *Fact Book.*

Standard and Poor's Corporation, 25 Broadway, New York, New York 10004 (212) 208-8000; *Standard and Poor's Outlook Weekly.*

U.S. Department of the Treasury, Fifteenth Street and Pennsylvania Avenue, NW, Washington, D.C. 20220 (202) 566-2000; *Treasury Bulletin.*

BONDS - UNITED STATES SAVINGS

Board of Governors of the Federal Reserve System, Twentieth Street and Constitution Avenue, NW, Washington, D.C. 20551 (202) 452-3000; *Federal Reserve Bulletin.*

U.S. Department of Commerce, Bureau of the Census, Suitland, Maryland 20233 (301) 763-4040; *Current Population Reports.*

U.S. Department of the Treasury, Fifteenth Street and Pennsylvania Avenue, NW, Washington, D.C. 20220 (202) 566-2000; *Treasury Bulletin.*

BONITO

U.S. Department of Commerce, National Oceanic and Atmospheric Administration, National Marine Fisheries Service, 1335 East- West Highway, Silver Spring, Maryland 20910 (301) 427-2239; *Fishery Statistics of the United States,* and *Fisheries of the United States.*

BOOKKEEPING - See ACCOUNTING, AUDITING AND BOOKKEEPING

BOOKS AND LIBRARIES - See also LIBRARIES and PRINTING AND PUBLISHING

BOOKS - FOREIGN TRADE

R.R. Bowker Company, 121 Chanlon Road, New Providence, New Jersey 07974 (908) 464-6800; *Publishers Weekly.*

BOOKS - PRICES

R.R. Bowker Company, 121 Chanlon Road, New Providence, New Jersey 07974 (908) 464-6800; *Publishers Weekly, Bowker Annual: Library and Book Trade Almanac,* and *Library Journal.*

BOOKS - READING

Veronis, Suhler and Associates, 350 Park Avenue, New York, New York 10022 (212) 935-4990; *Communications Industry Report.*

BOOKS - SALES

Book Industry Study Group, Incorporated, 160 Fifth Avenue, New York, New York 10010 (212) 929-1393; *Book Industry Trends,* and *Consumer Research Study of Book Purchasing.*

U.S. Department of Commerce, Bureau of Economic Analysis, Fourteenth Street between Constitution Avenue and E Street, NW, Washington, D.C. 20230 (202) 606-9900; *The National Income and Product Accounts of the United States,* and *Survey of Current Business.*

Veronis, Suhler and Associates, 350 Park Avenue, New York, New York 10022 (212) 935-4990; *Communications Industry Report.*

BOOTS - See FOOTWEAR

BORON

U.S. Department of the Interior, Bureau of Mines, 810 Seventh Street, NW, Washington, D.C. 20241 (202) 501-9649; *Annual Reports, Minerals Yearbook,* and *Mineral Commodity Summaries.*

BOSNIA AND HERCEGOVINA - See also YUGOSLAVIA

BOSNIA AND HERCEGOVINA - AGRICULTURE

Encyclopedia Britannica, Incorporated, 310 South Michigan Avenue, Chicago, Illinois 60604 (312) 347-7000; *Britannica World Data.*

BOSNIA AND HERCEGOVINA - AIRLINE SERVICE

Encyclopedia Britannica, Incorporated, 310 South Michigan Avenue, Chicago, Illinois 60604 (312) 347-7000; *Britannica World Data.*

BOSNIA AND HERCEGOVINA - BIRTH RATES

Encyclopedia Britannica, Incorporated, 310 South Michigan Avenue, Chicago, Illinois 60604 (312) 347-7000; *Britannica World Data.*

BOSNIA AND HERCEGOVINA - CONSTRUCTION INDUSTRY

Encyclopedia Britannica, Incorporated, 310 South Michigan Avenue, Chicago, Illinois 60604 (312) 347-7000; *Britannica World Data.*

BOSNIA AND HERCEGOVINA - DEMOGRAPHY

Encyclopedia Britannica, Incorporated, 310 South Michigan Avenue, Chicago, Illinois 60604 (312) 347-7000; *Britannica World Data.*

BOSNIA AND HERCEGOVINA - DIVORCE RATES

Encyclopedia Britannica, Incorporated, 310 South Michigan Avenue, Chicago, Illinois 60604 (312) 347-7000; *Britannica World Data.*

BOSNIA AND HERCEGOVINA - ECONOMY

Encyclopedia Britannica, Incorporated, 310 South Michigan Avenue, Chicago, Illinois 60604 (312) 347-7000; *Britannica World Data.*

BOSNIA AND HERCEGOVINA - EDUCATION

Encyclopedia Britannica, Incorporated, 310 South Michigan Avenue, Chicago, Illinois 60604 (312) 347-7000; *Britannica World Data.*

BOSNIA AND HERCEGOVINA - ENERGY PRODUCTION

Encyclopedia Britannica, Incorporated, 310 South Michigan Avenue, Chicago, Illinois 60604 (312) 347-7000; *Britannica World Data.*

BOSNIA AND HERCEGOVINA - EXPORTS

Encyclopedia Britannica, Incorporated, 310 South Michigan Avenue, Chicago, Illinois 60604 (312) 347-7000; *Britannica World Data.*

BOSNIA AND HERCEGOVINA - FERTILITY RATES

Encyclopedia Britannica, Incorporated, 310 South Michigan Avenue, Chicago, Illinois 60604 (312) 347-7000; *Britannica World Data.*

BOSNIA AND HERCEGOVINA - FISHERIES

Encyclopedia Britannica, Incorporated, 310 South Michigan Avenue, Chicago, Illinois 60604 (312) 347-7000; *Britannica World Data.*

BOSNIA AND HERCEGOVINA - FOREIGN TRADE

Encyclopedia Britannica, Incorporated, 310 South Michigan Avenue, Chicago, Illinois 60604 (312) 347-7000; *Britannica World Data.*

BOSNIA AND HERCEGOVINA - FORESTRY INDUSTRY AND FOREST PRODUCTS

Encyclopedia Britannica, Incorporated, 310 South Michigan Avenue, Chicago, Illinois 60604 (312) 347-7000; *Britannica World Data.*

BOSNIA AND HERCEGOVINA - HEALTH

Encyclopedia Britannica, Incorporated, 310 South Michigan Avenue, Chicago, Illinois 60604 (312) 347-7000; *Britannica World Data.*

BOSNIA AND HERCEGOVINA - HIGHWAYS

Encyclopedia Britannica, Incorporated, 310 South Michigan Avenue, Chicago, Illinois 60604 (312) 347-7000; *Britannica World Data.*

BOSNIA AND HERCEGOVINA - IMPORTS

Encyclopedia Britannica, Incorporated, 310 South Michigan Avenue, Chicago, Illinois 60604 (312) 347-7000; *Britannica World Data.*

BOSNIA AND HERCEGOVINA - LAND USE

Encyclopedia Britannica, Incorporated, 310 South Michigan Avenue, Chicago, Illinois 60604 (312) 347-7000; *Britannica World Data.*

BOSNIA AND HERCEGOVINA - LIVESTOCK AND POULTRY

Encyclopedia Britannica, Incorporated, 310 South Michigan Avenue, Chicago, Illinois 60604 (312) 347-7000; *Britannica World Data.*

BOSNIA AND HERCEGOVINA - MANUFACTURING

Encyclopedia Britannica, Incorporated, 310 South Michigan Avenue, Chicago, Illinois 60604 (312) 347-7000; *Britannica World Data.*

BOSNIA AND HERCEGOVINA - MARRIAGE RATES

Encyclopedia Britannica, Incorporated, 310 South Michigan Avenue, Chicago, Illinois 60604 (312) 347-7000; *Britannica World Data.*

BOSNIA AND HERCEGOVINA - MILITARY

The International Institute for Strategic Studies, 23 Tavistock Street, London WC2E 7NQ, England; *The Military Balance.*

BOSNIA AND HERCEGOVINA - MINING AND MINERAL PRODUCTS

Encyclopedia Britannica, Incorporated, 310 South Michigan Avenue, Chicago, Illinois 60604 (312) 347-7000; *Britannica World Data.*

BOSNIA AND HERCEGOVINA - POPULATION

Encyclopedia Britannica, Incorporated, 310 South Michigan Avenue, Chicago, Illinois 60604 (312) 347-7000; *Britannica World Data.*

BOSNIA AND HERCEGOVINA - RADIO RECEIVERS

Encyclopedia Britannica, Incorporated, 310 South Michigan Avenue, Chicago, Illinois 60604 (312) 347-7000; *Britannica World Data.*

BOSNIA AND HERCEGOVINA - RAILWAYS

Encyclopedia Britannica, Incorporated, 310 South Michigan Avenue, Chicago, Illinois 60604 (312) 347-7000; *Britannica World Data.*

BOSNIA AND HERCEGOVINA - TELEPHONES IN USE

Encyclopedia Britannica, Incorporated, 310 South Michigan Avenue, Chicago, Illinois 60604 (312) 347-7000; *Britannica World Data.*

BOSNIA AND HERCEGOVINA - TELEVISION RECEIVERS

Encyclopedia Britannica, Incorporated, 310 South Michigan Avenue, Chicago, Illinois 60604 (312) 347-7000; *Britannica World Data.*

BOSNIA AND HERCEGOVINA - TRANSPORTATION AND COMMUNICATION

Encyclopedia Britannica, Incorporated, 310 South Michigan Avenue, Chicago, Illinois 60604 (312) 347-7000; *Britannica World Data.*

BOSNIA AND HERCEGOVINA - VITAL STATISTICS

Encyclopedia Britannica, Incorporated, 310 South Michigan Avenue, Chicago, Illinois 60604 (312) 347-7000; *Britannica World Data.*

Botswana - National Statistical Office

Central Statistics Office, Private Bag 0024, Gaberone, Botswana.

Botswana - Primary Statistics Sources

Central Statistics Office, Government Printer, Post Office Box 87, Gaberone, Botswana, *Statistical Bulletin*, and *Botswana in Figures.*

BOTSWANA - AGRICULTURE

Facts on File, 460 Park Avenue South, New York, New York 10016 (800) 443-8323; *The New Book of World Rankings.*

Federal Statistical Office, Gustav - Stresemann - Ring 11, D-6200 Wiesbaden, Germany; *Botswana.*

Food and Agricultural Organization of the United Nations (FAO) Via delle Terme di Caracalla, 00100 Rome, Italy (Telephone Number in U.S. (202) 653-2400); *Production Yearbook, The State of Food and Agriculture*, and *Trade Yearbook.*

G.K. Hall and Company, 70 Lincoln Street, Boston, Massachusetts 02111 (617) 423-3990; *The World in Figures.*

Statistical Office of the United Nations, Publishing Service, New York, New York 10017 (800) 253-9646; *Statistical Yearbook*, and *Survey of Economic and Social Conditions in Africa.*

Times Books, 201 East 50th Street, New York, New York 10022 (212) 751-2600; *The Economist Book of Vital World Statistics.*

United Nations Economic Commission for Africa, Africa Hall, P.O. Box 3001, Addis Ababa, Ethiopia (Telephone Number in U.S. (800) 253-9646); *African Statistical Yearbook.*

The World Bank, 1818 H Street, NW, Washington, D.C. 20433 (202) 477-1234; *World Tables.*

BOTSWANA - AIRLINE SERVICE

Facts on File, 460 Park Avenue South, New York, New York 10016 (800) 443-8323; *The New Book of World Rankings.*

G.K. Hall and Company, 70 Lincoln Street, Boston, Massachusetts 02111 (617) 423-3990; *The World in Figures.*

Times Books, 201 East 50th Street, New York, New York 10022 (212) 751-2600; *The Economist Book of Vital World Statistics.*

United Nations Economic Commission for Africa, Africa Hall, P.O. Box 3001, Addis Ababa, Ethiopia (Telephone Number in U.S. (800) 253-9646); *African Statistical Yearbook.*

BOTSWANA - ALUMINUM PRODUCTION AND CONSUMPTION - See BOTSWANA - MINING AND MINERAL PRODUCTS

BOTSWANA - ANIMAL HEALTH

Food and Agricultural Organization of the United Nations (FAO), Via delle Terme di Caracalla, 00100 Rome, Italy (Telephone Number in U.S. (202) 653-2400); *Animal Health Yearbook.*

BOTSWANA - AREA AND DENSITY OF POPULATION

African Development Bank, 01 BP 1387, Abidjan 01, Cote D'Ivoire; *Selected Statistics on Regional Member Countries.*

Facts on File, 460 Park Avenue South, New York, New York 10016 (800) 443-8323; *The New Book of World Rankings.*

Federal Statistical Office, Gustav - Stresemann - Ring 11, D-6200 Wiesbaden, Germany; *Botswana.*

Food and Agricultural Organization of the United Nations (FAO) Via delle Terme di Caracalla, 00100 Rome, Italy (Telephone Number in U.S. (202) 653-2400); *The State of Food and Agriculture.*

G.K. Hall and Company, 70 Lincoln Street, Boston, Massachusetts 02111 (617) 423-3990; *The World in Figures.*

Statistical Office of the United Nations, Publishing Service, New York, New York 10017 (800) 253-9646; *Statistical Yearbook*, and *Survey of Economic and Social Conditions in Africa.*

Times Books, 201 East 50th Street, New York, New York 10022 (212) 751-2600; *The Economist Book of Vital World Statistics.*

BOTSWANA - ARMS EXPORTS AND IMPORTS

U.S. Arms Control and Disarmament Agency, 320 Twenty-first Street, NW, Washington, D.C. 20451 (202) 647-8677; *World Military Expenditures and Arms Transfers.*

BOTSWANA - BALANCE OF PAYMENTS

African Development Bank, 01 BP 1387, Abidjan 01, Cote D'Ivoire; *Selected Statistics on Regional Member Countries.*

The Economist Intelligence Unit, 111 West 57th Street, New York, New York 10019 (800) 938-4685; *The World Market Atlas.*

Federal Statistical Office, Gustav - Stresemann - Ring 11, D-6200 Wiesbaden, Germany; *Botswana.*

G.K. Hall and Company, 70 Lincoln Street, Boston, Massachusetts 02111 (617) 423-3990; *The World in Figures.*

International Monetary Fund, 700 Nineteenth Street, NW, Washington, D.C. 20431 (202) 623-7000; *Balance of Payments Yearbook.*

Times Books, 201 East 50th Street, New York, New York 10022 (212) 751-2600; *The Economist Book of Vital World Statistics.*

United Nations Economic Commission for Africa, Africa Hall, P.O. Box 3001, Addis Ababa, Ethiopia (Telephone Number in U.S. (800) 253-9646); *African Statistical Yearbook.*

The World Bank, 1818 H Street, NW, Washington, D.C. 20433 (202) 477-1234; *World Tables.*

BOTSWANA - BANKING

Facts on File, 460 Park Avenue South, New York, New York 10016 (800) 443-8323; *The New Book of World Rankings.*

G.K. Hall and Company, 70 Lincoln Street, Boston, Massachusetts 02111 (617) 423-3990; *The World in Figures*.

International Monetary Fund, 700 Nineteenth Street, NW, Washington, D.C. 20431 (202) 623-7000; *Government Finance Statistics Yearbook*, and *International Financial Statistics*.

United Nations Economic Commission for Africa, Africa Hall, P.O. Box 3001, Addis Ababa, Ethiopia (Telephone Number in U.S. (800) 253-9646); *African Statistical Yearbook*.

BOTSWANA - BARLEY PRODUCTION - See BOTSWANA - CROPS

BOTSWANA - BEER PRODUCTION

Facts on File, 460 Park Avenue South, New York, New York 10016 (800) 443-8323; *The New Book of World Rankings*.

Statistical Office of the United Nations, Publishing Service, New York, New York 10017 (800) 253-9646; *Statistical Yearbook*.

BOTSWANA - BIRTH RATES

Facts on File, 460 Park Avenue South, New York, New York 10016 (800) 443-8323; *The New Book of World Rankings*.

Statistical Office of the United Nations, Publishing Service, New York, New York 10017 (800) 253-9646; *Demographic Yearbook*, *Statistical Yearbook*, and *Survey of Economic and Social Conditions in Africa*.

Times Books, 201 East 50th Street, New York, New York 10022 (212) 751-2600; *The Economist Book of Vital World Statistics*.

The World Bank, 1818 H Street, NW, Washington, D.C. 20433 (202) 477-1234; *World Tables*.

BOTSWANA - BONDS

G.K. Hall and Company, 70 Lincoln Street, Boston, Massachusetts 02111 (617) 423-3990; *The World in Figures*.

International Monetary Fund, 700 Nineteenth Street, NW, Washington, D.C. 20431 (202) 623-7000; *Government Finance Statistics Yearbook*.

BOTSWANA - BOOK PRODUCTION

G.K. Hall and Company, 70 Lincoln Street, Boston, Massachusetts 02111 (617) 423-3990; *The World in Figures*.

United Nations Educational, Scientific and Cultural Organization (UNESCO), 7 Place de Fontenoy, F-75700 Paris, France (Telephone Number in U.S. (212) 963-5981); *Statistical Yearbook*.

BOTSWANA - BROADCASTING

Billboard Limited, P.O. Box 9027, 1006 AA Amsterdam, The Netherlands (Telephone Number in U.S. (212) 764-7300); *World Radio TV Handbook*.

Facts on File, 460 Park Avenue South, New York, New York 10016 (800) 443-8323; *The New Book of World Rankings*.

G.K. Hall and Company, 70 Lincoln Street, Boston, Massachusetts 02111 (617) 423-3990; *The World in Figures*.

Times Books, 201 East 50th Street, New York, New York 10022 (212) 751-2600; *The Economist Book of Vital World Statistics*.

BOTSWANA - BUILDING CONSTRUCTION - See BOTSWANA - CONSTRUCTION INDUSTRY

BOTSWANA - BUSINESS

G.K. Hall and Company, 70 Lincoln Street, Boston, Massachusetts 02111 (617) 423-3990; *The World in Figures*.

BOTSWANA - BUSINESS AND PROFESSIONAL LICENSES

International Monetary Fund, 700 Nineteenth Street, NW, Washington, D.C. 20431 (202) 623-7000; *Government Finance Statistics Yearbook*.

BOTSWANA - CALORIE SUPPLY

African Development Bank, 01 BP 1387, Abidjan 01, Cote D'Ivoire; *Selected Statistics on Regional Member Countries*.

Food and Agricultural Organization of the United Nations (FAO) Via delle Terme di Caracalla, 00100 Rome, Italy (Telephone Number in U.S. (202) 653-2400); *The State of Food and Agriculture*.

BOTSWANA - CAPITAL REVENUE

International Monetary Fund, 700 Nineteenth Street, NW, Washington, D.C. 20431 (202) 623-7000; *Government Finance Statistics Yearbook*.

BOTSWANA - CATTLE - See BOTSWANA - LIVESTOCK AND POULTRY

BOTSWANA - CEMENT PRODUCTION - See BOTSWANA - MINING AND MINERAL PRODUCTS

BOTSWANA - CHEMICAL (ORGANIC) PRODUCTION - See BOTSWANA - MINING AND MINERAL PRODUCTS

BOTSWANA - CHICKENS - See BOTSWANA - LIVESTOCK AND POULTRY

BOTSWANA - CIGARETTE PRODUCTION - See BOTSWANA - TOBACCO PRODUCTION

BOTSWANA - CLASS STRUCTURE

G.K. Hall and Company, 70 Lincoln Street, Boston, Massachusetts 02111 (617) 423-3990; *The World in Figures*.

BOTSWANA - CLIMATE

Facts on File, 460 Park Avenue South, New York, New York 10016 (800) 443-8323; *The New Book of World Rankings*.

G.K. Hall and Company, 70 Lincoln Street, Boston, Massachusetts 02111 (617) 423-3990; *The World in Figures*.

BOTSWANA - COAL PRODUCTION - See BOTSWANA - MINING AND MINERAL PRODUCTS

BOTSWANA - COFFEE PRODUCTION - See BOTSWANA - CROPS

BOTSWANA - COMMUNICATIONS

Federal Statistical Office, Gustav - Stresemann - Ring 11, D-6200 Wiesbaden, Germany; *Botswana*.

G.K. Hall and Company, 70 Lincoln Street, Boston, Massachusetts 02111 (617) 423-3990; *The World in Figures*.

United Nations Economic Commission for Africa, Africa Hall, P.O. Box 3001, Addis Ababa, Ethiopia (Telephone Number in U.S. (800) 253-9646); *African Statistical Yearbook.*

BOTSWANA - CONSTRUCTION INDUSTRY

Facts on File, 460 Park Avenue South, New York, New York 10016 (800) 443-8323; *The New Book of World Rankings.*

Statistical Office of the United Nations, Publishing Service, New York, New York 10017 (800) 253-9646; *Construction Statistics Yearbook,* and *Statistical Yearbook.*

United Nations Economic Commission for Africa, Africa Hall, P.O. Box 3001, Addis Ababa, Ethiopia (Telephone Number in U.S. (800) 253-9646); *African Statistical Yearbook.*

BOTSWANA - CONSUMER PRICE INDEX

African Development Bank, 01 BP 1387, Abidjan 01, Cote D'Ivoire; *Selected Statistics on Regional Member Countries.*

Federal Statistical Office, Gustav - Stresemann - Ring 11, D-6200 Wiesbaden, Germany; *Botswana.*

G.K. Hall and Company, 70 Lincoln Street, Boston, Massachusetts 02111 (617) 423-3990; *The World in Figures.*

Statistical Office of the United Nations, Publishing Service, New York, New York 10017 (800) 253-9646; *Statistical Yearbook,* and *Survey of Economic and Social Conditions in Africa.*

United Nations Economic Commission for Africa, Africa Hall, P.O. Box 3001, Addis Ababa, Ethiopia (Telephone Number in U.S. (800) 253-9646); *African Statistical Yearbook.*

BOTSWANA - CONSUMER PRICES

Federal Statistical Office, Gustav - Stresemann - Ring 11, D-6200 Wiesbaden, Germany; *Botswana.*

International Labour Office, I.L.O. Publications, CH-1211, Geneva 22, Switzerland; *Yearbook of Labour Statistics.*

International Monetary Fund, 700 Nineteenth Street, NW, Washington, D.C. 20431 (202) 623-7000; *International Financial Statistics.*

Times Books, 201 East 50th Street, New York, New York 10022 (212) 751-2600; *The Economist Book of Vital World Statistics.*

BOTSWANA - CONSUMPTION

African Development Bank, 01 BP 1387, Abidjan 01, Cote D'Ivoire; *Selected Statistics on Regional Member Countries.*

G.K. Hall and Company, 70 Lincoln Street, Boston, Massachusetts 02111 (617) 423-3990; *The World in Figures.*

Statistical Office of the United Nations, Publishing Service, New York, New York 10017 (800) 253-9646; *Survey of Economic and Social Conditions in Africa.*

BOTSWANA - COPPER AND COPPER ORE - See BOTSWANA - MINING AND MINERAL PRODUCTS

BOTSWANA - CORN PRODUCTION - See BOTSWANA - CROPS

BOTSWANA - CORPORATE TAXES - See BOTSWANA - TAXATION

BOTSWANA - COTTON - See BOTSWANA - CROPS

BOTSWANA - CRIME

Yale University Press, Yale Station, New Haven, Connecticut 06520 (203) 432-0940; *Violence and Crime in Cross-National Perspective.*

BOTSWANA - CROPS

Facts on File, 460 Park Avenue South, New York, New York 10016 (800) 443-8323; *The New Book of World Rankings.*

Food and Agricultural Organization of the United Nations (FAO) Via delle Terme di Caracalla, 00100 Rome, Italy (Telephone Number in U.S. (202) 653-2400); *Production Yearbook,* and *The State of Food and Agriculture.*

G.K. Hall and Company, 70 Lincoln Street, Boston, Massachusetts 02111 (617) 423-3990; *The World in Figures.*

Statistical Office of the United Nations, Publishing Service, New York, New York 10017 (800) 253-9646; *Statistical Yearbook.*

United Nations Economic Commission for Africa, Africa Hall, P.O. Box 3001, Addis Ababa, Ethiopia (Telephone Number in U.S. (800) 253-9646); *African Statistical Yearbook.*

BOTSWANA - CUSTOMS DUTIES

G.K. Hall and Company, 70 Lincoln Street, Boston, Massachusetts 02111 (617) 423-3990; *The World in Figures.*

International Monetary Fund, 700 Nineteenth Street, NW, Washington, D.C. 20431 (202) 623-7000; *Government Finance Statistics Yearbook.*

BOTSWANA - DAIRY PRODUCTS

Facts on File, 460 Park Avenue South, New York, New York 10016 (800) 443-8323; *The New Book of World Rankings.*

Food and Agricultural Organization of the United Nations (FAO) Via delle Terme di Caracalla, 00100 Rome, Italy (Telephone Number in U.S. (202) 653-2400); *The State of Food and Agriculture.*

Statistical Office of the United Nations, Publishing Service, New York, New York 10017 (800) 253-9646; *Statistical Yearbook.*

BOTSWANA - DEATH RATES

G.K. Hall and Company, 70 Lincoln Street, Boston, Massachusetts 02111 (617) 423-3990; *The World in Figures.*

Statistical Office of the United Nations, Publishing Service, New York, New York 10017 (800) 253-9646; *Statistical Yearbook,* and *Survey of Economic and Social Conditions in Africa.*

Times Books, 201 East 50th Street, New York, New York 10022 (212) 751-2600; *The Economist Book of Vital World Statistics.*

BOTSWANA - DEFENSE EXPENDITURES

G.K. Hall and Company, 70 Lincoln Street, Boston, Massachusetts 02111 (617) 423-3990; *The World in Figures.*

International Monetary Fund, 700 Nineteenth Street, NW, Washington, D.C. 20431 (202) 623-7000; *Government Finance Statistics Yearbook.*

U.S. Arms Control and Disarmament Agency, 320 Twenty-first Street, NW, Washington, D.C. 20451 (202) 647-8677; *World Military Expenditures and Arms Transfers.*

BOTSWANA - DEMOGRAPHY

The Economist Intelligence Unit, 111 West 57th Street, New York, New York 10019 (800) 938-4685; *The World Market Atlas.*

Facts on File, 460 Park Avenue South, New York, New York 10016 (800) 443-8323; *The New Book of World Rankings.*

Federal Statistical Office, Gustav - Stresemann - Ring 11, D-6200 Wiesbaden, Germany; *Botswana.*

G.K. Hall and Company, 70 Lincoln Street, Boston, Massachusetts 02111 (617) 423-3990; *The World in Figures.*

Statistical Office of the United Nations, Publishing Service, New York, New York 10017 (800) 253-9646; *Survey of Economic and Social Conditions in Africa.*

BOTSWANA - DEVELOPMENT ASSISTANCE

G.K. Hall and Company, 70 Lincoln Street, Boston, Massachusetts 02111 (617) 423-3990; *The World in Figures.*

Statistical Office of the United Nations, Publishing Service, New York, New York 10017 (800) 253-9646; *Statistical Yearbook.*

BOTSWANA - DIAMOND - See BOTSWANA - MINING AND MINERAL PRODUCTS

BOTSWANA - DISEASE

G.K. Hall and Company, 70 Lincoln Street, Boston, Massachusetts 02111 (617) 423-3990; *The World in Figures.*

BOTSWANA - DIVORCE RATES

Facts on File, 460 Park Avenue South, New York, New York 10016 (800) 443-8323; *The New Book of World Rankings.*

Statistical Office of the United Nations, Publishing Service, New York, New York 10017 (800) 253-9646; *Demographic Yearbook.*

BOTSWANA - DOMESTIC PRODUCT

G.K. Hall and Company, 70 Lincoln Street, Boston, Massachusetts 02111 (617) 423-3990; *The World in Figures.*

BOTSWANA - ECONOMY

African Development Bank, 01 BP 1387, Abidjan 01, Cote D'Ivoire; *Selected Statistics on Regional Member Countries.*

Facts on File, 460 Park Avenue South, New York, New York 10016 (800) 443-8323; *The New Book of World Rankings.*

Federal Statistical Office, Gustav - Stresemann - Ring 11, D-6200 Wiesbaden, Germany; *Botswana.*

G.K. Hall and Company, 70 Lincoln Street, Boston, Massachusetts 02111 (617) 423-3990; *The World in Figures.*

BOTSWANA - EDUCATION

African Development Bank, 01 BP 1387, Abidjan 01, Cote D'Ivoire; *Selected Statistics on Regional Member Countries.*

The Economist Intelligence Unit, 111 West 57th Street, New York, New York 10019 (800) 938-4685; *The World Market Atlas.*

Facts on File, 460 Park Avenue South, New York, New York 10016 (800) 443-8323; *The New Book of World Rankings.*

Federal Statistical Office, Gustav - Stresemann - Ring 11, D-6200 Wiesbaden, Germany; *Botswana.*

G.K. Hall and Company, 70 Lincoln Street, Boston, Massachusetts 02111 (617) 423-3990; *The World in Figures.*

International Monetary Fund, 700 Nineteenth Street, NW, Washington, D.C. 20431 (202) 623-7000; *Government Finance Statistics Yearbook.*

Statistical Office of the United Nations, Publishing Service, New York, New York 10017 (800) 253-9646; *Survey of Economic and Social Conditions in Africa.*

Times Books, 201 East 50th Street, New York, New York 10022 (212) 751-2600; *The Economist Book of Vital World Statistics.*

United Nations Economic Commission for Africa, Africa Hall, P.O. Box 3001, Addis Ababa, Ethiopia (Telephone Number in U.S. (800) 253-9646); *African Statistical Yearbook.*

United Nations Educational, Scientific and Cultural Organization (UNESCO), 7 Place de Fontenoy, F-75700 Paris, France (Telephone Number in U.S. (212) 963-5981); *Statistical Yearbook.*

The World Bank, 1818 H Street, NW, Washington, D.C. 20433 (202) 477-1234; *World Tables.*

BOTSWANA - EGG PRODUCTION - See BOTSWANA - DAIRY PRODUCTS

BOTSWANA - ELECTRICITY

Facts on File, 460 Park Avenue South, New York, New York 10016 (800) 443-8323; *The New Book of World Rankings.*

Statistical Office of the United Nations, Publishing Service, New York, New York 10017 (800) 253-9646; *Survey of Economic and Social Conditions in Africa.*

United Nations Economic Commission for Africa, Africa Hall, P.O. Box 3001, Addis Ababa, Ethiopia (Telephone Number in U.S. (800) 253-9646); *African Statistical Yearbook.*

BOTSWANA - EMPLOYMENT

Facts on File, 460 Park Avenue South, New York, New York 10016 (800) 443-8323; *The New Book of World Rankings.*

Federal Statistical Office, Gustav - Stresemann - Ring 11, D-6200 Wiesbaden, Germany; *Botswana.*

International Labour Office, I.L.O. Publications, CH-1211, Geneva 22, Switzerland; *Yearbook of Labour Statistics.*

Statistical Office of the United Nations, Publishing Service, New York, New York 10017 (800) 253-9646; *Statistical Yearbook,* and *Survey of Economic and Social Conditions in Africa.*

United Nations Economic Commission for Africa, Africa Hall, P.O. Box 3001, Addis Ababa, Ethiopia (Telephone Number in U.S. (800) 253-9646); *African Statistical Yearbook.*

BOTSWANA - ENERGY

Facts on File, 460 Park Avenue South, New York, New York 10016 (800) 443-8323; *The New Book of World Rankings.*

Food and Agricultural Organization of the United Nations (FAO) Via delle Terme di Caracalla, 00100 Rome, Italy (Telephone Number in U.S. (202) 653-2400); *The State of Food and Agriculture.*

G.K. Hall and Company, 70 Lincoln Street, Boston, Massachusetts 02111 (617) 423-3990; *The World in Figures.*

Statistical Office of the United Nations, Publishing Service, New York, New York 10017 (800) 253-9646; *Energy Statistics Yearbook,* and *Statistical Yearbook.*

United Nations Economic Commission for Africa, Africa Hall, P.O. Box 3001, Addis Ababa, Ethiopia (Telephone Number in U.S. (800) 253-9646); *African Statistical Yearbook.*

BOTSWANA - EXCHANGE RATES

African Development Bank, 01 BP 1387, Abidjan 01, Cote D'Ivoire; *Selected Statistics on Regional Member Countries.*

International Monetary Fund, 700 Nineteenth Street, NW, Washington, D.C. 20431 (202) 623-7000; *International Financial Statistics.*

BOTSWANA - EXPORTS

African Development Bank, 01 BP 1387, Abidjan 01, Cote D'Ivoire; *Selected Statistics on Regional Member Countries.*

The Economist Intelligence Unit, 111 West 57th Street, New York, New York 10019 (800) 938-4685; *The World Market Atlas.*

Food and Agricultural Organization of the United Nations (FAO) Via delle Terme di Caracalla, 00100 Rome, Italy (Telephone Number in U.S. (202) 653-2400); *The State of Food and Agriculture.*

G.K. Hall and Company, 70 Lincoln Street, Boston, Massachusetts 02111 (617) 423-3990; *The World in Figures.*

International Monetary Fund, 700 Nineteenth Street, NW, Washington, D.C. 20431 (202) 623-7000; *Direction of Trade Statistics, Government Finance Statistics Yearbook,* and *International Financial Statistics.*

Statistical Office of the United Nations, Publishing Service, New York, New York 10017 (800) 253-9646; *Survey of Economic and Social Conditions in Africa.*

United Nations Economic Commission for Africa, Africa Hall, P.O. Box 3001, Addis Ababa, Ethiopia (Telephone Number in U.S. (800) 253-9646); *African Statistical Yearbook.*

The World Bank, 1818 H Street, NW, Washington, D.C. 20433 (202) 477-1234; *World Tables.*

BOTSWANA - EXTERNAL INDEBTEDNESS

African Development Bank, 01 BP 1387, Abidjan 01, Cote D'Ivoire; *Selected Statistics on Regional Member Countries.*

Statistical Office of the United Nations, Publishing Service, New York, New York 10017 (800) 253-9646; *Survey of Economic and Social Conditions in Africa.*

The World Bank, 1818 H Street, NW, Washington, D.C. 20433 (202) 477-1234; *World Tables.*

BOTSWANA - EXTERNAL TRADE

African Development Bank, 01 BP 1387, Abidjan 01, Cote D'Ivoire; *Selected Statistics on Regional Member Countries.*

Food and Agricultural Organization of the United Nations (FAO) Via delle Terme di Caracalla, 00100 Rome, Italy (Telephone Number in U.S. (202) 653-2400); *The State of Food and Agriculture,* and *Trade Yearbook.*

G.K. Hall and Company, 70 Lincoln Street, Boston, Massachusetts 02111 (617) 423-3990; *The World in Figures.*

BOTSWANA - FARM CROPS - See BOTSWANA - CROPS

BOTSWANA - FERTILITY RATES

Facts on File, 460 Park Avenue South, New York, New York 10016 (800) 443-8323; *The New Book of World Rankings.*

Statistical Office of the United Nations, Publishing Service, New York, New York 10017 (800) 253-9646; *Survey of Economic and Social Conditions in Africa.*

Times Books, 201 East 50th Street, New York, New York 10022 (212) 751-2600; *The Economist Book of Vital World Statistics.*

The World Bank, 1818 H Street, NW, Washington, D.C. 20433 (202) 477-1234; *World Tables.*

BOTSWANA - FERTILIZER

Food and Agricultural Organization of the United Nations (FAO), Via delle Terme di Caracalla, 00100 Rome, Italy (Telephone Number in U.S. (202) 653-2400); *Fertilizer Yearbook,* and *The State of Food and Agriculture.*

Statistical Office of the United Nations, Publishing Service, New York, New York 10017 (800) 253-9646; *Statistical Yearbook.*

BOTSWANA - FETAL MORTALITY

Statistical Office of the United Nations, Publishing Service, New York, New York 10017 (800) 253-9646; *Demographic Yearbook.*

BOTSWANA - FINANCE

African Development Bank, 01 BP 1387, Abidjan 01, Cote D'Ivoire; *Selected Statistics on Regional Member Countries.*

Facts on File, 460 Park Avenue South, New York, New York 10016 (800) 443-8323; *The New Book of World Rankings.*

Federal Statistical Office, Gustav - Stresemann - Ring 11, D-6200 Wiesbaden, Germany; *Botswana.*

G.K. Hall and Company, 70 Lincoln Street, Boston, Massachusetts 02111 (617) 423-3990; *The World in Figures.*

International Monetary Fund, 700 Nineteenth Street, NW, Washington, D.C. 20431 (202) 623-7000; *Government Finance Statistics Yearbook,* and *International Financial Statistics.*

United Nations Economic Commission for Africa, Africa Hall, P.O. Box 3001, Addis Ababa, Ethiopia (Telephone Number in U.S. (800) 253-9646); *African Statistical Yearbook.*

BOTSWANA - FISHERIES

Facts on File, 460 Park Avenue South, New York, New York 10016 (800) 443-8323; *The New Book of World Rankings.*

Federal Statistical Office, Gustav - Stresemann - Ring 11, D-6200 Wiesbaden, Germany; *Botswana.*

Food and Agricultural Organization of the United Nations (FAO) Via delle Terme di Caracalla, 00100 Rome, Italy (Telephone Number in U.S. (202) 653-2400); *The State of Food and Agriculture,* and *Yearbook of Fishery Statistics.*

Statistical Office of the United Nations, Publishing Service, New York, New York 10017 (800) 253-9646; *Statistical Yearbook,* and *Survey of Economic and Social Conditions in Africa.*

United Nations Economic Commission for Africa, Africa Hall, P.O. Box 3001, Addis Ababa, Ethiopia (Telephone Number in U.S. (800) 253-9646); *African Statistical Yearbook.*

BOTSWANA - FOOD

African Development Bank, 01 BP 1387, Abidjan 01, Cote D'Ivoire; *Selected Statistics on Regional Member Countries.*

Food and Agricultural Organization of the United Nations (FAO) Via delle Terme di Caracalla, 00100 Rome, Italy (Telephone Number in U.S. (202) 653-2400); *Production Yearbook,* and *The State of Food and Agriculture.*

G.K. Hall and Company, 70 Lincoln Street, Boston, Massachusetts 02111 (617) 423-3990; *The World in Figures.*

BOTSWANA - FOREIGN AID

G.K. Hall and Company, 70 Lincoln Street, Boston, Massachusetts 02111 (617) 423-3990; *The World in Figures.*

BOTSWANA - FOREIGN DEBT

International Monetary Fund, 700 Nineteenth Street, NW, Washington, D.C. 20431 (202) 623-7000; *Government Finance Statistics Yearbook.*

BOTSWANA - FOREIGN TRADE

Facts on File, 460 Park Avenue South, New York, New York 10016 (800) 443-8323; *The New Book of World Rankings.*

Federal Statistical Office, Gustav - Stresemann - Ring 11, D-6200 Wiesbaden, Germany; *Botswana.*

Food and Agricultural Organization of the United Nations (FAO) Via delle Terme di Caracalla, 00100 Rome, Italy (Telephone Number in U.S. (202) 653-2400); *The State of Food and Agriculture.*

G.K. Hall and Company, 70 Lincoln Street, Boston, Massachusetts 02111 (617) 423-3990; *The World in Figures.*

Organisation for Economic Co-operation and Development (OECD), 2 rue Andre-Pascal, 75 Paris 16, France (Telephone Number in U.S. (202) 785-6323); *Trade by Commodities.*

United Nations Economic Commission for Africa, Africa Hall, P.O. Box 3001, Addis Ababa, Ethiopia (Telephone Number in U.S. (800) 253-9646); *African Statistical Yearbook.*

The World Bank, 1818 H Street, NW, Washington, D.C. 20433 (202) 477-1234; *World Tables.*

BOTSWANA - FORESTRY AND FOREST PRODUCTS

Facts on File, 460 Park Avenue South, New York, New York 10016 (800) 443-8323; *The New Book of World Rankings.*

Federal Statistical Office, Gustav - Stresemann - Ring 11, D-6200 Wiesbaden, Germany; *Botswana.*

Food and Agricultural Organization of the United Nations (FAO) Via delle Terme di Caracalla, 00100 Rome, Italy (Telephone Number in U.S. (202) 653-2400); *The State of Food and Agriculture,* and *Yearbook of Forest Products.*

G.K. Hall and Company, 70 Lincoln Street, Boston, Massachusetts 02111 (617) 423-3990; *The World in Figures.*

Statistical Office of the United Nations, Publishing Service, New York, New York 10017 (800) 253-9646; *Statistical Yearbook.*

United Nations Economic Commission for Africa, Africa Hall, P.O. Box 3001, Addis Ababa, Ethiopia (Telephone Number in U.S. (800) 253-9646); *African Statistical Yearbook.*

United Nations Educational, Scientific and Cultural Organization (UNESCO), 7 Place de Fontenoy, F-75700 Paris, France (Telephone Number in U.S. (212) 963-5981); *Statistical Yearbook.*

BOTSWANA - GAS PRODUCTION - See BOTSWANA - MINING AND MINERAL PRODUCTS

BOTSWANA - GENERAL INDUSTRIAL STATISTICS

Federal Statistical Office, Gustav - Stresemann - Ring 11, D-6200 Wiesbaden, Germany; *Botswana.*

BOTSWANA - GENERAL MORTALITY

Statistical Office of the United Nations, Publishing Service, New York, New York 10017 (800) 253-9646; *Demographic Yearbook.*

BOTSWANA - GEOGRAPHIC DATA

Facts on File, 460 Park Avenue South, New York, New York 10016 (800) 443-8323; *The New Book of World Rankings.*

Federal Statistical Office, Gustav - Stresemann - Ring 11, D-6200 Wiesbaden, Germany; *Botswana.*

BOTSWANA - GOATS - See BOTSWANA - LIVESTOCK AND POULTRY

BOTSWANA - GOLD HOLDINGS

International Monetary Fund, 700 Nineteenth Street, NW, Washington, D.C. 20431 (202) 623-7000; *International Financial Statistics.*

The World Bank, 1818 H Street, NW, Washington, D.C. 20433 (202) 477-1234; *World Tables.*

BOTSWANA - GOLD PRODUCTION AND CONSUMPTION - See BOTSWANA - MINING AND MINERAL PRODUCTS

BOTSWANA - GOVERNMENT

G.K. Hall and Company, 70 Lincoln Street, Boston, Massachusetts 02111 (617) 423-3990; *The World in Figures.*

BOTSWANA - GOVERNMENT EXPENDITURES

International Monetary Fund, 700 Nineteenth Street, NW, Washington, D.C. 20431 (202) 623-7000; *Government Finance Statistics Yearbook.*

Times Books, 201 East 50th Street, New York, New York 10022 (212) 751-2600; *The Economist Book of Vital World Statistics.*

The World Bank, 1818 H Street, NW, Washington, D.C. 20433 (202) 477-1234; *World Tables.*

BOTSWANA - GOVERNMENT FINANCE

International Monetary Fund, 700 Nineteenth Street, NW, Washington, D.C. 20431 (202) 623-7000; *International Financial Statistics.*

BOTSWANA - GOVERNMENT REVENUE

International Monetary Fund, 700 Nineteenth Street, NW, Washington, D.C. 20431 (202) 623-7000; *Government Finance Statistics Yearbook.*

Statistical Office of the United Nations, Publishing Service, New York, New York 10017 (800) 253-9646; *Survey of Economic and Social Conditions in Africa.*

Times Books, 201 East 50th Street, New York, New York 10022 (212) 751-2600; *The Economist Book of Vital World Statistics.*

The World Bank, 1818 H Street, NW, Washington, D.C. 20433 (202) 477-1234; *World Tables.*

BOTSWANA - GRAIN PRODUCTION - See BOTSWANA - CROPS

BOTSWANA - GRANTS

International Monetary Fund, 700 Nineteenth Street, NW, Washington, D.C. 20431 (202) 623-7000; *Government Finance Statistics Yearbook.*

BOTSWANA - GROSS DOMESTIC PRODUCT

African Development Bank, 01 BP 1387, Abidjan 01, Cote D'Ivoire; *Selected Statistics on Regional Member Countries.*

The Economist Intelligence Unit, 111 West 57th Street, New York, New York 10019 (800) 938-4685; *The World Market Atlas.*

Facts on File, 460 Park Avenue South, New York, New York 10016 (800) 443-8323; *The New Book of World Rankings.*

G.K. Hall and Company, 70 Lincoln Street, Boston, Massachusetts 02111 (617) 423-3990; *The World in Figures.*

Statistical Office of the United Nations, Publishing Service, New York, New York 10017 (800) 253-9646; *Statistical Yearbook,* and *Survey of Economic and Social Conditions in Africa.*

Times Books, 201 East 50th Street, New York, New York 10022 (212) 751-2600; *The Economist Book of Vital World Statistics.*

United Nations Economic Commission for Africa, Africa Hall, P.O. Box 3001, Addis Ababa, Ethiopia (Telephone Number in U.S. (800) 253-9646); *African Statistical Yearbook.*

The World Bank, 1818 H Street, NW, Washington, D.C. 20433 (202) 477-1234; *World Tables.*

BOTSWANA - GROSS NATIONAL PRODUCT

U.S. Arms Control and Disarmament Agency, 320 Twenty-first Street, NW, Washington, D.C. 20451 (202) 647-8677; *World Military Expenditures and Arms Transfers.*

The World Bank, 1818 H Street, NW, Washington, D.C. 20433 (202) 477-1234; *World Tables.*

BOTSWANA - GROUNDNUTS PRODUCTION - See BOTSWANA - CROPS

BOTSWANA - HEALTH

African Development Bank, 01 BP 1387, Abidjan 01, Cote D'Ivoire; *Selected Statistics on Regional Member Countries.*

Facts on File, 460 Park Avenue South, New York, New York 10016 (800) 443-8323; *The New Book of World Rankings.*

Federal Statistical Office, Gustav - Stresemann - Ring 11, D-6200 Wiesbaden, Germany; *Botswana.*

G.K. Hall and Company, 70 Lincoln Street, Boston, Massachusetts 02111 (617) 423-3990; *The World in Figures.*

Statistical Office of the United Nations, Publishing Service, New York, New York 10017 (800) 253-9646; *Statistical Yearbook.*

Times Books, 201 East 50th Street, New York, New York 10022 (212) 751-2600; *The Economist Book of Vital World Statistics.*

United Nations Economic Commission for Africa, Africa Hall, P.O. Box 3001, Addis Ababa, Ethiopia (Telephone Number in U.S. (800) 253-9646); *African Statistical Yearbook.*

BOTSWANA - HEALTH EXPENDITURES

International Monetary Fund, 700 Nineteenth Street, NW, Washington, D.C. 20431 (202) 623-7000; *Government Finance Statistics Yearbook.*

BOTSWANA - HIDE PRODUCTION

Food and Agricultural Organization of the United Nations (FAO), Via delle Terme di Caracalla, 00100 Rome, Italy (Telephone Number in U.S. (202) 653-2400); *Production Yearbook.*

BOTSWANA - HIGHWAYS

G.K. Hall and Company, 70 Lincoln Street, Boston, Massachusetts 02111 (617) 423-3990; *The World in Figures.*

International Road Federation, 525 School Street, SW, Washington, D.C. 20024 (202) 554-2106; *World Road Statistics.*

Statistical Office of the United Nations, Publishing Service, New York, New York 10017 (800) 253-9646; *Survey of Economic and Social Conditions in Africa.*

United Nations Economic Commission for Africa, Africa Hall, P.O. Box 3001, Addis Ababa, Ethiopia (Telephone Number in U.S. (800) 253-9646); *African Statistical Yearbook.*

BOTSWANA - HORSES - See BOTSWANA - LIVESTOCK AND POULTRY

BOTSWANA - HOURS OF WORK

International Labour Office, I.L.O. Publications, CH-1211, Geneva 22, Switzerland; *Yearbook of Labour Statistics*.

BOTSWANA - HOUSING AND HOUSING UNITS

Facts on File, 460 Park Avenue South, New York, New York 10016 (800) 443-8323; *The New Book of World Rankings*.

BOTSWANA - HOUSING EXPENDITURES

International Monetary Fund, 700 Nineteenth Street, NW, Washington, D.C. 20431 (202) 623-7000; *Government Finance Statistics Yearbook*.

BOTSWANA - ILLITERATE POPULATION

The Economist Intelligence Unit, 111 West 57th Street, New York, New York 10019 (800) 938-4685; *The World Market Atlas*.

G.K. Hall and Company, 70 Lincoln Street, Boston, Massachusetts 02111 (617) 423-3990; *The World in Figures*.

United Nations Educational, Scientific and Cultural Organization (UNESCO), 7 Place de Fontenoy, F-75700 Paris, France (Telephone Number in U.S. (212) 963-5981); *Statistical Yearbook*.

BOTSWANA - IMPORTS

African Development Bank, 01 BP 1387, Abidjan 01, Cote D'Ivoire; *Selected Statistics on Regional Member Countries*.

The Economist Intelligence Unit, 111 West 57th Street, New York, New York 10019 (800) 938-4685; *The World Market Atlas*.

Food and Agricultural Organization of the United Nations (FAO) Via delle Terme di Caracalla, 00100 Rome, Italy (Telephone Number in U.S. (202) 653-2400); *The State of Food and Agriculture*.

G.K. Hall and Company, 70 Lincoln Street, Boston, Massachusetts 02111 (617) 423-3990; *The World in Figures*.

International Monetary Fund, 700 Nineteenth Street, NW, Washington, D.C. 20431 (202) 623-7000; *Direction of Trade Statistics*, and *International Financial Statistics*.

Statistical Office of the United Nations, Publishing Service, New York, New York 10017 (800) 253-9646; *Survey of Economic and Social Conditions in Africa*.

United Nations Economic Commission for Africa, Africa Hall, P.O. Box 3001, Addis Ababa, Ethiopia (Telephone Number in U.S. (800) 253-9646); *African Statistical Yearbook*.

The World Bank, 1818 H Street, NW, Washington, D.C. 20433 (202) 477-1234; *World Tables*.

BOTSWANA - INCOME TAXES - See BOTSWANA - TAXATION

BOTSWANA - INDUSTRY

Facts on File, 460 Park Avenue South, New York, New York 10016 (800) 443-8323; *The New Book of World Rankings*.

Federal Statistical Office, Gustav - Stresemann - Ring 11, D-6200 Wiesbaden, Germany; *Botswana*.

G.K. Hall and Company, 70 Lincoln Street, Boston, Massachusetts 02111 (617) 423-3990; *The World in Figures*.

International Labour Office, I.L.O. Publications, CH-1211, Geneva 22, Switzerland; *Yearbook of Labour Statistics*.

Statistical Office of the United Nations, Publishing Service, New York, New York 10017 (800) 253-9646; *Survey of Economic and Social Conditions in Africa*.

Times Books, 201 East 50th Street, New York, New York 10022 (212) 751-2600; *The Economist Book of Vital World Statistics*.

United Nations Economic Commission for Africa, Africa Hall, P.O. Box 3001, Addis Ababa, Ethiopia (Telephone Number in U.S. (800) 253-9646); *African Statistical Yearbook*.

The World Bank, 1818 H Street, NW, Washington, D.C. 20433 (202) 477-1234; *World Tables*.

World Intellectual Property Organization, 34 Chemin des Colombettes, CH-1211 Geneva 20. Switzerland; *Industrial Property Statistics*.

BOTSWANA - INFANT AND MATERNAL MORTALITY

Statistical Office of the United Nations, Publishing Service, New York, New York 10017 (800) 253-9646; *Demographic Yearbook*, and *Survey of Economic and Social Conditions in Africa*.

Times Books, 201 East 50th Street, New York, New York 10022 (212) 751-2600; *The Economist Book of Vital World Statistics*.

The World Bank, 1818 H Street, NW, Washington, D.C. 20433 (202) 477-1234; *World Tables*.

BOTSWANA - INTERNATIONAL RESERVES EXCLUDING GOLD

African Development Bank, 01 BP 1387, Abidjan 01, Cote D'Ivoire; *Selected Statistics on Regional Member Countries*.

The World Bank, 1818 H Street, NW, Washington, D.C. 20433 (202) 477-1234; *World Tables*.

BOTSWANA - INTERNATIONAL LIQUIDITY

International Monetary Fund, 700 Nineteenth Street, NW, Washington, D.C. 20431 (202) 623-7000; *International Financial Statistics*.

BOTSWANA - IRON ORE PRODUCTION AND CONSUMPTION - See BOTSWANA - MINING AND MINERAL PRODUCTS

BOTSWANA - LABOR FORCE

African Development Bank, 01 BP 1387, Abidjan 01, Cote D'Ivoire; *Selected Statistics on Regional Member Countries*.

Facts on File, 460 Park Avenue South, New York, New York 10016 (800) 443-8323; *The New Book of World Rankings*.

Food and Agricultural Organization of the United Nations (FAO) Via delle Terme di Caracalla, 00100 Rome, Italy (Telephone Number in U.S. (202) 653-2400); *The State of Food and Agriculture*.

G.K. Hall and Company, 70 Lincoln Street, Boston, Massachusetts 02111 (617) 423-3990; *The World in Figures*.

Times Books, 201 East 50th Street, New York, New York 10022 (212) 751-2600; *The Economist Book of Vital World Statistics.*

The World Bank, 1818 H Street, NW, Washington, D.C. 20433 (202) 477-1234; *World Tables.*

BOTSWANA - LABOR PRODUCTIVITY

International Labour Office, I.L.O. Publications, CH-1211, Geneva 22, Switzerland; *Yearbook of Labour Statistics.*

BOTSWANA - LAND USE

Food and Agricultural Organization of the United Nations (FAO), Via delle Terme di Caracalla, 00100 Rome, Italy (Telephone Number in U.S. (202) 653-2400); *Production Yearbook.*

G.K. Hall and Company, 70 Lincoln Street, Boston, Massachusetts 02111 (617) 423-3990; *The World in Figures.*

BOTSWANA - LIBRARIES

Facts on File, 460 Park Avenue South, New York, New York 10016 (800) 443-8323; *The New Book of World Rankings.*

BOTSWANA - LIFE EXPECTANCY

African Development Bank, 01 BP 1387, Abidjan 01, Cote D'Ivoire; *Selected Statistics on Regional Member Countries.*

BOTSWANA - LITERACY RATE

Statistical Office of the United Nations, Publishing Service, New York, New York 10017 (800) 253-9646; *Survey of Economic and Social Conditions in Africa.*

BOTSWANA - LIVESTOCK AND POULTRY

Facts on File, 460 Park Avenue South, New York, New York 10016 (800) 443-8323; *The New Book of World Rankings.*

Food and Agricultural Organization of the United Nations (FAO), Via delle Terme di Caracalla, 00100 Rome, Italy (Telephone Number in U.S. (202) 653-2400); *Production Yearbook,* and *The State of Food and Agriculture.*

G.K. Hall and Company, 70 Lincoln Street, Boston, Massachusetts 02111 (617) 423-3990; *The World in Figures.*

Statistical Office of the United Nations, Publishing Service, New York, New York 10017 (800) 253-9646; *Statistical Yearbook,* and *Survey of Economic and Social Conditions in Africa.*

United Nations Economic Commission for Africa, Africa Hall, P.O. Box 3001, Addis Ababa, Ethiopia (Telephone Number in U.S. (800) 253-9646); *African Statistical Yearbook.*

BOTSWANA - LIVING LEVELS

G.K. Hall and Company, 70 Lincoln Street, Boston, Massachusetts 02111 (617) 423-3990; *The World in Figures.*

Times Books, 201 East 50th Street, New York, New York 10022 (212) 751-2600; *The Economist Book of Vital World Statistics.*

BOTSWANA - MAIL - NUMBER OF PIECES SENT OR RECEIVED

Statistical Office of the United Nations, Publishing Service, New York, New York 10017 (800) 253-9646; *Statistical Yearbook.*

BOTSWANA - MANGANESE ORE PRODUCTION AND CONSUMPTION - See BOTSWANA - MINING AND MINERAL PRODUCTS

BOTSWANA - MANUFACTURING

Facts on File, 460 Park Avenue South, New York, New York 10016 (800) 443-8323; *The New Book of World Rankings.*

G.K. Hall and Company, 70 Lincoln Street, Boston, Massachusetts 02111 (617) 423-3990; *The World in Figures.*

Statistical Office of the United Nations, Publishing Service, New York, New York 10017 (800) 253-9646; *Statistical Yearbook,* and *Survey of Economic and Social Conditions in Africa.*

Times Books, 201 East 50th Street, New York, New York 10022 (212) 751-2600; *The Economist Book of Vital World Statistics.*

United Nations Economic Commission for Africa, Africa Hall, P.O. Box 3001, Addis Ababa, Ethiopia (Telephone Number in U.S. (800) 253-9646); *African Statistical Yearbook.*

The World Bank, 1818 H Street, NW, Washington, D.C. 20433 (202) 477-1234; *World Tables.*

BOTSWANA - MARRIAGE RATES

Facts on File, 460 Park Avenue South, New York, New York 10016 (800) 443-8323; *The New Book of World Rankings.*

Statistical Office of the United Nations, Publishing Service, New York, New York 10017 (800) 253-9646; *Demographic Yearbook.*

BOTSWANA - MEAT PRODUCTION - See BOTSWANA - LIVESTOCK AND POULTRY

BOTSWANA - MERCHANT SHIPPING

G.K. Hall and Company, 70 Lincoln Street, Boston, Massachusetts 02111 (617) 423-3990; *The World in Figures.*

United Nations Economic Commission for Africa, Africa Hall, P.O. Box 3001, Addis Ababa, Ethiopia (Telephone Number in U.S. (800) 253-9646); *African Statistical Yearbook.*

BOTSWANA - MILITARY

G.K. Hall and Company, 70 Lincoln Street, Boston, Massachusetts 02111 (617) 423-3990; *The World in Figures.*

The International Institute for Strategic Studies, 23 Tavistock Street, London WC2E 7NQ, England; *The Military Balance.*

U.S. Arms Control and Disarmament Agency, 320 Twenty-first Street, NW, Washington, D.C. 20451 (202) 647-8677; *World Military Expenditures and Arms Transfers.*

BOTSWANA - MILK PRODUCTION - See BOTSWANA - DAIRY PRODUCTS

BOTSWANA - MILLET PRODUCTION - See BOTSWANA - CROPS

BOTSWANA - MINING AND MINERAL PRODUCTS

Facts on File, 460 Park Avenue South, New York, New York 10016 (800) 443-8323; *The New Book of World Rankings.*

G.K. Hall and Company, 70 Lincoln Street, Boston, Massachusetts 02111 (617) 423-3990; *The World in Figures.*

International Monetary Fund, 700 Nineteenth Street, NW, Washington, D.C. 20431 (202) 623-7000; *International Financial Statistics.*

Statistical Office of the United Nations, Publishing Service, New York, New York 10017 (800) 253-9646; *Statistical Yearbook.*

United Nations Economic Commission for Africa, Africa Hall, P.O. Box 3001, Addis Ababa, Ethiopia (Telephone Number in U.S. (800) 253-9646); *African Statistical Yearbook.*

BOTSWANA - MONEY EXCHANGE RATES

International Monetary Fund, 700 Nineteenth Street, NW, Washington, D.C. 20431 (202) 623-7000; *International Financial Statistics.*

Statistical Office of the United Nations, Publishing Service, New York, New York 10017 (800) 253-9646; *Statistical Yearbook.*

BOTSWANA - MONEY SUPPLY

African Development Bank, 01 BP 1387, Abidjan 01, Cote D'Ivoire; *Selected Statistics on Regional Member Countries.*

Federal Statistical Office, Gustav - Stresemann - Ring 11, D-6200 Wiesbaden, Germany; *Botswana.*

G.K. Hall and Company, 70 Lincoln Street, Boston, Massachusetts 02111 (617) 423-3990; *The World in Figures.*

International Monetary Fund, 700 Nineteenth Street, NW, Washington, D.C. 20431 (202) 623-7000; *International Financial Statistics.*

The World Bank, 1818 H Street, NW, Washington, D.C. 20433 (202) 477-1234; *World Tables.*

BOTSWANA - MONUMENTS AND HISTORICAL SITES

United Nations Educational, Scientific and Cultural Organization (UNESCO), 7 Place de Fontenoy, F-75700 Paris, France (Telephone Number in U.S. (212) 963-5981); *Statistical Yearbook.*

BOTSWANA - MOTION PICTURES

Statistical Office of the United Nations, Publishing Service, New York, New York 10017 (800) 253-9646; *Statistical Yearbook.*

BOTSWANA - MOTOR VEHICLE TAXES - See BOTSWANA - TAXATION

BOTSWANA - MOTOR VEHICLES IN USE

G.K. Hall and Company, 70 Lincoln Street, Boston, Massachusetts 02111 (617) 423-3990; *The World in Figures.*

International Road Federation, 525 School Street, SW, Washington, D.C. 20024 (202) 554-2106; *World Road Statistics.*

Statistical Office of the United Nations, Publishing Service, New York, New York 10017 (800) 253-9646; *Statistical Yearbook,* and *Survey of Economic and Social Conditions in Africa.*

Times Books, 201 East 50th Street, New York, New York 10022 (212) 751-2600; *The Economist Book of Vital World Statistics.*

BOTSWANA - MULES - See BOTSWANA - LIVESTOCK AND POULTRY

BOTSWANA - MUSEUMS

Facts on File, 460 Park Avenue South, New York, New York 10016 (800) 443-8323; *The New Book of World Rankings.*

United Nations Educational, Scientific and Cultural Organization (UNESCO), 7 Place de Fontenoy, F-75700 Paris, France (Telephone Number in U.S. (212) 963-5981); *Statistical Yearbook.*

BOTSWANA - NATALITY - See BOTSWANA - BIRTH RATE

BOTSWANA - NATIONAL ACCOUNTS

African Development Bank, 01 BP 1387, Abidjan 01, Cote D'Ivoire; *Selected Statistics on Regional Member Countries.*

Federal Statistical Office, Gustav - Stresemann - Ring 11, D-6200 Wiesbaden, Germany; *Botswana.*

Statistical Office of the United Nations, Publishing Service, New York, New York 10017 (800) 253-9646; *National Accounts Statistics,* and *Statistical Yearbook.*

United Nations Economic Commission for Africa, Africa Hall, P.O. Box 3001, Addis Ababa, Ethiopia (Telephone Number in U.S. (800) 253-9646); *African Statistical Yearbook.*

BOTSWANA - NATIONAL INCOME

Facts on File, 460 Park Avenue South, New York, New York 10016 (800) 443-8323; *The New Book of World Rankings.*

G.K. Hall and Company, 70 Lincoln Street, Boston, Massachusetts 02111 (617) 423-3990; *The World in Figures.*

Statistical Office of the United Nations, Publishing Service, New York, New York 10017 (800) 253-9646; *Statistical Yearbook.*

BOTSWANA - NATIONAL PRODUCT

Facts on File, 460 Park Avenue South, New York, New York 10016 (800) 443-8323; *The New Book of World Rankings.*

BOTSWANA - NATURAL GAS - PRODUCTION - See BOTSWANA - MINING AND MINERAL PRODUCTS

BOTSWANA - NET MATERIAL PRODUCT

Statistical Office of the United Nations, Publishing Service, New York, New York 10017 (800) 253-9646; *Statistical Yearbook.*

BOTSWANA - NEWSPAPER PRODUCTION - See BOTSWANA - FORESTRY AND FOREST PRODUCTS

BOTSWANA - NICKEL AND NICKEL ORE - See BOTSWANA - MINING AND MINERAL PRODUCTS

BOTSWANA - OCCUPATIONS - See BOTSWANA - LABOR FORCE

BOTSWANA - PATENTS

World Intellectual Property Organization, 34 Chemin des Colombettes, CH-1211 Geneva 20. Switzerland; *Industrial Property Statistics.*

BOTSWANA - PEANUT PRODUCTION - See BOTSWANA - CROPS

BOTSWANA - PESTICIDE USE

Food and Agricultural Organization of the United Nations (FAO) Via delle Terme di Caracalla, 00100 Rome, Italy (Telephone Number in U.S. (202) 653-2400); *The State of Food and Agriculture.*

BOTSWANA - PETROLEUM INDUSTRY

Facts on File, 460 Park Avenue South, New York, New York 10016 (800) 443-8323; *The New Book of World Rankings.*

Food and Agricultural Organization of the United Nations (FAO) Via delle Terme di Caracalla, 00100 Rome, Italy (Telephone Number in U.S. (202) 653-2400); *The State of Food and Agriculture.*

G.K. Hall and Company, 70 Lincoln Street, Boston, Massachusetts 02111 (617) 423-3990; *The World in Figures.*

BOTSWANA - PIGS - See BOTSWANA - LIVESTOCK AND POULTRY

BOTSWANA - POPULATION

African Development Bank, 01 BP 1387, Abidjan 01, Cote D'Ivoire; *Selected Statistics on Regional Member Countries.*

The Economist Intelligence Unit, 111 West 57th Street, New York, New York 10019 (800) 938-4685; *The World Market Atlas.*

Facts on File, 460 Park Avenue South, New York, New York 10016 (800) 443-8323; *The New Book of World Rankings.*

Federal Statistical Office, Gustav - Stresemann - Ring 11, D-6200 Wiesbaden, Germany; *Botswana.*

Food and Agricultural Organization of the United Nations (FAO), Via delle Terme di Caracalla, 00100 Rome, Italy (Telephone Number in U.S. (202) 653-2400); *Production Yearbook.*

G.K. Hall and Company, 70 Lincoln Street, Boston, Massachusetts 02111 (617) 423-3990; *The World in Figures.*

International Labour Office, I.L.O. Publications, CH-1211, Geneva 22, Switzerland; *Yearbook of Labour Statistics.*

Statistical Office of the United Nations, Publishing Service, New York, New York 10017 (800) 253-9646; *Demographic Yearbook,* and *Statistical Yearbook,* and *Survey of Economic and Social Conditions in Africa.*

Times Books, 201 East 50th Street, New York, New York 10022 (212) 751-2600; *The Economist Book of Vital World Statistics.*

United Nations Educational, Scientific and Cultural Organization (UNESCO), 7 Place de Fontenoy, F-75700 Paris, France (Telephone Number in U.S. (212) 963-5981); *Statistical Yearbook.*

U.S. Arms Control and Disarmament Agency, 320 Twenty-first Street, NW, Washington, D.C. 20451 (202) 647-8677; *World Military Expenditures and Arms Transfers.*

World Health Organization, Office of Publications, Avenue Appia, CH-1211 Geneva 27, Switzerland (Telephone Number in U.S. (518) 436-9686); *World Health Statistics Annual.*

BOTSWANA - POST OFFICES

Facts on File, 460 Park Avenue South, New York, New York 10016 (800) 443-8323; *The New Book of World Rankings.*

BOTSWANA - POTATO PRODUCTION - See BOTSWANA - CROPS

BOTSWANA - PRICES

Facts on File, 460 Park Avenue South, New York, New York 10016 (800) 443-8323; *The New Book of World Rankings.*

Federal Statistical Office, Gustav - Stresemann - Ring 11, D-6200 Wiesbaden, Germany; *Botswana.*

Food and Agricultural Organization of the United Nations (FAO), Via delle Terme di Caracalla, 00100 Rome, Italy (Telephone Number in U.S. (202) 653-2400); *Production Yearbook.*

G.K. Hall and Company, 70 Lincoln Street, Boston, Massachusetts 02111 (617) 423-3990; *The World in Figures.*

International Labour Office, I.L.O. Publications, CH-1211, Geneva 22, Switzerland; *Yearbook of Labour Statistics.*

International Monetary Fund, 700 Nineteenth Street, NW, Washington, D.C. 20431 (202) 623-7000; *International Financial Statistics.*

United Nations Economic Commission for Africa, Africa Hall, P.O. Box 3001, Addis Ababa, Ethiopia (Telephone Number in U.S. (800) 253-9646); *African Statistical Yearbook.*

BOTSWANA - PRODUCTION

Facts on File, 460 Park Avenue South, New York, New York 10016 (800) 443-8323; *The New Book of World Rankings.*

G.K. Hall and Company, 70 Lincoln Street, Boston, Massachusetts 02111 (617) 423-3990; *The World in Figures.*

BOTSWANA - PROPERTY TAXES - See BOTSWANA - TAXATION

BOTSWANA - PUBLIC FINANCE

Facts on File, 460 Park Avenue South, New York, New York 10016 (800) 443-8323; *The New Book of World Rankings.*

Federal Statistical Office, Gustav - Stresemann - Ring 11, D-6200 Wiesbaden, Germany; *Botswana.*

BOTSWANA - RADIO BROADCASTING - See BOTSWANA - BROADCASTING

BOTSWANA - RAILWAYS

G.K. Hall and Company, 70 Lincoln Street, Boston, Massachusetts 02111 (617) 423-3990; *The World in Figures.*

Jane's Information Group, Sentinel House, 163 Brighton Road, Coulsdon, Surrey CR5 2NH, England (Telephone Number in U.S. (703) 683-3700); *Jane's World Railways.*

Statistical Office of the United Nations, Publishing Service, New York, New York 10017 (800) 253-9646; *Statistical Yearbook,* and

Survey of Economic and Social Conditions in Africa.

United Nations Economic Commission for Africa, Africa Hall, P.O. Box 3001, Addis Ababa, Ethiopia (Telephone Number in U.S. (800) 253-9646); *African Statistical Yearbook.*

BOTSWANA - RELIGION

Facts on File, 460 Park Avenue South, New York, New York 10016 (800) 443-8323; *The New Book of World Rankings.*

BOTSWANA - RENT PRICES

International Labour Office, I.L.O. Publications, CH-1211, Geneva 22, Switzerland; *Yearbook of Labour Statistics.*

BOTSWANA - RETAIL TRADE

G.K. Hall and Company, 70 Lincoln Street, Boston, Massachusetts 02111 (617) 423-3990; *The World in Figures.*

BOTSWANA - RICE PRODUCTION - See BOTSWANA - CROPS

BOTSWANA - ROOT AND TUBER PRODUCTION - See BOTSWANA - CROPS

BOTSWANA - RUBBER PRODUCTION

Facts on File, 460 Park Avenue South, New York, New York 10016 (800) 443-8323; *The New Book of World Rankings.*

BOTSWANA - SAWNWOOD PRODUCTION - See BOTSWANA - FORESTRY AND FOREST PRODUCTS

BOTSWANA - SCIENCE AND TECHNOLOGY - EXPENDITURE FOR RESEARCH

Statistical Office of the United Nations, Publishing Service, New York, New York 10017 (800) 253-9646; *Statistical Yearbook.*

BOTSWANA - SCIENTISTS AND TECHNICIANS

Statistical Office of the United Nations, Publishing Service, New York, New York 10017 (800) 253-9646; *Statistical Yearbook.*

United Nations Educational, Scientific and Cultural Organization (UNESCO), 7 Place de Fontenoy, F-75700 Paris, France (Telephone Number in U.S. (212) 963-5981); *Statistical Yearbook.*

BOTSWANA - SENIOR CITIZENS

Facts on File, 460 Park Avenue South, New York, New York 10016 (800) 443-8323; *The New Book of World Rankings.*

BOTSWANA - SHEEP - See BOTSWANA - LIVESTOCK AND POULTRY

BOTSWANA - SILVER PRODUCTION AND CONSUMPTION - See BOTSWANA - MINING AND MINERAL PRODUCTS

BOTSWANA - SOCIAL DATA

African Development Bank, 01 BP 1387, Abidjan 01, Cote D'Ivoire; *Selected Statistics on Regional Member Countries.*

Facts on File, 460 Park Avenue South, New York, New York 10016 (800) 443-8323; *The New Book of World Rankings.*

G.K. Hall and Company, 70 Lincoln Street, Boston, Massachusetts 02111 (617) 423-3990; *The World in Figures.*

BOTSWANA - SOCIAL SECURITY

International Monetary Fund, 700 Nineteenth Street, NW, Washington, D.C. 20431 (202) 623-7000; *Government Finance Statistics Yearbook.*

BOTSWANA - STAMP TAXES AND DUTIES - See BOTSWANA - TAXATION

BOTSWANA - STEEL PRODUCTION - See BOTSWANA - MINING AND MINERAL PRODUCTS

BOTSWANA - STOCKS - COMMODITY - MARKET PRICE - INDEX

Food and Agricultural Organization of the United Nations (FAO) Via delle Terme di Caracalla, 00100 Rome, Italy (Telephone Number in U.S. (202) 653-2400); *The State of Food and Agriculture.*

BOTSWANA - SUGAR PRODUCTION - See BOTSWANA - CROPS

BOTSWANA - TAXATION

International Monetary Fund, 700 Nineteenth Street, NW, Washington, D.C. 20431 (202) 623-7000; *Government Finance Statistics Yearbook.*

International Road Federation, 525 School Street, SW, Washington, D.C. 20024 (202) 554-2106; *World Road Statistics.*

The World Bank, 1818 H Street, NW, Washington, D.C. 20433 (202) 477-1234; *World Tables.*

BOTSWANA - TELEPHONES IN USE

American Telephone and Telegraph Company, 26 Parsippany Road, Whippany, New Jersey 07981 (800) 338-4038; *The World's Telephones.*

G.K. Hall and Company, 70 Lincoln Street, Boston, Massachusetts 02111 (617) 423-3990; *The World in Figures.*

Statistical Office of the United Nations, Publishing Service, New York, New York 10017 (800) 253-9646; *Statistical Yearbook.*

BOTSWANA - TELEVISION BROADCASTING - See BOTSWANA - BROADCASTING

BOTSWANA - TEXTILE INDUSTRY

G.K. Hall and Company, 70 Lincoln Street, Boston, Massachusetts 02111 (617) 423-3990; *The World in Figures.*

BOTSWANA - THEATRE

United Nations Educational, Scientific and Cultural Organization (UNESCO), 7 Place de Fontenoy, F-75700 Paris, France (Telephone Number in U.S. (212) 963-5981); *Statistical Yearbook.*

BOTSWANA - TOBACCO PRODUCTION

Facts on File, 460 Park Avenue South, New York, New York 10016 (800) 443-8323; *The New Book of World Rankings.*

BOTSWANA - TOURISM

Facts on File, 460 Park Avenue South, New York, New York 10016 (800) 443-8323; *The New Book of World Rankings.*

Federal Statistical Office, Gustav - Stresemann - Ring 11, D-6200 Wiesbaden, Germany; *Botswana.*

G.K. Hall and Company, 70 Lincoln Street, Boston, Massachusetts 02111 (617) 423-3990; *The World in Figures.*

Times Books, 201 East 50th Street, New York, New York 10022 (212) 751-2600; *The Economist Book of Vital World Statistics.*

United Nations Economic Commission for Africa, Africa Hall, P.O. Box 3001, Addis Ababa, Ethiopia (Telephone Number in U.S. (800) 253-9646); *African Statistical Yearbook.*

World Tourism Organization, Calle Capitan Haya 42, E-28020 Madrid, Spain; *Yearbook of Tourism Statistics.*

BOTSWANA - TRACTORS IN USE

Statistical Office of the United Nations, Publishing Service, New York, New York 10017 (800) 253-9646; *Statistical Yearbook.*

BOTSWANA - TRADE - See BOTSWANA - FOREIGN TRADE

BOTSWANA - TRADEMARKS AND SERVICE MARKS

World Intellectual Property Organization, 34 Chemin des Colombettes, CH-1211 Geneva 20. Switzerland; *Industrial Property Statistics.*

BOTSWANA - TRANSPORTATION AND COMMUNICATIONS

Facts on File, 460 Park Avenue South, New York, New York 10016 (800) 443-8323; *The New Book of World Rankings.*

Federal Statistical Office, Gustav - Stresemann - Ring 11, D-6200 Wiesbaden, Germany; *Botswana.*

G.K. Hall and Company, 70 Lincoln Street, Boston, Massachusetts 02111 (617) 423-3990; *The World in Figures.*

United Nations Economic Commission for Africa, Africa Hall, P.O. Box 3001, Addis Ababa, Ethiopia (Telephone Number in U.S. (800) 253-9646); *African Statistical Yearbook.*

BOTSWANA - UNEMPLOYMENT

International Labour Office, I.L.O. Publications, CH-1211, Geneva 22, Switzerland; *Yearbook of Labour Statistics.*

BOTSWANA - VITAL STATISTICS

G.K. Hall and Company, 70 Lincoln Street, Boston, Massachusetts 02111 (617) 423-3990; *The World in Figures.*

World Health Organization, Office of Publications, Avenue Appia, CH-1211 Geneva 27, Switzerland (Telephone Number in U.S. (518) 436-9686); *World Health Statistics Annual.*

BOTSWANA - WAGES

Federal Statistical Office, Gustav - Stresemann - Ring 11, D-6200 Wiesbaden, Germany; *Botswana.*

G.K. Hall and Company, 70 Lincoln Street, Boston, Massachusetts 02111 (617) 423-3990; *The World in Figures.*

International Labour Office, I.L.O. Publications, CH-1211, Geneva 22, Switzerland; *Yearbook of Labour Statistics.*

BOTSWANA - WEATHER

Facts on File, 460 Park Avenue South, New York, New York 10016 (800) 443-8323; *The New Book of World Rankings.*

G.K. Hall and Company, 70 Lincoln Street, Boston, Massachusetts 02111 (617) 423-3990; *The World in Figures.*

BOTSWANA - WELFARE

International Monetary Fund, 700 Nineteenth Street, NW, Washington, D.C. 20431 (202) 623-7000; *Government Finance Statistics Yearbook.*

BOTSWANA - WHEAT - See BOTSWANA - CROPS

BOTSWANA - WINE PRODUCTION

Facts on File, 460 Park Avenue South, New York, New York 10016 (800) 443-8323; *The New Book of World Rankings.*

BOTSWANA - WOOL PRODUCTION

Facts on File, 460 Park Avenue South, New York, New York 10016 (800) 443-8323; *The New Book of World Rankings.*

BOTULISM

United States Department of Health and Human Services, Center for Disease Control, 1600 Clifton Road, NE, Atlanta, Georgia 30333 (404) 639-3311; *Summary of Notifiable Diseases, United States, Morbidity and Mortality Weekly Report.*

BOWLING

American Bowling Congress, 5301 South 76th Street, Greendale, Wisconsin 53129 (414) 421-6400.

National Bowling Council, 2300 Clarendon Boulevard, No. 1107, Arlington, Virginia 22201 (703) 841-1660.

National Sporting Goods Association, 1699 Wall Street, Mount Prospect, Illinois 60056 (708) 439-4000; *The Sporting Goods Market in 1993,* and *Sports Participation in 1992.*

BOY SCOUTS - MEMBERSHIP AND UNITS

Boy Scouts of America, 1325 Walnut Hill Lane, P.O. Box 152079, Irving, Texas 75015 (214) 580-2000; *Annual Report.*

Brazil - National Statistical Office

Fundacao Instituto Brasileiro de Geografia e Estatistica, Rva General Canabarro, 666 20271-Rio de Janeiro - RJ, Brazil.

Brazil - Primary Statistics Source

Fundacao Brasileiro de Geografia e Estatistica, Rva General Canabarro, 666 20271-Rio de Janeiro - RJ, Brazil; *Anuario estatistico do Brasil* (Statistical Yearbook of Brazil).

BRAZIL - AGRICULTURE

The Economist Intelligence Unit, 111 West 57th Street, New York, New York 10019 (800) 938-4685; *The New Latin America Market Atlas.*

Euromonitor Publications Limited, 87-88 Turnmill Street, London EC1M 5QU, England; *International Marketing Data and Statistics*, and *Third World Economic Handbook*.

Facts on File, 460 Park Avenue South, New York, New York 10016 (800) 443-8323; *The New Book of World Rankings*.

Federal Statistical Office, Gustav - Stresemann - Ring 11, D-6200 Wiesbaden, Germany; *Brazil*.

Food and Agricultural Organization of the United Nations (FAO) Via delle Terme di Caracalla, 00100 Rome, Italy (Telephone Number in U.S. (202) 653-2400); *Production Yearbook, The State of Food and Agriculture*, and *Trade Yearbook*.

Gale Research Incorporated, 835 Penobscot Building, Detroit, Michigan 48226 (800) 877-4253; *International Historical Statistics The Americas and Australasia*.

G.K. Hall and Company, 70 Lincoln Street, Boston, Massachusetts 02111 (617) 423-3990; *The World in Figures*.

Inter-American Development Bank, 1300 New York Avenue, NW, Washington, D.C. 20577 (202) 623-1753; *Economic and Social Progress in Latin America*.

Statistical Office of the United Nations, Publishing Service, New York, New York 10017 (800) 253-9646; *Statistical Yearbook*, and *Statistical Yearbook for Latin America and the Caribbean*.

Times Books, 201 East 50th Street, New York, New York 10022 (212) 751-2600; *The Economist Book of Vital World Statistics*.

U.C.L.A. Latin American Center Publications, University of California, Los Angeles, California 90024 (310) 825-6634; *Statistical Abstract of Latin America*.

The World Bank, 1818 H Street, NW, Washington, D.C. 20433 (202) 477-1234; *World Tables*.

BRAZIL - AIRLINE SERVICE

The Economist Intelligence Unit, 111 West 57th Street, New York, New York 10019 (800) 938-4685; *The New Latin America Market Atlas*.

Facts on File, 460 Park Avenue South, New York, New York 10016 (800) 443-8323; *The New Book of World Rankings*.

G.K. Hall and Company, 70 Lincoln Street, Boston, Massachusetts 02111 (617) 423-3990; *The World in Figures*.

International Civil Aviation Organization, 1000 Sherbrooke Street West, Suite 400, Montreal, Quebec, Canada H3A 2R2 (514) 285-8219; *Civil Aviation Statistics of the World*.

Statistical Office of the United Nations, Publishing Service, New York, New York 10017 (800) 253-9646; *Statistical Yearbook*.

Times Books, 201 East 50th Street, New York, New York 10022 (212) 751-2600; *The Economist Book of Vital World Statistics*.

BRAZIL - ALUMINUM PRODUCTION AND CONSUMPTION - See BRAZIL - MINING AND MINERAL PRODUCTS

BRAZIL - ANIMAL FEEDINGSTUFFS

Statistical Office of the United Nations, Publishing Service, New York, New York 10017 (800) 253-9646; *Statistical Yearbook*.

BRAZIL - ANIMAL HEALTH

Food and Agricultural Organization of the United Nations (FAO), Via delle Terme di Caracalla, 00100 Rome, Italy (Telephone Number in U.S. (202) 653-2400); *Animal Health Yearbook*.

BRAZIL - ANTIMONY AND ANTIMONY ORE - See BRAZIL - MINING AND MINERAL PRODUCTS

BRAZIL - AREA AND DENSITY OF POPULATION

Euromonitor Publications Limited, 87-88 Turnmill Street, London EC1M 5QU, England; *International Marketing Data and Statistics*.

Facts on File, 460 Park Avenue South, New York, New York 10016 (800) 443-8323; *The New Book of World Rankings*.

Federal Statistical Office, Gustav - Stresemann - Ring 11, D-6200 Wiesbaden, Germany; *Brazil*.

Food and Agricultural Organization of the United Nations (FAO) Via delle Terme di Caracalla, 00100 Rome, Italy (Telephone Number in U.S. (202) 653-2400); *The State of Food and Agriculture*.

G.K. Hall and Company, 70 Lincoln Street, Boston, Massachusetts 02111 (617) 423-3990; *The World in Figures*.

Inter-American Development Bank, 1300 New York Avenue, NW, Washington, D.C. 20577 (202) 623-1753; *Economic and Social Progress in Latin America*.

Statistical Office of the United Nations, Publishing Service, New York, New York 10017 (800) 253-9646; *Statistical Yearbook*.

Times Books, 201 East 50th Street, New York, New York 10022 (212) 751-2600; *The Economist Book of Vital World Statistics*.

BRAZIL - ARMS EXPORTS AND IMPORTS

U.S. Arms Control and Disarmament Agency, 320 Twenty-first Street, NW, Washington, D.C. 20451 (202) 647-8677; *World Military Expenditures and Arms Transfers*.

BRAZIL - ARSENIC PRODUCTION AND CONSUMPTION - See BRAZIL - MINING AND MINERAL PRODUCTS

BRAZIL - BALANCE OF PAYMENTS

The Economist Intelligence Unit, 111 West 57th Street, New York, New York 10019 (800) 938-4685; *The New Latin America Market Atlas*, and *The World Market Atlas*.

Euromonitor Publications Limited, 87-88 Turnmill Street, London EC1M 5QU, England; *Third World Economic Handbook*.

Federal Statistical Office, Gustav - Stresemann - Ring 11, D-6200 Wiesbaden, Germany; *Brazil*.

G.K. Hall and Company, 70 Lincoln Street, Boston, Massachusetts 02111 (617) 423-3990; *The World in Figures*.

Inter-American Development Bank, 1300 New York Avenue, NW, Washington, D.C. 20577 (202) 623-1753; *Economic and Social Progress in Latin America*.

International Monetary Fund, 700 Nineteenth Street, NW, Washington, D.C. 20431 (202) 623-7000; *Balance of Payments Yearbook*, and *International Financial Statistics*.

Organization of American States (OAS), General Secretariat, Washington, D.C. 20006 (202) 458-3533; *Statistical Bulletin of the OAS.*

Statistical Office of the United Nations, Publishing Service, New York, New York 10017 (800) 253-9646; *Economic Survey of Latin America and the Caribbean,* and *Statistical Yearbook for Latin America and the Caribbean.*

Times Books, 201 East 50th Street, New York, New York 10022 (212) 751-2600; *The Economist Book of Vital World Statistics.*

U.C.L.A. Latin American Center Publications, University of California, Los Angeles, California 90024 (310) 825-6634; *Statistical Abstract of Latin America.*

The World Bank, 1818 H Street, NW, Washington, D.C. 20433 (202) 477-1234; *World Tables.*

BRAZIL - BANKING

Facts on File, 460 Park Avenue South, New York, New York 10016 (800) 443-8323; *The New Book of World Rankings.*

G.K. Hall and Company, 70 Lincoln Street, Boston, Massachusetts 02111 (617) 423-3990; *The World in Figures.*

Inter-American Development Bank, 1300 New York Avenue, NW, Washington, D.C. 20577 (202) 623-1753; *Economic and Social Progress in Latin America.*

International Monetary Fund, 700 Nineteenth Street, NW, Washington, D.C. 20431 (202) 623-7000; *Government Finance Statistics Yearbook,* and *International Financial Statistics.*

Statistical Office of the United Nations, Publishing Service, New York, New York 10017; *Statistical Yearbook,* and *Statistical Yearbook for Latin American and the Caribbean.*

BRAZIL - BARLEY PRODUCTION - See BRAZIL - CROPS

BRAZIL - BAUXITE PRODUCTION AND CONSUMPTION -See BRAZIL - MINING AND MINERAL PRODUCTS

BRAZIL - BEER PRODUCTION

Facts on File, 460 Park Avenue South, New York, New York 10016 (800) 443-8323; *The New Book of World Rankings.*

Statistical Office of the United Nations, Publishing Service, New York, New York 10017 (800) 253-9646; *Statistical Yearbook.*

BRAZIL - BIRTH RATES

Euromonitor Publications Limited, 87-88 Turnmill Street, London EC1M 5QU, England; *Third World Economic Handbook.*

Facts on File, 460 Park Avenue South, New York, New York 10016 (800) 443-8323; *The New Book of World Rankings.*

Statistical Office of the United Nations, Publishing Service, New York, New York 10017 (800) 253-9646; *Demographic Yearbook, Statistical Yearbook,* and *Statistical Yearbook for Latin America and the Caribbean.*

Times Books, 201 East 50th Street, New York, New York 10022 (212) 751-2600; *The Economist Book of Vital World Statistics.*

The World Bank, 1818 H Street, NW, Washington, D.C. 20433 (202) 477-1234; *World Tables.*

World Health Organization, Office of Publications, Avenue Appia, CH-1211 Geneva 27, Switzerland (Telephone Number in U.S. (518) 436-9686); *World Health Statistics Annual.*

BRAZIL - BONDS

G.K. Hall and Company, 70 Lincoln Street, Boston, Massachusetts 02111 (617) 423-3990; *The World in Figures.*

Inter-American Development Bank, 1300 New York Avenue, NW, Washington, D.C. 20577 (202) 623-1753; *Economic and Social Progress in Latin America.*

International Monetary Fund, 700 Nineteenth Street, NW, Washington, D.C. 20431 (202) 623-7000; *Government Finance Statistics Yearbook.*

BRAZIL - BOOK PRODUCTION

G.K. Hall and Company, 70 Lincoln Street, Boston, Massachusetts 02111 (617) 423-3990; *The World in Figures.*

Statistical Office of the United Nations, Publishing Service, New York, New York 10017 (800) 253-9646; *Statistical Yearbook.*

BRAZIL - BROADCASTING

Billboard Limited, P.O. Box 9027, 1006 AA Amsterdam, The Netherlands (Telephone Number in U.S. (212) 764-7300); *World Radio TV Handbook.*

Facts on File, 460 Park Avenue South, New York, New York 10016 (800) 443-8323; *The New Book of World Rankings.*

G.K. Hall and Company, 70 Lincoln Street, Boston, Massachusetts 02111 (617) 423-3990; *The World in Figures.*

Times Books, 201 East 50th Street, New York, New York 10022 (212) 751-2600; *The Economist Book of Vital World Statistics.*

United Nations Educational, Scientific and Cultural Organization (UNESCO), 7 Place de Fontenoy, F-75700 Paris, France (Telephone Number in U.S. (212) 963-5981); *Statistical Yearbook.*

BRAZIL - BUILDING CONSTRUCTION - See BRAZIL - CONSTRUCTION INDUSTRY

BRAZIL - BUSINESS

G.K. Hall and Company, 70 Lincoln Street, Boston, Massachusetts 02111 (617) 423-3990; *The World in Figures.*

Inter-American Development Bank, 1300 New York Avenue, NW, Washington, D.C. 20577 (202) 623-1753; *Economic and Social Progress in Latin America.*

BRAZIL - BUSINESS AND PROFESSIONAL LICENSES

International Monetary Fund, 700 Nineteenth Street, NW, Washington, D.C. 20431 (202) 623-7000; *Government Finance Statistics Yearbook.*

BRAZIL - BUTTER PRODUCTION - See BRAZIL - DAIRY PRODUCTS

BRAZIL - CADMIUM PRODUCTION AND CONSUMPTION - See BRAZIL - MINING AND MINERAL PRODUCTS

BRAZIL - CALORIE SUPPLY

Food and Agricultural Organization of the United Nations (FAO) Via delle Terme di Caracalla, 00100 Rome, Italy (Telephone Number in U.S. (202) 653-2400); *The State of Food and Agriculture.*

Statistical Office of the United Nations, Publishing Service, New York, New York 10017 (800) 253-9646; *Statistical Yearbook for Latin America and the Caribbean.*

BRAZIL - CAPITAL INVESTMENT

Inter-American Development Bank, 1300 New York Avenue, NW, Washington, D.C. 20577 (202) 623-1753; *Economic and Social Progress in Latin America.*

BRAZIL - CAPITAL REVENUE

Inter-American Development Bank, 1300 New York Avenue, NW, Washington, D.C. 20577 (202) 623-1753; *Economic and Social Progress in Latin America.*

International Monetary Fund, 700 Nineteenth Street, NW, Washington, D.C. 20431 (202) 623-7000; *Government Finance Statistics Yearbook.*

BRAZIL - CASHEW NUT PRODUCTION - See BRAZIL - CROPS

BRAZIL - CASTOR BEAN PRODUCTION - See BRAZIL - CROPS

BRAZIL - CATTLE - See BRAZIL - LIVESTOCK AND POULTRY

BRAZIL - CAUSTIC SODA PRODUCTION

Statistical Office of the United Nations, Publishing Service, New York, New York 10017 (800) 253-9646; *Statistical Yearbook.*

BRAZIL - CEMENT PRODUCTION - See BRAZIL - MINING AND MINERAL PRODUCTS

BRAZIL - CHEESE PRODUCTION - See BRAZIL - DAIRY PRODUCTS

BRAZIL - CHEMICALS (ORGANIC) PRODUCTION - See BRAZIL - MINING AND MINERAL PRODUCTS

BRAZIL - CHESTNUT PRODUCTION - See BRAZIL - CROPS

BRAZIL - CHICKENS - See BRAZIL - LIVESTOCK AND POULTRY

BRAZIL - CHROMIUM ORE PRODUCTION AND CONSUMPTION - See BRAZIL - MINING AND MINERAL PRODUCTS

BRAZIL - CHROMITE PRODUCTION AND CONSUMPTION - See BRAZIL - MINING AND MINERAL PRODUCTS

BRAZIL - CIGAR PRODUCTION - See BRAZIL - TOBACCO PRODUCTION

BRAZIL - CIGARETTE PRODUCTION - See BRAZIL - TOBACCO PRODUCTS

BRAZIL - CLASS STRUCTURE

G.K. Hall and Company, 70 Lincoln Street, Boston, Massachusetts 02111 (617) 423-3990; *The World in Figures.*

BRAZIL - CLIMATE

Facts on File, 460 Park Avenue South, New York, New York 10016 (800) 443-8323; *The New Book of World Rankings.*

G.K. Hall and Company, 70 Lincoln Street, Boston, Massachusetts 02111 (617) 423-3990; *The World in Figures.*

BRAZIL - CLOTHING EXPORTS AND IMPORTS

Euromonitor Publications Limited, 87-88 Turnmill Street, London EC1M 5QU, England; *Third World Economic Handbook.*

Statistical Office of the United Nations, Publishing Service, New York, New York 10017 (800) 253-9646; *Trade in Manufactures of Developing Countries.*

BRAZIL - COAL PRODUCTION - See BRAZIL - MINING AND MINERAL PRODUCTS

BRAZIL - COCOA (BEANS) PRODUCTION - See BRAZIL - CROPS

BRAZIL - COFFEE - See BRAZIL - CROPS

BRAZIL - COKE OVEN COKE PRODUCTION - See BRAZIL - MINING AND MINERAL PRODUCTS

BRAZIL - COMMUNICATIONS

Euromonitor Publications Limited, 87-88 Turnmill Street, London EC1M 5QU, England; *Third World Economic Handbook.*

Federal Statistical Office, Gustav - Stresemann - Ring 11, D-6200 Wiesbaden, Germany; *Brazil.*

G.K. Hall and Company, 70 Lincoln Street, Boston, Massachusetts 02111 (617) 423-3990; *The World in Figures.*

Inter-American Development Bank, 1300 New York Avenue, NW, Washington, D.C. 20577 (202) 623-1753; *Economic and Social Progress in Latin America.*

U.C.L.A. Latin American Center Publications, University of California, Los Angeles, California 90024 (310) 825-6634; *Statistical Abstract of Latin America.*

BRAZIL - CONSTRUCTION INDUSTRY

The Economist Intelligence Unit, 111 West 57th Street, New York, New York 10019 (800) 938-4685; *The New Latin America Market Atlas.*

Facts on File, 460 Park Avenue South, New York, New York 10016 (800) 443-8323; *The New Book of World Rankings.*

Inter-American Development Bank, 1300 New York Avenue, NW, Washington, D.C. 20577 (202) 623-1753; *Economic and Social Progress in Latin America.*

Organization of American States (OAS), General Secretariat, Washington, D.C. 20006 (202) 458-3533; *Statistical Bulletin of the OAS.*

Statistical Office of the United Nations, Publishing Service, New York, New York 10017 (800) 253-9646; *Construction Statistics Yearbook,* and *Statistical Yearbook.*

U.C.L.A. Latin American Center Publications, University of California, Los Angeles, California 90024 (310) 825-6634; *Statistical*

Abstract of Latin America.

BRAZIL - CONSUMER PRICE INDEX

G.K. Hall and Company, 70 Lincoln Street, Boston, Massachusetts 02111 (617) 423-3990; *The World in Figures.*

Statistical Office of the United Nations, Publishing Service, New York, New York 10017 (800) 253-9646; *Statistical Yearbook.*

BRAZIL - CONSUMER PRICES

The Economist Intelligence Unit, 111 West 57th Street, New York, New York 10019 (800) 938-4685; *The New Latin America Market Atlas.*

International Labour Office, I.L.O. Publications, CH-1211, Geneva 22, Switzerland; *Yearbook of Labour Statistics.*

International Monetary Fund, 700 Nineteenth Street, NW, Washington, D.C. 20431 (202) 623-7000; *International Financial Statistics.*

Organization of American States (OAS), General Secretariat, Washington, D.C. 20006 (202) 458-3533; *Statistical Bulletin of the OAS.*

Times Books, 201 East 50th Street, New York, New York 10022 (212) 751-2600; *The Economist Book of Vital World Statistics.*

U.C.L.A. Latin American Center Publications, University of California, Los Angeles, California 90024 (310) 825-6634; *Statistical Abstract of Latin America.*

BRAZIL - CONSUMPTION

The Economist Intelligence Unit, 111 West 57th Street, New York, New York 10019 (800) 938-4685; *The New Latin America Market Atlas.*

G.K. Hall and Company, 70 Lincoln Street, Boston, Massachusetts 02111 (617) 423-3990; *The World in Figures.*

Inter-American Development Bank, 1300 New York Avenue, NW, Washington, D.C. 20577 (202) 623-1753; *Economic and Social Progress in Latin America.*

International Rubber Study Group, York House, 8th Floor, Empire Way, Wembley, London HA9 0PA, England; *Rubber Statistical Handbook.*

Statistical Office of the United Nations, Publishing Service, New York, New York 10017 (800) 253-9646; *Statistical Yearbook for Latin America and the Caribbean.*

BRAZIL - COOPERATIVES

U.C.L.A. Latin American Center Publications, University of California, Los Angeles, California 90024 (310) 825-6634; *Statistical Abstract of Latin America.*

BRAZIL - COPPER AND COPPER ORE - See BRAZIL - MINING AND MINERAL PRODUCTS

BRAZIL - CORN PRODUCTION - See BRAZIL - CROPS

BRAZIL - CORPORATE TAXES - See BRAZIL - TAXATION

BRAZIL - COTTON - See BRAZIL - CROPS

BRAZIL - CROPS

Commodity Research Bureau, Incorporated, 75 Wall Street, New York, New York 10005 (212) 504-7754; *Commodity Year Book.*

The Economist Intelligence Unit, 111 West 57th Street, New York, New York 10019 (800) 938-4685; *The New Latin America Market Atlas.*

Facts on File, 460 Park Avenue South, New York, New York 10016 (800) 443-8323; *The New Book of World Rankings.*

Food and Agricultural Organization of the United Nations (FAO) Via delle Terme di Caracalla, 00100 Rome, Italy (Telephone Number in U.S. (202) 653-2400); *Production Yearbook,* and *The State of Food and Agriculture.*

G.K. Hall and Company, 70 Lincoln Street, Boston, Massachusetts 02111 (617) 423-3990; *The World in Figures.*

International Monetary Fund, 700 Nineteenth Street, NW, Washington, D.C. 20431 (202) 623-7000; *Government Finance Statistics Yearbook.*

Organization of American States (OAS), General Secretariat, Washington, D.C. 20006 (202) 458-3533; *Statistical Bulletin of the OAS.*

Statistical Office of the United Nations, Publishing Service, New York, New York 10017 (800) 253-9646; *Statistical Yearbook.*

BRAZIL - CUSTOMS DUTIES

G.K. Hall and Company, 70 Lincoln Street, Boston, Massachusetts 02111 (617) 423-3990; *The World in Figures.*

Inter-American Development Bank, 1300 New York Avenue, NW, Washington, D.C. 20577 (202) 623-1753; *Economic and Social Progress in Latin America.*

International Monetary Fund, 700 Nineteenth Street, NW, Washington, D.C. 20431 (202) 623-7000; *Government Finance Statistics Yearbook.*

BRAZIL - DAIRY PRODUCTS

Commodity Research Bureau, Incorporated, 75 Wall Street, New York, New York 10005 (212) 504-7754; *Commodity Year Book.*

Facts on File, 460 Park Avenue South, New York, New York 10016 (800) 443-8323; *The New Book of World Rankings.*

Food and Agricultural Organization of the United Nations (FAO), Via delle Terme di Caracalla, 00100 Rome, Italy (Telephone Number in U.S. (202) 653-2400); *Production Yearbook,* and *The State of Food and Agriculture.*

Statistical Office of the United Nations, Publishing Service, New York, New York 10017 (800) 253-9646; *Statistical Yearbook.*

BRAZIL - DEATH RATES

Euromonitor Publications Limited, 87-88 Turnmill Street, London EC1M 5QU, England; *Third World Economic Handbook.*

G.K. Hall and Company, 70 Lincoln Street, Boston, Massachusetts 02111 (617) 423-3990; *The World in Figures.*

Statistical Office of the United Nations, Publishing Service, New York, New York 10017 (800) 253-9646; *Statistical Yearbook*, and *Statistical Yearbook for Latin America and the Caribbean.*

Times Books, 201 East 50th Street, New York, New York 10022 (212) 751-2600; *The Economist Book of Vital World Statistics.*

World Health Organization, Office of Publications, Avenue Appia, CH-1211 Geneva 27, Switzerland (Telephone Number in U.S. (518) 436-9686); *World Health Statistics Annual.*

BRAZIL - DEBT

The Economist Intelligence Unit, 111 West 57th Street, New York, New York 10019 (800) 938-4685; *The New Latin America Market Atlas.*

BRAZIL - DEFENSE EXPENDITURES

The Economist Intelligence Unit, 111 West 57th Street, New York, New York 10019 (800) 938-4685; *The New Latin America Market Atlas.*

G.K. Hall and Company, 70 Lincoln Street, Boston, Massachusetts 02111 (617) 423-3990; *The World in Figures.*

International Monetary Fund, 700 Nineteenth Street, NW, Washington, D.C. 20431 (202) 623-7000; *Government Finance Statistics Yearbook.*

U.S. Arms Control and Disarmament Agency, 320 Twenty-first Street, NW, Washington, D.C. 20451 (202) 647-8677; *World Military Expenditures and Arms Transfers.*

BRAZIL - DEMOGRAPHY

The Economist Intelligence Unit, 111 West 57th Street, New York, New York 10019 (800) 938-4685; *The World Market Atlas.*

Facts on File, 460 Park Avenue South, New York, New York 10016 (800) 443-8323; *The New Book of World Rankings.*

G.K. Hall and Company, 70 Lincoln Street, Boston, Massachusetts 02111 (617) 423-3990; *The World in Figures.*

U.C.L.A. Latin American Center Publications, University of California, Los Angeles, California 90024 (310) 825-6634; *Statistical Abstract of Latin America.*

BRAZIL - DEVELOPMENT ASSISTANCE

G.K. Hall and Company, 70 Lincoln Street, Boston, Massachusetts 02111 (617) 423-3990; *The World in Figures.*

Inter-American Development Bank, 1300 New York Avenue, NW, Washington, D.C. 20577 (202) 623-1753; *Economic and Social Progress in Latin America.*

Statistical Office of the United Nations, Publishing Service, New York, New York 10017 (800) 253-9646; *Statistical Yearbook.*

BRAZIL - DIAMOND PRODUCTION - See BRAZIL - MINING AND MINERAL PRODUCTS

BRAZIL - DISCOUNT RATES

Inter-American Development Bank, 1300 New York Avenue, NW, Washington, D.C. 20577 (202) 623-1753; *Economic and Social Progress in Latin America.*

BRAZIL - DISEASES

G.K. Hall and Company, 70 Lincoln Street, Boston, Massachusetts 02111 (617) 423-3990; *The World in Figures.*

World Health Organization, Office of Publications, Avenue Appia, CH-1211 Geneva 27, Switzerland (Telephone Number in U.S. (518) 436-9686); *World Health Statistics Annual.*

BRAZIL - DIVORCE RATES

Facts on File, 460 Park Avenue South, New York, New York 10016 (800) 443-8323; *The New Book of World Rankings.*

Statistical Office of the United Nations, Publishing Service, New York, New York 10017 (800) 253-9646; *Demographic Yearbook.*

BRAZIL - DOMESTIC PRODUCT

G.K. Hall and Company, 70 Lincoln Street, Boston, Massachusetts 02111 (617) 423-3990; *The World in Figures.*

BRAZIL - DUCKS - See BRAZIL - LIVESTOCK AND POULTRY

BRAZIL - ECONOMY

Euromonitor Publications Limited, 87-88 Turnmill Street, London EC1M 5QU, England; *International Marketing Data and Statistics*, and *Third World Economic Handbook.*

Facts on File, 460 Park Avenue South, New York, New York 10016 (800) 443-8323; *The New Book of World Rankings.*

G.K. Hall and Company, 70 Lincoln Street, Boston, Massachusetts 02111 (617) 423-3990; *The World in Figures.*

Inter-American Development Bank, 1300 New York Avenue, NW, Washington, D.C. 20577 (202) 623-1753; *Economic and Social Progress in Latin America.*

Organization of American States (OAS), General Secretariat, Washington, D.C. 20006 (202) 458-3533; *Statistical Bulletin of the OAS.*

Statistical Office of the United Nations, Publishing Service, New York, New York 10017 (800) 253-9646; *Economic Survey of Latin America and the Caribbean.*

U.C.L.A. Latin American Center Publications, University of California, Los Angeles, California 90024 (310) 825-6634; *Statistical Abstract of Latin America.*

BRAZIL - EDUCATION

The Economist Intelligence Unit, 111 West 57th Street, New York, New York 10019 (800) 938-4685; *The New Latin America Market Atlas*, and *The World Market Atlas.*

Facts on File, 460 Park Avenue South, New York, New York 10016 (800) 443-8323; *The New Book of World Rankings.*

Federal Statistical Office, Gustav - Stresemann - Ring 11, D-6200 Wiesbaden, Germany; *Brazil.*

Gale Research Incorporated, 835 Penobscot Building, Detroit, Michigan 48226 (800) 877-4253; *International Historical Statistics The Americas and Australasia.*

G.K. Hall and Company, 70 Lincoln Street, Boston, Massachusetts 02111 (617) 423-3990; *The World in Figures.*

International Monetary Fund, 700 Nineteenth Street, NW, Washington, D.C. 20431 (202) 623-7000; *Government Finance Statistics Yearbook.*

Statistical Office of the United Nations, Publishing Service, New York, New York 10017 (800) 253-9646; *Statistical Yearbook for Latin America and the Caribbean.*

Times Books, 201 East 50th Street, New York, New York 10022 (212) 751-2600; *The Economist Book of Vital World Statistics.*

U.C.L.A. Latin American Center Publications, University of California, Los Angeles, California 90024 (310) 825-6634; *Statistical Abstract of Latin America.*

United Nations Educational, Scientific and Cultural Organization (UNESCO), 7 Place de Fontenoy, F-75700 Paris, France (Telephone Number in U.S. (212) 963-5981); *Statistical Yearbook.*

The World Bank, 1818 H Street, NW, Washington, D.C. 20433 (202) 477-1234; *World Tables.*

BRAZIL - EGG PRODUCTION - See BRAZIL - DAIRY PRODUCTS

BRAZIL - ELECTRICITY

Commodity Research Bureau, Incorporated, 75 Wall Street, New York, New York 10005 (212) 504-7754; *Commodity Year Book.*

The Economist Intelligence Unit, 111 West 57th Street, New York, New York 10019 (800) 938-4685; *The New Latin America Market Atlas.*

Facts on File, 460 Park Avenue South, New York, New York 10016 (800) 443-8323; *The New Book of World Rankings.*

Inter-American Development Bank, 1300 New York Avenue, NW, Washington, D.C. 20577 (202) 623-1753; *Economic and Social Progress in Latin America.*

Organization of American States (OAS), General Secretariat, Washington, D.C. 20006 (202) 458-3533; *Statistical Bulletin of the OAS.*

Penn Well Publishing Company, 1421 South Sheridan Road, P.O. Box 1260, Tulsa, Oklahoma 74101 (800) 752-9764; *International Energy Statistics Sourcebook.*

Statistical Office of the United Nations, Publishing Service, New York, New York 10017 (800) 253-9646; *Statistical Yearbook.*

Times Books, 201 East 50th Street, New York, New York 10022 (212) 751-2600; *The Economist Book of Vital World Statistics.*

BRAZIL - EMPLOYMENT

Euromonitor Publications Limited, 87-88 Turnmill Street, London EC1M 5QU, England; *International Marketing Data and Statistics.*

Facts on File, 460 Park Avenue South, New York, New York 10016 (800) 443-8323; *The New Book of World Rankings.*

Federal Statistical Office, Gustav - Stresemann - Ring 11, D-6200 Wiesbaden, Germany; *Brazil.*

International Labour Office, I.L.O. Publications, CH-1211, Geneva 22, Switzerland; *Yearbook of Labour Statistics.*

Organization of American States (OAS), General Secretariat, Washington, D.C. 20006 (202) 458-3533; *Statistical Bulletin of the OAS.*

Statistical Office of the United Nations, Publishing Service, New York, New York 10017 (800) 253-9646; *Statistical Yearbook,* and *Statistical Yearbook for Latin America and the Caribbean.*

U.C.L.A. Latin American Center Publications, University of California, Los Angeles, California 90024 (310) 825-6634; *Statistical Abstract of Latin America.*

BRAZIL - ENERGY

The Economist Intelligence Unit, 111 West 57th Street, New York, New York 10019 (800) 938-4685; *The New Latin America Market Atlas.*

Facts on File, 460 Park Avenue South, New York, New York 10016 (800) 443-8323; *The New Book of World Rankings.*

Food and Agricultural Organization of the United Nations (FAO) Via delle Terme di Caracalla, 00100 Rome, Italy (Telephone Number in U.S. (202) 653-2400); *The State of Food and Agriculture.*

G.K. Hall and Company, 70 Lincoln Street, Boston, Massachusetts 02111 (617) 423-3990; *The World in Figures.*

Penn Well Publishing Company, 1421 South Sheridan Road, P.O. Box 1260, Tulsa, Oklahoma 74101 (800) 752-9764; *International Energy Statistics Sourcebook.*

Statistical Office of the United Nations, Publishing Service, New York, New York 10017 (800) 253-9646; *Energy Statistics Yearbook,* and *Statistical Yearbook for Latin America and the Caribbean.*

Times Books, 201 East 50th Street, New York, New York 10022 (212) 751-2600; *The Economist Book of Vital World Statistics.*

U.C.L.A. Latin American Center Publications, University of California, Los Angeles, California 90024 (310) 825-6634; *Statistical Abstract of Latin America.*

BRAZIL - ENGINEERING AND METAL PRODUCTS EXPORTS TO DEVELOPED COUNTRIES

Statistical Office of the United Nations, Publishing Service, New York, New York 10017 (800) 253-9646; *Trade in Manufactures of Developing Countries.*

BRAZIL - EXCHANGE RATES

Euromonitor Publications Limited, 87-88 Turnmill Street, London EC1M 5QU, England; *International Marketing Data and Statistics.*

Inter-American Development Bank, 1300 New York Avenue, NW, Washington, D.C. 20577 (202) 623-1753; *Economic and Social Progress in Latin America.*

International Civil Aviation Organization, 1000 Sherbrooke Street West, Suite 400, Montreal, Quebec, Canada H3A 2R2 (514) 285-8219; *Civil Aviation Statistics of the World.*

International Monetary Fund, 700 Nineteenth Street, NW, Washington, D.C. 20431 (202) 623-7000; *International Financial Statistics.*

Organization of American States (OAS), General Secretariat, Washington, D.C. 20006 (202) 458-3533; *Statistical Bulletin of the OAS.*

U.C.L.A. Latin American Center Publications, University of California, Los Angeles, California 90024 (310) 825-6634; *Statistical Abstract of Latin America.*

BRAZIL - EXCISE TAXES - See BRAZIL - TAXATION

BRAZIL - EXPORTS

American Automobile Manufacturers Association, 1401 H Street, NW, Suite 900, Washington, D.C. 20005 (202) 326-5500; *World Motor Vehicle Data.*

The Economist Intelligence Unit, 111 West 57th Street, New York, New York 10019 (800) 938-4685; *The New Latin America Market Atlas,* and *The World Market Atlas.*

Euromonitor Publications Limited, 87-88 Turnmill Street, London EC1M 5QU, England; *International Marketing Data and Statistics,* and *Third World Economic Handbook.*

Food and Agricultural Organization of the United Nations (FAO) Via delle Terme di Caracalla, 00100 Rome, Italy (Telephone Number in U.S. (202) 653-2400); *The State of Food and Agriculture.*

G.K. Hall and Company, 70 Lincoln Street, Boston, Massachusetts 02111 (617) 423-3990; *The World in Figures.*

Inter-American Development Bank, 1300 New York Avenue, NW, Washington, D.C. 20577 (202) 623-1753; *Economic and Social Progress in Latin America.*

International Monetary Fund, 700 Nineteenth Street, NW, Washington, D.C. 20431 (202) 623-7000; *Direction of Trade Statistics,* and *International Financial Statistics.*

International Rubber Study Group, York House, 8th Floor, Empire Way, Wembley, London HA9 0PA, England; *Rubber Statistical Bulletin.*

Organization of American States (OAS), General Secretariat, Washington, D.C. 20006 (202) 458-3533; *Statistical Bulletin of the OAS.*

Statistical Office of the United Nations, Publishing Service, New York, New York 10017 (800) 253-9646; *Statistical Yearbook for Latin America and the Caribbean,* and *Trade in Manufactures of Developing Countries.*

Times Books, 201 East 50th Street, New York, New York 10022 (212) 751-2600; *The Economist Book of Vital World Statistics.*

The World Bank, 1818 H Street, NW, Washington, D.C. 20433 (202) 477-1234; *World Tables.*

BRAZIL - EXTERNAL FINANCING

Inter-American Development Bank, 1300 New York Avenue, NW, Washington, D.C. 20577 (202) 623-1753; *Economic and Social Progress in Latin America.*

Statistical Office of the United Nations, Publishing Service, New York, New York 10017 (800) 253-9646; *Statistical Yearbook for Latin America and the Caribbean.*

BRAZIL - EXTERNAL INDEBTEDNESS

Euromonitor Publications Limited, 87-88 Turnmill Street, London EC1M 5QU, England; *Third World Economic Handbook.*

Inter-American Development Bank, 1300 New York Avenue, NW, Washington, D.C. 20577 (202) 623-1753; *Economic and Social Progress in Latin America.*

Statistical Office of the United Nations, Publishing Service, New York, New York 10017 (800) 253-9646; *Statistical Yearbook for Latin America and the Caribbean.*

The World Bank, 1818 H Street, NW, Washington, D.C. 20433 (202) 477-1234; *World Tables.*

BRAZIL - EXTERNAL TRADE

Food and Agricultural Organization of the United Nations (FAO) Via delle Terme di Caracalla, 00100 Rome, Italy (Telephone Number in U.S. (202) 653-2400); *The State of Food and Agriculture,* and *Trade Yearbook.*

Gale Research Incorporated, 835 Penobscot Building, Detroit, Michigan 48226 (800) 877-4253; *International Historical Statistics The Americas and Australasia.*

G.K. Hall and Company, 70 Lincoln Street, Boston, Massachusetts 02111 (617) 423-3990; *The World in Figures.*

Inter-American Development Bank, 1300 New York Avenue, NW, Washington, D.C. 20577 (202) 623-1753; *Economic and Social Progress in Latin America.*

Statistical Office of the United Nations, Publishing Service, New York, New York 10017 (800) 253-9646; *Statistical Yearbook,* and *Statistical Yearbook for Latin America and the Caribbean.*

BRAZIL - FABRIC PRODUCTION - See BRAZIL - TEXTILE INDUSTRY

BRAZIL - FAMILY PLANNING

U.C.L.A. Latin American Center Publications, University of California, Los Angeles, California 90024 (310) 825-6634; *Statistical Abstract of Latin America.*

BRAZIL - FARM CROPS - See BRAZIL - CROPS

BRAZIL - FEMALE WORKING POPULATION - See BRAZIL - EMPLOYMENT

BRAZIL - FERTILITY RATES

Facts on File, 460 Park Avenue South, New York, New York 10016 (800) 443-8323; *The New Book of World Rankings.*

Times Books, 201 East 50th Street, New York, New York 10022 (212) 751-2600; *The Economist Book of Vital World Statistics.*

The World Bank, 1818 H Street, NW, Washington, D.C. 20433 (202) 477-1234; *World Tables.*

BRAZIL - FERTILIZER

The Economist Intelligence Unit, 111 West 57th Street, New York, New York 10019 (800) 938-4685; *The New Latin America Market Atlas.*

Food and Agricultural Organization of the United Nations (FAO), Via delle Terme di Caracalla, 00100 Rome, Italy (Telephone Number in U.S. (202) 653-2400); *Fertilizer Yearbook*, and *The State of Food and Agriculture*.

Statistical Office of the United Nations, Publishing Service, New York, New York 10017 (800) 253-9646; *Statistical Yearbook*.

BRAZIL - FETAL MORTALITY

Statistical Office of the United Nations, Publishing Service, New York, New York 10017 (800) 253-9646; *Demographic Yearbook*.

World Health Organization, Office of Publications, Avenue Appia, CH-1211 Geneva 27, Switzerland (Telephone Number in U.S. (518) 436-9686); *World Health Statistics Annual*.

BRAZIL - FIBRE PRODUCTION - See BRAZIL - TEXTILE INDUSTRY

BRAZIL - FILAMENT PRODUCTION - See BRAZIL - TEXTILE INDUSTRY

BRAZIL - FILM - See BRAZIL - MOTION PICTURES

BRAZIL - FINANCE

Facts on File, 460 Park Avenue South, New York, New York 10016 (800) 443-8323; *The New Book of World Rankings*.

Federal Statistical Office, Gustav - Stresemann - Ring 11, D-6200 Wiesbaden, Germany; *Brazil*.

Gale Research Incorporated, 835 Penobscot Building, Detroit, Michigan 48226 (800) 877-4253; *International Historical Statistics The Americas and Australasia*.

G.K. Hall and Company, 70 Lincoln Street, Boston, Massachusetts 02111 (617) 423-3990; *The World in Figures*.

Inter-American Development Bank, 1300 New York Avenue, NW, Washington, D.C. 20577 (202) 623-1753; *Economic and Social Progress in Latin America*, and *International Financial Statistics*.

International Monetary Fund, 700 Nineteenth Street, NW, Washington, D.C. 20431 (202) 623-7000; *Government Finance Statistics Yearbook*.

Organization of American States (OAS), General Secretariat, Washington, D.C. 20006 (202) 458-3533; *Statistical Bulletin of the OAS*.

U.C.L.A. Latin American Center Publications, University of California, Los Angeles, California 90024 (310) 825-6634; *Statistical Abstract of Latin America*.

BRAZIL - FISHERIES

Facts on File, 460 Park Avenue South, New York, New York 10016 (800) 443-8323; *The New Book of World Rankings*.

Federal Statistical Office, Gustav - Stresemann - Ring 11, D-6200 Wiesbaden, Germany; *Brazil*.

Food and Agricultural Organization of the United Nations (FAO) Via delle Terme di Caracalla, 00100 Rome, Italy (Telephone Number in U.S. (202) 653-2400); *The State of Food and Agriculture*, and *Yearbook of Fishery Statistics*.

Inter-American Development Bank, 1300 New York Avenue, NW, Washington, D.C. 20577 (202) 623-1753; *Economic and Social Progress in Latin America*.

Statistical Office of the United Nations, Publishing Service, New York, New York 10017 (800) 253-9646; *Statistical Yearbook*.

U.C.L.A. Latin American Center Publications, University of California, Los Angeles, California 90024 (310) 825-6634; *Statistical Abstract of Latin America*.

BRAZIL - FLOUR PRODUCTION

Statistical Office of the United Nations, Publishing Service, New York, New York 10017 (800) 253-9646; *Statistical Yearbook*.

BRAZIL - FOOD

Food and Agricultural Organization of the United Nations (FAO) Via delle Terme di Caracalla, 00100 Rome, Italy (Telephone Number in U.S. (202) 653-2400); *The State of Food and Agriculture*.

G.K. Hall and Company, 70 Lincoln Street, Boston, Massachusetts 02111 (617) 423-3990; *The World in Figures*.

Statistical Office of the United Nations, Publishing Service, New York, New York 10017 (800) 253-9646; *Production Yearbook*, and *Trade in Manufactures of Developing Countries*.

BRAZIL - FOREIGN AID

G.K. Hall and Company, 70 Lincoln Street, Boston, Massachusetts 02111 (617) 423-3990; *The World in Figures*.

Inter-American Development Bank, 1300 New York Avenue, NW, Washington, D.C. 20577 (202) 623-1753; *Economic and Social Progress in Latin America*.

BRAZIL - FOREIGN DEBT

The Economist Intelligence Unit, 111 West 57th Street, New York, New York 10019 (800) 938-4685; *The New Latin America Market Atlas*.

Inter-American Development Bank, 1300 New York Avenue, NW, Washington, D.C. 20577 (202) 623-1753; *Economic and Social Progress in Latin America*.

International Monetary Fund, 700 Nineteenth Street, NW, Washington, D.C. 20431 (202) 623-7000; *Government Finance Statistics Yearbook*.

BRAZIL - FOREIGN FINANCE

Inter-American Development Bank, 1300 New York Avenue, NW, Washington, D.C. 20577 (202) 623-1753; *Economic and Social Progress in Latin America*.

BRAZIL - FOREIGN INDEBTEDNESS

Inter-American Development Bank, 1300 New York Avenue, NW, Washington, D.C. 20577 (202) 623-1753; *Economic and Social Progress in Latin America*.

Statistical Office of the United Nations, Publishing Service, New York, New York 10017 (800) 253-9646; *Economic Survey of Latin America and the Caribbean*.

BRAZIL - FOREIGN INVESTMENT

The Economist Intelligence Unit, 111 West 57th Street, New York, New York 10019 (800) 938-4685; *The New Latin America Market Atlas.*

BRAZIL - FOREIGN TRADE

The Economist Intelligence Unit, 111 West 57th Street, New York, New York 10019 (800) 938-4685; *The New Latin America Market Atlas.*

Euromonitor Publications Limited, 87-88 Turnmill Street, London EC1M 5QU, England; *International Marketing Data and Statistics,* and *Third World Economic Handbook.*

Facts on File, 460 Park Avenue South, New York, New York 10016 (800) 443-8323; *The New Book of World Rankings.*

Federal Statistical Office, Gustav - Stresemann - Ring 11, D-6200 Wiesbaden, Germany; *Brazil.*

Food and Agricultural Organization of the United Nations (FAO) Via delle Terme di Caracalla, 00100 Rome, Italy (Telephone Number in U.S. (202) 653-2400); *The State of Food and Agriculture.*

G.K. Hall and Company, 70 Lincoln Street, Boston, Massachusetts 02111 (617) 423-3990; *The World in Figures.*

Inter-American Development Bank, 1300 New York Avenue, NW, Washington, D.C. 20577 (202) 623-1753; *Economic and Social Progress in Latin America.*

Statistical Office of the United Nations, Publishing Service, New York, New York 10017 (800) 253-9646; *Economic Survey of Latin America and the Caribbean, International Trade Statistics Yearbook,* and *Statistical Yearbook.*

U.C.L.A. Latin American Center Publications, University of California, Los Angeles, California 90024 (310) 825-6634; *Statistical Abstract of Latin America.*

The World Bank, 1818 H Street, NW, Washington, D.C. 20433 (202) 477-1234 (202) 477-1234; *World Tables.*

World Bureau of Metal Statistics, 27-A High Street, Ware Hert SG12 9BA, England; *World Metal Statistics.*

BRAZIL - FORESTRY AND FOREST PRODUCTS

The Economist Intelligence Unit, 111 West 57th Street, New York, New York 10019 (800) 938-4685; *The New Latin America Market Atlas.*

Euromonitor Publications Limited, 87-88 Turnmill Street, London EC1M 5QU, England; *Third World Economic Handbook.*

Facts on File, 460 Park Avenue South, New York, New York 10016 (800) 443-8323; *The New Book of World Rankings.*

Federal Statistical Office, Gustav - Stresemann - Ring 11, D-6200 Wiesbaden, Germany; *Brazil.*

Food and Agricultural Organization of the United Nations (FAO) Via delle Terme di Caracalla, 00100 Rome, Italy (Telephone Number in U.S. (202) 653-2400); *The State of Food and Agriculture,* and *Yearbook of Forest Products.*

Forest and Paper Association, 1250 Connecticut Avenue, NW, Washington, D.C. 20036 (202) 463-2455; *Wood Pulp and Fiber Statistics.*

G.K. Hall and Company, 70 Lincoln Street, Boston, Massachusetts 02111 (617) 423-3990; *The World in Figures.*

Inter-American Development Bank, 1300 New York Avenue, NW, Washington, D.C. 20577 (202) 623-1753; *Economic and Social Progress in Latin America.*

U.C.L.A. Latin American Center Publications, University of California, Los Angeles, California 90024 (310) 825-6634; *Statistical Abstract of Latin America.*

United Nations Educational, Scientific and Cultural Organization (UNESCO), 7 Place de Fontenoy, F-75700 Paris, France (Telephone Number in U.S. (212) 963-5981); *Statistical Yearbook.*

BRAZIL - FURNITURE AND WOOD PRODUCTS - EXPORTS AND IMPORTS

Statistical Office of the United Nations, Publishing Service, New York, New York 10017 (800) 253-9646; *Trade in Manufactures of Developing Countries.*

BRAZIL - GARLIC PRODUCTION - See BRAZIL - CROPS

BRAZIL - GAS - See BRAZIL - MINING AND MINERAL PRODUCTS

BRAZIL - GENERAL INDUSTRIAL STATISTICS

Statistical Office of the United Nations, Publishing Service, New York, New York 10017 (800) 253-9646; *Industrial Statistics Yearbook.*

BRAZIL - GENERAL MORTALITY

Statistical Office of the United Nations, Publishing Service, New York, New York 10017 (800) 253-9646; *Demographic Yearbook.*

World Health Organization, Office of Publications, Avenue Appia, CH-1211 Geneva 27, Switzerland (Telephone Number in U.S. (518) 436-9686); *World Health Statistics Annual.*

BRAZIL - GEOGRAPHIC DATA

Facts on File, 460 Park Avenue South, New York, New York 10016 (800) 443-8323; *The New Book of World Rankings.*

U.C.L.A. Latin American Center Publications, University of California, Los Angeles, California 90024 (310) 825-6634; *Statistical Abstract of Latin America.*

BRAZIL - GOATS - See BRAZIL - LIVESTOCK AND POULTRY

BRAZIL - GOLD HOLDINGS

International Monetary Fund, 700 Nineteenth Street, NW, Washington, D.C. 20431 (202) 623-7000; *International Financial Statistics.*

Statistical Office of the United Nations, Publishing Service, New York, New York 10017 (800) 253-9646; *Statistical Yearbook.*

The World Bank, 1818 H Street, NW, Washington, D.C. 20433 (202) 477-1234; *World Tables.*

BRAZIL - GOLD PRODUCTION AND CONSUMPTION - See BRAZIL - MINING AND MINERAL PRODUCTS

BRAZIL - GOLD RESERVES

The Economist Intelligence Unit, 111 West 57th Street, New York, New York 10019 (800) 938-4685; *The New Latin America Market Atlas*.

BRAZIL - GOVERNMENT

G.K. Hall and Company, 70 Lincoln Street, Boston, Massachusetts 02111 (617) 423-3990; *The World in Figures*.

Inter-American Development Bank, 1300 New York Avenue, NW, Washington, D.C. 20577 (202) 623-1753; *Economic and Social Progress in Latin America*.

BRAZIL - GOVERNMENT BONDS - See BRAZIL - BONDS

BRAZIL - GOVERNMENT CONSUMPTION

Inter-American Development Bank, 1300 New York Avenue, NW, Washington, D.C. 20577 (202) 623-1753; *Economic and Social Progress in Latin America*.

BRAZIL - GOVERNMENT EXPENDITURES

Euromonitor Publications Limited, 87-88 Turnmill Street, London EC1M 5QU, England; *Third World Economic Handbook*.

Inter-American Development Bank, 1300 New York Avenue, NW, Washington, D.C. 20577 (202) 623-1753; *Economic and Social Progress in Latin America*.

International Monetary Fund, 700 Nineteenth Street, NW, Washington, D.C. 20431 (202) 623-7000; *Government Finance Statistics Yearbook*.

Times Books, 201 East 50th Street, New York, New York 10022 (212) 751-2600; *The Economist Book of Vital World Statistics*.

The World Bank, 1818 H Street, NW, Washington, D.C. 20433 (202) 477-1234; *World Tables*.

BRAZIL - GOVERNMENT FINANCES

Inter-American Development Bank, 1300 New York Avenue, NW, Washington, D.C. 20577 (202) 623-1753; *Economic and Social Progress in Latin America*.

International Monetary Fund, 700 Nineteenth Street, NW, Washington, D.C. 20431 (202) 623-7000; *International Financial Statistics*.

Statistical Office of the United Nations, Publishing Service, New York, New York 10017 (800) 253-9646; *Statistical Yearbook*.

BRAZIL - GOVERNMENT REVENUE

Inter-American Development Bank, 1300 New York Avenue, NW, Washington, D.C. 20577 (202) 623-1753; *Economic and Social Progress in Latin America*.

International Monetary Fund, 700 Nineteenth Street, NW, Washington, D.C. 20431 (202) 623-7000; *Government Finance Statistics Yearbook*.

Times Books, 201 East 50th Street, New York, New York 10022 (212) 751-2600; *The Economist Book of Vital World Statistics*.

U.C.L.A. Latin American Center Publications, University of California, Los Angeles, California 90024 (310) 825-6634; *Statistical Abstract of Latin America*.

The World Bank, 1818 H Street, NW, Washington, D.C. 20433 (202) 477-1234; *World Tables*.

BRAZIL - GRAIN PRODUCTION - See BRAZIL - CROPS

BRAZIL - GRANTS

International Monetary Fund, 700 Nineteenth Street, NW, Washington, D.C. 20431 (202) 623-7000; *Government Finance Statistics Yearbook*.

BRAZIL - GROSS DOMESTIC PRODUCT

The Economist Intelligence Unit, 111 West 57th Street, New York, New York 10019 (800) 938-4685; *The New Latin America Market Atlas*, and *The World Market Atlas*.

Euromonitor Publications Limited, 87-88 Turnmill Street, London EC1M 5QU, England; *International Marketing Data and Statistics*, and *Third World Economic Handbook*.

Facts on File, 460 Park Avenue South, New York, New York 10016 (800) 443-8323; *The New Book of World Rankings*.

G.K. Hall and Company, 70 Lincoln Street, Boston, Massachusetts 02111 (617) 423-3990; *The World in Figures*.

Inter-American Development Bank, 1300 New York Avenue, NW, Washington, D.C. 20577 (202) 623-1753; *Economic and Social Progress in Latin America*.

Organization of American States (OAS), General Secretariat, Washington, D.C. 20006 (202) 458-3533; *Statistical Bulletin of the OAS*.

Statistical Office of the United Nations, Publishing Service, New York, New York 10017 (800) 253-9646; *Statistical Yearbook*, and *Statistical Yearbook for Latin America and the Caribbean*.

Times Books, 201 East 50th Street, New York, New York 10022 (212) 751-2600; *The Economist Book of Vital World Statistics*.

U.C.L.A. Latin American Center Publications, University of California, Los Angeles, California 90024 (310) 825-6634; *Statistical Abstract of Latin America*.

The World Bank, 1818 H Street, NW, Washington, D.C. 20433 (202) 477-1234; *World Tables*.

BRAZIL - GROSS INDUSTRIAL PRODUCT

Euromonitor Publications Limited, 87-88 Turnmill Street, London EC1M 5QU, England; *Third World Economic Handbook*.

BRAZIL - GROSS NATIONAL PRODUCT

Euromonitor Publications Limited, 87-88 Turnmill Street, London EC1M 5QU, England; *International Marketing Data and Statistics*, and *Third World Economic Handbook*.

Inter-American Development Bank, 1300 New York Avenue, NW, Washington, D.C. 20577 (202) 623-1753; *Economic and Social*

Progress in Latin America.

U.S. Arms Control and Disarmament Agency, 320 Twenty-first Street, NW, Washington, D.C. 20451 (202) 647-8677; *World Military Expenditures and Arms Transfers.*

The World Bank, 1818 H Street, NW, Washington, D.C. 20433 (202) 477-1234; *World Tables.*

BRAZIL - GROUNDNUTS PRODUCTION - See BRAZIL - CROPS

BRAZIL - HEALTH

The Economist Intelligence Unit, 111 West 57th Street, New York, New York 10019 (800) 938-4685; *The New Latin America Market Atlas.*

Facts on File, 460 Park Avenue South, New York, New York 10016 (800) 443-8323; *The New Book of World Rankings.*

Federal Statistical Office, Gustav - Stresemann - Ring 11, D-6200 Wiesbaden, Germany; *Brazil.*

G.K. Hall and Company, 70 Lincoln Street, Boston, Massachusetts 02111 (617) 423-3990; *The World in Figures.*

Statistical Office of the United Nations, Publishing Service, New York, New York 10017 (800) 253-9646; *Statistical Yearbook.*

Times Books, 201 East 50th Street, New York, New York 10022 (212) 751-2600; *The Economist Book of Vital World Statistics.*

U.C.L.A. Latin American Center Publications, University of California, Los Angeles, California 90024 (310) 825-6634; *Statistical Abstract of Latin America.*

World Health Organization, Office of Publications, Avenue Appia, CH-1211 Geneva 27, Switzerland (Telephone Number in U.S. (518) 436-9686); *World Health Statistics Annual.*

BRAZIL - HEALTH EXPENDITURES

International Monetary Fund, 700 Nineteenth Street, NW, Washington, D.C. 20431 (202) 623-7000; *Government Finance Statistics Yearbook.*

BRAZIL - HIDE PRODUCTION

Food and Agricultural Organization of the United Nations (FAO), Via delle Terme di Caracalla, 00100 Rome, Italy (Telephone Number in U.S. (202) 653-2400); *Production Yearbook.*

BRAZIL - HIGHWAYS

The Economist Intelligence Unit, 111 West 57th Street, New York, New York 10019 (800) 938-4685; *The New Latin America Market Atlas.*

G.K. Hall and Company, 70 Lincoln Street, Boston, Massachusetts 02111 (617) 423-3990; *The World in Figures.*

International Road Federation, 525 School Street, SW, Washington, D.C. 20024 (202) 554-2106; *World Road Statistics.*

BRAZIL - HORSES - See BRAZIL - LIVESTOCK AND POULTRY

BRAZIL - HOURS OF WORK - See BRAZIL - EMPLOYMENT

BRAZIL - HOUSING AND HOUSING UNITS

Euromonitor Publications Limited, 87-88 Turnmill Street, London EC1M 5QU, England; *Third World Economic Handbook.*

Facts on File, 460 Park Avenue South, New York, New York 10016 (800) 443-8323; *The New Book of World Rankings.*

Statistical Office of the United Nations, Publishing Service, New York, New York 10017 (800) 253-9646; *Statistical Yearbook for Latin America and the Caribbean.*

U.C.L.A. Latin American Center Publications, University of California, Los Angeles, California 90024 (310) 825-6634; *Statistical Abstract of Latin America.*

BRAZIL - HOUSING EXPENDITURES

International Monetary Fund, 700 Nineteenth Street, NW, Washington, D.C. 20431 (202) 623-7000; *Government Finance Statistics Yearbook.*

BRAZIL - HYDROCHLORIC ACID PRODUCTION

Statistical Office of the United Nations, Publishing Service, New York, New York 10017 (800) 253-9646; *Statistical Yearbook.*

BRAZIL - ILLITERACY RATES

The Economist Intelligence Unit, 111 West 57th Street, New York, New York 10019 (800) 938-4685; *The New Latin America Market Atlas.*

BRAZIL - ILLITERATE POPULATION

The Economist Intelligence Unit, 111 West 57th Street, New York, New York 10019 (800) 938-4685; *The World Market Atlas.*

G.K. Hall and Company, 70 Lincoln Street, Boston, Massachusetts 02111 (617) 423-3990; *The World in Figures.*

Statistical Office of the United Nations, Publishing Service, New York, New York 10017 (800) 253-9646; *Statistical Yearbook for Latin America and the Caribbean.*

United Nations Educational, Scientific and Cultural Organization (UNESCO), 7 Place de Fontenoy, F-75700 Paris, France (Telephone Number in U.S. (212) 963-5981); *Statistical Yearbook.*

BRAZIL - IMMIGRATION

U.C.L.A. Latin American Center Publications, University of California, Los Angeles, California 90024 (310) 825-6634; *Statistical Abstract of Latin America.*

BRAZIL - IMPORTS

American Automobile Manufacturers Association, 1401 H Street, NW, Suite 900, Washington, D.C. 20005 (202) 326-5500; *World Motor Vehicle Data.*

The Economist Intelligence Unit, 111 West 57th Street, New York, New York 10019 (800) 938-4685; *The New Latin America Market Atlas*, and *The World Market Atlas.*

Euromonitor Publications Limited, 87-88 Turnmill Street, London EC1M 5QU, England; *International Marketing Data and Statistics*, and *Third World Economic Handbook.*

Food and Agricultural Organization of the United Nations (FAO) Via delle Terme di Caracalla, 00100 Rome, Italy (Telephone Number in U.S. (202) 653-2400); *The State of Food and Agriculture.*

G.K. Hall and Company, 70 Lincoln Street, Boston, Massachusetts 02111 (617) 423-3990; *The World in Figures.*

Inter-American Development Bank, 1300 New York Avenue, NW, Washington, D.C. 20577 (202) 623-1753; *Economic and Social Progress in Latin America.*

International Monetary Fund, 700 Nineteenth Street, NW, Washington, D.C. 20431 (202) 623-7000; *Direction of Trade Statistics, Government Finance Statistics Yearbook,* and *International Financial Statistics.*

International Rubber Study Group, York House, 8th Floor, Empire Way, Wembley, London HA9 0PA, England; *Rubber Statistical Bulletin.*

Organization of American States (OAS), General Secretariat, Washington, D.C. 20006 (202) 458-3533; *Statistical Bulletin of the OAS.*

Statistical Office of the United Nations, Publishing Service, New York, New York 10017 (800) 253-9646; *Statistical Yearbook for Latin America and the Caribbean,* and *Trade in Manufactures of Developing Countries.*

Times Books, 201 East 50th Street, New York, New York 10022 (212) 751-2600; *The Economist Book of Vital World Statistics.*

The World Bank, 1818 H Street, NW, Washington, D.C. 20433 (202) 477-1234; *World Tables.*

BRAZIL - INCOME DISTRIBUTION

Statistical Office of the United Nations, Publishing Service, New York, New York 10017 (800) 253-9646; *Statistical Yearbook for Latin America and the Caribbean.*

U.C.L.A. Latin American Center Publications, University of California, Los Angeles, California 90024 (310) 825-6634; *Statistical Abstract of Latin America.*

BRAZIL - INCOME TAXES - See BRAZIL - TAXATION

BRAZIL - INDUSTRIAL METALS PRODUCTION - See BRAZIL - MINING AND MINERAL PRODUCTS

BRAZIL - INDUSTRY

Euromonitor Publications Limited, 87-88 Turnmill Street, London EC1M 5QU, England; *Third World Economic Handbook.*

Facts on File, 460 Park Avenue South, New York, New York 10016 (800) 443-8323; *The New Book of World Rankings.*

Federal Statistical Office, Gustav - Stresemann - Ring 11, D-6200 Wiesbaden, Germany; *Brazil.*

Gale Research Incorporated, 835 Penobscot Building, Detroit, Michigan 48226 (800) 877-4253; *International Historical Statistics The Americas and Australasia.*

G.K. Hall and Company, 70 Lincoln Street, Boston, Massachusetts 02111 (617) 423-3990; *The World in Figures.*

International Labour Office, I.L.O. Publications, CH-1211, Geneva 22, Switzerland; *Yearbook of Labour Statistics.*

Statistical Office of the United Nations, Publishing Service, New York, New York 10017 (800) 253-9646; *Economic Survey of Latin America and the Caribbean.*

U.C.L.A. Latin American Center Publications, University of California, Los Angeles, California 90024 (310) 825-6634; *Statistical Abstract of Latin America.*

The World Bank, 1818 H Street, NW, Washington, D.C. 20433 (202) 477-1234; *World Tables.*

World Intellectual Property Organization, 34 Chemin des Colombettes, CH-1211 Geneva 20. Switzerland; *Industrial Property Statistics.*

BRAZIL - INFANT AND MATERNAL MORTALITY

The Economist Intelligence Unit, 111 West 57th Street, New York, New York 10019 (800) 938-4685; *The New Latin America Market Atlas.*

Statistical Office of the United Nations, Publishing Service, New York, New York 10017 (800) 253-9646; *Demographic Yearbook.*

Times Books, 201 East 50th Street, New York, New York 10022 (212) 751-2600; *The Economist Book of Vital World Statistics.*

The World Bank, 1818 H Street, NW, Washington, D.C. 20433 (202) 477-1234; *World Tables.*

World Health Organization, Office of Publications, Avenue Appia, CH-1211 Geneva 27, Switzerland (Telephone Number in U.S. (518) 436-9686); *World Health Statistics Annual.*

BRAZIL - INFLATIONARY FACTORS

Statistical Office of the United Nations, Publishing Service, New York, New York 10017 (800) 253-9646; *Economic Survey of Latin America and the Caribbean.*

BRAZIL - INTEREST RATES

Inter-American Development Bank, 1300 New York Avenue, NW, Washington, D.C. 20577 (202) 623-1753; *Economic and Social Progress in Latin America.*

Organization of American States (OAS), General Secretariat, Washington, D.C. 20006 (202) 458-3533; *Statistical Bulletin of the OAS.*

BRAZIL - INTERNAL TRADE

Statistical Office of the United Nations, Publishing Service, New York, New York 10017 (800) 253-9646; *Statistical Yearbook.*

BRAZIL - INTERNATIONAL FINANCE

Inter-American Development Bank, 1300 New York Avenue, NW, Washington, D.C. 20577 (202) 623-1753; *Economic and Social Progress in Latin America.*

U.C.L.A. Latin American Center Publications, University of California, Los Angeles, California 90024 (310) 825-6634; *Statistical Abstract of Latin America.*

BRAZIL - INTERNATIONAL LIQUIDITY

Inter-American Development Bank, 1300 New York Avenue, NW, Washington, D.C. 20577 (202) 623-1753; *Economic and Social Progress in Latin America.*

International Monetary Fund, 700 Nineteenth Street, NW, Washington, D.C. 20431 (202) 623-7000; *International Financial Statistics.*

BRAZIL - INTERNATIONAL RESERVES

Organization of American States (OAS), General Secretariat, Washington, D.C. 20006 (202) 458-3533; *Statistical Bulletin of the OAS.*

BRAZIL - INTERNATIONAL RESERVES EXCLUDING GOLD

Inter-American Development Bank, 1300 New York Avenue, NW, Washington, D.C. 20577 (202) 623-1753; *Economic and Social Progress in Latin America.*

The World Bank, 1818 H Street, NW, Washington, D.C. 20433 (202) 477-1234; *World Tables.*

BRAZIL - INTERNATIONAL STATISTICS

Inter-American Development Bank, 1300 New York Avenue, NW, Washington, D.C. 20577 (202) 623-1753; *Economic and Social Progress in Latin America.*

U.C.L.A. Latin American Center Publications, University of California, Los Angeles, California 90024 (310) 825-6634; *Statistical Abstract of Latin America.*

BRAZIL - INVESTMENT

Inter-American Development Bank, 1300 New York Avenue, NW, Washington, D.C. 20577 (202) 623-1753; *Economic and Social Progress in Latin America.*

International Monetary Fund, 700 Nineteenth Street, NW, Washington, D.C. 20431 (202) 623-7000; *International Financial Statistics.*

Statistical Office of the United Nations, Publishing Service, New York, New York 10017 (800) 253-9646; *Statistical Yearbook for Latin America and the Caribbean.*

BRAZIL - IRON ORE AND IRON ORE - See BRAZIL - MINING AND MINERAL PRODUCTS

BRAZIL - IRRIGATION

Euromonitor Publications Limited, 87-88 Turnmill Street, London EC1M 5QU, England; *International Marketing Data and Statistics.*

Inter-American Development Bank, 1300 New York Avenue, NW, Washington, D.C. 20577 (202) 623-1753; *Economic and Social Progress in Latin America.*

BRAZIL - JUTE PRODUCTION - See BRAZIL - CROPS

BRAZIL - LABOR FORCE

The Economist Intelligence Unit, 111 West 57th Street, New York, New York 10019 (800) 938-4685; *The New Latin America Market Atlas.*

Euromonitor Publications Limited, 87-88 Turnmill Street, London EC1M 5QU, England; *International Marketing Data and Statistics.*

Facts on File, 460 Park Avenue South, New York, New York 10016 (800) 443-8323; *The New Book of World Rankings.*

Food and Agricultural Organization of the United Nations (FAO) Via delle Terme di Caracalla, 00100 Rome, Italy (Telephone Number in U.S. (202) 653-2400); *The State of Food and Agriculture.*

Gale Research Incorporated, 835 Penobscot Building, Detroit, Michigan 48226 (800) 877-4253; *International Historical Statistics The Americas and Australasia.*

G.K. Hall and Company, 70 Lincoln Street, Boston, Massachusetts 02111 (617) 423-3990; *The World in Figures.*

Times Books, 201 East 50th Street, New York, New York 10022 (212) 751-2600; *The Economist Book of Vital World Statistics.*

The World Bank, 1818 H Street, NW, Washington, D.C. 20433 (202) 477-1234; *World Tables.*

BRAZIL - LABOR PRODUCTIVITY

International Labour Office, I.L.O. Publications, CH-1211, Geneva 22, Switzerland; *Yearbook of Labour Statistics.*

BRAZIL - LAND AREA

The Economist Intelligence Unit, 111 West 57th Street, New York, New York 10019 (800) 938-4685; *The New Latin America Market Atlas.*

BRAZIL - LAND USE

Euromonitor Publications Limited, 87-88 Turnmill Street, London EC1M 5QU, England; *International Marketing Data and Statistics.*

Food and Agricultural Organization of the United Nations (FAO), Via delle Terme di Caracalla, 00100 Rome, Italy (Telephone Number in U.S. (202) 653-2400); *Production Yearbook.*

G.K. Hall and Company, 70 Lincoln Street, Boston, Massachusetts 02111 (617) 423-3990; *The World in Figures.*

Inter-American Development Bank, 1300 New York Avenue, NW, Washington, D.C. 20577 (202) 623-1753; *Economic and Social Progress in Latin America.*

BRAZIL - LEAD AND LEAD ORE - See BRAZIL - MINING AND MINERAL PRODUCTS

BRAZIL - LEATHER AND FOOTWEAR - EXPORTS AND IMPORTS

Statistical Office of the United Nations, Publishing Service, New York, New York 10017 (800) 253-9646; *Trade in Manufactures of Developing Countries.*

BRAZIL - LIBRARIES

Facts on File, 460 Park Avenue South, New York, New York 10016 (800) 443-8323; *The New Book of World Rankings.*

United Nations Educational, Scientific and Cultural Organization (UNESCO), 7 Place de Fontenoy, F-75700 Paris, France (Telephone Number in U.S. (212) 963-5981); *Statistical Yearbook.*

BRAZIL - LIFE EXPECTANCY RATE

The Economist Intelligence Unit, 111 West 57th Street, New York, New York 10019 (800) 938-4685; *The New Latin America Market Atlas.*

BRAZIL - LIVESTOCK AND POULTRY

Commodity Research Bureau, Incorporated, 75 Wall Street, New York, New York 10005 (212) 504-7754; *Commodity Year Book.*

Euromonitor Publications Limited, 87-88 Turnmill Street, London EC1M 5QU, England; *International Marketing Data and Statistics.*

Facts on File, 460 Park Avenue South, New York, New York 10016 (800) 443-8323; *The New Book of World Rankings.*

Food and Agricultural Organization of the United Nations (FAO), Via delle Terme di Caracalla, 00100 Rome, Italy (Telephone Number in U.S. (202) 653-2400); *Production Yearbook,* and *The State of Food and Agriculture.*

G.K. Hall and Company, 70 Lincoln Street, Boston, Massachusetts 02111 (617) 423-3990; *The World in Figures.*

Statistical Office of the United Nations, Publishing Service, New York, New York 10017 (800) 253-9646; *Statistical Yearbook.*

BRAZIL - LIVING LEVELS

G.K. Hall and Company, 70 Lincoln Street, Boston, Massachusetts 02111 (617) 423-3990; *The World in Figures.*

Statistical Office of the United Nations, Publishing Service, New York, New York 10017 (800) 253-9646; *Statistical Yearbook for Latin America and the Caribbean.*

Times Books, 201 East 50th Street, New York, New York 10022 (212) 751-2600; *The Economist Book of Vital World Statistics.*

BRAZIL - MAIL - NUMBER OF PIECES SENT OR RECEIVED

Statistical Office of the United Nations, Publishing Service, New York, New York 10017 (800) 253-9646; *Statistical Yearbook.*

BRAZIL - MAIN ECONOMIC INDICATORS - See BRAZIL - ECONOMY

BRAZIL - MANGANESE ORE PRODUCTION AND CONSUMPTION - See BRAZIL - MINING AND MINERAL PRODUCTS

BRAZIL - MANUFACTURING

American Automobile Manufacturers Association, 1401 H Street, NW, Suite 900, Washington, D.C. 20005 (202) 326-5500; *World Motor Vehicle Data.*

The Economist Intelligence Unit, 111 West 57th Street, New York, New York 10019 (800) 938-4685; *The New Latin America Market Atlas.*

Euromonitor Publications Limited, 87-88 Turnmill Street, London EC1M 5QU, England; *Third World Economic Handbook.*

Facts on File, 460 Park Avenue South, New York, New York 10016 (800) 443-8323; *The New Book of World Rankings.*

G.K. Hall and Company, 70 Lincoln Street, Boston, Massachusetts 02111 (617) 423-3990; *The World in Figures.*

Inter-American Development Bank, 1300 New York Avenue, NW, Washington, D.C. 20577 (202) 623-1753; *Economic and Social Progress in Latin America.*

Statistical Office of the United Nations, Publishing Service, New York, New York 10017 (800) 253-9646; *Statistical Yearbook,* and *Statistical Yearbook for Latin America and the Caribbean.*

Times Books, 201 East 50th Street, New York, New York 10022 (212) 751-2600; *The Economist Book of Vital World Statistics.*

The World Bank, 1818 H Street, NW, Washington, D.C. 20433 (202) 477-1234; *World Tables.*

BRAZIL - MARRIAGE RATES

Facts on File, 460 Park Avenue South, New York, New York 10016 (800) 443-8323; *The New Book of World Rankings.*

Statistical Office of the United Nations, Publishing Service, New York, New York 10017 (800) 253-9646; *Demographic Yearbook.*

BRAZIL - MEAT PRODUCTION - See BRAZIL - LIVESTOCK AND POULTRY

BRAZIL - MEDICAL PERSONNEL

U.C.L.A. Latin American Center Publications, University of California, Los Angeles, California 90024 (310) 825-6634; *Statistical Abstract of Latin America.*

BRAZIL - MERCHANT SHIPPING

G.K. Hall and Company, 70 Lincoln Street, Boston, Massachusetts 02111 (617) 423-3990; *The World in Figures.*

Lloyd's Register of Shipping, 17 Battery Place, New York, New York 10004 (212) 425-8050; *Register of Ships.*

Statistical Office of the United Nations, Publishing Service, New York, New York 10017 (800) 253-9646; *Statistical Yearbook.*

Times Books, 201 East 50th Street, New York, New York 10022 (212) 751-2600; *The Economist Book of Vital World Statistics.*

U.S. Department of Transportation, Maritime Administration, 400 Seventh Street, SW, Washington, D.C. 20590; *A Statistical Analysis of the World's Merchant Fleets.*

BRAZIL - MILITARY

The Economist Intelligence Unit, 111 West 57th Street, New York, New York 10019 (800) 938-4685; *The New Latin America Market Atlas.*

G.K. Hall and Company, 70 Lincoln Street, Boston, Massachusetts 02111 (617) 423-3990; *The World in Figures.*

The International Institute for Strategic Studies, 23 Tavistock Street, London WC2E 7NQ, England; *The Military Balance.*

U.C.L.A. Latin American Center Publications, University of California, Los Angeles, California 90024 (310) 825-6634; *Statistical Abstract of Latin America.*

U.S. Arms Control and Disarmament Agency, 320 Twenty-first Street, NW, Washington, D.C. 20451 (202) 647-8677; *World Military Expenditures and Arms Transfers.*

BRAZIL - MILK PRODUCTION - See BRAZIL - DAIRY PRODUCTS

BRAZIL - MINING AND MINERAL PRODUCTS

Commodity Research Bureau, Incorporated, 75 Wall Street, New York, New York 10005 (212) 504-7754; *Commodity Year Book.*

The Economist Intelligence Unit, 111 West 57th Street, New York, New York 10019 (800) 938-4685; *The New Latin America Market Atlas.*

Euromonitor Publications Limited, 87-88 Turnmill Street, London EC1M 5QU, England; *Third World Economic Handbook.*

Facts on File, 460 Park Avenue South, New York, New York 10016 (800) 443-8323; *The New Book of World Rankings.*

G.K. Hall and Company, 70 Lincoln Street, Boston, Massachusetts 02111 (617) 423-3990; *The World in Figures.*

Inter-American Development Bank, 1300 New York Avenue, NW, Washington, D.C. 20577 (202) 623-1753; *Economic and Social Progress in Latin America.*

International Monetary Fund, 700 Nineteenth Street, NW, Washington, D.C. 20431 (202) 623-7000; *International Financial Statistics.*

Organization of American States (OAS), General Secretariat, Washington, D.C. 20006 (202) 458-3533; *Statistical Bulletin of the OAS.*

Penn Well Publishing Company, 1421 South Sheridan Road, P.O. Box 1260, Tulsa, Oklahoma 74101 (800) 752-9764; *International Energy Statistics Sourcebook.*

Statistical Office of the United Nations, Publishing Service, New York, New York 10017; *Statistical Yearbook,* and *Statistical Yearbook for Latin America and the Caribbean.*

U.C.L.A. Latin American Center Publications, University of California, Los Angeles, California 90024 (310) 825-6634; *Statistical Abstract of Latin America.*

World Bureau of Metal Statistics, 27-A High Street, Ware Hert SG12 9BA, England; *World Metal Statistics.*

BRAZIL - MOLASSES PRODUCTION - See BRAZIL - CROPS

BRAZIL - MOLYBDENUM AND MOLYBDENUM ORE - See BRAZIL - MINING AND MINERAL PRODUCTS

BRAZIL - MONEY EXCHANGE RATE

Euromonitor Publications Limited, 87-88 Turnmill Street, London EC1M 5QU, England; *International Marketing Data and Statistics.*

Inter-American Development Bank, 1300 New York Avenue, NW, Washington, D.C. 20577 (202) 623-1753; *Economic and Social Progress in Latin America.*

International Monetary Fund, 700 Nineteenth Street, NW, Washington, D.C. 20431 (202) 623-7000; *International Financial Statistics.*

Statistical Office of the United Nations, Publishing Service, New York, New York 10017 (800) 253-9646; *Statistical Yearbook.*

BRAZIL - MONEY RATES - MARKET

Inter-American Development Bank, 1300 New York Avenue, NW, Washington, D.C. 20577 (202) 623-1753; *Economic and Social Progress in Latin America.*

BRAZIL - MONEY RESERVES

Euromonitor Publications Limited, 87-88 Turnmill Street, London EC1M 5QU, England; *International Marketing Data and Statistics.*

Inter-American Development Bank, 1300 New York Avenue, NW, Washington, D.C. 20577 (202) 623-1753; *Economic and Social Progress in Latin America.*

BRAZIL - MONEY SUPPLY

Euromonitor Publications Limited, 87-88 Turnmill Street, London EC1M 5QU, England; *International Marketing Data and Statistics.*

G.K. Hall and Company, 70 Lincoln Street, Boston, Massachusetts 02111 (617) 423-3990; *The World in Figures.*

Inter-American Development Bank, 1300 New York Avenue, NW, Washington, D.C. 20577 (202) 623-1753; *Economic and Social Progress in Latin America.*

International Monetary Fund, 700 Nineteenth Street, NW, Washington, D.C. 20431 (202) 623-7000; *International Financial Statistics.*

Statistical Office of the United Nations, Publishing Service, New York, New York 10017 (800) 253-9646; *Statistical Yearbook.*

U.C.L.A. Latin American Center Publications, University of California, Los Angeles, California 90024 (310) 825-6634; *Statistical Abstract of Latin America.*

The World Bank, 1818 H Street, NW, Washington, D.C. 20433 (202) 477-1234; *World Tables.*

BRAZIL - MOTION PICTURES

Statistical Office of the United Nations, Publishing Service, New York, New York 10017 (800) 253-9646; *Statistical Yearbook.*

United Nations Educational, Scientific and Cultural Organization (UNESCO), 7 Place de Fontenoy, F-75700 Paris, France (Telephone Number in U.S. (212) 963-5981); *Statistical Yearbook.*

BRAZIL - MOTOR VEHICLE PRODUCTION AND ASSEMBLY

American Automobile Manufacturers Association, 1401 H Street, NW, Suite 900, Washington, D.C. 20005 (202) 326-5500; *World Motor Vehicle Data.*

Statistical Office of the United Nations, Publishing Service, New York, New York 10017 (800) 253-9646; *Statistical Yearbook.*

BRAZIL - MOTOR VEHICLE TAXES - See BRAZIL - TAXATION

BRAZIL - MOTOR VEHICLES IN USE

American Automobile Manufacturers Association, 1401 H Street, NW, Suite 900, Washington, D.C. 20005 (202) 326-5500; *World Motor Vehicle Data.*

The Economist Intelligence Unit, 111 West 57th Street, New York, New York 10019 (800) 938-4685; *The New Latin America Market*

Atlas.

G.K. Hall and Company, 70 Lincoln Street, Boston, Massachusetts 02111 (617) 423-3990; *The World in Figures.*

International Road Federation, 525 School Street, SW, Washington, D.C. 20024 (202) 554-2106; *World Road Statistics.*

Statistical Office of the United Nations, Publishing Service, New York, New York 10017 (800) 253-9646; *Statistical Yearbook.*

Times Books, 201 East 50th Street, New York, New York 10022 (212) 751-2600; *The Economist Book of Vital World Statistics.*

BRAZIL - MULES - See BRAZIL - LIVESTOCK AND POULTRY

BRAZIL - MUSEUMS

Facts on File, 460 Park Avenue South, New York, New York 10016 (800) 443-8323; *The New Book of World Rankings.*

United Nations Educational, Scientific and Cultural Organization (UNESCO), 7 Place de Fontenoy, F-75700 Paris, France (Telephone Number in U.S. (212) 963-5981); *Statistical Yearbook.*

BRAZIL - NATALITY - See BRAZIL - BIRTH RATE

BRAZIL - NATIONAL ACCOUNTS

Federal Statistical Office, Gustav - Stresemann - Ring 11, D-6200 Wiesbaden, Germany; *Brazil.*

Gale Research Incorporated, 835 Penobscot Building, Detroit, Michigan 48226 (800) 877-4253; *International Historical Statistics The Americas and Australasia.*

Inter-American Development Bank, 1300 New York Avenue, NW, Washington, D.C. 20577 (202) 623-1753; *Economic and Social Progress in Latin America.*

Organization of American States (OAS), General Secretariat, Washington, D.C. 20006 (202) 458-3533; *Statistical Bulletin of the OAS.*

Statistical Office of the United Nations, Publishing Service, New York, New York 10017 (800) 253-9646; *National Accounts Statistics,* and *Statistical Yearbook.*

U.C.L.A. Latin American Center Publications, University of California, Los Angeles, California 90024 (310) 825-6634; *Statistical Abstract of Latin America.*

BRAZIL - NATIONAL INCOME

Facts on File, 460 Park Avenue South, New York, New York 10016 (800) 443-8323; *The New Book of World Rankings.*

G.K. Hall and Company, 70 Lincoln Street, Boston, Massachusetts 02111 (617) 423-3990; *The World in Figures.*

Inter-American Development Bank, 1300 New York Avenue, NW, Washington, D.C. 20577 (202) 623-1753; *Economic and Social Progress in Latin America.*

Statistical Office of the United Nations, Publishing Service, New York, New York 10017 (800) 253-9646; *Statistical Yearbook,* and *Statistical Yearbook for Latin America and the Caribbean.*

BRAZIL - NATIONAL PRODUCT

Facts on File, 460 Park Avenue South, New York, New York 10016 (800) 443-8323; *The New Book of World Rankings.*

Statistical Office of the United Nations, Publishing Service, New York, New York 10017 (800) 253-9646; *Statistical Yearbook.*

BRAZIL - NATURAL GAS - PRODUCTION - See BRAZIL - MINING AND MINERAL PRODUCTS

BRAZIL - NATURAL RUBBER PRODUCTION

Euromonitor Publications Limited, 87-88 Turnmill Street, London EC1M 5QU, England; *Third World Economic Handbook.*

International Rubber Study Group, York House, 8th Floor, Empire Way, Wembley, London HA9 0PA, England; *Rubber Statistical Bulletin.*

Statistical Office of the United Nations, Publishing Service, New York, New York 10017 (800) 253-9646; *Statistical Yearbook.*

BRAZIL - NET MATERIAL PRODUCT

Statistical Office of the United Nations, Publishing Service, New York, New York 10017 (800) 253-9646; *Statistical Yearbook.*

BRAZIL - NEWSPAPER PRODUCTION - See BRAZIL - FORESTRY AND FOREST PRODUCTS

BRAZIL - NEWSPRINT - See BRAZIL - FORESTRY AND FOREST PRODUCTS

BRAZIL - NICKEL AND NICKEL ORE - See BRAZIL -MINING AND MINERAL PRODUCTS

BRAZIL - NITRIC ACID PRODUCTION - See BRAZIL - MINING AND MINERAL PRODUCTS

BRAZIL - NUTRITION

Statistical Office of the United Nations, Publishing Service, New York, New York 10017 (800) 253-9646; *Statistical Yearbook for Latin America and the Caribbean.*

BRAZIL - OATS PRODUCTION - See BRAZIL - CROPS

BRAZIL - OCCUPATIONS - See BRAZIL - LABOR FORCE

BRAZIL - ONIONS PRODUCTION - See BRAZIL - CROPS

BRAZIL - ORANGE PRODUCTION - See BRAZIL - CROPS

BRAZIL - PALM KERNELS PRODUCTION - See BRAZIL - CROPS

BRAZIL - PAPER - See BRAZIL - FORESTRY AND FOREST PRODUCTS

BRAZIL - PATENTS

Statistical Office of the United Nations, Publishing Service, New York, New York 10017 (800) 253-9646; *Statistical Yearbook.*

World Intellectual Property Organization, 34 Chemin des Colombettes, CH-1211 Geneva 20. Switzerland; *Industrial Property Statistics.*

BRAZIL - PEANUT PRODUCTION - See BRAZIL - CROPS

BRAZIL - PEPPER PRODUCTION - See BRAZIL - CROPS

BRAZIL - PERIODICALS

United Nations Educational, Scientific and Cultural Organization (UNESCO), 7 Place de Fontenoy, F-75700 Paris, France (Telephone Number in U.S. (212) 963-5981); *Statistical Yearbook.*

BRAZIL - PESTICIDE USE

Food and Agricultural Organization of the United Nations (FAO) Via delle Terme di Caracalla, 00100 Rome, Italy (Telephone Number in U.S. (202) 653-2400); *The State of Food and Agriculture.*

BRAZIL - PETROLEUM INDUSTRY

The Economist Intelligence Unit, 111 West 57th Street, New York, New York 10019 (800) 938-4685; *The New Latin America Market Atlas.*

Facts on File, 460 Park Avenue South, New York, New York 10016 (800) 443-8323; *The New Book of World Rankings.*

Food and Agricultural Organization of the United Nations (FAO) Via delle Terme di Caracalla, 00100 Rome, Italy (Telephone Number in U.S. (202) 653-2400); *The State of Food and Agriculture.*

G.K. Hall and Company, 70 Lincoln Street, Boston, Massachusetts 02111 (617) 423-3990; *The World in Figures.*

Inter-American Development Bank, 1300 New York Avenue, NW, Washington, D.C. 20577 (202) 623-1753; *Economic and Social Progress in Latin America.*

Organization of American States (OAS), General Secretariat, Washington, D.C. 20006 (202) 458-3533; *Statistical Bulletin of the OAS.*

Penn Well Publishing Company, 1421 South Sheridan Road, P.O. Box 1260, Tulsa, Oklahoma 74101 (800) 752-9764; *International Energy Statistics Sourcebook.*
Statistical Office of the United Nations, Publishing Service, New York, New York 10017 (800) 253-9646; *Statistical Yearbook.*

BRAZIL - PHOSPHATE ROCK PRODUCTION - See BRAZIL - MINING AND MINERAL PRODUCTS

BRAZIL - PHOSPHATES PRODUCTION - See BRAZIL - MINING AND MINERAL PRODUCTS

BRAZIL - PIG-IRON AND FERRO-ALLOY PRODUCTION - See BRAZIL - MINING AND MINERAL PRODUCTS

BRAZIL - PIGS - See BRAZIL - LIVESTOCK AND POULTRY

BRAZIL - PLASTIC AND RESIN PRODUCTION

Euromonitor Publications Limited, 87-88 Turnmill Street, London EC1M 5QU, England; *Third World Economic Handbook.*

Statistical Office of the United Nations, Publishing Service, New York, New York 10017 (800) 253-9646; *Statistical Yearbook.*

BRAZIL - POLITICAL DATA

U.C.L.A. Latin American Center Publications, University of California, Los Angeles, California 90024; *Statistical Abstract of Latin America.*

BRAZIL - POPULATION

The Economist Intelligence Unit, 111 West 57th Street, New York, New York 10019 (800) 938-4685; *The New Latin America Market Atlas*, and *The World Market Atlas.*

Euromonitor Publications Limited, 87-88 Turnmill Street, London EC1M 5QU, England; *International Marketing Data and Statistics*, and *Third World Economic Handbook.*

Facts on File, 460 Park Avenue South, New York, New York 10016 (800) 443-8323; *The New Book of World Rankings.*

Federal Statistical Office, Gustav - Stresemann - Ring 11, D-6200 Wiesbaden, Germany; *Brazil.*

Food and Agricultural Organization of the United Nations (FAO), Via delle Terme di Caracalla, 00100 Rome, Italy (Telephone Number in U.S. (202) 653-2400); *Production Yearbook.*

Gale Research Incorporated, 835 Penobscot Building, Detroit, Michigan 48226 (800) 877-4253; *International Historical Statistics The Americas and Australasia.*

G.K. Hall and Company, 70 Lincoln Street, Boston, Massachusetts 02111 (617) 423-3990; *The World in Figures.*

Inter-American Development Bank, 1300 New York Avenue, NW, Washington, D.C. 20577 (202) 623-1753; *Economic and Social Progress in Latin America.*

International Labour Office, I.L.O. Publications, CH-1211, Geneva 22, Switzerland; *Yearbook of Labour Statistics.*

Organization of American States (OAS), General Secretariat, Washington, D.C. 20006 (202) 458-3533; *Statistical Bulletin of the OAS.*

Statistical Office of the United Nations, Publishing Service, New York, New York 10017 (800) 253-9646; *Demographic Yearbook, Statistical Yearbook*, and *Statistical Yearbook for Latin America and the Caribbean.*

Times Books, 201 East 50th Street, New York, New York 10022 (212) 751-2600; *The Economist Book of Vital World Statistics.*

U.C.L.A. Latin American Center Publications, University of California, Los Angeles, California 90024 (310) 825-6634; *Statistical Abstract of Latin America.*

United Nations Educational, Scientific and Cultural Organization (UNESCO), 7 Place de Fontenoy, F-75700 Paris, France (Telephone Number in U.S. (212) 963-5981); *Statistical Yearbook.*

U.S. Arms Control and Disarmament Agency, 320 Twenty-first Street, NW, Washington, D.C. 20451 (202) 647-8677; *World Military Expenditures and Arms Transfers.*

World Health Organization, Office of Publications, Avenue Appia, CH-1211 Geneva 27, Switzerland (Telephone Number in U.S. (518) 436-9686); *World Health Statistics Annual.*

BRAZIL - POST OFFICES

Facts on File, 460 Park Avenue South, New York, New York 10016 (800) 443-8323; *The New Book of World Rankings.*

BRAZIL - POTATO PRODUCTION - See BRAZIL - CROPS

BRAZIL - PRICES

Facts on File, 460 Park Avenue South, New York, New York 10016 (800) 443-8323; *The New Book of World Rankings.*

Federal Statistical Office, Gustav - Stresemann - Ring 11, D-6200 Wiesbaden, Germany; *Brazil.*

Food and Agricultural Organization of the United Nations (FAO), Via delle Terme di Caracalla, 00100 Rome, Italy (Telephone Number in U.S. (202) 653-2400); *Production Yearbook,* and *The State of Food and Agriculture.*

Gale Research Incorporated, 835 Penobscot Building, Detroit, Michigan 48226 (800) 877-4253; *International Historical Statistics The Americas and Australasia.*

G.K. Hall and Company, 70 Lincoln Street, Boston, Massachusetts 02111 (617) 423-3990; *The World in Figures.*

International Labour Office, I.L.O. Publications, CH-1211, Geneva 22, Switzerland; *Yearbook of Labour Statistics.*

International Monetary Fund, 700 Nineteenth Street, NW, Washington, D.C. 20431 (202) 623-7000; *International Financial Statistics.*

International Rubber Study Group, York House, 8th Floor, Empire Way, Wembley, London HA9 0PA, England; *Rubber Statistical Bulletin.*

Statistical Office of the United Nations, Publishing Service, New York, New York 10017 (800) 253-9646; *Statistical Yearbook for Latin America and the Caribbean.*

World Bureau of Metal Statistics, 27-A High Street, Ware Herts SG12 9BA, England; *World Metal Statistics.*

BRAZIL - PRINTING AND WRITING PAPER - See BRAZIL - FORESTRY AND FOREST PRODUCTS

BRAZIL - PRODUCTION

American Automobile Manufacturers Association, 1401 H Street, NW, Suite 900, Washington, D.C. 20005 (202) 326-5500; *World Motor Vehicle Data.*

Euromonitor Publications Limited, 87-88 Turnmill Street, London EC1M 5QU, England; *Third World Economic Handbook.*

Facts on File, 460 Park Avenue South, New York, New York 10016 (800) 443-8323; *The New Book of World Rankings.*

G.K. Hall and Company, 70 Lincoln Street, Boston, Massachusetts 02111 (617) 423-3990; *The World in Figures.*

International Rubber Study Group, York House, 8th Floor, Empire Way, Wembley, London HA9 0PA, England; *Rubber Statistical Bulletin.*

BRAZIL - PRODUCTIVITY

Euromonitor Publications Limited, 87-88 Turnmill Street, London EC1M 5QU, England; *International Marketing Data and Statistics.*

BRAZIL - PROPERTY TAXES - See BRAZIL - TAXATION

BRAZIL - PUBLIC CONSUMPTION FUND

Inter-American Development Bank, 1300 New York Avenue, NW, Washington, D.C. 20577 (202) 623-1753; *Economic and Social Progress in Latin America.*

BRAZIL - PUBLIC EXPENDITURES

Inter-American Development Bank, 1300 New York Avenue, NW, Washington, D.C. 20577 (202) 623-1753; *Economic and Social Progress in Latin America.*

Organization of American States (OAS), General Secretariat, Washington, D.C. 20006 (202) 458-3533; *Statistical Bulletin of the OAS.*

Statistical Office of the United Nations, Publishing Service, New York, New York 10017 (800) 253-9646; *Statistical Yearbook for Latin America and the Caribbean.*

BRAZIL - PUBLIC FINANCE

Facts on File, 460 Park Avenue South, New York, New York 10016 (800) 443-8323; *The New Book of World Rankings.*

Inter-American Development Bank, 1300 New York Avenue, NW, Washington, D.C. 20577 (202) 623-1753; *Economic and Social Progress in Latin America.*

Organization of American States (OAS), General Secretariat, Washington, D.C. 20006 (202) 458-3533; *Statistical Bulletin of the OAS.*

BRAZIL - PUBLIC REVENUES

Inter-American Development Bank, 1300 New York Avenue, NW, Washington, D.C. 20577 (202) 623-1753; *Economic and Social Progress in Latin America.*

Organization of American States (OAS), General Secretariat, Washington, D.C. 20006 (202) 458-3533; *Statistical Bulletin of the OAS.*

BRAZIL - RADIO BROADCASTING - See BRAZIL - BROADCASTING

BRAZIL - RADIO RECEIVER PRODUCTION

Statistical Office of the United Nations, Publishing Service, New York, New York 10017 (800) 253-9646; *Statistical Yearbook.*

BRAZIL - RAILWAYS

The Economist Intelligence Unit, 111 West 57th Street, New York, New York 10019 (800) 938-4685; *The New Latin America Market Atlas.*

G.K. Hall and Company, 70 Lincoln Street, Boston, Massachusetts 02111 (617) 423-3990; *The World in Figures.*

Jane's Information Group, Sentinel House, 163 Brighton Road, Coulsdon, Surrey CR5 2NH, England (Telephone Number in U.S. (703) 683-3700); *Jane's World Railways.*

Statistical Office of the United Nations, Publishing Service, New York, New York 10017 (800) 253-9646; *Statistical Yearbook.*

BRAZIL - RANCHING

U.C.L.A. Latin American Center Publications, University of California, Los Angeles, California 90024 (310) 825-6634; *Statistical Abstract of Latin America.*

BRAZIL - RELIGION

Facts on File, 460 Park Avenue South, New York, New York 10016 (800) 443-8323; *The New Book of World Rankings.*

U.C.L.A. Latin American Center Publications, University of California, Los Angeles, California 90024 (310) 825-6634; *Statistical Abstract of Latin America.*

BRAZIL - RENT PRICES

International Labour Office, I.L.O. Publications, CH-1211, Geneva 22, Switzerland; *Yearbook of Labour Statistics.*

BRAZIL - RESERVES EXCLUDING GOLD

The Economist Intelligence Unit, 111 West 57th Street, New York, New York 10019 (800) 938-4685; *The New Latin America Market Atlas.*

BRAZIL - RETAIL TRADE

Euromonitor Publications Limited, 87-88 Turnmill Street, London EC1M 5QU, England; *Third World Economic Handbook.*

G.K. Hall and Company, 70 Lincoln Street, Boston, Massachusetts 02111 (617) 423-3990; *The World in Figures.*

Inter-American Development Bank, 1300 New York Avenue, NW, Washington, D.C. 20577 (202) 623-1753; *Economic and Social Progress in Latin America.*

Statistical Office of the United Nations, Publishing Service, New York, New York 10017 (800) 253-9646; *Statistical Yearbook.*

BRAZIL - RICE PRODUCTION - See BRAZIL - CROPS

BRAZIL - ROOT AND TUBER PRODUCTION - See BRAZIL - CROPS

BRAZIL - ROUNDWOOD - See BRAZIL - FORESTRY AND FOREST PRODUCTS

BRAZIL - RUBBER PRODUCTION AND CONSUMPTION

Commodity Research Bureau, Incorporated, 75 Wall Street, New York, New York 10005 (212) 504-7754; *Commodity Year Book.*

Euromonitor Publications Limited, 87-88 Turnmill Street, London EC1M 5QU, England; *Third World Economic Handbook.*

Facts on File, 460 Park Avenue South, New York, New York 10016 (800) 443-8323; *The New Book of World Rankings.*

International Rubber Study Group, York House, 8th Floor, Empire Way, Wembley, London HA9 0PA, England; *Rubber Statistical Bulletin.*

Statistical Office of the United Nations, Publishing Service, New York, New York 10017 (800) 253-9646; *Statistical Yearbook.*

BRAZIL - SALT PRODUCTION - See BRAZIL - MINING AND MINERAL PRODUCTS

BRAZIL - SAWNWOOD PRODUCTION - See BRAZIL - FORESTRY AND FOREST PRODUCTS

BRAZIL - SCIENCE AND TECHNOLOGY

U.C.L.A. Latin American Center Publications, University of California, Los Angeles, California 90024 (310) 825-6634; *Statistical Abstract of Latin America.*

BRAZIL - SCIENCE AND TECHNOLOGY - EXPENDITURE FOR RESEARCH

Statistical Office of the United Nations, Publishing Service, New York, New York 10017 (800) 253-9646; *Statistical Yearbook.*

BRAZIL - SCIENTISTS AND ENGINEERS

Statistical Office of the United Nations, Publishing Service, New York, New York 10017 (800) 253-9646; *Statistical Yearbook.*

BRAZIL - SENIOR CITIZENS

Facts on File, 460 Park Avenue South, New York, New York 10016 (800) 443-8323; *The New Book of World Rankings.*

BRAZIL - SESAME SEED PRODUCTION - See BRAZIL - CROPS

BRAZIL - SHEEP - See BRAZIL - LIVESTOCK AND POULTRY

BRAZIL - SILVER PRODUCTION AND CONSUMPTION - See BRAZIL - MINING AND MINERAL PRODUCTS

BRAZIL - SISAL PRODUCTION - See BRAZIL - CROPS

BRAZIL - SOCIAL DATA

Facts on File, 460 Park Avenue South, New York, New York 10016 (800) 443-8323; *The New Book of World Rankings.*

G.K. Hall and Company, 70 Lincoln Street, Boston, Massachusetts 02111 (617) 423-3990; *The World in Figures.*

U.C.L.A. Latin American Center Publications, University of California, Los Angeles, California 90024 (310) 825-6634; *Statistical Abstract of Latin America.*

BRAZIL - SOCIAL SECURITY

Inter-American Development Bank, 1300 New York Avenue, NW, Washington, D.C. 20577 (202) 623-1753; *Economic and Social Progress in Latin America.*

International Monetary Fund, 700 Nineteenth Street, NW, Washington, D.C. 20431 (202) 623-7000; *Government Finance Statistics Yearbook.*

BRAZIL - SOCIOECONOMIC DATA

Inter-American Development Bank, 1300 New York Avenue, NW, Washington, D.C. 20577 (202) 623-1753; *Economic and Social Progress in Latin America.*

U.C.L.A. Latin American Center Publications, University of California, Los Angeles, California 90024 (310) 825-6634; *Statistical Abstract of Latin America.*

BRAZIL - SOYBEAN - See BRAZIL - CROPS

BRAZIL - STAMP TAXES AND DUTIES - See BRAZIL - TAXATION

BRAZIL - STATE BUDGET REVENUE AND EXPENDITURES

Euromonitor Publications Limited, 87-88 Turnmill Street, London EC1M 5QU, England; *International Marketing Data and Statistics.*

Inter-American Development Bank, 1300 New York Avenue, NW, Washington, D.C. 20577 (202) 623-1753; *Economic and Social Progress in Latin America.*

BRAZIL - STEEL - See BRAZIL - MINING AND MINERAL PRODUCTS

BRAZIL - STOCKS - COMMODITY - MARKET PRICE - INDEX

Food and Agricultural Organization of the United Nations (FAO) Via delle Terme di Caracalla, 00100 Rome, Italy (Telephone Number in U.S. (202) 653-2400); *The State of Food and Agriculture.*

World Bureau of Metal Statistics, 27-A High Street, Ware Hert SG12 9BA, England; *World Metal Statistics.*

BRAZIL - SUGAR - See BRAZIL - CROPS

BRAZIL - SULPHURIC ACID PRODUCTION - See BRAZIL - MINING AND MINERAL PRODUCTS

BRAZIL - TAXATION

Inter-American Development Bank, 1300 New York Avenue, NW, Washington, D.C. 20577 (202) 623-1753; *Economic and Social Progress in Latin America.*

International Monetary Fund, 700 Nineteenth Street, NW, Washington, D.C. 20431 (202) 623-7000; *Government Finance Statistics Yearbook.*

International Road Federation, 525 School Street, SW, Washington, D.C. 20024 (202) 554-2106; *World Road Statistics.*

Statistical Office of the United Nations, Publishing Service, New York, New York 10017 (800) 253-9646; *Statistical Yearbook for Latin America and the Caribbean.*

The World Bank, 1818 H Street, NW, Washington, D.C. 20433 (202) 477-1234; *World Tables.*

BRAZIL - TEA PRODUCTION - See BRAZIL - CROPS

BRAZIL - TELEGRAPH SERVICE

Statistical Office of the United Nations, Publishing Service, New York, New York 10017 (800) 253-9646; *Statistical Yearbook.*

BRAZIL - TELEPHONES IN USE

American Telephone and Telegraph Company, 26 Parsippany Road, Whippany, New Jersey 07981 (800) 338-4038; *The World's Telephones.*

The Economist Intelligence Unit, 111 West 57th Street, New York, New York 10019 (800) 938-4685; *The New Latin America Market Atlas.*

Euromonitor Publications Limited, 87-88 Turnmill Street, London EC1M 5QU, England; *Third World Economic Handbook.*

G.K. Hall and Company, 70 Lincoln Street, Boston, Massachusetts 02111 (617) 423-3990; *The World in Figures.*

Statistical Office of the United Nations, Publishing Service, New York, New York 10017 (800) 253-9646; *Statistical Yearbook.*

BRAZIL - TELEVISION BROADCASTING - See BRAZIL - BROADCASTING

BRAZIL - TELEVISION RECEIVER PRODUCTION

Statistical Office of the United Nations, Publishing Service, New York, New York 10017 (800) 253-9646; *Statistical Yearbook.*

BRAZIL - TEXTILE INDUSTRY

Euromonitor Publications Limited, 87-88 Turnmill Street, London EC1M 5QU, England; *Third World Economic Handbook.*

G.K. Hall and Company, 70 Lincoln Street, Boston, Massachusetts 02111 (617) 423-3990; *The World in Figures.*

Statistical Office of the United Nations, Publishing Service, New York, New York 10017 (800) 253-9646; *Statistical Yearbook,* and *Trade in Manufactures of Developing Countries.*

BRAZIL - THEATRE

United Nations Educational, Scientific and Cultural Organization (UNESCO), 7 Place de Fontenoy, F-75700 Paris, France (Telephone Number in U.S. (212) 963-5981); *Statistical Yearbook.*

BRAZIL - TIN - See BRAZIL - MINING AND MINERAL PRODUCTS

BRAZIL - TIRE (MOTOR VEHICLE) PRODUCTION

International Rubber Study Group, York House, 8th Floor, Empire Way, Wembley, London HA9 0PA, England; *Rubber Statistical Bulletin.*

Statistical Office of the United Nations, Publishing Service, New York, New York 10017 (800) 253-9646; *Statistical Yearbook.*

BRAZIL - TOBACCO PRODUCTION

Commodity Research Bureau, Incorporated, 75 Wall Street, New York, New York 10005 (212) 504-7754; *Commodity Year Book.*

Euromonitor Publications Limited, 87-88 Turnmill Street, London EC1M 5QU, England; *Third World Economic Handbook.*

Facts on File, 460 Park Avenue South, New York, New York 10016 (800) 443-8323; *The New Book of World Rankings.*

Statistical Office of the United Nations, Publishing Service, New York, New York 10017 (800) 253-9646; *Statistical Yearbook.*

BRAZIL - TOURISM

The Economist Intelligence Unit, 111 West 57th Street, New York, New York 10019 (800) 938-4685; *The New Latin America Market Atlas.*

Euromonitor Publications Limited, 87-88 Turnmill Street, London EC1M 5QU, England; *Third World Economic Handbook.*

Facts on File, 460 Park Avenue South, New York, New York 10016 (800) 443-8323; *The New Book of World Rankings.*

Federal Statistical Office, Gustav - Stresemann - Ring 11, D-6200 Wiesbaden, Germany; *Brazil.*

G.K. Hall and Company, 70 Lincoln Street, Boston, Massachusetts 02111 (617) 423-3990; *The World in Figures.*

Statistical Office of the United Nations, Publishing Service, New York, New York 10017 (800) 253-9646; *Statistical Yearbook,* and *Statistical Yearbook for Latin America and the Caribbean.*

Times Books, 201 East 50th Street, New York, New York 10022 (212) 751-2600; *The Economist Book of Vital World Statistics.*

U.C.L.A. Latin American Center Publications, University of California, Los Angeles, California 90024 (310) 825-6634; *Statistical Abstract of Latin America.*

World Tourism Organization, Calle Capitan Haya 42, E-28020 Madrid, Spain; *Yearbook of Tourism Statistics.*

BRAZIL - TRACTORS IN USE

The Economist Intelligence Unit, 111 West 57th Street, New York, New York 10019 (800) 938-4685; *The New Latin America Market Atlas.*

Statistical Office of the United Nations, Publishing Service, New York, New York 10017 (800) 253-9646; *Statistical Yearbook.*

BRAZIL - TRADE - See BRAZIL - FOREIGN TRADE

BRAZIL - TRADEMARKS AND SERVICE MARKS

Statistical Office of the United Nations, Publishing Service, New York, New York 10017 (800) 253-9646; *Statistical Yearbook.*

World Intellectual Property Organization, 34 Chemin des Colombettes, CH-1211 Geneva 20. Switzerland; *Industrial Property Statistics.*

BRAZIL - TRANSPORTATION AND COMMUNICATIONS

The Economist Intelligence Unit, 111 West 57th Street, New York, New York 10019 (800) 938-4685; *The New Latin America Market Atlas.*

Euromonitor Publications Limited, 87-88 Turnmill Street, London EC1M 5QU, England; *Third World Economic Handbook.*

Facts on File, 460 Park Avenue South, New York, New York 10016 (800) 443-8323; *The New Book of World Rankings.*

Federal Statistical Office, Gustav - Stresemann - Ring 11, D-6200 Wiesbaden, Germany; *Brazil.*

Gale Research Incorporated, 835 Penobscot Building, Detroit, Michigan 48226 (800) 877-4253; *International Historical Statistics The Americas and Australasia.*

G.K. Hall and Company, 70 Lincoln Street, Boston, Massachusetts 02111 (617) 423-3990; *The World in Figures.*

Inter-American Development Bank, 1300 New York Avenue, NW, Washington, D.C. 20577 (202) 623-1753; *Economic and Social Progress in Latin America.*

Statistical Office of the United Nations, Publishing Service, New York, New York 10017 (800) 253-9646; *Statistical Yearbook for Latin America and the Caribbean.*

U.C.L.A. Latin American Center Publications, University of California, Los Angeles, California 90024 (310) 825-6634; *Statistical Abstract of Latin America.*

BRAZIL - TUNGSTEN PRODUCTION AND CONSUMPTION - See BRAZIL - MINING AND MINERAL PRODUCTS

BRAZIL - TURKEYS - See BRAZIL - LIVESTOCK AND POULTRY

BRAZIL - UNEMPLOYMENT

The Economist Intelligence Unit, 111 West 57th Street, New York, New York 10019 (800) 938-4685; *The New Latin America Market Atlas.*

Euromonitor Publications Limited, 87-88 Turnmill Street, London EC1M 5QU, England; *International Marketing Data and Statistics.*

International Labour Office, I.L.O. Publications, CH-1211, Geneva 22, Switzerland; *Yearbook of Labour Statistics.*

Statistical Office of the United Nations, Publishing Service, New York, New York 10017 (800) 253-9646; *Statistical Yearbook.*

U.C.L.A. Latin American Center Publications, University of California, Los Angeles, California 90024 (310) 825-6634; *Statistical Abstract of Latin America.*

BRAZIL - URANIUM PRODUCTION AND CONSUMPTION - See BRAZIL - MINING AND MINERAL PRODUCTS

BRAZIL - UTILITIES

U.C.L.A. Latin American Center Publications, University of California, Los Angeles, California 90024 (310) 825-6634; *Statistical Abstract of Latin America.*

BRAZIL - VITAL STATISTICS

Euromonitor Publications Limited, 87-88 Turnmill Street, London EC1M 5QU, England; *International Marketing Data and Statistics,* and *Third World Economic Handbook.*

Gale Research Incorporated, 835 Penobscot Building, Detroit, Michigan 48226 (800) 877-4253; *International Historical Statistics The Americas and Australasia.*

G.K. Hall and Company, 70 Lincoln Street, Boston, Massachusetts 02111 (617) 423-3990; *The World in Figures.*

Statistical Office of the United Nations, Publishing Service, New York, New York 10017 (800) 253-9646; *Statistical Yearbook.*

World Health Organization, Office of Publications, Avenue Appia, CH-1211 Geneva 27, Switzerland (Telephone Number in U.S. (518) 436-9686); *World Health Statistics Annual.*

BRAZIL - WAGES

Federal Statistical Office, Gustav - Stresemann - Ring 11, D-6200 Wiesbaden, Germany; *Brazil.*

G.K. Hall and Company, 70 Lincoln Street, Boston, Massachusetts 02111 (617) 423-3990; *The World in Figures.*

International Labour Office, I.L.O. Publications, CH-1211, Geneva 22, Switzerland; *Yearbook of Labour Statistics.*

Organization of American States (OAS), General Secretariat, Washington, D.C. 20006 (202) 458-3533; *Statistical Bulletin of the OAS.*

Statistical Office of the United Nations, Publishing Service, New York, New York 10017 (800) 253-9646; *Statistical Yearbook.*

U.C.L.A. Latin American Center Publications, University of California, Los Angeles, California 90024 (310) 825-6634; *Statistical Abstract of Latin America.*

BRAZIL - WALNUT PRODUCTION - See BRAZIL - CROPS

BRAZIL - WATERMELON PRODUCTION - See BRAZIL - CROPS

BRAZIL - WEATHER

Facts on File, 460 Park Avenue South, New York, New York 10016 (800) 443-8323; *The New Book of World Rankings.*

G.K. Hall and Company, 70 Lincoln Street, Boston, Massachusetts 02111 (617) 423-3990; *The World in Figures.*

BRAZIL - WELFARE

Inter-American Development Bank, 1300 New York Avenue, NW, Washington, D.C. 20577 (202) 623-1753; *Economic and Social Progress in Latin America.*

International Monetary Fund, 700 Nineteenth Street, NW, Washington, D.C. 20431 (202) 623-7000; *Government Finance Statistics Yearbook.*

BRAZIL - WHALES - See BRAZIL - FISHERIES

BRAZIL - WHEAT - See BRAZIL - CROPS

BRAZIL - WHOLESALE PRICES

Inter-American Development Bank, 1300 New York Avenue, NW, Washington, D.C. 20577 (202) 623-1753; *Economic and Social Progress in Latin America.*

International Monetary Fund, 700 Nineteenth Street, NW, Washington, D.C. 20431 (202) 623-7000; *International Financial Statistics.*

Organization of American States (OAS), General Secretariat, Washington, D.C. 20006 (202) 458-3533; *Statistical Bulletin of the OAS.*

Statistical Office of the United Nations, Publishing Service, New York, New York 10017 (800) 253-9646; *Statistical Yearbook.*

BRAZIL - WHOLESALE TRADE

Euromonitor Publications Limited, 87-88 Turnmill Street, London EC1M 5QU, England; *Third World Economic Handbook.*

Inter-American Development Bank, 1300 New York Avenue, NW, Washington, D.C. 20577 (202) 623-1753; *Economic and Social Progress in Latin America.*

Statistical Office of the United Nations, Publishing Service, New York, New York 10017 (800) 253-9646; *Statistical Yearbook.*

BRAZIL - WINE PRODUCTION

Facts on File, 460 Park Avenue South, New York, New York 10016 (800) 443-8323; *The New Book of World Rankings.*

Statistical Office of the United Nations, Publishing Service, New York, New York 10017 (800) 253-9646; *Statistical Yearbook.*

BRAZIL - WOOD AND WOOD PULP - See BRAZIL - FORESTRY AND FOREST PRODUCTS

BRAZIL - WOOL PRODUCTION

Facts on File, 460 Park Avenue South, New York, New York 10016 (800) 443-8323; *The New Book of World Rankings.*

Statistical Office of the United Nations, Publishing Service, New York, New York 10017 (800) 253-9646; *Statistical Yearbook.*

BRAZIL - YARN PRODUCTION

Statistical Office of the United Nations, Publishing Service, New York, New York 10017 (800) 253-9646; *Statistical Yearbook.*

BRAZIL - ZINC AND ZINC ORE - See BRAZIL - MINING AND MINERAL PRODUCTS

BRAZIL - ZOOS AND BOTANICAL GARDENS

United Nations Educational, Scientific and Cultural Organization (UNESCO), 7 Place de Fontenoy, F-75700 Paris, France (Telephone Number in U.S. (212) 963-5981); *Statistical Yearbook.*

BREAST IMPLANTS

U.S. Department of Health and Human Services, National Center for Health Statistics, 3700 East-West Highway, Hyattsville, Maryland 10782 (301) 436-8500; *National Health Interview Survey.*

BREAD

U.S. Department of Labor, Bureau of Labor Statistics, 2 Massachusetts Avenue, NE, Washington, D.C. 20212; *CPI Detailed Report,* and *Monthly Labor Review.*

BRITISH HONDURAS - See BELIZE

BRITISH INDIAN OCEAN TERRITORY - AGRICULTURE

Food and Agricultural Organization of the United Nations (FAO) Via delle Terme di Caracalla, 00100 Rome, Italy (Telephone Number in U.S. (202) 653-2400); *Production Yearbook, The State of Food and Agriculture,* and *Trade Yearbook.*

G.K. Hall and Company, 70 Lincoln Street, Boston, Massachusetts 02111 (617) 423-3990; *The World in Figures.*

BRITISH INDIAN OCEAN TERRITORY - AIRLINE SERVICE

G.K. Hall and Company, 70 Lincoln Street, Boston, Massachusetts 02111 (617) 423-3990; *The World in Figures.*

BRITISH INDIAN OCEAN TERRITORY - AREA AND DENSITY OF POPULATION

Food and Agricultural Organization of the United Nations (FAO) Via delle Terme di Caracalla, 00100 Rome, Italy (Telephone Number in U.S. (202) 653-2400); *The State of Food and Agriculture.*

G.K. Hall and Company, 70 Lincoln Street, Boston, Massachusetts 02111 (617) 423-3990; *The World in Figures.*

Statistical Office of the United Nations, Publishing Service, New York, New York 10017 (800) 253-9646; *Statistical Yearbook.*

BRITISH INDIAN OCEAN TERRITORY - BALANCE OF PAYMENTS

G.K. Hall and Company, 70 Lincoln Street, Boston, Massachusetts 02111 (617) 423-3990; *The World in Figures.*

BRITISH INDIAN OCEAN TERRITORY - BANKING

G.K. Hall and Company, 70 Lincoln Street, Boston, Massachusetts 02111 (617) 423-3990; *The World in Figures.*

BRITISH INDIAN OCEAN TERRITORY - BIRTH RATES

Statistical Office of the United Nations, Publishing Service, New York, New York 10017 (800) 253-9646; *Demographic Yearbook.*

BRITISH INDIAN OCEAN TERRITORY - BONDS

G.K. Hall and Company, 70 Lincoln Street, Boston, Massachusetts 02111 (617) 423-3990; *The World in Figures.*

BRITISH INDIAN OCEAN TERRITORY - BOOK PRODUCTION

G.K. Hall and Company, 70 Lincoln Street, Boston, Massachusetts 02111 (617) 423-3990; *The World in Figures.*

BRITISH INDIAN OCEAN TERRITORY - BROADCASTING

G.K. Hall and Company, 70 Lincoln Street, Boston, Massachusetts 02111 (617) 423-3990; *The World in Figures.*

BRITISH INDIAN OCEAN TERRITORY - BUSINESS

G.K. Hall and Company, 70 Lincoln Street, Boston, Massachusetts 02111 (617) 423-3990; *The World in Figures.*

BRITISH INDIAN OCEAN TERRITORY - CALORIE SUPPLY

Food and Agricultural Organization of the United Nations (FAO) Via delle Terme di Caracalla, 00100 Rome, Italy (Telephone Number in U.S. (202) 653-2400); *The State of Food and Agriculture.*

BRITISH INDIAN OCEAN TERRITORY - CHEMICAL (ORGANIC) PRODUCTION - See BRITISH INDIAN OCEAN TERRITORY - MINING AND MINERAL PRODUCTS

BRITISH INDIAN OCEAN TERRITORY - CLASS STRUCTURE

G.K. Hall and Company, 70 Lincoln Street, Boston, Massachusetts 02111 (617) 423-3990; *The World in Figures.*

BRITISH INDIAN OCEAN TERRITORY - CLIMATE

G.K. Hall and Company, 70 Lincoln Street, Boston, Massachusetts 02111 (617) 423-3990; *The World in Figures.*

BRITISH INDIAN OCEAN TERRITORY - COAL PRODUCTION - See BRITISH INDIAN OCEAN TERRITORY - MINING AND MINERAL PRODUCTS

BRITISH INDIAN OCEAN TERRITORY - COMMUNICATIONS

G.K. Hall and Company, 70 Lincoln Street, Boston, Massachusetts 02111 (617) 423-3990; *The World in Figures.*

BRITISH INDIAN OCEAN TERRITORY - CONSUMER PRICE INDEX

G.K. Hall and Company, 70 Lincoln Street, Boston, Massachusetts 02111 (617) 423-3990; *The World in Figures.*

BRITISH INDIAN OCEAN TERRITORY - CONSUMPTION

G.K. Hall and Company, 70 Lincoln Street, Boston, Massachusetts 02111 (617) 423-3990; *The World in Figures.*

BRITISH INDIAN OCEAN TERRITORY - CORN PRODUCTION - See BRITISH INDIAN OCEAN TERRITORY - CROPS

BRITISH INDIAN OCEAN TERRITORY - CORPORATE TAXES - See BRITISH INDIAN OCEAN TERRITORY - TAXATION

BRITISH INDIAN OCEAN TERRITORY - CROPS

Food and Agricultural Organization of the United Nations (FAO) Via delle Terme di Caracalla, 00100 Rome, Italy (Telephone Number in U.S. (202) 653-2400); *The State of Food and Agriculture.*

G.K. Hall and Company, 70 Lincoln Street, Boston, Massachusetts 02111 (617) 423-3990; *The World in Figures.*

BRITISH INDIAN OCEAN TERRITORY - CUSTOMS DUTIES

G.K. Hall and Company, 70 Lincoln Street, Boston, Massachusetts 02111 (617) 423-3990; *The World in Figures.*

BRITISH INDIAN OCEAN TERRITORY - DAIRY PRODUCTS

Food and Agricultural Organization of the United Nations (FAO) Via delle Terme di Caracalla, 00100 Rome, Italy (Telephone Number in U.S. (202) 653-2400); *The State of Food and Agriculture.*

BRITISH INDIAN OCEAN TERRITORY - DEATH RATES

G.K. Hall and Company, 70 Lincoln Street, Boston, Massachusetts 02111 (617) 423-3990; *The World in Figures.*

BRITISH INDIAN OCEAN TERRITORY - DEFENSE EXPENDITURES

G.K. Hall and Company, 70 Lincoln Street, Boston, Massachusetts 02111 (617) 423-3990; *The World in Figures.*

BRITISH INDIAN OCEAN TERRITORY - DEMOGRAPHY

G.K. Hall and Company, 70 Lincoln Street, Boston, Massachusetts 02111 (617) 423-3990; *The World in Figures.*

BRITISH INDIAN OCEAN TERRITORY - DEVELOPMENT ASSISTANCE

G.K. Hall and Company, 70 Lincoln Street, Boston, Massachusetts 02111 (617) 423-3990; *The World in Figures.*

BRITISH INDIAN OCEAN TERRITORY - DISEASE

G.K. Hall and Company, 70 Lincoln Street, Boston, Massachusetts 02111 (617) 423-3990; *The World in Figures.*

BRITISH INDIAN OCEAN TERRITORY - DIVORCE RATES

Statistical Office of the United Nations, Publishing Service, New York, New York 10017 (800) 253-9646; *Demographic Yearbook.*

BRITISH INDIAN OCEAN TERRITORY - DOMESTIC PRODUCT

G.K. Hall and Company, 70 Lincoln Street, Boston, Massachusetts 02111 (617) 423-3990; *The World in Figures.*

BRITISH INDIAN OCEAN TERRITORY - ECONOMY

G.K. Hall and Company, 70 Lincoln Street, Boston, Massachusetts 02111 (617) 423-3990; *The World in Figures.*

BRITISH INDIAN OCEAN TERRITORY - EDUCATION

G.K. Hall and Company, 70 Lincoln Street, Boston, Massachusetts 02111 (617) 423-3990; *The World in Figures.*

BRITISH INDIAN OCEAN TERRITORY - EGG PRODUCTION - See BRITISH INDIAN OCEAN TERRITORY - DAIRY PRODUCTS

BRITISH INDIAN OCEAN TERRITORY - ENERGY

Food and Agricultural Organization of the United Nations (FAO) Via delle Terme di Caracalla, 00100 Rome, Italy (Telephone Number in U.S. (202) 653-2400); *The State of Food and Agriculture.*

G.K. Hall and Company, 70 Lincoln Street, Boston, Massachusetts 02111 (617) 423-3990; *The World in Figures.*

BRITISH INDIAN OCEAN TERRITORY - EXPORTS

Food and Agricultural Organization of the United Nations (FAO) Via delle Terme di Caracalla, 00100 Rome, Italy (Telephone Number in U.S. (202) 653-2400); *The State of Food and Agriculture.*

G.K. Hall and Company, 70 Lincoln Street, Boston, Massachusetts 02111 (617) 423-3990; *The World in Figures.*

BRITISH INDIAN OCEAN TERRITORY - EXTERNAL TRADE

Food and Agricultural Organization of the United Nations (FAO) Via delle Terme di Caracalla, 00100 Rome, Italy (Telephone Number in U.S. (202) 653-2400); *The State of Food and Agriculture,* and *Trade Yearbook.*

G.K. Hall and Company, 70 Lincoln Street, Boston, Massachusetts 02111 (617) 423-3990; *The World in Figures.*

BRITISH INDIAN OCEAN TERRITORY - FARM CROPS - See BRITISH INDIAN OCEAN TERRITORY - CROPS

BRITISH INDIAN OCEAN TERRITORY - FETAL MORTALITY

Statistical Office of the United Nations, Publishing Service, New York, New York 10017 (800) 253-9646; *Demographic Yearbook.*

BRITISH INDIAN OCEAN TERRITORY - FERTILIZER

Food and Agricultural Organization of the United Nations (FAO) Via delle Terme di Caracalla, 00100 Rome, Italy (Telephone Number in U.S. (202) 653-2400); *The State of Food and Agriculture.*

BRITISH INDIAN OCEAN TERRITORY - FINANCE

G.K. Hall and Company, 70 Lincoln Street, Boston, Massachusetts 02111 (617) 423-3990; *The World in Figures.*

BRITISH INDIAN OCEAN TERRITORY - FISHERIES

Food and Agricultural Organization of the United Nations (FAO) Via delle Terme di Caracalla, 00100 Rome, Italy (Telephone Number in U.S. (202) 653-2400); *The State of Food and Agriculture,* and *Yearbook of Fishery Statistics.*

BRITISH INDIAN OCEAN TERRITORY - FOOD

Food and Agricultural Organization of the United Nations (FAO) Via delle Terme di Caracalla, 00100 Rome, Italy (Telephone Number in U.S. (202) 653-2400); *Production Yearbook,* and *The State of Food and Agriculture.*

G.K. Hall and Company, 70 Lincoln Street, Boston, Massachusetts 02111 (617) 423-3990; *The World in Figures.*

BRITISH INDIAN OCEAN TERRITORY - FOREIGN AID

G.K. Hall and Company, 70 Lincoln Street, Boston, Massachusetts 02111 (617) 423-3990; *The World in Figures.*

BRITISH INDIAN OCEAN TERRITORY - FOREIGN TRADE

Food and Agricultural Organization of the United Nations (FAO) Via delle Terme di Caracalla, 00100 Rome, Italy (Telephone Number in U.S. (202) 653-2400); *The State of Food and Agriculture.*

G.K. Hall and Company, 70 Lincoln Street, Boston, Massachusetts 02111 (617) 423-3990; *The World in Figures.*

BRITISH INDIAN OCEAN TERRITORY - FORESTRY AND FOREST PRODUCTS

Food and Agricultural Organization of the United Nations (FAO) Via delle Terme di Caracalla, 00100 Rome, Italy (Telephone Number in U.S. (202) 653-2400); *The State of Food and Agriculture.*

G.K. Hall and Company, 70 Lincoln Street, Boston, Massachusetts 02111 (617) 423-3990; *The World in Figures.*

BRITISH INDIAN OCEAN TERRITORY - GENERAL MORTALITY

Statistical Office of the United Nations, Publishing Service, New York, New York 10017 (800) 253-9646; *Demographic Yearbook.*

BRITISH INDIAN OCEAN TERRITORY - GOVERNMENT

G.K. Hall and Company, 70 Lincoln Street, Boston, Massachusetts 02111 (617) 423-3990; *The World in Figures.*

BRITISH INDIAN OCEAN TERRITORY - GRAIN PRODUCTION - See BRITISH INDIAN OCEAN TERRITORY - CROPS

BRITISH INDIAN OCEAN TERRITORY - GROSS DOMESTIC PRODUCT

G.K. Hall and Company, 70 Lincoln Street, Boston, Massachusetts 02111 (617) 423-3990; *The World in Figures.*

BRITISH INDIAN OCEAN TERRITORY - HEALTH

G.K. Hall and Company, 70 Lincoln Street, Boston, Massachusetts 02111 (617) 423-3990; *The World in Figures.*

BRITISH INDIAN OCEAN TERRITORY - HIGHWAYS

G.K. Hall and Company, 70 Lincoln Street, Boston, Massachusetts 02111 (617) 423-3990; *The World in Figures.*

BRITISH INDIAN OCEAN TERRITORY - ILLITERATE POPULATION

G.K. Hall and Company, 70 Lincoln Street, Boston, Massachusetts 02111 (617) 423-3990; *The World in Figures.*

BRITISH INDIAN OCEAN TERRITORY - IMPORTS

Food and Agricultural Organization of the United Nations (FAO) Via delle Terme di Caracalla, 00100 Rome, Italy (Telephone Number in U.S. (202) 653-2400); *The State of Food and Agriculture.*

G.K. Hall and Company, 70 Lincoln Street, Boston, Massachusetts 02111 (617) 423-3990; *The World in Figures.*

BRITISH INDIAN OCEAN TERRITORY - INDUSTRY

G.K. Hall and Company, 70 Lincoln Street, Boston, Massachusetts 02111 (617) 423-3990; *The World in Figures.*

BRITISH INDIAN OCEAN TERRITORY - INFANT AND MATERNAL MORTALITY

Statistical Office of the United Nations, Publishing Service, New York, New York 10017 (800) 253-9646; *Demographic Yearbook.*

BRITISH INDIAN OCEAN TERRITORY - LABOR FORCE

Food and Agricultural Organization of the United Nations (FAO) Via delle Terme di Caracalla, 00100 Rome, Italy (Telephone Number in U.S. (202) 653-2400); *The State of Food and Agriculture.*

G.K. Hall and Company, 70 Lincoln Street, Boston, Massachusetts 02111 (617) 423-3990; *The World in Figures.*

BRITISH INDIAN OCEAN TERRITORY - LAND USE

Food and Agricultural Organization of the United Nations (FAO), Via delle Terme di Caracalla, 00100 Rome, Italy (Telephone Number in U.S. (202) 653-2400); *Production Yearbook.*

G.K. Hall and Company, 70 Lincoln Street, Boston, Massachusetts 02111 (617) 423-3990; *The World in Figures.*

BRITISH INDIAN OCEAN TERRITORY - LIVESTOCK AND POULTRY

Food and Agricultural Organization of the United Nations (FAO), Via delle Terme di Caracalla, 00100 Rome, Italy (Telephone Number in U.S. (202) 653-2400); *Production Yearbook,* and *The State of Food and Agriculture.*

G.K. Hall and Company, 70 Lincoln Street, Boston, Massachusetts 02111 (617) 423-3990; *The World in Figures.*

BRITISH INDIAN OCEAN TERRITORY - LIVING LEVELS

G.K. Hall and Company, 70 Lincoln Street, Boston, Massachusetts 02111 (617) 423-3990; *The World in Figures.*

BRITISH INDIAN OCEAN TERRITORY - MANUFACTURING

G.K. Hall and Company, 70 Lincoln Street, Boston, Massachusetts 02111 (617) 423-3990; *The World in Figures.*

BRITISH INDIAN OCEAN TERRITORY - MARRIAGE RATES

Statistical Office of the United Nations, Publishing Service, New York, New York 10017 (800) 253-9646; *Demographic Yearbook.*

BRITISH INDIAN OCEAN TERRITORY - MEAT PRODUCTION - See BRITISH INDIAN OCEAN TERRITORY - LIVESTOCK AND POULTRY

BRITISH INDIAN OCEAN TERRITORY - MERCHANT SHIPPING

G.K. Hall and Company, 70 Lincoln Street, Boston, Massachusetts 02111 (617) 423-3990; *The World in Figures.*

BRITISH INDIAN OCEAN TERRITORY - MILITARY

G.K. Hall and Company, 70 Lincoln Street, Boston, Massachusetts 02111 (617) 423-3990; *The World in Figures.*

BRITISH INDIAN OCEAN TERRITORY - MINING AND MINERAL PRODUCTION

G.K. Hall and Company, 70 Lincoln Street, Boston, Massachusetts 02111 (617) 423-3990; *The World in Figures.*

BRITISH INDIAN OCEAN TERRITORY - MONEY SUPPLY

G.K. Hall and Company, 70 Lincoln Street, Boston, Massachusetts 02111 (617) 423-3990; *The World in Figures.*

BRITISH INDIAN OCEAN TERRITORY - MOTOR VEHICLES IN USE

G.K. Hall and Company, 70 Lincoln Street, Boston, Massachusetts 02111 (617) 423-3990; *The World in Figures.*

BRITISH INDIAN OCEAN TERRITORY - NATALITY - See BRITISH INDIAN OCEAN TERRITORY - BIRTH RATE

BRITISH INDIAN OCEAN TERRITORY - NATIONAL INCOME

G.K. Hall and Company, 70 Lincoln Street, Boston, Massachusetts 02111 (617) 423-3990; *The World in Figures.*

BRITISH INDIAN OCEAN TERRITORY - NEWSPAPER PRODUCTION - See BRITISH INDIAN OCEAN TERRITORY - FORESTRY AND FOREST PRODUCTS

BRITISH INDIAN OCEAN TERRITORY - OCCUPATIONS - See BRITISH INDIAN OCEAN TERRITORY - LABOR FORCE

BRITISH INDIAN OCEAN TERRITORY - PESTICIDE USE

Food and Agricultural Organization of the United Nations (FAO) Via delle Terme di Caracalla, 00100 Rome, Italy (Telephone Number in U.S. (202) 653-2400); *The State of Food and Agriculture.*

BRITISH INDIAN OCEAN TERRITORY - PETROLEUM INDUSTRY

Food and Agricultural Organization of the United Nations (FAO) Via delle Terme di Caracalla, 00100 Rome, Italy (Telephone Number in U.S. (202) 653-2400); *The State of Food and Agriculture.*

G.K. Hall and Company, 70 Lincoln Street, Boston, Massachusetts 02111 (617) 423-3990; *The World in Figures.*

BRITISH INDIAN OCEAN TERRITORY - POPULATION

Food and Agricultural Organization of the United Nations (FAO), Via delle Terme di Caracalla, 00100 Rome, Italy (Telephone Number in U.S. (202) 653-2400); *Production Yearbook.*

G.K. Hall and Company, 70 Lincoln Street, Boston, Massachusetts 02111 (617) 423-3990; *The World in Figures.*

Statistical Office of the United Nations, Publishing Service, New York, New York 10017 (800) 253-9646; *Demographic Yearbook,* and *Statistical Yearbook.*

World Health Organization, Office of Publications, Avenue Appia, CH-1211 Geneva 27, Switzerland (Telephone Number in U.S. (518) 436-9686); *World Health Statistics Annual.*

BRITISH INDIAN OCEAN TERRITORY - PRICES

Food and Agricultural Organization of the United Nations (FAO), Via delle Terme di Caracalla, 00100 Rome, Italy (Telephone Number in U.S. (202) 653-2400); *Production Yearbook,* and *The State of Food and Agriculture.*

G.K. Hall and Company, 70 Lincoln Street, Boston, Massachusetts 02111 (617) 423-3990; *The World in Figures.*

BRITISH INDIAN OCEAN TERRITORY - PRODUCTION

G.K. Hall and Company, 70 Lincoln Street, Boston, Massachusetts 02111 (617) 423-3990; *The World in Figures.*

BRITISH INDIAN OCEAN TERRITORY - RAILWAYS

G.K. Hall and Company, 70 Lincoln Street, Boston, Massachusetts 02111 (617) 423-3990; *The World in Figures.*

BRITISH INDIAN OCEAN TERRITORY - RETAIL TRADE

G.K. Hall and Company, 70 Lincoln Street, Boston, Massachusetts 02111 (617) 423-3990; *The World in Figures.*

BRITISH INDIAN OCEAN TERRITORY - SOCIAL DATA

G.K. Hall and Company, 70 Lincoln Street, Boston, Massachusetts 02111 (617) 423-3990; *The World in Figures.*

BRITISH INDIAN OCEAN TERRITORY - STOCKS - COMMODITY - MARKET PRICE - INDEX

Food and Agricultural Organization of the United Nations (FAO) Via delle Terme di Caracalla, 00100 Rome, Italy (Telephone Number in U.S. (202) 653-2400); *The State of Food and Agriculture.*

BRITISH INDIAN OCEAN TERRITORY - TAXATION

G.K. Hall and Company, 70 Lincoln Street, Boston, Massachusetts 02111 (617) 423-3990; *The World in Figures.*

BRITISH INDIAN OCEAN TERRITORY - TELEPHONES IN USE

G.K. Hall and Company, 70 Lincoln Street, Boston, Massachusetts 02111 (617) 423-3990; *The World in Figures.*

BRITISH INDIAN OCEAN TERRITORY - TEXTILE INDUSTRY

G.K. Hall and Company, 70 Lincoln Street, Boston, Massachusetts 02111 (617) 423-3990; *The World in Figures.*

BRITISH INDIAN OCEAN TERRITORY - TOURISM

G.K. Hall and Company, 70 Lincoln Street, Boston, Massachusetts 02111 (617) 423-3990; *The World in Figures.*

BRITISH INDIAN OCEAN TERRITORY - TRADE - See BRITISH INDIAN OCEAN TERRITORY - FOREIGN TRADE

BRITISH INDIAN OCEAN TERRITORY - TRANSPORTATION AND COMMUNICATIONS

G.K. Hall and Company, 70 Lincoln Street, Boston, Massachusetts 02111 (617) 423-3990; *The World in Figures.*

BRITISH INDIAN OCEAN TERRITORY - VITAL STATISTICS

G.K. Hall and Company, 70 Lincoln Street, Boston, Massachusetts 02111 (617) 423-3990; *The World in Figures.*

World Health Organization, Office of Publications, Avenue Appia, CH-1211 Geneva 27, Switzerland (Telephone Number in U.S. (518) 436-9686); *World Health Statistics Annual.*

BRITISH INDIAN OCEAN TERRITORY - WAGES

G.K. Hall and Company, 70 Lincoln Street, Boston, Massachusetts 02111 (617) 423-3990; *The World in Figures.*

BRITISH INDIAN OCEAN TERRITORY - WEATHER

G.K. Hall and Company, 70 Lincoln Street, Boston, Massachusetts 02111 (617) 423-3990; *The World in Figures.*

British Virgin Islands - Primary Statistics Sources

HM Stationery Office, Post Office Box 569, London, England SE1 9NH; *Report for the British Virgin Islands,* and Statistics Office, Ministry of Finance, Tortola, British Virgin Islands; *Statistical Abstract.*

BRITISH VIRGIN ISLANDS - AGRICULTURE

Food and Agricultural Organization of the United Nations (FAO) Via delle Terme di Caracalla, 00100 Rome, Italy (Telephone Number in U.S. (202) 653-2400); *Production Yearbook, The State of Food and Agriculture,* and *Trade Yearbook.*

G.K. Hall and Company, 70 Lincoln Street, Boston, Massachusetts 02111 (617) 423-3990; *The World in Figures.*

Statistical Office of the United Nations, Publishing Service, New York, New York 10017 (800) 253-9646; *Statistical Yearbook.*

BRITISH VIRGIN ISLANDS - AIRLINE SERVICE

G.K. Hall and Company, 70 Lincoln Street, Boston, Massachusetts 02111 (617) 423-3990; *The World in Figures.*

International Civil Aviation Organization, 1000 Sherbrooke Street West, Suite 400, Montreal, Quebec, Canada H3A 2R2; *Civil Aviation Statistics of the World.*

BRITISH VIRGIN ISLANDS - AREA AND DENSITY OF POPULATION

Food and Agricultural Organization of the United Nations (FAO) Via delle Terme di Caracalla, 00100 Rome, Italy (Telephone Number in U.S. (202) 653-2400); *The State of Food and Agriculture.*

G.K. Hall and Company, 70 Lincoln Street, Boston, Massachusetts 02111 (617) 423-3990; *The World in Figures.*

Statistical Office of the United Nations, Publishing Service, New York, New York 10017 (800) 253-9646; *Statistical Yearbook.*

BRITISH VIRGIN ISLANDS - BALANCE OF PAYMENTS

G.K. Hall and Company, 70 Lincoln Street, Boston, Massachusetts 02111 (617) 423-3990; *The World in Figures.*

BRITISH VIRGIN ISLANDS - BANKING

G.K. Hall and Company, 70 Lincoln Street, Boston, Massachusetts 02111 (617) 423-3990; *The World in Figures.*

BRITISH VIRGIN ISLANDS - BIRTH RATES

Statistical Office of the United Nations, Publishing Service, New York, New York 10017 (800) 253-9646; *Demographic Yearbook,* and *Statistical Yearbook.*

BRITISH VIRGIN ISLANDS - BONDS

G.K. Hall and Company, 70 Lincoln Street, Boston, Massachusetts 02111 (617) 423-3990; *The World in Figures.*

BRITISH VIRGIN ISLANDS - BOOK PRODUCTION

G.K. Hall and Company, 70 Lincoln Street, Boston, Massachusetts 02111 (617) 423-3990; *The World in Figures.*

BRITISH VIRGIN ISLANDS - BROADCASTING

Billboard Limited, P.O. Box 9027, 1006 AA Amsterdam, The Netherlands (Telephone Number in U.S. (212) 764-7300); *World Radio TV Handbook.*

G.K. Hall and Company, 70 Lincoln Street, Boston, Massachusetts 02111 (617) 423-3990; *The World in Figures.*

United Nations Educational, Scientific and Cultural Organization (UNESCO), 7 Place de Fontenoy, F-75700 Paris, France (Telephone Number in U.S. (212) 963-5981); *Statistical Yearbook.*

BRITISH VIRGIN ISLANDS - BUSINESS

G.K. Hall and Company, 70 Lincoln Street, Boston, Massachusetts 02111 (617) 423-3990; *The World in Figures.*

BRITISH VIRGIN ISLANDS - CALORIE SUPPLY

Food and Agricultural Organization of the United Nations (FAO) Via delle Terme di Caracalla, 00100 Rome, Italy (Telephone Number in U.S. (202) 653-2400); *The State of Food and Agriculture.*

BRITISH VIRGIN ISLANDS - CATTLE - See BRITISH VIRGIN ISLANDS - LIVESTOCK AND POULTRY

BRITISH VIRGIN ISLANDS - CHEMICAL (ORGANIC) PRODUCTION - See BRITISH VIRGIN ISLANDS - MINING AND MINERAL PRODUCTS

BRITISH VIRGIN ISLANDS - CLASS STRUCTURE

G.K. Hall and Company, 70 Lincoln Street, Boston, Massachusetts 02111 (617) 423-3990; *The World in Figures.*

BRITISH VIRGIN ISLANDS - CLIMATE

G.K. Hall and Company, 70 Lincoln Street, Boston, Massachusetts 02111 (617) 423-3990; *The World in Figures.*

BRITISH VIRGIN ISLANDS - COAL PRODUCTION - See BRITISH VIRGIN ISLANDS - MINING AND MINERAL PRODUCTS

BRITISH VIRGIN ISLANDS - COMMUNICATIONS

G.K. Hall and Company, 70 Lincoln Street, Boston, Massachusetts 02111 (617) 423-3990; *The World in Figures.*

BRITISH VIRGIN ISLANDS - CONSUMER PRICE INDEX

G.K. Hall and Company, 70 Lincoln Street, Boston, Massachusetts 02111 (617) 423-3990; *The World in Figures.*

Statistical Office of the United Nations, Publishing Service, New York, New York 10017 (800) 253-9646; *Statistical Yearbook.*

BRITISH VIRGIN ISLANDS - CONSUMER PRICES

International Labour Office, I.L.O. Publications, CH-1211, Geneva 22, Switzerland; *Yearbook of Labour Statistics.*

BRITISH VIRGIN ISLANDS - CONSUMPTION

G.K. Hall and Company, 70 Lincoln Street, Boston, Massachusetts 02111 (617) 423-3990; *The World in Figures.*

BRITISH VIRGIN ISLANDS - CORN PRODUCTION - See BRITISH VIRGIN ISLANDS - CROPS

BRITISH VIRGIN ISLANDS - CORPORATE TAXES - See BRITISH VIRGIN ISLANDS - TAXATION

BRITISH VIRGIN ISLANDS - CUSTOMS DUTIES

G.K. Hall and Company, 70 Lincoln Street, Boston, Massachusetts 02111 (617) 423-3990; *The World in Figures.*

BRITISH VIRGIN ISLANDS - CROPS

Food and Agricultural Organization of the United Nations (FAO) Via delle Terme di Caracalla, 00100 Rome, Italy (Telephone Number in U.S. (202) 653-2400); *The State of Food and Agriculture.*

G.K. Hall and Company, 70 Lincoln Street, Boston, Massachusetts 02111 (617) 423-3990; *The World in Figures.*

BRITISH VIRGIN ISLANDS - DAIRY PRODUCTS

Food and Agricultural Organization of the United Nations (FAO) Via delle Terme di Caracalla, 00100 Rome, Italy (Telephone Number in U.S. (202) 653-2400); *The State of Food and Agriculture.*

BRITISH VIRGIN ISLANDS - DEATH RATES

G.K. Hall and Company, 70 Lincoln Street, Boston, Massachusetts 02111 (617) 423-3990; *The World in Figures.*

Statistical Office of the United Nations, Publishing Service, New York, New York 10017 (800) 253-9646; *Statistical Yearbook.*

World Health Organization, Office of Publications, Avenue Appia, CH-1211 Geneva 27, Switzerland (Telephone Number in U.S. (518) 436-9686); *World Health Statistics Annual.*

BRITISH VIRGIN ISLANDS - DEFENSE EXPENDITURES

G.K. Hall and Company, 70 Lincoln Street, Boston, Massachusetts 02111 (617) 423-3990; *The World in Figures.*

BRITISH VIRGIN ISLANDS - DEMOGRAPHY

G.K. Hall and Company, 70 Lincoln Street, Boston, Massachusetts 02111 (617) 423-3990; *The World in Figures.*

BRITISH VIRGIN ISLANDS - DEVELOPMENT ASSISTANCE

G.K. Hall and Company, 70 Lincoln Street, Boston, Massachusetts 02111 (617) 423-3990; *The World in Figures.*

BRITISH VIRGIN ISLANDS - DISEASES

G.K. Hall and Company, 70 Lincoln Street, Boston, Massachusetts 02111 (617) 423-3990; *The World in Figures.*

World Health Organization, Office of Publications, Avenue Appia, CH-1211 Geneva 27, Switzerland (Telephone Number in U.S. (518) 436-9686); *World Health Statistics Annual.*

BRITISH VIRGIN ISLANDS - DIVORCE RATES

Statistical Office of the United Nations, Publishing Service, New York, New York 10017 (800) 253-9646; *Demographic Yearbook,* and *Statistical Yearbook.*

BRITISH VIRGIN ISLANDS - DOMESTIC PRODUCT

G.K. Hall and Company, 70 Lincoln Street, Boston, Massachusetts 02111 (617) 423-3990; *The World in Figures.*

BRITISH VIRGIN ISLANDS - ECONOMY

G.K. Hall and Company, 70 Lincoln Street, Boston, Massachusetts 02111 (617) 423-3990; *The World in Figures.*

BRITISH VIRGIN ISLANDS - EDUCATION

G.K. Hall and Company, 70 Lincoln Street, Boston, Massachusetts 02111 (617) 423-3990; *The World in Figures.*

United Nations Educational, Scientific and Cultural Organization (UNESCO), 7 Place de Fontenoy, F-75700 Paris, France (Telephone Number in U.S. (212) 963-5981); *Statistical Yearbook.*

BRITISH VIRGIN ISLANDS - EGG PRODUCTION - See BRITISH VIRGIN ISLANDS - DAIRY PRODUCTS

BRITISH VIRGIN ISLANDS - EMPLOYMENT

International Labour Office, I.L.O. Publications, CH-1211, Geneva 22, Switzerland; *Yearbook of Labour Statistics.*

BRITISH VIRGIN ISLANDS - ENERGY

Food and Agricultural Organization of the United Nations (FAO) Via delle Terme di Caracalla, 00100 Rome, Italy (Telephone Number in U.S. (202) 653-2400); *The State of Food and Agriculture.*

G.K. Hall and Company, 70 Lincoln Street, Boston, Massachusetts 02111 (617) 423-3990; *The World in Figures.*

Statistical Office of the United Nations, Publishing Service, New York, New York 10017 (800) 253-9646; *Energy Statistics Yearbook.*

BRITISH VIRGIN ISLANDS - EXPORTS

Food and Agricultural Organization of the United Nations (FAO) Via delle Terme di Caracalla, 00100 Rome, Italy (Telephone Number in U.S. (202) 653-2400); *The State of Food and Agriculture.*

G.K. Hall and Company, 70 Lincoln Street, Boston, Massachusetts 02111 (617) 423-3990; *The World in Figures.*

BRITISH VIRGIN ISLANDS - EXTERNAL TRADE

Food and Agricultural Organization of the United Nations (FAO) Via delle Terme di Caracalla, 00100 Rome, Italy (Telephone Number in U.S. (202) 653-2400); *The State of Food and Agriculture,* and *Trade Yearbook.*

G.K. Hall and Company, 70 Lincoln Street, Boston, Massachusetts 02111 (617) 423-3990; *The World in Figures.*

BRITISH VIRGIN ISLANDS - FARM CROPS - See BRITISH VIRGIN ISLANDS - CROPS

BRITISH VIRGIN ISLANDS - FERTILIZER

Food and Agricultural Organization of the United Nations (FAO) Via delle Terme di Caracalla, 00100 Rome, Italy (Telephone Number in U.S. (202) 653-2400); *The State of Food and Agriculture.*

BRITISH VIRGIN ISLANDS - FETAL MORTALITY

Statistical Office of the United Nations, Publishing Service, New York, New York 10017 (800) 253-9646; *Demographic Yearbook.*

BRITISH VIRGIN ISLANDS - FINANCE

G.K. Hall and Company, 70 Lincoln Street, Boston, Massachusetts 02111 (617) 423-3990; *The World in Figures.*

BRITISH VIRGIN ISLANDS - FISHERIES

Food and Agricultural Organization of the United Nations (FAO), Via delle Terme di Caracalla, 00100 Rome, Italy (Telephone Number in U.S. (202) 653-2400); *Fishery Commodities and Trade,* and *The State of Food and Agriculture.*

BRITISH VIRGIN ISLANDS - FOOD

Food and Agricultural Organization of the United Nations (FAO) Via delle Terme di Caracalla, 00100 Rome, Italy (Telephone Number in U.S. (202) 653-2400); *Production Yearbook,* and *The State of Food and Agriculture.*

G.K. Hall and Company, 70 Lincoln Street, Boston, Massachusetts 02111 (617) 423-3990; *The World in Figures.*

BRITISH VIRGIN ISLANDS - FOREIGN AID

G.K. Hall and Company, 70 Lincoln Street, Boston, Massachusetts 02111 (617) 423-3990; *The World in Figures.*

BRITISH VIRGIN ISLANDS - FOREIGN TRADE

Food and Agricultural Organization of the United Nations (FAO) Via delle Terme di Caracalla, 00100 Rome, Italy (Telephone Number in U.S. (202) 653-2400); *The State of Food and Agriculture.*

G.K. Hall and Company, 70 Lincoln Street, Boston, Massachusetts 02111 (617) 423-3990; *The World in Figures.*

Statistical Office of the United Nations, Publishing Service, New York, New York 10017 (800) 253-9646; *International Trade Statistics Yearbook.*

BRITISH VIRGIN ISLANDS - FORESTRY AND FOREST PRODUCTS

Food and Agricultural Organization of the United Nations (FAO) Via delle Terme di Caracalla, 00100 Rome, Italy (Telephone Number in U.S. (202) 653-2400); *The State of Food and Agriculture.*

G.K. Hall and Company, 70 Lincoln Street, Boston, Massachusetts 02111 (617) 423-3990; *The World in Figures.*

Statistical Office of the United Nations, Publishing Service, New York, New York 10017 (800) 253-9646; *Statistical Yearbook.*

BRITISH VIRGIN ISLANDS - GENERAL MORTALITY

Statistical Office of the United Nations, Publishing Service, New York, New York 10017 (800) 253-9646; *Demographic Yearbook.*

World Health Organization, Office of Publications, Avenue Appia, CH-1211 Geneva 27, Switzerland (Telephone Number in U.S. (518) 436-9686); *World Health Statistics Annual.*

BRITISH VIRGIN ISLANDS - GOVERNMENT

G.K. Hall and Company, 70 Lincoln Street, Boston, Massachusetts 02111 (617) 423-3990; *The World in Figures.*

BRITISH VIRGIN ISLANDS - GRAIN PRODUCTION - See BRITISH VIRGIN ISLANDS - CROPS

BRITISH VIRGIN ISLANDS - GROSS DOMESTIC PRODUCT

G.K. Hall and Company, 70 Lincoln Street, Boston, Massachusetts 02111 (617) 423-3990; *The World in Figures.*

Statistical Office of the United Nations, Publishing Service, New York, New York 10017 (800) 253-9646; *Statistical Yearbook.*

BRITISH VIRGIN ISLANDS - HEALTH

G.K. Hall and Company, 70 Lincoln Street, Boston, Massachusetts 02111 (617) 423-3990; *The World in Figures.*

Statistical Office of the United Nations, Publishing Service, New York, New York 10017 (800) 253-9646; *Statistical Yearbook.*

BRITISH VIRGIN ISLANDS - HIGHWAYS

G.K. Hall and Company, 70 Lincoln Street, Boston, Massachusetts 02111 (617) 423-3990; *The World in Figures.*

BRITISH VIRGIN ISLANDS - HIDE PRODUCTION

Food and Agricultural Organization of the United Nations (FAO), Via delle Terme di Caracalla, 00100 Rome, Italy (Telephone Number in U.S. (202) 653-2400); *Production Yearbook.*

BRITISH VIRGIN ISLANDS - HOURS OF WORK - See BRITISH VIRGIN ISLANDS - EMPLOYMENT

BRITISH VIRGIN ISLANDS - ILLITERATE POPULATION

G.K. Hall and Company, 70 Lincoln Street, Boston, Massachusetts 02111 (617) 423-3990; *The World in Figures.*

United Nations Educational, Scientific and Cultural Organization (UNESCO), 7 Place de Fontenoy, F-75700 Paris, France (Telephone Number in U.S. (212) 963-5981); *Statistical Yearbook.*

BRITISH VIRGIN ISLANDS - IMPORTS

Food and Agricultural Organization of the United Nations (FAO) Via delle Terme di Caracalla, 00100 Rome, Italy (Telephone Number in U.S. (202) 653-2400); *The State of Food and Agriculture.*

G.K. Hall and Company, 70 Lincoln Street, Boston, Massachusetts 02111 (617) 423-3990; *The World in Figures.*

BRITISH VIRGIN ISLANDS - INDUSTRY

G.K. Hall and Company, 70 Lincoln Street, Boston, Massachusetts 02111 (617) 423-3990; *The World in Figures.*

International Labour Office, I.L.O. Publications, CH-1211, Geneva 22, Switzerland; *Yearbook of Labour Statistics.*

BRITISH VIRGIN ISLANDS - INFANT AND MATERNAL MORTALITY

Statistical Office of the United Nations, Publishing Service, New York, New York 10017 (800) 253-9646; *Demographic Yearbook,* and *Statistical Yearbook.*

BRITISH VIRGIN ISLANDS - LABOR FORCE

Food and Agricultural Organization of the United Nations (FAO) Via delle Terme di Caracalla, 00100 Rome, Italy (Telephone Number in U.S. (202) 653-2400); *The State of Food and Agriculture.*

G.K. Hall and Company, 70 Lincoln Street, Boston, Massachusetts 02111 (617) 423-3990; *The World in Figures.*

BRITISH VIRGIN ISLANDS - LABOR PRODUCTIVITY

International Labour Office, I.L.O. Publications, CH-1211, Geneva 22, Switzerland; *Yearbook of Labour Statistics.*

BRITISH VIRGIN ISLANDS - LAND USE

Food and Agricultural Organization of the United Nations (FAO), Via delle Terme di Caracalla, 00100 Rome, Italy (Telephone Number in U.S. (202) 653-2400); *Production Yearbook.*

G.K. Hall and Company, 70 Lincoln Street, Boston, Massachusetts 02111 (617) 423-3990; *The World in Figures.*

BRITISH VIRGIN ISLANDS - LIBRARIES

United Nations Educational, Scientific and Cultural Organization (UNESCO), 7 Place de Fontenoy, F-75700 Paris, France (Telephone Number in U.S. (212) 963-5981); *Statistical Yearbook.*

BRITISH VIRGIN ISLANDS - LIVESTOCK AND POULTRY

Food and Agricultural Organization of the United Nations (FAO), Via delle Terme di Caracalla, 00100 Rome, Italy (Telephone Number in U.S. (202) 653-2400); *Production Yearbook,* and *The State of Food and Agriculture.*

G.K. Hall and Company, 70 Lincoln Street, Boston, Massachusetts 02111 (617) 423-3990; *The World in Figures.*

Statistical Office of the United Nations, Publishing Service, New York, New York 10017 (800) 253-9646; *Statistical Yearbook.*

BRITISH VIRGIN ISLANDS - LIVING LEVELS

G.K. Hall and Company, 70 Lincoln Street, Boston, Massachusetts 02111 (617) 423-3990; *The World in Figures.*

BRITISH VIRGIN ISLANDS - MANUFACTURING

G.K. Hall and Company, 70 Lincoln Street, Boston, Massachusetts 02111 (617) 423-3990; *The World in Figures.*

BRITISH VIRGIN ISLANDS - MARRIAGE RATES

Statistical Office of the United Nations, Publishing Service, New York, New York 10017 (800) 253-9646; *Demographic Yearbook*, and *Statistical Yearbook*.

BRITISH VIRGIN ISLANDS - MEAT PRODUCTION - See BRITISH VIRGIN ISLANDS - LIVESTOCK AND POULTRY

BRITISH VIRGIN ISLANDS - MERCHANT SHIPPING

G.K. Hall and Company, 70 Lincoln Street, Boston, Massachusetts 02111 (617) 423-3990; *The World in Figures*.

Statistical Office of the United Nations, Publishing Service, New York, New York 10017 (800) 253-9646; *Statistical Yearbook*.

BRITISH VIRGIN ISLANDS - MILITARY

G.K. Hall and Company, 70 Lincoln Street, Boston, Massachusetts 02111 (617) 423-3990; *The World in Figures*.

BRITISH VIRGIN ISLANDS - MINING AND MINERAL PRODUCTS

G.K. Hall and Company, 70 Lincoln Street, Boston, Massachusetts 02111 (617) 423-3990; *The World in Figures*.

BRITISH VIRGIN ISLANDS - MONEY SUPPLY

G.K. Hall and Company, 70 Lincoln Street, Boston, Massachusetts 02111 (617) 423-3990; *The World in Figures*.

BRITISH VIRGIN ISLANDS - MOTION PICTURES

Statistical Office of the United Nations, Publishing Service, New York, New York 10017 (800) 253-9646; *Statistical Yearbook*.

BRITISH VIRGIN ISLANDS - MOTOR VEHICLES IN USE

G.K. Hall and Company, 70 Lincoln Street, Boston, Massachusetts 02111 (617) 423-3990; *The World in Figures*.

Statistical Office of the United Nations, Publishing Service, New York, New York 10017 (800) 253-9646; *Statistical Yearbook*.

BRITISH VIRGIN ISLANDS - MUSEUMS

United Nations Educational, Scientific and Cultural Organization (UNESCO), 7 Place de Fontenoy, F-75700 Paris, France (Telephone Number in U.S. (212) 963-5981); *Statistical Yearbook*.

BRITISH VIRGIN ISLANDS - NATALITY - See BRITISH VIRGIN ISLANDS - BIRTH RATES

BRITISH VIRGIN ISLANDS - NATIONAL ACCOUNTS

Statistical Office of the United Nations, Publishing Service, New York, New York 10017 (800) 253-9646; *Demographic Yearbook, National Accounts Statistics*, and *Statistical Yearbook*.

BRITISH VIRGIN ISLANDS - NATIONAL INCOME

G.K. Hall and Company, 70 Lincoln Street, Boston, Massachusetts 02111 (617) 423-3990; *The World in Figures*.

BRITISH VIRGIN ISLANDS - NEWSPAPER PRODUCTION - See BRITISH VIRGIN ISLANDS - FORESTRY AND FOREST PRODUCTS

BRITISH VIRGIN ISLANDS - OCCUPATIONS - See BRITISH VIRGIN ISLANDS - LABOR FORCE

BRITISH VIRGIN ISLANDS - PERIODICALS

United Nations Educational, Scientific and Cultural Organization (UNESCO), 7 Place de Fontenoy, F-75700 Paris, France (Telephone Number in U.S. (212) 963-5981); *Statistical Yearbook*.

BRITISH VIRGIN ISLANDS - PESTICIDE USE

Food and Agricultural Organization of the United Nations (FAO) Via delle Terme di Caracalla, 00100 Rome, Italy (Telephone Number in U.S. (202) 653-2400); *The State of Food and Agriculture*.

BRITISH VIRGIN ISLANDS - PETROLEUM INDUSTRY

Food and Agricultural Organization of the United Nations (FAO) Via delle Terme di Caracalla, 00100 Rome, Italy (Telephone Number in U.S. (202) 653-2400); *The State of Food and Agriculture*.

G.K. Hall and Company, 70 Lincoln Street, Boston, Massachusetts 02111 (617) 423-3990; *The World in Figures*.

BRITISH VIRGIN ISLANDS - PIGS - See BRITISH VIRGIN ISLANDS - LIVESTOCK AND POULTRY

BRITISH VIRGIN ISLANDS - POPULATION

Food and Agricultural Organization of the United Nations (FAO), Via delle Terme di Caracalla, 00100 Rome, Italy (Telephone Number in U.S. (202) 653-2400); *Production Yearbook*.

G.K. Hall and Company, 70 Lincoln Street, Boston, Massachusetts 02111 (617) 423-3990; *The World in Figures*.

International Labour Office, I.L.O. Publications, CH-1211, Geneva 22, Switzerland; *Yearbook of Labour Statistics*.

Statistical Office of the United Nations, Publishing Service, New York, New York 10017 (800) 253-9646; *Demographic Yearbook*, and *Statistical Yearbook*.

World Health Organization, Office of Publications, Avenue Appia, CH-1211 Geneva 27, Switzerland (Telephone Number in U.S. (518) 436-9686); *World Health Statistics Annual*.

BRITISH VIRGIN ISLANDS - PRICES

Food and Agricultural Organization of the United Nations (FAO), Via delle Terme di Caracalla, 00100 Rome, Italy (Telephone Number in U.S. (202) 653-2400); *Production Yearbook*, and *The State of Food and Agriculture*.

G.K. Hall and Company, 70 Lincoln Street, Boston, Massachusetts 02111 (617) 423-3990; *The World in Figures*.

International Labour Office, I.L.O. Publications, CH-1211, Geneva 22, Switzerland; *Yearbook of Labour Statistics*.

BRITISH VIRGIN ISLANDS - PRODUCTION

G.K. Hall and Company, 70 Lincoln Street, Boston, Massachusetts 02111 (617) 423-3990; *The World in Figures*.

BRITISH VIRGIN ISLANDS - RADIO BROADCASTING - See BRITISH VIRGIN ISLANDS - BROADCASTING

BRITISH VIRGIN ISLANDS - RAILWAYS

G.K. Hall and Company, 70 Lincoln Street, Boston, Massachusetts 02111 (617) 423-3990; *The World in Figures.*

BRITISH VIRGIN ISLANDS - RENT PRICES

International Labour Office, I.L.O. Publications, CH-1211, Geneva 22, Switzerland; *Yearbook of Labour Statistics.*

BRITISH VIRGIN ISLANDS - RETAIL TRADE

G.K. Hall and Company, 70 Lincoln Street, Boston, Massachusetts 02111 (617) 423-3990; *The World in Figures.*

BRITISH VIRGIN ISLANDS - SOCIAL DATA

G.K. Hall and Company, 70 Lincoln Street, Boston, Massachusetts 02111 (617) 423-3990; *The World in Figures.*

BRITISH VIRGIN ISLANDS - STOCKS - COMMODITY - MARKET PRICE - INDEX

Food and Agricultural Organization of the United Nations (FAO) Via delle Terme di Caracalla, 00100 Rome, Italy (Telephone Number in U.S. (202) 653-2400); *The State of Food and Agriculture.*

BRITISH VIRGIN ISLANDS - TAXATION

G.K. Hall and Company, 70 Lincoln Street, Boston, Massachusetts 02111 (617) 423-3990; *The World in Figures.*

BRITISH VIRGIN ISLANDS - TELEPHONES IN USE

American Telephone and Telegraph Company, 26 Parsippany Road, Whippany, New Jersey 07981 (800) 338-4038; *The World's Telephones.*

G.K. Hall and Company, 70 Lincoln Street, Boston, Massachusetts 02111 (617) 423-3990; *The World in Figures.*

Statistical Office of the United Nations, Publishing Service, New York, New York 10017 (800) 253-9646; *Statistical Yearbook.*

BRITISH VIRGIN ISLANDS - TEXTILE INDUSTRY

G.K. Hall and Company, 70 Lincoln Street, Boston, Massachusetts 02111 (617) 423-3990; *The World in Figures.*

BRITISH VIRGIN ISLANDS - THEATRE

United Nations Educational, Scientific and Cultural Organization (UNESCO), 7 Place de Fontenoy, F-75700 Paris, France (Telephone Number in U.S. (212) 963-5981); *Statistical Yearbook.*

BRITISH VIRGIN ISLANDS - TOURISM

G.K. Hall and Company, 70 Lincoln Street, Boston, Massachusetts 02111 (617) 423-3990; *The World in Figures.*

BRITISH VIRGIN ISLANDS - TRACTORS IN USE

Statistical Office of the United Nations, Publishing Service, New York, New York 10017 (800) 253-9646; *Statistical Yearbook.*

BRITISH VIRGIN ISLANDS - TRADE - See BRITISH VIRGIN ISLANDS - FOREIGN TRADE

BRITISH VIRGIN ISLANDS - TRANSPORTATION AND COMMUNICATIONS

G.K. Hall and Company, 70 Lincoln Street, Boston, Massachusetts 02111 (617) 423-3990; *The World in Figures.*

BRITISH VIRGIN ISLANDS - UNEMPLOYMENT

International Labour Office, I.L.O. Publications, CH-1211, Geneva 22, Switzerland; *Yearbook of Labour Statistics.*

BRITISH VIRGIN ISLANDS - VITAL STATISTICS

G.K. Hall and Company, 70 Lincoln Street, Boston, Massachusetts 02111 (617) 423-3990; *The World in Figures.*

BRITISH VIRGIN ISLANDS - WAGES

G.K. Hall and Company, 70 Lincoln Street, Boston, Massachusetts 02111 (617) 423-3990; *The World in Figures.*

International Labour Office, I.L.O. Publications, CH-1211, Geneva 22, Switzerland; *Yearbook of Labour Statistics.*

BRITISH VIRGIN ISLANDS - WEATHER

G.K. Hall and Company, 70 Lincoln Street, Boston, Massachusetts 02111 (617) 423-3990; *The World in Figures.*

BROADCASTING STATIONS - See RADIO and TELEVISION BROADCASTING

BROADWAY AND OFF-BROADWAY SHOWS

Theatre Communications Group, 355 Lexington Avenue, New York, New York 10017 (212) 697-5230.

Variety, 249 West 17th Street, New York, New York 10011 (212) 779-1100; various June issues.

BROCCOLI

U.S. Department of Agriculture, National Agricultural Statistics Service, Fourteenth Street and Independence Avenue, SW, Washington, D.C. 20250 (202) 219-1504; *Economic Indicators of the Farm Sector: National Financial Summary, Agricultural Statistics, Food Consumption, Prices, and Expenditures, Vegetables,* and unpublished data.

BROILERS - See also POULTRY

BROILERS - PRODUCTION

U.S. Department of Agriculture, Economic Research Service, Fourteenth Street and Independence Avenue, SW, Washington, D.C. 20250 (202) 219-1504; *Economic Indicators of the Farm Sector: National Financial Summary.*

U.S. Department of Agriculture, National Agricultural Statistics Service, Fourteenth Street and Independence Avenue, SW, Washington, D.C. 20250 (202) 219-1504; *Layers and Egg Production, Poultry - Production and Value,* and *Turkeys, Chickens and Eggs.*

BROMINE

U.S. Department of the Interior, Bureau of Mines, 810 Seventh Street, NW, Washington, D.C. 20241 (202) 501-9649; *Mineral Commodity Summaries.*

BRONCHITIS, EMPHYSEMA, ETC. - DEATHS

U.S. Department of Health and Human Services, National Center for Health Statistics, 3700 East-West Highway, Hyattsville, Maryland 20782 (301) 436-8500; *Monthly Vital Statistics Report, Vital Statistics of the United States,* and unpublished data.

World Health Organization, Office of Publications, Avenue Appia, CH-1211 Geneva 27, Switzerland (Telephone Number in U.S. (518) 436-9686); *World Health Statistics Annual.*

Brunei - National Statistical Office

Chief Statistician, Economic Planning Unit, Bandar Seri Begawan, Brunei.

Brunei - Primary Statistics Source

Chief Statistician, Economic Planning Unit, Bandar Seri Begawan, Brunei; *Brunei Statistical Yearbook.*

BRUNEI - AGRICULTURE

Federal Statistical Office, Gustav - Stresemann - Ring 11, D-6200 Wiesbaden, Germany; *Brunei.*

Food and Agricultural Organization of the United Nations (FAO), Via delle Terme di Caracalla, 00100 Rome, Italy (Telephone Number in U.S. (202) 653-2400); *Production Yearbook, The State of Food and Agriculture,* and *Trade Yearbook.*

G.K. Hall and Company, 70 Lincoln Street, Boston, Massachusetts 02111 (617) 423-3990; *The World in Figures.*

Statistical Office of the United Nations, Publishing Service, New York, New York 10017 (800) 253-9646; *Statistical Yearbook,* and *Statistical Yearbook for Asia and the Pacific.*

Times Books, 201 East 50th Street, New York, New York 10022 (212) 751-2600; *The Economist Book of Vital World Statistics.*

BRUNEI - AIRLINE SERVICE

The Economist Intelligence Unit (Asia) Limited, 10th Floor, Luk Kwok Centre, 72 Gloucester Road, Wanchai, Hong Kong (Phone Number in U.S. (800) 938-4685); *Asian Market Atlas.*

G.K. Hall and Company, 70 Lincoln Street, Boston, Massachusetts 02111 (617) 423-3990; *The World in Figures.*

Times Books, 201 East 50th Street, New York, New York 10022 (212) 751-2600; *The Economist Book of Vital World Statistics.*

BRUNEI - AREA AND DENSITY OF POPULATION

Federal Statistical Office, Gustav - Stresemann - Ring 11, D-6200 Wiesbaden, Germany; *Brunei.*

Food and Agricultural Organization of the United Nations (FAO) Via delle Terme di Caracalla, 00100 Rome, Italy (Telephone Number in U.S. (202) 653-2400); *The State of Food and Agriculture.*

G.K. Hall and Company, 70 Lincoln Street, Boston, Massachusetts 02111 (617) 423-3990; *The World in Figures.*

Statistical Office of the United Nations, Publishing Service, New York, New York 10017 (800) 253-9646; *Statistical Yearbook.*

Times Books, 201 East 50th Street, New York, New York 10022 (212) 751-2600; *The Economist Book of Vital World Statistics.*

BRUNEI - BALANCE OF PAYMENTS

The Economist Intelligence Unit, 111 West 57th Street, New York, New York 10019 (800) 938-4685; *The World Market Atlas.*

Federal Statistical Office, Gustav - Stresemann - Ring 11, D-6200 Wiesbaden, Germany; *Brunei.*

G.K. Hall and Company, 70 Lincoln Street, Boston, Massachusetts 02111 (617) 423-3990; *The World in Figures.*

BRUNEI - BANKING

G.K. Hall and Company, 70 Lincoln Street, Boston, Massachusetts 02111 (617) 423-3990; *The World in Figures.*

BRUNEI - BIRTH RATES

The Economist Intelligence Unit (Asia) Limited, 10th Floor, Luk Kwok Centre, 72 Gloucester Road, Wanchai, Hong Kong (Phone Number in U.S. (800) 938-4685); *Asian Market Atlas.*

Statistical Office of the United Nations, Publishing Service, New York, New York 10017 (800) 253-9646; *Demographic Yearbook,* and *Statistical Yearbook.*

World Health Organization, Office of Publications, Avenue Appia, CH-1211 Geneva 27, Switzerland (Telephone Number in U.S. (518) 436-9686); *World Health Statistics Annual.*

BRUNEI - BONDS

G.K. Hall and Company, 70 Lincoln Street, Boston, Massachusetts 02111 (617) 423-3990; *The World in Figures.*

BRUNEI - BOOK PRODUCTION

G.K. Hall and Company, 70 Lincoln Street, Boston, Massachusetts 02111 (617) 423-3990; *The World in Figures.*

United Nations Educational, Scientific and Cultural Organization (UNESCO), 7 Place de Fontenoy, F-75700 Paris, France (Telephone Number in U.S. (212) 963-5981); *Statistical Yearbook.*

BRUNEI - BROADCASTING

Billboard Limited, P.O. Box 9027, 1006 AA Amsterdam, The Netherlands (Telephone Number in U.S. (212) 764-7300); *World Radio TV Handbook.*

The Economist Intelligence Unit (Asia) Limited, 10th Floor, Luk Kwok Centre, 72 Gloucester Road, Wanchai, Hong Kong (Phone Number in U.S. (800) 938-4685); *Asian Market Atlas.*

G.K. Hall and Company, 70 Lincoln Street, Boston, Massachusetts 02111 (617) 423-3990; *The World in Figures.*

Times Books, 201 East 50th Street, New York, New York 10022 (212) 751-2600; *The Economist Book of Vital World Statistics.*

United Nations Educational, Scientific and Cultural Organization (UNESCO), 7 Place de Fontenoy, F-75700 Paris, France (Telephone Number in U.S. (212) 963-5981); *Statistical Yearbook.*

BRUNEI - BUSINESS

G.K. Hall and Company, 70 Lincoln Street, Boston, Massachusetts 02111 (617) 423-3990; *The World in Figures.*

BRUNEI - CALORIE SUPPLY

Food and Agricultural Organization of the United Nations (FAO) Via delle Terme di Caracalla, 00100 Rome, Italy (Telephone Number in U.S. (202) 653-2400); *The State of Food and Agriculture.*

BRUNEI - CATTLE - See BRUNEI - LIVESTOCK AND POULTRY

BRUNEI - CHEMICAL (ORGANIC) PRODUCTION - See BRUNEI - MINING AND MINERAL PRODUCTS

BRUNEI - CLASS STRUCTURE

G.K. Hall and Company, 70 Lincoln Street, Boston, Massachusetts 02111 (617) 423-3990; *The World in Figures.*

BRUNEI - CLIMATE

G.K. Hall and Company, 70 Lincoln Street, Boston, Massachusetts 02111 (617) 423-3990; *The World in Figures.*

BRUNEI - COAL PRODUCTION - See BRUNEI - MINING AND MINERAL PRODUCTS

BRUNEI - COMMUNICATIONS

Federal Statistical Office, Gustav - Stresemann - Ring 11, D-6200 Wiesbaden, Germany; *Brunei.*

G.K. Hall and Company, 70 Lincoln Street, Boston, Massachusetts 02111 (617) 423-3990; *The World in Figures.*

Statistical Office of the United Nations, Publishing Service, New York, New York 10017 (800) 253-9646; *Statistical Yearbook for Asia and the Pacific.*

BRUNEI - CONSUMER PRICE INDEX

Federal Statistical Office, Gustav - Stresemann - Ring 11, D-6200 Wiesbaden, Germany; *Brunei.*

G.K. Hall and Company, 70 Lincoln Street, Boston, Massachusetts 02111 (617) 423-3990; *The World in Figures.*

Statistical Office of the United Nations, Publishing Service, New York, New York 10017 (800) 253-9646; *Statistical Yearbook.*

BRUNEI - CONSUMER PRICES

Federal Statistical Office, Gustav - Stresemann - Ring 11, D-6200 Wiesbaden, Germany; *Brunei.*

International Labour Office, I.L.O. Publications, CH-1211, Geneva 22, Switzerland; *Yearbook of Labour Statistics.*

BRUNEI - CONSUMPTION

G.K. Hall and Company, 70 Lincoln Street, Boston, Massachusetts 02111 (617) 423-3990; *The World in Figures.*

BRUNEI - CORN PRODUCTION - See BRUNEI - CROPS

BRUNEI - CORPORATE TAXES - See BRUNEI - TAXATION

BRUNEI - CROPS

Food and Agricultural Organization of the United Nations (FAO) Via delle Terme di Caracalla, 00100 Rome, Italy (Telephone Number in U.S. (202) 653-2400); *The State of Food and Agriculture.*

G.K. Hall and Company, 70 Lincoln Street, Boston, Massachusetts 02111 (617) 423-3990; *The World in Figures.*

Statistical Office of the United Nations, Publishing Service, New York, New York 10017 (800) 253-9646; *Statistical Yearbook.*

BRUNEI - CUSTOMS DUTIES

G.K. Hall and Company, 70 Lincoln Street, Boston, Massachusetts 02111 (617) 423-3990; *The World in Figures.*

BRUNEI - CRIME

International Criminal Police Organization (INTERPOL), 26 rue Armengaud, 92210 Saint Cloud, France; *International Crime Statistics.*

Yale University Press, Yale Station, New Haven, Connecticut 06520 (203) 432-0940; *Violence and Crime in Cross-National Perspective.*

BRUNEI - DAIRY PRODUCTS

Food and Agricultural Organization of the United Nations (FAO) Via delle Terme di Caracalla, 00100 Rome, Italy (Telephone Number in U.S. (202) 653-2400); *The State of Food and Agriculture.*

BRUNEI - DEATH RATES

The Economist Intelligence Unit (Asia) Limited, 10th Floor, Luk Kwok Centre, 72 Gloucester Road, Wanchai, Hong Kong (Phone Number in U.S. (800) 938-4685); *Asian Market Atlas.*

G.K. Hall and Company, 70 Lincoln Street, Boston, Massachusetts 02111 (617) 423-3990; *The World in Figures.*

Statistical Office of the United Nations, Publishing Service, New York, New York 10017 (800) 253-9646; *Statistical Yearbook.*

World Health Organization, Office of Publications, Avenue Appia, CH-1211 Geneva 27, Switzerland (Telephone Number in U.S. (518) 436-9686); *World Health Statistics Annual.*

BRUNEI - DEFENSE EXPENDITURES

G.K. Hall and Company, 70 Lincoln Street, Boston, Massachusetts 02111 (617) 423-3990; *The World in Figures.*

BRUNEI - DEMOGRAPHY

The Economist Intelligence Unit, 111 West 57th Street, New York, New York 10019 (800) 938-4685; *The World Market Atlas.*

The Economist Intelligence Unit (Asia) Limited, 10th Floor, Luk Kwok Centre, 72 Gloucester Road, Wanchai, Hong Kong (Phone Number in U.S. (800) 938-4685); *Asian Market Atlas.*

Federal Statistical Office, Gustav - Stresemann - Ring 11, D-6200 Wiesbaden, Germany; *Brunei.*

G.K. Hall and Company, 70 Lincoln Street, Boston, Massachusetts 02111 (617) 423-3990; *The World in Figures.*

BRUNEI - DEVELOPMENT ASSISTANCE

G.K. Hall and Company, 70 Lincoln Street, Boston, Massachusetts 02111 (617) 423-3990; *The World in Figures.*

Statistical Office of the United Nations, Publishing Service, New York, New York 10017 (800) 253-9646; *Statistical Yearbook.*

BRUNEI - DISEASES

G.K. Hall and Company, 70 Lincoln Street, Boston, Massachusetts 02111 (617) 423-3990; *The World in Figures.*

World Health Organization, Office of Publications, Avenue Appia, CH-1211 Geneva 27, Switzerland (Telephone Number in U.S. (518) 436-9686); *World Health Statistics Annual.*

BRUNEI - DIVORCE RATES

Statistical Office of the United Nations, Publishing Service, New York, New York 10017 (800) 253-9646; *Demographic Yearbook,* and *Statistical Yearbook.*

BRUNEI - DOMESTIC PRODUCT

G.K. Hall and Company, 70 Lincoln Street, Boston, Massachusetts 02111 (617) 423-3990; *The World in Figures.*

BRUNEI - DUCKS - See BRUNEI - LIVESTOCK AND POULTRY

BRUNEI - ECONOMY

Federal Statistical Office, Gustav - Stresemann - Ring 11, D-6200 Wiesbaden, Germany; *Brunei.*

G.K. Hall and Company, 70 Lincoln Street, Boston, Massachusetts 02111 (617) 423-3990; *The World in Figures.*

BRUNEI - EDUCATION

The Economist Intelligence Unit, 111 West 57th Street, New York, New York 10019 (800) 938-4685; *The World Market Atlas.*

The Economist Intelligence Unit (Asia) Limited, 10th Floor, Luk Kwok Centre, 72 Gloucester Road, Wanchai, Hong Kong (Phone Number in U.S. (800) 938-4685); *Asian Market Atlas.*

Federal Statistical Office, Gustav - Stresemann - Ring 11, D-6200 Wiesbaden, Germany; *Brunei.*

G.K. Hall and Company, 70 Lincoln Street, Boston, Massachusetts 02111 (617) 423-3990; *The World in Figures.*

Statistical Office of the United Nations, Publishing Service, New York, New York 10017; *Statistical Yearbook for Asia and the Pacific.*

Times Books, 201 East 50th Street, New York, New York 10022 (212) 751-2600; *The Economist Book of Vital World Statistics.*

United Nations Educational, Scientific and Cultural Organization (UNESCO), 7 Place de Fontenoy, F-75700 Paris, France (Telephone Number in U.S. (212) 963-5981); *Statistical Yearbook.*

BRUNEI - EGG PRODUCTION - See BRUNEI - DAIRY PRODUCTS

BRUNEI - ELECTRICITY

Penn Well Publishing Company, 1421 South Sheridan Road, P.O. Box 1260, Tulsa, Oklahoma 74101 (800) 752-9764; *International Energy Statistics Sourcebook.*

Statistical Office of the United Nations, Publishing Service, New York, New York 10017 (800) 253-9646; *Statistical Yearbook.*

Times Books, 201 East 50th Street, New York, New York 10022 (212) 751-2600; *The Economist Book of Vital World Statistics.*

BRUNEI - EMPLOYMENT

Federal Statistical Office, Gustav - Stresemann - Ring 11, D-6200 Wiesbaden, Germany; *Brunei.*

International Labour Office, I.L.O. Publications, CH-1211, Geneva 22, Switzerland; *Yearbook of Labour Statistics.*

Statistical Office of the United Nations, Publishing Service, New York, New York 10017 (800) 253-9646; *Statistical Yearbook.*

BRUNEI - ENERGY

Food and Agricultural Organization of the United Nations (FAO) Via delle Terme di Caracalla, 00100 Rome, Italy (Telephone Number in U.S. (202) 653-2400); *The State of Food and Agriculture.*

G.K. Hall and Company, 70 Lincoln Street, Boston, Massachusetts 02111 (617) 423-3990; *The World in Figures.*

Penn Well Publishing Company, 1421 South Sheridan Road, P.O. Box 1260, Tulsa, Oklahoma 74101 (800) 752-9764; *International Energy Statistics Sourcebook.*

Statistical Office of the United Nations, Publishing Service, New York, New York 10017 (800) 253-9646; *Energy Statistics Yearbook,* and *Statistical Yearbook for Asia and the Pacific.*

Times Books, 201 East 50th Street, New York, New York 10022 (212) 751-2600; *The Economist Book of Vital World Statistics.*

BRUNEI - EXCHANGE RATES

The Economist Intelligence Unit (Asia) Limited, 10th Floor, Luk Kwok Centre, 72 Gloucester Road, Wanchai, Hong Kong (Phone Number in U.S. (800) 938-4685); *Asian Market Atlas.*

BRUNEI - EXPORTS

The Economist Intelligence Unit, 111 West 57th Street, New York, New York 10019 (800) 938-4685; *The World Market Atlas.*

The Economist Intelligence Unit (Asia) Limited, 10th Floor, Luk Kwok Centre, 72 Gloucester Road, Wanchai, Hong Kong (Phone Number in U.S. (800) 938-4685); *Asian Market Atlas.*

Food and Agricultural Organization of the United Nations (FAO) Via delle Terme di Caracalla, 00100 Rome, Italy (Telephone Number in U.S. (202) 653-2400); *The State of Food and Agriculture.*

G.K. Hall and Company, 70 Lincoln Street, Boston, Massachusetts 02111 (617) 423-3990; *The World in Figures.*

International Monetary Fund, 700 Nineteenth Street, NW, Washington, D.C. 20431 (202) 623-7000; *Direction of Trade Statistics.*

Statistical Office of the United Nations, Publishing Service, New York, New York 10017 (800) 253-9646; *Foreign Trade Statistics of Asia and the Pacific, Trade in Manufactures of Developing Countries, Statistical Yearbook,* and *Statistical Yearbook for Asia and the Pacific.*

Times Books, 201 East 50th Street, New York, New York 10022 (212) 751-2600; *The Economist Book of Vital World Statistics.*

BRUNEI - EXTERNAL TRADE

Food and Agricultural Organization of the United Nations (FAO) Via delle Terme di Caracalla, 00100 Rome, Italy (Telephone Number in U.S. (202) 653-2400); *The State of Food and Agriculture,* and *Trade Yearbook.*

G.K. Hall and Company, 70 Lincoln Street, Boston, Massachusetts 02111 (617) 423-3990; *The World in Figures.*

Statistical Office of the United Nations, Publishing Service, New York, New York 10017 (800) 253-9646; *Statistical Yearbook.*

BRUNEI - FARM CROPS - See BRUNEI - CROPS

BRUNEI - FETAL MORTALITY

Statistical Office of the United Nations, Publishing Service, New York, New York 10017 (800) 253-9646; *Demographic Yearbook.*

BRUNEI - FERTILITY RATES

The Economist Intelligence Unit (Asia) Limited, 10th Floor, Luk Kwok Centre, 72 Gloucester Road, Wanchai, Hong Kong (Phone Number in U.S. (800) 938-4685); *Asian Market Atlas.*

BRUNEI - FERTILIZER

Food and Agricultural Organization of the United Nations (FAO) Via delle Terme di Caracalla, 00100 Rome, Italy (Telephone Number in U.S. (202) 653-2400); *The State of Food and Agriculture.*

BRUNEI - FILM - See BRUNEI - MOTION PICTURES

BRUNEI - FINANCE

Federal Statistical Office, Gustav - Stresemann - Ring 11, D-6200 Wiesbaden, Germany; *Brunei.*

G.K. Hall and Company, 70 Lincoln Street, Boston, Massachusetts 02111 (617) 423-3990; *The World in Figures.*

Statistical Office of the United Nations, Publishing Service, New York, New York 10017 (800) 253-9646; *Statistical Yearbook for Asia and the Pacific.*

BRUNEI - FISHERIES

Federal Statistical Office, Gustav - Stresemann - Ring 11, D-6200 Wiesbaden, Germany; *Brunei.*

Food and Agricultural Organization of the United Nations (FAO) Via delle Terme di Caracalla, 00100 Rome, Italy (Telephone Number in U.S. (202) 653-2400); *The State of Food and Agriculture,* and *Yearbook of Fishery Statistics.*

Statistical Office of the United Nations, Publishing Service, New York, New York 10017 (800) 253-9646; *Statistical Yearbook.*

BRUNEI - FOOD

Food and Agricultural Organization of the United Nations (FAO) Via delle Terme di Caracalla, 00100 Rome, Italy (Telephone Number in U.S. (202) 653-2400); *Production Yearbook,* and *The State of Food and Agriculture.*

G.K. Hall and Company, 70 Lincoln Street, Boston, Massachusetts 02111 (617) 423-3990; *The World in Figures.*

Statistical Office of the United Nations, Publishing Service, New York, New York 10017 (800) 253-9646; *Statistical Yearbook for Asia and the Pacific.*

BRUNEI - FOREIGN AID

G.K. Hall and Company, 70 Lincoln Street, Boston, Massachusetts 02111 (617) 423-3990; *The World in Figures.*

BRUNEI - FOREIGN TRADE

The Economist Intelligence Unit (Asia) Limited, 10th Floor, Luk Kwok Centre, 72 Gloucester Road, Wanchai, Hong Kong (Phone Number in U.S. (800) 938-4685); *Asian Market Atlas.*

Federal Statistical Office, Gustav - Stresemann - Ring 11, D-6200 Wiesbaden, Germany; *Brunei.*

Food and Agricultural Organization of the United Nations (FAO) Via delle Terme di Caracalla, 00100 Rome, Italy (Telephone Number in U.S. (202) 653-2400); *The State of Food and Agriculture.*

G.K. Hall and Company, 70 Lincoln Street, Boston, Massachusetts 02111 (617) 423-3990; *The World in Figures.*

Organisation for Economic Co-operation and Development (OECD), 2 rue Andre-Pascal, 75 Paris 16, France (Telephone Number in U.S. (202) 785-6323); *Trade by Commodities.*

Statistical Office of the United Nations, Publishing Service, New York, New York 10017 (800) 253-9646; *International Trade Statistics Yearbook,* and *Statistical Yearbook.*

BRUNEI - FORESTRY AND FOREST PRODUCTS

The Economist Intelligence Unit (Asia) Limited, 10th Floor, Luk Kwok Centre, 72 Gloucester Road, Wanchai, Hong Kong (Phone Number in U.S. (800) 938-4685); *Asian Market Atlas.*

Federal Statistical Office, Gustav - Stresemann - Ring 11, D-6200 Wiesbaden, Germany; *Brunei.*

Food and Agricultural Organization of the United Nations (FAO) Via delle Terme di Caracalla, 00100 Rome, Italy (Telephone Number in U.S. (202) 653-2400); *The State of Food and Agriculture,* and *Yearbook of Forest Statistics.*

G.K. Hall and Company, 70 Lincoln Street, Boston, Massachusetts 02111 (617) 423-3990; *The World in Figures.*

Statistical Office of the United Nations, Publishing Service, New York, New York 10017 (800) 253-9646; *Statistical Yearbook.*

United Nations Educational, Scientific and Cultural Organization (UNESCO), 7 Place de Fontenoy, F-75700 Paris, France (Telephone Number in U.S. (212) 963-5981); *Statistical Yearbook.*

BRUNEI - GAS PRODUCTION - See BRUNEI - MINING AND MINERAL PRODUCTS

BRUNEI - GENERAL INDUSTRIAL STATISTICS

Federal Statistical Office, Gustav - Stresemann - Ring 11, D-6200 Wiesbaden, Germany; *Brunei.*

BRUNEI - GENERAL MORTALITY

Statistical Office of the United Nations, Publishing Service, New York, New York 10017 (800) 253-9646; *Demographic Yearbook.*

World Health Organization, Office of Publications, Avenue Appia, CH-1211 Geneva 27, Switzerland (Telephone Number in U.S. (518) 436-9686); *World Health Statistics Annual.*

BRUNEI - GEOGRAPHIC DATA

Federal Statistical Office, Gustav - Stresemann - Ring 11, D-6200 Wiesbaden, Germany; *Brunei.*

BRUNEI - GOVERNMENT

G.K. Hall and Company, 70 Lincoln Street, Boston, Massachusetts 02111 (617) 423-3990; *The World in Figures.*

BRUNEI - GRAIN PRODUCTION - See BRUNEI - CROPS

BRUNEI - GROSS DOMESTIC PRODUCT

The Economist Intelligence Unit, 111 West 57th Street, New York, New York 10019 (800) 938-4685; *The World Market Atlas.*

The Economist Intelligence Unit (Asia) Limited, 10th Floor, Luk Kwok Centre, 72 Gloucester Road, Wanchai, Hong Kong (Phone Number in U.S. (800) 938-4685); *Asian Market Atlas.*

G.K. Hall and Company, 70 Lincoln Street, Boston, Massachusetts 02111 (617) 423-3990; *The World in Figures.*

Statistical Office of the United Nations, Publishing Service, New York, New York 10017 (800) 253-9646; *Statistical Yearbook.*

Times Books, 201 East 50th Street, New York, New York 10022 (212) 751-2600; *The Economist Book of Vital World Statistics.*

BRUNEI - HEALTH

The Economist Intelligence Unit (Asia) Limited, 10th Floor, Luk Kwok Centre, 72 Gloucester Road, Wanchai, Hong Kong (Phone Number in U.S. (800) 938-4685); *Asian Market Atlas.*

Federal Statistical Office, Gustav - Stresemann - Ring 11, D-6200 Wiesbaden, Germany; *Brunei.*

G.K. Hall and Company, 70 Lincoln Street, Boston, Massachusetts 02111 (617) 423-3990; *The World in Figures.*

Statistical Office of the United Nations, Publishing Service, New York, New York 10017 (800) 253-9646; *Statistical Yearbook.*

Times Books, 201 East 50th Street, New York, New York 10022 (212) 751-2600; *The Economist Book of Vital World Statistics.*

World Health Organization, Office of Publications, Avenue Appia, CH-1211 Geneva 27, Switzerland (Telephone Number in U.S. (518) 436-9686); *World Health Statistics Annual.*

BRUNEI - HIDE PRODUCTION

Food and Agricultural Organization of the United Nations (FAO), Via delle Terme di Caracalla, 00100 Rome, Italy (Telephone Number in U.S. (202) 653-2400); *Production Yearbook.*

BRUNEI - HIGHWAYS

The Economist Intelligence Unit (Asia) Limited, 10th Floor, Luk Kwok Centre, 72 Gloucester Road, Wanchai, Hong Kong (Phone Number in U.S. (800) 938-4685); *Asian Market Atlas.*

G.K. Hall and Company, 70 Lincoln Street, Boston, Massachusetts 02111 (617) 423-3990; *The World in Figures.*

BRUNEI - HOURS OF WORK - See BRUNEI - EMPLOYMENT

BRUNEI - ILLITERATE POPULATION

The Economist Intelligence Unit, 111 West 57th Street, New York, New York 10019 (800) 938-4685; *The World Market Atlas.*

G.K. Hall and Company, 70 Lincoln Street, Boston, Massachusetts 02111 (617) 423-3990; *The World in Figures.*

United Nations Educational, Scientific and Cultural Organization (UNESCO), 7 Place de Fontenoy, F-75700 Paris, France (Telephone Number in U.S. (212) 963-5981); *Statistical Yearbook.*

BRUNEI - IMPORTS

The Economist Intelligence Unit, 111 West 57th Street, New York, New York 10019 (800) 938-4685; *The World Market Atlas.*

The Economist Intelligence Unit (Asia) Limited, 10th Floor, Luk Kwok Centre, 72 Gloucester Road, Wanchai, Hong Kong (Phone Number in U.S. (800) 938-4685); *Asian Market Atlas.*

Food and Agricultural Organization of the United Nations (FAO) Via delle Terme di Caracalla, 00100 Rome, Italy (Telephone Number in U.S. (202) 653-2400); *The State of Food and Agriculture.*

G.K. Hall and Company, 70 Lincoln Street, Boston, Massachusetts 02111 (617) 423-3990; *The World in Figures.*

International Monetary Fund, 700 Nineteenth Street, NW, Washington, D.C. 20431 (202) 623-7000; *Direction of Trade Statistics.*

Statistical Office of the United Nations, Publishing Service, New York, New York 10017 (800) 253-9646; *Foreign Trade Statistics of Asia and the Pacific.*

Times Books, 201 East 50th Street, New York, New York 10022 (212) 751-2600; *The Economist Book of Vital World Statistics.*

BRUNEI - INDUSTRY

Federal Statistical Office, Gustav - Stresemann - Ring 11, D-6200 Wiesbaden, Germany; *Brunei.*

G.K. Hall and Company, 70 Lincoln Street, Boston, Massachusetts 02111 (617) 423-3990; *The World in Figures.*

International Labour Office, I.L.O. Publications, CH-1211, Geneva 22, Switzerland; *Yearbook of Labour Statistics.*

Statistical Office of the United Nations, Publishing Service, New York, New York 10017 (800) 253-9646; *Statistical Yearbook for Asia and the Pacific.*

Times Books, 201 East 50th Street, New York, New York 10022 (212) 751-2600; *The Economist Book of Vital World Statistics.*

BRUNEI - INFANT AND MATERNAL MORTALITY

The Economist Intelligence Unit (Asia) Limited, 10th Floor, Luk Kwok Centre, 72 Gloucester Road, Wanchai, Hong Kong (Phone Number in U.S. (800) 938-4685); *Asian Market Atlas.*

Statistical Office of the United Nations, Publishing Service, New York, New York 10017 (800) 253-9646; *Demographic Yearbook,* and *Statistical Yearbook.*

BRUNEI - INTERNAL TRADE

Statistical Office of the United Nations, Publishing Service, New York, New York 10017 (800) 253-9646; *Statistical Yearbook for Asia and the Pacific.*

BRUNEI - LABOR FORCE

The Economist Intelligence Unit (Asia) Limited, 10th Floor, Luk Kwok Centre, 72 Gloucester Road, Wanchai, Hong Kong (Phone Number in U.S. (800) 938-4685); *Asian Market Atlas.*

Food and Agricultural Organization of the United Nations (FAO) Via delle Terme di Caracalla, 00100 Rome, Italy (Telephone Number in U.S. (202) 653-2400); *The State of Food and Agriculture.*

G.K. Hall and Company, 70 Lincoln Street, Boston, Massachusetts 02111 (617) 423-3990; *The World in Figures.*

BRUNEI - LABOR PRODUCTIVITY

International Labour Office, I.L.O. Publications, CH-1211, Geneva 22, Switzerland; *Yearbook of Labour Statistics.*

BRUNEI - LAND USE

Food and Agricultural Organization of the United Nations (FAO), Via delle Terme di Caracalla, 00100 Rome, Italy (Telephone Number in U.S. (202) 653-2400); *Production Yearbook.*

G.K. Hall and Company, 70 Lincoln Street, Boston, Massachusetts 02111 (617) 423-3990; *The World in Figures.*

BRUNEI - LIBRARIES

United Nations Educational, Scientific and Cultural Organization (UNESCO), 7 Place de Fontenoy, F-75700 Paris, France (Telephone Number in U.S. (212) 963-5981); *Statistical Yearbook.*

BRUNEI - LIFE EXPECTANCY

The Economist Intelligence Unit (Asia) Limited, 10th Floor, Luk Kwok Centre, 72 Gloucester Road, Wanchai, Hong Kong (Phone Number in U.S. (800) 938-4685); *Asian Market Atlas.*

BRUNEI - LIVESTOCK AND POULTRY

Food and Agricultural Organization of the United Nations (FAO), Via delle Terme di Caracalla, 00100 Rome, Italy (Telephone Number in U.S. (202) 653-2400); *Production Yearbook,* and *The State of Food and Agriculture.*

G.K. Hall and Company, 70 Lincoln Street, Boston, Massachusetts 02111 (617) 423-3990; *The World in Figures.*

Statistical Office of the United Nations, Publishing Service, New York, New York 10017 (800) 253-9646; *Statistical Yearbook.*

BRUNEI - LIVING LEVELS

G.K. Hall and Company, 70 Lincoln Street, Boston, Massachusetts 02111 (617) 423-3990; *The World in Figures.*

BRUNEI - MAIL - NUMBER OF PIECES SENT OR RECEIVED

Statistical Office of the United Nations, Publishing Service, New York, New York 10017 (800) 253-9646; *Statistical Yearbook.*

BRUNEI - MANPOWER

Statistical Office of the United Nations, Publishing Service, New York, New York 10017 (800) 253-9646; *Statistical Yearbook for Asia and the Pacific.*

BRUNEI - MANUFACTURING

G.K. Hall and Company, 70 Lincoln Street, Boston, Massachusetts 02111 (617) 423-3990; *The World in Figures.*

Statistical Office of the United Nations, Publishing Service, New York, New York 10017 (800) 253-9646; *Statistical Yearbook.*

BRUNEI - MARRIAGE RATES

Statistical Office of the United Nations, Publishing Service, New York, New York 10017 (800) 253-9646; *Demographic Yearbook,* and *Statistical Yearbook.*

BRUNEI - MEAT PRODUCTION - See BRUNEI - LIVESTOCK AND POULTRY

BRUNEI - MERCHANT SHIPPING

G.K. Hall and Company, 70 Lincoln Street, Boston, Massachusetts 02111 (617) 423-3990; *The World in Figures.*

Statistical Office of the United Nations, Publishing Service, New York, New York 10017 (800) 253-9646; *Statistical Yearbook.*

Times Books, 201 East 50th Street, New York, New York 10022 (212) 751-2600; *The Economist Book of Vital World Statistics.*

BRUNEI - MILITARY

The Economist Intelligence Unit (Asia) Limited, 10th Floor, Luk Kwok Centre, 72 Gloucester Road, Wanchai, Hong Kong (Phone Number in U.S. (800) 938-4685); *Asian Market Atlas.*

G.K. Hall and Company, 70 Lincoln Street, Boston, Massachusetts 02111 (617) 423-3990; *The World in Figures.*

The International Institute for Strategic Studies, 23 Tavistock Street, London WC2E 7NQ, England; *The Military Balance.*

World Tourism Organization, Calle Capitan Haya 42, E-28020 Madrid, Spain; *Yearbook of Tourism Statistics.*

BRUNEI - MINING AND MINERAL PRODUCTS

G.K. Hall and Company, 70 Lincoln Street, Boston, Massachusetts 02111 (617) 423-3990; *The World in Figures.*

Penn Well Publishing Company, 1421 South Sheridan Road, P.O. Box 1260, Tulsa, Oklahoma 74101 (800) 752-9764; *International Energy*

Statistics Sourcebook.

Statistical Office of the United Nations, Publishing Service, New York, New York 10017 (800) 253-9646; *Statistical Yearbook.*

BRUNEI - MONEY SUPPLY

Federal Statistical Office, Gustav - Stresemann - Ring 11, D-6200 Wiesbaden, Germany; *Brunei.*

G.K. Hall and Company, 70 Lincoln Street, Boston, Massachusetts 02111 (617) 423-3990; *The World in Figures.*

BRUNEI - MOTION PICTURES

Statistical Office of the United Nations, Publishing Service, New York, New York 10017 (800) 253-9646; *Statistical Yearbook.*

United Nations Educational, Scientific and Cultural Organization (UNESCO), 7 Place de Fontenoy, F-75700 Paris, France (Telephone Number in U.S. (212) 963-5981); *Statistical Yearbook.*

BRUNEI - MOTOR VEHICLES IN USE

G.K. Hall and Company, 70 Lincoln Street, Boston, Massachusetts 02111 (617) 423-3990; *The World in Figures.*

Statistical Office of the United Nations, Publishing Service, New York, New York 10017 (800) 253-9646; *Statistical Yearbook.*

Times Books, 201 East 50th Street, New York, New York 10022 (212) 751-2600; *The Economist Book of Vital World Statistics.*

BRUNEI - MUSEUMS

United Nations Educational, Scientific and Cultural Organization (UNESCO), 7 Place de Fontenoy, F-75700 Paris, France (Telephone Number in U.S. (212) 963-5981); *Statistical Yearbook.*

BRUNEI - NATALITY - See BRUNEI - BIRTH RATES

BRUNEI - NATIONAL ACCOUNTS

Federal Statistical Office, Gustav - Stresemann - Ring 11, D-6200 Wiesbaden, Germany; *Brunei.*

Statistical Office of the United Nations, Publishing Service, New York, New York 10017 (800) 253-9646; *Statistical Yearbook,* and *Statistical Yearbook for Asia and the Pacific.*

BRUNEI - NATIONAL INCOME

G.K. Hall and Company, 70 Lincoln Street, Boston, Massachusetts 02111 (617) 423-3990; *The World in Figures.*

Statistical Office of the United Nations, Publishing Service, New York, New York 10017 (800) 253-9646; *Statistical Yearbook.*

BRUNEI - NATURAL GAS LIQUIDS - See BRUNEI - MINING AND MINERAL PRODUCTS

BRUNEI - NEWSPAPER PRODUCTION - See BRUNEI - FORESTRY AND FOREST PRODUCTS

BRUNEI - NEWSPRINT - See BRUNEI - FORESTRY AND FOREST PRODUCTS

BRUNEI - OCCUPATIONS - See BRUNEI - LABOR FORCE

BRUNEI - PAPER - See BRUNEI - FORESTRY AND FOREST PRODUCTS

BRUNEI - PERIODICALS

United Nations Educational, Scientific and Cultural Organization (UNESCO), 7 Place de Fontenoy, F-75700 Paris, France (Telephone Number in U.S. (212) 963-5981); *Statistical Yearbook.*

BRUNEI - PESTICIDE USE

Food and Agricultural Organization of the United Nations (FAO) Via delle Terme di Caracalla, 00100 Rome, Italy (Telephone Number in U.S. (202) 653-2400); *The State of Food and Agriculture.*

BRUNEI - PETROLEUM INDUSTRY

Food and Agricultural Organization of the United Nations (FAO) Via delle Terme di Caracalla, 00100 Rome, Italy (Telephone Number in U.S. (202) 653-2400); *The State of Food and Agriculture.*

G.K. Hall and Company, 70 Lincoln Street, Boston, Massachusetts 02111 (617) 423-3990; *The World in Figures.*

Penn Well Publishing Company, 1421 South Sheridan Road, P.O. Box 1260, Tulsa, Oklahoma 74101 (800) 752-9764; *International Energy Statistics Sourcebook.*

Statistical Office of the United Nations, Publishing Service, New York, New York 10017 (800) 253-9646; *Statistical Yearbook.*

BRUNEI - PIGS - See BRUNEI - LIVESTOCK AND POULTRY

BRUNEI - POPULATION

The Economist Intelligence Unit, 111 West 57th Street, New York, New York 10019 (800) 938-4685; *The World Market Atlas.*

The Economist Intelligence Unit (Asia) Limited, 10th Floor, Luk Kwok Centre, 72 Gloucester Road, Wanchai, Hong Kong (Phone Number in U.S. (800) 938-4685); *Asian Market Atlas.*

Federal Statistical Office, Gustav - Stresemann - Ring 11, D-6200 Wiesbaden, Germany; *Brunei.*

Food and Agricultural Organization of the United Nations (FAO), Via delle Terme di Caracalla, 00100 Rome, Italy (Telephone Number in U.S. (202) 653-2400); *Production Yearbook.*

G.K. Hall and Company, 70 Lincoln Street, Boston, Massachusetts 02111 (617) 423-3990; *The World in Figures.*

International Labour Office, I.L.O. Publications, CH-1211, Geneva 22, Switzerland; *Yearbook of Labour Statistics.*

Statistical Office of the United Nations, Publishing Service, New York, New York 10017 (800) 253-9646; *Demographic Yearbook, Statistical Yearbook,* and *Statistical Yearbook for Asia and the Pacific.*

Times Books, 201 East 50th Street, New York, New York 10022 (212) 751-2600; *The Economist Book of Vital World Statistics.*

United Nations Educational, Scientific and Cultural Organization (UNESCO), 7 Place de Fontenoy, F-75700 Paris, France (Telephone Number in U.S. (212) 963-5981); *Statistical Yearbook.*

World Health Organization, Office of Publications, Avenue Appia, CH-1211 Geneva 27, Switzerland (Telephone Number in U.S. (518) 436-9686); *World Health Statistics Annual.*

BRUNEI - PRICES

Federal Statistical Office, Gustav - Stresemann - Ring 11, D-6200 Wiesbaden, Germany; *Brunei.*

Food and Agricultural Organization of the United Nations (FAO), Via delle Terme di Caracalla, 00100 Rome, Italy (Telephone Number in U.S. (202) 653-2400); *Production Yearbook,* and *The State of Food and Agriculture.*

G.K. Hall and Company, 70 Lincoln Street, Boston, Massachusetts 02111 (617) 423-3990; *The World in Figures.*

International Labour Office, I.L.O. Publications, CH-1211, Geneva 22, Switzerland; *Yearbook of Labour Statistics.*

BRUNEI - PRINTING AND WRITING PAPER - See BRUNEI - FORESTRY AND FOREST PRODUCTS

BRUNEI - PRODUCTION

G.K. Hall and Company, 70 Lincoln Street, Boston, Massachusetts 02111 (617) 423-3990; *The World in Figures.*

BRUNEI - PUBLIC FINANCE

Federal Statistical Office, Gustav - Stresemann - Ring 11, D-6200 Wiesbaden, Germany; *Brunei.*

BRUNEI - RADIO BROADCASTING - See BRUNEI - BROADCASTING

BRUNEI - RAILWAYS

G.K. Hall and Company, 70 Lincoln Street, Boston, Massachusetts 02111 (617) 423-3990; *The World in Figures.*

BRUNEI - RENT PRICES

International Labour Office, I.L.O. Publications, CH-1211, Geneva 22, Switzerland; *Yearbook of Labour Statistics.*

BRUNEI - RETAIL TRADE

G.K. Hall and Company, 70 Lincoln Street, Boston, Massachusetts 02111 (617) 423-3990; *The World in Figures.*

BRUNEI - RICE PRODUCTION - See BRUNEI - CROPS

BRUNEI - ROUNDWOOD - See BRUNEI - FORESTRY AND FOREST PRODUCTS

BRUNEI - SAWNWOOD PRODUCTION - See BRUNEI - FORESTRY AND FOREST PRODUCTS

BRUNEI - SCIENCE AND TECHNOLOGY - EXPENDITURE FOR RESEARCH

Statistical Office of the United Nations, Publishing Service, New York, New York 10017 (800) 253-9646; *Statistical Yearbook.*

BRUNEI - SCIENTISTS AND TECHNICIANS

Statistical Office of the United Nations, Publishing Service, New York, New York 10017 (800) 253-9646; *Statistical Yearbook.*

United Nations Educational, Scientific and Cultural Organization (UNESCO), 7 Place de Fontenoy, F-75700 Paris, France (Telephone Number in U.S. (212) 963-5981); *Statistical Yearbook.*

BRUNEI - SOCIAL DATA

G.K. Hall and Company, 70 Lincoln Street, Boston, Massachusetts 02111 (617) 423-3990; *The World in Figures.*

BRUNEI - STOCKS - COMMODITY - MARKET PRICE - INDEX

Food and Agricultural Organization of the United Nations (FAO) Via delle Terme di Caracalla, 00100 Rome, Italy (Telephone Number in U.S. (202) 653-2400); *The State of Food and Agriculture.*

BRUNEI - TELEPHONES IN USE

American Telephone and Telegraph Company, 26 Parsippany Road, Whippany, New Jersey 07981 (800) 338-4038; *The World's Telephones.*

The Economist Intelligence Unit (Asia) Limited, 10th Floor, Luk Kwok Centre, 72 Gloucester Road, Wanchai, Hong Kong (Phone Number in U.S. (800) 938-4685); *Asian Market Atlas.*

G.K. Hall and Company, 70 Lincoln Street, Boston, Massachusetts 02111 (617) 423-3990; *The World in Figures.*

Statistical Office of the United Nations, Publishing Service, New York, New York 10017 (800) 253-9646; *Statistical Yearbook.*

BRUNEI - TELEVISION BROADCASTING - See BRUNEI - BROADCASTING

BRUNEI - TEXTILE INDUSTRY

G.K. Hall and Company, 70 Lincoln Street, Boston, Massachusetts 02111 (617) 423-3990; *The World in Figures.*

BRUNEI - THEATRE

United Nations Educational, Scientific and Cultural Organization (UNESCO), 7 Place de Fontenoy, F-75700 Paris, France (Telephone Number in U.S. (212) 963-5981); *Statistical Yearbook.*

BRUNEI - TOURISM

Federal Statistical Office, Gustav - Stresemann - Ring 11, D-6200 Wiesbaden, Germany; *Brunei.*

G.K. Hall and Company, 70 Lincoln Street, Boston, Massachusetts 02111 (617) 423-3990; *The World in Figures.*

Times Books, 201 East 50th Street, New York, New York 10022 (212) 751-2600; *The Economist Book of Vital World Statistics.*

World Tourism Organization, Calle Capitan Haya 42, E-28020 Madrid, Spain; *Yearbook of Tourism Statistics.*

BRUNEI - TRACTORS IN USE

Statistical Office of the United Nations, Publishing Service, New York, New York 10017 (800) 253-9646; *Statistical Yearbook.*

BRUNEI - TRADE - See BRUNEI - FOREIGN TRADE

BRUNEI - TRANSPORTATION AND COMMUNICATIONS

The Economist Intelligence Unit (Asia) Limited, 10th Floor, Luk Kwok Centre, 72 Gloucester Road, Wanchai, Hong Kong (Phone Number in U.S. (800) 938-4685); *Asian Market Atlas.*

Federal Statistical Office, Gustav - Stresemann - Ring 11, D-6200 Wiesbaden, Germany; *Brunei.*

G.K. Hall and Company, 70 Lincoln Street, Boston, Massachusetts 02111 (617) 423-3990; *The World in Figures.*

Statistical Office of the United Nations, Publishing Service, New York, New York 10017 (800) 253-9646; *Statistical Yearbook for Asia and the Pacific.*

BRUNEI - UNEMPLOYMENT

International Labour Office, I.L.O. Publications, CH-1211, Geneva 22, Switzerland; *Yearbook of Labour Statistics.*

Statistical Office of the United Nations, Publishing Service, New York, New York 10017 (800) 253-9646; *Statistical Yearbook.*

BRUNEI - VITAL STATISTICS

G.K. Hall and Company, 70 Lincoln Street, Boston, Massachusetts 02111 (617) 423-3990; *The World in Figures.*

Statistical Office of the United Nations, Publishing Service, New York, New York 10017 (800) 253-9646; *Statistical Yearbook.*

World Health Organization, Office of Publications, Avenue Appia, CH-1211 Geneva 27, Switzerland (Telephone Number in U.S. (518) 436-9686); *World Health Statistics Annual.*

BRUNEI - WAGES

Federal Statistical Office, Gustav - Stresemann - Ring 11, D-6200 Wiesbaden, Germany; *Brunei.*

G.K. Hall and Company, 70 Lincoln Street, Boston, Massachusetts 02111 (617) 423-3990; *The World in Figures.*

International Labour Office, I.L.O. Publications, CH-1211, Geneva 22, Switzerland; *Yearbook of Labour Statistics.*

Statistical Office of the United Nations, Publishing Service, New York, New York 10017; *Statistical Yearbook,* and *Statistical Yearbook for Asia and the Pacific.*

BRUNEI - WEATHER

G.K. Hall and Company, 70 Lincoln Street, Boston, Massachusetts 02111 (617) 423-3990; *The World in Figures.*

BRUNEI - ZOOS AND BOTANICAL GARDENS

United Nations Educational, Scientific and Cultural Organization (UNESCO), 7 Place de Fontenoy, F-75700 Paris, France (Telephone Number in U.S. (212) 963-5981); *Statistical Yearbook.*

BUDGET, FEDERAL - OUTLAYS

Executive Office of the President, Office of Management and Budget, Executive Office Building, Washington, D.C. 20503 (202) 395-3080; *Budget of the United States Government.*

BUDGET, FEDERAL - RECEIPTS

Executive Office of the President, Office of Management and Budget, Executive Office Building, Washington, D.C. 20503 (202) 395-3080; *Budget of the United States Government.*

BUDGET, FEDERAL - REVENUE LOSSES (TAX EXPENDITURES)

Executive Office of the President, Office of Management and Budget, Executive Office Building, Washington, D.C. 20503 (202) 395-3080; *Budget of the United States Government.*

BUDGET, FEDERAL - TAXES

Executive Office of the President, Office of Management and Budget, Executive Office Building, Washington, D.C. 20503 (202) 395-3080; *Budget of the United States Government.*

BUDGET, FEDERAL - TRUST FUNDS

Executive Office of the President, Office of Management and Budget, Executive Office Building, Washington, D.C. 20503 (202) 395-3080; *Budget of the United States Government.*

BUILDING CONTRACTORS, GENERAL - EARNINGS

U.S. Department of Commerce, Bureau of the Census, Suitland, Maryland 20233 (301) 763-4040; *County Business Patterns,* and *Census of Construction Industries.*

U.S. Department of Labor, Bureau of Labor Statistics, Two Massachusetts Avenue, NE, Washington, D.C. 20212 (202) 606-7828; *Employment and Earnings,* and Bulletins 2370 and 2429.

BUILDING CONTRACTORS, GENERAL - EMPLOYEES

U.S. Department of Commerce, Bureau of the Census, Suitland, Maryland 20233 (301) 763-4040; *Census of Construction Industries,* and *County Business Patterns.*

U.S. Department of Labor, Bureau of Labor Statistics, Two Massachusetts Avenue, NE, Washington, D.C. 20212 (202) 606-7828; *Employment and Earnings,* and Bulletins 2370 and 2429.

BUILDING CONTRACTORS, GENERAL - ESTABLISHMENTS

U.S. Department of Commerce, Bureau of the Census, Suitland, Maryland 20233 (301) 763-4040; *Census of Construction Industries,* and *County Business Patterns.*

BUILDING CONTRACTORS, GENERAL - OCCUPATIONAL SAFETY

U.S. Department of Labor, Bureau of Labor Statistics, Two Massachusetts Avenue, NE, Washington, D.C. 20212 (202) 606-7828; *Occupational Injuries and Illnesses in the United States by Industry.*

BUILDING CONTRACTORS, GENERAL - OUTPUT

U.S. Department of Commerce, Bureau of the Census, Suitland, Maryland 20233 (301) 763-4040; *Census of Construction Industries.*

BUILDING CONTRACTORS, GENERAL - RECEIPTS

U.S. Department of Commerce, Bureau of the Census, Suitland, Maryland 20233 (301) 763-4040; *Census of Construction Industries,* and *County Business Patterns.*

BUILDING CONTRACTORS, GENERAL - VALUE ADDED

U.S. Department of Commerce, Bureau of the Census, Suitland, Maryland 20233 (301) 763-4040; *Census of Construction Industries,* and *County Business Patterns.*

BUILDING MATERIALS, AND GARDEN SUPPLIES, RETAIL STORES - EARNINGS

U.S. Department of Commerce, Bureau of the Census, Suitland, Maryland 20233 (301) 763-4040; *Census of Retail Trade,* and *County Business Patterns.*

BUILDING MATERIALS, AND GARDEN SUPPLIES, RETAIL STORES - EMPLOYEES

U.S. Department of Commerce, Bureau of the Census, Suitland, Maryland 20233 (301) 763-4040; *Census of Retail Trade,* and *County Business Patterns.*

BUILDING MATERIALS, AND GARDEN SUPPLIES, RETAIL STORES - ESTABLISHMENTS

U.S. Department of Commerce, Bureau of the Census, Suitland, Maryland 20233 (301) 763-4040; *Census of Retail Trade, Census of Service Industries,* and *County Business Patterns.*

BUILDING MATERIALS, AND GARDEN SUPPLIES, RETAIL STORES - INVENTORIES

U.S. Department of Commerce, Bureau of the Census, Suitland, Maryland 20233 (301) 763-4040; *Current Business Reports, Combined Annual and Revised Monthly Retail Trade,* and *Monthly Retail Trade Reports.*

BUILDING MATERIALS, AND GARDEN SUPPLIES, RETAIL STORES - PRODUCTIVITY

U.S. Department of Labor, Bureau of Labor Statistics, Two Massachusetts Avenue, NE, Washington, D.C. 20212 (202) 606-7828; *Productivity Measures for Selected Industries and Government Services.*

BUILDING MATERIALS, AND GARDEN SUPPLIES, RETAIL STORES - SALES

Market Statistics, 633 Third Avenue, New York, New York 10017 (212) 986-4000; *The Survey of Buying Power Data.*

U.S. Department of Commerce, Bureau of the Census, Suitland, Maryland 20233 (301) 763-4040; *Census of Retail Trade, Current Business Reports, Combined Annual and Revised Monthly Retail Trade,* and *County Business Patterns.*

BUILDING PERMITS - See CONSTRUCTION INDUSTRY and HOUSING AND HOUSING UNITS

BUILDINGS - See also: CONSTRUCTION INDUSTRY and HOUSING AND HOUSING UNITS

BUILDINGS - CONSTRUCTION VALUE

F.W. Dodge Division, McGraw-Hill Information Systems Company, 1221 Avenue of the Americas, New York, New York 10020 (212) 512-2000; *Dodge Construction Potentials.*

U.S. Department of Commerce, Bureau of the Census, Suitland, Maryland 20233 (301) 763-4040; *Current Construction Reports,* and press release.

BUILDINGS - ENERGY CONSUMPTION AND EXPENDITURES

U.S. Department of Energy, Energy Information Administration, 1000 Independence Avenue, SW, Washington, D.C. 20585 (202) 586-8800; *Commercial Buildings, Energy Consumption and Expenditures.*

BUILDINGS - FEDERAL

U.S. General Services Administration, General Services Building, Eighteenth and F Streets, NW, Washington, D.C. 20405 (202) 708-5082; *Inventory Report on Real Property Owned by the United States Throughout the World.*

BUILDINGS - FIRE AND PROPERTY LOSS

National Fire Protection Association, One Batterymarch Park, Post Office Box 9101 Quincy, Massachusetts 02169 (617) 770-3000; *NFPA Reports on U.S. Fire Loss,* in *NFPA Journal.*

BUILDINGS - FLOOR SPACE

U.S. Department of Energy, Energy Information Administration, 1000 Independence Avenue, SW, Washington, D.C. 20585 (202) 586-8800; *Commercial Buildings, Energy Consumption and Expenditures,* and *Commercial Building Characteristics.*

BUILDINGS - OFFICE VACANCY RATE

ONCOR International, 3040 Post Oak Boulevard, Houston, Texas 77056 (713) 961-0600; *Office Market Data Book.*

Society of Industrial and Office Realtors, 777 14th Street, NW, Suite 400, Washington, D.C. 20005 (202) 383-1150; *Comparative Statistics of Industrial and Office Real Estate Markets.*

BUILDINGS - PRINCIPAL ACTIVITY

U.S. Department of Energy, Energy Information Administration, 1000 Independence Avenue, SW, Washington, D.C. 20585 (202) 586-8800; *Commercial Buildings, Energy Consumption and Expenditures,* and *Commercial Building Characteristics.*

Bulgaria - National Statistical Office

Central Statistical Office, Council of Ministers, 10, Sixth September Street, 1000, Sofia, Bulgaria.

Bulgaria - Primary Statistics Sources

Central Statistical Office, Council of Ministers, 10 Sixth September Street, 1000, Sofia, Bulgaria; *Statistical Yearbook of Bulgaria,* and *Statistical Pocketbook.*

BULGARIA - AGRICULTURE

Facts on File, 460 Park Avenue South, New York, New York 10016 (800) 443-8323; *The New Book of World Rankings.*

Federal Statistical Office, Gustav - Stresemann - Ring 11, D-6200 Wiesbaden, Germany; *Bulgarien.*

Food and Agricultural Organization of the United Nations (FAO), Via delle Terme di Caracalla, 00100 Rome, Italy (Telephone Number in U.S. (202) 653-2400); *Production Yearbook, The State of Food and Agriculture,* and *Trade Yearbook.*

G.K. Hall and Company, 70 Lincoln Street, Boston, Massachusetts 02111 (617) 423-3990; *The World in Figures.*

Statistical Office of the United Nations, Publishing Service, New York, New York 10017 (800) 253-9646; *Statistical Yearbook.*

Times Books, 201 East 50th Street, New York, New York 10022 (212) 751-2600; *The Economist Book of Vital World Statistics.*

BULGARIA - AIRLINE SERVICE

Facts on File, 460 Park Avenue South, New York, New York 10016 (800) 443-8323; *The New Book of World Rankings.*

G.K. Hall and Company, 70 Lincoln Street, Boston, Massachusetts 02111 (617) 423-3990; *The World in Figures.*

Statistical Office of the United Nations, Publishing Service, New York, New York 10017 (800) 253-9646; *Statistical Yearbook.*

Times Books, 201 East 50th Street, New York, New York 10022 (212) 751-2600; *The Economist Book of Vital World Statistics.*

BULGARIA - ALMOND PRODUCTION - See BULGARIA - CROPS

BULGARIA - ALUMINUM PRODUCTION AND CONSUMPTION - See BULGARIA - MINING AND MINERAL PRODUCTS

BULGARIA - ANIMAL HEALTH

Food and Agricultural Organization of the United Nations (FAO), Via delle Terme di Caracalla, 00100 Rome, Italy (Telephone Number in U.S. (202) 653-2400); *Animal Health Yearbook.*

BULGARIA - AREA AND DENSITY OF POPULATION

Facts on File, 460 Park Avenue South, New York, New York 10016 (800) 443-8323; *The New Book of World Rankings.*

Federal Statistical Office, Gustav - Stresemann - Ring 11, D-6200 Wiesbaden, Germany; *Bulgarien.*

Food and Agricultural Organization of the United Nations (FAO) Via delle Terme di Caracalla, 00100 Rome, Italy (Telephone Number in U.S. (202) 653-2400); *The State of Food and Agriculture.*

G.K. Hall and Company, 70 Lincoln Street, Boston, Massachusetts 02111 (617) 423-3990; *The World in Figures.*

Statistical Office of the United Nations, Publishing Service, New York, New York 10017 (800) 253-9646; *Statistical Yearbook.*

Times Books, 201 East 50th Street, New York, New York 10022 (212) 751-2600; *The Economist Book of Vital World Statistics.*

BULGARIA - BALANCE OF PAYMENTS

Business International Corporation, 215 Park Avenue South, New York, New York 10003 (800) 938-4685; *The World Market Atlas.*

Federal Statistical Office, Gustav- Stresemann - Ring 11, D-6200 Wiesbaden, Federal Republic of Germany; *Bulgarien.*

G.K. Hall and Company, 70 Lincoln Street, Boston, Massachusetts 02111 (617) 423-3990; *The World in Figures.*

Times Books, 201 East 50th Street, New York, New York 10022 (212) 751-2600; *The Economist Book of Vital World Statistics.*

BULGARIA - BANKING

Facts on File, 460 Park Avenue South, New York, New York 10016 (800) 443-8323; *The New Book of World Rankings.*

G.K. Hall and Company, 70 Lincoln Street, Boston, Massachusetts 02111 (617) 423-3990; *The World in Figures.*

BULGARIA - BARLEY PRODUCTION - See BULGARIA - CROPS

BULGARIA - BEER PRODUCTION

Facts on File, 460 Park Avenue South, New York, New York 10016 (800) 443-8323; *The New Book of World Rankings.*

Statistical Office of the United Nations, Publishing Service, New York, New York 10017 (800) 253-9646; *Statistical Yearbook.*

BULGARIA - BIRTH RATES

Facts on File, 460 Park Avenue South, New York, New York 10016 (800) 443-8323; *The New Book of World Rankings.*

Statistical Office of the United Nations, Publishing Service, New York, New York 10017 (800) 253-9646; *Demographic Yearbook,* and *Statistical Yearbook.*

Times Books, 201 East 50th Street, New York, New York 10022 (212) 751-2600; *The Economist Book of Vital World Statistics.*

World Health Organization, Office of Publications, Avenue Appia, CH-1211 Geneva 27, Switzerland (Telephone Number in U.S. (518) 436-9686); *World Health Statistics Annual.*

BULGARIA - BONDS

G.K. Hall and Company, 70 Lincoln Street, Boston, Massachusetts 02111 (617) 423-3990; *The World in Figures.*

BULGARIA - BOOK PRODUCTION

Euromonitor Publications Limited, 87-88 Turnmill Street, London EC1M 5QU, England; *European Marketing Data and Statistics.*

G.K. Hall and Company, 70 Lincoln Street, Boston, Massachusetts 02111 (617) 423-3990; *The World in Figures.*

United Nations Educational, Scientific and Cultural Organization (UNESCO), 7 Place de Fontenoy, F-75700 Paris, France (Telephone Number in U.S. (212) 963-5981); *Statistical Yearbook.*

BULGARIA - BROADCASTING

Billboard Limited, P.O. Box 9027, 1006 AA Amsterdam, The Netherlands (Telephone Number in U.S. (212) 764-7300); *World Radio TV Handbook.*

Facts on File, 460 Park Avenue South, New York, New York 10016 (800) 443-8323; *The New Book of World Rankings.*

G.K. Hall and Company, 70 Lincoln Street, Boston, Massachusetts 02111 (617) 423-3990; *The World in Figures.*

Times Books, 201 East 50th Street, New York, New York 10022 (212) 751-2600; *The Economist Book of Vital World Statistics.*

BULGARIA - BUILDING CONSTRUCTION - See BULGARIA - CONSTRUCTION INDUSTRY

BULGARIA - BUSINESS

G.K. Hall and Company, 70 Lincoln Street, Boston, Massachusetts 02111 (617) 423-3990; *The World in Figures.*

BULGARIA - BUTTER PRODUCTION - See BULGARIA - DAIRY PRODUCTS

BULGARIA - CABBAGE PRODUCTION - See BULGARIA - CROPS

BULGARIA - CALORIE SUPPLY

Food and Agricultural Organization of the United Nations (FAO) Via delle Terme di Caracalla, 00100 Rome, Italy (Telephone Number in U.S. (202) 653-2400); *The State of Food and Agriculture.*

BULGARIA - CASTOR BEAN PRODUCTION - See BULGARIA - CROPS

BULGARIA - CATTLE - See BULGARIA - LIVESTOCK AND POULTRY

BULGARIA - CAUSTIC SODA PRODUCTION

Statistical Office of the United Nations, Publishing Service, New York, New York 10017 (800) 253-9646; *Statistical Yearbook.*

BULGARIA - CEMENT PRODUCTION - See BULGARIA - MINING AND MINERAL PRODUCTS

BULGARIA - CEREALS PRODUCTION - See BULGARIA - CROPS

BULGARIA - CHEESE PRODUCTION - See BULGARIA - DAIRY PRODUCTS

BULGARIA - CHEMICAL (ORGANIC) PRODUCTION - See BULGARIA - MINING AND MINERAL PRODUCTS

BULGARIA - CHICK PEA PRODUCTION - See BULGARIA - CROPS

BULGARIA - CIGARETTE PRODUCTION - See BULGARIA - TOBACCO PRODUCTION

BULGARIA - CLASS STRUCTURE

Columbia University Press, 562 West 113th Street, New York, New York 10014 (212) 326-7100; *East European and Soviet Data Book.*

G.K. Hall and Company, 70 Lincoln Street, Boston, Massachusetts 02111 (617) 423-3990; *The World in Figures.*

BULGARIA - CLIMATE

Facts on File, 460 Park Avenue South, New York, New York 10016 (800) 433-8323; *The New Book of World Rankings.*

G.K. Hall and Company, 70 Lincoln Street, Boston, Massachusetts 02111 (617) 423-3990; *The World in Figures.*

BULGARIA - COAL PRODUCTION - See BULGARIA - MINING AND MINERAL PRODUCTS

BULGARIA - COFFEE PRODUCTION - See BULGARIA - CROPS

BULGARIA - COKE OVEN COKE PRODUCTION - See BULGARIA - MINING AND MINERAL PRODUCTS

BULGARIA - COMMUNICATIONS

Federal Statistical Office, Gustav- Stresemann - Ring 11, D-6200 Wiesbaden, Federal Republic of Germany; *Bulgarien.*

G.K. Hall and Company, 70 Lincoln Street, Boston, Massachusetts 02111 (617) 423-3990; *The World in Figures.*

BULGARIA - CONSTRUCTION INDUSTRY

Facts on File, 460 Park Avenue South, New York, New York 10016 (800) 443-8323; *The New Book of World Rankings.*

Statistical Office of the United Nations, Publishing Service, New York, New York 10017 (800) 253-9646; *Construction Statistics Yearbook,* and *Statistical Yearbook.*

BULGARIA - CONSUMER PRICE INDEX

Federal Statistical Office, Gustav - Stresemann - Ring 11, D-6200 Wiesbaden, Germany; *Bulgarien.*

G.K. Hall and Company, 70 Lincoln Street, Boston, Massachusetts 02111 (617) 423-3990; *The World in Figures.*

Statistical Office of the United Nations, Publishing Service, New York, New York 10017 (800) 253-9646; *Statistical Yearbook.*

BULGARIA - CONSUMER PRICES

Euromonitor Publications Limited, 87-88 Turnmill Street, London EC1M 5QU, England; *European Marketing Data and Statistics.*

Federal Statistical Office, Gustav - Stresemann - Ring 11, D-6200 Wiesbaden, Germany; *Bulgarien.*

International Labour Office, I.L.O. Publications, CH-1211, Geneva 22, Switzerland; *Yearbook of Labour Statistics.*

BULGARIA - CONSUMPTION

G.K. Hall and Company, 70 Lincoln Street, Boston, Massachusetts 02111 (617) 423-3990; *The World in Figures.*

International Lead and Zinc Study Group, Metro House, 58 St. James's Street, London SW1A 1LD, England; *Lead and Zinc Statistics.*

BULGARIA - COPPER AND COPPER ORE PRODUCTION - See BULGARIA - MINING AND MINERAL PRODUCTS

BULGARIA - CORN PRODUCTION - See BULGARIA - CROPS

BULGARIA - CORPORATE TAXES - See BULGARIA - TAXATION

BULGARIA - COTTON - See BULGARIA - CROPS

BULGARIA - CRIME

Yale University Press, Yale Station, New Haven, Connecticut 06520 (203) 432-0940; *Violence and Crime in Cross-National Perspective.*

BULGARIA - CROPS

Euromonitor Publications Limited, 87-88 Turnmill Street, London EC1M 5QU, England; *European Marketing Data and Statistics.*

Facts on File, 460 Park Avenue South, New York, New York 10016 (800) 443-8323; *The New Book of World Rankings.*

Food and Agricultural Organization of the United Nations (FAO) Via delle Terme di Caracalla, 00100 Rome, Italy (Telephone Number in U.S. (202) 653-2400); *The State of Food and Agriculture.*

G.K. Hall and Company, 70 Lincoln Street, Boston, Massachusetts 02111 (617) 423-3990; *The World in Figures.*

BULGARIA - CUSTOMS DUTIES

G.K. Hall and Company, 70 Lincoln Street, Boston, Massachusetts 02111 (617) 423-3990; *The World in Figures.*

BULGARIA - DAIRY PRODUCTS

Facts on File, 460 Park Avenue South, New York, New York 10016 (800) 443-8323; *The New Book of World Rankings.*

Food and Agricultural Organization of the United Nations (FAO), Via delle Terme di Caracalla, 00100 Rome, Italy (Telephone Number in U.S. (202) 653-2400); *Production Yearbook,* and *The State of Food and Agriculture.*

Statistical Office of the United Nations, Publishing Service, New York, New York 10017 (800) 253-9646; *Statistical Yearbook.*

BULGARIA - DEATH RATES

G.K. Hall and Company, 70 Lincoln Street, Boston, Massachusetts 02111 (617) 423-3990; *The World in Figures.*

Statistical Office of the United Nations, Publishing Service, New York, New York 10017 (800) 253-9646; *Statistical Yearbook.*

Times Books, 201 East 50th Street, New York, New York 10022 (212) 751-2600; *The Economist Book of Vital World Statistics.*

World Health Organization, Office of Publications, Avenue Appia, CH-1211 Geneva 27, Switzerland (Telephone Number in U.S. (518) 436-9686); *World Health Statistics Annual.*

BULGARIA - DEFENSE EXPENDITURES

G.K. Hall and Company, 70 Lincoln Street, Boston, Massachusetts 02111 (617) 423-3990; *The World in Figures.*

BULGARIA - DEMOGRAPHY

Business International Corporation, 215 Park Avenue South, New York, New York 10003 (800) 938-4685; *The World Market Atlas.*

Facts on File, 460 Park Avenue South, New York, New York 10016 (800) 443-8323; *The New Book of World Rankings.*

Federal Statistical Office, Gustav - Stresemann - Ring 11, D-6200 Wiesbaden, Germany; *Bulgarien.*

G.K. Hall and Company, 70 Lincoln Street, Boston, Massachusetts 02111 (617) 423-3990; *The World in Figures.*

BULGARIA - DEVELOPMENT ASSISTANCE

G.K. Hall and Company, 70 Lincoln Street, Boston, Massachusetts 02111 (617) 423-3990; *The World in Figures.*

Statistical Office of the United Nations, Publishing Service, New York, New York 10017 (800) 253-9646; *Statistical Yearbook.*

BULGARIA - DIAMOND PRODUCTION - See BULGARIA - MINING AND MINERAL PRODUCTS

BULGARIA - DISEASES

G.K. Hall and Company, 70 Lincoln Street, Boston, Massachusetts 02111 (617) 423-3990; *The World in Figures.*

World Health Organization, Office of Publications, Avenue Appia, CH-1211 Geneva 27, Switzerland (Telephone Number in U.S. (518) 436-9686); *World Health Statistics Annual.*

BULGARIA - DIVORCE RATES

Facts on File, 460 Park Avenue South, New York, New York 10016 (800) 443-8323; *The New Book of World Rankings.*

Statistical Office of the United Nations, Publishing Service, New York, New York 10017 (800) 253-9646; *Demographic Yearbook,* and *Statistical Yearbook.*

BULGARIA - DOMESTIC PRODUCT

G.K. Hall and Company, 70 Lincoln Street, Boston, Massachusetts 02111 (617) 423-3990; *The World in Figures.*

BULGARIA - DUCKS - See BULGARIA - LIVESTOCK AND POULTRY

BULGARIA - ECONOMY

Euromonitor Publications Limited, 87-88 Turnmill Street, London EC1M 5QU, England; *European Marketing Data and Statistics.*

Facts on File, 460 Park Avenue South, New York, New York 10016 (800) 443-8323; *The New Book of World Rankings.*

Federal Statistical Office, Gustav - Stresemann - Ring 11, D-6200 Wiesbaden, Germany; *Bulgarien.*

G.K. Hall and Company, 70 Lincoln Street, Boston, Massachusetts 02111 (617) 423-3990; *The World in Figures.*

BULGARIA - EDUCATION

Business International Corporation, 215 Park Avenue South, New York, New York 10003 (800) 938-4685; *The World Market Atlas.*

Columbia University Press, 562 West 113th Street, New York, New York 10014 (212) 316-7100; *East European and Soviet Data Book.*

Euromonitor Publications Limited, 87-88 Turnmill Street, London EC1M 5QU, England; *European Marketing Data and Statistics.*

Facts on File, 460 Park Avenue South, New York, New York 10016; *The New Book of World Rankings.*

Federal Statistical Office, Gustav - Stresemann - Ring 11, D-6200 Wiesbaden, Germany; *Bulgarien.*

G.K. Hall and Company, 70 Lincoln Street, Boston, Massachusetts 02111 (617) 423-3990; *The World in Figures.*

Times Books, 201 East 50th Street, New York, New York 10022 (212) 751-2600; *The Economist Book of Vital World Statistics.*

United Nations Educational, Scientific and Cultural Organization (UNESCO), 7 Place de Fontenoy, F-75700 Paris, France (Telephone Number in U.S. (212) 963-5981); *Statistical Yearbook.*

BULGARIA - EGG PRODUCTION - See BULGARIA - DAIRY PRODUCTS

BULGARIA - EGGPLANT PRODUCTION - See BULGARIA - CROPS

BULGARIA - ELECTRICITY

Facts on File, 460 Park Avenue South, New York, New York 10016 (800) 443-8323; *The New Book of World Rankings.*

Penn Well Publishing Company, 1421 South Sheridan Road, P.O. Box 1260, Tulsa, Oklahoma 74101 (800) 752-9764; *International Energy Statistics Sourcebook.*

Statistical Office of the United Nations, Publishing Service, New York, New York 10017 (800) 253-9646; *Statistical Yearbook.*

Times Books, 201 East 50th Street, New York, New York 10022 (212) 751-2600; *The Economist Book of Vital World Statistics.*

BULGARIA - EMPLOYMENT

Euromonitor Publications Limited, 87-88 Turnmill Street, London EC1M 5QU, England; *European Marketing Data and Statistics.*

Facts on File, 460 Park Avenue South, New York, New York 10016; *The New Book of World Rankings.*

Federal Statistical Office, Gustav - Stresemann - Ring 11, D-6200 Wiesbaden, Germany; *Bulgarien.*

International Labour Office, I.L.O. Publications, CH-1211, Geneva 22, Switzerland; *Yearbook of Labour Statistics.*

Statistical Office of the United Nations, Publishing Service, New York, New York 10017 (800) 253-9646; *Statistical Yearbook.*

BULGARIA - ENERGY

Euromonitor Publications Limited, 87-88 Turnmill Street, London EC1M 5QU, England; *European Marketing Data and Statistics.*

Facts on File, 460 Park Avenue South, New York, New York 10016 (800) 443-8323; *The New Book of World Rankings.*

Food and Agricultural Organization of the United Nations (FAO) Via delle Terme di Caracalla, 00100 Rome, Italy (Telephone Number in U.S. (202) 653-2400); *The State of Food and Agriculture.*

G.K. Hall and Company, 70 Lincoln Street, Boston, Massachusetts 02111 (617) 423-3990; *The World in Figures.*

Penn Well Publishing Company, 1421 South Sheridan Road, P.O. Box 1260, Tulsa, Oklahoma 74101 (800) 752-9764; *International Energy Statistics Sourcebook.*

Statistical Office of the United Nations, Publishing Service, New York, New York 10017 (800) 253-9646; *Energy Statistics Yearbook, Statistical Yearbook,* and *World Energy Supplies.*

Times Books, 201 East 50th Street, New York, New York 10022 (212) 751-2600; *The Economist Book of Vital World Statistics.*

BULGARIA - EXCHANGE RATES

Statistical Office of the United Nations, Publishing Service, New York, New York 10017 (800) 253-9646; *Statistical Yearbook.*

BULGARIA - EXPORTS

Business International Corporation, 215 Park Avenue South, New York, New York 10003 (800) 938-4685; *The World Market Atlas.*

Food and Agricultural Organization of the United Nations (FAO) Via delle Terme di Caracalla, 00100 Rome, Italy (Telephone Number in U.S. (202) 653-2400); *The State of Food and Agriculture.*

G.K. Hall and Company, 70 Lincoln Street, Boston, Massachusetts 02111 (617) 423-3990; *The World in Figures.*

International Lead and Zinc Study Group, Metro House, 58 St. James's Street, London SW1A 1LD, England; *Lead and Zinc Statistics.*

International Monetary Fund, 700 Nineteenth Street, NW, Washington, D.C. 20431 (202) 623-7000; *Direction of Trade Statistics.*

Times Books, 201 East 50th Street, New York, New York 10022 (212) 751-2600; *The Economist Book of Vital World Statistics.*

BULGARIA - EXTERNAL TRADE

Food and Agricultural Organization of the United Nations (FAO) Via delle Terme di Caracalla, 00100 Rome, Italy (Telephone Number in U.S. (202) 653-2400); *The State of Food and Agriculture,* and *Trade Yearbook.*

G.K. Hall and Company, 70 Lincoln Street, Boston, Massachusetts 02111 (617) 423-3990; *The World in Figures.*

Statistical Office of the United Nations, Publishing Service, New York, New York 10017 (800) 253-9646; *Statistical Yearbook.*

BULGARIA - FABRIC PRODUCTION - See BULGARIA - TEXTILE INDUSTRY

BULGARIA - FARM CROPS - See BULGARIA - CROPS

BULGARIA - FERTILITY RATES

Columbia University Press, 562 West 113th Street, New York, New York 10014 (212) 316-7100; *East European and Soviet Data Book.*

Facts on File, 460 Park Avenue South, New York, New York 10016 (800) 443-8323; *The New Book of World Rankings.*

Times Books, 201 East 50th Street, New York, New York 10022 (212) 751-2600; *The Economist Book of Vital World Statistics.*

BULGARIA - FERTILIZER

Food and Agricultural Organization of the United Nations (FAO), Via delle Terme di Caracalla, 00100 Rome, Italy (Telephone Number in U.S. (202) 653-2400); *Fertilizer Yearbook,* and *The State of Food and Agriculture.*

Statistical Office of the United Nations, Publishing Service, New York, New York 10017 (800) 253-9646; *Statistical Yearbook.*

BULGARIA - FETAL MORTALITY

Statistical Office of the United Nations, Publishing Service, New York, New York 10017 (800) 253-9646; *Demographic Yearbook.*

World Health Organization, Office of Publications, Avenue Appia, CH-1211 Geneva 27, Switzerland (Telephone Number in U.S. (518) 436-9686); *World Health Statistics Annual.*

BULGARIA - FIBRE PRODUCTION - See BULGARIA - TEXTILE INDUSTRY

BULGARIA - FILAMENT PRODUCTION - See BULGARIA - TEXTILE INDUSTRY

BULGARIA - FILM - See BULGARIA - MOTION PICTURES

BULGARIA - FINANCE

Facts on File, 460 Park Avenue South, New York, New York 10016 (800) 443-8323; *The New Book of World Rankings.*

Federal Statistical Office, Gustav - Stresemann - Ring 11, D-6200 Wiesbaden, Germany; *Bulgarien.*

G.K. Hall and Company, 70 Lincoln Street, Boston, Massachusetts 02111 (617) 423-3990; *The World in Figures.*

International Monetary Fund, 700 Nineteenth Street, NW, Washington, D.C. 20431 (202) 623-7000; *International Financial Statistics.*

BULGARIA - FISHERIES

Euromonitor Publications Limited, 87-88 Turnmill Street, London EC1M 5QU, England; *European Marketing Data and Statistics.*

Facts on File, 460 Park Avenue South, New York, New York 10016 (800) 443-8323; *The New Book of World Rankings.*

Federal Statistical Office, Gustav - Stresemann - Ring 11, D-6200 Wiesbaden, Germany; *Bulgarien.*

Food and Agricultural Organization of the United Nations (FAO) Via delle Terme di Caracalla, 00100 Rome, Italy (Telephone Number in U.S. (202) 653-2400); *The State of Food and Agriculture,* and *Yearbook of Fishery Statistics.*

Statistical Office of the United Nations, Publishing Service, New York, New York 10017 (800) 253-9646; *Statistical Yearbook.*

BULGARIA - FLAX FIBRE PRODUCTION - See BULGARIA - TEXTILE INDUSTRY

BULGARIA - FLOUR PRODUCTION

Statistical Office of the United Nations, Publishing Service, New York, New York 10017 (800) 253-9646; *Statistical Yearbook.*

BULGARIA - FOOD

Food and Agricultural Organization of the United Nations (FAO) Via delle Terme di Caracalla, 00100 Rome, Italy (Telephone Number in U.S. (202) 653-2400); *Production Yearbook,* and *The State of Food and Agriculture.*

G.K. Hall and Company, 70 Lincoln Street, Boston, Massachusetts 02111 (617) 423-3990; *The World in Figures.*

BULGARIA - FOREIGN AID

G.K. Hall and Company, 70 Lincoln Street, Boston, Massachusetts 02111 (617) 423-3990; *The World in Figures.*

BULGARIA - FOREIGN TRADE

Euromonitor Publications Limited, 87-88 Turnmill Street, London EC1M 5QU, England; *European Marketing Data and Statistics.*

Facts on File, 460 Park Avenue South, New York, New York 10016 (800) 443-8323; *The New Book of World Rankings.*

Federal Statistical Office, Gustav - Stresemann - Ring 11, D-6200 Wiesbaden, Germany; *Bulgarien.*

Food and Agricultural Organization of the United Nations (FAO) Via delle Terme di Caracalla, 00100 Rome, Italy (Telephone Number in U.S. (202) 653-2400); *The State of Food and Agriculture.*

G.K. Hall and Company, 70 Lincoln Street, Boston, Massachusetts 02111 (617) 423-3990; *The World in Figures.*

Statistical Office of the United Nations, Publishing Service, New York, New York 10017 (800) 253-9646; *Statistical Yearbook,* and *International Trade Statistics Yearbook.*

BULGARIA - FORESTRY AND FOREST PRODUCTS

Euromonitor Publications Limited, 87-88 Turnmill Street, London EC1M 5QU, England; *European Marketing Data and Statistics.*

Facts on File, 460 Park Avenue South, New York, New York 10016 (800) 443-8323; *The New Book of World Rankings.*

Federal Statistical Office, Gustav - Stresemann - Ring 11, D-6200 Wiesbaden, Germany; *Bulgarien.*

Food and Agricultural Organization of the United Nations (FAO) Via delle Terme di Caracalla, 00100 Rome, Italy (Telephone Number in U.S. (202) 653-2400); *The State of Food and Agriculture,* and *Yearbook of Forest Products.*

G.K. Hall and Company, 70 Lincoln Street, Boston, Massachusetts 02111 (617) 423-3990; *The World in Figures.*

Statistical Office of the United Nations, Publishing Service, New York, New York 10017 (800) 253-9646; *Statistical Yearbook.*

United Nations Educational, Scientific and Cultural Organization (UNESCO), 7 Place de Fontenoy, F-75700 Paris, France (Telephone Number in U.S. (212) 963-5981); *Statistical Yearbook.*

BULGARIA - GARLIC PRODUCTION - See BULGARIA - CROPS

BULGARIA - GAS PRODUCTION - See BULGARIA - MINING AND MINERAL PRODUCTS

BULGARIA - GENERAL INDUSTRIAL STATISTICS

Federal Statistical Office, Gustav - Stresemann - Ring 11, D-6200 Wiesbaden, Germany; *Bulgarien.*

Statistical Office of the United Nations, Publishing Service, New York, New York 10017 (800) 253-9646; *Industrial Statistics Yearbook.*

BULGARIA - GENERAL MORTALITY

Statistical Office of the United Nations, Publishing Service, New York, New York 10017 (800) 253-9646; *Demographic Yearbook.*

World Health Organization, Office of Publications, Avenue Appia, CH-1211 Geneva 27, Switzerland (Telephone Number in U.S. (518) 436-9686); *World Health Statistics Annual.*

BULGARIA - GEOGRAPHIC DATA

Facts on File, 460 Park Avenue South, New York, New York 10016 (800) 443-8323; *The New Book of World Rankings.*

Federal Statistical Office, Gustav - Stresemann - Ring 11, D-6200 Wiesbaden, Germany; *Bulgarien.*

BULGARIA - GOLD PRODUCTION AND CONSUMPTION - See BULGARIA - MINING AND MINERAL PRODUCTS

BULGARIA - GOVERNMENT

G.K. Hall and Company, 70 Lincoln Street, Boston, Massachusetts 02111 (617) 423-3990; *The World in Figures.*

BULGARIA - GOVERNMENT FINANCES

Statistical Office of the United Nations, Publishing Service, New York, New York 10017 (800) 253-9646; *Statistical Yearbook.*

BULGARIA - GRAIN PRODUCTION - See BULGARIA - CROPS

BULGARIA - GREEN PEPPER AND CHILIE PRODUCTION - See BULGARIA - CROPS

BULGARIA - GROSS DOMESTIC PRODUCT

Business International Corporation, 215 Park Avenue South, New York, New York 10003 (800) 938-4685; *The World Market Atlas.*

Facts on File, 460 Park Avenue South, New York, New York 10016 (800) 443-8323; *The New Book of World Rankings.*

G.K. Hall and Company, 70 Lincoln Street, Boston, Massachusetts 02111 (617) 423-3990; *The World in Figures.*

Statistical Office of the United Nations, Publishing Service, New York, New York 10017 (800) 253-9646; *Statistical Yearbook.*

Times Books, 201 East 50th Street, New York, New York 10022 (212) 751-2600; *The Economist Book of Vital World Statistics.*

BULGARIA - GROUNDNUT PRODUCTION - See BULGARIA - CROPS

BULGARIA - HAZELNUT PRODUCTION - See BULGARIA - CROPS

BULGARIA - HEALTH

Facts on File, 460 Park Avenue South, New York, New York 10016 (800) 443-8323; *The New Book of World Rankings.*

Federal Statistical Office, Gustav - Stresemann - Ring 11, D-6200 Wiesbaden, Germany; *Bulgarien.*

G.K. Hall and Company, 70 Lincoln Street, Boston, Massachusetts 02111 (617) 423-3990; *The World in Figures.*

Statistical Office of the United Nations, Publishing Service, New York, New York 10017 (800) 253-9646; *Statistical Yearbook.*

Times Books, 201 East 50th Street, New York, New York 10022 (212) 751-2600; *The Economist Book of Vital World Statistics.*

World Health Organization, Office of Publications, Avenue Appia, CH-1211 Geneva 27, Switzerland (Telephone Number in U.S. (518) 436-9686); *World Health Statistics Annual.*

BULGARIA - HEMP FIBRE PRODUCTION - See BULGARIA - TEXTILE INDUSTRY

BULGARIA - HIDE PRODUCTION

Food and Agricultural Organization of the United Nations (FAO), Via delle Terme di Caracalla, 00100 Rome, Italy (Telephone Number in U.S. (202) 653-2400); *Production Yearbook.*

BULGARIA - HIGHWAYS

G.K. Hall and Company, 70 Lincoln Street, Boston, Massachusetts 02111 (617) 423-3990; *The World in Figures.*

International Road Federation, 525 School Street, SW, Washington, D.C. 20024 (202) 554-2106; *World Road Statistics.*

Statistical Office of the United Nations, Publishing Service, New York, New York 10017 (800) 253-9646; *Annual Bulletin of Transport Statistics for Europe.*

BULGARIA - HOPS PRODUCTION - See BULGARIA - CROPS

BULGARIA - HORSES - See BULGARIA - LIVESTOCK AND POULTRY

BULGARIA - HOURS OF WORK - See BULGARIA - EMPLOYMENT

BULGARIA - HOUSING AND HOUSING UNITS

Columbia University Press, 562 West 113th Street, New York, New York 10014 (212) 316-7100; *East European and Soviet Data Book.*

Facts on File, 460 Park Avenue South, New York, New York 10016 (800) 443-8323; *The New Book of World Rankings.*

BULGARIA - HYDROCHLORIC ACID PRODUCTION

Statistical Office of the United Nations, Publishing Service, New York, New York 10017 (800) 253-9646; *Statistical Yearbook.*

BULGARIA - ILLITERATE POPULATION

Business International Corporation, 215 Park Avenue South, New York, New York 10003 (800) 938-4685; *The World Market Atlas.*

Columbia University Press, 562 West 113th Street, New York, New York 10014 (212) 316-7100; *East European and Soviet Data Book.*

G.K. Hall and Company, 70 Lincoln Street, Boston, Massachusetts 02111 (617) 423-3990; *The World in Figures.*

United Nations Educational, Scientific and Cultural Organization (UNESCO), 7 Place de Fontenoy, F-75700 Paris, France (Telephone Number in U.S. (212) 963-5981); *Statistical Yearbook.*

BULGARIA - IMPORTS

Business International Corporation, 215 Park Avenue South, New York, New York 10003 (800) 938-4685; *The World Market Atlas.*

Food and Agricultural Organization of the United Nations (FAO) Via delle Terme di Caracalla, 00100 Rome, Italy (Telephone Number in U.S. (202) 653-2400); *The State of Food and Agriculture.*

G.K. Hall and Company, 70 Lincoln Street, Boston, Massachusetts 02111 (617) 423-3990; *The World in Figures.*

International Lead and Zinc Study Group, Metro House, 58 St. James's Street, London SW1A 1LD, England; *Lead and Zinc Statistics.*

International Monetary Fund, 700 Nineteenth Street, NW, Washington, D.C. 20431 (202) 623-7000; *Direction of Trade Statistics.*

BULGARIA - INDUSTRIAL METALS PRODUCTION - See BULGARIA - MINING AND MINERAL PRODUCTS

BULGARIA - INDUSTRY

Facts on File, 460 Park Avenue South, New York, New York 10016 (800) 443-8323; *The New Book of World Rankings.*

Federal Statistical Office, Gustav - Stresemann - Ring 11, D-6200 Wiesbaden, Germany; *Bulgarien.*

G.K. Hall and Company, 70 Lincoln Street, Boston, Massachusetts 02111 (617) 423-3990; *The World in Figures.*

International Labour Office, I.L.O. Publications, CH-1211, Geneva 22, Switzerland; *Yearbook of Labour Statistics.*

Times Books, 201 East 50th Street, New York, New York 10022 (212) 751-2600; *The Economist Book of Vital World Statistics.*

World Intellectual Property Organization, 34 Chemin des Colombettes, CH-1211 Geneva 20. Switzerland; *Industrial Property Statistics.*

BULGARIA - INFANT AND MATERNAL MORTALITY

Statistical Office of the United Nations, Publishing Service, New York, New York 10017 (800) 253-9646; *Demographic Yearbook,* and *Statistical Yearbook.*

Times Books, 201 East 50th Street, New York, New York 10022 (212) 751-2600; *The Economist Book of Vital World Statistics.*

World Health Organization, Office of Publications, Avenue Appia, CH-1211 Geneva 27, Switzerland (Telephone Number in U.S. (518) 436-9686); *World Health Statistics Annual.*

BULGARIA - INTERNAL TRADE

Statistical Office of the United Nations, Publishing Service, New York, New York 10017 (800) 253-9646; *Statistical Yearbook.*

BULGARIA - IRON ORE PRODUCTION AND CONSUMPTION - See BULGARIA - MINING AND MINERAL PRODUCTS

BULGARIA - LABOR FORCE

Columbia University Press, 562 West 113th Street, New York, New York 10014 (212) 316-7100; *East European and Soviet Data Book.*

Facts on File, 460 Park Avenue South, New York, New York 10016 (800) 443-8323; *The New Book of World Rankings.*

Food and Agricultural Organization of the United Nations (FAO) Via delle Terme di Caracalla, 00100 Rome, Italy (Telephone Number in U.S. (202) 653-2400); *The State of Food and Agriculture.*

G.K. Hall and Company, 70 Lincoln Street, Boston, Massachusetts 02111 (617) 423-3990; *The World in Figures.*

Times Books, 201 East 50th Street, New York, New York 10022 (212) 751-2600; *The Economist Book of Vital World Statistics.*

BULGARIA - LABOR PRODUCTIVITY

International Labour Office, I.L.O. Publications, CH-1211, Geneva 22, Switzerland; *Yearbook of Labour Statistics.*

BULGARIA - LAND USE

Euromonitor Publications Limited, 87-88 Turnmill Street, London EC1M 5QU, England; *European Marketing Data and Statistics.*

Food and Agricultural Organization of the United Nations (FAO), Via delle Terme di Caracalla, 00100 Rome, Italy (Telephone Number in U.S. (202) 653-2400); *Production Yearbook.*

G.K. Hall and Company, 70 Lincoln Street, Boston, Massachusetts 02111 (617) 423-3990; *The World in Figures.*

BULGARIA - LEAD AND LEAD ORE PRODUCTION AND CONSUMPTION - See BULGARIA - MINING AND MINERAL PRODUCTS

BULGARIA - LIBRARIES

Euromonitor Publications Limited, 87-88 Turnmill Street, London EC1M 5QU, England; *European Marketing Data and Statistics.*

Facts on File, 460 Park Avenue South, New York, New York 10016 (800) 443-8323; *The New Book of World Rankings.*

United Nations Educational, Scientific and Cultural Organization (UNESCO), 7 Place de Fontenoy, F-75700 Paris, France (Telephone Number in U.S. (212) 963-5981); *Statistical Yearbook.*

BULGARIA - LIGNITE PRODUCTION - See BULGARIA - MINING AND MINERAL PRODUCTS

BULGARIA - LIVESTOCK AND POULTRY

Euromonitor Publications Limited, 87-88 Turnmill Street, London EC1M 5QU, England; *European Marketing Data and Statistics.*

Facts on File, 460 Park Avenue South, New York, New York 10016 (800) 443-8323; *The New Book of World Rankings.*

Food and Agricultural Organization of the United Nations (FAO), Via delle Terme di Caracalla, 00100 Rome, Italy (Telephone Number in U.S. (202) 653-2400); *Production Yearbook,* and *The State of Food and Agriculture.*

G.K. Hall and Company, 70 Lincoln Street, Boston, Massachusetts 02111 (617) 423-3990; *The World in Figures.*

Statistical Office of the United Nations, Publishing Service, New York, New York 10017 (800) 253-9646; *Statistical Yearbook.*

BULGARIA - LIVING LEVELS

G.K. Hall and Company, 70 Lincoln Street, Boston, Massachusetts 02111 (617) 423-3990; *The World in Figures.*

Times Books, 201 East 50th Street, New York, New York 10022 (212) 751-2600; *The Economist Book of Vital World Statistics.*

BULGARIA - MANGANESE ORE PRODUCTION AND CONSUMPTION -See BULGARIA - MINING AND MINERAL PRODUCTS

BULGARIA - MANUFACTURING

G.K. Hall and Company, 70 Lincoln Street, Boston, Massachusetts 02111 (617) 423-3990; *The World in Figures.*

Facts on File, 460 Park Avenue South, New York, New York 10016 (800) 443-8323; *The New Book of World Rankings.*

Statistical Office of the United Nations, Publishing Service, New York, New York 10017 (800) 253-9646; *Statistical Yearbook.*

Times Books, 201 East 50th Street, New York, New York 10022 (212) 751-2600; *The Economist Book of Vital World Statistics.*

BULGARIA - MARRIAGE RATES

Facts on File, 460 Park Avenue South, New York, New York 10016 (800) 443-8323; *The New Book of World Rankings.*

Statistical Office of the United Nations, Publishing Service, New York, New York 10017 (800) 253-9646; *Demographic Yearbook*, and *Statistical Yearbook*.

BULGARIA - MEAT PRODUCTION - See BULGARIA - LIVESTOCK AND POULTRY

BULGARIA - MERCHANT SHIPPING

G.K. Hall and Company, 70 Lincoln Street, Boston, Massachusetts 02111 (617) 423-3990; *The World in Figures*.

Lloyd's Register of Shipping, 17 Battery Place, New York, New York 10004 (212) 425-8050; *Register of Ships*.

Statistical Office of the United Nations, Publishing Service, New York, New York 10017 (800) 253-9646; *Annual Bulletin of Transport Statistics for Europe*, and *Statistical Yearbook*.

Times Books, 201 East 50th Street, New York, New York 10022 (212) 751-2600; *The Economist Book of Vital World Statistics*.

U.S. Department of Transportation, Maritime Administration, 400 Seventh Street, SW, Washington, D.C. 20590; *A Statistical Analysis of the World's Merchant Fleets*.

BULGARIA - MILITARY

G.K. Hall and Company, 70 Lincoln Street, Boston, Massachusetts 02111 (617) 423-3990; *The World in Figures*.

The International Institute for Strategic Studies, 23 Tavistock Street, London WC2E 7NQ, England; *The Military Balance*.

BULGARIA - MILK PRODUCTION - See BULGARIA - DAIRY PRODUCTS

BULGARIA - MILLET PRODUCTION - See BULGARIA - CROPS

BULGARIA - MINING AND MINERAL PRODUCTS

Commodity Research Bureau, Incorporated, 75 Wall Street, New York, New York 10005 (212) 504-7754; *Commodity Year Book*.

Facts on File, 460 Park Avenue South, New York, New York 10016 (800) 443-8323; *The New Book of World Rankings*.

G.K. Hall and Company, 70 Lincoln Street, Boston, Massachusetts 02111 (617) 423-3990; *The World in Figures*.

International Lead and Zinc Study Group, Metro House, 58 St. James's Street, London SW1A 1LD, England; *Lead and Zinc Statistics*.

Penn Well Publishing Company, 1421 South Sheridan Road, P.O. Box 1260, Tulsa, Oklahoma 74101 (800) 752-9764; *International Energy Statistics Sourcebook*.

Statistical Office of the United Nations, Publishing Service, New York, New York 10017 (800) 253-9646; *Statistical Yearbook*.

BULGARIA - MOLYBDENUM ORE PRODUCTION AND CONSUMPTION - See BULGARIA - MINING AND MINERAL PRODUCTS

BULGARIA - MONEY EXCHANGE RATES

Statistical Office of the United Nations, Publishing Service, New York, New York 10017 (800) 253-9646; *Statistical Yearbook*.

BULGARIA - MONEY SUPPLY

Federal Statistical Office, Gustav - Stresemann - Ring 11, D-6200 Wiesbaden, Germany; *Bulgarien*.

G.K. Hall and Company, 70 Lincoln Street, Boston, Massachusetts 02111 (617) 423-3990; *The World in Figures*.

BULGARIA - MOTION PICTURES

Statistical Office of the United Nations, Publishing Service, New York, New York 10017 (800) 253-9646; *Statistical Yearbook*.

United Nations Educational, Scientific and Cultural Organization (UNESCO), 7 Place de Fontenoy, F-75700 Paris, France (Telephone Number in U.S. (212) 963-5981); *Statistical Yearbook*.

BULGARIA - MOTOR VEHICLE PRODUCTION AND ASSEMBLY

Statistical Office of the United Nations, Publishing Service, New York, New York 10017 (800) 253-9646; *Statistical Yearbook*.

BULGARIA - MOTOR VEHICLES IN USE

G.K. Hall and Company, 70 Lincoln Street, Boston, Massachusetts 02111 (617) 423-3990; *The World in Figures*.

International Road Federation, 525 School Street, SW, Washington, D.C. 20024 (202) 554-2106; *World Road Statistics*.

Times Books, 201 East 50th Street, New York, New York 10022 (212) 751-2600; *The Economist Book of Vital World Statistics*.

BULGARIA - MULES - See BULGARIA - LIVESTOCK AND POULTRY

BULGARIA - MUSEUMS

Euromonitor Publications Limited, 87-88 Turnmill Street, London EC1M 5QU, England; *European Marketing Data and Statistics*.

Facts on File, 460 Park Avenue South, New York, New York 10016 (800) 443-8323; *The New Book of World Rankings*.

United Nations Educational, Scientific and Cultural Organization (UNESCO), 7 Place de Fontenoy, F-75700 Paris, France (Telephone Number in U.S. (212) 963-5981); *Statistical Yearbook*.

BULGARIA - NATALITY - See BULGARIA - BIRTH RATES

BULGARIA - NATIONAL ACCOUNTS

Federal Statistical Office, Gustav - Stresemann - Ring 11, D-6200 Wiesbaden, Germany; *Bulgarien*.

Statistical Office of the United Nations, Publishing Service, New York, New York 10017 (800) 253-9646; *National Accounts Statistics*, and *Statistical Yearbook*.

BULGARIA - NATIONAL INCOME

Facts on File, 460 Park Avenue South, New York, New York 10016 (800) 443-8323; *The New Book of World Rankings*.

G.K. Hall and Company, 70 Lincoln Street, Boston, Massachusetts 02111 (617) 423-3990; *The World in Figures*.

Statistical Office of the United Nations, Publishing Service, New York, New York 10017 (800) 253-9646; *Statistical Yearbook*.

BULGARIA - NATIONAL PRODUCT

Facts on File, 460 Park Avenue South, New York, New York 10016 (800) 443-8323; *The New Book of World Rankings*.

Statistical Office of the United Nations, Publishing Service, New York, New York 10017 (800) 253-9646; *Statistical Yearbook*.

BULGARIA - NATURAL GAS PRODUCTION - See BULGARIA - MINING AND MINERAL PRODUCTS

BULGARIA - NET MATERIAL PRODUCT

Statistical Office of the United Nations, Publishing Service, New York, New York 10017 (800) 253-9646; *Statistical Yearbook*.

BULGARIA - NEWSPAPER PRODUCTION - See BULGARIA - FORESTRY AND FOREST PRODUCTS

BULGARIA - NITRIC ACID PRODUCTION - See BULGARIA - MINING AND MINERAL PRODUCTS

BULGARIA - OATS PRODUCTION - See BULGARIA - CROPS

BULGARIA - OCCUPATIONS - See BULGARIA - LABOR FORCE

BULGARIA - PAPER PRODUCTION AND CONSUMPTION - See BULGARIA - FORESTRY AND FOREST PRODUCTS

BULGARIA - PARTY LEADERS

Columbia University Press, 562 West 113th Street, New York, New York 10014 (212) 316-7100; *East European and Soviet Data Book*.

BULGARIA - PARTY MEMBERSHIP

Columbia University Press, 562 West 113th Street, New York, New York 10014 (212) 316-7100; *East European and Soviet Data Book*.

BULGARIA - PATENTS

Statistical Office of the United Nations, Publishing Service, New York, New York 10017 (800) 253-9646; *Statistical Yearbook*.

World Intellectual Property Organization, 34 Chemin des Colombettes, CH-1211 Geneva 20. Switzerland; *Industrial Property Statistics*.

BULGARIA - PEANUT PRODUCTION - See BULGARIA - CROPS

BULGARIA - PERIODICALS

United Nations Educational, Scientific and Cultural Organization (UNESCO), 7 Place de Fontenoy, F-75700 Paris, France (Telephone Number in U.S. (212) 963-5981); *Statistical Yearbook*.

BULGARIA - PESTICIDE USE

Food and Agricultural Organization of the United Nations (FAO) Via delle Terme di Caracalla, 00100 Rome, Italy (Telephone Number in U.S. (202) 653-2400); *The State of Food and Agriculture*.

BULGARIA - PETROLEUM INDUSTRY

Euromonitor Publications Limited, 87-88 Turnmill Street, London EC1M 5QU, England; *European Marketing Data and Statistics*.

Facts on File, 460 Park Avenue South, New York, New York 10016 (800) 443-8323; *The New Book of World Rankings*.

Food and Agricultural Organization of the United Nations (FAO) Via delle Terme di Caracalla, 00100 Rome, Italy (Telephone Number in U.S. (202) 653-2400); *The State of Food and Agriculture*.

G.K. Hall and Company, 70 Lincoln Street, Boston, Massachusetts 02111 (617) 423-3990; *The World in Figures*.

Penn Well Publishing Company, 1421 South Sheridan Road, P.O. Box 1260, Tulsa, Oklahoma 74101 (800) 752-9764; *International Energy Statistics Sourcebook*.

Statistical Office of the United Nations, Publishing Service, New York, New York 10017 (800) 253-9646; *Statistical Yearbook*.

BULGARIA - PIG-IRON AND FERRO-ALLOY PRODUCTION - See BULGARIA - MINING AND MINERAL PRODUCTS

BULGARIA - PIGS - See BULGARIA - LIVESTOCK AND POULTRY

BULGARIA - PLASTIC AND RESIN PRODUCTION

Statistical Office of the United Nations, Publishing Service, New York, New York 10017 (800) 253-9646; *Statistical Yearbook*.

BULGARIA - POPULATION

Business International Corporation, 215 Park Avenue South, New York, New York 10003 (800) 938-4685; *The World Market Atlas*.

Columbia University Press, 562 West 113th Street, New York, New York 10014 (212) 316-7100; *East European and Soviet Data Book*.

Euromonitor Publications Limited, 87-88 Turnmill Street, London EC1M 5QU, England; *European Marketing Data and Statistics*.

Facts on File, 460 Park Avenue South, New York, New York 10016 (800) 443-8323; *The New Book of World Rankings*.

Federal Statistical Office, Gustav - Stresemann - Ring 11, D-6200 Wiesbaden, Germany; *Bulgarien*.

Food and Agricultural Organization of the United Nations (FAO), Via delle Terme di Caracalla, 00100 Rome, Italy (Telephone Number in U.S. (202) 653-2400); *Production Yearbook*.

G.K. Hall and Company, 70 Lincoln Street, Boston, Massachusetts 02111 (617) 423-3990; *The World in Figures*.

International Labour Office, I.L.O. Publications, CH-1211, Geneva 22, Switzerland; *Yearbook of Labour Statistics*.

Statistical Office of the United Nations, Publishing Service, New York, New York 10017 (800) 253-9646; *Demographic Yearbook*, and *Statistical Yearbook*.

Times Books, 201 East 50th Street, New York, New York 10022 (212) 751-2600; *The Economist Book of Vital World Statistics*.

United Nations Educational, Scientific and Cultural Organization (UNESCO), 7 Place de Fontenoy, F-75700 Paris, France (Telephone Number in U.S. (212) 963-5981); *Statistical Yearbook*.

World Health Organization, Office of Publications, Avenue Appia, CH-1211 Geneva 27, Switzerland (Telephone Number in U.S. (518) 436-9686); *World Health Statistics Annual*.

BULGARIA - POST OFFICES

Facts on File, 460 Park Avenue South, New York, New York 10016 (800) 443-8323; *The New Book of World Rankings.*

BULGARIA - POTATO PRODUCTION - See BULGARIA - CROPS

BULGARIA - POULTRY - See BULGARIA - LIVESTOCK AND POULTRY

BULGARIA - POWER PRODUCTION INDUSTRY

Statistical Office of the United Nations, Publishing Service, New York, New York 10017 (800) 253-9646; *Statistical Yearbook.*

BULGARIA - PRICES

Facts on File, 460 Park Avenue South, New York, New York 10016 (800) 443-8323; *The New Book of World Rankings.*

Federal Statistical Office, Gustav - Stresemann - Ring 11, D-6200 Wiesbaden, Germany; *Bulgarien.*

Food and Agricultural Organization of the United Nations (FAO), Via delle Terme di Caracalla, 00100 Rome, Italy (Telephone Number in U.S. (202) 653-2400); *Production Yearbook,* and *The State of Food and Agriculture.*

G.K. Hall and Company, 70 Lincoln Street, Boston, Massachusetts 02111 (617) 423-3990; *The World in Figures.*

International Labour Office, I.L.O. Publications, CH-1211, Geneva 22, Switzerland; *Yearbook of Labour Statistics.*

International Lead and Zinc Study Group, Metro House, 58 St. James's Street, London SW1A 1LD, England; *Lead and Zinc Statistics.*

BULGARIA - PRINTING AND WRITING PAPER - See BULGARIA - FORESTRY AND FOREST PRODUCTS

BULGARIA - PRODUCTION

Facts on File, 460 Park Avenue South, New York, New York 10016 (800) 443-8323; *The New Book of World Rankings.*

G.K. Hall and Company, 70 Lincoln Street, Boston, Massachusetts 02111 (617) 423-3990; *The World in Figures.*

International Lead and Zinc Study Group, Metro House, 58 St. James's Street, London SW1A 1LD, England; *Lead and Zinc Statistics.*

BULGARIA - PUBLIC FINANCE

Facts on File, 460 Park Avenue South, New York, New York 10016 (800) 443-8323; *The New Book of World Rankings.*

Federal Statistical Office, Gustav - Stresemann - Ring 11, D-6200 Wiesbaden, Germany; *Bulgarien.*

BULGARIA - RADIO BROADCASTING - See BULGARIA - BROADCASTING

BULGARIA - RADIO RECEIVER PRODUCTION

Statistical Office of the United Nations, Publishing Service, New York, New York 10017 (800) 253-9646; *Statistical Yearbook.*

BULGARIA - RAILWAYS

Euromonitor Publications Limited, 87-88 Turnmill Street, London EC1M 5QU, England; *European Marketing Data and Statistics.*

G.K. Hall and Company, 70 Lincoln Street, Boston, Massachusetts 02111 (617) 423-3990; *The World in Figures.*

Jane's Information Group, Sentinel House, 163 Brighton Road, Coulsdon, Surrey CR5 2NH, England (Telephone Number in U.S. (703) 683-3700); *Jane's World Railways.*

Statistical Office of the United Nations, Publishing Service, New York, New York 10017 (800) 253-9646; *Annual Bulletin of Transport Statistics for Europe,* and *Statistical Yearbook.*

BULGARIA - RELIGION

Facts on File, 460 Park Avenue South, New York, New York 10016 (800) 443-8323; *The New Book of World Rankings.*

BULGARIA - RETAIL TRADE

G.K. Hall and Company, 70 Lincoln Street, Boston, Massachusetts 02111 (617) 423-3990; *The World in Figures.*

BULGARIA - RETAIL TRADE - INDEX NUMBER

Statistical Office of the United Nations, Publishing Service, New York, New York 10017 (800) 253-9646; *Statistical Yearbook.*

BULGARIA - RICE PRODUCTION - See BULGARIA - CROPS

BULGARIA - ROOT AND TUBER PRODUCTION - See BULGARIA - CROPS

BULGARIA - ROUNDWOOD PRODUCTION - See BULGARIA - FORESTRY AND FOREST PRODUCTS

BULGARIA - RUBBER PRODUCTION

Facts on File, 460 Park Avenue South, New York, New York 10016 (800) 443-8323; *The New Book of World Rankings.*

Statistical Office of the United Nations, Publishing Service, New York, New York 10017 (800) 253-9646; *Statistical Yearbook.*

BULGARIA - SALT PRODUCTION - See BULGARIA - MINING AND MINERAL PRODUCTS

BULGARIA - SAWNWOOD PRODUCTION - See BULGARIA - FORESTRY AND FOREST PRODUCTS

BULGARIA - SCIENTISTS AND TECHNOLOGY

Statistical Office of the United Nations, Publishing Service, New York, New York 10017 (800) 253-9646; *Statistical Yearbook.*

BULGARIA - SENIOR CITIZENS

Facts on File, 460 Park Avenue South, New York, New York 10016 (800) 443-8323; *The New Book of World Rankings.*

BULGARIA - SESAME SEED PRODUCTION - See BULGARIA - CROPS

BULGARIA - SHEEP - See BULGARIA - LIVESTOCK AND POULTRY

BULGARIA - SILVER PRODUCTION AND CONSUMPTION - See BULGARIA - MINING AND MINERAL PRODUCTS

BULGARIA - SOCIAL DATA

Facts on File, 460 Park Avenue South, New York, New York 10016 (800) 443-8323; *The New Book of World Rankings.*

G.K. Hall and Company, 70 Lincoln Street, Boston, Massachusetts 02111 (617) 423-3990; *The World in Figures.*

BULGARIA - SOYBEAN PRODUCTION - See BULGARIA - CROPS

BULGARIA - STEEL - See BULGARIA -MINING AND MINERAL PRODUCTS

BULGARIA - STOCKS - COMMODITY - MARKET PRICE - INDEX

Food and Agricultural Organization of the United Nations (FAO) Via delle Terme di Caracalla, 00100 Rome, Italy (Telephone Number in U.S. (202) 653-2400); *The State of Food and Agriculture.*

International Lead and Zinc Study Group, Metro House, 58 St. James's Street, London SW1A 1LD, England; *Lead and Zinc Statistics.*

BULGARIA - SUGAR PRODUCTION AND CONSUMPTION - See BULGARIA - CROPS

BULGARIA - SULPHURIC ACID PRODUCTION - See BULGARIA - MINING AND MINERAL PRODUCTS

BULGARIA - TAXATION

G.K. Hall and Company, 70 Lincoln Street, Boston, Massachusetts 02111 (617) 423-3990; *The World in Figures.*

International Road Federation, 525 School Street, SW, Washington, D.C. 20024 (202) 554-2106; *World Road Statistics.*

BULGARIA - TELEGRAPH SERVICE

Statistical Office of the United Nations, Publishing Service, New York, New York 10017 (800) 253-9646; *Statistical Yearbook.*

BULGARIA - TELEPHONES IN USE

American Telephone and Telegraph Company, 26 Parsippany Road, Whippany, New Jersey 07981 (800) 338-4038; *The World's Telephones.*

G.K. Hall and Company, 70 Lincoln Street, Boston, Massachusetts 02111 (617) 423-3990; *The World in Figures.*

Statistical Office of the United Nations, Publishing Service, New York, New York 10017 (800) 253-9646; *Statistical Yearbook.*

BULGARIA - TELEVISION BROADCASTING - See BULGARIA - BROADCASTING

BULGARIA - TELEVISION RECEIVER PRODUCTION

Statistical Office of the United Nations, Publishing Service, New York, New York 10017 (800) 253-9646; *Statistical Yearbook.*

BULGARIA - TEXTILE INDUSTRY

Food and Agricultural Organization of the United Nations (FAO) Via delle Terme di Caracalla, 00100 Rome, Italy (Telephone Number in U.S. (202) 653-2400); *The State of Food and Agriculture.*

G.K. Hall and Company, 70 Lincoln Street, Boston, Massachusetts 02111 (617) 423-3990; *The World in Figures.*

Statistical Office of the United Nations, Publishing Service, New York, New York 10017 (800) 253-9646; *Statistical Yearbook.*

BULGARIA - THEATRE

United Nations Educational, Scientific and Cultural Organization (UNESCO), 7 Place de Fontenoy, F-75700 Paris, France (Telephone Number in U.S. (212) 963-5981); *Statistical Yearbook.*

BULGARIA - TIN - INDUSTRIAL CONSUMPTION - See BULGARIA - MINING AND MINERAL PRODUCTS

BULGARIA - TIRE (MOTOR VEHICLE) PRODUCTION

Statistical Office of the United Nations, Publishing Service, New York, New York 10017 (800) 253-9646; *Statistical Yearbook.*

BULGARIA - TOBACCO PRODUCTION

Euromonitor Publications Limited, 87-88 Turnmill Street, London EC1M 5QU, England; *European Marketing Data and Statistics.*

Facts on File, 460 Park Avenue South, New York, New York 10016 (800) 443-8323; *The New Book of World Rankings.*

Statistical Office of the United Nations, Publishing Service, New York, New York 10017 (800) 253-9646; *Statistical Yearbook.*

BULGARIA - TOURISM

Euromonitor Publications Limited, 87-88 Turnmill Street, London EC1M 5QU, England; *European Marketing Data and Statistics.*

Facts on File, 460 Park Avenue South, New York, New York 10016 (800) 443-8323; *The New Book of World Rankings.*

Federal Statistical Office, Gustav - Stresemann - Ring 11, D-6200 Wiesbaden, Germany; *Bulgarien.*

G.K. Hall and Company, 70 Lincoln Street, Boston, Massachusetts 02111 (617) 423-3990; *The World in Figures.*

World Tourism Organization, Calle Capitan Haya 42, E-28020 Madrid, Spain; *Yearbook of Tourism Statistics.*

Statistical Office of the United Nations, Publishing Service, New York, New York 10017 (800) 253-9646; *Statistical Yearbook.*

Times Books, 201 East 50th Street, New York, New York 10022 (212) 751-2600; *The Economist Book of Vital World Statistics.*

BULGARIA - TRACTORS IN USE

Statistical Office of the United Nations, Publishing Service, New York, New York 10017 (800) 253-9646; *Statistical Yearbook.*

BULGARIA - TRADE - See BULGARIA - FOREIGN TRADE

BULGARIA - TRADEMARKS AND SERVICE MARKS

Statistical Office of the United Nations, Publishing Service, New York, New York 10017 (800) 253-9646; *Statistical Yearbook.*

World Intellectual Property Organization, 34 Chemin des Colombettes, CH-1211 Geneva 20. Switzerland; *Industrial Property Statistics.*

BULGARIA - TRANSPORTATION AND COMMUNICATIONS

Facts on File, 460 Park Avenue South, New York, New York 10016 (800) 443-8323; *The New Book of World Rankings.*

Federal Statistical Office, Gustav - Stresemann - Ring 11, D-6200 Wiesbaden, Germany; *Bulgarien.*

G.K. Hall and Company, 70 Lincoln Street, Boston, Massachusetts 02111 (617) 423-3990; *The World in Figures.*

BULGARIA - TURKEYS - See BULGARIA - LIVESTOCK AND POULTRY

BULGARIA - UNEMPLOYMENT

Euromonitor Publications Limited, 87-88 Turnmill Street, London EC1M 5QU, England; *European Marketing Data and Statistics.*

International Labour Office, I.L.O. Publications, CH-1211, Geneva 22, Switzerland; *Yearbook of Labour Statistics.*

BULGARIA - VITAL STATISTICS

G.K. Hall and Company, 70 Lincoln Street, Boston, Massachusetts 02111 (617) 423-3990; *The World in Figures.*

Statistical Office of the United Nations, Publishing Service, New York, New York 10017 (800) 253-9646; *Statistical Yearbook.*

World Health Organization, Office of Publications, Avenue Appia, CH-1211 Geneva 27, Switzerland (Telephone Number in U.S. (518) 436-9686); *World Health Statistics Annual.*

BULGARIA - WAGES

Euromonitor Publications Limited, 87-88 Turnmill Street, London EC1M 5QU, England; *European Marketing Data and Statistics.*

Federal Statistical Office, Gustav - Stresemann - Ring 11, D-6200 Wiesbaden, Germany; *Bulgarien.*

G.K. Hall and Company, 70 Lincoln Street, Boston, Massachusetts 02111 (617) 423-3990; *The World in Figures.*

International Labour Office, I.L.O. Publications, CH-1211, Geneva 22, Switzerland; *Yearbook of Labour Statistics.*

Statistical Office of the United Nations, Publishing Service, New York, New York 10017 (800) 253-9646; *Statistical Yearbook.*

BULGARIA - WALNUT PRODUCTION - See BULGARIA - CROPS

BULGARIA - WATERMELON PRODUCTION - See BULGARIA - CROPS

BULGARIA - WATERWAYS IN USE

Statistical Office of the United Nations, Publishing Service, New York, New York 10017 (800) 253-9646; *Annual Bulletin of Transport Statistics for Europe.*

BULGARIA - WEATHER

Facts on File, 460 Park Avenue South, New York, New York 10016 (800) 443-8323; *The New Book of World Rankings.*

G.K. Hall and Company, 70 Lincoln Street, Boston, Massachusetts 02111 (617) 423-3990; *The World in Figures.*

BULGARIA - WHEAT PRODUCTION - See BULGARIA - CROPS

BULGARIA - WINE PRODUCTION

Facts on File, 460 Park Avenue South, New York, New York 10016 (800) 443-8323; *The New Book of World Rankings.*

Statistical Office of the United Nations, Publishing Service, New York, New York 10017 (800) 253-9646; *Statistical Yearbook.*

BULGARIA - WOOD - See BULGARIA - FORESTRY AND FOREST PRODUCTS

BULGARIA - WOOL PRODUCTION

Facts on File, 460 Park Avenue South, New York, New York 10016 (800) 443-8323; *The New Book of World Rankings.*

BULGARIA - YARN PRODUCTION

Statistical Office of the United Nations, Publishing Service, New York, New York 10017 (800) 253-9646; *Statistical Yearbook.*

BULGARIA - ZINC AND ZINC ORE PRODUCTION AND CONSUMPTION - See BULGARIA - MINING AND MINERAL PRODUCTS

BURGLARY

U.S. Department of Justice, Bureau of Justice Statistics, 633 Indiana Avenue, NW, Washington, D.C. 20531 (800) 732-3277; *Criminal Victimization in the United States.*

U.S. Department of Justice, Federal Bureau of Investigation, Ninth Street and Pennsylvania Avenue, NW, Washington, D.C. 20535 (202) 324-3000; *Crime in the United States, Population-at-Risk Rates and Selected Crime Indicators,* and unpublished data.

Burkina Faso - National Statistical Office

Institut National de la Statistique et de la Demographic, Ministere du Plan et de la Cooperation, BP 374, Ouagadougou, 01, Burkina Faso.

Burkina Faso - Primary Statistics Sources

Institut National de la Statistique et de la Demographic, Ministere du Plan et de la Cooperation BP 374, Ougadougou, 01, Burkina Faso; *Annuaire Statistique du Burkina Faso.*

BURKINA FASO - AGRICULTURE

Euromonitor Publications Limited, 87-88 Turnmill Street, London EC1M 5QU, England; *International Marketing Data and Statistics.*

Federal Statistical Office, Gustav - Stresemann - Ring 11, D-6200 Wiesbaden, Germany; *Burkina Faso.*

Food and Agricultural Organization of the United Nations (FAO) Via delle Terme di Caracalla, 00100 Rome, Italy (Telephone Number in U.S. (202) 653-2400); *The State of Food and Agriculture,* and *Trade Yearbook.*

G.K. Hall and Company, 70 Lincoln Street, Boston, Massachusetts 02111 (617) 423-3990; *The World in Figures.*

Statistical Office of the United Nations, Publishing Service, New York, New York 10017 (800) 253-9646; *Statistical Yearbook,* and *Survey of Economic and Social Conditions in Africa.*

Times Books, 201 East 50th Street, New York, New York 10022 (212) 751-2600; *The Economist Book of Vital World Statistics.*

United Nations Economic Commission for Africa, Africa Hall, P.O. Box 3001, Addis Ababa, Ethiopia (Telephone Number in U.S. (800) 253-9646); *African Statistical Yearbook.*

The World Bank, 1818 H Street, NW, Washington, D.C. 20433 (202) 477-1234; *World Tables.*

BURKINA FASO - AIRLINE SERVICE

G.K. Hall and Company, 70 Lincoln Street, Boston, Massachusetts 02111 (617) 423-3990; *The World in Figures.*

Statistical Office of the United Nations, Publishing Service, New York, New York 10017 (800) 253-9646; *Statistical Yearbook.*

Times Books, 201 East 50th Street, New York, New York 10022 (212) 751-2600; *The Economist Book of Vital World Statistics.*

United Nations Economic Commission for Africa, Africa Hall, P.O. Box 3001, Addis Ababa, Ethiopia (Telephone Number in U.S. (800) 253-9646); *African Statistical Yearbook.*

BURKINA FASO - ANIMAL HEALTH

Food and Agricultural Organization of the United Nations (FAO), Via delle Terme di Caracalla, 00100 Rome, Italy (Telephone Number in U.S. (202) 653-2400); *Animal Health Yearbook.*

BURKINA FASO - AREA AND DENSITY OF POPULATION

African Development Bank, 01 BP 1387, Abidjan 01, Cote D'Ivoire; *Selected Statistics on Regional Member Countries.*

Euromonitor Publications Limited, 87-88 Turnmill Street, London EC1M 5QU, England; *International Marketing Data and Statistics.*

Federal Statistical Office, Gustav - Stresemann - Ring 11, D-6200 Wiesbaden, Germany; *Burkina Faso.*

Food and Agricultural Organization of the United Nations (FAO) Via delle Terme di Caracalla, 00100 Rome, Italy (Telephone Number in U.S. (202) 653-2400); *The State of Food and Agriculture.*

G.K. Hall and Company, 70 Lincoln Street, Boston, Massachusetts 02111 (617) 423-3990; *The World in Figures.*

Statistical Office of the United Nations, Publishing Service, New York, New York 10017 (800) 253-9646; *Statistical Yearbook,* and *Survey of Economic and Social Conditions in Africa.*

Times Books, 201 East 50th Street, New York, New York 10022 (212) 751-2600; *The Economist Book of Vital World Statistics.*

United Nations Educational, Scientific and Cultural Organization (UNESCO), 7 Place de Fontenoy, F-75700 Paris, France (Telephone Number in U.S. (212) 963-5981); *Statistical Yearbook.*

BURKINA FASO - ARMS EXPORTS AND IMPORTS

U.S. Arms Control and Disarmament Agency, 320 Twenty-first Street, NW, Washington, D.C. 20451 (202) 647-8677; *World Military Expenditures and Arms Transfers.*

BURKINA FASO - BALANCE OF PAYMENTS

African Development Bank, 01 BP 1387, Abidjan 01, Cote D'Ivoire; *Selected Statistics on Regional Member Countries.*

Business International Corporation, 215 Park Avenue South, New York, New York 10003 (800) 938-4685; *The World Market Atlas.*

Federal Statistical Office, Gustav - Stresemann - Ring 11, D-6200 Wiesbaden, Germany; *Burkina Faso.*

G.K. Hall and Company, 70 Lincoln Street, Boston, Massachusetts 02111 (617) 423-3990; *The World in Figures.*

International Monetary Fund, 700 Nineteenth Street, NW, Washington, D.C. 20431 (202) 623-7000; *Balance of Payments Yearbook.*

Times Books, 201 East 50th Street, New York, New York 10022 (212) 751-2600; *The Economist Book of Vital World Statistics.*

United Nations Economic Commission for Africa, Africa Hall, P.O. Box 3001, Addis Ababa, Ethiopia (Telephone Number in U.S. (800) 253-9646); *African Statistical Yearbook.*

The World Bank, 1818 H Street, NW, Washington, D.C. 20433 (202) 477-1234; *World Tables.*

BURKINA FASO - BANKING

G.K. Hall and Company, 70 Lincoln Street, Boston, Massachusetts 02111 (617) 423-3990; *The World in Figures.*

International Monetary Fund, 700 Nineteenth Street, NW, Washington, D.C. 20431 (202) 623-7000; *International Financial Statistics.*

Statistical Office of the United Nations, Publishing Service, New York, New York 10017 (800) 253-9646; *Statistical Yearbook.*

United Nations Economic Commission for Africa, Africa Hall, P.O. Box 3001, Addis Ababa, Ethiopia (Telephone Number in U.S. (800) 253-9646); *African Statistical Yearbook.*

BURKINA FASO - BEER PRODUCTION

Statistical Office of the United Nations, Publishing Service, New York, New York 10017 (800) 253-9646; *Statistical Yearbook.*

BURKINA FASO - BIRTH RATES

Statistical Office of the United Nations, Publishing Service, New York, New York 10017 (800) 253-9646; *Demographic Yearbook, Statistical Yearbook,* and *Survey of Economic and Social Conditions in Africa.*

Times Books, 201 East 50th Street, New York, New York 10022 (212) 751-2600; *The Economist Book of Vital World Statistics.*

The World Bank, 1818 H Street, NW, Washington, D.C. 20433 (202) 477-1234; *World Tables.*

BURKINA FASO - BONDS

G.K. Hall and Company, 70 Lincoln Street, Boston, Massachusetts 02111 (617) 423-3990; *The World in Figures.*

BURKINA FASO - BOOK PRODUCTION

G.K. Hall and Company, 70 Lincoln Street, Boston, Massachusetts 02111 (617) 423-3990; *The World in Figures.*

BURKINA FASO - BROADCASTING

Billboard Limited, P.O. Box 9027, 1006 AA Amsterdam, The Netherlands (Telephone Number in U.S. (212) 764-7300); *World Radio TV Handbook.*

G.K. Hall and Company, 70 Lincoln Street, Boston, Massachusetts 02111 (617) 423-3990; *The World in Figures.*

Times Books, 201 East 50th Street, New York, New York 10022 (212) 751-2600; *The Economist Book of Vital World Statistics.*

United Nations Educational, Scientific and Cultural Organization (UNESCO), 7 Place de Fontenoy, F-75700 Paris, France (Telephone Number in U.S. (212) 963-5981; *Statistical Yearbook.*

BURKINA FASO - BUSINESS

G.K. Hall and Company, 70 Lincoln Street, Boston, Massachusetts 02111 (617) 423-3990; *The World in Figures.*

BURKINA FASO - BUSINESS AND PROFESSIONAL LICENSES

International Monetary Fund, 700 Nineteenth Street, NW, Washington, D.C. 20431 (202) 623-7000; *Government Finance Statistics Yearbook.*

BURKINA FASO - BUTTER PRODUCTION - See BURKINA FASO - DAIRY PRODUCTS

BURKINA FASO - CALORIE SUPPLY

African Development Bank, 01 BP 1387, Abidjan 01, Cote D'Ivoire; *Selected Statistics on Regional Member Countries.*

Food and Agricultural Organization of the United Nations (FAO) Via delle Terme di Caracalla, 00100 Rome, Italy (Telephone Number in U.S. (202) 653-2400); *The State of Food and Agriculture.*

BURKINA FASO - CAPITAL REVENUE

International Monetary Fund, 700 Nineteenth Street, NW, Washington, D.C. 20431 (202) 623-7000; *Government Finance Statistics Yearbook.*

BURKINA FASO - CATTLE - See BURKINA FASO - LIVESTOCK AND POULTRY

BURKINA FASO - CHEESE PRODUCTION - See BURKINA FASO - DAIRY PRODUCTS

BURKINA FASO - CHEMICAL (ORGANIC) PRODUCTION - See BURKINA FASO - MINING AND MINERAL PRODUCTS

BURKINA FASO - CHICKENS - See BURKINA FASO - LIVESTOCK AND POULTRY

BURKINA FASO - CIGARETTE PRODUCTION - See BURKINA FASO - TOBACCO PRODUCTION

BURKINA FASO - CLASS STRUCTURE

G.K. Hall and Company, 70 Lincoln Street, Boston, Massachusetts 02111 (617) 423-3990; *The World in Figures.*

BURKINA FASO - CLIMATE

G.K. Hall and Company, 70 Lincoln Street, Boston, Massachusetts 02111 (617) 423-3990; *The World in Figures.*

BURKINA FASO - COAL PRODUCTION - See BURKINA FASO - MINING AND MINERAL PRODUCTS

BURKINA FASO - COMMUNICATIONS

Federal Statistical Office, Gustav - Stresemann - Ring 11, D-6200 Wiesbaden, Germany; *Burkina Faso.*

G.K. Hall and Company, 70 Lincoln Street, Boston, Massachusetts 02111 (617) 423-3990; *The World in Figures.*

United Nations Economic Commission for Africa, Africa Hall, P.O. Box 3001, Addis Ababa, Ethiopia (Telephone Number in U.S. (800) 253-9646); *African Statistical Yearbook.*

BURKINA FASO - CONSTRUCTION INDUSTRY

United Nations Economic Commission for Africa, Africa Hall, P.O. Box 3001, Addis Ababa, Ethiopia (Telephone Number in U.S. (800) 253-9646); *African Statistical Yearbook.*

BURKINA FASO - CONSUMER PRICE INDEX

African Development Bank, 01 BP 1387, Abidjan 01, Cote D'Ivoire; *Selected Statistics on Regional Member Countries.*

Federal Statistical Office, Gustav - Stresemann - Ring 11, D-6200 Wiesbaden, Germany; *Burkina Faso.*

G.K. Hall and Company, 70 Lincoln Street, Boston, Massachusetts 02111 (617) 423-3990; *The World in Figures.*

Statistical Office of the United Nations, Publishing Service, New York, New York 10017 (800) 253-9646; *Survey of Economic and Social Conditions in Africa.*

United Nations Economic Commission for Africa, Africa Hall, P.O. Box 3001, Addis Ababa, Ethiopia (Telephone Number in U.S. (800) 253-9646); *African Statistical Yearbook.*

BURKINA FASO - CONSUMER PRICES

Federal Statistical Office, Gustav - Stresemann - Ring 11, D-6200 Wiesbaden, Germany; *Burkina Faso.*

International Labour Office, I.L.O. Publications, CH-1211, Geneva 22, Switzerland; *Yearbook of Labour Statistics.*

International Monetary Fund, 700 Nineteenth Street, NW, Washington, D.C. 20431 (202) 623-7000; *International Financial Statistics.*

Times Books, 201 East 50th Street, New York, New York 10022 (212) 751-2600; *The Economist Book of Vital World Statistics.*

BURKINA FASO - CONSUMPTION

African Development Bank, 01 BP 1387, Abidjan 01, Cote D'Ivoire; *Selected Statistics on Regional Member Countries.*

G.K. Hall and Company, 70 Lincoln Street, Boston, Massachusetts 02111 (617) 423-3990; *The World in Figures.*

Statistical Office of the United Nations, Publishing Service, New York, New York 10017 (800) 253-9646; *Survey of Economic and Social Conditions in Africa.*

BURKINA FASO - CORN PRODUCTION - See BURKINA FASO - CROPS

BURKINA FASO - CORPORATE TAXES - See BURKINA FASO - TAXATION

BURKINA FASO - COTTON - See BURKINA FASO - CROPS

BURKINA FASO - CROPS

Food and Agricultural Organization of the United Nations (FAO) Via delle Terme di Caracalla, 00100 Rome, Italy (Telephone Number in U.S. (202) 653-2400); *The State of Food and Agriculture.*

G.K. Hall and Company, 70 Lincoln Street, Boston, Massachusetts 02111 (617) 423-3990; *The World in Figures.*

International Monetary Fund, 700 Nineteenth Street, NW, Washington, D.C. 20431 (202) 623-7000; *International Financial Statistics.*

Statistical Office of the United Nations, Publishing Service, New York, New York 10017 (800) 253-9646; *Statistical Yearbook.*

United Nations Economic Commission for Africa, Africa Hall, P.O. Box 3001, Addis Ababa, Ethiopia (Telephone Number in U.S. (800) 253-9646); *African Statistical Yearbook.*

BURKINA FASO - CUSTOMS DUTIES

G.K. Hall and Company, 70 Lincoln Street, Boston, Massachusetts 02111 (617) 423-3990; *The World in Figures.*

International Monetary Fund, 700 Nineteenth Street, NW, Washington, D.C. 20431 (202) 623-7000; *Government Finance Statistics Yearbook.*

BURKINA FASO - DAIRY PRODUCTS

Food and Agricultural Organization of the United Nations (FAO) Via delle Terme di Caracalla, 00100 Rome, Italy (Telephone Number in U.S. (202) 653-2400); *The State of Food and Agriculture.*

Statistical Office of the United Nations, Publishing Service, New York, New York 10017 (800) 253-9646; *Statistical Yearbook.*

BURKINA FASO - DEATH RATES

G.K. Hall and Company, 70 Lincoln Street, Boston, Massachusetts 02111 (617) 423-3990; *The World in Figures.*

Statistical Office of the United Nations, Publishing Service, New York, New York 10017 (800) 253-9646; *Statistical Yearbook,* and *Survey of Economic and Social Conditions in Africa.*

Times Books, 201 East 50th Street, New York, New York 10022 (212) 751-2600; *The Economist Book of Vital World Statistics.*

World Health Organization, Office of Publications, Avenue Appia, CH-1211 Geneva 27, Switzerland (Telephone Number in U.S. (518) 436-9686); *World Health Statistics Annual.*

BURKINA FASO - DEFENSE EXPENDITURES

G.K. Hall and Company, 70 Lincoln Street, Boston, Massachusetts 02111 (617) 423-3990; *The World in Figures.*

International Monetary Fund, 700 Nineteenth Street, NW, Washington, D.C. 20431 (202) 623-7000; *Government Finance Statistics Yearbook.*

U.S. Arms Control and Disarmament Agency, 320 Twenty-first Street, NW, Washington, D.C. 20451 (202) 647-8677; *World Military Expenditures and Arms Transfers.*

BURKINA FASO - DEMOGRAPHY

Business International Corporation, 215 Park Avenue South, New York, New York 10003 (800) 938-4685; *The World Market Atlas.*

Federal Statistical Office, Gustav - Stresemann - Ring 11, D-6200 Wiesbaden, Germany; *Burkina Faso.*

G.K. Hall and Company, 70 Lincoln Street, Boston, Massachusetts 02111 (617) 423-3990; *The World in Figures.*

Statistical Office of the United Nations, Publishing Service, New York, New York 10017 (800) 253-9646; *Survey of Economic and Social Conditions in Africa.*

BURKINA FASO - DEVELOPMENT ASSISTANCE

G.K. Hall and Company, 70 Lincoln Street, Boston, Massachusetts 02111 (617) 423-3990; *The World in Figures.*

Statistical Office of the United Nations, Publishing Service, New York, New York 10017 (800) 253-9646; *Statistical Yearbook.*

BURKINA FASO - DISCOUNT RATES

Statistical Office of the United Nations, Publishing Service, New York, New York 10017 (800) 253-9646; *Statistical Yearbook.*

BURKINA FASO - DISEASES

G.K. Hall and Company, 70 Lincoln Street, Boston, Massachusetts 02111 (617) 423-3990; *The World in Figures.*

World Health Organization, Office of Publications, Avenue Appia, CH-1211 Geneva 27, Switzerland (Telephone Number in U.S. (518) 436-9686); *World Health Statistics Annual.*

BURKINA FASO - DIVORCE RATES

Statistical Office of the United Nations, Publishing Service, New York, New York 10017 (800) 253-9646; *Demographic Yearbook.*

BURKINA FASO - DOMESTIC PRODUCT

G.K. Hall and Company, 70 Lincoln Street, Boston, Massachusetts 02111 (617) 423-3990; *The World in Figures.*

BURKINA FASO - ECONOMY

African Development Bank, 01 BP 1387, Abidjan 01, Cote D'Ivoire; *Selected Statistics on Regional Member Countries.*

Euromonitor Publications Limited, 87-88 Turnmill Street, London EC1M 5QU, England; *International Marketing Data and Statistics.*

Federal Statistical Office, Gustav - Stresemann - Ring 11, D-6200 Wiesbaden, Germany; *Burkina Faso.*

G.K. Hall and Company, 70 Lincoln Street, Boston, Massachusetts 02111 (617) 423-3990; *The World in Figures.*

Statistical Office of the United Nations, Publishing Service, New York, New York 10017 (800) 253-9646; *Foreign Trade Statistics for Africa*.

BURKINA FASO - EDUCATION

African Development Bank, 01 BP 1387, Abidjan 01, Cote D'Ivoire; *Selected Statistics on Regional Member Countries*.

Business International Corporation, 215 Park Avenue South, New York, New York 10003 (800) 938-4685; *The World Market Atlas*.

Federal Statistical Office, Gustav - Stresemann - Ring 11, D-6200 Wiesbaden, Germany; *Burkina Faso*.

G.K. Hall and Company, 70 Lincoln Street, Boston, Massachusetts 02111 (617) 423-3990; *The World in Figures*.

International Monetary Fund, 700 Nineteenth Street, NW, Washington, D.C. 20431 (800) 623-7000; *Government Finance Statistics Yearbook*.

Statistical Office of the United Nations, Publishing Service, New York, New York 10017 (800) 253-9646; *Survey of Economic and Social Conditions in Africa*.

Times Books, 201 East 50th Street, New York, New York 10022 (212) 751-2600; *The Economist Book of Vital World Statistics*.

United Nations Economic Commission for Africa, Africa Hall, P.O. Box 3001, Addis Ababa, Ethiopia (Telephone Number in U.S. (800) 253-9646); *African Statistical Yearbook*.

United Nations Educational, Scientific and Cultural Organization (UNESCO), 7 Place de Fontenoy, F-75700 Paris, France (Telephone Number in U.S. ((212) 963-5981); *Statistical Yearbook*.

The World Bank, 1818 H Street, NW, Washington, D.C. 20433 (202) 477-1234; *World Tables*.

BURKINA FASO - EGG PRODUCTION - See BURKINA FASO - DAIRY PRODUCTS

BURKINA FASO - ELECTRICITY

Statistical Office of the United Nations, Publishing Service, New York, New York 10017 (800) 253-9646; *Statistical Yearbook*, and *Survey of Economic and Social Conditions in Africa*.

Times Books, 201 East 50th Street, New York, New York 10022 (212) 751-2600; *The Economist Book of Vital World Statistics*.

United Nations Economic Commission for Africa, Africa Hall, P.O. Box 3001, Addis Ababa, Ethiopia (Telephone Number in U.S. (800) 253-9646); *African Statistical Yearbook*.

BURKINA FASO - EMPLOYMENT

Euromonitor Publications Limited, 87-88 Turnmill Street, London EC1M 5QU, England; *International Marketing Data and Statistics*.

Federal Statistical Office, Gustav - Stresemann - Ring 11, D-6200 Wiesbaden, Germany; *Burkina Faso*.

International Labour Office, I.L.O. Publications, CH-1211, Geneva 22, Switzerland; *Yearbook of Labour Statistics*.

Statistical Office of the United Nations, Publishing Service, New York, New York 10017 (800) 253-9646; *Statistical Yearbook*, and *Survey of Economic and Social Conditions in Africa*.

United Nations Economic Commission for Africa, Africa Hall, P.O. Box 3001, Addis Ababa, Ethiopia (Telephone Number in U.S. (800) 253-9646); *African Statistical Yearbook*.

BURKINA FASO - ENERGY

Food and Agricultural Organization of the United Nations (FAO) Via delle Terme di Caracalla, 00100 Rome, Italy (Telephone Number in U.S. (202) 653-2400); *The State of Food and Agriculture*.

G.K. Hall and Company, 70 Lincoln Street, Boston, Massachusetts 02111 (617) 423-3990; *The World in Figures*.

Statistical Office of the United Nations, Publishing Service, New York, New York 10017 (800) 253-9646; *Energy Statistics Yearbook*, *Statistical Yearbook*, and *World Energy Supplies*.

Times Books, 201 East 50th Street, New York, New York 10022 (212) 751-2600; *The Economist Book of Vital World Statistics*.

United Nations Economic Commission for Africa, Africa Hall, P.O. Box 3001, Addis Ababa, Ethiopia (Telephone Number in U.S. (800) 253-9646); *African Statistical Yearbook*.

BURKINA FASO - EXCHANGE RATES

African Development Bank, 01 BP 1387, Abidjan 01, Cote D'Ivoire; *Selected Statistics on Regional Member Countries*.

Euromonitor Publications Limited, 87-88 Turnmill Street, London EC1M 5QU, England; *International Marketing Data and Statistics*.

International Monetary Fund, 700 Nineteenth Street, NW, Washington, D.C. 20431 (800) 623-7000; *International Financial Statistics*.

Statistical Office of the United Nations, Publishing Service, New York, New York 10017 (800) 253-9646; *Foreign Trade Statistics for Africa*, and *Statistical Yearbook*.

BURKINA FASO - EXCISE TAXES - See BURKINA FASO - TAXATION

BURKINA FASO - EXPORTS

African Development Bank, 01 BP 1387, Abidjan 01, Cote D'Ivoire; *Selected Statistics on Regional Member Countries*.

Business International Corporation, 215 Park Avenue South, New York, New York 10003 (800) 938-4685; *The World Market Atlas*.

Euromonitor Publications Limited, 87-88 Turnmill Street, London EC1M 5QU, England; *International Marketing Data and Statistics*.

Food and Agricultural Organization of the United Nations (FAO) Via delle Terme di Caracalla, 00100 Rome, Italy (Telephone Number in U.S. (202) 653-2400); *The State of Food and Agriculture*.

G.K. Hall and Company, 70 Lincoln Street, Boston, Massachusetts 02111 (617) 423-3990; *The World in Figures*.

International Monetary Fund, 700 Nineteenth Street, NW, Washington, D.C. 20431 (800) 623-7000; *Direction of Trade Statistics*, *Government Finance Statistics Yearbook*, and *International Financial Statistics*.

Statistical Office of the United Nations, Publishing Service, New York, New York 10017 (800) 253-9646; *Foreign Trade Statistics for*

Africa, and *Survey of Economic and Social Conditions in Africa.*

Times Books, 201 East 50th Street, New York, New York 10022 (212) 751-2600; *The Economist Book of Vital World Statistics.*

United Nations Economic Commission for Africa, Africa Hall, P.O. Box 3001, Addis Ababa, Ethiopia (Telephone Number in U.S. (800) 253-9646); *African Statistical Yearbook.*

The World Bank, 1818 H Street, NW, Washington, D.C. 20433 (202) 477-1234; *World Tables.*

BURKINA FASO - EXTERNAL INDEBTEDNESS

African Development Bank, 01 BP 1387, Abidjan 01, Cote D'Ivoire; *Selected Statistics on Regional Member Countries.*

Statistical Office of the United Nations, Publishing Service, New York, New York 10017 (800) 253-9646; *Survey of Economic and Social Conditions in Africa.*

The World Bank, 1818 H Street, NW, Washington, D.C. 20433 (202) 477-1234; *World Tables.*

BURKINA FASO - EXTERNAL TRADE

African Development Bank, 01 BP 1387, Abidjan 01, Cote D'Ivoire; *Selected Statistics on Regional Member Countries.*

Food and Agricultural Organization of the United Nations (FAO) Via delle Terme di Caracalla, 00100 Rome, Italy (Telephone Number in U.S. (202) 653-2400); *The State of Food and Agriculture*, and *Trade Yearbook.*

G.K. Hall and Company, 70 Lincoln Street, Boston, Massachusetts 02111 (617) 423-3990; *The World in Figures.*

Statistical Office of the United Nations, Publishing Service, New York, New York 10017 (800) 253-9646; *Statistical Yearbook.*

BURKINA FASO - FARM CROPS - See BURKINA FASO - CROPS

BURKINA FASO - FEMALE WORKING POPULATION - See BURKINA FASO - EMPLOYMENT

BURKINA FASO - FERTILITY RATES

Statistical Office of the United Nations, Publishing Service, New York, New York 10017 (800) 253-9646; *Survey of Economic and Social Conditions in Africa.*

Times Books, 201 East 50th Street, New York, New York 10022 (212) 751-2600; *The Economist Book of Vital World Statistics.*

The World Bank, 1818 H Street, NW, Washington, D.C. 20433 (202) 477-1234; *World Tables.*

BURKINA FASO - FERTILIZER

Food and Agricultural Organization of the United Nations (FAO), Via delle Terme di Caracalla, 00100 Rome, Italy (Telephone Number in U.S. (202) 653-2400); *Fertilizer Yearbook*, and *The State of Food and Agriculture.*

Statistical Office of the United Nations, Publishing Service, New York, New York 10017 (800) 253-9646; *Statistical Yearbook.*

BURKINA FASO - FETAL MORTALITY

Statistical Office of the United Nations, Publishing Service, New York, New York 10017 (800) 253-9646; *Demographic Yearbook.*

BURKINA FASO - FINANCE

African Development Bank, 01 BP 1387, Abidjan 01, Cote D'Ivoire; *Selected Statistics on Regional Member Countries.*

Federal Statistical Office, Gustav - Stresemann - Ring 11, D-6200 Wiesbaden, Germany; *Burkina Faso.*

G.K. Hall and Company, 70 Lincoln Street, Boston, Massachusetts 02111 (617) 423-3990; *The World in Figures.*

United Nations Economic Commission for Africa, Africa Hall, P.O. Box 3001, Addis Ababa, Ethiopia (Telephone Number in U.S. (800) 253-9646); *African Statistical Yearbook.*

BURKINA FASO - FISHERIES

Federal Statistical Office, Gustav - Stresemann - Ring 11, D-6200 Wiesbaden, Germany; *Burkina Faso.*

Food and Agricultural Organization of the United Nations (FAO) Via delle Terme di Caracalla, 00100 Rome, Italy (Telephone Number in U.S. (202) 653-2400); *The State of Food and Agriculture*, and *Yearbook of Fishery Statistics.*

Statistical Office of the United Nations, Publishing Service, New York, New York 10017 (800) 253-9646; *Statistical Yearbook*, and *Survey of Economic and Social Conditions in Africa.*

United Nations Economic Commission for Africa, Africa Hall, P.O. Box 3001, Addis Ababa, Ethiopia (Telephone Number in U.S. (800) 253-9646); *African Statistical Yearbook.*

BURKINA FASO - FOOD

African Development Bank, 01 BP 1387, Abidjan 01, Cote D'Ivoire; *Selected Statistics on Regional Member Countries.*

Food and Agricultural Organization of the United Nations (FAO) Via delle Terme di Caracalla, 00100 Rome, Italy (Telephone Number in U.S. (202) 653-2400); *Production Yearbook*, and *The State of Food and Agriculture.*

G.K. Hall and Company, 70 Lincoln Street, Boston, Massachusetts 02111 (617) 423-3990; *The World in Figures.*

BURKINA FASO - FOREIGN AID

G.K. Hall and Company, 70 Lincoln Street, Boston, Massachusetts 02111 (617) 423-3990; *The World in Figures.*

BURKINA FASO - FOREIGN TRADE

Euromonitor Publications Limited, 87-88 Turnmill Street, London EC1M 5QU, England; *International Marketing Data and Statistics.*

Federal Statistical Office, Gustav - Stresemann - Ring 11, D-6200 Wiesbaden, Germany; *Burkina Faso.*

Food and Agricultural Organization of the United Nations (FAO) Via delle Terme di Caracalla, 00100 Rome, Italy (Telephone Number in U.S. (202) 653-2400); *The State of Food and Agriculture.*

G.K. Hall and Company, 70 Lincoln Street, Boston, Massachusetts 02111 (617) 423-3990; *The World in Figures.*

Statistical Office of the United Nations, Publishing Service, New York, New York 10017 (800) 253-9646; *Foreign Trade Statistics for Africa, International Trade Statistics Yearbook, Statistical Yearbook,* and *Trade in Manufactures of Developing Countries.*

United Nations Economic Commission for Africa, Africa Hall, P.O. Box 3001, Addis Ababa, Ethiopia (Telephone Number in U.S. (800) 253-9646); *African Statistical Yearbook.*

The World Bank, 1818 H Street, NW, Washington, D.C. 20433 (202) 477-1234; *World Tables.*

BURKINA FASO - FORESTRY AND FOREST PRODUCTS

Federal Statistical Office, Gustav - Stresemann - Ring 11, D-6200 Wiesbaden, Germany; *Burkina Faso.*

Food and Agricultural Organization of the United Nations (FAO) Via delle Terme di Caracalla, 00100 Rome, Italy (Telephone Number in U.S. (202) 653-2400); *The State of Food and Agriculture,* and *Yearbook of Forest Products.*

G.K. Hall and Company, 70 Lincoln Street, Boston, Massachusetts 02111 (617) 423-3990; *The World in Figures.*

Organisation for Economic Co-operation and Development (OECD), 2 rue Andre-Pascal, 75 Paris 16, France; *Indicators of Industrial Activity.*

United Nations Economic Commission for Africa, Africa Hall, P.O. Box 3001, Addis Ababa, Ethiopia (Telephone Number in U.S. (800) 253-9646); *African Statistical Yearbook.*

BURKINA FASO - GENERAL INDUSTRIAL STATISTICS

Federal Statistical Office, Gustav - Stresemann - Ring 11, D-6200 Wiesbaden, Germany; *Burkina Faso.*

Statistical Office of the United Nations, Publishing Service, New York, New York 10017 (800) 253-9646; *Industrial Statistics Yearbook.*

BURKINA FASO - GENERAL MORTALITY

Statistical Office of the United Nations, Publishing Service, New York, New York 10017 (800) 253-9646; *Demographic Yearbook.*

BURKINA FASO - GEOGRAPHIC DATA

Federal Statistical Office, Gustav - Stresemann - Ring 11, D-6200 Wiesbaden, Germany; *Burkina Faso.*

BURKINA FASO - GOATS - See BURKINA FASO - LIVESTOCK AND POULTRY

BURKINA FASO - GOLD HOLDINGS

International Monetary Fund, 700 Nineteenth Street, NW, Washington, D.C. 20431 (800) 623-7000; *International Financial Statistics.*

Statistical Office of the United Nations, Publishing Service, New York, New York 10017 (800) 253-9646; *Statistical Yearbook.*

The World Bank, 1818 H Street, NW, Washington, D.C. 20433 (202) 477-1234; *World Tables.*

BURKINA FASO - GOVERNMENT

G.K. Hall and Company, 70 Lincoln Street, Boston, Massachusetts 02111 (617) 423-3990; *The World in Figures.*

BURKINA FASO - GOVERNMENT EXPENDITURES

International Monetary Fund, 700 Nineteenth Street, NW, Washington, D.C. 20431 (800 623-7000; *Government Finance Statistics Yearbook.*

Times Books, 201 East 50th Street, New York, New York 10022 (212) 751-2600; *The Economist Book of Vital World Statistics.*

The World Bank, 1818 H Street, NW, Washington, D.C. 20433 (202) 477-1234; *World Tables.*

BURKINA FASO - GOVERNMENT REVENUE

International Monetary Fund, 700 Nineteenth Street, NW, Washington, D.C. 20431 (800) 623-7000; *Government Finance Statistics Yearbook.*

Statistical Office of the United Nations, Publishing Service, New York, New York 10017 (800) 253-9646; *Survey of Economic and Social Conditions in Africa.*

Times Books, 201 East 50th Street, New York, New York 10022 (212) 751-2600; *The Economist Book of Vital World Statistics.*

The World Bank, 1818 H Street, NW, Washington, D.C. 20433 (202) 477-1234; *World Tables.*

BURKINA FASO - GRAIN PRODUCTION - See BURKINA FASO - CROPS

BURKINA FASO - GRANTS

International Monetary Fund, 700 Nineteenth Street, NW, Washington, D.C. 20431 (800) 623-7000; *Government Finance Statistics Yearbook.*

BURKINA FASO - GROSS DOMESTIC PRODUCT

African Development Bank, 01 BP 1387, Abidjan 01, Cote D'Ivoire; *Selected Statistics on Regional Member Countries.*

Business International Corporation, 215 Park Avenue South, New York, New York 10003 (800) 938-4685; *The World Market Atlas.*

Euromonitor Publications Limited, 87-88 Turnmill Street, London EC1M 5QU, England; *International Marketing Data and Statistics.*

G.K. Hall and Company, 70 Lincoln Street, Boston, Massachusetts 02111 (617) 423-3990; *The World in Figures.*

Statistical Office of the United Nations, Publishing Service, New York, New York 10017 (800) 253-9646; *Statistical Yearbook,* and *Survey of Economic and Social Conditions in Africa.*

Times Books, 201 East 50th Street, New York, New York 10022 (212) 751-2600; *The Economist Book of Vital World Statistics.*

United Nations Economic Commission for Africa, Africa Hall, P.O. Box 3001, Addis Ababa, Ethiopia (Telephone Number in U.S. (800) 253-9646); *African Statistical Yearbook.*

The World Bank, 1818 H Street, NW, Washington, D.C. 20433 (202) 477-1234; *World Tables.*

BURKINA FASO - GROSS NATIONAL PRODUCT

Euromonitor Publications Limited, 87-88 Turnmill Street, London EC1M 5QU, England; *International Marketing Data and Statistics.*

U.S. Arms Control and Disarmament Agency, 320 Twenty-first Street, NW, Washington, D.C. 20451 (202) 647-8677; *World Military Expenditures and Arms Transfers.*

The World Bank, 1818 H Street, NW, Washington, D.C. 20433 (202) 477-1234; *World Tables.*

BURKINA FASO - GROUNDNUTS PRODUCTION - See BURKINA FASO - CROPS

BURKINA FASO - HEALTH

African Development Bank, 01 BP 1387, Abidjan 01, Cote D'Ivoire; *Selected Statistics on Regional Member Countries.*

Federal Statistical Office, Gustav - Stresemann - Ring 11, D-6200 Wiesbaden, Germany; *Burkina Faso.*

G.K. Hall and Company, 70 Lincoln Street, Boston, Massachusetts 02111 (617) 423-3990; *The World in Figures.*

Statistical Office of the United Nations, Publishing Service, New York, New York 10017 (800) 253-9646; *Statistical Yearbook.*

Times Books, 201 East 50th Street, New York, New York 10022 (212) 751-2600; *The Economist Book of Vital World Statistics.*

United Nations Economic Commission for Africa, Africa Hall, P.O. Box 3001, Addis Ababa, Ethiopia (Telephone Number in U.S. (800) 253-9646); *African Statistical Yearbook.*

World Health Organization, Office of Publications, Avenue Appia, CH-1211 Geneva 27, Switzerland (Telephone Number in U.S. (518) 436-9686); *World Health Statistics Annual.*

BURKINA FASO - HEALTH EXPENDITURES

International Monetary Fund, 700 Nineteenth Street, NW, Washington, D.C. 20431 (800) 623-7000; *Government Finance Statistics Yearbook.*

BURKINA FASO - HIDE PRODUCTION

Food and Agricultural Organization of the United Nations (FAO), Via delle Terme di Caracalla, 00100 Rome, Italy (Telephone Number in U.S. (202) 653-2400); *Production Yearbook.*

BURKINA FASO - HIGHWAYS

G.K. Hall and Company, 70 Lincoln Street, Boston, Massachusetts 02111 (617) 423-3990; *The World in Figures.*

International Road Federation, 525 School Street, SW, Washington, D.C. 20024 (202) 554-2106; *World Road Statistics.*

Statistical Office of the United Nations, Publishing Service, New York, New York 10017 (800) 253-9646; *Survey of Economic and Social Conditions in Africa.*

United Nations Economic Commission for Africa, Africa Hall, P.O. Box 3001, Addis Ababa, Ethiopia (Telephone Number in U.S. (800) 253-9646); *African Statistical Yearbook.*

BURKINA FASO - HORSES - See BURKINA FASO - LIVESTOCK AND POULTRY

BURKINA FASO - HOURS OF WORK - See BURKINA FASO - EMPLOYMENT

BURKINA FASO - HOUSING EXPENDITURES

International Monetary Fund, 700 Nineteenth Street, NW, Washington, D.C. 20431 (800) 623-7000; *Government Finance Statistics.*

BURKINA FASO - ILLITERATE POPULATION

Business International Corporation, 215 Park Avenue South, New York, New York 10003 (800) 938-4685; *The World Market Atlas.*

G.K. Hall and Company, 70 Lincoln Street, Boston, Massachusetts 02111 (617) 423-3990; *The World in Figures.*

United Nations Educational, Scientific and Cultural Organization (UNESCO), 7 Place de Fontenoy, F-75700 Paris, France; *Statistical Yearbook.*

BURKINA FASO - IMPORTS

African Development Bank, 01 BP 1387, Abidjan 01, Cote D'Ivoire; *Selected Statistics on Regional Member Countries.*

Business International Corporation, 215 Park Avenue South, New York, New York 10003 (800) 938-4685; *The World Market Atlas.*

Euromonitor Publications Limited, 87-88 Turnmill Street, London EC1M 5QU, England; *International Marketing Data and Statistics.*

Food and Agricultural Organization of the United Nations (FAO) Via delle Terme di Caracalla, 00100 Rome, Italy (Telephone Number in U.S. (202) 653-2400); *The State of Food and Agriculture.*

G.K. Hall and Company, 70 Lincoln Street, Boston, Massachusetts 02111 (617) 423-3990; *The World in Figures.*

International Monetary Fund, 700 Nineteenth Street, NW, Washington, D.C. 20431 (800) 623-7000; *Direction of Trade Statistics, Government Finance Statistics Yearbook,* and *International Financial Statistics.*

Statistical Office of the United Nations, Publishing Service, New York, New York 10017 (800) 253-9646; *Foreign Trade Statistics for Africa, Trade in Manufactures of Developing Countries,* and *Survey of Economic and Social Conditions in Africa.*

Times Books, 201 East 50th Street, New York, New York 10022 (212) 751-2600; *The Economist Book of Vital World Statistics.*

United Nations Economic Commission for Africa, Africa Hall, P.O. Box 3001, Addis Ababa, Ethiopia (Telephone Number in U.S. (800) 253-9646); *African Statistical Yearbook.*

The World Bank, 1818 H Street, NW, Washington, D.C. 20433 (202) 477-1234; *World Tables.*

BURKINA FASO - INCOME TAXES - See BURKINA FASO - TAXATION

BURKINA FASO - INDUSTRY

Euromonitor Publications Limited, 87-88 Turnmill Street, London EC1M 5QU, England; *International Marketing Data and Statistics.*

Federal Statistical Office, Gustav - Stresemann - Ring 11, D-6200 Wiesbaden, Germany; *Burkina Faso.*

G.K. Hall and Company, 70 Lincoln Street, Boston, Massachusetts 02111 (617) 423-3990; *The World in Figures.*

International Labour Office, I.L.O. Publications, CH-1211, Geneva 22, Switzerland; *Yearbook of Labour Statistics.*

Statistical Office of the United Nations, Publishing Service, New York, New York 10017 (800) 253-9646; *Survey of Economic and Social Conditions in Africa.*

Times Books, 201 East 50th Street, New York, New York 10022 (212) 751-2600; *The Economist Book of Vital World Statistics.*

United Nations Economic Commission for Africa, Africa Hall, P.O. Box 3001, Addis Ababa, Ethiopia (Telephone Number in U.S. (800) 253-9646); *African Statistical Yearbook.*

The World Bank, 1818 H Street, NW, Washington, D.C. 20433 (202) 477-1234; *World Tables.*

BURKINA FASO - INFANT AND MATERNAL MORTALITY

Statistical Office of the United Nations, Publishing Service, New York, New York 10017 (800) 253-9646; *Demographic Yearbook, Statistical Yearbook,* and *Survey of Economic and Social Conditions in Africa.*

Times Books, 201 East 50th Street, New York, New York 10022 (212) 751-2600; *The Economist Book of Vital World Statistics.*

The World Bank, 1818 H Street, NW, Washington, D.C. 20433 (202) 477-1234; *World Tables.*

BURKINA FASO - INTERNATIONAL LIQUIDITY

International Monetary Fund, 700 Nineteenth Street, NW, Washington, D.C. 20431 (800) 623-7000; *International Financial Statistics.*

BURKINA FASO - INTERNATIONAL RESERVES - EXCLUDING GOLD

African Development Bank, 01 BP 1387, Abidjan 01, Cote D'Ivoire; *Selected Statistics on Regional Member Countries.*

Statistical Office of the United Nations, Publishing Service, New York, New York 10017 (800) 253-9646; *Statistical Yearbook.*

The World Bank, 1818 H Street, NW, Washington, D.C. 20433 (202) 477-1234; *World Tables.*

BURKINA FASO - IRRIGATION

Euromonitor Publications Limited, 87-88 Turnmill Street, London EC1M 5QU, England; *International Marketing Data and Statistics.*

BURKINA FASO - LABOR FORCE

African Development Bank, 01 BP 1387, Abidjan 01, Cote D'Ivoire; *Selected Statistics on Regional Member Countries.*

Euromonitor Publications Limited, 87-88 Turnmill Street, London EC1M 5QU, England; *International Marketing Data and Statistics.*

Food and Agricultural Organization of the United Nations (FAO) Via delle Terme di Caracalla, 00100 Rome, Italy (Telephone Number in U.S. (202) 653-2400); *The State of Food and Agriculture.*

G.K. Hall and Company, 70 Lincoln Street, Boston, Massachusetts 02111 (617) 423-3990; *The World in Figures.*

Times Books, 201 East 50th Street, New York, New York 10022 (212) 751-2600; *The Economist Book of Vital World Statistics.*

The World Bank, 1818 H Street, NW, Washington, D.C. 20433 (202) 477-1234; *World Tables.*

BURKINA FASO - LABOR PRODUCTIVITY

International Labour Office, I.L.O. Publications, CH-1211, Geneva 22, Switzerland; *Yearbook of Labour Statistics.*

BURKINA FASO - LAND USE

Euromonitor Publications Limited, 87-88 Turnmill Street, London EC1M 5QU, England; *International Marketing Data and Statistics.*

Food and Agricultural Organization of the United Nations (FAO), Via delle Terme di Caracalla, 00100 Rome, Italy (Telephone Number in U.S. (202) 653-2400); *Production Yearbook.*

G.K. Hall and Company, 70 Lincoln Street, Boston, Massachusetts 02111 (617) 423-3990; *The World in Figures.*

BURKINA FASO - LIBRARIES

United Nations Educational, Scientific and Cultural Organization (UNESCO), 7 Place de Fontenoy, F-75700 Paris, France (Telephone Number in U.S. (212) 963-5981); *Statistical Yearbook.*

BURKINA FASO - LIFE EXPECTANCY

African Development Bank, 01 BP 1387, Abidjan 01, Cote D'Ivoire; *Selected Statistics on Regional Member Countries.*

BURKINA FASO - LITERACY RATE

Statistical Office of the United Nations, Publishing Service, New York, New York 10017 (800) 253-9646; *Survey of Economic and Social Conditions in Africa.*

BURKINA FASO - LIVESTOCK AND POULTRY

Euromonitor Publications Limited, 87-88 Turnmill Street, London EC1M 5QU, England; *International Marketing Data and Statistics.*

Food and Agricultural Organization of the United Nations (FAO), Via delle Terme di Caracalla, 00100 Rome, Italy (Telephone Number in U.S. (202) 653-2400); *Production Yearbook,* and *The State of Food and Agriculture.*

G.K. Hall and Company, 70 Lincoln Street, Boston, Massachusetts 02111 (617) 423-3990; *The World in Figures.*

Statistical Office of the United Nations, Publishing Service, New York, New York 10017 (800) 253-9646; *Statistical Yearbook,* and *Survey of Economic and Social Conditions in Africa.*

United Nations Economic Commission for Africa, Africa Hall, P.O. Box 3001, Addis Ababa, Ethiopia (Telephone Number in U.S. (800) 253-9646); *African Statistical Yearbook.*

BURKINA FASO - LIVING LEVELS

G.K. Hall and Company, 70 Lincoln Street, Boston, Massachusetts 02111 (617) 423-3990; *The World in Figures*.

Times Books, 201 East 50th Street, New York, New York 10022 (212) 751-2600; *The Economist Book of Vital World Statistics*.

BURKINA FASO - MAIL - NUMBER OF ITEMS SENT AND RECEIVED

Statistical Office of the United Nations, Publishing Service, New York, New York 10017 (800) 253-9646; *Statistical Yearbook*.

BURKINA FASO - MANUFACTURING

G.K. Hall and Company, 70 Lincoln Street, Boston, Massachusetts 02111 (617) 423-3990; *The World in Figures*.

Statistical Office of the United Nations, Publishing Service, New York, New York 10017 (800) 253-9646; *Statistical Yearbook*, and *Survey of Economic and Social Conditions in Africa*.

Times Books, 201 East 50th Street, New York, New York 10022 (212) 751-2600; *The Economist Book of Vital World Statistics*.

United Nations Economic Commission for Africa, Africa Hall, P.O. Box 3001, Addis Ababa, Ethiopia (Telephone Number in U.S. (800) 253-9646); *African Statistical Yearbook*.

The World Bank, 1818 H Street, NW, Washington, D.C. 20433 (202) 477-1234; *World Tables*.

BURKINA FASO - MARRIAGE RATES

Statistical Office of the United Nations, Publishing Service, New York, New York 10017 (800) 253-9646; *Demographic Yearbook*.

BURKINA FASO - MEAT PRODUCTION - See BURKINA FASO - LIVESTOCK AND POULTRY

BURKINA FASO - MERCHANT SHIPPING

G.K. Hall and Company, 70 Lincoln Street, Boston, Massachusetts 02111 (617) 423-3990; *The World in Figures*.

United Nations Economic Commission for Africa, Africa Hall, P.O. Box 3001, Addis Ababa, Ethiopia (Telephone Number in U.S. (800) 253-9646); *African Statistical Yearbook*.

BURKINA FASO - MILITARY

G.K. Hall and Company, 70 Lincoln Street, Boston, Massachusetts 02111 (617) 423-3990; *The World in Figures*.

The International Institute for Strategic Studies, 23 Tavistock Street, London WC2E 7NQ, England; *The Military Balance*.

U.S. Arms Control and Disarmament Agency, 320 Twenty-first Street, NW, Washington, D.C. 20451 (202) 647-8677; *World Military Expenditures and Arms Transfers*.

BURKINA FASO - MILK PRODUCTION - See BURKINA FASO - DAIRY PRODUCTS

BURKINA FASO - MILLET PRODUCTION - See BURKINA FASO - CROPS

BURKINA FASO - MINING AND MINERAL PRODUCTS

G.K. Hall and Company, 70 Lincoln Street, Boston, Massachusetts 02111 (617) 423-3990; *The World in Figures*.

United Nations Economic Commission for Africa, Africa Hall, P.O. Box 3001, Addis Ababa, Ethiopia (Telephone Number in U.S. (800) 253-9646); *African Statistical Yearbook*.

BURKINA FASO - MONEY EXCHANGE RATES

Euromonitor Publications Limited, 87-88 Turnmill Street, London EC1M 5QU, England; *International Marketing Data and Statistics*.

Statistical Office of the United Nations, Publishing Service, New York, New York 10017 (800) 253-9646; *Statistical Yearbook*.

BURKINA FASO - MONEY RESERVES

Euromonitor Publications Limited, 87-88 Turnmill Street, London EC1M 5QU, England; *International Marketing Data and Statistics*.

BURKINA FASO - MONEY SUPPLY

African Development Bank, 01 BP 1387, Abidjan 01, Cote D'Ivoire; *Selected Statistics on Regional Member Countries*.

Euromonitor Publications Limited, 87-88 Turnmill Street, London EC1M 5QU, England; *International Marketing Data and Statistics*.

Federal Statistical Office, Gustav - Stresemann - Ring 11, D-6200 Wiesbaden, Germany; *Burkina Faso*.

G.K. Hall and Company, 70 Lincoln Street, Boston, Massachusetts 02111 (617) 423-3990; *The World in Figures*.

Statistical Office of the United Nations, Publishing Service, New York, New York 10017 (800) 253-9646; *Statistical Yearbook*.

The World Bank, 1818 H Street, NW, Washington, D.C. 20433 (202) 477-1234; *World Tables*.

BURKINA FASO - MOTOR VEHICLES IN USE

G.K. Hall and Company, 70 Lincoln Street, Boston, Massachusetts 02111 (617) 423-3990; *The World in Figures*.

International Road Federation, 525 School Street, SW, Washington, D.C. 20024 (202) 554-2106; *World Road Statistics*.

Statistical Office of the United Nations, Publishing Service, New York, New York 10017 (800) 253-9646; *Statistical Yearbook*, and *Survey of Economic and Social Conditions in Africa*.

Times Books, 201 East 50th Street, New York, New York 10022 (212) 751-2600; *The Economist Book of Vital World Statistics*.

BURKINA FASO - NATIONAL ACCOUNTS

African Development Bank, 01 BP 1387, Abidjan 01, Cote D'Ivoire; *Selected Statistics on Regional Member Countries*.

Federal Statistical Office, Gustav - Stresemann - Ring 11, D-6200 Wiesbaden, Germany; *Burkina Faso*.

Statistical Office of the United Nations, Publishing Service, New York, New York 10017 (800) 253-9646; *National Accounts Statistics*, and *Statistical Yearbook*.

United Nations Economic Commission for Africa, Africa Hall, P.O. Box 3001, Addis Ababa, Ethiopia (Telephone Number in U.S. (800) 253-9646); *African Statistical Yearbook.*

BURKINA FASO - NATIONAL INCOME

G.K. Hall and Company, 70 Lincoln Street, Boston, Massachusetts 02111 (617) 423-3990; *The World in Figures.*

Statistical Office of the United Nations, Publishing Service, New York, New York 10017 (800) 253-9646; *Statistical Yearbook.*

BURKINA FASO - NEWSPAPER PRODUCTION - See BURKINA FASO - FORESTRY AND FOREST PRODUCTS

BURKINA FASO - OCCUPATIONS - See BURKINA FASO - LABOR FORCE

BURKINA FASO - PERIODICALS

United Nations Educational, Scientific and Cultural Organization (UNESCO), 7 Place de Fontenoy, F-75700 Paris, France (Telephone Number in U.S. (212) 963-5981); *Statistical Yearbook.*

BURKINA FASO - PESTICIDE USE

Food and Agricultural Organization of the United Nations (FAO) Via delle Terme di Caracalla, 00100 Rome, Italy (Telephone Number in U.S. (202) 653-2400); *The State of Food and Agriculture.*

BURKINA FASO - PETROLEUM INDUSTRY

Food and Agricultural Organization of the United Nations (FAO) Via delle Terme di Caracalla, 00100 Rome, Italy (Telephone Number in U.S. (202) 653-2400); *The State of Food and Agriculture.*

G.K. Hall and Company, 70 Lincoln Street, Boston, Massachusetts 02111 (617) 423-3990; *The World in Figures.*

BURKINA FASO - PIGS - See BURKINA FASO - LIVESTOCK AND POULTRY

BURKINA FASO - POPULATION

African Development Bank, 01 BP 1387, Abidjan 01, Cote D'Ivoire; *Selected Statistics on Regional Member Countries.*

Business International Corporation, 215 Park Avenue South, New York, New York 10003 (800) 938-4685; *The World Market Atlas.*

Euromonitor Publications Limited, 87-88 Turnmill Street, London EC1M 5QU, England; *International Marketing Data and Statistics.*

Federal Statistical Office, Gustav - Stresemann - Ring 11, D-6200 Wiesbaden, Germany; *Burkina Faso.*

Food and Agricultural Organization of the United Nations (FAO), Via delle Terme di Caracalla, 00100 Rome, Italy (Telephone Number in U.S. (202) 653-2400); *Production Yearbook.*

G.K. Hall and Company, 70 Lincoln Street, Boston, Massachusetts 02111 (617) 423-3990; *The World in Figures.*

International Labour Office, I.L.O. Publications, CH-1211, Geneva 22, Switzerland; *Yearbook of Labour Statistics.*

Statistical Office of the United Nations, Publishing Service, New York, New York 10017 (800) 253-9646; *Demographic Yearbook, Statistical Yearbook,* and *Survey of Economic and Social Conditions in Africa.*

Times Books, 201 East 50th Street, New York, New York 10022 (212) 751-2600; *The Economist Book of Vital World Statistics.*

United Nations Educational, Scientific and Cultural Organization (UNESCO), 7 Place de Fontenoy, F-75700 Paris, France (Telephone Number in U.S. (212) 963-5981); *Statistical Yearbook.*

U.S. Arms Control and Disarmament Agency, 320 Twenty-first Street, NW, Washington, D.C. 20451 (202) 647-8677; *World Military Expenditures and Arms Transfers.*

World Health Organization, Office of Publications, Avenue Appia, CH-1211 Geneva 27, Switzerland (Telephone Number in U.S. (518) 436-9686); *World Health Statistics Annual.*

BURKINA FASO - PRICES

Federal Statistical Office, Gustav - Stresemann - Ring 11, D-6200 Wiesbaden, Germany; *Burkina Faso.*

Food and Agricultural Organization of the United Nations (FAO), Via delle Terme di Caracalla, 00100 Rome, Italy (Telephone Number in U.S. (202) 653-2400); *Production Yearbook,* and *The State of Food and Agriculture.*

G.K. Hall and Company, 70 Lincoln Street, Boston, Massachusetts 02111 (617) 423-3990; *The World in Figures.*

International Monetary Fund, 700 Nineteenth Street, NW, Washington, D.C. 20431 (800) 623-7000; *International Financial Statistics.*

United Nations Economic Commission for Africa, Africa Hall, P.O. Box 3001, Addis Ababa, Ethiopia (Telephone Number in U.S. (800) 253-9646); *African Statistical Yearbook.*

BURKINA FASO - PRODUCTION

G.K. Hall and Company, 70 Lincoln Street, Boston, Massachusetts 02111 (617) 423-3990; *The World in Figures.*

BURKINA FASO - PRODUCTIVITY

Euromonitor Publications Limited, 87-88 Turnmill Street, London EC1M 5QU, England; *International Marketing Data and Statistics.*

BURKINA FASO - PROPERTY TAXES - See BURKINA FASO - TAXATION

BURKINA FASO - PUBLIC FINANCE

Federal Statistical Office, Gustav - Stresemann - Ring 11, D-6200 Wiesbaden, Germany; *Burkina Faso.*

BURKINA FASO - RADIO BROADCASTING - See BURKINA FASO - BROADCASTING

BURKINA FASO - RAILWAYS

G.K. Hall and Company, 70 Lincoln Street, Boston, Massachusetts 02111 (617) 423-3990; *The World in Figures.*

Jane's Information Group, Sentinel House, 163 Brighton Road, Coulsdon, Surrey CR5 2NH, England (Telephone Number in U.S. (703) 683-3700); *Jane's World Railways.*

Statistical Office of the United Nations, Publishing Service, New York, New York 10017 (800) 253-9646; *Survey of Economic and Social Conditions in Africa.*

United Nations Economic Commission for Africa, Africa Hall, P.O. Box 3001, Addis Ababa, Ethiopia (Telephone Number in U.S. (800) 253-9646); *African Statistical Yearbook.*

BURKINA FASO - RETAIL TRADE

G.K. Hall and Company, 70 Lincoln Street, Boston, Massachusetts 02111 (617) 423-3990; *The World in Figures.*

BURKINA FASO - RICE PRODUCTION - See BURKINA FASO - CROPS

BURKINA FASO - ROOT AND TUBER PRODUCTION - See BURKINA FASO - CROPS

BURKINA FASO - ROUNDWOOD PRODUCTION - See BURKINA FASO - FORESTRY AND FOREST PRODUCTS

BURKINA FASO - SAVINGS

International Monetary Fund, 700 Nineteenth Street, NW, Washington, D.C. 20431 (800) 623-7000; *International Financial Statistics.*

BURKINA FASO - SAWNWOOD PRODUCTION - See BURKINA FASO - FORESTRY AND FOREST PRODUCTS

BURKINA FASO - SCIENCE AND TECHNOLOGY - EXPENDITURE FOR RESEARCH

Statistical Office of the United Nations, Publishing Service, New York, New York 10017 (800) 253-9646; *Statistical Yearbook.*

BURKINA FASO - SCIENTISTS AND TECHNICIANS

Statistical Office of the United Nations, Publishing Service, New York, New York 10017 (800) 253-9646; *Statistical Yearbook.*

United Nations Educational, Scientific and Cultural Organization (UNESCO), 7 Place de Fontenoy, F-75700 Paris, France (Telephone Number in U.S. (212) 963-5981); *Statistical Yearbook.*

BURKINA FASO - SESAME SEED PRODUCTION - See BURKINA FASO - CROPS

BURKINA FASO - SHEEP - See BURKINA FASO - LIVESTOCK AND POULTRY

BURKINA FASO - SOCIAL DATA

African Development Bank, 01 BP 1387, Abidjan 01, Cote D'Ivoire; *Selected Statistics on Regional Member Countries.*

G.K. Hall and Company, 70 Lincoln Street, Boston, Massachusetts 02111 (617) 423-3990; *The World in Figures.*

BURKINA FASO - SOCIAL SECURITY EXPENDITURES

International Monetary Fund, 700 Nineteenth Street, NW, Washington, D.C. 20431 (800) 623-7000; *Government Finance Statistics Yearbook.*

BURKINA FASO - STAMP TAXES AND DUTIES - See BURKINA FASO - TAXATION

BURKINA FASO - STATE BUDGET REVENUE AND EXPENDITURES

Euromonitor Publications Limited, 87-88 Turnmill Street, London EC1M 5QU, England; *International Marketing Data and Statistics.*

BURKINA FASO - STOCKS - COMMODITY - MARKET PRICE - INDEX

Food and Agricultural Organization of the United Nations (FAO) Via delle Terme di Caracalla, 00100 Rome, Italy (Telephone Number in U.S. (202) 653-2400); *The State of Food and Agriculture.*

BURKINA FASO - SUGAR PRODUCTION - See BURKINA FASO - CROPS

BURKINA FASO - TAXATION

G.K. Hall and Company, 70 Lincoln Street, Boston, Massachusetts 02111 (617) 423-3990; *The World in Figures.*

International Monetary Fund, 700 Nineteenth Street, NW, Washington, D.C. 20431 (800) 623-7000; *Government Finance Statistics Yearbook.*

International Road Federation, 525 School Street, SW, Washington, D.C. 20024 (202) 554-2106; *World Road Statistics.*

The World Bank, 1818 H Street, NW, Washington, D.C. 20433 (202) 477-1234; *World Tables.*

BURKINA FASO - TELEGRAPH SERVICE

Statistical Office of the United Nations, Publishing Service, New York, New York 10017 (800) 253-9646; *Statistical Yearbook.*

BURKINA FASO - TELEPHONES IN USE

American Telephone and Telegraph Company, 26 Parsippany Road, Whippany, New Jersey 07981 (800) 338-4038; *The World's Telephones.*

G.K. Hall and Company, 70 Lincoln Street, Boston, Massachusetts 02111 (617) 423-3990; *The World in Figures.*

Statistical Office of the United Nations, Publishing Service, New York, New York 10017 (800) 253-9646; *Statistical Yearbook.*

BURKINA FASO - TELEVISION BROADCASTING - See BURKINA FASO - BROADCASTING

BURKINA FASO - TEXTILE INDUSTRY

Food and Agricultural Organization of the United Nations (FAO) Via delle Terme di Caracalla, 00100 Rome, Italy (Telephone Number in U.S. (202) 653-2400); *The State of Food and Agriculture.*

G.K. Hall and Company, 70 Lincoln Street, Boston, Massachusetts 02111 (617) 423-3990; *The World in Figures.*

Statistical Office of the United Nations, Publishing Service, New York, New York 10017 (800) 253-9646; *Statistical Yearbook.*

BURKINA FASO - TOBACCO PRODUCTION

Facts on File, 460 Park Avenue South, New York, New York 10016 (800) 443-8323; *The New Book of World Rankings.*

Statistical Office of the United Nations, Publishing Service, New York, New York 10017 (800) 253-9646; *Statistical Yearbook.*

BURKINA FASO - TOURISM

Federal Statistical Office, Gustav - Stresemann - Ring 11, D-6200 Wiesbaden, Germany; *Burkina Faso.*

G.K. Hall and Company, 70 Lincoln Street, Boston, Massachusetts 02111 (617) 423-3990; *The World in Figures.*

Statistical Office of the United Nations, Publishing Service, New York, New York 10017 (800) 253-9646; *Statistical Yearbook.*

Times Books, 201 East 50th Street, New York, New York 10022 (212) 751-2600; *The Economist Book of Vital World Statistics.*

United Nations Economic Commission for Africa, Africa Hall, P.O. Box 3001, Addis Ababa, Ethiopia (Telephone Number in U.S. (800) 253-9646); *African Statistical Yearbook.*

World Tourism Organization, Calle Capitan Haya 42, E-28020 Madrid, Spain; *Yearbook of Tourism Statistics.*

BURKINA FASO - TRACTORS IN USE

Statistical Office of the United Nations, Publishing Service, New York, New York 10017 (800) 253-9646; *Statistical Yearbook.*

BURKINA FASO - TRADE - See BURKINA FASO - FOREIGN TRADE

BURKINA FASO - TRANSPORTATION AND COMMUNICATIONS

Federal Statistical Office, Gustav - Stresemann - Ring 11, D-6200 Wiesbaden, Germany; *Burkina Faso.*

G.K. Hall and Company, 70 Lincoln Street, Boston, Massachusetts 02111 (617) 423-3990; *The World in Figures.*

United Nations Economic Commission for Africa, Africa Hall, P.O. Box 3001, Addis Ababa, Ethiopia (Telephone Number in U.S. (800) 253-9646); *African Statistical Yearbook.*

BURKINA FASO - UNEMPLOYMENT

Euromonitor Publications Limited, 87-88 Turnmill Street, London EC1M 5QU, England; *International Marketing Data and Statistics.*

International Labour Office, I.L.O. Publications, CH-1211, Geneva 22, Switzerland; *Yearbook of Labour Statistics.*

Statistical Office of the United Nations, Publishing Service, New York, New York 10017 (800) 253-9646; *Statistical Yearbook.*

BURKINA FASO - VITAL STATISTICS

Euromonitor Publications Limited, 87-88 Turnmill Street, London EC1M 5QU, England; *International Marketing Data and Statistics.*

G.K. Hall and Company, 70 Lincoln Street, Boston, Massachusetts 02111 (617) 423-3990; *The World in Figures.*

World Health Organization, Office of Publications, Avenue Appia, CH-1211 Geneva 27, Switzerland (Telephone Number in U.S. (518) 436-9686); *World Health Statistics Annual.*

BURKINA FASO - WAGES

Federal Statistical Office, Gustav - Stresemann - Ring 11, D-6200 Wiesbaden, Germany; *Burkina Faso.*

G.K. Hall and Company, 70 Lincoln Street, Boston, Massachusetts 02111 (617) 423-3990; *The World in Figures.*

International Labour Office, I.L.O. Publications, CH-1211, Geneva 22, Switzerland; *Yearbook of Labour Statistics.*

Statistical Office of the United Nations, Publishing Service, New York, New York 10017 (800) 253-9646; *Statistical Yearbook.*

BURKINA FASO - WEATHER

G.K. Hall and Company, 70 Lincoln Street, Boston, Massachusetts 02111 (617) 423-3990; *The World in Figures.*

BURKINA FASO - WELFARE

International Monetary Fund, 700 Nineteenth Street, NW, Washington, D.C. 20431 (202) 623-7000; *Government Finance Statistics Yearbook.*

BURKINA FASO - YARN PRODUCTION

Statistical Office of the United Nations, Publishing Service, New York, New York 10017 (800) 253-9646; *Statistical Yearbook.*

BURMA - See MYANMAR

Burundi - National Statistical Office

Department des Statistiques, BP 1156, Bujumbura, Burundi.

Burundi - Primary Statistics Sources

Department de la Statistique, BP 1156, Bujumbura, Burundi; *Annuaire Statistique* (Statistical Yearbook), and *Bulletin Statistique* (Statistical Bulletin).

BURUNDI - AGRICULTURE

Euromonitor Publications Limited, 87-88 Turnmill Street, London EC1M 5QU, England; *International Marketing Data and Statistics.*

Federal Statistical Office, Gustav - Stresemann - Ring 11, D-6200 Wiesbaden, Germany; *Burundi.*

Food and Agricultural Organization of the United Nations (FAO), Via delle Terme di Caracalla, 00100 Rome, Italy (Telephone Number in U.S. (202) 653-2400); *Production Yearbook, The State of Food and Agriculture,* and *Trade Yearbook.*

G.K. Hall and Company, 70 Lincoln Street, Boston, Massachusetts 02111 (617) 423-3990; *The World in Figures.*

Statistical Office of the United Nations, Publishing Service, New York, New York 10017 (800) 253-9646; *Statistical Yearbook,* and *Survey of Economic and Social Conditions in Africa.*

Times Books, 201 East 50th Street, New York, New York 10022 (212) 751-2600; *The Economist Book of Vital World Statistics.*

United Nations Economic Commission for Africa, Africa Hall, P.O. Box 3001, Addis Ababa, Ethiopia (Telephone Number in U.S. (800) 253-9646); *African Statistical Yearbook.*

BURUNDI - AIRLINE SERVICE

G.K. Hall and Company, 70 Lincoln Street, Boston, Massachusetts 02111 (617) 423-3990; *The World in Figures.*

Times Books, 201 East 50th Street, New York, New York 10022 (212) 751-2600; *The Economist Book of Vital World Statistics.*

United Nations Economic Commission for Africa, Africa Hall, P.O. Box 3001, Addis Ababa, Ethiopia (Telephone Number in U.S. (800) 253-9646); *African Statistical Yearbook.*

BURUNDI - AREA AND DENSITY OF POPULATION

African Development Bank, 01 BP 1387, Abidjan 01, Cote D'Ivoire; *Selected Statistics on Regional Member Countries.*

Euromonitor Publications Limited, 87-88 Turnmill Street, London EC1M 5QU, England; *International Marketing Data and Statistics.*

Federal Statistical Office, Gustav - Stresemann - Ring 11, D-6200 Wiesbaden, Federal Republic of Germany; *Burundi.*

Food and Agricultural Organization of the United Nations (FAO) Via delle Terme di Caracalla, 00100 Rome, Italy (Telephone Number in U.S. (202) 653-2400); *The State of Food and Agriculture.*

G.K. Hall and Company, 70 Lincoln Street, Boston, Massachusetts 02111 (617) 423-3990; *The World in Figures.*

Statistical Office of the United Nations, Publishing Service, New York, New York 10017 (800) 253-9646; *Statistical Yearbook,* and *Survey of Economic and Social Conditions in Africa.*

Times Books, 201 East 50th Street, New York, New York 10022 (212) 751-2600; *The Economist Book of Vital World Statistics.*

BURUNDI - ARMS EXPORTS AND IMPORTS

U.S. Arms Control and Disarmament Agency, 320 Twenty-first Street, NW, Washington, D.C. 20451 (202) 647-8677; *World Military Expenditures and Arms Transfers.*

BURUNDI - BALANCE OF PAYMENTS

African Development Bank, 01 BP 1387, Abidjan 01, Cote D'Ivoire; *Selected Statistics on Regional Member Countries.*

The Economist Intelligence Unit, 111 West 57th Street, New York, New York 10019 (800) 938-4685; *The World Market Atlas.*

Federal Statistical Office, Gustav - Stresemann - Ring 11, D-6200 Wiesbaden, Germany; *Burundi.*

G.K. Hall and Company, 70 Lincoln Street, Boston, Massachusetts 02111 (617) 423-3990; *The World in Figures.*

Times Books, 201 East 50th Street, New York, New York 10022 (212) 751-2600; *The Economist Book of Vital World Statistics.*

United Nations Economic Commission for Africa, Africa Hall, P.O. Box 3001, Addis Ababa, Ethiopia (Telephone Number in U.S. (800) 253-9646); *African Statistical Yearbook.*

BURUNDI - BANKING

G.K. Hall and Company, 70 Lincoln Street, Boston, Massachusetts 02111 (617) 423-3990; *The World in Figures.*

International Monetary Fund, 700 Nineteenth Street, NW, Washington, D.C. 20431 (202) 623-7000; *International Financial Statistics.*

BURUNDI - BEER PRODUCTION

Statistical Office of the United Nations, Publishing Service, New York, New York 10017 (800) 253-9646; *Statistical Yearbook.*

BURUNDI - BIRTH RATES

Statistical Office of the United Nations, Publishing Service, New York, New York 10017 (800) 253-9646; *Demographic Yearbook, Statistical Yearbook,* and *Survey of Economic and Social Conditions in Africa.*

Times Books, 201 East 50th Street, New York, New York 10022 (212) 751-2600; *The Economist Book of Vital World Statistics.*

BURUNDI - BONDS

G.K. Hall and Company, 70 Lincoln Street, Boston, Massachusetts 02111 (617) 423-3990; *The World in Figures.*

BURUNDI - BOOK PRODUCTION

G.K. Hall and Company, 70 Lincoln Street, Boston, Massachusetts 02111 (617) 423-3990; *The World in Figures.*

BURUNDI - BROADCASTING

Billboard Limited, P.O. Box 9027, 1006 AA Amsterdam, The Netherlands (Telephone Number in U.S. (212) 764-7300); *World Radio TV Handbook.*

G.K. Hall and Company, 70 Lincoln Street, Boston, Massachusetts 02111 (617) 423-3990; *The World in Figures.*

Times Books, 201 East 50th Street, New York, New York 10022 (212) 751-2600; *The Economist Book of Vital World Statistics.*

BURUNDI - BUSINESS

G.K. Hall and Company, 70 Lincoln Street, Boston, Massachusetts 02111 (617) 423-3990; *The World in Figures.*

BURUNDI - CALORIE SUPPLY

African Development Bank, 01 BP 1387, Abidjan 01, Cote D'Ivoire; *Selected Statistics on Regional Member Countries.*

Food and Agricultural Organization of the United Nations (FAO) Via delle Terme di Caracalla, 00100 Rome, Italy (Telephone Number in U.S. (202) 653-2400); *The State of Food and Agriculture.*

BURUNDI - CATTLE - See BURUNDI - LIVESTOCK AND POULTRY

BURUNDI - CHEMICAL (ORGANIC) PRODUCTION - See BURUNDI - MINING AND MINERAL PRODUCTS

BURUNDI - CHICKENS - See BURUNDI - LIVESTOCK AND POULTRY

BURUNDI - CLASS STRUCTURE

G.K. Hall and Company, 70 Lincoln Street, Boston, Massachusetts 02111 (617) 423-3990; *The World in Figures.*

BURUNDI - CLIMATE

G.K. Hall and Company, 70 Lincoln Street, Boston, Massachusetts 02111 (617) 423-3990; *The World in Figures.*

BURUNDI - COAL PRODUCTION - See BURUNDI - MINING AND MINERAL PRODUCTS

BURUNDI - COFFEE - See BURUNDI - CROPS

BURUNDI - COMMERCIAL BANKS

International Monetary Fund, 700 Nineteenth Street, NW, Washington, D.C. 20431 (202) 623-7000; *International Financial Statistics.*

BURUNDI - COMMUNICATIONS

Federal Statistical Office, Gustav - Stresemann - Ring 11, D-6200 Wiesbaden, Germany; *Burundi.*

G.K. Hall and Company, 70 Lincoln Street, Boston, Massachusetts 02111 (617) 423-3990; *The World in Figures.*

United Nations Economic Commission for Africa, Africa Hall, P.O. Box 3001, Addis Ababa, Ethiopia (Telephone Number in U.S. (800) 253-9646); *African Statistical Yearbook.*

BURUNDI - CONSTRUCTION INDUSTRY

United Nations Economic Commission for Africa, Africa Hall, P.O. Box 3001, Addis Ababa, Ethiopia (Telephone Number in U.S. (800) 253-9646); *African Statistical Yearbook.*

BURUNDI - CONSUMER PRICE INDEX

African Development Bank, 01 BP 1387, Abidjan 01, Cote D'Ivoire; *Selected Statistics on Regional Member Countries.*

Federal Statistical Office, Gustav - Stresemann - Ring 11, D-6200 Wiesbaden, Germany; *Burundi.*

G.K. Hall and Company, 70 Lincoln Street, Boston, Massachusetts 02111 (617) 423-3990; *The World in Figures.*

Statistical Office of the United Nations, Publishing Service, New York, New York 10017 (800) 253-9646; *Statistical Yearbook,* and *Survey of Economic and Social Conditions in Africa.*

United Nations Economic Commission for Africa, Africa Hall, P.O. Box 3001, Addis Ababa, Ethiopia (Telephone Number in U.S. (800) 253-9646); *African Statistical Yearbook.*

BURUNDI - CONSUMER PRICES

Federal Statistical Office, Gustav - Stresemann - Ring 11, D-6200 Wiesbaden, Germany; *Burundi.*

International Labour Office, I.L.O. Publications, CH-1211, Geneva 22, Switzerland; *Yearbook of Labour Statistics.*

International Monetary Fund, 700 Nineteenth Street, NW, Washington, D.C. 20431 (202) 623-7000; *International Financial Statistics.*

Times Books, 201 East 50th Street, New York, New York 10022 (212) 751-2600; *The Economist Book of Vital World Statistics.*

BURUNDI - CONSUMPTION

African Development Bank, 01 BP 1387, Abidjan 01, Cote D'Ivoire; *Selected Statistics on Regional Member Countries.*

G.K. Hall and Company, 70 Lincoln Street, Boston, Massachusetts 02111 (617) 423-3990; *The World in Figures.*

Statistical Office of the United Nations, Publishing Service, New York, New York 10017 (800) 253-9646; *Survey of Economic and Social Conditions in Africa.*

BURUNDI - CORN PRODUCTION

Food and Agricultural Organization of the United Nations (FAO) Via delle Terme di Caracalla, 00100 Rome, Italy (Telephone Number in U.S. (202) 653-2400); *The State of Food and Agriculture.*

Statistical Office of the United Nations, Publishing Service, New York, New York 10017 (800) 253-9646; *Statistical Yearbook.*

BURUNDI - CORPORATE TAXES - See BURUNDI - TAXATION

BURUNDI - COTTON PRODUCTION - See BURUNDI - CROPS

BURUNDI - CRIME

International Criminal Police Organization (INTERPOL), 26 rue Armengaud, 92210 Saint Cloud, France; *International Crime Statistics.*

BURUNDI - CROPS

Food and Agricultural Organization of the United Nations (FAO) Via delle Terme di Caracalla, 00100 Rome, Italy (Telephone Number in U.S. (202) 653-2400); *The State of Food and Agriculture.*

G.K. Hall and Company, 70 Lincoln Street, Boston, Massachusetts 02111 (617) 423-3990; *The World in Figures.*

International Monetary Fund, 700 Nineteenth Street, NW, Washington, D.C. 20431 (202) 623-7000; *International Financial Statistics.*
Statistical Office of the United Nations, Publishing Service, New York, New York 10017 (800) 253-9646; *Statistical Yearbook.*

United Nations Economic Commission for Africa, Africa Hall, P.O. Box 3001, Addis Ababa, Ethiopia (Telephone Number in U.S. (800) 253-9646); *African Statistical Yearbook.*

BURUNDI - CUSTOMS RATES

G.K. Hall and Company, 70 Lincoln Street, Boston, Massachusetts 02111 (617) 423-3990; *The World in Figures.*

BURUNDI - DAIRY PRODUCTS

Food and Agricultural Organization of the United Nations (FAO) Via delle Terme di Caracalla, 00100 Rome, Italy (Telephone Number in U.S. (202) 653-2400); *Production Yearbook,* and *The State of Food and Agriculture.*

Statistical Office of the United Nations, Publishing Service, New York, New York 10017 (800) 253-9646; *Statistical Yearbook.*

BURUNDI - DEATH RATES

G.K. Hall and Company, 70 Lincoln Street, Boston, Massachusetts 02111 (617) 423-3990; *The World in Figures.*

Statistical Office of the United Nations, Publishing Service, New York, New York 10017 (800) 253-9646; *Statistical Yearbook,* and *Survey of Economic and Social Conditions in Africa.*

Times Books, 201 East 50th Street, New York, New York 10022 (212) 751-2600; *The Economist Book of Vital World Statistics.*

BURUNDI - DEFENSE EXPENDITURES

G.K. Hall and Company, 70 Lincoln Street, Boston, Massachusetts 02111 (617) 423-3990; *The World in Figures.*

U.S. Arms Control and Disarmament Agency, 320 Twenty-first Street, NW, Washington, D.C. 20451 (202) 647-8677; *World Military Expenditures and Arms Transfers.*

BURUNDI - DEMOGRAPHY

The Economist Intelligence Unit, 111 West 57th Street, New York, New York 10019 (800) 938-4685; *The World Market Atlas.*

Federal Statistical Office, Gustav - Stresemann - Ring 11, D-6200 Wiesbaden, Germany; *Burundi.*

G.K. Hall and Company, 70 Lincoln Street, Boston, Massachusetts 02111 (617) 423-3990; *The World in Figures.*

Statistical Office of the United Nations, Publishing Service, New York, New York 10017 (800) 253-9646; *Survey of Economic and Social Conditions in Africa.*

BURUNDI - DEVELOPMENT ASSISTANCE

G.K. Hall and Company, 70 Lincoln Street, Boston, Massachusetts 02111 (617) 423-3990; *The World in Figures.*

Statistical Office of the United Nations, Publishing Service, New York, New York 10017 (800) 253-9646; *Statistical Yearbook.*

BURUNDI - DISEASE

G.K. Hall and Company, 70 Lincoln Street, Boston, Massachusetts 02111 (617) 423-3990; *The World in Figures.*

BURUNDI - DIVORCE RATES

Statistical Office of the United Nations, Publishing Service, New York, New York 10017 (800) 253-9646; *Demographic Yearbook.*

BURUNDI - DOMESTIC PRODUCT

G.K. Hall and Company, 70 Lincoln Street, Boston, Massachusetts 02111 (617) 423-3990; *The World in Figures.*

BURUNDI - ECONOMY

African Development Bank, 01 BP 1387, Abidjan 01, Cote D'Ivoire; *Selected Statistics on Regional Member Countries.*

Euromonitor Publications Limited, 87-88 Turnmill Street, London EC1M 5QU, England; *International Marketing Data and Statistics.*

Federal Statistical Office, Gustav - Stresemann - Ring 11, D-6200 Wiesbaden, Germany; *Burundi.*

G.K. Hall and Company, 70 Lincoln Street, Boston, Massachusetts 02111 (617) 423-3990; *The World in Figures.*

Statistical Office of the United Nations, Publishing Service, New York, New York 10017 (800) 253-9646; *Foreign Trade Statistics for Africa.*

BURUNDI - EDUCATION

African Development Bank, 01 BP 1387, Abidjan 01, Cote D'Ivoire; *Selected Statistics on Regional Member Countries.*

The Economist Intelligence Unit, 111 West 57th Street, New York, New York 10019 (800) 938-4685; *The World Market Atlas.*

Federal Statistical Office, Gustav - Stresemann - Ring 11, D-6200 Wiesbaden, Germany; *Burundi.*

G.K. Hall and Company, 70 Lincoln Street, Boston, Massachusetts 02111 (617) 423-3990; *The World in Figures.*

Statistical Office of the United Nations, Publishing Service, New York, New York 10017 (800) 253-9646; *Survey of Economic and Social Conditions in Africa.*

Times Books, 201 East 50th Street, New York, New York 10022 (212) 751-2600; *The Economist Book of Vital World Statistics.*

United Nations Economic Commission for Africa, Africa Hall, P.O. Box 3001, Addis Ababa, Ethiopia (Telephone Number in U.S. (800) 253-9646); *African Statistical Yearbook.*

United Nations Educational, Scientific and Cultural Organization (UNESCO), 7 Place de Fontenoy, F-75700 Paris, France; *Statistical Yearbook.*

BURUNDI - EGG PRODUCTION - See BURUNDI - DAIRY PRODUCTS

BURUNDI - ELECTRICITY

Statistical Office of the United Nations, Publishing Service, New York, New York 10017 (800) 253-9646; *Survey of Economic and Social Conditions in Africa.*

Times Books, 201 East 50th Street, New York, New York 10022 (212) 751-2600; *The Economist Book of Vital World Statistics.*

United Nations Economic Commission for Africa, Africa Hall, P.O. Box 3001, Addis Ababa, Ethiopia (Telephone Number in U.S. (800) 253-9646); *African Statistical Yearbook.*

BURUNDI - EMPLOYMENT

Euromonitor Publications Limited, 87-88 Turnmill Street, London EC1M 5QU, England; *International Marketing Data and Statistics.*

Federal Statistical Office, Gustav - Stresemann - Ring 11, D-6200 Wiesbaden, Germany; *Burundi.*

International Labour Office, I.L.O. Publications, CH-1211, Geneva 22, Switzerland; *Yearbook of Labour Statistics.*

Statistical Office of the United Nations, Publishing Service, New York, New York 10017 (800) 253-9646; *Statistical Yearbook,* and *Survey of Economic and Social Conditions in Africa.*

United Nations Economic Commission for Africa, Africa Hall, P.O. Box 3001, Addis Ababa, Ethiopia (Telephone Number in U.S. (800) 253-9646); *African Statistical Yearbook.*

BURUNDI - ENERGY

Food and Agricultural Organization of the United Nations (FAO) Via delle Terme di Caracalla, 00100 Rome, Italy (Telephone Number in U.S. (202) 653-2400); *The State of Food and Agriculture.*

G.K. Hall and Company, 70 Lincoln Street, Boston, Massachusetts 02111 (617) 423-3990; *The World in Figures.*

Statistical Office of the United Nations, Publishing Service, New York, New York 10017 (800) 253-9646; *Energy Statistics Yearbook,* and *Statistical Yearbook.*

Times Books, 201 East 50th Street, New York, New York 10022 (212) 751-2600; *The Economist Book of Vital World Statistics.*

United Nations Economic Commission for Africa, Africa Hall, P.O. Box 3001, Addis Ababa, Ethiopia (Telephone Number in U.S. (800) 253-9646); *African Statistical Yearbook.*

BURUNDI - EXCHANGE RATES

African Development Bank, 01 BP 1387, Abidjan 01, Cote D'Ivoire; *Selected Statistics on Regional Member Countries.*

Euromonitor Publications Limited, 87-88 Turnmill Street, London EC1M 5QU, England; *International Marketing Data and Statistics.*

International Monetary Fund, 700 Nineteenth Street, NW, Washington, D.C. 20431 (202) 623-7000; *International Financial Statistics.*

Statistical Office of the United Nations, Publishing Service, New York, New York 10017 (800) 253-9646; *Foreign Trade Statistics for Africa,* and *Statistical Yearbook.*

BURUNDI - EXPORTS

African Development Bank, 01 BP 1387, Abidjan 01, Cote D'Ivoire; *Selected Statistics on Regional Member Countries.*

The Economist Intelligence Unit, 111 West 57th Street, New York, New York 10019 (800) 938-4685; *The World Market Atlas.*

Euromonitor Publications Limited, 87-88 Turnmill Street, London EC1M 5QU, England; *International Marketing Data and Statistics.*

Food and Agricultural Organization of the United Nations (FAO) Via delle Terme di Caracalla, 00100 Rome, Italy (Telephone Number in U.S. (202) 653-2400); *The State of Food and Agriculture.*

G.K. Hall and Company, 70 Lincoln Street, Boston, Massachusetts 02111 (617) 423-3990; *The World in Figures.*

International Monetary Fund, 700 Nineteenth Street, NW, Washington, D.C. 20431 (202) 623-7000; *Direction of Trade Statistics,* and *International Financial Statistics.*

Statistical Office of the United Nations, Publishing Service, New York, New York 10017 (800) 253-9646; *Foreign Trade Statistics for Africa,* and *Survey of Economic and Social Conditions in Africa.*

Times Books, 201 East 50th Street, New York, New York 10022 (212) 751-2600; *The Economist Book of Vital World Statistics.*

United Nations Economic Commission for Africa, Africa Hall, P.O. Box 3001, Addis Ababa, Ethiopia (Telephone Number in U.S. (800) 253-9646); *African Statistical Yearbook.*

BURUNDI - EXTERNAL INDEBTEDNESS

African Development Bank, 01 BP 1387, Abidjan 01, Cote D'Ivoire; *Selected Statistics on Regional Member Countries.*

Statistical Office of the United Nations, Publishing Service, New York, New York 10017 (800) 253-9646; *Survey of Economic and Social Conditions in Africa.*

BURUNDI - EXTERNAL TRADE

African Development Bank, 01 BP 1387, Abidjan 01, Cote D'Ivoire; *Selected Statistics on Regional Member Countries.*

Food and Agricultural Organization of the United Nations (FAO) Via delle Terme di Caracalla, 00100 Rome, Italy (Telephone Number in U.S. (202) 653-2400); *The State of Food and Agriculture,* and *Trade Yearbook.*

G.K. Hall and Company, 70 Lincoln Street, Boston, Massachusetts 02111 (617) 423-3990; *The World in Figures.*

Statistical Office of the United Nations, Publishing Service, New York, New York 10017 (800) 253-9646; *Statistical Yearbook.*

BURUNDI - FARM CROPS - See BURUNDI - CROPS
BURUNDI - FEMALE WORKING POPULATION - See BURUNDI - EMPLOYMENT

BURUNDI - FERTILITY RATES

Statistical Office of the United Nations, Publishing Service, New York, New York 10017 (800) 253-9646; *Survey of Economic and Social Conditions in Africa.*

Times Books, 201 East 50th Street, New York, New York 10022 (212) 751-2600; *The Economist Book of Vital World Statistics.*

BURUNDI - FERTILIZER

Food and Agricultural Organization of the United Nations (FAO) Via delle Terme di Caracalla, 00100 Rome, Italy (Telephone Number in U.S. (202) 653-2400); *The State of Food and Agriculture.*

Statistical Office of the United Nations, Publishing Service, New York, New York 10017 (800) 253-9646; *Statistical Yearbook.*

BURUNDI - FETAL MORTALITY

Statistical Office of the United Nations, Publishing Service, New York, New York 10017 (800) 253-9646; *Demographic Yearbook.*

BURUNDI - FINANCE

African Development Bank, 01 BP 1387, Abidjan 01, Cote D'Ivoire; *Selected Statistics on Regional Member Countries.*

Federal Statistical Office, Gustav - Stresemann - Ring 11, D-6200 Wiesbaden, Germany; *Burundi.*

G.K. Hall and Company, 70 Lincoln Street, Boston, Massachusetts 02111 (617) 423-3990; *The World in Figures.*

United Nations Economic Commission for Africa, Africa Hall, P.O. Box 3001, Addis Ababa, Ethiopia (Telephone Number in U.S. (800) 253-9646); *African Statistical Yearbook.*

BURUNDI - FISHERIES

Federal Statistical Office, Gustav - Stresemann - Ring 11, D-6200 Wiesbaden, Germany; *Burundi.*

Food and Agricultural Organization of the United Nations (FAO) Via delle Terme di Caracalla, 00100 Rome, Italy (Telephone Number in

U.S. (202) 653-2400); *The State of Food and Agriculture,* and *Yearbook of Fishery Statistics.*

Statistical Office of the United Nations, Publishing Service, New York, New York 10017 (800) 253-9646; *Statistical Yearbook,* and *Survey of Economic and Social Conditions in Africa.*

United Nations Economic Commission for Africa, Africa Hall, P.O. Box 3001, Addis Ababa, Ethiopia (Telephone Number in U.S. (800) 253-9646); *African Statistical Yearbook.*

BURUNDI - FOOD

African Development Bank, 01 BP 1387, Abidjan 01, Cote D'Ivoire; *Selected Statistics on Regional Member Countries.*

Food and Agricultural Organization of the United Nations (FAO) Via delle Terme di Caracalla, 00100 Rome, Italy (Telephone Number in U.S. (202) 653-2400); *Production Yearbook* and *The State of Food and Agriculture.*

G.K. Hall and Company, 70 Lincoln Street, Boston, Massachusetts 02111 (617) 423-3990; *The World in Figures.*

BURUNDI - FOREIGN AID

G.K. Hall and Company, 70 Lincoln Street, Boston, Massachusetts 02111 (617) 423-3990; *The World in Figures.*

BURUNDI - FOREIGN TRADE

Euromonitor Publications Limited, 87-88 Turnmill Street, London EC1M 5QU, England; *International Marketing Data and Statistics.*

Federal Statistical Office, Gustav - Stresemann - Ring 11, D-6200 Wiesbaden, Germany; *Burundi.*

Food and Agricultural Organization of the United Nations (FAO) Via delle Terme di Caracalla, 00100 Rome, Italy (Telephone Number in U.S. (202) 653-2400); *The State of Food and Agriculture.*

G.K. Hall and Company, 70 Lincoln Street, Boston, Massachusetts 02111 (617) 423-3990; *The World in Figures.*

Organisation for Economic Co-operation and Development (OECD), 2 rue Andre-Pascal, 75 Paris 16, France (Telephone Number in U.S. (202) 785-6323); *Trade by Commodities.*

Statistical Office of the United Nations, Publishing Service, New York, New York 10017 (800) 253-9646; *Foreign Trade Statistics for Africa, International Trade Statistics Yearbook, Statistical Yearbook,* and *Trade in Manufactures of Developing Countries.*

United Nations Economic Commission for Africa, Africa Hall, P.O. Box 3001, Addis Ababa, Ethiopia (Telephone Number in U.S. (800) 253-9646); *African Statistical Yearbook.*

BURUNDI - FORESTRY AND FOREST PRODUCTS

Federal Statistical Office, Gustav - Stresemann - Ring 11, D-6200 Wiesbaden, Germany; *Burundi.*

Food and Agricultural Organization of the United Nations (FAO) Via delle Terme di Caracalla, 00100 Rome, Italy (Telephone Number in U.S. (202) 653-2400); *The State of Food and Agriculture,* and *Yearbook of Forest Statistics.*

G.K. Hall and Company, 70 Lincoln Street, Boston, Massachusetts 02111 (617) 423-3990; *The World in Figures.*

Statistical Office of the United Nations, Publishing Service, New York, New York 10017 (800) 253-9646; *Statistical Yearbook.*

United Nations Economic Commission for Africa, Africa Hall, P.O. Box 3001, Addis Ababa, Ethiopia (Telephone Number in U.S. (800) 253-9646); *African Statistical Yearbook.*

United Nations Educational, Scientific and Cultural Organization (UNESCO), 7 Place de Fontenoy, F-75700 Paris, France (Telephone Number in U.S. (212) 963-5981); *Statistical Yearbook.*

BURUNDI - GENERAL INDUSTRIAL STATISTICS

Federal Statistical Office, Gustav - Stresemann - Ring 11, D-6200 Wiesbaden, Germany; *Burundi.*

BURUNDI - GENERAL MORTALITY

Statistical Office of the United Nations, Publishing Service, New York, New York 10017 (800) 253-9646; *Demographic Yearbook.*

BURUNDI - GEOGRAPHIC DATA

Federal Statistical Office, Gustav - Stresemann - Ring 11, D-6200 Wiesbaden, Germany; *Burundi.*

BURUNDI - GOATS - See BURUNDI - LIVESTOCK AND POULTRY

BURUNDI - GOLD HOLDINGS

International Monetary Fund, 700 Nineteenth Street, NW, Washington, D.C. 20431 (202) 623-7000; *International Financial Statistics.*

Statistical Office of the United Nations, Publishing Service, New York, New York 10017 (800) 253-9646; *Statistical Yearbook.*

BURUNDI - GOVERNMENT

G.K. Hall and Company, 70 Lincoln Street, Boston, Massachusetts 02111 (617) 423-3990; *The World in Figures.*

BURUNDI - GOVERNMENT FINANCE

International Monetary Fund, 700 Nineteenth Street, NW, Washington, D.C. 20431 (202) 623-7000; *International Financial Statistics.*

BURUNDI - GOVERNMENT REVENUE

Statistical Office of the United Nations, Publishing Service, New York, New York 10017 (800) 253-9646; *Survey of Economic and Social Conditions in Africa.*

Times Books, 201 East 50th Street, New York, New York 10022 (212) 751-2600; *The Economist Book of Vital World Statistics.*

BURUNDI - GRAIN PRODUCTION - See BURUNDI - CROPS

BURUNDI - GROSS DOMESTIC PRODUCT

African Development Bank, 01 BP 1387, Abidjan 01, Cote D'Ivoire; *Selected Statistics on Regional Member Countries.*

The Economist Intelligence Unit, 111 West 57th Street, New York, New York 10019 (800) 938-4685; *The World Market Atlas.*

Euromonitor Publications Limited, 87-88 Turnmill Street, London EC1M 5QU, England; *International Marketing Data and Statistics.*

G.K. Hall and Company, 70 Lincoln Street, Boston, Massachusetts 02111 (617) 423-3990; *The World in Figures.*

Statistical Office of the United Nations, Publishing Service, New York, New York 10017 (800) 253-9646; *Statistical Yearbook*, and *Survey of Economic and Social Conditions in Africa.*

Times Books, 201 East 50th Street, New York, New York 10022 (212) 751-2600; *The Economist Book of Vital World Statistics.*

United Nations Economic Commission for Africa, Africa Hall, P.O. Box 3001, Addis Ababa, Ethiopia (Telephone Number in U.S. (800) 253-9646); *African Statistical Yearbook.*

BURUNDI - GROSS NATIONAL PRODUCT

Euromonitor Publications Limited, 87-88 Turnmill Street, London EC1M 5QU, England; *International Marketing Data and Statistics.*

U.S. Arms Control and Disarmament Agency, 320 Twenty-first Street, NW, Washington, D.C. 20451 (202) 647-8677; *World Military Expenditures and Arms Transfers.*

BURUNDI - GROUNDNUTS PRODUCTION - See BURUNDI - CROPS

BURUNDI - HEALTH

African Development Bank, 01 BP 1387, Abidjan 01, Cote D'Ivoire; *Selected Statistics on Regional Member Countries.*

Federal Statistical Office, Gustav - Stresemann - Ring 11, D-6200 Wiesbaden, Germany; *Burundi.*

G.K. Hall and Company, 70 Lincoln Street, Boston, Massachusetts 02111 (617) 423-3990; *The World in Figures.*

Statistical Office of the United Nations, Publishing Service, New York, New York 10017 (800) 253-9646; *Statistical Yearbook.*

Times Books, 201 East 50th Street, New York, New York 10022 (212) 751-2600; *The Economist Book of Vital World Statistics.*

United Nations Economic Commission for Africa, Africa Hall, P.O. Box 3001, Addis Ababa, Ethiopia (Telephone Number in U.S. (800) 253-9646); *African Statistical Yearbook.*

BURUNDI - HIDE PRODUCTION

Food and Agricultural Organization of the United Nations (FAO), Via delle Terme di Caracalla, 00100 Rome, Italy (Telephone Number in U.S. (202) 653-2400); *Production Yearbook.*

BURUNDI - HIGHWAYS

G.K. Hall and Company, 70 Lincoln Street, Boston, Massachusetts 02111 (617) 423-3990; *The World in Figures.*

Statistical Office of the United Nations, Publishing Service, New York, New York 10017 (800) 253-9646; *Survey of Economic and Social Conditions in Africa.*

United Nations Economic Commission for Africa, Africa Hall, P.O. Box 3001, Addis Ababa, Ethiopia (Telephone Number in U.S. (800) 253-9646); *African Statistical Yearbook.*

BURUNDI - HOURS OF WORK - See BURUNDI - EMPLOYMENT

BURUNDI - ILLITERATE POPULATION

The Economist Intelligence Unit, 111 West 57th Street, New York, New York 10019 (800) 938-4685; *The World Market Atlas.*

G.K. Hall and Company, 70 Lincoln Street, Boston, Massachusetts 02111 (617) 423-3990; *The World in Figures.*

United Nations Educational, Scientific and Cultural Organization (UNESCO), 7 Place de Fontenoy, F-75700 Paris, France (Telephone Number in U.S. (212) 963-5981); *Statistical Yearbook.*

BURUNDI - IMPORTS

African Development Bank, 01 BP 1387, Abidjan 01, Cote D'Ivoire; *Selected Statistics on Regional Member Countries.*

The Economist Intelligence Unit, 111 West 57th Street, New York, New York 10019 (800) 938-4685; *The World Market Atlas.*

Euromonitor Publications Limited, 87-88 Turnmill Street, London EC1M 5QU, England; *International Marketing Data and Statistics.*

Food and Agricultural Organization of the United Nations (FAO) Via delle Terme di Caracalla, 00100 Rome, Italy (Telephone Number in U.S. (202) 653-2400); *The State of Food and Agriculture.*

G.K. Hall and Company, 70 Lincoln Street, Boston, Massachusetts 02111 (617) 423-3990; *The World in Figures.*

International Monetary Fund, 700 Nineteenth Street, NW, Washington, D.C. 20431 (202) 623-7000; *Direction of Trade Statistics*, and *International Financial Statistics.*

Statistical Office of the United Nations, Publishing Service, New York, New York 10017 (800) 253-9646; *Foreign Trade Statistics for Africa*, and *Survey of Economic and Social Conditions in Africa.*

Times Books, 201 East 50th Street, New York, New York 10022 (212) 751-2600; *The Economist Book of Vital World Statistics.*

United Nations Economic Commission for Africa, Africa Hall, P.O. Box 3001, Addis Ababa, Ethiopia (Telephone Number in U.S. (800) 253-9646); *African Statistical Yearbook.*

BURUNDI - INDUSTRY

Euromonitor Publications Limited, 87-88 Turnmill Street, London EC1M 5QU, England; *International Marketing Data and Statistics.*

Federal Statistical Office, Gustav - Stresemann - Ring 11, D-6200 Wiesbaden, Germany; *Burundi.*

G.K. Hall and Company, 70 Lincoln Street, Boston, Massachusetts 02111 (617) 423-3990; *The World in Figures.*

International Labour Office, I.L.O. Publications, CH-1211, Geneva 22, Switzerland; *Yearbook of Labour Statistics.*

Statistical Office of the United Nations, Publishing Service, New York, New York 10017 (800) 253-9646; *Survey of Economic and Social Conditions in Africa* and *Statistical Yearbook.*

Times Books, 201 East 50th Street, New York, New York 10022 (212) 751-2600; *The Economist Book of Vital World Statistics.*

United Nations Economic Commission for Africa, Africa Hall, P.O. Box 3001, Addis Ababa, Ethiopia (Telephone Number in U.S. (800) 253-9646); *African Statistical Yearbook.*

World Intellectual Property Organization, 34 Chemin des Colombettes, CH-1211 Geneva 20. Switzerland; *Industrial Property Statistics*.

BURUNDI - INFANT AND MATERNAL MORTALITY

Statistical Office of the United Nations, Publishing Service, New York, New York 10017 (800) 253-9646; *Demographic Yearbook*, *Statistical Yearbook*, and *Survey of Economic and Social Conditions in Africa*.

Times Books, 201 East 50th Street, New York, New York 10022 (212) 751-2600; *The Economist Book of Vital World Statistics*.

BURUNDI - INTERNATIONAL LIQUIDITY

International Monetary Fund, 700 Nineteenth Street, NW, Washington, D.C. 20431 (202) 623-7000; *International Financial Statistics*.

BURUNDI - INTERNATIONAL RESERVES EXCLUDING GOLD

African Development Bank, 01 BP 1387, Abidjan 01, Cote D'Ivoire; *Selected Statistics on Regional Member Countries*.

Statistical Office of the United Nations, Publishing Service, New York, New York 10017 (800) 253-9646; *Statistical Yearbook*.

BURUNDI - IRRIGATION

Euromonitor Publications Limited, 87-88 Turnmill Street, London EC1M 5QU, England; *International Marketing Data and Statistics*.

BURUNDI - LABOR FORCE

African Development Bank, 01 BP 1387, Abidjan 01, Cote D'Ivoire; *Selected Statistics on Regional Member Countries*.

Euromonitor Publications Limited, 87-88 Turnmill Street, London EC1M 5QU, England; *International Marketing Data and Statistics*.

Food and Agricultural Organization of the United Nations (FAO) Via delle Terme di Caracalla, 00100 Rome, Italy (Telephone Number in U.S. (202) 653-2400); *The State of Food and Agriculture*.

G.K. Hall and Company, 70 Lincoln Street, Boston, Massachusetts 02111 (617) 423-3990; *The World in Figures*.

Times Books, 201 East 50th Street, New York, New York 10022 (212) 751-2600; *The Economist Book of Vital World Statistics*.

BURUNDI - LABOR PRODUCTIVITY

International Labour Office, I.L.O. Publications, CH-1211, Geneva 22, Switzerland; *Yearbook of Labour Statistics*.

BURUNDI - LAND USE

Euromonitor Publications Limited, 87-88 Turnmill Street, London EC1M 5QU, England; *International Marketing Data and Statistics*.

Food and Agricultural Organization of the United Nations (FAO), Via delle Terme di Caracalla, 00100 Rome, Italy (Telephone Number in U.S. (202) 653-2400); *Production Yearbook*.

G.K. Hall and Company, 70 Lincoln Street, Boston, Massachusetts 02111 (617) 423-3990; *The World in Figures*.

BURUNDI - LIBRARIES

United Nations Educational, Scientific and Cultural Organization (UNESCO), 7 Place de Fontenoy, F-75700 Paris, France (Telephone Number in U.S. (212) 963-5981); *Statistical Yearbook*.

BURUNDI - LIFE EXPECTANCY

African Development Bank, 01 BP 1387, Abidjan 01, Cote D'Ivoire; *Selected Statistics on Regional Member Countries*.

BURUNDI - LITERACY RATE

Statistical Office of the United Nations, Publishing Service, New York, New York 10017 (800) 253-9646; *Survey of Economic and Social Conditions in Africa*.

BURUNDI - LIVESTOCK AND POULTRY

Euromonitor Publications Limited, 87-88 Turnmill Street, London EC1M 5QU, England; *International Marketing Data and Statistics*.

Food and Agricultural Organization of the United Nations (FAO), Via delle Terme di Caracalla, 00100 Rome, Italy (Telephone Number in U.S. (202) 653-2400); *Production Yearbook*, and *The State of Food and Agriculture*.

G.K. Hall and Company, 70 Lincoln Street, Boston, Massachusetts 02111 (617) 423-3990; *The World in Figures*.

Statistical Office of the United Nations, Publishing Service, New York, New York 10017 (800) 253-9646; *Statistical Yearbook*, and *Survey of Economic and Social Conditions in Africa*.

United Nations Economic Commission for Africa, Africa Hall, P.O. Box 3001, Addis Ababa, Ethiopia (Telephone Number in U.S. (800) 253-9646); *African Statistical Yearbook*.

BURUNDI - LIVING LEVELS

G.K. Hall and Company, 70 Lincoln Street, Boston, Massachusetts 02111 (617) 423-3990; *The World in Figures*.

Times Books, 201 East 50th Street, New York, New York 10022 (212) 751-2600; *The Economist Book of Vital World Statistics*.

BURUNDI - MAIL - NUMBER OF PIECES SENT OR RECEIVED

Statistical Office of the United Nations, Publishing Service, New York, New York 10017 (800) 253-9646; *Statistical Yearbook*.

BURUNDI - MANUFACTURING

G.K. Hall and Company, 70 Lincoln Street, Boston, Massachusetts 02111 (617) 423-3990; *The World in Figures*.

Statistical Office of the United Nations, Publishing Service, New York, New York 10017 (800) 253-9646; *Statistical Yearbook*, and *Survey of Economic and Social Conditions in Africa*.

United Nations Economic Commission for Africa, Africa Hall, P.O. Box 3001, Addis Ababa, Ethiopia (Telephone Number in U.S. (800) 253-9646); *African Statistical Yearbook*.

BURUNDI - MARRIAGE RATES

Statistical Office of the United Nations, Publishing Service, New York, New York 10017 (800) 253-9646; *Demographic Yearbook*.

BURUNDI - MEAT PRODUCTION - See BURUNDI - LIVESTOCK AND POULTRY

BURUNDI - MERCHANT SHIPPING

G.K. Hall and Company, 70 Lincoln Street, Boston, Massachusetts 02111 (617) 423-3990; *The World in Figures.*

United Nations Economic Commission for Africa, Africa Hall, P.O. Box 3001, Addis Ababa, Ethiopia (Telephone Number in U.S. (800) 253-9646); *African Statistical Yearbook.*

BURUNDI - MILITARY

G.K. Hall and Company, 70 Lincoln Street, Boston, Massachusetts 02111 (617) 423-3990; *The World in Figures.*

The International Institute for Strategic Studies, 23 Tavistock Street, London WC2E 7NQ, England; *The Military Balance.*

U.S. Arms Control and Disarmament Agency, 320 Twenty-first Street, NW, Washington, D.C. 20451 (202) 647-8677; *World Military Expenditures and Arms Transfers.*

BURUNDI - MILK PRODUCTION - See BURUNDI - DAIRY PRODUCTS

BURUNDI - MILLET PRODUCTION - See BURUNDI - CROPS

BURUNDI - MINING AND MINERAL PRODUCTS

G.K. Hall and Company, 70 Lincoln Street, Boston, Massachusetts 02111 (617) 423-3990; *The World in Figures.*

United Nations Economic Commission for Africa, Africa Hall, P.O. Box 3001, Addis Ababa, Ethiopia (Telephone Number in U.S. (800) 253-9646); *African Statistical Yearbook.*

BURUNDI - MONEY EXCHANGE RATE

Euromonitor Publications Limited, 87-88 Turnmill Street, London EC1M 5QU, England; *International Marketing Data and Statistics.*

International Monetary Fund, 700 Nineteenth Street, NW, Washington, D.C. 20431 (202) 623-7000; *International Financial Statistics.*

Statistical Office of the United Nations, Publishing Service, New York, New York 10017 (800) 253-9646; *Statistical Yearbook.*

BURUNDI - MONEY RESERVES

Euromonitor Publications Limited, 87-88 Turnmill Street, London EC1M 5QU, England; *International Marketing Data and Statistics.*

BURUNDI - MONEY SUPPLY

African Development Bank, 01 BP 1387, Abidjan 01, Cote D'Ivoire; *Selected Statistics on Regional Member Countries.*

Euromonitor Publications Limited, 87-88 Turnmill Street, London EC1M 5QU, England; *International Marketing Data and Statistics.*

Federal Statistical Office, Gustav - Stresemann - Ring 11, D-6200 Wiesbaden, Germany; *Burundi.*

G.K. Hall and Company, 70 Lincoln Street, Boston, Massachusetts 02111 (617) 423-3990; *The World in Figures.*

International Monetary Fund, 700 Nineteenth Street, NW, Washington, D.C. 20431 (202) 623-7000; *International Financial Statistics.*

Statistical Office of the United Nations, Publishing Service, New York, New York 10017 (800) 253-9646; *Statistical Yearbook.*

BURUNDI - MOTION PICTURES

Statistical Office of the United Nations, Publishing Service, New York, New York 10017 (800) 253-9646; *Statistical Yearbook.*

BURUNDI - MOTOR VEHICLES IN USE

G.K. Hall and Company, 70 Lincoln Street, Boston, Massachusetts 02111 (617) 423-3990; *The World in Figures.*

Statistical Office of the United Nations, Publishing Service, New York, New York 10017 (800) 253-9646; *Statistical Yearbook,* and *Survey of Economic and Social Conditions in Africa.*

Times Books, 201 East 50th Street, New York, New York 10022 (212) 751-2600; *The Economist Book of Vital World Statistics.*

BURUNDI - MUSEUMS

United Nations Educational, Scientific and Cultural Organization (UNESCO), 7 Place de Fontenoy, F-75700 Paris, France; *Statistical Yearbook.*

BURUNDI - NATALITY - See BURUNDI - BIRTH RATE
BURUNDI - NATIONAL ACCOUNTS

African Development Bank, 01 BP 1387, Abidjan 01, Cote D'Ivoire; *Selected Statistics on Regional Member Countries.*

Federal Statistical Office, Gustav - Stresemann - Ring 11, D-6200 Wiesbaden, Germany; *Burundi.*

Statistical Office of the United Nations, Publishing Service, New York, New York 10017 (800) 253-9646; *National Accounts Statistics,* and *Statistical Yearbook.*

United Nations Economic Commission for Africa, Africa Hall, P.O. Box 3001, Addis Ababa, Ethiopia (Telephone Number in U.S. (800) 253-9646); *African Statistical Yearbook.*

BURUNDI - NATIONAL INCOME

G.K. Hall and Company, 70 Lincoln Street, Boston, Massachusetts 02111 (617) 423-3990; *The World in Figures.*

Statistical Office of the United Nations, Publishing Service, New York, New York 10017 (800) 253-9646; *Statistical Yearbook.*

BURUNDI - NEWSPAPER PRODUCTION - See BURUNDI - FORESTRY AND FOREST PRODUCTS

BURUNDI - OCCUPATIONS - See BURUNDI - LABOR FORCE

BURUNDI - PATENTS

Statistical Office of the United Nations, Publishing Service, New York, New York 10017 (800) 253-9646; *Statistical Yearbook.*

U.S. Arms Control and Disarmament Agency, 320 Twenty-first Street, NW, Washington, D.C. 20451 (202) 647-8677; *World Military Expenditures and Arms Transfers.*

BURUNDI - PERIODICALS

United Nations Educational, Scientific and Cultural Organization (UNESCO), 7 Place de Fontenoy, F-75700 Paris, France (Telephone Number in U.S. (212) 963-5981); *Statistical Yearbook.*

BURUNDI - PESTICIDE USE

Food and Agricultural Organization of the United Nations (FAO) Via delle Terme di Caracalla, 00100 Rome, Italy (Telephone Number in U.S. (202) 653-2400); *The State of Food and Agriculture.*

BURUNDI - PETROLEUM INDUSTRY

Food and Agricultural Organization of the United Nations (FAO) Via delle Terme di Caracalla, 00100 Rome, Italy (Telephone Number in U.S. (202) 653-2400); *The State of Food and Agriculture.*

G.K. Hall and Company, 70 Lincoln Street, Boston, Massachusetts 02111 (617) 423-3990; *The World in Figures.*

BURUNDI - PIGS - See BURUNDI - LIVESTOCK AND POULTRY

BURUNDI - POPULATION

African Development Bank, 01 BP 1387, Abidjan 01, Cote D'Ivoire; *Selected Statistics on Regional Member Countries.*

The Economist Intelligence Unit, 111 West 57th Street, New York, New York 10019 (800) 938-4685; *The World Market Atlas.*

Euromonitor Publications Limited, 87-88 Turnmill Street, London EC1M 5QU, England; *International Marketing Data and Statistics.*

Federal Statistical Office, Gustav - Stresemann - Ring 11, D-6200 Wiesbaden, Germany; *Burundi.*

Food and Agricultural Organization of the United Nations (FAO), Via delle Terme di Caracalla, 00100 Rome, Italy (Telephone Number in U.S. (202) 653-2400); *Production Yearbook.*

G.K. Hall and Company, 70 Lincoln Street, Boston, Massachusetts 02111 (617) 423-3990; *The World in Figures.*

International Labour Office, I.L.O. Publications, CH-1211, Geneva 22, Switzerland; *Yearbook of Labour Statistics.*

Statistical Office of the United Nations, Publishing Service, New York, New York 10017 (800) 253-9646; *Demographic Yearbook, Statistical Yearbook,* and *Survey of Economic and Social Conditions in Africa.*

Times Books, 201 East 50th Street, New York, New York 10022 (212) 751-2600; *The Economist Book of Vital World Statistics.*

U.S. Arms Control and Disarmament Agency, 320 Twenty-first Street, NW, Washington, D.C. 20451 (202) 647-8677; *World Military Expenditures and Arms Transfers.*

World Health Organization, Office of Publications, Avenue Appia, CH-1211 Geneva 27, Switzerland (Telephone Number in U.S. (518) 436-9686); *World Health Statistics Annual.*

BURUNDI - POTATO PRODUCTION - See BURUNDI - CROPS

BURUNDI - PRICES

Federal Statistical Office, Gustav - Stresemann - Ring 11, D-6200 Wiesbaden, Germany; *Burundi.*

Food and Agricultural Organization of the United Nations (FAO), Via delle Terme di Caracalla, 00100 Rome, Italy (Telephone Number in U.S. (202) 653-2400); *Production Yearbook,* and *The State of Food and Agriculture.*

G.K. Hall and Company, 70 Lincoln Street, Boston, Massachusetts 02111 (617) 423-3990; *The World in Figures.*

International Labour Office, I.L.O. Publications, CH-1211, Geneva 22, Switzerland; *Yearbook of Labour Statistics.*

International Monetary Fund, 700 Nineteenth Street, NW, Washington, D.C. 20431 (202) 623-7000; *International Financial Statistics.*

United Nations Economic Commission for Africa, Africa Hall, P.O. Box 3001, Addis Ababa, Ethiopia (Telephone Number in U.S. (800) 253-9646); *African Statistical Yearbook.*

BURUNDI - PRODUCTION

G.K. Hall and Company, 70 Lincoln Street, Boston, Massachusetts 02111 (617) 423-3990; *The World in Figures.*

BURUNDI - PRODUCTIVITY

Euromonitor Publications Limited, 87-88 Turnmill Street, London EC1M 5QU, England; *International Marketing Data and Statistics.*

BURUNDI - PUBLIC FINANCE

Federal Statistical Office, Gustav - Stresemann - Ring 11, D-6200 Wiesbaden, Germany; *Burundi.*

BURUNDI - RADIO BROADCASTING - See BURUNDI - BROADCASTING

BURUNDI - RAILWAYS

G.K. Hall and Company, 70 Lincoln Street, Boston, Massachusetts 02111 (617) 423-3990; *The World in Figures.*

United Nations Economic Commission for Africa, Africa Hall, P.O. Box 3001, Addis Ababa, Ethiopia (Telephone Number in U.S. (800) 253-9646); *African Statistical Yearbook.*

BURUNDI - RENT PRICES

International Labour Office, I.L.O. Publications, CH-1211, Geneva 22, Switzerland; *Yearbook of Labour Statistics.*

BURUNDI - RETAIL TRADE

G.K. Hall and Company, 70 Lincoln Street, Boston, Massachusetts 02111 (617) 423-3990; *The World in Figures.*

BURUNDI - RICE PRODUCTION - See BURUNDI - CROPS

BURUNDI - ROOT AND TUBER PRODUCTION - See BURUNDI - CROPS

BURUNDI - ROUNDWOOD PRODUCTION - See BURUNDI - FORESTRY AND FOREST PRODUCTS

BURUNDI - SAWNWOOD PRODUCTION - See BURUNDI - FORESTRY AND FOREST PRODUCTS

BURUNDI - SHEEP - See BURUNDI - LIVESTOCK AND POULTRY

BURUNDI - SOCIAL DATA

African Development Bank, 01 BP 1387, Abidjan 01, Cote D'Ivoire; *Selected Statistics on Regional Member Countries.*

G.K. Hall and Company, 70 Lincoln Street, Boston, Massachusetts 02111 (617) 423-3990; *The World in Figures.*

BURUNDI - STATE BUDGET REVENUE AND EXPENDITURES

Euromonitor Publications Limited, 87-88 Turnmill Street, London EC1M 5QU, England; *International Marketing Data and Statistics.*

BURUNDI - STOCKS - COMMODITY - MARKET PRICE - INDEX

Food and Agricultural Organization of the United Nations (FAO) Via delle Terme di Caracalla, 00100 Rome, Italy (Telephone Number in U.S. (202) 653-2400); *The State of Food and Agriculture.*

BURUNDI - TAXATION

G.K. Hall and Company, 70 Lincoln Street, Boston, Massachusetts 02111 (617) 423-3990; *The World in Figures.*

BURUNDI - TEA PRODUCTION - See BURUNDI - CROPS

BURUNDI - TELEPHONES IN USE

American Telephone and Telegraph Company, 26 Parsippany Road, Whippany, New Jersey 07981 (800) 338-4038; *The World's Telephones.*

G.K. Hall and Company, 70 Lincoln Street, Boston, Massachusetts 02111 (617) 423-3990; *The World in Figures.*

Statistical Office of the United Nations, Publishing Service, New York, New York 10017 (800) 253-9646; *Statistical Yearbook,*

BURUNDI - TELEVISION BROADCASTING - See BURUNDI - BROADCASTING

BURUNDI - TEXTILE INDUSTRY

G.K. Hall and Company, 70 Lincoln Street, Boston, Massachusetts 02111 (617) 423-3990; *The World in Figures.*

BURUNDI - THEATRE

United Nations Educational, Scientific and Cultural Organization (UNESCO), 7 Place de Fontenoy, F-75700 Paris, France (Telephone Number in U.S. (212) 963-5981); *Statistical Yearbook.*

BURUNDI - TIN PRODUCTION - See BURUNDI - MINING AND MINERAL PRODUCTS

BURUNDI - TOBACCO PRODUCTION

Statistical Office of the United Nations, Publishing Service, New York, New York 10017 (800) 253-9646; *Statistical Yearbook.*

BURUNDI - TOURISM

Federal Statistical Office, Gustav - Stresemann - Ring 11, D-6200 Wiesbaden, Germany; *Burundi.*

G.K. Hall and Company, 70 Lincoln Street, Boston, Massachusetts 02111 (617) 423-3990; *The World in Figures.*

Statistical Office of the United Nations, Publishing Service, New York, New York 10017 (800) 253-9646; *Statistical Yearbook.*

Times Books, 201 East 50th Street, New York, New York 10022 (212) 751-2600; *The Economist Book of Vital World Statistics.*

United Nations Economic Commission for Africa, Africa Hall, P.O. Box 3001, Addis Ababa, Ethiopia (Telephone Number in U.S. (800) 253-9646); *African Statistical Yearbook.*

World Tourism Organization, Calle Capitan Haya 42, E-28020 Madrid, Spain; *Yearbook of Tourism Statistics.*

BURUNDI - TRACTORS IN USE

Statistical Office of the United Nations, Publishing Service, New York, New York 10017 (800) 253-9646; *Statistical Yearbook.*

BURUNDI - TRADE - See BURUNDI - FOREIGN TRADE

BURUNDI - TRADEMARKS AND SERVICE MARKS

Statistical Office of the United Nations, Publishing Service, New York, New York 10017 (800) 253-9646; *Statistical Yearbook.*

U.S. Arms Control and Disarmament Agency, 320 Twenty-first Street, NW, Washington, D.C. 20451 (202) 647-8677; *World Military Expenditures and Arms Transfers.*

BURUNDI - TRANSPORTATION AND COMMUNICATIONS

Federal Statistical Office, Gustav - Stresemann - Ring 11, D-6200 Wiesbaden, Germany; *Burundi.*

G.K. Hall and Company, 70 Lincoln Street, Boston, Massachusetts 02111 (617) 423-3990; *The World in Figures.*

United Nations Economic Commission for Africa, Africa Hall, P.O. Box 3001, Addis Ababa, Ethiopia (Telephone Number in U.S. (800) 253-9646); *African Statistical Yearbook.*

BURUNDI - UNEMPLOYMENT

Euromonitor Publications Limited, 87-88 Turnmill Street, London EC1M 5QU, England; *International Marketing Data and Statistics.*

International Labour Office, I.L.O. Publications, CH-1211, Geneva 22, Switzerland; *Yearbook of Labour Statistics.*

BURUNDI - VITAL STATISTICS

Euromonitor Publications Limited, 87-88 Turnmill Street, London EC1M 5QU, England; *International Marketing Data and Statistics.*

G.K. Hall and Company, 70 Lincoln Street, Boston, Massachusetts 02111 (617) 423-3990; *The World in Figures.*

Statistical Office of the United Nations, Publishing Service, New York, New York 10017 (800) 253-9646; *Statistical Yearbook.*

World Health Organization, Office of Publications, Avenue Appia, CH-1211 Geneva 27, Switzerland (Telephone Number in U.S. (518) 436-9686); *World Health Statistics Annual.*

BURUNDI - WAGES

Federal Statistical Office, Gustav - Stresemann - Ring 11, D-6200 Wiesbaden, Germany; *Burundi.*

G.K. Hall and Company, 70 Lincoln Street, Boston, Massachusetts 02111 (617) 423-3990; *The World in Figures.*

International Labour Office, I.L.O. Publications, CH-1211, Geneva 22, Switzerland; *Yearbook of Labour Statistics.*

Statistical Office of the United Nations, Publishing Service, New York, New York 10017 (800) 253-9646; *Statistical Yearbook.*

BURUNDI - WEATHER

G.K. Hall and Company, 70 Lincoln Street, Boston, Massachusetts 02111 (617) 423-3990; *The World in Figures.*

BURUNDI - WHEAT PRODUCTION - See BURUNDI - CROPS

BUSES AND BUS TRANSPORTATION - See also PASSENGER TRANSIT

BUSES AND BUS TRANSPORTATION

Eno Transportation Foundation, 44211 Statestone Court, Lansdowne, Virginia 22075 (703) 729-7200; *Transportation in America.*

U.S. Travel Data Center, Two Lafayette Center, 1133 21st Street, Washington, D.C. 20036 (202) 293-1040; *Impact of Travel on State Economies,* and *Economic Review of Travel in America.*

BUSES AND BUS TRANSPORTATION - FINANCES

American Bus Association, 1100 New York Avenue, NW, Washington, D.C. 20005 (202) 842-1645; *Annual Report,* and *Bus Facts.*

U.S. Interstate Commerce Commission, Twelfth Street and Constitution Avenue, NW, Washington, D.C. 20423 (202) 275-7119; *Transport Statistics in the United States.*

BUSES AND BUS TRANSPORTATION - INTERCITY OPERATIONS

American Bus Association, 1100 New York Avenue, NW, Washington, D.C. 20005 (202) 842-1645; *Bus Facts,* and *Annual Report.*

BUSES AND BUS TRANSPORTATION - PASSENGER TRAFFIC AND OUTLAYS

American Bus Association, 1100 New York Avenue, NW, Washington, D.C. 20005 (202) 842-1645; *Annual Report,* and *Bus Facts.*

Eno Transportation Foundation, 44211 Statestone Court, Lansdowne, Virginia 22075 (703) 729-7200; *Transportation in America.*

BUSES AND BUS TRANSPORTATION - PRODUCTION AND SALES

American Automobile Manufacturers Association, 1401 H Street, NW, Suite 900, Washington, D.C. 20005 (202) 326-5500; *Motor Vehicle Facts and Figures,* and *World Motor Vehicle Data.*

BUSES AND BUS TRANSPORTATION - RECEIPTS

American Bus Association, 1100 New York Avenue, NW, Washington, D.C. 20005 (202) 842-1645; *Bus Facts,* and *Annual Report.*

U.S. Interstate Commerce Commission, Twelfth Street and Constitution Avenue, NW, Washington, D.C. 20423 (202) 275-7119; *Transport Statistics in the United States.*

U.S. Travel Data Center, Two Lafayette Center, 1133 21st Street, NW, Washington, D.C. 20036 (202) 293-1040; *Economic Review of Travel in America.*

BUSINESS ENTERPRISE - See also Individual types of business and industry.

BUSINESS ENTERPRISE - BANKRUPTCIES FILED

Administrative Office of the United States Courts, United States Supreme Court Building, One Columbus Circle, NE, Washington, D.C. 20544 (202) 273-1120; *Annual Report of the Director,* and unpublished data.

BUSINESS ENTERPRISE - CAPITAL, FIXED BY INDUSTRY

U.S. Department of Commerce, Bureau of Economic Analysis, Fourteenth Street between Constitution Avenue and E Street, NW, Washington, D.C. 20230 (202) 606-9900; *Survey of Current Business.*

BUSINESS ENTERPRISE - CORPORATIONS - FOREIGN

Time Warner, 1675 Broadway, Rockefeller Center, New York, New York 10019 (212) 522-1212; *The Fortune Directories.*

U.S. Department of the Treasury, Internal Revenue Service, 111 Constitution Avenue, NW, Washington, D.C 20224 (202) 566-5000; *Statistics of Income Bulletin.*

BUSINESS ENTERPRISE - CORPORATIONS PHILANTHROPY

AAFRC Trust for Philanthropy, 25 West 43rd Street, Suite 820, New York, New York 10036 (212) 354-5799; *Giving U.S.A.*

The Conference Board, Incorporated, 845 Third Avenue, New York, New York 10022 (212) 759-0900; *Annual Survey of Corporate Contributions.*

BUSINESS ENTERPRISE - CORPORATIONS PROFITS AND SALES

Commodity Futures Trading Commission, 2033 K Street, NW, Washington, D.C. 20581 (202) 254-6387; *Annual Report.*

Forbes Incorporated, 60 Fifth Avenue, New York, New York 10011 212) 620-2200; *Forbes Annual Report on American Industry.*

Time Warner, 1675 Broadway, Rockefeller Center, New York, New York 10019 (212) 522-1212; *The Fortune Directories.*

U.S. Department of the Treasury, Internal Revenue Service, 1111 Constitution Avenue, NW, Washington, D.C. 20224 (202) 566-5000; *Statistics of Income Bulletin.*

BUSINESS ENTERPRISE - CORPORATIONS, PARTNERSHIPS, AND PROPRIETORSHIPS

U.S. Department of the Treasury, Internal Revenue Service, 1111 Constitution Avenue, NW, Washington, D.C. 20224 (202) 566-5000; *Statistics of Income, Partnership Returns, Statistics of Income Bulletin,* and unpublished data.

BUSINESS ENTERPRISE - CYCLES

U.S. Department of Commerce, Bureau of Economic Analysis, Fourteenth Street between Constitution Avenue and E Street, NW, Washington, D.C. 20230 (202) 606-9900; *Survey of Current Business.*

BUSINESS ENTERPRISE - DIVESTITURES

Securities Data Company, 1180 Raymond Boulevard, Newark, New Jersey 07102 (201) 622-3100; *Merger and Corporate Transactions Database*.

BUSINESS ENTERPRISE - ECONOMIC INDICATORS

U.S. Department of Commerce, Bureau of Economic Analysis, Fourteenth Street between Constitution Avenue and E Street, NW, Washington, D.C. 20230 (202) 606-9900; *Survey of Current Business*.

BUSINESS ENTERPRISE - EMPLOYEE STOCK OWNERSHIP PLANS

National Center for Employee Ownership, Inc., 2201 Broadway, Suite 807, Oakland, California 94612 (415) 272-9461; unpublished data.

BUSINESS ENTERPRISE - EMPLOYEES

Time Warner, 1675 Broadway, Rockefeller Center, New York, New York 10019 (212) 522-1212; *The Fortune Directories*.

U.S. Department of Commerce, Bureau of the Census, Suitland, Maryland 20233 (301) 763-4040; *County Business Patterns*.

BUSINESS ENTERPRISE - ESTABLISHMENTS

U.S. Department of Commerce, Bureau of the Census, Suitland, Maryland 20233 (301) 763-4040; *Census of Service Industries*, and *County Business Patterns*.

U.S. Department of the Treasury, Internal Revenue Service, 1111 Constitution Avenue, NW, Washington, D.C. 20224 (202) 566-5000; *Statistics of Income, Corporation Income Tax Returns*.

BUSINESS ENTERPRISE - EXPENDITURES - PLANT AND EQUIPMENT, NEW

U.S. Department of Commerce, Bureau of the Census, Suitland, Maryland 20233 (301) 763-4040; *Plant and Equipment Expenditures and Plans*.

BUSINESS ENTERPRISE - EXPENDITURES - RESEARCH AND DEVELOPMENT

National Science Foundation, 4201 Wilson Boulevard, Arlington, Virginia 22230 (703) 306-1234; *National Patterns of Science and Technology Resources*.

BUSINESS ENTERPRISE - FAILURES AND LIABILITIES

Dun and Bradstreet, Incorporated, 3 Century Drive, Parsippany, New Jersey 07054 (212) 593-6800; *Business Failure Record, New Business Incorporations*, and *Monthly Failure Report*.

BUSINESS ENTERPRISE - FINANCES

Board of Governors of the Federal Reserve System, Twentieth Street and Constitution Avenue, NW, Washington, D.C. 20551 (202) 452-3000; *Federal Reserve Bulletin*, and *Balance Sheets for U.S. Economy*.

U.S. Department of Commerce, Bureau of Economic Analysis, Fourteenth Street between Constitution Avenue and E Street, NW, Washington, D.C. 20230 (202) 606-9900; *Survey of Current Business*, and *The National Income and Product Accounts of the U.S.*

U.S. Department of Commerce, Bureau of the Census, Suitland, Maryland 20233 (301) 763-4040; *Plant and Equipment Expenditures and Plans*, and *Quarterly Financial Report for Manufacturing, Mining and Trade Corporations*.

U.S. Department of the Treasury, Internal Revenue Service, 1111 Constitution Avenue, NW, Washington, D.C. 20244 (202) 566-5000; *Statistics of Income, Statistics of Income Bulletin, Statistics of Income, Partnership Returns*, various publications and unpublished data.

BUSINESS ENTERPRISE - FLOW OF FUNDS

Board of Governors of the Federal Reserve System, Twentieth Street and Constitution Avenue, NW, Washington, D.C. 20551 (202) 452-3000; *Annual Statistical Digest*.

BUSINESS ENTERPRISE - FOREIGN INVESTMENT IN THE UNITED STATES

U.S. Department of Commerce, Bureau of Economic Analysis, Fourteenth Street between Constitution Avenue and E Street, NW, Washington, D.C. 20230 (202) 606-9900; *Foreign Direct Investment in the United States, Operation of U.S. Affiliates of Foreign Companies*, and *Survey of Current Business*.

BUSINESS ENTERPRISE - FRANCHISED ESTABLISHMENTS

National Automobile Dealers Association, 8400 Westpark Drive, McLean, Virginia 22102 (703) 827-7407; *NADA Data*, annual.

International Franchise Association, 1350 New York Avenue, Suite 900, Washington, D.C. 20005 (202) 628-8000; *Franchising in the Economy*.

BUSINESS ENTERPRISE - INCORPORATIONS

Dun and Bradstreet Corporation, 299 Park Avenue, 24th Floor, New York, New York 10171 (212) 593-6800; *Business Failure Record, Monthly Failure Report*, and *New Business Incorporations*.

BUSINESS ENTERPRISE - LAGGING INDICATORS

U.S. Department of Commerce, Bureau of Economic Analysis, Fourteenth Street between Constitution Avenue and E Street, NW, Washington, D.C. 20230 (202) 606-9900; *Survey of Current Business*.

BUSINESS ENTERPRISE - LEADING INDICATORS

U.S. Department of Commerce, Bureau of Economic Analysis, Fourteenth Street between Constitution Avenue and E Street, NW, Washington, D.C. 20230 (202) 606-9900; *Survey of Current Business*.

BUSINESS ENTERPRISE - LEVERAGED BUY-OUTS

Securities Data Company, 1180 Raymond Boulevard, Newark, New Jersey 07102 (201) 622-3100; *Merger and Corporate Transactions Database*.

BUSINESS ENTERPRISE - LOANS TO MINORITY - OPERATED SMALL BUSINESSES

U.S. Small Business Administration, 409 Third Street, SW, Washington, D.C. 20416 (800) 368-5855; unpublished data.

BUSINESS ENTERPRISE - MERGERS AND ACQUISITIONS

Securities Data Company, 1180 Raymond Boulevard, Newark, New Jersey 07102 (201) 622-3100; *Merger and Corporate Transactions*

Database.

BUSINESS ENTERPRISE - MULTINATIONAL COMPANIES

Time Warner, 1675 Broadway, Rockefeller Center, New York, New York 10019 (212) 522-1212; *The Fortune Directories.*

U.S. Department of Commerce, Bureau of Economic Analysis, Fourteenth Street between Constitution Avenue and E Street, NW, Washington, D.C. 20230 (202) 606-9900; *Survey of Current Business.*

BUSINESS ENTERPRISE - NATIONAL INCOME - ORIGIN IN

U.S. Department of Commerce, Bureau of Economic Analysis, Fourteenth Street between Constitution Avenue and E Street, NW, Washington, D.C. 20230 (202) 606-9900; *The National Income and Product Accounts of the United States,* and *Survey of Current Business.*

BUSINESS ENTERPRISE - NEW PRODUCT INTRODUCTIONS

Marketing Intelligence Service Limited, 33 Academy Street, Naples, New York 14512 (716) 374-6326; *Product Alert Weekly.*

BUSINESS ENTERPRISE - PATENTS

U.S. Department of Commerce, Patent and Trademark Office, 2011 Crystal Drive, Arlington, Virginia 22202 (703) 305-8341; *Patenting Trends in the United States, State Country Report, Commissioner of Patents and Trademarks Annual Report,* and *Technology Assessment and Forecast Database.*

BUSINESS ENTERPRISE - PAYROLL

U.S. Department of Commerce, Bureau of the Census, Suitland, Maryland 20233 (301) 763-4040; *County Business Patterns.*

BUSINESS ENTERPRISE - POLLUTION ABATEMENT EXPENDITURES

U.S. Department of Commerce, Bureau of Economic Analysis, Fourteenth Street between Constitution Avenue and E Street, NW, Washington,D.C. 20230 (202) 606-9900; *Survey of Current Business.*

BUSINESS ENTERPRISE - PROFITS

Time Warner, 1675 Broadway, Rockefeller Center, New York, New York 10019 (212) 522-1212; *The Fortune Directories.*

U.S. Department of Commerce, Bureau of Economic Analysis, Fourteenth Street between Constitution Avenue and E Street, NW, Washington, D.C. 20230 (202) 606-9900; *The National Income and Product Accounts of the U.S.,* and *Survey of Current Business.*

U.S. Department of Commerce, Bureau of the Census, Suitland, Maryland 20233 (301) 763-4040; *Quarterly Financial Report for Manufacturing, Mining, and Trade Corporations.*

BUSINESS ENTERPRISE - SALES, SHIPMENTS AND RECEIPTS

Time Warner, 1675 Broadway, Rockefeller Center, New York, New York 10019 (212) 522-1212; *The Fortune Directories.*

U.S. Department of Commerce, Bureau of the Census, Suitland, Maryland 20233 (301) 763-4040; *Quarterly Financial Report for Manufacturing, Mining, and Trade Corporations.*

BUSINESS ENTERPRISE - SMALL BUSINESS

U.S. Small Business Administration, 409 Third Street, Washington, D.C. 20416 (800) 368-5855; unpublished data.

BUSINESS ENTERPRISE - VENTURE CAPITAL

Venture Economics Investor Services, 30 Pittsburgh Street, Boston, Massachusetts 02210 (617) 345-2824; *Venture Capital Journal.*

BUSINESS MANAGEMENT - DEGREES CONFERRED

U.S. Department of Education, 400 Maryland Avenue, SW, Washington, D.C. 20202 (202) 708-5366; *Digest of Education Statistics.*

BUSINESS MANAGEMENT - SALARY OFFERS

College Placement Council, 62 Highland Avenue, Bethlehem, Pennsylvania 18017 (212) 868-1421; *A Study of Beginning Offers.*

Northwestern University Placement Center, 633 Clark Street, Evanston, Illinois 60201 (708) 491-3741; *The Northwestern Lindquist-Endicott Report.*

BUSINESS SERVICES - CAPITAL

U.S. Department of Commerce, Bureau of Economic Analysis, Fourteenth Street between Constitution Avenue and E Street, NW, Washington, D.C. 20230 (202) 606-9900; *Survey of Current Business.*

BUSINESS SERVICES - EARNINGS

U.S. Department of Commerce, Bureau of the Census, Suitland, Maryland 20233 (301) 763-4040; *County Business Patterns,* and *Census of Service Industries.*

U.S. Department of Labor, Bureau of Labor Statistics, Two Massachusetts Avenue, NE, Washington, D.C. 20212 (202) 606-7828; *Employment and Earnings,* and Bulletins 2370 and 2429.

BUSINESS SERVICES - ESTABLISHMENTS

U.S. Department of Commerce, Bureau of the Census, Suitland, Maryland 20233 (301) 763-4040; *Census of Service Industries,* and *County Business Patterns.*

International Franchise Association, 1350 New York Avenue, Suite 900, Washington, D.C. 20005 (202) 628-8000; *Franchising in the Economy.*

BUSINESS SERVICES - EMPLOYEES

U.S. Department of Commerce, Bureau of Economic Analysis, Fourteenth Street between Constitution Avenue and E Street, NW, Washington, D.C. 20230 (202) 606-9900; *The National Income and Product Accounts of the United States,* and *Survey of Current Business.*

U.S. Department of Commerce, Bureau of the Census, Suitland, Maryland 20233 (301) 763-4040; *Census of Manufactures, Census of Service Industries, Annual Survey of Manufactures, Origin of Exports of Manufactured Products, County Business Patterns,* and unpublished data.

U.S. Department of Labor, Bureau of Labor Statistics, Two Massachusetts Avenue, NE, Washington, D.C. 20212 (202) 606-7828; *Employment and Earnings, Monthly Labor Review,* and Bulletins 2370 and 2429.

BUSINESS SERVICES - GROSS DOMESTIC PRODUCT

Fiber Economics Bureau, Inc., 101 Eisenhower Parkway, Roseland, New Jersey 07068 (201) 228-1107; *Textile Organon*.

U.S. Department of Commerce, Bureau of Economic Analysis, Fourteenth Street between Constitution Avenue and E Street, NW, Washington, D.C. 20230 (202) 606-9900; *Survey of Current Business*.

BUSINESS SERVICES - MERGERS AND ACQUISITIONS

Securities Data Company, 1180 Raymond Boulevard, Newark, New Jersey 07102 (201) 622-3100; *Merger and Corporate Transactions Database*.

BUSINESS SERVICES - OCCUPATIONAL SAFETY

U.S. Department of Labor, Bureau of Labor Statistics, Two Massachusetts Avenue, NE, Washington, D.C. 20212 (202) 606-7828; *Occupational Injuries and Illnesses in the United States by Industry*.

BUSINESS SERVICES - RECEIPTS

U.S. Department of Commerce, Bureau of the Census, Suitland, Maryland 20233 (301) 763-4040; *Current Business Reports, Service Annual Survey, Census of Service Industries*, and *County Business Patterns*.

International Franchise Association, 1350 New York Avenue, Suite 900, Washington, D.C. 20005 (202) 628-8000; *Franchising in the Economy*.

BUTTER

U.S. Department of Agriculture, Economic Research Service, Fourteenth Street and Independence Avenue, SW, Washington, D.C. 20250 (202) 219-1504; *Food Consumption, Prices, and Expenditures, Production of Manufactured Dairy Products*, and *Milk Production Disposition, and Income*.

BUTTERFISH

U.S. Department of Commerce, National Oceanic and Atmospheric Administration, National Marine Fisheries Service, 1335 East-West Highway, Silver Spring, Maryland 20910 (301) 427-2239; *Fisheries of the United States*.

BYELORUSSIA - See BELARUS

C

CABLE AND OTHER PAY TELEVISION SERVICES

A. C. Nielsen Company, Nielsen Plaza, Northbrook, Illinois 60062 (708) 498-6300; *Nielsen Station Index.*

Paul Kagan Associates, Incorporated, 126 Clock Tower Place, Carmel, California 93923 (408) 624-1536; *The Cable TV Financial Databook, The Kagan Census of Cable and Pay TV,* and *The Cable TV Investor.*

Warren Publishing, Incorporated, 2115 Ward Court, NW, Washington, D.C. 20037 (202) 872-9200; *Television and Cable Factbook.*

CABLE AND OTHER PAY TELEVISION SERVICES - ADVERTISING EXPENDITURES

McCann-Erickson, Incorporated 750 Third Avenue, New York, New York 10017 (212) 697-6000; compiled for Crain Communications, Incorporated, 740 North Rush Street, Chicago, Illinois 60611 (312) 649-5200; *Advertising Age.*

CABLE AND OTHER PAY TELEVISION SERVICES - RECEIPTS

U.S. Department of Commerce, Bureau of the Census, Suitland, Maryland 20233 (301) 763-4040; *Annual Survey of Communication Services.*

Veronis, Suhler and Associates, 350 Park Avenue, New York, New York 10022 (212) 935-4990; *Communications Industry Report.*

CABLE AND OTHER PAY TELEVISION SERVICES - VIEWING

Mediamark Research Incorporated, 708 Third Avenue, New York, New York 10017 (212) 599-0444; *Multimedia Audiences.*

Veronis, Suhler and Associates, 350 Park Avenue, New York, New York 10022 (212) 935-4990; *Communications Industry Report.*

CADMIUM

U.S. Department of the Interior, Bureau of Mines, 810 Seventh Street, NW, Washington, D.C. 20241 (202) 501-9649; *Annual Reports,* and *Minerals Commodity Summaries.*

CAFETERIAS - See EATING AND DRINKING PLACES

CALCIUM - AVAILABLE FOR CONSUMPTION

U.S. Department of Health and Human Services, National Center for Health Statistics, 3700 East-West Highway, Hyattsville, Maryland 20782 (301) 436-8500; *Vital and Health Statistics,* and unpublished data.

CALCIUM - CHLORIDE

U.S. Department of the Interior, Bureau of Mines, 810 Seventh Street, NW, Washington, D.C. 20241 (202) 501-9649; *Annual Reports,* and *Mineral Commodity Summaries.*

CALIFORNIA - See also STATE DATA (FOR INDIVIDUAL STATES)

California - Primary Statistics Sources

Department of Finance, 915 L Street, 8th Floor, State Government of California, Sacramento, California 95814 (916) 322-2263; *California Statistical Abstract.*

Pacific Data Resources, Post Office Box 1922, Santa Barbara, California 93116-1922 (800) 422-2546; *California Almanac.*

California - State Data Centers

State Census Data Center, Department of Finance, 915 L Street, Sacramento, California 95814, Ms. Linda Gage, Director (916) 322-4651.

Sacramento Area COG, 106 K Street, Suite 200, Sacramento, California 95814, Mr. Bob Faseler (916) 457-2264.

Association of Bay Area Governments, Metro Center, 8th and Oak Streets, Post Office Box 2050, Oakland, California 94604-2050, Ms. Patricia Perry (415) 464-7937.

Southern California Association of Governments, 818 West 7th Street, 12th Floor, Los Angeles, California 90017, Mr. Javier Minjares (213) 236-1800.

San Diego Association of Governments, First Federal Plaza, 401 B Street, Suite 800, San Diego, California 92101, Ms. Karen Lamphere (619) 236-5300.

State Data Center Program, University of California-Berkeley, 2538 Channing Way, Berkeley, California 94720, Ms. Ilona Einowski/Fred Gey (415) 642-6571.

Association of Monterey Bay Area Governments, 445 Reservation Road, Post Office Box 838, Marina, California 93933, Mr. Steve Williams (408) 883-3750.

CALISTHENICS

National Sporting Goods Organization, Lake Center Plaza Building, 1699 Wall Street, Mount Prospect, Illinois 60056 (708) 439-4000; *Sports Participation in 1992.*

CALVES

U.S. Department of Agriculture, Economic Research Service, Fourteenth Street and Independence Avenue, SW, Washington, D.C. 20250 (202) 219-1504; *Economic Indicators of the Farm Sector: National Financial Summary, Livestock and Meat Statistics,* and *Agricultural Outlook.*

U.S. Department of Agriculture, National Agricultural Statistics Service, Fourteenth Street and Independence Avenue, SW, Washington, D.C. 20250 (202) 219-1504; *Agricultural Statistics,* and *Meat Animals - Production, Disposition, and Income.*

Cambodia - National Statistical Office

Directorate of Statistics, Ministry of Planning, Phnom Penh, Cambodia.

Cambodia - Primary Statistic Sources

Institut National de la Statistique et des Recherches Economiques, Phnom-Penh, Cambodia; *Bulletin Mensuel Statistique.*

CAMBODIA - AGRICULTURE

Euromonitor Publications Limited, 87-88 Turnmill Street, London EC1M 5QU, England; *International Marketing Data and Statistics.*

Food and Agricultural Organization of the United Nations (FAO) Via delle Terme di Caracalla, 00100 Rome, Italy (Telephone Number in U.S. (202) 653-2400); *The State of Food and Agriculture.*

G.K. Hall and Company, 70 Lincoln Street, Boston, Massachusetts 02111 (617) 423-3990; *The World in Figures.*

Statistical Office of the United Nations, Publishing Service, New York, New York 10017 (800) 253-9646; *Statistical Yearbook,* and *Statistical Yearbook for Asia and the Pacific.*

Times Books, 201 East 50th Street, New York, New York 10022 (212) 751-2600; *The Economist Book of Vital World Statistics.*

CAMBODIA - AIRLINE SERVICE

The Economist Intelligence Unit (Asia) Limited, 10th Floor, Luk Kwok Centre, 72 Gloucester Road, Wanchai, Hong Kong (Phone Number in U.S. (800) 938-4685); *Asian Market Atlas.*

G.K. Hall and Company, 70 Lincoln Street, Boston, Massachusetts 02111 (617) 423-3990; *The World in Figures.*

Statistical Office of the United Nations, Publishing Service, New York, New York 10017 (800) 253-9646; *Statistical Yearbook.*

CAMBODIA - AREA AND DENSITY OF POPULATION

Euromonitor Publications Limited, 87-88 Turnmill Street, London EC1M 5QU, England; *International Marketing Data and Statistics.*

Food and Agricultural Organization of the United Nations (FAO) Via delle Terme di Caracalla, 00100 Rome, Italy (Telephone Number in U.S. (202) 653-2400); *The State of Food and Agriculture.*

G.K. Hall and Company, 70 Lincoln Street, Boston, Massachusetts 02111 (617) 423-3990; *The World in Figures.*

Statistical Office of the United Nations, Publishing Service, New York, New York 10017 (800) 253-9646; *Statistical Yearbook.*

Times Books, 201 East 50th Street, New York, New York 10022 (212) 751-2600; *The Economist Book of Vital World Statistics.*

CAMBODIA - ARMS EXPORTS AND IMPORTS

U.S. Arms Control and Disarmament Agency, 320 Twenty-first Street, NW, Washington, D.C. 20451 (202) 647-8677; *World Military Expenditures and Arms Transfers.*

CAMBODIA - BALANCE OF PAYMENTS

The Economist Intelligence Unit, 111 West 57th Street, New York, New York 10019 (800) 938-4685; *The World Market Atlas.*

G.K. Hall and Company, 70 Lincoln Street, Boston, Massachusetts 02111 (617) 423-3990; *The World in Figures.*

CAMBODIA - BANKING

G.K. Hall and Company, 70 Lincoln Street, Boston, Massachusetts 02111 (617) 423-3990; *The World in Figures.*

CAMBODIA - BEER PRODUCTION

Statistical Office of the United Nations, Publishing Service, New York, New York 10017 (800) 253-9646; *Statistical Yearbook.*

CAMBODIA - BIRTH RATE

The Economist Intelligence Unit (Asia) Limited, 10th Floor, Luk Kwok Centre, 72 Gloucester Road, Wanchai, Hong Kong (Phone Number in U.S. (800) 938-4685); *Asian Market Atlas.*

Statistical Office of the United Nations, Publishing Service, New York, New York 10017 (800) 253-9646; *Demographic Yearbook,* and *Statistical Yearbook.*

Times Books, 201 East 50th Street, New York, New York 10022 (212) 751-2600; *The Economist Book of Vital World Statistics.*

CAMBODIA - BONDS

G.K. Hall and Company, 70 Lincoln Street, Boston, Massachusetts 02111 (617) 423-3990; *The World in Figures.*

CAMBODIA - BOOK PRODUCTION

G.K. Hall and Company, 70 Lincoln Street, Boston, Massachusetts 02111 (617) 423-3990; *The World in Figures.*

CAMBODIA - BROADCASTING

Billboard Limited, P.O. Box 9027, 1006 AA Amsterdam, The Netherlands (Telephone Number in U.S. (212) 764-7300); *World Radio TV Handbook.*

G.K. Hall and Company, 70 Lincoln Street, Boston, Massachusetts 02111 (617) 423-3990; *The World in Figures.*

CAMBODIA - BUSINESS

G.K. Hall and Company, 70 Lincoln Street, Boston, Massachusetts 02111 (617) 423-3990; *The World in Figures.*

CAMBODIA - CALORIE SUPPLY

Food and Agricultural Organization of the United Nations (FAO) Via delle Terme di Caracalla, 00100 Rome, Italy (Telephone Number in U.S. (202) 653-2400); *The State of Food and Agriculture.*

CAMBODIA - CATTLE - See CAMBODIA - LIVESTOCK AND POULTRY

CAMBODIA - CEMENT PRODUCTION - See CAMBODIA - MINING AND MINERAL PRODUCTS

CAMBODIA - CHEMICAL (ORGANIC) PRODUCTION - See CAMBODIA - MINING AND MINERAL PRODUCTS

CAMBODIA - CHICKENS - See CAMBODIA - LIVESTOCK AND POULTRY

CAMBODIA - CIGARETTE PRODUCTION - See CAMBODIA - TOBACCO PRODUCTION

CAMBODIA - CLASS STRUCTURE

G.K. Hall and Company, 70 Lincoln Street, Boston, Massachusetts 02111 (617) 423-3990; *The World in Figures.*

CAMBODIA - CLIMATE

G.K. Hall and Company, 70 Lincoln Street, Boston, Massachusetts 02111 (617) 423-3990; *The World in Figures.*

CAMBODIA - COAL PRODUCTION - See CAMBODIA - MINING AND MINERAL PRODUCTS

CAMBODIA - COMMUNICATIONS

G.K. Hall and Company, 70 Lincoln Street, Boston, Massachusetts 02111 (617) 423-3990; *The World in Figures.*

Statistical Office of the United Nations, Publishing Service, New York, New York 10017 (800) 253-9646; *Statistical Yearbook for Asia and the Pacific.*

CAMBODIA - CONSUMER PRICE INDEX

G.K. Hall and Company, 70 Lincoln Street, Boston, Massachusetts 02111 (617) 423-3990; *The World in Figures.*

Statistical Office of the United Nations, Publishing Service, New York, New York 10017 (800) 253-9646; *Statistical Yearbook.*

CAMBODIA - CONSUMPTION

G.K. Hall and Company, 70 Lincoln Street, Boston, Massachusetts 02111 (617) 423-3990; *The World in Figures.*

CAMBODIA - CORN PRODUCTION - See CAMBODIA - CROPS

CAMBODIA - CORPORATE TAXES - See CAMBODIA - TAXATION

CAMBODIA - COTTON PRODUCTION - See CAMBODIA - CROPS

CAMBODIA - CROPS

Food and Agricultural Organization of the United Nations (FAO) Via delle Terme di Caracalla, 00100 Rome, Italy (Telephone Number in U.S. (202) 653-2400); *Production Yearbook,* and *The State of Food and Agriculture.*

G.K. Hall and Company, 70 Lincoln Street, Boston, Massachusetts 02111 (617) 423-3990; *The World in Figures.*

Statistical Office of the United Nations, Publishing Service, New York, New York 10017 (800) 253-9646; *Statistical Yearbook.*

CAMBODIA - CUSTOMS DUTIES

G.K. Hall and Company, 70 Lincoln Street, Boston, Massachusetts 02111 (617) 423-3990; *The World in Figures.*

CAMBODIA - DAIRY PRODUCTS

Food and Agricultural Organization of the United Nations (FAO) Via delle Terme di Caracalla, 00100 Rome, Italy (Telephone Number in U.S. (202) 653-2400); *The State of Food and Agriculture.*

Statistical Office of the United Nations, Publishing Service, New York, New York 10017 (800) 253-9646; *Statistical Yearbook.*

CAMBODIA - DEATH RATES

The Economist Intelligence Unit (Asia) Limited, 10th Floor, Luk Kwok Centre, 72 Gloucester Road, Wanchai, Hong Kong (Phone Number in U.S. (800) 938-4685); *Asian Market Atlas.*

G.K. Hall and Company, 70 Lincoln Street, Boston, Massachusetts 02111 (617) 423-3990; *The World in Figures.*

Statistical Office of the United Nations, Publishing Service, New York, New York 10017 (800) 253-9646; *Statistical Yearbook.*

Times Books, 201 East 50th Street, New York, New York 10022 (212) 751-2600; *The Economist Book of Vital World Statistics.*

CAMBODIA - DEFENSE EXPENDITURES

G.K. Hall and Company, 70 Lincoln Street, Boston, Massachusetts 02111 (617) 423-3990; *The World in Figures.*

U.S. Arms Control and Disarmament Agency, 320 Twenty-first Street, NW, Washington, D.C. 20451 (202) 647-8677; *World Military Expenditures and Arms Transfers.*

CAMBODIA - DEMOGRAPHY

The Economist Intelligence Unit, 111 West 57th Street, New York, New York 10019 (800) 938-4685; *The World Market Atlas.*

The Economist Intelligence Unit (Asia) Limited, 10th Floor, Luk Kwok Centre, 72 Gloucester Road, Wanchai, Hong Kong (Phone Number in U.S. (800) 938-4685); *Asian Market Atlas.*

G.K. Hall and Company, 70 Lincoln Street, Boston, Massachusetts 02111 (617) 423-3990; *The World in Figures.*

CAMBODIA - DEVELOPMENT ASSISTANCE

G.K. Hall and Company, 70 Lincoln Street, Boston, Massachusetts 02111 (617) 423-3990; *The World in Figures.*

Statistical Office of the United Nations, Publishing Service, New York, New York 10017 (800) 253-9646; *Statistical Yearbook.*

CAMBODIA - DISEASE

G.K. Hall and Company, 70 Lincoln Street, Boston, Massachusetts 02111 (617) 423-3990; *The World in Figures.*

CAMBODIA - DIVORCE RATES

Statistical Office of the United Nations, Publishing Service, New York, New York 10017 (800) 253-9646; *Demographic Yearbook.*

CAMBODIA - DOMESTIC PRODUCT

G.K. Hall and Company, 70 Lincoln Street, Boston, Massachusetts 02111 (617) 423-3990; *The World in Figures.*

CAMBODIA - DUCKS - See CAMBODIA - LIVESTOCK AND POULTRY

CAMBODIA - ECONOMY

Euromonitor Publications Limited, 87-88 Turnmill Street, London EC1M 5QU, England; *International Marketing Data and Statistics.*

G.K. Hall and Company, 70 Lincoln Street, Boston, Massachusetts 02111 (617) 423-3990; *The World in Figures.*

CAMBODIA - EDUCATION

The Economist Intelligence Unit, 111 West 57th Street, New York, New York 10019 (800) 938-4685; *The World Market Atlas.*

The Economist Intelligence Unit (Asia) Limited, 10th Floor, Luk Kwok Centre, 72 Gloucester Road, Wanchai, Hong Kong (Phone Number in U.S. (800) 938-4685); *Asian Market Atlas.*

G.K. Hall and Company, 70 Lincoln Street, Boston, Massachusetts 02111 (617) 423-3990; *The World in Figures.*

Statistical Office of the United Nations, Publishing Service, New York, New York 10017 (800) 253-9646; *Statistical Yearbook for Asia and the Pacific.*

CAMBODIA - EGG PRODUCTION - See CAMBODIA - DAIRY PRODUCTS

CAMBODIA - ELECTRICITY

Statistical Office of the United Nations, Publishing Service, New York, New York 10017 (800) 253-9646; *Statistical Yearbook.*

CAMBODIA - EMPLOYMENT

Euromonitor Publications Limited, 87-88 Turnmill Street, London EC1M 5QU, England; *International Marketing Data and Statistics.*

CAMBODIA - ENERGY

Food and Agricultural Organization of the United Nations (FAO) Via delle Terme di Caracalla, 00100 Rome, Italy (Telephone Number in U.S. (202) 653-2400); *The State of Food and Agriculture.*

G.K. Hall and Company, 70 Lincoln Street, Boston, Massachusetts 02111 (617) 423-3990; *The World in Figures.*

Statistical Office of the United Nations, Publishing Service, New York, New York 10017 (800) 253-9646; *Energy Statistics Yearbook,* and *Statistical Yearbook.*

Times Books, 201 East 50th Street, New York, New York 10022 (212) 751-2600; *The Economist Book of Vital World Statistics.*

CAMBODIA - EXCHANGE RATES

The Economist Intelligence Unit (Asia) Limited, 10th Floor, Luk Kwok Centre, 72 Gloucester Road, Wanchai, Hong Kong (Phone Number in U.S. (800) 938-4685); *Asian Market Atlas.*

Euromonitor Publications Limited, 87-88 Turnmill Street, London EC1M 5QU, England; *International Marketing Data and Statistics.*

Statistical Office of the United Nations, Publishing Service, New York, New York 10017 (800) 253-9646; *Statistical Yearbook.*

CAMBODIA - EXPORTS

The Economist Intelligence Unit, 111 West 57th Street, New York, New York 10019 (800) 938-4685; *The World Market Atlas.*

The Economist Intelligence Unit (Asia) Limited, 10th Floor, Luk Kwok Centre, 72 Gloucester Road, Wanchai, Hong Kong (Phone Number in U.S. (800) 938-4685); *Asian Market Atlas.*

Euromonitor Publications Limited, 87-88 Turnmill Street, London EC1M 5QU, England; *International Marketing Data and Statistics.*

Food and Agricultural Organization of the United Nations (FAO) Via delle Terme di Caracalla, 00100 Rome, Italy (Telephone Number in U.S. (202) 653-2400); *The State of Food and Agriculture.*

G.K. Hall and Company, 70 Lincoln Street, Boston, Massachusetts 02111 (617) 423-3990; *The World in Figures.*

International Monetary Fund, 700 Nineteenth Street, NW, Washington, D.C. 20431 (202) 623-7000; *Direction of Trade Statistics.*

CAMBODIA - EXTERNAL TRADE

Food and Agricultural Organization of the United Nations (FAO) Via delle Terme di Caracalla, 00100 Rome, Italy (Telephone Number in U.S. (202) 653-2400); *The State of Food and Agriculture.*

G.K. Hall and Company, 70 Lincoln Street, Boston, Massachusetts 02111 (617) 423-3990; *The World in Figures.*

Statistical Office of the United Nations, Publishing Service, New York, New York 10017 (800) 253-9646; *Statistical Yearbook,* and *Statistical Yearbook for Asia and the Pacific.*

CAMBODIA - FARM CROPS - See CAMBODIA - CROPS

CAMBODIA - FEMALE WORKING POPULATION - See CAMBODIA - EMPLOYMENT

CAMBODIA - FERTILITY RATES

The Economist Intelligence Unit (Asia) Limited, 10th Floor, Luk Kwok Centre, 72 Gloucester Road, Wanchai, Hong Kong (Phone Number in U.S. (800) 938-4685); *Asian Market Atlas.*

Times Books, 201 East 50th Street, New York, New York 10022 (212) 751-2600; *The Economist Book of Vital World Statistics.*

CAMBODIA - FERTILIZER

Food and Agricultural Organization of the United Nations (FAO) Via delle Terme di Caracalla, 00100 Rome, Italy (Telephone Number in U.S. (202) 653-2400); *The State of Food and Agriculture.*

Statistical Office of the United Nations, Publishing Service, New York, New York 10017 (800) 253-9646; *Statistical Yearbook.*

CAMBODIA - FETAL MORTALITY

Statistical Office of the United Nations, Publishing Service, New York, New York 10017 (800) 253-9646; *Demographic Yearbook.*

CAMBODIA - FINANCE

G.K. Hall and Company, 70 Lincoln Street, Boston, Massachusetts 02111 (617) 423-3990; *The World in Figures.*

Statistical Office of the United Nations, Publishing Service, New York, New York 10017 (800) 253-9646; *Statistical Yearbook for Asia and the Pacific.*

CAMBODIA - FISHERIES

Food and Agricultural Organization of the United Nations (FAO) Via delle Terme di Caracalla, 00100 Rome, Italy (Telephone Number in U.S. (202) 653-2400); *The State of Food and Agriculture.*

Statistical Office of the United Nations, Publishing Service, New York, New York 10017 (800) 253-9646; *Statistical Yearbook.*

CAMBODIA - FOOD

Food and Agricultural Organization of the United Nations (FAO) Via delle Terme di Caracalla, 00100 Rome, Italy (Telephone Number in U.S. (202) 653-2400); *The State of Food and Agriculture.*

G.K. Hall and Company, 70 Lincoln Street, Boston, Massachusetts 02111 (617) 423-3990; *The World in Figures.*

Statistical Office of the United Nations, Publishing Service, New York, New York 10017 (800) 253-9646; *Statistical Yearbook for Asia and the Pacific.*

CAMBODIA - FOREIGN AID

G.K. Hall and Company, 70 Lincoln Street, Boston, Massachusetts 02111 (617) 423-3990; *The World in Figures.*

CAMBODIA - FOREIGN TRADE

The Economist Intelligence Unit (Asia) Limited, 10th Floor, Luk Kwok Centre, 72 Gloucester Road, Wanchai, Hong Kong (Phone Number in U.S. (800) 938-4685); *Asian Market Atlas.*

Euromonitor Publications Limited, 87-88 Turnmill Street, London EC1M 5QU, England; *International Marketing Data and Statistics.*

Food and Agricultural Organization of the United Nations (FAO) Via delle Terme di Caracalla, 00100 Rome, Italy (Telephone Number in U.S. (202) 653-2400); *The State of Food and Agriculture.*

G.K. Hall and Company, 70 Lincoln Street, Boston, Massachusetts 02111 (617) 423-3990; *The World in Figures.*

Statistical Office of the United Nations, Publishing Service, New York, New York 10017 (800) 253-9646; *International Trade Statistics Yearbook,* and *Statistical Yearbook.*

CAMBODIA - FORESTRY AND FOREST PRODUCTS

The Economist Intelligence Unit (Asia) Limited, 10th Floor, Luk Kwok Centre, 72 Gloucester Road, Wanchai, Hong Kong (Phone Number in U.S. (800) 938-4685); *Asian Market Atlas.*

Food and Agricultural Organization of the United Nations (FAO) Via delle Terme di Caracalla, 00100 Rome, Italy (Telephone Number in U.S. (202) 653-2400); *The State of Food and Agriculture,* and *Yearbook of Forest Products.*

G.K. Hall and Company, 70 Lincoln Street, Boston, Massachusetts 02111 (617) 423-3990; *The World in Figures.*

Statistical Office of the United Nations, Publishing Service, New York, New York 10017 (800) 253-9646; *Statistical Yearbook.*

United Nations Educational, Scientific and Cultural Organization (UNESCO), 7 Place de Fontenoy, F-75700 Paris, France (Telephone Number in U.S. (212) 963-5981); *Statistical Yearbook.*

CAMBODIA - GENERAL MORTALITY

Statistical Office of the United Nations, Publishing Service, New York, New York 10017 (800) 253-9646; *Demographic Yearbook.*

CAMBODIA - GOATS - See CAMBODIA - LIVESTOCK AND POULTRY

CAMBODIA - GOVERNMENT

G.K. Hall and Company, 70 Lincoln Street, Boston, Massachusetts 02111 (617) 423-3990; *The World in Figures.*

CAMBODIA - GRAIN PRODUCTION - See CAMBODIA - CROPS

CAMBODIA - GROSS DOMESTIC PRODUCT

The Economist Intelligence Unit, 111 West 57th Street, New York, New York 10019 (800) 938-4685; *The World Market Atlas.*

The Economist Intelligence Unit (Asia) Limited, 10th Floor, Luk Kwok Centre, 72 Gloucester Road, Wanchai, Hong Kong (Phone Number in U.S. (800) 938-4685); *Asian Market Atlas.*

Euromonitor Publications Limited, 87-88 Turnmill Street, London EC1M 5QU, England; *International Marketing Data and Statistics.*

G.K. Hall and Company, 70 Lincoln Street, Boston, Massachusetts 02111 (617) 423-3990; *The World in Figures.*

Statistical Office of the United Nations, Publishing Service, New York, New York 10017 (800) 253-9646; *Statistical Yearbook.*

Times Books, 201 East 50th Street, New York, New York 10022 (212) 751-2600; *The Economist Book of Vital World Statistics.*

CAMBODIA - GROSS NATIONAL PRODUCT

Euromonitor Publications Limited, 87-88 Turnmill Street, London EC1M 5QU, England; *International Marketing Data and Statistics.*

U.S. Arms Control and Disarmament Agency, 320 Twenty-first Street, NW, Washington, D.C. 20451 (202) 647-8677; *World Military Expenditures and Arms Transfers.*

CAMBODIA - GROUNDNUTS (IN SHELL) - See CAMBODIA - CROPS

CAMBODIA - HEALTH

The Economist Intelligence Unit (Asia) Limited, 10th Floor, Luk Kwok Centre, 72 Gloucester Road, Wanchai, Hong Kong (Phone Number in U.S. (800) 938-4685); *Asian Market Atlas.*

G.K. Hall and Company, 70 Lincoln Street, Boston, Massachusetts 02111 (617) 423-3990; *The World in Figures.*

Statistical Office of the United Nations, Publishing Service, New York, New York 10017 (800) 253-9646; *Statistical Yearbook.*

Times Books, 201 East 50th Street, New York, New York 10022 (212) 751-2600; *The Economist Book of Vital World Statistics.*

CAMBODIA - HIDE PRODUCTION

Food and Agricultural Organization of the United Nations (FAO), Via delle Terme di Caracalla, 00100 Rome, Italy (Telephone Number in U.S. (202) 653-2400); *Production Yearbook.*

CAMBODIA - HIGHWAYS

The Economist Intelligence Unit (Asia) Limited, 10th Floor, Luk Kwok Centre, 72 Gloucester Road, Wanchai, Hong Kong (Phone Number in U.S. (800) 938-4685); *Asian Market Atlas.*

G.K. Hall and Company, 70 Lincoln Street, Boston, Massachusetts 02111 (617) 423-3990; *The World in Figures.*

CAMBODIA - HORSES - See CAMBODIA - LIVESTOCK AND POULTRY

CAMBODIA - HOURS OF WORK - See CAMBODIA - EMPLOYMENT

CAMBODIA - ILLITERATE POPULATION

The Economist Intelligence Unit, 111 West 57th Street, New York, New York 10019 (800) 938-4685; *The World Market Atlas.*

G.K. Hall and Company, 70 Lincoln Street, Boston, Massachusetts 02111 (617) 423-3990; *The World in Figures.*

United Nations Educational, Scientific and Cultural Organization (UNESCO), 7 Place de Fontenoy, F-75700 Paris, France (Telephone Number in U.S. (212) 963-5981); *Statistical Yearbook.*

CAMBODIA - IMPORTS

The Economist Intelligence Unit, 111 West 57th Street, New York, New York 10019 (800) 938-4685; *The World Market Atlas.*

The Economist Intelligence Unit (Asia) Limited, 10th Floor, Luk Kwok Centre, 72 Gloucester Road, Wanchai, Hong Kong (Phone Number in U.S. (800) 938-4685); *Asian Market Atlas.*

Euromonitor Publications Limited, 87-88 Turnmill Street, London EC1M 5QU, England; *International Marketing Data and Statistics.*

Food and Agricultural Organization of the United Nations (FAO) Via delle Terme di Caracalla, 00100 Rome, Italy (Telephone Number in U.S. (202) 653-2400); *The State of Food and Agriculture.*

G.K. Hall and Company, 70 Lincoln Street, Boston, Massachusetts 02111 (617) 423-3990; *The World in Figures.*

International Monetary Fund, 700 Nineteenth Street, NW, Washington, D.C. 20431 (202) 623-7000; *Direction of Trade Statistics.*

CAMBODIA - INDUSTRY

Euromonitor Publications Limited, 87-88 Turnmill Street, London EC1M 5QU, England; *International Marketing Data and Statistics.*

G.K. Hall and Company, 70 Lincoln Street, Boston, Massachusetts 02111 (617) 423-3990; *The World in Figures.*

Statistical Office of the United Nations, Publishing Service, New York, New York 10017 (800) 253-9646; *Statistical Yearbook for Asia and the Pacific.*

Times Books, 201 East 50th Street, New York, New York 10022 (212) 751-2600; *The Economist Book of Vital World Statistics.*

CAMBODIA - INFANT AND MATERNAL MORTALITY

The Economist Intelligence Unit (Asia) Limited, 10th Floor, Luk Kwok Centre, 72 Gloucester Road, Wanchai, Hong Kong (Phone Number in U.S. (800) 938-4685); *Asian Market Atlas.*

Statistical Office of the United Nations, Publishing Service, New York, New York 10017 (800) 253-9646; *Demographic Yearbook,* and *Statistical Yearbook.*

Times Books, 201 East 50th Street, New York, New York 10022 (212) 751-2600; *The Economist Book of Vital World Statistics.*

CAMBODIA - INTERNAL TRADE

Statistical Office of the United Nations, Publishing Service, New York, New York 10017 (800) 253-9646; *Statistical Yearbook for Asia and the Pacific.*

CAMBODIA - IRRIGATION

Euromonitor Publications Limited, 87-88 Turnmill Street, London EC1M 5QU, England; *International Marketing Data and Statistics.*

CAMBODIA - JUTE PRODUCTION - See CAMBODIA - CROPS

CAMBODIA - LABOR FORCE

The Economist Intelligence Unit (Asia) Limited, 10th Floor, Luk Kwok Centre, 72 Gloucester Road, Wanchai, Hong Kong (Phone Number in U.S. (800) 938-4685); *Asian Market Atlas.*

Euromonitor Publications Limited, 87-88 Turnmill Street, London EC1M 5QU, England; *International Marketing Data and Statistics.*

Food and Agricultural Organization of the United Nations (FAO) Via delle Terme di Caracalla, 00100 Rome, Italy (Telephone Number in U.S. (202) 653-2400); *The State of Food and Agriculture.*

G.K. Hall and Company, 70 Lincoln Street, Boston, Massachusetts 02111 (617) 423-3990; *The World in Figures.*

CAMBODIA - LAND USE

Euromonitor Publications Limited, 87-88 Turnmill Street, London EC1M 5QU, England; *International Marketing Data and Statistics.*

G.K. Hall and Company, 70 Lincoln Street, Boston, Massachusetts 02111 (617) 423-3990; *The World in Figures.*

CAMBODIA - LIFE EXPECTANCY

The Economist Intelligence Unit (Asia) Limited, 10th Floor, Luk Kwok Centre, 72 Gloucester Road, Wanchai, Hong Kong (Phone Number in U.S. (800) 938-4685); *Asian Market Atlas.*

CAMBODIA - LIVESTOCK AND POULTRY

Euromonitor Publications Limited, 87-88 Turnmill Street, London EC1M 5QU, England; *International Marketing Data and Statistics.*

Food and Agricultural Organization of the United Nations (FAO) Via delle Terme di Caracalla, 00100 Rome, Italy (Telephone Number in U.S. (202) 653-2400); *Production Yearbook,* and *The State of Food and Agriculture.*

G.K. Hall and Company, 70 Lincoln Street, Boston, Massachusetts 02111 (617) 423-3990; *The World in Figures.*

Statistical Office of the United Nations, Publishing Service, New York, New York 10017 (800) 253-9646; *Statistical Yearbook.*

CAMBODIA - LIVING LEVELS

G.K. Hall and Company, 70 Lincoln Street, Boston, Massachusetts 02111 (617) 423-3990; *The World in Figures.*

Times Books, 201 East 50th Street, New York, New York 10022 (212) 751-2600; *The Economist Book of Vital World Statistics.*

CAMBODIA - MAIL TRAFFIC

Statistical Office of the United Nations, Publishing Service, New York, New York 10017 (800) 253-9646; *Statistical Yearbook.*

CAMBODIA - MANPOWER

Statistical Office of the United Nations, Publishing Service, New York, New York 10017 (800) 253-9646; *Statistical Yearbook for Asia and the Pacific.*

CAMBODIA - MANUFACTURING

G.K. Hall and Company, 70 Lincoln Street, Boston, Massachusetts 02111 (617) 423-3990; *The World in Figures.*

CAMBODIA - MARRIAGE RATES

Statistical Office of the United Nations, Publishing Service, New York, New York 10017 (800) 253-9646; *Demographic Yearbook.*

CAMBODIA - MEAT PRODUCTION - See CAMBODIA - LIVESTOCK AND POULTRY

CAMBODIA - MERCHANT SHIPPING

G.K. Hall and Company, 70 Lincoln Street, Boston, Massachusetts 02111 (617) 423-3990; *The World in Figures.*

Statistical Office of the United Nations, Publishing Service, New York, New York 10017 (800) 253-9646; *Statistical Yearbook.*

Times Books, 201 East 50th Street, New York, New York 10022 (212) 751-2600; *The Economist Book of Vital World Statistics.*

CAMBODIA - MILITARY

The Economist Intelligence Unit (Asia) Limited, 10th Floor, Luk Kwok Centre, 72 Gloucester Road, Wanchai, Hong Kong (Phone Number in U.S. (800) 938-4685); *Asian Market Atlas.*

G.K. Hall and Company, 70 Lincoln Street, Boston, Massachusetts 02111 (617) 423-3990; *The World in Figures.*

The International Institute for Strategic Studies, 23 Tavistock Street, London WC2E 7NQ, England; *The Military Balance.*

U.S. Arms Control and Disarmament Agency, 320 Twenty-first Street, NW, Washington, D.C. 20451 (202) 647-8677; *World Military Expenditures and Arms Transfers.*

CAMBODIA - MINING AND MINERAL PRODUCTS

G.K. Hall and Company, 70 Lincoln Street, Boston, Massachusetts 02111 (617) 423-3990; *The World in Figures.*

Organisation for Economic Cooperation and Development (OECD), 2 rue Andre-Pascal, 75 Paris 16, France (Telephone Number in U.S. (202) 785-6323); *OECD Economic Surveys: Cambodia.*

Statistical Office of the United Nations, Publishing Service, New York, New York 10017 (800) 253-9646; *Statistical Yearbook.*

CAMBODIA - MONEY AND CREDIT

Organisation for Economic Cooperation and Development (OECD), 2 rue Andre-Pascal, 75 Paris 16, France (Telephone Number in U.S. (202) 785-6323); *OECD Economic Surveys: Cambodia.*

CAMBODIA - MONEY EXCHANGE RATES

Euromonitor Publications Limited, 87-88 Turnmill Street, London EC1M 5QU, England; *International Marketing Data and Statistics.*

Statistical Office of the United Nations, Publishing Service, New York, New York 10017 (800) 253-9646; *Statistical Yearbook.*

CAMBODIA - MONEY RESERVES

Euromonitor Publications Limited, 87-88 Turnmill Street, London EC1M 5QU, England; *International Marketing Data and Statistics.*

CAMBODIA - MONEY SUPPLY

Euromonitor Publications Limited, 87-88 Turnmill Street, London EC1M 5QU, England; *International Marketing Data and Statistics.*

G.K. Hall and Company, 70 Lincoln Street, Boston, Massachusetts 02111 (617) 423-3990; *The World in Figures.*

CAMBODIA - MOTOR VEHICLES IN USE

G.K. Hall and Company, 70 Lincoln Street, Boston, Massachusetts 02111 (617) 423-3990; *The World in Figures.*

Statistical Office of the United Nations, Publishing Service, New York, New York 10017 (800) 253-9646; *Statistical Yearbook.*

Times Books, 201 East 50th Street, New York, New York 10022 (212) 751-2600; *The Economist Book of Vital World Statistics.*

CAMBODIA - NATALITY - See CAMBODIA - BIRTH RATE

CAMBODIA - NATIONAL ACCOUNTS

Statistical Office of the United Nations, Publishing Service, New York, New York 10017 (800) 253-9646; *National Accounts Statistics, Statistical Yearbook,* and *Statistical Yearbook for Asia and the Pacific.*

CAMBODIA - NATIONAL INCOME

G.K. Hall and Company, 70 Lincoln Street, Boston, Massachusetts 02111 (617) 423-3990; *The World in Figures.*

Statistical Office of the United Nations, Publishing Service, New York, New York 10017 (800) 253-9646; *Statistical Yearbook.*

CAMBODIA - NATIONAL PRODUCT

Statistical Office of the United Nations, Publishing Service, New York, New York 10017 (800) 253-9646; *Statistical Yearbook.*

CAMBODIA - NEWSPAPER PRODUCTION - See CAMBODIA - FORESTRY AND FOREST PRODUCTS

CAMBODIA - NEWSPRINT PRODUCTION AND CONSUMPTION - See CAMBODIA - FORESTRY AND FOREST PRODUCTS

CAMBODIA - OCCUPATIONS - See CAMBODIA - LABOR FORCE

CAMBODIA - PAPER PRODUCTION AND CONSUMPTION - See CAMBODIA - FORESTRY AND FOREST PRODUCTS

CAMBODIA - PATENTS

Statistical Office of the United Nations, Publishing Service, New York, New York 10017 (800) 253-9646; *Statistical Yearbook.*

CAMBODIA - PESTICIDE USE

Food and Agricultural Organization of the United Nations (FAO) Via delle Terme di Caracalla, 00100 Rome, Italy (Telephone Number in U.S. (202) 653-2400); *The State of Food and Agriculture.*

CAMBODIA - PETROLEUM INDUSTRY

Food and Agricultural Organization of the United Nations (FAO) Via delle Terme di Caracalla, 00100 Rome, Italy (Telephone Number in U.S. (202) 653-2400); *The State of Food and Agriculture.*

G.K. Hall and Company, 70 Lincoln Street, Boston, Massachusetts 02111 (617) 423-3990; *The World in Figures.*

Statistical Office of the United Nations, Publishing Service, New York, New York 10017 (800) 253-9646; *Statistical Yearbook.*

CAMBODIA - PIGS - See CAMBODIA - LIVESTOCK AND POULTRY

CAMBODIA - POPULATION

The Economist Intelligence Unit, 111 West 57th Street, New York, New York 10019 (800) 938-4685; *The World Market Atlas.*

The Economist Intelligence Unit (Asia) Limited, 10th Floor, Luk Kwok Centre, 72 Gloucester Road, Wanchai, Hong Kong (Phone Number in U.S. (800) 938-4685); *Asian Market Atlas.*

Euromonitor Publications Limited, 87-88 Turnmill Street, London EC1M 5QU, England; *International Marketing Data and Statistics.*

G.K. Hall and Company, 70 Lincoln Street, Boston, Massachusetts 02111 (617) 423-3990; *The World in Figures.*

Statistical Office of the United Nations, Publishing Service, New York, New York 10017 (800) 253-9646; *Demographic Yearbook, Statistical Yearbook,* and *Statistical Yearbook for Asia and the Pacific.*

Times Books, 201 East 50th Street, New York, New York 10022 (212) 751-2600; *The Economist Book of Vital World Statistics.*

U.S. Arms Control and Disarmament Agency, 320 Twenty-first Street, NW, Washington, D.C. 20451 (202) 647-8677; *World Military Expenditures and Arms Transfers.*

World Health Organization, Office of Publications, Avenue Appia, CH-1211 Geneva 27, Switzerland (Telephone Number in U.S. (518) 436-9686); *World Health Statistics Annual.*

CAMBODIA - POULTRY - See CAMBODIA - LIVESTOCK AND POULTRY

CAMBODIA - PRICES

Food and Agricultural Organization of the United Nations (FAO) Via delle Terme di Caracalla, 00100 Rome, Italy (Telephone Number in U.S. (202) 653-2400); *The State of Food and Agriculture.*

G.K. Hall and Company, 70 Lincoln Street, Boston, Massachusetts 02111 (617) 423-3990; *The World in Figures.*

CAMBODIA - PRINTING AND WRITING PAPER - See CAMBODIA - FORESTRY AND FOREST PRODUCTS

CAMBODIA - PRODUCTION

G.K. Hall and Company, 70 Lincoln Street, Boston, Massachusetts 02111 (617) 423-3990; *The World in Figures.*

CAMBODIA - PRODUCTIVITY

Euromonitor Publications Limited, 87-88 Turnmill Street, London EC1M 5QU, England; *International Marketing Data and Statistics.*

CAMBODIA - RADIO

The Economist Intelligence Unit (Asia) Limited, 10th Floor, Luk Kwok Centre, 72 Gloucester Road, Wanchai, Hong Kong (Phone Number in U.S. (800) 938-4685); *Asian Market Atlas.*

CAMBODIA - RAILWAYS

G.K. Hall and Company, 70 Lincoln Street, Boston, Massachusetts 02111 (617) 423-3990; *The World in Figures.*

Jane's Information Group, Sentinel House, 163 Brighton Road, Coulsdon, Surrey CR5 2NH, England (Telephone Number in U.s. (703) 683-3700); *Jane's World Railways.*

Statistical Office of the United Nations, Publishing Service, New York, New York 10017 (800) 253-9646; *Statistical Yearbook.*

CAMBODIA - RETAIL TRADE

G.K. Hall and Company, 70 Lincoln Street, Boston, Massachusetts 02111 (617) 423-3990; *The World in Figures.*

CAMBODIA - RICE PRODUCTION - See CAMBODIA - CROPS

CAMBODIA - ROOT AND TUBER PRODUCTION - See CAMBODIA - CROPS

CAMBODIA - ROUNDWOOD PRODUCTION - See CAMBODIA - FORESTRY AND FOREST PRODUCTS

CAMBODIA - RUBBER PRODUCTION

Statistical Office of the United Nations, Publishing Service, New York, New York 10017 (800) 253-9646; *Statistical Yearbook.*

CAMBODIA - SALT PRODUCTION - See CAMBODIA - MINING AND MINERAL PRODUCTS

CAMBODIA - SAWNWOOD PRODUCTION - See CAMBODIA - FORESTRY AND FOREST PRODUCTS

CAMBODIA - SESAME SEED PRODUCTION - See CAMBODIA - CROPS

CAMBODIA - SHEEP - See CAMBODIA - LIVESTOCK AND POULTRY

CAMBODIA - SOCIAL DATA

G.K. Hall and Company, 70 Lincoln Street, Boston, Massachusetts 02111 (617) 423-3990; *The World in Figures.*

CAMBODIA - SOYBEANS PRODUCTION - See CAMBODIA - CROPS

CAMBODIA - STATE BUDGET REVENUE AND EXPENDITURES

Euromonitor Publications Limited, 87-88 Turnmill Street, London EC1M 5QU, England; *International Marketing Data and Statistics.*

CAMBODIA - STEEL - See CAMBODIA - MINING AND MINERAL PRODUCTS

CAMBODIA - STOCKS - COMMODITY - MARKET PRICE - INDEX

Food and Agricultural Organization of the United Nations (FAO) Via delle Terme di Caracalla, 00100 Rome, Italy (Telephone Number in U.S. (202) 653-2400); *The State of Food and Agriculture.*

CAMBODIA - TAXATION

G.K. Hall and Company, 70 Lincoln Street, Boston, Massachusetts 02111 (617) 423-3990; *The World in Figures.*

CAMBODIA - TELEPHONES IN USE

The Economist Intelligence Unit (Asia) Limited, 10th Floor, Luk Kwok Centre, 72 Gloucester Road, Wanchai, Hong Kong (Phone Number in U.S. (800) 938-4685); *Asian Market Atlas.*

Forest and Paper Association, 1250 Connecticut Avenue, NW, Washington, D.C. 20036 (202) 463-2455; *Wood Pulp and Fiber Statistics.*

G.K. Hall and Company, 70 Lincoln Street, Boston, Massachusetts 02111 (617) 423-3990; *The World in Figures.*

Statistical Office of the United Nations, Publishing Service, New York, New York 10017 (800) 253-9646; *Statistical Yearbook.*

CAMBODIA - TELEVISION

The Economist Intelligence Unit (Asia) Limited, 10th Floor, Luk Kwok Centre, 72 Gloucester Road, Wanchai, Hong Kong (Phone Number in U.S. (800) 938-4685); *Asian Market Atlas.*

CAMBODIA - TEXTILE INDUSTRY

G.K. Hall and Company, 70 Lincoln Street, Boston, Massachusetts 02111 (617) 423-3990; *The World in Figures.*

CAMBODIA - TOBACCO PRODUCTION

Statistical Office of the United Nations, Publishing Service, New York, New York 10017 (800) 253-9646; *Statistical Yearbook.*

CAMBODIA - TOURISM

G.K. Hall and Company, 70 Lincoln Street, Boston, Massachusetts 02111 (617) 423-3990; *The World in Figures.*

CAMBODIA - TRACTORS IN USE

Statistical Office of the United Nations, Publishing Service, New York, New York 10017 (800) 253-9646; *Statistical Yearbook.*

CAMBODIA - TRADE - See CAMBODIA - FOREIGN TRADE

CAMBODIA - TRADEMARKS AND SERVICE MARKS

Statistical Office of the United Nations, Publishing Service, New York, New York 10017 (800) 253-9646; *Statistical Yearbook.*

CAMBODIA - TRANSPORTATION AND COMMUNICATIONS

The Economist Intelligence Unit (Asia) Limited, 10th Floor, Luk Kwok Centre, 72 Gloucester Road, Wanchai, Hong Kong (Phone Number in U.S. (800) 938-4685); *Asian Market Atlas.*

G.K. Hall and Company, 70 Lincoln Street, Boston, Massachusetts 02111 (617) 423-3990; *The World in Figures.*

CAMBODIA - UNEMPLOYMENT

Euromonitor Publications Limited, 87-88 Turnmill Street, London EC1M 5QU, England; *International Marketing Data and Statistics.*

Organisation for Economic Cooperation and Development (OECD), 2 rue Andre-Pascal, 75 Paris 16, France (Telephone Number in U.S. (202) 785-6323); *OECD Economic Surveys: Cambodia.*

Statistical Office of the United Nations, Publishing Service, New York, New York 10017 (800) 253-9646; *Statistical Yearbook for Asia and the Pacific.*

CAMBODIA - VITAL STATISTICS

Euromonitor Publications Limited, 87-88 Turnmill Street, London EC1M 5QU, England; *International Marketing Data and Statistics.*

G.K. Hall and Company, 70 Lincoln Street, Boston, Massachusetts 02111 (617) 423-3990; *The World in Figures.*

Statistical Office of the United Nations, Publishing Service, New York, New York 10017 (800) 253-9646; *Statistical Yearbook.*

World Health Organization, Office of Publications, Avenue Appia, CH-1211 Geneva 27, Switzerland (Telephone Number in U.S. (518) 436-9686); *World Health Statistics Annual.*

CAMBODIA - WAGES

G.K. Hall and Company, 70 Lincoln Street, Boston, Massachusetts 02111 (617) 423-3990; *The World in Figures.*

Statistical Office of the United Nations, Publishing Service, New York, New York 10017 (800) 253-9646; *Statistical Yearbook for Asia and the Pacific.*

CAMBODIA - WEATHER

G.K. Hall and Company, 70 Lincoln Street, Boston, Massachusetts 02111 (617) 423-3990; *The World in Figures.*

CAMBODIA - YARN PRODUCTION

Statistical Office of the United Nations, Publishing Service, New York, New York 10017 (800) 253-9646; *Statistical Yearbook.*

Cameroon - National Statistical Office

Direction de la Statistique et de la Comptabilite Nationale, Ministere de Plan et de l'Amenagement du Territoire, Yaounde, Cameroon.

Cameroon - Primary Statistics Sources

Direction de la Statistique et de la Comptabilite Nationale (Department of Statistics and National Accounts), BP 660, Yaounde, Cameroon; *Bulletin mensuel de statistique* (Monthly Bulletin of Statistics), *Note Annuelle de Statistique* (Annual Statistical Note), and *Le Cameroon en Chiffres* (Cameroon in figures).

CAMEROON - AGRICULTURE

Euromonitor Publications Limited, 41 Russell Square, London EC1M 5QU, England; *International Marketing Data and Statistics.*

Facts on File, 460 Park Avenue South, New York, New York 10016 (800) 443-8323; *The New Book of World Rankings.*

Federal Statistical Office, Gustav - Stresemann - Ring 11, D-6200 Wiesbaden, Germany; *Kamerun.*

Food and Agricultural Organization of the United Nations (FAO) Via delle Terme di Caracalla, 00100 Rome, Italy (Telephone Number in U.S. (202) 653-2400); *Production Yearbook, The State of Food and Agriculture,* and *Trade Yearbook.*

G.K. Hall and Company, 70 Lincoln Street, Boston, Massachusetts 02111 (617) 423-3990; *The World in Figures.*

Statistical Office of the United Nations, Publishing Service, New York, New York 10017 (800) 253-9646; *Statistical Yearbook,* and *Survey of Economic and Social Conditions in Africa.*

Times Books, 201 East 50th Street, New York, New York 10022 (212) 751-2600; *The Economist Book of Vital World Statistics.*

United Nations Economic Commission for Africa, Africa Hall, P.O. Box 3001, Addis Ababa, Ethiopia (Telephone Number in U.S. (800) 253-9646); *African Statistical Yearbook.*

The World Bank, 1818 H Street, NW, Washington, D.C. 20433 (202) 477-1234; *World Tables.*

CAMEROON - AIRLINE SERVICE

Facts on File, 460 Park Avenue South, New York, New York 10016 (800) 443-8323; *The New Book of World Rankings.*

G.K. Hall and Company, 70 Lincoln Street, Boston, Massachusetts 02111 (617) 423-3990; *The World in Figures.*

International Civil Aviation Organization, 1000 Sherbrooke Street West, Suite 400, Montreal, Quebec, Canada H3A 2R2 (514) 285-8219; *Civil Aviation Statistics of the World.*

Statistical Office of the United Nations, Publishing Service, New York, New York 10017 (800) 253-9646; *Statistical Yearbook.*

United Nations Economic Commission for Africa, Africa Hall, P.O. Box 3001, Addis Ababa, Ethiopia (Telephone Number in U.S. (800) 253-9646); *African Statistical Yearbook.*

Times Books, 201 East 50th Street, New York, New York 10022 (212) 751-2600; *The Economist Book of Vital World Statistics.*

CAMEROON - ALUMINUM PRODUCTION AND CONSUMPTION - See CAMEROON - MINING AND MINERAL PRODUCTS

CAMEROON - ANIMAL HEALTH

Food and Agricultural Organization of the United Nations (FAO), Via delle Terme di Caracalla, 00100 Rome, Italy (Telephone Number in U.S. (202) 653-2400); *Animal Health Yearbook.*

CAMEROON - AREA AND DENSITY OF POPULATION

African Development Bank, 01 BP 1387, Abidjan 01, Cote D'Ivoire; *Selected Statistics on Regional Member Countries.*

Euromonitor Publications Limited, 87-88 Turnmill Street, London EC1M 5QU, England; *International Marketing Data and Statistics.*

Facts on File, 460 Park Avenue South, New York, New York 10016 (800) 443-8323; *The New Book of World Rankings.*

Federal Statistical Office, Gustav - Stresemann - Ring 11, D-6200 Wiesbaden, Germany; *Kamerun.*

Food and Agricultural Organization of the United Nations (FAO) Via delle Terme di Caracalla, 00100 Rome, Italy (Telephone Number in U.S. (202) 653-2400); *The State of Food and Agriculture.*

G.K. Hall and Company, 70 Lincoln Street, Boston, Massachusetts 02111 (617) 423-3990; *The World in Figures.*

Statistical Office of the United Nations, Publishing Service, New York, New York 10017 (800) 253-9646; *Statistical Yearbook,* and *Survey of Economic and Social Conditions in Africa.*

Times Books, 201 East 50th Street, New York, New York 10022 (212) 751-2600; *The Economist Book of Vital World Statistics.*

United Nations Educational, Scientific and Cultural Organization (UNESCO), 7 Place de Fontenoy, F-75700 Paris, France (Telephone Number in U.S. (212) 963-5981); *Statistical Yearbook.*

CAMEROON - ARMS EXPORTS AND IMPORTS

U.S. Arms Control and Disarmament Agency, 320 Twenty-first Street, NW, Washington, D.C. 20451 (202) 647-8677; *World Military Expenditures and Arms Transfers.*

CAMEROON - BALANCE OF PAYMENTS

African Development Bank, 01 BP 1387, Abidjan 01, Cote D'Ivoire; *Selected Statistics on Regional Member Countries.*

The Economist Intelligence Unit, 111 West 57th Street, New York, New York 10019 (800) 938-4685; *The World Market Atlas.*

Federal Statistical Office, Gustav - Stresemann - Ring 11, D-6200 Wiesbaden, Germany; *Kamerun.*

G.K. Hall and Company, 70 Lincoln Street, Boston, Massachusetts 02111 (617) 423-3990; *The World in Figures.*

Times Books, 201 East 50th Street, New York, New York 10022 (212) 751-2600; *The Economist Book of Vital World Statistics.*

United Nations Economic Commission for Africa, Africa Hall, P.O. Box 3001, Addis Ababa, Ethiopia (Telephone Number in U.S. (800) 253-9646); *African Statistical Yearbook.*

The World Bank, 1818 H Street, NW, Washington, D.C. 20433 (202) 477-1234; *World Tables.*

CAMEROON - BANKING

Facts on File, 460 Park Avenue South, New York, New York 10016 (800) 443-8323; *The New Book of World Rankings.*

G.K. Hall and Company, 70 Lincoln Street, Boston, Massachusetts 02111 (617) 423-3990; *The World in Figures.*

International Monetary Fund, 700 Nineteenth Street, NW, Washington, D.C. 20431 (202) 623-7000; *Government Finance Statistics Yearbook,* and *International Financial Statistics.*

United Nations Economic Commission for Africa, Africa Hall, P.O. Box 3001, Addis Ababa, Ethiopia (Telephone Number in U.S. (800) 253-9646); *African Statistical Yearbook.*

CAMEROON - BARLEY PRODUCTION - See CAMEROON - CROPS

CAMEROON - BEER PRODUCTION

Facts on File, 460 Park Avenue South, New York, New York 10016 (800) 443-8323; *The New Book of World Rankings.*

Statistical Office of the United Nations, Publishing Service, New York, New York 10017 (800) 253-9646; *Statistical Yearbook.*

CAMEROON - BIRTH RATES

Facts on File, 460 Park Avenue South, New York, New York 10016 (800) 443-8323; *The New Book of World Rankings.*

Statistical Office of the United Nations, Publishing Service, New York, New York 10017 (800) 253-9646; *Demographic Yearbook, Statistical Yearbook,* and *Survey of Economic and Social Conditions in Africa.*

Times Books, 201 East 50th Street, New York, New York 10022 (212) 751-2600; *The Economist Book of Vital World Statistics.*

The World Bank, 1818 H Street, NW, Washington, D.C. 20433 (202) 477-1234; *World Tables.*

CAMEROON - BONDS

G.K. Hall and Company, 70 Lincoln Street, Boston, Massachusetts 02111 (617) 423-3990; *The World in Figures.*

International Monetary Fund, 700 Nineteenth Street, NW, Washington, D.C. 20431 (202) 623-7000; *Government Finance Statistics Yearbook.*

CAMEROON - BOOK PRODUCTION

G.K. Hall and Company, 70 Lincoln Street, Boston, Massachusetts 02111 (617) 423-3990; *The World in Figures.*

United Nations Educational, Scientific and Cultural Organization (UNESCO), 7 Place de Fontenoy, F-75700 Paris, France (Telephone Number in U.S. (212) 963-5981); *Statistical Yearbook.*

CAMEROON - BROADCASTING

Billboard Limited, P.O. Box 9027, 1006 AA Amsterdam, The Netherlands (Telephone Number in U.S. (212) 764-7300); *World Radio TV Handbook.*

Facts on File, 460 Park Avenue South, New York, New York 10016 (800) 443-8323; *The New Book of World Rankings.*

G.K. Hall and Company, 70 Lincoln Street, Boston, Massachusetts 02111 (617) 423-3990; *The World in Figures.*

Times Books, 201 East 50th Street, New York, New York 10022 (212) 751-2600; *The Economist Book of Vital World Statistics.*

CAMEROON - BUILDING CONSTRUCTION - See CAMEROON - CONSTRUCTION INDUSTRY

CAMEROON - BUSINESS

G.K. Hall and Company, 70 Lincoln Street, Boston, Massachusetts 02111 (617) 423-3990; *The World in Figures.*

CAMEROON - BUSINESS AND PROFESSIONAL LICENSES

International Monetary Fund, 700 Nineteenth Street, NW, Washington, D.C. 20431 (202) 623-7000; *Government Finance Statistics Yearbook.*

CAMEROON - CACAO - See CAMEROON - CROPS

CAMEROON - CALORIE SUPPLY

African Development Bank, 01 BP 1387, Abidjan 01, Cote D'Ivoire; *Selected Statistics on Regional Member Countries.*

Food and Agricultural Organization of the United Nations (FAO) Via delle Terme di Caracalla, 00100 Rome, Italy (Telephone Number in U.S. (202) 653-2400); *The State of Food and Agriculture.*

CAMEROON - CAPITAL REVENUE

International Monetary Fund, 700 Nineteenth Street, NW, Washington, D.C. 20431 (202) 623-7000; *Government Finance Statistics Yearbook.*

CAMEROON - CATTLE - See CAMEROON - LIVESTOCK AND POULTRY

CAMEROON - CEMENT PRODUCTION - See CAMEROON - MINING AND MINERAL PRODUCTS

CAMEROON - CHEMICAL (ORGANIC) PRODUCTION - See CAMEROON - MINING AND MINERAL PRODUCTS

CAMEROON - CHICKENS - See CAMEROON - LIVESTOCK AND POULTRY

CAMEROON - CIGARETTE PRODUCTION - See CAMEROON - TOBACCO PRODUCTION

CAMEROON - CLASS STRUCTURE

G.K. Hall and Company, 70 Lincoln Street, Boston, Massachusetts 02111 (617) 423-3990; *The World in Figures.*

CAMEROON - CLIMATE

Facts on File, 460 Park Avenue South, New York, New York 10016 (800) 443-8323; *The New Book of World Rankings.*

G.K. Hall and Company, 70 Lincoln Street, Boston, Massachusetts 02111 (617) 423-3990; *The World in Figures.*

CAMEROON - COAL PRODUCTION - See CAMEROON - MINING AND MINERAL PRODUCTS

CAMEROON - COCOA (BEANS) PRODUCTION - See CAMEROON - CROPS

CAMEROON - COFFEE - See CAMEROON - CROPS

CAMEROON - COMMUNICATIONS

Federal Statistical Office, Gustav - Stresemann - Ring 11, D-6200 Wiesbaden, Germany; *Kamerun.*

G.K. Hall and Company, 70 Lincoln Street, Boston, Massachusetts 02111 (617) 423-3990; *The World in Figures.*

United Nations Economic Commission for Africa, Africa Hall, P.O. Box 3001, Addis Ababa, Ethiopia (Telephone Number in U.S. (800) 253-9646); *African Statistical Yearbook.*

CAMEROON - CONSTRUCTION INDUSTRY

Facts on File, 460 Park Avenue South, New York, New York 10016 (800) 443-8323; *The New Book of World Rankings.*

Statistical Office of the United Nations, Publishing Service, New York, New York 10017 (800) 253-9646; *Construction Statistics Yearbook,* and *Statistical Yearbook.*

United Nations Economic Commission for Africa, Africa Hall, P.O. Box 3001, Addis Ababa, Ethiopia (Telephone Number in U.S. (800) 253-9646); *African Statistical Yearbook.*

CAMEROON - CONSUMER PRICE INDEX

African Development Bank, 01 BP 1387, Abidjan 01, Cote D'Ivoire; *Selected Statistics on Regional Member Countries.*

Federal Statistical Office, Gustav - Stresemann - Ring 11, D-6200 Wiesbaden, Germany; *Kamerun.*

G.K. Hall and Company, 70 Lincoln Street, Boston, Massachusetts 02111 (617) 423-3990; *The World in Figures.*

Statistical Office of the United Nations, Publishing Service, New York, New York 10017 (800) 253-9646; *Statistical Yearbook,* and *Survey of Economic and Social Conditions in Africa.*

United Nations Economic Commission for Africa, Africa Hall, P.O. Box 3001, Addis Ababa, Ethiopia (Telephone Number in U.S. (800) 253-9646); *African Statistical Yearbook.*

CAMEROON - CONSUMER PRICES

Federal Statistical Office, Gustav - Stresemann - Ring 11, D-6200 Wiesbaden, Germany; *Kamerun.*

International Labour Office, I.L.O. Publications, CH-1211, Geneva 22, Switzerland; *Yearbook of Labour Statistics.*

International Monetary Fund, 700 Nineteenth Street, NW, Washington, D.C. 20431 (202) 623-7000; *International Financial Statistics.*

Times Books, 201 East 50th Street, New York, New York 10022 (212) 751-2600; *The Economist Book of Vital World Statistics.*

CAMEROON - CONSUMPTION

African Development Bank, 01 BP 1387, Abidjan 01, Cote D'Ivoire; *Selected Statistics on Regional Member Countries.*

G.K. Hall and Company, 70 Lincoln Street, Boston, Massachusetts 02111 (617) 423-3990; *The World in Figures.*

International Rubber Study Group, York House, Eighth Floor, Empire Way, Wembley, London HA9 0PA, England; *Rubber Statistical Bulletin.*

Statistical Office of the United Nations, Publishing Service, New York, New York 10017 (800) 253-9646; *Survey of Economic and Social Conditions in Africa.*

CAMEROON - COPPER PRODUCTION - See CAMEROON - MINING AND MINERAL PRODUCTS

CAMEROON - CORN PRODUCTION - See CAMEROON - CROPS

CAMEROON - CORPORATE TAXES - See CAMEROON - TAXATION

CAMEROON - COTTON PRODUCTION - See CAMEROON - CROPS

CAMEROON - CRIME

Yale University Press, Yale Station, New Haven, Connecticut 06520 (203) 432-0940; *Violence and Crime in Cross-National Perspective.*

CAMEROON - CROPS

Commodity Research Bureau, Incorporated, 75 Wall Street, New York, New York 10005 (212) 504-7754; *Commodity Year Book.*

Facts on File, 460 Park Avenue South, New York, New York 10016 (800) 443-8323; *The New Book of World Rankings.*

Food and Agricultural Organization of the United Nations (FAO) Via delle Terme di Caracalla, 00100 Rome, Italy (Telephone Number in U.S. (202) 653-2400); *The State of Food and Agriculture.*

G.K. Hall and Company, 70 Lincoln Street, Boston, Massachusetts 02111 (617) 423-3990; *The World in Figures.*

International Monetary Fund, 700 Nineteenth Street, NW, Washington, D.C. 20431 (202) 623-7000; *International Financial Statistics.*

Statistical Office of the United Nations, Publishing Service, New York, New York 10017 (800) 253-9646; *Statistical Yearbook.*

United Nations Economic Commission for Africa, Africa Hall, P.O. Box 3001, Addis Ababa, Ethiopia (Telephone Number in U.S. (800) 253-9646); *African Statistical Yearbook.*

CAMEROON - CUSTOMS DUTIES

G.K. Hall and Company, 70 Lincoln Street, Boston, Massachusetts 02111 (617) 423-3990; *The World in Figures.*

International Monetary Fund, 700 Nineteenth Street, NW, Washington, D.C. 20431 (202) 623-7000; *Government Finance Statistics Yearbook.*

CAMEROON - DAIRY PRODUCTS

Facts on File, 460 Park Avenue South, New York, New York 10016 (800) 443-8323; *The New Book of World Rankings.*

Food and Agricultural Organization of the United Nations (FAO) Via delle Terme di Caracalla, 00100 Rome, Italy (Telephone Number in U.S. (202) 653-2400); *The State of Food and Agriculture.*

Statistical Office of the United Nations, Publishing Service, New York, New York 10017 (800) 253-9646; *Statistical Yearbook.*

CAMEROON - DEATH RATES

G.K. Hall and Company, 70 Lincoln Street, Boston, Massachusetts 02111 (617) 423-3990; *The World in Figures.*

Statistical Office of the United Nations, Publishing Service, New York, New York 10017 (800) 253-9646; *Statistical Yearbook,* and *Survey of Economic and Social Conditions in Africa.*

Times Books, 201 East 50th Street, New York, New York 10022 (212) 751-2600; *The Economist Book of Vital World Statistics.*

CAMEROON - DEFENSE EXPENDITURES

G.K. Hall and Company, 70 Lincoln Street, Boston, Massachusetts 02111 (617) 423-3990; *The World in Figures.*

International Monetary Fund, 700 Nineteenth Street, NW, Washington, D.C. 20431 (202) 623-7000; *Government Finance Statistics Yearbook.*

U.S. Arms Control and Disarmament Agency, 320 Twenty-first Street, NW, Washington, D.C. 20451 (202) 647-8677; *World Military Expenditures and Arms Transfers.*

CAMEROON - DEMOGRAPHY

The Economist Intelligence Unit, 111 West 57th Street, New York, New York 10019 (800) 938-4685; *The World Market Atlas.*

Facts on File, 460 Park Avenue South, New York, New York 10016 (800) 443-8323; *The New Book of World Rankings.*

Federal Statistical Office, Gustav - Stresemann - Ring 11, D-6200 Wiesbaden, Germany; *Kamerun.*

G.K. Hall and Company, 70 Lincoln Street, Boston, Massachusetts 02111 (617) 423-3990; *The World in Figures.*

Statistical Office of the United Nations, Publishing Service, New York, New York 10017 (800) 253-9646; *Survey of Economic and Social Conditions in Africa.*

CAMEROON - DEVELOPMENT ASSISTANCE

G.K. Hall and Company, 70 Lincoln Street, Boston, Massachusetts 02111 (617) 423-3990; *The World in Figures.*

Statistical Office of the United Nations, Publishing Service, New York, New York 10017 (800) 253-9646; *Statistical Yearbook.*

CAMEROON - DIAMOND PRODUCTION - See CAMEROON - MINING AND MINERAL PRODUCTS

CAMEROON - DIVORCE RATES

Facts on File, 460 Park Avenue South, New York, New York 10016 (800) 443-8323; *The New Book of World Rankings.*

Statistical Office of the United Nations, Publishing Service, New York, New York 10017 (800) 253-9646; *Demographic Yearbook.*

CAMEROON - DISEASE

G.K. Hall and Company, 70 Lincoln Street, Boston, Massachusetts 02111 (617) 423-3990; *The World in Figures.*

CAMEROON - DOMESTIC PRODUCT

G.K. Hall and Company, 70 Lincoln Street, Boston, Massachusetts 02111 (617) 423-3990; *The World in Figures.*

CAMEROON - ECONOMY

African Development Bank, 01 BP 1387, Abidjan 01, Cote D'Ivoire; *Selected Statistics on Regional Member Countries.*

Euromonitor Publications Limited, 87-88 Turnmill Street, London EC1M 5QU, England; *International Marketing Data and Statistics.*

Facts on File, 460 Park Avenue South, New York, New York 10016 (800) 443-8323; *The New Book of World Rankings.*

Federal Statistical Office, Gustav - Stresemann - Ring 11, D-6200 Wiesbaden, Germany; *Kamerun.*

G.K. Hall and Company, 70 Lincoln Street, Boston, Massachusetts 02111 (617) 423-3990; *The World in Figures.*

Statistical Office of the United Nations, Publishing Service, New York, New York 10017 (800) 253-9646; *Foreign Trade Statistics for Africa.*

CAMEROON - ECONOMICALLY ACTIVE POPULATION

Euromonitor Publications Limited, 87-88 Turnmill Street, London EC1M 5QU, England; *International Marketing Data and Statistics.*

CAMEROON - EDUCATION

African Development Bank, 01 BP 1387, Abidjan 01, Cote D'Ivoire; *Selected Statistics on Regional Member Countries.*

The Economist Intelligence Unit, 111 West 57th Street, New York, New York 10019 (800) 938-4685; *The World Market Atlas.*

Facts on File, 460 Park Avenue South, New York, New York 10016 (800) 443-8323; *The New Book of World Rankings.*

Federal Statistical Office, Gustav - Stresemann - Ring 11, D-6200 Wiesbaden, Germany; *Kamerun.*

G.K. Hall and Company, 70 Lincoln Street, Boston, Massachusetts 02111 (617) 423-3990; *The World in Figures.*

International Monetary Fund, 700 Nineteenth Street, NW, Washington, D.C. 20431 (202) 623-7000; *Government Finance Statistics Yearbook.*

Statistical Office of the United Nations, Publishing Service, New York, New York 10017 (800) 253-9646; *Survey of Economic and Social Conditions in Africa.*

Times Books, 201 East 50th Street, New York, New York 10022 (212) 751-2600; *The Economist Book of Vital World Statistics.*

United Nations Economic Commission for Africa, Africa Hall, P.O. Box 3001, Addis Ababa, Ethiopia (Telephone Number in U.S. (800) 253-9646); *African Statistical Yearbook.*

United Nations Educational, Scientific and Cultural Organization (UNESCO), 7 Place de Fontenoy, F-75700 Paris, France (Telephone Number in U.S. (212) 963-5981); *Statistical Yearbook.*

The World Bank, 1818 H Street, NW, Washington, D.C. 20433 (202) 477-1234; *World Tables.*

CAMEROON - EGG PRODUCTION - See CAMEROON - DAIRY PRODUCTS

CAMEROON - ELECTRICITY

Facts on File, 460 Park Avenue South, New York, New York 10016 (800) 443-8323; *The New Book of World Rankings.*

Penn Well Publishing Company, 1421 South Sheridan Road, P.O. Box 1260, Tulsa, Oklahoma 74101 (800) 752-9764; *International Energy Statistics Sourcebook.*

Statistical Office of the United Nations, Publishing Service, New York, New York 10017 (800) 253-9646; *Statistical Yearbook,* and *Survey of Economic and Social Conditions in Africa.*

United Nations Economic Commission for Africa, Africa Hall, P.O. Box 3001, Addis Ababa, Ethiopia (Telephone Number in U.S. (800) 253-9646); *African Statistical Yearbook.*

Times Books, 201 East 50th Street, New York, New York 10022 (212) 751-2600; *The Economist Book of Vital World Statistics.*

CAMEROON - EMPLOYMENT

Euromonitor Publications Limited, 87-88 Turnmill Street, London EC1M 5QU, England; *International Marketing Data and Statistics.*

Facts on File, 460 Park Avenue South, New York, New York 10016 (800) 443-8323; *The New Book of World Rankings.*

Federal Statistical Office, Gustav - Stresemann - Ring 11, D-6200 Wiesbaden, Germany; *Kamerun.*

International Labour Office, I.L.O. Publications, CH-1211, Geneva 22, Switzerland; *Yearbook of Labour Statistics.*

Statistical Office of the United Nations, Publishing Service, New York, New York 10017 (800) 253-9646; *Statistical Yearbook,* and *Survey of Economic and Social Conditions in Africa.*

United Nations Economic Commission for Africa, Africa Hall, P.O. Box 3001, Addis Ababa, Ethiopia (Telephone Number in U.S. (800) 253-9646); *African Statistical Yearbook.*

CAMEROON - ENERGY

Facts on File, 460 Park Avenue South, New York, New York 10016 (800) 443-8323; *The New Book of World Rankings.*

Food and Agricultural Organization of the United Nations (FAO) Via delle Terme di Caracalla, 00100 Rome, Italy (Telephone Number in U.S. (202) 653-2400); *The State of Food and Agriculture.*

G.K. Hall and Company, 70 Lincoln Street, Boston, Massachusetts 02111 (617) 423-3990; *The World in Figures.*

Penn Well Publishing Company, 1421 South Sheridan Road, P.O. Box 1260, Tulsa, Oklahoma 74101 (800) 752-9764; *International Energy Statistics Sourcebook.*

Statistical Office of the United Nations, Publishing Service, New York, New York 10017 (800) 253-9646; *Statistical Yearbook.*

Times Books, 201 East 50th Street, New York, New York 10022 (212) 751-2600; *The Economist Book of Vital World Statistics.*

United Nations Economic Commission for Africa, Africa Hall, P.O. Box 3001, Addis Ababa, Ethiopia (Telephone Number in U.S. (800) 253-9646); *African Statistical Yearbook.*

CAMEROON - EXCHANGE RATES

African Development Bank, 01 BP 1387, Abidjan 01, Cote D'Ivoire; *Selected Statistics on Regional Member Countries.*

Euromonitor Publications Limited, 87-88 Turnmill Street, London EC1M 5QU, England; *International Marketing Data and Statistics.*

International Civil Aviation Organization, 1000 Sherbrooke Street West, Suite 400, Montreal, Quebec, Canada H3A 2R2 (514) 285-8219; *Civil Aviation Statistics of the World.*

International Monetary Fund, 700 Nineteenth Street, NW, Washington, D.C. 20431 (202) 623-7000; *International Financial Statistics.*

Statistical Office of the United Nations, Publishing Service, New York, New York 10017 (800) 253-9646; *Foreign Trade Statistics for Africa.*

CAMEROON - EXCISE TAXES - See CAMEROON - TAXATION

CAMEROON - EXPORTS

African Development Bank, 01 BP 1387, Abidjan 01, Cote D'Ivoire; *Selected Statistics on Regional Member Countries.*

The Economist Intelligence Unit, 111 West 57th Street, New York, New York 10019 (800) 938-4685; *The World Market Atlas.*

Euromonitor Publications Limited, 87-88 Turnmill Street, London EC1M 5QU, England; *International Marketing Data and Statistics.*

Food and Agricultural Organization of the United Nations (FAO) Via delle Terme di Caracalla, 00100 Rome, Italy (Telephone Number in U.S. (202) 653-2400); *The State of Food and Agriculture.*

G.K. Hall and Company, 70 Lincoln Street, Boston, Massachusetts 02111 (617) 423-3990; *The World in Figures.*

International Monetary Fund, 700 Nineteenth Street, NW, Washington, D.C. 20431 (202) 623-7000; *Direction of Trade Statistics, Government Finance Statistics Yearbook,* and *International Financial Statistics.*

International Rubber Study Group, York House, Eighth Floor, Empire Way, Wembley, London HA9 0PA, England; *Rubber Statistical Bulletin.*

Statistical Office of the United Nations, Publishing Service, New York, New York 10017 (800) 253-9646; *Foreign Trade Statistics for Africa, Trade in Manufactures of Developing Countries,* and *Survey of Economic and Social Conditions in Africa.*

Times Books, 201 East 50th Street, New York, New York 10022 (212) 751-2600; *The Economist Book of Vital World Statistics.*

United Nations Economic Commission for Africa, Africa Hall, P.O. Box 3001, Addis Ababa, Ethiopia (Telephone Number in U.S. (800) 253-9646); *African Statistical Yearbook.*

The World Bank, 1818 H Street, NW, Washington, D.C. 20433 (202) 477-1234; *World Tables.*

CAMEROON - EXTERNAL INDEBTEDNESS

African Development Bank, 01 BP 1387, Abidjan 01, Cote D'Ivoire; *Selected Statistics on Regional Member Countries.*

Statistical Office of the United Nations, Publishing Service, New York, New York 10017 (800) 253-9646; *Survey of Economic and Social Conditions in Africa.*

The World Bank, 1818 H Street, NW, Washington, D.C. 20433 (202) 477-1234; *World Tables.*

CAMEROON - EXTERNAL TRADE

African Development Bank, 01 BP 1387, Abidjan 01, Cote D'Ivoire; *Selected Statistics on Regional Member Countries.*

Food and Agricultural Organization of the United Nations (FAO), Via delle Terme di Caracalla, 00100 Rome, Italy (Telephone Number in U.S. (202) 653-2400); *Trade Yearbook, The State of Food and Agriculture,* and *Trade Yearbook.*

G.K. Hall and Company, 70 Lincoln Street, Boston, Massachusetts 02111 (617) 423-3990; *The World in Figures.*

Statistical Office of the United Nations, Publishing Service, New York, New York 10017 (800) 253-9646; *Statistical Yearbook.*

CAMEROON - FARM CROPS - See CAMEROON - CROPS

CAMEROON - FEMALE WORKING POPULATION - See CAMEROON - EMPLOYMENT

CAMEROON - FERTILITY RATES

Facts on File, 460 Park Avenue South, New York, New York 10016 (800) 443-8323; *The New Book of World Rankings.*

Statistical Office of the United Nations, Publishing Service, New York, New York 10017 (800) 253-9646; *Survey of Economic and Social Conditions in Africa.*

Times Books, 201 East 50th Street, New York, New York 10022 (212) 751-2600; *The Economist Book of Vital World Statistics.*

The World Bank, 1818 H Street, NW, Washington, D.C. 20433 (202) 477-1234; *World Tables.*

CAMEROON - FERTILIZER

Food and Agricultural Organization of the United Nations (FAO), Via delle Terme di Caracalla, 00100 Rome, Italy (Telephone Number in U.S. (202) 653-2400); *Fertilizer Yearbook,* and *The State of Food and Agriculture.*

Statistical Office of the United Nations, Publishing Service, New York, New York 10017 (800) 253-9646; *Statistical Yearbook.*

CAMEROON - FETAL MORTALITY

Statistical Office of the United Nations, Publishing Service, New York, New York 10017 (800) 253-9646; *Demographic Yearbook.*

CAMEROON - FILM - See CAMEROON - MOTION PICTURES

CAMEROON - FINANCE

African Development Bank, 01 BP 1387, Abidjan 01, Cote D'Ivoire; *Selected Statistics on Regional Member Countries.*

Facts on File, 460 Park Avenue South, New York, New York 10016 (800) 443-8323; *The New Book of World Rankings.*

Federal Statistical Office, Gustav - Stresemann - Ring 11, D-6200 Wiesbaden, Germany; *Kamerun.*

G.K. Hall and Company, 70 Lincoln Street, Boston, Massachusetts 02111 (617) 423-3990; *The World in Figures.*

International Monetary Fund, 700 Nineteenth Street, NW, Washington, D.C. 20431 (202) 623-7000; *Government Finance Statistics Yearbook,* and *International Financial Statistics.*

United Nations Economic Commission for Africa, Africa Hall, P.O. Box 3001, Addis Ababa, Ethiopia (Telephone Number in U.S. (800) 253-9646); *African Statistical Yearbook.*

CAMEROON - FISHERIES

Facts on File, 460 Park Avenue South, New York, New York 10016 (800) 443-8323; *The New Book of World Rankings.*

Federal Statistical Office, Gustav - Stresemann - Ring 11, D-6200 Wiesbaden, Germany; *Kamerun.*

Food and Agricultural Organization of the United Nations (FAO) Via delle Terme di Caracalla, 00100 Rome, Italy (Telephone Number in U.S. (202) 653-2400); *The State of Food and Agriculture,* and *Yearbook of Fishery Statistics.*

Statistical Office of the United Nations, Publishing Service, New York, New York 10017 (800) 253-9646; *Statistical Yearbook,* and *Survey of Economic and Social Conditions in Africa.*

United Nations Economic Commission for Africa, Africa Hall, P.O. Box 3001, Addis Ababa, Ethiopia (Telephone Number in U.S. (800) 253-9646); *African Statistical Yearbook.*

CAMEROON - FLOUR PRODUCTION

Statistical Office of the United Nations, Publishing Service, New York, New York 10017 (800) 253-9646; *Statistical Yearbook.*

CAMEROON - FOOD

African Development Bank, 01 BP 1387, Abidjan 01, Cote D'Ivoire; *Selected Statistics on Regional Member Countries.*

Food and Agricultural Organization of the United Nations (FAO) Via delle Terme di Caracalla, 00100 Rome, Italy (Telephone Number in U.S. (202) 653-2400); *Production Yearbook,* and *The State of Food and Agriculture.*

G.K. Hall and Company, 70 Lincoln Street, Boston, Massachusetts 02111 (617) 423-3990; *The World in Figures.*

Statistical Office of the United Nations, Publishing Service, New York, New York 10017 (800) 253-9646; *Trade in Manufactures of Developing Countries*.

CAMEROON - FOREIGN AID

G.K. Hall and Company, 70 Lincoln Street, Boston, Massachusetts 02111 (617) 423-3990; *The World in Figures*.

CAMEROON - FOREIGN DEBT

International Monetary Fund, 700 Nineteenth Street, NW, Washington, D.C. 20431 (202) 623-7000; *Government Finance Statistics Yearbook*.

CAMEROON - FOREIGN TRADE

Euromonitor Publications Limited, 87-88 Turnmill Street, London EC1M 5QU, England; *International Marketing Data and Statistics*.

Facts on File, 460 Park Avenue South, New York, New York 10016 (800) 443-8323; *The New Book of World Rankings*.

Federal Statistical Office, Gustav - Stresemann - Ring 11, D-6200 Wiesbaden, Germany; *Kamerun*.

Food and Agricultural Organization of the United Nations (FAO) Via delle Terme di Caracalla, 00100 Rome, Italy (Telephone Number in U.S. (202) 653-2400); *The State of Food and Agriculture*.

G.K. Hall and Company, 70 Lincoln Street, Boston, Massachusetts 02111 (617) 423-3990; *The World in Figures*.

Organisation for Economic Co-operation and Development (OECD), 2 rue Andre-Pascal, 75 Paris 16, France (Telephone Number in U.S. (202) 785-6323); *Economic Outlook*.

Statistical Office of the United Nations, Publishing Service, New York, New York 10017 (800) 253-9646; *Foreign Trade Statistics for Africa, International Trade Statistics Yearbook*, and *Statistical Yearbook*.

United Nations Economic Commission for Africa, Africa Hall, P.O. Box 3001, Addis Ababa, Ethiopia (Telephone Number in U.S. (800) 253-9646); *African Statistical Yearbook*.

The World Bank, 1818 H Street, NW, Washington, D.C. 20433 (202) 477-1234; *World Tables*.

CAMEROON - FORESTRY AND FOREST PRODUCTS

Facts on File, 460 Park Avenue South, New York, New York 10016 (800) 443-8323; *The New Book of World Rankings*.

Federal Statistical Office, Gustav - Stresemann - Ring 11, D-6200 Wiesbaden, Germany; *Kamerun*.

Food and Agricultural Organization of the United Nations (FAO) Via delle Terme di Caracalla, 00100 Rome, Italy (Telephone Number in U.S. (202) 653-2400); *The State of Food and Agriculture*, and *Yearbook of Forest Products*.

G.K. Hall and Company, 70 Lincoln Street, Boston, Massachusetts 02111 (617) 423-3990; *The World in Figures*.

International Monetary Fund, 700 Nineteenth Street, NW, Washington, D.C. 20431 (202) 623-7000; *International Financial Statistics*.

Statistical Office of the United Nations, Publishing Service, New York, New York 10017 (800) 253-9646; *Statistical Yearbook*.

United Nations Economic Commission for Africa, Africa Hall, P.O. Box 3001, Addis Ababa, Ethiopia (Telephone Number in U.S. (800) 253-9646); *African Statistical Yearbook*.

United Nations Educational, Scientific and Cultural Organization (UNESCO), 7 Place de Fontenoy, F-75700 Paris, France (Telephone Number in U.S. (212) 963-5981); *Statistical Yearbook*.

CAMEROON - FURNITURE AND WOOD PRODUCTS - EXPORTS AND IMPORTS

Statistical Office of the United Nations, Publishing Service, New York, New York 10017 (800) 253-9646; *Trade in Manufactures of Developing Countries*.

CAMEROON - GAS PRODUCTION - See CAMEROON - MINING AND MINERAL PRODUCTS

CAMEROON - GENERAL INDUSTRIAL STATISTICS

Federal Statistical Office, Gustav - Stresemann - Ring 11, D-6200 Wiesbaden, Germany; *Kamerun*.

CAMEROON - GENERAL MORTALITY

Statistical Office of the United Nations, Publishing Service, New York, New York 10017 (800) 253-9646; *Demographic Yearbook*.

CAMEROON - GEOGRAPHIC DATA

Facts on File, 460 Park Avenue South, New York, New York 10016 (800) 443-8323; *The New Book of World Rankings*.

Federal Statistical Office, Gustav - Stresemann - Ring 11, D-6200 Wiesbaden, Germany; *Kamerun*.

CAMEROON - GOATS - See CAMEROON - LIVESTOCK AND POULTRY

CAMEROON - GOLD HOLDINGS

International Monetary Fund, 700 Nineteenth Street, NW, Washington, D.C. 20431 (202) 623-7000; *International Financial Statistics*.

The World Bank, 1818 H Street, NW, Washington, D.C. 20433 (202) 477-1234; *World Tables*.

CAMEROON - GOLD PRODUCTION AND CONSUMPTION - See CAMEROON - MINING AND MINERALS

CAMEROON - GOVERNMENT

G.K. Hall and Company, 70 Lincoln Street, Boston, Massachusetts 02111 (617) 423-3990; *The World in Figures*.

CAMEROON - GOVERNMENT EXPENDITURES

International Monetary Fund, 700 Nineteenth Street, NW, Washington, D.C. 20431 (202) 623-7000; *Government Finance Statistics Yearbook*.

The World Bank, 1818 H Street, NW, Washington, D.C. 20433 (202) 477-1234; *World Tables*.

Times Books, 201 East 50th Street, New York, New York 10022 (212) 751-2600; *The Economist Book of Vital World Statistics*.

CAMEROON - GOVERNMENT FINANCE

International Monetary Fund, 700 Nineteenth Street, NW, Washington, D.C. 20431 (202) 623-7000; *International Financial Statistics*.

CAMEROON - GOVERNMENT REVENUE

International Monetary Fund, 700 Nineteenth Street, NW, Washington, D.C. 20431 (202) 623-7000; *Government Finance Statistics Yearbook*.

Statistical Office of the United Nations, Publishing Service, New York, New York 10017 (800) 253-9646; *Survey of Economic and Social Conditions in Africa*.

Times Books, 201 East 50th Street, New York, New York 10022 (212) 751-2600; *The Economist Book of Vital World Statistics*.

The World Bank, 1818 H Street, NW, Washington, D.C. 20433 (202) 477-1234; *World Tables*.

CAMEROON - GRAIN PRODUCTION - See CAMEROON - CROPS

CAMEROON - GRANTS

International Monetary Fund, 700 Nineteenth Street, NW, Washington, D.C. 20431 (202) 623-7000; *Government Finance Statistics Yearbook*.

CAMEROON - GROSS DOMESTIC PRODUCT

African Development Bank, 01 BP 1387, Abidjan 01, Cote D'Ivoire; *Selected Statistics on Regional Member Countries*.

The Economist Intelligence Unit, 111 West 57th Street, New York, New York 10019 (800) 938-4685; *The World Market Atlas*.

Facts on File, 460 Park Avenue South, New York, New York 10016 (800) 443-8323; *The New Book of World Rankings*.

G.K. Hall and Company, 70 Lincoln Street, Boston, Massachusetts 02111 (617) 423-3990; *The World in Figures*.

International Monetary Fund, 700 Nineteenth Street, NW, Washington, D.C. 20431 (202) 623-7000; *International Financial Statistics*.

Statistical Office of the United Nations, Publishing Service, New York, New York 10017 (800) 253-9646; *Statistical Yearbook*, and *Survey of Economic and Social Conditions in Africa*.

Times Books, 201 East 50th Street, New York, New York 10022 (212) 751-2600; *The Economist Book of Vital World Statistics*.

United Nations Economic Commission for Africa, Africa Hall, P.O. Box 3001, Addis Ababa, Ethiopia (Telephone Number in U.S. (800) 253-9646); *African Statistical Yearbook*.

The World Bank, 1818 H Street, NW, Washington, D.C. 20433 (202) 477-1234; *World Tables*.

CAMEROON - GROSS NATIONAL PRODUCT

Euromonitor Publications Limited, 87-88 Turnmill Street, London EC1M 5QU, England; *International Marketing Data and Statistics*.

U.S. Arms Control and Disarmament Agency, 320 Twenty-first Street, NW, Washington, D.C. 20451 (202) 647-8677; *World Military Expenditures and Arms Transfers*.

The World Bank, 1818 H Street, NW, Washington, D.C. 20433 (202) 477-1234; *World Tables*.

CAMEROON - GROUNDNUTS PRODUCTION - See CAMEROON - CROPS

CAMEROON - HEALTH

African Development Bank, 01 BP 1387, Abidjan 01, Cote D'Ivoire; *Selected Statistics on Regional Member Countries*.

Facts on File, 460 Park Avenue South, New York, New York 10016 (800) 443-8323; *The New Book of World Rankings*.

Federal Statistical Office, Gustav - Stresemann - Ring 11, D-6200 Wiesbaden, Germany; *Kamerun*.

G.K. Hall and Company, 70 Lincoln Street, Boston, Massachusetts 02111 (617) 423-3990; *The World in Figures*.

Statistical Office of the United Nations, Publishing Service, New York, New York 10017 (800) 253-9646; *Statistical Yearbook*.

United Nations Economic Commission for Africa, Africa Hall, P.O. Box 3001, Addis Ababa, Ethiopia (Telephone Number in U.S. (800) 253-9646); *African Statistical Yearbook*.

Times Books, 201 East 50th Street, New York, New York 10022 (212) 751-2600; *The Economist Book of Vital World Statistics*.

CAMEROON - HEALTH EXPENDITURES

International Monetary Fund, 700 Nineteenth Street, NW, Washington, D.C. 20431 (202) 623-7000; *Government Finance Statistics Yearbook*.

CAMEROON - HIDE PRODUCTION

Food and Agricultural Organization of the United Nations (FAO), Via delle Terme di Caracalla, 00100 Rome, Italy (Telephone Number in U.S. (202) 653-2400); *Production Yearbook*.

CAMEROON - HIGHWAYS

G.K. Hall and Company, 70 Lincoln Street, Boston, Massachusetts 02111 (617) 423-3990; *The World in Figures*.

International Road Federation, 525 School Street, SW, Washington, D.C. 20024 (202) 554-2106; *World Road Statistics*.

Statistical Office of the United Nations, Publishing Service, New York, New York 10017 (800) 253-9646; *Survey of Economic and Social Conditions in Africa*.

United Nations Economic Commission for Africa, Africa Hall, P.O. Box 3001, Addis Ababa, Ethiopia (Telephone Number in U.S. (800) 253-9646); *African Statistical Yearbook*.

CAMEROON - HORSES - See CAMEROON - LIVESTOCK AND POULTRY

CAMEROON - HOURS OF WORK - See CAMEROON - EMPLOYMENT

CAMEROON - HOUSING AND HOUSING UNITS

Facts on File, 460 Park Avenue South, New York, New York 10016 (800) 443-8323; *The New Book of World Rankings*.

Statistical Office of the United Nations, Publishing Service, New York, New York 10017 (800) 253-9646; *Statistical Yearbook.*

CAMEROON - ILLITERATE POPULATION

The Economist Intelligence Unit, 111 West 57th Street, New York, New York 10019 (800) 938-4685; *The World Market Atlas.*

G.K. Hall and Company, 70 Lincoln Street, Boston, Massachusetts 02111 (617) 423-3990; *The World in Figures.*

United Nations Educational, Scientific and Cultural Organization (UNESCO), 7 Place de Fontenoy, F-75700 Paris, France (Telephone Number in U.S. (212) 963-5981); *Statistical Yearbook.*

CAMEROON - IMPORTS

African Development Bank, 01 BP 1387, Abidjan 01, Cote D'Ivoire; *Selected Statistics on Regional Member Countries.*

The Economist Intelligence Unit, 111 West 57th Street, New York, New York 10019 (800) 938-4685; *The World Market Atlas.*

Euromonitor Publications Limited, 87-88 Turnmill Street, London EC1M 5QU, England; *International Marketing Data and Statistics.*

Food and Agricultural Organization of the United Nations (FAO) Via delle Terme di Caracalla, 00100 Rome, Italy (Telephone Number in U.S. (202) 653-2400); *The State of Food and Agriculture.*

G.K. Hall and Company, 70 Lincoln Street, Boston, Massachusetts 02111 (617) 423-3990; *The World in Figures.*

International Monetary Fund, 700 Nineteenth Street, NW, Washington, D.C. 20431 (202) 623-7000; *Direction of Trade Statistics,* and *Government Finance Statistics Yearbook.*

International Rubber Study Group, York House, Eighth Floor, Empire Way, Wembley, London HA9 0PA, England; *Rubber Statistical Bulletin.*

Statistical Office of the United Nations, Publishing Service, New York, New York 10017 (800) 253-9646; *Foreign Trade Statistics for Africa, Survey of Economic and Social Conditions in Africa,* and *Trade in Manufactures of Developing Countries.*

Times Books, 201 East 50th Street, New York, New York 10022 (212) 751-2600; *The Economist Book of Vital World Statistics.*

United Nations Economic Commission for Africa, Africa Hall, P.O. Box 3001, Addis Ababa, Ethiopia (Telephone Number in U.S. (800) 253-9646); *African Statistical Yearbook.*

The World Bank, 1818 H Street, NW, Washington, D.C. 20433 (202) 477-1234; *World Tables.*

CAMEROON - INCOME TAXES - See CAMEROON - TAXATION

CAMEROON - INDUSTRIAL METALS PRODUCTION - See CAMEROON - MINING AND MINERAL PRODUCTS

CAMEROON - INDUSTRY

Euromonitor Publications Limited, 87-88 Turnmill Street, London EC1M 5QU, England; *International Marketing Data and Statistics.*

Facts on File, 460 Park Avenue South, New York, New York 10016 (800) 443-8323; *The New Book of World Rankings.*

Federal Statistical Office, Gustav - Stresemann - Ring 11, D-6200 Wiesbaden, Germany; *Kamerun.*

G.K. Hall and Company, 70 Lincoln Street, Boston, Massachusetts 02111 (617) 423-3990; *The World in Figures.*

International Labour Office, I.L.O. Publications, CH-1211, Geneva 22, Switzerland; *Yearbook of Labour Statistics.*

Statistical Office of the United Nations, Publishing Service, New York, New York 10017 (800) 253-9646; *Survey of Economic and Social Conditions in Africa.*

Times Books, 201 East 50th Street, New York, New York 10022 (212) 751-2600; *The Economist Book of Vital World Statistics.*

United Nations Economic Commission for Africa, Africa Hall, P.O. Box 3001, Addis Ababa, Ethiopia (Telephone Number in U.S. (800) 253-9646); *African Statistical Yearbook.*

The World Bank, 1818 H Street, NW, Washington, D.C. 20433 (202) 477-1234; *World Tables.*

CAMEROON - INFANT AND MATERNAL MORTALITY

Statistical Office of the United Nations, Publishing Service, New York, New York 10017 (800) 253-9646; *Demographic Yearbook, Statistical Yearbook,* and *Survey of Economic and Social Conditions in Africa.*

Times Books, 201 East 50th Street, New York, New York 10022 (212) 751-2600; *The Economist Book of Vital World Statistics.*

The World Bank, 1818 H Street, NW, Washington, D.C. 20433 (202) 477-1234; *World Tables.*

CAMEROON - INTERNATIONAL LIQUIDITY

International Monetary Fund, 700 Nineteenth Street, NW, Washington, D.C. 20431 (202) 623-7000; *International Financial Statistics.*

CAMEROON - INTERNATIONAL RESERVES EXCLUDING GOLD

African Development Bank, 01 BP 1387, Abidjan 01, Cote D'Ivoire; *Selected Statistics on Regional Member Countries.*

The World Bank, 1818 H Street, NW, Washington, D.C. 20433 (202) 477-1234; *World Tables.*

CAMEROON - IRON ORE PRODUCTION AND CONSUMPTION - See CAMEROON - MINING AND MINERAL PRODUCTS

CAMEROON - IRRIGATION

Euromonitor Publications Limited, 87-88 Turnmill Street, London EC1M 5QU, England; *International Marketing Data and Statistics.*

CAMEROON - LABOR FORCE

African Development Bank, 01 BP 1387, Abidjan 01, Cote D'Ivoire; *Selected Statistics on Regional Member Countries.*

Euromonitor Publications Limited, 87-88 Turnmill Street, London EC1M 5QU, England; *International Marketing Data and Statistics.*

Facts on File, 460 Park Avenue South, New York, New York 10016 (800) 443-8323; *The New Book of World Rankings.*

Food and Agricultural Organization of the United Nations (FAO) Via delle Terme di Caracalla, 00100 Rome, Italy (Telephone Number in U.S. (202) 653-2400); *The State of Food and Agriculture.*

G.K. Hall and Company, 70 Lincoln Street, Boston, Massachusetts 02111 (617) 423-3990; *The World in Figures.*

Times Books, 201 East 50th Street, New York, New York 10022 (212) 751-2600; *The Economist Book of Vital World Statistics.*

The World Bank, 1818 H Street, NW, Washington, D.C. 20433 (202) 477-1234; *World Tables.*

CAMEROON - LABOR PRODUCTIVITY

International Labour Office, I.L.O. Publications, CH-1211, Geneva 22, Switzerland; *Yearbook of Labour Statistics.*

CAMEROON - LAND USE

Euromonitor Publications Limited, 87-88 Turnmill Street, London EC1M 5QU, England; *International Marketing Data and Statistics.*

Food and Agricultural Organization of the United Nations (FAO), Via delle Terme di Caracalla, 00100 Rome, Italy (Telephone Number in U.S. (202) 653-2400); *Production Yearbook.*

G.K. Hall and Company, 70 Lincoln Street, Boston, Massachusetts 02111 (617) 423-3990; *The World in Figures.*

CAMEROON - LIBRARIES

Facts on File, 460 Park Avenue South, New York, New York 10016 (800) 443-8323; *The New Book of World Rankings.*

CAMEROON - LIFE EXPECTANCY

African Development Bank, 01 BP 1387, Abidjan 01, Cote D'Ivoire; *Selected Statistics on Regional Member Countries.*

CAMEROON - LITERACY RATE

Statistical Office of the United Nations, Publishing Service, New York, New York 10017 (800) 253-9646; *Survey of Economic and Social Conditions in Africa.*

CAMEROON - LIVESTOCK AND POULTRY

Euromonitor Publications Limited, 87-88 Turnmill Street, London EC1M 5QU, England; *International Marketing Data and Statistics.*

Facts on File, 460 Park Avenue South, New York, New York 10016 (800) 443-8323; *The New Book of World Rankings.*

Food and Agricultural Organization of the United Nations (FAO), Via delle Terme di Caracalla, 00100 Rome, Italy (Telephone Number in U.S. (202) 653-2400); *Production Yearbook,* and *The State of Food and Agriculture.*

G.K. Hall and Company, 70 Lincoln Street, Boston, Massachusetts 02111 (617) 423-3990; *The World in Figures.*

Statistical Office of the United Nations, Publishing Service, New York, New York 10017 (800) 253-9646; *Statistical Yearbook,* and *Survey of Economic and Social Conditions in Africa.*

United Nations Economic Commission for Africa, Africa Hall, P.O. Box 3001, Addis Ababa, Ethiopia (Telephone Number in U.S. (800) 253-9646); *African Statistical Yearbook.*

CAMEROON - LIVING LEVELS

G.K. Hall and Company, 70 Lincoln Street, Boston, Massachusetts 02111 (617) 423-3990; *The World in Figures.*

Times Books, 201 East 50th Street, New York, New York 10022 (212) 751-2600; *The Economist Book of Vital World Statistics.*

CAMEROON - MAIL TRAFFIC - NUMBER OF ITEMS

Statistical Office of the United Nations, Publishing Service, New York, New York 10017 (800) 253-9646; *Statistical Yearbook.*

CAMEROON - MANUFACTURING

Facts on File, 460 Park Avenue South, New York, New York 10016 (800) 443-8323; *The New Book of World Rankings.*

G.K. Hall and Company, 70 Lincoln Street, Boston, Massachusetts 02111 (617) 423-3990; *The World in Figures.*

Statistical Office of the United Nations, Publishing Service, New York, New York 10017 (800) 253-9646; *Statistical Yearbook,* and *Survey of Economic and Social Conditions in Africa.*

Times Books, 201 East 50th Street, New York, New York 10022 (212) 751-2600; *The Economist Book of Vital World Statistics.*

United Nations Economic Commission for Africa, Africa Hall, P.O. Box 3001, Addis Ababa, Ethiopia (Telephone Number in U.S. (800) 253-9646); *African Statistical Yearbook.*

The World Bank, 1818 H Street, NW, Washington, D.C. 20433 (202) 477-1234; *World Tables.*

CAMEROON - MARRIAGE RATES

Facts on File, 460 Park Avenue South, New York, New York 10016 (800) 443-8323; *The New Book of World Rankings.*

Statistical Office of the United Nations, Publishing Service, New York, New York 10017 (800) 253-9646; *Demographic Yearbook.*

CAMEROON - MEAT PRODUCTION - See CAMEROON - LIVESTOCK AND POULTRY

CAMEROON - MERCHANT SHIPPING

G.K. Hall and Company, 70 Lincoln Street, Boston, Massachusetts 02111 (617) 423-3990; *The World in Figures.*

Statistical Office of the United Nations, Publishing Service, New York, New York 10017 (800) 253-9646; *Statistical Yearbook.*

Times Books, 201 East 50th Street, New York, New York 10022 (212) 751-2600; *The Economist Book of Vital World Statistics.*

United Nations Economic Commission for Africa, Africa Hall, P.O. Box 3001, Addis Ababa, Ethiopia (Telephone Number in U.S. (800) 253-9646); *African Statistical Yearbook.*

U.S. Department of Transportation, Maritime Administration, 400 Seventh Street, SW, Washington, D.C. 20590; *A Statistical Analysis of the World's Merchant Fleets.*

CAMEROON - MILITARY

G.K. Hall and Company, 70 Lincoln Street, Boston, Massachusetts 02111 (617) 423-3990; *The World in Figures.*

The International Institute for Strategic Studies, 23 Tavistock Street, London WC2E 7NQ, England; *The Military Balance.*

U.S. Arms Control and Disarmament Agency, 320 Twenty-first Street, NW, Washington, D.C. 20451 (202) 647-8677; *World Military Expenditures and Arms Transfers.*

CAMEROON - MILK PRODUCTION - See CAMEROON - DAIRY PRODUCTS

CAMEROON - MILLET PRODUCTION - See CAMEROON - CROPS

CAMEROON - MINING AND MINERAL PRODUCTS

Commodity Research Bureau, Incorporated, 75 Wall Street, New York, New York 10005 (212) 504-7754; *Commodity Year Book.*

Facts on File, 460 Park Avenue South, New York, New York 10016 (800) 443-8323; *The New Book of World Rankings.*

G.K. Hall and Company, 70 Lincoln Street, Boston, Massachusetts 02111 (617) 423-3990; *The World in Figures.*

Penn Well Publishing Company, 1421 South Sheridan Road, P.O. Box 1260, Tulsa, Oklahoma 74101 (800) 752-9764; *International Energy Statistics Sourcebook.*

Statistical Office of the United Nations, Publishing Service, New York, New York 10017 (800) 253-9646; *Statistical Yearbook.*

United Nations Economic Commission for Africa, Africa Hall, P.O. Box 3001, Addis Ababa, Ethiopia (Telephone Number in U.S. (800) 253-9646); *African Statistical Yearbook.*

CAMEROON - MONEY EXCHANGE RATE

Euromonitor Publications Limited, 87-88 Turnmill Street, London EC1M 5QU, England; *International Marketing Data and Statistics.*

International Monetary Fund, 700 Nineteenth Street, NW, Washington, D.C. 20431 (202) 623-7000; *International Financial Statistics.*

CAMEROON - MONEY RESERVES

Euromonitor Publications Limited, 87-88 Turnmill Street, London EC1M 5QU, England; *International Marketing Data and Statistics.*

CAMEROON - MONEY SUPPLY

African Development Bank, 01 BP 1387, Abidjan 01, Cote D'Ivoire; *Selected Statistics on Regional Member Countries.*

Euromonitor Publications Limited, 87-88 Turnmill Street, London EC1M 5QU, England; *International Marketing Data and Statistics.*

Federal Statistical Office, Gustav - Stresemann - Ring 11, D-6200 Wiesbaden, Germany; *Kamerun.*

G.K. Hall and Company, 70 Lincoln Street, Boston, Massachusetts 02111 (617) 423-3990; *The World in Figures.*

International Monetary Fund, 700 Nineteenth Street, NW, Washington, D.C. 20431 (202) 623-7000; *International Financial Statistics.*

The World Bank, 1818 H Street, NW, Washington, D.C. 20433 (202) 477-1234; *World Tables.*

CAMEROON - MOTION PICTURES

Statistical Office of the United Nations, Publishing Service, New York, New York 10017 (800) 253-9646; *Statistical Yearbook.*

United Nations Educational, Scientific and Cultural Organization (UNESCO), 7 Place de Fontenoy, F-75700 Paris, France (Telephone Number in U.S. (212) 963-5981); *Statistical Yearbook.*

CAMEROON - MOTOR VEHICLE TAXES - See CAMEROON - TAXATION

CAMEROON - MOTOR VEHICLES IN USE

G.K. Hall and Company, 70 Lincoln Street, Boston, Massachusetts 02111 (617) 423-3990; *The World in Figures.*

International Road Federation, 525 School Street, SW, Washington, D.C. 20024 (202) 554-2106; *World Road Statistics.*

Statistical Office of the United Nations, Publishing Service, New York, New York 10017 (800) 253-9646; *Statistical Yearbook,* and *Survey of Economic and Social Conditions in Africa.*

Times Books, 201 East 50th Street, New York, New York 10022 (212) 751-2600; *The Economist Book of Vital World Statistics.*

CAMEROON - MUSEUMS

Facts on File, 460 Park Avenue South, New York, New York 10016 (800) 443-8323; *The New Book of World Rankings.*

United Nations Educational, Scientific and Cultural Organization (UNESCO), 7 Place de Fontenoy, F-75700 Paris, France (Telephone Number in U.S. (212) 963-5981); *Statistical Yearbook.*

CAMEROON - NATALITY - See CAMEROON - BIRTH RATE

CAMEROON - NATIONAL ACCOUNTS

African Development Bank, 01 BP 1387, Abidjan 01, Cote D'Ivoire; *Selected Statistics on Regional Member Countries.*

Federal Statistical Office, Gustav - Stresemann - Ring 11, D-6200 Wiesbaden, Germany; *Kamerun.*

Statistical Office of the United Nations, Publishing Service, New York, New York 10017 (800) 253-9646; *National Accounts Statistics,* and *Statistical Yearbook.*

United Nations Economic Commission for Africa, Africa Hall, P.O. Box 3001, Addis Ababa, Ethiopia (Telephone Number in U.S. (800) 253-9646); *African Statistical Yearbook.*

CAMEROON - NATIONAL INCOME

Facts on File, 460 Park Avenue South, New York, New York 10016 (800) 443-8323; *The New Book of World Rankings.*

G.K. Hall and Company, 70 Lincoln Street, Boston, Massachusetts 02111 (617) 423-3990; *The World in Figures.*

Statistical Office of the United Nations, Publishing Service, New York, New York 10017 (800) 253-9646; *Statistical Yearbook.*

CAMEROON - NATIONAL PRODUCT

Facts on File, 460 Park Avenue South, New York, New York 10016 (800) 443-8323; *The New Book of World Rankings.*

Statistical Office of the United Nations, Publishing Service, New York, New York 10017 (800) 253-9646; *Statistical Yearbook.*

CAMEROON - NATURAL GAS PRODUCTION - See CAMEROON - MINING AND MINERAL PRODUCTS

CAMEROON - NATURAL RUBBER PRODUCTION

International Rubber Study Group, York House, Eighth Floor, Empire Way, Wembley, London HA9 0PA, England; *Rubber Statistical Bulletin.*

Statistical Office of the United Nations, Publishing Service, New York, New York 10017 (800) 253-9646; *Statistical Yearbook.*

CAMEROON - NEWSPAPER PRODUCTION - See CAMEROON - FORESTRY AND FOREST PRODUCTS

CAMEROON - NEWSPRINT - See CAMEROON - FORESTRY AND FOREST PRODUCTS

CAMEROON - OCCUPATIONS - See CAMEROON - LABOR FORCE

CAMEROON - PALM OIL AND PALM KERNELS PRODUCTION - See CAMEROON - CROPS

CAMEROON - PAPER

United Nations Educational, Scientific and Cultural Organization (UNESCO), 7 Place de Fontenoy, F-75700 Paris, France (Telephone Number in U.S. (212) 963-5981); *Statistical Yearbook.*

CAMEROON - PEANUT PRODUCTION - See CAMEROON - CROPS

CAMEROON - PERIODICALS

United Nations Educational, Scientific and Cultural Organization (UNESCO), 7 Place de Fontenoy, F-75700 Paris, France (Telephone Number in U.S. (212) 963-5981); *Statistical Yearbook.*

CAMEROON - PESTICIDE USE

Food and Agricultural Organization of the United Nations (FAO) Via delle Terme di Caracalla, 00100 Rome, Italy (Telephone Number in U.S. (202) 653-2400); *The State of Food and Agriculture.*

CAMEROON - PETROLEUM INDUSTRY

Facts on File, 460 Park Avenue South, New York, New York 10016 (800) 443-8323; *The New Book of World Rankings.*

Food and Agricultural Organization of the United Nations (FAO) Via delle Terme di Caracalla, 00100 Rome, Italy (Telephone Number in U.S. (202) 653-2400); *The State of Food and Agriculture.*

G.K. Hall and Company, 70 Lincoln Street, Boston, Massachusetts 02111 (617) 423-3990; *The World in Figures.*

Penn Well Publishing Company, 1421 South Sheridan Road, P.O. Box 1260, Tulsa, Oklahoma 74101 (800) 752-9764; *International Energy Statistics Sourcebook.*

CAMEROON - PIGS - See CAMEROON - LIVESTOCK AND POULTRY

CAMEROON - POPULATION

African Development Bank, 01 BP 1387, Abidjan 01, Cote D'Ivoire; *Selected Statistics on Regional Member Countries.*

The Economist Intelligence Unit, 111 West 57th Street, New York, New York 10019 (800) 938-4685; *The World Market Atlas.*

Euromonitor Publications Limited, 87-88 Turnmill Street, London EC1M 5QU, England; *International Marketing Data and Statistics.*

Facts on File, 460 Park Avenue South, New York, New York 10016 (800) 443-8323; *The New Book of World Rankings.*

Federal Statistical Office, Gustav - Stresemann - Ring 11, D-6200 Wiesbaden, Germany; *Kamerun.*

Food and Agricultural Organization of the United Nations (FAO), Via delle Terme di Caracalla, 00100 Rome, Italy (Telephone Number in U.S. (202) 653-2400); *Production Yearbook.*

G.K. Hall and Company, 70 Lincoln Street, Boston, Massachusetts 02111 (617) 423-3990; *The World in Figures.*

International Labour Office, I.L.O. Publications, CH-1211, Geneva 22, Switzerland; *Yearbook of Labour Statistics.*

Statistical Office of the United Nations, Publishing Service, New York, New York 10017 (800) 253-9646; *Statistical Yearbook,* and *Survey of Economic and Social Conditions in Africa.*

Times Books, 201 East 50th Street, New York, New York 10022 (212) 751-2600; *The Economist Book of Vital World Statistics.*

United Nations Educational, Scientific and Cultural Organization (UNESCO), 7 Place de Fontenoy, F-75700 Paris, France (Telephone Number in U.S. (212) 963-5981); *Statistical Yearbook.*

U.S. Arms Control and Disarmament Agency, 320 Twenty-first Street, NW, Washington, D.C. 20451 (202) 647-8677; *World Military Expenditures and Arms Transfers.*

CAMEROON - POST OFFICES

Facts on File, 460 Park Avenue South, New York, New York 10016 (800) 443-8323; *The New Book of World Rankings.*

CAMEROON - POTATO PRODUCTION - See CAMEROON - CROPS

CAMEROON - PRICES

Facts on File, 460 Park Avenue South, New York, New York 10016 (800) 443-8323; *The New Book of World Rankings.*

Federal Statistical Office, Gustav - Stresemann - Ring 11, D-6200 Wiesbaden, Germany; *Kamerun.*

Food and Agricultural Organization of the United Nations (FAO), Via delle Terme di Caracalla, 00100 Rome, Italy (Telephone Number in U.S. (202) 653-2400); *Production Yearbook,* and *The State of Food and Agriculture.*

G.K. Hall and Company, 70 Lincoln Street, Boston, Massachusetts 02111 (617) 423-3990; *The World in Figures.*

International Labour Office, I.L.O. Publications, CH-1211, Geneva 22, Switzerland; *Yearbook of Labour Statistics.*

International Monetary Fund, 700 Nineteenth Street, NW, Washington, D.C. 20431 (202) 623-7000; *International Financial Statistics.*

International Rubber Study Group, York House, Eighth Floor, Empire Way, Wembley, London HA9 0PA, England; *Rubber Statistical*

Bulletin.

United Nations Economic Commission for Africa, Africa Hall, P.O. Box 3001, Addis Ababa, Ethiopia (Telephone Number in U.S. (800) 253-9646); *African Statistical Yearbook.*

CAMEROON - PRINTING AND WRITING PAPER - See CAMEROON - FORESTRY AND FOREST PRODUCTS

CAMEROON - PRODUCTION

Facts on File, 460 Park Avenue South, New York, New York 10016 (800) 443-8323; *The New Book of World Rankings.*

G.K. Hall and Company, 70 Lincoln Street, Boston, Massachusetts 02111 (617) 423-3990; *The World in Figures.*

International Rubber Study Group, York House, Eighth Floor, Empire Way, Wembley, London HA9 0PA, England; *Rubber Statistical Bulletin.*

CAMEROON - PRODUCTIVITY

Euromonitor Publications Limited, 87-88 Turnmill Street, London EC1M 5QU, England; *International Marketing Data and Statistics.*

CAMEROON - PROPERTY TAXES - See CAMEROON - TAXATION

CAMEROON - PUBLIC FINANCE

Facts on File, 460 Park Avenue South, New York, New York 10016 (800) 443-8323; *The New Book of World Rankings.*

Federal Statistical Office, Gustav - Stresemann - Ring 11, D-6200 Wiesbaden, Germany; *Kamerun.*

CAMEROON - RADIO BROADCASTING - See CAMEROON - BROADCASTING

CAMEROON - RADIO RECEIVER PRODUCTION

Statistical Office of the United Nations, Publishing Service, New York, New York 10017 (800) 253-9646; *Statistical Yearbook.*

CAMEROON - RAILWAYS

G.K. Hall and Company, 70 Lincoln Street, Boston, Massachusetts 02111 (617) 423-3990; *The World in Figures.*

Jane's Information Group, Sentinel House, 163 Brighton Road, Coulsdon, Surrey CR5 2NH, England (Telephone Number in U.S. (703) 683-3700); *Jane's World Railways.*

Statistical Office of the United Nations, Publishing Service, New York, New York 10017 (800) 253-9646; *Statistical Yearbook,* and *Survey of Economic and Social Conditions in Africa.*

United Nations Economic Commission for Africa, Africa Hall, P.O. Box 3001, Addis Ababa, Ethiopia (Telephone Number in U.S. (800) 253-9646); *African Statistical Yearbook.*

CAMEROON - RELIGION

Facts on File, 460 Park Avenue South, New York, New York 10016 (800) 443-8323; *The New Book of World Rankings.*

CAMEROON - RENT PRICES

International Labour Office, I.L.O. Publications, CH-1211, Geneva 22, Switzerland; *Yearbook of Labour Statistics.*

CAMEROON - RETAIL TRADE

G.K. Hall and Company, 70 Lincoln Street, Boston, Massachusetts 02111 (617) 423-3990; *The World in Figures.*

CAMEROON - RICE PRODUCTION - See CAMEROON - CROPS

CAMEROON - ROOT AND TUBER PRODUCTION - See CAMEROON - CROPS

CAMEROON - ROUNDWOOD PRODUCTION - See CAMEROON - FORESTRY AND FOREST PRODUCTS

CAMEROON - RUBBER PRODUCTION AND CONSUMPTION

Facts on File, 460 Park Avenue South, New York, New York 10016 (800) 443-8323; *The New Book of World Rankings.*

International Rubber Study Group, York House, Eighth Floor, Empire Way, Wembley, London HA9 0PA, England; *Rubber Statistical Bulletin.*

Statistical Office of the United Nations, Publishing Service, New York, New York 10017 (800) 253-9646; *Statistical Yearbook.*

CAMEROON - SAWNWOOD PRODUCTION - See CAMEROON - FORESTRY AND FOREST PRODUCTS

CAMEROON - SCIENCE AND TECHNOLOGY - EXPENDITURE FOR RESEARCH

Statistical Office of the United Nations, Publishing Service, New York, New York 10017 (800) 253-9646; *Statistical Yearbook.*

CAMEROON - SCIENTISTS AND TECHNICIANS

Statistical Office of the United Nations, Publishing Service, New York, New York 10017 (800) 253-9646; *Statistical Yearbook.*

United Nations Educational, Scientific and Cultural Organization (UNESCO), 7 Place de Fontenoy, F-75700 Paris, France (Telephone Number in U.S. (212) 963-5981); *Statistical Yearbook.*

CAMEROON - SENIOR CITIZENS

Facts on File, 460 Park Avenue South, New York, New York 10016 (800) 443-8323; *The New Book of World Rankings.*

CAMEROON - SESAME SEED PRODUCTION - See CAMEROON - CROPS

CAMEROON - SHEEP - See CAMEROON - LIVESTOCK AND POULTRY

CAMEROON - SILVER PRODUCTION - See CAMEROON - MINING AND MINERAL PRODUCTS

CAMEROON - SOCIAL DATA

African Development Bank, 01 BP 1387, Abidjan 01, Cote D'Ivoire; *Selected Statistics on Regional Member Countries.*

Facts on File, 460 Park Avenue South, New York, New York 10016 (800) 443-8323; *The New Book of World Rankings.*

G.K. Hall and Company, 70 Lincoln Street, Boston, Massachusetts 02111 (617) 423-3990; *The World in Figures.*

CAMEROON - SOCIAL SECURITY

International Monetary Fund, 700 Nineteenth Street, NW, Washington, D.C. 20431 (202) 623-7000; *Government Finance Statistics Yearbook.*

CAMEROON - STAMP TAXES AND DUTIES - See CAMEROON - TAXATION

CAMEROON - STATE BUDGET REVENUE AND EXPENDITURES

Euromonitor Publications Limited, 87-88 Turnmill Street, London EC1M 5QU, England; *International Marketing Data and Statistics.*

CAMEROON - STEEL PRODUCTION - See CAMEROON - MINING AND MINERAL PRODUCTS

CAMEROON - STOCKS - COMMODITY - MARKET PRICE - INDEX

Food and Agricultural Organization of the United Nations (FAO) Via delle Terme di Caracalla, 00100 Rome, Italy (Telephone Number in U.S. (202) 653-2400); *The State of Food and Agriculture.*

CAMEROON - SUGAR PRODUCTION - See CAMEROON - CROPS

CAMEROON - TAXATION

G.K. Hall and Company, 70 Lincoln Street, Boston, Massachusetts 02111 (617) 423-3990; *The World in Figures.*

International Monetary Fund, 700 Nineteenth Street, NW, Washington, D.C. 20431 (202) 623-7000; *Government Finance Statistics Yearbook.*

International Road Federation, 525 School Street, SW, Washington, D.C. 20024 (202) 554-2106; *World Road Statistics.*

The World Bank, 1818 H Street, NW, Washington, D.C. 20433 (202) 477-1234; *World Tables.*

CAMEROON - TEA PRODUCTION - See CAMEROON - CROPS

CAMEROON - TELEGRAPH SERVICE

Statistical Office of the United Nations, Publishing Service, New York, New York 10017 (800) 253-9646; *Statistical Yearbook.*

CAMEROON - TELEPHONES IN USE

American Telephone and Telegraph Company, 26 Parsippany Road, Whippany, New Jersey 07981 (800) 338-4038; *The World's Telephones.*

G.K. Hall and Company, 70 Lincoln Street, Boston, Massachusetts 02111 (617) 423-3990; *The World in Figures.*

CAMEROON - TELEVISION BROADCASTING - See CAMEROON - BROADCASTING

CAMEROON - TEXTILE INDUSTRY

G.K. Hall and Company, 70 Lincoln Street, Boston, Massachusetts 02111 (617) 423-3990; *The World in Figures.*

CAMEROON - THEATRE

United Nations Educational, Scientific and Cultural Organization (UNESCO), 7 Place de Fontenoy, F-75700 Paris, France (Telephone Number in U.S. (212) 963-5981); *Statistical Yearbook.*

CAMEROON - TIN PRODUCTION - See CAMEROON - MINING AND MINERAL PRODUCTS

CAMEROON - TIRE (MOTOR VEHICLE) PRODUCTION

International Rubber Study Group, York House, Eighth Floor, Empire Way, Wembley, London HA9 0PA, England; *Rubber Statistical Bulletin.*

CAMEROON - TOBACCO PRODUCTION

Facts on File, 460 Park Avenue South, New York, New York 10016 (800) 443-8323; *The New Book of World Rankings.*

Statistical Office of the United Nations, Publishing Service, New York, New York 10017 (800) 253-9646; *Statistical Yearbook.*

CAMEROON - TOURISM

Facts on File, 460 Park Avenue South, New York, New York 10016 (800) 443-8323; *The New Book of World Rankings.*

Federal Statistical Office, Gustav - Stresemann - Ring 11, D-6200 Wiesbaden, Germany; *Kamerun.*

G.K. Hall and Company, 70 Lincoln Street, Boston, Massachusetts 02111 (617) 423-3990; *The World in Figures.*

Statistical Office of the United Nations, Publishing Service, New York, New York 10017 (800) 253-9646; *Statistical Yearbook.*

Times Books, 201 East 50th Street, New York, New York 10022 (212) 751-2600; *The Economist Book of Vital World Statistics.*

United Nations Economic Commission for Africa, Africa Hall, P.O. Box 3001, Addis Ababa, Ethiopia (Telephone Number in U.S. (800) 253-9646); *African Statistical Yearbook.*

CAMEROON - TRACTORS IN USE

Statistical Office of the United Nations, Publishing Service, New York, New York 10017 (800) 253-9646; *Statistical Yearbook.*

CAMEROON - TRADE - See CAMEROON - FOREIGN TRADE

CAMEROON - TRANSPORTATION AND COMMUNICATIONS

Facts on File, 460 Park Avenue South, New York, New York 10016 (800) 443-8323; *The New Book of World Rankings.*

Federal Statistical Office, Gustav - Stresemann - Ring 11, D-6200 Wiesbaden, Germany; *Kamerun.*

G.K. Hall and Company, 70 Lincoln Street, Boston, Massachusetts 02111 (617) 423-3990; *The World in Figures.*

United Nations Economic Commission for Africa, Africa Hall, P.O. Box 3001, Addis Ababa, Ethiopia (Telephone Number in U.S. (800) 253-9646); *African Statistical Yearbook.*

CAMEROON - TRAVEL FARES ABROAD

International Monetary Fund, 700 Nineteenth Street, NW, Washington, D.C. 20431 (202) 623-7000; *Government Finance Statistics Yearbook.*

CAMEROON - UNEMPLOYMENT

Euromonitor Publications Limited, 87-88 Turnmill Street, London EC1M 5QU, England; *International Marketing Data and Statistics.*

International Labour Office, I.L.O. Publications, CH-1211, Geneva 22, Switzerland; *Yearbook of Labour Statistics.*

Statistical Office of the United Nations, Publishing Service, New York, New York 10017 (800) 253-9646; *Statistical Yearbook.*

CAMEROON - VITAL STATISTICS

Euromonitor Publications Limited, 87-88 Turnmill Street, London EC1M 5QU, England; *International Marketing Data and Statistics.*

G.K. Hall and Company, 70 Lincoln Street, Boston, Massachusetts 02111 (617) 423-3990; *The World in Figures.*

Statistical Office of the United Nations, Publishing Service, New York, New York 10017 (800) 253-9646; *Statistical Yearbook.*

CAMEROON - WAGES

Federal Statistical Office, Gustav - Stresemann - Ring 11, D-6200 Wiesbaden, Germany; *Kamerun.*

G.K. Hall and Company, 70 Lincoln Street, Boston, Massachusetts 02111 (617) 423-3990; *The World in Figures.*

International Labour Office, I.L.O. Publications, CH-1211, Geneva 22, Switzerland; *Yearbook of Labour Statistics.*

CAMEROON - WEATHER

Facts on File, 460 Park Avenue South, New York, New York 10016 (800) 443-8323; *The New Book of World Rankings.*

G.K. Hall and Company, 70 Lincoln Street, Boston, Massachusetts 02111 (617) 423-3990; *The World in Figures.*

CAMEROON - WHEAT PRODUCTION - See CAMEROON - CROPS

CAMEROON - WINE PRODUCTION

Facts on File, 460 Park Avenue South, New York, New York 10016 (800) 443-8323; *The New Book of World Rankings.*

CAMEROON - WOOL PRODUCTION

Facts on File, 460 Park Avenue South, New York, New York 10016 (800) 443-8323; *The New Book of World Rankings.*

CAMEROON - WOOD EXPORTS - See CAMEROON - FORESTRY AND FOREST PRODUCTS

CAMPAIGNS - FUND RAISING

U.S. Federal Election Commission, 999 E Street, NW, Washington, D.C. 20463 (800) 424-9530; *FEC Reports on Financial Activity, Final Report, United States Senate and House Campaigns, FEC Index of Independent Expenditures, FEC Reports on Financial Activity, Final Report, Party and Non-Party Political Committees,* and press release.

CAMPERS - TRUCKS AND TRAILERS

American Automobile Manufacturers Association, 1401 H Street, NW, Suite 900, Washington, D.C. 20005 (202) 326-5500; *Motor Vehicle Facts and Figures.*

Recreation Vehicle Industry Association, P.O. Box 2999, 1896 Preston White Drive, Reston, Virginia 22090 (703) 620-6003; *RV's...The Family Camping Vehicle, A Year End Report.*

CAMPING, ETC.

National Sporting Goods Association, 1699 Wall Street, Mount Prospect, Illinois 60056 (708) 439-4000; *The Sporting Goods Market in 1993,* and *Sports Participation in 1992.*

U.S. Department of Agriculture, Forest Service, Fourteenth Street and Independence Avenue, SW, Washington, D.C. 20250 (202) 720-3760; unpublished data.

U.S. Department of the Interior, Bureau of Land Management, C Street between Eighteenth and Nineteenth Street, NW, Washington, D.C. 20240 (202) 208-3435; *Public Land Statistics.*

Canada - Databases

CANSIM (Canadian Socio-Economic Information Management System),Statistics Canada, R.H. Coats Building, 8th Floor, Tunney's Pasture, Ottawa, Ontario, Canada K1A 0T6 (613) 951-1365; Subject coverage: social, demographic, and financial data.

Alberta Statistical Information System (ASIST), Alberta Treasury, Park Plaza, Suite 600, 10611 98th Avenue, Edmonton, Alberta, Canada T5K 2R7 (403) 427-3099; Subject coverage: statistical information on Alberta, other provinces, and Canada including population, prices, economic accounts, income, industries and trade, and other topics.

BC STATS, Central Statistics Branch, British Columbia Ministry of Government Services, 553 Superior Street, Victoria, British Columbia, Canada V8V 1X4 (604) 387-1502; Subject coverage: British Columbia statistics.

The Conference Board Online System, The Conference Board of Canada, Applied Economic Research and Information Centre (AERIC), 255 Smyth Road, Ottawa, Ontario, Canada K1H 8M7 (613) 526-3280; Offers the following databases: (1) Conference Board International Database. Subject coverage: key economic market and trade indicators for 75 of the world's economies. (2) Conference Board National Database. Subject coverage: time series providing detailed quarterly forecasts of the Canadian economy for five years. (3) Conference Board Provincial Database. Subject coverage: time series for each of the ten provinces.

The WEFA Group, 401 City Line Avenue, Suite 300, Bala Cynwyd, Pennsylvania 19004 (215) 660-6300; Offers the following databases: (1) Canadian Agriculture Forecast. Subject coverage: agricultural forecast data. (2) Canadian Macroeconomic Forecast. Subject coverage: macroeconomic forecasts covering the real and financial sectors of the Canadian economy.

Canada - National Statistical Office

Statistics Canada, Ottawa, Ontario K1A 0T6, Canada.

Canada - Primary Statistics Sources

Publications Distribution, Statistics Canada, Ottawa, Ontario K1A 0T6, Canada; *The Canada Yearbook*, and *Canadian Statistical Review*.

Canada - Provincial Statistical Offices

Alberta

Bureau of Statistics, Alberta Treasury, 6th Floor, Park Plaza, 10611 98 Avenue, Edmondton, Alberta T5K 2R7, Canada (403) 427-3058.

British Columbia

Ministry of Finance and Corporate Relations,Central Statistics Branch, 553 Superior Street, First Floor, Victoria, British Columbia V8V 1X4, Canada (604) 387-1502.

Manitoba

Manitoba Bureau of Statistics, #333, 260 St. Mary Avenue, Winnipeg, Manitoba R3C 0M6, Canada (204) 945-2985.

New Brunswick

New Brunswick Statistics Agency, PO Box 6000, Fredericton, New Brunswick E3B 5H1, Canada (506) 453-2381.

Newfoundland

Newfoundland Statistics Agency, Executive Council, 10th Floor, Confederation Building, PO Box 8700, St. John's Newfoundland A1B 4J6, Canada (709) 729-2913.

Northwest Territories

Bureau of Statistics, Department of Executive Finance, Post Office Box 1320, Yellowknife, Northwest Territories X1A 2L9, Canada (403) 873-7147.

Nova Scotia

Statistical Services Branch, Department of Economic Development, PO Box 519, Halifax, Nova Scotia B3J 2R7, Canada (902) 424-5691.

Ontario

Statistics Group, Sectoral and Community Economic Policy Branch, Ministry of Treasury and Economics, Frost Building, North, 3rd Floor, Toronto, Ontario M7A 1Y9, Canada (416) 325-1544.

Prince Edward Island

Economics, Statistics & Fiscal Analysis Division, Department of Provincial Treasury, PO Box 2000, Charlottetown, Prince Edward Island C1A 7N8, Canada (902) 368-4030.

Quebec

Bureau de la statistique du Quebec, Centre d'information et de documentation, 117 St. Andre, 1er etage, Quebec, PQG1K 3Y3, Canada (418) 691-2401 and 1-800-463-4090.

Saskatchewan

Saskatchewan Bureau of Statistics, 5th Floor, 2350 Albert Street, Regina, Saskatchewan S4P 4A6, Canada (306) 787-6327.

Yukon

Executive Council Office, Bureau of Statistics, PO Box 2703, Whitehorse, Yukon Territory Y1A 2C6, Canada (403) 667-5640.

CANADA - AGRICULTURE

Euromonitor Publications Limited, 87-88 Turnmill Street, London EC1M 5QU, England; *International Marketing Data and Statistics*.

Facts on File, 460 Park Avenue South, New York, New York 10016 (800) 443-8323; *The New Book of World Rankings*.

Federal Statistical Office, Gustav - Stresemann - Ring 11, D-6200 Wiesbaden, Germany; *Kanada*.

Food and Agricultural Organization of the United Nations (FAO) Via delle Terme di Caracalla, 00100 Rome, Italy (Telephone Number in U.S. (202) 653-2400); *Production Yearbook, The State of Food and Agriculture*, and *Trade Yearbook*.

Gale Research Incorporated, 835 Penobscot Building, Detroit, Michigan 48226 (800) 877-4253; *International Historical Statistics The Americas and Australasia*.

G.K. Hall and Company, 70 Lincoln Street, Boston, Massachusetts 02111 (617) 423-3990; *The World in Figures*.

National Technical Information Service, 5285 Port Royal Road, Springfield, Virginia 22161 (703) 487-4600; *Handbook of Economic Statistics*.

Organisation for Economic Co-operation and Development (OECD), 2 rue Andre-Pascal, 75 Paris 16, France (Telephone Number in U.S. (202) 785-6323); *Economic Accounts for Agriculture, Indicators of Industrial Activity, Industrial Structure Statistics*, and *OECD Economic Surveys: Canada*.

Statistical Office of the United Nations, Publishing Service, New York, New York 10017 (800) 253-9646; *Statistical Yearbook*.

Times Books, 201 East 50th Street, New York, New York 10022 (212) 751-2600; *The Economist Book of Vital World Statistics*.

The World Bank, 1818 H Street, NW, Washington, D.C. 20433 (202) 477-1234; *World Tables*.

CANADA - AIRLINE SERVICE

Facts on File, 460 Park Avenue South, New York, New York 10016 (800) 443-8323; *The New Book of World Rankings*.

G.K. Hall and Company, 70 Lincoln Street, Boston, Massachusetts 02111 (617) 423-3990; *The World in Figures*.

International Civil Aviation Organization, 1000 Sherbrooke Street West, Suite 400, Montreal, Quebec, Canada H3A 2R2 (514) 285-8219; *Civil Aviation Statistics of the World*.

National Technical Information Service, 5285 Port Royal Road, Springfield, Virginia 22161 (703) 487-4600; *Handbook of Economic Statistics*.

Organisation for Economic Co-operation and Development (OECD), 2 rue Andre-Pascal, 75 Paris 16, France (Telephone Number in U.S. (202) 785-6323); *Tourism Policy and International Tourism in OECD Member Countries*.

Statistical Office of the United Nations, Publishing Service, New York, New York 10017 (800) 253-9646; *Statistical Yearbook.*

Times Books, 201 East 50th Street, New York, New York 10022 (212) 751-2600; *The Economist Book of Vital World Statistics.*

CANADA - ALUMINUM PRODUCTION AND CONSUMPTION - See CANADA - MINING AND MINERAL PRODUCTS

CANADA - ANIMAL FEEDINGSTUFFS

Organisation for Economic Co-operation and Development (OECD), 2 rue Andre-Pascal, 75 Paris 16, France (Telephone Number in U.S. (202) 785-6323); *Foreign Trade by Commodities.*

Statistical Office of the United Nations, Publishing Service, New York, New York 10017 (800) 253-9646; *Statistical Yearbook.*

CANADA - ANIMAL HEALTH

Food and Agricultural Organization of the United Nations (FAO), Via delle Terme di Caracalla, 00100 Rome, Italy (Telephone Number in U.S. (202) 653-2400); *Animal Health Yearbook.*

CANADA - ANTIMONY AND ANTIMONY ORE PRODUCTION AND CONSUMPTION - See CANADA - MINING AND MINERAL PRODUCTS

CANADA - APPLE PRODUCTION - See CANADA - CROPS

CANADA - AREA AND DENSITY OF POPULATION

Euromonitor Publications Limited, 87-88 Turnmill Street, London EC1M 5QU, England; *International Marketing Data and Statistics.*

Facts on File, 460 Park Avenue South, New York, New York 10016 (800) 443-8323; *The New Book of World Rankings.*

Federal Statistical Office, Gustav - Stresemann - Ring 11, D-6200 Wiesbaden, Germany; *Kanada.*

Food and Agricultural Organization of the United Nations (FAO) Via delle Terme di Caracalla, 00100 Rome, Italy (Telephone Number in U.S. (202) 653-2400); *The State of Food and Agriculture.*

G.K. Hall and Company, 70 Lincoln Street, Boston, Massachusetts 02111 (617) 423-3990; *The World in Figures.*

National Technical Information Service, 5285 Port Royal Road, Springfield, Virginia 22161 (703) 487-4600; *Handbook of Economic Statistics.*

Statistical Office of the United Nations, Publishing Service, New York, New York 10017 (800) 253-9646; *Statistical Yearbook.*

Times Books, 201 East 50th Street, New York, New York 10022 (212) 751-2600; *The Economist Book of Vital World Statistics.*

United Nations Educational, Scientific and Cultural Organization (UNESCO), 7 Place de Fontenoy, F-75700 Paris, France (Telephone Number in U.S. (212) 963-5981); *Statistical Yearbook.*

CANADA - ARMS EXPORTS AND IMPORTS

U.S. Arms Control and Disarmament Agency, 320 Twenty-first Street, NW, Washington, D.C. 20451 (202) 647-8677; *World Military Expenditures and Arms Transfers.*

CANADA - ARSENIC PRODUCTION AND CONSUMPTION - See CANADA - MINING AND MINERAL PRODUCTS

CANADA - BALANCE OF PAYMENTS

The Economist Intelligence Unit, 111 West 57th Street, New York, New York 10019 (800) 938-4685; *The World Market Atlas.*

Federal Statistical Office, Gustav - Stresemann - Ring 11, D-6200 Wiesbaden, Germany; *Kanada.*

G.K. Hall and Company, 70 Lincoln Street, Boston, Massachusetts 02111 (617) 423-3990; *The World in Figures.*

International Monetary Fund, 700 Nineteenth Street, NW, Washington, D.C. 20431 (202) 623-7000; *Balance of Payments Yearbook,* and *International Financial Statistics.*

National Technical Information Service, 5285 Port Royal Road, Springfield, Virginia 22161 (703) 487-4600; *Handbook of Economic Statistics.*

Organisation for Economic Co-operation and Development (OECD), 2 rue Andre-Pascal, 75 Paris 16, France (Telephone Number in U.S. (202) 785-6323); *Economic Outlook, Geographical Distribution of Financial Flows to Developing Countries, Main Economic Indicators - Historical Statistics,* and *OECD Economic Surveys: Canada.*

Times Books, 201 East 50th Street, New York, New York 10022 (212) 751-2600; *The Economist Book of Vital World Statistics.*

The World Bank, 1818 H Street, NW, Washington, D.C. 20433 (202) 477-1234; *World Tables.*

CANADA - BANKING

Facts on File, 460 Park Avenue South, New York, New York 10016 (800) 443-8323; *The New Book of World Rankings.*

G.K. Hall and Company, 70 Lincoln Street, Boston, Massachusetts 02111 (617) 423-3990; *The World in Figures.*

International Monetary Fund, 700 Nineteenth Street, NW, Washington, D.C. 20431 (202) 623-7000; *International Financial Statistics.*

Organisation for Economic Co-operation and Development (OECD), 2 rue Andre-Pascal, 75 Paris 16, France (Telephone Number in U.S. (202) 785-6323); *Economic Outlook, Financial Market Trends,* and *OECD Economic Surveys: Canada.*

National Technical Information Service, 5285 Port Royal Road, Springfield, Virginia 22161 (703) 487-4600; *Handbook of Economic Statistics.*

Statistical Office of the United Nations, Publishing Service, New York, New York 10017 (800) 253-9646; *Statistical Yearbook.*

CANADA - BARLEY PRODUCTION - See CANADA - CROPS

CANADA - BAUXITE PRODUCTION AND CONSUMPTION - See CANADA - MINING AND MINERAL PRODUCTS

CANADA - BEER PRODUCTION

Facts on File, 460 Park Avenue South, New York, New York 10016 (800) 443-8323; *The New Book of World Rankings.*

Statistical Office of the United Nations, Publishing Service, New York, New York 10017 (800) 253-9646; *Statistical Yearbook.*

CANADA - BEVERAGES - PRODUCTION INDEX

Organisation for Economic Co-operation and Development (OECD), 2 rue Andre-Pascal, 75 Paris 16, France (Telephone Number in U.S. (202) 785-6323); *Indicators of Industrial Activity.*

CANADA - BIRTH RATES

Facts on File, 460 Park Avenue South, New York, New York 10016 (800) 443-8323; *The New Book of World Rankings.*

Statistical Office of the United Nations, Publishing Service, New York, New York 10017 (800) 253-9646; *Demographic Yearbook*, and *Statistical Yearbook.*

Times Books, 201 East 50th Street, New York, New York 10022 (212) 751-2600; *The Economist Book of Vital World Statistics.*

The World Bank, 1818 H Street, NW, Washington, D.C. 20433 (202) 477-1234; *World Tables.*

World Health Organization, Office of Publications, Avenue Appia, CH-1211 Geneva 27, Switzerland (Telephone Number in U.S. (518) 436-9686); *World Health Statistics Annual.*

CANADA - BISMUTH PRODUCTION AND CONSUMPTION - See CANADA - MINING AND MINERAL PRODUCTS

CANADA - BONDS

G.K. Hall and Company, 70 Lincoln Street, Boston, Massachusetts 02111 (617) 423-3990; *The World in Figures.*

International Monetary Fund, 700 Nineteenth Street, NW, Washington, D.C. 20431 (202) 623-7000; *Government Finance Statistics Yearbook.*

Organisation for Economic Co-operation and Development (OECD), 2 rue Andre-Pascal, 75 Paris 16, France (Telephone Number in U.S. (202) 785-6323); *Financial Market Trends.*

Statistical Office of the United Nations, Publishing Service, New York, New York 10017 (800) 253-9646; *Statistical Yearbook.*

CANADA - BOOK PRODUCTION

G.K. Hall and Company, 70 Lincoln Street, Boston, Massachusetts 02111 (617) 423-3990; *The World in Figures.*

Organisation for Economic Co-operation and Development (OECD), 2 rue Andre-Pascal, 75 Paris 16, France (Telephone Number in U.S. (202) 785-6323); *Indicators of Industrial Activity.*

United Nations Educational, Scientific and Cultural Organization (UNESCO), 7 Place de Fontenoy, F-75700 Paris, France (Telephone Number in U.S. (212) 963-5981); *Statistical Yearbook.*

CANADA - BROADCASTING

Billboard Limited, P.O. Box 9027, 1006 AA Amsterdam, The Netherlands (Telephone Number in U.S. (212) 764-7300); *World Radio TV Handbook.*

Facts on File, 460 Park Avenue South, New York, New York 10016 (800) 443-8323; *The New Book of World Rankings.*

G.K. Hall and Company, 70 Lincoln Street, Boston, Massachusetts 02111 (617) 423-3990; *The World in Figures.*

Times Books, 201 East 50th Street, New York, New York 10022 (212) 751-2600; *The Economist Book of Vital World Statistics.*

United Nations Educational, Scientific and Cultural Organization (UNESCO), 7 Place de Fontenoy, F-75700 Paris, France (Telephone Number in U.S. (212) 963-5981); *Statistical Yearbook.*

CANADA - BUILDING CONSTRUCTION - See CANADA - CONSTRUCTION INDUSTRY

CANADA - BUSINESS

G.K. Hall and Company, 70 Lincoln Street, Boston, Massachusetts 02111 (617) 423-3990; *The World in Figures.*

CANADA - BUTTER - See CANADA - DAIRY PRODUCTS

CANADA - CABBAGE PRODUCTION - See CANADA - CROPS

CANADA - CADMIUM PRODUCTION AND CONSUMPTION - See CANADA - MINING AND MINERAL PRODUCTS

CANADA - CALORIE SUPPLY

Food and Agricultural Organization of the United Nations (FAO) Via delle Terme di Caracalla, 00100 Rome, Italy (Telephone Number in U.S. (202) 653-2400); *The State of Food and Agriculture.*

CANADA - CAPITAL INVESTMENT

National Technical Information Service, 5285 Port Royal Road, Springfield, Virginia 22161 (703) 487-4600; *Handbook of Economic Statistics.*

Organisation for Economic Co-operation and Development (OECD), 2 rue Andre-Pascal, 75 Paris 16, France (Telephone Number in U.S. (202) 785-6323); *Financial Market Trends*, and *Economic Outlook.*

CANADA - CAPITAL REVENUE

International Monetary Fund, 700 Nineteenth Street, NW, Washington, D.C. 20431 (202) 623-7000; *Government Finance Statistics Yearbook.*

Organisation for Economic Co-operation and Development (OECD), 2 rue Andre-Pascal, 75 Paris 16, France (Telephone Number in U.S. (202) 785-6323); *Economic Outlook*, and *Financial Market Trends.*

CANADA - CATTLE - See CANADA - LIVESTOCK AND POULTRY

CANADA - CAULIFLOWER PRODUCTION - See CANADA - CROPS

CANADA - CAUSTIC SODA PRODUCTION

Food and Agricultural Organization of the United Nations (FAO) Via delle Terme di Caracalla, 00100 Rome, Italy (Telephone Number in U.S. (202) 653-2400); *The State of Food and Agriculture.*

National Technical Information Service, 5285 Port Royal Road, Springfield, Virginia 22161 (703) 487-4600; *Handbook of Economic Statistics.*

Statistical Office of the United Nations, Publishing Service, New York, New York 10017 (800) 253-9646; *Statistical Yearbook.*

CANADA - CEMENT PRODUCTION - See CANADA - MINING AND MINERAL PRODUCTS

CANADA - CEREAL PRODUCTION - See CANADA - CROPS

CANADA - CHEESE - See CANADA - DAIRY PRODUCTS

CANADA - CHEMICAL (ORGANIC) PRODUCTION - See CANADA - MINING AND MINERAL PRODUCTS

CANADA - CHICKENS - See CANADA - LIVESTOCK AND POULTRY

CANADA - CHROMITE PRODUCTION AND CONSUMPTION - See CANADA - MINING AND MINERAL PRODUCTS

CANADA - CHROMIUM ORE PRODUCTION AND CONSUMPTION - See CANADA - MINING AND MINERAL PRODUCTS

CANADA - CIGAR PRODUCTION - See CANADA - TOBACCO PRODUCTION

CANADA - CIGARETTE PRODUCTION - See CANADA - TOBACCO PRODUCTION

CANADA - CLASS STRUCTURE

G.K. Hall and Company, 70 Lincoln Street, Boston, Massachusetts 02111 (617) 423-3990; *The World in Figures.*

CANADA - CLIMATE

Facts on File, 460 Park Avenue South, New York, New York 10016 (800) 443-8323; *The New Book of World Rankings.*

G.K. Hall and Company, 70 Lincoln Street, Boston, Massachusetts 02111 (617) 423-3990; *The World in Figures.*

CANADA - CLOTHING - PRODUCTION INDEX

Organisation for Economic Co-operation and Development (OECD), 2 rue Andre-Pascal, 75 Paris 16, France (Telephone Number in U.S. (202) 785-6323); *Indicators of Industrial Activity.*

CANADA - CLOTHING EXPORTS AND IMPORTS

Organisation for Economic Co-operation and Development (OECD), 2 rue Andre-Pascal, 75 Paris 16, France (Telephone Number in U.S. (202) 785-6323); *Textile Industry in OECD Countries.*

Statistical Office of the United Nations, Publishing Service, New York, New York 10017 (800) 253-9646; *Trade in Manufactures of Developing Countries.*

CANADA - COAL PRODUCTION - See CANADA - MINING AND MINERAL PRODUCTS

CANADA - COBALT PRODUCTION AND CONSUMPTION - See CANADA - MINING AND MINERAL PRODUCTS

CANADA - COFFEE CONSUMPTION

Statistical Office of the United Nations, Publishing Service, New York, New York 10017 (800) 253-9646; *Statistical Yearbook.*

CANADA - COFFEE PRODUCTION - See CANADA - CROPS

CANADA - COKE AND COKE OVEN COKE PRODUCTION - See CANADA - MINING AND MINERAL PRODUCTS

CANADA - COKE OVEN ORE PRODUCTION AND CONSUMPTION - See CANADA - MINING AND MINERAL PRODUCTS

CANADA - COMMUNICATIONS

Federal Statistical Office, Gustav - Stresemann - Ring 11, D-6200 Wiesbaden, Germany; *Kanada.*

G.K. Hall and Company, 70 Lincoln Street, Boston, Massachusetts 02111 (617) 423-3990; *The World in Figures.*

CANADA - CONSTRUCTION INDUSTRY

Facts on File, 460 Park Avenue South, New York, New York 10016 (800) 443-8323; *The New Book of World Rankings.*

Organisation for Economic Co-operation and Development (OECD), 2 rue Andre-Pascal, 75 Paris 16, France (Telephone Number in U.S. (202) 785-6323); *Industrial Structure Statistics, The Iron and Steel Industry, Main Economic Indicators - Historical Statistics,* and *OECD Economic Surveys: Canada.*

Statistical Office of the United Nations, Publishing Service, New York, New York 10017 (800) 253-9646; *Construction Statistics Yearbook,* and *Statistical Yearbook.*

CANADA - CONSUMER PRICE INDEX

Federal Statistical Office, Gustav - Stresemann - Ring 11, D-6200 Wiesbaden, Germany; *Kanada.*

G.K. Hall and Company, 70 Lincoln Street, Boston, Massachusetts 02111 (617) 423-3990; *The World in Figures.*

National Technical Information Service, 5285 Port Royal Road, Springfield, Virginia 22161 (703) 487-4600; *Handbook of Economic Statistics.*

Organisation for Economic Co-operation and Development (OECD), 2 rue Andre-Pascal, 75 Paris 16, France (Telephone Number in U.S. (202) 785-6323); *Economic Outlook.*

Statistical Office of the United Nations, Publishing Service, New York, New York 10017 (800) 253-9646; *Statistical Yearbook.*

CANADA - CONSUMER PRICES

Federal Statistical Office, Gustav - Stresemann - Ring 11, D-6200 Wiesbaden, Germany; *Kanada.*

International Labour Office, I.L.O. Publications, CH-1211, Geneva 22, Switzerland; *Yearbook of Labour Statistics.*

International Monetary Fund, 700 Nineteenth Street, NW, Washington, D.C. 20431 (202) 623-7000; *International Financial Statistics.*

Organisation for Economic Co-operation and Development (OECD), 2 rue Andre-Pascal, 75 Paris 16, France (Telephone Number in U.S. (202) 785-6323); *Economic Outlook.*

Times Books, 201 East 50th Street, New York, New York 10022 (212) 751-2600; *The Economist Book of Vital World Statistics.*

CANADA - CONSUMPTION

G.K. Hall and Company, 70 Lincoln Street, Boston, Massachusetts 02111 (617) 423-3990; *The World in Figures.*

International Iron and Steel Institute, 120, rue Colonel Bourg, B-1140, Brussels, Belgium; *Steel Statistical Yearbook.*

International Lead and Zinc Study Group, Metro House, 58 St. James's Street, London SW1A 1LD, England; *Lead and Zinc Statistics.*

International Monetary Fund, 700 Nineteenth Street, NW, Washington, D.C. 20431 (202) 623-7000; *International Financial Statistics.*

International Rubber Study Group, York House, Eighth Floor, Empire Way, Wembley, London HA9 0PA, England; *Rubber Statistical Bulletin.*

National Technical Information Service, 5285 Port Royal Road, Springfield, Virginia 22161 (703) 487-4600; *Handbook of Economic Statistics.*

Organisation for Economic Co-operation and Development (OECD), 2 rue Andre-Pascal, 75 Paris 16, France (Telephone Number in U.S. (202) 785-6323); *The Footwear, Raw Hides and Skins, and Leather Industry in OECD Countries, The Iron and Steel Industry, Meat Balances in OECD Member Countries, The Non-Ferrous Metals Industry, The Pulp and Paper Industry,* and *Textile Industry in OECD Countries.*

CANADA - COPPER AND COPPER ORE PRODUCTION - See CANADA - MINING AND MINERAL PRODUCTS

CANADA - CORN PRODUCTION - See CANADA - CROPS

CANADA - CORPORATE INCOME TAXES - See CANADA - TAXATION

CANADA - CORPORATE TAXES - See CANADA - TAXATION

CANADA - COTTON - See CANADA - CROPS

CANADA - CRIME

International Criminal Police Organization (INTERPOL), 26 rue Armengaud, 92210 Saint Cloud, France; *International Crime Statistics.*

Yale University Press, Yale Station, New Haven, Connecticut 06520 (203) 432-0940; *Violence and Crime in Cross-National Perspective.*

CANADA - CROPS

Commodity Research Bureau, Incorporated, 75 Wall Street, New York, New York 10005 (212) 504-7754; *Commodity Year Book.*

Facts on File, 460 Park Avenue South, New York, New York 10016 (800) 443-8323; *The New Book of World Rankings.*

Food and Agricultural Organization of the United Nations (FAO) Via delle Terme di Caracalla, 00100 Rome, Italy (Telephone Number in U.S. (202) 653-2400); *Production Yearbook,* and *The State of Food and Agriculture.*

G.K. Hall and Company, 70 Lincoln Street, Boston, Massachusetts 02111 (617) 423-3990; *The World in Figures.*

International Monetary Fund, 700 Nineteenth Street, NW, Washington, D.C. 20431 (202) 623-7000; *International Financial Statistics.*

National Technical Information Service, 5285 Port Royal Road, Springfield, Virginia 22161 (703) 487-4600; *Handbook of Economic Statistics.*

Organisation for Economic Co-operation and Development (OECD), 2 rue Andre-Pascal, 75 Paris 16, France (Telephone Number in U.S. (202) 785-6323); *Economic Accounts for Agriculture,* and *Foreign Trade by Commodities,* and *Textile Industry in OECD Countries.*

Statistical Office of the United Nations, Publishing Service, New York, New York 10017 (800) 253-9646; *Statistical Yearbook.*

CANADA - CUSTOMS DUTIES

G.K. Hall and Company, 70 Lincoln Street, Boston, Massachusetts 02111 (617) 423-3990; *The World in Figures.*

International Monetary Fund, 700 Nineteenth Street, NW, Washington, D.C. 20431 (202) 623-7000; *Government Finance Statistics Yearbook.*

Organisation for Economic Co-operation and Development (OECD), 2 rue Andre-Pascal, 75 Paris 16, France (Telephone Number in U.S. (202) 785-6323); *The Non-Ferrous Metals Industry.*

CANADA - DAIRY PRODUCTS

Commodity Research Bureau, Incorporated, 75 Wall Street, New York, New York 10005 (212) 504-7754; *Commodity Year Book.*

Facts on File, 460 Park Avenue South, New York, New York 10016 (800) 443-8323; *The New Book of World Rankings.*

Food and Agricultural Organization of the United Nations (FAO) Via delle Terme di Caracalla, 00100 Rome, Italy (Telephone Number in U.S. (202) 653-2400); *Production Yearbook,* and *The State of Food and Agriculture.*

National Technical Information Service, 5285 Port Royal Road, Springfield, Virginia 22161 (703) 487-4600; *Handbook of Economic Statistics.*

Organisation for Economic Co-operation and Development (OECD), 2 rue Andre-Pascal, 75 Paris 16, France (Telephone Number in U.S. (202) 785-6323); *Economic Accounts for Agriculture,* and *Milk, Milk Products, and Egg Balances in OECD Member Countries.*

Statistical Office of the United Nations, Publishing Service, New York, New York 10017 (800) 253-9646; *Statistical Yearbook.*

CANADA - DEATH RATE

G.K. Hall and Company, 70 Lincoln Street, Boston, Massachusetts 02111 (617) 423-3990; *The World in Figures.*

Statistical Office of the United Nations, Publishing Service, New York, New York 10017 (800) 253-9646; *Statistical Yearbook.*

Times Books, 201 East 50th Street, New York, New York 10022 (212) 751-2600; *The Economist Book of Vital World Statistics.*

World Health Organization, Office of Publications, Avenue Appia, CH-1211 Geneva 27, Switzerland (Telephone Number in U.S. (518) 436-9686); *World Health Statistics Annual.*

CANADA - DEFENSE EXPENDITURES

G.K. Hall and Company, 70 Lincoln Street, Boston, Massachusetts 02111 (617) 423-3990; *The World in Figures.*

International Monetary Fund, 700 Nineteenth Street, NW, Washington, D.C. 20431 (202) 623-7000; *Government Finance Statistics Yearbook.*

National Technical Information Service, 5285 Port Royal Road, Springfield, Virginia 22161 (703) 487-4600; *Handbook of Economic Statistics.*

U.S. Arms Control and Disarmament Agency, 320 Twenty-first Street, NW, Washington, D.C. 20451 (202) 647-8677; *World Military Expenditures and Arms Transfers.*

CANADA - DEMOGRAPHY

The Economist Intelligence Unit, 111 West 57th Street, New York, New York 10019 (800) 938-4685; *The World Market Atlas.*

Facts on File, 460 Park Avenue South, New York, New York 10016 (800) 443-8323; *The New Book of World Rankings.*

Federal Statistical Office, Gustav - Stresemann - Ring 11, D-6200 Wiesbaden, Germany; *Kanada.*

G.K. Hall and Company, 70 Lincoln Street, Boston, Massachusetts 02111 (617) 423-3990; *The World in Figures.*

CANADA - DEVELOPMENT ASSISTANCE

G.K. Hall and Company, 70 Lincoln Street, Boston, Massachusetts 02111 (617) 423-3990; *The World in Figures.*

Organisation for Economic Co-operation and Development (OECD), 2 rue Andre-Pascal, 75 Paris 16, France (Telephone Number in U.S. (202) 785-6323); *Geographical Distribution of Financial Flows to Developing Countries.*

Statistical Office of the United Nations, Publishing Service, New York, New York 10017 (800) 253-9646; *Statistical Yearbook.*

CANADA - DIAMOND PRODUCTION - See CANADA - MINING AND MINERAL PRODUCTS

CANADA - DISCOUNT RATES

Organisation for Economic Co-operation and Development (OECD), 2 rue Andre-Pascal, 75 Paris 16, France (Telephone Number in U.S. (202) 785-6323); *Financial Market Trends.*

Statistical Office of the United Nations, Publishing Service, New York, New York 10017 (800) 253-9646; *Statistical Yearbook.*

CANADA - DISEASE

G.K. Hall and Company, 70 Lincoln Street, Boston, Massachusetts 02111 (617) 423-3990; *The World in Figures.*

World Health Organization, Office of Publications, Avenue Appia, CH-1211 Geneva 27, Switzerland (Telephone Number in U.S. (518) 436-9686); *World Health Statistics Annual.*

CANADA - DIVORCE RATES

Facts on File, 460 Park Avenue South, New York, New York 10016 (800) 443-8323; *The New Book of World Rankings.*

Statistical Office of the United Nations, Publishing Service, New York, New York 10017 (800) 253-9646; *Demographic Yearbook,* and *Statistical Yearbook.*

CANADA - DOMESTIC PRODUCT

G.K. Hall and Company, 70 Lincoln Street, Boston, Massachusetts 02111 (617) 423-3990; *The World in Figures.*

Organisation for Economic Co-operation and Development (OECD), 2 rue Andre-Pascal, 75 Paris 16, France; *Main Economic Indicators - Historical Statistics.*

CANADA - DUCKS - See CANADA - LIVESTOCK AND POULTRY

CANADA - ECONOMY

Euromonitor Publications Limited, 87-88 Turnmill Street, London EC1M 5QU, England; *International Marketing Data and Statistics.*

Facts on File, 460 Park Avenue South, New York, New York 10016 (800) 443-8323; *The New Book of World Rankings.*

Federal Statistical Office, Gustav - Stresemann - Ring 11, D-6200 Wiesbaden, Germany; *Kanada.*

G.K. Hall and Company, 70 Lincoln Street, Boston, Massachusetts 02111 (617) 423-3990; *The World in Figures.*

National Technical Information Service, 5285 Port Royal Road, Springfield, Virginia 22161 (703) 487-4600; *Handbook of Economic Statistics.*

Organisation for Economic Co-operation and Development (OECD), 2 rue Andre-Pascal, 75 Paris 16, France (Telephone Number in U.S. (202) 785-6323); *Economic Outlook, Geographical Distribution of Financial Flows to Developing Countries, Main Economic Indicators - Historical Statistics, OECD Economic Surveys: Canada,* and *OECD Employment Outlook.*

CANADA - EDUCATION

The Economist Intelligence Unit, 111 West 57th Street, New York, New York 10019 (800) 938-4685; *The World Market Atlas.*

Facts on File, 460 Park Avenue South, New York, New York 10016 (800) 443-8323; *The New Book of World Rankings.*

Federal Statistical Office, Gustav - Stresemann - Ring 11, D-6200 Wiesbaden, Germany; *Kanada.*

Gale Research Incorporated, 835 Penobscot Building, Detroit, Michigan 48226 (800) 877-4253; *International Historical Statistics The Americas and Australasia.*

G.K. Hall and Company, 70 Lincoln Street, Boston, Massachusetts 02111 (617) 423-3990; *The World in Figures.*

International Monetary Fund, 700 Nineteenth Street, NW, Washington, D.C. 20431 (202) 623-7000; *Government Finance Statistics Yearbook.*

Organisation for Economic Co-operation and Development (OECD), 2 rue Andre-Pascal, 75 Paris 16, France (Telephone Number in U.S. (202) 785-6323); *Education in OECD Countries.*

Times Books, 201 East 50th Street, New York, New York 10022 (212) 751-2600; *The Economist Book of Vital World Statistics.*

United Nations Educational, Scientific and Cultural Organization (UNESCO), 7 Place de Fontenoy, F-75700 Paris, France (Telephone Number in U.S. (212) 963-5981); *Statistical Yearbook.*

The World Bank, 1818 H Street, NW, Washington, D.C. 20433 (202) 477-1234; *World Tables.*

CANADA - EGG PRODUCTION AND CONSUMPTION - See CANADA - DAIRY PRODUCTS

CANADA - ELECTRICITY

Commodity Research Bureau, Incorporated, 75 Wall Street, New York, New York 10005 (212) 504-7754; *Commodity Year Book.*

Facts on File, 460 Park Avenue South, New York, New York 10016 (800) 443-8323; *The New Book of World Rankings.*

National Technical Information Service, 5285 Port Royal Road, Springfield, Virginia 22161 (703) 487-4600; *Handbook of Economic Statistics.*

Organisation for Economic Co-operation and Development (OECD), 2 rue Andre-Pascal, 75 Paris 16, France (Telephone Number in U.S. (202) 785-6323); *Coal Information, Energy Statistics of OECD Countries, Indicators of Industrial Activity,* and *Industrial Structure Statistics.*

Penn Well Publishing Company, 1421 South Sheridan Road, P.O. Box 1260, Tulsa, Oklahoma 74101 (800) 752-9764; *International Energy Statistics Sourcebook.*

Statistical Office of the United Nations, Publishing Service, New York, New York 10017 (800) 253-9646; *Statistical Yearbook.*

Times Books, 201 East 50th Street, New York, New York 10022 (212) 751-2600; *The Economist Book of Vital World Statistics.*

CANADA - EMPLOYMENT

Euromonitor Publications Limited, 87-88 Turnmill Street, London EC1M 5QU, England; *International Marketing Data and Statistics.*

Facts on File, 460 Park Avenue South, New York, New York 10016 (800) 443-8323; *The New Book of World Rankings.*

Federal Statistical Office, Gustav - Stresemann - Ring 11, D-6200 Wiesbaden, Germany; *Kanada.*

International Labour Office, I.L.O. Publications, CH-1211, Geneva 22, Switzerland; *Yearbook of Labour Statistics.*

National Technical Information Service, 5285 Port Royal Road, Springfield, Virginia 22161 (703) 487-4600; *Handbook of Economic Statistics.*

Organisation for Economic Co-operation and Development (OECD), 2 rue Andre-Pascal, 75 Paris 16, France (Telephone Number in U.S. (202) 785-6323); *Economic Outlook, The Iron and Steel Industry, Labour Force Statistics, OECD Economic Surveys: Canada, OECD Employment Outlook,* and *Textile Industries in OECD Countries.*

Statistical Office of the United Nations, Publishing Service, New York, New York 10017 (800) 253-9646; *Statistical Yearbook.*

CANADA - ENERGY

Facts on File, 460 Park Avenue South, New York, New York 10016 (800) 443-8323; *The New Book of World Rankings.*

G.K. Hall and Company, 70 Lincoln Street, Boston, Massachusetts 02111 (617) 423-3990; *The World in Figures.*

National Technical Information Service, 5285 Port Royal Road, Springfield, Virginia 22161 (703) 487-4600; *Handbook of Economic Statistics.*

Organisation for Economic Co-operation and Development (OECD), 2 rue Andre-Pascal, 75 Paris 16, France (Telephone Number in U.S. (202) 785-6323); *Coal Information, Energy Statistics of OECD Countries, OECD Environmental Data,* and *Oil and Gas Information.*

Penn Well Publishing Company, 1421 South Sheridan Road, P.O. Box 1260, Tulsa, Oklahoma 74101 (800) 752-9764; *International Energy Statistics Sourcebook.*

Statistical Office of the United Nations, Publishing Service, New York, New York 10017 (800) 253-9646; *Energy Statistics Yearbook, Statistical Yearbook,* and *World Energy Supplies.*

Times Books, 201 East 50th Street, New York, New York 10022 (212) 751-2600; *The Economist Book of Vital World Statistics.*

CANADA - ENGINEERING AND METAL PRODUCTS IMPORTS FROM DEVELOPING COUNTRIES

Statistical Office of the United Nations, Publishing Service, New York, New York 10017 (800) 253-9646; *Trade in Manufactures of Developing Countries.*

CANADA - ENVIRONMENT

Organization for Economic Co-operation and Development (OECD), 2 rue Andre-Pascal, 75 Paris 16, France (Telephone Number in U.S. (202) 785-6323); *OECD Environmental Data.*

CANADA - EXCHANGE RATES

Euromonitor Publications Limited, 87-88 Turnmill Street, London EC1M 5QU, England; *International Marketing Data and Statistics.*

International Civil Aviation Organization, 1000 Sherbrooke Street West, Suite 400, Montreal, Quebec, Canada H3A 2R2 (514) 285-8219; *Civil Aviation Statistics of the World.*

International Monetary Fund, 700 Nineteenth Street, NW, Washington, D.C. 20431 (202) 623-7000; *International Financial Statistics.*

National Technical Information Service, 5285 Port Royal Road, Springfield, Virginia 22161 (703) 487-4600; *Handbook of Economic Statistics.*

Organisation for Economic Co-operation and Development (OECD), 2 rue Andre-Pascal, 75 Paris 16, France (Telephone Number in U.S. (202) 785-6323); *Economic Outlook, Financial Market Trends, Revenue Statistics of OECD Member Countries,* and *Tourism Policy and International Tourism in OECD Member Countries.*

Statistical Office of the United Nations, Publishing Service, New York, New York 10017 (800) 253-9646; *Statistical Yearbook.*

CANADA - EXCISE TAXES - See CANADA - TAXATION

CANADA - EXPORTS

American Automobile Manufacturers Association, 1401 H Street, NW, Suite 900, Washington, D.C. 20005 (202) 326-5500; *World Motor Vehicle Data.*

The Economist Intelligence Unit, 111 West 57th Street, New York, New York 10019 (800) 938-4685; *The World Market Atlas.*

Euromonitor Publications Limited, 87-88 Turnmill Street, London EC1M 5QU, England; *International Marketing Data and Statistics.*

Food and Agricultural Organization of the United Nations (FAO) Via delle Terme di Caracalla, 00100 Rome, Italy (Telephone Number in U.S. (202) 653-2400); *The State of Food and Agriculture.*

G.K. Hall and Company, 70 Lincoln Street, Boston, Massachusetts 02111 (617) 423-3990; *The World in Figures.*

International Iron and Steel Institute, 120, rue Colonel Bourg, B-1140, Brussels, Belgium; *Steel Statistical Yearbook.*

International Lead and Zinc Study Group, Metro House, 58 St. James's Street, London SW1A 1LD, England; *Lead and Zinc Statistics.*

International Monetary Fund, 700 Nineteenth Street, NW, Washington, D.C. 20431 (202) 623-7000; *Direction of Trade Statistics, Government Finance Statistics Yearbook,* and *International Financial Statistics.*

International Rubber Study Group, York House, Eighth Floor, Empire Way, Wembley, London HA9 0PA, England; *Rubber Statistical Bulletin.*

National Technical Information Service, 5285 Port Royal Road, Springfield, Virginia 22161 (703) 487-4600; *Handbook of Economic Statistics.*

Organisation for Economic Co-operation and Development (OECD), 2 rue Andre-Pascal, 75 Paris 16, France (Telephone Number in U.S. (202) 785-6323); *Economic Outlook, The Footwear, Raw Hides and Skins, and Leather Industry in OECD Countries, Foreign Trade by Commodities, Geographical Distribution of Financial Flows to Developing Countries, Industrial Structure Statistics, The Iron and Steel Industry,Milk, Milk Products, and Egg Balances in OECD Member Countries, OECD Economic Surveys: Canada, The Pulp and Paper Industry,* and *Review of Fisheries in OECD Member Countries.*

Times Books, 201 East 50th Street, New York, New York 10022 (212) 751-2600; *The Economist Book of Vital World Statistics.*

The World Bank, 1818 H Street, NW, Washington, D.C. 20433 (202) 477-1234; *World Tables.*

CANADA - EXTERNAL FINANCING

Organisation for Economic Co-operation and Development (OECD), 2 rue Andre-Pascal, 75 Paris 16, France (Telephone Number in U.S. (202) 785-6323); *Economic Outlook,* and *Financial Market Trends.*

CANADA - EXTERNAL INDEBTEDNESS

National Technical Information Service, 5285 Port Royal Road, Springfield, Virginia 22161 (703) 487-4600; *Handbook of Economic Statistics.*

Organisation for Economic Co-operation and Development (OECD), 2 rue Andre-Pascal, 75 Paris 16, France (Telephone Number in U.S. (202) 785-6323); *Financial Market Trends,* and *Geographical Distribution of Financial Flows to Developing Countries.*

The World Bank, 1818 H Street, NW, Washington, D.C. 20433 (202) 477-1234; *World Tables.*

CANADA - EXTERNAL TRADE

Food and Agricultural Organization of the United Nations (FAO) Via delle Terme di Caracalla, 00100 Rome, Italy (Telephone Number in U.S. (202) 653-2400); *The State of Food and Agriculture,* and *Trade Yearbook.*

Gale Research Incorporated, 835 Penobscot Building, Detroit, Michigan 48226 (800) 877-4253; *International Historical Statistics The Americas and Australasia.*

G.K. Hall and Company, 70 Lincoln Street, Boston, Massachusetts 02111 (617) 423-3990; *The World in Figures.*

National Technical Information Service, 5285 Port Royal Road, Springfield, Virginia 22161 (703) 487-4600; *Handbook of Economic Statistics.*

Statistical Office of the United Nations, Publishing Service, New York, New York 10017 (800) 253-9646; *Statistical Yearbook.*

CANADA - FABRIC PRODUCTION - See CANADA - TEXTILE INDUSTRY

CANADA - FARM CROPS - See CANADA - CROPS

CANADA - FEMALE WORKING POPULATION - See CANADA - EMPLOYMENT

CANADA - FERTILITY RATES

Facts on File, 460 Park Avenue South, New York, New York 10016 (800) 443-8323; *The New Book of World Rankings.*

Times Books, 201 East 50th Street, New York, New York 10022 (212) 751-2600; *The Economist Book of Vital World Statistics.*

The World Bank, 1818 H Street, NW, Washington, D.C. 20433 (202) 477-1234; *World Tables.*

CANADA - FERTILIZER

Food and Agricultural Organization of the United Nations (FAO), Via delle Terme di Caracalla, 00100 Rome, Italy (Telephone Number in U.S. (202) 653-2400); *Fertilizer Yearbook,* and *The State of Food and Agriculture.*

National Technical Information Service, 5285 Port Royal Road, Springfield, Virginia 22161 (703) 487-4600; *Handbook of Economic Statistics.*

Organisation for Economic Co-operation and Development (OECD), 2 rue Andre-Pascal, 75 Paris 16, France (Telephone Number in U.S. (202) 785-6323); *Economic Accounts for Agriculture, Foreign Trade by Commodities.*

Statistical Office of the United Nations, Publishing Service, New York, New York 10017 (800) 253-9646; *Statistical Yearbook.*

CANADA - FETAL MORTALITY

Statistical Office of the United Nations, Publishing Service, New York, New York 10017 (800) 253-9646; *Demographic Yearbook.*

World Health Organization, Office of Publications, Avenue Appia, CH-1211 Geneva 27, Switzerland (Telephone Number in U.S. (518) 436-9686); *World Health Statistics Annual.*

CANADA - FIBRE PRODUCTION - See CANADA - TEXTILE INDUSTRY

CANADA - FILAMENT PRODUCTION - See CANADA - TEXTILE INDUSTRY

CANADA - FILM - See CANADA - MOTION PICTURES

CANADA - FINANCE

Facts on File, 460 Park Avenue South, New York, New York 10016 (800) 443-8323; *The New Book of World Rankings*.

Federal Statistical Office, Gustav - Stresemann - Ring 11, D-6200 Wiesbaden, Germany; *Kanada*.

Gale Research Incorporated, 835 Penobscot Building, Detroit, Michigan 48226 (800) 877-4253; *International Historical Statistics The Americas and Australasia*.

G.K. Hall and Company, 70 Lincoln Street, Boston, Massachusetts 02111 (617) 423-3990; *The World in Figures*.

International Monetary Fund, 700 Nineteenth Street, NW, Washington, D.C. 20431 (202) 623-7000; *Government Finance Statistics Yearbook*, and *International Financial Statistics*.

Organisation for Economic Co-operation and Development (OECD), 2 rue Andre-Pascal, 75 Paris 16, France (Telephone Number in U.S. (202) 785-6323); *Economic Outlook, Financial Market Trends, Geographical Distribution of Financial Flows to Developing Countries*, and *OECD Financial Statistics*.

CANADA - FISHERIES

Facts on File, 460 Park Avenue South, New York, New York 10016 (800) 443-8323; *The New Book of World Rankings*.

Federal Statistical Office, Gustav - Stresemann - Ring 11, D-6200 Wiesbaden, Germany; *Kanada*.

Food and Agricultural Organization of the United Nations (FAO) Via delle Terme di Caracalla, 00100 Rome, Italy (Telephone Number in U.S. (202) 653-2400); *The State of Food and Agriculture*, and *Yearbook of Fishery Statistics*.

National Technical Information Service, 5285 Port Royal Road, Springfield, Virginia 22161 (703) 487-4600; *Handbook of Economic Statistics*.

Organisation for Economic Co-operation and Development (OECD), 2 rue Andre-Pascal, 75 Paris 16, France (Telephone Number in U.S. (202) 785-6323); *Foreign Trade by Commodities, Industrial Structure Statistics*, and *Review of Fisheries in OECD Member Countries*.

Statistical Office of the United Nations, Publishing Service, New York, New York 10017 (800) 253-9646; *Statistical Yearbook*.

CANADA - FLOUR PRODUCTION

Commodity Research Bureau, Incorporated, 75 Wall Street, New York, New York 10005 (212) 504-7754; *Commodity Year Book*.

Statistical Office of the United Nations, Publishing Service, New York, New York 10017 (800) 253-9646; *Statistical Yearbook*.

CANADA - FOOD

Food and Agricultural Organization of the United Nations (FAO) Via delle Terme di Caracalla, 00100 Rome, Italy (Telephone Number in U.S. (202) 653-2400); *The State of Food and Agriculture*.

G.K. Hall and Company, 70 Lincoln Street, Boston, Massachusetts 02111 (617) 423-3990; *The World in Figures*.

Organisation for Economic Co-operation and Development (OECD), 2 rue Andre-Pascal, 75 Paris 16, France (Telephone Number in U.S. (202) 785-6323); *Food Consumption Statistics*, and *Foreign Trade by Commodities*.

Statistical Office of the United Nations, Publishing Service, New York, New York 10017 (800) 253-9646; *Trade in Manufactures of Developing Countries*.

CANADA - FOOTWEAR - PRODUCTION INDEX

Organisation for Economic Co-operation and Development (OECD), 2 rue Andre-Pascal, 75 Paris 16, France (Telephone Number in U.S. (202) 785-6323); *Indicators of Industrial Activity*.

CANADA - FOREIGN AID

G.K. Hall and Company, 70 Lincoln Street, Boston, Massachusetts 02111 (617) 423-3990; *The World in Figures*.

National Technical Information Service, 5285 Port Royal Road, Springfield, Virginia 22161 (703) 487-4600; *Handbook of Economic Statistics*.

CANADA - FOREIGN DEBT

International Monetary Fund, 700 Nineteenth Street, NW, Washington, D.C. 20431 (202) 623-7000; *Government Finance Statistics Yearbook*.

Organisation for Economic Co-operation and Development (OECD), 2 rue Andre-Pascal, 75 Paris 16, France (Telephone Number in U.S. (202) 785-6323); *Economic Outlook*.

CANADA - FOREIGN FINANCE

Organisation for Economic Co-operation and Development (OECD), 2 rue Andre-Pascal, 75 Paris 16, France (Telephone Number in U.S. (202) 785-6323); *Economic Outlook, Financial Market Trends*, and *Main Economic Indicators - Historical Statistics*.

CANADA - FOREIGN INDEBTEDNESS

Organisation for Economic Co-operation and Development (OECD), 2 rue Andre-Pascal, 75 Paris 16, France (Telephone Number in U.S. (202) 785-6323); *Economic Outlook*, and *Financial Market Trends*.

CANADA - FOREIGN TRADE

Euromonitor Publications Limited, 87-88 Turnmill Street, London EC1M 5QU, England; *International Marketing Data and Statistics*.

Facts on File, 460 Park Avenue South, New York, New York 10016 (800) 443-8323; *The New Book of World Rankings*.

Federal Statistical Office, Gustav - Stresemann - Ring 11, D-6200 Wiesbaden, Germany; *Kanada*.

Food and Agricultural Organization of the United Nations (FAO) Via delle Terme di Caracalla, 00100 Rome, Italy (Telephone Number in

U.S. (202) 653-2400); *The State of Food and Agriculture.*

G.K. Hall and Company, 70 Lincoln Street, Boston, Massachusetts 02111 (617) 423-3990; *The World in Figures.*

International Iron and Steel Institute, 120, rue Colonel Bourg, B-1140, Brussels, Belgium; *Steel Statistical Yearbook.*

National Technical Information Service, 5285 Port Royal Road, Springfield, Virginia 22161 (703) 487-4600; *Handbook of Economic Statistics.*

Organisation for Economic Co-operation and Development (OECD), 2 rue Andre-Pascal, 75 Paris 16, France (Telephone Number in U.S. (202) 785-6323); *Economic Outlook, The Footwear, Raw Hides and Skins, and Leather Industry in OECD Countries, Foreign Trade by Commodities, Main Economic Indicators - Historical Statistics, Maritime Transport, Meat Balances in OECD Member Countries,* and *OECD Economic Surveys: Canada.*

Statistical Office of the United Nations, Publishing Service, New York, New York 10017 (800) 253-9646; *International Trade Statistics Yearbook, Statistical Yearbook,* and *Trade in Manufactures of Developing Countries.*

The World Bank, 1818 H Street, NW, Washington, D.C. 20433 (202) 477-1234; *World Tables.*

World Bureau of Metal Statistics, 27-A High Street, Ware Hert SG12 9BA, England; *World Metal Statistics.*

CANADA - FORESTRY AND FOREST PRODUCTS

Facts on File, 460 Park Avenue South, New York, New York 10016 (800) 443-8323; *The New Book of World Rankings.*

Federal Statistical Office, Gustav - Stresemann - Ring 11, D-6200 Wiesbaden, Germany; *Kanada.*

Food and Agricultural Organization of the United Nations (FAO) Via delle Terme di Caracalla, 00100 Rome, Italy (Telephone Number in U.S. (202) 653-2400); *The State of Food and Agriculture,* and *Yearbook of Forest Products.*

Forest and Paper Association, 1250 Connecticut Avenue, NW, Washington, D.C. 20036 (202) 463-2455; *Pulp and Fiber Statistics.*

G.K. Hall and Company, 70 Lincoln Street, Boston, Massachusetts 02111 (617) 423-3990; *The World in Figures.*

International Monetary Fund, 700 Nineteenth Street, NW, Washington, D.C. 20431 (202) 623-7000; *International Financial Statistics.*

National Technical Information Service, 5285 Port Royal Road, Springfield, Virginia 22161 (703) 487-4600; *Handbook of Economic Statistics.*

Organisation for Economic Co-operation and Development (OECD), 2 rue Andre-Pascal, 75 Paris 16, France (Telephone Number in U.S. (202) 785-6323); *Foreign Trade by Commodities, Indicators of Industrial Activity, Industrial Structure Statistics,* and *The Pulp and Paper Industry.*

Statistical Office of the United Nations, Publishing Service, New York, New York 10017 (800) 253-9646; *Statistical Yearbook.*

CANADA - FRUIT PRODUCTION - See CANADA - CROPS

CANADA - FURNITURE AND WOOD PRODUCTS - EXPORTS AND IMPORTS

Organisation for Economic Co-operation and Development (OECD), 2 rue Andre-Pascal, 75 Paris 16, France (Telephone Number in U.S. (202) 785-6323); *Foreign Trade by Commodities,* and *Industrial Structure Statistics.*

CANADA - GAS AND GAS LIQUIDS PRODUCTION - See CANADA - MINING AND MINERAL PRODUCTS

CANADA - GENERAL INDUSTRIAL STATISTICS

Federal Statistical Office, Gustav - Stresemann - Ring 11, D-6200 Wiesbaden, Germany; *Kanada.*

Statistical Office of the United Nations, Publishing Service, New York, New York 10017 (800) 253-9646; *Industrial Statistics Yearbook.*

CANADA - GENERAL MORTALITY

Statistical Office of the United Nations, Publishing Service, New York, New York 10017 (800) 253-9646; *Demographic Yearbook.*

World Health Organization, Office of Publications, Avenue Appia, CH-1211 Geneva 27, Switzerland (Telephone Number in U.S. (518) 436-9686); *World Health Statistics Annual.*

CANADA - GEOGRAPHIC DATA

Facts on File, 460 Park Avenue South, New York, New York 10016 (800) 443-8323; *The New Book of World Rankings.*

Federal Statistical Office, Gustav - Stresemann - Ring 11, D-6200 Wiesbaden, Germany; *Kanada.*

CANADA - GLASS AND GLASS PRODUCTS - See CANADA - MINING AND MINERAL PRODUCTS

CANADA - GOATS - See CANADA - LIVESTOCK AND POULTRY

CANADA - GOLD HOLDINGS

International Monetary Fund, 700 Nineteenth Street, NW, Washington, D.C. 20431 (202) 623-7000; *International Financial Statistics.*

Statistical Office of the United Nations, Publishing Service, New York, New York 10017 (800) 253-9646; *Statistical Yearbook.*

The World Bank, 1818 H Street, NW, Washington, D.C. 20433 (202) 477-1234; *World Tables.*

CANADA - GOLD PRODUCTION AND CONSUMPTION - See CANADA - MINING AND MINERAL PRODUCTS

CANADA - GOVERNMENT

G.K. Hall and Company, 70 Lincoln Street, Boston, Massachusetts 02111 (617) 423-3990; *The World in Figures.*

CANADA - GOVERNMENT BONDS - See CANADA - BONDS

CANADA - GOVERNMENT CONSUMPTION

International Monetary Fund, 700 Nineteenth Street, NW, Washington, D.C. 20431 (202) 623-7000; *International Financial Statistics.*

CANADA - GOVERNMENT EXPENDITURES

International Monetary Fund, 700 Nineteenth Street, NW, Washington, D.C. 20431 (202) 623-7000; *Government Finance Statistics Yearbook.*

Organisation for Economic Co-operation and Development (OECD), 2 rue Andre-Pascal, 75 Paris 16, France (Telephone Number in U.S. (202) 785-6323); *Economic Outlook.*

Times Books, 201 East 50th Street, New York, New York 10022 (212) 751-2600; *The Economist Book of Vital World Statistics.*

The World Bank, 1818 H Street, NW, Washington, D.C. 20433 (202) 477-1234; *World Tables.*

CANADA - GOVERNMENT FINANCES

International Monetary Fund, 700 Nineteenth Street, NW, Washington, D.C. 20431 (202) 623-7000; *International Financial Statistics.*

Organisation for Economic Co-operation and Development (OECD), 2 rue Andre-Pascal, 75 Paris 16, France (Telephone Number in U.S. (202) 785-6323); *Economic Outlook.*

Statistical Office of the United Nations, Publishing Service, New York, New York 10017 (800) 253-9646; *Statistical Yearbook.*

CANADA - GOVERNMENT REVENUE

International Monetary Fund, 700 Nineteenth Street, NW, Washington, D.C. 20431 (202) 623-7000; *Government Finance Statistics Yearbook.*

Organisation for Economic Co-operation and Development (OECD), 2 rue Andre-Pascal, 75 Paris 16, France (Telephone Number in U.S. (202) 785-6323); *Economic Outlook,* and *Revenue Statistics of OECD Member Countries.*

Times Books, 201 East 50th Street, New York, New York 10022 (212) 751-2600; *The Economist Book of Vital World Statistics.*

The World Bank, 1818 H Street, NW, Washington, D.C. 20433 (202) 477-1234; *World Tables.*

CANADA - GRAIN PRODUCTION - See CANADA - CROPS

CANADA - GRANTS

International Monetary Fund, 700 Nineteenth Street, NW, Washington, D.C. 20431 (202) 623-7000; *Government Finance Statistics Yearbook.*

National Technical Information Service, 5285 Port Royal Road, Springfield, Virginia 22161 (703) 487-4600; *Handbook of Economic Statistics.*

Organisation for Economic Co-operation and Development (OECD), 2 rue Andre-Pascal, 75 Paris 16, France (Telephone Number in U.S. (202) 785-6323); *Geographical Distribution of Financial Flows to Developing Countries.*

CANADA - GREEN PEPPER AND CHILIE PRODUCTION - See CANADA - CROPS

CANADA - GROSS DOMESTIC PRODUCT

The Economist Intelligence Unit, 111 West 57th Street, New York, New York 10019 (800) 938-4685; *The World Market Atlas.*

Euromonitor Publications Limited, 87-88 Turnmill Street, London EC1M 5QU, England; *International Marketing Data and Statistics.*

Facts on File, 460 Park Avenue South, New York, New York 10016 (800) 443-8323; *The New Book of World Rankings.*

G.K. Hall and Company, 70 Lincoln Street, Boston, Massachusetts 02111 (617) 423-3990; *The World in Figures.*

International Monetary Fund, 700 Nineteenth Street, NW, Washington, D.C. 20431 (202) 623-7000; *International Financial Statistics.*

National Technical Information Service, 5285 Port Royal Road, Springfield, Virginia 22161 (703) 487-4600; *Handbook of Economic Statistics.*

Organisation for Economic Co-operation and Development (OECD), 2 rue Andre-Pascal, 75 Paris 16, France (Telephone Number in U.S. (202) 785-6323); *Economic Outlook, Geographical Distribution of Financial Flows to Developing Countries,* and *Revenue Statistics of OECD Member Countries.*

Statistical Office of the United Nations, Publishing Service, New York, New York 10017 (800) 253-9646; *Statistical Yearbook.*

Times Books, 201 East 50th Street, New York, New York 10022 (212) 751-2600; *The Economist Book of Vital World Statistics.*

The World Bank, 1818 H Street, NW, Washington, D.C. 20433 (202) 477-1234; *World Tables.*

CANADA - GROSS NATIONAL PRODUCT

Euromonitor Publications Limited, 87-88 Turnmill Street, London EC1M 5QU, England; *International Marketing Data and Statistics.*

National Technical Information Service, 5285 Port Royal Road, Springfield, Virginia 22161 (703) 487-4600; *Handbook of Economic Statistics.*

Organisation for Economic Co-operation and Development (OECD), 2 rue Andre-Pascal, 75 Paris 16, France (Telephone Number in U.S. (202) 785-6323); *Economic Outlook,* and *Geographical Distribution of Financial Flows to Developing Countries.*

U.S. Arms Control and Disarmament Agency, 320 Twenty-first Street, NW, Washington, D.C. 20451 (202) 647-8677; *World Military Expenditures and Arms Transfers.*

The World Bank, 1818 H Street, NW, Washington, D.C. 20433 (202) 477-1234; *World Tables.*

CANADA - HEALTH

Facts on File, 460 Park Avenue South, New York, New York 10016 (800) 443-8323; *The New Book of World Rankings.*

Federal Statistical Office, Gustav - Stresemann - Ring 11, D-6200 Wiesbaden, Germany; *Kanada.*

G.K. Hall and Company, 70 Lincoln Street, Boston, Massachusetts 02111 (617) 423-3990; *The World in Figures.*

Statistical Office of the United Nations, Publishing Service, New York, New York 10017 (800) 253-9646; *Statistical Yearbook.*

Organisation for Economic Co-operation and Development (OECD), 2 rue Andre-Pascal, 75 Paris 16, France (Telephone Number in U.S. (202) 785-6323); *OECD Health Systems: Facts and Trends.*

Times Books, 201 East 50th Street, New York, New York 10022 (212) 751-2600; *The Economist Book of Vital World Statistics.*

World Health Organization, Office of Publications, Avenue Appia, CH-1211 Geneva 27, Switzerland (Telephone Number in U.S. (518) 436-9686); *World Health Statistics Annual.*

CANADA - HEALTH EXPENDITURES

International Monetary Fund, 700 Nineteenth Street, NW, Washington, D.C. 20431 (202) 623-7000; *Government Finance Statistics Yearbook.*

CANADA - HIDE PRODUCTION

Food and Agricultural Organization of the United Nations (FAO), Via delle Terme di Caracalla, 00100 Rome, Italy (Telephone Number in U.S. (202) 653-2400); *Production Yearbook.*

Organisation for Economic Co-operation and Development (OECD), 2 rue Andre-Pascal, 75 Paris 16, France (Telephone Number in U.S. (202) 785-6323); *The Footwear, Raw Hides and Skins, and Leather Industry in OECD Countries, Foreign Trade by Commodities,* and *Indicators of Industrial Activity.*

CANADA - HIGHWAYS

G.K. Hall and Company, 70 Lincoln Street, Boston, Massachusetts 02111 (617) 423-3990; *The World in Figures.*

International Road Federation, 525 School Street, SW, Washington, D.C. 20024 (202) 554-2106; *World Road Statistics.*

Statistical Office of the United Nations, Publishing Service, New York, New York 10017 (800) 253-9646; *Annual Bulletin of Transport Statistics for Europe.*

CANADA - HOME FINANCE

Organisation for Economic Co-operation and Development (OECD), 2 rue Andre-Pascal, 75 Paris 16, France (Telephone Number in U.S. (202) 785-6323); *Main Economic Indicators - Historical Statistics.*

CANADA - HONEY PRODUCTION

Commodity Research Bureau, Incorporated, 75 Wall Street, New York, New York 10005 (212) 504-7754; *Commodity Year Book.*

CANADA - HORSES - See CANADA - LIVESTOCK AND POULTRY

CANADA - HOURS OF WORK - See CANADA - EMPLOYMENT

CANADA - HOUSING AND HOUSING UNITS

Facts on File, 460 Park Avenue South, New York, New York 10016 (800) 443-8323; *The New Book of World Rankings.*

National Technical Information Service, 5285 Port Royal Road, Springfield, Virginia 22161 (703) 487-4600; *Handbook of Economic Statistics.*

Statistical Office of the United Nations, Publishing Service, New York, New York 10017 (800) 253-9646; *Statistical Yearbook.*

CANADA - HOUSING CONSTRUCTION - See CANADA - CONSTRUCTION

CANADA - HOUSING EXPENDITURES

International Monetary Fund, 700 Nineteenth Street, NW, Washington, D.C. 20431 (202) 623-7000; *Government Finance Statistics Yearbook.*

CANADA - HYDROCHLORIC ACID

Statistical Office of the United Nations, Publishing Service, New York, New York 10017 (800) 253-9646; *Statistical Yearbook.*

CANADA - ILLITERATE POPULATION

The Economist Intelligence Unit, 111 West 57th Street, New York, New York 10019 (800) 938-4685; *The World Market Atlas.*

G.K. Hall and Company, 70 Lincoln Street, Boston, Massachusetts 02111 (617) 423-3990; *The World in Figures.*

CANADA - IMPORTS

American Automobile Manufacturers Association, 1401 H Street, NW, Suite 900, Washington, D.C. 20005 (202) 326-5500; *World Motor Vehicle Data.*

The Economist Intelligence Unit, 111 West 57th Street, New York, New York 10019 (800) 938-4685; *The World Market Atlas.*

Euromonitor Publications Limited, 87-88 Turnmill Street, London EC1M 5QU, England; *International Marketing Data and Statistics.*

Food and Agricultural Organization of the United Nations (FAO) Via delle Terme di Caracalla, 00100 Rome, Italy (Telephone Number in U.S. (202) 653-2400); *The State of Food and Agriculture.*

G.K. Hall and Company, 70 Lincoln Street, Boston, Massachusetts 02111 (617) 423-3990; *The World in Figures.*

International Iron and Steel Institute, 120, rue Colonel Bourg, B-1140, Brussels, Belgium; *Steel Statistical Yearbook.*

International Lead and Zinc Study Group, Metro House, 58 St. James's Street, London SW1A 1LD, England; *Lead and Zinc Statistics.*

International Monetary Fund, 700 Nineteenth Street, NW, Washington, D.C. 20431 (202) 623-7000; *Direction of Trade Statistics, Government Finance Statistics Yearbook,* and *International Financial Statistics.*

International Rubber Study Group, York House, Eighth Floor, Empire Way, Wembley, London HA9 0PA, England; *Rubber Statistical Bulletin.*

National Technical Information Service, 5285 Port Royal Road, Springfield, Virginia 22161 (703) 487-4600; *Handbook of Economic Statistics.*

Organisation for Economic Co-operation and Development (OECD), 2 rue Andre-Pascal, 75 Paris 16, France (Telephone Number in U.S. (202) 785-6323); *Economic Outlook, The Footwear, Raw Hides and Skins, and Leather Industry in OECD Countries, Industrial Structure Statistics, The Iron and Steel Industry, Milk, Milk Products, and Egg*

Balances in OECD Member Countries, OECD Economic Surveys: Canada, The Pulp and Paper Industry, and *Review of Fisheries in OECD Member Countries.*

Times Books, 201 East 50th Street, New York, New York 10022 (212) 751-2600; *The Economist Book of Vital World Statistics.*

The World Bank, 1818 H Street, NW, Washington, D.C. 20433 (202) 477-1234; *World Tables.*

CANADA - INCOME TAXES - See CANADA - TAXATION

CANADA - INDUSTRIAL METALS PRODUCTION - See CANADA - MINING AND MINERAL PRODUCTS

CANADA - INDUSTRY

Euromonitor Publications Limited, 87-88 Turnmill Street, London EC1M 5QU, England; *International Marketing Data and Statistics.*

Facts on File, 460 Park Avenue South, New York, New York 10016 (800) 443-8323; *The New Book of World Rankings.*

Federal Statistical Office, Gustav - Stresemann - Ring 11, D-6200 Wiesbaden, Germany; *Kanada.*

Gale Research Incorporated, 835 Penobscot Building, Detroit, Michigan 48226 (800) 877-4253; *International Historical Statistics The Americas and Australasia.*

G.K. Hall and Company, 70 Lincoln Street, Boston, Massachusetts 02111 (617) 423-3990; *The World in Figures.*

International Labour Office, I.L.O. Publications, CH-1211, Geneva 22, Switzerland; *Yearbook of Labour Statistics.*

National Technical Information Service, 5285 Port Royal Road, Springfield, Virginia 22161 (703) 487-4600; *Handbook of Economic Statistics.*

Organization for Economic Co-operation and Development (OECD), 2 rue Andre-Pascal, 75 Paris 16, France (Telephone Number in U.S. (202) 785-6323); *Economic Outlook, Indicators of Industrial Activity, Industrial Structure Statistics,* and *OECD Environmental Data.*

Statistical Office of the United Nations, Publishing Service, New York, New York 10017 (800) 253-9646; *Statistical Yearbook.*

Times Books, 201 East 50th Street, New York, New York 10022 (212) 751-2600; *The Economist Book of Vital World Statistics.*

The World Bank, 1818 H Street, NW, Washington, D.C. 20433 (202) 477-1234; *World Tables.*

World Intellectual Property Organization, 34 Chemin des Colombettes, CH-1211 Geneva 20. Switzerland; *Industrial Property Statistics.*

CANADA - INFANT AND MATERNAL MORTALITY

Statistical Office of the United Nations, Publishing Service, New York, New York 10017 (800) 253-9646; *Demographic Yearbook,* and *Statistical Yearbook.*

Times Books, 201 East 50th Street, New York, New York 10022 (212) 751-2600; *The Economist Book of Vital World Statistics.*

The World Bank, 1818 H Street, NW, Washington, D.C. 20433 (202) 477-1234; *World Tables.*

World Health Organization, Office of Publications, Avenue Appia, CH-1211 Geneva 27, Switzerland (Telephone Number in U.S. (518) 436-9686); *World Health Statistics Annual.*

CANADA - INFLATIONARY FACTORS

National Technical Information Service, 5285 Port Royal Road, Springfield, Virginia 22161 (703) 487-4600; *Handbook of Economic Statistics.*

CANADA - INTEREST RATES

National Technical Information Service, 5285 Port Royal Road, Springfield, Virginia 22161 (703) 487-4600; *Handbook of Economic Statistics.*

Organisation for Economic Co-operation and Development (OECD), 2 rue Andre-Pascal, 75 Paris 16, France (Telephone Number in U.S. (202) 785-6323); *Economic Outlook, Financial Market Trends, Main Economic Indicators - Historical Statistics,* and *OECD Financial Statistics.*

CANADA - INTERNAL TRADE

Organisation for Economic Co-operation and Development (OECD), 2 rue Andre-Pascal, 75 Paris 16, France (Telephone Number in U.S. (202) 785-6323); *Main Economic Indicators - Historical Statistics.*

CANADA - INTERNATIONAL FINANCE

Organisation for Economic Co-operation and Development (OECD), 2 rue Andre-Pascal, 75 Paris 16, France (Telephone Number in U.S. (202) 785-6323); *Economic Outlook,* and *Financial Market Trends.*

CANADA - INTERNATIONAL LIQUIDITY

International Monetary Fund, 700 Nineteenth Street, NW, Washington, D.C. 20431 (202) 623-7000; *International Financial Statistics.*

Organisation for Economic Co-operation and Development (OECD), 2 rue Andre-Pascal, 75 Paris 16, France (Telephone Number in U.S. (202) 785-6323); *Economic Outlook,* and *Financial Market Trends.*

CANADA - INTERNATIONAL RESERVES EXCLUDING GOLD

National Technical Information Service, 5285 Port Royal Road, Springfield, Virginia 22161 (703) 487-4600; *Handbook of Economic Statistics.*

The World Bank, 1818 H Street, NW, Washington, D.C. 20433 (202) 477-1234; *World Tables.*

CANADA - INTERNATIONAL STATISTICS

Organisation for Economic Co-operation and Development (OECD), 2 rue Andre-Pascal, 75 Paris 16, France (Telephone Number in U.S. (202) 785-6323); *Financial Market Trends,* and *Tourism Policy and International Tourism in OECD Member Countries.*

CANADA - INVESTMENTS

International Monetary Fund, 700 Nineteenth Street, NW, Washington, D.C. 20431 (202) 623-7000; *International Financial Statistics.*

Organisation for Economic Co-operation and Development (OECD), 2 rue Andre-Pascal, 75 Paris 16, France (Telephone Number in U.S. (202) 785-6323); *Economic Outlook, Financial Market Trends,*

Industrial Structure Statistics, The Iron and Steel Industry, and *Textile Industry in OECD Countries.*

CANADA - IRON ORE - See CANADA - MINING AND MINERAL PRODUCTS

CANADA - IRRIGATION

Euromonitor Publications Limited, 87-88 Turnmill Street, London EC1M 5QU, England; *International Marketing Data and Statistics.*

CANADA - LABOR FORCE

Euromonitor Publications Limited, 87-88 Turnmill Street, London EC1M 5QU, England; *International Marketing Data and Statistics.*

Facts on File, 460 Park Avenue South, New York, New York 10016 (800) 443-8323; *The New Book of World Rankings.*

Food and Agricultural Organization of the United Nations (FAO) Via delle Terme di Caracalla, 00100 Rome, Italy (Telephone Number in U.S. (202) 653-2400); *The State of Food and Agriculture.*

Gale Research Incorporated, 835 Penobscot Building, Detroit, Michigan 48226 (800) 877-4253; *International Historical Statistics The Americas and Australasia.*

G.K. Hall and Company, 70 Lincoln Street, Boston, Massachusetts 02111 (617) 423-3990; *The World in Figures.*

National Technical Information Service, 5285 Port Royal Road, Springfield, Virginia 22161 (703) 487-4600; *Handbook of Economic Statistics.*

Organisation for Economic Co-operation and Development (OECD), 2 rue Andre-Pascal, 75 Paris 16, France (Telephone Number in U.S. (202) 785-6323); *Economic Outlook, The Iron and Steel Industry, Labour Force Statistics, Main Economic Indicators - Historical Statistics, Maritime Transport, OECD Economic Surveys: Canada, OECD Employment Outlook,* and *Textile Industry in OECD Countries.*

Times Books, 201 East 50th Street, New York, New York 10022 (212) 751-2600; *The Economist Book of Vital World Statistics.*

The World Bank, 1818 H Street, NW, Washington, D.C. 20433 (202) 477-1234; *World Tables.*

CANADA - LABOR PRODUCTIVITY

International Labour Office, I.L.O. Publications, CH-1211, Geneva 22, Switzerland; *Yearbook of Labour Statistics.*

Organisation for Economic Co-operation and Development (OECD), 2 rue Andre-Pascal, 75 Paris 16, France (Telephone Number in U.S. (202) 785-6323); *Economic Outlook,* and *OECD Employment Outlook.*

CANADA - LAND USE

Euromonitor Publications Limited, 87-88 Turnmill Street, London EC1M 5QU, England; *International Marketing Data and Statistics.*

Food and Agricultural Organization of the United Nations (FAO), Via delle Terme di Caracalla, 00100 Rome, Italy (Telephone Number in U.S. (202) 653-2400); *Production Yearbook.*

G.K. Hall and Company, 70 Lincoln Street, Boston, Massachusetts 02111 (617) 423-3990; *The World in Figures.*

CANADA - LEAD AND LEAD ORE PRODUCTION AND CONSUMPTION - See CANADA - MINING AND MINERAL PRODUCTS

CANADA - LEATHER - PRODUCTION INDEX

Organisation for Economic Co-operation and Development (OECD), 2 rue Andre-Pascal, 75 Paris 16, France (Telephone Number in U.S. (202) 785-6323); *Indicators of Industrial Activity.*

CANADA - LEATHER AND FOOTWEAR EXPORTS AND IMPORTS

Organisation for Economic Co-operation and Development (OECD), 2 rue Andre-Pascal, 75 Paris 16, France (Telephone Number in U.S. (202) 785-6323); *The Footwear, Raw Hides and Skins, and Leather Industry in OECD Countries.*

Statistical Office of the United Nations, Publishing Service, New York, New York 10017 (800) 253-9646; *Trade in Manufactures of Developing Countries.*

CANADA - LIBRARIES

Facts on File, 460 Park Avenue South, New York, New York 10016 (800) 443-8323; *The New Book of World Rankings.*

United Nations Educational, Scientific and Cultural Organization (UNESCO), 7 Place de Fontenoy, F-75700 Paris, France (Telephone Number in U.S. (212) 963-5981); *Statistical Yearbook.*

CANADA - LIGNITE PRODUCTION - See CANADA - MINING AND MINERAL PRODUCTS

CANADA - LIVESTOCK AND POULTRY

Commodity Research Bureau, Incorporated, 75 Wall Street, New York, New York 10005 (212) 504-7754; *Commodity Year Book.*

Euromonitor Publications Limited, 87-88 Turnmill Street, London EC1M 5QU, England; *International Marketing Data and Statistics.*

Facts on File, 460 Park Avenue South, New York, New York 10016 (800) 443-8323; *The New Book of World Rankings.*

Food and Agricultural Organization of the United Nations (FAO), Via delle Terme di Caracalla, 00100 Rome, Italy (Telephone Number in U.S. (202) 653-2400); *Production Yearbook,* and *The State of Food and Agriculture.*

G.K. Hall and Company, 70 Lincoln Street, Boston, Massachusetts 02111 (617) 423-3990; *The World in Figures.*

National Technical Information Service, 5285 Port Royal Road, Springfield, Virginia 22161 (703) 487-4600; *Handbook of Economic Statistics.*

Organisation for Economic Co-operation and Development (OECD), 2 rue Andre-Pascal, 75 Paris 16, France (Telephone Number in U.S. (202) 785-6323); *Economic Accounts for Agriculture,* and *Meat Balances in OECD Member Countries.*

Statistical Office of the United Nations, Publishing Service, New York, New York 10017 (800) 253-9646; *Statistical Yearbook.*

CANADA - LIVING LEVELS

G.K. Hall and Company, 70 Lincoln Street, Boston, Massachusetts 02111 (617) 423-3990; *The World in Figures.*

Organisation for Economic Co-operation and Development (OECD), 2 rue Andre-Pascal, 75 Paris 16, France (Telephone Number in U.S. (202) 785-6323); *Economic Outlook.*

Times Books, 201 East 50th Street, New York, New York 10022 (212) 751-2600; *The Economist Book of Vital World Statistics.*

CANADA - MACHINERY - PRODUCTION INDEX

Organisation for Economic Co-operation and Development (OECD), 2 rue Andre-Pascal, 75 Paris 16, France (Telephone Number in U.S. (202) 785-6323); *Indicators of Industrial Activity.*

CANADA - MAGNESIUM PRODUCTION AND CONSUMPTION - See CANADA - MINING AND MINERAL PRODUCTS

CANADA - MAIL - NUMBER OF PIECES SENT OR RECEIVED

Statistical Office of the United Nations, Publishing Service, New York, New York 10017 (800) 253-9646; *Statistical Yearbook.*

CANADA - MANGANESE PRODUCTION AND CONSUMPTION - See CANADA - MINING AND MINERAL PRODUCTS

CANADA - MANUFACTURING

American Automobile Manufacturers Association, 1401 H Street, NW, Suite 900, Washington, D.C. 20005 (202) 326-5500; *World Motor Vehicle Data.*

Facts on File, 460 Park Avenue South, New York, New York 10016 (800) 443-8323; *The New Book of World Rankings.*

G.K. Hall and Company, 70 Lincoln Street, Boston, Massachusetts 02111 (617) 423-3990; *The World in Figures.*

National Technical Information Service, 5285 Port Royal Road, Springfield, Virginia 22161 (703) 487-4600; *Handbook of Economic Statistics.*

Organisation for Economic Co-operation and Development (OECD), 2 rue Andre-Pascal, 75 Paris 16, France (Telephone Number in U.S. (202) 785-6323); *Foreign Trade by Commodities, Indicators of Industrial Activity, Industrial Structure Statistics, Main Economic Indicators - Historical Statistics,* and *OECD Economic Surveys: Canada.*

Statistical Office of the United Nations, Publishing Service, New York, New York 10017 (800) 253-9646; *Statistical Yearbook.*

Times Books, 201 East 50th Street, New York, New York 10022 (212) 751-2600; *The Economist Book of Vital World Statistics.*

The World Bank, 1818 H Street, NW, Washington, D.C. 20433 (202) 477-1234; *World Tables.*

CANADA - MARRIAGE RATES

Facts on File, 460 Park Avenue South, New York, New York 10016 (800) 443-8323; *The New Book of World Rankings.*

Statistical Office of the United Nations, Publishing Service, New York, New York 10017 (800) 253-9646; *Demographic Yearbook.*

CANADA - MEAT PRODUCTION - See CANADA - LIVESTOCK AND POULTRY

CANADA - MERCHANT SHIPPING

G.K. Hall and Company, 70 Lincoln Street, Boston, Massachusetts 02111 (617) 423-3990; *The World in Figures.*

Lloyd's Register of Shipping, 17 Battery Place, New York, New York 10004 (212) 425-8050; *Register of Ships.*

National Technical Information Service, 5285 Port Royal Road, Springfield, Virginia 22161 (703) 487-4600; *Handbook of Economic Statistics.*

Organisation for Economic Co-operation and Development (OECD), 2 rue Andre-Pascal, 75 Paris 16, France (Telephone Number in U.S. (202) 785-6323); *Maritime Transport.*

Statistical Office of the United Nations, Publishing Service, New York, New York 10017 (800) 253-9646; *Statistical Yearbook.*

Times Books, 201 East 50th Street, New York, New York 10022 (212) 751-2600; *The Economist Book of Vital World Statistics.*

U.S. Department of Transportation, Maritime Administration, 400 Seventh Street, SW, Washington, D.C. 20590 (202) 366-5807; *A Statistical Analysis of the World's Merchant Fleets.*

CANADA - MERCURY PRODUCTION AND CONSUMPTION - See CANADA MINING AND MINERAL PRODUCTS

CANADA - MILITARY

G.K. Hall and Company, 70 Lincoln Street, Boston, Massachusetts 02111 (617) 423-3990; *The World in Figures.*

The International Institute for Strategic Studies, 23 Tavistock Street, London WC2E 7NQ, England; *The Military Balance.*

U.S. Arms Control and Disarmament Agency, 320 Twenty-first Street, NW, Washington, D.C. 20451 (202) 647-8677; *World Military Expenditures and Arms Transfers.*

CANADA - MILK PRODUCTION - See CANADA - DAIRY PRODUCTS

CANADA - MINING AND MINERAL PRODUCTS

Commodity Research Bureau, Incorporated, 75 Wall Street, New York, New York 10005 (212) 504-7754; *Commodity Year Book.*

Facts on File, 460 Park Avenue South, New York, New York 10016 (800) 443-8323; *The New Book of World Rankings.*

G.K. Hall and Company, 70 Lincoln Street, Boston, Massachusetts 02111 (617) 423-3990; *The World in Figures.*

International Iron and Steel Institute, 120, rue Colonel Bourg, B-1140, Brussels, Belgium; *Steel Statistical Yearbook.*

International Lead and Zinc Study Group, Metro House, 58 St. James's Street, London SW1A 1LD, England; *Lead and Zinc Statistics.*

International Monetary Fund, 700 Nineteenth Street, NW, Washington, D.C. 20431 (202) 623-7000; *International Financial Statistics.*

National Technical Information Service, 5285 Port Royal Road, Springfield, Virginia 22161 (703) 487-4600; *Handbook of Economic Statistics.*

Organisation for Economic Co-operation and Development (OECD), 2 rue Andre-Pascal, 75 Paris 16, France (Telephone Number in U.S. (202) 785-6323); *Coal Information, Energy Statistics of OECD Countries, Foreign Trade by Commodities, Indicators of Industrial Activity, Industrial Structure Statistics, The Iron and Steel Industry, The Non-Ferrous Metals Industry,* and *Statistical Yearbook.*

Penn Well Publishing Company, 1421 South Sheridan Road, P.O. Box 1260, Tulsa, Oklahoma 74101 (800) 752-9764; *International Energy Statistics Sourcebook.*

Statistical Office of the United Nations, Publishing Service, New York, New York 10017 (800) 253-9646; *Statistical Yearbook.*

World Bureau of Metal Statistics, 27-A High Street, Ware Hert SG12 9BA, England; *World Metal Statistics.*

CANADA - MINING OUTPUT - See CANADA - MINING AND MINERAL PRODUCTS

CANADA - MOLYBDENUM AND MOLYBDENUM ORE PRODUCTION AND CONSUMPTION - See CANADA - MINING AND MINERAL PRODUCTS

CANADA - MONEY EXCHANGE RATE

Euromonitor Publications Limited, 87-88 Turnmill Street, London EC1M 5QU, England; *International Marketing Data and Statistics.*

International Monetary Fund, 700 Nineteenth Street, NW, Washington, D.C. 20431 (202) 623-7000; *International Financial Statistics.*

Organisation for Economic Co-operation and Development (OECD), 2 rue Andre-Pascal, 75 Paris 16, France (Telephone Number in U.S. (202) 785-6323); *Economic Outlook, Financial Market Trends,* and *Tourism Policy and International Tourism in OECD Member Countries.*

Statistical Office of the United Nations, Publishing Service, New York, New York 10017 (800) 253-9646; *Statistical Yearbook.*

CANADA - MONEY RATES - MARKET

Organisation for Economic Co-operation and Development (OECD), 2 rue Andre-Pascal, 75 Paris 16, France (Telephone Number in U.S. (202) 785-6323); *Economic Outlook,* and *Financial Market Trends.*

Statistical Office of the United Nations, Publishing Service, New York, New York 10017 (800) 253-9646; *Statistical Yearbook.*

CANADA - MONEY RESERVES

Euromonitor Publications Limited, 87-88 Turnmill Street, London EC1M 5QU, England; *International Marketing Data and Statistics.*

Organisation for Economic Co-operation and Development (OECD), 2 rue Andre-Pascal, 75 Paris 16, France (Telephone Number in U.S. (202) 785-6323); *Economic Outlook,* and *Financial Market Trends.*

CANADA - MONEY SUPPLY

Euromonitor Publications Limited, 87-88 Turnmill Street, London EC1M 5QU, England; *International Marketing Data and Statistics.*

Federal Statistical Office, Gustav - Stresemann - Ring 11, D-6200 Wiesbaden, Germany; *Kanada.*

G.K. Hall and Company, 70 Lincoln Street, Boston, Massachusetts 02111 (617) 423-3990; *The World in Figures.*

International Monetary Fund, 700 Nineteenth Street, NW, Washington, D.C. 20431 (202) 623-7000; *International Financial Statistics.*

Organisation for Economic Co-operation and Development (OECD), 2 rue Andre-Pascal, 75 Paris 16, France (Telephone Number in U.S. (202) 785-6323); *Economic Outlook.*

Statistical Office of the United Nations, Publishing Service, New York, New York 10017 (800) 253-9646; *Statistical Yearbook.*

The World Bank, 1818 H Street, NW, Washington, D.C. 20433 (202) 477-1234; *World Tables.*

CANADA - MONUMENTS AND HISTORICAL SITES

United Nations Educational, Scientific and Cultural Organization (UNESCO), 7 Place de Fontenoy, F-75700 Paris, France (Telephone Number in U.S. (212) 963-5981); *Statistical Yearbook.*

CANADA - MOTION PICTURES

Statistical Office of the United Nations, Publishing Service, New York, New York 10017 (800) 253-9646; *Statistical Yearbook.*

United Nations Educational, Scientific and Cultural Organization (UNESCO), 7 Place de Fontenoy, F-75700 Paris, France (Telephone Number in U.S. (212) 963-5981); *Statistical Yearbook.*

CANADA - MOTOR VEHICLE PRODUCTION

American Automobile Manufacturers Association, 1401 H Street, NW, Suite 900, Washington, D.C. 20005 (202) 326-5500 *World Motor Vehicle Data.*

National Technical Information Service, 5285 Port Royal Road, Springfield, Virginia 22161 (703) 487-4600; *Handbook of Economic Statistics.*

Organisation for Economic Co-operation and Development (OECD), 2 rue Andre-Pascal, 75 Paris 16, France (Telephone Number in U.S. (202) 785-6323); *Foreign Trade by Commodities,* and *Indicators of Industrial Activity.*

Statistical Office of the United Nations, Publishing Service, New York, New York 10017 (800) 253-9646; *Statistical Yearbook.*

CANADA - MOTOR VEHICLES IN USE

American Automobile Manufacturers Association, 1401 H Street, NW, Suite 900, Washington, D.C. 20005 (202) 326-5500; *World Motor Vehicle Data.*

G.K. Hall and Company, 70 Lincoln Street, Boston, Massachusetts 02111 (617) 423-3990; *The World in Figures.*

International Road Federation, 525 School Street, SW, Washington, D.C. 20024 (202) 554-2106; *World Road Statistics.*

Statistical Office of the United Nations, Publishing Service, New York, New York 10017 (800) 253-9646; *Statistical Yearbook.*

Times Books, 201 East 50th Street, New York, New York 10022 (212) 751-2600; *The Economist Book of Vital World Statistics.*

CANADA - MULES - See CANADA - LIVESTOCK AND POULTRY

CANADA - MUSEUMS

Facts on File, 460 Park Avenue South, New York, New York 10016 (800) 443-8323; *The New Book of World Rankings.*

United Nations Educational, Scientific and Cultural Organization (UNESCO), 7 Place de Fontenoy, F-75700 Paris, France (Telephone Number in U.S. (212) 963-5981); *Statistical Yearbook.*

CANADA - NATALITY - See CANADA - BIRTH RATE

CANADA - NATIONAL ACCOUNTS

Federal Statistical Office, Gustav - Stresemann - Ring 11, D-6200 Wiesbaden, Germany; *Kanada.*

Gale Research Incorporated, 835 Penobscot Building, Detroit, Michigan 48226 (800) 877-4253; *International Historical Statistics The Americas and Australasia.*

International Monetary Fund, 700 Nineteenth Street, NW, Washington, D.C. 20431 (202) 623-7000; *International Financial Statistics.*

Organisation for Economic Co-operation and Development (OECD), 2 rue Andre-Pascal, 75 Paris 16, France (Telephone Number in U.S. (202) 785-6323); *Economic Outlook.*

Statistical Office of the United Nations, Publishing Service, New York, New York 10017 (800) 253-9646; *National Accounts Statistics,* and *Statistical Yearbook.*

CANADA - NATIONAL INCOME

Facts on File, 460 Park Avenue South, New York, New York 10016 (800) 443-8323; *The New Book of World Rankings.*

G.K. Hall and Company, 70 Lincoln Street, Boston, Massachusetts 02111 (617) 423-3990; *The World in Figures.*

Organisation for Economic Co-operation and Development (OECD), 2 rue Andre-Pascal, 75 Paris 16, France (Telephone Number in U.S. (202) 785-6323); *Economic Outlook.*

Statistical Office of the United Nations, Publishing Service, New York, New York 10017 (800) 253-9646; *Statistical Yearbook.*

CANADA - NATIONAL PRODUCT

Facts on File, 460 Park Avenue South, New York, New York 10016 (800) 443-8323; *The New Book of World Rankings.*

Organisation for Economic Co-operation and Development (OECD), 2 rue Andre-Pascal, 75 Paris 16, France (Telephone Number in U.S. (202) 785-6323); *Economic Outlook,* and *Main Economic Indicators - Historical Statistics.*

Statistical Office of the United Nations, Publishing Service, New York, New York 10017 (800) 253-9646; *Statistical Yearbook.*

CANADA - NATURAL GAS PRODUCTION - See CANADA - MINING AND MINERAL PRODUCTS

CANADA - NATURAL RUBBER PRODUCTION

International Rubber Study Group, York House, Eighth Floor, Empire Way, Wembley, London HA9 0PA, England; *Rubber Statistical Bulletin.*

National Technical Information Service, 5285 Port Royal Road, Springfield, Virginia 22161 (703) 487-4600; *Handbook of Economic Statistics.*

CANADA - NET MATERIAL PRODUCT

Statistical Office of the United Nations, Publishing Service, New York, New York 10017 (800) 253-9646; *Statistical Yearbook.*

CANADA - NEWSPAPER PRODUCTION - See CANADA - FORESTRY AND FOREST PRODUCTS

CANADA - NEWSPRINT - See CANADA - FORESTRY AND FOREST PRODUCTS

CANADA - NICKEL AND NICKEL ORE PRODUCTION AND CONSUMPTION - See CANADA - MINING AND MINERAL PRODUCTS

CANADA - NITRIC ACID PRODUCTION - See CANADA - MINING AND MINERAL PRODUCTS

CANADA - OATS PRODUCTION - See CANADA - CROPS

CANADA - OCCUPATIONS - See CANADA - LABOR FORCE

CANADA - OIL PRODUCING CROPS

Organisation for Economic Co-operation and Development (OECD), 2 rue Andre-Pascal, 75 Paris 16, France (Telephone Number in U.S. (202) 785-6323); *Foreign Trade by Commodities.*

CANADA - PAPER - See CANADA - FORESTRY AND FOREST PRODUCTS

CANADA - PATENTS

Statistical Office of the United Nations, Publishing Service, New York, New York 10017 (800) 253-9646; *Statistical Yearbook.*

World Intellectual Property Organization, 34 Chemin des Colombettes, CH-1211 Geneva 20. Switzerland; *Industrial Property Statistics.*

CANADA - PEANUT PRODUCTION - See CANADA - CROPS

CANADA - PERIODICALS

United Nations Educational, Scientific and Cultural Organization (UNESCO), 7 Place de Fontenoy, F-75700 Paris, France (Telephone Number in U.S. (212) 963-5981); *Statistical Yearbook.*

CANADA - PESTICIDE USE

Food and Agricultural Organization of the United Nations (FAO) Via delle Terme di Caracalla, 00100 Rome, Italy (Telephone Number in U.S. (202) 653-2400); *The State of Food and Agriculture.*

CANADA - PETROLEUM INDUSTRY

Commodity Research Bureau, Incorporated, 75 Wall Street, New York, New York 10005 (212) 504-7754; *Commodity Year Book.*

Facts on File, 460 Park Avenue South, New York, New York 10016 (800) 443-8323; *The New Book of World Rankings.*

Food and Agricultural Organization of the United Nations (FAO) Via delle Terme di Caracalla, 00100 Rome, Italy (Telephone Number in

U.S. (202) 653-2400); *The State of Food and Agriculture.*

G.K. Hall and Company, 70 Lincoln Street, Boston, Massachusetts 02111 (617) 423-3990; *The World in Figures.*

International Monetary Fund, 700 Nineteenth Street, NW, Washington, D.C. 20431 (202) 623-7000; *International Financial Statistics.*

National Technical Information Service, 5285 Port Royal Road, Springfield, Virginia 22161 (703) 487-4600; *Handbook of Economic Statistics.*

Organisation for Economic Co-operation and Development (OECD), 2 rue Andre-Pascal, 75 Paris 16, France (Telephone Number in U.S. (202) 785-6323); *Energy Statistics of OECD Countries, Foreign Trade by Commodities, Indicators of Industrial Activity,* and *Oil and Gas Information.*

Penn Well Publishing Company, 1421 South Sheridan Road, P.O. Box 1260, Tulsa, Oklahoma 74101 (800) 752-9764; *International Energy Statistics Sourcebook.*

Statistical Office of the United Nations, Publishing Service, New York, New York 10017 (800) 253-9646; *Statistical Yearbook.*

CANADA - PHOSPHATE AND PHOSPHATE ROCK PRODUCTION - See CANADA - MINING AND MINERAL PRODUCTS

CANADA - PIG-IRON AND FERRO-ALLOY PRODUCTION - See CANADA - MINING AND MINERAL PRODUCTS

CANADA - PIGS - See CANADA - LIVESTOCK AND POULTRY

CANADA - PIPELINES FOR OIL AND PETROLEUM PRODUCTS

National Technical Information Service, 5285 Port Royal Road, Springfield, Virginia 22161 (703) 487-4600; *Handbook of Economic Statistics.*

Statistical Office of the United Nations, Publishing Service, New York, New York 10017 (800) 253-9646; *Annual Bulletin of Transport Statistics for Europe.*

CANADA - PLASTIC AND RESIN PRODUCTION

Organisation for Economic Co-operation and Development (OECD), 2 rue Andre-Pascal, 75 Paris 16, France (Telephone Number in U.S. (202) 785-6323); *Foreign Trade by Commodities.*

Statistical Office of the United Nations, Publishing Service, New York, New York 10017 (800) 253-9646; *Statistical Yearbook.*

CANADA - PLATINUM PRODUCTION - See CANADA - MINING AND MINERAL PRODUCTS

CANADA - POPULATION

The Economist Intelligence Unit, 111 West 57th Street, New York, New York 10019 (800) 938-4685; *The World Market Atlas.*

Euromonitor Publications Limited, 87-88 Turnmill Street, London EC1M 5QU, England; *International Marketing Data and Statistics.*

Facts on File, 460 Park Avenue South, New York, New York 10016 (800) 443-8323; *The New Book of World Rankings.*

Federal Statistical Office, Gustav - Stresemann - Ring 11, D-6200 Wiesbaden, Germany; *Kanada.*

Food and Agricultural Organization of the United Nations (FAO), Via delle Terme di Caracalla, 00100 Rome, Italy (Telephone Number in U.S. (202) 653-2400); *Production Yearbook.*

Gale Research Incorporated, 835 Penobscot Building, Detroit, Michigan 48226 (800) 877-4253; *International Historical Statistics The Americas and Australasia.*

G.K. Hall and Company, 70 Lincoln Street, Boston, Massachusetts 02111 (617) 423-3990; *The World in Figures.*

International Labour Office, I.L.O. Publications, CH-1211, Geneva 22, Switzerland; *Yearbook of Labour Statistics.*

National Technical Information Service, 5285 Port Royal Road, Springfield, Virginia 22161 (703) 487-4600; *Handbook of Economic Statistics.*

Statistical Office of the United Nations, Publishing Service, New York, New York 10017 (800) 253-9646; *Demographic Yearbook,* and *Statistical Yearbook.*

Times Books, 201 East 50th Street, New York, New York 10022 (212) 751-2600; *The Economist Book of Vital World Statistics.*

United Nations Educational, Scientific and Cultural Organization (UNESCO), 7 Place de Fontenoy, F-75700 Paris, France (Telephone Number in U.S. (212) 963-5981); *Statistical Yearbook.*

U.S. Arms Control and Disarmament Agency, 320 Twenty-first Street, NW, Washington, D.C. 20451 (202) 647-8677; *World Military Expenditures and Arms Transfers.*

World Health Organization, Office of Publications, Avenue Appia, CH-1211 Geneva 27, Switzerland (Telephone Number in U.S. (518) 436-9686); *World Health Statistics Annual.*

CANADA - POST OFFICES

Facts on File, 460 Park Avenue South, New York, New York 10016 (800) 443-8323; *The New Book of World Rankings.*

CANADA - POTATO PRODUCTION - See CANADA - CROPS

CANADA - POWER PRODUCTION INDUSTRY - EMPLOYMENT

Statistical Office of the United Nations, Publishing Service, New York, New York 10017 (800) 253-9646; *Statistical Yearbook.*

CANADA - PRICES

Facts on File, 460 Park Avenue South, New York, New York 10016 (800) 443-8323; *The New Book of World Rankings.*

Federal Statistical Office, Gustav - Stresemann - Ring 11, D-6200 Wiesbaden, Germany; *Kanada.*

Food and Agricultural Organization of the United Nations (FAO), Via delle Terme di Caracalla, 00100 Rome, Italy (Telephone Number in U.S. (202) 653-2400); *Production Yearbook,* and *The State of Food and Agriculture.*

Gale Research Incorporated, 835 Penobscot Building, Detroit, Michigan 48226 (800) 877-4253; *International Historical Statistics The Americas and Australasia.*

G.K. Hall and Company, 70 Lincoln Street, Boston, Massachusetts 02111 (617) 423-3990; *The World in Figures.*

International Labour Office, I.L.O. Publications, CH-1211, Geneva 22, Switzerland; *Yearbook of Labour Statistics.*

International Lead and Zinc Study Group, Metro House, 58 St. James's Street, London SW1A 1LD, England; *Lead and Zinc Statistics.*

International Rubber Study Group, York House, Eighth Floor, Empire Way, Wembley, London HA9 0PA, England; *Rubber Statistical Bulletin.*

National Technical Information Service, 5285 Port Royal Road, Springfield, Virginia 22161 (703) 487-4600; *Handbook of Economic Statistics.*

Organisation for Economic Co-operation and Development (OECD), 2 rue Andre-Pascal, 75 Paris 16, France (Telephone Number in U.S. (202) 785-6323); *Economic Outlook, The Footwear, Raw Hides and Skins, and Leather Industry in OECD Countries, Indicators of Industrial Activity, The Iron and Steel Industry, Main Economic Indicators - Historical Statistics,* and *The Pulp and Paper Industry.*

World Bureau of Metal Statistics, 27-A High Street, Ware Hert SG12 9BA, England; *World Metal Statistics.*

CANADA - PRINTING AND WRITING PAPER - See CANADA - FORESTRY AND FOREST PRODUCTS

CANADA - PRODUCTION

American Automobile Manufacturers Association, 1401 H Street, NW, Suite 900, Washington, D.C. 20005 (202) 326-5500; *World Motor Vehicle Data.*

Facts on File, 460 Park Avenue South, New York, New York 10016 (800) 443-8323; *The New Book of World Rankings.*

G.K. Hall and Company, 70 Lincoln Street, Boston, Massachusetts 02111 (617) 423-3990; *The World in Figures.*

International Iron and Steel Institute, 120, rue Colonel Bourg, B-1140, Brussels, Belgium; *Steel Statistical Yearbook.*

International Lead and Zinc Study Group, Metro House, 58 St. James's Street, London SW1A 1LD, England; *Lead and Zinc Statistics.*

International Rubber Study Group, York House, Eighth Floor, Empire Way, Wembley, London HA9 0PA, England; *Rubber Statistical Bulletin.*

National Technical Information Service, 5285 Port Royal Road, Springfield, Virginia 22161 (703) 487-4600; *Handbook of Economic Statistics.*

Organisation for Economic Co-operation and Development (OECD), 2 rue Andre-Pascal, 75 Paris 16, France (Telephone Number in U.S. (202) 785-6323); *Economic Outlook, The Footwear, Raw Hides and Skins, and Leather Industry in OECD Countries, Indicators of Industrial Activity, Industrial Structure Statistics, The Iron and Steel Industry, Main Economic Indicators - Historical Statistics, Meat Balances in OECD Member Countries, Milk, Milk Products, and Egg Balances in OECD Member Countries, The Non-Ferrous Metals Industry, The Pulp and Paper Industry,* and *Textile Industry in OECD Countries.*

CANADA - PRODUCTIVITY

Euromonitor Publications Limited, 87-88 Turnmill Street, London EC1M 5QU, England; *International Marketing Data and Statistics.*

Organisation for Economic Co-operation and Development (OECD), 2 rue Andre-Pascal, 75 Paris 16, France (Telephone Number in U.S. (202) 785-6323); *Economic Outlook.*

CANADA - PROPERTY TAXES

International Monetary Fund, 700 Nineteenth Street, NW, Washington, D.C. 20431 (202) 623-7000; *Government Finance Statistics Yearbook.*

Organisation for Economic Co-operation and Development (OECD), 2 rue Andre-Pascal, 75 Paris 16, France (Telephone Number in U.S. (202) 785-6323); *Revenue Statistics of OECD Member Countries.*

CANADA - PUBLIC CONSUMPTION FUND

Organisation for Economic Co-operation and Development (OECD), 2 rue Andre-Pascal, 75 Paris 16, France (Telephone Number in U.S. (202) 785-6323); *Revenue Statistics of OECD Member Countries.*

CANADA - PUBLIC EXPENDITURES

National Technical Information Service, 5285 Port Royal Road, Springfield, Virginia 22161 (703) 487-4600; *Handbook of Economic Statistics.*

Organisation for Economic Co-operation and Development (OECD), 2 rue Andre-Pascal, 75 Paris 16, France (Telephone Number in U.S. (202) 785-6323); *Revenue Statistics of OECD Member Countries.*

CANADA - PUBLIC FINANCE

Facts on File, 460 Park Avenue South, New York, New York 10016 (800) 443-8323; *The New Book of World Rankings.*

Federal Statistical Office, Gustav - Stresemann - Ring 11, D-6200 Wiesbaden, Germany; *Kanada.*

National Technical Information Service, 5285 Port Royal Road, Springfield, Virginia 22161 (703) 487-4600; *Handbook of Economic Statistics.*

Organisation for Economic Co-operation and Development (OECD), 2 rue Andre-Pascal, 75 Paris 16, France (Telephone Number in U.S. (202) 785-6323); *Revenue Statistics of OECD Member Countries.*

CANADA - PUBLIC REVENUES

National Technical Information Service, 5285 Port Royal Road, Springfield, Virginia 22161 (703) 487-4600; *Handbook of Economic Statistics.*

Organisation for Economic Co-operation and Development (OECD), 2 rue Andre-Pascal, 75 Paris 16, France (Telephone Number in U.S. (202) 785-6323); *Revenue Statistics of OECD Member Countries.*

CANADA - RADIO BROADCASTING - See CANADA - BROADCASTING

CANADA - RADIO RECEIVER PRODUCTION

Statistical Office of the United Nations, Publishing Service, New York, New York 10017 (800) 253-9646; *Statistical Yearbook.*

CANADA - RAILWAYS

G.K. Hall and Company, 70 Lincoln Street, Boston, Massachusetts 02111 (617) 423-3990; *The World in Figures.*

Jane's Information Group, Sentinel House, 163 Brighton Road, Coulsdon, Surrey CR5 2NH, England (Telephone Number in U.S. (703) 683-3700); *Jane's World of Railways.*

National Technical Information Service, 5285 Port Royal Road, Springfield, Virginia 22161 (703) 487-4600; *Handbook of Economic Statistics.*

Statistical Office of the United Nations, Publishing Service, New York, New York 10017 (800) 253-9646; *Annual Bulletin of Transport Statistics for Europe,* and *Statistical Yearbook.*

CANADA - RAPESEED PRODUCTION - See CANADA - CROPS

CANADA - RELIGION

Facts on File, 460 Park Avenue South, New York, New York 10016 (800) 443-8323; *The New Book of World Rankings.*

CANADA - RETAIL TRADE

G.K. Hall and Company, 70 Lincoln Street, Boston, Massachusetts 02111 (617) 423-3990; *The World in Figures.*

Statistical Office of the United Nations, Publishing Service, New York, New York 10017 (800) 253-9646; *Statistical Yearbook.*

CANADA - RICE PRODUCTION - See CANADA - CROPS

CANADA - ROOT AND TUBER PRODUCTION - See CANADA - CROPS

CANADA - ROUNDWOOD PRODUCTION - See CANADA - FORESTRY AND FOREST PRODUCTS

CANADA - RUBBER PRODUCTION AND CONSUMPTION

Commodity Research Bureau, Incorporated, 75 Wall Street, New York, New York 10005 (212) 504-7754; *Commodity Year Book.*

Facts on File, 460 Park Avenue South, New York, New York 10016 (800) 443-8323; *The New Book of World Rankings.*

International Rubber Study Group, York House, Eighth Floor, Empire Way, Wembley, London HA9 0PA, England; *Rubber Statistical Bulletin.*

National Technical Information Service, 5285 Port Royal Road, Springfield, Virginia 22161 (703) 487-4600; *Handbook of Economic Statistics.*

Organisation for Economic Co-operation and Development (OECD), 2 rue Andre-Pascal, 75 Paris 16, France (Telephone Number in U.S. (202) 785-6323); *Foreign Trade by Commodities.*

Statistical Office of the United Nations, Publishing Service, New York, New York 10017 (800) 253-9646; *Statistical Yearbook.*

CANADA - RYE PRODUCTION - See CANADA - CROPS

CANADA - SALT PRODUCTION - See CANADA - MINING AND MINERAL PRODUCTS

CANADA - SAWNWOOD PRODUCTION - See CANADA - FORESTRY AND FOREST PRODUCTS

CANADA - SCIENCE AND TECHNOLOGY - EXPENDITURE FOR RESEARCH

Statistical Office of the United Nations, Publishing Service, New York, New York 10017 (800) 253-9646; *Statistical Yearbook.*

CANADA - SCIENTISTS AND TECHNICIANS

Statistical Office of the United Nations, Publishing Service, New York, New York 10017 (800) 253-9646; *Statistical Yearbook.*

CANADA - SENIOR CITIZENS

Facts on File, 460 Park Avenue South, New York, New York 10016 (800) 443-8323; *The New Book of World Rankings.*

CANADA - SHEEP - See CANADA - LIVESTOCK AND POULTRY

CANADA - SHIPBUILDING - PRODUCTION INDEX

Organisation for Economic Co-operation and Development (OECD), 2 rue Andre-Pascal, 75 Paris 16, France (Telephone Number in U.S. (202) 785-6323); *Indicators of Industrial Activity.*

CANADA - SILVER PRODUCTION AND CONSUMPTION - See CANADA - MINING AND MINERAL PRODUCTS

CANADA - SOCIAL DATA

Facts on File, 460 Park Avenue South, New York, New York 10016 (800) 443-8323; *The New Book of World Rankings.*

G.K. Hall and Company, 70 Lincoln Street, Boston, Massachusetts 02111 (617) 423-3990; *The World in Figures.*

CANADA - SOCIAL SECURITY

International Monetary Fund, 700 Nineteenth Street, NW, Washington, D.C. 20431 (202) 623-7000; *Government Finance Statistics Yearbook.*

Organisation for Economic Co-operation and Development (OECD), 2 rue Andre-Pascal, 75 Paris 16, France (Telephone Number in U.S. (202) 785-6323); *Revenue Statistics of OECD Member Countries.*

CANADA - SOCIOECONOMIC DATA

Organisation for Economic Co-operation and Development (OECD), 2 rue Andre-Pascal, 75 Paris 16, France (Telephone Number in U.S. (202) 785-6323); *Economic Outlook.*

CANADA - SOYBEAN PRODUCTION - See CANADA - CROPS

CANADA - STATE BUDGET REVENUE AND EXPENDITURES

Euromonitor Publications Limited, 87-88 Turnmill Street, London EC1M 5QU, England; *International Marketing Data and Statistics.*

CANADA - STEEL - See CANADA - MINING AND MINERAL PRODUCTS

CANADA - STOCKS - COMMODITY - MARKET PRICE - INDEXES

Food and Agricultural Organization of the United Nations (FAO) Via delle Terme di Caracalla, 00100 Rome, Italy (Telephone Number in U.S. (202) 653-2400); *The State of Food and Agriculture.*

International Lead and Zinc Study Group, Metro House, 58 St. James's Street, London SW1A 1LD, England; *Lead and Zinc Statistics.*

Statistical Office of the United Nations, Publishing Service, New York, New York 10017 (800) 253-9646; *Statistical Yearbook.*

World Bureau of Metal Statistics, 27-A High Street, Ware Hert SG12 9BA, England; *World Metal Statistics.*

CANADA - SUGAR - See CANADA - CROPS

CANADA - SULPHUR AND SULPHURIC ACID PRODUCTION - See CANADA - MINING AND MINERAL PRODUCTS

CANADA - TAXATION

G.K. Hall and Company, 70 Lincoln Street, Boston, Massachusetts 02111 (617) 423-3990; *The World in Figures.*

International Monetary Fund, 700 Nineteenth Street, NW, Washington, D.C. 20431 (202) 623-7000; *Government Finance Statistics Yearbook.*

International Road Federation, 525 School Street, SW, Washington, D.C. 20024 (202) 554-2106; *World Road Statistics.*

Organisation for Economic Co-operation and Development (OECD), 2 rue Andre-Pascal, 75 Paris 16, France (Telephone Number in U.S. (202) 785-6323); *Revenue Statistics of OECD Member Countries.*

The World Bank, 1818 H Street, NW, Washington, D.C. 20433 (202) 477-1234; *World Tables.*

CANADA - TELEGRAPH SERVICE

Statistical Office of the United Nations, Publishing Service, New York, New York 10017 (800) 253-9646; *Statistical Yearbook.*

CANADA - TELEPHONES IN USE

American Telephone and Telegraph Company, 26 Parsippany Road, Whippany, New Jersey 07981 (800) 338-4038; *The World's Telephones.*

G.K. Hall and Company, 70 Lincoln Street, Boston, Massachusetts 02111 (617) 423-3990; *The World in Figures.*

Statistical Office of the United Nations, Publishing Service, New York, New York 10017 (800) 253-9646; *Statistical Yearbook.*

CANADA - TELEVISION BROADCASTING - See CANADA - BROADCASTING

CANADA - TELEVISION RECEIVER PRODUCTION

National Technical Information Service, 5285 Port Royal Road, Springfield, Virginia 22161 (703) 487-4600; *Handbook of Economic Statistics.*

Statistical Office of the United Nations, Publishing Service, New York, New York 10017 (800) 253-9646; *Statistical Yearbook.*

CANADA - TEXTILE INDUSTRY

Forest and Paper Association, 1250 Connecticut Avenue, NW, Washington, D.C. 20036 (202) 463-2455; *Pulp and Fiber Statistics.*

G.K. Hall and Company, 70 Lincoln Street, Boston, Massachusetts 02111 (617) 423-3990; *The World in Figures.*

National Technical Information Service, 5285 Port Royal Road, Springfield, Virginia 22161 (703) 487-4600; *Handbook of Economic Statistics.*

Organisation for Economic Co-operation and Development (OECD), 2 rue Andre-Pascal, 75 Paris 16, France (Telephone Number in U.S. (202) 785-6323); *Foreign Trade by Commodities, Indicators of Industrial Activity, Industrial Structure Statistics,* and *Textile Industry in OECD Countries.*

Statistical Office of the United Nations, Publishing Service, New York, New York 10017 (800) 253-9646; *Trade in Manufactures of Developing Countries,* and *Statistical Yearbook.*

CANADA - THEATRE

United Nations Educational, Scientific and Cultural Organization (UNESCO), 7 Place de Fontenoy, F-75700 Paris, France (Telephone Number in U.S. (212) 963-5981); *Statistical Yearbook.*

CANADA - TIN - See CANADA - MINING AND MINERAL PRODUCTS

CANADA - TIRE (MOTOR VEHICLE) PRODUCTION

International Rubber Study Group, York House, Eighth Floor, Empire Way, Wembley, London HA9 0PA, England; *Rubber Statistical Bulletin.*

National Technical Information Service, 5285 Port Royal Road, Springfield, Virginia 22161 (703) 487-4600; *Handbook of Economic Statistics.*

Statistical Office of the United Nations, Publishing Service, New York, New York 10017 (800) 253-9646; *Statistical Yearbook.*

CANADA - TOBACCO PRODUCTION

Commodity Research Bureau, Incorporated, 75 Wall Street, New York, New York 10005 (212) 504-7754; *Commodity Year Book.*

Facts on File, 460 Park Avenue South, New York, New York 10016 (800) 443-8323; *The New Book of World Rankings.*

Organisation for Economic Co-operation and Development (OECD), 2 rue Andre-Pascal, 75 Paris 16, France (Telephone Number in U.S. (202) 785-6323); *Foreign Trade by Commodities, Indicators of Industrial Activity,* and *Industrial Structure Statistics.*

Statistical Office of the United Nations, Publishing Service, New York, New York 10017 (800) 253-9646; *Statistical Yearbook.*

CANADA - TOURISM

Facts on File, 460 Park Avenue South, New York, New York 10016 (800) 443-8323; *The New Book of World Rankings.*

Federal Statistical Office, Gustav - Stresemann - Ring 11, D-6200 Wiesbaden, Germany; *Kanada.*

G.K. Hall and Company, 70 Lincoln Street, Boston, Massachusetts 02111 (617) 423-3990; *The World in Figures.*

Organisation for Economic Co-operation and Development (OECD), 2 rue Andre-Pascal, 75 Paris 16, France (Telephone Number in U.S. (202) 785-6323); *Tourism Policy and International Tourism in OECD Member Countries.*

Statistical Office of the United Nations, Publishing Service, New York, New York 10017 (800) 253-9646; *Statistical Yearbook.*

Times Books, 201 East 50th Street, New York, New York 10022 (212) 751-2600; *The Economist Book of Vital World Statistics.*

World Tourism Organization, Calle Capitan Haya 42, E-28020 Madrid, Spain; *Yearbook of Tourism Statistics.*

CANADA - TRACTORS IN USE

Statistical Office of the United Nations, Publishing Service, New York, New York 10017 (800) 253-9646; *Statistical Yearbook.*

CANADA - TRADE - See CANADA - FOREIGN TRADE

CANADA - TRADEMARKS AND SERVICE MARKS

Statistical Office of the United Nations, Publishing Service, New York, New York 10017 (800) 253-9646; *Statistical Yearbook.*

World Intellectual Property Organization, 34 Chemin des Colombettes, CH-1211 Geneva 20. Switzerland; *Industrial Property Statistics.*

CANADA - TRANSPORTATION AND COMMUNICATIONS

Facts on File, 460 Park Avenue South, New York, New York 10016 (800) 443-8323; *The New Book of World Rankings.*

Federal Statistical Office, Gustav - Stresemann - Ring 11, D-6200 Wiesbaden, Germany; *Kanada.*

Gale Research Incorporated, 835 Penobscot Building, Detroit, Michigan 48226 (800) 877-4253; *International Historical Statistics The Americas and Australasia.*

G.K. Hall and Company, 70 Lincoln Street, Boston, Massachusetts 02111 (617) 423-3990; *The World in Figures.*

CANADA - TUNGSTEN PRODUCTION AND CONSUMPTION - See CANADA - MINING AND MINERAL PRODUCTS

CANADA - TURKEYS - See CANADA - LIVESTOCK AND POULTRY

CANADA - UNEMPLOYMENT

Euromonitor Publications Limited, 87-88 Turnmill Street, London EC1M 5QU, England; *International Marketing Data and Statistics.*

International Labour Office, I.L.O. Publications, CH-1211, Geneva 22, Switzerland; *Yearbook of Labour Statistics.*

National Technical Information Service, 5285 Port Royal Road, Springfield, Virginia 22161 (703) 487-4600; *Handbook of Economic Statistics.*

Organisation for Economic Co-operation and Development (OECD), 2 rue Andre-Pascal, 75 Paris 16, France (Telephone Number in U.S. (202) 785-6323); *Economic Outlook, Labour Force Statistics,* and *OECD Employment Outlook.*

Statistical Office of the United Nations, Publishing Service, New York, New York 10017 (800) 253-9646; *Statistical Yearbook.*

CANADA - URANIUM PRODUCTION AND CONSUMPTION - See CANADA - MINING AND MINERAL PRODUCTS

CANADA - VANADIUM AND VANADIUM ORE PRODUCTION AND CONSUMPTION - See CANADA - MINING AND MINERAL PRODUCTS

CANADA - VITAL STATISTICS

Euromonitor Publications Limited, 87-88 Turnmill Street, London EC1M 5QU, England; *International Marketing Data and Statistics.*

Gale Research Incorporated, 835 Penobscot Building, Detroit, Michigan 48226 (800) 877-4253; *International Historical Statistics The Americas and Australasia.*

G.K. Hall and Company, 70 Lincoln Street, Boston, Massachusetts 02111 (617) 423-3990; *The World in Figures.*

Statistical Office of the United Nations, Publishing Service, New York, New York 10017 (800) 253-9646; *Statistical Yearbook.*

World Health Organization, Office of Publications, Avenue Appia, CH-1211 Geneva 27, Switzerland (Telephone Number in U.S. (518) 436-9686); *World Health Statistics Annual.*

CANADA - WAGES

Federal Statistical Office, Gustav - Stresemann - Ring 11, D-6200 Wiesbaden, Germany; *Kanada.*

G.K. Hall and Company, 70 Lincoln Street, Boston, Massachusetts 02111 (617) 423-3990; *The World in Figures.*

International Labour Office, I.L.O. Publications, CH-1211, Geneva 22, Switzerland; *Yearbook of Labour Statistics.*

Organisation for Economic Co-operation and Development (OECD), 2 rue Andre-Pascal, 75 Paris 16, France (Telephone Number in U.S. (202) 785-6323); *Economic Outlook, Industrial Structure Statistics,* and *Main Economic Indicators - Historical Statistics.*

Statistical Office of the United Nations, Publishing Service, New York, New York 10017 (800) 253-9646; *Statistical Yearbook.*

CANADA - WATERWAYS IN USE - See CANADA - MERCHANT SHIPPING

CANADA - WEATHER

Facts on File, 460 Park Avenue South, New York, New York 10016 (800) 443-8323; *The New Book of World Rankings.*

G.K. Hall and Company, 70 Lincoln Street, Boston, Massachusetts 02111 (617) 423-3990; *The World in Figures.*

CANADA - WHALES - See CANADA - FISHERIES

CANADA - WHEAT - See CANADA - CROPS

Facts on File, 460 Park Avenue South, New York, New York 10016 (800) 443-8323; *The New Book of World Rankings.*

National Technical Information Service, 5285 Port Royal Road, Springfield, Virginia 22161 (703) 487-4600; *Handbook of Economic Statistics.*

Statistical Office of the United Nations, Publishing Service, New York, New York 10017 (800) 253-9646; *Statistical Yearbook.*

CANADA - WHOLESALE PRICES

National Technical Information Service, 5285 Port Royal Road, Springfield, Virginia 22161 (703) 487-4600; *Handbook of Economic Statistics*.

Statistical Office of the United Nations, Publishing Service, New York, New York 10017 (800) 253-9646; *Statistical Yearbook*.

CANADA - WHOLESALE TRADE

Statistical Office of the United Nations, Publishing Service, New York, New York 10017 (800) 253-9646; *Statistical Yearbook*.

CANADA - WINE PRODUCTION

Facts on File, 460 Park Avenue South, New York, New York 10016 (800) 443-8323; *The New Book of World Rankings*.

Statistical Office of the United Nations, Publishing Service, New York, New York 10017 (800) 253-9646; *Statistical Yearbook*.

CANADA - WOOD EXPORTS - See CANADA - FORESTRY AND FOREST PRODUCTS

CANADA - WOOL PRODUCTION

Facts on File, 460 Park Avenue South, New York, New York 10016 (800) 443-8323; *The New Book of World Rankings*.

National Technical Information Service, 5285 Port Royal Road, Springfield, Virginia 22161 (703) 487-4600; *Handbook of Economic Statistics*.

Organisation for Economic Co-operation and Development (OECD), 2 rue Andre-Pascal, 75 Paris 16, France (Telephone Number in U.S. (202) 785-6323); *Economic Accounts for Agriculture*, and *Textile Industry in OECD Countries*.

Statistical Office of the United Nations, Publishing Service, New York, New York 10017 (800) 253-9646; *Statistical Yearbook*.

CANADA - YARN PRODUCTION

Organisation for Economic Co-operation and Development (OECD), 2 rue Andre-Pascal, 75 Paris 16, France (Telephone Number in U.S. (202) 785-6323); *Foreign Trade by Commodities*, and *Textile Industry in OECD Countries*.

Statistical Office of the United Nations, Publishing Service, New York, New York 10017 (800) 253-9646; *Statistical Yearbook*.

CANADA - ZINC AND ZINC ORE PRODUCTION AND CONSUMPTION - See CANADA - MINING AND MINERAL PRODUCTS

CANADA - ZOOS AND BOTANICAL GARDENS

United Nations Educational, Scientific and Cultural Organization (UNESCO), 7 Place de Fontenoy, F-75700 Paris, France (Telephone Number in U.S. (212) 963-5981); *Statistical Yearbook*.

CANAL ZONE - BIRTH RATE

Statistical Office of the United Nations, Publishing Service, New York, New York 10017 (800) 253-9646; *Demographic Yearbook*, and *Statistical Yearbook*.

World Health Organization, Office of Publications, Avenue Appia, CH-1211 Geneva 27, Switzerland (Telephone Number in U.S. (518) 436-9686); *World Health Statistics Annual*.

CANAL ZONE - DIVORCE RATES

Statistical Office of the United Nations, Publishing Service, New York, New York 10017 (800) 253-9646; *Demographic Yearbook*.

CANAL ZONE - EDUCATION

United Nations Educational, Scientific and Cultural Organization (UNESCO), 7 Place de Fontenoy, F-75700 Paris, France (Telephone Number in U.S. (212) 963-5981); *Statistical Yearbook*.

CANAL ZONE - ENERGY

Statistical Office of the United Nations, Publishing Service, New York, New York 10017 (800) 253-9646; *Statistical Yearbook*.

CANAL ZONE - FETAL MORTALITY

Statistical Office of the United Nations, Publishing Service, New York, New York 10017 (800) 253-9646; *Demographic Yearbook*.

World Health Organization, Office of Publications, Avenue Appia, CH-1211 Geneva 27, Switzerland (Telephone Number in U.S. (518) 436-9686); *World Health Statistics Annual*.

CANAL ZONE - GENERAL MORTALITY

Statistical Office of the United Nations, Publishing Service, New York, New York 10017 (800) 253-9646; *Demographic Yearbook*.

World Health Organization, Office of Publications, Avenue Appia, CH-1211 Geneva 27, Switzerland (Telephone Number in U.S. (518) 436-9686); *World Health Statistics Annual*.

CANAL ZONE - HEALTH

Statistical Office of the United Nations, Publishing Service, New York, New York 10017 (800) 253-9646; *Statistical Yearbook*.

CANAL ZONE - INFANT AND MATERNAL MORTALITY

Statistical Office of the United Nations, Publishing Service, New York, New York 10017 (800) 253-9646; *Demographic Yearbook*, and *Statistical Yearbook*.

World Health Organization, Office of Publications, Avenue Appia, CH-1211 Geneva 27, Switzerland (Telephone Number in U.S. (518) 436-9686); *World Health Statistics Annual*.

CANAL ZONE - LIBRARIES

United Nations Educational, Scientific and Cultural Organization (UNESCO), 7 Place de Fontenoy, F-75700 Paris, France (Telephone Number in U.S. (212) 963-5981); *Statistical Yearbook*.

CANAL ZONE - MARRIAGE RATES

Statistical Office of the United Nations, Publishing Service, New York, New York 10017 (800) 253-9646; *Demographic Yearbook*.

CANAL ZONE - MERCHANT SHIPPING

Statistical Office of the United Nations, Publishing Service, New York, New York 10017 (800) 253-9646; *Statistical Yearbook*.

CANAL ZONE - MOTION PICTURE THEATRES

Statistical Office of the United Nations, Publishing Service, New York, New York 10017 (800) 253-9646; *Statistical Yearbook.*

CANAL ZONE - MOTOR VEHICLES IN USE

Statistical Office of the United Nations, Publishing Service, New York, New York 10017 (800) 253-9646; *Statistical Yearbook.*

CANAL ZONE - NATALITY - See CANAL ZONE - BIRTH RATE

CANAL ZONE - POPULATION

Statistical Office of the United Nations, Publishing Service, New York, New York 10017 (800) 253-9646; *Demographic Yearbook,* and *Statistical Yearbook.*

World Health Organization, Office of Publications, Avenue Appia, CH-1211 Geneva 27, Switzerland (Telephone Number in U.S. (518) 436-9686); *World Health Statistics Annual.*

CANAL ZONE - SCIENTISTS AND TECHNOLOGISTS

Statistical Office of the United Nations, Publishing Service, New York, New York 10017 (800) 253-9646; *Statistical Yearbook.*

CANAL ZONE - VITAL STATISTICS

World Health Organization, Office of Publications, Avenue Appia, CH-1211 Geneva 27, Switzerland (Telephone Number in U.S. (518) 436-9686); *World Health Statistics Annual.*

World Health Organization, Avenue Appia, Office of Publications, CH-1211 Geneva 27, Switzerland (Telephone Number in U.S. (518) 436-9686); *World Health Statistics Annual.*

CANCER - (MALIGNANCIES)

U.S. Department of Health and Human Services, National Institutes of Health, National Cancer Institute, 9000 Rockville Pike, Bethesda, Maryland 20892 (301) 496-5737; *Cancer Statistics Review.*

U.S. Department of Health and Human Services, National Center for Health Statistics, 3700 East-West Highway, Hyattsville, Maryland 20782 (301) 436-8500; *Monthly Vital Statistics Report, Vital Statistics of the United States, Health, United States, Monthly Vital Statistics Report, Health Promotion and Disease Prevention,* and unpublished data.

CANCER - (MALIGNANCIES) - DEATHS

U.S. Department of Health and Human Services, National Institutes of Health, National Cancer Institute, 9000 Rockville Pike, Bethesda, Maryland 20892 (301) 496-5737; *Cancer Statistics Review.*

U.S. Department of Health and Human Services, National Center for Health Statistics, 3700 East-West Highway, Hyattsville, Maryland 20782 (301) 436-8500; *Vital Statistics of the United States,* and unpublished data.

CANCER - (MALIGNANCIES) FOREIGN COUNTRIES

World Health Organization, Avenue Appia, Office of Publications, CH-1211 Geneva, 27, Switzerland (Telephone Number in U.S. (518) 436-9686); *World Health Statistics Annual.*

CANTON AND ENDERBURY ISLANDS - AGRICULTURE

Food and Agricultural Organization of the United Nations (FAO) Via delle Terme di Caracalla, 00100 Rome, Italy (Telephone Number in U.S. (202) 653-2400); *Production Yearbook, The State of Food and Agriculture,* and *Trade Yearbook.*

G.K. Hall and Company, 70 Lincoln Street, Boston, Massachusetts 02111 (617) 423-3990; *The World in Figures.*

CANTON AND ENDERBURY ISLANDS - AIRLINE SERVICE

G.K. Hall and Company, 70 Lincoln Street, Boston, Massachusetts 02111 (617) 423-3990; *The World in Figures.*

CANTON AND ENDERBURY ISLANDS - AREA AND DENSITY OF POPULATION

G.K. Hall and Company, 70 Lincoln Street, Boston, Massachusetts 02111 (617) 423-3990; *The World in Figures.*

CANTON AND ENDERBURY ISLANDS - BALANCE OF PAYMENTS

G.K. Hall and Company, 70 Lincoln Street, Boston, Massachusetts 02111 (617) 423-3990; *The World in Figures.*

CANTON AND ENDERBURY ISLANDS - BANKING

G.K. Hall and Company, 70 Lincoln Street, Boston, Massachusetts 02111 (617) 423-3990; *The World in Figures.*

CANTON AND ENDERBURY ISLANDS - BIRTH RATES

Statistical Office of the United Nations, Publishing Service, New York, New York 10017 (800) 253-9646; *Demographic Yearbook.*

CANTON AND ENDERBURY ISLANDS - BONDS

G.K. Hall and Company, 70 Lincoln Street, Boston, Massachusetts 02111 (617) 423-3990; *The World in Figures.*

CANTON AND ENDERBURY ISLANDS - BOOK PRODUCTION

G.K. Hall and Company, 70 Lincoln Street, Boston, Massachusetts 02111 (617) 423-3990; *The World in Figures.*

CANTON AND ENDERBURY ISLANDS - BROADCASTING

G.K. Hall and Company, 70 Lincoln Street, Boston, Massachusetts 02111 (617) 423-3990; *The World in Figures.*

CANTON AND ENDERBURY ISLANDS - BUSINESS

G.K. Hall and Company, 70 Lincoln Street, Boston, Massachusetts 02111 (617) 423-3990; *The World in Figures.*

CANTON AND ENDERBURY ISLANDS - CALORIE SUPPLY

Food and Agricultural Organization of the United Nations (FAO) Via delle Terme di Caracalla, 00100 Rome, Italy (Telephone Number in U.S. (202) 653-2400); *The State of Food and Agriculture.*

CANTON AND ENDERBURY ISLANDS - CLASS STRUCTURE

G.K. Hall and Company, 70 Lincoln Street, Boston, Massachusetts 02111 (617) 423-3990; *The World in Figures.*

CANTON AND ENDERBURY ISLANDS - CLIMATE

G.K. Hall and Company, 70 Lincoln Street, Boston, Massachusetts 02111 (617) 423-3990; *The World in Figures.*

CANTON AND ENDERBURY ISLANDS - COAL PRODUCTION - See CANTON AND ENDERBURY ISLANDS - MINING AND MINERAL PRODUCTS

CANTON AND ENDERBURY ISLANDS - COMMUNICATIONS

G.K. Hall and Company, 70 Lincoln Street, Boston, Massachusetts 02111 (617) 423-3990; *The World in Figures.*

CANTON AND ENDERBURY ISLANDS - CONSUMER PRICE INDEX

G.K. Hall and Company, 70 Lincoln Street, Boston, Massachusetts 02111 (617) 423-3990; *The World in Figures.*

CANTON AND ENDERBURY ISLANDS - CONSUMPTION

G.K. Hall and Company, 70 Lincoln Street, Boston, Massachusetts 02111 (617) 423-3990; *The World in Figures.*

CANTON AND ENDERBURY ISLANDS - CORN PRODUCTION - See CANTON AND ENDERBURY ISLANDS - CROPS

CANTON AND ENDERBURY ISLANDS - CORPORATE TAXES

G.K. Hall and Company, 70 Lincoln Street, Boston, Massachusetts 02111 (617) 423-3990; *The World in Figures.*

CANTON AND ENDERBURY ISLANDS - CROPS

Food and Agricultural Organization of the United Nations (FAO) Via delle Terme di Caracalla, 00100 Rome, Italy (Telephone Number in U.S. (202) 653-2400); *The State of Food and Agriculture.*

G.K. Hall and Company, 70 Lincoln Street, Boston, Massachusetts 02111 (617) 423-3990; *The World in Figures.*

CANTON AND ENDERBURY ISLANDS - CUSTOMS DUTIES

G.K. Hall and Company, 70 Lincoln Street, Boston, Massachusetts 02111 (617) 423-3990; *The World in Figures.*

CANTON AND ENDERBURY ISLANDS - DAIRY PRODUCTS

Food and Agricultural Organization of the United Nations (FAO) Via delle Terme di Caracalla, 00100 Rome, Italy (Telephone Number in U.S. (202) 653-2400); *The State of Food and Agriculture.*

CANTON AND ENDERBURY ISLANDS - DEATH RATES

G.K. Hall and Company, 70 Lincoln Street, Boston, Massachusetts 02111 (617) 423-3990; *The World in Figures.*

CANTON AND ENDERBURY ISLANDS - DEFENSE EXPENDITURES

G.K. Hall and Company, 70 Lincoln Street, Boston, Massachusetts 02111 (617) 423-3990; *The World in Figures.*

CANTON AND ENDERBURY ISLANDS - DEMOGRAPHY

G.K. Hall and Company, 70 Lincoln Street, Boston, Massachusetts 02111 (617) 423-3990; *The World in Figures.*

CANTON AND ENDERBURY ISLANDS - DEVELOPMENT ASSISTANCE

G.K. Hall and Company, 70 Lincoln Street, Boston, Massachusetts 02111 (617) 423-3990; *The World in Figures.*

CANTON AND ENDERBURY ISLANDS - DISEASE

G.K. Hall and Company, 70 Lincoln Street, Boston, Massachusetts 02111 (617) 423-3990; *The World in Figures.*

CANTON AND ENDERBURY ISLANDS - DIVORCE RATES

Statistical Office of the United Nations, Publishing Service, New York, New York 10017 (800) 253-9646; *Demographic Yearbook.*

CANTON AND ENDERBURY ISLANDS - DOMESTIC PRODUCT

G.K. Hall and Company, 70 Lincoln Street, Boston, Massachusetts 02111 (617) 423-3990; *The World in Figures.*

CANTON AND ENDERBURY ISLANDS - ECONOMY

G.K. Hall and Company, 70 Lincoln Street, Boston, Massachusetts 02111 (617) 423-3990; *The World in Figures.*

CANTON AND ENDERBURY ISLANDS - EDUCATION

G.K. Hall and Company, 70 Lincoln Street, Boston, Massachusetts 02111 (617) 423-3990; *The World in Figures.*

CANTON AND ENDERBURY ISLANDS - EGG PRODUCTION - See CANTON AND ENDERBURY ISLANDS - DAIRY PRODUCTS

CANTON AND ENDERBURY ISLANDS - ENERGY

Food and Agricultural Organization of the United Nations (FAO) Via delle Terme di Caracalla, 00100 Rome, Italy (Telephone Number in U.S. (202) 653-2400); *The State of Food and Agriculture.*

G.K. Hall and Company, 70 Lincoln Street, Boston, Massachusetts 02111 (617) 423-3990; *The World in Figures.*

CANTON AND ENDERBURY ISLANDS - EXPORTS

Food and Agricultural Organization of the United Nations (FAO) Via delle Terme di Caracalla, 00100 Rome, Italy (Telephone Number in U.S. (202) 653-2400); *The State of Food and Agriculture.*

G.K. Hall and Company, 70 Lincoln Street, Boston, Massachusetts 02111 (617) 423-3990; *The World in Figures.*

CANTON AND ENDERBURY ISLANDS - EXTERNAL TRADE

Food and Agricultural Organization of the United Nations (FAO) Via delle Terme di Caracalla, 00100 Rome, Italy (Telephone Number in U.S. (202) 653-2400); *The State of Food and Agriculture*, and *Trade Yearbook.*

G.K. Hall and Company, 70 Lincoln Street, Boston, Massachusetts 02111 (617) 423-3990; *The World in Figures.*

CANTON AND ENDERBURY ISLANDS - FARM CROPS - See CANTON AND ENDERBURY ISLANDS - CROPS

CANTON AND ENDERBURY ISLANDS - FERTILIZER

Food and Agricultural Organization of the United Nations (FAO) Via delle Terme di Caracalla, 00100 Rome, Italy (Telephone Number in U.S. (202) 653-2400); *The State of Food and Agriculture.*

CANTON AND ENDERBURY ISLANDS - FETAL MORTALITY

Statistical Office of the United Nations, Publishing Service, New York, New York 10017 (800) 253-9646; *Demographic Yearbook.*

CANTON AND ENDERBURY ISLANDS - FINANÇE

G.K. Hall and Company, 70 Lincoln Street, Boston, Massachusetts 02111 (617) 423-3990; *The World in Figures.*

CANTON AND ENDERBURY ISLANDS - FISHERIES

Food and Agricultural Organization of the United Nations (FAO) Via delle Terme di Caracalla, 00100 Rome, Italy (Telephone Number in U.S. (202) 653-2400); *The State of Food and Agriculture,* and *Yearbook of Fishery Statistics.*

CANTON AND ENDERBURY ISLANDS - FOOD

Food and Agricultural Organization of the United Nations (FAO) Via delle Terme di Caracalla, 00100 Rome, Italy (Telephone Number in U.S. (202) 653-2400); *Production Yearbook,* and *The State of Food and Agriculture.*

G.K. Hall and Company, 70 Lincoln Street, Boston, Massachusetts 02111 (617) 423-3990; *The World in Figures.*

CANTON AND ENDERBURY ISLANDS - FOREIGN AID

G.K. Hall and Company, 70 Lincoln Street, Boston, Massachusetts 02111 (617) 423-3990; *The World in Figures.*

CANTON AND ENDERBURY ISLANDS - FOREIGN TRADE

Food and Agricultural Organization of the United Nations (FAO) Via delle Terme di Caracalla, 00100 Rome, Italy (Telephone Number in U.S. (202) 653-2400); *The State of Food and Agriculture.*

G.K. Hall and Company, 70 Lincoln Street, Boston, Massachusetts 02111 (617) 423-3990; *The World in Figures.*

Organisation for Economic Co-operation and Development (OECD), 2 rue Andre-Pascal, 75 Paris 16, France (Telephone Number in U.S. (202) 785-6323); *Trade by Commodities.*

CANTON AND ENDERBURY ISLANDS - FORESTRY AND FOREST PRODUCTS

Food and Agricultural Organization of the United Nations (FAO) Via delle Terme di Caracalla, 00100 Rome, Italy (Telephone Number in U.S. (202) 653-2400); *The State of Food and Agriculture.*

G.K. Hall and Company, 70 Lincoln Street, Boston, Massachusetts 02111 (617) 423-3990; *The World in Figures.*

CANTON AND ENDERBURY ISLANDS - GENERAL MORTALITY

Statistical Office of the United Nations, Publishing Service, New York, New York 10017 (800) 253-9646; *Demographic Yearbook.*

CANTON AND ENDERBURY ISLANDS - GOVERNMENT

G.K. Hall and Company, 70 Lincoln Street, Boston, Massachusetts 02111 (617) 423-3990; *The World in Figures.*

CANTON AND ENDERBURY ISLANDS - GRAIN PRODUCTION - See CANTON AND ENDERBURY ISLANDS - CROPS

CANTON AND ENDERBURY ISLANDS - GROSS DOMESTIC PRODUCT

G.K. Hall and Company, 70 Lincoln Street, Boston, Massachusetts 02111 (617) 423-3990; *The World in Figures.*

CANTON AND ENDERBURY ISLANDS - HEALTH

G.K. Hall and Company, 70 Lincoln Street, Boston, Massachusetts 02111 (617) 423-3990; *The World in Figures.*

CANTON AND ENDERBURY ISLANDS - HIGHWAYS

G.K. Hall and Company, 70 Lincoln Street, Boston, Massachusetts 02111 (617) 423-3990; *The World in Figures.*

CANTON AND ENDERBURY ISLANDS - ILLITERATE POPULATION

G.K. Hall and Company, 70 Lincoln Street, Boston, Massachusetts 02111 (617) 423-3990; *The World in Figures.*

CANTON AND ENDERBURY ISLANDS - IMPORTS

Food and Agricultural Organization of the United Nations (FAO) Via delle Terme di Caracalla, 00100 Rome, Italy (Telephone Number in U.S. (202) 653-2400); *The State of Food and Agriculture.*

G.K. Hall and Company, 70 Lincoln Street, Boston, Massachusetts 02111 (617) 423-3990; *The World in Figures.*

CANTON AND ENDERBURY ISLANDS - INDUSTRY

G.K. Hall and Company, 70 Lincoln Street, Boston, Massachusetts 02111 (617) 423-3990; *The World in Figures.*

CANTON AND ENDERBURY ISLANDS - INFANT AND MATERNAL MORTALITY

Statistical Office of the United Nations, Publishing Service, New York, New York 10017 (800) 253-9646; *Demographic Yearbook.*

CANTON AND ENDERBURY ISLANDS - LABOR FORCE

Food and Agricultural Organization of the United Nations (FAO) Via delle Terme di Caracalla, 00100 Rome, Italy (Telephone Number in U.S. (202) 653-2400); *The State of Food and Agriculture.*

G.K. Hall and Company, 70 Lincoln Street, Boston, Massachusetts 02111 (617) 423-3990; *The World in Figures.*

CANTON AND ENDERBURY ISLANDS - LAND USE

Food and Agricultural Organization of the United Nations (FAO), Via delle Terme di Caracalla, 00100 Rome, Italy (Telephone Number in U.S. (202) 653-2400); *Production Yearbook.*

G.K. Hall and Company, 70 Lincoln Street, Boston, Massachusetts 02111 (617) 423-3990; *The World in Figures.*

CANTON AND ENDERBURY ISLANDS - LIVESTOCK AND POULTRY

Food and Agricultural Organization of the United Nations (FAO), Via delle Terme di Caracalla, 00100 Rome, Italy (Telephone Number in U.S. (202) 653-2400); *Production Yearbook,* and *The State of Food and Agriculture.*

G.K. Hall and Company, 70 Lincoln Street, Boston, Massachusetts 02111 (617) 423-3990; *The World in Figures.*

CANTON AND ENDERBURY ISLANDS - LIVING LEVELS

G.K. Hall and Company, 70 Lincoln Street, Boston, Massachusetts 02111 (617) 423-3990; *The World in Figures.*

CANTON AND ENDERBURY ISLANDS - MANUFACTURING

G.K. Hall and Company, 70 Lincoln Street, Boston, Massachusetts 02111 (617) 423-3990; *The World in Figures.*

CANTON AND ENDERBURY ISLANDS - MARRIAGE RATES

Statistical Office of the United Nations, Publishing Service, New York, New York 10017 (800) 253-9646; *Demographic Yearbook.*

CANTON AND ENDERBURY ISLANDS - MEAT PRODUCTION - See CANTON AND ENDERBURY ISLANDS - LIVESTOCK AND POULTRY

CANTON AND ENDERBURY ISLANDS - MERCHANT SHIPPING

G.K. Hall and Company, 70 Lincoln Street, Boston, Massachusetts 02111 (617) 423-3990; *The World in Figures.*

CANTON AND ENDERBURY ISLANDS - MILITARY

G.K. Hall and Company, 70 Lincoln Street, Boston, Massachusetts 02111 (617) 423-3990; *The World in Figures.*

CANTON AND ENDERBURY ISLANDS - MINING AND MINERAL PRODUCTS

G.K. Hall and Company, 70 Lincoln Street, Boston, Massachusetts 02111 (617) 423-3990; *The World in Figures.*

CANTON AND ENDERBURY ISLANDS - MONEY SUPPLY

G.K. Hall and Company, 70 Lincoln Street, Boston, Massachusetts 02111 (617) 423-3990; *The World in Figures.*

CANTON AND ENDERBURY ISLANDS - MOTOR VEHICLES IN USE

G.K. Hall and Company, 70 Lincoln Street, Boston, Massachusetts 02111 (617) 423-3990; *The World in Figures.*

CANTON AND ENDERBURY ISLANDS - NATALITY - See CANTON AND ENDERBURY ISLANDS - BIRTH RATES

CANTON AND ENDERBURY ISLANDS - NATIONAL INCOME

G.K. Hall and Company, 70 Lincoln Street, Boston, Massachusetts 02111 (617) 423-3990; *The World in Figures.*

CANTON AND ENDERBURY ISLANDS - NEWSPAPER PRODUCTION - See CANTON AND ENDERBURY ISLANDS - FORESTRY AND FOREST PRODUCTS

CANTON AND ENDERBURY ISLANDS - OCCUPATIONS - See CANTON AND ENDERBURY ISLANDS - LABOR FORCE

CANTON AND ENDERBURY ISLANDS - PESTICIDE USE

Food and Agricultural Organization of the United Nations (FAO) Via delle Terme di Caracalla, 00100 Rome, Italy (Telephone Number in U.S. (202) 653-2400); *The State of Food and Agriculture.*

CANTON AND ENDERBURY ISLANDS - PETROLEUM INDUSTRY

Food and Agricultural Organization of the United Nations (FAO) Via delle Terme di Caracalla, 00100 Rome, Italy (Telephone Number in U.S. (202) 653-2400); *The State of Food and Agriculture.*

G.K. Hall and Company, 70 Lincoln Street, Boston, Massachusetts 02111 (617) 423-3990; *The World in Figures.*

CANTON AND ENDERBURY ISLANDS - POPULATION

Food and Agricultural Organization of the United Nations (FAO), Via delle Terme di Caracalla, 00100 Rome, Italy (Telephone Number in U.S. (202) 653-2400); *Production Yearbook.*

G.K. Hall and Company, 70 Lincoln Street, Boston, Massachusetts 02111 (617) 423-3990; *The World in Figures.*

Statistical Office of the United Nations, Publishing Service, New York, New York 10017 (800) 253-9646; *Demographic Yearbook,* and *Statistical Yearbook.*

United Nations Educational, Scientific and Cultural Organization (UNESCO), 7 Place de Fontenoy, F-75700 Paris, France (Telephone Number in U.S. (212) 963-5981); *Statistical Yearbook.*

CANTON AND ENDERBURY ISLANDS - PRICES

Food and Agricultural Organization of the United Nations (FAO), Via delle Terme di Caracalla, 00100 Rome, Italy (Telephone Number in U.S. (202) 653-2400); *Production Yearbook,* and *The State of Food and Agriculture.*

G.K. Hall and Company, 70 Lincoln Street, Boston, Massachusetts 02111 (617) 423-3990; *The World in Figures.*

CANTON AND ENDERBURY ISLANDS - PRODUCTION

G.K. Hall and Company, 70 Lincoln Street, Boston, Massachusetts 02111 (617) 423-3990; *The World in Figures.*

CANTON AND ENDERBURY ISLANDS - RAILWAYS

G.K. Hall and Company, 70 Lincoln Street, Boston, Massachusetts 02111 (617) 423-3990; *The World in Figures.*

CANTON AND ENDERBURY ISLANDS - RETAIL TRADE

G.K. Hall and Company, 70 Lincoln Street, Boston, Massachusetts 02111 (617) 423-3990; *The World in Figures.*

CANTON AND ENDERBURY ISLANDS - SOCIAL DATA

G.K. Hall and Company, 70 Lincoln Street, Boston, Massachusetts 02111 (617) 423-3990; *The World in Figures.*

CANTON AND ENDERBURY ISLANDS - STOCKS - COMMODITY - MARKET PRICE - INDEX

Food and Agricultural Organization of the United Nations (FAO) Via delle Terme di Caracalla, 00100 Rome, Italy (Telephone Number in U.S. (202) 653-2400); *The State of Food and Agriculture.*

CANTON AND ENDERBURY ISLANDS - TELEPHONES IN USE

G.K. Hall and Company, 70 Lincoln Street, Boston, Massachusetts 02111 (617) 423-3990; *The World in Figures.*

CANTON AND ENDERBURY ISLANDS - TEXTILE INDUSTRY

G.K. Hall and Company, 70 Lincoln Street, Boston, Massachusetts 02111 (617) 423-3990; *The World in Figures.*

CANTON AND ENDERBURY ISLANDS - TOURISM

G.K. Hall and Company, 70 Lincoln Street, Boston, Massachusetts 02111 (617) 423-3990; *The World in Figures.*

CANTON AND ENDERBURY ISLANDS - TRADE - See CANTON AND ENDERBURY ISLANDS - FOREIGN TRADE

CANTON AND ENDERBURY ISLANDS - TRANSPORTATION AND COMMUNICATIONS

G.K. Hall and Company, 70 Lincoln Street, Boston, Massachusetts 02111 (617) 423-3990; *The World in Figures.*

CANTON AND ENDERBURY ISLANDS - VITAL STATISTICS

G.K. Hall and Company, 70 Lincoln Street, Boston, Massachusetts 02111 (617) 423-3990; *The World in Figures.*

CANTON AND ENDERBURY ISLANDS - WAGES

G.K. Hall and Company, 70 Lincoln Street, Boston, Massachusetts 02111 (617) 423-3990; *The World in Figures.*

CANTON AND ENDERBURY ISLANDS - WEATHER

G.K. Hall and Company, 70 Lincoln Street, Boston, Massachusetts 02111 (617) 423-3990; *The World in Figures.*

CAPACITY UTILIZATION INDEX

Board of Governors of the Federal Reserve System, Twentieth Street and Constitution Avenue, NW, Washington, D.C. 20551 (202) 452-3000; *Capacity Utilization in Manufacturing, Mining, Utilities, and Industrial Materials.* Based on data from the Federal Reserve Board, U.S. Department of Commerce, U.S. Bureau of Labor Statistics, and McGraw-Hill Information Systems Company, and other sources.

Cape Verde - National Statistical Office

Direccao-Geral de Estatistica, C.P. 116, Praia, Cape Verde.

Cape Verde - Primary Statistics Source

Servico Nacional de Estatistica, CP 116, Praia, Cape Verde; *Boletin Anual de estatistica.*

CAPE VERDE - AGRICULTURE

Food and Agricultural Organization of the United Nations (FAO) Via delle Terme di Caracalla, 00100 Rome, Italy (Telephone Number in U.S. (202) 653-2400); *Production Yearbook, The State of Food and Agriculture,* and *Trade Yearbook.*

G.K. Hall and Company, 70 Lincoln Street, Boston, Massachusetts 02111 (617) 423-3990; *The World in Figures.*

Statistical Office of the United Nations, Publishing Service, New York, New York 10017 (800) 253-9646; *Statistical Yearbook,* and *Survey of Economic and Social Conditions in Africa.*

United Nations Economic Commission for Africa, Africa Hall, P.O. Box 3001, Addis Ababa, Ethiopia (Telephone Number in U.S. (800) 253-9646); *African Statistical Yearbook.*

The World Bank, 1818 H Street, NW, Washington, D.C. 20433 (202) 477-1234; *World Tables.*

CAPE VERDE - AIRLINE SERVICE

G.K. Hall and Company, 70 Lincoln Street, Boston, Massachusetts 02111 (617) 423-3990; *The World in Figures.*

United Nations Economic Commission for Africa, Africa Hall, P.O. Box 3001, Addis Ababa, Ethiopia (Telephone Number in U.S. (800) 253-9646); *African Statistical Yearbook.*

CAPE VERDE - ANIMAL HEALTH

Food and Agricultural Organization of the United Nations (FAO), Via delle Terme di Caracalla, 00100 Rome, Italy (Telephone Number in U.S. (202) 653-2400); *Animal Health Yearbook.*

CAPE VERDE - AREA AND DENSITY OF POPULATION

African Development Bank, 01 BP 1387, Abidjan 01, Cote D'Ivoire; *Selected Statistics on Regional Member Countries.*

Food and Agricultural Organization of the United Nations (FAO) Via delle Terme di Caracalla, 00100 Rome, Italy (Telephone Number in U.S. (202) 653-2400); *The State of Food and Agriculture.*

G.K. Hall and Company, 70 Lincoln Street, Boston, Massachusetts 02111 (617) 423-3990; *The World in Figures.*

Statistical Office of the United Nations, Publishing Service, New York, New York 10017 (800) 253-9646; *Statistical Yearbook,* and *Survey of Economic and Social Conditions in Africa.*

United Nations Educational, Scientific and Cultural Organization (UNESCO), 7 Place de Fontenoy, F-75700 Paris, France (Telephone Number in U.S. (212) 963-5981); *Statistical Yearbook.*

CAPE VERDE - ARMS EXPORTS AND IMPORTS

U.S. Arms Control and Disarmament Agency, 320 Twenty-first Street, NW, Washington, D.C. 20451 (202) 647-8677; *World Military Expenditures and Arms Transfers.*

CAPE VERDE - BALANCE OF PAYMENTS

African Development Bank, 01 BP 1387, Abidjan 01, Cote D'Ivoire; *Selected Statistics on Regional Member Countries.*

The Economist Intelligence Unit, 111 West 57th Street, New York, New York 10019 (800) 938-4685; *The World Market Atlas.*

G.K. Hall and Company, 70 Lincoln Street, Boston, Massachusetts 02111 (617) 423-3990; *The World in Figures.*

United Nations Economic Commission for Africa, Africa Hall, P.O. Box 3001, Addis Ababa, Ethiopia (Telephone Number in U.S. (800) 253-9646); *African Statistical Yearbook.*

The World Bank, 1818 H Street, NW, Washington, D.C. 20433 (202) 477-1234; *World Tables.*

CAPE VERDE - BANKING

G.K. Hall and Company, 70 Lincoln Street, Boston, Massachusetts 02111 (617) 423-3990; *The World in Figures.*

United Nations Economic Commission for Africa, Africa Hall, P.O. Box 3001, Addis Ababa, Ethiopia (Telephone Number in U.S. (800) 253-9646); *African Statistical Yearbook.*

CAPE VERDE - BIRTH RATES

Statistical Office of the United Nations, Publishing Service, New York, New York 10017 (800) 253-9646; *Demographic Yearbook, Statistical Yearbook*, and *Survey of Economic and Social Conditions in Africa*.

World Health Organization, Office of Publications, Avenue Appia, CH-1211 Geneva 27, Switzerland (Telephone Number in U.S. (518) 436-9686); *World Health Statistics Annual*.

The World Bank, 1818 H Street, NW, Washington, D.C. 20433 (202) 477-1234; *World Tables*.

CAPE VERDE - BONDS

G.K. Hall and Company, 70 Lincoln Street, Boston, Massachusetts 02111 (617) 423-3990; *The World in Figures*.

CAPE VERDE - BOOK PRODUCTION

G.K. Hall and Company, 70 Lincoln Street, Boston, Massachusetts 02111 (617) 423-3990; *The World in Figures*.

CAPE VERDE - BROADCASTING

Billboard Limited, P.O. Box 9027, 1006 AA Amsterdam, The Netherlands (Telephone Number in U.S. (212) 764-7300); *World Radio TV Handbook*.

G.K. Hall and Company, 70 Lincoln Street, Boston, Massachusetts 02111 (617) 423-3990; *The World in Figures*.

CAPE VERDE - BUSINESS

G.K. Hall and Company, 70 Lincoln Street, Boston, Massachusetts 02111 (617) 423-3990; *The World in Figures*.

CAPE VERDE - CALORIE SUPPLY

African Development Bank, 01 BP 1387, Abidjan 01, Cote D'Ivoire; *Selected Statistics on Regional Member Countries*.

Food and Agricultural Organization of the United Nations (FAO) Via delle Terme di Caracalla, 00100 Rome, Italy (Telephone Number in U.S. (202) 653-2400); *The State of Food and Agriculture*.

CAPE VERDE - CATTLE - See CAPE VERDE - LIVESTOCK AND POULTRY

CAPE VERDE - CEMENT PRODUCTION - See CAPE VERDE - MINING AND MINERAL PRODUCTS

CAPE VERDE - CHEMICAL (ORGANIC) PRODUCTION - See CAPE VERDE - MINING AND MINERAL PRODUCTS

CAPE VERDE - CLASS STRUCTURE

G.K. Hall and Company, 70 Lincoln Street, Boston, Massachusetts 02111 (617) 423-3990; *The World in Figures*.

CAPE VERDE - CLIMATE

G.K. Hall and Company, 70 Lincoln Street, Boston, Massachusetts 02111 (617) 423-3990; *The World in Figures*.

CAPE VERDE - COAL PRODUCTION - See CAPE VERDE - MINING AND MINERAL PRODUCTS

CAPE VERDE - COMMUNICATIONS

G.K. Hall and Company, 70 Lincoln Street, Boston, Massachusetts 02111 (617) 423-3990; *The World in Figures*.

United Nations Economic Commission for Africa, Africa Hall, P.O. Box 3001, Addis Ababa, Ethiopia (Telephone Number in U.S. (800) 253-9646); *African Statistical Yearbook*.

CAPE VERDE - CONSTRUCTION INDUSTRY

Statistical Office of the United Nations, Publishing Service, New York, New York 10017 (800) 253-9646; *Construction Statistics Yearbook*, and *Statistical Yearbook*.

United Nations Economic Commission for Africa, Africa Hall, P.O. Box 3001, Addis Ababa, Ethiopia (Telephone Number in U.S. (800) 253-9646); *African Statistical Yearbook*.

CAPE VERDE - CONSUMER PRICE INDEX

African Development Bank, 01 BP 1387, Abidjan 01, Cote D'Ivoire; *Selected Statistics on Regional Member Countries*.

G.K. Hall and Company, 70 Lincoln Street, Boston, Massachusetts 02111 (617) 423-3990; *The World in Figures*.

Statistical Office of the United Nations, Publishing Service, New York, New York 10017 (800) 253-9646; *Statistical Yearbook*, and *Survey of Economic and Social Conditions in Africa*.

CAPE VERDE - CONSUMER PRICES

International Labour Office, I.L.O. Publications, CH-1211, Geneva 22, Switzerland; *Yearbook of Labour Statistics*.

CAPE VERDE - CONSUMPTION

African Development Bank, 01 BP 1387, Abidjan 01, Cote D'Ivoire; *Selected Statistics on Regional Member Countries*.

G.K. Hall and Company, 70 Lincoln Street, Boston, Massachusetts 02111 (617) 423-3990; *The World in Figures*.

Statistical Office of the United Nations, Publishing Service, New York, New York 10017 (800) 253-9646; *Survey of Economic and Social Conditions in Africa*.

CAPE VERDE - CORN PRODUCTION - See CAPE VERDE - CROPS

CAPE VERDE - CORPORATE TAXES - See CAPE VERDE - TAXATION

CAPE VERDE - CROPS

Food and Agricultural Organization of the United Nations (FAO) Via delle Terme di Caracalla, 00100 Rome, Italy (Telephone Number in U.S. (202) 653-2400); *The State of Food and Agriculture*.

G.K. Hall and Company, 70 Lincoln Street, Boston, Massachusetts 02111 (617) 423-3990; *The World in Figures*.

Statistical Office of the United Nations, Publishing Service, New York, New York 10017 (800) 253-9646; *Statistical Yearbook*.

United Nations Economic Commission for Africa, Africa Hall, P.O. Box 3001, Addis Ababa, Ethiopia (Telephone Number in U.S. (800) 253-9646); *African Statistical Yearbook*.

CAPE VERDE - CUSTOMS DUTIES

G.K. Hall and Company, 70 Lincoln Street, Boston, Massachusetts 02111 (617) 423-3990; *The World in Figures.*

CAPE VERDE - DAIRY PRODUCTS

Food and Agricultural Organization of the United Nations (FAO) Via delle Terme di Caracalla, 00100 Rome, Italy (Telephone Number in U.S. (202) 653-2400); *The State of Food and Agriculture.*

CAPE VERDE - DEATH RATES

G.K. Hall and Company, 70 Lincoln Street, Boston, Massachusetts 02111 (617) 423-3990; *The World in Figures.*

Statistical Office of the United Nations, Publishing Service, New York, New York 10017 (800) 253-9646; *Statistical Yearbook,* and *Survey of Economic and Social Conditions in Africa.*

World Health Organization, Office of Publications, Avenue Appia, CH-1211 Geneva 27, Switzerland (Telephone Number in U.S. (518) 436-9686); *World Health Statistics Annual.*

CAPE VERDE - DEFENSE EXPENDITURES

G.K. Hall and Company, 70 Lincoln Street, Boston, Massachusetts 02111 (617) 423-3990; *The World in Figures.*

U.S. Arms Control and Disarmament Agency, 320 Twenty-first Street, NW, Washington, D.C. 20451 (202) 647-8677; *World Military Expenditures and Arms Transfers.*

CAPE VERDE - DEMOGRAPHY

The Economist Intelligence Unit, 111 West 57th Street, New York, New York 10019 (800) 938-4685; *The World Market Atlas.*

G.K. Hall and Company, 70 Lincoln Street, Boston, Massachusetts 02111 (617) 423-3990; *The World in Figures.*

Statistical Office of the United Nations, Publishing Service, New York, New York 10017 (800) 253-9646; *Survey of Economic and Social Conditions in Africa.*

CAPE VERDE - DEVELOPMENT ASSISTANCE

G.K. Hall and Company, 70 Lincoln Street, Boston, Massachusetts 02111 (617) 423-3990; *The World in Figures.*

Statistical Office of the United Nations, Publishing Service, New York, New York 10017 (800) 253-9646; *Statistical Yearbook.*

CAPE VERDE - DISEASE

G.K. Hall and Company, 70 Lincoln Street, Boston, Massachusetts 02111 (617) 423-3990; *The World in Figures.*

World Health Organization, Office of Publications, Avenue Appia, CH-1211 Geneva 27, Switzerland (Telephone Number in U.S. (518) 436-9686); *World Health Statistics Annual.*

CAPE VERDE - DIVORCE RATES

G.K. Hall and Company, 70 Lincoln Street, Boston, Massachusetts 02111 (617) 423-3990; *The World in Figures.*

Statistical Office of the United Nations, Publishing Service, New York, New York 10017 (800) 253-9646; *Demographic Yearbook.*

CAPE VERDE - DOMESTIC PRODUCT

G.K. Hall and Company, 70 Lincoln Street, Boston, Massachusetts 02111 (617) 423-3990; *The World in Figures.*

CAPE VERDE - ECONOMY

African Development Bank, 01 BP 1387, Abidjan 01, Cote D'Ivoire; *Selected Statistics on Regional Member Countries.*

G.K. Hall and Company, 70 Lincoln Street, Boston, Massachusetts 02111 (617) 423-3990; *The World in Figures.*

Statistical Office of the United Nations, Publishing Service, New York, New York 10017 (800) 253-9646; *Foreign Trade Statistics for Africa.*

CAPE VERDE - EDUCATION

African Development Bank, 01 BP 1387, Abidjan 01, Cote D'Ivoire; *Selected Statistics on Regional Member Countries.*

The Economist Intelligence Unit, 111 West 57th Street, New York, New York 10019 (800) 938-4685; *The World Market Atlas.*

G.K. Hall and Company, 70 Lincoln Street, Boston, Massachusetts 02111 (617) 423-3990; *The World in Figures.*

Statistical Office of the United Nations, Publishing Service, New York, New York 10017 (800) 253-9646; *Survey of Economic and Social Conditions in Africa.*

United Nations Economic Commission for Africa, Africa Hall, P.O. Box 3001, Addis Ababa, Ethiopia (Telephone Number in U.S. (800) 253-9646); *African Statistical Yearbook.*

United Nations Educational, Scientific and Cultural Organization (UNESCO), 7 Place de Fontenoy, F-75700 Paris, France (Telephone Number in U.S. (212) 963-5981); *Statistical Yearbook.*

The World Bank, 1818 H Street, NW, Washington, D.C. 20433 (202) 477-1234; *World Tables.*

CAPE VERDE - EGG PRODUCTION - See CAPE VERDE - DAIRY PRODUCTS

CAPE VERDE - ELECTRICITY

Statistical Office of the United Nations, Publishing Service, New York, New York 10017 (800) 253-9646; *Survey of Economic and Social Conditions in Africa.*

United Nations Economic Commission for Africa, Africa Hall, P.O. Box 3001, Addis Ababa, Ethiopia (Telephone Number in U.S. (800) 253-9646); *African Statistical Yearbook.*

CAPE VERDE - EMPLOYMENT

International Labour Office, I.L.O. Publications, CH-1211, Geneva 22, Switzerland; *Yearbook of Labour Statistics.*

Statistical Office of the United Nations, Publishing Service, New York, New York 10017 (800) 253-9646; *Survey of Economic and Social Conditions in Africa.*

United Nations Economic Commission for Africa, Africa Hall, P.O. Box 3001, Addis Ababa, Ethiopia (Telephone Number in U.S. (800) 253-9646); *African Statistical Yearbook.*

CAPE VERDE - ENERGY

Food and Agricultural Organization of the United Nations (FAO) Via delle Terme di Caracalla, 00100 Rome, Italy (Telephone Number in U.S. (202) 653-2400); *The State of Food and Agriculture.*

G.K. Hall and Company, 70 Lincoln Street, Boston, Massachusetts 02111 (617) 423-3990; *The World in Figures.*

Statistical Office of the United Nations, Publishing Service, New York, New York 10017 (800) 253-9646; *Energy Statistics Yearbook.*

United Nations Economic Commission for Africa, Africa Hall, P.O. Box 3001, Addis Ababa, Ethiopia (Telephone Number in U.S. (800) 253-9646); *African Statistical Yearbook.*

CAPE VERDE - EXCHANGE RATES

African Development Bank, 01 BP 1387, Abidjan 01, Cote D'Ivoire; *Selected Statistics on Regional Member Countries.*

Statistical Office of the United Nations, Publishing Service, New York, New York 10017 (800) 253-9646; *Foreign Trade Statistics for Africa,* and *Statistical Yearbook.*

CAPE VERDE - EXPORTS

African Development Bank, 01 BP 1387, Abidjan 01, Cote D'Ivoire; *Selected Statistics on Regional Member Countries.*

The Economist Intelligence Unit, 111 West 57th Street, New York, New York 10019 (800) 938-4685; *The World Market Atlas.*

Food and Agricultural Organization of the United Nations (FAO) Via delle Terme di Caracalla, 00100 Rome, Italy (Telephone Number in U.S. (202) 653-2400); *The State of Food and Agriculture.*

G.K. Hall and Company, 70 Lincoln Street, Boston, Massachusetts 02111 (617) 423-3990; *The World in Figures.*

International Monetary Fund, 700 Nineteenth Street, NW, Washington, D.C. 20431 (202) 623-7000; *Direction of Trade Statistics.*

Statistical Office of the United Nations, Publishing Service, New York, New York 10017 (800) 253-9646; *Foreign Trade Statistics for Africa,* and *Survey of Economic and Social Conditions in Africa.*

United Nations Economic Commission for Africa, Africa Hall, P.O. Box 3001, Addis Ababa, Ethiopia (Telephone Number in U.S. (800) 253-9646); *African Statistical Yearbook.*

The World Bank, 1818 H Street, NW, Washington, D.C. 20433 (202) 477-1234; *World Tables.*

CAPE VERDE - EXTERNAL INDEBTEDNESS

African Development Bank, 01 BP 1387, Abidjan 01, Cote D'Ivoire; *Selected Statistics on Regional Member Countries.*

Facts on File, 460 Park Avenue South, New York, New York 10016; *The New Book of World Rankings.*

Statistical Office of the United Nations, Publishing Service, New York, New York 10017 (800) 253-9646; *Survey of Economic and Social Conditions in Africa.*

CAPE VERDE - EXTERNAL TRADE

African Development Bank, 01 BP 1387, Abidjan 01, Cote D'Ivoire; *Selected Statistics on Regional Member Countries.*

Food and Agricultural Organization of the United Nations (FAO) Via delle Terme di Caracalla, 00100 Rome, Italy (Telephone Number in U.S. (202) 653-2400); *The State of Food and Agriculture,* and *Trade Yearbook.*

G.K. Hall and Company, 70 Lincoln Street, Boston, Massachusetts 02111 (617) 423-3990; *The World in Figures.*

Statistical Office of the United Nations, Publishing Service, New York, New York 10017 (800) 253-9646; *Statistical Yearbook.*

CAPE VERDE - FARM CROPS - See CAPE VERDE - CROPS

CAPE VERDE - FERTILITY RATES

Statistical Office of the United Nations, Publishing Service, New York, New York 10017 (800) 253-9646; *Survey of Economic and Social Conditions in Africa.*

The World Bank, 1818 H Street, NW, Washington, D.C. 20433 (202) 477-1234; *World Tables.*

CAPE VERDE - FERTILIZER

Food and Agricultural Organization of the United Nations (FAO) Via delle Terme di Caracalla, 00100 Rome, Italy (Telephone Number in U.S. (202) 653-2400); *The State of Food and Agriculture.*

CAPE VERDE - FETAL MORTALITY

Statistical Office of the United Nations, Publishing Service, New York, New York 10017 (800) 253-9646; *Demographic Yearbook.*

World Health Organization, Office of Publications, Avenue Appia, CH-1211 Geneva 27, Switzerland (Telephone Number in U.S. (518) 436-9686); *World Health Statistics Annual.*

CAPE VERDE - FINANCE

African Development Bank, 01 BP 1387, Abidjan 01, Cote D'Ivoire; *Selected Statistics on Regional Member Countries.*

G.K. Hall and Company, 70 Lincoln Street, Boston, Massachusetts 02111 (617) 423-3990; *The World in Figures.*

United Nations Economic Commission for Africa, Africa Hall, P.O. Box 3001, Addis Ababa, Ethiopia (Telephone Number in U.S. (800) 253-9646); *African Statistical Yearbook.*

CAPE VERDE - FISHERIES

Food and Agricultural Organization of the United Nations (FAO) Via delle Terme di Caracalla, 00100 Rome, Italy (Telephone Number in U.S. (202) 653-2400); *The State of Food and Agriculture,* and *Yearbook of Fishery Statistics.*

Statistical Office of the United Nations, Publishing Service, New York, New York 10017 (800) 253-9646; *Statistical Yearbook,* and *Survey of Economic and Social Conditions in Africa.*

United Nations Economic Commission for Africa, Africa Hall, P.O. Box 3001, Addis Ababa, Ethiopia (Telephone Number in U.S. (800) 253-9646); *African Statistical Yearbook.*

CAPE VERDE - FOOD

African Development Bank, 01 BP 1387, Abidjan 01, Cote D'Ivoire; *Selected Statistics on Regional Member Countries.*

Food and Agricultural Organization of the United Nations (FAO) Via delle Terme di Caracalla, 00100 Rome, Italy (Telephone Number in U.S. (202) 653-2400); *Production Yearbook,* and *The State of Food and Agriculture.*

G.K. Hall and Company, 70 Lincoln Street, Boston, Massachusetts 02111 (617) 423-3990; *The World in Figures.*

CAPE VERDE - FOREIGN AID

G.K. Hall and Company, 70 Lincoln Street, Boston, Massachusetts 02111 (617) 423-3990; *The World in Figures.*

CAPE VERDE - FOREIGN TRADE

G.K. Hall and Company, 70 Lincoln Street, Boston, Massachusetts 02111 (617) 423-3990; *The World in Figures.*

Organisation for Economic Co-operation and Development (OECD), 2 rue Andre-Pascal, 75 Paris 16, France (Telephone Number in U.S. (202) 785-6323); *Trade by Commodities.*

Statistical Office of the United Nations, Publishing Service, New York, New York 10017 (800) 253-9646; *Foreign Trade Statistics for Africa, International Trade Statistics Yearbook,* and *Statistical Yearbook.*

United Nations Economic Commission for Africa, Africa Hall, P.O. Box 3001, Addis Ababa, Ethiopia (Telephone Number in U.S. (800) 253-9646); *African Statistical Yearbook.*

The World Bank, 1818 H Street, NW, Washington, D.C. 20433 (202) 477-1234; *World Tables.*

CAPE VERDE - FORESTRY AND FOREST PRODUCTS

Food and Agricultural Organization of the United Nations (FAO) Via delle Terme di Caracalla, 00100 Rome, Italy (Telephone Number in U.S. (202) 653-2400); *The State of Food and Agriculture,* and *Yearbook of Forest Products.*

G.K. Hall and Company, 70 Lincoln Street, Boston, Massachusetts 02111 (617) 423-3990; *The World in Figures.*

United Nations Economic Commission for Africa, Africa Hall, P.O. Box 3001, Addis Ababa, Ethiopia (Telephone Number in U.S. (800) 253-9646); *African Statistical Yearbook.*

CAPE VERDE - GENERAL MORTALITY

Statistical Office of the United Nations, Publishing Service, New York, New York 10017 (800) 253-9646; *Demographic Yearbook.*

World Health Organization, Office of Publications, Avenue Appia, CH-1211 Geneva 27, Switzerland (Telephone Number in U.S. (518) 436-9686); *World Health Statistics Annual.*

CAPE VERDE - GOATS - See CAPE VERDE - LIVESTOCK AND POULTRY

CAPE VERDE - GOLD HOLDINGS

The World Bank, 1818 H Street, NW, Washington, D.C. 20433 (202) 477-1234; *World Tables.*

CAPE VERDE - GOVERNMENT

G.K. Hall and Company, 70 Lincoln Street, Boston, Massachusetts 02111 (617) 423-3990; *The World in Figures.*

CAPE VERDE - GOVERNMENT EXPENDITURE

The World Bank, 1818 H Street, NW, Washington, D.C. 20433 (202) 477-1234; *World Tables.*

CAPE VERDE - GOVERNMENT REVENUE

Statistical Office of the United Nations, Publishing Service, New York, New York 10017 (800) 253-9646; *Survey of Economic and Social Conditions in Africa.*

The World Bank, 1818 H Street, NW, Washington, D.C. 20433 (202) 477-1234; *World Tables.*

CAPE VERDE - GRAIN PRODUCTION - See CAPE VERDE - CROPS

CAPE VERDE - GROSS DOMESTIC PRODUCT

African Development Bank, 01 BP 1387, Abidjan 01, Cote D'Ivoire; *Selected Statistics on Regional Member Countries.*

The Economist Intelligence Unit, 111 West 57th Street, New York, New York 10019 (800) 938-4685; *The World Market Atlas.*

G.K. Hall and Company, 70 Lincoln Street, Boston, Massachusetts 02111 (617) 423-3990; *The World in Figures.*

Statistical Office of the United Nations, Publishing Service, New York, New York 10017 (800) 253-9646; *Survey of Economic and Social Conditions in Africa.*

United Nations Economic Commission for Africa, Africa Hall, P.O. Box 3001, Addis Ababa, Ethiopia (Telephone Number in U.S. (800) 253-9646); *African Statistical Yearbook.*

The World Bank, 1818 H Street, NW, Washington, D.C. 20433 (202) 477-1234; *World Tables.*

CAPE VERDE - GROSS NATIONAL PRODUCT

U.S. Arms Control and Disarmament Agency, 320 Twenty-first Street, NW, Washington, D.C. 20451 (202) 647-8677; *World Military Expenditures and Arms Transfers.*

The World Bank, 1818 H Street, NW, Washington, D.C. 20433 (202) 477-1234; *World Tables.*

CAPE VERDE - GROUNDNUTS PRODUCTION - See CAPE VERDE - CROPS

CAPE VERDE - HEALTH

African Development Bank, 01 BP 1387, Abidjan 01, Cote D'Ivoire; *Selected Statistics on Regional Member Countries.*

G.K. Hall and Company, 70 Lincoln Street, Boston, Massachusetts 02111 (617) 423-3990; *The World in Figures.*

Statistical Office of the United Nations, Publishing Service, New York, New York 10017 (800) 253-9646; *Statistical Yearbook.*

United Nations Economic Commission for Africa, Africa Hall, P.O. Box 3001, Addis Ababa, Ethiopia (Telephone Number in U.S. (800) 253-9646); *African Statistical Yearbook.*

World Health Organization, Office of Publications, Avenue Appia, CH-1211 Geneva 27, Switzerland (Telephone Number in U.S. (518) 436-9686); *World Health Statistics Annual.*

CAPE VERDE - HIGHWAYS

G.K. Hall and Company, 70 Lincoln Street, Boston, Massachusetts 02111 (617) 423-3990; *The World in Figures.*

Statistical Office of the United Nations, Publishing Service, New York, New York 10017 (800) 253-9646; *Survey of Economic and Social Conditions in Africa.*

United Nations Economic Commission for Africa, Africa Hall, P.O. Box 3001, Addis Ababa, Ethiopia (Telephone Number in U.S. (800) 253-9646); *African Statistical Yearbook.*

CAPE VERDE - HIDE PRODUCTION

Food and Agricultural Organization of the United Nations (FAO), Via delle Terme di Caracalla, 00100 Rome, Italy (Telephone Number in U.S. (202) 653-2400); *Production Yearbook.*

CAPE VERDE - HORSES - See CAPE VERDE - LIVESTOCK AND POULTRY

CAPE VERDE - HOURS OF WORK - See CAPE VERDE - EMPLOYMENT

CAPE VERDE - ILLITERATE POPULATION

The Economist Intelligence Unit, 111 West 57th Street, New York, New York 10019 (800) 938-4685; *The World Market Atlas.*

G.K. Hall and Company, 70 Lincoln Street, Boston, Massachusetts 02111 (617) 423-3990; *The World in Figures.*

United Nations Educational, Scientific and Cultural Organization (UNESCO), 7 Place de Fontenoy, F-75700 Paris, France (Telephone Number in U.S. (212) 963-5981); *Statistical Yearbook.*

CAPE VERDE - IMPORTS

African Development Bank, 01 BP 1387, Abidjan 01, Cote D'Ivoire; *Selected Statistics on Regional Member Countries.*

The Economist Intelligence Unit, 111 West 57th Street, New York, New York 10019 (800) 938-4685; *The World Market Atlas.*

Food and Agricultural Organization of the United Nations (FAO) Via delle Terme di Caracalla, 00100 Rome, Italy (Telephone Number in U.S. (202) 653-2400); *The State of Food and Agriculture.*

G.K. Hall and Company, 70 Lincoln Street, Boston, Massachusetts 02111 (617) 423-3990; *The World in Figures.*

International Monetary Fund, 700 Nineteenth Street, NW, Washington, D.C. 20431 (202) 623-7000; *Direction of Trade Statistics.*

Statistical Office of the United Nations, Publishing Service, New York, New York 10017 (800) 253-9646; *Foreign Trade Statistics for Africa,* and *Survey of Economic and Social Conditions in Africa.*

United Nations Economic Commission for Africa, Africa Hall, P.O. Box 3001, Addis Ababa, Ethiopia (Telephone Number in U.S. (800) 253-9646); *African Statistical Yearbook.*

The World Bank, 1818 H Street, NW, Washington, D.C. 20433 (202) 477-1234; *World Tables.*

CAPE VERDE - INDUSTRY

G.K. Hall and Company, 70 Lincoln Street, Boston, Massachusetts 02111 (617) 423-3990; *The World in Figures.*

International Labour Office, I.L.O. Publications, CH-1211, Geneva 22, Switzerland; *Yearbook of Labour Statistics.*

Statistical Office of the United Nations, Publishing Service, New York, New York 10017 (800) 253-9646; *Survey of Economic and Social Conditions in Africa.*

United Nations Economic Commission for Africa, Africa Hall, P.O. Box 3001, Addis Ababa, Ethiopia (Telephone Number in U.S. (800) 253-9646); *African Statistical Yearbook.*

The World Bank, 1818 H Street, NW, Washington, D.C. 20433 (202) 477-1234; *World Tables.*

CAPE VERDE - INFANT AND MATERNAL MORTALITY

Statistical Office of the United Nations, Publishing Service, New York, New York 10017 (800) 253-9646; *Demographic Yearbook, Statistical Yearbook,* and *Survey of Economic and Social Conditions in Africa.*

The World Bank, 1818 H Street, NW, Washington, D.C. 20433 (202) 477-1234; *World Tables.*

World Health Organization, Office of Publications, Avenue Appia, CH-1211 Geneva 27, Switzerland (Telephone Number in U.S. (518) 436-9686); *World Health Statistics Annual.*

CAPE VERDE - INTERNATIONAL RESERVES EXCLUDING GOLD

African Development Bank, 01 BP 1387, Abidjan 01, Cote D'Ivoire; *Selected Statistics on Regional Member Countries.*

The World Bank, 1818 H Street, NW, Washington, D.C. 20433 (202) 477-1234; *World Tables.*

CAPE VERDE - LABOR FORCE

African Development Bank, 01 BP 1387, Abidjan 01, Cote D'Ivoire; *Selected Statistics on Regional Member Countries.*

Food and Agricultural Organization of the United Nations (FAO) Via delle Terme di Caracalla, 00100 Rome, Italy (Telephone Number in U.S. (202) 653-2400); *The State of Food and Agriculture.*

G.K. Hall and Company, 70 Lincoln Street, Boston, Massachusetts 02111 (617) 423-3990; *The World in Figures.*

The World Bank, 1818 H Street, NW, Washington, D.C. 20433 (202) 477-1234; *World Tables.*

CAPE VERDE - LABOR PRODUCTIVITY

International Labour Office, I.L.O. Publications, CH-1211, Geneva 22, Switzerland; *Yearbook of Labour Statistics.*

CAPE VERDE - LAND USE

Food and Agricultural Organization of the United Nations (FAO), Via delle Terme di Caracalla, 00100 Rome, Italy (Telephone Number in U.S. (202) 653-2400); *Production Yearbook.*

G.K. Hall and Company, 70 Lincoln Street, Boston, Massachusetts 02111 (617) 423-3990; *The World in Figures.*

CAPE VERDE - LIFE EXPECTANCY

African Development Bank, 01 BP 1387, Abidjan 01, Cote D'Ivoire; *Selected Statistics on Regional Member Countries.*

CAPE VERDE - LITERACY RATE

Statistical Office of the United Nations, Publishing Service, New York, New York 10017 (800) 253-9646; *Survey of Economic and Social Conditions in Africa.*

CAPE VERDE - LIVESTOCK AND POULTRY

Food and Agricultural Organization of the United Nations (FAO), Via delle Terme di Caracalla, 00100 Rome, Italy (Telephone Number in U.S. (202) 653-2400); *Production Yearbook,* and *The State of Food and Agriculture.*

G.K. Hall and Company, 70 Lincoln Street, Boston, Massachusetts 02111 (617) 423-3990; *The World in Figures.*

Statistical Office of the United Nations, Publishing Service, New York, New York 10017 (800) 253-9646; *Statistical Yearbook,* and *Survey of Economic and Social Conditions in Africa.*

United Nations Economic Commission for Africa, Africa Hall, P.O. Box 3001, Addis Ababa, Ethiopia (Telephone Number in U.S. (800) 253-9646); *African Statistical Yearbook.*

CAPE VERDE - LIVING LEVELS

G.K. Hall and Company, 70 Lincoln Street, Boston, Massachusetts 02111 (617) 423-3990; *The World in Figures.*

CAPE VERDE - MAIL - NUMBER OF PIECES SENT OR RECEIVED

Statistical Office of the United Nations, Publishing Service, New York, New York 10017 (800) 253-9646; *Statistical Yearbook.*

CAPE VERDE - MANUFACTURING

G.K. Hall and Company, 70 Lincoln Street, Boston, Massachusetts 02111 (617) 423-3990; *The World in Figures.*

Statistical Office of the United Nations, Publishing Service, New York, New York 10017 (800) 253-9646; *Survey of Economic and Social Conditions in Africa.*

United Nations Economic Commission for Africa, Africa Hall, P.O. Box 3001, Addis Ababa, Ethiopia (Telephone Number in U.S. (800) 253-9646); *African Statistical Yearbook.*

The World Bank, 1818 H Street, NW, Washington, D.C. 20433 (202) 477-1234; *World Tables.*

CAPE VERDE - MARRIAGE RATES

Statistical Office of the United Nations, Publishing Service, New York, New York 10017 (800) 253-9646; *Demographic Yearbook,* and *Statistical Yearbook.*

CAPE VERDE - MEAT PRODUCTION - See CAPE VERDE - LIVESTOCK AND POULTRY

CAPE VERDE - MERCHANT SHIPPING

G.K. Hall and Company, 70 Lincoln Street, Boston, Massachusetts 02111 (617) 423-3990; *The World in Figures.*

Statistical Office of the United Nations, Publishing Service, New York, New York 10017 (800) 253-9646; *Statistical Yearbook.*

United Nations Economic Commission for Africa, Africa Hall, P.O. Box 3001, Addis Ababa, Ethiopia (Telephone Number in U.S. (800) 253-9646); *African Statistical Yearbook.*

CAPE VERDE - MILITARY

G.K. Hall and Company, 70 Lincoln Street, Boston, Massachusetts 02111 (617) 423-3990; *The World in Figures.*

The International Institute for Strategic Studies, 23 Tavistock Street, London WC2E 7NQ, England; *The Military Balance.*

U.S. Arms Control and Disarmament Agency, 320 Twenty-first Street, NW, Washington, D.C. 20451 (202) 647-8677; *World Military Expenditures and Arms Transfers.*

CAPE VERDE - MINING AND MINERAL PRODUCTS

G.K. Hall and Company, 70 Lincoln Street, Boston, Massachusetts 02111 (617) 423-3990; *The World in Figures.*

Statistical Office of the United Nations, Publishing Service, New York, New York 10017 (800) 253-9646; *Statistical Yearbook.*

United Nations Economic Commission for Africa, Africa Hall, P.O. Box 3001, Addis Ababa, Ethiopia (Telephone Number in U.S. (800) 253-9646); *African Statistical Yearbook.*

CAPE VERDE - MONEY EXCHANGE RATES

Statistical Office of the United Nations, Publishing Service, New York, New York 10017 (800) 253-9646; *Statistical Yearbook.*

CAPE VERDE - MONEY SUPPLY

African Development Bank, 01 BP 1387, Abidjan 01, Cote D'Ivoire; *Selected Statistics on Regional Member Countries.*

G.K. Hall and Company, 70 Lincoln Street, Boston, Massachusetts 02111 (617) 423-3990; *The World in Figures.*

The World Bank, 1818 H Street, NW, Washington, D.C. 20433 (202) 477-1234; *World Tables.*

CAPE VERDE - MOTION PICTURES

Statistical Office of the United Nations, Publishing Service, New York, New York 10017 (800) 253-9646; *Statistical Yearbook.*

CAPE VERDE - MOTOR VEHICLES IN USE

G.K. Hall and Company, 70 Lincoln Street, Boston, Massachusetts 02111 (617) 423-3990; *The World in Figures.*

Statistical Office of the United Nations, Publishing Service, New York, New York 10017 (800) 253-9646; *Statistical Yearbook,* and *Survey of Economic and Social Conditions in Africa,* and *Survey of Economic and Social Conditions in Africa.*

CAPE VERDE - MULES - See CAPE VERDE - LIVESTOCK AND POULTRY

CAPE VERDE - NATALITY - See CAPE VERDE - BIRTH RATE

CAPE VERDE - NATIONAL ACCOUNTS

African Development Bank, 01 BP 1387, Abidjan 01, Cote D'Ivoire; *Selected Statistics on Regional Member Countries.*

United Nations Economic Commission for Africa, Africa Hall, P.O. Box 3001, Addis Ababa, Ethiopia (Telephone Number in U.S. (800) 253-9646); *African Statistical Yearbook.*

CAPE VERDE - NATIONAL INCOME

G.K. Hall and Company, 70 Lincoln Street, Boston, Massachusetts 02111 (617) 423-3990; *The World in Figures.*

CAPE VERDE - NEWSPAPER PRODUCTION - See CAPE VERDE - FORESTRY AND FOREST PRODUCTS

CAPE VERDE - OCCUPATIONS - See CAPE VERDE - LABOR FORCE

CAPE VERDE - PESTICIDE USE

Food and Agricultural Organization of the United Nations (FAO) Via delle Terme di Caracalla, 00100 Rome, Italy (Telephone Number in U.S. (202) 653-2400); *The State of Food and Agriculture.*

CAPE VERDE - PETROLEUM INDUSTRY

Food and Agricultural Organization of the United Nations (FAO) Via delle Terme di Caracalla, 00100 Rome, Italy (Telephone Number in U.S. (202) 653-2400); *The State of Food and Agriculture.*

G.K. Hall and Company, 70 Lincoln Street, Boston, Massachusetts 02111 (617) 423-3990; *The World in Figures.*

CAPE VERDE - PIGS - See CAPE VERDE - LIVESTOCK AND POULTRY

CAPE VERDE - POPULATION

African Development Bank, 01 BP 1387, Abidjan 01, Cote D'Ivoire; *Selected Statistics on Regional Member Countries.*

The Economist Intelligence Unit, 111 West 57th Street, New York, New York 10019 (800) 938-4685; *The World Market Atlas.*

Food and Agricultural Organization of the United Nations (FAO), Via delle Terme di Caracalla, 00100 Rome, Italy (Telephone Number in U.S. (202) 653-2400); *Production Yearbook.*

G.K. Hall and Company, 70 Lincoln Street, Boston, Massachusetts 02111 (617) 423-3990; *The World in Figures.*

International Labour Office, I.L.O. Publications, CH-1211, Geneva 22, Switzerland; *Yearbook of Labour Statistics.*

Statistical Office of the United Nations, Publishing Service, New York, New York 10017 (800) 253-9646; *Demographic Yearbook, Statistical Yearbook,* and *Survey of Economic and Social Conditions in Africa.*

United Nations Educational, Scientific and Cultural Organization (UNESCO), 7 Place de Fontenoy, F-75700 Paris, France (Telephone Number in U.S. (212) 963-5981); *Statistical Yearbook.*

U.S. Arms Control and Disarmament Agency, 320 Twenty-first Street, NW, Washington, D.C. 20451 (202) 647-8677; *World Military Expenditures and Arms Transfers.*

World Health Organization, Office of Publications, Avenue Appia, CH-1211 Geneva 27, Switzerland (Telephone Number in U.S. (518) 436-9686); *World Health Statistics Annual.*

CAPE VERDE - POTATO PRODUCTION - See CAPE VERDE - CROPS

CAPE VERDE - PRICES

Food and Agricultural Organization of the United Nations (FAO), Via delle Terme di Caracalla, 00100 Rome, Italy (Telephone Number in U.S. (202) 653-2400); *Production Yearbook,* and *The State of Food and Agriculture.*

G.K. Hall and Company, 70 Lincoln Street, Boston, Massachusetts 02111 (617) 423-3990; *The World in Figures.*

CAPE VERDE - PRODUCTION

G.K. Hall and Company, 70 Lincoln Street, Boston, Massachusetts 02111 (617) 423-3990; *The World in Figures.*

CAPE VERDE - RAILWAYS

G.K. Hall and Company, 70 Lincoln Street, Boston, Massachusetts 02111 (617) 423-3990; *The World in Figures.*

United Nations Economic Commission for Africa, Africa Hall, P.O. Box 3001, Addis Ababa, Ethiopia (Telephone Number in U.S. (800) 253-9646); *African Statistical Yearbook.*

CAPE VERDE - RETAIL TRADE

G.K. Hall and Company, 70 Lincoln Street, Boston, Massachusetts 02111 (617) 423-3990; *The World in Figures.*

CAPE VERDE - ROOT AND TUBER PRODUCTION - See CAPE VERDE - CROPS

CAPE VERDE - ROUNDWOOD PRODUCTION - See CAPE VERDE - FORESTRY AND FOREST PRODUCTS

CAPE VERDE - SALT PRODUCTION - See CAPE VERDE - MINING AND MINERAL PRODUCTS

CAPE VERDE - SAWNWOOD PRODUCTION - See CAPE VERDE - FORESTRY AND FOREST PRODUCTS

CAPE VERDE - SHEEP - See CAPE VERDE - LIVESTOCK AND POULTRY

CAPE VERDE - SOCIAL DATA

African Development Bank, 01 BP 1387, Abidjan 01, Cote D'Ivoire; *Selected Statistics on Regional Member Countries.*

G.K. Hall and Company, 70 Lincoln Street, Boston, Massachusetts 02111 (617) 423-3990; *The World in Figures.*

CAPE VERDE - STOCKS - COMMODITY - MARKET PRICE - INDEX

Food and Agricultural Organization of the United Nations (FAO) Via delle Terme di Caracalla, 00100 Rome, Italy (Telephone Number in U.S. (202) 653-2400); *The State of Food and Agriculture.*

CAPE VERDE - TELEGRAPH SERVICE

Statistical Office of the United Nations, Publishing Service, New York, New York 10017 (800) 253-9646; *Statistical Yearbook.*

CAPE VERDE - TELEPHONES IN USE

American Telephone and Telegraph Company, 26 Parsippany Road, Whippany, New Jersey 07981 (800) 338-4038; *The World's Telephones*.

G.K. Hall and Company, 70 Lincoln Street, Boston, Massachusetts 02111 (617) 423-3990; *The World in Figures*.

Statistical Office of the United Nations, Publishing Service, New York, New York 10017 (800) 253-9646; *Statistical Yearbook*.

CAPE VERDE - TAXATION

G.K. Hall and Company, 70 Lincoln Street, Boston, Massachusetts 02111 (617) 423-3990; *The World in Figures*.

The World Bank, 1818 H Street, NW, Washington, D.C. 20433 (202) 477-1234; *World Tables*.

CAPE VERDE - TEXTILE INDUSTRY

G.K. Hall and Company, 70 Lincoln Street, Boston, Massachusetts 02111 (617) 423-3990; *The World in Figures*.

CAPE VERDE - TOBACCO PRODUCTION

Statistical Office of the United Nations, Publishing Service, New York, New York 10017 (800) 253-9646; *Statistical Yearbook*.

CAPE VERDE - TOURISM

G.K. Hall and Company, 70 Lincoln Street, Boston, Massachusetts 02111 (617) 423-3990; *The World in Figures*.

United Nations Economic Commission for Africa, Africa Hall, P.O. Box 3001, Addis Ababa, Ethiopia (Telephone Number in U.S. (800) 253-9646); *African Statistical Yearbook*.

CAPE VERDE - TRACTORS IN USE

Statistical Office of the United Nations, Publishing Service, New York, New York 10017 (800) 253-9646; *Statistical Yearbook*.

CAPE VERDE - TRADE - See CAPE VERDE - FOREIGN TRADE

CAPE VERDE - TRANSPORTATION AND COMMUNICATIONS

G.K. Hall and Company, 70 Lincoln Street, Boston, Massachusetts 02111 (617) 423-3990; *The World in Figures*.

United Nations Economic Commission for Africa, Africa Hall, P.O. Box 3001, Addis Ababa, Ethiopia (Telephone Number in U.S. (800) 253-9646); *African Statistical Yearbook*.

CAPE VERDE - UNEMPLOYMENT

International Labour Office, I.L.O. Publications, CH-1211, Geneva 22, Switzerland; *Yearbook of Labour Statistics*.

CAPE VERDE - VITAL STATISTICS

G.K. Hall and Company, 70 Lincoln Street, Boston, Massachusetts 02111 (617) 423-3990; *The World in Figures*.

Statistical Office of the United Nations, Publishing Service, New York, New York 10017 (800) 253-9646; *Statistical Yearbook*.

World Health Organization, Office of Publications, Avenue Appia, CH-1211 Geneva 27, Switzerland (Telephone Number in U.S. (518) 436-9686); *World Health Statistics Annual*.

CAPE VERDE - WAGES

G.K. Hall and Company, 70 Lincoln Street, Boston, Massachusetts 02111 (617) 423-3990; *The World in Figures*.

International Labour Office, I.L.O. Publications, CH-1211, Geneva 22, Switzerland; *Yearbook of Labour Statistics*.

CAPE VERDE - WEATHER

G.K. Hall and Company, 70 Lincoln Street, Boston, Massachusetts 02111 (617) 423-3990; *The World in Figures*.

CAPITAL - AGE OF STOCKS

U.S. Department of Commerce, Bureau of Economic Analysis, Fourteenth Street between Constitution Avenue and E Street, NW, Washington, D.C. 20230 (202) 606-9900; *Fixed Reproducible Tangible Wealth in the United States*, and *Survey of Current Business*.

CAPITAL - BANKING

Federal Deposit Insurance Corporation, 550 Seventeenth Street, NW, Washington, D.C. 20429 (202) 393-8400; *The FDIC Quarterly Banking Profile*, *Annual Report*, and *Statistics on Banking*.

CAPITAL - EXPENDITURES

U.S. Department of Commerce, Bureau of the Census, Suitland, Maryland 20233 (301) 763-4040; *Annual Survey of Manufactures*, *Census of Manufactures*, *Plant and Equipment Expenditures and Plans*, and *Current Industrial Reports*.

CAPITAL - NEW SECURITY ISSUES

Board of Governors of the Federal Reserve System, Twentieth Street and Constitution Avenue, NW, Washington, D.C. 20551 (202) 452-3000; *Annual Statistical Digest*, and *Federal Reserve Bulletin*.

CAPITAL - STOCKS

U.S. Department of Commerce, Bureau of Economic Analysis, Fourteenth Street between Constitution Avenue and E Street, NW, Washington, D.C. 20230 (202) 606-9900; *Current Industrial Reports*, *Manufacturers' Shipments, Inventories and Orders*, *Fixed Reproducible Tangible Wealth in the U.S.*, and *Survey of Current Business*.

CAPITAL - UTILITIES

American Gas Association, 1515 Wilson Boulevard, Arlington, Virginia 22209 (703) 841-8400; *Gas Facts*.

U.S. Department of Energy, Energy Information Administration, Washington, D.C. 20585 (202) 586-8800; *Financial Statistics of Major U.S. Investor-Owned Electric Utilities*.

U.S. Federal Communications Commission, 1919 M Street, NW, Washington, D.C. 20554 (202) 632-7000; *Statistics of Communications Common Carriers*, and unpublished data.

CAPITAL EQUIPMENT - PRODUCER PRICE INDEXES

U.S. Department of Labor, Bureau of Labor Statistics, Two Massachusetts Avenue, NE, Washington, D.C. 20212 (202) 606-7828; *Monthly Labor Review*.

CARBON DIOXIDE (NATURAL) - PRODUCTION AND VALUE

U.S. Department of the Interior, Bureau of Mines, 810 Seventh Street, NW, Washington, D.C. 20241 (202) 501-9649; *Annual Reports* and *Mineral Commodity Summaries*.

CARDIOVASCULAR DISEASE - See HEART DISEASE

CARGO TONNAGE - See TONNAGE VESSELS

CARPETS AND RUGS

U.S. Department of Commerce, Bureau of the Census, Suitland, Maryland 20233 (301) 763-4040; *Current Industrial Reports*.

CARROTS

U.S. Department of Agriculture, National Agricultural Statistics Service, Fourteenth Street and Independence Avenue, SW, Washington, D.C. 20250 (202) 219-1504; *Agricultural Statistics, Economic Indicators of the Farm Sector: National Financial Summary*, and *Vegetables*.

U.S. Department of Agriculture, Economic Research Service, Fourteenth Street, and Independence Avenue, SW, Washington, D.C. 20250 (202) 219-1504; *Food Consumption, Prices, and Expenditures, Agricultural Outlook*, and unpublished data.

CASSETTES

Recording Industry Association of America, 1020 19th Street, N.W., Washington, D.C. 20036 (202) 775-0101; *Inside the Recording Industry: A Statistical Overview*.

CASUALTIES - VIETNAM CONFLICT

National Archives and Records Administration, Seventh Street and Pennsylvania Avenue, NW, Washington, D.C. 20408 (202) 501-5400; unpublished data from Combat Area Casualties database.

CASUALTY INSURANCE

U.S. Department of Commerce, International Trade Administration, Fourteenth Street between Constitution Avenue and E Street, NW, Washington, D.C 20230 (202) 482-3809; *U.S. Industrial Outlook*.

CATALOG AND MAIL ORDER HOUSES - EARNINGS

U.S. Department of Commerce, Bureau of the Census, Suitland, Maryland 20233 (301) 763-4040; *County Business Patterns*, and *Census of Retail Trade*.

CATALOG AND MAIL ORDER HOUSES - EMPLOYEES

U.S. Department of Commerce, Bureau of the Census, Suitland, Maryland 20233 (301) 763-4040; *Census of Retail Trade*, and *County Business Patterns*.

CATALOG AND MAIL ORDER HOUSES - ESTABLISHMENTS

U.S. Department of Commerce, Bureau of the Census, Suitland, Maryland 20233 (301) 763-4040; *Census of Retail Trade*, and *County Business Patterns*.

CATALOG AND MAIL ORDER HOUSES - SALES

U.S. Department of Commerce, Bureau of the Census, Suitland, Maryland 20233 (301) 763-4040; *County Business Patterns, Census of Retail Trade*, and *Current Business Reports, Combined Annual and Revised Monthly Retail Trade*, and unpublished data.

CAT - OWNERSHIP

American Veterinary Medical Association, 930 North Meacham Road, Schaumburg, Illinois 60196 (708) 605-8070; *U.S. Pet Ownership and Demographics Sourcebook*.

CATFISH

U.S. Department of Agriculture, National Agricultural Statistics Service, Fourteenth Street and Independence Avenue, SW, Washington, D.C. 20250 (202) 219-1504; *USDA*.

CATTLE - FARM MARKETINGS, SALES

U.S. Department of Agriculture, Economic Research Service, Fourteenth Street and Independence Avenue, SW, Washington, D.C. 20250 (202) 219-1504; *Economic Indicators of the Farm Sector: National Financial Summary*.

CATTLE - NUMBER - ON FARMS

U.S. Department of Agriculture, National Agricultural Statistics Service, Fourteenth Street and Independence Avenue, SW, Washington, D.C. 20250 (202) 219-1504; *Agricultural Statistics, Meat Animals - Production, Disposition, and Income*, and annual livestock summaries.

CATTLE - PRICES

U.S. Department of Agriculture, National Agricultural Statistics Service, Fourteenth Street and Independence Avenue, SW, Washington, D.C. 20250 (202) 219-1504; *Agricultural Statistics, Meat Animals - Production, Disposition, and Income*, and annual livestock summaries.

CATTLE - PRODUCTION

U.S. Department of Agriculture, National Agricultural Statistics Service, Fourteenth Street and Independence Avenue, SW, Washington, D.C. 20250 (202) 219-1504; *Agricultural Statistics, Meat Animals - Production, Disposition, and Income*, and annual livestock summaries.

CATTLE - SLAUGHTER

U.S. Department of Agriculture, National Agricultural Statistics Service, Fourteenth Street and Independence Avenue, SW, Washington, D.C. 20250 (202) 219-1504; *Agricultural Outlook, Livestock and Meat Statistics*, and *Meat Animals - Production, Disposition, and Income*.

CATTLE - VALUE ON FARMS

U.S. Department of Agriculture, National Agricultural Statistics Service, Fourteenth Street and Independence Avenue, SW, Washington, D.C. 20250 (202) 219-1504; *Agricultural Statistics*, and *Meat Animals - Production, Disposition, and Income*.

CAULIFLOWER

U.S. Department of Agriculture, Economic Research Service, Fourteenth Street, and Independence Avenue, SW, Washington, D.C.

20250 (202) 219-1504; *Food Consumption Prices, and Expenditures, Agricultural Outlook,* and unpublished data.

U.S. Department of Agriculture, National Agricultural Statistics Service, Fourteenth Street and Independence Avenue, SW, Washington, D.C. 20250 (202) 219-1504; *Agricultural Statistics,* and *Vegetables.*

Cayman Islands - National Statistical Office

Department of Finance and Development, Administration Building, George Town, Grand Cayman, Cayman Islands.

Cayman Islands - Primary Statistics Source

Department of Finance and Development, Administration Building, George Town, Grand Cayman; *Statistical Abstract of the Government of the Cayman Islands.*

CAYMAN ISLANDS - AGRICULTURE

Food and Agricultural Organization of the United Nations (FAO) Via delle Terme di Caracalla, 00100 Rome, Italy (Telephone Number in U.S. (202) 653-2400); *Production Yearbook, The State of Food and Agriculture,* and *Trade Yearbook.*
G.K. Hall and Company, 70 Lincoln Street, Boston, Massachusetts 02111 (617) 423-3990; *The World in Figures.*

CAYMAN ISLANDS - AIRLINE SERVICE

G.K. Hall and Company, 70 Lincoln Street, Boston, Massachusetts 02111 (617) 423-3990; *The World in Figures.*

CAYMAN ISLANDS - AREA AND DENSITY OF POPULATION

Food and Agricultural Organization of the United Nations (FAO) Via delle Terme di Caracalla, 00100 Rome, Italy (Telephone Number in U.S. (202) 653-2400); *The State of Food and Agriculture.*

G.K. Hall and Company, 70 Lincoln Street, Boston, Massachusetts 02111 (617) 423-3990; *The World in Figures.*

Statistical Office of the United Nations, Publishing Service, New York, New York 10017 (800) 253-9646; *Statistical Yearbook.*

United Nations Educational, Scientific and Cultural Organization (UNESCO), 7 Place de Fontenoy, F-75700 Paris, France (Telephone Number in U.S. (212) 963-5981); *Statistical Yearbook.*

CAYMAN ISLANDS - BALANCE OF PAYMENTS

G.K. Hall and Company, 70 Lincoln Street, Boston, Massachusetts 02111 (617) 423-3990; *The World in Figures.*

CAYMAN ISLANDS - BANKING

G.K. Hall and Company, 70 Lincoln Street, Boston, Massachusetts 02111 (617) 423-3990; *The World in Figures.*

CAYMAN ISLANDS - BIRTH RATE

Statistical Office of the United Nations, Publishing Service, New York, New York 10017 (800) 253-9646; *Demographic Yearbook,* and *Statistical Yearbook.*

CAYMAN ISLANDS - BONDS

G.K. Hall and Company, 70 Lincoln Street, Boston, Massachusetts 02111 (617) 423-3990; *The World in Figures.*

CAYMAN ISLANDS - BOOK PRODUCTION

G.K. Hall and Company, 70 Lincoln Street, Boston, Massachusetts 02111 (617) 423-3990; *The World in Figures.*

CAYMAN ISLANDS - BROADCASTING

Billboard Limited, P.O. Box 9027, 1006 AA Amsterdam, The Netherlands (Telephone Number in U.S. (212) 764-7300); *World Radio TV Handbook.*

G.K. Hall and Company, 70 Lincoln Street, Boston, Massachusetts 02111 (617) 423-3990; *The World in Figures.*

United Nations Educational, Scientific and Cultural Organization (UNESCO), 7 Place de Fontenoy, F-75700 Paris, France (Telephone Number in U.S. (212) 963-5981); *Statistical Yearbook.*

CAYMAN ISLANDS - BUSINESS

G.K. Hall and Company, 70 Lincoln Street, Boston, Massachusetts 02111 (617) 423-3990; *The World in Figures.*

CAYMAN ISLANDS - CALORIE SUPPLY

Food and Agricultural Organization of the United Nations (FAO) Via delle Terme di Caracalla, 00100 Rome, Italy (Telephone Number in U.S. (202) 653-2400); *The State of Food and Agriculture.*

CAYMAN ISLANDS - CLASS STRUCTURE

G.K. Hall and Company, 70 Lincoln Street, Boston, Massachusetts 02111 (617) 423-3990; *The World in Figures.*

CAYMAN ISLANDS - CLIMATE

G.K. Hall and Company, 70 Lincoln Street, Boston, Massachusetts 02111 (617) 423-3990; *The World in Figures.*

CAYMAN ISLANDS - COAL PRODUCTION - See CAYMAN ISLANDS - MINING AND MINERAL PRODUCTS

CAYMAN ISLANDS - CORN PRODUCTION - See CAYMAN ISLANDS - CROPS

CAYMAN ISLANDS - COMMUNICATIONS

G.K. Hall and Company, 70 Lincoln Street, Boston, Massachusetts 02111 (617) 423-3990; *The World in Figures.*

CAYMAN ISLANDS - CONSUMER PRICE INDEX

G.K. Hall and Company, 70 Lincoln Street, Boston, Massachusetts 02111 (617) 423-3990; *The World in Figures.*

CAYMAN ISLANDS - CONSUMPTION

G.K. Hall and Company, 70 Lincoln Street, Boston, Massachusetts 02111 (617) 423-3990; *The World in Figures.*

CAYMAN ISLANDS - CORPORATE TAXES - See CAYMAN ISLANDS - TAXATION

CAYMAN ISLANDS - CROPS

Food and Agricultural Organization of the United Nations (FAO) Via delle Terme di Caracalla, 00100 Rome, Italy (Telephone Number in U.S. (202) 653-2400); *The State of Food and Agriculture*.

G.K. Hall and Company, 70 Lincoln Street, Boston, Massachusetts 02111 (617) 423-3990; *The World in Figures*.

CAYMAN ISLANDS - CUSTOMS DUTIES

G.K. Hall and Company, 70 Lincoln Street, Boston, Massachusetts 02111 (617) 423-3990; *The World in Figures*.

CAYMAN ISLANDS - DAIRY PRODUCTS

Food and Agricultural Organization of the United Nations (FAO) Via delle Terme di Caracalla, 00100 Rome, Italy (Telephone Number in U.S. (202) 653-2400); *The State of Food and Agriculture*.

CAYMAN ISLANDS - DEATH RATES

G.K. Hall and Company, 70 Lincoln Street, Boston, Massachusetts 02111 (617) 423-3990; *The World in Figures*.

Statistical Office of the United Nations, Publishing Service, New York, New York 10017 (800) 253-9646; *Statistical Yearbook*.

World Health Organization, Office of Publications, Avenue Appia, CH-1211 Geneva 27, Switzerland (Telephone Number in U.S. (518) 436-9686); *World Health Statistics Annual*.

CAYMAN ISLANDS - DEFENSE EXPENDITURES

G.K. Hall and Company, 70 Lincoln Street, Boston, Massachusetts 02111 (617) 423-3990; *The World in Figures*.

CAYMAN ISLANDS - DEMOGRAPHY

G.K. Hall and Company, 70 Lincoln Street, Boston, Massachusetts 02111 (617) 423-3990; *The World in Figures*.

CAYMAN ISLANDS - DEVELOPMENT ASSISTANCE

G.K. Hall and Company, 70 Lincoln Street, Boston, Massachusetts 02111 (617) 423-3990; *The World in Figures*.

CAYMAN ISLANDS - DISEASE

G.K. Hall and Company, 70 Lincoln Street, Boston, Massachusetts 02111 (617) 423-3990; *The World in Figures*.

World Health Organization, Office of Publications, Avenue Appia, CH-1211 Geneva 27, Switzerland (Telephone Number in U.S. (518) 436-9686); *World Health Statistics Annual*.

CAYMAN ISLANDS - DIVORCE RATES

Statistical Office of the United Nations, Publishing Service, New York, New York 10017 (800) 253-9646; *Demographic Yearbook*, and *Statistical Yearbook*.

CAYMAN ISLANDS - DOMESTIC PRODUCT

G.K. Hall and Company, 70 Lincoln Street, Boston, Massachusetts 02111 (617) 423-3990; *The World in Figures*.

CAYMAN ISLANDS - ECONOMY

G.K. Hall and Company, 70 Lincoln Street, Boston, Massachusetts 02111 (617) 423-3990; *The World in Figures*.

CAYMAN ISLANDS - EDUCATION

G.K. Hall and Company, 70 Lincoln Street, Boston, Massachusetts 02111 (617) 423-3990; *The World in Figures*.

United Nations Educational, Scientific and Cultural Organization (UNESCO), 7 Place de Fontenoy, F-75700 Paris, France (Telephone Number in U.S. (212) 963-5981); *Statistical Yearbook*.

CAYMAN ISLANDS - EGG PRODUCTION - See CAYMAN ISLANDS - DAIRY PRODUCTS

CAYMAN ISLANDS - ELECTRICITY

Statistical Office of the United Nations, Publishing Service, New York, New York 10017 (800) 253-9646; *Statistical Yearbook*.

CAYMAN ISLANDS - ENERGY

Food and Agricultural Organization of the United Nations (FAO) Via delle Terme di Caracalla, 00100 Rome, Italy (Telephone Number in U.S. (202) 653-2400); *The State of Food and Agriculture*.

G.K. Hall and Company, 70 Lincoln Street, Boston, Massachusetts 02111 (617) 423-3990; *The World in Figures*.

Statistical Office of the United Nations, Publishing Service, New York, New York 10017 (800) 253-9646; *Energy Statistics Yearbook*.

CAYMAN ISLANDS - EXPORTS

Food and Agricultural Organization of the United Nations (FAO) Via delle Terme di Caracalla, 00100 Rome, Italy (Telephone Number in U.S. (202) 653-2400); *The State of Food and Agriculture*.

G.K. Hall and Company, 70 Lincoln Street, Boston, Massachusetts 02111 (617) 423-3990; *The World in Figures*.

CAYMAN ISLANDS - EXTERNAL TRADE

Food and Agricultural Organization of the United Nations (FAO) Via delle Terme di Caracalla, 00100 Rome, Italy (Telephone Number in U.S. (202) 653-2400); *The State of Food and Agriculture*, and *Trade Yearbook*.

G.K. Hall and Company, 70 Lincoln Street, Boston, Massachusetts 02111 (617) 423-3990; *The World in Figures*.

CAYMAN ISLANDS - FARM CROPS - See CAYMAN ISLANDS - CROPS

CAYMAN ISLANDS - FETAL MORTALITY

Statistical Office of the United Nations, Publishing Service, New York, New York 10017 (800) 253-9646; *Demographic Yearbook*.

CAYMAN ISLANDS - FERTILIZER

Food and Agricultural Organization of the United Nations (FAO) Via delle Terme di Caracalla, 00100 Rome, Italy (Telephone Number in U.S. (202) 653-2400); *The State of Food and Agriculture*.

CAYMAN ISLANDS - FINANCE

G.K. Hall and Company, 70 Lincoln Street, Boston, Massachusetts 02111 (617) 423-3990; *The World in Figures.*

CAYMAN ISLANDS - FISHERIES

Food and Agricultural Organization of the United Nations (FAO) Via delle Terme di Caracalla, 00100 Rome, Italy (Telephone Number in U.S. (202) 653-2400); *The State of Food and Agriculture,* and *Yearbook of Fishery Statistics.*

CAYMAN ISLANDS - FOOD

Food and Agricultural Organization of the United Nations (FAO) Via delle Terme di Caracalla, 00100 Rome, Italy (Telephone Number in U.S. (202) 653-2400); *Production Yearbook,* and *The State of Food and Agriculture.*

G.K. Hall and Company, 70 Lincoln Street, Boston, Massachusetts 02111 (617) 423-3990; *The World in Figures.*

CAYMAN ISLANDS - FOREIGN AID

G.K. Hall and Company, 70 Lincoln Street, Boston, Massachusetts 02111 (617) 423-3990; *The World in Figures.*

CAYMAN ISLANDS - FORESTRY AND FOREST PRODUCTS

Food and Agricultural Organization of the United Nations (FAO) Via delle Terme di Caracalla, 00100 Rome, Italy (Telephone Number in U.S. (202) 653-2400); *The State of Food and Agriculture.*

G.K. Hall and Company, 70 Lincoln Street, Boston, Massachusetts 02111 (617) 423-3990; *The World in Figures.*

Statistical Office of the United Nations, Publishing Service, New York, New York 10017 (800) 253-9646; *Statistical Yearbook.*

CAYMAN ISLANDS - FOREIGN TRADE

Food and Agricultural Organization of the United Nations (FAO) Via delle Terme di Caracalla, 00100 Rome, Italy (Telephone Number in U.S. (202) 653-2400); *The State of Food and Agriculture.*

G.K. Hall and Company, 70 Lincoln Street, Boston, Massachusetts 02111 (617) 423-3990; *The World in Figures.*

Organisation for Economic Co-operation and Development (OECD), 2 rue Andre-Pascal, 75 Paris 16, France Telephone Number in U.S. (202) 785-6323; *Trade by Commodities.*

CAYMAN ISLANDS - GENERAL MORTALITY

Statistical Office of the United Nations, Publishing Service, New York, New York 10017 (800) 253-9646; *Demographic Yearbook.*

CAYMAN ISLANDS - GOVERNMENT

G.K. Hall and Company, 70 Lincoln Street, Boston, Massachusetts 02111 (617) 423-3990; *The World in Figures.*

CAYMAN ISLANDS - GRAIN PRODUCTION - See CAYMAN ISLANDS - CROPS

CAYMAN ISLANDS - GROSS DOMESTIC PRODUCT

G.K. Hall and Company, 70 Lincoln Street, Boston, Massachusetts 02111 (617) 423-3990; *The World in Figures.*

CAYMAN ISLANDS - HEALTH

G.K. Hall and Company, 70 Lincoln Street, Boston, Massachusetts 02111 (617) 423-3990; *The World in Figures.*

Statistical Office of the United Nations, Publishing Service, New York, New York 10017 (800) 253-9646; *Statistical Yearbook.*

World Health Organization, Office of Publications, Avenue Appia, CH-1211 Geneva 27, Switzerland (Telephone Number in U.S. (518) 436-9686); *World Health Statistics Annual.*

CAYMAN ISLANDS - HIGHWAYS

G.K. Hall and Company, 70 Lincoln Street, Boston, Massachusetts 02111 (617) 423-3990; *The World in Figures.*

CAYMAN ISLANDS - ILLITERATE POPULATION

G.K. Hall and Company, 70 Lincoln Street, Boston, Massachusetts 02111 (617) 423-3990; *The World in Figures.*

United Nations Educational, Scientific and Cultural Organization (UNESCO), 7 Place de Fontenoy, F-75700 Paris, France (Telephone Number in U.S. (212) 963-5981); *Statistical Yearbook.*

CAYMAN ISLANDS - IMPORTS

Food and Agricultural Organization of the United Nations (FAO) Via delle Terme di Caracalla, 00100 Rome, Italy (Telephone Number in U.S. (202) 653-2400); *The State of Food and Agriculture.*

G.K. Hall and Company, 70 Lincoln Street, Boston, Massachusetts 02111 (617) 423-3990; *The World in Figures.*

CAYMAN ISLANDS - INDUSTRY

G.K. Hall and Company, 70 Lincoln Street, Boston, Massachusetts 02111 (617) 423-3990; *The World in Figures.*

CAYMAN ISLANDS - INFANT AND MATERNAL MORTALITY

Statistical Office of the United Nations, Publishing Service, New York, New York 10017 (800) 253-9646; *Demographic Yearbook,* and *Statistical Yearbook.*

CAYMAN ISLANDS - LABOR FORCE

Food and Agricultural Organization of the United Nations (FAO) Via delle Terme di Caracalla, 00100 Rome, Italy (Telephone Number in U.S. (202) 653-2400); *The State of Food and Agriculture.*

G.K. Hall and Company, 70 Lincoln Street, Boston, Massachusetts 02111 (617) 423-3990; *The World in Figures.*

CAYMAN ISLANDS - LAND USE

Food and Agricultural Organization of the United Nations (FAO), Via delle Terme di Caracalla, 00100 Rome, Italy (Telephone Number in U.S. (202) 653-2400); *Production Yearbook.*

G.K. Hall and Company, 70 Lincoln Street, Boston, Massachusetts 02111 (617) 423-3990; *The World in Figures.*

CAYMAN ISLANDS - LIVESTOCK AND POULTRY

Food and Agricultural Organization of the United Nations (FAO), Via delle Terme di Caracalla, 00100 Rome, Italy (Telephone Number in U.S. (202) 653-2400); *Production Yearbook,* and *The State of Food and*

Agriculture.

G.K. Hall and Company, 70 Lincoln Street, Boston, Massachusetts 02111 (617) 423-3990; *The World in Figures.*

CAYMAN ISLANDS - LIVING LEVELS

G.K. Hall and Company, 70 Lincoln Street, Boston, Massachusetts 02111 (617) 423-3990; *The World in Figures.*

CAYMAN ISLANDS - MAIL - NUMBER OF PIECES SENT OR RECEIVED

Statistical Office of the United Nations, Publishing Service, New York, New York 10017 (800) 253-9646; *Statistical Yearbook.*

CAYMAN ISLANDS - MANUFACTURING

G.K. Hall and Company, 70 Lincoln Street, Boston, Massachusetts 02111 (617) 423-3990; *The World in Figures.*

CAYMAN ISLANDS - MARRIAGE RATES

Statistical Office of the United Nations, Publishing Service, New York, New York 10017 (800) 253-9646; *Demographic Yearbook,* and *Statistical Yearbook.*

CAYMAN ISLANDS - MEAT PRODUCTION - See CAYMAN ISLANDS - LIVESTOCK AND POULTRY

CAYMAN ISLANDS - MERCHANT SHIPPING

G.K. Hall and Company, 70 Lincoln Street, Boston, Massachusetts 02111 (617) 423-3990; *The World in Figures.*

Statistical Office of the United Nations, Publishing Service, New York, New York 10017 (800) 253-9646; *Statistical Yearbook.*

CAYMAN ISLANDS - MILITARY

G.K. Hall and Company, 70 Lincoln Street, Boston, Massachusetts 02111 (617) 423-3990; *The World in Figures.*

CAYMAN ISLANDS - MINING AND MINERAL PRODUCTS

G.K. Hall and Company, 70 Lincoln Street, Boston, Massachusetts 02111 (617) 423-3990; *The World in Figures.*

Statistical Office of the United Nations, Publishing Service, New York, New York 10017 (800) 253-9646; *Statistical Yearbook.*

CAYMAN ISLANDS - MOTION PICTURES

Statistical Office of the United Nations, Publishing Service, New York, New York 10017 (800) 253-9646; *Statistical Yearbook.*

CAYMAN ISLANDS - MONEY SUPPLY

G.K. Hall and Company, 70 Lincoln Street, Boston, Massachusetts 02111 (617) 423-3990; *The World in Figures.*

CAYMAN ISLANDS - MOTOR VEHICLES IN USE

G.K. Hall and Company, 70 Lincoln Street, Boston, Massachusetts 02111 (617) 423-3990; *The World in Figures.*

CAYMAN ISLANDS - NATALITY - See CAYMAN ISLANDS - BIRTH RATE

CAYMAN ISLANDS - NATIONAL INCOME

G.K. Hall and Company, 70 Lincoln Street, Boston, Massachusetts 02111 (617) 423-3990; *The World in Figures.*

CAYMAN ISLANDS - NEWSPAPER PRODUCTION - See CAYMAN ISLANDS - FORESTRY AND FOREST PRODUCTS

CAYMAN ISLANDS - OCCUPATIONS - See CAYMAN ISLANDS - LABOR FORCE

CAYMAN ISLANDS - PERIODICALS

United Nations Educational, Scientific and Cultural Organization (UNESCO), 7 Place de Fontenoy, F-75700 Paris, France (Telephone Number in U.S. (212) 963-5981); *Statistical Yearbook.*

CAYMAN ISLANDS - PESTICIDE USE

Food and Agricultural Organization of the United Nations (FAO) Via delle Terme di Caracalla, 00100 Rome, Italy (Telephone Number in U.S. (202) 653-2400); *The State of Food and Agriculture.*

CAYMAN ISLANDS - PETROLEUM INDUSTRY

Food and Agricultural Organization of the United Nations (FAO) Via delle Terme di Caracalla, 00100 Rome, Italy (Telephone Number in U.S. (202) 653-2400); *The State of Food and Agriculture.*

G.K. Hall and Company, 70 Lincoln Street, Boston, Massachusetts 02111 (617) 423-3990; *The World in Figures.*

CAYMAN ISLANDS - POPULATION

Food and Agricultural Organization of the United Nations (FAO), Via delle Terme di Caracalla, 00100 Rome, Italy (Telephone Number in U.S. (202) 653-2400); *Production Yearbook.*

G.K. Hall and Company, 70 Lincoln Street, Boston, Massachusetts 02111 (617) 423-3990; *The World in Figures.*

Statistical Office of the United Nations, Publishing Service, New York, New York 10017 (800) 253-9646; *Demographic Yearbook,* and *Statistical Yearbook.*

United Nations Educational, Scientific and Cultural Organization (UNESCO), 7 Place de Fontenoy, F-75700 Paris, France (Telephone Number in U.S. (212) 963-5981); *Statistical Yearbook.*

World Health Organization, Office of Publications, Avenue Appia, CH-1211 Geneva 27, Switzerland (Telephone Number in U.S. (518) 436-9686); *World Health Statistics Annual.*

CAYMAN ISLANDS - PRICES

Food and Agricultural Organization of the United Nations (FAO), Via delle Terme di Caracalla, 00100 Rome, Italy (Telephone Number in U.S. (202) 653-2400); *Production Yearbook,* and *The State of Food and Agriculture.*

G.K. Hall and Company, 70 Lincoln Street, Boston, Massachusetts 02111 (617) 423-3990; *The World in Figures.*

CAYMAN ISLANDS - PRODUCTION

G.K. Hall and Company, 70 Lincoln Street, Boston, Massachusetts 02111 (617) 423-3990; *The World in Figures.*

CAYMAN ISLANDS - RADIO BROADCASTING - See CAYMAN ISLANDS - BROADCASTING

CAYMAN ISLANDS - RAILWAYS

G.K. Hall and Company, 70 Lincoln Street, Boston, Massachusetts 02111 (617) 423-3990; *The World in Figures.*

CAYMAN ISLANDS - RETAIL TRADE

G.K. Hall and Company, 70 Lincoln Street, Boston, Massachusetts 02111 (617) 423-3990; *The World in Figures.*

CAYMAN ISLANDS - SCIENTISTS AND TECHNICIANS

Statistical Office of the United Nations, Publishing Service, New York, New York 10017 (800) 253-9646; *Statistical Yearbook.*

CAYMAN ISLANDS - SOCIAL DATA

G.K. Hall and Company, 70 Lincoln Street, Boston, Massachusetts 02111 (617) 423-3990; *The World in Figures.*

CAYMAN ISLANDS - STOCKS - COMMODITY - MARKET PRICE - INDEX

Food and Agricultural Organization of the United Nations (FAO) Via delle Terme di Caracalla, 00100 Rome, Italy (Telephone Number in U.S. (202) 653-2400); *The State of Food and Agriculture.*

CAYMAN ISLANDS - TAXATION

G.K. Hall and Company, 70 Lincoln Street, Boston, Massachusetts 02111 (617) 423-3990; *The World in Figures.*

CAYMAN ISLANDS - TELEPHONES IN USE

American Telephone and Telegraph Company, 26 Parsippany Road, Whippany, New Jersey 07981 (800) 338-4038; *The World's Telephones.*

G.K. Hall and Company, 70 Lincoln Street, Boston, Massachusetts 02111 (617) 423-3990; *The World in Figures.*

Statistical Office of the United Nations, Publishing Service, New York, New York 10017 (800) 253-9646; *Statistical Yearbook.*

CAYMAN ISLANDS - TEXTILE INDUSTRY

G.K. Hall and Company, 70 Lincoln Street, Boston, Massachusetts 02111 (617) 423-3990; *The World in Figures.*

CAYMAN ISLANDS - TOURISM

G.K. Hall and Company, 70 Lincoln Street, Boston, Massachusetts 02111 (617) 423-3990; *The World in Figures.*

Statistical Office of the United Nations, Publishing Service, New York, New York 10017 (800) 253-9646; *Statistical Yearbook.*

World Tourism Organization, Calle Capitan Haya 42, E-28020 Madrid, Spain; *Yearbook of Tourism Statistics.*

CAYMAN ISLANDS - TRADE - See CAYMAN ISLANDS - FOREIGN TRADE

CAYMAN ISLANDS - TRANSPORTATION AND COMMUNICATIONS

G.K. Hall and Company, 70 Lincoln Street, Boston, Massachusetts 02111 (617) 423-3990; *The World in Figures.*

CAYMAN ISLANDS - VITAL STATISTICS RATES

G.K. Hall and Company, 70 Lincoln Street, Boston, Massachusetts 02111 (617) 423-3990; *The World in Figures.*

Statistical Office of the United Nations, Publishing Service, New York, New York 10017 (800) 253-9646; *Statistical Yearbook.*

World Health Organization, Office of Publications, Avenue Appia, CH-1211 Geneva 27, Switzerland (Telephone Number in U.S. (518) 436-9686); *World Health Statistics Annual.*

CAYMAN ISLANDS - WAGES

G.K. Hall and Company, 70 Lincoln Street, Boston, Massachusetts 02111 (617) 423-3990; *The World in Figures.*

CAYMAN ISLANDS - WEATHER

G.K. Hall and Company, 70 Lincoln Street, Boston, Massachusetts 02111 (617) 423-3990; *The World in Figures.*

CD-ROMS IN SCHOOLS

Quality Education Data, Inc., 1600 Broadway, 12th Floor, Denver, Colorado 80202 (303) 860-1832; *Technology in Public Schools.*

CELERY

U.S. Department of Agriculture, Economic Research Service, Fourteenth Street, and Independence Avenue, SW, Washington, D.C. 20250 (202) 219-1504; *Economic Indicators of the Farm Sector: National Financial Summary, Food Consumption Prices, and Expenditures, Agricultural Outlook,* and unpublished data.

U.S. Department of Agriculture, National Agricultural Statistics Service, Fourteenth Street and Independence Avenue, SW, Washington, D.C. 20250 (202) 219-1504; *Agricultural Statistics,* and *Vegetables.*

CELLULAR TELEPHONES - See TELEPHONE COMMUNICATION

CEMENT - See also STONE, CLAY, AND GLASS PRODUCTS

CEMENT - CONSUMPTION

U.S. Department of the Interior, Bureau of Mines, 810 Seventh Street, NW, Washington, D.C. 20241 (202) 501-9649; *Annual Reports* and *Mineral Commodity Summaries.*

CEMENT - EMPLOYMENT

U.S. Department of Commerce, Bureau of the Census, Suitland, Maryland 20233 (301) 763-4040; *Mineral Commodity Summaries.*

CEMENT - FOREIGN TRADE

U.S. Department of the Interior, Bureau of Mines, 810 Seventh Street, NW, Washington, D.C. 20241 (202) 501-9649; *Mineral Commodity Summaries.*

CEMENT - PRICE INDEXES

U.S. Department of Labor, Bureau of Labor Statistics, Two Massachusetts Avenue, NE, Washington, D.C. 20212 (202) 606-7828; *Producer Price Indexes.*

CEMENT - PRICES

U.S. Department of the Interior, Bureau of Mines, 810 Seventh Street, NW, Washington, D.C. 20241 (202) 501-9649; *Mineral Commodity Summaries.*

CEMENT - PRODUCTION AND VALUE

U.S. Department of the Interior, Bureau of Mines, 810 Seventh Street, NW, Washington, D.C. 20241 (202) 501-9649; *Annual Reports* and *Mineral Commodities Summaries.*

CEMENT - WORLD PRODUCTION

Statistical Office of the United Nations, New York, New York 10017 (800) 253-9646; *Monthly Bulletin of Statistics.*

U.S. Department of the Interior, Bureau of Mines, 810 Seventh Street, NW, Washington, D.C. 20241 (202) 501-9649; *Mineral Commodities Summaries.*

CENTER OF POPULATION

U.S. Department of Commerce, Bureau of the Census, Suitland, Maryland 20233 (301) 763-4040; *Census of Population and Housing,* and *Population and Housing Unit Counts.*

Central African Republic - National Statistical Office

Direction de la Statistique Generale et des Etudes Economiques, BP 732, Bangui, Central African Republic.

Central African Republic - Primary Statistics Sources

Direction de la Statistique Generale et des Etudes Economiques, BP 732, Bangui, Central African Republic; *Annuaire statistique* (Statistical Yearbook), *Bulletin Trimes triel de Statistique,* (Quarterly Bulletin of Statistics), and *Bulletin d'informations statistiques,* (Bulletin of Statistical Information).

CENTRAL AFRICAN REPUBLIC - AGRICULTURE

Billboard Limited, P.O. Box 9027, 1006 AA Amsterdam, The Netherlands (Telephone Number in U.S. (212) 764-7300); *World Radio TV Handbook.*

Facts on File, 460 Park Avenue South, New York, New York 10016 (800) 443-8323; *The New Book of World Rankings.*

Federal Statistical Office, Gustav - Stresemann - Ring 11, D-6200 Wiesbaden, Germany; *Zentralafrikanische Republik.*

Food and Agricultural Organization of the United Nations (FAO) Via delle Terme di Caracalla, 00100 Rome, Italy (Telephone Number in U.S. (202) 653-2400); *Production Yearbook, The State of Food and Agriculture,* and *Trade Yearbook.*

G.K. Hall and Company, 70 Lincoln Street, Boston, Massachusetts 02111 (617) 423-3990; *The World in Figures.*

Statistical Office of the United Nations, Publishing Service, New York, New York 10017 (800) 253-9646; *Statistical Yearbook,* and *Survey of Economic and Social Conditions in Africa.*

United Nations Economic Commission for Africa, Africa Hall, P.O. Box 3001, Addis Ababa, Ethiopia (Telephone Number in U.S. (800) 253-9646); *African Statistical Yearbook.*

Times Books, 201 East 50th Street, New York, New York 10022 (212) 751-2600; *The Economist Book of Vital World Statistics.*

The World Bank, 1818 H Street, NW, Washington, D.C. 20433 (202) 477-1234; *World Tables.*

CENTRAL AFRICAN REPUBLIC - AIRLINE SERVICE

Facts on File, 460 Park Avenue South, New York, New York 10016 (800) 443-8323; *The New Book of World Rankings.*

G.K. Hall and Company, 70 Lincoln Street, Boston, Massachusetts 02111 (617) 423-3990; *The World in Figures.*

Statistical Office of the United Nations, Publishing Service, New York, New York 10017 (800) 253-9646; *Statistical Yearbook.*

Times Books, 201 East 50th Street, New York, New York 10022 (212) 751-2600; *The Economist Book of Vital World Statistics.*

United Nations Economic Commission for Africa, Africa Hall, P.O. Box 3001, Addis Ababa, Ethiopia (Telephone Number in U.S. (800) 253-9646); *African Statistical Yearbook.*

CENTRAL AFRICAN REPUBLIC - ALUMINUM PRODUCTION AND CONSUMPTION - See CENTRAL AFRICAN REPUBLIC - MINING AND MINERAL PRODUCTS

CENTRAL AFRICAN REPUBLIC - ANIMAL HEALTH

Food and Agricultural Organization of the United Nations (FAO), Via delle Terme di Caracalla, 00100 Rome, Italy (Telephone Number in U.S. (202) 653-2400); *Animal Health Yearbook.*

CENTRAL AFRICAN REPUBLIC - AREA AND DENSITY OF POPULATION

African Development Bank, 01 BP 1387, Abidjan 01, Cote D'Ivoire; *Selected Statistics on Regional Member Countries.*

Facts on File, 460 Park Avenue South, New York, New York 10016 (800) 443-8323; *The New Book of World Rankings.*

Federal Statistical Office, Gustav - Stresemann - Ring 11, D-6200 Wiesbaden, Germany; *Zentralafrikanische Republik.*

Food and Agricultural Organization of the United Nations (FAO) Via delle Terme di Caracalla, 00100 Rome, Italy (Telephone Number in U.S. (202) 653-2400); *The State of Food and Agriculture.*

G.K. Hall and Company, 70 Lincoln Street, Boston, Massachusetts 02111 (617) 423-3990; *The World in Figures.*

Statistical Office of the United Nations, Publishing Service, New York, New York 10017 (800) 253-9646; *Statistical Yearbook, Survey of Economic and Social Conditions in Africa.*

Times Books, 201 East 50th Street, New York, New York 10022 (212) 751-2600; *The Economist Book of Vital World Statistics.*

United Nations Educational, Scientific and Cultural Organization (UNESCO), 7 Place de Fontenoy, F-75700 Paris, France (Telephone Number in U.S. (212) 963-5981); *Statistical Yearbook.*

CENTRAL AFRICAN REPUBLIC - ARMS EXPORTS AND IMPORTS

U.S. Arms Control and Disarmament Agency, 320 Twenty-first Street, NW, Washington, D.C. 20451 (202) 647-8677; *World Military Expenditures and Arms Transfers.*

CENTRAL AFRICAN REPUBLIC - BALANCE OF PAYMENTS

African Development Bank, 01 BP 1387, Abidjan 01, Cote D'Ivoire; *Selected Statistics on Regional Member Countries.*

The Economist Intelligence Unit, 111 West 57th Street, New York, New York 10019 (800) 938-4685; *The World Market Atlas.*

Federal Statistical Office, Gustav - Stresemann - Ring 11, D-6200 Wiesbaden, Germany; *Zentralafrikanische Republik.*

G.K. Hall and Company, 70 Lincoln Street, Boston, Massachusetts 02111 (617) 423-3990; *The World in Figures.*

International Monetary Fund, 700 Nineteenth Street, NW, Washington, D.C. 20431 (202) 623-7000; *Balance of Payments Yearbook.*

Times Books, 201 East 50th Street, New York, New York 10022 (212) 751-2600; *The Economist Book of Vital World Statistics.*

United Nations Economic Commission for Africa, Africa Hall, P.O. Box 3001, Addis Ababa, Ethiopia (Telephone Number in U.S. (800) 253-9646); *African Statistical Yearbook.*

The World Bank, 1818 H Street, NW, Washington, D.C. 20433 (202) 477-1234; *World Tables.*

CENTRAL AFRICAN REPUBLIC - BANKING

Facts on File, 460 Park Avenue South, New York, New York 10016 (800) 443-8323; *The New Book of World Rankings.*

G.K. Hall and Company, 70 Lincoln Street, Boston, Massachusetts 02111 (617) 423-3990; *The World in Figures.*

International Monetary Fund, 700 Nineteenth Street, NW, Washington, D.C. 20431 (202) 623-7000; *International Financial Statistics.*

United Nations Economic Commission for Africa, Africa Hall, P.O. Box 3001, Addis Ababa, Ethiopia (Telephone Number in U.S. (800) 253-9646); *African Statistical Yearbook.*

CENTRAL AFRICAN REPUBLIC - BARLEY PRODUCTION - See CENTRAL AFRICAN REPUBLIC - CROPS

CENTRAL AFRICAN REPUBLIC - BEER PRODUCTION

Facts on File, 460 Park Avenue South, New York, New York 10016 (800) 443-8323; *The New Book of World Rankings.*

Statistical Office of the United Nations, Publishing Service, New York, New York 10017 (800) 253-9646; *Statistical Yearbook.*

CENTRAL AFRICAN REPUBLIC - BIRTH RATES

Facts on File, 460 Park Avenue South, New York, New York 10016 (800) 443-8323; *The New Book of World Rankings.*

Statistical Office of the United Nations, Publishing Service, New York, New York 10017 (800) 253-9646; *Demographic Yearbook, Statistical Yearbook,* and *Survey of Economic and Social Conditions in Africa.*

Times Books, 201 East 50th Street, New York, New York 10022 (212) 751-2600; *The Economist Book of Vital World Statistics.*

The World Bank, 1818 H Street, NW, Washington, D.C. 20433 (202) 477-1234; *World Tables.*

CENTRAL AFRICAN REPUBLIC - BONDS

G.K. Hall and Company, 70 Lincoln Street, Boston, Massachusetts 02111 (617) 423-3990; *The World in Figures.*

CENTRAL AFRICAN REPUBLIC - BOOK PRODUCTION

G.K. Hall and Company, 70 Lincoln Street, Boston, Massachusetts 02111 (617) 423-3990; *The World in Figures.*

CENTRAL AFRICAN REPUBLIC - BROADCASTING

Facts on File, 460 Park Avenue South, New York, New York 10016 (800) 443-8323; *The New Book of World Rankings.*

G.K. Hall and Company, 70 Lincoln Street, Boston, Massachusetts 02111 (617) 423-3990; *The World in Figures.*

Times Books, 201 East 50th Street, New York, New York 10022 (212) 751-2600; *The Economist Book of Vital World Statistics.*

CENTRAL AFRICAN REPUBLIC - BUSINESS

G.K. Hall and Company, 70 Lincoln Street, Boston, Massachusetts 02111 (617) 423-3990; *The World in Figures.*

CENTRAL AFRICAN REPUBLIC - CALORIE SUPPLY

African Development Bank, 01 BP 1387, Abidjan 01, Cote d'Ivoire; *Selected Statistics on Regional Member Countries.*

Food and Agricultural Organization of the United Nations (FAO) Via delle Terme di Caracalla, 00100 Rome, Italy (Telephone Number in U.S. (202) 653-2400); *The State of Food and Agriculture.*

CENTRAL AFRICAN REPUBLIC - CATTLE - See CENTRAL AFRICAN REPUBLIC - LIVESTOCK AND POULTRY

CENTRAL AFRICAN REPUBLIC - CEMENT PRODUCTION - See CENTRAL AFRICAN REPUBLIC - MINING AND MINERAL PRODUCTS

CENTRAL AFRICAN REPUBLIC - CHICKENS - See CENTRAL AFRICAN REPUBLIC - LIVESTOCK AND POULTRY

CENTRAL AFRICAN REPUBLIC - CHEMICAL (ORGANIC) PRODUCTION - See CENTRAL AFRICAN REPUBLIC - MINING AND MINERAL PRODUCTS

CENTRAL AFRICAN REPUBLIC - CIGARETTE PRODUCTION - See CENTRAL AFRICAN REPUBLIC - TOBACCO INDUSTRY

CENTRAL AFRICAN REPUBLIC - CLASS STRUCTURE

G.K. Hall and Company, 70 Lincoln Street, Boston, Massachusetts 02111 (617) 423-3990; *The World in Figures.*

CENTRAL AFRICAN REPUBLIC - CLIMATE

Facts on File, 460 Park Avenue South, New York, New York 10016 (800) 443-8323; *The New Book of World Rankings.*

G.K. Hall and Company, 70 Lincoln Street, Boston, Massachusetts 02111 (617) 423-3990; *The World in Figures.*

CENTRAL AFRICAN REPUBLIC - COAL PRODUCTION - See CENTRAL AFRICAN REPUBLIC - MINING AND MINERAL PRODUCTS

CENTRAL AFRICAN REPUBLIC - COCOA PRODUCTION - See CENTRAL AFRICAN REPUBLIC - CROPS

CENTRAL AFRICAN REPUBLIC - COFFEE PRODUCTION - See CENTRAL AFRICAN REPUBLIC - CROPS

CENTRAL AFRICAN REPUBLIC - COMMERCIAL BANKS

International Monetary Fund, 700 Nineteenth H Street, NW, Washington, D.C. 20431 (202) 623-7000; *International Financial Statistics.*

CENTRAL AFRICAN REPUBLIC - COMMUNICATIONS

Federal Statistical Office, Gustav - Stresemann - Ring 11, D-6200 Wiesbaden, Germany; *Zentralafrikanische Republik.*

G.K. Hall and Company, 70 Lincoln Street, Boston, Massachusetts 02111 (617) 423-3990; *The World in Figures.*

United Nations Economic Commission for Africa, Africa Hall, P.O. Box 3001, Addis Ababa, Ethiopia (Telephone Number in U.S. (800) 253-9646); *African Statistical Yearbook.*

CENTRAL AFRICAN REPUBLIC - CONSTRUCTION INDUSTRY

Facts on File, 460 Park Avenue South, New York, New York 10016 (800) 443-8323; *The New Book of World Rankings.*

Statistical Office of the United Nations, Publishing Service, New York, New York 10017 (800) 253-9646; *Construction Statistics Yearbook.*

United Nations Economic Commission for Africa, Africa Hall, P.O. Box 3001, Addis Ababa, Ethiopia (Telephone Number in U.S. (800) 253-9646); *African Statistical Yearbook.*

CENTRAL AFRICAN REPUBLIC - CONSUMER PRICE INDEX

African Development Bank, 01 BP 1387, Abidjan 01, Cote D'Ivoire; *Selected Statistics on Regional Member Countries.*

Federal Statistical Office, Gustav - Stresemann - Ring 11, D-6200 Wiesbaden, Germany; *Zentralafrikanische Republik.*

G.K. Hall and Company, 70 Lincoln Street, Boston, Massachusetts 02111 (617) 423-3990; *The World in Figures.*

Statistical Office of the United Nations, Publishing Service, New York, New York 10017 (800) 253-9646; *Statistical Yearbook,* and *Survey of Economic and Social Conditions in Africa.*

United Nations Economic Commission for Africa, Africa Hall, P.O. Box 3001, Addis Ababa, Ethiopia (Telephone Number in U.S. (800) 253-9646); *African Statistical Yearbook.*

CENTRAL AFRICAN REPUBLIC - CONSUMER PRICES

Federal Statistical Office, Gustav - Stresemann - Ring 11, D-6200 Wiesbaden, Germany; *Zentralafrikanische Republik.*

International Labour Office, I.L.O. Publications, CH-1211, Geneva 22, Switzerland; *Yearbook of Labour Statistics.*

International Monetary Fund, 700 Nineteenth Street, NW, Washington, D.C. 20431 (202) 623-7000; *International Financial Statistics.*

Times Books, 201 East 50th Street, New York, New York 10022 (212) 751-2600; *The Economist Book of Vital World Statistics.*

CENTRAL AFRICAN REPUBLIC - CONSUMPTION

African Development Bank, 01 BP 1387, Abidjan 01, Cote D'Ivoire; *Selected Statistics on Regional Member Countries.*

G.K. Hall and Company, 70 Lincoln Street, Boston, Massachusetts 02111 (617) 423-3990; *The World in Figures.*

Statistical Office of the United Nations, Publishing Service, New York, New York 10017 (800) 253-9646; *Survey of Economic and Social Conditions in Africa.*

CENTRAL AFRICAN REPUBLIC - COPPER PRODUCTION - See CENTRAL AFRICAN REPUBLIC - MINING AND MINERAL PRODUCTS

CENTRAL AFRICAN REPUBLIC - CORN PRODUCTION - See CENTRAL AFRICAN REPUBLIC - CROPS

CENTRAL AFRICAN REPUBLIC - CORPORATE TAXES - See CENTRAL AFRICAN REPUBLIC - TAXATION

CENTRAL AFRICAN REPUBLIC - COTTON PRODUCTION - See CENTRAL AFRICAN REPUBLIC - CROPS

CENTRAL AFRICAN REPUBLIC - CRIME

International Criminal Police Organization (INTERPOL), 26 rue Armengaud, 92210 Saint Cloud, France; *International Crime Statistics.*

Yale University Press, Yale Station, New Haven, Connecticut 06520 (203) 432-0940; *Violence and Crime in Cross-National Perspective.*

CENTRAL AFRICAN REPUBLIC - CROPS

Facts on File, 460 Park Avenue South, New York, New York 10016 (800) 443-8323; *The New Book of World Rankings.*

Food and Agricultural Organization of the United Nations (FAO) Via delle Terme di Caracalla, 00100 Rome, Italy (Telephone Number in U.S. (202) 653-2400); *Production Yearbook,* and *The State of Food and Agriculture.*

G.K. Hall and Company, 70 Lincoln Street, Boston, Massachusetts 02111 (617) 423-3990; *The World in Figures.*

Statistical Office of the United Nations, Publishing Service, New York, New York 10017 (800) 253-9646; *Statistical Yearbook.*

United Nations Economic Commission for Africa, Africa Hall, P.O. Box 3001, Addis Ababa, Ethiopia (Telephone Number in U.S. (800) 253-9646); *African Statistical Yearbook.*

CENTRAL AFRICAN REPUBLIC - CUSTOMS RATES

G.K. Hall and Company, 70 Lincoln Street, Boston, Massachusetts 02111 (617) 423-3990; *The World in Figures.*

CENTRAL AFRICAN REPUBLIC - DAIRY PRODUCTS

Facts on File, 460 Park Avenue South, New York, New York 10016 (800) 443-8323; *The New Book of World Rankings.*

Food and Agricultural Organization of the United Nations (FAO) Via delle Terme di Caracalla, 00100 Rome, Italy (Telephone Number in U.S. (202) 653-2400); *The State of Food and Agriculture.*

CENTRAL AFRICAN REPUBLIC - DEATH RATES

G.K. Hall and Company, 70 Lincoln Street, Boston, Massachusetts 02111 (617) 423-3990; *The World in Figures.*

Statistical Office of the United Nations, Publishing Service, New York, New York 10017 (800) 253-9646; *Statistical Yearbook,* and *Survey of Economic and Social Conditions in Africa.*

Times Books, 201 East 50th Street, New York, New York 10022 (212) 751-2600; *The Economist Book of Vital World Statistics.*

World Health Organization, Office of Publications, Avenue Appia, CH-1211 Geneva 27, Switzerland (Telephone Number in U.S. (518) 436-9686); *World Health Statistics Annual.*

CENTRAL AFRICAN REPUBLIC - DEFENSE EXPENDITURES

G.K. Hall and Company, 70 Lincoln Street, Boston, Massachusetts 02111 (617) 423-3990; *The World in Figures.*

U.S. Arms Control and Disarmament Agency, 320 Twenty-first Street, NW, Washington, D.C. 20451 (202) 647-8677; *World Military Expenditures and Arms Transfers.*

CENTRAL AFRICAN REPUBLIC - DEMOGRAPHY

The Economist Intelligence Unit, 111 West 57th Street, New York, New York 10019 (800) 938-4685; *The World Market Atlas.*

Facts on File, 460 Park Avenue South, New York, New York 10016 (800) 443-8323; *The New Book of World Rankings.*

Federal Statistical Office, Gustav - Stresemann - Ring 11, D-6200 Wiesbaden, Germany; *Zentralafrikanische Republik.*

G.K. Hall and Company, 70 Lincoln Street, Boston, Massachusetts 02111 (617) 423-3990; *The World in Figures.*

Statistical Office of the United Nations, Publishing Service, New York, New York 10017 (800) 253-9646; *Survey of Economic and Social Conditions in Africa.*

CENTRAL AFRICAN REPUBLIC - DEVELOPMENT ASSISTANCE

G.K. Hall and Company, 70 Lincoln Street, Boston, Massachusetts 02111 (617) 423-3990; *The World in Figures.*

Statistical Office of the United Nations, Publishing Service, New York, New York 10017 (800) 253-9646; *Statistical Yearbook.*

CENTRAL AFRICAN REPUBLIC - DIAMOND PRODUCTION - See CENTRAL AFRICAN REPUBLIC - MINING AND MINERAL PRODUCTS

CENTRAL AFRICAN REPUBLIC - DISEASE

G.K. Hall and Company, 70 Lincoln Street, Boston, Massachusetts 02111 (617) 423-3990; *The World in Figures.*

World Health Organization, Office of Publications, Avenue Appia, CH-1211 Geneva 27, Switzerland (Telephone Number in U.S. (518) 436-9686); *World Health Statistics Annual.*

CENTRAL AFRICAN REPUBLIC - DIVORCE RATES

Facts on File, 460 Park Avenue South, New York, New York 10016 (800) 443-8323; *The New Book of World Rankings.*

Statistical Office of the United Nations, Publishing Service, New York, New York 10017 (800) 253-9646; *Demographic Yearbook.*

CENTRAL AFRICAN REPUBLIC - DOMESTIC PRODUCT

G.K. Hall and Company, 70 Lincoln Street, Boston, Massachusetts 02111 (617) 423-3990; *The World in Figures.*

CENTRAL AFRICAN REPUBLIC - DUCKS - See CENTRAL AFRICAN REPUBLIC - LIVESTOCK AND POULTRY

CENTRAL AFRICAN REPUBLIC - ECONOMY

African Development Bank, 01 BP 1387, Abidjan 01, Cote D'Ivoire; *Selected Statistics on Regional Member Countries.*

Facts on File, 460 Park Avenue South, New York, New York 10016 (800) 443-8323; *The New Book of World Rankings.*

Federal Statistical Office, Gustav - Stresemann - Ring 11, D-6200 Wiesbaden, Germany; *Zentralafrikanische Republik.*

G.K. Hall and Company, 70 Lincoln Street, Boston, Massachusetts 02111 (617) 423-3990; *The World in Figures.*

Statistical Office of the United Nations, Publishing Service, New York, New York 10017 (800) 253-9646; *Foreign Trade Statistics for Africa.*

CENTRAL AFRICAN REPUBLIC - EDUCATION

African Development Bank, 01 BP 1387, Abidjan 01, Cote D'Ivoire; *Selected Statistics on Regional Member Countries.*

The Economist Intelligence Unit, 111 West 57th Street, New York, New York 10019 (800) 938-4685; *The World Market Atlas.*

Facts on File, 460 Park Avenue South, New York, New York 10016 (800) 443-8323; *The New Book of World Rankings.*

Federal Statistical Office, Gustav - Stresemann - Ring 11, D-6200 Wiesbaden, Germany; *Zentralafrikanische Republik.*

G.K. Hall and Company, 70 Lincoln Street, Boston, Massachusetts 02111 (617) 423-3990; *The World in Figures.*

Statistical Office of the United Nations, Publishing Service, New York, New York 10017 (800) 253-9646; *Survey of Economic and Social Conditions in Africa.*

Times Books, 201 East 50th Street, New York, New York 10022 (212) 751-2600; *The Economist Book of Vital World Statistics.*

United Nations Economic Commission for Africa, Africa Hall, P.O. Box 3001, Addis Ababa, Ethiopia (Telephone Number in U.S. (800)

253-9646); *African Statistical Yearbook.*

United Nations Educational, Scientific and Cultural Organization (UNESCO), 7 Place de Fontenoy, F-75700 Paris, France (Telephone Number in U.S. (212) 963-5981); *Statistical Yearbook.*

The World Bank, 1818 H Street, NW, Washington, D.C. 20433 (202) 477-1234; *World Tables.*

CENTRAL AFRICAN REPUBLIC - EGG PRODUCTION - See CENTRAL AFRICAN REPUBLIC - DAIRY PRODUCTS

CENTRAL AFRICAN REPUBLIC - ELECTRICITY

Facts on File, 460 Park Avenue South, New York, New York 10016 (800) 443-8323; *The New Book of World Rankings.*

Statistical Office of the United Nations, Publishing Service, New York, New York 10017 (800) 253-9646; *Statistical Yearbook,* and *Survey of Economic and Social Conditions in Africa.*

Times Books, 201 East 50th Street, New York, New York 10022 (212) 751-2600; *The Economist Book of Vital World Statistics.*

United Nations Economic Commission for Africa, Africa Hall, P.O. Box 3001, Addis Ababa, Ethiopia (Telephone Number in U.S. (800) 253-9646); *African Statistical Yearbook.*

CENTRAL AFRICAN REPUBLIC - EMPLOYMENT

Facts on File, 460 Park Avenue South, New York, New York 10016 (800) 443-8323; *The New Book of World Rankings.*

Federal Statistical Office, Gustav - Stresemann - Ring 11, D-6200 Wiesbaden, Germany; *Zentralafrikanische Republik.*

International Labour Office, I.L.O. Publications, CH-1211, Geneva 22, Switzerland; *Yearbook of Labour Statistics.*

Statistical Office of the United Nations, Publishing Service, New York, New York 10017 (800) 253-9646; *Statistical Yearbook,* and *Survey of Economic and Social Conditions in Africa.*

United Nations Economic Commission for Africa, Africa Hall, P.O. Box 3001, Addis Ababa, Ethiopia (Telephone Number in U.S. (800) 253-9646); *African Statistical Yearbook.*

CENTRAL AFRICAN REPUBLIC - ENERGY

Facts on File, 460 Park Avenue South, New York, New York 10016 (800) 443-8323; *The New Book of World Rankings.*

Food and Agricultural Organization of the United Nations (FAO) Via delle Terme di Caracalla, 00100 Rome, Italy (Telephone Number in U.S. (202) 653-2400); *The State of Food and Agriculture.*

G.K. Hall and Company, 70 Lincoln Street, Boston, Massachusetts 02111 (617) 423-3990; *The World in Figures.*

Statistical Office of the United Nations, Publishing Service, New York, New York 10017 (800) 253-9646; *Energy Statistics Yearbook,* and *Statistical Yearbook.*

Times Books, 201 East 50th Street, New York, New York 10022 (212) 751-2600; *The Economist Book of Vital World Statistics.*

United Nations Economic Commission for Africa, Africa Hall, P.O. Box 3001, Addis Ababa, Ethiopia (Telephone Number in U.S. (800) 253-9646); *African Statistical Yearbook.*

CENTRAL AFRICAN REPUBLIC - EXCHANGE RATES

African Development Bank, 01 BP 1387, Abidjan 01, Cote D'Ivoire; *Selected Statistics on Regional Member Countries.*

International Monetary Fund, 700 Nineteenth Street, NW, Washington, D.C. 20431 (202) 623-7000; *International Financial Statistics.*

Statistical Office of the United Nations, Publishing Service, New York, New York 10017 (800) 253-9646; *Foreign Trade Statistics for Africa,* and *Statistical Yearbook.*

CENTRAL AFRICAN REPUBLIC - EXPORTS

African Development Bank, 01 BP 1387, Abidjan 01, Cote D'Ivoire; *Selected Statistics on Regional Member Countries.*

The Economist Intelligence Unit, 111 West 57th Street, New York, New York 10019 (800) 938-4685; *The World Market Atlas.*

Food and Agricultural Organization of the United Nations (FAO) Via delle Terme di Caracalla, 00100 Rome, Italy (Telephone Number in U.S. (202) 653-2400); *The State of Food and Agriculture.*

G.K. Hall and Company, 70 Lincoln Street, Boston, Massachusetts 02111 (617) 423-3990; *The World in Figures.*

International Monetary Fund, 700 Nineteenth Street, NW, Washington, D.C. 20431 (202) 623-7000; *Direction of Trade Statistics.*

Statistical Office of the United Nations, Publishing Service, New York, New York 10017 (800) 253-9646; *Foreign Trade Statistics for Africa,* and *Survey of Economic and Social Conditions in Africa.*

Times Books, 201 East 50th Street, New York, New York 10022 (212) 751-2600; *The Economist Book of Vital World Statistics.*

United Nations Economic Commission for Africa, Africa Hall, P.O. Box 3001, Addis Ababa, Ethiopia (Telephone Number in U.S. (800) 253-9646); *African Statistical Yearbook.*

The World Bank, 1818 H Street, NW, Washington, D.C. 20433 (202) 477-1234; *World Tables.*

CENTRAL AFRICAN REPUBLIC - EXTERNAL INDEBTEDNESS

African Development Bank, 01 BP 1387, Abidjan 01, Cote D'Ivoire; *Selected Statistics on Regional Member Countries.*

Statistical Office of the United Nations, Publishing Service, New York, New York 10017 (800) 253-9646; *Survey of Economic and Social Conditions in Africa.*

The World Bank, 1818 H Street, NW, Washington, D.C. 20433 (202) 477-1234; *World Tables.*

CENTRAL AFRICAN REPUBLIC - EXTERNAL TRADE

African Development Bank, 01 BP 1387, Abidjan 01, Cote D'Ivoire; *Selected Statistics on Regional Member Countries.*

Food and Agricultural Organization of the United Nations (FAO) Via delle Terme di Caracalla, 00100 Rome, Italy (Telephone Number in U.S. (202) 653-2400); *The State of Food and Agriculture,* and *Trade Yearbook.*

G.K. Hall and Company, 70 Lincoln Street, Boston, Massachusetts 02111 (617) 423-3990; *The World in Figures.*

Statistical Office of the United Nations, Publishing Service, New York, New York 10017 (800) 253-9646; *Statistical Yearbook.*

CENTRAL AFRICAN REPUBLIC - FABRIC PRODUCTION - See CENTRAL AFRICAN REPUBLIC - TEXTILE INDUSTRY

CENTRAL AFRICAN REPUBLIC - FARM CROPS - See CENTRAL AFRICAN REPUBLIC - CROPS

CENTRAL AFRICAN REPUBLIC - FERTILITY RATES

Facts on File, 460 Park Avenue South, New York, New York 10016 (800) 443-8323; *The New Book of World Rankings.*

Statistical Office of the United Nations, Publishing Service, New York, New York 10017 (800) 253-9646; *Survey of Economic and Social Conditions in Africa.*

Times Books, 201 East 50th Street, New York, New York 10022 (212) 751-2600; *The Economist Book of Vital World Statistics.*

The World Bank, 1818 H Street, NW, Washington, D.C. 20433 (202) 477-1234; *World Tables.*

CENTRAL AFRICAN REPUBLIC - FERTILIZER

Food and Agricultural Organization of the United Nations (FAO), Via delle Terme di Caracalla, 00100 Rome, Italy (Telephone Number in U.S. (202) 653-2400); *Fertilizer Yearbook,* and *The State of Food and Agriculture.*

Statistical Office of the United Nations, Publishing Service, New York, New York 10017 (800) 253-9646; *Statistical Yearbook.*

CENTRAL AFRICAN REPUBLIC - FETAL MORTALITY

Statistical Office of the United Nations, Publishing Service, New York, New York 10017 (800) 253-9646; *Demographic Yearbook.*

CENTRAL AFRICAN REPUBLIC - FINANCE

African Development Bank, 01 BP 1387, Abidjan 01, Cote D'Ivoire; *Selected Statistics on Regional Member Countries.*

Facts on File, 460 Park Avenue South, New York, New York 10016 (800) 443-8323; *The New Book of World Rankings.*

Federal Statistical Office, Gustav - Stresemann - Ring 11, D-6200 Wiesbaden, Germany; *Zentralafrikanische Republik.*

G.K. Hall and Company, 70 Lincoln Street, Boston, Massachusetts 02111 (617) 423-3990; *The World in Figures.*

International Monetary Fund, 700 Nineteenth Street, NW, Washington, D.C. 20431 (202) 623-7000; *International Financial Statistics.*

United Nations Economic Commission for Africa, Africa Hall, P.O. Box 3001, Addis Ababa, Ethiopia (Telephone Number in U.S. (800) 253-9646); *African Statistical Yearbook.*

CENTRAL AFRICAN REPUBLIC - FISHERIES

Facts on File, 460 Park Avenue South, New York, New York 10016 (800) 443-8323; *The New Book of World Rankings.*

Federal Statistical Office, Gustav - Stresemann - Ring 11, D-6200 Wiesbaden, Germany; *Zentralafrikanische Republik.*

Food and Agricultural Organization of the United Nations (FAO) Via delle Terme di Caracalla, 00100 Rome, Italy (Telephone Number in U.S. (202) 653-2400); *The State of Food and Agriculture,* and *Yearbook of Fishery Statistics.*

Statistical Office of the United Nations, Publishing Service, New York, New York 10017 (800) 253-9646; *Statistical Yearbook,* and *Survey of Economic and Social Conditions in Africa.*

United Nations Economic Commission for Africa, Africa Hall, P.O. Box 3001, Addis Ababa, Ethiopia (Telephone Number in U.S. (800) 253-9646); *African Statistical Yearbook.*

CENTRAL AFRICAN REPUBLIC - FLOUR PRODUCTION

Statistical Office of the United Nations, Publishing Service, New York, New York 10017 (800) 253-9646; *Statistical Yearbook.*

CENTRAL AFRICAN REPUBLIC - FOOD

African Development Bank, 01 BP 1387, Abidjan 01, Cote D'Ivoire; *Selected Statistics on Regional Member Countries.*

Food and Agricultural Organization of the United Nations (FAO) Via delle Terme di Caracalla, 00100 Rome, Italy (Telephone Number in U.S. (202) 653-2400); *Production Yearbook,* and *The State of Food and Agriculture.*

G.K. Hall and Company, 70 Lincoln Street, Boston, Massachusetts 02111 (617) 423-3990; *The World in Figures.*

CENTRAL AFRICAN REPUBLIC - FOREIGN AID

G.K. Hall and Company, 70 Lincoln Street, Boston, Massachusetts 02111 (617) 423-3990; *The World in Figures.*

CENTRAL AFRICAN REPUBLIC - FOREIGN TRADE

Facts on File, 460 Park Avenue South, New York, New York 10016 (800) 443-8323; *The New Book of World Rankings.*

Federal Statistical Office, Gustav - Stresemann - Ring 11, D-6200 Wiesbaden, Germany; *Zentralafrikanische Republik.*

Food and Agricultural Organization of the United Nations (FAO) Via delle Terme di Caracalla, 00100 Rome, Italy (Telephone Number in U.S. (202) 653-2400); *The State of Food and Agriculture.*

G.K. Hall and Company, 70 Lincoln Street, Boston, Massachusetts 02111 (617) 423-3990; *The World in Figures.*

Organisation for Economic Co-operation and Development (OECD), 2 rue Andre-Pascal, 75 Paris 16, France (Telephone Number in U.S. (202 785-6323; *Trade by Commodities.*

Statistical Office of the United Nations, Publishing Service, New York, New York 10017 (800) 253-9646; *Foreign Trade Statistics for Africa, Statistical Yearbook,* and *Trade in Manufactures of Developing Countries.*

United Nations Economic Commission for Africa, Africa Hall, P.O. Box 3001, Addis Ababa, Ethiopia (Telephone Number in U.S. (800) 253-9646); *African Statistical Yearbook.*

The World Bank, 1818 H Street, NW, Washington, D.C. 20433 (202) 477-1234; *World Tables.*

CENTRAL AFRICAN REPUBLIC - FORESTRY AND FOREST PRODUCTS

Facts on File, 460 Park Avenue South, New York, New York 10016 (800) 443-8323; *The New Book of World Rankings.*

Federal Statistical Office, Gustav - Stresemann - Ring 11, D-6200 Wiesbaden, Germany; *Zentralafrikanische Republik.*

Food and Agricultural Organization of the United Nations (FAO) Via delle Terme di Caracalla, 00100 Rome, Italy (Telephone Number in U.S. (202) 653-2400); *The State of Food and Agriculture,* and *Yearbook of Forest Products.*

G.K. Hall and Company, 70 Lincoln Street, Boston, Massachusetts 02111 (617) 423-3990; *The World in Figures.*

Statistical Office of the United Nations, Publishing Service, New York, New York 10017 (800) 253-9646; *Statistical Yearbook.*

United Nations Economic Commission for Africa, Africa Hall, P.O. Box 3001, Addis Ababa, Ethiopia (Telephone Number in U.S. (800) 253-9646); *African Statistical Yearbook.*

United Nations Educational, Scientific and Cultural Organization (UNESCO), 7 Place de Fontenoy, F-75700 Paris, France (Telephone Number in U.S. (212) 963-5981); *Statistical Yearbook.*

CENTRAL AFRICAN REPUBLIC - GAS PRODUCTION

Facts on File, 460 Park Avenue South, New York, New York 10016 (800) 443-8323; *The New Book of World Rankings.*

CENTRAL AFRICAN REPUBLIC - GENERAL INDUSTRIAL STATISTICS

Federal Statistical Office, Gustav - Stresemann - Ring 11, D-6200 Wiesbaden, Germany; *Zentralafrikanische Republik.*

Statistical Office of the United Nations, Publishing Service, New York, New York 10017 (800) 253-9646; *Industrial Statistics Yearbook.*

CENTRAL AFRICAN REPUBLIC - GENERAL MORTALITY

Statistical Office of the United Nations, Publishing Service, New York, New York 10017 (800) 253-9646; *Demographic Yearbook.*

CENTRAL AFRICAN REPUBLIC - GEOGRAPHIC DATA

Facts on File, 460 Park Avenue South, New York, New York 10016 (800) 443-8323; *The New Book of World Rankings.*

Federal Statistical Office, Gustav - Stresemann - Ring 11, D-6200 Wiesbaden, Germany; *Zentralafrikanische Republik.*

CENTRAL AFRICAN REPUBLIC - GOATS - See CENTRAL AFRICAN REPUBLIC - LIVESTOCK AND POULTRY

CENTRAL AFRICAN REPUBLIC - GOLD HOLDINGS

International Monetary Fund, 700 Nineteenth Street, NW, Washington, D.C. 20431 (202) 623-7000; *International Financial Statistics.*

Statistical Office of the United Nations, Publishing Service, New York, New York 10017 (800) 253-9646; *Statistical Yearbook.*

The World Bank, 1818 H Street, NW, Washington, D.C. 20433 (202) 477-1234; *World Tables.*

CENTRAL AFRICAN REPUBLIC - GOLD PRODUCTION AND CONSUMPTION - See CENTRAL AFRICAN REPUBLIC - MINING AND MINERAL PRODUCTS

CENTRAL AFRICAN REPUBLIC - GOVERNMENT

G.K. Hall and Company, 70 Lincoln Street, Boston, Massachusetts 02111 (617) 423-3990; *The World in Figures.*

CENTRAL AFRICAN REPUBLIC - GOVERNMENT EXPENDITURES

The World Bank, 1818 H Street, NW, Washington, D.C. 20433 (202) 477-1234; *World Tables.*

CENTRAL AFRICAN REPUBLIC - GOVERNMENT FINANCES

International Monetary Fund, 700 Nineteenth Street, NW, Washington, D.C. 20431 (202) 623-7000; *International Financial Statistics.*

Statistical Office of the United Nations, Publishing Service, New York, New York 10017 (800) 253-9646; *Statistical Yearbook.*

CENTRAL AFRICAN REPUBLIC - GOVERNMENT REVENUE

Statistical Office of the United Nations, Publishing Service, New York, New York 10017 (800) 253-9646; *Survey of Economic and Social Conditions in Africa.*

The World Bank, 1818 H Street, NW, Washington, D.C. 20433 (202) 477-1234; *World Tables.*

CENTRAL AFRICAN REPUBLIC - GRAIN PRODUCTION - See CENTRAL AFRICAN REPUBLIC - CROPS

CENTRAL AFRICAN REPUBLIC - GROSS DOMESTIC PRODUCT

African Development Bank, 01 BP 1387, Abidjan 01, Cote D'Ivoire; *Selected Statistics on Regional Member Countries.*

The Economist Intelligence Unit, 111 West 57th Street, New York, New York 10019 (800) 938-4685; *The World Market Atlas.*

Facts on File, 460 Park Avenue South, New York, New York 10016 (800) 443-8323; *The New Book of World Rankings.*

G.K. Hall and Company, 70 Lincoln Street, Boston, Massachusetts 02111 (617) 423-3990; *The World in Figures.*

Statistical Office of the United Nations, Publishing Service, New York, New York 10017 (800) 253-9646; *Statistical Yearbook,* and *Survey of Economic and Social Conditions in Africa.*

Times Books, 201 East 50th Street, New York, New York 10022 (212) 751-2600; *The Economist Book of Vital World Statistics.*

United Nations Economic Commission for Africa, Africa Hall, P.O. Box 3001, Addis Ababa, Ethiopia (Telephone Number in U.S. (800) 253-9646); *African Statistical Yearbook.*

The World Bank, 1818 H Street, NW, Washington, D.C. 20433 (202) 477-1234; *World Tables.*

CENTRAL AFRICAN REPUBLIC - GROSS NATIONAL PRODUCT

U.S. Arms Control and Disarmament Agency, 320 Twenty-first Street, NW, Washington, D.C. 20451 (202) 647-8677; *World Military Expenditures and Arms Transfers.*

The World Bank, 1818 H Street, NW, Washington, D.C. 20433 (202) 477-1234; *World Tables.*

CENTRAL AFRICAN REPUBLIC - GROUNDNUTS PRODUCTION - See CENTRAL AFRICAN REPUBLIC - CROPS

CENTRAL AFRICAN REPUBLIC - HEALTH

African Development Bank, 01 BP 1387, Abidjan 01, Cote D'Ivoire; *Selected Statistics on Regional Member Countries.*

Facts on File, 460 Park Avenue South, New York, New York 10016 (800) 443-8323; *The New Book of World Rankings.*

Federal Statistical Office, Gustav - Stresemann - Ring 11, D-6200 Wiesbaden, Germany; *Zentralafrikanische Republik.*

G.K. Hall and Company, 70 Lincoln Street, Boston, Massachusetts 02111 (617) 423-3990; *The World in Figures.*

Statistical Office of the United Nations, Publishing Service, New York, New York 10017 (800) 253-9646; *Statistical Yearbook.*

United Nations Economic Commission for Africa, Africa Hall, P.O. Box 3001, Addis Ababa, Ethiopia (Telephone Number in U.S. (800) 253-9646); *African Statistical Yearbook.*

World Health Organization, Office of Publications, Avenue Appia, CH-1211 Geneva 27, Switzerland (Telephone Number in U.S. (518) 436-9686); *World Health Statistics Annual.*

CENTRAL AFRICAN REPUBLIC - HIDE PRODUCTION

Food and Agricultural Organization of the United Nations (FAO), Via delle Terme di Caracalla, 00100 Rome, Italy (Telephone Number in U.S. (202) 653-2400); *Production Yearbook.*

CENTRAL AFRICAN REPUBLIC - HIGHWAYS

G.K. Hall and Company, 70 Lincoln Street, Boston, Massachusetts 02111 (617) 423-3990; *The World in Figures.*

International Road Federation, 525 School Street, SW, Washington, D.C. 20024 (202) 554-2106; *World Road Statistics.*

Statistical Office of the United Nations, Publishing Service, New York, New York 10017 (800) 253-9646; *Survey of Economic and Social Conditions in Africa.*

United Nations Economic Commission for Africa, Africa Hall, P.O. Box 3001, Addis Ababa, Ethiopia (Telephone Number in U.S. (800) 253-9646); *African Statistical Yearbook.*

CENTRAL AFRICAN REPUBLIC - HORSES - See CENTRAL AFRICAN REPUBLIC - LIVESTOCK AND POULTRY

CENTRAL AFRICAN REPUBLIC - HOURS OF WORK - See CENTRAL AFRICAN REPUBLIC - EMPLOYMENT

CENTRAL AFRICAN REPUBLIC - HOUSING AND HOUSING UNITS

Facts on File, 460 Park Avenue South, New York, New York 10016 (800) 443-8323; *The New Book of World Rankings.*

CENTRAL AFRICAN REPUBLIC - ILLITERATE POPULATION

The Economist Intelligence Unit, 111 West 57th Street, New York, New York 10019 (800) 938-4685; *The World Market Atlas.*

G.K. Hall and Company, 70 Lincoln Street, Boston, Massachusetts 02111 (617) 423-3990; *The World in Figures.*

United Nations Educational, Scientific and Cultural Organization (UNESCO), 7 Place de Fontenoy, F-75700 Paris, France (Telephone Number in U.S. (212) 963-5981); *Statistical Yearbook.*

CENTRAL AFRICAN REPUBLIC - IMPORTS

African Development Bank, 01 BP 1387, Abidjan 01, Cote D'Ivoire; *Selected Statistics on Regional Member Countries.*

The Economist Intelligence Unit, 111 West 57th Street, New York, New York 10019 (800) 938-4685; *The World Market Atlas.*

Food and Agricultural Organization of the United Nations (FAO) Via delle Terme di Caracalla, 00100 Rome, Italy (Telephone Number in U.S. (202) 653-2400); *The State of Food and Agriculture.*

G.K. Hall and Company, 70 Lincoln Street, Boston, Massachusetts 02111 (617) 423-3990; *The World in Figures.*

International Monetary Fund, 700 Nineteenth Street, NW, Washington, D.C. 20431 (202) 623-7000; *Direction of Trade Statistics.*

Statistical Office of the United Nations, Publishing Service, New York, New York 10017 (800) 253-9646; *Foreign Trade Statistics for Africa, Survey of Economic and Social Conditions in Africa,* and *Trade in Manufactures of Developing Countries.*

United Nations Economic Commission for Africa, Africa Hall, P.O. Box 3001, Addis Ababa, Ethiopia (Telephone Number in U.S. (800) 253-9646); *African Statistical Yearbook.*

The World Bank, 1818 H Street, NW, Washington, D.C. 20433 (202) 477-1234; *World Tables.*

CENTRAL AFRICAN REPUBLIC - INDUSTRY

Facts on File, 460 Park Avenue South, New York, New York 10016 (800) 443-8323; *The New Book of World Rankings.*

Federal Statistical Office, Gustav - Stresemann - Ring 11, D-6200 Wiesbaden, Germany; *Zentralafrikanische Republik.*

G.K. Hall and Company, 70 Lincoln Street, Boston, Massachusetts 02111 (617) 423-3990; *The World in Figures.*

International Labour Office, I.L.O. Publications, CH-1211, Geneva 22, Switzerland; *Yearbook of Labour Statistics.*

Statistical Office of the United Nations, Publishing Service, New York, New York 10017 (800) 253-9646; *Survey of Economic and Social Conditions in Africa.*

Times Books, 201 East 50th Street, New York, New York 10022 (212) 751-2600; *The Economist Book of Vital World Statistics.*

United Nations Economic Commission for Africa, Africa Hall, P.O. Box 3001, Addis Ababa, Ethiopia (Telephone Number in U.S. (800) 253-9646); *African Statistical Yearbook.*

The World Bank, 1818 H Street, NW, Washington, D.C. 20433 (202) 477-1234; *World Tables.*

CENTRAL AFRICAN REPUBLIC - INFANT AND MATERNAL MORTALITY

Statistical Office of the United Nations, Publishing Service, New York, New York 10017 (800) 253-9646; *Demographic Yearbook, Statistical Yearbook,* and *Survey of Economic and Social Conditions in Africa.*

Times Books, 201 East 50th Street, New York, New York 10022 (212) 751-2600; *The Economist Book of Vital World Statistics.*

The World Bank, 1818 H Street, NW, Washington, D.C. 20433 (202) 477-1234; *World Tables.*

CENTRAL AFRICAN REPUBLIC - INTERNATIONAL LIQUIDITY

International Monetary Fund, 700 Nineteenth Street, NW, Washington, D.C. 20431 (202) 623-7000; *International Financial Statistics.*

CENTRAL AFRICAN REPUBLIC - INTERNATIONAL RESERVES EXCLUDING GOLD

African Development Bank, 01 BP 1387, Abidjan 01, Cote D'Ivoire; *Selected Statistics on Regional Member Countries.*

The World Bank, 1818 H Street, NW, Washington, D.C. 20433 (202) 477-1234; *World Tables.*

CENTRAL AFRICAN REPUBLIC - IRON PRODUCTION - See CENTRAL AFRICAN REPUBLIC - MINING AND MINERAL PRODUCTS

CENTRAL AFRICAN REPUBLIC - LABOR FORCE

African Development Bank, 01 BP 1387, Abidjan 01, Cote D'Ivoire; *Selected Statistics on Regional Member Countries.*

Facts on File, 460 Park Avenue South, New York, New York 10016 (800) 443-8323; *The New Book of World Rankings.*

Food and Agricultural Organization of the United Nations (FAO) Via delle Terme di Caracalla, 00100 Rome, Italy (Telephone Number in U.S. (202) 653-2400); *The State of Food and Agriculture.*

G.K. Hall and Company, 70 Lincoln Street, Boston, Massachusetts 02111 (617) 423-3990; *The World in Figures.*

The World Bank, 1818 H Street, NW, Washington, D.C. 20433 (202) 477-1234; *World Tables.*

CENTRAL AFRICAN REPUBLIC - LABOR PRODUCTIVITY

International Labour Office, I.L.O. Publications, CH-1211, Geneva 22, Switzerland; *Yearbook of Labour Statistics.*

CENTRAL AFRICAN REPUBLIC - LAND USE

Food and Agricultural Organization of the United Nations (FAO), Via delle Terme di Caracalla, 00100 Rome, Italy (Telephone Number in U.S. (202) 653-2400); *Production Yearbook.*

G.K. Hall and Company, 70 Lincoln Street, Boston, Massachusetts 02111 (617) 423-3990; *The World in Figures.*

CENTRAL AFRICAN REPUBLIC - LIBRARIES

Facts on File, 460 Park Avenue South, New York, New York 10016 (800) 443-8323; *The New Book of World Rankings.*

CENTRAL AFRICAN REPUBLIC - LIFE EXPECTANCY

African Development Bank, 01 BP 1387, Abidjan 01, Cote D'Ivoire; *Selected Statistics on Regional Member Countries.*

CENTRAL AFRICAN REPUBLIC - LITERACY RATE

Statistical Office of the United Nations, Publishing Service, New York, New York 10017 (800) 253-9646; *Survey of Economic and Social Conditions in Africa.*

CENTRAL AFRICAN REPUBLIC - LIVESTOCK AND POULTRY

Facts on File, 460 Park Avenue South, New York, New York 10016 (800) 443-8323; *The New Book of World Rankings.*

Food and Agricultural Organization of the United Nations (FAO), Via delle Terme di Caracalla, 00100 Rome, Italy (Telephone Number in U.S. (202) 653-2400); *Production Yearbook,* and *The State of Food and Agriculture.*

G.K. Hall and Company, 70 Lincoln Street, Boston, Massachusetts 02111 (617) 423-3990; *The World in Figures.*

Statistical Office of the United Nations, Publishing Service, New York, New York 10017 (800) 253-9646; *Statistical Yearbook,* and *Survey of Economic and Social Conditions in Africa.*

United Nations Economic Commission for Africa, Africa Hall, P.O. Box 3001, Addis Ababa, Ethiopia (Telephone Number in U.S. (800) 253-9646); *African Statistical Yearbook.*

CENTRAL AFRICAN REPUBLIC - LIVING LEVELS

G.K. Hall and Company, 70 Lincoln Street, Boston, Massachusetts 02111 (617) 423-3990; *The World in Figures.*

Times Books, 201 East 50th Street, New York, New York 10022 (212) 751-2600; *The Economist Book of Vital World Statistics.*

CENTRAL AFRICAN REPUBLIC - MAIL - NUMBER OF PIECES SENT OR RECEIVED

Statistical Office of the United Nations, Publishing Service, New York, New York 10017 (800) 253-9646; *Statistical Yearbook.*

CENTRAL AFRICAN REPUBLIC - MANUFACTURING

Facts on File, 460 Park Avenue South, New York, New York 10016 (800) 443-8323; *The New Book of World Rankings.*

G.K. Hall and Company, 70 Lincoln Street, Boston, Massachusetts 02111 (617) 423-3990; *The World in Figures.*

Statistical Office of the United Nations, Publishing Service, New York, New York 10017 (800) 253-9646; *Statistical Yearbook,* and *Survey of Economic and Social Conditions in Africa.*

United Nations Economic Commission for Africa, Africa Hall, P.O. Box 3001, Addis Ababa, Ethiopia (Telephone Number in U.S. (800) 253-9646); *African Statistical Yearbook.*

The World Bank, 1818 H Street, NW, Washington, D.C. 20433 (202) 477-1234; *World Tables.*

CENTRAL AFRICAN REPUBLIC - MARRIAGE RATES

Facts on File, 460 Park Avenue South, New York, New York 10016 (800) 443-8323; *The New Book of World Rankings.*

Statistical Office of the United Nations, Publishing Service, New York, New York 10017 (800) 253-9646; *Demographic Yearbook.*

CENTRAL AFRICAN REPUBLIC - MEAT PRODUCTION - See CENTRAL AFRICAN REPUBLIC - LIVESTOCK AND POULTRY

CENTRAL AFRICAN REPUBLIC - MERCHANT SHIPPING

G.K. Hall and Company, 70 Lincoln Street, Boston, Massachusetts 02111 (617) 423-3990; *The World in Figures.*

United Nations Economic Commission for Africa, Africa Hall, P.O. Box 3001, Addis Ababa, Ethiopia (Telephone Number in U.S. (800) 253-9646); *African Statistical Yearbook.*

CENTRAL AFRICAN REPUBLIC - MILITARY

G.K. Hall and Company, 70 Lincoln Street, Boston, Massachusetts 02111 (617) 423-3990; *The World in Figures.*

The International Institute for Strategic Studies, 23 Tavistock Street, London WC2E 7NQ, England; *The Military Balance.*

U.S. Arms Control and Disarmament Agency, 320 Twenty-first Street, NW, Washington, D.C. 20451 (202) 647-8677; *World Military Expenditures and Arms Transfers.*

CENTRAL AFRICAN REPUBLIC - MILK PRODUCTION - See CENTRAL AFRICAN REPUBLIC - DAIRY PRODUCTS

CENTRAL AFRICAN REPUBLIC - MILLET PRODUCTION - See CENTRAL AFRICAN REPUBLIC - CROPS

CENTRAL AFRICAN REPUBLIC - MINING AND MINERAL PRODUCTS

Facts on File, 460 Park Avenue South, New York, New York 10016 (800) 443-8323; *The New Book of World Rankings.*

G.K. Hall and Company, 70 Lincoln Street, Boston, Massachusetts 02111 (617) 423-3990; *The World in Figures.*

Statistical Office of the United Nations, Publishing Service, New York, New York 10017 (800) 253-9646; *Statistical Yearbook.*

United Nations Economic Commission for Africa, Africa Hall, P.O. Box 3001, Addis Ababa, Ethiopia (Telephone Number in U.S. (800) 253-9646); *African Statistical Yearbook.*

CENTRAL AFRICAN REPUBLIC - MONEY EXCHANGE RATES

International Monetary Fund, 700 Nineteenth Street, NW, Washington, D.C. 20431 (202) 623-7000; *International Financial Statistics.*

Statistical Office of the United Nations, Publishing Service, New York, New York 10017 (800) 253-9646; *Statistical Yearbook.*

CENTRAL AFRICAN REPUBLIC - MONEY SUPPLY

African Development Bank, 01 BP 1387, Abidjan 01, Cote D'Ivoire; *Selected Statistics on Regional Member Countries.*

Federal Statistical Office, Gustav - Stresemann - Ring 11, D-6200 Wiesbaden, Germany; *Zentralafrikanische Republik.*

G.K. Hall and Company, 70 Lincoln Street, Boston, Massachusetts 02111 (617) 423-3990; *The World in Figures.*

International Monetary Fund, 700 Nineteenth Street, NW, Washington, D.C. 20431 (202) 623-7000; *International Financial Statistics.*

Statistical Office of the United Nations, Publishing Service, New York, New York 10017 (800) 253-9646; *Statistical Yearbook.*

The World Bank, 1818 H Street, NW, Washington, D.C. 20433 (202) 477-1234; *World Tables.*

CENTRAL AFRICAN REPUBLIC - MONUMENTS AND HISTORICAL SITES

United Nations Educational, Scientific and Cultural Organization (UNESCO), 7 Place de Fontenoy, F-75700 Paris, France (Telephone Number in U.S. (212) 963-5981); *Statistical Yearbook.*

CENTRAL AFRICAN REPUBLIC - MOTOR VEHICLES IN USE

G.K. Hall and Company, 70 Lincoln Street, Boston, Massachusetts 02111 (617) 423-3990; *The World in Figures.*

International Road Federation, 525 School Street, SW, Washington, D.C. 20024 (202) 554-2106; *World Road Statistics.*

Statistical Office of the United Nations, Publishing Service, New York, New York 10017 (800) 253-9646; *Statistical Yearbook,* and *Survey of Economic and Social Conditions in Africa.*

Times Books, 201 East 50th Street, New York, New York 10022 (212) 751-2600; *The Economist Book of Vital World Statistics.*

CENTRAL AFRICAN REPUBLIC - MUSEUMS

Facts on File, 460 Park Avenue South, New York, New York 10016 (800) 443-8323; *The New Book of World Rankings.*

United Nations Educational, Scientific and Cultural Organization (UNESCO), 7 Place de Fontenoy, F-75700 Paris, France (Telephone Number in U.S. (212) 963-5981); *Statistical Yearbook.*

CENTRAL AFRICAN REPUBLIC - NATALITY - See CENTRAL AFRICAN REPUBLIC - BIRTH RATES

CENTRAL AFRICAN REPUBLIC - NATIONAL ACCOUNTS

African Development Bank, 01 BP 1387, Abidjan 01, Cote D'Ivoire; *Selected Statistics on Regional Member Countries.*

Federal Statistical Office, Gustav - Stresemann - Ring 11, D-6200 Wiesbaden, Germany; *Zentralafrikanische Republik.*

Statistical Office of the United Nations, Publishing Service, New York, New York 10017 (800) 253-9646; *National Accounts Statistics,* and *Statistical Yearbook.*

United Nations Economic Commission for Africa, Africa Hall, P.O. Box 3001, Addis Ababa, Ethiopia (Telephone Number in U.S. (800) 253-9646); *African Statistical Yearbook.*

CENTRAL AFRICAN REPUBLIC - NATIONAL INCOME

Facts on File, 460 Park Avenue South, New York, New York 10016 (800) 443-8323; *The New Book of World Rankings.*

G.K. Hall and Company, 70 Lincoln Street, Boston, Massachusetts 02111 (617) 423-3990; *The World in Figures.*

Statistical Office of the United Nations, Publishing Service, New York, New York 10017 (800) 253-9646; *Statistical Yearbook.*

CENTRAL AFRICAN REPUBLIC - NATIONAL PRODUCT

Facts on File, 460 Park Avenue South, New York, New York 10016 (800) 443-8323; *The New Book of World Rankings.*

CENTRAL AFRICAN REPUBLIC - NATURAL GAS PRODUCTION - See CENTRAL AFRICAN REPUBLIC - MINING AND MINERAL PRODUCTS

CENTRAL AFRICAN REPUBLIC - NATURAL RUBBER PRODUCTION

Statistical Office of the United Nations, Publishing Service, New York, New York 10017 (800) 253-9646; *Statistical Yearbook.*

CENTRAL AFRICAN REPUBLIC - NET MATERIAL PRODUCT

Statistical Office of the United Nations, Publishing Service, New York, New York 10017 (800) 253-9646; *Statistical Yearbook.*

CENTRAL AFRICAN REPUBLIC - NEWSPAPER PRODUCTION - See CENTRAL AFRICAN REPUBLIC - FORESTRY AND FOREST PRODUCTS

CENTRAL AFRICAN REPUBLIC - OCCUPATIONS - See CENTRAL AFRICAN REPUBLIC

CENTRAL AFRICAN REPUBLIC - PALM KERNELS AND PALM OIL - See CENTRAL AFRICAN REPUBLIC - CROPS

CENTRAL AFRICAN REPUBLIC - PAPER - See CENTRAL AFRICAN REPUBLIC - FORESTRY AND FOREST PRODUCTS

CENTRAL AFRICAN REPUBLIC - PEANUT PRODUCTION - See CENTRAL AFRICAN REPUBLIC - CROPS

CENTRAL AFRICAN REPUBLIC - PERIODICALS

United Nations Educational, Scientific and Cultural Organization (UNESCO), 7 Place de Fontenoy, F-75700 Paris, France (Telephone Number in U.S. (212) 963-5981); *Statistical Yearbook.*

CENTRAL AFRICAN REPUBLIC - PESTICIDE USE

Food and Agricultural Organization of the United Nations (FAO) Via delle Terme di Caracalla, 00100 Rome, Italy (Telephone Number in U.S. (202) 653-2400); *The State of Food and Agriculture.*

CENTRAL AFRICAN REPUBLIC - PETROLEUM INDUSTRY

Facts on File, 460 Park Avenue South, New York, New York 10016 (800) 443-8323; *The New Book of World Rankings.*

Food and Agricultural Organization of the United Nations (FAO) Via delle Terme di Caracalla, 00100 Rome, Italy (Telephone Number in U.S. (202) 653-2400); *The State of Food and Agriculture.*

G.K. Hall and Company, 70 Lincoln Street, Boston, Massachusetts 02111 (617) 423-3990; *The World in Figures.*

CENTRAL AFRICAN REPUBLIC - PIGS - See CENTRAL AFRICAN REPUBLIC - LIVESTOCK AND POULTRY

CENTRAL AFRICAN REPUBLIC - POPULATION

African Development Bank, 01 BP 1387, Abidjan 01, Cote D'Ivoire; *Selected Statistics on Regional Member Countries.*

The Economist Intelligence Unit, 111 West 57th Street, New York, New York 10019 (800) 938-4685; *The World Market Atlas.*

Facts on File, 460 Park Avenue South, New York, New York 10016 (800) 443-8323; *The New Book of World Rankings.*

Federal Statistical Office, Gustav - Stresemann - Ring 11, D-6200 Wiesbaden, Germany; *Zentralafrikanische Republik.*

Food and Agricultural Organization of the United Nations (FAO), Via delle Terme di Caracalla, 00100 Rome, Italy (Telephone Number in U.S. (202) 653-2400); *Production Yearbook.*

G.K. Hall and Company, 70 Lincoln Street, Boston, Massachusetts 02111 (617) 423-3990; *The World in Figures.*

International Labour Office, I.L.O. Publications, CH-1211, Geneva 22, Switzerland; *Yearbook of Labour Statistics.*

Statistical Office of the United Nations, Publishing Service, New York, New York 10017 (800) 253-9646; *Demographic Yearbook, Statistical Yearbook,* and *Survey of Economic and Social Conditions in Africa.*

Times Books, 201 East 50th Street, New York, New York 10022 (212) 751-2600; *The Economist Book of Vital World Statistics.*

United Nations Educational, Scientific and Cultural Organization (UNESCO), 7 Place de Fontenoy, F-75700 Paris, France (Telephone Number in U.S. (212) 963-5981); *Statistical Yearbook.*

U.S. Arms Control and Disarmament Agency, 320 Twenty-first Street, NW, Washington, D.C. 20451 (202) 647-8677; *World Military Expenditures and Arms Transfers.*

World Health Organization, Office of Publications, Avenue Appia, CH-1211 Geneva 27, Switzerland (Telephone Number in U.S. (518) 436-9686); *World Health Statistics Annual.*

CENTRAL AFRICAN REPUBLIC - POST OFFICES

Facts on File, 460 Park Avenue South, New York, New York 10016 (800) 443-8323; *The New Book of World Rankings.*

CENTRAL AFRICAN REPUBLIC - POTATO PRODUCTION - See CENTRAL AFRICAN REPUBLIC - CROPS

CENTRAL AFRICAN REPUBLIC - PRICES

Facts on File, 460 Park Avenue South, New York, New York 10016 (800) 443-8323; *The New Book of World Rankings.*

Federal Statistical Office, Gustav - Stresemann - Ring 11, D-6200 Wiesbaden, Germany; *Zentralafrikanische Republik.*

Food and Agricultural Organization of the United Nations (FAO), Via delle Terme di Caracalla, 00100 Rome, Italy (Telephone Number in U.S. (202) 653-2400); *Production Yearbook,* and *The State of Food and Agriculture.*

G.K. Hall and Company, 70 Lincoln Street, Boston, Massachusetts 02111 (617) 423-3990; *The World in Figures.*

International Labour Office, I.L.O. Publications, CH-1211, Geneva 22, Switzerland; *Yearbook of Labour Statistics.*

International Monetary Fund, 700 Nineteenth Street, NW, Washington, D.C. 20431 (202) 623-7000; *International Financial Statistics.*

United Nations Economic Commission for Africa, Africa Hall, P.O. Box 3001, Addis Ababa, Ethiopia (Telephone Number in U.S. (800) 253-9646); *African Statistical Yearbook.*

CENTRAL AFRICAN REPUBLIC - PRINTING AND WRITING PAPER - See CENTRAL AFRICAN REPUBLIC - FORESTRY AND FOREST PRODUCTS

CENTRAL AFRICAN REPUBLIC - PRODUCTION

Facts on File, 460 Park Avenue South, New York, New York 10016 (800) 443-8323; *The New Book of World Rankings.*

G.K. Hall and Company, 70 Lincoln Street, Boston, Massachusetts 02111 (617) 423-3990; *The World in Figures.*

CENTRAL AFRICAN REPUBLIC - PUBLIC FINANCE

Facts on File, 460 Park Avenue South, New York, New York 10016 (800) 443-8323; *The New Book of World Rankings.*

Federal Statistical Office, Gustav - Stresemann - Ring 11, D-6200 Wiesbaden, Germany; *Zentralafrikanische Republik.*

CENTRAL AFRICAN REPUBLIC - RADIO BROADCASTING - See CENTRAL AFRICAN REPUBLIC - BROADCASTING

CENTRAL AFRICAN REPUBLIC - RADIO RECEIVER PRODUCTION

Statistical Office of the United Nations, Publishing Service, New York, New York 10017 (800) 253-9646; *Statistical Yearbook.*

CENTRAL AFRICAN REPUBLIC - RAILWAYS

G.K. Hall and Company, 70 Lincoln Street, Boston, Massachusetts 02111 (617) 423-3990; *The World in Figures.*

United Nations Economic Commission for Africa, Africa Hall, P.O. Box 3001, Addis Ababa, Ethiopia (Telephone Number in U.S. (800) 253-9646); *African Statistical Yearbook.*

CENTRAL AFRICAN REPUBLIC - RELIGION

Facts on File, 460 Park Avenue South, New York, New York 10016 (800) 443-8323; *The New Book of World Rankings.*

CENTRAL AFRICAN REPUBLIC - RETAIL TRADE

G.K. Hall and Company, 70 Lincoln Street, Boston, Massachusetts 02111 (617) 423-3990; *The World in Figures.*

CENTRAL AFRICAN REPUBLIC - RICE PRODUCTION - See CENTRAL AFRICAN REPUBLIC - CROPS

CENTRAL AFRICAN REPUBLIC - ROOT AND TUBER PRODUCTION - See CENTRAL AFRICAN REPUBLIC - CROPS

CENTRAL AFRICAN REPUBLIC - ROUNDWOOD PRODUCTION - See CENTRAL AFRICAN REPUBLIC - FORESTRY AND FOREST PRODUCTS

CENTRAL AFRICAN REPUBLIC - RUBBER PRODUCTION

Facts on File, 460 Park Avenue South, New York, New York 10016 (800) 443-8323; *The New Book of World Rankings.*

CENTRAL AFRICAN REPUBLIC - RUBBER (NATURAL) PRODUCTION

Statistical Office of the United Nations, Publishing Service, New York, New York 10017 (800) 253-9646; *Statistical Yearbook.*

CENTRAL AFRICAN REPUBLIC - SAWNWOOD PRODUCTION - See CENTRAL AFRICAN REPUBLIC - FORESTRY AND FOREST PRODUCTS

CENTRAL AFRICAN REPUBLIC - SCIENTISTS AND TECHNICIANS

United Nations Educational, Scientific and Cultural Organization (UNESCO), 7 Place de Fontenoy, F-75700 Paris, France (Telephone Number in U.S. (212) 963-5981); *Statistical Yearbook.*

CENTRAL AFRICAN REPUBLIC - SENIOR CITIZENS

Facts on File, 460 Park Avenue South, New York, New York 10016 (800) 443-8323; *The New Book of World Rankings.*

CENTRAL AFRICAN REPUBLIC - SESAME SEED PRODUCTION - See CENTRAL AFRICAN REPUBLIC - CROPS

CENTRAL AFRICAN REPUBLIC - SHEEP - See CENTRAL AFRICAN REPUBLIC - LIVESTOCK AND POULTRY

CENTRAL AFRICAN REPUBLIC - SILVER PRODUCTION AND CONSUMPTION - See CENTRAL AFRICAN REPUBLIC - MINING AND MINERAL PRODUCTS

CENTRAL AFRICAN REPUBLIC - SISAL PRODUCTION - See CENTRAL AFRICAN REPUBLIC - CROPS

CENTRAL AFRICAN REPUBLIC - SOCIAL DATA

African Development Bank, 01 BP 1387, Abidjan 01, Cote D'Ivoire; *Selected Statistics on Regional Member Countries.*

Facts on File, 460 Park Avenue South, New York, New York 10016 (800) 443-8323; *The New Book of World Rankings.*

G.K. Hall and Company, 70 Lincoln Street, Boston, Massachusetts 02111 (617) 423-3990; *The World in Figures.*

CENTRAL AFRICAN REPUBLIC - STEEL PRODUCTION - See CENTRAL AFRICAN REPUBLIC - MINING AND MINERAL PRODUCTS

CENTRAL AFRICAN REPUBLIC - STOCKS - COMMODITY - MARKET PRICE - INDEX

Food and Agricultural Organization of the United Nations (FAO) Via delle Terme di Caracalla, 00100 Rome, Italy (Telephone Number in U.S. (202) 653-2400); *The State of Food and Agriculture.*

CENTRAL AFRICAN REPUBLIC - SUGAR PRODUCTION - See CENTRAL AFRICAN REPUBLIC - CROPS

CENTRAL AFRICAN REPUBLIC - TAXATION

G.K. Hall and Company, 70 Lincoln Street, Boston, Massachusetts 02111 (617) 423-3990; *The World in Figures.*

International Road Federation, 525 School Street, SW, Washington, D.C. 20024 (202) 554-2106; *World Road Statistics.*

The World Bank, 1818 H Street, NW, Washington, D.C. 20433 (202) 477-1234; *World Tables*.

CENTRAL AFRICAN REPUBLIC - TELEGRAPH SERVICE

Statistical Office of the United Nations, Publishing Service, New York, New York 10017 (800) 253-9646; *Statistical Yearbook*.

CENTRAL AFRICAN REPUBLIC - TELEPHONES IN USE

American Telephone and Telegraph Company, 26 Parsippany Road, Whippany, New Jersey 07981 (800) 338-4038; *The World's Telephones*.

G.K. Hall and Company, 70 Lincoln Street, Boston, Massachusetts 02111 (617) 423-3990; *The World in Figures*.

CENTRAL AFRICAN REPUBLIC - TELEVISION BROADCASTING - See CENTRAL AFRICAN REPUBLIC - BROADCASTING

CENTRAL AFRICAN REPUBLIC - TEXTILE INDUSTRY

G.K. Hall and Company, 70 Lincoln Street, Boston, Massachusetts 02111 (617) 423-3990; *The World in Figures*.

Statistical Office of the United Nations, Publishing Service, New York, New York 10017 (800) 253-9646; *Statistical Yearbook*.

CENTRAL AFRICAN REPUBLIC - TOBACCO PRODUCTION

Facts on File, 460 Park Avenue South, New York, New York 10016 (800) 443-8323; *The New Book of World Rankings*.

Statistical Office of the United Nations, Publishing Service, New York, New York 10017 (800) 253-9646; *Statistical Yearbook*.

CENTRAL AFRICAN REPUBLIC - TOURISM

Facts on File, 460 Park Avenue South, New York, New York 10016 (800) 443-8323; *The New Book of World Rankings*.

Federal Statistical Office, Gustav - Stresemann - Ring 11, D-6200 Wiesbaden, Germany; *Zentralafrikanische Republik*.

G.K. Hall and Company, 70 Lincoln Street, Boston, Massachusetts 02111 (617) 423-3990; *The World in Figures*.

Statistical Office of the United Nations, Publishing Service, New York, New York 10017 (800) 253-9646; *Statistical Yearbook*.

Times Books, 201 East 50th Street, New York, New York 10022 (212) 751-2600; *The Economist Book of Vital World Statistics*.

United Nations Economic Commission for Africa, Africa Hall, P.O. Box 3001, Addis Ababa, Ethiopia (Telephone Number in U.S. (800) 253-9646); *African Statistical Yearbook*.

CENTRAL AFRICAN REPUBLIC - TRACTORS IN USE

Statistical Office of the United Nations, Publishing Service, New York, New York 10017 (800) 253-9646; *Statistical Yearbook*.

CENTRAL AFRICAN REPUBLIC - TRADE - See CENTRAL AFRICAN REPUBLIC - FOREIGN TRADE

CENTRAL AFRICAN REPUBLIC - TRANSPORTATION AND COMMUNICATIONS

Facts on File, 460 Park Avenue South, New York, New York 10016 (800) 443-8323; *The New Book of World Rankings*.

Federal Statistical Office, Gustav - Stresemann - Ring 11, D-6200 Wiesbaden, Germany; *Zentralafrikanische Republik*.

G.K. Hall and Company, 70 Lincoln Street, Boston, Massachusetts 02111 (617) 423-3990; *The World in Figures*.

United Nations Economic Commission for Africa, Africa Hall, P.O. Box 3001, Addis Ababa, Ethiopia (Telephone Number in U.S. (800) 253-9646); *African Statistical Yearbook*.

CENTRAL AFRICAN REPUBLIC - UNEMPLOYMENT

International Labour Office, I.L.O. Publications, CH-1211, Geneva 22, Switzerland; *Yearbook of Labour Statistics*.

Statistical Office of the United Nations, Publishing Service, New York, New York 10017 (800) 253-9646; *Statistical Yearbook*.

CENTRAL AFRICAN REPUBLIC - URANIUM PRODUCTION AND CONSUMPTION - See CENTRAL AFRICAN REPUBLIC - MINING AND MINERAL PRODUCTS

CENTRAL AFRICAN REPUBLIC - VITAL STATISTICS

G.K. Hall and Company, 70 Lincoln Street, Boston, Massachusetts 02111 (617) 423-3990; *The World in Figures*.

Statistical Office of the United Nations, Publishing Service, New York, New York 10017 (800) 253-9646; *Statistical Yearbook*.

World Health Organization, Office of Publications, Avenue Appia, CH-1211 Geneva 27, Switzerland (Telephone Number in U.S. (518) 436-9686); *World Health Statistics Annual*.

CENTRAL AFRICAN REPUBLIC - WAGES

Federal Statistical Office, Gustav - Stresemann - Ring 11, D-6200 Wiesbaden, Germany; *Zentralafrikanische Republik*.

G.K. Hall and Company, 70 Lincoln Street, Boston, Massachusetts 02111 (617) 423-3990; *The World in Figures*.

International Labour Office, I.L.O. Publications, CH-1211, Geneva 22, Switzerland; *Yearbook of Labour Statistics*.

CENTRAL AFRICAN REPUBLIC - WEATHER

Facts on File, 460 Park Avenue South, New York, New York 10016 (800) 443-8323; *The New Book of World Rankings*.

G.K. Hall and Company, 70 Lincoln Street, Boston, Massachusetts 02111 (617) 423-3990; *The World in Figures*.

CENTRAL AFRICAN REPUBLIC - WHEAT PRODUCTION - See CENTRAL AFRICAN REPUBLIC - CROPS

CENTRAL AFRICAN REPUBLIC - WHOLESALE PRICES

International Monetary Fund, 700 Nineteenth Street, NW, Washington, D.C. 20431 (202) 623-7000; *International Financial Statistics*.

Statistical Office of the United Nations, Publishing Service, New York, New York 10017 (800) 253-9646; *Statistical Yearbook.*

CENTRAL AFRICAN REPUBLIC - WINE PRODUCTION

Facts on File, 460 Park Avenue South, New York, New York 10016 (800) 443-8323; *The New Book of World Rankings.*

CENTRAL AFRICAN REPUBLIC - WOOL PRODUCTION

Facts on File, 460 Park Avenue South, New York, New York 10016 (800) 443-8323; *The New Book of World Rankings.*

CEREAL - CONSUMPTION, BREAKFAST

U.S. Department of Agriculture, Economic Research Service, Fourteenth Street and Independence Avenue, SW, Washington, D.C. 20250 (202) 219-1504; *Food Consumption, Prices, and Expenditures.*

CEREAL AND BAKERY PRODUCTS - EXPENDITURES - PRICES

U.S. Department of Agriculture, Economic Research Service, Fourteenth Street and Independence Avenue, SW, Washington, D.C. 20250 (202) 219-1504; *Food Cost Review, National Food Review,* and *Agricultural Statistics.*

U.S. Department of Labor, Bureau of Labor Statistics, Two Massachusetts Avenue, NE, Washington, D.C. 20212 (202) 606-7828; *Monthly Labor Review, Consumer Price Indexes, Detailed Report, Consumer Expenditures in 1992.*

CEREBROVASCULAR DISEASES - DEATHS

U.S. Department of Health and Human Services, National Center for Health Statistics, 3700 East-West Highway, Hyattsville, Maryland 20782 (301) 436-8500; *Vital Statistics of the United States, Health, United States, Monthly Vital Statistics Report,* and unpublished data.

CEREBROVASCULAR DISEASES - FOREIGN COUNTRIES

World Health Organisation, Avenue Appia, CH-1211 Geneva 27, Switzerland (Telephone Number in U.S. (518) 436-9686); *World Health Statistics Annual,* and unpublished data.

CERTIFICATES OF DEPOSIT

Board of Governors of the Federal Reserve System, Twentieth Street and Constitution Avenue, NW, Washington, D.C. 20551 (202) 452-3000; *Federal Reserve Bulletin, Annual Statistical Digest,* and *Money Stock, Liquid Assets, and Debt Measures.*

CESAREAN SECTION DELIVERIES

U.S. Department of Health and Human Services, National Center for Health Statistics, 3700 East-West Highway, Hyattsville, Maryland 20782 (301) 436-8500; *Vital and Health Statistics,* and unpublished data.

CESIUM

U.S. Department of Interior, Bureau of Mines, 810 Seventh Street, NW, Washington, D.C. 20241 (202) 501-9649; *Mineral Commodity Summaries.*

Chad - National Statistical Office

Direction de la Statistique, BP 453, N' Djamena, Chad.

Chad - Primary Statistics Sources

Direction de la Statistique, BP 453, N' Djamena, Chad; *Annuaire Statistique du Tchad (Statistical Yearbook of Chad),* and *Bulletin de Statistique,* (Bulletin of Statistics).

CHAD - AGRICULTURE

Billboard Limited, P.O. Box 9027, 1006 AA Amsterdam, The Netherlands (Telephone Number in U.S. (212) 764-7300); *World Radio TV Handbook.*

Euromonitor Publications Limited, 87-88 Turnmill Street, London EC1M 5QU, England; *International Marketing Data and Statistics.*

Facts on File, 460 Park Avenue South, New York, New York 10016 (800) 443-8323; *The New Book of World Rankings.*

Food and Agricultural Organization of the United Nations (FAO) Via delle Terme di Caracalla, 00100 Rome, Italy (Telephone Number in U.S. (202) 653-2400); *Production Yearbook, The State of Food and Agriculture,* and *Trade Yearbook.*

G.K. Hall and Company, 70 Lincoln Street, Boston, Massachusetts 02111 (617) 423-3990; *The World in Figures.*

Statistical Office of the United Nations, Publishing Service, New York, New York 10017 (800) 253-9646; *Statistical Yearbook,* and *Survey of Economic and Social Conditions in Africa.*

Times Books, 201 East 50th Street, New York, New York 10022 (212) 751-2600; *The Economist Book of Vital World Statistics.*

United Nations Economic Commission for Africa, Africa Hall, P.O. Box 3001, Addis Ababa, Ethiopia (Telephone Number in U.S. (800) 253-9646); *African Statistical Yearbook.*

The World Bank, 1818 H Street, NW, Washington, D.C. 20433 (202) 477-1234; *World Tables.*

CHAD - AIRLINE SERVICE

Facts on File, 460 Park Avenue South, New York, New York 10016 (800) 443-8323; *The New Book of World Rankings.*

G.K. Hall and Company, 70 Lincoln Street, Boston, Massachusetts 02111 (617) 423-3990; *The World in Figures.*

Statistical Office of the United Nations, Publishing Service, New York, New York 10017 (800) 253-9646; *Statistical Yearbook.*

Times Books, 201 East 50th Street, New York, New York 10022 (212) 751-2600; *The Economist Book of Vital World Statistics.*

United Nations Economic Commission for Africa, Africa Hall, P.O. Box 3001, Addis Ababa, Ethiopia (Telephone Number in U.S. (800) 253-9646); *African Statistical Yearbook.*

CHAD - ALUMINUM PRODUCTION AND CONSUMPTION - See CHAD - MINING AND MINERAL PRODUCTS

CHAD - ANIMAL HEALTH

Food and Agricultural Organization of the United Nations (FAO), Via delle Terme di Caracalla, 00100 Rome, Italy (Telephone Number in U.S. (202) 653-2400); *Animal Health Yearbook.*

CHAD - AREA AND DENSITY OF POPULATION

African Development Bank, 01 BP 1387, Abidjan 01, Cote D'Ivoire; *Selected Statistics on Regional Member Countries.*

Euromonitor Publications Limited, 87-88 Turnmill Street, London EC1M 5QU, England; *International Marketing Data and Statistics.*

Facts on File, 460 Park Avenue South, New York, New York 10016 (800) 443-8323; *The New Book of World Rankings.*

Food and Agricultural Organization of the United Nations (FAO) Via delle Terme di Caracalla, 00100 Rome, Italy (Telephone Number in U.S. (202) 653-2400); *The State of Food and Agriculture.*

G.K. Hall and Company, 70 Lincoln Street, Boston, Massachusetts 02111 (617) 423-3990; *The World in Figures.*

Statistical Office of the United Nations, Publishing Service, New York, New York 10017 (800) 253-9646; *Statistical Yearbook,* and *Survey of Economic and Social Conditions in Africa.*

Times Books, 201 East 50th Street, New York, New York 10022 (212) 751-2600; *The Economist Book of Vital World Statistics.*

United Nations Educational, Scientific and Cultural Organization (UNESCO), 7 Place de Fontenoy, F-75700 Paris, France (Telephone Number in U.S. (212) 963-5981); *Statistical Yearbook.*

CHAD - ARMS EXPORTS AND IMPORTS

U.S. Arms Control and Disarmament Agency, 320 Twenty-first Street, NW, Washington, D.C. 20451 (202) 647-8677; *World Military Expenditures and Arms Transfers.*

CHAD - BALANCE OF PAYMENTS

African Development Bank, 01 BP 1387, Abidjan 01, Cote D'Ivoire; *Selected Statistics on Regional Member Countries.*

The Economist Intelligence Unit, 111 West 57th Street, New York, New York 10019 (800) 938-4685; *The World Market Atlas.*

G.K. Hall and Company, 70 Lincoln Street, Boston, Massachusetts 02111 (617) 423-3990; *The World in Figures.*

International Monetary Fund, 700 Nineteenth Street, NW, Washington, D.C. 20431 (202) 623-7000; *Balance of Payments Yearbook.*

Times Books, 201 East 50th Street, New York, New York 10022 (212) 751-2600; *The Economist Book of Vital World Statistics.*

United Nations Economic Commission for Africa, Africa Hall, P.O. Box 3001, Addis Ababa, Ethiopia (Telephone Number in U.S. (800) 253-9646); *African Statistical Yearbook.*

The World Bank, 1818 H Street, NW, Washington, D.C. 20433 (202) 477-1234; *World Tables.*

CHAD - BANKING

Facts on File, 460 Park Avenue South, New York, New York 10016 (800) 443-8323; *The New Book of World Rankings.*

G.K. Hall and Company, 70 Lincoln Street, Boston, Massachusetts 02111 (617) 423-3990; *The World in Figures.*

International Monetary Fund, 700 Nineteenth Street, NW, Washington, D.C. 20431 (202) 623-7000; *Government Finance Statistics Yearbook,* and *International Financial Statistics.*

United Nations Economic Commission for Africa, Africa Hall, P.O. Box 3001, Addis Ababa, Ethiopia (Telephone Number in U.S. (800) 253-9646); *African Statistical Yearbook.*

CHAD - BARLEY PRODUCTION - See CHAD - CROPS

CHAD - BEER PRODUCTION

Facts on File, 460 Park Avenue South, New York, New York 10016 (800) 443-8323; *The New Book of World Rankings.*

Statistical Office of the United Nations, Publishing Service, New York, New York 10017 (800) 253-9646; *Statistical Yearbook.*

CHAD - BIRTH RATES

Facts on File, 460 Park Avenue South, New York, New York 10016 (800) 443-8323; *The New Book of World Rankings.*

Statistical Office of the United Nations, Publishing Service, New York, New York 10017 (800) 253-9646; *Demographic Yearbook, Statistical Yearbook,* and *Survey of Economic and Social Conditions in Africa.*

Times Books, 201 East 50th Street, New York, New York 10022 (212) 751-2600; *The Economist Book of Vital World Statistics.*

The World Bank, 1818 H Street, NW, Washington, D.C. 20433 (202) 477-1234; *World Tables.*

CHAD - BONDS

G.K. Hall and Company, 70 Lincoln Street, Boston, Massachusetts 02111 (617) 423-3990; *The World in Figures.*

International Monetary Fund, 700 Nineteenth Street, NW, Washington, D.C. 20431 (202) 623-7000; *Government Finance Statistics Yearbook.*

CHAD - BOOK PRODUCTION

G.K. Hall and Company, 70 Lincoln Street, Boston, Massachusetts 02111 (617) 423-3990; *The World in Figures.*

CHAD - BROADCASTING

Facts on File, 460 Park Avenue South, New York, New York 10016 (800) 443-8323; *The New Book of World Rankings.*

G.K. Hall and Company, 70 Lincoln Street, Boston, Massachusetts 02111 (617) 423-3990; *The World in Figures.*

Times Books, 201 East 50th Street, New York, New York 10022 (212) 751-2600; *The Economist Book of Vital World Statistics.*

CHAD - BUSINESS

G.K. Hall and Company, 70 Lincoln Street, Boston, Massachusetts 02111 (617) 423-3990; *The World in Figures.*

CHAD - BUSINESS AND PROFESSIONAL LICENSES

International Monetary Fund, 700 Nineteenth Street, NW, Washington, D.C. 20431 (202) 623-7000; *Government Finance Statistics Yearbook.*

CHAD - BUTTER PRODUCTION - See CHAD - DAIRY PRODUCTS

CHAD - CALORIE SUPPLY

African Development Bank, 01 BP 1387, Abidjan 01, Cote D'Ivoire; *Selected Statistics on Regional Member Countries.*

Food and Agricultural Organization of the United Nations (FAO) Via delle Terme di Caracalla, 00100 Rome, Italy (Telephone Number in U.S. (202) 653-2400); *The State of Food and Agriculture.*

CHAD - CAPITAL REVENUE

International Monetary Fund, 700 Nineteenth Street, NW, Washington, D.C. 20431 (202) 623-7000; *Government Finance Statistics Yearbook.*

CHAD - CATTLE - See CHAD - LIVESTOCK AND POULTRY

CHAD - CEMENT PRODUCTION - See CHAD - MINING AND MINERAL PRODUCTS

CHAD - CHEMICAL (ORGANIC) PRODUCTION - See CHAD - MINING AND MINERAL PRODUCTS

CHAD - CHICKENS - See CHAD - LIVESTOCK AND POULTRY

CHAD - CIGARETTE PRODUCTION - See CHAD - TOBACCO PRODUCTION

CHAD - CLASS STRUCTURE

G.K. Hall and Company, 70 Lincoln Street, Boston, Massachusetts 02111 (617) 423-3990; *The World in Figures.*

CHAD - CLIMATE

Facts on File, 460 Park Avenue South, New York, New York 10016 (800) 443-8323; *The New Book of World Rankings.*

G.K. Hall and Company, 70 Lincoln Street, Boston, Massachusetts 02111 (617) 423-3990; *The World in Figures.*

CHAD - COAL PRODUCTION - See CHAD - MINING AND MINERAL PRODUCTS

CHAD - COFFEE PRODUCTION - See CHAD - CROPS

CHAD - COMMUNICATIONS

G.K. Hall and Company, 70 Lincoln Street, Boston, Massachusetts 02111 (617) 423-3990; *The World in Figures.*

United Nations Economic Commission for Africa, Africa Hall, P.O. Box 3001, Addis Ababa, Ethiopia (Telephone Number in U.S. (800) 253-9646); *African Statistical Yearbook.*

CHAD - CONSTRUCTION INDUSTRY

Facts on File, 460 Park Avenue South, New York, New York 10016 (800) 443-8323; *The New Book of World Rankings.*

United Nations Economic Commission for Africa, Africa Hall, P.O. Box 3001, Addis Ababa, Ethiopia (Telephone Number in U.S. (800) 253-9646); *African Statistical Yearbook.*

CHAD - CONSUMER PRICE INDEX

African Development Bank, 01 BP 1387, Abidjan 01, Cote D'Ivoire; *Selected Statistics on Regional Member Countries.*

G.K. Hall and Company, 70 Lincoln Street, Boston, Massachusetts 02111 (617) 423-3990; *The World in Figures.*

Statistical Office of the United Nations, Publishing Service, New York, New York 10017 (800) 253-9646; *Statistical Yearbook*, and *Survey of Economic and Social Conditions in Africa.*

United Nations Economic Commission for Africa, Africa Hall, P.O. Box 3001, Addis Ababa, Ethiopia (Telephone Number in U.S. (800) 253-9646); *African Statistical Yearbook.*

CHAD - CONSUMER PRICES

International Labour Office, I.L.O. Publications, CH-1211, Geneva 22, Switzerland; *Yearbook of Labour Statistics.*

International Monetary Fund, 700 Nineteenth Street, NW, Washington, D.C. 20431 (202) 623-7000; *International Financial Statistics.*

Times Books, 201 East 50th Street, New York, New York 10022 (212) 751-2600; *The Economist Book of Vital World Statistics.*

CHAD - CONSUMPTION

African Development Bank, 01 BP 1387, Abidjan 01, Cote D'Ivoire; *Selected Statistics on Regional Member Countries.*

G.K. Hall and Company, 70 Lincoln Street, Boston, Massachusetts 02111 (617) 423-3990; *The World in Figures.*

Statistical Office of the United Nations, Publishing Service, New York, New York 10017 (800) 253-9646; *Survey of Economic and Social Conditions in Africa.*

CHAD - COPPER PRODUCTION - See CHAD - MINING AND MINERAL PRODUCTS

CHAD - CORN PRODUCTION - See CHAD - CROPS

CHAD - CORPORATE TAXES - See CHAD - TAXATION

CHAD - COTTON - See CHAD - CROPS

CHAD - CRIME

Yale University Press, Yale Station, New Haven, Connecticut 06520 (203) 432-0940; *Violence and Crime in Cross-National Perspective.*

CHAD - CROPS

Facts on File, 460 Park Avenue South, New York, New York 10016 (800) 443-8323; *The New Book of World Rankings.*

Food and Agricultural Organization of the United Nations (FAO) Via delle Terme di Caracalla, 00100 Rome, Italy (Telephone Number in U.S. (202) 653-2400); *Production Yearbook,* and *The State of Food and Agriculture.*

G.K. Hall and Company, 70 Lincoln Street, Boston, Massachusetts 02111 (617) 423-3990; *The World in Figures.*

International Monetary Fund, 700 Nineteenth Street, NW, Washington, D.C. 20431 (202) 623-7000; *International Financial Statistics.*

Statistical Office of the United Nations, Publishing Service, New York, New York 10017 (800) 253-9646; *Statistical Yearbook.*

United Nations Economic Commission for Africa, Africa Hall, P.O. Box 3001, Addis Ababa, Ethiopia (Telephone Number in U.S. (800) 253-9646); *African Statistical Yearbook.*

CHAD - CUSTOMS DUTIES

G.K. Hall and Company, 70 Lincoln Street, Boston, Massachusetts 02111 (617) 423-3990; *The World in Figures.*

International Monetary Fund, 700 Nineteenth Street, NW, Washington, D.C. 20431 (202) 623-7000; *Government Finance Statistics Yearbook.*

CHAD - DAIRY PRODUCTS

Facts on File, 460 Park Avenue South, New York, New York 10016 (800) 443-8323; *The New Book of World Rankings.*

Food and Agricultural Organization of the United Nations (FAO) Via delle Terme di Caracalla, 00100 Rome, Italy (Telephone Number in U.S. (202) 653-2400); *The State of Food and Agriculture.*

Statistical Office of the United Nations, Publishing Service, New York, New York 10017 (800) 253-9646; *Statistical Yearbook.*

CHAD - DEATH RATES

G.K. Hall and Company, 70 Lincoln Street, Boston, Massachusetts 02111 (617) 423-3990; *The World in Figures.*

Statistical Office of the United Nations, Publishing Service, New York, New York 10017 (800) 253-9646; *Statistical Yearbook,* and *Survey of Economic and Social Conditions in Africa.*

Times Books, 201 East 50th Street, New York, New York 10022 (212) 751-2600; *The Economist Book of Vital World Statistics.*

World Health Organization, Office of Publications, Avenue Appia, CH-1211 Geneva 27, Switzerland (Telephone Number in U.S. (518) 436-9686); *World Health Statistics Annual.*

CHAD - DEFENSE EXPENDITURES

G.K. Hall and Company, 70 Lincoln Street, Boston, Massachusetts 02111 (617) 423-3990; *The World in Figures.*

International Monetary Fund, 700 Nineteenth Street, NW, Washington, D.C. 20431 (202) 623-7000; *Government Finance Statistics Yearbook.*

U.S. Arms Control and Disarmament Agency, 320 Twenty-first Street, NW, Washington, D.C. 20451 (202) 647-8677; *World Military Expenditures and Arms Transfers.*

CHAD - DEMOGRAPHY

The Economist Intelligence Unit, 111 West 57th Street, New York, New York 10019 (800) 938-4685; *The World Market Atlas.*

Facts on File, 460 Park Avenue South, New York, New York 10016 (800) 443-8323; *The New Book of World Rankings.*

G.K. Hall and Company, 70 Lincoln Street, Boston, Massachusetts 02111 (617) 423-3990; *The World in Figures.*

Statistical Office of the United Nations, Publishing Service, New York, New York 10017 (800) 253-9646; *Survey of Economic and Social Conditions in Africa.*

CHAD - DEVELOPMENT ASSISTANCE

G.K. Hall and Company, 70 Lincoln Street, Boston, Massachusetts 02111 (617) 423-3990; *The World in Figures.*

Statistical Office of the United Nations, Publishing Service, New York, New York 10017 (800) 253-9646; *Statistical Yearbook.*

CHAD - DIAMOND PRODUCTION - See CHAD - MINING AND MINERAL PRODUCTS

CHAD - DISEASE

G.K. Hall and Company, 70 Lincoln Street, Boston, Massachusetts 02111 (617) 423-3990; *The World in Figures.*

World Health Organization, Office of Publications, Avenue Appia, CH-1211 Geneva 27, Switzerland (Telephone Number in U.S. (518) 436-9686); *World Health Statistics Annual.*

CHAD - DIVORCE RATES

Facts on File, 460 Park Avenue South, New York, New York 10016 (800) 443-8323; *The New Book of World Rankings.*

Statistical Office of the United Nations, Publishing Service, New York, New York 10017 (800) 253-9646; *Demographic Yearbook.*

CHAD - DOMESTIC PRODUCT

G.K. Hall and Company, 70 Lincoln Street, Boston, Massachusetts 02111 (617) 423-3990; *The World in Figures.*

CHAD - ECONOMY

African Development Bank, 01 BP 1387, Abidjan 01, Cote D'Ivoire; *Selected Statistics on Regional Member Countries.*

Euromonitor Publications Limited, 87-88 Turnmill Street, London EC1M 5QU, England; *International Marketing Data and Statistics.*

Facts on File, 460 Park Avenue South, New York, New York 10016 (800) 443-8323; *The New Book of World Rankings.*

G.K. Hall and Company, 70 Lincoln Street, Boston, Massachusetts 02111 (617) 423-3990; *The World in Figures.*

Statistical Office of the United Nations, Publishing Service, New York, New York 10017 (800) 253-9646; *Foreign Trade Statistics for Africa.*

CHAD - EDUCATION

African Development Bank, 01 BP 1387, Abidjan 01, Cote D'Ivoire; *Selected Statistics on Regional Member Countries.*

The Economist Intelligence Unit, 111 West 57th Street, New York, New York 10019 (800) 938-4685; *The World Market Atlas.*

Facts on File, 460 Park Avenue South, New York, New York 10016 (800) 443-8323; *The New Book of World Rankings.*

G.K. Hall and Company, 70 Lincoln Street, Boston, Massachusetts 02111 (617) 423-3990; *The World in Figures.*

International Monetary Fund, 700 Nineteenth Street, NW, Washington, D.C. 20431 (202) 623-7000; *Government Finance Statistics Yearbook.*

Statistical Office of the United Nations, Publishing Service, New York, New York 10017 (800) 253-9646; *Survey of Economic and Social Conditions in Africa.*

Times Books, 201 East 50th Street, New York, New York 10022 (212) 751-2600; *The Economist Book of Vital World Statistics.*

United Nations Economic Commission for Africa, Africa Hall, P.O. Box 3001, Addis Ababa, Ethiopia (Telephone Number in U.S. (800) 253-9646); *African Statistical Yearbook.*

United Nations Educational, Scientific and Cultural Organization (UNESCO), 7 Place de Fontenoy, F-75700 Paris, France (Telephone Number in U.S. (212) 963-5981); *Statistical Yearbook.*

The World Bank, 1818 H Street, NW, Washington, D.C. 20433 (202) 477-1234; *World Tables.*

CHAD - EGG PRODUCTION - See CHAD - DAIRY PRODUCTS

CHAD - ELECTRICITY

Facts on File, 460 Park Avenue South, New York, New York 10016 (800) 443-8323; *The New Book of World Rankings.*

Statistical Office of the United Nations, Publishing Service, New York, New York 10017 (800) 253-9646; *Statistical Yearbook,* and *Survey of Economic and Social Conditions in Africa.*

Times Books, 201 East 50th Street, New York, New York 10022 (212) 751-2600; *The Economist Book of Vital World Statistics.*

United Nations Economic Commission for Africa, Africa Hall, P.O. Box 3001, Addis Ababa, Ethiopia (Telephone Number in U.S. (800) 253-9646); *African Statistical Yearbook.*

CHAD - EMPLOYMENT

Euromonitor Publications Limited, 87-88 Turnmill Street, London EC1M 5QU, England; *International Marketing Data and Statistics.*

Facts on File, 460 Park Avenue South, New York, New York 10016 (800) 443-8323; *The New Book of World Rankings.*

International Labour Office, I.L.O. Publications, CH-1211, Geneva 22, Switzerland; *Yearbook of Labour Statistics.*

Statistical Office of the United Nations, Publishing Service, New York, New York 10017 (800) 253-9646; *Survey of Economic and Social Conditions in Africa.*

United Nations Economic Commission for Africa, Africa Hall, P.O. Box 3001, Addis Ababa, Ethiopia (Telephone Number in U.S. (800) 253-9646); *African Statistical Yearbook.*

CHAD - ENERGY

Facts on File, 460 Park Avenue South, New York, New York 10016 (800) 443-8323; *The New Book of World Rankings.*

Food and Agricultural Organization of the United Nations (FAO) Via delle Terme di Caracalla, 00100 Rome, Italy (Telephone Number in U.S. (202) 653-2400); *The State of Food and Agriculture.*

G.K. Hall and Company, 70 Lincoln Street, Boston, Massachusetts 02111 (617) 423-3990; *The World in Figures.*

Statistical Office of the United Nations, Publishing Service, New York, New York 10017 (800) 253-9646; *Energy Statistics Yearbook.*

Times Books, 201 East 50th Street, New York, New York 10022 (212) 751-2600; *The Economist Book of Vital World Statistics.*

United Nations Economic Commission for Africa, Africa Hall, P.O. Box 3001, Addis Ababa, Ethiopia (Telephone Number in U.S. (800) 253-9646); *African Statistical Yearbook.*

CHAD - EXCHANGE RATES

African Development Bank, 01 BP 1387, Abidjan 01, Cote D'Ivoire; *Selected Statistics on Regional Member Countries.*

Euromonitor Publications Limited, 87-88 Turnmill Street, London EC1M 5QU, England; *International Marketing Data and Statistics.*

International Monetary Fund, 700 Nineteenth Street, NW, Washington, D.C. 20431 (202) 623-7000; *International Financial Statistics.*

Statistical Office of the United Nations, Publishing Service, New York, New York 10017 (800) 253-9646; *Foreign Trade Statistics for Africa,* and *Statistical Yearbook.*

CHAD - EXPORTS

African Development Bank, 01 BP 1387, Abidjan 01, Cote D'Ivoire; *Selected Statistics on Regional Member Countries.*

The Economist Intelligence Unit, 111 West 57th Street, New York, New York 10019 (800) 938-4685; *The World Market Atlas.*

Euromonitor Publications Limited, 87-88 Turnmill Street, London EC1M 5QU, England; *International Marketing Data and Statistics.*

Food and Agricultural Organization of the United Nations (FAO) Via delle Terme di Caracalla, 00100 Rome, Italy (Telephone Number in U.S. (202) 653-2400); *The State of Food and Agriculture.*

G.K. Hall and Company, 70 Lincoln Street, Boston, Massachusetts 02111 (617) 423-3990; *The World in Figures.*

International Monetary Fund, 700 Nineteenth Street, NW, Washington, D.C. 20431 (202) 623-7000; *Direction of Trade Statistics, Government Finance Statistics Yearbook,* and *International Financial Statistics.*

Statistical Office of the United Nations, Publishing Service, New York, New York 10017 (800) 253-9646; *Foreign Trade Statistics for Africa,* and *Survey of Economic and Social Conditions in Africa.*

Times Books, 201 East 50th Street, New York, New York 10022 (212) 751-2600; *The Economist Book of Vital World Statistics*.

United Nations Economic Commission for Africa, Africa Hall, P.O. Box 3001, Addis Ababa, Ethiopia (Telephone Number in U.S. (800) 253-9646); *African Statistical Yearbook*.

The World Bank, 1818 H Street, NW, Washington, D.C. 20433 (202) 477-1234; *World Tables*.

CHAD - EXTERNAL INDEBTEDNESS

African Development Bank, 01 BP 1387, Abidjan 01, Cote D'Ivoire; *Selected Statistics on Regional Member Countries*.

Statistical Office of the United Nations, Publishing Service, New York, New York 10017 (800) 253-9646; *Survey of Economic and Social Conditions in Africa*.

The World Bank, 1818 H Street, NW, Washington, D.C. 20433 (202) 477-1234; *World Tables*.

CHAD - EXTERNAL TRADE

African Development Bank, 01 BP 1387, Abidjan 01, Cote D'Ivoire; *Selected Statistics on Regional Member Countries*.

Food and Agricultural Organization of the United Nations (FAO) Via delle Terme di Caracalla, 00100 Rome, Italy (Telephone Number in U.S. (202) 653-2400); *The State of Food and Agriculture*, and *Trade Yearbook*.

G.K. Hall and Company, 70 Lincoln Street, Boston, Massachusetts 02111 (617) 423-3990; *The World in Figures*.

Statistical Office of the United Nations, Publishing Service, New York, New York 10017 (800) 253-9646; *Statistical Yearbook*.

CHAD - FABRIC PRODUCTION - See CHAD - TEXTILE INDUSTRY

CHAD - FARM CROPS - See CHAD - CROPS

CHAD - FEMALE WORKING POPULATION - See CHAD - EMPLOYMENT

CHAD - FERTILITY RATES

Facts on File, 460 Park Avenue South, New York, New York 10016 (800) 443-8323; *The New Book of World Rankings*.

Statistical Office of the United Nations, Publishing Service, New York, New York 10017 (800) 253-9646; *Survey of Economic and Social Conditions in Africa*.

Times Books, 201 East 50th Street, New York, New York 10022 (212) 751-2600; *The Economist Book of Vital World Statistics*.

The World Bank, 1818 H Street, NW, Washington, D.C. 20433 (202) 477-1234; *World Tables*.

CHAD - FERTILIZER

Food and Agricultural Organization of the United Nations (FAO), Via delle Terme di Caracalla, 00100 Rome, Italy (Telephone Number in U.S. (202) 653-2400); *Fertilizer Yearbook*, and *The State of Food and Agriculture*.

Statistical Office of the United Nations, Publishing Service, New York, New York 10017 (800) 253-9646; *Statistical Yearbook*.

CHAD - FETAL MORTALITY

Statistical Office of the United Nations, Publishing Service, New York, New York 10017 (800) 253-9646; *Demographic Yearbook*.

CHAD - FINANCE

African Development Bank, 01 BP 1387, Abidjan 01, Cote D'Ivoire; *Selected Statistics on Regional Member Countries*.

Facts on File, 460 Park Avenue South, New York, New York 10016 (800) 443-8323; *The New Book of World Rankings*.

G.K. Hall and Company, 70 Lincoln Street, Boston, Massachusetts 02111 (617) 423-3990; *The World in Figures*.

International Monetary Fund, 700 Nineteenth Street, NW, Washington, D.C. 20431 (202) 623-7000; *Government Finance Statistics Yearbook*, and *International Financial Statistics*.

United Nations Economic Commission for Africa, Africa Hall, P.O. Box 3001, Addis Ababa, Ethiopia (Telephone Number in U.S. (800) 253-9646); *African Statistical Yearbook*.

CHAD - FISHERIES

Facts on File, 460 Park Avenue South, New York, New York 10016 (800) 443-8323; *The New Book of World Rankings*.

Food and Agricultural Organization of the United Nations (FAO) Via delle Terme di Caracalla, 00100 Rome, Italy (Telephone Number in U.S. (202) 653-2400); *The State of Food and Agriculture*, and *Yearbook of Fishery Statistics*.

Statistical Office of the United Nations, Publishing Service, New York, New York 10017 (800) 253-9646; *Statistical Yearbook*, and *Survey of Economic and Social Conditions in Africa*.

United Nations Economic Commission for Africa, Africa Hall, P.O. Box 3001, Addis Ababa, Ethiopia (Telephone Number in U.S. (800) 253-9646); *African Statistical Yearbook*.

CHAD - FLOUR PRODUCTION

Statistical Office of the United Nations, Publishing Service, New York, New York 10017 (800) 253-9646; *Statistical Yearbook*.

CHAD - FOOD

African Development Bank, 01 BP 1387, Abidjan 01, Cote D'Ivoire; *Selected Statistics on Regional Member Countries*.

Food and Agricultural Organization of the United Nations (FAO) Via delle Terme di Caracalla, 00100 Rome, Italy (Telephone Number in U.S. (202) 653-2400); *Production Yearbook*, and *The State of Food and Agriculture*.

G.K. Hall and Company, 70 Lincoln Street, Boston, Massachusetts 02111 (617) 423-3990; *The World in Figures*.

CHAD - FOREIGN AID

G.K. Hall and Company, 70 Lincoln Street, Boston, Massachusetts 02111 (617) 423-3990; *The World in Figures*.

CHAD - FOREIGN DEBT

International Monetary Fund, 700 Nineteenth Street, NW, Washington, D.C. 20431 (202) 623-7000; *Government Finance*

Statistics Yearbook.

CHAD - FOREIGN TRADE

Euromonitor Publications Limited, 87-88 Turnmill Street, London EC1M 5QU, England; *International Marketing Data and Statistics.*

Facts on File, 460 Park Avenue South, New York, New York 10016 (800) 443-8323; *The New Book of World Rankings.*

Food and Agricultural Organization of the United Nations (FAO) Via delle Terme di Caracalla, 00100 Rome, Italy (Telephone Number in U.S. (202) 653-2400); *The State of Food and Agriculture.*

G.K. Hall and Company, 70 Lincoln Street, Boston, Massachusetts 02111 (617) 423-3990; *The World in Figures.*

Organisation for Economic Co-operation and Development (OECD), 2 rue Andre-Pascal, 75 Paris 16, France (Telephone Number in U.S. (202) 785-6323); *Trade by Commodities.*

Statistical Office of the United Nations, Publishing Service, New York, New York 10017 (800) 253-9646; *Foreign Trade Statistics for Africa, International Trade Statistics Yearbook, Statistical Yearbook,* and *Trade in Manufactures of Developing Countries.*

United Nations Economic Commission for Africa, Africa Hall, P.O. Box 3001, Addis Ababa, Ethiopia (Telephone Number in U.S. (800) 253-9646); *African Statistical Yearbook.*

The World Bank, 1818 H Street, NW, Washington, D.C. 20433 (202) 477-1234; *World Tables.*

CHAD - FORESTRY AND FOREST PRODUCTS

Facts on File, 460 Park Avenue South, New York, New York 10016 (800) 443-8323; *The New Book of World Rankings.*

Food and Agricultural Organization of the United Nations (FAO) Via delle Terme di Caracalla, 00100 Rome, Italy (Telephone Number in U.S. (202) 653-2400); *The State of Food and Agriculture,* and *Yearbook of Forest Products.*

G.K. Hall and Company, 70 Lincoln Street, Boston, Massachusetts 02111 (617) 423-3990; *The World in Figures.*

Statistical Office of the United Nations, Publishing Service, New York, New York 10017 (800) 253-9646; *Demographic Yearbook.*

United Nations Economic Commission for Africa, Africa Hall, P.O. Box 3001, Addis Ababa, Ethiopia (Telephone Number in U.S. (800) 253-9646); *African Statistical Yearbook.*

CHAD - GAS PRODUCTION

Facts on File, 460 Park Avenue South, New York, New York 10016 (800) 443-8323; *The New Book of World Rankings.*

CHAD - GENERAL MORTALITY

Statistical Office of the United Nations, Publishing Service, New York, New York 10017 (800) 253-9646; *Demographic Yearbook.*

CHAD - GEOGRAPHIC DATA

Facts on File, 460 Park Avenue South, New York, New York 10016 (800) 443-8323; *The New Book of World Rankings.*

CHAD - GOATS - See CHAD - LIVESTOCK AND POULTRY

CHAD - GOLD HOLDINGS

International Monetary Fund, 700 Nineteenth Street, NW, Washington, D.C. 20431 (202) 623-7000; *International Financial Statistics.*

Statistical Office of the United Nations, Publishing Service, New York, New York 10017 (800) 253-9646; *Statistical Yearbook.*

The World Bank, 1818 H Street, NW, Washington, D.C. 20433 (202) 477-1234; *World Tables.*

CHAD - GOLD PRODUCTION AND CONSUMPTION - See CHAD - MINING AND MINERAL PRODUCTS

CHAD - GOVERNMENT

G.K. Hall and Company, 70 Lincoln Street, Boston, Massachusetts 02111 (617) 423-3990; *The World in Figures.*

Statistical Office of the United Nations, Publishing Service, New York, New York 10017 (800) 253-9646; *Survey of Economic and Social Conditions in Africa.*

CHAD - GOVERNMENT EXPENDITURES

International Monetary Fund, 700 Nineteenth Street, NW, Washington, D.C. 20431 (202) 623-7000; *Government Finance Statistics Yearbook.*

The World Bank, 1818 H Street, NW, Washington, D.C. 20433 (202) 477-1234; *World Tables.*

CHAD - GOVERNMENT FINANCES

International Monetary Fund, 700 Nineteenth Street, NW, Washington, D.C. 20431 (202) 623-7000; *International Financial Statistics.*

CHAD - GOVERNMENT REVENUE

International Monetary Fund, 700 Nineteenth Street, NW, Washington, D.C. 20431 (202) 623-7000; *Government Finance Statistics Yearbook.*

Statistical Office of the United Nations, Publishing Service, New York, New York 10017 (800) 253-9646; *Survey of Economic and Social Conditions in Africa.*

The World Bank, 1818 H Street, NW, Washington, D.C. 20433 (202) 477-1234; *World Tables.*

CHAD - GRAIN PRODUCTION - See CHAD - CROPS

CHAD - GRANTS

International Monetary Fund, 700 Nineteenth Street, NW, Washington, D.C. 20431 (202) 623-7000; *Government Finance Statistics Yearbook.*

CHAD - GROSS DOMESTIC PRODUCT

African Development Bank, 01 BP 1387, Abidjan 01, Cote D'Ivoire; *Selected Statistics on Regional Member Countries.*

The Economist Intelligence Unit, 111 West 57th Street, New York, New York 10019 (800) 938-4685; *The World Market Atlas.*

Euromonitor Publications Limited, 87-88 Turnmill Street, London EC1M 5QU, England; *International Marketing Data and Statistics.*

Facts on File, 460 Park Avenue South, New York, New York 10016 (800) 443-8323; *The New Book of World Rankings.*

G.K. Hall and Company, 70 Lincoln Street, Boston, Massachusetts 02111 (617) 423-3990; *The World in Figures.*

Statistical Office of the United Nations, Publishing Service, New York, New York 10017 (800) 253-9646; *Statistical Yearbook*, and *Survey of Economic and Social Conditions in Africa.*

Times Books, 201 East 50th Street, New York, New York 10022 (212) 751-2600; *The Economist Book of Vital World Statistics.*

United Nations Economic Commission for Africa, Africa Hall, P.O. Box 3001, Addis Ababa, Ethiopia (Telephone Number in U.S. (800) 253-9646); *African Statistical Yearbook.*

The World Bank, 1818 H Street, NW, Washington, D.C. 20433 (202) 477-1234; *World Tables.*

CHAD - GROSS NATIONAL PRODUCT

Euromonitor Publications Limited, 87-88 Turnmill Street, London EC1M 5QU, England; *International Marketing Data and Statistics.*

U.S. Arms Control and Disarmament Agency, 320 Twenty-first Street, NW, Washington, D.C. 20451 (202) 647-8677; *World Military Expenditures and Arms Transfers.*

The World Bank, 1818 H Street, NW, Washington, D.C. 20433 (202) 477-1234; *World Tables.*

CHAD - GROUNDNUTS PRODUCTION - See CHAD - CROPS

CHAD - HEALTH

African Development Bank, 01 BP 1387, Abidjan 01, Cote D'Ivoire; *Selected Statistics on Regional Member Countries.*

Facts on File, 460 Park Avenue South, New York, New York 10016 (800) 443-8323; *The New Book of World Rankings.*

G.K. Hall and Company, 70 Lincoln Street, Boston, Massachusetts 02111 (617) 423-3990; *The World in Figures.*

Statistical Office of the United Nations, Publishing Service, New York, New York 10017 (800) 253-9646; *Statistical Yearbook.*

Times Books, 201 East 50th Street, New York, New York 10022 (212) 751-2600; *The Economist Book of Vital World Statistics.*

United Nations Economic Commission for Africa, Africa Hall, P.O. Box 3001, Addis Ababa, Ethiopia (Telephone Number in U.S. (800) 253-9646); *African Statistical Yearbook.*

World Health Organization, Office of Publications, Avenue Appia, CH-1211 Geneva 27, Switzerland (Telephone Number in U.S. (518) 436-9686); *World Health Statistics Annual.*

CHAD - HEALTH EXPENDITURES

International Monetary Fund, 700 Nineteenth Street, NW, Washington, D.C. 20431 (202) 623-7000; *Government Finance Statistics Yearbook.*

CHAD - HIDE PRODUCTION

Food and Agricultural Organization of the United Nations (FAO), Via delle Terme di Caracalla, 00100 Rome, Italy (Telephone Number in U.S. (202) 653-2400); *Production Yearbook.*

CHAD - HIGHWAYS

G.K. Hall and Company, 70 Lincoln Street, Boston, Massachusetts 02111 (617) 423-3990; *The World in Figures.*

International Road Federation, 525 School Street, SW, Washington, D.C. 20024 (202) 554-2106; *World Road Statistics.*

Statistical Office of the United Nations, Publishing Service, New York, New York 10017 (800) 253-9646; *Survey of Economic and Social Conditions in Africa.*

United Nations Economic Commission for Africa, Africa Hall, P.O. Box 3001, Addis Ababa, Ethiopia (Telephone Number in U.S. (800) 253-9646); *African Statistical Yearbook.*

CHAD - HORSES - See CHAD - LIVESTOCK AND POULTRY

CHAD - HOURS OF WORK - See CHAD - EMPLOYMENT

CHAD - HOUSING AND HOUSING UNITS

Facts on File, 460 Park Avenue South, New York, New York 10016 (800) 443-8323; *The New Book of World Rankings.*

CHAD - HOUSING EXPENDITURES

International Monetary Fund, 700 Nineteenth Street, NW, Washington, D.C. 20431 (202) 623-7000; *Government Finance Statistics Yearbook.*

CHAD - ILLITERATE POPULATION

The Economist Intelligence Unit, 111 West 57th Street, New York, New York 10019 (800) 938-4685; *The World Market Atlas.*

G.K. Hall and Company, 70 Lincoln Street, Boston, Massachusetts 02111 (617) 423-3990; *The World in Figures.*

United Nations Educational, Scientific and Cultural Organization (UNESCO), 7 Place de Fontenoy, F-75700 Paris, France (Telephone Number in U.S. (212) 963-5981); *Statistical Yearbook.*

CHAD - IMPORTS

African Development Bank, 01 BP 1387, Abidjan 01, Cote D'Ivoire; *Selected Statistics on Regional Member Countries.*

The Economist Intelligence Unit, 111 West 57th Street, New York, New York 10019 (800) 938-4685; *The World Market Atlas.*

Euromonitor Publications Limited, 87-88 Turnmill Street, London EC1M 5QU, England; *International Marketing Data and Statistics.*

Food and Agricultural Organization of the United Nations (FAO) Via delle Terme di Caracalla, 00100 Rome, Italy (Telephone Number in U.S. (202) 653-2400); *The State of Food and Agriculture.*

G.K. Hall and Company, 70 Lincoln Street, Boston, Massachusetts 02111 (617) 423-3990; *The World in Figures.*

International Monetary Fund, 700 Nineteenth Street, NW, Washington, D.C. 20431 (202) 623-7000; *Direction of Trade*

Statistics, Government Finance Statistics Yearbook, and *International Financial Statistics.*

Statistical Office of the United Nations, Publishing Service, New York, New York 10017 (800) 253-9646; *Foreign Trade Statistics for Africa,* and *Survey of Economic and Social Conditions in Africa.*

United Nations Economic Commission for Africa, Africa Hall, P.O. Box 3001, Addis Ababa, Ethiopia (Telephone Number in U.S. (800) 253-9646); *African Statistical Yearbook.*

The World Bank, 1818 H Street, NW, Washington, D.C. 20433 (202) 477-1234; *World Tables.*

CHAD - INCOME TAXES - See CHAD - TAXATION

CHAD - INDUSTRY

Euromonitor Publications Limited, 87-88 Turnmill Street, London EC1M 5QU, England; *International Marketing Data and Statistics.*

Facts on File, 460 Park Avenue South, New York, New York 10016 (800) 443-8323; *The New Book of World Rankings.*

G.K. Hall and Company, 70 Lincoln Street, Boston, Massachusetts 02111 (617) 423-3990; *The World in Figures.*

International Labour Office, I.L.O. Publications, CH-1211, Geneva 22, Switzerland; *Yearbook of Labour Statistics.*

Statistical Office of the United Nations, Publishing Service, New York, New York 10017 (800) 253-9646; *Survey of Economic and Social Conditions in Africa.*

Times Books, 201 East 50th Street, New York, New York 10022 (212) 751-2600; *The Economist Book of Vital World Statistics.*

United Nations Economic Commission for Africa, Africa Hall, P.O. Box 3001, Addis Ababa, Ethiopia (Telephone Number in U.S. (800) 253-9646); *African Statistical Yearbook.*

The World Bank, 1818 H Street, NW, Washington, D.C. 20433 (202) 477-1234; *World Tables.*

CHAD - INFANT AND MATERNAL MORTALITY

Statistical Office of the United Nations, Publishing Service, New York, New York 10017 (800) 253-9646; *Demographic Yearbook, Statistical Yearbook,* and *Survey of Economic and Social Conditions in Africa.*

Times Books, 201 East 50th Street, New York, New York 10022 (212) 751-2600; *The Economist Book of Vital World Statistics.*

The World Bank, 1818 H Street, NW, Washington, D.C. 20433 (202) 477-1234; *World Tables.*

CHAD - INTERNATIONAL LIQUIDITY

International Monetary Fund, 700 Nineteenth Street, NW, Washington, D.C. 20431 (202) 623-7000; *International Financial Statistics.*

CHAD - INTERNATIONAL RESERVES EXCLUDING GOLD

African Development Bank, 01 BP 1387, Abidjan 01, Cote D'Ivoire; *Selected Statistics on Regional Member Countries.*

The World Bank, 1818 H Street, NW, Washington, D.C. 20433 (202) 477-1234; *World Tables.*

CHAD - IRON ORE PRODUCTION AND CONSUMPTION - See CHAD - MINING AND MINERAL PRODUCTS

CHAD - IRRIGATION

Euromonitor Publications Limited, 87-88 Turnmill Street, London EC1M 5QU, England; *International Marketing Data and Statistics.*

CHAD - LABOR FORCE

African Development Bank, 01 BP 1387, Abidjan 01, Cote D'Ivoire; *Selected Statistics on Regional Member Countries.*

Euromonitor Publications Limited, 87-88 Turnmill Street, London EC1M 5QU, England; *International Marketing Data and Statistics.*

Facts on File, 460 Park Avenue South, New York, New York 10016 (800) 443-8323; *The New Book of World Rankings.*

Food and Agricultural Organization of the United Nations (FAO) Via delle Terme di Caracalla, 00100 Rome, Italy (Telephone Number in U.S. (202) 653-2400); *The State of Food and Agriculture.*

G.K. Hall and Company, 70 Lincoln Street, Boston, Massachusetts 02111 (617) 423-3990; *The World in Figures.*

The World Bank, 1818 H Street, NW, Washington, D.C. 20433 (202) 477-1234; *World Tables.*

CHAD - LABOR PRODUCTIVITY

International Labour Office, I.L.O. Publications, CH-1211, Geneva 22, Switzerland; *Yearbook of Labour Statistics.*

CHAD - LAND USE

Euromonitor Publications Limited, 87-88 Turnmill Street, London EC1M 5QU, England; *International Marketing Data and Statistics.*

Food and Agricultural Organization of the United Nations (FAO), Via delle Terme di Caracalla, 00100 Rome, Italy (Telephone Number in U.S. (202) 653-2400); *Production Yearbook.*

G.K. Hall and Company, 70 Lincoln Street, Boston, Massachusetts 02111 (617) 423-3990; *The World in Figures.*

CHAD - LIBRARIES

Facts on File, 460 Park Avenue South, New York, New York 10016 (800) 443-8323; *The New Book of World Rankings.*

CHAD - LIFE EXPECTANCY

African Development Bank, 01 BP 1387, Abidjan 01, Cote D'Ivoire; *Selected Statistics on Regional Member Countries.*

CHAD - LITERACY RATE

Statistical Office of the United Nations, Publishing Service, New York, New York 10017 (800) 253-9646; *Survey of Economic and Social Conditions in Africa.*

CHAD - LIVESTOCK AND POULTRY

Euromonitor Publications Limited, 87-88 Turnmill Street, London EC1M 5QU, England; *International Marketing Data and Statistics.*

Facts on File, 460 Park Avenue South, New York, New York 10016 (800) 443-8323; *The New Book of World Rankings*.

Food and Agricultural Organization of the United Nations (FAO), Via delle Terme di Caracalla, 00100 Rome, Italy (Telephone Number in U.S. (202) 653-2400); *Production Yearbook*, and *The State of Food and Agriculture*.

G.K. Hall and Company, 70 Lincoln Street, Boston, Massachusetts 02111 (617) 423-3990; *The World in Figures*.

Statistical Office of the United Nations, Publishing Service, New York, New York 10017 (800) 253-9646; *Statistical Yearbook*, and *Survey of Economic and Social Conditions in Africa*.

United Nations Economic Commission for Africa, Africa Hall, P.O. Box 3001, Addis Ababa, Ethiopia (Telephone Number in U.S. (800) 253-9646); *African Statistical Yearbook*.

CHAD - LIVING LEVELS

G.K. Hall and Company, 70 Lincoln Street, Boston, Massachusetts 02111 (617) 423-3990; *The World in Figures*.

Times Books, 201 East 50th Street, New York, New York 10022 (212) 751-2600; *The Economist Book of Vital World Statistics*.

CHAD - MAIL - NUMBER OF PIECES SENT OR RECEIVED

Statistical Office of the United Nations, Publishing Service, New York, New York 10017 (800) 253-9646; *Statistical Yearbook*.

CHAD - MANUFACTURING

Facts on File, 460 Park Avenue South, New York, New York 10016 (800) 443-8323; *The New Book of World Rankings*.

G.K. Hall and Company, 70 Lincoln Street, Boston, Massachusetts 02111 (617) 423-3990; *The World in Figures*.

Statistical Office of the United Nations, Publishing Service, New York, New York 10017 (800) 253-9646; *Survey of Economic and Social Conditions in Africa*.

Times Books, 201 East 50th Street, New York, New York 10022 (212) 751-2600; *The Economist Book of Vital World Statistics*.

United Nations Economic Commission for Africa, Africa Hall, P.O. Box 3001, Addis Ababa, Ethiopia (Telephone Number in U.S. (800) 253-9646); *African Statistical Yearbook*.

The World Bank, 1818 H Street, NW, Washington, D.C. 20433 (202) 477-1234; *World Tables*.

CHAD - MARRIAGE RATES

Facts on File, 460 Park Avenue South, New York, New York 10016 (800) 443-8323; *The New Book of World Rankings*.

Statistical Office of the United Nations, Publishing Service, New York, New York 10017 (800) 253-9646; *Demographic Yearbook*.

CHAD - MEAT PRODUCTION - See CHAD - LIVESTOCK AND POULTRY

CHAD - MERCHANT SHIPPING

G.K. Hall and Company, 70 Lincoln Street, Boston, Massachusetts 02111 (617) 423-3990; *The World in Figures*.

United Nations Economic Commission for Africa, Africa Hall, P.O. Box 3001, Addis Ababa, Ethiopia (Telephone Number in U.S. (800) 253-9646); *African Statistical Yearbook*.

CHAD - MILITARY

G.K. Hall and Company, 70 Lincoln Street, Boston, Massachusetts 02111 (617) 423-3990; *The World in Figures*.

The International Institute for Strategic Studies, 23 Tavistock Street, London WC2E 7NQ, England; *The Military Balance*.

U.S. Arms Control and Disarmament Agency, 320 Twenty-first Street, NW, Washington, D.C. 20451 (202) 647-8677; *World Military Expenditures and Arms Transfers*.

CHAD - MILK PRODUCTION - See CHAD - DAIRY PRODUCTS

CHAD - MILLET PRODUCTION - See CHAD - CROPS

CHAD - MINING AND MINERAL PRODUCTS

Facts on File, 460 Park Avenue South, New York, New York 10016 (800) 443-8323; *The New Book of World Rankings*.

G.K. Hall and Company, 70 Lincoln Street, Boston, Massachusetts 02111 (617) 423-3990; *The World in Figures*.

United Nations Economic Commission for Africa, Africa Hall, P.O. Box 3001, Addis Ababa, Ethiopia (Telephone Number in U.S. (800) 253-9646); *African Statistical Yearbook*.

CHAD - MONEY EXCHANGE RATES

Euromonitor Publications Limited, 87-88 Turnmill Street, London EC1M 5QU, England; *International Marketing Data and Statistics*.

International Monetary Fund, 700 Nineteenth Street, NW, Washington, D.C. 20431 (202) 623-7000; *International Financial Statistics*.

Statistical Office of the United Nations, Publishing Service, New York, New York 10017 (800) 253-9646; *Statistical Yearbook*.

CHAD - MONEY RESERVES

Euromonitor Publications Limited, 87-88 Turnmill Street, London EC1M 5QU, England; *International Marketing Data and Statistics*.

CHAD - MONEY SUPPLY

African Development Bank, 01 BP 1387, Abidjan 01, Cote D'Ivoire; *Selected Statistics on Regional Member Countries*.

G.K. Hall and Company, 70 Lincoln Street, Boston, Massachusetts 02111 (617) 423-3990; *The World in Figures*.

International Monetary Fund, 700 Nineteenth Street, NW, Washington, D.C. 20431 (202) 623-7000; *International Financial Statistics*.

Statistical Office of the United Nations, Publishing Service, New York, New York 10017 (800) 253-9646; *Statistical Yearbook*.

The World Bank, 1818 H Street, NW, Washington, D.C. 20433 (202) 477-1234; *World Tables*.

CHAD - MOTOR VEHICLE TAXES - See CHAD - TAXATION

CHAD - MOTOR VEHICLES IN USE

G.K. Hall and Company, 70 Lincoln Street, Boston, Massachusetts 02111 (617) 423-3990; *The World in Figures.*

International Road Federation, 525 School Street, SW, Washington, D.C. 20024 (202) 554-2106; *World Road Statistics.*

Statistical Office of the United Nations, Publishing Service, New York, New York 10017 (800) 253-9646; *Statistical Yearbook,* and *Survey of Economic and Social Conditions in Africa.*

Times Books, 201 East 50th Street, New York, New York 10022 (212) 751-2600; *The Economist Book of Vital World Statistics.*

CHAD - MUSEUMS

Facts on File, 460 Park Avenue South, New York, New York 10016 (800) 443-8323; *The New Book of World Rankings.*

United Nations Educational, Scientific and Cultural Organization (UNESCO), 7 Place de Fontenoy, F-75700 Paris, France (Telephone Number in U.S. (212) 963-5981); *Statistical Yearbook.*

CHAD - NATALITY - See CHAD - BIRTH RATE

CHAD - NATIONAL ACCOUNTS

African Development Bank, 01 BP 1387, Abidjan 01, Cote D'Ivoire; *Selected Statistics on Regional Member Countries.*

Statistical Office of the United Nations, Publishing Service, New York, New York 10017 (800) 253-9646; *National Accounts Statistics,* and *Statistical Yearbook.*

United Nations Economic Commission for Africa, Africa Hall, P.O. Box 3001, Addis Ababa, Ethiopia (Telephone Number in U.S. (800) 253-9646); *African Statistical Yearbook.*

CHAD - NATIONAL INCOME

Facts on File, 460 Park Avenue South, New York, New York 10016 (800) 443-8323; *The New Book of World Rankings.*

G.K. Hall and Company, 70 Lincoln Street, Boston, Massachusetts 02111 (617) 423-3990; *The World in Figures.*

Statistical Office of the United Nations, Publishing Service, New York, New York 10017 (800) 253-9646; *Statistical Yearbook.*

CHAD - NATIONAL PRODUCT

Facts on File, 460 Park Avenue South, New York, New York 10016 (800) 443-8323; *The New Book of World Rankings.*

Statistical Office of the United Nations, Publishing Service, New York, New York 10017 (800) 253-9646; *Statistical Yearbook.*

CHAD - NATURAL GAS PRODUCTION - See CHAD - MINING AND MINERAL PRODUCTS

CHAD - NEWSPAPER PRODUCTION - See CHAD - FORESTRY AND FOREST PRODUCTS

CHAD - OCCUPATIONS - See CHAD - LABOR FORCE

CHAD - PAPER - See CHAD - FORESTRY AND FOREST PRODUCTS

CHAD - PEANUT PRODUCTION - See CHAD - CROPS

CHAD - PESTICIDE USE

Food and Agricultural Organization of the United Nations (FAO) Via delle Terme di Caracalla, 00100 Rome, Italy (Telephone Number in U.S. (202) 653-2400); *The State of Food and Agriculture.*

CHAD - PETROLEUM INDUSTRY

Facts on File, 460 Park Avenue South, New York, New York 10016 (800) 443-8323; *The New Book of World Rankings.*

Food and Agricultural Organization of the United Nations (FAO) Via delle Terme di Caracalla, 00100 Rome, Italy (Telephone Number in U.S. (202) 653-2400); *The State of Food and Agriculture.*

G.K. Hall and Company, 70 Lincoln Street, Boston, Massachusetts 02111 (617) 423-3990; *The World in Figures.*

CHAD - PIGS - See CHAD - LIVESTOCK AND POULTRY

CHAD - POPULATION

African Development Bank, 01 BP 1387, Abidjan 01, Cote D'Ivoire; *Selected Statistics on Regional Member Countries.*

The Economist Intelligence Unit, 111 West 57th Street, New York, New York 10019 (800) 938-4685; *The World Market Atlas.*

Euromonitor Publications Limited, 87-88 Turnmill Street, London EC1M 5QU, England; *International Marketing Data and Statistics.*

Facts on File, 460 Park Avenue South, New York, New York 10016 (800) 443-8323; *The New Book of World Rankings.*

Food and Agricultural Organization of the United Nations (FAO), Via delle Terme di Caracalla, 00100 Rome, Italy (Telephone Number in U.S. (202) 653-2400); *Production Yearbook.*

G.K. Hall and Company, 70 Lincoln Street, Boston, Massachusetts 02111 (617) 423-3990; *The World in Figures.*

International Labour Office, I.L.O. Publications, CH-1211, Geneva 22, Switzerland; *Yearbook of Labour Statistics.*

Statistical Office of the United Nations, Publishing Service, New York, New York 10017 (800) 253-9646; *Demographic Yearbook, Statistical Yearbook,* and *Survey of Economic and Social Conditions in Africa.*

Times Books, 201 East 50th Street, New York, New York 10022 (212) 751-2600; *The Economist Book of Vital World Statistics.*

United Nations Educational, Scientific and Cultural Organization (UNESCO), 7 Place de Fontenoy, F-75700 Paris, France (Telephone Number in U.S. (212) 963-5981); *Statistical Yearbook.*

U.S. Arms Control and Disarmament Agency, 320 Twenty-first Street, NW, Washington, D.C. 20451 (202) 647-8677; *World Military Expenditures and Arms Transfers.*

World Health Organization, Office of Publications, Avenue Appia, CH-1211 Geneva 27, Switzerland (Telephone Number in U.S. (518) 436-9686); *World Health Statistics Annual.*

CHAD - POST OFFICES

Facts on File, 460 Park Avenue South, New York, New York 10016 (800) 443-8323; *The New Book of World Rankings.*

CHAD - POTATO PRODUCTION - See CHAD - CROPS

CHAD - PRICES

Facts on File, 460 Park Avenue South, New York, New York 10016 (800) 443-8323; *The New Book of World Rankings*.

Food and Agricultural Organization of the United Nations (FAO), Via delle Terme di Caracalla, 00100 Rome, Italy (Telephone Number in U.S. (202) 653-2400); *Production Yearbook*, and *The State of Food and Agriculture*.

G.K. Hall and Company, 70 Lincoln Street, Boston, Massachusetts 02111 (617) 423-3990; *The World in Figures*.

International Monetary Fund, 700 Nineteenth Street, NW, Washington, D.C. 20431 (202) 623-7000; *International Financial Statistics*.

United Nations Economic Commission for Africa, Africa Hall, P.O. Box 3001, Addis Ababa, Ethiopia (Telephone Number in U.S. (800) 253-9646); *African Statistical Yearbook*.

CHAD - PRINTING AND WRITING PAPER

United Nations Educational, Scientific and Cultural Organization (UNESCO), 7 Place de Fontenoy, F-75700 Paris, France (Telephone Number in U.S. (212) 963-5981); *Statistical Yearbook*.

CHAD - PRODUCTION

Facts on File, 460 Park Avenue South, New York, New York 10016 (800) 443-8323; *The New Book of World Rankings*.

G.K. Hall and Company, 70 Lincoln Street, Boston, Massachusetts 02111 (617) 423-3990; *The World in Figures*.

CHAD - PRODUCTIVITY

Euromonitor Publications Limited, 87-88 Turnmill Street, London EC1M 5QU, England; *International Marketing Data and Statistics*.

CHAD - PROPERTY TAXES

International Monetary Fund, 700 Nineteenth Street, NW, Washington, D.C. 20431 (202) 623-7000; *Government Finance Statistics Yearbook*.

CHAD - PUBLIC FINANCE

Facts on File, 460 Park Avenue South, New York, New York 10016 (800) 443-8323; *The New Book of World Rankings*.

CHAD - RADIO BROADCASTING - See CHAD - BROADCASTING

CHAD - RAILWAYS

G.K. Hall and Company, 70 Lincoln Street, Boston, Massachusetts 02111 (617) 423-3990; *The World in Figures*.

United Nations Economic Commission for Africa, Africa Hall, P.O. Box 3001, Addis Ababa, Ethiopia (Telephone Number in U.S. (800) 253-9646); *African Statistical Yearbook*.

CHAD - RELIGION

Facts on File, 460 Park Avenue South, New York, New York 10016 (800) 443-8323; *The New Book of World Rankings*.

CHAD - RETAIL TRADE

G.K. Hall and Company, 70 Lincoln Street, Boston, Massachusetts 02111 (617) 423-3990; *The World in Figures*.

CHAD - RICE PRODUCTION - See CHAD - CROPS

CHAD - ROOT AND TUBER PRODUCTION - See CHAD - CROPS

CHAD - ROUNDWOOD PRODUCTION - See CHAD - FORESTRY AND FOREST PRODUCTS

CHAD - RUBBER PRODUCTION

Facts on File, 460 Park Avenue South, New York, New York 10016 (800) 443-8323; *The New Book of World Rankings*.

CHAD - SAWNWOOD PRODUCTION - See CHAD - FORESTRY AND FOREST PRODUCTS

CHAD - SCIENCE AND TECHNOLOGY - EXPENDITURE FOR RESEARCH

Statistical Office of the United Nations, Publishing Service, New York, New York 10017 (800) 253-9646; *Statistical Yearbook*.

CHAD - SCIENTISTS AND TECHNICIANS

Statistical Office of the United Nations, Publishing Service, New York, New York 10017 (800) 253-9646; *Statistical Yearbook*.

United Nations Educational, Scientific and Cultural Organization (UNESCO), 7 Place de Fontenoy, F-75700 Paris, France (Telephone Number in U.S. (212) 963-5981); *Statistical Yearbook*.

CHAD - SENIOR CITIZENS

Facts on File, 460 Park Avenue South, New York, New York 10016 (800) 443-8323; *The New Book of World Rankings*.

CHAD - SESAME SEED PRODUCTION - See CHAD - CROPS

CHAD - SHEEP - See CHAD - LIVESTOCK AND POULTRY

CHAD - SILVER PRODUCTION AND CONSUMPTION - See CHAD - MINING AND MINERAL PRODUCTS

CHAD - SOCIAL DATA

African Development Bank, 01 BP 1387, Abidjan 01, Cote D'Ivoire; *Selected Statistics on Regional Member Countries*.

Facts on File, 460 Park Avenue South, New York, New York 10016 (800) 443-8323; *The New Book of World Rankings*.

G.K. Hall and Company, 70 Lincoln Street, Boston, Massachusetts 02111 (617) 423-3990; *The World in Figures*.

CHAD - SOCIAL SECURITY

International Monetary Fund, 700 Nineteenth Street, NW, Washington, D.C. 20431 (202) 623-7000; *Government Finance Statistics Yearbook*.

CHAD - STAMP TAXES AND DUTIES - See CHAD - TAXATION

CHAD - STATE BUDGET REVENUE AND EXPENDITURES

Euromonitor Publications Limited, 87-88 Turnmill Street, London EC1M 5QU, England; *International Marketing Data and Statistics.*

CHAD - STEEL PRODUCTION - See CHAD - MINING AND MINERAL PRODUCTS

CHAD - STOCKS - COMMODITY - MARKET PRICE - INDEX

Food and Agricultural Organization of the United Nations (FAO) Via delle Terme di Caracalla, 00100 Rome, Italy (Telephone Number in U.S. (202) 653-2400); *The State of Food and Agriculture.*

CHAD - SUGAR PRODUCTION - See CHAD - CROPS

CHAD - TAXATION

G.K. Hall and Company, 70 Lincoln Street, Boston, Massachusetts 02111 (617) 423-3990; *The World in Figures.*

International Monetary Fund, 700 Nineteenth Street, NW, Washington, D.C. 20431 (202) 623-7000; *Government Finance Statistics Yearbook.*

International Road Federation, 525 School Street, SW, Washington, D.C. 20024 (202) 554-2106; *World Road Statistics.*

The World Bank, 1818 H Street, NW, Washington, D.C. 20433 (202) 477-1234; *World Tables.*

CHAD - TELEGRAPH SERVICE

Statistical Office of the United Nations, Publishing Service, New York, New York 10017 (800) 253-9646; *Statistical Yearbook.*

CHAD - TELEPHONES IN USE

American Telephone and Telegraph Company, 26 Parsippany Road, Whippany, New Jersey 07981 (800) 338-4038; *The World's Telephones.*

G.K. Hall and Company, 70 Lincoln Street, Boston, Massachusetts 02111 (617) 423-3990; *The World in Figures.*

Statistical Office of the United Nations, Publishing Service, New York, New York 10017 (800) 253-9646; *Statistical Yearbook.*

CHAD - TELEVISION BROADCASTING - See CHAD - BROADCASTING

CHAD - TEXTILE INDUSTRY

G.K. Hall and Company, 70 Lincoln Street, Boston, Massachusetts 02111 (617) 423-3990; *The World in Figures.*

Statistical Office of the United Nations, Publishing Service, New York, New York 10017 (800) 253-9646; *Statistical Yearbook.*

CHAD - THEATRE

United Nations Educational, Scientific and Cultural Organization (UNESCO), 7 Place de Fontenoy, F-75700 Paris, France (Telephone Number in U.S. (212) 963-5981); *Statistical Yearbook.*

CHAD - TOBACCO PRODUCTION

Facts on File, 460 Park Avenue South, New York, New York 10016 (800) 443-8323; *The New Book of World Rankings.*

Statistical Office of the United Nations, Publishing Service, New York, New York 10017 (800) 253-9646; *Statistical Yearbook.*

CHAD - TOURISM

Facts on File, 460 Park Avenue South, New York, New York 10016 (800) 443-8323; *The New Book of World Rankings.*

G.K. Hall and Company, 70 Lincoln Street, Boston, Massachusetts 02111 (617) 423-3990; *The World in Figures.*

Statistical Office of the United Nations, Publishing Service, New York, New York 10017 (800) 253-9646; *Statistical Yearbook.*

Times Books, 201 East 50th Street, New York, New York 10022 (212) 751-2600; *The Economist Book of Vital World Statistics.*

United Nations Economic Commission for Africa, Africa Hall, P.O. Box 3001, Addis Ababa, Ethiopia (Telephone Number in U.S. (800) 253-9646); *African Statistical Yearbook.*

World Tourism Organization, Calle Capitan Haya 42, E-28020 Madrid, Spain; *Yearbook of Tourism Statistics.*

CHAD - TRACTORS IN USE

Statistical Office of the United Nations, Publishing Service, New York, New York 10017 (800) 253-9646; *Statistical Yearbook.*

CHAD - TRADE - See CHAD - FOREIGN TRADE

CHAD - TRANSPORTATION AND COMMUNICATIONS

Facts on File, 460 Park Avenue South, New York, New York 10016 (800) 443-8323; *The New Book of World Rankings.*

G.K. Hall and Company, 70 Lincoln Street, Boston, Massachusetts 02111 (617) 423-3990; *The World in Figures.*

United Nations Economic Commission for Africa, Africa Hall, P.O. Box 3001, Addis Ababa, Ethiopia (Telephone Number in U.S. (800) 253-9646); *African Statistical Yearbook.*

CHAD - UNEMPLOYMENT

Euromonitor Publications Limited, 87-88 Turnmill Street, London EC1M 5QU, England; *International Marketing Data and Statistics.*

International Labour Office, I.L.O. Publications, CH-1211, Geneva 22, Switzerland; *Yearbook of Labour Statistics.*

CHAD - VITAL STATISTICS

Euromonitor Publications Limited, 87-88 Turnmill Street, London EC1M 5QU, England; *International Marketing Data and Statistics.*

G.K. Hall and Company, 70 Lincoln Street, Boston, Massachusetts 02111 (617) 423-3990; *The World in Figures.*

Statistical Office of the United Nations, Publishing Service, New York, New York 10017 (800) 253-9646; *Statistical Yearbook.*

World Health Organization, Office of Publications, Avenue Appia, CH-1211 Geneva 27, Switzerland (Telephone Number in U.S. (518) 436-9686); *World Health Statistics Annual.*

CHAD - WAGES

G.K. Hall and Company, 70 Lincoln Street, Boston, Massachusetts 02111 (617) 423-3990; *The World in Figures*.

International Labour Office, I.L.O. Publications, CH-1211, Geneva 22, Switzerland; *Yearbook of Labour Statistics*.

CHAD - WEATHER

Facts on File, 460 Park Avenue South, New York, New York 10016 (800) 443-8323; *The New Book of World Rankings*.

G.K. Hall and Company, 70 Lincoln Street, Boston, Massachusetts 02111 (617) 423-3990; *The World in Figures*.

CHAD - WELFARE

G.K. Hall and Company, 70 Lincoln Street, Boston, Massachusetts 02111 (617) 423-3990; *The World in Figures*.

International Monetary Fund, 700 Nineteenth Street, NW, Washington, D.C. 20431 (202) 623-7000; *Government Finance Statistics Yearbook*.

CHAD - WHEAT PRODUCTION - See CHAD - CROPS

CHAD - WINE PRODUCTION

Facts on File, 460 Park Avenue South, New York, New York 10016 (800) 443-8323; *The New Book of World Rankings*.

CHAD - WOOL PRODUCTION

Facts on File, 460 Park Avenue South, New York, New York 10016 (800) 443-8323; *The New Book of World Rankings*.

CHAMBERS OF COMMERCE

Gale Research Incorporated, 835 Penobscot Building, Detroit, Michigan 48226 (800) 877-4253; compiled from *Encyclopedia of Associations*.

CHANNEL ISLANDS - AREA AND DENSITY OF POPULATION

Statistical Office of the United Nations, Publishing Service, New York, New York 10017 (800) 253-9646; *Statistical Yearbook*.

United Nations Educational, Scientific and Cultural Organization (UNESCO), 7 Place de Fontenoy, F-75700 Paris, France (Telephone Number in U.S. (212) 963-5981); *Statistical Yearbook*.

CHANNEL ISLANDS - BIRTH RATES

Statistical Office of the United Nations, Publishing Service, New York, New York 10017 (800) 253-9646; *Demographic Yearbook*, and *Statistical Yearbook*.

CHANNEL ISLANDS - DEATH RATES

Statistical Office of the United Nations, Publishing Service, New York, New York 10017 (800) 253-9646; *Statistical Yearbook*.

World Health Organization, Office of Publications, Avenue Appia, CH-1211 Geneva 27, Switzerland (Telephone Number in U.S. (518) 436-9686); *World Health Statistics Annual*.

CHANNEL ISLANDS - DISEASE

World Health Organization, Office of Publications, Avenue Appia, CH-1211 Geneva 27, Switzerland (Telephone Number in U.S. (518) 436-9686); *World Health Statistics Annual*.

CHANNEL ISLANDS - DIVORCE RATES

Statistical Office of the United Nations, Publishing Service, New York, New York 10017 (800) 253-9646; *Demographic Yearbook*, and *Statistical Yearbook*.

CHANNEL ISLANDS - FETAL MORTALITY

Statistical Office of the United Nations, Publishing Service, New York, New York 10017 (800) 253-9646; *Demographic Yearbook*.

World Health Organization, Office of Publications, Avenue Appia, CH-1211 Geneva 27, Switzerland (Telephone Number in U.S. (518) 436-9686); *World Health Statistics Annual*.

CHANNEL ISLANDS - FOREIGN TRADE

Organisation for Economic Co-operation and Development (OECD), 2 rue Andre-Pascal, 75 Paris 16, France (Telephone Number in U.S. (202) 785-6323); *Trade by Commodities*.

CHANNEL ISLANDS - GENERAL MORTALITY

Statistical Office of the United Nations, Publishing Service, New York, New York 10017 (800) 253-9646; *Demographic Yearbook*.

World Health Organization, Office of Publications, Avenue Appia, CH-1211 Geneva 27, Switzerland (Telephone Number in U.S. (518) 436-9686); *World Health Statistics Annual*.

CHANNEL ISLANDS - HEALTH

Statistical Office of the United Nations, Publishing Service, New York, New York 10017 (800) 253-9646; *Statistical Yearbook*.

World Health Organization, Office of Publications, Avenue Appia, CH-1211 Geneva 27, Switzerland (Telephone Number in U.S. (518) 436-9686); *World Health Statistics Annual*.

CHANNEL ISLANDS - INFANT AND MATERNAL MORTALITY

Statistical Office of the United Nations, Publishing Service, New York, New York 10017 (800) 253-9646; *Demographic Yearbook*, and *Statistical Yearbook*.

World Health Organization, Office of Publications, Avenue Appia, CH-1211 Geneva 27, Switzerland (Telephone Number in U.S. (518) 436-9686); *World Health Statistics Annual*.

CHANNEL ISLANDS - MAIL TRAFFIC - NUMBER OF ITEMS

Statistical Office of the United Nations, Publishing Service, New York, New York 10017 (800) 253-9646; *Statistical Yearbook*.

CHANNEL ISLANDS - MARRIAGE RATES

Statistical Office of the United Nations, Publishing Service, New York, New York 10017 (800) 253-9646; *Demographic Yearbook*, and *Statistical Yearbook*.

CHANNEL ISLANDS - NATALITY

Statistical Office of the United Nations, Publishing Service, New York, New York 10017 (800) 253-9646; *Demographic Yearbook.*

World Health Organization, Office of Publications, Avenue Appia, CH-1211 Geneva 27, Switzerland (Telephone Number in U.S. (518) 436-9686); *World Health Statistics Annual.*

CHANNEL ISLANDS - POPULATION

Statistical Office of the United Nations, Publishing Service, New York, New York 10017 (800) 253-9646; *Demographic Yearbook,* and *Statistical Yearbook.*

United Nations Educational, Scientific and Cultural Organization (UNESCO), 7 Place de Fontenoy, F-75700 Paris, France (Telephone Number in U.S. (212) 963-5981); *Statistical Yearbook.*

World Health Organization, Office of Publications, Avenue Appia, CH-1211 Geneva 27, Switzerland (Telephone Number in U.S. (518) 436-9686); *World Health Statistics Annual.*

CHANNEL ISLANDS - TELEPHONES IN USE

Statistical Office of the United Nations, Publishing Service, New York, New York 10017 (800) 253-9646; *Statistical Yearbook.*

CHANNEL ISLANDS - VITAL STATISTICS

Statistical Office of the United Nations, Publishing Service, New York, New York 10017 (800) 253-9646; *Statistical Yearbook.*

World Health Organization, Office of Publications, Avenue Appia, CH-1211 Geneva 27, Switzerland (Telephone Number in U.S. (518) 436-9686); *World Health Statistics Annual.*

CHARITABLE CONTRIBUTIONS - See also PHILANTHROPY

CHARITABLE CONTRIBUTIONS

American Association of Fund-Raising Counsel, Incorporated, 25 West 43rd Street, New York, New York 10036 (212) 354-5799; *Giving USA.*

Independent Sector, 1828 L Street, NW, Washington, D.C. 20036 (202) 223-8100; *Giving and Volunteering in the United States.*

CHEESE - See also DAIRY PRODUCTS

CHEESE

U.S. Department of Agriculture, Economic Research Service, Fourteenth Street and Independence Avenue, SW, Washington, D.C. 20250 (202) 219-1504; *Food Consumption, Prices, and Expenditures,* and unpublished data.

U.S. Department of Agriculture, National Agricultural Statistics Service, Fourteenth Street and Independence Avenue, SW, Washington, D.C. 20250 (202) 219-1504; *Dairy Products,* and *Milk Production, Disposition, and Income.*

CHEMICALS AND ALLIED PRODUCTS - MANUFACTURING - See also Individual Chemicals

CHEMICALS AND ALLIED PRODUCTS - MANUFACTURING - CAPITAL

U.S. Department of Commerce, Bureau of the Census, Suitland, Maryland 20233 (301) 763-4040; *Current Industrial Reports.*

CHEMICALS AND ALLIED PRODUCTS - MANUFACTURING - EARNINGS

U.S. Department of Commerce, Bureau of the Census, Suitland, Maryland 20233 (301) 763-4040; *County Business Patterns, Census of Manufactures,* and *Annual Survey of Manufactures.*

U.S. Department of Labor, Bureau of Labor Statistics, Two Massachusetts Avenue, NE, Washington, D.C. 20212 (202) 606-7828; *Employment and Earnings, Employment and Wages, Annual Averages,* and Bulletins 2370 and 2429.

CHEMICALS AND ALLIED PRODUCTS - MANUFACTURING - EMPLOYEES

U.S. Department of Commerce, Bureau of the Census, Suitland, Maryland 20233 (301) 763-4040; *United States Census of Manufactures, Annual Survey of Manufactures,* and *County Business Patterns.*

U.S. Department of Labor, Bureau of Labor Statistics, Two Massachusetts Avenue, NE, Washington, D.C. 20212 (202) 606-7828; *Employment and Earnings, Monthly Labor Review, Employment and Wages, Annual Averages,* and Bulletins 2370 and 2429.

CHEMICALS AND ALLIED PRODUCTS - MANUFACTURING - ENERGY CONSUMPTION

U.S. Department of Energy, Energy Information Administration, 1000 Independence Avenue, SW, Washington, D.C. 20585 (202) 586-8000; *Manufacturing Energy Consumption.*

CHEMICALS AND ALLIED PRODUCTS - MANUFACTURING - ESTABLISHMENTS

U.S. Department of Commerce, Bureau of the Census, Suitland, Maryland 20233 (301) 763-4040; *Census of Manufactures, Annual Survey of Manufactures,* and *County Business Patterns.*

CHEMICALS AND ALLIED PRODUCTS - MANUFACTURING - FAILURES

Dun and Bradstreet Corporation, 299 Park Avenue, 24th Floor, New York, New York 10171 (212) 593-6800; *Business Failure Record.*

CHEMICALS AND ALLIED PRODUCTS - MANUFACTURING - FOREIGN TRADE

U.S. Department of Commerce, Bureau of the Census, Suitland, Maryland 20233 (301) 763-4040; *Annual Survey of Manufactures, Census of Manufactures,* and *U.S. Merchandise Trade.*

U.S. Department of Commerce, International Trade Administration, Fourteenth Street between Constitution Avenue and E Street, NW, Washington, D.C. 20230 (202) 482-5487; *Business America, Market Share Reports,* and unpublished data.

U.S. Department of the Army, Corps of Engineers, The Pentagon, Washington, D.C. 20310 (202) 545-6700; *Waterborne Commerce of the United States.*

CHEMICALS AND ALLIED PRODUCTS - MANUFACTURING - GROSS DOMESTIC PRODUCT

U.S. Department of Commerce, Bureau of Economic Analysis, Fourteenth Street between Constitution Avenue and E Street, NW, Washington, D.C. 20230 (202) 606-9900; *Survey of Current Business.*

CHEMICALS AND ALLIED PRODUCTS - MANUFACTURING - INVENTORIES

U.S. Department of Commerce, Bureau of the Census, Suitland, Maryland 20233 (301) 763-4040; *Current Industrial Reports, Manufactures' Shipments, Inventories, and Orders.*

CHEMICALS AND ALLIED PRODUCTS - MANUFACTURING - OCCUPATIONAL SAFETY

U.S. Department of Labor, Bureau of Labor Statistics, Two Massachusetts Avenue, NE, Washington, D.C. 20212 (202) 606-7828; *Occupational Injuries and Illnesses in the United States by Industry.*

CHEMICALS AND ALLIED PRODUCTS - MANUFACTURING - PATENTS

U.S. Department of Commerce, Patent and Trademark Office, 2011 Crystal Drive, Arlington, Virginia 22202 (703) 305-8341; *Patenting Trends in the United States, State Country Report.*

CHEMICALS AND ALLIED PRODUCTS - MANUFACTURING - POLLUTION ABATEMENT

U.S. Department of Commerce, Bureau of the Census, Suitland, Maryland 20233 (301) 763-4040; *Current Industrial Reports.*

CHEMICALS AND ALLIED PRODUCTS - MANUFACTURING - PRODUCTIVITY

U.S. Department of Labor, Bureau of Labor Statistics, Two Massachusetts Avenue, NE, Washington, D.C. 20212 (202) 606-7828; *Productivity Measures for Selected Industries and Government Services*, and unpublished data.

CHEMICALS AND ALLIED PRODUCTS - MANUFACTURING - PROFITS

Executive Office of the President, Council of Economic Advisers, Old Executive Office Building, Washington, D.C. 20500 (202) 395-5084; *Economic Report of the President.*

Forbes, Incorporated, 60 Fifth Avenue, New York, New York 10011 (212) 620-2200; *Forbes Annual Report on American Industry.*

Time Warner, 1675 Broadway, Rockefeller Center, New York, New York 10020 (212) 522-1212; *The Fortune Directories.*

U.S. Department of Commerce, Bureau of Economic Analysis, Fourteenth Street between Constitution Avenue and E Street, NW, Washington, D.C. 20230 (202) 606-9900; *The National Income and Product Accounts of the United States*, and *Survey of Current Business.*

U.S. Department of Commerce, Bureau of the Census, Suitland, Maryland 20233 (301) 763-4040; *Quarterly Financial Report for Manufacturing, Mining and Trade Corporations.*

CHEMICALS AND ALLIED PRODUCTS - MANUFACTURING - RESEARCH AND DEVELOPMENT

U.S. National Science Foundation, 4201 Wilson Boulevard, Arlington, Virginia 22230 (703) 306-1234; *Research and Development in Industry.*

CHEMICALS AND ALLIED PRODUCTS - MANUFACTURING - SHIPMENTS

U.S. Department of Commerce, Bureau of the Census, Suitland, Maryland 20233 (301) 763-4040; *Annual Survey of Manufactures, Census of Manufactures*, and *Current Industrial Reports, Manufactures' Shipments, Inventories, and Orders.*

U.S. Department of Commerce, International Trade Administration, Fourteenth Street between Constitution Avenue and E Street, NW, Washington, D.C. 20230 (202) 482-5487; *U.S. Industrial Outlook.*

CHEMICALS AND ALLIED PRODUCTS - MANUFACTURING - TOXIC CHEMICAL RELEASES

U.S. Environmental Protection Agency, 401 M Street, NW, Washington, D.C. 20460 (202) 382-2090; *Toxics Release Inventory Public Data Release.*

CHEMICALS AND ALLIED PRODUCTS - MANUFACTURING - VALUE ADDED

U.S. Department of Commerce, Bureau of the Census, Suitland, Maryland 20233 (301) 763-4040; *United States Census of Manufactures*, and *Annual Survey of Manufactures.*

CHEMISTRY - See also PHYSICAL SCIENCES

CHEMISTRY - EMPLOYMENT

U.S. Department of Labor, Bureau of Labor Statistics, Two Massachusetts Avenue, NE, Washington, D.C. 20212 (202) 606-7828; *Employment and Earnings.*

CHEMISTRY - NOBEL PRIZE LAUREATES

U.S. National Science Foundation, 4201 Wilson Boulevard, Arlington, Virginia 22230 (703) 306-1234; unpublished data.

CHEMISTRY - SALARY OFFERS

College Placement Council, Inc., 62 Highland Avenue, Bethlehem, Pennsylvania 18017 (212) 868-1421; *Salary Survey, A Study of Beginning Offers.*

Northwestern University, 633 Clark Street, Evanston, Illinois 60201 (708) 491-3741; *The Northwestern Endicott-Lindquist Report.*

CHERRIES

U.S. Department of Agriculture, National Agricultural Statistics Service, Fourteenth Street and Independence Avenue, SW, Washington, D.C. 20250 (202) 219-1504; *Economic Indicators of the Farm Sector: National Financial Summary*, and *Noncitrus Fruits and Nuts.*

CHICKEN POX

U.S. Department of Health and Human Services, Center for Disease Control, 1600 Clifton Road, NE, Atlanta, Georgia 30333 (404) 639-3311; *Summary of Notifiable Diseases, United States Morbidity and Mortality Weekly Report.*

CHICKENS - See POULTRY

CHILD ABUSE

U.S. Department of Health and Human Services, National Center on Child Abuse and Neglect, 370 L'Enfant Promenade, SW, Washington, D.C. 20447 (202) 205-8586; *National Child Abuse and Neglect Data System*, and *Child Maltreatment*.

CHILD CARE

U.S. Department of Commerce, Bureau of the Census, Suitland, Maryland 20233 (301) 763-4040; *Current Population Reports, Census of Service Industries*, and unpublished data.

CHILD SUPPORT

U.S. Department of Commerce, Bureau of the Census, Suitland, Maryland 20233 (301) 763-4040; *Current Population Reports*.

U.S. Department of Health and Human Services, Office of Child Support Enforcement, 370 L'Enfant Promenade, SW, Washington, D.C. 20447 (202) 401-9373; *Annual Report to Congress*.

CHILDREN - See also POPULATION and VITAL STATISTICS

CHILDREN - ACUTE CONDITIONS

U.S. Department of Health and Human Services, National Center for Health Statistics, 3700 East-West Highway, Hyattsville, Maryland 20782 (301) 436-8500; *Vital and Health Statistics*, and unpublished data.

CHILDREN - ADOPTIVE FAMILIES

U.S. Department of Commerce, Bureau of the Census, Suitland, Maryland 20233 (301) 763-4040; *Current Population Reports*.

CHILDREN - AGE AND/OR SEX

U.S. Department of Commerce, Bureau of the Census, Suitland, Maryland 20233 (301) 763-4040; *Current Population Reports*.

CHILDREN - AID - SOCIAL WELFARE PROGRAMS

U.S. Department of Health and Human Services, Administration for Children and Families, 370 L'Enfant Promenade, SW, Washington, D.C. 20447 (202) 401-9200; *Quarterly Public Assistance Statistics*.

U.S. Department of Health and Human Services, Social Security Administration, 6401 Security Boulevard, Baltimore, Maryland 21235 (410) 965-1234; *Social Security Bulletin, Annual Statistical Supplement to the Social Security Bulletin*, and unpublished data.

U.S. Library of Congress, 10 First Street, SE, Washington, D.C. 20540 (202) 707-5000; *Cash and Non-Cash Benefits for Persons With Limited Income: Eligibility Rules, Recipient and Expenditure Data*.

CHILDREN - AID TO FAMILIES WITH DEPENDENT CHILDREN, RECIPIENTS AND PAYMENTS

U.S. Department of Health and Human Services, Administration for Children and Families, 370 L'Enfant Promenade, SW, Washington, D.C. 20447 (202) 401-9200; *Quarterly Public Assistance Statistics*.

U.S. Department of Health and Human Services, Social Security Administration, 6401 Security Boulevard, Baltimore, Maryland 21235 (410) 965-1234; *Annual Statistical Supplement to the Social Security Bulletin*, and *Social Security Bulletin*.

CHILDREN - AIDS

U.S. Department of Health and Human Services, Center for Disease Control, 1600 Clifton Road, NE, Atlanta, Georgia 30333 (404) 639-3311; *Surveillance Report*, and unpublished data.

CHILDREN - ALCOHOL USE

U.S. Department of Health and Human Services, National Center for Health Statistics, 3700 East-West Highway, Hyattsville, Maryland 20782 (301) 436-8500; *Vital and Health Statistics*, and unpublished data.

U.S. Department of Health and Human Services, Substance Abuse and Mental Health Services Administration, 5600 Fishers Lane, Rockville, Maryland 20857 (301) 443-4797; *National Household Survey on Drug Abuse*.

CHILDREN - ASTHMA

U.S. Department of Health and Human Services, National Center for Health Statistics, 3700 East-West Highway, Hyattsville, Maryland 20782 (301) 436-8500; *Vital and Health Statistics*, and unpublished data.

CHILDREN - BRONCHITIS, EMPHYSEMA

U.S. Department of Health and Human Services, National Center for Health Statistics, 3700 East-West Highway, Hyattsville, Maryland 20782 (301) 436-8500; *Health, United States*, and unpublished data.

CHILDREN - CHILD ABUSE

U.S. Department of Health and Human Services, National Center on Child Abuse and Neglect, 370 L'Enfant Promenade, SW, Washington, D.C. 20447 (202) 205-8586; *National Child Abuse and Neglect Data System*, and *Child Maltreatment*.

CHILDREN - CHILD DAY CARE

U.S. Department of Commerce, Bureau of the Census, Suitland, Maryland 20233 (301) 763-4040; *Current Population Reports, Census of Service Industries*, and unpublished data.

CHILDREN - CHILD SUPPORT

U.S. Department of Commerce, Bureau of the Census, Suitland, Maryland 20233 (301) 763-4040; *Current Population Reports*.

U.S. Department of Health and Human Services, Office of Child Support Enforcement, 370 L'Enfant Promenade, SW, Washington, D.C. 20447 (202) 401-9373; *Annual Report to Congress*.

CHILDREN - CHRONIC CONDITIONS

U.S. Department of Health and Human Services, National Center for Health Statistics, 3700 East-West Highway, Hyattsville, Maryland 20782 (301) 436-8500; *Vital and Health Statistics*, and unpublished data.

CHILDREN - CONGENITAL ABNORMALITIES

U.S. Department of Health and Human Services, National Center for Health Statistics, 3700 East-West Highway, Hyattsville, Maryland 20782 (301) 436-8500; *Health, United States*, and unpublished data.

CHILDREN - DAYS LOST FROM SCHOOL

U.S. Department of Health and Human Services, National Center for Health Statistics, 3700 East-West Highway, Hyattsville, Maryland 20782 (301) 436-8500; *Vital and Health Statistics,* and unpublished data.

CHILDREN - DEATHS AND DEATH RATES

Institute for Health and Aging, University of California, San Francisco, San Francisco, California 94143 (415) 476-9483; unpublished data.

U.S. Department of Health and Human Services, Centers for Disease Control, 1600 Clifton Road, NE, Atlanta, Georgia 30333 (404) 639-3311; *Surveillance Report,* and unpublished data.

U.S. Department of Health and Human Services, National Center for Health Statistics, 3700 East-West Highway, Hyattsville, Maryland 20782 (301) 436-8500; *Advance Data from Vital and Health Statistics, Monthly Vital Statistics Report,* and *Vital Statistics of the United States.*

CHILDREN - DEPENDENT AND NEGLECTED - IN INSTITUTIONS

U.S. Department of Commerce, Bureau of the Census, Suitland, Maryland 20233 (301) 763-4040; *Census of Population, General Population Characteristics.*

CHILDREN - DIABETES

U.S. Department of Health and Human Services, National Center for Health Statistics, 3700 East-West Highway, Hyattsville, Maryland 20782 (301) 436-8500; *Vital and Health Statistics,* and unpublished data.

CHILDREN - DIVORCE, INVOLVED IN

U.S. Department of Health and Human Services, National Center for Health Statistics, 3700 East West Highway, Hyattsville, Maryland 20782 (301) 436-8500; *Vital Statistics of the United States, Monthly Vital Statistics Report,* and unpublished data.

CHILDREN - DRUG USE

U.S. Department of Health and Human Services, Substance Abuse and Mental Health Services Administration, 5600 Fishers Lane. Rockville, Maryland 20857 (301) 443-4797; *National Household Survey on Drug Abuse.*

CHILDREN - FAMILIES WITH

U.S. Department of Commerce, Bureau of the Census, Suitland, Maryland 20233 (301) 763-4040; *Current Population Reports,* and *Census of Population.*

CHILDREN - FARM WORKERS

U.S. Department of Agriculture, Economic Research Service, Fourteenth Street and Independence Avenue, SW, Washington, D.C. 20250 (202) 219-1504; unpublished data.

CHILDREN - HEALTH INSURANCE COVERAGE

U.S. Department of Commerce, Bureau of the Census, Suitland, Maryland 20233 (301) 763-4040; *Current Population Reports,* and unpublished data.

U.S. Department of Health and Human Services, National Center for Health Statistics, 3700 East-West Highway, Hyattsville, Maryland 20782 (301) 436-8500; *Advance Data from Vital and Health Statistics.*

CHILDREN - HIGH SCHOOL DROPOUT

U.S. Department of Commerce, Bureau of the Census, Suitland, Maryland 20233 (301) 763-4040; *Current Population Reports,* and unpublished data.

CHILDREN - HISPANIC ORIGIN POPULATION

U.S. Department of Commerce, Bureau of the Census, Suitland, Maryland 20233 (301) 763-4040; *Census of Population, Current Population Reports,* and unpublished data.

CHILDREN - HOSPITAL USE

U.S. Department of Health and Human Services, National Center for Health Statistics, 3700 East-West Highway, Hyattsville, Maryland 20782 (301) 436-8500; *Vital and Health Statistics, Health, United States,* and unpublished data.

CHILDREN - IMMIGRANTS

U.S. Department of Justice, Immigration and Naturalization Service, 421 I Street, NW, Washington, D.C. 20536 (202) 514-4316; *Statistical Yearbook.*

CHILDREN - IMMUNIZATION AGAINST DISEASES

U.S. Department of Health and Human Services, Centers for Disease Control, 1600 Clifton Road, NE, Atlanta, Georgia 30333 (404) 639-3311; *National Health Interview Survey.*

CHILDREN - INJURIES

U.S. Department of Health and Human Services, National Center for Health Statistics, 3700 East-West Highway, Hyattsville, Maryland 20782 (301) 436-8500; *Vital and Health Statistics,* and unpublished data.

CHILDREN - JUVENILE DELINQUENCY

National Center for Juvenile Justice, 701 Forbes Avenue, Pittsburgh, Pennsylvania 15219 (412) 227-6950; *Juvenile Court Statistics.*

CHILDREN - LABOR FORCE (16 TO 19 YEARS OLD) - EMPLOYED

U.S. Department of Labor, Bureau of Labor Statistics, Two Massachusetts Avenue, NE, Washington, D.C. 20212 (202) 606-7828; *Employment and Earnings,* Bulletin 2307, and unpublished data.

CHILDREN - LABOR FORCE (16 TO 19 YEARS OLD) - EMPLOYMENT STATUS

U.S. Department of Labor, Bureau of Labor Statistics, Two Massachusetts Avenue, NE, Washington, D.C. 20212 (202) 606-7828; *Employment and Earnings.*

CHILDREN - LABOR FORCE (16 TO 19 YEARS OLD) - MINIMUM WAGE WORKERS

U.S. Department of Labor, Bureau of Labor Statistics, Two Massachusetts Avenue, NE, Washington, D.C. 20212 (202) 606-7828; unpublished data.

CHILDREN - LABOR FORCE (16 TO 19 YEARS OLD) -PARTICIPATION RATES

U.S. Department of Labor, Bureau of Labor Statistics, Two Massachusetts Avenue, NE, Washington, D.C. 20212 (202) 606-7828; *Bulletin 2217, Bulletin 2340*, and unpublished data.

CHILDREN - LABOR FORCE (16 TO 19 YEARS OLD) - RACE

U.S. Department of Labor, Bureau of Labor Statistics, Two Massachusetts Avenue, NE, Washington, D.C. 20212 (202) 606-7828; *Employment and Earnings*, and unpublished data.

CHILDREN - LABOR FORCE (16 TO 19 YEARS OLD) - SEX

U.S. Department of Labor, Bureau of Labor Statistics, Two Massachusetts Avenue, NE, Washington, D.C. 20212 (202) 606-7828; *Employment and Earnings, Monthly Labor Review*, and unpublished data.

CHILDREN - LABOR FORCE (16 TO 19 YEARS OLD) - UNEMPLOYED

U.S. Department of Labor, Bureau of Labor Statistics, Two Massachusetts Avenue, NE, Washington, D.C. 20212 (202) 606-7828; *Employment and Earnings*.

CHILDREN - MEDICAL DEVICE IMPLANTS

U.S. Department of Health and Human Services, National Center for Health Statistics, 3700 East-West Highway, Hyattsville, Maryland 20782 (301) 436-8500; *National Health Interview Survey*, and unpublished data.

CHILDREN - MOBILITY STATUS

U.S. Department of Commerce, Bureau of the Census, Suitland, Maryland 20233 (301) 763-4040; *Current Population Reports*.

CHILDREN - MOTHERS IN LABOR FORCE - BY AGE OF CHILDREN

U.S. Department of Labor, Bureau of Labor Statistics, *Employment and Earnings*, Bulletin 2307, and unpublished data.

CHILDREN - PNEUMONIA

U.S. Department of Health and Human Services, National Center for Health Statistics, 3700 East-West Highway, Hyattsville, Maryland 20782 (301) 436-8500; *Vital and Health Statistics, Health, United States*, and unpublished data.

CHILDREN - POVERTY

National Center for Children in Poverty, Columbia University, 154 Haven Avenue, Manhattan, New York 10032 (212) 927-8793; unpublished data.

U.S. Department of Commerce, Bureau of the Census, Suitland, Maryland 20233 (301) 763-4040; *Current Population Reports*.

CHILDREN - PRESENCE OF PARENTS

U.S. Department of Commerce, Bureau of the Census, Suitland, Maryland 20233 (301) 763-4040; *Current Population Reports*.

CHILDREN - PROJECTIONS

U.S. Department of Commerce, Bureau of the Census, Suitland, Maryland 20233 (301) 763-4040; *Current Population Reports*.

CHILDREN - RESPIRATORY INFECTION - ACUTE

U.S. Department of Health and Human Services, National Center for Health Statistics, 3700 East-West Highway, Hyattsville, Maryland 20782 (301) 436-8500; *Vital and Health Statistics, Health, United States*, and unpublished data.

CHILDREN - SCHOOL ENROLLMENT

U.S. Department of Commerce, Bureau of the Census, Suitland, Maryland 20233 (301) 763-4040; *Current Population Reports*, and unpublished data.

U.S. Department of Education, 400 Maryland Avenue, SW, Washington, D.C. 20202 (202) 708-5366; *Projections of Education Statistics*, and *Digest of Education Statistics*.

CHILDREN - SCHOOL ENROLLMENT - PREPRIMARY SCHOOL ENROLLMENT

U.S. Department of Commerce, Bureau of the Census, Suitland, Maryland 20233 (301) 763-4040; *Current Population Reports*, and unpublished data.

CHILDREN - SCHOOL ENROLLMENT - PROJECTIONS

U.S. Department of Education, 400 Maryland Avenue, SW, Washington, D.C. 20202 (202) 708-5366; *Digest of Education Statistics*, and *Projections of Education Statistics*.

CHILDREN - SOCIAL SECURITY BENEFICIARIES AND PAYMENTS

U.S. Department of Health and Human Services, Social Security Administration, 6401 Security Boulevard, Baltimore, Maryland 21235 (410) 965-1234; *Annual Statistical Supplement to the Social Security Bulletin*, and unpublished data.

CHILDREN - SUICIDES

U.S. Department of Health and Human Services, National Center for Health Statistics, 3700 East-West Highway, Hyattsville, Maryland 20782 (301) 436-8500; *Vital Statistics of the United States, Monthly Vital Statistics Report*, and *Advance Data from Vital and Health Statistics*.

Chile - National Statistical Office

Instituto Nacional de Estadisticas, Casilla 498-3, Santiago, Chile.

Chile - Primary Statistics Sources

Instituto Nacional de Estadisticas, Casilla 498-3, Santiago, Chile; *Anuario estadistico de Chile* (Statistical Yearbook of Chile), and *Sintesis Estadistica*, and *Compendio Estadistica*.

CHILE - AGRICULTURE

The Economist Intelligence Unit, 111 West 57th Street, New York, New York 10019 (800) 938-4685; *The New Latin America Market Atlas*.

Euromonitor Publications Limited, 87-88 Turnmill Street, London EC1M 5QU, England; *International Marketing Data and Statistics*, and *Third World Economic Handbook*.

Facts on File, 460 Park Avenue South, New York, New York 10016 (800) 443-8323; *The New Book of World Rankings*.

Federal Statistical Office, Gustav - Stresemann - Ring 11, D-6200 Wiesbaden, Germany; *Chile.*

Food and Agricultural Organization of the United Nations (FAO) Via delle Terme di Caracalla, 00100 Rome, Italy (Telephone Number in U.S. (202) 653-2400); *Production Yearbook, The State of Food and Agriculture,* and *Trade Yearbook.*

Gale Research Incorporated, 835 Penobscot Building, Detroit, Michigan 48226 (800) 877-4253; *International Historical Statistics The Americas and Australasia.*

G.K. Hall and Company, 70 Lincoln Street, Boston, Massachusetts 02111 (617) 423-3990; *The World in Figures.*

Inter-American Development Bank, 1300 New York Avenue, NW, Washington, D.C. 20577 (202) 623-1753; *Economic and Social Progress in Latin America.*

Statistical Office of the United Nations, Publishing Service, New York, New York 10017 (800) 253-9646; *Statistical Yearbook,* and *Statistical Yearbook for Latin America and the Caribbean.*

Times Books, 201 East 50th Street, New York, New York 10022 (212) 751-2600; *The Economist Book of Vital World Statistics.*

U.C.L.A. Latin American Center Publications, University of California, Los Angeles, California 90024 (310) 825-6634; *Statistical Abstract of Latin America.*

The World Bank, 1818 H Street, NW, Washington, D.C. 20433 (202) 477-1234; *World Tables.*

CHILE - AIRLINE SERVICE

The Economist Intelligence Unit, 111 West 57th Street, New York, New York 10019 (800) 938-4685; *The New Latin America Market Atlas.*

Facts on File, 460 Park Avenue South, New York, New York 10016 (800) 443-8323; *The New Book of World Rankings.*

G.K. Hall and Company, 70 Lincoln Street, Boston, Massachusetts 02111 (617) 423-3990; *The World in Figures.*

International Civil Aviation Organization, 1000 Sherbrooke Street West, Suite 400, Montreal, Quebec, Canada H3A 2R2 (514) 285-8219; *Civil Aviation Statistics of the World.*

Statistical Office of the United Nations, Publishing Service, New York, New York 10017 (800) 253-9646; *Statistical Yearbook.*

Times Books, 201 East 50th Street, New York, New York 10022 (212) 751-2600; *The Economist Book of Vital World Statistics.*

CHILE - ALUMINUM PRODUCTION AND CONSUMPTION - See CHILE - MINING AND MINERAL PRODUCTS

CHILE - ANIMAL FEEDINGSTUFFS OF AQUATIC ANIMAL ORIGIN

Statistical Office of the United Nations, Publishing Service, New York, New York 10017 (800) 253-9646; *Statistical Yearbook.*

CHILE - ANIMAL HEALTH

Food and Agricultural Organization of the United Nations (FAO), Via delle Terme di Caracalla, 00100 Rome, Italy (Telephone Number in U.S. (202) 653-2400); *Animal Health Yearbook.*

CHILE - ANTIMONY AND ANTIMONY ORE PRODUCTION AND CONSUMPTION - See CHILE - MINING AND MINERAL PRODUCTS

CHILE - AREA AND DENSITY OF POPULATION

Euromonitor Publications Limited, 87-88 Turnmill Street, London EC1M 5QU, England; *International Marketing Data and Statistics.*

Facts on File, 460 Park Avenue South, New York, New York 10016 (800) 443-8323; *The New Book of World Rankings.*

Federal Statistical Office, Gustav - Stresemann - Ring 11, D-6200 Wiesbaden, Germany; *Chile.*

Food and Agricultural Organization of the United Nations (FAO) Via delle Terme di Caracalla, 00100 Rome, Italy (Telephone Number in U.S. (202) 653-2400); *The State of Food and Agriculture.*

G.K. Hall and Company, 70 Lincoln Street, Boston, Massachusetts 02111 (617) 423-3990; *The World in Figures.*

Inter-American Development Bank, 1300 New York Avenue, NW, Washington, D.C. 20577 (202) 623-1753; *Economic and Social Progress in Latin America.*

Statistical Office of the United Nations, Publishing Service, New York, New York 10017 (800) 253-9646; *Statistical Yearbook.*

Times Books, 201 East 50th Street, New York, New York 10022 (212) 751-2600; *The Economist Book of Vital World Statistics.*

United Nations Educational, Scientific and Cultural Organization (UNESCO), 7 Place de Fontenoy, F-75700 Paris France (Telephone Number in U.S. (212) 963-5981); *Statistical Yearbook.*

CHILE - ARMS EXPORTS AND IMPORTS

U.S. Arms Control and Disarmament Agency, 320 Twenty-first Street, NW, Washington, D.C. 20451 (202) 647-8677; *World Military Expenditures and Arms Transfers.*

CHILE - ARTICHOKE PRODUCTION - See CHILE - CROPS

CHILE - BALANCE OF PAYMENTS

The Economist Intelligence Unit, 111 West 57th Street, New York, New York 10019 (800) 938-4685; *The New Latin America Market Atlas,* and *The World Market Atlas.*

Euromonitor Publications Limited, 87-88 Turnmill Street, London EC1M 5QU, England; *Third World Economic Handbook.*

Federal Statistical Office, Gustav - Stresemann - Ring 11, D-6200 Wiesbaden, Germany; *Chile.*

G.K. Hall and Company, 70 Lincoln Street, Boston, Massachusetts 02111 (617) 423-3990; *The World in Figures.*

Inter-American Development Bank, 1300 New York Avenue, NW, Washington, D.C. 20577 (202) 623-1753; *Economic and Social Progress in Latin America.*

International Monetary Fund, 700 Nineteenth Street, NW, Washington, D.C. 20431 (202) 623-7000; *Balance of Payments Yearbook.*

Organization of American States (OAS), General Secretariat, Washington, D.C. 20006 (202) 458-3533; *Statistical Bulletin of the OAS.*

Statistical Office of the United Nations, Publishing Service, New York, New York 10017 (800) 253-9646; *Economic Survey of Latin America and the Caribbean,* and *Statistical Yearbook for Latin America and the Caribbean.*

Times Books, 201 East 50th Street, New York, New York 10022 (212) 751-2600; *The Economist Book of Vital World Statistics.*

U.C.L.A. Latin American Center Publications, University of California, Los Angeles, California 90024 (310) 825-6634; *Statistical Abstract of Latin America.*

The World Bank, 1818 H Street, NW, Washington, D.C. 20433 (202) 477-1234; *World Tables.*

CHILE - BANKING

Facts on File, 460 Park Avenue South, New York, New York 10016 (800) 443-8323; *The New Book of World Rankings.*

G.K. Hall and Company, 70 Lincoln Street, Boston, Massachusetts 02111 (617) 423-3990; *The World in Figures.*

Inter-American Development Bank, 1300 New York Avenue, NW, Washington, D.C. 20577 (202) 623-1753; *Economic and Social Progress in Latin America,* and *Government Finance Statistics Yearbook,* and *International Financial Statistics.*

International Monetary Fund, 700 Nineteenth Street, NW, Washington, D.C. 20431 (202) 623-7000; *International Financial Statistics.*

Statistical Office of the United Nations, Publishing Service, New York, New York 10017 (800) 253-9646; *Statistical Yearbook for Latin America and the Caribbean.*

CHILE - BARLEY PRODUCTION - See CHILE - CROPS

CHILE - BAUXITE PRODUCTION AND CONSUMPTION - See CHILE - MINING AND MINERAL PRODUCTS

CHILE - BEER PRODUCTION

Facts on File, 460 Park Avenue South, New York, New York 10016 (800) 443-8323; *The New Book of World Rankings.*

Statistical Office of the United Nations, Publishing Service, New York, New York 10017 (800) 253-9646; *Statistical Yearbook.*

CHILE - BIRTH RATES

Euromonitor Publications Limited, 87-88 Turnmill Street, London EC1M 5QU, England; *Third World Economic Handbook.*

Facts on File, 460 Park Avenue South, New York, New York 10016 (800) 443-8323; *The New Book of World Rankings.*

Statistical Office of the United Nations, Publishing Service, New York, New York 10017 (800) 253-9646; *Demographic Yearbook, Statistical Yearbook,* and *Statistical Yearbook for Latin America and the Caribbean.*

Times Books, 201 East 50th Street, New York, New York 10022 (212) 751-2600; *The Economist Book of Vital World Statistics.*

The World Bank, 1818 H Street, NW, Washington, D.C. 20433 (202) 477-1234; *World Tables.*

World Health Organization, Office of Publications, Avenue Appia, CH-1211 Geneva 27, Switzerland (Telephone Number in U.S. (518) 436-9686); *World Health Statistics Annual.*

CHILE - BONDS

G.K. Hall and Company, 70 Lincoln Street, Boston, Massachusetts 02111 (617) 423-3990; *The World in Figures.*

Inter-American Development Bank, 1300 New York Avenue, NW, Washington, D.C. 20577 (202) 623-1753; *Economic and Social Progress in Latin America.*

International Monetary Fund, 700 Nineteenth Street, NW, Washington, D.C. 20431 (202) 623-7000; *Government Finance Statistics Yearbook.*

CHILE - BOOK PRODUCTION

G.K. Hall and Company, 70 Lincoln Street, Boston, Massachusetts 02111 (617) 423-3990; *The World in Figures.*

United Nations Educational, Scientific and Cultural Organization (UNESCO), 7 Place de Fontenoy, F-75700 Paris France (Telephone Number in U.S. (212) 963-5981); *Statistical Yearbook.*

CHILE - BROADCASTING

Billboard Limited, P.O. Box 9027, 1006 AA Amsterdam, The Netherlands (Telephone Number in U.S. (212) 764-7300); *World Radio TV Handbook.*

Facts on File, 460 Park Avenue South, New York, New York 10016 (800) 443-8323; *The New Book of World Rankings.*

G.K. Hall and Company, 70 Lincoln Street, Boston, Massachusetts 02111 (617) 423-3990; *The World in Figures.*

Times Books, 201 East 50th Street, New York, New York 10022 (212) 751-2600; *The Economist Book of Vital World Statistics.*

CHILE - BUSINESS

G.K. Hall and Company, 70 Lincoln Street, Boston, Massachusetts 02111 (617) 423-3990; *The World in Figures.*

Inter-American Development Bank, 1300 New York Avenue, NW, Washington, D.C. 20577 (202) 623-1753; *Economic and Social Progress in Latin America.*

CHILE - BUTTER - See CHILE - DAIRY PRODUCTS

CHILE - CABBAGE PRODUCTION - See CHILE - CROPS

CHILE - CADMIUM PRODUCTION AND CONSUMPTION - See CHILE - MINING AND MINERAL PRODUCTS

CHILE - CALORIE SUPPLY

Food and Agricultural Organization of the United Nations (FAO) Via delle Terme di Caracalla, 00100 Rome, Italy (Telephone Number in U.S. (202) 653-2400); *The State of Food and Agriculture.*

Statistical Office of the United Nations, Publishing Service, New York, New York 10017 (800) 253-9646; *Statistical Yearbook for Latin America and the Caribbean.*

CHILE - CAPITAL INVESTMENT

Inter-American Development Bank, 1300 New York Avenue, NW, Washington, D.C. 20577 (202) 623-1753; *Economic and Social Progress in Latin America.*

CHILE - CAPITAL REVENUE

Inter-American Development Bank, 1300 New York Avenue, NW, Washington, D.C. 20577 (202) 623-1753; *Economic and Social Progress in Latin America.*

International Monetary Fund, 700 Nineteenth Street, NW, Washington, D.C. 20431 (202) 623-7000; *Government Finance Statistics Yearbook.*

CHILE - CATTLE - See CHILE - LIVESTOCK AND POULTRY

CHILE - CAULIFLOWER PRODUCTION - See CHILE - CROPS

CHILE - CAUSTIC SODA PRODUCTION

Statistical Office of the United Nations, Publishing Service, New York, New York 10017 (800) 253-9646; *Statistical Yearbook.*

CHILE - CEMENT PRODUCTION - See CHILE - MINING AND MINERAL PRODUCTS

CHILE - CHEESE PRODUCTION - See CHILE - DAIRY PRODUCTS

CHILE - CHEMICAL (ORGANIC) PRODUCTION - See CHILE - MINING AND MINERAL PRODUCTS

CHILE - CHICK PEA PRODUCTION - See CHILE - CROPS

CHILE - CHICKENS - See CHILE - LIVESTOCK AND POULTRY

CHILE - CIGAR PRODUCTION - See CHILE - TOBACCO PRODUCTION

CHILE - CIGARETTE PRODUCTION - See CHILE - TOBACCO PRODUCTION

CHILE - CLASS STRUCTURE

G.K. Hall and Company, 70 Lincoln Street, Boston, Massachusetts 02111 (617) 423-3990; *The World in Figures.*

CHILE - CLIMATE

Facts on File, 460 Park Avenue South, New York, New York 10016 (800) 443-8323; *The New Book of World Rankings.*

G.K. Hall and Company, 70 Lincoln Street, Boston, Massachusetts 02111 (617) 423-3990; *The World in Figures.*

CHILE - CLOTHING EXPORTS AND IMPORTS

Euromonitor Publications Limited, 87-88 Turnmill Street, London EC1M 5QU, England; *Third World Economic Handbook.*

CHILE - COAL PRODUCTION - See CHILE - MINING AND MINERAL PRODUCTS

CHILE - COFFEE PRODUCTION - See CHILE - CROPS

CHILE - COKE OVEN COKE PRODUCTION AND CONSUMPTION - See CHILE - MINING AND MINERAL PRODUCTS

CHILE - COMMUNICATIONS

Euromonitor Publications Limited, 87-88 Turnmill Street, London EC1M 5QU, England; *Third World Economic Handbook.*

Federal Statistical Office, Gustav - Stresemann - Ring 11, D-6200 Wiesbaden, Germany; *Chile.*

G.K. Hall and Company, 70 Lincoln Street, Boston, Massachusetts 02111 (617) 423-3990; *The World in Figures.*

Inter-American Development Bank, 1300 New York Avenue, NW, Washington, D.C. 20577 (202) 623-1753; *Economic and Social Progress in Latin America.*

U.C.L.A. Latin American Center Publications, University of California, Los Angeles, California 90024 (310) 825-6634; *Statistical Abstract of Latin America.*

CHILE - CONSTRUCTION INDUSTRY

The Economist Intelligence Unit, 111 West 57th Street, New York, New York 10019 (800) 938-4685; *The New Latin America Market Atlas.*

Facts on File, 460 Park Avenue South, New York, New York 10016 (800) 443-8323; *The New Book of World Rankings.*

Inter-American Development Bank, 1300 New York Avenue, NW, Washington, D.C. 20577 (202) 623-1753; *Economic and Social Progress in Latin America.*

Organization of American States (OAS), General Secretariat, Washington, D.C. 20006 (202) 458-3533; *Statistical Bulletin of the OAS.*

Statistical Office of the United Nations, Publishing Service, New York, New York 10017 (800) 253-9646; *Construction Statistics Yearbook,* and *Statistical Yearbook.*

U.C.L.A. Latin American Center Publications, University of California, Los Angeles, California 90024 (310) 825-6634; *Statistical Abstract of Latin America.*

CHILE - CONSUMER PRICE INDEX

Federal Statistical Office, Gustav - Stresemann - Ring 11, D-6200 Wiesbaden, Germany; *Chile.*

G.K. Hall and Company, 70 Lincoln Street, Boston, Massachusetts 02111 (617) 423-3990; *The World in Figures.*

Statistical Office of the United Nations, Publishing Service, New York, New York 10017 (800) 253-9646; *Statistical Yearbook.*

CHILE - CONSUMER PRICES

The Economist Intelligence Unit, 111 West 57th Street, New York, New York 10019 (800) 938-4685; *The New Latin America Market Atlas.*

Federal Statistical Office, Gustav - Stresemann - Ring 11, D-6200 Wiesbaden, Germany; *Chile.*

International Labour Office, I.L.O. Publications, CH-1211, Geneva 22, Switzerland; *Yearbook of Labour Statistics.*

International Monetary Fund, 700 Nineteenth Street, NW, Washington, D.C. 20431 (202) 623-7000; *International Financial*

Statistics.

Organization of American States (OAS), General Secretariat, Washington, D.C. 20006 (202) 458-3533; *Statistical Bulletin of the OAS.*

Times Books, 201 East 50th Street, New York, New York 10022 (212) 751-2600; *The Economist Book of Vital World Statistics.*

U.C.L.A. Latin American Center Publications, University of California, Los Angeles, California 90024 (310) 825-6634; *Statistical Abstract of Latin America.*

CHILE - CONSUMPTION

The Economist Intelligence Unit, 111 West 57th Street, New York, New York 10019 (800) 938-4685; *The New Latin America Market Atlas.*

G.K. Hall and Company, 70 Lincoln Street, Boston, Massachusetts 02111 (617) 423-3990; *The World in Figures.*

Inter-American Development Bank, 1300 New York Avenue, NW, Washington, D.C. 20577 (202) 623-1753; *Economic and Social Progress in Latin America.*

Statistical Office of the United Nations, Publishing Service, New York, New York 10017 (800) 253-9646; *Statistical Yearbook for Latin America and the Caribbean.*

CHILE - COOPERATIVES

U.C.L.A. Latin American Center Publications, University of California, Los Angeles, California 90024 (310) 825-6634; *Statistical Abstract of Latin America.*

CHILE - COPPER - See CHILE - MINING AND MINERAL PRODUCTS

CHILE - CORPORATE INCOME TAXES - See CHILE - TAXATION

CHILE - CORPORATE TAXES - See CHILE - TAXATION

CHILE - CORN PRODUCTION - See CHILE - CROPS

CHILE - COTTON - See CHILE - CROPS

CHILE - CRIME

International Criminal Police Organization (INTERPOL), 26 rue Armengaud, 92210 Saint Cloud, France; *International Crime Statistics.*

Yale University Press, Yale Station, New Haven, Connecticut 06520 (203) 432-0940; *Violence and Crime in Cross-National Perspective.*

CHILE - CROPS

The Economist Intelligence Unit, 111 West 57th Street, New York, New York 10019 (800) 938-4685; *The New Latin America Market Atlas.*

Facts on File, 460 Park Avenue South, New York, New York 10016 (800) 443-8323; *The New Book of World Rankings.*

Food and Agricultural Organization of the United Nations (FAO) Via delle Terme di Caracalla, 00100 Rome, Italy (Telephone Number in U.S. (202) 653-2400); *Production Yearbook,* and *The State of Food and Agriculture.*

G.K. Hall and Company, 70 Lincoln Street, Boston, Massachusetts 02111 (617) 423-3990; *The World in Figures.*

Statistical Office of the United Nations, Publishing Service, New York, New York 10017 (800) 253-9646; *Statistical Yearbook.*

CHILE - CUSTOMS DUTIES

G.K. Hall and Company, 70 Lincoln Street, Boston, Massachusetts 02111 (617) 423-3990; *The World in Figures.*

Inter-American Development Bank, 1300 New York Avenue, NW, Washington, D.C. 20577 (202) 623-1753; *Economic and Social Progress in Latin America.*

International Monetary Fund, 700 Nineteenth Street, NW, Washington, D.C. 20431 (202) 623-7000; *Government Finance Statistics Yearbook.*

CHILE - DAIRY PRODUCTS

Facts on File, 460 Park Avenue South, New York, New York 10016 (800) 443-8323; *The New Book of World Rankings.*

Food and Agricultural Organization of the United Nations (FAO) Via delle Terme di Caracalla, 00100 Rome, Italy (Telephone Number in U.S. (202) 653-2400); *The State of Food and Agriculture.*

Statistical Office of the United Nations, Publishing Service, New York, New York 10017 (800) 253-9646; *Statistical Yearbook.*

CHILE - DEATH RATE

Euromonitor Publications Limited, 87-88 Turnmill Street, London EC1M 5QU, England; *Third World Economic Handbook.*

G.K. Hall and Company, 70 Lincoln Street, Boston, Massachusetts 02111 (617) 423-3990; *The World in Figures.*

Statistical Office of the United Nations, Publishing Service, New York, New York 10017 (800) 253-9646; *Statistical Yearbook,* and *Statistical Yearbook for Latin America and the Caribbean.*

Times Books, 201 East 50th Street, New York, New York 10022 (212) 751-2600; *The Economist Book of Vital World Statistics.*

World Health Organization, Office of Publications, Avenue Appia, CH-1211 Geneva 27, Switzerland (Telephone Number in U.S. (518) 436-9686); *World Health Statistics Annual.*

CHILE - DEBT

The Economist Intelligence Unit, 111 West 57th Street, New York, New York 10019 (800) 938-4685; *The New Latin America Market Atlas.*

CHILE - DEFENSE EXPENDITURES

The Economist Intelligence Unit, 111 West 57th Street, New York, New York 10019 (800) 938-4685; *The New Latin America Market Atlas.*

G.K. Hall and Company, 70 Lincoln Street, Boston, Massachusetts 02111 (617) 423-3990; *The World in Figures.*

International Monetary Fund, 700 Nineteenth Street, NW, Washington, D.C. 20431 (202) 623-7000; *Government Finance Statistics Yearbook.*

U.S. Arms Control and Disarmament Agency, 320 Twenty-first Street, NW, Washington, D.C. 20451 (202) 647-8677; *World Military Expenditures and Arms Transfers.*

CHILE - DEMOGRAPHY

The Economist Intelligence Unit, 111 West 57th Street, New York, New York 10019 (800) 938-4685; *The World Market Atlas.*

Facts on File, 460 Park Avenue South, New York, New York 10016 (800) 443-8323; *The New Book of World Rankings.*

Federal Statistical Office, Gustav - Stresemann - Ring 11, D-6200 Wiesbaden, Germany; *Chile.*

G.K. Hall and Company, 70 Lincoln Street, Boston, Massachusetts 02111 (617) 423-3990; *The World in Figures.*

CHILE - DEVELOPMENT ASSISTANCE

G.K. Hall and Company, 70 Lincoln Street, Boston, Massachusetts 02111 (617) 423-3990; *The World in Figures.*

Inter-American Development Bank, 1300 New York Avenue, NW, Washington, D.C. 20577 (202) 623-1753; *Economic and Social Progress in Latin America.*

Statistical Office of the United Nations, Publishing Service, New York, New York 10017 (800) 253-9646; *Statistical Yearbook.*

CHILE - DIAMOND PRODUCTION - See CHILE - MINING AND MINERAL PRODUCTS

CHILE - DISCOUNT RATES

Inter-American Development Bank, 1300 New York Avenue, NW, Washington, D.C. 20577 (202) 623-1753; *Economic and Social Progress in Latin America.*

CHILE - DISEASE

G.K. Hall and Company, 70 Lincoln Street, Boston, Massachusetts 02111 (617) 423-3990; *The World in Figures.*

World Health Organization, Office of Publications, Avenue Appia, CH-1211 Geneva 27, Switzerland (Telephone Number in U.S. (518) 436-9686); *World Health Statistics Annual.*

CHILE - DIVORCE RATES

Facts on File, 460 Park Avenue South, New York, New York 10016 (800) 443-8323; *The New Book of World Rankings.*

Statistical Office of the United Nations, Publishing Service, New York, New York 10017 (800) 253-9646; *Demographic Yearbook,* and *Statistical Yearbook.*

CHILE - DOMESTIC PRODUCT

G.K. Hall and Company, 70 Lincoln Street, Boston, Massachusetts 02111 (617) 423-3990; *The World in Figures.*

CHILE - ECONOMY

Euromonitor Publications Limited, 87-88 Turnmill Street, London EC1M 5QU, England; *International Marketing Data and Statistics,* and *Third World Economic Handbook.*

Facts on File, 460 Park Avenue South, New York, New York 10016 (800) 443-8323; *The New Book of World Rankings.*

Federal Statistical Office, Gustav - Stresemann - Ring 11, D-6200 Wiesbaden, Germany; *Chile.*

G.K. Hall and Company, 70 Lincoln Street, Boston, Massachusetts 02111 (617) 423-3990; *The World in Figures.*

Inter-American Development Bank, 1300 New York Avenue, NW, Washington, D.C. 20577 (202) 623-1753; *Economic and Social Progress in Latin America.*

Organization of American States (OAS), General Secretariat, Washington, D.C. 20006 (202) 458-3533; *Statistical Bulletin of the OAS.*

Statistical Office of the United Nations, Publishing Service, New York, New York 10017 (800) 253-9646; *Economic Survey of Latin America and the Caribbean.*

U.C.L.A. Latin American Center Publications, University of California, Los Angeles, California 90024 (310) 825-6634; *Statistical Abstract of Latin America.*

CHILE - EDUCATION

The Economist Intelligence Unit, 111 West 57th Street, New York, New York 10019 (800) 938-4685; *The New Latin America Market Atlas,* and *The World Market Atlas.*

Facts on File, 460 Park Avenue South, New York, New York 10016 (800) 443-8323; *The New Book of World Rankings.*

Federal Statistical Office, Gustav - Stresemann - Ring 11, D-6200 Wiesbaden, Germany; *Chile.*

Gale Research Incorporated, 835 Penobscot Building, Detroit, Michigan 48226 (800) 877-4253; *International Historical Statistics The Americas and Australasia.*

G.K. Hall and Company, 70 Lincoln Street, Boston, Massachusetts 02111 (617) 423-3990; *The World in Figures.*

International Monetary Fund, 700 Nineteenth Street, NW, Washington, D.C. 20431 (202) 623-7000; *Government Finance Statistics Yearbook.*

Statistical Office of the United Nations, Publishing Service, New York, New York 10017 (800) 253-9646; *Statistical Yearbook for Latin America and the Caribbean.*

Times Books, 201 East 50th Street, New York, New York 10022 (212) 751-2600; *The Economist Book of Vital World Statistics.*

U.C.L.A. Latin American Center Publications, University of California, Los Angeles, California 90024 (310) 825-6634; *Statistical Abstract of Latin America.*

United Nations Educational, Scientific and Cultural Organization (UNESCO), 7 Place de Fontenoy, F-75700 Paris France (Telephone Number in U.S. (212) 963-5981); *Statistical Yearbook.*

The World Bank, 1818 H Street, NW, Washington, D.C. 20433 (202) 477-1234; *World Tables.*

CHILE - EGG PRODUCTION - See CHILE - DAIRY PRODUCTS

CHILE - ELECTRICITY

The Economist Intelligence Unit, 111 West 57th Street, New York, New York 10019 (800) 938-4685; *The New Latin America Market Atlas.*

Facts on File, 460 Park Avenue South, New York, New York 10016 (800) 443-8323; *The New Book of World Rankings.*

Inter-American Development Bank, 1300 New York Avenue, NW, Washington, D.C. 20577 (202) 623-1753; *Economic and Social Progress in Latin America.*

Organization of American States (OAS), General Secretariat, Washington, D.C. 20006 (202) 458-3533; *Statistical Bulletin of the OAS.*

Penn Well Publishing Company, 1421 South Sheridan Road, P.O. Box 1260, Tulsa, Oklahoma 74101 (800) 752-9764; *International Energy Statistics Sourcebook.*

Statistical Office of the United Nations, Publishing Service, New York, New York 10017 (800) 253-9646; *Statistical Yearbook.*

Times Books, 201 East 50th Street, New York, New York 10022 (212) 751-2600; *The Economist Book of Vital World Statistics.*

CHILE - EMPLOYMENT

Euromonitor Publications Limited, 87-88 Turnmill Street, London EC1M 5QU, England; *International Marketing Data and Statistics.*

Facts on File, 460 Park Avenue South, New York, New York 10016 (800) 443-8323; *The New Book of World Rankings.*

Federal Statistical Office, Gustav - Stresemann - Ring 11, D-6200 Wiesbaden, Germany; *Chile.*

International Labour Office, I.L.O. Publications, CH-1211, Geneva 22, Switzerland; *Yearbook of Labour Statistics.*

Organization of American States (OAS), General Secretariat, Washington, D.C. 20006 (202) 458-3533; *Statistical Bulletin of the OAS.*

Statistical Office of the United Nations, Publishing Service, New York, New York 10017 (800) 253-9646; *Statistical Yearbook for Latin America and the Caribbean.*

U.C.L.A. Latin American Center Publications, University of California, Los Angeles, California 90024 (310) 825-6634; *Statistical Abstract of Latin America.*

CHILE - ENERGY

The Economist Intelligence Unit, 111 West 57th Street, New York, New York 10019 (800) 938-4685; *The New Latin America Market Atlas.*

Facts on File, 460 Park Avenue South, New York, New York 10016 (800) 443-8323; *The New Book of World Rankings.*

Food and Agricultural Organization of the United Nations (FAO) Via delle Terme di Caracalla, 00100 Rome, Italy (Telephone Number in U.S. (202) 653-2400); *The State of Food and Agriculture.*

G.K. Hall and Company, 70 Lincoln Street, Boston, Massachusetts 02111 (617) 423-3990; *The World in Figures.*

Penn Well Publishing Company, 1421 South Sheridan Road, P.O. Box 1260, Tulsa, Oklahoma 74101 (800) 752-9764; *International Energy Statistics Sourcebook.*

Statistical Office of the United Nations, Publishing Service, New York, New York 10017 (800) 253-9646; *Energy Statistics Yearbook,* and *Statistical Yearbook for Latin America and the Caribbean.*

Times Books, 201 East 50th Street, New York, New York 10022 (212) 751-2600; *The Economist Book of Vital World Statistics.*

U.C.L.A. Latin American Center Publications, University of California, Los Angeles, California 90024 (310) 825-6634; *Statistical Abstract of Latin America.*

CHILE - EXCHANGE RATES

Euromonitor Publications Limited, 87-88 Turnmill Street, London EC1M 5QU, England; *International Marketing Data and Statistics.*

Inter-American Development Bank, 1300 New York Avenue, NW, Washington, D.C. 20577 (202) 623-1753; *Economic and Social Progress in Latin America.*

International Civil Aviation Organization, 1000 Sherbrooke Street West, Suite 400, Montreal, Quebec, Canada H3A 2R2 (514) 285-8219; *Civil Aviation Statistics of the World.*

International Monetary Fund, 700 Nineteenth Street, NW, Washington, D.C. 20431 (202) 623-7000; *International Financial Statistics.*

Organization of American States (OAS), General Secretariat, Washington, D.C. 20006 (202) 458-3533; *Statistical Bulletin of the OAS.*

Statistical Office of the United Nations, Publishing Service, New York, New York 10017 (800) 253-9646; *Statistical Yearbook.*

U.C.L.A. Latin American Center Publications, University of California, Los Angeles, California 90024 (310) 825-6634; *Statistical Abstract of Latin America.*

CHILE - EXCISE TAXES - See CHILE - TAXATION

CHILE - EXPORTS

American Automobile Manufacturers Association, 1401 H Street, NW, Suite 900, Washington, D.C. 20005 (202) 326-5500; *World Motor Vehicle Data.*

The Economist Intelligence Unit, 111 West 57th Street, New York, New York 10019 (800) 938-4685; *The New Latin America Market Atlas,* and *The World Market Atlas.*

Euromonitor Publications Limited, 87-88 Turnmill Street, London EC1M 5QU, England; *International Marketing Data and Statistics,* and *Third World Economic Handbook.*

Food and Agricultural Organization of the United Nations (FAO) Via delle Terme di Caracalla, 00100 Rome, Italy (Telephone Number in U.S. (202) 653-2400); *The State of Food and Agriculture.*

G.K. Hall and Company, 70 Lincoln Street, Boston, Massachusetts 02111 (617) 423-3990; *The World in Figures.*

Inter-American Development Bank, 1300 New York Avenue, NW, Washington, D.C. 20577 (202) 623-1753; *Economic and Social Progress in Latin America.*

International Monetary Fund, 700 Nineteenth Street, NW, Washington, D.C. 20431 (202) 623-7000; *Direction of Trade Statistics*, and *International Financial Statistics*.

Organization of American States (OAS), General Secretariat, Washington, D.C. 20006 (202) 458-3533; *Statistical Bulletin of the OAS*.

Statistical Office of the United Nations, Publishing Service, New York, New York 10017 (800) 253-9646; *Statistical Yearbook for Latin America and the Caribbean*, and *Trade in Manufactures of Developing Countries*.

Times Books, 201 East 50th Street, New York, New York 10022 (212) 751-2600; *The Economist Book of Vital World Statistics*.

The World Bank, 1818 H Street, NW, Washington, D.C. 20433 (202) 477-1234; *World Tables*.

CHILE - EXTERNAL FINANCING

Inter-American Development Bank, 1300 New York Avenue, NW, Washington, D.C. 20577 (202) 623-1753; *Economic and Social Progress in Latin America*.

Statistical Office of the United Nations, Publishing Service, New York, New York 10017 (800) 253-9646; *Statistical Yearbook for Latin America and the Caribbean*.

CHILE - EXTERNAL INDEBTEDNESS

Euromonitor Publications Limited, 87-88 Turnmill Street, London EC1M 5QU, England; *Third World Economic Handbook*.

Inter-American Development Bank, 1300 New York Avenue, NW, Washington, D.C. 20577 (202) 623-1753; *Economic and Social Progress in Latin America*.

Statistical Office of the United Nations, Publishing Service, New York, New York 10017 (800) 253-9646; *Statistical Yearbook for Latin America and the Caribbean*.

The World Bank, 1818 H Street, NW, Washington, D.C. 20433 (202) 477-1234; *World Tables*.

CHILE - EXTERNAL TRADE

Food and Agricultural Organization of the United Nations (FAO) Via delle Terme di Caracalla, 00100 Rome, Italy (Telephone Number in U.S. (202) 653-2400); *The State of Food and Agriculture*, and *Trade Yearbook*.

Gale Research Incorporated, 835 Penobscot Building, Detroit, Michigan 48226 (800) 877-4253; *International Historical Statistics The Americas and Australasia*.

G.K. Hall and Company, 70 Lincoln Street, Boston, Massachusetts 02111 (617) 423-3990; *The World in Figures*.

Inter-American Development Bank, 1300 New York Avenue, NW, Washington, D.C. 20577 (202) 623-1753; *Economic and Social Progress in Latin America*.

Statistical Office of the United Nations, Publishing Service, New York, New York 10017 (800) 253-9646; *Statistical Yearbook*, and *Statistical Yearbook for Latin America and the Caribbean*.

CHILE - FABRIC PRODUCTION - See CHILE - TEXTILE INDUSTRY

CHILE - FAMILY PLANNING

U.C.L.A. Latin American Center Publications, University of California, Los Angeles, California 90024 (310) 825-6634; *Statistical Abstract of Latin America*.

CHILE - FARM CROPS - See CHILE - CROPS

CHILE - FEMALE WORKING POPULATION - See CHILE - EMPLOYMENT

CHILE - FERTILITY RATES

Facts on File, 460 Park Avenue South, New York, New York 10016 (800) 443-8323; *The New Book of World Rankings*.

Times Books, 201 East 50th Street, New York, New York 10022 (212) 751-2600; *The Economist Book of Vital World Statistics*.

The World Bank, 1818 H Street, NW, Washington, D.C. 20433 (202) 477-1234; *World Tables*.

CHILE - FERTILIZER

The Economist Intelligence Unit, 111 West 57th Street, New York, New York 10019 (800) 938-4685; *The New Latin America Market Atlas*.

Food and Agricultural Organization of the United Nations (FAO), Via delle Terme di Caracalla, 00100 Rome, Italy (Telephone Number in U.S. (202) 653-2400); *Fertilizer Yearbook*, and *The State of Food and Agriculture*.

Statistical Office of the United Nations, Publishing Service, New York, New York 10017 (800) 253-9646; *Statistical Yearbook*.

CHILE - FETAL MORTALITY

Statistical Office of the United Nations, Publishing Service, New York, New York 10017 (800) 253-9646; *Demographic Yearbook*.

CHILE - FIBRE PRODUCTION - See CHILE - TEXTILE INDUSTRY

CHILE - FILAMENT PRODUCTION - See CHILE - TEXTILE INDUSTRY

CHILE - FINANCE

Facts on File, 460 Park Avenue South, New York, New York 10016 (800) 443-8323; *The New Book of World Rankings*.

Federal Statistical Office, Gustav - Stresemann - Ring 11, D-6200 Wiesbaden, Germany; *Chile*.

Gale Research Incorporated, 835 Penobscot Building, Detroit, Michigan 48226 (800) 877-4253; *International Historical Statistics The Americas and Australasia*.

G.K. Hall and Company, 70 Lincoln Street, Boston, Massachusetts 02111 (617) 423-3990; *The World in Figures*.

Inter-American Development Bank, 1300 New York Avenue, NW, Washington, D.C. 20577 (202) 623-1753; *Economic and Social Progress in Latin America*.

International Monetary Fund, 700 Nineteenth Street, NW, Washington, D.C. 20431 (202) 623-7000; *Government Finance Statistics Yearbook*, and *International Financial Statistics*.

Organization of American States (OAS), General Secretariat, Washington, D.C. 20006 (202) 458-3533; *Statistical Bulletin of the OAS.*

U.C.L.A. Latin American Center Publications, University of California, Los Angeles, California 90024 (310) 825-6634; *Statistical Abstract of Latin America.*

CHILE - FISHERIES

Facts on File, 460 Park Avenue South, New York, New York 10016 (800) 443-8323; *The New Book of World Rankings.*

Federal Statistical Office, Gustav - Stresemann - Ring 11, D-6200 Wiesbaden, Germany; *Chile.*

Food and Agricultural Organization of the United Nations (FAO) Via delle Terme di Caracalla, 00100 Rome, Italy (Telephone Number in U.S. (202) 653-2400); *The State of Food and Agriculture,* and *Yearbook of Fishery Statistics.*

Inter-American Development Bank, 1300 New York Avenue, NW, Washington, D.C. 20577 (202) 623-1753; *Economic and Social Progress in Latin America.*

Statistical Office of the United Nations, Publishing Service, New York, New York 10017 (800) 253-9646; *Statistical Yearbook.*

U.C.L.A. Latin American Center Publications, University of California, Los Angeles, California 90024 (310) 825-6634; *Statistical Abstract of Latin America.*

CHILE - FLAX FIBRE PRODUCTION - See CHILE - TEXTILE INDUSTRY

CHILE - FLOUR PRODUCTION

Statistical Office of the United Nations, Publishing Service, New York, New York 10017 (800) 253-9646; *Statistical Yearbook.*

CHILE - FOOD

Food and Agricultural Organization of the United Nations (FAO) Via delle Terme di Caracalla, 00100 Rome, Italy (Telephone Number in U.S. (202) 653-2400); *Production Yearbook,* and *The State of Food and Agriculture.*

G.K. Hall and Company, 70 Lincoln Street, Boston, Massachusetts 02111 (617) 423-3990; *The World in Figures.*

CHILE - FOREIGN AID

G.K. Hall and Company, 70 Lincoln Street, Boston, Massachusetts 02111 (617) 423-3990; *The World in Figures.*

Inter-American Development Bank, 1300 New York Avenue, NW, Washington, D.C. 20577 (202) 623-1753; *Economic and Social Progress in Latin America.*

CHILE - FOREIGN DEBT

The Economist Intelligence Unit, 111 West 57th Street, New York, New York 10019 (800) 938-4685; *The New Latin America Market Atlas.*

Inter-American Development Bank, 1300 New York Avenue, NW, Washington, D.C. 20577 (202) 623-1753; *Economic and Social Progress in Latin America.*

International Monetary Fund, 700 Nineteenth Street, NW, Washington, D.C. 20431 (202) 623-7000; *Government Finance Statistics Yearbook.*

CHILE - FOREIGN FINANCE

Inter-American Development Bank, 1300 New York Avenue, NW, Washington, D.C. 20577 (202) 623-1753; *Economic and Social Progress in Latin America.*

CHILE - FOREIGN INDEBTEDNESS

Inter-American Development Bank, 1300 New York Avenue, NW, Washington, D.C. 20577 (202) 623-1753; *Economic and Social Progress in Latin America.*

Statistical Office of the United Nations, Publishing Service, New York, New York 10017 (800) 253-9646; *Economic Survey of Latin America and the Caribbean.*

CHILE - FOREIGN INVESTMENT

The Economist Intelligence Unit, 111 West 57th Street, New York, New York 10019 (800) 938-4685; *The New Latin America Market Atlas.*

CHILE - FOREIGN TRADE

The Economist Intelligence Unit, 111 West 57th Street, New York, New York 10019 (800) 938-4685; *The New Latin America Market Atlas.*

Euromonitor Publications Limited, 87-88 Turnmill Street, London EC1M 5QU, England; *Third World Economic Handbook.*

Facts on File, 460 Park Avenue South, New York, New York 10016 (800) 443-8323; *The New Book of World Rankings.*

Food and Agricultural Organization of the United Nations (FAO), Via delle Terme di Caracalla, 00100 Rome, Italy (Telephone Number in U.S. (202) 653-2400); *Production Yearbook.*

Federal Statistical Office, Gustav - Stresemann - Ring 11, D-6200 Wiesbaden, Germany; *Chile.*

G.K. Hall and Company, 70 Lincoln Street, Boston, Massachusetts 02111 (617) 423-3990; *The World in Figures.*

Inter-American Development Bank, 1300 New York Avenue, NW, Washington, D.C. 20577 (202) 623-1753; *Economic and Social Progress in Latin America.*

International Monetary Fund, 700 Nineteenth Street, NW, Washington, D.C. 20431 (202) 623-7000; *International Financial Statistics.*

Organisation for Economic Co-operation and Development (OECD), 2 rue Andre-Pascal, 75 Paris 16, France; *Trade by Commodities.*

Statistical Office of the United Nations, Publishing Service, New York, New York 10017 (800) 253-9646; *Economic Survey of Latin America and the Caribbean, International Trade Statistics Yearbook,* and *Statistical Yearbook.*

U.C.L.A. Latin American Center Publications, University of California, Los Angeles, California 90024 (310) 825-6634; *Statistical Abstract of Latin America.*

The World Bank, 1818 H Street, NW, Washington, D.C. 20433 (202) 477-1234; *World Tables*.

World Bureau of Metal Statistics, 27-A High Street, Ware Hert SG12 9BA, England; *World Metal Statistics*.

CHILE - FORESTRY AND FOREST PRODUCTS

The Economist Intelligence Unit, 111 West 57th Street, New York, New York 10019 (800) 938-4685; *The New Latin America Market Atlas*.

Euromonitor Publications Limited, 87-88 Turnmill Street, London EC1M 5QU, England; *Third World Economic Handbook*.

Facts on File, 460 Park Avenue South, New York, New York 10016 (800) 443-8323; *The New Book of World Rankings*.

Federal Statistical Office, Gustav - Stresemann - Ring 11, D-6200 Wiesbaden, Germany; *Chile*.

Food and Agricultural Organization of the United Nations (FAO) Via delle Terme di Caracalla, 00100 Rome, Italy (Telephone Number in U.S. (202) 653-2400); *The State of Food and Agriculture*, and *Yearbook of Forest Products*.

Forest and Paper Association, 1250 Connecticut Avenue, NW, Washington, D.C. 20036 (202) 463-2455; *Wood Pulp and Fiber Statistics*.

G.K. Hall and Company, 70 Lincoln Street, Boston, Massachusetts 02111 (617) 423-3990; *The World in Figures*.

Inter-American Development Bank, 1300 New York Avenue, NW, Washington, D.C. 20577 (202) 623-1753; *Economic and Social Progress in Latin America*.

Statistical Office of the United Nations, Publishing Service, New York, New York 10017 (800) 253-9646; *Statistical Yearbook*.

U.C.L.A. Latin American Center Publications, University of California, Los Angeles, California 90024 (310) 825-6634; *Statistical Abstract of Latin America*.

United Nations Educational, Scientific and Cultural Organization (UNESCO), 7 Place de Fontenoy, F-75700 Paris France (Telephone Number in U.S. (212) 963-5981); *Statistical Yearbook*.

CHILE - GARLIC PRODUCTION - See CHILE - CROPS

CHILE - GAS LIQUIDS (NATURAL) PRODUCTION - See CHILE - MINING AND MINERAL PRODUCTS

CHILE - GAS PRODUCTION - See CHILE - MINING AND MINERAL PRODUCTS

CHILE - GENERAL INDUSTRIAL STATISTICS

Federal Statistical Office, Gustav - Stresemann - Ring 11, D-6200 Wiesbaden, Germany; *Chile*.

Statistical Office of the United Nations, Publishing Service, New York, New York 10017 (800) 253-9646; *Industrial Statistics Yearbook*.

CHILE - GENERAL MORTALITY

Statistical Office of the United Nations, Publishing Service, New York, New York 10017 (800) 253-9646; *Demographic Yearbook*.

World Health Organization, Office of Publications, Avenue Appia, CH-1211 Geneva 27, Switzerland (Telephone Number in U.S. (518) 436-9686); *World Health Statistics Annual*.

CHILE - GEOGRAPHIC DATA

Facts on File, 460 Park Avenue South, New York, New York 10016 (800) 443-8323; *The New Book of World Rankings*.

Federal Statistical Office, Gustav - Stresemann - Ring 11, D-6200 Wiesbaden, Germany; *Chile*.

U.C.L.A. Latin American Center Publications, University of California, Los Angeles, California 90024 (310) 825-6634; *Statistical Abstract of Latin America*.

CHILE - GOATS - See CHILE - LIVESTOCK AND POULTRY

CHILE - GOLD HOLDINGS

International Monetary Fund, 700 Nineteenth Street, NW, Washington, D.C. 20431 (202) 623-7000; *International Financial Statistics*.

Statistical Office of the United Nations, Publishing Service, New York, New York 10017 (800) 253-9646; *Statistical Yearbook*.

The World Bank, 1818 H Street, NW, Washington, D.C. 20433 (202) 477-1234; *World Tables*.

CHILE - GOLD PRODUCTION AND CONSUMPTION - See CHILE - MINING AND MINERAL PRODUCTS

CHILE - GOLD RESERVES

The Economist Intelligence Unit, 111 West 57th Street, New York, New York 10019 (800) 938-4685; *The New Latin America Market Atlas*.

CHILE - GOVERNMENT

G.K. Hall and Company, 70 Lincoln Street, Boston, Massachusetts 02111 (617) 423-3990; *The World in Figures*.

Inter-American Development Bank, 1300 New York Avenue, NW, Washington, D.C. 20577 (202) 623-1753; *Economic and Social Progress in Latin America*.

CHILE - GOVERNMENT BONDS - See CHILE - BONDS

CHILE - GOVERNMENT CONSUMPTION

Inter-American Development Bank, 1300 New York Avenue, NW, Washington, D.C. 20577 (202) 623-1753; *Economic and Social Progress in Latin America*.

CHILE - GOVERNMENT EXPENDITURES

Euromonitor Publications Limited, 87-88 Turnmill Street, London EC1M 5QU, England; *Third World Economic Handbook*.

Inter-American Development Bank, 1300 New York Avenue, NW, Washington, D.C. 20577 (202) 623-1753; *Economic and Social Progress in Latin America*.

International Monetary Fund, 700 Nineteenth Street, NW, Washington, D.C. 20431 (202) 623-7000; *Government Finance Statistics Yearbook*.

The World Bank, 1818 H Street, NW, Washington, D.C. 20433 (202) 477-1234; *World Tables.*

CHILE - GOVERNMENT FINANCES

Inter-American Development Bank, 1300 New York Avenue, NW, Washington, D.C. 20577 (202) 623-1753; *Economic and Social Progress in Latin America.*

International Monetary Fund, 700 Nineteenth Street, NW, Washington, D.C. 20431 (202) 623-7000; *International Financial Statistics.*

Statistical Office of the United Nations, Publishing Service, New York, New York 10017 (800) 253-9646; *Statistical Yearbook.*

CHILE - GOVERNMENT REVENUE

Inter-American Development Bank, 1300 New York Avenue, NW, Washington, D.C. 20577 (202) 623-1753; *Economic and Social Progress in Latin America.*

International Monetary Fund, 700 Nineteenth Street, NW, Washington, D.C. 20431 (202) 623-7000; *Government Finance Statistics Yearbook.*

Times Books, 201 East 50th Street, New York, New York 10022 (212) 751-2600; *The Economist Book of Vital World Statistics.*

U.C.L.A. Latin American Center Publications, University of California, Los Angeles, California 90024 (310) 825-6634; *Statistical Abstract of Latin America.*

The World Bank, 1818 H Street, NW, Washington, D.C. 20433 (202) 477-1234; *World Tables.*

CHILE - GRAIN PRODUCTION - See CHILE - CROPS

CHILE - GRANTS

International Monetary Fund, 700 Nineteenth Street, NW, Washington, D.C. 20431 (202) 623-7000; *Government Finance Statistics Yearbook.*

CHILE - GREEN PEPPER AND CHILIE PRODUCTION - See CHILE - CROPS

CHILE - GROSS DOMESTIC PRODUCT

The Economist Intelligence Unit, 111 West 57th Street, New York, New York 10019 (800) 938-4685; *The New Latin America Market Atlas,* and *The World Market Atlas.*

Euromonitor Publications Limited, 87-88 Turnmill Street, London EC1M 5QU, England; *International Marketing Data and Statistics,* and *Third World Economic Handbook.*

Facts on File, 460 Park Avenue South, New York, New York 10016 (800) 443-8323; *The New Book of World Rankings.*

G.K. Hall and Company, 70 Lincoln Street, Boston, Massachusetts 02111 (617) 423-3990; *The World in Figures.*

Inter-American Development Bank, 1300 New York Avenue, NW, Washington, D.C. 20577 (202) 623-1753; *Economic and Social Progress in Latin America.*

Organization of American States (OAS), General Secretariat, Washington, D.C. 20006 (202) 458-3533; *Statistical Bulletin of the OAS.*

Statistical Office of the United Nations, Publishing Service, New York, New York 10017 (800) 253-9646; *Statistical Yearbook,* and *Statistical Yearbook for Latin America and the Caribbean.*

Times Books, 201 East 50th Street, New York, New York 10022 (212) 751-2600; *The Economist Book of Vital World Statistics.*

U.C.L.A. Latin American Center Publications, University of California, Los Angeles, California 90024 (310) 825-6634; *Statistical Abstract of Latin America.*

The World Bank, 1818 H Street, NW, Washington, D.C. 20433 (202) 477-1234; *World Tables.*

CHILE - GROSS INDUSTRIAL PRODUCT

Euromonitor Publications Limited, 87-88 Turnmill Street, London EC1M 5QU, England; *Third World Economic Handbook.*

CHILE - GROSS NATIONAL PRODUCT

Euromonitor Publications Limited, 87-88 Turnmill Street, London EC1M 5QU, England; *International Marketing Data and Statistics,* and *Third World Economic Handbook.*

Inter-American Development Bank, 1300 New York Avenue, NW, Washington, D.C. 20577 (202) 623-1753; *Economic and Social Progress in Latin America.*

U.S. Arms Control and Disarmament Agency, 320 Twenty-first Street, NW, Washington, D.C. 20451 (202) 647-8677; *World Military Expenditures and Arms Transfers.*

The World Bank, 1818 H Street, NW, Washington, D.C. 20433 (202) 477-1234; *World Tables.*

CHILE - HEALTH

The Economist Intelligence Unit, 111 West 57th Street, New York, New York 10019 (800) 938-4685; *The New Latin America Market Atlas.*

Facts on File, 460 Park Avenue South, New York, New York 10016 (800) 443-8323; *The New Book of World Rankings.*

Federal Statistical Office, Gustav - Stresemann - Ring 11, D-6200 Wiesbaden, Germany; *Chile.*

G.K. Hall and Company, 70 Lincoln Street, Boston, Massachusetts 02111 (617) 423-3990; *The World in Figures.*

Statistical Office of the United Nations, Publishing Service, New York, New York 10017 (800) 253-9646; *Statistical Yearbook.*

Times Books, 201 East 50th Street, New York, New York 10022 (212) 751-2600; *The Economist Book of Vital World Statistics.*

U.C.L.A. Latin American Center Publications, University of California, Los Angeles, California 90024 (310) 825-6634; *Statistical Abstract of Latin America.*

World Health Organization, Office of Publications, Avenue Appia, CH-1211 Geneva 27, Switzerland (Telephone Number in U.S. (518) 436-9686); *World Health Statistics Annual.*

CHILE - HEALTH EXPENDITURES

International Monetary Fund, 700 Nineteenth Street, NW, Washington, D.C. 20431 (202) 623-7000; *Government Finance Statistics Yearbook.*

Statistical Office of the United Nations, Publishing Service, New York, New York 10017 (800) 253-9646; *Statistical Yearbook for Latin America and the Caribbean.*

CHILE - HIDE PRODUCTION

Food and Agricultural Organization of the United Nations (FAO), Via delle Terme di Caracalla, 00100 Rome, Italy (Telephone Number in U.S. (202) 653-2400); *Production Yearbook.*

CHILE - HIGHWAYS

The Economist Intelligence Unit, 111 West 57th Street, New York, New York 10019 (800) 938-4685; *The New Latin America Market Atlas.*

G.K. Hall and Company, 70 Lincoln Street, Boston, Massachusetts 02111 (617) 423-3990; *The World in Figures.*

International Road Federation, 525 School Street, SW, Washington, D.C. 20024 (202) 554-2106; *World Road Statistics.*

CHILE - HORSES - See CHILE - LIVESTOCK AND POULTRY

CHILE - HOURS OF WORK - See CHILE - EMPLOYMENT

CHILE - HOUSING AND HOUSING UNITS

Euromonitor Publications Limited, 87-88 Turnmill Street, London EC1M 5QU, England; *Third World Economic Handbook.*

Facts on File, 460 Park Avenue South, New York, New York 10016 (800) 443-8323; *The New Book of World Rankings.*

Statistical Office of the United Nations, Publishing Service, New York, New York 10017 (800) 253-9646; *Statistical Yearbook for Latin America and the Caribbean.*

U.C.L.A. Latin American Center Publications, University of California, Los Angeles, California 90024 (310) 825-6634; *Statistical Abstract of Latin America.*

CHILE - HOUSING EXPENDITURES

International Monetary Fund, 700 Nineteenth Street, NW, Washington, D.C. 20431 (202) 623-7000; *Government Finance Statistics Yearbook.*

CHILE - HYDROCHLORIC ACID PRODUCTION

Statistical Office of the United Nations, Publishing Service, New York, New York 10017 (800) 253-9646; *Statistical Yearbook.*

CHILE - ILLITERATE POPULATION

The Economist Intelligence Unit, 111 West 57th Street, New York, New York 10019 (800) 938-4685; *The New Latin America Market Atlas,* and *The World Market Atlas.*

G.K. Hall and Company, 70 Lincoln Street, Boston, Massachusetts 02111 (617) 423-3990; *The World in Figures.*

Statistical Office of the United Nations, Publishing Service, New York, New York 10017 (800) 253-9646; *Statistical Yearbook for Latin America and the Caribbean.*

United Nations Educational, Scientific and Cultural Organization (UNESCO), 7 Place de Fontenoy, F-75700 Paris France (Telephone Number in U.S. (212) 963-5981); *Statistical Yearbook.*

CHILE - IMMIGRATION

U.C.L.A. Latin American Center Publications, University of California, Los Angeles, California 90024 (310) 825-6634; *Statistical Abstract of Latin America.*

CHILE - IMPORTS

American Automobile Manufacturers Association, 1401 H Street, NW, Suite 900, Washington, D.C. 20005 (202) 326-5500; *World Motor Vehicle Data.*

The Economist Intelligence Unit, 111 West 57th Street, New York, New York 10019 (800) 938-4685; *The New Latin America Market Atlas,* and *The World Market Atlas.*

Euromonitor Publications Limited, 87-88 Turnmill Street, London EC1M 5QU, England; *International Marketing Data and Statistics,* and *Third World Economic Handbook.*

Food and Agricultural Organization of the United Nations (FAO) Via delle Terme di Caracalla, 00100 Rome, Italy (Telephone Number in U.S. (202) 653-2400); *The State of Food and Agriculture.*

G.K. Hall and Company, 70 Lincoln Street, Boston, Massachusetts 02111 (617) 423-3990; *The World in Figures.*

Inter-American Development Bank, 1300 New York Avenue, NW, Washington, D.C. 20577 (202) 623-1753; *Economic and Social Progress in Latin America.*

International Monetary Fund, 700 Nineteenth Street, NW, Washington, D.C. 20431 (202) 623-7000; *Direction of Trade Statistics, Government Finance Statistics Yearbook,* and *International Financial Statistics.*

Organization of American States (OAS), General Secretariat, Washington, D.C. 20006 (202) 458-3533; *Statistical Bulletin of the OAS.*

Statistical Office of the United Nations, Publishing Service, New York, New York 10017 (800) 253-9646; *Statistical Yearbook for Latin America and the Caribbean.*

Times Books, 201 East 50th Street, New York, New York 10022 (212) 751-2600; *The Economist Book of Vital World Statistics.*

The World Bank, 1818 H Street, NW, Washington, D.C. 20433 (202) 477-1234; *World Tables.*

CHILE - INCOME DISTRIBUTION

Statistical Office of the United Nations, Publishing Service, New York, New York 10017 (800) 253-9646; *Statistical Yearbook for Latin America and the Caribbean.*

U.C.L.A. Latin American Center Publications, University of California, Los Angeles, California 90024 (310) 825-6634; *Statistical Abstract of Latin America.*

CHILE - INCOME TAXES - See CHILE - TAXATION

CHILE - INDUSTRIAL METALS PRODUCTION - See CHILE - MINING AND MINERAL PRODUCTS

CHILE - INDUSTRY

Euromonitor Publications Limited, 87-88 Turnmill Street, London EC1M 5QU, England; *Third World Economic Handbook.*

Facts on File, 460 Park Avenue South, New York, New York 10016 (800) 443-8323; *The New Book of World Rankings.*

Federal Statistical Office, Gustav - Stresemann - Ring 11, D-6200 Wiesbaden, Germany; *Chile.*

Gale Research Incorporated, 835 Penobscot Building, Detroit, Michigan 48226 (800) 877-4253; *International Historical Statistics The Americas and Australasia.*

G.K. Hall and Company, 70 Lincoln Street, Boston, Massachusetts 02111 (617) 423-3990; *The World in Figures.*

Penn Well Publishing Company, 1421 South Sheridan Road, P.O. Box 1260, Tulsa, Oklahoma 74101 (800) 752-9764; *International Energy Statistics Sourcebook.*

Statistical Office of the United Nations, Publishing Service, New York, New York 10017 (800) 253-9646; *Economic Survey of Latin America and the Caribbean,* and *Statistical Yearbook.*

Times Books, 201 East 50th Street, New York, New York 10022 (212) 751-2600; *The Economist Book of Vital World Statistics.*

U.C.L.A. Latin American Center Publications, University of California, Los Angeles, California 90024 (310) 825-6634; *Statistical Abstract of Latin America.*

The World Bank, 1818 H Street, NW, Washington, D.C. 20433 (202) 477-1234; *World Tables.*

CHILE - INFANT AND MATERNAL MORTALITY

The Economist Intelligence Unit, 111 West 57th Street, New York, New York 10019 (800) 938-4685; *The New Latin America Market Atlas.*

Statistical Office of the United Nations, Publishing Service, New York, New York 10017 (800) 253-9646; *Demographic Yearbook,* and *Statistical Yearbook.*

Times Books, 201 East 50th Street, New York, New York 10022 (212) 751-2600; *The Economist Book of Vital World Statistics.*

The World Bank, 1818 H Street, NW, Washington, D.C. 20433 (202) 477-1234; *World Tables.*

World Health Organization, Office of Publications, Avenue Appia, CH-1211 Geneva 27, Switzerland (Telephone Number in U.S. (518) 436-9686); *World Health Statistics Annual.*

CHILE - INFLATIONARY FACTORS

Statistical Office of the United Nations, Publishing Service, New York, New York 10017 (800) 253-9646; *Economic Survey of Latin America and the Caribbean.*

CHILE - INTEREST RATES

Inter-American Development Bank, 1300 New York Avenue, NW, Washington, D.C. 20577 (202) 623-1753; *Economic and Social Progress in Latin America.*

CHILE - INTERNATIONAL FINANCE

Inter-American Development Bank, 1300 New York Avenue, NW, Washington, D.C. 20577 (202) 623-1753; *Economic and Social Progress in Latin America.*

U.C.L.A. Latin American Center Publications, University of California, Los Angeles, California 90024 (310) 825-6634; *Statistical Abstract of Latin America.*

CHILE - INTERNATIONAL LIQUIDITY

Inter-American Development Bank, 1300 New York Avenue, NW, Washington, D.C. 20577 (202) 623-1753; *Economic and Social Progress in Latin America.*

International Monetary Fund, 700 Nineteenth Street, NW, Washington, D.C. 20431 (202) 623-7000; *International Financial Statistics.*

CHILE - INTERNATIONAL RESERVES

Organization of American States (OAS), General Secretariat, Washington, D.C. 20006 (202) 458-3533; *Statistical Bulletin of the OAS.*

CHILE - INTERNATIONAL RESERVES EXCLUDING GOLD

Inter-American Development Bank, 1300 New York Avenue, NW, Washington, D.C. 20577 (202) 623-1753; *Economic and Social Progress in Latin America.*

The World Bank, 1818 H Street, NW, Washington, D.C. 20433 (202) 477-1234; *World Tables.*

CHILE - INTERNATIONAL STATISTICS

Inter-American Development Bank, 1300 New York Avenue, NW, Washington, D.C. 20577 (202) 623-1753; *Economic and Social Progress in Latin America.*

U.C.L.A. Latin American Center Publications, University of California, Los Angeles, California 90024 (310) 825-6634; *Statistical Abstract of Latin America.*

CHILE - INVESTMENTS

Inter-American Development Bank, 1300 New York Avenue, NW, Washington, D.C. 20577 (202) 623-1753; *Economic and Social Progress in Latin America.*

Statistical Office of the United Nations, Publishing Service, New York, New York 10017 (800) 253-9646; *Statistical Yearbook for Latin America and the Caribbean.*

CHILE - IRON ORE - See CHILE - MINING AND MINERAL PRODUCTS

CHILE - IRRIGATION

Euromonitor Publications Limited, 87-88 Turnmill Street, London EC1M 5QU, England; *International Marketing Data and Statistics.*

Inter-American Development Bank, 1300 New York Avenue, NW, Washington, D.C. 20577 (202) 623-1753; *Economic and Social Progress in Latin America.*

CHILE - LABOR FORCE

The Economist Intelligence Unit, 111 West 57th Street, New York, New York 10019 (800) 938-4685; *The New Latin America Market Atlas.*

Euromonitor Publications Limited, 87-88 Turnmill Street, London EC1M 5QU, England; *International Marketing Data and Statistics.*

Facts on File, 460 Park Avenue South, New York, New York 10016 (800) 443-8323; *The New Book of World Rankings.*

Food and Agricultural Organization of the United Nations (FAO) Via delle Terme di Caracalla, 00100 Rome, Italy (Telephone Number in U.S. (202) 653-2400); *The State of Food and Agriculture.*

Gale Research Incorporated, 835 Penobscot Building, Detroit, Michigan 48226 (800) 877-4253; *International Historical Statistics The Americas and Australasia.*

G.K. Hall and Company, 70 Lincoln Street, Boston, Massachusetts 02111 (617) 423-3990; *The World in Figures.*

Times Books, 201 East 50th Street, New York, New York 10022 (212) 751-2 600; *The Economist Book of Vital World Statistics.*

The World Bank, 1818 H Street, NW, Washington, D.C. 20433 (202) 477-1234; *World Tables.*

CHILE - LABOR PRODUCTIVITY

International Labour Office, I.L.O. Publications, CH-1211, Geneva 22, Switzerland; *Yearbook of Labour Statistics.*

CHILE - LAND AREA

The Economist Intelligence Unit, 111 West 57th Street, New York, New York 10019 (800) 938-4685; *The New Latin America Market Atlas.*

CHILE - LAND USE

Euromonitor Publications Limited, 87-88 Turnmill Street, London EC1M 5QU, England; *International Marketing Data and Statistics.*

Food and Agricultural Organization of the United Nations (FAO), Via delle Terme di Caracalla, 00100 Rome, Italy (Telephone Number in U.S. (202) 653-2400); *Production Yearbook.*

G.K. Hall and Company, 70 Lincoln Street, Boston, Massachusetts 02111 (617) 423-3990; *The World in Figures.*

Inter-American Development Bank, 1300 New York Avenue, NW, Washington, D.C. 20577 (202) 623-1753; *Economic and Social Progress in Latin America.*

CHILE - LEAD - See CHILE - MINING AND MINERAL PRODUCTS

CHILE - LIBRARIES

Facts on File, 460 Park Avenue South, New York, New York 10016 (800) 443-8323; *The New Book of World Rankings.*

United Nations Educational, Scientific and Cultural Organization (UNESCO), 7 Place de Fontenoy, F-75700 Paris France (Telephone Number in U.S. (212) 963-5981); *Statistical Yearbook.*

CHILE - LIFE EXPECTANCY

The Economist Intelligence Unit, 111 West 57th Street, New York, New York 10019 (800) 938-4685; *The New Latin America Market Atlas.*

CHILE - LIGNITE PRODUCTION - See CHILE - MINING AND MINERAL PRODUCTS

CHILE - LIVESTOCK AND POULTRY

Euromonitor Publications Limited, 87-88 Turnmill Street, London EC1M 5QU, England; *Third World Economic Handbook.*

Facts on File, 460 Park Avenue South, New York, New York 10016 (800) 443-8323; *The New Book of World Rankings.*

Food and Agricultural Organization of the United Nations (FAO), Via delle Terme di Caracalla, 00100 Rome, Italy (Telephone Number in U.S. (202) 653-2400); *Production Yearbook,* and *The State of Food and Agriculture.*

G.K. Hall and Company, 70 Lincoln Street, Boston, Massachusetts 02111 (617) 423-3990; *The World in Figures.*

Statistical Office of the United Nations, Publishing Service, New York, New York 10017 (800) 253-9646; *Statistical Yearbook.*

CHILE - LIVING LEVELS

G.K. Hall and Company, 70 Lincoln Street, Boston, Massachusetts 02111 (617) 423-3990; *The World in Figures.*

Statistical Office of the United Nations, Publishing Service, New York, New York 10017 (800) 253-9646; *Statistical Yearbook for Latin America and the Caribbean.*

Times Books, 201 East 50th Street, New York, New York 10022 (212) 751-2600; *The Economist Book of Vital World Statistics.*

CHILE - MAIL - NUMBER OF PIECES SENT OR RECEIVED

Statistical Office of the United Nations, Publishing Service, New York, New York 10017 (800) 253-9646; *Statistical Yearbook.*

CHILE - MAIN ECONOMIC INDICATORS - See CHILE - ECONOMY

CHILE - MAIN INDICATORS - See CHILE - ECONOMY

CHILE - MANGANESE AND MANGANESE ORE - See CHILE - MINING AND MINERAL PRODUCTS

CHILE - MANUFACTURING

American Automobile Manufacturers Association, 1401 H Street, NW, Suite 900, Washington, D.C. 20005 (202) 326-5500; *World Motor Vehicle Data.*

The Economist Intelligence Unit, 111 West 57th Street, New York, New York 10019 (800) 938-4685; *The New Latin America Market Atlas.*

Euromonitor Publications Limited, 87-88 Turnmill Street, London EC1M 5QU, England; *Third World Economic Handbook.*

Facts on File, 460 Park Avenue South, New York, New York 10016 (800) 443-8323; *The New Book of World Rankings.*

G.K. Hall and Company, 70 Lincoln Street, Boston, Massachusetts 02111 (617) 423-3990; *The World in Figures.*

Inter-American Development Bank, 1300 New York Avenue, NW, Washington, D.C. 20577 (202) 623-1753; *Economic and Social Progress in Latin America.*

International Monetary Fund, 700 Nineteenth Street, NW, Washington, D.C. 20431 (202) 623-7000; *International Financial Statistics.*

Organization of American States (OAS), General Secretariat, Washington, D.C. 20006 (202) 458-3533; *Statistical Bulletin of the OAS.*

Statistical Office of the United Nations, Publishing Service, New York, New York 10017 (800) 253-9646; *Statistical Yearbook,* and *Statistical Yearbook for Latin America and the Caribbean.*

Times Books, 201 East 50th Street, New York, New York 10022 (212) 751-2600; *The Economist Book of Vital World Statistics.*

The World Bank, 1818 H Street, NW, Washington, D.C. 20433 (202) 477-1234; *World Tables.*

CHILE - MARRIAGE RATES

Facts on File, 460 Park Avenue South, New York, New York 10016 (800) 443-8323; *The New Book of World Rankings.*

Statistical Office of the United Nations, Publishing Service, New York, New York 10017 (800) 253-9646; *Demographic Yearbook,* and *Statistical Yearbook.*

CHILE - MEAT PRODUCTION - See CHILE - LIVESTOCK AND POULTRY

CHILE - MEDICAL PERSONNEL

U.C.L.A. Latin American Center Publications, University of California, Los Angeles, California 90024 (310) 825-6634; *Statistical Abstract of Latin America.*

CHILE - MERCHANT SHIPPING

G.K. Hall and Company, 70 Lincoln Street, Boston, Massachusetts 02111 (617) 423-3990; *The World in Figures.*

Lloyd's Register of Shipping, 17 Battery Place, New York, New York 10004 (212) 425-8050; *Register of Ships.*

Statistical Office of the United Nations, Publishing Service, New York, New York 10017 (800) 253-9646; *Statistical Yearbook.*

Times Books, 201 East 50th Street, New York, New York 10022 (212) 751-2600; *The Economist Book of Vital World Statistics.*

U.S. Department of Transportation, Maritime Administration, 400 Seventh Street, SW, Washington, D.C. 20590 (202) 366-5807; *A Statistical Analysis of the World's Merchant Fleets.*

CHILE - MERCURY PRODUCTION AND CONSUMPTION - See CHILE - MINING AND MINERALS

CHILE - MILITARY

The Economist Intelligence Unit, 111 West 57th Street, New York, New York 10019 (800) 938-4685; *The New Latin America Market Atlas.*

G.K. Hall and Company, 70 Lincoln Street, Boston, Massachusetts 02111 (617) 423-3990; *The World in Figures.*

The International Institute for Strategic Studies, 23 Tavistock Street, London WC2E 7NQ, England; *The Military Balance.*

U.C.L.A. Latin American Center Publications, University of California, Los Angeles, California 90024 (310) 825-6634; *Statistical Abstract of Latin America.*

U.S. Arms Control and Disarmament Agency, 320 Twenty-first Street, NW, Washington, D.C. 20451 (202) 647-8677; *World Military Expenditures and Arms Transfers.*

CHILE - MILK PRODUCTION - See CHILE - DAIRY PRODUCTS

CHILE - MINING AND MINERAL PRODUCTS

Commodity Research Bureau, Incorporated, 75 Wall Street, New York, New York 10005 (212) 504-7754; *Commodity Year Book.*

The Economist Intelligence Unit, 111 West 57th Street, New York, New York 10019 (800) 938-4685; *The New Latin America Market Atlas.*

Euromonitor Publications Limited, 87-88 Turnmill Street, London EC1M 5QU, England; *Third World Economic Handbook.*

G.K. Hall and Company, 70 Lincoln Street, Boston, Massachusetts 02111 (617) 423-3990; *The World in Figures.*

Inter-American Development Bank, 1300 New York Avenue, NW, Washington, D.C. 20577 (202) 623-1753; *Economic and Social Progress in Latin America.*

International Monetary Fund, 700 Nineteenth Street, NW, Washington, D.C. 20431 (202) 623-7000; *International Financial Statistics.*

Organization of American States (OAS), General Secretariat, Washington, D.C. 20006 (202) 458-3533; *Statistical Bulletin of the OAS.*

Penn Well Publishing Company, 1421 South Sheridan Road, P.O. Box 1260, Tulsa, Oklahoma 74101 (800) 752-9764; *International Energy Statistics Sourcebook.*

Statistical Office of the United Nations, Publishing Service, New York, New York 10017 (800) 253-9646; *Statistical Yearbook,* and *Statistical Yearbook for Latin America and the Caribbean.*

U.C.L.A. Latin American Center Publications, University of California, Los Angeles, California 90024 (310) 825-6634; *Statistical Abstract of Latin America.*

World Bureau of Metal Statistics, 27-A High Street, Ware Hert SG12 9BA, England; *World Metal Statistics.*

CHILE - MOLYBDENUM AND MOLYBDENUM ORE - See CHILE - MINING AND MINERAL PRODUCTS

CHILE - MONEY EXCHANGE RATE

Euromonitor Publications Limited, 87-88 Turnmill Street, London EC1M 5QU, England; *International Marketing Data and Statistics.*

Inter-American Development Bank, 1300 New York Avenue, NW, Washington, D.C. 20577 (202) 623-1753; *Economic and Social Progress in Latin America.*

International Monetary Fund, 700 Nineteenth Street, NW, Washington, D.C. 20431 (202) 623-7000; *International Financial Statistics*.

Statistical Office of the United Nations, Publishing Service, New York, New York 10017 (800) 253-9646; *Statistical Yearbook*.

CHILE - MONEY RATES - MARKET

Inter-American Development Bank, 1300 New York Avenue, NW, Washington, D.C. 20577 (202) 623-1753; *Economic and Social Progress in Latin America*.

CHILE - MONEY RESERVES

Euromonitor Publications Limited, 87-88 Turnmill Street, London EC1M 5QU, England; *International Marketing Data and Statistics*.

Inter-American Development Bank, 1300 New York Avenue, NW, Washington, D.C. 20577 (202) 623-1753; *Economic and Social Progress in Latin America*.

CHILE - MONEY SUPPLY

Euromonitor Publications Limited, 87-88 Turnmill Street, London EC1M 5QU, England; *International Marketing Data and Statistics*.

Federal Statistical Office, Gustav - Stresemann - Ring 11, D-6200 Wiesbaden, Germany; *Chile*.

G.K. Hall and Company, 70 Lincoln Street, Boston, Massachusetts 02111 (617) 423-3990; *The World in Figures*.

Inter-American Development Bank, 1300 New York Avenue, NW, Washington, D.C. 20577 (202) 623-1753; *Economic and Social Progress in Latin America*.

International Monetary Fund, 700 Nineteenth Street, NW, Washington, D.C. 20431 (202) 623-7000; *International Financial Statistics*.

Statistical Office of the United Nations, Publishing Service, New York, New York 10017 (800) 253-9646; *Statistical Yearbook*.

U.C.L.A. Latin American Center Publications, University of California, Los Angeles, California 90024 (310) 825-6634; *Statistical Abstract of Latin America*.

The World Bank, 1818 H Street, NW, Washington, D.C. 20433 (202) 477-1234; *World Tables*.

CHILE - MOTION PICTURE THEATRES

Statistical Office of the United Nations, Publishing Service, New York, New York 10017 (800) 253-9646; *Statistical Yearbook*.

CHILE - MOTOR VEHICLE PRODUCTION

American Automobile Manufacturers Association, 1401 H Street, NW, Suite 900, Washington, D.C. 20005 (202) 326-5500; *World Motor Vehicle Data*.

CHILE - MOTOR VEHICLE TAXES - See CHILE - TAXATION

CHILE - MOTOR VEHICLES IN USE

American Automobile Manufacturers Association, 1401 H Street, NW, Suite 900, Washington, D.C. 20005 (202) 326-5500; *World Motor Vehicle Data*.

The Economist Intelligence Unit, 111 West 57th Street, New York, New York 10019 (800) 938-4685; *The New Latin America Market Atlas*.

G.K. Hall and Company, 70 Lincoln Street, Boston, Massachusetts 02111 (617) 423-3990; *The World in Figures*.

International Road Federation, 525 School Street, SW, Washington, D.C. 20024 (202) 554-2106; *World Road Statistics*.

Statistical Office of the United Nations, Publishing Service, New York, New York 10017 (800) 253-9646; *Statistical Yearbook*.

Times Books, 201 East 50th Street, New York, New York 10022 (212) 751-2600; *The Economist Book of Vital World Statistics*.

CHILE - MULES - See CHILE - LIVESTOCK AND POULTRY

CHILE - MUSEUMS

Facts on File, 460 Park Avenue South, New York, New York 10016 (800) 443-8323; *The New Book of World Rankings*.

United Nations Educational, Scientific and Cultural Organization (UNESCO), 7 Place de Fontenoy, F-75700 Paris France (Telephone Number in U.S. (212) 963-5981); *Statistical Yearbook*.

CHILE - NATALITY - See CHILE - BIRTH RATE

CHILE - NATIONAL ACCOUNTS

Federal Statistical Office, Gustav - Stresemann - Ring 11, D-6200 Wiesbaden, Germany; *Chile*.

Gale Research Incorporated, 835 Penobscot Building, Detroit, Michigan 48226 (800) 877-4253; *International Historical Statistics The Americas and Australasia*.

Inter-American Development Bank, 1300 New York Avenue, NW, Washington, D.C. 20577 (202) 623-1753; *Economic and Social Progress in Latin America*.

Organization of American States (OAS), General Secretariat, Washington, D.C. 20006 (202) 458-3533; *Statistical Bulletin of the OAS*.

Statistical Office of the United Nations, Publishing Service, New York, New York 10017 (800) 253-9646; *National Accounts Statistics*, and *Statistical Yearbook*.

U.C.L.A. Latin American Center Publications, University of California, Los Angeles, California 90024 (310) 825-6634; *Statistical Abstract of Latin America*.

CHILE - NATIONAL INCOME

Facts on File, 460 Park Avenue South, New York, New York 10016 (800) 443-8323; *The New Book of World Rankings*.

G.K. Hall and Company, 70 Lincoln Street, Boston, Massachusetts 02111 (617) 423-3990; *The World in Figures*.

Inter-American Development Bank, 1300 New York Avenue, NW, Washington, D.C. 20577 (202) 623-1753; *Economic and Social Progress in Latin America*.

Statistical Office of the United Nations, Publishing Service, New York, New York 10017 (800) 253-9646; *Statistical Yearbook for Latin America and the Caribbean*.

CHILE - NATIONAL PRODUCT

Facts on File, 460 Park Avenue South, New York, New York 10016 (800) 443-8323; *The New Book of World Rankings.*

Statistical Office of the United Nations, Publishing Service, New York, New York 10017 (800) 253-9646; *Statistical Yearbook.*

CHILE - NATURAL GAS PRODUCTION - See CHILE - MINING AND MINERAL PRODUCTS

CHILE - NEWSPAPER PRODUCTION - See CHILE - FORESTRY AND FOREST PRODUCTS

CHILE - NEWSPRINT - See CHILE - FORESTRY AND FOREST PRODUCTS

CHILE - NICKEL AND NICKEL ORE - See CHILE - MINING AND MINERAL PRODUCTS

CHILE - NUTRITION

Statistical Office of the United Nations, Publishing Service, New York, New York 10017 (800) 253-9646; *Statistical Yearbook for Latin America and the Caribbean.*

CHILE - OATS PRODUCTION - See CHILE - CROPS

CHILE - OCCUPATIONS - See CHILE - LABOR FORCE

CHILE - PAPER - See CHILE - FORESTRY AND FOREST PRODUCTS

CHILE - PATENTS

Penn Well Publishing Company, 1421 South Sheridan Road, P.O. Box 1260, Tulsa, Oklahoma 74101 (800) 752-9764; *International Energy Statistics Sourcebook.*

Statistical Office of the United Nations, Publishing Service, New York, New York 10017 (800) 253-9646; *Statistical Yearbook.*

CHILE - PEANUT PRODUCTION - See CHILE - CROPS

CHILE - PERIODICALS

United Nations Educational, Scientific and Cultural Organization (UNESCO), 7 Place de Fontenoy, F-75700 Paris France (Telephone Number in U.S. (212) 963-5981); *Statistical Yearbook.*

CHILE - PESTICIDE USE

Food and Agricultural Organization of the United Nations (FAO) Via delle Terme di Caracalla, 00100 Rome, Italy (Telephone Number in U.S. (202) 653-2400); *The State of Food and Agriculture.*

CHILE - PETROLEUM INDUSTRY

The Economist Intelligence Unit, 111 West 57th Street, New York, New York 10019 (800) 938-4685; *The New Latin America Market Atlas.*

Facts on File, 460 Park Avenue South, New York, New York 10016 (800) 443-8323; *The New Book of World Rankings.*

Food and Agricultural Organization of the United Nations (FAO) Via delle Terme di Caracalla, 00100 Rome, Italy (Telephone Number in U.S. (202) 653-2400); *The State of Food and Agriculture.*

G.K. Hall and Company, 70 Lincoln Street, Boston, Massachusetts 02111 (617) 423-3990; *The World in Figures.*

Inter-American Development Bank, 1300 New York Avenue, NW, Washington, D.C. 20577 (202) 623-1753; *Economic and Social Progress in Latin America.*

Penn Well Publishing Company, 1421 South Sheridan Road, P.O. Box 1260, Tulsa, Oklahoma 74101 (800) 752-9764; *International Energy Statistics Sourcebook.*

Statistical Office of the United Nations, Publishing Service, New York, New York 10017 (800) 253-9646; *Statistical Yearbook.*

CHILE - PIG-IRON AND FERRO-ALLOY PRODUCTION - See CHILE - MINING AND MINERAL PRODUCTS

CHILE - PIGS - See CHILE - LIVESTOCK AND POULTRY

CHILE - PLASTIC AND RESIN PRODUCTION

Euromonitor Publications Limited, 87-88 Turnmill Street, London EC1M 5QU, England; *Third World Economic Handbook.*

Statistical Office of the United Nations, Publishing Service, New York, New York 10017 (800) 253-9646; *Statistical Yearbook.*

CHILE - POLITICAL DATA

U.C.L.A. Latin American Center Publications, University of California, Los Angeles, California 90024 (310) 825-6634; *Statistical Abstract of Latin America.*

CHILE - POPULATION

The Economist Intelligence Unit, 111 West 57th Street, New York, New York 10019 (800) 938-4685; *The New Latin America Market Atlas,* and *The World Market Atlas.*

Euromonitor Publications Limited, 87-88 Turnmill Street, London EC1M 5QU, England; *International Marketing Data and Statistics,* and *Third World Economic Handbook.*

Facts on File, 460 Park Avenue South, New York, New York 10016 (800) 443-8323; *The New Book of World Rankings.*

Federal Statistical Office, Gustav - Stresemann - Ring 11, D-6200 Wiesbaden, Germany; *Chile.*

Food and Agricultural Organization of the United Nations (FAO), Via delle Terme di Caracalla, 00100 Rome, Italy (Telephone Number in U.S. (202) 653-2400); *Production Yearbook.*

Gale Research Incorporated, 835 Penobscot Building, Detroit, Michigan 48226 (800) 877-4253; *International Historical Statistics The Americas and Australasia.*

G.K. Hall and Company, 70 Lincoln Street, Boston, Massachusetts 02111 (617) 423-3990; *The World in Figures.*

Inter-American Development Bank, 1300 New York Avenue, NW, Washington, D.C. 20577 (202) 623-1753; *Economic and Social Progress in Latin America.*

International Labour Office, I.L.O. Publications, CH-1211, Geneva 22, Switzerland; *Yearbook of Labour Statistics.*

Organization of American States (OAS), General Secretariat, Washington, D.C. 20006 (202) 458-3533; *Statistical Bulletin of the*

OAS.

Statistical Office of the United Nations, Publishing Service, New York, New York 10017 (800) 253-9646; *Demographic Yearbook, Statistical Yearbook,* and *Statistical Yearbook for Latin America and the Caribbean.*

Times Books, 201 East 50th Street, New York, New York 10022 (212) 751-2600; *The Economist Book of Vital World Statistics.*

U.C.L.A. Latin American Center Publications, University of California, Los Angeles, California 90024 (310) 825-6634; *Statistical Abstract of Latin America.*

United Nations Educational, Scientific and Cultural Organization (UNESCO), 7 Place de Fontenoy, F-75700 Paris France (Telephone Number in U.S. (212) 963-5981); *Statistical Yearbook.*

U.S. Arms Control and Disarmament Agency, 320 Twenty-first Street, NW, Washington, D.C. 20451 (202) 647-8677; *World Military Expenditures and Arms Transfers.*

World Health Organization, Office of Publications, Avenue Appia, CH-1211 Geneva 27, Switzerland (Telephone Number in U.S. (518) 436-9686); *World Health Statistics Annual.*

CHILE - POST OFFICES

Facts on File, 460 Park Avenue South, New York, New York 10016 (800) 443-8323; *The New Book of World Rankings.*

CHILE - POTATO PRODUCTION - See CHILE - CROPS

CHILE - PRICES

Facts on File, 460 Park Avenue South, New York, New York 10016 (800) 443-8323; *The New Book of World Rankings.*

Federal Statistical Office, Gustav - Stresemann - Ring 11, D-6200 Wiesbaden, Germany; *Chile.*

Food and Agricultural Organization of the United Nations (FAO), Via delle Terme di Caracalla, 00100 Rome, Italy (Telephone Number in U.S. (202) 653-2400); *Production Yearbook,* and *The State of Food and Agriculture.*

Gale Research Incorporated, 835 Penobscot Building, Detroit, Michigan 48226 (800) 877-4253; *International Historical Statistics The Americas and Australasia.*

G.K. Hall and Company, 70 Lincoln Street, Boston, Massachusetts 02111 (617) 423-3990; *The World in Figures.*

International Labour Office, I.L.O. Publications, CH-1211, Geneva 22, Switzerland; *Yearbook of Labour Statistics.*

International Monetary Fund, 700 Nineteenth Street, NW, Washington, D.C. 20431 (202) 623-7000; *International Financial Statistics.*

Statistical Office of the United Nations, Publishing Service, New York, New York 10017 (800) 253-9646; *Statistical Yearbook for Latin America and the Caribbean.*

World Bureau of Metal Statistics, 27-A High Street, Ware Hert SG12 9BA, England; *World Metal Statistics.*

CHILE - PRINTING AND WRITING PAPER - See CHILE - FORESTRY AND FOREST PRODUCTS

CHILE - PRODUCTION

American Automobile Manufacturers Association, 1401 H Street, NW, Suite 900, Washington, D.C. 20005 (202) 326-5500; *World Motor Vehicle Data.*

Euromonitor Publications Limited, 87-88 Turnmill Street, London EC1M 5QU, England; *Third World Economic Handbook.*

Facts on File, 460 Park Avenue South, New York, New York 10016 (800) 443-8323; *The New Book of World Rankings.*

G.K. Hall and Company, 70 Lincoln Street, Boston, Massachusetts 02111 (617) 423-3990; *The World in Figures.*

CHILE - PRODUCTIVITY

Euromonitor Publications Limited, 87-88 Turnmill Street, London EC1M 5QU, England; *International Marketing Data and Statistics.*

CHILE - PROPERTY TAXES - See CHILE - TAXATION

CHILE - PUBLIC CONSUMPTION FUND

Inter-American Development Bank, 1300 New York Avenue, NW, Washington, D.C. 20577 (202) 623-1753; *Economic and Social Progress in Latin America.*

CHILE - PUBLIC EXPENDITURE

Inter-American Development Bank, 1300 New York Avenue, NW, Washington, D.C. 20577 (202) 623-1753; *Economic and Social Progress in Latin America.*

Organization of American States (OAS), General Secretariat, Washington, D.C. 20006 (202) 458-3533; *Statistical Bulletin of the OAS.*

Statistical Office of the United Nations, Publishing Service, New York, New York 10017 (800) 253-9646; *Statistical Yearbook for Latin America and the Caribbean.*

CHILE - PUBLIC FINANCE

Facts on File, 460 Park Avenue South, New York, New York 10016 (800) 443-8323; *The New Book of World Rankings.*

Federal Statistical Office, Gustav - Stresemann - Ring 11, D-6200 Wiesbaden, Germany; *Chile.*

Inter-American Development Bank, 1300 New York Avenue, NW, Washington, D.C. 20577 (202) 623-1753; *Economic and Social Progress in Latin America.*

Organization of American States (OAS), General Secretariat, Washington, D.C. 20006 (202) 458-3533; *Statistical Bulletin of the OAS.*

CHILE - PUBLIC REVENUES

Inter-American Development Bank, 1300 New York Avenue, NW, Washington, D.C. 20577 (202) 623-1753; *Economic and Social Progress in Latin America.*

Organization of American States (OAS), General Secretariat, Washington, D.C. 20006 (202) 458-3533; *Statistical Bulletin of the*

OAS.

CHILE - RADIO BROADCASTING - See CHILE - BROADCASTING

CHILE - RADIO RECEIVER PRODUCTION

Statistical Office of the United Nations, Publishing Service, New York, New York 10017 (800) 253-9646; *Statistical Yearbook.*

CHILE - RAILWAYS

The Economist Intelligence Unit, 111 West 57th Street, New York, New York 10019 (800) 938-4685; *The New Latin America Market Atlas.*

G.K. Hall and Company, 70 Lincoln Street, Boston, Massachusetts 02111 (617) 423-3990; *The World in Figures.*

Jane's Information Group, Sentinel House, 163 Brighton Road, Coulsdon, Surrey CR5 2NH, England (Telephone Number in U.S. (703) 683-3700); *Jane's World Railways.*

Statistical Office of the United Nations, Publishing Service, New York, New York 10017 (800) 253-9646; *Statistical Yearbook.*

CHILE - RAPESEED PRODUCTION - See CHILE - CROPS

CHILE - RELIGION

Facts on File, 460 Park Avenue South, New York, New York 10016 (800) 443-8323; *The New Book of World Rankings.*

U.C.L.A. Latin American Center Publications, University of California, Los Angeles, California 90024 (310) 825-6634; *Statistical Abstract of Latin America.*

CHILE - RENT PRICES

International Labour Office, I.L.O. Publications, CH-1211, Geneva 22, Switzerland; *Yearbook of Labour Statistics.*

CHILE - RESERVES EXCLUDING GOLD

The Economist Intelligence Unit, 111 West 57th Street, New York, New York 10019 (800) 938-4685; *The New Latin America Market Atlas.*

CHILE - RETAIL TRADE

Euromonitor Publications Limited, 87-88 Turnmill Street, London EC1M 5QU, England; *Third World Economic Handbook.*

G.K. Hall and Company, 70 Lincoln Street, Boston, Massachusetts 02111 (617) 423-3990; *The World in Figures.*

Inter-American Development Bank, 1300 New York Avenue, NW, Washington, D.C. 20577 (202) 623-1753; *Economic and Social Progress in Latin America.*

CHILE - RICE PRODUCTION - See CHILE - CROPS

CHILE - ROOT AND TUBER PRODUCTION - See CHILE - CROPS

CHILE - ROUNDWOOD PRODUCTION - See CHILE - FORESTRY AND FOREST PRODUCTS

CHILE - RUBBER PRODUCTION

Euromonitor Publications Limited, 87-88 Turnmill Street, London EC1M 5QU, England; *Third World Economic Handbook.*

Facts on File, 460 Park Avenue South, New York, New York 10016 (800) 443-8323; *The New Book of World Rankings.*

CHILE - SALT PRODUCTION - See CHILE - MINING AND MINERAL PRODUCTS

CHILE - SAWNWOOD PRODUCTION - See CHILE - FORESTRY AND FOREST PRODUCTS

CHILE - SCIENCE AND TECHNOLOGY

U.C.L.A. Latin American Center Publications, University of California, Los Angeles, California 90024 (310) 825-6634; *Statistical Abstract of Latin America.*

CHILE - SCIENTISTS AND TECHNICIANS

Statistical Office of the United Nations, Publishing Service, New York, New York 10017 (800) 253-9646; *Statistical Yearbook.*

CHILE - SENIOR CITIZENS

Facts on File, 460 Park Avenue South, New York, New York 10016 (800) 443-8323; *The New Book of World Rankings.*

CHILE - SHEEP - See CHILE - LIVESTOCK AND POULTRY

CHILE - SILVER PRODUCTION AND CONSUMPTION - See CHILE - MINING AND MINERAL PRODUCTS

CHILE - SOCIAL DATA

Facts on File, 460 Park Avenue South, New York, New York 10016 (800) 443-8323; *The New Book of World Rankings.*

G.K. Hall and Company, 70 Lincoln Street, Boston, Massachusetts 02111 (617) 423-3990; *The World in Figures.*

U.C.L.A. Latin American Center Publications, University of California, Los Angeles, California 90024 (310) 825-6634; *Statistical Abstract of Latin America.*

CHILE - SOCIAL SECURITY

Inter-American Development Bank, 1300 New York Avenue, NW, Washington, D.C. 20577 (202) 623-1753; *Economic and Social Progress in Latin America.*

International Monetary Fund, 700 Nineteenth Street, NW, Washington, D.C. 20431 (202) 623-7000; *Government Finance Statistics Yearbook.*

CHILE - SOCIOECONOMIC DATA

Inter-American Development Bank, 1300 New York Avenue, NW, Washington, D.C. 20577 (202) 623-1753; *Economic and Social Progress in Latin America.*

U.C.L.A. Latin American Center Publications, University of California, Los Angeles, California 90024 (310) 825-6634; *Statistical Abstract of Latin America.*

CHILE - SOYBEAN PRODUCTION - See CHILE - CROPS

CHILE - STAMP TAXES AND DUTIES - See CHILE - TAXATION

CHILE - STATE BUDGET REVENUE AND EXPENDITURES

Euromonitor Publications Limited, 87-88 Turnmill Street, London EC1M 5QU, England; *International Marketing Data and Statistics.*

Inter-American Development Bank, 1300 New York Avenue, NW, Washington, D.C. 20577 (202) 623-1753; *Economic and Social Progress in Latin America.*

CHILE - STEEL - See CHILE - MINING AND MINERAL PRODUCTS

CHILE - STOCKS - COMMODITY - MARKET PRICE - INDEXES

Food and Agricultural Organization of the United Nations (FAO) Via delle Terme di Caracalla, 00100 Rome, Italy (Telephone Number in U.S. (202) 653-2400); *The State of Food and Agriculture.*

Statistical Office of the United Nations, Publishing Service, New York, New York 10017 (800) 253-9646; *Statistical Yearbook.*

World Bureau of Metal Statistics, 27-A High Street, Ware Hert SG12 9BA, England; *World Metal Statistics.*

CHILE - SUGAR - See CHILE - CROPS

CHILE - SULPHUR AND SULPHURIC ACID PRODUCTION - See CHILE - MINING AND MINERAL PRODUCTS

CHILE - TAXATION

G.K. Hall and Company, 70 Lincoln Street, Boston, Massachusetts 02111 (617) 423-3990; *The World in Figures.*

Inter-American Development Bank, 1300 New York Avenue, NW, Washington, D.C. 20577 (202) 623-1753; *Economic and Social Progress in Latin America.*

International Monetary Fund, 700 Nineteenth Street, NW, Washington, D.C. 20431 (202) 623-7000; *Government Finance Statistics Yearbook.*

International Road Federation, 525 School Street, SW, Washington, D.C. 20024 (202) 554-2106; *World Road Statistics.*

Statistical Office of the United Nations, Publishing Service, New York, New York 10017 (800) 253-9646; *Statistical Yearbook for Latin America and the Caribbean.*

The World Bank, 1818 H Street, NW, Washington, D.C. 20433 (202) 477-1234; *World Tables.*

CHILE - TEA - See CHILE - CROPS

CHILE - TELEGRAPH SERVICE

Statistical Office of the United Nations, Publishing Service, New York, New York 10017 (800) 253-9646; *Statistical Yearbook.*

CHILE - TELEPHONES IN USE

American Telephone and Telegraph Company, 26 Parsippany Road, Whippany, New Jersey 07981 (800) 338-4038; *The World's Telephones.*

The Economist Intelligence Unit, 111 West 57th Street, New York, New York 10019 (800) 938-4685; *The New Latin America Market Atlas.*

Euromonitor Publications Limited, 87-88 Turnmill Street, London EC1M 5QU, England; *Third World Economic Handbook.*

G.K. Hall and Company, 70 Lincoln Street, Boston, Massachusetts 02111 (617) 423-3990; *The World in Figures.*

Statistical Office of the United Nations, Publishing Service, New York, New York 10017 (800) 253-9646; *Statistical Yearbook.*

CHILE - TELEVISION BROADCASTING - See CHILE - BROADCASTING

CHILE - TELEVISION RECEIVER PRODUCTION

Statistical Office of the United Nations, Publishing Service, New York, New York 10017 (800) 253-9646; *Statistical Yearbook.*

CHILE - TEXTILE INDUSTRY

Euromonitor Publications Limited, 87-88 Turnmill Street, London EC1M 5QU, England; *Third World Economic Handbook.*

Food and Agricultural Organization of the United Nations (FAO), Via delle Terme di Caracalla, 00100 Rome, Italy (Telephone Number in U.S. (202) 653-2400); *Production Yearbook.*

Forest and Paper Association, 1250 Connecticut Avenue, N.W., Washington, D.C. 20036 (202) 463-2455; *Wood Pulp and Fiber Statistics.*

G.K. Hall and Company, 70 Lincoln Street, Boston, Massachusetts 02111 (617) 423-3990; *The World in Figures.*

Statistical Office of the United Nations, Publishing Service, New York, New York 10017 (800) 253-9646; *Statistical Yearbook.*

CHILE - THEATRE

United Nations Educational, Scientific and Cultural Organization (UNESCO), 7 Place de Fontenoy, F-75700 Paris France (Telephone Number in U.S. (212) 963-5981); *Statistical Yearbook.*

CHILE - TIN - See CHILE - MINING AND MINERAL PRODUCTS

CHILE - TIRE (MOTOR VEHICLE) PRODUCTION

Statistical Office of the United Nations, Publishing Service, New York, New York 10017 (800) 253-9646; *Statistical Yearbook.*

CHILE - TOBACCO PRODUCTION

Euromonitor Publications Limited, 87-88 Turnmill Street, London EC1M 5QU, England; *Third World Economic Handbook.*

Facts on File, 460 Park Avenue South, New York, New York 10016 (800) 443-8323; *The New Book of World Rankings.*

Statistical Office of the United Nations, Publishing Service, New York, New York 10017 (800) 253-9646; *Statistical Yearbook.*

CHILE - TOURISM

The Economist Intelligence Unit, 111 West 57th Street, New York, New York 10019 (800) 938-4685; *The New Latin America Market Atlas.*

Euromonitor Publications Limited, 87-88 Turnmill Street, London EC1M 5QU, England; *Third World Economic Handbook.*

Facts on File, 460 Park Avenue South, New York, New York 10016 (800) 443-8323; *The New Book of World Rankings.*

Federal Statistical Office, Gustav - Stresemann - Ring 11, D-6200 Wiesbaden, Germany; *Chile.*

G.K. Hall and Company, 70 Lincoln Street, Boston, Massachusetts 02111 (617) 423-3990; *The World in Figures.*

Statistical Office of the United Nations, Publishing Service, New York, New York 10017 (800) 253-9646; *Statistical Yearbook,* and *Statistical Yearbook for Latin America and the Caribbean.*

Times Books, 201 East 50th Street, New York, New York 10022 (212) 751-2600; *The Economist Book of Vital World Statistics.*

U.C.L.A. Latin American Center Publications, University of California, Los Angeles, California 90024 (310) 825-6634; *Statistical Abstract of Latin America.*

World Tourism Organization, Calle Capitan Haya 42, E-28020 Madrid, Spain; *Yearbook of Tourism Statistics.*

CHILE - TRACTORS IN USE

The Economist Intelligence Unit, 111 West 57th Street, New York, New York 10019 (800) 938-4685; *The New Latin America Market Atlas.*

Statistical Office of the United Nations, Publishing Service, New York, New York 10017 (800) 253-9646; *Statistical Yearbook.*

CHILE - TRADE - See CHILE - FOREIGN TRADE

CHILE - TRADEMARKS AND SERVICE MARKS

Statistical Office of the United Nations, Publishing Service, New York, New York 10017 (800) 253-9646; *Statistical Yearbook.*

World Intellectual Property Organization, 34 Chemin des Colombettes, CH-1211 Geneva 20. Switzerland; *Industrial Property Statistics.*

CHILE - TRANSPORTATION AND COMMUNICATIONS

The Economist Intelligence Unit (Asia) Limited, 10th Floor, Luk Kwok Centre, 72 Gloucester Road, Wanchai, Hong Kong (Phone Number in U.S. (800) 938-4685); *Asian Market Atlas.*

Euromonitor Publications Limited, 87-88 Turnmill Street, London EC1M 5QU, England; *Third World Economic Handbook.*

Facts on File, 460 Park Avenue South, New York, New York 10016 (800) 443-8323; *The New Book of World Rankings.*

Federal Statistical Office, Gustav - Stresemann - Ring 11, D-6200 Wiesbaden, Germany; *Chile.*

Gale Research Incorporated, 835 Penobscot Building, Detroit, Michigan 48226 (800) 877-4253; *International Historical Statistics The Americas and Australasia.*

G.K. Hall and Company, 70 Lincoln Street, Boston, Massachusetts 02111 (617) 423-3990; *The World in Figures.*

Inter-American Development Bank, 1300 New York Avenue, NW, Washington, D.C. 20577 (202) 623-1753; *Economic and Social Progress in Latin America.*

Statistical Office of the United Nations, Publishing Service, New York, New York 10017 (800) 253-9646; *Statistical Yearbook for Latin America and the Caribbean.*

U.C.L.A. Latin American Center Publications, University of California, Los Angeles, California 90024 (310) 825-6634; *Statistical Abstract of Latin America.*

CHILE - UNEMPLOYMENT

The Economist Intelligence Unit (Asia) Limited, 10th Floor, Luk Kwok Centre, 72 Gloucester Road, Wanchai, Hong Kong (Phone Number in U.S. (800) 938-4685); *Asian Market Atlas.*

Euromonitor Publications Limited, 87-88 Turnmill Street, London EC1M 5QU, England; *International Marketing Data and Statistics.*

International Labour Office, I.L.O. Publications, CH-1211, Geneva 22, Switzerland; *Yearbook of Labour Statistics.*

Organization of American States (OAS), General Secretariat, Washington, D.C. 20006 (202) 458-3533; *Statistical Bulletin of the OAS.*

Statistical Office of the United Nations, Publishing Service, New York, New York 10017 (800) 253-9646; *Statistical Yearbook.*

U.C.L.A. Latin American Center Publications, University of California, Los Angeles, California 90024 (310) 825-6634; *Statistical Abstract of Latin America.*

CHILE - UTILITIES

U.C.L.A. Latin American Center Publications, University of California, Los Angeles, California 90024 (310) 825-6634; *Statistical Abstract of Latin America.*

CHILE - VANADIUM AND VANADIUM ORE - See CHILE - MINING AND MINERAL PRODUCTS

CHILE - VITAL STATISTICS

Euromonitor Publications Limited, 87-88 Turnmill Street, London EC1M 5QU, England; *International Marketing Data and Statistics,* and *Third World Economic Handbook.*

Gale Research Incorporated, 835 Penobscot Building, Detroit, Michigan 48226 (800) 877-4253; *International Historical Statistics The Americas and Australasia.*

G.K. Hall and Company, 70 Lincoln Street, Boston, Massachusetts 02111 (617) 423-3990; *The World in Figures.*

Statistical Office of the United Nations, Publishing Service, New York, New York 10017 (800) 253-9646; *Statistical Yearbook.*

World Health Organization, Office of Publications, Avenue Appia, CH-1211 Geneva 27, Switzerland (Telephone Number in U.S. (518) 436-9686); *World Health Statistics Annual.*

CHILE - WAGES

Federal Statistical Office, Gustav - Stresemann - Ring 11, D-6200 Wiesbaden, Germany; *Chile.*

G.K. Hall and Company, 70 Lincoln Street, Boston, Massachusetts 02111 (617) 423-3990; *The World in Figures*.

International Labour Office, I.L.O. Publications, CH-1211, Geneva 22, Switzerland; *Yearbook of Labour Statistics*.

Organization of American States (OAS), General Secretariat, Washington, D.C. 20006 (202) 458-3533; *Statistical Bulletin of the OAS*.

Statistical Office of the United Nations, Publishing Service, New York, New York 10017 (800) 253-9646; *Statistical Yearbook*.

U.C.L.A. Latin American Center Publications, University of California, Los Angeles, California 90024 (310) 825-6634; *Statistical Abstract of Latin America*.

CHILE - WATERMELON PRODUCTION - See CHILE - CROPS

CHILE - WEATHER

Facts on File, 460 Park Avenue South, New York, New York 10016 (800) 443-8323; *The New Book of World Rankings*.

G.K. Hall and Company, 70 Lincoln Street, Boston, Massachusetts 02111 (617) 423-3990; *The World in Figures*.

CHILE - WELFARE

Inter-American Development Bank, 1300 New York Avenue, NW, Washington, D.C. 20577 (202) 623-1753; *Economic and Social Progress in Latin America*.

International Monetary Fund, 700 Nineteenth Street, NW, Washington, D.C. 20431 (202) 623-7000; *Government Finance Statistics Yearbook*.

CHILE - WHALES - See CHILE - FISHERIES

CHILE - WHEAT PRODUCTION - See CHILE - CROPS

CHILE - WHOLESALE PRICES

Inter-American Development Bank, 1300 New York Avenue, NW, Washington, D.C. 20577 (202) 623-1753; *Economic and Social Progress in Latin America*.

Organization of American States (OAS), General Secretariat, Washington, D.C. 20006 (202) 458-3533; *Statistical Bulletin of the OAS*.

Statistical Office of the United Nations, Publishing Service, New York, New York 10017 (800) 253-9646; *Statistical Yearbook*.

CHILE - WHOLESALE TRADE

Euromonitor Publications Limited, 87-88 Turnmill Street, London EC1M 5QU, England; *Third World Economic Handbook*.

Inter-American Development Bank, 1300 New York Avenue, NW, Washington, D.C. 20577 (202) 623-1753; *Economic and Social Progress in Latin America*.

Statistical Office of the United Nations, Publishing Service, New York, New York 10017 (800) 253-9646; *Statistical Yearbook*.

CHILE - WINE PRODUCTION

Facts on File, 460 Park Avenue South, New York, New York 10016 (800) 443-8323; *The New Book of World Rankings*.

Statistical Office of the United Nations, Publishing Service, New York, New York 10017 (800) 253-9646; *Statistical Yearbook*.

CHILE - WOOD - See CHILE - FORESTRY AND FOREST PRODUCTS

CHILE - WOOL PRODUCTION

Facts on File, 460 Park Avenue South, New York, New York 10016 (800) 443-8323; *The New Book of World Rankings*.

Statistical Office of the United Nations, Publishing Service, New York, New York 10017 (800) 253-9646; *Statistical Yearbook*.

CHILE - YARN PRODUCTION

Statistical Office of the United Nations, Publishing Service, New York, New York 10017 (800) 253-9646; *Statistical Yearbook*.

CHILE - ZINC AND ZINC ORE - See CHILE -MINING AND MINERAL PRODUCTS

China, People's Republic of - National Statistical Office

State Statistical Bureau, 38 Yuetan Nanjie, Sanlihe, Beijing, People's Republic of China.

China, People's Republic of - Primary Statistics Source

The University of Illinois at Chicago, China Statistics Archives, Suite 700 South, 1033 West Van Buren Street, Chicago, Illinois 60607-9940 (312) 413-0001 and China Statistical Information and Consultancy Service Center, 38 Yuetan Nanjie, Sanlihe, Beijing, People's Republic of China; *China Statistics Monthly*, and *China Statistics Yearbook*.

CHINA, PEOPLE'S REPUBLIC OF - AGRICULTURE

Asian Development Bank, P.O. Box 789, 1099 Manila, Philippines; *Key Indicators of Developing Asian and Pacific Countries*.

The Economist Intelligence Unit (Asia) Limited, 10th Floor, Luk Kwok Centre, 72 Gloucester Road, Wanchai, Hong Kong (Phone Number in U.S. (800) 938-4685); *China Market Atlas*.

Euromonitor Publications Limited, 87-88 Turnmill Street, London EC1M 5QU, England; *International Marketing Data and Statistics*, and *Third World Economic Handbook*.

Facts on File, 460 Park Avenue South, New York, New York 10016 (800) 443-8323; *The New Book of World Rankings*.

Food and Agricultural Organization of the United Nations (FAO) Via delle Terme di Caracalla, 00100 Rome, Italy (Telephone Number in U.S. (202) 653-2400); *Production Yearbook*, *The State of Food and Agriculture*, and *Trade Yearbook*.

G.K. Hall and Company, 70 Lincoln Street, Boston, Massachusetts 02111 (617) 423-3990; *The World in Figures*.

Statistical Office of the United Nations, Publishing Service, New York, New York 10017 (800) 253-9646; *Statistical Yearbook*, and

Statistical Yearbook for Asia and the Pacific.

Times Books, 201 East 50th Street, New York, New York 10022 (212) 751-2600; *The Economist Book of Vital World Statistics.*

The University of Illinois at Chicago, China Statistics Archives, Suite 700 South, 1033 West Van Buren Street, Chicago, Illinois 60607-9940 (312) 413-0001 and China Statistical Information and Consultancy Service Center, 38 Yuetan Nanjie, Sanlihe, Beijing, People's Republic of China; *China Rural Statistics, China Social Statistics, China Statistical Abstract,* and *China Trade and Price Statistics.*

The World Bank, 1818 H Street, NW, Washington, D.C. 20433 (202) 477-1234; *World Tables.*

CHINA, PEOPLE'S REPUBLIC OF - AIRLINE SERVICE

The Economist Intelligence Unit (Asia) Limited, 10th Floor, Luk Kwok Centre, 72 Gloucester Road, Wanchai, Hong Kong (Phone Number in U.S. (800) 938-4685); *Asian Market Atlas,* and *China Market Atlas.*

Facts on File, 460 Park Avenue South, New York, New York 10016 (800) 443-8323; *The New Book of World Rankings.*

G.K. Hall and Company, 70 Lincoln Street, Boston, Massachusetts 02111 (617) 423-3990; *The World in Figures.*

Times Books, 201 East 50th Street, New York, New York 10022 (212) 751-2600; *The Economist Book of Vital World Statistics.*

CHINA, PEOPLE'S REPUBLIC OF - ALUMINUM PRODUCTION AND CONSUMPTION - See CHINA, PEOPLE'S REPUBLIC OF - MINING AND MINERAL PRODUCTS

CHINA, PEOPLE'S REPUBLIC OF - ANIMAL HEALTH

Food and Agricultural Organization of the United Nations (FAO), Via delle Terme di Caracalla, 00100 Rome, Italy (Telephone Number in U.S. (202) 653-2400); *Animal Health Yearbook.*

CHINA, PEOPLE'S REPUBLIC OF - ANTIMONY AND ANTIMONY ORE - See CHINA, PEOPLE'S REPUBLIC OF - MINING AND MINERAL PRODUCTS

CHINA, PEOPLE'S REPUBLIC OF - AREA AND DENSITY OF POPULATION

The Economist Intelligence Unit (Asia) Limited, 10th Floor, Luk Kwok Centre, 72 Gloucester Road, Wanchai, Hong Kong (Phone Number in U.S. (800) 938-4685); *China Market Atlas.*

Euromonitor Publications Limited, 87-88 Turnmill Street, London EC1M 5QU, England; *International Marketing Data and Statistics.*

Facts on File, 460 Park Avenue South, New York, New York 10016 (800) 443-8323; *The New Book of World Rankings.*

Food and Agricultural Organization of the United Nations (FAO) Via delle Terme di Caracalla, 00100 Rome, Italy (Telephone Number in U.S. (202) 653-2400); *The State of Food and Agriculture.*

G.K. Hall and Company, 70 Lincoln Street, Boston, Massachusetts 02111 (617) 423-3990; *The World in Figures.*

Statistical Office of the United Nations, Publishing Service, New York, New York 10017 (800) 253-9646; *Statistical Yearbook.*

Times Books, 201 East 50th Street, New York, New York 10022 (212) 751-2600; *The Economist Book of Vital World Statistics.*

United Nations Educational, Scientific and Cultural Organization (UNESCO), 7 Place de Fontenoy, F-75700 Paris, France (Telephone Number in U.S. (212) 963-5981; *Statistical Yearbook.*

The University of Illinois at Chicago, China Statistics Archives, Suite 700 South, 1033 West Van Buren Street, Chicago, Illinois 60607-9940 (312) 413-0001 and China Statistical Information and Consultancy Service Center, 38 Yuetan Nanjie, Sanlihe, Beijing, People's Republic of China; *China Rural Statistics, China Social Statistics,* and *China Statistical Abstract.*

CHINA, PEOPLE'S REPUBLIC OF - ARMS EXPORTS AND IMPORTS

U.S. Arms Control and Disarmament Agency, 320 Twenty-first Street, NW, Washington, D.C. 20451 (202) 647-8677; *World Military Expenditures and Arms Transfers.*

CHINA, PEOPLE'S REPUBLIC OF - BALANCE OF PAYMENTS

The Economist Intelligence Unit, 111 West 57th Street, New York, New York 10019 (800) 938-4685; *The World Market Atlas.*

Euromonitor Publications Limited, 87-88 Turnmill Street, London EC1M 5QU, England; *Third World Economic Handbook.*

G.K. Hall and Company, 70 Lincoln Street, Boston, Massachusetts 02111 (617) 423-3990; *The World in Figures.*

International Monetary Fund, 700 Nineteenth Street, NW, Washington, D.C. 20431 (202) 623-7000; *Balance of Payments Yearbook.*

Times Books, 201 East 50th Street, New York, New York 10022 (212) 751-2600; *The Economist Book of Vital World Statistics.*

The University of Illinois at Chicago, China Statistics Archives, Suite 700 South, 1033 West Van Buren Street, Chicago, Illinois 60607-9940 (312) 413-0001 and China Statistical Information and Consultancy Service Center, 38 Yuetan Nanjie, Sanlihe, Beijing, People's Republic of China; *China Statistical Abstract,* and *China Trade and Price Statistics.*

The World Bank, 1818 H Street, NW, Washington, D.C. 20433 (202) 477-1234; *World Tables.*

CHINA, PEOPLE'S REPUBLIC OF - BANKING

Asian Development Bank, P.O. Box 789, 1099 Manila, Philippines; *Key Indicators of Developing Asian and Pacific Countries.*

The Economist Intelligence Unit (Asia) Limited, 10th Floor, Luk Kwok Centre, 72 Gloucester Road, Wanchai, Hong Kong (Phone Number in U.S. (800) 938-4685); *China Market Atlas.*

Facts on File, 460 Park Avenue South, New York, New York 10016 (800) 443-8323; *The New Book of World Rankings.*

G.K. Hall and Company, 70 Lincoln Street, Boston, Massachusetts 02111 (617) 423-3990; *The World in Figures.*

The University of Illinois at Chicago, China Statistics Archives, Suite 700 South, 1033 West Van Buren Street, Chicago, Illinois 60607-9940 (312) 413-0001 and China Statistical Information and Consultancy Service Center, 38 Yuetan Nanjie, Sanlihe, Beijing, People's Republic of China: *China Social Statistics,* and *China Statistical Abstract.*

CHINA, PEOPLE'S REPUBLIC OF - BARLEY PRODUCTION - See CHINA, PEOPLE'S REPUBLIC OF - CROPS

CHINA, PEOPLE'S REPUBLIC OF - BAUXITE PRODUCTION AND CONSUMPTION - See CHINA, PEOPLE'S REPUBLIC OF - MINING AND MINERAL PRODUCTS

CHINA, PEOPLE'S REPUBLIC OF - BEER PRODUCTION

Facts on File, 460 Park Avenue South, New York, New York 10016 (800) 443-8323; *The New Book of World Rankings.*

Statistical Office of the United Nations, Publishing Service, New York, New York 10017 (800) 253-9646; *Statistical Yearbook.*

The University of Illinois at Chicago, China Statistics Archives, Suite 700 South, 1033 West Van Buren Street, Chicago, Illinois 60607-9940 (312) 413-0001 and China Statistical Information and Consultancy Service Center, 38 Yuetan Nanjie, Sanlihe, Beijing, People's Republic of China; *China Statistical Abstract.*

CHINA, PEOPLE'S REPUBLIC OF - BIRTH RATES

The Economist Intelligence Unit (Asia) Limited, 10th Floor, Luk Kwok Centre, 72 Gloucester Road, Wanchai, Hong Kong (Phone Number in U.S. (800) 938-4685); *Asian Market Atlas,* and *China Market Atlas.*

Euromonitor Publications Limited, 87-88 Turnmill Street, London EC1M 5QU, England; *Third World Economic Handbook.*

Facts on File, 460 Park Avenue South, New York, New York 10016 (800) 443-8323; *The New Book of World Rankings.*

Statistical Office of the United Nations, Publishing Service, New York, New York 10017 (800) 253-9646; *Demographic Yearbook,* and *Statistical Yearbook.*

Times Books, 201 East 50th Street, New York, New York 10022 (212) 751-2600; *The Economist Book of Vital World Statistics.*

The University of Illinois at Chicago, China Statistics Archives, Suite 700 South, 1033 West Van Buren Street, Chicago, Illinois 60607-9940 (312) 413-0001 and China Statistical Information and Consultancy Service Center, 38 Yuetan Nanjie, Sanlihe, Beijing, People's Republic of China; *China Rural Statistics, China Social Statistics,* and *China Statistical Abstract.*

The World Bank, 1818 H Street, NW, Washington, D.C. 20433 (202) 477-1234; *World Tables.*

World Health Organization, Office of Publications, Avenue Appia, CH-1211 Geneva 27, Switzerland (Telephone Number in U.S. (518) 436-9686); *World Health Statistics Annual.*

CHINA, PEOPLE'S REPUBLIC OF - BISMUTH PRODUCTION AND CONSUMPTION - See CHINA, PEOPLE'S REPUBLIC OF - MINING AND MINERAL PRODUCTS

CHINA, PEOPLE'S REPUBLIC OF - BONDS

G.K. Hall and Company, 70 Lincoln Street, Boston, Massachusetts 02111 (617) 423-3990; *The World in Figures.*

Asian Development Bank, P.O. Box 789, 1099 Manila, Philippines; *Key Indicators of Developing Asian and Pacific Countries.*

CHINA, PEOPLE'S REPUBLIC OF - BOOK PRODUCTION

G.K. Hall and Company, 70 Lincoln Street, Boston, Massachusetts 02111 (617) 423-3990; *The World in Figures.*

United Nations Educational, Scientific and Cultural Organization (UNESCO), 7 Place de Fontenoy, F-75700 Paris, France (Telephone Number in U.S. (212) 963-5981; *Statistical Yearbook.*

The University of Illinois at Chicago, China Statistics Archives, Suite 700 South, 1033 West Van Buren Street, Chicago, Illinois 60607-9940 (312) 413-0001 and China Statistical Information and Consultancy Service Center, 38 Yuetan Nanjie, Sanlihe, Beijing, People's Republic of China; *China Statistical Abstract.*

CHINA, PEOPLE'S REPUBLIC OF - BROADCASTING

Billboard Limited, P.O. Box 9027, 1006 AA Amsterdam, The Netherlands (Telephone Number in U.S. (212) 764-7300); *World Radio TV Handbook.*

The Economist Intelligence Unit (Asia) Limited, 10th Floor, Luk Kwok Centre, 72 Gloucester Road, Wanchai, Hong Kong (Phone Number in U.S. (800) 938-4685); *Asian Market Atlas.*

Facts on File, 460 Park Avenue South, New York, New York 10016 (800) 443-8323; *The New Book of World Rankings.*

G.K. Hall and Company, 70 Lincoln Street, Boston, Massachusetts 02111 (617) 423-3990; *The World in Figures.*

Times Books, 201 East 50th Street, New York, New York 10022 (212) 751-2600; *The Economist Book of Vital World Statistics.*

CHINA, PEOPLE'S REPUBLIC OF - BUSINESS

G.K. Hall and Company, 70 Lincoln Street, Boston, Massachusetts 02111 (617) 423-3990; *The World in Figures.*

CHINA, PEOPLE'S REPUBLIC OF - BUSINESS - COMPANIES BY TYPE OF INDUSTRY

The University of Illinois at Chicago, China Statistics Archives, Suite 700 South, 1033 West Van Buren Street, Chicago, Illinois 60607-9940 (312) 413-0001 and China Statistical Information and Consultancy Service Center, 38 Yuetan Nanjie, Sanlihe, Beijing, People's Republic of China; *China Statistical Abstract.*

CHINA, PEOPLE'S REPUBLIC OF - BUTTER PRODUCTION - See CHINA, PEOPLE'S REPUBLIC OF - DAIRY PRODUCTS

CHINA, PEOPLE'S REPUBLIC OF - CABBAGE PRODUCTION - See CHINA, PEOPLE'S REPUBLIC OF - CROPS

CHINA, PEOPLE'S REPUBLIC OF - CALORIE SUPPLY

Asian Development Bank, P.O. Box 789, 1099 Manila, Philippines; *Key Indicators of Developing Asian and Pacific Countries.*

Food and Agricultural Organization of the United Nations (FAO) Via delle Terme di Caracalla, 00100 Rome, Italy (Telephone Number in U.S. (202) 653-2400); *The State of Food and Agriculture.*

CHINA, PEOPLE'S REPUBLIC OF - CAPITAL INVESTMENT

Asian Development Bank, P.O. Box 789, 1099 Manila, Philippines; *Key Indicators of Developing Asian and Pacific Countries.*

The Economist Intelligence Unit (Asia) Limited, 10th Floor, Luk Kwok Centre, 72 Gloucester Road, Wanchai, Hong Kong (Phone Number in U.S. (800) 938-4685); *China Market Atlas.*

The University of Illinois at Chicago, China Statistics Archives, Suite 700 South, 1033 West Van Buren Street, Chicago, Illinois 60607-9940 (312) 413-0001 and China Statistical Information and Consultancy Service Center, 38 Yuetan Nanjie, Sanlihe, Beijing, People's Republic of China; *China Statistical Abstract.*

CHINA, PEOPLE'S REPUBLIC OF - CAPITAL REVENUE

Asian Development Bank, P.O. Box 789, 1099 Manila, Philippines; *Key Indicators of Developing Asian and Pacific Countries.*

The University of Illinois at Chicago, China Statistics Archives, Suite 700 South, 1033 West Van Buren Street, Chicago, Illinois 60607-9940 (312) 413-0001 and China Statistical Information and Consultancy Service Center, 38 Yuetan Nanjie, Sanlihe, Beijing, People's Republic of China; *China Statistical Abstract.*

CHINA, PEOPLE'S REPUBLIC OF - CATTLE - See CHINA, PEOPLE'S REPUBLIC OF - LIVESTOCK AND POULTRY

CHINA, PEOPLE'S REPUBLIC OF - CAULIFLOWER PRODUCTION - See CHINA, PEOPLE'S REPUBLIC OF - CROPS

CHINA, PEOPLE'S REPUBLIC OF - CEMENT PRODUCTION - See CHINA, PEOPLE'S REPUBLIC OF - MINING AND MINERAL PRODUCTS

CHINA, PEOPLE'S REPUBLIC OF - CHEESE PRODUCTION - See CHINA, PEOPLE'S REPUBLIC OF - DAIRY PRODUCTS

CHINA, PEOPLE'S REPUBLIC OF - CHEMICAL (ORGANIC) PRODUCTION - See CHINA, PEOPLE'S REPUBLIC OF - MINING AND MINERAL PRODUCTS

CHINA, PEOPLE'S REPUBLIC OF - CHESTNUT PRODUCTION - See CHINA, PEOPLE'S REPUBLIC OF - CROPS

CHINA, PEOPLE'S REPUBLIC OF - CHICKENS - See CHINA, PEOPLE'S REPUBLIC OF - LIVESTOCK AND POULTRY

CHINA, PEOPLE'S REPUBLIC OF - CIGARETTE PRODUCTION - See CHINA, PEOPLE'S REPUBLIC OF - TOBACCO PRODUCTION

CHINA, PEOPLE'S REPUBLIC OF - CLASS STRUCTURE

G.K. Hall and Company, 70 Lincoln Street, Boston, Massachusetts 02111 (617) 423-3990; *The World in Figures.*

CHINA, PEOPLE'S REPUBLIC OF - CLIMATE

Facts on File, 460 Park Avenue South, New York, New York 10016 (800) 443-8323; *The New Book of World Rankings.*

G.K. Hall and Company, 70 Lincoln Street, Boston, Massachusetts 02111 (617) 423-3990; *The World in Figures.*

CHINA, PEOPLE'S REPUBLIC OF - CLOTHING EXPORTS AND IMPORTS

The Economist Intelligence Unit (Asia) Limited, 10th Floor, Luk Kwok Centre, 72 Gloucester Road, Wanchai, Hong Kong (Phone Number in U.S. (800) 938-4685); *China Market Atlas.*

Euromonitor Publications Limited, 87-88 Turnmill Street, London EC1M 5QU, England; *Third World Economic Handbook.*

The University of Illinois at Chicago, China Statistics Archives, Suite 700 South, 1033 West Van Buren Street, Chicago, Illinois 60607-9940 (312) 413-0001 and China Statistical Information and Consultancy Service Center, 38 Yuetan Nanjie, Sanlihe, Beijing, People's Republic of China; *China Statistical Abstract,* and *China Trade and Price Statistics.*

CHINA, PEOPLE'S REPUBLIC OF - COAL PRODUCTION - See CHINA, PEOPLE'S REPUBLIC OF - MINING AND MINERAL PRODUCTS

CHINA, PEOPLE'S REPUBLIC OF - COFFEE - See CHINA, PEOPLE'S REPUBLIC OF - CROPS

CHINA, PEOPLE'S REPUBLIC OF - COKE OVEN COKE - See CHINA, PEOPLE'S REPUBLIC OF - MINING AND MINERAL PRODUCTS

CHINA, PEOPLE'S REPUBLIC OF - COMMUNICATIONS

The Economist Intelligence Unit (Asia) Limited, 10th Floor, Luk Kwok Centre, 72 Gloucester Road, Wanchai, Hong Kong (Phone Number in U.S. (800) 938-4685); *China Market Atlas.*

Euromonitor Publications Limited, 87-88 Turnmill Street, London EC1M 5QU, England; *Third World Economic Handbook.*

G.K. Hall and Company, 70 Lincoln Street, Boston, Massachusetts 02111 (617) 423-3990; *The World in Figures.*

Statistical Office of the United Nations, Publishing Service, New York, New York 10017 (800) 253-9646; *Statistical Yearbook for Asia and the Pacific.*

The University of Illinois at Chicago, China Statistics Archives, Suite 700 South, 1033 West Van Buren Street, Chicago, Illinois 60607-9940 (312) 413-0001 and China Statistical Information and Consultancy Service Center, 38 Yuetan Nanjie, Sanlihe, Beijing, People's Republic of China; *China Rural Statistics, China Social Statistics,* and *China Statistical Abstract.*

CHINA, PEOPLE'S REPUBLIC OF - CONSTRUCTION INDUSTRY

The Economist Intelligence Unit (Asia) Limited, 10th Floor, Luk Kwok Centre, 72 Gloucester Road, Wanchai, Hong Kong (Phone Number in U.S. (800) 938-4685); *China Market Atlas.*

Facts on File, 460 Park Avenue South, New York, New York 10016 (800) 443-8323; *The New Book of World Rankings.*

The University of Illinois at Chicago, China Statistics Archives, Suite 700 South, 1033 West Van Buren Street, Chicago, Illinois 60607-9940 (312) 413-0001 and China Statistical Information and Consultancy Service Center, 38 Yuetan Nanjie, Sanlihe, Beijing, People's Republic of China; *China Statistical Abstract.*

CHINA, PEOPLE'S REPUBLIC OF - CONSUMER PRICE INDEX

Asian Development Bank, P.O. Box 789, 1099 Manila, Philippines; *Key Indicators of Developing Asian and Pacific Countries.*

G.K. Hall and Company, 70 Lincoln Street, Boston, Massachusetts 02111 (617) 423-3990; *The World in Figures.*

CHINA, PEOPLE'S REPUBLIC OF - CONSUMER PRICES

International Monetary Fund, 700 Nineteenth Street, NW, Washington, D.C. 20431 (202) 623-7000; *International Financial Statistics.*

Times Books, 201 East 50th Street, New York, New York 10022 (212) 751-2600; *The Economist Book of Vital World Statistics.*

The University of Illinois at Chicago, China Statistics Archives, Suite 700 South, 1033 West Van Buren Street, Chicago, Illinois 60607-9940 (312) 413-0001 and China Statistical Information and Consultancy Service Center, 38 Yuetan Nanjie, Sanlihe, Beijing, People's Republic of China: *China Social Statistics, China Statistical Abstract,* and *China Trade and Price Statistics.*

CHINA, PEOPLE'S REPUBLIC OF - CONSUMER PRODUCTS

The Economist Intelligence Unit (Asia) Limited, 10th Floor, Luk Kwok Centre, 72 Gloucester Road, Wanchai, Hong Kong (Phone Number in U.S. (800) 938-4685); *China Market Atlas.*

CHINA, PEOPLE'S REPUBLIC OF - CONSUMPTION

The Economist Intelligence Unit (Asia) Limited, 10th Floor, Luk Kwok Centre, 72 Gloucester Road, Wanchai, Hong Kong (Phone Number in U.S. (800) 938-4685); *China Market Atlas.*

G.K. Hall and Company, 70 Lincoln Street, Boston, Massachusetts 02111 (617) 423-3990; *The World in Figures.*

CHINA, PEOPLE'S REPUBLIC OF - COPPER PRODUCTION - See CHINA, PEOPLE'S REPUBLIC OF - MINING AND MINERAL PRODUCTS

CHINA, PEOPLE'S REPUBLIC OF - CORN PRODUCTION - See CHINA, PEOPLE'S REPUBLIC OF - CROPS

CHINA, PEOPLE'S REPUBLIC OF - CORPORATE TAXES - See CHINA, PEOPLE'S REPUBLIC OF - TAXATION

CHINA, PEOPLE'S REPUBLIC OF - COTTON - See CHINA, PEOPLE'S REPUBLIC OF - CROPS

CHINA, PEOPLE'S REPUBLIC OF - CRIME

International Criminal Police Organization (INTERPOL), 26 rue Armengaud, 92210 Saint Cloud, France; *International Crime Statistics.*

The University of Illinois at Chicago, China Statistics Archives, Suite 700 South, 1033 West Van Buren Street, Chicago, Illinois 60607-9940 (312) 413-0001 and China Statistical Information and Consultancy Service Center, 38 Yuetan Nanjie, Sanlihe, Beijing, People's Republic of China: *China Social Statistics,* and *China Statistical Abstract.*

Yale University Press, Yale Station, New Haven, Connecticut 06520 (203) 432-0940; *Violence and Crime in Cross-National Perspective.*

CHINA, PEOPLE'S REPUBLIC OF - CROPS

Asian Development Bank, P.O. Box 789, 1099 Manila, Philippines; *Key Indicators of Developing Asian and Pacific Countries.*

Commodity Research Bureau, Incorporated, 75 Wall Street, New York, New York 10005 (212) 504-7754; *Commodity Year Book.*

The Economist Intelligence Unit (Asia) Limited, 10th Floor, Luk Kwok Centre, 72 Gloucester Road, Wanchai, Hong Kong (Phone Number in U.S. (800) 938-4685); *China Market Atlas.*

Facts on File, 460 Park Avenue South, New York, New York 10016 (800) 443-8323; *The New Book of World Rankings.*

Food and Agricultural Organization of the United Nations (FAO) Via delle Terme di Caracalla, 00100 Rome, Italy (Telephone Number in U.S. (202) 653-2400); *The State of Food and Agriculture.*

G.K. Hall and Company, 70 Lincoln Street, Boston, Massachusetts 02111 (617) 423-3990; *The World in Figures.*

Statistical Office of the United Nations, Publishing Service, New York, New York 10017 (800) 253-9646; *Statistical Yearbook.*

The University of Illinois at Chicago, China Statistics Archives, Suite 700 South, 1033 West Van Buren Street, Chicago, Illinois 60607-9940 (312) 413-0001 and China Statistical Information and Consultancy Service Center, 38 Yuetan Nanjie, Sanlihe, Beijing, People's Republic of China; *China Rural Statistics,* and *China Statistical Abstract.*

CHINA, PEOPLE'S REPUBLIC OF - CUSTOMS DUTIES

G.K. Hall and Company, 70 Lincoln Street, Boston, Massachusetts 02111 (617) 423-3990; *The World in Figures.*

CHINA, PEOPLE'S REPUBLIC OF - DAIRY PRODUCTS

Commodity Research Bureau, Incorporated, 75 Wall Street, New York, New York 10005 (212) 504-7754; *Commodity Year Book.*

The Economist Intelligence Unit (Asia) Limited, 10th Floor, Luk Kwok Centre, 72 Gloucester Road, Wanchai, Hong Kong (Phone Number in U.S. (800) 938-4685); *China Market Atlas.*

Facts on File, 460 Park Avenue South, New York, New York 10016 (800) 443-8323; *The New Book of World Rankings.*

Food and Agricultural Organization of the United Nations (FAO), Via delle Terme di Caracalla, 00100 Rome, Italy (Telephone Number in U.S. (202) 653-2400); *Production Yearbook,* and *The State of Food and Agriculture.*

Statistical Office of the United Nations, Publishing Service, New York, New York 10017 (800) 253-9646; *Statistical Yearbook.*

The University of Illinois at Chicago, China Statistics Archives, Suite 700 South, 1033 West Van Buren Street, Chicago, Illinois 60607-9940 (312) 413-0001 and China Statistical Information and Consultancy Service Center, 38 Yuetan Nanjie, Sanlihe, Beijing, People's Republic of China; *China Rural Statistics,* and *China Statistical Abstract.* Commodity Research Bureau, Incorporated, 75 Wall Street, New York, New York 10005 (212) 504-7754; *Commodity Year Book.*

CHINA, PEOPLE'S REPUBLIC OF - DEATH RATE

The Economist Intelligence Unit (Asia) Limited, 10th Floor, Luk Kwok Centre, 72 Gloucester Road, Wanchai, Hong Kong (Phone Number in U.S. (800) 938-4685); *Asian Market Atlas,* and *China Market Atlas.*

Euromonitor Publications Limited, 87-88 Turnmill Street, London EC1M 5QU, England; *Third World Economic Handbook.*

G.K. Hall and Company, 70 Lincoln Street, Boston, Massachusetts 02111 (617) 423-3990; *The World in Figures.*

Statistical Office of the United Nations, Publishing Service, New York, New York 10017 (800) 253-9646; *Statistical Yearbook.*

Times Books, 201 East 50th Street, New York, New York 10022 (212) 751-2600; *The Economist Book of Vital World Statistics.*

The University of Illinois at Chicago, China Statistics Archives, Suite 700 South, 1033 West Van Buren Street, Chicago, Illinois 60607-9940 (312) 413-0001 and China Statistical Information and Consultancy Service Center, 38 Yuetan Nanjie, Sanlihe, Beijing, People's Republic of China; *China Rural Statistics, China Social Statistics,* and *China Statistical Abstract.*

World Health Organization, Office of Publications, Avenue Appia, CH-1211 Geneva 27, Switzerland (Telephone Number in U.S. (518) 436-9686); *World Health Statistics Annual.*

CHINA, PEOPLE'S REPUBLIC OF - DEFENSE EXPENDITURES

G.K. Hall and Company, 70 Lincoln Street, Boston, Massachusetts 02111 (617) 423-3990; *The World in Figures.*

U.S. Arms Control and Disarmament Agency, 320 Twenty-first Street, NW, Washington, D.C. 20451 (202) 647-8677; *World Military Expenditures and Arms Transfers.*

CHINA, PEOPLE'S REPUBLIC OF - DEMOGRAPHY

The Economist Intelligence Unit, 111 West 57th Street, New York, New York 10019 (800) 938-4685; *The World Market Atlas.*

The Economist Intelligence Unit (Asia) Limited, 10th Floor, Luk Kwok Centre, 72 Gloucester Road, Wanchai, Hong Kong (Phone Number in U.S. (800) 938-4685); *Asian Market Atlas.*

Facts on File, 460 Park Avenue South, New York, New York 10016 (800) 443-8323; *The New Book of World Rankings.*

G.K. Hall and Company, 70 Lincoln Street, Boston, Massachusetts 02111 (617) 423-3990; *The World in Figures.*

CHINA, PEOPLE'S REPUBLIC OF - DEVELOPMENT ASSISTANCE

Asian Development Bank, P.O. Box 789, 1099 Manila, Philippines; *Key Indicators of Developing Asian and Pacific Countries.*

G.K. Hall and Company, 70 Lincoln Street, Boston, Massachusetts 02111 (617) 423-3990; *The World in Figures.*

Statistical Office of the United Nations, Publishing Service, New York, New York 10017 (800) 253-9646; *Statistical Yearbook.*

The University of Illinois at Chicago, China Statistics Archives, Suite 700 South, 1033 West Van Buren Street, Chicago, Illinois 60607-9940 (312) 413-0001 and China Statistical Information and Consultancy Service Center, 38 Yuetan Nanjie, Sanlihe, Beijing, People's Republic of China; *China Statistical Abstract.*

CHINA, PEOPLE'S REPUBLIC OF - DIAMOND PRODUCTION - See CHINA, PEOPLE'S REPUBLIC OF - MINING AND MINERAL PRODUCTS

CHINA, PEOPLE'S REPUBLIC OF - DISEASE

G.K. Hall and Company, 70 Lincoln Street, Boston, Massachusetts 02111 (617) 423-3990; *The World in Figures.*

The University of Illinois at Chicago, China Statistics Archives, Suite 700 South, 1033 West Van Buren Street, Chicago, Illinois 60607-9940 (312) 413-0001 and China Statistical Information and Consultancy Service Center, 38 Yuetan Nanjie, Sanlihe, Beijing, People's Republic of China; *China Statistical Abstract.*

World Health Organization, Office of Publications, Avenue Appia, CH-1211 Geneva 27, Switzerland (Telephone Number in U.S. (518) 436-9686); *World Health Statistics Annual.*

CHINA, PEOPLE'S REPUBLIC OF - DIVORCE RATES

Facts on File, 460 Park Avenue South, New York, New York 10016 (800) 443-8323; *The New Book of World Rankings.*

Statistical Office of the United Nations, Publishing Service, New York, New York 10017 (800) 253-9646; *Demographic Yearbook.*

The University of Illinois at Chicago, China Statistics Archives, Suite 700 South, 1033 West Van Buren Street, Chicago, Illinois 60607-9940 (312) 413-0001 and China Statistical Information and Consultancy Service Center, 38 Yuetan Nanjie, Sanlihe, Beijing, People's Republic of China: *China Social Statistics,* and *China Statistical Abstract.*

CHINA, PEOPLE'S REPUBLIC OF - DOMESTIC PRODUCT

G.K. Hall and Company, 70 Lincoln Street, Boston, Massachusetts 02111 (617) 423-3990; *The World in Figures.*

CHINA, PEOPLE'S REPUBLIC OF - DUCKS - See CHINA, PEOPLE'S REPUBLIC OF - LIVESTOCK AND POULTRY

CHINA, PEOPLE'S REPUBLIC OF - ECONOMY

Asian Development Bank, P.O. Box 789, 1099 Manila, Philippines; *Key Indicators of Developing Asian and Pacific Countries.*

The Economist Intelligence Unit (Asia) Limited, 10th Floor, Luk Kwok Centre, 72 Gloucester Road, Wanchai, Hong Kong (Phone Number in U.S. (800) 938-4685); *China Market Atlas.*

Euromonitor Publications Limited, 87-88 Turnmill Street, London EC1M 5QU, England; *International Marketing Data and Statistics,* and *Third World Economic Handbook.*

Facts on File, 460 Park Avenue South, New York, New York 10016 (800) 443-8323; *The New Book of World Rankings.*

G.K. Hall and Company, 70 Lincoln Street, Boston, Massachusetts 02111 (617) 423-3990; *The World in Figures.*

The University of Illinois at Chicago, China Statistics Archives, Suite 700 South, 1033 West Van Buren Street, Chicago, Illinois 60607-9940 (312) 413-0001 and China Statistical Information and Consultancy Service Center, 38 Yuetan Nanjie, Sanlihe, Beijing, People's Republic of China; *China Rural Statistics, China Social Statistics,* and *China Statistical Abstract, China Trade and Price Statistics.*

CHINA, PEOPLE'S REPUBLIC OF - EDUCATION

The Economist Intelligence Unit, 111 West 57th Street, New York, New York 10019 (800) 938-4685; *The World Market Atlas.*

The Economist Intelligence Unit (Asia) Limited, 10th Floor, Luk Kwok Centre, 72 Gloucester Road, Wanchai, Hong Kong (Phone Number in U.S. (800) 938-4685); *Asian Market Atlas,* and *China Market Atlas.*

Facts on File, 460 Park Avenue South, New York, New York 10016 (800) 443-8323; *The New Book of World Rankings.*

G.K. Hall and Company, 70 Lincoln Street, Boston, Massachusetts 02111 (617) 423-3990; *The World in Figures.*

Statistical Office of the United Nations, Publishing Service, New York, New York 10017; *Statistical Yearbook for Asia and the Pacific.*

Times Books, 201 East 50th Street, New York, New York 10022 (212) 751-2600; *The Economist Book of Vital World Statistics.*

United Nations Educational, Scientific and Cultural Organization (UNESCO), 7 Place de Fontenoy, F-75700 Paris, France (Telephone Number in U.S. (212) 963-5981; *Statistical Yearbook.*

The University of Illinois at Chicago, China Statistics Archives, Suite 700 South, 1033 West Van Buren Street, Chicago, Illinois 60607-9940 (312) 413-0001 and China Statistical Information and Consultancy Service Center, 38 Yuetan Nanjie, Sanlihe, Beijing, People's Republic of China; *China Rural Statistics, China Social Statistics,* and *China Statistical Abstract.*

The World Bank, 1818 H Street, NW, Washington, D.C. 20433 (202) 477-1234; *World Tables.*

CHINA, PEOPLE'S REPUBLIC OF - EGG PRODUCTION - See CHINA, PEOPLE'S REPUBLIC OF - DAIRY PRODUCTS

CHINA, PEOPLE'S REPUBLIC OF - EGGPLANT PRODUCTION - SeeCHINA, PEOPLE'S REPUBLIC OF - CROPS

CHINA, PEOPLE'S REPUBLIC OF - ELECTRICITY

Asian Development Bank, P.O. Box 789, 1099 Manila, Philippines; *Key Indicators of Developing Asian and Pacific Countries.*

Facts on File, 460 Park Avenue South, New York, New York 10016 (800) 443-8323; *The New Book of World Rankings.*

Penn Well Publishing Company, 1421 South Sheridan Road, P.O. Box 1260, Tulsa, Oklahoma 74101 (800) 752-9764; *International Energy Statistics Sourcebook.*

Statistical Office of the United Nations, Publishing Service, New York, New York 10017 (800) 253-9646; *Electric Power in Asia and the Pacific,* and *Statistical Yearbook.*

Times Books, 201 East 50th Street, New York, New York 10022 (212) 751-2600; *The Economist Book of Vital World Statistics.*

The University of Illinois at Chicago, China Statistics Archives, Suite 700 South, 1033 West Van Buren Street, Chicago, Illinois 60607-9940 (312) 413-0001 and China Statistical Information and Consultancy Service Center, 38 Yuetan Nanjie, Sanlihe, Beijing, People's Republic of China; *China Statistical Abstract.*

The World Bank, 1818 H Street, NW, Washington, D.C. 20433 (202) 477-1234; *World Tables.*

CHINA, PEOPLE'S REPUBLIC OF - ELECTRONICS

The Economist Intelligence Unit (Asia) Limited, 10th Floor, Luk Kwok Centre, 72 Gloucester Road, Wanchai, Hong Kong (Phone Number in U.S. (800) 938-4685); *China Market Atlas.*

CHINA, PEOPLE'S REPUBLIC OF - EMPLOYMENT

Euromonitor Publications Limited, 87-88 Turnmill Street, London EC1M 5QU, England; *International Marketing Data and Statistics.*

Facts on File, 460 Park Avenue South, New York, New York 10016 (800) 443-8323; *The New Book of World Rankings.*

The University of Illinois at Chicago, China Statistics Archives, Suite 700 South, 1033 West Van Buren Street, Chicago, Illinois 60607-9940 (312) 413-0001 and China Statistical Information and Consultancy Service Center, 38 Yuetan Nanjie, Sanlihe, Beijing, People's Republic of China; *China Rural Statistics, China Social Statistics,* and *China Statistical Abstract.*

The World Bank, 1818 H Street, NW, Washington, D.C. 20433 (202) 477-1234; *World Tables.*

CHINA, PEOPLE'S REPUBLIC OF - ENERGY

Facts on File, 460 Park Avenue South, New York, New York 10016 (800) 443-8323; *The New Book of World Rankings.*

G.K. Hall and Company, 70 Lincoln Street, Boston, Massachusetts 02111 (617) 423-3990; *The World in Figures.*

Statistical Office of the United Nations, Publishing Service, New York, New York 10017 (800) 253-9646; *Statistical Yearbook.*

Times Books, 201 East 50th Street, New York, New York 10022 (212) 751-2600; *The Economist Book of Vital World Statistics.*

The University of Illinois at Chicago, China Statistics Archives, Suite 700 South, 1033 West Van Buren Street, Chicago, Illinois 60607-9940 (312) 413-0001 and China Statistical Information and Consultancy Service Center, 38 Yuetan Nanjie, Sanlihe, Beijing, People's Republic of China; *China Statistical Abstract.*

Penn Well Publishing Company, 1421 South Sheridan Road, P.O. Box 1260, Tulsa, Oklahoma 74101 (800) 752-9764; *International Energy Statistics Sourcebook.*

CHINA, PEOPLE'S REPUBLIC OF - EXCHANGE RATE

Asian Development Bank, P.O. Box 789, 1099 Manila, Philippines; *Key Indicators of Developing Asian and Pacific Countries.*

The Economist Intelligence Unit (Asia) Limited, 10th Floor, Luk Kwok Centre, 72 Gloucester Road, Wanchai, Hong Kong (Phone Number in U.S. (800) 938-4685); *Asian Market Atlas.*

Euromonitor Publications Limited, 87-88 Turnmill Street, London EC1M 5QU, England; *International Marketing Data and Statistics.*

International Monetary Fund, 700 Nineteenth Street, NW, Washington, D.C. 20431 (202) 623-7000; *International Financial Statistics.*

Statistical Office of the United Nations, Publishing Service, New York, New York 10017 (800) 253-9646; *Statistical Yearbook.*

The University of Illinois at Chicago, China Statistics Archives, Suite 700 South, 1033 West Van Buren Street, Chicago, Illinois 60607-9940 (312) 413-0001 and China Statistical Information and Consultancy Service Center, 38 Yuetan Nanjie, Sanlihe, Beijing, People's Republic of China; *China Statistical Abstract,* and *China Trade and Price Statistics.*

CHINA, PEOPLE'S REPUBLIC OF - EXPORTS

American Automobile Manufacturers Association, 1401 H Street, NW, Suite 900, Washington, D.C. 20005 (202) 326-5500; *World Motor Vehicle Data.*

Asian Development Bank, P.O. Box 789, 1099 Manila, Philippines; *Key Indicators of Developing Asian and Pacific Countries.*

The Economist Intelligence Unit, 111 West 57th Street, New York, New York 10019 (800) 938-4685; *The World Market Atlas.*

The Economist Intelligence Unit (Asia) Limited, 10th Floor, Luk Kwok Centre, 72 Gloucester Road, Wanchai, Hong Kong (Phone Number in U.S. (800) 938-4685); *Asian Market Atlas,* and *China Market Atlas.*

Euromonitor Publications Limited, 87-88 Turnmill Street, London EC1M 5QU, England; *International Marketing Data and Statistics,* and *Third World Economic Handbook.*

Food and Agricultural Organization of the United Nations (FAO) Via delle Terme di Caracalla, 00100 Rome, Italy (Telephone Number in U.S. (202) 653-2400); *The State of Food and Agriculture.*

G.K. Hall and Company, 70 Lincoln Street, Boston, Massachusetts 02111 (617) 423-3990; *The World in Figures.*

International Monetary Fund, 700 Nineteenth Street, NW, Washington, D.C. 20431 (202) 623-7000; *Direction of Trade Statistics,* and *International Financial Statistics.*

Times Books, 201 East 50th Street, New York, New York 10022 (212) 751-2600; *The Economist Book of Vital World Statistics.*

The University of Illinois at Chicago, China Statistics Archives, Suite 700 South, 1033 West Van Buren Street, Chicago, Illinois 60607-9940 (312) 413-0001 and China Statistical Information and Consultancy Service Center, 38 Yuetan Nanjie, Sanlihe, Beijing, People's Republic of China; *China Statistical Abstract,* and *China Trade and Price Statistics.*

The World Bank, 1818 H Street, NW, Washington, D.C. 20433 (202) 477-1234; *World Tables.*

CHINA, PEOPLE'S REPUBLIC OF - EXTERNAL FINANCING

Asian Development Bank, P.O. Box 789, 1099 Manila, Philippines; *Key Indicators of Developing Asian and Pacific Countries.*

CHINA, PEOPLE'S REPUBLIC OF - EXTERNAL INDEBTEDNESS

Asian Development Bank, P.O. Box 789, 1099 Manila, Philippines; *Key Indicators of Developing Asian and Pacific Countries.*

Euromonitor Publications Limited, 87-88 Turnmill Street, London EC1M 5QU, England; *Third World Economic Handbook.*

The World Bank, 1818 H Street, NW, Washington, D.C. 20433 (202) 477-1234; *World Tables.*

CHINA, PEOPLE'S REPUBLIC OF - EXTERNAL TRADE

Asian Development Bank, P.O. Box 789, 1099 Manila, Philippines; *Key Indicators of Developing Asian and Pacific Countries.*

Food and Agricultural Organization of the United Nations (FAO) Via delle Terme di Caracalla, 00100 Rome, Italy (Telephone Number in U.S. (202) 653-2400); *The State of Food and Agriculture,* and *Trade Yearbook.*

G.K. Hall and Company, 70 Lincoln Street, Boston, Massachusetts 02111 (617) 423-3990; *The World in Figures.*

Statistical Office of the United Nations, Publishing Service, New York, New York 10017 (800) 253-9646; *Statistical Yearbook for Asia and the Pacific.*

The University of Illinois at Chicago, China Statistics Archives, Suite 700 South, 1033 West Van Buren Street, Chicago, Illinois 60607-9940 (312) 413-0001 and China Statistical Information and Consultancy Service Center, 38 Yuetan Nanjie, Sanlihe, Beijing, People's Republic of China; *China Statistical Abstract,* and *China Trade and Price Statistics.*

CHINA, PEOPLE'S REPUBLIC OF - FARM CROPS - See CHINA, PEOPLE'S REPUBLIC OF - CROPS

CHINA, PEOPLE'S REPUBLIC OF - FEMALE WORKING POPULATION - See CHINA, PEOPLE'S REPUBLIC OF - EMPLOYMENT

CHINA, PEOPLE'S REPUBLIC OF - FERTILITY RATES

The Economist Intelligence Unit (Asia) Limited, 10th Floor, Luk Kwok Centre, 72 Gloucester Road, Wanchai, Hong Kong (Phone Number in U.S. (800) 938-4685); *Asian Market Atlas.*

Facts on File, 460 Park Avenue South, New York, New York 10016 (800) 443-8323; *The New Book of World Rankings.*

Times Books, 201 East 50th Street, New York, New York 10022 (212) 751-2600; *The Economist Book of Vital World Statistics.*

The World Bank, 1818 H Street, NW, Washington, D.C. 20433 (202) 477-1234; *World Tables.*

CHINA, PEOPLE'S REPUBLIC OF - FERTILIZER

The Economist Intelligence Unit (Asia) Limited, 10th Floor, Luk Kwok Centre, 72 Gloucester Road, Wanchai, Hong Kong (Phone Number in U.S. (800) 938-4685); *China Market Atlas.*

Food and Agricultural Organization of the United Nations (FAO), Via delle Terme di Caracalla, 00100 Rome, Italy (Telephone Number in U.S. (202) 653-2400); *Fertilizer Yearbook,* and *The State of Food and Agriculture.*

Statistical Office of the United Nations, Publishing Service, New York, New York 10017 (800) 253-9646; *Statistical Yearbook.*

The University of Illinois at Chicago, China Statistics Archives, Suite 700 South, 1033 West Van Buren Street, Chicago, Illinois 60607-9940 (312) 413-0001 and China Statistical Information and Consultancy Service Center, 38 Yuetan Nanjie, Sanlihe, Beijing, People's Republic of China; *China Rural Statistics,* and *China Statistical Abstract.*

CHINA, PEOPLE'S REPUBLIC OF - FETAL MORTALITY

Statistical Office of the United Nations, Publishing Service, New York, New York 10017 (800) 253-9646; *Demographic Yearbook.*

The University of Illinois at Chicago, China Statistics Archives, Suite 700 South, 1033 West Van Buren Street, Chicago, Illinois 60607-9940 (312) 413-0001 and China Statistical Information and Consultancy Service Center, 38 Yuetan Nanjie, Sanlihe, Beijing, People's Republic of China: *China Social Statistics.*

The University of Illinois at Chicago, China Statistics Archives, Suite 700 South, 1033 West Van Buren Street, Chicago, Illinois 60607-9940 (312) 413-0001 and China Statistical Information and Consultancy Service Center, 38 Yuetan Nanjie, Sanlihe, Beijing, People's Republic of China; *China Statistical Abstract.*

CHINA, PEOPLE'S REPUBLIC OF - FIBRE PRODUCTION - See CHINA, PEOPLE'S REPUBLIC OF - TEXTILE INDUSTRY

CHINA, PEOPLE'S REPUBLIC OF - FILAMENT PRODUCTION - See CHINA, PEOPLE'S REPUBLIC OF - TEXTILE INDUSTRY

CHINA, PEOPLE'S REPUBLIC OF - FINANCE

Asian Development Bank, P.O. Box 789, 1099 Manila, Philippines; *Key Indicators of Developing Asian and Pacific Countries.*

The Economist Intelligence Unit (Asia) Limited, 10th Floor, Luk Kwok Centre, 72 Gloucester Road, Wanchai, Hong Kong (Phone Number in U.S. (800) 938-4685); *China Market Atlas.*

Facts on File, 460 Park Avenue South, New York, New York 10016 (800) 443-8323; *The New Book of World Rankings.*

G.K. Hall and Company, 70 Lincoln Street, Boston, Massachusetts 02111 (617) 423-3990; *The World in Figures.*

International Monetary Fund, 700 Nineteenth Street, NW, Washington, D.C. 20431 (202) 623-7000; *International Financial Statistics.*

Statistical Office of the United Nations, Publishing Service, New York, New York 10017 (800) 253-9646; *Statistical Yearbook for Asia and the Pacific.*

The University of Illinois at Chicago, China Statistics Archives, Suite 700 South, 1033 West Van Buren Street, Chicago, Illinois 60607-9940 (312) 413-0001 and China Statistical Information and Consultancy Service Center, 38 Yuetan Nanjie, Sanlihe, Beijing, People's Republic of China: *China Social Statistics, China Statistical Abstract,* and *China Trade and Price Statistics.*

CHINA, PEOPLE'S REPUBLIC OF - FISHERIES

The Economist Intelligence Unit (Asia) Limited, 10th Floor, Luk Kwok Centre, 72 Gloucester Road, Wanchai, Hong Kong (Phone Number in U.S. (800) 938-4685); *China Market Atlas.*

Facts on File, 460 Park Avenue South, New York, New York 10016 (800) 443-8323; *The New Book of World Rankings.*

Food and Agricultural Organization of the United Nations (FAO) Via delle Terme di Caracalla, 00100 Rome, Italy (Telephone Number in U.S. (202) 653-2400); *The State of Food and Agriculture,* and *Yearbook of Fishery Statistics.*

Statistical Office of the United Nations, Publishing Service, New York, New York 10017 (800) 253-9646; *Statistical Yearbook.*

The University of Illinois at Chicago, China Statistics Archives, Suite 700 South, 1033 West Van Buren Street, Chicago, Illinois 60607-9940 (312) 413-0001 and China Statistical Information and Consultancy Service Center, 38 Yuetan Nanjie, Sanlihe, Beijing, People's Republic of China; *China Rural Statistics, China Statistical Abstract,* and *China Trade and Price Statistics.*

CHINA, PEOPLE'S REPUBLIC OF - FLAX FIBRE PRODUCTION - See CHINA, PEOPLE'S REPUBLIC OF - TEXTILE INDUSTRY

CHINA, PEOPLE'S REPUBLIC OF - FOOD

Food and Agricultural Organization of the United Nations (FAO) Via delle Terme di Caracalla, 00100 Rome, Italy (Telephone Number in U.S. (202) 653-2400); *Production Yearbook,* and *The State of Food and Agriculture.*

G.K. Hall and Company, 70 Lincoln Street, Boston, Massachusetts 02111 (617) 423-3990; *The World in Figures.*

Statistical Office of the United Nations, Publishing Service, New York, New York 10017 (800) 253-9646; *Statistical Yearbook for Asia and the Pacific.*

The University of Illinois at Chicago, China Statistics Archives, Suite 700 South, 1033 West Van Buren Street, Chicago, Illinois 60607-9940 (312) 413-0001 and China Statistical Information and Consultancy Service Center, 38 Yuetan Nanjie, Sanlihe, Beijing, People's Republic of China; *China Rural Statistics, China Social Statistics, China Statistical Abstract,* and *China Trade and Price Statistics.*

CHINA, PEOPLE'S REPUBLIC OF - FOREIGN AID

G.K. Hall and Company, 70 Lincoln Street, Boston, Massachusetts 02111 (617) 423-3990; *The World in Figures.*

CHINA, PEOPLE'S REPUBLIC OF - FOREIGN TRADE

Asian Development Bank, P.O. Box 789, 1099 Manila, Philippines; *Key Indicators of Developing Asian and Pacific Countries.*

The Economist Intelligence Unit (Asia) Limited, 10th Floor, Luk Kwok Centre, 72 Gloucester Road, Wanchai, Hong Kong (Phone Number in U.S. (800) 938-4685); *Asian Market Atlas,* and *China Market Atlas.*

Euromonitor Publications Limited, 87-88 Turnmill Street, London EC1M 5QU, England; *International Marketing Data and Statistics,* and *Third World Economic Handbook.*

Facts on File, 460 Park Avenue South, New York, New York 10016 (800) 443-8323; *The New Book of World Rankings.*

Food and Agricultural Organization of the United Nations (FAO) Via delle Terme di Caracalla, 00100 Rome, Italy (Telephone Number in U.S. (202) 653-2400); *The State of Food and Agriculture.*

G.K. Hall and Company, 70 Lincoln Street, Boston, Massachusetts 02111 (617) 423-3990; *The World in Figures.*

Organisation for Economic Co-operation and Development (OECD), 2 rue Andre-Pascal, 75 Paris 16, France; *Trade by Commodities.*

Statistical Office of the United Nations, Publishing Service, New York, New York 10017 (800) 253-9646; *Statistical Yearbook.*

The University of Illinois at Chicago, China Statistics Archives, Suite 700 South, 1033 West Van Buren Street, Chicago, Illinois 60607-9940 (312) 413-0001 and China Statistical Information and Consultancy Service Center, 38 Yuetan Nanjie, Sanlihe, Beijing, People's Republic of China; *China Statistical Abstract,* and *China Trade and Price Statistics.*

The World Bank, 1818 H Street, NW, Washington, D.C. 20433 (202) 477-1234; *World Tables.*

CHINA, PEOPLE'S REPUBLIC OF - FORESTRY AND FOREST PRODUCTS

The Economist Intelligence Unit (Asia) Limited, 10th Floor, Luk Kwok Centre, 72 Gloucester Road, Wanchai, Hong Kong (Phone Number in U.S. (800) 938-4685); *China Market Atlas.*

Euromonitor Publications Limited, 87-88 Turnmill Street, London EC1M 5QU, England; *Third World Economic Handbook.*

Facts on File, 460 Park Avenue South, New York, New York 10016 (800) 443-8323; *The New Book of World Rankings.*

Food and Agricultural Organization of the United Nations (FAO) Via delle Terme di Caracalla, 00100 Rome, Italy (Telephone Number in

U.S. (202) 653-2400); *The State of Food and Agriculture*, and *Yearbook of Forest Products*.

Forest and Paper Association, 1250 Connecticut Avenue, NW, Washington, D.C. 20036 (202) 463-2455; *Wood Pulp and Fiber Statistics*.

G.K. Hall and Company, 70 Lincoln Street, Boston, Massachusetts 02111 (617) 423-3990; *The World in Figures*.

United Nations Educational, Scientific and Cultural Organization (UNESCO), 7 Place de Fontenoy, F-75700 Paris, France (Telephone Number in U.S. (212) 963-5981; *Statistical Yearbook*.

The University of Illinois at Chicago, China Statistics Archives, Suite 700 South, 1033 West Van Buren Street, Chicago, Illinois 60607-9940 (312) 413-0001 and China Statistical Information and Consultancy Service Center, 38 Yuetan Nanjie, Sanlihe, Beijing, People's Republic of China; *China Rural Statistics, China Statistical Abstract*, and *China Trade and Price Statistics*.

CHINA, PEOPLE'S REPUBLIC OF - FRUIT PRODUCTION - See CHINA, PEOPLE'S REPUBLIC OF - CROPS

CHINA, PEOPLE'S REPUBLIC OF - GARLIC PRODUCTION - See CHINA, PEOPLE'S REPUBLIC OF - CROPS

CHINA, PEOPLE'S REPUBLIC OF - GAS PRODUCTION - See CHINA, PEOPLE'S REPUBLIC OF - MINING AND MINERAL PRODUCTS

CHINA, PEOPLE'S REPUBLIC OF - GENERAL MORTALITY

Statistical Office of the United Nations, Publishing Service, New York, New York 10017 (800) 253-9646; *Demographic Yearbook*.

The University of Illinois at Chicago, China Statistics Archives, Suite 700 South, 1033 West Van Buren Street, Chicago, Illinois 60607-9940 (312) 413-0001 and China Statistical Information and Consultancy Service Center, 38 Yuetan Nanjie, Sanlihe, Beijing, People's Republic of China: *China Social Statistics*, and *China Statistical Abstract*.

World Health Organization, Office of Publications, Avenue Appia, CH-1211 Geneva 27, Switzerland (Telephone Number in U.S. (518) 436-9686); *World Health Statistics Annual*.

CHINA, PEOPLE'S REPUBLIC OF - GEOGRAPHIC DATA

Facts on File, 460 Park Avenue South, New York, New York 10016 (800) 443-8323; *The New Book of World Rankings*.

CHINA, PEOPLE'S REPUBLIC OF - GOATS - See CHINA, PEOPLE'S REPUBLIC OF - LIVESTOCK AND POULTRY

CHINA, PEOPLE'S REPUBLIC OF - GOLD HOLDINGS

International Monetary Fund, 700 Nineteenth Street, NW, Washington, D.C. 20431 (202) 623-7000; *International Financial Statistics*.

The University of Illinois at Chicago, China Statistics Archives, Suite 700 South, 1033 West Van Buren Street, Chicago, Illinois 60607-9940 (312) 413-0001 and China Statistical Information and Consultancy Service Center, 38 Yuetan Nanjie, Sanlihe, Beijing, People's Republic of China; *China Statistical Abstract*.

The World Bank, 1818 H Street, NW, Washington, D.C. 20433 (202) 477-1234; *World Tables*.

CHINA, PEOPLE'S REPUBLIC OF - GOLD PRODUCTION AND CONSUMPTION - See CHINA, PEOPLE'S REPUBLIC OF - MINING AND MINERAL PRODUCTS

CHINA, PEOPLE'S REPUBLIC OF - GOVERNMENT

Asian Development Bank, P.O. Box 789, 1099 Manila, Philippines; *Key Indicators of Developing Asian and Pacific Countries*.

G.K. Hall and Company, 70 Lincoln Street, Boston, Massachusetts 02111 (617) 423-3990; *The World in Figures*.

CHINA, PEOPLE'S REPUBLIC OF - GOVERNMENT BONDS - See CHINA, PEOPLE'S REPUBLIC OF - BONDS

CHINA, PEOPLE'S REPUBLIC OF - GOVERNMENT EXPENDITURE

Asian Development Bank, P.O. Box 789, 1099 Manila, Philippines; *Key Indicators of Developing Asian and Pacific Countries*.

The Economist Intelligence Unit (Asia) Limited, 10th Floor, Luk Kwok Centre, 72 Gloucester Road, Wanchai, Hong Kong (Phone Number in U.S. (800) 938-4685); *China Market Atlas*.

Euromonitor Publications Limited, 87-88 Turnmill Street, London EC1M 5QU, England; *Third World Economic Handbook*.

The World Bank, 1818 H Street, NW, Washington, D.C. 20433 (202) 477-1234; *World Tables*.

CHINA, PEOPLE'S REPUBLIC OF - GOVERNMENT FINANCE

Asian Development Bank, P.O. Box 789, 1099 Manila, Philippines; *Key Indicators of Developing Asian and Pacific Countries*.

International Monetary Fund, 700 Nineteenth Street, NW, Washington, D.C. 20431 (202) 623-7000; *International Financial Statistics*.

CHINA, PEOPLE'S REPUBLIC OF - GOVERNMENT REVENUE

Asian Development Bank, P.O. Box 789, 1099 Manila, Philippines; *Key Indicators of Developing Asian and Pacific Countries*.

The World Bank, 1818 H Street, NW, Washington, D.C. 20433 (202) 477-1234; *World Tables*.

CHINA, PEOPLE'S REPUBLIC OF - GRAIN PRODUCTION - See CHINA, PEOPLE'S REPUBLIC OF - CROPS

CHINA, PEOPLE'S REPUBLIC OF - GREEN PEPPER AND CHILIE PRODUCTION - See CHINA, PEOPLE'S REPUBLIC OF - CROPS

CHINA, PEOPLE'S REPUBLIC OF - GROSS DOMESTIC PRODUCT

Asian Development Bank, P.O. Box 789, 1099 Manila, Philippines; *Key Indicators of Developing Asian and Pacific Countries*.

The Economist Intelligence Unit, 111 West 57th Street, New York, New York 10019 (800) 938-4685; *The World Market Atlas*.

The Economist Intelligence Unit (Asia) Limited, 10th Floor, Luk Kwok Centre, 72 Gloucester Road, Wanchai, Hong Kong (Phone Number in U.S. (800) 938-4685); *Asian Market Atlas*, and *China Market Atlas*.

Euromonitor Publications Limited, 87-88 Turnmill Street, London EC1M 5QU, England; *International Marketing Data and Statistics*, and *Third World Economic Handbook*.

Facts on File, 460 Park Avenue South, New York, New York 10016 (800) 443-8323; *The New Book of World Rankings*.

G.K. Hall and Company, 70 Lincoln Street, Boston, Massachusetts 02111 (617) 423-3990; *The World in Figures*.

Times Books, 201 East 50th Street, New York, New York 10022 (212) 751-2600; *The Economist Book of Vital World Statistics*.

The World Bank, 1818 H Street, NW, Washington, D.C. 20433 (202) 477-1234; *World Tables*.

CHINA, PEOPLE'S REPUBLIC OF - GROSS INDUSTRIAL PRODUCT

Euromonitor Publications Limited, 87-88 Turnmill Street, London EC1M 5QU, England; *Third World Economic Handbook*.

The University of Illinois at Chicago, China Statistics Archives, Suite 700 South, 1033 West Van Buren Street, Chicago, Illinois 60607-9940 (312) 413-0001 and China Statistical Information and Consultancy Service Center, 38 Yuetan Nanjie, Sanlihe, Beijing, People's Republic of China; *China Trade and Price Statistics*.

CHINA, PEOPLE'S REPUBLIC OF - GROSS NATIONAL PRODUCT

Asian Development Bank, P.O. Box 789, 1099 Manila, Philippines; *Key Indicators of Developing Asian and Pacific Countries*.

The Economist Intelligence Unit (Asia) Limited, 10th Floor, Luk Kwok Centre, 72 Gloucester Road, Wanchai, Hong Kong (Phone Number in U.S. (800) 938-4685); *China Market Atlas*.

Euromonitor Publications Limited, 87-88 Turnmill Street, London EC1M 5QU, England; *International Marketing Data and Statistics*, and *Third World Economic Handbook*.

The University of Illinois at Chicago, China Statistics Archives, Suite 700 South, 1033 West Van Buren Street, Chicago, Illinois 60607-9940 (312) 413-0001 and China Statistical Information and Consultancy Service Center, 38 Yuetan Nanjie, Sanlihe, Beijing, People's Republic of China; *China Statistical Abstract*.

U.S. Arms Control and Disarmament Agency, 320 Twenty-first Street, NW, Washington, D.C. 20451 (202) 647-8677; *World Military Expenditures and Arms Transfers*.

The World Bank, 1818 H Street, NW, Washington, D.C. 20433 (202) 477-1234; *World Tables*.

CHINA, PEOPLE'S REPUBLIC OF - GROUNDNUTS PRODUCTION - See CHINA, PEOPLE'S REPUBLIC OF - CROPS

CHINA, PEOPLE'S REPUBLIC OF - HEALTH

The Economist Intelligence Unit (Asia) Limited, 10th Floor, Luk Kwok Centre, 72 Gloucester Road, Wanchai, Hong Kong (Phone Number in U.S. (800) 938-4685); *Asian Market Atlas*, and *China Market Atlas*.

Facts on File, 460 Park Avenue South, New York, New York 10016 (800) 443-8323; *The New Book of World Rankings*.

G.K. Hall and Company, 70 Lincoln Street, Boston, Massachusetts 02111 (617) 423-3990; *The World in Figures*.

Statistical Office of the United Nations, Publishing Service, New York, New York 10017 (800) 253-9646; *Statistical Yearbook*.

Times Books, 201 East 50th Street, New York, New York 10022 (212) 751-2600; *The Economist Book of Vital World Statistics*.

The University of Illinois at Chicago, China Statistics Archives, Suite 700 South, 1033 West Van Buren Street, Chicago, Illinois 60607-9940 (312) 413-0001 and China Statistical Information and Consultancy Service Center, 38 Yuetan Nanjie, Sanlihe, Beijing, People's Republic of China; *China Rural Statistics*, *China Social Statistics*, and *China Statistical Abstract*.

CHINA, PEOPLE'S REPUBLIC OF - HEMP FIBRE PRODUCTION - See CHINA, PEOPLE'S REPUBLIC OF - TEXTILE INDUSTRY

CHINA, PEOPLE'S REPUBLIC OF - HIDE PRODUCTION

Food and Agricultural Organization of the United Nations (FAO), Via delle Terme di Caracalla, 00100 Rome, Italy (Telephone Number in U.S. (202) 653-2400); *Production Yearbook*.

The University of Illinois at Chicago, China Statistics Archives, Suite 700 South, 1033 West Van Buren Street, Chicago, Illinois 60607-9940 (312) 413-0001 and China Statistical Information and Consultancy Service Center, 38 Yuetan Nanjie, Sanlihe, Beijing, People's Republic of China; *China Rural Statistics*, and *China Statistical Abstract*.

CHINA, PEOPLE'S REPUBLIC OF - HIGHWAYS

The Economist Intelligence Unit (Asia) Limited, 10th Floor, Luk Kwok Centre, 72 Gloucester Road, Wanchai, Hong Kong (Phone Number in U.S. (800) 938-4685); *Asian Market Atlas*, and *China Market Atlas*.

G.K. Hall and Company, 70 Lincoln Street, Boston, Massachusetts 02111 (617) 423-3990; *The World in Figures*.

CHINA, PEOPLE'S REPUBLIC OF - HONEY PRODUCTION

Commodity Research Bureau, Incorporated, 75 Wall Street, New York, New York 10005 (212) 504-7754; *Commodity Year Book*.

The University of Illinois at Chicago, China Statistics Archives, Suite 700 South, 1033 West Van Buren Street, Chicago, Illinois 60607-9940 (312) 413-0001 and China Statistical Information and Consultancy Service Center, 38 Yuetan Nanjie, Sanlihe, Beijing, People's Republic of China; *China Rural Statistics*, and *China Statistical Abstract*.

CHINA, PEOPLE'S REPUBLIC OF - HORSES - See CHINA, PEOPLE'S REPUBLIC OF - LIVESTOCK AND POULTRY

CHINA, PEOPLE'S REPUBLIC OF - HOURS OF WORK - See CHINA, PEOPLE'S REPUBLIC OF

CHINA, PEOPLE'S REPUBLIC OF - HOUSING AND HOUSING UNITS

The Economist Intelligence Unit (Asia) Limited, 10th Floor, Luk Kwok Centre, 72 Gloucester Road, Wanchai, Hong Kong (Phone Number in U.S. (800) 938-4685); *China Market Atlas*.

Euromonitor Publications Limited, 87-88 Turnmill Street, London EC1M 5QU, England; *Third World Economic Handbook*.

Facts on File, 460 Park Avenue South, New York, New York 10016 (800) 443-8323; *The New Book of World Rankings.*

The University of Illinois at Chicago, China Statistics Archives, Suite 700 South, 1033 West Van Buren Street, Chicago, Illinois 60607-9940 (312) 413-0001 and China Statistical Information and Consultancy Service Center, 38 Yuetan Nanjie, Sanlihe, Beijing, People's Republic of China; *China Rural Statistics, China Social Statistics,* and *China Statistical Abstract.*

CHINA, PEOPLE'S REPUBLIC OF - ILLITERATE POPULATION

The Economist Intelligence Unit, 111 West 57th Street, New York, New York 10019 (800) 938-4685; *The World Market Atlas.*

The Economist Intelligence Unit (Asia) Limited, 10th Floor, Luk Kwok Centre, 72 Gloucester Road, Wanchai, Hong Kong (Phone Number in U.S. (800) 938-4685); *China Market Atlas.*

G.K. Hall and Company, 70 Lincoln Street, Boston, Massachusetts 02111 (617) 423-3990; *The World in Figures.*

CHINA, PEOPLE'S REPUBLIC OF - IMPORTS

Asian Development Bank, P.O. Box 789, 1099 Manila, Philippines; *Key Indicators of Developing Asian and Pacific Countries.*

The Economist Intelligence Unit, 111 West 57th Street, New York, New York 10019 (800) 938-4685; *The World Market Atlas.*

The Economist Intelligence Unit (Asia) Limited, 10th Floor, Luk Kwok Centre, 72 Gloucester Road, Wanchai, Hong Kong (Phone Number in U.S. (800) 938-4685); *Asian Market Atlas,* and *China Market Atlas.*

Euromonitor Publications Limited, 87-88 Turnmill Street, London EC1M 5QU, England; *International Marketing Data and Statistics,* and *Third World Economic Handbook.*

Food and Agricultural Organization of the United Nations (FAO) Via delle Terme di Caracalla, 00100 Rome, Italy (Telephone Number in U.S. (202) 653-2400); *The State of Food and Agriculture.*

G.K. Hall and Company, 70 Lincoln Street, Boston, Massachusetts 02111 (617) 423-3990; *The World in Figures.*

International Monetary Fund, 700 Nineteenth Street, NW, Washington, D.C. 20431 (202) 623-7000; *Direction of Trade Statistics,* and *International Financial Statistics.*

The University of Illinois at Chicago, China Statistics Archives, Suite 700 South, 1033 West Van Buren Street, Chicago, Illinois 60607-9940 (312) 413-0001 and China Statistical Information and Consultancy Service Center, 38 Yuetan Nanjie, Sanlihe, Beijing, People's Republic of China; *China Statistical Abstract,* and *China Trade and Price Statistics.*

The World Bank, 1818 H Street, NW, Washington, D.C. 20433 (202) 477-1234; *World Tables.*

CHINA, PEOPLE'S REPUBLIC OF - INDUSTRIAL METALS PRODUCTION - See CHINA, PEOPLE'S REPUBLIC OF - MINING AND MINERAL PRODUCTS

CHINA, PEOPLE'S REPUBLIC OF - INDUSTRY

The Economist Intelligence Unit (Asia) Limited, 10th Floor, Luk Kwok Centre, 72 Gloucester Road, Wanchai, Hong Kong (Phone Number in U.S. (800) 938-4685); *China Market Atlas.*

Euromonitor Publications Limited, 87-88 Turnmill Street, London EC1M 5QU, England; *Third World Economic Handbook.*

Facts on File, 460 Park Avenue South, New York, New York 10016 (800) 443-8323; *The New Book of World Rankings.*

G.K. Hall and Company, 70 Lincoln Street, Boston, Massachusetts 02111 (617) 423-3990; *The World in Figures.*

Statistical Office of the United Nations, Publishing Service, New York, New York 10017 (800) 253-9646; *Statistical Yearbook for Asia and the Pacific.*

Times Books, 201 East 50th Street, New York, New York 10022 (212) 751-2600; *The Economist Book of Vital World Statistics.*

The University of Illinois at Chicago, China Statistics Archives, Suite 700 South, 1033 West Van Buren Street, Chicago, Illinois 60607-9940 (312) 413-0001 and China Statistical Information and Consultancy Service Center, 38 Yuetan Nanjie, Sanlihe, Beijing, People's Republic of China; *China Statistical Abstract.*

The World Bank, 1818 H Street, NW, Washington, D.C. 20433 (202) 477-1234; *World Tables.*

World Intellectual Property Organization, 34 Chemin des Colombettes, CH-1211 Geneva 20. Switzerland; *Industrial Property Statistics.*

CHINA, PEOPLE'S REPUBLIC OF - INFANT AND MATERNAL MORTALITY

The Economist Intelligence Unit (Asia) Limited, 10th Floor, Luk Kwok Centre, 72 Gloucester Road, Wanchai, Hong Kong (Phone Number in U.S. (800) 938-4685); *Asian Market Atlas.*

Statistical Office of the United Nations, Publishing Service, New York, New York 10017 (800) 253-9646; *Demographic Yearbook.*

Times Books, 201 East 50th Street, New York, New York 10022 (212) 751-2600; *The Economist Book of Vital World Statistics.*

The University of Illinois at Chicago, China Statistics Archives, Suite 700 South, 1033 West Van Buren Street, Chicago, Illinois 60607-9940 (312) 413-0001 and China Statistical Information and Consultancy Service Center, 38 Yuetan Nanjie, Sanlihe, Beijing, People's Republic of China: *China Social Statistics,* and *China Statistical Abstract.*

The World Bank, 1818 H Street, NW, Washington, D.C. 20433 (202) 477-1234; *World Tables.*

CHINA, PEOPLE'S REPUBLIC OF - INTERNAL TRADE

Statistical Office of the United Nations, Publishing Service, New York, New York 10017 (800) 253-9646; *Statistical Yearbook for Asia and the Pacific.*

The University of Illinois at Chicago, China Statistics Archives, Suite 700 South, 1033 West Van Buren Street, Chicago, Illinois 60607-9940 (312) 413-0001 and China Statistical Information and Consultancy Service Center, 38 Yuetan Nanjie, Sanlihe, Beijing, People's Republic of China; *China Statistical Abstract,* and *China Trade and Price Statistics.*

CHINA, PEOPLE'S REPUBLIC OF - INTERNATIONAL LIQUIDITY

International Monetary Fund, 700 Nineteenth Street, NW, Washington, D.C. 20431 (202) 623-7000; *International Financial*

Statistics.

CHINA, PEOPLE'S REPUBLIC OF - INTERNATIONAL RESERVES

Asian Development Bank, P.O. Box 789, 1099 Manila, Philippines; *Key Indicators of Developing Asian and Pacific Countries.*

The University of Illinois at Chicago, China Statistics Archives, Suite 700 South, 1033 West Van Buren Street, Chicago, Illinois 60607-9940 (312) 413-0001 and China Statistical Information and Consultancy Service Center, 38 Yuetan Nanjie, Sanlihe, Beijing, People's Republic of China; *China Statistical Abstract.*

CHINA, PEOPLE'S REPUBLIC OF - INTERNATIONAL RESERVES EXCLUDING GOLD

The World Bank, 1818 H Street, NW, Washington, D.C. 20433 (202) 477-1234; *World Tables.*

CHINA, PEOPLE'S REPUBLIC OF - INTERNATIONAL STATISTICS

Asian Development Bank, P.O. Box 789, 1099 Manila, Philippines; *Key Indicators of Developing Asian and Pacific Countries.*

CHINA, PEOPLE'S REPUBLIC OF - IRON ORE PRODUCTION AND CONSUMPTION - See CHINA, PEOPLE'S REPUBLIC OF - MINING AND MINERAL PRODUCTS

CHINA, PEOPLE'S REPUBLIC OF - IRRIGATION

Euromonitor Publications Limited, 87-88 Turnmill Street, London EC1M 5QU, England; *International Marketing Data and Statistics.*

The University of Illinois at Chicago, China Statistics Archives, Suite 700 South, 1033 West Van Buren Street, Chicago, Illinois 60607-9940 (312) 413-0001 and China Statistical Information and Consultancy Service Center, 38 Yuetan Nanjie, Sanlihe, Beijing, People's Republic of China; *China Rural Statistics.*

CHINA, PEOPLE'S REPUBLIC OF - JUTE PRODUCTION - See CHINA, PEOPLE'S REPUBLIC OF - CROPS

CHINA, PEOPLE'S REPUBLIC OF - LABOR FORCE

The Economist Intelligence Unit (Asia) Limited, 10th Floor, Luk Kwok Centre, 72 Gloucester Road, Wanchai, Hong Kong (Phone Number in U.S. (800) 938-4685); *Asian Market Atlas,* and *China Market Atlas.*

Euromonitor Publications Limited, 87-88 Turnmill Street, London EC1M 5QU, England; *International Marketing Data and Statistics.*

Facts on File, 460 Park Avenue South, New York, New York 10016 (800) 443-8323; *The New Book of World Rankings.*

Food and Agricultural Organization of the United Nations (FAO) Via delle Terme di Caracalla, 00100 Rome, Italy (Telephone Number in U.S. (202) 653-2400); *The State of Food and Agriculture.*

G.K. Hall and Company, 70 Lincoln Street, Boston, Massachusetts 02111 (617) 423-3990; *The World in Figures.*

The University of Illinois at Chicago, China Statistics Archives, Suite 700 South, 1033 West Van Buren Street, Chicago, Illinois 60607-9940 (312) 413-0001 and China Statistical Information and Consultancy Service Center, 38 Yuetan Nanjie, Sanlihe, Beijing, People's Republic of China; *China Rural Statistics, China Social Statistics,* and *China Statistical Abstract.*

The World Bank, 1818 H Street, NW, Washington, D.C. 20433 (202) 477-1234; *World Tables.*

CHINA, PEOPLE'S REPUBLIC OF - LAND USE

Euromonitor Publications Limited, 87-88 Turnmill Street, London EC1M 5QU, England; *International Marketing Data and Statistics.*

Food and Agricultural Organization of the United Nations (FAO), Via delle Terme di Caracalla, 00100 Rome, Italy (Telephone Number in U.S. (202) 653-2400); *Production Yearbook.*

G.K. Hall and Company, 70 Lincoln Street, Boston, Massachusetts 02111 (617) 423-3990; *The World in Figures.*

The University of Illinois at Chicago, China Statistics Archives, Suite 700 South, 1033 West Van Buren Street, Chicago, Illinois 60607-9940 (312) 413-0001 and China Statistical Information and Consultancy Service Center, 38 Yuetan Nanjie, Sanlihe, Beijing, People's Republic of China; *China Rural Statistics, China Social Statistics,* and *China Statistical Abstract.*

CHINA, PEOPLE'S REPUBLIC OF - LEAD AND LEAD ORE - See CHINA, PEOPLE'S REPUBLIC OF - MINING AND MINERAL PRODUCTS

CHINA, PEOPLE'S REPUBLIC OF - LIBRARIES

Facts on File, 460 Park Avenue South, New York, New York 10016 (800) 443-8323; *The New Book of World Rankings.*

CHINA, PEOPLE'S REPUBLIC OF - LIFE EXPECTANCY

The Economist Intelligence Unit (Asia) Limited, 10th Floor, Luk Kwok Centre, 72 Gloucester Road, Wanchai, Hong Kong (Phone Number in U.S. (800) 938-4685); *Asian Market Atlas,* and *China Market Atlas.*

CHINA, PEOPLE'S REPUBLIC OF - LIGNITE PRODUCTION - See CHINA, PEOPLE'S REPUBLIC OF - MINING AND MINERAL PRODUCTS

CHINA, PEOPLE'S REPUBLIC OF - LIVESTOCK AND POULTRY

Commodity Research Bureau, Incorporated, 75 Wall Street, New York, New York 10005 (212) 504-7754; *Commodity Year Book.*

The Economist Intelligence Unit (Asia) Limited, 10th Floor, Luk Kwok Centre, 72 Gloucester Road, Wanchai, Hong Kong (Phone Number in U.S. (800) 938-4685); *China Market Atlas.*

Euromonitor Publications Limited, 87-88 Turnmill Street, London EC1M 5QU, England; *Third World Economic Handbook.*

Facts on File, 460 Park Avenue South, New York, New York 10016 (800) 443-8323; *The New Book of World Rankings.*

Food and Agricultural Organization of the United Nations (FAO), Via delle Terme di Caracalla, 00100 Rome, Italy (Telephone Number in U.S. (202) 653-2400); *Production Yearbook,* and *The State of Food and Agriculture.*

G.K. Hall and Company, 70 Lincoln Street, Boston, Massachusetts 02111 (617) 423-3990; *The World in Figures.*

Statistical Office of the United Nations, Publishing Service, New York, New York 10017 (800) 253-9646; *Statistical Yearbook.*

The University of Illinois at Chicago, China Statistics Archives, Suite 700 South, 1033 West Van Buren Street, Chicago, Illinois 60607-9940 (312) 413-0001 and China Statistical Information and Consultancy Service Center, 38 Yuetan Nanjie, Sanlihe, Beijing, People's Republic of China; *China Rural Statistics*, and *China Statistical Abstract*.

CHINA, PEOPLE'S REPUBLIC OF - LIVING LEVELS

G.K. Hall and Company, 70 Lincoln Street, Boston, Massachusetts 02111 (617) 423-3990; *The World in Figures*.

Times Books, 201 East 50th Street, New York, New York 10022 (212) 751-2600; *The Economist Book of Vital World Statistics*.

CHINA, PEOPLE'S REPUBLIC OF - MAGAZINES

The University of Illinois at Chicago, China Statistics Archives, Suite 700 South, 1033 West Van Buren Street, Chicago, Illinois 60607-9940 (312) 413-0001 and China Statistical Information and Consultancy Service Center, 38 Yuetan Nanjie, Sanlihe, Beijing, People's Republic of China: *China Social Statistics*, and *China Statistical Abstract*.

CHINA, PEOPLE'S REPUBLIC OF - MAGNESIUM PRODUCTION AND CONSUMPTION - See CHINA, PEOPLE'S REPUBLIC OF - MINING AND MINERAL PRODUCTS

CHINA, PEOPLE'S REPUBLIC OF - MAIL TRAFFIC

The University of Illinois at Chicago, China Statistics Archives, Suite 700 South, 1033 West Van Buren Street, Chicago, Illinois 60607-9940 (312) 413-0001 and China Statistical Information and Consultancy Service Center, 38 Yuetan Nanjie, Sanlihe, Beijing, People's Republic of China; *China Statistical Abstract*.

CHINA, PEOPLE'S REPUBLIC OF - MANGANESE AND MANGANESE ORE - See CHINA, PEOPLE'S REPUBLIC OF - MINING AND MINERAL PRODUCTS

CHINA, PEOPLE'S REPUBLIC OF - MANPOWER

Statistical Office of the United Nations, Publishing Service, New York, New York 10017 (800) 253-9646; *Statistical Yearbook for Asia and the Pacific*.

The University of Illinois at Chicago, China Statistics Archives, Suite 700 South, 1033 West Van Buren Street, Chicago, Illinois 60607-9940 (312) 413-0001 and China Statistical Information and Consultancy Service Center, 38 Yuetan Nanjie, Sanlihe, Beijing, People's Republic of China; *China Rural Statistics, China Social Statistics*, and *China Statistical Abstract*.

CHINA, PEOPLE'S REPUBLIC OF - MANUFACTURING

American Automobile Manufacturers Association, 1401 H Street, NW, Suite 900, Washington, D.C. 20005 (202) 326-5500; *World Motor Vehicle Data*.

Asian Development Bank, P.O. Box 789, 1099 Manila, Philippines; *Key Indicators of Developing Asian and Pacific Countries*.

Euromonitor Publications Limited, 87-88 Turnmill Street, London EC1M 5QU, England; *Third World Economic Handbook*.

Facts on File, 460 Park Avenue South, New York, New York 10016 (800) 443-8323; *The New Book of World Rankings*.

G.K. Hall and Company, 70 Lincoln Street, Boston, Massachusetts 02111 (617) 423-3990; *The World in Figures*.

Times Books, 201 East 50th Street, New York, New York 10022 (212) 751-2600; *The Economist Book of Vital World Statistics*.

The University of Illinois at Chicago, China Statistics Archives, Suite 700 South, 1033 West Van Buren Street, Chicago, Illinois 60607-9940 (312) 413-0001 and China Statistical Information and Consultancy Service Center, 38 Yuetan Nanjie, Sanlihe, Beijing, People's Republic of China; *China Rural Statistics, China Social Statistics*, and *China Statistical Abstract*.

The World Bank, 1818 H Street, NW, Washington, D.C. 20433 (202) 477-1234; *World Tables*.

CHINA, PEOPLE'S REPUBLIC OF - MARRIAGE RATES

Facts on File, 460 Park Avenue South, New York, New York 10016 (800) 443-8323; *The New Book of World Rankings*.

Statistical Office of the United Nations, Publishing Service, New York, New York 10017 (800) 253-9646; *Demographic Yearbook*.

The University of Illinois at Chicago, China Statistics Archives, Suite 700 South, 1033 West Van Buren Street, Chicago, Illinois 60607-9940 (312) 413-0001 and China Statistical Information and Consultancy Service Center, 38 Yuetan Nanjie, Sanlihe, Beijing, People's Republic of China: *China Social Statistics*, and *China Statistical Abstract*.

CHINA, PEOPLE'S REPUBLIC OF - MEAT PRODUCTION - See CHINA, PEOPLE'S REPUBLIC OF - LIVESTOCK AND POULTRY

CHINA, PEOPLE'S REPUBLIC OF - MERCHANT SHIPPING

G.K. Hall and Company, 70 Lincoln Street, Boston, Massachusetts 02111 (617) 423-3990; *The World in Figures*.

Lloyd's Register of Shipping, 17 Battery Place, New York, New York 10004 (212) 752-0055; *Register of Ships*.

Statistical Office of the United Nations, Publishing Service, New York, New York 10017 (800) 253-9646; *Statistical Yearbook*.

Times Books, 201 East 50th Street, New York, New York 10022 (212) 751-2600; *The Economist Book of Vital World Statistics*.

The University of Illinois at Chicago, China Statistics Archives, Suite 700 South, 1033 West Van Buren Street, Chicago, Illinois 60607-9940 (312) 413-0001 and China Statistical Information and Consultancy Service Center, 38 Yuetan Nanjie, Sanlihe, Beijing, People's Republic of China; *China Statistical Abstract*.

U.S. Department of Transportation, Maritime Administration, 400 Seventh Street, SW, Washington, D.C. 20590 (202) 366-5807; *A Statistical Analysis of the World's Merchant Fleets*.

CHINA, PEOPLE'S REPUBLIC OF - MERCURY PRODUCTION AND CONSUMPTION - See CHINA, PEOPLE'S REPUBLIC OF - MINING AND MINERAL PRODUCTS

CHINA, PEOPLE'S REPUBLIC OF - MILITARY

The Economist Intelligence Unit (Asia) Limited, 10th Floor, Luk Kwok Centre, 72 Gloucester Road, Wanchai, Hong Kong (Phone Number in U.S. (800) 938-4685); *Asian Market Atlas*.

G.K. Hall and Company, 70 Lincoln Street, Boston, Massachusetts 02111 (617) 423-3990; *The World in Figures*.

The International Institute for Strategic Studies, 23 Tavistock Street, London WC2E 7NQ, England; *The Military Balance.*

U.S. Arms Control and Disarmament Agency, 320 Twenty-first Street, NW, Washington, D.C. 20451 (202) 647-8677; *World Military Expenditures and Arms Transfers.*

CHINA, PEOPLE'S REPUBLIC OF - MILK - See CHINA, PEOPLE'S REPUBLIC OF - DAIRY PRODUCTS

CHINA, PEOPLE'S REPUBLIC OF - MILLET PRODUCTION- See CHINA, PEOPLE'S REPUBLIC OF - CROPS

CHINA, PEOPLE'S REPUBLIC OF - MINING AND MINERAL PRODUCTS

Asian Development Bank, P.O. Box 789, 1099 Manila, Philippines; *Key Indicators of Developing Asian and Pacific Countries.*

Commodity Research Bureau, Incorporated, 75 Wall Street, New York, New York 10005 (212) 504-7754; *Commodity Year Book.*

The Economist Intelligence Unit (Asia) Limited, 10th Floor, Luk Kwok Centre, 72 Gloucester Road, Wanchai, Hong Kong (Phone Number in U.S. (800) 938-4685); *China Market Atlas.*

Euromonitor Publications Limited, 87-88 Turnmill Street, London EC1M 5QU, England; *Third World Economic Handbook.*

Facts on File, 460 Park Avenue South, New York, New York 10016 (800) 443-8323; *The New Book of World Rankings.*

G.K. Hall and Company, 70 Lincoln Street, Boston, Massachusetts 02111 (617) 423-3990; *The World in Figures.*

Penn Well Publishing Company, 1421 South Sheridan Road, P.O. Box 1260, Tulsa, Oklahoma 74101 (800) 752-9764; *International Energy Statistics Sourcebook.*

Statistical Office of the United Nations, Publishing Service, New York, New York 10017 (800) 253-9646; *Statistical Yearbook.*

The University of Illinois at Chicago, China Statistics Archives, Suite 700 South, 1033 West Van Buren Street, Chicago, Illinois 60607-9940 (312) 413-0001 and China Statistical Information and Consultancy Service Center, 38 Yuetan Nanjie, Sanlihe, Beijing, People's Republic of China; *China Statistical Abstract.*

CHINA, PEOPLE'S REPUBLIC OF - MOLYBDENUM AND MOLYBDENUM ORE - See CHINA, PEOPLE'S REPUBLIC OF - MINING AND MINERAL PRODUCTS

CHINA, PEOPLE'S REPUBLIC OF - MONEY EXCHANGE RATE

Euromonitor Publications Limited, 87-88 Turnmill Street, London EC1M 5QU, England; *International Marketing Data and Statistics.*

International Monetary Fund, 700 Nineteenth Street, NW, Washington, D.C. 20431 (202) 623-7000; *International Financial Statistics.*

Statistical Office of the United Nations, Publishing Service, New York, New York 10017 (800) 253-9646; *Statistical Yearbook.*

CHINA, PEOPLE'S REPUBLIC OF - MONEY RESERVES

Euromonitor Publications Limited, 87-88 Turnmill Street, London EC1M 5QU, England; *International Marketing Data and Statistics.*

The University of Illinois at Chicago, China Statistics Archives, Suite 700 South, 1033 West Van Buren Street, Chicago, Illinois 60607-9940 (312) 413-0001 and China Statistical Information and Consultancy Service Center, 38 Yuetan Nanjie, Sanlihe, Beijing, People's Republic of China; *China Statistical Abstract.*

CHINA, PEOPLE'S REPUBLIC OF - MONEY SUPPLY

Asian Development Bank, P.O. Box 789, 1099 Manila, Philippines; *Key Indicators of Developing Asian and Pacific Countries.*

Euromonitor Publications Limited, 87-88 Turnmill Street, London EC1M 5QU, England; *International Marketing Data and Statistics.*

G.K. Hall and Company, 70 Lincoln Street, Boston, Massachusetts 02111 (617) 423-3990; *The World in Figures.*

International Monetary Fund, 700 Nineteenth Street, NW, Washington, D.C. 20431 (202) 623-7000; *International Financial Statistics.*

The University of Illinois at Chicago, China Statistics Archives, Suite 700 South, 1033 West Van Buren Street, Chicago, Illinois 60607-9940 (312) 413-0001 and China Statistical Information and Consultancy Service Center, 38 Yuetan Nanjie, Sanlihe, Beijing, People's Republic of China; *China Statistical Abstract.*

The World Bank, 1818 H Street, NW, Washington, D.C. 20433 (202) 477-1234; *World Tables.*

CHINA, PEOPLE'S REPUBLIC OF - MOTOR VEHICLE PRODUCTION

American Automobile Manufacturers Association, 1401 H Street, NW, Suite 900, Washington, D.C. 20005 (202) 326-5500; *World Motor Vehicle Data.*

The Economist Intelligence Unit (Asia) Limited, 10th Floor, Luk Kwok Centre, 72 Gloucester Road, Wanchai, Hong Kong (Phone Number in U.S. (800) 938-4685); *China Market Atlas.*

The University of Illinois at Chicago, China Statistics Archives, Suite 700 South, 1033 West Van Buren Street, Chicago, Illinois 60607-9940 (312) 413-0001 and China Statistical Information and Consultancy Service Center, 38 Yuetan Nanjie, Sanlihe, Beijing, People's Republic of China; *China Statistical Abstract.*

CHINA, PEOPLE'S REPUBLIC OF - MOTOR VEHICLES IN USE

American Automobile Manufacturers Association, 1401 H Street, NW, Suite 900, Washington, D.C. 20005 (202) 326-5500; *World Motor Vehicle Data.*

G.K. Hall and Company, 70 Lincoln Street, Boston, Massachusetts 02111 (617) 423-3990; *The World in Figures.*

Times Books, 201 East 50th Street, New York, New York 10022 (212) 751-2600; *The Economist Book of Vital World Statistics.*

CHINA, PEOPLE'S REPUBLIC OF - MULES - See CHINA, PEOPLE'S REPUBLIC OF - LIVESTOCK AND POULTRY

CHINA, PEOPLE'S REPUBLIC OF - MUSEUMS

Facts on File, 460 Park Avenue South, New York, New York 10016 (800) 443-8323; *The New Book of World Rankings.*

CHINA, PEOPLE'S REPUBLIC OF - NATALITY - See CHINA, PEOPLE'S REPUBLIC OF - BIRTH RATE

CHINA, PEOPLE'S REPUBLIC OF - NATIONAL ACCOUNTS

International Monetary Fund, 700 Nineteenth Street, NW, Washington, D.C. 20431 (202) 623-7000; *International Financial Statistics.*

Statistical Office of the United Nations, Publishing Service, New York, New York 10017 (800) 253-9646; *Statistical Yearbook for Asia and the Pacific.*

The University of Illinois at Chicago, China Statistics Archives, Suite 700 South, 1033 West Van Buren Street, Chicago, Illinois 60607-9940 (312) 413-0001 and China Statistical Information and Consultancy Service Center, 38 Yuetan Nanjie, Sanlihe, Beijing, People's Republic of China; *China Statistical Abstract.*

CHINA, PEOPLE'S REPUBLIC OF - NATIONAL INCOME

Facts on File, 460 Park Avenue South, New York, New York 10016 (800) 443-8323; *The New Book of World Rankings.*

G.K. Hall and Company, 70 Lincoln Street, Boston, Massachusetts 02111 (617) 423-3990; *The World in Figures.*

CHINA, PEOPLE'S REPUBLIC OF - NATIONAL PRODUCT

Facts on File, 460 Park Avenue South, New York, New York 10016 (800) 443-8323; *The New Book of World Rankings.*

CHINA, PEOPLE'S REPUBLIC OF - NATURAL GAS PRODUCTION - See CHINA, PEOPLE'S REPUBLIC OF - MINING AND MINERAL PRODUCTS

CHINA, PEOPLE'S REPUBLIC OF - NEWSPAPER PRODUCTION - SeeCHINA, PEOPLE'S REPUBLIC OF - FORESTRY AND FOREST PRODUCTS

CHINA, PEOPLE'S REPUBLIC OF - NEWSPRINT - See CHINA, PEOPLE'S REPUBLIC OF - FORESTRY AND FOREST PRODUCTS

CHINA, PEOPLE'S REPUBLIC OF - OATS PRODUCTION - See CHINA, PEOPLE'S REPUBLIC OF - CROPS

CHINA, PEOPLE'S REPUBLIC OF - OCCUPATIONS - See CHINA, PEOPLE'S REPUBLIC OF - LABOR FORCE

CHINA, PEOPLE'S REPUBLIC OF - PALM KERNELS AND PALM OIL PRODUCTION - See CHINA, PEOPLE'S REPUBLIC OF - CROPS

CHINA, PEOPLE'S REPUBLIC OF - PAPER - See CHINA, PEOPLE'S REPUBLIC OF - FORESTRY AND FOREST PRODUCTS

CHINA, PEOPLE'S REPUBLIC OF - PATENTS

World Intellectual Property Organization, 34 Chemin des Colombettes, CH-1211 Geneva 20. Switzerland; *Industrial Property Statistics.*

CHINA, PEOPLE'S REPUBLIC OF - PEANUT PRODUCTION - See CHINA, PEOPLE'S REPUBLIC OF - CROPS

CHINA, PEOPLE'S REPUBLIC OF - PESTICIDE USE

The Economist Intelligence Unit (Asia) Limited, 10th Floor, Luk Kwok Centre, 72 Gloucester Road, Wanchai, Hong Kong (Phone Number in U.S. (800) 938-4685); *China Market Atlas.*

Food and Agricultural Organization of the United Nations (FAO) Via delle Terme di Caracalla, 00100 Rome, Italy (Telephone Number in U.S. (202) 653-2400); *The State of Food and Agriculture.*

CHINA, PEOPLE'S REPUBLIC OF - PETROLEUM INDUSTRY

Asian Development Bank, P.O. Box 789, 1099 Manila, Philippines; *Key Indicators of Developing Asian and Pacific Countries.*

Commodity Research Bureau, Incorporated, 75 Wall Street, New York, New York 10005 (212) 504-7754; *Commodity Year Book.*

The Economist Intelligence Unit (Asia) Limited, 10th Floor, Luk Kwok Centre, 72 Gloucester Road, Wanchai, Hong Kong (Phone Number in U.S. (800) 938-4685); *China Market Atlas.*

Facts on File, 460 Park Avenue South, New York, New York 10016 (800) 443-8323; *The New Book of World Rankings.*

Food and Agricultural Organization of the United Nations (FAO) Via delle Terme di Caracalla, 00100 Rome, Italy (Telephone Number in U.S. (202) 653-2400); *The State of Food and Agriculture.*

G.K. Hall and Company, 70 Lincoln Street, Boston, Massachusetts 02111 (617) 423-3990; *The World in Figures.*

Penn Well Publishing Company, 1421 South Sheridan Road, P.O. Box 1260, Tulsa, Oklahoma 74101 (800) 752-9764; *International Energy Statistics Sourcebook.*

Statistical Office of the United Nations, Publishing Service, New York, New York 10017 (800) 253-9646; *Statistical Yearbook.*

The University of Illinois at Chicago, China Statistics Archives, Suite 700 South, 1033 West Van Buren Street, Chicago, Illinois 60607-9940 (312) 413-0001 and China Statistical Information and Consultancy Service Center, 38 Yuetan Nanjie, Sanlihe, Beijing, People's Republic of China; *China Statistical Abstract.*

CHINA, PEOPLE'S REPUBLIC OF - PHOSPHATE AND PHOSPHATE ROCK PRODUCTION - See CHINA, PEOPLE'S REPUBLIC OF - MINING AND MINERAL PRODUCTS

CHINA, PEOPLE'S REPUBLIC OF - PIG-IRON AND FERRO-ALLOY PRODUCTION - See CHINA, PEOPLE'S REPUBLIC OF - MINING AND MINERAL PRODUCTS

CHINA, PEOPLE'S REPUBLIC OF - PIGS - See CHINA, PEOPLE'S REPUBLIC OF - LIVESTOCK AND POULTRY

CHINA, PEOPLE'S REPUBLIC OF - PLASTICS AND RESINS PRODUCTION

The Economist Intelligence Unit (Asia) Limited, 10th Floor, Luk Kwok Centre, 72 Gloucester Road, Wanchai, Hong Kong (Phone Number in U.S. (800) 938-4685); *China Market Atlas.*

Euromonitor Publications Limited, 87-88 Turnmill Street, London EC1M 5QU, England; *Third World Economic Handbook.*

The University of Illinois at Chicago, China Statistics Archives, Suite 700 South, 1033 West Van Buren Street, Chicago, Illinois 60607-9940 (312) 413-0001 and China Statistical Information and Consultancy Service Center, 38 Yuetan Nanjie, Sanlihe, Beijing, People's Republic of China; *China Statistical Abstract.*

CHINA, PEOPLE'S REPUBLIC OF - POLLUTION

The Economist Intelligence Unit (Asia) Limited, 10th Floor, Luk Kwok Centre, 72 Gloucester Road, Wanchai, Hong Kong (Phone Number in U.S. (800) 938-4685); *China Market Atlas.*

CHINA, PEOPLE'S REPUBLIC OF - POPULATION

Asian Development Bank, P.O. Box 789, 1099 Manila, Philippines; *Key Indicators of Developing Asian and Pacific Countries.*

The Economist Intelligence Unit, 111 West 57th Street, New York, New York 10019 (800) 938-4685; *The World Market Atlas.*

The Economist Intelligence Unit (Asia) Limited, 10th Floor, Luk Kwok Centre, 72 Gloucester Road, Wanchai, Hong Kong (Phone Number in U.S. (800) 938-4685); *Asian Market Atlas,* and *China Market Atlas.*

Euromonitor Publications Limited, 87-88 Turnmill Street, London EC1M 5QU, England; *International Marketing Data and Statistics,* and *Third World Economic Handbook.*

Facts on File, 460 Park Avenue South, New York, New York 10016 (800) 443-8323; *The New Book of World Rankings.*

Food and Agricultural Organization of the United Nations (FAO), Via delle Terme di Caracalla, 00100 Rome, Italy (Telephone Number in U.S. (202) 653-2400); *Production Yearbook.*

G.K. Hall and Company, 70 Lincoln Street, Boston, Massachusetts 02111 (617) 423-3990; *The World in Figures.*

Statistical Office of the United Nations, Publishing Service, New York, New York 10017 (800) 253-9646; *Demographic Yearbook, Statistical Yearbook,* and *Statistical Yearbook for Asia and the Pacific.*

Times Books, 201 East 50th Street, New York, New York 10022 (212) 751-2600; *The Economist Book of Vital World Statistics.*

United Nations Educational, Scientific and Cultural Organization (UNESCO), 7 Place de Fontenoy, F-75700 Paris, France (Telephone Number in U.S. (212) 963-5981; *Statistical Yearbook.*

The University of Illinois at Chicago, China Statistics Archives, Suite 700 South, 1033 West Van Buren Street, Chicago, Illinois 60607-9940 (312) 413-0001 and China Statistical Information and Consultancy Service Center, 38 Yuetan Nanjie, Sanlihe, Beijing, People's Republic of China; *China Rural Statistics, China Social Statistics,* and *China Statistical Abstract.*

U.S. Arms Control and Disarmament Agency, 320 Twenty-first Street, NW, Washington, D.C. 20451 (202) 647-8677; *World Military Expenditures and Arms Transfers.*

World Health Organization, Office of Publications, Avenue Appia, CH-1211 Geneva 27, Switzerland (Telephone Number in U.S. (518) 436-9686); *World Health Statistics Annual.*

CHINA, PEOPLE'S REPUBLIC OF - POST OFFICES

Facts on File, 460 Park Avenue South, New York, New York 10016 (800) 443-8323; *The New Book of World Rankings.*

CHINA, PEOPLE'S REPUBLIC OF - POTATO PRODUCTION - See CHINA, PEOPLE'S REPUBLIC OF - CROPS

CHINA, PEOPLE'S REPUBLIC OF - POWER PRODUCTION INDUSTRY

The Economist Intelligence Unit (Asia) Limited, 10th Floor, Luk Kwok Centre, 72 Gloucester Road, Wanchai, Hong Kong (Phone Number in U.S. (800) 938-4685); *China Market Atlas.*

Statistical Office of the United Nations, Publishing Service, New York, New York 10017 (800) 253-9646; *Electric Power in Asia and the Pacific.*

The University of Illinois at Chicago, China Statistics Archives, Suite 700 South, 1033 West Van Buren Street, Chicago, Illinois 60607-9940 (312) 413-0001 and China Statistical Information and Consultancy Service Center, 38 Yuetan Nanjie, Sanlihe, Beijing, People's Republic of China; *China Statistical Abstract.*

CHINA, PEOPLE'S REPUBLIC OF - PRICES

Asian Development Bank, P.O. Box 789, 1099 Manila, Philippines; *Key Indicators of Developing Asian and Pacific Countries.*

Facts on File, 460 Park Avenue South, New York, New York 10016 (800) 443-8323; *The New Book of World Rankings.*

Food and Agricultural Organization of the United Nations (FAO), Via delle Terme di Caracalla, 00100 Rome, Italy (Telephone Number in U.S. (202) 653-2400); *Production Yearbook,* and *The State of Food and Agriculture.*

G.K. Hall and Company, 70 Lincoln Street, Boston, Massachusetts 02111 (617) 423-3990; *The World in Figures.*

International Monetary Fund, 700 Nineteenth Street, NW, Washington, D.C. 20431 (202) 623-7000; *International Financial Statistics.*

The University of Illinois at Chicago, China Statistics Archives, Suite 700 South, 1033 West Van Buren Street, Chicago, Illinois 60607-9940 (312) 413-0001 and China Statistical Information and Consultancy Service Center, 38 Yuetan Nanjie, Sanlihe, Beijing, People's Republic of China; *China Statistical Abstract,* and *China Trade and Price Statistics.*

CHINA, PEOPLE'S REPUBLIC OF - PRINTING AND WRITING PAPER - See CHINA, PEOPLE'S REPUBLIC OF - FORESTRY AND FOREST PRODUCTS

CHINA, PEOPLE'S REPUBLIC OF - PRODUCTION

American Automobile Manufacturers Association, 1401 H Street, NW, Suite 900, Washington, D.C. 20005 (202) 326-5500; *World Motor Vehicle Data.*

Euromonitor Publications Limited, 87-88 Turnmill Street, London EC1M 5QU, England; *Third World Economic Handbook.*

Facts on File, 460 Park Avenue South, New York, New York 10016 (800) 443-8323; *The New Book of World Rankings.*

G.K. Hall and Company, 70 Lincoln Street, Boston, Massachusetts 02111 (617) 423-3990; *The World in Figures.*

The University of Illinois at Chicago, China Statistics Archives, Suite 700 South, 1033 West Van Buren Street, Chicago, Illinois 60607-9940 (312) 413-0001 and China Statistical Information and Consultancy Service Center, 38 Yuetan Nanjie, Sanlihe, Beijing, People's Republic of China; *China Statistical Abstract.*

CHINA, PEOPLE'S REPUBLIC OF - PRODUCTIVITY

Euromonitor Publications Limited, 87-88 Turnmill Street, London EC1M 5QU, England; *International Marketing Data and Statistics*.

CHINA, PEOPLE'S REPUBLIC OF - PUBLIC FINANCE

Facts on File, 460 Park Avenue South, New York, New York 10016 (800) 443-8323; *The New Book of World Rankings*.

CHINA, PEOPLE'S REPUBLIC OF - RADIO BROADCASTING - See CHINA, PEOPLE'S REPUBLIC OF - BROADCASTING

CHINA, PEOPLE'S REPUBLIC OF - RAILWAYS

The Economist Intelligence Unit (Asia) Limited, 10th Floor, Luk Kwok Centre, 72 Gloucester Road, Wanchai, Hong Kong (Phone Number in U.S. (800) 938-4685); *China Market Atlas*.

G.K. Hall and Company, 70 Lincoln Street, Boston, Massachusetts 02111 (617) 423-3990; *The World in Figures*.

Jane's Information Group, Sentinel House, 163 Brighton Road, Coulsdon, Surrey CR5 2NH, England (Telephone Number in U.S. (703) 683-3700); *Jane's World Railways*.

Statistical Office of the United Nations, Publishing Service, New York, New York 10017 (800) 253-9646; *Statistical Yearbook*.

The University of Illinois at Chicago, China Statistics Archives, Suite 700 South, 1033 West Van Buren Street, Chicago, Illinois 60607-9940 (312) 413-0001 and China Statistical Information and Consultancy Service Center, 38 Yuetan Nanjie, Sanlihe, Beijing, People's Republic of China: *China Social Statistics*, and *China Statistical Abstract*.

CHINA, PEOPLE'S REPUBLIC OF - RAPESEED PRODUCTION - See CHINA, PEOPLE'S REPUBLIC OF - CROPS

CHINA, PEOPLE'S REPUBLIC OF - RELIGION

Facts on File, 460 Park Avenue South, New York, New York 10016 (800) 443-8323; *The New Book of World Rankings*.

CHINA, PEOPLE'S REPUBLIC OF - RETAIL TRADE

The Economist Intelligence Unit (Asia) Limited, 10th Floor, Luk Kwok Centre, 72 Gloucester Road, Wanchai, Hong Kong (Phone Number in U.S. (800) 938-4685); *China Market Atlas*.

Euromonitor Publications Limited, 87-88 Turnmill Street, London EC1M 5QU, England; *Third World Economic Handbook*.

G.K. Hall and Company, 70 Lincoln Street, Boston, Massachusetts 02111 (617) 423-3990; *The World in Figures*.

The University of Illinois at Chicago, China Statistics Archives, Suite 700 South, 1033 West Van Buren Street, Chicago, Illinois 60607-9940 (312) 413-0001 and China Statistical Information and Consultancy Service Center, 38 Yuetan Nanjie, Sanlihe, Beijing, People's Republic of China; *China Statistical Abstract*, and *China Trade and Price Statistics*.

CHINA, PEOPLE'S REPUBLIC OF - RICE PRODUCTION - See CHINA, PEOPLE'S REPUBLIC OF - CROPS

CHINA, PEOPLE'S REPUBLIC OF - ROOT AND TUBER PRODUCTION - See CHINA, PEOPLE'S REPUBLIC OF - CROPS

CHINA, PEOPLE'S REPUBLIC OF - ROUNDWOOD PRODUCTION - See CHINA, PEOPLE'S REPUBLIC OF - FORESTRY AND FOREST PRODUCTS

CHINA, PEOPLE'S REPUBLIC OF - RUBBER PRODUCTION AND CONSUMPTION

Euromonitor Publications Limited, 87-88 Turnmill Street, London EC1M 5QU, England; *Third World Economic Handbook*.

Facts on File, 460 Park Avenue South, New York, New York 10016 (800) 443-8323; *The New Book of World Rankings*.

Statistical Office of the United Nations, Publishing Service, New York, New York 10017 (800) 253-9646; *Statistical Yearbook*.

The University of Illinois at Chicago, China Statistics Archives, Suite 700 South, 1033 West Van Buren Street, Chicago, Illinois 60607-9940 (312) 413-0001 and China Statistical Information and Consultancy Service Center, 38 Yuetan Nanjie, Sanlihe, Beijing, People's Republic of China; *China Rural Statistics*, and *China Statistical Abstract*.

CHINA, PEOPLE'S REPUBLIC OF - SALT PRODUCTION - See CHINA, PEOPLE'S REPUBLIC OF - MINING AND MINERAL PRODUCTS

CHINA, PEOPLE'S REPUBLIC OF - SAWNWOOD PRODUCTION - SeeCHINA, PEOPLE'S REPUBLIC OF - FORESTRY AND FOREST PRODUCTS

CHINA, PEOPLE'S REPUBLIC OF - SENIOR CITIZENS

Facts on File, 460 Park Avenue South, New York, New York 10016 (800) 443-8323; *The New Book of World Rankings*.

CHINA, PEOPLE'S REPUBLIC OF - SESAME SEED PRODUCTION - See CHINA, PEOPLE'S REPUBLIC OF - CROPS

CHINA, PEOPLE'S REPUBLIC OF - SHEEP - See CHINA, PEOPLE'S REPUBLIC OF - LIVESTOCK AND POULTRY

CHINA, PEOPLE'S REPUBLIC OF - SILVER PRODUCTION AND CONSUMPTION - See CHINA, PEOPLE'S REPUBLIC OF - MINING AND MINERAL PRODUCTS

CHINA, PEOPLE'S REPUBLIC OF - SISAL PRODUCTION - See CHINA, PEOPLE'S REPUBLIC OF - CROPS

CHINA, PEOPLE'S REPUBLIC OF - SOCIAL DATA

Asian Development Bank, P.O. Box 789, 1099 Manila, Philippines; *Key Indicators of Developing Asian and Pacific Countries*.

Facts on File, 460 Park Avenue South, New York, New York 10016 (800) 443-8323; *The New Book of World Rankings*.

G.K. Hall and Company, 70 Lincoln Street, Boston, Massachusetts 02111 (617) 423-3990; *The World in Figures*.

The University of Illinois at Chicago, China Statistics Archives, Suite 700 South, 1033 West Van Buren Street, Chicago, Illinois 60607-9940 (312) 413-0001 and China Statistical Information and Consultancy Service Center, 38 Yuetan Nanjie, Sanlihe, Beijing, People's Republic of China: *China Social Statistics*, and *China Statistical Abstract*.

CHINA, PEOPLE'S REPUBLIC OF - SOYBEAN PRODUCTION - See CHINA, PEOPLE'S REPUBLIC OF - CROPS

CHINA, PEOPLE'S REPUBLIC OF - STATE BUDGET REVENUE AND EXPENDITURES

Euromonitor Publications Limited, 87-88 Turnmill Street, London EC1M 5QU, England; *International Marketing Data and Statistics.*

CHINA, PEOPLE'S REPUBLIC OF - STEEL - See CHINA, PEOPLE'S REPUBLIC OF - MINING AND MINERAL PRODUCTS

CHINA, PEOPLE'S REPUBLIC OF - STOCKS - COMMODITY - MARKET PRICE - INDEX

Food and Agricultural Organization of the United Nations (FAO) Via delle Terme di Caracalla, 00100 Rome, Italy (Telephone Number in U.S. (202) 653-2400); *The State of Food and Agriculture.*

The University of Illinois at Chicago, China Statistics Archives, Suite 700 South, 1033 West Van Buren Street, Chicago, Illinois 60607-9940 (312) 413-0001 and China Statistical Information and Consultancy Service Center, 38 Yuetan Nanjie, Sanlihe, Beijing, People's Republic of China; *China Statistical Abstract,* and *China Trade and Price Statistics.*

CHINA, PEOPLE'S REPUBLIC OF - SUGAR - See CHINA, PEOPLE'S REPUBLIC OF - CROPS

CHINA, PEOPLE'S REPUBLIC OF - SULPHUR PRODUCTION - See CHINA, PEOPLE'S REPUBLIC OF - MINING AND MINERAL PRODUCTS

CHINA, PEOPLE'S REPUBLIC OF - TAXATION

The Economist Intelligence Unit (Asia) Limited, 10th Floor, Luk Kwok Centre, 72 Gloucester Road, Wanchai, Hong Kong (Phone Number in U.S. (800) 938-4685); *China Market Atlas.*

G.K. Hall and Company, 70 Lincoln Street, Boston, Massachusetts 02111 (617) 423-3990; *The World in Figures.*

The World Bank, 1818 H Street, NW, Washington, D.C. 20433 (202) 477-1234; *World Tables.*

CHINA, PEOPLE'S REPUBLIC OF - TEA - See CHINA, PEOPLE'S REPUBLIC OF - CROPS

CHINA, PEOPLE'S REPUBLIC OF - TELEPHONES IN USE

American Telephone and Telegraph Company, 26 Parsippany Road, Whippany, New Jersey 07981 (800) 338-4038; *The World's Telephones.*

The Economist Intelligence Unit (Asia) Limited, 10th Floor, Luk Kwok Centre, 72 Gloucester Road, Wanchai, Hong Kong (Phone Number in U.S. (800) 938-4685); *Asian Market Atlas,* and *China Market Atlas.*

Euromonitor Publications Limited, 87-88 Turnmill Street, London EC1M 5QU, England; *Third World Economic Handbook.*

G.K. Hall and Company, 70 Lincoln Street, Boston, Massachusetts 02111 (617) 423-3990; *The World in Figures.*

CHINA, PEOPLE'S REPUBLIC OF - TELEVISION BROADCASTING - See CHINA, PEOPLE'S REPUBLIC OF - BROADCASTING

CHINA, PEOPLE'S REPUBLIC OF - TEXTILE INDUSTRY

The Economist Intelligence Unit (Asia) Limited, 10th Floor, Luk Kwok Centre, 72 Gloucester Road, Wanchai, Hong Kong (Phone Number in U.S. (800) 938-4685); *China Market Atlas.*

Euromonitor Publications Limited, 87-88 Turnmill Street, London EC1M 5QU, England; *Third World Economic Handbook.*

Food and Agricultural Organization of the United Nations (FAO), Via delle Terme di Caracalla, 00100 Rome, Italy (Telephone Number in U.S. (202) 653-2400); *Production Yearbook.*

Forest and Paper Association, 1250 Connecticut Avenue, NW, Washington, D.C. 20036 (202) 463-2455; *Wood Pulp and Fiber Statistics.*

G.K. Hall and Company, 70 Lincoln Street, Boston, Massachusetts 02111 (617) 423-3990; *The World in Figures.*

Statistical Office of the United Nations, Publishing Service, New York, New York 10017 (800) 253-9646; *Statistical Yearbook.*

The University of Illinois at Chicago, China Statistics Archives, Suite 700 South, 1033 West Van Buren Street, Chicago, Illinois 60607-9940 (312) 413-0001 and China Statistical Information and Consultancy Service Center, 38 Yuetan Nanjie, Sanlihe, Beijing, People's Republic of China; *China Rural Statistics,* and *China Statistical Abstract.*

CHINA, PEOPLE'S REPUBLIC OF - TOBACCO PRODUCTION

Commodity Research Bureau, Incorporated, 75 Wall Street, New York, New York 10005 (212) 504-7754; *Commodity Year Book.*

The Economist Intelligence Unit (Asia) Limited, 10th Floor, Luk Kwok Centre, 72 Gloucester Road, Wanchai, Hong Kong (Phone Number in U.S. (800) 938-4685); *China Market Atlas.*

Euromonitor Publications Limited, 87-88 Turnmill Street, London EC1M 5QU, England; *Third World Economic Handbook.*

Facts on File, 460 Park Avenue South, New York, New York 10016 (800) 443-8323; *The New Book of World Rankings.*

Statistical Office of the United Nations, Publishing Service, New York, New York 10017 (800) 253-9646; *Statistical Yearbook.*

The University of Illinois at Chicago, China Statistics Archives, Suite 700 South, 1033 West Van Buren Street, Chicago, Illinois 60607-9940 (312) 413-0001 and China Statistical Information and Consultancy Service Center, 38 Yuetan Nanjie, Sanlihe, Beijing, People's Republic of China; *China Rural Statistics,* and *China Statistical Abstract.*

CHINA, PEOPLE'S REPUBLIC OF - TOBACCO PRODUCTS PRODUCTION

The University of Illinois at Chicago, China Statistics Archives, Suite 700 South, 1033 West Van Buren Street, Chicago, Illinois 60607-9940 (312) 413-0001 and China Statistical Information and Consultancy Service Center, 38 Yuetan Nanjie, Sanlihe, Beijing, People's Republic of China; *China Rural Statistics,* and *China Statistical Abstract.*

CHINA, PEOPLE'S REPUBLIC OF - TOURISM

The Economist Intelligence Unit (Asia) Limited, 10th Floor, Luk Kwok Centre, 72 Gloucester Road, Wanchai, Hong Kong (Phone Number in U.S. (800) 938-4685); *China Market Atlas.*

Euromonitor Publications Limited, 87-88 Turnmill Street, London EC1M 5QU, England; *Third World Economic Handbook.*

Facts on File, 460 Park Avenue South, New York, New York 10016 (800) 443-8323; *The New Book of World Rankings.*

G.K. Hall and Company, 70 Lincoln Street, Boston, Massachusetts 02111 (617) 423-3990; *The World in Figures.*

Times Books, 201 East 50th Street, New York, New York 10022 (212) 751-2600; *The Economist Book of Vital World Statistics.*

The University of Illinois at Chicago, China Statistics Archives, Suite 700 South, 1033 West Van Buren Street, Chicago, Illinois 60607-9940 (312) 413-0001 and China Statistical Information and Consultancy Service Center, 38 Yuetan Nanjie, Sanlihe, Beijing, People's Republic of China; *China Statistical Abstract,* and *China Trade and Price Statistics.*

World Tourism Organization, Calle Capitan Haya 42, E-28020 Madrid, Spain; *Yearbook of Tourism Statistics.*

CHINA, PEOPLE'S REPUBLIC OF - TRACTORS IN USE

Statistical Office of the United Nations, Publishing Service, New York, New York 10017 (800) 253-9646; *Statistical Yearbook.*

The University of Illinois at Chicago, China Statistics Archives, Suite 700 South, 1033 West Van Buren Street, Chicago, Illinois 60607-9940 (312) 413-0001 and China Statistical Information and Consultancy Service Center, 38 Yuetan Nanjie, Sanlihe, Beijing, People's Republic of China; *China Rural Statistics,* and *China Statistical Abstract.*

CHINA, PEOPLE'S REPUBLIC OF - TRADE - See CHINA, PEOPLE'S REPUBLIC OF - FOREIGN TRADE

CHINA, PEOPLE'S REPUBLIC OF - TRANSPORTATION AND COMMUNICATIONS

The Economist Intelligence Unit (Asia) Limited, 10th Floor, Luk Kwok Centre, 72 Gloucester Road, Wanchai, Hong Kong (Phone Number in U.S. (800) 938-4685); *Asian Market Atlas,* and *China Market Atlas.*

Euromonitor Publications Limited, 87-88 Turnmill Street, London EC1M 5QU, England; *Third World Economic Handbook.*

Facts on File, 460 Park Avenue South, New York, New York 10016 (800) 443-8323; *The New Book of World Rankings.*

G.K. Hall and Company, 70 Lincoln Street, Boston, Massachusetts 02111 (617) 423-3990; *The World in Figures.*

Statistical Office of the United Nations, Publishing Service, New York, New York 10017 (800) 253-9646; *Statistical Yearbook for Asia and the Pacific.*

The University of Illinois at Chicago, China Statistics Archives, Suite 700 South, 1033 West Van Buren Street, Chicago, Illinois 60607-9940 (312) 413-0001 and China Statistical Information and Consultancy Service Center, 38 Yuetan Nanjie, Sanlihe, Beijing, People's Republic of China; *China Rural Statistics, China Social Statistics,* and *China Statistical Abstract.*

CHINA, PEOPLE'S REPUBLIC OF - TUNGSTEN PRODUCTION AND CONSUMPTION - See CHINA, PEOPLE'S REPUBLIC OF - MINING AND MINERAL PRODUCTS

CHINA, PEOPLE'S REPUBLIC OF - TURKEYS - See CHINA, PEOPLE'S REPUBLIC OF - LIVESTOCK AND POULTRY

CHINA, PEOPLE'S REPUBLIC OF - UNEMPLOYMENT

Euromonitor Publications Limited, 87-88 Turnmill Street, London EC1M 5QU, England; *International Marketing Data and Statistics.*

The University of Illinois at Chicago, China Statistics Archives, Suite 700 South, 1033 West Van Buren Street, Chicago, Illinois 60607-9940 (312) 413-0001 and China Statistical Information and Consultancy Service Center, 38 Yuetan Nanjie, Sanlihe, Beijing, People's Republic of China: *China Social Statistics,* and *China Statistical Abstract.*

CHINA, PEOPLE'S REPUBLIC OF - UTILITIES

Statistical Office of the United Nations, Publishing Service, New York, New York 10017; *Electric Power in Asia and the Pacific.*

The University of Illinois at Chicago, China Statistics Archives, Suite 700 South, 1033 West Van Buren Street, Chicago, Illinois 60607-9940 (312) 413-0001 and China Statistical Information and Consultancy Service Center, 38 Yuetan Nanjie, Sanlihe, Beijing, People's Republic of China; *China Statistical Abstract.*

CHINA, PEOPLE'S REPUBLIC OF - VANADIUM PRODUCTION AND CONSUMPTION - See CHINA, PEOPLE'S REPUBLIC OF - MINING AND MINERAL PRODUCTS

CHINA, PEOPLE'S REPUBLIC OF - VITAL STATISTICS

Euromonitor Publications Limited, 87-88 Turnmill Street, London EC1M 5QU, England; *International Marketing Data and Statistics,* and *Third World Economic Handbook.*

G.K. Hall and Company, 70 Lincoln Street, Boston, Massachusetts 02111 (617) 423-3990; *The World in Figures.*

Statistical Office of the United Nations, Publishing Service, New York, New York 10017 (800) 253-9646; *Statistical Yearbook.*

The University of Illinois at Chicago, China Statistics Archives, Suite 700 South, 1033 West Van Buren Street, Chicago, Illinois 60607-9940 (312) 413-0001 and China Statistical Information and Consultancy Service Center, 38 Yuetan Nanjie, Sanlihe, Beijing, People's Republic of China; *China Rural Statistics, China Social Statistics,* and *China Statistical Abstract.*

World Health Organization, Office of Publications, Avenue Appia, CH-1211 Geneva 27, Switzerland (Telephone Number in U.S. (518) 436-9686); *World Health Statistics Annual.*

CHINA, PEOPLE'S REPUBLIC OF - WAGES

The Economist Intelligence Unit (Asia) Limited, 10th Floor, Luk Kwok Centre, 72 Gloucester Road, Wanchai, Hong Kong (Phone Number in U.S. (800) 938-4685); *China Market Atlas.*

G.K. Hall and Company, 70 Lincoln Street, Boston, Massachusetts 02111 (617) 423-3990; *The World in Figures.*

Statistical Office of the United Nations, Publishing Service, New York, New York 10017 (800) 253-9646; *Statistical Yearbook for Asia and the Pacific.*

The University of Illinois at Chicago, China Statistics Archives, Suite 700 South, 1033 West Van Buren Street, Chicago, Illinois 60607-9940 (312) 413-0001 and China Statistical Information and Consultancy Service Center, 38 Yuetan Nanjie, Sanlihe, Beijing, People's Republic of China; *China Rural Statistics, China Social Statistics, China Statistical Abstract,* and *China Trade and Price Statistics.*

CHINA, PEOPLE'S REPUBLIC OF - WALNUT PRODUCTION - See CHINA, PEOPLE'S REPUBLIC OF - CROPS

CHINA, PEOPLE'S REPUBLIC OF - WATERMELON - See CHINA, PEOPLE'S REPUBLIC OF - CROPS

CHINA, PEOPLE'S REPUBLIC OF - WEATHER

Facts on File, 460 Park Avenue South, New York, New York 10016 (800) 443-8323; *The New Book of World Rankings.*

G.K. Hall and Company, 70 Lincoln Street, Boston, Massachusetts 02111 (617) 423-3990; *The World in Figures.*

CHINA, PEOPLE'S REPUBLIC OF - WHEAT PRODUCTION - See CHINA, PEOPLE'S REPUBLIC OF - CROPS

CHINA, PEOPLE'S REPUBLIC OF - WHOLESALE PRICES

Asian Development Bank, P.O. Box 789, 1099 Manila, Philippines; *Key Indicators of Developing Asian and Pacific Countries.*

International Monetary Fund, 700 Nineteenth Street, NW, Washington, D.C. 20431 (202) 623-7000; *Government Finance Statistics Yearbook.*

The University of Illinois at Chicago, China Statistics Archives, Suite 700 South, 1033 West Van Buren Street, Chicago, Illinois 60607-9940 (312) 413-0001 and China Statistical Information and Consultancy Service Center, 38 Yuetan Nanjie, Sanlihe, Beijing, People's Republic of China; *China Trade and Price Statistics.*

CHINA, PEOPLE'S REPUBLIC OF - WHOLESALE TRADE

Euromonitor Publications Limited, 87-88 Turnmill Street, London EC1M 5QU, England; *Third World Economic Handbook.*

The University of Illinois at Chicago, China Statistics Archives, Suite 700 South, 1033 West Van Buren Street, Chicago, Illinois 60607-9940 (312) 413-0001 and China Statistical Information and Consultancy Service Center, 38 Yuetan Nanjie, Sanlihe, Beijing, People's Republic of China; *China Trade and Price Statistics.*

CHINA, PEOPLE'S REPUBLIC OF - WINE PRODUCTION

Facts on File, 460 Park Avenue South, New York, New York 10016 (800) 443-8323; *The New Book of World Rankings.*

CHINA, PEOPLE'S REPUBLIC OF - WOOD EXPORTS - See CHINA, PEOPLE'S REPUBLIC OF - FORESTRY AND FOREST PRODUCTS

CHINA, PEOPLE'S REPUBLIC OF - WOOL PRODUCTION

The Economist Intelligence Unit (Asia) Limited, 10th Floor, Luk Kwok Centre, 72 Gloucester Road, Wanchai, Hong Kong (Phone Number in U.S. (800) 938-4685); *China Market Atlas.*

Facts on File, 460 Park Avenue South, New York, New York 10016 (800) 443-8323; *The New Book of World Rankings.*

CHINA, PEOPLE'S REPUBLIC OF - YARN PRODUCTION

The Economist Intelligence Unit (Asia) Limited, 10th Floor, Luk Kwok Centre, 72 Gloucester Road, Wanchai, Hong Kong (Phone Number in U.S. (800) 938-4685); *China Market Atlas.*

Statistical Office of the United Nations, Publishing Service, New York, New York 10017 (800) 253-9646; *Statistical Yearbook.*

The University of Illinois at Chicago, China Statistics Archives, Suite 700 South, 1033 West Van Buren Street, Chicago, Illinois 60607-9940 (312) 413-0001 (312) 413-0001 and China Statistical Information and Consultancy Service Center, 38 Yuetan Nanjie, Sanlihe, Beijing, People's Republic of China; *China Statistical Abstract.*

CHINA, PEOPLE'S REPUBLIC OF - ZINC AND ZINC ORE - See CHINA, PEOPLE'S REPUBLIC OF - MINING AND MINERAL PRODUCTS

CHINA, REPUBLIC OF (TAIWAN) - See TAIWAN

CHIROPRACTOR'S OFFICES

U.S. Department of Commerce, Bureau of the Census, Suitland, Maryland 20233 (301) 763-4040; *County Business Patterns.*

CHOCOLATE - See COCOA AND CONFECTIONERY PRODUCTS

CHOLELITHIASIS - DEATHS

U.S. Department of Health and Human Services, National Center for Health Statistics, 3700 East-West Highway, Hyattsville, Maryland 20782 (301) 436-8500; *Monthly Vital Statistics Report,* and *Vital Statistics of the United States.*

Christmas Island - Primary Statistics Source

Sales and Distribution, Australian Government Publishing Service, Post Office Box 84, Canberra ACT 2601, Australia; *Annual Report on the Territory of Christmas Island.*

CHRISTMAS ISLAND - AGRICULTURE

Food and Agricultural Organization of the United Nations (FAO) Via delle Terme di Caracalla, 00100 Rome, Italy (Telephone Number in U.S. (202) 653-2400); *Production Yearbook, The State of Food and Agriculture,* and *Trade Yearbook.*

G.K. Hall and Company, 70 Lincoln Street, Boston, Massachusetts 02111 (617) 423-3990; *The World in Figures.*

CHRISTMAS ISLAND - AIRLINE SERVICE

G.K. Hall and Company, 70 Lincoln Street, Boston, Massachusetts 02111 (617) 423-3990; *The World in Figures.*

CHRISTMAS ISLAND - AREA AND DENSITY OF POPULATION

Food and Agricultural Organization of the United Nations (FAO) Via delle Terme di Caracalla, 00100 Rome, Italy (Telephone Number in U.S. (202) 653-2400); *The State of Food and Agriculture.*

G.K. Hall and Company, 70 Lincoln Street, Boston, Massachusetts 02111 (617) 423-3990; *The World in Figures.*

Statistical Office of the United Nations, Publishing Service, New York, New York 10017 (800) 253-9646; *Statistical Yearbook.*

United Nations Educational, Scientific and Cultural Organization (UNESCO), 7 Place de Fontenoy, F-75700 Paris, France (Telephone Number in U.S. (212) 963-5081; *Statistical Yearbook.*

CHRISTMAS ISLAND - BALANCE OF PAYMENTS

G.K. Hall and Company, 70 Lincoln Street, Boston, Massachusetts 02111 (617) 423-3990; *The World in Figures.*

CHRISTMAS ISLAND - BANKING

G.K. Hall and Company, 70 Lincoln Street, Boston, Massachusetts 02111 (617) 423-3990; *The World in Figures*.

CHRISTMAS ISLAND - BIRTH RATES

Statistical Office of the United Nations, Publishing Service, New York, New York 10017 (800) 253-9646; *Demographic Yearbook*, and *Statistical Yearbook*.

World Health Organization, Office of Publications, Avenue Appia, CH-1211 Geneva 27, Switzerland (Telephone Number in U.S. (518) 436-9686; *World Health Statistics Annual*.

CHRISTMAS ISLAND - BONDS

G.K. Hall and Company, 70 Lincoln Street, Boston, Massachusetts 02111 (617) 423-3990; *The World in Figures*.

CHRISTMAS ISLAND - BOOK PRODUCTION

G.K. Hall and Company, 70 Lincoln Street, Boston, Massachusetts 02111 (617) 423-3990; *The World in Figures*.

CHRISTMAS ISLAND - BROADCASTING

Billboard Limited, P.O. Box 9027, 1006 AA Amsterdam, The Netherlands (Telephone Number in U.S. (212) 764-7300); *World Radio TV Handbook*.

G.K. Hall and Company, 70 Lincoln Street, Boston, Massachusetts 02111 (617) 423-3990; *The World in Figures*.

CHRISTMAS ISLAND - BUSINESS

G.K. Hall and Company, 70 Lincoln Street, Boston, Massachusetts 02111 (617) 423-3990; *The World in Figures*.

CHRISTMAS ISLAND - CALORIE SUPPLY

Food and Agricultural Organization of the United Nations (FAO) Via delle Terme di Caracalla, 00100 Rome, Italy (Telephone Number in U.S. (202) 653-2400); *The State of Food and Agriculture*.

CHRISTMAS ISLAND - CENTRAL BANKS

G.K. Hall and Company, 70 Lincoln Street, Boston, Massachusetts 02111 (617) 423-3990; *The World in Figures*.

CHRISTMAS ISLAND - CHEMICAL (ORGANIC) PRODUCTION - See CHRISTMAS ISLAND - MINING AND MINERAL PRODUCTS

CHRISTMAS ISLAND - CLASS STRUCTURE

G.K. Hall and Company, 70 Lincoln Street, Boston, Massachusetts 02111 (617) 423-3990; *The World in Figures*.

CHRISTMAS ISLAND - CLIMATE

G.K. Hall and Company, 70 Lincoln Street, Boston, Massachusetts 02111 (617) 423-3990; *The World in Figures*.

CHRISTMAS ISLAND - COAL PRODUCTION - See CHRISTMAS ISLAND - MINING AND MINERAL PRODUCTS

CHRISTMAS ISLAND - COMMUNICATIONS

G.K. Hall and Company, 70 Lincoln Street, Boston, Massachusetts 02111 (617) 423-3990; *The World in Figures*.

CHRISTMAS ISLAND - CONSUMER PRICE INDEX

G.K. Hall and Company, 70 Lincoln Street, Boston, Massachusetts 02111 (617) 423-3990; *The World in Figures*.

CHRISTMAS ISLAND - CONSUMPTION

G.K. Hall and Company, 70 Lincoln Street, Boston, Massachusetts 02111 (617) 423-3990; *The World in Figures*.

CHRISTMAS ISLAND - CORN PRODUCTION - See CHRISTMAS ISLAND - CROPS

CHRISTMAS ISLAND - CORPORATE TAXES - See CHRISTMAS ISLAND - TAXATION

CHRISTMAS ISLAND - CROPS

Food and Agricultural Organization of the United Nations (FAO) Via delle Terme di Caracalla, 00100 Rome, Italy (Telephone Number in U.S. (202) 653-2400); *The State of Food and Agriculture*.

G.K. Hall and Company, 70 Lincoln Street, Boston, Massachusetts 02111 (617) 423-3990; *The World in Figures*.

CHRISTMAS ISLAND - CUSTOMS DUTIES

G.K. Hall and Company, 70 Lincoln Street, Boston, Massachusetts 02111 (617) 423-3990; *The World in Figures*.

CHRISTMAS ISLAND - DAIRY PRODUCTS

Food and Agricultural Organization of the United Nations (FAO) Via delle Terme di Caracalla, 00100 Rome, Italy (Telephone Number in U.S. (202) 653-2400); *The State of Food and Agriculture*.

CHRISTMAS ISLAND - DEATH RATES

G.K. Hall and Company, 70 Lincoln Street, Boston, Massachusetts 02111 (617) 423-3990; *The World in Figures*.

Statistical Office of the United Nations, Publishing Service, New York, New York 10017 (800) 253-9646; *Statistical Yearbook*.

CHRISTMAS ISLAND - DEFENSE EXPENDITURES

G.K. Hall and Company, 70 Lincoln Street, Boston, Massachusetts 02111 (617) 423-3990; *The World in Figures*.

CHRISTMAS ISLAND - DEMOGRAPHY

G.K. Hall and Company, 70 Lincoln Street, Boston, Massachusetts 02111 (617) 423-3990; *The World in Figures*.

CHRISTMAS ISLAND - DEVELOPMENT ASSISTANCE

G.K. Hall and Company, 70 Lincoln Street, Boston, Massachusetts 02111 (617) 423-3990; *The World in Figures*.

CHRISTMAS ISLAND - DISEASE

G.K. Hall and Company, 70 Lincoln Street, Boston, Massachusetts 02111 (617) 423-3990; *The World in Figures*.

CHRISTMAS ISLAND - DIVORCE RATES

Statistical Office of the United Nations, Publishing Service, New York, New York 10017 (800) 253-9646; *Statistical Yearbook.*

CHRISTMAS ISLAND - DOMESTIC PRODUCT

G.K. Hall and Company, 70 Lincoln Street, Boston, Massachusetts 02111 (617) 423-3990; *The World in Figures.*

CHRISTMAS ISLAND - ECONOMY

G.K. Hall and Company, 70 Lincoln Street, Boston, Massachusetts 02111 (617) 423-3990; *The World in Figures.*

CHRISTMAS ISLAND - EDUCATION

G.K. Hall and Company, 70 Lincoln Street, Boston, Massachusetts 02111 (617) 423-3990; *The World in Figures.*

CHRISTMAS ISLAND - EGG PRODUCTION - See CHRISTMAS ISLAND - DAIRY PRODUCTS

CHRISTMAS ISLAND - ENERGY

Food and Agricultural Organization of the United Nations (FAO) Via delle Terme di Caracalla, 00100 Rome, Italy (Telephone Number in U.S. (202) 653-2400); *The State of Food and Agriculture.*

G.K. Hall and Company, 70 Lincoln Street, Boston, Massachusetts 02111 (617) 423-3990; *The World in Figures.*

Statistical Office of the United Nations, Publishing Service, New York, New York 10017 (800) 253-9646; *Statistical Yearbook,* and *World Energy Supplies.*

CHRISTMAS ISLAND - EXPORTS

Food and Agricultural Organization of the United Nations (FAO) Via delle Terme di Caracalla, 00100 Rome, Italy (Telephone Number in U.S. (202) 653-2400); *The State of Food and Agriculture.*

G.K. Hall and Company, 70 Lincoln Street, Boston, Massachusetts 02111 (617) 423-3990; *The World in Figures.*

CHRISTMAS ISLAND - EXTERNAL TRADE

Food and Agricultural Organization of the United Nations (FAO) Via delle Terme di Caracalla, 00100 Rome, Italy (Telephone Number in U.S. (202) 653-2400); *The State of Food and Agriculture,* and *Trade Yearbook.*

G.K. Hall and Company, 70 Lincoln Street, Boston, Massachusetts 02111 (617) 423-3990; *The World in Figures.*

CHRISTMAS ISLAND - FARM CROPS - See CHRISTMAS ISLAND - CROPS

CHRISTMAS ISLAND - FETAL MORTALITY

Statistical Office of the United Nations, Publishing Service, New York, New York 10017 (800) 253-9646; *Demographic Yearbook.*

CHRISTMAS ISLAND - FERTILIZER

Food and Agricultural Organization of the United Nations (FAO) Via delle Terme di Caracalla, 00100 Rome, Italy (Telephone Number in U.S. (202) 653-2400); *The State of Food and Agriculture.*

CHRISTMAS ISLAND - FINANCE

G.K. Hall and Company, 70 Lincoln Street, Boston, Massachusetts 02111 (617) 423-3990; *The World in Figures.*

CHRISTMAS ISLAND - FISHERIES

Food and Agricultural Organization of the United Nations (FAO) Via delle Terme di Caracalla, 00100 Rome, Italy (Telephone Number in U.S. (202) 653-2400); *The State of Food and Agriculture,* and *Yearbook of Fishery Statistics.*

CHRISTMAS ISLAND - FOOD

Food and Agricultural Organization of the United Nations (FAO), Via delle Terme di Caracalla, 00100 Rome, Italy (Telephone Number in U.S. (202) 653-2400); *Production Yearbook,* and *The State of Food and Agriculture.*

G.K. Hall and Company, 70 Lincoln Street, Boston, Massachusetts 02111 (617) 423-3990; *The World in Figures.*

CHRISTMAS ISLAND - FOREIGN AID

G.K. Hall and Company, 70 Lincoln Street, Boston, Massachusetts 02111 (617) 423-3990; *The World in Figures.*

CHRISTMAS ISLAND - FOREIGN TRADE

Food and Agricultural Organization of the United Nations (FAO) Via delle Terme di Caracalla, 00100 Rome, Italy (Telephone Number in U.S. (202) 653-2400); *The State of Food and Agriculture.*

G.K. Hall and Company, 70 Lincoln Street, Boston, Massachusetts 02111 (617) 423-3990; *The World in Figures.*

Organisation for Economic Co-operation and Development (OECD), 2 rue Andre-Pascal, 75 Paris 16, France (Telephone Number in U.S. (202) 785-6323; *Trade by Commodities.*

CHRISTMAS ISLAND - FORESTRY AND FOREST PRODUCTS

Food and Agricultural Organization of the United Nations (FAO) Via delle Terme di Caracalla, 00100 Rome, Italy (Telephone Number in U.S. (202) 653-2400); *The State of Food and Agriculture.*

G.K. Hall and Company, 70 Lincoln Street, Boston, Massachusetts 02111 (617) 423-3990; *The World in Figures.*

CHRISTMAS ISLAND - GENERAL MORTALITY

Statistical Office of the United Nations, Publishing Service, New York, New York 10017 (800) 253-9646; *Demographic Yearbook.*

World Health Organization, Office of Publications, Avenue Appia, CH-1211 Geneva 27, Switzerland (Telephone Number in U.S. (518) 436-9686; *World Health Statistics Annual.*

CHRISTMAS ISLAND - GOVERNMENT

G.K. Hall and Company, 70 Lincoln Street, Boston, Massachusetts 02111 (617) 423-3990; *The World in Figures.*

CHRISTMAS ISLAND - GRAIN PRODUCTION - See CHRISTMAS ISLAND - CROPS

CHRISTMAS ISLAND - GROSS DOMESTIC PRODUCT

G.K. Hall and Company, 70 Lincoln Street, Boston, Massachusetts 02111 (617) 423-3990; *The World in Figures.*

CHRISTMAS ISLAND - HEALTH

G.K. Hall and Company, 70 Lincoln Street, Boston, Massachusetts 02111 (617) 423-3990; *The World in Figures.*

CHRISTMAS ISLAND - HIGHWAYS

G.K. Hall and Company, 70 Lincoln Street, Boston, Massachusetts 02111 (617) 423-3990; *The World in Figures.*

CHRISTMAS ISLAND - ILLITERATE POPULATION

G.K. Hall and Company, 70 Lincoln Street, Boston, Massachusetts 02111 (617) 423-3990; *The World in Figures.*

CHRISTMAS ISLAND - IMPORTS

Food and Agricultural Organization of the United Nations (FAO) Via delle Terme di Caracalla, 00100 Rome, Italy (Telephone Number in U.S. (202) 653-2400); *The State of Food and Agriculture.*

G.K. Hall and Company, 70 Lincoln Street, Boston, Massachusetts 02111 (617) 423-3990; *The World in Figures.*

CHRISTMAS ISLAND - INDUSTRY

G.K. Hall and Company, 70 Lincoln Street, Boston, Massachusetts 02111 (617) 423-3990; *The World in Figures.*

CHRISTMAS ISLAND - LABOR FORCE

Food and Agricultural Organization of the United Nations (FAO) Via delle Terme di Caracalla, 00100 Rome, Italy (Telephone Number in U.S. (202) 653-2400); *The State of Food and Agriculture.*

G.K. Hall and Company, 70 Lincoln Street, Boston, Massachusetts 02111 (617) 423-3990; *The World in Figures.*

CHRISTMAS ISLAND - LAND USE

Food and Agricultural Organization of the United Nations (FAO), Via delle Terme di Caracalla, 00100 Rome, Italy (Telephone Number in U.S. (202) 653-2400); *Production Yearbook.*

G.K. Hall and Company, 70 Lincoln Street, Boston, Massachusetts 02111 (617) 423-3990; *The World in Figures.*

CHRISTMAS ISLAND - LIVESTOCK AND POULTRY

Food and Agricultural Organization of the United Nations (FAO), Via delle Terme di Caracalla, 00100 Rome, Italy (Telephone Number in U.S. (202) 653-2400); *Production Yearbook,* and *The State of Food and Agriculture.*

G.K. Hall and Company, 70 Lincoln Street, Boston, Massachusetts 02111 (617) 423-3990; *The World in Figures.*

CHRISTMAS ISLAND - LIVING LEVELS

G.K. Hall and Company, 70 Lincoln Street, Boston, Massachusetts 02111 (617) 423-3990; *The World in Figures.*

CHRISTMAS ISLAND - MANUFACTURING

G.K. Hall and Company, 70 Lincoln Street, Boston, Massachusetts 02111 (617) 423-3990; *The World in Figures.*

CHRISTMAS ISLAND - MARRIAGE RATES

Statistical Office of the United Nations, Publishing Service, New York, New York 10017 (800) 253-9646; *Demographic Yearbook,* and *Statistical Yearbook.*

CHRISTMAS ISLAND - MEAT PRODUCTION - See CHRISTMAS ISLAND - LIVESTOCK AND POULTRY

CHRISTMAS ISLAND - MERCHANT SHIPPING

G.K. Hall and Company, 70 Lincoln Street, Boston, Massachusetts 02111 (617) 423-3990; *The World in Figures.*

Statistical Office of the United Nations, Publishing Service, New York, New York 10017 (800) 253-9646; *Statistical Yearbook.*

CHRISTMAS ISLAND - MILITARY

G.K. Hall and Company, 70 Lincoln Street, Boston, Massachusetts 02111 (617) 423-3990; *The World in Figures.*

CHRISTMAS ISLAND - MINING AND MINERAL PRODUCTS

G.K. Hall and Company, 70 Lincoln Street, Boston, Massachusetts 02111 (617) 423-3990; *The World in Figures.*

CHRISTMAS ISLAND - MONEY SUPPLY

G.K. Hall and Company, 70 Lincoln Street, Boston, Massachusetts 02111 (617) 423-3990; *The World in Figures.*

CHRISTMAS ISLAND - MOTOR VEHICLES IN USE

G.K. Hall and Company, 70 Lincoln Street, Boston, Massachusetts 02111 (617) 423-3990; *The World in Figures.*

CHRISTMAS ISLAND - NATALITY - See CHRISTMAS ISLAND - BIRTH RATE

CHRISTMAS ISLAND - NATIONAL INCOME

G.K. Hall and Company, 70 Lincoln Street, Boston, Massachusetts 02111 (617) 423-3990; *The World in Figures.*

CHRISTMAS ISLAND - NEWSPAPER PRODUCTION - See CHRISTMAS ISLAND - FORESTRY AND FOREST PRODUCTS

CHRISTMAS ISLAND - OCCUPATIONS - See CHRISTMAS ISLAND - LABOR FORCE

CHRISTMAS ISLAND - PESTICIDE USE

Food and Agricultural Organization of the United Nations (FAO) Via delle Terme di Caracalla, 00100 Rome, Italy (Telephone Number in U.S. (202) 653-2400); *The State of Food and Agriculture.*

CHRISTMAS ISLAND - PETROLEUM INDUSTRY

Food and Agricultural Organization of the United Nations (FAO) Via delle Terme di Caracalla, 00100 Rome, Italy (Telephone Number in U.S. (202) 653-2400); *The State of Food and Agriculture.*

G.K. Hall and Company, 70 Lincoln Street, Boston, Massachusetts 02111 (617) 423-3990; *The World in Figures.*

CHRISTMAS ISLAND - PHOSPHATE ROCK PRODUCTION - See CHRISTMAS ISLAND, PEOPLE'S REPUBLIC OF - MINING AND MINERAL PRODUCTS

CHRISTMAS ISLAND - POPULATION

Food and Agricultural Organization of the United Nations (FAO), Via delle Terme di Caracalla, 00100 Rome, Italy (Telephone Number in U.S. (202) 653-2400); *Production Yearbook.*

G.K. Hall and Company, 70 Lincoln Street, Boston, Massachusetts 02111 (617) 423-3990; *The World in Figures.*

Statistical Office of the United Nations, Publishing Service, New York, New York 10017 (800) 253-9646; *Demographic Yearbook, Statistical Yearbook.*

United Nations Educational, Scientific and Cultural Organization (UNESCO), 7 Place de Fontenoy, F-75700 Paris, France (Telephone Number in U.S. (212) 963-5981; *Statistical Yearbook.*

World Health Organization, Office of Publications, Avenue Appia, CH-1211 Geneva 27, Switzerland (Telephone Number in U.S. (518) 436-9686; *World Health Statistics Annual.*

CHRISTMAS ISLAND - PRICES

Food and Agricultural Organization of the United Nations (FAO), Via delle Terme di Caracalla, 00100 Rome, Italy (Telephone Number in U.S. (202) 653-2400); *Production Yearbook,* and *The State of Food and Agriculture.*

G.K. Hall and Company, 70 Lincoln Street, Boston, Massachusetts 02111 (617) 423-3990; *The World in Figures.*

CHRISTMAS ISLAND - PRODUCTION

G.K. Hall and Company, 70 Lincoln Street, Boston, Massachusetts 02111 (617) 423-3990; *The World in Figures.*

CHRISTMAS ISLAND - RAILWAYS

G.K. Hall and Company, 70 Lincoln Street, Boston, Massachusetts 02111 (617) 423-3990; *The World in Figures.*

CHRISTMAS ISLAND - RETAIL TRADE

G.K. Hall and Company, 70 Lincoln Street, Boston, Massachusetts 02111 (617) 423-3990; *The World in Figures.*

CHRISTMAS ISLAND - SOCIAL DATA

G.K. Hall and Company, 70 Lincoln Street, Boston, Massachusetts 02111 (617) 423-3990; *The World in Figures.*

CHRISTMAS ISLAND - STOCKS - COMMODITY - MARKET PRICE - INDEX

Food and Agricultural Organization of the United Nations (FAO) Via delle Terme di Caracalla, 00100 Rome, Italy (Telephone Number in U.S. (202) 653-2400); *The State of Food and Agriculture.*

CHRISTMAS ISLAND - TAXATION

G.K. Hall and Company, 70 Lincoln Street, Boston, Massachusetts 02111 (617) 423-3990; *The World in Figures.*

CHRISTMAS ISLAND - TELEPHONES IN USE

American Telephone and Telegraph Company, 26 Parsippany Road, Whippany, New Jersey 07981 (800) 338-4038; *The World's Telephones.*

G.K. Hall and Company, 70 Lincoln Street, Boston, Massachusetts 02111 (617) 423-3990; *The World in Figures.*

CHRISTMAS ISLAND - TEXTILE INDUSTRY

G.K. Hall and Company, 70 Lincoln Street, Boston, Massachusetts 02111 (617) 423-3990; *The World in Figures.*

CHRISTMAS ISLAND - TOURISM

G.K. Hall and Company, 70 Lincoln Street, Boston, Massachusetts 02111 (617) 423-3990; *The World in Figures.*

CHRISTMAS ISLAND - TRADE - See CHRISTMAS ISLAND - FOREIGN TRADE

CHRISTMAS ISLAND - TRANSPORTATION AND COMMUNICATIONS

G.K. Hall and Company, 70 Lincoln Street, Boston, Massachusetts 02111 (617) 423-3990; *The World in Figures.*

CHRISTMAS ISLAND - VITAL STATISTICS

G.K. Hall and Company, 70 Lincoln Street, Boston, Massachusetts 02111 (617) 423-3990; *The World in Figures.*

Statistical Office of the United Nations, Publishing Service, New York, New York 10017 (800) 253-9646; *Statistical Yearbook.*

World Health Organization, Office of Publications, Avenue Appia, CH-1211 Geneva 27, Switzerland (Telephone Number in U.S. (518) 436-9686; *World Health Statistics Annual.*

CHRISTMAS ISLAND - WAGES

G.K. Hall and Company, 70 Lincoln Street, Boston, Massachusetts 02111 (617) 423-3990; *The World in Figures.*

CHRISTMAS ISLAND - WEATHER

G.K. Hall and Company, 70 Lincoln Street, Boston, Massachusetts 02111 (617) 423-3990; *The World in Figures.*

CHROMITE

U.S. Department of the Interior, Bureau of Mines, 810 Seventh Street, NW, Washington, D.C. 20241 (202) 501-9649; *Mineral Commodities Summaries.*

CHROMIUM

U.S. Department of the Interior, Bureau of Mines, 810 Seventh Street, NW, Washington, D.C. 20241 (202) 501-9649; *Mineral Commodity Summaries.*

CHURCHES - ATTENDANCE

Princeton Religion Research Center, 47 Hulfish Street, Princeton, New Jersey 08542 (609) 921-8112; *Emerging Trends,* based on surveys conducted by the Gallup Organization, Inc., 100 Palmer Square, Princeton, New Jersey 08542 (609) 924-9600.

CHURCHES - CONSTRUCTION VALUE

F.W. Dodge Division, McGraw-Hill Information Systems Company, 1221 Avenue of the Americas, New York, New York 10020 (212) 512-2000; *Dodge Construction Potentials.*

U.S. Department of Commerce, Bureau of the Census, Suitland, Maryland 20233 (301) 763-4040; *Current Construction Reports.*

CHURCHES - GRANTS, FOUNDATIONS

The Foundation Center, 79 Fifth Avenue, New York, New York 10003 (212) 620-4230; *Foundation Grants Index.*

CHURCHES - NUMBER AND MEMBERSHIP

Encyclopedia Britannica, Incorporated, 310 South Michigan Avenue, Chicago, Illinois 60604 (312) 347-7000; *Britannica Book of the Year.*

National Council of the Churches of Christ in the United States of America, 475 Riverside Drive, New York, New York 10027 (212) 870-2227; *Yearbook of American and Canadian Churches.*

Princeton Religion Research Center, 47 Hulfish Street, Princeton, New Jersey 08542 (609) 921-8112; *Emerging Trends,* based on surveys conducted by the Gallup Organization, Inc., 100 Palmer Square, Princeton, New Jersey 08542 (609) 924-9600.

CHURCHES - VOLUNTEERS

Independent Sector, 1828 L Street, NW, Washington, D.C. 20036 (202) 223-8100; *Giving and Volunteering in the U.S.*

CIGARETTES - See also TOBACCO PRODUCTS

CIGARETTES - FOREIGN TRADE

U.S. Department of Commerce, Bureau of the Census, Suitland, Maryland 20233 (301) 763-4040; *U.S. Merchandise Trade: Selected Highlights.*

CIGARETTES - PRODUCTION

U.S. Department of Agriculture, Economic Research Service, Fourteenth Street and Independence Avenue, SW, Washington, D.C. 20005-4789 (202) 219-1504; *Tobacco Situation and Outlook.*

CIGARETTES - SMOKERS AND USE

U.S. Department of Health and Human Services, National Center for Health Statistics, 3700 East West Highway, Hyattsville, Maryland 20782 (301) 436-8500; *Health Promotion and Disease Prevention, United States, Health, United States, Vital and Health Statistics,* and unpublished data.

U.S. Department of Health and Human Services, Substance Abuse and Mental Health Services Administration, 5600 Fishers Lane, Rockville, Maryland 20857 (301) 443-4797; *National Household Survey on Drug Abuse.*

CIGARETTES - TAXES - EXCISE

U.S. Department of Commerce, Bureau of the Census, Suitland, Maryland 20233 (301) 763-4040; *State Government Tax Collections.*

CIRCULATION OF NEWSPAPERS AND PERIODICALS

Editor and Publisher Company, 11 West 19th Street, New York, New York 10011 (212) 675-4380; *Editor and Publisher International Year Book.*

Gale Research Incorporated, 835 Penobscot Building, Detroit, Michigan 48226 (800) 877-4253; *Gale Directory of Publications and Broadcast Media.*

CIRCULATION OF NEWSPAPERS AND PERIODICALS - FOREIGN COUNTRIES

United Nations Educational, Scientific and Cultural Organization, 7 Place de Fontenoy, F-F-75700 Paris, France (Telephone Number in U.S. (212) 963-5981); *Statistical Yearbook.*

CIRRHOSIS OF THE LIVER - DEATHS

U.S. Department of Health and Human Services, National Center for Health Statistics, 3700 East-West Highway, Hyattsville, Maryland 20782 (301) 436-8500; *Vital Statistics of the United States, Monthly Vital Statistics Report,* and unpublished data.

CIRRHOSIS OF THE LIVER - DEATHS - FOREIGN COUNTRIES

World Health Organization, Avenue Appia, Office of Publications, CH-1211 Geneva, 27, Switzerland (Telephone Number in U.S. (518) 436-9686); *World Health Statistics Annual.*

CITIES - CLIMATE

U.S. Department of Commerce, National Oceanic and Atmospheric Administration, National Climatic Data Center, Federal Building, Asheville, North Carolina 28801 (704) 259-2850; *Comparative Climatic Data,* and *Climatography of the United States.*

CITIES - CRIME

U.S. Department of Justice, Federal Bureau of Investigation, Ninth Street and Pennsylvania Avenue, NW, Washington, D.C. 20585 (202) 324-3000; *Crime in the United States.*

U.S. Department of Justice, National Institute of Justice, 633 Indiana Avenue, NW, Washington, D.C. 20531 (202) 307-0781; *Drug Use Forecasting.*

CITIES - DEBT

U.S. Department of Commerce, Bureau of the Census, Suitland, Maryland 20233 (301) 763-4040; *City Government Finances.*

CITIES - EMPLOYEES, EARNINGS, PAYROLLS

U.S. Department of Commerce, Bureau of the Census, Suitland, Maryland 20233 (301) 763-4040; *City Employment,* and *Compendium of Public Employment.*

CITIES - FINANCES OF CITY GOVERNMENTS

U.S. Department of Commerce, Bureau of the Census, Suitland, Maryland 20233 (301 763-4040; *City Government Finances.*

CITIES - GOVERNMENTAL UNITS

U.S. Department of Commerce, Bureau of the Census, Suitland, Maryland 20233 (301) 763-4040; *Census of Governments, Government Organization.*

CITIES - OFFICE VACANCY RATES

ONCOR International, 3040 Post Oak Boulevard, Houston, Texas 77056 (713) 961-0600; *Office Market Data Book.*

CITIES - OFFICIALS - ELECTED

Joint Center for Political and Economic Studies, 1090 Vermont Avenue, NW, Washington, D.C. 20005 (202) 789-3500; *Black Elected Officials - A National Roster.*

CITIES - POPULATION

U.S. Department of Commerce, Bureau of the Census, Suitland, Maryland 20233 (301) 763-4040; *Census of Population, Current Population Reports,* and unpublished data.

CITIES - POPULATION - FOREIGN COUNTRIES

U.S. Department of Commerce, Bureau of the Census, Suitland, Maryland 20233 (301) 763-4040; *International Data Base.*

CITIES - PROPERTY TAX RATES

Government of the District of Columbia, Department of Finance and Revenue, 300 Indiana Avenue, NW, Washington, D.C. 20001 (202) 727-6103; *Tax Rates and Tax Burdens in the District of Columbia: A Nationwide Comparison.*

CITIES - TAXES PAID - BY FAMILY INCOME LEVEL

Government of the District of Columbia, Department of Finance and Revenue, 300 Indiana Avenue, NW, Washington, D.C. 20001 (202) 727-6103; *Tax Rates and Tax Burdens in the District of Columbia: A Nationwide Comparison.*

CITIES - WOMEN PUBLIC OFFICIALS

Center of the American Woman and Politics, Eagleton Institute of Politics, Rutgers University, New Brunswick, New Jersey 08901 (908) 828-2210; information releases.

CITIZENS - NATURALIZED

U.S. Department of Commerce, Bureau of the Census, Suitland, Maryland 20233 (301) 763-4040; *Census of Population, The Foreign Born Population in the U.S.*

CITRUS FRUITS - CONSUMPTION

U.S. Department of Agriculture, Economic Research Service, Fourteenth Street and Independence Avenue, SW, Washington, D.C. 20005-4789 (202) 219-1504; *Food Consumption, Prices and Expenditures, Agricultural Outlook,* and unpublished data.

CITRUS FRUITS - PRODUCTION

U.S. Department of Agriculture, National Agricultural Statistics Service, Fourteenth Street and Independence Avenue, SW, Washington, D.C. 20250 (202) 219-1504; *Citrus Fruits.*

CIVIL AVIATION - See AIR TRANSPORTATION

CIVIL CASES - U.S. DISTRICT COURTS

Administrative Office of the United States Courts, United States Supreme Court Building, One First Street, NW, Washington, D.C. 20544 (202) 633-6094; *Annual Report of the Director.*

CIVIL CASES - U.S. DISTRICT COURTS - PRODUCT LIABILITY CASES

Administrative Office of the United States Courts, United States Supreme Court Building, One First Street, NW, Washington, D.C. 20544 (202) 633-6094; *Annual Report of the Director.*

CIVIL SERVICE EMPLOYEES - See GOVERNMENT

CIVIL WAR - COST

U.S. Congress, Joint Economic Committee, The Capitol, Washington, D.C. 20515 (202) 275-2051; *The Military Budget and National Economic Priorities,* 91st Congress, 1st Session (Statement of James L. Clayton, University of Utah), subsequently revised and updated by James L. Clayton.

CLAMS

U.S. Department of Commerce, National Oceanic and Atmospheric Administration, National Marine Fisheries Service, 1335 East-West Highway, Silver Spring, Maryland 20910 (301) 427-2239; *Fishery Statistics of the United States,* and *Fisheries of the United States.*

CLERGYMEN

National Council of the Churches of Christ in the U.S.A., 475 Riverside Drive, New York, New York 10115 (212) 870-2227; *Yearbook of American and Canadian Churches.*

CLERGYMEN - EMPLOYMENT

U.S. Department of Labor, Bureau of Labor Statistics, Two Massachusetts Avenue, NE, Washington, D.C. 20212 (202) 606-7828; *Employment and Earnings.*

CLERGYMEN - PASTORS WITH CHARGES

National Council of the Churches of Christ in the United States of America, 475 Riverside Avenue, New York, New York 10027 (212) 870-2227; *Yearbook of American and Canadian Churches.*

CLIMATE - SELECTED CITIES

U.S. Department of Commerce, National Oceanic and Atmospheric Administration, National Climatic Data Center, Federal Building, Asheville, North Carolina 28801 (704) 259-2850; *Comparative Climatic Data,* and *Climatography of the United States.*

CLIMATE - SELECTED CITIES - PRECIPITATION

U.S. Department of Commerce, National Oceanic and Atmospheric Administration, National Climatic Data Center, Federal Building, Asheville, North Carolina 28801 (704) 259-2850; *Comparative Climatic Data,* and *Climatography of the United States.*

CLIMATE - SELECTED CITIES - TEMPERATURE

U.S. Department of Commerce, National Oceanic and Atmospheric Administration, National Climatic Data Center, Federal Building, Asheville, North Carolina 28801 (704) 259-2850; *Comparative Climatic Data,* and *Climatography of the United States.*

CLOTHING - See APPAREL GOODS

COAL - See also PETROLEUM AND COAL PRODUCTS and COAL MINING INDUSTRY

COAL - CAR LOADINGS

Association of American Railroads, American Railroads Building, 50 F Street, NW, Washington, D.C. 20001 (202) 639-2100; *Freight Commodity Statistics,* and *Weekly Railroad Traffic.*

COAL - CONSUMPTION

U.S. Department of Energy, Energy Information Administration, Washington, D.C. 20585 (202) 586-8800; *State Energy Data Report, Annual Energy Review,* and *Monthly Energy Review.*

COAL - CONSUMPTION - ELECTRIC UTILITIES

U.S. Department of Energy, Energy Information Administration, Washington, D.C. 20585 (202) 586-8800; *Annual Energy Review, Electric Power Annual, Electric Power Monthly,* and *Inventory of Power Plants in the U.S.*

COAL - EXPENDITURES

U.S. Department of Energy, Energy Information Administration, Washington, D.C. 20585 (202) 586-8800; *State Energy Price and Expenditure Report.*

COAL - FOREIGN TRADE

U.S. Department of Commerce, Bureau of the Census, Suitland, Maryland 20233 (301) 763-4040; *U.S. Merchandise Trade, Exports, General Imports, and Imports for Consumption, U.S. Exports of Merchandise* and *U.S. Imports of Merchandise,* compact discs.

U.S. Department of Energy, Energy Information Administration, Washington, D.C. 20585 (202) 586-8800; *Energy Data Reports, Weekly Coal Production, Coal Production, Annual Energy Review, Monthly Energy Review, Coke Plant Report, Quarterly Coal Report, Annual Prospects for World Coal Trade.*

COAL - PRICES

U.S. Department of Energy, Energy Information Administration, Washington, D.C. 20585 (202) 586-8800; *Annual Energy Review,* and *Monthly Energy Review.*

U.S. Department of the Interior, Bureau of Mines, 810 Seventh Street, NW, Washington, D.C. 20241 (202) 501-9649; *Minerals Yearbook,* and *Mineral Commodity Summaries.*

COAL - PRODUCTION AND VALUE

U.S. Department of Energy, Energy Information Administration, Washington, D.C. 20585 (202) 586-8800; *Annual Energy Review, Monthly Energy Review, Quarterly Coal Report,* and *Coal Production.*

COAL - WORLD PRODUCTION

Statistical Office of the United Nations, New York, New York 10017 (800) 253-9646; *Monthly Bulletin of Statistics.*

U.S. Department of the Interior, Bureau of Mines, 810 Seventh Street, NW, Washington, D.C. 20241 (202) 501-9649; *Annual Reports,* and *Mineral Commodity Summaries.*

COAL MINING INDUSTRY - CAPITAL

U.S. Department of Commerce, Bureau of the Census, Suitland, Maryland 20233 (301) 763-4040; *Census of Mineral Industries.*

COAL MINING INDUSTRY - EARNINGS

U.S. Department of Labor, Bureau of Labor Statistics, Two Massachusetts Avenue, NE, Washington, D.C. 20212 (202) 606-7828; *Employment and Earnings,* and Bulletins 2370 and 2429.

COAL MINING INDUSTRY - EMPLOYMENT

U.S. Department of Labor, Bureau of Labor Statistics, Two Massachusetts Avenue, NE, Washington, D.C. 20212 (202) 606-7828; *Monthly Labor Review, Employment and Earnings,* and Bulletin 2370.

COAL MINING INDUSTRY - ESTABLISHMENTS

U.S. Department of Commerce, Bureau of the Census, Suitland, Maryland 20233 (301) 763-4040; *Census of Mineral Industries.*

COAL MINING INDUSTRY - GROSS DOMESTIC PRODUCT ORIGINATING IN

U.S. Department of Commerce, Bureau of Economic Analysis, Fourteenth Street between Constitution Avenue and E Street, NW, Washington, D.C. 20230 (202) 606-9900; *Survey of Current Business.*

COAL MINING INDUSTRY - MINES

U.S. Department of Energy, Energy Information Administration, 1000 Independence Avenue, SW, Washington, D.C. 20585 (202) 586-8800; *Coal Production, Coke Plant Report, Annual Energy Review, Energy Data Reports, Weekly Coal Production,* and *Quarterly Coal Report.*

COAL MINING INDUSTRY - MINES - INJURIES

U.S. Department of Labor, Bureau of Labor Statistics, Two Massachusetts Avenue, NE, Washington, D.C. 20212 (202) 606-7828; *Occupational Injuries and Illnesses in the United States by Industry.*

U.S. Department of Labor, Mine Safety and Health Administration, 4015 Wilson Boulevard, Arlington, Virginia 22203 (703) 235-1452; unpublished data.

COAL MINING INDUSTRY - OCCUPATIONAL SAFETY

U.S. Department of Labor, Bureau of Labor Statistics, Two Massachusetts Avenue, NE, Washington, D.C. 20212 (202) 606-7828; *Occupational Injuries and Illnesses in the United States by Industry.*

U.S. Department of Labor, Mine Safety and Health Administration, 4015 Wilson Boulevard, Arlington, Virginia 22203 (703) 235-1452; unpublished data.

COAL MINING INDUSTRY - OUTPUT

Board of Governors of the Federal Reserve System, Twentieth Street and Constitution Avenue, NW, Washington, D.C. 20551 (202) 452-3000; *Federal Reserve Bulletin.*

U.S. Department of Energy, Energy Information Administration, 1000 Independence Avenue, SW, Washington, D.C. 20585 (202) 586-8800; *Annual Energy Review, Monthly Energy Review, Quarterly Coal Report,* and *State Energy Data Report.*

U.S. Department of the Interior, Bureau of Mines, 810 Seventh Street, NW, Washington, D.C. 20241 (202) 501-9649; *Annual Reports,* and *Mineral Commodities Summaries.*

COAL MINING INDUSTRY - PRODUCTIVITY

U.S. Department of Energy, Energy Information Administration, 1000 Independence Avenue, SW, Washington, D.C. 20585 (202) 285-8800; *Coal Production, Coke Plant Report, Annual Energy Review,* and *Quarterly Coal Report.*

U.S. Department of Labor, Bureau of Labor Statistics, Two Massachusetts Avenue, NE, Washington, D.C. 20212 (202) 606-7828; *Productivity Measures for Selected Industries and Government Services.*

COAL MINING INDUSTRY - SHIPMENTS

U.S. Department of Commerce, Bureau of the Census, Suitland, Maryland 20233 (301) 763-4040; *Census of Mineral Industries.*

COAL MINING INDUSTRY - VALUE ADDED

U.S. Department of Commerce, Bureau of the Census, Suitland, Maryland 20233 (301) 763-4040; *Census of Mineral Industries.*

COAST GUARD PERSONNEL

U.S. Department of Transportation, United States Coast Guard, 2100 Second Street, SW, Washington, D.C. 20593 (202) 267-1587; *Annual Report of the Secretary of Transportation.*

COASTAL POPULATION

U.S. Department of Commerce, Bureau of the Census, Suitland, Maryland 20233 (301) 763-4040; *Census of Population and Housing,* and press release.

COBALT

U.S. Department of Defense, The Pentagon, Washington, D.C. 20301 (703) 545-6700; *Statistical Supplement, Stockpile Report to the Congress.*

U.S. Department of Energy, Energy Information Administration, Washington, D.C. 20585 (202) 586-8800; *Annual Energy Review.*

U.S. Department of the Interior, Bureau of Mines, 810 Seventh Street, NW, Washington, D.C. 20241 (202) 501-9649; *Annual Reports,* and *Mineral Commodity Summaries.*

COCAINE - ARRESTS AND USE

U.S. Department of Health and Human Services, Substance Abuse and Mental Health Services Administration, 5600 Fishers Lane, Rockville, Maryland 29857 (301) 443-4797; *National Household Survey on Drug Abuse.*

U.S. Department of Justice, Federal Bureau of Investigation, Ninth Street and Pennsylvania Avenue, NW, Washington, D.C. 20535 (202) 324-3000; *Crime in the United States.*

COCOA AND CONFECTIONERY PRODUCTS

U.S. Department of Agriculture, Economic Research Service, Fourteenth and Independence Avenue, SW, Washington, D.C. 20005 (202) 219-1504; *Agricultural Outlook, Food Consumption, Prices, and Expenditures, Foreign Agricultural Trade of the U.S.,* and unpublished data.

U.S. Department of Commerce, Bureau of the Census, Suitland, Maryland 20233 (301) 763-4040; *U.S. Merchandise Trade.*

Cocos (Keeling) Islands - Primary Statistics Source

Sales and Distribution, Australian Government Publishing Service, Post Office Box 84, Canberra ACT 2600, Australia; *Annual Report on the Territory of Cocos (Keeling) Islands.*

COCOS (KEELING) ISLANDS - ABORTIONS

Statistical Office of the United Nations, Publishing Service, New York, New York 10017 (800) 253-9646; *Demographic Yearbook.*

COCOS (KEELING) ISLANDS - AGRICULTURE

Food and Agricultural Organization of the United Nations (FAO) Via delle Terme di Caracalla, 00100 Rome, Italy (Telephone Number in U.S. (202) 653-2400); *Production Yearbook, The State of Food and Agriculture,* and *Trade Yearbook.*

G.K. Hall and Company, 70 Lincoln Street, Boston, Massachusetts 02111 (617) 423-3990; *The World in Figures.*

COCOS (KEELING) ISLANDS - AIRLINE SERVICE

G.K. Hall and Company, 70 Lincoln Street, Boston, Massachusetts 02111 (617) 423-3990; *The World in Figures.*

COCOS (KEELING) ISLANDS - AREA AND DENSITY OF POPULATION

Food and Agricultural Organization of the United Nations (FAO) Via delle Terme di Caracalla, 00100 Rome, Italy (Telephone Number in U.S. (202) 653-2400); *The State of Food and Agriculture.*

G.K. Hall and Company, 70 Lincoln Street, Boston, Massachusetts 02111 (617) 423-3990; *The World in Figures.*

Statistical Office of the United Nations, Publishing Service, New York, New York 10017 (800) 253-9646; *Statistical Yearbook.*

COCOS (KEELING) ISLANDS - BALANCE OF PAYMENTS

G.K. Hall and Company, 70 Lincoln Street, Boston, Massachusetts 02111 (617) 423-3990; *The World in Figures.*

COCOS (KEELING) ISLANDS - BANKING

G.K. Hall and Company, 70 Lincoln Street, Boston, Massachusetts 02111 (617) 423-3990; *The World in Figures.*

COCOS (KEELING) ISLANDS - BIRTH RATES

Statistical Office of the United Nations, Publishing Service, New York, New York 10017 (800) 253-9646; *Demographic Yearbook,* and *Statistical Yearbook.*

World Health Organization, Office of Publications, Avenue Appia, CH-1211 Geneva 27, Switzerland (Telephone Number in U.S. (518) 436-9686); *World Health Statistics Annual.*

COCOS (KEELING) ISLANDS - BONDS

G.K. Hall and Company, 70 Lincoln Street, Boston, Massachusetts 02111 (617) 423-3990; *The World in Figures.*

COCOS (KEELING) ISLANDS - BOOK PRODUCTION

G.K. Hall and Company, 70 Lincoln Street, Boston, Massachusetts 02111 (617) 423-3990; *The World in Figures.*

COCOS (KEELING) ISLANDS - BROADCASTING

Billboard Limited, P.O. Box 9027, 1006 AA Amsterdam, The Netherlands (Telephone Number in U.S. (212) 764-7300); *World Radio TV Handbook.*

G.K. Hall and Company, 70 Lincoln Street, Boston, Massachusetts 02111 (617) 423-3990; *The World in Figures.*

COCOS (KEELING) ISLANDS - BUSINESS

G.K. Hall and Company, 70 Lincoln Street, Boston, Massachusetts 02111 (617) 423-3990; *The World in Figures.*

COCOS (KEELING) ISLANDS - CALORIE SUPPLY

Food and Agricultural Organization of the United Nations (FAO) Via delle Terme di Caracalla, 00100 Rome, Italy (Telephone Number in U.S. (202) 653-2400); *The State of Food and Agriculture.*

COCOS (KEELING) ISLANDS - CHEMICAL (ORGANIC) PRODUCTION - See COCOS (KEELING) ISLANDS - MINING AND MINERAL PRODUCTS

COCOS (KEELING) ISLANDS - CLASS STRUCTURE

G.K. Hall and Company, 70 Lincoln Street, Boston, Massachusetts 02111 (617) 423-3990; *The World in Figures.*

COCOS (KEELING) ISLANDS - CLIMATE

G.K. Hall and Company, 70 Lincoln Street, Boston, Massachusetts 02111 (617) 423-3990; *The World in Figures.*

COCOS (KEELING) ISLANDS - COAL PRODUCTION - See COCOS (KEELING) ISLANDS - MINING AND MINERAL PRODUCTS

COCOS (KEELING) ISLANDS - COMMUNICATIONS

G.K. Hall and Company, 70 Lincoln Street, Boston, Massachusetts 02111 (617) 423-3990; *The World in Figures.*

COCOS (KEELING) ISLANDS - CONSUMER PRICE INDEX

G.K. Hall and Company, 70 Lincoln Street, Boston, Massachusetts 02111 (617) 423-3990; *The World in Figures.*

COCOS (KEELING) ISLANDS - CONSUMPTION

G.K. Hall and Company, 70 Lincoln Street, Boston, Massachusetts 02111 (617) 423-3990; *The World in Figures.*

COCOS (KEELING) ISLANDS - CORN PRODUCTION - See COCOS (KEELING) ISLANDS - CROPS

COCOS (KEELING) ISLANDS - CORPORATE TAXES

G.K. Hall and Company, 70 Lincoln Street, Boston, Massachusetts 02111 (617) 423-3990; *The World in Figures.*

COCOS (KEELING) ISLANDS - CROPS

Food and Agricultural Organization of the United Nations (FAO) Via delle Terme di Caracalla, 00100 Rome, Italy (Telephone Number in U.S. (202) 653-2400); *The State of Food and Agriculture.*

G.K. Hall and Company, 70 Lincoln Street, Boston, Massachusetts 02111 (617) 423-3990; *The World in Figures.*

COCOS (KEELING) ISLANDS - CUSTOMS DUTIES

G.K. Hall and Company, 70 Lincoln Street, Boston, Massachusetts 02111 (617) 423-3990; *The World in Figures.*

COCOS (KEELING) ISLANDS - DAIRY PRODUCTS

Food and Agricultural Organization of the United Nations (FAO) Via delle Terme di Caracalla, 00100 Rome, Italy (Telephone Number in U.S. (202) 653-2400); *The State of Food and Agriculture.*

COCOS (KEELING) ISLANDS - DEATH RATES

G.K. Hall and Company, 70 Lincoln Street, Boston, Massachusetts 02111 (617) 423-3990; *The World in Figures.*

Statistical Office of the United Nations, Publishing Service, New York, New York 10017 (800) 253-9646; *Statistical Yearbook.*

COCOS (KEELING) ISLANDS - DEFENSE EXPENDITURES

G.K. Hall and Company, 70 Lincoln Street, Boston, Massachusetts 02111 (617) 423-3990; *The World in Figures.*

COCOS (KEELING) ISLANDS - DEMOGRAPHY

G.K. Hall and Company, 70 Lincoln Street, Boston, Massachusetts 02111 (617) 423-3990; *The World in Figures.*

COCOS (KEELING) ISLANDS - DEVELOPMENT ASSISTANCE

G.K. Hall and Company, 70 Lincoln Street, Boston, Massachusetts 02111 (617) 423-3990; *The World in Figures.*

COCOS (KEELING) ISLANDS - DISEASE

G.K. Hall and Company, 70 Lincoln Street, Boston, Massachusetts 02111 (617) 423-3990; *The World in Figures.*

COCOS (KEELING) ISLANDS - DIVORCE RATES

Statistical Office of the United Nations, Publishing Service, New York, New York 10017 (800) 253-9646; *Demographic Yearbook.*

COCOS (KEELING) ISLANDS - DOMESTIC PRODUCT

G.K. Hall and Company, 70 Lincoln Street, Boston, Massachusetts 02111 (617) 423-3990; *The World in Figures.*

COCOS (KEELING) ISLANDS - ECONOMY

G.K. Hall and Company, 70 Lincoln Street, Boston, Massachusetts 02111 (617) 423-3990; *The World in Figures.*

COCOS (KEELING) ISLANDS - EDUCATION

G.K. Hall and Company, 70 Lincoln Street, Boston, Massachusetts 02111 (617) 423-3990; *The World in Figures.*

COCOS (KEELING) ISLANDS - EGG PRODUCTION - See COCOS (KEELING) ISLANDS - DAIRY PRODUCTS

COCOS (KEELING) ISLANDS - ENERGY

Food and Agricultural Organization of the United Nations (FAO) Via delle Terme di Caracalla, 00100 Rome, Italy (Telephone Number in U.S. (202) 653-2400); *The State of Food and Agriculture.*

G.K. Hall and Company, 70 Lincoln Street, Boston, Massachusetts 02111 (617) 423-3990; *The World in Figures.*

COCOS (KEELING) ISLANDS - EXPORTS

Food and Agricultural Organization of the United Nations (FAO) Via delle Terme di Caracalla, 00100 Rome, Italy (Telephone Number in U.S. (202) 653-2400); *The State of Food and Agriculture.*

G.K. Hall and Company, 70 Lincoln Street, Boston, Massachusetts 02111 (617) 423-3990; *The World in Figures.*

COCOS (KEELING) ISLANDS - EXTERNAL TRADE

Food and Agricultural Organization of the United Nations (FAO) Via delle Terme di Caracalla, 00100 Rome, Italy (Telephone Number in U.S. (202) 653-2400); *The State of Food and Agriculture,* and *Trade Yearbook.*

G.K. Hall and Company, 70 Lincoln Street, Boston, Massachusetts 02111 (617) 423-3990; *The World in Figures.*

COCOS (KEELING) ISLANDS - FARM CROPS - See COCOS (KEELING) ISLANDS - CROPS

COCOS (KEELING) ISLANDS - FETAL MORTALITY

Statistical Office of the United Nations, Publishing Service, New York, New York 10017 (800) 253-9646; *Demographic Yearbook.*

COCOS (KEELING) ISLANDS - FERTILIZER

Food and Agricultural Organization of the United Nations (FAO) Via delle Terme di Caracalla, 00100 Rome, Italy (Telephone Number in U.S. (202) 653-2400); *The State of Food and Agriculture.*

COCOS (KEELING) ISLANDS - FINANCE

G.K. Hall and Company, 70 Lincoln Street, Boston, Massachusetts 02111 (617) 423-3990; *The World in Figures.*

COCOS (KEELING) ISLANDS - FISHERIES

Food and Agricultural Organization of the United Nations (FAO) Via delle Terme di Caracalla, 00100 Rome, Italy (Telephone Number in U.S. (202) 653-2400); *The State of Food and Agriculture,* and *Yearbook of Fishery Statistics.*

COCOS (KEELING) ISLANDS - FOOD

Food and Agricultural Organization of the United Nations (FAO) Via delle Terme di Caracalla, 00100 Rome, Italy (Telephone Number in U.S. (202) 653-2400); *Production Yearbook,* and *The State of Food and Agriculture.*

G.K. Hall and Company, 70 Lincoln Street, Boston, Massachusetts 02111 (617) 423-3990; *The World in Figures.*

COCOS (KEELING) ISLANDS - FOREIGN AID

G.K. Hall and Company, 70 Lincoln Street, Boston, Massachusetts 02111 (617) 423-3990; *The World in Figures.*

COCOS (KEELING) ISLANDS - FOREIGN TRADE

Food and Agricultural Organization of the United Nations (FAO) Via delle Terme di Caracalla, 00100 Rome, Italy (Telephone Number in U.S. (202) 653-2400); *The State of Food and Agriculture.*

G.K. Hall and Company, 70 Lincoln Street, Boston, Massachusetts 02111 (617) 423-3990; *The World in Figures.*

Organisation for Economic Co-operation and Development (OECD), 2 rue Andre-Pascal, 75 Paris 16, France (Telephone Number in U.S. (202) 785-6323); *Trade by Commodities.*

COCOS (KEELING) ISLANDS - FORESTRY AND FOREST PRODUCTS

Food and Agricultural Organization of the United Nations (FAO) Via delle Terme di Caracalla, 00100 Rome, Italy (Telephone Number in U.S. (202) 653-2400); *The State of Food and Agriculture.*

G.K. Hall and Company, 70 Lincoln Street, Boston, Massachusetts 02111 (617) 423-3990; *The World in Figures.*

COCOS (KEELING) ISLANDS - GENERAL MORTALITY

World Health Organization, Office of Publications, Avenue Appia, CH-1211 Geneva 27, Switzerland (Telephone Number in U.S. (518) 436-9686); *World Health Statistics Annual.*

COCOS (KEELING) ISLANDS - GOVERNMENT

G.K. Hall and Company, 70 Lincoln Street, Boston, Massachusetts 02111 (617) 423-3990; *The World in Figures.*

COCOS (KEELING) ISLANDS - GRAIN PRODUCTION - See COCOS (KEELING) ISLANDS - CROPS

COCOS (KEELING) ISLANDS - GROSS DOMESTIC PRODUCT

G.K. Hall and Company, 70 Lincoln Street, Boston, Massachusetts 02111 (617) 423-3990; *The World in Figures.*

COCOS (KEELING) ISLANDS - HEALTH

G.K. Hall and Company, 70 Lincoln Street, Boston, Massachusetts 02111 (617) 423-3990; *The World in Figures.*

COCOS (KEELING) ISLANDS - HIGHWAYS

G.K. Hall and Company, 70 Lincoln Street, Boston, Massachusetts 02111 (617) 423-3990; *The World in Figures.*

COCOS (KEELING) ISLANDS - ILLITERATE POPULATION

G.K. Hall and Company, 70 Lincoln Street, Boston, Massachusetts 02111 (617) 423-3990; *The World in Figures.*

COCOS (KEELING) ISLANDS - IMPORTS

Food and Agricultural Organization of the United Nations (FAO) Via delle Terme di Caracalla, 00100 Rome, Italy (Telephone Number in U.S. (202) 653-2400); *The State of Food and Agriculture.*

G.K. Hall and Company, 70 Lincoln Street, Boston, Massachusetts 02111 (617) 423-3990; *The World in Figures.*

COCOS (KEELING) ISLANDS - INDUSTRY

G.K. Hall and Company, 70 Lincoln Street, Boston, Massachusetts 02111 (617) 423-3990; *The World in Figures.*

COCOS (KEELING) ISLANDS - INFANT AND MATERNAL MORTALITY

Statistical Office of the United Nations, Publishing Service, New York, New York 10017 (800) 253-9646; *Demographic Yearbook.*

COCOS (KEELING) ISLANDS - LABOR FORCE

Food and Agricultural Organization of the United Nations (FAO) Via delle Terme di Caracalla, 00100 Rome, Italy (Telephone Number in U.S. (202) 653-2400); *The State of Food and Agriculture.*

G.K. Hall and Company, 70 Lincoln Street, Boston, Massachusetts 02111 (617) 423-3990; *The World in Figures.*

COCOS (KEELING) ISLANDS - LAND USE

Food and Agricultural Organization of the United Nations (FAO), Via delle Terme di Caracalla, 00100 Rome, Italy (Telephone Number in U.S. (202) 653-2400); *Production Yearbook.*

G.K. Hall and Company, 70 Lincoln Street, Boston, Massachusetts 02111 (617) 423-3990; *The World in Figures.*

COCOS (KEELING) ISLANDS - LIVESTOCK AND POULTRY

Food and Agricultural Organization of the United Nations (FAO), Via delle Terme di Caracalla, 00100 Rome, Italy (Telephone Number in U.S. (202) 653-2400); *Production Yearbook,* and *The State of Food and Agriculture.*

G.K. Hall and Company, 70 Lincoln Street, Boston, Massachusetts 02111 (617) 423-3990; *The World in Figures.*

COCOS (KEELING) ISLANDS - LIVING LEVELS

G.K. Hall and Company, 70 Lincoln Street, Boston, Massachusetts 02111 (617) 423-3990; *The World in Figures.*

COCOS (KEELING) ISLANDS - MANUFACTURING

G.K. Hall and Company, 70 Lincoln Street, Boston, Massachusetts 02111 (617) 423-3990; *The World in Figures.*

COCOS (KEELING) ISLANDS - MARRIAGE RATES

Statistical Office of the United Nations, Publishing Service, New York, New York 10017 (800) 253-9646; *Demographic Yearbook,* and *Statistical Yearbook.*

COCOS (KEELING) ISLANDS - MEAT PRODUCTION - See COCOS (KEELING) ISLANDS - LIVESTOCK AND POULTRY

COCOS (KEELING) ISLANDS - MERCHANT SHIPPING

G.K. Hall and Company, 70 Lincoln Street, Boston, Massachusetts 02111 (617) 423-3990; *The World in Figures.*

COCOS (KEELING) ISLANDS - MILITARY

G.K. Hall and Company, 70 Lincoln Street, Boston, Massachusetts 02111 (617) 423-3990; *The World in Figures.*

COCOS (KEELING) ISLANDS - MINING AND MINERAL PRODUCTS

G.K. Hall and Company, 70 Lincoln Street, Boston, Massachusetts 02111 (617) 423-3990; *The World in Figures.*

COCOS (KEELING) ISLANDS - MONEY SUPPLY

G.K. Hall and Company, 70 Lincoln Street, Boston, Massachusetts 02111 (617) 423-3990; *The World in Figures.*

COCOS (KEELING) ISLANDS - MOTOR VEHICLES IN USE

G.K. Hall and Company, 70 Lincoln Street, Boston, Massachusetts 02111 (617) 423-3990; *The World in Figures.*

COCOS (KEELING) ISLANDS - NATALITY - See COCOS (KEELING) ISLANDS - BIRTH RATE

COCOS (KEELING) ISLANDS - NATIONAL INCOME

G.K. Hall and Company, 70 Lincoln Street, Boston, Massachusetts 02111 (617) 423-3990; *The World in Figures.*

COCOS (KEELING) ISLANDS - NEWSPAPER PRODUCTION - See COCOS (KEELING) ISLANDS - FORESTRY AND FOREST PRODUCTS

COCOS (KEELING) ISLANDS - OCCUPATIONS - See COCOS (KEELING) ISLANDS - LABOR FORCE

COCOS (KEELING) ISLANDS - PESTICIDE USE

Food and Agricultural Organization of the United Nations (FAO) Via delle Terme di Caracalla, 00100 Rome, Italy (Telephone Number in U.S. (202) 653-2400); *The State of Food and Agriculture.*

COCOS (KEELING) ISLANDS - PETROLEUM INDUSTRY

Food and Agricultural Organization of the United Nations (FAO) Via delle Terme di Caracalla, 00100 Rome, Italy (Telephone Number in U.S. (202) 653-2400); *The State of Food and Agriculture.*

G.K. Hall and Company, 70 Lincoln Street, Boston, Massachusetts 02111 (617) 423-3990; *The World in Figures.*

COCOS (KEELING) ISLANDS - POPULATION

Food and Agricultural Organization of the United Nations (FAO), Via delle Terme di Caracalla, 00100 Rome, Italy (Telephone Number in U.S. (202) 653-2400); *Production Yearbook.*

G.K. Hall and Company, 70 Lincoln Street, Boston, Massachusetts 02111 (617) 423-3990; *The World in Figures.*

Statistical Office of the United Nations, Publishing Service, New York, New York 10017 (800) 253-9646; *Demographic Yearbook,* and *Statistical Yearbook.*

United Nations Educational, Scientific and Cultural Organization (UNESCO), 7 Place de Fontenoy, F-75700 Paris, France (Telephone Number in U.S. (212) 963-5981); *Statistical Yearbook.*

World Health Organization, Office of Publications, Avenue Appia, CH-1211 Geneva 27, Switzerland (Telephone Number in U.S. (518) 436-9686); *World Health Statistics Annual.*

COCOS (KEELING) ISLANDS - PRICES

Food and Agricultural Organization of the United Nations (FAO), Via delle Terme di Caracalla, 00100 Rome, Italy (Telephone Number in U.S. (202) 653-2400); *Production Yearbook,* and *The State of Food and Agriculture.*

G.K. Hall and Company, 70 Lincoln Street, Boston, Massachusetts 02111 (617) 423-3990; *The World in Figures.*

COCOS (KEELING) ISLANDS - PRODUCTION

G.K. Hall and Company, 70 Lincoln Street, Boston, Massachusetts 02111 (617) 423-3990; *The World in Figures.*

COCOS (KEELING) ISLANDS - RAILWAYS

G.K. Hall and Company, 70 Lincoln Street, Boston, Massachusetts 02111 (617) 423-3990; *The World in Figures.*

COCOS (KEELING) ISLANDS - RETAIL TRADE

G.K. Hall and Company, 70 Lincoln Street, Boston, Massachusetts 02111 (617) 423-3990; *The World in Figures.*

COCOS (KEELING) ISLANDS - SOCIAL DATA

G.K. Hall and Company, 70 Lincoln Street, Boston, Massachusetts 02111 (617) 423-3990; *The World in Figures.*

COCOS (KEELING) ISLANDS - STOCKS - COMMODITY - MARKET PRICE - INDEX

Food and Agricultural Organization of the United Nations (FAO) Via delle Terme di Caracalla, 00100 Rome, Italy (Telephone Number in U.S. (202) 653-2400); *The State of Food and Agriculture.*

COCOS (KEELING) ISLANDS - TELEPHONES IN USE

American Telephone and Telegraph Company, 26 Parsippany Road, Whippany, New Jersey 07981 (800) 3348-4038; *The World's Telephones.*

G.K. Hall and Company, 70 Lincoln Street, Boston, Massachusetts 02111 (617) 423-3990; *The World in Figures.*

COCOS (KEELING) ISLANDS - TEXTILE INDUSTRY

G.K. Hall and Company, 70 Lincoln Street, Boston, Massachusetts 02111 (617) 423-3990; *The World in Figures.*

COCOS (KEELING) ISLANDS - TOURISM

G.K. Hall and Company, 70 Lincoln Street, Boston, Massachusetts 02111 (617) 423-3990; *The World in Figures.*

COCOS (KEELING) ISLANDS - TRADE - See COCOS (KEELING) ISLANDS - FOREIGN TRADE

COCOS (KEELING) ISLANDS - TRANSPORTATION AND COMMUNICATIONS

G.K. Hall and Company, 70 Lincoln Street, Boston, Massachusetts 02111 (617) 423-3990; *The World in Figures.*

COCOS (KEELING) ISLANDS - VITAL STATISTICS

G.K. Hall and Company, 70 Lincoln Street, Boston, Massachusetts 02111 (617) 423-3990; *The World in Figures.*

Statistical Office of the United Nations, Publishing Service, New York, New York 10017 (800) 253-9646; *Statistical Yearbook.*

World Health Organization, Office of Publications, Avenue Appia, CH-1211 Geneva 27, Switzerland (Telephone Number in U.S. (518) 436-9686); *World Health Statistics Annual.*

COCOS (KEELING) ISLANDS - WAGES

G.K. Hall and Company, 70 Lincoln Street, Boston, Massachusetts 02111 (617) 423-3990; *The World in Figures.*

COCOS (KEELING) ISLANDS - WEATHER

G.K. Hall and Company, 70 Lincoln Street, Boston, Massachusetts 02111 (617) 423-3990; *The World in Figures.*

COD

U.S. Department of Commerce, National Oceanic and Atmospheric Administration, National Marine Fisheries Service, 1335 East-West Highway, Silver Spring, Maryland 20910 (301) 427-2239; *Fishery Statistics of the United States,* and *Fisheries of the United States.*

COFFEE - CONSUMPTION

U.S. Department of Agriculture, Economic Research Service, Fourteenth Street and Independence Avenue, SW, Washington, D.C. 20005 (202) 219-1504; *Food Consumption, Prices, and Expenditures,* and unpublished data.

COFFEE - FOREIGN TRADE

U.S. Department of Agriculture, Economic Research Service, Fourteenth Street and Independence Avenue, SW, Washington, D.C. 20005-4789 (202) 219-1504; *Foreign Agricultural Trade of the United States.*

U.S. Department of Commerce, Bureau of the Census, Suitland, Maryland 20233 (301) 763-4040; *U.S. Merchandise Trade.*

COFFEE - PRICE INDEXES

U.S. Department of Labor, Bureau of Labor Statistics, Two Massachusetts Avenue, NE, Washington, D.C. 20212 (202) 606-7828; *Monthly Labor Review,* and *CPI Detailed Report.*

COFFEE - WORLD PRODUCTION

Statistical Office of the United Nations, Publishing Service, New York, New York 10017 (800) 253-9646; *Monthly Bulletin of Statistics.*

COKE - See also COAL

COKE

U.S. Department of Energy, Energy Information Administration, Washington, D.C. 20585 (202) 586-8800; *Coal Production, Annual Energy Review,* and quarterly *Coal Report.*

COKE - CAR LOADINGS AND FREIGHT CARRIED

Association of American Railroads, American Railroads Buildings, 50 F Street, NW, Washington, D.C. 20001 (202) 639-2100; *Weekly Railroad Traffic.*

COLLECTIVE BARGAINING SETTLEMENTS

U.S. Department of Labor, Bureau of Labor Statistics, Two Massachusetts Avenue, NE, Washington, D.C. 20212 (202) 606-7828; *Compensation and Working Conditions.*

COLLECTIVE BARGAINING SETTLEMENTS - STATE AND LOCAL GOVERNMENTS

U.S. Department of Labor, Bureau of Labor Statistics, Two Massachusetts Avenue, NE, Washington, D.C. 20212 (202) 606-7828; *Current Wage Developments.*

COLLEGES AND UNIVERSITIES - See EDUCATION - HIGHER EDUCATION INSTITUTIONS

Colombia - National Statistical Office

Departmento Administrativo Nacional de Estadistica, Avenida Eldorado, Bogota D.E., Colombia.

Colombia - Primary Statistics Source

DANE, Avenida El Dorado, Bogota, D.E., Colombia; *Anuario general de estadistica (General Statistical Yearbook); Boletin mensual de estadistica* (Monthly Bulletin of Statistics), and *Colombia estadistica,* (Statistics Columbia).

COLOMBIA - AGRICULTURE

The Economist Intelligence Unit, 111 West 57th Street, New York, New York 10019 (800) 938-4685; *The New Latin America Market Atlas.*

Euromonitor Publications Limited, 87-88 Turnmill Street, London EC1M 5QU, England; *International Marketing Data and Statistics,* and *Third World Economic Handbook.*

Facts on File, 460 Park Avenue South, New York, New York 10016 (800) 443-8323; *The New Book of World Rankings.*

Federal Statistical Office, Gustav - Stresemann - Ring 11, D-6200 Wiesbaden, Germany; *Kolumbien.*

Food and Agricultural Organization of the United Nations (FAO) Via delle Terme di Caracalla, 00100 Rome, Italy (Telephone Number in U.S. (202) 653-2400); *Production Yearbook, The State of Food and Agriculture,* and *Trade Yearbook.*

Gale Research Incorporated, 835 Penobscot Building, Detroit, Michigan 48226 (800) 877-4253; *International Historical Statistics The Americas and Australasia.*

G.K. Hall and Company, 70 Lincoln Street, Boston, Massachusetts 02111 (617) 423-3990; *The World in Figures.*

Inter-American Development Bank, 1300 New York Avenue, NW, Washington, D.C. 20577 (202) 623-1753; *Economic and Social Progress in Latin America.*

Statistical Office of the United Nations, Publishing Service, New York, New York 10017 (800) 253-9646; *Statistical Yearbook,* and *Statistical Yearbook for Latin America and the Caribbean.*

Times Books, 201 East 50th Street, New York, New York 10022 (212) 751-2600; *The Economist Book of Vital World Statistics.*

U.C.L.A. Latin American Center Publications, University of California, Los Angeles, California 90024 (310) 825-6634; *Statistical Abstract of Latin America.*

COLOMBIA - AIRLINE SERVICE

The Economist Intelligence Unit, 111 West 57th Street, New York, New York 10019 (800) 938-4685; *The New Latin America Market Atlas.*

Facts on File, 460 Park Avenue South, New York, New York 10016 (800) 443-8323; *The New Book of World Rankings.*

G.K. Hall and Company, 70 Lincoln Street, Boston, Massachusetts 02111 (617) 423-3990; *The World in Figures.*

International Civil Aviation Organization, 1000 Sherbrooke Street West, Suite 400, Montreal, Quebec, Canada H3A 2R2 (514) 285-8219; *Civil Aviation Statistics of the World.*

Statistical Office of the United Nations, Publishing Service, New York, New York 10017 (800) 253-9646; *Statistical Yearbook.*

Times Books, 201 East 50th Street, New York, New York 10022 (212) 751-2600; *The Economist Book of Vital World Statistics.*

COLOMBIA - ALUMINUM PRODUCTION AND CONSUMPTION - See COLOMBIA - MINING AND MINERAL PRODUCTS

COLOMBIA - ANIMAL HEALTH

Food and Agricultural Organization of the United Nations (FAO), Via delle Terme di Caracalla, 00100 Rome, Italy (Telephone Number in U.S. (202) 653-2400); *Animal Health Yearbook.*

COLOMBIA - AREA AND DENSITY OF POPULATION

Euromonitor Publications Limited, 87-88 Turnmill Street, London EC1M 5QU, England; *International Marketing Data and Statistics.*

Facts on File, 460 Park Avenue South, New York, New York 10016 (800) 443-8323; *The New Book of World Rankings.*

Federal Statistical Office, Gustav - Stresemann - Ring 11, D-6200 Wiesbaden, Germany; *Kolumbien.*

Food and Agricultural Organization of the United Nations (FAO) Via delle Terme di Caracalla, 00100 Rome, Italy (Telephone Number in U.S. (202) 653-2400); *The State of Food and Agriculture.*

G.K. Hall and Company, 70 Lincoln Street, Boston, Massachusetts 02111 (617) 423-3990; *The World in Figures.*

Inter-American Development Bank, 1300 New York Avenue, NW, Washington, D.C. 20577 (202) 623-1753; *Economic and Social Progress in Latin America.*

Statistical Office of the United Nations, Publishing Service, New York, New York 10017 (800) 253-9646; *Statistical Yearbook.*

Times Books, 201 East 50th Street, New York, New York 10022 212 751-2600; *The Economist Book of Vital World Statistics.*

United Nations Educational, Scientific and Cultural Organization (UNESCO), 7 Place de Fontenoy, F-75700 Paris, France (Telephone Number in U.S (212) 963-5981; *Statistical Yearbook.*

COLOMBIA - ARMS EXPORTS AND IMPORTS

U.S. Arms Control and Disarmament Agency, 320 Twenty-first Street, NW, Washington, D.C. 20451 (202) 647-8677; *World Military Expenditures and Arms Transfers.*

COLOMBIA - BALANCE OF PAYMENTS

The Economist Intelligence Unit, 111 West 57th Street, New York, New York 10019 (800) 938-4685; *The World Market Atlas.*

Euromonitor Publications Limited, 87-88 Turnmill Street, London EC1M 5QU, England; *Third World Economic Handbook.*

Federal Statistical Office, Gustav - Stresemann - Ring 11, D-6200 Wiesbaden, Germany; *Kolumbien.*

G.K. Hall and Company, 70 Lincoln Street, Boston, Massachusetts 02111 (617) 423-3990; *The World in Figures.*

Inter-American Development Bank, 1300 New York Avenue, NW, Washington, D.C. 20577 (202) 623-1753; *Economic and Social Progress in Latin America.*

International Monetary Fund, 700 Nineteenth Street, NW, Washington, D.C. 20431 (202) 623-7000; *Balance of Payments Yearbook.*

Organization of American States (OAS), General Secretariat, Washington, D.C. 20006 (202) 458-3533; *Statistical Bulletin of the OAS.*

Statistical Office of the United Nations, Publishing Service, New York, New York 10017 (800) 253-9646; *Economic Survey of Latin America and the Caribbean,* and *Statistical Yearbook for Latin America and the Caribbean.*

Times Books, 201 East 50th Street, New York, New York 10022 (212) 751-2600; *The Economist Book of Vital World Statistics.*

U.C.L.A. Latin American Center Publications, University of California, Los Angeles, California 90024 (310) 825-6634; *Statistical Abstract of Latin America.*

COLOMBIA - BANKING

Facts on File, 460 Park Avenue South, New York, New York 10016 (800) 443-8323; *The New Book of World Rankings.*

G.K. Hall and Company, 70 Lincoln Street, Boston, Massachusetts 02111 (617) 423-3990; *The World in Figures.*

Inter-American Development Bank, 1300 New York Avenue, NW, Washington, D.C. 20577 (202) 623-1753; *Economic and Social Progress in Latin America.*

International Monetary Fund, 700 Nineteenth Street, NW, Washington, D.C. 20431 (202) 623-7000; *International Financial Statistics.*

Statistical Office of the United Nations, Publishing Service, New York, New York 10017 (800) 253-9646; *Statistical Yearbook,* and *Statistical Yearbook for Latin America and the Caribbean.*

COLOMBIA - BARLEY PRODUCTION - See COLOMBIA - CROPS

COLOMBIA - BEER PRODUCTION

Facts on File, 460 Park Avenue South, New York, New York 10016 (800) 443-8323; *The New Book of World Rankings.*

Statistical Office of the United Nations, Publishing Service, New York, New York 10017 (800) 253-9646; *Statistical Yearbook.*

COLOMBIA - BIRTH RATES

Euromonitor Publications Limited, 87-88 Turnmill Street, London EC1M 5QU, England; *Third World Economic Handbook.*

Facts on File, 460 Park Avenue South, New York, New York 10016 (800) 443-8323; *The New Book of World Rankings.*

Statistical Office of the United Nations, Publishing Service, New York, New York 10017 (800) 253-9646; *Demographic Yearbook, Statistical Yearbook,* and *Statistical Yearbook for Latin America and the Caribbean.*

Times Books, 201 East 50th Street, New York, New York 10022 (212) 751-2600; *The Economist Book of Vital World Statistics.*

World Health Organization, Office of Publications, Avenue Appia, CH-1211 Geneva 27, Switzerland (Telephone Number in U.S. (518) 436-9686); *World Health Statistics Annual.*

COLOMBIA - BONDS

G.K. Hall and Company, 70 Lincoln Street, Boston, Massachusetts 02111 (617) 423-3990; *The World in Figures.*

Inter-American Development Bank, 1300 New York Avenue, NW, Washington, D.C. 20577 (202) 623-1753; *Economic and Social Progress in Latin America.*

COLOMBIA - BOOK PRODUCTION

G.K. Hall and Company, 70 Lincoln Street, Boston, Massachusetts 02111 (617) 423-3990; *The World in Figures.*

United Nations Educational, Scientific and Cultural Organization (UNESCO), 7 Place de Fontenoy, F-75700 Paris, France (Telephone Number in U.S. (212) 963-5981); *Statistical Yearbook.*

COLOMBIA - BROADCASTING

Billboard Limited, P.O. Box 9027, 1006 AA Amsterdam, The Netherlands (Telephone Number in U.S. (212) 764-7300); *World Radio TV Handbook.*

Facts on File, 460 Park Avenue South, New York, New York 10016 (800) 443-8323; *The New Book of World Rankings.*

G.K. Hall and Company, 70 Lincoln Street, Boston, Massachusetts 02111 (617) 423-3990; *The World in Figures.*

Times Books, 201 East 50th Street, New York, New York 10022 (212) 751-2600; *The Economist Book of Vital World Statistics.*

United Nations Educational, Scientific and Cultural Organization (UNESCO), 7 Place de Fontenoy, F-75700 Paris, France (Telephone Number in U.S. (518) 436-9686); *Statistical Yearbook.*

COLOMBIA - BUILDING CONSTRUCTION - See COLOMBIA - CONSTRUCTION INDUSTRY

COLOMBIA - BUSINESS

G.K. Hall and Company, 70 Lincoln Street, Boston, Massachusetts 02111 (617) 423-3990; *The World in Figures.*

Inter-American Development Bank, 1300 New York Avenue, NW, Washington, D.C. 20577 (202) 623-1753; *Economic and Social Progress in Latin America.*

COLOMBIA - BUTTER PRODUCTION - See COLOMBIA - DAIRY PRODUCTS

COLOMBIA - CABBAGE PRODUCTION - See COLOMBIA - CROPS

COLOMBIA - CALORIE SUPPLY

Food and Agricultural Organization of the United Nations (FAO) Via delle Terme di Caracalla, 00100 Rome, Italy (Telephone Number in U.S. (202) 653-2400); *The State of Food and Agriculture.*

Statistical Office of the United Nations, Publishing Service, New York, New York 10017 (800) 253-9646; *Statistical Yearbook for Latin*

America and the Caribbean.

COLOMBIA - CAPITAL INVESTMENT

Inter-American Development Bank, 1300 New York Avenue, NW, Washington, D.C. 20577 (202) 623-1753; *Economic and Social Progress in Latin America.*

COLOMBIA - CAPITAL REVENUE

Inter-American Development Bank, 1300 New York Avenue, NW, Washington, D.C. 20577 (202) 623-1753; *Economic and Social Progress in Latin America.*

International Monetary Fund, 700 Nineteenth Street, NW, Washington, D.C. 20431 (202) 623-7000; *Government Finance Statistics Yearbook.*

COLOMBIA - CATTLE - See COLOMBIA - LIVESTOCK AND POULTRY

COLOMBIA - CAULIFLOWER PRODUCTION - See COLOMBIA - CROPS

COLOMBIA - CAUSTIC SODA PRODUCTION

Statistical Office of the United Nations, Publishing Service, New York, New York 10017 (800) 253-9646; *Statistical Yearbook.*

COLOMBIA - CEMENT PRODUCTION - See COLOMBIA - MINING AND MINERAL PRODUCTS

COLOMBIA - CHEESE PRODUCTION - See COLOMBIA - DAIRY PRODUCTS

COLOMBIA - CHEMICALS (ORGANIC) PRODUCTION - See COLOMBIA - MINING AND MINERAL PRODUCTS

COLOMBIA - CHICK PEA PRODUCTION - See COLOMBIA - CROPS

COLOMBIA - CHICKENS - See COLOMBIA - LIVESTOCK AND POULTRY

COLOMBIA - CIGAR PRODUCTION - See COLOMBIA - TOBACCO PRODUCTION

COLOMBIA - CIGARETTE PRODUCTION - See COLOMBIA - TOBACCO PRODUCTION

COLOMBIA - CLASS STRUCTURE

G.K. Hall and Company, 70 Lincoln Street, Boston, Massachusetts 02111 (617) 423-3990; *The World in Figures.*

COLOMBIA - CLIMATE

Facts on File, 460 Park Avenue South, New York, New York 10016 (800) 443-8323; *The New Book of World Rankings.*

G.K. Hall and Company, 70 Lincoln Street, Boston, Massachusetts 02111 (617) 423-3990; *The World in Figures.*

COLOMBIA - CLOTHING EXPORTS AND IMPORTS

Euromonitor Publications Limited, 87-88 Turnmill Street, London EC1M 5QU, England; *Third World Economic Handbook.*

Statistical Office of the United Nations, Publishing Service, New York, New York 10017 (800) 253-9646; *Trade in Manufactures of Developing Countries.*

COLOMBIA - COAL PRODUCTION - See COLOMBIA - MINING AND MINERAL PRODUCTS

COLOMBIA - COCOA (BEANS) PRODUCTION - See COLOMBIA - CROPS

COLOMBIA - COFFEE - See COLOMBIA - CROPS

COLOMBIA - COKE OVEN COKE PRODUCTION - See COLOMBIA - MINING AND MINERAL PRODUCTS

COLOMBIA - COMMUNICATIONS

Euromonitor Publications Limited, 87-88 Turnmill Street, London EC1M 5QU, England; *Third World Economic Handbook.*

Federal Statistical Office, Gustav - Stresemann - Ring 11, D-6200 Wiesbaden, Germany; *Kolumbien.*

G.K. Hall and Company, 70 Lincoln Street, Boston, Massachusetts 02111 (617) 423-3990; *The World in Figures.*

Inter-American Development Bank, 1300 New York Avenue, NW, Washington, D.C. 20577 (202) 623-1753; *Economic and Social Progress in Latin America.*

U.C.L.A. Latin American Center Publications, University of California, Los Angeles, California 90024 (310) 825-6634; *Statistical Abstract of Latin America.*

COLOMBIA - CONSTRUCTION INDUSTRY

The Economist Intelligence Unit, 111 West 57th Street, New York, New York 10019 (800) 938-4685; *The New Latin America Market Atlas.*

Facts on File, 460 Park Avenue South, New York, New York 10016 (800) 443-8323; *The New Book of World Rankings.*

Inter-American Development Bank, 1300 New York Avenue, NW, Washington, D.C. 20577 (202) 623-1753; *Economic and Social Progress in Latin America.*

Statistical Office of the United Nations, Publishing Service, New York, New York 10017 (800) 253-9646; *Construction Statistics Yearbook*, and *Statistical Yearbook.*

U.C.L.A. Latin American Center Publications, University of California, Los Angeles, California 90024 (310) 825-6634; *Statistical Abstract of Latin America.*

COLOMBIA - CONSUMER PRICE INDEX

The Economist Intelligence Unit, 111 West 57th Street, New York, New York 10019 (800) 938-4685; *The New Latin America Market Atlas.*

Federal Statistical Office, Gustav - Stresemann - Ring 11, D-6200 Wiesbaden, Germany; *Kolumbien.*

G.K. Hall and Company, 70 Lincoln Street, Boston, Massachusetts 02111 (617) 423-3990; *The World in Figures.*

Statistical Office of the United Nations, Publishing Service, New York, New York 10017 (800) 253-9646; *Statistical Yearbook.*

COLOMBIA - CONSUMER PRICES

Federal Statistical Office, Gustav - Stresemann - Ring 11, D-6200 Wiesbaden, Germany; *Kolumbien.*

International Labour Office, I.L.O. Publications, CH-1211, Geneva 22, Switzerland; *Yearbook of Labour Statistics.*

International Monetary Fund, 700 Nineteenth Street, NW, Washington, D.C. 20431 (202) 623-7000; *International Financial Statistics.*

Organization of American States (OAS), General Secretariat, Washington, D.C. 20006 (202) 458-3533; *Statistical Bulletin of the OAS.*

Times Books, 201 East 50th Street, New York, New York 10022 (212) 751-2600; *The Economist Book of Vital World Statistics.*

U.C.L.A. Latin American Center Publications, University of California, Los Angeles, California 90024 (310) 825-6634; *Statistical Abstract of Latin America.*

COLOMBIA - CONSUMPTION

The Economist Intelligence Unit, 111 West 57th Street, New York, New York 10019 (800) 938-4685; *The New Latin America Market Atlas.*

G.K. Hall and Company, 70 Lincoln Street, Boston, Massachusetts 02111 (617) 423-3990; *The World in Figures.*

Inter-American Development Bank, 1300 New York Avenue, NW, Washington, D.C. 20577 (202) 623-1753; *Economic and Social Progress in Latin America.*

Statistical Office of the United Nations, Publishing Service, New York, New York 10017 (800) 253-9646; *Statistical Yearbook for Latin America and the Caribbean.*

COLOMBIA - COOPERATIVES

U.C.L.A. Latin American Center Publications, University of California, Los Angeles, California 90024 (310) 825-6634; *Statistical Abstract of Latin America.*

COLOMBIA - COPPER PRODUCTION - See COLOMBIA - MINING AND MINERAL PRODUCTS

COLOMBIA - CORN PRODUCTION - See COLOMBIA - CROPS

COLOMBIA - CORPORATE TAXES - See COLOMBIA - TAXATION

COLOMBIA - COTTON - See COLOMBIA - CROPS

COLOMBIA - CRIME

Yale University Press, Yale Station, New Haven, Connecticut 06520 (203) 432-0940; *Violence and Crime in Cross-National Perspective.*

COLOMBIA - CROPS

Commodity Research Bureau, Incorporated, 75 Wall Street, New York, New York 10005 (212) 504-7754; *Commodity Year Book.*

The Economist Intelligence Unit, 111 West 57th Street, New York, New York 10019 (800) 938-4685; *The New Latin America Market Atlas.*

Facts on File, 460 Park Avenue South, New York, New York 10016 (800) 443-8323; *The New Book of World Rankings.*

Food and Agricultural Organization of the United Nations (FAO) Via delle Terme di Caracalla, 00100 Rome, Italy (Telephone Number in U.S. (202) 653-2400); *Production Yearbook,* and *The State of Food and Agriculture.*

G.K. Hall and Company, 70 Lincoln Street, Boston, Massachusetts 02111 (617) 423-3990; *The World in Figures.*

International Monetary Fund, 700 Nineteenth Street, NW, Washington, D.C. 20431 (202) 623-7000; *International Financial Statistics.*

Organization of American States (OAS), General Secretariat, Washington, D.C. 20006 (202) 458-3533; *Statistical Bulletin of the OAS.*

Statistical Office of the United Nations, Publishing Service, New York, New York 10017 (800) 253-9646; *Statistical Yearbook.*

COLOMBIA - CUSTOMS DUTIES

G.K. Hall and Company, 70 Lincoln Street, Boston, Massachusetts 02111 (617) 423-3990; *The World in Figures.*

Inter-American Development Bank, 1300 New York Avenue, NW, Washington, D.C. 20577 (202) 623-1753; *Economic and Social Progress in Latin America.*

International Monetary Fund, 700 Nineteenth Street, NW, Washington, D.C. 20431 (202) 623-7000; *Government Finance Statistics Yearbook.*

COLOMBIA - DAIRY PRODUCTS

Facts on File, 460 Park Avenue South, New York, New York 10016 (800) 443-8323; *The New Book of World Rankings.*

Food and Agricultural Organization of the United Nations (FAO) Via delle Terme di Caracalla, 00100 Rome, Italy (Telephone Number in U.S. (202) 653-2400); *The State of Food and Agriculture.*

Statistical Office of the United Nations, Publishing Service, New York, New York 10017 (800) 253-9646; *Statistical Yearbook.*

COLOMBIA - DEATH RATES

Euromonitor Publications Limited, 87-88 Turnmill Street, London EC1M 5QU, England; *Third World Economic Handbook.*

G.K. Hall and Company, 70 Lincoln Street, Boston, Massachusetts 02111 (617) 423-3990; *The World in Figures.*

Statistical Office of the United Nations, Publishing Service, New York, New York 10017 (800) 253-9646; *Statistical Yearbook,* and *Statistical Yearbook for Latin America and the Caribbean.*

Times Books, 201 East 50th Street, New York, New York 10022 (212) 751-2600; *The Economist Book of Vital World Statistics.*

World Health Organization, Office of Publications, Avenue Appia, CH-1211 Geneva 27, Switzerland (Telephone Number in U.S. (518) 436-9686); *World Health Statistics Annual.*

COLOMBIA - DEBT

The Economist Intelligence Unit, 111 West 57th Street, New York, New York 10019 (800) 938-4685; *The New Latin America Market Atlas*.

COLOMBIA - DEFENSE EXPENDITURES

The Economist Intelligence Unit, 111 West 57th Street, New York, New York 10019 (800) 938-4685; *The New Latin America Market Atlas*.

G.K. Hall and Company, 70 Lincoln Street, Boston, Massachusetts 02111 (617) 423-3990; *The World in Figures*.

U.S. Arms Control and Disarmament Agency, 320 Twenty-first Street, NW, Washington, D.C. 20451 (202) 647-8677; *World Military Expenditures and Arms Transfers*.

COLOMBIA - DEMOGRAPHY

The Economist Intelligence Unit, 111 West 57th Street, New York, New York 10019 (800) 938-4685; *The World Market Atlas*.

Facts on File, 460 Park Avenue South, New York, New York 10016 (800) 443-8323; *The New Book of World Rankings*.

Federal Statistical Office, Gustav - Stresemann - Ring 11, D-6200 Wiesbaden, Germany; *Kolumbien*.

G.K. Hall and Company, 70 Lincoln Street, Boston, Massachusetts 02111 (617) 423-3990; *The World in Figures*.

COLOMBIA - DEVELOPMENT ASSISTANCE

G.K. Hall and Company, 70 Lincoln Street, Boston, Massachusetts 02111 (617) 423-3990; *The World in Figures*.

Inter-American Development Bank, 1300 New York Avenue, NW, Washington, D.C. 20577 (202) 623-1753; *Economic and Social Progress in Latin America*.

Statistical Office of the United Nations, Publishing Service, New York, New York 10017 (800) 253-9646; *Statistical Yearbook*.

COLOMBIA - DIAMOND PRODUCTION - See COLOMBIA - MINING AND MINERAL PRODUCTS

COLOMBIA - DISCOUNT RATES

Inter-American Development Bank, 1300 New York Avenue, NW, Washington, D.C. 20577 (202) 623-1753; *Economic and Social Progress in Latin America*.

Statistical Office of the United Nations, Publishing Service, New York, New York 10017 (800) 253-9646; *Statistical Yearbook*.

COLOMBIA - DISEASE

G.K. Hall and Company, 70 Lincoln Street, Boston, Massachusetts 02111 (617) 423-3990; *The World in Figures*.

World Health Organization, Office of Publications, Avenue Appia, CH-1211 Geneva 27, Switzerland (Telephone Number in U.S. (518) 436-9686); *World Health Statistics Annual*.

COLOMBIA - DIVORCE RATES

Facts on File, 460 Park Avenue South, New York, New York 10016 (800) 443-8323; *The New Book of World Rankings*.

Statistical Office of the United Nations, Publishing Service, New York, New York 10017 (800) 253-9646; *Demographic Yearbook*, and *Statistical Yearbook*.

COLOMBIA - DOMESTIC PRODUCT

G.K. Hall and Company, 70 Lincoln Street, Boston, Massachusetts 02111 (617) 423-3990; *The World in Figures*.

COLOMBIA - ECONOMY

Euromonitor Publications Limited, 87-88 Turnmill Street, London, EC1M 5QU, England; *International Marketing Data and Statistics*, and *Third World Economic Handbook*.

Facts on File, 460 Park Avenue South, New York, New York 10016 (800) 443-8323; *The New Book of World Rankings*.

Federal Statistical Office, Gustav - Stresemann - Ring 11, D-6200 Wiesbaden, Germany; *Kolumbien*.

G.K. Hall and Company, 70 Lincoln Street, Boston, Massachusetts 02111 (617) 423-3990; *The World in Figures*.

Inter-American Development Bank, 1300 New York Avenue, NW, Washington, D.C. 20577 (202) 623-1753; *Economic and Social Progress in Latin America*.

Organization of American States (OAS), General Secretariat, Washington, D.C. 20006 (202) 458-3533; *Statistical Bulletin of the OAS*.

Statistical Office of the United Nations, Publishing Service, New York, New York 10017 (800) 253-9646; *Economic Survey of Latin America and the Caribbean*.

U.C.L.A. Latin American Center Publications, University of California, Los Angeles, California 90024 (310) 825-6634; *Statistical Abstract of Latin America*.

COLOMBIA - EDUCATION

The Economist Intelligence Unit, 111 West 57th Street, New York, New York 10019 (800) 938-4685; *The New Latin America Market Atlas*, and *The World Market Atlas*.

Facts on File, 460 Park Avenue South, New York, New York 10016 (800) 443-8323; *The New Book of World Rankings*.

Federal Statistical Office, Gustav - Stresemann - Ring 11, D-6200 Wiesbaden, Germany; *Kolumbien*.

Gale Research Incorporated, 835 Penobscot Building, Detroit, Michigan 48226 (800) 877-4253; *International Historical Statistics The Americas and Australasia*.

G.K. Hall and Company, 70 Lincoln Street, Boston, Massachusetts 02111 (617) 423-3990; *The World in Figures*.

Statistical Office of the United Nations, Publishing Service, New York, New York 10017 (800) 253-9646; *Statistical Yearbook for Latin America and the Caribbean*.

Times Books, 201 East 50th Street, New York, New York 10022 (212) 751-2600; *The Economist Book of Vital World Statistics.*

U.C.L.A. Latin American Center Publications, University of California, Los Angeles, California 90024 (310) 825-6634; *Statistical Abstract of Latin America.*

United Nations Educational, Scientific and Cultural Organization (UNESCO), 7 Place de Fontenoy, F-75700 Paris, France (Telephone Number in U.S. (212) 963-5981); *Statistical Yearbook.*

COLOMBIA - EGG PRODUCTION - See COLOMBIA - DAIRY PRODUCTS

COLOMBIA - ELECTRICITY

The Economist Intelligence Unit, 111 West 57th Street, New York, New York 10019 (800) 938-4685; *The New Latin America Market Atlas.*

Facts on File, 460 Park Avenue South, New York, New York 10016 (800) 443-8323; *The New Book of World Rankings.*

Inter-American Development Bank, 1300 New York Avenue, NW, Washington, D.C. 20577 (202) 623-1753; *Economic and Social Progress in Latin America.*

Penn Well Publishing Company, 1421 South Sheridan Road, P.O. Box 1260, Tulsa, Oklahoma 74101 (800) 752-9764; *International Energy Statistics Sourcebook.*

Statistical Office of the United Nations, Publishing Service, New York, New York 10017 (800) 253-9646; *Statistical Yearbook.*

Times Books, 201 East 50th Street, New York, New York 10022 (212) 751-2600; *The Economist Book of Vital World Statistics.*

COLOMBIA - EMPLOYMENT

Euromonitor Publications Limited, 87-88 Turnmill Street, London, EC1M 5QU, England; *International Marketing Data and Statistics.*

Facts on File, 460 Park Avenue South, New York, New York 10016 (800) 443-8323; *The New Book of World Rankings.*

Federal Statistical Office, Gustav - Stresemann - Ring 11, D-6200 Wiesbaden, Germany; *Kolumbien.*

International Labour Office, I.L.O. Publications, CH-1211, Geneva 22, Switzerland; *Yearbook of Labour Statistics.*

Organization of American States (OAS), General Secretariat, Washington, D.C. 20006 (202) 458-3533; *Statistical Bulletin of the OAS.*

Statistical Office of the United Nations, Publishing Service, New York, New York 10017 (800) 253-9646; *Statistical Yearbook for Latin America and the Caribbean.*

U.C.L.A. Latin American Center Publications, University of California, Los Angeles, California 90024 (310) 825-6634; *Statistical Abstract of Latin America.*

COLOMBIA - ENERGY

The Economist Intelligence Unit, 111 West 57th Street, New York, New York 10019 (800) 938-4685; *The New Latin America Market Atlas.*

Facts on File, 460 Park Avenue South, New York, New York 10016 (800) 443-8323; *The New Book of World Rankings.*

Food and Agricultural Organization of the United Nations (FAO) Via delle Terme di Caracalla, 00100 Rome, Italy (Telephone Number in U.S. (202) 653-2400); *The State of Food and Agriculture.*

G.K. Hall and Company, 70 Lincoln Street, Boston, Massachusetts 02111 (617) 423-3990; *The World in Figures.*

Statistical Office of the United Nations, Publishing Service, New York, New York 10017 (800) 253-9646; *Energy Statistics Yearbook, Statistical Yearbook,* and *Statistical Yearbook for Latin America and the Caribbean.*

Times Books, 201 East 50th Street, New York, New York 10022 (212) 751-2600; *The Economist Book of Vital World Statistics.*

U.C.L.A. Latin American Center Publications, University of California, Los Angeles, California 90024 (310) 825-6634; *Statistical Abstract of Latin America.*

Penn Well Publishing Company, 1421 South Sheridan Road, P.O. Box 1260, Tulsa, Oklahoma 74101 (800) 752-9764; *International Energy Statistics Sourcebook.*

COLOMBIA - EXCHANGE RATE

Euromonitor Publications Limited, 87-88 Turnmill Street, London, EC1M 5QU, England; *International Marketing Data and Statistics.*

Inter-American Development Bank, 1300 New York Avenue, NW, Washington, D.C. 20577 (202) 623-1753; *Economic and Social Progress in Latin America.*

International Civil Aviation Organization, 1000 Sherbrooke Street West, Suite 400, Montreal, Quebec, Canada H3A 2R2 (514) 285-8219; *Civil Aviation Statistics of the World.*

International Monetary Fund, 700 Nineteenth Street, NW, Washington, D.C. 20431 (202) 623-7000; *International Financial Statistics.*

Organization of American States (OAS), General Secretariat, Washington, D.C. 20006 (202) 458-3533; *Statistical Bulletin of the OAS.*

Statistical Office of the United Nations, Publishing Service, New York, New York 10017 (800) 253-9646; *Statistical Yearbook.*

U.C.L.A. Latin American Center Publications, University of California, Los Angeles, California 90024 (310) 825-6634; *Statistical Abstract of Latin America.*

COLOMBIA - EXCISE TAXES

Inter-American Development Bank, 1300 New York Avenue, NW, Washington, D.C. 20577 (202) 623-1753; *Economic and Social Progress in Latin America.*

International Monetary Fund, 700 Nineteenth Street, NW, Washington, D.C. 20431 (202) 623-7000; *Government Finance Statistics Yearbook.*

COLOMBIA - EXPORTS

American Automobile Manufacturers Association, 1401 H Street, NW, Suite 900, Washington, D.C. 20005 (202) 326-5500; *World Motor Vehicle Data.*

The Economist Intelligence Unit, 111 West 57th Street, New York, New York 10019 (800) 938-4685; *The New Latin America Market Atlas*, and *The World Market Atlas*.

Euromonitor Publications Limited, 87-88 Turnmill Street, London, EC1M 5QU, England; *International Marketing Data and Statistics*, and *Third World Economic Handbook*.

Food and Agricultural Organization of the United Nations (FAO) Via delle Terme di Caracalla, 00100 Rome, Italy (Telephone Number in U.S. (202) 653-2400); *The State of Food and Agriculture*.

G.K. Hall and Company, 70 Lincoln Street, Boston, Massachusetts 02111 (617) 423-3990; *The World in Figures*.

Inter-American Development Bank, 1300 New York Avenue, NW, Washington, D.C. 20577 (202) 623-1753; *Economic and Social Progress in Latin America*.

International Monetary Fund, 700 Nineteenth Street, NW, Washington, D.C. 20431 (202) 623-7000; *Direction of Trade Statistics*, and *International Financial Statistics*.

Organization of American States (OAS), General Secretariat, Washington, D.C. 20006 (202) 458-3533; *Statistical Bulletin of the OAS*.

Statistical Office of the United Nations, Publishing Service, New York, New York 10017 (800) 253-9646; *Statistical Yearbook for Latin America and the Caribbean*, and *Trade in Manufactures of Developing Countries*.

Times Books, 201 East 50th Street, New York, New York 10022 (212) 751-2600; *The Economist Book of Vital World Statistics*.

COLOMBIA - EXTERNAL FINANCING

Inter-American Development Bank, 1300 New York Avenue, NW, Washington, D.C. 20577 (202) 623-1753; *Economic and Social Progress in Latin America*.

Statistical Office of the United Nations, Publishing Service, New York, New York 10017 (800) 253-9646; *Statistical Yearbook for Latin America and the Caribbean*.

COLOMBIA - EXTERNAL INDEBTEDNESS

Euromonitor Publications Limited, 87-88 Turnmill Street, London EC1M 5QU, England; *Third World Economic Handbook*.

Inter-American Development Bank, 1300 New York Avenue, NW, Washington, D.C. 20577 (202) 623-1753; *Economic and Social Progress in Latin America*.

Statistical Office of the United Nations, Publishing Service, New York, New York 10017 (800) 253-9646; *Statistical Yearbook for Latin America and the Caribbean*.

COLOMBIA - EXTERNAL TRADE

Food and Agricultural Organization of the United Nations (FAO) Via delle Terme di Caracalla, 00100 Rome, Italy (Telephone Number in U.S. (202) 653-2400); *The State of Food and Agriculture*, and *Trade Yearbook*.

Gale Research Incorporated, 835 Penobscot Building, Detroit, Michigan 48226 (800) 877-4253; *International Historical Statistics The Americas and Australasia*.

G.K. Hall and Company, 70 Lincoln Street, Boston, Massachusetts 02111 (617) 423-3990; *The World in Figures*.

Inter-American Development Bank, 1300 New York Avenue, NW, Washington, D.C. 20577 (202) 623-1753; *Economic and Social Progress in Latin America*.

Statistical Office of the United Nations, Publishing Service, New York, New York 10017 (800) 253-9646; *Statistical Yearbook*, and *Statistical Yearbook for Latin America and the Caribbean*.

COLOMBIA - FABRIC PRODUCTION - See COLOMBIA - TEXTILE INDUSTRY

COLOMBIA - FAMILY PLANNING

U.C.L.A. Latin American Center Publications, University of California, Los Angeles, California 90024 (310) 825-6634; *Statistical Abstract of Latin America*.

COLOMBIA - FARM CROPS - See COLOMBIA - CROPS

COLOMBIA - FEMALE WORKING POPULATION - See COLOMBIA - EMPLOYMENT

COLOMBIA - FERTILITY RATES

Facts on File, 460 Park Avenue South, New York, New York 10016 (800) 443-8323; *The New Book of World Rankings*.

Times Books, 201 East 50th Street, New York, New York 10022 (212) 751-2600; *The Economist Book of Vital World Statistics*.

COLOMBIA - FERTILIZER

The Economist Intelligence Unit, 111 West 57th Street, New York, New York 10019 (800) 938-4685; *The New Latin America Market Atlas*.

Food and Agricultural Organization of the United Nations (FAO), Via delle Terme di Caracalla, 00100 Rome, Italy (Telephone Number in U.S. (202) 653-2400); *Fertilizer Yearbook*, and *The State of Food and Agriculture*.

Statistical Office of the United Nations, Publishing Service, New York, New York 10017 (800) 253-9646; *Statistical Yearbook*.

COLOMBIA - FETAL MORTALITY

Statistical Office of the United Nations, Publishing Service, New York, New York 10017 (800) 253-9646; *Demographic Yearbook*.

World Health Organization, Office of Publications, Avenue Appia, CH-1211 Geneva 27, Switzerland (Telephone Number in U.S. (518) 436-9686); *World Health Statistics Annual*.

COLOMBIA - FIBRE PRODUCTION - See COLOMBIA - TEXTILE INDUSTRY

COLOMBIA - FILAMENT PRODUCTION - See COLOMBIA - LIVESTOCK AND POULTRY

COLOMBIA - FILM - See COLOMBIA - MOTION PICTURES

COLOMBIA - FINANCE

Facts on File, 460 Park Avenue South, New York, New York 10016 (800) 443-8323; *The New Book of World Rankings*.

Federal Statistical Office, Gustav - Stresemann - Ring 11, D-6200 Wiesbaden, Germany; *Kolumbien.*

Gale Research Incorporated, 835 Penobscot Building, Detroit, Michigan 48226 (800) 877-4253; *International Historical Statistics The Americas and Australasia.*

G.K. Hall and Company, 70 Lincoln Street, Boston, Massachusetts 02111 (617) 423-3990; *The World in Figures.*

Inter-American Development Bank, 1300 New York Avenue, NW, Washington, D.C. 20577 (202) 623-1753; *Economic and Social Progress in Latin America.*

International Monetary Fund, 700 Nineteenth Street, NW, Washington, D.C. 20431 (202) 623-7000; *International Financial Statistics.*

Organization of American States (OAS), General Secretariat, Washington, D.C. 20006 (202) 458-3533; *Statistical Bulletin of the OAS.*

U.C.L.A. Latin American Center Publications, University of California, Los Angeles, California 90024 (310) 825-6634; *Statistical Abstract of Latin America.*

COLOMBIA - FISHERIES

Facts on File, 460 Park Avenue South, New York, New York 10016 (800) 443-8323; *The New Book of World Rankings.*

Federal Statistical Office, Gustav - Stresemann - Ring 11, D-6200 Wiesbaden, Germany; *Kolumbien.*

Food and Agricultural Organization of the United Nations (FAO) Via delle Terme di Caracalla, 00100 Rome, Italy (Telephone Number in U.S. (202) 653-2400); *The State of Food and Agriculture,* and *Yearbook of Fishery Statistics.*

Inter-American Development Bank, 1300 New York Avenue, NW, Washington, D.C. 20577 (202) 623-1753; *Economic and Social Progress in Latin America.*

Statistical Office of the United Nations, Publishing Service, New York, New York 10017 (800) 253-9646; *Statistical Yearbook,* and *Survey of Economic and Social Conditions in Africa.*

U.C.L.A. Latin American Center Publications, University of California, Los Angeles, California 90024 (310) 825-6634; *Statistical Abstract of Latin America.*

COLOMBIA - FLOUR PRODUCTION

Statistical Office of the United Nations, Publishing Service, New York, New York 10017 (800) 253-9646; *Statistical Yearbook.*

COLOMBIA - FOOD

Food and Agricultural Organization of the United Nations (FAO) Via delle Terme di Caracalla, 00100 Rome, Italy (Telephone Number in U.S. (202) 653-2400); *Production Yearbook,* and *The State of Food and Agriculture.*

G.K. Hall and Company, 70 Lincoln Street, Boston, Massachusetts 02111 (617) 423-3990; *The World in Figures.*

COLOMBIA - FOREIGN AID

G.K. Hall and Company, 70 Lincoln Street, Boston, Massachusetts 02111 (617) 423-3990; *The World in Figures.*

Inter-American Development Bank, 1300 New York Avenue, NW, Washington, D.C. 20577 (202) 623-1753; *Economic and Social Progress in Latin America.*

COLOMBIA - FOREIGN DEBT

The Economist Intelligence Unit, 111 West 57th Street, New York, New York 10019 (800) 938-4685; *The New Latin America Market Atlas.*

Inter-American Development Bank, 1300 New York Avenue, NW, Washington, D.C. 20577 (202) 623-1753; *Economic and Social Progress in Latin America.*

COLOMBIA - FOREIGN FINANCE

Inter-American Development Bank, 1300 New York Avenue, NW, Washington, D.C. 20577 (202) 623-1753; *Economic and Social Progress in Latin America.*

COLOMBIA - FOREIGN INDEBTEDNESS

Inter-American Development Bank, 1300 New York Avenue, NW, Washington, D.C. 20577 (202) 623-1753; *Economic and Social Progress in Latin America.*

Statistical Office of the United Nations, Publishing Service, New York, New York 10017 (800) 253-9646; *Economic Survey of Latin America and the Caribbean.*

COLOMBIA - FOREIGN INVESTMENT

The Economist Intelligence Unit, 111 West 57th Street, New York, New York 10019 (800) 938-4685; *The New Latin America Market Atlas.*

COLOMBIA - FOREIGN TRADE

The Economist Intelligence Unit, 111 West 57th Street, New York, New York 10019 (800) 938-4685; *The New Latin America Market Atlas.*

Euromonitor Publications Limited, 87-88 Turnmill Street, London, EC1M 5QU, England; *International Marketing Data and Statistics,* and *Third World Economic Handbook.*

Facts on File, 460 Park Avenue South, New York, New York 10016 (800) 443-8323; *The New Book of World Rankings.*

Federal Statistical Office, Gustav - Stresemann - Ring 11, D-6200 Wiesbaden, Germany; *Kolumbien.*

Food and Agricultural Organization of the United Nations (FAO) Via delle Terme di Caracalla, 00100 Rome, Italy (Telephone Number in U.S. (202) 653-2400); *The State of Food and Agriculture.*

G.K. Hall and Company, 70 Lincoln Street, Boston, Massachusetts 02111 (617) 423-3990; *The World in Figures.*

Inter-American Development Bank, 1300 New York Avenue, NW, Washington, D.C. 20577 (202) 623-1753; *Economic and Social Progress in Latin America.*

International Monetary Fund, 700 Nineteenth Street, NW, Washington, D.C. 20431 (202) 623-7000; *International Financial Statistics.*

Organisation for Economic Co-operation and Development (OECD), 2 rue Andre-Pascal, 75 Paris 16, France (Telephone Number in U.S. (202) 785-6323); *Trade by Commodities.*

Statistical Office of the United Nations, Publishing Service, New York, New York 10017 (800) 253-9646; *Economic Survey of Latin America and the Caribbean, International Trade Statistics Yearbook,* and *Statistical Yearbook.*

U.C.L.A. Latin American Center Publications, University of California, Los Angeles, California 90024 (310) 825-6634; *Statistical Abstract of Latin America.*

COLOMBIA - FORESTRY AND FOREST PRODUCTS

The Economist Intelligence Unit, 111 West 57th Street, New York, New York 10019 (800) 938-4685; *The New Latin America Market Atlas.*

Euromonitor Publications Limited, 87-88 Turnmill Street, London EC1M 5QU, England; *Third World Economic Handbook.*

Facts on File, 460 Park Avenue South, New York, New York 10016 (800) 443-8323; *The New Book of World Rankings.*

Federal Statistical Office, Gustav - Stresemann - Ring 11, D-6200 Wiesbaden, Germany; *Kolumbien.*

Food and Agricultural Organization of the United Nations (FAO) Via delle Terme di Caracalla, 00100 Rome, Italy (Telephone Number in U.S. (202) 653-2400); *The State of Food and Agriculture,* and *Yearbook of Forest Products.*

Forest and Paper Association, 1250 Connecticut Avenue, NW, Washington, D.C. 20036 (202) 463-2455; *Wood Pulp and Fiber Statistics.*

G.K. Hall and Company, 70 Lincoln Street, Boston, Massachusetts 02111 (617) 423-3990; *The World in Figures.*

Inter-American Development Bank, 1300 New York Avenue, NW, Washington, D.C. 20577 (202) 623-1753; *Economic and Social Progress in Latin America.*

Statistical Office of the United Nations, Publishing Service, New York, New York 10017 (800) 253-9646; *Statistical Yearbook.*

U.C.L.A. Latin American Center Publications, University of California, Los Angeles, California 90024 (310) 825-6634; *Statistical Abstract of Latin America.*

United Nations Educational, Scientific and Cultural Organization (UNESCO), 7 Place de Fontenoy, F-75700 Paris, France (Telephone Number in U.S. (518) 436-9686); *Statistical Yearbook.*

COLOMBIA - FUEL OIL EXPORTS

International Monetary Fund, 700 Nineteenth Street, NW, Washington, D.C. 20431 (202) 623-7000; *International Financial Statistics.*

COLOMBIA - GAS AND GAS LIQUIDS PRODUCTION - See COLOMBIA - MINING AND MINERAL PRODUCTS

COLOMBIA - GENERAL INDUSTRIAL STATISTICS

Federal Statistical Office, Gustav - Stresemann - Ring 11, D-6200 Wiesbaden, Germany; *Kolumbien.*

Statistical Office of the United Nations, Publishing Service, New York, New York 10017 (800) 253-9646; *Industrial Statistics Yearbook.*

COLOMBIA - GENERAL MORTALITY

Statistical Office of the United Nations, Publishing Service, New York, New York 10017 (800) 253-9646; *Demographic Yearbook.*

World Health Organization, Office of Publications, Avenue Appia, CH-1211 Geneva 27, Switzerland (Telephone Number in U.S. (518) 436-9686); *World Health Statistics Annual.*

COLOMBIA - GEOGRAPHIC DATA

Facts on File, 460 Park Avenue South, New York, New York 10016 (800) 443-8323; *The New Book of World Rankings.*

Federal Statistical Office, Gustav - Stresemann - Ring 11, D-6200 Wiesbaden, Germany; *Kolumbien.*

U.C.L.A. Latin American Center Publications, University of California, Los Angeles, California 90024 (310) 825-6634; *Statistical Abstract of Latin America.*

COLOMBIA - GOATS - See COLOMBIA - LIVESTOCK AND POULTRY

COLOMBIA - GOLD HOLDINGS

International Monetary Fund, 700 Nineteenth Street, NW, Washington, D.C. 20431 (202) 623-7000; *International Financial Statistics.*

Statistical Office of the United Nations, Publishing Service, New York, New York 10017 (800) 253-9646; *Statistical Yearbook.*

COLOMBIA - GOLD PRODUCTION - See COLOMBIA - MINING AND MINERAL PRODUCTS

COLOMBIA - GOLD RESERVES

The Economist Intelligence Unit, 111 West 57th Street, New York, New York 10019 (800) 938-4685; *The New Latin America Market Atlas.*

COLOMBIA - GOVERNMENT

G.K. Hall and Company, 70 Lincoln Street, Boston, Massachusetts 02111 (617) 423-3990; *The World in Figures.*

Inter-American Development Bank, 1300 New York Avenue, NW, Washington, D.C. 20577 (202) 623-1753; *Economic and Social Progress in Latin America.*

COLOMBIA - GOVERNMENT BONDS - See COLOMBIA - BONDS

COLOMBIA - GOVERNMENT CONSUMPTION

Inter-American Development Bank, 1300 New York Avenue, NW, Washington, D.C. 20577 (202) 623-1753; *Economic and Social Progress in Latin America.*

COLOMBIA - GOVERNMENT EXPENDITURE

Euromonitor Publications Limited, 87-88 Turnmill Street, London EC1M 5QU, England; *Third World Economic Handbook.*

Inter-American Development Bank, 1300 New York Avenue, NW, Washington, D.C. 20577 (202) 623-1753; *Economic and Social Progress in Latin America.*

Times Books, 201 East 50th Street, New York, New York 10022 (212) 751-2600; *The Economist Book of Vital World Statistics.*

COLOMBIA - GOVERNMENT FINANCES

Inter-American Development Bank, 1300 New York Avenue, NW, Washington, D.C. 20577 (202) 623-1753; *Economic and Social Progress in Latin America.*

International Monetary Fund, 700 Nineteenth Street, NW, Washington, D.C. 20431 (202) 623-7000; *International Financial Statistics.*

Statistical Office of the United Nations, Publishing Service, New York, New York 10017 (800) 253-9646; *Statistical Yearbook.*

COLOMBIA - GOVERNMENT REVENUE

Inter-American Development Bank, 1300 New York Avenue, NW, Washington, D.C. 20577 (202) 623-1753; *Economic and Social Progress in Latin America.*

International Monetary Fund, 700 Nineteenth Street, NW, Washington, D.C. 20431 (202) 623-7000; *Government Finance Statistics Yearbook.*

Times Books, 201 East 50th Street, New York, New York 10022 (212) 751-2600; *The Economist Book of Vital World Statistics.*

U.C.L.A. Latin American Center Publications, University of California, Los Angeles, California 90024 (310) 825-6634; *Statistical Abstract of Latin America.*

COLOMBIA - GRAIN PRODUCTION - See COLOMBIA - CROPS

COLOMBIA - GRANTS

International Monetary Fund, 700 Nineteenth Street, NW, Washington, D.C. 20431 (202) 623-7000; *Government Finance Statistics Yearbook.*

COLOMBIA - GREEN PEPPER AND CHILIE PRODUCTION - See COLOMBIA - CROPS

COLOMBIA - GROSS DOMESTIC PRODUCT

The Economist Intelligence Unit, 111 West 57th Street, New York, New York 10019 (800) 938-4685; *The New Latin America Market Atlas,* and *The World Market Atlas.*

Euromonitor Publications Limited, 87-88 Turnmill Street, London, EC1M 5QU, England; *International Marketing Data and Statistics,* and *Third World Economic Handbook.*

G.K. Hall and Company, 70 Lincoln Street, Boston, Massachusetts 02111 (617) 423-3990; *The World in Figures.*

Inter-American Development Bank, 1300 New York Avenue, NW, Washington, D.C. 20577 (202) 623-1753; *Economic and Social Progress in Latin America.*

Organization of American States (OAS), General Secretariat, Washington, D.C. 20006 (202) 458-3533; *Statistical Bulletin of the OAS.*

Statistical Office of the United Nations, Publishing Service, New York, New York 10017 (800) 253-9646; *Statistical Yearbook,* and *Statistical Yearbook for Latin America and the Caribbean.*

Times Books, 201 East 50th Street, New York, New York 10022 (212) 751-2600; *The Economist Book of Vital World Statistics.*

U.C.L.A. Latin American Center Publications, University of California, Los Angeles, California 90024 (310) 825-6634; *Statistical Abstract of Latin America.*

COLOMBIA - GROSS INDUSTRIAL PRODUCT

Euromonitor Publications Limited, 87-88 Turnmill Street, London EC1M 5QU, England; *Third World Economic Handbook.*

COLOMBIA - GROSS NATIONAL PRODUCT

Euromonitor Publications Limited, 87-88 Turnmill Street, London, EC1M 5QU, England; *International Marketing Data and Statistics,* and *Third World Economic Handbook.*

Inter-American Development Bank, 1300 New York Avenue, NW, Washington, D.C. 20577 (202) 623-1753; *Economic and Social Progress in Latin America.*

U.S. Arms Control and Disarmament Agency, 320 Twenty-first Street, NW, Washington, D.C. 20451 (202) 647-8677; *World Military Expenditures and Arms Transfers.*

COLOMBIA - GROUNDNUTS PRODUCTION - See COLOMBIA - CROPS

COLOMBIA - GROWTH - DOMESTIC PRODUCT

Facts on File, 460 Park Avenue South, New York, New York 10016 (800) 443-8323; *The New Book of World Rankings.*

COLOMBIA - HEALTH

The Economist Intelligence Unit, 111 West 57th Street, New York, New York 10019 (800) 938-4685; *The New Latin America Market Atlas.*

Facts on File, 460 Park Avenue South, New York, New York 10016 (800) 443-8323; *The New Book of World Rankings.*

Federal Statistical Office, Gustav - Stresemann - Ring 11, D-6200 Wiesbaden, Germany; *Kolumbien.*

G.K. Hall and Company, 70 Lincoln Street, Boston, Massachusetts 02111 (617) 423-3990; *The World in Figures.*

Statistical Office of the United Nations, Publishing Service, New York, New York 10017 (800) 253-9646; *Statistical Yearbook.*

Times Books, 201 East 50th Street, New York, New York 10022 (212) 751-2600; *The Economist Book of Vital World Statistics.*

U.C.L.A. Latin American Center Publications, University of California, Los Angeles, California 90024 (310) 825-6634; *Statistical Abstract of Latin America.*

World Health Organization, Office of Publications, Avenue Appia, CH-1211 Geneva 27, Switzerland (Telephone Number in U.S. (518) 436-9686); *World Health Statistics Annual.*

COLOMBIA - HEALTH EXPENDITURES

Statistical Office of the United Nations, Publishing Service, New York, New York 10017 (800) 253-9646; *Statistical Yearbook for Latin America and the Caribbean.*

COLOMBIA - HIDE PRODUCTION

Food and Agricultural Organization of the United Nations (FAO), Via delle Terme di Caracalla, 00100 Rome, Italy (Telephone Number in U.S. (202) 653-2400); *Production Yearbook.*

COLOMBIA - HIGHWAYS

The Economist Intelligence Unit, 111 West 57th Street, New York, New York 10019 (800) 938-4685; *The New Latin America Market Atlas.*

G.K. Hall and Company, 70 Lincoln Street, Boston, Massachusetts 02111 (617) 423-3990; *The World in Figures.*

International Road Federation, 525 School Street, SW, Washington, D.C. 20024 (202) 554-2106; *World Road Statistics.*

COLOMBIA - HORSES - See COLOMBIA - LIVESTOCK AND POULTRY

COLOMBIA - HOURS OF WORK - See COLOMBIA - EMPLOYMENT

COLOMBIA - HOUSING AND HOUSING UNITS

Euromonitor Publications Limited, 87-88 Turnmill Street, London EC1M 5QU, England; *Third World Economic Handbook.*

Facts on File, 460 Park Avenue South, New York, New York 10016 (800) 443-8323; *The New Book of World Rankings.*

Statistical Office of the United Nations, Publishing Service, New York, New York 10017 (800) 253-9646; *Statistical Yearbook for Latin America and the Caribbean.*

U.C.L.A. Latin American Center Publications, University of California, Los Angeles, California 90024 (310) 825-6634; *Statistical Abstract of Latin America.*

COLOMBIA - HYDROCHLORIC ACID PRODUCTION

Statistical Office of the United Nations, Publishing Service, New York, New York 10017 (800) 253-9646; *Statistical Yearbook.*

COLOMBIA - ILLITERACY RATES

The Economist Intelligence Unit, 111 West 57th Street, New York, New York 10019 (800) 938-4685; *The New Latin America Market Atlas.*

COLOMBIA - ILLITERATE POPULATION

The Economist Intelligence Unit, 111 West 57th Street, New York, New York 10019 (800) 938-4685; *The World Market Atlas.*

G.K. Hall and Company, 70 Lincoln Street, Boston, Massachusetts 02111 (617) 423-3990; *The World in Figures.*

Statistical Office of the United Nations, Publishing Service, New York, New York 10017 (800) 253-9646; *Statistical Yearbook for Latin America and the Caribbean.*

United Nations Educational, Scientific and Cultural Organization (UNESCO), 7 Place de Fontenoy, F-75700 Paris, France (Telephone Number in U.S. (518) 436-9686); *Statistical Yearbook.*

COLOMBIA - IMMIGRATION

U.C.L.A. Latin American Center Publications, University of California, Los Angeles, California 90024 (310) 825-6634; *Statistical Abstract of Latin America.*

COLOMBIA - IMPORTS

American Automobile Manufacturers Association, 1401 H Street, NW, Suite 900, Washington, D.C. 20005 (202) 326-5500; *World Motor Vehicle Data.*

The Economist Intelligence Unit, 111 West 57th Street, New York, New York 10019 (800) 938-4685; *The New Latin America Market Atlas*, and *The World Market Atlas.*

Euromonitor Publications Limited, 87-88 Turnmill Street, London, EC1M 5QU, England; *International Marketing Data and Statistics*, and *Third World Economic Handbook.*

Food and Agricultural Organization of the United Nations (FAO) Via delle Terme di Caracalla, 00100 Rome, Italy (Telephone Number in U.S. (202) 653-2400); *The State of Food and Agriculture.*

G.K. Hall and Company, 70 Lincoln Street, Boston, Massachusetts 02111 (617) 423-3990; *The World in Figures.*

Inter-American Development Bank, 1300 New York Avenue, NW, Washington, D.C. 20577 (202) 623-1753; *Economic and Social Progress in Latin America.*

International Monetary Fund, 700 Nineteenth Street, NW, Washington, D.C. 20431 (202) 623-7000; *Direction of Trade Statistics*, and *International Financial Statistics.*

Organization of American States (OAS), General Secretariat, Washington, D.C. 20006 (202) 458-3533; *Statistical Bulletin of the OAS.*

Statistical Office of the United Nations, Publishing Service, New York, New York 10017 (800) 253-9646; *Statistical Yearbook for Latin America and the Caribbean*, and *Trade in Manufactures of Developing Countries.*

Times Books, 201 East 50th Street, New York, New York 10022 (212) 751-2600; *The Economist Book of Vital World Statistics.*

COLOMBIA - INCOME DISTRIBUTION

Statistical Office of the United Nations, Publishing Service, New York, New York 10017 (800) 253-9646; *Statistical Yearbook for Latin America and the Caribbean.*

U.C.L.A. Latin American Center Publications, University of California, Los Angeles, California 90024 (310) 825-6634; *Statistical Abstract of Latin America.*

COLOMBIA - INCOME TAXES

Inter-American Development Bank, 1300 New York Avenue, NW, Washington, D.C. 20577 (202) 623-1753; *Economic and Social Progress in Latin America.*

International Monetary Fund, 700 Nineteenth Street, NW, Washington, D.C. 20431 (202) 623-7000; *Government Finance Statistics Yearbook.*

COLOMBIA - INDUSTRIAL METALS PRODUCTIONS - See COLOMBIA - MINING AND MINERAL PRODUCTS

COLOMBIA - INDUSTRY

Euromonitor Publications Limited, 87-88 Turnmill Street, London EC1M 5QU, England; *Third World Economic Handbook*.

Facts on File, 460 Park Avenue South, New York, New York 10016 (800) 443-8323; *The New Book of World Rankings*.

Federal Statistical Office, Gustav - Stresemann - Ring 11, D-6200 Wiesbaden, Germany; *Kolumbien*.

Gale Research Incorporated, 835 Penobscot Building, Detroit, Michigan 48226 (800) 877-4253; *International Historical Statistics The Americas and Australasia*.

G.K. Hall and Company, 70 Lincoln Street, Boston, Massachusetts 02111 (617) 423-3990; *The World in Figures*.

International Labour Office, I.L.O. Publications, CH-1211, Geneva 22, Switzerland; *Yearbook of Labour Statistics*.

Statistical Office of the United Nations, Publishing Service, New York, New York 10017 (800) 253-9646; *Economic Survey of Latin America and the Caribbean*, and *Statistical Yearbook*.

Times Books, 201 East 50th Street, New York, New York 10022 (212) 751-2600; *The Economist Book of Vital World Statistics*.

U.C.L.A. Latin American Center Publications, University of California, Los Angeles, California 90024 (310) 825-6634; *Statistical Abstract of Latin America*.

World Intellectual Property Organization, 34 Chemin des Colombettes, CH-1211 Geneva 20. Switzerland; *Industrial Property Statistics*.

COLOMBIA - INFANT AND MATERNAL MORTALITY

The Economist Intelligence Unit, 111 West 57th Street, New York, New York 10019 (800) 938-4685; *The New Latin America Market Atlas*.

Statistical Office of the United Nations, Publishing Service, New York, New York 10017 (800) 253-9646; *Demographic Yearbook*, and *Statistical Yearbook*.

Times Books, 201 East 50th Street, New York, New York 10022 (212) 751-2600; *The Economist Book of Vital World Statistics*.

World Health Organization, Office of Publications, Avenue Appia, CH-1211 Geneva 27, Switzerland (Telephone Number in U.S. (518) 436-9686); *World Health Statistics Annual*.

COLOMBIA - INFLATIONARY FACTORS

Statistical Office of the United Nations, Publishing Service, New York, New York 10017 (800) 253-9646; *Economic Survey of Latin America and the Caribbean*.

COLOMBIA - INTEREST RATES

Inter-American Development Bank, 1300 New York Avenue, NW, Washington, D.C. 20577 (202) 623-1753; *Economic and Social Progress in Latin America*.

Organization of American States (OAS), General Secretariat, Washington, D.C. 20006 (202) 458-3533; *Statistical Bulletin of the OAS*.

COLOMBIA - INTERNATIONAL FINANCE

Inter-American Development Bank, 1300 New York Avenue, NW, Washington, D.C. 20577 (202) 623-1753; *Economic and Social Progress in Latin America*.

U.C.L.A. Latin American Center Publications, University of California, Los Angeles, California 90024 (310) 825-6634; *Statistical Abstract of Latin America*.

COLOMBIA - INTERNATIONAL LIQUIDITY

Inter-American Development Bank, 1300 New York Avenue, NW, Washington, D.C. 20577 (202) 623-1753; *Economic and Social Progress in Latin America*.

International Monetary Fund, 700 Nineteenth Street, NW, Washington, D.C. 20431 (202) 623-7000; *International Financial Statistics*.

COLOMBIA - INTERNATIONAL RESERVES

Organization of American States (OAS), General Secretariat, Washington, D.C. 20006 (202) 458-3533; *Statistical Bulletin of the OAS*.

COLOMBIA - INTERNATIONAL RESERVES EXCLUDING GOLD

Inter-American Development Bank, 1300 New York Avenue, NW, Washington, D.C. 20577 (202) 623-1753; *Economic and Social Progress in Latin America*.

COLOMBIA - INTERNATIONAL STATISTICS

Inter-American Development Bank, 1300 New York Avenue, NW, Washington, D.C. 20577 (202) 623-1753; *Economic and Social Progress in Latin America*.

U.C.L.A. Latin American Center Publications, University of California, Los Angeles, California 90024 (310) 825-6634; *Statistical Abstract of Latin America*.

COLOMBIA - INVESTMENTS

Inter-American Development Bank, 1300 New York Avenue, NW, Washington, D.C. 20577 (202) 623-1753; *Economic and Social Progress in Latin America*.

Statistical Office of the United Nations, Publishing Service, New York, New York 10017 (800) 253-9646; *Statistical Yearbook for Latin America and the Caribbean*.

COLOMBIA - IRON ORE PRODUCTION AND CONSUMPTION - See COLOMBIA - MINING AND MINERAL PRODUCTS

COLOMBIA - IRRIGATION

Euromonitor Publications Limited, 87-88 Turnmill Street, London, EC1M 5QU, England; *International Marketing Data and Statistics*.

Inter-American Development Bank, 1300 New York Avenue, NW, Washington, D.C. 20577 (202) 623-1753; *Economic and Social Progress in Latin America*.

COLOMBIA - LABOR FORCE

The Economist Intelligence Unit, 111 West 57th Street, New York, New York 10019 (800) 938-4685; *The New Latin America Market Atlas.*

Euromonitor Publications Limited, 87-88 Turnmill Street, London, EC1M 5QU, England; *International Marketing Data and Statistics.*

Facts on File, 460 Park Avenue South, New York, New York 10016 (800) 443-8323; *The New Book of World Rankings.*

Food and Agricultural Organization of the United Nations (FAO) Via delle Terme di Caracalla, 00100 Rome, Italy (Telephone Number in U.S. (202) 653-2400); *The State of Food and Agriculture.*

Gale Research Incorporated, 835 Penobscot Building, Detroit, Michigan 48226 (800) 877-4253; *International Historical Statistics The Americas and Australasia.*

G.K. Hall and Company, 70 Lincoln Street, Boston, Massachusetts 02111 (617) 423-3990; *The World in Figures.*

Times Books, 201 East 50th Street, New York, New York 10022 (212) 751-2600; *The Economist Book of Vital World Statistics.*

COLOMBIA - LABOR PRODUCTIVITY

International Labour Office, I.L.O. Publications, CH-1211, Geneva 22, Switzerland; *Yearbook of Labour Statistics.*

COLOMBIA - LAND AREA

The Economist Intelligence Unit, 111 West 57th Street, New York, New York 10019 (800) 938-4685; *The New Latin America Market Atlas.*

COLOMBIA - LAND USE

Euromonitor Publications Limited, 87-88 Turnmill Street, London, EC1M 5QU, England; *International Marketing Data and Statistics.*

Food and Agricultural Organization of the United Nations (FAO), Via delle Terme di Caracalla, 00100 Rome, Italy (Telephone Number in U.S. (202) 653-2400); *Production Yearbook.*

G.K. Hall and Company, 70 Lincoln Street, Boston, Massachusetts 02111 (617) 423-3990; *The World in Figures.*

Inter-American Development Bank, 1300 New York Avenue, NW, Washington, D.C. 20577 (202) 623-1753; *Economic and Social Progress in Latin America.*

COLOMBIA - LEAD PRODUCTION AND CONSUMPTION - See COLOMBIA - MINING AND MINERAL PRODUCTS

COLOMBIA - LEATHER AND FOOTWEAR - EXPORTS AND IMPORTS

Statistical Office of the United Nations, Publishing Service, New York, New York 10017 (800) 253-9646; *Trade in Manufactures of Developing Countries.*

COLOMBIA - LIBRARIES

Facts on File, 460 Park Avenue South, New York, New York 10016 (800) 443-8323; *The New Book of World Rankings.*

United Nations Educational, Scientific and Cultural Organization (UNESCO), 7 Place de Fontenoy, F-75700 Paris, France (Telephone Number in U.S. (518) 436-9686); *Statistical Yearbook.*

COLOMBIA - LIFE EXPECTANCY RATE

The Economist Intelligence Unit, 111 West 57th Street, New York, New York 10019 (800) 938-4685; *The New Latin America Market Atlas.*

COLOMBIA - LIGNITE PRODUCTION - See COLOMBIA - MINING AND MINERAL PRODUCTS

COLOMBIA - LIVESTOCK AND POULTRY

Commodity Research Bureau, Incorporated, 75 Wall Street, New York, New York 10005 (212) 504-7754; *Commodity Year Book.*

Euromonitor Publications Limited, 87-88 Turnmill Street, London, EC1M 5QU, England; *International Marketing Data and Statistics.*

Facts on File, 460 Park Avenue South, New York, New York 10016 (800) 443-8323; *The New Book of World Rankings.*

Food and Agricultural Organization of the United Nations (FAO), Via delle Terme di Caracalla, 00100 Rome, Italy (Telephone Number in U.S. (202) 653-2400); *Production Yearbook,* and *The State of Food and Agriculture.*

G.K. Hall and Company, 70 Lincoln Street, Boston, Massachusetts 02111 (617) 423-3990; *The World in Figures.*

Statistical Office of the United Nations, Publishing Service, New York, New York 10017 (800) 253-9646; *Statistical Yearbook,* and *Survey of Economic and Social Conditions in Africa.*

COLOMBIA - LIVING LEVELS

G.K. Hall and Company, 70 Lincoln Street, Boston, Massachusetts 02111 (617) 423-3990; *The World in Figures.*

Statistical Office of the United Nations, Publishing Service, New York, New York 10017 (800) 253-9646; *Statistical Yearbook for Latin America and the Caribbean.*

Times Books, 201 East 50th Street, New York, New York 10022 (212) 751-2600; *The Economist Book of Vital World Statistics.*

COLOMBIA - MAIL TRAFFIC - NUMBER OF ITEMS

Statistical Office of the United Nations, Publishing Service, New York, New York 10017 (800) 253-9646; *Statistical Yearbook.*

COLOMBIA - MAIN ECONOMIC INDICATORS - See COLOMBIA - ECONOMY

COLOMBIA - MAIN INDICATORS - See COLOMBIA - ECONOMY

COLOMBIA - MANUFACTURING

American Automobile Manufacturers Association, 1401 H Street, NW, Suite 900, Washington, D.C. 20005 (202) 326-5500; *World Motor Vehicle Data.*

The Economist Intelligence Unit, 111 West 57th Street, New York, New York 10019 (800) 938-4685; *The New Latin America Market Atlas.*

Euromonitor Publications Limited, 87-88 Turnmill Street, London EC1M 5QU, England; *Third World Economic Handbook.*

Facts on File, 460 Park Avenue South, New York, New York 10016 (800) 443-8323; *The New Book of World Rankings*.

G.K. Hall and Company, 70 Lincoln Street, Boston, Massachusetts 02111 (617) 423-3990; *The World in Figures*.

Inter-American Development Bank, 1300 New York Avenue, NW, Washington, D.C. 20577 (202) 623-1753; *Economic and Social Progress in Latin America*.

Statistical Office of the United Nations, Publishing Service, New York, New York 10017 (800) 253-9646; *Statistical Yearbook*, and *Statistical Yearbook for Latin America and the Caribbean*.

Times Books, 201 East 50th Street, New York, New York 10022 (212) 751-2600; *The Economist Book of Vital World Statistics*.

COLOMBIA - MARRIAGE RATES

Facts on File, 460 Park Avenue South, New York, New York 10016 (800) 443-8323; *The New Book of World Rankings*.

Statistical Office of the United Nations, Publishing Service, New York, New York 10017 (800) 253-9646; *Demographic Yearbook*, and *Statistical Yearbook*.

COLOMBIA - MEAT PRODUCTION - See COLOMBIA - LIVESTOCK AND POULTRY

COLOMBIA - MEDICAL PERSONNEL

U.C.L.A. Latin American Center Publications, University of California, Los Angeles, California 90024 (310) 825-6634; *Statistical Abstract of Latin America*.

COLOMBIA - MERCHANT SHIPPING

G.K. Hall and Company, 70 Lincoln Street, Boston, Massachusetts 02111 (617) 423-3990; *The World in Figures*.

Lloyd's Register of Shipping, 17 Battery Place, New York, New York 10004 (212) 425-8050; *Register of Ships*.

Statistical Office of the United Nations, Publishing Service, New York, New York 10017 (800) 253-9646; *Statistical Yearbook*.

Times Books, 201 East 50th Street, New York, New York 10022 (212) 751-2600; *The Economist Book of Vital World Statistics*.

U.S. Department of Transportation, Maritime Administration, 400 Seventh Street, SW, Washington, D.C. 20590; *A Statistical Analysis of the World's Merchant Fleets*.

COLOMBIA - MERCURY PRODUCTION AND CONSUMPTION - See COLOMBIA - MINING AND MINERAL PRODUCTS

COLOMBIA - MILITARY

The Economist Intelligence Unit, 111 West 57th Street, New York, New York 10019 (800) 938-4685; *The New Latin America Market Atlas*.

G.K. Hall and Company, 70 Lincoln Street, Boston, Massachusetts 02111 (617) 423-3990; *The World in Figures*.

The International Institute for Strategic Studies, 23 Tavistock Street, London WC2E 7NQ, England; *The Military Balance*.

U.C.L.A. Latin American Center Publications, University of California, Los Angeles, California 90024 (310) 825-6634; *Statistical Abstract of Latin America*.

U.S. Arms Control and Disarmament Agency, 320 Twenty-first Street, NW, Washington, D.C. 20451 (202) 647-8677; *World Military Expenditures and Arms Transfers*.

COLOMBIA - MILK PRODUCTION - See COLOMBIA - DAIRY PRODUCTS

COLOMBIA - MINING AND MINERAL PRODUCTS

Commodity Research Bureau, Incorporated, 75 Wall Street, New York, New York 10005 (212) 504-7754; *Commodity Year Book*.

The Economist Intelligence Unit, 111 West 57th Street, New York, New York 10019 (800) 938-4685; *The New Latin America Market Atlas*.

Facts on File, 460 Park Avenue South, New York, New York 10016 (800) 443-8323; *The New Book of World Rankings*.

G.K. Hall and Company, 70 Lincoln Street, Boston, Massachusetts 02111 (617) 423-3990; *The World in Figures*.

Inter-American Development Bank, 1300 New York Avenue, NW, Washington, D.C. 20577 (202) 623-1753; *Economic and Social Progress in Latin America*.

Penn Well Publishing Company, 1421 South Sheridan Road, P.O. Box 1260, Tulsa, Oklahoma 74101 (800) 752-9764; *International Energy Statistics Sourcebook*.

Statistical Office of the United Nations, Publishing Service, New York, New York 10017 (800) 253-9646; *Statistical Yearbook*.

U.C.L.A. Latin American Center Publications, University of California, Los Angeles, California 90024 (310) 825-6634; *Statistical Abstract of Latin America*.

COLOMBIA - MONEY EXCHANGE RATE

Euromonitor Publications Limited, 87-88 Turnmill Street, London, EC1M 5QU, England; *International Marketing Data and Statistics*.

Inter-American Development Bank, 1300 New York Avenue, NW, Washington, D.C. 20577 (202) 623-1753; *Economic and Social Progress in Latin America*.

International Monetary Fund, 700 Nineteenth Street, NW, Washington, D.C. 20431 (202) 623-7000; *International Financial Statistics*.

Statistical Office of the United Nations, Publishing Service, New York, New York 10017 (800) 253-9646; *Statistical Yearbook*.

COLOMBIA - MONEY RATES - MARKET

Inter-American Development Bank, 1300 New York Avenue, NW, Washington, D.C. 20577 (202) 623-1753; *Economic and Social Progress in Latin America*.

COLOMBIA - MONEY RESERVES

Euromonitor Publications Limited, 87-88 Turnmill Street, London, EC1M 5QU, England; *International Marketing Data and Statistics*.

Inter-American Development Bank, 1300 New York Avenue, NW, Washington, D.C. 20577 (202) 623-1753; *Economic and Social Progress in Latin America.*

COLOMBIA - MONEY SUPPLY

Euromonitor Publications Limited, 87-88 Turnmill Street, London, EC1M 5QU, England; *International Marketing Data and Statistics.*

Federal Statistical Office, Gustav - Stresemann - Ring 11, D-6200 Wiesbaden, Germany; *Kolumbien.*

G.K. Hall and Company, 70 Lincoln Street, Boston, Massachusetts 02111 (617) 423-3990; *The World in Figures.*

Inter-American Development Bank, 1300 New York Avenue, NW, Washington, D.C. 20577 (202) 623-1753; *Economic and Social Progress in Latin America.*

International Monetary Fund, 700 Nineteenth Street, NW, Washington, D.C. 20431 (202) 623-7000; *International Financial Statistics.*

Statistical Office of the United Nations, Publishing Service, New York, New York 10017 (800) 253-9646; *Statistical Yearbook.*

U.C.L.A. Latin American Center Publications, University of California, Los Angeles, California 90024 (310) 825-6634; *Statistical Abstract of Latin America.*

COLOMBIA - MONUMENTS AND HISTORICAL SITES

United Nations Educational, Scientific and Cultural Organization (UNESCO), 7 Place de Fontenoy, F-75700 Paris, France (Telephone Number in U.S. (518) 436-9686); *Statistical Yearbook.*

COLOMBIA - MOTION PICTURES

Statistical Office of the United Nations, Publishing Service, New York, New York 10017 (800) 253-9646; *Statistical Yearbook.*

United Nations Educational, Scientific and Cultural Organization (UNESCO), 7 Place de Fontenoy, F-75700 Paris, France (Telephone Number in U.S. (518) 436-9686); *Statistical Yearbook.*

COLOMBIA - MOTOR VEHICLE ASSEMBLY

Statistical Office of the United Nations, Publishing Service, New York, New York 10017 (800) 253-9646; *Statistical Yearbook.*

COLOMBIA - MOTOR VEHICLE PRODUCTION

American Automobile Manufacturers Association, 1401 H Street, NW, Washington, D.C. 20005 (202) 326-5500; *World Motor Vehicle Data.*

COLOMBIA - MOTOR VEHICLE TAXES - See COLOMBIA - TAXATION

COLOMBIA - MOTOR VEHICLES IN USE

American Automobile Manufacturers Association, 1401 H Street, NW, Suite 900, Washington, D.C. 20005 (202) 326-5500; *World Motor Vehicle Data.*

The Economist Intelligence Unit, 111 West 57th Street, New York, New York 10019 (800) 938-4685; *The New Latin America Market Atlas.*

G.K. Hall and Company, 70 Lincoln Street, Boston, Massachusetts 02111 (617) 423-3990; *The World in Figures.*

International Road Federation, 525 School Street, SW, Washington, D.C. 20024 (202) 554-2106; *World Road Statistics.*

Statistical Office of the United Nations, Publishing Service, New York, New York 10017 (800) 253-9646; *Statistical Yearbook.*

Times Books, 201 East 50th Street, New York, New York 10022 (212) 751-2600; *The Economist Book of Vital World Statistics.*

COLOMBIA - MULES - See COLOMBIA - LIVESTOCK AND POULTRY

COLOMBIA - MUSEUMS

Facts on File, 460 Park Avenue South, New York, New York 10016 (800) 443-8323; *The New Book of World Rankings.*

United Nations Educational, Scientific and Cultural Organization (UNESCO), 7 Place de Fontenoy, F-75700 Paris, France (Telephone Number in U.S. (518) 436-9686); *Statistical Yearbook.*

COLOMBIA - NATALITY - See COLOMBIA - BIRTH RATE

COLOMBIA - NATIONAL ACCOUNTS

Federal Statistical Office, Gustav - Stresemann - Ring 11, D-6200 Wiesbaden, Germany; *Kolumbien.*

Gale Research Incorporated, 835 Penobscot Building, Detroit, Michigan 48226 (800) 877-4253; *International Historical Statistics The Americas and Australasia.*

Inter-American Development Bank, 1300 New York Avenue, NW, Washington, D.C. 20577 (202) 623-1753; *Economic and Social Progress in Latin America.*

Organization of American States (OAS), General Secretariat, Washington, D.C. 20006 (202) 458-3533; *Statistical Bulletin of the OAS.*

Statistical Office of the United Nations, Publishing Service, New York, New York 10017 (800) 253-9646; *National Accounts Statistics,* and *Statistical Yearbook.*

U.C.L.A. Latin American Center Publications, University of California, Los Angeles, California 90024 (310) 825-6634; *Statistical Abstract of Latin America.*

COLOMBIA - NATIONAL INCOME

Facts on File, 460 Park Avenue South, New York, New York 10016 (800) 443-8323; *The New Book of World Rankings.*

G.K. Hall and Company, 70 Lincoln Street, Boston, Massachusetts 02111 (617) 423-3990; *The World in Figures.*

Inter-American Development Bank, 1300 New York Avenue, NW, Washington, D.C. 20577 (202) 623-1753; *Economic and Social Progress in Latin America.*

Statistical Office of the United Nations, Publishing Service, New York, New York 10017 (800) 253-9646; *Statistical Yearbook,* and *Statistical Yearbook for Latin America and the Caribbean.*

COLOMBIA - NATIONAL PRODUCT

Facts on File, 460 Park Avenue South, New York, New York 10016 (800) 443-8323; *The New Book of World Rankings*.

Statistical Office of the United Nations, Publishing Service, New York, New York 10017 (800) 253-9646; *Statistical Yearbook*.

COLOMBIA - NATURAL GAS PRODUCTION - See COLOMBIA - MINING AND MINERAL PRODUCTS

COLOMBIA - NEWSPAPER PRODUCTION - See COLOMBIA - FORESTRY AND FOREST PRODUCTS

COLOMBIA - NITRIC ACID PRODUCTION - See COLOMBIA - MINING AND MINERAL PRODUCTS

COLOMBIA - NUTRITION

Statistical Office of the United Nations, Publishing Service, New York, New York 10017 (800) 253-9646; *Statistical Yearbook for Latin America and the Caribbean*.

COLOMBIA - OCCUPATIONS - See COLOMBIA - LABOR FORCE

COLOMBIA - PALM OIL PRODUCTION - See COLOMBIA - CROPS

COLOMBIA - PAPER PRODUCTION AND CONSUMPTION - See COLOMBIA - FORESTRY AND FOREST PRODUCTS

COLOMBIA - PATENTS

Statistical Office of the United Nations, Publishing Service, New York, New York 10017 (800) 253-9646; *Statistical Yearbook*.

World Intellectual Property Organization, 34 Chemin des Colombettes, CH-1211 Geneva 20. Switzerland; *Industrial Property Statistics*.

COLOMBIA - PEANUT PRODUCTION - See COLOMBIA - CROPS

COLOMBIA - PERIODICALS

United Nations Educational, Scientific and Cultural Organization (UNESCO), 7 Place de Fontenoy, F-75700 Paris, France (Telephone Number in U.S. (518) 436-9686); *Statistical Yearbook*, section on Printed Materials.

COLOMBIA - PESTICIDE USE

Food and Agricultural Organization of the United Nations (FAO) Via delle Terme di Caracalla, 00100 Rome, Italy (Telephone Number in U.S. (202) 653-2400); *The State of Food and Agriculture*.

COLOMBIA - PETROLEUM INDUSTRY

The Economist Intelligence Unit, 111 West 57th Street, New York, New York 10019 (800) 938-4685; *The New Latin America Market Atlas*.

Facts on File, 460 Park Avenue South, New York, New York 10016 (800) 443-8323; *The New Book of World Rankings*.

Food and Agricultural Organization of the United Nations (FAO) Via delle Terme di Caracalla, 00100 Rome, Italy (Telephone Number in U.S. (202) 653-2400); *The State of Food and Agriculture*.

G.K. Hall and Company, 70 Lincoln Street, Boston, Massachusetts 02111 (617) 423-3990; *The World in Figures*.

Inter-American Development Bank, 1300 New York Avenue, NW, Washington, D.C. 20577 (202) 623-1753; *Economic and Social Progress in Latin America*.

International Monetary Fund, 700 Nineteenth Street, NW, Washington, D.C. 20431 (202) 623-7000; *International Financial Statistics*.

Penn Well Publishing Company, 1421 South Sheridan Road, P.O. Box 1260, Tulsa, Oklahoma 74101 (800) 752-9764; *International Energy Statistics Sourcebook*.

Statistical Office of the United Nations, Publishing Service, New York, New York 10017 (800) 253-9646; *Statistical Yearbook*.

Organization of American States (OAS), General Secretariat, Washington, D.C. 20006 (202) 458-3533; *Statistical Bulletin of the OAS*.

Statistical Office of the United Nations, Publishing Service, New York, New York 10017 (800) 253-9646; *Statistical Yearbook*.

COLOMBIA - PHOSPHATE ROCK PRODUCTION - See COLOMBIA - MINING AND MINERAL PRODUCTS

COLOMBIA - PIG-IRON AND FERRO-ALLOY PRODUCTION - See COLOMBIA - MINING AND MINERAL PRODUCTS

COLOMBIA - PIGS - See COLOMBIA - LIVESTOCK AND POULTRY

COLOMBIA - PLASTIC AND RESIN PRODUCTION

Euromonitor Publications Limited, 87-88 Turnmill Street, London EC1M 5QU, England; *Third World Economic Handbook*.

Statistical Office of the United Nations, Publishing Service, New York, New York 10017 (800) 253-9646; *Statistical Yearbook*.

COLOMBIA - PLATINUM PRODUCTION - See COLOMBIA - MINING AND MINERAL PRODUCTS

COLOMBIA - POLITICAL DATA

U.C.L.A. Latin American Center Publications, University of California, Los Angeles, California 90024 (310) 825-6634; *Statistical Abstract of Latin America*.

COLOMBIA - POPULATION

The Economist Intelligence Unit, 111 West 57th Street, New York, New York 10019 (800) 938-4685; *The New Latin America Market Atlas*, and *The World Market Atlas*.

Euromonitor Publications Limited, 87-88 Turnmill Street, London, EC1M 5QU, England; *International Marketing Data and Statistics*, and *Third World Economic Handbook*.

Facts on File, 460 Park Avenue South, New York, New York 10016 (800) 443-8323; *The New Book of World Rankings*.

Federal Statistical Office, Gustav - Stresemann - Ring 11, D-6200 Wiesbaden, Germany; *Kolumbien*.

Food and Agricultural Organization of the United Nations (FAO), Via delle Terme di Caracalla, 00100 Rome, Italy (Telephone Number in U.S. (202) 653-2400); *Production Yearbook*.

Gale Research Incorporated, 835 Penobscot Building, Detroit, Michigan 48226 (800) 877-4253; *International Historical Statistics*

The Americas and Australasia.

G.K. Hall and Company, 70 Lincoln Street, Boston, Massachusetts 02111 (617) 423-3990; *The World in Figures.*

Inter-American Development Bank, 1300 New York Avenue, NW, Washington, D.C. 20577 (202) 623-1753; *Economic and Social Progress in Latin America.*

International Labour Office, I.L.O. Publications, CH-1211, Geneva 22, Switzerland; *Yearbook of Labour Statistics.*

Organization of American States (OAS), General Secretariat, Washington, D.C. 20006 (202) 458-3533; *Statistical Bulletin of the OAS.*

Statistical Office of the United Nations, Publishing Service, New York, New York 10017 (800) 253-9646; *Demographic Yearbook, Statistical Yearbook,* and *Statistical Yearbook for Latin America and the Caribbean.*

Times Books, 201 East 50th Street, New York, New York 10022 (212) 751-2600; *The Economist Book of Vital World Statistics.*

U.C.L.A. Latin American Center Publications, University of California, Los Angeles, California 90024 (310) 825-6634; *Statistical Abstract of Latin America.*

United Nations Educational, Scientific and Cultural Organization (UNESCO), 7 Place de Fontenoy, F-75700 Paris, France (Telephone Number in U.S. (518) 436-9686); *Statistical Yearbook.*

U.S. Arms Control and Disarmament Agency, 320 Twenty-first Street, NW, Washington, D.C. 20451 (202) 647-8677; *World Military Expenditures and Arms Transfers.*

World Health Organization, Office of Publications, Avenue Appia, CH-1211 Geneva 27, Switzerland (Telephone Number in U.S. (518) 436-9686); *World Health Statistics Annual.*

COLOMBIA - POST OFFICES

Facts on File, 460 Park Avenue South, New York, New York 10016 (800) 443-8323; *The New Book of World Rankings.*

COLOMBIA - POTATO PRODUCTION - See COLOMBIA - CROPS

COLOMBIA - PRICES

Facts on File, 460 Park Avenue South, New York, New York 10016 (800) 443-8323; *The New Book of World Rankings.*

Federal Statistical Office, Gustav - Stresemann - Ring 11, D-6200 Wiesbaden, Germany; *Kolumbien.*

Food and Agricultural Organization of the United Nations (FAO), Via delle Terme di Caracalla, 00100 Rome, Italy (Telephone Number in U.S. (202) 653-2400); *Production Yearbook,* and *The State of Food and Agriculture.*

Gale Research Incorporated, 835 Penobscot Building, Detroit, Michigan 48226 (800) 877-4253; *International Historical Statistics The Americas and Australasia.*

G.K. Hall and Company, 70 Lincoln Street, Boston, Massachusetts 02111 (617) 423-3990; *The World in Figures.*

International Labour Office, I.L.O. Publications, CH-1211, Geneva 22, Switzerland; *Yearbook of Labour Statistics.*

International Monetary Fund, 700 Nineteenth Street, NW, Washington, D.C. 20431 (202) 623-7000; *International Financial Statistics.*

Statistical Office of the United Nations, Publishing Service, New York, New York 10017 (800) 253-9646; *Economic Survey of Latin America and the Caribbean,* and *Statistical Yearbook for Latin America and the Caribbean.*

COLOMBIA - PRINTING AND WRITING PAPER - See COLOMBIA - FORESTRY AND FOREST PRODUCTS

COLOMBIA - PRODUCTION

American Automobile Manufacturers Association, 1401 H Street, NW, Suite 900, Washington, D.C. 20005 (202) 326-5500;; *World Motor Vehicle Data.*

Euromonitor Publications Limited, 87-88 Turnmill Street, London EC1M 5QU, England; *Third World Economic Handbook.*

Facts on File, 460 Park Avenue South, New York, New York 10016 (800) 443-8323; *The New Book of World Rankings.*

G.K. Hall and Company, 70 Lincoln Street, Boston, Massachusetts 02111 (617) 423-3990; *The World in Figures.*

COLOMBIA - PRODUCTIVITY

Euromonitor Publications Limited, 87-88 Turnmill Street, London, EC1M 5QU, England; *International Marketing Data and Statistics.*

COLOMBIA - PROPERTY TAXES - See COLOMBIA - TAXATION

COLOMBIA - PUBLIC CONSUMPTION FUND

Inter-American Development Bank, 1300 New York Avenue, NW, Washington, D.C. 20577 (202) 623-1753; *Economic and Social Progress in Latin America.*

COLOMBIA - PUBLIC EXPENDITURES

Inter-American Development Bank, 1300 New York Avenue, NW, Washington, D.C. 20577 (202) 623-1753; *Economic and Social Progress in Latin America.*

Organization of American States (OAS), General Secretariat, Washington, D.C. 20006 (202) 458-3533; *Statistical Bulletin of the OAS.*

Statistical Office of the United Nations, Publishing Service, New York, New York 10017 (800) 253-9646; *Statistical Yearbook for Latin America and the Caribbean.*

COLOMBIA - PUBLIC FINANCES

Facts on File, 460 Park Avenue South, New York, New York 10016 (800) 443-8323; *The New Book of World Rankings.*

Federal Statistical Office, Gustav - Stresemann - Ring 11, D-6200 Wiesbaden, Germany; *Kolumbien.*

Inter-American Development Bank, 1300 New York Avenue, NW, Washington, D.C. 20577 (202) 623-1753; *Economic and Social Progress in Latin America.*

Organization of American States (OAS), General Secretariat, Washington, D.C. 20006 (202) 458-3533; *Statistical Bulletin of the OAS.*

COLOMBIA - PUBLIC REVENUES

Inter-American Development Bank, 1300 New York Avenue, NW, Washington, D.C. 20577 (202) 623-1753; *Economic and Social Progress in Latin America.*

Organization of American States (OAS), General Secretariat, Washington, D.C. 20006 (202) 458-3533; *Statistical Bulletin of the OAS.*

COLOMBIA - RADIO BROADCASTING - See COLOMBIA - BROADCASTING

COLOMBIA - RADIO RECEIVER PRODUCTION

Statistical Office of the United Nations, Publishing Service, New York, New York 10017 (800) 253-9646; *Statistical Yearbook.*

COLOMBIA - RAILWAYS

The Economist Intelligence Unit, 111 West 57th Street, New York, New York 10019 (800) 938-4685; *The New Latin America Market Atlas.*

G.K. Hall and Company, 70 Lincoln Street, Boston, Massachusetts 02111 (617) 423-3990; *The World in Figures.*

Jane's Information Group, Sentinel House, 163 Brighton Road, Coulsdon, Surrey CR5 2NH, England (Telephone Number in U.S. (703) 683-3700); *Jane's World Railways.*

Statistical Office of the United Nations, Publishing Service, New York, New York 10017 (800) 253-9646; *Statistical Yearbook.*

COLOMBIA - RELIGION

Facts on File, 460 Park Avenue South, New York, New York 10016 (800) 443-8323; *The New Book of World Rankings.*

U.C.L.A. Latin American Center Publications, University of California, Los Angeles, California 90024 (310) 825-6634; *Statistical Abstract of Latin America.*

COLOMBIA - RENT PRICES

International Labour Office, I.L.O. Publications, CH-1211, Geneva 22, Switzerland; *Yearbook of Labour Statistics.*

COLOMBIA - RESERVES EXCLUDING GOLD

The Economist Intelligence Unit, 111 West 57th Street, New York, New York 10019 (800) 938-4685; *The New Latin America Market Atlas.*

COLOMBIA - RETAIL TRADE

Euromonitor Publications Limited, 87-88 Turnmill Street, London EC1M 5QU, England; *Third World Economic Handbook.*

G.K. Hall and Company, 70 Lincoln Street, Boston, Massachusetts 02111 (617) 423-3990; *The World in Figures.*

Inter-American Development Bank, 1300 New York Avenue, NW, Washington, D.C. 20577 (202) 623-1753; *Economic and Social Progress in Latin America.*

Statistical Office of the United Nations, Publishing Service, New York, New York 10017 (800) 253-9646; *Statistical Yearbook.*

COLOMBIA - RICE PRODUCTION - See COLOMBIA - CROPS

COLOMBIA - ROOT AND TUBER PRODUCTION - See COLOMBIA - CROPS

COLOMBIA - ROUNDWOOD PRODUCTION - See COLOMBIA - FORESTRY AND FOREST PRODUCTS

COLOMBIA - RUBBER PRODUCTION

Euromonitor Publications Limited, 87-88 Turnmill Street, London EC1M 5QU, England; *Third World Economic Handbook.*

Facts on File, 460 Park Avenue South, New York, New York 10016 (800) 443-8323; *The New Book of World Rankings.*

COLOMBIA - SALT PRODUCTION - See COLOMBIA - MINING AND MINERAL PRODUCTS

COLOMBIA - SAWNWOOD PRODUCTION - See COLOMBIA - FORESTRY AND FOREST PRODUCTS

COLOMBIA - SCIENCE AND TECHNOLOGY

U.C.L.A. Latin American Center Publications, University of California, Los Angeles, California 90024 (310) 825-6634; *Statistical Abstract of Latin America.*

COLOMBIA - SCIENTISTS AND TECHNICIANS

Statistical Office of the United Nations, Publishing Service, New York, New York 10017 (800) 253-9646; *Statistical Yearbook.*

COLOMBIA - SENIOR CITIZENS

Facts on File, 460 Park Avenue South, New York, New York 10016 (800) 443-8323; *The New Book of World Rankings.*

COLOMBIA - SESAME SEED PRODUCTION - See COLOMBIA - CROPS

COLOMBIA - SHEEP - See COLOMBIA - LIVESTOCK AND POULTRY

COLOMBIA - SILVER PRODUCTION AND CONSUMPTION - See COLOMBIA - MINING AND MINERAL PRODUCTS

COLOMBIA - SOCIAL DATA

Facts on File, 460 Park Avenue South, New York, New York 10016 (800) 443-8323; *The New Book of World Rankings.*

G.K. Hall and Company, 70 Lincoln Street, Boston, Massachusetts 02111 (617) 423-3990; *The World in Figures.*

U.C.L.A. Latin American Center Publications, University of California, Los Angeles, California 90024 (310) 825-6634; *Statistical Abstract of Latin America.*

COLOMBIA - SOCIAL SECURITY

Inter-American Development Bank, 1300 New York Avenue, NW, Washington, D.C. 20577 (202) 623-1753; *Economic and Social Progress in Latin America.*

COLOMBIA - SOCIOECONOMIC DATA

Inter-American Development Bank, 1300 New York Avenue, NW, Washington, D.C. 20577 (202) 623-1753; *Economic and Social Progress in Latin America.*

U.C.L.A. Latin American Center Publications, University of California, Los Angeles, California 90024 (310) 825-6634; *Statistical Abstract of Latin America.*

COLOMBIA - SOYBEAN PRODUCTION - See COLOMBIA - CROPS

COLOMBIA - STAMP TAXES AND DUTIES - See COLOMBIA - TAXATION

COLOMBIA - STATE BUDGET REVENUE AND EXPENDITURES

Euromonitor Publications Limited, 87-88 Turnmill Street, London, EC1M 5QU, England; *International Marketing Data and Statistics.*

Inter-American Development Bank, 1300 New York Avenue, NW, Washington, D.C. 20577 (202) 623-1753; *Economic and Social Progress in Latin America.*

COLOMBIA - STEEL - See COLOMBIA - MINING AND MINERAL PRODUCTS

COLOMBIA - STOCKS - COMMODITY - MARKET PRICE - INDEXES

Food and Agricultural Organization of the United Nations (FAO) Via delle Terme di Caracalla, 00100 Rome, Italy (Telephone Number in U.S. (202) 653-2400); *The State of Food and Agriculture.*

Statistical Office of the United Nations, Publishing Service, New York, New York 10017 (800) 253-9646; *Statistical Yearbook.*

COLOMBIA - SUGAR - See COLOMBIA - CROPS

COLOMBIA - SULPHURIC ACID PRODUCTION - See COLOMBIA - MINING AND MINERAL PRODUCTS

COLOMBIA - TAXATION

G.K. Hall and Company, 70 Lincoln Street, Boston, Massachusetts 02111 (617) 423-3990; *The World in Figures.*

Inter-American Development Bank, 1300 New York Avenue, NW, Washington, D.C. 20577 (202) 623-1753; *Economic and Social Progress in Latin America.*

International Monetary Fund, 700 Nineteenth Street, NW, Washington, D.C. 20431 (202) 623-7000; *Government Finance Statistics Yearbook.*

International Road Federation, 525 School Street, SW, Washington, D.C. 20024 (202) 554-2106; *World Road Statistics.*

Statistical Office of the United Nations, Publishing Service, New York, New York 10017 (800) 253-9646; *Statistical Yearbook for Latin America and the Caribbean.*

COLOMBIA - TELEGRAPH SERVICE

Statistical Office of the United Nations, Publishing Service, New York, New York 10017 (800) 253-9646; *Statistical Yearbook.*

COLOMBIA - TELEPHONES IN USE

American Telephone and Telegraph Company, 26 Parsippany Road, Whippany, New Jersey 07981; *The World's Telephones.*

The Economist Intelligence Unit, 111 West 57th Street, New York, New York 10019 (800) 938-4685; *The New Latin America Market Atlas.*

Euromonitor Publications Limited, 87-88 Turnmill Street, London EC1M 5QU, England; *Third World Economic Handbook.*

G.K. Hall and Company, 70 Lincoln Street, Boston, Massachusetts 02111 (617) 423-3990; *The World in Figures.*

Statistical Office of the United Nations, Publishing Service, New York, New York 10017 (800) 253-9646; *Statistical Yearbook.*

COLOMBIA - TELEVISION BROADCASTING - See COLOMBIA - BROADCASTING

COLOMBIA - TELEVISION RECEIVER PRODUCTION

Statistical Office of the United Nations, Publishing Service, New York, New York 10017 (800) 253-9646; *Statistical Yearbook.*

COLOMBIA - TEXTILE INDUSTRY

Euromonitor Publications Limited, 87-88 Turnmill Street, London EC1M 5QU, England; *Third World Economic Handbook.*

Forest and Paper Association, 1250 Connecticut Avenue, NW, Washington, D.C. 20036 (202) 463-2455; *Wood Pulp and Fiber Statistics.*

G.K. Hall and Company, 70 Lincoln Street, Boston, Massachusetts 02111 (617) 423-3990; *The World in Figures.*

Statistical Office of the United Nations, Publishing Service, New York, New York 10017 (800) 253-9646; *Trade in Manufactures of Developing Countries,* and *Statistical Yearbook.*

COLOMBIA - THEATRE

United Nations Educational, Scientific and Cultural Organization (UNESCO), 7 Place de Fontenoy, F-75700 Paris, France (Telephone Number in U.S. (518) 436-9686); *Statistical Yearbook.*

COLOMBIA - TIN - INDUSTRIAL CONSUMPTION - See COLOMBIA - MINING AND MINERAL PRODUCTS

COLOMBIA - TIRE (MOTOR VEHICLE) PRODUCTION

Statistical Office of the United Nations, Publishing Service, New York, New York 10017 (800) 253-9646; *Statistical Yearbook.*

COLOMBIA - TOBACCO PRODUCTION

Euromonitor Publications Limited, 87-88 Turnmill Street, London EC1M 5QU, England; *Third World Economic Handbook.*

Facts on File, 460 Park Avenue South, New York, New York 10016 (800) 443-8323; *The New Book of World Rankings.*

Statistical Office of the United Nations, Publishing Service, New York, New York 10017 (800) 253-9646; *Statistical Yearbook.*

COLOMBIA - TOURISM

The Economist Intelligence Unit, 111 West 57th Street, New York, New York 10019 (800) 938-4685; *The New Latin America Market Atlas.*

Euromonitor Publications Limited, 87-88 Turnmill Street, London EC1M 5QU, England; *Third World Economic Handbook.*

Facts on File, 460 Park Avenue South, New York, New York 10016 (800) 443-8323; *The New Book of World Rankings.*

Federal Statistical Office, Gustav - Stresemann - Ring 11, D-6200 Wiesbaden, Germany; *Kolumbien.*

G.K. Hall and Company, 70 Lincoln Street, Boston, Massachusetts 02111 (617) 423-3990; *The World in Figures.*

Statistical Office of the United Nations, Publishing Service, New York, New York 10017 (800) 253-9646; *Statistical Yearbook,* and *Statistical Yearbook for Latin America and the Caribbean.*

Times Books, 201 East 50th Street, New York, New York 10022 (212) 751-2600; *The Economist Book of Vital World Statistics.*

U.C.L.A. Latin American Center Publications, University of California, Los Angeles, California 90024 (310) 825-6634; *Statistical Abstract of Latin America.*

World Tourism Organization, Calle Capitan Haya 42, E-28020 Madrid, Spain; *Yearbook of Tourism Statistics.*

COLOMBIA - TRACTORS IN USE

The Economist Intelligence Unit, 111 West 57th Street, New York, New York 10019 (800) 938-4685; *The New Latin America Market Atlas.*

Statistical Office of the United Nations, Publishing Service, New York, New York 10017 (800) 253-9646; *Statistical Yearbook.*

COLOMBIA - TRADE - See COLOMBIA - FOREIGN TRADE

COLOMBIA - TRADEMARKS AND SERVICE MARKS

Statistical Office of the United Nations, Publishing Service, New York, New York 10017 (800) 253-9646; *Statistical Yearbook.*

World Intellectual Property Organization, 34 Chemin des Colombettes, CH-1211 Geneva 20. Switzerland; *Industrial Property Statistics.*

COLOMBIA - TRANSPORTATION AND COMMUNICATIONS

The Economist Intelligence Unit, 111 West 57th Street, New York, New York 10019 (800) 938-4685; *The New Latin America Market Atlas.*

Euromonitor Publications Limited, 87-88 Turnmill Street, London EC1M 5QU, England; *Third World Economic Handbook.*

Facts on File, 460 Park Avenue South, New York, New York 10016 (800) 443-8323; *The New Book of World Rankings.*

Federal Statistical Office, Gustav - Stresemann - Ring 11, D-6200 Wiesbaden, Germany; *Kolumbien.*

Gale Research Incorporated, 835 Penobscot Building, Detroit, Michigan 48226 (800) 877-4253; *International Historical Statistics The Americas and Australasia.*

G.K. Hall and Company, 70 Lincoln Street, Boston, Massachusetts 02111 (617) 423-3990; *The World in Figures.*

Inter-American Development Bank, 1300 New York Avenue, NW, Washington, D.C. 20577 (202) 623-1753; *Economic and Social Progress in Latin America.*

Statistical Office of the United Nations, Publishing Service, New York, New York 10017 (800) 253-9646; *Statistical Yearbook for Latin America and the Caribbean.*

U.C.L.A. Latin American Center Publications, University of California, Los Angeles, California 90024 (310) 825-6634; *Statistical Abstract of Latin America.*

COLOMBIA - UNEMPLOYMENT

The Economist Intelligence Unit, 111 West 57th Street, New York, New York 10019 (800) 938-4685; *The New Latin America Market Atlas.*

Euromonitor Publications Limited, 87-88 Turnmill Street, London, EC1M 5QU, England; *International Marketing Data and Statistics.*

International Labour Office, I.L.O. Publications, CH-1211, Geneva 22, Switzerland; *Yearbook of Labour Statistics.*

Statistical Office of the United Nations, Publishing Service, New York, New York 10017 (800) 253-9646; *Statistical Yearbook.*

U.C.L.A. Latin American Center Publications, University of California, Los Angeles, California 90024 (310) 825-6634; *Statistical Abstract of Latin America.*

COLOMBIA - UTILITIES

U.C.L.A. Latin American Center Publications, University of California, Los Angeles, California 90024 (310) 825-6634; *Statistical Abstract of Latin America.*

COLOMBIA - VITAL STATISTICS

Euromonitor Publications Limited, 87-88 Turnmill Street, London, EC1M 5QU, England; *International Marketing Data and Statistics,* and *Third World Economic Handbook,* and *Third World Economic Handbook.*

G.K. Hall and Company, 70 Lincoln Street, Boston, Massachusetts 02111 (617) 423-3990; *The World in Figures.*

Gale Research Incorporated, 835 Penobscot Building, Detroit, Michigan 48226 (800) 877-4253; *International Historical Statistics The Americas and Australasia.*

Statistical Office of the United Nations, Publishing Service, New York, New York 10017 (800) 253-9646; *Statistical Yearbook.*

World Health Organization, Office of Publications, Avenue Appia, CH-1211 Geneva 27, Switzerland (Telephone Number in U.S. (518) 436-9686); *World Health Statistics Annual.*

COLOMBIA - WAGES

Federal Statistical Office, Gustav - Stresemann - Ring 11, D-6200 Wiesbaden, Germany; *Kolumbien.*

G.K. Hall and Company, 70 Lincoln Street, Boston, Massachusetts 02111 (617) 423-3990; *The World in Figures.*

International Labour Office, I.L.O. Publications, CH-1211, Geneva 22, Switzerland; *Yearbook of Labour Statistics.*

Organization of American States (OAS), General Secretariat, Washington, D.C. 20006 (202) 458-3533; *Statistical Bulletin of the OAS.*

Statistical Office of the United Nations, Publishing Service, New York, New York 10017 (800) 253-9646; *Statistical Yearbook.*

U.C.L.A. Latin American Center Publications, University of California, Los Angeles, California 90024 (310) 825-6634; *Statistical Abstract of Latin America.*

COLOMBIA - WEATHER

Facts on File, 460 Park Avenue South, New York, New York 10016 (800) 443-8323; *The New Book of World Rankings.*

G.K. Hall and Company, 70 Lincoln Street, Boston, Massachusetts 02111 (617) 423-3990; *The World in Figures.*

COLOMBIA - WELFARE

Inter-American Development Bank, 1300 New York Avenue, NW, Washington, D.C. 20577 (202) 623-1753; *Economic and Social Progress in Latin America.*

COLOMBIA - WHEAT PRODUCTION - See COLOMBIA - CROPS

COLOMBIA - WHOLESALE PRICES

Inter-American Development Bank, 1300 New York Avenue, NW, Washington, D.C. 20577 (202) 623-1753; *Economic and Social Progress in Latin America.*

International Monetary Fund, 700 Nineteenth Street, NW, Washington, D.C. 20431 (202) 623-7000; *International Financial Statistics.*

Organization of American States (OAS), General Secretariat, Washington, D.C. 20006 (202) 458-3533; *Statistical Bulletin of the OAS.*

Statistical Office of the United Nations, Publishing Service, New York, New York 10017 (800) 253-9646; *Statistical Yearbook.*

COLOMBIA - WHOLESALE TRADE

Euromonitor Publications Limited, 87-88 Turnmill Street, London EC1M 5QU, England; *Third World Economic Handbook.*

Inter-American Development Bank, 1300 New York Avenue, NW, Washington, D.C. 20577 (202) 623-1753; *Economic and Social Progress in Latin America.*

Statistical Office of the United Nations, Publishing Service, New York, New York 10017 (800) 253-9646; *Statistical Yearbook.*

COLOMBIA - WINE PRODUCTION

Facts on File, 460 Park Avenue South, New York, New York 10016 (800) 443-8323; *The New Book of World Rankings.*

COLOMBIA - WOOD - See COLOMBIA - FORESTRY AND FOREST PRODUCTS

COLOMBIA - WOOL PRODUCTION

Facts on File, 460 Park Avenue South, New York, New York 10016 (800) 443-8323; *The New Book of World Rankings.*

COLOMBIA - YARN PRODUCTION

Statistical Office of the United Nations, Publishing Service, New York, New York 10017 (800) 253-9646; *Statistical Yearbook.*

COLOMBIA - ZINC ORE PRODUCTION AND CONSUMPTION - See COLOMBIA - MINING AND MINERAL PRODUCTS

COLOMBIA - ZOOS AND BOTANICAL GARDENS

United Nations Educational, Scientific and Cultural Organization (UNESCO), 7 Place de Fontenoy, F-75700 Paris, France (Telephone Number in U.S. (518) 436-9686); *Statistical Yearbook.*

COLORADO - See also STATE DATA (FOR INDIVIDUAL STATES)

Colorado - Primary Statistics Source

University of Colorado, Business Research Division, Campus Box 420, Boulder, Colorado 80309 (303) 492-8227; *Statistical Abstract of Colorado.*

Colorado - State Data Centers

Colorado Division of Local Government, Colorado Department of Local Affairs, 1313 Sherman Street, Room 521, Denver, Colorado 80203, Ms. Rebecca Picaso (303) 866-2156.

Business Research Division, Graduate School of Business Administration, University of Colorado-Boulder, Boulder, Colorado 80309, Ms. Ginny Hayden (303) 492-8227.

Natural Resources and Economics, Department of Agriculture, Colorado State University, Fort Collins, Colorado 80523, Ms. Sue Anderson (303) 491-5706.

Documents Department, The Libraries, Colorado State University, Fort Collins, Colorado 80523, Ms. Suzanne Taylor (303) 491-1880.

COLUMBIUM - TANTALUM

U.S. Department of the Interior, Bureau of Mines, 810 Seventh Street, NW, Washington, D.C. 20241 (202) 501-9649; *Minerals Commodity Summaries,* and *Annual Reports.*

COMMERCE - DOMESTIC - BY RAIL

Association of American Railroads, American Railroads Building, 50 F Street, NW, Washington, D.C. 20001 (202) 639-2100; *Weekly Railroad Traffic.*

COMMERCE - DOMESTIC - BY WATER

U.S. Department of the Army, Corps of Engineers, The Pentagon, Washington, D.C. 20310 (202) 545-6700; *Waterborne Commerce of the United States.*

COMMERCE - FOREIGN - See FOREIGN TRADE

COMMERCE AND HOUSING CREDIT

Executive Office of the President, Office of Management and Budget, Executive Office Building, Washington, D.C. 20503 (202) 395-3080; *Budget of the United States Government.*

COMMERCIAL BUILDINGS - BUILDERS

U.S. Department of Commerce, Bureau of the Census, Suitland, Maryland 20233 (301) 763-4040; *Census of Construction Industries.*

COMMERCIAL BUILDINGS - BUILDING PERMIT VALUE

U.S. Department of Commerce, Bureau of the Census, Suitland, Maryland 20233 (301) 763-4040; unpublished data.

COMMERCIAL BUILDINGS - CONSTRUCTION VALUE

F.W. Dodge Division, McGraw-Hill Information Systems Company, 1221 Avenue of the Americas, New York, New York 10020 (212) 512-2000; *Dodge Construction Potentials.*

U.S. Department of Commerce, Bureau of the Census, Suitland, Maryland 20233 (301) 763-4040; *Current Construction Reports.*

COMMERCIAL BUILDINGS - COST OF CONSTRUCTION

U.S. Department of Commerce, Bureau of the Census, Suitland, Maryland 20233 (301) 763-4040; *Current Construction Reports.*

COMMERCIAL BUILDINGS - CRIME INCIDENTS

U.S. Department of Justice, Bureau of Justice Statistics, 633 Indiana Avenue, NW, Washington, D.C. 20531 (800) 732-3277; *Criminal Victimization in the United States.*

COMMERCIAL BUILDINGS - EDUCATION

U.S. Department of Energy, Energy Information Administration, 1000 Independence Avenue, SW, Washington, D.C. 20585 (202) 586-8800; *Commercial Building Characteristics.*

COMMERCIAL BUILDINGS - ENERGY CHARACTERISTICS

U.S. Department of Energy, Energy Information Administration, Washington, D.C. 20585 (202) 586-8800; *Commercial Buildings Characteristics.*

COMMERCIAL BUILDINGS - FLOOR SPACE

F.W. Dodge Division, McGraw-Hill Information Systems Company, 1221 Avenue of the Americas, New York, New York 10020 (212) 512-2000; *Dodge Construction Potentials.*

U.S. Department of Energy, Energy Information Administration, Washington, D.C. 20585 (202) 586-8800; *Commercial Building Characteristics.*

COMMERCIAL BUILDINGS - HEALTH CARE

U.S. Department of Energy, Energy Information Administration, 1000 Independence Avenue, SW, Washington, D.C. 20585 (202) 586-8800; *Commercial Building Characteristics.*

COMMERCIAL BUILDINGS - INVENTORY

U.S. Department of Energy, Energy Information Administration, Washington, D.C. 20585 (202) 586-8800; *Commercial Building Characteristics.*

COMMERCIAL BUILDINGS - OFFICE BUILDINGS

U.S. Department of Energy, Energy Information Administration, 1000 Independence Avenue, SW, Washington, D.C. 20585 (202) 586-8800; *Commercial Building Characteristics.*

COMMERCIAL BUILDINGS - OFFICE BUILDINGS - VACANCY RATES

ONCOR International, 3040 Post Oak Boulevard, Houston, Texas 77056 (713) 961-0600; *Office Market Data Book.*

Society of Industrial and Office Realtors, 777 Fourteenth Street, NW, Suite 400, Washington, D.C. 20005 (202) 383-1150; *Comparative Statistics to Industrial and Office Real Estate Markets.*

COMMERCIAL PAPER

Board of Governors of the Federal Reserve System, Twentieth Street and Constitution Avenue, NW, Washington, D.C. 20551 (202) 452-3000; *Federal Reserve Bulletin.*

COMMODITIES - See Individual Types of Commodities

COMMODITY CREDIT CORPORATION

U.S. Department of Agriculture, Agricultural Stabilization and Conservation Service, Fourteenth Street and Independence Avenue, SW, Washington, D.C. 20250 (202) 720-5237; *Commodity Credit Corporation Report of Financial Conditions and Operations,* and *Agricultural Outlook.*

U.S. Department of Agriculture, Economic Research Service, Fourteenth Street and Independence Avenue, SW, Washington, D.C. 20005-4789 (202) 219-1504; *Economic Indicators of the Farm Sector: National Financial Summary.*

COMMODITY FUTURES TRADING

U.S. Commodity Futures Trading Commission, 2033 K Street, NW, Washington, D.C. 20581 (202) 254-6387; *Annual Report.*

COMMONWEALTH OF INDEPENDENT STATES - See UNION OF SOVIET SOCIALIST REPUBLICS

COMMUNICATIONS - DEGREES CONFERRED

U.S. Department of Education, National Center for Education Statistics, 400 Maryland Avenue, SW, Washington, D.C. 20202 (202) 708-5366; *Digest of Education Statistics.*

COMMUNICATIONS EQUIPMENT - MANUFACTURE - EARNINGS

U.S. Department of Commerce, Bureau of the Census, Suitland, Maryland 20233 (301) 763-4040; *Census of Manufactures,* and *Annual Survey of Manufactures.*

U.S. Department of Labor, Bureau of Labor Statistics, Two Massachusetts Avenue, NE, Washington, D.C. 20212 (202) 606-7828; *Employment and Wages, Annual Averages, Employment and Earnings,* and Bulletins 2370 and 2429.

COMMUNICATIONS EQUIPMENT - MANUFACTURE - EMPLOYEES

U.S. Department of Labor, Bureau of Labor Statistics, Two Massachusetts Avenue, NE, Washington, D.C. 20212 (202) 606-7828; *Employment, and Wages, Annual Averages, Employment and Earnings,* and Bulletins 2370 and 2429.

COMMUNICATIONS EQUIPMENT - MANUFACTURE - ESTABLISHMENTS

U.S. Department of Commerce, Bureau of the Census, Suitland, Maryland 20233 (301) 763-4040; *Annual Survey of Manufactures,* and *Census of Manufactures.*

COMMUNICATIONS EQUIPMENT - MANUFACTURE - INVENTORIES

U.S. Department of Commerce, Bureau of the Census, Suitland, Maryland 20233 (301) 763-4040; *Current Industrial Reports, Manufactures' Shipments, Inventories, and Orders.*

COMMUNICATIONS EQUIPMENT - MANUFACTURE - SHIPMENTS

U.S. Department of Commerce, Bureau of the Census, Suitland, Maryland 20233 (301) 763-4040; *Annual Survey of Manufactures, Census of Manufactures,* and *Current Industrial Reports, Manufacturers' Shipments, Inventories and Orders.*

COMMUNICATIONS EQUIPMENT - MANUFACTURE - VALUE ADDED

U.S. Department of Commerce, Bureau of the Census, Suitland, Maryland 20233 (301) 763-4040; *Annual Survey of Manufactures,* and *Census of Manufactures.*

COMMUNICATIONS INDUSTRY - See also TELEPHONE, TELEVISION AND RADIO

COMMUNICATIONS INDUSTRY - CAPITAL

Board of Governors of the Federal Reserve System, Twentieth Street and Constitution Avenue, NW, Washington, D.C. 20551 (202) 452-3000; *Federal Reserve Bulletin,* and *Annual Statistical Digest.*

U.S. Department of Commerce, Bureau of the Census, Suitland, Maryland 20233 (301) 763-4040; *Plant and Equipment Expenditures and Plans.*

COMMUNICATIONS INDUSTRY - EARNINGS

U.S. Department of Commerce, Bureau of Economic Analysis, Fourteenth Street between Constitution Avenue and E Street, NW, Washington, D.C. 20230 (202) 606-9900; *The National Income and Product Accounts of the United States,* and *Survey of Current Business.*

U.S. Department of Commerce, Bureau of the Census, Suitland, Maryland 20233 (301) 763-4040; *County Business Patterns.*

U.S. Department of Labor, Bureau of Labor Statistics, Two Massachusetts Avenue, NE, Washington, D.C. 20212 (202) 606-7828; *Employment and Earnings,* and Bulletins 2370 and 2429.

COMMUNICATIONS INDUSTRY - EMPLOYEES

U.S. Department of Labor, Bureau of Labor Statistics, Two Massachusetts Avenue, NE, Washington, D.C. 20212 (202) 606-7828; *Employment and Earnings, Monthly Labor Review,* and Bulletins 2370 and 2429.

COMMUNICATIONS INDUSTRY - FOREIGN COUNTRIES

United Nations Educational, Scientific and Cultural Organization, Department of State, Washington, D.C. 20520 (Telephone Number in U.S. (212) 963-5981); *Statistical Yearbook.*

COMMUNICATIONS INDUSTRY - OCCUPATIONAL SAFETY

U.S. Department of Labor, Bureau of Labor Statistics, Two Massachusetts Avenue, NE, Washington, D.C. 20212 (202) 606-7828; *Occupational Injuries and Illnesses in the United States by Industry.*

COMMUNICATIONS INDUSTRY - PROFITS

U.S. Department of Commerce, Bureau of Economic Analysis, Fourteenth Street between Constitution Avenue and E Street, NW, Washington, D.C. 20230 (202) 606-9900; *The National Income and Product Accounts of the U.S.,* and *Survey of Current Business.*

U.S. Department of the Treasury, Internal Revenue Service, 1111 Constitution Avenue, NW, Washington, D.C. 20224 (202) 566-5000; *Statistics of Income,* various publications, and unpublished data.

COMMUNICATIONS INDUSTRY - SALES, SHIPMENTS, RECEIPTS

Veronis, Suhler and Associates, 350 Park Avenue, New York, New York 10022 (212) 935-4990; *Communications Industry Report.*

U.S. Department of the Treasury, Internal Revenue Service, 1111 Constitution Avenue, NW, Washington, D.C. 20224 (202) 566-5000; *Statistics of Income,* and unpublished data.

COMMUNITY DEVELOPMENT - FEDERAL OUTLAYS

Executive Office of the President, Office of Management and Budget, Executive Office Building, Washington, D.C. 20503 (202) 395-3080; *Budget of the United States Government.*

COMMUTER/REGIONAL AIRLINES OPERATIONS

Regional Airline Association, 1101 Connecticut Avenue, NW, Suite 700, Washington, D.C. 20036 (202) 857-1170; *Annual Report of the Regional Airline Industry.*

Comoros - Primary Statistics Sources

Imprimerie Nationale, 2 rue Paul-Hervieu, 75732 Paris Cedex 15, France; *Annuaire statistique des territories d'outre-mer* (Statistical Yearbook for the Overseas Territories).

COMOROS - AGRICULTURE

Food and Agricultural Organization of the United Nations (FAO) Via delle Terme di Caracalla, 00100 Rome, Italy (Telephone Number in U.S. (202) 653-2400); *Production Yearbook, The State of Food and Agriculture,* and *Trade Yearbook.*

G.K. Hall and Company, 70 Lincoln Street, Boston, Massachusetts 02111 (617) 423-3990; *The World in Figures.*

Statistical Office of the United Nations, Publishing Service, New York, New York 10017 (800) 253-9646; *Survey of Economic and Social Conditions in Africa.*

United Nations Economic Commission for Africa, Africa Hall, P.O. Box 3001, Addis Ababa, Ethiopia (Telephone Number in U.S. (800) 253-9646); *African Statistical Yearbook.*

COMOROS - AIRLINE SERVICE

G.K. Hall and Company, 70 Lincoln Street, Boston, Massachusetts 02111 (617) 423-3990; *The World in Figures.*

United Nations Economic Commission for Africa, Africa Hall, P.O. Box 3001, Addis Ababa, Ethiopia (Telephone Number in U.S. (800) 253-9646); *African Statistical Yearbook.*

COMOROS - ANIMAL HEALTH

Food and Agricultural Organization of the United Nations (FAO), Via delle Terme di Caracalla, 00100 Rome, Italy (Telephone Number in U.S. (202) 653-2400); *Animal Health Yearbook.*

COMOROS - AREA AND DENSITY OF POPULATION

African Development Bank, 01 BP 1387, Abidjan 01, Cote D'Ivoire; *Selected Statistics on Regional Member Countries.*

Food and Agricultural Organization of the United Nations (FAO) Via delle Terme di Caracalla, 00100 Rome, Italy (Telephone Number in U.S. (202) 653-2400); *The State of Food and Agriculture.*

G.K. Hall and Company, 70 Lincoln Street, Boston, Massachusetts 02111 (617) 423-3990; *The World in Figures.*

Statistical Office of the United Nations, Publishing Service, New York, New York 10017 (800) 253-9646; *Statistical Yearbook,* and *Survey of Economic and Social Conditions in Africa.*

United Nations Educational, Scientific and Cultural Organization (UNESCO), 7 Place de Fontenoy, F-75700 Paris, France (Telephone Number in U.S. (518) 436-9686); *Statistical Yearbook.*

COMOROS - BALANCE OF PAYMENTS

African Development Bank, 01 BP 1387, Abidjan 01, Cote D'Ivoire; *Selected Statistics on Regional Member Countries.*

G.K. Hall and Company, 70 Lincoln Street, Boston, Massachusetts 02111 (617) 423-3990; *The World in Figures.*

United Nations Economic Commission for Africa, Africa Hall, P.O. Box 3001, Addis Ababa, Ethiopia (Telephone Number in U.S. (800) 253-9646); *African Statistical Yearbook.*

COMOROS - BANKING

G.K. Hall and Company, 70 Lincoln Street, Boston, Massachusetts 02111 (617) 423-3990; *The World in Figures.*

United Nations Economic Commission for Africa, Africa Hall, P.O. Box 3001, Addis Ababa, Ethiopia (Telephone Number in U.S. (800) 253-9646); *African Statistical Yearbook.*

COMOROS - BIRTH RATES

Statistical Office of the United Nations, Publishing Service, New York, New York 10017 (800) 253-9646; *Demographic Yearbook, Statistical Yearbook,* and *Survey of Economic and Social Conditions in Africa.*

COMOROS - BONDS

G.K. Hall and Company, 70 Lincoln Street, Boston, Massachusetts 02111 (617) 423-3990; *The World in Figures.*

COMOROS - BOOK PRODUCTION

G.K. Hall and Company, 70 Lincoln Street, Boston, Massachusetts 02111 (617) 423-3990; *The World in Figures.*

COMOROS - BROADCASTING

Billboard Limited, P.O. Box 9027, 1006 AA Amsterdam, The Netherlands (Telephone Number in U.S. (212) 764-7300); *World Radio TV Handbook.*

G.K. Hall and Company, 70 Lincoln Street, Boston, Massachusetts 02111 (617) 423-3990; *The World in Figures.*

COMOROS - BUSINESS

G.K. Hall and Company, 70 Lincoln Street, Boston, Massachusetts 02111 (617) 423-3990; *The World in Figures.*

COMOROS - CALORIE SUPPLY

African Development Bank, 01 BP 1387, Abidjan 01, Cote D'Ivoire; *Selected Statistics on Regional Member Countries.*

Food and Agricultural Organization of the United Nations (FAO) Via delle Terme di Caracalla, 00100 Rome, Italy (Telephone Number in U.S. (202) 653-2400); *The State of Food and Agriculture.*

COMOROS - CATTLE - See COMOROS - LIVESTOCK AND POULTRY

COMOROS - CHEMICAL (ORGANIC) PRODUCTION - See COMOROS - MINING AND MINERAL PRODUCTS

COMOROS - CLASS STRUCTURE

G.K. Hall and Company, 70 Lincoln Street, Boston, Massachusetts 02111 (617) 423-3990; *The World in Figures.*

COMOROS - CLIMATE

G.K. Hall and Company, 70 Lincoln Street, Boston, Massachusetts 02111 (617) 423-3990; *The World in Figures.*

COMOROS - COAL PRODUCTION - See COMOROS - MINING AND MINERAL PRODUCTS

COMOROS - COCOA PRODUCTION - See COMOROS - CROPS

COMOROS - COMMUNICATIONS

G.K. Hall and Company, 70 Lincoln Street, Boston, Massachusetts 02111 (617) 423-3990; *The World in Figures.*

United Nations Economic Commission for Africa, Africa Hall, P.O. Box 3001, Addis Ababa, Ethiopia (Telephone Number in U.S. (800) 253-9646); *African Statistical Yearbook.*

COMOROS - CONSTRUCTION INDUSTRY

United Nations Economic Commission for Africa, Africa Hall, P.O. Box 3001, Addis Ababa, Ethiopia (Telephone Number in U.S. (800) 253-9646); *African Statistical Yearbook.*

COMOROS - CONSUMER PRICE INDEX

African Development Bank, 01 BP 1387, Abidjan 01, Cote D'Ivoire; *Selected Statistics on Regional Member Countries.*

G.K. Hall and Company, 70 Lincoln Street, Boston, Massachusetts 02111 (617) 423-3990; *The World in Figures.*

Statistical Office of the United Nations, Publishing Service, New York, New York 10017 (800) 253-9646; *Survey of Economic and Social Conditions in Africa.*

COMOROS - CONSUMPTION

African Development Bank, 01 BP 1387, Abidjan 01, Cote D'Ivoire; *Selected Statistics on Regional Member Countries.*

G.K. Hall and Company, 70 Lincoln Street, Boston, Massachusetts 02111 (617) 423-3990; *The World in Figures.*

Statistical Office of the United Nations, Publishing Service, New York, New York 10017 (800) 253-9646; *Survey of Economic and Social Conditions in Africa.*

COMOROS - CORN PRODUCTION - See COMOROS - CROPS

COMOROS - CORPORATE TAXES - See COMOROS - TAXATION

COMOROS - CROPS

Food and Agricultural Organization of the United Nations (FAO) Via delle Terme di Caracalla, 00100 Rome, Italy (Telephone Number in U.S. (202) 653-2400); *Production Yearbook*, and *The State of Food and Agriculture*.

G.K. Hall and Company, 70 Lincoln Street, Boston, Massachusetts 02111 (617) 423-3990; *The World in Figures*.

Statistical Office of the United Nations, Publishing Service, New York, New York 10017 (800) 253-9646; *Statistical Yearbook*.

United Nations Economic Commission for Africa, Africa Hall, P.O. Box 3001, Addis Ababa, Ethiopia (Telephone Number in U.S. (800) 253-9646); *African Statistical Yearbook*.

COMOROS - CUSTOMS DUTIES

G.K. Hall and Company, 70 Lincoln Street, Boston, Massachusetts 02111 (617) 423-3990; *The World in Figures*.

COMOROS - DAIRY PRODUCTS

Food and Agricultural Organization of the United Nations (FAO) Via delle Terme di Caracalla, 00100 Rome, Italy (Telephone Number in U.S. (202) 653-2400); *The State of Food and Agriculture*.

COMOROS - DEATH RATES

G.K. Hall and Company, 70 Lincoln Street, Boston, Massachusetts 02111 (617) 423-3990; *The World in Figures*.

Statistical Office of the United Nations, Publishing Service, New York, New York 10017 (800) 253-9646; *Statistical Yearbook*, and *Survey of Economic and Social Conditions in Africa*.

COMOROS - DEFENSE EXPENDITURES

G.K. Hall and Company, 70 Lincoln Street, Boston, Massachusetts 02111 (617) 423-3990; *The World in Figures*.

COMOROS - DEMOGRAPHY

G.K. Hall and Company, 70 Lincoln Street, Boston, Massachusetts 02111 (617) 423-3990; *The World in Figures*.

Statistical Office of the United Nations, Publishing Service, New York, New York 10017 (800) 253-9646; *Survey of Economic and Social Conditions in Africa*.

COMOROS - DEVELOPMENT ASSISTANCE

G.K. Hall and Company, 70 Lincoln Street, Boston, Massachusetts 02111 (617) 423-3990; *The World in Figures*.

Statistical Office of the United Nations, Publishing Service, New York, New York 10017 (800) 253-9646; *Statistical Yearbook*.

COMOROS - DISEASE

G.K. Hall and Company, 70 Lincoln Street, Boston, Massachusetts 02111 (617) 423-3990; *The World in Figures*.

COMOROS - DIVORCE RATES

Statistical Office of the United Nations, Publishing Service, New York, New York 10017 (800) 253-9646; *Demographic Yearbook*, and *Statistical Yearbook*.

COMOROS - DOMESTIC PRODUCT

G.K. Hall and Company, 70 Lincoln Street, Boston, Massachusetts 02111 (617) 423-3990; *The World in Figures*.

COMOROS - ECONOMY

African Development Bank, 01 BP 1387, Abidjan 01, Cote D'Ivoire; *Selected Statistics on Regional Member Countries*.

G.K. Hall and Company, 70 Lincoln Street, Boston, Massachusetts 02111 (617) 423-3990; *The World in Figures*.

COMOROS - EDUCATION

African Development Bank, 01 BP 1387, Abidjan 01, Cote D'Ivoire; *Selected Statistics on Regional Member Countries*.

G.K. Hall and Company, 70 Lincoln Street, Boston, Massachusetts 02111 (617) 423-3990; *The World in Figures*.

Statistical Office of the United Nations, Publishing Service, New York, New York 10017 (800) 253-9646; *Survey of Economic and Social Conditions in Africa*.

United Nations Economic Commission for Africa, Africa Hall, P.O. Box 3001, Addis Ababa, Ethiopia (Telephone Number in U.S. (800) 253-9646); *African Statistical Yearbook*.

COMOROS - EGG PRODUCTION - See COMOROS - DAIRY PRODUCTS

COMOROS - ELECTRICITY

Statistical Office of the United Nations, Publishing Service, New York, New York 10017 (800) 253-9646; *Survey of Economic and Social Conditions in Africa*.

United Nations Economic Commission for Africa, Africa Hall, P.O. Box 3001, Addis Ababa, Ethiopia (Telephone Number in U.S. (800) 253-9646); *African Statistical Yearbook*.

COMOROS - EMPLOYMENT

Statistical Office of the United Nations, Publishing Service, New York, New York 10017 (800) 253-9646; *Survey of Economic and Social Conditions in Africa*.

United Nations Economic Commission for Africa, Africa Hall, P.O. Box 3001, Addis Ababa, Ethiopia (Telephone Number in U.S. (800) 253-9646); *African Statistical Yearbook*.

COMOROS - ENERGY

Food and Agricultural Organization of the United Nations (FAO) Via delle Terme di Caracalla, 00100 Rome, Italy (Telephone Number in U.S. (202) 653-2400); *The State of Food and Agriculture*.

G.K. Hall and Company, 70 Lincoln Street, Boston, Massachusetts 02111 (617) 423-3990; *The World in Figures*.

Statistical Office of the United Nations, Publishing Service, New York, New York 10017 (800) 253-9646; *Energy Statistics Yearbook*, *Statistical Yearbook*, and *World Energy Supplies*.

United Nations Economic Commission for Africa, Africa Hall, P.O. Box 3001, Addis Ababa, Ethiopia (Telephone Number in U.S. (800) 253-9646); *African Statistical Yearbook.*

COMOROS - EXCHANGE RATES

African Development Bank, 01 BP 1387, Abidjan 01, Cote D'Ivoire; *Selected Statistics on Regional Member Countries.*

Statistical Office of the United Nations, Publishing Service, New York, New York 10017 (800) 253-9646; *Statistical Yearbook.*

COMOROS - EXPORTS

African Development Bank, 01 BP 1387, Abidjan 01, Cote D'Ivoire; *Selected Statistics on Regional Member Countries.*

Food and Agricultural Organization of the United Nations (FAO) Via delle Terme di Caracalla, 00100 Rome, Italy (Telephone Number in U.S. (202) 653-2400); *The State of Food and Agriculture.*

G.K. Hall and Company, 70 Lincoln Street, Boston, Massachusetts 02111 (617) 423-3990; *The World in Figures.*

International Monetary Fund, 700 Nineteenth Street, NW, Washington, D.C. 20431 (202) 623-7000; *Direction of Trade Statistics.*

Statistical Office of the United Nations, Publishing Service, New York, New York 10017 (800) 253-9646; *Survey of Economic and Social Conditions in Africa.*

United Nations Economic Commission for Africa, Africa Hall, P.O. Box 3001, Addis Ababa, Ethiopia (Telephone Number in U.S. (800) 253-9646); *African Statistical Yearbook.*

COMOROS - EXTERNAL INDEBTEDNESS

African Development Bank, 01 BP 1387, Abidjan 01, Cote D'Ivoire; *Selected Statistics on Regional Member Countries.*

Statistical Office of the United Nations, Publishing Service, New York, New York 10017 (800) 253-9646; *Survey of Economic and Social Conditions in Africa.*

COMOROS - EXTERNAL TRADE

African Development Bank, 01 BP 1387, Abidjan 01, Cote D'Ivoire; *Selected Statistics on Regional Member Countries.*

Food and Agricultural Organization of the United Nations (FAO) Via delle Terme di Caracalla, 00100 Rome, Italy (Telephone Number in U.S. (202) 653-2400); *The State of Food and Agriculture,* and *Trade Yearbook.*

G.K. Hall and Company, 70 Lincoln Street, Boston, Massachusetts 02111 (617) 423-3990; *The World in Figures.*

COMOROS - FARM CROPS - See COMOROS - CROPS

COMOROS - FETAL MORTALITY

Statistical Office of the United Nations, Publishing Service, New York, New York 10017 (800) 253-9646; *Demographic Yearbook.*

COMOROS - FERTILITY RATES

Statistical Office of the United Nations, Publishing Service, New York, New York 10017 (800) 253-9646; *Survey of Economic and Social Conditions in Africa.*

COMOROS - FERTILIZER

Food and Agricultural Organization of the United Nations (FAO) Via delle Terme di Caracalla, 00100 Rome, Italy (Telephone Number in U.S. (202) 653-2400); *The State of Food and Agriculture.*

COMOROS - FINANCE

African Development Bank, 01 BP 1387, Abidjan 01, Cote D'Ivoire; *Selected Statistics on Regional Member Countries.*

G.K. Hall and Company, 70 Lincoln Street, Boston, Massachusetts 02111 (617) 423-3990; *The World in Figures.*

United Nations Economic Commission for Africa, Africa Hall, P.O. Box 3001, Addis Ababa, Ethiopia (Telephone Number in U.S. (800) 253-9646); *African Statistical Yearbook.*

COMOROS - FISHERIES

Food and Agricultural Organization of the United Nations (FAO) Via delle Terme di Caracalla, 00100 Rome, Italy (Telephone Number in U.S. (202) 653-2400); *The State of Food and Agriculture,* and *Yearbook of Fishery Statistics.*

Statistical Office of the United Nations, Publishing Service, New York, New York 10017 (800) 253-9646; *Statistical Yearbook,* and *Survey of Economic and Social Conditions in Africa.*

United Nations Economic Commission for Africa, Africa Hall, P.O. Box 3001, Addis Ababa, Ethiopia (Telephone Number in U.S. (800) 253-9646); *African Statistical Yearbook.*

COMOROS - FOOD

African Development Bank, 01 BP 1387, Abidjan 01, Cote D'Ivoire; *Selected Statistics on Regional Member Countries.*

Food and Agricultural Organization of the United Nations (FAO) Via delle Terme di Caracalla, 00100 Rome, Italy (Telephone Number in U.S. (202) 653-2400); *Production Yearbook,* and *The State of Food and Agriculture.*

G.K. Hall and Company, 70 Lincoln Street, Boston, Massachusetts 02111 (617) 423-3990; *The World in Figures.*

COMOROS - FOREIGN AID

G.K. Hall and Company, 70 Lincoln Street, Boston, Massachusetts 02111 (617) 423-3990; *The World in Figures.*

COMOROS - FOREIGN TRADE

Food and Agricultural Organization of the United Nations (FAO) Via delle Terme di Caracalla, 00100 Rome, Italy (Telephone Number in U.S. (202) 653-2400); *The State of Food and Agriculture.*

G.K. Hall and Company, 70 Lincoln Street, Boston, Massachusetts 02111 (617) 423-3990; *The World in Figures.*

Organisation for Economic Co-operation and Development (OECD), 2 rue Andre-Pascal, 75 Paris 16, France (Telephone Number in U.S. (202) 785-6323); *Trade by Commodities.*

Statistical Office of the United Nations, Publishing Service, New York, New York 10017 (800) 253-9646; *International Trade Statistics Yearbook,* and *International Trade Statistics Yearbook.*

United Nations Economic Commission for Africa, Africa Hall, P.O. Box 3001, Addis Ababa, Ethiopia (Telephone Number in U.S. (800) 253-9646); *African Statistical Yearbook.*

COMOROS - FORESTRY AND FOREST PRODUCTS

Food and Agricultural Organization of the United Nations (FAO) Via delle Terme di Caracalla, 00100 Rome, Italy (Telephone Number in U.S. (202) 653-2400); *The State of Food and Agriculture.*

G.K. Hall and Company, 70 Lincoln Street, Boston, Massachusetts 02111 (617) 423-3990; *The World in Figures.*

United Nations Economic Commission for Africa, Africa Hall, P.O. Box 3001, Addis Ababa, Ethiopia (Telephone Number in U.S. (800) 253-9646); *African Statistical Yearbook.*

COMOROS - GENERAL MORTALITY

Statistical Office of the United Nations, Publishing Service, New York, New York 10017 (800) 253-9646; *Demographic Yearbook.*

COMOROS - GOATS - See COMOROS - LIVESTOCK AND POULTRY

COMOROS - GOVERNMENT

G.K. Hall and Company, 70 Lincoln Street, Boston, Massachusetts 02111 (617) 423-3990; *The World in Figures.*

COMOROS - GOVERNMENT REVENUE

Statistical Office of the United Nations, Publishing Service, New York, New York 10017 (800) 253-9646; *Survey of Economic and Social Conditions in Africa.*

COMOROS - GRAIN PRODUCTION - See COMOROS - CROPS

COMOROS - GROSS DOMESTIC PRODUCT

African Development Bank, 01 BP 1387, Abidjan 01, Cote D'Ivoire; *Selected Statistics on Regional Member Countries.*

G.K. Hall and Company, 70 Lincoln Street, Boston, Massachusetts 02111 (617) 423-3990; *The World in Figures.*

Statistical Office of the United Nations, Publishing Service, New York, New York 10017 (800) 253-9646; *Statistical Yearbook,* and *Survey of Economic and Social Conditions in Africa.*

United Nations Economic Commission for Africa, Africa Hall, P.O. Box 3001, Addis Ababa, Ethiopia (Telephone Number in U.S. (800) 253-9646); *African Statistical Yearbook.*

COMOROS - HEALTH

African Development Bank, 01 BP 1387, Abidjan 01, Cote D'Ivoire; *Selected Statistics on Regional Member Countries.*

G.K. Hall and Company, 70 Lincoln Street, Boston, Massachusetts 02111 (617) 423-3990; *The World in Figures.*

Statistical Office of the United Nations, Publishing Service, New York, New York 10017 (800) 253-9646; *Statistical Yearbook.*

United Nations Economic Commission for Africa, Africa Hall, P.O. Box 3001, Addis Ababa, Ethiopia (Telephone Number in U.S. (800) 253-9646); *African Statistical Yearbook.*

COMOROS - HIDE PRODUCTION

Food and Agricultural Organization of the United Nations (FAO), Via delle Terme di Caracalla, 00100 Rome, Italy (Telephone Number in U.S. (202) 653-2400); *Production Yearbook.*

COMOROS - HIGHWAYS

G.K. Hall and Company, 70 Lincoln Street, Boston, Massachusetts 02111 (617) 423-3990; *The World in Figures.*

Statistical Office of the United Nations, Publishing Service, New York, New York 10017 (800) 253-9646; *Survey of Economic and Social Conditions in Africa.*

United Nations Economic Commission for Africa, Africa Hall, P.O. Box 3001, Addis Ababa, Ethiopia (Telephone Number in U.S. (800) 253-9646); *African Statistical Yearbook.*

COMOROS - ILLITERATE POPULATION

G.K. Hall and Company, 70 Lincoln Street, Boston, Massachusetts 02111 (617) 423-3990; *The World in Figures.*

United Nations Educational, Scientific and Cultural Organization (UNESCO), 7 Place de Fontenoy, F-75700 Paris, France (Telephone Number in U.S. (518) 436-9686); *Statistical Yearbook.*

COMOROS - IMPORTS

African Development Bank, 01 BP 1387, Abidjan 01, Cote D'Ivoire; *Selected Statistics on Regional Member Countries.*

Food and Agricultural Organization of the United Nations (FAO) Via delle Terme di Caracalla, 00100 Rome, Italy (Telephone Number in U.S. (202) 653-2400); *The State of Food and Agriculture.*

G.K. Hall and Company, 70 Lincoln Street, Boston, Massachusetts 02111 (617) 423-3990; *The World in Figures.*

International Monetary Fund, 700 Nineteenth Street, NW, Washington, D.C. 20431 (202) 623-7000; *Direction of Trade Statistics.*

Statistical Office of the United Nations, Publishing Service, New York, New York 10017 (800) 253-9646; *Survey of Economic and Social Conditions in Africa.*

United Nations Economic Commission for Africa, Africa Hall, P.O. Box 3001, Addis Ababa, Ethiopia (Telephone Number in U.S. (800) 253-9646); *African Statistical Yearbook.*

COMOROS - INDUSTRY

G.K. Hall and Company, 70 Lincoln Street, Boston, Massachusetts 02111 (617) 423-3990; *The World in Figures.*

Statistical Office of the United Nations, Publishing Service, New York, New York 10017 (800) 253-9646; *Survey of Economic and Social Conditions in Africa.*

United Nations Economic Commission for Africa, Africa Hall, P.O. Box 3001, Addis Ababa, Ethiopia (Telephone Number in U.S. (800) 253-9646); *African Statistical Yearbook.*

COMOROS - INFANT AND MATERNAL MORTALITY

Statistical Office of the United Nations, Publishing Service, New York, New York 10017 (800) 253-9646; *Demographic Yearbook,*

Statistical Yearbook, and *Survey of Economic and Social Conditions in Africa*.

COMOROS - INTERNATIONAL RESERVES EXCLUDING GOLD

African Development Bank, 01 BP 1387, Abidjan 01, Cote D'Ivoire; *Selected Statistics on Regional Member Countries*.

COMOROS - LABOR FORCE

African Development Bank, 01 BP 1387, Abidjan 01, Cote D'Ivoire; *Selected Statistics on Regional Member Countries*.

Food and Agricultural Organization of the United Nations (FAO) Via delle Terme di Caracalla, 00100 Rome, Italy (Telephone Number in U.S. (202) 653-2400); *The State of Food and Agriculture*.

G.K. Hall and Company, 70 Lincoln Street, Boston, Massachusetts 02111 (617) 423-3990; *The World in Figures*.

COMOROS - LAND USE

Food and Agricultural Organization of the United Nations (FAO), Via delle Terme di Caracalla, 00100 Rome, Italy (Telephone Number in U.S. (202) 653-2400); *Production Yearbook*.

G.K. Hall and Company, 70 Lincoln Street, Boston, Massachusetts 02111 (617) 423-3990; *The World in Figures*.

COMOROS - LIBRARIES

United Nations Educational, Scientific and Cultural Organization (UNESCO), 7 Place de Fontenoy, F-75700 Paris, France (Telephone Number in U.S. (518) 436-9686); *Statistical Yearbook*.

COMOROS - LIFE EXPECTANCY

African Development Bank, 01 BP 1387, Abidjan 01, Cote D'Ivoire; *Selected Statistics on Regional Member Countries*.

COMOROS - LITERACY RATE

Statistical Office of the United Nations, Publishing Service, New York, New York 10017 (800) 253-9646; *Survey of Economic and Social Conditions in Africa*.

COMOROS - LIVESTOCK AND POULTRY

Food and Agricultural Organization of the United Nations (FAO), Via delle Terme di Caracalla, 00100 Rome, Italy (Telephone Number in U.S. (202) 653-2400); *Production Yearbook*, and *The State of Food and Agriculture*.

G.K. Hall and Company, 70 Lincoln Street, Boston, Massachusetts 02111 (617) 423-3990; *The World in Figures*.

Statistical Office of the United Nations, Publishing Service, New York, New York 10017 (800) 253-9646; *Statistical Yearbook*, and *Survey of Economic and Social Conditions in Africa*.

United Nations Economic Commission for Africa, Africa Hall, P.O. Box 3001, Addis Ababa, Ethiopia (Telephone Number in U.S. (800) 253-9646); *African Statistical Yearbook*.

COMOROS - LIVING LEVELS

G.K. Hall and Company, 70 Lincoln Street, Boston, Massachusetts 02111 (617) 423-3990; *The World in Figures*.

COMOROS - MAIL - NUMBER OF PIECES SENT OR RECEIVED

Statistical Office of the United Nations, Publishing Service, New York, New York 10017 (800) 253-9646; *Statistical Yearbook*.

COMOROS - MANUFACTURING

G.K. Hall and Company, 70 Lincoln Street, Boston, Massachusetts 02111 (617) 423-3990; *The World in Figures*.

Statistical Office of the United Nations, Publishing Service, New York, New York 10017 (800) 253-9646; *Survey of Economic and Social Conditions in Africa*.

United Nations Economic Commission for Africa, Africa Hall, P.O. Box 3001, Addis Ababa, Ethiopia (Telephone Number in U.S. (800) 253-9646); *African Statistical Yearbook*.

COMOROS - MARRIAGE RATES

Statistical Office of the United Nations, Publishing Service, New York, New York 10017 (800) 253-9646; *Demographic Yearbook*, and *Statistical Yearbook*.

COMOROS - MEAT PRODUCTION - See COMOROS - LIVESTOCK AND POULTRY

COMOROS - MERCHANT SHIPPING

G.K. Hall and Company, 70 Lincoln Street, Boston, Massachusetts 02111 (617) 423-3990; *The World in Figures*.

Lloyd's Register of Shipping, 17 Battery Place, New York, New York 10004 (212) 425-8050; *Register of Ships*.

Statistical Office of the United Nations, Publishing Service, New York, New York 10017 (800) 253-9646; *Statistical Yearbook*.

United Nations Economic Commission for Africa, Africa Hall, P.O. Box 3001, Addis Ababa, Ethiopia (Telephone Number in U.S. (800) 253-9646); *African Statistical Yearbook*.

COMOROS - MILITARY

G.K. Hall and Company, 70 Lincoln Street, Boston, Massachusetts 02111 (617) 423-3990; *The World in Figures*.

COMOROS - MINING AND MINERAL PRODUCTS

G.K. Hall and Company, 70 Lincoln Street, Boston, Massachusetts 02111 (617) 423-3990; *The World in Figures*.

United Nations Economic Commission for Africa, Africa Hall, P.O. Box 3001, Addis Ababa, Ethiopia (Telephone Number in U.S. (800) 253-9646); *African Statistical Yearbook*.

COMOROS - MONEY EXCHANGE RATES

Statistical Office of the United Nations, Publishing Service, New York, New York 10017 (800) 253-9646; *Statistical Yearbook*.

COMOROS - MONEY SUPPLY

African Development Bank, 01 BP 1387, Abidjan 01, Cote D'Ivoire; *Selected Statistics on Regional Member Countries*.

G.K. Hall and Company, 70 Lincoln Street, Boston, Massachusetts 02111 (617) 423-3990; *The World in Figures*.

COMOROS - MOTION PICTURES

Statistical Office of the United Nations, Publishing Service, New York, New York 10017 (800) 253-9646; *Statistical Yearbook.*

COMOROS - MOTOR VEHICLES IN USE

G.K. Hall and Company, 70 Lincoln Street, Boston, Massachusetts 02111 (617) 423-3990; *The World in Figures.*

Statistical Office of the United Nations, Publishing Service, New York, New York 10017 (800) 253-9646; *Survey of Economic and Social Conditions in Africa.*

COMOROS - NATALITY - See COMOROS - BIRTH RATE

COMOROS - NATIONAL ACCOUNTS

African Development Bank, 01 BP 1387, Abidjan 01, Cote D'Ivoire; *Selected Statistics on Regional Member Countries.*

Statistical Office of the United Nations, Publishing Service, New York, New York 10017 (800) 253-9646; *Statistical Yearbook.*

United Nations Economic Commission for Africa, Africa Hall, P.O. Box 3001, Addis Ababa, Ethiopia (Telephone Number in U.S. (800) 253-9646); *African Statistical Yearbook.*

COMOROS - NATIONAL INCOME

G.K. Hall and Company, 70 Lincoln Street, Boston, Massachusetts 02111 (617) 423-3990; *The World in Figures.*

Statistical Office of the United Nations, Publishing Service, New York, New York 10017 (800) 253-9646; *Statistical Yearbook.*

COMOROS - NEWSPAPER PRODUCTION - See COMOROS - FORESTRY AND FOREST PRODUCTS

COMOROS - OCCUPATIONS - See COMOROS - LABOR FORCE

COMOROS - PESTICIDE USE

Food and Agricultural Organization of the United Nations (FAO) Via delle Terme di Caracalla, 00100 Rome, Italy (Telephone Number in U.S. (202) 653-2400); *The State of Food and Agriculture.*

COMOROS - PETROLEUM INDUSTRY

Food and Agricultural Organization of the United Nations (FAO) Via delle Terme di Caracalla, 00100 Rome, Italy (Telephone Number in U.S. (202) 653-2400); *The State of Food and Agriculture.*

G.K. Hall and Company, 70 Lincoln Street, Boston, Massachusetts 02111 (617) 423-3990; *The World in Figures.*

COMOROS - POPULATION

African Development Bank, 01 BP 1387, Abidjan 01, Cote D'Ivoire; *Selected Statistics on Regional Member Countries.*

Food and Agricultural Organization of the United Nations (FAO), Via delle Terme di Caracalla, 00100 Rome, Italy (Telephone Number in U.S. (202) 653-2400); *Production Yearbook.*

G.K. Hall and Company, 70 Lincoln Street, Boston, Massachusetts 02111 (617) 423-3990; *The World in Figures.*

Statistical Office of the United Nations, Publishing Service, New York, New York 10017 (800) 253-9646; *Demographic Yearbook, Statistical Yearbook,* and *Survey of Economic and Social Conditions in Africa.*

United Nations Educational, Scientific and Cultural Organization (UNESCO), 7 Place de Fontenoy, F-75700 Paris, France (Telephone Number in U.S. (518) 436-9686); *Statistical Yearbook.*

World Health Organization, Office of Publications, Avenue Appia, CH-1211 Geneva 27, Switzerland (Telephone Number in U.S. (518) 436-9686); *World Health Statistics Annual.*

COMOROS - PRICES

Food and Agricultural Organization of the United Nations (FAO), Via delle Terme di Caracalla, 00100 Rome, Italy (Telephone Number in U.S. (202) 653-2400); *Production Yearbook,* and *The State of Food and Agriculture.*

G.K. Hall and Company, 70 Lincoln Street, Boston, Massachusetts 02111 (617) 423-3990; *The World in Figures.*

United Nations Economic Commission for Africa, Africa Hall, P.O. Box 3001, Addis Ababa, Ethiopia (Telephone Number in U.S. (800) 253-9646); *African Statistical Yearbook.*

COMOROS - PRODUCTION

G.K. Hall and Company, 70 Lincoln Street, Boston, Massachusetts 02111 (617) 423-3990; *The World in Figures.*

COMOROS - RAILWAYS

G.K. Hall and Company, 70 Lincoln Street, Boston, Massachusetts 02111 (617) 423-3990; *The World in Figures.*

United Nations Economic Commission for Africa, Africa Hall, P.O. Box 3001, Addis Ababa, Ethiopia (Telephone Number in U.S. (800) 253-9646); *African Statistical Yearbook.*

COMOROS - RETAIL TRADE

G.K. Hall and Company, 70 Lincoln Street, Boston, Massachusetts 02111 (617) 423-3990; *The World in Figures.*

COMOROS - RICE PRODUCTION - See COMOROS - CROPS

COMOROS - ROOT AND TUBER PRODUCTION - See COMOROS - CROPS

COMOROS - SHEEP - See COMOROS - LIVESTOCK AND POULTRY

COMOROS - SISAL PRODUCTION - See COMOROS - CROPS

COMOROS - SOCIAL DATA

African Development Bank, 01 BP 1387, Abidjan 01, Cote D'Ivoire; *Selected Statistics on Regional Member Countries.*

G.K. Hall and Company, 70 Lincoln Street, Boston, Massachusetts 02111 (617) 423-3990; *The World in Figures.*

COMOROS - STOCKS - COMMODITY - MARKET PRICE -INDEX

Food and Agricultural Organization of the United Nations (FAO) Via delle Terme di Caracalla, 00100 Rome, Italy (Telephone Number in U.S. (202) 653-2400); *The State of Food and Agriculture.*

COMOROS - TELEPHONES IN USE

American Telephone and Telegraph Company, 26 Parsippany Road, Whippany, New Jersey 07981 (800) 338-4038; *The World's Telephones*.

G.K. Hall and Company, 70 Lincoln Street, Boston, Massachusetts 02111 (617) 423-3990; *The World in Figures*.

Statistical Office of the United Nations, Publishing Service, New York, New York 10017 (800) 253-9646; *Statistical Yearbook*.

COMOROS - TEXTILE INDUSTRY

G.K. Hall and Company, 70 Lincoln Street, Boston, Massachusetts 02111 (617) 423-3990; *The World in Figures*.

COMOROS - TOURISM

G.K. Hall and Company, 70 Lincoln Street, Boston, Massachusetts 02111 (617) 423-3990; *The World in Figures*.

United Nations Economic Commission for Africa, Africa Hall, P.O. Box 3001, Addis Ababa, Ethiopia (Telephone Number in U.S. (800) 253-9646); *African Statistical Yearbook*.

World Tourism Organization, Calle Capitan Haya 42, E-28020 Madrid, Spain; *Yearbook of Tourism Statistics*.

COMOROS - TRADE - See COMOROS - FOREIGN TRADE

COMOROS - TRANSPORTATION AND COMMUNICATIONS

G.K. Hall and Company, 70 Lincoln Street, Boston, Massachusetts 02111 (617) 423-3990; *The World in Figures*.

United Nations Economic Commission for Africa, Africa Hall, P.O. Box 3001, Addis Ababa, Ethiopia (Telephone Number in U.S. (800) 253-9646); *African Statistical Yearbook*.

COMOROS - VITAL STATISTICS

G.K. Hall and Company, 70 Lincoln Street, Boston, Massachusetts 02111 (617) 423-3990; *The World in Figures*.

Statistical Office of the United Nations, Publishing Service, New York, New York 10017 (800) 253-9646; *Statistical Yearbook*.

World Health Organization, Office of Publications, Avenue Appia, CH-1211 Geneva 27, Switzerland (Telephone Number in U.S. (518) 436-9686); *World Health Statistics Annual*.

COMOROS - WAGES

G.K. Hall and Company, 70 Lincoln Street, Boston, Massachusetts 02111 (617) 423-3990; *The World in Figures*.

COMOROS - WEATHER

G.K. Hall and Company, 70 Lincoln Street, Boston, Massachusetts 02111 (617) 423-3990; *The World in Figures*.

COMPACT DISCS (AUDIO)

Recording Industry Association of America, 1020 19th Street, NW, Suite 200, Washington, D.C. 20036 (202) 775-0101; *Inside the Recording Industry: A Statistical Overview*.

COMPUTER - See also COMPUTER AND OFFICE EQUIPMENT

COMPUTER - ADVERTISING EXPENDITURES

Publishers Information Bureau, 575 Lexington Avenue, New York, New York 10022 (212) 752-0055.

Television Bureau of Advertising, Incorporated, 850 Third Avenue, New York, New York 10022 (212) 486-1111; data compiled by Competitive Media Reporting, 11 West 42nd Street, New York, New York 10036 (212) 789-1400.

COMPUTER - SALES

Dataquest, Incorporated, 1290 Ridder Park Drive, San Jose, California 95131 (408) 437-8000; *Consolidated Data Base*.

COMPUTER - SOFTWARE

Software Publishers Association, 1730 M Street, NW, Washington, D.C. 20036 (202) 452-1600; *SPA Software Sales Report*.

COMPUTER - USE

Market Data Retrieval, 16 Progress Drive, Shelton, Connecticut 06484 (203) 926-4800; *Microcomputers in Schools*, and unpublished data.

University of Minnesota, Department of Sociology, Minneapolis, Minnesota 55455 (612) 625-5000; *IEA Computers in Education Study*.

U.S. Department of Education, National Center for Education Statistics, 400 Maryland Avenue, SW, Washington, D.C. 20202 (202) 708-5366; *Digest of Education Statistics*.

U.S. Department of Energy, Energy Information Administration, 1000 Independence Avenue, SW, Washington, D.C. 20585 (202) 586-8800; *Housing Characteristics*.

COMPUTER AND OFFICE EQUIPMENT, MANUFACTURING - EARNINGS

U.S. Department of Commerce, Bureau of the Census, Suitland, Maryland 20233 (301) 763-4040; *Annual Survey of Manufactures*, and *Census of Manufactures*.

U.S. Department of Labor, Bureau of Labor Statistics, Two Massachusetts Avenue, NE, Washington, D.C. 20212 (202) 606-7828; *Employment and Earnings*, and Bulletins 2370 and 2429.

COMPUTER AND OFFICE EQUIPMENT, MANUFACTURING - EMPLOYEES

U.S. Department of Commerce, Bureau of the Census, Suitland, Maryland 20233 (301) 763-4040; *Annual Survey of Manufactures*, and *Census of Manufactures*.

U.S. Department of Labor, Bureau of Labor Statistics, Two Massachusetts Avenue, NE, Washington, D.C. 20212 (202) 606-7828; *Employment and Earnings*, *Monthly Labor Review*, and Bulletins 2370 and 2429.

COMPUTER AND OFFICE EQUIPMENT, MANUFACTURING - ESTABLISHMENTS

U.S. Department of Commerce, Bureau of the Census, Suitland, Maryland 20233 (301) 763-4040; *Census of Manufactures*, and *Annual Survey of Manufactures*.

COMPUTER AND OFFICE EQUIPMENT, MANUFACTURING - PROFITS

Forbes, Incorporated, 60 Fifth Avenue, New York, New York 10011 (212) 620-2200; *Forbes Annual Report on American Industry.*

COMPUTER AND OFFICE EQUIPMENT, MANUFACTURING - SHIPMENTS

Electronic Industries Association, 2001 Pennsylvania Avenue, NW, Washington, D.C. 20006 (202) 457-4900; *Electronic Market Data Book.*

U.S. Department of Commerce, Bureau of the Census, Suitland, Maryland 20233 (301) 763-4040; *Census of Service Industries, Current Business Reports, Service Annual Survey, Census of Manufactures, Current Industrial Reports*, and *Annual Survey of Manufactures.*

COMPUTER AND OFFICE EQUIPMENT, MANUFACTURING - VALUE ADDED

U.S. Department of Commerce, Bureau of the Census, Suitland, Maryland 20233 (301) 763-4040; *Census of Manufactures*, and *Annual Survey of Manufactures.*

COMPUTER PROGRAMMING AND DATA PROCESSING SERVICES - EARNINGS

U.S. Department of Commerce, Bureau of the Census, Suitland, Maryland 20233 (301) 763-4040; *Census of Service Industries*, and *County Business Patterns.*

U.S. Department of Labor, Bureau of Labor Statistics, Two Massachusetts Avenue, NE, Washington, D.C. 20212 (202) 606-7828; *Employment and Earnings, Employment and Wages, Annual Averages*, and Bulletins 2370 and 2429.

COMPUTER PROGRAMMING AND DATA PROCESSING SERVICES - EMPLOYEES

U.S. Department of Commerce, Bureau of the Census, Suitland, Maryland 20233 (301) 763-4040; *County Business Patterns*, and *Census of Service Industries.*

U.S. Department of Labor, Bureau of Labor Statistics, Two Massachusetts Avenue, NE, Washington, D.C. 20212 (202) 606-7828; *Employment and Earnings, Employment and Wages, Annual Averages, Monthly Labor Review*, and Bulletins 2370 and 2429.

COMPUTER PROGRAMMING AND DATA PROCESSING SERVICES - ESTABLISHMENTS

U.S. Department of Commerce, Bureau of the Census, Suitland, Maryland 20233 (301) 763-4040; *County Business Patterns*, and *Census of Service Industries.*

COMPUTER PROGRAMMING AND DATA PROCESSING SERVICES - RECEIPTS

U.S. Department of Commerce, Bureau of the Census, Suitland, Maryland 20233 (301) 763-4040; *Census of Service Industries, Current Business Reports*, and *Service Annual Survey.*

COMPUTER SPECIALISTS - DEGREES CONFERRED

U.S. Department of Education, National Center for Education Statistics, 400 Maryland Avenue, SW, Washington, D.C. 20202 (202) 708-5366; *Digest of Education Statistics.*

U.S. National Science Foundation, 4201 Wilson Boulevard, Arlington, Virginia 22230 (703) 306-1234; *Survey of Earned Doctorates*, and *Characteristics of Recent Science and Engineering Graduates.*

COMPUTER SPECIALISTS - LABOR FORCE - SALARY OFFERS

College Placement Council, 62 Highland Avenue, Bethlehem, Pennsylvania 18017 (212) 316-7100; *A Study of Beginning Offers.*

Northwestern University, 633 Clark Street, Evanston, Illinois 60201 (708) 491-3741; *The Northwestern Lindquist-Endicott Report.*

COMPUTER SPECIALISTS - FEDERAL OBLIGATIONS FOR RESEARCH

U.S. National Science Foundation, 4201 Wilson Boulevard, Arlington, Virginia 22230 (703) 306-1234; *Federal Funds for Research and Development.*

COMPUTER USE BY STUDENTS

Quality Education Data, Inc., 1600 Broadway, 12th Floor, Denver, Colorado 80202 (303) 860-1832; *Technology in Public Schools.*

University of Minnesota, Department of Sociology, Minneapolis, Minnesota 55455 (612) 625-5000; *IEA Computers in Education Study.*

U.S. Department of Education, National Center for Education Statistics, 400 Maryland Avenue, SW, Washington, D.C. 20202 (202) 708-5366; *Digest of Education Statistics.*

CONCERTS - SYMPHONY ORCHESTRAS

American Symphony Orchestra League, 777 Fourteenth Street, NW, Washington, D.C. 20005 (202) 628-0099.

CONDENSED AND EVAPORATED MILK

U.S. Department of Agriculture, Economic Research Service, Fourteenth Street and Independence Avenue, SW, Washington, D.C. 20005-4789 (202) 219-1504; *Dairy Products, Milk Production, Disposition, and Income, Food Consumption, Prices, and Expenditures*, and unpublished data.

CONDOMINIUMS

Chicago Title Insurance Company, 111 West Washington Street, Chicago, Illinois 60602 (312) 630-2000; *The Guarantor.*

U.S. Department of Commerce, Bureau of the Census, Suitland, Maryland 20233 (301) 763-4040; *Current Construction Reports.*

CONFECTIONERY PRODUCTS

Television Bureau of Advertising, Inc., 850 Third Avenue, New York, New York 10022 (212) 486-1111. Data compiled by Competitive Media Reporting, 11 West 42nd Street, New York, New York 10036 (212) 789-1400.

CONGENITAL ANOMALIES

U.S. Department of Health and Human Services, National Center for Health Statistics, 3700 East-West Highway, Hyattsville, Maryland 20782 (301) 436-8500; *Monthly Vital Statistics Report*, and *Vital Statistics of the United States.*

CONGESTION ON ROAD

Texas Transportation Institute, Texas A&M University, Riverside Campus, Building 7751, Safety Division, College Station, Texas 77843 (409) 845-8408; *Roadway Congestion in Major Urban Areas.*

Congo - National Statistical Office

Centre National de la Statistique et des Etudes Economiques, BP 2031, Brazzaville, Congo.

Congo - Primary Statistics Source

Centre National de la Statistique et des Etudes Economiques, BP 2031, Brazzaville, Congo; *Annuaire statistique* (Statistical Yearbook); and *Bulletin mensuel des statistique* (Monthly Bulletin of Statistics).

CONGO - AGRICULTURE

Facts on File, 460 Park Avenue South, New York, New York 10016 (800) 443-8323; *The New Book of World Rankings.*

Federal Statistical Office, Gustav - Stresemann - Ring 11, D-6200 Wiesbaden, Germany; *Kongo.*

Food and Agricultural Organization of the United Nations (FAO) Via delle Terme di Caracalla, 00100 Rome, Italy (Telephone Number in U.S. (202) 653-2400); *Production Yearbook, The State of Food and Agriculture,* and *Trade Yearbook.*

G.K. Hall and Company, 70 Lincoln Street, Boston, Massachusetts 02111 (617) 423-3990; *The World in Figures.*

Statistical Office of the United Nations, Publishing Service, New York, New York 10017 (800) 253-9646; *Statistical Yearbook,* and *Survey of Economic and Social Conditions in Africa.*

Times Books, 201 East 50th Street, New York, New York 10022 (212) 751-2600; *The Economist Book of Vital World Statistics.*

United Nations Economic Commission for Africa, Africa Hall, P.O. Box 3001, Addis Ababa, Ethiopia (Telephone Number in U.S. (800) 253-9646); *African Statistical Yearbook.*

The World Bank, 1818 H Street, NW, Washington, D.C. 20433 (202) 477-1234; *World Tables.*

CONGO - AIRLINE SERVICE

Facts on File, 460 Park Avenue South, New York, New York 10016 (800) 443-8323; *The New Book of World Rankings.*

G.K. Hall and Company, 70 Lincoln Street, Boston, Massachusetts 02111 (617) 423-3990; *The World in Figures.*

Statistical Office of the United Nations, Publishing Service, New York, New York 10017 (800) 253-9646; *Statistical Yearbook.*

Times Books, 201 East 50th Street, New York, New York 10022 (212) 751-2600; *The Economist Book of Vital World Statistics.*

United Nations Economic Commission for Africa, Africa Hall, P.O. Box 3001, Addis Ababa, Ethiopia (Telephone Number in U.S. (800) 253-9646); *African Statistical Yearbook.*

CONGO - ALUMINUM PRODUCTION AND CONSUMPTION - See CONGO - MINING AND MINERAL PRODUCTS

CONGO - ANIMAL HEALTH

Food and Agricultural Organization of the United Nations (FAO), Via delle Terme di Caracalla, 00100 Rome, Italy (Telephone Number in U.S. (202) 653-2400); *Animal Health Yearbook.*

CONGO - AREA AND DENSITY OF POPULATION

African Development Bank, 01 BP 1387, Abidjan 01, Cote D'Ivoire; *Selected Statistics on Regional Member Countries.*

Facts on File, 460 Park Avenue South, New York, New York 10016 (800) 443-8323; *The New Book of World Rankings.*

Federal Statistical Office, Gustav - Stresemann - Ring 11, D-6200 Wiesbaden, Germany; *Kongo.*

Food and Agricultural Organization of the United Nations (FAO) Via delle Terme di Caracalla, 00100 Rome, Italy (Telephone Number in U.S. (202) 653-2400); *The State of Food and Agriculture.*

G.K. Hall and Company, 70 Lincoln Street, Boston, Massachusetts 02111 (617) 423-3990; *The World in Figures.*

Statistical Office of the United Nations, Publishing Service, New York, New York 10017 (800) 253-9646; *Statistical Yearbook,* and *Survey of Economic and Social Conditions in Africa.*

Times Books, 201 East 50th Street, New York, New York 10022 (212) 751-2600; *The Economist Book of Vital World Statistics.*

United Nations Educational, Scientific and Cultural Organization (UNESCO), 7 Place de Fontenoy, F-75700 Paris, France (Telephone Number in U.S. (212) 963-5981); *Statistical Yearbook.*

CONGO - ARMS EXPORTS AND IMPORTS

U.S. Arms Control and Disarmament Agency, 320 Twenty-first Street, NW, Washington, D.C. 20451 (202) 647-8677; *World Military Expenditures and Arms Transfers.*

CONGO - BALANCE OF PAYMENTS

African Development Bank, 01 BP 1387, Abidjan 01, Cote D'Ivoire; *Selected Statistics on Regional Member Countries.*

The Economist Intelligence Unit, 111 West 57th Street, New York, New York 10019 (800) 938-4685; *The World Market Atlas.*

Federal Statistical Office, Gustav - Stresemann - Ring 11, D-6200 Wiesbaden, Germany; *Kongo.*

G.K. Hall and Company, 70 Lincoln Street, Boston, Massachusetts 02111 (617) 423-3990; *The World in Figures.*

International Monetary Fund, 700 Nineteenth Street, NW, Washington, D.C. 20431 (202) 623-7000; *Balance of Payments Yearbook.*

Times Books, 201 East 50th Street, New York, New York 10022 (212) 751-2600; *The Economist Book of Vital World Statistics.*

United Nations Economic Commission for Africa, Africa Hall, P.O. Box 3001, Addis Ababa, Ethiopia (Telephone Number in U.S. (800) 253-9646); *African Statistical Yearbook.*

The World Bank, 1818 H Street, NW, Washington, D.C. 20433 (202) 477-1234; *World Tables.*

CONGO - BANKING

Facts on File, 460 Park Avenue South, New York, New York 10016 (800) 443-8323; *The New Book of World Rankings*.

G.K. Hall and Company, 70 Lincoln Street, Boston, Massachusetts 02111 (617) 423-3990; *The World in Figures*.

International Monetary Fund, 700 Nineteenth Street, NW, Washington, D.C. 20431 (202) 623-7000; *International Financial Statistics*.

United Nations Economic Commission for Africa, Africa Hall, P.O. Box 3001, Addis Ababa, Ethiopia (Telephone Number in U.S. (800) 253-9646); *African Statistical Yearbook*.

CONGO - BARLEY PRODUCTION - See CONGO - CROPS

CONGO - BEER PRODUCTION

Facts on File, 460 Park Avenue South, New York, New York 10016 (800) 443-8323; *The New Book of World Rankings*.

Statistical Office of the United Nations, Publishing Service, New York, New York 10017 (800) 253-9646; *Statistical Yearbook*.

CONGO - BIRTH RATES

Facts on File, 460 Park Avenue South, New York, New York 10016 (800) 443-8323; *The New Book of World Rankings*.

Statistical Office of the United Nations, Publishing Service, New York, New York 10017 (800) 253-9646; *Demographic Yearbook*, *Statistical Yearbook*, and *Survey of Economic and Social Conditions in Africa*.

Times Books, 201 East 50th Street, New York, New York 10022 (212) 751-2600; *The Economist Book of Vital World Statistics*.

The World Bank, 1818 H Street, NW, Washington, D.C. 20433 (202) 477-1234; *World Tables*.

CONGO - BONDS

G.K. Hall and Company, 70 Lincoln Street, Boston, Massachusetts 02111 (617) 423-3990; *The World in Figures*.

CONGO - BOOK PRODUCTION

G.K. Hall and Company, 70 Lincoln Street, Boston, Massachusetts 02111 (617) 423-3990; *The World in Figures*.

United Nations Educational, Scientific and Cultural Organization (UNESCO), 7 Place de Fontenoy, F-75700 Paris, France (Telephone Number in U.S. (212) 963-5981); *Statistical Yearbook*.

CONGO - BROADCASTING

Billboard Limited, P.O. Box 9027, 1006 AA Amsterdam, The Netherlands (Telephone Number in U.S. (212) 764-7300); *World Radio TV Handbook*.

Facts on File, 460 Park Avenue South, New York, New York 10016 (800) 443-8323; *The New Book of World Rankings*.

G.K. Hall and Company, 70 Lincoln Street, Boston, Massachusetts 02111 (617) 423-3990; *The World in Figures*.

Times Books, 201 East 50th Street, New York, New York 10022 (212) 751-2600; *The Economist Book of Vital World Statistics*.

CONGO - BUSINESS

G.K. Hall and Company, 70 Lincoln Street, Boston, Massachusetts 02111 (617) 423-3990; *The World in Figures*.

CONGO - BUSINESS AND PROFESSIONAL LICENSES

International Monetary Fund, 700 Nineteenth Street, NW, Washington, D.C. 20431 (202) 623-7000; *Government Finance Statistics Yearbook*.

CONGO - CALORIE SUPPLY

African Development Bank, 01 BP 1387, Abidjan 01, Cote D'Ivoire; *Selected Statistics on Regional Member Countries*.

Food and Agricultural Organization of the United Nations (FAO) Via delle Terme di Caracalla, 00100 Rome, Italy (Telephone Number in U.S. (202) 653-2400); *The State of Food and Agriculture*.

CONGO - CAPITAL REVENUE

International Monetary Fund, 700 Nineteenth Street, NW, Washington, D.C. 20431 (202) 623-7000; *Government Finance Statistics Yearbook*.

CONGO - CATTLE - See CONGO - LIVESTOCK AND POULTRY

CONGO - CEMENT PRODUCTION - See CONGO - MINING AND MINERAL PRODUCTS

CONGO - CHEMICAL (ORGANIC) PRODUCTION - See CONGO - MINING AND MINERAL PRODUCTS

CONGO - CHICKENS - See CONGO - LIVESTOCK AND POULTRY

CONGO - CIGARETTE PRODUCTION - SEE CONGO - TOBACCO PRODUCTION

CONGO - CLASS STRUCTURE

G.K. Hall and Company, 70 Lincoln Street, Boston, Massachusetts 02111 (617) 423-3990; *The World in Figures*.

CONGO - CLIMATE

Facts on File, 460 Park Avenue South, New York, New York 10016 (800) 443-8323; *The New Book of World Rankings*.

G.K. Hall and Company, 70 Lincoln Street, Boston, Massachusetts 02111 (617) 423-3990; *The World in Figures*.

CONGO - COAL PRODUCTION - See CONGO - MINING AND MINERAL PRODUCTS

CONGO - COCOA (BEANS) PRODUCTION - See CONGO - CROPS

CONGO - COFFEE PRODUCTION - See CONGO - CROPS

CONGO - COMMUNICATIONS

Federal Statistical Office, Gustav - Stresemann - Ring 11, D-6200 Wiesbaden, Germany; *Kongo*.

G.K. Hall and Company, 70 Lincoln Street, Boston, Massachusetts 02111 (617) 423-3990; *The World in Figures*.

United Nations Economic Commission for Africa, Africa Hall, P.O. Box 3001, Addis Ababa, Ethiopia (Telephone Number in U.S. (800) 253-9646); *African Statistical Yearbook.*

CONGO - CONSTRUCTION INDUSTRY

Facts on File, 460 Park Avenue South, New York, New York 10016 (800) 443-8323; *The New Book of World Rankings.*

United Nations Economic Commission for Africa, Africa Hall, P.O. Box 3001, Addis Ababa, Ethiopia (Telephone Number in U.S. (800) 253-9646); *African Statistical Yearbook.*

CONGO - CONSUMER PRICE INDEX

African Development Bank, 01 BP 1387, Abidjan 01, Cote D'Ivoire; *Selected Statistics on Regional Member Countries.*

Federal Statistical Office, Gustav - Stresemann - Ring 11, D-6200 Wiesbaden, Germany; *Kongo.*

G.K. Hall and Company, 70 Lincoln Street, Boston, Massachusetts 02111 (617) 423-3990; *The World in Figures.*

Statistical Office of the United Nations, Publishing Service, New York, New York 10017 (800) 253-9646; *Statistical Yearbook,* and *Survey of Economic and Social Conditions in Africa.*

Times Books, 201 East 50th Street, New York, New York 10022 (212) 751-2600; *The Economist Book of Vital World Statistics.*

United Nations Economic Commission for Africa, Africa Hall, P.O. Box 3001, Addis Ababa, Ethiopia (Telephone Number in U.S. (800) 253-9646); *African Statistical Yearbook.*

CONGO - CONSUMER PRICES

Federal Statistical Office, Gustav - Stresemann - Ring 11, D-6200 Wiesbaden, Germany; *Kongo.*

International Labour Office, I.L.O. Publications, CH-1211, Geneva 22, Switzerland; *Yearbook of Labour Statistics.*

International Monetary Fund, 700 Nineteenth Street, NW, Washington, D.C. 20431 (202) 623-7000; *International Financial Statistics.*

CONGO - CONSUMPTION

African Development Bank, 01 BP 1387, Abidjan 01, Cote D'Ivoire; *Selected Statistics on Regional Member Countries.*

G.K. Hall and Company, 70 Lincoln Street, Boston, Massachusetts 02111 (617) 423-3990; *The World in Figures.*

Statistical Office of the United Nations, Publishing Service, New York, New York 10017 (800) 253-9646; *Survey of Economic and Social Conditions in Africa.*

CONGO - COPPER AND COPPER ORE - See CONGO - MINING AND MINERAL PRODUCTS

CONGO - CORN PRODUCTION - See CONGO - CROPS

CONGO - CORPORATE TAXES - See CONGO - TAXATION

CONGO - COTTON - See CONGO - CROPS

CONGO - CRIME

Yale University Press, Yale Station, New Haven, Connecticut 06520 (203) 432-0940; *Violence and Crime in Cross-National Perspective.*

CONGO - CROPS

Facts on File, 460 Park Avenue South, New York, New York 10016 (800) 443-8323; *The New Book of World Rankings.*

Food and Agricultural Organization of the United Nations (FAO) Via delle Terme di Caracalla, 00100 Rome, Italy (Telephone Number in U.S. (202) 653-2400); *The State of Food and Agriculture.*

G.K. Hall and Company, 70 Lincoln Street, Boston, Massachusetts 02111 (617) 423-3990; *The World in Figures.*

Statistical Office of the United Nations, Publishing Service, New York, New York 10017 (800) 253-9646; *Statistical Yearbook.*

United Nations Economic Commission for Africa, Africa Hall, P.O. Box 3001, Addis Ababa, Ethiopia (Telephone Number in U.S. (800) 253-9646); *African Statistical Yearbook.*

CONGO - CUSTOMS DUTIES

G.K. Hall and Company, 70 Lincoln Street, Boston, Massachusetts 02111 (617) 423-3990; *The World in Figures.*

International Monetary Fund, 700 Nineteenth Street, NW, Washington, D.C. 20431 (202) 623-7000; *Government Finance Statistics Yearbook.*

CONGO - DAIRY PRODUCTS

Facts on File, 460 Park Avenue South, New York, New York 10016 (800) 443-8323; *The New Book of World Rankings.*

Food and Agricultural Organization of the United Nations (FAO) Via delle Terme di Caracalla, 00100 Rome, Italy (Telephone Number in U.S. (202) 653-2400); *The State of Food and Agriculture.*

CONGO - DEATH RATES

G.K. Hall and Company, 70 Lincoln Street, Boston, Massachusetts 02111 (617) 423-3990; *The World in Figures.*

Statistical Office of the United Nations, Publishing Service, New York, New York 10017 (800) 253-9646; *Statistical Yearbook,* and *Survey of Economic and Social Conditions in Africa.*

Times Books, 201 East 50th Street, New York, New York 10022 (212) 751-2600; *The Economist Book of Vital World Statistics.*

World Health Organization, Office of Publications, Avenue Appia, CH-1211 Geneva 27, Switzerland (Telephone Number in U.S. (518) 436-9686); *World Health Statistics Annual.*

CONGO - DEFENSE EXPENDITURES

G.K. Hall and Company, 70 Lincoln Street, Boston, Massachusetts 02111 (617) 423-3990; *The World in Figures.*

International Monetary Fund, 700 Nineteenth Street, NW, Washington, D.C. 20431 (202) 623-7000; *Government Finance Statistics Yearbook.*

U.S. Arms Control and Disarmament Agency, 320 Twenty-first Street, NW, Washington, D.C. 20451 (202) 647-8677; *World Military*

Expenditures and Arms Transfers.

CONGO - DEMOGRAPHY

The Economist Intelligence Unit, 111 West 57th Street, New York, New York 10019 (800) 938-4685; *The World Market Atlas.*

Facts on File, 460 Park Avenue South, New York, New York 10016 (800) 443-8323; *The New Book of World Rankings.*

Federal Statistical Office, Gustav - Stresemann - Ring 11, D-6200 Wiesbaden, Germany; *Kongo.*

G.K. Hall and Company, 70 Lincoln Street, Boston, Massachusetts 02111 (617) 423-3990; *The World in Figures.*

Statistical Office of the United Nations, Publishing Service, New York, New York 10017 (800) 253-9646; *Survey of Economic and Social Conditions in Africa.*

CONGO - DEVELOPMENT ASSISTANCE

G.K. Hall and Company, 70 Lincoln Street, Boston, Massachusetts 02111 (617) 423-3990; *The World in Figures.*

Statistical Office of the United Nations, Publishing Service, New York, New York 10017 (800) 253-9646; *Statistical Yearbook.*

CONGO - DIAMOND - See CONGO - MINING AND MINERAL PRODUCTS

CONGO - DISEASE

G.K. Hall and Company, 70 Lincoln Street, Boston, Massachusetts 02111 (617) 423-3990; *The World in Figures.*

World Health Organization, Office of Publications, Avenue Appia, CH-1211 Geneva 27, Switzerland (Telephone Number in U.S. (518) 436-9686); *World Health Statistics Annual.*

CONGO - DIVORCE RATES

Facts on File, 460 Park Avenue South, New York, New York 10016 (800) 443-8323; *The New Book of World Rankings.*

Statistical Office of the United Nations, Publishing Service, New York, New York 10017 (800) 253-9646; *Demographic Yearbook,* and *Statistical Yearbook.*

CONGO - DOMESTIC PRODUCT

G.K. Hall and Company, 70 Lincoln Street, Boston, Massachusetts 02111 (617) 423-3990; *The World in Figures.*

CONGO - ECONOMY

African Development Bank, 01 BP 1387, Abidjan 01, Cote D'Ivoire; *Selected Statistics on Regional Member Countries.*

Facts on File, 460 Park Avenue South, New York, New York 10016 (800) 443-8323; *The New Book of World Rankings.*

Federal Statistical Office, Gustav - Stresemann - Ring 11, D-6200 Wiesbaden, Germany; *Kongo.*

G.K. Hall and Company, 70 Lincoln Street, Boston, Massachusetts 02111 (617) 423-3990; *The World in Figures.*

Statistical Office of the United Nations, Publishing Service, New York, New York 10017 (800) 253-9646; *Foreign Trade Statistics for Africa.*

CONGO - EDUCATION

African Development Bank, 01 BP 1387, Abidjan 01, Cote D'Ivoire; *Selected Statistics on Regional Member Countries.*

The Economist Intelligence Unit, 111 West 57th Street, New York, New York 10019 (800) 938-4685; *The World Market Atlas.*

Facts on File, 460 Park Avenue South, New York, New York 10016 (800) 443-8323; *The New Book of World Rankings.*

Federal Statistical Office, Gustav - Stresemann - Ring 11, D-6200 Wiesbaden, Germany; *Kongo.*

G.K. Hall and Company, 70 Lincoln Street, Boston, Massachusetts 02111 (617) 423-3990; *The World in Figures.*

International Monetary Fund, 700 Nineteenth Street, NW, Washington, D.C. 20431 (202) 623-7000; *Government Finance Statistics Yearbook.*

Statistical Office of the United Nations, Publishing Service, New York, New York 10017 (800) 253-9646; *Survey of Economic and Social Conditions in Africa.*

Times Books, 201 East 50th Street, New York, New York 10022 (212) 751-2600; *The Economist Book of Vital World Statistics.*

United Nations Economic Commission for Africa, Africa Hall, P.O. Box 3001, Addis Ababa, Ethiopia (Telephone Number in U.S. (800) 253-9646); *African Statistical Yearbook.*

United Nations Educational, Scientific and Cultural Organization (UNESCO), 7 Place de Fontenoy, F-75700 Paris, France (Telephone Number in U.S. (212) 963-5981); *Statistical Yearbook.*

The World Bank, 1818 H Street, NW, Washington, D.C. 20433 (202) 477-1234; *World Tables.*

CONGO - EGG PRODUCTION - See CONGO - DAIRY PRODUCTS

CONGO - ELECTRICITY

Facts on File, 460 Park Avenue South, New York, New York 10016 (800) 443-8323; *The New Book of World Rankings.*

Penn Well Publishing Company, 1421 South Sheridan Road, P.O. Box 1260, Tulsa, Oklahoma 74101 (800) 752-9764; *International Energy Statistics Sourcebook.*

Statistical Office of the United Nations, Publishing Service, New York, New York 10017 (800) 253-9646; *Statistical Yearbook,* and *Survey of Economic and Social Conditions in Africa.*

Times Books, 201 East 50th Street, New York, New York 10022 (212) 751-2600; *The Economist Book of Vital World Statistics.*

United Nations Economic Commission for Africa, Africa Hall, P.O. Box 3001, Addis Ababa, Ethiopia (Telephone Number in U.S. (800) 253-9646); *African Statistical Yearbook.*

CONGO - EMPLOYMENT

Facts on File, 460 Park Avenue South, New York, New York 10016 (800) 443-8323; *The New Book of World Rankings.*

Federal Statistical Office, Gustav - Stresemann - Ring 11, D-6200 Wiesbaden, Germany; *Kongo.*

International Labour Office, I.L.O. Publications, CH-1211, Geneva 22, Switzerland; *Yearbook of Labour Statistics.*

Statistical Office of the United Nations, Publishing Service, New York, New York 10017 (800) 253-9646; *Statistical Yearbook,* and *Survey of Economic and Social Conditions in Africa.*

United Nations Economic Commission for Africa, Africa Hall, P.O. Box 3001, Addis Ababa, Ethiopia (Telephone Number in U.S. (800) 253-9646); *African Statistical Yearbook.*

CONGO - ENERGY

Facts on File, 460 Park Avenue South, New York, New York 10016 (800) 443-8323; *The New Book of World Rankings.*

Food and Agricultural Organization of the United Nations (FAO) Via delle Terme di Caracalla, 00100 Rome, Italy (Telephone Number in U.S. (202) 653-2400); *The State of Food and Agriculture.*

G.K. Hall and Company, 70 Lincoln Street, Boston, Massachusetts 02111 (617) 423-3990; *The World in Figures.*

Penn Well Publishing Company, 1421 South Sheridan Road, P.O. Box 1260, Tulsa, Oklahoma 74101 (800) 752-9764; *International Energy Statistics Sourcebook.*

Statistical Office of the United Nations, Publishing Service, New York, New York 10017 (800) 253-9646; *Energy Statistics Yearbook,* and *Statistical Yearbook.*

Times Books, 201 East 50th Street, New York, New York 10022 (212) 751-2600; *The Economist Book of Vital World Statistics.*

United Nations Economic Commission for Africa, Africa Hall, P.O. Box 3001, Addis Ababa, Ethiopia (Telephone Number in U.S. (800) 253-9646); *African Statistical Yearbook.*

CONGO - EXCHANGE RATES

African Development Bank, 01 BP 1387, Abidjan 01, Cote D'Ivoire; *Selected Statistics on Regional Member Countries.*

International Monetary Fund, 700 Nineteenth Street, NW, Washington, D.C. 20431 (202) 623-7000; *International Financial Statistics.*

Statistical Office of the United Nations, Publishing Service, New York, New York 10017 (800) 253-9646; *Foreign Trade Statistics for Africa,* and *Statistical Yearbook.*

CONGO - EXCISE TAXES - See CONGO - TAXATION

CONGO - EXPORTS

African Development Bank, 01 BP 1387, Abidjan 01, Cote D'Ivoire; *Selected Statistics on Regional Member Countries.*

The Economist Intelligence Unit, 111 West 57th Street, New York, New York 10019 (800) 938-4685; *The World Market Atlas.*

Food and Agricultural Organization of the United Nations (FAO) Via delle Terme di Caracalla, 00100 Rome, Italy (Telephone Number in U.S. (202) 653-2400); *The State of Food and Agriculture.*

G.K. Hall and Company, 70 Lincoln Street, Boston, Massachusetts 02111 (617) 423-3990; *The World in Figures.*

International Monetary Fund, 700 Nineteenth Street, NW, Washington, D.C. 20431 (202) 623-7000; *Direction of Trade Statistics, Government Finance Statistics Yearbook,* and *International Financial Statistics.*

Statistical Office of the United Nations, Publishing Service, New York, New York 10017 (800) 253-9646; *Foreign Trade Statistics for Africa,* and *Survey of Economic and Social Conditions in Africa.*

Times Books, 201 East 50th Street, New York, New York 10022 (212) 751-2600; *The Economist Book of Vital World Statistics.*

United Nations Economic Commission for Africa, Africa Hall, P.O. Box 3001, Addis Ababa, Ethiopia (Telephone Number in U.S. (800) 253-9646); *African Statistical Yearbook.*

The World Bank, 1818 H Street, NW, Washington, D.C. 20433 (202) 477-1234; *World Tables.*

CONGO - EXTERNAL INDEBTEDNESS

African Development Bank, 01 BP 1387, Abidjan 01, Cote D'Ivoire; *Selected Statistics on Regional Member Countries.*

Statistical Office of the United Nations, Publishing Service, New York, New York 10017 (800) 253-9646; *Survey of Economic and Social Conditions in Africa.*

The World Bank, 1818 H Street, NW, Washington, D.C. 20433 (202) 477-1234; *World Tables.*

CONGO - EXTERNAL TRADE

African Development Bank, 01 BP 1387, Abidjan 01, Cote D'Ivoire; *Selected Statistics on Regional Member Countries.*

Food and Agricultural Organization of the United Nations (FAO) Via delle Terme di Caracalla, 00100 Rome, Italy (Telephone Number in U.S. (202) 653-2400); *The State of Food and Agriculture,* and *Trade Yearbook.*

G.K. Hall and Company, 70 Lincoln Street, Boston, Massachusetts 02111 (617) 423-3990; *The World in Figures.*

Statistical Office of the United Nations, Publishing Service, New York, New York 10017 (800) 253-9646; *Statistical Yearbook.*

CONGO - FARM CROPS - See CONGO - CROPS

CONGO - FERTILITY RATES

Facts on File, 460 Park Avenue South, New York, New York 10016 (800) 443-8323; *The New Book of World Rankings.*

Statistical Office of the United Nations, Publishing Service, New York, New York 10017 (800) 253-9646; *Survey of Economic and Social Conditions in Africa.*

Times Books, 201 East 50th Street, New York, New York 10022 (212) 751-2600; *The Economist Book of Vital World Statistics.*

The World Bank, 1818 H Street, NW, Washington, D.C. 20433 (202) 477-1234; *World Tables.*

CONGO - FERTILIZER

Food and Agricultural Organization of the United Nations (FAO), Via delle Terme di Caracalla, 00100 Rome, Italy (Telephone Number in U.S. (202) 653-2400); *Fertilizer Yearbook*, and *The State of Food and Agriculture*.

Statistical Office of the United Nations, Publishing Service, New York, New York 10017 (800) 253-9646; *Statistical Yearbook*.

CONGO - FETAL MORTALITY

Statistical Office of the United Nations, Publishing Service, New York, New York 10017 (800) 253-9646; *Demographic Yearbook*.

CONGO - FINANCE

African Development Bank, 01 BP 1387, Abidjan 01, Cote D'Ivoire; *Selected Statistics on Regional Member Countries*.

Facts on File, 460 Park Avenue South, New York, New York 10016 (800) 443-8323; *The New Book of World Rankings*.

Federal Statistical Office, Gustav - Stresemann - Ring 11, D-6200 Wiesbaden, Germany; *Kongo*.

G.K. Hall and Company, 70 Lincoln Street, Boston, Massachusetts 02111 (617) 423-3990; *The World in Figures*.

International Monetary Fund, 700 Nineteenth Street, NW, Washington, D.C. 20431 (202) 623-7000; *International Financial Statistics*.

United Nations Economic Commission for Africa, Africa Hall, P.O. Box 3001, Addis Ababa, Ethiopia (Telephone Number in U.S. (800) 253-9646); *African Statistical Yearbook*.

CONGO - FISHERIES

Facts on File, 460 Park Avenue South, New York, New York 10016 (800) 443-8323; *The New Book of World Rankings*.

Federal Statistical Office, Gustav - Stresemann - Ring 11, D-6200 Wiesbaden, Germany; *Kongo*.

Food and Agricultural Organization of the United Nations (FAO) Via delle Terme di Caracalla, 00100 Rome, Italy (Telephone Number in U.S. (202) 653-2400); *The State of Food and Agriculture*, and *Yearbook of Fishery Statistics*.

Statistical Office of the United Nations, Publishing Service, New York, New York 10017 (800) 253-9646; *Statistical Yearbook*, and *Survey of Economic and Social Conditions in Africa*.

United Nations Economic Commission for Africa, Africa Hall, P.O. Box 3001, Addis Ababa, Ethiopia (Telephone Number in U.S. (800) 253-9646); *African Statistical Yearbook*.

CONGO - FLOUR PRODUCTION

Statistical Office of the United Nations, Publishing Service, New York, New York 10017 (800) 253-9646; *Statistical Yearbook*.

CONGO - FOOD

African Development Bank, 01 BP 1387, Abidjan 01, Cote D'Ivoire; *Selected Statistics on Regional Member Countries*.

Food and Agricultural Organization of the United Nations (FAO) Via delle Terme di Caracalla, 00100 Rome, Italy (Telephone Number in U.S. (202) 653-2400); *Production Yearbook*, and *The State of Food and Agriculture*.

G.K. Hall and Company, 70 Lincoln Street, Boston, Massachusetts 02111 (617) 423-3990; *The World in Figures*.

CONGO - FOREIGN AID

G.K. Hall and Company, 70 Lincoln Street, Boston, Massachusetts 02111 (617) 423-3990; *The World in Figures*.

CONGO - FOREIGN TRADE

Facts on File, 460 Park Avenue South, New York, New York 10016 (800) 443-8323; *The New Book of World Rankings*.

Federal Statistical Office, Gustav - Stresemann - Ring 11, D-6200 Wiesbaden, Germany; *Kongo*.

Food and Agricultural Organization of the United Nations (FAO) Via delle Terme di Caracalla, 00100 Rome, Italy (Telephone Number in U.S. (202) 653-2400); *The State of Food and Agriculture*.

G.K. Hall and Company, 70 Lincoln Street, Boston, Massachusetts 02111 (617) 423-3990; *The World in Figures*.

Organisation for Economic Co-operation and Development (OECD), 2 rue Andre-Pascal, 75 Paris 16, France (Telephone Number in U.S. (202) 785-6323); *Trade by Commodities*.

Statistical Office of the United Nations, Publishing Service, New York, New York 10017 (800) 253-9646; *Foreign Trade Statistics for Africa*, *International Trade Statistics Yearbook*, and *Statistical Yearbook*.

United Nations Economic Commission for Africa, Africa Hall, P.O. Box 3001, Addis Ababa, Ethiopia (Telephone Number in U.S. (800) 253-9646); *African Statistical Yearbook*.

The World Bank, 1818 H Street, NW, Washington, D.C. 20433 (202) 477-1234; *World Tables*.

CONGO - FORESTRY AND FOREST PRODUCTS

Facts on File, 460 Park Avenue South, New York, New York 10016 (800) 443-8323; *The New Book of World Rankings*.

Federal Statistical Office, Gustav - Stresemann - Ring 11, D-6200 Wiesbaden, Germany; *Kongo*.

Food and Agricultural Organization of the United Nations (FAO) Via delle Terme di Caracalla, 00100 Rome, Italy (Telephone Number in U.S. (202) 653-2400); *The State of Food and Agriculture*, and *Yearbook of Forest Products*.

G.K. Hall and Company, 70 Lincoln Street, Boston, Massachusetts 02111 (617) 423-3990; *The World in Figures*.

International Monetary Fund, 700 Nineteenth Street, NW, Washington, D.C. 20431 (202) 623-7000; *International Financial Statistics*.

United Nations Economic Commission for Africa, Africa Hall, P.O. Box 3001, Addis Ababa, Ethiopia (Telephone Number in U.S. (800) 253-9646); *African Statistical Yearbook*.

United Nations Educational, Scientific and Cultural Organization (UNESCO), 7 Place de Fontenoy, F-75700 Paris, France (Telephone Number in U.S. (212) 963-5981); *Statistical Yearbook.*

CONGO - GAS PRODUCTION - See CONGO - MINING AND MINERAL PRODUCTS

CONGO - GENERAL INDUSTRIAL STATISTICS

Federal Statistical Office, Gustav - Stresemann - Ring 11, D-6200 Wiesbaden, Germany; *Kongo.*

CONGO - GENERAL MORTALITY

Statistical Office of the United Nations, Publishing Service, New York, New York 10017 (800) 253-9646; *Demographic Yearbook.*

CONGO - GEOGRAPHIC DATA

Facts on File, 460 Park Avenue South, New York, New York 10016 (800) 443-8323; *The New Book of World Rankings.*

Federal Statistical Office, Gustav - Stresemann - Ring 11, D-6200 Wiesbaden, Germany; *Kongo.*

CONGO - GOATS - See CONGO - LIVESTOCK AND POULTRY

CONGO - GOLD HOLDINGS

International Monetary Fund, 700 Nineteenth Street, NW, Washington, D.C. 20431 (202) 623-7000; *International Financial Statistics.*

Statistical Office of the United Nations, Publishing Service, New York, New York 10017 (800) 253-9646; *Statistical Yearbook.*

The World Bank, 1818 H Street, NW, Washington, D.C. 20433 (202) 477-1234; *World Tables.*

CONGO - GOLD PRODUCTION AND CONSUMPTION - See CONGO - MINING AND MINERAL PRODUCTS

CONGO - GOVERNMENT

G.K. Hall and Company, 70 Lincoln Street, Boston, Massachusetts 02111 (617) 423-3990; *The World in Figures.*

CONGO - GOVERNMENT EXPENDITURES

International Monetary Fund, 700 Nineteenth Street, NW, Washington, D.C. 20431 (202) 623-7000; *Government Finance Statistics Yearbook.*

Times Books, 201 East 50th Street, New York, New York 10022 (212) 751-2600; *The Economist Book of Vital World Statistics.*

The World Bank, 1818 H Street, NW, Washington, D.C. 20433 (202) 477-1234; *World Tables.*

CONGO - GOVERNMENT FINANCE

International Monetary Fund, 700 Nineteenth Street, NW, Washington, D.C. 20431 (202) 623-7000; *International Financial Statistics.*

CONGO - GOVERNMENT REVENUE

International Monetary Fund, 700 Nineteenth Street, NW, Washington, D.C. 20431 (202) 623-7000; *Government Finance Statistics Yearbook.*

Statistical Office of the United Nations, Publishing Service, New York, New York 10017 (800) 253-9646; *Survey of Economic and Social Conditions in Africa.*

Times Books, 201 East 50th Street, New York, New York 10022 (212) 751-2600; *The Economist Book of Vital World Statistics.*

The World Bank, 1818 H Street, NW, Washington, D.C. 20433 (202) 477-1234; *World Tables.*

CONGO - GRAIN PRODUCTION - See CONGO - CROPS

CONGO - GRANTS

International Monetary Fund, 700 Nineteenth Street, NW, Washington, D.C. 20431 (202) 623-7000; *Government Finance Statistics Yearbook.*

CONGO - GROSS DOMESTIC PRODUCT

African Development Bank, 01 BP 1387, Abidjan 01, Cote D'Ivoire; *Selected Statistics on Regional Member Countries.*

The Economist Intelligence Unit, 111 West 57th Street, New York, New York 10019 (800) 938-4685; *The World Market Atlas.*

Facts on File, 460 Park Avenue South, New York, New York 10016 (800) 443-8323; *The New Book of World Rankings.*

G.K. Hall and Company, 70 Lincoln Street, Boston, Massachusetts 02111 (617) 423-3990; *The World in Figures.*

Statistical Office of the United Nations, Publishing Service, New York, New York 10017 (800) 253-9646; *Statistical Yearbook,* and *Survey of Economic and Social Conditions in Africa.*

Times Books, 201 East 50th Street, New York, New York 10022 (212) 751-2600; *The Economist Book of Vital World Statistics.*

United Nations Economic Commission for Africa, Africa Hall, P.O. Box 3001, Addis Ababa, Ethiopia (Telephone Number in U.S. (800) 253-9646); *African Statistical Yearbook.*

The World Bank, 1818 H Street, NW, Washington, D.C. 20433 (202) 477-1234; *World Tables.*

CONGO - GROSS NATIONAL PRODUCT

U.S. Arms Control and Disarmament Agency, 320 Twenty-first Street, NW, Washington, D.C. 20451 (202) 647-8677; *World Military Expenditures and Arms Transfers.*

The World Bank, 1818 H Street, NW, Washington, D.C. 20433 (202) 477-1234; *World Tables.*

CONGO - GROUNDNUTS PRODUCTION - See CONGO - CROPS

CONGO - HEALTH

African Development Bank, 01 BP 1387, Abidjan 01, Cote D'Ivoire; *Selected Statistics on Regional Member Countries.*

Facts on File, 460 Park Avenue South, New York, New York 10016 (800) 443-8323; *The New Book of World Rankings.*

Federal Statistical Office, Gustav - Stresemann - Ring 11, D-6200 Wiesbaden, Germany; *Kongo.*

G.K. Hall and Company, 70 Lincoln Street, Boston, Massachusetts 02111 (617) 423-3990; *The World in Figures.*

Statistical Office of the United Nations, Publishing Service, New York, New York 10017 (800) 253-9646; *Statistical Yearbook.*

Times Books, 201 East 50th Street, New York, New York 10022 (212) 751-2600; *The Economist Book of Vital World Statistics.*

United Nations Economic Commission for Africa, Africa Hall, P.O. Box 3001, Addis Ababa, Ethiopia (Telephone Number in U.S. (800) 253-9646); *African Statistical Yearbook.*

World Health Organization, Office of Publications, Avenue Appia, CH-1211 Geneva 27, Switzerland (Telephone Number in U.S. (518) 436-9686); *World Health Statistics Annual.*

CONGO - HEALTH EXPENDITURE

International Monetary Fund, 700 Nineteenth Street, NW, Washington, D.C. 20431 (202) 623-7000; *Government Finance Statistics Yearbook.*

CONGO - HIDE PRODUCTION

Food and Agricultural Organization of the United Nations (FAO), Via delle Terme di Caracalla, 00100 Rome, Italy (Telephone Number in U.S. (202) 653-2400); *Production Yearbook.*

CONGO - HIGHWAYS

G.K. Hall and Company, 70 Lincoln Street, Boston, Massachusetts 02111 (617) 423-3990; *The World in Figures.*

International Road Federation, 525 School Street, SW, Washington, D.C. 20024 (202) 554-2106; *World Road Statistics.*

Statistical Office of the United Nations, Publishing Service, New York, New York 10017 (800) 253-9646; *Survey of Economic and Social Conditions in Africa.*

United Nations Economic Commission for Africa, Africa Hall, P.O. Box 3001, Addis Ababa, Ethiopia (Telephone Number in U.S. (800) 253-9646); *African Statistical Yearbook.*

CONGO - HOURS OF WORK - See CONGO - EMPLOYMENT

CONGO - HORSES - See CONGO - LIVESTOCK AND POULTRY

CONGO - HOUSING AND HOUSING UNITS

Facts on File, 460 Park Avenue South, New York, New York 10016 (800) 443-8323; *The New Book of World Rankings.*

Statistical Office of the United Nations, Publishing Service, New York, New York 10017 (800) 253-9646; *Statistical Yearbook.*

CONGO - HOUSING EXPENDITURES

International Monetary Fund, 700 Nineteenth Street, NW, Washington, D.C. 20431 (202) 623-7000; *Government Finance Statistics Yearbook.*

CONGO - ILLITERATE POPULATION

The Economist Intelligence Unit, 111 West 57th Street, New York, New York 10019 (800) 938-4685; *The World Market Atlas.*

G.K. Hall and Company, 70 Lincoln Street, Boston, Massachusetts 02111 (617) 423-3990; *The World in Figures.*

United Nations Educational, Scientific and Cultural Organization (UNESCO), 7 Place de Fontenoy, F-75700 Paris, France (Telephone Number in U.S. (212) 963-5981); *Statistical Yearbook.*

CONGO - IMPORTS

African Development Bank, 01 BP 1387, Abidjan 01, Cote D'Ivoire; *Selected Statistics on Regional Member Countries.*

The Economist Intelligence Unit, 111 West 57th Street, New York, New York 10019 (800) 938-4685; *The World Market Atlas.*

Food and Agricultural Organization of the United Nations (FAO) Via delle Terme di Caracalla, 00100 Rome, Italy (Telephone Number in U.S. (202) 653-2400); *The State of Food and Agriculture.*

G.K. Hall and Company, 70 Lincoln Street, Boston, Massachusetts 02111 (617) 423-3990; *The World in Figures.*

International Monetary Fund, 700 Nineteenth Street, NW, Washington, D.C. 20431 (202) 623-7000; *Direction of Trade Statistics, Government Finance Statistics Yearbook,* and *International Financial Statistics.*

Statistical Office of the United Nations, Publishing Service, New York, New York 10017 (800) 253-9646; *Foreign Trade Statistics for Africa, Survey of Economic and Social Conditions in Africa,* and *Trade in Manufactures of Developing Countries.*

Times Books, 201 East 50th Street, New York, New York 10022 (212) 751-2600; *The Economist Book of Vital World Statistics.*

United Nations Economic Commission for Africa, Africa Hall, P.O. Box 3001, Addis Ababa, Ethiopia (Telephone Number in U.S. (800) 253-9646); *African Statistical Yearbook.*

The World Bank, 1818 H Street, NW, Washington, D.C. 20433 (202) 477-1234; *World Tables.*

CONGO - INCOME TAXES - See CONGO - TAXATION

CONGO - INDUSTRY

Facts on File, 460 Park Avenue South, New York, New York 10016 (800) 443-8323; *The New Book of World Rankings.*

Federal Statistical Office, Gustav - Stresemann - Ring 11, D-6200 Wiesbaden, Germany; *Kongo.*

G.K. Hall and Company, 70 Lincoln Street, Boston, Massachusetts 02111 (617) 423-3990; *The World in Figures.*

International Labour Office, I.L.O. Publications, CH-1211, Geneva 22, Switzerland; *Yearbook of Labour Statistics.*

Statistical Office of the United Nations, Publishing Service, New York, New York 10017 (800) 253-9646; *Survey of Economic and Social Conditions in Africa.*

Times Books, 201 East 50th Street, New York, New York 10022 (212) 751-2600; *The Economist Book of Vital World Statistics.*

United Nations Economic Commission for Africa, Africa Hall, P.O. Box 3001, Addis Ababa, Ethiopia (Telephone Number in U.S. (800) 253-9646); *African Statistical Yearbook.*

The World Bank, 1818 H Street, NW, Washington, D.C. 20433 (202) 477-1234; *World Tables.*

CONGO - INFANT AND MATERNAL MORTALITY

Statistical Office of the United Nations, Publishing Service, New York, New York 10017 (800) 253-9646; *Demographic Yearbook, Statistical Yearbook,* and *Survey of Economic and Social Conditions in Africa.*

Times Books, 201 East 50th Street, New York, New York 10022 (212) 751-2600; *The Economist Book of Vital World Statistics.*

The World Bank, 1818 H Street, NW, Washington, D.C. 20433 (202) 477-1234; *World Tables.*

CONGO - INTERNATIONAL LIQUIDITY

International Monetary Fund, 700 Nineteenth Street, NW, Washington, D.C. 20431 (202) 623-7000; *International Financial Statistics.*

CONGO - INTERNATIONAL RESERVES EXCLUDING GOLD

African Development Bank, 01 BP 1387, Abidjan 01, Cote D'Ivoire; *Selected Statistics on Regional Member Countries.*

The World Bank, 1818 H Street, NW, Washington, D.C. 20433 (202) 477-1234; *World Tables.*

CONGO - IRON ORE PRODUCTION AND CONSUMPTION - See CONGO - MINING AND MINERAL PRODUCTS

CONGO - LABOR FORCE

African Development Bank, 01 BP 1387, Abidjan 01, Cote D'Ivoire; *Selected Statistics on Regional Member Countries.*

Facts on File, 460 Park Avenue South, New York, New York 10016 (800) 443-8323; *The New Book of World Rankings.*

Food and Agricultural Organization of the United Nations (FAO) Via delle Terme di Caracalla, 00100 Rome, Italy (Telephone Number in U.S. (202) 653-2400); *The State of Food and Agriculture.*

G.K. Hall and Company, 70 Lincoln Street, Boston, Massachusetts 02111 (617) 423-3990; *The World in Figures.*

The World Bank, 1818 H Street, NW, Washington, D.C. 20433 (202) 477-1234; *World Tables.*

CONGO - LABOR PRODUCTIVITY

International Labour Office, I.L.O. Publications, CH-1211, Geneva 22, Switzerland; *Yearbook of Labour Statistics.*

CONGO - LAND USE

Food and Agricultural Organization of the United Nations (FAO), Via delle Terme di Caracalla, 00100 Rome, Italy (Telephone Number in U.S. (202) 653-2400); *Production Yearbook.*

G.K. Hall and Company, 70 Lincoln Street, Boston, Massachusetts 02111 (617) 423-3990; *The World in Figures.*

CONGO - LEAD ORE PRODUCTION AND CONSUMPTION - See CONGO - MINING AND MINERAL PRODUCTS

CONGO - LIBRARIES

Facts on File, 460 Park Avenue South, New York, New York 10016 (800) 443-8323; *The New Book of World Rankings.*

CONGO - LIFE EXPECTANCY

African Development Bank, 01 BP 1387, Abidjan 01, Cote D'Ivoire; *Selected Statistics on Regional Member Countries.*

CONGO- LITERACY RATE

Statistical Office of the United Nations, Publishing Service, New York, New York 10017 (800) 253-9646; *Survey of Economic and Social Conditions in Africa.*

CONGO - LIVESTOCK AND POULTRY

Facts on File, 460 Park Avenue South, New York, New York 10016 (800) 443-8323; *The New Book of World Rankings.*

Food and Agricultural Organization of the United Nations (FAO), Via delle Terme di Caracalla, 00100 Rome, Italy (Telephone Number in U.S. (202) 653-2400); *Production Yearbook,* and *The State of Food and Agriculture.*

G.K. Hall and Company, 70 Lincoln Street, Boston, Massachusetts 02111 (617) 423-3990; *The World in Figures.*

Statistical Office of the United Nations, Publishing Service, New York, New York 10017 (800) 253-9646; *Survey of Economic and Social Conditions in Africa,* and *Statistical Yearbook.*

United Nations Economic Commission for Africa, Africa Hall, P.O. Box 3001, Addis Ababa, Ethiopia (Telephone Number in U.S. (800) 253-9646); *African Statistical Yearbook.*

CONGO - LIVING LEVELS

G.K. Hall and Company, 70 Lincoln Street, Boston, Massachusetts 02111 (617) 423-3990; *The World in Figures.*

Times Books, 201 East 50th Street, New York, New York 10022 (212) 751-2600; *The Economist Book of Vital World Statistics.*

CONGO - MAIL - NUMBER OF ITEMS SENT AND RECEIVED

Statistical Office of the United Nations, Publishing Service, New York, New York 10017 (800) 253-9646; *Statistical Yearbook.*

CONGO - MANUFACTURING

Facts on File, 460 Park Avenue South, New York, New York 10016 (800) 443-8323; *The New Book of World Rankings.*

G.K. Hall and Company, 70 Lincoln Street, Boston, Massachusetts 02111 (617) 423-3990; *The World in Figures.*

Statistical Office of the United Nations, Publishing Service, New York, New York 10017 (800) 253-9646; *Statistical Yearbook,* and *Survey of Economic and Social Conditions in Africa.*

Times Books, 201 East 50th Street, New York, New York 10022 (212) 751-2600; *The Economist Book of Vital World Statistics.*

United Nations Economic Commission for Africa, Africa Hall, P.O. Box 3001, Addis Ababa, Ethiopia (Telephone Number in U.S. (800) 253-9646); *African Statistical Yearbook.*

The World Bank, 1818 H Street, NW, Washington, D.C. 20433 (202) 477-1234; *World Tables.*

CONGO - MARRIAGE RATES

Facts on File, 460 Park Avenue South, New York, New York 10016 (800) 443-8323; *The New Book of World Rankings.*

Statistical Office of the United Nations, Publishing Service, New York, New York 10017 (800) 253-9646; *Demographic Yearbook,* and *Statistical Yearbook.*

CONGO - MEAT PRODUCTION - See CONGO - LIVESTOCK AND POULTRY

CONGO - MERCHANT SHIPPING

G.K. Hall and Company, 70 Lincoln Street, Boston, Massachusetts 02111 (617) 423-3990; *The World in Figures.*

Lloyd's Register of Shipping, 17 Battery Place, New York, New York 10004 (212) 425-8050; *Register of Ships.*

Statistical Office of the United Nations, Publishing Service, New York, New York 10017 (800) 253-9646; *Statistical Yearbook.*

Times Books, 201 East 50th Street, New York, New York 10022 (212) 751-2600; *The Economist Book of Vital World Statistics.*

United Nations Economic Commission for Africa, Africa Hall, P.O. Box 3001, Addis Ababa, Ethiopia (Telephone Number in U.S. (800) 253-9646); *African Statistical Yearbook.*

CONGO - MILK - See CONGO - DAIRY PRODUCTS

CONGO - MILITARY

G.K. Hall and Company, 70 Lincoln Street, Boston, Massachusetts 02111 (617) 423-3990; *The World in Figures.*

The International Institute for Strategic Studies, 23 Tavistock Street, London WC2E 7NQ, England; *The Military Balance.*

U.S. Arms Control and Disarmament Agency, 320 Twenty-first Street, NW, Washington, D.C. 20451 (202) 647-8677; *World Military Expenditures and Arms Transfers.*

CONGO - MINING AND MINERAL PRODUCTS

Facts on File, 460 Park Avenue South, New York, New York 10016 (800) 443-8323; *The New Book of World Rankings.*

G.K. Hall and Company, 70 Lincoln Street, Boston, Massachusetts 02111 (617) 423-3990; *The World in Figures.*

Penn Well Publishing Company, 1421 South Sheridan Road, P.O. Box 1260, Tulsa, Oklahoma 74101 (800) 752-9764; *International Energy Statistics Sourcebook.*

Statistical Office of the United Nations, Publishing Service, New York, New York 10017 (800) 253-9646; *Statistical Yearbook.*

United Nations Economic Commission for Africa, Africa Hall, P.O. Box 3001, Addis Ababa, Ethiopia (Telephone Number in U.S. (800) 253-9646); *African Statistical Yearbook.*

CONGO - MONEY EXCHANGE RATE

International Monetary Fund, 700 Nineteenth Street, NW, Washington, D.C. 20431 (202) 623-7000; *International Financial Statistics.*

Statistical Office of the United Nations, Publishing Service, New York, New York 10017 (800) 253-9646; *Statistical Yearbook.*

CONGO - MONEY SUPPLY

African Development Bank, 01 BP 1387, Abidjan 01, Cote D'Ivoire; *Selected Statistics on Regional Member Countries.*

Federal Statistical Office, Gustav - Stresemann - Ring 11, D-6200 Wiesbaden, Germany; *Kongo.*

G.K. Hall and Company, 70 Lincoln Street, Boston, Massachusetts 02111 (617) 423-3990; *The World in Figures.*

International Monetary Fund, 700 Nineteenth Street, NW, Washington, D.C. 20431 (202) 623-7000; *International Financial Statistics.*

Statistical Office of the United Nations, Publishing Service, New York, New York 10017 (800) 253-9646; *Statistical Yearbook.*

The World Bank, 1818 H Street, NW, Washington, D.C. 20433 (202) 477-1234; *World Tables.*

CONGO - MOTION PICTURES

Statistical Office of the United Nations, Publishing Service, New York, New York 10017 (800) 253-9646; *Statistical Yearbook.*

CONGO - MOTOR VEHICLE TAXES - See CONGO - TAXATION

CONGO - MOTOR VEHICLES IN USE

G.K. Hall and Company, 70 Lincoln Street, Boston, Massachusetts 02111 (617) 423-3990; *The World in Figures.*

International Road Federation, 525 School Street, SW, Washington, D.C. 20024 (202) 554-2106; *World Road Statistics.*

Statistical Office of the United Nations, Publishing Service, New York, New York 10017 (800) 253-9646; *Statistical Yearbook,* and *Survey of Economic and Social Conditions in Africa.*

Times Books, 201 East 50th Street, New York, New York 10022 (212) 751-2600; *The Economist Book of Vital World Statistics.*

CONGO - MUSEUMS

Facts on File, 460 Park Avenue South, New York, New York 10016 (800) 443-8323; *The New Book of World Rankings.*

United Nations Educational, Scientific and Cultural Organization (UNESCO), 7 Place de Fontenoy, F-75700 Paris, France (Telephone Number in U.S. (212) 963-5981); *Statistical Yearbook.*

CONGO - NATALITY - See CONGO - BIRTH RATE

CONGO - NATIONAL ACCOUNTS

African Development Bank, 01 BP 1387, Abidjan 01, Cote D'Ivoire; *Selected Statistics on Regional Member Countries.*

Federal Statistical Office, Gustav - Stresemann - Ring 11, D-6200 Wiesbaden, Germany; *Kongo.*

Statistical Office of the United Nations, Publishing Service, New York, New York 10017 (800) 253-9646; *National Accounts Statistics,* and *Statistical Yearbook.*

United Nations Economic Commission for Africa, Africa Hall, P.O. Box 3001, Addis Ababa, Ethiopia (Telephone Number in U.S. (800) 253-9646); *African Statistical Yearbook.*

CONGO - NATIONAL INCOME

Facts on File, 460 Park Avenue South, New York, New York 10016 (800) 443-8323; *The New Book of World Rankings.*

G.K. Hall and Company, 70 Lincoln Street, Boston, Massachusetts 02111 (617) 423-3990; *The World in Figures.*

Statistical Office of the United Nations, Publishing Service, New York, New York 10017 (800) 253-9646; *Statistical Yearbook.*

CONGO - NATIONAL PRODUCT

Facts on File, 460 Park Avenue South, New York, New York 10016 (800) 443-8323; *The New Book of World Rankings.*

CONGO - NATURAL GAS PRODUCTION - See CONGO - MINING AND MINERAL PRODUCTS

CONGO - NEWSPAPER PRODUCTION - See CONGO - FORESTRY AND FOREST PRODUCTS

CONGO - OCCUPATIONS - See CONGO - LABOR FORCE

CONGO - PALM OIL AND PALM KERNELS PRODUCTION - See CONGO - CROPS

CONGO - PAPER - See CONGO - FORESTRY AND FOREST PRODUCTS

CONGO - PEANUT PRODUCTION - See CONGO - CROPS

CONGO - PERIODICALS

United Nations Educational, Scientific and Cultural Organization (UNESCO), 7 Place de Fontenoy, F-75700 Paris, France (Telephone Number in U.S. (212) 963-5981); *Statistical Yearbook.*

CONGO - PESTICIDE USE

Food and Agricultural Organization of the United Nations (FAO) Via delle Terme di Caracalla, 00100 Rome, Italy (Telephone Number in U.S. (202) 653-2400); *The State of Food and Agriculture.*

CONGO - PETROLEUM INDUSTRY

Facts on File, 460 Park Avenue South, New York, New York 10016 (800) 443-8323; *The New Book of World Rankings.*

Food and Agricultural Organization of the United Nations (FAO) Via delle Terme di Caracalla, 00100 Rome, Italy (Telephone Number in U.S. (202) 653-2400); *The State of Food and Agriculture.*

G.K. Hall and Company, 70 Lincoln Street, Boston, Massachusetts 02111 (617) 423-3990; *The World in Figures.*

International Monetary Fund, 700 Nineteenth Street, NW, Washington, D.C. 20431 (202) 623-7000; *International Financial Statistics.*

Penn Well Publishing Company, 1421 South Sheridan Road, P.O. Box 1260, Tulsa, Oklahoma 74101 (800) 752-9764; *International Energy Statistics Sourcebook.*

Statistical Office of the United Nations, Publishing Service, New York, New York 10017 (800) 253-9646; *Statistical Yearbook.* Quarrying - Crude petroleum.

CONGO - PIGS - See CONGO - LIVESTOCK AND POULTRY

CONGO - POPULATION

African Development Bank, 01 BP 1387, Abidjan 01, Cote D'Ivoire; *Selected Statistics on Regional Member Countries.*

The Economist Intelligence Unit, 111 West 57th Street, New York, New York 10019 (800) 938-4685; *The World Market Atlas.*

Facts on File, 460 Park Avenue South, New York, New York 10016 (800) 443-8323; *The New Book of World Rankings.*

Federal Statistical Office, Gustav - Stresemann - Ring 11, D-6200 Wiesbaden, Germany; *Kongo.*

Food and Agricultural Organization of the United Nations (FAO), Via delle Terme di Caracalla, 00100 Rome, Italy (Telephone Number in U.S. (202) 653-2400); *Production Yearbook.*

G.K. Hall and Company, 70 Lincoln Street, Boston, Massachusetts 02111 (617) 423-3990; *The World in Figures.*

International Labour Office, I.L.O. Publications, CH-1211, Geneva 22, Switzerland; *Yearbook of Labour Statistics.*

Statistical Office of the United Nations, Publishing Service, New York, New York 10017 (800) 253-9646; *Demographic Yearbook, Statistical Yearbook,* and *Survey of Economic and Social Conditions in Africa.*

Times Books, 201 East 50th Street, New York, New York 10022 (212) 751-2600; *The Economist Book of Vital World Statistics.*

United Nations Educational, Scientific and Cultural Organization (UNESCO), 7 Place de Fontenoy, F-75700 Paris, France (Telephone Number in U.S. (212) 963-5981); *Statistical Yearbook.*

U.S. Arms Control and Disarmament Agency, 320 Twenty-first Street, NW, Washington, D.C. 20451 (202) 647-8677; *World Military Expenditures and Arms Transfers.*

World Health Organization, Office of Publications, Avenue Appia, CH-1211 Geneva 27, Switzerland (Telephone Number in U.S. (518) 436-9686); *World Health Statistics Annual.*

CONGO - POST OFFICES

Facts on File, 460 Park Avenue South, New York, New York 10016 (800) 443-8323; *The New Book of World Rankings.*

CONGO - POTATO PRODUCTION - See CONGO - CROPS

CONGO - PRICES

Facts on File, 460 Park Avenue South, New York, New York 10016 (800) 443-8323; *The New Book of World Rankings.*

Federal Statistical Office, Gustav - Stresemann - Ring 11, D-6200 Wiesbaden, Germany; *Kongo.*

Food and Agricultural Organization of the United Nations (FAO), Via delle Terme di Caracalla, 00100 Rome, Italy (Telephone Number in U.S. (202) 653-2400); *Production Yearbook*, and *The State of Food and Agriculture*.

G.K. Hall and Company, 70 Lincoln Street, Boston, Massachusetts 02111 (617) 423-3990; *The World in Figures*.

International Labour Office, I.L.O. Publications, CH-1211, Geneva 22, Switzerland; *Yearbook of Labour Statistics*.

International Monetary Fund, 700 Nineteenth Street, NW, Washington, D.C. 20431 (202) 623-7000; *International Financial Statistics*.

United Nations Economic Commission for Africa, Africa Hall, P.O. Box 3001, Addis Ababa, Ethiopia (Telephone Number in U.S. (800) 253-9646); *African Statistical Yearbook*.

CONGO - PRINTING AND WRITING PAPER - See CONGO - FORESTRY AND FOREST PRODUCTS

CONGO - PRODUCTION

Facts on File, 460 Park Avenue South, New York, New York 10016 (800) 443-8323; *The New Book of World Rankings*.

G.K. Hall and Company, 70 Lincoln Street, Boston, Massachusetts 02111 (617) 423-3990; *The World in Figures*.

CONGO - PROPERTY TAXES - See CONGO - TAXATION

CONGO - PUBLIC FINANCE

Facts on File, 460 Park Avenue South, New York, New York 10016 (800) 443-8323; *The New Book of World Rankings*.

Federal Statistical Office, Gustav - Stresemann - Ring 11, D-6200 Wiesbaden, Germany; *Kongo*.

CONGO - RADIO BROADCASTING - See CONGO - BROADCASTING

CONGO - RAILWAYS

G.K. Hall and Company, 70 Lincoln Street, Boston, Massachusetts 02111 (617) 423-3990; *The World in Figures*.

Jane's Information Group, Sentinel House, 163 Brighton Road, Coulsdon, Surrey CR5 2NH, England (Telephone Number in U.S. (703) 683-3700); *Jane's World Railways*.

Statistical Office of the United Nations, Publishing Service, New York, New York 10017 (800) 253-9646; *Statistical Yearbook*, and *Survey of Economic and Social Conditions in Africa*.

United Nations Economic Commission for Africa, Africa Hall, P.O. Box 3001, Addis Ababa, Ethiopia (Telephone Number in U.S. (800) 253-9646); *African Statistical Yearbook*.

CONGO - RELIGION

Facts on File, 460 Park Avenue South, New York, New York 10016 (800) 443-8323; *The New Book of World Rankings*.

CONGO - RETAIL TRADE

G.K. Hall and Company, 70 Lincoln Street, Boston, Massachusetts 02111 (617) 423-3990; *The World in Figures*.

CONGO - RICE PRODUCTION - See CONGO - CROPS

CONGO - ROOT AND TUBER PRODUCTION - See CONGO - CROPS

CONGO - ROUNDWOOD PRODUCTION - See CONGO - FORESTRY AND FOREST PRODUCTS

CONGO - RUBBER PRODUCTION

Facts on File, 460 Park Avenue South, New York, New York 10016 (800) 443-8323; *The New Book of World Rankings*.

CONGO - SAWNWOOD PRODUCTION - See CONGO - FORESTRY AND FOREST PRODUCTS

CONGO - SCIENTISTS AND TECHNICIANS

United Nations Educational, Scientific and Cultural Organization (UNESCO), 7 Place de Fontenoy, F-75700 Paris, France (Telephone Number in U.S. (212) 963-5981); *Statistical Yearbook*.

CONGO - SENIOR CITIZENS

Facts on File, 460 Park Avenue South, New York, New York 10016 (800) 443-8323; *The New Book of World Rankings*.

CONGO - SHEEP - See CONGO - LIVESTOCK AND POULTRY

CONGO - SILVER PRODUCTION AND CONSUMPTION - See CONGO - MINING AND MINERAL PRODUCTS

CONGO - SOCIAL DATA

African Development Bank, 01 BP 1387, Abidjan 01, Cote D'Ivoire; *Selected Statistics on Regional Member Countries*.

Facts on File, 460 Park Avenue South, New York, New York 10016 (800) 443-8323; *The New Book of World Rankings*.

G.K. Hall and Company, 70 Lincoln Street, Boston, Massachusetts 02111 (617) 423-3990; *The World in Figures*.

International Monetary Fund, 700 Nineteenth Street, NW, Washington, D.C. 20431 (202) 623-7000; *Government Finance Statistics Yearbook*.

CONGO - STAMP TAXES AND DUTIES - See CONGO - TAXATION

CONGO - STEEL - See CONGO - MINING AND MINERAL PRODUCTS

CONGO - STOCKS - COMMODITY - MARKET PRICE - INDEX

Food and Agricultural Organization of the United Nations (FAO) Via delle Terme di Caracalla, 00100 Rome, Italy (Telephone Number in U.S. (202) 653-2400); *The State of Food and Agriculture*.

CONGO - SUGAR PRODUCTION - See CONGO - CROPS

CONGO - TAXATION

G.K. Hall and Company, 70 Lincoln Street, Boston, Massachusetts 02111 (617) 423-3990; *The World in Figures*.

International Monetary Fund, 700 Nineteenth Street, NW, Washington, D.C. 20431 (202) 623-7000; *Government Finance Statistics Yearbook*.

International Road Federation, 525 School Street, SW, Washington, D.C. 20024 (202) 554-2106; *World Road Statistics*.

The World Bank, 1818 H Street, NW, Washington, D.C. 20433 (202) 477-1234; *World Tables.*

CONGO - TELEGRAPH SERVICE

Statistical Office of the United Nations, Publishing Service, New York, New York 10017 (800) 253-9646; *Statistical Yearbook.*

CONGO - TELEPHONES IN USE

American Telephone and Telegraph Company, 26 Parsippany Road, Whippany, New Jersey 07981 (800) 338-4038; *The World's Telephones.*

G.K. Hall and Company, 70 Lincoln Street, Boston, Massachusetts 02111 (617) 423-3990; *The World in Figures.*

Statistical Office of the United Nations, Publishing Service, New York, New York 10017 (800) 253-9646; *Statistical Yearbook.*

CONGO - TELEVISION BROADCASTING - See CONGO - BROADCASTING

CONGO - TEXTILE INDUSTRY

G.K. Hall and Company, 70 Lincoln Street, Boston, Massachusetts 02111 (617) 423-3990; *The World in Figures.*

CONGO - THEATRE

United Nations Educational, Scientific and Cultural Organization (UNESCO), 7 Place de Fontenoy, F-75700 Paris, France (Telephone Number in U.S. (212) 963-5981); *Statistical Yearbook.*

CONGO - TIN PRODUCTION - See CONGO - MINING AND MINERAL PRODUCTS

CONGO - TOBACCO PRODUCTION

Facts on File, 460 Park Avenue South, New York, New York 10016 (800) 443-8323; *The New Book of World Rankings.*

Statistical Office of the United Nations, Publishing Service, New York, New York 10017 (800) 253-9646; *Statistical Yearbook.*

CONGO - TOBACCO PRODUCTS PRODUCTION

Statistical Office of the United Nations, Publishing Service, New York, New York 10017 (800) 253-9646; *Statistical Yearbook.*

CONGO - TOURISM

Facts on File, 460 Park Avenue South, New York, New York 10016 (800) 443-8323; *The New Book of World Rankings.*

Federal Statistical Office, Gustav - Stresemann - Ring 11, D-6200 Wiesbaden, Germany; *Kongo.*

G.K. Hall and Company, 70 Lincoln Street, Boston, Massachusetts 02111 (617) 423-3990; *The World in Figures.*

Statistical Office of the United Nations, Publishing Service, New York, New York 10017 (800) 253-9646; *Statistical Yearbook.*

Times Books, 201 East 50th Street, New York, New York 10022 (212) 751-2600; *The Economist Book of Vital World Statistics.*

United Nations Economic Commission for Africa, Africa Hall, P.O. Box 3001, Addis Ababa, Ethiopia (Telephone Number in U.S. (800) 253-9646); *African Statistical Yearbook.*

World Tourism Organization, Calle Capitan Haya 42, E-28020 Madrid, Spain; *Yearbook of Tourism Statistics.*

CONGO - TRACTORS IN USE

Statistical Office of the United Nations, Publishing Service, New York, New York 10017 (800) 253-9646; *Statistical Yearbook.*

CONGO - TRADE - See CONGO - FOREIGN TRADE

CONGO - TRANSPORTATION AND COMMUNICATIONS

Facts on File, 460 Park Avenue South, New York, New York 10016 (800) 443-8323; *The New Book of World Rankings.*

Federal Statistical Office, Gustav - Stresemann - Ring 11, D-6200 Wiesbaden, Germany; *Kongo.*

G.K. Hall and Company, 70 Lincoln Street, Boston, Massachusetts 02111 (617) 423-3990; *The World in Figures.*

United Nations Economic Commission for Africa, Africa Hall, P.O. Box 3001, Addis Ababa, Ethiopia (Telephone Number in U.S. (800) 253-9646); *African Statistical Yearbook.*

CONGO - UNEMPLOYMENT

International Labour Office, I.L.O. Publications, CH-1211, Geneva 22, Switzerland; *Yearbook of Labour Statistics.*

CONGO - VITAL STATISTICS

G.K. Hall and Company, 70 Lincoln Street, Boston, Massachusetts 02111 (617) 423-3990; *The World in Figures.*

Statistical Office of the United Nations, Publishing Service, New York, New York 10017 (800) 253-9646; *Statistical Yearbook.*

World Health Organization, Office of Publications, Avenue Appia, CH-1211 Geneva 27, Switzerland (Telephone Number in U.S. (518) 436-9686); *World Health Statistics Annual.*

CONGO - WAGES

Federal Statistical Office, Gustav - Stresemann - Ring 11, D-6200 Wiesbaden, Germany; *Kongo.*

G.K. Hall and Company, 70 Lincoln Street, Boston, Massachusetts 02111 (617) 423-3990; *The World in Figures.*

International Labour Office, I.L.O. Publications, CH-1211, Geneva 22, Switzerland; *Yearbook of Labour Statistics.*

Statistical Office of the United Nations, Publishing Service, New York, New York 10017 (800) 253-9646; *Statistical Yearbook.*

CONGO - WEATHER

Facts on File, 460 Park Avenue South, New York, New York 10016 (800) 443-8323; *The New Book of World Rankings.*

G.K. Hall and Company, 70 Lincoln Street, Boston, Massachusetts 02111 (617) 423-3990; *The World in Figures.*

CONGO - WELFARE

International Monetary Fund, 700 Nineteenth Street, NW, Washington, D.C. 20431 (202) 623-7000; *Government Finance Statistics Yearbook.*

CONGO - WHEAT - See CONGO - CROPS

CONGO - WHOLESALE PRICES

International Monetary Fund, 700 Nineteenth Street, NW, Washington, D.C. 20431 (202) 623-7000; *International Financial Statistics.*

Statistical Office of the United Nations, Publishing Service, New York, New York 10017 (800) 253-9646; *Statistical Yearbook.*

CONGO - WINE PRODUCTION

Facts on File, 460 Park Avenue South, New York, New York 10016 (800) 443-8323; *The New Book of World Rankings.*

CONGO - WOOD - See CONGO - FORESTRY AND FOREST PRODUCTS

CONGO - WOOL PRODUCTION

Facts on File, 460 Park Avenue South, New York, New York 10016 (800) 443-8323; *The New Book of World Rankings.*

CONGO - ZINC ORE PRODUCTION AND CONSUMPTION - See CONGO - MINING AND MINERAL PRODUCTS

CONGRESS OF INDUSTRIAL ORGANIZATIONS (CIO) - See AFL-CIO

CONGRESS, UNITED STATES - BILLS, ACTS, RESOLUTIONS

U.S. Congress, The Capitol, Washington, D.C. 20510 (202) 224-3121; *Calendars of the United States House of Representatives and History of Legislation, Presidential Vetoes, Congressional Record,* and *Daily Calendar.*

CONGRESS, UNITED STATES - BLACK MEMBERS

Joint Center for Political and Economic Studies, 1090 Vermont Avenue, NW, Washington, D.C. 20005 (202) 789-3500; *Black Elected Officials, A National Roster.*

U.S. Department of Commerce, Bureau of the Census, Suitland, Maryland 20233 (301) 763-4040; data published in *Congressional Directory.*

CONGRESS, UNITED STATES - CAMPAIGN FINANCES

U.S. Federal Election Commission, 999 E Street, NW, Washington, D.C. 20463 (800) 424-9530; *FEC Reports on Financial Activity, Final Report, U.S. Senate and House Campaigns, FEC Index of Independent Expenditures, FEC Reports on Financial Activity, Final Report, Party and Non-Party Political Committees,* unpublished data and press releases.

CONGRESS, UNITED STATES - COMPOSITION

U.S. Congress, Joint Committee on Printing, North Capitol and H Streets, NW, Washington, D.C. 20401 (202) 275-2051; *Congressional Directory,* and unpublished data.

CONGRESS, UNITED STATES - CONGRESSIONAL DISTRICTS - CANDIDATES, VOTES CAST

Elections Research Center, 5508 Greystone Street, Chevy Case, Maryland 20815 (202) 659-9490; *America Votes.*

CONGRESS, UNITED STATES - HISPANIC MEMBERS

National Association of Latino Elected and Appointed Officials, 3409 Garnet Street, Los Angeles, California 90023 (213) 262-8503; *National Roster of Hispanic Elected Officials.*

U.S. Congress, Joint Committee on Printing, North Capitol and H Streets, NW, Washington, D.C. 20401 (202) 275-2051; *Congressional Directory.*

CONGRESS, UNITED STATES - MEMBERS CHARACTERISTICS

Congressional Quarterly, Incorporated, 1414 Twenty-second Street, NW, Washington, D.C. 20037 (202) 887-8500; *Congressional Quarterly Weekly Report.*

U.S. Congress, Joint Committee on Printing, North Capitol and H Streets, NW, Washington, D.C. 20510 (202) 275-2051; *Congressional Directory.*

CONGRESS, UNITED STATES - REPRESENTATIVES - VOTE CAST

Congressional Quarterly, Incorporated, 1414 Twenty-second Street, NW, Washington, D.C. 20037 (202) 887-8500; *Congressional Quarterly Weekly Report.*

Elections Research Center, 5508 Greystone Street, Chevy Chase, Maryland 20815 (202) 659-9490; *America Votes,* biennial.

U.S. Department of Commerce, Bureau of the Census, Suitland, Maryland 20233 (301) 763-4040; *Current Population Reports.*

CONGRESS, UNITED STATES - SENATORS - VOTE CAST

Congressional Quarterly, Incorporated, 1414 Twenty-second Street, NW, Washington, D.C. 20037 (202) 887-8500; *Congressional Quarterly Weekly Report.*

Elections Research Center, 5508 Greystone Street, Chevy Chase, Maryland 20815 (202) 659-9490; *America Votes.*

CONGRESS, UNITED STATES - SENIORITY

U.S. Department of Commerce, Bureau of the Census, Suitland, Maryland 20233 (301) 763-4040; data published in *Congressional Directory.*

CONGRESS, UNITED STATES - STAFF

Congressional Quarterly, Incorporated, 1414 Twenty-second Street, NW, Washington, D.C. 20037 (202) 887-8500; *Vital Statistics on Congress.*

CONGRESS, UNITED STATES - TIME IN SESSION

U.S. Congress, The Capitol, Washington, D.C. 20510 (202) 224-3121; *Congressional Record,* and *Daily Calendar.*

CONGRESS, UNITED STATES - WOMEN MEMBERS

U.S. Department of Commerce, Bureau of the Census, Suitland, Maryland 20233 (301) 763-4040; data published in *Congressional*

Directory.

CONNECTICUT - See also STATE DATA (FOR INDIVIDUAL STATES)

Connecticut - Primary Statistics Sources

Connecticut Department of Economic Development, 865 Brook Street, Rocky Hill, Connecticut 06067-3405 (800) 392-2122; *Connecticut Market Data.*

Connecticut - State Data Centers

Capitol Region Council of Governments, 221 Main Street, Hartford, Connecticut 06106, Barbara MacFarland (203) 522-2217.

Connecticut Department of Economic Development, 865 Brook Street, Rocky Hill, Connecticut 06067-3405, Mr. Jeff Blodgett (203) 258-4219.

Government Documents, Connecticut State Library, 231 Capitol Avenue, Hartford, Connecticut 06106, Mr. Albert Palko (203) 566-4971.

Policy Development and Planning Division, Connecticut Office of Policy and Management, 80 Washington Street, Hartford, Connecticut 06106, Mr. Bill Kraynak (203) 566-8285.

CONSTRUCTION INDUSTRY - BUILDING PERMITS - VALUE

U.S. Department of Commerce, Bureau of the Census, Suitland, Maryland 20233 (301) 763-4040; *Construction Reports,* and unpublished data.

CONSTRUCTION INDUSTRY - BUILDINGS AUTHORIZED

U.S. Department of Commerce, Bureau of the Census, Suitland, Maryland 20233 (301) 763-4040; *Construction Reports.*

CONSTRUCTION INDUSTRY - CAPITAL

U.S. Department of Commerce, Bureau of Economic Analysis, Fourteenth Street between Constitution Avenue and E Street, NW, Washington, D.C. 20230 (202) 606-9900; *Survey of Current Business.*

CONSTRUCTION INDUSTRY - COLLECTIVE BARGAINING SETTLEMENTS

U.S. Department of Labor, Bureau of Labor Statistics, Two Massachusetts Avenue, NE, Washington, D.C. 20212 (202) 606-7828; *Compensation and Working Conditions.*

CONSTRUCTION INDUSTRY - CONSTRUCTION CONTRACTS

F.W. Dodge Division, McGraw-Hill Information Systems Company, 1221 Avenue of the Americas, New York, New York 10020 (212) 512-2000; *Dodge Construction Potentials.*

U.S. Department of Commerce, Bureau of the Census, Suitland, Maryland 20233 (301) 763-4040; *County Business Patterns.*

U.S. Department of Housing and Urban Development, 451 Seventh Street, SW, Washington, D.C. 20410 (202) 708-1422; unpublished data.

CONSTRUCTION INDUSTRY - COST

U.S. Department of Commerce, Bureau of the Census, Suitland, Maryland 20233 (301) 763-4040; *Construction Review,* and *Current Construction Reports.*

CONSTRUCTION INDUSTRY - EARNINGS

U.S. Department of Commerce, Bureau of the Census, Suitland, Maryland 20233 (301) 763-4040; *County Business Patterns, Census of Construction Industries,* and *Economic Census of Outlying Areas.*

U.S. Department of Commerce, Bureau of Economic Analysis, Fourteenth Street between Constitution Avenue and E Street, NW, Washington, D.C. 20230 (202) 606-9900; *The National Income and Product Accounts of the United States,* and *Survey of Current Business.*

U.S. Department of Labor, Bureau of Labor Statistics, Two Massachusetts Avenue, NE, Washington, D.C. 20212 (202) 606-7828; *Employment and Earnings,* and Bulletins 2370 and 2429.

CONSTRUCTION INDUSTRY - EMPLOYEES

U.S. Department of Commerce, Bureau of the Census, Suitland, Maryland 20233 (301) 763-4040; *Census of Construction Industries, County Business Patterns,* and *Economic Census of Outlying Areas.*

U.S. Department of Labor, Bureau of Labor Statistics, Two Massachusetts Avenue, NE, Washington, D.C. 20212 (202) 606-7828; *Employment and Earnings, Monthly Labor Review,* and unpublished data.

CONSTRUCTION INDUSTRY - ESTABLISHMENTS

U.S. Department of Commerce, Bureau of the Census, Suitland, Maryland 20233 (301) 763-4040; *Census of Construction Industries, County Business Patterns,* and *Economic Census of Outlying Areas.*

CONSTRUCTION INDUSTRY - FINANCES

U.S. Department of the Treasury, Internal Revenue Service, 1111 Constitution Avenue, NW, Washington, D.C. 20224 (202) 566-5000; *Statistics of Income, Corporation Income Tax Returns, Statistics of Income Bulletin,* and *Statistics of Income, Partnership Returns.*

CONSTRUCTION INDUSTRY - GROSS DOMESTIC PRODUCT

Puerto Rico Planning Board, San Juan, Puerto Rico; *Economic Report of the Governor.*

U.S. Department of Commerce, Bureau of Economic Analysis, Fourteenth Street between Constitution Avenue and E Street, NW, Washington, D.C. 20230 (202) 606-9900; *The National Income and Product Accounts of the United States,* and *Survey of Current Business.*

CONSTRUCTION INDUSTRY - MERGERS AND ACQUISITIONS

Securities Data Company, 1180 Raymond Boulevard, Newark, New Jersey 07102 (201) 622-3100; *Merger and Corporate Transactions Database.*

CONSTRUCTION INDUSTRY - NON-RESIDENTIAL BUILDING PROJECTS

U.S. Department of Commerce, Bureau of the Census, Suitland, Maryland 20233 (301) 763-4040; *Current Construction Reports.*

CONSTRUCTION INDUSTRY - OCCUPATIONAL SAFETY

National Safety Council, 1121 Spring Lake Drive, Itasca, Illinois 60143-3201 (708) 285-1121; *Accident Facts.*

U.S. Department of Labor, Bureau of Labor Statistics, Two Massachusetts Avenue, NE, Washington, D.C. 20212 (202) 606-7828; *Occupational Injuries and Illnesses in the United States.*

CONSTRUCTION INDUSTRY - PRODUCER PRICE INDEXES

U.S. Department of Labor, Bureau of Labor Statistics, Two Massachusetts Avenue, NE, Washington, D.C. 20212 (202) 606-7828; *Producer Price Indexes.*

CONSTRUCTION INDUSTRY - PROFITS

Forbes, Incorporated, 60 Fifth Avenue, New York, New York 10011 (212) 620-2200; *Forbes Annual Report on American Industry.*

U.S. Department of Commerce, Bureau of Economic Analysis, Fourteenth Street between Constitution Avenue and E Street, NW, Washington, D.C. 20230 (202) 606-9900; *The National Income and Product Accounts of the United States,* and *Survey of Current Business.*

U.S. Department of the Treasury, Internal Revenue Service, 1111 Constitution Avenue, NW, Washington, D.C. 20224 (202) 566-5000; *Statistics of Income,* various publications, *Statistics of Income, Corporation Tax Returns,* and unpublished data.

CONSTRUCTION INDUSTRY - RESIDENTIAL

National Association of Home Builders of the United States, 1201 Fifteenth Street, NW, Washington, D.C. 20005 (202) 822-0200; *Forecast of Housing Activity.*

U.S. Department of Commerce, Bureau of the Census, Suitland, Maryland 20233 (301) 763-4040; *Construction Reports,* and unpublished data.

U.S. Department of Housing and Urban Development, 451 Seventh Street, SW, Washington, D.C. 20410 (202) 708-1422; *Characteristics of New Housing,* and *New One-Family Houses Sold.*

CONSTRUCTION INDUSTRY - SHIPMENTS, RECEIPTS

Forbes Incorporated, 60 Fifth Avenue, New York, New York 10011 (202) 620-2200; *Forbes Annual Report on American Industry.*

U.S. Department of Commerce, Bureau of the Census, Suitland, Maryland 20233 (301) 763-4040; *Census of Construction Industries,* and *Economic Censuses of Outlying Areas.*

CONSTRUCTION INDUSTRY - UNIONS

U.S. Department of Labor, Bureau of Labor Statistics, Two Massachusetts Avenue, NE, Washington, D.C. 20212 (202) 606-7828; *Employment and Earnings.*

CONSTRUCTION INDUSTRY - VALUE ADDED

U.S. Department of Commerce, Bureau of the Census, Suitland, Maryland 20233 (301) 763-4040; *Current Construction Reports,* and *Census of Construction Industries.*

CONSTRUCTION MACHINERY - MANUFACTURING - EARNINGS

U.S. Department of Commerce, Bureau of the Census, Suitland, Maryland 20233 (301) 763-4040; *Census of Manufactures,* and *Annual Survey of Manufactures.*

U.S. Department of Labor, Bureau of Labor Statistics, Two Massachusetts Avenue, NE, Washington, D.C. 20212 (202) 606-7828; *Employment and Earnings,* and Bulletins 2370 and 2429.

CONSTRUCTION MACHINERY - MANUFACTURING - EMPLOYEES

U.S. Department of Commerce, Bureau of the Census, Suitland, Maryland 20233 (301) 763-4040; *Census of Manufactures,* and *Annual Survey of Manufactures.*

U.S. Department of Labor, Bureau of Labor Statistics, Two Massachusetts Avenue, NE, Washington, D.C. 20212 (202) 606-7828; *Employment and Earnings,* and Bulletins 2370 and 2429.

CONSTRUCTION MACHINERY - MANUFACTURING - ESTABLISHMENTS

U.S. Department of Commerce, Bureau of the Census, Suitland, Maryland 20233 (301) 763-4040; *Census of Manufactures,* and *Annual Survey of Manufactures.*

CONSTRUCTION MACHINERY - MANUFACTURING - INVENTORIES

U.S. Department of Commerce, Bureau of the Census, Suitland, Maryland 20233 (301) 763-4040; *Current Industrial Reports, Manufactures' Shipments, Inventories, and Orders.*

CONSTRUCTION MACHINERY - MANUFACTURING - SHIPMENTS

U.S. Department of Commerce, Bureau of the Census, Suitland, Maryland 20233 (301) 763-4040; *Annual Survey of Manufactures, Census of Manufactures,* and *Current Industrial Reports, Manufactures' Shipments, Inventories and Orders.*

CONSTRUCTION MACHINERY - MANUFACTURING - VALUE ADDED

U.S. Department of Commerce, Bureau of the Census, Suitland, Maryland 20233 (301) 763-4040; *Census of Manufactures,* and *Annual Survey of Manufactures.*

CONSTRUCTION MATERIALS - See BUILDING MATERIALS

CONSUMER - CONSUMER GOODS - PRODUCER PRICES

U.S. Department of Labor, Bureau of Labor Statistics, Two Massachusetts Avenue, NE, Washington, D.C. 20212 (202) 606-7828; *Monthly Labor Review.*

CONSUMER - CREDIT

Board of Governors of the Federal Reserve System, Twentieth Street and Constitution Avenue, NW, Washington, D.C. 20551 (202) 452-3000; *Federal Reserve Bulletin, Annual Statistical Digest,* and unpublished data.

CONSUMER - DELINQUENCY RATES

American Bankers Association, 1120 Connecticut Avenue, NW, Washington, D.C. 20036 (202) 663-5000; *Consumer Credit Delinquency Bulletin.*

CONSUMER - ELECTRONICS

Recording Industry Association of America, 1020 Nineteenth Street, NW, Washington, D.C. 20036 (202) 775-0101; *Inside the Recording Industry: A Statistical Overview.*

CONSUMER - EXPENDITURES

U.S. Department of Commerce, Bureau of Economic Analysis, Fourteenth Street between Constitution Avenue and E Street, NW, Washington, D.C. 20230 (202) 606-9900; *The National Income and Product Accounts of the United States*, and *Survey of Current Business*.

U.S. Department of Labor, Bureau of Labor Statistics, Two Massachusetts Avenue, NE, Washington, D.C. 20212 (202) 606-7828; *Consumer Expenditures in 1992*.

CONSUMER - EXPENDITURES - BOOKS

Book Industry Study Group, 160 Fifth Avenue, New York, New York 10010 (212) 929-1393; *Book Industry Trends*.

CONSUMER - EXPENDITURES - ENTERTAINMENT

U.S. Department of Labor, Bureau of Labor Statistics, Two Massachusetts Avenue, NE, Washington, D.C. 20212 (202) 606-7828; *Consumer Expenditure Survey*.

CONSUMER - EXPENDITURES - FOOD

U.S. Department of Agriculture, Economic Research Service, Fourteenth Street and Independence Avenue, SW, Washington, D.C. 20005-4789 (202) 219-1504; *Agricultural Statistics*, *Food Cost Review*, and *Food Review*.

U.S. Department of Labor, Bureau of Labor Statistics, Two Massachusetts Avenue, NE, Washington, D.C. 20212 (202) 606-7828; *Consumer Expenditures in 1992*, and *Consumer Expenditure Survey*.

CONSUMER - EXPENDITURES - HOUSING

U.S. Department of Labor, Bureau of Labor Statistics, Two Massachusetts Avenue, NE, Washington, D.C. 20212 (202) 606-7828; *Consumer Expenditures in 1992*, and *Consumer Expenditure Survey*.

CONSUMER - EXPENDITURES - MEDICAL CARE

U.S. Department of Health and Human Services, Health Care Financing Administration, 200 Independence Avenue, SW, Washington, D.C. 20201 (202) 245-6113; *Health Care Financing Review*.

U.S. Department of Labor, Bureau of Labor Statistics, Two Massachusetts Avenue, NE, Washington, D.C. 20212 (202) 606-7828; *Consumer Expenditures in 1991*, and *Consumer Expenditure Survey*.

CONSUMER - EXPENDITURES - METROPOLITAN AREAS

U.S. Department of Labor, Bureau of Labor Statistics, Two Massachusetts Avenue, NE, Washington, D.C. 20212 (202) 606-7828; *Consumer Expenditure Survey*.

CONSUMER - EXPENDITURES - READING MATERIALS

Book Industry Study Group, 160 Fifth Avenue, New York, New York 10010 (212) 929-1393; *Consumer Research Study on Book Purchasing*.

U.S. Department of Labor, Bureau of Labor Statistics, Two Massachusetts Avenue, NE, Washington, D.C. 20212 (202) 606-7828; *Consumer Expenditure Survey*.

CONSUMER - EXPENDITURES - SPORTING GOODS

National Sporting Goods Association, 1699 Wall Street, Mount Prospect, Illinois 60056 (708) 439-4000; *The Sporting Goods Market in 1993*.

CONSUMER - EXPENDITURES - TRANSPORTATION

U.S. Department of Labor, Bureau of Labor Statistics, Two Massachusetts Avenue, NE, Washington, D.C. 20212 (202) 606-7828; *Consumer Expenditures in 1992*, and *Consumer Expenditure Survey*.

CONSUMER PRICE INDEXES

U.S. Department of Commerce, Bureau Economic Analysis, Fourteenth Street between Constitution Avenue and E Street, NW, Washington, D.C. 20230 (202) 523-0777; *Survey of Current Business*.

U.S. Department of Labor, Bureau of Labor Statistics, Two Massachusetts Avenue, NE, Washington, D.C. 20212 (202) 606-7828; *Monthly Labor Review*, *Consumer Price Indexes, Detailed Report*, and *Handbook of Labor Statistics*.

CONSUMER PRICE INDEXES - BY COMMODITY GROUPS

U.S. Department of Labor, Bureau of Labor Statistics, Two Massachusetts Avenue, NE, Washington, D.C. 20212 (202) 606-7828; *Monthly Labor Review*, *Handbook of Labor Statistics*, and *Consumer Price Indexes, Detailed Report*.

CONSUMER PRICE INDEXES - FOREIGN COUNTRIES

International Monetary Fund, 700 Nineteenth Street, NW, Washington, D.C. 20431 (202) 623-7000; *International Financial Statistics*.

Organization for Economic Co-operation and Development, Publication and Information Center, 2001 L Street, NW, Washington, D.C. 20036 (202) 785-6323; *Main Economic Indicators*.

U.S. Department of Labor, Bureau of Labor Statistics, Two Massachusetts Avenue, NE, Washington, D.C. 20212 (202) 606-7828; *Handbook of Labor Statistics*.

CONSUMER PRICE INDEXES - MEDICAL CARE

U.S. Department of Labor, Bureau of Labor Statistics, Two Massachusetts Avenue, NE, Washington, D.C. 20212 (202) 606-7828; *CPI Detailed Report*, *Handbook of Labor Statistics*, *Monthly Labor Review*, and unpublished data.

CONSUMER PRICE INDEXES - PURCHASING POWER OF THE DOLLAR

U.S. Department of Commerce, Bureau of Economic Analysis, Fourteenth Street between Constitution Avenue and E Street, NW, Washington, D.C. 20230 (202) 606-9900; *Survey of Current Business*.

CONSUMER PRICE INDEXES - YEAR TO YEAR CHANGES

U.S. Department of Labor, Bureau of Labor Statistics, Two Massachusetts Avenue, NE, Washington, D.C. 20212 (202) 606-7828; *Monthly Labor Review*.

CONTINENTS - POPULATION AND VITAL STATISTICS

U.S. Department of Commerce, Bureau of the Census, Suitland, Maryland 20233 (301) 763-4040; *International Data Base*, and *World Population Profile*.

CONTRACEPTIVE USE

U.S. Department of Health and Human Services, National Center for Health Statistics, 3700 East-West Highway, Hyattsville, Maryland 20782 (301) 436-8500; *Advance Data from Vital and Health Statistics.*

CONVENIENCE STORES

International Franchise Association, 1350 New York Avenue, Suite 900, Washington, D.C. 20005 (202) 628-8000; *Franchising in the Economy.*

Maclean Hunter Media Inc., Post Office Box 10246, Stamford, Connecticut 06904 (203) 325-3500; *Progressive Grocer, Annual Report of the Grocery Industry.*

U.S. Department of Agriculture, Economic Research Service, Fourteenth Street and Independence Avenue, SW, Washington, D.C. 20005-4789 (202) 219-1504; *Food Marketing Review.*

Cook Islands - National Statistical Office

Statistics Office, Post Office Box 125, Rarotonga, Cook Islands.

Cook Islands - Primary Statistics Source

Statistics Office, Post Office Box 125, Rarotonga, Cook Islands; *Quarterly Abstract of Statistics.*

COOK ISLANDS - AGRICULTURE

Asian Development Bank, P.O. Box 789, 1099 Manila, Philippines; *Key Indicators of Developing Asian and Pacific Countries.*

Food and Agricultural Organization of the United Nations (FAO) Via delle Terme di Caracalla, 00100 Rome, Italy (Telephone Number in U.S. (202) 653-2400); *Production Yearbook, The State of Food and Agriculture,* and *Trade Yearbook.*

G.K. Hall and Company, 70 Lincoln Street, Boston, Massachusetts 02111 (617) 423-3990; *The World in Figures.*

Statistical Office of the United Nations, Publishing Service, New York, New York 10017 (800) 253-9646; *Statistical Yearbook,* and *Statistical Yearbook for Asia and the Pacific.*

COOK ISLANDS - AIRLINE SERVICE

G.K. Hall and Company, 70 Lincoln Street, Boston, Massachusetts 02111 (617) 423-3990; *The World in Figures.*

COOK ISLANDS - AREA AND DENSITY OF POPULATION

Food and Agricultural Organization of the United Nations (FAO) Via delle Terme di Caracalla, 00100 Rome, Italy (Telephone Number in U.S. (202) 653-2400); *The State of Food and Agriculture.*

G.K. Hall and Company, 70 Lincoln Street, Boston, Massachusetts 02111 (617) 423-3990; *The World in Figures.*

Statistical Office of the United Nations, Publishing Service, New York, New York 10017 (800) 253-9646; *Statistical Yearbook.*

United Nations Educational, Scientific and Cultural Organization (UNESCO), 7 Place de Fontenoy, F-75700 Paris, France (Telephone Number in U.S. (212) 963-5981); *Statistical Yearbook.*

COOK ISLANDS - BALANCE OF PAYMENTS

G.K. Hall and Company, 70 Lincoln Street, Boston, Massachusetts 02111 (617) 423-3990; *The World in Figures.*

COOK ISLANDS - BANKING

Asian Development Bank, P.O. Box 789, 1099 Manila, Philippines; *Key Indicators of Developing Asian and Pacific Countries.*

G.K. Hall and Company, 70 Lincoln Street, Boston, Massachusetts 02111 (617) 423-3990; *The World in Figures.*

COOK ISLANDS - BIRTH RATES

Statistical Office of the United Nations, Publishing Service, New York, New York 10017 (800) 253-9646; *Demographic Yearbook,* and *Statistical Yearbook.*

World Health Organization, Office of Publications, Avenue Appia, CH-1211 Geneva 27, Switzerland (Telephone Number in U.S. (518) 436-9686); *World Health Statistics Annual.*

COOK ISLANDS - BONDS

Asian Development Bank, P.O. Box 789, 1099 Manila, Philippines; *Key Indicators of Developing Asian and Pacific Countries.*

G.K. Hall and Company, 70 Lincoln Street, Boston, Massachusetts 02111 (617) 423-3990; *The World in Figures.*

COOK ISLANDS - BOOK PRODUCTION

G.K. Hall and Company, 70 Lincoln Street, Boston, Massachusetts 02111 (617) 423-3990; *The World in Figures.*

COOK ISLANDS - BROADCASTING

Billboard Limited, P.O. Box 9027, 1006 AA Amsterdam, The Netherlands (Telephone Number in U.S. (212) 764-7300); *World Radio TV Handbook.*

G.K. Hall and Company, 70 Lincoln Street, Boston, Massachusetts 02111 (617) 423-3990; *The World in Figures.*

United Nations Educational, Scientific and Cultural Organization (UNESCO), 7 Place de Fontenoy, F-75700 Paris, France (Telephone Number in U.S. (212) 963-5981); *Statistical Yearbook.*

COOK ISLANDS - BUSINESS

G.K. Hall and Company, 70 Lincoln Street, Boston, Massachusetts 02111 (617) 423-3990; *The World in Figures.*

COOK ISLANDS - CALORIE SUPPLY

Asian Development Bank, P.O. Box 789, 1099 Manila, Philippines; *Key Indicators of Developing Asian and Pacific Countries.*

Food and Agricultural Organization of the United Nations (FAO) Via delle Terme di Caracalla, 00100 Rome, Italy (Telephone Number in U.S. (202) 653-2400); *The State of Food and Agriculture.*

COOK ISLANDS - CAPITAL INVESTMENT

Asian Development Bank, P.O. Box 789, 1099 Manila, Philippines; *Key Indicators of Developing Asian and Pacific Countries.*

COOK ISLANDS - CAPITAL REVENUE

Asian Development Bank, P.O. Box 789, 1099 Manila, Philippines; *Key Indicators of Developing Asian and Pacific Countries.*

COOK ISLANDS - CATTLE - See COOK ISLANDS - LIVESTOCK AND POULTRY

COOK ISLANDS - CHEMICAL (ORGANIC) PRODUCTION - See COOK ISLANDS - MINING AND MINERAL PRODUCTS

COOK ISLANDS - CLASS STRUCTURE

G.K. Hall and Company, 70 Lincoln Street, Boston, Massachusetts 02111 (617) 423-3990; *The World in Figures.*

COOK ISLANDS - CLIMATE

G.K. Hall and Company, 70 Lincoln Street, Boston, Massachusetts 02111 (617) 423-3990; *The World in Figures.*

COOK ISLANDS - CLOTHING EXPORTS AND IMPORTS

South Pacific Commission, Post Box D5, Noumea Cedex, New Caledonia; *Statistical Bulletin of the South Pacific: Retail Price Indexes.*

COOK ISLANDS - COAL PRODUCTION - See COOK ISLANDS - MINING AND MINERAL PRODUCTS

COOK ISLANDS - COMMUNICATIONS

G.K. Hall and Company, 70 Lincoln Street, Boston, Massachusetts 02111 (617) 423-3990; *The World in Figures.*

Statistical Office of the United Nations, Publishing Service, New York, New York 10017 (800) 253-9646; *Statistical Yearbook for Asia and the Pacific.*

COOK ISLANDS - CONSUMER PRICE INDEX

Asian Development Bank, P.O. Box 789, 1099 Manila, Philippines; *Key Indicators of Developing Asian and Pacific Countries.*

G.K. Hall and Company, 70 Lincoln Street, Boston, Massachusetts 02111 (617) 423-3990; *The World in Figures.*

Statistical Office of the United Nations, Publishing Service, New York, New York 10017 (800) 253-9646; *Statistical Yearbook.*

COOK ISLANDS - CONSUMER PRICES

International Labour Office, I.L.O. Publications, CH-1211, Geneva 22, Switzerland; *Yearbook of Labour Statistics.*

COOK ISLANDS - CONSUMPTION

G.K. Hall and Company, 70 Lincoln Street, Boston, Massachusetts 02111 (617) 423-3990; *The World in Figures.*

South Pacific Commission, Post Box D5, Noumea Cedex, New Caledonia; *Statistical Bulletin of the South Pacific: Retail Price Indexes.*

COOK ISLANDS - CORN PRODUCTION - See COOK ISLANDS - CROPS

COOK ISLANDS - CORPORATE TAXES - See COOK ISLANDS - TAXATION

COOK ISLANDS - CROPS

Asian Development Bank, P.O. Box 789, 1099 Manila, Philippines; *Key Indicators of Developing Asian and Pacific Countries.*

Food and Agricultural Organization of the United Nations (FAO) Via delle Terme di Caracalla, 00100 Rome, Italy (Telephone Number in U.S. (202) 653-2400); *The State of Food and Agriculture.*

G.K. Hall and Company, 70 Lincoln Street, Boston, Massachusetts 02111 (617) 423-3990; *The World in Figures.*

COOK ISLANDS - CUSTOMS DUTIES

G.K. Hall and Company, 70 Lincoln Street, Boston, Massachusetts 02111 (617) 423-3990; *The World in Figures.*

COOK ISLANDS - DAIRY PRODUCTS

Facts on File, 460 Park Avenue South, New York, New York 10016 (800) 443-8323; *The New Book of World Rankings.*

Food and Agricultural Organization of the United Nations (FAO) Via delle Terme di Caracalla, 00100 Rome, Italy (Telephone Number in U.S. (202) 653-2400); *The State of Food and Agriculture.*

COOK ISLANDS - DEATH RATES

G.K. Hall and Company, 70 Lincoln Street, Boston, Massachusetts 02111 (617) 423-3990; *The World in Figures.*

Statistical Office of the United Nations, Publishing Service, New York, New York 10017 (800) 253-9646; *Statistical Yearbook.*

World Health Organization, Office of Publications, Avenue Appia, CH-1211 Geneva 27, Switzerland (Telephone Number in U.S. (518) 436-9686); *World Health Statistics Annual.*

COOK ISLANDS - DEFENSE EXPENDITURES

G.K. Hall and Company, 70 Lincoln Street, Boston, Massachusetts 02111 (617) 423-3990; *The World in Figures.*

COOK ISLANDS - DEMOGRAPHY

G.K. Hall and Company, 70 Lincoln Street, Boston, Massachusetts 02111 (617) 423-3990; *The World in Figures.*

COOK ISLANDS - DEVELOPMENT ASSISTANCE

Asian Development Bank, P.O. Box 789, 1099 Manila, Philippines; *Key Indicators of Developing Asian and Pacific Countries.*

G.K. Hall and Company, 70 Lincoln Street, Boston, Massachusetts 02111 (617) 423-3990; *The World in Figures.*

Statistical Office of the United Nations, Publishing Service, New York, New York 10017 (800) 253-9646; *Statistical Yearbook.*

COOK ISLANDS - DISEASE

G.K. Hall and Company, 70 Lincoln Street, Boston, Massachusetts 02111 (617) 423-3990; *The World in Figures.*

World Health Organization, Office of Publications, Avenue Appia, CH-1211 Geneva 27, Switzerland (Telephone Number in U.S. (518) 436-9686); *World Health Statistics Annual.*

COOK ISLANDS - DIVORCE RATES

Statistical Office of the United Nations, Publishing Service, New York, New York 10017 (800) 253-9646; *Demographic Yearbook*, and *Statistical Yearbook*.

COOK ISLANDS - DOMESTIC PRODUCT

G.K. Hall and Company, 70 Lincoln Street, Boston, Massachusetts 02111 (617) 423-3990; *The World in Figures*.

COOK ISLANDS - ECONOMY

Asian Development Bank, P.O. Box 789, 1099 Manila, Philippines; *Key Indicators of Developing Asian and Pacific Countries*.

G.K. Hall and Company, 70 Lincoln Street, Boston, Massachusetts 02111 (617) 423-3990; *The World in Figures*.

COOK ISLANDS - EDUCATION

G.K. Hall and Company, 70 Lincoln Street, Boston, Massachusetts 02111 (617) 423-3990; *The World in Figures*.

Statistical Office of the United Nations, Publishing Service, New York, New York 10017 (800) 253-9646; *Statistical Yearbook for Asia and the Pacific*.

United Nations Educational, Scientific and Cultural Organization (UNESCO), 7 Place de Fontenoy, F-75700 Paris, France (Telephone Number in U.S. (212) 963-5981); *Statistical Yearbook*.

COOK ISLANDS - EGG PRODUCTION - See COOK ISLANDS - DAIRY PRODUCTS

COOK ISLANDS - ELECTRICITY

Asian Development Bank, P.O. Box 789, 1099 Manila, Philippines; *Key Indicators of Developing Asian and Pacific Countries*.

Statistical Office of the United Nations, Publishing Service, New York, New York 10017 (800) 253-9646; *Electric Power in Asia and the Pacific*.

COOK ISLANDS - EMPLOYMENT

International Labour Office, I.L.O. Publications, CH-1211, Geneva 22, Switzerland; *Yearbook of Labour Statistics*.

COOK ISLANDS - ENERGY

Food and Agricultural Organization of the United Nations (FAO) Via delle Terme di Caracalla, 00100 Rome, Italy (Telephone Number in U.S. (202) 653-2400); *The State of Food and Agriculture*.

G.K. Hall and Company, 70 Lincoln Street, Boston, Massachusetts 02111 (617) 423-3990; *The World in Figures*.

Statistical Office of the United Nations, Publishing Service, New York, New York 10017 (800) 253-9646; *Energy Statistics Yearbook*, *Statistical Yearbook*, and *Statistical Yearbook for Asia and the Pacific*.

COOK ISLANDS - EXCHANGE RATES

Asian Development Bank, P.O. Box 789, 1099 Manila, Philippines; *Key Indicators of Developing Asian and Pacific Countries*.

COOK ISLANDS - EXPORTS

Asian Development Bank, P.O. Box 789, 1099 Manila, Philippines; *Key Indicators of Developing Asian and Pacific Countries*.

Food and Agricultural Organization of the United Nations (FAO) Via delle Terme di Caracalla, 00100 Rome, Italy (Telephone Number in U.S. (202) 653-2400); *The State of Food and Agriculture*.

G.K. Hall and Company, 70 Lincoln Street, Boston, Massachusetts 02111 (617) 423-3990; *The World in Figures*.

South Pacific Commission, Post Box D5, Noumea Cedex, New Caledonia; *Statistical Bulletin of the South Pacific: Overseas Trade*.

COOK ISLANDS - EXTERNAL FINANCING

Asian Development Bank, P.O. Box 789, 1099 Manila, Philippines; *Key Indicators of Developing Asian and Pacific Countries*.

COOK ISLANDS - EXTERNAL INDEBTEDNESS

Asian Development Bank, P.O. Box 789, 1099 Manila, Philippines; *Key Indicators of Developing Asian and Pacific Countries*.

COOK ISLANDS - EXTERNAL TRADE

Asian Development Bank, P.O. Box 789, 1099 Manila, Philippines; *Key Indicators of Developing Asian and Pacific Countries*.

Food and Agricultural Organization of the United Nations (FAO) Via delle Terme di Caracalla, 00100 Rome, Italy (Telephone Number in U.S. (202) 653-2400); *The State of Food and Agriculture*, and *Trade Yearbook*.

G.K. Hall and Company, 70 Lincoln Street, Boston, Massachusetts 02111 (617) 423-3990; *The World in Figures*.

Statistical Office of the United Nations, Publishing Service, New York, New York 10017 (800) 253-9646; *Statistical Yearbook*, and *Statistical Yearbook for Asia and the Pacific*.

COOK ISLANDS - FARM CROPS - See COOK ISLANDS - CROPS

COOK ISLANDS - FETAL MORTALITY

Statistical Office of the United Nations, Publishing Service, New York, New York 10017 (800) 253-9646; *Demographic Yearbook*.

World Health Organization, Office of Publications, Avenue Appia, CH-1211 Geneva 27, Switzerland (Telephone Number in U.S. (518) 436-9686); *World Health Statistics Annual*.

COOK ISLANDS - FERTILIZER

Food and Agricultural Organization of the United Nations (FAO) Via delle Terme di Caracalla, 00100 Rome, Italy (Telephone Number in U.S. (202) 653-2400); *The State of Food and Agriculture*.

COOK ISLANDS - FINANCE

Asian Development Bank, P.O. Box 789, 1099 Manila, Philippines; *Key Indicators of Developing Asian and Pacific Countries*.

G.K. Hall and Company, 70 Lincoln Street, Boston, Massachusetts 02111 (617) 423-3990; *The World in Figures*.

Statistical Office of the United Nations, Publishing Service, New York, New York 10017 (800) 253-9646; *Statistical Yearbook for Asia and the Pacific.*

COOK ISLANDS - FISHERIES

Food and Agricultural Organization of the United Nations (FAO) Via delle Terme di Caracalla, 00100 Rome, Italy (Telephone Number in U.S. (202) 653-2400); *The State of Food and Agriculture,* and *Yearbook of Fishery Statistics.*

Statistical Office of the United Nations, Publishing Service, New York, New York 10017 (800) 253-9646; *Statistical Yearbook.*

COOK ISLANDS - FOOD

Food and Agricultural Organization of the United Nations (FAO) Via delle Terme di Caracalla, 00100 Rome, Italy (Telephone Number in U.S. (202) 653-2400); *Production Yearbook,* and *The State of Food and Agriculture.*

G.K. Hall and Company, 70 Lincoln Street, Boston, Massachusetts 02111 (617) 423-3990; *The World in Figures.*

South Pacific Commission, Post Box D5, Noumea Cedex, New Caledonia; *Statistical Bulletin of the South Pacific: Retail Price Indexes.*

Statistical Office of the United Nations, Publishing Service, New York, New York 10017 (800) 253-9646; *Statistical Yearbook for Asia and the Pacific.*

COOK ISLANDS - FOREIGN AID

G.K. Hall and Company, 70 Lincoln Street, Boston, Massachusetts 02111 (617) 423-3990; *The World in Figures.*

COOK ISLANDS - FOREIGN TRADE

Asian Development Bank, P.O. Box 789, 1099 Manila, Philippines; *Key Indicators of Developing Asian and Pacific Countries.*

Food and Agricultural Organization of the United Nations (FAO) Via delle Terme di Caracalla, 00100 Rome, Italy (Telephone Number in U.S. (202) 653-2400); *The State of Food and Agriculture.*

G.K. Hall and Company, 70 Lincoln Street, Boston, Massachusetts 02111 (617) 423-3990; *The World in Figures.*

Organisation for Economic Co-operation and Development (OECD), 2 rue Andre-Pascal, 75 Paris 16, France (Telephone Number in U.S. (202) 785-6323); *Trade by Commodities.*

South Pacific Commission, Post Box D5, Noumea Cedex, New Caledonia; *Statistical Bulletin of the South Pacific: Overseas Trade.*

Statistical Office of the United Nations, Publishing Service, New York, New York 10017 (800) 253-9646; *International Trade Statistics Yearbook, Statistical Yearbook,* and *Statistical Yearbook for Asia and the Pacific.*

COOK ISLANDS - FORESTRY AND FOREST PRODUCTS

Food and Agricultural Organization of the United Nations (FAO) Via delle Terme di Caracalla, 00100 Rome, Italy (Telephone Number in U.S. (202) 653-2400); *The State of Food and Agriculture.*

G.K. Hall and Company, 70 Lincoln Street, Boston, Massachusetts 02111 (617) 423-3990; *The World in Figures.*

Statistical Office of the United Nations, Publishing Service, New York, New York 10017 (800) 253-9646; *Statistical Yearbook.*

United Nations Educational, Scientific and Cultural Organization (UNESCO), 7 Place de Fontenoy, F-75700 Paris, France (Telephone Number in U.S. (212) 963-5981); *Statistical Yearbook.*

COOK ISLANDS - GENERAL MORTALITY

Statistical Office of the United Nations, Publishing Service, New York, New York 10017 (800) 253-9646; *Demographic Yearbook.*

World Health Organization, Office of Publications, Avenue Appia, CH-1211 Geneva 27, Switzerland (Telephone Number in U.S. (518) 436-9686); *World Health Statistics Annual.*

COOK ISLANDS - GOVERNMENT

Asian Development Bank, P.O. Box 789, 1099 Manila, Philippines; *Key Indicators of Developing Asian and Pacific Countries.*

G.K. Hall and Company, 70 Lincoln Street, Boston, Massachusetts 02111 (617) 423-3990; *The World in Figures.*

COOK ISLANDS - GOVERNMENT BONDS - See COOK ISLANDS - BONDS

COOK ISLANDS - GOVERNMENT EXPENDITURE

Asian Development Bank, P.O. Box 789, 1099 Manila, Philippines; *Key Indicators of Developing Asian and Pacific Countries.*

COOK ISLANDS - GOVERNMENT FINANCES

Asian Development Bank, P.O. Box 789, 1099 Manila, Philippines; *Key Indicators of Developing Asian and Pacific Countries.*

COOK ISLANDS - GOVERNMENT REVENUE

Asian Development Bank, P.O. Box 789, 1099 Manila, Philippines; *Key Indicators of Developing Asian and Pacific Countries.*

COOK ISLANDS - GRAIN PRODUCTION - See COOK ISLANDS - CROPS

COOK ISLANDS - GROSS DOMESTIC PRODUCT

Asian Development Bank, P.O. Box 789, 1099 Manila, Philippines; *Key Indicators of Developing Asian and Pacific Countries.*

G.K. Hall and Company, 70 Lincoln Street, Boston, Massachusetts 02111 (617) 423-3990; *The World in Figures.*

Statistical Office of the United Nations, Publishing Service, New York, New York 10017 (800) 253-9646; *Statistical Yearbook.*

COOK ISLANDS - GROSS DOMESTIC PRODUCT

Asian Development Bank, P.O. Box 789, 1099 Manila, Philippines; *Key Indicators of Developing Asian and Pacific Countries.*

Statistical Office of the United Nations, Publishing Service, New York, New York 10017 (800) 253-9646; *Statistical Yearbook.*

COOK ISLANDS - GROSS NATIONAL PRODUCT

Asian Development Bank, P.O. Box 789, 1099 Manila, Philippines; *Key Indicators of Developing Asian and Pacific Countries.*

COOK ISLANDS - HEALTH

G.K. Hall and Company, 70 Lincoln Street, Boston, Massachusetts 02111 (617) 423-3990; *The World in Figures.*

South Pacific Commission, Post Box D5, Noumea Cedex, New Caledonia; *Statistical Bulletin of the South Pacific: Retail Price Indexes.*

Statistical Office of the United Nations, Publishing Service, New York, New York 10017 (800) 253-9646; *Statistical Yearbook.*

World Health Organization, Office of Publications, Avenue Appia, CH-1211 Geneva 27, Switzerland (Telephone Number in U.S. (518) 436-9686); *World Health Statistics Annual.*

COOK ISLANDS - HEALTH AND MEDICAL SERVICES

Statistical Office of the United Nations, Publishing Service, New York, New York 10017 (800) 253-9646; *Statistical Yearbook.*

COOK ISLANDS - HIDE PRODUCTION

Food and Agricultural Organization of the United Nations (FAO), Via delle Terme di Caracalla, 00100 Rome, Italy (Telephone Number in U.S. (202) 653-2400); *Production Yearbook.*

COOK ISLANDS - HIGHWAYS

G.K. Hall and Company, 70 Lincoln Street, Boston, Massachusetts 02111 (617) 423-3990; *The World in Figures.*

COOK ISLANDS - HORSES - See COOK ISLAND - LIVESTOCK AND POULTRY

COOK ISLANDS - HOURS OF WORK - See COOK ISLANDS - EMPLOYMENT

COOK ISLANDS - HOUSING AND HOUSING UNITS

South Pacific Commission, Post Box D5, Noumea Cedex, New Caledonia; *Statistical Bulletin of the South Pacific: Retail Price Indexes.*

Statistical Office of the United Nations, Publishing Service, New York, New York 10017 (800) 253-9646; *Statistical Yearbook.*

COOK ISLANDS - HOUSING EXPENDITURES

South Pacific Commission, Post Box D5, Noumea Cedex, New Caledonia; *Statistical Bulletin of the South Pacific: Retail Price Indexes.*

COOK ISLANDS - ILLITERATE POPULATION

G.K. Hall and Company, 70 Lincoln Street, Boston, Massachusetts 02111 (617) 423-3990; *The World in Figures.*

United Nations Educational, Scientific and Cultural Organization (UNESCO), 7 Place de Fontenoy, F-75700 Paris, France (Telephone Number in U.S. (212) 963-5981); *Statistical Yearbook.*

COOK ISLANDS - IMPORTS

Asian Development Bank, P.O. Box 789, 1099 Manila, Philippines; *Key Indicators of Developing Asian and Pacific Countries.*

Food and Agricultural Organization of the United Nations (FAO) Via delle Terme di Caracalla, 00100 Rome, Italy (Telephone Number in U.S. (202) 653-2400); *The State of Food and Agriculture.*

G.K. Hall and Company, 70 Lincoln Street, Boston, Massachusetts 02111 (617) 423-3990; *The World in Figures.*

South Pacific Commission, Post Box D5, Noumea Cedex, New Caledonia; *Statistical Bulletin of the South Pacific: Overseas Trade.*

COOK ISLANDS - INDUSTRY

G.K. Hall and Company, 70 Lincoln Street, Boston, Massachusetts 02111 (617) 423-3990; *The World in Figures.*

International Labour Office, I.L.O. Publications, CH-1211, Geneva 22, Switzerland; *Yearbook of Labour Statistics.*

Statistical Office of the United Nations, Publishing Service, New York, New York 10017 (800) 253-9646; *Statistical Yearbook for Asia and the Pacific.*

COOK ISLANDS - INFANT AND MATERNAL MORTALITY

Statistical Office of the United Nations, Publishing Service, New York, New York 10017 (800) 253-9646; *Demographic Yearbook,* and *Statistical Yearbook.*

World Health Organization, Office of Publications, Avenue Appia, CH-1211 Geneva 27, Switzerland (Telephone Number in U.S. (518) 436-9686); *World Health Statistics Annual.*

COOK ISLANDS - INTERNAL TRADE

Statistical Office of the United Nations, Publishing Service, New York, New York 10017 (800) 253-9646; *Statistical Yearbook for Asia and the Pacific.*

COOK ISLANDS - INTERNATIONAL RESERVES EXCLUDING GOLD

Asian Development Bank, P.O. Box 789, 1099 Manila, Philippines; *Key Indicators of Developing Asian and Pacific Countries.*

COOK ISLANDS - INTERNATIONAL STATISTICS

Asian Development Bank, P.O. Box 789, 1099 Manila, Philippines; *Key Indicators of Developing Asian and Pacific Countries.*

COOK ISLANDS - LABOR FORCE

Food and Agricultural Organization of the United Nations (FAO) Via delle Terme di Caracalla, 00100 Rome, Italy (Telephone Number in U.S. (202) 653-2400); *The State of Food and Agriculture.*

G.K. Hall and Company, 70 Lincoln Street, Boston, Massachusetts 02111 (617) 423-3990; *The World in Figures.*

COOK ISLANDS - LABOR PRODUCTIVITY

International Labour Office, I.L.O. Publications, CH-1211, Geneva 22, Switzerland; *Yearbook of Labour Statistics.*

COOK ISLANDS - LAND USE

Food and Agricultural Organization of the United Nations (FAO), Via delle Terme di Caracalla, 00100 Rome, Italy (Telephone Number in U.S. (202) 653-2400); *Production Yearbook.*

G.K. Hall and Company, 70 Lincoln Street, Boston, Massachusetts 02111 (617) 423-3990; *The World in Figures.*

COOK ISLANDS - LIBRARIES

United Nations Educational, Scientific and Cultural Organization (UNESCO), 7 Place de Fontenoy, F-75700 Paris, France (Telephone Number in U.S. (212) 963-5981); *Statistical Yearbook.*

COOK ISLANDS - LIVESTOCK AND POULTRY

Food and Agricultural Organization of the United Nations (FAO), Via delle Terme di Caracalla, 00100 Rome, Italy (Telephone Number in U.S. (202) 653-2400); *Production Yearbook,* and *The State of Food and Agriculture.*

G.K. Hall and Company, 70 Lincoln Street, Boston, Massachusetts 02111 (617) 423-3990; *The World in Figures.*

Statistical Office of the United Nations, Publishing Service, New York, New York 10017 (800) 253-9646; *Statistical Yearbook.*

COOK ISLANDS - LIVING LEVELS

G.K. Hall and Company, 70 Lincoln Street, Boston, Massachusetts 02111 (617) 423-3990; *The World in Figures.*

COOK ISLANDS - MANPOWER

Statistical Office of the United Nations, Publishing Service, New York, New York 10017 (800) 253-9646; *Statistical Yearbook for Asia and the Pacific.*

COOK ISLANDS - MANUFACTURING

Asian Development Bank, P.O. Box 789, 1099 Manila, Philippines; *Key Indicators of Developing Asian and Pacific Countries.*

G.K. Hall and Company, 70 Lincoln Street, Boston, Massachusetts 02111 (617) 423-3990; *The World in Figures.*

COOK ISLANDS - MARRIAGE RATES

Statistical Office of the United Nations, Publishing Service, New York, New York 10017 (800) 253-9646; *Demographic Yearbook,* and *Statistical Yearbook.*

COOK ISLANDS - MEAT PRODUCTION - See COOK ISLANDS - LIVESTOCK AND POULTRY

COOK ISLANDS - MERCHANT SHIPPING

G.K. Hall and Company, 70 Lincoln Street, Boston, Massachusetts 02111 (617) 423-3990; *The World in Figures.*

Statistical Office of the United Nations, Publishing Service, New York, New York 10017 (800) 253-9646; *Statistical Yearbook.*

COOK ISLANDS - MILITARY

G.K. Hall and Company, 70 Lincoln Street, Boston, Massachusetts 02111 (617) 423-3990; *The World in Figures.*

COOK ISLANDS - MINING AND MINERAL PRODUCTS

Asian Development Bank, P.O. Box 789, 1099 Manila, Philippines; *Key Indicators of Developing Asian and Pacific Countries.*

G.K. Hall and Company, 70 Lincoln Street, Boston, Massachusetts 02111 (617) 423-3990; *The World in Figures.*

COOK ISLANDS - MONEY SUPPLY

Asian Development Bank, P.O. Box 789, 1099 Manila, Philippines; *Key Indicators of Developing Asian and Pacific Countries.*

G.K. Hall and Company, 70 Lincoln Street, Boston, Massachusetts 02111 (617) 423-3990; *The World in Figures.*

COOK ISLANDS - MOTOR VEHICLES IN USE

G.K. Hall and Company, 70 Lincoln Street, Boston, Massachusetts 02111 (617) 423-3990; *The World in Figures.*

COOK ISLANDS - MUSEUMS

United Nations Educational, Scientific and Cultural Organization (UNESCO), 7 Place de Fontenoy, F-75700 Paris, France (Telephone Number in U.S. (212) 963-5981); *Statistical Yearbook.*

COOK ISLANDS - NATALITY - See COOK ISLANDS - BIRTH RATES

COOK ISLANDS - NATIONAL ACCOUNTS

Statistical Office of the United Nations, Publishing Service, New York, New York 10017 (800) 253-9646; *National Accounts Statistics, Statistical Yearbook,* and *Statistical Yearbook for Asia and the Pacific.*

COOK ISLANDS - NATIONAL INCOME

G.K. Hall and Company, 70 Lincoln Street, Boston, Massachusetts 02111 (617) 423-3990; *The World in Figures.*

Statistical Office of the United Nations, Publishing Service, New York, New York 10017 (800) 253-9646; *Statistical Yearbook.*

COOK ISLANDS - NATIONAL PRODUCT

Statistical Office of the United Nations, Publishing Service, New York, New York 10017 (800) 253-9646; *Statistical Yearbook.*

COOK ISLANDS - NEWSPAPER PRODUCTION - See COOK ISLANDS - FORESTRY AND FOREST PRODUCTS

COOK ISLANDS - OCCUPATIONS - See COOK ISLANDS - LABOR FORCE

COOK ISLANDS - PESTICIDE USE

Food and Agricultural Organization of the United Nations (FAO) Via delle Terme di Caracalla, 00100 Rome, Italy (Telephone Number in U.S. (202) 653-2400); *The State of Food and Agriculture.*

COOK ISLANDS - PETROLEUM INDUSTRY

Asian Development Bank, P.O. Box 789, 1099 Manila, Philippines; *Key Indicators of Developing Asian and Pacific Countries.*

Food and Agricultural Organization of the United Nations (FAO) Via delle Terme di Caracalla, 00100 Rome, Italy (Telephone Number in U.S. (202) 653-2400); *The State of Food and Agriculture.*

G.K. Hall and Company, 70 Lincoln Street, Boston, Massachusetts 02111 (617) 423-3990; *The World in Figures.*

COOK ISLANDS - PIGS - See COOK ISLANDS - LIVESTOCK AND POULTRY

COOK ISLANDS - POPULATION

Asian Development Bank, P.O. Box 789, 1099 Manila, Philippines; *Key Indicators of Developing Asian and Pacific Countries.*

Food and Agricultural Organization of the United Nations (FAO), Via delle Terme di Caracalla, 00100 Rome, Italy (Telephone Number in U.S. (202) 653-2400); *Production Yearbook.*

G.K. Hall and Company, 70 Lincoln Street, Boston, Massachusetts 02111 (617) 423-3990; *The World in Figures.*

International Labour Office, I.L.O. Publications, CH-1211, Geneva 22, Switzerland; *Yearbook of Labour Statistics.*

Statistical Office of the United Nations, Publishing Service, New York, New York 10017 (800) 253-9646; *Demographic Yearbook, Statistical Yearbook,* and *Statistical Yearbook for Asia and the Pacific.*

United Nations Educational, Scientific and Cultural Organization (UNESCO), 7 Place de Fontenoy, F-75700 Paris, France (Telephone Number in U.S. (212) 963-5981); *Statistical Yearbook.*

World Health Organization, Office of Publications, Avenue Appia, CH-1211 Geneva 27, Switzerland (Telephone Number in U.S. (518) 436-9686); *World Health Statistics Annual.*

COOK ISLANDS - POWER PRODUCTION INDUSTRY

Statistical Office of the United Nations, Publishing Service, New York, New York 10017 (800) 253-9646; *Electric Power in Asia and the Pacific.*

COOK ISLANDS - PRICES

Asian Development Bank, P.O. Box 789, 1099 Manila, Philippines; *Key Indicators of Developing Asian and Pacific Countries.*

Food and Agricultural Organization of the United Nations (FAO), Via delle Terme di Caracalla, 00100 Rome, Italy (Telephone Number in U.S. (202) 653-2400); *Production Yearbook,* and *The State of Food and Agriculture.*

G.K. Hall and Company, 70 Lincoln Street, Boston, Massachusetts 02111 (617) 423-3990; *The World in Figures.*

International Labour Office, I.L.O. Publications, CH-1211, Geneva 22, Switzerland; *Yearbook of Labour Statistics.*

South Pacific Commission, Post Box D5, Noumea Cedex, New Caledonia; *Statistical Bulletin of the South Pacific: Overseas Trade,* and *Statistical Bulletin of the South Pacific: Retail Price Indexes.*

COOK ISLANDS - PRODUCTION

G.K. Hall and Company, 70 Lincoln Street, Boston, Massachusetts 02111 (617) 423-3990; *The World in Figures.*

COOK ISLANDS - RADIO BROADCASTING - See COOK ISLANDS - BROADCASTING

COOK ISLANDS - RAILWAYS

G.K. Hall and Company, 70 Lincoln Street, Boston, Massachusetts 02111 (617) 423-3990; *The World in Figures.*

COOK ISLANDS - RENT PRICES

International Labour Office, I.L.O. Publications, CH-1211, Geneva 22, Switzerland; *Yearbook of Labour Statistics.*

COOK ISLANDS - RETAIL TRADE

G.K. Hall and Company, 70 Lincoln Street, Boston, Massachusetts 02111 (617) 423-3990; *The World in Figures.*

COOK ISLANDS - RICE PRODUCTION - See COOK ISLANDS - CROPS

COOK ISLANDS - SCIENCE AND TECHNOLOGY - EXPENDITURE FOR RESEARCH

Statistical Office of the United Nations, Publishing Service, New York, New York 10017 (800) 253-9646; *Statistical Yearbook.*

COOK ISLANDS - SCIENTISTS AND TECHNICIANS

Statistical Office of the United Nations, Publishing Service, New York, New York 10017 (800) 253-9646; *Statistical Yearbook.*

COOK ISLANDS - SOCIAL DATA

Asian Development Bank, P.O. Box 789, 1099 Manila, Philippines; *Key Indicators of Developing Asian and Pacific Countries.*

G.K. Hall and Company, 70 Lincoln Street, Boston, Massachusetts 02111 (617) 423-3990; *The World in Figures.*

COOK ISLANDS - STOCKS - COMMODITY - MARKET PRICE - INDEX

Food and Agricultural Organization of the United Nations (FAO) Via delle Terme di Caracalla, 00100 Rome, Italy (Telephone Number in U.S. (202) 653-2400); *The State of Food and Agriculture.*

COOK ISLANDS - TAXATION

G.K. Hall and Company, 70 Lincoln Street, Boston, Massachusetts 02111 (617) 423-3990; *The World in Figures.*

Inter-American Development Bank, 1300 New York Avenue, NW, Washington, D.C. 20577 (202) 623-1753; *Economic and Social Progress in Latin America.*

International Monetary Fund, 700 Nineteenth Street, NW, Washington, D.C. 20431 (202) 623-7000; *Government Finance Statistics Yearbook.*

COOK ISLANDS - TELEPHONES IN USE

American Telephone and Telegraph Company, 26 Parsippany Road, Whippany, New Jersey 07981 (800) 338-4038; *The World's Telephones.*

G.K. Hall and Company, 70 Lincoln Street, Boston, Massachusetts 02111 (617) 423-3990; *The World in Figures.*

COOK ISLANDS - TEXTILE INDUSTRY

G.K. Hall and Company, 70 Lincoln Street, Boston, Massachusetts 02111 (617) 423-3990; *The World in Figures.*

COOK ISLANDS - TOBACCO PRODUCTION

South Pacific Commission, Post Box D5, Noumea Cedex, New Caledonia; *Statistical Bulletin of the South Pacific: Retail Price Indexes.*

COOK ISLANDS - TOURISM

G.K. Hall and Company, 70 Lincoln Street, Boston, Massachusetts 02111 (617) 423-3990; *The World in Figures.*

Statistical Office of the United Nations, Publishing Service, New York, New York 10017 (800) 253-9646; *Statistical Yearbook.*

World Tourism Organization, Calle Capitan Haya 42, E-28020 Madrid, Spain; *Yearbook of Tourism Statistics.*

COOK ISLANDS - TRACTORS IN USE

Statistical Office of the United Nations, Publishing Service, New York, New York 10017 (800) 253-9646; *Statistical Yearbook.*

COOK ISLANDS - TRADE - See COOK ISLANDS - FOREIGN TRADE

COOK ISLANDS - TRANSPORTATION AND COMMUNICATIONS

G.K. Hall and Company, 70 Lincoln Street, Boston, Massachusetts 02111 (617) 423-3990; *The World in Figures.*

South Pacific Commission, Post Box D5, Noumea Cedex, New Caledonia; *Statistical Bulletin of the South Pacific: Overseas Trade.*

Statistical Office of the United Nations, Publishing Service, New York, New York 10017 (800) 253-9646; *Statistical Yearbook for Asia and the Pacific.*

COOK ISLANDS - UNEMPLOYMENT

International Labour Office, I.L.O. Publications, CH-1211, Geneva 22, Switzerland; *Yearbook of Labour Statistics.*

COOK ISLANDS - UTILITIES

Statistical Office of the United Nations, Publishing Service, New York, New York 10017 (800) 253-9646; *Electric Power in Asia and the Pacific.*

COOK ISLANDS - VITAL STATISTICS

G.K. Hall and Company, 70 Lincoln Street, Boston, Massachusetts 02111 (617) 423-3990; *The World in Figures.*

World Health Organization, Office of Publications, Avenue Appia, CH-1211 Geneva 27, Switzerland (Telephone Number in U.S. (518) 436-9686); *World Health Statistics Annual.*

COOK ISLANDS - WAGES

G.K. Hall and Company, 70 Lincoln Street, Boston, Massachusetts 02111 (617) 423-3990; *The World in Figures.*

International Labour Office, I.L.O. Publications, CH-1211, Geneva 22, Switzerland; *Yearbook of Labour Statistics.*

Statistical Office of the United Nations, Publishing Service, New York, New York 10017 (800) 253-9646; *Statistical Yearbook for Asia and the Pacific.*

COOK ISLANDS - WEATHER

G.K. Hall and Company, 70 Lincoln Street, Boston, Massachusetts 02111 (617) 423-3990; *The World in Figures.*

COOK ISLANDS - WHOLESALE PRICES

Asian Development Bank, P.O. Box 789, 1099 Manila, Philippines; *Key Indicators of Developing Asian and Pacific Countries.*

COOKING OILS CONSUMPTION

U.S. Department of Agriculture, Economic Research Service, Fourteenth Street and Independence Avenue, SW, Washington, D.C. 20005-4789 (202) 219-1504; *Food Consumption, Prices, and Expenditures,* annual, and unpublished data.

COOLING DEGREE DAYS

U.S. Department of Commerce, National Oceanic and Atmospheric Administration, National Climatic Data Center, Federal Building, Asheville, North Carolina 28801 (704) 259-2850; *Climatography of the United States.*

COOPERATIVES - BANKS

Congressional Budget Office, Second and D Streets, SW, Washington, D.C. 20515 (202) 226-2621; *Controlling the Risks of Government-Sponsored Enterprises.*

COOPERATIVES - FARM

U.S. Department of Agriculture, Economic Research Service, Fourteenth Street and Independence Avenue, SW, Washington, D.C. 20005-4789 (202) 219-1504; *Economic Indicators of the Farm Sector: National Financial Summary.*

COPPER - CONSUMPTION

U.S. Department of the Interior, Bureau of Mines, 810 Seventh Street, NW, Washington, D.C. 20241 (202) 501-9649; *Mineral Commodity Summaries.*

COPPER - FOREIGN TRADE

U.S. Department of the Interior, Bureau of Mines, 810 Seventh Street, NW, Washington, D.C. 20241 (202) 501-9649; *Minerals Yearbook, Mineral Commodity Summaries,* and Annual Reports.

COPPER - PRICES

U.S. Department of the Interior, Bureau of Mines, 810 Seventh Street, NW, Washington, D.C. 20241 (202) 501-9649; *Mineral Commodity Summaries.*

COPPER - PRODUCTION - WORLD

U.S. Department of the Interior, Bureau of Mines, 810 Seventh Street, NW, Washington, D.C. 20241 (202) 501-9649; Annual Reports, and *Mineral Commodities Summaries.*

COPPER - PRODUCTION AND VALUE

U.S. Department of the Interior, Bureau of Mines, 810 Seventh Street, NW, Washington, D.C. 20241 (202) 501-9649; Annual Reports, and *Mineral Commodities Summaries.*

COPYRIGHTS - REGISTRATION

U.S. Library of Congress, 10 First Street, SE, Washington, D.C. 20540 (202) 707-5000; *Annual Report.*

CORN - ACREAGE

U.S. Department of Agriculture, Economic Research Service, Fourteenth Street and Independence Avenue, SW, Washington, D.C. 20005-4789 (202) 219-1504; *Agricultural Statistics*, and *Agricultural Outlook*.

U.S. Department of Agriculture, National Agricultural Statistics Service, Fourteenth Street and Independence Avenue, SW, Washington, D.C. 20250 (202) 219-1504; *Crop Production, Crop Values*, and *Field Crops*.

CORN - CONSUMPTION

U.S. Department of Agriculture, Economic Research Service, Fourteenth Street and Independence Avenue, SW, Washington, D.C. 20005-4789 (202) 219-1504; *Agricultural Outlook, Food Consumption, Prices, and Expenditures*, and unpublished data.

CORN - FARM MARKETINGS, SALES

U.S. Department of Agriculture, Economic Research Service, Fourteenth Street and Independence Avenue, SW, Washington, D.C. 20005 (202) 219-1504; *Economic Indicators of the Farm Sector: National Financial Summary*.

CORN - FOREIGN TRADE

Food and Agricultural Organization of the United States, Via delle Terme di Caracalla, 00100 Rome, Italy (Telephone Number in U.S. (202) 653-2400); *FAO Trade Yearbook*.

U.S. Department of Agriculture, Economic Research Service, Fourteenth Street and Independence Avenue, SW, Washington, D.C. 20005-4789 (202) 219-1504; *Agricultural Outlook, Agricultural Statistics, Foreign Agricultural Trade of the U.S*, and *World Agriculture - Trends and Indicators*.

U.S. Department of Agriculture, Foreign Agricultural Service, Fourteenth Street and Independence Avenue, SW, Washington, D.C. 20250 (202) 720-3448; *Foreign Agricultural Commodity Circular Series*.

U.S. Department of Commerce, Bureau of the Census, Suitland, Maryland 20233 (301) 763-4040; *U.S. Merchandise Trade*.

CORN - PRICES

U.S. Department of Agriculture, National Agricultural Statistics Service, Fourteenth Street and Independence Avenue, SW, Washington, D.C. 20250 (202) 219-1504; *Crop Production, Field Crops, Crop Values, Agricultural Statistics*, and *Agricultural Outlook*.

CORN - PRODUCTION

U.S. Department of Agriculture, Economic Research Service, Fourteenth Street and Independence Avenue, SW, Washington, D.C. 20005-4789 (202) 219-1504; *Agricultural Statistics*.

U.S. Department of Agriculture, Foreign Agricultural Service, Fourteenth Street and Independence Avenue, SW, Washington, D.C. 20250 (202) 720-3448; *Foreign Agricultural Commodity Circular Series*.

U.S. Department of Agriculture, National Agricultural Statistics Service, Fourteenth Street and Independence Avenue, SW, Washington, D.C. 20250 (202) 219-1504; *Crop Production, Crop Values, Field Crops*, and *Vegetables*.

CORN - PRODUCTION - WORLD PRODUCTION

Food and Agricultural Organization of the United Nations (FAO), Via della Terme di Caracalla, 00100 Rome, Italy (Telephone Number in U.S. (202) 653-2400); *FAO Production Yearbook*.

Statistical Office of the United Nations, New York, New York 10017 (800) 253-9646; *Monthly Bulletin of Statistics*.

U.S. Department of Agriculture, Foreign Agricultural Service, Fourteenth Street and Independence Avenue, SW, Washington, D.C. 20250 (202) 720-3448; *Foreign Agricultural Commodity Circular Series*.

CORN - SUPPLY AND DISAPPEARANCE

U.S. Department of Agriculture, Economic Research Service, Fourteenth Street and Independence Avenue, SW, Washington, D.C. 20005-4789 (202) 219-1504; *Agricultural Statistics, Agricultural Outlook*, and *Agricultural Supply and Demand Estimates*.

CORPORATE BUSINESS SECTOR

Board of Governors of the Federal Reserve System, Twentieth Street and Constitution Avenue, NW, Washington, D.C. 20551 (202) 452-3000; *Balance Sheets for the United States Economy*, and *Flow of Funds Accounts*.

CORPORATE BUSINESS SECTOR - POLITICAL ACTION COMMITTEES

Federal Election Commission, 999 E Street, NW, Washington, D.C. 20463 (800) 424-9530; Press releases, and *FEC Reports on Financial Activity, Final Report, Party and Non-Party Political Committees*.

CORPORATIONS - CAPITAL

Board of Governors of the Federal Reserve System, Twentieth Street and Constitution Avenue, NW, Washington, D.C. 20551 (202) 452-3000; *Annual Statistical Digest*.

U.S. Department of the Treasury, Internal Revenue Service, 1111 Constitution Avenue, NW, Washington, D.C. 20224 (202) 566-5000; *Statistics of Income, Corporation Income Tax Returns*.

CORPORATIONS - DIVIDEND PAYMENTS

U.S. Department of Commerce, Bureau of Economic Analysis, Fourteenth Street between Constitution Avenue and E Street, NW, Washington, D.C. 20230 (202) 606-9900; *The National Income and Product Accounts of the United States*, and *Survey of Current Business*.

CORPORATIONS - FINANCES

Board of Governors of the Federal Reserve System, Twentieth Street and Constitution Avenue, NW, Washington, D.C. 20551 (202) 452-3000; *Annual Statistical Digest, Flow of Funds Accounts*, and *Balance Sheets for the U.S. Economy*.

Time Warner, 1675 Broadway, Rockefeller Center, New York, New York 10019 (212) 522-1212; *The Fortune Directories*.

U.S. Department of the Treasury, Internal Revenue Service, 1111 Constitution Avenue, NW, Washington, D.C. 20224 (202) 566-5000; *Statistics of Income, Corporation Income Tax Returns, Statistics of Income Bulletins* and *Statistics of Income*, various publications.

CORPORATIONS - FOREIGN

Time Warner, 1675 Broadway, Rockefeller Center, New York, New York 10019 (212) 522-1212; *The Fortune Directories.*

U.S. Department of Commerce, Bureau of Economic Analysis, Fourteenth Street between Constitution Avenue and E Street, NW, Washington, D.C. 20230 (202) 606-9900; *Survey of Current Business.*

U.S. Department of the Treasury, Internal Revenue Service, 1111 Constitution Avenue, NW, Washington, D.C. 20224 (202) 566-5000; *Statistics of Income Bulletin.*

CORPORATIONS - INTEREST

U.S. Department of Commerce, Bureau of Economic Analysis, Fourteenth Street between Constitution Avenue and E Street, NW, Washington, D.C. 20230 (202) 606-9900; *The National Income and Product Accounts of the United States,* and *Survey of Current Business.*

CORPORATIONS - INVENTORIES

U.S. Department of Commerce, Bureau of Economic Analysis, Fourteenth Street between Constitution Avenue and E Street, NW, Washington, D.C. 20230 (202) 606-9900; *The National Income and Product Accounts of the United States,* and *Survey of Current Business.*

CORPORATIONS - MANUFACTURING

U.S. Department of Commerce, Bureau of the Census, Suitland, Maryland 20233 (301) 763-4040; *Quarterly Financial Report for Manufacturing, Mining, and Trade Corporations.*

CORPORATIONS - NONFINANCIAL

Board of Governors of the Federal Reserve System, Twentieth Street and Constitution Avenue, NW, Washington, D.C. 20551 (202) 452-3000; *Federal Reserve Bulletin, Flow of Funds Accounts,* and *Balance Sheets for the U.S. Economy.*

The Conference Board, 845 Third Avenue, New York, New York 10022 (212) 759-0900; *Quarterly Survey of Capital Appropriations.*

CORPORATIONS - PHILANTHROPY

American Association of Fund Raising Counsel, Incorporated, 25 West Forty-third Street, New York, New York 10036 (212) 354-5799; *Giving USA.*

The Conference Board, 845 Third Avenue, New York, New York 10022 (212) 759-0900; *Annual Survey of Corporate Contributions.*

Independent Sector, 1828 L Street, NW, Washington, D.C. 20036 (202) 857-4722; *Giving and Volunteering in the United States.*

CORPORATIONS - PROFITS

Board of Governors of the Federal Reserve System, Twentieth Street and Constitution Avenue, NW, Washington, D.C. 20551 (202) 452-3000; annual report, *Flow of Funds Accounts.*

Executive Office of the President, Council of Economic Advisers, Old Executive Office Building, Washington, D.C. 20500 (202) 395-5084; *Economic Report of the President.*

Forbes, Incorporated, 60 Fifth Avenue, New York, New York 10011 (202) 620-2200; *Forbes Annual Report on American Industry.*

Time Warner, 1675 Broadway, Rockefeller Center, New York, New York 10019 (212) 522-1212; *The Fortune Directories.*

U.S. Department of Commerce, Bureau of Economic Analysis, Fourteenth Street between Constitution Avenue and E Street, NW, Washington, D.C. 20230 (202) 606-9900; *Survey of Current Business,* July issues, and *The National Income and Product Accounts of the United States.*

U.S. Department of Commerce, Bureau of the Census, Suitland, Maryland 20233 (301) 763-4040; *Quarterly Financial Report for Manufacturing Corporations.*

U.S. Department of the Treasury, Internal Revenue Service, 1111 Constitution Avenue, NW, Washington, D.C. 20224 (202) 566-5000; *Statistics of Income, Corporation Income Tax Returns,* and *Statistics of Income Bulletin.*

CORPORATIONS - RECEIPTS

U.S. Department of the Treasury, Internal Revenue Service, 1111 Constitution Avenue, NW, Washington, D.C. 20224 (202) 566-5000; *Statistics of Income, Corporation Income Tax Returns, Statistics of Income,* various publications, and *Statistics of Income Bulletin.*

CORPORATIONS - SALES

Forbes, Incorporated, 60 Fifth Avenue, New York, New York 10011 (202) 620-2200; *Forbes Annual Report on American Industry.*

Time Warner, 1675 Broadway, Rockefeller Center, New York, New York 10019 (212) 522-1212; *The Fortune Directories.*

U.S. Department of Commerce, Bureau of the Census, Suitland, Maryland 20233 (301) 763-4040; *Quarterly Financial Report for Manufacturing, Mining and Trade Corporations.*

U.S. Department of the Treasury, Internal Revenue Service, 1111 Constitution Avenue, NW, Washington, D.C. 20224 (202) 566-5000; *Statistics of Income, Corporation Income Tax Returns.*

CORPORATIONS - STOCKS AND BONDS

Board of Governors of the Federal Reserve System, Twentieth Street and Constitution Avenue, NW, Washington, D.C. 20551 (202) 452-3000; *Federal Reserve Bulletin.*

CORPORATIONS - TAXES - CORPORATE INCOME TAX

U.S. Department of the Treasury, Internal Revenue Service, 1111 Constitution Avenue, NW, Washington, D.C. 20224 (202) 566-5000; *Statistics of Income, Corporation Income Tax Returns,* and *Statistics of Income Bulletin.*

CORPORATIONS - TAXES - RETURNS

U.S. Department of the Treasury, Internal Revenue Service, 1111 Constitution Avenue, NW, Washington, D.C. 20224 (202) 566-5000; *Statistics of Income, Corporation Income Tax Returns.*

CORPORATIONS - TAXES - STATE TAX COLLECTIONS

U.S. Department of Commerce, Bureau of the Census, Suitland, Maryland 20233 (301) 763-4040; *State Government Tax Collections.*

CORRECTIONAL INSTITUTIONS - See also PRISONS AND PRISONERS

CORRECTIONAL INSTITUTIONS

U.S. Department of Commerce, Bureau of the Census, Suitland, Maryland 20233 (301) 763-4040; *Census of Population, General Population Characteristics.*

CORRECTIONAL INSTITUTIONS - EMPLOYEES

U.S. Department of Commerce, Bureau of the Census, Suitland, Maryland 20233 (301) 763-4040; *Public Employment,* and *Government Finances.*

U.S. Department of Justice, Bureau of Justice Statistics, 633 Indiana Avenue, NW, Washington, D.C. 20531 (800) 732-3277; *Justice Expenditure and Employment in the U.S.*

CORRECTIONAL INSTITUTIONS - EXPENDITURES

U.S. Department of Commerce, Bureau of the Census, Suitland, Maryland 20233 (301) 763-4040; *Public Employment,* and *Government Finances.*

U.S. Department of Justice, Bureau of Justice Statistics, 633 Indiana Avenue, NW, Washington, D.C. 20531 (800) 732-3277; *Justice Expenditure and Employment in the U.S.*

CORRECTIONAL INSTITUTIONS - PRISONERS

U.S. Department of Justice, Bureau of Justice Statistics, 633 Indiana Avenue, NW, Washington, D.C. 20531 (800) 732-3277; *Prisoners in State and Federal Institutions on December 31, Probation and Parole, Prisoners in 1991, Correctional Populations in the U.S.,* and *Survey of State Prison Inmates.*

COSMETICS, PERFUME, ETC. - ADVERTISING EXPENDITURES

Publishers Information Bureau, 575 Lexington Avenue, New York, New York 10022 (212) 752-0055; as compiled by Leading National Advertisers, Inc., 11 West 42nd Street, New York, New York 10036 (212) 789-1400.

Television Bureau of Advertising, Inc., 850 Third Avenue, New York, New York 10022 (212) 486-1111; data compiled by Competitive Media Reporting, 11 West 42nd Street, New York, New York 10036 (212) 789-1400.

COST-OF-LIVING INDEXES - See CONSUMER PRICE INDEXES

Costa Rica - National Statistical Office

Direccion General de Estadistica y Censos, Apartado 10216, San Jose, Costa Rica.

Costa Rica - Primary Statistics Source

Direccion General de Estadistica y Censos, Apartado 10216, San Jose, Costa Rica; Centra para la promocion de las Exportaciones y la Inversiones, *Datos Y Cifras de Costa Rica.*

COSTA RICA - AGRICULTURE

The Economist Intelligence Unit, 111 West 57th Street, New York, New York 10019 (800) 938-4685; *The New Latin America Market Atlas.*

Euromonitor Publications Limited, 87-88 Turnmill Street, London, EC1M 5QU, England; *International Marketing Data and Statistics.*

Facts on File, 460 Park Avenue South, New York, New York 10016 (800) 443-8323; *The New Book of World Rankings.*

Federal Statistical Office, Gustav - Stresemann - Ring 11, D-6200 Wiesbaden, Germany; *Costa Rica.*

Food and Agricultural Organization of the United Nations (FAO) Via delle Terme di Caracalla, 00100 Rome, Italy (Telephone Number in U.S. (202) 653-2400); *Production Yearbook, The State of Food and Agriculture,* and *Trade Yearbook.*

Gale Research Incorporated, 835 Penobscot Building, Detroit, Michigan 48226 (800) 877-4253; *International Historical Statistics The Americas and Australasia.*

G.K. Hall and Company, 70 Lincoln Street, Boston, Massachusetts 02111 (617) 423-3990; *The World in Figures.*

Inter-American Development Bank, 1300 New York Avenue, NW, Washington, D.C. 20577 (202) 623-1753; *Economic and Social Progress in Latin America.*

Statistical Office of the United Nations, Publishing Service, New York, New York 10017 (800) 253-9646; *Statistical Yearbook,* and *Statistical Yearbook for Latin America and the Caribbean.*

Times Books, 201 East 50th Street, New York, New York 10022 (212) 751-2600; *The Economist Book of Vital World Statistics.*

The World Bank, 1818 H Street, NW, Washington, D.C. 20433 (202) 477-1234; *World Tables.*

COSTA RICA - AIRLINE SERVICE

The Economist Intelligence Unit, 111 West 57th Street, New York, New York 10019 (800) 938-4685; *The New Latin America Market Atlas.*

Facts on File, 460 Park Avenue South, New York, New York 10016 (800) 443-8323; *The New Book of World Rankings.*

G.K. Hall and Company, 70 Lincoln Street, Boston, Massachusetts 02111 (617) 423-3990; *The World in Figures.*

International Civil Aviation Organization, 1000 Sherbrooke Street West, Suite 400, Montreal, Quebec, Canada H3A 2R2 (514) 285-8219; *Civil Aviation Statistics of the World.*

Times Books, 201 East 50th Street, New York, New York 10022 (212) 751-2600; *The Economist Book of Vital World Statistics.*

COSTA RICA - ALUMINUM PRODUCTION AND CONSUMPTION - See COSTA RICA - MINING AND MINERAL PRODUCTS

COSTA RICA - ANIMAL HEALTH

Food and Agricultural Organization of the United Nations (FAO), Via delle Terme di Caracalla, 00100 Rome, Italy (Telephone Number in U.S. (202) 653-2400); *Animal Health Yearbook.*

COSTA RICA - AREA AND DENSITY OF POPULATION

Euromonitor Publications Limited, 87-88 Turnmill Street, London, EC1M 5QU, England; *International Marketing Data and Statistics.*

Facts on File, 460 Park Avenue South, New York, New York 10016 (800) 443-8323; *The New Book of World Rankings.*

Federal Statistical Office, Gustav - Stresemann - Ring 11, D-6200 Wiesbaden, Germany; *Costa Rica*.

Food and Agricultural Organization of the United Nations (FAO) Via delle Terme di Caracalla, 00100 Rome, Italy (Telephone Number in U.S. (202) 653-2400); *The State of Food and Agriculture*.

G.K. Hall and Company, 70 Lincoln Street, Boston, Massachusetts 02111 (617) 423-3990; *The World in Figures*.

Inter-American Development Bank, 1300 New York Avenue, NW, Washington, D.C. 20577 (202) 623-1753; *Economic and Social Progress in Latin America*.

Statistical Office of the United Nations, Publishing Service, New York, New York 10017 (800) 253-9646; *Statistical Yearbook*.

Times Books, 201 East 50th Street, New York, New York 10022 (212) 751-2600; *The Economist Book of Vital World Statistics*.

United Nations Educational, Scientific and Cultural Organization (UNESCO), 7 Place de Fontenoy, F-75700 Paris, France (Telephone Number in U.S. (212) 963-5981); *Statistical Yearbook*.

COSTA RICA - ARMS EXPORTS AND IMPORTS

U.S. Arms Control and Disarmament Agency, 320 Twenty-first Street, NW, Washington, D.C. 20451 (202) 647-8677; *World Military Expenditures and Arms Transfers*.

COSTA RICA - BALANCE OF PAYMENTS

The Economist Intelligence Unit, 111 West 57th Street, New York, New York 10019 (800) 938-4685; *The New Latin America Market Atlas*, and *The World Market Atlas*.

Federal Statistical Office, Gustav - Stresemann - Ring 11, D-6200 Wiesbaden, Germany; *Costa Rica*.

G.K. Hall and Company, 70 Lincoln Street, Boston, Massachusetts 02111 (617) 423-3990; *The World in Figures*.

Inter-American Development Bank, 1300 New York Avenue, NW, Washington, D.C. 20577 (202) 623-1753; *Economic and Social Progress in Latin America*.

International Monetary Fund, 700 Nineteenth Street, NW, Washington, D.C. 20431 (202) 623-7000; *Balance of Payments Yearbook*.

Organization of American States (OAS), General Secretariat, Washington, D.C. 20006 (202) 458-3533; *Statistical Bulletin of the OAS*.

Statistical Office of the United Nations, Publishing Service, New York, New York 10017 (800) 253-9646; *Economic Survey of Latin America and the Caribbean*, and *Statistical Yearbook for Latin America and the Caribbean*.

U.C.L.A. Latin American Center Publications, University of California, Los Angeles, California 90024 (310) 825-6634; *Statistical Abstract of Latin America*.

The World Bank, 1818 H Street, NW, Washington, D.C. 20433 (202) 477-1234; *World Tables*.

COSTA RICA - BANANA EXPORTS - See COSTA RICA - CROPS

COSTA RICA - BANKING

Facts on File, 460 Park Avenue South, New York, New York 10016 (800) 443-8323; *The New Book of World Rankings*.

G.K. Hall and Company, 70 Lincoln Street, Boston, Massachusetts 02111 (617) 423-3990; *The World in Figures*.

Inter-American Development Bank, 1300 New York Avenue, NW, Washington, D.C. 20577 (202) 623-1753; *Economic and Social Progress in Latin America*.

International Monetary Fund, 700 Nineteenth Street, NW, Washington, D.C. 20431 (202) 623-7000; *Government Finance Statistics Yearbook*, and *International Financial Statistics*.

Statistical Office of the United Nations, Publishing Service, New York, New York 10017 (800) 253-9646; *Statistical Yearbook*, and *Statistical Yearbook for Latin America and the Caribbean*.

COSTA RICA - BARLEY PRODUCTION - See COSTA RICA - CROPS

COSTA RICA - BEEF EXPORTS

International Monetary Fund, 700 Nineteenth Street, NW, Washington, D.C. 20431 (202) 623-7000; *International Financial Statistics*.

COSTA RICA - BEER PRODUCTION

Facts on File, 460 Park Avenue South, New York, New York 10016 (800) 443-8323; *The New Book of World Rankings*.

Statistical Office of the United Nations, Publishing Service, New York, New York 10017 (800) 253-9646; *Statistical Yearbook*.

COSTA RICA - BIRTH RATES

Facts on File, 460 Park Avenue South, New York, New York 10016 (800) 443-8323; *The New Book of World Rankings*.

Statistical Office of the United Nations, Publishing Service, New York, New York 10017 (800) 253-9646; *Demographic Yearbook*, and *Statistical Yearbook*.

Times Books, 201 East 50th Street, New York, New York 10022 (212) 751-2600; *The Economist Book of Vital World Statistics*.

The World Bank, 1818 H Street, NW, Washington, D.C. 20433 (202) 477-1234; *World Tables*.

World Health Organization, Office of Publications, Avenue Appia, CH-1211 Geneva 27, Switzerland (Telephone Number in U.S. (518) 436-9686); *World Health Statistics Annual*.

COSTA RICA - BONDS

G.K. Hall and Company, 70 Lincoln Street, Boston, Massachusetts 02111 (617) 423-3990; *The World in Figures*.

Inter-American Development Bank, 1300 New York Avenue, NW, Washington, D.C. 20577 (202) 623-1753; *Economic and Social Progress in Latin America*.

International Monetary Fund, 700 Nineteenth Street, NW, Washington, D.C. 20431 (202) 623-7000; *Government Finance Statistics Yearbook*.

COSTA RICA - BOOK PRODUCTION

G.K. Hall and Company, 70 Lincoln Street, Boston, Massachusetts 02111 (617) 423-3990; *The World in Figures*.

United Nations Educational, Scientific and Cultural Organization (UNESCO), 7 Place de Fontenoy, F-75700 Paris, France (Telephone Number in U.S. (212) 963-5981); *Statistical Yearbook*.

COSTA RICA - BROADCASTING

Billboard Limited, P.O. Box 9027, 1006 AA Amsterdam, The Netherlands (Telephone Number in U.S. (212) 764-7300); *World Radio TV Handbook*.

Facts on File, 460 Park Avenue South, New York, New York 10016 (800) 443-8323; *The New Book of World Rankings*.

G.K. Hall and Company, 70 Lincoln Street, Boston, Massachusetts 02111 (617) 423-3990; *The World in Figures*.

Times Books, 201 East 50th Street, New York, New York 10022 (212) 751-2600; *The Economist Book of Vital World Statistics*.

COSTA RICA - BUILDING CONSTRUCTION - See COSTA RICA - CONSTRUCTION INDUSTRY

COSTA RICA - BUSINESS

G.K. Hall and Company, 70 Lincoln Street, Boston, Massachusetts 02111 (617) 423-3990; *The World in Figures*.

Inter-American Development Bank, 1300 New York Avenue, NW, Washington, D.C. 20577 (202) 623-1753; *Economic and Social Progress in Latin America*.

COSTA RICA - BUTTER PRODUCTION - See COSTA RICA - DAIRY PRODUCTS

COSTA RICA - CABBAGE PRODUCTION - See COSTA RICA - CROPS

COSTA RICA - CALORIE SUPPLY

Food and Agricultural Organization of the United Nations (FAO) Via delle Terme di Caracalla, 00100 Rome, Italy (Telephone Number in U.S. (202) 653-2400); *The State of Food and Agriculture*.

Statistical Office of the United Nations, Publishing Service, New York, New York 10017 (800) 253-9646; *Statistical Yearbook for Latin America and the Caribbean*.

COSTA RICA - CAPITAL INVESTMENT

Inter-American Development Bank, 1300 New York Avenue, NW, Washington, D.C. 20577 (202) 623-1753; *Economic and Social Progress in Latin America*.

COSTA RICA - CAPITAL REVENUE

Inter-American Development Bank, 1300 New York Avenue, NW, Washington, D.C. 20577 (202) 623-1753; *Economic and Social Progress in Latin America*.

International Monetary Fund, 700 Nineteenth Street, NW, Washington, D.C. 20431 (202) 623-7000; *Government Finance Statistics Yearbook*.

COSTA RICA - CATTLE - See COSTA RICA - LIVESTOCK AND POULTRY

COSTA RICA - CEMENT PRODUCTION - See COSTA RICA - MINING AND MINERAL PRODUCTS

COSTA RICA - CHEESE PRODUCTION - See COSTA RICA - DAIRY PRODUCTS

COSTA RICA - CHEMICAL (ORGANIC) PRODUCTION - See COSTA RICA - MINING AND MINERAL PRODUCTS

COSTA RICA - CHICKENS - See COSTA RICA - LIVESTOCK AND POULTRY

COSTA RICA - CIGARETTE PRODUCTION - See COSTA RICA - TOBACCO PRODUCTION

COSTA RICA - CLASS STRUCTURE

G.K. Hall and Company, 70 Lincoln Street, Boston, Massachusetts 02111 (617) 423-3990; *The World in Figures*.

COSTA RICA - CLIMATE

Facts on File, 460 Park Avenue South, New York, New York 10016 (800) 443-8323; *The New Book of World Rankings*.

G.K. Hall and Company, 70 Lincoln Street, Boston, Massachusetts 02111 (617) 423-3990; *The World in Figures*.

COSTA RICA - CLOTHING EXPORTS AND IMPORTS

Statistical Office of the United Nations, Publishing Service, New York, New York 10017 (800) 253-9646; *Trade in Manufactures of Developing Countries*.

COSTA RICA - COAL PRODUCTION - See COSTA RICA - MINING AND MINERAL PRODUCTS

COSTA RICA - COCOA (BEANS) PRODUCTION - See COSTA RICA - CROPS

COSTA RICA - COFFEE - See COSTA RICA - CROPS

COSTA RICA - COMMUNICATIONS

Federal Statistical Office, Gustav - Stresemann - Ring 11, D-6200 Wiesbaden, Germany; *Costa Rica*.

G.K. Hall and Company, 70 Lincoln Street, Boston, Massachusetts 02111 (617) 423-3990; *The World in Figures*.

Inter-American Development Bank, 1300 New York Avenue, NW, Washington, D.C. 20577 (202) 623-1753; *Economic and Social Progress in Latin America*.

U.C.L.A. Latin American Center Publications, University of California, Los Angeles, California 90024 (310) 825-6634; *Statistical Abstract of Latin America*.

COSTA RICA - CONSTRUCTION INDUSTRY

The Economist Intelligence Unit, 111 West 57th Street, New York, New York 10019 (800) 938-4685; *The New Latin America Market Atlas*.

Facts on File, 460 Park Avenue South, New York, New York 10016 (800) 443-8323; *The New Book of World Rankings*.

Inter-American Development Bank, 1300 New York Avenue, NW, Washington, D.C. 20577 (202) 623-1753; *Economic and Social*

Progress in Latin America.

Statistical Office of the United Nations, Publishing Service, New York, New York 10017 (800) 253-9646; *Construction Statistics Yearbook.*

U.C.L.A. Latin American Center Publications, University of California, Los Angeles, California 90024 (310) 825-6634; *Statistical Abstract of Latin America.*

COSTA RICA - CONSUMER PRICE INDEX

Federal Statistical Office, Gustav - Stresemann - Ring 11, D-6200 Wiesbaden, Germany; *Costa Rica.*

G.K. Hall and Company, 70 Lincoln Street, Boston, Massachusetts 02111 (617) 423-3990; *The World in Figures.*

Statistical Office of the United Nations, Publishing Service, New York, New York 10017 (800) 253-9646; *Statistical Yearbook.*

COSTA RICA - CONSUMER PRICES

The Economist Intelligence Unit, 111 West 57th Street, New York, New York 10019 (800) 938-4685; *The New Latin America Market Atlas.*

Federal Statistical Office, Gustav - Stresemann - Ring 11, D-6200 Wiesbaden, Germany; *Costa Rica.*

International Labour Office, I.L.O. Publications, CH-1211, Geneva 22, Switzerland; *Yearbook of Labour Statistics.*

Organization of American States (OAS), General Secretariat, Washington, D.C. 20006 (202) 458-3533; *Statistical Bulletin of the OAS.*

Times Books, 201 East 50th Street, New York, New York 10022 (212) 751-2600; *The Economist Book of Vital World Statistics.*

U.C.L.A. Latin American Center Publications, University of California, Los Angeles, California 90024 (310) 825-6634; *Statistical Abstract of Latin America.*

COSTA RICA - CONSUMPTION

The Economist Intelligence Unit, 111 West 57th Street, New York, New York 10019 (800) 938-4685; *The New Latin America Market Atlas.*

G.K. Hall and Company, 70 Lincoln Street, Boston, Massachusetts 02111 (617) 423-3990; *The World in Figures.*

Inter-American Development Bank, 1300 New York Avenue, NW, Washington, D.C. 20577 (202) 623-1753; *Economic and Social Progress in Latin America.*

Statistical Office of the United Nations, Publishing Service, New York, New York 10017 (800) 253-9646; *Statistical Yearbook for Latin America and the Caribbean.*

COSTA RICA - COOPERATIVES

U.C.L.A. Latin American Center Publications, University of California, Los Angeles, California 90024 (310) 825-6634; *Statistical Abstract of Latin America.*

COSTA RICA - COPPER PRODUCTION - See COSTA RICA - MINING AND MINERAL PRODUCTS

COSTA RICA - CORN PRODUCTION - See COSTA RICA - CROPS

COSTA RICA - CORPORATE TAXES - See COSTA RICA - TAXATION

COSTA RICA - COTTON - See COSTA RICA - CROPS

COSTA RICA - CRIME

International Criminal Police Organization (INTERPOL), 26 rue Armengaud, 92210 Saint Cloud, France; *International Crime Statistics.*

COSTA RICA - CROPS

Commodity Research Bureau, Incorporated, 75 Wall Street, New York, New York 10005 (212) 504-7754; *Commodity Year Book.*

The Economist Intelligence Unit, 111 West 57th Street, New York, New York 10019 (800) 938-4685; *The New Latin America Market Atlas.*

Facts on File, 460 Park Avenue South, New York, New York 10016 (800) 443-8323; *The New Book of World Rankings.*

Food and Agricultural Organization of the United Nations (FAO) Via delle Terme di Caracalla, 00100 Rome, Italy (Telephone Number in U.S. (202) 653-2400); *Production Yearbook,* and *The State of Food and Agriculture.*

G.K. Hall and Company, 70 Lincoln Street, Boston, Massachusetts 02111 (617) 423-3990; *The World in Figures.*

International Monetary Fund, 700 Nineteenth Street, NW, Washington, D.C. 20431 (202) 623-7000; *International Financial Statistics.*

Organization of American States (OAS), General Secretariat, Washington, D.C. 20006 (202) 458-3533; *Statistical Bulletin of the OAS.*

Statistical Office of the United Nations, Publishing Service, New York, New York 10017 (800) 253-9646; *Statistical Yearbook.*

COSTA RICA - CUSTOMS DUTIES

G.K. Hall and Company, 70 Lincoln Street, Boston, Massachusetts 02111 (617) 423-3990; *The World in Figures.*

Inter-American Development Bank, 1300 New York Avenue, NW, Washington, D.C. 20577 (202) 623-1753; *Economic and Social Progress in Latin America.*

International Monetary Fund, 700 Nineteenth Street, NW, Washington, D.C. 20431 (202) 623-7000; *Government Finance Statistics Yearbook.*

COSTA RICA - DAIRY PRODUCTS

Facts on File, 460 Park Avenue South, New York, New York 10016 (800) 443-8323; *The New Book of World Rankings.*

Food and Agricultural Organization of the United Nations (FAO) Via delle Terme di Caracalla, 00100 Rome, Italy (Telephone Number in U.S. (202) 653-2400); *The State of Food and Agriculture.*

Statistical Office of the United Nations, Publishing Service, New York, New York 10017 (800) 253-9646; *Statistical Yearbook.*

COSTA RICA - DEATH RATES

G.K. Hall and Company, 70 Lincoln Street, Boston, Massachusetts 02111 (617) 423-3990; *The World in Figures.*

Statistical Office of the United Nations, Publishing Service, New York, New York 10017 (800) 253-9646; *Statistical Yearbook,* and *Statistical Yearbook for Latin America and the Caribbean.*

Times Books, 201 East 50th Street, New York, New York 10022 (212) 751-2600; *The Economist Book of Vital World Statistics.*

World Health Organization, Office of Publications, Avenue Appia, CH-1211 Geneva 27, Switzerland (Telephone Number in U.S. (518) 436-9686); *World Health Statistics Annual.*

COSTA RICA - DEBT

The Economist Intelligence Unit, 111 West 57th Street, New York, New York 10019 (800) 938-4685; *The New Latin America Market Atlas.*

COSTA RICA - DEFENSE EXPENDITURES

The Economist Intelligence Unit, 111 West 57th Street, New York, New York 10019 (800) 938-4685; *The New Latin America Market Atlas.*

G.K. Hall and Company, 70 Lincoln Street, Boston, Massachusetts 02111 (617) 423-3990; *The World in Figures.*

International Monetary Fund, 700 Nineteenth Street, NW, Washington, D.C. 20431 (202) 623-7000; *Government Finance Statistics Yearbook.*

U.S. Arms Control and Disarmament Agency, 320 Twenty-first Street, NW, Washington, D.C. 20451 (202) 647-8677; *World Military Expenditures and Arms Transfers.*

COSTA RICA - DEMOGRAPHY

The Economist Intelligence Unit, 111 West 57th Street, New York, New York 10019 (800) 938-4685; *The World Market Atlas.*

Facts on File, 460 Park Avenue South, New York, New York 10016 (800) 443-8323; *The New Book of World Rankings.*

Federal Statistical Office, Gustav - Stresemann - Ring 11, D-6200 Wiesbaden, Germany; *Costa Rica.*

G.K. Hall and Company, 70 Lincoln Street, Boston, Massachusetts 02111 (617) 423-3990; *The World in Figures.*

COSTA RICA - DEVELOPMENT ASSISTANCE

G.K. Hall and Company, 70 Lincoln Street, Boston, Massachusetts 02111 (617) 423-3990; *The World in Figures.*

Inter-American Development Bank, 1300 New York Avenue, NW, Washington, D.C. 20577 (202) 623-1753; *Economic and Social Progress in Latin America.*

Statistical Office of the United Nations, Publishing Service, New York, New York 10017 (800) 253-9646; *Statistical Yearbook.*

COSTA RICA - DIAMOND PRODUCTION - See COSTA RICA - MINING AND MINERAL PRODUCTS

COSTA RICA - DISCOUNT RATES

Inter-American Development Bank, 1300 New York Avenue, NW, Washington, D.C. 20577 (202) 623-1753; *Economic and Social Progress in Latin America.*

Statistical Office of the United Nations, Publishing Service, New York, New York 10017 (800) 253-9646; *Statistical Yearbook.*

COSTA RICA - DISEASE

G.K. Hall and Company, 70 Lincoln Street, Boston, Massachusetts 02111 (617) 423-3990; *The World in Figures.*

World Health Organization, Office of Publications, Avenue Appia, CH-1211 Geneva 27, Switzerland (Telephone Number in U.S. (518) 436-9686); *World Health Statistics Annual.*

COSTA RICA - DIVORCE RATES

Facts on File, 460 Park Avenue South, New York, New York 10016 (800) 443-8323; *The New Book of World Rankings.*

Statistical Office of the United Nations, Publishing Service, New York, New York 10017 (800) 253-9646; *Demographic Yearbook,* and *Statistical Yearbook.*

COSTA RICA - DOMESTIC PRODUCT

G.K. Hall and Company, 70 Lincoln Street, Boston, Massachusetts 02111 (617) 423-3990; *The World in Figures.*

COSTA RICA - ECONOMY

Euromonitor Publications Limited, 87-88 Turnmill Street, London, EC1M 5QU, England; *International Marketing Data and Statistics.*

Facts on File, 460 Park Avenue South, New York, New York 10016 (800) 443-8323; *The New Book of World Rankings.*

Federal Statistical Office, Gustav - Stresemann - Ring 11, D-6200 Wiesbaden, Germany; *Costa Rica.*

G.K. Hall and Company, 70 Lincoln Street, Boston, Massachusetts 02111 (617) 423-3990; *The World in Figures.*

Inter-American Development Bank, 1300 New York Avenue, NW, Washington, D.C. 20577 (202) 623-1753; *Economic and Social Progress in Latin America.*

Organization of American States (OAS), General Secretariat, Washington, D.C. 20006 (202) 458-3533; *Statistical Bulletin of the OAS.*

Statistical Office of the United Nations, Publishing Service, New York, New York 10017 (800) 253-9646; *Economic Survey of Latin America and the Caribbean.*

U.C.L.A. Latin American Center Publications, University of California, Los Angeles, California 90024 (310) 825-6634; *Statistical Abstract of Latin America.*

COSTA RICA - EDUCATION

The Economist Intelligence Unit, 111 West 57th Street, New York, New York 10019 (800) 938-4685; *The New Latin America Market Atlas,* and *The World Market Atlas.*

Facts on File, 460 Park Avenue South, New York, New York 10016 (800) 443-8323; *The New Book of World Rankings.*

Federal Statistical Office, Gustav - Stresemann - Ring 11, D-6200 Wiesbaden, Germany; *Costa Rica.*

Gale Research Incorporated, 835 Penobscot Building, Detroit, Michigan 48226 (800) 877-4253; *International Historical Statistics The Americas and Australasia.*

G.K. Hall and Company, 70 Lincoln Street, Boston, Massachusetts 02111 (617) 423-3990; *The World in Figures.*

International Monetary Fund, 700 Nineteenth Street, NW, Washington, D.C. 20431 (202) 623-7000; *Government Finance Statistics Yearbook.*

Statistical Office of the United Nations, Publishing Service, New York, New York 10017 (800) 253-9646; *Statistical Yearbook for Latin America and the Caribbean.*

Times Books, 201 East 50th Street, New York, New York 10022 (212) 751-2600; *The Economist Book of Vital World Statistics.*

U.C.L.A. Latin American Center Publications, University of California, Los Angeles, California 90024 (310) 825-6634; *Statistical Abstract of Latin America.*

United Nations Educational, Scientific and Cultural Organization (UNESCO), 7 Place de Fontenoy, F-75700 Paris, France (Telephone Number in U.S. (212) 963-5981); *Statistical Yearbook.*

The World Bank, 1818 H Street, NW, Washington, D.C. 20433 (202) 477-1234; *World Tables.*

COSTA RICA - EGG PRODUCTION - See COSTA RICA - DAIRY PRODUCTS

COSTA RICA - ELECTRICITY

The Economist Intelligence Unit, 111 West 57th Street, New York, New York 10019 (800) 938-4685; *The New Latin America Market Atlas.*

Facts on File, 460 Park Avenue South, New York, New York 10016 (800) 443-8323; *The New Book of World Rankings.*

Inter-American Development Bank, 1300 New York Avenue, NW, Washington, D.C. 20577 (202) 623-1753; *Economic and Social Progress in Latin America.*

Organization of American States (OAS), General Secretariat, Washington, D.C. 20006 (202) 458-3533; *Statistical Bulletin of the OAS.*

Statistical Office of the United Nations, Publishing Service, New York, New York 10017 (800) 253-9646; *Statistical Yearbook.*

Times Books, 201 East 50th Street, New York, New York 10022 (212) 751-2600; *The Economist Book of Vital World Statistics.*

COSTA RICA - EMPLOYMENT

Euromonitor Publications Limited, 87-88 Turnmill Street, London, EC1M 5QU, England; *International Marketing Data and Statistics.*

Facts on File, 460 Park Avenue South, New York, New York 10016 (800) 443-8323; *The New Book of World Rankings.*

Federal Statistical Office, Gustav - Stresemann - Ring 11, D-6200 Wiesbaden, Germany; *Costa Rica.*

International Labour Office, I.L.O. Publications, CH-1211, Geneva 22, Switzerland; *Yearbook of Labour Statistics.*

Organization of American States (OAS), General Secretariat, Washington, D.C. 20006 (202) 458-3533; *Statistical Bulletin of the OAS.*

Statistical Office of the United Nations, Publishing Service, New York, New York 10017 (800) 253-9646; *Statistical Yearbook for Latin America and the Caribbean.*

U.C.L.A. Latin American Center Publications, University of California, Los Angeles, California 90024 (310) 825-6634; *Statistical Abstract of Latin America.*

COSTA RICA - ENERGY

The Economist Intelligence Unit, 111 West 57th Street, New York, New York 10019 (800) 938-4685; *The New Latin America Market Atlas.*

Facts on File, 460 Park Avenue South, New York, New York 10016 (800) 443-8323; *The New Book of World Rankings.*

Food and Agricultural Organization of the United Nations (FAO) Via delle Terme di Caracalla, 00100 Rome, Italy (Telephone Number in U.S. (202) 653-2400); *The State of Food and Agriculture.*

G.K. Hall and Company, 70 Lincoln Street, Boston, Massachusetts 02111 (617) 423-3990; *The World in Figures.*

Statistical Office of the United Nations, Publishing Service, New York, New York 10017 (800) 253-9646; *Energy Statistics Yearbook, Statistical Yearbook,* and *Statistical Yearbook for Latin America and the Caribbean.*

Times Books, 201 East 50th Street, New York, New York 10022 (212) 751-2600; *The Economist Book of Vital World Statistics.*

U.C.L.A. Latin American Center Publications, University of California, Los Angeles, California 90024 (310) 825-6634; *Statistical Abstract of Latin America.*

COSTA RICA - EXCHANGE RATES

Euromonitor Publications Limited, 87-88 Turnmill Street, London, EC1M 5QU, England; *International Marketing Data and Statistics.*

Inter-American Development Bank, 1300 New York Avenue, NW, Washington, D.C. 20577 (202) 623-1753; *Economic and Social Progress in Latin America.*

International Civil Aviation Organization, 1000 Sherbrooke Street West, Suite 400, Montreal, Quebec, Canada H3A 2R2 (514) 285-8219; *Civil Aviation Statistics of the World.*

International Monetary Fund, 700 Nineteenth Street, NW, Washington, D.C. 20431 (202) 623-7000; *International Financial Statistics.*

Organization of American States (OAS), General Secretariat, Washington, D.C. 20006 (202) 458-3533; *Statistical Bulletin of the OAS.*

Statistical Office of the United Nations, Publishing Service, New York, New York 10017 (800) 253-9646; *Statistical Yearbook.*

U.C.L.A. Latin American Center Publications, University of California, Los Angeles, California 90024 (310) 825-6634; *Statistical Abstract of Latin America.*

COSTA RICA - EXCISE TAXES - See COSTA RICA - TAXATION

COSTA RICA - EXPORTS

The Economist Intelligence Unit, 111 West 57th Street, New York, New York 10019 (800) 938-4685; *The New Latin America Market Atlas,* and *The World Market Atlas.*

Euromonitor Publications Limited, 87-88 Turnmill Street, London, EC1M 5QU, England; *International Marketing Data and Statistics.*

Food and Agricultural Organization of the United Nations (FAO) Via delle Terme di Caracalla, 00100 Rome, Italy (Telephone Number in U.S. (202) 653-2400); *The State of Food and Agriculture.*

G.K. Hall and Company, 70 Lincoln Street, Boston, Massachusetts 02111 (617) 423-3990; *The World in Figures.*

Inter-American Development Bank, 1300 New York Avenue, NW, Washington, D.C. 20577 (202) 623-1753; *Economic and Social Progress in Latin America.*

International Monetary Fund, 700 Nineteenth Street, NW, Washington, D.C. 20431 (202) 623-7000; *Direction of Trade Statistics, Government Finance Statistics Yearbook,* and *International Financial Statistics.*

Organization of American States (OAS), General Secretariat, Washington, D.C. 20006 (202) 458-3533; *Statistical Bulletin of the OAS.*

Statistical Office of the United Nations, Publishing Service, New York, New York 10017 (800) 253-9646; *Statistical Yearbook for Latin America and the Caribbean.*

Times Books, 201 East 50th Street, New York, New York 10022 (212) 751-2600; *The Economist Book of Vital World Statistics.*

The World Bank, 1818 H Street, NW, Washington, D.C. 20433 (202) 477-1234; *World Tables.*

COSTA RICA - EXTERNAL FINANCING

Inter-American Development Bank, 1300 New York Avenue, NW, Washington, D.C. 20577 (202) 623-1753; *Economic and Social Progress in Latin America.*

Statistical Office of the United Nations, Publishing Service, New York, New York 10017 (800) 253-9646; *Statistical Yearbook for Latin America and the Caribbean.*

COSTA RICA - EXTERNAL INDEBTEDNESS

Inter-American Development Bank, 1300 New York Avenue, NW, Washington, D.C. 20577 (202) 623-1753; *Economic and Social Progress in Latin America.*

Statistical Office of the United Nations, Publishing Service, New York, New York 10017 (800) 253-9646; *Statistical Yearbook for Latin America and the Caribbean.*

The World Bank, 1818 H Street, NW, Washington, D.C. 20433 (202) 477-1234; *World Tables.*

COSTA RICA - EXTERNAL TRADE

Food and Agricultural Organization of the United Nations (FAO) Via delle Terme di Caracalla, 00100 Rome, Italy (Telephone Number in U.S. (202) 653-2400); *The State of Food and Agriculture.*

Gale Research Incorporated, 835 Penobscot Building, Detroit, Michigan 48226 (800) 877-4253; *International Historical Statistics The Americas and Australasia.*

G.K. Hall and Company, 70 Lincoln Street, Boston, Massachusetts 02111 (617) 423-3990; *The World in Figures.*

Inter-American Development Bank, 1300 New York Avenue, NW, Washington, D.C. 20577 (202) 623-1753; *Economic and Social Progress in Latin America.*

Statistical Office of the United Nations, Publishing Service, New York, New York 10017 (800) 253-9646; *Statistical Yearbook,* and *Statistical Yearbook for Latin America and the Caribbean.*

COSTA RICA - FAMILY PLANNING

U.C.L.A. Latin American Center Publications, University of California, Los Angeles, California 90024 (310) 825-6634; *Statistical Abstract of Latin America.*

COSTA RICA - FARM CROPS - See COSTA RICA - CROPS

COSTA RICA - FEMALE WORKING POPULATION - See COSTA RICA - EMPLOYMENT

COSTA RICA - FERTILITY RATES

Facts on File, 460 Park Avenue South, New York, New York 10016 (800) 443-8323; *The New Book of World Rankings.*

Times Books, 201 East 50th Street, New York, New York 10022 (212) 751-2600; *The Economist Book of Vital World Statistics.*

The World Bank, 1818 H Street, NW, Washington, D.C. 20433 (202) 477-1234; *World Tables.*

COSTA RICA - FERTILIZER

The Economist Intelligence Unit, 111 West 57th Street, New York, New York 10019 (800) 938-4685; *The New Latin America Market Atlas.*

Food and Agricultural Organization of the United Nations (FAO), Via delle Terme di Caracalla, 00100 Rome, Italy (Telephone Number in U.S. (202) 653-2400); *Fertilizer Yearbook,* and *The State of Food and Agriculture.*

Statistical Office of the United Nations, Publishing Service, New York, New York 10017 (800) 253-9646; *Statistical Yearbook.*

COSTA RICA - FETAL MORTALITY

Statistical Office of the United Nations, Publishing Service, New York, New York 10017 (800) 253-9646; *Demographic Yearbook.*

World Health Organization, Office of Publications, Avenue Appia, CH-1211 Geneva 27, Switzerland (Telephone Number in U.S. (518) 436-9686); *World Health Statistics Annual.*

COSTA RICA - FINANCE

Facts on File, 460 Park Avenue South, New York, New York 10016 (800) 443-8323; *The New Book of World Rankings.*

Federal Statistical Office, Gustav - Stresemann - Ring 11, D-6200 Wiesbaden, Germany; *Costa Rica.*

Gale Research Incorporated, 835 Penobscot Building, Detroit, Michigan 48226 (800) 877-4253; *International Historical Statistics The Americas and Australasia.*

G.K. Hall and Company, 70 Lincoln Street, Boston, Massachusetts 02111 (617) 423-3990; *The World in Figures.*

Inter-American Development Bank, 1300 New York Avenue, NW, Washington, D.C. 20577 (202) 623-1753; *Economic and Social Progress in Latin America.*

International Monetary Fund, 700 Nineteenth Street, NW, Washington, D.C. 20431 (202) 623-7000; *Government Finance Statistics Yearbook,* and *International Financial Statistics.*

Organization of American States (OAS), General Secretariat, Washington, D.C. 20006 (202) 458-3533; *Statistical Bulletin of the OAS.*

U.C.L.A. Latin American Center Publications, University of California, Los Angeles, California 90024 (310) 825-6634; *Statistical Abstract of Latin America.*

COSTA RICA - FISHERIES

Facts on File, 460 Park Avenue South, New York, New York 10016 (800) 443-8323; *The New Book of World Rankings.*

Federal Statistical Office, Gustav - Stresemann - Ring 11, D-6200 Wiesbaden, Germany; *Costa Rica.*

Food and Agricultural Organization of the United Nations (FAO) Via delle Terme di Caracalla, 00100 Rome, Italy (Telephone Number in U.S. (202) 653-2400); *The State of Food and Agriculture,* and *Yearbook of Fishery Statistics.*

Inter-American Development Bank, 1300 New York Avenue, NW, Washington, D.C. 20577 (202) 623-1753; *Economic and Social Progress in Latin America.*

Statistical Office of the United Nations, Publishing Service, New York, New York 10017 (800) 253-9646; *Statistical Yearbook.*

U.C.L.A. Latin American Center Publications, University of California, Los Angeles, California 90024 (310) 825-6634; *Statistical Abstract of Latin America.*

COSTA RICA - FOOD

Food and Agricultural Organization of the United Nations (FAO) Via delle Terme di Caracalla, 00100 Rome, Italy (Telephone Number in U.S. (202) 653-2400); *Production Yearbook,* and *The State of Food and Agriculture.*

G.K. Hall and Company, 70 Lincoln Street, Boston, Massachusetts 02111 (617) 423-3990; *The World in Figures.*

COSTA RICA - FOREIGN AID

G.K. Hall and Company, 70 Lincoln Street, Boston, Massachusetts 02111 (617) 423-3990; *The World in Figures.*

Inter-American Development Bank, 1300 New York Avenue, NW, Washington, D.C. 20577 (202) 623-1753; *Economic and Social Progress in Latin America.*

COSTA RICA - FOREIGN DEBT

The Economist Intelligence Unit, 111 West 57th Street, New York, New York 10019 (800) 938-4685; *The New Latin America Market Atlas.*

Inter-American Development Bank, 1300 New York Avenue, NW, Washington, D.C. 20577 (202) 623-1753; *Economic and Social Progress in Latin America.*

International Monetary Fund, 700 Nineteenth Street, NW, Washington, D.C. 20431 (202) 623-7000; *Government Finance Statistics Yearbook.*

COSTA RICA - FOREIGN INDEBTEDNESS

Inter-American Development Bank, 1300 New York Avenue, NW, Washington, D.C. 20577 (202) 623-1753; *Economic and Social Progress in Latin America.*

Statistical Office of the United Nations, Publishing Service, New York, New York 10017 (800) 253-9646; *Economic Survey of Latin America and the Caribbean.*

COSTA RICA - FOREIGN INVESTMENT

The Economist Intelligence Unit, 111 West 57th Street, New York, New York 10019 (800) 938-4685; *The New Latin America Market Atlas.*

COSTA RICA - FOREIGN TRADE

The Economist Intelligence Unit, 111 West 57th Street, New York, New York 10019 (800) 938-4685; *The New Latin America Market Atlas.*

Euromonitor Publications Limited, 87-88 Turnmill Street, London EC1M 5QU, England; *International Marketing Data and Statistics.*

Facts on File, 460 Park Avenue South, New York, New York 10016 (800) 443-8323; *The New Book of World Rankings.*

Federal Statistical Office, Gustav - Stresemann - Ring 11, D-6200 Wiesbaden, Germany; *Costa Rica.*

Food and Agricultural Organization of the United Nations (FAO) Via delle Terme di Caracalla, 00100 Rome, Italy (Telephone Number in U.S. (202) 653-2400); *The State of Food and Agriculture.*

G.K. Hall and Company, 70 Lincoln Street, Boston, Massachusetts 02111 (617) 423-3990; *The World in Figures.*

Inter-American Development Bank, 1300 New York Avenue, NW, Washington, D.C. 20577 (202) 623-1753; *Economic and Social Progress in Latin America.*

International Monetary Fund, 700 Nineteenth Street, NW, Washington, D.C. 20431 (202) 623-7000; *International Financial Statistics.*

Organisation for Economic Co-operation and Development (OECD), 2 rue Andre-Pascal, 75 Paris 16, France (Telephone Number in U.S. (202) 785-6323); *Trade by Commodities.*

Statistical Office of the United Nations, Publishing Service, New York, New York 10017 (800) 253-9646; *Economic Survey of Latin America and the Caribbean*, *International Trade Statistics Yearbook*, and *Statistical Yearbook*.

U.C.L.A. Latin American Center Publications, University of California, Los Angeles, California 90024 (310) 825-6634; *Statistical Abstract of Latin America*.

The World Bank, 1818 H Street, NW, Washington, D.C. 20433 (202) 477-1234; *World Tables*.

COSTA RICA - FORESTRY AND FOREST PRODUCTS

The Economist Intelligence Unit, 111 West 57th Street, New York, New York 10019 (800) 938-4685; *The New Latin America Market Atlas*.

Facts on File, 460 Park Avenue South, New York, New York 10016 (800) 443-8323; *The New Book of World Rankings*.

Federal Statistical Office, Gustav - Stresemann - Ring 11, D-6200 Wiesbaden, Germany; *Costa Rica*.

Food and Agricultural Organization of the United Nations (FAO) Via delle Terme di Caracalla, 00100 Rome, Italy (Telephone Number in U.S. (202) 653-2400); *The State of Food and Agriculture*, and *Yearbook of Forest Products*.

G.K. Hall and Company, 70 Lincoln Street, Boston, Massachusetts 02111 (617) 423-3990; *The World in Figures*.

Inter-American Development Bank, 1300 New York Avenue, NW, Washington, D.C. 20577 (202) 623-1753; *Economic and Social Progress in Latin America*.

Statistical Office of the United Nations, Publishing Service, New York, New York 10017 (800) 253-9646; *Statistical Yearbook*.

U.C.L.A. Latin American Center Publications, University of California, Los Angeles, California 90024 (310) 825-6634; *Statistical Abstract of Latin America*.

United Nations Educational, Scientific and Cultural Organization (UNESCO), 7 Place de Fontenoy, F-75700 Paris, France (Telephone Number in U.S. (212) 963-5981); *Statistical Yearbook*.

COSTA RICA - GAS PRODUCTION - See COSTA RICA - MINING AND MINERAL PRODUCTS

COSTA RICA - GENERAL INDUSTRIAL STATISTICS

Federal Statistical Office, Gustav - Stresemann - Ring 11, D-6200 Wiesbaden, Germany; *Costa Rica*.

COSTA RICA - GENERAL MORTALITY

Statistical Office of the United Nations, Publishing Service, New York, New York 10017 (800) 253-9646; *Demographic Yearbook*.

World Health Organization, Office of Publications, Avenue Appia, CH-1211 Geneva 27, Switzerland (Telephone Number in U.S. (518) 436-9686); *World Health Statistics Annual*.

COSTA RICA - GEOGRAPHIC DATA

Facts on File, 460 Park Avenue South, New York, New York 10016 (800) 443-8323; *The New Book of World Rankings*.

Federal Statistical Office, Gustav - Stresemann - Ring 11, D-6200 Wiesbaden, Germany; *Costa Rica*.

U.C.L.A. Latin American Center Publications, University of California, Los Angeles, California 90024 (310) 825-6634; *Statistical Abstract of Latin America*.

COSTA RICA - GOATS - See COSTA RICA - LIVESTOCK AND POULTRY

COSTA RICA - GOLD HOLDINGS

International Monetary Fund, 700 Nineteenth Street, NW, Washington, D.C. 20431 (202) 623-7000; *International Financial Statistics*.

Statistical Office of the United Nations, Publishing Service, New York, New York 10017 (800) 253-9646; *Statistical Yearbook*.

The World Bank, 1818 H Street, NW, Washington, D.C. 20433 (202) 477-1234; *World Tables*.

COSTA RICA - GOLD PRODUCTION AND CONSUMPTION - See COSTA RICA - MINING AND MINERAL PRODUCTS

COSTA RICA - GOLD RESERVES

The Economist Intelligence Unit, 111 West 57th Street, New York, New York 10019 (800) 938-4685; *The New Latin America Market Atlas*.

COSTA RICA - GOVERNMENT

G.K. Hall and Company, 70 Lincoln Street, Boston, Massachusetts 02111 (617) 423-3990; *The World in Figures*.

Inter-American Development Bank, 1300 New York Avenue, NW, Washington, D.C. 20577 (202) 623-1753; *Economic and Social Progress in Latin America*.

COSTA RICA - GOVERNMENT BONDS - See COSTA RICA - BONDS

COSTA RICA - GOVERNMENT CONSUMPTION

Inter-American Development Bank, 1300 New York Avenue, NW, Washington, D.C. 20577 (202) 623-1753; *Economic and Social Progress in Latin America*.

COSTA RICA - GOVERNMENT EXPENDITURES

Inter-American Development Bank, 1300 New York Avenue, NW, Washington, D.C. 20577 (202) 623-1753; *Economic and Social Progress in Latin America*.

International Monetary Fund, 700 Nineteenth Street, NW, Washington, D.C. 20431 (202) 623-7000; *Government Finance Statistics Yearbook*.

Times Books, 201 East 50th Street, New York, New York 10022 (212) 751-2600; *The Economist Book of Vital World Statistics*.

The World Bank, 1818 H Street, NW, Washington, D.C. 20433 (202) 477-1234; *World Tables*.

COSTA RICA - GOVERNMENT FINANCES

Inter-American Development Bank, 1300 New York Avenue, NW, Washington, D.C. 20577 (202) 623-1753; *Economic and Social Progress in Latin America*.

International Monetary Fund, 700 Nineteenth Street, NW, Washington, D.C. 20431 (202) 623-7000; *International Financial Statistics.*

Statistical Office of the United Nations, Publishing Service, New York, New York 10017 (800) 253-9646; *Statistical Yearbook.*

COSTA RICA - GOVERNMENT REVENUES

Inter-American Development Bank, 1300 New York Avenue, NW, Washington, D.C. 20577 (202) 623-1753; *Economic and Social Progress in Latin America.*

International Monetary Fund, 700 Nineteenth Street, NW, Washington, D.C. 20431 (202) 623-7000; *Government Finance Statistics Yearbook.*

U.C.L.A. Latin American Center Publications, University of California, Los Angeles, California 90024 (310) 825-6634; *Statistical Abstract of Latin America.*

Times Books, 201 East 50th Street, New York, New York 10022 (212) 751-2600; *The Economist Book of Vital World Statistics.*

The World Bank, 1818 H Street, NW, Washington, D.C. 20433 (202) 477-1234; *World Tables.*

COSTA RICA - GRAIN PRODUCTION - See COSTA RICA - CROPS

COSTA RICA - GRANTS

International Monetary Fund, 700 Nineteenth Street, NW, Washington, D.C. 20431 (202) 623-7000; *Government Finance Statistics Yearbook.*

COSTA RICA - GROSS DOMESTIC PRODUCT

The Economist Intelligence Unit, 111 West 57th Street, New York, New York 10019 (800) 938-4685; *The New Latin America Market Atlas,* and *The World Market Atlas.*

Euromonitor Publications Limited, 87-88 Turnmill Street, London, EC1M 5QU, England; *International Marketing Data and Statistics.*

Facts on File, 460 Park Avenue South, New York, New York 10016 (800) 443-8323; *The New Book of World Rankings.*

G.K. Hall and Company, 70 Lincoln Street, Boston, Massachusetts 02111 (617) 423-3990; *The World in Figures.*

Inter-American Development Bank, 1300 New York Avenue, NW, Washington, D.C. 20577 (202) 623-1753; *Economic and Social Progress in Latin America.*

Organization of American States (OAS), General Secretariat, Washington, D.C. 20006 (202) 458-3533; *Statistical Bulletin of the OAS.*

Statistical Office of the United Nations, Publishing Service, New York, New York 10017 (800) 253-9646; *Statistical Yearbook,* and *Statistical Yearbook for Latin America and the Caribbean.*

Times Books, 201 East 50th Street, New York, New York 10022 (212) 751-2600; *The Economist Book of Vital World Statistics.*

U.C.L.A. Latin American Center Publications, University of California, Los Angeles, California 90024 (310) 825-6634; *Statistical Abstract of Latin America.*

The World Bank, 1818 H Street, NW, Washington, D.C. 20433 (202) 477-1234; *World Tables.*

COSTA RICA - GROSS NATIONAL PRODUCT

Euromonitor Publications Limited, 87-88 Turnmill Street, London, EC1M 5QU, England; *International Marketing Data and Statistics.*

Inter-American Development Bank, 1300 New York Avenue, NW, Washington, D.C. 20577 (202) 623-1753; *Economic and Social Progress in Latin America.*

U.S. Arms Control and Disarmament Agency, 320 Twenty-first Street, NW, Washington, D.C. 20451 (202) 647-8677; *World Military Expenditures and Arms Transfers.*

The World Bank, 1818 H Street, NW, Washington, D.C. 20433 (202) 477-1234; *World Tables.*

COSTA RICA - HEALTH

The Economist Intelligence Unit, 111 West 57th Street, New York, New York 10019 (800) 938-4685; *The New Latin America Market Atlas.*

Facts on File, 460 Park Avenue South, New York, New York 10016 (800) 443-8323; *The New Book of World Rankings.*

Federal Statistical Office, Gustav - Stresemann - Ring 11, D-6200 Wiesbaden, Germany; *Costa Rica.*

G.K. Hall and Company, 70 Lincoln Street, Boston, Massachusetts 02111 (617) 423-3990; *The World in Figures.*

Statistical Office of the United Nations, Publishing Service, New York, New York 10017 (800) 253-9646; *Statistical Yearbook.*

Times Books, 201 East 50th Street, New York, New York 10022 (212) 751-2600; *The Economist Book of Vital World Statistics.*

U.C.L.A. Latin American Center Publications, University of California, Los Angeles, California 90024 (310) 825-6634; *Statistical Abstract of Latin America.*

World Health Organization, Office of Publications, Avenue Appia, CH-1211 Geneva 27, Switzerland (Telephone Number in U.S. (518) 436-9686); *World Health Statistics Annual.*

COSTA RICA - HEALTH EXPENDITURES

International Monetary Fund, 700 Nineteenth Street, NW, Washington, D.C. 20431 (202) 623-7000; *Government Finance Statistics Yearbook.*

Statistical Office of the United Nations, Publishing Service, New York, New York 10017 (800) 253-9646; *Statistical Yearbook for Latin America and the Caribbean.*

COSTA RICA - HIDE PRODUCTION

Food and Agricultural Organization of the United Nations (FAO), Via delle Terme di Caracalla, 00100 Rome, Italy (Telephone Number in U.S. (202) 653-2400); *Production Yearbook.*

COSTA RICA - HIGHWAYS

The Economist Intelligence Unit, 111 West 57th Street, New York, New York 10019 (800) 938-4685; *The New Latin America Market Atlas.*

G.K. Hall and Company, 70 Lincoln Street, Boston, Massachusetts 02111 (617) 423-3990; *The World in Figures*.

International Road Federation, 525 School Street, SW, Washington, D.C. 20024 (202) 554-2106; *World Road Statistics*.

COSTA RICA - HORSES - See COSTA RICA - LIVESTOCK AND POULTRY

COSTA RICA - HOURS OF WORK - See COSTA RICA - EMPLOYMENT

COSTA RICA - HOUSING AND HOUSING UNITS

Facts on File, 460 Park Avenue South, New York, New York 10016 (800) 443-8323; *The New Book of World Rankings*.

Statistical Office of the United Nations, Publishing Service, New York, New York 10017 (800) 253-9646; *Statistical Yearbook for Latin America and the Caribbean*.

U.C.L.A. Latin American Center Publications, University of California, Los Angeles, California 90024 (310) 825-6634; *Statistical Abstract of Latin America*.

COSTA RICA - HOUSING EXPENDITURES

International Monetary Fund, 700 Nineteenth Street, NW, Washington, D.C. 20431 (202) 623-7000; *Government Finance Statistics Yearbook*.

COSTA RICA - ILLITERACY RATES

The Economist Intelligence Unit, 111 West 57th Street, New York, New York 10019 (800) 938-4685; *The New Latin America Market Atlas*.

COSTA RICA - ILLITERATE POPULATION

The Economist Intelligence Unit, 111 West 57th Street, New York, New York 10019 (800) 938-4685; *The World Market Atlas*.

G.K. Hall and Company, 70 Lincoln Street, Boston, Massachusetts 02111 (617) 423-3990; *The World in Figures*.

Statistical Office of the United Nations, Publishing Service, New York, New York 10017 (800) 253-9646; *Statistical Yearbook for Latin America and the Caribbean*.

United Nations Educational, Scientific and Cultural Organization (UNESCO), 7 Place de Fontenoy, F-75700 Paris, France (Telephone Number in U.S. (212) 963-5981); *Statistical Yearbook*.

COSTA RICA - IMMIGRATION

U.C.L.A. Latin American Center Publications, University of California, Los Angeles, California 90024 (310) 825-6634; *Statistical Abstract of Latin America*.

COSTA RICA - IMPORTS

The Economist Intelligence Unit, 111 West 57th Street, New York, New York 10019 (800) 938-4685; *The New Latin America Market Atlas*, and *The World Market Atlas*.

Euromonitor Publications Limited, 87-88 Turnmill Street, London, EC1M 5QU, England; *International Marketing Data and Statistics*.

Food and Agricultural Organization of the United Nations (FAO) Via delle Terme di Caracalla, 00100 Rome, Italy (Telephone Number in U.S. (202) 653-2400); *The State of Food and Agriculture*.

G.K. Hall and Company, 70 Lincoln Street, Boston, Massachusetts 02111 (617) 423-3990; *The World in Figures*.

Inter-American Development Bank, 1300 New York Avenue, NW, Washington, D.C. 20577 (202) 623-1753; *Economic and Social Progress in Latin America*.

International Monetary Fund, 700 Nineteenth Street, NW, Washington, D.C. 20431 (202) 623-7000; *Direction of Trade Statistics*, *Government Finance Statistics Yearbook*, and *International Financial Statistics*.

Organization of American States (OAS), General Secretariat, Washington, D.C. 20006 (202) 458-3533; *Statistical Bulletin of the OAS*.

Statistical Office of the United Nations, Publishing Service, New York, New York 10017 (800) 253-9646; *Statistical Yearbook for Latin America and the Caribbean*, and *Trade in Manufactures of Developing Countries*.

Times Books, 201 East 50th Street, New York, New York 10022 (212) 751-2600; *The Economist Book of Vital World Statistics*.

The World Bank, 1818 H Street, NW, Washington, D.C. 20433 (202) 477-1234; *World Tables*.

COSTA RICA - INCOME DISTRIBUTION

Statistical Office of the United Nations, Publishing Service, New York, New York 10017 (800) 253-9646; *Statistical Yearbook for Latin America and the Caribbean*.

U.C.L.A. Latin American Center Publications, University of California, Los Angeles, California 90024 (310) 825-6634; *Statistical Abstract of Latin America*.

COSTA RICA - INCOME TAXES - See COSTA RICA - TAXATION

COSTA RICA - INDUSTRY

Euromonitor Publications Limited, 87-88 Turnmill Street, London, EC1M 5QU, England; *International Marketing Data and Statistics*.

Facts on File, 460 Park Avenue South, New York, New York 10016 (800) 443-8323; *The New Book of World Rankings*.

Federal Statistical Office, Gustav - Stresemann - Ring 11, D-6200 Wiesbaden, Germany; *Costa Rica*.

Gale Research Incorporated, 835 Penobscot Building, Detroit, Michigan 48226 (800) 877-4253; *International Historical Statistics The Americas and Australasia*.

G.K. Hall and Company, 70 Lincoln Street, Boston, Massachusetts 02111 (617) 423-3990; *The World in Figures*.

International Labour Office, I.L.O. Publications, CH-1211, Geneva 22, Switzerland; *Yearbook of Labour Statistics*.

Statistical Office of the United Nations, Publishing Service, New York, New York 10017 (800) 253-9646; *Economic Survey of Latin America and the Caribbean*, and *Statistical Yearbook*.

Times Books, 201 East 50th Street, New York, New York 10022 (212) 751-2600; *The Economist Book of Vital World Statistics*.

U.C.L.A. Latin American Center Publications, University of California, Los Angeles, California 90024 (310) 825-6634; *Statistical Abstract of Latin America.*

The World Bank, 1818 H Street, NW, Washington, D.C. 20433 (202) 477-1234; *World Tables.*

COSTA RICA - INFANT AND MATERNAL MORTALITY

The Economist Intelligence Unit, 111 West 57th Street, New York, New York 10019 (800) 938-4685; *The New Latin America Market Atlas.*

Statistical Office of the United Nations, Publishing Service, New York, New York 10017 (800) 253-9646; *Demographic Yearbook,* and *Statistical Yearbook.*

Times Books, 201 East 50th Street, New York, New York 10022 (212) 751-2600; *The Economist Book of Vital World Statistics.*

The World Bank, 1818 H Street, NW, Washington, D.C. 20433 (202) 477-1234; *World Tables.*

World Health Organization, Office of Publications, Avenue Appia, CH-1211 Geneva 27, Switzerland (Telephone Number in U.S. (518) 436-9686); *World Health Statistics Annual.*

COSTA RICA - INFLATIONARY FACTORS

Statistical Office of the United Nations, Publishing Service, New York, New York 10017 (800) 253-9646; *Economic Survey of Latin America and the Caribbean.*

COSTA RICA - INTEREST RATES

Inter-American Development Bank, 1300 New York Avenue, NW, Washington, D.C. 20577 (202) 623-1753; *Economic and Social Progress in Latin America.*

Organization of American States (OAS), General Secretariat, Washington, D.C. 20006 (202) 458-3533; *Statistical Bulletin of the OAS.*

COSTA RICA - INTERNAL STATISTICS

U.C.L.A. Latin American Center Publications, University of California, Los Angeles, California 90024 (310) 825-6634; *Statistical Abstract of Latin America.*

COSTA RICA - INTERNATIONAL FINANCE

Inter-American Development Bank, 1300 New York Avenue, NW, Washington, D.C. 20577 (202) 623-1753; *Economic and Social Progress in Latin America.*

U.C.L.A. Latin American Center Publications, University of California, Los Angeles, California 90024 (310) 825-6634; *Statistical Abstract of Latin America.*

COSTA RICA - INTERNATIONAL LIQUIDITY

Inter-American Development Bank, 1300 New York Avenue, NW, Washington, D.C. 20577 (202) 623-1753; *Economic and Social Progress in Latin America.*

International Monetary Fund, 700 Nineteenth Street, NW, Washington, D.C. 20431 (202) 623-7000; *International Financial Statistics.*

COSTA RICA - INTERNATIONAL RESERVES

Organization of American States (OAS), General Secretariat, Washington, D.C. 20006 (202) 458-3533; *Statistical Bulletin of the OAS.*

COSTA RICA - INTERNATIONAL RESERVES EXCLUDING GOLD

Inter-American Development Bank, 1300 New York Avenue, NW, Washington, D.C. 20577 (202) 623-1753; *Economic and Social Progress in Latin America.*

The World Bank, 1818 H Street, NW, Washington, D.C. 20433 (202) 477-1234; *World Tables.*

COSTA RICA - INTERNATIONAL STATISTICS

Inter-American Development Bank, 1300 New York Avenue, NW, Washington, D.C. 20577 (202) 623-1753; *Economic and Social Progress in Latin America.*

U.C.L.A. Latin American Center Publications, University of California, Los Angeles, California 90024 (310) 825-6634; *Statistical Abstract of Latin America.*

COSTA RICA - INVESTMENT

Inter-American Development Bank, 1300 New York Avenue, NW, Washington, D.C. 20577 (202) 623-1753; *Economic and Social Progress in Latin America.*

Statistical Office of the United Nations, Publishing Service, New York, New York 10017 (800) 253-9646; *Statistical Yearbook for Latin America and the Caribbean.*

COSTA RICA - IRON ORE PRODUCTION AND CONSUMPTION - See COSTA RICA - MINING AND MINERAL PRODUCTS

COSTA RICA - IRRIGATION

Euromonitor Publications Limited, 87-88 Turnmill Street, London, EC1M 5QU, England; *International Marketing Data and Statistics.*

Inter-American Development Bank, 1300 New York Avenue, NW, Washington, D.C. 20577 (202) 623-1753; *Economic and Social Progress in Latin America.*

COSTA RICA - LABOR FORCE

The Economist Intelligence Unit, 111 West 57th Street, New York, New York 10019 (800) 938-4685; *The New Latin America Market Atlas.*

Euromonitor Publications Limited, 87-88 Turnmill Street, London, EC1M 5QU, England; *International Marketing Data and Statistics.*

Facts on File, 460 Park Avenue South, New York, New York 10016 (800) 443-8323; *The New Book of World Rankings.*

Food and Agricultural Organization of the United Nations (FAO) Via delle Terme di Caracalla, 00100 Rome, Italy (Telephone Number in U.S. (202) 653-2400); *The State of Food and Agriculture.*

Gale Research Incorporated, 835 Penobscot Building, Detroit, Michigan 48226 (800) 877-4253; *International Historical Statistics The Americas and Australasia.*

G.K. Hall and Company, 70 Lincoln Street, Boston, Massachusetts 02111 (617) 423-3990; *The World in Figures.*

Times Books, 201 East 50th Street, New York, New York 10022 (212) 751-2600; *The Economist Book of Vital World Statistics.*

The World Bank, 1818 H Street, NW, Washington, D.C. 20433 (202) 477-1234; *World Tables.*

COSTA RICA - LABOR PRODUCTIVITY

International Labour Office, I.L.O. Publications, CH-1211, Geneva 22, Switzerland; *Yearbook of Labour Statistics.*

COSTA RICA - LAND AREA

The Economist Intelligence Unit, 111 West 57th Street, New York, New York 10019 (800) 938-4685; *The New Latin America Market Atlas.*

COSTA RICA - LAND USE

Euromonitor Publications Limited, 87-88 Turnmill Street, London, EC1M 5QU, England; *International Marketing Data and Statistics.*

Food and Agricultural Organization of the United Nations (FAO), Via delle Terme di Caracalla, 00100 Rome, Italy (Telephone Number in U.S. (202) 653-2400); *Production Yearbook.*

G.K. Hall and Company, 70 Lincoln Street, Boston, Massachusetts 02111 (617) 423-3990; *The World in Figures.*

Inter-American Development Bank, 1300 New York Avenue, NW, Washington, D.C. 20577 (202) 623-1753; *Economic and Social Progress in Latin America.*

COSTA RICA - LIBRARIES

Facts on File, 460 Park Avenue South, New York, New York 10016 (800) 443-8323; *The New Book of World Rankings.*

United Nations Educational, Scientific and Cultural Organization (UNESCO), 7 Place de Fontenoy, F-75700 Paris, France (Telephone Number in U.S. (212) 963-5981); *Statistical Yearbook.*

COSTA RICA - LIFE EXPECTANCY RATE

The Economist Intelligence Unit, 111 West 57th Street, New York, New York 10019 (800) 938-4685; *The New Latin America Market Atlas.*

COSTA RICA - LIVESTOCK AND POULTRY

Euromonitor Publications Limited, 87-88 Turnmill Street, London, EC1M 5QU, England; *International Marketing Data and Statistics.*

Facts on File, 460 Park Avenue South, New York, New York 10016 (800) 443-8323; *The New Book of World Rankings.*

Food and Agricultural Organization of the United Nations (FAO), Via delle Terme di Caracalla, 00100 Rome, Italy (Telephone Number in U.S. (202) 653-2400); *Production Yearbook,* and *The State of Food and Agriculture.*

G.K. Hall and Company, 70 Lincoln Street, Boston, Massachusetts 02111 (617) 423-3990; *The World in Figures.*

Statistical Office of the United Nations, Publishing Service, New York, New York 10017 (800) 253-9646; *Statistical Yearbook.*

COSTA RICA - LIVING LEVELS

G.K. Hall and Company, 70 Lincoln Street, Boston, Massachusetts 02111 (617) 423-3990; *The World in Figures.*

Statistical Office of the United Nations, Publishing Service, New York, New York 10017 (800) 253-9646; *Statistical Yearbook for Latin America and the Caribbean.*

Times Books, 201 East 50th Street, New York, New York 10022 (212) 751-2600; *The Economist Book of Vital World Statistics.*

COSTA RICA - MAIN ECONOMIC INDICATORS - See COSTA RICA - ECONOMY

COSTA RICA - MAIN INDICATORS - See COSTA RICA - ECONOMY

COSTA RICA - MANUFACTURING

The Economist Intelligence Unit, 111 West 57th Street, New York, New York 10019 (800) 938-4685; *The New Latin America Market Atlas.*

Facts on File, 460 Park Avenue South, New York, New York 10016 (800) 443-8323; *The New Book of World Rankings.*

G.K. Hall and Company, 70 Lincoln Street, Boston, Massachusetts 02111 (617) 423-3990; *The World in Figures.*

Inter-American Development Bank, 1300 New York Avenue, NW, Washington, D.C. 20577 (202) 623-1753; *Economic and Social Progress in Latin America.*

Statistical Office of the United Nations, Publishing Service, New York, New York 10017 (800) 253-9646; *Statistical Yearbook,* and *Statistical Yearbook for Latin America and the Caribbean.*

Times Books, 201 East 50th Street, New York, New York 10022 (212) 751-2600; *The Economist Book of Vital World Statistics.*

The World Bank, 1818 H Street, NW, Washington, D.C. 20433 (202) 477-1234; *World Tables.*

COSTA RICA - MARRIAGE RATES

Facts on File, 460 Park Avenue South, New York, New York 10016 (800) 443-8323; *The New Book of World Rankings.*

Statistical Office of the United Nations, Publishing Service, New York, New York 10017 (800) 253-9646; *Demographic Yearbook,* and *Statistical Yearbook.*

COSTA RICA - MEAT EXPORTS

Organization of American States (OAS), General Secretariat, Washington, D.C. 20006 (202) 458-3533; *Statistical Bulletin of the OAS.*

COSTA RICA - MEAT PRODUCTION - See COSTA RICA - LIVESTOCK AND POULTRY

COSTA RICA - MEDICAL PERSONNEL

U.C.L.A. Latin American Center Publications, University of California, Los Angeles, California 90024 (310) 825-6634; *Statistical Abstract of Latin America.*

COSTA RICA - MERCHANT SHIPPING

G.K. Hall and Company, 70 Lincoln Street, Boston, Massachusetts 02111 (617) 423-3990; *The World in Figures.*

Statistical Office of the United Nations, Publishing Service, New York, New York 10017 (800) 253-9646; *Statistical Yearbook.*

Times Books, 201 East 50th Street, New York, New York 10022 (212) 751-2600; *The Economist Book of Vital World Statistics.*

COSTA RICA - MILITARY

The Economist Intelligence Unit, 111 West 57th Street, New York, New York 10019 (800) 938-4685; *The New Latin America Market Atlas.*

G.K. Hall and Company, 70 Lincoln Street, Boston, Massachusetts 02111 (617) 423-3990; *The World in Figures.*

The International Institute for Strategic Studies, 23 Tavistock Street, London WC2E 7NQ, England; *The Military Balance.*

U.C.L.A. Latin American Center Publications, University of California, Los Angeles, California 90024 (310) 825-6634; *Statistical Abstract of Latin America.*

U.S. Arms Control and Disarmament Agency, 320 Twenty-first Street, NW, Washington, D.C. 20451 (202) 647-8677; *World Military Expenditures and Arms Transfers.*

COSTA RICA - MILK - See COSTA RICA - DAIRY PRODUCTS

COSTA RICA - MINING AND MINERAL PRODUCTS

The Economist Intelligence Unit, 111 West 57th Street, New York, New York 10019 (800) 938-4685; *The New Latin America Market Atlas.*

G.K. Hall and Company, 70 Lincoln Street, Boston, Massachusetts 02111 (617) 423-3990; *The World in Figures.*

Inter-American Development Bank, 1300 New York Avenue, NW, Washington, D.C. 20577 (202) 623-1753; *Economic and Social Progress in Latin America.*

Statistical Office of the United Nations, Publishing Service, New York, New York 10017 (800) 253-9646; *Statistical Yearbook for Latin America and the Caribbean.*

U.C.L.A. Latin American Center Publications, University of California, Los Angeles, California 90024 (310) 825-6634; *Statistical Abstract of Latin America.*

COSTA RICA - MONEY EXCHANGE RATES

Euromonitor Publications Limited, 87-88 Turnmill Street, London, EC1M 5QU, England; *International Marketing Data and Statistics.*

Inter-American Development Bank, 1300 New York Avenue, NW, Washington, D.C. 20577 (202) 623-1753; *Economic and Social Progress in Latin America.*

International Monetary Fund, 700 Nineteenth Street, NW, Washington, D.C. 20431 (202) 623-7000; *International Financial Statistics.*

Statistical Office of the United Nations, Publishing Service, New York, New York 10017 (800) 253-9646; *Statistical Yearbook.*

COSTA RICA - MONEY RATES - MARKET

Inter-American Development Bank, 1300 New York Avenue, NW, Washington, D.C. 20577 (202) 623-1753; *Economic and Social Progress in Latin America.*

COSTA RICA - MONEY RESERVES

Euromonitor Publications Limited, 87-88 Turnmill Street, London, EC1M 5QU, England; *International Marketing Data and Statistics.*

Inter-American Development Bank, 1300 New York Avenue, NW, Washington, D.C. 20577 (202) 623-1753; *Economic and Social Progress in Latin America.*

COSTA RICA - MONEY SUPPLY

Euromonitor Publications Limited, 87-88 Turnmill Street, London, EC1M 5QU, England; *International Marketing Data and Statistics.*

Federal Statistical Office, Gustav - Stresemann - Ring 11, D-6200 Wiesbaden, Germany; *Costa Rica.*

G.K. Hall and Company, 70 Lincoln Street, Boston, Massachusetts 02111 (617) 423-3990; *The World in Figures.*

Inter-American Development Bank, 1300 New York Avenue, NW, Washington, D.C. 20577 (202) 623-1753; *Economic and Social Progress in Latin America.*

International Monetary Fund, 700 Nineteenth Street, NW, Washington, D.C. 20431 (202) 623-7000; *International Financial Statistics.*

Statistical Office of the United Nations, Publishing Service, New York, New York 10017 (800) 253-9646; *Statistical Yearbook.*

U.C.L.A. Latin American Center Publications, University of California, Los Angeles, California 90024 (310) 825-6634; *Statistical Abstract of Latin America.*

The World Bank, 1818 H Street, NW, Washington, D.C. 20433 (202) 477-1234; *World Tables.*

COSTA RICA - MOTOR VEHICLE TAXES - See COSTA RICA - TAXATION

COSTA RICA - MOTOR VEHICLES IN USE

The Economist Intelligence Unit, 111 West 57th Street, New York, New York 10019 (800) 938-4685; *The New Latin America Market Atlas.*

G.K. Hall and Company, 70 Lincoln Street, Boston, Massachusetts 02111 (617) 423-3990; *The World in Figures.*

Statistical Office of the United Nations, Publishing Service, New York, New York 10017 (800) 253-9646; *Statistical Yearbook.*

Times Books, 201 East 50th Street, New York, New York 10022 (212) 751-2600; *The Economist Book of Vital World Statistics.*

COSTA RICA - MULES - See COSTA RICA - LIVESTOCK AND POULTRY

COSTA RICA - MUSEUMS

Facts on File, 460 Park Avenue South, New York, New York 10016 (800) 443-8323; *The New Book of World Rankings.*

United Nations Educational, Scientific and Cultural Organization (UNESCO), 7 Place de Fontenoy, F-75700 Paris, France (Telephone Number in U.S. (212) 963-5981); *Statistical Yearbook*.

COSTA RICA - NATALITY - See COSTA RICA - BIRTH RATES

COSTA RICA - NATIONAL ACCOUNTS

Federal Statistical Office, Gustav - Stresemann - Ring 11, D-6200 Wiesbaden, Germany; *Costa Rica*.

Gale Research Incorporated, 835 Penobscot Building, Detroit, Michigan 48226 (800) 877-4253; *International Historical Statistics The Americas and Australasia*.

Inter-American Development Bank, 1300 New York Avenue, NW, Washington, D.C. 20577 (202) 623-1753; *Economic and Social Progress in Latin America*.

Organization of American States (OAS), General Secretariat, Washington, D.C. 20006 (202) 458-3533; *Statistical Bulletin of the OAS*.

Statistical Office of the United Nations, Publishing Service, New York, New York 10017 (800) 253-9646; *National Accounts Statistics*, and *Statistical Yearbook*.

U.C.L.A. Latin American Center Publications, University of California, Los Angeles, California 90024 (310) 825-6634; *Statistical Abstract of Latin America*.

COSTA RICA - NATIONAL INCOME

Facts on File, 460 Park Avenue South, New York, New York 10016 (800) 443-8323; *The New Book of World Rankings*.

G.K. Hall and Company, 70 Lincoln Street, Boston, Massachusetts 02111 (617) 423-3990; *The World in Figures*.

Inter-American Development Bank, 1300 New York Avenue, NW, Washington, D.C. 20577 (202) 623-1753; *Economic and Social Progress in Latin America*.

Statistical Office of the United Nations, Publishing Service, New York, New York 10017 (800) 253-9646; *Statistical Yearbook*, and *Statistical Yearbook for Latin America and the Caribbean*.

COSTA RICA - NATIONAL PRODUCT

Facts on File, 460 Park Avenue South, New York, New York 10016 (800) 443-8323; *The New Book of World Rankings*.

Statistical Office of the United Nations, Publishing Service, New York, New York 10017 (800) 253-9646; *Statistical Yearbook*.

COSTA RICA - NATURAL GAS - PRODUCTION - See COSTA RICA - MINING AND MINERAL PRODUCTS

COSTA RICA - NEWSPAPER PRODUCTION - See COSTA RICA - FORESTRY AND FOREST PRODUCTS

COSTA RICA - NEWSPRINT - See COSTA RICA - FORESTRY AND FOREST PRODUCTS

COSTA RICA - NUTRITION

Statistical Office of the United Nations, Publishing Service, New York, New York 10017 (800) 253-9646; *Statistical Yearbook for Latin America and the Caribbean*.

COSTA RICA - OCCUPATIONS - See COSTA RICA - LABOR FORCE

COSTA RICA - PALM OIL AND PALM KERNELS PRODUCTION - See COSTA RICA - CROPS

COSTA RICA - PAPER - See COSTA RICA - FORESTRY AND FOREST PRODUCTS

COSTA RICA - PATENTS

Statistical Office of the United Nations, Publishing Service, New York, New York 10017 (800) 253-9646; *Statistical Yearbook*.

COSTA RICA - PEANUT PRODUCTION - See COSTA RICA - CROPS

COSTA RICA - PESTICIDE USE

Food and Agricultural Organization of the United Nations (FAO) Via delle Terme di Caracalla, 00100 Rome, Italy (Telephone Number in U.S. (202) 653-2400); *The State of Food and Agriculture*.

COSTA RICA - PETROLEUM INDUSTRY

The Economist Intelligence Unit, 111 West 57th Street, New York, New York 10019 (800) 938-4685; *The New Latin America Market Atlas*.

Facts on File, 460 Park Avenue South, New York, New York 10016 (800) 443-8323; *The New Book of World Rankings*.

Food and Agricultural Organization of the United Nations (FAO) Via delle Terme di Caracalla, 00100 Rome, Italy (Telephone Number in U.S. (202) 653-2400); *The State of Food and Agriculture*.

G.K. Hall and Company, 70 Lincoln Street, Boston, Massachusetts 02111 (617) 423-3990; *The World in Figures*.

Inter-American Development Bank, 1300 New York Avenue, NW, Washington, D.C. 20577 (202) 623-1753; *Economic and Social Progress in Latin America*.

Statistical Office of the United Nations, Publishing Service, New York, New York 10017 (800) 253-9646; *Statistical Yearbook*.

COSTA RICA - PIGS - See COSTA RICA - LIVESTOCK AND POULTRY

COSTA RICA - POLITICAL DATA

U.C.L.A. Latin American Center Publications, University of California, Los Angeles, California 90024 (310) 825-6634; *Statistical Abstract of Latin America*.

COSTA RICA - POPULATION

The Economist Intelligence Unit, 111 West 57th Street, New York, New York 10019 (800) 938-4685; *The New Latin America Market Atlas*, and *The World Market Atlas*.

Euromonitor Publications Limited, 87-88 Turnmill Street, London EC1M 5QU, England; *International Marketing Data and Statistics*.

Facts on File, 460 Park Avenue South, New York, New York 10016 (800) 443-8323; *The New Book of World Rankings*.

Federal Statistical Office, Gustav - Stresemann - Ring 11, D-6200 Wiesbaden, Germany; *Costa Rica*.

Food and Agricultural Organization of the United Nations (FAO), Via delle Terme di Caracalla, 00100 Rome, Italy (Telephone Number in

U.S. (202) 653-2400); *Production Yearbook.*

Gale Research Incorporated, 835 Penobscot Building, Detroit, Michigan 48226 (800) 877-4253; *International Historical Statistics The Americas and Australasia.*

G.K. Hall and Company, 70 Lincoln Street, Boston, Massachusetts 02111 (617) 423-3990; *The World in Figures.*

Inter-American Development Bank, 1300 New York Avenue, NW, Washington, D.C. 20577 (202) 623-1753; *Economic and Social Progress in Latin America.*

International Labour Office, I.L.O. Publications, CH-1211, Geneva 22, Switzerland; *Yearbook of Labour Statistics.*

Organization of American States (OAS), General Secretariat, Washington, D.C. 20006 (202) 458-3533; *Statistical Bulletin of the OAS.*

Statistical Office of the United Nations, Publishing Service, New York, New York 10017 (800) 253-9646; *Demographic Yearbook, Statistical Yearbook,* and *Statistical Yearbook for Latin America and the Caribbean.*

Times Books, 201 East 50th Street, New York, New York 10022 (212) 751-2600; *The Economist Book of Vital World Statistics.*

U.C.L.A. Latin American Center Publications, University of California, Los Angeles, California 90024 (310) 825-6634; *Statistical Abstract of Latin America.*

U.S. Arms Control and Disarmament Agency, 320 Twenty-first Street, NW, Washington, D.C. 20451 (202) 647-8677; *World Military Expenditures and Arms Transfers.*

World Health Organization, Office of Publications, Avenue Appia, CH-1211 Geneva 27, Switzerland (Telephone Number in U.S. (518) 436-9686); *World Health Statistics Annual.*

COSTA RICA - POST OFFICES

Facts on File, 460 Park Avenue South, New York, New York 10016 (800) 443-8323; *The New Book of World Rankings.*

COSTA RICA - POTATO PRODUCTION - See COSTA RICA - CROPS

COSTA RICA - PRICES

Facts on File, 460 Park Avenue South, New York, New York 10016 (800) 443-8323; *The New Book of World Rankings.*

Federal Statistical Office, Gustav - Stresemann - Ring 11, D-6200 Wiesbaden, Germany; *Costa Rica.*

Food and Agricultural Organization of the United Nations (FAO), Via delle Terme di Caracalla, 00100 Rome, Italy (Telephone Number in U.S. (202) 653-2400); *Production Yearbook,* and *The State of Food and Agriculture.*

Gale Research Incorporated, 835 Penobscot Building, Detroit, Michigan 48226 (800) 877-4253; *International Historical Statistics The Americas and Australasia.*

G.K. Hall and Company, 70 Lincoln Street, Boston, Massachusetts 02111 (617) 423-3990; *The World in Figures.*

International Labour Office, I.L.O. Publications, CH-1211, Geneva 22, Switzerland; *Yearbook of Labour Statistics.*

International Monetary Fund, 700 Nineteenth Street, NW, Washington, D.C. 20431 (202) 623-7000; *International Financial Statistics.*

Statistical Office of the United Nations, Publishing Service, New York, New York 10017 (800) 253-9646; *Economic Survey of Latin America and the Caribbean,* and *Statistical Yearbook for Latin America and the Caribbean.*

COSTA RICA - PRINTING AND WRITING PAPER - See COSTA RICA - FORESTRY AND FOREST PRODUCTS

COSTA RICA - PRODUCTION

Facts on File, 460 Park Avenue South, New York, New York 10016 (800) 443-8323; *The New Book of World Rankings.*

G.K. Hall and Company, 70 Lincoln Street, Boston, Massachusetts 02111 (617) 423-3990; *The World in Figures.*

COSTA RICA - PRODUCTIVITY

Euromonitor Publications Limited, 87-88 Turnmill Street, London EC1M 5QU, England; *International Marketing Data and Statistics.*

COSTA RICA - PROPERTY TAXES - See COSTA RICA - TAXATION

COSTA RICA - PUBLIC CONSUMPTION FUNDS

Inter-American Development Bank, 1300 New York Avenue, NW, Washington, D.C. 20577 (202) 623-1753; *Economic and Social Progress in Latin America.*

COSTA RICA - PUBLIC DEBT

Statistical Office of the United Nations, Publishing Service, New York, New York 10017 (800) 253-9646; *Statistical Yearbook.*

COSTA RICA - PUBLIC EXPENDITURES

Inter-American Development Bank, 1300 New York Avenue, NW, Washington, D.C. 20577 (202) 623-1753; *Economic and Social Progress in Latin America.*

Organization of American States (OAS), General Secretariat, Washington, D.C. 20006 (202) 458-3533; *Statistical Bulletin of the OAS.*

Statistical Office of the United Nations, Publishing Service, New York, New York 10017 (800) 253-9646; *Statistical Yearbook for Latin America and the Caribbean.*

COSTA RICA - PUBLIC FINANCE

Facts on File, 460 Park Avenue South, New York, New York 10016 (800) 443-8323; *The New Book of World Rankings.*

Federal Statistical Office, Gustav - Stresemann - Ring 11, D-6200 Wiesbaden, Germany; *Costa Rica.*

Inter-American Development Bank, 1300 New York Avenue, NW, Washington, D.C. 20577 (202) 623-1753; *Economic and Social Progress in Latin America.*

Organization of American States (OAS), General Secretariat, Washington, D.C. 20006 (202) 458-3533; *Statistical Bulletin of the OAS.*

COSTA RICA - PUBLIC REVENUE

Inter-American Development Bank, 1300 New York Avenue, NW, Washington, D.C. 20577 (202) 623-1753; *Economic and Social Progress in Latin America.*

Organization of American States (OAS), General Secretariat, Washington, D.C. 20006 (202) 458-3533; *Statistical Bulletin of the OAS.*

COSTA RICA - RADIO BROADCASTING - See COSTA RICA - BROADCASTING

COSTA RICA - RAILWAYS

The Economist Intelligence Unit, 111 West 57th Street, New York, New York 10019 (800) 938-4685; *The New Latin America Market Atlas.*

G.K. Hall and Company, 70 Lincoln Street, Boston, Massachusetts 02111 (617) 423-3990; *The World in Figures.*

Jane's Information Group, Sentinel House, 163 Brighton Road, Coulsdon, Surrey CR5 2NH, England (Telephone Number in U.S. (703) 683-3700); *Jane's World Railways.*

Statistical Office of the United Nations, Publishing Service, New York, New York 10017 (800) 253-9646; *Statistical Yearbook.*

COSTA RICA - RANCHING

U.C.L.A. Latin American Center Publications, University of California, Los Angeles, California 90024 (310) 825-6634; *Statistical Abstract of Latin America.*

COSTA RICA - RELIGION

Facts on File, 460 Park Avenue South, New York, New York 10016 (800) 443-8323; *The New Book of World Rankings.*

U.C.L.A. Latin American Center Publications, University of California, Los Angeles, California 90024 (310) 825-6634; *Statistical Abstract of Latin America.*

COSTA RICA - RENT PRICES

International Labour Office, I.L.O. Publications, CH-1211, Geneva 22, Switzerland; *Yearbook of Labour Statistics.*

COSTA RICA - RESERVES EXCLUDING GOLD

The Economist Intelligence Unit, 111 West 57th Street, New York, New York 10019 (800) 938-4685; *The New Latin America Market Atlas.*

COSTA RICA - RETAIL TRADE

The Economist Intelligence Unit, 111 West 57th Street, New York, New York 10019 (800) 938-4685; *The New Latin America Market Atlas.*

Facts on File, 460 Park Avenue South, New York, New York 10016 (800) 443-8323; *The New Book of World Rankings.*

G.K. Hall and Company, 70 Lincoln Street, Boston, Massachusetts 02111 (617) 423-3990; *The World in Figures.*

Inter-American Development Bank, 1300 New York Avenue, NW, Washington, D.C. 20577 (202) 623-1753; *Economic and Social Progress in Latin America.*

COSTA RICA - RICE PRODUCTION

Statistical Office of the United Nations, Publishing Service, New York, New York 10017 (800) 253-9646; *Statistical Yearbook.*

COSTA RICA - ROOT AND TUBER PRODUCTION - See COSTA RICA - CROPS

COSTA RICA - ROUNDWOOD PRODUCTION - See COSTA RICA - FORESTRY AND FOREST PRODUCTS

COSTA RICA - RUBBER PRODUCTION

Facts on File, 460 Park Avenue South, New York, New York 10016 (800) 443-8323; *The New Book of World Rankings.*

COSTA RICA - SALT PRODUCTION - See COSTA RICA - MINING AND MINERAL PRODUCTS

COSTA RICA - SAWNWOOD PRODUCTION - See COSTA RICA - FORESTRY AND FOREST PRODUCTS

COSTA RICA - SCIENCE AND TECHNOLOGY

U.C.L.A. Latin American Center Publications, University of California, Los Angeles, California 90024 (310) 825-6634; *Statistical Abstract of Latin America.*

COSTA RICA - SENIOR CITIZENS

Facts on File, 460 Park Avenue South, New York, New York 10016 (800) 443-8323; *The New Book of World Rankings.*

COSTA RICA - SHEEP - See COSTA RICA - LIVESTOCK AND POULTRY

COSTA RICA - SILVER PRODUCTION AND CONSUMPTION - See COSTA RICA - MINING AND MINERAL PRODUCTS

COSTA RICA - SOCIAL DATA

Facts on File, 460 Park Avenue South, New York, New York 10016 (800) 443-8323; *The New Book of World Rankings.*

G.K. Hall and Company, 70 Lincoln Street, Boston, Massachusetts 02111 (617) 423-3990; *The World in Figures.*

U.C.L.A. Latin American Center Publications, University of California, Los Angeles, California 90024 (310) 825-6634; *Statistical Abstract of Latin America.*

COSTA RICA - SOCIAL SECURITY

Inter-American Development Bank, 1300 New York Avenue, NW, Washington, D.C. 20577 (202) 623-1753; *Economic and Social Progress in Latin America.*

International Monetary Fund, 700 Nineteenth Street, NW, Washington, D.C. 20431 (202) 623-7000; *Government Finance Statistics Yearbook.*

COSTA RICA - SOCIOECONOMIC DATA

Inter-American Development Bank, 1300 New York Avenue, NW, Washington, D.C. 20577 (202) 623-1753; *Economic and Social Progress in Latin America.*

U.C.L.A. Latin American Center Publications, University of California, Los Angeles, California 90024 (310) 825-6634; *Statistical Abstract of Latin America.*

Inter-American Development Bank, 1300 New York Avenue, NW, Washington, D.C. 20577 (202) 623-1753; *Economic and Social Progress in Latin America.*

COSTA RICA - SOYBEAN PRODUCTION - See COSTA RICA - CROPS

COSTA RICA - STEEL - See COSTA RICA - MINING AND MINERAL PRODUCTS

COSTA RICA - STOCKS - COMMODITY - MARKET PRICE - INDEX

Food and Agricultural Organization of the United Nations (FAO) Via delle Terme di Caracalla, 00100 Rome, Italy (Telephone Number in U.S. (202) 653-2400); *The State of Food and Agriculture.*

COSTA RICA - SUGAR - See COSTA RICA - CROPS

COSTA RICA - TAXATION

Inter-American Development Bank, 1300 New York Avenue, NW, Washington, D.C. 20577 (202) 623-1753; *Economic and Social Progress in Latin America.*

International Monetary Fund, 700 Nineteenth Street, NW, Washington, D.C. 20431 (202) 623-7000; *Government Finance Statistics Yearbook.*

International Road Federation, 525 School Street, SW, Washington, D.C. 20024 (202) 554-2106; *World Road Statistics.*

Statistical Office of the United Nations, Publishing Service, New York, New York 10017 (800) 253-9646; *Statistical Yearbook for Latin America and the Caribbean.*

The World Bank, 1818 H Street, NW, Washington, D.C. 20433 (202) 477-1234; *World Tables.*

COSTA RICA - TELEGRAPH SERVICE

Statistical Office of the United Nations, Publishing Service, New York, New York 10017 (800) 253-9646; *Statistical Yearbook.*

COSTA RICA - TELEPHONES IN USE

American Telephone and Telegraph Company, 26 Parsippany Road, Whippany, New Jersey 07981 (800) 338-4038; *The World's Telephones.*

The Economist Intelligence Unit, 111 West 57th Street, New York, New York 10019 (800) 938-4685; *The New Latin America Market Atlas.*

G.K. Hall and Company, 70 Lincoln Street, Boston, Massachusetts 02111 (617) 423-3990; *The World in Figures.*

Statistical Office of the United Nations, Publishing Service, New York, New York 10017 (800) 253-9646; *Statistical Yearbook.*

COSTA RICA - TELEVISION BROADCASTING - See COSTA RICA - BROADCASTING

COSTA RICA - TEXTILE INDUSTRY

G.K. Hall and Company, 70 Lincoln Street, Boston, Massachusetts 02111 (617) 423-3990; *The World in Figures.*

COSTA RICA - THEATRE

United Nations Educational, Scientific and Cultural Organization (UNESCO), 7 Place de Fontenoy, F-75700 Paris, France (Telephone Number in U.S. (212) 963-5981; *Statistical Yearbook.*

COSTA RICA - TOBACCO PRODUCTION

Facts on File, 460 Park Avenue South, New York, New York 10016 (800) 443-8323; *The New Book of World Rankings.*

Statistical Office of the United Nations, Publishing Service, New York, New York 10017 (800) 253-9646; *Statistical Yearbook.*

COSTA RICA - TOURISM

The Economist Intelligence Unit, 111 West 57th Street, New York, New York 10019 (800) 938-4685; *The New Latin America Market Atlas.*

Facts on File, 460 Park Avenue South, New York, New York 10016 (800) 443-8323; *The New Book of World Rankings.*

Federal Statistical Office, Gustav - Stresemann - Ring 11, D-6200 Wiesbaden, Germany; *Costa Rica.*

G.K. Hall and Company, 70 Lincoln Street, Boston, Massachusetts 02111 (617) 423-3990; *The World in Figures.*

Organization of American States (OAS), General Secretariat, Washington, D.C. 20006 (202) 458-3533; *Statistical Bulletin of the OAS.*

Statistical Office of the United Nations, Publishing Service, New York, New York 10017 (800) 253-9646; *Statistical Yearbook,* and *Statistical Yearbook for Latin America and the Caribbean.*

Times Books, 201 East 50th Street, New York, New York 10022 (212) 751-2600; *The Economist Book of Vital World Statistics.*

U.C.L.A. Latin American Center Publications, University of California, Los Angeles, California 90024 (310) 825-6634; *Statistical Abstract of Latin America.*

World Tourism Organization, Calle Capitan Haya 42, E-28020 Madrid, Spain; *Yearbook of Tourism Statistics.*

COSTA RICA - TRACTORS IN USE

The Economist Intelligence Unit, 111 West 57th Street, New York, New York 10019 (800) 938-4685; *The New Latin America Market Atlas.*

Statistical Office of the United Nations, Publishing Service, New York, New York 10017 (800) 253-9646; *Statistical Yearbook.*

COSTA RICA - TRADE - See COSTA RICA - FOREIGN TRADE

COSTA RICA - TRADEMARKS AND SERVICE MARKS

Statistical Office of the United Nations, Publishing Service, New York, New York 10017 (800) 253-9646; *Statistical Yearbook.*

COSTA RICA - TRANSPORTATION AND COMMUNICATIONS

The Economist Intelligence Unit, 111 West 57th Street, New York, New York 10019 (800) 938-4685; *The New Latin America Market Atlas.*

Facts on File, 460 Park Avenue South, New York, New York 10016 (800) 443-8323; *The New Book of World Rankings.*

Federal Statistical Office, Gustav - Stresemann - Ring 11, D-6200 Wiesbaden, Germany; *Costa Rica.*

Gale Research Incorporated, 835 Penobscot Building, Detroit, Michigan 48226 (800) 877-4253; *International Historical Statistics The Americas and Australasia.*

G.K. Hall and Company, 70 Lincoln Street, Boston, Massachusetts 02111 (617) 423-3990; *The World in Figures.*

Inter-American Development Bank, 1300 New York Avenue, NW, Washington, D.C. 20577 (202) 623-1753; *Economic and Social Progress in Latin America.*

Statistical Office of the United Nations, Publishing Service, New York, New York 10017 (800) 253-9646; *Statistical Yearbook for Latin America and the Caribbean.*

U.C.L.A. Latin American Center Publications, University of California, Los Angeles, California 90024 (310) 825-6634; *Statistical Abstract of Latin America.*

COSTA RICA - UNEMPLOYMENT

The Economist Intelligence Unit, 111 West 57th Street, New York, New York 10019 (800) 938-4685; *The New Latin America Market Atlas.*

Euromonitor Publications Limited, 87-88 Turnmill Street, London EC1M 5QU, England; *International Marketing Data and Statistics.*

International Labour Office, I.L.O. Publications, CH-1211, Geneva 22, Switzerland; *Yearbook of Labour Statistics.*

Statistical Office of the United Nations, Publishing Service, New York, New York 10017 (800) 253-9646; *Statistical Yearbook.*

U.C.L.A. Latin American Center Publications, University of California, Los Angeles, California 90024 (310) 825-6634; *Statistical Abstract of Latin America.*

COSTA RICA - UTILITIES

U.C.L.A. Latin American Center Publications, University of California, Los Angeles, California 90024 (310) 825-6634; *Statistical Abstract of Latin America.*

COSTA RICA - VITAL STATISTICS

Euromonitor Publications Limited, 87-88 Turnmill Street, London EC1M 5QU, England; *International Marketing Data and Statistics.*

G.K. Hall and Company, 70 Lincoln Street, Boston, Massachusetts 02111 (617) 423-3990; *The World in Figures.*

Statistical Office of the United Nations, Publishing Service, New York, New York 10017 (800) 253-9646; *Statistical Yearbook.*

World Health Organization, Office of Publications, Avenue Appia, CH-1211 Geneva 27, Switzerland (Telephone Number in U.S. (518) 436-9686); *World Health Statistics Annual.*

COSTA RICA - WAGES

Federal Statistical Office, Gustav - Stresemann - Ring 11, D-6200 Wiesbaden, Germany; *Costa Rica.*

G.K. Hall and Company, 70 Lincoln Street, Boston, Massachusetts 02111 (617) 423-3990; *The World in Figures.*

International Labour Office, I.L.O. Publications, CH-1211, Geneva 22, Switzerland; *Yearbook of Labour Statistics.*

Organization of American States (OAS), General Secretariat, Washington, D.C. 20006 (202) 458-3533; *Statistical Bulletin of the OAS.*

U.C.L.A. Latin American Center Publications, University of California, Los Angeles, California 90024 (310) 825-6634; *Statistical Abstract of Latin America.*

COSTA RICA - WEATHER

Facts on File, 460 Park Avenue South, New York, New York 10016 (800) 443-8323; *The New Book of World Rankings.*

G.K. Hall and Company, 70 Lincoln Street, Boston, Massachusetts 02111 (617) 423-3990; *The World in Figures.*

COSTA RICA - WELFARE

Inter-American Development Bank, 1300 New York Avenue, NW, Washington, D.C. 20577 (202) 623-1753; *Economic and Social Progress in Latin America.*

International Monetary Fund, 700 Nineteenth Street, NW, Washington, D.C. 20431 (202) 623-7000; *Government Finance Statistics Yearbook.*

COSTA RICA - WHEAT PRODUCTION - See COSTA RICA - CROPS

COSTA RICA - WHOLESALE PRICES

Inter-American Development Bank, 1300 New York Avenue, NW, Washington, D.C. 20577 (202) 623-1753; *Economic and Social Progress in Latin America.*

International Monetary Fund, 700 Nineteenth Street, NW, Washington, D.C. 20431 (202) 623-7000; *International Financial Statistics.*

Organization of American States (OAS), General Secretariat, Washington, D.C. 20006 (202) 458-3533; *Statistical Bulletin of the OAS.*

Statistical Office of the United Nations, Publishing Service, New York, New York 10017 (800) 253-9646; *Statistical Yearbook.*

COSTA RICA - WHOLESALE TRADE

Inter-American Development Bank, 1300 New York Avenue, NW, Washington, D.C. 20577 (202) 623-1753; *Economic and Social Progress in Latin America.*

COSTA RICA - WINE PRODUCTION

Facts on File, 460 Park Avenue South, New York, New York 10016 (800) 443-8323; *The New Book of World Rankings.*

COSTA RICA - WOOL PRODUCTION

Facts on File, 460 Park Avenue South, New York, New York 10016 (800) 443-8323; *The New Book of World Rankings*.

COSTUME JEWELRY AND NOTIONS - MANUFACTURING - EARNINGS

U.S. Department of Commerce, Bureau of the Census, Suitland, Maryland 20233 (310) 763-4040; *Census of Manufactures*, and *Annual Survey of Manufactures*.

U.S. Department of Labor, Bureau of Labor Statistics, Two Massachusetts Avenue, NE, Washington, D.C. 20212 (202) 606-7828; *Employment and Earnings*, and Bulletins 2370 and 2429.

COSTUME JEWELRY AND NOTIONS - MANUFACTURING - EMPLOYEES

U.S. Department of Commerce, Bureau of the Census, Suitland, Maryland 20233 (310) 763-4040; *Census of Manufactures*, and *Annual Survey of Manufactures*.

U.S. Department of Labor, Bureau of Labor Statistics, Two Massachusetts Avenue, NE, Washington, D.C. 20212 (202) 606-7828; *Employment and Earnings*, and Bulletins 2370 and 2429.

COSTUME JEWELRY AND NOTIONS - MANUFACTURING - ESTABLISHMENTS

U.S. Department of Commerce, Bureau of the Census, Suitland, Maryland 20233 (310) 763-4040; *Annual Survey of Manufactures*, and *Census of Manufactures*.

COSTUME JEWELRY AND NOTIONS - MANUFACTURING - SHIPMENTS

U.S. Department of Commerce, Bureau of the Census, Suitland, Maryland 20233 (310) 763-4040; *Census of Manufactures*, and *Annual Survey of Manufactures*.

COSTUME JEWELRY AND NOTIONS - MANUFACTURING - VALUE ADDED

U.S. Department of Commerce, Bureau of the Census, Suitland, Maryland 20233 (310) 763-4040; *Census of Manufactures*, and *Annual Survey of Manufacturers*.

Cote d'Ivoire - National Statistical Office

Direction de la Statistique, BP V55, Abidjan, Cote d'Ivoire.

Cote d'Ivoire - Primary Statistics Source

Direction de la Statistique, BP 222, Abidjan, Cote d'Ivoire; *Bulletin mensuel de statistique* (Monthly Bulletin of Statistics).

COTE d'IVOIRE - AGRICULTURE

Euromonitor Publications Limited, 87-88 Turnmill Street, London EC1M 5QU, England; *International Marketing Data and Statistics*.

Facts on File, 460 Park Avenue South, New York, New York 10016 (800) 443-8323; *The New Book of World Rankings*.

Food and Agricultural Organization of the United Nations (FAO), Via delle Terme di Caracalla, 00100 Rome, Italy (Telephone Number in U.S. (202) 653-2400); *Production Yearbook, The State of Food and Agriculture*, and *Trade Yearbook*.

G.K. Hall and Company, 70 Lincoln Street, Boston, Massachusetts 02111 (617) 423-3990; *The World in Figures*.

Statistical Office of the United Nations, Publishing Service, New York, New York 10017 (800) 253-9646; *Statistical Yearbook*, and *Survey of Economic and Social Conditions in Africa*.

Times Books, 201 East 50th Street, New York, New York 10022 (212) 751-2600; *The Economist Book of Vital World Statistics*.

United Nations Economic Commission for Africa, Africa Hall, P.O. Box 3001, Addis Ababa, Ethiopia (Telephone Number in U.S. (800) 253-9646); *African Statistical Yearbook*.

The World Bank, 1818 H Street, NW, Washington, D.C. 20433 (202) 477-1234; *World Tables*.

COTE d'IVOIRE - AIRLINE SERVICE

Facts on File, 460 Park Avenue South, New York, New York 10016 (800) 443-8323; *The New Book of World Rankings*.

G.K. Hall and Company, 70 Lincoln Street, Boston, Massachusetts 02111 (617) 423-3990; *The World in Figures*.

Statistical Office of the United Nations, Publishing Service, New York, New York 10017 (800) 253-9646; *Statistical Yearbook*.

Times Books, 201 East 50th Street, New York, New York 10022 (212) 751-2600; *The Economist Book of Vital World Statistics*.

United Nations Economic Commission for Africa, Africa Hall, P.O. Box 3001, Addis Ababa, Ethiopia (Telephone Number in U.S. (800) 253-9646); *African Statistical Yearbook*.

COTE d'IVOIRE - ALUMINUM PRODUCTION AND CONSUMPTION - See COTE d'IVOIRE - MINING AND MINERAL PRODUCTS

COTE d'IVOIRE - ANIMAL HEALTH

Food and Agricultural Organization of the United Nations (FAO), Via delle Terme di Caracalla, 00100 Rome, Italy (Telephone Number in U.S. (202) 653-2400); *Animal Health Yearbook*.

COTE d'IVOIRE - AREA AND DENSITY OF POPULATION

African Development Bank, 01 BP 1387, Abidjan 01, Cote D'Ivoire; *Selected Statistics on Regional Member Countries*.

Euromonitor Publications Limited, 87-88 Turnmill Street, London EC1M 5QU, England; *International Marketing Data and Statistics*.

Facts on File, 460 Park Avenue South, New York, New York 10016 (800) 443-8323; *The New Book of World Rankings*.

Food and Agricultural Organization of the United Nations (FAO) Via delle Terme di Caracalla, 00100 Rome, Italy (Telephone Number in U.S. (202) 653-2400); *The State of Food and Agriculture*.

G.K. Hall and Company, 70 Lincoln Street, Boston, Massachusetts 02111 (617) 423-3990; *The World in Figures*.

Statistical Office of the United Nations, Publishing Service, New York, New York 10017 (800) 253-9646; *Statistical Yearbook*, and *Survey of Economic and Social Conditions in Africa*.

Times Books, 201 East 50th Street, New York, New York 10022 (212) 751-2600; *The Economist Book of Vital World Statistics.*

United Nations Educational, Scientific and Cultural Organization (UNESCO), 7 Place de Fontenoy, F-75700 Paris, France (Telephone Number in U.S. (212) 963-5981; *Statistical Yearbook.*

COTE d'IVOIRE - ARMS EXPORTS AND IMPORTS

U.S. Arms Control and Disarmament Agency, 320 Twenty-first Street, NW, Washington, D.C. 20451 (202) 647-8677; *World Military Expenditures and Arms Transfers.*

COTE d'IVOIRE - BALANCE OF PAYMENTS

African Development Bank, 01 BP 1387, Abidjan 01, Cote D'Ivoire; *Selected Statistics on Regional Member Countries.*

The Economist Intelligence Unit, 111 West 57th Street, New York, New York 10019 (800) 938-4685; *The World Market Atlas.*

G.K. Hall and Company, 70 Lincoln Street, Boston, Massachusetts 02111 (617) 423-3990; *The World in Figures.*

International Monetary Fund, 700 Nineteenth Street, NW, Washington, D.C. 20431 (202) 623-7000; *Balance of Payments Yearbook.*

Times Books, 201 East 50th Street, New York, New York 10022 (212) 751-2600; *The Economist Book of Vital World Statistics.*

United Nations Economic Commission for Africa, Africa Hall, P.O. Box 3001, Addis Ababa, Ethiopia (Telephone Number in U.S. (800) 253-9646); *African Statistical Yearbook.*

The World Bank, 1818 H Street, NW, Washington, D.C. 20433 (202) 477-1234; *World Tables.*

COTE d'IVOIRE - BANKING

Facts on File, 460 Park Avenue South, New York, New York 10016 (800) 443-8323; *The New Book of World Rankings.*

G.K. Hall and Company, 70 Lincoln Street, Boston, Massachusetts 02111 (617) 423-3990; *The World in Figures.*

Statistical Office of the United Nations, Publishing Service, New York, New York 10017 (800) 253-9646; *Statistical Yearbook.*

United Nations Economic Commission for Africa, Africa Hall, P.O. Box 3001, Addis Ababa, Ethiopia (Telephone Number in U.S. (800) 253-9646); *African Statistical Yearbook.*

COTE d'IVOIRE - BARLEY PRODUCTION - See COTE d'IVOIRE - CROPS

COTE d'IVOIRE - BEER PRODUCTION

Facts on File, 460 Park Avenue South, New York, New York 10016 (800) 443-8323; *The New Book of World Rankings.*

Statistical Office of the United Nations, Publishing Service, New York, New York 10017 (800) 253-9646; *Statistical Yearbook.*

COTE d'IVOIRE - BIRTH RATES

Facts on File, 460 Park Avenue South, New York, New York 10016 (800) 443-8323; *The New Book of World Rankings.*

Statistical Office of the United Nations, Publishing Service, New York, New York 10017 (800) 253-9646; *Demographic Yearbook, Statistical Yearbook,* and *Survey of Economic and Social Conditions in Africa.*

Times Books, 201 East 50th Street, New York, New York 10022 (212) 751-2600; *The Economist Book of Vital World Statistics.*

The World Bank, 1818 H Street, NW, Washington, D.C. 20433 (202) 477-1234; *World Tables.*

COTE d'IVOIRE - BONDS

G.K. Hall and Company, 70 Lincoln Street, Boston, Massachusetts 02111 (617) 423-3990; *The World in Figures.*

COTE d'IVOIRE - BOOK PRODUCTION

G.K. Hall and Company, 70 Lincoln Street, Boston, Massachusetts 02111 (617) 423-3990; *The World in Figures.*

United Nations Educational, Scientific and Cultural Organization (UNESCO), 7 Place de Fontenoy, F-75700 Paris, France (Telephone Number in U.S. (212) 963-5981); *Statistical Yearbook.*

COTE d'IVOIRE - BROADCASTING

Billboard Limited, P.O. Box 9027, 1006 AA Amsterdam, The Netherlands (Telephone Number in U.S. (212) 764-7300); *World Radio TV Handbook.*

Facts on File, 460 Park Avenue South, New York, New York 10016 (800) 443-8323; *The New Book of World Rankings.*

G.K. Hall and Company, 70 Lincoln Street, Boston, Massachusetts 02111 (617) 423-3990; *The World in Figures.*

Times Books, 201 East 50th Street, New York, New York 10022 (212) 751-2600; *The Economist Book of Vital World Statistics.*

United Nations Educational, Scientific and Cultural Organization (UNESCO), 7 Place de Fontenoy, F-75700 Paris, France (Telephone Number in U.S. (212) 963-5981); *Statistical Yearbook.*

COTE d'IVOIRE - BUSINESS

G.K. Hall and Company, 70 Lincoln Street, Boston, Massachusetts 02111 (617) 423-3990; *The World in Figures.*

COTE d'IVOIRE - CALORIE SUPPLY

African Development Bank, 01 BP 1387, Abidjan 01, Cote D'Ivoire; *Selected Statistics on Regional Member Countries.*

Food and Agricultural Organization of the United Nations (FAO) Via delle Terme di Caracalla, 00100 Rome, Italy (Telephone Number in U.S. (202) 653-2400); *The State of Food and Agriculture.*

COTE d'IVOIRE - CASHEW NUT PRODUCTION - See COTE d'IVOIRE - CROPS

COTE d'IVOIRE - CATTLE - See COTE d'IVOIRE - LIVESTOCK AND POULTRY

COTE d'IVOIRE - CEMENT PRODUCTION - See COTE d'IVOIRE - MINING AND MINERAL PRODUCTS

COTE d'IVOIRE - CHEMICAL (ORGANIC) PRODUCTION - See COTE d'IVOIRE - MINING AND MINERAL PRODUCTS

COTE d'IVOIRE - CHICKENS - See COTE d'IVOIRE - LIVESTOCK AND POULTRY

COTE d'IVOIRE - CIGAR PRODUCTION - See COTE d'IVOIRE - TOBACCO PRODUCTION

COTE d'IVOIRE - CIGARETTE PRODUCTION - See COTE d'IVOIRE - TOBACCO PRODUCTION

COTE d'IVOIRE - CLASS STRUCTURE

G.K. Hall and Company, 70 Lincoln Street, Boston, Massachusetts 02111 (617) 423-3990; *The World in Figures.*

COTE d'IVOIRE - CLIMATE

Facts on File, 460 Park Avenue South, New York, New York 10016 (800) 443-8323; *The New Book of World Rankings.*

G.K. Hall and Company, 70 Lincoln Street, Boston, Massachusetts 02111 (617) 423-3990; *The World in Figures.*

COTE d'IVOIRE - COAL PRODUCTION - See COTE d'IVOIRE - MINING AND MINERAL PRODUCTS

COTE d'IVOIRE - COCOA (BEANS) PRODUCTION - See COTE d'IVOIRE - CROPS

COTE d'IVOIRE - COFFEE PRODUCTION - See COTE d'IVOIRE - CROPS

COTE d'IVOIRE - COMMUNICATIONS

G.K. Hall and Company, 70 Lincoln Street, Boston, Massachusetts 02111 (617) 423-3990; *The World in Figures.*

United Nations Economic Commission for Africa, Africa Hall, P.O. Box 3001, Addis Ababa, Ethiopia (Telephone Number in U.S. (800) 253-9646); *African Statistical Yearbook.*

COTE d'IVOIRE - CONSTRUCTION INDUSTRY

Facts on File, 460 Park Avenue South, New York, New York 10016 (800) 443-8323; *The New Book of World Rankings.*

Statistical Office of the United Nations, Publishing Service, New York, New York 10017 (800) 253-9646; *Construction Statistics Yearbook, Statistical Yearbook.*

United Nations Economic Commission for Africa, Africa Hall, P.O. Box 3001, Addis Ababa, Ethiopia (Telephone Number in U.S. (800) 253-9646); *African Statistical Yearbook.*

COTE d'IVOIRE - CONSUMER PRICE INDEX

African Development Bank, 01 BP 1387, Abidjan 01, Cote D'Ivoire; *Selected Statistics on Regional Member Countries.*

G.K. Hall and Company, 70 Lincoln Street, Boston, Massachusetts 02111 (617) 423-3990; *The World in Figures.*

Statistical Office of the United Nations, Publishing Service, New York, New York 10017 (800) 253-9646; *Statistical Yearbook,* and *Survey of Economic and Social Conditions in Africa.*

United Nations Economic Commission for Africa, Africa Hall, P.O. Box 3001, Addis Ababa, Ethiopia (Telephone Number in U.S. (800) 253-9646); *African Statistical Yearbook.*

COTE d'IVOIRE - CONSUMER PRICES

International Labour Office, I.L.O. Publications, CH-1211, Geneva 22, Switzerland; *Yearbook of Labour Statistics.*

Times Books, 201 East 50th Street, New York, New York 10022 (212) 751-2600; *The Economist Book of Vital World Statistics.*

COTE d'IVOIRE - CONSUMPTION

African Development Bank, 01 BP 1387, Abidjan 01, Cote D'Ivoire; *Selected Statistics on Regional Member Countries.*

G.K. Hall and Company, 70 Lincoln Street, Boston, Massachusetts 02111 (617) 423-3990; *The World in Figures.*

International Rubber Study Group, York House, 8th Floor, Empire Way, Wembley, London HA9 0PA, England; *Rubber Statistical Bulletin.*

Statistical Office of the United Nations, Publishing Service, New York, New York 10017 (800) 253-9646; *Survey of Economic and Social Conditions in Africa.*

COTE d'IVOIRE - COPPER PRODUCTION - See COTE d'IVOIRE - MINING AND MINERAL PRODUCTS

COTE d'IVOIRE - CORN PRODUCTION - See COTE d'IVOIRE - CROPS

COTE d'IVOIRE - CORPORATE TAXES - See COTE d'IVOIRE - TAXATION

COTE d'IVOIRE - COTTON - See COTE d'IVOIRE - CROPS

COTE d'IVOIRE - CRIME

International Criminal Police Organization (INTERPOL), 26 rue Armengaud, 92210 Saint Cloud, France; *International Crime Statistics.*

Yale University Press, Yale Station, New Haven, Connecticut 06520 (203) 432-0940; *Violence and Crime in Cross-National Perspective.*

COTE d'IVOIRE - CROPS

Commodity Research Bureau, Incorporated, 75 Wall Street, New York, New York 10005 (212) 504-7754; *Commodity Year Book.*

Facts on File, 460 Park Avenue South, New York, New York 10016 (800) 443-8323; *The New Book of World Rankings.*

Food and Agricultural Organization of the United Nations (FAO), Via delle Terme di Caracalla, 00100 Rome, Italy (Telephone Number in U.S. (202) 653-2400); *Production Yearbook,* and *State of Food and Agriculture.*

G.K. Hall and Company, 70 Lincoln Street, Boston, Massachusetts 02111 (617) 423-3990; *The World in Figures.*

Statistical Office of the United Nations, Publishing Service, New York, New York 10017 (800) 253-9646; *Statistical Yearbook.*

United Nations Economic Commission for Africa, Africa Hall, P.O. Box 3001, Addis Ababa, Ethiopia (Telephone Number in U.S. (800) 253-9646); *African Statistical Yearbook.*

COTE d'IVOIRE - CUSTOMS DUTIES

G.K. Hall and Company, 70 Lincoln Street, Boston, Massachusetts 02111 (617) 423-3990; *The World in Figures.*

COTE d'IVOIRE - DAIRY PRODUCTS

Facts on File, 460 Park Avenue South, New York, New York 10016 (800) 443-8323; *The New Book of World Rankings.*

Food and Agricultural Organization of the United Nations (FAO) Via delle Terme di Caracalla, 00100 Rome, Italy (Telephone Number in U.S. (202) 653-2400); *The State of Food and Agriculture.*

Statistical Office of the United Nations, Publishing Service, New York, New York 10017 (800) 253-9646; *Statistical Yearbook.*

COTE d'IVOIRE - DEATH RATES

G.K. Hall and Company, 70 Lincoln Street, Boston, Massachusetts 02111 (617) 423-3990; *The World in Figures.*

Statistical Office of the United Nations, Publishing Service, New York, New York 10017 (800) 253-9646; *Statistical Yearbook,* and *Survey of Economic and Social Conditions in Africa.*

Times Books, 201 East 50th Street, New York, New York 10022 (212) 751-2600; *The Economist Book of Vital World Statistics.*

COTE d'IVOIRE - DEFENSE EXPENDITURES

G.K. Hall and Company, 70 Lincoln Street, Boston, Massachusetts 02111 (617) 423-3990; *The World in Figures.*

U.S. Arms Control and Disarmament Agency, 320 Twenty-first Street, NW, Washington, D.C. 20451 (202) 647-8677; *World Military Expenditures and Arms Transfers.*

COTE d'IVOIRE - DEMOGRAPHY

The Economist Intelligence Unit, 111 West 57th Street, New York, New York 10019 (800) 938-4685; *The World Market Atlas.*

Facts on File, 460 Park Avenue South, New York, New York 10016 (800) 443-8323; *The New Book of World Rankings.*

G.K. Hall and Company, 70 Lincoln Street, Boston, Massachusetts 02111 (617) 423-3990; *The World in Figures.*

Statistical Office of the United Nations, Publishing Service, New York, New York 10017 (800) 253-9646; *Survey of Economic and Social Conditions in Africa.*

COTE d'IVOIRE - DEVELOPMENT ASSISTANCE

G.K. Hall and Company, 70 Lincoln Street, Boston, Massachusetts 02111 (617) 423-3990; *The World in Figures.*

Statistical Office of the United Nations, Publishing Service, New York, New York 10017 (800) 253-9646; *Statistical Yearbook.*

COTE d'IVOIRE - DIAMOND PRODUCTION - See COTE d'IVOIRE - MINING AND MINERAL PRODUCTS

COTE d'IVOIRE - DISCOUNT RATES

Statistical Office of the United Nations, Publishing Service, New York, New York 10017 (800) 253-9646; *Statistical Yearbook.*

COTE d'IVOIRE - DISEASE

G.K. Hall and Company, 70 Lincoln Street, Boston, Massachusetts 02111 (617) 423-3990; *The World in Figures.*

COTE d'IVOIRE - DIVORCE RATES

Facts on File, 460 Park Avenue South, New York, New York 10016 (800) 443-8323; *The New Book of World Rankings.*

Statistical Office of the United Nations, Publishing Service, New York, New York 10017 (800) 253-9646; *Demographic Yearbook.*

COTE d'IVOIRE - DOMESTIC PRODUCT

G.K. Hall and Company, 70 Lincoln Street, Boston, Massachusetts 02111 (617) 423-3990; *The World in Figures.*

COTE d'IVOIRE - ECONOMY

African Development Bank, 01 BP 1387, Abidjan 01, Cote D'Ivoire; *Selected Statistics on Regional Member Countries.*

Euromonitor Publications Limited, 87-88 Turnmill Street, London EC1M 5QU, England; *International Marketing Data and Statistics.*

Facts on File, 460 Park Avenue South, New York, New York 10016 (800) 443-8323; *The New Book of World Rankings.*

G.K. Hall and Company, 70 Lincoln Street, Boston, Massachusetts 02111 (617) 423-3990; *The World in Figures.*

Statistical Office of the United Nations, Publishing Service, New York, New York 10017 (800) 253-9646; *Foreign Trade Statistics for Africa.*

COTE d'IVOIRE - EDUCATION

African Development Bank, 01 BP 1387, Abidjan 01, Cote D'Ivoire; *Selected Statistics on Regional Member Countries.*

The Economist Intelligence Unit, 111 West 57th Street, New York, New York 10019 (800) 938-4685; *The World Market Atlas.*

Facts on File, 460 Park Avenue South, New York, New York 10016 (800) 443-8323; *The New Book of World Rankings.*

G.K. Hall and Company, 70 Lincoln Street, Boston, Massachusetts 02111 (617) 423-3990; *The World in Figures.*

Statistical Office of the United Nations, Publishing Service, New York, New York 10017 (800) 253-9646; *Survey of Economic and Social Conditions in Africa.*

Times Books, 201 East 50th Street, New York, New York 10022 (212) 751-2600; *The Economist Book of Vital World Statistics.*

United Nations Economic Commission for Africa, Africa Hall, P.O. Box 3001, Addis Ababa, Ethiopia (Telephone Number in U.S. (800) 253-9646); *African Statistical Yearbook.*

United Nations Educational, Scientific and Cultural Organization (UNESCO), 7 Place de Fontenoy, F-75700 Paris, France (Telephone Number in U.S. (212) 963-5981); *Statistical Yearbook.*

The World Bank, 1818 H Street, NW, Washington, D.C. 20433 (202) 477-1234; *World Tables.*

COTE d'IVOIRE - EGG PRODUCTION - See COTE d'IVOIRE - DAIRY PRODUCTS

COTE d'IVOIRE - EGGPLANT PRODUCTION - See COTE d'IVOIRE - CROPS

COTE d'IVOIRE - ELECTRICITY

Facts on File, 460 Park Avenue South, New York, New York 10016 (800) 443-8323; *The New Book of World Rankings.*

Penn Well Publishing Company, 1421 South Sheridan Road, P.O. Box 1260, Tulsa, Oklahoma 74101 (800) 752-9764; *International Energy Statistics Sourcebook.*

Statistical Office of the United Nations, Publishing Service, New York, New York 10017 (800) 253-9646; *Statistical Yearbook,* and *Survey of Economic and Social Conditions in Africa.*

Times Books, 201 East 50th Street, New York, New York 10022 (212) 751-2600; *The Economist Book of Vital World Statistics.*

United Nations Economic Commission for Africa, Africa Hall, P.O. Box 3001, Addis Ababa, Ethiopia (Telephone Number in U.S. (800) 253-9646); *African Statistical Yearbook.*

COTE d'IVOIRE - EMPLOYMENT

Euromonitor Publications Limited, 87-88 Turnmill Street, London EC1M 5QU, England; *International Marketing Data and Statistics.*

Facts on File, 460 Park Avenue South, New York, New York 10016 (800) 443-8323; *The New Book of World Rankings.*

Statistical Office of the United Nations, Publishing Service, New York, New York 10017 (800) 253-9646; *Statistical Yearbook,* and *Survey of Economic and Social Conditions in Africa.*

United Nations Economic Commission for Africa, Africa Hall, P.O. Box 3001, Addis Ababa, Ethiopia (Telephone Number in U.S. (800) 253-9646); *African Statistical Yearbook.*

COTE d'IVOIRE - ENERGY

Facts on File, 460 Park Avenue South, New York, New York 10016 (800) 443-8323; *The New Book of World Rankings.*

Food and Agricultural Organization of the United Nations (FAO) Via delle Terme di Caracalla, 00100 Rome, Italy (Telephone Number in U.S. (202) 653-2400); *The State of Food and Agriculture.*

G.K. Hall and Company, 70 Lincoln Street, Boston, Massachusetts 02111 (617) 423-3990; *The World in Figures.*

Penn Well Publishing Company, 1421 South Sheridan Road, P.O. Box 1260, Tulsa, Oklahoma 74101 (800) 752-9764; *International Energy Statistics Sourcebook.*

Statistical Office of the United Nations, Publishing Service, New York, New York 10017 (800) 253-9646; *Energy Statistics Yearbook, Statistical Yearbook,* and *World Energy Supplies.*

Times Books, 201 East 50th Street, New York, New York 10022 (212) 751-2600; *The Economist Book of Vital World Statistics.*

United Nations Economic Commission for Africa, Africa Hall, P.O. Box 3001, Addis Ababa, Ethiopia (Telephone Number in U.S. (800) 253-9646); *African Statistical Yearbook.*

COTE d'IVOIRE - EXCHANGE RATES

African Development Bank, 01 BP 1387, Abidjan 01, Cote D'Ivoire; *Selected Statistics on Regional Member Countries.*

Euromonitor Publications Limited, 87-88 Turnmill Street, London EC1M 5QU, England; *International Marketing Data and Statistics.*

Statistical Office of the United Nations, Publishing Service, New York, New York 10017 (800) 253-9646; *Foreign Trade Statistics for Africa,* and *Statistical Yearbook.*

COTE d'IVOIRE - EXPORTS

African Development Bank, 01 BP 1387, Abidjan 01, Cote D'Ivoire; *Selected Statistics on Regional Member Countries.*

The Economist Intelligence Unit, 111 West 57th Street, New York, New York 10019 (800) 938-4685; *The World Market Atlas.*

Euromonitor Publications Limited, 87-88 Turnmill Street, London EC1M 5QU, England; *International Marketing Data and Statistics.*

Food and Agricultural Organization of the United Nations (FAO) Via delle Terme di Caracalla, 00100 Rome, Italy (Telephone Number in U.S. (202) 653-2400); *The State of Food and Agriculture.*

G.K. Hall and Company, 70 Lincoln Street, Boston, Massachusetts 02111 (617) 423-3990; *The World in Figures.*

International Monetary Fund, 700 Nineteenth Street, NW, Washington, D.C. 20431 (202) 623-7000; *Direction of Trade Statistics.*

International Rubber Study Group, York House, 8th Floor, Empire Way, Wembley, London HA9 0PA, England; *Rubber Statistical Bulletin.*

Statistical Office of the United Nations, Publishing Service, New York, New York 10017 (800) 253-9646; *Foreign Trade Statistics for Africa, Survey of Economic and Social Conditions in Africa,* and *Trade in Manufactures of Developing Countries.*

Times Books, 201 East 50th Street, New York, New York 10022 (212) 751-2600; *The Economist Book of Vital World Statistics.*

United Nations Economic Commission for Africa, Africa Hall, P.O. Box 3001, Addis Ababa, Ethiopia (Telephone Number in U.S. (800) 253-9646); *African Statistical Yearbook.*

The World Bank, 1818 H Street, NW, Washington, D.C. 20433 (202) 477-1234; *World Tables.*

COTE d'IVOIRE - EXTERNAL INDEBTEDNESS

African Development Bank, 01 BP 1387, Abidjan 01, Cote D'Ivoire; *Selected Statistics on Regional Member Countries.*

Statistical Office of the United Nations, Publishing Service, New York, New York 10017 (800) 253-9646; *Survey of Economic and Social Conditions in Africa.*

The World Bank, 1818 H Street, NW, Washington, D.C. 20433 (202) 477-1234; *World Tables.*

COTE d'IVOIRE - EXTERNAL TRADE

African Development Bank, 01 BP 1387, Abidjan 01, Cote D'Ivoire; *Selected Statistics on Regional Member Countries.*

Food and Agricultural Organization of the United Nations (FAO) Via delle Terme di Caracalla, 00100 Rome, Italy (Telephone Number in U.S. (202) 653-2400); *The State of Food and Agriculture*, and *Trade Yearbook*.

G.K. Hall and Company, 70 Lincoln Street, Boston, Massachusetts 02111 (617) 423-3990; *The World in Figures*.

Statistical Office of the United Nations, Publishing Service, New York, New York 10017 (800) 253-9646; *Statistical Yearbook*.

COTE d'IVOIRE - FARM CROPS - See COTE d'IVOIRE - CROPS

COTE d'IVOIRE - FEMALE WORKING POPULATION - See COTE d'IVOIRE - EMPLOYMENT

COTE d'IVOIRE - FERTILITY RATES

Facts on File, 460 Park Avenue South, New York, New York 10016 (800) 443-8323; *The New Book of World Rankings*.

Statistical Office of the United Nations, Publishing Service, New York, New York 10017 (800) 253-9646; *Survey of Economic and Social Conditions in Africa*.

Times Books, 201 East 50th Street, New York, New York 10022 (212) 751-2600; *The Economist Book of Vital World Statistics*.

The World Bank, 1818 H Street, NW, Washington, D.C. 20433 (202) 477-1234; *World Tables*.

COTE d'IVOIRE - FERTILIZER

Food and Agricultural Organization of the United Nations (FAO), Via delle Terme di Caracalla, 00100 Rome, Italy (Telephone Number in U.S. (202) 653-2400); *Fertilizer Yearbook*, and *The State of Food and Agriculture*.

Statistical Office of the United Nations, Publishing Service, New York, New York 10017 (800) 253-9646; *Statistical Yearbook*.

COTE d'IVOIRE - FETAL MORTALITY

Statistical Office of the United Nations, Publishing Service, New York, New York 10017 (800) 253-9646; *Demographic Yearbook*.

COTE d'IVOIRE - FILM - See COTE d'IVOIRE - MOTION PICTURES

COTE d'IVOIRE - FINANCE

African Development Bank, 01 BP 1387, Abidjan 01, Cote D'Ivoire; *Selected Statistics on Regional Member Countries*.

Facts on File, 460 Park Avenue South, New York, New York 10016 (800) 443-8323; *The New Book of World Rankings*.

G.K. Hall and Company, 70 Lincoln Street, Boston, Massachusetts 02111 (617) 423-3990; *The World in Figures*.

International Monetary Fund, 700 Nineteenth Street, NW, Washington, D.C. 20431 (202) 623-7000; *International Financial Statistics*.

United Nations Economic Commission for Africa, Africa Hall, P.O. Box 3001, Addis Ababa, Ethiopia (Telephone Number in U.S. (800) 253-9646); *African Statistical Yearbook*.

COTE d'IVOIRE - FISHERIES

Facts on File, 460 Park Avenue South, New York, New York 10016 (800) 443-8323; *The New Book of World Rankings*.

Food and Agricultural Organization of the United Nations (FAO) Via delle Terme di Caracalla, 00100 Rome, Italy (Telephone Number in U.S. (202) 653-2400); *The State of Food and Agriculture*, and *Yearbook of Fishery Statistics*.

Statistical Office of the United Nations, Publishing Service, New York, New York 10017 (800) 253-9646; *Statistical Yearbook*, and *Survey of Economic and Social Conditions in Africa*.

United Nations Economic Commission for Africa, Africa Hall, P.O. Box 3001, Addis Ababa, Ethiopia (Telephone Number in U.S. (800) 253-9646); *African Statistical Yearbook*.

COTE d'IVOIRE - FLOUR PRODUCTION

Statistical Office of the United Nations, Publishing Service, New York, New York 10017 (800) 253-9646; *Statistical Yearbook*.

COTE d'IVOIRE - FOOD

African Development Bank, 01 BP 1387, Abidjan 01, Cote D'Ivoire; *Selected Statistics on Regional Member Countries*.

Food and Agricultural Organization of the United Nations (FAO) Via delle Terme di Caracalla, 00100 Rome, Italy (Telephone Number in U.S. (202) 653-2400); *Production Yearbook*, and *The State of Food and Agriculture*.

G.K. Hall and Company, 70 Lincoln Street, Boston, Massachusetts 02111 (617) 423-3990; *The World in Figures*.

Statistical Office of the United Nations, Publishing Service, New York, New York 10017 (800) 253-9646; *Trade in Manufactures of Developing Countries*.

COTE d'IVOIRE - FOREIGN AID

G.K. Hall and Company, 70 Lincoln Street, Boston, Massachusetts 02111 (617) 423-3990; *The World in Figures*.

COTE d'IVOIRE - FOREIGN TRADE

Euromonitor Publications Limited, 87-88 Turnmill Street, London EC1M 5QU, England; *International Marketing Data and Statistics*.

Facts on File, 460 Park Avenue South, New York, New York 10016 (800) 443-8323; *The New Book of World Rankings*.

Food and Agricultural Organization of the United Nations (FAO) Via delle Terme di Caracalla, 00100 Rome, Italy (Telephone Number in U.S. (202) 653-2400); *The State of Food and Agriculture*.

G.K. Hall and Company, 70 Lincoln Street, Boston, Massachusetts 02111 (617) 423-3990; *The World in Figures*.

Statistical Office of the United Nations, Publishing Service, New York, New York 10017 (800) 253-9646; *Foreign Trade Statistics for Africa*, *International Trade Statistics Yearbook*, and *Statistical Yearbook*.

United Nations Economic Commission for Africa, Africa Hall, P.O. Box 3001, Addis Ababa, Ethiopia (Telephone Number in U.S. (800) 253-9646); *African Statistical Yearbook*.

The World Bank, 1818 H Street, NW, Washington, D.C. 20433 (202) 477-1234; *World Tables.*

COTE d'IVOIRE - FORESTRY AND FOREST PRODUCTS

Facts on File, 460 Park Avenue South, New York, New York 10016 (800) 443-8323; *The New Book of World Rankings.*

Food and Agricultural Organization of the United Nations (FAO) Via delle Terme di Caracalla, 00100 Rome, Italy (Telephone Number in U.S. (202) 653-2400); *The State of Food and Agriculture,* and *Yearbook of Forest Products.*

G.K. Hall and Company, 70 Lincoln Street, Boston, Massachusetts 02111 (617) 423-3990; *The World in Figures.*

Statistical Office of the United Nations, Publishing Service, New York, New York 10017 (800) 253-9646; *Statistical Yearbook.*

United Nations Economic Commission for Africa, Africa Hall, P.O. Box 3001, Addis Ababa, Ethiopia (Telephone Number in U.S. (800) 253-9646); *African Statistical Yearbook.*

United Nations Educational, Scientific and Cultural Organization (UNESCO), 7 Place de Fontenoy, F-75700 Paris, France (Telephone Number in U.S. (212) 963-5981); *Statistical Yearbook.*

COTE d'IVOIRE - FURNITURE AND WOOD PRODUCTS - EXPORTS AND IMPORTS

Statistical Office of the United Nations, Publishing Service, New York, New York 10017 (800) 253-9646; *Trade in Manufactures of Developed Countries.*

COTE d'IVOIRE - GAS PRODUCTION - See COTE d'IVOIRE - MINING AND MINERAL PRODUCTS

COTE d'IVOIRE - GENERAL INDUSTRIAL STATISTICS

Statistical Office of the United Nations, Publishing Service, New York, New York 10017 (800) 253-9646; *Industrial Statistics Yearbook.*

COTE d'IVOIRE - GENERAL MORTALITY

Statistical Office of the United Nations, Publishing Service, New York, New York 10017 (800) 253-9646; *Demographic Yearbook.*

COTE d'IVOIRE - GEOGRAPHIC DATA

Facts on File, 460 Park Avenue South, New York, New York 10016 (800) 443-8323; *The New Book of World Rankings.*

COTE d'IVOIRE - GOATS - See COTE d'IVOIRE - LIVESTOCK AND POULTRY

COTE d'IVOIRE - GOLD HOLDINGS

Statistical Office of the United Nations, Publishing Service, New York, New York 10017 (800) 253-9646; *Statistical Yearbook.*

The World Bank, 1818 H Street, NW, Washington, D.C. 20433 (202) 477-1234; *World Tables.*

COTE d'IVOIRE - GOLD PRODUCTION AND CONSUMPTION - See COTE d'IVOIRE - MINING AND MINERAL PRODUCTS

COTE d'IVOIRE - GOVERNMENT

G.K. Hall and Company, 70 Lincoln Street, Boston, Massachusetts 02111 (617) 423-3990; *The World in Figures.*

COTE d'IVOIRE - GOVERNMENT EXPENDITURE

Times Books, 201 East 50th Street, New York, New York 10022 (212) 751-2600; *The Economist Book of Vital World Statistics.*

The World Bank, 1818 H Street, NW, Washington, D.C. 20433 (202) 477-1234; *World Tables.*

COTE d'IVOIRE - GOVERNMENT FINANCES

Statistical Office of the United Nations, Publishing Service, New York, New York 10017 (800) 253-9646; *Statistical Yearbook.*

COTE d'IVOIRE - GOVERNMENT REVENUE

Statistical Office of the United Nations, Publishing Service, New York, New York 10017 (800) 253-9646; *Survey of Economic and Social Conditions in Africa.*

Times Books, 201 East 50th Street, New York, New York 10022 (212) 751-2600; *The Economist Book of Vital World Statistics.*

The World Bank, 1818 H Street, NW, Washington, D.C. 20433 (202) 477-1234; *World Tables.*

COTE d'IVOIRE - GRAIN PRODUCTION - See COTE d'IVOIRE - CROPS

COTE d'IVOIRE - GREEN PEPPER AND CHILIE PRODUCTION - See COTE d'IVOIRE - CROPS

COTE d'IVOIRE - GROSS DOMESTIC PRODUCT

African Development Bank, 01 BP 1387, Abidjan 01, Cote D'Ivoire; *Selected Statistics on Regional Member Countries.*

The Economist Intelligence Unit, 111 West 57th Street, New York, New York 10019 (800) 938-4685; *The World Market Atlas.*

Euromonitor Publications Limited, 87-88 Turnmill Street, London EC1M 5QU, England; *International Marketing Data and Statistics.*

Facts on File, 460 Park Avenue South, New York, New York 10016 (800) 443-8323; *The New Book of World Rankings.*

G.K. Hall and Company, 70 Lincoln Street, Boston, Massachusetts 02111 (617) 423-3990; *The World in Figures.*

Statistical Office of the United Nations, Publishing Service, New York, New York 10017 (800) 253-9646; *Statistical Yearbook,* and *Survey of Economic and Social Conditions in Africa.*

United Nations Economic Commission for Africa, Africa Hall, P.O. Box 3001, Addis Ababa, Ethiopia (Telephone Number in U.S. (800) 253-9646); *African Statistical Yearbook.*

Times Books, 201 East 50th Street, New York, New York 10022 (212) 751-2600; *The Economist Book of Vital World Statistics.*

The World Bank, 1818 H Street, NW, Washington, D.C. 20433 (202) 477-1234; *World Tables.*

COTE d'IVOIRE - GROSS NATIONAL PRODUCT

Euromonitor Publications Limited, 87-88 Turnmill Street, London EC1M 5QU, England; *International Marketing Data and Statistics.*

U.S. Arms Control and Disarmament Agency, 320 Twenty-first Street, NW, Washington, D.C. 20451 (202) 647-8677; *World Military Expenditures and Arms Transfers.*

The World Bank, 1818 H Street, NW, Washington, D.C. 20433 (202) 477-1234; *World Tables.*

COTE d'IVOIRE - GROUNDNUTS PRODUCTION - See COTE d'IVOIRE - CROPS

COTE d'IVOIRE - HEALTH

African Development Bank, 01 BP 1387, Abidjan 01, Cote D'Ivoire; *Selected Statistics on Regional Member Countries.*

Facts on File, 460 Park Avenue South, New York, New York 10016 (800) 443-8323; *The New Book of World Rankings.*

G.K. Hall and Company, 70 Lincoln Street, Boston, Massachusetts 02111 (617) 423-3990; *The World in Figures.*

Statistical Office of the United Nations, Publishing Service, New York, New York 10017 (800) 253-9646; *Statistical Yearbook.*

Times Books, 201 East 50th Street, New York, New York 10022 (212) 751-2600; *The Economist Book of Vital World Statistics.*

United Nations Economic Commission for Africa, Africa Hall, P.O. Box 3001, Addis Ababa, Ethiopia (Telephone Number in U.S. (800) 253-9646); *African Statistical Yearbook.*

COTE d'IVOIRE - HIDE PRODUCTION

Food and Agricultural Organization of the United Nations (FAO), Via delle Terme di Caracalla, 00100 Rome, Italy (Telephone Number in U.S. (202) 653-2400); *Production Yearbook.*

COTE d'IVOIRE - HIGHWAYS

G.K. Hall and Company, 70 Lincoln Street, Boston, Massachusetts 02111 (617) 423-3990; *The World in Figures.*

International Road Federation, 525 School Street, SW, Washington, D.C. 20024 (202) 554-2106; *World Road Statistics.*

Statistical Office of the United Nations, Publishing Service, New York, New York 10017 (800) 253-9646; *Survey of Economic and Social Conditions in Africa.*

United Nations Economic Commission for Africa, Africa Hall, P.O. Box 3001, Addis Ababa, Ethiopia (Telephone Number in U.S. (800) 253-9646); *African Statistical Yearbook.*

COTE d'IVOIRE - HORSES - See COTE d'IVOIRE - LIVESTOCK AND POULTRY

COTE d'IVOIRE - HOURS OF WORK - See COTE d'IVOIRE - EMPLOYMENT

COTE d'IVOIRE - HOUSING

Facts on File, 460 Park Avenue South, New York, New York 10016 (800) 443-8323; *The New Book of World Rankings.*

COTE d'IVOIRE - ILLITERATE POPULATION

The Economist Intelligence Unit, 111 West 57th Street, New York, New York 10019 (800) 938-4685; *The World Market Atlas.*

G.K. Hall and Company, 70 Lincoln Street, Boston, Massachusetts 02111 (617) 423-3990; *The World in Figures.*

United Nations Educational, Scientific and Cultural Organization (UNESCO), 7 Place de Fontenoy, F-75700 Paris, France (Telephone Number in U.S. (212) 963-5981); *Statistical Yearbook.*

COTE d'IVOIRE - IMPORTS

African Development Bank, 01 BP 1387, Abidjan 01, Cote D'Ivoire; *Selected Statistics on Regional Member Countries.*

The Economist Intelligence Unit, 111 West 57th Street, New York, New York 10019 (800) 938-4685; *The World Market Atlas.*

Euromonitor Publications Limited, 87-88 Turnmill Street, London EC1M 5QU, England; *International Marketing Data and Statistics.*

Food and Agricultural Organization of the United Nations (FAO) Via delle Terme di Caracalla, 00100 Rome, Italy (Telephone Number in U.S. (202) 653-2400); *The State of Food and Agriculture.*

G.K. Hall and Company, 70 Lincoln Street, Boston, Massachusetts 02111 (617) 423-3990; *The World in Figures.*

International Monetary Fund, 700 Nineteenth Street, NW, Washington, D.C. 20431 (202) 623-7000; *Direction of Trade Statistics.*

International Rubber Study Group, York House, 8th Floor, Empire Way, Wembley, London HA9 0PA, England; *Rubber Statistical Bulletin.*

Statistical Office of the United Nations, Publishing Service, New York, New York 10017 (800) 253-9646; *Foreign Trade Statistics for Africa, Survey of Economic and Social Conditions in Africa,* and *Trade in Manufactures of Developing Countries.*

Times Books, 201 East 50th Street, New York, New York 10022 (212) 751-2600; *The Economist Book of Vital World Statistics.*

United Nations Economic Commission for Africa, Africa Hall, P.O. Box 3001, Addis Ababa, Ethiopia (Telephone Number in U.S. (800) 253-9646); *African Statistical Yearbook.*

The World Bank, 1818 H Street, NW, Washington, D.C. 20433 (202) 477-1234; *World Tables.*

COTE d'IVOIRE - INDUSTRY

Euromonitor Publications Limited, 87-88 Turnmill Street, London EC1M 5QU, England; *International Marketing Data and Statistics.*

Facts on File, 460 Park Avenue South, New York, New York 10016 (800) 443-8323; *The New Book of World Rankings.*

G.K. Hall and Company, 70 Lincoln Street, Boston, Massachusetts 02111 (617) 423-3990; *The World in Figures.*

Statistical Office of the United Nations, Publishing Service, New York, New York 10017 (800) 253-9646; *Survey of Economic and Social Conditions in Africa.*

Times Books, 201 East 50th Street, New York, New York 10022 (212) 751-2600; *The Economist Book of Vital World Statistics.*

United Nations Economic Commission for Africa, Africa Hall, P.O. Box 3001, Addis Ababa, Ethiopia (Telephone Number in U.S. (800) 253-9646); *African Statistical Yearbook.*

The World Bank, 1818 H Street, NW, Washington, D.C. 20433 (202) 477-1234; *World Tables.*

COTE d'IVOIRE - INFANT AND MATERNAL MORTALITY

Statistical Office of the United Nations, Publishing Service, New York, New York 10017 (800) 253-9646; *Demographic Yearbook, Statistical Yearbook,* and *Survey of Economic and Social Conditions in Africa.*

Times Books, 201 East 50th Street, New York, New York 10022 (212) 751-2600; *The Economist Book of Vital World Statistics.*

The World Bank, 1818 H Street, NW, Washington, D.C. 20433 (202) 477-1234; *World Tables.*

COTE d'IVOIRE - INTERNATIONAL RESERVES EXCLUDING GOLD

African Development Bank, 01 BP 1387, Abidjan 01, Cote D'Ivoire; *Selected Statistics on Regional Member Countries.*

Statistical Office of the United Nations, Publishing Service, New York, New York 10017 (800) 253-9646; *Statistical Yearbook.*

The World Bank, 1818 H Street, NW, Washington, D.C. 20433 (202) 477-1234; *World Tables.*

COTE d'IVOIRE - IRON ORE PRODUCTION AND CONSUMPTION - See COTE d'IVOIRE - MINING AND MINERAL PRODUCTS

COTE d'IVOIRE - IRRIGATION

Euromonitor Publications Limited, 87-88 Turnmill Street, London EC1M 5QU, England; *International Marketing Data and Statistics.*

COTE d'IVOIRE - LABOR FORCE

African Development Bank, 01 BP 1387, Abidjan 01, Cote D'Ivoire; *Selected Statistics on Regional Member Countries.*

Euromonitor Publications Limited, 87-88 Turnmill Street, London EC1M 5QU, England; *International Marketing Data and Statistics.*

Facts on File, 460 Park Avenue South, New York, New York 10016 (800) 443-8323; *The New Book of World Rankings.*

Food and Agricultural Organization of the United Nations (FAO) Via delle Terme di Caracalla, 00100 Rome, Italy (Telephone Number in U.S. (202) 653-2400); *The State of Food and Agriculture.*

G.K. Hall and Company, 70 Lincoln Street, Boston, Massachusetts 02111 (617) 423-3990; *The World in Figures.*

The World Bank, 1818 H Street, NW, Washington, D.C. 20433 (202) 477-1234; *World Tables.*

COTE d'IVOIRE - LAND USE

Euromonitor Publications Limited, 87-88 Turnmill Street, London EC1M 5QU, England; *International Marketing Data and Statistics.*

Food and Agricultural Organization of the United Nations (FAO), Via delle Terme di Caracalla, 00100 Rome, Italy (Telephone Number in U.S. (202) 653-2400); *Production Yearbook.*

G.K. Hall and Company, 70 Lincoln Street, Boston, Massachusetts 02111 (617) 423-3990; *The World in Figures.*

COTE d'IVOIRE - LIBRARIES

Facts on File, 460 Park Avenue South, New York, New York 10016 (800) 443-8323; *The New Book of World Rankings.*

United Nations Educational, Scientific and Cultural Organization (UNESCO), 7 Place de Fontenoy, F-75700 Paris, France (Telephone Number in U.S. (212) 963-5981); *Statistical Yearbook.*

COTE d'IVOIRE - LIFE EXPECTANCY

African Development Bank, 01 BP 1387, Abidjan 01, Cote D'Ivoire; *Selected Statistics on Regional Member Countries.*

COTE d'IVOIRE - LITERACY RATE

Statistical Office of the United Nations, Publishing Service, New York, New York 10017 (800) 253-9646; *Survey of Economic and Social Conditions in Africa.*

COTE d'IVOIRE - LIVESTOCK AND POULTRY

Euromonitor Publications Limited, 87-88 Turnmill Street, London EC1M 5QU, England; *International Marketing Data and Statistics.*

Facts on File, 460 Park Avenue South, New York, New York 10016 (800) 443-8323; *The New Book of World Rankings.*

Food and Agricultural Organization of the United Nations (FAO), Via delle Terme di Caracalla, 00100 Rome, Italy (Telephone Number in U.S. (202) 653-2400); *Production Yearbook,* and *The State of Food and Agriculture.*

G.K. Hall and Company, 70 Lincoln Street, Boston, Massachusetts 02111 (617) 423-3990; *The World in Figures.*

Statistical Office of the United Nations, Publishing Service, New York, New York 10017 (800) 253-9646; *Statistical Yearbook,* and *Survey of Economic and Social Conditions in Africa.*

United Nations Economic Commission for Africa, Africa Hall, P.O. Box 3001, Addis Ababa, Ethiopia (Telephone Number in U.S. (800) 253-9646); *African Statistical Yearbook.*

COTE d'IVOIRE - LIVING LEVELS

G.K. Hall and Company, 70 Lincoln Street, Boston, Massachusetts 02111 (617) 423-3990; *The World in Figures.*

Times Books, 201 East 50th Street, New York, New York 10022 (212) 751-2600; *The Economist Book of Vital World Statistics.*

COTE d'IVOIRE - MAIL TRAFFIC - NUMBER OF ITEMS SENT AND RECEIVED

Statistical Office of the United Nations, Publishing Service, New York, New York 10017 (800) 253-9646; *Statistical Yearbook.*

COTE d'IVOIRE - MANGANESE ORE PRODUCTION AND CONSUMPTION - See COTE d'IVOIRE - MINING AND MINERAL PRODUCTS

COTE d'IVOIRE - MANUFACTURING

Facts on File, 460 Park Avenue South, New York, New York 10016 (800) 443-8323; *The New Book of World Rankings.*

G.K. Hall and Company, 70 Lincoln Street, Boston, Massachusetts 02111 (617) 423-3990; *The World in Figures.*

Statistical Office of the United Nations, Publishing Service, New York, New York 10017 (800) 253-9646; *Statistical Yearbook,* and *Survey of Economic and Social Conditions in Africa.*

United Nations Economic Commission for Africa, Africa Hall, P.O. Box 3001, Addis Ababa, Ethiopia (Telephone Number in U.S. (800) 253-9646); *African Statistical Yearbook.*

The World Bank, 1818 H Street, NW, Washington, D.C. 20433 (202) 477-1234; *World Tables.*

COTE d'IVOIRE - MARRIAGE RATES

Facts on File, 460 Park Avenue South, New York, New York 10016 (800) 443-8323; *The New Book of World Rankings.*

Statistical Office of the United Nations, Publishing Service, New York, New York 10017 (800) 253-9646; *Demographic Yearbook.*

COTE d'IVOIRE - MEAT PRODUCTION - See COTE d'IVOIRE - LIVESTOCK AND POULTRY

COTE d'IVOIRE - MERCHANT SHIPPING

G.K. Hall and Company, 70 Lincoln Street, Boston, Massachusetts 02111 (617) 423-3990; *The World in Figures.*

Statistical Office of the United Nations, Publishing Service, New York, New York 10017 (800) 253-9646; *Statistical Yearbook.*

Times Books, 201 East 50th Street, New York, New York 10022 (212) 751-2600; *The Economist Book of Vital World Statistics.*

United Nations Economic Commission for Africa, Africa Hall, P.O. Box 3001, Addis Ababa, Ethiopia (Telephone Number in U.S. (800) 253-9646); *African Statistical Yearbook.*

U.S. Department of Transportation, Maritime Administration, 400 Seventh Street, SW, Washington, D.C. 20590 (202) 366-5807; *A Statistical Analysis of the World's Merchant Fleets.*

COTE d'IVOIRE - MILITARY

G.K. Hall and Company, 70 Lincoln Street, Boston, Massachusetts 02111 (617) 423-3990; *The World in Figures.*

The International Institute for Strategic Studies, 23 Tavistock Street, London WC2E 7NQ, England; *The Military Balance.*

U.S. Arms Control and Disarmament Agency, 320 Twenty-first Street, NW, Washington, D.C. 20451 (202) 647-8677; *World Military Expenditures and Arms Transfers.*

COTE d'IVOIRE - MILK PRODUCTION - See COTE d'IVOIRE - DAIRY PRODUCTS

COTE d'IVOIRE - MILLET PRODUCTION - See COTE d'IVOIRE - CROPS

COTE d'IVOIRE - MINING AND MINERAL PRODUCTS

Facts on File, 460 Park Avenue South, New York, New York 10016 (800) 443-8323; *The New Book of World Rankings.*

G.K. Hall and Company, 70 Lincoln Street, Boston, Massachusetts 02111 (617) 423-3990; *The World in Figures.*

Penn Well Publishing Company, 1421 South Sheridan Road, P.O. Box 1260, Tulsa, Oklahoma 74101 (800) 752-9764; *International Energy Statistics Sourcebook.*

Statistical Office of the United Nations, Publishing Service, New York, New York 10017 (800) 253-9646; *Statistical Yearbook.*

United Nations Economic Commission for Africa, Africa Hall, P.O. Box 3001, Addis Ababa, Ethiopia (Telephone Number in U.S. (800) 253-9646); *African Statistical Yearbook.*

COTE d'IVOIRE - MONEY EXCHANGE RATE

Euromonitor Publications Limited, 87-88 Turnmill Street, London EC1M 5QU, England; *International Marketing Data and Statistics.*

Statistical Office of the United Nations, Publishing Service, New York, New York 10017 (800) 253-9646; *Statistical Yearbook.*

COTE d'IVOIRE - MONEY RESERVES

Euromonitor Publications Limited, 87-88 Turnmill Street, London EC1M 5QU, England; *International Marketing Data and Statistics.*

COTE d'IVOIRE - MONEY SUPPLY

African Development Bank, 01 BP 1387, Abidjan 01, Cote D'Ivoire; *Selected Statistics on Regional Member Countries.*

Euromonitor Publications Limited, 87-88 Turnmill Street, London EC1M 5QU, England; *International Marketing Data and Statistics.*

G.K. Hall and Company, 70 Lincoln Street, Boston, Massachusetts 02111 (617) 423-3990; *The World in Figures.*

Statistical Office of the United Nations, Publishing Service, New York, New York 10017 (800) 253-9646; *Statistical Yearbook.*

The World Bank, 1818 H Street, NW, Washington, D.C. 20433 (202) 477-1234; *World Tables.*

COTE d'IVOIRE - MOTION PICTURES

Statistical Office of the United Nations, Publishing Service, New York, New York 10017 (800) 253-9646; *Statistical Yearbook.*

United Nations Educational, Scientific and Cultural Organization (UNESCO), 7 Place de Fontenoy, F-75700 Paris, France (Telephone Number in U.S. (212) 963-5981); *Statistical Yearbook.*

COTE d'IVOIRE - MOTOR VEHICLE PRODUCTION

Statistical Office of the United Nations, Publishing Service, New York, New York 10017 (800) 253-9646; *Statistical Yearbook.*

COTE d'IVOIRE - MOTOR VEHICLES IN USE

G.K. Hall and Company, 70 Lincoln Street, Boston, Massachusetts 02111 (617) 423-3990; *The World in Figures.*

International Road Federation, 525 School Street, SW, Washington, D.C. 20024 (202) 554-2106; *World Road Statistics.*

Statistical Office of the United Nations, Publishing Service, New York, New York 10017 (800) 253-9646; *Statistical Yearbook,* and *Survey of Economic and Social Conditions in Africa.*

Times Books, 201 East 50th Street, New York, New York 10022 (212) 751-2600; *The Economist Book of Vital World Statistics.*

COTE d'IVOIRE - MUSEUMS

Facts on File, 460 Park Avenue South, New York, New York 10016 (800) 443-8323; *The New Book of World Rankings.*

COTE d'IVOIRE - NATALITY - See COTE d'IVOIRE - BIRTH RATES

COTE d'IVOIRE - NATIONAL ACCOUNTS

African Development Bank, 01 BP 1387, Abidjan 01, Cote D'Ivoire; *Selected Statistics on Regional Member Countries.*

Statistical Office of the United Nations, Publishing Service, New York, New York 10017 (800) 253-9646; *National Accounts Statistics,* and *Statistical Yearbook.*

United Nations Economic Commission for Africa, Africa Hall, P.O. Box 3001, Addis Ababa, Ethiopia (Telephone Number in U.S. (800) 253-9646); *African Statistical Yearbook.*

COTE d'IVOIRE - NATIONAL INCOME

Facts on File, 460 Park Avenue South, New York, New York 10016 (800) 443-8323; *The New Book of World Rankings.*

G.K. Hall and Company, 70 Lincoln Street, Boston, Massachusetts 02111 (617) 423-3990; *The World in Figures.*

Statistical Office of the United Nations, Publishing Service, New York, New York 10017 (800) 253-9646; *Statistical Yearbook.*

COTE d'IVOIRE - NATIONAL PRODUCT

Facts on File, 460 Park Avenue South, New York, New York 10016 (800) 443-8323; *The New Book of World Rankings.*

Statistical Office of the United Nations, Publishing Service, New York, New York 10017 (800) 253-9646; *Statistical Yearbook.*

COTE d'IVOIRE - NATURAL GAS PRODUCTION - See COTE d'IVOIRE - MINING AND MINERAL PRODUCTS

COTE d'IVOIRE - NATURAL RUBBER PRODUCTION

International Rubber Study Group, York House, 8th Floor, Empire Way, Wembley, London HA9 0PA, England; *Rubber Statistical Bulletin.*

COTE d'IVOIRE - NEWSPAPER PRODUCTION - See COTE d'IVOIRE - FORESTRY AND FOREST PRODUCTS

COTE d'IVOIRE - NEWSPRINT CONSUMPTION - See COTE d'IVOIRE - FORESTRY AND FOREST PRODUCTS

COTE d'IVOIRE - OCCUPATIONS - See COTE d'IVOIRE - LABOR FORCE

COTE d'IVOIRE - PALM OIL AND PALM KERNELS PRODUCTION - See COTE d'IVOIRE - CROPS

COTE d'IVOIRE - PAPER - See COTE d'IVOIRE - FORESTRY AND FOREST PRODUCTS

COTE d'IVOIRE - PEANUT PRODUCTION - See COTE d'IVOIRE - CROPS

COTE d'IVOIRE - PERIODICALS

United Nations Educational, Scientific and Cultural Organization (UNESCO), 7 Place de Fontenoy, F-75700 Paris, France (Telephone Number in U.S. (212) 963-5981); *Statistical Yearbook.*

COTE d'IVOIRE - PESTICIDE USE

Food and Agricultural Organization of the United Nations (FAO) Via delle Terme di Caracalla, 00100 Rome, Italy (Telephone Number in U.S. (202) 653-2400); *The State of Food and Agriculture.*

COTE d'IVOIRE - PETROLEUM INDUSTRY

Facts on File, 460 Park Avenue South, New York, New York 10016 (800) 443-8323; *The New Book of World Rankings.*

Food and Agricultural Organization of the United Nations (FAO) Via delle Terme di Caracalla, 00100 Rome, Italy (Telephone Number in U.S. (202) 653-2400); *The State of Food and Agriculture.*

G.K. Hall and Company, 70 Lincoln Street, Boston, Massachusetts 02111 (617) 423-3990; *The World in Figures.*

Penn Well Publishing Company, 1421 South Sheridan Road, P.O. Box 1260, Tulsa, Oklahoma 74101 (800) 752-9764; *International Energy Statistics Sourcebook.*

Statistical Office of the United Nations, Publishing Service, New York, New York 10017 (800) 253-9646; *Statistical Yearbook.*

COTE d'IVOIRE - PIGS - See COTE d'IVOIRE - LIVESTOCK AND POULTRY

COTE d'IVOIRE - POPULATION

African Development Bank, 01 BP 1387, Abidjan 01, Cote D'Ivoire; *Selected Statistics on Regional Member Countries.*

The Economist Intelligence Unit, 111 West 57th Street, New York, New York 10019 (800) 938-4685; *The World Market Atlas.*

Euromonitor Publications Limited, 87-88 Turnmill Street, London EC1M 5QU, England; *International Marketing Data and Statistics.*

Facts on File, 460 Park Avenue South, New York, New York 10016 (800) 443-8323; *The New Book of World Rankings.*

Food and Agricultural Organization of the United Nations (FAO), Via delle Terme di Caracalla, 00100 Rome, Italy (Telephone Number in U.S. (202) 653-2400); *Production Yearbook.*

G.K. Hall and Company, 70 Lincoln Street, Boston, Massachusetts 02111 (617) 423-3990; *The World in Figures.*

International Labour Office, I.L.O. Publications, CH-1211, Geneva 22, Switzerland; *Yearbook of Labour Statistics.*

Statistical Office of the United Nations, Publishing Service, New York, New York 10017 (800) 253-9646; *Demographic Yearbook, Statistical Yearbook,* and *Survey of Economic and Social Conditions in Africa.*

Times Books, 201 East 50th Street, New York, New York 10022 (212) 751-2600; *The Economist Book of Vital World Statistics.*

United Nations Educational, Scientific and Cultural Organization (UNESCO), 7 Place de Fontenoy, F-75700 Paris, France (Telephone Number in U.S. (212) 963-5981; *Statistical Yearbook.*

U.S. Arms Control and Disarmament Agency, 320 Twenty-first Street, NW, Washington, D.C. 20451 (202) 647-8677; *World Military Expenditures and Arms Transfers.*

World Health Organization, Office of Publications, Avenue Appia, CH-1211 Geneva 27, Switzerland (Telephone Number in U.S. (518) 436-9686); *World Health Statistics Annual.*

COTE d'IVOIRE - POST OFFICES

Facts on File, 460 Park Avenue South, New York, New York 10016 (800) 443-8323; *The New Book of World Rankings.*

COTE d'IVOIRE - POTATO PRODUCTION - See COTE d'IVOIRE - CROPS

COTE d'IVOIRE - PRICES

Facts on File, 460 Park Avenue South, New York, New York 10016 (800) 443-8323; *The New Book of World Rankings.*

Food and Agricultural Organization of the United Nations (FAO), Via delle Terme di Caracalla, 00100 Rome, Italy (Telephone Number in U.S. (202) 653-2400); *Production Yearbook,* and *The State of Food and Agriculture.*

G.K. Hall and Company, 70 Lincoln Street, Boston, Massachusetts 02111 (617) 423-3990; *The World in Figures.*

International Rubber Study Group, York House, 8th Floor, Empire Way, Wembley, London HA9 0PA, England; *Rubber Statistical Bulletin.*

United Nations Economic Commission for Africa, Africa Hall, P.O. Box 3001, Addis Ababa, Ethiopia (Telephone Number in U.S. (800) 253-9646); *African Statistical Yearbook.*

COTE d'IVOIRE - PRINTING AND WRITING PAPER - See COTE d'IVOIRE - FORESTRY AND FOREST PRODUCTS

COTE d'IVOIRE - PRODUCTION

Facts on File, 460 Park Avenue South, New York, New York 10016 (800) 443-8323; *The New Book of World Rankings.*

G.K. Hall and Company, 70 Lincoln Street, Boston, Massachusetts 02111 (617) 423-3990; *The World in Figures.*

International Rubber Study Group, York House, 8th Floor, Empire Way, Wembley, London HA9 0PA, England; *Rubber Statistical Bulletin.*

COTE d'IVOIRE - PRODUCTIVITY

Euromonitor Publications Limited, 87-88 Turnmill Street, London EC1M 5QU, England; *International Marketing Data and Statistics.*

COTE d'IVOIRE - PUBLIC FINANCE

Facts on File, 460 Park Avenue South, New York, New York 10016 (800) 443-8323; *The New Book of World Rankings.*

COTE d'IVOIRE - RADIO BROADCASTING - See COTE d'IVOIRE - BROADCASTING

COTE d'IVOIRE - RADIO RECEIVER PRODUCTION

Statistical Office of the United Nations, Publishing Service, New York, New York 10017 (800) 253-9646; *Statistical Yearbook.*

COTE d'IVOIRE - RAILWAYS

G.K. Hall and Company, 70 Lincoln Street, Boston, Massachusetts 02111 (617) 423-3990; *The World in Figures.*

Jane's Information Group, Sentinel House, 163 Brighton Road, Coulsdon, Surrey CR5 2NH, England (Telephone Number in U.S. (703) 683-3700); *Jane's World Railways.*

Statistical Office of the United Nations, Publishing Service, New York, New York 10017 (800) 253-9646; *Statistical Yearbook,* and *Survey of Economic and Social Conditions in Africa.*

United Nations Economic Commission for Africa, Africa Hall, P.O. Box 3001, Addis Ababa, Ethiopia (Telephone Number in U.S. (800) 253-9646); *African Statistical Yearbook.*

COTE d'IVOIRE - RELIGION

Facts on File, 460 Park Avenue South, New York, New York 10016 (800) 443-8323; *The New Book of World Rankings.*

COTE d'IVOIRE - RETAIL TRADE

G.K. Hall and Company, 70 Lincoln Street, Boston, Massachusetts 02111 (617) 423-3990; *The World in Figures.*

COTE d'IVOIRE - RICE PRODUCTION - See COTE d'IVOIRE - CROPS

COTE d'IVOIRE - ROOT AND TUBER PRODUCTION - See COTE d'IVOIRE - CROPS

COTE d'IVOIRE - ROUNDWOOD PRODUCTION - See COTE d'IVOIRE - FORESTRY AND FOREST PRODUCTS

COTE d'IVOIRE - RUBBER PRODUCTION AND CONSUMPTION

Facts on File, 460 Park Avenue South, New York, New York 10016 (800) 443-8323; *The New Book of World Rankings.*

International Rubber Study Group, York House, 8th Floor, Empire Way, Wembley, London HA9 0PA, England; *Rubber Statistical Bulletin.*

Statistical Office of the United Nations, Publishing Service, New York, New York 10017 (800) 253-9646; *Statistical Yearbook.*

COTE d'IVOIRE - SAWNWOOD PRODUCTION - See COTE d'IVOIRE - FORESTRY AND FOREST PRODUCTS

COTE d'IVOIRE - SCIENCE AND TECHNOLOGY - EXPENDITURE FOR RESEARCH

Statistical Office of the United Nations, Publishing Service, New York, New York 10017 (800) 253-9646; *Statistical Yearbook.*

COTE d'IVOIRE - SCIENTISTS AND ENGINEERS

United Nations Educational, Scientific and Cultural Organization (UNESCO), 7 Place de Fontenoy, F-75700 Paris, France (Telephone Number in U.S. (212) 963-5981); *Statistical Yearbook.*

COTE d'IVOIRE - SCIENTISTS AND TECHNICIANS

Statistical Office of the United Nations, Publishing Service, New York, New York 10017 (800) 253-9646; *Statistical Yearbook.*

COTE d'IVOIRE - SENIOR CITIZENS

Facts on File, 460 Park Avenue South, New York, New York 10016 (800) 443-8323; *The New Book of World Rankings.*

COTE d'IVOIRE - SESAME SEED PRODUCTION - See COTE d'IVOIRE - CROPS

COTE d'IVOIRE - SHEEP - See COTE d'IVOIRE - LIVESTOCK AND POULTRY

COTE d'IVOIRE - SILVER PRODUCTION AND CONSUMPTION - See COTE d'IVOIRE - MINING AND MINERAL PRODUCTS

COTE d'IVOIRE - SOCIAL DATA

African Development Bank, 01 BP 1387, Abidjan 01, Cote D'Ivoire; *Selected Statistics on Regional Member Countries.*

Facts on File, 460 Park Avenue South, New York, New York 10016 (800) 443-8323; *The New Book of World Rankings.*

COTE d'IVOIRE - STATE BUDGET REVENUE AND EXPENDITURES

Euromonitor Publications Limited, 87-88 Turnmill Street, London EC1M 5QU, England; *International Marketing Data and Statistics.*

COTE d'IVOIRE - STEEL - See COTE d'IVOIRE - MINING AND MINERAL PRODUCTS

COTE d'IVOIRE - SOCIAL DATA

G.K. Hall and Company, 70 Lincoln Street, Boston, Massachusetts 02111 (617) 423-3990; *The World in Figures.*

COTE d'IVOIRE - STOCKS - COMMODITY - MARKET PRICE - INDEX

Food and Agricultural Organization of the United Nations (FAO) Via delle Terme di Caracalla, 00100 Rome, Italy (Telephone Number in U.S. (202) 653-2400); *The State of Food and Agriculture.*

COTE d'IVOIRE - SUGAR PRODUCTION - See COTE d'IVOIRE - CROPS

COTE d'IVOIRE - TAXATION

G.K. Hall and Company, 70 Lincoln Street, Boston, Massachusetts 02111 (617) 423-3990; *The World in Figures.*

International Road Federation, 525 School Street, SW, Washington, D.C. 20024 (202) 554-2106; *World Road Statistics.*

The World Bank, 1818 H Street, NW, Washington, D.C. 20433 (202) 477-1234; *World Tables.*

COTE d'IVOIRE - TELEGRAPH SERVICE

Statistical Office of the United Nations, Publishing Service, New York, New York 10017 (800) 253-9646; *Statistical Yearbook.*

COTE d'IVOIRE - TELEPHONES IN USE

American Telephone and Telegraph Company, 26 Parsippany Road, Indianapolis, Indiana 46219 (800) 338-4058; *The World's Telephones.*

G.K. Hall and Company, 70 Lincoln Street, Boston, Massachusetts 02111 (617) 423-3990; *The World in Figures.*

Statistical Office of the United Nations, Publishing Service, New York, New York 10017 (800) 253-9646; *Statistical Yearbook.*

COTE d'IVOIRE - TELEVISION BROADCASTING - See COTE d'IVOIRE - BROADCASTING

COTE d'IVOIRE - TEXTILE INDUSTRY

G.K. Hall and Company, 70 Lincoln Street, Boston, Massachusetts 02111 (617) 423-3990; *The World in Figures.*

COTE d'IVOIRE - TIRE (MOTOR VEHICLE) PRODUCTION

International Rubber Study Group, York House, 8th Floor, Empire Way, Wembley, London HA9 0PA, England; *Rubber Statistical Bulletin.*

COTE d'IVOIRE - TOBACCO PRODUCTION

Facts on File, 460 Park Avenue South, New York, New York 10016 (800) 443-8323; *The New Book of World Rankings.*

Statistical Office of the United Nations, Publishing Service, New York, New York 10017 (800) 253-9646; *Statistical Yearbook.*

COTE d'IVOIRE - TOURISM

Facts on File, 460 Park Avenue South, New York, New York 10016 (800) 443-8323; *The New Book of World Rankings.*

G.K. Hall and Company, 70 Lincoln Street, Boston, Massachusetts 02111 (617) 423-3990; *The World in Figures.*

Statistical Office of the United Nations, Publishing Service, New York, New York 10017 (800) 253-9646; *Statistical Yearbook.*

Times Books, 201 East 50th Street, New York, New York 10022 (212) 751-2600; *The Economist Book of Vital World Statistics.*

World Tourism Organization, Calle Capitan Haya 42, E-28020 Madrid, Spain; *Yearbook of Tourism Statistics.*

United Nations Economic Commission for Africa, Africa Hall, P.O. Box 3001, Addis Ababa, Ethiopia (Telephone Number in U.S. (800) 253-9646); *African Statistical Yearbook.*

COTE d'IVOIRE - TRACTORS IN USE

Statistical Office of the United Nations, Publishing Service, New York, New York 10017 (800) 253-9646; *Statistical Yearbook.*

COTE d'IVOIRE - TRADE - See COTE d'IVOIRE - FOREIGN TRADE

COTE d'IVOIRE - TRANSPORTATION AND COMMUNICATIONS

Facts on File, 460 Park Avenue South, New York, New York 10016 (800) 443-8323; *The New Book of World Rankings.*

G.K. Hall and Company, 70 Lincoln Street, Boston, Massachusetts 02111 (617) 423-3990; *The World in Figures.*

United Nations Economic Commission for Africa, Africa Hall, P.O. Box 3001, Addis Ababa, Ethiopia (Telephone Number in U.S. (800) 253-9646); *African Statistical Yearbook.*

COTE d'IVOIRE - UNEMPLOYMENT

Euromonitor Publications Limited, 87-88 Turnmill Street, London EC1M 5QU, England; *International Marketing Data and Statistics.*

COTE d'IVOIRE - VITAL STATISTICS

Euromonitor Publications Limited, 87-88 Turnmill Street, London EC1M 5QU, England; *International Marketing Data and Statistics.*

G.K. Hall and Company, 70 Lincoln Street, Boston, Massachusetts 02111 (617) 423-3990; *The World in Figures.*

Statistical Office of the United Nations, Publishing Service, New York, New York 10017 (800) 253-9646; *Statistical Yearbook.*

World Health Organization, Office of Publications, Avenue Appia, CH-1211 Geneva 27, Switzerland; *World Health Statistics Annual.*

COTE d'IVOIRE - WAGES

G.K. Hall and Company, 70 Lincoln Street, Boston, Massachusetts 02111 (617) 423-3990; *The World in Figures.*

COTE d'IVOIRE - WEATHER

Facts on File, 460 Park Avenue South, New York, New York 10016 (800) 443-8323; *The New Book of World Rankings.*

G.K. Hall and Company, 70 Lincoln Street, Boston, Massachusetts 02111 (617) 423-3990; *The World in Figures.*

COTE d'IVOIRE - WHEAT - See COTE d'IVOIRE - CROPS

COTE d'IVOIRE - WHOLESALE PRICES

Statistical Office of the United Nations, Publishing Service, New York, New York 10017 (800) 253-9646; *Statistical Yearbook.*

COTE d'IVOIRE - WINE PRODUCTION

Facts on File, 460 Park Avenue South, New York, New York 10016 (800) 443-8323; *The New Book of World Rankings.*

COTE d'IVOIRE - WOOL PRODUCTION

Facts on File, 460 Park Avenue South, New York, New York 10016 (800) 443-8323; *The New Book of World Rankings.*

COTE d'IVOIRE - YARN PRODUCTION

Statistical Office of the United Nations, Publishing Service, New York, New York 10017 (800) 253-9646; *Statistical Yearbook.*

COTTON - ACREAGE

U.S. Department of Agriculture, National Agricultural Statistics Service, Fourteenth Street and Independence Avenue, SW, Washington, D.C. 20250 (202) 219-1504; *Agricultural Statistics, Crop Production, Crop Values, Field Crops,* and *Cotton and Wool Outlook Statistics.*

COTTON - COMMODITY CREDIT CORPORATION TRANSACTIONS

U.S. Department of Agriculture, Agricultural Stabilization and Conservation Service, Fourteenth Street and Independence Avenue, SW, Washington, D.C. 20250 (202) 720-5237; *Agricultural Outlook,* and *Commodity Credit Corporation Report of Financial Condition and Operations.*

COTTON - CONSUMPTION

Fiber Economics Bureau, Incorporated, 101 Eisenhower Parkway, Roseland, New Jersey 07068 (201) 228-1107; *Textile Organon.*

U.S. Department of Agriculture, Economic Research Service, Fourteenth Street and Independence Avenue, SW, Washington, D.C. 20005-4789 (202) 219-1504; *Cotton and Wool Outlook and Situation.*

COTTON - FARM MARKETINGS - SALES

U.S. Department of Agriculture, Economic Research Service, Fourteenth Street and Independence Avenue, SW, Washington, D.C. 20004-4789 (202) 219-1504; *Economic Indicators of the Farm Sector: National Financial Summary,* and *Economic Indicators of the Farm Sector: State Financial Summary.*

COTTON - FOREIGN TRADE

Fiber Economics Bureau, 101 Eisenhower Parkway, Roseland, New Jersey 07068 (201) 228-1107; *Textile Organon.*

U.S. Department of Agriculture, Economic Research Service, Fourteenth Street and Independence Avenue, SW, Washington, D.C. 20005-4789 (202) 219-1504; *Cotton and Wool Outlook Statistics, Foreign Agricultural Trade of the U.S., Agricultural Statistics,* and unpublished data.

U.S. Department of Agriculture, Foreign Agricultural Service, Fourteenth Street and Independence Avenue, SW, Washington, D.C. 20250 (202) 720-3448; *Foreign Agricultural Commodity Circular Series.*

U.S. Department of Agriculture, National Agricultural Statistics Service, Fourteenth Street and Independence Avenue, SW, Washington, D.C. 20250 (202) 219-1504; *Crop Production,* and *Crop Values.*

U.S. Department of Commerce, Bureau of the Census, Suitland, Maryland 20233 (310) 763-4040; *U.S. Merchandise Trade.*

COTTON - PRICES

U.S. Department of Agriculture, National Agricultural Statistics Service, Fourteenth Street and Independence Avenue, SW, Washington, D.C. 20250 (202) 219-1504; *Agricultural Statistics, Crop Production, Crop Values, Field Crops,* and *Agricultural Prices: Annual Summary.*

COTTON - PRODUCTION

U.S. Department of Agriculture, Economic Research Service, Fourteenth Street and Independence Avenue, SW, Washington, D.C. 20005-4789 (202) 219-1504; *Agricultural Statistics, Crop Production, Crop Values, Field Crops, Cotton and Wool Outlook Statistics, Agricultural Outlook,* and *Economic Indicators of the Farm Sector: Production and Efficiency Statistics.*

U.S. Department of Agriculture, Foreign Agricultural Service, Fourteenth Street and Independence Avenue, SW, Washington, D.C. 20250 (202) 720-3448; *Foreign Agricultural Commodity Circular Series.*

COTTON - PRODUCTION - WORLD

Food and Agricultural Organization of the U.N. (FAO), Via delle Terme di Caracalla, 00100 Rome, Italy (Telephone Number in U.S.

(202) 653-2400); *FAO Production Yearbook.*

Statistical Office of the United Nations, Publishing Service, New York, New York 10017 (800) 253-9646; *Monthly Bulletin of Statistics.*

U.S. Department of Agriculture, Foreign Agricultural Service, Fourteenth Street and Independence Avenue, SW, Washington, D.C. 20250 (202) 720-3448; *Foreign Agricultural Commodity Circular Series.*

COTTON - SUPPLY AND DISAPPEARANCE

U.S. Department of Agriculture, Economic Research Service, Fourteenth Street and Independence Avenue, SW, Washington, D.C. 20005-4789 (202) 219-1504; *Cotton and Wool Outlook Statistics,* and *Agricultural Supply and Demand Estimates.*

COUNTY GOVERNMENTS

U.S. Department of Commerce, Bureau of the Census, Suitland, Maryland 20233 (310) 763-4040; *Census of Governments, Government Organization, Government Units,* and *County Government Finances.*

COUNTY GOVERNMENTS - ELECTED OFFICIALS

Center for the American Woman and Politics, The Eagleton Institute of Politics, Rutgers University, New Brunswick, New Jersey 08901 (908) 828-2210; Information releases.

Joint Center for Political and Economic Studies, 1090 Vermont Avenue, NW, Suite 1100, Washington, D.C. 20005 (202) 789-3500; *Black Elected Officials: A National Roster.*

National Association of Latino Elected and Appointed Officials, NALEO Education Fund, 3409 Garnet Street, Los Angeles, California 90023 (213) 262-8503; *National Roster of Hispanic Elected Officials.*

COUNTY GOVERNMENTS - FINANCES

U.S. Department of Commerce, Bureau of the Census, Suitland, Maryland 20233 (310) 763-4040; *County Government Finances.*

COURTS

Administrative Office of the United States Courts, United States Supreme Court Building, Columbus Circle, NE, Washington, D.C. 20544 (202) 273-1120; *Annual Report of the Director,* and unpublished data.

National Center for Juvenile Justice, 701 Forbes Avenue, Pittsburgh, Pennsylvania 15219 (412) 227-6950; *Juvenile Court Statistics.*

U.S. Department Of Justice, Bureau of Justice Statistics, 633 Indiana Avenue, NW, Washington, D.C. 20531 (800) 732-3277; *Justice Expenditure and Employment in the U.S.*

COURTS - APPEALS COURTS, UNITED STATES

Administrative Office of the United States Courts, United States Supreme Court Building, Columbus Circle, NE, Washington, D.C. 20544 (202) 273-1120; *Annual Report of the Director.*

COURTS - DISTRICT COURTS, UNITED STATES

Administrative Office of the United States Courts, United States Supreme Court Building, Columbus Circle, NE, Washington, D.C. 20544 (202) 273-1120; *Annual Report of the Director.*

COURTS - JUVENILE COURT CASES HANDLED

National Center for Juvenile Justice, 701 Forbes Avenue, Pittsburgh, Pennsylvania 15219 (412) 227-6950; *Juvenile Court Statistics.*

COURTS - PUBLIC OFFICIALS - PROSECUTIONS

U.S. Department of Justice, Constitution Avenue and Tenth Street, NW, Washington, D.C. 20530 (202) 514-2000; *Federal Prosecutions of Corrupt Public Officials,* and *Report to Congress on the Activities and Operations of the Public Integrity Section.*

COURTS - SENTENCING

U.S. Department of Justice, Bureau of Justice Statistics, 633 Indiana Avenue, NW, Washington, D.C. 20531 (800) 732-3277; *Federal Criminal Case Processing.*

COURTS - SUPREME COURT, UNITED STATES

Administrative Office of the United States Courts, United States Supreme Court Building, Columbus Circle, NE, Washington, D.C. 20544 (202) 273-1120; unpublished data.

COWS - See also DAIRY PRODUCTS

COWS

U.S. Department of Agriculture, National Agricultural Statistics Service, Fourteenth Street and Independence Avenue, SW, Washington, D.C. 20250 (202) 219-1504; *Agricultural Statistics, Meat Animals - Production, Disposition, and Income, Dairy Products,* and *Milk Production, Disposition, and Income.*

CRABS

U.S. Department of Commerce, National Oceanic and Atmospheric Administration, National Marine Fisheries Service, 1335 East-West Highway, Silver Spring, Maryland 20910 (301) 427-2239; *Fishery Statistics of the United States,* and *Fisheries of the United States.*

CRACK

U.S. Department of Health and Human Services, Substance Abuse and Mental Health Administration, 5600 Fishers Lane, Rockville, Maryland 20857 (301) 443-4797; *National Household Survey on Drug Abuse.*

CRANBERRIES

U.S. Department of Agriculture, National Agricultural Statistics Service, Fourteenth Street and Independence Avenue, SW, Washington, D.C. 20250 (202) 219-1504; *Agricultural Outlook,* and *Noncitrus Fruits and Nuts.*

CREDIT CARDS

American Bankers Association, 1120 Connecticut Avenue, NW, Washington, D.C. 20036 (202) 663-5000; *Consumer Credit Delinquency Bulletin.*

Board of Governors of the Federal Reserve System, Twentieth Street and Constitution Avenue, NW, Washington, D.C. 20551 (202) 452-3000; *Federal Reserve Bulletin, Annual Statistical Digest,* and unpublished data.

HSN Consultants, Incorporated, 300 Esplanade Drive, Suite 1790, Oxnard, California 93030 (310) 392-8478; *The Nilson Report.*

CREDIT MARKETS

Board of Governors of the Federal Reserve System, Twentieth Street and Constitution Avenue, NW, Washington, D.C. 20551 (202) 452-3000; *Federal Reserve Bulletin, Annual Statistical Digest,* and unpublished data.

Executive Office of the President, Office of Management and Budget, Executive Office Building, Washington, D.C. 20503 (202) 395-3080; *Analytical Perspectives, Budget of the United States Government.*

CREDIT UNIONS

Board of Governors of the Federal Reserve System, Twentieth Street and Constitution Avenue, NW, Washington, D.C. 20551 (202) 452-3000; *Annual Statistical Digest,* and *Federal Reserve Bulletin.*

National Credit Union Administration, 1776 G Street, NW, Washington, D.C. 20456 (202) 682-9600; *Annual Report of the National Credit Union Administration, National Credit Union Administration Year End Statistics,* and unpublished data.

CREDIT UNIONS - ESTABLISHMENTS

National Credit Union Administration, 1776 G Street, NW, Washington, D.C. 20456 (202) 682-9600; *Annual Report of the National Credit Union Administration, National Credit Union Administration Year End Statistics,* and unpublished data.

CREDIT UNIONS - FINANCES

Board of Governors of the Federal Reserve System, Twentieth Street and Constitution Avenue, NW, Washington, D.C. 20551 (202) 452-3000; *Annual Statistical Digest, Federal Reserve Bulletin,* and unpublished data.

National Credit Union Administration, 1776 G Street, NW, Washington, D.C. 20456 (202) 682-9600; *Annual Report of the National Credit Union Administration, National Credit Union Administration Year End Statistics,* and unpublished data.

CREDIT UNIONS - INDIVIDUAL RETIREMENT ACCOUNTS

Investment Company Institute, 1600 M Street, NW, Suite 600, Washington, D.C. 20036 (202) 293-7700; *Mutual Fund Fact Book.*

CRIME - See also CRIMINAL VICTIMIZATION and LAW ENFORCEMENT

CRIME - ASSAULT

U.S. Department of Justice, Bureau of Justice Statistics, 633 Indiana Avenue, NW, Washington, D.C. 20531 (800) 732-3277; *Criminal Victimization in the United States,* and unpublished data.

U.S. Department of Justice, Federal Bureau of Investigation, Ninth Street and Pennsylvania Avenue, NW, Washington, D.C. 20535 (202) 324-3000; *Crime in the United States.*

CRIME - AVERAGE VALUE LOST

U.S. Department of Justice, Federal Bureau of Investigation, Ninth Street and Pennsylvania Avenue, NW, Washington, D.C. 20535 (202) 324-3000; *Population at Risk Rates and Selected Crime Indicators.*

CRIME - BURGLARY

U.S. Department of Justice, Bureau of Justice Statistics, 633 Indiana Avenue, NW, Washington, D.C. 20531 (800) 732-3277; *Crime and the Nation's Households,* and *Criminal Victimization in the U.S.*

U.S. Department of Justice, Federal Bureau of Investigation, Ninth Street and Pennsylvania Avenue, NW, Washington, D.C. 20535 (202) 324-3000; *Crime in the United States,* and *Population at Risk Rates and Selected Crime Indicators.*

CRIME - CHILD ABUSE AND NEGLECT

U.S. Department of Health and Human Services, National Center on Child Abuse and Neglect, 370 L'Enfant Promenade, SW, Washington, D.C. 20447 (202) 205-8586; *National Child Abuse and Neglect Data System, Working Paper 2, Summary Data Component,* and *Child Maltreatment.*

CRIME - DRUG ABUSE VIOLATIONS

Administrative Office of the United States Courts, United States Supreme Court Building, Columbus Circle, NE, Washington, D.C. 20544 (202) 273-1120; *Annual Report of the Director.*

U.S. Department of Justice, Bureau of Justice Statistics, 633 Indiana Avenue, NW, Washington, D.C. 20531 (800) 732-3277; *Drug Use Forecasting,* and *Federal Criminal Case Processing.*

CRIME - HOMICIDES - RACE AND SEX

U.S. Department of Health and Human Services, National Center for Health Statistics, 3700 East-West Highway, Hyattsville, Maryland 20782 (301) 436-8500; *Vital Statistics of the United States,* and unpublished data.

CRIME - IMMIGRATION VIOLATIONS

U.S. Department of Justice, Immigration and Naturalization Service, 425 I Street, NW, Washington, D.C. 20536 (202) 514-4316; *Statistical Yearbook,* and unpublished data.

CRIME - LARCENY - THEFT

U.S. Department of Justice, Bureau of Justice Statistics, 633 Indiana Avenue, NW, Washington, D.C. 20531 (800) 732-3277; *Criminal Victimization in the U.S.*

U.S. Department of Justice, Federal Bureau of Investigation, Ninth Street and Pennsylvania Avenue, NW, Washington, D.C. 20535 (202) 324-3000; *Crime in the United States,* and *Population at Risk Rates and Selected Crime Indicators.*

CRIME - MOTOR VEHICLE THEFT

U.S. Department of Justice, Bureau of Justice Statistics, 633 Indiana Avenue, NW, Washington, D.C. 20531 (800) 732-3277; *Crime and the Nation's Households,* and *Criminal Victimization in the U.S.*

U.S. Department of Justice, Federal Bureau of Investigation, Ninth Street and Pennsylvania Avenue, NW, Washington, D.C. 20535 (202) 324-3000; *Crime in the United States.*

CRIME - MURDER - MURDER CIRCUMSTANCES

U.S. Department of Justice, Federal Bureau of Investigation, Ninth Street and Pennsylvania Avenue, NW, Washington, D.C. 20535 (202) 324-3000; *Crime in the United States.*

CRIME - PLACE AND TIME OF OCCURRENCE

U.S. Department of Justice, Bureau of Justice Statistics, 633 Indiana Avenue, NW, Washington, D.C. 20531 (800) 732-3277; *Criminal Victimization in the United States.*

CRIME - POLICE OFFICERS ASSAULTED, KILLED

U.S. Department of Justice, Federal Bureau of Investigation, Ninth Street and Pennsylvania Avenue, NW, Washington, D.C. 20535 (202) 324-3000; *Law Enforcement Officers Killed and Assaulted.*

CRIME - PROPERTY CRIME

U.S. Department of Justice, Federal Bureau of Investigation, Ninth Street and Pennsylvania Avenue, NW, Washington, D.C. 20535 (202) 324-3000; *Crime in the United States.*

CRIME - RAPE, FORCIBLE

U.S. Department of Justice, Federal Bureau of Investigation, Ninth Street and Pennsylvania Avenue, NW, Washington, D.C. 20535 (202) 324-3000; *Crime in the United States,* and *Population at Risk Rates and Selected Crime Indicators.*

CRIME - ROBBERY

U.S. Department of Justice, Federal Bureau of Investigation, Ninth Street and Pennsylvania Avenue, NW, Washington, D.C. 20535 (202) 324-3000; *Crime in the United States,* and *Population at Risk Rates and Selected Crime Indicators.*

CRIME - SHOPLIFTING

U.S. Department of Justice, Federal Bureau of Investigation, Ninth Street and Pennsylvania Avenue, NW, Washington, D.C. 20535 (202) 324-3000; *Crime in the United States,* and *Population at Risk Rates and Selected Crime Indicators.*

CRIME - VIOLENT CRIME

U.S. Department of Justice, Federal Bureau of Investigation, Ninth Street and Pennsylvania Avenue, NW, Washington, D.C. 20535 (202) 324-3000; *Crime in the United States,* and *Criminal Victimization in the United States.*

CRIMINAL VICTIMIZATION

U.S. Department of Justice, Bureau of Justice Statistics, 633 Indiana Avenue, NW, Washington, D.C. 20531 (800) 732-3277; *Crime and the Nation's Households,* and *Criminal Victimization in the United States.*

CRIMINAL VICTIMIZATION - HOUSEHOLDS

U.S. Department of Justice, Bureau of Justice Statistics, 633 Indiana Avenue, NW, Washington, D.C. 20531 (800) 732-3277; *Crime and the Nation's Households.*

CROAKER

U.S. Department of Commerce, National Oceanic and Atmospheric Administration, National Marine Fisheries Service, 1335 East-West Highway, Silver Spring, Maryland 20910 (301) 427-2239; *Fisheries of the United States.*

CROATIA - See also YUGOSLAVIA

CROATIA - AGRICULTURE

Encyclopedia Britannica, Incorporated, 310 South Michigan Avenue, Chicago, Illinois 60604 (312) 347-7000; *Britannica World Data.*

CROATIA - AIRLINE SERVICE

Encyclopedia Britannica, Incorporated, 310 South Michigan Avenue, Chicago, Illinois 60604 (312) 347-7000; *Britannica World Data.*

CROATIA - BIRTH RATES

Encyclopedia Britannica, Incorporated, 310 South Michigan Avenue, Chicago, Illinois 60604 (312) 347-7000; *Britannica World Data.*

CROATIA - CONSTRUCTION

Encyclopedia Britannica, Incorporated, 310 South Michigan Avenue, Chicago, Illinois 60604 (312) 347-7000; *Britannica World Data.*

CROATIA - DEMOGRAPHY

Encyclopedia Britannica, Incorporated, 310 South Michigan Avenue, Chicago, Illinois 60604 (312) 347-7000; *Britannica World Data.*

CROATIA - DIVORCE RATES

Encyclopedia Britannica, Incorporated, 310 South Michigan Avenue, Chicago, Illinois 60604 (312) 347-7000; *Britannica World Data.*

CROATIA - ECONOMY

Encyclopedia Britannica, Incorporated, 310 South Michigan Avenue, Chicago, Illinois 60604 (312) 347-7000; *Britannica World Data.*

CROATIA - EDUCATION

Encyclopedia Britannica, Incorporated, 310 South Michigan Avenue, Chicago, Illinois 60604 (312) 347-7000; *Britannica World Data.*

CROATIA - ENERGY PRODUCTION

Encyclopedia Britannica, Incorporated, 310 South Michigan Avenue, Chicago, Illinois 60604 (312) 347-7000; *Britannica World Data.*

CROATIA - EXPORTS

Encyclopedia Britannica, Incorporated, 310 South Michigan Avenue, Chicago, Illinois 60604 (312) 347-7000; *Britannica World Data.*

CROATIA - FERTILITY RATES

Encyclopedia Britannica, Incorporated, 310 South Michigan Avenue, Chicago, Illinois 60604 (312) 347-7000; *Britannica World Data.*

CROATIA - FISHERIES

Encyclopedia Britannica, Incorporated, 310 South Michigan Avenue, Chicago, Illinois 60604 (312) 347-7000; *Britannica World Data.*

CROATIA - FOREIGN TRADE

Encyclopedia Britannica, Incorporated, 310 South Michigan Avenue, Chicago, Illinois 60604 (312) 347-7000; *Britannica World Data.*

CROATIA - FORESTRY AND FOREST PRODUCTS

Encyclopedia Britannica, Incorporated, 310 South Michigan Avenue, Chicago, Illinois 60604 (312) 347-7000; *Britannica World Data.*

CROATIA - HEALTH

Encyclopedia Britannica, Incorporated, 310 South Michigan Avenue, Chicago, Illinois 60604 (312) 347-7000; *Britannica World Data.*

CROATIA - HIGHWAYS

Encyclopedia Britannica, Incorporated, 310 South Michigan Avenue, Chicago, Illinois 60604 (312) 347-7000; *Britannica World Data.*

CROATIA - IMPORTS

Encyclopedia Britannica, Incorporated, 310 South Michigan Avenue, Chicago, Illinois 60604 (312) 347-7000; *Britannica World Data.*

CROATIA - LAND USE

Encyclopedia Britannica, Incorporated, 310 South Michigan Avenue, Chicago, Illinois 60604 (312) 347-7000; *Britannica World Data.*

CROATIA - LIVESTOCK AND POULTRY

Encyclopedia Britannica, Incorporated, 310 South Michigan Avenue, Chicago, Illinois 60604 (312) 347-7000; *Britannica World Data.*

CROATIA - MANUFACTURING

Encyclopedia Britannica, Incorporated, 310 South Michigan Avenue, Chicago, Illinois 60604 (312) 347-7000; *Britannica World Data.*

CROATIA - MARRIAGE RATES

Encyclopedia Britannica, Incorporated, 310 South Michigan Avenue, Chicago, Illinois 60604 (312) 347-7000; *Britannica World Data.*

CROATIA - MILITARY

The International Institute for Strategic Studies, 23 Tavistock Street, London WC2E 7NQ, England; *The Military Balance.*

CROATIA - MINING AND MINERAL PRODUCTS

Encyclopedia Britannica, Incorporated, 310 South Michigan Avenue, Chicago, Illinois 60604 (312) 347-7000; *Britannica World Data.*

CROATIA - POPULATION

Encyclopedia Britannica, Incorporated, 310 South Michigan Avenue, Chicago, Illinois 60604 (312) 347-7000; *Britannica World Data.*

CROATIA - RADIO RECEIVERS

Encyclopedia Britannica, Incorporated, 310 South Michigan Avenue, Chicago, Illinois 60604 (312) 347-7000; *Britannica World Data.*

CROATIA - RAILWAYS

Encyclopedia Britannica, Incorporated, 310 South Michigan Avenue, Chicago, Illinois 60604 (312) 347-7000; *Britannica World Data.*

CROATIA - TELEPHONES IN USE

Encyclopedia Britannica, Incorporated, 310 South Michigan Avenue, Chicago, Illinois 60604 (312) 347-7000; *Britannica World Data.*

CROATIA - TELEVISION RECEIVERS

Encyclopedia Britannica, Incorporated, 310 South Michigan Avenue, Chicago, Illinois 60604 (312) 347-7000; *Britannica World Data.*

CROATIA - TRANSPORTATION AND COMMUNICATION

Encyclopedia Britannica, Incorporated, 310 South Michigan Avenue, Chicago, Illinois 60604 (312) 347-7000; *Britannica World Data.*

CROATIA - VITAL STATISTICS

Encyclopedia Britannica, Incorporated, 310 South Michigan Avenue, Chicago, Illinois 60604 (312) 347-7000; *Britannica World Data.*

CROPS - See also: FARMS and Individual Crops

CROPS - ACREAGE

U.S. Department of Agriculture, Economic Research Service, Fourteenth Street and Independence Avenue, SW, Washington, D.C. 20005-4789 (202) 219-1504; *Feed Situation, Fats and Oils Situation, Wheat Situation, Tobacco Situation, Cotton and Wool Outlook Statistics, Agricultural Supply and Demand Estimates, Agricultural Statistics,* and *Agricultural Outlook.*

U.S. Department of Agriculture, National Agricultural Statistics Service, Fourteenth Street and Independence Avenue, SW, Washington, D.C. 20005-4789 (202) 219-1504; *Crop Production, Field Crops,* and *Crop Values.*

CROPS - FARM MARKETINGS, SALES

U.S. Department of Agriculture, Economic Research Service, Fourteenth Street and Independence Avenue, SW, Washington, D.C. 20005-4789 (202) 219-1504; *Economic Indicators of the Farm Sector: State Financial Summary.*

U.S. Department of Commerce, Bureau of the Census, Suitland, Maryland 20233 (310) 763-4040; *Census of Agriculture.*

CROPS - FOREIGN TRADE

U.S. Department of Agriculture, Economic Research Service, Fourteenth Street and Independence Avenue, SW, Washington, D.C. 20005-4789 (202) 219-1504; *Agricultural Statistics,* and, *Foreign Agricultural Trade of the United States.*

U.S. Department of Commerce, Bureau of the Census, Suitland, Maryland 20233 (310) 763-4040; *U.S. Merchandise Trade.*

CROPS - PRICES

U.S. Department of Agriculture, National Agricultural Statistics Service, Fourteenth Street and Independence Avenue, SW, Washington, D.C. 20250 (202) 219-1504; *Agricultural Outlook, Agricultural Prices: Annual Summary,* and *Agricultural Statistics.*

CROPS - PRODUCTION

U.S. Department of Agriculture, Economic Research Service, Fourteenth Street and Independence Avenue, SW, Washington, D.C. 20005-4789 (202) 219-1504; *Agricultural Statistics,* and *Agricultural Outlook.*

U.S. Department of Agriculture, National Agricultural Statistics Service, Fourteenth Street and Independence Avenue, SW, Washington, D.C. 20250 (202) 219-1504; *Crop Production, Crop Values,* and *Field Crops.*

CROPS - PRODUCTIVITY

U.S. Department of Agriculture, Economic Research Service, Fourteenth Street and Independence Avenue, SW, Washington, D.C. 20005-4789 (202) 219-1504; *Agricultural Statistics*, and *Agricultural Resources: Cropland, Water, and Conservation Situation and Outlook Report.*

CROPS - SUPPLY AND DISAPPEARANCE

U.S. Department of Agriculture, Economic Research Service, Fourteenth Street and Independence Avenue, SW, Washington, D.C. 20005-4789 (202) 219-1504; *Agricultural Outlook, Agricultural Statistics, Agricultural Supply and Demand Estimates, Fats and Oils Situation, Feed Situation, Cotton and Wool Outlook Statistics, Tobacco Situation*, and *Wheat Situation.*

CRUDE MATERIALS - PRODUCER PRICE INDEXES

U.S. Department of Labor, Bureau of Labor Statistics, Two Massachusetts Avenue, NE, Washington, D.C. 20212 (202) 606-7828; *Monthly Labor Review.*

CRUDE MATERIALS - PRODUCTION

Statistical Office of the United Nations, Publishing Service, New York, New York 10017 (800) 253-9646; *Statistical Yearbook*, and *Monthly Bulletin of Statistics.*

U.S. Department of Energy, Energy Information Administration, 1000 Independence Avenue, SW, Washington, D.C. 20585 (202) 586-8800; *International Energy Annual*, and *Monthly Energy Review.*

CRUDE OIL - See also PETROLEUM AND PRODUCTS

CRUDE OIL - FOREIGN TRADE

U.S. Department of Commerce, Bureau of the Census, Suitland, Maryland 20233 (310) 763-4040; *U.S. Merchandise Trade.*

U.S. Department of Energy, Energy Information Administration, 1000 Independence Avenue, SW, Washington, D.C. 20585 (202) 586-8800; *U.S. Crude Oil, Natural Gas, and Natural Gas Liquids, Annual Energy Review, International Energy Annual, Monthly Energy Review*, and *Petroleum Supply Annual.*

CRUDE OIL - PRODUCTION

American Petroleum Institute, 1220 L Street, NW, Washington, D.C. 20005 (202) 682-8000; *Joint Association Survey of Drilling Costs.*

U.S. Department of Energy, Energy Information Administration, 1000 Independence Avenue, SW, Washington, D.C. 20585 (202) 586-8800; *Monthly Energy Review, Annual Energy Review, Crude Oil, Natural Gas, and Natural Gas Liquids*, and *Petroleum Supply Annual.*

U.S. Department of the Interior, Minerals Management Service, 1849 C Street, NW, Washington, D.C. 20240 (202) 208-3983; *Federal Offshore Statistics.*

Cuba - National Statistical Office

Comite Estatal de Estadisticas, Almendares No. 156, Ciudad de la Habana, Cuba.

Cuba - Primary Statistics Sources

Comite Estatal de Estadisticas, Almendares No. 156, Gaveta Postal 6016 Ciudad de la Habana, Cuba; *Anuario estadistico de Cuba* (Statistical Yearbook of Cuba).

CUBA - AGRICULTURE

Euromonitor Publications Limited, 87-88 Turnmill Street, London EC1M 5QU, England; *International Marketing Data and Statistics.*

Facts on File, 460 Park Avenue South, New York, New York 10016 (800) 443-8323; *The New Book of World Rankings.*

Federal Statistical Office, Gustav - Stresemann - Ring 11, D-6200 Wiesbaden, Germany; *Kuba.*

Food and Agricultural Organization of the United Nations (FAO), Via delle Terme di Caracalla, 00100 Rome, Italy (Telephone Number in U.S. (202) 653-2400); *Production Yearbook, The State of Food and Agriculture*, and *Trade Yearbook.*

Gale Research Incorporated, 835 Penobscot Building, Detroit, Michigan 48226 (800) 877-4253; *International Historical Statistics The Americas and Australasia.*

G.K. Hall and Company, 70 Lincoln Street, Boston, Massachusetts 02111 (617) 423-3990; *The World in Figures.*

Statistical Office of the United Nations, Publishing Service, New York, New York 10017 (800) 253-9646; *Statistical Yearbook.*

Times Books, 201 East 50th Street, New York, New York 10022 (212) 751-2600; *The Economist Book of Vital World Statistics.*

U.C.L.A. Latin American Center Publications, University of California, Los Angeles, California 90024 (310) 825-6634; *Statistical Abstract of Latin America.*

CUBA - AIRLINE SERVICE

Facts on File, 460 Park Avenue South, New York, New York 10016 (800) 443-8323; *The New Book of World Rankings.*

G.K. Hall and Company, 70 Lincoln Street, Boston, Massachusetts 02111 (617) 423-3990; *The World in Figures.*

Statistical Office of the United Nations, Publishing Service, New York, New York 10017 (800) 253-9646; *Statistical Yearbook.*

Times Books, 201 East 50th Street, New York, New York 10022 (212) 751-2600; *The Economist Book of Vital World Statistics.*

CUBA - ALUMINUM PRODUCTION AND CONSUMPTION - See CUBA - MINING AND MINERAL PRODUCTS

CUBA - ANIMAL HEALTH

Food and Agricultural Organization of the United Nations (FAO), Via delle Terme di Caracalla, 00100 Rome, Italy (Telephone Number in U.S. (202) 653-2400); *Animal Health Yearbook.*

CUBA - AREA AND DENSITY OF POPULATION

Euromonitor Publications Limited, 87-88 Turnmill Street, London EC1M 5QU, England; *International Marketing Data and Statistics.*

Facts on File, 460 Park Avenue South, New York, New York 10016 (800) 443-8323; *The New Book of World Rankings.*

Federal Statistical Office, Gustav - Stresemann - Ring 11, D-6200 Wiesbaden, Germany; *Kuba.*

Food and Agricultural Organization of the United Nations (FAO) Via delle Terme di Caracalla, 00100 Rome, Italy (Telephone Number in U.S. (202) 653-2400); *The State of Food and Agriculture.*

G.K. Hall and Company, 70 Lincoln Street, Boston, Massachusetts 02111 (617) 423-3990; *The World in Figures.*

Statistical Office of the United Nations, Publishing Service, New York, New York 10017 (800) 253-9646; *Statistical Yearbook.*

Times Books, 201 East 50th Street, New York, New York 10022 (212) 751-2600; *The Economist Book of Vital World Statistics.*

United Nations Educational, Scientific and Cultural Organization (UNESCO), 7 Place de Fontenoy, F-75700 Paris, France (Telephone Number in U.S. (212) 963-5981); *Statistical Yearbook.*

CUBA - ARMS EXPORTS AND IMPORTS

U.S. Arms Control and Disarmament Agency, 320 Twenty-first Street, NW, Washington, D.C. 20451 (202) 647-8677; *World Military Expenditures and Arms Transfers.*

CUBA - BALANCE OF PAYMENTS

The Economist Intelligence Unit, 111 West 57th Street, New York, New York 10019 (800) 938-4685; *The World Market Atlas.*

Federal Statistical Office, Gustav - Stresemann - Ring 11, D-6200 Wiesbaden, Germany; *Kuba.*

G.K. Hall and Company, 70 Lincoln Street, Boston, Massachusetts 02111 (617) 423-3990; *The World in Figures.*

Statistical Office of the United Nations, Publishing Service, New York, New York 10017 (800) 253-9646; *Economic Survey of Latin America and the Caribbean.*

Times Books, 201 East 50th Street, New York, New York 10022 (212) 751-2600; *The Economist Book of Vital World Statistics.*

CUBA - BANKING

Facts on File, 460 Park Avenue South, New York, New York 10016 (800) 443-8323; *The New Book of World Rankings.*

G.K. Hall and Company, 70 Lincoln Street, Boston, Massachusetts 02111 (617) 423-3990; *The World in Figures.*

CUBA - BARLEY PRODUCTION - See CUBA - CROPS

CUBA - BEER PRODUCTION

Facts on File, 460 Park Avenue South, New York, New York 10016 (800) 443-8323; *The New Book of World Rankings.*

Statistical Office of the United Nations, Publishing Service, New York, New York 10017 (800) 253-9646; *Statistical Yearbook.*

CUBA - BIRTH RATES

Facts on File, 460 Park Avenue South, New York, New York 10016 (800) 443-8323; *The New Book of World Rankings.*

Statistical Office of the United Nations, Publishing Service, New York, New York 10017 (800) 253-9646; *Demographic Yearbook,* and *Statistical Yearbook.*

Times Books, 201 East 50th Street, New York, New York 10022 (212) 751-2600; *The Economist Book of Vital World Statistics.*

World Health Organization, Office of Publications, Avenue Appia, CH-1211 Geneva 27, Switzerland (Telephone Number in U.S. (518) 436-9686); *World Health Statistics Annual.*

CUBA - BONDS

G.K. Hall and Company, 70 Lincoln Street, Boston, Massachusetts 02111 (617) 423-3990; *The World in Figures.*

CUBA - BOOK PRODUCTION

G.K. Hall and Company, 70 Lincoln Street, Boston, Massachusetts 02111 (617) 423-3990; *The World in Figures.*

United Nations Educational, Scientific and Cultural Organization (UNESCO), 7 Place de Fontenoy, F-75700 Paris, France (Telephone Number in U.S. (212) 963-5981); *Statistical Yearbook.*

CUBA - BROADCASTING

Billboard Limited, P.O. Box 9027, 1006 AA Amsterdam, The Netherlands (Telephone Number in U.S. (212) 764-7300); *World Radio TV Handbook.*

Facts on File, 460 Park Avenue South, New York, New York 10016 (800) 443-8323; *The New Book of World Rankings.*

G.K. Hall and Company, 70 Lincoln Street, Boston, Massachusetts 02111 (617) 423-3990; *The World in Figures.*

Times Books, 201 East 50th Street, New York, New York 10022 (212) 751-2600; *The Economist Book of Vital World Statistics.*

United Nations Educational, Scientific and Cultural Organization (UNESCO), 7 Place de Fontenoy, F-75700 Paris, France (Telephone Number in U.S. (212) 963-5981); *Statistical Yearbook.*

CUBA - BUILDING CONSTRUCTION - See CUBA - CONSTRUCTION INDUSTRY

CUBA - BUSINESS

G.K. Hall and Company, 70 Lincoln Street, Boston, Massachusetts 02111 (617) 423-3990; *The World in Figures.*

CUBA - BUTTER PRODUCTION - See CUBA - DAIRY PRODUCTS

CUBA - CABBAGE PRODUCTION - See CUBA - CROPS

CUBA - CALORIE SUPPLY

Food and Agricultural Organization of the United Nations (FAO) Via delle Terme di Caracalla, 00100 Rome, Italy (Telephone Number in U.S. (202) 653-2400); *The State of Food and Agriculture.*

CUBA - CATTLE - See CUBA - LIVESTOCK AND POULTRY

CUBA - CAUSTIC SODA PRODUCTION

Statistical Office of the United Nations, Publishing Service, New York, New York 10017 (800) 253-9646; *Statistical Yearbook.*

CUBA - CEMENT PRODUCTION - See CUBA - MINING AND MINERAL PRODUCTS

CUBA - CHEESE PRODUCTION - See CUBA - DAIRY PRODUCTS

CUBA - CHEMICAL (ORGANIC) PRODUCTION - See CUBA - MINING AND MINERAL PRODUCTS

CUBA - CHICKENS - See CUBA - LIVESTOCK AND POULTRY

CUBA - CHROMITE PRODUCTION AND CONSUMPTION - See CUBA - MINING AND MINERAL PRODUCTS

CUBA - CHROMIUM ORE PRODUCTION AND CONSUMPTION - See CUBA - MINING AND MINERAL PRODUCTS

CUBA - CIGAR PRODUCTION - See CUBA - TOBACCO PRODUCTION

CUBA - CIGARETTE PRODUCTION - See CUBA - TOBACCO PRODUCTION

CUBA - CLASS STRUCTURE

G.K. Hall and Company, 70 Lincoln Street, Boston, Massachusetts 02111 (617) 423-3990; *The World in Figures.*

CUBA - CLIMATE

Facts on File, 460 Park Avenue South, New York, New York 10016 (800) 443-8323; *The New Book of World Rankings.*

G.K. Hall and Company, 70 Lincoln Street, Boston, Massachusetts 02111 (617) 423-3990; *The World in Figures.*

CUBA - COAL PRODUCTION - See CUBA - MINING AND MINERAL PRODUCTS

CUBA - COBALT PRODUCTION AND CONSUMPTION - See CUBA - MINING AND MINERAL PRODUCTS

CUBA - COCOA (BEANS) PRODUCTION - See CUBA - CROPS

CUBA - COFFEE PRODUCTION - See CUBA - CROPS

CUBA - COMMUNICATIONS

Federal Statistical Office, Gustav - Stresemann - Ring 11, D-6200 Wiesbaden, Germany; *Kuba.*

G.K. Hall and Company, 70 Lincoln Street, Boston, Massachusetts 02111 (617) 423-3990; *The World in Figures.*

U.C.L.A. Latin American Center Publications, University of California, Los Angeles, California 90024 (310) 825-6634; *Statistical Abstract of Latin America.*

CUBA - CONSTRUCTION INDUSTRY

Facts on File, 460 Park Avenue South, New York, New York 10016 (800) 443-8323; *The New Book of World Rankings.*

U.C.L.A. Latin American Center Publications, University of California, Los Angeles, California 90024 (310) 825-6634; *Statistical Abstract of Latin America.*

Statistical Office of the United Nations, Publishing Service, New York, New York 10017 (800) 253-9646; *Construction Statistics Yearbook,* and *Statistical Yearbook.*

CUBA - CONSUMER PRICE INDEX

Federal Statistical Office, Gustav - Stresemann - Ring 11, D-6200 Wiesbaden, Germany; *Kuba.*

G.K. Hall and Company, 70 Lincoln Street, Boston, Massachusetts 02111 (617) 423-3990; *The World in Figures.*

CUBA - CONSUMER PRICES

Federal Statistical Office, Gustav - Stresemann - Ring 11, D-6200 Wiesbaden, Germany; *Kuba.*

International Labour Office, I.L.O. Publications, CH-1211, Geneva 22, Switzerland; *Yearbook of Labour Statistics.*

Times Books, 201 East 50th Street, New York, New York 10022 (212) 751-2600; *The Economist Book of Vital World Statistics.*

CUBA - CONSUMPTION

G.K. Hall and Company, 70 Lincoln Street, Boston, Massachusetts 02111 (617) 423-3990; *The World in Figures.*

CUBA - COOPERATIVES

U.C.L.A. Latin American Center Publications, University of California, Los Angeles, California 90024 (310) 825-6634; *Statistical Abstract of Latin America.*

CUBA - COPPER AND COPPER ORE PRODUCTION - See CUBA - MINING AND MINERAL PRODUCTS

CUBA - CORN PRODUCTION - See CUBA - CROPS

CUBA - CORPORATE TAXES - See CUBA - TAXATION

CUBA - COTTON - See CUBA - CROPS

CUBA - CRIME

Yale University Press, Yale Station, New Haven, Connecticut 06520 (203) 432-0940; *Violence and Crime in Cross-National Perspective.*

CUBA - CROPS

Commodity Research Bureau, Incorporated, 75 Wall Street, New York, New York 10005 (212) 504-7754; *Commodity Year Book.*

Facts on File, 460 Park Avenue South, New York, New York 10016 (800) 443-8323; *The New Book of World Rankings.*

Food and Agricultural Organization of the United Nations (FAO) Via delle Terme di Caracalla, 00100 Rome, Italy (Telephone Number in U.S. (202) 653-2400); *Production Yearbook,* and *The State of Food and Agriculture.*

G.K. Hall and Company, 70 Lincoln Street, Boston, Massachusetts 02111 (617) 423-3990; *The World in Figures.*

Statistical Office of the United Nations, Publishing Service, New York, New York 10017 (800) 253-9646; *Statistical Yearbook.*

CUBA - CUSTOMS DUTIES

G.K. Hall and Company, 70 Lincoln Street, Boston, Massachusetts 02111 (617) 423-3990; *The World in Figures.*

CUBA - DAIRY PRODUCTS

Facts on File, 460 Park Avenue South, New York, New York 10016 (800) 443-8323; *The New Book of World Rankings*.

Food and Agricultural Organization of the United Nations (FAO) Via delle Terme di Caracalla, 00100 Rome, Italy (Telephone Number in U.S. (202) 653-2400); *Production Yearbook*, and *The State of Food and Agriculture*.

Statistical Office of the United Nations, Publishing Service, New York, New York 10017 (800) 253-9646; *Statistical Yearbook*.

CUBA - DEATH RATES

G.K. Hall and Company, 70 Lincoln Street, Boston, Massachusetts 02111 (617) 423-3990; *The World in Figures*.

Statistical Office of the United Nations, Publishing Service, New York, New York 10017 (800) 253-9646; *Statistical Yearbook*.

Times Books, 201 East 50th Street, New York, New York 10022 (212) 751-2600; *The Economist Book of Vital World Statistics*.

World Health Organization, Office of Publications, Avenue Appia, CH-1211 Geneva 27, Switzerland (Telephone Number in U.S. (518) 436-9686); *World Health Statistics Annual*.

CUBA - DEFENSE EXPENDITURES

G.K. Hall and Company, 70 Lincoln Street, Boston, Massachusetts 02111 (617) 423-3990; *The World in Figures*.

U.S. Arms Control and Disarmament Agency, 320 Twenty-first Street, NW, Washington, D.C. 20451 (202) 647-8677; *World Military Expenditures and Arms Transfers*.

CUBA - DEMOGRAPHY

The Economist Intelligence Unit, 111 West 57th Street, New York, New York 10019 (800) 938-4685; *The World Market Atlas*.

Facts on File, 460 Park Avenue South, New York, New York 10016 (800) 443-8323; *The New Book of World Rankings*.

Federal Statistical Office, Gustav - Stresemann - Ring 11, D-6200 Wiesbaden, Germany; *Kuba*.

G.K. Hall and Company, 70 Lincoln Street, Boston, Massachusetts 02111 (617) 423-3990; *The World in Figures*.

CUBA - DEVELOPMENT ASSISTANCE

G.K. Hall and Company, 70 Lincoln Street, Boston, Massachusetts 02111 (617) 423-3990; *The World in Figures*.

Statistical Office of the United Nations, Publishing Service, New York, New York 10017 (800) 253-9646; *Statistical Yearbook*.

CUBA - DIAMOND PRODUCTION - See CUBA - MINING AND MINERAL PRODUCTS

CUBA - DISEASE

G.K. Hall and Company, 70 Lincoln Street, Boston, Massachusetts 02111 (617) 423-3990; *The World in Figures*.

World Health Organization, Office of Publications, Avenue Appia, CH-1211 Geneva 27, Switzerland (Telephone Number in U.S. (518) 436-9686); *World Health Statistics Annual*.

CUBA - DIVORCE RATES

Facts on File, 460 Park Avenue South, New York, New York 10016 (800) 443-8323; *The New Book of World Rankings*.

Statistical Office of the United Nations, Publishing Service, New York, New York 10017 (800) 253-9646; *Demographic Yearbook*, and *Statistical Yearbook*.

CUBA - DOMESTIC PRODUCT

G.K. Hall and Company, 70 Lincoln Street, Boston, Massachusetts 02111 (617) 423-3990; *The World in Figures*.

CUBA - ECONOMY

Euromonitor Publications Limited, 87-88 Turnmill Street, London EC1M 5QU, England; *International Marketing Data and Statistics*.

Facts on File, 460 Park Avenue South, New York, New York 10016 (800) 443-8323; *The New Book of World Rankings*.

Federal Statistical Office, Gustav - Stresemann - Ring 11, D-6200 Wiesbaden, Germany; *Kuba*.

G.K. Hall and Company, 70 Lincoln Street, Boston, Massachusetts 02111 (617) 423-3990; *The World in Figures*.

Statistical Office of the United Nations, Publishing Service, New York, New York 10017 (800) 253-9646; *Economic Survey of Latin America and the Caribbean*.

U.C.L.A. Latin American Center Publications, University of California, Los Angeles, California 90024 (310) 825-6634; *Statistical Abstract of Latin America*.

CUBA - EDUCATION

The Economist Intelligence Unit, 111 West 57th Street, New York, New York 10019 (800) 938-4685; *The World Market Atlas*.

Facts on File, 460 Park Avenue South, New York, New York 10016 (800) 443-8323; *The New Book of World Rankings*.

Federal Statistical Office, Gustav - Stresemann - Ring 11, D-6200 Wiesbaden, Germany; *Kuba*.

Gale Research Incorporated, 835 Penobscot Building, Detroit, Michigan 48226 (800) 877-4253; *International Historical Statistics The Americas and Australasia*.

G.K. Hall and Company, 70 Lincoln Street, Boston, Massachusetts 02111 (617) 423-3990; *The World in Figures*.

Times Books, 201 East 50th Street, New York, New York 10022 (212) 751-2600; *The Economist Book of Vital World Statistics*.

U.C.L.A. Latin American Center Publications, University of California, Los Angeles, California 90024 (310) 825-6634; *Statistical Abstract of Latin America*.

United Nations Educational, Scientific and Cultural Organization (UNESCO), 7 Place de Fontenoy, F-75700 Paris, France (Telephone Number in U.S. (212) 963-5981); *Statistical Yearbook*.

CUBA - EGG PRODUCTION - See CUBA - DAIRY PRODUCTS

CUBA - ELECTRICITY

Facts on File, 460 Park Avenue South, New York, New York 10016 (800) 443-8323; *The New Book of World Rankings.*

Penn Well Publishing Company, 1421 South Sheridan Road, P.O. Box 1260, Tulsa, Oklahoma 74101 (800) 752-9764; *International Energy Statistics Sourcebook.*

Statistical Office of the United Nations, Publishing Service, New York, New York 10017 (800) 253-9646; *Statistical Yearbook.*

Times Books, 201 East 50th Street, New York, New York 10022 (212) 751-2600; *The Economist Book of Vital World Statistics.*

CUBA - EMPLOYMENT

Euromonitor Publications Limited, 87-88 Turnmill Street, London EC1M 5QU, England; *International Marketing Data and Statistics.*

Facts on File, 460 Park Avenue South, New York, New York 10016 (800) 443-8323; *The New Book of World Rankings.*

Federal Statistical Office, Gustav - Stresemann - Ring 11, D-6200 Wiesbaden, Germany; *Kuba.*

International Labour Office, I.L.O. Publications, CH-1211, Geneva 22, Switzerland; *Yearbook of Labour Statistics.*

Statistical Office of the United Nations, Publishing Service, New York, New York 10017 (800) 253-9646; *Statistical Yearbook.*

U.C.L.A. Latin American Center Publications, University of California, Los Angeles, California 90024 (310) 825-6634; *Statistical Abstract of Latin America.*

CUBA - ENERGY

Facts on File, 460 Park Avenue South, New York, New York 10016 (800) 443-8323; *The New Book of World Rankings.*

Food and Agricultural Organization of the United Nations (FAO) Via delle Terme di Caracalla, 00100 Rome, Italy (Telephone Number in U.S. (202) 653-2400); *The State of Food and Agriculture.*

G.K. Hall and Company, 70 Lincoln Street, Boston, Massachusetts 02111 (617) 423-3990; *The World in Figures.*

Penn Well Publishing Company, 1421 South Sheridan Road, P.O. Box 1260, Tulsa, Oklahoma 74101 (800) 752-9764; *International Energy Statistics Sourcebook.*

Statistical Office of the United Nations, Publishing Service, New York, New York 10017 (800) 253-9646; *Energy Statistics Yearbook,* and *Statistical Yearbook.*

Times Books, 201 East 50th Street, New York, New York 10022 (212) 751-2600; *The Economist Book of Vital World Statistics.*

U.C.L.A. Latin American Center Publications, University of California, Los Angeles, California 90024 (310) 825-6634; *Statistical Abstract of Latin America.*

CUBA - EXCHANGE RATES

Euromonitor Publications Limited, 87-88 Turnmill Street, London EC1M 5QU, England; *International Marketing Data and Statistics.*

Statistical Office of the United Nations, Publishing Service, New York, New York 10017 (800) 253-9646; *Statistical Yearbook.*

U.C.L.A. Latin American Center Publications, University of California, Los Angeles, California 90024 (310) 825-6634; *Statistical Abstract of Latin America.*

CUBA - EXPORTS

The Economist Intelligence Unit, 111 West 57th Street, New York, New York 10019 (800) 938-4685; *The World Market Atlas.*

Euromonitor Publications Limited, 87-88 Turnmill Street, London EC1M 5QU, England; *International Marketing Data and Statistics.*

Food and Agricultural Organization of the United Nations (FAO) Via delle Terme di Caracalla, 00100 Rome, Italy (Telephone Number in U.S. (202) 653-2400); *The State of Food and Agriculture.*

G.K. Hall and Company, 70 Lincoln Street, Boston, Massachusetts 02111 (617) 423-3990; *The World in Figures.*

International Monetary Fund, 700 Nineteenth Street, NW, Washington, D.C. 20431 (202) 623-7000; *Direction of Trade Statistics.*

Times Books, 201 East 50th Street, New York, New York 10022 (212) 751-2600; *The Economist Book of Vital World Statistics.*

CUBA - EXTERNAL TRADE

Food and Agricultural Organization of the United Nations (FAO) Via delle Terme di Caracalla, 00100 Rome, Italy (Telephone Number in U.S. (202) 653-2400); *The State of Food and Agriculture,* and *Trade Yearbook.*

Gale Research Incorporated, 835 Penobscot Building, Detroit, Michigan 48226 (800) 877-4253; *International Historical Statistics The Americas and Australasia.*

G.K. Hall and Company, 70 Lincoln Street, Boston, Massachusetts 02111 (617) 423-3990; *The World in Figures.*

Statistical Office of the United Nations, Publishing Service, New York, New York 10017 (800) 253-9646; *Statistical Yearbook.*

CUBA - FABRIC PRODUCTION - See CUBA - TEXTILE INDUSTRY

CUBA - FAMILY PLANNING

U.C.L.A. Latin American Center Publications, University of California, Los Angeles, California 90024 (310) 825-6634; *Statistical Abstract of Latin America.*

CUBA - FARM CROPS - See CUBA - CROPS

CUBA - FEMALE WORKING POPULATION - See CUBA - EMPLOYMENT

CUBA - FERTILITY RATES

Facts on File, 460 Park Avenue South, New York, New York 10016 (800) 443-8323; *The New Book of World Rankings.*

Times Books, 201 East 50th Street, New York, New York 10022 (212) 751-2600; *The Economist Book of Vital World Statistics.*

CUBA - FERTILIZER

Food and Agricultural Organization of the United Nations (FAO), Via delle Terme di Caracalla, 00100 Rome, Italy (Telephone Number in U.S. (202) 653-2400); *Fertilizer Yearbook*, and *The State of Food and Agriculture*.

Statistical Office of the United Nations, Publishing Service, New York, New York 10017 (800) 253-9646; *Statistical Yearbook*.

CUBA - FETAL MORTALITY

Statistical Office of the United Nations, Publishing Service, New York, New York 10017 (800) 253-9646; *Demographic Yearbook*.

World Health Organization, Office of Publications, Avenue Appia, CH-1211 Geneva 27, Switzerland (Telephone Number in U.S. (518) 436-9686); *World Health Statistics Annual*.

CUBA - FILM - See CUBA - MOTION PICTURES

CUBA - FINANCE

Facts on File, 460 Park Avenue South, New York, New York 10016 (800) 443-8323; *The New Book of World Rankings*.

Federal Statistical Office, Gustav - Stresemann - Ring 11, D-6200 Wiesbaden, Germany; *Kuba*.

Gale Research Incorporated, 835 Penobscot Building, Detroit, Michigan 48226 (800) 877-4253; *International Historical Statistics The Americas and Australasia*.

G.K. Hall and Company, 70 Lincoln Street, Boston, Massachusetts 02111 (617) 423-3990; *The World in Figures*.

U.C.L.A. Latin American Center Publications, University of California, Los Angeles, California 90024 (310) 825-6634; *Statistical Abstract of Latin America*.

CUBA - FISHERIES

Facts on File, 460 Park Avenue South, New York, New York 10016 (800) 443-8323; *The New Book of World Rankings*.

Federal Statistical Office, Gustav - Stresemann - Ring 11, D-6200 Wiesbaden, Germany; *Kuba*.

Food and Agricultural Organization of the United Nations (FAO) Via delle Terme di Caracalla, 00100 Rome, Italy (Telephone Number in U.S. (202) 653-2400); *The State of Food and Agriculture*, and *Yearbook of Fishery Statistics*.

Statistical Office of the United Nations, Publishing Service, New York, New York 10017 (800) 253-9646; *Statistical Yearbook*.

U.C.L.A. Latin American Center Publications, University of California, Los Angeles, California 90024 (310) 825-6634; *Statistical Abstract of Latin America*.

CUBA - FLOUR PRODUCTION

Statistical Office of the United Nations, Publishing Service, New York, New York 10017 (800) 253-9646; *Statistical Yearbook*.

CUBA - FOOD

Food and Agricultural Organization of the United Nations (FAO) Via delle Terme di Caracalla, 00100 Rome, Italy (Telephone Number in U.S. (202) 653-2400); *Production Yearbook*, and *The State of Food and Agriculture*.

G.K. Hall and Company, 70 Lincoln Street, Boston, Massachusetts 02111 (617) 423-3990; *The World in Figures*.

CUBA - FOREIGN AID

G.K. Hall and Company, 70 Lincoln Street, Boston, Massachusetts 02111 (617) 423-3990; *The World in Figures*.

CUBA - FOREIGN INDEBTEDNESS

Statistical Office of the United Nations, Publishing Service, New York, New York 10017 (800) 253-9646; *Economic Survey of Latin America and the Caribbean*.

CUBA - FOREIGN TRADE

Euromonitor Publications Limited, 87-88 Turnmill Street, London EC1M 5QU, England; *International Marketing Data and Statistics*.

Facts on File, 460 Park Avenue South, New York, New York 10016 (800) 443-8323; *The New Book of World Rankings*.

Federal Statistical Office, Gustav - Stresemann - Ring 11, D-6200 Wiesbaden, Germany; *Kuba*.

Food and Agricultural Organization of the United Nations (FAO) Via delle Terme di Caracalla, 00100 Rome, Italy (Telephone Number in U.S. (202) 653-2400); *The State of Food and Agriculture*.

G.K. Hall and Company, 70 Lincoln Street, Boston, Massachusetts 02111 (617) 423-3990; *The World in Figures*.

Organisation for Economic Co-operation and Development (OECD), 2 rue Andre-Pascal, 75 Paris 16, France; *Trade by Commodities*.

Statistical Office of the United Nations, Publishing Service, New York, New York 10017 (800) 253-9646; *Economic Survey of Latin America and the Caribbean, International Trade Statistics Yearbook*, and *Statistical Yearbook*.

U.C.L.A. Latin American Center Publications, University of California, Los Angeles, California 90024 (310) 825-6634; *Statistical Abstract of Latin America*.

CUBA - FORESTRY AND FOREST PRODUCTS

Facts on File, 460 Park Avenue South, New York, New York 10016 (800) 443-8323; *The New Book of World Rankings*.

Federal Statistical Office, Gustav - Stresemann - Ring 11, D-6200 Wiesbaden, Germany; *Kuba*.

Food and Agricultural Organization of the United Nations (FAO) Via delle Terme di Caracalla, 00100 Rome, Italy (Telephone Number in U.S. (202) 653-2400); *The State of Food and Agriculture*, and *Yearbook of Forest Products*.

G.K. Hall and Company, 70 Lincoln Street, Boston, Massachusetts 02111 (617) 423-3990; *The World in Figures*.

Statistical Office of the United Nations, Publishing Service, New York, New York 10017 (800) 253-9646; *Statistical Yearbook*.

U.C.L.A. Latin American Center Publications, University of California, Los Angeles, California 90024 (310) 825-6634; *Statistical Abstract of Latin America*.

United Nations Educational, Scientific and Cultural Organization (UNESCO), 7 Place de Fontenoy, F-75700 Paris, France (Telephone Number in U.S. (212) 963-5981); *Statistical Yearbook.*

CUBA - GAS PRODUCTION - See CUBA - MINING AND MINERAL PRODUCTS

CUBA - GENERAL INDUSTRIAL STATISTICS

Federal Statistical Office, Gustav - Stresemann - Ring 11, D-6200 Wiesbaden, Germany; *Kuba.*

CUBA - GENERAL MORTALITY

Statistical Office of the United Nations, Publishing Service, New York, New York 10017 (800) 253-9646; *Demographic Yearbook.*

World Health Organization, Office of Publications, Avenue Appia, CH-1211 Geneva 27, Switzerland (Telephone Number in U.S. (518) 436-9686); *World Health Statistics Annual.*

CUBA - GEOGRAPHIC DATA

Facts on File, 460 Park Avenue South, New York, New York 10016 (800) 443-8323; *The New Book of World Rankings.*

Federal Statistical Office, Gustav - Stresemann - Ring 11, D-6200 Wiesbaden, Germany; *Kuba.*

U.C.L.A. Latin American Center Publications, University of California, Los Angeles, California 90024 (310) 825-6634; *Statistical Abstract of Latin America.*

CUBA - GOATS

Euromonitor Publications Limited, 87-88 Turnmill Street, London EC1M 5QU, England; *International Marketing Data and Statistics.*

CUBA - GOLD PRODUCTION - See CUBA - MINING AND MINERAL PRODUCTS

CUBA - GOVERNMENT

G.K. Hall and Company, 70 Lincoln Street, Boston, Massachusetts 02111 (617) 423-3990; *The World in Figures.*

CUBA - GRAIN PRODUCTION - See CUBA - CROPS

CUBA - GREEN PEPPER AND CHILIE PRODUCTION - See CUBA - CROPS

CUBA - GROSS DOMESTIC PRODUCT

The Economist Intelligence Unit, 111 West 57th Street, New York, New York 10019 (800) 938-4685; *The World Market Atlas.*

Euromonitor Publications Limited, 87-88 Turnmill Street, London EC1M 5QU, England; *International Marketing Data and Statistics.*

Facts on File, 460 Park Avenue South, New York, New York 10016 (800) 443-8323; *The New Book of World Rankings.*

G.K. Hall and Company, 70 Lincoln Street, Boston, Massachusetts 02111 (617) 423-3990; *The World in Figures.*

Statistical Office of the United Nations, Publishing Service, New York, New York 10017 (800) 253-9646; *Statistical Yearbook.*

Times Books, 201 East 50th Street, New York, New York 10022 (212) 751-2600; *The Economist Book of Vital World Statistics.*

CUBA - GROSS NATIONAL PRODUCT

Euromonitor Publications Limited, 87-88 Turnmill Street, London EC1M 5QU, England; *International Marketing Data and Statistics.*

U.S. Arms Control and Disarmament Agency, 320 Twenty-first Street, NW, Washington, D.C. 20451 (202) 647-8677; *World Military Expenditures and Arms Transfers.*

CUBA - GROUNDNUTS PRODUCTION - See CUBA - CROPS

CUBA - HEALTH

Facts on File, 460 Park Avenue South, New York, New York 10016 (800) 443-8323; *The New Book of World Rankings.*

Federal Statistical Office, Gustav - Stresemann - Ring 11, D-6200 Wiesbaden, Germany; *Kuba.*

G.K. Hall and Company, 70 Lincoln Street, Boston, Massachusetts 02111 (617) 423-3990; *The World in Figures.*

Statistical Office of the United Nations, Publishing Service, New York, New York 10017 (800) 253-9646; *Statistical Yearbook.*

Times Books, 201 East 50th Street, New York, New York 10022 (212) 751-2600; *The Economist Book of Vital World Statistics.*

U.C.L.A. Latin American Center Publications, University of California, Los Angeles, California 90024 (310) 825-6634; *Statistical Abstract of Latin America.*

World Health Organization, Office of Publications, Avenue Appia, CH-1211 Geneva 27, Switzerland (Telephone Number in U.S. (518) 436-9686); *World Health Statistics Annual.*

CUBA - HIDE PRODUCTION

Food and Agricultural Organization of the United Nations (FAO), Via delle Terme di Caracalla, 00100 Rome, Italy (Telephone Number in U.S. (202) 653-2400); *Production Yearbook.*

CUBA - HIGHWAYS

G.K. Hall and Company, 70 Lincoln Street, Boston, Massachusetts 02111 (617) 423-3990; *The World in Figures.*

CUBA - HORSES - See CUBA - LIVESTOCK AND POULTRY

CUBA - HOURS OF WORK - See CUBA - EMPLOYMENT

CUBA - HOUSING AND HOUSING UNITS

Facts on File, 460 Park Avenue South, New York, New York 10016 (800) 443-8323; *The New Book of World Rankings.*

U.C.L.A. Latin American Center Publications, University of California, Los Angeles, California 90024 (310) 825-6634; *Statistical Abstract of Latin America.*

CUBA - HYDROCHLORIC ACID PRODUCTION

Statistical Office of the United Nations, Publishing Service, New York, New York 10017 (800) 253-9646; *Statistical Yearbook.*

CUBA - ILLITERATE POPULATION

The Economist Intelligence Unit, 111 West 57th Street, New York, New York 10019 (800) 938-4685; *The World Market Atlas.*

G.K. Hall and Company, 70 Lincoln Street, Boston, Massachusetts 02111 (617) 423-3990; *The World in Figures.*

United Nations Educational, Scientific and Cultural Organization (UNESCO), 7 Place de Fontenoy, F-75700 Paris, France (Telephone Number in U.S. (212) 963-5981); *Statistical Yearbook.*

CUBA - IMMIGRATION

U.C.L.A. Latin American Center Publications, University of California, Los Angeles, California 90024 (310) 825-6634; *Statistical Abstract of Latin America.*

CUBA - IMPORTS

The Economist Intelligence Unit, 111 West 57th Street, New York, New York 10019 (800) 938-4685; *The World Market Atlas.*

Euromonitor Publications Limited, 87-88 Turnmill Street, London EC1M 5QU, England; *International Marketing Data and Statistics.*

Food and Agricultural Organization of the United Nations (FAO) Via delle Terme di Caracalla, 00100 Rome, Italy (Telephone Number in U.S. (202) 653-2400); *The State of Food and Agriculture.*

G.K. Hall and Company, 70 Lincoln Street, Boston, Massachusetts 02111 (617) 423-3990; *The World in Figures.*

International Monetary Fund, 700 Nineteenth Street, NW, Washington, D.C. 20431 (202) 623-7000; *Direction of Trade Statistics.*

Times Books, 201 East 50th Street, New York, New York 10022 (212) 751-2600; *The Economist Book of Vital World Statistics.*

CUBA - INCOME DISTRIBUTION

U.C.L.A. Latin American Center Publications, University of California, Los Angeles, California 90024 (310) 825-6634; *Statistical Abstract of Latin America.*

CUBA - INDUSTRIAL METALS PRODUCTION - See CUBA - MINING AND MINERAL PRODUCTS

CUBA - INDUSTRY

Euromonitor Publications Limited, 87-88 Turnmill Street, London EC1M 5QU, England; *International Marketing Data and Statistics.*

Facts on File, 460 Park Avenue South, New York, New York 10016 (800) 443-8323; *The New Book of World Rankings.*

Federal Statistical Office, Gustav - Stresemann - Ring 11, D-6200 Wiesbaden, Germany; *Kuba.*

Gale Research Incorporated, 835 Penobscot Building, Detroit, Michigan 48226 (800) 877-4253; *International Historical Statistics The Americas and Australasia.*

G.K. Hall and Company, 70 Lincoln Street, Boston, Massachusetts 02111 (617) 423-3990; *The World in Figures.*

International Labour Office, I.L.O. Publications, CH-1211, Geneva 22, Switzerland; *Yearbook of Labour Statistics.*

Statistical Office of the United Nations, Publishing Service, New York, New York 10017 (800) 253-9646; *Economic Survey of Latin America and the Caribbean.*

Times Books, 201 East 50th Street, New York, New York 10022 (212) 751-2600; *The Economist Book of Vital World Statistics.*

U.C.L.A. Latin American Center Publications, University of California, Los Angeles, California 90024 (310) 825-6634; *Statistical Abstract of Latin America.*

World Intellectual Property Organization, 34 Chemin des Colombettes, CH-1211 Geneva 20. Switzerland; *Industrial Property Statistics.*

CUBA - INFANT AND MATERNAL MORTALITY

Statistical Office of the United Nations, Publishing Service, New York, New York 10017 (800) 253-9646; *Demographic Yearbook,* and *Statistical Yearbook.*

Times Books, 201 East 50th Street, New York, New York 10022 (212) 751-2600; *The Economist Book of Vital World Statistics.*

World Health Organization, Office of Publications, Avenue Appia, CH-1211 Geneva 27, Switzerland (Telephone Number in U.S. (518) 436-9686); *World Health Statistics Annual.*

CUBA - INFLATIONARY FACTORS

Statistical Office of the United Nations, Publishing Service, New York, New York 10017 (800) 253-9646; *Economic Survey of Latin America and the Caribbean.*

CUBA - INTERNATIONAL FINANCE

U.C.L.A. Latin American Center Publications, University of California, Los Angeles, California 90024 (310) 825-6634; *Statistical Abstract of Latin America.*

CUBA - INTERNATIONAL STATISTICS

U.C.L.A. Latin American Center Publications, University of California, Los Angeles, California 90024 (310) 825-6634; *Statistical Abstract of Latin America.*

CUBA - IRON ORE PRODUCTION AND CONSUMPTION - See CUBA - MINING AND MINERAL PRODUCTS

CUBA - IRRIGATION

Euromonitor Publications Limited, 87-88 Turnmill Street, London EC1M 5QU, England; *International Marketing Data and Statistics.*

CUBA - JUTE PRODUCTION - See CUBA - CROPS

CUBA - LABOR FORCE

Euromonitor Publications Limited, 87-88 Turnmill Street, London EC1M 5QU, England; *International Marketing Data and Statistics.*

Facts on File, 460 Park Avenue South, New York, New York 10016 (800) 443-8323; *The New Book of World Rankings.*

Food and Agricultural Organization of the United Nations (FAO) Via delle Terme di Caracalla, 00100 Rome, Italy (Telephone Number in U.S. (202) 653-2400); *The State of Food and Agriculture.*

Gale Research Incorporated, 835 Penobscot Building, Detroit, Michigan 48226 (800) 877-4253; *International Historical Statistics The Americas and Australasia.*

G.K. Hall and Company, 70 Lincoln Street, Boston, Massachusetts 02111 (617) 423-3990; *The World in Figures.*

Times Books, 201 East 50th Street, New York, New York 10022 (212) 751-2600; *The Economist Book of Vital World Statistics.*

CUBA - LABOR PRODUCTIVITY

International Labour Office, I.L.O. Publications, CH-1211, Geneva 22, Switzerland; *Yearbook of Labour Statistics.*

CUBA - LAND USE

Euromonitor Publications Limited, 87-88 Turnmill Street, London EC1M 5QU, England; *International Marketing Data and Statistics.*

Food and Agricultural Organization of the United Nations (FAO), Via delle Terme di Caracalla, 00100 Rome, Italy (Telephone Number in U.S. (202) 653-2400); *Production Yearbook.*

G.K. Hall and Company, 70 Lincoln Street, Boston, Massachusetts 02111 (617) 423-3990; *The World in Figures.*

CUBA - LIBRARIES

Facts on File, 460 Park Avenue South, New York, New York 10016 (800) 443-8323; *The New Book of World Rankings.*

CUBA - LIVESTOCK AND POULTRY

Euromonitor Publications Limited, 87-88 Turnmill Street, London EC1M 5QU, England; *International Marketing Data and Statistics.*

Facts on File, 460 Park Avenue South, New York, New York 10016 (800) 443-8323; *The New Book of World Rankings.*

Food and Agricultural Organization of the United Nations (FAO) Via delle Terme di Caracalla, 00100 Rome, Italy (Telephone Number in U.S. (202) 653-2400); *Production Yearbook,* and *The State of Food and Agriculture.*

G.K. Hall and Company, 70 Lincoln Street, Boston, Massachusetts 02111 (617) 423-3990; *The World in Figures.*

Statistical Office of the United Nations, Publishing Service, New York, New York 10017 (800) 253-9646; *Statistical Yearbook.*

CUBA - LIVING LEVELS

G.K. Hall and Company, 70 Lincoln Street, Boston, Massachusetts 02111 (617) 423-3990; *The World in Figures.*

Times Books, 201 East 50th Street, New York, New York 10022 (212) 751-2600; *The Economist Book of Vital World Statistics.*

CUBA - MAIL - NUMBER OF PIECES SENT OR RECEIVED

Statistical Office of the United Nations, Publishing Service, New York, New York 10017 (800) 253-9646; *Statistical Yearbook.*

CUBA - MAIN INDICATORS - See CUBA - ECONOMY

CUBA - MANGANESE ORE PRODUCTION AND CONSUMPTION - See CUBA - MINING AND MINERAL PRODUCTS

CUBA - MANUFACTURING

Facts on File, 460 Park Avenue South, New York, New York 10016 (800) 443-8323; *The New Book of World Rankings.*

G.K. Hall and Company, 70 Lincoln Street, Boston, Massachusetts 02111 (617) 423-3990; *The World in Figures.*

CUBA - MARRIAGE RATES

Facts on File, 460 Park Avenue South, New York, New York 10016 (800) 443-8323; *The New Book of World Rankings.*

Statistical Office of the United Nations, Publishing Service, New York, New York 10017 (800) 253-9646; *Demographic Yearbook,* and *Statistical Yearbook.*

CUBA - MEAT PRODUCTION - See CUBA - LIVESTOCK AND POULTRY

CUBA - MEDICAL PERSONNEL

U.C.L.A. Latin American Center Publications, University of California, Los Angeles, California 90024 (310) 825-6634; *Statistical Abstract of Latin America.*

CUBA - MERCHANT SHIPPING

G.K. Hall and Company, 70 Lincoln Street, Boston, Massachusetts 02111 (617) 423-3990; *The World in Figures.*

Statistical Office of the United Nations, Publishing Service, New York, New York 10017 (800) 253-9646; *Statistical Yearbook.*

Times Books, 201 East 50th Street, New York, New York 10022 (212) 751-2600; *The Economist Book of Vital World Statistics.*

U.S. Department of Transportation, Maritime Administration, 400 Seventh Street, SW, Washington, D.C. 20590 (202) (202) 366-5807; *A Statistical Analysis of the World's Merchant Fleets.*

CUBA - MILITARY

G.K. Hall and Company, 70 Lincoln Street, Boston, Massachusetts 02111 (617) 423-3990; *The World in Figures.*

The International Institute for Strategic Studies, 23 Tavistock Street, London WC2E 7NQ, England; *The Military Balance.*

U.C.L.A. Latin American Center Publications, University of California, Los Angeles, California 90024 (310) 825-6634; *Statistical Abstract of Latin America.*

U.S. Arms Control and Disarmament Agency, 320 Twenty-first Street, NW, Washington, D.C. 20451 (202) 647-8677; *World Military Expenditures and Arms Transfers.*

CUBA - MILK - See CUBA - DAIRY PRODUCTS

CUBA - MINING AND MINERAL PRODUCTS

Commodity Research Bureau, Incorporated, 75 Wall Street, New York, New York 10005 (212) 504-7754; *Commodity Year Book.*

Facts on File, 460 Park Avenue South, New York, New York 10016 (800) 443-8323; *The New Book of World Rankings.*

G.K. Hall and Company, 70 Lincoln Street, Boston, Massachusetts 02111 (617) 423-3990; *The World in Figures.*

Penn Well Publishing Company, 1421 South Sheridan Road, P.O. Box 1260, Tulsa, Oklahoma 74101 (800) 752-9764; *International Energy Statistics Sourcebook.*

Statistical Office of the United Nations, Publishing Service, New York, New York 10017 (800) 253-9646; *Statistical Yearbook.*

U.C.L.A. Latin American Center Publications, University of California, Los Angeles, California 90024 (310) 825-6634; *Statistical Abstract of Latin America.*

CUBA - MOLASSES PRODUCTION - See CUBA - CROPS

CUBA - MONEY EXCHANGE RATES

Euromonitor Publications Limited, 87-88 Turnmill Street, London EC1M 5QU, England; *International Marketing Data and Statistics.*

Statistical Office of the United Nations, Publishing Service, New York, New York 10017 (800) 253-9646; *Statistical Yearbook.*

CUBA - MONEY RESERVES

Euromonitor Publications Limited, 87-88 Turnmill Street, London EC1M 5QU, England; *International Marketing Data and Statistics.*

CUBA - MONEY SUPPLY

Euromonitor Publications Limited, 87-88 Turnmill Street, London EC1M 5QU, England; *International Marketing Data and Statistics.*

Federal Statistical Office, Gustav - Stresemann - Ring 11, D-6200 Wiesbaden, Germany; *Kuba.*

G.K. Hall and Company, 70 Lincoln Street, Boston, Massachusetts 02111 (617) 423-3990; *The World in Figures.*

U.C.L.A. Latin American Center Publications, University of California, Los Angeles, California 90024 (310) 825-6634; *Statistical Abstract of Latin America.*

CUBA - MOTION PICTURES

Statistical Office of the United Nations, Publishing Service, New York, New York 10017 (800) 253-9646; *Statistical Yearbook.*

United Nations Educational, Scientific and Cultural Organization (UNESCO), 7 Place de Fontenoy, F-75700 Paris, France (Telephone Number in U.S. (212) 963-5981); *Statistical Yearbook.*

CUBA - MOTOR VEHICLES IN USE

G.K. Hall and Company, 70 Lincoln Street, Boston, Massachusetts 02111 (617) 423-3990; *The World in Figures.*

Statistical Office of the United Nations, Publishing Service, New York, New York 10017 (800) 253-9646; *Statistical Yearbook.*

Times Books, 201 East 50th Street, New York, New York 10022 (212) 751-2600; *The Economist Book of Vital World Statistics.*

CUBA - MULES - See CUBA - LIVESTOCK AND POULTRY

CUBA - MUSEUMS

Facts on File, 460 Park Avenue South, New York, New York 10016 (800) 443-8323; *The New Book of World Rankings.*

United Nations Educational, Scientific and Cultural Organization (UNESCO), 7 Place de Fontenoy, F-75700 Paris, France (Telephone Number in U.S. (212) 963-5981); *Statistical Yearbook.*

CUBA - NATALITY - See CUBA - BIRTH RATES

CUBA - NATIONAL ACCOUNTS

Federal Statistical Office, Gustav - Stresemann - Ring 11, D-6200 Wiesbaden, Germany; *Kuba.*

Gale Research Incorporated, 835 Penobscot Building, Detroit, Michigan 48226 (800) 877-4253; *International Historical Statistics The Americas and Australasia.*

Statistical Office of the United Nations, Publishing Service, New York, New York 10017 (800) 253-9646; *National Accounts Statistics,* and *Statistical Yearbook.*

U.C.L.A. Latin American Center Publications, University of California, Los Angeles, California 90024 (310) 825-6634; *Statistical Abstract of Latin America.*

CUBA - NATIONAL INCOME

Facts on File, 460 Park Avenue South, New York, New York 10016 (800) 443-8323; *The New Book of World Rankings.*

G.K. Hall and Company, 70 Lincoln Street, Boston, Massachusetts 02111 (617) 423-3990; *The World in Figures.*

Statistical Office of the United Nations, Publishing Service, New York, New York 10017 (800) 253-9646; *Statistical Yearbook.*

CUBA - NATIONAL PRODUCT

Facts on File, 460 Park Avenue South, New York, New York 10016 (800) 443-8323; *The New Book of World Rankings.*

Statistical Office of the United Nations, Publishing Service, New York, New York 10017 (800) 253-9646; *Statistical Yearbook.*

CUBA - NATURAL GAS PRODUCTION - See CUBA - MINING AND MINERAL PRODUCTS

CUBA - NET MATERIAL PRODUCT

Statistical Office of the United Nations, Publishing Service, New York, New York 10017 (800) 253-9646; *Statistical Yearbook.*

CUBA - NEWSPAPER PRODUCTION - See CUBA - FORESTRY AND FOREST PRODUCTS

CUBA - NEWSPRINT - See CUBA - FORESTRY AND FOREST PRODUCTS

CUBA - NICKEL ORE PRODUCTION AND CONSUMPTION - See CUBA - MINING AND MINERAL PRODUCTS

CUBA - OCCUPATIONS - See CUBA - LABOR FORCE

CUBA - PAPER - See CUBA - FORESTRY AND FOREST PRODUCTS

CUBA - PATENTS

Statistical Office of the United Nations, Publishing Service, New York, New York 10017 (800) 253-9646; *Statistical Yearbook.*

World Intellectual Property Organization, 34 Chemin des Colombettes, CH-1211 Geneva 20. Switzerland; *Industrial Property Statistics*.

CUBA - PEANUT PRODUCTION - See CUBA - CROPS

CUBA - PERIODICALS

United Nations Educational, Scientific and Cultural Organization (UNESCO), 7 Place de Fontenoy, F-75700 Paris, France (Telephone Number in U.S. (212) 963-5981); *Statistical Yearbook*.

CUBA - PESTICIDE USE

Food and Agricultural Organization of the United Nations (FAO) Via delle Terme di Caracalla, 00100 Rome, Italy (Telephone Number in U.S. (202) 653-2400); *The State of Food and Agriculture*.

CUBA - PETROLEUM INDUSTRY

Facts on File, 460 Park Avenue South, New York, New York 10016 (800) 443-8323; *The New Book of World Rankings*.

Food and Agricultural Organization of the United Nations (FAO) Via delle Terme di Caracalla, 00100 Rome, Italy (Telephone Number in U.S. (202) 653-2400); *The State of Food and Agriculture*.

G.K. Hall and Company, 70 Lincoln Street, Boston, Massachusetts 02111 (617) 423-3990; *The World in Figures*.

Penn Well Publishing Company, 1421 South Sheridan Road, P.O. Box 1260, Tulsa, Oklahoma 74101 (800) 752-9764; *International Energy Statistics Sourcebook*.

Statistical Office of the United Nations, Publishing Service, New York, New York 10017 (800) 253-9646; *Statistical Yearbook*.

CUBA - PIGS - See CUBA - LIVESTOCK AND POULTRY

CUBA - POLITICAL DATA

U.C.L.A. Latin American Center Publications, University of California, Los Angeles, California 90024 (310) 825-6634; *Statistical Abstract of Latin America*.

CUBA - POPULATION

The Economist Intelligence Unit, 111 West 57th Street, New York, New York 10019 (800) 938-4685; *The World Market Atlas*.

Euromonitor Publications Limited, 87-88 Turnmill Street, London EC1M 5QU, England; *International Marketing Data and Statistics*.

Facts on File, 460 Park Avenue South, New York, New York 10016 (800) 443-8323; *The New Book of World Rankings*.

Federal Statistical Office, Gustav - Stresemann - Ring 11, D-6200 Wiesbaden, Germany; *Kuba*.

Food and Agricultural Organization of the United Nations (FAO), Via delle Terme di Caracalla, 00100 Rome, Italy (Telephone Number in U.S. (202) 653-2400); *Production Yearbook*.

Gale Research Incorporated, 835 Penobscot Building, Detroit, Michigan 48226 (800) 877-4253; *International Historical Statistics The Americas and Australasia*.

G.K. Hall and Company, 70 Lincoln Street, Boston, Massachusetts 02111 (617) 423-3990; *The World in Figures*.

International Labour Office, I.L.O. Publications, CH-1211, Geneva 22, Switzerland; *Yearbook of Labour Statistics*.

Statistical Office of the United Nations, Publishing Service, New York, New York 10017 (800) 253-9646; *Demographic Yearbook*, and *Statistical Yearbook*.

Times Books, 201 East 50th Street, New York, New York 10022 (212) 751-2600; *The Economist Book of Vital World Statistics*.

U.C.L.A. Latin American Center Publications, University of California, Los Angeles, California 90024 (310) 825-6634; *Statistical Abstract of Latin America*.

United Nations Educational, Scientific and Cultural Organization (UNESCO), 7 Place de Fontenoy, F-75700 Paris, France (Telephone Number in U.S. (212) 963-5981); *Statistical Yearbook*.

U.S. Arms Control and Disarmament Agency, 320 Twenty-first Street, NW, Washington, D.C. 20451 (202) 647-8677; *World Military Expenditures and Arms Transfers*.

World Health Organization, Office of Publications, Avenue Appia, CH-1211 Geneva 27, Switzerland (Telephone Number in U.S. (518) 436-9686); *World Health Statistics Annual*.

CUBA - POST OFFICES

Facts on File, 460 Park Avenue South, New York, New York 10016 (800) 443-8323; *The New Book of World Rankings*.

CUBA - POTATO PRODUCTION - See CUBA - CROPS

CUBA - PRICES

Facts on File, 460 Park Avenue South, New York, New York 10016 (800) 443-8323; *The New Book of World Rankings*.

Federal Statistical Office, Gustav - Stresemann - Ring 11, D-6200 Wiesbaden, Germany; *Kuba*.

Food and Agricultural Organization of the United Nations (FAO), Via delle Terme di Caracalla, 00100 Rome, Italy (Telephone Number in U.S. (202) 653-2400); *Production Yearbook*, and *The State of Food and Agriculture*.

Gale Research Incorporated, 835 Penobscot Building, Detroit, Michigan 48226 (800) 877-4253; *International Historical Statistics The Americas and Australasia*.

G.K. Hall and Company, 70 Lincoln Street, Boston, Massachusetts 02111 (617) 423-3990; *The World in Figures*.

International Labour Office, I.L.O. Publications, CH-1211, Geneva 22, Switzerland; *Yearbook of Labour Statistics*.

Statistical Office of the United Nations, Publishing Service, New York, New York 10017 (800) 253-9646; *Economic Survey of Latin America and the Caribbean*.

CUBA - PRINTING AND WRITING PAPER - See CUBA - FORESTRY AND FOREST PRODUCTS

CUBA - PRODUCTION

Facts on File, 460 Park Avenue South, New York, New York 10016 (800) 443-8323; *The New Book of World Rankings*.

G.K. Hall and Company, 70 Lincoln Street, Boston, Massachusetts 02111 (617) 423-3990; *The World in Figures.*

CUBA - PRODUCTIVITY

Euromonitor Publications Limited, 87-88 Turnmill Street, London EC1M 5QU, England; *International Marketing Data and Statistics.*

CUBA - PUBLIC FINANCE

Facts on File, 460 Park Avenue South, New York, New York 10016 (800) 443-8323; *The New Book of World Rankings.*

Federal Statistical Office, Gustav - Stresemann - Ring 11, D-6200 Wiesbaden, Germany; *Kuba.*

CUBA - RADIO BROADCASTING - See CUBA - BROADCASTING

CUBA - RADIO RECEIVER PRODUCTION

Statistical Office of the United Nations, Publishing Service, New York, New York 10017 (800) 253-9646; *Statistical Yearbook.*

CUBA - RAILWAYS

G.K. Hall and Company, 70 Lincoln Street, Boston, Massachusetts 02111 (617) 423-3990; *The World in Figures.*

Jane's Information Group, Sentinel House, 163 Brighton Road, Coulsdon, Surrey CR5 2NH, England (Telephone Number in U.S. (703) 683-3700); *Jane's World Railways.*

Statistical Office of the United Nations, Publishing Service, New York, New York 10017 (800) 253-9646; *Statistical Yearbook.*

CUBA - RANCHING

U.C.L.A. Latin American Center Publications, University of California, Los Angeles, California 90024 (310) 825-6634; *Statistical Abstract of Latin America.*

CUBA - RELIGION

Facts on File, 460 Park Avenue South, New York, New York 10016 (800) 443-8323; *The New Book of World Rankings.*

U.C.L.A. Latin American Center Publications, University of California, Los Angeles, California 90024 (310) 825-6634; *Statistical Abstract of Latin America.*

CUBA - RETAIL TRADE

G.K. Hall and Company, 70 Lincoln Street, Boston, Massachusetts 02111 (617) 423-3990; *The World in Figures.*

Statistical Office of the United Nations, Publishing Service, New York, New York 10017 (800) 253-9646; *Statistical Yearbook.*

CUBA - RICE PRODUCTION - See CUBA - CROPS

CUBA - ROOT AND TUBER PRODUCTION - See CUBA - CROPS

CUBA - ROUNDWOOD PRODUCTION - See CUBA - FORESTRY AND FOREST PRODUCTS

CUBA - RUBBER PRODUCTION

Facts on File, 460 Park Avenue South, New York, New York 10016 (800) 443-8323; *The New Book of World Rankings.*

CUBA - SALT PRODUCTION - See CUBA - MINING AND MINERAL PRODUCTS

CUBA - SAWNWOOD PRODUCTION - See CUBA - FORESTRY AND FOREST PRODUCTS

CUBA - SCIENCE AND TECHNOLOGY

U.C.L.A. Latin American Center Publications, University of California, Los Angeles, California 90024 (310) 825-6634; *Statistical Abstract of Latin America.*

CUBA - SENIOR CITIZENS

Facts on File, 460 Park Avenue South, New York, New York 10016 (800) 443-8323; *The New Book of World Rankings.*

CUBA - SHEEP - See CUBA - LIVESTOCK AND POULTRY

CUBA - SILVER PRODUCTION AND CONSUMPTION - See CUBA - MINING AND MINERAL PRODUCTS

CUBA - SOCIAL DATA

Facts on File, 460 Park Avenue South, New York, New York 10016 (800) 443-8323; *The New Book of World Rankings.*

G.K. Hall and Company, 70 Lincoln Street, Boston, Massachusetts 02111 (617) 423-3990; *The World in Figures.*

U.C.L.A. Latin American Center Publications, University of California, Los Angeles, California 90024 (310) 825-6634; *Statistical Abstract of Latin America.*

CUBA - SOCIOECONOMIC DATA

U.C.L.A. Latin American Center Publications, University of California, Los Angeles, California 90024 (310) 825-6634; *Statistical Abstract of Latin America.*

CUBA - STATE BUDGET REVENUE AND EXPENDITURES

Euromonitor Publications Limited, 87-88 Turnmill Street, London EC1M 5QU, England; *International Marketing Data and Statistics.*

CUBA - STEEL - See CUBA - MINING AND MINERAL PRODUCTS

CUBA - STOCKS - COMMODITY - MARKET PRICE - INDEX

Food and Agricultural Organization of the United Nations (FAO) Via delle Terme di Caracalla, 00100 Rome, Italy (Telephone Number in U.S. (202) 653-2400); *The State of Food and Agriculture.*

CUBA - SUGAR - See CUBA - CROPS

CUBA - TAXATION

G.K. Hall and Company, 70 Lincoln Street, Boston, Massachusetts 02111 (617) 423-3990; *The World in Figures.*

CUBA - TELEGRAPH SERVICE

Statistical Office of the United Nations, Publishing Service, New York, New York 10017 (800) 253-9646; *Statistical Yearbook.*

CUBA - TELEPHONES IN USE

American Telephone and Telegraph Company, 26 Parsippany Road, Whippany, New Jersey 07981 (800) 338-4038; *The World's Telephones.*

G.K. Hall and Company, 70 Lincoln Street, Boston, Massachusetts 02111 (617) 423-3990; *The World in Figures.*

Statistical Office of the United Nations, Publishing Service, New York, New York 10017 (800) 253-9646; *Statistical Yearbook.*

CUBA - TELEVISION BROADCASTING - See CUBA - BROADCASTING

CUBA - TEXTILE INDUSTRY

G.K. Hall and Company, 70 Lincoln Street, Boston, Massachusetts 02111 (617) 423-3990; *The World in Figures.*

Statistical Office of the United Nations, Publishing Service, New York, New York 10017 (800) 253-9646; *Statistical Yearbook.*

CUBA - TIN - INDUSTRIAL CONSUMPTION - See CUBA - MINING AND MINERAL PRODUCTS

CUBA - TIRE (MOTOR VEHICLE) PRODUCTION

Statistical Office of the United Nations, Publishing Service, New York, New York 10017 (800) 253-9646; *Statistical Yearbook.*

CUBA - TOBACCO PRODUCTION

Facts on File, 460 Park Avenue South, New York, New York 10016 (800) 443-8323; *The New Book of World Rankings.*

Statistical Office of the United Nations, Publishing Service, New York, New York 10017 (800) 253-9646; *Statistical Yearbook.*

CUBA - TOURISM

Facts on File, 460 Park Avenue South, New York, New York 10016 (800) 443-8323; *The New Book of World Rankings.*

Federal Statistical Office, Gustav - Stresemann - Ring 11, D-6200 Wiesbaden, Germany; *Kuba.*

G.K. Hall and Company, 70 Lincoln Street, Boston, Massachusetts 02111 (617) 423-3990; *The World in Figures.*

Times Books, 201 East 50th Street, New York, New York 10022 (212) 751-2600; *The Economist Book of Vital World Statistics.*

U.C.L.A. Latin American Center Publications, University of California, Los Angeles, California 90024 (310) 825-6634; *Statistical Abstract of Latin America.*

World Tourism Organization, Calle Capitan Haya 42, E-28020 Madrid, Spain; *Yearbook of Tourism Statistics.*

CUBA - TRACTORS IN USE

Statistical Office of the United Nations, Publishing Service, New York, New York 10017 (800) 253-9646; *Statistical Yearbook.*

CUBA - TRADE - See CUBA - FOREIGN TRADE

CUBA - TRADEMARKS AND SERVICE MARKS

Statistical Office of the United Nations, Publishing Service, New York, New York 10017 (800) 253-9646; *Statistical Yearbook.*

World Intellectual Property Organization, 34 Chemin des Colombettes, CH-1211 Geneva 20. Switzerland; *Industrial Property Statistics.*

CUBA - TRANSPORTATION AND COMMUNICATIONS

Facts on File, 460 Park Avenue South, New York, New York 10016 (800) 443-8323; *The New Book of World Rankings.*

Federal Statistical Office, Gustav - Stresemann - Ring 11, D-6200 Wiesbaden, Germany; *Kuba.*

Gale Research Incorporated, 835 Penobscot Building, Detroit, Michigan 48226 (800) 877-4253; *International Historical Statistics The Americas and Australasia.*

G.K. Hall and Company, 70 Lincoln Street, Boston, Massachusetts 02111 (617) 423-3990; *The World in Figures.*

U.C.L.A. Latin American Center Publications, University of California, Los Angeles, California 90024 (310) 825-6634; *Statistical Abstract of Latin America.*

CUBA - UNEMPLOYMENT

Euromonitor Publications Limited, 87-88 Turnmill Street, London EC1M 5QU, England; *International Marketing Data and Statistics.*

International Labour Office, I.L.O. Publications, CH-1211, Geneva 22, Switzerland; *Yearbook of Labour Statistics.*

Statistical Office of the United Nations, Publishing Service, New York, New York 10017 (800) 253-9646; *Statistical Yearbook.*

U.C.L.A. Latin American Center Publications, University of California, Los Angeles, California 90024 (310) 825-6634; *Statistical Abstract of Latin America.*

CUBA - UTILITIES

U.C.L.A. Latin American Center Publications, University of California, Los Angeles, California 90024 (310) 825-6634; *Statistical Abstract of Latin America.*

CUBA - VITAL STATISTICS

Euromonitor Publications Limited, 87-88 Turnmill Street, London EC1M 5QU, England; *International Marketing Data and Statistics.*

Gale Research Incorporated, 835 Penobscot Building, Detroit, Michigan 48226 (800) 877-4253; *International Historical Statistics The Americas and Australasia.*

G.K. Hall and Company, 70 Lincoln Street, Boston, Massachusetts 02111 (617) 423-3990; *The World in Figures.*

World Health Organization, Office of Publications, Avenue Appia, CH-1211 Geneva 27, Switzerland (Telephone Number in U.S. (518) 436-9686); *World Health Statistics Annual.*

CUBA - WAGES

Federal Statistical Office, Gustav - Stresemann - Ring 11, D-6200 Wiesbaden, Germany; *Kuba.*

G.K. Hall and Company, 70 Lincoln Street, Boston, Massachusetts 02111 (617) 423-3990; *The World in Figures.*

International Labour Office, I.L.O. Publications, CH-1211, Geneva 22, Switzerland; *Yearbook of Labour Statistics.*

Statistical Office of the United Nations, Publishing Service, New York, New York 10017 (800) 253-9646; *Statistical Yearbook.*

U.C.L.A. Latin American Center Publications, University of California, Los Angeles, California 90024 (310) 825-6634; *Statistical Abstract of Latin America*.

CUBA - WEATHER

Facts on File, 460 Park Avenue South, New York, New York 10016 (800) 443-8323; *The New Book of World Rankings*.

G.K. Hall and Company, 70 Lincoln Street, Boston, Massachusetts 02111 (617) 423-3990; *The World in Figures*.

CUBA - WHEAT - See CUBA - CROPS

CUBA - WHOLESALE TRADE

Statistical Office of the United Nations, Publishing Service, New York, New York 10017 (800) 253-9646; *Statistical Yearbook*.

CUBA - WINE PRODUCTION

Facts on File, 460 Park Avenue South, New York, New York 10016 (800) 443-8323; *The New Book of World Rankings*.

CUBA - WOOL PRODUCTION

Facts on File, 460 Park Avenue South, New York, New York 10016 (800) 443-8323; *The New Book of World Rankings*.

CUBA - YARN PRODUCTION

Statistical Office of the United Nations, Publishing Service, New York, New York 10017 (800) 253-9646; *Statistical Yearbook*.

CUBAN POPULATION - See also: HISPANIC ORIGIN POPULATION

CUBAN POPULATION

U.S. Department of Commerce, Bureau of the Census, Suitland, Maryland 20233 (310) 763-4040; *Current Population Reports*, and *Census of Population, General Population Characteristics*.

CUBAN POPULATION - LABOR FORCE

U.S. Department of Labor, Bureau of Labor Statistics, Two Massachusetts Avenue, NE, Washington, D.C. 20212 (202) 606-7828; *Employment and Earnings*, and Bulletin 2307.

CUCUMBERS

U.S. Department of Agriculture, Economic Research Service, 14th Street and Independence Avenue, SW, Washington, D.C. 20250 (202) 219-1504; *Economic Indicators of the Farm Sector: National Financial Summary*, and *Agricultural Outlook*.

U.S. Department of Agriculture, National Agricultural Statistics Service, Fourteenth Street and Independence Avenue, SW, Washington, D.C. 20250 (202) 219-1504; *Vegetables*, and *Agricultural Statistics*.

CULTURAL ASSOCIATIONS

Gale Research, Incorporated, 835 Penobscot Building, Detroit, Michigan 48226 (800) 877-4253; *Encyclopedia of Associations*.

CURRENCY - COMMODITY FUTURES TRADING

U.S. Commodity Futures Trading Commission, 2033 K Street, NW, Washington, D.C. 20581 (202) 254-6387; *Annual Report*.

CURRENCY - FOREIGN EXCHANGE RATE

Board of Governors of the Federal Reserve System, Twentieth Street and Constitution Avenue, NW, Washington, D.C. 20551 (202) 452-3000; *Federal Reserve Bulletin*.

U.S. Department of Labor, Bureau of Labor Statistics, Two Massachusetts Avenue, NE, Washington, D.C. 20212 (202) 606-7828; *Monthly Labor Review*.

CURRENCY - PERSONAL SAVING COMPONENT

U.S. Department of Commerce, Bureau of Economic Analysis, Fourteenth Street between Constitution Avenue and E Street, NW, Washington, D.C. 20230 (202) 606-9900; *The National Income and Product Accounts of the United States*, and *Survey of Current Business*.

CURRENCY - SUPPLY

Board of Governors of the Federal Reserve System, Twentieth Street and Constitution Avenue, NW, Washington, D.C. 20551 (202) 452-3000; *Federal Reserve Bulletin*, *Annual Statistical Digest*, and *Money Stock, Liquid Assets and Debt Measures*.

CUSK - IMPORTS

U.S. Department of Commerce, National Oceanic and Atmospheric Administration, National Marine Fisheries Service, 1335 East-West Highway, Silver Spring, Maryland 20910 (301) 427-2239; *Fishery Statistics of the United States*, and *Fisheries of the United States*.

CUSTOMS OUTLAYS

Executive Office of the President, Office of Management and Budget, Executive Office Building, Washington, D.C. 20503 (202) 395-3080; *Budget of the United States Government*.

CUSTOMS OUTLAYS - DUTIES AND PERCENT OF VALUE

U.S. Department of Commerce, Bureau of the Census, Suitland, Maryland 20233 (310) 763-4040; *U.S. Merchandise Trade: Selected Highlights*, and unpublished data.

CUSTOMS REGIONS - IMPORTS AND EXPORTS

U.S. Department of Commerce, Bureau of the Census, Suitland, Maryland 20233 (310) 763-4040; *U.S. Merchandise Trade: Selected Highlights*.

CYCLONES

U.S. Department of Commerce, National Oceanic and Atmospheric Administration, National Climatic Data Center, Federal Building, Asheville, North Carolina 28801 (704) 259-2850; *Storm Data*.

Cyprus - National Statistical Office

Statistics and Research Department, Ministry of Finance, 13 Lord Byron Avenue, Nicosia, Cyprus.

Cyprus - Primary Statistics Sources

Statistics and Research Department, Nicosia, Cyprus; *Statistical Abstract* and *Quarterly Statistical Digest*.

CYPRUS - AGRICULTURE

Facts on File, 460 Park Avenue South, New York, New York 10016 (800) 443-8323; *The New Book of World Rankings.*

Food and Agricultural Organization of the United Nations (FAO) Via delle Terme di Caracalla, 00100 Rome, Italy (Telephone Number in U.S. (202) 653-2400); *Production Yearbook, The State of Food and Agriculture,* and *Trade Yearbook.*

G.K. Hall and Company, 70 Lincoln Street, Boston, Massachusetts 02111 (617) 423-3990; *The World in Figures.*

Statistical Office of the United Nations, Publishing Service, New York, New York 10017 (800) 253-9646; *Statistical Yearbook.*

Times Books, 201 East 50th Street, New York, New York 10022 (212) 751-2600; *The Economist Book of Vital World Statistics.*

The World Bank, 1818 H Street, NW, Washington, D.C. 20433 (202) 477-1234; *World Tables.*

CYPRUS - AIRLINE SERVICE

Facts on File, 460 Park Avenue South, New York, New York 10016 (800) 443-8323; *The New Book of World Rankings.*

G.K. Hall and Company, 70 Lincoln Street, Boston, Massachusetts 02111 (617) 423-3990; *The World in Figures.*

International Civil Aviation Organization, 1000 Sherbrooke Street West, Suite 400, Montreal, Quebec, Canada H3A 2R2 (514) 285-8219; *Civil Aviation Statistics of the World.*

Statistical Office of the United Nations, Publishing Service, New York, New York 10017 (800) 253-9646; *Statistical Yearbook.*

Times Books, 201 East 50th Street, New York, New York 10022 (212) 751-2600; *The Economist Book of Vital World Statistics.*

CYPRUS - ALMOND PRODUCTION - See CYPRUS - CROPS

CYPRUS - ALUMINUM PRODUCTION AND CONSUMPTION - See CYPRUS - MINING AND MINERAL PRODUCTS

CYPRUS - ANIMAL HEALTH

Food and Agricultural Organization of the United Nations (FAO), Via delle Terme di Caracalla, 00100 Rome, Italy (Telephone Number in U.S. (202) 653-2400); *Animal Health Yearbook.*

CYPRUS - AREA AND DENSITY OF POPULATION

Facts on File, 460 Park Avenue South, New York, New York 10016 (800) 443-8323; *The New Book of World Rankings.*

Food and Agricultural Organization of the United Nations (FAO) Via delle Terme di Caracalla, 00100 Rome, Italy (Telephone Number in U.S. (202) 653-2400); *The State of Food and Agriculture.*

G.K. Hall and Company, 70 Lincoln Street, Boston, Massachusetts 02111 (617) 423-3990; *The World in Figures.*

Statistical Office of the United Nations, Publishing Service, New York, New York 10017 (800) 253-9646; *Statistical Yearbook.*

Times Books, 201 East 50th Street, New York, New York 10022 (212) 751-2600; *The Economist Book of Vital World Statistics.*

United Nations Educational, Scientific and Cultural Organization (UNESCO), 7 Place de Fontenoy, F-75700 Paris, France (Telephone Number in U.S. (212) 963-5981); *Statistical Yearbook.*

CYPRUS - ARMS EXPORTS AND IMPORTS

U.S. Arms Control and Disarmament Agency, 320 Twenty-first Street, NW, Washington, D.C. 20451 (202) 647-8677; *World Military Expenditures and Arms Transfers.*

CYPRUS - ARTICHOKE PRODUCTION - See CYPRUS - CROPS

CYPRUS - BALANCE OF PAYMENTS

The Economist Intelligence Unit, 111 West 57th Street, New York, New York 10019 (800) 938-4685; *The World Market Atlas.*

G.K. Hall and Company, 70 Lincoln Street, Boston, Massachusetts 02111 (617) 423-3990; *The World in Figures.*

International Monetary Fund, 700 Nineteenth Street, NW, Washington, D.C. 20431 (202) 623-7000; *Balance of Payments Yearbook.*

Times Books, 201 East 50th Street, New York, New York 10022 (212) 751-2600; *The Economist Book of Vital World Statistics.*

The World Bank, 1818 H Street, NW, Washington, D.C. 20433 (202) 477-1234; *World Tables.*

CYPRUS - BANKING

Facts on File, 460 Park Avenue South, New York, New York 10016 (800) 443-8323; *The New Book of World Rankings.*

G.K. Hall and Company, 70 Lincoln Street, Boston, Massachusetts 02111 (617) 423-3990; *The World in Figures.*

International Monetary Fund, 700 Nineteenth Street, NW, Washington, D.C. 20431 (202) 623-7000; *Government Finance Statistics Yearbook,* and *International Financial Statistics.*

CYPRUS - BARLEY PRODUCTION - See CYPRUS - CROPS

CYPRUS - BEER PRODUCTION

Facts on File, 460 Park Avenue South, New York, New York 10016 (800) 443-8323; *The New Book of World Rankings.*

Statistical Office of the United Nations, Publishing Service, New York, New York 10017 (800) 253-9646; *Statistical Yearbook.*

CYPRUS - BIRTH RATES

Facts on File, 460 Park Avenue South, New York, New York 10016 (800) 443-8323; *The New Book of World Rankings.*

Statistical Office of the United Nations, Publishing Service, New York, New York 10017 (800) 253-9646; *Demographic Yearbook,* and *Statistical Yearbook.*

Times Books, 201 East 50th Street, New York, New York 10022 (212) 751-2600; *The Economist Book of Vital World Statistics.*

The World Bank, 1818 H Street, NW, Washington, D.C. 20433 (202) 477-1234; *World Tables.*

World Health Organization, Office of Publications, Avenue Appia, CH-1211 Geneva 27, Switzerland (Telephone Number in U.S. (518)

436-9686); *World Health Statistics Annual.*

CYPRUS - BONDS

G.K. Hall and Company, 70 Lincoln Street, Boston, Massachusetts 02111 (617) 423-3990; *The World in Figures.*

International Monetary Fund, 700 Nineteenth Street, NW, Washington, D.C. 20431 (202) 623-7000; *Government Finance Statistics Yearbook.*

CYPRUS - BOOK PRODUCTION

Euromonitor Publications Limited, 87-88 Turnmill Street, London EC1M 5QU, England; *European Marketing Data and Statistics.*

G.K. Hall and Company, 70 Lincoln Street, Boston, Massachusetts 02111 (617) 423-3990; *The World in Figures.*

United Nations Educational, Scientific and Cultural Organization (UNESCO), 7 Place de Fontenoy, F-75700 Paris, France (Telephone Number in U.S. (212) 963-5981); *Statistical Yearbook.*

CYPRUS - BROADCASTING

Billboard Limited, P.O. Box 9027, 1006 AA Amsterdam, The Netherlands (Telephone Number in U.S. (212) 764-7300); *World Radio TV Handbook.*

G.K. Hall and Company, 70 Lincoln Street, Boston, Massachusetts 02111 (617) 423-3990; *The World in Figures.*

Times Books, 201 East 50th Street, New York, New York 10022 (212) 751-2600; *The Economist Book of Vital World Statistics.*

United Nations Educational, Scientific and Cultural Organization (UNESCO), 7 Place de Fontenoy, F-75700 Paris, France (Telephone Number in U.S. (212) 963-5981); *Statistical Yearbook.*

CYPRUS - BUILDING CONSTRUCTION - See CYPRUS - CONSTRUCTION INDUSTRY

CYPRUS - BUSINESS

G.K. Hall and Company, 70 Lincoln Street, Boston, Massachusetts 02111 (617) 423-3990; *The World in Figures.*

CYPRUS - BUSINESS AND PROFESSIONAL LICENSES

International Monetary Fund, 700 Nineteenth Street, NW, Washington, D.C. 20431 (202) 623-7000; *Government Finance Statistics Yearbook.*

CYPRUS - CALORIE SUPPLY

Food and Agricultural Organization of the United Nations (FAO) Via delle Terme di Caracalla, 00100 Rome, Italy (Telephone Number in U.S. (202) 653-2400); *The State of Food and Agriculture.*

CYPRUS - CAPITAL REVENUES

International Monetary Fund, 700 Nineteenth Street, NW, Washington, D.C. 20431 (202) 623-7000; *Government Finance Statistics Yearbook.*

CYPRUS - CATTLE - See CYPRUS - LIVESTOCK AND POULTRY

CYPRUS - CEMENT PRODUCTION - See CYPRUS - MINING AND MINERAL PRODUCTS

CYPRUS - CEREAL PRODUCTION - See CYPRUS - CROPS

CYPRUS - CHEESE PRODUCTION - See CYPRUS - DAIRY PRODUCTS

CYPRUS - CHEMICAL (ORGANIC) PRODUCTION - See CYPRUS - MINING AND MINERAL PRODUCTS

CYPRUS - CHICK PEA PRODUCTION - See CYPRUS - CROPS

CYPRUS - CHROMIUM ORE PRODUCTION AND CONSUMPTION - See CYPRUS - MINING AND MINERAL PRODUCTS

CYPRUS - CIGARETTE PRODUCTION - See CYPRUS - TOBACCO PRODUCTION

CYPRUS - CLASS STRUCTURE

G.K. Hall and Company, 70 Lincoln Street, Boston, Massachusetts 02111 (617) 423-3990; *The World in Figures.*

CYPRUS - CLIMATE

Facts on File, 460 Park Avenue South, New York, New York 10016 (800) 443-8323; *The New Book of World Rankings.*

G.K. Hall and Company, 70 Lincoln Street, Boston, Massachusetts 02111 (617) 423-3990; *The World in Figures.*

CYPRUS - COAL PRODUCTION - See CYPRUS - MINING AND MINERAL PRODUCTS

CYPRUS - COFFEE - See CYPRUS - CROPS

CYPRUS - COMMUNICATIONS

G.K. Hall and Company, 70 Lincoln Street, Boston, Massachusetts 02111 (617) 423-3990; *The World in Figures.*

CYPRUS - CONSTRUCTION INDUSTRY

Facts on File, 460 Park Avenue South, New York, New York 10016 (800) 443-8323; *The New Book of World Rankings.*

Statistical Office of the United Nations, Publishing Service, New York, New York 10017 (800) 253-9646; *Construction Statistics Yearbook,* and *Statistical Yearbook.*

CYPRUS - CONSUMER PRICE INDEX

G.K. Hall and Company, 70 Lincoln Street, Boston, Massachusetts 02111 (617) 423-3990; *The World in Figures.*

Statistical Office of the United Nations, Publishing Service, New York, New York 10017 (800) 253-9646; *Statistical Yearbook.*

CYPRUS - CONSUMER PRICES

Euromonitor Publications Limited, 87-88 Turnmill Street, London EC1M 5QU, England; *European Marketing Data and Statistics.*

International Labour Office, I.L.O. Publications, CH-1211, Geneva 22, Switzerland; *Yearbook of Labour Statistics.*

International Monetary Fund, 700 Nineteenth Street, NW, Washington, D.C. 20431 (202) 623-7000; *International Financial Statistics.*

Times Books, 201 East 50th Street, New York, New York 10022 (212) 751-2600; *The Economist Book of Vital World Statistics.*

CYPRUS - CONSUMPTION

G.K. Hall and Company, 70 Lincoln Street, Boston, Massachusetts 02111 (617) 423-3990; *The World in Figures*.

CYPRUS - COPPER AND COPPER ORE PRODUCTION - See CYPRUS - MINING AND MINERAL PRODUCTS

CYPRUS - CORN PRODUCTION - See CYPRUS - CROPS

CYPRUS - CORPORATE TAXES - See CYPRUS - TAXATION

CYPRUS - COTTON - See CYPRUS - CROPS

CYPRUS - CRIME

International Criminal Police Organization (INTERPOL), 26 rue Armengaud, 92210 Saint Cloud, France; *International Crime Statistics*.

Yale University Press, Yale Station, New Haven, Connecticut 06520 (203) 432-0940; *Violence and Crime in Cross-National Perspective*.

CYPRUS - CROPS

Euromonitor Publications Limited, 87-88 Turnmill Street, London EC1M 5QU, England; *European Marketing Data and Statistics*.

Facts on File, 460 Park Avenue South, New York, New York 10016 (800) 443-8323; *The New Book of World Rankings*.

Food and Agricultural Organization of the United Nations (FAO) Via delle Terme di Caracalla, 00100 Rome, Italy (Telephone Number in U.S. (202) 653-2400); *Production Yearbook*, and *The State of Food and Agriculture*.

G.K. Hall and Company, 70 Lincoln Street, Boston, Massachusetts 02111 (617) 423-3990; *The World in Figures*.

International Monetary Fund, 700 Nineteenth Street, NW, Washington, D.C. 20431 (202) 623-7000; *International Financial Statistics*.

Statistical Office of the United Nations, Publishing Service, New York, New York 10017 (800) 253-9646; *Statistical Yearbook*.

CYPRUS - CUSTOMS DUTIES

G.K. Hall and Company, 70 Lincoln Street, Boston, Massachusetts 02111 (617) 423-3990; *The World in Figures*.

International Monetary Fund, 700 Nineteenth Street, NW, Washington, D.C. 20431 (202) 623-7000; *Government Finance Statistics Yearbook*.

CYPRUS - DAIRY PRODUCTS

Facts on File, 460 Park Avenue South, New York, New York 10016 (800) 443-8323; *The New Book of World Rankings*.

Food and Agricultural Organization of the United Nations (FAO) Via delle Terme di Caracalla, 00100 Rome, Italy (Telephone Number in U.S. (202) 653-2400); *Production Yearbook*, and *The State of Food and Agriculture*.

Statistical Office of the United Nations, Publishing Service, New York, New York 10017 (800) 253-9646; *Statistical Yearbook*.

CYPRUS - DEATH RATES

G.K. Hall and Company, 70 Lincoln Street, Boston, Massachusetts 02111 (617) 423-3990; *The World in Figures*.

Statistical Office of the United Nations, Publishing Service, New York, New York 10017 (800) 253-9646; *Statistical Yearbook*.

Times Books, 201 East 50th Street, New York, New York 10022 (212) 751-2600; *The Economist Book of Vital World Statistics*.

World Health Organization, Office of Publications, Avenue Appia, CH-1211 Geneva 27, Switzerland (Telephone Number in U.S. (518) 436-9686); *World Health Statistics Annual*.

CYPRUS - DEFENSE EXPENDITURES

G.K. Hall and Company, 70 Lincoln Street, Boston, Massachusetts 02111 (617) 423-3990; *The World in Figures*.

International Monetary Fund, 700 Nineteenth Street, NW, Washington, D.C. 20431 (202) 623-7000; *Government Finance Statistics Yearbook*.

U.S. Arms Control and Disarmament Agency, 320 Twenty-first Street, NW, Washington, D.C. 20451 (202) 647-8677; *World Military Expenditures and Arms Transfers*.

CYPRUS - DEMOGRAPHY

The Economist Intelligence Unit, 111 West 57th Street, New York, New York 10019 (800) 938-4685; *The World Market Atlas*.

Facts on File, 460 Park Avenue South, New York, New York 10016 (800) 443-8323; *The New Book of World Rankings*.

G.K. Hall and Company, 70 Lincoln Street, Boston, Massachusetts 02111 (617) 423-3990; *The World in Figures*.

CYPRUS - DEVELOPMENT ASSISTANCE

G.K. Hall and Company, 70 Lincoln Street, Boston, Massachusetts 02111 (617) 423-3990; *The World in Figures*.

Statistical Office of the United Nations, Publishing Service, New York, New York 10017 (800) 253-9646; *Statistical Yearbook*.

CYPRUS - DIAMOND PRODUCTION - See CYPRUS - MINING AND MINERAL PRODUCTS

CYPRUS - DISEASE

G.K. Hall and Company, 70 Lincoln Street, Boston, Massachusetts 02111 (617) 423-3990; *The World in Figures*.

World Health Organization, Office of Publications, Avenue Appia, CH-1211 Geneva 27, Switzerland (Telephone Number in U.S. (518) 436-9686); *World Health Statistics Annual*.

CYPRUS - DIVORCE RATES

Facts on File, 460 Park Avenue South, New York, New York 10016 (800) 443-8323; *The New Book of World Rankings*.

Statistical Office of the United Nations, Publishing Service, New York, New York 10017 (800) 253-9646; *Demographic Yearbook*, and *Statistical Yearbook*.

CYPRUS - DOMESTIC PRODUCT

G.K. Hall and Company, 70 Lincoln Street, Boston, Massachusetts 02111 (617) 423-3990; *The World in Figures.*

CYPRUS - DUCKS - See CYPRUS - LIVESTOCK AND POULTRY

CYPRUS - ECONOMY

Euromonitor Publications Limited, 87-88 Turnmill Street, London EC1M 5QU, England; *European Marketing Data and Statistics.*

Facts on File, 460 Park Avenue South, New York, New York 10016 (800) 443-8323; *The New Book of World Rankings.*

G.K. Hall and Company, 70 Lincoln Street, Boston, Massachusetts 02111 (617) 423-3990; *The World in Figures.*

CYPRUS - EDUCATION

The Economist Intelligence Unit, 111 West 57th Street, New York, New York 10019 (800) 938-4685; *The World Market Atlas.*

Euromonitor Publications Limited, 87-88 Turnmill Street, London EC1M 5QU, England; *European Marketing Data and Statistics.*

Facts on File, 460 Park Avenue South, New York, New York 10016 (800) 443-8323; *The New Book of World Rankings.*

G.K. Hall and Company, 70 Lincoln Street, Boston, Massachusetts 02111 (617) 423-3990; *The World in Figures.*

International Monetary Fund, 700 Nineteenth Street, NW, Washington, D.C. 20431 (202) 623-7000; *Government Finance Statistics Yearbook.*

Times Books, 201 East 50th Street, New York, New York 10022 (212) 751-2600; *The Economist Book of Vital World Statistics.*

United Nations Educational, Scientific and Cultural Organization (UNESCO), 7 Place de Fontenoy, F-75700 Paris, France (Telephone Number in U.S. (212) 963-5981); *Statistical Yearbook.*

The World Bank, 1818 H Street, NW, Washington, D.C. 20433 (202) 477-1234; *World Tables.*

CYPRUS - EGG PRODUCTION - See CYPRUS - DAIRY PRODUCTS

CYPRUS - ELECTRICITY

Facts on File, 460 Park Avenue South, New York, New York 10016 (800) 443-8323; *The New Book of World Rankings.*

Statistical Office of the United Nations, Publishing Service, New York, New York 10017 (800) 253-9646; *Statistical Yearbook.*

Times Books, 201 East 50th Street, New York, New York 10022 (212) 751-2600; *The Economist Book of Vital World Statistics.*

CYPRUS - EMPLOYMENT

Euromonitor Publications Limited, 87-88 Turnmill Street, London EC1M 5QU, England; *European Marketing Data and Statistics.*

Facts on File, 460 Park Avenue South, New York, New York 10016 (800) 443-8323; *The New Book of World Rankings.*

International Labour Office, I.L.O. Publications, CH-1211, Geneva 22, Switzerland; *Yearbook of Labour Statistics.*

Statistical Office of the United Nations, Publishing Service, New York, New York 10017 (800) 253-9646; *Statistical Yearbook.*

CYPRUS - ENERGY

Euromonitor Publications Limited, 87-88 Turnmill Street, London EC1M 5QU, England; *European Marketing Data and Statistics.*

Facts on File, 460 Park Avenue South, New York, New York 10016 (800) 443-8323; *The New Book of World Rankings.*

Food and Agricultural Organization of the United Nations (FAO) Via delle Terme di Caracalla, 00100 Rome, Italy (Telephone Number in U.S. (202) 653-2400); *The State of Food and Agriculture.*

G.K. Hall and Company, 70 Lincoln Street, Boston, Massachusetts 02111 (617) 423-3990; *The World in Figures.*

Statistical Office of the United Nations, Publishing Service, New York, New York 10017 (800) 253-9646; *Energy Statistics Yearbook,* and *Statistical Yearbook.*

Times Books, 201 East 50th Street, New York, New York 10022 (212) 751-2600; *The Economist Book of Vital World Statistics.*

CYPRUS - EXCHANGE RATES

International Civil Aviation Organization, 1000 Sherbrooke Street West, Suite 400, Montreal, Quebec, Canada H3A 2R2 (514) 285-8219; *Civil Aviation Statistics of the World.*

International Monetary Fund, 700 Nineteenth Street, NW, Washington, D.C. 20431 (202) 623-7000; *International Financial Statistics.*

Statistical Office of the United Nations, Publishing Service, New York, New York 10017 (800) 253-9646; *Statistical Yearbook.*

CYPRUS - EXCISE TAXES - See CYPRUS - TAXATION

CYPRUS - EXPORTS

The Economist Intelligence Unit, 111 West 57th Street, New York, New York 10019 (800) 938-4685; *The World Market Atlas.*

Food and Agricultural Organization of the United Nations (FAO) Via delle Terme di Caracalla, 00100 Rome, Italy (Telephone Number in U.S. (202) 653-2400); *The State of Food and Agriculture.*

G.K. Hall and Company, 70 Lincoln Street, Boston, Massachusetts 02111 (617) 423-3990; *The World in Figures.*

International Monetary Fund, 700 Nineteenth Street, NW, Washington, D.C. 20431 (202) 623-7000; *Direction of Trade Statistics,* and *International Financial Statistics.*

Times Books, 201 East 50th Street, New York, New York 10022 (212) 751-2600; *The Economist Book of Vital World Statistics.*

The World Bank, 1818 H Street, NW, Washington, D.C. 20433 (202) 477-1234; *World Tables.*

CYPRUS - EXTERNAL INDEBTEDNESS

The World Bank, 1818 H Street, NW, Washington, D.C. 20433 (202) 477-1234; *World Tables.*

CYPRUS - EXTERNAL TRADE

Food and Agricultural Organization of the United Nations (FAO) Via delle Terme di Caracalla, 00100 Rome, Italy (Telephone Number in U.S. (202) 653-2400); *The State of Food and Agriculture*, and *Trade Yearbook*.

G.K. Hall and Company, 70 Lincoln Street, Boston, Massachusetts 02111 (617) 423-3990; *The World in Figures*.

Statistical Office of the United Nations, Publishing Service, New York, New York 10017 (800) 253-9646; *Statistical Yearbook*.

CYPRUS - FARM CROPS - See CYPRUS - CROPS

CYPRUS - FERTILITY RATES

Facts on File, 460 Park Avenue South, New York, New York 10016 (800) 443-8323; *The New Book of World Rankings*.

Times Books, 201 East 50th Street, New York, New York 10022 (212) 751-2600; *The Economist Book of Vital World Statistics*.

The World Bank, 1818 H Street, NW, Washington, D.C. 20433 (202) 477-1234; *World Tables*.

CYPRUS - FERTILIZER

Food and Agricultural Organization of the United Nations (FAO), Via delle Terme di Caracalla, 00100 Rome, Italy (Telephone Number in U.S. (202) 653-2400); *Fertilizer Yearbook*, and *The State of Food and Agriculture*.

Statistical Office of the United Nations, Publishing Service, New York, New York 10017 (800) 253-9646; *Statistical Yearbook*.

CYPRUS - FETAL MORTALITY

Statistical Office of the United Nations, Publishing Service, New York, New York 10017 (800) 253-9646; *Demographic Yearbook*.

World Health Organization, Office of Publications, Avenue Appia, CH-1211 Geneva 27, Switzerland (Telephone Number in U.S. (518) 436-9686); *World Health Statistics Annual*.

CYPRUS - FINANCE

Facts on File, 460 Park Avenue South, New York, New York 10016 (800) 443-8323; *The New Book of World Rankings*.

G.K. Hall and Company, 70 Lincoln Street, Boston, Massachusetts 02111 (617) 423-3990; *The World in Figures*.

International Monetary Fund, 700 Nineteenth Street, NW, Washington, D.C. 20431 (202) 623-7000; *Government Finance Statistics Yearbook*, and *International Financial Statistics*.

CYPRUS - FISHERIES

Euromonitor Publications Limited, 87-88 Turnmill Street, London EC1M 5QU, England; *European Marketing Data and Statistics*.

Facts on File, 460 Park Avenue South, New York, New York 10016 (800) 443-8323; *The New Book of World Rankings*.

Food and Agricultural Organization of the United Nations (FAO) Via delle Terme di Caracalla, 00100 Rome, Italy (Telephone Number in U.S. (202) 653-2400); *The State of Food and Agriculture*, and *Yearbook of Fishery Statistics*.

Statistical Office of the United Nations, Publishing Service, New York, New York 10017 (800) 253-9646; *Statistical Yearbook*.

CYPRUS - FOOD

Food and Agricultural Organization of the United Nations (FAO) Via delle Terme di Caracalla, 00100 Rome, Italy (Telephone Number in U.S. (202) 653-2400); *Production Yearbook*, and *The State of Food and Agriculture*.

G.K. Hall and Company, 70 Lincoln Street, Boston, Massachusetts 02111 (617) 423-3990; *The World in Figures*.

CYPRUS - FOREIGN AID

G.K. Hall and Company, 70 Lincoln Street, Boston, Massachusetts 02111 (617) 423-3990; *The World in Figures*.

CYPRUS - FOREIGN DEBT

International Monetary Fund, 700 Nineteenth Street, NW, Washington, D.C. 20431 (202) 623-7000; *Government Finance Statistics Yearbook*.

CYPRUS - FOREIGN TRADE

Euromonitor Publications Limited, 87-88 Turnmill Street, London EC1M 5QU, England; *European Marketing Data and Statistics*.

Facts on File, 460 Park Avenue South, New York, New York 10016 (800) 443-8323; *The New Book of World Rankings*.

Food and Agricultural Organization of the United Nations (FAO) Via delle Terme di Caracalla, 00100 Rome, Italy (Telephone Number in U.S. (202) 653-2400); *The State of Food and Agriculture*.

G.K. Hall and Company, 70 Lincoln Street, Boston, Massachusetts 02111 (617) 423-3990; *The World in Figures*.

International Monetary Fund, 700 Nineteenth Street, NW, Washington, D.C. 20431 (202) 623-7000; *International Financial Statistics*.

Statistical Office of the United Nations, Publishing Service, New York, New York 10017 (800) 253-9646; *International Trade Statistics Yearbook*, and *Statistical Yearbook*.

The World Bank, 1818 H Street, NW, Washington, D.C. 20433 (202) 477-1234; *World Tables*.

CYPRUS - FORESTRY AND FOREST PRODUCTS

Euromonitor Publications Limited, 87-88 Turnmill Street, London EC1M 5QU, England; *European Marketing Data and Statistics*.

Facts on File, 460 Park Avenue South, New York, New York 10016 (800) 443-8323; *The New Book of World Rankings*.

Food and Agricultural Organization of the United Nations (FAO) Via delle Terme di Caracalla, 00100 Rome, Italy (Telephone Number in U.S. (202) 653-2400); *The State of Food and Agriculture*, and *Yearbook of Forest Products*.

G.K. Hall and Company, 70 Lincoln Street, Boston, Massachusetts 02111 (617) 423-3990; *The World in Figures*.

Statistical Office of the United Nations, Publishing Service, New York, New York 10017 (800) 253-9646; *Statistical Yearbook*.

United Nations Educational, Scientific and Cultural Organization (UNESCO), 7 Place de Fontenoy, F-75700 Paris, France (Telephone Number in U.S. (212) 963-5981); *Statistical Yearbook.*

CYPRUS - FRUIT PRODUCTION

International Monetary Fund, 700 Nineteenth Street, NW, Washington, D.C. 20431 (202) 623-7000; *International Financial Statistics.*

CYPRUS - GAS PRODUCTION - See CYPRUS - MINING AND MINERAL PRODUCTS

CYPRUS - GENERAL INDUSTRIAL STATISTICS

Statistical Office of the United Nations, Publishing Service, New York, New York 10017 (800) 253-9646; *Industrial Statistics Yearbook.*

CYPRUS - GENERAL MORTALITY

Statistical Office of the United Nations, Publishing Service, New York, New York 10017 (800) 253-9646; *Demographic Yearbook.*

World Health Organization, Office of Publications, Avenue Appia, CH-1211 Geneva 27, Switzerland (Telephone Number in U.S. (518) 436-9686); *World Health Statistics Annual.*

CYPRUS - GEOGRAPHIC DATA

Facts on File, 460 Park Avenue South, New York, New York 10016 (800) 443-8323; *The New Book of World Rankings.*

CYPRUS - GOLD HOLDINGS

International Monetary Fund, 700 Nineteenth Street, NW, Washington, D.C. 20431 (202) 623-7000; *International Financial Statistics.*

Statistical Office of the United Nations, Publishing Service, New York, New York 10017 (800) 253-9646; *Statistical Yearbook.*

The World Bank, 1818 H Street, NW, Washington, D.C. 20433 (202) 477-1234; *World Tables.*

CYPRUS - GOLD PRODUCTION AND CONSUMPTION - See CYPRUS - MINING AND MINERAL PRODUCTS

CYPRUS - GOVERNMENT

G.K. Hall and Company, 70 Lincoln Street, Boston, Massachusetts 02111 (617) 423-3990; *The World in Figures.*

CYPRUS - GOVERNMENT EXPENDITURES

International Monetary Fund, 700 Nineteenth Street, NW, Washington, D.C. 20431 (202) 623-7000; *Government Finance Statistics Yearbook.*

Times Books, 201 East 50th Street, New York, New York 10022 (212) 751-2600; *The Economist Book of Vital World Statistics.*

The World Bank, 1818 H Street, NW, Washington, D.C. 20433 (202) 477-1234; *World Tables.*

CYPRUS - GOVERNMENT FINANCES

International Monetary Fund, 700 Nineteenth Street, NW, Washington, D.C. 20431 (202) 623-7000; *International Financial Statistics.*

Statistical Office of the United Nations, Publishing Service, New York, New York 10017 (800) 253-9646; *Statistical Yearbook.*

CYPRUS - GOVERNMENT REVENUES

International Monetary Fund, 700 Nineteenth Street, NW, Washington, D.C. 20431 (202) 623-7000; *Government Finance Statistics Yearbook.*

Times Books, 201 East 50th Street, New York, New York 10022 (212) 751-2600; *The Economist Book of Vital World Statistics.*

The World Bank, 1818 H Street, NW, Washington, D.C. 20433 (202) 477-1234; *World Tables.*

CYPRUS - GRAIN PRODUCTION - See CYPRUS - CROPS

CYPRUS - GRANTS

International Monetary Fund, 700 Nineteenth Street, NW, Washington, D.C. 20431 (202) 623-7000; *Government Finance Statistics Yearbook.*

CYPRUS - GROSS DOMESTIC PRODUCT

The Economist Intelligence Unit, 111 West 57th Street, New York, New York 10019 (800) 938-4685; *The World Market Atlas.*

Facts on File, 460 Park Avenue South, New York, New York 10016 (800) 443-8323; *The New Book of World Rankings.*

G.K. Hall and Company, 70 Lincoln Street, Boston, Massachusetts 02111 (617) 423-3990; *The World in Figures.*

Statistical Office of the United Nations, Publishing Service, New York, New York 10017 (800) 253-9646; *Statistical Yearbook.*

Times Books, 201 East 50th Street, New York, New York 10022 (212) 751-2600; *The Economist Book of Vital World Statistics.*

The World Bank, 1818 H Street, NW, Washington, D.C. 20433 (202) 477-1234; *World Tables.*

CYPRUS - GROSS NATIONAL PRODUCT

U.S. Arms Control and Disarmament Agency, 320 Twenty-first Street, NW, Washington, D.C. 20451 (202) 647-8677; *World Military Expenditures and Arms Transfers.*

The World Bank, 1818 H Street, NW, Washington, D.C. 20433 (202) 477-1234; *World Tables.*

CYPRUS - GROUNDNUTS PRODUCTION - See CYPRUS - CROPS

CYPRUS - HAZELNUT PRODUCTION - See CYPRUS - CROPS

CYPRUS - HEALTH

Facts on File, 460 Park Avenue South, New York, New York 10016 (800) 443-8323; *The New Book of World Rankings.*

G.K. Hall and Company, 70 Lincoln Street, Boston, Massachusetts 02111 (617) 423-3990; *The World in Figures.*

Statistical Office of the United Nations, Publishing Service, New York, New York 10017 (800) 253-9646; *Statistical Yearbook.*

Times Books, 201 East 50th Street, New York, New York 10022 (212) 751-2600; *The Economist Book of Vital World Statistics.*

World Health Organization, Office of Publications, Avenue Appia, CH-1211 Geneva 27, Switzerland (Telephone Number in U.S. (518) 436-9686); *World Health Statistics Annual.*

CYPRUS - HEALTH EXPENDITURES

International Monetary Fund, 700 Nineteenth Street, NW, Washington, D.C. 20431 (202) 623-7000; *Government Finance Statistics Yearbook.*

CYPRUS - HIDE PRODUCTION

Food and Agricultural Organization of the United Nations (FAO), Via delle Terme di Caracalla, 00100 Rome, Italy (Telephone Number in U.S. (202) 653-2400); *Production Yearbook.*

CYPRUS - HIGHWAYS

G.K. Hall and Company, 70 Lincoln Street, Boston, Massachusetts 02111 (617) 423-3990; *The World in Figures.*

International Road Federation, 525 School Street, SW, Washington, D.C. 20024 (202) 554-2106; *World Road Statistics.*

Statistical Office of the United Nations, Publishing Service, New York, New York 10017 (800) 253-9646; *Annual Bulletin of Transport Statistics for Europe.*

CYPRUS - HORSES - See CYPRUS - LIVESTOCK AND POULTRY

CYPRUS - HOURS OF WORK - See CYPRUS - EMPLOYMENT

CYPRUS - HOUSING AND HOUSING UNITS

Facts on File, 460 Park Avenue South, New York, New York 10016 (800) 443-8323; *The New Book of World Rankings.*

CYPRUS - HOUSING EXPENDITURES

International Monetary Fund, 700 Nineteenth Street, NW, Washington, D.C. 20431 (202) 623-7000; *Government Finance Statistics Yearbook.*

CYPRUS - ILLITERATE POPULATION

The Economist Intelligence Unit, 111 West 57th Street, New York, New York 10019 (800) 938-4685; *The World Market Atlas.*

G.K. Hall and Company, 70 Lincoln Street, Boston, Massachusetts 02111 (617) 423-3990; *The World in Figures.*

United Nations Educational, Scientific and Cultural Organization (UNESCO), 7 Place de Fontenoy, F-75700 Paris, France (Telephone Number in U.S. (212) 963-5981); *Statistical Yearbook.*

CYPRUS - IMPORTS

The Economist Intelligence Unit, 111 West 57th Street, New York, New York 10019 (800) 938-4685; *The World Market Atlas.*

Food and Agricultural Organization of the United Nations (FAO) Via delle Terme di Caracalla, 00100 Rome, Italy (Telephone Number in U.S. (202) 653-2400); *The State of Food and Agriculture.*

G.K. Hall and Company, 70 Lincoln Street, Boston, Massachusetts 02111 (617) 423-3990; *The World in Figures.*

International Monetary Fund, 700 Nineteenth Street, NW, Washington, D.C. 20431 (202) 623-7000; *Direction of Trade Statistics, Government Finance Statistics Yearbook,* and *International Financial Statistics.*

Statistical Office of the United Nations, Publishing Service, New York, New York 10017 (800) 253-9646; *Trade in Manufactures of Developing Countries.*

Times Books, 201 East 50th Street, New York, New York 10022 (212) 751-2600; *The Economist Book of Vital World Statistics.*

The World Bank, 1818 H Street, NW, Washington, D.C. 20433 (202) 477-1234; *World Tables.*

CYPRUS - INCOME TAXES - See CYPRUS - TAXATION

CYPRUS - INDUSTRY

Facts on File, 460 Park Avenue South, New York, New York 10016 (800) 443-8323; *The New Book of World Rankings.*

G.K. Hall and Company, 70 Lincoln Street, Boston, Massachusetts 02111 (617) 423-3990; *The World in Figures.*

International Labour Office, I.L.O. Publications, CH-1211, Geneva 22, Switzerland; *Yearbook of Labour Statistics.*

International Monetary Fund, 700 Nineteenth Street, NW, Washington, D.C. 20431 (202) 623-7000; *International Financial Statistics.*

Times Books, 201 East 50th Street, New York, New York 10022 (212) 751-2600; *The Economist Book of Vital World Statistics.*

The World Bank, 1818 H Street, NW, Washington, D.C. 20433 (202) 477-1234; *World Tables.*

World Intellectual Property Organization, 34 Chemin des Colombettes, CH-1211 Geneva 20. Switzerland; *Industrial Property Statistics.*

CYPRUS - INFANT AND MATERNAL MORTALITY

Statistical Office of the United Nations, Publishing Service, New York, New York 10017 (800) 253-9646; *Demographic Yearbook.*

Times Books, 201 East 50th Street, New York, New York 10022 (212) 751-2600; *The Economist Book of Vital World Statistics.*

The World Bank, 1818 H Street, NW, Washington, D.C. 20433 (202) 477-1234; *World Tables.*

World Health Organization, Office of Publications, Avenue Appia, CH-1211 Geneva 27, Switzerland (Telephone Number in U.S. (518) 436-9686); *World Health Statistics Annual.*

CYPRUS - INTERNATIONAL LIQUIDITY

International Monetary Fund, 700 Nineteenth Street, NW, Washington, D.C. 20431 (202) 623-7000; *International Financial Statistics.*

CYPRUS - INTERNATIONAL RESERVES EXCLUDING GOLD

The World Bank, 1818 H Street, NW, Washington, D.C. 20433 (202) 477-1234; *World Tables.*

CYPRUS - IRON ORE PRODUCTION AND CONSUMPTION - See CYPRUS - MINING AND MINERAL PRODUCTS

CYPRUS - LABOR FORCE

Facts on File, 460 Park Avenue South, New York, New York 10016 (800) 443-8323; *The New Book of World Rankings.*

Food and Agricultural Organization of the United Nations (FAO) Via delle Terme di Caracalla, 00100 Rome, Italy (Telephone Number in U.S. (202) 653-2400); *The State of Food and Agriculture.*

G.K. Hall and Company, 70 Lincoln Street, Boston, Massachusetts 02111 (617) 423-3990; *The World in Figures.*

Times Books, 201 East 50th Street, New York, New York 10022 (212) 751-2600; *The Economist Book of Vital World Statistics.*

The World Bank, 1818 H Street, NW, Washington, D.C. 20433 (202) 477-1234; *World Tables.*

CYPRUS - LABOR PRODUCTIVITY

International Labour Office, I.L.O. Publications, CH-1211, Geneva 22, Switzerland; *Yearbook of Labour Statistics.*

CYPRUS - LAND USE

Euromonitor Publications Limited, 87-88 Turnmill Street, London EC1M 5QU, England; *European Marketing Data and Statistics.*

Food and Agricultural Organization of the United Nations (FAO), Via delle Terme di Caracalla, 00100 Rome, Italy (Telephone Number in U.S. (202) 653-2400); *Production Yearbook.*

G.K. Hall and Company, 70 Lincoln Street, Boston, Massachusetts 02111 (617) 423-3990; *The World in Figures.*

CYPRUS - LIBRARIES

Euromonitor Publications Limited, 87-88 Turnmill Street, London EC1M 5QU, England; *European Marketing Data and Statistics.*

Facts on File, 460 Park Avenue South, New York, New York 10016 (800) 443-8323; *The New Book of World Rankings.*

United Nations Educational, Scientific and Cultural Organization (UNESCO), 7 Place de Fontenoy, F-75700 Paris, France (Telephone Number in U.S. (212) 963-5981); *Statistical Yearbook.*

CYPRUS - LIVESTOCK AND POULTRY

Euromonitor Publications Limited, 87-88 Turnmill Street, London EC1M 5QU, England; *European Marketing Data and Statistics.*

Facts on File, 460 Park Avenue South, New York, New York 10016 (800) 443-8323; *The New Book of World Rankings.*

Food and Agricultural Organization of the United Nations (FAO), Via delle Terme di Caracalla, 00100 Rome, Italy (Telephone Number in U.S. (202) 653-2400); *Production Yearbook,* and *The State of Food and Agriculture.*

G.K. Hall and Company, 70 Lincoln Street, Boston, Massachusetts 02111 (617) 423-3990; *The World in Figures.*

Statistical Office of the United Nations, Publishing Service, New York, New York 10017 (800) 253-9646; *Statistical Yearbook.*

CYPRUS - LIVING LEVELS

G.K. Hall and Company, 70 Lincoln Street, Boston, Massachusetts 02111 (617) 423-3990; *The World in Figures.*

Times Books, 201 East 50th Street, New York, New York 10022 (212) 751-2600; *The Economist Book of Vital World Statistics.*

CYPRUS - MAIL - NUMBER OF PIECES SENT OR RECEIVED

Statistical Office of the United Nations, Publishing Service, New York, New York 10017 (800) 253-9646; *Statistical Yearbook.*

CYPRUS - MANUFACTURING

Facts on File, 460 Park Avenue South, New York, New York 10016 (800) 443-8323; *The New Book of World Rankings.*

G.K. Hall and Company, 70 Lincoln Street, Boston, Massachusetts 02111 (617) 423-3990; *The World in Figures.*

Statistical Office of the United Nations, Publishing Service, New York, New York 10017 (800) 253-9646; *Statistical Yearbook.*

The World Bank, 1818 H Street, NW, Washington, D.C. 20433 (202) 477-1234; *World Tables.*

CYPRUS - MARRIAGE RATES

Facts on File, 460 Park Avenue South, New York, New York 10016 (800) 443-8323; *The New Book of World Rankings.*

Statistical Office of the United Nations, Publishing Service, New York, New York 10017 (800) 253-9646; *Demographic Yearbook,* and *Statistical Yearbook.*

CYPRUS - MEAT PRODUCTION - See CYPRUS - LIVESTOCK AND POULTRY

CYPRUS - MERCHANT SHIPPING

G.K. Hall and Company, 70 Lincoln Street, Boston, Massachusetts 02111 (617) 423-3990; *The World in Figures.*

Lloyd's Register of Shipping, 17 Battery Place, New York, New York 10004 (212) 425-8050; *Register of Ships.*

Statistical Office of the United Nations, Publishing Service, New York, New York 10017 (800) 253-9646; *Statistical Yearbook.*

Times Books, 201 East 50th Street, New York, New York 10022 (212) 751-2600; *The Economist Book of Vital World Statistics.*

U.S. Department of Transportation, Maritime Administration, 400 Seventh Street, SW, Washington, D.C. 20590 (202) 366-5807; *A Statistical Analysis of the World's Merchant Fleets.*

CYPRUS - MILITARY

G.K. Hall and Company, 70 Lincoln Street, Boston, Massachusetts 02111 (617) 423-3990; *The World in Figures.*

The International Institute for Strategic Studies, 23 Tavistock Street, London WC2E 7NQ, England; *The Military Balance.*

U.S. Arms Control and Disarmament Agency, 320 Twenty-first Street, NW, Washington, D.C. 20451 (202) 647-8677; *World Military Expenditures and Arms Transfers.*

CYPRUS - MILK - See CYPRUS - DAIRY PRODUCTS

CYPRUS - MINING AND MINERAL PRODUCTS

Facts on File, 460 Park Avenue South, New York, New York 10016 (800) 443-8323; *The New Book of World Rankings.*

G.K. Hall and Company, 70 Lincoln Street, Boston, Massachusetts 02111 (617) 423-3990; *The World in Figures.*

International Monetary Fund, 700 Nineteenth Street, NW, Washington, D.C. 20431 (202) 623-7000; *International Financial Statistics.*

Statistical Office of the United Nations, Publishing Service, New York, New York 10017 (800) 253-9646; *Statistical Yearbook.*

CYPRUS - MONEY EXCHANGE RATES

International Monetary Fund, 700 Nineteenth Street, NW, Washington, D.C. 20431 (202) 623-7000; *International Financial Statistics.*

Statistical Office of the United Nations, Publishing Service, New York, New York 10017 (800) 253-9646; *Statistical Yearbook.*

CYPRUS - MONEY SUPPLY

G.K. Hall and Company, 70 Lincoln Street, Boston, Massachusetts 02111 (617) 423-3990; *The World in Figures.*

International Monetary Fund, 700 Nineteenth Street, NW, Washington, D.C. 20431 (202) 623-7000; *International Financial Statistics.*

Statistical Office of the United Nations, Publishing Service, New York, New York 10017 (800) 253-9646; *Statistical Yearbook.*

The World Bank, 1818 H Street, NW, Washington, D.C. 20433 (202) 477-1234; *World Tables.*

CYPRUS - MONUMENTS AND HISTORICAL SITES

United Nations Educational, Scientific and Cultural Organization (UNESCO), 7 Place de Fontenoy, F-75700 Paris, France (Telephone Number in U.S. (212) 963-5981); *Statistical Yearbook.*

CYPRUS - MOTION PICTURES

Statistical Office of the United Nations, Publishing Service, New York, New York 10017 (800) 253-9646; *Statistical Yearbook.*

CYPRUS - MOTOR VEHICLE TAXES - See CYPRUS - TAXATION

CYPRUS - MOTOR VEHICLES IN USE

G.K. Hall and Company, 70 Lincoln Street, Boston, Massachusetts 02111 (617) 423-3990; *The World in Figures.*

International Road Federation, 525 School Street, SW, Washington, D.C. 20024 (202) 554-2106; *World Road Statistics.*

Statistical Office of the United Nations, Publishing Service, New York, New York 10017 (800) 253-9646; *Statistical Yearbook.*

Times Books, 201 East 50th Street, New York, New York 10022 (212) 751-2600; *The Economist Book of Vital World Statistics.*

CYPRUS - MULES - See CYPRUS - LIVESTOCK AND POULTRY

CYPRUS - MUSEUMS

Euromonitor Publications Limited, 87-88 Turnmill Street, London EC1M 5QU, England; *European Marketing Data and Statistics.*

Facts on File, 460 Park Avenue South, New York, New York 10016 (800) 443-8323; *The New Book of World Rankings.*

United Nations Educational, Scientific and Cultural Organization (UNESCO), 7 Place de Fontenoy, F-75700 Paris, France (Telephone Number in U.S. (212) 963-5981); *Statistical Yearbook.*

CYPRUS - NATALITY - See CYPRUS - BIRTH RATES

CYPRUS - NATIONAL ACCOUNTS

Statistical Office of the United Nations, Publishing Service, New York, New York 10017 (800) 253-9646; *National Accounts Statistics,* and *Statistical Yearbook.*

CYPRUS - NATIONAL INCOME

Facts on File, 460 Park Avenue South, New York, New York 10016 (800) 443-8323; *The New Book of World Rankings.*

G.K. Hall and Company, 70 Lincoln Street, Boston, Massachusetts 02111 (617) 423-3990; *The World in Figures.*

Statistical Office of the United Nations, Publishing Service, New York, New York 10017 (800) 253-9646; *Statistical Yearbook.*

CYPRUS - NATIONAL PRODUCT

Facts on File, 460 Park Avenue South, New York, New York 10016 (800) 443-8323; *The New Book of World Rankings.*

Statistical Office of the United Nations, Publishing Service, New York, New York 10017 (800) 253-9646; *Statistical Yearbook.*

CYPRUS - NATURAL GAS PRODUCTION - See CYPRUS - MINING AND MINERAL PRODUCTS

CYPRUS - NEWSPAPER PRODUCTION - See CYPRUS - FORESTRY AND FOREST PRODUCTS

CYPRUS - NEWSPRINT CONSUMPTION - See CYPRUS - FORESTRY AND FOREST PRODUCTS

CYPRUS - NUPTIALITY - See CYPRUS - MARRIAGE RATES

CYPRUS - OCCUPATIONS - See CYPRUS - LABOR FORCE

CYPRUS - PAPER - See CYPRUS - FORESTRY AND FOREST PRODUCTS

CYPRUS - PATENTS

Statistical Office of the United Nations, Publishing Service, New York, New York 10017 (800) 253-9646; *Statistical Yearbook.*

World Intellectual Property Organization, 34 Chemin des Colombettes, CH-1211 Geneva 20. Switzerland; *Industrial Property Statistics.*

CYPRUS - PEANUT PRODUCTION - See CYPRUS - CROPS

CYPRUS - PERIODICALS

United Nations Educational, Scientific and Cultural Organization (UNESCO), 7 Place de Fontenoy, F-75700 Paris, France (Telephone Number in U.S. (212) 963-5981); *Statistical Yearbook.*

CYPRUS - PESTICIDE USE

Food and Agricultural Organization of the United Nations (FAO) Via delle Terme di Caracalla, 00100 Rome, Italy (Telephone Number in U.S. (202) 653-2400); *The State of Food and Agriculture.*

CYPRUS - PETROLEUM INDUSTRY

Euromonitor Publications Limited, 87-88 Turnmill Street, London EC1M 5QU, England; *European Marketing Data and Statistics.*

Facts on File, 460 Park Avenue South, New York, New York 10016 (800) 443-8323; *The New Book of World Rankings.*

Food and Agricultural Organization of the United Nations (FAO) Via delle Terme di Caracalla, 00100 Rome, Italy (Telephone Number in U.S. (202) 653-2400); *The State of Food and Agriculture.*

G.K. Hall and Company, 70 Lincoln Street, Boston, Massachusetts 02111 (617) 423-3990; *The World in Figures.*

Statistical Office of the United Nations, Publishing Service, New York, New York 10017 (800) 253-9646; *Statistical Yearbook.*

CYPRUS - PIGS - See CYPRUS - LIVESTOCK AND POULTRY

CYPRUS - POPULATION

The Economist Intelligence Unit, 111 West 57th Street, New York, New York 10019 (800) 938-4685; *The World Market Atlas.*

Euromonitor Publications Limited, 87-88 Turnmill Street, London EC1M 5QU, England; *European Marketing Data and Statistics.*

Facts on File, 460 Park Avenue South, New York, New York 10016 (800) 443-8323; *The New Book of World Rankings.*

Food and Agricultural Organization of the United Nations (FAO), Via delle Terme di Caracalla, 00100 Rome, Italy (Telephone Number in U.S. (202) 653-2400); *Production Yearbook.*

G.K. Hall and Company, 70 Lincoln Street, Boston, Massachusetts 02111 (617) 423-3990; *The World in Figures.*

International Labour Office, I.L.O. Publications, CH-1211, Geneva 22, Switzerland; *Yearbook of Labour Statistics.*

Statistical Office of the United Nations, Publishing Service, New York, New York 10017 (800) 253-9646; *Demographic Yearbook,* and *Statistical Yearbook.*

Times Books, 201 East 50th Street, New York, New York 10022 (212) 751-2600; *The Economist Book of Vital World Statistics.*

United Nations Educational, Scientific and Cultural Organization (UNESCO), 7 Place de Fontenoy, F-75700 Paris, France (Telephone Number in U.S. (212) 963-5981); *Statistical Yearbook.*

U.S. Arms Control and Disarmament Agency, 320 Twenty-first Street, NW, Washington, D.C. 20451 (202) 647-8677; *World Military Expenditures and Arms Transfers.*

World Health Organization, Office of Publications, Avenue Appia, CH-1211 Geneva 27, Switzerland (Telephone Number in U.S. (518) 436-9686); *World Health Statistics Annual.*

CYPRUS - POST OFFICES

Facts on File, 460 Park Avenue South, New York, New York 10016 (800) 443-8323; *The New Book of World Rankings.*

CYPRUS - POTATO PRODUCTION - See CYPRUS - CROPS

CYPRUS - PRICES

Facts on File, 460 Park Avenue South, New York, New York 10016 (800) 443-8323; *The New Book of World Rankings.*

Food and Agricultural Organization of the United Nations (FAO), Via delle Terme di Caracalla, 00100 Rome, Italy (Telephone Number in U.S. (202) 653-2400); *Production Yearbook,* and *The State of Food and Agriculture.*

G.K. Hall and Company, 70 Lincoln Street, Boston, Massachusetts 02111 (617) 423-3990; *The World in Figures.*

International Labour Office, I.L.O. Publications, CH-1211, Geneva 22, Switzerland; *Yearbook of Labour Statistics.*

International Monetary Fund, 700 Nineteenth Street, NW, Washington, D.C. 20431 (202) 623-7000; *International Financial Statistics.*

CYPRUS - PRINTING AND WRITING PAPER - See CYPRUS - FORESTRY AND FOREST PRODUCTS

CYPRUS - PRODUCTION

Facts on File, 460 Park Avenue South, New York, New York 10016 (800) 443-8323; *The New Book of World Rankings.*

G.K. Hall and Company, 70 Lincoln Street, Boston, Massachusetts 02111 (617) 423-3990; *The World in Figures.*

CYPRUS - PROPERTY TAXES - See CYPRUS - TAXATION

CYPRUS - PUBLIC FINANCE

Facts on File, 460 Park Avenue South, New York, New York 10016 (800) 443-8323; *The New Book of World Rankings.*

CYPRUS - RADIO BROADCASTING - See CYPRUS - BROADCASTING

CYPRUS - RAILWAYS

Euromonitor Publications Limited, 87-88 Turnmill Street, London EC1M 5QU, England; *European Marketing Data and Statistics.*

G.K. Hall and Company, 70 Lincoln Street, Boston, Massachusetts 02111 (617) 423-3990; *The World in Figures.*

CYPRUS - RELIGION

Facts on File, 460 Park Avenue South, New York, New York 10016 (800) 443-8323; *The New Book of World Rankings.*

CYPRUS - RENT PRICES

International Labour Office, I.L.O. Publications, CH-1211, Geneva 22, Switzerland; *Yearbook of Labour Statistics.*

CYPRUS - RETAIL TRADE

G.K. Hall and Company, 70 Lincoln Street, Boston, Massachusetts 02111 (617) 423-3990; *The World in Figures.*

Statistical Office of the United Nations, Publishing Service, New York, New York 10017 (800) 253-9646; *Statistical Yearbook.*

CYPRUS - RICE PRODUCTION - See CYPRUS - CROPS

CYPRUS - ROOT AND TUBER PRODUCTION - See CYPRUS - CROPS

CYPRUS - ROUNDWOOD PRODUCTION - See CYPRUS - FORESTRY AND FOREST PRODUCTS

CYPRUS - RUBBER PRODUCTION

Facts on File, 460 Park Avenue South, New York, New York 10016 (800) 443-8323; *The New Book of World Rankings.*

CYPRUS - SALT PRODUCTION - See CYPRUS - MINING AND MINERAL PRODUCTS

CYPRUS - SAWNWOOD PRODUCTION - See CYPRUS - FORESTRY AND FOREST PRODUCTS

CYPRUS - SCIENTISTS AND TECHNICIANS

Statistical Office of the United Nations, Publishing Service, New York, New York 10017 (800) 253-9646; *Statistical Yearbook.*

CYPRUS - SENIOR CITIZENS

Facts on File, 460 Park Avenue South, New York, New York 10016 (800) 443-8323; *The New Book of World Rankings.*

CYPRUS - SHEEP - See CYPRUS - LIVESTOCK AND POULTRY

CYPRUS - SILVER PRODUCTION AND CONSUMPTION - See CYPRUS - MINING AND MINERAL PRODUCTS

CYPRUS - SOCIAL DATA

Facts on File, 460 Park Avenue South, New York, New York 10016 (800) 443-8323; *The New Book of World Rankings.*

G.K. Hall and Company, 70 Lincoln Street, Boston, Massachusetts 02111 (617) 423-3990; *The World in Figures.*

CYPRUS - SOCIAL SECURITY

International Monetary Fund, 700 Nineteenth Street, NW, Washington, D.C. 20431 (202) 623-7000; *Government Finance Statistics Yearbook.*

CYPRUS - STAMP TAXES AND DUTIES - See CYPRUS - TAXATION

CYPRUS - STEEL PRODUCTION - See CYPRUS - MINING AND MINERAL PRODUCTS

CYPRUS - STOCKS - COMMODITY - MARKET PRICE - INDEX

Food and Agricultural Organization of the United Nations (FAO) Via delle Terme di Caracalla, 00100 Rome, Italy (Telephone Number in U.S. (202) 653-2400); *The State of Food and Agriculture.*

CYPRUS - SUGAR PRODUCTION - See CYPRUS - CROPS

CYPRUS - TAXATION

International Monetary Fund, 700 Nineteenth Street, NW, Washington, D.C. 20431 (202) 623-7000; *Government Finance Statistics Yearbook.*

The World Bank, 1818 H Street, NW, Washington, D.C. 20433 (202) 477-1234; *World Tables.*

CYPRUS - TELEGRAPH SERVICE

Statistical Office of the United Nations, Publishing Service, New York, New York 10017 (800) 253-9646; *Statistical Yearbook.*

CYPRUS - TELEPHONES IN USE

American Telephone and Telegraph Company, 26 Parsippany Road, Whippany, New Jersey 07981 (800) 338-4038; *The World's Telephones.*

G.K. Hall and Company, 70 Lincoln Street, Boston, Massachusetts 02111 (617) 423-3990; *The World in Figures.*

Statistical Office of the United Nations, Publishing Service, New York, New York 10017 (800) 253-9646; *Statistical Yearbook.*

CYPRUS - TELEVISION BROADCASTING - See CYPRUS - BROADCASTING

CYPRUS - TEXTILE INDUSTRY

G.K. Hall and Company, 70 Lincoln Street, Boston, Massachusetts 02111 (617) 423-3990; *The World in Figures.*

CYPRUS - THEATRE

United Nations Educational, Scientific and Cultural Organization (UNESCO), 7 Place de Fontenoy, F-75700 Paris, France (Telephone Number in U.S. (212) 963-5981); *Statistical Yearbook.*

CYPRUS - TOBACCO PRODUCTION

Euromonitor Publications Limited, 87-88 Turnmill Street, London EC1M 5QU, England; *European Marketing Data and Statistics.*

Facts on File, 460 Park Avenue South, New York, New York 10016 (800) 443-8323; *The New Book of World Rankings.*

Statistical Office of the United Nations, Publishing Service, New York, New York 10017 (800) 253-9646; *Statistical Yearbook.*

CYPRUS - TOURISM

Euromonitor Publications Limited, 87-88 Turnmill Street, London EC1M 5QU, England; *European Marketing Data and Statistics.*

Facts on File, 460 Park Avenue South, New York, New York 10016 (800) 443-8323; *The New Book of World Rankings.*

G.K. Hall and Company, 70 Lincoln Street, Boston, Massachusetts 02111 (617) 423-3990; *The World in Figures.*

International Road Federation, 525 School Street, SW, Washington, D.C. 20024 (202) 554-2106; *World Road Statistics.*

Statistical Office of the United Nations, Publishing Service, New York, New York 10017 (800) 253-9646; *Statistical Yearbook.*

Times Books, 201 East 50th Street, New York, New York 10022 ((212) 751-2600; *The Economist Book of Vital World Statistics*.

World Tourism Organization, Calle Capitan Haya 42, E-28020 Madrid, Spain; *Yearbook of Tourism Statistics*.

CYPRUS - TRACTORS IN USE

Statistical Office of the United Nations, Publishing Service, New York, New York 10017 (800) 253-9646; *Statistical Yearbook*.

CYPRUS - TRADE - See CYPRUS - FOREIGN TRADE

CYPRUS - TRADEMARKS AND SERVICE MARKS

Statistical Office of the United Nations, Publishing Service, New York, New York 10017 (800) 253-9646; *Statistical Yearbook*.

World Intellectual Property Organization, 34 Chemin des Colombettes, CH-1211 Geneva 20. Switzerland; *Industrial Property Statistics*.

CYPRUS - TRANSPORTATION AND COMMUNICATIONS

Facts on File, 460 Park Avenue South, New York, New York 10016 (800) 443-8323; *The New Book of World Rankings*.

G.K. Hall and Company, 70 Lincoln Street, Boston, Massachusetts 02111 (617) 423-3990; *The World in Figures*.

CYPRUS - TURKEYS - See CYPRUS - LIVESTOCK AND POULTRY

CYPRUS - UNEMPLOYMENT

Euromonitor Publications Limited, 87-88 Turnmill Street, London EC1M 5QU, England; *European Marketing Data and Statistics*.

International Labour Office, I.L.O. Publications, CH-1211, Geneva 22, Switzerland; *Yearbook of Labour Statistics*.

Statistical Office of the United Nations, Publishing Service, New York, New York 10017 (800) 253-9646; *Statistical Yearbook*.

CYPRUS - VITAL STATISTICS

G.K. Hall and Company, 70 Lincoln Street, Boston, Massachusetts 02111 (617) 423-3990; *The World in Figures*.

Statistical Office of the United Nations, Publishing Service, New York, New York 10017 (800) 253-9646; *Statistical Yearbook*.

World Health Organization, Office of Publications, Avenue Appia, CH-1211 Geneva 27, Switzerland (Telephone Number in U.S. (518) 436-9686); *World Health Statistics Annual*.

CYPRUS - WAGES

Euromonitor Publications Limited, 87-88 Turnmill Street, London EC1M 5QU, England; *European Marketing Data and Statistics*.

G.K. Hall and Company, 70 Lincoln Street, Boston, Massachusetts 02111 (617) 423-3990; *The World in Figures*.

International Labour Office, I.L.O. Publications, CH-1211, Geneva 22, Switzerland; *Yearbook of Labour Statistics*.

Statistical Office of the United Nations, Publishing Service, New York, New York 10017 (800) 253-9646; *Statistical Yearbook*.

CYPRUS - WALNUT PRODUCTION - See CYPRUS - CROPS

CYPRUS - WATERMELON PRODUCTION - See CYPRUS - CROPS

CYPRUS - WEATHER

Facts on File, 460 Park Avenue South, New York, New York 10016 (800) 443-8323; *The New Book of World Rankings*.

G.K. Hall and Company, 70 Lincoln Street, Boston, Massachusetts 02111 (617) 423-3990; *The World in Figures*.

CYPRUS - WELFARE

International Monetary Fund, 700 Nineteenth Street, NW, Washington, D.C. 20431 (202) 623-7000; *Government Finance Statistics Yearbook*.

CYPRUS - WHEAT PRODUCTION - See CYPRUS - CROPS

CYPRUS - WHOLESALE PRICES

International Monetary Fund, 700 Nineteenth Street, NW, Washington, D.C. 20431 (202) 623-7000; *International Financial Statistics*.

Statistical Office of the United Nations, Publishing Service, New York, New York 10017 (800) 253-9646; *Statistical Yearbook*.

CYPRUS - WHOLESALE TRADE

Statistical Office of the United Nations, Publishing Service, New York, New York 10017 (800) 253-9646; *Statistical Yearbook*.

CYPRUS - WINE EXPORTS

International Monetary Fund, 700 Nineteenth Street, NW, Washington, D.C. 20431 (202) 623-7000; *International Financial Statistics*.

CYPRUS - WINE PRODUCTION

Facts on File, 460 Park Avenue South, New York, New York 10016 (800) 443-8323; *The New Book of World Rankings*.

Statistical Office of the United Nations, Publishing Service, New York, New York 10017 (800) 253-9646; *Statistical Yearbook*.

CYPRUS - WOOL PRODUCTION

Facts on File, 460 Park Avenue South, New York, New York 10016 (800) 443-8323; *The New Book of World Rankings*.

CZECH REPUBLIC - See also CZECHOSLOVAKIA

CZECH REPUBLIC - AGRICULTURE

Encyclopedia Britannica, Incorporated, 310 South Michigan Avenue, Chicago, Illinois 60604 (312) 347-7000; *Britannica World Data*.

CZECH REPUBLIC - AIRLINE SERVICE

Encyclopedia Britannica, Incorporated, 310 South Michigan Avenue, Chicago, Illinois 60604 (312) 347-7000; *Britannica World Data*.

CZECH REPUBLIC - BIRTH RATES

Encyclopedia Britannica, Incorporated, 310 South Michigan Avenue, Chicago, Illinois 60604 (312) 347-7000; *Britannica World Data*.

CZECH REPUBLIC - CONSTRUCTION INDUSTRY

Encyclopedia Britannica, Incorporated, 310 South Michigan Avenue, Chicago, Illinois 60604 (312) 347-7000; *Britannica World Data.*

CZECH REPUBLIC - DEMOGRAPHY

Encyclopedia Britannica, Incorporated, 310 South Michigan Avenue, Chicago, Illinois 60604 (312) 347-7000; *Britannica World Data.*

CZECH REPUBLIC - DIVORCE RATES

Encyclopedia Britannica, Incorporated, 310 South Michigan Avenue, Chicago, Illinois 60604 (312) 347-7000; *Britannica World Data.*

CZECH REPUBLIC - ECONOMY

Encyclopedia Britannica, Incorporated, 310 South Michigan Avenue, Chicago, Illinois 60604 (312) 347-7000; *Britannica World Data.*

CZECH REPUBLIC - ENERGY PRODUCTION

Encyclopedia Britannica, Incorporated, 310 South Michigan Avenue, Chicago, Illinois 60604 (312) 347-7000; *Britannica World Data.*

CZECH REPUBLIC - ENERGY

Encyclopedia Britannica, Incorporated, 310 South Michigan Avenue, Chicago, Illinois 60604 (312) 347-7000; *Britannica World Data.*

CZECH REPUBLIC - EXPORTS

Encyclopedia Britannica, Incorporated, 310 South Michigan Avenue, Chicago, Illinois 60604 (312) 347-7000; *Britannica World Data.*

CZECH REPUBLIC - FERTILITY RATES

Encyclopedia Britannica, Incorporated, 310 South Michigan Avenue, Chicago, Illinois 60604 (312) 347-7000; *Britannica World Data.*

CZECH REPUBLIC - FISHERIES

Encyclopedia Britannica, Incorporated, 310 South Michigan Avenue, Chicago, Illinois 60604 (312) 347-7000; *Britannica World Data.*

CZECH REPUBLIC - FOREIGN TRADE

Encyclopedia Britannica, Incorporated, 310 South Michigan Avenue, Chicago, Illinois 60604 (312) 347-7000; *Britannica World Data.*

CZECH REPUBLIC - FORESTRY AND FOREST PRODUCTS

Encyclopedia Britannica, Incorporated, 310 South Michigan Avenue, Chicago, Illinois 60604 (312) 347-7000; *Britannica World Data.*

CZECH REPUBLIC - HEALTH

Encyclopedia Britannica, Incorporated, 310 South Michigan Avenue, Chicago, Illinois 60604 (312) 347-7000; *Britannica World Data.*

CZECH REPUBLIC - IMPORTS

Encyclopedia Britannica, Incorporated, 310 South Michigan Avenue, Chicago, Illinois 60604 (312) 347-7000; *Britannica World Data.*

CZECH REPUBLIC - LAND USE

Encyclopedia Britannica, Incorporated, 310 South Michigan Avenue, Chicago, Illinois 60604 (312) 347-7000; *Britannica World Data.*

CZECH REPUBLIC - LIVESTOCK AND POULTRY

Encyclopedia Britannica, Incorporated, 310 South Michigan Avenue, Chicago, Illinois 60604 (312) 347-7000; *Britannica World Data.*

CZECH REPUBLIC - MANUFACTURING

Encyclopedia Britannica, Incorporated, 310 South Michigan Avenue, Chicago, Illinois 60604 (312) 347-7000; *Britannica World Data.*

CZECH REPUBLIC - MARRIAGE RATES

Encyclopedia Britannica, Incorporated, 310 South Michigan Avenue, Chicago, Illinois 60604 (312) 347-7000; *Britannica World Data.*

CZECH REPUBLIC - MILITARY

Encyclopedia Britannica, Incorporated, 310 South Michigan Avenue, Chicago, Illinois 60604 (312) 347-7000; *Britannica World Data.*

CZECH REPUBLIC - MINING AND MINERAL PRODUCTS

Encyclopedia Britannica, Incorporated, 310 South Michigan Avenue, Chicago, Illinois 60604 (312) 347-7000; *Britannica World Data.*

CZECH REPUBLIC - TRANSPORTATION AND COMMUNICATIONS

Encyclopedia Britannica, Incorporated, 310 South Michigan Avenue, Chicago, Illinois 60604 (312) 347-7000; *Britannica World Data.*

CZECH REPUBLIC - VITAL STATISTICS

Encyclopedia Britannica, Incorporated, 310 South Michigan Avenue, Chicago, Illinois 60604 (312) 347-7000; *Britannica World Data.*

Czechoslovakia - National Statistical Office

Federalni Statisticky Urad (Federal Statistical Office), Sokolovska 142, 186 13 Prague 8, Czechoslovakia; for federal statistics.

Czechoslovakia - Primary Statistics Sources

Federalni Statisticky Urad (Federal Statistical Office), Sokolovska 142, Praha 8-Karlin, Czechoslovakia; *Statisticka rocenka Ceske A Slovenske Federativni Republiky,* and *Statisticke prehledy* (Statistical Surveys).

CZECHOSLOVAKIA - ABORTIONS

Statistical Office of the United Nations, Publishing Service, New York, New York 10017 (800) 253-9646; *Demographic Yearbook.*

CZECHOSLOVAKIA - AGRICULTURE

Facts on File, 460 Park Avenue South, New York, New York 10016; *The New Book of World Rankings.*

Federal Statistical Office, Gustav - Stresemann - Ring 11, D-6200 Wiesbaden, Germany; *Tschechoslowakei.*

Food and Agricultural Organization of the United Nations (FAO) Via delle Terme di Caracalla, 00100 Rome, Italy (Telephone Number in U.S. (202) 653-2400); *Production Yearbook, The State of Food and Agriculture,* and *Trade Yearbook.*

G.K. Hall and Company, 70 Lincoln Street, Boston, Massachusetts 02111 (617) 423-3990; *The World in Figures.*

Statistical Office of the United Nations, Publishing Service, New York, New York 10017 (800) 253-9646; *Statistical Yearbook.*

Times Books, 201 East 50th Street, New York, New York 10022 (212) 751-2600; *The Economist Book of Vital World Statistics.*

CZECHOSLOVAKIA - AIRLINE SERVICE

Facts on File, 460 Park Avenue South, New York, New York 10016 (800) 443-8323; *The New Book of World Rankings.*

G.K. Hall and Company, 70 Lincoln Street, Boston, Massachusetts 02111 (617) 423-3990; *The World in Figures.*

Statistical Office of the United Nations, Publishing Service, New York, New York 10017 (800) 253-9646; *Statistical Yearbook.*

Times Books, 201 East 50th Street, New York, New York 10022 (212) 751-2600; *The Economist Book of Vital World Statistics.*

CZECHOSLOVAKIA - ALUMINUM PRODUCTION - See CZECHOSLOVAKIA - MINING AND MINERAL PRODUCTS

CZECHOSLOVAKIA - ANIMAL HEALTH

Food and Agricultural Organization of the United Nations (FAO), Via delle Terme di Caracalla, 00100 Rome, Italy (Telephone Number in U.S. (202) 653-2400); *Animal Health Yearbook.*

CZECHOSLOVAKIA - ANTIMONY AND ANTIMONY ORE PRODUCTION AND CONSUMPTION - See CZECHOSLOVAKIA - MINING AND MINERAL PRODUCTS

CZECHOSLOVAKIA - AREA AND DENSITY OF POPULATION

Facts on File, 460 Park Avenue South, New York, New York 10016 (800) 443-8323; *The New Book of World Rankings.*

Federal Statistical Office, Gustav - Stresemann - Ring 11, D-6200 Wiesbaden, Germany; *Tschechoslowakei.*

Food and Agricultural Organization of the United Nations (FAO) Via delle Terme di Caracalla, 00100 Rome, Italy (Telephone Number in U.S. (202) 653-2400); *The State of Food and Agriculture.*

G.K. Hall and Company, 70 Lincoln Street, Boston, Massachusetts 02111 (617) 423-3990; *The World in Figures.*

Statistical Office of the United Nations, Publishing Service, New York, New York 10017 (800) 253-9646; *Statistical Yearbook.*

Times Books, 201 East 50th Street, New York, New York 10022 (212) 751-2600; *The Economist Book of Vital World Statistics.*

CZECHOSLOVAKIA - ARMS EXPORTS AND IMPORTS

U.S. Arms Control and Disarmament Agency, 320 Twenty-first Street, NW, Washington, D.C. 20451 (202) 647-8677; *World Military Expenditures and Arms Transfers.*

CZECHOSLOVAKIA - BALANCE OF PAYMENTS

The Economist Intelligence Unit, 111 West 57th Street, New York, New York 10019 (800) 938-4685; *The World Market Atlas.*

Federal Statistical Office, Gustav - Stresemann - Ring 11, D-6200 Wiesbaden, Germany; *Tschechoslowakei.*

G.K. Hall and Company, 70 Lincoln Street, Boston, Massachusetts 02111 (617) 423-3990; *The World in Figures.*

Times Books, 201 East 50th Street, New York, New York 10022 (212) 751-2600; *The Economist Book of Vital World Statistics.*

CZECHOSLOVAKIA - BANKING

Facts on File, 460 Park Avenue South, New York, New York 10016 (800) 443-8323; *The New Book of World Rankings.*

G.K. Hall and Company, 70 Lincoln Street, Boston, Massachusetts 02111 (617) 423-3990; *The World in Figures.*

CZECHOSLOVAKIA - BARLEY PRODUCTION - See CZECHOSLOVAKIA - CROPS

CZECHOSLOVAKIA - BEER PRODUCTION

Facts on File, 460 Park Avenue South, New York, New York 10016; *The New Book of World Rankings.*

Statistical Office of the United Nations, Publishing Service, New York, New York 10017 (800) 253-9646; *Statistical Yearbook.*

CZECHOSLOVAKIA - BIRTH RATES

Facts on File, 460 Park Avenue South, New York, New York 10016; *The New Book of World Rankings.*

Statistical Office of the United Nations, Publishing Service, New York, New York 10017 (800) 253-9646; *Demographic Yearbook,* and *Statistical Yearbook.*

Times Books, 201 East 50th Street, New York, New York 10022 (212) 751-2600; *The Economist Book of Vital World Statistics.*

World Health Organization, Office of Publications, Avenue Appia, CH-1211 Geneva 27, Switzerland (Telephone Number in U.S. (518) 436-9686); *World Health Statistics Annual.*

CZECHOSLOVAKIA - BONDS

G.K. Hall and Company, 70 Lincoln Street, Boston, Massachusetts 02111 (617) 423-3990; *The World in Figures.*

CZECHOSLOVAKIA - BOOK PRODUCTION

Euromonitor Publications Limited, 87-88 Turnmill Street, London EC1M 5QU, England; *European Marketing Data and Statistics.*

G.K. Hall and Company, 70 Lincoln Street, Boston, Massachusetts 02111 (617) 423-3990; *The World in Figures.*

United Nations Educational, Scientific and Cultural Organization (UNESCO), 7 Place de Fontenoy, F-75700 Paris, France (Telephone Number in U.S. (212) 963-5981); *Statistical Yearbook.*

CZECHOSLOVAKIA - BROADCASTING

Billboard Limited, P.O. Box 9027, 1006 AA Amsterdam, The Netherlands (Telephone Number in U.S. (212) 764-7300); *World Radio TV Handbook.*

Facts on File, 460 Park Avenue South, New York, New York 10016 (800) 443-8323; *The New Book of World Rankings.*

G.K. Hall and Company, 70 Lincoln Street, Boston, Massachusetts 02111 (617) 423-3990; *The World in Figures.*

Times Books, 201 East 50th Street, New York, New York 10022 (212) 751-2600; *The Economist Book of Vital World Statistics.*

CZECHOSLOVAKIA - BUILDING CONSTRUCTION - See CZECHOSLOVAKIA - CONSTRUCTION INDUSTRY

CZECHOSLOVAKIA - BUSINESS

G.K. Hall and Company, 70 Lincoln Street, Boston, Massachusetts 02111 (617) 423-3990; *The World in Figures.*

CZECHOSLOVAKIA - BUTTER PRODUCTION - See CZECHOSLOVAKIA - DAIRY PRODUCTS

CZECHOSLOVAKIA - CABBAGE PRODUCTION - See CZECHOSLOVAKIA - CROPS

CZECHOSLOVAKIA - CALORIE SUPPLY

Food and Agricultural Organization of the United Nations (FAO) Via delle Terme di Caracalla, 00100 Rome, Italy (Telephone Number in U.S. (202) 653-2400); *The State of Food and Agriculture.*

CZECHOSLOVAKIA - CATTLE - See CZECHOSLOVAKIA - LIVESTOCK AND POULTRY

CZECHOSLOVAKIA - CAULIFLOWER PRODUCTION - See CZECHOSLOVAKIA - CROPS

CZECHOSLOVAKIA - CAUSTIC SODA PRODUCTION

Statistical Office of the United Nations, Publishing Service, New York, New York 10017 (800) 253-9646; *Statistical Yearbook.*

CZECHOSLOVAKIA - CEMENT PRODUCTION - See CZECHOSLOVAKIA - MINING AND MINERAL PRODUCTS

CZECHOSLOVAKIA - CHEESE PRODUCTION - See CZECHOSLOVAKIA - DAIRY PRODUCTS

CZECHOSLOVAKIA - CHEMICAL (ORGANIC) PRODUCTION - See CZECHOSLOVAKIA - MINING AND MINERAL PRODUCTS

CZECHOSLOVAKIA - CIGAR PRODUCTION - See CZECHOSLOVAKIA - TOBACCO PRODUCTION

CZECHOSLOVAKIA - CIGARETTE PRODUCTION - See CZECHOSLOVAKIA - TOBACCO PRODUCTION

CZECHOSLOVAKIA - CLASS STRUCTURE

Columbia University Press, 562 West 113th Street, New York, New York 10014; *East European and Soviet Data Book.*

G.K. Hall and Company, 70 Lincoln Street, Boston, Massachusetts 02111 (617) 423-3990; *The World in Figures.*

CZECHOSLOVAKIA - CLIMATE

G.K. Hall and Company, 70 Lincoln Street, Boston, Massachusetts 02111 (617) 423-3990; *The World in Figures.*

CZECHOSLOVAKIA - COAL PRODUCTION - See CZECHOSLOVAKIA - MINING AND MINERAL PRODUCTS

CZECHOSLOVAKIA - COFFEE - See CZECHOSLOVAKIA - CROPS

CZECHOSLOVAKIA - COKE OVEN COKE PRODUCTION - See CZECHOSLOVAKIA - MINING AND MINERAL PRODUCTS

CZECHOSLOVAKIA - COMMUNICATIONS

Federal Statistical Office, Gustav - Stresemann - Ring 11, D-6200 Wiesbaden, Germany; *Tschechoslowakei.*

G.K. Hall and Company, 70 Lincoln Street, Boston, Massachusetts 02111 (617) 423-3990; *The World in Figures.*

CZECHOSLOVAKIA - CONSTRUCTION INDUSTRY

Facts on File, 460 Park Avenue South, New York, New York 10016 (800) 443-8323; *The New Book of World Rankings.*

Statistical Office of the United Nations, Publishing Service, New York, New York 10017; *Construction Statistics Yearbook,* and *Statistical Yearbook.*

CZECHOSLOVAKIA - CONSUMER PRICE INDEX

Federal Statistical Office, Gustav - Stresemann - Ring 11, D-6200 Wiesbaden, Germany; *Tschechoslowakei.*

G.K. Hall and Company, 70 Lincoln Street, Boston, Massachusetts 02111 (617) 423-3990; *The World in Figures.*

Statistical Office of the United Nations, Publishing Service, New York, New York 10017 (800) 253-9646; *Statistical Yearbook,*

CZECHOSLOVAKIA - CONSUMER PRICES

Euromonitor Publications Limited, 87-88 Turnmill Street, London EC1M 5QU, England; *European Marketing Data and Statistics.*

Federal Statistical Office, Gustav - Stresemann - Ring 11, D-6200 Wiesbaden, Germany; *Tschechoslowakei.*

International Labour Office, I.L.O. Publications, CH-1211, Geneva 22, Switzerland; *Yearbook of Labour Statistics.*

CZECHOSLOVAKIA - CONSUMPTION

G.K. Hall and Company, 70 Lincoln Street, Boston, Massachusetts 02111 (617) 423-3990; *The World in Figures.*

International Lead and Zinc Study Group, Metro House, 58 St. James's Street, London SW1A 1LD, England; *Lead and Zinc Statistics.*

International Rubber Study Group, York House, 8th Floor, Empire Way, Wembley, London HA9 0PA, England; *Rubber Statistical Bulletin.*

CZECHOSLOVAKIA - COPPER AND COPPER ORE PRODUCTION - See CZECHOSLOVAKIA - MINING AND MINERAL PRODUCTS

CZECHOSLOVAKIA - CORN PRODUCTION - See CZECHOSLOVAKIA - CROPS

CZECHOSLOVAKIA - CORPORATE TAXES - See CZECHOSLOVAKIA - TAXATION

CZECHOSLOVAKIA - COTTON - See CZECHOSLOVAKIA - CROPS

CZECHOSLOVAKIA - CROPS

Commodity Research Bureau, Incorporated, 75 Wall Street, New York, New York 10005 (212) 504-7754; *Commodity Year Book.*

Euromonitor Publications Limited, 87-88 Turnmill Street, London EC1M 5QU, England; *European Marketing Data and Statistics.*

Facts on File, 460 Park Avenue South, New York, New York 10016 (800) 443-8323; *The New Book of World Rankings.*

Food and Agricultural Organization of the United Nations (FAO), Via delle Terme di Caracalla, 00100 Rome, Italy (Telephone Number in U.S. (202) 653-2400); *Production Yearbook,* and *State of Food and Agriculture.*

G.K. Hall and Company, 70 Lincoln Street, Boston, Massachusetts 02111 (617) 423-3990; *The World in Figures.*

Statistical Office of the United Nations, Publishing Service, New York, New York 10017 (800) 253-9646; *Statistical Yearbook.*

CZECHOSLOVAKIA - CUSTOMS DUTIES

G.K. Hall and Company, 70 Lincoln Street, Boston, Massachusetts 02111 (617) 423-3990; *The World in Figures.*

CZECHOSLOVAKIA - DAIRY PRODUCTS

Commodity Research Bureau, Incorporated, 75 Wall Street, New York, New York 10005 (212) 504-7754; *Commodity Year Book.*

Facts on File, 460 Park Avenue South, New York, New York 10016 (800) 443-8323; *The New Book of World Rankings.*

Food and Agricultural Organization of the United Nations (FAO), Via delle Terme di Caracalla, 00100 Rome, Italy (Telephone Number in U.S. (202) 653-2400); *Production Yearbook,* and *The State of Food and Agriculture.*

Statistical Office of the United Nations, Publishing Service, New York, New York 10017 (800) 253-9646; *Statistical Yearbook.*

CZECHOSLOVAKIA - DEATH RATE

G.K. Hall and Company, 70 Lincoln Street, Boston, Massachusetts 02111 (617) 423-3990; *The World in Figures.*

Times Books, 201 East 50th Street, New York, New York 10022 (212) 751-2600; *The Economist Book of Vital World Statistics.*

CZECHOSLOVAKIA - DEFENSE EXPENDITURES

G.K. Hall and Company, 70 Lincoln Street, Boston, Massachusetts 02111 (617) 423-3990; *The World in Figures.*

U.S. Arms Control and Disarmament Agency, 320 Twenty-first Street, NW, Washington, D.C. 20451 (202) 647-8677; *World Military Expenditures and Arms Transfers.*

CZECHOSLOVAKIA - DEMOGRAPHY

The Economist Intelligence Unit, 111 West 57th Street, New York, New York 10019 (800) 938-4685; *The World Market Atlas.*

Facts on File, 460 Park Avenue South, New York, New York 10016 (800) 443-8323; *The New Book of World Rankings.*

Federal Statistical Office, Gustav - Stresemann - Ring 11, D-6200 Wiesbaden, Germany; *Tschechoslowakei.*

G.K. Hall and Company, 70 Lincoln Street, Boston, Massachusetts 02111 (617) 423-3990; *The World in Figures.*

CZECHOSLOVAKIA - DEVELOPMENT ASSISTANCE

G.K. Hall and Company, 70 Lincoln Street, Boston, Massachusetts 02111 (617) 423-3990; *The World in Figures.*

Statistical Office of the United Nations, Publishing Service, New York, New York 10017 (800) 253-9646; *Statistical Yearbook.*

CZECHOSLOVAKIA - DIAMOND PRODUCTION - See CZECHOSLOVAKIA - MINING AND MINERAL PRODUCTS

CZECHOSLOVAKIA - DISEASE

G.K. Hall and Company, 70 Lincoln Street, Boston, Massachusetts 02111 (617) 423-3990; *The World in Figures.*

CZECHOSLOVAKIA - DIVORCE RATES

Facts on File, 460 Park Avenue South, New York, New York 10016 (800) 443-8323; *The New Book of World Rankings.*

Statistical Office of the United Nations, Publishing Service, New York, New York 10017 (800) 253-9646; *Demographic Yearbook,* and *Statistical Yearbook.*

CZECHOSLOVAKIA - DOMESTIC PRODUCT

G.K. Hall and Company, 70 Lincoln Street, Boston, Massachusetts 02111 (617) 423-3990; *The World in Figures.*

CZECHOSLOVAKIA - DUCKS - See CZECHOSLOVAKIA - LIVESTOCK AND POULTRY

CZECHOSLOVAKIA - ECONOMY

Euromonitor Publications Limited, 87-88 Turnmill Street, London EC1M 5QU, England; *European Marketing Data and Statistics.*

Facts on File, 460 Park Avenue South, New York, New York 10016 (800) 443-8323; *The New Book of World Rankings.*

Federal Statistical Office, Gustav - Stresemann - Ring 11, D-6200 Wiesbaden, Germany; *Tschechoslowakei.*

G.K. Hall and Company, 70 Lincoln Street, Boston, Massachusetts 02111 (617) 423-3990; *The World in Figures.*

CZECHOSLOVAKIA - EDUCATION

Columbia University Press, 562 West 113th Street, New York, New York 10014 (212) 316-7100; *East European and Soviet Data Book.*

The Economist Intelligence Unit, 111 West 57th Street, New York, New York 10019 (800) 938-4685; *The World Market Atlas.*

Euromonitor Publications Limited, 87-88 Turnmill Street, London EC1M 5QU, England; *European Marketing Data and Statistics.*

Facts on File, 460 Park Avenue South, New York, New York 10016; *The New Book of World Rankings.*

Federal Statistical Office, Gustav - Stresemann - Ring 11, D-6200 Wiesbaden, Germany; *Tschechoslowakei.*

G.K. Hall and Company, 70 Lincoln Street, Boston, Massachusetts 02111 (617) 423-3990; *The World in Figures.*

Times Books, 201 East 50th Street, New York, New York 10022 (212) 751-2600; *The Economist Book of Vital World Statistics.*

United Nations Educational, Scientific and Cultural Organization (UNESCO), 7 Place de Fontenoy, F-75700 Paris, France (Telephone Number in U.S. (212) 963-5981); *Statistical Yearbook.*

CZECHOSLOVAKIA - EGG PRODUCTION - See CZECHOSLOVAKIA - DAIRY PRODUCTS

CZECHOSLOVAKIA - ELECTRICITY

Commodity Research Bureau, Incorporated, 75 Wall Street, New York, New York 10005 (212) 504-7754; *Commodity Year Book.*

Facts on File, 460 Park Avenue South, New York, New York 10016 (800) 443-8323; *The New Book of World Rankings.*

Penn Well Publishing Company, 1421 South Sheridan Road, P.O. Box 1260, Tulsa, Oklahoma 74101 (800) 752-9764; *International Energy Statistics Sourcebook.*

Statistical Office of the United Nations, Publishing Service, New York, New York 10017 (800) 253-9646; *Statistical Yearbook.*

Times Books, 201 East 50th Street, New York, New York 10022 (212) 751-2600; *The Economist Book of Vital World Statistics.*

CZECHOSLOVAKIA - EMPLOYMENT

Euromonitor Publications Limited, 87-88 Turnmill Street, London EC1M 5QU, England; *European Marketing Data and Statistics.*

Facts on File, 460 Park Avenue South, New York, New York 10016 (800) 443-8323; *The New Book of World Rankings.*

Federal Statistical Office, Gustav - Stresemann - Ring 11, D-6200 Wiesbaden, Germany; *Tschechoslowakei.*

International Labour Office, I.L.O. Publications, CH-1211, Geneva 22, Switzerland; *Yearbook of Labour Statistics.*

Statistical Office of the United Nations, Publishing Service, New York, New York 10017 (800) 253-9646; *Statistical Yearbook.*

CZECHOSLOVAKIA - ENERGY

Euromonitor Publications Limited, 87-88 Turnmill Street, London EC1M 5QU, England; *European Marketing Data and Statistics.*

Facts on File, 460 Park Avenue South, New York, New York 10016 (800) 443-8323; *The New Book of World Rankings.*

Food and Agricultural Organization of the United Nations (FAO) Via delle Terme di Caracalla, 00100 Rome, Italy (Telephone Number in U.S. (202) 653-2400); *The State of Food and Agriculture.*

G.K. Hall and Company, 70 Lincoln Street, Boston, Massachusetts 02111 (617) 423-3990; *The World in Figures.*

Penn Well Publishing Company, 1421 South Sheridan Road, P.O. Box 1260, Tulsa, Oklahoma 74101 (800) 752-9764; *International Energy Statistics Sourcebook.*

Statistical Office of the United Nations, Publishing Service, New York, New York 10017 (800) 253-9646; *Energy Statistics Yearbook,* and *Statistical Yearbook.*

Times Books, 201 East 50th Street, New York, New York 10022 (212) 751-2600; *The Economist Book of Vital World Statistics.*

CZECHOSLOVAKIA - EXCHANGE RATES

Statistical Office of the United Nations, Publishing Service, New York, New York 10017 (800) 253-9646; *Statistical Yearbook.*

CZECHOSLOVAKIA - EXPORTS

American Automobile Manufacturers Association, 1401 H Street, NW, Suite 900, Washington, D.C. 20005 (202) 326-5500; *World Motor Vehicle Data.*

The Economist Intelligence Unit, 111 West 57th Street, New York, New York 10019 (800) 938-4685; *The World Market Atlas.*

Food and Agricultural Organization of the United Nations (FAO) Via delle Terme di Caracalla, 00100 Rome, Italy (Telephone Number in U.S. (202) 653-2400); *The State of Food and Agriculture.*

G.K. Hall and Company, 70 Lincoln Street, Boston, Massachusetts 02111 (617) 423-3990; *The World in Figures.*

International Lead and Zinc Study Group, Metro House, 58 St. James's Street, London SW1A 1LD, England; *Lead and Zinc Statistics.*

International Monetary Fund, 700 Nineteenth Street, NW, Washington, D.C. 20431 (202) 623-7000; *Direction of Trade Statistics.*

International Rubber Study Group, York House, 8th Floor, Empire Way, Wembley, London HA9 0PA, England; *Rubber Statistical Bulletin.*

Times Books, 201 East 50th Street, New York, New York 10022 (212) 751-2600; *The Economist Book of Vital World Statistics.*

CZECHOSLOVAKIA - EXTERNAL TRADE

Food and Agricultural Organization of the United Nations (FAO) Via delle Terme di Caracalla, 00100 Rome, Italy (Telephone Number in U.S. (202) 653-2400); *The State of Food and Agriculture,* and *Trade Yearbook.*

G.K. Hall and Company, 70 Lincoln Street, Boston, Massachusetts 02111 (617) 423-3990; *The World in Figures.*

Statistical Office of the United Nations, Publishing Service, New York, New York 10017 (800) 253-9646; *Statistical Yearbook.*

CZECHOSLOVAKIA - FABRIC PRODUCTION - See CZECHOSLOVAKIA - TEXTILE INDUSTRY

CZECHOSLOVAKIA - FARM CROPS - See CZECHOSLOVAKIA - CROPS

CZECHOSLOVAKIA - FERTILITY RATES

Columbia University Press, 562 West 113th Street, New York, New York 10014 (212) 316-7100; *East European and Soviet Data Book.*

Facts on File, 460 Park Avenue South, New York, New York 10016 (800) 443-8323; *The New Book of World Rankings.*

Times Books, 201 East 50th Street, New York, New York 10022 (212) 751-2600; *The Economist Book of Vital World Statistics.*

CZECHOSLOVAKIA - FERTILIZER

Food and Agricultural Organization of the United Nations (FAO), Via delle Terme di Caracalla, 00100 Rome, Italy (Telephone Number in

U.S. (202) 653-2400); *Fertilizer Yearbook*, and *The State of Food and Agriculture*.

Statistical Office of the United Nations, Publishing Service, New York, New York 10017 (800) 253-9646; *Statistical Yearbook*.

CZECHOSLOVAKIA - FETAL MORTALITY

Statistical Office of the United Nations, Publishing Service, New York, New York 10017 (800) 253-9646; *Demographic Yearbook*.

World Health Organization, Office of Publications, Avenue Appia, CH-1211 Geneva 27, Switzerland (Telephone Number in U.S. (518) 436-9686); *World Health Statistics Annual*.

CZECHOSLOVAKIA - FIBRE PRODUCTION - See CZECHOSLOVAKIA - TEXTILE INDUSTRY

CZECHOSLOVAKIA - FILAMENT PRODUCTION - See CZECHOSLOVAKIA - TEXTILE INDUSTRY

CZECHOSLOVAKIA - FILM - See CZECHOSLOVAKIA - MOTION PICTURES

CZECHOSLOVAKIA - FINANCE

Facts on File, 460 Park Avenue South, New York, New York 10016; *The New Book of World Rankings*.

Federal Statistical Office, Gustav - Stresemann - Ring 11, D-6200 Wiesbaden, Germany; *Tschechoslowakei*.

G.K. Hall and Company, 70 Lincoln Street, Boston, Massachusetts 02111 (617) 423-3990; *The World in Figures*.

CZECHOSLOVAKIA - FISHERIES

Euromonitor Publications Limited, 87-88 Turnmill Street, London EC1M 5QU, England; *European Marketing Data and Statistics*.

Facts on File, 460 Park Avenue South, New York, New York 10016 (800) 443-8323; *The New Book of World Rankings*.

Federal Statistical Office, Gustav - Stresemann - Ring 11, D-6200 Wiesbaden, Germany; *Tschechoslowakei*.

Food and Agricultural Organization of the United Nations (FAO) Via delle Terme di Caracalla, 00100 Rome, Italy (Telephone Number in U.S. (202) 653-2400); *The State of Food and Agriculture*, and *Yearbook of Fishery Statistics*.

Statistical Office of the United Nations, Publishing Service, New York, New York 10017 (800) 253-9646; *Statistical Yearbook*.

CZECHOSLOVAKIA - FLAX FIBRE PRODUCTION - See CZECHOSLOVAKIA - TEXTILE INDUSTRY

CZECHOSLOVAKIA - FLOUR PRODUCTION

Statistical Office of the United Nations, Publishing Service, New York, New York 10017 (800) 253-9646; *Statistical Yearbook*.

CZECHOSLOVAKIA - FOOD

Food and Agricultural Organization of the United Nations (FAO) Via delle Terme di Caracalla, 00100 Rome, Italy (Telephone Number in U.S. (202) 653-2400); *Production Yearbook*, and *The State of Food and Agriculture*.

G.K. Hall and Company, 70 Lincoln Street, Boston, Massachusetts 02111 (617) 423-3990; *The World in Figures*.

CZECHOSLOVAKIA - FOREIGN AID

G.K. Hall and Company, 70 Lincoln Street, Boston, Massachusetts 02111 (617) 423-3990; *The World in Figures*.

CZECHOSLOVAKIA - FOREIGN TRADE

Euromonitor Publications Limited, 87-88 Turnmill Street, London EC1M 5QU, England; *European Marketing Data and Statistics*.

Facts on File, 460 Park Avenue South, New York, New York 10016 (800) 443-8323; *The New Book of World Rankings*.

Federal Statistical Office, Gustav - Stresemann - Ring 11, D-6200 Wiesbaden, Germany; *Tschechoslowakei*.

Food and Agricultural Organization of the United Nations (FAO) Via delle Terme di Caracalla, 00100 Rome, Italy (Telephone Number in U.S. (202) 653-2400); *The State of Food and Agriculture*.

G.K. Hall and Company, 70 Lincoln Street, Boston, Massachusetts 02111 (617) 423-3990; *The World in Figures*.

Statistical Office of the United Nations, Publishing Service, New York, New York 10017 (800) 253-9646; *International Trade Statistics Yearbook*, and *Statistical Yearbook*.

CZECHOSLOVAKIA - FORESTRY AND FOREST PRODUCTS

Euromonitor Publications Limited, 87-88 Turnmill Street, London EC1M 5QU, England; *European Marketing Data and Statistics*.

Facts on File, 460 Park Avenue South, New York, New York 10016 (800) 443-8323; *The New Book of World Rankings*.

Federal Statistical Office, Gustav - Stresemann - Ring 11, D-6200 Wiesbaden, Germany; *Tschechoslowakei*.

Food and Agricultural Organization of the United Nations (FAO) Via delle Terme di Caracalla, 00100 Rome, Italy (Telephone Number in U.S. (202) 653-2400); *The State of Food and Agriculture*, and *Yearbook of Forest Products*.

G.K. Hall and Company, 70 Lincoln Street, Boston, Massachusetts 02111 (617) 423-3990; *The World in Figures*.

Statistical Office of the United Nations, Publishing Service, New York, New York 10017 (800) 253-9646; *Statistical Yearbook*.

United Nations Educational, Scientific and Cultural Organization (UNESCO), 7 Place de Fontenoy, F-75700 Paris, France (Telephone Number in U.S. (212) 963-5981); *Statistical Yearbook*.

CZECHOSLOVAKIA - GARLIC PRODUCTION - See CZECHOSLOVAKIA - CROPS

CZECHOSLOVAKIA - GAS LIQUIDS PRODUCTION - See CZECHOSLOVAKIA - MINING AND MINERAL PRODUCTS

CZECHOSLOVAKIA - GAS PRODUCTION - See CZECHOSLOVAKIA - MINING AND MINERAL PRODUCTS

CZECHOSLOVAKIA - GENERAL INDUSTRIAL STATISTICS

Federal Statistical Office, Gustav - Stresemann - Ring 11, D-6200 Wiesbaden, Germany; *Tschechoslowakei*.

Statistical Office of the United Nations, Publishing Service, New York, New York 10017 (800) 253-9646; *Industrial Statistics Yearbook.*

CZECHOSLOVAKIA - GENERAL MORTALITY

Statistical Office of the United Nations, Publishing Service, New York, New York 10017 (800) 253-9646; *Demographic Yearbook.*

World Health Organization, Office of Publications, Avenue Appia, CH-1211 Geneva 27, Switzerland (Telephone Number in U.S. (518) 436-9686); *World Health Statistics Annual.*

CZECHOSLOVAKIA - GEOGRAPHIC DATA

Facts on File, 460 Park Avenue South, New York, New York 10016 (800) 443-8323; *The New Book of World Rankings.*

Federal Statistical Office, Gustav - Stresemann - Ring 11, D-6200 Wiesbaden, Germany; *Tschechoslowakei.*

CZECHOSLOVAKIA - GOLD PRODUCTION AND CONSUMPTION - See CZECHOSLOVAKIA - MINING AND MINERAL PRODUCTS

CZECHOSLOVAKIA - GOVERNMENT

G.K. Hall and Company, 70 Lincoln Street, Boston, Massachusetts 02111 (617) 423-3990; *The World in Figures.*

CZECHOSLOVAKIA - GOVERNMENT FINANCES

Statistical Office of the United Nations, Publishing Service, New York, New York 10017 (800) 253-9646; *Statistical Yearbook.*

CZECHOSLOVAKIA - GRAIN PRODUCTION - See CZECHOSLOVAKIA - CROPS

CZECHOSLOVAKIA - GREEN PEPPER AND CHILIE PRODUCTION - See CZECHOSLOVAKIA - CROPS

CZECHOSLOVAKIA - GROSS DOMESTIC PRODUCT

The Economist Intelligence Unit, 111 West 57th Street, New York, New York 10019 (800) 938-4685; *The World Market Atlas.*

Facts on File, 460 Park Avenue South, New York, New York 10016 (800) 443-8323; *The New Book of World Rankings.*

G.K. Hall and Company, 70 Lincoln Street, Boston, Massachusetts 02111 (617) 423-3990; *The World in Figures.*

Statistical Office of the United Nations, Publishing Service, New York, New York 10017 (800) 253-9646; *Statistical Yearbook.*

Times Books, 201 East 50th Street, New York, New York 10022 (212) 751-2600; *The Economist Book of Vital World Statistics.*

CZECHOSLOVAKIA - GROSS NATIONAL PRODUCT

U.S. Arms Control and Disarmament Agency, 320 Twenty-first Street, NW, Washington, D.C. 20451 (202) 647-8677; *World Military Expenditures and Arms Transfers.*

CZECHOSLOVAKIA - HEALTH

Facts on File, 460 Park Avenue South, New York, New York 10016 (800) 443-8323; *The New Book of World Rankings.*

Federal Statistical Office, Gustav - Stresemann - Ring 11, D-6200 Wiesbaden, Germany; *Tschechoslowakei.*

G.K. Hall and Company, 70 Lincoln Street, Boston, Massachusetts 02111 (617) 423-3990; *The World in Figures.*

Statistical Office of the United Nations, Publishing Service, New York, New York 10017 (800) 253-9646; *Statistical Yearbook.*

Times Books, 201 East 50th Street, New York, New York 10022 (212) 751-2600; *The Economist Book of Vital World Statistics.*

CZECHOSLOVAKIA - HEMP FIBRE PRODUCTION - See CZECHOSLOVAKIA - TEXTILE INDUSTRY

CZECHOSLOVAKIA - HIDE PRODUCTION

Food and Agricultural Organization of the United Nations (FAO), Via delle Terme di Caracalla, 00100 Rome, Italy (Telephone Number in U.S. (202) 653-2400); *Production Yearbook.*

CZECHOSLOVAKIA - HIGHWAYS

G.K. Hall and Company, 70 Lincoln Street, Boston, Massachusetts 02111 (617) 423-3990; *The World in Figures.*

International Road Federation, 525 School Street, SW, Washington, D.C. 20024 (202) 554-2106; *World Road Statistics.*

Statistical Office of the United Nations, Publishing Service, New York, New York 10017 (800) 253-9646; *Annual Bulletin of Transport Statistics for Europe.*

CZECHOSLOVAKIA - HOPS PRODUCTION - See CZECHOSLOVAKIA - CROPS

CZECHOSLOVAKIA - HORSES - See CZECHOSLOVAKIA - LIVESTOCK AND POULTRY

CZECHOSLOVAKIA - HOURS OF WORK - See CZECHOSLOVAKIA - EMPLOYMENT

CZECHOSLOVAKIA - HOUSING AND HOUSING UNITS

Columbia University Press, 562 West 113th Street, New York, New York 10014; *East European and Soviet Data Book.*

Facts on File, 460 Park Avenue South, New York, New York 10016 (800) 443-8323; *The New Book of World Rankings.*

CZECHOSLOVAKIA - HYDROCHLORIC ACID PRODUCTION

Statistical Office of the United Nations, Publishing Service, New York, New York 10017 (800) 253-9646; *Statistical Yearbook.*

CZECHOSLOVAKIA - ILLITERATE POPULATION

The Economist Intelligence Unit, 111 West 57th Street, New York, New York 10019 (800) 938-4685; *The World Market Atlas.*

G.K. Hall and Company, 70 Lincoln Street, Boston, Massachusetts 02111 (617) 423-3990; *The World in Figures.*

CZECHOSLOVAKIA - IMPORTS

American Automobile Manufacturers Association, 1401 H Street, NW, Suite 900, Washington, D.C. 20005 (202) 326-5500; *World Motor Vehicle Data.*

The Economist Intelligence Unit, 111 West 57th Street, New York, New York 10019 (800) 938-4685; *The World Market Atlas.*

Food and Agricultural Organization of the United Nations (FAO) Via delle Terme di Caracalla, 00100 Rome, Italy (Telephone Number in U.S. (202) 653-2400); *The State of Food and Agriculture.*

G.K. Hall and Company, 70 Lincoln Street, Boston, Massachusetts 02111 (617) 423-3990; *The World in Figures.*

International Lead and Zinc Study Group, Metro House, 58 St. James's Street, London SW1A 1LD, England; *Lead and Zinc Statistics.*

International Monetary Fund, 700 Nineteenth Street, NW, Washington, D.C. 20431 (202) 623-7000; *Direction of Trade Statistics.*

International Rubber Study Group, York House, 8th Floor, Empire Way, Wembley, London HA9 0PA, England; *Rubber Statistical Bulletin.*

Times Books, 201 East 50th Street, New York, New York 10022 (212) 751-2600; *The Economist Book of Vital World Statistics.*

CZECHOSLOVAKIA - INDUSTRIAL METALS PRODUCTION - See CZECHOSLOVAKIA - MINING AND MINERAL PRODUCTS

CZECHOSLOVAKIA - INDUSTRY

Facts on File, 460 Park Avenue South, New York, New York 10016; *The New Book of World Rankings.*

Federal Statistical Office, Gustav - Stresemann - Ring 11, D-6200 Wiesbaden, Germany; *Tschechoslowakei.*

G.K. Hall and Company, 70 Lincoln Street, Boston, Massachusetts 02111 (617) 423-3990; *The World in Figures.*

International Labour Office, I.L.O. Publications, CH-1211, Geneva 22, Switzerland; *Yearbook of Labour Statistics.*

Statistical Office of the United Nations, Publishing Service, New York, New York 10017 (800) 253-9646; *Statistical Yearbook.*

Times Books, 201 East 50th Street, New York, New York 10022 (212) 751-2600; *The Economist Book of Vital World Statistics.*

World Intellectual Property Organization, 34 Chemin des Colombettes, CH-1211 Geneva 20. Switzerland; *Industrial Property Statistics.*

CZECHOSLOVAKIA - INFANT AND MATERNAL MORTALITY

Statistical Office of the United Nations, Publishing Service, New York, New York 10017 (800) 253-9646; *Demographic Yearbook,* and *Statistical Yearbook.*

Times Books, 201 East 50th Street, New York, New York 10022 (212) 751-2600; *The Economist Book of Vital World Statistics.*

World Health Organization, Office of Publications, Avenue Appia, CH-1211 Geneva 27, Switzerland (Telephone Number in U.S. (518) 436-9686); *World Health Statistics Annual.*

CZECHOSLOVAKIA - INTERNAL TRADE

Statistical Office of the United Nations, Publishing Service, New York, New York 10017 (800) 253-9646; *Statistical Yearbook.*

CZECHOSLOVAKIA - IRON ORE PRODUCTION AND CONSUMPTION - See CZECHOSLOVAKIA - MINING AND MINERAL PRODUCTS

CZECHOSLOVAKIA - LABOR FORCE

Columbia University Press, 562 West 113th Street, New York, New York 10014; *East European and Soviet Data Book.*

Facts on File, 460 Park Avenue South, New York, New York 10016; *The New Book of World Rankings.*

Food and Agricultural Organization of the United Nations (FAO) Via delle Terme di Caracalla, 00100 Rome, Italy (Telephone Number in U.S. (202) 653-2400); *The State of Food and Agriculture.*

G.K. Hall and Company, 70 Lincoln Street, Boston, Massachusetts 02111 (617) 423-3990; *The World in Figures.*

CZECHOSLOVAKIA - LABOR PRODUCTIVITY

International Labour Office, I.L.O. Publications, CH-1211, Geneva 22, Switzerland; *Yearbook of Labour Statistics.*

CZECHOSLOVAKIA - LAND USE

Euromonitor Publications Limited, 87-88 Turnmill Street, London EC1M 5QU, England; *European Marketing Data and Statistics.*

Food and Agricultural Organization of the United Nations (FAO), Via delle Terme di Caracalla, 00100 Rome, Italy (Telephone Number in U.S. (202) 653-2400); *Production Yearbook.*

G.K. Hall and Company, 70 Lincoln Street, Boston, Massachusetts 02111 (617) 423-3990; *The World in Figures.*

CZECHOSLOVAKIA - LEAD AND LEAD ORE PRODUCTION AND CONSUMPTION - See CZECHOSLOVAKIA - MINING AND MINERAL PRODUCTS

CZECHOSLOVAKIA - LIBRARIES

Euromonitor Publications Limited, 87-88 Turnmill Street, London EC1M 5QU, England; *European Marketing Data and Statistics.*

Facts on File, 460 Park Avenue South, New York, New York 10016 (800) 443-8323; *The New Book of World Rankings.*

United Nations Educational, Scientific and Cultural Organization (UNESCO), 7 Place de Fontenoy, F-75700 Paris, France (Telephone Number in U.S. (212) 963-5981); *Statistical Yearbook.*

CZECHOSLOVAKIA - LIGNITE PRODUCTION - See CZECHOSLOVAKIA - MINING AND MINERAL PRODUCTS

CZECHOSLOVAKIA - LIVESTOCK AND POULTRY

Commodity Research Bureau, Incorporated, 75 Wall Street, New York, New York 10005 (212) 504-7754; *Commodity Year Book.*

Euromonitor Publications Limited, 87-88 Turnmill Street, London EC1M 5QU, England; *European Marketing Data and Statistics.*

Facts on File, 460 Park Avenue South, New York, New York 10016 (800) 443-8323; *The New Book of World Rankings.*

Food and Agricultural Organization of the United Nations (FAO), Via delle Terme di Caracalla, 00100 Rome, Italy (Telephone Number in U.S. (202) 653-2400); *Production Yearbook,* and *The State of Food and*

Agriculture.

G.K. Hall and Company, 70 Lincoln Street, Boston, Massachusetts 02111 (617) 423-3990; *The World in Figures.*

Statistical Office of the United Nations, Publishing Service, New York, New York 10017 (800) 253-9646; *Statistical Yearbook.*

CZECHOSLOVAKIA - LIVING LEVELS

G.K. Hall and Company, 70 Lincoln Street, Boston, Massachusetts 02111 (617) 423-3990; *The World in Figures.*

Times Books, 201 East 50th Street, New York, New York 10022 (212) 751-2600; *The Economist Book of Vital World Statistics.*

CZECHOSLOVAKIA - MAIL - NUMBER OF PIECES SENT OR RECEIVED

Statistical Office of the United Nations, Publishing Service, New York, New York 10017 (800) 253-9646; *Statistical Yearbook.*

CZECHOSLOVAKIA - MANGANESE ORE PRODUCTION AND CONSUMPTION - See CZECHOSLOVAKIA - MINING AND MINERAL PRODUCTS

CZECHOSLOVAKIA - MANUFACTURING

American Automobile Manufacturers Association, 1401 H Street, NW, Suite 900, Washington, D.C. 20005 (202) 326-5500; *World Motor Vehicle Data.*

Facts on File, 460 Park Avenue South, New York, New York 10016 (800) 443-8323; *The New Book of World Rankings.*

G.K. Hall and Company, 70 Lincoln Street, Boston, Massachusetts 02111 (617) 423-3990; *The World in Figures.*

Statistical Office of the United Nations, Publishing Service, New York, New York 10017 (800) 253-9646; *Statistical Yearbook.*

Times Books, 201 East 50th Street, New York, New York 10022 (212) 751-2600; *The Economist Book of Vital World Statistics.*

CZECHOSLOVAKIA - MARRIAGE RATES

Facts on File, 460 Park Avenue South, New York, New York 10016; *The New Book of World Rankings.*

Statistical Office of the United Nations, Publishing Service, New York, New York 10017 (800) 253-9646; *Demographic Yearbook,* and *Statistical Yearbook.*

United Nations Educational, Scientific and Cultural Organization (UNESCO), 7 Place de Fontenoy, F-75700 Paris, France (Telephone Number in U.S. (212) 963-5981); *Statistical Yearbook.*

CZECHOSLOVAKIA - MEAT PRODUCTION - See CZECHOSLOVAKIA - LIVESTOCK AND POULTRY

CZECHOSLOVAKIA - MERCHANT SHIPPING

G.K. Hall and Company, 70 Lincoln Street, Boston, Massachusetts 02111 (617) 423-3990; *The World in Figures.*

Statistical Office of the United Nations, Publishing Service, New York, New York 10017 (800) 253-9646; *Annual Bulletin of Transport Statistics for Europe,* and *Statistical Yearbook.*

Times Books, 201 East 50th Street, New York, New York 10022 (212) 751-2600; *The Economist Book of Vital World Statistics.*

U.S. Department of Transportation, Maritime Administration, 400 Seventh Street, SW, Washington, D.C. 20590; *A Statistical Analysis of the World's Merchant Fleets.*

CZECHOSLOVAKIA - MERCURY PRODUCTION AND CONSUMPTION - See CZECHOSLOVAKIA - MINING AND MINERAL PRODUCTS

CZECHOSLOVAKIA - MILITARY

The International Institute for Strategic Studies, 23 Tavistock Street, London WC2E 7NQ, England; *The Military Balance.*

G.K. Hall and Company, 70 Lincoln Street, Boston, Massachusetts 02111 (617) 423-3990; *The World in Figures.*

U.S. Arms Control and Disarmament Agency, 320 Twenty-first Street, NW, Washington, D.C. 20451 (202) 647-8677; *World Military Expenditures and Arms Transfers.*

CZECHOSLOVAKIA - MILK - See CZECHOSLOVAKIA - DAIRY PRODUCTS

CZECHOSLOVAKIA - MILLET PRODUCTION - See CZECHOSLOVAKIA - CROPS

CZECHOSLOVAKIA - MINING AND MINERAL PRODUCTS

Commodity Research Bureau, Incorporated, 75 Wall Street, New York, New York 10005 (212) 504-7754; *Commodity Year Book.*

Facts on File, 460 Park Avenue South, New York, New York 10016; *The New Book of World Rankings.*

G.K. Hall and Company, 70 Lincoln Street, Boston, Massachusetts 02111 (617) 423-3990; *The World in Figures.*

International Lead and Zinc Study Group, Metro House, 58 St. James's Street, London SW1A 1LD, England; *Lead and Zinc Statistics.*

Penn Well Publishing Company, 1421 South Sheridan Road, P.O. Box 1260, Tulsa, Oklahoma 74101 (800) 752-9764; *International Energy Statistics Sourcebook.*

Statistical Office of the United Nations, Publishing Service, New York, New York 10017 (800) 253-9646; *Statistical Yearbook.*

CZECHOSLOVAKIA - MONEY EXCHANGE RATES

Statistical Office of the United Nations, Publishing Service, New York, New York 10017 (800) 253-9646; *Statistical Yearbook.*

CZECHOSLOVAKIA - MONEY SUPPLY

Federal Statistical Office, Gustav - Stresemann - Ring 11, D-6200 Wiesbaden, Germany; *Tschechoslowakei.*

G.K. Hall and Company, 70 Lincoln Street, Boston, Massachusetts 02111 (617) 423-3990; *The World in Figures.*

CZECHOSLOVAKIA - MOTION PICTURES

Statistical Office of the United Nations, Publishing Service, New York, New York 10017 (800) 253-9646; *Statistical Yearbook.*

CZECHOSLOVAKIA - MOTOR VEHICLE PRODUCTION

American Automobile Manufacturers Association, 1401 H Street, NW, Suite 900, Washington, D.C. 20005 (202) 326-5500; *World Motor Vehicle Data.*

Statistical Office of the United Nations, Publishing Service, New York, New York 10017 (800) 253-9646; *Statistical Yearbook.*

CZECHOSLOVAKIA - MOTOR VEHICLES IN USE

American Automobile Manufacturers Association, 1401 H Street, NW, Suite 900, Washington, D.C. 20005 (202) 326-5500; *World Motor Vehicle Data.*

G.K. Hall and Company, 70 Lincoln Street, Boston, Massachusetts 02111 (617) 423-3990; *The World in Figures.*

International Road Federation, 525 School Street, SW, Washington, D.C. 20024 (202) 554-2106; *World Road Statistics.*

Statistical Office of the United Nations, Publishing Service, New York, New York 10017 (800) 253-9646; *Statistical Yearbook.*

Times Books, 201 East 50th Street, New York, New York 10022 (212) 751-2600; *The Economist Book of Vital World Statistics.*

CZECHOSLOVAKIA - MUSEUMS

Euromonitor Publications Limited, 87-88 Turnmill Street, London EC1M 5QU, England; *European Marketing Data and Statistics.*

Facts on File, 460 Park Avenue South, New York, New York 10016 (800) 443-8323; *The New Book of World Rankings.*

United Nations Educational, Scientific and Cultural Organization (UNESCO), 7 Place de Fontenoy, F-75700 Paris, France (Telephone Number in U.S. (212) 963-5981); *Statistical Yearbook.*

CZECHOSLOVAKIA - NATALITY - See CZECHOSLOVAKIA - BIRTH RATES

CZECHOSLOVAKIA - NATIONAL ACCOUNTS

Federal Statistical Office, Gustav - Stresemann - Ring 11, D-6200 Wiesbaden, Germany; *Tschechoslowakei.*

Statistical Office of the United Nations, Publishing Service, New York, New York 10017 (800) 253-9646; *National Accounts Statistics,* and *Statistical Yearbook.*

CZECHOSLOVAKIA - NATIONAL INCOME

Facts on File, 460 Park Avenue South, New York, New York 10016 (800) 443-8323; *The New Book of World Rankings.*

G.K. Hall and Company, 70 Lincoln Street, Boston, Massachusetts 02111 (617) 423-3990; *The World in Figures.*

Statistical Office of the United Nations, Publishing Service, New York, New York 10017 (800) 253-9646; *Statistical Yearbook.*

CZECHOSLOVAKIA - NATIONAL PRODUCT

Facts on File, 460 Park Avenue South, New York, New York 10016 (800) 443-8323; *The New Book of World Rankings.*

Statistical Office of the United Nations, Publishing Service, New York, New York 10017 (800) 253-9646; *Statistical Yearbook.*

CZECHOSLOVAKIA - NATURAL GAS PRODUCTION - See CZECHOSLOVAKIA - MINING AND MINERAL PRODUCTS

CZECHOSLOVAKIA - NATURAL RUBBER PRODUCTION

International Rubber Study Group, York House, 8th Floor, Empire Way, Wembley, London HA9 0PA, England; *Rubber Statistical Bulletin.*

CZECHOSLOVAKIA - NET MATERIAL PRODUCT

Statistical Office of the United Nations, Publishing Service, New York, New York 10017 (800) 253-9646; *Statistical Yearbook.*

CZECHOSLOVAKIA - NEWSPAPER PRODUCTION - See CZECHOSLOVAKIA - FORESTRY AND FOREST PRODUCTS

CZECHOSLOVAKIA - NEWSPRINT CONSUMPTION - See CZECHOSLOVAKIA - FORESTRY AND FOREST PRODUCTS

CZECHOSLOVAKIA - NICKEL PRODUCTION AND CONSUMPTION - See CZECHOSLOVAKIA - MINING AND MINERAL PRODUCTS

CZECHOSLOVAKIA - OATS PRODUCTION - See CZECHOSLOVAKIA - CROPS

CZECHOSLOVAKIA - OCCUPATIONS - See CZECHOSLOVAKIA - LABOR FORCE

CZECHOSLOVAKIA - PAPER - See CZECHOSLOVAKIA - FORESTRY AND FOREST PRODUCTS

CZECHOSLOVAKIA - PARTY LEADERS

Columbia University Press, 562 West 113th Street, New York, New York 10014; *East European and Soviet Data Book.*

CZECHOSLOVAKIA - PARTY MEMBERSHIP

Columbia University Press, 562 West 113th Street, New York, New York 10014; *East European and Soviet Data Book.*

CZECHOSLOVAKIA - PATENTS

Statistical Office of the United Nations, Publishing Service, New York, New York 10017 (800) 253-9646; *Statistical Yearbook.*

World Intellectual Property Organization, 34 Chemin des Colombettes, CH-1211 Geneva 20. Switzerland; *Industrial Property Statistics.*

CZECHOSLOVAKIA - PEANUT PRODUCTION - See CZECHOSLOVAKIA - CROPS

CZECHOSLOVAKIA - PERIODICALS

United Nations Educational, Scientific and Cultural Organization (UNESCO), 7 Place de Fontenoy, F-75700 Paris, France (Telephone Number in U.S. (212) 963-5981); *Statistical Yearbook.*

CZECHOSLOVAKIA - PESTICIDE USE

Food and Agricultural Organization of the United Nations (FAO) Via delle Terme di Caracalla, 00100 Rome, Italy (Telephone Number in U.S. (202) 653-2400); *The State of Food and Agriculture.*

CZECHOSLOVAKIA - PETROLEUM INDUSTRY

Euromonitor Publications Limited, 87-88 Turnmill Street, London EC1M 5QU, England; *European Marketing Data and Statistics.*

Facts on File, 460 Park Avenue South, New York, New York 10016 (800) 443-8323; *The New Book of World Rankings.*

Food and Agricultural Organization of the United Nations (FAO) Via delle Terme di Caracalla, 00100 Rome, Italy (Telephone Number in U.S. (202) 653-2400); *The State of Food and Agriculture.*

G.K. Hall and Company, 70 Lincoln Street, Boston, Massachusetts 02111 (617) 423-3990; *The World in Figures.*

Penn Well Publishing Company, 1421 South Sheridan Road, P.O. Box 1260, Tulsa, Oklahoma 74101 (800) 752-9764; *International Energy Statistics Sourcebook.*

Statistical Office of the United Nations, Publishing Service, New York, New York 10017 (800) 253-9646; *Statistical Yearbook.*

CZECHOSLOVAKIA - PIG-IRON AND FERRO-ALLOY PRODUCTION - See CZECHOSLOVAKIA - MINING AND MINERAL PRODUCTS

CZECHOSLOVAKIA - PIGS - See CZECHOSLOVAKIA - LIVESTOCK AND POULTRY

CZECHOSLOVAKIA - PIPELINES FOR OIL AND PETROLEUM PRODUCTS

Statistical Office of the United Nations, Publishing Service, New York, New York 10017 (800) 253-9646; *Annual Bulletin of Transport Statistics for Europe.*

CZECHOSLOVAKIA - PLASTIC AND RESIN PRODUCTION

Commodity Research Bureau, Incorporated, 75 Wall Street, New York, New York 10005 (212) 504-7754; *Commodity Year Book.*

Statistical Office of the United Nations, Publishing Service, New York, New York 10017 (800) 253-9646; *Statistical Yearbook.*

CZECHOSLOVAKIA - POPULATION

Columbia University Press, 562 West 113th Street, New York, New York 10014; *East European and Soviet Data Book.*

The Economist Intelligence Unit, 111 West 57th Street, New York, New York 10019 (800) 938-4685; *The World Market Atlas.*

Encyclopedia Britannica, Incorporated, 310 South Michigan Avenue, Chicago, Illinois 60604 (312) 347-7000; *Britannica World Data.*

Euromonitor Publications Limited, 87-88 Turnmill Street, London EC1M 5QU, England; *European Marketing Data and Statistics.*

Facts on File, 460 Park Avenue South, New York, New York 10016 (800) 443-8323; *The New Book of World Rankings.*

Federal Statistical Office, Gustav - Stresemann - Ring 11, D-6200 Wiesbaden, Germany; *Tschechoslowakei.*

Food and Agricultural Organization of the United Nations (FAO), Via delle Terme di Caracalla, 00100 Rome, Italy (Telephone Number in U.S. (202) 653-2400); *Production Yearbook.*

G.K. Hall and Company, 70 Lincoln Street, Boston, Massachusetts 02111 (617) 423-3990; *The World in Figures.*

International Labour Office, I.L.O. Publications, CH-1211, Geneva 22, Switzerland; *Yearbook of Labour Statistics.*

Statistical Office of the United Nations, Publishing Service, New York, New York 10017 (800) 253-9646; *Demographic Yearbook,* and *Statistical Yearbook.*

Times Books, 201 East 50th Street, New York, New York 10022 (212) 751-2600; *The Economist Book of Vital World Statistics.*

United Nations Educational, Scientific and Cultural Organization (UNESCO), 7 Place de Fontenoy, F-75700 Paris, France (Telephone Number in U.S. (212) 963-5981); *Statistical Yearbook.*

U.S. Arms Control and Disarmament Agency, 320 Twenty-first Street, NW, Washington, D.C. 20451 (202) 647-8677; *World Military Expenditures and Arms Transfers.*

World Health Organization, Office of Publications, Avenue Appia, CH-1211 Geneva 27, Switzerland (Telephone Number in U.S. (518) 436-9686); *World Health Statistics Annual.*

CZECHOSLOVAKIA - POST OFFICES

Facts on File, 460 Park Avenue South, New York, New York 10016 (800) 443-8323; *The New Book of World Rankings.*

CZECHOSLOVAKIA - POTATO PRODUCTION - See CZECHOSLOVAKIA - CROPS

CZECHOSLOVAKIA - POWER PRODUCTION INDUSTRY

Statistical Office of the United Nations, Publishing Service, New York, New York 10017 (800) 253-9646; *Statistical Yearbook.*

CZECHOSLOVAKIA - PRICES

Facts on File, 460 Park Avenue South, New York, New York 10016 (800) 443-8323; and *The New Book of World Rankings.*

Federal Statistical Office, Gustav - Stresemann - Ring 11, D-6200 Wiesbaden, Germany; *Tschechoslowakei.*

Food and Agricultural Organization of the United Nations (FAO), Via delle Terme di Caracalla, 00100 Rome, Italy (Telephone Number in U.S. (202) 653-2400); *Production Yearbook,* and *The State of Food and Agriculture.*

G.K. Hall and Company, 70 Lincoln Street, Boston, Massachusetts 02111 (617) 423-3990; *The World in Figures.*

International Labour Office, I.L.O. Publications, CH-1211, Geneva 22, Switzerland; *Yearbook of Labour Statistics.*

International Lead and Zinc Study Group, Metro House, 58 St. James's Street, London SW1A 1LD, England; *Lead and Zinc Statistics.*

International Rubber Study Group, York House, 8th Floor, Empire Way, Wembley, London HA9 0PA, England; *Rubber Statistical Bulletin.*

CZECHOSLOVAKIA - PRODUCTION

American Automobile Manufacturers Association, 1401 H Street, NW, Suite 900, Washington, D.C. 20005 (202) 326-5500; *World*

Motor Vehicle Data.

Facts on File, 460 Park Avenue South, New York, New York 10016 (800) 443-8323; *The New Book of World Rankings.*

G.K. Hall and Company, 70 Lincoln Street, Boston, Massachusetts 02111 (617) 423-3990; *The World in Figures.*

International Lead and Zinc Study Group, Metro House, 58 St. James's Street, London SW1A 1LD, England; *Lead and Zinc Statistics.*

International Rubber Study Group, York House, 8th Floor, Empire Way, Wembley, London HA9 0PA, England; *Rubber Statistical Bulletin.*

CZECHOSLOVAKIA - PUBLIC FINANCE

Facts on File, 460 Park Avenue South, New York, New York 10016 (800) 443-8323; *The New Book of World Rankings.*

Federal Statistical Office, Gustav - Stresemann - Ring 11, D-6200 Wiesbaden, Germany; *Tschechoslowakei.*

CZECHOSLOVAKIA - RADIO BROADCASTING - See CZECHOSLOVAKIA - BROADCASTING

CZECHOSLOVAKIA - RADIO RECEIVER PRODUCTION

Encyclopedia Britannica, Incorporated, 310 South Michigan Avenue, Chicago, Illinois 60604 (312) 347-7000; *Britannica World Data.*

Statistical Office of the United Nations, Publishing Service, New York, New York 10017 (800) 253-9646; *Statistical Yearbook.*

CZECHOSLOVAKIA - RAILWAYS

Encyclopedia Britannica, Incorporated, 310 South Michigan Avenue, Chicago, Illinois 60604 (312) 347-7000; *Britannica World Data.*

Euromonitor Publications Limited, 87-88 Turnmill Street, London EC1M 5QU, England; *European Marketing Data and Statistics.*

Jane's Information Group, Sentinel House, 163 Brighton Road, Coulsdon, Surrey CR5 2NH, England (Telephone Number in U.S. (703) 683-3700); *Jane's World Railways.*

Statistical Office of the United Nations, Publishing Service, New York, New York 10017 (800) 253-9646; *Annual Bulletin of Transport Statistics for Europe,* and *Statistical Yearbook.*

CZECHOSLOVAKIA - RAPESEED PRODUCTION - See CZECHOSLOVAKIA - CROPS

CZECHOSLOVAKIA - RELIGION

Facts on File, 460 Park Avenue South, New York, New York 10016 (800) 443-8323; *The New Book of World Rankings.*

CZECHOSLOVAKIA - RETAIL TRADE

G.K. Hall and Company, 70 Lincoln Street, Boston, Massachusetts 02111 (617) 423-3990; *The World in Figures.*

Statistical Office of the United Nations, Publishing Service, New York, New York 10017 (800) 253-9646; *Statistical Yearbook.*

CZECHOSLOVAKIA - RICE PRODUCTION - See CZECHOSLOVAKIA - CROPS

CZECHOSLOVAKIA - ROADS

Encyclopedia Britannica, Incorporated, 310 South Michigan Avenue, Chicago, Illinois 60604 (312) 347-7000; *Britannica World Data.*

CZECHOSLOVAKIA - ROOT AND TUBER PRODUCTION - See CZECHOSLOVAKIA - CROPS

CZECHOSLOVAKIA - ROUNDWOOD PRODUCTION - See CZECHOSLOVAKIA - FORESTRY AND FOREST PRODUCTS

CZECHOSLOVAKIA - RUBBER PRODUCTION AND CONSUMPTION

Facts on File, 460 Park Avenue South, New York, New York 10016 (800) 443-8323; *The New Book of World Rankings.*

International Rubber Study Group, York House, 8th Floor, Empire Way, Wembley, London HA9 0PA, England; *Rubber Statistical Bulletin.*

Statistical Office of the United Nations, Publishing Service, New York, New York 10017 (800) 253-9646; *Statistical Yearbook.*

CZECHOSLOVAKIA - RYE PRODUCTION - See CZECHOSLOVAKIA - CROPS

CZECHOSLOVAKIA - SALT PRODUCTION - See CZECHOSLOVAKIA - MINING AND MINERAL PRODUCTS

CZECHOSLOVAKIA - SAWNWOOD PRODUCTION - See CZECHOSLOVAKIA - FORESTRY AND FOREST PRODUCTS

CZECHOSLOVAKIA - SCIENTISTS AND TECHNICIANS

Statistical Office of the United Nations, Publishing Service, New York, New York 10017 (800) 253-9646; *Statistical Yearbook,* section on Science and Technology.

CZECHOSLOVAKIA - SENIOR CITIZENS

Facts on File, 460 Park Avenue South, New York, New York 10016 (800) 443-8323; *The New Book of World Rankings.*

CZECHOSLOVAKIA - SHEEP - See CZECHOSLOVAKIA - LIVESTOCK AND POULTRY

CZECHOSLOVAKIA - SILVER PRODUCTION AND CONSUMPTION - See CZECHOSLOVAKIA - MINING AND MINERAL PRODUCTS

CZECHOSLOVAKIA - SOCIAL DATA

Facts on File, 460 Park Avenue South, New York, New York 10016 (800) 443-8323; *The New Book of World Rankings.*

G.K. Hall and Company, 70 Lincoln Street, Boston, Massachusetts 02111 (617) 423-3990; *The World in Figures.*

CZECHOSLOVAKIA - STEEL - See CZECHOSLOVAKIA - MINING AND MINERAL PRODUCTS

CZECHOSLOVAKIA - STOCKS - COMMODITY - MARKET PRICE - INDEX

Food and Agricultural Organization of the United Nations (FAO) Via delle Terme di Caracalla, 00100 Rome, Italy (Telephone Number in U.S. (202) 653-2400); *The State of Food and Agriculture.*

International Lead and Zinc Study Group, Metro House, 58 St. James's Street, London SW1A 1LD, England; *Lead and Zinc*

Statistics.

CZECHOSLOVAKIA - SUGAR - See CZECHOSLOVAKIA - CROPS

CZECHOSLOVAKIA - SULPHURIC ACID PRODUCTION

Statistical Office of the United Nations, Publishing Service, New York, New York 10017 (800) 253-9646; *Statistical Yearbook.*

CZECHOSLOVAKIA - TAXATION

G.K. Hall and Company, 70 Lincoln Street, Boston, Massachusetts 02111 (617) 423-3990; *The World in Figures.*

International Road Federation, 525 School Street, SW, Washington, D.C. 20024 (202) 554-2106; *World Road Statistics.*

CZECHOSLOVAKIA - TEA - See CZECHOSLOVAKIA - CROPS

CZECHOSLOVAKIA - TELEGRAPH SERVICE

Statistical Office of the United Nations, Publishing Service, New York, New York 10017 (800) 253-9646; *Statistical Yearbook.*

CZECHOSLOVAKIA - TELEPHONES IN USE

American Telephone and Telegraph Company, 26 Parsippany Road, Whippany, New Jersey 07981 (800) 338-4038; *The World's Telephones.*

Encyclopedia Britannica, Incorporated, 310 South Michigan Avenue, Chicago, Illinois 60604 (312) 347-7000; *Britannica World Data.*

G.K. Hall and Company, 70 Lincoln Street, Boston, Massachusetts 02111 (617) 423-3990; *The World in Figures.*

Statistical Office of the United Nations, Publishing Service, New York, New York 10017 (800) 253-9646; *Statistical Yearbook.*

CZECHOSLOVAKIA - TELEVISION BROADCASTING - See CZECHOSLOVAKIA - BROADCASTING

CZECHOSLOVAKIA - TELEVISION RECEIVER PRODUCTION

Encyclopedia Britannica, Incorporated, 310 South Michigan Avenue, Chicago, Illinois 60604 (312) 347-7000; *Britannica World Data.*

Statistical Office of the United Nations, Publishing Service, New York, New York 10017 (800) 253-9646; *Statistical Yearbook.*

CZECHOSLOVAKIA - TEXTILE INDUSTRY

Food and Agricultural Organization of the United Nations (FAO), Via delle Terme di Caracalla, 00100 Rome, Italy (Telephone Number in U.S. (202) 653-2400); *Production Yearbook.*

G.K. Hall and Company, 70 Lincoln Street, Boston, Massachusetts 02111 (617) 423-3990; *The World in Figures.*

Statistical Office of the United Nations, Publishing Service, New York, New York 10017 (800) 253-9646; *Statistical Yearbook.*

CZECHOSLOVAKIA - THEATRE

United Nations Educational, Scientific and Cultural Organization (UNESCO), 7 Place de Fontenoy, F-75700 Paris, France (Telephone Number in U.S. (212) 963-5981); *Statistical Yearbook.*

CZECHOSLOVAKIA - TIN - See CZECHOSLOVAKIA - MINING AND MINERAL PRODUCTS

CZECHOSLOVAKIA - TIRE (MOTOR VEHICLE) PRODUCTION

International Rubber Study Group, York House, 8th Floor, Empire Way, Wembley, London HA9 0PA, England; *Rubber Statistical Bulletin.*

Statistical Office of the United Nations, Publishing Service, New York, New York 10017 (800) 253-9646; *Statistical Yearbook.*

CZECHOSLOVAKIA - TOBACCO PRODUCTION

Facts on File, 460 Park Avenue South, New York, New York 10016 (800) 443-8323; *The New Book of World Rankings.*

Euromonitor Publications Limited, 87-88 Turnmill Street, London EC1M 5QU, England; *European Marketing Data and Statistics.*

Statistical Office of the United Nations, Publishing Service, New York, New York 10017 (800) 253-9646; *Statistical Yearbook.*

CZECHOSLOVAKIA - TOURISM

Euromonitor Publications Limited, 87-88 Turnmill Street, London EC1M 5QU, England; *European Marketing Data and Statistics.*

Facts on File, 460 Park Avenue South, New York, New York 10016 (800) 443-8323; *The New Book of World Rankings.*

Federal Statistical Office, Gustav - Stresemann - Ring 11, D-6200 Wiesbaden, Germany; *Tschechoslowakei.*

G.K. Hall and Company, 70 Lincoln Street, Boston, Massachusetts 02111 (617) 423-3990; *The World in Figures.*

International Road Federation, 525 School Street, SW, Washington, D.C. 20024 (202) 554-2106; *World Road Statistics.*

Statistical Office of the United Nations, Publishing Service, New York, New York 10017 (800) 253-9646; *Statistical Yearbook.*

Times Books, 201 East 50th Street, New York, New York 10022 (212) 751-2600; *The Economist Book of Vital World Statistics.*

World Tourism Organization, Calle Capitan Haya 42, E-28020 Madrid, Spain; *Yearbook of Tourism Statistics.*

CZECHOSLOVAKIA - TRACTORS IN USE

Statistical Office of the United Nations, Publishing Service, New York, New York 10017 (800) 253-9646; *Statistical Yearbook.*

CZECHOSLOVAKIA - TRADE - See CZECHOSLOVAKIA - FOREIGN TRADE

CZECHOSLOVAKIA - TRADEMARKS AND SERVICE MARKS

Statistical Office of the United Nations, Publishing Service, New York, New York 10017 (800) 253-9646; *Statistical Yearbook.*

World Intellectual Property Organization, 34 Chemin des Colombettes, CH-1211 Geneva 20. Switzerland; *Industrial Property Statistics.*

CZECHOSLOVAKIA - TRANSPORTATION AND COMMUNICATIONS

Encyclopedia Britannica, Incorporated, 310 South Michigan Avenue, Chicago, Illinois 60604 (312) 347-7000; *Britannica World Data.*

Facts on File, 460 Park Avenue South, New York, New York 10016 (800) 443-8323; *The New Book of World Rankings.*

Federal Statistical Office, Gustav - Stresemann - Ring 11, D-6200 Wiesbaden, Germany; *Tschechoslowakei.*

G.K. Hall and Company, 70 Lincoln Street, Boston, Massachusetts 02111 (617) 423-3990; *The World in Figures.*

CZECHOSLOVAKIA - TURKEYS - See CZECHOSLOVAKIA - LIVESTOCK AND POULTRY

CZECHOSLOVAKIA - UNEMPLOYMENT

Euromonitor Publications Limited, 87-88 Turnmill Street, London EC1M 5QU, England; *European Marketing Data and Statistics.*

International Labour Office, I.L.O. Publications, CH-1211, Geneva 22, Switzerland; *Yearbook of Labour Statistics.*

Statistical Office of the United Nations, Publishing Service, New York, New York 10017 (800) 253-9646; *Statistical Yearbook.*

CZECHOSLOVAKIA - VITAL STATISTICS

G.K. Hall and Company, 70 Lincoln Street, Boston, Massachusetts 02111 (617) 423-3990; *The World in Figures.*

Statistical Office of the United Nations, Publishing Service, New York, New York 10017 (800) 253-9646; *Statistical Yearbook.*

World Health Organization, Office of Publications, Avenue Appia, CH-1211 Geneva 27, Switzerland (Telephone Number in U.S. (518) 436-9686); *World Health Statistics Annual.*

CZECHOSLOVAKIA - WAGES

Euromonitor Publications Limited, 87-88 Turnmill Street, London EC1M 5QU, England; *European Marketing Data and Statistics.*

Federal Statistical Office, Gustav - Stresemann - Ring 11, D-6200 Wiesbaden, Germany; *Tschechoslowakei.*

G.K. Hall and Company, 70 Lincoln Street, Boston, Massachusetts 02111 (617) 423-3990; *The World in Figures.*

International Labour Office, I.L.O. Publications, CH-1211, Geneva 22, Switzerland; *Yearbook of Labour Statistics.*

Statistical Office of the United Nations, Publishing Service, New York, New York 10017 (800) 253-9646; *Statistical Yearbook.*

CZECHOSLOVAKIA - WALNUT PRODUCTION - See CZECHOSLOVAKIA - CROPS

CZECHOSLOVAKIA - WATERWAYS IN USE

Statistical Office of the United Nations, Publishing Service, New York, New York 10017 (800) 253-9646; *Annual Bulletin of Transport Statistics for Europe.*

CZECHOSLOVAKIA - WEATHER

Facts on File, 460 Park Avenue South, New York, New York 10016 (800) 443-8323; *The New Book of World Rankings.*

G.K. Hall and Company, 70 Lincoln Street, Boston, Massachusetts 02111 (617) 423-3990; *The World in Figures.*

CZECHOSLOVAKIA - WHEAT - See CZECHOSLOVAKIA - CROPS

CZECHOSLOVAKIA - WHOLESALE TRADE

Statistical Office of the United Nations, Publishing Service, New York, New York 10017 (800) 253-9646; *Statistical Yearbook.*

CZECHOSLOVAKIA - WINE PRODUCTION

Facts on File, 460 Park Avenue South, New York, New York 10016 (800) 443-8323; *The New Book of World Rankings.*

Statistical Office of the United Nations, Publishing Service, New York, New York 10017 (800) 253-9646; *Statistical Yearbook.*

CZECHOSLOVAKIA - WOOD - See CZECHOSLOVAKIA - FORESTRY AND FOREST PRODUCTS

CZECHOSLOVAKIA - YARN PRODUCTION

Statistical Office of the United Nations, Publishing Service, New York, New York 10017 (800) 253-9646; *Statistical Yearbook.*

CZECHOSLOVAKIA - ZINC PRODUCTION AND CONSUMPTION - See CZECHOSLOVAKIA - MINING AND MINERAL PRODUCTS

D

DAIRY PRODUCTS - See also Individual Products

DAIRY PRODUCTS - COMMODITY CREDIT CORPORATION TRANSACTIONS

U.S. Department of Agriculture, Agricultural Stabilization and Conservation Service, Fourteenth Street and Independence Avenue, SW, Washington, D.C. 20250 (202) 720-5237; *Commodity Credit Corporation Report of Financial Condition and Operations*, and *Agricultural Outlook*.

DAIRY PRODUCTS - CONSUMER EXPENDITURES

U.S. Department of Agriculture, Economic Research Service, Fourteenth and Independence Avenue, SW, Washington, D.C. 20250 (202) 219-1504; *Food Cost Review*, *Food Review*, and *Agricultural Statistics*.

U.S. Department of Labor, Bureau of Labor Statistics, Two Massachusetts Avenue, NE, Washington, D.C. 20212 (202) 606-7828; *Consumer Expenditures in 1992*.

DAIRY PRODUCTS - CONSUMPTION

U.S. Department of Agriculture, Economic Research Service, Fourteenth Street and Independence Avenue, SW, Washington, D.C. 20250 (202) 219-1504; *Food Consumption, Prices and Expenditures*, and unpublished data.

DAIRY PRODUCTS - FARM MARKETINGS

U.S. Department of Agriculture, Economic Research Service, Fourteenth Street and Independence Avenue, SW, Washington, D.C. 20250 (202) 219-1504; *Economic Indicators of the Farm Sector: National Financial Summary*, and unpublished data.

U.S. Department of Agriculture, National Agricultural Statistics Service, Fourteenth Street and Independence Avenue, SW, Washington, D.C. 20250 (202) 219-1504; *Dairy Products*, and *Milk Production, Disposition, and Income*.

DAIRY PRODUCTS - FOREIGN TRADE

U.S. Department of Agriculture, Economic Research Service, Fourteenth Street and Independence Avenue, SW, Washington, D.C. 20250 (202) 219-1504; *Foreign Agricultural Trade of the United States*, and *Agricultural Outlook*.

U.S. Department of Commerce, Bureau of the Census, Suitland, Maryland 20233 (301) 763-4040; *Current Business Reports*, *Combined Annual and Revised Monthly Wholesale Trade*, and *U.S. Merchandise Trade*.

DAIRY PRODUCTS - MANUFACTURE

U.S. Department of Commerce, Bureau of the Census, Suitland, Maryland 20233 (301) 763-4040; *Census of Manufactures*, and *Annual Survey of Manufactures*.

DAIRY PRODUCTS - PRICES

U.S. Department of Agriculture, National Agricultural Statistics Service, Fourteenth Street and Independence Avenue, SW, Washington, D.C. 20250 (202) 219-1504; *Milk Production, Disposition and Income*, *Dairy Products*, and *Agricultural Prices: Annual Summary*.

DAIRY PRODUCTS - PRODUCTION

U.S. Department of Agriculture, Economic Research Service, Fourteenth Street and Independence Avenue, SW, Washington, D.C. 20250 (202) 219-1504; *Agricultural Outlook*.

U.S. Department of Agriculture, National Agricultural Statistics Service, Fourteenth Street and Independence Avenue, SW, Washington, D.C. 20250 (202) 219-1504; *Dairy Products*, and *Milk Production, Disposition, and Income*.

DATA PROCESSING SERVICES - See COMPUTER PROGRAMMING AND DATA PROCESSING SERVICES

DATES

U.S. Department of Agriculture, National Agricultural Statistics Service, Fourteenth Street and Independence Avenue, SW, Washington, D.C. 20250 (202) 219-1504; *Noncitrus Fruits and Nuts*.

DEAF PERSONS

U.S. Department of Health and Human Services, National Center for Health Statistics, 3700 East-West Highway, Hyattsville, Maryland 20782 (301) 436-8500; *Vital and Health Statistics*, and unpublished data.

DEATHS AND DEATH RATES - See also ACCIDENTS AND FATALITIES

DEATHS AND DEATH RATES - AGE AND SEX

U.S. Department of Health and Human Services, National Center for Health Statistics, 3700 East-West Highway, Hyattsville, Maryland 20782 (301) 436-8500; *Advance Data from Vital and Health Statistics, Monthly Vital Statistics Report, Vital Statistics of the United States*, and unpublished data.

World Health Organization, Avenue Appia, Office of Publications, CH-1211 Geneva, 27, Switzerland (Telephone Number in U.S. (518) 436-9686); *World Health Statistics Annual.*

DEATHS AND DEATH RATES - AIDS

U.S. Department of Health and Human Services, Centers for Disease Control, 1600 Clifton Road, NE, Atlanta, Georgia 30333 (404) 639-3311; *Surveillance Report.*

U.S. Department of Health and Human Services, National Center for Health Statistics, 3700 East-West Highway, Hyattsville, Maryland 20782 (301) 436-8500; *Monthly Vital Statistics Report, Vital Statistics of the United States*, and unpublished data.

DEATHS AND DEATH RATES - BLACK POPULATION

U.S. Department of Health and Human Services, Centers for Disease Control, 1600 Clifton Road, NE, Atlanta, Georgia 30333 (404) 639-3311; *Surveillance Report.*

U.S. Department of Health and Human Services, National Center for Health Statistics, 3700 East-West Highway, Hyattsville, Maryland 20782 (301) 436-8500; *Advance Data from Vital and Health Statistics, Monthly Vital Statistics Report, Vital Statistics of the United States*, and unpublished data.

DEATHS AND DEATH RATES - CANCER

U.S. Department of Health and Human Services, National Center for Health Statistics, 3700 East-West Highway, Hyattsville, Maryland 20782 (301) 436-8500; *Monthly Vital Statistics Report, Vital Statistics of the United States*, and unpublished data.

DEATHS AND DEATH RATES - CANCER - FOREIGN COUNTRIES

World Health Organization, Avenue Appia, Office of Publications, CH-1211 Geneva, 27, Switzerland (Telephone Number in U.S. (518) 436-9686; *World Health Statistics Annual.*

DEATHS AND DEATH RATES - CAUSE

U.S. Department of Health and Human Services, Centers for Disease Control, 1600 Clifton Road, NE, Atlanta, Georgia 30333 (404) 639-3311; unpublished data.

U.S. Department of Health and Human Services, National Center for Health Statistics, 3700 East-West Highway, Hyattsville, Maryland 20782 (301) 436-8500; *Monthly Vital Statistics Report, Vital Statistics of the United States*, and unpublished data.

U.S. Department of Transportation, Federal Railroad Administration, 400 Seventh Street, SW, Washington, D.C. 20591 (202) 366-0881; *Accident Bulletin.*

U.S. Department of Transportation, Bureau of Transportation Statistics, 400 Seventh Street, SW, Washington, D.C. 20590 (202) 366-DATA; *National Transportation Statistics Annual, Historical Compendium Information Report.*

U.S. Department of Transportation, Transportation Systems Center, Kendall Square, Cambridge, Massachusetts, 02142 (617) 494-2224; *Transportation Safety Information Report.*

DEATHS AND DEATH RATES - CAUSE - FOREIGN COUNTRIES

World Health Organization, Avenue Appia, Office of Publications, CH-1211 Geneva, 27, Switzerland (Telephone Number in U.S. (518) 436-9686); *World Health Statistics Annual.*

DEATHS AND DEATH RATES - FETAL AND NEONATAL

U.S. Department of Health and Human Services, National Center for Health Statistics, 3700 East-West Highway, Hyattsville, Maryland 20782 (301) 436-8500; *Monthly Vital Statistics Report*, and *Vital Statistics of the United States.*

DEATHS AND DEATH RATES - FOREIGN COUNTRIES

American Automobile Manufacturers Association, 1401 H Street, NW, Suite 900, Washington, D.C. 20006 (202) 326-5500; *AAMA Motor Vehicle Facts and Figures.*

World Health Organization, Office of Publications, Avenue Appia CH-1211 Geneva, 27, Switzerland (Telephone Number in U.S. (518) 436-9686); *World Health Statistics Annual*, and unpublished data.

DEATHS AND DEATH RATES - INDUSTRIAL

National Safety Council, 1121 Spring Lake Drive, Itasca, Illinois 60143-3201 (708) 285-1121; *Accident Facts.*

DEATHS AND DEATH RATES - INFANT

U.S. Department of Health and Human Services, National Center for Health Statistics, 3700 East-West Highway, Hyattsville, Maryland 20782 (301) 436-8500; *Monthly Vital Statistics Reports, Vital Statistics of the United States*, and unpublished data.

DEATHS AND DEATH RATES - MATERNAL

U.S. Department of Health and Human Services, National Center for Health Statistics, 3700 East-West Highway, Hyattsville, Maryland 20782 (301) 436-8500; *Monthly Vital Statistics Report*, and *Vital Statistics of the United States.*

DEATHS AND DEATH RATES - METROPOLITAN AREAS

U.S. Department of Health and Human Services, National Center for Health Statistics, 3700 East-West Highway, Hyattsville, Maryland 20782 (301) 436-8500; *Vital Statistics of the United States*, and unpublished data.

DEATHS AND DEATH RATES - OUTLYING AREAS OF UNITED STATES

U.S. Department of Commerce, Bureau of the Census, Suitland, Maryland 20233 (301) 763-4040; *Current Population Reports.*

U.S. Department of Health and Human Services, National Center for Health Statistics, 3700 East-West Highway, Hyattsville, Maryland 20782 (301) 436-8500; *Vital Statistics of the United States.*

DEATHS AND DEATH RATES - PROJECTIONS

U.S. Department of Commerce, Bureau of the Census, Suitland, Maryland 20233 (301) 763-4040; *Current Population Reports.*

DEATHS AND DEATH RATES - RACE

U.S. Department of Health and Human Services, National Center for Health Statistics, 3700 East-West Highway, Hyattsville, Maryland 20782 (301) 436-8500; *Monthly Vital Statistics Report, Advance Data from Vital and Health Statistics, Vital Statistics of the United States*, and unpublished data.

DEATHS AND DEATH RATES - SUMMARY

U.S. Department of Health and Human Services, National Center for Health Statistics, 3700 East-West Highway, Hyattsville, Maryland 20782 (301) 436-8500; *Monthly Vital Statistics Report, Vital Statistics of the United States*, and unpublished data.

DEBT - See also LOANS AND MORTGAGES

DEBT - CITY GOVERNMENTS

U.S. Department of Commerce, Bureau of the Census, Suitland, Maryland 20233 (301) 763-4040; *City Government Finances*.

DEBT - CONSUMER

American Bankers Association, 1120 Connecticut Avenue, NW, Washington, D.C. 20036 (202) 663-5000; *Consumer Credit Delinquency Bulletin*.

Board of Governors of the Federal Reserve System, Twentieth Street and Constitution Avenue, NW, Washington, D.C 20551 (202) 452-3000; *Annual Statistical Digest, Federal Reserve Bulletin*, and unpublished data.

DEBT - COUNTY GOVERNMENTS

U.S. Department of Commerce, Bureau of the Census, Suitland, Maryland 20233 (301) 763-4040; *County Government Finances*.

DEBT - FARM

U.S. Department of Agriculture, Economic Research Service, Fourteenth Street and Independence Avenue, SW, Washington, D.C. 20250 (202) 219-1504; *Economic Indicators of the Farm Sector: National Financial Summary*, and *Economic Indicators of the Farm Sector: State Financial Summary*.

DEBT - FEDERAL GOVERNMENT

Executive Office of the President, Office of Management and Budget, Executive Office Building, Washington, D.C. 20503 (202) 395-3080; *Budget of the United States Government*.

U.S. Department of Commerce, Bureau of the Census, Suitland, Maryland 20233 (301) 763-4040; *Government Finances*.

U.S. Department of the Treasury, Fifteenth Street and Pennsylvania Avenue, NW, Washington, D.C. 20220 (202) 566-2000; *Treasury Bulletin*.

U.S. Department of the Treasury, Internal Revenue Service, 1111 Constitution Avenue, NW, Washington, D.C. 20224 (202) 566-5000; *Statistics of Income, Individual Income Tax Returns*.

DEBT - FOREIGN COUNTRIES

Central Intelligence Agency, Washington, D.C. 20505 (703) 482-1100; *Handbook of International Economic Statistics*, and unpublished data.

The World Bank, 1818 H Street, NW, Washington, D.C. 20006 (202) 447-1234; *World Debt Tables*.

DEBT - LOCAL GOVERNMENTS

Advisory Commission on Intergovernmental Relations, 800 K Street, NW, Suite 450 South, Washington, D.C. 20575 (202) 653-5540; *Significant Features of Fiscal Federalism*, based on *Budget of the U.S. Government*.

Executive Office of the President, Office of Management and Budget, Executive Office Building, Washington, D.C. 20503 (202) 395-3080; *Historical Tables, Budget of the U.S. Government*, and *Budget of the U.S. Government*.

Securities Data Company, Inc., 1180 Raymond Boulevard, Newark, New Jersey 07102 (201) 622-3100; Municipal New Issues Database.

U.S. Department of Commerce, Bureau of the Census, Suitland, Maryland 20233 (301) 763-4040; *Historical Statistics on Government Finances and Employment, Government Finances, State Government Finances, Census of Governments, Survey of Current Business, The National Income and Product Accounts of the U.S.*, and *Federal Expenditures by State for Fiscal Year*.

DEBT - STATE AND LOCAL GOVERNMENT

U.S. Department of Commerce, Bureau of the Census, Suitland, Maryland 20233 (301) 763-4040; *Historical Statistics on Governmental Finances and Employment, Government Finances, State Government Finances*, and unpublished data.

DEBT - PUBLIC - STATE AND LOCAL GOVERNMENT - HIGHWAYS

U.S. Department of Transportation, Federal Highway Administration, 400 Seventh Street, SW, Washington, D.C. 20590 (202) 366-0660; *Highway Statistics*.

DEBT - PUBLIC - STATE GOVERNMENT

U.S. Department of Commerce, Bureau of the Census, Suitland, Maryland 20233 (301) 763-4040; *Government Finances, Historical Statistics on Governmental Finances and Employment, State Government Finances, Census of Governments*, and unpublished data.

DEFENSE, DEPARTMENT OF - See also ARMY, NAVY, and AIR FORCE

DEFENSE, DEPARTMENT OF - BUDGET AUTHORITY, OUTLAYS

Executive Office of the President, Office of Management and Budget, Executive Office Building, Washington, D.C. 20503 (202) 395-3080; *Budget of the U.S. Government*.

DEFENSE, DEPARTMENT OF - CONTRACT AWARDS - STATES

U.S. Department of Defense, Office of the Secretary, The Pentagon, Washington, D.C. 20301 (703) 545-6700; *Atlas/Data Abstract for the United States and Selected Areas*.

DEFENSE, DEPARTMENT OF - EMPLOYEES - CIVILIAN

U.S. Department of Defense, Office of the Secretary, The Pentagon, Washington, D.C. 20301 (703) 545-6700; *Selected Manpower Statistics*, and *Atlas/Data Abstract for the United States and Selected Areas*.

DEFENSE, DEPARTMENT OF - EXPENDITURES

Executive Office of the President, Office of Management and Budget, Executive Office Building, Washington, D.C. 20503 (202) 395-3080; *The Budget of the United States Government.*

U.S. Department of Defense, Office of the Secretary, The Pentagon, Washington, D.C. 20301 (703) 545-6700; *Atlas/Data Abstract for the United States and Selected Areas.*

DEFENSE, DEPARTMENT OF - EXPENDITURES - HEALTH AND MEDICAL CARE

U.S. Department of Health and Human Services, Health Care Financing Administration, 200 Independence Avenue, SW, Washington, D.C. 20201 (202) 245-6113; *Health Care Financing Review.*

DEFENSE, DEPARTMENT OF - EXPENDITURES - MILITARY RETIREES

U.S. Department of Defense, Office of the Secretary, The Pentagon, Washington, D.C. 20301-1155 (703) 545-6700; *Selected Manpower Statistics.*

DEFENSE, DEPARTMENT OF - EXPENDITURES - SPACE PROGRAM

U.S. National Aeronautics and Space Administration, 600 Independence Avenue, SW, Washington, D.C. 20546 (202) 453-1000; *Aeronautics and Space Report of the President,* data from Executive Office of the President, Office of Management and Budget, Executive Office Building, Washington, D.C. 20503 (202) 395-3080.

DEFENSE, DEPARTMENT OF - FUNDS AVAILABLE AND OUTLAYS

Executive Office of the President, Office of Management and Budget, Executive Office Building, Washington, D.C. 20503 (202) 395-3080; *The Budget of the United States Government.*

DEFENSE, DEPARTMENT OF - MILITARY BASES

Army Times Publishing Company, 6883 Commercial Drive, Springfield, Virginia 22159 (703) 750-9000; *Guide to Military Installations in the U.S.*

DEFENSE, DEPARTMENT OF - MILITARY PERSONNEL

U.S. Department of Defense, Office of the Secretary, The Pentagon, Washington, D.C. 20301 (703) 545-6700; *Selected Manpower Statistics, Official Guard and Reserve Manpower Strengths and Statistics,* and unpublished data.

DEFENSE, DEPARTMENT OF - PROPERTY - REAL AND PERSONAL

U.S. General Services Administration, General Services Building, Eighteenth and F Streets, NW, Washington, D.C. 20405 (202) 708-5082; *Inventory Report on Real Property Owned by the United States Throughout the World.*

DEGREES CONFERRED - See also individual field

National Science Foundation, 4201 Wilson Boulevard, Arlington, Virginia 22230 (703) 306-1234; *Characteristics of Recent Science and Engineering Graduates,* and *Survey of Earned Doctorates, Selected Data on Science and Engineering Doctorate Awards.*

U.S. Department of Education, 400 Maryland Avenue, SW, Washington, D.C. 20202 (202) 708-5366; *Digest of Education Statistics,* and *Projections of Education Statistics to 2003.*

DEGREES CONFERRED - SALARY OFFERS

College Placement Council, 62 Highland Avenue, Bethlehem, Pennsylvania 18017(212) 868-1421; *Salary Survey, A Study of Beginning Offers.*

Northwestern University Placement Center, 633 Clark Street, Evanston, Illinois 60201 (708) 491-3741; *The Northwestern Endicott-Lindquist Report.*

DEHUMIDIFIERS

U.S. Department of Energy, Energy Information Administration, Washington, D.C. 20585 (202) 586-8800; *Housing Characteristics.*

DELAWARE - See also STATE DATA (FOR INDIVIDUAL STATES)

Delaware - Primary Statistics Source

Delaware Development Office, 99 Kings Highway, P.O. Box 1401, Dover, Delaware 19903 (302) 739-4271; *Delaware Data Book.*

University of Delaware, Bureau of Economic Research, College of Business and Economics, Newark, New Jersey 19716-2730 (302) 831-8401; *Delaware Economic Report.*

Delaware - State Data Centers

Delaware Development Office, 99 Kings Highway, P.O. Box 1401, Dover, Delaware 19903, Ms. Judy McKinney-Cherry (302) 739-4271.

College of Urban Affairs and Public Policy, University of Delaware, Graham Hall, Room 286, Academy Street, Newark, Delaware 19716, Mr. Ed Ratledge (302) 415-8406.

DEMOCRATIC KAMPUCHEA - See CAMBODIA

Denmark - National Statistical Office

Danmarks Statistik, Post Boks 2550, Sejrogade 11, 2100 Copenhagen, 0, Denmark.

Denmark - Primary Statistics Source

Danmarks Statistik, Sejrogade 11, Postboks 2250, 2100 Kobenhavn 0, Denmark; *Statistisk Arbog* (Statistical Yearbook), *Statistiske Efterretninger* (Statistical News), and *Statistisk Manedsoversigt* (Monthly review of statistics).

Denmark - Databases

Arbejdsloshed statistikkens Bruger-Bank (ABBA), Danmarks Statistik, Sejrogade 11, Post Office Box 2550, DK-2100 Copenhagen, Denmark; Subject coverage: Labor market data.

Danmarks Statistisk's Time-Series Data Bank, Danmarks Statistik, Sejrodage 11, Post Office Box 2550, DK-2100 Copenhagen, Denmark. Subject coverage: Time series economic statistics.

Kommunal Statistisk Data Bank (KSDB), Danmarks Statistik, Sejrogade 11, Post Office Box 2550, DK-2100 Copenhagen, Denmark. Subject coverage: Time series of demographic data on all municipalities.

VE-DATABASEN, Energy and Environmental Data, Niels Jernes Jey 10, Dk-9220 Aalborg O, Denmark. Subject coverage: Historical and current information on renewable energy in Denmark.

DENMARK - ABORTIONS

European Community Information Service, 2100 M Street, NW, Washington, D.C. 20037 (202) 862-9500; *Demographic Statistics.*

Nordic Council of Ministers, Store Strandstraede 18, DK-1255 Copenhagen K, Denmark and the Nordic Statistical Secretariat, Postboks 2550, DK-2100 Copenhagen 0, Denmark; *The Yearbook of Nordic Statistics.*

Statistical Office of the United Nations, Publishing Service, New York, New York 10017 (800) 253-9646; *Demographic Yearbook.*

DENMARK - AGRICULTURAL CONSUMPTION

European Community Information Service, 2100 M Street, NW, Washington, D.C. 20037 (202) 862-9500; *Basic Statistics of the Community.*

DENMARK - AGRICULTURE

European Community Information Service, 2100 M Street, NW, Washington, D.C. 20037 (202) 862-9500; *Agriculture: Statistical Yearbook, Basic Statistics of the Community, Eurostatistics: Data for Short-Term Economic Analysis, Labor Force Sample Survey,* and *Regions: Statistical Yearbook.*

Facts on File, 460 Park Avenue South, New York, New York 10016 (800) 443-8323; *The New Book of World Rankings.*

Federal Statistical Office, Gustav - Stresemann - Ring 11, D-6200 Wiesbaden, Germany; *Danemark.*

Food and Agricultural Organization of the United Nations (FAO), Via delle Terme di Caracalla, 00100 Rome, Italy (Telephone Number in U.S. (202) 653-2400); *Production Yearbook, The State of Food and Agriculture,* and *Trade Yearbook.*

G.K. Hall and Company, 70 Lincoln Street, Boston, Massachusetts 02111 (617) 423-3990; *The World in Figures.*

International Monetary Fund, 700 Nineteenth Street, NW, Washington, D.C. 20431 (202) 623-7000; *International Financial Statistics.*

Nordic Council of Ministers, Store Strandstraede 18, DK-1255 Copenhagen K, Denmark and the Nordic Statistical Secretariat, Postboks 2550, DK-2100 Copenhagen 0, Denmark; *The Yearbook of Nordic Statistics.*

Organisation for Economic Co-operation and Development (OECD), 2 rue Andre-Pascal, 75 Paris 16, France (Telephone Number in U.S. (202) 785-6323); *Economic Accounts for Agriculture, Indicators of Industrial Activity, Industrial Structure Statistics,* and *OECD Economic Surveys: Denmark.*

Statistical Office of the United Nations, Publishing Service, New York, New York 10017 (800) 253-9646; *Statistical Yearbook.*

Times Books, 201 East 50th Street, New York, New York 10022 (212) 751-2600; *The Economist Book of Vital World Statistics.*

The World Bank, 1818 H Street, NW, Washington, D.C. 20433 (202) 477-1234; *World Tables.*

DENMARK - AIRLINE SERVICE

European Community Information Service, 2100 M Street, NW, Washington, D.C. 20037 (202) 862-9500; *Basic Statistics of the Community, Regions: Statistical Yearbook,* and *Transport Annual Statistics.*

Facts on File, 460 Park Avenue South, New York, New York 10016 (800) 443-8323; *The New Book of World Rankings.*

G.K. Hall and Company, 70 Lincoln Street, Boston, Massachusetts 02111 (617) 423-3990; *The World in Figures.*

International Civil Aviation Organization, 1000 Sherbrooke Street West, Suite 400, Montreal, Quebec, Canada H3A 2R2 (514) 285-8219; *Civil Aviation Statistics of the World.*

Nordic Council of Ministers, Store Strandstraede 18, DK-1255 Copenhagen K, Denmark and the Nordic Statistical Secretariat, Postboks 2550, DK-2100 Copenhagen 0, Denmark; *The Yearbook of Nordic Statistics.*

Organisation for Economic Co-operation and Development (OECD), 2 rue Andre-Pascal, 75 Paris 16, France (Telephone Number in U.S. (202) 785-6323); *Tourism Policy and International Tourism in OECD Member Countries.*

Statistical Office of the United Nations, Publishing Service, New York, New York 10017 (800) 253-9646; *Statistical Yearbook.*

DENMARK - ALMOND PRODUCTION - See DENMARK - CROPS

DENMARK - ALUMINUM PRODUCTION AND CONSUMPTION - See DENMARK - MINING AND MINERAL PRODUCTS

DENMARK - ANIMAL FEEDINGSTUFFS

Organisation for Economic Co-operation and Development (OECD), 2 rue Andre-Pascal, 75 Paris 16, France (Telephone Number in U.S. (202) 785-6323); *Foreign Trade by Commodities.*

Statistical Office of the United Nations, Publishing Service, New York, New York 10017 (800) 253-9646; *Statistical Yearbook.*

DENMARK - ANIMAL HEALTH

Food and Agricultural Organization of the United Nations (FAO), Via delle Terme di Caracalla, 00100 Rome, Italy (Telephone Number in U.S. (202) 653-2400); *Animal Health Yearbook.*

DENMARK - ANTIMONY AND ANTIMONY ORE - See DENMARK - MINING AND MINERAL PRODUCTS

DENMARK - APPLE PRODUCTION - See DENMARK - CROPS

DENMARK - AREA AND DENSITY OF POPULATION

European Community Information Service, 2100 M Street, NW, Washington, D.C. 20037 (202) 862-9500; *Basic Statistics of the Community,* and *Demographic Statistics.*

Facts on File, 460 Park Avenue South, New York, New York 10016; *The New Book of World Rankings.*

Federal Statistical Office, Gustav - Stresemann - Ring 11, D-6200 Wiesbaden, Germany; *Danemark.*

Food and Agricultural Organization of the United Nations (FAO) Via delle Terme di Caracalla, 00100 Rome, Italy (Telephone Number in

U.S. (202) 653-2400); *The State of Food and Agriculture.*

G.K. Hall and Company, 70 Lincoln Street, Boston, Massachusetts 02111 (617) 423-3990; *The World in Figures.*

Nordic Council of Ministers, Store Strandstraede 18, DK-1255 Copenhagen K, Denmark and the Nordic Statistical Secretariat, Postboks 2550, DK-2100 Copenhagen 0, Denmark; *The Yearbook of Nordic Statistics.*

Statistical Office of the United Nations, Publishing Service, New York, New York 10017 (800) 253-9646; *Statistical Yearbook.*

Times Books, 201 East 50th Street, New York, New York 10022 (212) 751-2600; *The Economist Book of Vital World Statistics.*

United Nations Educational, Scientific and Cultural Organization (UNESCO), 7 Place de Fontenoy, F-75700 Paris, France (Telephone Number in U.S. (212) 963-5981); *Statistical Yearbook.*

DENMARK - ARMS EXPORTS AND IMPORTS

U.S. Arms Control and Disarmament Agency, 320 Twenty-first Street, NW, Washington, D.C. 20451 (202) 647-8677; *World Military Expenditures and Arms Transfers.*

DENMARK - ARSENIC - See DENMARK - MINING AND MINERAL PRODUCTS

DENMARK - BALANCE OF PAYMENTS

The Economist Intelligence Unit, 111 West 57th Street, New York, New York 10019 (800) 938-4685; *The World Market Atlas.*

European Community Information Service, 2100 M Street, NW, Washington, D.C. 20037 (202) 862-9500; *ACP: Basic Statistics, Basic Statistics of the Community, Energy Statistics Yearbook,* and *Eurostatistics: Data for Short-Term Economic Analysis.*

Federal Statistical Office, Gustav - Stresemann - Ring 11, D-6200 Wiesbaden, Germany; *Danemark.*

G.K. Hall and Company, 70 Lincoln Street, Boston, Massachusetts 02111 (617) 423-3990; *The World in Figures.*

International Monetary Fund, 700 Nineteenth Street, NW, Washington, D.C. 20431 (202) 623-7000; *Balance of Payments Yearbook,* and *International Financial Statistics.*

Nordic Council of Ministers, Store Strandstraede 18, DK-1255 Copenhagen K, Denmark and the Nordic Statistical Secretariat, Postboks 2550, DK-2100 Copenhagen 0, Denmark; *The Yearbook of Nordic Statistics.*

Organisation for Economic Co-operation and Development (OECD), 2 rue Andre-Pascal, 75 Paris 16, France (Telephone Number in U.S. (202) 785-6323); *Economic Outlook, Geographical Distribution of Financial Flows to Developing Countries,* and *OECD Economic Surveys: Denmark.*

Times Books, 201 East 50th Street, New York, New York 10022 (212) 751-2600; *The Economist Book of Vital World Statistics.*

The World Bank, 1818 H Street, NW, Washington, D.C. 20433 (202) 477-1234; *World Tables.*

DENMARK - BANANA PRODUCTION - See DENMARK - CROPS

DENMARK - BANKING

European Community Information Service, 2100 M Street, NW, Washington, D.C. 20037 (202) 862-9500; *ACP: Basic Statistics.*

Facts on File, 460 Park Avenue South, New York, New York 10016 (800) 443-8323; *The New Book of World Rankings.*

G.K. Hall and Company, 70 Lincoln Street, Boston, Massachusetts 02111 (617) 423-3990; *The World in Figures.*

International Monetary Fund, 700 Nineteenth Street, NW, Washington, D.C. 20431 (202) 623-7000; *International Financial Statistics.*

Nordic Council of Ministers, Store Strandstraede 18, DK-1255 Copenhagen K, Denmark and the Nordic Statistical Secretariat, Postboks 2550, DK-2100 Copenhagen 0, Denmark; *The Yearbook of Nordic Statistics.*

Organisation for Economic Co-operation and Development (OECD), 2 rue Andre-Pascal, 75 Paris 16, France (Telephone Number in U.S. (202) 785-6323); *Economic Outlook, Financial Market Trends,* and *OECD Economic Surveys: Denmark.*

Statistical Office of the United Nations, Publishing Service, New York, New York 10017 (800) 253-9646; *Statistical Yearbook.*

DENMARK - BARLEY PRODUCTION - See DENMARK - CROPS

DENMARK - BAUXITE PRODUCTION AND CONSUMPTION - See DENMARK - MINING AND MINERAL PRODUCTS

DENMARK - BEER PRODUCTION

Facts on File, 460 Park Avenue South, New York, New York 10016 (800) 443-8323; *The New Book of World Rankings.*

Statistical Office of the United Nations, Publishing Service, New York, New York 10017 (800) 253-9646; *Statistical Yearbook.*

DENMARK - BEVERAGES - PRODUCTION INDEX

Organisation for Economic Co-operation and Development (OECD), 2 rue Andre-Pascal, 75 Paris 16, France (Telephone Number in U.S. (202) 785-6323); *Indicators of Industrial Activity.*

DENMARK - BIRTH RATE

European Community Information Service, 2100 M Street, NW, Washington, D.C. 20037 (202) 862-9500; *Basic Statistics of the Community,* and *Demographic Statistics.*

Facts on File, 460 Park Avenue South, New York, New York 10016 (800) 443-8323; *The New Book of World Rankings.*

Nordic Council of Ministers, Store Strandstraede 18, DK-1255 Copenhagen K, Denmark and the Nordic Statistical Secretariat, Postboks 2550, DK-2100 Copenhagen 0, Denmark; *The Yearbook of Nordic Statistics.*

Organisation for Economic Co-operation and Development (OECD), 2 rue Andre-Pascal, 75 Paris 16, France; (Telephone Number in U.S. (202) 785-6323); *Labour Force Statistics.*

Statistical Office of the United Nations, Publishing Service, New York, New York 10017 (800) 253-9646; *Demographic Yearbook,* and *Statistical Yearbook.*

Times Books, 201 East 50th Street, New York, New York 10022 (212) 751-2600; *The Economist Book of Vital World Statistics.*

The World Bank, 1818 H Street, NW, Washington, D.C. 20433 (202) 477-1234; *World Tables.*

World Health Organization, Office of Publications, Avenue Appia, CH-1211 Geneva 27, Switzerland (Telephone Number in U.S. (518) 436-9686); *World Health Statistics Annual.*

DENMARK - BISMUTH PRODUCTION AND CONSUMPTION - See DENMARK - MINING AND MINERAL PRODUCTS

DENMARK - BONDS

European Community Information Service, 2100 M Street, NW, Washington, D.C. 20037 (202) 862-9500; *Basic Statistics of the Community.*

G.K. Hall and Company, 70 Lincoln Street, Boston, Massachusetts 02111 (617) 423-3990; *The World in Figures.*

Organisation for Economic Co-operation and Development (OECD), 2 rue Andre-Pascal, 75 Paris 16, France (Telephone Number in U.S. (202) 785-6323); *Financial Market Trends.*

Statistical Office of the United Nations, Publishing Service, New York, New York 10017 (800) 253-9646; *Statistical Yearbook.*

DENMARK - BOOK PRODUCTION

Euromonitor Publications Limited, 87-88 Turnmill Street, London EC1M 5QU, England; *European Marketing Data and Statistics.*

G.K. Hall and Company, 70 Lincoln Street, Boston, Massachusetts 02111 (617) 423-3990; *The World in Figures.*

Nordic Council of Ministers, Store Strandstraede 18, DK-1255 Copenhagen K, Denmark and the Nordic Statistical Secretariat, Postboks 2550, DK-2100 Copenhagen 0, Denmark; *The Yearbook of Nordic Statistics.*

Organisation for Economic Co-operation and Development (OECD), 2 rue Andre-Pascal, 75 Paris 16, France (Telephone Number in U.S. (202) 785-6323); *Indicators of Industrial Activity.*

United Nations Educational, Scientific and Cultural Organization (UNESCO), 7 Place de Fontenoy, F-75700 Paris, France (Telephone Number in U.S. (212) 963-5981); *Statistical Yearbook.*

DENMARK - BROADCASTING

Billboard Limited, P.O. Box 9027, 1006 AA Amsterdam, The Netherlands (Telephone Number in U.S. (212) 764-7300); *World Radio TV Handbook.*

European Community Information Service, 2100 M Street, NW, Washington, D.C. 20037 (202) 862-9500; *Basic Statistics of the Community.*

Facts on File, 460 Park Avenue South, New York, New York 10016 (800) 443-8323; *The New Book of World Rankings.*

G.K. Hall and Company, 70 Lincoln Street, Boston, Massachusetts 02111 (617) 423-3990; *The World in Figures.*

Nordic Council of Ministers, Store Strandstraede 18, DK-1255 Copenhagen K, Denmark and the Nordic Statistical Secretariat, Postboks 2550, DK-2100 Copenhagen 0, Denmark; *The Yearbook of Nordic Statistics.*

Times Books, 201 East 50th Street, New York, New York 10022 (212) 751-2600; *The Economist Book of Vital World Statistics.*

United Nations Educational, Scientific and Cultural Organization (UNESCO), 7 Place de Fontenoy, F-75700 Paris, France (Telephone Number in U.S. (212) 963-5981); *Statistical Yearbook.*

DENMARK - BUILDING CONSTRUCTION - See DENMARK - CONSTRUCTION INDUSTRY

DENMARK - BUSINESS

European Community Information Service, 2100 M Street, NW, Washington, D.C. 20037 (202) 862-9500; *Basic Statistics of the Community.*

G.K. Hall and Company, 70 Lincoln Street, Boston, Massachusetts 02111 (617) 423-3990; *The World in Figures.*

DENMARK - BUSINESS AND PROFESSIONAL LICENSES

International Monetary Fund, 700 Nineteenth Street, NW, Washington, D.C. 20431 (202) 623-7000; *Government Finance Statistics Yearbook.*

DENMARK - BUTTER - See DENMARK - DAIRY PRODUCTS

DENMARK - CABBAGE PRODUCTION - See DENMARK - CROPS

DENMARK - CADMIUM PRODUCTION - See DENMARK - MINING AND MINERAL PRODUCTS

DENMARK - CALORIE SUPPLY

Food and Agricultural Organization of the United Nations (FAO) Via delle Terme di Caracalla, 00100 Rome, Italy (Telephone Number in U.S. (202) 653-2400); *The State of Food and Agriculture.*

DENMARK - CAPITAL INVESTMENT

Organisation for Economic Co-operation and Development (OECD), 2 rue Andre-Pascal, 75 Paris 16, France (Telephone Number in U.S. (202) 785-6323); *Economic Outlook,* and *Financial Market Trends.*

DENMARK - CAPITAL REVENUE

International Monetary Fund, 700 Nineteenth Street, NW, Washington, D.C. 20431 (202) 623-7000; *Government Finance Statistics Yearbook.*

Organisation for Economic Co-operation and Development (OECD), 2 rue Andre-Pascal, 75 Paris 16, France (Telephone Number in U.S. (202) 785-6323); *Economic Outlook,* and *Financial Market Trends.*

DENMARK - CASHEW NUT PRODUCTION - See DENMARK - CROPS

DENMARK - CASTOR BEAN PRODUCTION - See DENMARK - CROPS

DENMARK - CATTLE - See DENMARK - LIVESTOCK AND POULTRY

DENMARK - CAULIFLOWER PRODUCTION - See DENMARK - CROPS

DENMARK - CAUSTIC SODA PRODUCTION

European Community Information Service, 2100 M Street, NW, Washington, D.C. 20037 (202) 862-9500; *Basic Statistics of the Community.*

Organisation for Economic Co-operation and Development (OECD), 2 rue Andre-Pascal, 75 Paris 16, France (Telephone Number in U.S. (202) 785-6323); *Indicators of Industrial Activity.*

Statistical Office of the United Nations, Publishing Service, New York, New York 10017 (800) 253-9646; *Statistical Yearbook.*

DENMARK - CEMENT PRODUCTION - See DENMARK - MINING AND MINERAL PRODUCTS

DENMARK - CEREAL PRODUCTION - See DENMARK - CROPS

DENMARK - CHEESE - See DENMARK - DAIRY PRODUCTS

DENMARK - CHEMICAL INDUSTRY

European Community Information Service, 2100 M Street, NW, Washington, D.C. 20037 (202) 862-9500; *Industrial Production: Quarterly Statistics.*

DENMARK - CHEMICAL (ORGANIC) PRODUCTION - See DENMARK - MINING AND MINERAL PRODUCTS

DENMARK - CHESTNUT PRODUCTION - See DENMARK - CROPS

DENMARK - CHICKENS - See DENMARK - LIVESTOCK AND POULTRY

DENMARK - CHROMITE PRODUCTION AND CONSUMPTION - See DENMARK - MINING AND MINERAL PRODUCTS

DENMARK - CHROMIUM ORE PRODUCTION AND CONSUMPTION - See DENMARK - MINING AND MINERAL PRODUCTS

DENMARK - CIGAR PRODUCTION - See DENMARK - TOBACCO PRODUCTION

DENMARK - CIGARETTE PRODUCTION - See DENMARK - TOBACCO PRODUCTION

DENMARK - CLASS STRUCTURE

European Community Information Service, 2100 M Street, NW, Washington, D.C. 20037 (202) 862-9500; *Basic Statistics of the Community,* and *Labor Force Sample Survey.*

G.K. Hall and Company, 70 Lincoln Street, Boston, Massachusetts 02111 (617) 423-3990; *The World in Figures.*

DENMARK - CLIMATE

Facts on File, 460 Park Avenue South, New York, New York 10016 (800) 443-8323; *The New Book of World Rankings.*

G.K. Hall and Company, 70 Lincoln Street, Boston, Massachusetts 02111 (617) 423-3990; *The World in Figures.*

DENMARK - CLOTHING - PRODUCTION INDEX

Organisation for Economic Co-operation and Development (OECD), 2 rue Andre-Pascal, 75 Paris 16, France (Telephone Number in U.S. (202) 785-6323); *Indicators of Industrial Activity.*

DENMARK - CLOTHING EXPORTS AND IMPORTS

European Community Information Service, 2100 M Street, NW, Washington, D.C. 20037 (202) 862-9500; *Basic Statistics of the Community.*

Organisation for Economic Co-operation and Development (OECD), 2 rue Andre-Pascal, 75 Paris 16, France (Telephone Number in U.S. (202) 785-6323); *Textile Industry in OECD Countries.*

Statistical Office of the United Nations, Publishing Service, New York, New York 10017 (800) 253-9646; *Trade in Manufactures of Developing Countries.*

DENMARK - COAL PRODUCTION - See DENMARK - MINING AND MINERAL PRODUCTS

DENMARK - COBALT PRODUCTION AND CONSUMPTION - See DENMARK - MINING AND MINERAL PRODUCTS

DENMARK - COCOA (BEANS) PRODUCTION - See DENMARK - CROPS

DENMARK - COFFEE EXPORTS - See DENMARK - CROPS

DENMARK - COKE AND COKE OVEN ORE - See DENMARK - MINING AND MINERAL PRODUCTS

DENMARK - COMMUNICATIONS

European Community Information Service, 2100 M Street, NW, Washington, D.C. 20037 (202) 862-9500; *Basic Statistics of the Community,* and *Transport Annual Statistics.*

Federal Statistical Office, Gustav - Stresemann - Ring 11, D-6200 Wiesbaden, Germany; *Danemark.*

G.K. Hall and Company, 70 Lincoln Street, Boston, Massachusetts 02111 (617) 423-3990; *The World in Figures.*

DENMARK - CONSTRUCTION INDUSTRY

European Community Information Service, 2100 M Street, NW, Washington, D.C. 20037 (202) 862-9500; *Basic Statistics of the Community,* and *Labor Force Sample Survey.*

Facts on File, 460 Park Avenue South, New York, New York 10016 (800) 443-8323; *The New Book of World Rankings.*

Nordic Council of Ministers, Store Strandstraede 18, DK-1255 Copenhagen K, Denmark and the Nordic Statistical Secretariat, Postboks 2550, DK-2100 Copenhagen 0, Denmark; *The Yearbook of Nordic Statistics.*

Organisation for Economic Co-operation and Development (OECD), 2 rue Andre-Pascal, 75 Paris 16, France (Telephone Number in U.S. (202) 785-6323); *Industrial Structure Statistics, The Iron and Steel Industry,* and *OECD Economic Surveys: Australia.*

Statistical Office of the United Nations, Publishing Service, New York, New York 10017 (800) 253-9646; *Construction Statistics Yearbook,* and *Statistical Yearbook.*

DENMARK - CONSUMER PRICE INDEX

European Community Information Service, 2100 M Street, NW, Washington, D.C. 20037 (202) 862-9500; *Basic Statistics of the Community.*

Federal Statistical Office, Gustav - Stresemann - Ring 11, D-6200 Wiesbaden, Germany; *Danemark.*

G.K. Hall and Company, 70 Lincoln Street, Boston, Massachusetts 02111 (617) 423-3990; *The World in Figures.*

Nordic Council of Ministers, Store Strandstraede 18, DK-1255 Copenhagen K, Denmark and the Nordic Statistical Secretariat, Postboks 2550, DK-2100 Copenhagen 0, Denmark; *The Yearbook of Nordic Statistics*.

Organisation for Economic Co-operation and Development (OECD), 2 rue Andre-Pascal, 75 Paris 16, France (Telephone Number in U.S. (202) 785-6323); *Economic Outlook*.

Statistical Office of the United Nations, Publishing Service, New York, New York 10017 (800) 253-9646; *Statistical Yearbook*.

DENMARK - CONSUMER PRICES

Euromonitor Publications Limited, 87-88 Turnmill Street, London EC1M 5QU, England; *European Marketing Data and Statistics*.

European Community Information Service, 2100 M Street, NW, Washington, D.C. 20037 (202) 862-9500; *Basic Statistics of the Community, Eurostatistics: Data for Short-Term Economic Analysis*, and *Money and Finance*.

Federal Statistical Office, Gustav - Stresemann - Ring 11, D-6200 Wiesbaden, Germany; *Danemark*.

International Labour Office, I.L.O. Publications, CH-1211, Geneva 22, Switzerland; *Yearbook of Labour Statistics*.

International Monetary Fund, 700 Nineteenth Street, NW, Washington, D.C. 20431 (202) 623-7000; *International Financial Statistics*.

Organisation for Economic Co-operation and Development (OECD), 2 rue Andre-Pascal, 75 Paris 16, France (Telephone Number in U.S. (202) 785-6323); *Economic Outlook*.

Times Books, 201 East 50th Street, New York, New York 10022 (212) 751-2600; *The Economist Book of Vital World Statistics*.

DENMARK - CONSUMPTION

European Community Information Service, 2100 M Street, NW, Washington, D.C. 20037 (202) 862-9500; *Basic Statistics of the Community*.

G.K. Hall and Company, 70 Lincoln Street, Boston, Massachusetts 02111 (617) 423-3990; *The World in Figures*.

International Lead and Zinc Study Group, Metro House, 58 St. James's Street, London SW1A 1LD, England; *Lead and Zinc Statistics*.

International Rubber Study Group, York House, 8th Floor, Empire Way, Wembley, London HA9 0PA, England; *Rubber Statistical Bulletin*.

Nordic Council of Ministers, Store Strandstraede 18, DK-1255 Copenhagen K, Denmark and the Nordic Statistical Secretariat, Postboks 2550, DK-2100 Copenhagen 0, Denmark; *The Yearbook of Nordic Statistics*.

Organisation for Economic Co-operation and Development (OECD), 2 rue Andre-Pascal, 75 Paris 16, France (Telephone Number in U.S. (202) 785-6323); *The Footwear, Raw Hides and Skins, and Leather Industry in OECD Countries, The Iron and Steel Industry, Meat Balances in OECD Member Countries, The Non-Ferrous Metals Industry, The Pulp and Paper Industry*, and *Textile Industry in OECD Countries*.

DENMARK - COPPER AND COPPER ORE PRODUCTION - See DENMARK - MINING AND MINERAL PRODUCTS

DENMARK - CORN PRODUCTION - See DENMARK - CROPS

DENMARK - CORPORATE TAXES - See DENMARK - TAXATION

DENMARK - COTTON - See DENMARK - CROPS

DENMARK - CRIME

International Criminal Police Organization (INTERPOL), 26 rue Armengaud, 92210 Saint Cloud, France; *International Crime Statistics*.

Nordic Council of Ministers, Store Strandstraede 18, DK-1255 Copenhagen K, Denmark and the Nordic Statistical Secretariat, Postboks 2550, DK-2100 Copenhagen 0, Denmark; *The Yearbook of Nordic Statistics*.

Yale University Press, Yale Station, New Haven, Connecticut 06520 (203) 432-0940; *Violence and Crime in Cross-National Perspective*.

DENMARK - CROPS

Commodity Research Bureau, Incorporated, 75 Wall Street, New York, New York 10005 (212) 504-7754; *Commodity Year Book*.

Euromonitor Publications Limited, 87-88 Turnmill Street, London EC1M 5QU, England; *European Marketing Data and Statistics*.

European Community Information Service, 2100 M Street, NW, Washington, D.C. 20037 (202) 862-9500; *ACP: Basic Statistics, Agriculture: Statistical Yearbook, Basic Statistics of the Community, Crop Production: Quarterly Statistics, Eurostatistics: Data for Short-Term Economic Analysis*, and *Regions: Statistical Yearbook*.

Facts on File, 460 Park Avenue South, New York, New York 10016 (800) 443-8323; *The New Book of World Rankings*.

Food and Agricultural Organization of the United Nations (FAO), Via delle Terme di Caracalla, 00100 Rome, Italy (Telephone Number in U.S. (202) 653-2400); *Production Yearbook*, and *State of Food and Agriculture*.

G.K. Hall and Company, 70 Lincoln Street, Boston, Massachusetts 02111 (617) 423-3990; *The World in Figures*.

International Wheat Statistics, 28 Haymarket, London SW1Y 4SS, England; *World Wheat Statistics*.

Organisation for Economic Co-operation and Development (OECD), 2 rue Andre-Pascal, 75 Paris 16, France (Telephone Number in U.S. (202) 785-6323); *Economic Accounts for Agriculture, Foreign Trade by Commodities*, and *Textile Industry in OECD Countries*.

Statistical Office of the United Nations, Publishing Service, New York, New York 10017 (800) 253-9646; *Statistical Yearbook*.

DENMARK - CUSTOMS DUTIES

European Community Information Service, 2100 M Street, NW, Washington, D.C. 20037 (202) 862-9500; *Basic Statistics of the Community*.

G.K. Hall and Company, 70 Lincoln Street, Boston, Massachusetts 02111 (617) 423-3990; *The World in Figures*.

International Monetary Fund, 700 Nineteenth Street, NW, Washington, D.C. 20431 (202) 623-7000; *Government Finance Statistics Yearbook.*

Organisation for Economic Co-operation and Development (OECD), 2 rue Andre-Pascal, 75 Paris 16, France (Telephone Number in U.S. (202) 785-6323); *The Non-Ferrous Metals Industry.*

DENMARK - DAIRY PRODUCTS

Commodity Research Bureau, Incorporated, 75 Wall Street, New York, New York 10005 (212) 504-7754; *Commodity Year Book.*

European Community Information Service, 2100 M Street, NW, Washington, D.C. 20037 (202) 862-9500; *Basic Statistics of the Community,* and *Eurostatistics: Data for Short-Term Economic Analysis.*

Facts on File, 460 Park Avenue South, New York, New York 10016 (800) 443-8323; *The New Book of World Rankings.*

Food and Agricultural Organization of the United Nations (FAO) Via delle Terme di Caracalla, 00100 Rome, Italy (Telephone Number in U.S. (202) 653-2400); *Production Yearbook,* and *The State of Food and Agriculture.*

Organisation for Economic Co-operation and Development (OECD), 2 rue Andre-Pascal, 75 Paris 16, France (Telephone Number in U.S. (202) 785-6323); *Economic Accounts for Agriculture, Milk, Milk Products, and Egg Balances in OECD Member Countries.*

Statistical Office of the United Nations, Publishing Service, New York, New York 10017 (800) 253-9646; *Statistical Yearbook.*

DENMARK - DEATH RATES

European Community Information Service, 2100 M Street, NW, Washington, D.C. 20037 (202) 862-9500; *Basic Statistics of the Community,* and *Demographic Statistics.*

G.K. Hall and Company, 70 Lincoln Street, Boston, Massachusetts 02111 (617) 423-3990; *The World in Figures.*

Nordic Council of Ministers, Store Strandstraede 18, DK-1255 Copenhagen K, Denmark and the Nordic Statistical Secretariat, Postboks 2550, DK-2100 Copenhagen 0, Denmark; *The Yearbook of Nordic Statistics.*

Statistical Office of the United Nations, Publishing Service, New York, New York 10017 (800) 253-9646; *Statistical Yearbook.*

Times Books, 201 East 50th Street, New York, New York 10022 (212) 751-2600; *The Economist Book of Vital World Statistics.*

World Health Organization, Office of Publications, Avenue Appia, CH-1211 Geneva 27, Switzerland (Telephone Number in U.S. (518) 436-9686); *World Health Statistics Annual.*

DENMARK - DEFENSE EXPENDITURES

European Community Information Service, 2100 M Street, NW, Washington, D.C. 20037 (202) 862-9500; *Government Financing of Research and Development.*

G.K. Hall and Company, 70 Lincoln Street, Boston, Massachusetts 02111 (617) 423-3990; *The World in Figures.*

International Monetary Fund, 700 Nineteenth Street, NW, Washington, D.C. 20431 (202) 623-7000; *Government Finance Statistics Yearbook.*

U.S. Arms Control and Disarmament Agency, 320 Twenty-first Street, NW, Washington, D.C. 20451 (202) 647-8677; *World Military Expenditures and Arms Transfers.*

DENMARK - DEMOGRAPHY

The Economist Intelligence Unit, 111 West 57th Street, New York, New York 10019 (800) 938-4685; *The World Market Atlas.*

European Community Information Service, 2100 M Street, NW, Washington, D.C. 20037 (202) 862-9500; *Basic Statistics of the Community, Demographic Statistics, Employment and Unemployment,* and *Regions: Statistical Yearbook.*

Facts on File, 460 Park Avenue South, New York, New York 10016 (800) 443-8323; *The New Book of World Rankings.*

Federal Statistical Office, Gustav - Stresemann - Ring 11, D-6200 Wiesbaden, Germany; *Danemark.*

G.K. Hall and Company, 70 Lincoln Street, Boston, Massachusetts 02111 (617) 423-3990; *The World in Figures.*

Nordic Council of Ministers, Store Strandstraede 18, DK-1255 Copenhagen K, Denmark and the Nordic Statistical Secretariat, Postboks 2550, DK-2100 Copenhagen 0, Denmark; *The Yearbook of Nordic Statistics.*

DENMARK - DEVELOPMENT ASSISTANCE

European Community Information Service, 2100 M Street, NW, Washington, D.C. 20037 (202) 862-9500; *ACP: Basic Statistics, Basic Statistics of the Community,* and *Government Financing of Research and Development.*

G.K. Hall and Company, 70 Lincoln Street, Boston, Massachusetts 02111 (617) 423-3990; *The World in Figures.*

Organisation for Economic Co-operation and Development (OECD), 2 rue Andre-Pascal, 75 Paris 16, France (Telephone Number in U.S. (202) 785-6323); *Geographical Distribution of Financial Flows to Developing Countries.*

Statistical Office of the United Nations, Publishing Service, New York, New York 10017 (800) 253-9646; *Statistical Yearbook.*

DENMARK - DIAMOND - See DENMARK - MINING AND MINERAL PRODUCTS

DENMARK - DISCOUNT RATES

Organisation for Economic Co-operation and Development (OECD), 2 rue Andre-Pascal, 75 Paris 16, France (Telephone Number in U.S. (202) 785-6323); *Financial Market Trends.*

Statistical Office of the United Nations, Publishing Service, New York, New York 10017 (800) 253-9646; *Statistical Yearbook.*

DENMARK - DISEASES

G.K. Hall and Company, 70 Lincoln Street, Boston, Massachusetts 02111 (617) 423-3990; *The World in Figures.*

World Health Organization, Office of Publications, Avenue Appia, CH-1211 Geneva 27, Switzerland (Telephone Number in U.S. (518) 436-9686); *World Health Statistics Annual.*

DENMARK - DIVORCE RATES

European Community Information Service, 2100 M Street, NW, Washington, D.C. 20037 (202) 862-9500; *Demographic Statistics.*

Facts on File, 460 Park Avenue South, New York, New York 10016 (800) 443-8323; *The New Book of World Rankings.*

Nordic Council of Ministers, Store Strandstraede 18, DK-1255 Copenhagen K, Denmark and the Nordic Statistical Secretariat, Postboks 2550, DK-2100 Copenhagen 0, Denmark; *The Yearbook of Nordic Statistics.*

Statistical Office of the United Nations, Publishing Service, New York, New York 10017 (800) 253-9646; *Demographic Yearbook,* and *Statistical Yearbook.*

DENMARK - DOMESTIC PRODUCT

European Community Information Service, 2100 M Street, NW, Washington, D.C. 20037 (202) 862-9500; *Basic Statistics of the Community.*

G.K. Hall and Company, 70 Lincoln Street, Boston, Massachusetts 02111 (617) 423-3990; *The World in Figures.*

DENMARK - DUCKS - See DENMARK - LIVESTOCK AND POULTRY

DENMARK - ECONOMY

Euromonitor Publications Limited, 87-88 Turnmill Street, London EC1M 5QU, England; *European Marketing Data and Statistics.*

European Community Information Service, 2100 M Street, NW, Washington, D.C. 20037 (202) 862-9500; *ACP: Basic Statistics, Basic Statistics of the Community, Energy Statistics Yearbook, Labor Force Sample Survey, Money and Finance,* and *OECD Economic Surveys: Denmark.*

Facts on File, 460 Park Avenue South, New York, New York 10016 (800) 443-8323; *The New Book of World Rankings.*

Federal Statistical Office, Gustav - Stresemann - Ring 11, D-6200 Wiesbaden, Germany; *Danemark.*

G.K. Hall and Company, 70 Lincoln Street, Boston, Massachusetts 02111 (617) 423-3990; *The World in Figures.*

Organisation for Economic Co-operation and Development (OECD), 2 rue Andre-Pascal, 75 Paris 16, France (Telephone Number in U.S. (202) 785-6323); *Economic Outlook, Geographical Distribution of Financial Flows to Developing Countries, Main Economic Indicators Historical Statistics,* and *OECD Employment Outlook.*

Statistical Office of the United Nations, Publishing Service, New York, New York 10017 (800) 253-9646; *Statistical Yearbook.*

DENMARK - EDUCATION

The Economist Intelligence Unit, 111 West 57th Street, New York, New York 10019 (800) 938-4685; *The World Market Atlas.*

Euromonitor Publications Limited, 87-88 Turnmill Street, London EC1M 5QU, England; *European Marketing Data and Statistics.*

European Community Information Service, 2100 M Street, NW, Washington, D.C. 20037 (202) 862-9500; *Basic Statistics of the Community,* and *Regions: Statistical Yearbook.*

Facts on File, 460 Park Avenue South, New York, New York 10016 (800) 443-8323; *The New Book of World Rankings.*

Federal Statistical Office, Gustav - Stresemann - Ring 11, D-6200 Wiesbaden, Germany; *Danemark.*

G.K. Hall and Company, 70 Lincoln Street, Boston, Massachusetts 02111 (617) 423-3990; *The World in Figures.*

International Monetary Fund, 700 Nineteenth Street, NW, Washington, D.C. 20431 (202) 623-7000; *Government Finance Statistics Yearbook.*

Nordic Council of Ministers, Store Strandstraede 18, DK-1255 Copenhagen K, Denmark and the Nordic Statistical Secretariat, Postboks 2550, DK-2100 Copenhagen 0, Denmark; *The Yearbook of Nordic Statistics.*

Organisation for Economic Co-operation and Development (OECD), 2 rue Andre-Pascal, 75 Paris 16, France (Telephone Number in U.S. (202) 785-6323); *Education in OECD Countries.*

Times Books, 201 East 50th Street, New York, New York 10022 (212) 751-2600; *The Economist Book of Vital World Statistics.*

United Nations Educational, Scientific and Cultural Organization (UNESCO), 7 Place de Fontenoy, F-75700 Paris, France (Telephone Number in U.S. (212) 963-5981); *Statistical Yearbook.*

The World Bank, 1818 H Street, NW, Washington, D.C. 20433 (202) 477-1234; *World Tables.*

DENMARK - EGG PRODUCTION AND CONSUMPTION - See DENMARK - DAIRY PRODUCTS

DENMARK - ELECTRICITY

European Community Information Service, 2100 M Street, NW, Washington, D.C. 20037 (202) 862-9500; *Basic Statistics of the Community, Energy: Monthly Statistics, Energy Statistics Yearbook, Eurostatistics: Data for Short-Term Economic Analysis,* and *Regions: Statistical Yearbook.*

Facts on File, 460 Park Avenue South, New York, New York 10016 (800) 443-8323; *The New Book of World Rankings.*

Nordic Council of Ministers, Store Strandstraede 18, DK-1255 Copenhagen K, Denmark and the Nordic Statistical Secretariat, Postboks 2550, DK-2100 Copenhagen 0, Denmark; *The Yearbook of Nordic Statistics.*

Organisation for Economic Co-operation and Development (OECD), 2 rue Andre-Pascal, 75 Paris 16, France (Telephone Number in U.S. (202) 785-6323); *Coal Information, Energy Statistics of OECD Countries, Indicators of Industrial Activity,* and *Industrial Structure Statistics.*

Penn Well Publishing Company, 1421 South Sheridan Road, P.O. Box 1260, Tulsa, Oklahoma 74101 (800) 752-9764; *International Energy Statistics Sourcebook.*

Statistical Office of the United Nations, Publishing Service, New York, New York 10017 (800) 253-9646; *Statistical Yearbook.*

Times Books, 201 East 50th Street, New York, New York 10022 (212) 751-2600; *The Economist Book of Vital World Statistics.*

DENMARK - EMPLOYMENT

Euromonitor Publications Limited, 87-88 Turnmill Street, London EC1M 5QU, England; *European Marketing Data and Statistics.*

European Community Information Service, 2100 M Street, NW, Washington, D.C. 20037 (202) 862-9500; *Basic Statistics of the Community, Earnings in Agriculture, Employment and Unemployment, Eurostatistics: Data for Short-Term Economic Analysis, Iron and Steel: Statistical Yearbook,* and *Labor Force Sample Survey.*

Facts on File, 460 Park Avenue South, New York, New York 10016 (800) 443-8323; *The New Book of World Rankings.*

Federal Statistical Office, Gustav - Stresemann - Ring 11, D-6200 Wiesbaden, Germany; *Danemark.*

International Labour Office, I.L.O. Publications, CH-1211, Geneva 22, Switzerland; *Yearbook of Labour Statistics.*

Nordic Council of Ministers, Store Strandstraede 18, DK-1255 Copenhagen K, Denmark and the Nordic Statistical Secretariat, Postboks 2550, DK-2100 Copenhagen 0, Denmark; *The Yearbook of Nordic Statistics.*

Organisation for Economic Co-operation and Development (OECD), 2 rue Andre-Pascal, 75 Paris 16, France (Telephone Number in U.S. (202) 785-6323); *Economic Outlook, The Iron and Steel Industry, OECD Economic Surveys: Denmark, OECD Employment Outlook,* and *Textile Industry in OECD Countries.*

Statistical Office of the United Nations, Publishing Service, New York, New York 10017 (800) 253-9646; *Statistical Yearbook.*

DENMARK - ENERGY

Euromonitor Publications Limited, 87-88 Turnmill Street, London EC1M 5QU, England; *European Marketing Data and Statistics.*

European Community Information Service, 2100 M Street, NW, Washington, D.C. 20037 (202) 862-9500; *Basic Statistics of the Community, Energy: Monthly Statistics, Energy Statistics Yearbook, Regions: Statistical Yearbook,* and *Transport Annual Statistics.*

Facts on File, 460 Park Avenue South, New York, New York 10016 (800) 443-8323; *The New Book of World Rankings.*

Food and Agricultural Organization of the United Nations (FAO) Via delle Terme di Caracalla, 00100 Rome, Italy (Telephone Number in U.S. (202) 653-2400); *The State of Food and Agriculture.*

G.K. Hall and Company, 70 Lincoln Street, Boston, Massachusetts 02111 (617) 423-3990; *The World in Figures.*

Nordic Council of Ministers, Store Strandstraede 18, DK-1255 Copenhagen K, Denmark and the Nordic Statistical Secretariat, Postboks 2550, DK-2100 Copenhagen 0, Denmark; *The Yearbook of Nordic Statistics.*

Organisation for Economic Co-operation and Development (OECD), 2 rue Andre-Pascal, 75 Paris 16, France (Telephone Number in U.S. (202) 785-6323); *Coal Information, Energy Statistics of OECD Countries, OECD Environmental Data,* and *Oil and Gas Information.*

Penn Well Publishing Company, 1421 South Sheridan Road, P.O. Box 1260, Tulsa, Oklahoma 74101 (800) 752-9764; *International Energy Statistics Sourcebook.*

Statistical Office of the United Nations, Publishing Service, New York, New York 10017 (800) 253-9646; *Energy Statistics Yearbook, Statistical Yearbook,* and *World Energy Supplies.*

Times Books, 201 East 50th Street, New York, New York 10022 (212) 751-2600; *The Economist Book of Vital World Statistics.*

DENMARK - ENGINEERING AND METAL PRODUCTS - EXPORTS AND IMPORTS

European Community Information Service, 2100 M Street, NW, Washington, D.C. 20037 (202) 862-9500; *Basic Statistics of the Community,* and *Industrial Production: Quarterly Statistics.*

DENMARK - ENVIRONMENT

Organization for Economic Co-operation and Development (OECD), 2 rue Andre-Pascal, 75 Paris 16, France (Telephone Number in U.S. (202) 785-6323); *OECD Environmental Data.*

DENMARK - EXCHANGE RATES

European Community Information Service, 2100 M Street, NW, Washington, D.C. 20037 (202) 862-9500; *Eurostatistics: Data for Short-Term Economic Analysis,* and *Money and Finance.*

International Civil Aviation Organization, 1000 Sherbrooke Street West, Suite 400, Montreal, Quebec, Canada H3A 2R2 (514) 285-8219; *Civil Aviation Statistics of the World.*

International Monetary Fund, 700 Nineteenth Street, NW, Washington, D.C. 20431 (202) 623-7000; *International Financial Statistics.*

Nordic Council of Ministers, Store Strandstraede 18, DK-1255 Copenhagen K, Denmark and the Nordic Statistical Secretariat, Postboks 2550, DK-2100 Copenhagen 0, Denmark; *The Yearbook of Nordic Statistics.*

Organisation for Economic Co-operation and Development (OECD), 2 rue Andre-Pascal, 75 Paris 16, France (Telephone Number in U.S. (202) 785-6323); *Economic Outlook, Financial Market Trends, Revenue Statistics of OECD Member Countries,* and *Tourism Policy and International Tourism in OECD Member Countries.*

Statistical Office of the United Nations, Publishing Service, New York, New York 10017 (800) 253-9646; *Statistical Yearbook.*

DENMARK - EXCISE TAXES - See DENMARK - TAXATION

DENMARK - EXPORTS

American Automobile Manufacturers Association, 1401 H Street, NW, Suite 900, Washington, D.C. 20005 (202) 326-5500; *World Motor Vehicle Data.*

The Economist Intelligence Unit, 111 West 57th Street, New York, New York 10019 (800) 938-4685; *The World Market Atlas.*

European Community Information Service, 2100 M Street, NW, Washington, D.C. 20037 (202) 862-9500; *Basic Statistics of the Community, Energy: Monthly Statistics, Energy Statistics Yearbook, Eurostatistics: Data for Short-Term Economic Analysis, External Trade: Monthly Statistics, External Trade: Statistical Yearbook,* and *Fisheries: Yearly Statistic.*

Food and Agricultural Organization of the United Nations (FAO) Via delle Terme di Caracalla, 00100 Rome, Italy (Telephone Number in U.S. (202) 653-2400); *The State of Food and Agriculture.*

G.K. Hall and Company, 70 Lincoln Street, Boston, Massachusetts 02111 (617) 423-3990; *The World in Figures.*

International Lead and Zinc Study Group, Metro House, 58 St. James's Street, London SW1A 1LD, England; *Lead and Zinc Statistics.*

International Monetary Fund, 700 Nineteenth Street, NW, Washington, D.C. 20431 (202) 623-7000; *Direction of Trade Statistics, Government Finance Statistics Yearbook,* and *International Financial Statistics.*

International Rubber Study Group, York House, 8th Floor, Empire Way, Wembley, London HA9 0PA, England; *Rubber Statistical Bulletin.*

Nordic Council of Ministers, Store Strandstraede 18, DK-1255 Copenhagen K, Denmark and the Nordic Statistical Secretariat, Postboks 2550, DK-2100 Copenhagen 0, Denmark; *The Yearbook of Nordic Statistics.*

Organisation for Economic Co-operation and Development (OECD), 2 rue Andre-Pascal, 75 Paris 16, France (Telephone Number in U.S. (202) 785-6323); *Economic Outlook, The Footwear, Raw Hides and Skins, and Leather Industry in OECD Countries, Foreign Trade by Commodities, Geographical Distribution of Financial Flows to Developing Countries, Industrial Structure Statistics, The Iron and Steel Industry, Milk, Milk Products, and Egg Balances in OECD Member Countries, OECD Economic Surveys: Denmark, The Pulp and Paper Industry,* and *Review of Fisheries in OECD Member Countries.*

Times Books, 201 East 50th Street, New York, New York 10022 (212) 751-2600; *The Economist Book of Vital World Statistics.*

The World Bank, 1818 H Street, NW, Washington, D.C. 20433 (202) 477-1234; *World Tables.*

DENMARK - EXTERNAL FINANCING

Organisation for Economic Co-operation and Development (OECD), 2 rue Andre-Pascal, 75 Paris 16, France (Telephone Number in U.S. (202) 785-6323); *Economic Outlook,* and *Financial Market Trends.*

DENMARK - EXTERNAL INDEBTEDNESS

Organisation for Economic Co-operation and Development (OECD), 2 rue Andre-Pascal, 75 Paris 16, France (Telephone Number in U.S. (202) 785-6323); *Financial Market Trends,* and *Geographical Distribution of Financial Flows to Developing Countries.*

The World Bank, 1818 H Street, NW, Washington, D.C. 20433 (202) 477-1234; *World Tables.*

DENMARK - EXTERNAL TRADE

European Community Information Service, 2100 M Street, NW, Washington, D.C. 20037 (202) 862-9500; *ACP: Basic Statistics, Basic Statistics of the Community, Eurostatistics: Data for Short-Term Economic Analysis, External Trade: Monthly Statistics,* and *External Trade: Statistical Yearbook.*

Food and Agricultural Organization of the United Nations (FAO) Via delle Terme di Caracalla, 00100 Rome, Italy (Telephone Number in U.S. (202) 653-2400); *The State of Food and Agriculture,* and *Trade Yearbook.*

G.K. Hall and Company, 70 Lincoln Street, Boston, Massachusetts 02111 (617) 423-3990; *The World in Figures.*

Nordic Council of Ministers, Store Strandstraede 18, DK-1255 Copenhagen K, Denmark and the Nordic Statistical Secretariat, Postboks 2550, DK-2100 Copenhagen 0, Denmark; *The Yearbook of Nordic Statistics.*

Statistical Office of the United Nations, Publishing Service, New York, New York 10017 (800) 253-9646; *Statistical Yearbook.*

DENMARK - FABRIC PRODUCTION - See DENMARK - TEXTILE INDUSTRY

DENMARK - FARM CROPS - See DENMARK - CROPS

DENMARK - FEMALE WORKING POPULATION - See DENMARK - EMPLOYMENT

DENMARK - FERTILITY RATES

European Community Information Service, 2100 M Street, NW, Washington, D.C. 20037 (202) 862-9500; *Demographic Statistics.*

Facts on File, 460 Park Avenue South, New York, New York 10016 (800) 443-8323; *The New Book of World Rankings.*

Nordic Council of Ministers, Store Strandstraede 18, DK-1255 Copenhagen K, Denmark and the Nordic Statistical Secretariat, Postboks 2550, DK-2100 Copenhagen 0, Denmark; *The Yearbook of Nordic Statistics.*

Times Books, 201 East 50th Street, New York, New York 10022 (212) 751-2600; *The Economist Book of Vital World Statistics.*

The World Bank, 1818 H Street, NW, Washington, D.C. 20433 (202) 477-1234; *World Tables.*

DENMARK - FERTILIZER

European Community Information Service, 2100 M Street, NW, Washington, D.C. 20037 (202) 862-9500; *Basic Statistics of the Community.*

Food and Agricultural Organization of the United Nations (FAO), Via delle Terme di Caracalla, 00100 Rome, Italy (Telephone Number in U.S. (202) 653-2400); *Fertilizer Yearbook,* and *The State of Food and Agriculture.*

Organisation for Economic Co-operation and Development (OECD), 2 rue Andre-Pascal, 75 Paris 16, France (Telephone Number in U.S. (202) 785-6323); *Economic Accounts for Agriculture,* and *Foreign Trade by Commodities.*

Statistical Office of the United Nations, Publishing Service, New York, New York 10017 (800) 253-9646; *Statistical Yearbook.*

DENMARK - FETAL MORTALITY

European Community Information Service, 2100 M Street, NW, Washington, D.C. 20037 (202) 862-9500; *Basic Statistics of the Community,* and *Demographic Statistics.*

Nordic Council of Ministers, Store Strandstraede 18, DK-1255 Copenhagen K, Denmark and the Nordic Statistical Secretariat, Postboks 2550, DK-2100 Copenhagen 0, Denmark; *The Yearbook of Nordic Statistics.*

Statistical Office of the United Nations, Publishing Service, New York, New York 10017 (800) 253-9646; *Demographic Yearbook.*

World Health Organization, Office of Publications, Avenue Appia, CH-1211 Geneva 27, Switzerland (Telephone Number in U.S. (518) 436-9686); *World Health Statistics Annual.*

DENMARK - FIBRE PRODUCTION - See DENMARK - TEXTILE INDUSTRY

DENMARK - FILAMENT PRODUCTION - See DENMARK - TEXTILE INDUSTRY

DENMARK - FILM - See DENMARK - MOTION PICTURES

DENMARK - FINANCE

European Community Information Service, 2100 M Street, NW, Washington, D.C. 20037 (202) 862-9500; *ACP: Basic Statistics, Basic Statistics of the Community, Eurostatistics: Data for Short-Term Economic Analysis,* and *Money and Finance.*

Facts on File, 460 Park Avenue South, New York, New York 10016 (800) 443-8323; *The New Book of World Rankings.*

Federal Statistical Office, Gustav - Stresemann - Ring 11, D-6200 Wiesbaden, Germany; *Danemark.*

G.K. Hall and Company, 70 Lincoln Street, Boston, Massachusetts 02111 (617) 423-3990; *The World in Figures.*

International Monetary Fund, 700 Nineteenth Street, NW, Washington, D.C. 20431 (202) 623-7000; *International Financial Statistics.*

Organisation for Economic Co-operation and Development (OECD), 2 rue Andre-Pascal, 75 Paris 16, France (Telephone Number in U.S. (202) 785-6323); *Economic Outlook, Financial Market Trends, Geographical Distribution of Financial Flows to Developing Countries,* and *OECD Financial Statistics.*

DENMARK - FISHERIES

Euromonitor Publications Limited, 87-88 Turnmill Street, London EC1M 5QU, England; *European Marketing Data and Statistics.*

European Community Information Service, 2100 M Street, NW, Washington, D.C. 20037 (202) 862-9500; *Agriculture: Statistical Yearbook, Basic Statistics of the Community,* and *Fisheries: Yearly Statistics.*

Facts on File, 460 Park Avenue South, New York, New York 10016 (800) 443-8323; *The New Book of World Rankings.*

Federal Statistical Office, Gustav - Stresemann - Ring 11, D-6200 Wiesbaden, Germany; *Danemark.*

Food and Agricultural Organization of the United Nations (FAO) Via delle Terme di Caracalla, 00100 Rome, Italy (Telephone Number in U.S. (202) 653-2400); *The State of Food and Agriculture,* and *Yearbook of Fishery Statistics.*

Nordic Council of Ministers, Store Strandstraede 18, DK-1255 Copenhagen K, Denmark and the Nordic Statistical Secretariat, Postboks 2550, DK-2100 Copenhagen 0, Denmark; *The Yearbook of Nordic Statistics.*

Organisation for Economic Co-operation and Development (OECD), 2 rue Andre-Pascal, 75 Paris 16, France (Telephone Number in U.S. (202) 785-6323); *Foreign Trade by Commodities, Industrial Structure Statistics,* and *Review of Fisheries in OECD Member Countries.*

Statistical Office of the United Nations, Publishing Service, New York, New York 10017 (800) 253-9646; *Statistical Yearbook.*

DENMARK - FLAX AND FLAX FIBRE PRODUCTION - See DENMARK - TEXTILE INDUSTRY

DENMARK - FLOUR PRODUCTION

European Community Information Service, 2100 M Street, NW, Washington, D.C. 20037 (202) 862-9500; *Basic Statistics of the Community.*

Statistical Office of the United Nations, Publishing Service, New York, New York 10017 (800) 253-9646; *Statistical Yearbook.*

DENMARK - FOOD

European Community Information Service, 2100 M Street, NW, Washington, D.C. 20037 (202) 862-9500; *Basic Statistics of the Community.*

Food and Agricultural Organization of the United Nations (FAO) Via delle Terme di Caracalla, 00100 Rome, Italy (Telephone Number in U.S. (202) 653-2400); *The State of Food and Agriculture.*

G.K. Hall and Company, 70 Lincoln Street, Boston, Massachusetts 02111 (617) 423-3990; *The World in Figures.*

Organisation for Economic Co-operation and Development (OECD), 2 rue Andre-Pascal, 75 Paris, 16, France; *Food Consumption Statistics,* and *Foreign Trade by Commodities.*

DENMARK - FOOTWEAR - PRODUCTION INDEX

Organisation for Economic Co-operation and Development (OECD), 2 rue Andre-Pascal, 75 Paris 16, France (Telephone Number in U.S. (202) 785-6323); *Indicators of Industrial Activity.*

DENMARK - FOREIGN AID

G.K. Hall and Company, 70 Lincoln Street, Boston, Massachusetts 02111 (617) 423-3990; *The World in Figures.*

DENMARK - FOREIGN DEBT

Organisation for Economic Co-operation and Development (OECD), 2 rue Andre-Pascal, 75 Paris 16, France (Telephone Number in U.S. (202) 785-6323); *Economic Outlook.*

DENMARK - FOREIGN FINANCE

Organisation for Economic Co-operation and Development (OECD), 2 rue Andre-Pascal, 75 Paris 16, France (Telephone Number in U.S. (202) 785-6323); *Economic Outlook,* and *Financial Market Trends.*

DENMARK - FOREIGN INDEBTEDNESS

Organisation for Economic Co-operation and Development (OECD), 2 rue Andre-Pascal, 75 Paris 16, France (Telephone Number in U.S. (202) 785-6323); *Economic Outlook,* and *Financial Market Trends.*

DENMARK - FOREIGN OFFICIAL RESERVES

European Community Information Service, 2100 M Street, NW, Washington, D.C. 20037 (202) 862-9500; *Money and Finance.*

DENMARK - FOREIGN TRADE

European Community Information Service, 2100 M Street, NW, Washington, D.C. 20037 (202) 862-9500; *Basic Statistics of the Community*, and *Iron and Steel: Statistical Yearbook*.

Facts on File, 460 Park Avenue South, New York, New York 10016 (800) 443-8323; *The New Book of World Rankings*.

Federal Statistical Office, Gustav - Stresemann - Ring 11, D-6200 Wiesbaden, Germany; *Danemark*.

Food and Agricultural Organization of the United Nations (FAO) Via delle Terme di Caracalla, 00100 Rome, Italy (Telephone Number in U.S. (202) 653-2400); *The State of Food and Agriculture*.

G.K. Hall and Company, 70 Lincoln Street, Boston, Massachusetts 02111 (617) 423-3990; *The World in Figures*.

International Monetary Fund, 700 Nineteenth Street, NW, Washington, D.C. 20431 (202) 623-7000; *International Financial Statistics*.

Organisation for Economic Co-operation and Development (OECD), 2 rue Andre-Pascal, 75 Paris 16, France (Telephone Number in U.S. (202) 785-6323); *Economic Outlook, The Footwear, Raw Hides and Skins, and Leather Industry in OECD Countries, Foreign Trade by Commodities, Maritime Transport, Meat Balances in OECD Member Countries*, and *OECD Economic Surveys: Denmark*.

Statistical Office of the United Nations, Publishing Service, New York, New York 10017 (800) 253-9646; *International Trade Statistics Yearbook*, and *Statistical Yearbook*.

The World Bank, 1818 H Street, NW, Washington, D.C. 20433 (202) 477-1234; *World Tables*.

World Bureau of Metal Statistics, 27-A High Street, Ware Hert SG12 9BA, England; *World Metal Statistics*.

DENMARK - FORESTRY AND FOREST PRODUCTS

Euromonitor Publications Limited, 87-88 Turnmill Street, London EC1M 5QU, England; *European Marketing Data and Statistics*.

European Community Information Service, 2100 M Street, NW, Washington, D.C. 20037 (202) 862-9500; *Agriculture: Statistical Yearbook, Basic Statistics of the Community, European Marketing Data and Statistics*, and *Industrial Production: Quarterly Statistics*.

Facts on File, 460 Park Avenue South, New York, New York 10016 (800) 443-8323; *The New Book of World Rankings*.

Federal Statistical Office, Gustav - Stresemann - Ring 11, D-6200 Wiesbaden, Germany; *Danemark*.

Food and Agricultural Organization of the United Nations (FAO) Via delle Terme di Caracalla, 00100 Rome, Italy (Telephone Number in U.S. (202) 653-2400); *The State of Food and Agriculture*, and *Yearbook of Forest Products*.

Forest and Paper Association, 1250 Connecticut Avenue, NW, Washington, D.C. 20036 (202) 463-2455; *Wood Pulp and Fiber Statistics*.

G.K. Hall and Company, 70 Lincoln Street, Boston, Massachusetts 02111 (617) 423-3990; *The World in Figures*.

Nordic Council of Ministers, Store Strandstraede 18, DK-1255 Copenhagen K, Denmark and the Nordic Statistical Secretariat, Postboks 2550, DK-2100 Copenhagen 0, Denmark; *The Yearbook of Nordic Statistics*.

Organisation for Economic Co-operation and Development (OECD), 2 rue Andre-Pascal, 75 Paris 16, France (Telephone Number in U.S. (202) 785-6323); *Foreign Trade by Commodities, Indicators of Industrial Activity, Industrial Structure Statistics*, and *The Pulp and Paper Industry*.

Statistical Office of the United Nations, Publishing Service, New York, New York 10017 (800) 253-9646; *Statistical Yearbook*.

United Nations Educational, Scientific and Cultural Organization (UNESCO), 7 Place de Fontenoy, F-75700 Paris, France (Telephone Number in U.S. (212) 963-5981); *Statistical Yearbook*.

DENMARK - FRUIT PRODUCTION - See DENMARK - CROPS

DENMARK - FURNITURE AND WOOD PRODUCTS - EXPORTS AND IMPORTS

European Community Information Service, 2100 M Street, NW, Washington, D.C. 20037 (202) 862-9500; *Basic Statistics of the Community*.

Organisation for Economic Co-operation and Development (OECD), 2 rue Andre-Pascal, 75 Paris 16, France (Telephone Number in U.S. (202) 785-6323); *Foreign Trade by Commodities*, and *Industrial Structure Statistics*.

DENMARK - GARLIC PRODUCTION - See DENMARK - CROPS

DENMARK - GAS AND GAS LIQUIDS - See DENMARK - MINING AND MINERAL PRODUCTS

DENMARK - GENERAL INDUSTRIAL STATISTICS

European Community Information Service, 2100 M Street, NW, Washington, D.C. 20037 (202) 862-9500; *Basic Statistics of the Community*.

Federal Statistical Office, Gustav - Stresemann - Ring 11, D-6200 Wiesbaden, Germany; *Danemark*.

Statistical Office of the United Nations, Publishing Service, New York, New York 10017 (800) 253-9646; *Industrial Statistics Yearbook*.

DENMARK - GENERAL MORTALITY

European Community Information Service, 2100 M Street, NW, Washington, D.C. 20037 (202) 862-9500; *Basic Statistics of the Community, Demographic Statistics*.

Nordic Council of Ministers, Store Strandstraede 18, DK-1255 Copenhagen K, Denmark and the Nordic Statistical Secretariat, Postboks 2550, DK-2100 Copenhagen 0, Denmark; *The Yearbook of Nordic Statistics*.

Statistical Office of the United Nations, Publishing Service, New York, New York 10017 (800) 253-9646; *Demographic Yearbook*.

World Health Organization, Office of Publications, Avenue Appia, CH-1211 Geneva 27, Switzerland (Telephone Number in U.S. (518) 436-9686); *World Health Statistics Annual*.

DENMARK - GEOGRAPHIC DATA

European Community Information Service, 2100 M Street, NW, Washington, D.C. 20037 (202) 862-9500; *Basic Statistics of the Community.*

Facts on File, 460 Park Avenue South, New York, New York 10016 (800) 443-8323; *The New Book of World Rankings.*

Federal Statistical Office, Gustav - Stresemann - Ring 11, D-6200 Wiesbaden, Germany; *Danemark.*

DENMARK - GLASS AND GLASS PRODUCTS - PRODUCTION INDEX

Organisation for Economic Co-operation and Development (OECD), 2 rue Andre-Pascal, 75 Paris 16, France (Telephone Number in U.S. (202) 785-6323); *Indicators of Industrial Activity.*

DENMARK - GOATS - See DENMARK - LIVESTOCK AND POULTRY

DENMARK - GOLD HOLDINGS

International Monetary Fund, 700 Nineteenth Street, NW, Washington, D.C. 20431 (202) 623-7000; *International Financial Statistics.*

Statistical Office of the United Nations, Publishing Service, New York, New York 10017 (800) 253-9646; *Statistical Yearbook.*

The World Bank, 1818 H Street, NW, Washington, D.C. 20433 (202) 477-1234; *World Tables.*

DENMARK - GOLD PRODUCTION AND CONSUMPTION - See DENMARK - MINING AND MINERAL PRODUCTS

DENMARK - GOVERNMENT

European Community Information Service, 2100 M Street, NW, Washington, D.C. 20037 (202) 862-9500; *Basic Statistics of the Community.*

G.K. Hall and Company, 70 Lincoln Street, Boston, Massachusetts 02111 (617) 423-3990; *The World in Figures.*

Organisation for Economic Co-operation and Development (OECD), 2 rue Andre-Pascal, 75 Paris 16, France (Telephone Number in U.S. (202) 785-6323); *Revenue Statistics of OECD Member Countries.*

DENMARK - GOVERNMENT BONDS - See DENMARK - BONDS

DENMARK - GOVERNMENT CONSUMPTION

European Community Information Service, 2100 M Street, NW, Washington, D.C. 20037 (202) 862-9500; *Basic Statistics of the Community.*

DENMARK - GOVERNMENT EXPENDITURES

European Community Information Service, 2100 M Street, NW, Washington, D.C. 20037 (202) 862-9500; *Basic Statistics of the Community,* and *Government Financing of Research and Development.*

International Monetary Fund, 700 Nineteenth Street, NW, Washington, D.C. 20431 (202) 623-7000; *Government Finance Statistics Yearbook.*

Nordic Council of Ministers, Store Strandstraede 18, DK-1255 Copenhagen K, Denmark and the Nordic Statistical Secretariat, Postboks 2550, DK-2100 Copenhagen 0, Denmark; *The Yearbook of Nordic Statistics.*

Organisation for Economic Co-operation and Development (OECD), 2 rue Andre-Pascal, 75 Paris 16, France (Telephone Number in U.S. (202) 785-6323); *Economic Outlook.*

Times Books, 201 East 50th Street, New York, New York 10022 (212) 751-2600; *The Economist Book of Vital World Statistics.*

The World Bank, 1818 H Street, NW, Washington, D.C. 20433 (202) 477-1234; *World Tables.*

DENMARK - GOVERNMENT FINANCES

European Community Information Service, 2100 M Street, NW, Washington, D.C. 20037 (202) 862-9500; *Basic Statistics of the Community, Government Financing of Research and Development,* and *Money and Finance.*

International Monetary Fund, 700 Nineteenth Street, NW, Washington, D.C. 20431 (202) 623-7000; *International Financial Statistics.*

Organisation for Economic Co-operation and Development (OECD), 2 rue Andre-Pascal, 75 Paris 16, France (Telephone Number in U.S. (202) 785-6323); *Economic Outlook.*

Statistical Office of the United Nations, Publishing Service, New York, New York 10017 (800) 253-9646; *Statistical Yearbook.*

DENMARK - GOVERNMENT REVENUES

European Community Information Service, 2100 M Street, NW, Washington, D.C. 20037 (202) 862-9500; *Basic Statistics of the Community,* and *Government Financing of Research and Development.*

International Monetary Fund, 700 Nineteenth Street, NW, Washington, D.C. 20431 (202) 623-7000; *Government Finance Statistics Yearbook.*

Nordic Council of Ministers, Store Strandstraede 18, DK-1255 Copenhagen K, Denmark and the Nordic Statistical Secretariat, Postboks 2550, DK-2100 Copenhagen 0, Denmark; *The Yearbook of Nordic Statistics.*

Organisation for Economic Co-operation and Development (OECD), 2 rue Andre-Pascal, 75 Paris 16, France (Telephone Number in U.S. (202) 785-6323); *Economic Outlook.*

Times Books, 201 East 50th Street, New York, New York 10022 (212) 751-2600; *The Economist Book of Vital World Statistics.*

The World Bank, 1818 H Street, NW, Washington, D.C. 20433 (202) 477-1234; *World Tables.*

DENMARK - GRAIN PRODUCTION - See DENMARK - CROPS

DENMARK - GRANTS

International Monetary Fund, 700 Nineteenth Street, NW, Washington, D.C. 20431 (202) 623-7000; *Government Finance Statistics Yearbook.*

Organisation for Economic Co-operation and Development (OECD), 2 rue Andre-Pascal, 75 Paris 16, France (Telephone Number in U.S. (202) 785-6323); *Geographical Distribution of Financial Flows to Developing Countries.*

DENMARK - GREEN PEPPER AND CHILIE PRODUCTION - See DENMARK - CROPS

DENMARK - GROSS DOMESTIC PRODUCT

The Economist Intelligence Unit, 111 West 57th Street, New York, New York 10019 (800) 938-4685; *The World Market Atlas*.

European Community Information Service, 2100 M Street, NW, Washington, D.C. 20037 (202) 862-9500; *Basic Statistics of the Community*, *Eurostatistics: Data for Short-Term Economic Analysis*, *Government Financing of Research and Development*, *Iron and Steel: Statistical Yearbook*, and *Money and Finance*.

Facts on File, 460 Park Avenue South, New York, New York 10016 (800) 443-8323; *The New Book of World Rankings*.

G.K. Hall and Company, 70 Lincoln Street, Boston, Massachusetts 02111 (617) 423-3990; *The World in Figures*.

Nordic Council of Ministers, Store Strandstraede 18, DK-1255 Copenhagen K, Denmark and the Nordic Statistical Secretariat, Postboks 2550, DK-2100 Copenhagen 0, Denmark; *The Yearbook of Nordic Statistics*.

Organisation for Economic Co-operation and Development (OECD), 2 rue Andre-Pascal, 75 Paris 16, France (Telephone Number in U.S. (202) 785-6323); *Economic Outlook*, *Geographical Distribution of Financial Flows to Developing Countries*, and *Revenue Statistics of OECD Member Countries*.

Statistical Office of the United Nations, Publishing Service, New York, New York 10017 (800) 253-9646; *Statistical Yearbook*.

Times Books, 201 East 50th Street, New York, New York 10022 (212) 751-2600; *The Economist Book of Vital World Statistics*.

The World Bank, 1818 H Street, NW, Washington, D.C. 20433 (202) 477-1234; *World Tables*.

DENMARK - GROSS INDUSTRIAL PRODUCT

European Community Information Service, 2100 M Street, NW, Washington, D.C. 20037 (202) 862-9500; *Government Financing of Research and Development*.

DENMARK - GROSS NATIONAL PRODUCT

European Community Information Service, 2100 M Street, NW, Washington, D.C. 20037 (202) 862-9500; *ACP: Basic Statistics*, and *Basic Statistics of the Community*.

Organisation for Economic Co-operation and Development (OECD), 2 rue Andre-Pascal, 75 Paris 16, France (Telephone Number in U.S. (202) 785-6323); *Economic Outlook*, and *Geographical Distribution of Financial Flows to Developing Countries*.

U.S. Arms Control and Disarmament Agency, 320 Twenty-first Street, NW, Washington, D.C. 20451 (202) 647-8677; *World Military Expenditures and Arms Transfers*.

The World Bank, 1818 H Street, NW, Washington, D.C. 20433 (202) 477-1234; *World Tables*.

DENMARK - GROUNDNUT PRODUCTION - See DENMARK - CROPS

DENMARK - GROWTH - DOMESTIC PRODUCT

Facts on File, 460 Park Avenue South, New York, New York 10016 (800) 443-8323; *The New Book of World Rankings*.

DENMARK - HAY PRODUCTION - See DENMARK - CROPS

DENMARK - HAZELNUT PRODUCTION - See DENMARK - CROPS

DENMARK - HEALTH

European Community Information Service, 2100 M Street, NW, Washington, D.C. 20037 (202) 862-9500; *Basic Statistics of the Community*, and *Regions: Statistical Yearbook*.

Facts on File, 460 Park Avenue South, New York, New York 10016 (800) 443-8323; *The New Book of World Rankings*.

Federal Statistical Office, Gustav - Stresemann - Ring 11, D-6200 Wiesbaden, Germany; *Danemark*.

G.K. Hall and Company, 70 Lincoln Street, Boston, Massachusetts 02111 (617) 423-3990; *The World in Figures*.

Nordic Council of Ministers, Store Strandstraede 18, DK-1255 Copenhagen K, Denmark and the Nordic Statistical Secretariat, Postboks 2550, DK-2100 Copenhagen 0, Denmark; *The Yearbook of Nordic Statistics*.

Organisation for Economic Co-operation and Development (OECD), 2 rue Andre-Pascal, 75 Paris 16, France (Telephone Number in U.S. (202) 785-6323); *OECD Health Systems: Facts and Trends*.

Statistical Office of the United Nations, Publishing Service, New York, New York 10017 (800) 253-9646; *Statistical Yearbook*.

Times Books, 201 East 50th Street, New York, New York 10022 (212) 751-2600; *The Economist Book of Vital World Statistics*.

World Health Organization, Office of Publications, Avenue Appia, CH-1211 Geneva 27, Switzerland (Telephone Number in U.S. (518) 436-9686); *World Health Statistics Annual*.

DENMARK - HEMP FIBRE PRODUCTION - See DENMARK - TEXTILE INDUSTRY

DENMARK - HIDE PRODUCTION

Food and Agricultural Organization of the United Nations (FAO), Via delle Terme di Caracalla, 00100 Rome, Italy (Telephone Number in U.S. (202) 653-2400); *Production Yearbook*.

Organisation for Economic Co-operation and Development (OECD), 2 rue Andre-Pascal, 75 Paris 16, France (Telephone Number in U.S. (202) 785-6323); *The Footwear, Raw Hides and Skins, and Leather Industry in OECD Countries*, *Foreign Trade by Commodities*, and *Indicators of Industrial Activity*.

DENMARK - HIGHWAYS

European Community Information Service, 2100 M Street, NW, Washington, D.C. 20037 (202) 862-9500; *Basic Statistics of the Community*, and *Transport Annual Statistics*.

G.K. Hall and Company, 70 Lincoln Street, Boston, Massachusetts 02111 (617) 423-3990; *The World in Figures*.

International Road Federation, 525 School Street, SW, Washington, D.C. 20024 (202) 554-2106; *World Road Statistics*.

Nordic Council of Ministers, Store Strandstraede 18, DK-1255 Copenhagen K, Denmark and the Nordic Statistical Secretariat, Postboks 2550, DK-2100 Copenhagen 0, Denmark; *The Yearbook of Nordic Statistics.*

Statistical Office of the United Nations, Publishing Service, New York, New York 10017 (800) 253-9646; *Annual Bulletin of Transport Statistics for Europe.*

DENMARK - HOPS PRODUCTION - See DENMARK - CROPS

DENMARK - HORSES - See DENMARK - LIVESTOCK AND POULTRY

DENMARK - HOURS OF WORK - See DENMARK - EMPLOYMENT

DENMARK - HOUSING AND HOUSING UNITS

European Community Information Service, 2100 M Street, NW, Washington, D.C. 20037 (202) 862-9500; *Basic Statistics of the Community, Labor Force Sample Survey,* and *Regions: Statistical Yearbook.*

Facts on File, 460 Park Avenue South, New York, New York 10016 (800) 443-8323; *The New Book of World Rankings.*

Nordic Council of Ministers, Store Strandstraede 18, DK-1255 Copenhagen K, Denmark and the Nordic Statistical Secretariat, Postboks 2550, DK-2100 Copenhagen 0, Denmark; *The Yearbook of Nordic Statistics.*

DENMARK - HOUSING CONSTRUCTION - See DENMARK - CONSTRUCTION INDUSTRY

DENMARK - HOUSING EXPENDITURES

European Community Information Service, 2100 M Street, NW, Washington, D.C. 20037 (202) 862-9500; *Basic Statistics of the Community.*

International Monetary Fund, 700 Nineteenth Street, NW, Washington, D.C. 20431 (202) 623-7000; *Government Finance Statistics Yearbook.*

DENMARK - HYDROCHLORIC ACID PRODUCTION

European Community Information Service, 2100 M Street, NW, Washington, D.C. 20037 (202) 862-9500; *Basic Statistics of the Community.*

Statistical Office of the United Nations, Publishing Service, New York, New York 10017 (800) 253-9646; *Statistical Yearbook.*

DENMARK - ILLITERATE POPULATION

The Economist Intelligence Unit, 111 West 57th Street, New York, New York 10019 (800) 938-4685; *The World Market Atlas.*

G.K. Hall and Company, 70 Lincoln Street, Boston, Massachusetts 02111 (617) 423-3990; *The World in Figures.*

DENMARK - IMPORTS

American Automobile Manufacturers Association, 1401 H Street, NW, Suite 900, Washington, D.C. 20005 (202) 326-5500; *World Motor Vehicle Data.*

The Economist Intelligence Unit, 111 West 57th Street, New York, New York 10019 (800) 938-4685; *The World Market Atlas.*

European Community Information Service, 2100 M Street, NW, Washington, D.C. 20037 (202) 862-9500; *Basic Statistics of the Community, Energy: Monthly Statistics, Energy Statistics Yearbook, Eurostatistics: Data for Short-Term Economic Analysis, External Trade: Monthly Statistics, External Trade: Statistical Yearbook,* and *Fisheries: Yearly Statistics.*

Food and Agricultural Organization of the United Nations (FAO) Via delle Terme di Caracalla, 00100 Rome, Italy (Telephone Number in U.S. (202) 653-2400); *The State of Food and Agriculture.*

G.K. Hall and Company, 70 Lincoln Street, Boston, Massachusetts 02111 (617) 423-3990; *The World in Figures.*

International Lead and Zinc Study Group, Metro House, 58 St. James's Street, London SW1A 1LD, England; *Lead and Zinc Statistics.*

International Monetary Fund, 700 Nineteenth Street, NW, Washington, D.C. 20431 (202) 623-7000; *Direction of Trade Statistics, Government Finance Statistics Yearbook,* and *International Financial Statistics.*

International Rubber Study Group, York House, 8th Floor, Empire Way, Wembley, London HA9 0PA, England; *Rubber Statistical Bulletin.*

Nordic Council of Ministers, Store Strandstraede 18, DK-1255 Copenhagen K, Denmark and the Nordic Statistical Secretariat, Postboks 2550, DK-2100 Copenhagen 0, Denmark; *The Yearbook of Nordic Statistics.*

Organisation for Economic Co-operation and Development (OECD), 2 rue Andre-Pascal, 75 Paris 16, France (Telephone Number in U.S. (202) 785-6323); *Economic Outlook, The Footwear, Raw Hides and Skins, and Leather Industry in OECD Countries, Industrial Structure Statistics,* and *The Iron and Steel Industry, Milk, Milk Products, and Egg Balances in OECD Member Countries, OECD Economic Surveys: Denmark, The Pulp and Paper Industry,* and *Review of Fisheries in OECD Member Countries.*

Times Books, 201 East 50th Street, New York, New York 10022 (212) 751-2600; *The Economist Book of Vital World Statistics.*

The World Bank, 1818 H Street, NW, Washington, D.C. 20433 (202) 477-1234; *World Tables.*

DENMARK - INCOME TAXES - See DENMARK - TAXATION

DENMARK - INDUSTRIAL METALS PRODUCTION - See DENMARK - MINING AND MINERAL PRODUCTS

DENMARK - INDUSTRY

European Community Information Service, 2100 M Street, NW, Washington, D.C. 20037 (202) 862-9500; *Basic Statistics of the Community, Employment and Unemployment, Eurostatistics: Data for Short-Term Economic Analysis,* and *Labor Force Sample Survey.*

Facts on File, 460 Park Avenue South, New York, New York 10016 (800) 443-8323; *The New Book of World Rankings.*

Federal Statistical Office, Gustav - Stresemann - Ring 11, D-6200 Wiesbaden, Germany; *Danemark.*

G.K. Hall and Company, 70 Lincoln Street, Boston, Massachusetts 02111 (617) 423-3990; *The World in Figures.*

International Labour Office, I.L.O. Publications, CH-1211, Geneva 22, Switzerland; *Yearbook of Labour Statistics.*

Nordic Council of Ministers, Store Strandstraede 18, DK-1255 Copenhagen K, Denmark and the Nordic Statistical Secretariat, Postboks 2550, DK-2100 Copenhagen 0, Denmark; *The Yearbook of Nordic Statistics.*

Organization for Economic Co-operation and Development (OECD), 2 rue Andre-Pascal, 75 Paris 16, France (Telephone Number in U.S. (202) 785-6323); *Economic Outlook, Industrial Structure Statistics,* and *OECD Environmental Data.*

Statistical Office of the United Nations, Publishing Service, New York, New York 10017 (800) 253-9646; *Statistical Yearbook.*

Times Books, 201 East 50th Street, New York, New York 10022 (212) 751-2600; *The Economist Book of Vital World Statistics.*

The World Bank, 1818 H Street, NW, Washington, D.C. 20433 (202) 477-1234; *World Tables.*

World Intellectual Property Organization, 34 Chemin des Colombettes, CH-1211 Geneva 20. Switzerland; *Industrial Property Statistics.*

DENMARK - INFANT AND MATERNAL MORTALITY

European Community Information Service, 2100 M Street, NW, Washington, D.C. 20037 (202) 862-9500; *Basic Statistics of the Community,* and *Demographic Statistics.*

Nordic Council of Ministers, Store Strandstraede 18, DK-1255 Copenhagen K, Denmark and the Nordic Statistical Secretariat, Postboks 2550, DK-2100 Copenhagen 0, Denmark; *The Yearbook of Nordic Statistics.*

Statistical Office of the United Nations, Publishing Service, New York, New York 10017 (800) 253-9646; *Demographic Yearbook,* and *Statistical Yearbook.*

The World Bank, 1818 H Street, NW, Washington, D.C. 20433 (202) 477-1234; *World Tables.*

World Health Organization, Office of Publications, Avenue Appia, CH-1211 Geneva 27, Switzerland (Telephone Number in U.S. (518) 436-9686); *World Health Statistics Annual.*

DENMARK - INTEREST RATES

European Community Information Service, 2100 M Street, NW, Washington, D.C. 20037 (202) 862-9500; *Money and Finance.*

Organisation for Economic Co-operation and Development (OECD), 2 rue Andre-Pascal, 75 Paris 16, France (Telephone Number in U.S. (202) 785-6323); *Economic Outlook, Financial Market Trends,* and *OECD Financial Statistics.*

DENMARK - INTERNAL TRADE

European Community Information Service, 2100 M Street, NW, Washington, D.C. 20037 (202) 862-9500; *Basic Statistics of the Community.*

Nordic Council of Ministers, Store Strandstraede 18, DK-1255 Copenhagen K, Denmark and the Nordic Statistical Secretariat, Postboks 2550, DK-2100 Copenhagen 0, Denmark; *The Yearbook of Nordic Statistics.*

DENMARK - INTERNATIONAL FINANCE

European Community Information Service, 2100 M Street, NW, Washington, D.C. 20037 (202) 862-9500; *Basic Statistics of the Community.*

Organisation for Economic Co-operation and Development (OECD), 2 rue Andre-Pascal, 75 Paris 16, France (Telephone Number in U.S. (202) 785-6323); *Economic Outlook,* and *Financial Market Trends.*

DENMARK - INTERNATIONAL LIQUIDITY

International Monetary Fund, 700 Nineteenth Street, NW, Washington, D.C. 20431 (202) 623-7000; *International Financial Statistics.*

Organisation for Economic Co-operation and Development (OECD), 2 rue Andre-Pascal, 75 Paris 16, France (Telephone Number in U.S. (202) 785-6323); *Economic Outlook,* and *Financial Market Trends.*

DENMARK - INTERNATIONAL RESERVES EXCLUDING GOLD

The World Bank, 1818 H Street, NW, Washington, D.C. 20433 (202) 477-1234; *World Tables.*

DENMARK - INTERNATIONAL STATISTICS

Organisation for Economic Co-operation and Development (OECD), 2 rue Andre-Pascal, 75 Paris 16, France (Telephone Number in U.S. (202) 785-6323); *Financial Market Trends,* and *Tourism Policy and International Tourism in OECD Member Countries.*

DENMARK - INVESTMENTS

International Monetary Fund, 700 Nineteenth Street, NW, Washington, D.C. 20431 (202) 623-7000; *International Financial Statistics.*

Organisation for Economic Co-operation and Development (OECD), 2 rue Andre-Pascal, 75 Paris 16, France (Telephone Number in U.S. (202) 785-6323); *Economic Outlook, Financial Market Trends, Industrial Structure Statistics, The Iron and Steel Industry,* and *Textile Industry in OECD Countries.*

DENMARK - IRON ORE - See DENMARK - MINING AND MINERAL PRODUCTS

DENMARK - JUTE PRODUCTION - See DENMARK - CROPS

DENMARK - LABOR FORCE

European Community Information Service, 2100 M Street, NW, Washington, D.C. 20037 (202) 862-9500; *Basic Statistics of the Community, Labor Force Sample Survey,* and *Regions: Statistical Yearbook.*

Facts on File, 460 Park Avenue South, New York, New York 10016 (800) 443-8323; *The New Book of World Rankings.*

Food and Agricultural Organization of the United Nations (FAO) Via delle Terme di Caracalla, 00100 Rome, Italy (Telephone Number in U.S. (202) 653-2400); *The State of Food and Agriculture.*

G.K. Hall and Company, 70 Lincoln Street, Boston, Massachusetts 02111 (617) 423-3990; *The World in Figures.*

Nordic Council of Ministers, Store Strandstraede 18, DK-1255 Copenhagen K, Denmark and the Nordic Statistical Secretariat, Postboks 2550, DK-2100 Copenhagen 0, Denmark; *The Yearbook of*

Nordic Statistics.

Organisation for Economic Co-operation and Development (OECD), 2 rue Andre-Pascal, 75 Paris 16, France (Telephone Number in U.S. (202) 785-6323); *Economic Outlook, The Iron and Steel Industry, Maritime Transport, OECD Economic Surveys: Denmark, OECD Employment Outlook,* and *Textile Industry in OECD Countries.*

Times Books, 201 East 50th Street, New York, New York 10022 (212) 751-2600; *The Economist Book of Vital World Statistics.*

The World Bank, 1818 H Street, NW, Washington, D.C. 20433 (202) 477-1234; *World Tables.*

DENMARK - LABOR PRODUCTIVITY

International Labour Office, I.L.O. Publications, CH-1211, Geneva 22, Switzerland; *Yearbook of Labour Statistics.*

Organisation for Economic Co-operation and Development (OECD), 2 rue Andre-Pascal, 75 Paris 16, France (Telephone Number in U.S. (202) 785-6323); *Economic Outlook,* and *OECD Employment Outlook.*

DENMARK - LAND USE

Euromonitor Publications Limited, 87-88 Turnmill Street, London EC1M 5QU, England; *European Marketing Data and Statistics.*

European Community Information Service, 2100 M Street, NW, Washington, D.C. 20037 (202) 862-9500; *Agriculture: Statistical Yearbook, Basic Statistics of the Community, Crop Production: Quarterly Statistics,* and *Regions: Statistical Yearbook.*

Food and Agricultural Organization of the United Nations (FAO), Via delle Terme di Caracalla, 00100 Rome, Italy (Telephone Number in U.S. (202) 653-2400); *Production Yearbook.*

G.K. Hall and Company, 70 Lincoln Street, Boston, Massachusetts 02111 (617) 423-3990; *The World in Figures.*

DENMARK - LEAD AND LEAD ORE - See DENMARK - MINING AND MINERAL PRODUCTS

DENMARK - LEATHER - PRODUCTION INDEX

Organisation for Economic Co-operation and Development (OECD), 2 rue Andre-Pascal, 75 Paris 16, France (Telephone Number in U.S. (202) 785-6323); *Indicators of Industrial Activity.*

DENMARK - LEATHER AND FOOTWEAR - EXPORTS AND IMPORTS

European Community Information Service, 2100 M Street, NW, Washington, D.C. 20037 (202) 862-9500; *Basic Statistics of the Community.*

Organisation for Economic Co-operation and Development (OECD), 2 rue Andre-Pascal, 75 Paris 16, France (Telephone Number in U.S. (202) 785-6323); *The Footwear, Raw Hides and Skins, and Leather Industry in OECD Countries.*

DENMARK - LIBRARIES

Euromonitor Publications Limited, 87-88 Turnmill Street, London EC1M 5QU, England; *European Marketing Data and Statistics.*

Facts on File, 460 Park Avenue South, New York, New York 10016 (800) 443-8323; *The New Book of World Rankings.*

Nordic Council of Ministers, Store Strandstraede 18, DK-1255 Copenhagen K, Denmark and the Nordic Statistical Secretariat, Postboks 2550, DK-2100 Copenhagen 0, Denmark; *The Yearbook of Nordic Statistics.*

United Nations Educational, Scientific and Cultural Organization (UNESCO), 7 Place de Fontenoy, F-75700 Paris, France (Telephone Number in U.S. (212) 963-5981); *Statistical Yearbook.*

DENMARK - LIGNITE PRODUCTION - See DENMARK - MINING AND MINERAL PRODUCTS

DENMARK - LIVESTOCK AND POULTRY

Commodity Research Bureau, Incorporated, 75 Wall Street, New York, New York 10005 (212) 504-7754; *Commodity Year Book.*

Euromonitor Publications Limited, 87-88 Turnmill Street, London EC1M 5QU, England; *European Marketing Data and Statistics.*

European Community Information Service, 2100 M Street, NW, Washington, D.C. 20037 (202) 862-9500; *Agriculture: Statistical Yearbook, Basic Statistics of the Community, Eurostatistics: Data for Short-Term Economic Analysis,* and *Regions: Statistical Yearbook.*

Facts on File, 460 Park Avenue South, New York, New York 10016 (800) 443-8323; *The New Book of World Rankings.*

Food and Agricultural Organization of the United Nations (FAO), Via delle Terme di Caracalla, 00100 Rome, Italy (Telephone Number in U.S. (202) 653-2400); *Production Yearbook,* and *The State of Food and Agriculture.*

G.K. Hall and Company, 70 Lincoln Street, Boston, Massachusetts 02111 (617) 423-3990; *The World in Figures.*

Nordic Council of Ministers, Store Strandstraede 18, DK-1255 Copenhagen K, Denmark and the Nordic Statistical Secretariat, Postboks 2550, DK-2100 Copenhagen 0, Denmark; *The Yearbook of Nordic Statistics.*

Organisation for Economic Co-operation and Development (OECD), 2 rue Andre-Pascal, 75 Paris 16, France (Telephone Number in U.S. (202) 785-6323); *Economic Accounts for Agriculture,* and *Meat Balances in OECD Member Countries.*

Statistical Office of the United Nations, Publishing Service, New York, New York 10017 (800) 253-9646; *Statistical Yearbook.*

DENMARK - LIVING LEVELS

G.K. Hall and Company, 70 Lincoln Street, Boston, Massachusetts 02111 (617) 423-3990; *The World in Figures.*

Organisation for Economic Co-operation and Development (OECD), 2 rue Andre-Pascal, 75 Paris 16, France (Telephone Number in U.S. (202) 785-6323); *Economic Outlook.*

Times Books, 201 East 50th Street, New York, New York 10022 (212) 751-2600; *The Economist Book of Vital World Statistics.*

DENMARK - MACHINERY - PRODUCTION INDEX

Organisation for Economic Co-operation and Development (OECD), 2 rue Andre-Pascal, 75 Paris 16, France (Telephone Number in U.S. (202) 785-6323); *Indicators of Industrial Activity.*

DENMARK - MAGNESIUM PRODUCTION AND CONSUMPTION - See DENMARK - MINING AND MINERAL PRODUCTS

DENMARK - MAIL - NUMBER OF PIECES SENT OR RECEIVED

European Community Information Service, 2100 M Street, NW, Washington, D.C. 20037 (202) 862-9500; *Transport Annual Statistics.*

Nordic Council of Ministers, Store Strandstraede 18, DK-1255 Copenhagen K, Denmark and the Nordic Statistical Secretariat, Postboks 2550, DK-2100 Copenhagen 0, Denmark; *The Yearbook of Nordic Statistics.*

Statistical Office of the United Nations, Publishing Service, New York, New York 10017 (800) 253-9646; *Statistical Yearbook.*

DENMARK - MAIN ECONOMIC INDICATORS - See DENMARK - ECONOMY

DENMARK - MANGANESE PRODUCTION - See DENMARK - MINING AND MINERAL PRODUCTS

DENMARK - MANUFACTURING

American Automobile Manufacturers Association, 1401 H Street, NW, Suite 900, Washington, D.C. 20005 (202) 326-5500; *World Motor Vehicle Data.*

European Community Information Service, 2100 M Street, NW, Washington, D.C. 20037 (202) 862-9500; *Basic Statistics of the Community, Eurostatistics: Data for Short-Term Economic Analysis, Industrial Production: Quarterly Statistics,* and *Labor Force Sample Survey.*

Facts on File, 460 Park Avenue South, New York, New York 10016 (800) 443-8323; *The New Book of World Rankings.*

G.K. Hall and Company, 70 Lincoln Street, Boston, Massachusetts 02111 (617) 423-3990; *The World in Figures.*

International Monetary Fund, 700 Nineteenth Street, NW, Washington, D.C. 20431 (202) 623-7000; *International Financial Statistics.*

Nordic Council of Ministers, Store Strandstraede 18, DK-1255 Copenhagen K, Denmark and the Nordic Statistical Secretariat, Postboks 2550, DK-2100 Copenhagen 0, Denmark; *The Yearbook of Nordic Statistics.*

Organisation for Economic Co-operation and Development (OECD), 2 rue Andre-Pascal, 75 Paris 16, France (Telephone Number in U.S. (202) 785-6323); *Foreign Trade by Commodities, Indicators of Industrial Activity, Industrial Structure Statistics,* and *OECD Economic Surveys: Australia.*

Statistical Office of the United Nations, Publishing Service, New York, New York 10017 (800) 253-9646; *Statistical Yearbook.*

Times Books, 201 East 50th Street, New York, New York 10022 (212) 751-2600; *The Economist Book of Vital World Statistics.*

The World Bank, 1818 H Street, NW, Washington, D.C. 20433 (202) 477-1234; *World Tables.*

DENMARK - MARRIAGE RATES

European Community Information Service, 2100 M Street, NW, Washington, D.C. 20037 (202) 862-9500; *Basic Statistics of the Community.*

Facts on File, 460 Park Avenue South, New York, New York 10016 (800) 443-8323; *The New Book of World Rankings.*

Nordic Council of Ministers, Store Strandstraede 18, DK-1255 Copenhagen K, Denmark and the Nordic Statistical Secretariat, Postboks 2550, DK-2100 Copenhagen 0, Denmark; *The Yearbook of Nordic Statistics.*

Statistical Office of the United Nations, Publishing Service, New York, New York 10017 (800) 253-9646; *Demographic Yearbook,* and *Statistical Yearbook.*

DENMARK - MEAT PRODUCTION - See DENMARK - LIVESTOCK AND POULTRY

DENMARK - MERCHANT SHIPPING

European Community Information Service, 2100 M Street, NW, Washington, D.C. 20037 (202) 862-9500; *Basic Statistics of the Community, Fisheries: Yearly Statistics, Regions: Statistical Yearbook,* and *Transport Annual Statistics.*

G.K. Hall and Company, 70 Lincoln Street, Boston, Massachusetts 02111 (617) 423-3990; *The World in Figures.*

Lloyd's Register of Shipping, 17 Battery Place, New York, New York 10004 (212) 425-8050; *Register of Ships.*

Nordic Council of Ministers, Store Strandstraede 18, DK-1255 Copenhagen K, Denmark and the Nordic Statistical Secretariat, Postboks 2550, DK-2100 Copenhagen 0, Denmark; *The Yearbook of Nordic Statistics.*

Organisation for Economic Co-operation and Development (OECD), 2 rue Andre-Pascal, 75 Paris 16, France (Telephone Number in U.S. (202) 785-6323); *Maritime Transport.*

Statistical Office of the United Nations, Publishing Service, New York, New York 10017 (800) 253-9646; *Statistical Yearbook.*

Times Books, 201 East 50th Street, New York, New York 10022 (212) 751-2600; *The Economist Book of Vital World Statistics.*

U.S. Department of Transportation, Maritime Administration, 400 Seventh Street, SW, Washington, D.C. 20590; *A Statistical Analysis of the World's Merchant Fleets.*

DENMARK - MERCURY PRODUCTION AND CONSUMPTION - See DENMARK - MINING AND MINERAL PRODUCTS

DENMARK - MILITARY

G.K. Hall and Company, 70 Lincoln Street, Boston, Massachusetts 02111 (617) 423-3990; *The World in Figures.*

The International Institute for Strategic Studies, 23 Tavistock Street, London WC2E 7NQ, England; *The Military Balance.*

Nordic Council of Ministers, Store Strandstraede 18, DK-1255 Copenhagen K, Denmark and the Nordic Statistical Secretariat, Postboks 2550, DK-2100 Copenhagen 0, Denmark; *The Yearbook of Nordic Statistics.*

U.S. Arms Control and Disarmament Agency, 320 Twenty-first Street, NW, Washington, D.C. 20451 (202) 647-8677; *World Military Expenditures and Arms Transfers.*

DENMARK - MILK PRODUCTION - See DENMARK - DAIRY PRODUCTS

DENMARK - MILLET PRODUCTION - See DENMARK - CROPS

DENMARK - MINING AND MINERAL PRODUCTS

European Community Information Service, 2100 M Street, NW, Washington, D.C. 20037 (202) 862-9500; *ACP: Basic Statistics, Basic Statistics of the Community, Energy: Monthly Statistics, Energy Statistics Yearbook, Eurostatistics: Data for Short-Term Economic Analysis, Industrial Production: Quarterly Statistics, Iron and Steel: Statistical Yearbook,* and *Regions: Statistical Yearbook.*

Facts on File, 460 Park Avenue South, New York, New York 10016 (800) 443-8323; *The New Book of World Rankings.*

G.K. Hall and Company, 70 Lincoln Street, Boston, Massachusetts 02111 (617) 423-3990; *The World in Figures.*

International Lead and Zinc Study Group, Metro House, 58 St. James's Street, London SW1A 1LD, England; *Lead and Zinc Statistics.*

Nordic Council of Ministers, Store Strandstraede 18, DK-1255 Copenhagen K, Denmark and the Nordic Statistical Secretariat, Postboks 2550, DK-2100 Copenhagen 0, Denmark; *The Yearbook of Nordic Statistics.*

Organisation for Economic Co-operation and Development (OECD), 2 rue Andre-Pascal, 75 Paris 16, France (Telephone Number in U.S. (202) 785-6323); *Coal Information, Energy Statistics of OECD Countries, Foreign Trade by Commodities, Indicators of Industrial Activity, Industrial Structure Statistics, The Iron and Steel Industry, The Non-Ferrous Metals Industry,* and *OECD Economic Surveys: Denmark.*

Penn Well Publishing Company, 1421 South Sheridan Road, P.O. Box 1260, Tulsa, Oklahoma 74101 (800) 752-9764; *International Energy Statistics Sourcebook.*

Statistical Office of the United Nations, Publishing Service, New York, New York 10017 (800) 253-9646; *Statistical Yearbook.*

World Bureau of Metal Statistics, 27-A High Street, Ware Hert SG12 9BA, England; *World Metal Statistics.*

DENMARK - MOLYBDENUM AND MOLYBDENUM ORE PRODUCTION AND CONSUMPTION - See DENMARK - MINING AND MINERAL PRODUCTS

DENMARK - MONEY AND CREDIT

Organisation for Economic Cooperation and Development (OECD), 2 rue Andre-Pascal, 75 Paris 16, France (Telephone Number in U.S. (202) 785-6323); *OECD Economic Surveys: Denmark.*

DENMARK - MONEY EXCHANGE RATE

European Community Information Service, 2100 M Street, NW, Washington, D.C. 20037 (202) 862-9500; *Basic Statistics of the Community.*

International Monetary Fund, 700 Nineteenth Street, NW, Washington, D.C. 20431 (202) 623-7000; *International Financial Statistics.*

Organisation for Economic Co-operation and Development (OECD), 2 rue Andre-Pascal, 75 Paris 16, France (Telephone Number in U.S. (202) 785-6323); *Economic Outlook, Financial Market Trends,* and *Tourism Policy and International Tourism in OECD Member Countries.*

Statistical Office of the United Nations, Publishing Service, New York, New York 10017 (800) 253-9646; *Statistical Yearbook.*

DENMARK - MONEY RATES - MARKET

European Community Information Service, 2100 M Street, NW, Washington, D.C. 20037 (202) 862-9500; *Basic Statistics of the Community.*

Organisation for Economic Co-operation and Development (OECD), 2 rue Andre-Pascal, 75 Paris 16, France (Telephone Number in U.S. (202) 785-6323); *Economic Outlook,* and *Financial Market Trends.*

DENMARK - MONEY RESERVES

European Community Information Service, 2100 M Street, NW, Washington, D.C. 20037 (202) 862-9500; *Basic Statistics of the Community.*

Organisation for Economic Co-operation and Development (OECD), 2 rue Andre-Pascal, 75 Paris 16, France (Telephone Number in U.S. (202) 785-6323); *Economic Outlook,* and *Financial Market Trends.*

DENMARK - MONEY SUPPLY

European Community Information Service, 2100 M Street, NW, Washington, D.C. 20037 (202) 862-9500; *Basic Statistics of the Community, Eurostatistics: Data for Short-Term Economic Analysis,* and *Money and Finance.*

Federal Statistical Office, Gustav - Stresemann - Ring 11, D-6200 Wiesbaden, Germany; *Danemark.*

G.K. Hall and Company, 70 Lincoln Street, Boston, Massachusetts 02111 (617) 423-3990; *The World in Figures.*

International Monetary Fund, 700 Nineteenth Street, NW, Washington, D.C. 20431 (202) 623-7000; *International Financial Statistics.*

Nordic Council of Ministers, Store Strandstraede 18, DK-1255 Copenhagen K, Denmark and the Nordic Statistical Secretariat, Postboks 2550, DK-2100 Copenhagen 0, Denmark; *The Yearbook of Nordic Statistics.*

Organisation for Economic Co-operation and Development (OECD), 2 rue Andre-Pascal, 75 Paris 16, France (Telephone Number in U.S. (202) 785-6323); *Economic Outlook.*

Statistical Office of the United Nations, Publishing Service, New York, New York 10017 (800) 253-9646; *Statistical Yearbook.*

The World Bank, 1818 H Street, NW, Washington, D.C. 20433 (202) 477-1234; *World Tables.*

DENMARK - MONUMENTS AND HISTORICAL SITES

United Nations Educational, Scientific and Cultural Organization (UNESCO), 7 Place de Fontenoy, F-75700 Paris, France (Telephone Number in U.S. (212) 963-5981); *Statistical Yearbook.*

DENMARK - MOTION PICTURES

Statistical Office of the United Nations, Publishing Service, New York, New York 10017 (800) 253-9646; *Statistical Yearbook.*

United Nations Educational, Scientific and Cultural Organization (UNESCO), 7 Place de Fontenoy, F-75700 Paris, France (Telephone Number in U.S. (212) 963-5981); *Statistical Yearbook.*

DENMARK - MOTOR VEHICLE PRODUCTION

American Automobile Manufacturers Association, 1401 H Street, NW, Suite 900, Washington, D.C. 20005 (202) 326-5500; *World Motor Vehicle Data.*

European Community Information Service, 2100 M Street, NW, Washington, D.C. 20037 (202) 862-9500; *Basic Statistics of the Community,* and *Eurostatistics: Data for Short-Term Economic Analysis.*

Organisation for Economic Co-operation and Development (OECD), 2 rue Andre-Pascal, 75 Paris 16, France (Telephone Number in U.S. (202) 785-6323); *Foreign Trade by Commodities,* and *Indicators of Industrial Activity.*

Statistical Office of the United Nations, Publishing Service, New York, New York 10017 (800) 253-9646; *Statistical Yearbook.*

DENMARK - MOTOR VEHICLE TAXES - See DENMARK - TAXATION

DENMARK - MOTOR VEHICLES IN USE

American Automobile Manufacturers Association, 1401 H Street, NW, Suite 900, Washington, D.C. 20005 (202) 326-5500; *World Motor Vehicle Data.*

European Community Information Service, 2100 M Street, NW, Washington, D.C. 20037 (202) 862-9500; *Basic Statistics of the Community,* and *Transport Annual Statistics.*

G.K. Hall and Company, 70 Lincoln Street, Boston, Massachusetts 02111 (617) 423-3990; *The World in Figures.*

International Road Federation, 525 School Street, SW, Washington, D.C. 20024 (202) 554-2106; *World Road Statistics.*

Nordic Council of Ministers, Store Strandstraede 18, DK-1255 Copenhagen K, Denmark and the Nordic Statistical Secretariat, Postboks 2550, DK-2100 Copenhagen 0, Denmark; *The Yearbook of Nordic Statistics.*

Statistical Office of the United Nations, Publishing Service, New York, New York 10017 (800) 253-9646; *Statistical Yearbook.*

Times Books, 201 East 50th Street, New York, New York 10022 (212) 751-2600; *The Economist Book of Vital World Statistics.*

DENMARK - MULES - See DENMARK - LIVESTOCK AND POULTRY

DENMARK - MUSEUMS

Euromonitor Publications Limited, 87-88 Turnmill Street, London EC1M 5QU, England; *European Marketing Data and Statistics.*

Facts on File, 460 Park Avenue South, New York, New York 10016 (800) 443-8323; *The New Book of World Rankings.*

Nordic Council of Ministers, Store Strandstraede 18, DK-1255 Copenhagen K, Denmark and the Nordic Statistical Secretariat, Postboks 2550, DK-2100 Copenhagen 0, Denmark; *The Yearbook of Nordic Statistics.*

United Nations Educational, Scientific and Cultural Organization (UNESCO), 7 Place de Fontenoy, F-75700 Paris, France (Telephone Number in U.S. (212) 963-5981); *Statistical Yearbook.*

DENMARK - NATALITY - See DENMARK - BIRTH RATES

DENMARK - NATIONAL ACCOUNTS

European Community Information Service, 2100 M Street, NW, Washington, D.C. 20037 (202) 862-9500; *Basic Statistics of the Community,* and *Eurostatistics: Data for Short-Term Economic Analysis.*

Federal Statistical Office, Gustav - Stresemann - Ring 11, D-6200 Wiesbaden, Germany; *Danemark.*

International Monetary Fund, 700 Nineteenth Street, NW, Washington, D.C. 20431 (202) 623-7000; *International Financial Statistics.*

Nordic Council of Ministers, Store Strandstraede 18, DK-1255 Copenhagen K, Denmark and the Nordic Statistical Secretariat, Postboks 2550, DK-2100 Copenhagen 0, Denmark; *The Yearbook of Nordic Statistics.*

Organisation for Economic Co-operation and Development (OECD), 2 rue Andre-Pascal, 75 Paris 16, France (Telephone Number in U.S. (202) 785-6323); *Economic Outlook.*

Statistical Office of the United Nations, Publishing Service, New York, New York 10017 (800) 253-9646; *National Accounts Statistics,* and *Statistical Yearbook.*

DENMARK - NATIONAL INCOME

Facts on File, 460 Park Avenue South, New York, New York 10016 (800) 443-8323; *The New Book of World Rankings.*

G.K. Hall and Company, 70 Lincoln Street, Boston, Massachusetts 02111 (617) 423-3990; *The World in Figures.*

Nordic Council of Ministers, Store Strandstraede 18, DK-1255 Copenhagen K, Denmark and the Nordic Statistical Secretariat, Postboks 2550, DK-2100 Copenhagen 0, Denmark; *The Yearbook of Nordic Statistics.*

Organisation for Economic Co-operation and Development (OECD), 2 rue Andre-Pascal, 75 Paris 16, France (Telephone Number in U.S. (202) 785-6323); *Economic Outlook.*

Statistical Office of the United Nations, Publishing Service, New York, New York 10017 (800) 253-9646; *Statistical Yearbook.*

DENMARK - NATIONAL PRODUCT

European Community Information Service, 2100 M Street, NW, Washington, D.C. 20037 (202) 862-9500; *Basic Statistics of the Community.*

Facts on File, 460 Park Avenue South, New York, New York 10016 (800) 443-8323; *The New Book of World Rankings.*

Organisation for Economic Co-operation and Development (OECD), 2 rue Andre-Pascal, 75 Paris 16, France (Telephone Number in U.S. (202) 785-6323); *Economic Outlook.*

Statistical Office of the United Nations, Publishing Service, New York, New York 10017 (800) 253-9646; *Statistical Yearbook.*

DENMARK - NATURAL GAS - PRODUCTION - See DENMARK - MINING AND MINERAL PRODUCTS

DENMARK - NATURAL RUBBER PRODUCTION

European Community Information Service, 2100 M Street, NW, Washington, D.C. 20037 (202) 862-9500; *Basic Statistics of the Community.*

International Rubber Study Group, York House, 8th Floor, Empire Way, Wembley, London HA9 0PA, England; *Rubber Statistical Bulletin.*

DENMARK - NEWSPAPER PRODUCTION - See DENMARK - FORESTRY AND FOREST PRODUCTS

DENMARK - NEWSPRINT - See DENMARK - FORESTRY AND FOREST PRODUCTS

DENMARK - NICKEL AND NICKEL ORE - See DENMARK - MINING AND MINERAL PRODUCTS

DENMARK - NITRIC ACID PRODUCTION - See DENMARK - MINING AND MINERAL PRODUCTS

DENMARK - OATS PRODUCTION - See DENMARK - CROPS

DENMARK - OCCUPATIONS - See DENMARK - LABOR FORCE

DENMARK - OIL PRODUCING CROPS

European Community Information Service, 2100 M Street, NW, Washington, D.C. 20037 (202) 862-9500; *Basic Statistics of the Community.*

Organisation for Economic Co-operation and Development (OECD), 2 rue Andre-Pascal, 75 Paris 16, France (Telephone Number in U.S. (202) 785-6323); *Foreign Trade by Commodities.*

DENMARK - ONION PRODUCTION - See DENMARK - CROPS

DENMARK - PALM KERNEL PRODUCTION - See DENMARK - CROPS

DENMARK - PAPER - See DENMARK - FORESTRY AND FOREST PRODUCTS

DENMARK - PATENTS

Nordic Council of Ministers, Store Strandstraede 18, DK-1255 Copenhagen K, Denmark and the Nordic Statistical Secretariat, Postboks 2550, DK-2100 Copenhagen 0, Denmark; *The Yearbook of Nordic Statistics.*

Statistical Office of the United Nations, Publishing Service, New York, New York 10017 (800) 253-9646; *Statistical Yearbook.*

World Intellectual Property Organization, 34 Chemin des Colombettes, CH-1211 Geneva 20. Switzerland; *Industrial Property Statistics.*

DENMARK - PEANUT PRODUCTION - See DENMARK - CROPS

DENMARK - PEPPER PRODUCTION - See DENMARK - CROPS

DENMARK - PERIODICALS

United Nations Educational, Scientific and Cultural Organization (UNESCO), 7 Place de Fontenoy, F-75700 Paris, France (Telephone Number in U.S. (212) 963-5981); *Statistical Yearbook.*

DENMARK - PESTICIDE USE

Food and Agricultural Organization of the United Nations (FAO) Via delle Terme di Caracalla, 00100 Rome, Italy (Telephone Number in U.S. (202) 653-2400); *The State of Food and Agriculture.*

DENMARK - PETROLEUM INDUSTRY

Euromonitor Publications Limited, 87-88 Turnmill Street, London EC1M 5QU, England; *European Marketing Data and Statistics.*

European Community Information Service, 2100 M Street, NW, Washington, D.C. 20037 (202) 862-9500; *ACP: Basic Statistics, Basic Statistics of the Community, Energy Statistics Yearbook.*

Facts on File, 460 Park Avenue South, New York, New York 10016 (800) 443-8323; *The New Book of World Rankings.*

Food and Agricultural Organization of the United Nations (FAO) Via delle Terme di Caracalla, 00100 Rome, Italy (Telephone Number in U.S. (202) 653-2400); *The State of Food and Agriculture.*

G.K. Hall and Company, 70 Lincoln Street, Boston, Massachusetts 02111 (617) 423-3990; *The World in Figures.*

Organisation for Economic Co-operation and Development (OECD), 2 rue Andre-Pascal, 75 Paris 16, France (Telephone Number in U.S. (202) 785-6323); *Energy Statistics of OECD Countries, Foreign Trade by Commodities, Indicators of Industrial Activity,* and *Oil and Gas Information.*

Penn Well Publishing Company, 1421 South Sheridan Road, P.O. Box 1260, Tulsa, Oklahoma 74101 (800) 752-9764; *International Energy Statistics Sourcebook.*

Statistical Office of the United Nations, Publishing Service, New York, New York 10017 (800) 253-9646; *Statistical Yearbook.*

DENMARK - PHOSPHATE ROCK PRODUCTION - See DENMARK - MINING AND MINERAL PRODUCTS

DENMARK - PHOSPHATES PRODUCTION - See DENMARK - MINING AND MINERAL PRODUCTS

DENMARK - PIG-IRON AND FERRO-ALLOY PRODUCTION - See DENMARK - MINING AND MINERAL PRODUCTS

DENMARK - PIGS - See DENMARK - LIVESTOCK AND POULTRY

DENMARK - PIPELINES FOR OIL AND PETROLEUM PRODUCTS

European Community Information Service, 2100 M Street, NW, Washington, D.C. 20037 (202) 862-9500; *Transport Annual Statistics.*

Statistical Office of the United Nations, Publishing Service, New York, New York 10017 (800) 253-9646; *Annual Bulletin of Transport Statistics for Europe.*

DENMARK - PLASTIC AND RESIN PRODUCTION

European Community Information Service, 2100 M Street, NW, Washington, D.C. 20037 (202) 862-9500; *Basic Statistics of the Community.*

Organisation for Economic Co-operation and Development (OECD), 2 rue Andre-Pascal, 75 Paris 16, France (Telephone Number in U.S. (202) 785-6323); *Foreign Trade by Commodities.*

Statistical Office of the United Nations, Publishing Service, New York, New York 10017 (800) 253-9646; *Statistical Yearbook.*

DENMARK - PLATINUM PRODUCTION - See DENMARK - MINING AND MINERAL PRODUCTS

DENMARK - POPULATION

The Economist Intelligence Unit, 111 West 57th Street, New York, New York 10019 (800) 938-4685; *The World Market Atlas.*

Euromonitor Publications Limited, 87-88 Turnmill Street, London EC1M 5QU, England; *European Marketing Data and Statistics.*

European Community Information Service, 2100 M Street, NW, Washington, D.C. 20037 (202) 862-9500; *ACP: Basic Statistics, Basic Statistics of the Community, Demographic Statistics, Employment and Unemployment, Fisheries: Yearly Statistics, Iron and Steel: Statistical Yearbook, Labor Force Sample Survey,* and *Regions: Statistical Yearbook.*

Facts on File, 460 Park Avenue South, New York, New York 10016 (800) 443-8323; *The New Book of World Rankings.*

Federal Statistical Office, Gustav - Stresemann - Ring 11, D-6200 Wiesbaden, Germany; *Danemark.*

Food and Agricultural Organization of the United Nations (FAO), Via delle Terme di Caracalla, 00100 Rome, Italy (Telephone Number in U.S. (202) 653-2400); *Production Yearbook.*

G.K. Hall and Company, 70 Lincoln Street, Boston, Massachusetts 02111 (617) 423-3990; *The World in Figures.*

International Labour Office, I.L.O. Publications, CH-1211, Geneva 22, Switzerland; *Yearbook of Labour Statistics.*

Nordic Council of Ministers, Store Strandstraede 18, DK-1255 Copenhagen K, Denmark and the Nordic Statistical Secretariat, Postboks 2550, DK-2100 Copenhagen 0, Denmark; *The Yearbook of Nordic Statistics.*

Statistical Office of the United Nations, Publishing Service, New York, New York 10017 (800) 253-9646; *Demographic Yearbook,* and *Statistical Yearbook.*

Times Books, 201 East 50th Street, New York, New York 10022 (212) 751-2600; *The Economist Book of Vital World Statistics.*

United Nations Educational, Scientific and Cultural Organization (UNESCO), 7 Place de Fontenoy, F-75700 Paris, France (Telephone Number in U.S. (212) 963-5981); *Statistical Yearbook.*

U.S. Arms Control and Disarmament Agency, 320 Twenty-first Street, NW, Washington, D.C. 20451 (202) 647-8677; *World Military Expenditures and Arms Transfers.*

World Health Organization, Office of Publications, Avenue Appia, CH-1211 Geneva 27, Switzerland (Telephone Number in U.S. (518) 436-9686); *World Health Statistics Annual.*

DENMARK - POST OFFICES

Facts on File, 460 Park Avenue South, New York, New York 10016 (800) 443-8323; *The New Book of World Rankings.*

DENMARK - POTATO PRODUCTION - See DENMARK - CROPS

DENMARK - POULTRY - See DENMARK - LIVESTOCK AND POULTRY

DENMARK - POWER PRODUCTION INDUSTRY

European Community Information Service, 2100 M Street, NW, Washington, D.C. 20037 (202) 862-9500; *Basic Statistics of the Community.*

DENMARK - PRICES

European Community Information Service, 2100 M Street, NW, Washington, D.C. 20037 (202) 862-9500; *Basic Statistics of the Community,* and *Eurostatistics: Data for Short-Term Economic Analysis.*

Facts on File, 460 Park Avenue South, New York, New York 10016 (800) 443-8323; *The New Book of World Rankings.*

Federal Statistical Office, Gustav - Stresemann - Ring 11, D-6200 Wiesbaden, Germany; *Danemark.*

Food and Agricultural Organization of the United Nations (FAO), Via delle Terme di Caracalla, 00100 Rome, Italy (Telephone Number in U.S. (202) 653-2400); *Production Yearbook,* and *The State of Food and Agriculture.*

G.K. Hall and Company, 70 Lincoln Street, Boston, Massachusetts 02111 (617) 423-3990; *The World in Figures.*

International Labour Office, I.L.O. Publications, CH-1211, Geneva 22, Switzerland; *Yearbook of Labour Statistics.*

International Lead and Zinc Study Group, Metro House, 58 St. James's Street, London SW1A 1LD, England; *Lead and Zinc Statistics.*

International Monetary Fund, 700 Nineteenth Street, NW, Washington, D.C. 20431 (202) 623-7000; *International Financial Statistics.*

International Rubber Study Group, York House, 8th Floor, Empire Way, Wembley, London HA9 0PA, England; *Rubber Statistical Bulletin.*

Nordic Council of Ministers, Store Strandstraede 18, DK-1255 Copenhagen K, Denmark and the Nordic Statistical Secretariat, Postboks 2550, DK-2100 Copenhagen 0, Denmark; *The Yearbook of Nordic Statistics.*

Organisation for Economic Co-operation and Development (OECD), 2 rue Andre-Pascal, 75 Paris 16, France (Telephone Number in U.S. (202) 785-6323); *Economic Outlook, The Footwear, Raw Hides and Skins, and Leather Industry in OECD Countries, Indicators of Industrial Activity, The Iron and Steel Industry,* and *The Pulp and Paper Industry.*

World Bureau of Metal Statistics, 27-A High Street, Ware Hert SG12 9BA, England; *World Metal Statistics.*

DENMARK - PRINTING AND WRITING PAPER - See DENMARK - FORESTRY AND FOREST PRODUCTS

DENMARK - PRODUCTION

American Automobile Manufacturers Association, 1401 H Eye Street, NW, Suite 900, Washington, D.C. 20005 (202) 326-5500; *World Motor Vehicle Data.*

European Community Information Service, 2100 M Street, NW, Washington, D.C. 20037 (202) 862-9500; *Basic Statistics of the Community, Eurostatistics: Data for Short-Term Economic Analysis,* and *Fisheries: Yearly Statistics.*

Facts on File, 460 Park Avenue South, New York, New York 10016 (800) 443-8323; *The New Book of World Rankings.*

G.K. Hall and Company, 70 Lincoln Street, Boston, Massachusetts 02111 (617) 423-3990; *The World in Figures.*

International Lead and Zinc Study Group, Metro House, 58 St. James's Street, London SW1A 1LD, England; *Lead and Zinc Statistics.*

International Rubber Study Group, York House, 8th Floor, Empire Way, Wembley, London HA9 0PA, England; *Rubber Statistical Bulletin.*

Organisation for Economic Co-operation and Development (OECD), 2 rue Andre-Pascal, 75 Paris 16, France (Telephone Number in U.S. (202) 785-6323); *Economic Outlook, The Footwear, Raw Hides and Skins, and Leather Industry in OECD Countries, Indicators of Industrial Activity, Industrial Structure Statistics, The Iron and Steel Industry, Meat Balances in OECD Member Countries, Milk, Milk Products, and Egg Balances in OECD Member Countries, The Non-Ferrous Metals Industry, The Pulp and Paper Industry,* and *Textile Industry in OECD Countries.*

DENMARK - PRODUCTIVITY

European Community Information Service, 2100 M Street, NW, Washington, D.C. 20037 (202) 862-9500; *Basic Statistics of the Community.*

Organisation for Economic Co-operation and Development (OECD), 2 rue Andre-Pascal, 75 Paris 16, France (Telephone Number in U.S. (202) 785-6323); *Economic Outlook.*

DENMARK - PROPERTY TAXES - See DENMARK - TAXATION

DENMARK - PUBLIC CONSUMPTION FUND

European Community Information Service, 2100 M Street, NW, Washington, D.C. 20037 (202) 862-9500; *Basic Statistics of the Community.*

Nordic Council of Ministers, Store Strandstraede 18, DK-1255 Copenhagen K, Denmark and the Nordic Statistical Secretariat, Postboks 2550, DK-2100 Copenhagen 0, Denmark; *The Yearbook of Nordic Statistics.*

Organisation for Economic Co-operation and Development (OECD), 2 rue Andre-Pascal, 75 Paris 16, France (Telephone Number in U.S. (202) 785-6323); *Revenue Statistics of OECD Member Countries.*

DENMARK - PUBLIC EXPENDITURES

European Community Information Service, 2100 M Street, NW, Washington, D.C. 20037 (202) 862-9500; *Basic Statistics of the Community.*

Organisation for Economic Co-operation and Development (OECD), 2 rue Andre-Pascal, 75 Paris 16, France (Telephone Number in U.S. (202) 785-6323); *Revenue Statistics of OECD Member Countries.*

DENMARK - PUBLIC FINANCE

Facts on File, 460 Park Avenue South, New York, New York 10016 (800) 443-8323; *The New Book of World Rankings.*

Federal Statistical Office, Gustav - Stresemann - Ring 11, D-6200 Wiesbaden, Germany; *Danemark.*

Organisation for Economic Co-operation and Development (OECD), 2 rue Andre-Pascal, 75 Paris 16, France (Telephone Number in U.S. (202) 785-6323); *Revenue Statistics of OECD Member Countries.*

DENMARK - PUBLIC HEALTH

European Community Information Service, 2100 M Street, NW, Washington, D.C. 20037 (202) 862-9500; *Basic Statistics of the Community.*

DENMARK - PUBLIC REVENUES

Organisation for Economic Co-operation and Development (OECD), 2 rue Andre-Pascal, 75 Paris 16, France (Telephone Number in U.S. (202) 785-6323); *Revenue Statistics of OECD Member Countries.*

DENMARK - RADIO BROADCASTING - See DENMARK - BROADCASTING

DENMARK - RADIO RECEIVER PRODUCTION

Statistical Office of the United Nations, Publishing Service, New York, New York 10017 (800) 253-9646; *Statistical Yearbook.*

DENMARK - RAILWAYS

Euromonitor Publications Limited, 87-88 Turnmill Street, London EC1M 5QU, England; *European Marketing Data and Statistics.*

European Community Information Service, 2100 M Street, NW, Washington, D.C. 20037 (202) 862-9500; *Basic Statistics of the Community, Regions: Statistical Yearbook,* and *Transport Annual Statistics.*

G.K. Hall and Company, 70 Lincoln Street, Boston, Massachusetts 02111 (617) 423-3990; *The World in Figures.*

Jane's Information Group, Sentinel House, 163 Brighton Road, Coulsdon, Surrey CR5 2NH, England (Telephone Number in U.S. (703) 683-3700); *Jane's World Railways.*

Nordic Council of Ministers, Store Strandstraede 18, DK-1255 Copenhagen K, Denmark and the Nordic Statistical Secretariat, Postboks 2550, DK-2100 Copenhagen 0, Denmark; *The Yearbook of Nordic Statistics.*

Statistical Office of the United Nations, Publishing Service, New York, New York 10017 (800) 253-9646; *Annual Bulletin of Transport Statistics for Europe,* and *Statistical Yearbook.*

DENMARK - RANCHING

European Community Information Service, 2100 M Street, NW, Washington, D.C. 20037 (202) 862-9500; *Basic Statistics of the Community.*

DENMARK - RAPESEED PRODUCTION - See DENMARK - CROPS

DENMARK - RELIGION

Facts on File, 460 Park Avenue South, New York, New York 10016 (800) 443-8323; *The New Book of World Rankings.*

DENMARK - RENT PRICES

International Labour Office, I.L.O. Publications, CH-1211, Geneva 22, Switzerland; *Yearbook of Labour Statistics.*

DENMARK - RETAIL TRADE

European Community Information Service, 2100 M Street, NW, Washington, D.C. 20037 (202) 862-9500; *Basic Statistics of the Community,* and *Eurostatistics: Data for Short-Term Economic Analysis.*

G.K. Hall and Company, 70 Lincoln Street, Boston, Massachusetts 02111 (617) 423-3990; *The World in Figures.*

Statistical Office of the United Nations, Publishing Service, New York, New York 10017 (800) 253-9646; *Statistical Yearbook.*

DENMARK - RICE PRODUCTION - See DENMARK - CROPS

DENMARK - ROOT AND TUBER PRODUCTION - See DENMARK - CROPS

DENMARK - ROUNDWOOD PRODUCTION - See DENMARK - FORESTRY AND FOREST PRODUCTS

DENMARK - RUBBER PRODUCTION AND CONSUMPTION

European Community Information Service, 2100 M Street, NW, Washington, D.C. 20037 (202) 862-9500; *Basic Statistics of the Community.*

Facts on File, 460 Park Avenue South, New York, New York 10016 (800) 443-8323; *The New Book of World Rankings.*

International Rubber Study Group, York House, 8th Floor, Empire Way, Wembley, London HA9 0PA, England; *Rubber Statistical Bulletin.*

Organisation for Economic Co-operation and Development (OECD), 2 rue Andre-Pascal, 75 Paris 16, France (Telephone Number in U.S. (202) 785-6323); *Foreign Trade by Commodities.*

DENMARK - RYE PRODUCTION - See DENMARK - CROPS

DENMARK - SAFFLOWER SEED PRODUCTION - See DENMARK - CROPS

DENMARK - SALT PRODUCTION - See DENMARK - MINING AND MINERAL PRODUCTS

DENMARK - SAVINGS ACCOUNT DEPOSITS

European Community Information Service, 2100 M Street, NW, Washington, D.C. 20037 (202) 862-9500; *Eurostatistics: Data for Short-Term Economic Analysis.*

DENMARK - SAWNWOOD PRODUCTION - See DENMARK - FORESTRY AND FOREST PRODUCTS

DENMARK - SCIENCE AND TECHNOLOGY - EXPENDITURE FOR RESEARCH

European Community Information Service, 2100 M Street, NW, Washington, D.C. 20037 (202) 862-9500; *Basic Statistics of the Community.*

DENMARK - SCIENTISTS, ENGINEERS AND TECHNICIANS

European Community Information Service, 2100 M Street, NW, Washington, D.C. 20037 (202) 862-9500; *Basic Statistics of the Community.*

Statistical Office of the United Nations, Publishing Service, New York, New York 10017 (800) 253-9646; *Statistical Yearbook.*

DENMARK - SENIOR CITIZENS

Facts on File, 460 Park Avenue South, New York, New York 10016 (800) 443-8323; *The New Book of World Rankings.*

DENMARK - SESAME SEED PRODUCTION - See DENMARK - CROPS

DENMARK - SHEEP - See DENMARK - LIVESTOCK AND POULTRY

DENMARK - SHIPBUILDING - PRODUCTION INDEX

Organisation for Economic Co-operation and Development (OECD), 2 rue Andre-Pascal, 75 Paris 16, France (Telephone Number in U.S. (202) 785-6323); *Indicators of Industrial Activity.*

DENMARK - SILVER PRODUCTION AND CONSUMPTION - See DENMARK - MINING AND MINERAL PRODUCTS

DENMARK - SISAL PRODUCTION - See DENMARK - CROPS

DENMARK - SOCIAL DATA

European Community Information Service, 2100 M Street, NW, Washington, D.C. 20037 (202) 862-9500; *ACP: Basic Statistics, Basic Statistics of the Community.*

Facts on File, 460 Park Avenue South, New York, New York 10016 (800) 443-8323; *The New Book of World Rankings.*

G.K. Hall and Company, 70 Lincoln Street, Boston, Massachusetts 02111 (617) 423-3990; *The World in Figures.*

DENMARK - SOCIAL SECURITY

European Community Information Service, 2100 M Street, NW, Washington, D.C. 20037 (202) 862-9500; *Basic Statistics of the Community.*

International Monetary Fund, 700 Nineteenth Street, NW, Washington, D.C. 20431 (202) 623-7000; *Government Finance Statistics Yearbook.*

Nordic Council of Ministers, Store Strandstraede 18, DK-1255 Copenhagen K, Denmark and the Nordic Statistical Secretariat, Postboks 2550, DK-2100 Copenhagen 0, Denmark; *The Yearbook of Nordic Statistics.*

Organisation for Economic Co-operation and Development (OECD), 2 rue Andre-Pascal, 75 Paris 16, France (Telephone Number in U.S. (202) 785-6323); *Revenue Statistics of OECD Member Countries.*

DENMARK - SOCIOECONOMIC DATA

European Community Information Service, 2100 M Street, NW, Washington, D.C. 20037 (202) 862-9500; *Basic Statistics of the Community.*

Organisation for Economic Co-operation and Development (OECD), 2 rue Andre-Pascal, 75 Paris 16, France (Telephone Number in U.S. (202) 785-6323); *Economic Outlook.*

DENMARK - SOYBEAN PRODUCTION - See DENMARK - CROPS

DENMARK - STAMP TAXES AND DUTIES - See DENMARK - TAXATION

DENMARK - STEEL - See DENMARK -MINING AND MINERAL PRODUCTS

DENMARK - STOCKS - COMMODITY - MARKET PRICE - INDEX

Food and Agricultural Organization of the United Nations (FAO) Via delle Terme di Caracalla, 00100 Rome, Italy (Telephone Number in U.S. (202) 653-2400); *The State of Food and Agriculture.*

International Lead and Zinc Study Group, Metro House, 58 St. James's Street, London SW1A 1LD, England; *Lead and Zinc Statistics.*

World Bureau of Metal Statistics, 27-A High Street, Ware Hert SG12 9BA, England; *World Metal Statistics.*

DENMARK - STRAW PRODUCTION - See DENMARK - CROPS

DENMARK - SUGAR - See DENMARK - CROPS

DENMARK - SUGARBEET PRODUCTION - See DENMARK - CROPS

DENMARK - SULPHUR AND SULPHURIC ACID PRODUCTION - See DENMARK - MINING AND MINERAL PRODUCTS

DENMARK - SUNFLOWER PRODUCTION - See DENMARK - CROPS

DENMARK - TAXATION

European Community Information Service, 2100 M Street, NW, Washington, D.C. 20037 (202) 862-9500; *Basic Statistics of the Community.*

G.K. Hall and Company, 70 Lincoln Street, Boston, Massachusetts 02111 (617) 423-3990; *The World in Figures.*

International Monetary Fund, 700 Nineteenth Street, NW, Washington, D.C. 20431 (202) 623-7000; *Government Finance Statistics Yearbook.*

International Road Federation, 525 School Street, SW, Washington, D.C. 20024 (202) 554-2106; *World Road Statistics.*

Nordic Council of Ministers, Store Strandstraede 18, DK-1255 Copenhagen K, Denmark and the Nordic Statistical Secretariat, Postboks 2550, DK-2100 Copenhagen 0, Denmark; *The Yearbook of Nordic Statistics.*

Organisation for Economic Co-operation and Development (OECD), 2 rue Andre-Pascal, 75 Paris 16, France (Telephone Number in U.S. (202) 785-6323); *Revenue Statistics of OECD Member Countries.*

The World Bank, 1818 H Street, NW, Washington, D.C. 20433 (202) 477-1234; *World Tables.*

DENMARK - TEA - See DENMARK - CROPS

DENMARK - TELEGRAPH SERVICE

European Community Information Service, 2100 M Street, NW, Washington, D.C. 20037 (202) 862-9500; *Transport Annual Statistics.*

Nordic Council of Ministers, Store Strandstraede 18, DK-1255 Copenhagen K, Denmark and the Nordic Statistical Secretariat, Postboks 2550, DK-2100 Copenhagen 0, Denmark; *The Yearbook of Nordic Statistics.*

Statistical Office of the United Nations, Publishing Service, New York, New York 10017 (800) 253-9646; *Statistical Yearbook.*

DENMARK - TELEPHONES IN USE

American Telephone and Telegraph Company, 26 Parsippany Road, Whippany, New Jersey 07981 (800) 338-4038; *The World's Telephones.*

European Community Information Service, 2100 M Street, NW, Washington, D.C. 20037 (202) 862-9500; *Basic Statistics of the Community,* and *Transport Annual Statistics.*

G.K. Hall and Company, 70 Lincoln Street, Boston, Massachusetts 02111 (617) 423-3990; *The World in Figures.*

Nordic Council of Ministers, Store Strandstraede 18, DK-1255 Copenhagen K, Denmark and the Nordic Statistical Secretariat, Postboks 2550, DK-2100 Copenhagen 0, Denmark; *The Yearbook of Nordic Statistics.*

Statistical Office of the United Nations, Publishing Service, New York, New York 10017 (800) 253-9646; *Statistical Yearbook.*

DENMARK - TELEVISION BROADCASTING - See DENMARK - BROADCASTING

DENMARK - TELEVISION RECEIVER PRODUCTION

European Community Information Service, 2100 M Street, NW, Washington, D.C. 20037 (202) 862-9500; *Basic Statistics of the Community.*

Statistical Office of the United Nations, Publishing Service, New York, New York 10017 (800) 253-9646; *Statistical Yearbook.*

DENMARK - TEXTILE INDUSTRY

European Community Information Service, 2100 M Street, NW, Washington, D.C. 20037 (202) 862-9500; *Basic Statistics of the Community, Eurostatistics: Data for Short-Term Economic Analysis,* and *Industrial Production: Quarterly Statistics.*

Forest and Paper Association, 1250 Connecticut Avenue, NW, Washington, D.C. 20036 (202) 463-2455; *Wood Pulp and Fiber Statistics.*

G.K. Hall and Company, 70 Lincoln Street, Boston, Massachusetts 02111 (617) 423-3990; *The World in Figures.*

Organisation for Economic Co-operation and Development (OECD), 2 rue Andre-Pascal, 75 Paris 16, France (Telephone Number in U.S. (202) 785-6323); *Foreign Trade by Commodities, Indicators of*

Industrial Activity, Industrial Structure Statistics, and *Textile Industry in OECD Countries.*

Statistical Office of the United Nations, Publishing Service, New York, New York 10017 (800) 253-9646; *Statistical Yearbook,* and *Trade in Manufactures of Developing Countries.*

DENMARK - TIMBER - DENMARK - FORESTRY AND FOREST PRODUCTS

DENMARK - TIN - See DENMARK - MINING AND MINERAL PRODUCTS

DENMARK - TIRE (MOTOR VEHICLE) PRODUCTION

International Rubber Study Group, York House, 8th Floor, Empire Way, Wembley, London HA9 0PA, England; *Rubber Statistical Bulletin.*

DENMARK - TOBACCO PRODUCTION

Euromonitor Publications Limited, 87-88 Turnmill Street, London EC1M 5QU, England; *European Marketing Data and Statistics.*

European Community Information Service, 2100 M Street, NW, Washington, D.C. 20037 (202) 862-9500; *Basic Statistics of the Community,* and *Industrial Production: Quarterly Statistics.*

Facts on File, 460 Park Avenue South, New York, New York 10016 (800) 443-8323; *The New Book of World Rankings.*

Organisation for Economic Co-operation and Development (OECD), 2 rue Andre-Pascal, 75 Paris 16, France (Telephone Number in U.S. (202) 785-6323); *Foreign Trade by Commodities, Indicators of Industrial Activity,* and *Industrial Structure Statistics.*

Statistical Office of the United Nations, Publishing Service, New York, New York 10017 (800) 253-9646; *Statistical Yearbook.*

DENMARK - TOURISM

Euromonitor Publications Limited, 87-88 Turnmill Street, London EC1M 5QU, England; *European Marketing Data and Statistics.*

European Community Information Service, 2100 M Street, NW, Washington, D.C. 20037 (202) 862-9500; *Transport Annual Statistics.*

Facts on File, 460 Park Avenue South, New York, New York 10016 (800) 443-8323; *The New Book of World Rankings.*

Federal Statistical Office, Gustav - Stresemann - Ring 11, D-6200 Wiesbaden, Germany; *Danemark.*

G.K. Hall and Company, 70 Lincoln Street, Boston, Massachusetts 02111 (617) 423-3990; *The World in Figures.*

Organisation for Economic Co-operation and Development (OECD), 2 rue Andre-Pascal, 75 Paris 16, France (Telephone Number in U.S. (202) 785-6323); *Tourism Policy and International Tourism in OECD Member Countries.*

Statistical Office of the United Nations, Publishing Service, New York, New York 10017 (800) 253-9646; *Statistical Yearbook.*

Times Books, 201 East 50th Street, New York, New York 10022 (212) 751-2600; *The Economist Book of Vital World Statistics.*

World Tourism Organization, Calle Capitan Haya 42, E-28020 Madrid, Spain; *Yearbook of Tourism Statistics.*

DENMARK - TRACTORS IN USE

European Community Information Service, 2100 M Street, NW, Washington, D.C. 20037 (202) 862-9500; *Transport Annual Statistics.*

Statistical Office of the United Nations, Publishing Service, New York, New York 10017 (800) 253-9646; *Statistical Yearbook.*

DENMARK - TRADE - See DENMARK - FOREIGN TRADE

DENMARK - TRADEMARKS AND SERVICE MARKS

Statistical Office of the United Nations, Publishing Service, New York, New York 10017 (800) 253-9646; *Statistical Yearbook.*

World Intellectual Property Organization, 34 Chemin des Colombettes, CH-1211 Geneva 20. Switzerland; *Industrial Property Statistics.*

DENMARK - TRANSPORTATION AND COMMUNICATIONS

European Community Information Service, 2100 M Street, NW, Washington, D.C. 20037 (202) 862-9500; *Basic Statistics of the Community, Energy Statistics Yearbook, Regions: Statistical Yearbook,* and *Transport Annual Statistics.*

Facts on File, 460 Park Avenue South, New York, New York 10016 (800) 443-8323; *The New Book of World Rankings.*

Federal Statistical Office, Gustav - Stresemann - Ring 11, D-6200 Wiesbaden, Germany; *Danemark.*

G.K. Hall and Company, 70 Lincoln Street, Boston, Massachusetts 02111 (617) 423-3990; *The World in Figures.*

Nordic Council of Ministers, Store Strandstraede 18, DK-1255 Copenhagen K, Denmark and the Nordic Statistical Secretariat, Postboks 2550, DK-2100 Copenhagen 0, Denmark; *The Yearbook of Nordic Statistics.*

DENMARK - TUNGSTEN PRODUCTION - See DENMARK - MINING AND MINERAL PRODUCTS

DENMARK - TURKEYS - See DENMARK - LIVESTOCK AND POULTRY

DENMARK - UNEMPLOYMENT

Euromonitor Publications Limited, 87-88 Turnmill Street, London EC1M 5QU, England; *European Marketing Data and Statistics.*

European Community Information Service, 2100 M Street, NW, Washington, D.C. 20037 (202) 862-9500; *Basic Statistics of the Community, Employment and Unemployment, Eurostatistics: Data for Short-Term Economic Analysis, Labor Force Sample Survey,* and *Regions: Statistical Yearbook.*

International Labour Office, I.L.O. Publications, CH-1211, Geneva 22, Switzerland; *Yearbook of Labour Statistics.*

Nordic Council of Ministers, Store Strandstraede 18, DK-1255 Copenhagen K, Denmark and the Nordic Statistical Secretariat, Postboks 2550, DK-2100 Copenhagen 0, Denmark; *The Yearbook of Nordic Statistics.*

Organisation for Economic Co-operation and Development (OECD), 2 rue Andre-Pascal, 75 Paris 16, France (Telephone Number in U.S. (202) 785-6323); *Economic Outlook, Labour Force Statistics, OECD Economic Surveys: Denmark,* and *OECD Employment Outlook.*

Statistical Office of the United Nations, Publishing Service, New York, New York 10017 (800) 253-9646; *Statistical Yearbook.*

DENMARK - URANIUM PRODUCTION AND CONSUMPTION - See DENMARK - MINING AND MINERAL PRODUCTS

DENMARK - UTILITIES

European Community Information Service, 2100 M Street, NW, Washington, D.C. 20037 (202) 862-9500; *Basic Statistics of the Community.*

DENMARK - VANADIUM AND VANADIUM ORE - See DENMARK - MINING AND MINERAL PRODUCTS

DENMARK - VITAL STATISTICS

European Community Information Service, 2100 M Street, NW, Washington, D.C. 20037 (202) 862-9500; *Basic Statistics of the Community.*

G.K. Hall and Company, 70 Lincoln Street, Boston, Massachusetts 02111 (617) 423-3990; *The World in Figures.*

Nordic Council of Ministers, Store Strandstraede 18, DK-1255 Copenhagen K, Denmark and the Nordic Statistical Secretariat, Postboks 2550, DK-2100 Copenhagen 0, Denmark; *The Yearbook of Nordic Statistics.*

Statistical Office of the United Nations, Publishing Service, New York, New York 10017 (800) 253-9646; *Statistical Yearbook.*

World Health Organization, Office of Publications, Avenue Appia, CH-1211 Geneva 27, Switzerland (Telephone Number in U.S. (518) 436-9686); *World Health Statistics Annual.*

DENMARK - WAGES

Euromonitor Publications Limited, 87-88 Turnmill Street, London EC1M 5QU, England; *European Marketing Data and Statistics.*

European Community Information Service, 2100 M Street, NW, Washington, D.C. 20037 (202) 862-9500; *Basic Statistics of the Community, Earnings in Agriculture,* and *Eurostatistics: Data for Short-Term Economic Analysis.*

Federal Statistical Office, Gustav - Stresemann - Ring 11, D-6200 Wiesbaden, Germany; *Danemark.*

G.K. Hall and Company, 70 Lincoln Street, Boston, Massachusetts 02111 (617) 423-3990; *The World in Figures.*

International Labour Office, I.L.O. Publications, CH-1211, Geneva 22, Switzerland; *Yearbook of Labour Statistics.*

Nordic Council of Ministers, Store Strandstraede 18, DK-1255 Copenhagen K, Denmark and the Nordic Statistical Secretariat, Postboks 2550, DK-2100 Copenhagen 0, Denmark; *The Yearbook of Nordic Statistics.*

Organisation for Economic Co-operation and Development (OECD), 2 rue Andre-Pascal, 75 Paris 16, France (Telephone Number in U.S. (202) 785-6323); *Economic Outlook,* and *Industrial Structure Statistics.*

Statistical Office of the United Nations, Publishing Service, New York, New York 10017 (800) 253-9646; *Statistical Yearbook.*

DENMARK - WALNUT PRODUCTION - See DENMARK - CROPS

DENMARK - WATERWAYS IN USE

European Community Information Service, 2100 M Street, NW, Washington, D.C. 20037 (202) 862-9500; *Basic Statistics of the Community,* and *Transport Annual Statistics.*

Organisation for Economic Co-operation and Development (OECD), 2 rue Andre-Pascal, 75 Paris 16, France (Telephone Number in U.S. (202) 785-6323); *Maritime Transport.*

DENMARK - WEATHER

Facts on File, 460 Park Avenue South, New York, New York 10016 (800) 443-8323; *The New Book of World Rankings.*

G.K. Hall and Company, 70 Lincoln Street, Boston, Massachusetts 02111 (617) 423-3990; *The World in Figures.*

Nordic Council of Ministers, Store Strandstraede 18, DK-1255 Copenhagen K, Denmark and the Nordic Statistical Secretariat, Postboks 2550, DK-2100 Copenhagen 0, Denmark; *The Yearbook of Nordic Statistics.*

DENMARK - WELFARE

European Community Information Service, 2100 M Street, NW, Washington, D.C. 20037 (202) 862-9500; *Basic Statistics of the Community.*

International Monetary Fund, 700 Nineteenth Street, NW, Washington, D.C. 20431 (202) 623-7000; *Government Finance Statistics Yearbook.*

Nordic Council of Ministers, Store Strandstraede 18, DK-1255 Copenhagen K, Denmark and the Nordic Statistical Secretariat, Postboks 2550, DK-2100 Copenhagen 0, Denmark; *The Yearbook of Nordic Statistics.*

DENMARK - WHALES - See DENMARK - FISHERIES

DENMARK - WHEAT PRODUCTION - See DENMARK - CROPS

DENMARK - WHOLESALE PRICES

European Community Information Service, 2100 M Street, NW, Washington, D.C. 20037 (202) 862-9600; *Basic Statistics of the Community.*

Nordic Council of Ministers, Store Strandstraede 18, DK-1255 Copenhagen K, Denmark and the Nordic Statistical Secretariat, Postboks 2550, DK-2100 Copenhagen 0, Denmark; *The Yearbook of Nordic Statistics.*

Statistical Office of the United Nations, Publishing Service, New York, New York 10017 (800) 253-9646; *Statistical Yearbook.*

DENMARK - WHOLESALE TRADE

European Community Information Service, 2100 M Street, NW, Washington, D.C. 20037 (202) 862-9500; *Basic Statistics of the Community.*

Statistical Office of the United Nations, Publishing Service, New York, New York 10017 (800) 253-9646; *Statistical Yearbook.*

DENMARK - WINE PRODUCTION

European Community Information Service, 2100 M Street, NW, Washington, D.C. 20037 (202) 862-9500; *Basic Statistics of the Community.*

Facts on File, 460 Park Avenue South, New York, New York 10016 (800) 443-8323; *The New Book of World Rankings.*

DENMARK - WOOD - See DENMARK - FORESTRY AND FOREST PRODUCTS

DENMARK - WOOL - INDUSTRIAL CONSUMPTION

Organisation for Economic Co-operation and Development (OECD), 2 rue Andre-Pascal, 75 Paris 16, France (Telephone Number in U.S. (202) 785-6323; *Textile Industry in OECD Countries.*

Statistical Office of the United Nations, Publishing Service, New York, New York 10017 (800) 253-9646; *Statistical Yearbook.*

DENMARK - WOOL PRODUCTION

European Community Information Service, 2100 M Street, NW, Washington, D.C. 20037 (202) 862-9500; *Basic Statistics of the Community.*

Facts on File, 460 Park Avenue South, New York, New York 10016 (800) 443-8323; *The New Book of World Rankings.*

Organisation for Economic Co-operation and Development (OECD), 2 rue Andre-Pascal, 75 Paris 16, France (Telephone Number in U.S. (202) 785-6323; *Economic Accounts for Agriculture,* and *Textile Industry in OECD Countries.*

DENMARK - YARN PRODUCTION

European Community Information Service, 2100 M Street, NW, Washington, D.C. 20037 (202) 862-9500; *Basic Statistics of the Community.*

Organisation for Economic Co-operation and Development (OECD), 2 rue Andre-Pascal, 75 Paris 16, France (Telephone Number in U.S. (202) 785-6323; *Foreign Trade by Commodities,* and *Textile Industry in OECD Countries.*

Statistical Office of the United Nations, Publishing Service, New York, New York 10017 (800) 253-9646; *Statistical Yearbook.*

DENMARK - ZINC AND ZINC ORE - See DENMARK - MINING AND MINERAL PRODUCTS

DENMARK - ZOOS AND BOTANICAL GARDENS

United Nations Educational, Scientific and Cultural Organization (UNESCO), 7 Place de Fontenoy, F-75700 Paris, France (Telephone Number in U.S. (212) 963-5981); *Statistical Yearbook.*

DENTISTS

American Dental Association, 211 East Chicago Avenue, Chicago, Illinois 60611 (312) 440-2500; *Annual Report on Dental Education.*

U.S. Department of Health and Human Services, Health Resources and Services Administration, 5600 Fishers Lane, Rockville, Maryland 20857 (301) 443-2086; unpublished data.

U.S. Department of Labor, Bureau of Labor Statistics, Two Massachusetts Avenue, NE, Washington, D.C. 20212 (202) 606-7828; *Employment and Earnings,* and Bulletins 2370 and 2429.

DENTISTS - CHARGES AND EXPENDITURES FOR

U.S. Department of Health and Human Services, Health Care Financing Administration, 200 Independence Avenue, SW, Washington, D.C. 20201 (202) 245-6113; *Health Care Financing Review.*

U.S. Department of Labor, Bureau of Labor Statistics, Two Massachusetts Avenue, NE, Washington, D.C. 20212 (202) 606-7828; *Consumer Price Indexes Detailed Report,* and unpublished data.

DENTISTS - DENTAL SCHOOLS - STUDENTS, AND GRADUATES

American Dental Association, 211 East Chicago Avenue, Chicago, Illinois 60611 (312) 440-2500; *Annual Report on Dental Education.*

U.S. Department of Education, National Center for Education Statistics, 400 Maryland Avenue, SW, Washington, D.C. 20202 (202) 708-5366; *Digest of Education Statistics.*

U.S. Department of Health and Human Services, Health Resources and Services Administration, 5600 Fishers Lane, Rockville, Maryland 20857 (301) 443-2086; unpublished data.

DENTISTS - MEDICAID PAYMENTS, RECIPIENTS

U.S. Department of Health and Human Services, Health Care Financing Administration, 200 Independence Avenue, SW, Washington, D.C. 20201 (202) 245-6113; *Health Care Financing Review.*

DENTISTS - OFFICES

U.S. Department of Commerce, Bureau of the Census, Suitland, Maryland 20233 (301) 763-4040; *County Business Patterns, Census of Service Industries, Current Business Reports,* and *Service Annual Survey.*

DENTISTS - VISITS TO

U.S. Department of Health and Human Services, National Center for Health Statistics, 3700 East-West Highway, Hyattsville, Maryland 20782 (301) 436-8500; *Vital and Health Statistics,* and unpublished data.

DEPARTMENT STORES - ADVERTISING EXPENDITURES

Television Bureau of Advertising, Incorporated, 850 Third Avenue, New York, New York 10022 (212) 486-111; data compiled by Competitive Media Reporting, 11 West 42nd Street, New York, New York 10036 (212) 789-1400.

DEPARTMENT STORES - EARNINGS

U.S. Department of Commerce, Bureau of the Census, Suitland, Maryland 20233 (301) 763-4040; *Census of Retail Trade,* and *County Business Patterns.*

DEPARTMENT STORES - EMPLOYEES

U.S. Department of Commerce, Bureau of the Census, Suitland, Maryland 20233 (301) 763-4040; *Census of Retail Trade,* and *County Business Patterns.*

DEPARTMENT STORES - ESTABLISHMENTS

U.S. Department of Commerce, Bureau of the Census, Suitland, Maryland 20233 (301) 763-4040; *Census of Retail Trade*, and *County Business Patterns*.

DEPARTMENT STORES - INVENTORIES

U.S. Department of Commerce, Bureau of the Census, Suitland, Maryland 20233 (301) 763-4040; *Current Business Reports, Combined Annual and Revised Monthly Retail Trade*.

DEPARTMENT STORES - SALES

Market Statistics, 633 Third Avenue, New York, New York 10017 (212) 986-4000; *The Survey of Buying Power Data Service*.

U.S. Department of Commerce, Bureau of the Census, Suitland, Maryland 20233 (301) 763-4040; *Census of Retail Trade, Current Business Reports, Combined Annual and Revised Monthly Retail Trade*, and unpublished data.

DEPOSITS - See BANKS

DETECTIVE AND PROTECTIVE SERVICES

U.S. Department of Commerce, Bureau of the Census, Suitland, Maryland 20233 (301) 763-4040; *County Business Patterns, Current Business Reports, Service Annual Survey*, and *Census of Service Industries*.

DIABETES

U.S. Department of Health and Human Services, National Center for Health Statistics, 3700 East-West Highway, Hyattsville, Maryland 20782 (301) 436-8500; *Monthly Vital Statistics Report, Vital and Health Statistics, Vital Statistics of the United States*, and unpublished data.

DIAGNOSTIC HEALTH PROCEDURES

U.S. Department of Health and Human Services, National Center for Health Statistics, 3700 East-West Highway, Hyattsville, Maryland 20782 (301) 436-8500; *Vital and Health Statistics*, and unpublished data.

DIAMONDS

U.S. Department of the Interior, Bureau of Mines, 810 Seventh Street, NW, Washington, D.C. 20241 (202) 501-9649; *Annual Reports*, and *Mineral Commodity Summaries*.

DIAMONDS - FOREIGN TRADE

U.S. Department of Commerce, Bureau of the Census, Suitland, Maryland 20233 (301) 763-4040; *U.S. Merchandise Trade*.

U.S. Department of the Interior, Bureau of Mines, 810 Seventh Street, NW, Washington, D.C. 20241 (202) 501-9649; *Annual Reports*, and *Mineral Commodity Summaries*.

DIAMONDS - WORLD PRODUCTION

U.S. Department of Interior, Bureau of Mines, 810 Seventh Street, NW, Washington, D.C. 20241 (202) 501-9649; *Annual Reports*, and *Mineral Commodity Summaries*.

DIATOMITE

U.S. Department of the Interior, Bureau of Mines, 810 Seventh Street, NW, Washington, D.C. 20241 (202) 501-9649; *Annual Reports*, and *Mineral Commodity Summaries*.

DIETICIANS AND THERAPISTS

U.S. Department of Labor, Bureau of Labor Statistics, Two Massachusetts Avenue, NE, Washington, D.C. 20212 (202) 606-7828; *Employment and Earnings*.

DIPHTHERIA

U.S. Department of Health and Human Services, Center for Disease Control, 1600 Clifton Road, NE, Atlanta, Georgia 30333 (404) 639-3311; *National Health Interview Survey*.

DIRECT MAIL ADVERTISING EXPENDITURES

McCann - Erickson, Incorporated, 750 Third Avenue, New York, New York 10017 (212) 697-6000; compiled for Crain Communications, Incorporated, 740 North Rush Street, Chicago, Illinois 60611 (312) 649-5200; in *Advertising Age*.

DISABILITY - BED - DISABILITY DAYS

U.S. Department of Health and Human Services, National Center for Health Statistics, 3700 East-West Highway, Hyattsville, Maryland 20782 (301) 436-8500; *Vital and Health Statistics*, and unpublished data.

DISABILITY - BENEFICIARIES

U.S. Department of Health and Human Services, Social Security Administration, 6401 Security Boulevard, Baltimore, Maryland 21235 (410) 965-1234; *Annual Statistical Supplement to the Social Security Bulletin, Social Security Bulletin*, and unpublished data.

DISABILITY - BENEFITS PAID

U.S. Department of Health and Human Services, Social Security Administration, 6401 Security Boulevard, Baltimore, Maryland 21235 (410) 965-1234; *Social Security Bulletin, Annual Report of the Board of Trustees, OASI, DI, HI, and SMI Trust Funds, Annual Statistical Supplement to the Social Security Bulletin*, and unpublished data.

DISABILITY - DAYS LOST FROM WORK AND SCHOOL

U.S. Department of Health and Human Services, National Center for Health Statistics, 3700 East-West Highway, Hyattsville, Maryland 20782 (301) 436-8500; *Vital and Health Statistics*, and unpublished data.

DISABILITY - MEDICAID PAYMENTS AND/OR RECIPIENTS

U.S. Department of Commerce, Bureau of the Census, Suitland, Maryland 20233 (301) 763-4040; *Current Population Reports*, and unpublished data.

U.S. Department of Health and Human Services, Health Care Financing Administration, 200 Independence Avenue, SW, Washington, D.C. 20201 (202) 245-6113; *Health Care Financing Review*, and unpublished data.

DISABILITY - PAYMENTS

U.S. Department of Health and Human Services, Social Security Administration, 6401 Security Boulevard, Baltimore, Maryland 21235

(410) 965-1234; *Annual Report of Board of Trustees, OASI, DI, HI, and SMI Trust Funds, Annual Statistical Supplement to the Social Security Bulletin, Social Security Bulletin,* and unpublished data.

DISABILITY - PERSONS WITH WORK DISABILITY

U.S. Department of Commerce, Bureau of the Census, Suitland, Maryland 20233 (301) 763-4040; unpublished data.

DISABILITY - PUBLIC ASSISTANCE RECIPIENTS AND/OR PAYMENTS

U.S. Department of Commerce, Bureau of the Census, Suitland, Maryland 20233 (301) 763-4040; unpublished data.

U.S. Department of Health and Human Services, Administration for Children and Families, 370 L,Enfant Promenade, SW, Washington, D.C. 20447 (202) 401-9200; *Quarterly Public Assistance Statistics.*

U.S. Department of Health and Human Services, Social Security Administration, 6401 Security Boulevard, Baltimore, Maryland 21235 (410) 965-1234; *Social Security Bulletin,* and *Annual Statistical Supplement to the Social Security Bulletin.*

DISABILITY - SOCIAL SECURITY RECIPIENTS

U.S. Department of Health and Human Services, Social Security Administration, 6401 Security Boulevard, Baltimore, Maryland 21235 (410) 965-1234; *Annual Statistical Supplement to the Social Security Bulletin, Social Security Bulletin,* and unpublished data.

DISABILITY - SUPPLEMENTAL SECURITY INCOME RECIPIENTS AND PAYMENTS

U.S. Department of Health and Human Services, Administration for Children and Families, 370 L'Enfant Promenade, SW, Washington, D.C. 20447 (202) 401-9200; *Quarterly Public Assistance Statistics.*

U.S. Department of Health and Human Services, Social Security Administration, 6401 Security Boulevard, Baltimore, Maryland 21235 (410) 965-1234; *Annual Statistical Supplement to the Social Security Bulletin,* and *Social Security Bulletin.*

DISABILITY - VETERANS RECEIVING COMPENSATION

U.S. Department of Veterans Affairs, 810 Vermont Avenue, NW, Washington, D.C. 20420 (212) 223-2300; *Annual Report of the Secretary of Veterans Affairs,* and unpublished data.

DISABILITY - VOCATIONAL REHABILITATION

U.S. Department of Education, Rehabilitation Services Administration, 400 Maryland Avenue, SW, Washington, D.C. 20202 (202) 708-5366; *Caseload Statistics of State Vocational Rehabilitation Agencies in Fiscal Years,* and *State Vocational Rehabilitation Agency Program Data in Fiscal Years.*

DISABILITY INSURANCE TRUST FUND (SOCIAL SECURITY)

Executive Office of the President, Office of Management and Budget, Executive Office Building, Washington, D.C. 20503 (202) 395-3080; *Budget of the United States Government.*

U.S. Department of Health and Human Services, Social Security Administration, 6401 Security Boulevard, Baltimore, Maryland 21235 (410) 965-1234; *Annual Report of Board of Trustees, OASI, DI, HI, and SMI Trust Funds, Social Security Bulletin,* and *Annual Statistical Supplement to the Social Security Bulletin.*

DISASTERS (TORNADOES, FLOODS, ETC.)

U.S. Department of Commerce, National Oceanic and Atmospheric Administration, National Climatic Data Center, Federal Building, Asheville, North Carolina 28801 (704) 259-2850; *Storm Data.*

DISCOUNT RATES - FEDERAL RESERVE BANK OF NEW YORK

Board of Governors of the Federal Reserve System, Twentieth Street and Constitution Avenue, NW, Washington, D.C. 20551 (202) 452-3000; *Federal Reserve Bulletin,* and *Annual Statistical Digest.*

DISEASES - See also DEATHS AND DEATH RATES and specific diseases

DISEASES

U.S. Department of Health and Human Services, Center for Disease Control, 1600 Clifton Road, NE, Atlanta, Georgia 30333 (404) 639-3311; *Summary of Notifiable Diseases, U.S. Morbidity and Mortality Weekly Report.*

U.S. Department of Health and Human Services, National Institutes of Health, National Cancer Institute, 9000 Rockville Pike, Bethesda, Maryland 20892 (301) 496-5737; *Cancer Statistics Review.*

U.S. Department of Health and Human Services, National Center for Health Statistics, 3700 East-West Highway, Hyattsville, Maryland 20782 (301) 436-8500; *Vital and Health Statistics, Health, United States,* and unpublished data.

DISEASES - DEATHS FROM

U.S. Department of Health and Human Services, Centers for Disease Control, 1600 Clifton Road, NE, Atlanta, Georgia 30333 (404) 639-3311; *Surveillance Report.*

U.S. Department of Health and Human Services, National Center for Health Statistics, 3700 East-West Highway, Hyattsville, Maryland 20782 (301) 436-8500; *Monthly Vital Statistics Report, Vital Statistics of the United States,* and unpublished data.

DISHWASHERS

Euromonitor Publications Limited, 87 - 88 Turnmill Street, London EC1M 5QU, England; *European Marketing Data and Statistics.*

U.S. Department of Energy, Energy Information Administration, Washington, D.C. 20585 (202) 586-8800; *Housing Characteristics,* and *Annual Energy Review.*

DISPOSABLE PERSONAL INCOME - See also: INCOME AND NATIONAL INCOME

U.S. Department of Commerce, Bureau of Economic Analysis, Fourteenth Street between Constitution Avenue and E Street, NW, Washington, D.C. 20230 (202) 606-9900; *The National Income and Product Accounts of the United States, Survey of Current Business,* and unpublished data.

DISTRICT COURTS, UNITED STATES

Administrative Office of the United States Courts, United States Supreme Court Building, Columbus Circle, NE, Washington, D.C. 20544 (202) 273-1120; *Annual Report of the Director.*

DISTRICT COURTS - UNITED STATES - CRIMINAL CASES

Administrative Office of the United States Courts, United States Supreme Court Building, Columbus Circle, NE, Washington, D.C. 20544 (202) 273-1120; *Annual Report of the Director.*

DISTRICT OF COLUMBIA - See also STATE DATA (FOR INDIVIDUAL STATES)

District of Columbia - Primary Statistics Sources

Office of Planning, Data Management Division, Presidential Building, Suite 500, 415 Twelfth Street, NW, Washington, D.C. 20004 (202) 727-6533; *1990 Census, Population and Housing for the District of Columbia, 1990 Census: Social, Economic Indicators by Census Tract,* and *Socio-Economic Indicators of Change by Census Tract.*

Office of Policy and Evaluation, Executive Office of the Mayor, One Judiciary Square, Suite 1000, 441 Fourth Street, NW, Washington, D.C. 20001 (202) 727-4016; *Indices - A Statistical Index to DC Services.*

District of Columbia - State Data Centers

Data Services Division, Mayor's Office of Planning, Room 570 Presidential Building, 415 Twelfth Street, NW, Washington, D.C. 20004, Mr. Gan Ahuja, (202) 727-6533.

Metropolitan Washington Council of Governments, 777 North Capitol Street, Suite 300, Washington, D.C. 20002-4201, Mr. Robert Griffiths, Ms. Jenean Johanningmeier, (202) 962-3200.

DIVESTITURES

Securities Data Company, 1180 Raymond Boulevard, Newark, New Jersey 07102 (201) 622-3100; *Merger and Corporate Transactions Database.*

DIVIDENDS - CORPORATION

U.S. Department of Commerce, Bureau of Economic Analysis, Fourteenth Street between Constitution Avenue and E Street, NW, Washington, D.C. 20230 (202) 606-9900; *The National Income and Product Accounts of the United States,* and *Survey of Current Business.*

DIVIDENDS - INDIVIDUAL INCOME TAX RETURNS

U.S. Department of the Treasury, Internal Revenue Service, 1111 Constitution Avenue, NW, Washington, D.C. 20224 (202) 566-5000; *Statistics of Income, Individual Income Tax Returns.*

DIVIDENDS - NATIONAL AND/OR PERSONAL INCOME COMPONENTS

U.S. Department of Commerce, Bureau of Economic Analysis, Fourteenth Street between Constitution Avenue and E Street, NW, Washington, D.C. 20230 (202) 606-9900; *The National Income and Product Accounts of the United States,* and *Survey of Current Business.*

DIVIDENDS - RAILROAD STOCK

Association of American Railroads, American Railroads Building, 50 F Street, NW, Washington, D.C. 20001 (202) 639-2333; *Railroad Facts, Statistics of Railroads of Class I,* and *Analysis of Class I Railroads.*

DIVORCE - See - MARRIAGE AND DIVORCE and MARITAL STATUS

Djibouti - National Statistical Office

Direction Nationale de la Statistique, BP 67, Djibouti.

Djibouti - Primary Statistics Sources

Djibouti Direction Nationale de la Statistique, BP 67, Djibouti; *Annuaire Statistique de Djibouti* (Statistical Yearbook), and *Bulletin trimestriel de Statistique,* (Quarterly Bulletin of Statistics).

DJIBOUTI - AGRICULTURE

Federal Statistical Office, Gustav - Stresemann - Ring 11, D-6200 Wiesbaden, Germany; *Dschibuti.*

Food and Agricultural Organization of the United Nations (FAO) Via delle Terme di Caracalla, 00100 Rome, Italy (Telephone Number in U.S. (202) 653-2400); *Production Yearbook, The State of Food and Agriculture,* and *Trade Yearbook.*

G.K. Hall and Company, 70 Lincoln Street, Boston, Massachusetts 02111 (617) 423-3990; *The World in Figures.*

Statistical Office of the United Nations, Publishing Service, New York, New York 10017 (800) 253-9646; *Statistical Yearbook,* and *Survey of Economic and Social Conditions in Africa.*

United Nations Economic Commission for Africa, Africa Hall, P.O. Box 3001, Addis Ababa, Ethiopia (Telephone Number in U.S. (800) 253-9646); *African Statistical Yearbook.*

DJIBOUTI - AIRLINE SERVICE

G.K. Hall and Company, 70 Lincoln Street, Boston, Massachusetts 02111 (617) 423-3990; *The World in Figures.*

United Nations Economic Commission for Africa, Africa Hall, P.O. Box 3001, Addis Ababa, Ethiopia (Telephone Number in U.S. (800) 253-9646); *African Statistical Yearbook.*

DJIBOUTI - ANIMAL HEALTH

Food and Agricultural Organization of the United Nations (FAO), Via delle Terme di Caracalla, 00100 Rome, Italy (Telephone Number in U.S. (202) 653-2400); *Animal Health Yearbook.*

DJIBOUTI - AREA AND DENSITY OF POPULATION

African Development Bank, 01 BP 1387, Abidjan 01, Cote D'Ivoire; *Selected Statistics on Regional Member Countries.*

Federal Statistical Office, Gustav - Stresemann - Ring 11, D-6200 Wiesbaden, Germany; *Dschibuti.*

Food and Agricultural Organization of the United Nations (FAO) Via delle Terme di Caracalla, 00100 Rome, Italy (Telephone Number in U.S. (202) 653-2400); *The State of Food and Agriculture.*

G.K. Hall and Company, 70 Lincoln Street, Boston, Massachusetts 02111 (617) 423-3990; *The World in Figures.*

Statistical Office of the United Nations, Publishing Service, New York, New York 10017 (800) 253-9646; *Statistical Yearbook*, and *Survey of Economic and Social Conditions in Africa.*

DJIBOUTI - BALANCE OF PAYMENTS

African Development Bank, 01 BP 1387, Abidjan 01, Cote D'Ivoire; *Selected Statistics on Regional Member Countries.*

The Economist Intelligence Unit, 111 West 57th Street, New York, New York 10019 (800) 938-4685; *The World Market Atlas.*

Federal Statistical Office, Gustav - Stresemann - Ring 11, D-6200 Wiesbaden, Germany; *Dschibuti.*

G.K. Hall and Company, 70 Lincoln Street, Boston, Massachusetts 02111 (617) 423-3990; *The World in Figures.*

United Nations Economic Commission for Africa, Africa Hall, P.O. Box 3001, Addis Ababa, Ethiopia (Telephone Number in U.S. (800) 253-9646); *African Statistical Yearbook.*

DJIBOUTI - BANKING

G.K. Hall and Company, 70 Lincoln Street, Boston, Massachusetts 02111 (617) 423-3990; *The World in Figures.*

United Nations Economic Commission for Africa, Africa Hall, P.O. Box 3001, Addis Ababa, Ethiopia (Telephone Number in U.S. (800) 253-9646); *African Statistical Yearbook.*

DJIBOUTI - BIRTH RATES

Statistical Office of the United Nations, Publishing Service, New York, New York 10017 (800) 253-9646; *Demographic Yearbook, Statistical Yearbook*, and *Survey of Economic and Social Conditions in Africa.*

DJIBOUTI - BONDS

G.K. Hall and Company, 70 Lincoln Street, Boston, Massachusetts 02111 (617) 423-3990; *The World in Figures.*

DJIBOUTI - BOOK PRODUCTION

G.K. Hall and Company, 70 Lincoln Street, Boston, Massachusetts 02111 (617) 423-3990; *The World in Figures.*

DJIBOUTI - BROADCASTING

Billboard Limited, P.O. Box 9027, 1006 AA Amsterdam, The Netherlands (Telephone Number in U.S. (212) 764-7300); *World Radio TV Handbook.*

G.K. Hall and Company, 70 Lincoln Street, Boston, Massachusetts 02111 (617) 423-3990; *The World in Figures.*

DJIBOUTI - BUSINESS

G.K. Hall and Company, 70 Lincoln Street, Boston, Massachusetts 02111 (617) 423-3990; *The World in Figures.*

DJIBOUTI - BUSINESS AND PROFESSIONAL LICENSES

International Monetary Fund, 700 Nineteenth Street, NW, Washington, D.C. 20431 (202) 623-7000; *Government Finance Statistics Yearbook.*

DJIBOUTI - CALORIE SUPPLY

African Development Bank, 01 BP 1387, Abidjan 01, Cote D'Ivoire; *Selected Statistics on Regional Member Countries.*

Food and Agricultural Organization of the United Nations (FAO) Via delle Terme di Caracalla, 00100 Rome, Italy (Telephone Number in U.S. (202) 653-2400); *The State of Food and Agriculture.*

DJIBOUTI - CAPITAL REVENUE

International Monetary Fund, 700 Nineteenth Street, NW, Washington, D.C. 20431 (202) 623-7000; *Government Finance Statistics Yearbook.*

DJIBOUTI - CATTLE - See DJIBOUTI - LIVESTOCK AND POULTRY

DJIBOUTI - CHEMICAL (ORGANIC) PRODUCTION - See DJIBOUTI - MINING AND MINERAL PRODUCTS

DJIBOUTI - CLASS STRUCTURE

G.K. Hall and Company, 70 Lincoln Street, Boston, Massachusetts 02111 (617) 423-3990; *The World in Figures.*

DJIBOUTI - CLIMATE

G.K. Hall and Company, 70 Lincoln Street, Boston, Massachusetts 02111 (617) 423-3990; *The World in Figures.*

DJIBOUTI - COAL PRODUCTION - See DJIBOUTI - MINING AND MINERAL PRODUCTS

DJIBOUTI - COMMUNICATIONS

Federal Statistical Office, Gustav - Stresemann - Ring 11, D-6200 Wiesbaden, Germany; *Dschibuti.*

G.K. Hall and Company, 70 Lincoln Street, Boston, Massachusetts 02111 (617) 423-3990; *The World in Figures.*

United Nations Economic Commission for Africa, Africa Hall, P.O. Box 3001, Addis Ababa, Ethiopia (Telephone Number in U.S. (800) 253-9646); *African Statistical Yearbook.*

DJIBOUTI - CONSTRUCTION INDUSTRY

Statistical Office of the United Nations, Publishing Service, New York, New York 10017 (800) 253-9646; *Statistical Yearbook.*

United Nations Economic Commission for Africa, Africa Hall, P.O. Box 3001, Addis Ababa, Ethiopia (Telephone Number in U.S. (800) 253-9646); *African Statistical Yearbook.*

DJIBOUTI - CONSUMER PRICE INDEX

African Development Bank, 01 BP 1387, Abidjan 01, Cote D'Ivoire; *Selected Statistics on Regional Member Countries.*

Federal Statistical Office, Gustav - Stresemann - Ring 11, D-6200 Wiesbaden, Germany; *Dschibuti.*

G.K. Hall and Company, 70 Lincoln Street, Boston, Massachusetts 02111 (617) 423-3990; *The World in Figures.*

Statistical Office of the United Nations, Publishing Service, New York, New York 10017 (800) 253-9646; *Survey of Economic and Social Conditions in Africa.*

United Nations Economic Commission for Africa, Africa Hall, P.O. Box 3001, Addis Ababa, Ethiopia (Telephone Number in U.S. (800) 253-9646); *African Statistical Yearbook.*

DJIBOUTI - CONSUMER PRICES

Federal Statistical Office, Gustav - Stresemann - Ring 11, D-6200 Wiesbaden, Germany; *Dschibuti.*

International Labour Office, I.L.O. Publications, CH-1211, Geneva 22, Switzerland; *Yearbook of Labour Statistics.*

DJIBOUTI - CONSUMPTION

African Development Bank, 01 BP 1387, Abidjan 01, Cote D'Ivoire; *Selected Statistics on Regional Member Countries.*

G.K. Hall and Company, 70 Lincoln Street, Boston, Massachusetts 02111 (617) 423-3990; *The World in Figures.*

Statistical Office of the United Nations, Publishing Service, New York, New York 10017 (800) 253-9646; *Survey of Economic and Social Conditions in Africa.*

DJIBOUTI - CORN PRODUCTION - See DJIBOUTI - CROPS

DJIBOUTI - CORPORATE TAXES - See DJIBOUTI - TAXATION

DJIBOUTI - CROPS

Food and Agricultural Organization of the United Nations (FAO) Via delle Terme di Caracalla, 00100 Rome, Italy (Telephone Number in U.S. (202) 653-2400); *The State of Food and Agriculture.*

G.K. Hall and Company, 70 Lincoln Street, Boston, Massachusetts 02111 (617) 423-3990; *The World in Figures.*

United Nations Economic Commission for Africa, Africa Hall, P.O. Box 3001, Addis Ababa, Ethiopia (Telephone Number in U.S. (800) 253-9646); *African Statistical Yearbook.*

DJIBOUTI - CUSTOMS DUTIES

G.K. Hall and Company, 70 Lincoln Street, Boston, Massachusetts 02111 (617) 423-3990; *The World in Figures.*

DJIBOUTI - DAIRY PRODUCTS

Food and Agricultural Organization of the United Nations (FAO) Via delle Terme di Caracalla, 00100 Rome, Italy (Telephone Number in U.S. (202) 653-2400); *The State of Food and Agriculture.*

DJIBOUTI - DEATH RATES

G.K. Hall and Company, 70 Lincoln Street, Boston, Massachusetts 02111 (617) 423-3990; *The World in Figures.*

Statistical Office of the United Nations, Publishing Service, New York, New York 10017 (800) 253-9646; *Statistical Yearbook,* and *Survey of Economic and Social Conditions in Africa.*

DJIBOUTI - DEFENSE EXPENDITURES

G.K. Hall and Company, 70 Lincoln Street, Boston, Massachusetts 02111 (617) 423-3990; *The World in Figures.*

International Monetary Fund, 700 Nineteenth Street, NW, Washington, D.C. 20431 (202) 623-7000; *Government Finance Statistics Yearbook.*

DJIBOUTI - DEMOGRAPHY

The Economist Intelligence Unit, 111 West 57th Street, New York, New York 10019 (800) 938-4685; *The World Market Atlas.*

Federal Statistical Office, Gustav - Stresemann - Ring 11, D-6200 Wiesbaden, Germany; *Dschibuti.*

G.K. Hall and Company, 70 Lincoln Street, Boston, Massachusetts 02111 (617) 423-3990; *The World in Figures.*

Statistical Office of the United Nations, Publishing Service, New York, New York 10017 (800) 253-9646; *Survey of Economic and Social Conditions in Africa.*

DJIBOUTI - DEVELOPMENT ASSISTANCE

G.K. Hall and Company, 70 Lincoln Street, Boston, Massachusetts 02111 (617) 423-3990; *The World in Figures.*

Statistical Office of the United Nations, Publishing Service, New York, New York 10017 (800) 253-9646; *Statistical Yearbook.*

DJIBOUTI - DISEASE

G.K. Hall and Company, 70 Lincoln Street, Boston, Massachusetts 02111 (617) 423-3990; *The World in Figures.*

DJIBOUTI - DIVORCE RATES

Statistical Office of the United Nations, Publishing Service, New York, New York 10017 (800) 253-9646; *Demographic Yearbook,* and *Statistical Yearbook.*

DJIBOUTI - DOMESTIC PRODUCT

G.K. Hall and Company, 70 Lincoln Street, Boston, Massachusetts 02111 (617) 423-3990; *The World in Figures.*

DJIBOUTI - ECONOMY

African Development Bank, 01 BP 1387, Abidjan 01, Cote D'Ivoire; *Selected Statistics on Regional Member Countries.*

Federal Statistical Office, Gustav - Stresemann - Ring 11, D-6200 Wiesbaden, Germany; *Dschibuti.*

G.K. Hall and Company, 70 Lincoln Street, Boston, Massachusetts 02111 (617) 423-3990; *The World in Figures.*

Statistical Office of the United Nations, Publishing Service, New York, New York 10017 (800) 253-9646; *Foreign Trade Statistics for Africa.*

DJIBOUTI - EDUCATION

African Development Bank, 01 BP 1387, Abidjan 01, Cote D'Ivoire; *Selected Statistics on Regional Member Countries.*

The Economist Intelligence Unit, 111 West 57th Street, New York, New York 10019 (800) 938-4685; *The World Market Atlas.*

Federal Statistical Office, Gustav - Stresemann - Ring 11, D-6200 Wiesbaden, Germany; *Dschibuti.*

G.K. Hall and Company, 70 Lincoln Street, Boston, Massachusetts 02111 (617) 423-3990; *The World in Figures.*

International Monetary Fund, 700 Nineteenth Street, NW, Washington, D.C. 20431 (202) 623-7000; *Government Finance Statistics Yearbook.*

Statistical Office of the United Nations, Publishing Service, New York, New York 10017 (800) 253-9646; *Survey of Economic and Social Conditions in Africa.*

United Nations Economic Commission for Africa, Africa Hall, P.O. Box 3001, Addis Ababa, Ethiopia (Telephone Number in U.S. (800) 253-9646); *African Statistical Yearbook.*

United Nations Educational, Scientific and Cultural Organization (UNESCO), 7 Place de Fontenoy, F-75700 Paris, France (Telephone Number in U.S. (212) 963-5981; *Statistical Yearbook.*

DJIBOUTI - EGG PRODUCTION - See DJIBOUTI - DAIRY PRODUCTS

DJIBOUTI - ELECTRICITY

Statistical Office of the United Nations, Publishing Service, New York, New York 10017 (800) 253-9646; *Statistical Yearbook,* and *Survey of Economic and Social Conditions in Africa.*

United Nations Economic Commission for Africa, Africa Hall, P.O. Box 3001, Addis Ababa, Ethiopia (Telephone Number in U.S. (800) 253-9646); *African Statistical Yearbook.*

DJIBOUTI - EMPLOYMENT

Federal Statistical Office, Gustav - Stresemann - Ring 11, D-6200 Wiesbaden, Germany; *Dschibuti.*

International Labour Office, I.L.O. Publications, CH-1211, Geneva 22, Switzerland; *Yearbook of Labour Statistics.*

Statistical Office of the United Nations, Publishing Service, New York, New York 10017 (800) 253-9646; *Survey of Economic and Social Conditions in Africa.*

United Nations Economic Commission for Africa, Africa Hall, P.O. Box 3001, Addis Ababa, Ethiopia (Telephone Number in U.S. (800) 253-9646); *African Statistical Yearbook.*

DJIBOUTI - ENERGY

Food and Agricultural Organization of the United Nations (FAO) Via delle Terme di Caracalla, 00100 Rome, Italy (Telephone Number in U.S. (202) 653-2400); *The State of Food and Agriculture.*

G.K. Hall and Company, 70 Lincoln Street, Boston, Massachusetts 02111 (617) 423-3990; *The World in Figures.*

Statistical Office of the United Nations, Publishing Service, New York, New York 10017 (800) 253-9646; *Statistical Yearbook.*

United Nations Economic Commission for Africa, Africa Hall, P.O. Box 3001, Addis Ababa, Ethiopia (Telephone Number in U.S. (800) 253-9646); *African Statistical Yearbook.*

DJIBOUTI - EXCHANGE RATES

African Development Bank, 01 BP 1387, Abidjan 01, Cote D'Ivoire; *Selected Statistics on Regional Member Countries.*

Inter-American Development Bank, 1300 New York Avenue, NW, Washington, D.C. 20577 (202) 623-1753; *Economic and Social Progress in Latin America.*

Statistical Office of the United Nations, Publishing Service, New York, New York 10017 (800) 253-9646; *Foreign Trade Statistics for Africa.*

DJIBOUTI - EXPORTS

African Development Bank, 01 BP 1387, Abidjan 01, Cote D'Ivoire; *Selected Statistics on Regional Member Countries.*

The Economist Intelligence Unit, 111 West 57th Street, New York, New York 10019 (800) 938-4685; *The World Market Atlas.*

Food and Agricultural Organization of the United Nations (FAO) Via delle Terme di Caracalla, 00100 Rome, Italy (Telephone Number in U.S. (202) 653-2400); *The State of Food and Agriculture.*

G.K. Hall and Company, 70 Lincoln Street, Boston, Massachusetts 02111 (617) 423-3990; *The World in Figures.*

Inter-American Development Bank, 1300 New York Avenue, NW, Washington, D.C. 20577 (202) 623-1753; *Economic and Social Progress in Latin America.*

International Monetary Fund, 700 Nineteenth Street, NW, Washington, D.C. 20431 (202) 623-7000; *Foreign Trade Statistics for Africa,* and *Government Finance Statistics Yearbook.*

Statistical Office of the United Nations, Publishing Service, New York, New York 10017 (800) 253-9646; *Foreign Trade Statistics for Africa,* and *Survey of Economic and Social Conditions in Africa.*

United Nations Economic Commission for Africa, Africa Hall, P.O. Box 3001, Addis Ababa, Ethiopia (Telephone Number in U.S. (800) 253-9646); *African Statistical Yearbook.*

DJIBOUTI - EXTERNAL INDEBTEDNESS

African Development Bank, 01 BP 1387, Abidjan 01, Cote D'Ivoire; *Selected Statistics on Regional Member Countries.*

Statistical Office of the United Nations, Publishing Service, New York, New York 10017 (800) 253-9646; *Survey of Economic and Social Conditions in Africa.*

DJIBOUTI - EXTERNAL TRADE

African Development Bank, 01 BP 1387, Abidjan 01, Cote D'Ivoire; *Selected Statistics on Regional Member Countries.*

Food and Agricultural Organization of the United Nations (FAO) Via delle Terme di Caracalla, 00100 Rome, Italy (Telephone Number in U.S. (202) 653-2400); *The State of Food and Agriculture,* and *Trade Yearbook.*

G.K. Hall and Company, 70 Lincoln Street, Boston, Massachusetts 02111 (617) 423-3990; *The World in Figures.*

Statistical Office of the United Nations, Publishing Service, New York, New York 10017 (800) 253-9646; *Statistical Yearbook.*

DJIBOUTI - FARM CROPS - See DJIBOUTI - CROPS

DJIBOUTI - FETAL MORTALITY

Statistical Office of the United Nations, Publishing Service, New York, New York 10017 (800) 253-9646; *Demographic Yearbook.*

DJIBOUTI - FERTILITY RATES

Statistical Office of the United Nations, Publishing Service, New York, New York 10017 (800) 253-9646; *Survey of Economic and Social Conditions in Africa.*

DJIBOUTI - FERTILIZER

Food and Agricultural Organization of the United Nations (FAO) Via delle Terme di Caracalla, 00100 Rome, Italy (Telephone Number in U.S. (202) 653-2400); *The State of Food and Agriculture.*

DJIBOUTI - FINANCE

African Development Bank, 01 BP 1387, Abidjan 01, Cote D'Ivoire; *Selected Statistics on Regional Member Countries.*

Federal Statistical Office, Gustav - Stresemann - Ring 11, D-6200 Wiesbaden, Germany; *Dschibuti.*

G.K. Hall and Company, 70 Lincoln Street, Boston, Massachusetts 02111 (617) 423-3990; *The World in Figures.*

International Monetary Fund, 700 Nineteenth Street, NW, Washington, D.C. 20431 (202) 623-7000; *Government Finance Statistics Yearbook.*

United Nations Economic Commission for Africa, Africa Hall, P.O. Box 3001, Addis Ababa, Ethiopia (Telephone Number in U.S. (800) 253-9646); *African Statistical Yearbook.*

DJIBOUTI - FISHERIES

Federal Statistical Office, Gustav - Stresemann - Ring 11, D-6200 Wiesbaden, Germany; *Dschibuti.*

Food and Agricultural Organization of the United Nations (FAO) Via delle Terme di Caracalla, 00100 Rome, Italy (Telephone Number in U.S. (202) 653-2400); *The State of Food and Agriculture,* and *Yearbook of Fishery Statistics.*

United Nations Economic Commission for Africa, Africa Hall, P.O. Box 3001, Addis Ababa, Ethiopia (Telephone Number in U.S. (800) 253-9646); *African Statistical Yearbook.*

DJIBOUTI - FOOD

African Development Bank, 01 BP 1387, Abidjan 01, Cote D'Ivoire; *Selected Statistics on Regional Member Countries.*

Food and Agricultural Organization of the United Nations (FAO) Via delle Terme di Caracalla, 00100 Rome, Italy (Telephone Number in U.S. (202) 653-2400); *Production Yearbook,* and *The State of Food and Agriculture.*

G.K. Hall and Company, 70 Lincoln Street, Boston, Massachusetts 02111 (617) 423-3990; *The World in Figures.*

DJIBOUTI - FOREIGN AID

G.K. Hall and Company, 70 Lincoln Street, Boston, Massachusetts 02111 (617) 423-3990; *The World in Figures.*

DJIBOUTI - FOREIGN TRADE

Federal Statistical Office, Gustav - Stresemann - Ring 11, D-6200 Wiesbaden, Germany; *Dschibuti.*

Food and Agricultural Organization of the United Nations (FAO) Via delle Terme di Caracalla, 00100 Rome, Italy (Telephone Number in U.S. (202) 653-2400); *The State of Food and Agriculture.*

G.K. Hall and Company, 70 Lincoln Street, Boston, Massachusetts 02111 (617) 423-3990; *The World in Figures.*

Inter-American Development Bank, 1300 New York Avenue, NW, Washington, D.C. 20577 (202) 623-1753; *Economic and Social Progress in Latin America.*

Statistical Office of the United Nations, Publishing Service, New York, New York 10017 (800) 253-9646; *Foreign Trade Statistics for Africa,* and *Statistical Yearbook.*

United Nations Economic Commission for Africa, Africa Hall, P.O. Box 3001, Addis Ababa, Ethiopia (Telephone Number in U.S. (800) 253-9646); *African Statistical Yearbook.*

DJIBOUTI - FORESTRY AND FOREST PRODUCTS

Federal Statistical Office, Gustav - Stresemann - Ring 11, D-6200 Wiesbaden, Germany; *Dschibuti.*

Food and Agricultural Organization of the United Nations (FAO) Via delle Terme di Caracalla, 00100 Rome, Italy (Telephone Number in U.S. (202) 653-2400); *The State of Food and Agriculture,* and *Yearbook of Forest Products.*

G.K. Hall and Company, 70 Lincoln Street, Boston, Massachusetts 02111 (617) 423-3990; *The World in Figures.*

Statistical Office of the United Nations, Publishing Service, New York, New York 10017 (800) 253-9646; *Statistical Yearbook.*

United Nations Economic Commission for Africa, Africa Hall, P.O. Box 3001, Addis Ababa, Ethiopia (Telephone Number in U.S. (800) 253-9646); *African Statistical Yearbook.*

United Nations Educational, Scientific and Cultural Organization (UNESCO), 7 Place de Fontenoy, F-75700 Paris, France (Telephone Number in U.S. (212) 963-5981; *Statistical Yearbook.*

DJIBOUTI - GENERAL INDUSTRIAL STATISTICS

Federal Statistical Office, Gustav - Stresemann - Ring 11, D-6200 Wiesbaden, Germany; *Dschibuti.*

DJIBOUTI - GENERAL MORTALITY

Statistical Office of the United Nations, Publishing Service, New York, New York 10017 (800) 253-9646; *Demographic Yearbook.*

DJIBOUTI - GEOGRAPHIC DATA

Federal Statistical Office, Gustav - Stresemann - Ring 11, D-6200 Wiesbaden, Germany; *Dschibuti.*

DJIBOUTI - GOATS - See DJIBOUTI - LIVESTOCK AND POULTRY

DJIBOUTI - GOVERNMENT

G.K. Hall and Company, 70 Lincoln Street, Boston, Massachusetts 02111 (617) 423-3990; *The World in Figures.*

DJIBOUTI - GOVERNMENT EXPENDITURES

International Monetary Fund, 700 Nineteenth Street, NW, Washington, D.C. 20431 (202) 623-7000; *Government Finance*

Statistics Yearbook.

DJIBOUTI - GOVERNMENT REVENUE

International Monetary Fund, 700 Nineteenth Street, NW, Washington, D.C. 20431 (202) 623-7000; *Government Finance Statistics Yearbook.*

Statistical Office of the United Nations, Publishing Service, New York, New York 10017 (800) 253-9646; *Survey of Economic and Social Conditions in Africa.*

DJIBOUTI - GRAIN PRODUCTION - See DJIBOUTI - CROPS

DJIBOUTI - GRANTS

International Monetary Fund, 700 Nineteenth Street, NW, Washington, D.C. 20431 (202) 623-7000; *Government Finance Statistics Yearbook.*

DJIBOUTI - GROSS DOMESTIC PRODUCT

African Development Bank, 01 BP 1387, Abidjan 01, Cote D'Ivoire; *Selected Statistics on Regional Member Countries.*

The Economist Intelligence Unit, 111 West 57th Street, New York, New York 10019 (800) 938-4685; *The World Market Atlas.*

G.K. Hall and Company, 70 Lincoln Street, Boston, Massachusetts 02111 (617) 423-3990; *The World in Figures.*

Statistical Office of the United Nations, Publishing Service, New York, New York 10017 (800) 253-9646; *Statistical Yearbook,* and *Survey of Economic and Social Conditions in Africa.*

United Nations Economic Commission for Africa, Africa Hall, P.O. Box 3001, Addis Ababa, Ethiopia (Telephone Number in U.S. (800) 253-9646); *African Statistical Yearbook.*

DJIBOUTI - HEALTH

African Development Bank, 01 BP 1387, Abidjan 01, Cote D'Ivoire; *Selected Statistics on Regional Member Countries.*

Federal Statistical Office, Gustav - Stresemann - Ring 11, D-6200 Wiesbaden, Germany; *Dschibuti.*

G.K. Hall and Company, 70 Lincoln Street, Boston, Massachusetts 02111 (617) 423-3990; *The World in Figures.*

Statistical Office of the United Nations, Publishing Service, New York, New York 10017 (800) 253-9646; *Statistical Yearbook.*

United Nations Economic Commission for Africa, Africa Hall, P.O. Box 3001, Addis Ababa, Ethiopia (Telephone Number in U.S. (800) 253-9646); *African Statistical Yearbook.*

DJIBOUTI - HEALTH EXPENDITURES

International Monetary Fund, 700 Nineteenth Street, NW, Washington, D.C. 20431 (202) 623-7000; *Government Finance Statistics Yearbook.*

DJIBOUTI - HIDE PRODUCTION

Food and Agricultural Organization of the United Nations (FAO), Via delle Terme di Caracalla, 00100 Rome, Italy (Telephone Number in U.S. (202) 653-2400); *Production Yearbook.*

DJIBOUTI - HIGHWAYS

G.K. Hall and Company, 70 Lincoln Street, Boston, Massachusetts 02111 (617) 423-3990; *The World in Figures.*

Statistical Office of the United Nations, Publishing Service, New York, New York 10017 (800) 253-9646; *Survey of Economic and Social Conditions in Africa.*

United Nations Economic Commission for Africa, Africa Hall, P.O. Box 3001, Addis Ababa, Ethiopia (Telephone Number in U.S. (800) 253-9646); *African Statistical Yearbook.*

DJIBOUTI - HOURS OF WORK - See DJIBOUTI - EMPLOYMENT

DJIBOUTI - HOUSING EXPENDITURES

International Monetary Fund, 700 Nineteenth Street, NW, Washington, D.C. 20431 (202) 623-7000; *Government Finance Statistics Yearbook.*

DJIBOUTI - ILLITERATE POPULATION

The Economist Intelligence Unit, 111 West 57th Street, New York, New York 10019 (800) 938-4685; *The World Market Atlas.*

G.K. Hall and Company, 70 Lincoln Street, Boston, Massachusetts 02111 (617) 423-3990; *The World in Figures.*

DJIBOUTI - IMPORTS

African Development Bank, 01 BP 1387, Abidjan 01, Cote D'Ivoire; *Selected Statistics on Regional Member Countries.*

The Economist Intelligence Unit, 111 West 57th Street, New York, New York 10019 (800) 938-4685; *The World Market Atlas.*

Food and Agricultural Organization of the United Nations (FAO) Via delle Terme di Caracalla, 00100 Rome, Italy (Telephone Number in U.S. (202) 653-2400); *The State of Food and Agriculture.*

G.K. Hall and Company, 70 Lincoln Street, Boston, Massachusetts 02111 (617) 423-3990; *The World in Figures.*

Inter-American Development Bank, 1300 New York Avenue, NW, Washington, D.C. 20577 (202) 623-1753; *Economic and Social Progress in Latin America.*

International Monetary Fund, 700 Nineteenth Street, NW, Washington, D.C. 20431 (202) 623-7000; *Direction of Trade Statistics.*

Statistical Office of the United Nations, Publishing Service, New York, New York 10017 (800) 253-9646; *Foreign Trade Statistics for Africa,* and *Survey of Economic and Social Conditions in Africa.*

United Nations Economic Commission for Africa, Africa Hall, P.O. Box 3001, Addis Ababa, Ethiopia (Telephone Number in U.S. (800) 253-9646); *African Statistical Yearbook.*

DJIBOUTI - INDUSTRY

Federal Statistical Office, Gustav - Stresemann - Ring 11, D-6200 Wiesbaden, Germany; *Dschibuti.*

G.K. Hall and Company, 70 Lincoln Street, Boston, Massachusetts 02111 (617) 423-3990; *The World in Figures.*

International Labour Office, I.L.O. Publications, CH-1211, Geneva 22, Switzerland; *Yearbook of Labour Statistics.*

Statistical Office of the United Nations, Publishing Service, New York, New York 10017 (800) 253-9646; *Survey of Economic and Social Conditions in Africa.*

United Nations Economic Commission for Africa, Africa Hall, P.O. Box 3001, Addis Ababa, Ethiopia (Telephone Number in U.S. (800) 253-9646); *African Statistical Yearbook.*

DJIBOUTI - INFANT AND MATERNAL MORTALITY

Statistical Office of the United Nations, Publishing Service, New York, New York 10017 (800) 253-9646; *Demographic Yearbook,* and *Survey of Economic and Social Conditions in Africa.*

DJIBOUTI - INTERNATIONAL RESERVES EXCLUDING GOLD

African Development Bank, 01 BP 1387, Abidjan 01, Cote D'Ivoire; *Selected Statistics on Regional Member Countries.*

DJIBOUTI - LABOR FORCE

African Development Bank, 01 BP 1387, Abidjan 01, Cote D'Ivoire; *Selected Statistics on Regional Member Countries.*

Food and Agricultural Organization of the United Nations (FAO) Via delle Terme di Caracalla, 00100 Rome, Italy (Telephone Number in U.S. (202) 653-2400); *The State of Food and Agriculture.*

G.K. Hall and Company, 70 Lincoln Street, Boston, Massachusetts 02111 (617) 423-3990; *The World in Figures.*

DJIBOUTI - LABOR PRODUCTIVITY

International Labour Office, I.L.O. Publications, CH-1211, Geneva 22, Switzerland; *Yearbook of Labour Statistics.*

DJIBOUTI - LAND USE

Food and Agricultural Organization of the United Nations (FAO), Via delle Terme di Caracalla, 00100 Rome, Italy (Telephone Number in U.S. (202) 653-2400); *Production Yearbook.*

G.K. Hall and Company, 70 Lincoln Street, Boston, Massachusetts 02111 (617) 423-3990; *The World in Figures.*

DJIBOUTI - LIBRARIES

United Nations Educational, Scientific and Cultural Organization (UNESCO), 7 Place de Fontenoy, F-75700 Paris, France (Telephone Number in U.S. (212) 963-5981; *Statistical Yearbook.*

DJIBOUTI - LIFE EXPECTANCY

African Development Bank, 01 BP 1387, Abidjan 01, Cote D'Ivoire; *Selected Statistics on Regional Member Countries.*

DJIBOUTI - LITERACY RATE

Statistical Office of the United Nations, Publishing Service, New York, New York 10017 (800) 253-9646; *Survey of Economic and Social Conditions in Africa.*

DJIBOUTI - LIVESTOCK AND POULTRY

Food and Agricultural Organization of the United Nations (FAO), Via delle Terme di Caracalla, 00100 Rome, Italy (Telephone Number in U.S. (202) 653-2400); *Production Yearbook,* and *The State of Food and Agriculture.*

G.K. Hall and Company, 70 Lincoln Street, Boston, Massachusetts 02111 (617) 423-3990; *The World in Figures.*

Statistical Office of the United Nations, Publishing Service, New York, New York 10017 (800) 253-9646; *Statistical Yearbook,* and *Survey of Economic and Social Conditions in Africa.*

United Nations Economic Commission for Africa, Africa Hall, P.O. Box 3001, Addis Ababa, Ethiopia (Telephone Number in U.S. (800) 253-9646); *African Statistical Yearbook.*

DJIBOUTI - LIVING LEVELS

G.K. Hall and Company, 70 Lincoln Street, Boston, Massachusetts 02111 (617) 423-3990; *The World in Figures.*

DJIBOUTI - MAIL - NUMBER OF ITEMS

Statistical Office of the United Nations, Publishing Service, New York, New York 10017 (800) 253-9646; *Statistical Yearbook.*

DJIBOUTI - MANUFACTURING

G.K. Hall and Company, 70 Lincoln Street, Boston, Massachusetts 02111 (617) 423-3990; *The World in Figures.*

Statistical Office of the United Nations, Publishing Service, New York, New York 10017 (800) 253-9646; *Survey of Economic and Social Conditions in Africa.*

DJIBOUTI - MARRIAGE RATES

Statistical Office of the United Nations, Publishing Service, New York, New York 10017 (800) 253-9646; *Demographic Yearbook.*

DJIBOUTI - MEAT PRODUCTION - See DJIBOUTI - LIVESTOCK AND POULTRY

DJIBOUTI - MERCHANT SHIPPING

G.K. Hall and Company, 70 Lincoln Street, Boston, Massachusetts 02111 (617) 423-3990; *The World in Figures.*

Statistical Office of the United Nations, Publishing Service, New York, New York 10017 (800) 253-9646; *Statistical Yearbook.*

United Nations Economic Commission for Africa, Africa Hall, P.O. Box 3001, Addis Ababa, Ethiopia (Telephone Number in U.S. (800) 253-9646); *African Statistical Yearbook.*

DJIBOUTI - MILITARY

G.K. Hall and Company, 70 Lincoln Street, Boston, Massachusetts 02111 (617) 423-3990; *The World in Figures.*

The International Institute for Strategic Studies, 23 Tavistock Street, London WC2E 7NQ, England; *The Military Balance.*

DJIBOUTI - MINING AND MINERAL PRODUCTS

G.K. Hall and Company, 70 Lincoln Street, Boston, Massachusetts 02111 (617) 423-3990; *The World in Figures.*

United Nations Economic Commission for Africa, Africa Hall, P.O. Box 3001, Addis Ababa, Ethiopia (Telephone Number in U.S. (800) 253-9646); *African Statistical Yearbook.*

DJIBOUTI - MONEY SUPPLY

African Development Bank, 01 BP 1387, Abidjan 01, Cote D'Ivoire; *Selected Statistics on Regional Member Countries.*

Federal Statistical Office, Gustav - Stresemann - Ring 11, D-6200 Wiesbaden, Germany; *Dschibuti.*

G.K. Hall and Company, 70 Lincoln Street, Boston, Massachusetts 02111 (617) 423-3990; *The World in Figures.*

DJIBOUTI - MOTION PICTURES

Statistical Office of the United Nations, Publishing Service, New York, New York 10017 (800) 253-9646; *Statistical Yearbook.*

DJIBOUTI - MOTOR VEHICLE TAXES - See DJIBOUTI - TAXATION

DJIBOUTI - MOTOR VEHICLES IN USE

G.K. Hall and Company, 70 Lincoln Street, Boston, Massachusetts 02111 (617) 423-3990; *The World in Figures.*

Statistical Office of the United Nations, Publishing Service, New York, New York 10017 (800) 253-9646; *Statistical Yearbook,* and *Survey of Economic and Social Conditions in Africa.*

DJIBOUTI - NATALITY - See DJIBOUTI - BIRTH RATES

DJIBOUTI - NATIONAL ACCOUNTS

African Development Bank, 01 BP 1387, Abidjan 01, Cote D'Ivoire; *Selected Statistics on Regional Member Countries.*

Federal Statistical Office, Gustav - Stresemann - Ring 11, D-6200 Wiesbaden, Germany; *Dschibuti.*

Statistical Office of the United Nations, Publishing Service, New York, New York 10017 (800) 253-9646; *National Accounts Statistics.*

United Nations Economic Commission for Africa, Africa Hall, P.O. Box 3001, Addis Ababa, Ethiopia (Telephone Number in U.S. (800) 253-9646); *African Statistical Yearbook.*

DJIBOUTI - NATIONAL INCOME

G.K. Hall and Company, 70 Lincoln Street, Boston, Massachusetts 02111 (617) 423-3990; *The World in Figures.*

Statistical Office of the United Nations, Publishing Service, New York, New York 10017 (800) 253-9646; *Statistical Yearbook.*

DJIBOUTI - NATIONAL PRODUCT

Statistical Office of the United Nations, Publishing Service, New York, New York 10017 (800) 253-9646; *Statistical Yearbook.*

DJIBOUTI - NEWSPAPER PRODUCTION - See DJIBOUTI - FORESTRY AND FOREST PRODUCTS

DJIBOUTI - NEWSPRINT - See DOMINICAN REPUBLIC - CROPS

DJIBOUTI - OCCUPATIONS - See DJIBOUTI - LABOR FORCE

DJIBOUTI - PAPER - See DJIBOUTI - FORESTRY AND FOREST PRODUCTS

DJIBOUTI - PERIODICALS

United Nations Educational, Scientific and Cultural Organization (UNESCO), 7 Place de Fontenoy, F-75700 Paris, France (Telephone Number in U.S. (212) 963-5981; *Statistical Yearbook.*

DJIBOUTI - PESTICIDE USE

Food and Agricultural Organization of the United Nations (FAO) Via delle Terme di Caracalla, 00100 Rome, Italy (Telephone Number in U.S. (202) 653-2400); *The State of Food and Agriculture.*

DJIBOUTI - PETROLEUM INDUSTRY

Food and Agricultural Organization of the United Nations (FAO) Via delle Terme di Caracalla, 00100 Rome, Italy (Telephone Number in U.S. (202) 653-2400); *The State of Food and Agriculture.*

G.K. Hall and Company, 70 Lincoln Street, Boston, Massachusetts 02111 (617) 423-3990; *The World in Figures.*

DJIBOUTI - POPULATION

African Development Bank, 01 BP 1387, Abidjan 01, Cote D'Ivoire; *Selected Statistics on Regional Member Countries.*

The Economist Intelligence Unit, 111 West 57th Street, New York, New York 10019 (800) 938-4685; *The World Market Atlas.*

Federal Statistical Office, Gustav - Stresemann - Ring 11, D-6200 Wiesbaden, Germany; *Dschibuti.*

Food and Agricultural Organization of the United Nations (FAO), Via delle Terme di Caracalla, 00100 Rome, Italy (Telephone Number in U.S. (202) 653-2400); *Production Yearbook.*

G.K. Hall and Company, 70 Lincoln Street, Boston, Massachusetts 02111 (617) 423-3990; *The World in Figures.*

International Labour Office, I.L.O. Publications, CH-1211, Geneva 22, Switzerland; *Yearbook of Labour Statistics.*

Statistical Office of the United Nations, Publishing Service, New York, New York 10017 (800) 253-9646; *Demographic Yearbook, Statistical Yearbook,* and *Survey of Economic and Social Conditions in Africa.*

World Health Organization, Office of Publications, Avenue Appia, CH-1211 Geneva 27, Switzerland (Telephone Number in U.S. (518) 436-9686); *World Health Statistics Annual.*

DJIBOUTI - PRICES

Federal Statistical Office, Gustav - Stresemann - Ring 11, D-6200 Wiesbaden, Germany; *Dschibuti.*

Food and Agricultural Organization of the United Nations (FAO), Via delle Terme di Caracalla, 00100 Rome, Italy (Telephone Number in U.S. (202) 653-2400); *Production Yearbook,* and *The State of Food and Agriculture.*

G.K. Hall and Company, 70 Lincoln Street, Boston, Massachusetts 02111 (617) 423-3990; *The World in Figures.*

International Labour Office, I.L.O. Publications, CH-1211, Geneva 22, Switzerland; *Yearbook of Labour Statistics.*

United Nations Economic Commission for Africa, Africa Hall, P.O. Box 3001, Addis Ababa, Ethiopia (Telephone Number in U.S. (800)

253-9646); *African Statistical Yearbook.*

DJIBOUTI - PRODUCTION

G.K. Hall and Company, 70 Lincoln Street, Boston, Massachusetts 02111 (617) 423-3990; *The World in Figures.*

DJIBOUTI - PROPERTY TAXES - See DJIBOUTI - TAXATION

DJIBOUTI - PUBLIC FINANCE

Federal Statistical Office, Gustav - Stresemann - Ring 11, D-6200 Wiesbaden, Germany; *Dschibuti.*

DJIBOUTI - RAILWAYS

G.K. Hall and Company, 70 Lincoln Street, Boston, Massachusetts 02111 (617) 423-3990; *The World in Figures.*

Statistical Office of the United Nations, Publishing Service, New York, New York 10017 (800) 253-9646; *Survey of Economic and Social Conditions in Africa.*

United Nations Economic Commission for Africa, Africa Hall, P.O. Box 3001, Addis Ababa, Ethiopia (Telephone Number in U.S. (800) 253-9646); *African Statistical Yearbook.*

DJIBOUTI - RETAIL TRADE

G.K. Hall and Company, 70 Lincoln Street, Boston, Massachusetts 02111 (617) 423-3990; *The World in Figures.*

DJIBOUTI - ROUNDWOOD PRODUCTION - See DJIBOUTI - FORESTRY AND FOREST PRODUCTS

DJIBOUTI - SAWNWOOD PRODUCTION - See DJIBOUTI - FORESTRY AND FOREST PRODUCTS

DJIBOUTI - SCIENTISTS AND TECHNICIANS

Statistical Office of the United Nations, Publishing Service, New York, New York 10017 (800) 253-9646; *Statistical Yearbook.*

DJIBOUTI - SHEEP - See DJIBOUTI - LIVESTOCK AND POULTRY

DJIBOUTI - SOCIAL DATA

African Development Bank, 01 BP 1387, Abidjan 01, Cote D'Ivoire; *Selected Statistics on Regional Member Countries.*

G.K. Hall and Company, 70 Lincoln Street, Boston, Massachusetts 02111 (617) 423-3990; *The World in Figures.*

DJIBOUTI - SOCIAL SECURITY

International Monetary Fund, 700 Nineteenth Street, NW, Washington, D.C. 20431 (202) 623-7000; *Government Finance Statistics Yearbook.*

DJIBOUTI - STAMP TAXES AND DUTIES

International Monetary Fund, 700 Nineteenth Street, NW, Washington, D.C. 20431 (202) 623-7000; *Government Finance Statistics Yearbook.*

DJIBOUTI - STOCKS - COMMODITY - MARKET PRICE - INDEX

Food and Agricultural Organization of the United Nations (FAO) Via delle Terme di Caracalla, 00100 Rome, Italy (Telephone Number in U.S. (202) 653-2400); *The State of Food and Agriculture.*

DJIBOUTI - TAXATION

International Monetary Fund, 700 Nineteenth Street, NW, Washington, D.C. 20431 (202) 623-7000; *Government Finance Statistics Yearbook.*

DJIBOUTI - TELEGRAPH SERVICE

Statistical Office of the United Nations, Publishing Service, New York, New York 10017 (800) 253-9646; *Statistical Yearbook.*

DJIBOUTI - TELEPHONES IN USE

American Telephone and Telegraph Company, 26 Parsippany Road, Whippany, New Jersey 07981 (800) 339-4038; *The World's Telephones.*

G.K. Hall and Company, 70 Lincoln Street, Boston, Massachusetts 02111 (617) 423-3990; *The World in Figures.*

Statistical Office of the United Nations, Publishing Service, New York, New York 10017 (800) 253-9646; *Statistical Yearbook.*

DJIBOUTI - TEXTILE INDUSTRY

G.K. Hall and Company, 70 Lincoln Street, Boston, Massachusetts 02111 (617) 423-3990; *The World in Figures.*

DJIBOUTI - TOURISM

Federal Statistical Office, Gustav - Stresemann - Ring 11, D-6200 Wiesbaden, Germany; *Dschibuti.*

G.K. Hall and Company, 70 Lincoln Street, Boston, Massachusetts 02111 (617) 423-3990; *The World in Figures.*

United Nations Economic Commission for Africa, Africa Hall, P.O. Box 3001, Addis Ababa, Ethiopia (Telephone Number in U.S. (800) 253-9646); *African Statistical Yearbook.*

DJIBOUTI - TRACTORS IN USE

Statistical Office of the United Nations, Publishing Service, New York, New York 10017 (800) 253-9646; *Statistical Yearbook.*

DJIBOUTI - TRADE - See DJIBOUTI - FOREIGN TRADE

DJIBOUTI - TRANSPORTATION AND COMMUNICATIONS

Federal Statistical Office, Gustav - Stresemann - Ring 11, D-6200 Wiesbaden, Germany; *Dschibuti.*

G.K. Hall and Company, 70 Lincoln Street, Boston, Massachusetts 02111 (617) 423-3990; *The World in Figures.*

United Nations Economic Commission for Africa, Africa Hall, P.O. Box 3001, Addis Ababa, Ethiopia (Telephone Number in U.S. (800) 253-9646); *African Statistical Yearbook.*

DJIBOUTI - UNEMPLOYMENT

International Labour Office, I.L.O. Publications, CH-1211, Geneva 22, Switzerland; *Yearbook of Labour Statistics.*

DJIBOUTI - VITAL STATISTICS

G.K. Hall and Company, 70 Lincoln Street, Boston, Massachusetts 02111 (617) 423-3990; *The World in Figures.*

Statistical Office of the United Nations, Publishing Service, New York, New York 10017 (800) 253-9646; *Statistical Yearbook.*

World Health Organization, Office of Publications, Avenue Appia, CH-1211 Geneva 27, Switzerland (Telephone Number in U.S. (518) 436-9686); *World Health Statistics Annual.*

DJIBOUTI - WAGES

Federal Statistical Office, Gustav - Stresemann - Ring 11, D-6200 Wiesbaden, Germany; *Dschibuti.*

G.K. Hall and Company, 70 Lincoln Street, Boston, Massachusetts 02111 (617) 423-3990; *The World in Figures.*

International Labour Office, I.L.O. Publications, CH-1211, Geneva 22, Switzerland; *Yearbook of Labour Statistics.*

DJIBOUTI - WEATHER

G.K. Hall and Company, 70 Lincoln Street, Boston, Massachusetts 02111 (617) 423-3990; *The World in Figures.*

DJIBOUTI - WELFARE

International Monetary Fund, 700 Nineteenth Street, NW, Washington, D.C. 20431 (202) 623-7000; *Government Finance Statistics Yearbook.*

DOCTORS, M.D.'s - See PHYSICIANS

DOG OWNERSHIP

American Veterinary Medical Association, 930 North Meacham Road, Schaumburg, Illinois 60196 (708) 605-8070; *U.S. Pet Ownership and Demographics Sourcebook.*

DOG RACING - GREYHOUND

Association of Racing Commissioners International, 4067 Iron Works Pike, Lexington, Kentucky 40511 (606) 254-4060.

DOMESTIC SERVICE - EMPLOYEES

U.S. Department of Labor, Bureau of Labor Statistics, Two Massachusetts Avenue, NE, Washington, D.C. 20212 (202) 606-7828; *Employment and Earnings,* and *Monthly Labor Review.*

DOMESTIC SERVICE - GROSS DOMESTIC PRODUCT

U.S. Department of Commerce, Bureau of Economic Analysis, Fourteenth Street between Constitution Avenue and E Street, NW, Washington, D.C. 20230 (202) 606-9900; *The National Income and Product Accounts of the U.S.,* and *Survey of Current Business.*

Dominica - National Statistical Office

Statistical Office, Ministry of Finance, 22 Bath Road, Roseau, Dominica.

Dominica - Primary Statistics Source

Statistical Office, Ministry of Finance, 22 Bath Road, Roseau, Dominica; *Statistical Digest.*

DOMINICA - AGRICULTURE

Food and Agricultural Organization of the United Nations (FAO) Via delle Terme di Caracalla, 00100 Rome, Italy (Telephone Number in U.S. (202) 653-2400); *Production Yearbook, The State of Food and Agriculture, Trade Yearbook.*

G.K. Hall and Company, 70 Lincoln Street, Boston, Massachusetts 02111 (617) 423-3990; *The World in Figures.*

Statistical Office of the United Nations, Publishing Service, New York, New York 10017 (800) 253-9646; *Statistical Yearbook.*

The World Bank, 1818 H Street, NW, Washington, D.C. 20433 (202) 477-1234; *World Tables.*

DOMINICA - AIRLINE SERVICE

G.K. Hall and Company, 70 Lincoln Street, Boston, Massachusetts 02111 (617) 423-3990; *The World in Figures.*

DOMINICA - ANIMAL HEALTH

Food and Agricultural Organization of the United Nations (FAO), Via delle Terme di Caracalla, 00100 Rome, Italy (Telephone Number in U.S. (202) 653-2400); *Animal Health Yearbook.*

DOMINICA - AREA AND DENSITY OF POPULATION

Food and Agricultural Organization of the United Nations (FAO) Via delle Terme di Caracalla, 00100 Rome, Italy (Telephone Number in U.S. (202) 653-2400); *The State of Food and Agriculture.*

G.K. Hall and Company, 70 Lincoln Street, Boston, Massachusetts 02111 (617) 423-3990; *The World in Figures.*

Statistical Office of the United Nations, Publishing Service, New York, New York 10017 (800) 253-9646; *Statistical Yearbook.*

United Nations Educational, Scientific and Cultural Organization (UNESCO), 7 Place de Fontenoy, F-75700 Paris, France (Telephone Number in U.S. (212) 963-5981; *Statistical Yearbook.*

DOMINICA - BALANCE OF PAYMENTS

G.K. Hall and Company, 70 Lincoln Street, Boston, Massachusetts 02111 (617) 423-3990; *The World in Figures.*

Statistical Office of the United Nations, Publishing Service, New York, New York 10017 (800) 253-9646; *Economic Survey of Latin America and the Caribbean.*

The World Bank, 1818 H Street, NW, Washington, D.C. 20433 (202) 477-1234; *World Tables.*

DOMINICA - BANKING

G.K. Hall and Company, 70 Lincoln Street, Boston, Massachusetts 02111 (617) 423-3990; *The World in Figures.*

DOMINICA - BIRTH RATES

Statistical Office of the United Nations, Publishing Service, New York, New York 10017 (800) 253-9646; *Demographic Yearbook,* and

Statistical Yearbook.

The World Bank, 1818 H Street, NW, Washington, D.C. 20433 (202) 477-1234; *World Tables.*

World Health Organization, Office of Publications, Avenue Appia, CH-1211 Geneva 27, Switzerland (Telephone Number in U.S. (518) 436-9686); *World Health Statistics Annual.*

DOMINICA - BONDS

G.K. Hall and Company, 70 Lincoln Street, Boston, Massachusetts 02111 (617) 423-3990; *The World in Figures.*

DOMINICA - BOOK PRODUCTION

G.K. Hall and Company, 70 Lincoln Street, Boston, Massachusetts 02111 (617) 423-3990; *The World in Figures.*

DOMINICA - BROADCASTING

Billboard Limited, P.O. Box 9027, 1006 AA Amsterdam, The Netherlands (Telephone Number in U.S. (212) 764-7300); *World Radio TV Handbook.*

G.K. Hall and Company, 70 Lincoln Street, Boston, Massachusetts 02111 (617) 423-3990; *The World in Figures.*

DOMINICA - BUSINESS

G.K. Hall and Company, 70 Lincoln Street, Boston, Massachusetts 02111 (617) 423-3990; *The World in Figures.*

DOMINICA - BUSINESS AND PROFESSIONAL LICENSES

International Monetary Fund, 700 Nineteenth Street, NW, Washington, D.C. 20431 (202) 623-7000; *Government Finance Statistics Yearbook.*

DOMINICA - CALORIE SUPPLY

Food and Agricultural Organization of the United Nations (FAO) Via delle Terme di Caracalla, 00100 Rome, Italy (Telephone Number in U.S. (202) 653-2400); *The State of Food and Agriculture.*

DOMINICA - CAPITAL REVENUE

International Monetary Fund, 700 Nineteenth Street, NW, Washington, D.C. 20431 (202) 623-7000; *Government Finance Statistics Yearbook.*

DOMINICA - CATTLE - See DOMINICA - LIVESTOCK AND POULTRY

DOMINICA - CHEMICAL (ORGANIC) PRODUCTION - See DOMINICA - MINING AND MINERAL PRODUCTS

DOMINICA - CLASS STRUCTURE

G.K. Hall and Company, 70 Lincoln Street, Boston, Massachusetts 02111 (617) 423-3990; *The World in Figures.*

DOMINICA - CLIMATE

G.K. Hall and Company, 70 Lincoln Street, Boston, Massachusetts 02111 (617) 423-3990; *The World in Figures.*

DOMINICA - COAL PRODUCTION - See DOMINICA - MINING AND MINERAL PRODUCTS

DOMINICA - COCOA BEANS PRODUCTION - See DOMINICA - CROPS

DOMINICA - COMMUNICATIONS

G.K. Hall and Company, 70 Lincoln Street, Boston, Massachusetts 02111 (617) 423-3990; *The World in Figures.*

DOMINICA - CONSUMER PRICE INDEX

G.K. Hall and Company, 70 Lincoln Street, Boston, Massachusetts 02111 (617) 423-3990; *The World in Figures.*

Statistical Office of the United Nations, Publishing Service, New York, New York 10017 (800) 253-9646; *Statistical Yearbook.*

DOMINICA - CONSUMER PRICES

International Labour Office, I.L.O. Publications, CH-1211, Geneva 22, Switzerland; *Yearbook of Labour Statistics.*

DOMINICA - CONSUMPTION

G.K. Hall and Company, 70 Lincoln Street, Boston, Massachusetts 02111 (617) 423-3990; *The World in Figures.*

DOMINICA - CORN PRODUCTION - See DOMINICA - CROPS

DOMINICA - CORPORATE TAXES

G.K. Hall and Company, 70 Lincoln Street, Boston, Massachusetts 02111 (617) 423-3990; *The World in Figures.*

International Monetary Fund, 700 Nineteenth Street, NW, Washington, D.C. 20431 (202) 623-7000; *Government Finance Statistics Yearbook.*

DOMINICA - CROPS

Food and Agricultural Organization of the United Nations (FAO) Via delle Terme di Caracalla, 00100 Rome, Italy (Telephone Number in U.S. (202) 653-2400); *Production Yearbook,* and *The State of Food and Agriculture.*

G.K. Hall and Company, 70 Lincoln Street, Boston, Massachusetts 02111 (617) 423-3990; *The World in Figures.*

Statistical Office of the United Nations, Publishing Service, New York, New York 10017 (800) 253-9646; *Statistical Yearbook.*

DOMINICA - CUSTOMS DUTIES

G.K. Hall and Company, 70 Lincoln Street, Boston, Massachusetts 02111 (617) 423-3990; *The World in Figures.*

International Monetary Fund, 700 Nineteenth Street, NW, Washington, D.C. 20431 (202) 623-7000; *Government Finance Statistics Yearbook.*

DOMINICA - DAIRY PRODUCTS

Food and Agricultural Organization of the United Nations (FAO) Via delle Terme di Caracalla, 00100 Rome, Italy (Telephone Number in U.S. (202) 653-2400); *The State of Food and Agriculture.*

DOMINICA - DEATH RATES

G.K. Hall and Company, 70 Lincoln Street, Boston, Massachusetts 02111 (617) 423-3990; *The World in Figures.*

Statistical Office of the United Nations, Publishing Service, New York, New York 10017 (800) 253-9646; *Statistical Yearbook.*

World Health Organization, Office of Publications, Avenue Appia, CH-1211 Geneva 27, Switzerland (Telephone Number in U.S. (518) 436-9686); *World Health Statistics Annual.*

DOMINICA - DEFENSE EXPENDITURES

G.K. Hall and Company, 70 Lincoln Street, Boston, Massachusetts 02111 (617) 423-3990; *The World in Figures.*

International Monetary Fund, 700 Nineteenth Street, NW, Washington, D.C. 20431 (202) 623-7000; *Government Finance Statistics Yearbook.*

DOMINICA - DEMOGRAPHY

G.K. Hall and Company, 70 Lincoln Street, Boston, Massachusetts 02111 (617) 423-3990; *The World in Figures.*

DOMINICA - DEVELOPMENT ASSISTANCE

G.K. Hall and Company, 70 Lincoln Street, Boston, Massachusetts 02111 (617) 423-3990; *The World in Figures.*

DOMINICA - DISEASES

G.K. Hall and Company, 70 Lincoln Street, Boston, Massachusetts 02111 (617) 423-3990; *The World in Figures.*

World Health Organization, Office of Publications, Avenue Appia, CH-1211 Geneva 27, Switzerland (Telephone Number in U.S. (518) 436-9686); *World Health Statistics Annual.*

DOMINICA - DIVORCE RATES

Statistical Office of the United Nations, Publishing Service, New York, New York 10017 (800) 253-9646; *Demographic Yearbook,* and *Statistical Yearbook.*

DOMINICA - DOMESTIC PRODUCT

G.K. Hall and Company, 70 Lincoln Street, Boston, Massachusetts 02111 (617) 423-3990; *The World in Figures.*

DOMINICA - ECONOMY

G.K. Hall and Company, 70 Lincoln Street, Boston, Massachusetts 02111 (617) 423-3990; *The World in Figures.*

Statistical Office of the United Nations, Publishing Service, New York, New York 10017; *Economic Survey of Latin America and the Caribbean.*

DOMINICA - EDUCATION

G.K. Hall and Company, 70 Lincoln Street, Boston, Massachusetts 02111 (617) 423-3990; *The World in Figures.*

International Monetary Fund, 700 Nineteenth Street, NW, Washington, D.C. 20431 (202) 623-7000; *Government Finance Statistics Yearbook.*

United Nations Educational, Scientific and Cultural Organization (UNESCO), 7 Place de Fontenoy, F-75700 Paris, France (Telephone Number in U.S. (212) 963-5981; *Statistical Yearbook.*

The World Bank, 1818 H Street, NW, Washington, D.C. 20433 (202) 477-1234; *World Tables.*

DOMINICA - EGG PRODUCTION - See DOMINICA - DAIRY PRODUCTS

DOMINICA - EMPLOYMENT

International Labour Office, I.L.O. Publications, CH-1211, Geneva 22, Switzerland; *Yearbook of Labour Statistics.*

DOMINICA - ENERGY

Food and Agricultural Organization of the United Nations (FAO) Via delle Terme di Caracalla, 00100 Rome, Italy (Telephone Number in U.S. (202) 653-2400); *The State of Food and Agriculture.*

G.K. Hall and Company, 70 Lincoln Street, Boston, Massachusetts 02111 (617) 423-3990; *The World in Figures.*

Statistical Office of the United Nations, Publishing Service, New York, New York 10017 (800) 253-9646; *Energy Statistics Yearbook.*

DOMINICA - EXCHANGE TAXES

International Monetary Fund, 700 Nineteenth Street, NW, Washington, D.C. 20431 (202) 623-7000; *Government Finance Statistics Yearbook.*

DOMINICA - EXCISE TAXES - See DOMINICA - TAXATION

DOMINICA - EXPORTS

Food and Agricultural Organization of the United Nations (FAO) Via delle Terme di Caracalla, 00100 Rome, Italy (Telephone Number in U.S. (202) 653-2400); *The State of Food and Agriculture.*

G.K. Hall and Company, 70 Lincoln Street, Boston, Massachusetts 02111 (617) 423-3990; *The World in Figures.*

International Monetary Fund, 700 Nineteenth Street, NW, Washington, D.C. 20431 (202) 623-7000; *Government Finance Statistics Yearbook.*

The World Bank, 1818 H Street, NW, Washington, D.C. 20433 (202) 477-1234; *World Tables.*

DOMINICA - EXTERNAL INDEBTEDNESS

The World Bank, 1818 H Street, NW, Washington, D.C. 20433 (202) 477-1234; *World Tables.*

DOMINICA - EXTERNAL TRADE

Food and Agricultural Organization of the United Nations (FAO) Via delle Terme di Caracalla, 00100 Rome, Italy (Telephone Number in U.S. (202) 653-2400); *The State of Food and Agriculture,* and *Trade Yearbook.*

G.K. Hall and Company, 70 Lincoln Street, Boston, Massachusetts 02111 (617) 423-3990; *The World in Figures.*

DOMINICA - FARM CROPS - See DOMINICA - CROPS

DOMINICA - FERTILITY RATES

The World Bank, 1818 H Street, NW, Washington, D.C. 20433 (202) 477-1234; *World Tables.*

DOMINICA - FETAL MORTALITY

Statistical Office of the United Nations, Publishing Service, New York, New York 10017 (800) 253-9646; *Demographic Yearbook.*

World Health Organization, Office of Publications, Avenue Appia, CH-1211 Geneva 27, Switzerland (Telephone Number in U.S. (518) 436-9686); *World Health Statistics Annual.*

DOMINICA - FERTILIZER

Food and Agricultural Organization of the United Nations (FAO) Via delle Terme di Caracalla, 00100 Rome, Italy (Telephone Number in U.S. (202) 653-2400); *The State of Food and Agriculture.*

DOMINICA - FINANCE

G.K. Hall and Company, 70 Lincoln Street, Boston, Massachusetts 02111 (617) 423-3990; *The World in Figures.*

DOMINICA - FISHERIES

Food and Agricultural Organization of the United Nations (FAO) Via delle Terme di Caracalla, 00100 Rome, Italy (Telephone Number in U.S. (202) 653-2400); *The State of Food and Agriculture,* and *Yearbook of Fishery Statistics.*

DOMINICA - FOOD

Food and Agricultural Organization of the United Nations (FAO) Via delle Terme di Caracalla, 00100 Rome, Italy (Telephone Number in U.S. (202) 653-2400); *The State of Food and Agriculture.*

G.K. Hall and Company, 70 Lincoln Street, Boston, Massachusetts 02111 (617) 423-3990; *The World in Figures.*

DOMINICA - FOREIGN AID

G.K. Hall and Company, 70 Lincoln Street, Boston, Massachusetts 02111 (617) 423-3990; *The World in Figures.*

DOMINICA - FOREIGN INDEBTEDNESS

Statistical Office of the United Nations, Publishing Service, New York, New York 10017 (800) 253-9646; *Economic Survey of Latin America and the Caribbean.*

DOMINICA - FOREIGN TRADE

Food and Agricultural Organization of the United Nations (FAO) Via delle Terme di Caracalla, 00100 Rome, Italy (Telephone Number in U.S. (202) 653-2400); *The State of Food and Agriculture.*

G.K. Hall and Company, 70 Lincoln Street, Boston, Massachusetts 02111 (617) 423-3990; *The World in Figures.*

Organisation for Economic Co-operation and Development (OECD), 2 rue Andre-Pascal, 75 Paris 16, France; *Trade by Commodities.*

Statistical Office of the United Nations, Publishing Service, New York, New York 10017 (800) 253-9646; *Economic Survey of Latin America and the Caribbean,* and *International Trade Statistics Yearbook.*

The World Bank, 1818 H Street, NW, Washington, D.C. 20433 (202) 477-1234; *World Tables.*

DOMINICA - FORESTRY AND FOREST PRODUCTS

Food and Agricultural Organization of the United Nations (FAO) Via delle Terme di Caracalla, 00100 Rome, Italy (Telephone Number in U.S. (202) 653-2400); *The State of Food and Agriculture,* and *Yearbook of Forest Products.*

G.K. Hall and Company, 70 Lincoln Street, Boston, Massachusetts 02111 (617) 423-3990; *The World in Figures.*

DOMINICA - GENERAL MORTALITY

Statistical Office of the United Nations, Publishing Service, New York, New York 10017 (800) 253-9646; *Demographic Yearbook.*

World Health Organization, Office of Publications, Avenue Appia, CH-1211 Geneva 27, Switzerland (Telephone Number in U.S. (518) 436-9686); *World Health Statistics Annual.*

DOMINICA - GOLD HOLDINGS

The World Bank, 1818 H Street, NW, Washington, D.C. 20433 (202) 477-1234; *World Tables.*

DOMINICA - GOVERNMENT

G.K. Hall and Company, 70 Lincoln Street, Boston, Massachusetts 02111 (617) 423-3990; *The World in Figures.*

DOMINICA - GOVERNMENT EXPENDITURES

International Monetary Fund, 700 Nineteenth Street, NW, Washington, D.C. 20431 (202) 623-7000; *Government Finance Statistics Yearbook.*

The World Bank, 1818 H Street, NW, Washington, D.C. 20433 (202) 477-1234; *World Tables.*

DOMINICA - GOVERNMENT REVENUES

International Monetary Fund, 700 Nineteenth Street, NW, Washington, D.C. 20431 (202) 623-7000; *Government Finance Statistics Yearbook.*

The World Bank, 1818 H Street, NW, Washington, D.C. 20433 (202) 477-1234; *World Tables.*

DOMINICA - GRAIN PRODUCTION - See DOMINICA - CROPS

DOMINICA - GRANTS

International Monetary Fund, 700 Nineteenth Street, NW, Washington, D.C. 20431 (202) 623-7000; *Government Finance Statistics Yearbook.*

DOMINICA - GROSS DOMESTIC PRODUCT

G.K. Hall and Company, 70 Lincoln Street, Boston, Massachusetts 02111 (617) 423-3990; *The World in Figures.*

Statistical Office of the United Nations, Publishing Service, New York, New York 10017 (800) 253-9646; *Statistical Yearbook.*

The World Bank, 1818 H Street, NW, Washington, D.C. 20433 (202) 477-1234; *World Tables.*

DOMINICA - GROSS NATIONAL PRODUCT

The World Bank, 1818 H Street, NW, Washington, D.C. 20433 (202) 477-1234; *World Tables.*

DOMINICA - HEALTH

G.K. Hall and Company, 70 Lincoln Street, Boston, Massachusetts 02111 (617) 423-3990; *The World in Figures.*

Statistical Office of the United Nations, Publishing Service, New York, New York 10017 (800) 253-9646; *Statistical Yearbook.*

World Health Organization, Office of Publications, Avenue Appia, CH-1211 Geneva 27, Switzerland (Telephone Number in U.S. (518) 436-9686); *World Health Statistics Annual.*

DOMINICA - HEALTH EXPENDITURES

International Monetary Fund, 700 Nineteenth Street, NW, Washington, D.C. 20431 (202) 623-7000; *Government Finance Statistics Yearbook.*

DOMINICA - HIDE PRODUCTION

Food and Agricultural Organization of the United Nations (FAO), Via delle Terme di Caracalla, 00100 Rome, Italy (Telephone Number in U.S. (202) 653-2400); *Production Yearbook.*

DOMINICA - HIGHWAYS

G.K. Hall and Company, 70 Lincoln Street, Boston, Massachusetts 02111 (617) 423-3990; *The World in Figures.*

DOMINICA - HOURS OF WORK - See DOMINICA - EMPLOYMENT

DOMINICA - HOUSING AND HOUSING UNITS

Statistical Office of the United Nations, Publishing Service, New York, New York 10017 (800) 253-9646; *Statistical Yearbook.*

DOMINICA - HOUSING EXPENDITURES

International Monetary Fund, 700 Nineteenth Street, NW, Washington, D.C. 20431 (202) 623-7000; *Government Finance Statistics Yearbook.*

DOMINICA - ILLITERATE POPULATION

G.K. Hall and Company, 70 Lincoln Street, Boston, Massachusetts 02111 (617) 423-3990; *The World in Figures.*

United Nations Educational, Scientific and Cultural Organization (UNESCO), 7 Place de Fontenoy, F-75700 Paris, France (Telephone Number in U.S. (212) 963-5981; *Statistical Yearbook.*

DOMINICA - IMPORTS

Food and Agricultural Organization of the United Nations (FAO) Via delle Terme di Caracalla, 00100 Rome, Italy (Telephone Number in U.S. (202) 653-2400); *The State of Food and Agriculture.*

G.K. Hall and Company, 70 Lincoln Street, Boston, Massachusetts 02111 (617) 423-3990; *The World in Figures.*

International Monetary Fund, 700 Nineteenth Street, NW, Washington, D.C. 20431 (202) 623-7000; *Government Finance Statistics Yearbook.*

The World Bank, 1818 H Street, NW, Washington, D.C. 20433 (202) 477-1234; *World Tables.*

DOMINICA - INCOME TAXES - See DOMINICA - TAXATION

DOMINICA - INDUSTRY

G.K. Hall and Company, 70 Lincoln Street, Boston, Massachusetts 02111 (617) 423-3990; *The World in Figures.*

International Labour Office, I.L.O. Publications, CH-1211, Geneva 22, Switzerland; *Yearbook of Labour Statistics.*

Statistical Office of the United Nations, Publishing Service, New York, New York 10017 (800) 253-9646; *Economic Survey of Latin America and the Caribbean.*

The World Bank, 1818 H Street, NW, Washington, D.C. 20433 (202) 477-1234; *World Tables.*

DOMINICA - INFANT AND MATERNAL MORTALITY

Statistical Office of the United Nations, Publishing Service, New York, New York 10017 (800) 253-9646; *Demographic Yearbook,* and *Statistical Yearbook.*

The World Bank, 1818 H Street, NW, Washington, D.C. 20433 (202) 477-1234; *World Tables.*

World Health Organization, Office of Publications, Avenue Appia, CH-1211 Geneva 27, Switzerland (Telephone Number in U.S. (518) 436-9686); *World Health Statistics Annual.*

DOMINICA - INFLATIONARY FACTORS

Statistical Office of the United Nations, Publishing Service, New York, New York 10017 (800) 253-9646; *Economic Survey of Latin America and the Caribbean.*

DOMINICA - INTERNATIONAL RESERVES EXCLUDING GOLD

The World Bank, 1818 H Street, NW, Washington, D.C. 20433 (202) 477-1234; *World Tables.*

DOMINICA - LABOR FORCE

Food and Agricultural Organization of the United Nations (FAO) Via delle Terme di Caracalla, 00100 Rome, Italy (Telephone Number in U.S. (202) 653-2400); *The State of Food and Agriculture.*

G.K. Hall and Company, 70 Lincoln Street, Boston, Massachusetts 02111 (617) 423-3990; *The World in Figures.*

The World Bank, 1818 H Street, NW, Washington, D.C. 20433 (202) 477-1234; *World Tables.*

DOMINICA - LABOR PRODUCTIVITY

International Labour Office, I.L.O. Publications, CH-1211, Geneva 22, Switzerland; *Yearbook of Labour Statistics.*

DOMINICA - LAND USE

Food and Agricultural Organization of the United Nations (FAO), Via delle Terme di Caracalla, 00100 Rome, Italy (Telephone Number in U.S. (202) 653-2400); *Production Yearbook.*

G.K. Hall and Company, 70 Lincoln Street, Boston, Massachusetts 02111 (617) 423-3990; *The World in Figures.*

DOMINICA - LIVESTOCK AND POULTRY

Food and Agricultural Organization of the United Nations (FAO), Via delle Terme di Caracalla, 00100 Rome, Italy (Telephone Number in U.S. (202) 653-2400); *Production Yearbook*, and *The State of Food and Agriculture*.

G.K. Hall and Company, 70 Lincoln Street, Boston, Massachusetts 02111 (617) 423-3990; *The World in Figures*.

Statistical Office of the United Nations, Publishing Service, New York, New York 10017 (800) 253-9646; *Statistical Yearbook*.

DOMINICA - LIVING LEVELS

G.K. Hall and Company, 70 Lincoln Street, Boston, Massachusetts 02111 (617) 423-3990; *The World in Figures*.

DOMINICA - MANUFACTURING

G.K. Hall and Company, 70 Lincoln Street, Boston, Massachusetts 02111 (617) 423-3990; *The World in Figures*.

The World Bank, 1818 H Street, NW, Washington, D.C. 20433 (202) 477-1234; *World Tables*.

DOMINICA - MARRIAGE RATES

Statistical Office of the United Nations, Publishing Service, New York, New York 10017 (800) 253-9646; *Demographic Yearbook*, and *Statistical Yearbook*.

DOMINICA - MEAT PRODUCTION - See DOMINICA - LIVESTOCK AND POULTRY

DOMINICA - MERCHANT SHIPPING

G.K. Hall and Company, 70 Lincoln Street, Boston, Massachusetts 02111 (617) 423-3990; *The World in Figures*.

Statistical Office of the United Nations, Publishing Service, New York, New York 10017 (800) 253-9646; *Statistical Yearbook*.

DOMINICA - MILITARY

G.K. Hall and Company, 70 Lincoln Street, Boston, Massachusetts 02111 (617) 423-3990; *The World in Figures*.

DOMINICA - MINING AND MINERAL PRODUCTS

G.K. Hall and Company, 70 Lincoln Street, Boston, Massachusetts 02111 (617) 423-3990; *The World in Figures*.

DOMINICA - MONEY SUPPLY

G.K. Hall and Company, 70 Lincoln Street, Boston, Massachusetts 02111 (617) 423-3990; *The World in Figures*.

The World Bank, 1818 H Street, NW, Washington, D.C. 20433 (202) 477-1234; *World Tables*.

DOMINICA - MOTOR VEHICLES IN USE

G.K. Hall and Company, 70 Lincoln Street, Boston, Massachusetts 02111 (617) 423-3990; *The World in Figures*.

DOMINICA - MOTOR VEHICLES TAXES - See DOMINICA - TAXATION

DOMINICA - NATALITY - See DOMINICA - BIRTH RATE

DOMINICA - NATIONAL ACCOUNTS

Statistical Office of the United Nations, Publishing Service, New York, New York 10017 (800) 253-9646; *National Accounts Statistics*, and *Statistical Yearbook*.

DOMINICA - NATIONAL INCOME

G.K. Hall and Company, 70 Lincoln Street, Boston, Massachusetts 02111 (617) 423-3990; *The World in Figures*.

Statistical Office of the United Nations, Publishing Service, New York, New York 10017 (800) 253-9646; *Statistical Yearbook*.

DOMINICA - NEWSPAPER PRODUCTION - See DOMINICA - FORESTRY AND FOREST PRODUCTS

DOMINICA - OCCUPATIONS - See DOMINICA - LABOR FORCE

DOMINICA - PESTICIDE USE

Food and Agricultural Organization of the United Nations (FAO) Via delle Terme di Caracalla, 00100 Rome, Italy (Telephone Number in U.S. (202) 653-2400); *The State of Food and Agriculture*.

DOMINICA - PETROLEUM INDUSTRY

Food and Agricultural Organization of the United Nations (FAO) Via delle Terme di Caracalla, 00100 Rome, Italy (Telephone Number in U.S. (202) 653-2400); *The State of Food and Agriculture*.

G.K. Hall and Company, 70 Lincoln Street, Boston, Massachusetts 02111 (617) 423-3990; *The World in Figures*.

DOMINICA - PIGS - See DOMINICA - LIVESTOCK AND POULTRY

DOMINICA - POPULATION

Food and Agricultural Organization of the United Nations (FAO), Via delle Terme di Caracalla, 00100 Rome, Italy (Telephone Number in U.S. (202) 653-2400); *Production Yearbook*.

G.K. Hall and Company, 70 Lincoln Street, Boston, Massachusetts 02111 (617) 423-3990; *The World in Figures*.

International Labour Office, I.L.O. Publications, CH-1211, Geneva 22, Switzerland; *Yearbook of Labour Statistics*.

Organization of American States (OAS), General Secretariat, Washington, D.C. 20006; *Statistical Bulletin of the OAS*.

Statistical Office of the United Nations, Publishing Service, New York, New York 10017 (800) 253-9646; *Demographic Yearbook*, and *Statistical Yearbook*.

United Nations Educational, Scientific and Cultural Organization (UNESCO), 7 Place de Fontenoy, F-75700 Paris, France (Telephone Number in U.S. (212) 963-5981; *Statistical Yearbook*.

World Health Organization, Office of Publications, Avenue Appia, CH-1211 Geneva 27, Switzerland (Telephone Number in U.S. (518) 436-9686); *World Health Statistics Annual*.

DOMINICA - PRICES

Food and Agricultural Organization of the United Nations (FAO), Via delle Terme di Caracalla, 00100 Rome, Italy (Telephone Number in

U.S. (202) 653-2400); *Production Yearbook*, and *The State of Food and Agriculture*.

G.K. Hall and Company, 70 Lincoln Street, Boston, Massachusetts 02111 (617) 423-3990; *The World in Figures*.

International Labour Office, I.L.O. Publications, CH-1211, Geneva 22, Switzerland; *Yearbook of Labour Statistics*.

Statistical Office of the United Nations, Publishing Service, New York, New York 10017 (800) 253-9646; *Economic Survey of Latin America and the Caribbean*.

DOMINICA - PRODUCTION

G.K. Hall and Company, 70 Lincoln Street, Boston, Massachusetts 02111 (617) 423-3990; *The World in Figures*.

DOMINICA - PROPERTY TAXES - See DOMINICA - TAXATION

DOMINICA - RAILWAYS

G.K. Hall and Company, 70 Lincoln Street, Boston, Massachusetts 02111 (617) 423-3990; *The World in Figures*.

DOMINICA - RENT PRICES

International Labour Office, I.L.O. Publications, CH-1211, Geneva 22, Switzerland; *Yearbook of Labour Statistics*.

DOMINICA - RETAIL TRADE

G.K. Hall and Company, 70 Lincoln Street, Boston, Massachusetts 02111 (617) 423-3990; *The World in Figures*.

DOMINICA - ROOT AND TUBER PRODUCTION - See DOMINICA - CROPS

DOMINICA - ROUNDWOOD PRODUCTION - See DOMINICA - FORESTRY AND FOREST PRODUCTS

DOMINICA - SAWNWOOD PRODUCTION - See DOMINICA - FORESTRY AND FOREST PRODUCTS

DOMINICA - SHEEP - See DOMINICA - LIVESTOCK AND POULTRY

DOMINICA - SOCIAL DATA

G.K. Hall and Company, 70 Lincoln Street, Boston, Massachusetts 02111 (617) 423-3990; *The World in Figures*.

DOMINICA - SOCIAL SECURITY

International Monetary Fund, 700 Nineteenth Street, NW, Washington, D.C. 20431 (202) 623-7000; *Government Finance Statistics Yearbook*.

DOMINICA - STAMP TAXES AND DUTIES - See DOMINICA - TAXATION

DOMINICA - STOCKS - COMMODITY - MARKET PRICE - INDEX

Food and Agricultural Organization of the United Nations (FAO) Via delle Terme di Caracalla, 00100 Rome, Italy (Telephone Number in U.S. (202) 653-2400); *The State of Food and Agriculture*.

DOMINICA - TAXATION

G.K. Hall and Company, 70 Lincoln Street, Boston, Massachusetts 02111 (617) 423-3990; *The World in Figures*.

International Monetary Fund, 700 Nineteenth Street, NW, Washington, D.C. 20431 (202) 623-7000; *Government Finance Statistics Yearbook*.

The World Bank, 1818 H Street, NW, Washington, D.C. 20433 (202) 477-1234; *World Tables*.

DOMINICA - TELEPHONES IN USE

American Telephone and Telegraph Company, 26 Parsippany Road, Whippany, New Jersey 07981 (800) 338-4038; *The World's Telephones*.

G.K. Hall and Company, 70 Lincoln Street, Boston, Massachusetts 02111 (617) 423-3990; *The World in Figures*.

Statistical Office of the United Nations, Publishing Service, New York, New York 10017 (800) 253-9646; *Statistical Yearbook*.

DOMINICA - TEXTILE INDUSTRY

G.K. Hall and Company, 70 Lincoln Street, Boston, Massachusetts 02111 (617) 423-3990; *The World in Figures*.

DOMINICA - TOURISM

G.K. Hall and Company, 70 Lincoln Street, Boston, Massachusetts 02111 (617) 423-3990; *The World in Figures*.

World Tourism Organization, Calle Capitan Haya 42, E-28020 Madrid, Spain; *Yearbook of Tourism Statistics*.

DOMINICA - TRACTORS IN USE

Statistical Office of the United Nations, Publishing Service, New York, New York 10017 (800) 253-9646; *Statistical Yearbook*.

DOMINICA - TRADE - See DOMINICA - FOREIGN TRADE

DOMINICA - TRANSPORTATION AND COMMUNICATIONS

G.K. Hall and Company, 70 Lincoln Street, Boston, Massachusetts 02111 (617) 423-3990; *The World in Figures*.

DOMINICA - UNEMPLOYMENT

International Labour Office, I.L.O. Publications, CH-1211, Geneva 22, Switzerland; *Yearbook of Labour Statistics*.

DOMINICA - VITAL STATISTICS

G.K. Hall and Company, 70 Lincoln Street, Boston, Massachusetts 02111 (617) 423-3990; *The World in Figures*.

World Health Organization, Office of Publications, Avenue Appia, CH-1211 Geneva 27, Switzerland (Telephone Number in U.S. (518) 436-9686); *World Health Statistics Annual*.

DOMINICA - WAGES

G.K. Hall and Company, 70 Lincoln Street, Boston, Massachusetts 02111 (617) 423-3990; *The World in Figures*.

International Labour Office, I.L.O. Publications, CH-1211, Geneva 22, Switzerland; *Yearbook of Labour Statistics*.

DOMINICA - WEATHER

G.K. Hall and Company, 70 Lincoln Street, Boston, Massachusetts 02111 (617) 423-3990; *The World in Figures.*

DOMINICA - WELFARE

International Monetary Fund, 700 Nineteenth Street, NW, Washington, D.C. 20431 (202) 623-7000; *Government Finance Statistics Yearbook.*

Dominican Republic - National Statistical Office

Oficina Nacional de Estadistica Apartado de Correos No. 1342, Santo Domingo, D.N., Dominican Republic.

Dominican Republic - Primary Statistics Source

Oficina Nacional de Estadistica Apartado do Correos No. 1342, Santo Domingo, D.N., Dominican Republic; *Republica Dominicana en Cifras (The Dominican Republic in Figures).*

DOMINICAN REPUBLIC - AGRICULTURE

The Economist Intelligence Unit, 111 West 57th Street, New York, New York 10019 (800) 938-4685; *The New Latin America Market Atlas.*

Euromonitor Publications Limited, 87-88 Turnmill Street, London EC1M 5QU, England; *International Marketing Data and Statistics.*

Facts on File, 460 Park Avenue South, New York, New York 10016 (800) 443-8323; *The New Book of World Rankings.*

Federal Statistical Office, Gustav - Stresemann - Ring 11, D-6200 Wiesbaden, Germany; *Dominikanische Republik.*

Food and Agricultural Organization of the United Nations (FAO) Via delle Terme di Caracalla, 00100 Rome, Italy (Telephone Number in U.S. (202) 653-2400); *Production Yearbook, The State of Food and Agriculture,* and *Trade Yearbook.*

Gale Research Incorporated, 835 Penobscot Building, Detroit, Michigan 48226 (800) 877-4253; *International Historical Statistics The Americas and Australasia.*

G.K. Hall and Company, 70 Lincoln Street, Boston, Massachusetts 02111 (617) 423-3990; *The World in Figures.*

Inter-American Development Bank, 1300 New York Avenue, NW, Washington, D.C. 20577 (202) 623-1753; *Economic and Social Progress in Latin America.*

Statistical Office of the United Nations, Publishing Service, New York, New York 10017 (800) 253-9646; *Statistical Yearbook,* and *Statistical Yearbook for Latin America and the Caribbean.*

Times Books, 201 East 50th Street, New York, New York 10022 (212) 751-2600; *The Economist Book of Vital World Statistics.*

U.C.L.A. Latin American Center Publications, University of California, Los Angeles, California 90024 (310) 825-6634; *Statistical Abstract of Latin America.*

The World Bank, 1818 H Street, NW, Washington, D.C. 20433 (202) 477-1234; *World Tables.*

DOMINICAN REPUBLIC - AIRLINE SERVICE

The Economist Intelligence Unit, 111 West 57th Street, New York, New York 10019 (800) 938-4685; *The New Latin America Market Atlas.*

Facts on File, 460 Park Avenue South, New York, New York 10016 (800) 443-8323; *The New Book of World Rankings.*

G.K. Hall and Company, 70 Lincoln Street, Boston, Massachusetts 02111 (617) 423-3990; *The World in Figures.*

International Civil Aviation Organization, 1000 Sherbrooke Street West, Suite 400, Montreal, Quebec, Canada H3A 2R2 (514) 285-8219; *Civil Aviation Statistics of the World.*

Times Books, 201 East 50th Street, New York, New York 10022 (212) 751-2600; *The Economist Book of Vital World Statistics.*

DOMINICAN REPUBLIC - ALUMINUM PRODUCTION AND CONSUMPTION - See DOMINICAN REPUBLIC - MINING AND MINERAL PRODUCTS

DOMINICAN REPUBLIC - ANIMAL HEALTH

Food and Agricultural Organization of the United Nations (FAO), Via delle Terme di Caracalla, 00100 Rome, Italy (Telephone Number in U.S. (202) 653-2400); *Animal Health Yearbook.*

DOMINICAN REPUBLIC - AREA AND DENSITY OF POPULATION

Euromonitor Publications Limited, 87-88 Turnmill Street, London EC1M 5QU, England; *International Marketing Data and Statistics.*

Facts on File, 460 Park Avenue South, New York, New York 10016 (800) 443-8323; *The New Book of World Rankings.*

Federal Statistical Office, Gustav - Stresemann - Ring 11, D-6200 Wiesbaden, Germany; *Dominikanische Republik.*

Food and Agricultural Organization of the United Nations (FAO) Via delle Terme di Caracalla, 00100 Rome, Italy (Telephone Number in U.S. (202) 653-2400); *The State of Food and Agriculture.*

G.K. Hall and Company, 70 Lincoln Street, Boston, Massachusetts 02111 (617) 423-3990; *The World in Figures.*

Inter-American Development Bank, 1300 New York Avenue, NW, Washington, D.C. 20577 (202) 623-1753; *Economic and Social Progress in Latin America.*

Times Books, 201 East 50th Street, New York, New York 10022 (212) 751-2600; *The Economist Book of Vital World Statistics.*

DOMINICAN REPUBLIC - ARMS EXPORTS AND IMPORTS

U.S. Arms Control and Disarmament Agency, 320 Twenty-first Street, NW, Washington, D.C. 20451 (202) 647-8677; *World Military Expenditures and Arms Transfers.*

DOMINICAN REPUBLIC - BALANCE OF PAYMENTS

The Economist Intelligence Unit, 111 West 57th Street, New York, New York 10019 (800) 938-4685; *The New Latin America Market Atlas,* and *The World Market Atlas.*

Federal Statistical Office, Gustav - Stresemann - Ring 11, D-6200 Wiesbaden, Germany; *Dominikanische Republik.*

G.K. Hall and Company, 70 Lincoln Street, Boston, Massachusetts 02111 (617) 423-3990; *The World in Figures*.

Inter-American Development Bank, 1300 New York Avenue, NW, Washington, D.C. 20577 (202) 623-1753; *Economic and Social Progress in Latin America*.

International Monetary Fund, 700 Nineteenth Street, NW, Washington, D.C. 20431 (202) 623-7000; *Balance of Payments Yearbook*.

Organization of American States (OAS), General Secretariat, Washington, D.C. 20006 (202) 458-3533; *Statistical Bulletin of the OAS*.

Statistical Office of the United Nations, Publishing Service, New York, New York 10017 (800) 253-9646; *Statistical Yearbook for Latin America and the Caribbean*.

Times Books, 201 East 50th Street, New York, New York 10022 (212) 751-2600; *The Economist Book of Vital World Statistics*.

U.C.L.A. Latin American Center Publications, University of California, Los Angeles, California 90024 (310) 825-6634; *Statistical Abstract of Latin America*.

The World Bank, 1818 H Street, NW, Washington, D.C. 20433 (202) 477-1234; *World Tables*.

DOMINICAN REPUBLIC - BANKING

Facts on File, 460 Park Avenue South, New York, New York 10016 (800) 443-8323; *The New Book of World Rankings*.

G.K. Hall and Company, 70 Lincoln Street, Boston, Massachusetts 02111 (617) 423-3990; *The World in Figures*.

Inter-American Development Bank, 1300 New York Avenue, NW, Washington, D.C. 20577 (202) 623-1753; *Economic and Social Progress in Latin America*.

International Monetary Fund, 700 Nineteenth Street, NW, Washington, D.C. 20431 (202) 623-7000; *International Financial Statistics*.

Statistical Office of the United Nations, Publishing Service, New York, New York 10017 (800) 253-9646; *Statistical Yearbook for Latin America and the Caribbean*.

DOMINICAN REPUBLIC - BARLEY PRODUCTION - See DOMINICAN REPUBLIC - CROPS

DOMINICAN REPUBLIC - BAUXITE - See DOMINICAN REPUBLIC - MINING AND MINERAL PRODUCTS

DOMINICAN REPUBLIC - BEER PRODUCTION

Facts on File, 460 Park Avenue South, New York, New York 10016 (800) 443-8323; *The New Book of World Rankings*.

Statistical Office of the United Nations, Publishing Service, New York, New York 10017 (800) 253-9646; *Statistical Yearbook*.

DOMINICAN REPUBLIC - BIRTH RATES

Facts on File, 460 Park Avenue South, New York, New York 10016 (800) 443-8323; *The New Book of World Rankings*.

Statistical Office of the United Nations, Publishing Service, New York, New York 10017 (800) 253-9646; *Demographic Yearbook*, *Statistical Yearbook*, and *Statistical Yearbook for Latin America and the Caribbean*.

Times Books, 201 East 50th Street, New York, New York 10022 (212) 751-2600; *The Economist Book of Vital World Statistics*.

The World Bank, 1818 H Street, NW, Washington, D.C. 20433 (202) 477-1234; *World Tables*.

World Health Organization, Office of Publications, Avenue Appia, CH-1211 Geneva 27, Switzerland (Telephone Number in U.S. (518) 436-9686); *World Health Statistics Annual*.

DOMINICAN REPUBLIC - BONDS

G.K. Hall and Company, 70 Lincoln Street, Boston, Massachusetts 02111 (617) 423-3990; *The World in Figures*.

Inter-American Development Bank, 1300 New York Avenue, NW, Washington, D.C. 20577 (202) 623-1753; *Economic and Social Progress in Latin America*.

DOMINICAN REPUBLIC - BOOK PRODUCTION

G.K. Hall and Company, 70 Lincoln Street, Boston, Massachusetts 02111 (617) 423-3990; *The World in Figures*.

DOMINICAN REPUBLIC - BROADCASTING

Billboard Limited, P.O. Box 9027, 1006 AA Amsterdam, The Netherlands (Telephone Number in U.S. (212) 764-7300); *World Radio TV Handbook*.

Facts on File, 460 Park Avenue South, New York, New York 10016 (800) 443-8323; *The New Book of World Rankings*.

G.K. Hall and Company, 70 Lincoln Street, Boston, Massachusetts 02111 (617) 423-3990; *The World in Figures*.

Times Books, 201 East 50th Street, New York, New York 10022 (212) 751-2600; *The Economist Book of Vital World Statistics*.

DOMINICAN REPUBLIC - BUILDING CONSTRUCTION - See DOMINICAN REPUBLIC - CONSTRUCTION INDUSTRY

DOMINICAN REPUBLIC - BUSINESS

G.K. Hall and Company, 70 Lincoln Street, Boston, Massachusetts 02111 (617) 423-3990; *The World in Figures*.

Inter-American Development Bank, 1300 New York Avenue, NW, Washington, D.C. 20577 (202) 623-1753; *Economic and Social Progress in Latin America*.

DOMINICAN REPUBLIC - BUSINESS AND PROFESSIONAL LICENSES

International Monetary Fund, 700 Nineteenth Street, NW, Washington, D.C. 20431 (202) 623-7000; *Government Finance Statistics Yearbook*.

DOMINICAN REPUBLIC - CACAO - See DOMINICAN REPUBLIC - CROPS

DOMINICAN REPUBLIC - CALORIE SUPPLY

Food and Agricultural Organization of the United Nations (FAO) Via delle Terme di Caracalla, 00100 Rome, Italy (Telephone Number in U.S. (202) 653-2400); *The State of Food and Agriculture.*

Statistical Office of the United Nations, Publishing Service, New York, New York 10017 (800) 253-9646; *Statistical Yearbook for Latin America and the Caribbean.*

DOMINICAN REPUBLIC - CAPITAL INVESTMENT

Inter-American Development Bank, 1300 New York Avenue, NW, Washington, D.C. 20577 (202) 623-1753; *Economic and Social Progress in Latin America.*

DOMINICAN REPUBLIC - CAPITAL REVENUE

Inter-American Development Bank, 1300 New York Avenue, NW, Washington, D.C. 20577 (202) 623-1753; *Economic and Social Progress in Latin America.*

International Monetary Fund, 700 Nineteenth Street, NW, Washington, D.C. 20431 (202) 623-7000; *Government Finance Statistics Yearbook.*

DOMINICAN REPUBLIC - CASHEW NUT PRODUCTION - See DOMINICAN REPUBLIC - CROPS

DOMINICAN REPUBLIC - CATTLE - See DOMINICAN REPUBLIC - LIVESTOCK AND POULTRY

DOMINICAN REPUBLIC - CEMENT PRODUCTION - See DOMINICAN REPUBLIC - MINING AND MINERAL PRODUCTS

DOMINICAN REPUBLIC - CHEESE PRODUCTION - See DOMINICAN REPUBLIC - DAIRY PRODUCTS

DOMINICAN REPUBLIC - CHEMICAL (ORGANIC) PRODUCTION - See DOMINICAN REPUBLIC - MINING AND MINERAL PRODUCTS

DOMINICAN REPUBLIC - CHICKENS - See DOMINICAN REPUBLIC - LIVESTOCK AND POULTRY

DOMINICAN REPUBLIC - CIGAR PRODUCTION - See DOMINICAN REPUBLIC - TOBACCO PRODUCTION

DOMINICAN REPUBLIC - CIGARETTE PRODUCTION - See DOMINICAN REPUBLIC - TOBACCO PRODUCTION

DOMINICAN REPUBLIC - CLASS STRUCTURE

G.K. Hall and Company, 70 Lincoln Street, Boston, Massachusetts 02111 (617) 423-3990; *The World in Figures.*

DOMINICAN REPUBLIC - CLIMATE

Facts on File, 460 Park Avenue South, New York, New York 10016 (800) 443-8323; *The New Book of World Rankings.*

G.K. Hall and Company, 70 Lincoln Street, Boston, Massachusetts 02111 (617) 423-3990; *The World in Figures.*

DOMINICAN REPUBLIC - CLOTHING EXPORTS AND IMPORTS

Statistical Office of the United Nations, Publishing Service, New York, New York 10017 (800) 253-9646; *Trade in Manufactures of Developing Countries.*

DOMINICAN REPUBLIC - COAL PRODUCTION - See DOMINICAN REPUBLIC - MINING AND MINERAL PRODUCTS

DOMINICAN REPUBLIC - COCOA (BEANS) PRODUCTION - See DOMINICAN REPUBLIC - CROPS

DOMINICAN REPUBLIC - COFFEE - See DOMINICAN REPUBLIC - CROPS

DOMINICAN REPUBLIC - COMMUNICATIONS

Federal Statistical Office, Gustav - Stresemann - Ring 11, D-6200 Wiesbaden, Germany; *Dominikanische Republik.*

G.K. Hall and Company, 70 Lincoln Street, Boston, Massachusetts 02111 (617) 423-3990; *The World in Figures.*

Inter-American Development Bank, 1300 New York Avenue, NW, Washington, D.C. 20577 (202) 623-1753; *Economic and Social Progress in Latin America.*

U.C.L.A. Latin American Center Publications, University of California, Los Angeles, California 90024 (310) 825-6634; *Statistical Abstract of Latin America.*

DOMINICAN REPUBLIC - CONSTRUCTION INDUSTRY

The Economist Intelligence Unit, 111 West 57th Street, New York, New York 10019 (800) 938-4685; *The New Latin America Market Atlas.*

Facts on File, 460 Park Avenue South, New York, New York 10016 (800) 443-8323; *The New Book of World Rankings.*

Inter-American Development Bank, 1300 New York Avenue, NW, Washington, D.C. 20577 (202) 623-1753; *Economic and Social Progress in Latin America.*

Statistical Office of the United Nations, Publishing Service, New York, New York 10017 (800) 253-9646; *Construction Statistics Yearbook,* and *Statistical Yearbook.*

U.C.L.A. Latin American Center Publications, University of California, Los Angeles, California 90024 (310) 825-6634; *Statistical Abstract of Latin America.*

DOMINICAN REPUBLIC - CONSUMER PRICE INDEX

Federal Statistical Office, Gustav - Stresemann - Ring 11, D-6200 Wiesbaden, Germany; *Dominikanische Republik.*

G.K. Hall and Company, 70 Lincoln Street, Boston, Massachusetts 02111 (617) 423-3990; *The World in Figures.*

International Labour Office, I.L.O. Publications, CH-1211, Geneva 22, Switzerland; *Yearbook of Labour Statistics.*

Statistical Office of the United Nations, Publishing Service, New York, New York 10017 (800) 253-9646; *Statistical Yearbook.*

DOMINICAN REPUBLIC - CONSUMER PRICES

The Economist Intelligence Unit, 111 West 57th Street, New York, New York 10019 (800) 938-4685; *The New Latin America Market Atlas.*

Federal Statistical Office, Gustav - Stresemann - Ring 11, D-6200 Wiesbaden, Germany; *Dominikanische Republik.*

International Labour Office, I.L.O. Publications, CH-1211, Geneva 22, Switzerland; *Yearbook of Labour Statistics.*

International Monetary Fund, 700 Nineteenth Street, NW, Washington, D.C. 20431 (202) 623-7000; *International Financial Statistics.*

Organization of American States (OAS), General Secretariat, Washington, D.C. 20006 (202) 458-3533; *Statistical Bulletin of the OAS.*

Times Books, 201 East 50th Street, New York, New York 10022 (212) 751-2600; *The Economist Book of Vital World Statistics.*

U.C.L.A. Latin American Center Publications, University of California, Los Angeles, California 90024 (310) 825-6634; *Statistical Abstract of Latin America.*

DOMINICAN REPUBLIC - CONSUMPTION

The Economist Intelligence Unit, 111 West 57th Street, New York, New York 10019 (800) 938-4685; *The New Latin America Market Atlas.*

G.K. Hall and Company, 70 Lincoln Street, Boston, Massachusetts 02111 (617) 423-3990; *The World in Figures.*

Inter-American Development Bank, 1300 New York Avenue, NW, Washington, D.C. 20577 (202) 623-1753; *Economic and Social Progress in Latin America.*

Statistical Office of the United Nations, Publishing Service, New York, New York 10017 (800) 253-9646; *Statistical Yearbook for Latin America and the Caribbean.*

DOMINICAN REPUBLIC - COOPERATIVES

U.C.L.A. Latin American Center Publications, University of California, Los Angeles, California 90024 (310) 825-6634; *Statistical Abstract of Latin America.*

DOMINICAN REPUBLIC - COPPER AND COPPER ORE - See DOMINICAN REPUBLIC - MINING AND MINERAL PRODUCTS

DOMINICAN REPUBLIC - CORN PRODUCTION - See DOMINICAN REPUBLIC - CROPS

DOMINICAN REPUBLIC - CORPORATE INCOME TAXES - See DOMINICAN REPUBLIC - TAXATION

DOMINICAN REPUBLIC - CORPORATE TAXES - See DOMINICAN REPUBLIC - TAXATION

DOMINICAN REPUBLIC - COTTON PRODUCTION - See DOMINICAN REPUBLIC - CROPS

DOMINICAN REPUBLIC - CRIME

Yale University Press, Yale Station, New Haven, Connecticut 06520 (203) 432-0940; *Violence and Crime in Cross-National Perspective.*

DOMINICAN REPUBLIC - CROPS

Commodity Research Bureau, Incorporated, 75 Wall Street, New York, New York 10005 (212) 504-7754; *Commodity Year Book.*

The Economist Intelligence Unit, 111 West 57th Street, New York, New York 10019 (800) 938-4685; *The New Latin America Market Atlas.*

Facts on File, 460 Park Avenue South, New York, New York 10016 (800) 443-8323; *The New Book of World Rankings.*

Food and Agricultural Organization of the United Nations (FAO) Via delle Terme di Caracalla, 00100 Rome, Italy (Telephone Number in U.S. (202) 653-2400); *Production Yearbook,* and *The State of Food and Agriculture.*

G.K. Hall and Company, 70 Lincoln Street, Boston, Massachusetts 02111 (617) 423-3990; *The World in Figures.*

International Monetary Fund, 700 Nineteenth Street, NW, Washington, D.C. 20431 (202) 623-7000; *International Financial Statistics.*

Organization of American States (OAS), General Secretariat, Washington, D.C. 20006 (202) 458-3533; *Statistical Bulletin of the OAS.*

Statistical Office of the United Nations, Publishing Service, New York, New York 10017 (800) 253-9646; *Statistical Yearbook.*

DOMINICAN REPUBLIC - CUSTOMS DUTIES

G.K. Hall and Company, 70 Lincoln Street, Boston, Massachusetts 02111 (617) 423-3990; *The World in Figures.*

Inter-American Development Bank, 1300 New York Avenue, NW, Washington, D.C. 20577 (202) 623-1753; *Economic and Social Progress in Latin America.*

International Monetary Fund, 700 Nineteenth Street, NW, Washington, D.C. 20431 (202) 623-7000; *Government Finance Statistics Yearbook.*

DOMINICAN REPUBLIC - DAIRY PRODUCTS

Facts on File, 460 Park Avenue South, New York, New York 10016 (800) 443-8323; *The New Book of World Rankings.*

Food and Agricultural Organization of the United Nations (FAO) Via delle Terme di Caracalla, 00100 Rome, Italy (Telephone Number in U.S. (202) 653-2400); *The State of Food and Agriculture.*

Statistical Office of the United Nations, Publishing Service, New York, New York 10017 (800) 253-9646; *Statistical Yearbook.*

DOMINICAN REPUBLIC - DEATH RATE

G.K. Hall and Company, 70 Lincoln Street, Boston, Massachusetts 02111 (617) 423-3990; *The World in Figures.*

Statistical Office of the United Nations, Publishing Service, New York, New York 10017 (800) 253-9646; *Statistical Yearbook,* and *Statistical Yearbook for Latin America and the Caribbean.*

Times Books, 201 East 50th Street, New York, New York 10022 (212) 751-2600; *The Economist Book of Vital World Statistics.*

World Health Organization, Office of Publications, Avenue Appia, CH-1211 Geneva 27, Switzerland (Telephone Number in U.S. (518) 436-9686); *World Health Statistics Annual.*

DOMINICAN REPUBLIC - DEBT

The Economist Intelligence Unit, 111 West 57th Street, New York, New York 10019 (800) 938-4685; *The New Latin America Market Atlas.*

DOMINICAN REPUBLIC - DEFENSE EXPENDITURES

The Economist Intelligence Unit, 111 West 57th Street, New York, New York 10019 (800) 938-4685; *The New Latin America Market Atlas.*

G.K. Hall and Company, 70 Lincoln Street, Boston, Massachusetts 02111 (617) 423-3990; *The World in Figures.*

International Monetary Fund, 700 Nineteenth Street, NW, Washington, D.C. 20431 (202) 623-7000; *Government Finance Statistics Yearbook.*

U.S. Arms Control and Disarmament Agency, 320 Twenty-first Street, NW, Washington, D.C. 20451 (202) 647-8677; *World Military Expenditures and Arms Transfers.*

DOMINICAN REPUBLIC - DEMOGRAPHY

The Economist Intelligence Unit, 111 West 57th Street, New York, New York 10019 (800) 938-4685; *The World Market Atlas.*

Facts on File, 460 Park Avenue South, New York, New York 10016 (800) 443-8323; *The New Book of World Rankings.*

Federal Statistical Office, Gustav - Stresemann - Ring 11, D-6200 Wiesbaden, Germany; *Dominikanische Republik.*

G.K. Hall and Company, 70 Lincoln Street, Boston, Massachusetts 02111 (617) 423-3990; *The World in Figures.*

DOMINICAN REPUBLIC - DEVELOPMENT ASSISTANCE

G.K. Hall and Company, 70 Lincoln Street, Boston, Massachusetts 02111 (617) 423-3990; *The World in Figures.*

Inter-American Development Bank, 1300 New York Avenue, NW, Washington, D.C. 20577 (202) 623-1753; *Economic and Social Progress in Latin America.*

Statistical Office of the United Nations, Publishing Service, New York, New York 10017 (800) 253-9646; *Statistical Yearbook.*

DOMINICAN REPUBLIC - DIAMOND PRODUCTION - See DOMINICAN REPUBLIC - MINING AND MINERAL PRODUCTS

DOMINICAN REPUBLIC - DISCOUNT RATES

Inter-American Development Bank, 1300 New York Avenue, NW, Washington, D.C. 20577 (202) 623-1753; *Economic and Social Progress in Latin America.*

DOMINICAN REPUBLIC - DISEASES

G.K. Hall and Company, 70 Lincoln Street, Boston, Massachusetts 02111 (617) 423-3990; *The World in Figures.*

World Health Organization, Office of Publications, Avenue Appia, CH-1211 Geneva 27, Switzerland (Telephone Number in U.S. (518) 436-9686); *World Health Statistics Annual.*

DOMINICAN REPUBLIC - DIVORCE RATES

Facts on File, 460 Park Avenue South, New York, New York 10016 (800) 443-8323; *The New Book of World Rankings.*

Statistical Office of the United Nations, Publishing Service, New York, New York 10017 (800) 253-9646; *Demographic Yearbook,* and *Statistical Yearbook.*

DOMINICAN REPUBLIC - DOMESTIC PRODUCT

G.K. Hall and Company, 70 Lincoln Street, Boston, Massachusetts 02111 (617) 423-3990; *The World in Figures.*

DOMINICAN REPUBLIC - DUCKS - See DOMINICAN REPUBLIC - LIVESTOCK AND POULTRY

DOMINICAN REPUBLIC - ECONOMY

Euromonitor Publications Limited, 87-88 Turnmill Street, London EC1M 5QU, England; *International Marketing Data and Statistics.*

Facts on File, 460 Park Avenue South, New York, New York 10016 (800) 443-8323; *The New Book of World Rankings.*

Federal Statistical Office, Gustav - Stresemann - Ring 11, D-6200 Wiesbaden, Germany; *Dominikanische Republik.*

G.K. Hall and Company, 70 Lincoln Street, Boston, Massachusetts 02111 (617) 423-3990; *The World in Figures.*

Inter-American Development Bank, 1300 New York Avenue, NW, Washington, D.C. 20577 (202) 623-1753; *Economic and Social Progress in Latin America.*

Organization of American States (OAS), General Secretariat, Washington, D.C. 20006 (202) 458-3533; *Statistical Bulletin of the OAS.*

U.C.L.A. Latin American Center Publications, University of California, Los Angeles, California 90024 (310) 825-6634; *Statistical Abstract of Latin America.*

DOMINICAN REPUBLIC - EDUCATION

The Economist Intelligence Unit, 111 West 57th Street, New York, New York 10019 (800) 938-4685; *The New Latin America Market Atlas,* and *The World Market Atlas.*

Facts on File, 460 Park Avenue South, New York, New York 10016 (800) 443-8323; *The New Book of World Rankings.*

Federal Statistical Office, Gustav - Stresemann - Ring 11, D-6200 Wiesbaden, Germany; *Dominikanische Republik.*

Gale Research Incorporated, 835 Penobscot Building, Detroit, Michigan 48226 (800) 877-4253; *International Historical Statistics The Americas and Australasia.*

G.K. Hall and Company, 70 Lincoln Street, Boston, Massachusetts 02111 (617) 423-3990; *The World in Figures.*

International Monetary Fund, 700 Nineteenth Street, NW, Washington, D.C. 20431 (202) 623-7000; *Government Finance Statistics Yearbook.*

Statistical Office of the United Nations, Publishing Service, New York, New York 10017 (800) 253-9646; *Statistical Yearbook for Latin America and the Caribbean.*

Times Books, 201 East 50th Street, New York, New York 10022 (212) 751-2600; *The Economist Book of Vital World Statistics.*

U.C.L.A. Latin American Center Publications, University of California, Los Angeles, California 90024 (310) 825-6634; *Statistical Abstract of Latin America.*

United Nations Educational, Scientific and Cultural Organization (UNESCO), 7 Place de Fontenoy, F-75700 Paris, France (Telephone Number in U.S. (212) 963-5981; *Statistical Yearbook.*

The World Bank, 1818 H Street, NW, Washington, D.C. 20433 (202) 477-1234; *World Tables.*

DOMINICAN REPUBLIC - EGG PRODUCTION - See DOMINICAN REPUBLIC - DAIRY PRODUCTS

DOMINICAN REPUBLIC - ELECTRICITY

The Economist Intelligence Unit, 111 West 57th Street, New York, New York 10019 (800) 938-4685; *The New Latin America Market Atlas.*

Facts on File, 460 Park Avenue South, New York, New York 10016 (800) 443-8323; *The New Book of World Rankings.*

Inter-American Development Bank, 1300 New York Avenue, NW, Washington, D.C. 20577 (202) 623-1753; *Economic and Social Progress in Latin America.*

Statistical Office of the United Nations, Publishing Service, New York, New York 10017 (800) 253-9646; *Statistical Yearbook.*

Times Books, 201 East 50th Street, New York, New York 10022 (212) 751-2600; *The Economist Book of Vital World Statistics.*

DOMINICAN REPUBLIC - EMPLOYMENT

Euromonitor Publications Limited, 87-88 Turnmill Street, London EC1M 5QU, England; *International Marketing Data and Statistics.*

Facts on File, 460 Park Avenue South, New York, New York 10016 (800) 443-8323; *The New Book of World Rankings.*

Federal Statistical Office, Gustav - Stresemann - Ring 11, D-6200 Wiesbaden, Germany; *Dominikanische Republik.*

International Labour Office, I.L.O. Publications, CH-1211, Geneva 22, Switzerland; *Yearbook of Labour Statistics.*

Statistical Office of the United Nations, Publishing Service, New York, New York 10017 (800) 253-9646; *Statistical Yearbook,* and *Statistical Yearbook for Latin America and the Caribbean.*

U.C.L.A. Latin American Center Publications, University of California, Los Angeles, California 90024 (310) 825-6634; *Statistical Abstract of Latin America.*

DOMINICAN REPUBLIC - ENERGY

The Economist Intelligence Unit, 111 West 57th Street, New York, New York 10019 (800) 938-4685; *The New Latin America Market Atlas.*

Facts on File, 460 Park Avenue South, New York, New York 10016 (800) 443-8323; *The New Book of World Rankings.*

Food and Agricultural Organization of the United Nations (FAO) Via delle Terme di Caracalla, 00100 Rome, Italy (Telephone Number in U.S. (202) 653-2400); *The State of Food and Agriculture.*

G.K. Hall and Company, 70 Lincoln Street, Boston, Massachusetts 02111 (617) 423-3990; *The World in Figures.*

Statistical Office of the United Nations, Publishing Service, New York, New York 10017 (800) 253-9646; *Energy Statistics Yearbook, Statistical Yearbook,* and *Statistical Yearbook for Latin America and the Caribbean.*

Times Books, 201 East 50th Street, New York, New York 10022 (212) 751-2600; *The Economist Book of Vital World Statistics.*

U.C.L.A. Latin American Center Publications, University of California, Los Angeles, California 90024 (310) 825-6634; *Statistical Abstract of Latin America.*

DOMINICAN REPUBLIC - EXCHANGE RATES

Euromonitor Publications Limited, 87-88 Turnmill Street, London EC1M 5QU, England; *International Marketing Data and Statistics.*

Inter-American Development Bank, 1300 New York Avenue, NW, Washington, D.C. 20577 (202) 623-1753; *Economic and Social Progress in Latin America.*

International Civil Aviation Organization, 1000 Sherbrooke Street West, Suite 400, Montreal, Quebec, Canada H3A 2R2 (514) 285-8219; *Civil Aviation Statistics of the World.*

International Monetary Fund, 700 Nineteenth Street, NW, Washington, D.C. 20431 (202) 623-7000; *International Financial Statistics.*

Organization of American States (OAS), General Secretariat, Washington, D.C. 20006 (202) 458-3533; *Statistical Bulletin of the OAS.*

Statistical Office of the United Nations, Publishing Service, New York, New York 10017 (800) 253-9646; *Statistical Yearbook.*

U.C.L.A. Latin American Center Publications, University of California, Los Angeles, California 90024 (310) 825-6634; *Statistical Abstract of Latin America.*

DOMINICAN REPUBLIC - EXCISE TAXES - See DOMINICAN REPUBLIC - TAXATION

DOMINICAN REPUBLIC - EXPORTS

The Economist Intelligence Unit, 111 West 57th Street, New York, New York 10019 (800) 938-4685; *The New Latin America Market Atlas,* and *The World Market Atlas.*

Euromonitor Publications Limited, 87-88 Turnmill Street, London EC1M 5QU, England; *International Marketing Data and Statistics.*

Food and Agricultural Organization of the United Nations (FAO) Via delle Terme di Caracalla, 00100 Rome, Italy (Telephone Number in U.S. (202) 653-2400); *The State of Food and Agriculture.*

G.K. Hall and Company, 70 Lincoln Street, Boston, Massachusetts 02111 (617) 423-3990; *The World in Figures.*

Inter-American Development Bank, 1300 New York Avenue, NW, Washington, D.C. 20577 (202) 623-1753; *Economic and Social Progress in Latin America.*

International Monetary Fund, 700 Nineteenth Street, NW, Washington, D.C. 20431 (202) 623-7000; *Direction of Trade Statistics,* and *International Financial Statistics.*

Organization of American States (OAS), General Secretariat, Washington, D.C. 20006 (202) 458-3533; *Statistical Bulletin of the OAS.*

Statistical Office of the United Nations, Publishing Service, New York, New York 10017 (800) 253-9646; *Statistical Yearbook for Latin America and the Caribbean*, and *Trade in Manufactures of Developing Countries*.

Times Books, 201 East 50th Street, New York, New York 10022 (212) 751-2600; *The Economist Book of Vital World Statistics*.

The World Bank, 1818 H Street, NW, Washington, D.C. 20433 (202) 477-1234; *World Tables*.

DOMINICAN REPUBLIC - EXTERNAL FINANCING

Inter-American Development Bank, 1300 New York Avenue, NW, Washington, D.C. 20577 (202) 623-1753; *Economic and Social Progress in Latin America*.

Statistical Office of the United Nations, Publishing Service, New York, New York 10017 (800) 253-9646; *Statistical Yearbook for Latin America and the Caribbean*.

DOMINICAN REPUBLIC - EXTERNAL INDEBTEDNESS

Inter-American Development Bank, 1300 New York Avenue, NW, Washington, D.C. 20577 (202) 623-1753; *Economic and Social Progress in Latin America*.

Statistical Office of the United Nations, Publishing Service, New York, New York 10017 (800) 253-9646; *Statistical Yearbook for Latin America and the Caribbean*.

The World Bank, 1818 H Street, NW, Washington, D.C. 20433 (202) 477-1234; *World Tables*.

DOMINICAN REPUBLIC - EXTERNAL TRADE

Food and Agricultural Organization of the United Nations (FAO) Via delle Terme di Caracalla, 00100 Rome, Italy (Telephone Number in U.S. (202) 653-2400); *The State of Food and Agriculture*, and *Trade Yearbook*.

Gale Research Incorporated, 835 Penobscot Building, Detroit, Michigan 48226 (800) 877-4253; *International Historical Statistics The Americas and Australasia*.

G.K. Hall and Company, 70 Lincoln Street, Boston, Massachusetts 02111 (617) 423-3990; *The World in Figures*.

Inter-American Development Bank, 1300 New York Avenue, NW, Washington, D.C. 20577 (202) 623-1753; *Economic and Social Progress in Latin America*.

Statistical Office of the United Nations, Publishing Service, New York, New York 10017 (800) 253-9646; *Statistical Yearbook*, and *Statistical Yearbook for Latin America and the Caribbean*.

DOMINICAN REPUBLIC - FABRIC PRODUCTION - See DOMINICAN REPUBLIC - TEXTILE INDUSTRY

DOMINICAN REPUBLIC - FAMILY PLANNING

U.C.L.A. Latin American Center Publications, University of California, Los Angeles, California 90024 (310) 825-6634; *Statistical Abstract of Latin America*.

DOMINICAN REPUBLIC - FARM CROPS - See DOMINICAN REPUBLIC - CROPS

DOMINICAN REPUBLIC - FEMALE WORKING POPULATION - See DOMINICAN REPUBLIC - EMPLOYMENT

DOMINICAN REPUBLIC - FERTILITY RATES

Facts on File, 460 Park Avenue South, New York, New York 10016 (800) 443-8323; *The New Book of World Rankings*.

Times Books, 201 East 50th Street, New York, New York 10022 (212) 751-2600; *The Economist Book of Vital World Statistics*.

The World Bank, 1818 H Street, NW, Washington, D.C. 20433 (202) 477-1234; *World Tables*.

DOMINICAN REPUBLIC - FERTILIZER

The Economist Intelligence Unit, 111 West 57th Street, New York, New York 10019 (800) 938-4685; *The New Latin America Market Atlas*.

Food and Agricultural Organization of the United Nations (FAO), Via delle Terme di Caracalla, 00100 Rome, Italy (Telephone Number in U.S. (202) 653-2400); *Fertilizer Yearbook*, and *The State of Food and Agriculture*.

Statistical Office of the United Nations, Publishing Service, New York, New York 10017 (800) 253-9646; *Statistical Yearbook*.

DOMINICAN REPUBLIC - FETAL MORTALITY

Statistical Office of the United Nations, Publishing Service, New York, New York 10017 (800) 253-9646; *Demographic Yearbook*.

World Health Organization, Office of Publications, Avenue Appia, CH-1211 Geneva 27, Switzerland (Telephone Number in U.S. (518) 436-9686); *World Health Statistics Annual*.

DOMINICAN REPUBLIC - FINANCE

Facts on File, 460 Park Avenue South, New York, New York 10016 (800) 443-8323; *The New Book of World Rankings*.

Federal Statistical Office, Gustav - Stresemann - Ring 11, D-6200 Wiesbaden, Germany; *Dominikanische Republik*.

Gale Research Incorporated, 835 Penobscot Building, Detroit, Michigan 48226 (800) 877-4253; *International Historical Statistics The Americas and Australasia*.

G.K. Hall and Company, 70 Lincoln Street, Boston, Massachusetts 02111 (617) 423-3990; *The World in Figures*.

Inter-American Development Bank, 1300 New York Avenue, NW, Washington, D.C. 20577 (202) 623-1753; *Economic and Social Progress in Latin America*.

International Monetary Fund, 700 Nineteenth Street, NW, Washington, D.C. 20431 (202) 623-7000; *International Financial Statistics*.

Organization of American States (OAS), General Secretariat, Washington, D.C. 20006 (202) 458-3533; *Statistical Bulletin of the OAS*.

U.C.L.A. Latin American Center Publications, University of California, Los Angeles, California 90024 (310) 825-6634; *Statistical Abstract of Latin America*.

DOMINICAN REPUBLIC - FISHERIES

Facts on File, 460 Park Avenue South, New York, New York 10016 (800) 443-8323; *The New Book of World Rankings.*

Federal Statistical Office, Gustav - Stresemann - Ring 11, D-6200 Wiesbaden, Germany; *Dominikanische Republik.*

Food and Agricultural Organization of the United Nations (FAO) Via delle Terme di Caracalla, 00100 Rome, Italy (Telephone Number in U.S. (202) 653-2400); *The State of Food and Agriculture,* and *Yearbook of Fishery Statistics.*

Inter-American Development Bank, 1300 New York Avenue, NW, Washington, D.C. 20577 (202) 623-1753; *Economic and Social Progress in Latin America.*

Statistical Office of the United Nations, Publishing Service, New York, New York 10017 (800) 253-9646; *Statistical Yearbook.*

U.C.L.A. Latin American Center Publications, University of California, Los Angeles, California 90024 (310) 825-6634; *Statistical Abstract of Latin America.*

DOMINICAN REPUBLIC - FLOUR PRODUCTION

Statistical Office of the United Nations, Publishing Service, New York, New York 10017 (800) 253-9646; *Statistical Yearbook.*

DOMINICAN REPUBLIC - FOOD

Food and Agricultural Organization of the United Nations (FAO) Via delle Terme di Caracalla, 00100 Rome, Italy (Telephone Number in U.S. (202) 653-2400); *Production Yearbook,* and *The State of Food and Agriculture.*

G.K. Hall and Company, 70 Lincoln Street, Boston, Massachusetts 02111 (617) 423-3990; *The World in Figures.*

DOMINICAN REPUBLIC - FOREIGN AID

G.K. Hall and Company, 70 Lincoln Street, Boston, Massachusetts 02111 (617) 423-3990; *The World in Figures.*

Inter-American Development Bank, 1300 New York Avenue, NW, Washington, D.C. 20577 (202) 623-1753; *Economic and Social Progress in Latin America.*

DOMINICAN REPUBLIC - FOREIGN DEBT

The Economist Intelligence Unit, 111 West 57th Street, New York, New York 10019 (800) 938-4685; *The New Latin America Market Atlas.*

Inter-American Development Bank, 1300 New York Avenue, NW, Washington, D.C. 20577 (202) 623-1753; *Economic and Social Progress in Latin America.*

DOMINICAN REPUBLIC - FOREIGN FINANCE

Inter-American Development Bank, 1300 New York Avenue, NW, Washington, D.C. 20577 (202) 623-1753; *Economic and Social Progress in Latin America.*

DOMINICAN REPUBLIC - FOREIGN INDEBTEDNESS

Inter-American Development Bank, 1300 New York Avenue, NW, Washington, D.C. 20577 (202) 623-1753; *Economic and Social Progress in Latin America.*

DOMINICAN REPUBLIC - FOREIGN INVESTMENTS

The Economist Intelligence Unit, 111 West 57th Street, New York, New York 10019 (800) 938-4685; *The New Latin America Market Atlas.*

DOMINICAN REPUBLIC - FOREIGN TRADE

The Economist Intelligence Unit, 111 West 57th Street, New York, New York 10019 (800) 938-4685; *The New Latin America Market Atlas.*

Euromonitor Publications Limited, 87-88 Turnmill Street, London EC1M 5QU, England; *International Marketing Data and Statistics.*

Facts on File, 460 Park Avenue South, New York, New York 10016 (800) 443-8323; *The New Book of World Rankings.*

Federal Statistical Office, Gustav - Stresemann - Ring 11, D-6200 Wiesbaden, Germany; *Dominikanische Republik.*

Food and Agricultural Organization of the United Nations (FAO) Via delle Terme di Caracalla, 00100 Rome, Italy (Telephone Number in U.S. (202) 653-2400); *The State of Food and Agriculture,*

G.K. Hall and Company, 70 Lincoln Street, Boston, Massachusetts 02111 (617) 423-3990; *The World in Figures.*

Inter-American Development Bank, 1300 New York Avenue, NW, Washington, D.C. 20577 (202) 623-1753; *Economic and Social Progress in Latin America.*

International Monetary Fund, 700 Nineteenth Street, NW, Washington, D.C. 20431 (202) 623-7000; *International Financial Statistics.*

Organisation for Economic Co-operation and Development (OECD), 2 rue Andre-Pascal, 75 Paris 16, France (Telephone Number in U.S. (202) 785-6323); *Trade by Commodities.*

Statistical Office of the United Nations, Publishing Service, New York, New York 10017 (800) 253-9646; *International Trade Statistics Yearbook,* and *Statistical Yearbook.*

U.C.L.A. Latin American Center Publications, University of California, Los Angeles, California 90024 (310) 825-6634; *Statistical Abstract of Latin America.*

The World Bank, 1818 H Street, NW, Washington, D.C. 20433 (202) 477-1234; *World Tables.*

DOMINICAN REPUBLIC - FORESTRY AND FOREST PRODUCTS

The Economist Intelligence Unit, 111 West 57th Street, New York, New York 10019 (800) 938-4685; *The New Latin America Market Atlas.*

Facts on File, 460 Park Avenue South, New York, New York 10016 (800) 443-8323; *The New Book of World Rankings.*

Federal Statistical Office, Gustav - Stresemann - Ring 11, D-6200 Wiesbaden, Germany; *Dominikanische Republik.*

Food and Agricultural Organization of the United Nations (FAO) Via delle Terme di Caracalla, 00100 Rome, Italy (Telephone Number in U.S. (202) 653-2400); *The State of Food and Agriculture,* and *Yearbook of Forest Products.*

G.K. Hall and Company, 70 Lincoln Street, Boston, Massachusetts 02111 (617) 423-3990; *The World in Figures.*

Inter-American Development Bank, 1300 New York Avenue, NW, Washington, D.C. 20577 (202) 623-1753; *Economic and Social Progress in Latin America.*

Statistical Office of the United Nations, Publishing Service, New York, New York 10017 (800) 253-9646; *Statistical Yearbook.*

U.C.L.A. Latin American Center Publications, University of California, Los Angeles, California 90024 (310) 825-6634; *Statistical Abstract of Latin America.*

United Nations Educational, Scientific and Cultural Organization (UNESCO), 7 Place de Fontenoy, F-75700 Paris, France (Telephone Number in U.S. (212) 963-5981; *Statistical Yearbook.*

DOMINICAN REPUBLIC - GAS PRODUCTION - See DOMINICAN REPUBLIC - MINING AND MINERAL PRODUCTS

DOMINICAN REPUBLIC - GENERAL INDUSTRIAL STATISTICS

Federal Statistical Office, Gustav - Stresemann - Ring 11, D-6200 Wiesbaden, Germany; *Dominikanische Republik.*

Statistical Office of the United Nations, Publishing Service, New York, New York 10017 (800) 253-9646; *Industrial Statistics Yearbook.*

DOMINICAN REPUBLIC - GENERAL MORTALITY

Statistical Office of the United Nations, Publishing Service, New York, New York 10017 (800) 253-9646; *Demographic Yearbook.*

World Health Organization, Office of Publications, Avenue Appia, CH-1211 Geneva 27, Switzerland (Telephone Number in U.S. (518) 436-9686); *World Health Statistics Annual.*

DOMINICAN REPUBLIC - GEOGRAPHIC DATA

Facts on File, 460 Park Avenue South, New York, New York 10016 (800) 443-8323; *The New Book of World Rankings.*

Federal Statistical Office, Gustav - Stresemann - Ring 11, D-6200 Wiesbaden, Germany; *Dominikanische Republik.*

U.C.L.A. Latin American Center Publications, University of California, Los Angeles, California 90024 (310) 825-6634; *Statistical Abstract of Latin America.*

DOMINICAN REPUBLIC - GOATS - See DOMINICAN REPUBLIC - LIVESTOCK AND POULTRY

DOMINICAN REPUBLIC - GOLD HOLDINGS

International Monetary Fund, 700 Nineteenth Street, NW, Washington, D.C. 20431 (202) 623-7000; *International Financial Statistics.*

Statistical Office of the United Nations, Publishing Service, New York, New York 10017 (800) 253-9646; *Statistical Yearbook.*

The World Bank, 1818 H Street, NW, Washington, D.C. 20433 (202) 477-1234; *World Tables.*

DOMINICAN REPUBLIC - GOLD PRODUCTION AND CONSUMPTION - See DOMINICAN REPUBLIC - MINING AND MINERAL PRODUCTS

DOMINICAN REPUBLIC - GOLD RESERVES

The Economist Intelligence Unit, 111 West 57th Street, New York, New York 10019 (800) 938-4685; *The New Latin America Market Atlas.*

DOMINICAN REPUBLIC - GOVERNMENT

G.K. Hall and Company, 70 Lincoln Street, Boston, Massachusetts 02111 (617) 423-3990; *The World in Figures.*

Inter-American Development Bank, 1300 New York Avenue, NW, Washington, D.C. 20577 (202) 623-1753; *Economic and Social Progress in Latin America.*

DOMINICAN REPUBLIC - GOVERNMENT BONDS - See DOMINICAN REPUBLIC - BONDS

DOMINICAN REPUBLIC - GOVERNMENT CONSUMPTION

Inter-American Development Bank, 1300 New York Avenue, NW, Washington, D.C. 20577 (202) 623-1753; *Economic and Social Progress in Latin America.*

DOMINICAN REPUBLIC - GOVERNMENT EXPENDITURES

Inter-American Development Bank, 1300 New York Avenue, NW, Washington, D.C. 20577 (202) 623-1753; *Economic and Social Progress in Latin America.*

International Monetary Fund, 700 Nineteenth Street, NW, Washington, D.C. 20431 (202) 623-7000; *Government Finance Statistics Yearbook.*

Times Books, 201 East 50th Street, New York, New York 10022 (212) 751-2600; *The Economist Book of Vital World Statistics.*

The World Bank, 1818 H Street, NW, Washington, D.C. 20433 (202) 477-1234; *World Tables.*

DOMINICAN REPUBLIC - GOVERNMENT FINANCES

Inter-American Development Bank, 1300 New York Avenue, NW, Washington, D.C. 20577 (202) 623-1753; *Economic and Social Progress in Latin America.*

International Monetary Fund, 700 Nineteenth Street, NW, Washington, D.C. 20431 (202) 623-7000; *International Financial Statistics.*

Statistical Office of the United Nations, Publishing Service, New York, New York 10017 (800) 253-9646; *Statistical Yearbook.*

DOMINICAN REPUBLIC - GOVERNMENT REVENUES

Inter-American Development Bank, 1300 New York Avenue, NW, Washington, D.C. 20577 (202) 623-1753; *Economic and Social Progress in Latin America.*

International Monetary Fund, 700 Nineteenth Street, NW, Washington, D.C. 20431 (202) 623-7000; *Government Finance Statistics Yearbook.*

Times Books, 201 East 50th Street, New York, New York 10022 (212) 751-2600; *The Economist Book of Vital World Statistics.*

U.C.L.A. Latin American Center Publications, University of California, Los Angeles, California 90024 (310) 825-6634; *Statistical Abstract of Latin America.*

The World Bank, 1818 H Street, NW, Washington, D.C. 20433 (202) 477-1234; *World Tables.*

DOMINICAN REPUBLIC - GRAIN PRODUCTION - See DOMINICAN REPUBLIC - CROPS

DOMINICAN REPUBLIC - GRANTS

International Monetary Fund, 700 Nineteenth Street, NW, Washington, D.C. 20431 (202) 623-7000; *Government Finance Statistics Yearbook.*

DOMINICAN REPUBLIC - GREEN PEPPER AND CHILIE PRODUCTION - See DOMINICAN REPUBLIC - CROPS

DOMINICAN REPUBLIC - GROSS DOMESTIC PRODUCT

The Economist Intelligence Unit, 111 West 57th Street, New York, New York 10019 (800) 938-4685; *The New Latin America Market Atlas,* and *The World Market Atlas.*

Euromonitor Publications Limited, 87-88 Turnmill Street, London EC1M 5QU, England; *International Marketing Data and Statistics.*

Facts on File, 460 Park Avenue South, New York, New York 10016 (212) 340-0600; *The New Book of World Rankings.*

G.K. Hall and Company, 70 Lincoln Street, Boston, Massachusetts 02111 (617) 423-3990; *The World in Figures.*

Inter-American Development Bank, 1300 New York Avenue, NW, Washington, D.C. 20577 (202) 623-1753; *Economic and Social Progress in Latin America.*

Organization of American States (OAS), General Secretariat, Washington, D.C. 20006 (202) 458-3533; *Statistical Bulletin of the OAS.*

Statistical Office of the United Nations, Publishing Service, New York, New York 10017 (800) 253-9646; *Statistical Yearbook,* and *Statistical Yearbook for Latin America and the Caribbean.*

Times Books, 201 East 50th Street, New York, New York 10022 (212) 751-2600; *The Economist Book of Vital World Statistics.*

U.C.L.A. Latin American Center Publications, University of California, Los Angeles, California 90024 (310) 825-6634; *Statistical Abstract of Latin America.*

The World Bank, 1818 H Street, NW, Washington, D.C. 20433 (202) 477-1234; *World Tables.*

DOMINICAN REPUBLIC - GROSS NATIONAL PRODUCT

Euromonitor Publications Limited, 87-88 Turnmill Street, London EC1M 5QU, England; *International Marketing Data and Statistics.*

Inter-American Development Bank, 1300 New York Avenue, NW, Washington, D.C. 20577 (202) 623-1753; *Economic and Social Progress in Latin America.*

U.S. Arms Control and Disarmament Agency, 320 Twenty-first Street, NW, Washington, D.C. 20451 (202) 647-8677; *World Military Expenditures and Arms Transfers.*

The World Bank, 1818 H Street, NW, Washington, D.C. 20433 (202) 477-1234; *World Tables.*

DOMINICAN REPUBLIC - GROUNDNUTS PRODUCTION - See DOMINICAN REPUBLIC - CROPS

DOMINICAN REPUBLIC - HEALTH

The Economist Intelligence Unit, 111 West 57th Street, New York, New York 10019 (800) 938-4685; *The New Latin America Market Atlas.*

Facts on File, 460 Park Avenue South, New York, New York 10016 (800) 443-8323; *The New Book of World Rankings.*

Federal Statistical Office, Gustav - Stresemann - Ring 11, D-6200 Wiesbaden, Germany; *Dominikanische Republik.*

G.K. Hall and Company, 70 Lincoln Street, Boston, Massachusetts 02111 (617) 423-3990; *The World in Figures.*

Statistical Office of the United Nations, Publishing Service, New York, New York 10017 (800) 253-9646; *Statistical Yearbook.*

Times Books, 201 East 50th Street, New York, New York 10022 (212) 751-2600; *The Economist Book of Vital World Statistics.*

U.C.L.A. Latin American Center Publications, University of California, Los Angeles, California 90024 (310) 825-6634; *Statistical Abstract of Latin America.*

World Health Organization, Office of Publications, Avenue Appia, CH-1211 Geneva 27, Switzerland (Telephone Number in U.S. (518) 436-9686); *World Health Statistics Annual.*

DOMINICAN REPUBLIC - HEALTH EXPENDITURES

International Monetary Fund, 700 Nineteenth Street, NW, Washington, D.C. 20431 (202) 623-7000; *Government Finance Statistics Yearbook.*

Statistical Office of the United Nations, Publishing Service, New York, New York 10017 (800) 253-9646; *Statistical Yearbook for Latin America and the Caribbean.*

DOMINICAN REPUBLIC - HIDE PRODUCTION

Food and Agricultural Organization of the United Nations (FAO), Via delle Terme di Caracalla, 00100 Rome, Italy (Telephone Number in U.S. (202) 653-2400); *Production Yearbook.*

DOMINICAN REPUBLIC - HIGHWAYS

The Economist Intelligence Unit, 111 West 57th Street, New York, New York 10019 (800) 938-4685; *The New Latin America Market Atlas.*

G.K. Hall and Company, 70 Lincoln Street, Boston, Massachusetts 02111 (617) 423-3990; *The World in Figures.*

International Road Federation, 525 School Street, SW, Washington, D.C. 20024 (202) 554-2106; *World Road Statistics.*

DOMINICAN REPUBLIC - HORSES - See DOMINICAN REPUBLIC - LIVESTOCK AND POULTRY

DOMINICAN REPUBLIC - HOURS OF WORK - See DOMINICAN REPUBLIC - EMPLOYMENT

DOMINICAN REPUBLIC - HOUSING AND HOUSING UNITS

Facts on File, 460 Park Avenue South, New York, New York 10016 (800) 443-8323; *The New Book of World Rankings.*

Statistical Office of the United Nations, Publishing Service, New York, New York 10017 (800) 253-9646; *Statistical Yearbook for Latin America and the Caribbean.*

U.C.L.A. Latin American Center Publications, University of California, Los Angeles, California 90024 (310) 825-6634; *Statistical Abstract of Latin America.*

DOMINICAN REPUBLIC - HOUSING EXPENDITURES

International Monetary Fund, 700 Nineteenth Street, NW, Washington, D.C. 20431 (202) 623-7000; *Government Finance Statistics Yearbook.*

DOMINICAN REPUBLIC - ILLITERATE POPULATION

The Economist Intelligence Unit, 111 West 57th Street, New York, New York 10019 (800) 938-4685; *The New Latin America Market Atlas,* and *The World Market Atlas.*

G.K. Hall and Company, 70 Lincoln Street, Boston, Massachusetts 02111 (617) 423-3990; *The World in Figures.*

Statistical Office of the United Nations, Publishing Service, New York, New York 10017 (800) 253-9646; *Statistical Yearbook for Latin America and the Caribbean.*

United Nations Educational, Scientific and Cultural Organization (UNESCO), 7 Place de Fontenoy, F-75700 Paris, France (Telephone Number in U.S. (212) 963-5981; *Statistical Yearbook.*

DOMINICAN REPUBLIC - IMMIGRATION

U.C.L.A. Latin American Center Publications, University of California, Los Angeles, California 90024 (310) 825-6634; *Statistical Abstract of Latin America.*

DOMINICAN REPUBLIC - IMPORTS

The Economist Intelligence Unit, 111 West 57th Street, New York, New York 10019 (800) 938-4685; *The New Latin America Market Atlas,* and *The World Market Atlas.*

Euromonitor Publications Limited, 87-88 Turnmill Street, London EC1M 5QU, England; *International Marketing Data and Statistics.*

Food and Agricultural Organization of the United Nations (FAO) Via delle Terme di Caracalla, 00100 Rome, Italy (Telephone Number in U.S. (202) 653-2400); *The State of Food and Agriculture.*

G.K. Hall and Company, 70 Lincoln Street, Boston, Massachusetts 02111 (617) 423-3990; *The World in Figures.*

Inter-American Development Bank, 1300 New York Avenue, NW, Washington, D.C. 20577 (202) 623-1753; *Economic and Social Progress in Latin America.*

International Monetary Fund, 700 Nineteenth Street, NW, Washington, D.C. 20431 (202) 623-7000; *Direction of Trade Statistics, Government Finance Statistics Yearbook,* and *International Financial Statistics.*

Organization of American States (OAS), General Secretariat, Washington, D.C. 20006 (202) 458-3533; *Statistical Bulletin of the OAS.*

Statistical Office of the United Nations, Publishing Service, New York, New York 10017 (800) 253-9646; *Statistical Yearbook for Latin America and the Caribbean.*

Times Books, 201 East 50th Street, New York, New York 10022 (212) 751-2600; *The Economist Book of Vital World Statistics.*

The World Bank, 1818 H Street, NW, Washington, D.C. 20433 (202) 477-1234; *World Tables.*

DOMINICAN REPUBLIC - INCOME DISTRIBUTION

Statistical Office of the United Nations, Publishing Service, New York, New York 10017 (800) 253-9646; *Statistical Yearbook for Latin America and the Caribbean.*

U.C.L.A. Latin American Center Publications, University of California, Los Angeles, California 90024 (310) 825-6634; *Statistical Abstract of Latin America.*

DOMINICAN REPUBLIC - INCOME TAXES - See DOMINICAN REPUBLIC - TAXATION

DOMINICAN REPUBLIC - INDUSTRY

Facts on File, 460 Park Avenue South, New York, New York 10016 (800) 443-8323; *The New Book of World Rankings.*

Federal Statistical Office, Gustav - Stresemann - Ring 11, D-6200 Wiesbaden, Germany; *Dominikanische Republik.*

Euromonitor Publications Limited, 87-88 Turnmill Street, London EC1M 5QU, England; *International Marketing Data and Statistics.*

Facts on File, 460 Park Avenue South, New York, New York 10016 (800) 443-8323; *The New Book of World Rankings.*

Federal Statistical Office, Gustav - Stresemann - Ring 11, D-6200 Wiesbaden, Germany; *Dominikanische Republik.*

Gale Research Incorporated, 835 Penobscot Building, Detroit, Michigan 48226 (800) 877-4253; *International Historical Statistics The Americas and Australasia.*

G.K. Hall and Company, 70 Lincoln Street, Boston, Massachusetts 02111 (617) 423-3990; *The World in Figures.*

International Labour Office, I.L.O. Publications, CH-1211, Geneva 22, Switzerland; *Yearbook of Labour Statistics.*

Statistical Office of the United Nations, Publishing Service, New York, New York 10017 (800) 253-9646; *Statistical Yearbook.*

Times Books, 201 East 50th Street, New York, New York 10022 (212) 751-2600; *The Economist Book of Vital World Statistics.*

U.C.L.A. Latin American Center Publications, University of California, Los Angeles, California 90024 (310) 825-6634; *Statistical Abstract of Latin America.*

The World Bank, 1818 H Street, NW, Washington, D.C. 20433 (202) 477-1234; *World Tables.*

DOMINICAN REPUBLIC - INFANT AND MATERNAL MORTALITY

The Economist Intelligence Unit, 111 West 57th Street, New York, New York 10019 (800) 938-4685; *The New Latin America Market*

Atlas.

Statistical Office of the United Nations, Publishing Service, New York, New York 10017 (800) 253-9646; *Demographic Yearbook*, and *Statistical Yearbook.*

Times Books, 201 East 50th Street, New York, New York 10022 (212) 751-2600; *The Economist Book of Vital World Statistics.*

The World Bank, 1818 H Street, NW, Washington, D.C. 20433 (202) 477-1234; *World Tables.*

World Health Organization, Office of Publications, Avenue Appia, CH-1211 Geneva 27, Switzerland (Telephone Number in U.S. (518) 436-9686); *World Health Statistics Annual.*

DOMINICAN REPUBLIC - INTEREST RATES

Inter-American Development Bank, 1300 New York Avenue, NW, Washington, D.C. 20577 (202) 623-1753; *Economic and Social Progress in Latin America.*

DOMINICAN REPUBLIC - INTERNAL TRADE

Statistical Office of the United Nations, Publishing Service, New York, New York 10017 (800) 253-9646; *Statistical Yearbook.*

DOMINICAN REPUBLIC - INTERNATIONAL FINANCE

Inter-American Development Bank, 1300 New York Avenue, NW, Washington, D.C. 20577 (202) 623-1753; *Economic and Social Progress in Latin America.*

U.C.L.A. Latin American Center Publications, University of California, Los Angeles, California 90024 (310) 825-6634; *Statistical Abstract of Latin America.*

DOMINICAN REPUBLIC - INTERNATIONAL LIQUIDITY

Inter-American Development Bank, 1300 New York Avenue, NW, Washington, D.C. 20577 (202) 623-1753; *Economic and Social Progress in Latin America.*

International Monetary Fund, 700 Nineteenth Street, NW, Washington, D.C. 20431 (202) 623-7000; *International Financial Statistics.*

DOMINICAN REPUBLIC - INTERNATIONAL RESERVES

Organization of American States (OAS), General Secretariat, Washington, D.C. 20006 (202) 458-3533; *Statistical Bulletin of the OAS.*

DOMINICAN REPUBLIC - INTERNATIONAL RESERVES EXCLUDING GOLD

Inter-American Development Bank, 1300 New York Avenue, NW, Washington, D.C. 20577 (202) 623-1753; *Economic and Social Progress in Latin America.*

The World Bank, 1818 H Street, NW, Washington, D.C. 20433 (202) 477-1234; *World Tables.*

DOMINICAN REPUBLIC - INTERNATIONAL STATISTICS

Inter-American Development Bank, 1300 New York Avenue, NW, Washington, D.C. 20577 (202) 623-1753; *Economic and Social Progress in Latin America.*

U.C.L.A. Latin American Center Publications, University of California, Los Angeles, California 90024 (310) 825-6634; *Statistical Abstract of Latin America.*

DOMINICAN REPUBLIC - INVESTMENT

Inter-American Development Bank, 1300 New York Avenue, NW, Washington, D.C. 20577 (202) 623-1753; *Economic and Social Progress in Latin America.*

Statistical Office of the United Nations, Publishing Service, New York, New York 10017 (800) 253-9646; *Statistical Yearbook for Latin America and the Caribbean.*

DOMINICAN REPUBLIC - IRON ORE PRODUCTION AND CONSUMPTION - See DOMINICAN REPUBLIC - MINING AND MINERAL PRODUCTS

DOMINICAN REPUBLIC - IRRIGATION

Euromonitor Publications Limited, 87-88 Turnmill Street, London EC1M 5QU, England; *International Marketing Data and Statistics.*

Inter-American Development Bank, 1300 New York Avenue, NW, Washington, D.C. 20577 (202) 623-1753; *Economic and Social Progress in Latin America.*

DOMINICAN REPUBLIC - LABOR FORCE

The Economist Intelligence Unit, 111 West 57th Street, New York, New York 10019 (800) 938-4685; *The New Latin America Market Atlas.*

Euromonitor Publications Limited, 87-88 Turnmill Street, London EC1M 5QU, England; *International Marketing Data and Statistics.*

Facts on File, 460 Park Avenue South, New York, New York 10016 (800) 443-8323; *The New Book of World Rankings.*

Food and Agricultural Organization of the United Nations (FAO) Via delle Terme di Caracalla, 00100 Rome, Italy (Telephone Number in U.S. (202) 653-2400); *The State of Food and Agriculture.*

Gale Research Incorporated, 835 Penobscot Building, Detroit, Michigan 48226 (800) 877-4253; *International Historical Statistics The Americas and Australasia.*

G.K. Hall and Company, 70 Lincoln Street, Boston, Massachusetts 02111 (617) 423-3990; *The World in Figures.*

The World Bank, 1818 H Street, NW, Washington, D.C. 20433 (202) 477-1234; *World Tables.*

DOMINICAN REPUBLIC - LABOR PRODUCTIVITY

International Labour Office, I.L.O. Publications, CH-1211, Geneva 22, Switzerland; *Yearbook of Labour Statistics.*

DOMINICAN REPUBLIC - LAND AREA

The Economist Intelligence Unit, 111 West 57th Street, New York, New York 10019 (800) 938-4685; *The New Latin America Market Atlas.*

DOMINICAN REPUBLIC - LAND USE

Euromonitor Publications Limited, 87-88 Turnmill Street, London EC1M 5QU, England; *International Marketing Data and Statistics.*

Food and Agricultural Organization of the United Nations (FAO), Via delle Terme di Caracalla, 00100 Rome, Italy (Telephone Number in U.S. (202) 653-2400); *Production Yearbook.*

G.K. Hall and Company, 70 Lincoln Street, Boston, Massachusetts 02111 (617) 423-3990; *The World in Figures.*

Inter-American Development Bank, 1300 New York Avenue, NW, Washington, D.C. 20577 (202) 623-1753; *Economic and Social Progress in Latin America.*

DOMINICAN REPUBLIC - LIBRARIES

Facts on File, 460 Park Avenue South, New York, New York 10016 (800) 443-8323; *The New Book of World Rankings.*

DOMINICAN REPUBLIC - LIFE EXPECTANCY RATE

The Economist Intelligence Unit, 111 West 57th Street, New York, New York 10019 (800) 938-4685; *The New Latin America Market Atlas.*

DOMINICAN REPUBLIC - LIVESTOCK AND POULTRY

Euromonitor Publications Limited, 87-88 Turnmill Street, London EC1M 5QU, England; *International Marketing Data and Statistics.*

Facts on File, 460 Park Avenue South, New York, New York 10016 (800) 443-8323; *The New Book of World Rankings.*

Food and Agricultural Organization of the United Nations (FAO), Via delle Terme di Caracalla, 00100 Rome, Italy (Telephone Number in U.S. (202) 653-2400); *Production Yearbook,* and *The State of Food and Agriculture.*

G.K. Hall and Company, 70 Lincoln Street, Boston, Massachusetts 02111 (617) 423-3990; *The World in Figures.*

Statistical Office of the United Nations, Publishing Service, New York, New York 10017 (800) 253-9646; *Statistical Yearbook.*

DOMINICAN REPUBLIC - LIVING LEVELS

G.K. Hall and Company, 70 Lincoln Street, Boston, Massachusetts 02111 (617) 423-3990; *The World in Figures.*

Statistical Office of the United Nations, Publishing Service, New York, New York 10017 (800) 253-9646; *Statistical Yearbook for Latin America and the Caribbean.*

Times Books, 201 East 50th Street, New York, New York 10022 (212) 751-2600; *The Economist Book of Vital World Statistics.*

DOMINICAN REPUBLIC - MAIL - NUMBER OF ITEMS

Statistical Office of the United Nations, Publishing Service, New York, New York 10017 (800) 253-9646; *Statistical Yearbook.*

DOMINICAN REPUBLIC - MAIN ECONOMIC INDICATORS - See DOMINICAN REPUBLIC - ECONOMY

DOMINICAN REPUBLIC - MAIN INDICATORS - See DOMINICAN REPUBLIC - ECONOMY

DOMINICAN REPUBLIC - MANUFACTURING

The Economist Intelligence Unit, 111 West 57th Street, New York, New York 10019 (800) 938-4685; *The New Latin America Market Atlas.*

Facts on File, 460 Park Avenue South, New York, New York 10016 (800) 443-8323; *The New Book of World Rankings.*

G.K. Hall and Company, 70 Lincoln Street, Boston, Massachusetts 02111 (617) 423-3990; *The World in Figures.*

Inter-American Development Bank, 1300 New York Avenue, NW, Washington, D.C. 20577 (202) 623-1753; *Economic and Social Progress in Latin America.*

Statistical Office of the United Nations, Publishing Service, New York, New York 10017 (800) 253-9646; *Statistical Yearbook,* and *Statistical Yearbook for Latin America and the Caribbean.*

Times Books, 201 East 50th Street, New York, New York 10022 (212) 751-2600; *The Economist Book of Vital World Statistics.*

The World Bank, 1818 H Street, NW, Washington, D.C. 20433 (202) 477-1234; *World Tables.*

DOMINICAN REPUBLIC - MARRIAGE RATES

Facts on File, 460 Park Avenue South, New York, New York 10016 (800) 443-8323; *The New Book of World Rankings.*

Statistical Office of the United Nations, Publishing Service, New York, New York 10017 (800) 253-9646; *Demographic Yearbook,* and *Statistical Yearbook.*

DOMINICAN REPUBLIC - MEAT PRODUCTION - See DOMINICAN REPUBLIC - LIVESTOCK AND POULTRY

DOMINICAN REPUBLIC - MEDICAL PERSONNEL

U.C.L.A. Latin American Center Publications, University of California, Los Angeles, California 90024 (310) 825-6634; *Statistical Abstract of Latin America.*

DOMINICAN REPUBLIC - MERCHANT SHIPPING

G.K. Hall and Company, 70 Lincoln Street, Boston, Massachusetts 02111 (617) 423-3990; *The World in Figures.*

Statistical Office of the United Nations, Publishing Service, New York, New York 10017 (800) 253-9646; *Statistical Yearbook.*

Times Books, 201 East 50th Street, New York, New York 10022 (212) 751-2600; *The Economist Book of Vital World Statistics.*

U.S. Department of Transportation, Maritime Administration, 400 Seventh Street, SW, Washington, D.C. 20590; *A Statistical Analysis of the World's Merchant Fleets.*

DOMINICAN REPUBLIC - MILITARY

The Economist Intelligence Unit, 111 West 57th Street, New York, New York 10019 (800) 938-4685; *The New Latin America Market Atlas.*

G.K. Hall and Company, 70 Lincoln Street, Boston, Massachusetts 02111 (617) 423-3990; *The World in Figures.*

The International Institute for Strategic Studies, 23 Tavistock Street, London WC2E 7NQ, England; *The Military Balance.*

U.C.L.A. Latin American Center Publications, University of California, Los Angeles, California 90024 (310) 825-6634; *Statistical Abstract of Latin America.*

U.S. Arms Control and Disarmament Agency, 320 Twenty-first Street, NW, Washington, D.C. 20451 (202) 647-8677; *World Military Expenditures and Arms Transfers.*

DOMINICAN REPUBLIC - MILK PRODUCTION - See DOMINICAN REPUBLIC - DAIRY PRODUCTS

DOMINICAN REPUBLIC - MINING AND MINERAL PRODUCTS

The Economist Intelligence Unit, 111 West 57th Street, New York, New York 10019 (800) 938-4685; *The New Latin America Market Atlas.*

Facts on File, 460 Park Avenue South, New York, New York 10016 (800) 443-8323; *The New Book of World Rankings.*

G.K. Hall and Company, 70 Lincoln Street, Boston, Massachusetts 02111 (617) 423-3990; *The World in Figures.*

Inter-American Development Bank, 1300 New York Avenue, NW, Washington, D.C. 20577 (202) 623-1753; *Economic and Social Progress in Latin America.*

International Monetary Fund, 700 Nineteenth Street, NW, Washington, D.C. 20431 (202) 623-7000; *International Financial Statistics.*

Organization of American States (OAS), General Secretariat, Washington, D.C. 20006 (202) 458-3533; *Statistical Bulletin of the OAS.*

Statistical Office of the United Nations, Publishing Service, New York, New York 10017; *Statistical Yearbook,* and *Statistical Yearbook for Latin America and the Caribbean.*

U.C.L.A. Latin American Center Publications, University of California, Los Angeles, California 90024 (310) 825-6634; *Statistical Abstract of Latin America.*

DOMINICAN REPUBLIC - MONEY EXCHANGE RATE

Euromonitor Publications Limited, 87-88 Turnmill Street, London EC1M 5QU, England; *International Marketing Data and Statistics.*

Inter-American Development Bank, 1300 New York Avenue, NW, Washington, D.C. 20577 (202) 623-1753; *Economic and Social Progress in Latin America.*

International Monetary Fund, 700 Nineteenth Street, NW, Washington, D.C. 20431 (202) 623-7000; *International Financial Statistics.*

Statistical Office of the United Nations, Publishing Service, New York, New York 10017 (800) 253-9646; *Statistical Yearbook.*

DOMINICAN REPUBLIC - MONEY RATES - MARKET

Inter-American Development Bank, 1300 New York Avenue, NW, Washington, D.C. 20577 (202) 623-1753; *Economic and Social Progress in Latin America.*

DOMINICAN REPUBLIC - MONEY RESERVES

Euromonitor Publications Limited, 87-88 Turnmill Street, London EC1M 5QU, England; *International Marketing Data and Statistics.*

Inter-American Development Bank, 1300 New York Avenue, NW, Washington, D.C. 20577 (202) 623-1753; *Economic and Social Progress in Latin America.*

DOMINICAN REPUBLIC - MONEY SUPPLY

Euromonitor Publications Limited, 87-88 Turnmill Street, London EC1M 5QU, England; *International Marketing Data and Statistics.*

Federal Statistical Office, Gustav - Stresemann - Ring 11, D-6200 Wiesbaden, Germany; *Dominikanische Republik.*

G.K. Hall and Company, 70 Lincoln Street, Boston, Massachusetts 02111 (617) 423-3990; *The World in Figures.*

Inter-American Development Bank, 1300 New York Avenue, NW, Washington, D.C. 20577 (202) 623-1753; *Economic and Social Progress in Latin America.*

International Monetary Fund, 700 Nineteenth Street, NW, Washington, D.C. 20431 (202) 623-7000; *International Financial Statistics.*

Statistical Office of the United Nations, Publishing Service, New York, New York 10017 (800) 253-9646; *Statistical Yearbook.*

U.C.L.A. Latin American Center Publications, University of California, Los Angeles, California 90024 (310) 825-6634; *Statistical Abstract of Latin America.*

The World Bank, 1818 H Street, NW, Washington, D.C. 20433 (202) 477-1234; *World Tables.*

DOMINICAN REPUBLIC - MOTOR VEHICLE TAXES - See DOMINICAN REPUBLIC - TAXATION

DOMINICAN REPUBLIC - MOTOR VEHICLES IN USE

The Economist Intelligence Unit, 111 West 57th Street, New York, New York 10019 (800) 938-4685; *The New Latin America Market Atlas.*

G.K. Hall and Company, 70 Lincoln Street, Boston, Massachusetts 02111 (617) 423-3990; *The World in Figures.*

International Road Federation, 525 School Street, SW, Washington, D.C. 20024 (202) 554-2106; *World Road Statistics.*

Statistical Office of the United Nations, Publishing Service, New York, New York 10017 (800) 253-9646; *Statistical Yearbook.*

Times Books, 201 East 50th Street, New York, New York 10022 (212) 751-2600; *The Economist Book of Vital World Statistics.*

DOMINICAN REPUBLIC - MULES - See DOMINICAN REPUBLIC - LIVESTOCK AND POULTRY

DOMINICAN REPUBLIC - MUSEUMS

Facts on File, 460 Park Avenue South, New York, New York 10016 (800) 443-8323; *The New Book of World Rankings.*

United Nations Educational, Scientific and Cultural Organization (UNESCO), 7 Place de Fontenoy, F-75700 Paris, France (Telephone Number in U.S. (212) 963-5981; *Statistical Yearbook.*

DOMINICAN REPUBLIC - NATALITY - See DOMINICAN REPUBLIC - BIRTH RATE

DOMINICAN REPUBLIC - NATIONAL ACCOUNTS

Federal Statistical Office, Gustav - Stresemann - Ring 11, D-6200 Wiesbaden, Germany; *Dominikanische Republik.*

Gale Research Incorporated, 835 Penobscot Building, Detroit, Michigan 48226 (800) 877-4253; *International Historical Statistics The Americas and Australasia.*

Inter-American Development Bank, 1300 New York Avenue, NW, Washington, D.C. 20577 (202) 623-1753; *Economic and Social Progress in Latin America.*

International Monetary Fund, 700 Nineteenth Street, NW, Washington, D.C. 20431 (202) 623-7000; *International Financial Statistics.*

Organization of American States (OAS), General Secretariat, Washington, D.C. 20006 (202) 458-3533; *Statistical Bulletin of the OAS.*

Statistical Office of the United Nations, Publishing Service, New York, New York 10017 (800) 253-9646; *National Accounts Statistics,* and *Statistical Yearbook.*

U.C.L.A. Latin American Center Publications, University of California, Los Angeles, California 90024 (310) 825-6634; *Statistical Abstract of Latin America.*

DOMINICAN REPUBLIC - NATIONAL INCOME

Facts on File, 460 Park Avenue South, New York, New York 10016 (800) 443-8323; *The New Book of World Rankings.*

G.K. Hall and Company, 70 Lincoln Street, Boston, Massachusetts 02111 (617) 423-3990; *The World in Figures.*

Inter-American Development Bank, 1300 New York Avenue, NW, Washington, D.C. 20577 (202) 623-1753; *Economic and Social Progress in Latin America.*

Statistical Office of the United Nations, Publishing Service, New York, New York 10017 (800) 253-9646; *Statistical Yearbook.*

DOMINICAN REPUBLIC - NATIONAL PRODUCT

Facts on File, 460 Park Avenue South, New York, New York 10016 (800) 443-8323; *The New Book of World Rankings.*

Statistical Office of the United Nations, Publishing Service, New York, New York 10017 (800) 253-9646; *Statistical Yearbook.*

DOMINICAN REPUBLIC - NATURAL GAS PRODUCTION - See DOMINICAN REPUBLIC - MINING AND MINERAL PRODUCTS

DOMINICAN REPUBLIC - NEWSPAPER PRODUCTION - See DOMINICAN REPUBLIC - FORESTRY AND FOREST PRODUCTs

DOMINICAN REPUBLIC - NEWSPRINT CONSUMPTION - See DOMINICAN REPUBLIC - FORESTRY AND FOREST PRODUCTS

DOMINICAN REPUBLIC - NICKEL ORE PRODUCTION AND CONSUMPTION - See DOMINICAN REPUBLIC - MINING AND MINERAL PRODUCTS

DOMINICAN REPUBLIC - NUTRITION

Statistical Office of the United Nations, Publishing Service, New York, New York 10017 (800) 253-9646; *Statistical Yearbook for Latin America and the Caribbean.*

DOMINICAN REPUBLIC - OCCUPATIONS - See DOMINICAN REPUBLIC - LABOR FORCE

DOMINICAN REPUBLIC - PAPER - See DOMINICAN REPUBLIC - FORESTRY AND FOREST PRODUCTs

DOMINICAN REPUBLIC - PATENTS

Statistical Office of the United Nations, Publishing Service, New York, New York 10017 (800) 253-9646; *Statistical Yearbook.*

DOMINICAN REPUBLIC - PEANUT PRODUCTION - See DOMINICAN REPUBLIC - CROPS

DOMINICAN REPUBLIC - PESTICIDE USE

Food and Agricultural Organization of the United Nations (FAO) Via delle Terme di Caracalla, 00100 Rome, Italy (Telephone Number in U.S. (202) 653-2400); *The State of Food and Agriculture.*

DOMINICAN REPUBLIC - PETROLEUM INDUSTRY

The Economist Intelligence Unit, 111 West 57th Street, New York, New York 10019 (800) 938-4685; *The New Latin America Market Atlas.*

Facts on File, 460 Park Avenue South, New York, New York 10016 (212) 340-0600; *The New Book of World Rankings.*

Food and Agricultural Organization of the United Nations (FAO) Via delle Terme di Caracalla, 00100 Rome, Italy (Telephone Number in U.S. (202) 653-2400); *The State of Food and Agriculture.*

G.K. Hall and Company, 70 Lincoln Street, Boston, Massachusetts 02111 (617) 423-3990; *The World in Figures.*

Inter-American Development Bank, 1300 New York Avenue, NW, Washington, D.C. 20577 (202) 623-1753; *Economic and Social Progress in Latin America.*

Statistical Office of the United Nations, Publishing Service, New York, New York 10017 (800) 253-9646; *Statistical Yearbook.*

DOMINICAN REPUBLIC - PIGS - See DOMINICAN REPUBLIC - LIVESTOCK AND POULTRY

DOMINICAN REPUBLIC - POLITICAL DATA

U.C.L.A. Latin American Center Publications, University of California, Los Angeles, California 90024 (310) 825-6634; *Statistical Abstract of Latin America.*

DOMINICAN REPUBLIC - POPULATION

The Economist Intelligence Unit, 111 West 57th Street, New York, New York 10019 (800) 938-4685; *The New Latin America Market Atlas,* and *The World Market Atlas.*

Euromonitor Publications Limited, 87-88 Turnmill Street, London EC1M 5QU, England; *International Marketing Data and Statistics.*

Facts on File, 460 Park Avenue South, New York, New York 10016 (800) 443-8323; *The New Book of World Rankings.*

Federal Statistical Office, Gustav - Stresemann - Ring 11, D-6200 Wiesbaden, Germany; *Dominikanische Republik.*

Food and Agricultural Organization of the United Nations (FAO), Via delle Terme di Caracalla, 00100 Rome, Italy (Telephone Number in U.S. (202) 653-2400); *Production Yearbook.*

Gale Research Incorporated, 835 Penobscot Building, Detroit, Michigan 48226 (800) 877-4253; *International Historical Statistics The Americas and Australasia.*

G.K. Hall and Company, 70 Lincoln Street, Boston, Massachusetts 02111 (617) 423-3990; *The World in Figures.*

Inter-American Development Bank, 1300 New York Avenue, NW, Washington, D.C. 20577 (202) 623-1753; *Economic and Social Progress in Latin America.*

International Labour Office, I.L.O. Publications, CH-1211, Geneva 22, Switzerland; *Yearbook of Labour Statistics.*

Organization of American States (OAS), General Secretariat, Washington, D.C. 20006 (202) 458-3533; *Statistical Bulletin of the OAS.*

Statistical Office of the United Nations, Publishing Service, New York, New York 10017 (800) 253-9646; *Demographic Yearbook, Statistical Yearbook,* and *Statistical Yearbook for Latin America and the Caribbean.*

Times Books, 201 East 50th Street, New York, New York 10022 (212) 751-2600; *The Economist Book of Vital World Statistics.*

U.C.L.A. Latin American Center Publications, University of California, Los Angeles, California 90024 (310) 825-6634; *Statistical Abstract of Latin America.*

United Nations Educational, Scientific and Cultural Organization (UNESCO), 7 Place de Fontenoy, F-75700 Paris, France (Telephone Number in U.S. (212) 963-5981; *Statistical Yearbook.*

U.S. Arms Control and Disarmament Agency, 320 Twenty-first Street, NW, Washington, D.C. 20451 (202) 647-8677; *World Military Expenditures and Arms Transfers.*

World Health Organization, Office of Publications, Avenue Appia, CH-1211 Geneva 27, Switzerland (Telephone Number in U.S. (518) 436-9686); *World Health Statistics Annual.*

DOMINICAN REPUBLIC - POST OFFICES

Facts on File, 460 Park Avenue South, New York, New York 10016 (800) 443-8323; *The New Book of World Rankings.*

DOMINICAN REPUBLIC - POTATO PRODUCTION - See DOMINICAN REPUBLIC - CROPS

DOMINICAN REPUBLIC - POWER PRODUCTION INDUSTRY

Statistical Office of the United Nations, Publishing Service, New York, New York 10017 (800) 253-9646; *Statistical Yearbook.*

DOMINICAN REPUBLIC - PRICES

Facts on File, 460 Park Avenue South, New York, New York 10016 (800) 443-8323; *The New Book of World Rankings.*

Federal Statistical Office, Gustav - Stresemann - Ring 11, D-6200 Wiesbaden, Germany; *Dominikanische Republik.*

Food and Agricultural Organization of the United Nations (FAO), Via delle Terme di Caracalla, 00100 Rome, Italy (Telephone Number in U.S. (202) 653-2400); *Production Yearbook,* and *The State of Food and Agriculture.*

Gale Research Incorporated, 835 Penobscot Building, Detroit, Michigan 48226 (800) 877-4253; *International Historical Statistics The Americas and Australasia.*

G.K. Hall and Company, 70 Lincoln Street, Boston, Massachusetts 02111 (617) 423-3990; *The World in Figures.*

International Labour Office, I.L.O. Publications, CH-1211, Geneva 22, Switzerland; *Yearbook of Labour Statistics.*

International Monetary Fund, 700 Nineteenth Street, NW, Washington, D.C. 20431 (202) 623-7000; *International Financial Statistics.*

Statistical Office of the United Nations, Publishing Service, New York, New York 10017 (800) 253-9646; *Statistical Yearbook for Latin America and the Caribbean.*

DOMINICAN REPUBLIC - PRINTING AND WRITING PAPER - See DOMINICAN REPUBLIC - FORESTRY AND FOREST PRODUCTS

DOMINICAN REPUBLIC - PRODUCTION

Facts on File, 460 Park Avenue South, New York, New York 10016 (800) 443-8323; *The New Book of World Rankings.*

G.K. Hall and Company, 70 Lincoln Street, Boston, Massachusetts 02111 (617) 423-3990; *The World in Figures.*

DOMINICAN REPUBLIC - PRODUCTIVITY

Euromonitor Publications Limited, 87-88 Turnmill Street, London EC1M 5QU, England; *International Marketing Data and Statistics.*

DOMINICAN REPUBLIC - PROPERTY TAXES - See DOMINICAN REPUBLIC - TAXATION

DOMINICAN REPUBLIC - PUBLIC CONSUMPTION FUND

Inter-American Development Bank, 1300 New York Avenue, NW, Washington, D.C. 20577 (202) 623-1753; *Economic and Social Progress in Latin America.*

DOMINICAN REPUBLIC - PUBLIC EXPENDITURES

Inter-American Development Bank, 1300 New York Avenue, NW, Washington, D.C. 20577 (202) 623-1753; *Economic and Social Progress in Latin America.*

Organization of American States (OAS), General Secretariat, Washington, D.C. 20006 (202) 458-3533; *Statistical Bulletin of the OAS.*

Statistical Office of the United Nations, Publishing Service, New York, New York 10017 (800) 253-9646; *Statistical Yearbook for Latin America and the Caribbean.*

DOMINICAN REPUBLIC - PUBLIC FINANCE

Facts on File, 460 Park Avenue South, New York, New York 10016 (800) 443-8323; *The New Book of World Rankings.*

Federal Statistical Office, Gustav - Stresemann - Ring 11, D-6200 Wiesbaden, Germany; *Dominikanische Republik.*

Inter-American Development Bank, 1300 New York Avenue, NW, Washington, D.C. 20577 (202) 623-1753; *Economic and Social Progress in Latin America.*

Organization of American States (OAS), General Secretariat, Washington, D.C. 20006 (202) 458-3533; *Statistical Bulletin of the OAS.*

DOMINICAN REPUBLIC - PUBLIC REVENUE

Inter-American Development Bank, 1300 New York Avenue, NW, Washington, D.C. 20577 (202) 623-1753; *Economic and Social Progress in Latin America.*

Organization of American States (OAS), General Secretariat, Washington, D.C. 20006 (202) 458-3533; *Statistical Bulletin of the OAS.*

DOMINICAN REPUBLIC - RADIO BROADCASTING - See DOMINICAN REPUBLIC - BROADCASTING

DOMINICAN REPUBLIC - RAILWAYS

The Economist Intelligence Unit, 111 West 57th Street, New York, New York 10019 (800) 938-4685; *The New Latin America Market Atlas.*

G.K. Hall and Company, 70 Lincoln Street, Boston, Massachusetts 02111 (617) 423-3990; *The World in Figures.*

Jane's Information Group, Sentinel House, 163 Brighton Road, Coulsdon, Surrey CR5 2NH, England (Telephone Number in U.S. (703) 683-3700); *Jane's World Railways.*

DOMINICAN REPUBLIC - RANCHING

U.C.L.A. Latin American Center Publications, University of California, Los Angeles, California 90024 (310) 825-6634; *Statistical Abstract of Latin America.*

DOMINICAN REPUBLIC - RELIGION

Facts on File, 460 Park Avenue South, New York, New York 10016 (800) 443-8323; *The New Book of World Rankings.*

U.C.L.A. Latin American Center Publications, University of California, Los Angeles, California 90024 (310) 825-6634; *Statistical Abstract of Latin America.*

DOMINICAN REPUBLIC - RENT PRICES

International Labour Office, I.L.O. Publications, CH-1211, Geneva 22, Switzerland; *Yearbook of Labour Statistics.*

DOMINICAN REPUBLIC - RESERVES EXCLUDING GOLD

The Economist Intelligence Unit, 111 West 57th Street, New York, New York 10019 (800) 938-4685; *The New Latin America Market Atlas.*

DOMINICAN REPUBLIC - RETAIL TRADE

G.K. Hall and Company, 70 Lincoln Street, Boston, Massachusetts 02111 (617) 423-3990; *The World in Figures.*

Inter-American Development Bank, 1300 New York Avenue, NW, Washington, D.C. 20577 (202) 623-1753; *Economic and Social Progress in Latin America.*

DOMINICAN REPUBLIC - RICE PRODUCTION - See DOMINICAN REPUBLIC - CROPS

DOMINICAN REPUBLIC - ROOT AND TUBER PRODUCTION - See DOMINICAN REPUBLIC - CROPS

DOMINICAN REPUBLIC - ROUNDWOOD PRODUCTION - See DOMINICAN REPUBLIC - FORESTRY AND FOREST PRODUCTS

Food and Agricultural Organization of the United Nations (FAO), Via delle Terme di Caracalla, 00100 Rome, Italy (Telephone Number in U.S. (202) 653-2400); *Yearbook of Forest Products.*

Inter-American Development Bank, 1300 New York Avenue, NW, Washington, D.C. 20577 (202) 623-1753; *Economic and Social Progress in Latin America.*

Statistical Office of the United Nations, Publishing Service, New York, New York 10017 (800) 253-9646; *Statistical Yearbook.*

DOMINICAN REPUBLIC - RUBBER PRODUCTION

Facts on File, 460 Park Avenue South, New York, New York 10016 (800) 443-8323; *The New Book of World Rankings.*

DOMINICAN REPUBLIC - SALT PRODUCTION - See DOMINICAN REPUBLIC - MINING AND MINERAL PRODUCTS

DOMINICAN REPUBLIC - SAWNWOOD PRODUCTION - See DOMINICAN REPUBLIC - FORESTRY AND FOREST PRODUCTS

DOMINICAN REPUBLIC - SCIENCE AND TECHNOLOGY

U.C.L.A. Latin American Center Publications, University of California, Los Angeles, California 90024 (310) 825-6634; *Statistical Abstract of Latin America.*

DOMINICAN REPUBLIC - SENIOR CITIZENS

Facts on File, 460 Park Avenue South, New York, New York 10016 (800) 443-8323; *The New Book of World Rankings.*

DOMINICAN REPUBLIC - SESAME SEED PRODUCTION - See DOMINICAN REPUBLIC - CROPS

DOMINICAN REPUBLIC - SHEEP - See DOMINICAN REPUBLIC - LIVESTOCK AND POULTRY

DOMINICAN REPUBLIC - SILVER PRODUCTION AND CONSUMPTION - See DOMINICAN REPUBLIC - MINING AND MINERAL PRODUCTS

DOMINICAN REPUBLIC - SISAL PRODUCTION - See DOMINICAN REPUBLIC - CROPS

DOMINICAN REPUBLIC - SOCIAL DATA

Facts on File, 460 Park Avenue South, New York, New York 10016 (800) 443-8323; *The New Book of World Rankings.*

G.K. Hall and Company, 70 Lincoln Street, Boston, Massachusetts 02111 (617) 423-3990; *The World in Figures.*

U.C.L.A. Latin American Center Publications, University of California, Los Angeles, California 90024 (310) 825-6634; *Statistical Abstract of Latin America.*

DOMINICAN REPUBLIC - SOCIAL SECURITY

Inter-American Development Bank, 1300 New York Avenue, NW, Washington, D.C. 20577 (202) 623-1753; *Economic and Social Progress in Latin America.*

International Monetary Fund, 700 Nineteenth Street, NW, Washington, D.C. 20431 (202) 623-7000; *Government Finance Statistics Yearbook.*

DOMINICAN REPUBLIC - SOCIOECONOMIC DATA

Inter-American Development Bank, 1300 New York Avenue, NW, Washington, D.C. 20577 (202) 623-1753; *Economic and Social Progress in Latin America.*

U.C.L.A. Latin American Center Publications, University of California, Los Angeles, California 90024 (310) 825-6634; *Statistical Abstract of Latin America.*

DOMINICAN REPUBLIC - SOYBEAN PRODUCTION - See DOMINICAN REPUBLIC - CROPS

DOMINICAN REPUBLIC - STAMP TAXES AND DUTIES - See DOMINICAN REPUBLIC - TAXATION

DOMINICAN REPUBLIC - STATE BUDGET REVENUE AND EXPENDITURES

Euromonitor Publications Limited, 87-88 Turnmill Street, London EC1M 5QU, England; *International Marketing Data and Statistics.*

Inter-American Development Bank, 1300 New York Avenue, NW, Washington, D.C. 20577 (202) 623-1753; *Economic and Social Progress in Latin America.*

DOMINICAN REPUBLIC - STEEL - See DOMINICAN REPUBLIC - MINING AND MINERAL PRODUCTS

DOMINICAN REPUBLIC - STOCKS - COMMODITY - MARKET PRICE - INDEX

Food and Agricultural Organization of the United Nations (FAO) Via delle Terme di Caracalla, 00100 Rome, Italy (Telephone Number in U.S. (202) 653-2400); *The State of Food and Agriculture.*

DOMINICAN REPUBLIC - SUGAR - See DOMINICAN REPUBLIC - CROPS

DOMINICAN REPUBLIC - TAXATION

G.K. Hall and Company, 70 Lincoln Street, Boston, Massachusetts 02111 (617) 423-3990; *The World in Figures.*

Inter-American Development Bank, 1300 New York Avenue, NW, Washington, D.C. 20577 (202) 623-1753; *Economic and Social Progress in Latin America.*

International Monetary Fund, 700 Nineteenth Street, NW, Washington, D.C. 20431 (202) 623-7000; *Government Finance Statistics Yearbook.*

International Road Federation, 525 School Street, SW, Washington, D.C. 20024 (202) 554-2106; *World Road Statistics.*

Statistical Office of the United Nations, Publishing Service, New York, New York 10017 (800) 253-9646; *Statistical Yearbook for Latin America and the Caribbean.*

The World Bank, 1818 H Street, NW, Washington, D.C. 20433 (202) 477-1234; *World Tables.*

DOMINICAN REPUBLIC - TELEPHONES IN USE

American Telephone and Telegraph Company, 26 Parsippany Road, Whippany, New Jersey 07981 (800) 338-4038; *The World's Telephones.*

The Economist Intelligence Unit, 111 West 57th Street, New York, New York 10019 (800) 938-4685; *The New Latin America Market Atlas.*

G.K. Hall and Company, 70 Lincoln Street, Boston, Massachusetts 02111 (617) 423-3990; *The World in Figures.*

DOMINICAN REPUBLIC - TELEVISION BROADCASTING - See DOMINICAN REPUBLIC - BROADCASTING

DOMINICAN REPUBLIC - TEXTILE INDUSTRY

G.K. Hall and Company, 70 Lincoln Street, Boston, Massachusetts 02111 (617) 423-3990; *The World in Figures.*

Statistical Office of the United Nations, Publishing Service, New York, New York 10017 (800) 253-9646; *Statistical Yearbook.*

DOMINICAN REPUBLIC - TOBACCO EXPORTS

International Monetary Fund, 700 Nineteenth Street, NW, Washington, D.C. 20431 (202) 623-7000; *International Financial Statistics.*

DOMINICAN REPUBLIC - TOBACCO PRODUCTION

Facts on File, 460 Park Avenue South, New York, New York 10016 (800) 443-8323; *The New Book of World Rankings.*

Statistical Office of the United Nations, Publishing Service, New York, New York 10017 (800) 253-9646; *Statistical Yearbook.*

DOMINICAN REPUBLIC - TOURISM

The Economist Intelligence Unit, 111 West 57th Street, New York, New York 10019 (800) 938-4685; *The New Latin America Market Atlas.*

Facts on File, 460 Park Avenue South, New York, New York 10016 (800) 443-8323; *The New Book of World Rankings.*

Federal Statistical Office, Gustav - Stresemann - Ring 11, D-6200 Wiesbaden, Germany; *Dominikanische Republik.*

G.K. Hall and Company, 70 Lincoln Street, Boston, Massachusetts 02111 (617) 423-3990; *The World in Figures.*

Statistical Office of the United Nations, Publishing Service, New York, New York 10017 (800) 253-9646; *Statistical Yearbook,* and *Statistical Yearbook for Latin America and the Caribbean.*

Times Books, 201 East 50th Street, New York, New York 10022 (212) 751-2600; *The Economist Book of Vital World Statistics.*

U.C.L.A. Latin American Center Publications, University of California, Los Angeles, California 90024 (310) 825-6634; *Statistical Abstract of Latin America.*

World Tourism Organization, Calle Capitan Haya 42, E-28020 Madrid, Spain; *Yearbook of Tourism Statistics.*

DOMINICAN REPUBLIC - TRACTORS IN USE

The Economist Intelligence Unit, 111 West 57th Street, New York, New York 10019 (800) 938-4685; *The New Latin America Market Atlas.*

Statistical Office of the United Nations, Publishing Service, New York, New York 10017 (800) 253-9646; *Statistical Yearbook.*

DOMINICAN REPUBLIC - TRADE - See DOMINICAN REPUBLIC - FOREIGN TRADE

DOMINICAN REPUBLIC - TRADEMARKS AND SERVICE MARKS

Statistical Office of the United Nations, Publishing Service, New York, New York 10017 (800) 253-9646; *Statistical Yearbook.*

DOMINICAN REPUBLIC - TRANSPORTATION AND COMMUNICATIONS

The Economist Intelligence Unit, 111 West 57th Street, New York, New York 10019 (800) 938-4685; *The New Latin America Market Atlas.*

Facts on File, 460 Park Avenue South, New York, New York 10016 (800) 443-8323; *The New Book of World Rankings.*

Federal Statistical Office, Gustav - Stresemann - Ring 11, D-6200 Wiesbaden, Germany; *Dominikanische Republik.*

Gale Research Incorporated, 835 Penobscot Building, Detroit, Michigan 48226 (800) 877-4253; *International Historical Statistics The Americas and Australasia.*

G.K. Hall and Company, 70 Lincoln Street, Boston, Massachusetts 02111 (617) 423-3990; *The World in Figures.*

Inter-American Development Bank, 1300 New York Avenue, NW, Washington, D.C. 20577 (202) 623-1753; *Economic and Social Progress in Latin America.*

Statistical Office of the United Nations, Publishing Service, New York, New York 10017 (800) 253-9646; *Statistical Yearbook for Latin America and the Caribbean.*

U.C.L.A. Latin American Center Publications, University of California, Los Angeles, California 90024 (310) 825-6634; *Statistical Abstract of Latin America.*

DOMINICAN REPUBLIC - TRAVEL FARES ABROAD

International Monetary Fund, 700 Nineteenth Street, NW, Washington, D.C. 20431 (202) 623-7000; *Government Finance Statistics Yearbook.*

DOMINICAN REPUBLIC - TURKEYS - See DOMINICAN REPUBLIC - LIVESTOCK AND POULTRY

DOMINICAN REPUBLIC - UNEMPLOYMENT

The Economist Intelligence Unit, 111 West 57th Street, New York, New York 10019 (800) 938-4685; *The New Latin America Market Atlas.*

Euromonitor Publications Limited, 87-88 Turnmill Street, London EC1M 5QU, England; *International Marketing Data and Statistics.*

International Labour Office, I.L.O. Publications, CH-1211, Geneva 22, Switzerland; *Yearbook of Labour Statistics.*

U.C.L.A. Latin American Center Publications, University of California, Los Angeles, California 90024 (310) 825-6634; *Statistical Abstract of Latin America.*

DOMINICAN REPUBLIC - UTILITIES

U.C.L.A. Latin American Center Publications, University of California, Los Angeles, California 90024 (310) 825-6634; *Statistical Abstract of Latin America.*

DOMINICAN REPUBLIC - VITAL STATISTICS

Euromonitor Publications Limited, 87-88 Turnmill Street, London EC1M 5QU, England; *International Marketing Data and Statistics.*

Gale Research Incorporated, 835 Penobscot Building, Detroit, Michigan 48226 (800) 877-4253; *International Historical Statistics The Americas and Australasia.*

G.K. Hall and Company, 70 Lincoln Street, Boston, Massachusetts 02111 (617) 423-3990; *The World in Figures.*

Statistical Office of the United Nations, Publishing Service, New York, New York 10017 (800) 253-9646; *Statistical Yearbook.*

World Health Organization, Office of Publications, Avenue Appia, CH-1211 Geneva 27, Switzerland (Telephone Number in U.S. (518) 436-9686); *World Health Statistics Annual.*

DOMINICAN REPUBLIC - WAGES

Federal Statistical Office, Gustav - Stresemann - Ring 11, D-6200 Wiesbaden, Germany; *Dominikanische Republik.*

G.K. Hall and Company, 70 Lincoln Street, Boston, Massachusetts 02111 (617) 423-3990; *The World in Figures.*

International Labour Office, I.L.O. Publications, CH-1211, Geneva 22, Switzerland; *Yearbook of Labour Statistics.*

Statistical Office of the United Nations, Publishing Service, New York, New York 10017 (800) 253-9646; *Statistical Yearbook.*

U.C.L.A. Latin American Center Publications, University of California, Los Angeles, California 90024 (310) 825-6634; *Statistical Abstract of Latin America.*

DOMINICAN REPUBLIC - WEATHER

Facts on File, 460 Park Avenue South, New York, New York 10016 (800) 443-8323; *The New Book of World Rankings.*

G.K. Hall and Company, 70 Lincoln Street, Boston, Massachusetts 02111 (617) 423-3990; *The World in Figures.*

DOMINICAN REPUBLIC - WELFARE

Inter-American Development Bank, 1300 New York Avenue, NW, Washington, D.C. 20577 (202) 623-1753; *Economic and Social Progress in Latin America.*

International Monetary Fund, 700 Nineteenth Street, NW, Washington, D.C. 20431 (202) 623-7000; *Government Finance Statistics Yearbook.*

DOMINICAN REPUBLIC - WHEAT PRODUCTION - See DOMINICAN REPUBLIC - CROPS

DOMINICAN REPUBLIC - WHOLESALE PRICES

Inter-American Development Bank, 1300 New York Avenue, NW, Washington, D.C. 20577 (202) 623-1753; *Economic and Social Progress in Latin America.*

Organization of American States (OAS), General Secretariat, Washington, D.C. 20006 (202) 458-3533; *Statistical Bulletin of the OAS.*

Statistical Office of the United Nations, Publishing Service, New York, New York 10017 (800) 253-9646; *Statistical Yearbook.*

DOMINICAN REPUBLIC - WHOLESALE TRADE

Inter-American Development Bank, 1300 New York Avenue, NW, Washington, D.C. 20577 (202) 623-1753; *Economic and Social Progress in Latin America.*

DOMINICAN REPUBLIC - WINE PRODUCTION

Facts on File, 460 Park Avenue South, New York, New York 10016 (800) 443-8323; *The New Book of World Rankings.*

DOMINICAN REPUBLIC - WOOL PRODUCTION

Facts on File, 460 Park Avenue South, New York, New York 10016 (800) 443-8323; *The New Book of World Rankings.*

DOMINICAN REPUBLIC - YARN PRODUCTION

Statistical Office of the United Nations, Publishing Service, New York, New York 10017 (800) 253-9646; *Statistical Yearbook.*

DORMITORY POPULATION

U.S. Department of Commerce, Bureau of the Census, Suitland, Maryland 20233 (301) 763-4040; *Census of Population, General Population Characteristics.*

DRINKING PLACES - See EATING AND DRINKING PLACES

DRIVERS LICENSES

U.S. Department of Transportation, Federal Highway Administration, 400 Seventh Street, SW, Washington, D.C. 20590 (202) 366-0660; *Highway Statistics,* and *Selected Highway Statistics and Charts.*

DRIVING WHILE INTOXICATED

U.S. Department of Justice, Bureau of Justice Statistics, 633 Indiana Avenue, NW, Washington, D.C. 20531 (800) 732-3277; *Drunk Driving, Special Report.*

U.S. Department of Justice, Federal Bureau of Investigation, Ninth Street and Pennsylvania Avenue, NW, Washington, D.C. 20535 (202) 324-3000; *Crime in the United States.*

DRIVING WHILE INTOXICATED - FATAL ACCIDENTS, BY AGE

U.S. Department of Transportation, National Highway Traffic Safety Administration, 400 Seventh Street, SW, Washington, D.C. 20590 (202) 366-9550; *General Estimates System,* and unpublished data.

DRUG STORES AND PROPRIETARY STORES - EARNINGS

U.S. Department of Commerce, Bureau of the Census, Suitland, Maryland 20233 (301) 763-4040; *Census of Retail Trade,* and *County Business Patterns.*

DRUG STORES AND PROPRIETARY STORES - EMPLOYEES

U.S. Department of Commerce, Bureau of the Census, Suitland, Maryland 20233 (301) 763-4040; *Census of Retail Trade,* and *County Business Patterns.*

DRUG STORES AND PROPRIETARY STORES - ESTABLISHMENTS

U.S. Department of Commerce, Bureau of the Census, Suitland, Maryland 20233 (301) 763-4040; *Census of Retail Trade,* and *County Business Patterns.*

DRUG STORES AND PROPRIETARY STORES - PRODUCTIVITY

U.S. Department of Labor, Bureau of Labor Statistics, Two Massachusetts Avenue, NE, Washington, D.C. 20212 (202) 606-7828; *Productivity Measures for Selected Industries and Government Services,* and unpublished data.

DRUG STORES AND PROPRIETARY STORES - SALES

U.S. Department of Commerce, Bureau of the Census, Suitland, Maryland 20233 (301) 763-4040; *Census of Retail Trade, Current Business Reports, Combined Annual Revised Monthly Retail Trade,* and unpublished data.

DRUGS AND MEDICINES - ACCIDENTAL POISONINGS

National Safety Council, 1121 Spring Lake Drive, Itasca, Illinois 60143-3201 (708) 285-1121; *Accident Facts.*

U.S. Department of Health and Human Services, National Center for Health Statistics, 3700 East-West Highway, Hyattsville, Maryland 20782 (301) 436-8500; *Vital Statistics of the United States,* and unpublished data.

DRUGS AND MEDICINES - ADVERTISING EXPENDITURES

Publishers Information Bureau, Incorporated, 575 Lexington Avenue, New York, New York 10022 (212) 752-0055; data complied by Leading National Advertisers, 11 West 42nd Street, New York, New York 10036 (212) 789-1400.

Television Bureau of Advertising, Incorporated, 850 Third Avenue, New York, New York 10022 (212) 486-1111; from data compiled by Competition Media, 11 West 42nd Street, New York, New York 10036 (212) 789-1400.

DRUGS AND MEDICINES - CONSUMER PRICE INDEXES

U.S. Department of Labor, Bureau of Labor Statistics, Two Massachusetts Avenue, NE, Washington, D.C. 20212 (202) 606-7828; *Monthly Labor Review,* and *Consumer Price Indexes, Detailed Report.*

DRUGS AND MEDICINES - DRUG ABUSE TREATMENT

U.S. Department of Health and Human Services, Substance Abuse and Mental Health Administration, 5600 Fishers Lane, Rockville, Maryland 20857 (301) 443-4797; *Highlights from the National Drug and Alcoholism Treatment Unit Survey, Selected Trends.*

DRUGS AND MEDICINES - EXPENDITURES FOR

U.S. Department of Health and Human Services, Health Care Financing Administration, 200 Independence Avenue, SW, Washington, D.C. 20201 (202) 245-6113; *Health Care Financing Review.*

U.S. Department of Labor, Bureau of Labor Statistics, Two Massachusetts Avenue, NE, Washington, D.C. 20212 (202) 606-7828; *Consumer Expenditure Survey.*

DRUGS AND MEDICINES - FOREIGN TRADE

U.S. Department of Commerce, Bureau of the Census, Suitland, Maryland 20233 (301) 763-4040; *U.S. Merchandise Trade: Exports, General Imports, and Imports for Consumption.*

DRUGS AND MEDICINES - MEDICAID PAYMENTS

U.S. Department of Health and Human Services, Health Care Financing Administration, 200 Independence Avenue, SW, Washington, D.C. 20201 (202) 245-6113; *Health Care Financing Review.*

DRUGS AND MEDICINES INDUSTRY - MANUFACTURING - EARNINGS

U.S. Department of Commerce, Bureau of the Census, Suitland, Maryland 20233 (301) 763-4040; *Census of Manufactures,* and *Annual Survey of Manufactures.*

U.S. Department of Labor, Bureau of Labor Statistics, Two Massachusetts Avenue, NE, Washington, D.C. 20212 (202) 606-7828; *Employment and Earnings, Employment and Wages, Annual Averages,* and Bulletins 2370, 2429, and 2433.

DRUGS AND MEDICINES INDUSTRY - MANUFACTURING - EMPLOYEES

U.S. Department of Commerce, Bureau of the Census, Suitland, Maryland 20233 (301) 763-4040; *Census of Manufactures,* and *Annual Survey of Manufactures.*

U.S. Department of Labor, Bureau of Labor Statistics, Two Massachusetts Avenue, NE, Washington, D.C. 20212 (202) 606-7828; *Employment and Earnings, Employment and Wages, Annual Averages,* and Bulletins 2370, 2429, and 2433.

DRUGS AND MEDICINES INDUSTRY - MANUFACTURING - ESTABLISHMENTS

U.S. Department of Commerce, Bureau of the Census, Suitland, Maryland 20233 (301) 763-4040; *Census of Manufactures,* and *Annual Survey of Manufactures.*

DRUGS AND MEDICINES INDUSTRY - MANUFACTURING - SHIPMENTS

U.S. Department of Commerce, Bureau of the Census, Suitland, Maryland 20233 (301) 763-4040; *Census of Manufactures,* and *Annual Survey of Manufactures.*

DRUGS AND MEDICINES INDUSTRY - MANUFACTURING - VALUE ADDED

U.S. Department of Commerce, Bureau of the Census, Suitland, Maryland 20233 (301) 763-4040; *Census of Manufactures,* and *Annual Survey of Manufactures.*

DRUGS (ILLEGAL) - ARRESTS

U.S. Department of Justice, Federal Bureau of Investigation, Ninth Street and Pennsylvania Avenue, NW, Washington, D.C. 20530 (202) 324-3000; *Crime in the United States.*

U.S. Department of Justice, Immigration and Naturalization Service, 425 I Street, NW, Washington, D.C. 20536 (202) 514-4316; *Statistical Yearbook,* and unpublished data.

U.S. Department of Justice, National Institute of Justice, 633 Indiana Avenue, NW, Washington, D.C. 20531 (202) 307-0781; *Drug Use Forecasting.*

DRUGS (ILLEGAL) - COURT CASES

Administrative Office of the United States Courts, United States Supreme Court Building, Columbus Circle, NE, Washington, D.C. 20544 (202) 273-1120; *Annual Report of the Director.*

U.S. Department of Justice, Bureau of Justice Statistics, 633 Indiana Avenue, NW, Washington, D.C. 20531 (800) 732-3277; *Federal Criminal Case Processing.*

DRUGS (ILLEGAL) - DRUG ABUSE TREATMENT

U.S. Department of Health and Human Services, Substance Abuse and Mental Health Administration, 5600 Fishers Lane, Rockville, Maryland 20857 (301) 443-4797; *Highlights from the National Drug and Alcoholism Treatment Unit Survey, Selected Trends.*

U.S. Department of Labor, Bureau of Labor Statistics, Two Massachusetts Avenue, NE, Washington, D.C. 20212 (202) 606-7828; *Employee Benefits in State and Local Governments, Employee Benefits in Medium and Large Private Establishments,* and *Employee Benefits in Small Private Establishments.*

DRUGS (ILLEGAL) - ENFORCEMENT ACTIVITIES

U.S. Department of Justice, Drug Enforcement Administration, 600-700 Army Navy Drive, Arlington, Virginia 22202 (202) 307-1000; *Annual Report.*

U.S. Department of Justice, Immigration and Naturalization Service, 425 I Street, NW, Washington, D.C. 20536 (202) 514-4316; *Statistical Yearbook,* and unpublished data.

DRUGS (ILLEGAL) - USAGE

U.S. Department of Health and Human Services, Substance Abuse and Mental Health Administration, 5600 Fishers Lane, Rockville, Maryland 20857 (301) 443-4797; *National Household Survey on Drug Abuse.*

U.S. Department of Justice, Federal Bureau of Investigation, Ninth Street and Pennsylvania Avenue, NW, Washington, D.C. 20530 (202) 324-3000; *Crime in the U.S.*

U.S. Department of Justice, National Institute of Justice, 633 Indiana Avenue, NW, Washington, D.C. 20531 (202) 307-0781; *Drug Use Forecasting.*

DRUNK DRIVING

U.S. Department of Justice, Bureau of Justice Statistics, 633 Indiana Avenue, NW, Washington, D.C. 20531 (202) 732-3277; *Drunk Driving, Special Report.*

U.S. Department of Transportation, Federal Highway Administration, 400 Seventh Street, SW, Washington, D.C. 20590 (202) 366-0660; *Selected Highway Statistics and Charts.*

U.S. Department of Transportation, National Highway Traffic Safety Administration, 400 Seventh Street, SW, Washington, D.C. 20590 (202) 366-9550; *General Estimates System*, and unpublished data.

DRUNK DRIVING - ARRESTS

U.S. Department of Justice, Bureau of Justice Statistics, 633 Indiana Avenue, NW, Washington, D.C. 20531 (800) 732-3277; *Drunk Driving, Special Report.*

U.S. Department of Justice, Federal Bureau of Investigation, Ninth Street and Pennsylvania Avenue, NW, Washington, D.C. 20535 (202) 324-3000; *Crime in the United States.*

DRYERS - CLOTHES

U.S. Department of Energy, Energy Information Administration, Washington, D.C. 20585 (202) 586-8800; *Housing Characteristics.*

DUTIABLE IMPORTS AND DUTIES

U.S. Department of Commerce, Bureau of the Census, Suitland, Maryland 20233 (301) 763-4040; *U.S. Merchandise Trade: Selected Highlights*, and unpublished data.

DWELLINGS - See HOUSING AND HOUSING UNITS and HOUSEHOLDS OR FAMILIES

E

EARNINGS - AGRICULTURE, FORESTRY, FISHERIES

U.S. Department of Commerce, Bureau of the Census, Suitland, Maryland 20233 (301) 763-4040; *County Business Patterns.*

EARNINGS - AIRLINES

Air Transport Association of America, 1301 Pennsylvania Avenue, Suite 1100, Washington, D.C. 20004-7017 (202) 626-4000; *Air Transport*, and *Air Transport Facts and Figures.*

EARNINGS - COLLECTIVE BARGAINING SETTLEMENTS

U.S. Department of Labor, Bureau of Labor Statistics, Two Massachusetts Avenue, NE, Washington, D.C. 20212 (202) 606-7828; *Compensation and Working Conditions.*

EARNINGS - COLLEGE FACULTY

Maryse Eymonerie Associates/American Association of University Professors, 1012 Fourteenth Street, NW, Suite 500, Washington, D.C. 20005 (202) 737-5900; *AAUP Annual Report on the Economic Status of the Profession.*

EARNINGS - COLLEGE GRADUATES, STARTING SALARIES

College Placement Council, 62 Highland Avenue, Bethlehem, Pennsylvania 18017 (212) 868-1421; *Salary Survey, A Study of Beginning Offers.*

Northwestern University, 633 Clark Street, Evanston, Illinois 60201 (708) 491-3741; *The Northwestern Lindquist-Endicott Report.*

EARNINGS - CONSTRUCTION INDUSTRY

U.S. Department of Commerce, Bureau of the Census, Suitland, Maryland 20233 (301) 763-4040; *Census of Construction Industries*, and *County Business Patterns.*

EARNINGS - EMPLOYMENT COVERED BY SOCIAL INSURANCE

U.S. Department of Health and Human Services, Social Security Administration, 6401 Security Boulevard, Baltimore, Maryland 21235 (410) 965-1234; *Annual Statistical Supplement to the Social Security Bulletin*, and unpublished data.

U.S. Department of Labor, Employment and Training Administration, 200 Constitution Avenue, NW, Washington, D.C. 20210 (202) 219-0600; *Unemployment Insurance Data Summary.*

EARNINGS - FAMILY TYPE

U.S. Department of Labor, Bureau of Labor Statistics, Two Massachusetts Avenue, NE, Washington, D.C. 20212 (202) 606-7828; *Bulletin 2307*, and *Employment and Earnings.*

EARNINGS - FINANCE, INSURANCE, REAL ESTATE

U.S. Department of Commerce, Bureau of the Census, Suitland, Maryland 20233 (301) 763-4040; *County Business Patterns.*

EARNINGS - GOVERNMENT EMPLOYEES - FEDERAL

U.S. Department of Commerce, Bureau of the Census, Suitland, Maryland 20233 (301) 763-4040; *Historical Statistics on Governmental Finances and Employment*, and *Public Employment.*

U.S. Office of Personnel Management, 1900 E Street, NW, Washington, D.C. 20415 (202) 606-1800; *The Pay Structure of the Federal Civil Service, Federal Civilian Workforce Statistics Employment and Trends*, and *Central Personnel Data File.*

EARNINGS - GOVERNMENT EMPLOYEES - STATE AND LOCAL

U.S. Department of Commerce, Bureau of the Census, Suitland, Maryland 20233 (301) 763-4040; *Historical Statistics on Governmental Finances and Employment*, and *Public Employment.*

U.S. Equal Employment Opportunity Commission, 1801 L Street, NW, Washington, D.C. 20507 (800) USA-EEOC; *State and Local Government Information Report.*

EARNINGS - HUSBAND-WIFE FAMILIES

U.S. Department of Commerce, Bureau of the Census, Suitland, Maryland 20233 (301) 763-4040; *Current Population Reports.*

U.S. Department of Labor, Bureau of Labor Statistics, Two Massachusetts Avenue, NE, Washington, D.C. 20212 (202) 606-7828; *Employment and Earnings*, and Bulletin 2370.

EARNINGS - INCOME TAX RETURNS (REPORTED TOTALS)

U.S. Department of the Treasury, Internal Revenue Service, 1111 Constitution Avenue, NW, Washington, D.C. 20224 (202) 566-5000; *Statistics of Income Bulletin*, and *Statistics of Income, Individual Income Tax Returns.*

EARNINGS - INDUSTRY

U.S. Department of Commerce, Bureau of Economic Analysis, Fourteenth Street between Constitution Avenue and E Street, NW,

Washington, D.C. 20230 (202) 606-9900; *The National Income and Product Accounts of the U.S.*, and *Survey of Current Business.*

U.S. Department of Commerce, Bureau of the Census, Suitland, Maryland 20233 (301) 763-4040; *County Business Patterns.*

U.S. Department of Labor, Bureau of Labor Statistics, Two Massachusetts Avenue, NE, Washington, D.C. 20212 (202) 606-7828; *Employment and Earnings, Monthly Labor Review,* Bulletins 2370 and 2429, and unpublished data.

EARNINGS - MANUFACTURING

U.S. Department of Commerce, Bureau of the Census, Suitland, Maryland 20233 (301) 763-4040; *County Business Patterns.*

EARNINGS - METROPOLITAN AREAS

U.S. Department of Labor, Bureau of Labor Statistics, Two Massachusetts Avenue, NE, Washington, D.C. 20212 (202) 606-7828; *Average Annual Pay Levels in Metropolitan Areas.*

EARNINGS - MINERAL INDUSTRIES

U.S. Department of Commerce, Bureau of the Census, Suitland, Maryland 20233 (301) 763-4040; *Census of Mineral Industries.*

EARNINGS - MINIMUM WAGE EARNERS

U.S. Department of Labor, Employment Standards Administration, 200 Constitution Avenue, NW, Washington, D.C. 20210 (202) 219-7320; *Minimum Wage and Maximum Hours Standards Under the Fair Labor Standards Act,* and unpublished data.

EARNINGS - MINING INDUSTRY

U.S. Department of Commerce, Bureau of the Census, Suitland, Maryland 20233 (301) 763-4040; *Census of Mineral Industries,* and *County Business Patterns.*

EARNINGS - MUNICIPAL EMPLOYEES

U.S. Department of Commerce, Bureau of the Census, Suitland, Maryland 20233 (301) 763-4040; *City Employment,* and *Compendium of Public Employment.*

EARNINGS - NATIONAL INCOME COMPONENTS

U.S. Department of Commerce, Bureau of Economic Analysis, Fourteenth Street between Constitution Avenue and E Street, NW, Washington, D.C. 20230 (202) 606-9900; *Survey of Current Business,* and *The National Income and Product Accounts of the United States.*

EARNINGS - OCCUPATIONS

U.S. Department of Commerce, Bureau of the Census, Suitland, Maryland 20233 (301) 763-4040; *Current Population Reports.*

U.S. Department of Labor, Bureau of Labor Statistics, Two Massachusetts Avenue, NE, Washington, D.C. 20212 (202) 606-7828; *Bulletin 2307,* and *Employment and Earnings.*

EARNINGS - PERSONAL INCOME

U.S. Department of Commerce, Bureau of Economic Analysis, Fourteenth Street between Constitution Avenue and E Street, NW, Washington, D.C. 20230 (202) 606-9900; *The National Income and Product Accounts of the U.S., Survey of Current Business,* and unpublished data.

EARNINGS - PHYSICIANS

American Medical Association, 515 North State Street, Chicago, Illinois 60610 (312) 464-5000; *Socioeconomic Characteristics of Medical Practice.*

EARNINGS - PUBLIC SCHOOL TEACHERS

National Education Association, 1201 Sixteenth Street, NW, Washington, D.C. 20036 (202) 833-4000; *Estimates of School Statistics,* and *Rankings of the States.*

Northwestern University Placement Center, 633 Clark Street, Evanston, Illinois 60201 (708) 491-3741; *The Northwestern Lindquist - Endicott Report.*

EARNINGS - RAILROADS

Association of American Railroads, American Railroads Building, 50 F Street, NW, Washington, D.C. 20001 (202) 639-2100; *Railroad Facts, Statistics of Railroads of Class I,* and *Analysis of Class I Railroads.*

EARNINGS - RETAIL TRADE

U.S. Department of Commerce, Bureau of the Census, Suitland, Maryland 20233 (301) 763-4040; *County Business Patterns.*

EARNINGS - SEAMEN

U.S. Department of Transportation, Maritime Administration, 400 Seventh Street, SW, Washington, D.C. 20590 (202) 366-5807; *U.S. Merchant Marine Data Sheet,* and unpublished data.

EARNINGS - SERVICES

U.S. Department of Commerce, Bureau of the Census, Suitland, Maryland 20233 (301) 763-4040; *County Business Patterns.*

EARNINGS - STATES

U.S. Department of Labor, Bureau of Labor Statistics, Two Massachusetts Avenue, NE, Washington, D.C. 20212 (202) 606-7828; *Employment and Wages, Annual Averages,* and *Average Annual Pay by State and Industry.*

EARNINGS - TELEPHONE SYSTEMS, EMPLOYEES

U.S. Federal Communications Commission, 1919 M Street, NW, Washington, D.C. 20554 (202) 632-7000; *Statistics of Communications Common Carriers,* and unpublished data.

U.S. Telephone Association, 900 Nineteenth Street, NW, Washington, D.C. 20006 (202) 835-3100; *Statistics of the Local Exchange Carriers.*

EARNINGS - TRANSPORTATION

U.S. Department of Commerce, Bureau of the Census, Suitland, Maryland 20233 (301) 763-4040; *County Business Patterns.*

EARNINGS - UNION MEMBERS

U.S. Department of Labor, Bureau of Labor Statistics, Two Massachusetts Avenue, NE, Washington, D.C. 20212 (202) 606-7828; *Employment and Earnings.*

EARNINGS - WHOLESALE TRADE

U.S. Department of Commerce, Bureau of the Census, Suitland, Maryland 20233 (301) 763-4040; *Census of Wholesale Trade*, and *County Business Patterns*.

EARTH SCIENCES - DEGREES CONFERRED

U.S. National Science Foundation, 4201 Wilson Boulevard, Arlington, Virginia 22230 (703) 306-1234; *Survey of Earned Doctorates, Selected Data on Science and Engineering Doctorate Awards*.

EAST TIMOR - AGRICULTURE

Food and Agricultural Organization of the United Nations (FAO) Via delle Terme di Caracalla, 00100 Rome, Italy (Telephone Number in U.S. (202) 653-2400); *Production Yearbook, The State of Food and Agriculture*, and *Trade Yearbook*.

G.K. Hall and Company, 70 Lincoln Street, Boston, Massachusetts 02111 (617) 423-3990; *The World in Figures*.

Statistical Office of the United Nations, Publishing Service, New York, New York 10017 (800) 253-9646; *Statistical Yearbook*.

EAST TIMOR - AIRLINE SERVICE

G.K. Hall and Company, 70 Lincoln Street, Boston, Massachusetts 02111 (617) 423-3990; *The World in Figures*.

EAST TIMOR - ANIMAL HEALTH

Food and Agricultural Organization of the United Nations (FAO), Via delle Terme di Caracalla, 00100 Rome, Italy (Telephone Number in U.S. (202) 653-2400); *Animal Health Yearbook*.

EAST TIMOR - AREA AND DENSITY OF POPULATION

Food and Agricultural Organization of the United Nations (FAO) Via delle Terme di Caracalla, 00100 Rome, Italy (Telephone Number in U.S. (202) 653-2400); *The State of Food and Agriculture*.

G.K. Hall and Company, 70 Lincoln Street, Boston, Massachusetts 02111 (617) 423-3990; *The World in Figures*.

Statistical Office of the United Nations, Publishing Service, New York, New York 10017 (800) 253-9646; *Statistical Yearbook*.

EAST TIMOR - BALANCE OF PAYMENTS

G.K. Hall and Company, 70 Lincoln Street, Boston, Massachusetts 02111 (617) 423-3990; *The World in Figures*.

EAST TIMOR - BANKING

G.K. Hall and Company, 70 Lincoln Street, Boston, Massachusetts 02111 (617) 423-3990; *The World in Figures*.

EAST TIMOR - BIRTH RATES

Statistical Office of the United Nations, Publishing Service, New York, New York 10017 (800) 253-9646; *Demographic Yearbook*, and *Statistical Yearbook*.

EAST TIMOR - BONDS

G.K. Hall and Company, 70 Lincoln Street, Boston, Massachusetts 02111 (617) 423-3990; *The World in Figures*.

EAST TIMOR - BOOK PRODUCTION

G.K. Hall and Company, 70 Lincoln Street, Boston, Massachusetts 02111 (617) 423-3990; *The World in Figures*.

EAST TIMOR - BROADCASTING

G.K. Hall and Company, 70 Lincoln Street, Boston, Massachusetts 02111 (617) 423-3990; *The World in Figures*.

EAST TIMOR - BUSINESS

G.K. Hall and Company, 70 Lincoln Street, Boston, Massachusetts 02111 (617) 423-3990; *The World in Figures*.

EAST TIMOR - CALORIE SUPPLY

Food and Agricultural Organization of the United Nations (FAO) Via delle Terme di Caracalla, 00100 Rome, Italy (Telephone Number in U.S. (202) 653-2400); *The State of Food and Agriculture*.

EAST TIMOR - CATTLE - See EAST TIMOR - LIVESTOCK AND POULTRY

EAST TIMOR - CHEMICAL (ORGANIC) PRODUCTION - See EAST TIMOR - MINING AND MINERAL PRODUCTS

EAST TIMOR - CLASS STRUCTURE

G.K. Hall and Company, 70 Lincoln Street, Boston, Massachusetts 02111 (617) 423-3990; *The World in Figures*.

EAST TIMOR - CLIMATE

G.K. Hall and Company, 70 Lincoln Street, Boston, Massachusetts 02111 (617) 423-3990; *The World in Figures*.

EAST TIMOR - COAL PRODUCTION - See EAST TIMOR - MINING AND MINERAL PRODUCTS

EAST TIMOR - COFFEE PRODUCTION - See EAST TIMOR - CROPS

EAST TIMOR - COMMUNICATIONS

G.K. Hall and Company, 70 Lincoln Street, Boston, Massachusetts 02111 (617) 423-3990; *The World in Figures*.

EAST TIMOR - CONSUMER PRICE INDEX

G.K. Hall and Company, 70 Lincoln Street, Boston, Massachusetts 02111 (617) 423-3990; *The World in Figures*.

EAST TIMOR - CONSUMPTION

G.K. Hall and Company, 70 Lincoln Street, Boston, Massachusetts 02111 (617) 423-3990; *The World in Figures*.

EAST TIMOR - CORN PRODUCTION - See EAST TIMOR - CROPS

EAST TIMOR - CORPORATE TAXES - See EAST TIMOR - TAXATION

EAST TIMOR - CROPS

Food and Agricultural Organization of the United Nations (FAO) Via delle Terme di Caracalla, 00100 Rome, Italy (Telephone Number in U.S. (202) 653-2400); *Production Yearbook*, and *The State of Food and Agriculture*.

G.K. Hall and Company, 70 Lincoln Street, Boston, Massachusetts 02111 (617) 423-3990; *The World in Figures*.

Statistical Office of the United Nations, Publishing Service, New York, New York 10017 (800) 253-9646; *Statistical Yearbook.*

EAST TIMOR - CUSTOMS DUTIES

G.K. Hall and Company, 70 Lincoln Street, Boston, Massachusetts 02111 (617) 423-3990; *The World in Figures.*

EAST TIMOR - DAIRY PRODUCTS

Food and Agricultural Organization of the United Nations (FAO) Via delle Terme di Caracalla, 00100 Rome, Italy (Telephone Number in U.S. (202) 653-2400); *Production Yearbook,* and *The State of Food and Agriculture.*

EAST TIMOR - DEATH RATES

G.K. Hall and Company, 70 Lincoln Street, Boston, Massachusetts 02111 (617) 423-3990; *The World in Figures.*

Statistical Office of the United Nations, Publishing Service, New York, New York 10017 (800) 253-9646; *Statistical Yearbook.*

EAST TIMOR - DEFENSE EXPENDITURES

G.K. Hall and Company, 70 Lincoln Street, Boston, Massachusetts 02111 (617) 423-3990; *The World in Figures.*

EAST TIMOR - DEMOGRAPHY

G.K. Hall and Company, 70 Lincoln Street, Boston, Massachusetts 02111 (617) 423-3990; *The World in Figures.*

EAST TIMOR - DEVELOPMENT ASSISTANCE

G.K. Hall and Company, 70 Lincoln Street, Boston, Massachusetts 02111 (617) 423-3990; *The World in Figures.*

Statistical Office of the United Nations, Publishing Service, New York, New York 10017 (800) 253-9646; *Statistical Yearbook.*

EAST TIMOR - DISEASE

G.K. Hall and Company, 70 Lincoln Street, Boston, Massachusetts 02111 (617) 423-3990; *The World in Figures.*

EAST TIMOR - DIVORCE RATES

Statistical Office of the United Nations, Publishing Service, New York, New York 10017 (800) 253-9646; *Demographic Yearbook.*

EAST TIMOR - DOMESTIC PRODUCT

G.K. Hall and Company, 70 Lincoln Street, Boston, Massachusetts 02111 (617) 423-3990; *The World in Figures.*

EAST TIMOR - ECONOMY

G.K. Hall and Company, 70 Lincoln Street, Boston, Massachusetts 02111 (617) 423-3990; *The World in Figures.*

EAST TIMOR - EDUCATION

G.K. Hall and Company, 70 Lincoln Street, Boston, Massachusetts 02111 (617) 423-3990; *The World in Figures.*

EAST TIMOR - EGG PRODUCTION - See EAST TIMOR - DAIRY PRODUCTS

EAST TIMOR - ENERGY

Food and Agricultural Organization of the United Nations (FAO) Via delle Terme di Caracalla, 00100 Rome, Italy (Telephone Number in U.S. (202) 653-2400); *The State of Food and Agriculture.*

G.K. Hall and Company, 70 Lincoln Street, Boston, Massachusetts 02111 (617) 423-3990; *The World in Figures.*

Statistical Office of the United Nations, Publishing Service, New York, New York 10017 (800) 253-9646; *Statistical Yearbook.*

EAST TIMOR - EXPORTS

Food and Agricultural Organization of the United Nations (FAO) Via delle Terme di Caracalla, 00100 Rome, Italy (Telephone Number in U.S. (202) 653-2400); *The State of Food and Agriculture.*

G.K. Hall and Company, 70 Lincoln Street, Boston, Massachusetts 02111 (617) 423-3990; *The World in Figures.*

EAST TIMOR - EXTERNAL TRADE

Food and Agricultural Organization of the United Nations (FAO) Via delle Terme di Caracalla, 00100 Rome, Italy (Telephone Number in U.S. (202) 653-2400); *The State of Food and Agriculture,* and *Trade Yearbook.*

G.K. Hall and Company, 70 Lincoln Street, Boston, Massachusetts 02111 (617) 423-3990; *The World in Figures.*

EAST TIMOR - FARM CROPS - See EAST TIMOR - CROPS

EAST TIMOR - FETAL MORTALITY

Statistical Office of the United Nations, Publishing Service, New York, New York 10017 (800) 253-9646; *Demographic Yearbook.*

EAST TIMOR - FERTILIZER

Food and Agricultural Organization of the United Nations (FAO) Via delle Terme di Caracalla, 00100 Rome, Italy (Telephone Number in U.S. (202) 653-2400); *The State of Food and Agriculture.*

EAST TIMOR - FINANCE

G.K. Hall and Company, 70 Lincoln Street, Boston, Massachusetts 02111 (617) 423-3990; *The World in Figures.*

EAST TIMOR - FISHERIES

Food and Agricultural Organization of the United Nations (FAO) Via delle Terme di Caracalla, 00100 Rome, Italy (Telephone Number in U.S. (202) 653-2400); *The State of Food and Agriculture,* and *Yearbook of Fishery Statistics.*

EAST TIMOR - FOOD

Food and Agricultural Organization of the United Nations (FAO) Via delle Terme di Caracalla, 00100 Rome, Italy (Telephone Number in U.S. (202) 653-2400); *Production Yearbook,* and *The State of Food and Agriculture.*

G.K. Hall and Company, 70 Lincoln Street, Boston, Massachusetts 02111 (617) 423-3990; *The World in Figures.*

EAST TIMOR - FOREIGN AID

G.K. Hall and Company, 70 Lincoln Street, Boston, Massachusetts 02111 (617) 423-3990; *The World in Figures.*

EAST TIMOR - FOREIGN TRADE

Food and Agricultural Organization of the United Nations (FAO) Via delle Terme di Caracalla, 00100 Rome, Italy (Telephone Number in U.S. (202) 653-2400); *The State of Food and Agriculture.*

G.K. Hall and Company, 70 Lincoln Street, Boston, Massachusetts 02111 (617) 423-3990; *The World in Figures.*

EAST TIMOR - FORESTRY AND FOREST PRODUCTS

Food and Agricultural Organization of the United Nations (FAO) Via delle Terme di Caracalla, 00100 Rome, Italy (Telephone Number in U.S. (202) 653-2400); *The State of Food and Agriculture,* and *Yearbook of Forest Products.*

G.K. Hall and Company, 70 Lincoln Street, Boston, Massachusetts 02111 (617) 423-3990; *The World in Figures.*

Statistical Office of the United Nations, Publishing Service, New York, New York 10017 (800) 253-9646; *Demographic Yearbook.*

United Nations Educational, Scientific and Cultural Organization (UNESCO), 7 Place de Fontenoy, F-75700 Paris, France (Telephone Number in U.S. (212) 963-5981); *Statistical Yearbook.*

EAST TIMOR - GENERAL MORTALITY

Statistical Office of the United Nations, Publishing Service, New York, New York 10017 (800) 253-9646; *Demographic Yearbook.*

EAST TIMOR - GOVERNMENT

G.K. Hall and Company, 70 Lincoln Street, Boston, Massachusetts 02111 (617) 423-3990; *The World in Figures.*

EAST TIMOR - GRAIN PRODUCTION - See EAST TIMOR - CROPS

EAST TIMOR - GROSS DOMESTIC PRODUCT

G.K. Hall and Company, 70 Lincoln Street, Boston, Massachusetts 02111 (617) 423-3990; *The World in Figures.*

Statistical Office of the United Nations, Publishing Service, New York, New York 10017 (800) 253-9646; *Statistical Yearbook.*

EAST TIMOR - GROUNDNUTS PRODUCTION - See EAST TIMOR - CROPS

EAST TIMOR - HEALTH

G.K. Hall and Company, 70 Lincoln Street, Boston, Massachusetts 02111 (617) 423-3990; *The World in Figures.*

Statistical Office of the United Nations, Publishing Service, New York, New York 10017 (800) 253-9646; *Statistical Yearbook.*

EAST TIMOR - HIDE PRODUCTION

Food and Agricultural Organization of the United Nations (FAO), Via delle Terme di Caracalla, 00100 Rome, Italy (Telephone Number in U.S. (202) 653-2400); *Production Yearbook.*

EAST TIMOR - HIGHWAYS

G.K. Hall and Company, 70 Lincoln Street, Boston, Massachusetts 02111 (617) 423-3990; *The World in Figures.*

EAST TIMOR - HORSES - See EAST TIMOR - LIVESTOCK AND POULTRY

EAST TIMOR - ILLITERATE POPULATION

G.K. Hall and Company, 70 Lincoln Street, Boston, Massachusetts 02111 (617) 423-3990; *The World in Figures.*

EAST TIMOR - IMPORTS

Food and Agricultural Organization of the United Nations (FAO) Via delle Terme di Caracalla, 00100 Rome, Italy (Telephone Number in U.S. (202) 653-2400); *The State of Food and Agriculture.*

G.K. Hall and Company, 70 Lincoln Street, Boston, Massachusetts 02111 (617) 423-3990; *The World in Figures.*

EAST TIMOR - INDUSTRY

G.K. Hall and Company, 70 Lincoln Street, Boston, Massachusetts 02111 (617) 423-3990; *The World in Figures.*

EAST TIMOR - INFANT AND MATERNAL MORTALITY

Statistical Office of the United Nations, Publishing Service, New York, New York 10017 (800) 253-9646; *Demographic Yearbook,* and *Statistical Yearbook.*

EAST TIMOR - LABOR FORCE

Food and Agricultural Organization of the United Nations (FAO) Via delle Terme di Caracalla, 00100 Rome, Italy (Telephone Number in U.S. (202) 653-2400); *The State of Food and Agriculture.*

G.K. Hall and Company, 70 Lincoln Street, Boston, Massachusetts 02111 (617) 423-3990; *The World in Figures.*

EAST TIMOR - LAND USE

Food and Agricultural Organization of the United Nations (FAO), Via delle Terme di Caracalla, 00100 Rome, Italy (Telephone Number in U.S. (202) 653-2400); *Production Yearbook.*

G.K. Hall and Company, 70 Lincoln Street, Boston, Massachusetts 02111 (617) 423-3990; *The World in Figures.*

EAST TIMOR - LIBRARIES

United Nations Educational, Scientific and Cultural Organization (UNESCO), 7 Place de Fontenoy, F-75700 Paris, France (Telephone Number in U.S. (212) 963-5981); *Statistical Yearbook.*

EAST TIMOR - LIVESTOCK AND POULTRY

Food and Agricultural Organization of the United Nations (FAO), Via delle Terme di Caracalla, 00100 Rome, Italy (Telephone Number in U.S. (202) 653-2400); *Production Yearbook,* and *The State of Food and Agriculture.*

G.K. Hall and Company, 70 Lincoln Street, Boston, Massachusetts 02111 (617) 423-3990; *The World in Figures.*

Statistical Office of the United Nations, Publishing Service, New York, New York 10017 (800) 253-9646; *Statistical Yearbook.*

EAST TIMOR - LIVING LEVELS

G.K. Hall and Company, 70 Lincoln Street, Boston, Massachusetts 02111 (617) 423-3990; *The World in Figures.*

EAST TIMOR - MAIL - NUMBER OF ITEMS SENT AND RECEIVED

Statistical Office of the United Nations, Publishing Service, New York, New York 10017 (800) 253-9646; *Statistical Yearbook.*

EAST TIMOR - MANUFACTURING

G.K. Hall and Company, 70 Lincoln Street, Boston, Massachusetts 02111 (617) 423-3990; *The World in Figures.*

EAST TIMOR - MARRIAGE RATES

Statistical Office of the United Nations, Publishing Service, New York, New York 10017 (800) 253-9646; *Demographic Yearbook,* and *Statistical Yearbook.*

EAST TIMOR - MEAT PRODUCTION - See EAST TIMOR - LIVESTOCK AND POULTRY

EAST TIMOR - MERCHANT SHIPPING

G.K. Hall and Company, 70 Lincoln Street, Boston, Massachusetts 02111 (617) 423-3990; *The World in Figures.*

Statistical Office of the United Nations, Publishing Service, New York, New York 10017 (800) 253-9646; *Statistical Yearbook.*

EAST TIMOR - MILITARY

G.K. Hall and Company, 70 Lincoln Street, Boston, Massachusetts 02111 (617) 423-3990; *The World in Figures.*

EAST TIMOR - MILK - See EAST TIMOR - DAIRY PRODUCTS

EAST TIMOR - MINING AND MINERAL PRODUCTS

G.K. Hall and Company, 70 Lincoln Street, Boston, Massachusetts 02111 (617) 423-3990; *The World in Figures.*

EAST TIMOR - MONEY SUPPLY

G.K. Hall and Company, 70 Lincoln Street, Boston, Massachusetts 02111 (617) 423-3990; *The World in Figures.*

EAST TIMOR - MOTOR VEHICLES IN USE

G.K. Hall and Company, 70 Lincoln Street, Boston, Massachusetts 02111 (617) 423-3990; *The World in Figures.*

EAST TIMOR - NATALITY - See EAST TIMOR - BIRTH RATES

EAST TIMOR - NATIONAL INCOME

G.K. Hall and Company, 70 Lincoln Street, Boston, Massachusetts 02111 (617) 423-3990; *The World in Figures.*

Statistical Office of the United Nations, Publishing Service, New York, New York 10017 (800) 253-9646; *Statistical Yearbook.*

EAST TIMOR - NEWSPAPER PRODUCTION - See EAST TIMOR - FORESTRY AND FOREST PRODUCTS

EAST TIMOR - NEWSPRINT - See EAST TIMOR - FORESTRY AND FOREST PRODUCTS

EAST TIMOR - OCCUPATIONS - See EAST TIMOR - LABOR FORCE

EAST TIMOR - PALM KERNELS AND PALM OIL - See EAST TIMOR - CROPS

EAST TIMOR - PAPER - See EAST TIMOR - FORESTRY AND FOREST PRODUCTS

EAST TIMOR - PESTICIDE USE

Food and Agricultural Organization of the United Nations (FAO) Via delle Terme di Caracalla, 00100 Rome, Italy (Telephone Number in U.S. (202) 653-2400); *The State of Food and Agriculture.*

EAST TIMOR - PETROLEUM INDUSTRY

Food and Agricultural Organization of the United Nations (FAO) Via delle Terme di Caracalla, 00100 Rome, Italy (Telephone Number in U.S. (202) 653-2400); *The State of Food and Agriculture.*

G.K. Hall and Company, 70 Lincoln Street, Boston, Massachusetts 02111 (617) 423-3990; *The World in Figures.*

EAST TIMOR - PIGS - See EAST TIMOR - LIVESTOCK AND POULTRY

EAST TIMOR - POPULATION

Food and Agricultural Organization of the United Nations (FAO), Via delle Terme di Caracalla, 00100 Rome, Italy (Telephone Number in U.S. (202) 653-2400); *Production Yearbook.*

G.K. Hall and Company, 70 Lincoln Street, Boston, Massachusetts 02111 (617) 423-3990; *The World in Figures.*

Statistical Office of the United Nations, Publishing Service, New York, New York 10017 (800) 253-9646; *Demographic Yearbook,* and *Statistical Yearbook.*

World Health Organization, Office of Publications, Avenue Appia, CH-1211 Geneva 27, Switzerland (Telephone Number in U.S. (518) 436-9686); *World Health Statistics Annual.*

EAST TIMOR - POTATO PRODUCTION - See EAST TIMOR - CROPS

EAST TIMOR - PRICES

Food and Agricultural Organization of the United Nations (FAO), Via delle Terme di Caracalla, 00100 Rome, Italy (Telephone Number in U.S. (202) 653-2400); *Production Yearbook,* and *The State of Food and Agriculture.*

G.K. Hall and Company, 70 Lincoln Street, Boston, Massachusetts 02111 (617) 423-3990; *The World in Figures.*

EAST TIMOR - PRODUCTION

G.K. Hall and Company, 70 Lincoln Street, Boston, Massachusetts 02111 (617) 423-3990; *The World in Figures.*

EAST TIMOR - RAILWAYS

G.K. Hall and Company, 70 Lincoln Street, Boston, Massachusetts 02111 (617) 423-3990; *The World in Figures.*

EAST TIMOR - RETAIL TRADE

G.K. Hall and Company, 70 Lincoln Street, Boston, Massachusetts 02111 (617) 423-3990; *The World in Figures.*

EAST TIMOR - RICE PRODUCTION - See EAST TIMOR - CROPS

EAST TIMOR - ROOT AND TUBER PRODUCTION - See EAST TIMOR - CROPS

EAST TIMOR - ROUNDWOOD PRODUCTION - See EAST TIMOR - FORESTRY AND FOREST PRODUCTS

EAST TIMOR - SAWNWOOD PRODUCTION - See EAST TIMOR - FORESTRY AND FOREST PRODUCTS

EAST TIMOR - SOCIAL DATA

G.K. Hall and Company, 70 Lincoln Street, Boston, Massachusetts 02111 (617) 423-3990; *The World in Figures.*

EAST TIMOR - STOCKS - COMMODITY - MARKET PRICE - INDEX

Food and Agricultural Organization of the United Nations (FAO) Via delle Terme di Caracalla, 00100 Rome, Italy (Telephone Number in U.S. (202) 653-2400); *The State of Food and Agriculture.*

EAST TIMOR - TAXATION

G.K. Hall and Company, 70 Lincoln Street, Boston, Massachusetts 02111 (617) 423-3990; *The World in Figures.*

EAST TIMOR - TELEPHONES IN USE

G.K. Hall and Company, 70 Lincoln Street, Boston, Massachusetts 02111 (617) 423-3990; *The World in Figures.*

EAST TIMOR - TEXTILE INDUSTRY

G.K. Hall and Company, 70 Lincoln Street, Boston, Massachusetts 02111 (617) 423-3990; *The World in Figures.*

EAST TIMOR - TOBACCO PRODUCTION

Statistical Office of the United Nations, Publishing Service, New York, New York 10017 (800) 253-9646; *Statistical Yearbook.*

EAST TIMOR - TOURISM

G.K. Hall and Company, 70 Lincoln Street, Boston, Massachusetts 02111 (617) 423-3990; *The World in Figures.*

EAST TIMOR - TRACTORS IN USE

Statistical Office of the United Nations, Publishing Service, New York, New York 10017 (800) 253-9646; *Statistical Yearbook.*

EAST TIMOR - TRADE - See EAST TIMOR - FOREIGN TRADE

EAST TIMOR - TRANSPORTATION AND COMMUNICATIONS

G.K. Hall and Company, 70 Lincoln Street, Boston, Massachusetts 02111 (617) 423-3990; *The World in Figures.*

EAST TIMOR - VITAL STATISTICS

G.K. Hall and Company, 70 Lincoln Street, Boston, Massachusetts 02111 (617) 423-3990; *The World in Figures.*

Statistical Office of the United Nations, Publishing Service, New York, New York 10017 (800) 253-9646; *Statistical Yearbook.*

World Health Organization, Office of Publications, Avenue Appia, CH-1211 Geneva 27, Switzerland; *World Health Statistics Annual.*

EAST TIMOR - WAGES

G.K. Hall and Company, 70 Lincoln Street, Boston, Massachusetts 02111 (617) 423-3990; *The World in Figures.*

EAST TIMOR - WEATHER

G.K. Hall and Company, 70 Lincoln Street, Boston, Massachusetts 02111 (617) 423-3990; *The World in Figures.*

EATING AND DRINKING PLACES - EARNINGS

U.S. Department of Commerce, Bureau of the Census, Suitland, Maryland 20233 (301) 763-4040; *Census of Retail Trade,* and *County Business Patterns.*

U.S. Department of Labor, Bureau of Labor Statistics, Two Massachusetts Avenue, NE, Washington, D.C. 20212 (202) 606-7828; *Employment and Earnings,* and Bulletins 2370 and 2429.

EATING AND DRINKING PLACES - EMPLOYEES

U.S. Department of Commerce, Bureau of the Census, Suitland, Maryland 20233 (301) 763-4040; *Census of Retail Trade,* and *County Business Patterns.*

U.S. Department of Labor, Bureau of Labor Statistics, Two Massachusetts Avenue, NE, Washington, D.C. 20212 (202) 606-7828; *Monthly Labor Review, Employment and Earnings,* and Bulletins 2370 and 2429.

EATING AND DRINKING PLACES - ESTABLISHMENTS

U.S. Department of Commerce, Bureau of the Census, Suitland, Maryland 20233 (301) 763-4040; *Census of Retail Trade,* and *County Business Patterns.*

International Franchise Association, 1350 New York Avenue, Suite 900, Washington, D.C 20005 (202) 628-8000; *Franchising in the Economy.*

EATING AND DRINKING PLACES - FRANCHISES

International Franchise Association, 1350 New York Avenue, Suite 900, Washington, D.C. 20005 (202) 628-8000; *Franchising in the Economy.*

EATING AND DRINKING PLACES - PRODUCTIVITY

U.S. Department of Labor, Bureau of Labor Statistics, Two Massachusetts Avenue, NE, Washington, D.C. 20212 (202) 606-7828; *Productivity Measures for Selected Industries and Government Services,* and unpublished data.

EATING AND DRINKING PLACES - SALES

U.S. Department of Commerce, Bureau of the Census, Suitland, Maryland 20233 (301) 763-4040; *Current Business Reports, Combined Annual and Revised Monthly Retail Trade,* and *Census of Retail Trade.*

ECONOMIC ASSISTANCE - FOREIGN

U.S. International Development Cooperation Agency, Agency for International Development, 320 Twenty-first Street, NW, Washington, D.C. 20523 (202) 647-9620; *United States Overseas Loans and Grants and Assistance from International Organizations,* and unpublished data.

ECONOMIC GROWTH RATES

Organization for Economic Cooperation and Development, Publication and Information Center, 2001 L Street, NW, Washington, D.C. 20036 (202) 785-6323; *National Accounts.*

U.S. Department of Commerce, Bureau of Economic Analysis, Fourteenth Street between Constitution Avenue and E Street, NW, Washington, D.C. 20230 (202) 606-9900; *The National Income and Product Accounts of the United States, Survey of Current Business,* and unpublished data.

U.S. Department of Commerce, International Trade Administration, Fourteenth Street between Constitution Avenue and E Street, NW, Washington, D.C. 20230 (202) 482-3809.

ECONOMIC GROWTH RATES - FOREIGN COUNTRIES

U.S. Department of State, Bureau of Intelligence and Research, 2201 C Street, NW, Washington, D.C. 20520 (202) 647-1080; *Economic Growth of OECD Countries,* and unpublished data.

ECONOMIC INDICATORS

Center for International Business Cycle Research, Columbia University, Graduate School of Business, 808 Uris Hall, New York, New York 10027 (202) 280-2916; *International Economic Indicators.*

U.S. Department of Commerce, Bureau of Economic Analysis, Fourteenth Street between Constitution Avenue and E Street, NW, Washington, D.C. 20230 (202) 606-9900; *Survey of Current Business.*

ECONOMIC INDICATORS - FOREIGN COUNTRIES

Center for International Business Cycle Research, Columbia Business School, 808 Uris Hall, New York, New York 10027 (202) 280-2916; *International Economic Indicators.*

Organization for Economic Cooperation and Development, Publication and Information Center, 2001 L Street, NW, Washington, D.C. 20036 (202) 785-6323; *National Accounts.*

ECONOMISTS - LABOR FORCE

U.S. Department of Labor, Bureau of Labor Statistics, Two Massachusetts Avenue, NE, Washington, D.C. 20212 (202) 606-7828; *Employment and Earnings.*

Ecuador - National Statistical Offices

Banco Central de Ecuador, Division de Investigacciones Economicas, AV 10 de Agosto y Briceno, Quito, Ecuador.

Instituto Nacional de Estadistica, 10 de Agosto 229, Quito, Ecuador.

Ecuador - Primary Statistics Sources

Banco Central del Ecuador, Casilla 339, Quito, Ecuador; *Boletin anuario (Annual Bulletin).*

Instituto Nacional de Estadistica, 10 de Agosto 229, Quito, Ecuador; *Anuario de estadistica* (Statistical Yearbook), and *Serie estadistica* (Statistical Series).

ECUADOR - AGRICULTURE

The Economist Intelligence Unit, 111 West 57th Street, New York, New York 10019 (800) 938-4685; *The New Latin America Market Atlas.*

Euromonitor Publications Limited, 87-88 Turnmill Street, London EC1M 5QU England; *International Marketing Data and Statistics.*

Facts on File, 460 Park Avenue South, New York, New York 10016 (800) 443-8323; *The New Book of World Rankings.*

Federal Statistical Office, Gustav - Stresemann - Ring 11, D-6200 Wiesbaden, Germany; *Ecuador.*

Food and Agricultural Organization of the United Nations (FAO), Via delle Terme di Caracalla, 00100 Rome, Italy (Telephone Number in U.S. (202) 653-2400); *Production Yearbook, The State of Food and Agriculture,* and *Trade Yearbook.*

Gale Research Incorporated, 835 Penobscot Building, Detroit, Michigan 48226 (800) 877-4253; *International Historical Statistics The Americas and Australasia.*

G.K. Hall and Company, 70 Lincoln Street, Boston, Massachusetts 02111 (617) 423-3990; *The World in Figures.*

Inter-American Development Bank, 1300 New York Avenue, NW, Washington, D.C. 20577 (202) 623-1753; *Economic and Social Progress in Latin America.*

Statistical Office of the United Nations, Publishing Service, New York, New York 10017 (800) 253-9646; *Statistical Yearbook,* and *Statistical Yearbook for Latin America and the Caribbean.*

Times Books, 201 East 50th Street, New York, New York 10022 (202) 751-2600; *The Economist Book of Vital World Statistics.*

U.C.L.A. Latin American Center Publications, University of California, Los Angeles, California 90024 (310) 825-6634; *Statistical Abstract of Latin America.*

The World Bank, 1818 H Street, NW, Washington, D.C. 20433 (202) 477-1234; *World Tables.*

ECUADOR - AIRLINE SERVICE

The Economist Intelligence Unit, 111 West 57th Street, New York, New York 10019 (800) 938-4685; *The New Latin America Market Atlas.*

Facts on File, 460 Park Avenue South, New York, New York 10016 (800) 443-8323; *The New Book of World Rankings.*

G.K. Hall and Company, 70 Lincoln Street, Boston, Massachusetts 02111 (617) 423-3990; *The World in Figures.*

International Civil Aviation Organization, 1000 Sherbrooke Street West, Suite 400, Montreal, Quebec, Canada H3A 2R2 (514) 285-8219; *Civil Aviation Statistics of the World.*

Statistical Office of the United Nations, Publishing Service, New York, New York 10017 (800) 253-9646; *Statistical Yearbook.*

Times Books, 201 East 50th Street, New York, New York 10022 (202) 751-2600; *The Economist Book of Vital World Statistics.*

ECUADOR - ALUMINUM PRODUCTION AND CONSUMPTION - See ECUADOR - MINING AND MINERAL PRODUCTS

ECUADOR - ANIMAL HEALTH

Food and Agricultural Organization of the United Nations (FAO), Via delle Terme di Caracalla, 00100 Rome, Italy (Telephone Number in U.S. (202) 653-2400); *Animal Health Yearbook.*

ECUADOR - AREA AND DENSITY OF POPULATION

Euromonitor Publications Limited, 87-88 Turnmill Street, London EC1M 5QU, England; *International Marketing Data and Statistics.*

Facts on File, 460 Park Avenue South, New York, New York 10016 (800) 443-8323; *The New Book of World Rankings.*

Federal Statistical Office, Gustav - Stresemann - Ring 11, D-6200 Wiesbaden, Germany; *Ecuador.*

Food and Agricultural Organization of the United Nations (FAO) Via delle Terme di Caracalla, 00100 Rome, Italy (Telephone Number in U.S. (202) 653-2400); *The State of Food and Agriculture.*

G.K. Hall and Company, 70 Lincoln Street, Boston, Massachusetts 02111 (617) 423-3990; *The World in Figures.*

Inter-American Development Bank, 1300 New York Avenue, NW, Washington, D.C. 20577 (202) 623-1753; *Economic and Social Progress in Latin America.*

Statistical Office of the United Nations, Publishing Service, New York, New York 10017 (800) 253-9646; *Statistical Yearbook.*

Times Books, 201 East 50th Street, New York, New York 10022 (202) 751-2600; *The Economist Book of Vital World Statistics.*

United Nations Educational, Scientific and Cultural Organization (UNESCO), 7 Place de Fontenoy, F-75700 Paris, France (Telephone Number in U.S. (212) 963-5981); *Statistical Yearbook.*

ECUADOR - ARMS EXPORTS AND IMPORTS

U.S. Arms Control and Disarmament Agency, 320 Twenty-first Street, NW, Washington, D.C. 20451 (202) 647-8677; *World Military Expenditures and Arms Transfers.*

ECUADOR - BALANCE OF PAYMENTS

The Economist Intelligence Unit, 111 West 57th Street, New York, New York 10019 (800) 938-4685; *The New Latin America Market Atlas,* and *The World Market Atlas.*

Federal Statistical Office, Gustav - Stresemann - Ring 11, D-6200 Wiesbaden, Germany; *Ecuador.*

G.K. Hall and Company, 70 Lincoln Street, Boston, Massachusetts 02111 (617) 423-3990; *The World in Figures.*

Inter-American Development Bank, 1300 New York Avenue, NW, Washington, D.C. 20577 (202) 623-1753; *Economic and Social Progress in Latin America.*

International Monetary Fund, 700 Nineteenth Street, NW, Washington, D.C. 20431 (202) 623-7000; *Balance of Payments Yearbook,* and *International Financial Statistics.*

Organization of American States (OAS), General Secretariat, Washington, D.C. 20006 (202) 458-3533; *Statistical Bulletin of the OAS.*

Statistical Office of the United Nations, Publishing Service, New York, New York 10017 (800) 253-9646; *Economic Survey of Latin America and the Caribbean,* and *Statistical Yearbook for Latin America and the Caribbean.*

Times Books, 201 East 50th Street, New York, New York 10022 (202) 751-2600; *The Economist Book of Vital World Statistics.*

U.C.L.A. Latin American Center Publications, University of California, Los Angeles, California 90024 (310) 825-6634; *Statistical Abstract of Latin America.*

The World Bank, 1818 H Street, NW, Washington, D.C. 20433 (202) 477-1234; *World Tables.*

ECUADOR - BANANA EXPORTS - See ECUADOR - CROPS

ECUADOR - BANKING

Facts on File, 460 Park Avenue South, New York, New York 10016 (800) 443-8323; *The New Book of World Rankings.*

G.K. Hall and Company, 70 Lincoln Street, Boston, Massachusetts 02111 (617) 423-3990; *The World in Figures.*

Inter-American Development Bank, 1300 New York Avenue, NW, Washington, D.C. 20577 (202) 623-1753; *Economic and Social Progress in Latin America.*

International Monetary Fund, 700 Nineteenth Street, NW, Washington, D.C. 20431 (202) 623-7000; *International Financial Statistics.*

Statistical Office of the United Nations, Publishing Service, New York, New York 10017 (800) 253-9646; *Statistical Yearbook,* and *Statistical Yearbook for Latin America and the Caribbean.*

ECUADOR - BARLEY PRODUCTION - See ECUADOR - CROPS

ECUADOR - BEER PRODUCTION

Facts on File, 460 Park Avenue South, New York, New York 10016 (800) 443-8323; *The New Book of World Rankings.*

Statistical Office of the United Nations, Publishing Service, New York, New York 10017 (800) 253-9646; *Statistical Yearbook.*

ECUADOR - BIRTH RATES

Facts on File, 460 Park Avenue South, New York, New York 10016 (800) 443-8323; *The New Book of World Rankings.*

Statistical Office of the United Nations, Publishing Service, New York, New York 10017 (800) 253-9646; *Demographic Yearbook.*

Times Books, 201 East 50th Street, New York, New York 10022 (202) 751-2600; *The Economist Book of Vital World Statistics.*

The World Bank, 1818 H Street, NW, Washington, D.C. 20433 (202) 477-1234; *World Tables.*

World Health Organization, Office of Publications, Avenue Appia, CH-1211 Geneva 27, Switzerland (Telephone Number in U.S. (518) 436-9686); *World Health Statistics Annual.*

ECUADOR - BONDS

G.K. Hall and Company, 70 Lincoln Street, Boston, Massachusetts 02111 (617) 423-3990; *The World in Figures.*

Inter-American Development Bank, 1300 New York Avenue, NW, Washington, D.C. 20577 (202) 623-1753; *Economic and Social Progress in Latin America.*

ECUADOR - BOOK PRODUCTION

G.K. Hall and Company, 70 Lincoln Street, Boston, Massachusetts 02111 (617) 423-3990; *The World in Figures.*

ECUADOR - BROADCASTING

Billboard Limited, P.O. Box 9027, 1006 AA Amsterdam, The Netherlands (Telephone Number in U.S. (212) 764-7300); *World Radio TV Handbook.*

Facts on File, 460 Park Avenue South, New York, New York 10016 (800) 443-8323; *The New Book of World Rankings.*

G.K. Hall and Company, 70 Lincoln Street, Boston, Massachusetts 02111 (617) 423-3990; *The World in Figures.*

Times Books, 201 East 50th Street, New York, New York 10022 (202) 751-2600; *The Economist Book of Vital World Statistics.*

ECUADOR - BUILDING CONSTRUCTION - See ECUADOR - CONSTRUCTION INDUSTRY

ECUADOR - BUSINESS

G.K. Hall and Company, 70 Lincoln Street, Boston, Massachusetts 02111 (617) 423-3990; *The World in Figures.*

Inter-American Development Bank, 1300 New York Avenue, NW, Washington, D.C. 20577 (202) 623-1753; *Economic and Social Progress in Latin America.*

ECUADOR - BUTTER PRODUCTION - See ECUADOR - DAIRY PRODUCTS

ECUADOR - CABBAGE PRODUCTION - See ECUADOR - CROPS

ECUADOR - CACAO EXPORTS - See ECUADOR - CROPS

ECUADOR - CALORIE SUPPLY

Food and Agricultural Organization of the United Nations (FAO) Via delle Terme di Caracalla, 00100 Rome, Italy (Telephone Number in U.S. (202) 653-2400); *The State of Food and Agriculture.*

Statistical Office of the United Nations, Publishing Service, New York, New York 10017 (800) 253-9646; *Statistical Yearbook for Latin America and the Caribbean.*

ECUADOR - CAPITAL INVESTMENT

Inter-American Development Bank, 1300 New York Avenue, NW, Washington, D.C. 20577 (202) 623-1753; *Economic and Social Progress in Latin America.*

ECUADOR - CAPITAL REVENUE

Inter-American Development Bank, 1300 New York Avenue, NW, Washington, D.C. 20577 (202) 623-1753; *Economic and Social Progress in Latin America.*

International Monetary Fund, 700 Nineteenth Street, NW, Washington, D.C. 20431 (202) 623-7000; *Government Finance Statistics Yearbook.*

ECUADOR - CASTOR BEAN PRODUCTION - See ECUADOR - CROPS

ECUADOR - CATTLE - See ECUADOR - LIVESTOCK AND POULTRY

ECUADOR - CAULIFLOWER PRODUCTION - See ECUADOR - CROPS

ECUADOR - CEMENT PRODUCTION - See ECUADOR - MINING AND MINERAL PRODUCTS

ECUADOR - CHEESE PRODUCTION - See ECUADOR - DAIRY PRODUCTS

ECUADOR - CHEMICAL (ORGANIC) PRODUCTION - See ECUADOR - MINING AND MINERAL PRODUCTS

ECUADOR - CHICKENS - See ECUADOR - LIVESTOCK AND POULTRY

ECUADOR - CIGAR PRODUCTION - See ECUADOR - TOBACCO PRODUCTION

ECUADOR - CIGARETTE PRODUCTION - See ECUADOR - TOBACCO PRODUCTION

ECUADOR - CLASS STRUCTURE

G.K. Hall and Company, 70 Lincoln Street, Boston, Massachusetts 02111 (617) 423-3990; *The World in Figures.*

ECUADOR - CLIMATE

Facts on File, 460 Park Avenue South, New York, New York 10016 (800) 443-8323; *The New Book of World Rankings.*

G.K. Hall and Company, 70 Lincoln Street, Boston, Massachusetts 02111 (617) 423-3990; *The World in Figures.*

ECUADOR - COAL PRODUCTION - See ECUADOR - MINING AND MINERAL PRODUCTS

ECUADOR - COCOA (BEANS) PRODUCTION - See ECUADOR - CROPS

ECUADOR - COFFEE - See ECUADOR - CROPS

ECUADOR - COMMUNICATIONS

Federal Statistical Office, Gustav - Stresemann - Ring 11, D-6200 Wiesbaden, Germany; *Ecuador.*

G.K. Hall and Company, 70 Lincoln Street, Boston, Massachusetts 02111 (617) 423-3990; *The World in Figures.*

Inter-American Development Bank, 1300 New York Avenue, NW, Washington, D.C. 20577 (202) 623-1753; *Economic and Social Progress in Latin America.*

U.C.L.A. Latin American Center Publications, University of California, Los Angeles, California 90024 (310) 825-6634; *Statistical Abstract of Latin America.*

ECUADOR - CONSTRUCTION INDUSTRY

The Economist Intelligence Unit, 111 West 57th Street, New York, New York 10019 (800) 938-4685; *The New Latin America Market Atlas.*

Facts on File, 460 Park Avenue South, New York, New York 10016 (800) 443-8323; *The New Book of World Rankings.*

Inter-American Development Bank, 1300 New York Avenue, NW, Washington, D.C. 20577 (202) 623-1753; *Economic and Social Progress in Latin America.*

Statistical Office of the United Nations, Publishing Service, New York, New York 10017 (800) 253-9646; *Construction Statistics Yearbook,* and *Statistical Yearbook.*

U.C.L.A. Latin American Center Publications, University of California, Los Angeles, California 90024 (310) 825-6634; *Statistical Abstract of Latin America.*

ECUADOR - CONSUMER PRICE INDEX

Federal Statistical Office, Gustav - Stresemann - Ring 11, D-6200 Wiesbaden, Germany; *Ecuador.*

G.K. Hall and Company, 70 Lincoln Street, Boston, Massachusetts 02111 (617) 423-3990; *The World in Figures.*

International Labour Office, I.L.O. Publications, CH-1211, Geneva 22, Switzerland; *Yearbook of Labour Statistics.*

Statistical Office of the United Nations, Publishing Service, New York, New York 10017 (800) 253-9646; *Statistical Yearbook.*

ECUADOR - CONSUMER PRICES

The Economist Intelligence Unit, 111 West 57th Street, New York, New York 10019 (800) 938-4685; *The New Latin America Market Atlas.*

Federal Statistical Office, Gustav - Stresemann - Ring 11, D-6200 Wiesbaden, Germany; *Ecuador.*

International Labour Office, I.L.O. Publications, CH-1211, Geneva 22, Switzerland; *Yearbook of Labour Statistics.*

International Monetary Fund, 700 Nineteenth Street, NW, Washington, D.C. 20431 (202) 623-7000; *International Financial Statistics.*

Organization of American States (OAS), General Secretariat, Washington, D.C. 20006 (202) 458-3533; *Statistical Bulletin of the OAS.*

Times Books, 201 East 50th Street, New York, New York 10022 (202) 751-2600; *The Economist Book of Vital World Statistics.*

U.C.L.A. Latin American Center Publications, University of California, Los Angeles, California 90024 (310) 825-6634; *Statistical Abstract of Latin America.*

ECUADOR - CONSUMPTION

The Economist Intelligence Unit, 111 West 57th Street, New York, New York 10019 (800) 938-4685; *The New Latin America Market Atlas.*

G.K. Hall and Company, 70 Lincoln Street, Boston, Massachusetts 02111 (617) 423-3990; *The World in Figures.*

Inter-American Development Bank, 1300 New York Avenue, NW, Washington, D.C. 20577 (202) 623-1753; *Economic and Social Progress in Latin America.*

Statistical Office of the United Nations, Publishing Service, New York, New York 10017 (800) 253-9646; *Statistical Yearbook for Latin America and the Caribbean.*

ECUADOR - COOPERATIVES

U.C.L.A. Latin American Center Publications, University of California, Los Angeles, California 90024 (310) 825-6634; *Statistical Abstract of Latin America.*

ECUADOR - COPPER AND COPPER ORE - See ECUADOR - MINING AND MINERAL PRODUCTS

ECUADOR - CORN PRODUCTION - See ECUADOR - CROPS

ECUADOR - CORPORATE INCOME TAXES - See ECUADOR - TAXATION

ECUADOR - CORPORATE TAXES - See ECUADOR - TAXATION

ECUADOR - COTTON - See ECUADOR - CROPS

ECUADOR - CRIME

International Criminal Police Organization (INTERPOL), 26 rue Armengaud, 92210 Saint Cloud, France; *International Crime Statistics.*

ECUADOR - CROPS

Commodity Research Bureau, Incorporated, 75 Wall Street, New York, New York 10005 (212) 504-7754; *Commodity Year Book.*

The Economist Intelligence Unit, 111 West 57th Street, New York, New York 10019 (800) 938-4685; *The New Latin America Market Atlas.*

Facts on File, 460 Park Avenue South, New York, New York 10016 (800) 443-8323; *The New Book of World Rankings.*

Food and Agricultural Organization of the United Nations (FAO) Via delle Terme di Caracalla, 00100 Rome, Italy (Telephone Number in U.S. (202) 653-2400); *Production Yearbook* and *The State of Food and Agriculture.*

G.K. Hall and Company, 70 Lincoln Street, Boston, Massachusetts 02111 (617) 423-3990; *The World in Figures.*

International Monetary Fund, 700 Nineteenth Street, NW, Washington, D.C. 20431 (202) 623-7000; *International Financial Statistics.*

Organization of American States (OAS), General Secretariat, Washington, D.C. 20006 (202) 458-3533; *Statistical Bulletin of the OAS.*

Statistical Office of the United Nations, Publishing Service, New York, New York 10017 (800) 253-9646; *Statistical Yearbook.*

ECUADOR - CUSTOMS DUTIES

G.K. Hall and Company, 70 Lincoln Street, Boston, Massachusetts 02111 (617) 423-3990; *The World in Figures.*

Inter-American Development Bank, 1300 New York Avenue, NW, Washington, D.C. 20577 (202) 623-1753; *Economic and Social Progress in Latin America.*

International Monetary Fund, 700 Nineteenth Street, NW, Washington, D.C. 20431 (202) 623-7000; *Government Finance Statistics Yearbook.*

ECUADOR - DAIRY PRODUCTS

Facts on File, 460 Park Avenue South, New York, New York 10016 (800) 443-8323; *The New Book of World Rankings.*

Food and Agricultural Organization of the United Nations (FAO) Via delle Terme di Caracalla, 00100 Rome, Italy (Telephone Number in U.S. (202) 653-2400); *The State of Food and Agriculture.*

Statistical Office of the United Nations, Publishing Service, New York, New York 10017 (800) 253-9646; *Statistical Yearbook.*

ECUADOR - DEATH RATES

G.K. Hall and Company, 70 Lincoln Street, Boston, Massachusetts 02111 (617) 423-3990; *The World in Figures.*

Statistical Office of the United Nations, Publishing Service, New York, New York 10017 (800) 253-9646; *Statistical Yearbook,* and *Statistical Yearbook for Latin America and the Caribbean.*

Times Books, 201 East 50th Street, New York, New York 10022 (202) 751-2600; *The Economist Book of Vital World Statistics.*

World Health Organization, Office of Publications, Avenue Appia, CH-1211 Geneva 27, Switzerland (Telephone Number in U.S. (518) 436-9686); *World Health Statistics Annual.*

ECUADOR - DEBT

The Economist Intelligence Unit, 111 West 57th Street, New York, New York 10019 (800) 938-4685; *The New Latin America Market Atlas.*

ECUADOR - DEFENSE EXPENDITURES

The Economist Intelligence Unit, 111 West 57th Street, New York, New York 10019 (800) 938-4685; *The New Latin America Market Atlas.*

G.K. Hall and Company, 70 Lincoln Street, Boston, Massachusetts 02111 (617) 423-3990; *The World in Figures.*

International Monetary Fund, 700 Nineteenth Street, NW, Washington, D.C. 20431 (202) 623-7000; *Government Finance Statistics Yearbook.*

U.S. Arms Control and Disarmament Agency, 320 Twenty-first Street, NW, Washington, D.C. 20451 (202) 647-8677; *World Military Expenditures and Arms Transfers.*

ECUADOR - DEMOGRAPHY

The Economist Intelligence Unit, 111 West 57th Street, New York, New York 10019 (800) 938-4685; *The World Market Atlas.*

Facts on File, 460 Park Avenue South, New York, New York 10016 (800) 443-8323; *The New Book of World Rankings.*

Federal Statistical Office, Gustav - Stresemann - Ring 11, D-6200 Wiesbaden, Germany; *Ecuador.*

G.K. Hall and Company, 70 Lincoln Street, Boston, Massachusetts 02111 (617) 423-3990; *The World in Figures.*

U.C.L.A. Latin American Center Publications, University of California, Los Angeles, California 90024 (310) 825-6634; *Statistical Abstract of Latin America.*

ECUADOR - DEVELOPMENT ASSISTANCE

G.K. Hall and Company, 70 Lincoln Street, Boston, Massachusetts 02111 (617) 423-3990; *The World in Figures.*

Inter-American Development Bank, 1300 New York Avenue, NW, Washington, D.C. 20577 (202) 623-1753; *Economic and Social Progress in Latin America.*

Statistical Office of the United Nations, Publishing Service, New York, New York 10017 (800) 253-9646; *Statistical Yearbook.*

ECUADOR - DIAMOND PRODUCTION - See ECUADOR - MINING AND MINERAL PRODUCTS

ECUADOR - DISCOUNT RATES

Inter-American Development Bank, 1300 New York Avenue, NW, Washington, D.C. 20577 (202) 623-1753; *Economic and Social Progress in Latin America.*

Statistical Office of the United Nations, Publishing Service, New York, New York 10017 (800) 253-9646; *Statistical Yearbook.*

ECUADOR - DISEASES

G.K. Hall and Company, 70 Lincoln Street, Boston, Massachusetts 02111 (617) 423-3990; *The World in Figures.*

World Health Organization, Office of Publications, Avenue Appia, CH-1211 Geneva 27, Switzerland (Telephone Number in U.S. (518) 436-9686); *World Health Statistics Annual.*

ECUADOR - DIVORCE RATES

Facts on File, 460 Park Avenue South, New York, New York 10016 (800) 443-8323; *The New Book of World Rankings.*

Statistical Office of the United Nations, Publishing Service, New York, New York 10017 (800) 253-9646; *Demographic Yearbook,* and *Statistical Yearbook.*

ECUADOR - DOMESTIC PRODUCT

G.K. Hall and Company, 70 Lincoln Street, Boston, Massachusetts 02111 (617) 423-3990; *The World in Figures.*

ECUADOR - DUCKS - See ECUADOR - LIVESTOCK AND POULTRY

ECUADOR - ECONOMY

Euromonitor Publications Limited, 87-88 Turnmill Street, London EC1M 5QU, England; *International Marketing Data and Statistics.*

Facts on File, 460 Park Avenue South, New York, New York 10016 (800) 443-8323; *The New Book of World Rankings.*

Federal Statistical Office, Gustav - Stresemann - Ring 11, D-6200 Wiesbaden, Germany; *Ecuador.*

G.K. Hall and Company, 70 Lincoln Street, Boston, Massachusetts 02111 (617) 423-3990; *The World in Figures.*

Inter-American Development Bank, 1300 New York Avenue, NW, Washington, D.C. 20577 (202) 623-1753; *Economic and Social*

Progress in Latin America.

Organization of American States (OAS), General Secretariat, Washington, D.C. 20006 (202) 458-3533; *Statistical Bulletin of the OAS.*

Statistical Office of the United Nations, Publishing Service, New York, New York 10017 (800) 253-9646; *Economic Survey of Latin America and the Caribbean.*

U.C.L.A. Latin American Center Publications, University of California, Los Angeles, California 90024 (310) 825-6634; *Statistical Abstract of Latin America.*

ECUADOR - EDUCATION

The Economist Intelligence Unit, 111 West 57th Street, New York, New York 10019 (800) 938-4685; *The New Latin America Market Atlas*, and *The World Market Atlas.*

Facts on File, 460 Park Avenue South, New York, New York 10016 (800) 443-8323; *The New Book of World Rankings.*

Federal Statistical Office, Gustav - Stresemann - Ring 11, D-6200 Wiesbaden, Germany; *Ecuador.*

Gale Research Incorporated, 835 Penobscot Building, Detroit, Michigan 48226 (800) 877-4253; *International Historical Statistics The Americas and Australasia.*

G.K. Hall and Company, 70 Lincoln Street, Boston, Massachusetts 02111 (617) 423-3990; *The World in Figures.*

International Monetary Fund, 700 Nineteenth Street, NW, Washington, D.C. 20431 (202) 623-7000; *Government Finance Statistics Yearbook.*

Statistical Office of the United Nations, Publishing Service, New York, New York 10017 (800) 253-9646; *Statistical Yearbook for Latin America and the Caribbean.*

Times Books, 201 East 50th Street, New York, New York 10022 (202) 751-2600; *The Economist Book of Vital World Statistics.*

U.C.L.A. Latin American Center Publications, University of California, Los Angeles, California 90024 (310) 825-6634; *Statistical Abstract of Latin America.*

United Nations Educational, Scientific and Cultural Organization (UNESCO), 7 Place de Fontenoy, F-75700 Paris, France (Telephone Number in U.S. (212) 963-5981); *Statistical Yearbook.*

The World Bank, 1818 H Street, NW, Washington, D.C. 20433 (202) 477-1234; *World Tables.*

ECUADOR - EGG PRODUCTION - See ECUADOR - DAIRY PRODUCTS

ECUADOR - ELECTRICITY

The Economist Intelligence Unit, 111 West 57th Street, New York, New York 10019 (800) 938-4685; *The New Latin America Market Atlas.*

Facts on File, 460 Park Avenue South, New York, New York 10016 (800) 443-8323; *The New Book of World Rankings.*

Inter-American Development Bank, 1300 New York Avenue, NW, Washington, D.C. 20577 (202) 623-1753; *Economic and Social Progress in Latin America.*

Penn Well Publishing Company, 1421 South Sheridan Road, P.O. Box 1260, Tulsa, Oklahoma 74101 (800) 752-9764; *International Energy Statistics Sourcebook.*

Statistical Office of the United Nations, Publishing Service, New York, New York 10017 (800) 253-9646; *Statistical Yearbook.*

Times Books, 201 East 50th Street, New York, New York 10022 (202) 751-2600; *The Economist Book of Vital World Statistics.*

ECUADOR - EMPLOYMENT

Euromonitor Publications Limited, 87-88 Turnmill Street, London EC1M 5QU, England; *International Marketing Data and Statistics.*

Facts on File, 460 Park Avenue South, New York, New York 10016 (800) 443-8323; *The New Book of World Rankings.*

Federal Statistical Office, Gustav - Stresemann - Ring 11, D-6200 Wiesbaden, Germany; *Ecuador.*

International Labour Office, I.L.O. Publications, CH-1211, Geneva 22, Switzerland; *Yearbook of Labour Statistics.*

Organization of American States (OAS), General Secretariat, Washington, D.C. 20006 (202) 458-3533; *Statistical Bulletin of the OAS.*

Statistical Office of the United Nations, Publishing Service, New York, New York 10017 (800) 253-9646; *Statistical Yearbook*, and *Statistical Yearbook for Latin America and the Caribbean.*

U.C.L.A. Latin American Center Publications, University of California, Los Angeles, California 90024 (310) 825-6634; *Statistical Abstract of Latin America.*

ECUADOR - ENERGY

The Economist Intelligence Unit, 111 West 57th Street, New York, New York 10019 (800) 938-4685; *The New Latin America Market Atlas.*

Facts on File, 460 Park Avenue South, New York, New York 10016 (800) 443-8323; *The New Book of World Rankings.*

Food and Agricultural Organization of the United Nations (FAO) Via delle Terme di Caracalla, 00100 Rome, Italy (Telephone Number in U.S. (202) 653-2400); *The State of Food and Agriculture.*

G.K. Hall and Company, 70 Lincoln Street, Boston, Massachusetts 02111 (617) 423-3990; *The World in Figures.*

Penn Well Publishing Company, 1421 South Sheridan Road, P.O. Box 1260, Tulsa, Oklahoma 74101 (800) 752-9764; *International Energy Statistics Sourcebook.*

Statistical Office of the United Nations, Publishing Service, New York, New York 10017 (800) 253-9646; *Energy Statistics Yearbook, Statistical Yearbook*, and *Statistical Yearbook for Latin America and the Caribbean.*

Times Books, 201 East 50th Street, New York, New York 10022 (202) 751-2600; *The Economist Book of Vital World Statistics.*

U.C.L.A. Latin American Center Publications, University of California, Los Angeles, California 90024 (310) 825-6634; *Statistical Abstract of Latin America.*

ECUADOR - EXCHANGE RATES

Euromonitor Publications Limited, 87-88 Turnmill Street, London EC1M 5QU, England; *International Marketing Data and Statistics.*

Inter-American Development Bank, 1300 New York Avenue, NW, Washington, D.C. 20577 (202) 623-1753; *Economic and Social Progress in Latin America.*

International Civil Aviation Organization, 1000 Sherbrooke Street West, Suite 400, Montreal, Quebec, Canada H3A 2R2 (514) 285-8219; *Civil Aviation Statistics of the World.*

International Monetary Fund, 700 Nineteenth Street, NW, Washington, D.C. 20431 (202) 623-7000; *International Financial Statistics.*

Organization of American States (OAS), General Secretariat, Washington, D.C. 20006 (202) 458-3533; *Statistical Bulletin of the OAS.*

Organization of Petroleum Exporting Countries, Obere Donaustrasse 93, 1020 Vienna 2, Austria; *OPEC Annual Statistical Bulletin.*

Statistical Office of the United Nations, Publishing Service, New York, New York 10017 (800) 253-9646; *Statistical Yearbook.*

U.C.L.A. Latin American Center Publications, University of California, Los Angeles, California 90024 (310) 825-6634; *Statistical Abstract of Latin America.*

ECUADOR - EXCISE TAXES

Inter-American Development Bank, 1300 New York Avenue, NW, Washington, D.C. 20577 (202) 623-1753; *Economic and Social Progress in Latin America.*

International Monetary Fund, 700 Nineteenth Street, NW, Washington, D.C. 20431 (202) 623-7000; *Government Finance Statistics Yearbook.*

ECUADOR - EXPORTS

The Economist Intelligence Unit, 111 West 57th Street, New York, New York 10019 (800) 938-4685; *The New Latin America Market Atlas,* and *The World Market Atlas.*

Euromonitor Publications Limited, 87-88 Turnmill Street, London EC1M 5QU, England; *International Marketing Data and Statistics.*

Food and Agricultural Organization of the United Nations (FAO) Via delle Terme di Caracalla, 00100 Rome, Italy (Telephone Number in U.S. (202) 653-2400); *The State of Food and Agriculture.*

G.K. Hall and Company, 70 Lincoln Street, Boston, Massachusetts 02111 (617) 423-3990; *The World in Figures.*

Inter-American Development Bank, 1300 New York Avenue, NW, Washington, D.C. 20577 (202) 623-1753; *Economic and Social Progress in Latin America.*

International Monetary Fund, 700 Nineteenth Street, NW, Washington, D.C. 20431 (202) 623-7000; *Direction of Trade Statistics,* and *International Financial Statistics.*

Organization of American States (OAS), General Secretariat, Washington, D.C. 20006 (202) 458-3533; *Statistical Bulletin of the OAS.*

Organization of Petroleum Exporting Countries, Obere Donaustrasse 93, 1020 Vienna 2, Austria; *OPEC Annual Statistical Bulletin.*

Statistical Office of the United Nations, Publishing Service, New York, New York 10017 (800) 253-9646; *Statistical Yearbook for Latin America and the Caribbean,* and *Trade in Manufactures of Developing Countries.*

Times Books, 201 East 50th Street, New York, New York 10022 (202) 751-2600; *The Economist Book of Vital World Statistics.*

The World Bank, 1818 H Street, NW, Washington, D.C. 20433 (202) 477-1234; *World Tables.*

ECUADOR - EXTERNAL FINANCING

Inter-American Development Bank, 1300 New York Avenue, NW, Washington, D.C. 20577 (202) 623-1753; *Economic and Social Progress in Latin America.*

Statistical Office of the United Nations, Publishing Service, New York, New York 10017 (800) 253-9646; *Statistical Yearbook for Latin America and the Caribbean.*

ECUADOR - EXTERNAL INDEBTEDNESS

Inter-American Development Bank, 1300 New York Avenue, NW, Washington, D.C. 20577 (202) 623-1753; *Economic and Social Progress in Latin America.*

The World Bank, 1818 H Street, NW, Washington, D.C. 20433 (202) 477-1234; *World Tables.*

ECUADOR - EXTERNAL TRADE

Food and Agricultural Organization of the United Nations (FAO) Via delle Terme di Caracalla, 00100 Rome, Italy (Telephone Number in U.S. (202) 653-2400); *The State of Food and Agriculture* and *Trade Yearbook.*

Gale Research Incorporated, 835 Penobscot Building, Detroit, Michigan 48226 (800) 877-4253; *International Historical Statistics The Americas and Australasia.*

G.K. Hall and Company, 70 Lincoln Street, Boston, Massachusetts 02111 (617) 423-3990; *The World in Figures.*

Inter-American Development Bank, 1300 New York Avenue, NW, Washington, D.C. 20577 (202) 623-1753; *Economic and Social Progress in Latin America.*

Statistical Office of the United Nations, Publishing Service, New York, New York 10017 (800) 253-9646; *Statistical Yearbook,* and *Statistical Yearbook for Latin America and the Caribbean.*

ECUADOR - FABRIC PRODUCTION - See ECUADOR - TEXTILE INDUSTRY

ECUADOR - FAMILY PLANNING

U.C.L.A. Latin American Center Publications, University of California, Los Angeles, California 90024 (310) 825-6634; *Statistical Abstract of Latin America.*

ECUADOR - FARM CROPS - See ECUADOR - CROPS

ECUADOR - FEMALE WORKING POPULATION - See ECUADOR - EMPLOYMENT

ECUADOR - FERTILITY RATES

Facts on File, 460 Park Avenue South, New York, New York 10016 (800) 443-8323; *The New Book of World Rankings.*

Times Books, 201 East 50th Street, New York, New York 10022 (202) 751-2600; *The Economist Book of Vital World Statistics.*

The World Bank, 1818 H Street, NW, Washington, D.C. 20433 (202) 477-1234; *World Tables.*

ECUADOR - FERTILIZER

The Economist Intelligence Unit, 111 West 57th Street, New York, New York 10019 (800) 938-4685; *The New Latin America Market Atlas.*

Food and Agricultural Organization of the United Nations (FAO), Via delle Terme di Caracalla, 00100 Rome, Italy (Telephone Number in U.S. (202) 653-2400); *Fertilizer Yearbook,* and *The State of Food and Agriculture.*

Statistical Office of the United Nations, Publishing Service, New York, New York 10017 (800) 253-9646; *Statistical Yearbook.*

ECUADOR - FETAL MORTALITY

Statistical Office of the United Nations, Publishing Service, New York, New York 10017 (800) 253-9646; *Demographic Yearbook.*

World Health Organization, Office of Publications, Avenue Appia, CH-1211 Geneva 27, Switzerland (Telephone Number in U.S (518) 436-9686); *World Health Statistics Annual.*

ECUADOR - FIBRE PRODUCTION - See ECUADOR - TEXTILE INDUSTRY

ECUADOR - FINANCE

Facts on File, 460 Park Avenue South, New York, New York 10016 (800) 443-8323; *The New Book of World Rankings.*

Federal Statistical Office, Gustav - Stresemann - Ring 11, D-6200 Wiesbaden, Germany; *Ecuador.*

Gale Research Incorporated, 835 Penobscot Building, Detroit, Michigan 48226 (800) 877-4253; *International Historical Statistics The Americas and Australasia.*

G.K. Hall and Company, 70 Lincoln Street, Boston, Massachusetts 02111 (617) 423-3990; *The World in Figures.*

Inter-American Development Bank, 1300 New York Avenue, NW, Washington, D.C. 20577 (202) 623-1753; *Economic and Social Progress in Latin America.*

International Monetary Fund, 700 Nineteenth Street, NW, Washington, D.C. 20431 (202) 623-7000; *International Financial Statistics.*

Organization of American States (OAS), General Secretariat, Washington, D.C. 20006 (202) 458-3533; *Statistical Bulletin of the OAS.*

U.C.L.A. Latin American Center Publications, University of California, Los Angeles, California 90024 (310) 825-6634; *Statistical Abstract of Latin America.*

ECUADOR - FISHERIES

Facts on File, 460 Park Avenue South, New York, New York 10016 (800) 443-8323; *The New Book of World Rankings.*

Federal Statistical Office, Gustav - Stresemann - Ring 11, D-6200 Wiesbaden, Germany; *Ecuador.*

Food and Agricultural Organization of the United Nations (FAO) Via delle Terme di Caracalla, 00100 Rome, Italy (Telephone Number in U.S. (202) 653-2400); *The State of Food and Agriculture,* and *Yearbook of Fishery Statistics.*

Inter-American Development Bank, 1300 New York Avenue, NW, Washington, D.C. 20577 (202) 623-1753; *Economic and Social Progress in Latin America.*

Statistical Office of the United Nations, Publishing Service, New York, New York 10017 (800) 253-9646; *Statistical Yearbook.*

U.C.L.A. Latin American Center Publications, University of California, Los Angeles, California 90024 (310) 825-6634; *Statistical Abstract of Latin America.*

ECUADOR - FLOUR PRODUCTION

Statistical Office of the United Nations, Publishing Service, New York, New York 10017 (800) 253-9646; *Statistical Yearbook.*

ECUADOR - FOOD

Food and Agricultural Organization of the United Nations (FAO) Via delle Terme di Caracalla, 00100 Rome, Italy (Telephone Number in U.S. (202) 653-2400); *Production Yearbook,* and *The State of Food and Agriculture.*

G.K. Hall and Company, 70 Lincoln Street, Boston, Massachusetts 02111 (617) 423-3990; *The World in Figures.*

Statistical Office of the United Nations, Publishing Service, New York, New York 10017 (800) 253-9646; *Trade in Manufactures of Developing Countries.*

ECUADOR - FOREIGN AID

G.K. Hall and Company, 70 Lincoln Street, Boston, Massachusetts 02111 (617) 423-3990; *The World in Figures.*

Inter-American Development Bank, 1300 New York Avenue, NW, Washington, D.C. 20577 (202) 623-1753; *Economic and Social Progress in Latin America.*

ECUADOR - FOREIGN DEBT

The Economist Intelligence Unit, 111 West 57th Street, New York, New York 10019 (800) 938-4685; *The New Latin America Market Atlas.*

Inter-American Development Bank, 1300 New York Avenue, NW, Washington, D.C. 20577 (202) 623-1753; *Economic and Social Progress in Latin America.*

ECUADOR - FOREIGN FINANCE

Inter-American Development Bank, 1300 New York Avenue, NW, Washington, D.C. 20577 (202) 623-1753; *Economic and Social Progress in Latin America.*

ECUADOR - FOREIGN INDEBTEDNESS

Inter-American Development Bank, 1300 New York Avenue, NW, Washington, D.C. 20577 (202) 623-1753; *Economic and Social Progress in Latin America*.

Statistical Office of the United Nations, Publishing Service, New York, New York 10017 (800) 253-9646; *Economic Survey of Latin America and the Caribbean*.

ECUADOR - FOREIGN INVESTMENT

The Economist Intelligence Unit, 111 West 57th Street, New York, New York 10019 (800) 938-4685; *The New Latin America Market Atlas*.

ECUADOR - FOREIGN TRADE

The Economist Intelligence Unit, 111 West 57th Street, New York, New York 10019 (800) 938-4685; *The New Latin America Market Atlas*.

Euromonitor Publications Limited, 87-88 Turnmill Street, London EC1M 5QU, England; *International Marketing Data and Statistics*.

Facts on File, 460 Park Avenue South, New York, New York 10016 (800) 443-8323; *The New Book of World Rankings*.

Federal Statistical Office, Gustav - Stresemann - Ring 11, D-6200 Wiesbaden, Germany; *Ecuador*.

Food and Agricultural Organization of the United Nations (FAO) Via delle Terme di Caracalla, 00100 Rome, Italy (Telephone Number in U.S. (202) 653-2400); *The State of Food and Agriculture*.

G.K. Hall and Company, 70 Lincoln Street, Boston, Massachusetts 02111 (617) 423-3990; *The World in Figures*.

Inter-American Development Bank, 1300 New York Avenue, NW, Washington, D.C. 20577 (202) 623-1753; *Economic and Social Progress in Latin America*.

International Monetary Fund, 700 Nineteenth Street, NW, Washington, D.C. 20431 (202) 623-7000; *International Financial Statistics*.

Organisation for Economic Co-operation and Development (OECD), 2 rue Andre-Pascal, 75 Paris 16, France (Telephone Number in U.S. (202) 785-6323); *Trade by Commodities*.

Statistical Office of the United Nations, Publishing Service, New York, New York 10017 (800) 253-9646; *Economic Survey of Latin America and the Caribbean*, *International Trade Statistics Yearbook*, and *Statistical Yearbook*.

U.C.L.A. Latin American Center Publications, University of California, Los Angeles, California 90024 (310) 825-6634; *Statistical Abstract of Latin America*.

The World Bank, 1818 H Street, NW, Washington, D.C. 20433 (202) 477-1234; *World Tables*.

ECUADOR - FORESTRY AND FOREST PRODUCTS

Facts on File, 460 Park Avenue South, New York, New York 10016 (800) 443-8323; *The New Book of World Rankings*.

Federal Statistical Office, Gustav - Stresemann - Ring 11, D-6200 Wiesbaden, Germany; *Ecuador*.

Food and Agricultural Organization of the United Nations (FAO) Via delle Terme di Caracalla, 00100 Rome, Italy (Telephone Number in U.S. (202) 653-2400); *The State of Food and Agriculture*, and *Yearbook of Forest Products*.

Forest and Paper Association, 1250 Connecticut Avenue, NW, Washington, D.C. 20036 (202) 463-2455; *Wood Pulp and Fiber Statistics*.

G.K. Hall and Company, 70 Lincoln Street, Boston, Massachusetts 02111 (617) 423-3990; *The World in Figures*.

Inter-American Development Bank, 1300 New York Avenue, NW, Washington, D.C. 20577 (202) 623-1753; *Economic and Social Progress in Latin America*.

U.C.L.A. Latin American Center Publications, University of California, Los Angeles, California 90024 (310) 825-6634; *Statistical Abstract of Latin America*.

United Nations Educational, Scientific and Cultural Organization (UNESCO), 7 Place de Fontenoy, F-75700 Paris, France (Telephone Number in U.S. (212) 963-5981); *Statistical Yearbook*.

ECUADOR - GARLIC PRODUCTION - See ECUADOR - CROPS

ECUADOR - GAS AND GAS LIQUIDS PRODUCTION - See ECUADOR - MINING AND MINERAL PRODUCTS

ECUADOR - GENERAL INDUSTRIAL STATISTICS

Federal Statistical Office, Gustav - Stresemann - Ring 11, D-6200 Wiesbaden, Germany; *Ecuador*.

Statistical Office of the United Nations, Publishing Service, New York, New York 10017 (800) 253-9646; *Industrial Statistics Yearbook*.

ECUADOR - GENERAL MORTALITY

Statistical Office of the United Nations, Publishing Service, New York, New York 10017 (800) 253-9646; *Demographic Yearbook*.

World Health Organization, Office of Publications, Avenue Appia, CH-1211 Geneva 27, Switzerland (Telephone Number in U.S. (518) 436-9686); *World Health Statistics Annual*.

ECUADOR - GEOGRAPHIC DATA

Facts on File, 460 Park Avenue South, New York, New York 10016 (800) 443-8323; *The New Book of World Rankings*.

Federal Statistical Office, Gustav - Stresemann - Ring 11, D-6200 Wiesbaden, Germany; *Ecuador*.

U.C.L.A. Latin American Center Publications, University of California, Los Angeles, California 90024 (310) 825-6634; *Statistical Abstract of Latin America*.

ECUADOR - GOATS - See ECUADOR - LIVESTOCK AND POULTRY

ECUADOR - GOLD HOLDINGS

International Monetary Fund, 700 Nineteenth Street, NW, Washington, D.C. 20431 (202) 623-7000; *International Financial Statistics*.

Statistical Office of the United Nations, Publishing Service, New York, New York 10017 (800) 253-9646; *Statistical Yearbook*.

The World Bank, 1818 H Street, NW, Washington, D.C. 20433 (202) 477-1234; *World Tables.*

ECUADOR - GOLD PRODUCTION - See ECUADOR - MINING AND MINERAL PRODUCTS

ECUADOR - GOLD RESERVES

The Economist Intelligence Unit, 111 West 57th Street, New York, New York 10019 (800) 938-4685; *The New Latin America Market Atlas.*

ECUADOR - GOVERNMENT

G.K. Hall and Company, 70 Lincoln Street, Boston, Massachusetts 02111 (617) 423-3990; *The World in Figures.*

Inter-American Development Bank, 1300 New York Avenue, NW, Washington, D.C. 20577 (202) 623-1753; *Economic and Social Progress in Latin America.*

ECUADOR - GOVERNMENT BONDS - See ECUADOR - BONDS

ECUADOR - GOVERNMENT CONSUMPTION

Inter-American Development Bank, 1300 New York Avenue, NW, Washington, D.C. 20577 (202) 623-1753; *Economic and Social Progress in Latin America.*

ECUADOR - GOVERNMENT EXPENDITURES

Inter-American Development Bank, 1300 New York Avenue, NW, Washington, D.C. 20577 (202) 623-1753; *Economic and Social Progress in Latin America.*

International Monetary Fund, 700 Nineteenth Street, NW, Washington, D.C. 20431 (202) 623-7000; *Government Finance Statistics Yearbook.*

Times Books, 201 East 50th Street, New York, New York 10022 (202) 751-2600; *The Economist Book of Vital World Statistics.*

The World Bank, 1818 H Street, NW, Washington, D.C. 20433 (202) 477-1234; *World Tables.*

ECUADOR - GOVERNMENT FINANCES

Inter-American Development Bank, 1300 New York Avenue, NW, Washington, D.C. 20577 (202) 623-1753; *Economic and Social Progress in Latin America.*

Statistical Office of the United Nations, Publishing Service, New York, New York 10017 (800) 253-9646; *Statistical Yearbook.*

ECUADOR - GOVERNMENT REVENUES

Inter-American Development Bank, 1300 New York Avenue, NW, Washington, D.C. 20577 (202) 623-1753; *Economic and Social Progress in Latin America.*

International Monetary Fund, 700 Nineteenth Street, NW, Washington, D.C. 20431 (202) 623-7000; *Government Finance Statistics Yearbook.*

Times Books, 201 East 50th Street, New York, New York 10022 (202) 751-2600; *The Economist Book of Vital World Statistics.*

U.C.L.A. Latin American Center Publications, University of California, Los Angeles, California 90024 (310) 825-6634; *Statistical Abstract of Latin America.*

The World Bank, 1818 H Street, NW, Washington, D.C. 20433 (202) 477-1234; *World Tables.*

ECUADOR - GRAIN PRODUCTION - See ECUADOR - CROPS

ECUADOR - GRANTS

International Monetary Fund, 700 Nineteenth Street, NW, Washington, D.C. 20431 (202) 623-7000; *Government Finance Statistics Yearbook.*

ECUADOR - GREEN PEPPER AND CHILIE PRODUCTION - See ECUADOR - CROPS

ECUADOR - GROSS DOMESTIC PRODUCT

The Economist Intelligence Unit, 111 West 57th Street, New York, New York 10019 (800) 938-4685; *The New Latin America Market Atlas,* and *The World Market Atlas.*

Euromonitor Publications Limited, 87-88 Turnmill Street, London EC1M 5QU, England; *International Marketing Data and Statistics.*

Facts on File, 460 Park Avenue South, New York, New York 10016; *The New Book of World Rankings.*

G.K. Hall and Company, 70 Lincoln Street, Boston, Massachusetts 02111 (617) 423-3990; *The World in Figures.*

Inter-American Development Bank, 1300 New York Avenue, NW, Washington, D.C. 20577 (202) 623-1753; *Economic and Social Progress in Latin America.*

Organization of American States (OAS), General Secretariat, Washington, D.C. 20006 (202) 458-3533; *Statistical Bulletin of the OAS.*

Statistical Office of the United Nations, Publishing Service, New York, New York 10017 (800) 253-9646; *Statistical Yearbook,* and *Statistical Yearbook for Latin America and the Caribbean.*

Times Books, 201 East 50th Street, New York, New York 10022 (202) 751-2600; *The Economist Book of Vital World Statistics.*

U.C.L.A. Latin American Center Publications, University of California, Los Angeles, California 90024 (310) 825-6634; *Statistical Abstract of Latin America.*

The World Bank, 1818 H Street, NW, Washington, D.C. 20433 (202) 477-1234; *World Tables.*

ECUADOR - GROSS NATIONAL PRODUCT

Euromonitor Publications Limited, 87-88 Turnmill Street, London EC1M 5QU, England; *International Marketing Data and Statistics.*

Inter-American Development Bank, 1300 New York Avenue, NW, Washington, D.C. 20577 (202) 623-1753; *Economic and Social Progress in Latin America.*

Organization of Petroleum Exporting Countries, Obere Donaustrasse 93, 1020 Vienna 2, Austria; *OPEC Annual Statistical Bulletin.*

U.S. Arms Control and Disarmament Agency, 320 Twenty-first Street, NW, Washington, D.C. 20451 (202) 647-8677; *World Military Expenditures and Arms Transfers.*

The World Bank, 1818 H Street, NW, Washington, D.C. 20433 (202) 477-1234; *World Tables.*

ECUADOR - GROUNDNUTS PRODUCTION - See ECUADOR - CROPS

ECUADOR - HEALTH

The Economist Intelligence Unit, 111 West 57th Street, New York, New York 10019 (800) 938-4685; *The New Latin America Market Atlas.*

Facts on File, 460 Park Avenue South, New York, New York 10016 (800) 443-8323; *The New Book of World Rankings.*

Federal Statistical Office, Gustav - Stresemann - Ring 11, D-6200 Wiesbaden, Germany; *Ecuador.*

G.K. Hall and Company, 70 Lincoln Street, Boston, Massachusetts 02111 (617) 423-3990; *The World in Figures.*

Statistical Office of the United Nations, Publishing Service, New York, New York 10017 (800) 253-9646; *Statistical Yearbook.*

Times Books, 201 East 50th Street, New York, New York 10022 (202) 751-2600; *The Economist Book of Vital World Statistics.*

U.C.L.A. Latin American Center Publications, University of California, Los Angeles, California 90024 (310) 825-6634; *Statistical Abstract of Latin America.*

World Health Organization, Office of Publications, Avenue Appia, CH-1211 Geneva 27, Switzerland (Telephone Number in U.S. (518) 436-9686); *World Health Statistics Annual.*

ECUADOR - HEALTH EXPENDITURES

International Monetary Fund, 700 Nineteenth Street, NW, Washington, D.C. 20431 (202) 623-7000; *Government Finance Statistics Yearbook.*

Statistical Office of the United Nations, Publishing Service, New York, New York 10017 (800) 253-9646; *Statistical Yearbook for Latin America and the Caribbean.*

ECUADOR - HIDE PRODUCTION

Food and Agricultural Organization of the United Nations (FAO), Via delle Terme di Caracalla, 00100 Rome, Italy (Telephone Number in U.S. (202) 653-2400); *Production Yearbook.*

ECUADOR - HIGHWAYS

The Economist Intelligence Unit, 111 West 57th Street, New York, New York 10019 (800) 938-4685; *The New Latin America Market Atlas.*

G.K. Hall and Company, 70 Lincoln Street, Boston, Massachusetts 02111 (617) 423-3990; *The World in Figures.*

International Road Federation, 525 School Street, SW, Washington, D.C. 20024 (202) 554-2106; *World Road Statistics.*

ECUADOR - HORSES - See ECUADOR - LIVESTOCK AND POULTRY

ECUADOR - HOURS OF WORK - See ECUADOR - EMPLOYMENT

ECUADOR - HOUSING AND HOUSING UNITS

Facts on File, 460 Park Avenue South, New York, New York 10016 (800) 443-8323; *The New Book of World Rankings.*

Statistical Office of the United Nations, Publishing Service, New York, New York 10017 (800) 253-9646; *Statistical Yearbook for Latin America and the Caribbean.*

U.C.L.A. Latin American Center Publications, University of California, Los Angeles, California 90024 (310) 825-6634; *Statistical Abstract of Latin America.*

ECUADOR - ILLITERACY RATES

The Economist Intelligence Unit, 111 West 57th Street, New York, New York 10019 (800) 938-4685; *The New Latin America Market Atlas.*

ECUADOR - ILLITERATE POPULATION

The Economist Intelligence Unit, 111 West 57th Street, New York, New York 10019 (800) 938-4685; *The World Market Atlas.*

G.K. Hall and Company, 70 Lincoln Street, Boston, Massachusetts 02111 (617) 423-3990; *The World in Figures.*

Statistical Office of the United Nations, Publishing Service, New York, New York 10017 (800) 253-9646; *Statistical Yearbook for Latin America and the Caribbean.*

United Nations Educational, Scientific and Cultural Organization (UNESCO), 7 Place de Fontenoy, F-75700 Paris, France (Telephone Number in U.S. (212) 963-5981); *Statistical Yearbook.*

ECUADOR - IMMIGRATION

U.C.L.A. Latin American Center Publications, University of California, Los Angeles, California 90024 (310) 825-6634; *Statistical Abstract of Latin America.*

ECUADOR - IMPORTS

The Economist Intelligence Unit, 111 West 57th Street, New York, New York 10019 (800) 938-4685; *The New Latin America Market Atlas,* and *The World Market Atlas.*

Euromonitor Publications Limited, 87-88 Turnmill Street, London EC1M 5QU, England; *International Marketing Data and Statistics.*

Food and Agricultural Organization of the United Nations (FAO) Via delle Terme di Caracalla, 00100 Rome, Italy (Telephone Number in U.S. (202) 653-2400); *The State of Food and Agriculture.*

G.K. Hall and Company, 70 Lincoln Street, Boston, Massachusetts 02111 (617) 423-3990; *The World in Figures.*

Inter-American Development Bank, 1300 New York Avenue, NW, Washington, D.C. 20577 (202) 623-1753; *Economic and Social Progress in Latin America.*

International Monetary Fund, 700 Nineteenth Street, NW, Washington, D.C. 20431 (202) 623-7000; *Direction of Trade Statistics, Government Finance Statistics Yearbook,* and *International Financial Statistics.*

Organization of American States (OAS), General Secretariat, Washington, D.C. 20006 (202) 458-3533; *Statistical Bulletin of the OAS.*

Statistical Office of the United Nations, Publishing Service, New York, New York 10017 (800) 253-9646; *Statistical Yearbook for Latin America and the Caribbean.*

Times Books, 201 East 50th Street, New York, New York 10022 (202) 751-2600; *The Economist Book of Vital World Statistics.*

The World Bank, 1818 H Street, NW, Washington, D.C. 20433 (202) 477-1234; *World Tables.*

ECUADOR - INCOME DISTRIBUTION

Statistical Office of the United Nations, Publishing Service, New York, New York 10017 (800) 253-9646; *Statistical Yearbook for Latin America and the Caribbean.*

U.C.L.A. Latin American Center Publications, University of California, Los Angeles, California 90024 (310) 825-6634; *Statistical Abstract of Latin America.*

ECUADOR - INCOME TAXES - See ECUADOR - TAXATION

ECUADOR - INDUSTRY

Euromonitor Publications Limited, 87-88 Turnmill Street, London EC1M 5QU, England; *International Marketing Data and Statistics.*

Facts on File, 460 Park Avenue South, New York, New York 10016 (800) 443-8323; *The New Book of World Rankings.*

Federal Statistical Office, Gustav - Stresemann - Ring 11, D-6200 Wiesbaden, Germany; *Ecuador.*

Gale Research Incorporated, 835 Penobscot Building, Detroit, Michigan 48226 (800) 877-4253; *International Historical Statistics The Americas and Australasia.*

G.K. Hall and Company, 70 Lincoln Street, Boston, Massachusetts 02111 (617) 423-3990; *The World in Figures.*

International Labour Office, I.L.O. Publications, CH-1211, Geneva 22, Switzerland; *Yearbook of Labour Statistics.*

Statistical Office of the United Nations, Publishing Service, New York, New York 10017 (800) 253-9646; *Economic Survey of Latin America and the Caribbean,* and *Statistical Yearbook.*

Times Books, 201 East 50th Street, New York, New York 10022 (202) 751-2600; *The Economist Book of Vital World Statistics.*

U.C.L.A. Latin American Center Publications, University of California, Los Angeles, California 90024 (310) 825-6634; *Statistical Abstract of Latin America.*

The World Bank, 1818 H Street, NW, Washington, D.C. 20433 (202) 477-1234; *World Tables.*

ECUADOR - INFANT AND MATERNAL MORTALITY

The Economist Intelligence Unit, 111 West 57th Street, New York, New York 10019 (800) 938-4685; *The New Latin America Market Atlas.*

Statistical Office of the United Nations, Publishing Service, New York, New York 10017 (800) 253-9646; *Demographic Yearbook,* and *Statistical Yearbook.*

Times Books, 201 East 50th Street, New York, New York 10022 (202) 751-2600; *The Economist Book of Vital World Statistics.*

The World Bank, 1818 H Street, NW, Washington, D.C. 20433 (202) 477-1234; *World Tables.*

World Health Organization, Office of Publications, Avenue Appia, CH-1211 Geneva 27, Switzerland (Telephone Number in U.S. (518) 436-9686); *World Health Statistics Annual.*

ECUADOR - INFLATIONARY FACTORS

Statistical Office of the United Nations, Publishing Service, New York, New York 10017 (800) 253-9646; *Economic Survey of Latin America and the Caribbean.*

ECUADOR - INTEREST RATES

Inter-American Development Bank, 1300 New York Avenue, NW, Washington, D.C. 20577 (202) 623-1753; *Economic and Social Progress in Latin America.*

Organization of American States (OAS), General Secretariat, Washington, D.C. 20006 (202) 458-3533; *Statistical Bulletin of the OAS.*

ECUADOR - INTERNAL TRADE

Statistical Office of the United Nations, Publishing Service, New York, New York 10017 (800) 253-9646; *Statistical Yearbook.*

ECUADOR - INTERNATIONAL FINANCE

Inter-American Development Bank, 1300 New York Avenue, NW, Washington, D.C. 20577 (202) 623-1753; *Economic and Social Progress in Latin America.*

U.C.L.A. Latin American Center Publications, University of California, Los Angeles, California 90024 (310) 825-6634; *Statistical Abstract of Latin America.*

ECUADOR - INTERNATIONAL LIQUIDITY

Inter-American Development Bank, 1300 New York Avenue, NW, Washington, D.C. 20577 (202) 623-1753; *Economic and Social Progress in Latin America.*

International Monetary Fund, 700 Nineteenth Street, NW, Washington, D.C. 20431 (202) 623-7000; *International Financial Statistics.*

ECUADOR - INTERNATIONAL RESERVES

Organization of American States (OAS), General Secretariat, Washington, D.C. 20006 (202) 458-3533; *Statistical Bulletin of the OAS.*

ECUADOR - INTERNATIONAL RESERVES EXCLUDING GOLD

The World Bank, 1818 H Street, NW, Washington, D.C. 20433 (202) 477-1234; *World Tables.*

Inter-American Development Bank, 1300 New York Avenue, NW, Washington, D.C. 20577 (202) 623-1753; *Economic and Social Progress in Latin America.*

Statistical Office of the United Nations, Publishing Service, New York, New York 10017 (800) 253-9646; *Statistical Yearbook.*

ECUADOR - INTERNATIONAL STATISTICS

Inter-American Development Bank, 1300 New York Avenue, NW, Washington, D.C. 20577 (202) 623-1753; *Economic and Social Progress in Latin America.*

U.C.L.A. Latin American Center Publications, University of California, Los Angeles, California 90024 (310) 825-6634; *Statistical Abstract of Latin America.*

ECUADOR - INVESTMENT

Inter-American Development Bank, 1300 New York Avenue, NW, Washington, D.C. 20577 (202) 623-1753; *Economic and Social Progress in Latin America.*

Statistical Office of the United Nations, Publishing Service, New York, New York 10017 (800) 253-9646; *Statistical Yearbook for Latin America and the Caribbean.*

ECUADOR - IRON ORE PRODUCTION - See ECUADOR - MINING AND MINERAL PRODUCTS

ECUADOR - IRRIGATION

Euromonitor Publications Limited, 87-88 Turnmill Street, London EC1M 5QU, England; *International Marketing Data and Statistics.*

Inter-American Development Bank, 1300 New York Avenue, NW, Washington, D.C. 20577 (202) 623-1753; *Economic and Social Progress in Latin America.*

ECUADOR - LABOR FORCE

The Economist Intelligence Unit, 111 West 57th Street, New York, New York 10019 (800) 938-4685; *The New Latin America Market Atlas.*

Euromonitor Publications Limited, 87-88 Turnmill Street, London EC1M 5QU, England; *International Marketing Data and Statistics.*

Facts on File, 460 Park Avenue South, New York, New York 10016 (800) 443-8323; *The New Book of World Rankings.*

Food and Agricultural Organization of the United Nations (FAO) Via delle Terme di Caracalla, 00100 Rome, Italy (Telephone Number in U.S. (202) 653-2400); *The State of Food and Agriculture.*

Gale Research Incorporated, 835 Penobscot Building, Detroit, Michigan 48226 (800) 877-4253; *International Historical Statistics The Americas and Australasia.*

G.K. Hall and Company, 70 Lincoln Street, Boston, Massachusetts 02111 (617) 423-3990; *The World in Figures.*

Times Books, 201 East 50th Street, New York, New York 10022 (202) 751-2600; *The Economist Book of Vital World Statistics.*

The World Bank, 1818 H Street, NW, Washington, D.C. 20433 (202) 477-1234; *World Tables.*

ECUADOR - LABOR PRODUCTIVITY

International Labour Office, I.L.O. Publications, CH-1211, Geneva 22, Switzerland; *Yearbook of Labour Statistics.*

ECUADOR - LAND AREA

The Economist Intelligence Unit, 111 West 57th Street, New York, New York 10019 (800) 938-4685; *The New Latin America Market Atlas.*

ECUADOR - LAND USE

Euromonitor Publications Limited, 87-88 Turnmill Street, London EC1M 5QU, England; *International Marketing Data and Statistics.*

Food and Agricultural Organization of the United Nations (FAO), Via delle Terme di Caracalla, 00100 Rome, Italy (Telephone Number in U.S. (202) 653-2400); *Production Yearbook.*

G.K. Hall and Company, 70 Lincoln Street, Boston, Massachusetts 02111 (617) 423-3990; *The World in Figures.*

Inter-American Development Bank, 1300 New York Avenue, NW, Washington, D.C. 20577 (202) 623-1753; *Economic and Social Progress in Latin America.*

ECUADOR - LIBRARIES

Facts on File, 460 Park Avenue South, New York, New York 10016 (800) 443-8323; *The New Book of World Rankings.*

ECUADOR - LIFE EXPECTANCY RATE

The Economist Intelligence Unit, 111 West 57th Street, New York, New York 10019 (800) 938-4685; *The New Latin America Market Atlas.*

ECUADOR - LIVESTOCK AND POULTRY

Euromonitor Publications Limited, 87-88 Turnmill Street, London EC1M 5QU, England; *International Marketing Data and Statistics.*

Facts on File, 460 Park Avenue South, New York, New York 10016 (800) 443-8323; *The New Book of World Rankings.*

Food and Agricultural Organization of the United Nations (FAO), Via delle Terme di Caracalla, 00100 Rome, Italy (Telephone Number in U.S. (202) 653-2400); *Production Yearbook,* and *The State of Food and Agriculture.*

G.K. Hall and Company, 70 Lincoln Street, Boston, Massachusetts 02111 (617) 423-3990; *The World in Figures.*

Statistical Office of the United Nations, Publishing Service, New York, New York 10017 (800) 253-9646; *Statistical Yearbook.*

ECUADOR - LIVING LEVELS

G.K. Hall and Company, 70 Lincoln Street, Boston, Massachusetts 02111 (617) 423-3990; *The World in Figures.*

Statistical Office of the United Nations, Publishing Service, New York, New York 10017 (800) 253-9646; *Statistical Yearbook for Latin America and the Caribbean.*

Times Books, 201 East 50th Street, New York, New York 10022 (202) 751-2600; *The Economist Book of Vital World Statistics.*

ECUADOR - MAIL - NUMBER OF ITEMS SENT AND RECEIVED

Statistical Office of the United Nations, Publishing Service, New York, New York 10017 (800) 253-9646; *Statistical Yearbook.*

ECUADOR - MAIN ECONOMIC INDICATORS - See ECUADOR - ECONOMY

ECUADOR - MAIN INDICATORS - See ECUADOR - ECONOMY

ECUADOR - MANUFACTURING

The Economist Intelligence Unit, 111 West 57th Street, New York, New York 10019 (800) 938-4685; *The New Latin America Market Atlas*.

Facts on File, 460 Park Avenue South, New York, New York 10016 (800) 443-8323; *The New Book of World Rankings*.

G.K. Hall and Company, 70 Lincoln Street, Boston, Massachusetts 02111 (617) 423-3990; *The World in Figures*.

Inter-American Development Bank, 1300 New York Avenue, NW, Washington, D.C. 20577 (202) 623-1753; *Economic and Social Progress in Latin America*.

Statistical Office of the United Nations, Publishing Service, New York, New York 10017 (800) 253-9646; *Statistical Yearbook*, and *Statistical Yearbook for Latin America and the Caribbean*.

Times Books, 201 East 50th Street, New York, New York 10022 (202) 751-2600; *The Economist Book of Vital World Statistics*.

The World Bank, 1818 H Street, NW, Washington, D.C. 20433 (202) 477-1234; *World Tables*.

ECUADOR - MARRIAGE RATES

Facts on File, 460 Park Avenue South, New York, New York 10016 (800) 443-8323; *The New Book of World Rankings*.

Statistical Office of the United Nations, Publishing Service, New York, New York 10017 (800) 253-9646; *Demographic Yearbook*, and *Statistical Yearbook*.

ECUADOR - MEAT PRODUCTION - See ECUADOR - LIVESTOCK AND POULTRY

ECUADOR - MEDICAL PERSONNEL

U.C.L.A. Latin American Center Publications, University of California, Los Angeles, California 90024 (310) 825-6634; *Statistical Abstract of Latin America*.

ECUADOR - MERCHANT SHIPPING

G.K. Hall and Company, 70 Lincoln Street, Boston, Massachusetts 02111 (617) 423-3990; *The World in Figures*.

Organization of Petroleum Exporting Countries, Obere Donaustrasse 93, 1020 Vienna 2, Austria; *OPEC Annual Statistical Bulletin*.

Statistical Office of the United Nations, Publishing Service, New York, New York 10017 (800) 253-9646; *Statistical Yearbook*.

Times Books, 201 East 50th Street, New York, New York 10022 (202) 751-2600; *The Economist Book of Vital World Statistics*.

U.S. Department of Transportation, Maritime Administration, 400 Seventh Street, SW, Washington, D.C. 20590 (202) 366-5807; *A Statistical Analysis of the World's Merchant Fleets*.

ECUADOR - MILITARY

The Economist Intelligence Unit, 111 West 57th Street, New York, New York 10019 (800) 938-4685; *The New Latin American Market Atlas*.

G.K. Hall and Company, 70 Lincoln Street, Boston, Massachusetts 02111 (617) 423-3990; *The World in Figures*.

The International Institute for Strategic Studies, 23 Tavistock Street, London WC2E 7NQ, England; *The Military Balance*.

U.C.L.A. Latin American Center Publications, University of California, Los Angeles, California 90024 (310) 825-6634; *Statistical Abstract of Latin America*.

U.S. Arms Control and Disarmament Agency, 320 Twenty-first Street, NW, Washington, D.C. 20451 (202) 647-8677; *World Military Expenditures and Arms Transfers*.

ECUADOR - MILK - See ECUADOR - DAIRY PRODUCTS

ECUADOR - MINING AND MINERAL PRODUCTS

The Economist Intelligence Unit, 111 West 57th Street, New York, New York 10019 (800) 938-4685; *The New Latin America Market Atlas*.

Facts on File, 460 Park Avenue South, New York, New York 10016 (800) 443-8323; *The New Book of World Rankings*.

G.K. Hall and Company, 70 Lincoln Street, Boston, Massachusetts 02111 (617) 423-3990; *The World in Figures*.

Inter-American Development Bank, 1300 New York Avenue, NW, Washington, D.C. 20577 (202) 623-1753; *Economic and Social Progress in Latin America*.

Organization of Petroleum Exporting Countries, Obere Donaustrasse 93, 1020 Vienna 2, Austria; *OPEC Annual Statistical Bulletin*.

Penn Well Publishing Company, 1421 South Sheridan Road, P.O. Box 1260, Tulsa, Oklahoma 74101 (800) 752-9764; *International Energy Statistics Sourcebook*.

Statistical Office of the United Nations, Publishing Service, New York, New York 10017 (800) 253-9646; *Statistical Yearbook*, and *Statistical Yearbook for Latin America and the Caribbean*.

U.C.L.A. Latin American Center Publications, University of California, Los Angeles, California 90024 (310) 825-6634; *Statistical Abstract of Latin America*.

ECUADOR - MONEY EXCHANGE RATE

Euromonitor Publications Limited, 87-88 Turnmill Street, London EC1M 5QU, England; *International Marketing Data and Statistics*.

Inter-American Development Bank, 1300 New York Avenue, NW, Washington, D.C. 20577 (202) 623-1753; *Economic and Social Progress in Latin America*.

International Monetary Fund, 700 Nineteenth Street, NW, Washington, D.C. 20431 (202) 623-7000; *International Financial Statistics*.

Statistical Office of the United Nations, Publishing Service, New York, New York 10017 (800) 253-9646; *Statistical Yearbook*.

ECUADOR - MONEY RATES - MARKET

Inter-American Development Bank, 1300 New York Avenue, NW, Washington, D.C. 20577 (202) 623-1753; *Economic and Social Progress in Latin America*.

ECUADOR - MONEY RESERVES

Euromonitor Publications Limited, 87-88 Turnmill Street, London EC1M 5QU, England; *International Marketing Data and Statistics*.

Inter-American Development Bank, 1300 New York Avenue, NW, Washington, D.C. 20577 (202) 623-1753; *Economic and Social Progress in Latin America*.

ECUADOR - MONEY SUPPLY

Euromonitor Publications Limited, 87-88 Turnmill Street, London EC1M 5QU, England; *International Marketing Data and Statistics*.

Federal Statistical Office, Gustav - Stresemann - Ring 11, D-6200 Wiesbaden, Germany; *Ecuador*.

G.K. Hall and Company, 70 Lincoln Street, Boston, Massachusetts 02111 (617) 423-3990; *The World in Figures*.

Inter-American Development Bank, 1300 New York Avenue, NW, Washington, D.C. 20577 (202) 623-1753; *Economic and Social Progress in Latin America*.

International Monetary Fund, 700 Nineteenth Street, NW, Washington, D.C. 20431 (202) 623-7000; *International Financial Statistics*.

Statistical Office of the United Nations, Publishing Service, New York, New York 10017 (800) 253-9646; *Statistical Yearbook*.

U.C.L.A. Latin American Center Publications, University of California, Los Angeles, California 90024 (310) 825-6634; *Statistical Abstract of Latin America*.

The World Bank, 1818 H Street, NW, Washington, D.C. 20433 (202) 477-1234; *World Tables*.

ECUADOR - MOTION PICTURES

Statistical Office of the United Nations, Publishing Service, New York, New York 10017 (800) 253-9646; *Statistical Yearbook*.

ECUADOR - MOTOR VEHICLE TAXES - See ECUADOR - TAXATION

ECUADOR - MOTOR VEHICLES IN USE

The Economist Intelligence Unit, 111 West 57th Street, New York, New York 10019 (800) 938-4685; *The New Latin America Market Atlas*.

G.K. Hall and Company, 70 Lincoln Street, Boston, Massachusetts 02111 (617) 423-3990; *The World in Figures*.

International Road Federation, 525 School Street, SW, Washington, D.C. 20024 (202) 554-2106; *World Road Statistics*.

Statistical Office of the United Nations, Publishing Service, New York, New York 10017 (800) 253-9646; *Statistical Yearbook*.

Times Books, 201 East 50th Street, New York, New York 10022 (202) 751-2600; *The Economist Book of Vital World Statistics*.

ECUADOR - MULES - See ECUADOR - LIVESTOCK AND POULTRY

ECUADOR - MUSEUMS

Facts on File, 460 Park Avenue South, New York, New York 10016 (800) 443-8323; *The New Book of World Rankings*.

ECUADOR - NATALITY - See ECUADOR - BIRTH RATE

ECUADOR - NATIONAL ACCOUNTS

Federal Statistical Office, Gustav - Stresemann - Ring 11, D-6200 Wiesbaden, Germany; *Ecuador*.

Gale Research Incorporated, 835 Penobscot Building, Detroit, Michigan 48226 (800) 877-4253; *International Historical Statistics The Americas and Australasia*.

Inter-American Development Bank, 1300 New York Avenue, NW, Washington, D.C. 20577 (202) 623-1753; *Economic and Social Progress in Latin America*.

International Monetary Fund, 700 Nineteenth Street, NW, Washington, D.C. 20431 (202) 623-7000; *International Financial Statistics*.

Organization of American States (OAS), General Secretariat, Washington, D.C. 20006 (202) 458-3533; *Statistical Bulletin of the OAS*.

Statistical Office of the United Nations, Publishing Service, New York, New York 10017 (800) 253-9646; *National Accounts Statistics*, and *Statistical Yearbook*.

U.C.L.A. Latin American Center Publications, University of California, Los Angeles, California 90024 (310) 825-6634; *Statistical Abstract of Latin America*.

ECUADOR - NATIONAL INCOME

Facts on File, 460 Park Avenue South, New York, New York 10016 (800) 443-8323; *The New Book of World Rankings*.

G.K. Hall and Company, 70 Lincoln Street, Boston, Massachusetts 02111 (617) 423-3990; *The World in Figures*.

Inter-American Development Bank, 1300 New York Avenue, NW, Washington, D.C. 20577 (202) 623-1753; *Economic and Social Progress in Latin America*.

International Monetary Fund, 700 Nineteenth Street, NW, Washington, D.C. 20431 (202) 623-7000; *International Financial Statistics*.

Statistical Office of the United Nations, Publishing Service, New York, New York 10017 (800) 253-9646; *Statistical Yearbook*, and *Statistical Yearbook for Latin America and the Caribbean*.

ECUADOR - NATIONAL PRODUCT

Facts on File, 460 Park Avenue South, New York, New York 10016 (800) 443-8323; *The New Book of World Rankings*.

Statistical Office of the United Nations, Publishing Service, New York, New York 10017 (800) 253-9646; *Statistical Yearbook*.

ECUADOR - NATURAL GAS PRODUCTION - See ECUADOR - MINING AND MINERAL PRODUCTS

ECUADOR - NEWSPAPER PRODUCTION

G.K. Hall and Company, 70 Lincoln Street, Boston, Massachusetts 02111 (617) 423-3990; *The World in Figures.*

Statistical Office of the United Nations, Publishing Service, New York, New York 10017 (800) 253-9646; *Statistical Yearbook.*

United Nations Educational, Scientific and Cultural Organization (UNESCO), 7 Place de Fontenoy, F-75700 Paris, France (Telephone Number in U.S. (212) 963-5981); *Statistical Yearbook.*

ECUADOR - NEWSPRINT CONSUMPTION - See ECUADOR - FORESTRY AND FOREST PRODUCTS

ECUADOR - NUTRITION

Statistical Office of the United Nations, Publishing Service, New York, New York 10017 (800) 253-9646; *Statistical Yearbook for Latin America and the Caribbean.*

ECUADOR - OCCUPATIONS - See ECUADOR - LABOR FORCE

ECUADOR - PALM KERNEL PRODUCTION - See ECUADOR - CROPS

ECUADOR - PAPER

United Nations Educational, Scientific and Cultural Organization (UNESCO), 7 Place de Fontenoy, F-75700 Paris, France (Telephone Number in U.S. (212) 963-5981); *Statistical Yearbook.*

ECUADOR - PATENTS

Statistical Office of the United Nations, Publishing Service, New York, New York 10017 (800) 253-9646; *Statistical Yearbook.*

ECUADOR - PEANUT PRODUCTION - See ECUADOR - CROPS

ECUADOR - PERIODICALS

United Nations Educational, Scientific and Cultural Organization (UNESCO), 7 Place de Fontenoy, F-75700 Paris, France (Telephone Number in U.S. (212) 963-5981); *Statistical Yearbook.*

ECUADOR - PESTICIDE USE

Food and Agricultural Organization of the United Nations (FAO) Via delle Terme di Caracalla, 00100 Rome, Italy (Telephone Number in U.S. (202) 653-2400); *The State of Food and Agriculture.*

ECUADOR - PETROLEUM INDUSTRY

The Economist Intelligence Unit, 111 West 57th Street, New York, New York 10019 (800) 938-4685; *The New Latin America Market Atlas.*

Facts on File, 460 Park Avenue South, New York, New York 10016 (800) 443-8323; *The New Book of World Rankings.*

Food and Agricultural Organization of the United Nations (FAO) Via delle Terme di Caracalla, 00100 Rome, Italy (Telephone Number in U.S. (202) 653-2400); *The State of Food and Agriculture.*

G.K. Hall and Company, 70 Lincoln Street, Boston, Massachusetts 02111 (617) 423-3990; *The World in Figures.*

Inter-American Development Bank, 1300 New York Avenue, NW, Washington, D.C. 20577 (202) 623-1753; *Economic and Social Progress in Latin America.*

Organization of American States (OAS), General Secretariat, Washington, D.C. 20006 (202) 458-3533; *Statistical Bulletin of the OAS,* and *Statistical Yearbook.*

Organization of Petroleum Exporting Countries, Obere Donaustrasse 93, 1020 Vienna 2, Austria; *OPEC Annual Statistical Bulletin.*

Penn Well Publishing Company, 1421 South Sheridan Road, P.O. Box 1260, Tulsa, Oklahoma 74101 (800) 752-9764; *International Energy Statistics Sourcebook.*

Statistical Office of the United Nations, Publishing Service, New York, New York 10017 (800) 253-9646; *Statistical Yearbook.*

ECUADOR - PIGS - See ECUADOR - LIVESTOCK AND POULTRY

ECUADOR - PIPELINES FOR OIL AND PETROLEUM PRODUCTS

Organization of Petroleum Exporting Countries, Obere Donaustrasse 93, 1020 Vienna 2, Austria; *OPEC Annual Statistical Bulletin.*

ECUADOR - POLITICAL DATA

U.C.L.A. Latin American Center Publications, University of California, Los Angeles, California 90024 (310) 825-6634; *Statistical Abstract of Latin America.*

ECUADOR - POPULATION

The Economist Intelligence Unit, 111 West 57th Street, New York, New York 10019 (800) 938-4685; *The New Latin America Market Atlas,* and *The World Market Atlas.*

Euromonitor Publications Limited, 87-88 Turnmill Street, London EC1M 5QU, England; *International Marketing Data and Statistics.*

Facts on File, 460 Park Avenue South, New York, New York 10016 (800) 443-8323; *The New Book of World Rankings.*

Federal Statistical Office, Gustav - Stresemann - Ring 11, D-6200 Wiesbaden, Germany; *Ecuador.*

Food and Agricultural Organization of the United Nations (FAO), Via delle Terme di Caracalla, 00100 Rome, Italy (Telephone Number in U.S. (202) 653-2400); *Production Yearbook.*

Gale Research Incorporated, 835 Penobscot Building, Detroit, Michigan 48226 (800) 877-4253; *International Historical Statistics The Americas and Australasia.*

G.K. Hall and Company, 70 Lincoln Street, Boston, Massachusetts 02111 (617) 423-3990; *The World in Figures.*

Inter-American Development Bank, 1300 New York Avenue, NW, Washington, D.C. 20577 (202) 623-1753; *Economic and Social Progress in Latin America.*

International Labour Office, I.L.O. Publications, CH-1211, Geneva 22, Switzerland; *Yearbook of Labour Statistics.*

Organization of American States (OAS), General Secretariat, Washington, D.C. 20006 (202) 458-3533; *Statistical Bulletin of the OAS.*

Statistical Office of the United Nations, Publishing Service, New York, New York 10017 (800) 253-9646; *Demographic Yearbook, Statistical Yearbook,* and *Statistical Yearbook for Latin America and the Caribbean.*

Times Books, 201 East 50th Street, New York, New York 10022 (202) 751-2600; *The Economist Book of Vital World Statistics.*

U.C.L.A. Latin American Center Publications, University of California, Los Angeles, California 90024 (310) 825-6634; *Statistical Abstract of Latin America.*

United Nations Educational, Scientific and Cultural Organization (UNESCO), 7 Place de Fontenoy, F-75700 Paris, France (Telephone Number in U.S. (212) 963-5981); *Statistical Yearbook.*

U.S. Arms Control and Disarmament Agency, 320 Twenty-first Street, NW, Washington, D.C. 20451 (202) 647-8677; *World Military Expenditures and Arms Transfers.*

World Health Organization, Office of Publications, Avenue Appia, CH-1211 Geneva 27, Switzerland (Telephone Number in U.S. (518) 436-9686); *World Health Statistics Annual.*

ECUADOR - POST OFFICES

Facts on File, 460 Park Avenue South, New York, New York 10016 (800) 443-8323; *The New Book of World Rankings.*

ECUADOR - POTATO PRODUCTION - See ECUADOR - CROPS

ECUADOR - PRICE TRENDS

Statistical Office of the United Nations, Publishing Service, New York, New York 10017 (800) 253-9646; *Economic Survey of Latin America and the Caribbean.*

ECUADOR - PRICES

Facts on File, 460 Park Avenue South, New York, New York 10016 (800) 443-8323; *The New Book of World Rankings.*

Federal Statistical Office, Gustav - Stresemann - Ring 11, D-6200 Wiesbaden, Germany; *Ecuador.*

Food and Agricultural Organization of the United Nations (FAO), Via delle Terme di Caracalla, 00100 Rome, Italy (Telephone Number in U.S. (202) 653-2400); *Production Yearbook,* and *The State of Food and Agriculture.*

Gale Research Incorporated, 835 Penobscot Building, Detroit, Michigan 48226 (800) 877-4253; *International Historical Statistics The Americas and Australasia.*

G.K. Hall and Company, 70 Lincoln Street, Boston, Massachusetts 02111 (617) 423-3990; *The World in Figures.*

International Labour Office, I.L.O. Publications, CH-1211, Geneva 22, Switzerland; *Yearbook of Labour Statistics.*

International Monetary Fund, 700 Nineteenth Street, NW, Washington, D.C. 20431 (202) 623-7000; *International Financial Statistics.*

Statistical Office of the United Nations, Publishing Service, New York, New York 10017 (800) 253-9646; *Statistical Yearbook for Latin America and the Caribbean.*

ECUADOR - PRINTING AND WRITING PAPER - See ECUADOR - FORESTRY AND FOREST PRODUCTS

ECUADOR - PRODUCTION

Facts on File, 460 Park Avenue South, New York, New York 10016 (800) 443-8323; *The New Book of World Rankings.*

G.K. Hall and Company, 70 Lincoln Street, Boston, Massachusetts 02111 (617) 423-3990; *The World in Figures.*

ECUADOR - PRODUCTIVITY

Euromonitor Publications Limited, 87-88 Turnmill Street, London EC1M 5QU, England; *International Marketing Data and Statistics.*

ECUADOR - PROPERTY TAXES - See ECUADOR - TAXATION

ECUADOR - PUBLIC CONSUMPTION FUND

Inter-American Development Bank, 1300 New York Avenue, NW, Washington, D.C. 20577 (202) 623-1753; *Economic and Social Progress in Latin America.*

ECUADOR - PUBLIC EXPENDITURE

Inter-American Development Bank, 1300 New York Avenue, NW, Washington, D.C. 20577 (202) 623-1753; *Economic and Social Progress in Latin America.*

Organization of American States (OAS), General Secretariat, Washington, D.C. 20006 (202) 458-3533; *Statistical Bulletin of the OAS.*

Statistical Office of the United Nations, Publishing Service, New York, New York 10017 (800) 253-9646; *Statistical Yearbook for Latin America and the Caribbean.*

ECUADOR - PUBLIC FINANCE

Facts on File, 460 Park Avenue South, New York, New York 10016 (800) 443-8323; *The New Book of World Rankings.*

Federal Statistical Office, Gustav - Stresemann - Ring 11, D-6200 Wiesbaden, Germany; *Ecuador.*

Inter-American Development Bank, 1300 New York Avenue, NW, Washington, D.C. 20577 (202) 623-1753; *Economic and Social Progress in Latin America.*

Organization of American States (OAS), General Secretariat, Washington, D.C. 20006 (202) 458-3533; *Statistical Bulletin of the OAS.*

ECUADOR - PUBLIC REVENUES

Inter-American Development Bank, 1300 New York Avenue, NW, Washington, D.C. 20577 (202) 623-1753; *Economic and Social Progress in Latin America.*

Organization of American States (OAS), General Secretariat, Washington, D.C. 20006 (202) 458-3533; *Statistical Bulletin of the OAS.*

ECUADOR - RADIO BROADCASTING - See ECUADOR - BROADCASTING

ECUADOR - RADIO RECEIVER PRODUCTION

Statistical Office of the United Nations, Publishing Service, New York, New York 10017 (800) 253-9646; *Statistical Yearbook.*

ECUADOR - RAILWAYS

The Economist Intelligence Unit, 111 West 57th Street, New York, New York 10019 (800) 938-4685; *The New Latin America Market Atlas.*

G.K. Hall and Company, 70 Lincoln Street, Boston, Massachusetts 02111 (617) 423-3990; *The World in Figures.*

Jane's Information Group, Sentinel House, 163 Brighton Road, Coulsdon, Surrey CR5 2NH, England (Telephone Number in U.S. (703) 683-3700); *Jane's World Railways.*

Statistical Office of the United Nations, Publishing Service, New York, New York 10017 (800) 253-9646; *Statistical Yearbook.*

ECUADOR - RANCHING

U.C.L.A. Latin American Center Publications, University of California, Los Angeles, California 90024 (310) 825-6634; *Statistical Abstract of Latin America.*

ECUADOR - RELIGION

Facts on File, 460 Park Avenue South, New York, New York 10016 (800) 443-8323; *The New Book of World Rankings.*

U.C.L.A. Latin American Center Publications, University of California, Los Angeles, California 90024 (310) 825-6634; *Statistical Abstract of Latin America.*

ECUADOR - RESERVES EXCLUDING GOLD

The Economist Intelligence Unit, 111 West 57th Street, New York, New York 10019 (800) 938-4685; *The New Latin America Market Atlas.*

ECUADOR - RENT PRICES

International Labour Office, I.L.O. Publications, CH-1211, Geneva 22, Switzerland; *Yearbook of Labour Statistics.*

ECUADOR - RETAIL TRADE

G.K. Hall and Company, 70 Lincoln Street, Boston, Massachusetts 02111 (617) 423-3990; *The World in Figures.*

Inter-American Development Bank, 1300 New York Avenue, NW, Washington, D.C. 20577 (202) 623-1753; *Economic and Social Progress in Latin America.*

Statistical Office of the United Nations, Publishing Service, New York, New York 10017 (800) 253-9646; *Statistical Yearbook.*

ECUADOR - RICE PRODUCTION - See ECUADOR - CROPS

ECUADOR - ROOT AND TUBER PRODUCTION - See ECUADOR - CROPS

ECUADOR - ROUNDWOOD PRODUCTION

The Economist Intelligence Unit, 111 West 57th Street, New York, New York 10019 (800) 938-4685; *The New Latin America Market Atlas.*

Food and Agricultural Organization of the United Nations (FAO), Via delle Terme di Caracalla, 00100 Rome, Italy (Telephone Number in U.S. (202) 653-2400); *Yearbook of Forest Products.*

Inter-American Development Bank, 1300 New York Avenue, NW, Washington, D.C. 20577 (202) 623-1753; *Economic and Social Progress in Latin America.*

Statistical Office of the United Nations, Publishing Service, New York, New York 10017 (800) 253-9646; *Statistical Yearbook.*

ECUADOR - RUBBER PRODUCTION

Facts on File, 460 Park Avenue South, New York, New York 10016 (800) 443-8323; *The New Book of World Rankings.*

ECUADOR - SALT PRODUCTION - See ECUADOR - MINING AND MINERAL PRODUCTS

ECUADOR - SAWNWOOD PRODUCTION

Food and Agricultural Organization of the United Nations (FAO), Via delle Terme di Caracalla, 00100 Rome, Italy (Telephone Number in U.S. (202) 653-2400); *Yearbook of Forest Products.*

Statistical Office of the United Nations, Publishing Service, New York, New York 10017 (800) 253-9646; *Statistical Yearbook.*

ECUADOR - SCIENCE AND TECHNOLOGY

U.C.L.A. Latin American Center Publications, University of California, Los Angeles, California 90024 (310) 825-6634; *Statistical Abstract of Latin America.*

ECUADOR - SCIENTISTS AND TECHNICIANS

Statistical Office of the United Nations, Publishing Service, New York, New York 10017 (800) 253-9646; *Statistical Yearbook.*

ECUADOR - SENIOR CITIZENS

Facts on File, 460 Park Avenue South, New York, New York 10016 (800) 443-8323; *The New Book of World Rankings.*

ECUADOR - SESAME SEED PRODUCTION - See ECUADOR - CROPS

ECUADOR - SHEEP - See ECUADOR - LIVESTOCK AND POULTRY

ECUADOR - SILVER PRODUCTION AND CONSUMPTION - See ECUADOR - MINING AND MINERAL PRODUCTS

ECUADOR - SOCIAL DATA

Facts on File, 460 Park Avenue South, New York, New York 10016 (800) 443-8323; *The New Book of World Rankings.*

G.K. Hall and Company, 70 Lincoln Street, Boston, Massachusetts 02111 (617) 423-3990; *The World in Figures.*

U.C.L.A. Latin American Center Publications, University of California, Los Angeles, California 90024 (310) 825-6634; *Statistical Abstract of Latin America.*

ECUADOR - SOCIAL SECURITY

Inter-American Development Bank, 1300 New York Avenue, NW, Washington, D.C. 20577 (202) 623-1753; *Economic and Social Progress in Latin America.*

International Monetary Fund, 700 Nineteenth Street, NW, Washington, D.C. 20431 (202) 623-7000; *Government Finance Statistics Yearbook.*

ECUADOR - SOCIOECONOMIC DATA

Inter-American Development Bank, 1300 New York Avenue, NW, Washington, D.C. 20577 (202) 623-1753; *Economic and Social Progress in Latin America.*

U.C.L.A. Latin American Center Publications, University of California, Los Angeles, California 90024 (310) 825-6634; *Statistical Abstract of Latin America.*

ECUADOR - SOYBEAN PRODUCTION - See ECUADOR - CROPS

ECUADOR - STAMP TAXES AND DUTIES - See ECUADOR - TAXATION

ECUADOR - STATE BUDGET REVENUE AND EXPENDITURES

Euromonitor Publications Limited, 87-88 Turnmill Street, London EC1M 5QU, England; *International Marketing Data and Statistics.*

Inter-American Development Bank, 1300 New York Avenue, NW, Washington, D.C. 20577 (202) 623-1753; *Economic and Social Progress in Latin America.*

ECUADOR - STEEL - See ECUADOR - MINING AND MINERAL PRODUCTS

ECUADOR - STOCKS - COMMODITY - MARKET PRICE - INDEX

Food and Agricultural Organization of the United Nations (FAO) Via delle Terme di Caracalla, 00100 Rome, Italy (Telephone Number in U.S. (202) 653-2400); *The State of Food and Agriculture.*

ECUADOR - SUGAR PRODUCTION AND CONSUMPTION - See ECUADOR - CROPS

ECUADOR - TAXATION

G.K. Hall and Company, 70 Lincoln Street, Boston, Massachusetts 02111 (617) 423-3990; *The World in Figures.*

Inter-American Development Bank, 1300 New York Avenue, NW, Washington, D.C. 20577 (202) 623-1753; *Economic and Social Progress in Latin America.*

International Monetary Fund, 700 Nineteenth Street, NW, Washington, D.C. 20431 (202) 623-7000; *Government Finance Statistics Yearbook.*

Statistical Office of the United Nations, Publishing Service, New York, New York 10017 (800) 253-9646; *Statistical Yearbook for Latin America and the Caribbean.*

The World Bank, 1818 H Street, NW, Washington, D.C. 20433 (202) 477-1234; *World Tables.*

ECUADOR - TELEGRAPH SERVICE

Statistical Office of the United Nations, Publishing Service, New York, New York 10017 (800) 253-9646; *Statistical Yearbook.*

ECUADOR - TELEPHONES IN USE

American Telephone and Telegraph Company, 26 Parsippany Road, Whippany, New Jersey 07981 (800) 338-4038; *The World's Telephones.*

The Economist Intelligence Unit, 111 West 57th Street, New York, New York 10019 (800) 938-4685; *The New Latin America Market Atlas.*

G.K. Hall and Company, 70 Lincoln Street, Boston, Massachusetts 02111 (617) 423-3990; *The World in Figures.*

Statistical Office of the United Nations, Publishing Service, New York, New York 10017 (800) 253-9646; *Statistical Yearbook.*

ECUADOR - TELEVISION BROADCASTING - See ECUADOR - BROADCASTING

ECUADOR - TELEVISION RECEIVER PRODUCTION

Statistical Office of the United Nations, Publishing Service, New York, New York 10017 (800) 253-9646; *Statistical Yearbook.*

ECUADOR - TEXTILE INDUSTRY

Forest and Paper Association, 1250 Connecticut Avenue, NW, Washington, D.C. 20036 (202) 463-2455; *Wood Pulp and Fiber Statistics.*

G.K. Hall and Company, 70 Lincoln Street, Boston, Massachusetts 02111 (617) 423-3990; *The World in Figures.*

Statistical Office of the United Nations, Publishing Service, New York, New York 10017 (800) 253-9646; *Statistical Yearbook.*

ECUADOR - TIRE (MOTOR VEHICLE) PRODUCTION

Statistical Office of the United Nations, Publishing Service, New York, New York 10017 (800) 253-9646; *Statistical Yearbook.*

ECUADOR - TOBACCO PRODUCTION

Facts on File, 460 Park Avenue South, New York, New York 10016 (800) 443-8323; *The New Book of World Rankings.*

Statistical Office of the United Nations, Publishing Service, New York, New York 10017 (800) 253-9646; *Statistical Yearbook.*

ECUADOR - TOURISM

The Economist Intelligence Unit, 111 West 57th Street, New York, New York 10019 (800) 938-4685; *The New Latin America Market Atlas.*

Facts on File, 460 Park Avenue South, New York, New York 10016 (800) 443-8323; *The New Book of World Rankings.*

Federal Statistical Office, Gustav - Stresemann - Ring 11, D-6200 Wiesbaden, Germany; *Ecuador.*

G.K. Hall and Company, 70 Lincoln Street, Boston, Massachusetts 02111 (617) 423-3990; *The World in Figures.*

Statistical Office of the United Nations, Publishing Service, New York, New York 10017 (800) 253-9646; *Statistical Yearbook*, and *Statistical Yearbook for Latin America and the Caribbean.*

Times Books, 201 East 50th Street, New York, New York 10022 (202) 751-2600; *The Economist Book of Vital World Statistics.*

U.C.L.A. Latin American Center Publications, University of California, Los Angeles, California 90024 (310) 825-6634; *Statistical Abstract of Latin America.*

World Tourism Organization, Calle Capitan Haya 42, E-28020 Madrid, Spain; *Yearbook of Tourism Statistics.*

ECUADOR - TRACTORS IN USE

The Economist Intelligence Unit, 111 West 57th Street, New York, New York 10019 (800) 938-4685; *The New Latin America Market Atlas.*

Statistical Office of the United Nations, Publishing Service, New York, New York 10017 (800) 253-9646; *Statistical Yearbook.*

ECUADOR - TRADE - See ECUADOR - FOREIGN TRADE

ECUADOR - TRADEMARKS AND SERVICE MARKS

Statistical Office of the United Nations, Publishing Service, New York, New York 10017 (800) 253-9646; *Statistical Yearbook.*

ECUADOR - TRANSPORTATION AND COMMUNICATIONS

The Economist Intelligence Unit, 111 West 57th Street, New York, New York 10019 (800) 938-4685; *The New Latin America Market Atlas.*

Facts on File, 460 Park Avenue South, New York, New York 10016 (800) 443-8323; *The New Book of World Rankings.*

Federal Statistical Office, Gustav - Stresemann - Ring 11, D-6200 Wiesbaden, Germany; *Ecuador.*

Gale Research Incorporated, 835 Penobscot Building, Detroit, Michigan 48226 (800) 877-4253; *International Historical Statistics The Americas and Australasia.*

G.K. Hall and Company, 70 Lincoln Street, Boston, Massachusetts 02111 (617) 423-3990; *The World in Figures.*

Inter-American Development Bank, 1300 New York Avenue, NW, Washington, D.C. 20577 (202) 623-1753; *Economic and Social Progress in Latin America.*

Statistical Office of the United Nations, Publishing Service, New York, New York 10017; *Statistical Yearbook for Latin America and the Caribbean.*

U.C.L.A. Latin American Center Publications, University of California, Los Angeles, California 90024 (310) 825-6634; *Statistical Abstract of Latin America.*

ECUADOR - TURKEYS - See ECUADOR - LIVESTOCK AND POULTRY

ECUADOR - UNEMPLOYMENT

The Economist Intelligence Unit, 111 West 57th Street, New York, New York 10019 (800) 938-4685; *The New Latin America Market Atlas.*

Euromonitor Publications Limited, 87-88 Turnmill Street, London EC1M 5QU, England; *International Marketing Data and Statistics.*

International Labour Office, I.L.O. Publications, CH-1211, Geneva 22, Switzerland; *Yearbook of Labour Statistics.*

U.C.L.A. Latin American Center Publications, University of California, Los Angeles, California 90024 (310) 825-6634; *Statistical Abstract of Latin America.*

ECUADOR - UTILITIES

U.C.L.A. Latin American Center Publications, University of California, Los Angeles, California 90024 (310) 825-6634; *Statistical Abstract of Latin America.*

ECUADOR - VITAL STATISTICS

Euromonitor Publications Limited, 87-88 Turnmill Street, London EC1M 5QU, England; *International Marketing Data and Statistics.*

Gale Research Incorporated, 835 Penobscot Building, Detroit, Michigan 48226 (800) 877-4253; *International Historical Statistics The Americas and Australasia.*

G.K. Hall and Company, 70 Lincoln Street, Boston, Massachusetts 02111 (617) 423-3990; *The World in Figures.*

Statistical Office of the United Nations, Publishing Service, New York, New York 10017 (800) 253-9646; *Statistical Yearbook.*

World Health Organization, Office of Publications, Avenue Appia, CH-1211 Geneva 27, Switzerland (Telephone Number in U.S. (518) 436-9686); *World Health Statistics Annual.*

ECUADOR - WAGES

Federal Statistical Office, Gustav - Stresemann - Ring 11, D-6200 Wiesbaden, Germany; *Ecuador.*

G.K. Hall and Company, 70 Lincoln Street, Boston, Massachusetts 02111 (617) 423-3990; *The World in Figures.*

International Labour Office, I.L.O. Publications, CH-1211, Geneva 22, Switzerland; *Yearbook of Labour Statistics.*

Organization of American States (OAS), General Secretariat, Washington, D.C. 20006 (202) 458-3533; *Statistical Bulletin of the OAS.*

Statistical Office of the United Nations, Publishing Service, New York, New York 10017 (800) 253-9646; *Statistical Yearbook.*

U.C.L.A. Latin American Center Publications, University of California, Los Angeles, California 90024 (310) 825-6634; *Statistical Abstract of Latin America.*

ECUADOR - WATERMELON PRODUCTION - See ECUADOR - CROPS

ECUADOR - WEATHER

Facts on File, 460 Park Avenue South, New York, New York 10016 (800) 443-8323; *The New Book of World Rankings.*

G.K. Hall and Company, 70 Lincoln Street, Boston, Massachusetts 02111 (617) 423-3990; *The World in Figures.*

ECUADOR - WELFARE

Inter-American Development Bank, 1300 New York Avenue, NW, Washington, D.C. 20577 (202) 623-1753; *Economic and Social Progress in Latin America.*

International Monetary Fund, 700 Nineteenth Street, NW, Washington, D.C. 20431 (202) 623-7000; *Government Finance Statistics Yearbook.*

ECUADOR - WHEAT PRODUCTION - See ECUADOR - CROPS

ECUADOR - WHOLESALE PRICES

Inter-American Development Bank, 1300 New York Avenue, NW, Washington, D.C. 20577 (202) 623-1753; *Economic and Social Progress in Latin America.*

International Monetary Fund, 700 Nineteenth Street, NW, Washington, D.C. 20431 (202) 623-7000; *International Financial Statistics.*

Organization of American States (OAS), General Secretariat, Washington, D.C. 20006 (202) 458-3533; *Statistical Bulletin of the OAS.*

ECUADOR - WHOLESALE TRADE

Inter-American Development Bank, 1300 New York Avenue, NW, Washington, D.C. 20577 (202) 623-1753; *Economic and Social Progress in Latin America.*

Statistical Office of the United Nations, Publishing Service, New York, New York 10017 (800) 253-9646; *Statistical Yearbook.*

ECUADOR - WINE PRODUCTION

Facts on File, 460 Park Avenue South, New York, New York 10016 (800) 443-8323; *The New Book of World Rankings.*

ECUADOR - WOOD AND WOOD PULP - See ECUADOR - FORESTRY AND FOREST PRODUCTS

ECUADOR - WOOL PRODUCTION

Facts on File, 460 Park Avenue South, New York, New York 10016 (800) 443-8323; *The New Book of World Rankings.*

ECUADOR - YARN PRODUCTION

Statistical Office of the United Nations, Publishing Service, New York, New York 10017 (800) 253-9646; *Statistical Yearbook.*

EDUCATION - ADULT EDUCATION

U.S. Department of Education, National Center for Education Statistics, 400 Maryland Avenue, SW, Washington, D.C. 20202 (202) 708-5366; *Adult Education Profile,* and unpublished data.

EDUCATION - AMERICAN COLLEGE TESTING (ACT) PROGRAM

The American College Testing Program, Box 168, Iowa City, Iowa 52243 (319) 337-1000; *High School Profile Report.*

EDUCATION - ATTAINMENT

U.S. Department of Commerce, Bureau of the Census, Suitland, Maryland 20233 (301) 763-4040; *Current Population Reports, Census of Population,* and unpublished data.

U.S. Department of Education, 400 Maryland Avenue, SW, Washington, D.C. 20202 (202) 708-5366; *Digest of Education Statistics.*

EDUCATION - ATTAINMENT - AMERICAN INDIAN, ESKIMO, ALEUT POPULATION

U.S. Department of Commerce, Bureau of the Census, Suitland, Maryland 20233 (301) 763-4040; *Current Population Reports.*

U.S. Department of Education, National Center for Education Statistics, 400 Maryland Avenue, SW, Washington, D.C. 20202 (202) 708-5366; *Digest of Education Statistics.*

EDUCATION - ATTAINMENT - ASIAN AND PACIFIC ISLANDER POPULATION

U.S. Department of Commerce, Bureau of the Census, Suitland, Maryland 20233 (301) 763-4040; *Current Population Reports.*

U.S. Department of Education, National Center for Education Statistics, 400 Maryland Avenue, SW, Washington, D.C. 20202 (202) 708-5366; *Digest of Education Statistics.*

EDUCATION - ATTAINMENT - BLACK POPULATION

U.S. Department of Commerce, Bureau of the Census, Suitland, Maryland 20233 (301) 763-4040; *Census of Population,* and *Current Population Reports.*

U.S. Department of Education, National Center for Education Statistics, 400 Maryland Avenue, SW, Washington, D.C. 20202 (202) 708-5366; *Digest of Education Statistics.*

EDUCATION - ATTAINMENT - CIGARETTE SMOKING

U.S. Department of Health and Human Services, Centers for Disease Control, 1600 Clifton Road, NE, Atlanta, Georgia 30333 (404) 639-3311; *Reducing the Health Consequences of Smoking.*

EDUCATION - ATTAINMENT - ELDERLY

U.S. Department of Commerce, Bureau of the Census, Suitland, Maryland 20233 (301) 763-4040; *Census of Population, Current Population Reports,* and unpublished data.

EDUCATION - ATTAINMENT - FOREIGN BORN POPULATION

U.S. Department of Commerce, Bureau of the Census, Suitland, Maryland 20233 (301) 763-4040; *Census of Population,* and unpublished data.

EDUCATION - ATTAINMENT - GENERAL EDUCATION DEVELOPMENT CERTIFICATES (GED's)

U.S. Department of Education, National Center for Education Statistics, 400 Maryland Avenue, SW, Washington, D.C. 20202 (202) 708-5366; *Digest of Education Statistics.*

EDUCATION - ATTAINMENT - HISPANIC ORIGIN POPULATION

U.S. Department of Commerce, Bureau of the Census, Suitland, Maryland 20233 (301) 763-4040; *Census of Population,* and *Current Population Reports.*

U.S. Department of Education, National Center for Education Statistics, 400 Maryland Avenue, SW, Washington, D.C. 20202 (202) 708-5366; *Digest of Education Statistics.*

EDUCATION - ATTAINMENT - INCOME

U.S. Department of Commerce, Bureau of the Census, Suitland, Maryland 20233 (301) 763-4040; *Current Population Reports.*

EDUCATION - ATTAINMENT - LABOR FORCE STATUS

U.S. Department of Labor, Bureau of Labor Statistics, Two Massachusetts Avenue, NE, Washington, D.C. 20212 (202) 606-7828; Bulletin 2307, and unpublished data.

EDUCATION - ATTAINMENT - MULTIMEDIA USERS

Mediamark Research, Incorporated, 708 Third Avenue, New York, New York 10017 (212) 599-0444; *Multimedia Audiences.*

EDUCATION - ATTAINMENT - OCCUPATION

U.S. Department of Labor, Bureau of Labor Statistics, Two Massachusetts Avenue, NE, Washington, D.C. 20212 (202) 606-7828; unpublished data.

EDUCATION - ATTAINMENT - OUTLYING AREAS OF THE UNITED STATES

U.S. Department of Commerce, Bureau of the Census, Suitland, Maryland 20233 (301) 763-4040; *Census of Population and Housing.*

EDUCATION - ATTAINMENT - POVERTY

U.S. Department of Commerce, Bureau of the Census, Suitland, Maryland 20233 (301) 763-4040; *Current Population Reports.*

EDUCATION - ATTAINMENT - RACE

U.S. Department of Commerce, Bureau of the Census, Suitland, Maryland 20233 (301) 763-4040; *Current Population Reports, Census of Population,* and unpublished data.

EDUCATION - ATTAINMENT - RECREATION ACTIVITIES

National Sporting Goods Association, Lake Center Plaza Building, 1699 Wall Street, Mount Prospect, Illinois 60056 (708) 439-4000; *The Sporting Goods Market in 1993.*

EDUCATION - ATTAINMENT - UNEMPLOYMENT RATE BY RACE, SEX

U.S. Department of Labor, Bureau of Labor Statistics, Two Massachusetts Avenue, NE, Washington, D.C. 20212 (202) 606-7828; Bulletin 2307 and unpublished data.

EDUCATION - ATTAINMENT - WOMEN

U.S. Department of Commerce, Bureau of the Census, Suitland, Maryland 20233 (301) 763-4040; *Census of Population, Current Population Reports,* and unpublished data.

U.S. Department of Education, National Center for Education Statistics, 400 Maryland Avenue, SW, Washington, D.C. 20202 (202) 708-5366; *Digest of Education Statistics.*

EDUCATION - CATHOLIC SCHOOLS

National Catholic Educational Association, 1077 Thirtieth Street, NW, Washington, D.C. 20007 (202) 337-6232; *Ganley's Catholic Schools in America.*

EDUCATION - CHARITABLE CONTRIBUTIONS

The Gallup Organization, Incorporated, 100 Palmer Square, Princeton, New Jersey 08542 (609) 924-9600; *Giving and Volunteering in the United States.*

EDUCATION - COMPUTER USE

Quality Education Data, Inc., 1600 Broadway, 12th Floor, Denver, Colorado 80202 (303) 860-1832; *Technology in Public Schools.*

U.S. Department of Education, National Center for Education Statistics, 400 Maryland Avenue, SW, Washington, D.C. 20202 (202) 708-5366; *Digest of Education Statistics.*

University of Minnesota, Department of Sociology, Minneapolis, Minnesota 55455 (612) 625-5000; *IEA Computers in Education Study.*

EDUCATION - CRIME INCIDENTS

U.S. Department of Justice, Bureau of Justice Statistics, 633 Indiana Avenue, NW, Washington, D.C. 20531 (800) 732-3277; *Criminal Victimization in the United States.*

EDUCATION - DAYS LOST FROM SCHOOL

U.S. Department of Health and Human Services, National Center for Health Statistics, 3700 East-West Highway, Hyattsville, Maryland 20782 (301) 436-8500; *Vital and Health Statistics,* and unpublished data.

EDUCATION - DEGREES CONFERRED

U.S. Department of Education, 400 Maryland Avenue, SW, Washington, D.C. 20202 (202) 708-5366; *Digest of Education Statistics.*

EDUCATION - DEGREES CONFERRED - NON-RESIDENT ALIENS

U.S. Department of Education, National Center for Education Statistics, 400 Maryland Avenue, SW, Washington, D.C. 20202 (202) 708-5366; *Digest of Education Statistics.*

EDUCATION - DEGREES CONFERRED - SALARY OFFERS

College Placement Council, Incorporated, 62 Highland Avenue, Bethlehem, Pennsylvania 18017 (212) 868-1421; *Salary Survey, A Study of Beginning Offers.*

EDUCATION - DENTAL SCHOOLS - STUDENTS - GRADUATES

American Dental Association, 211 East Chicago Avenue, Chicago, Illinois 60611 (312) 440-2500; *Annual Report on Dental Education.*

EDUCATION - EMPLOYMENT - STATE AND LOCAL GOVERNMENT

U.S. Department of Commerce, Bureau of the Census, Suitland, Maryland 20233 (301) 763-4040; *Public Employment.*

EDUCATION - EMPLOYMENT STATUS OF HIGH SCHOOL GRADUATES AND DROPOUTS

U.S. Department of Labor, Bureau of Labor Statistics, Two Massachusetts Avenue, NE, Washington, D.C. 20212 (202) 606-7828; *Bulletin 2307, News,* and unpublished data.

EDUCATION - ENROLLMENT

National Education Association, 1201 Sixteenth Street, NW, Washington, D.C. 20036 (212) 833-4000; *Estimates of School Statistics, Rankings of the States,* and unpublished data.

U.S. Department of Commerce, Bureau of the Census, Suitland, Maryland 20233 (301) 763-4040; *Current Population Reports, Census of Population*, and unpublished data.

U.S. Department of Education, 400 Maryland Avenue, SW, Washington, D.C. 20202 (202) 708-5366; *Digest of Education Statistics, Projections of Education Statistics*, and unpublished data.

EDUCATION - ENROLLMENT - CATHOLIC SCHOOLS

National Catholic Educational Association, 1077 30th Street, NW, Washington, D.C. 20007 (202) 337-6232; *Ganley's Catholic Schools in America*.

EDUCATION - ENROLLMENT - OUTLYING AREAS OF THE UNITED STATES

Puerto Rico Planning Board, San Juan, Puerto Rico; *Income and Product*, and *Socioeconomic Statistics*.

U.S. Department of Commerce, Bureau of the Census, Suitland, Maryland 20233 (301) 763-4040; unpublished data.

EDUCATION - ENROLLMENT - PREPRIMARY SCHOOLS

U.S. Department of Commerce, Bureau of the Census, Suitland, Maryland 20233 (301) 763-4040; *Current Population Reports*, and unpublished data.

EDUCATION - ENROLLMENT - PROJECTIONS

U.S. Department of Education, 400 Maryland Avenue, SW, Washington, D.C. 20202 (202) 708-5366; *Digest of Education Statistics*, and *Projections of Education Statistics*.

EDUCATION - ENROLLMENT - STATES

U.S. Department of Education, 400 Maryland Avenue, SW, Washington, D.C. 20202 (202) 708-5366; *Digest of Education Statistics*, and *Projections of Education Statistics*.

EDUCATION - EXPENDITURES - ASSISTANCE FOR PERSONS WITH LIMITED INCOME

U.S. Library of Congress, Congressional Research Service, 10 First Street, SE, Washington, D.C. 20540 (202) 707-5000; *Cash and Noncash Benefits for Persons with Limited Income: Eligibility Rules, Recipient and Expenditure Data*.

EDUCATION - EXPENDITURES - CITY GOVERNMENT

U.S. Department of Commerce, Bureau of the Census, Suitland, Maryland 20233 (301) 763-4040; *City Government Finances*.

EDUCATION - EXPENDITURES - PRIVATE

U.S. Department of Health and Human Services, Social Security Administration, 6401 Security Boulevard, Baltimore, Maryland 21235 (410) 965-1234; *Annual Statistical Supplement to the Social Security Bulletin*.

EDUCATION - EXPENDITURES - STATE AND LOCAL GOVERNMENTS

U.S. Department of Commerce, Bureau of the Census, Suitland, Maryland 20233 (301) 763-4040; *State Government Finances, Historical Statistics on Governmental Finances and Employment*, and *Government Finances*.

U.S. Department of Education, 400 Maryland Avenue, SW, Washington, D.C. 20202 (202) 708-5366; *Digest of Education Statistics*, and unpublished data.

EDUCATION - FEDERAL AID

National Science Foundation, 4201 Wilson Boulevard, Arlington, Virginia 22230 (703) 306-1234; *Federal Funds for Research and Development*.

U.S. Department of Education, National Center for Education Statistics, 400 Maryland Avenue, SW, Washington, D.C. 20202 (202) 708-5366; *Digest of Education Statistics*, and unpublished data.

EDUCATION - GRADUATES - COLLEGE

U.S. Department of Commerce, Bureau of the Census, Suitland, Maryland 20233 (301) 763-4040; *Census of Population*, and *Current Population Reports*.

U.S. Department of Education, 400 Maryland Avenue, SW, Washington, D.C. 20202 (202) 708-5366; *Digest of Education Statistics*.

EDUCATION - GRADUATES - HIGH SCHOOL

U.S. Department of Commerce, Bureau of the Census, Suitland, Maryland 20233 (301) 763-4040; *Census of Population, Current Population Reports*, and unpublished data.

U.S. Department of Education, 400 Maryland Avenue, SW, Washington, D.C. 20202 (202) 708-5366; *Digest of Education Statistics*.

EDUCATION - GRANTS TO INSTITUTIONS FROM FOUNDATIONS

The Foundation Center, 79 Fifth Avenue, New York, New York 10002 (212) 620-4230; *Foundation Grants Index*.

EDUCATION - HANDICAPPED STUDENTS

U.S. Department of Education, Office of Special Education Programs, 400 Maryland Avenue, SW, Washington, D.C. 20202 (202) 708-5366; *Annual Report to Congress*.

EDUCATION - HIGH SCHOOL DROPOUTS

U.S. Department of Labor, Bureau of Labor Statistics, Two Massachusetts Avenue, NE, Washington, D.C. 20212 (202) 606-7828; *Bulletin 2307* and unpublished data.

EDUCATION - HIGHER EDUCATION INSTITUTIONS - BEGINNING SALARY OFFERS, COLLEGE GRADUATES

College Placement Council, 62 Highland Avenue, Bethlehem, Pennsylvania 18017 (212) 868-1421; *Salary Survey, A Study of Beginning Offers*.

Northwestern University, 633 Clark Street, Evanston, Illinois 60201 (708) 491-3741; *The Northwestern Lindquist-Endicott Report*.

EDUCATION - HIGHER EDUCATION INSTITUTIONS - CHARGES FOR ROOM AND BOARD

U.S. Department of Education, 400 Maryland Avenue, SW, Washington, D.C. 20202 (202) 708-5366; *Digest of Education Statistics*.

EDUCATION - HIGHER EDUCATION INSTITUTIONS - DEGREES CONFERRED

National Science Foundation, 4201 Wilson Boulevard, Arlington, Virginia 22230 (703) 306-1234; *Survey of Earned Doctorates, Selected Data on Science and Engineering Doctorate Awards,* and *Characteristics of Recent Science and Engineering Graduates.*

U.S. Department of Education, 400 Maryland Avenue, SW, Washington, D.C. 20202 (202) 708-5366; *Digest of Education Statistics,* and *Projections of Education Statistics.*

EDUCATION - HIGHER EDUCATION INSTITUTIONS - DEGREES CONFERRED - NON-RESIDENT ALIENS

U.S. Department of Education, National Center for Education Statistics, 400 Maryland Avenue, SW, Washington, D.C. 20202 (202) 708-5366; *Digest of Education Statistics.*

EDUCATION - HIGHER EDUCATION INSTITUTIONS - DORMITORY POPULATION

U.S. Department of Commerce, Bureau of the Census, Suitland, Maryland 20233 (301) 763-4040; *Census of Population, General Population Characteristics.*

EDUCATION - HIGHER EDUCATION INSTITUTIONS - ENROLLMENT

Institute of International Education, 809 United Nations Plaza, New York, New York 10017 (212) 883-8200; *Open Doors.*

U.S. Department of Commerce, Bureau of the Census, Suitland, Maryland 20233 (301) 763-4040; *Current Population Reports, Census of Population,* and unpublished data.

U.S. Department of Education, 400 Maryland Avenue, SW, Washington, D.C. 20202 (202) 708-5366; *Digest of Education Statistics, Projections of Education Statistics,* and unpublished data.

EDUCATION - HIGHER EDUCATION INSTITUTIONS - ENROLLMENT - COLLEGE FRESHMEN

The Higher Education Research Institute, University of California, Graduate School of Education, Los Angeles, California 90024 (213) 825-1925; *The American Freshman: National Norms.*

EDUCATION - HIGHER EDUCATION INSTITUTIONS - ENROLLMENT - FOREIGN LANGUAGES

Association of Departments of Foreign Languages, 10 Astor Place, New York, New York 10003 (212) 614-6319; *ADFL Bulletin.*

EDUCATION - HIGHER EDUCATION INSTITUTIONS - ENROLLMENT - FOREIGN STUDENTS

Institute of International Education, 809 United Nations Plaza, New York, New York 10017 (212) 883-8200; *Open Doors.*

U.S. Department of Education, National Center for Education Statistics, 400 Maryland Avenue, SW, Washington, D.C. 20202 (202) 708-5366; *Digest of Education Statistics.*

EDUCATION - HIGHER EDUCATION INSTITUTIONS - ENROLLMENT - PROJECTIONS

U.S. Department of Education, 400 Maryland Avenue, SW, Washington, D.C. 20202 (202) 708-5366; *Digest of Education Statistics, Projections of Education Statistics,* and unpublished data.

EDUCATION - HIGHER EDUCATION INSTITUTIONS - ENROLLMENT - STATES

Research Associates of Washington, 2605 Klingle Road, NW, Washington, D.C. 20008 (202) 966-3326; *State Profiles: Financing Public Higher Education.*

U.S. Department of Education, 400 Maryland Avenue, SW, Washington, D.C. 20202 (202) 708-5366; *Digest of Education Statistics.*

EDUCATION - HIGHER EDUCATION INSTITUTIONS - ENROLLMENT - UNITED STATES SERVICE SCHOOLS

U.S. Department of Education, 400 Maryland Avenue, SW, Washington, D.C. 20202 (202) 708-5366; *Digest of Education Statistics.*

EDUCATION - HIGHER EDUCATION INSTITUTIONS - EXPENDITURES

Council for Aid to Education, 51 Madison Avenue, Suite 2200, New York, New York 10010 (212) 689-2400; *Voluntary Support of Education.*

Research Associates of Washington, 2605 Klingle Road, NW, Washington, D.C. 20008 (202) 966-3326; *State Profiles: Financing Public Higher Education.*

U.S. Department of Education, 400 Maryland Avenue, SW, Washington, D.C. 20202 (202) 708-5366; *Digest of Education Statistics, Projections of Education Statistics,* and unpublished data.

EDUCATION - HIGHER EDUCATION INSTITUTIONS - EXPENDITURES - PRICE INDEXES

Research Associates of Washington, 2605 Klingle Road, NW, Washington, D.C. 20008 (202) 966-3326; *Inflation Measures for Schools and Colleges.*

EDUCATION - HIGHER EDUCATION INSTITUTIONS - EXPENDITURES - SCIENTIFIC PURPOSES BY TYPE

U.S. National Science Foundation, 4201 Wilson Boulevard, Arlington, Virginia 22230 (703) 306-1234; *Survey of Scientific and Engineering Expenditures at Universities and Colleges.*

EDUCATION - HIGHER EDUCATION INSTITUTIONS - FACULTY

Maryse Eymonerie Associates/American Association of University Professors, 1012 Fourteenth Street, NW, Suite 500, Washington, D.C. 20005 (202) 737-5900; *AAUP Annual Report on the Economic Status of the Profession.*

U.S. Department of Education, 400 Maryland Avenue, SW, Washington, D.C. 20202 (202) 708-5366; *Digest of Education Statistics, Projections of Education Statistics,* and unpublished data.

EDUCATION - HIGHER EDUCATION INSTITUTIONS - FINANCES

Research Association of Washington, 2605 Klingle Road, NW, Washington, D.C. 20008 (202) 996-3326; *State Profiles: Financing Public Higher Education.*

U.S. Department of Education, 400 Maryland Avenue, SW, Washington, D.C. 20202 (202) 708-5366; *Digest of Education Statistics, Projections of Educational Statistics,* and unpublished data.

EDUCATION - HIGHER EDUCATION INSTITUTIONS - FINANCIAL AID

U.S. Department of Education, 400 Maryland Avenue, SW, Washington, D.C. 20202 (202) 708-5366; *Digest of Education Statistics*, and unpublished data.

EDUCATION - HIGHER EDUCATION INSTITUTIONS - LIBRARIES

R.R. Bowker Company, 121 Chanlon Road, New Providence, New Jersey 07974 (908) 464-6800; *The Bowker Annual: Library and Book Trade Almanac*, and *American Library Directory*.

U.S. Department of Education, 400 Maryland Avenue, SW, Washington, D.C. 20202 (202) 708-5366; *Digest of Education Statistics*, and *Academic Libraries*.

EDUCATION - HIGHER EDUCATION INSTITUTIONS - NUMBER

U.S. Department of Education, 400 Maryland Avenue, SW, Washington, D.C. 20202 (202) 708-5366; *Digest of Education Statistics*, *Projections of Education Statistics*, and unpublished data.

EDUCATION - HIGHER EDUCATION INSTITUTIONS - PRICE INDEXES

Research Associates of Washington, 2605 Klingle Road, NW, Washington, D.C. 20008 (202) 966-3326; *Inflation Measures for Schools and Colleges*.

EDUCATION - HIGHER EDUCATION INSTITUTIONS - EXPENDITURES - SCIENTIFIC PURPOSES BY TYPE

U.S. National Science Foundation, 4201 Wilson Boulevard, Arlington, Virginia 22230 (703) 306-1234; "Survey of Scientific and Engineering Expenditures at Universities and Colleges."

EDUCATION - HIGHER EDUCATION INSTITUTIONS - FACULTY

Maryse Eymonerie Associates/American Association of University Professors, 1012 Fourteenth Street, NW, Suite 500, Washington, D.C. 20005 (202) 737-5900; "AAUP Annual Report on the Economic Status of the Profession."

U.S. Department of Education, 400 Maryland Avenue, SW, Washington, D.C. 20202 (202) 708-5366; "Digest of Education Statistics," "Projections of Education Statistics," and unpublished data.

EDUCATION - HIGHER EDUCATION INSTITUTIONS - FINANCES

Research Association of Washington, 2605 Klingle Road, NW, Washington, D.C. 20008 (202) 996-3326; "State Profiles: Financing Public Higher Education."

U.S. Department of Education, 400 Maryland Avenue, SW, Washington, D.C. 20202 (202) 708-5366; "Digest of Education Statistics," "Financial Statistics of Institutions of Higher Education," "Projections of Educational Statistics," and unpublished data.

EDUCATION - HIGHER EDUCATION INSTITUTIONS - FINANCIAL AID

U.S. Department of Education, 400 Maryland Avenue, SW, Washington, D.C. 20202 (202) 708-5366; "Digest of Education Statistics," and unpublished data.

EDUCATION - HIGHER EDUCATION INSTITUTIONS - LIBRARIES

R.R. Bowker Company, 245 West Seventeenth Street, New York, New York 10011 (212) 645-9700; "The Bowker Annual: Library and Book Trade Almanac," and "American Library Directory."

U.S. Department of Education, 400 Maryland Avenue, SW, Washington, D.C. 20202 (202) 708-5366; "Digest of Education Statistics," and "Academic Libraries."

EDUCATION - HIGHER EDUCATION INSTITUTIONS - NUMBER

U.S. Department of Education, 400 Maryland Avenue, SW, Washington, D.C. 20202 (202) 708-5366; "Digest of Education Statistics," "Projections of Education Statistics," and unpublished data.

EDUCATION - HIGHER EDUCATION INSTITUTIONS - PRICE INDEXES

Research Associates of Washington, 2605 Klingle Road, NW, Washington, D.C. 20008 (202) 966-3326; "Inflation Measures for Schools and Colleges."

EDUCATION - HIGHER EDUCATION INSTITUTIONS - SCIENTISTS AND ENGINEERS EMPLOYED

U.S. National Science Foundation, 4201 Wilson Boulevard, Arlington, Virginia 22230 (703) 306-1234; "National Patterns of R & D Resources."

EDUCATION - HIGHER EDUCATION INSTITUTIONS - TUITION AND FEES

U.S. Department of Education, 400 Maryland Avenue, SW, Washington, D.C. 20202 (202) 708-5366; "Digest of Education Statistics."

EDUCATION - HIGHER EDUCATION INSTITUTIONS - VOLUNTARY FINANCIAL SUPPORT

Council for Financial Aid to Education, 51 Madison Avenue, Suite 2200, New York, New York 10010 (212) 689-2400; "Voluntary Support of Education."

EDUCATION - LOANS AND GRANTS - FEDERAL GOVERNMENT

U.S. Department of Education, 400 Maryland Avenue, SW, Washington, D.C. 20202 (202) 708-5366; unpublished data.

EDUCATION - MEDICAL SCHOOLS - STUDENTS - GRADUATES

American Dental Association, 211 East Chicago Avenue, Chicago, Illinois 60611 (312) 440-2500; "Annual Report on Dental Education."

American Medical Association, 515 North State Street, Chicago, Illinois 60610 (312) 464-4818; "Physician Characteristics and Distribution in the United States."

U.S. Department of Health and Human Services, National Center for Health Statistics, 3700 East-West Highway, Hyattsville, Maryland 20782 (301) 436-8500; unpublished data.

EDUCATION - NURSING PROGRAMS - STUDENTS - GRADUATES

National League for Nursing, 350 Hudson Street, New York, New York 10014 (212) 989-9393; "NLN Data Book," and "State Approved Schools of Nursing, RN."

U.S. Department of Health and Human Services, National Center for Health Statistics, 3700 East-West Highway, Hyattsville, Maryland 20782 (301) 436-8500; unpublished data.

EDUCATION - OUTLYING AREAS OF THE UNITED STATES

Puerto Rico Planning Board, San Juan, Puerto Rico; "Socioeconomic Statistics."

U.S. Department of Commerce, Bureau of the Census, Suitland, Maryland 20233 (301) 763-4040; "Census of Population," and unpublished data.

U.S. Department of Education, National Center for Education Statistics, 400 Maryland Avenue, SW, Washington, D.C. 20202 (202) 708-5366; unpublished data.

EDUCATION - PHILANTHROPY

American Association of Fund Raising Counsel, 25 West Forty-third Street, New York, New York 10036 (212) 354-5799; "Giving USA."

The Conference Board, 845 Third Avenue, New York, New York 10022 (212) 759-0900; "Annual Survey of Corporate Contributions."

The Foundation Center, 79 Fifth Avenue, New York, New York 10003 (212) 620-4230; "Foundation Grants Index."

The Gallup Organization, Incorporated, 100 Palmer Square, Princeton, New Jersey 08542 (609) 924-9600; "Giving and Volunteering in the United States."

EDUCATION - PRIVATE SCHOOLS - COMPUTER USE

Market Data Retrieval, 16 Progress Drive, Shelton, Connecticut 06484 (203) 926-4800; "Microcomputers in Schools," and unpublished data.

EDUCATION - PRIVATE SCHOOLS - ELEMENTARY AND SECONDARY

National Catholic Educational Association, 1077 Thirtieth Street, NW, Suite 100, Washington, D.C. 20007 (202) 337-6232; "Ganley's Catholic Schools in America."

U.S. Department of Commerce, Bureau of the Census, Suitland, Maryland 20233 (301) 763-4040; "Current Population Reports," and unpublished data.

U.S. Department of Education, 400 Maryland Avenue, SW, Washington, D.C. 20202 (202) 708-5366; "Projections of Education Statistics," "Digest of Education Statistics," and unpublished data.

EDUCATION - PRIVATE SCHOOLS - ELEMENTARY AND SECONDARY - PROJECTIONS - (ENROLLMENT)

U.S. Department of Education, 400 Maryland Avenue, SW, Washington, D.C. 20202 (202) 708-5366; "Digest of Education Statistics," "Projections of Education Statistics," and unpublished data.

EDUCATION - PRIVATE SCHOOLS - EXPENDITURES

U.S. Department of Education, 400 Maryland Avenue, SW, Washington, D.C. 20202 (202) 708-5366; "Digest of Education Statistics," and unpublished data.

EDUCATION - PRIVATE SCHOOLS - NUMBER

U.S. Department of Education, 400 Maryland Avenue, SW, Washington, D.C. 20202 (202) 708-5366; "Digest of Education Statistics," and "Projections of Education Statistics."

EDUCATION - PRIVATE SCHOOLS - TEACHERS

U.S. Department of Education, 400 Maryland Avenue, SW, Washington, D.C. 20202 (202) 708-5366; "Digest of Education Statistics."

EDUCATION - PUBLIC ELEMENTARY AND SECONDARY SCHOOLS - COMPUTER USE

Market Data Retrieval, 16 Progress Drive, Shelton, Connecticut 06484 (203) 926-4800; "Microcomputers in Schools," and unpublished data.

EDUCATION - PUBLIC ELEMENTARY AND SECONDARY SCHOOLS - ENROLLMENT

National Education Association, 1201 Sixteenth Street, NW, Washington, D.C. 20036 (202) 833-4000; "Estimates of School Statistics," "Rankings of the States," and unpublished data.

U.S. Department of Commerce, Bureau of the Census, Suitland, Maryland 20233 (301) 763-4040; "Current Population Reports," and unpublished data.

U.S. Department of Education, 400 Maryland Avenue, SW, Washington, D.C. 20202 (202) 708-5366; "Digest of Education Statistics," "Projections of Education Statistics," and unpublished data.

EDUCATION - PUBLIC ELEMENTARY AND SECONDARY SCHOOLS - ENROLLMENT - PROJECTIONS

U.S. Department of Education, 400 Maryland Avenue, SW, Washington, D.C. 20202 (202) 708-5366; *Digest of Education Statistics, Projections of Education Statistics,* and unpublished data.

EDUCATION - PUBLIC ELEMENTARY AND SECONDARY SCHOOLS - ENROLLMENT - SIZE

U.S. Department of Education, 400 Maryland Avenue, SW, Washington, D.C. 20202 (202) 708-5366; *Digest of Education Statistics.*

EDUCATION - PUBLIC ELEMENTARY AND SECONDARY SCHOOLS - ENROLLMENT - STATES

U.S. Department of Education, 400 Maryland Avenue, SW, Washington, D.C. 20202 (202) 708-5366; *Digest of Education Statistics,* and *Projections of Education Statistics.*

EDUCATION - PUBLIC ELEMENTARY AND SECONDARY SCHOOLS - FINANCES

National Education Association, 1201 Sixteenth Street, NW, Washington, D.C. 20036 (202) 883-4000; *Estimates of School Statistics* and unpublished data.

U.S. Department of Commerce, Bureau of the Census, Suitland, Maryland 20233 (301) 763-4040; *Public Education Finances.*

U.S. Department of Education, 400 Maryland Avenue, SW, Washington, D.C. 20202 (202) 708-5366; *Digest of Education Statistics, Projections of Education Statistics,* and unpublished data.

EDUCATION - PUBLIC ELEMENTARY AND SECONDARY SCHOOLS - HIGH SCHOOL GRADUATES

U.S. Department of Education, 400 Maryland Avenue, SW, Washington, D.C. 20202 (202) 708-5366; *Digest of Education Statistics,* and *Projections of Education Statistics.*

EDUCATION - PUBLIC ELEMENTARY AND SECONDARY SCHOOLS - NUMBER

U.S. Department of Education, 400 Maryland Avenue, SW, Washington, D.C. 20202 (202) 708-5366; *Digest of Education Statistics,* and *Projections of Education Statistics.*

EDUCATION - PUBLIC ELEMENTARY AND SECONDARY SCHOOLS - PERSONNEL

Equal Employment Opportunity Commission, 1801 L Street, NW, Washington, D.C. 20507 (800) USA-EEOC; *Elementary-Secondary Staff Information.*

EDUCATION - PUBLIC ELEMENTARY AND SECONDARY SCHOOLS - PERSONNEL SALARIES

Educational Research Service, 2000 Clarendon Boulevard, Arlington, Virginia 22209 (703) 243-2100; *National Survey of Salaries and Wages in Public Schools.*

EDUCATION - PUBLIC ELEMENTARY AND SECONDARY SCHOOLS - PRICE INDEXES

Research Associates of Washington, 2605 Klingle Road, NW, Washington, D.C. 20008 (202) 966-3326; *Inflation Measures for Schools and Colleges.*

EDUCATION - PUBLIC ELEMENTARY AND SECONDARY SCHOOLS - SPECIAL EDUCATION PROGRAMS

U.S. Department of Education, Office of Special Education Programs, 400 Maryland Avenue, SW, Washington, D.C. 20202 (202) 708-5366; *Annual Report to Congress.*

EDUCATION - PUBLIC ELEMENTARY AND SECONDARY SCHOOLS - TEACHERS

Equal Employment Opportunity Commission, 1801 L Street, NW, Washington, D.C. 20507 (800) USA-EEOC; *Elementary-Secondary Staff Information.*

National Education Association, 1201 Sixteenth Street, NW, Washington, D.C. 20036 (202) 833-4000; *Estimates of School Statistics, Rankings of the States,* and unpublished data.

U.S. Department of Education, 400 Maryland Avenue, SW, Washington, D.C. 20202 (202) 708-5366; *Projections of Education Statistics, Digest of Education Statistics,* and unpublished data.

EDUCATION - SCHOLASTIC APTITUDE TEST

College Entrance Examination Board, 45 Columbus Avenue, New York, New York 10023 (212) 713-8000; *National College - Bound Senior.*

EDUCATION - SCHOOL DISTRICTS

U.S. Department of Commerce, Bureau of the Census, Suitland, Maryland 20233 (301) 763-4040; *Census of Governments,* and *Government Organization.*

EDUCATION - SCHOOL LOSS DAYS

U.S. Department of Health and Human Services, National Center for Health Statistics, 3700 East-West Highway, Hyattsville, Maryland 20782 (301) 436-8500; *Vital and Health Statistics,* and unpublished data.

EDUCATION - SCHOOL YEARS COMPLETED - See EDUCATION ATTAINMENT

EDUCATION - SPECIAL EDUCATION PROGRAMS

U.S. Department of Education, Office of Special Education Programs, 400 Maryland Avenue, SW, Washington, D.C. 20202 (202) 708-5366; *Annual Report to Congress.*

EDUCATION - STATE DATA - ELEMENTARY AND SECONDARY SCHOOLS

National Education Association, 1201 Sixteenth Street, NW, Washington, D.C. 20036 (202) 833-4000; *Estimates of School Statistics,* and unpublished data.

U.S. Department of Education, 400 Maryland Avenue, SW, Washington, D.C. 20202 (202) 708-5366; *Digest of Education Statistics,* and *Projections of Education.*

EDUCATION - STATE DATA - HIGHER EDUCATION

Research Associates of Washington, 2605 Klingle Road, NW, Washington, D.C. 20008 (202) 966-3326; *State Profiles: Financing Public Higher Education.*

U.S. Department of Education, 400 Maryland Avenue, SW, Washington, D.C. 20202 (202) 708-5366; *Digest of Education Statistics.*

EDUCATION - TEACHERS - CATHOLIC SCHOOLS

National Catholic Education Association, 1077 Thirtieth Street, NW, Washington, D.C. 20007 (202) 337-6232; *Ganley's Catholic Schools in America.*

EDUCATION - TEACHERS - ELEMENTARY AND SECONDARY

National Education Association, 1201 Sixteenth Street, NW, Washington, D.C. 20036 (202) 833-4000; *Estimates of School Statistics, Rankings of the States,* and unpublished data.

U.S. Department of Education, 400 Maryland Avenue, SW, Washington, D.C. 20202 (202) 708-5366; *Digest of Education Statistics,* and *Projections of Education Statistics.*

EDUCATION - TEACHERS - EMPLOYMENT PROJECTIONS

U.S. Department of Education, 400 Maryland Avenue, SW, Washington, D.C. 20202 (202) 708-5366; *Digest of Education Statistics*, and *Projections of Educations Statistics*.

U.S. Department of Labor, Bureau of Labor Statistics, Two Massachusetts Avenue, NE, Washington, D.C. 20212 (202) 606-7828; *Monthly Labor Review*.

EDUCATION - TEACHERS - HIGHER EDUCATION

Maryse Eymonerie Associates/American Association of University Professors, 1012 Fourteenth Street, NW, Suite 500, Washington, D.C. 20005 (202) 737-5900; *AAUP Annual Report on the Economic Status of the Profession*.

U.S. Department of Education, 400 Maryland Avenue, SW, Washington, D.C. 20202 (202) 708-5366; *Digest of Education Statistics*, and unpublished data.

EDUCATION, DEPARTMENT OF, BUDGET OUTLAYS

Executive Office of the President, Office of Management and Budget, Executive Office Building, Washington, D.C. 20503 (202) 395-3080; *Budget of the United States Government*.

EDUCATIONAL SERVICES

Gale Research Incorporated, 835 Penobscot Building, Detroit, Michigan 48226 (800) 877-4253; *Encyclopedia of Associations*.

EDUCATIONAL SERVICES - ADVERTISING EXPENDITURES

Television Bureau of Advertising, Incorporated, 850 Third Avenue, New York, New York 10022 (212) 486-1111; based on data from Competitive Media Reporting, 11 West 42nd Street, New York, New York 10036 (212) 789-1400.

EDUCATIONAL SERVICES - EARNINGS

U.S. Department of Commerce, Bureau of the Census, Suitland, Maryland 20233 (301) 763-4040; *Census of Service Industries*, *County Business Patterns*, and unpublished data.

U.S. Department of Labor, Bureau of Labor Statistics, Two Massachusetts Avenue, NE, Washington, D.C. 20212 (202) 606-7828; *Employment and Earnings*, and Bulletins 2370 and 2429.

EDUCATIONAL SERVICES - EMPLOYEES

U.S. Department of Commerce, Bureau of the Census, Suitland, Maryland 20233 (301) 763-4040; *Census of Service Industries*, *County Business Patterns*, and unpublished data.

EDUCATIONAL SERVICES - ESTABLISHMENTS

International Franchise Association, 1350 New York Avenue, NW, Suite 900, Washington, D.C. 20005 (202) 628-8000; *Franchising in the Economy*.

U.S. Department of Commerce, Bureau of the Census, Suitland, Maryland 20233 (301) 763-4040; *Census of the Service Industries*, *County Business Patterns*, and unpublished data.

EDUCATIONAL SERVICES - FINANCES

U.S. Department of Commerce, Bureau of the Census, Suitland, Maryland 20233 (301) 763-4040; *Census of Service Industries*, and unpublished data.

EDUCATIONAL SERVICES - GROSS DOMESTIC PRODUCT

U.S. Department of Commerce, Bureau of Economic Analysis, Fourteenth Street between Constitution Avenue and E Street, NW, Washington, D.C. 20230 (202) 606-9900; *Survey of Current Business*, and *The National Income and Product Accounts of the United States*.

EDUCATIONAL SERVICES - RECEIPTS

International Franchise Association, 1350 New York Avenue, NW, Suite 900, Washington, D.C. 20005 (202) 628-8000; *Franchising in the Economy*.

U.S. Department of Commerce, Bureau of the Census, Suitland, Maryland 20233 (301) 763-4040; *Census of Service Industries*.

EGGPLANT

U.S. Department of Agriculture, Economic Research Service, 14th Street and Independence Avenue, SW, Washington, D.C. 20250 (202) 219-1504; unpublished data.

EGGS - See also POULTRY

EGGS - CONSUMPTION

U.S. Department of Agriculture, Economic Research Service, Fourteenth Street and Independence Avenue, SW, Washington, D.C. 20250 (202) 219-1504; *Layers and Egg Production - Annual*, and *Food Consumption Prices and Expenditures*.

EGGS - FARM MARKETINGS, SALES

U.S. Department of Agriculture, Economic Research Service, Fourteenth Street and Independence Avenue, SW, Washington, D.C. 20250 (202) 219-1504; *Economic Indicators of the Farm Sector: National Financial Summary*, and unpublished data.

EGGS - PRICES

U.S. Department of Agriculture, National Agricultural Statistics Service, Fourteenth Street and Independence Avenue, SW, Washington, D.C. 20250 (202) 219-1504; *Layers and Egg Production - Annual*, *Turkeys*, *Food Cost Review*, and *Agricultural Outlook*.

U.S. Department of Labor, Bureau of Labor Statistics, 2 Massachusetts Avenue, NE, Washington, D.C. 20212 (202) 606-7828; *CPI Detailed Report*, and *Monthly Labor Review*.

EGGS - PRODUCTION

U.S. Department of Agriculture, National Agricultural Statistics Service, Fourteenth Street and Independence Avenue, SW, Washington, D.C. 20250 (202) 219-1504; *Layers and Egg Production - Annual*, *Turkeys*, and *Agricultural Outlook*.

Egypt - National Statistical Office

Central Agency for Public Mobilization and Statistics, Post Office Box 2086, Nasr City, Cairo, Egypt.

Egypt - Primary Statistics Sources

Central Agency for Public Mobilization and Statistics, Post Office Box 2086, Cairo, Egypt; *Statistical Abstract of the Arab Republic of*

Egypt, and *Statistical Yearbook: Arab Republic of Egypt.*

EGYPT - AGRICULTURE

Economic Commission for Western Asia, Post Office Box 27, Baghdad, Iraq; *Statistical Abstract of Western Asia.*

Euromonitor Publications Limited, 87-88 Turnmill Street, London EC1M 5QU, England; *International Marketing Data and Statistics*, and *Middle East Economic Handbook.*

Facts on File, 460 Park Avenue South, New York, New York 10016 (800) 443-8323; *The New Book of World Rankings.*

Food and Agricultural Organization of the United Nations (FAO) Via delle Terme di Caracalla, 00100 Rome, Italy (Telephone Number in U.S. (202) 653-2400); *The State of Food and Agriculture*, and *Trade Yearbook.*

G.K. Hall and Company, 70 Lincoln Street, Boston, Massachusetts 02111 (617) 423-3990; *The World in Figures.*

Statistical Office of the United Nations, Publishing Service, New York, New York 10017 (800) 253-9646; *Statistical Yearbook*, and *Survey of Economic and Social Conditions in Africa.*

Times Books, 201 East 50th Street, New York, New York 10022 (212) 751-2600; *The Economist Book of Vital World Statistics.*

United Nations Economic Commission for Africa, Africa Hall, P.O. Box 3001, Addis Ababa, Ethiopia (Telephone Number in U.S. (800) 253-9646); *African Statistical Yearbook.*

EGYPT - AIRLINE SERVICE

Economic Commission for Western Asia, Post Office Box 27, Baghdad, Iraq; *Statistical Abstract of Western Asia.*

Facts on File, 460 Park Avenue South, New York, New York 10016 (800) 443-8323; *The New Book of World Rankings.*

G.K. Hall and Company, 70 Lincoln Street, Boston, Massachusetts 02111 (617) 423-3990; *The World in Figures.*

International Civil Aviation Organization, 1000 Sherbrooke Street West, Suite 400, Montreal, Quebec, Canada H3A 2R2 (514) 285-8219; *Civil Aviation Statistics of the World.*

Statistical Office of the United Nations, Publishing Service, New York, New York 10017 (800) 253-9646; *Statistical Yearbook.*

Times Books, 201 East 50th Street, New York, New York 10022 (212) 751-2600; *The Economist Book of Vital World Statistics.*

United Nations Economic Commission for Africa, Africa Hall, P.O. Box 3001, Addis Ababa, Ethiopia (Telephone Number in U.S. (800) 253-9646); *African Statistical Yearbook.*

EGYPT - ALUMINUM PRODUCTION AND CONSUMPTION - See EGYPT - MINING AND MINERAL PRODUCTS

EGYPT - ANIMAL HEALTH

Food and Agricultural Organization of the United Nations (FAO), Via delle Terme di Caracalla, 00100 Rome, Italy (Telephone Number in U.S. (202) 653-2400); *Animal Health Yearbook.*

EGYPT - AREA AND DENSITY OF POPULATION

African Development Bank, 01 BP 1387, Abidjan 01, Cote D'Ivoire; *Selected Statistics on Regional Member Countries.*

Economic Commission for Western Asia, Post Office Box 27, Baghdad, Iraq; *Statistical Abstract of Western Asia.*

Euromonitor Publications Limited, 87-88 Turnmill Street, London EC1M 5QU, England; *International Marketing Data and Statistics*, and *Middle East Economic Handbook.*

Facts on File, 460 Park Avenue South, New York, New York 10016 (800) 443-8323; *The New Book of World Rankings.*

Food and Agricultural Organization of the United Nations (FAO) Via delle Terme di Caracalla, 00100 Rome, Italy (Telephone Number in U.S. (202) 653-2400); *The State of Food and Agriculture.*

G.K. Hall and Company, 70 Lincoln Street, Boston, Massachusetts 02111 (617) 423-3990; *The World in Figures.*

Statistical Office of the United Nations, Publishing Service, New York, New York 10017 (800) 253-9646; *Statistical Yearbook*, and *Survey of Economic and Social Conditions in Africa.*

Times Books, 201 East 50th Street, New York, New York 10022 (212) 751-2600; *The Economist Book of Vital World Statistics.*

United Nations Educational, Scientific and Cultural Organization (UNESCO), 7 Place de Fontenoy, F-75700 Paris, France (Telephone Number in U.S. (212) 963-5981); *Statistical Yearbook.*

EGYPT - ARMS EXPORTS AND IMPORTS

U.S. Arms Control and Disarmament Agency, 320 Twenty-first Street, NW, Washington, D.C. 20451 (202) 647-8677; *World Military Expenditures and Arms Transfers.*

EGYPT - ARTICHOKE PRODUCTION - See EGYPT - CROPS

EGYPT - BALANCE OF PAYMENTS

African Development Bank, 01 BP 1387, Abidjan 01, Cote D'Ivoire; *Selected Statistics on Regional Member Countries.*

Economic Commission for Western Asia, Post Office Box 27, Baghdad, Iraq; *Statistical Abstract of Western Asia.*

The Economist Intelligence Unit, 111 West 57th Street, New York, New York 10019 (800) 938-4685; *The World Market Atlas.*

G.K. Hall and Company, 70 Lincoln Street, Boston, Massachusetts 02111 (617) 423-3990; *The World in Figures.*

International Monetary Fund, 700 Nineteenth Street, NW, Washington, D.C. 20431 (202) 623-7000; *Balance of Payments Yearbook.*

Times Books, 201 East 50th Street, New York, New York 10022 (212) 751-2600; *The Economist Book of Vital World Statistics.*

United Nations Economic Commission for Africa, Africa Hall, P.O. Box 3001, Addis Ababa, Ethiopia (Telephone Number in U.S. (800) 253-9646); *African Statistical Yearbook.*

EGYPT - BALANCE OF TRADE

Economic Commission for Western Asia, Post Office Box 27, Baghdad, Iraq; *Statistical Abstract of Western Asia.*

EGYPT - BANKING

Economic Commission for Western Asia, Post Office Box 27, Baghdad, Iraq; *Statistical Abstract of Western Asia.*

Facts on File, 460 Park Avenue South, New York, New York 10016 (800) 443-8323; *The New Book of World Rankings.*

G.K. Hall and Company, 70 Lincoln Street, Boston, Massachusetts 02111 (617) 423-3990; *The World in Figures.*

International Monetary Fund, 700 Nineteenth Street, NW, Washington, D.C. 20431 (202) 623-7000; *International Financial Statistics.*

Statistical Office of the United Nations, Publishing Service, New York, New York 10017 (800) 253-9646; *Statistical Yearbook.*

United Nations Economic Commission for Africa, Africa Hall, P.O. Box 3001, Addis Ababa, Ethiopia (Telephone Number in U.S. (800) 253-9646); *African Statistical Yearbook.*

EGYPT - BARLEY PRODUCTION - See EGYPT - CROPS

EGYPT - BEER PRODUCTION

Facts on File, 460 Park Avenue South, New York, New York 10016 (800) 443-8323; *The New Book of World Rankings.*

Statistical Office of the United Nations, Publishing Service, New York, New York 10017 (800) 253-9646; *Statistical Yearbook.*

EGYPT - BIRTH RATES

Euromonitor Publications Limited, 87-88 Turnmill Street, London EC1M 5QU, England; *Middle East Economic Handbook.*

Facts on File, 460 Park Avenue South, New York, New York 10016 (800) 443-8323; *The New Book of World Rankings.*

Statistical Office of the United Nations, Publishing Service, New York, New York 10017 (800) 253-9646; *Demographic Yearbook, Statistical Yearbook,* and *Survey of Economic and Social Conditions in Africa.*

Times Books, 201 East 50th Street, New York, New York 10022 (212) 751-2600; *The Economist Book of Vital World Statistics.*

World Health Organization, Office of Publications, Avenue Appia, CH-1211, Geneva, 27, Switzerland (Telephone Number in U.S. (518) 436-9686); *World Health Statistics Annual.*

EGYPT - BONDS

G.K. Hall and Company, 70 Lincoln Street, Boston, Massachusetts 02111 (617) 423-3990; *The World in Figures.*

International Monetary Fund, 700 Nineteenth Street, NW, Washington, D.C. 20431 (202) 623-7000; *Government Finance Statistics Yearbook.*

Statistical Office of the United Nations, Publishing Service, New York, New York 10017 (800) 253-9646; *Statistical Yearbook.*

EGYPT - BOOK PRODUCTION

G.K. Hall and Company, 70 Lincoln Street, Boston, Massachusetts 02111 (617) 423-3990; *The World in Figures.*

United Nations Educational, Scientific and Cultural Organization (UNESCO), 7 Place de Fontenoy, F-75700 Paris, France (Telephone Number in U.S. (212) 963-5981); *Statistical Yearbook.*

EGYPT - BROADCASTING

Billboard Limited, P.O. Box 9027, 1006 AA Amsterdam, The Netherlands (Telephone Number in U.S. (212) 764-7300); *World Radio TV Handbook.*

G.K. Hall and Company, 70 Lincoln Street, Boston, Massachusetts 02111 (617) 423-3990; *The World in Figures.*

Facts on File, 460 Park Avenue South, New York, New York 10016 (800) 443-8323; *The New Book of World Rankings.*

Times Books, 201 East 50th Street, New York, New York 10022 (212) 751-2600; *The Economist Book of Vital World Statistics.*

EGYPT - BUILDING CONSTRUCTION - See EGYPT - CONSTRUCTION INDUSTRY

EGYPT - BUSINESS

G.K. Hall and Company, 70 Lincoln Street, Boston, Massachusetts 02111 (617) 423-3990; *The World in Figures.*

EGYPT - BUSINESS AND PROFESSIONAL LICENSES

International Monetary Fund, 700 Nineteenth Street, NW, Washington, D.C. 20431 (202) 623-7000; *Government Finance Statistics Yearbook.*

EGYPT - BUTTER PRODUCTION - See EGYPT - DAIRY PRODUCTS

EGYPT - CABBAGE PRODUCTION - See EGYPT - CROPS

EGYPT - CALORIE SUPPLY

African Development Bank, 01 BP 1387, Abidjan 01, Cote D'Ivoire; *Selected Statistics on Regional Member Countries.*

Food and Agricultural Organization of the United Nations (FAO) Via delle Terme di Caracalla, 00100 Rome, Italy (Telephone Number in U.S. (202) 653-2400); *The State of Food and Agriculture.*

EGYPT - CAPITAL REVENUE

International Monetary Fund, 700 Nineteenth Street, NW, Washington, D.C. 20431 (202) 623-7000; *Government Finance Statistics Yearbook.*

EGYPT - CATTLE - See EGYPT - LIVESTOCK AND POULTRY

EGYPT - CAULIFLOWER PRODUCTION - See EGYPT - CROPS

EGYPT - CAUSTIC SODA PRODUCTION

Statistical Office of the United Nations, Publishing Service, New York, New York 10017 (800) 253-9646; *Statistical Yearbook.*

EGYPT - CEMENT PRODUCTION - See EGYPT - MINING AND MINERAL PRODUCTS

EGYPT - CHEESE PRODUCTION - See EGYPT - DAIRY PRODUCTS

EGYPT - CHEMICAL (ORGANIC) PRODUCTION - See EGYPT - MINING AND MINERAL PRODUCTS

EGYPT - CHICK PEA PRODUCTION - See EGYPT - CROPS

EGYPT - CHICKENS - See EGYPT - LIVESTOCK AND POULTRY

EGYPT - CIGAR PRODUCTION - See EGYPT - TOBACCO PRODUCTION

EGYPT - CIGARETTE PRODUCTION - See EGYPT - TOBACCO PRODUCTION

EGYPT - CLASS STRUCTURE

G.K. Hall and Company, 70 Lincoln Street, Boston, Massachusetts 02111 (617) 423-3990; *The World in Figures.*

EGYPT - CLIMATE

Facts on File, 460 Park Avenue South, New York, New York 10016 (800) 443-8323; *The New Book of World Rankings.*

G.K. Hall and Company, 70 Lincoln Street, Boston, Massachusetts 02111 (617) 423-3990; *The World in Figures.*

EGYPT - COAL PRODUCTION - See EGYPT - MINING AND MINERAL PRODUCTS

EGYPT - COFFEE PRODUCTION - See EGYPT - CROPS

EGYPT - COKE OVEN COKE PRODUCTION - See EGYPT - MINING AND MINERAL PRODUCTS

EGYPT - COMMUNICATIONS

Economic Commission for Western Asia, Post Office Box 27, Baghdad, Iraq; *Statistical Abstract of Western Asia.*

G.K. Hall and Company, 70 Lincoln Street, Boston, Massachusetts 02111 (617) 423-3990; *The World in Figures.*

United Nations Economic Commission for Africa, Africa Hall, P.O. Box 3001, Addis Ababa, Ethiopia (Telephone Number in U.S. (800) 253-9646); *African Statistical Yearbook.*

EGYPT - CONSTRUCTION INDUSTRY

Facts on File, 460 Park Avenue South, New York, New York 10016 (800) 443-8323; *The New Book of World Rankings.*

Statistical Office of the United Nations, Publishing Service, New York, New York 10017 (800) 253-9646; *Statistical Yearbook.*

United Nations Economic Commission for Africa, Africa Hall, P.O. Box 3001, Addis Ababa, Ethiopia (Telephone Number in U.S. (800) 253-9646); *African Statistical Yearbook.*

EGYPT - CONSUMER PRICE INDEX

African Development Bank, 01 BP 1387, Abidjan 01, Cote D'Ivoire; *Selected Statistics on Regional Member Countries.*

G.K. Hall and Company, 70 Lincoln Street, Boston, Massachusetts 02111 (617) 423-3990; *The World in Figures.*

Statistical Office of the United Nations, Publishing Service, New York, New York 10017 (800) 253-9646; *Statistical Yearbook,* and *Survey of Economic and Social Conditions in Africa.*

United Nations Economic Commission for Africa, Africa Hall, P.O. Box 3001, Addis Ababa, Ethiopia (Telephone Number in U.S. (800) 253-9646); *African Statistical Yearbook.*

EGYPT - CONSUMER PRICES

International Labour Office, I.L.O. Publications, CH-1211, Geneva 22, Switzerland; *Yearbook of Labour Statistics.*

International Monetary Fund, 700 Nineteenth Street, NW, Washington, D.C. 20431 (202) 623-7000; *International Financial Statistics.*

Times Books, 201 East 50th Street, New York, New York 10022 (212) 751-2600; *The Economist Book of Vital World Statistics.*

EGYPT - CONSUMPTION

African Development Bank, 01 BP 1387, Abidjan 01, Cote D'Ivoire; *Selected Statistics on Regional Member Countries.*

Euromonitor Publications Limited, 87-88 Turnmill Street, London EC1M 5QU, England; *Middle East Economic Handbook.*

G.K. Hall and Company, 70 Lincoln Street, Boston, Massachusetts 02111 (617) 423-3990; *The World in Figures.*

Statistical Office of the United Nations, Publishing Service, New York, New York 10017 (800) 253-9646; *Survey of Economic and Social Conditions in Africa.*

EGYPT - COPPER PRODUCTION - See EGYPT - MINING AND MINERAL PRODUCTS

EGYPT - CORN PRODUCTION - See EGYPT - CROPS

EGYPT - CORPORATE TAXES - See EGYPT - TAXATION

EGYPT - COTTON - See EGYPT - CROPS

EGYPT - CRIME

International Criminal Police Organization (INTERPOL), 26 rue Armengaud, 92210 Saint Cloud, France; *International Crime Statistics.*

Yale University Press, Yale Station, New Haven, Connecticut 06520 (203) 432-0940; *Violence and Crime in Cross-National Perspective.*

EGYPT - CROPS

Commodity Research Bureau, Incorporated, 75 Wall Street, New York, New York 10005 (212) 504-7754; *Commodity Year Book.*

Facts on File, 460 Park Avenue South, New York, New York 10016 (800) 443-8323; *The New Book of World Rankings.*

Food and Agricultural Organization of the United Nations (FAO) Via delle Terme di Caracalla, 00100 Rome, Italy (Telephone Number in U.S. (202) 653-2400); *Production Yearbook,* and *The State of Food and Agriculture.*

G.K. Hall and Company, 70 Lincoln Street, Boston, Massachusetts 02111 (617) 423-3990; *The World in Figures.*

International Monetary Fund, 700 Nineteenth Street, NW, Washington, D.C. 20431 (202) 623-7000; *International Financial Statistics*.

Statistical Office of the United Nations, Publishing Service, New York, New York 10017 (800) 253-9646; *Statistical Yearbook*.

United Nations Economic Commission for Africa, Africa Hall, P.O. Box 3001, Addis Ababa, Ethiopia (Telephone Number in U.S. (800) 253-9646); *African Statistical Yearbook*.

EGYPT - CUSTOMS DUTIES

G.K. Hall and Company, 70 Lincoln Street, Boston, Massachusetts 02111 (617) 423-3990; *The World in Figures*.

International Monetary Fund, 700 Nineteenth Street, NW, Washington, D.C. 20431 (202) 623-7000; *Government Finance Statistics Yearbook*.

EGYPT - DAIRY PRODUCTS

Economic Commission for Western Asia, Post Office Box 27, Baghdad, Iraq; *Statistical Abstract of Western Asia*.

Facts on File, 460 Park Avenue South, New York, New York 10016 (800) 443-8323; *The New Book of World Rankings*.

Food and Agricultural Organization of the United Nations (FAO) Via delle Terme di Caracalla, 00100 Rome, Italy (Telephone Number in U.S. (202) 653-2400); *Production Yearbook*, and *The State of Food and Agriculture*.

Statistical Office of the United Nations, Publishing Service, New York, New York 10017 (800) 253-9646; *Statistical Yearbook*.

EGYPT - DEATH RATES

Euromonitor Publications Limited, 87-88 Turnmill Street, London EC1M 5QU, England; *Middle East Economic Handbook*.

G.K. Hall and Company, 70 Lincoln Street, Boston, Massachusetts 02111 (617) 423-3990; *The World in Figures*.

Statistical Office of the United Nations, Publishing Service, New York, New York 10017 (800) 253-9646; *Statistical Yearbook*, and *Survey of Economic and Social Conditions in Africa*.

Times Books, 201 East 50th Street, New York, New York 10022 (212) 751-2600; *The Economist Book of Vital World Statistics*.

World Health Organization, Office of Publications, Avenue Appia, CH-12117 Geneva, 27, Switzerland (Telephone Number in U.S. (518) 436-9686); *World Health Statistics Annual*.

EGYPT - DEFENSE EXPENDITURES

G.K. Hall and Company, 70 Lincoln Street, Boston, Massachusetts 02111 (617) 423-3990; *The World in Figures*.

International Monetary Fund, 700 Nineteenth Street, NW, Washington, D.C. 20431 (202) 623-7000; *Government Finance Statistics Yearbook*.

U.S. Arms Control and Disarmament Agency, 320 Twenty-first Street, NW, Washington, D.C. 20451 (202) 647-8677; *World Military Expenditures and Arms Transfers*.

EGYPT - DEMOGRAPHY

The Economist Intelligence Unit, 111 West 57th Street, New York, New York 10019 (800) 938-4685; *The World Market Atlas*.

Facts on File, 460 Park Avenue South, New York, New York 10016 (800) 443-8323; *The New Book of World Rankings*.

G.K. Hall and Company, 70 Lincoln Street, Boston, Massachusetts 02111 (617) 423-3990; *The World in Figures*.

Statistical Office of the United Nations, Publishing Service, New York, New York 10017 (800) 253-9646; *Survey of Economic and Social Conditions in Africa*.

EGYPT - DEVELOPMENT ASSISTANCE

G.K. Hall and Company, 70 Lincoln Street, Boston, Massachusetts 02111 (617) 423-3990; *The World in Figures*.

Statistical Office of the United Nations, Publishing Service, New York, New York 10017 (800) 253-9646; *Statistical Yearbook*.

EGYPT - DIAMOND PRODUCTION - See EGYPT - MINING AND MINERAL PRODUCTS

EGYPT - DISCOUNT RATES

Statistical Office of the United Nations, Publishing Service, New York, New York 10017 (800) 253-9646; *Statistical Yearbook*.

EGYPT - DISEASES

G.K. Hall and Company, 70 Lincoln Street, Boston, Massachusetts 02111 (617) 423-3990; *The World in Figures*.

World Health Organization, Office of Publications, Avenue Appia, Ch-1211 Geneva, 27, Switzerland (Telephone Number in U.S. (518) 436-9686); *World Health Statistics Annual*.

EGYPT - DIVORCE RATES

Facts on File, 460 Park Avenue South, New York, New York 10016 (800) 443-8323; *The New Book of World Rankings*.

Statistical Office of the United Nations, Publishing Service, New York, New York 10017 (800) 253-9646; *Demographic Yearbook*, and *Statistical Yearbook*.

EGYPT - DOMESTIC PRODUCT

G.K. Hall and Company, 70 Lincoln Street, Boston, Massachusetts 02111 (617) 423-3990; *The World in Figures*.

EGYPT - DUCKS - See EGYPT - LIVESTOCK AND POULTRY

EGYPT - ECONOMY

African Development Bank, 01 BP 1387, Abidjan 01, Cote D'Ivoire; *Selected Statistics on Regional Member Countries*.

Euromonitor Publications Limited, 87-88 Turnmill Street, London EC1M 5QU, England; *International Marketing Data and Statistics*.

Facts on File, 460 Park Avenue South, New York, New York 10016 (800) 443-8323; *The New Book of World Rankings*.

G.K. Hall and Company, 70 Lincoln Street, Boston, Massachusetts 02111 (617) 423-3990; *The World in Figures*.

Statistical Office of the United Nations, Publishing Service, New York, New York 10017 (800) 253-9646; *Foreign Trade Statistics for Africa.*

EGYPT - EDUCATION

African Development Bank, 01 BP 1387, Abidjan 01, Cote D'Ivoire; *Selected Statistics on Regional Member Countries.*

Economic Commission for Western Asia, Post Office Box 27, Baghdad, Iraq; *Statistical Abstract of Western Asia.*

The Economist Intelligence Unit, 111 West 57th Street, New York, New York 10019 (800) 938-4685; *The World Market Atlas.*

Euromonitor Publications Limited, 87-88 Turnmill Street, London EC1M 5QU, England; *Middle East Economic Handbook.*

Facts on File, 460 Park Avenue South, New York, New York 10016 (800) 443-8323; *The New Book of World Rankings.*

G.K. Hall and Company, 70 Lincoln Street, Boston, Massachusetts 02111 (617) 423-3990; *The World in Figures.*

International Monetary Fund, 700 Nineteenth Street, NW, Washington, D.C. 20431 (202) 623-7000; *Government Finance Statistics Yearbook.*

Statistical Office of the United Nations, Publishing Service, New York, New York 10017 (800) 253-9646; *Survey of Economic and Social Conditions in Africa.*

Times Books, 201 East 50th Street, New York, New York 10022 (212) 751-2600; *The Economist Book of Vital World Statistics.*

United Nations Economic Commission for Africa, Africa Hall, P.O. Box 3001, Addis Ababa, Ethiopia (Telephone Number in U.S. (800) 253-9646); *African Statistical Yearbook.*

United Nations Educational, Scientific and Cultural Organization (UNESCO), 7 Place de Fontenoy, F-75700 Paris, France (Telephone Number in U.S. (212) 963-5981); *Statistical Yearbook.*

EGYPT - EGG PRODUCTION - See EGYPT - DAIRY PRODUCTS

EGYPT - EGGPLANT PRODUCTION - See EGYPT - CROPS

EGYPT - ELECTRICITY

Facts on File, 460 Park Avenue South, New York, New York 10016 (800) 443-8323; *The New Book of World Rankings.*

Penn Well Publishing Company, 1421 South Sheridan Road, P.O. Box 1260, Tulsa, Oklahoma 74101 (800) 752-9764; *International Energy Statistics Sourcebook.*

Statistical Office of the United Nations, Publishing Service, New York, New York 10017 (800) 253-9646; *Statistical Yearbook,* and *Survey of Economic and Social Conditions in Africa.*

Times Books, 201 East 50th Street, New York, New York 10022 (212) 751-2600; *The Economist Book of Vital World Statistics.*

United Nations Economic Commission for Africa, Africa Hall, P.O. Box 3001, Addis Ababa, Ethiopia (Telephone Number in U.S. (800) 253-9646); *African Statistical Yearbook.*

EGYPT - EMPLOYMENT

Economic Commission for Western Asia, Post Office Box 27, Baghdad, Iraq; *Statistical Abstract of Western Asia.*

Euromonitor Publications Limited, 87-88 Turnmill Street, London EC1M 5QU, England; *International Marketing Data and Statistics,* and *Middle East Economic Handbook.*

Facts on File, 460 Park Avenue South, New York, New York 10016 (800) 443-8323; *The New Book of World Rankings.*

International Labour Office, I.L.O. Publications, CH-1211, Geneva 22, Switzerland; *Yearbook of Labour Statistics.*

Statistical Office of the United Nations, Publishing Service, New York, New York 10017 (800) 253-9646; *Statistical Yearbook,* and *Survey of Economic and Social Conditions in Africa.*

United Nations Economic Commission for Africa, Africa Hall, P.O. Box 3001, Addis Ababa, Ethiopia (Telephone Number in U.S. (800) 253-9646); *African Statistical Yearbook.*

EGYPT - ENERGY

Economic Commission for Western Asia, Post Office Box 27, Baghdad, Iraq; *Statistical Abstract of Western Asia.*

Euromonitor Publications Limited, 87-88 Turnmill Street, London EC1M 5QU, England; *Middle East Economic Handbook.*

Facts on File, 460 Park Avenue South, New York, New York 10016 (800) 443-8323; *The New Book of World Rankings.*

Food and Agricultural Organization of the United Nations (FAO) Via delle Terme di Caracalla, 00100 Rome, Italy (Telephone Number in U.S. (202) 653-2400); *The State of Food and Agriculture.*

G.K. Hall and Company, 70 Lincoln Street, Boston, Massachusetts 02111 (617) 423-3990; *The World in Figures.*

Penn Well Publishing Company, 1421 South Sheridan Road, P.O. Box 1260, Tulsa, Oklahoma 74101 (800) 752-9764; *International Energy Statistics Sourcebook.*

Statistical Office of the United Nations, Publishing Service, New York, New York 10017 (800) 253-9646; *Energy Statistics Yearbook,* and *Statistical Yearbook.*

Times Books, 201 East 50th Street, New York, New York 10022 (212) 751-2600; *The Economist Book of Vital World Statistics.*

United Nations Economic Commission for Africa, Africa Hall, P.O. Box 3001, Addis Ababa, Ethiopia (Telephone Number in U.S. (800) 253-9646); *African Statistical Yearbook.*

EGYPT - EXCHANGE RATES

African Development Bank, 01 BP 1387, Abidjan 01, Cote D'Ivoire; *Selected Statistics on Regional Member Countries.*

Euromonitor Publications Limited, 87-88 Turnmill Street, London EC1M 5QU, England; *International Marketing Data and Statistics,* and *Middle East Economic Handbook.*

International Civil Aviation Organization, 1000 Sherbrooke Street West, Suite 400, Montreal, Quebec, Canada H3A 2R2 (514) 285-8219; *Civil Aviation Statistics of the World.*

International Monetary Fund, 700 Nineteenth Street, NW, Washington, D.C. 20431 (202) 623-7000; *International Financial Statistics.*

Statistical Office of the United Nations, Publishing Service, New York, New York 10017 (800) 253-9646; *Foreign Trade Statistics for Africa,* and *Statistical Yearbook.*

EGYPT - EXCISE TAXES - See EGYPT - TAXATION

EGYPT - EXPORTS

African Development Bank, 01 BP 1387, Abidjan 01, Cote D'Ivoire; *Selected Statistics on Regional Member Countries.*

Economic Commission for Western Asia, Post Office Box 27, Baghdad, Iraq; *Statistical Abstract of Western Asia.*

The Economist Intelligence Unit, 111 West 57th Street, New York, New York 10019 (800) 938-4685; *The World Market Atlas.*

Euromonitor Publications Limited, 87-88 Turnmill Street, London EC1M 5QU, England; *International Marketing Data and Statistics,* and *Middle East Economic Handbook.*

Food and Agricultural Organization of the United Nations (FAO) Via delle Terme di Caracalla, 00100 Rome, Italy (Telephone Number in U.S. (202) 653-2400); *The State of Food and Agriculture.*

G.K. Hall and Company, 70 Lincoln Street, Boston, Massachusetts 02111 (617) 423-3990; *The World in Figures.*

International Monetary Fund, 700 Nineteenth Street, NW, Washington, D.C. 20431 (202) 623-7000; *Direction of Trade Statistics,* and *International Financial Statistics.*

Statistical Office of the United Nations, Publishing Service, New York, New York 10017 (800) 253-9646; *Foreign Trade Statistics for Africa, Survey of Economic and Social Conditions in Africa,* and *Trade in Manufactures of Developing Countries.*

Times Books, 201 East 50th Street, New York, New York 10022 (212) 751-2600; *The Economist Book of Vital World Statistics.*

United Nations Economic Commission for Africa, Africa Hall, P.O. Box 3001, Addis Ababa, Ethiopia (Telephone Number in U.S. (800) 253-9646); *African Statistical Yearbook.*

EGYPT - EXTERNAL INDEBTEDNESS

African Development Bank, 01 BP 1387, Abidjan 01, Cote D'Ivoire; *Selected Statistics on Regional Member Countries.*

Statistical Office of the United Nations, Publishing Service, New York, New York 10017 (800) 253-9646; *Survey of Economic and Social Conditions in Africa.*

EGYPT - EXTERNAL TRADE

African Development Bank, 01 BP 1387, Abidjan 01, Cote D'Ivoire; *Selected Statistics on Regional Member Countries.*

Food and Agricultural Organization of the United Nations (FAO) Via delle Terme di Caracalla, 00100 Rome, Italy (Telephone Number in U.S. (202) 653-2400); *The State of Food and Agriculture,* and *Trade Yearbook.*

G.K. Hall and Company, 70 Lincoln Street, Boston, Massachusetts 02111 (617) 423-3990; *The World in Figures.*

Statistical Office of the United Nations, Publishing Service, New York, New York 10017 (800) 253-9646; *Statistical Yearbook.*

EGYPT - FABRIC PRODUCTION - See EGYPT - TEXTILE INDUSTRY

EGYPT - FARM CROPS - See EGYPT - CROPS

EGYPT - FEMALE WORKING POPULATION - See EGYPT - EMPLOYMENT

EGYPT - FERTILITY RATES

Facts on File, 460 Park Avenue South, New York, New York 10016 (800) 443-8323; *The New Book of World Rankings.*

Statistical Office of the United Nations, Publishing Service, New York, New York 10017 (800) 253-9646; *Survey of Economic and Social Conditions in Africa.*

Times Books, 201 East 50th Street, New York, New York 10022 (212) 751-2600; *The Economist Book of Vital World Statistics.*

EGYPT - FERTILIZER

Food and Agricultural Organization of the United Nations (FAO), Via delle Terme di Caracalla, 00100 Rome, Italy (Telephone Number in U.S. (202) 653-2400); *Fertilizer Yearbook,* and *The State of Food and Agriculture.*

Statistical Office of the United Nations, Publishing Service, New York, New York 10017 (800) 253-9646; *Statistical Yearbook.*

EGYPT - FETAL MORTALITY

Statistical Office of the United Nations, Publishing Service, New York, New York 10017 (800) 253-9646; *Demographic Yearbook.*

World Health Organization, Office of Publications, Avenue Appia, CH-1211 Geneva, 27, Switzerland (Telephone Number in U.S. (518) 436-9686); *World Health Statistics Annual.*

EGYPT - FIBRE PRODUCTION - See EGYPT - TEXTILE INDUSTRY

EGYPT - FILAMENT PRODUCTION - See EGYPT - TEXTILE INDUSTRY

EGYPT - FILM - See EGYPT - MOTION PICTURES

EGYPT - FINANCE

African Development Bank, 01 BP 1387, Abidjan 01, Cote D'Ivoire; *Selected Statistics on Regional Member Countries.*

Economic Commission for Western Asia, Post Office Box 27, Baghdad, Iraq; *Statistical Abstract of Western Asia.*

Euromonitor Publications Limited, 87-88 Turnmill Street, London EC1M 5QU, England; *Middle East Economic Handbook.*

Facts on File, 460 Park Avenue South, New York, New York 10016 (800) 443-8323; *The New Book of World Rankings.*

G.K. Hall and Company, 70 Lincoln Street, Boston, Massachusetts 02111 (617) 423-3990; *The World in Figures.*

International Monetary Fund, 700 Nineteenth Street, NW, Washington, D.C. 20431 (202) 623-7000; *Government Finance Statistics Yearbook,* and *International Financial Statistics.*

United Nations Economic Commission for Africa, Africa Hall, P.O. Box 3001, Addis Ababa, Ethiopia (Telephone Number in U.S. (800) 253-9646); *African Statistical Yearbook.*

EGYPT - FISHERIES

Economic Commission for Western Asia, Post Office Box 27, Baghdad, Iraq; *Statistical Abstract of Western Asia.*

Facts on File, 460 Park Avenue South, New York, New York 10016 (800) 443-8323; *The New Book of World Rankings.*

Food and Agricultural Organization of the United Nations (FAO) Via delle Terme di Caracalla, 00100 Rome, Italy (Telephone Number in U.S. (202) 653-2400); *The State of Food and Agriculture,* and *Yearbook of Fishery Statistics.*

Statistical Office of the United Nations, Publishing Service, New York, New York 10017 (800) 253-9646; *Statistical Yearbook,* and *Survey of Economic and Social Conditions in Africa.*

United Nations Economic Commission for Africa, Africa Hall, P.O. Box 3001, Addis Ababa, Ethiopia (Telephone Number in U.S. (800) 253-9646); *African Statistical Yearbook.*

EGYPT - FLAX FIBRE PRODUCTION - See EGYPT - TEXTILE INDUSTRY

EGYPT - FLOUR PRODUCTION

Commodity Research Bureau, Incorporated, 75 Wall Street, New York, New York 10005 (212) 504-7754; *Commodity Year Book.*

Statistical Office of the United Nations, Publishing Service, New York, New York 10017 (800) 253-9646; *Statistical Yearbook.*

EGYPT - FOOD

African Development Bank, 01 BP 1387, Abidjan 01, Cote D'Ivoire; *Selected Statistics on Regional Member Countries.*

Food and Agricultural Organization of the United Nations (FAO) Via delle Terme di Caracalla, 00100 Rome, Italy (Telephone Number in U.S. (202) 653-2400); *Production Yearbook,* and *The State of Food and Agriculture.*

G.K. Hall and Company, 70 Lincoln Street, Boston, Massachusetts 02111 (617) 423-3990; *The World in Figures.*

EGYPT - FOREIGN AID

G.K. Hall and Company, 70 Lincoln Street, Boston, Massachusetts 02111 (617) 423-3990; *The World in Figures.*

EGYPT - FOREIGN INDEBTEDNESS

Euromonitor Publications Limited, 87-88 Turnmill Street, London EC1M 5QU, England; *Middle East Economic Handbook.*

EGYPT - FOREIGN TRADE

Economic Commission for Western Asia, Post Office Box 27, Baghdad, Iraq; *Statistical Abstract of Western Asia.*

Euromonitor Publications Limited, 87-88 Turnmill Street, London EC1M 5QU, England; *International Marketing Data and Statistics.*

Facts on File, 460 Park Avenue South, New York, New York 10016 (800) 443-8323; *The New Book of World Rankings.*

Food and Agricultural Organization of the United Nations (FAO) Via delle Terme di Caracalla, 00100 Rome, Italy (Telephone Number in U.S. (202) 653-2400); *The State of Food and Agriculture.*

G.K. Hall and Company, 70 Lincoln Street, Boston, Massachusetts 02111 (617) 423-3990; *The World in Figures.*

International Monetary Fund, 700 Nineteenth Street, NW, Washington, D.C. 20431 (202) 623-7000; *International Financial Statistics.*

Statistical Office of the United Nations, Publishing Service, New York, New York 10017 (800) 253-9646; *Foreign Trade Statistics for Africa, International Trade Statistics Yearbook,* and *Statistical Yearbook.*

United Nations Economic Commission for Africa, Africa Hall, P.O. Box 3001, Addis Ababa, Ethiopia (Telephone Number in U.S. (800) 253-9646); *African Statistical Yearbook.*

EGYPT - FORESTRY AND FOREST PRODUCTS

Facts on File, 460 Park Avenue South, New York, New York 10016 (800) 443-8323; *The New Book of World Rankings.*

Food and Agricultural Organization of the United Nations (FAO) Via delle Terme di Caracalla, 00100 Rome, Italy (Telephone Number in U.S. (202) 653-2400); *The State of Food and Agriculture,* and *Yearbook of Forest Products.*

Forest and Paper Association, 1250 Connecticut Avenue, NW, Washington, D.C. 20036 (202) 463-2455; *Wood Pulp and Fiber Statistics.*

G.K. Hall and Company, 70 Lincoln Street, Boston, Massachusetts 02111 (617) 423-3990; *The World in Figures.*

Statistical Office of the United Nations, Publishing Service, New York, New York 10017 (800) 253-9646; *Statistical Yearbook.*

United Nations Economic Commission for Africa, Africa Hall, P.O. Box 3001, Addis Ababa, Ethiopia (Telephone Number in U.S. (800) 253-9646); *African Statistical Yearbook.*

United Nations Educational, Scientific and Cultural Organization (UNESCO), 7 Place de Fontenoy, F-75700 Paris, France (Telephone Number in U.S. (212) 963-5981); *Statistical Yearbook.*

EGYPT - GARLIC PRODUCTION - See EGYPT - CROPS

EGYPT - GAS AND GAS LIQUIDS - See EGYPT - MINING AND MINERAL PRODUCTS

EGYPT - GENERAL INDUSTRIAL STATISTICS

Statistical Office of the United Nations, Publishing Service, New York, New York 10017 (800) 253-9646; *Industrial Statistics Yearbook.*

EGYPT - GENERAL MORTALITY

Statistical Office of the United Nations, Publishing Service, New York, New York 10017 (800) 253-9646; *Demographic Yearbook.*

World Health Organization, Office of Publications, Avenue Appia, CH-1211 Geneva, 27, Switzerland (Telephone Number in U.S. (518) 436-9686; *World Health Statistics Annual.*

EGYPT - GEOGRAPHIC DATA

Facts on File, 460 Park Avenue South, New York, New York 10016 (800) 443-8323; *The New Book of World Rankings.*

EGYPT - GOATS - See EGYPT - LIVESTOCK AND POULTRY

EGYPT - GOLD HOLDINGS

International Monetary Fund, 700 Nineteenth Street, NW, Washington, D.C. 20431 (202) 623-7000; *International Financial Statistics.*

Statistical Office of the United Nations, Publishing Service, New York, New York 10017 (800) 253-9646; *Statistical Yearbook.*

EGYPT - GOLD PRODUCTION AND CONSUMPTION - See EGYPT - MINING AND MINERAL PRODUCTS

EGYPT - GOVERNMENT

G.K. Hall and Company, 70 Lincoln Street, Boston, Massachusetts 02111 (617) 423-3990; *The World in Figures.*

EGYPT - GOVERNMENT EXPENDITURES

Economic Commission for Western Asia, Post Office Box 27, Baghdad, Iraq; *Statistical Abstract of Western Asia.*

International Monetary Fund, 700 Nineteenth Street, NW, Washington, D.C. 20431 (202) 623-7000; *Government Finance Statistics Yearbook.*

Times Books, 201 East 50th Street, New York, New York 10022 (212) 751-2600; *The Economist Book of Vital World Statistics.*

EGYPT - GOVERNMENT FINANCES

Statistical Office of the United Nations, Publishing Service, New York, New York 10017 (800) 253-9646; *Statistical Yearbook.*

EGYPT - GOVERNMENT REVENUES

Economic Commission for Western Asia, Post Office Box 27, Baghdad, Iraq; *Statistical Abstract of Western Asia.*

International Monetary Fund, 700 Nineteenth Street, NW, Washington, D.C. 20431 (202) 623-7000; *Government Finance Statistics Yearbook.*

Statistical Office of the United Nations, Publishing Service, New York, New York 10017 (800) 253-9646; *Survey of Economic and Social Conditions in Africa.*

Times Books, 201 East 50th Street, New York, New York 10022 (212) 751-2600; *The Economist Book of Vital World Statistics.*

EGYPT - GRAIN PRODUCTION - See EGYPT - CROPS

EGYPT - GRANTS

International Monetary Fund, 700 Nineteenth Street, NW, Washington, D.C. 20431 (202) 623-7000; *Government Finance Statistics Yearbook.*

EGYPT - GREEN PEPPER AND CHILIE PRODUCTION - See EGYPT - CROPS

EGYPT - GROSS DOMESTIC PRODUCT

African Development Bank, 01 BP 1387, Abidjan 01, Cote D'Ivoire; *Selected Statistics on Regional Member Countries.*

Economic Commission for Western Asia, Post Office Box 27, Baghdad, Iraq; *Statistical Abstract of Western Asia.*

The Economist Intelligence Unit, 111 West 57th Street, New York, New York 10019 (800) 938-4685; *The World Market Atlas.*

Euromonitor Publications Limited, 87-88 Turnmill Street, London EC1M 5QU, England; *International Marketing Data and Statistics,* and *Middle East Economic Handbook.*

G.K. Hall and Company, 70 Lincoln Street, Boston, Massachusetts 02111 (617) 423-3990; *The World in Figures.*

Statistical Office of the United Nations, Publishing Service, New York, New York 10017 (800) 253-9646; *Statistical Yearbook,* and *Survey of Economic and Social Conditions in Africa.*

Times Books, 201 East 50th Street, New York, New York 10022 (212) 751-2600; *The Economist Book of Vital World Statistics.*

United Nations Economic Commission for Africa, Africa Hall, P.O. Box 3001, Addis Ababa, Ethiopia (Telephone Number in U.S. (800) 253-9646); *African Statistical Yearbook.*

EGYPT - GROSS NATIONAL PRODUCT

Euromonitor Publications Limited, 87-88 Turnmill Street, London EC1M 5QU, England; *International Marketing Data and Statistics.*

U.S. Arms Control and Disarmament Agency, 320 Twenty-first Street, NW, Washington, D.C. 20451 (202) 647-8677; *World Military Expenditures and Arms Transfers.*

EGYPT - GROUNDNUTS PRODUCTION - See EGYPT - CROPS

EGYPT - GROWTH - DOMESTIC PRODUCT

Facts on File, 460 Park Avenue South, New York, New York 10016 (800) 443-8323; *The New Book of World Rankings.*

EGYPT - HEALTH

African Development Bank, 01 BP 1387, Abidjan 01, Cote D'Ivoire; *Selected Statistics on Regional Member Countries.*

Economic Commission for Western Asia, Post Office Box 27, Baghdad, Iraq; *Statistical Abstract of Western Asia.*

Euromonitor Publications Limited, 87-88 Turnmill Street, London EC1M 5QU, England; *Middle East Economic Handbook.*

Facts on File, 460 Park Avenue South, New York, New York 10016 (800) 443-8323; *The New Book of World Rankings.*

G.K. Hall and Company, 70 Lincoln Street, Boston, Massachusetts 02111 (617) 423-3990; *The World in Figures.*

Statistical Office of the United Nations, Publishing Service, New York, New York 10017 (800) 253-9646; *Statistical Yearbook.*

Times Books, 201 East 50th Street, New York, New York 10022 (212) 751-2600; *The Economist Book of Vital World Statistics.*

United Nations Economic Commission for Africa, Africa Hall, P.O. Box 3001, Addis Ababa, Ethiopia (Telephone Number in U.S. (800) 253-9646); *African Statistical Yearbook.*

World Health Organization, Office of Publications, Avenue Appia, CH-1211 Geneva, 27, Switzerland (Telephone Number in U.S. (518) 436-9686); *World Health Statistics Annual.*

EGYPT - HEALTH EXPENDITURES

International Monetary Fund, 700 Nineteenth Street, NW, Washington, D.C. 20431 (202) 623-7000; *Government Finance Statistics Yearbook.*

EGYPT - HIDE PRODUCTION

Food and Agricultural Organization of the United Nations (FAO), Via delle Terme di Caracalla, 00100 Rome, Italy (Telephone Number in U.S. (202) 653-2400); *Production Yearbook.*

EGYPT - HIGHWAYS

Economic Commission for Western Asia, Post Office Box 27, Baghdad, Iraq; *Statistical Abstract of Western Asia.*

G.K. Hall and Company, 70 Lincoln Street, Boston, Massachusetts 02111 (617) 423-3990; *The World in Figures.*

International Road Federation, 525 School Street, SW, Washington, D.C. 20024 (202) 554-2106; *World Road Statistics.*

Statistical Office of the United Nations, Publishing Service, New York, New York 10017 (800) 253-9646; *Survey of Economic and Social Conditions in Africa.*

United Nations Economic Commission for Africa, Africa Hall, P.O. Box 3001, Addis Ababa, Ethiopia (Telephone Number in U.S. (800) 253-9646); *African Statistical Yearbook.*

EGYPT - HORSES - See EGYPT - LIVESTOCK AND POULTRY

EGYPT - HOURS OF WORK - See EGYPT - EMPLOYMENT

EGYPT - HOUSING AND HOUSING UNITS

Facts on File, 460 Park Avenue South, New York, New York 10016 (800) 443-8323; *The New Book of World Rankings.*

Statistical Office of the United Nations, Publishing Service, New York, New York 10017 (800) 253-9646; *Statistical Yearbook.*

EGYPT - HOUSING EXPENDITURES

International Monetary Fund, 700 Nineteenth Street, NW, Washington, D.C. 20431 (202) 623-7000; *Government Finance Statistics Yearbook.*

EGYPT - HYDROCHLORIC ACID PRODUCTION

Statistical Office of the United Nations, Publishing Service, New York, New York 10017 (800) 253-9646; *Statistical Yearbook.*

EGYPT - ILLITERATE POPULATION

The Economist Intelligence Unit, 111 West 57th Street, New York, New York 10019 (800) 938-4685; *The World Market Atlas.*

G.K. Hall and Company, 70 Lincoln Street, Boston, Massachusetts 02111 (617) 423-3990; *The World in Figures.*

United Nations Educational, Scientific and Cultural Organization (UNESCO), 7 Place de Fontenoy, F-75700 Paris, France (Telephone Number in U.S. (212) 963-5981); *Statistical Yearbook.*

EGYPT - IMPORTS

African Development Bank, 01 BP 1387, Abidjan 01, Cote D'Ivoire; *Selected Statistics on Regional Member Countries.*

Economic Commission for Western Asia, Post Office Box 27, Baghdad, Iraq; *Statistical Abstract of Western Asia.*

The Economist Intelligence Unit, 111 West 57th Street, New York, New York 10019 (800) 938-4685; *The World Market Atlas.*

Euromonitor Publications Limited, 87-88 Turnmill Street, London EC1M 5QU, England; *International Marketing Data and Statistics,* and *Middle East Economic Handbook.*

Food and Agricultural Organization of the United Nations (FAO) Via delle Terme di Caracalla, 00100 Rome, Italy (Telephone Number in U.S. (202) 653-2400); *The State of Food and Agriculture.*

G.K. Hall and Company, 70 Lincoln Street, Boston, Massachusetts 02111 (617) 423-3990; *The World in Figures.*

International Monetary Fund, 700 Nineteenth Street, NW, Washington, D.C. 20431 (202) 623-7000; *Direction of Trade Statistics, Government Finance Statistics Yearbook,* and *International Financial Statistics.*

Statistical Office of the United Nations, Publishing Service, New York, New York 10017 (800) 253-9646; *Foreign Trade Statistics for Africa, Foreign Trade Statistics for Africa, Survey of Economic and Social Conditions in Africa,* and *Trade in Manufactures of Developing Countries.*

Times Books, 201 East 50th Street, New York, New York 10022 (212) 751-2600; *The Economist Book of Vital World Statistics.*

United Nations Economic Commission for Africa, Africa Hall, P.O. Box 3001, Addis Ababa, Ethiopia (Telephone Number in U.S. (800) 253-9646); *African Statistical Yearbook.*

EGYPT - INCOME TAXES - See EGYPT - TAXATION

EGYPT - INDUSTRY

Euromonitor Publications Limited, 87-88 Turnmill Street, London EC1M 5QU, England; *International Marketing Data and Statistics.*

Facts on File, 460 Park Avenue South, New York, New York 10016 (800) 443-8323; *The New Book of World Rankings.*

G.K. Hall and Company, 70 Lincoln Street, Boston, Massachusetts 02111 (617) 423-3990; *The World in Figures.*

International Labour Office, I.L.O. Publications, CH-1211, Geneva 22, Switzerland; *Yearbook of Labour Statistics.*

Statistical Office of the United Nations, Publishing Service, New York, New York 10017 (800) 253-9646; *Survey of Economic and Social Conditions in Africa.*

Times Books, 201 East 50th Street, New York, New York 10022 (212) 751-2600; *The Economist Book of Vital World Statistics.*

United Nations Economic Commission for Africa, Africa Hall, P.O. Box 3001, Addis Ababa, Ethiopia (Telephone Number in U.S. (800)

253-9646); *African Statistical Yearbook.*

EGYPT - INFANT AND MATERNAL MORTALITY

Statistical Office of the United Nations, Publishing Service, New York, New York 10017 (800) 253-9646; *Demographic Yearbook, Statistical Yearbook,* and *Survey of Economic and Social Conditions in Africa.*

Times Books, 201 East 50th Street, New York, New York 10022 (212) 751-2600; *The Economist Book of Vital World Statistics.*

World Health Organization, Office of Publications, Avenue Appia, CH-1211 Geneva, 27, Switzerland (Telephone Number in U.S. (518) 436-9686); *World Health Statistics Annual.*

EGYPT - INTERNATIONAL LIQUIDITY

International Monetary Fund, 700 Nineteenth Street, NW, Washington, D.C. 20431 (202) 623-7000; *International Financial Statistics.*

EGYPT - INTERNATIONAL RESERVES EXCLUDING GOLD

African Development Bank, 01 BP 1387, Abidjan 01, Cote D'Ivoire; *Selected Statistics on Regional Member Countries.*

EGYPT - IRON ORE PRODUCTION AND CONSUMPTION - See EGYPT - MINING AND MINERAL PRODUCTS

EGYPT - IRRIGATION

Euromonitor Publications Limited, 87-88 Turnmill Street, London EC1M 5QU, England; *International Marketing Data and Statistics.*

EGYPT - LABOR FORCE

African Development Bank, 01 BP 1387, Abidjan 01, Cote D'Ivoire; *Selected Statistics on Regional Member Countries.*

Economic Commission for Western Asia, Post Office Box 27, Baghdad, Iraq; *Statistical Abstract of Western Asia.*

Euromonitor Publications Limited, 87-88 Turnmill Street, London EC1M 5QU, England; *International Marketing Data and Statistics,* and *Middle East Economic Handbook.*

Facts on File, 460 Park Avenue South, New York, New York 10016 (800) 443-8323; *The New Book of World Rankings.*

Food and Agricultural Organization of the United Nations (FAO) Via delle Terme di Caracalla, 00100 Rome, Italy (Telephone Number in U.S. (202) 653-2400); *The State of Food and Agriculture.*

G.K. Hall and Company, 70 Lincoln Street, Boston, Massachusetts 02111 (617) 423-3990; *The World in Figures.*

Times Books, 201 East 50th Street, New York, New York 10022 (212) 751-2600; *The Economist Book of Vital World Statistics.*

EGYPT - LABOR PRODUCTIVITY

International Labour Office, I.L.O. Publications, CH-1211, Geneva 22, Switzerland; *Yearbook of Labour Statistics.*

EGYPT - LAND USE

Economic Commission for Western Asia, Post Office Box 27, Baghdad, Iraq; *Statistical Abstract of Western Asia.*

Euromonitor Publications Limited, 87-88 Turnmill Street, London EC1M 5QU, England; *International Marketing Data and Statistics.*

Food and Agricultural Organization of the United Nations (FAO), Via delle Terme di Caracalla, 00100 Rome, Italy (Telephone Number in U.S. (202) 653-2400); *Production Yearbook.*

G.K. Hall and Company, 70 Lincoln Street, Boston, Massachusetts 02111 (617) 423-3990; *The World in Figures.*

EGYPT - LEAD PRODUCTION AND CONSUMPTION - See EGYPT - MINING AND MINERAL PRODUCTS

EGYPT - LIBRARIES

Facts on File, 460 Park Avenue South, New York, New York 10016 (800) 443-8323; *The New Book of World Rankings.*

United Nations Educational, Scientific and Cultural Organization (UNESCO), 7 Place de Fontenoy, F-75700 Paris, France (Telephone Number in U.S. (212) 963-5981); *Statistical Yearbook.*

EGYPT - LIFE EXPECTANCY

African Development Bank, 01 BP 1387, Abidjan 01, Cote D'Ivoire; *Selected Statistics on Regional Member Countries.*

EGYPT - LITERACY RATE

Statistical Office of the United Nations, Publishing Service, New York, New York 10017 (800) 253-9646; *Survey of Economic and Social Conditions in Africa.*

EGYPT - LIVESTOCK AND POULTRY AND POULTRY

Economic Commission for Western Asia, Post Office Box 27, Baghdad, Iraq; *Statistical Abstract of Western Asia.*

Euromonitor Publications Limited, 87-88 Turnmill Street, London EC1M 5QU, England; *International Marketing Data and Statistics.*

Facts on File, 460 Park Avenue South, New York, New York 10016 (800) 443-8323; *The New Book of World Rankings.*

Food and Agricultural Organization of the United Nations (FAO), Via delle Terme di Caracalla, 00100 Rome, Italy (Telephone Number in U.S. (202) 653-2400); *Production Yearbook,* and *The State of Food and Agriculture.*

G.K. Hall and Company, 70 Lincoln Street, Boston, Massachusetts 02111 (617) 423-3990; *The World in Figures.*

Statistical Office of the United Nations, Publishing Service, New York, New York 10017 (800) 253-9646; *Statistical Yearbook,* and *Survey of Economic and Social Conditions in Africa.*

United Nations Economic Commission for Africa, Africa Hall, P.O. Box 3001, Addis Ababa, Ethiopia (Telephone Number in U.S. (800) 253-9646); *African Statistical Yearbook.*

EGYPT - LIVING LEVELS

G.K. Hall and Company, 70 Lincoln Street, Boston, Massachusetts 02111 (617) 423-3990; *The World in Figures.*

Times Books, 201 East 50th Street, New York, New York 10022 (212) 751-2600; *The Economist Book of Vital World Statistics.*

EGYPT - MAIL - NUMBER OF PIECES SENT OR RECEIVED

Statistical Office of the United Nations, Publishing Service, New York, New York 10017 (800) 253-9646; *Statistical Yearbook*.

EGYPT - MANGANESE ORE PRODUCTION AND CONSUMPTION - See EGYPT - MINING AND MINERAL PRODUCTS

EGYPT - MANUFACTURED GAS PRODUCTION - See EGYPT - MINING AND MINERAL PRODUCTS

EGYPT - MANUFACTURING

Facts on File, 460 Park Avenue South, New York, New York 10016 (800) 443-8323; *The New Book of World Rankings*.

G.K. Hall and Company, 70 Lincoln Street, Boston, Massachusetts 02111 (617) 423-3990; *The World in Figures*.

Statistical Office of the United Nations, Publishing Service, New York, New York 10017 (800) 253-9646; *Statistical Yearbook*, and *Survey of Economic and Social Conditions in Africa*.

Times Books, 201 East 50th Street, New York, New York 10022 (212) 751-2600; *The Economist Book of Vital World Statistics*.

United Nations Economic Commission for Africa, Africa Hall, P.O. Box 3001, Addis Ababa, Ethiopia (Telephone Number in U.S. (800) 253-9646); *African Statistical Yearbook*.

EGYPT - MARRIAGE RATES

Facts on File, 460 Park Avenue South, New York, New York 10016 (800) 443-8323; *The New Book of World Rankings*.

Statistical Office of the United Nations, Publishing Service, New York, New York 10017 (800) 253-9646; *Demographic Yearbook*, and *Statistical Yearbook*.

EGYPT - MEAT PRODUCTION - See EGYPT - LIVESTOCK AND POULTRY

EGYPT - MERCHANT SHIPPING

Economic Commission for Western Asia, Post Office Box 27, Baghdad, Iraq; *Statistical Abstract of Western Asia*.

G.K. Hall and Company, 70 Lincoln Street, Boston, Massachusetts 02111 (617) 423-3990; *The World in Figures*.

Lloyd's Register of Shipping, 17 Battery Place, New York, New York 10004 (212) 425-8050; *Register of Ships*.

Statistical Office of the United Nations, Publishing Service, New York, New York 10017 (800) 253-9646; *Statistical Yearbook*.

Times Books, 201 East 50th Street, New York, New York 10022 (212) 751-2600; *The Economist Book of Vital World Statistics*.

United Nations Economic Commission for Africa, Africa Hall, P.O. Box 3001, Addis Ababa, Ethiopia (Telephone Number in U.S. (800) 253-9646); *African Statistical Yearbook*.

EGYPT - MERCHANT VESSELS - TONNAGE LAUNCHED

Lloyd's Register of Shipping, 17 Battery Place, New York, New York 10004 (212) 425-8050; *Register of Ships*.

EGYPT - MILITARY

G.K. Hall and Company, 70 Lincoln Street, Boston, Massachusetts 02111 (617) 423-3990; *The World in Figures*.

The International Institute for Strategic Studies, 23 Tavistock Street, London WC2E 7NQ, England; *The Military Balance*.

U.S. Arms Control and Disarmament Agency, 320 Twenty-first Street, NW, Washington, D.C. 20451 (202) 647-8677; *World Military Expenditures and Arms Transfers*.

EGYPT - MILK PRODUCTION - See EL SALVADOR - FORESTRY AND FOREST PRODUCTS

EGYPT - MILLET PRODUCTION - See EGYPT - CROPS

EGYPT - MINING AND MINERAL PRODUCTS

Economic Commission for Western Asia, Post Office Box 27, Baghdad, Iraq; *Statistical Abstract of Western Asia*.

Facts on File, 460 Park Avenue South, New York, New York 10016 (800) 443-8323; *The New Book of World Rankings*.

G.K. Hall and Company, 70 Lincoln Street, Boston, Massachusetts 02111 (617) 423-3990; *The World in Figures*.

Penn Well Publishing Company, 1421 South Sheridan Road, P.O. Box 1260, Tulsa, Oklahoma 74101 (800) 752-9764; *International Energy Statistics Sourcebook*.

Statistical Office of the United Nations, Publishing Service, New York, New York 10017 (800) 253-9646; *Statistical Yearbook*.

United Nations Economic Commission for Africa, Africa Hall, P.O. Box 3001, Addis Ababa, Ethiopia (Telephone Number in U.S. (800) 253-9646); *African Statistical Yearbook*.

EGYPT - MONEY EXCHANGE RATE

Euromonitor Publications Limited, 87-88 Turnmill Street, London EC1M 5QU, England; *International Marketing Data and Statistics*.

International Monetary Fund, 700 Nineteenth Street, NW, Washington, D.C. 20431 (202) 623-7000; *International Financial Statistics*.

Statistical Office of the United Nations, Publishing Service, New York, New York 10017 (800) 253-9646; *Statistical Yearbook*.

EGYPT - MONEY RESERVES

Euromonitor Publications Limited, 87-88 Turnmill Street, London EC1M 5QU, England; *International Marketing Data and Statistics*.

EGYPT - MONEY SUPPLY

African Development Bank, 01 BP 1387, Abidjan 01, Cote D'Ivoire; *Selected Statistics on Regional Member Countries*.

Economic Commission for Western Asia, Post Office Box 27, Baghdad, Iraq; *Statistical Abstract of Western Asia*.

Euromonitor Publications Limited, 87-88 Turnmill Street, London EC1M 5QU, England; *International Marketing Data and Statistics*.

G.K. Hall and Company, 70 Lincoln Street, Boston, Massachusetts 02111 (617) 423-3990; *The World in Figures*.

International Monetary Fund, 700 Nineteenth Street, NW, Washington, D.C. 20431 (202) 623-7000; *International Financial Statistics*.

Statistical Office of the United Nations, Publishing Service, New York, New York 10017 (800) 253-9646; *Statistical Yearbook*.

EGYPT - MOTION PICTURES

United Nations Educational, Scientific and Cultural Organization (UNESCO), 7 Place de Fontenoy, F-75700 Paris, France (Telephone Number in U.S. (212) 963-5981); *Statistical Yearbook*.

EGYPT - MOTOR VEHICLE ASSEMBLY

Statistical Office of the United Nations, Publishing Service, New York, New York 10017 (800) 253-9646; *Statistical Yearbook*.

EGYPT - MOTOR VEHICLE TAXES - See EGYPT - TAXATION

EGYPT - MOTOR VEHICLES

Economic Commission for Western Asia, Post Office Box 27, Baghdad, Iraq; *Statistical Abstract of Western Asia*.

International Road Federation, 525 School Street, SW, Washington, D.C. 20024 (202) 554-2106; *World Road Statistics*.

EGYPT - MOTOR VEHICLES IN USE

G.K. Hall and Company, 70 Lincoln Street, Boston, Massachusetts 02111 (617) 423-3990; *The World in Figures*.

Statistical Office of the United Nations, Publishing Service, New York, New York 10017 (800) 253-9646; *Statistical Yearbook*, and *Survey of Economic and Social Conditions in Africa*.

Times Books, 201 East 50th Street, New York, New York 10022 (212) 751-2600; *The Economist Book of Vital World Statistics*.

EGYPT - MULES - See EGYPT - LIVESTOCK AND POULTRY

EGYPT - MUSEUMS

Facts on File, 460 Park Avenue South, New York, New York 10016 (800) 443-8323; *The New Book of World Rankings*.

United Nations Educational, Scientific and Cultural Organization (UNESCO), 7 Place de Fontenoy, F-75700 Paris, France (Telephone Number in U.S. (212) 963-5981); *Statistical Yearbook*.

EGYPT - NATALITY - See EGYPT - BIRTH RATES

EGYPT - NATIONAL ACCOUNTS

African Development Bank, 01 BP 1387, Abidjan 01, Cote D'Ivoire; *Selected Statistics on Regional Member Countries*.

Economic Commission for Western Asia, Post Office Box 27, Baghdad, Iraq; *Statistical Abstract of Western Asia*.

International Monetary Fund, 700 Nineteenth Street, NW, Washington, D.C. 20431 (202) 623-7000; *International Financial Statistics*.

Statistical Office of the United Nations, Publishing Service, New York, New York 10017 (800) 253-9646; *National Accounts Statistics*, and *Statistical Yearbook*.

United Nations Economic Commission for Africa, Africa Hall, P.O. Box 3001, Addis Ababa, Ethiopia (Telephone Number in U.S. (800) 253-9646); *African Statistical Yearbook*.

EGYPT - NATIONAL INCOME

Facts on File, 460 Park Avenue South, New York, New York 10016 (800) 443-8323; *The New Book of World Rankings*.

G.K. Hall and Company, 70 Lincoln Street, Boston, Massachusetts 02111 (617) 423-3990; *The World in Figures*.

International Monetary Fund, 700 Nineteenth Street, NW, Washington, D.C. 20431 (202) 623-7000; *International Financial Statistics*.

Statistical Office of the United Nations, Publishing Service, New York, New York 10017 (800) 253-9646; *Statistical Yearbook*.

EGYPT - NATIONAL PRODUCT

Facts on File, 460 Park Avenue South, New York, New York 10016 (800) 443-8323; *The New Book of World Rankings*.

Statistical Office of the United Nations, Publishing Service, New York, New York 10017 (800) 253-9646; *Statistical Yearbook*.

EGYPT - NATURAL GAS PRODUCTION - See EGYPT - MINING AND MINERAL PRODUCTS

EGYPT - NEWSPAPER PRODUCTION - See EGYPT - FORESTRY AND FOREST PRODUCTS

EGYPT - NEWSPRINT CONSUMPTION - See EGYPT - FORESTRY AND FOREST PRODUCTS

EGYPT - NITRIC ACID PRODUCTION

Statistical Office of the United Nations, Publishing Service, New York, New York 10017 (800) 253-9646; *Statistical Yearbook*.

EGYPT - OCCUPATIONS - See EGYPT - LABOR FORCE

EGYPT - ONION PRODUCTION - See EGYPT - CROPS

EGYPT - PAPER - See EGYPT - FORESTRY AND FOREST PRODUCTS

EGYPT - PATENTS

Statistical Office of the United Nations, Publishing Service, New York, New York 10017 (800) 253-9646; *Statistical Yearbook*.

EGYPT - PEANUTS - See EGYPT - CROPS

EGYPT - PERIODICALS

United Nations Educational, Scientific and Cultural Organization (UNESCO), 7 Place de Fontenoy, F-75700 Paris, France (Telephone Number in U.S. (212) 963-5981); *Statistical Yearbook*.

EGYPT - PESTICIDE USE

Food and Agricultural Organization of the United Nations (FAO) Via delle Terme di Caracalla, 00100 Rome, Italy (Telephone Number in U.S. (202) 653-2400); *The State of Food and Agriculture*.

EGYPT - PETROLEUM INDUSTRY

Euromonitor Publications Limited, 87-88 Turnmill Street, London EC1M 5QU, England; *Middle East Economic Handbook.*

Facts on File, 460 Park Avenue South, New York, New York 10016 (800) 443-8323; *The New Book of World Rankings.*

Food and Agricultural Organization of the United Nations (FAO) Via delle Terme di Caracalla, 00100 Rome, Italy (Telephone Number in U.S. (202) 653-2400); *The State of Food and Agriculture.*

G.K. Hall and Company, 70 Lincoln Street, Boston, Massachusetts 02111 (617) 423-3990; *The World in Figures.*

Penn Well Publishing Company, 1421 South Sheridan Road, P.O. Box 1260, Tulsa, Oklahoma 74101 (800) 752-9764; *International Energy Statistics Sourcebook.*

Statistical Office of the United Nations, Publishing Service, New York, New York 10017 (800) 253-9646; *Statistical Yearbook.*

EGYPT - PHOSPHATE ROCK PRODUCTION - See EGYPT - MINING AND MINERAL PRODUCTS

EGYPT - PIG-IRON AND FERRO-ALLOY PRODUCTION - See EGYPT - MINING AND MINERAL PRODUCTS

EGYPT - PIGS - See EGYPT - LIVESTOCK AND POULTRY

EGYPT - POPULATION

African Development Bank, 01 BP 1387, Abidjan 01, Cote D'Ivoire; *Selected Statistics on Regional Member Countries.*

Economic Commission for Western Asia, Post Office Box 27, Baghdad, Iraq; *Statistical Abstract of Western Asia.*

The Economist Intelligence Unit, 111 West 57th Street, New York, New York 10019 (800) 938-4685; *The World Market Atlas.*

Euromonitor Publications Limited, 87-88 Turnmill Street, London EC1M 5QU, England; *International Marketing Data and Statistics.*

Facts on File, 460 Park Avenue South, New York, New York 10016 (800) 443-8323; *The New Book of World Rankings.*

Food and Agricultural Organization of the United Nations (FAO), Via delle Terme di Caracalla, 00100 Rome, Italy (Telephone Number in U.S. (202) 653-2400); *Production Yearbook.*

G.K. Hall and Company, 70 Lincoln Street, Boston, Massachusetts 02111 (617) 423-3990; *The World in Figures.*

International Labour Office, I.L.O. Publications, CH-1211, Geneva 22, Switzerland; *Yearbook of Labour Statistics.*

Statistical Office of the United Nations, Publishing Service, New York, New York 10017 (800) 253-9646; *Demographic Yearbook, Statistical Yearbook,* and *Survey of Economic and Social Conditions in Africa.*

Times Books, 201 East 50th Street, New York, New York 10022 (212) 751-2600; *The Economist Book of Vital World Statistics.*

United Nations Educational, Scientific and Cultural Organization (UNESCO), 7 Place de Fontenoy, F-75700 Paris, France (Telephone Number in U.S. (212) 963-5981); *Statistical Yearbook.*

U.S. Arms Control and Disarmament Agency, 320 Twenty-first Street, NW, Washington, D.C. 20451 (202) 647-8677; *World Military Expenditures and Arms Transfers.*

World Health Organization, Office of Publications, Avenue Appia, CH-1211 Geneva, 27, Switzerland (Telephone Number in U.S. (518) 436-9686); *World Health Statistics Annual.*

EGYPT - POST OFFICES

Facts on File, 460 Park Avenue South, New York, New York 10016 (800) 443-8323; *The New Book of World Rankings.*

EGYPT - POTATO PRODUCTION - See EGYPT - CROPS

EGYPT - POWER PRODUCTION INDUSTRY

Statistical Office of the United Nations, Publishing Service, New York, New York 10017 (800) 253-9646; *Statistical Yearbook.*

EGYPT - PRICES

Economic Commission for Western Asia, Post Office Box 27, Baghdad, Iraq; *Statistical Abstract of Western Asia.*

Facts on File, 460 Park Avenue South, New York, New York 10016 (800) 443-8323; *The New Book of World Rankings.*

Food and Agricultural Organization of the United Nations (FAO), Via delle Terme di Caracalla, 00100 Rome, Italy (Telephone Number in U.S. (202) 653-2400); *Production Yearbook,* and *The State of Food and Agriculture.*

G.K. Hall and Company, 70 Lincoln Street, Boston, Massachusetts 02111 (617) 423-3990; *The World in Figures.*

International Labour Office, I.L.O. Publications, CH-1211, Geneva 22, Switzerland; *Yearbook of Labour Statistics.*

International Monetary Fund, 700 Nineteenth Street, NW, Washington, D.C. 20431 (202) 623-7000; *International Financial Statistics.*

United Nations Economic Commission for Africa, Africa Hall, P.O. Box 3001, Addis Ababa, Ethiopia (Telephone Number in U.S. (800) 253-9646); *African Statistical Yearbook.*

EGYPT - PRINTING AND WRITING PAPER - See EGYPT - FORESTRY AND FOREST PRODUCTS

EGYPT - PRODUCTION

Facts on File, 460 Park Avenue South, New York, New York 10016 (800) 443-8323; *The New Book of World Rankings.*

G.K. Hall and Company, 70 Lincoln Street, Boston, Massachusetts 02111 (617) 423-3990; *The World in Figures.*

EGYPT - PRODUCTIVITY

Euromonitor Publications Limited, 87-88 Turnmill Street, London EC1M 5QU, England; *International Marketing Data and Statistics.*

EGYPT - PROPERTY TAXES - See EGYPT - TAXATION

EGYPT - PUBLIC FINANCE

Facts on File, 460 Park Avenue South, New York, New York 10016 (800) 443-8323; *The New Book of World Rankings.*

EGYPT - RADIO BROADCASTING - See EGYPT - BROADCASTING

EGYPT - RADIO RECEIVER PRODUCTION

Statistical Office of the United Nations, Publishing Service, New York, New York 10017 (800) 253-9646; *Statistical Yearbook.*

EGYPT - RAILWAYS

G.K. Hall and Company, 70 Lincoln Street, Boston, Massachusetts 02111 (617) 423-3990; *The World in Figures.*

Jane's Information Group, Sentinel House, 163 Brighton Road, Coulsdon, Surrey CR5 2NH, England (Telephone Number in U.S. (703) 683-3700); *Jane's World Railways.*

Statistical Office of the United Nations, Publishing Service, New York, New York 10017 (800) 253-9646; *Statistical Yearbook,* and *Survey of Economic and Social Conditions in Africa.*

United Nations Economic Commission for Africa, Africa Hall, P.O. Box 3001, Addis Ababa, Ethiopia (Telephone Number in U.S. (800) 253-9646); *African Statistical Yearbook.*

EGYPT - RELIGION

Facts on File, 460 Park Avenue South, New York, New York 10016 (800) 443-8323; *The New Book of World Rankings.*

EGYPT - RENT PRICES

International Labour Office, I.L.O. Publications, CH-1211, Geneva 22, Switzerland; *Yearbook of Labour Statistics.*

EGYPT - RETAIL TRADE

G.K. Hall and Company, 70 Lincoln Street, Boston, Massachusetts 02111 (617) 423-3990; *The World in Figures.*

Statistical Office of the United Nations, Publishing Service, New York, New York 10017 (800) 253-9646; *Statistical Yearbook.*

EGYPT - RICE - See EGYPT - CROPS

EGYPT - ROOT AND TUBER PRODUCTION - See EGYPT - CROPS

EGYPT - ROUNDWOOD PRODUCTION - See EGYPT - FORESTRY AND FOREST PRODUCTS

EGYPT - RUBBER PRODUCTION

Facts on File, 460 Park Avenue South, New York, New York 10016 (800) 443-8323; *The New Book of World Rankings.*

EGYPT - SALT PRODUCTION - See EGYPT - MINING AND MINERAL PRODUCTS

EGYPT - SAWNWOOD PRODUCTION - See EGYPT - FORESTRY AND FOREST PRODUCTS

EGYPT - SCIENTISTS AND ENGINEERS

Statistical Office of the United Nations, Publishing Service, New York, New York 10017 (800) 253-9646; *Statistical Yearbook.*

United Nations Educational, Scientific and Cultural Organization (UNESCO), 7 Place de Fontenoy, F-75700 Paris, France (Telephone Number in U.S. (212) 963-5981); *Statistical Yearbook.*

EGYPT - SENIOR CITIZENS

Facts on File, 460 Park Avenue South, New York, New York 10016 (800) 443-8323; *The New Book of World Rankings.*

EGYPT - SESAME SEED PRODUCTION - See EGYPT - CROPS

EGYPT - SHEEP - See EGYPT - LIVESTOCK AND POULTRY

EGYPT - SILVER PRODUCTION AND CONSUMPTION - See EGYPT - MINING AND MINERAL PRODUCTS

EGYPT - SOCIAL DATA

African Development Bank, 01 BP 1387, Abidjan 01, Cote D'Ivoire; *Selected Statistics on Regional Member Countries.*

Facts on File, 460 Park Avenue South, New York, New York 10016 (800) 443-8323; *The New Book of World Rankings.*

G.K. Hall and Company, 70 Lincoln Street, Boston, Massachusetts 02111 (617) 423-3990; *The World in Figures.*

EGYPT - SOCIAL SECURITY

International Monetary Fund, 700 Nineteenth Street, NW, Washington, D.C. 20431 (202) 623-7000; *Government Finance Statistics Yearbook.*

EGYPT - SOYBEAN PRODUCTION - See EGYPT - CROPS

EGYPT - STAMP TAXES AND DUTIES - See EGYPT - TAXATION

EGYPT - STATE BUDGET REVENUE AND EXPENDITURES

Euromonitor Publications Limited, 87-88 Turnmill Street, London EC1M 5QU, England; *International Marketing Data and Statistics.*

EGYPT - STEEL - See EGYPT - MINING AND MINERAL PRODUCTS

EGYPT - STOCKS - COMMODITY - MARKET PRICE - INDEX

Food and Agricultural Organization of the United Nations (FAO) Via delle Terme di Caracalla, 00100 Rome, Italy (Telephone Number in U.S. (202) 653-2400); *The State of Food and Agriculture.*

EGYPT - SUGAR - See EGYPT - CROPS

EGYPT - SULPHURIC ACID PRODUCTION

Statistical Office of the United Nations, Publishing Service, New York, New York 10017 (800) 253-9646; *Statistical Yearbook.*

EGYPT - TAXATION

G.K. Hall and Company, 70 Lincoln Street, Boston, Massachusetts 02111 (617) 423-3990; *The World in Figures.*

International Monetary Fund, 700 Nineteenth Street, NW, Washington, D.C. 20431 (202) 623-7000; *Government Finance Statistics Yearbook.*

International Road Federation, 525 School Street, SW, Washington, D.C. 20024 (202) 554-2106; *World Road Statistics.*

EGYPT - TEA - See EGYPT - CROPS

EGYPT - TELEPHONES IN USE

American Telephone and Telegraph Company, 26 Parsippany Road, Whippany, New Jersey 07981 (800) 338-4038; *The World's Telephones*.

Euromonitor Publications Limited, 87-88 Turnmill Street, London EC1M 5QU, England; *Middle East Economic Handbook*.

G.K. Hall and Company, 70 Lincoln Street, Boston, Massachusetts 02111 (617) 423-3990; *The World in Figures*.

Statistical Office of the United Nations, Publishing Service, New York, New York 10017 (800) 253-9646; *Statistical Yearbook*.

EGYPT - TELEVISION BROADCASTING - See EGYPT - BROADCASTING

EGYPT - TELEVISION RECEIVER PRODUCTION

Statistical Office of the United Nations, Publishing Service, New York, New York 10017 (800) 253-9646; *Statistical Yearbook*.

EGYPT - TEXTILE INDUSTRY

Forest and Paper Association, 1250 Connecticut Avenue, NW, Washington, D.C. 20036 (202) 463-2455; *Wood Pulp and Fiber Statistics*.

G.K. Hall and Company, 70 Lincoln Street, Boston, Massachusetts 02111 (617) 423-3990; *The World in Figures*.

Statistical Office of the United Nations, Publishing Service, New York, New York 10017 (800) 253-9646; *Statistical Yearbook*, and *Trade in Manufactures of Developing Countries*.

EGYPT - THEATRE

United Nations Educational, Scientific and Cultural Organization (UNESCO), 7 Place de Fontenoy, F-75700 Paris, France (Telephone Number in U.S. (212) 963-5981); *Statistical Yearbook*.

EGYPT - TIN - INDUSTRIAL CONSUMPTION - See EGYPT - MINING AND MINERAL PRODUCTS

EGYPT - TIRE (MOTOR VEHICLE) PRODUCTION

Statistical Office of the United Nations, Publishing Service, New York, New York 10017 (800) 253-9646; *Statistical Yearbook*.

EGYPT - TOBACCO PRODUCTION

Facts on File, 460 Park Avenue South, New York, New York 10016 (800) 443-8323; *The New Book of World Rankings*.

Statistical Office of the United Nations, Publishing Service, New York, New York 10017 (800) 253-9646; *Statistical Yearbook*.

EGYPT - TOURISM

Economic Commission for Western Asia, Post Office Box 27, Baghdad, Iraq; *Statistical Abstract of Western Asia*.

Euromonitor Publications Limited, 87-88 Turnmill Street, London EC1M 5QU, England; *Middle East Economic Handbook*.

Facts on File, 460 Park Avenue South, New York, New York 10016 (800) 443-8323; *The New Book of World Rankings*.

G.K. Hall and Company, 70 Lincoln Street, Boston, Massachusetts 02111 (617) 423-3990; *The World in Figures*.

Statistical Office of the United Nations, Publishing Service, New York, New York 10017 (800) 253-9646; *Statistical Yearbook*.

Times Books, 201 East 50th Street, New York, New York 10022 (212) 751-2600; *The Economist Book of Vital World Statistics*.

United Nations Economic Commission for Africa, Africa Hall, P.O. Box 3001, Addis Ababa, Ethiopia (Telephone Number in U.S. (800) 253-9646); *African Statistical Yearbook*.

EGYPT - TRADE - See EGYPT - FOREIGN TRADE

EGYPT - TRADEMARKS AND SERVICE MARKS

Statistical Office of the United Nations, Publishing Service, New York, New York 10017 (800) 253-9646; *Statistical Yearbook*.

EGYPT - TRANSPORTATION AND COMMUNICATIONS

Economic Commission for Western Asia, Post Office Box 27, Baghdad, Iraq; *Statistical Abstract of Western Asia*.

Euromonitor Publications Limited, 87-88 Turnmill Street, London EC1M 5QU, England; *Middle East Economic Handbook*.

Facts on File, 460 Park Avenue South, New York, New York 10016 (800) 443-8323; *The New Book of World Rankings*.

G.K. Hall and Company, 70 Lincoln Street, Boston, Massachusetts 02111 (617) 423-3990; *The World in Figures*.

United Nations Economic Commission for Africa, Africa Hall, P.O. Box 3001, Addis Ababa, Ethiopia (Telephone Number in U.S. (800) 253-9646); *African Statistical Yearbook*.

EGYPT - TRAVEL FARES ABROAD

International Monetary Fund, 700 Nineteenth Street, NW, Washington, D.C. 20431 (202) 623-7000; *Government Finance Statistics Yearbook*.

EGYPT - TURKEYS - See EGYPT - LIVESTOCK AND POULTRY

EGYPT - UNEMPLOYMENT

Euromonitor Publications Limited, 87-88 Turnmill Street, London EC1M 5QU, England; *International Marketing Data and Statistics*, and *Middle East Economic Handbook*.

International Labour Office, I.L.O. Publications, CH-1211, Geneva 22, Switzerland; *Yearbook of Labour Statistics*.

Statistical Office of the United Nations, Publishing Service, New York, New York 10017 (800) 253-9646; *Statistical Yearbook*.

EGYPT - VITAL STATISTICS

Euromonitor Publications Limited, 87-88 Turnmill Street, London EC1M 5QU, England; *International Marketing Data and Statistics*, and *Middle East Economic Handbook*.

G.K. Hall and Company, 70 Lincoln Street, Boston, Massachusetts 02111 (617) 423-3990; *The World in Figures*.

World Health Organization, Office of Publications, Avenue Appia, CH-1211 Geneva, 27, Switzerland (Telephone Number in U.S. (518)

436-9686); *World Health Statistics Annual.*

EGYPT - WAGES

G.K. Hall and Company, 70 Lincoln Street, Boston, Massachusetts 02111 (617) 423-3990; *The World in Figures.*

International Labour Office, I.L.O. Publications, CH-1211, Geneva 22, Switzerland; *Yearbook of Labour Statistics.*

Statistical Office of the United Nations, Publishing Service, New York, New York 10017 (800) 253-9646; *Statistical Yearbook.*

EGYPT - WATERMELON PRODUCTION - See EGYPT - CROPS

EGYPT - WEATHER

Facts on File, 460 Park Avenue South, New York, New York 10016 (800) 443-8323; *The New Book of World Rankings.*

G.K. Hall and Company, 70 Lincoln Street, Boston, Massachusetts 02111 (617) 423-3990; *The World in Figures.*

EGYPT - WELFARE

International Monetary Fund, 700 Nineteenth Street, NW, Washington, D.C. 20431 (202) 623-7000; *Government Finance Statistics Yearbook.*

EGYPT - WHEAT - See EGYPT - CROPS

EGYPT - WHOLESALE PRICES

International Monetary Fund, 700 Nineteenth Street, NW, Washington, D.C. 20431 (202) 623-7000; *International Financial Statistics.*

Statistical Office of the United Nations, Publishing Service, New York, New York 10017 (800) 253-9646; *Statistical Yearbook.*

EGYPT - WHOLESALE TRADE

Statistical Office of the United Nations, Publishing Service, New York, New York 10017 (800) 253-9646; *Statistical Yearbook.*

EGYPT - WINE PRODUCTION

Facts on File, 460 Park Avenue South, New York, New York 10016 (800) 443-8323; *The New Book of World Rankings.*

Statistical Office of the United Nations, Publishing Service, New York, New York 10017 (800) 253-9646; *Statistical Yearbook.*

EGYPT - WOOD - See EGYPT - FORESTRY AND FOREST PRODUCTS

EGYPT - WOOL PRODUCTION

Facts on File, 460 Park Avenue South, New York, New York 10016 (800) 443-8323; *The New Book of World Rankings.*

EGYPT - YARN PRODUCTION

Statistical Office of the United Nations, Publishing Service, New York, New York 10017 (800) 253-9646; *Statistical Yearbook.*

EGYPT - ZOOS AND BOTANICAL GARDENS

United Nations Educational, Scientific and Cultural Organization (UNESCO), 7 Place de Fontenoy, F-75700 Paris, France (Telephone Number in U.S. (212) 963-5981); *Statistical Yearbook.*

EIRE - See IRELAND

El Salvador - National Statistical Office

Direccion General de Estadistica y Censos, Calle Pte. Y43 Av Nte., Apartado Postal 2670, San Salvador, El Salvador.

El Salvador - Primary Statistics Sources

Direccion General de Estadistica y Censos, Pte. Y43 Av Nte., Apartado Postal 2670, San Salvador, El Salvador; *Anuario Estadistico,* (Statistical Yearbook), and *Boletin estadistico (Statistical Bulletin).*

EL SALVADOR - AGRICULTURE

The Economist Intelligence Unit, 111 West 57th Street, New York, New York 10019 (800) 938-4685; *The New Latin America Market Atlas.*

Euromonitor Publications Limited, 87-88 Turnmill Street, London EC1M 5QU, England; *International Marketing Data and Statistics.*

Facts on File, 460 Park Avenue South, New York, New York 10016 (800) 443-8323; *The New Book of World Rankings.*

Federal Statistical Office, Gustav - Stresemann - Ring 11, D-6200 Wiesbaden, Germany; *El Salvador.*

Food and Agricultural Organization of the United Nations (FAO), Via delle Terme di Caracalla, 00100 Rome, Italy (Telephone Number in U.S. (202) 653-2400); *Production Yearbook, The State of Food and Agriculture,* and *Trade Yearbook.*

Gale Research Incorporated, 835 Penobscot Building, Detroit, Michigan 48226 (800) 877-4253; *International Historical Statistics The Americas and Australasia.*

G.K. Hall and Company, 70 Lincoln Street, Boston, Massachusetts 02111 (617) 423-3990; *The World in Figures.*

Inter-American Development Bank, 1300 New York Avenue, NW, Washington, D.C. 20577 (202) 623-1753; *Economic and Social Progress in Latin America.*

Statistical Office of the United Nations, Publishing Service, New York, New York 10017 (800) 253-9646; *Statistical Yearbook,* and *Statistical Yearbook for Latin America and the Caribbean.*

Times Books, 201 East 50th Street, New York, New York 10022 (212) 751-2600; *The Economist Book of Vital World Statistics.*

U.C.L.A. Latin American Center Publications, University of California, Los Angeles, California 90024 (310) 825-6634; *Statistical Abstract of Latin America.*

EL SALVADOR - AIRLINE SERVICE

The Economist Intelligence Unit, 111 West 57th Street, New York, New York 10019 (800) 938-4685; *The New Latin America Market Atlas.*

Facts on File, 460 Park Avenue South, New York, New York 10016 (800) 443-8323; *The New Book of World Rankings.*

G.K. Hall and Company, 70 Lincoln Street, Boston, Massachusetts 02111 (617) 423-3990; *The World in Figures.*

International Civil Aviation Organization, 1000 Sherbrooke Street West, Suite 400, Montreal, Quebec, Canada H3A 2R2 (514) 285-8219; *Civil Aviation Statistics of the World.*

Times Books, 201 East 50th Street, New York, New York 10022 (212) 751-2600; *The Economist Book of Vital World Statistics.*

EL SALVADOR - ALUMINUM PRODUCTION AND CONSUMPTION - See EL SALVADOR - MINING AND MINERAL PRODUCTS

EL SALVADOR - ANIMAL HEALTH

Food and Agricultural Organization of the United Nations (FAO), Via delle Terme di Caracalla, 00100 Rome, Italy (Telephone Number in U.S. (202) 653-2400); *Animal Health Yearbook.*

EL SALVADOR - AREA AND DENSITY OF POPULATION

Euromonitor Publications Limited, 87-88 Turnmill Street, London EC1M 5QU, England; *International Marketing Data and Statistics.*

Facts on File, 460 Park Avenue South, New York, New York 10016 (800) 443-8323; *The New Book of World Rankings.*

Federal Statistical Office, Gustav - Stresemann - Ring 11, D-6200 Wiesbaden, Germany; *El Salvador.*

Food and Agricultural Organization of the United Nations (FAO) Via delle Terme di Caracalla, 00100 Rome, Italy (Telephone Number in U.S. (202) 653-2400); *The State of Food and Agriculture.*

G.K. Hall and Company, 70 Lincoln Street, Boston, Massachusetts 02111 (617) 423-3990; *The World in Figures.*

Inter-American Development Bank, 1300 New York Avenue, NW, Washington, D.C. 20577 (202) 623-1753; *Economic and Social Progress in Latin America.*

Statistical Office of the United Nations, Publishing Service, New York, New York 10017 (800) 253-9646; *Statistical Yearbook.*

Times Books, 201 East 50th Street, New York, New York 10022 (212) 751-2600; *The Economist Book of Vital World Statistics.*

United Nations Educational, Scientific and Cultural Organization (UNESCO), 7 Place de Fontenoy, F-75700 Paris, France (Telephone Number in U.S. (212) 963-5981); *Statistical Yearbook.*

EL SALVADOR - ARMS EXPORTS AND IMPORTS

U.S. Arms Control and Disarmament Agency, 320 Twenty-first Street, NW, Washington, D.C. 20451 (202) 647-8677; *World Military Expenditures and Arms Transfers.*

EL SALVADOR - BALANCE OF PAYMENTS

The Economist Intelligence Unit, 111 West 57th Street, New York, New York 10019 (800) 938-4685; *The New Latin America Market Atlas,* and *The World Market Atlas.*

Federal Statistical Office, Gustav - Stresemann - Ring 11, D-6200 Wiesbaden, Germany; *El Salvador.*

G.K. Hall and Company, 70 Lincoln Street, Boston, Massachusetts 02111 (617) 423-3990; *The World in Figures.*

Inter-American Development Bank, 1300 New York Avenue, NW, Washington, D.C. 20577 (202) 623-1753; *Economic and Social Progress in Latin America.*

International Monetary Fund, 700 Nineteenth Street, NW, Washington, D.C. 20431 (202) 623-7000; *Balance of Payments Yearbook,* and *International Financial Statistics.*

Organization of American States (OAS), General Secretariat, Washington, D.C. 20006 (202) 458-3533; *Statistical Bulletin of the OAS.*

Statistical Office of the United Nations, Publishing Service, New York, New York 10017 (800) 253-9646; *Economic Survey of Latin America and the Caribbean,* and *Statistical Yearbook for Latin America and the Caribbean.*

Times Books, 201 East 50th Street, New York, New York 10022 (212) 751-2600; *The Economist Book of Vital World Statistics.*

U.C.L.A. Latin American Center Publications, University of California, Los Angeles, California 90024 (310) 825-6634; *Statistical Abstract of Latin America.*

EL SALVADOR - BANKING

Facts on File, 460 Park Avenue South, New York, New York 10016 (800) 443-8323; *The New Book of World Rankings.*

G.K. Hall and Company, 70 Lincoln Street, Boston, Massachusetts 02111 (617) 423-3990; *The World in Figures.*

Inter-American Development Bank, 1300 New York Avenue, NW, Washington, D.C. 20577 (202) 623-1753; *Economic and Social Progress in Latin America.*

International Monetary Fund, 700 Nineteenth Street, NW, Washington, D.C. 20431 (202) 623-7000; *Government Finance Statistics Yearbook,* and *International Financial Statistics.*

EL SALVADOR - BARLEY PRODUCTION - See EL SALVADOR - CROPS

EL SALVADOR - BEER PRODUCTION

Facts on File, 460 Park Avenue South, New York, New York 10016 (800) 443-8323; *The New Book of World Rankings.*

Statistical Office of the United Nations, Publishing Service, New York, New York 10017 (800) 253-9646; *Statistical Yearbook.*

EL SALVADOR - BIRTH RATE

Facts on File, 460 Park Avenue South, New York, New York 10016 (800) 443-8323; *The New Book of World Rankings.*

Statistical Office of the United Nations, Publishing Service, New York, New York 10017 (800) 253-9646; *Demographic Yearbook, Statistical Yearbook,* and *Statistical Yearbook for Latin America and the Caribbean.*

Times Books, 201 East 50th Street, New York, New York 10022 (212) 751-2600; *The Economist Book of Vital World Statistics.*

World Health Organization, Office of Publications, Avenue Appia, CH-1211 Geneva, 27, Switzerland (Telephone Number in U.S. (518) 436-9686); *World Health Statistics Annual.*

EL SALVADOR - BONDS

G.K. Hall and Company, 70 Lincoln Street, Boston, Massachusetts 02111 (617) 423-3990; *The World in Figures*.

Inter-American Development Bank, 1300 New York Avenue, NW, Washington, D.C. 20577 (202) 623-1753; *Economic and Social Progress in Latin America*.

International Monetary Fund, 700 Nineteenth Street, NW, Washington, D.C. 20431 (202) 623-7000; *Government Finance Statistics Yearbook*.

EL SALVADOR - BOOK PRODUCTION

G.K. Hall and Company, 70 Lincoln Street, Boston, Massachusetts 02111 (617) 423-3990; *The World in Figures*.

United Nations Educational, Scientific and Cultural Organization (UNESCO), 7 Place de Fontenoy, F-75700 Paris, France (Telephone Number in U.S. (212) 963-5981); *Statistical Yearbook*.

EL SALVADOR - BROADCASTING

Billboard Limited, P.O. Box 9027, 1006 AA Amsterdam, The Netherlands (Telephone Number in U.S. (212) 764-7300); *World Radio TV Handbook*.

G.K. Hall and Company, 70 Lincoln Street, Boston, Massachusetts 02111 (617) 423-3990; *The World in Figures*.

Facts on File, 460 Park Avenue South, New York, New York 10016 (800) 443-8323; *The New Book of World Rankings*.

Times Books, 201 East 50th Street, New York, New York 10022 (212) 751-2600; *The Economist Book of Vital World Statistics*.

EL SALVADOR - BUILDING CONSTRUCTION - See EL SALVADOR - CONSTRUCTION INDUSTRY

EL SALVADOR - BUSINESS

G.K. Hall and Company, 70 Lincoln Street, Boston, Massachusetts 02111 (617) 423-3990; *The World in Figures*.

Inter-American Development Bank, 1300 New York Avenue, NW, Washington, D.C. 20577 (202) 623-1753; *Economic and Social Progress in Latin America*.

EL SALVADOR - BUSINESS AND PROFESSIONAL LICENSES

International Monetary Fund, 700 Nineteenth Street, NW, Washington, D.C. 20431 (202) 623-7000; *Government Finance Statistics Yearbook*.

EL SALVADOR - BUTTER - See EL SALVADOR - DAIRY PRODUCTS

EL SALVADOR - CALORIE SUPPLY

Food and Agricultural Organization of the United Nations (FAO) Via delle Terme di Caracalla, 00100 Rome, Italy (Telephone Number in U.S. (202) 653-2400); *The State of Food and Agriculture*.

Statistical Office of the United Nations, Publishing Service, New York, New York 10017 (800) 253-9646; *Statistical Yearbook for Latin America and the Caribbean*.

EL SALVADOR - CAPITAL INVESTMENT

Inter-American Development Bank, 1300 New York Avenue, NW, Washington, D.C. 20577 (202) 623-1753; *Economic and Social Progress in Latin America*.

EL SALVADOR - CAPITAL REVENUE

Inter-American Development Bank, 1300 New York Avenue, NW, Washington, D.C. 20577 (202) 623-1753; *Economic and Social Progress in Latin America*.

International Monetary Fund, 700 Nineteenth Street, NW, Washington, D.C. 20431 (202) 623-7000; *Government Finance Statistics Yearbook*.

EL SALVADOR - CATTLE - See EL SALVADOR - LIVESTOCK AND POULTRY

EL SALVADOR - CEMENT PRODUCTION - See EL SALVADOR - MINING AND MINERAL PRODUCTS

EL SALVADOR - CHEESE PRODUCTION - See EL SALVADOR - DAIRY PRODUCTS

EL SALVADOR - CHEMICAL (ORGANIC) PRODUCTION - See EL SALVADOR - MINING AND MINERAL PRODUCTS

EL SALVADOR - CHICKENS - See EL SALVADOR - LIVESTOCK AND POULTRY

EL SALVADOR - CIGARETTE PRODUCTION - See EL SALVADOR - TOBACCO PRODUCTION

EL SALVADOR - CLASS STRUCTURE

G.K. Hall and Company, 70 Lincoln Street, Boston, Massachusetts 02111 (617) 423-3990; *The World in Figures*.

EL SALVADOR - CLIMATE

Facts on File, 460 Park Avenue South, New York, New York 10016 (800) 443-8323; *The New Book of World Rankings*.

G.K. Hall and Company, 70 Lincoln Street, Boston, Massachusetts 02111 (617) 423-3990; *The World in Figures*.

EL SALVADOR - CLOTHING EXPORTS AND IMPORTS

Statistical Office of the United Nations, Publishing Service, New York, New York 10017 (800) 253-9646; *Trade in Manufactures of Developing Countries*.

EL SALVADOR - COAL PRODUCTION - See EL SALVADOR - MINING AND MINERAL PRODUCTS

EL SALVADOR - COCOA (BEANS) PRODUCTION - See EL SALVADOR - CROPS

EL SALVADOR - COFFEE - See EL SALVADOR - CROPS

EL SALVADOR - COMMUNICATIONS

Federal Statistical Office, Gustav - Stresemann - Ring 11, D-6200 Wiesbaden, Germany; *El Salvador*.

G.K. Hall and Company, 70 Lincoln Street, Boston, Massachusetts 02111 (617) 423-3990; *The World in Figures*.

Inter-American Development Bank, 1300 New York Avenue, NW, Washington, D.C. 20577 (202) 623-1753; *Economic and Social Progress in Latin America.*

U.C.L.A. Latin American Center Publications, University of California, Los Angeles, California 90024 (310) 825-6634; *Statistical Abstract of Latin America.*

EL SALVADOR - CONSTRUCTION INDUSTRY

The Economist Intelligence Unit, 111 West 57th Street, New York, New York 10019 (800) 938-4685; *The New Latin America Market Atlas.*

Facts on File, 460 Park Avenue South, New York, New York 10016 (800) 443-8323; *The New Book of World Rankings.*

Organization of American States (OAS), General Secretariat, Washington, D.C. 20006 (202) 458-3533; *Statistical Bulletin of the OAS.*

Inter-American Development Bank, 1300 New York Avenue, NW, Washington, D.C. 20577 (202) 623-1753; *Economic and Social Progress in Latin America.*

Statistical Office of the United Nations, Publishing Service, New York, New York 10017 (800) 253-9646; *Construction Statistics Yearbook,* and *Statistical Yearbook.*

EL SALVADOR - CONSUMER PRICE INDEX

Federal Statistical Office, Gustav - Stresemann - Ring 11, D-6200 Wiesbaden, Germany; *El Salvador.*

G.K. Hall and Company, 70 Lincoln Street, Boston, Massachusetts 02111 (617) 423-3990; *The World in Figures.*

Statistical Office of the United Nations, Publishing Service, New York, New York 10017 (800) 253-9646; *Statistical Yearbook.*

EL SALVADOR - CONSUMER PRICES

The Economist Intelligence Unit, 111 West 57th Street, New York, New York 10019 (800) 938-4685; *The New Latin America Market Atlas.*

Federal Statistical Office, Gustav - Stresemann - Ring 11, D-6200 Wiesbaden, Germany; *El Salvador.*

International Labour Office, I.L.O. Publications, CH-1211, Geneva 22, Switzerland; *Yearbook of Labour Statistics.*

International Monetary Fund, 700 Nineteenth Street, NW, Washington, D.C. 20431 (202) 623-7000; *International Financial Statistics.*

Organization of American States (OAS), General Secretariat, Washington, D.C. 20006 (202) 458-3533; *Statistical Bulletin of the OAS.*

Times Books, 201 East 50th Street, New York, New York 10022 (212) 751-2600; *The Economist Book of Vital World Statistics.*

U.C.L.A. Latin American Center Publications, University of California, Los Angeles, California 90024 (310) 825-6634; *Statistical Abstract of Latin America.*

EL SALVADOR - CONSUMPTION

The Economist Intelligence Unit, 111 West 57th Street, New York, New York 10019 (800) 938-4685; *The New Latin America Market Atlas.*

G.K. Hall and Company, 70 Lincoln Street, Boston, Massachusetts 02111 (617) 423-3990; *The World in Figures.*

Inter-American Development Bank, 1300 New York Avenue, NW, Washington, D.C. 20577 (202) 623-1753; *Economic and Social Progress in Latin America.*

Statistical Office of the United Nations, Publishing Service, New York, New York 10017 (800) 253-9646; *Statistical Yearbook for Latin America and the Caribbean.*

EL SALVADOR - COOPERATIVES

U.C.L.A. Latin American Center Publications, University of California, Los Angeles, California 90024 (310) 825-6634; *Statistical Abstract of Latin America.*

EL SALVADOR - COPPER PRODUCTION - See EL SALVADOR - MINING AND MINERAL PRODUCTS

EL SALVADOR - CORN PRODUCTION - See EL SALVADOR - CROPS

EL SALVADOR - CORPORATE INCOME TAXES - See EL SALVADOR - TAXATION

EL SALVADOR - CORPORATE TAXES - See EL SALVADOR - TAXATION

EL SALVADOR - COTTON - See EL SALVADOR - CROPS

EL SALVADOR - CRIME

Yale University Press, Yale Station, New Haven, Connecticut 06520 (203) 432-0940; *Violence and Crime in Cross-National Perspective.*

EL SALVADOR - CROPS

The Economist Intelligence Unit, 111 West 57th Street, New York, New York 10019 (800) 938-4685; *The New Latin America Market Atlas.*

Facts on File, 460 Park Avenue South, New York, New York 10016 (800) 443-8323; *The New Book of World Rankings.*

Food and Agricultural Organization of the United Nations (FAO) Via delle Terme di Caracalla, 00100 Rome, Italy (Telephone Number in U.S. (202) 653-2400); *Production Yearbook,* and *The State of Food and Agriculture.*

G.K. Hall and Company, 70 Lincoln Street, Boston, Massachusetts 02111 (617) 423-3990; *The World in Figures.*

International Monetary Fund, 700 Nineteenth Street, NW, Washington, D.C. 20431 (202) 623-7000; *International Financial Statistics.*

Organization of American States (OAS), General Secretariat, Washington, D.C. 20006 (202) 458-3533; *Statistical Bulletin of the OAS.*

Statistical Office of the United Nations, Publishing Service, New York, New York 10017 (800) 253-9646; *Statistical Yearbook.*

EL SALVADOR - CUSTOMS DUTIES

G.K. Hall and Company, 70 Lincoln Street, Boston, Massachusetts 02111 (617) 423-3990; *The World in Figures*.

Inter-American Development Bank, 1300 New York Avenue, NW, Washington, D.C. 20577 (202) 623-1753; *Economic and Social Progress in Latin America*.

International Monetary Fund, 700 Nineteenth Street, NW, Washington, D.C. 20431 (202) 623-7000; *Government Finance Statistics Yearbook*.

EL SALVADOR - DAIRY PRODUCTS

Facts on File, 460 Park Avenue South, New York, New York 10016 (800) 443-8323; *The New Book of World Rankings*.

Food and Agricultural Organization of the United Nations (FAO) Via delle Terme di Caracalla, 00100 Rome, Italy (Telephone Number in U.S. (202) 653-2400); *Production Yearbook*, and *The State of Food and Agriculture*.

Statistical Office of the United Nations, Publishing Service, New York, New York 10017 (800) 253-9646; *Statistical Yearbook*.

EL SALVADOR - DEATH RATE

G.K. Hall and Company, 70 Lincoln Street, Boston, Massachusetts 02111 (617) 423-3990; *The World in Figures*.

Statistical Office of the United Nations, Publishing Service, New York, New York 10017 (800) 253-9646; *Statistical Yearbook*, and *Statistical Yearbook for Latin America and the Caribbean*.

Times Books, 201 East 50th Street, New York, New York 10022 (212) 751-2600; *The Economist Book of Vital World Statistics*.

World Health Organization, Office of Publications, Avenue Appia, CH-1211 Geneva, 27, Switzerland (Telephone Number in U.S. (518) 436-9686); *World Health Statistics Annual*.

EL SALVADOR - DEBT

The Economist Intelligence Unit, 111 West 57th Street, New York, New York 10019 (800) 938-4685; *The New Latin America Market Atlas*.

EL SALVADOR - DEFENSE EXPENDITURES

The Economist Intelligence Unit, 111 West 57th Street, New York, New York 10019 (800) 938-4685; *The New Latin America Market Atlas*.

G.K. Hall and Company, 70 Lincoln Street, Boston, Massachusetts 02111 (617) 423-3990; *The World in Figures*.

International Monetary Fund, 700 Nineteenth Street, NW, Washington, D.C. 20431 (202) 623-7000; *Government Finance Statistics Yearbook*.

U.S. Arms Control and Disarmament Agency, 320 Twenty-first Street, NW, Washington, D.C. 20451 (202) 647-8677; *World Military Expenditures and Arms Transfers*.

EL SALVADOR - DEMOGRAPHY

The Economist Intelligence Unit, 111 West 57th Street, New York, New York 10019 (800) 938-4685; *The World Market Atlas*.

Facts on File, 460 Park Avenue South, New York, New York 10016 (800) 443-8323; *The New Book of World Rankings*.

Federal Statistical Office, Gustav - Stresemann - Ring 11, D-6200 Wiesbaden, Germany; *El Salvador*.

G.K. Hall and Company, 70 Lincoln Street, Boston, Massachusetts 02111 (617) 423-3990; *The World in Figures*.

EL SALVADOR - DEVELOPMENT ASSISTANCE

G.K. Hall and Company, 70 Lincoln Street, Boston, Massachusetts 02111 (617) 423-3990; *The World in Figures*.

Inter-American Development Bank, 1300 New York Avenue, NW, Washington, D.C. 20577 (202) 623-1753; *Economic and Social Progress in Latin America*.

Statistical Office of the United Nations, Publishing Service, New York, New York 10017 (800) 253-9646; *Statistical Yearbook*.

EL SALVADOR - DIAMOND PRODUCTION - See EL SALVADOR - MINING AND MINERAL PRODUCTS

EL SALVADOR - DISCOUNT RATES

Inter-American Development Bank, 1300 New York Avenue, NW, Washington, D.C. 20577 (202) 623-1753; *Economic and Social Progress in Latin America*.

EL SALVADOR - DISEASES

G.K. Hall and Company, 70 Lincoln Street, Boston, Massachusetts 02111 (617) 423-3990; *The World in Figures*.

World Health Organization, Office of Publications, Avenue Appia, CH-1211 Geneva, 27, Switzerland (Telephone Number in U.S. (518) 4367-9686); *World Health Statistics Annual*.

EL SALVADOR - DIVORCE RATES

Facts on File, 460 Park Avenue South, New York, New York 10016 (800) 443-8323; *The New Book of World Rankings*.

Statistical Office of the United Nations, Publishing Service, New York, New York 10017 (800) 253-9646; *Demographic Yearbook*, and *Statistical Yearbook*.

EL SALVADOR - DOMESTIC PRODUCT

G.K. Hall and Company, 70 Lincoln Street, Boston, Massachusetts 02111 (617) 423-3990; *The World in Figures*.

EL SALVADOR - ECONOMY

Euromonitor Publications Limited, 87-88 Turnmill Street, London EC1M 5QU, England; *International Marketing Data and Statistics*.

Facts on File, 460 Park Avenue South, New York, New York 10016 (800) 443-8323; *The New Book of World Rankings*.

Federal Statistical Office, Gustav - Stresemann - Ring 11, D-6200 Wiesbaden, Germany; *El Salvador*.

G.K. Hall and Company, 70 Lincoln Street, Boston, Massachusetts 02111 (617) 423-3990; *The World in Figures*.

Inter-American Development Bank, 1300 New York Avenue, NW, Washington, D.C. 20577 (202) 623-1753; *Economic and Social*

Progress in Latin America.

Organization of American States (OAS), General Secretariat, Washington, D.C. 20006 (202) 458-3533; *Statistical Bulletin of the OAS.*

Statistical Office of the United Nations, Publishing Service, New York, New York 10017 (800) 253-9646; *Economic Survey of Latin America and the Caribbean.*

U.C.L.A. Latin American Center Publications, University of California, Los Angeles, California 90024 (310) 825-6634; *Statistical Abstract of Latin America.*

EL SALVADOR - EDUCATION

The Economist Intelligence Unit, 111 West 57th Street, New York, New York 10019 (800) 938-4685; *The New Latin America Market Atlas,* and *The World Market Atlas.*

Facts on File, 460 Park Avenue South, New York, New York 10016 (800) 443-8323; *The New Book of World Rankings.*

Federal Statistical Office, Gustav - Stresemann - Ring 11, D-6200 Wiesbaden, Germany; *El Salvador.*

Gale Research Incorporated, 835 Penobscot Building, Detroit, Michigan 48226 (800) 877-4253; *International Historical Statistics The Americas and Australasia.*

G.K. Hall and Company, 70 Lincoln Street, Boston, Massachusetts 02111 (617) 423-3990; *The World in Figures.*

International Monetary Fund, 700 Nineteenth Street, NW, Washington, D.C. 20431 (202) 623-7000; *Government Finance Statistics Yearbook.*

Statistical Office of the United Nations, Publishing Service, New York, New York 10017 (800) 253-9646; *Statistical Yearbook for Latin America and the Caribbean.*

Times Books, 201 East 50th Street, New York, New York 10022 (212) 751-2600; *The Economist Book of Vital World Statistics.*

U.C.L.A. Latin American Center Publications, University of California, Los Angeles, California 90024 (310) 825-6634; *Statistical Abstract of Latin America.*

United Nations Educational, Scientific and Cultural Organization (UNESCO), 7 Place de Fontenoy, F-75700 Paris, France (Telephone Number in U.S. (212) 963-5981); *Statistical Yearbook.*

EL SALVADOR - EGG PRODUCTION - See EL SALVADOR - DAIRY PRODUCTS

EL SALVADOR - ELECTRICITY

The Economist Intelligence Unit, 111 West 57th Street, New York, New York 10019 (800) 938-4685; *The New Latin America Market Atlas.*

Facts on File, 460 Park Avenue South, New York, New York 10016 (800) 443-8323; *The New Book of World Rankings.*

Inter-American Development Bank, 1300 New York Avenue, NW, Washington, D.C. 20577 (202) 623-1753; *Economic and Social Progress in Latin America.*

Organization of American States (OAS), General Secretariat, Washington, D.C. 20006 (202) 458-3533; *Statistical Bulletin of the OAS.*

Times Books, 201 East 50th Street, New York, New York 10022 (212) 751-2600; *The Economist Book of Vital World Statistics.*

EL SALVADOR - EMPLOYMENT

Euromonitor Publications Limited, 87-88 Turnmill Street, London EC1M 5QU, England; *International Marketing Data and Statistics.*

Facts on File, 460 Park Avenue South, New York, New York 10016 (800) 443-8323; *The New Book of World Rankings.*

Federal Statistical Office, Gustav - Stresemann - Ring 11, D-6200 Wiesbaden, Germany; *El Salvador.*

International Labour Office, I.L.O. Publications, CH-1211, Geneva 22, Switzerland; *Yearbook of Labour Statistics.*

Organization of American States (OAS), General Secretariat, Washington, D.C. 20006 (202) 458-3533; *Statistical Bulletin of the OAS.*

Statistical Office of the United Nations, Publishing Service, New York, New York 10017 (800) 253-9646; *Statistical Yearbook for Latin America and the Caribbean.*

U.C.L.A. Latin American Center Publications, University of California, Los Angeles, California 90024 (310) 825-6634; *Statistical Abstract of Latin America.*

EL SALVADOR - ENERGY

The Economist Intelligence Unit, 111 West 57th Street, New York, New York 10019 (800) 938-4685; *The New Latin America Market Atlas.*

Facts on File, 460 Park Avenue South, New York, New York 10016 (800) 443-8323; *The New Book of World Rankings.*

Food and Agricultural Organization of the United Nations (FAO) Via delle Terme di Caracalla, 00100 Rome, Italy (Telephone Number in U.S. (202) 653-2400); *The State of Food and Agriculture.*

G.K. Hall and Company, 70 Lincoln Street, Boston, Massachusetts 02111 (617) 423-3990; *The World in Figures.*

Statistical Office of the United Nations, Publishing Service, New York, New York 10017 (800) 253-9646; *Statistical Yearbook, Statistical Yearbook for Latin America and the Caribbean,* and *Energy Statistics Yearbook.*

Times Books, 201 East 50th Street, New York, New York 10022 (212) 751-2600; *The Economist Book of Vital World Statistics.*

U.C.L.A. Latin American Center Publications, University of California, Los Angeles, California 90024 (310) 825-6634; *Statistical Abstract of Latin America.*

EL SALVADOR - ENGINEERING AND METAL PRODUCTS EXPORTS TO DEVELOPED COUNTRIES

Statistical Office of the United Nations, Publishing Service, New York, New York 10017 (800) 253-9646; *Trade in Manufactures of Developing Countries.*

EL SALVADOR - EXCHANGE RATES

Euromonitor Publications Limited, 87-88 Turnmill Street, London EC1M 5QU, England; *International Marketing Data and Statistics*.

Inter-American Development Bank, 1300 New York Avenue, NW, Washington, D.C. 20577 (202) 623-1753; *Economic and Social Progress in Latin America*.

International Civil Aviation Organization, 1000 Sherbrooke Street West, Suite 400, Montreal, Quebec, Canada H3A 2R2 (514) 285-8219; *Civil Aviation Statistics of the World*.

International Monetary Fund, 700 Nineteenth Street, NW, Washington, D.C. 20431 (202) 623-7000; *International Financial Statistics*.

Organization of American States (OAS), General Secretariat, Washington, D.C. 20006 (202) 458-3533; *Statistical Bulletin of the OAS*.

Statistical Office of the United Nations, Publishing Service, New York, New York 10017 (800) 253-9646; *Statistical Yearbook*.

U.C.L.A. Latin American Center Publications, University of California, Los Angeles, California 90024 (310) 825-6634; *Statistical Abstract of Latin America*.

EL SALVADOR - EXCISE TAXES - See EL SALVADOR - TAXATION

EL SALVADOR - EXPORTS

The Economist Intelligence Unit, 111 West 57th Street, New York, New York 10019 (800) 938-4685; *The New Latin America Market Atlas*, and *The World Market Atlas*.

Euromonitor Publications Limited, 87-88 Turnmill Street, London EC1M 5QU, England; *International Marketing Data and Statistics*.

Food and Agricultural Organization of the United Nations (FAO) Via delle Terme di Caracalla, 00100 Rome, Italy (Telephone Number in U.S. (202) 653-2400); *The State of Food and Agriculture*.

G.K. Hall and Company, 70 Lincoln Street, Boston, Massachusetts 02111 (617) 423-3990; *The World in Figures*.

Inter-American Development Bank, 1300 New York Avenue, NW, Washington, D.C. 20577 (202) 623-1753; *Economic and Social Progress in Latin America*.

International Monetary Fund, 700 Nineteenth Street, NW, Washington, D.C. 20431 (202) 623-7000; *Direction of Trade Statistics, Government Finance Statistics Yearbook*, and *International Financial Statistics*.

Organization of American States (OAS), General Secretariat, Washington, D.C. 20006 (202) 458-3533; *Statistical Bulletin of the OAS*.

Statistical Office of the United Nations, Publishing Service, New York, New York 10017 (800) 253-9646; *Statistical Yearbook for Latin America and the Caribbean*, and *Trade in Manufactures of Developing Countries*.

Times Books, 201 East 50th Street, New York, New York 10022 (212) 751-2600; *The Economist Book of Vital World Statistics*.

EL SALVADOR - EXTERNAL FINANCING

Inter-American Development Bank, 1300 New York Avenue, NW, Washington, D.C. 20577 (202) 623-1753; *Economic and Social Progress in Latin America*.

Statistical Office of the United Nations, Publishing Service, New York, New York 10017 (800) 253-9646; *Statistical Yearbook for Latin America and the Caribbean*.

EL SALVADOR - EXTERNAL INDEBTEDNESS

Inter-American Development Bank, 1300 New York Avenue, NW, Washington, D.C. 20577 (202) 623-1753; *Economic and Social Progress in Latin America*.

Statistical Office of the United Nations, Publishing Service, New York, New York 10017 (800) 253-9646; *Statistical Yearbook for Latin America and the Caribbean*.

EL SALVADOR - EXTERNAL TRADE

Food and Agricultural Organization of the United Nations (FAO) Via delle Terme di Caracalla, 00100 Rome, Italy (Telephone Number in U.S. (202) 653-2400); *The State of Food and Agriculture*, and *Trade Yearbook*.

Gale Research Incorporated, 835 Penobscot Building, Detroit, Michigan 48226 (800) 877-4253; *International Historical Statistics The Americas and Australasia*.

G.K. Hall and Company, 70 Lincoln Street, Boston, Massachusetts 02111 (617) 423-3990; *The World in Figures*.

Inter-American Development Bank, 1300 New York Avenue, NW, Washington, D.C. 20577 (202) 623-1753; *Economic and Social Progress in Latin America*.

Statistical Office of the United Nations, Publishing Service, New York, New York 10017 (800) 253-9646; *Statistical Yearbook*, and *Statistical Yearbook for Latin America and the Caribbean*.

EL SALVADOR - FABRIC PRODUCTION - See EL SALVADOR - TEXTILE INDUSTRY

EL SALVADOR - FAMILY PLANNING

U.C.L.A. Latin American Center Publications, University of California, Los Angeles, California 90024 (310) 825-6634; *Statistical Abstract of Latin America*.

EL SALVADOR - FARM CROPS - See EL SALVADOR - CROPS

EL SALVADOR - FEMALE WORKING POPULATION - See EL SALVADOR - EMPLOYMENT

EL SALVADOR - FERTILITY RATES

Facts on File, 460 Park Avenue South, New York, New York 10016 (800) 443-8323; *The New Book of World Rankings*.

Times Books, 201 East 50th Street, New York, New York 10022 (212) 751-2600; *The Economist Book of Vital World Statistics*.

EL SALVADOR - FERTILIZER

The Economist Intelligence Unit, 111 West 57th Street, New York, New York 10019 (800) 938-4685; *The New Latin America Market Atlas*.

Food and Agricultural Organization of the United Nations (FAO), Via delle Terme di Caracalla, 00100 Rome, Italy (Telephone Number in U.S. (202) 653-2400); *Fertilizer Yearbook*, and *The State of Food and Agriculture*.

Statistical Office of the United Nations, Publishing Service, New York, New York 10017 (800) 253-9646; *Statistical Yearbook*.

EL SALVADOR - FETAL MORTALITY

Statistical Office of the United Nations, Publishing Service, New York, New York 10017 (800) 253-9646; *Demographic Yearbook*.

World Health Organization, Office of Publications, Avenue Appia, CH-1211, Geneva, 27, Switzerland (Telephone Number in U.S. (518) 436-9686); *World Health Statistics Annual*.

EL SALVADOR - FINANCE

Facts on File, 460 Park Avenue South, New York, New York 10016 (800) 443-8323; *The New Book of World Rankings*.

Federal Statistical Office, Gustav - Stresemann - Ring 11, D-6200 Wiesbaden, Germany; *El Salvador*.

Gale Research Incorporated, 835 Penobscot Building, Detroit, Michigan 48226 (800) 877-4253; *International Historical Statistics The Americas and Australasia*.

G.K. Hall and Company, 70 Lincoln Street, Boston, Massachusetts 02111 (617) 423-3990; *The World in Figures*.

Inter-American Development Bank, 1300 New York Avenue, NW, Washington, D.C. 20577 (202) 623-1753; *Economic and Social Progress in Latin America*.

International Monetary Fund, 700 Nineteenth Street, NW, Washington, D.C. 20431 (202) 623-7000; *Government Finance Statistics Yearbook*, and *International Financial Statistics*.

Organization of American States (OAS), General Secretariat, Washington, D.C. 20006 (202) 458-3533; *Statistical Bulletin of the OAS*.

U.C.L.A. Latin American Center Publications, University of California, Los Angeles, California 90024 (310) 825-6634; *Statistical Abstract of Latin America*.

EL SALVADOR - FISHERIES

Facts on File, 460 Park Avenue South, New York, New York 10016 (800) 443-8323; *The New Book of World Rankings*.

Federal Statistical Office, Gustav - Stresemann - Ring 11, D-6200 Wiesbaden, Germany; *El Salvador*.

Food and Agricultural Organization of the United Nations (FAO) Via delle Terme di Caracalla, 00100 Rome, Italy (Telephone Number in U.S. (202) 653-2400); *The State of Food and Agriculture*, and *Yearbook of Fishery Statistics*.

Inter-American Development Bank, 1300 New York Avenue, NW, Washington, D.C. 20577 (202) 623-1753; *Economic and Social Progress in Latin America*.

Statistical Office of the United Nations, Publishing Service, New York, New York 10017 (800) 253-9646; *Statistical Yearbook*.

U.C.L.A. Latin American Center Publications, University of California, Los Angeles, California 90024 (310) 825-6634; *Statistical Abstract of Latin America*.

EL SALVADOR - FLOUR PRODUCTION

Statistical Office of the United Nations, Publishing Service, New York, New York 10017 (800) 253-9646; *Statistical Yearbook*.

EL SALVADOR - FOOD

Food and Agricultural Organization of the United Nations (FAO) Via delle Terme di Caracalla, 00100 Rome, Italy (Telephone Number in U.S. (202) 653-2400); *Production Yearbook*, and *The State of Food and Agriculture*.

G.K. Hall and Company, 70 Lincoln Street, Boston, Massachusetts 02111 (617) 423-3990; *The World in Figures*.

EL SALVADOR - FOREIGN AID

G.K. Hall and Company, 70 Lincoln Street, Boston, Massachusetts 02111 (617) 423-3990; *The World in Figures*.

Inter-American Development Bank, 1300 New York Avenue, NW, Washington, D.C. 20577 (202) 623-1753; *Economic and Social Progress in Latin America*.

EL SALVADOR - FOREIGN DEBT

The Economist Intelligence Unit, 111 West 57th Street, New York, New York 10019 (800) 938-4685; *The New Latin America Market Atlas*.

Inter-American Development Bank, 1300 New York Avenue, NW, Washington, D.C. 20577 (202) 623-1753; *Economic and Social Progress in Latin America*.

International Monetary Fund, 700 Nineteenth Street, NW, Washington, D.C. 20431 (202) 623-7000; *Government Finance Statistics Yearbook*.

EL SALVADOR - FOREIGN FINANCE

Inter-American Development Bank, 1300 New York Avenue, NW, Washington, D.C. 20577 (202) 623-1753; *Economic and Social Progress in Latin America*.

EL SALVADOR - FOREIGN INDEBTEDNESS

Inter-American Development Bank, 1300 New York Avenue, NW, Washington, D.C. 20577 (202) 623-1753; *Economic and Social Progress in Latin America*.

Statistical Office of the United Nations, Publishing Service, New York, New York 10017 (800) 253-9646; *Economic Survey of Latin America and the Caribbean*.

EL SALVADOR - FOREIGN INVESTMENT

The Economist Intelligence Unit, 111 West 57th Street, New York, New York 10019 (800) 938-4685; *The New Latin America Market Atlas*.

EL SALVADOR - FOREIGN TRADE

The Economist Intelligence Unit, 111 West 57th Street, New York, New York 10019 (800) 938-4685; *The New Latin America Market Atlas*.

Euromonitor Publications Limited, 87-88 Turnmill Street, London EC1M 5QU, England; *International Marketing Data and Statistics.*

Facts on File, 460 Park Avenue South, New York, New York 10016 (800) 443-8323; *The New Book of World Rankings.*

Federal Statistical Office, Gustav - Stresemann - Ring 11, D-6200 Wiesbaden, Germany; *El Salvador.*

Food and Agricultural Organization of the United Nations (FAO) Via delle Terme di Caracalla, 00100 Rome, Italy (Telephone Number in U.S. (202) 653-2400), *The State of Food and Agriculture.*

G.K. Hall and Company, 70 Lincoln Street, Boston, Massachusetts 02111 (617) 423-3990; *The World in Figures.*

Inter-American Development Bank, 1300 New York Avenue, NW, Washington, D.C. 20577 (202) 623-1753; *Economic and Social Progress in Latin America.*

International Monetary Fund, 700 Nineteenth Street, NW, Washington, D.C. 20431 (202) 623-7000; *International Financial Statistics.*

Statistical Office of the United Nations, Publishing Service, New York, New York 10017 (800) 253-9646; *Economic Survey of Latin America and the Caribbean, International Trade Statistics Yearbook, Statistical Yearbook,* and *Yearbook of International Statistics.*

U.C.L.A. Latin American Center Publications, University of California, Los Angeles, California 90024 (310) 825-6634; *Statistical Abstract of Latin America.*

EL SALVADOR - FORESTRY AND FOREST PRODUCTS

The Economist Intelligence Unit, 111 West 57th Street, New York, New York 10019 (800) 938-4685; *The New Latin America Market Atlas.*

Facts on File, 460 Park Avenue South, New York, New York 10016 (800) 443-8323; *The New Book of World Rankings.*

Federal Statistical Office, Gustav - Stresemann - Ring 11, D-6200 Wiesbaden, Germany; *El Salvador.*

Food and Agricultural Organization of the United Nations (FAO) Via delle Terme di Caracalla, 00100 Rome, Italy (Telephone Number in U.S. (202) 653-2400); *The State of Food and Agriculture,* and *Yearbook of Forest Products.*

G.K. Hall and Company, 70 Lincoln Street, Boston, Massachusetts 02111 (617) 423-3990; *The World in Figures.*

Inter-American Development Bank, 1300 New York Avenue, NW, Washington, D.C. 20577 (202) 623-1753; *Economic and Social Progress in Latin America.*

Statistical Office of the United Nations, Publishing Service, New York, New York 10017 (800) 253-9646; *Statistical Yearbook.*

U.C.L.A. Latin American Center Publications, University of California, Los Angeles, California 90024 (310) 825-6634; *Statistical Abstract of Latin America.*

United Nations Educational, Scientific and Cultural Organization (UNESCO), 7 Place de Fontenoy, F-75700 Paris, France (Telephone Number in U.S. (212) 963-5981); *Statistical Yearbook.*

EL SALVADOR - GAS PRODUCTION - See EL SALVADOR - MINING AND MINERAL PRODUCTS

EL SALVADOR - GENERAL INDUSTRIAL STATISTICS

Federal Statistical Office, Gustav - Stresemann - Ring 11, D-6200 Wiesbaden, Germany; *El Salvador.*

Statistical Office of the United Nations, Publishing Service, New York, New York 10017 (800) 253-9646; *Industrial Statistics Yearbook.*

EL SALVADOR - GENERAL MORTALITY

Statistical Office of the United Nations, Publishing Service, New York, New York 10017 (800) 253-9646; *Demographic Yearbook.*

World Health Organization, Office of Publications, Avenue Appia, CH-1211 Geneva, 27, Switzerland (Telephone Number in U.S. (518) 436-9686); *World Health Statistics Annual.*

EL SALVADOR - GEOGRAPHIC DATA

Facts on File, 460 Park Avenue South, New York, New York 10016 (800) 443-8323; *The New Book of World Rankings.*

Federal Statistical Office, Gustav - Stresemann - Ring 11, D-6200 Wiesbaden, Germany; *El Salvador.*

U.C.L.A. Latin American Center Publications, University of California, Los Angeles, California 90024 (310) 825-6634; *Statistical Abstract of Latin America.*

EL SALVADOR - GOATS - See EL SALVADOR - LIVESTOCK AND POULTRY

EL SALVADOR - GOLD HOLDINGS

International Monetary Fund, 700 Nineteenth Street, NW, Washington, D.C. 20431 (202) 623-7000; *International Financial Statistics.*

Statistical Office of the United Nations, Publishing Service, New York, New York 10017 (800) 253-9646; *Statistical Yearbook.*

EL SALVADOR - GOLD PRODUCTION AND CONSUMPTION - See EL SALVADOR - MINING AND MINERAL PRODUCTS

EL SALVADOR - GOLD RESERVES

The Economist Intelligence Unit, 111 West 57th Street, New York, New York 10019 (800) 938-4685; *The New Latin America Market Atlas.*

EL SALVADOR - GOVERNMENT

G.K. Hall and Company, 70 Lincoln Street, Boston, Massachusetts 02111 (617) 423-3990; *The World in Figures.*

Inter-American Development Bank, 1300 New York Avenue, NW, Washington, D.C. 20577 (202) 623-1753; *Economic and Social Progress in Latin America.*

EL SALVADOR - GOVERNMENT BONDS - See EL SALVADOR - BONDS

EL SALVADOR - GOVERNMENT CONSUMPTION

Inter-American Development Bank, 1300 New York Avenue, NW, Washington, D.C. 20577 (202) 623-1753; *Economic and Social Progress in Latin America.*

EL SALVADOR - GOVERNMENT EXPENDITURES

Inter-American Development Bank, 1300 New York Avenue, NW, Washington, D.C. 20577 (202) 623-1753; *Economic and Social Progress in Latin America.*

International Monetary Fund, 700 Nineteenth Street, NW, Washington, D.C. 20431 (202) 623-7000; *Government Finance Statistics Yearbook.*

Times Books, 201 East 50th Street, New York, New York 10022 (212) 751-2600; *The Economist Book of Vital World Statistics.*

EL SALVADOR - GOVERNMENT FINANCES

Inter-American Development Bank, 1300 New York Avenue, NW, Washington, D.C. 20577 (202) 623-1753; *Economic and Social Progress in Latin America.*

International Monetary Fund, 700 Nineteenth Street, NW, Washington, D.C. 20431 (202) 623-7000; *International Financial Statistics.*

Statistical Office of the United Nations, Publishing Service, New York, New York 10017 (800) 253-9646; *Statistical Yearbook.*

EL SALVADOR - GOVERNMENT REVENUES

Inter-American Development Bank, 1300 New York Avenue, NW, Washington, D.C. 20577 (202) 623-1753; *Economic and Social Progress in Latin America.*

International Monetary Fund, 700 Nineteenth Street, NW, Washington, D.C. 20431 (202) 623-7000; *Government Finance Statistics Yearbook.*

Times Books, 201 East 50th Street, New York, New York 10022 (212) 751-2600; *The Economist Book of Vital World Statistics.*

U.C.L.A. Latin American Center Publications, University of California, Los Angeles, California 90024 (310) 825-6634; *Statistical Abstract of Latin America.*

EL SALVADOR - GRAIN PRODUCTION - See EL SALVADOR - CROPS

EL SALVADOR - GRANTS

International Monetary Fund, 700 Nineteenth Street, NW, Washington, D.C. 20431 (202) 623-7000; *Government Finance Statistics Yearbook.*

EL SALVADOR - GROSS DOMESTIC PRODUCT

The Economist Intelligence Unit, 111 West 57th Street, New York, New York 10019 (800) 938-4685; *The New Latin America Market Atlas,* and *The World Market Atlas.*

Euromonitor Publications Limited, 87-88 Turnmill Street, London EC1M 5QU, England; *International Marketing Data and Statistics.*

G.K. Hall and Company, 70 Lincoln Street, Boston, Massachusetts 02111 (617) 423-3990; *The World in Figures.*

Inter-American Development Bank, 1300 New York Avenue, NW, Washington, D.C. 20577 (202) 623-1753; *Economic and Social Progress in Latin America.*

Organization of American States (OAS), General Secretariat, Washington, D.C. 20006 (202) 458-3533; *Statistical Bulletin of the OAS.*

Statistical Office of the United Nations, Publishing Service, New York, New York 10017 (800) 253-9646; *Statistical Yearbook,* and *Statistical Yearbook for Latin America and the Caribbean.*

Times Books, 201 East 50th Street, New York, New York 10022 (212) 751-2600; *The Economist Book of Vital World Statistics.*

U.C.L.A. Latin American Center Publications, University of California, Los Angeles, California 90024 (310) 825-6634; *Statistical Abstract of Latin America.*

EL SALVADOR - GROSS NATIONAL PRODUCT

Euromonitor Publications Limited, 87-88 Turnmill Street, London EC1M 5QU, England; *International Marketing Data and Statistics.*

Inter-American Development Bank, 1300 New York Avenue, NW, Washington, D.C. 20577 (202) 623-1753; *Economic and Social Progress in Latin America.*

U.S. Arms Control and Disarmament Agency, 320 Twenty-first Street, NW, Washington, D.C. 20451 (202) 647-8677; *World Military Expenditures and Arms Transfers.*

EL SALVADOR - GROUNDNUTS PRODUCTION - See EL SALVADOR - CROPS

EL SALVADOR - GROWTH - DOMESTIC PRODUCT

Facts on File, 460 Park Avenue South, New York, New York 10016 (800) 443-8323; *The New Book of World Rankings.*

EL SALVADOR - HEALTH

The Economist Intelligence Unit, 111 West 57th Street, New York, New York 10019 (800) 938-4685; *The New Latin America Market Atlas.*

Facts on File, 460 Park Avenue South, New York, New York 10016 (800) 443-8323; *The New Book of World Rankings.*

Federal Statistical Office, Gustav - Stresemann - Ring 11, D-6200 Wiesbaden, Germany; *El Salvador.*

G.K. Hall and Company, 70 Lincoln Street, Boston, Massachusetts 02111 (617) 423-3990; *The World in Figures.*

Statistical Office of the United Nations, Publishing Service, New York, New York 10017 (800) 253-9646; *Statistical Yearbook.*

Times Books, 201 East 50th Street, New York, New York 10022 (212) 751-2600; *The Economist Book of Vital World Statistics.*

U.C.L.A. Latin American Center Publications, University of California, Los Angeles, California 90024 (310) 825-6634; *Statistical Abstract of Latin America.*

World Health Organization, Office of Publications, Avenue Appia, CH-1211 Geneva, 27, Switzerland (Telephone Number in U.S. (518) 436-9686); *World Health Statistics Annual.*

EL SALVADOR - HEALTH EXPENDITURES

International Monetary Fund, 700 Nineteenth Street, NW, Washington, D.C. 20431 (202) 623-7000; *Government Finance Statistics Yearbook.*

Statistical Office of the United Nations, Publishing Service, New York, New York 10017 (800) 253-9646; *Statistical Yearbook for Latin America and the Caribbean.*

EL SALVADOR - HIDE PRODUCTION

Food and Agricultural Organization of the United Nations (FAO), Via delle Terme di Caracalla, 00100 Rome, Italy (Telephone Number in U.S. (202) 653-2400); *Production Yearbook.*

EL SALVADOR - HIGHWAYS

The Economist Intelligence Unit, 111 West 57th Street, New York, New York 10019 (800) 938-4685; *The New Latin America Market Atlas.*

G.K. Hall and Company, 70 Lincoln Street, Boston, Massachusetts 02111 (617) 423-3990; *The World in Figures.*

International Road Federation, 525 School Street, SW, Washington, D.C. 20024 (202) 554-2106; *World Road Statistics.*

EL SALVADOR - HORSES - See EL SALVADOR - LIVESTOCK AND POULTRY

EL SALVADOR - HOURS OF WORK - See EL SALVADOR - EMPLOYMENT

EL SALVADOR - HOUSING AND HOUSING UNITS

Facts on File, 460 Park Avenue South, New York, New York 10016 (800) 443-8323; *The New Book of World Rankings.*

Statistical Office of the United Nations, Publishing Service, New York, New York 10017 (800) 253-9646; *Statistical Yearbook for Latin America and the Caribbean.*

U.C.L.A. Latin American Center Publications, University of California, Los Angeles, California 90024 (310) 825-6634; *Statistical Abstract of Latin America.*

EL SALVADOR - HOUSING EXPENDITURES

International Monetary Fund, 700 Nineteenth Street, NW, Washington, D.C. 20431 (202) 623-7000; *Government Finance Statistics Yearbook.*

EL SALVADOR - ILLITERATE POPULATION

The Economist Intelligence Unit, 111 West 57th Street, New York, New York 10019 (800) 938-4685; *The New Latin America Market Atlas,* and *The World Market Atlas.*

G.K. Hall and Company, 70 Lincoln Street, Boston, Massachusetts 02111 (617) 423-3990; *The World in Figures.*

Statistical Office of the United Nations, Publishing Service, New York, New York 10017 (800) 253-9646; *Statistical Yearbook for Latin America and the Caribbean.*

United Nations Educational, Scientific and Cultural Organization (UNESCO), 7 Place de Fontenoy, F-75700 Paris, France (Telephone Number in U.S. (212) 963-5981); *Statistical Yearbook.*

EL SALVADOR - IMMIGRATION

U.C.L.A. Latin American Center Publications, University of California, Los Angeles, California 90024 (310) 825-6634; *Statistical Abstract of Latin America.*

EL SALVADOR - IMPORTS

The Economist Intelligence Unit, 111 West 57th Street, New York, New York 10019 (800) 938-4685; *The New Latin America Market Atlas,* and *The World Market Atlas.*

Euromonitor Publications Limited, 87-88 Turnmill Street, London EC1M 5QU, England; *International Marketing Data and Statistics.*

Food and Agricultural Organization of the United Nations (FAO) Via delle Terme di Caracalla, 00100 Rome, Italy (Telephone Number in U.S. (202) 653-2400); *The State of Food and Agriculture.*

G.K. Hall and Company, 70 Lincoln Street, Boston, Massachusetts 02111 (617) 423-3990; *The World in Figures.*

Inter-American Development Bank, 1300 New York Avenue, NW, Washington, D.C. 20577 (202) 623-1753; *Economic and Social Progress in Latin America.*

International Monetary Fund, 700 Nineteenth Street, NW, Washington, D.C. 20431 (202) 623-7000; *Direction of Trade Statistics, Government Finance Statistics Yearbook,* and *International Financial Statistics.*

Organization of American States (OAS), General Secretariat, Washington, D.C. 20006 (202) 458-3533; *Statistical Bulletin of the OAS.*

Statistical Office of the United Nations, Publishing Service, New York, New York 10017 (800) 253-9646; *Statistical Yearbook for Latin America and the Caribbean,* and *Trade in Manufactures of Developing Countries.*

Times Books, 201 East 50th Street, New York, New York 10022 (212) 751-2600; *The Economist Book of Vital World Statistics.*

EL SALVADOR - INCOME DISTRIBUTION

Statistical Office of the United Nations, Publishing Service, New York, New York 10017 (800) 253-9646; *Statistical Yearbook for Latin America and the Caribbean.*

U.C.L.A. Latin American Center Publications, University of California, Los Angeles, California 90024 (310) 825-6634; *Statistical Abstract of Latin America.*

EL SALVADOR - INCOME TAXES - See EL SALVADOR - TAXATION

EL SALVADOR - INDUSTRY

Euromonitor Publications Limited, 87-88 Turnmill Street, London EC1M 5QU, England; *International Marketing Data and Statistics.*

Facts on File, 460 Park Avenue South, New York, New York 10016 (800) 443-8323; *The New Book of World Rankings.*

Federal Statistical Office, Gustav - Stresemann - Ring 11, D-6200 Wiesbaden, Germany; *El Salvador.*

Gale Research Incorporated, 835 Penobscot Building, Detroit, Michigan 48226 (800) 877-4253; *International Historical Statistics The Americas and Australasia.*

G.K. Hall and Company, 70 Lincoln Street, Boston, Massachusetts 02111 (617) 423-3990; *The World in Figures.*

International Labour Office, I.L.O. Publications, CH-1211, Geneva 22, Switzerland; *Yearbook of Labour Statistics.*

Statistical Office of the United Nations, Publishing Service, New York, New York 10017 (800) 253-9646; *Economic Survey of Latin America and the Caribbean,* and *Statistical Yearbook.*

Times Books, 201 East 50th Street, New York, New York 10022 (212) 751-2600; *The Economist Book of Vital World Statistics.*

U.C.L.A. Latin American Center Publications, University of California, Los Angeles, California 90024 (310) 825-6634; *Statistical Abstract of Latin America.*

World Intellectual Property Organization, 34 Chemin des Colombettes, CH-1211 Geneva 20. Switzerland; *Industrial Property Statistics.*

EL SALVADOR - INFANT AND MATERNAL MORTALITY

The Economist Intelligence Unit, 111 West 57th Street, New York, New York 10019 (800) 938-4685; *The New Latin America Market Atlas.*

Statistical Office of the United Nations, Publishing Service, New York, New York 10017 (800) 253-9646; *Demographic Yearbook,* and *Statistical Yearbook.*

Times Books, 201 East 50th Street, New York, New York 10022 (212) 751-2600; *The Economist Book of Vital World Statistics.*

World Health Organization, Office of Publications, Avenue Appia, CH-1211 Geneva, 27, Switzerland (Telephone Number in U.S. (518) 436-9686); *World Health Statistics Annual.*

EL SALVADOR - INFLATIONARY FACTORS

Statistical Office of the United Nations, Publishing Service, New York, New York 10017 (800) 253-9646; *Economic Survey of Latin America and the Caribbean.*

EL SALVADOR - INTEREST RATES

Inter-American Development Bank, 1300 New York Avenue, NW, Washington, D.C. 20577 (202) 623-1753; *Economic and Social Progress in Latin America.*

EL SALVADOR - INTERNATIONAL FINANCE

Inter-American Development Bank, 1300 New York Avenue, NW, Washington, D.C. 20577 (202) 623-1753; *Economic and Social Progress in Latin America.*

U.C.L.A. Latin American Center Publications, University of California, Los Angeles, California 90024 (310) 825-6634; *Statistical Abstract of Latin America.*

EL SALVADOR - INTERNATIONAL LIQUIDITY

Inter-American Development Bank, 1300 New York Avenue, NW, Washington, D.C. 20577 (202) 623-1753; *Economic and Social Progress in Latin America.*

International Monetary Fund, 700 Nineteenth Street, NW, Washington, D.C. 20431 (202) 623-7000; *International Financial Statistics.*

EL SALVADOR - INTERNATIONAL RESERVES EXCLUDING GOLD

Inter-American Development Bank, 1300 New York Avenue, NW, Washington, D.C. 20577 (202) 623-1753; *Economic and Social Progress in Latin America.*

Statistical Office of the United Nations, Publishing Service, New York, New York 10017 (800) 253-9646; *Statistical Yearbook.*

EL SALVADOR - INTERNATIONAL STATISTICS

Inter-American Development Bank, 1300 New York Avenue, NW, Washington, D.C. 20577 (202) 623-1753; *Economic and Social Progress in Latin America.*

U.C.L.A. Latin American Center Publications, University of California, Los Angeles, California 90024 (310) 825-6634; *Statistical Abstract of Latin America.*

EL SALVADOR - INVESTMENT

Inter-American Development Bank, 1300 New York Avenue, NW, Washington, D.C. 20577 (202) 623-1753; *Economic and Social Progress in Latin America.*

Statistical Office of the United Nations, Publishing Service, New York, New York 10017 (800) 253-9646; *Statistical Yearbook for Latin America and the Caribbean.*

EL SALVADOR - IRON ORE PRODUCTION AND CONSUMPTION - See EL SALVADOR - MINING AND MINERAL PRODUCTS

EL SALVADOR - IRRIGATION

Euromonitor Publications Limited, 87-88 Turnmill Street, London EC1M 5QU, England; *International Marketing Data and Statistics.*

Inter-American Development Bank, 1300 New York Avenue, NW, Washington, D.C. 20577 (202) 623-1753; *Economic and Social Progress in Latin America.*

EL SALVADOR - JUTE PRODUCTION - See EL SALVADOR - CROPS

EL SALVADOR - LABOR FORCE

The Economist Intelligence Unit, 111 West 57th Street, New York, New York 10019 (800) 938-4685; *The New Latin America Market Atlas.*

Euromonitor Publications Limited, 87-88 Turnmill Street, London EC1M 5QU, England; *International Marketing Data and Statistics.*

Facts on File, 460 Park Avenue South, New York, New York 10016 (800) 443-8323; *The New Book of World Rankings.*

Food and Agricultural Organization of the United Nations (FAO) Via delle Terme di Caracalla, 00100 Rome, Italy (Telephone Number in U.S. (202) 653-2400); *The State of Food and Agriculture.*

G.K. Hall and Company, 70 Lincoln Street, Boston, Massachusetts 02111 (617) 423-3990; *The World in Figures.*

Gale Research Incorporated, 835 Penobscot Building, Detroit, Michigan 48226 (800) 877-4253; *International Historical Statistics The Americas and Australasia.*

EL SALVADOR - LABOR PRODUCTIVITY

International Labour Office, I.L.O. Publications, CH-1211, Geneva 22, Switzerland; *Yearbook of Labour Statistics.*

EL SALVADOR - LAND AREA

The Economist Intelligence Unit, 111 West 57th Street, New York, New York 10019 (800) 938-4685; *The New Latin America Market Atlas.*

EL SALVADOR - LAND USE

Euromonitor Publications Limited, 87-88 Turnmill Street, London EC1M 5QU, England; *International Marketing Data and Statistics.*

Food and Agricultural Organization of the United Nations (FAO), Via delle Terme di Caracalla, 00100 Rome, Italy (Telephone Number in U.S. (202) 653-2400); *Production Yearbook.*

G.K. Hall and Company, 70 Lincoln Street, Boston, Massachusetts 02111 (617) 423-3990; *The World in Figures.*

Inter-American Development Bank, 1300 New York Avenue, NW, Washington, D.C. 20577 (202) 623-1753; *Economic and Social Progress in Latin America.*

EL SALVADOR - LIBRARIES

Facts on File, 460 Park Avenue South, New York, New York 10016 (800) 443-8323; *The New Book of World Rankings.*

United Nations Educational, Scientific and Cultural Organization (UNESCO), 7 Place de Fontenoy, F-75700 Paris, France (Telephone Number in U.S. (212) 963-5981); *Statistical Yearbook.*

EL SALVADOR - LIFE EXPECTANCY RATE

The Economist Intelligence Unit, 111 West 57th Street, New York, New York 10019 (800) 938-4685; *The New Latin America Market Atlas.*

EL SALVADOR - LIVESTOCK AND POULTRY AND POULTRY

Euromonitor Publications Limited, 87-88 Turnmill Street, London EC1M 5QU, England; *International Marketing Data and Statistics.*

Facts on File, 460 Park Avenue South, New York, New York 10016 (800) 443-8323; *The New Book of World Rankings.*

Food and Agricultural Organization of the United Nations (FAO), Via delle Terme di Caracalla, 00100 Rome, Italy (Telephone Number in U.S. (202) 653-2400); *Production Yearbook*, and *The State of Food and Agriculture.*

G.K. Hall and Company, 70 Lincoln Street, Boston, Massachusetts 02111 (617) 423-3990; *The World in Figures.*

Statistical Office of the United Nations, Publishing Service, New York, New York 10017 (800) 253-9646; *Statistical Yearbook.*

EL SALVADOR - LIVING LEVELS

G.K. Hall and Company, 70 Lincoln Street, Boston, Massachusetts 02111 (617) 423-3990; *The World in Figures.*

Statistical Office of the United Nations, Publishing Service, New York, New York 10017 (800) 253-9646; *Statistical Yearbook for Latin America and the Caribbean.*

Times Books, 201 East 50th Street, New York, New York 10022 (212) 751-2600; *The Economist Book of Vital World Statistics.*

EL SALVADOR - MAIL - NUMBER OF PIECES SENT OR RECEIVED

Statistical Office of the United Nations, Publishing Service, New York, New York 10017 (800) 253-9646; *Statistical Yearbook.*

EL SALVADOR - MAIN ECONOMIC INDICATORS - See EL SALVADOR - ECONOMY

EL SALVADOR - MANUFACTURING

The Economist Intelligence Unit, 111 West 57th Street, New York, New York 10019 (800) 938-4685; *The New Latin America Market Atlas.*

Facts on File, 460 Park Avenue South, New York, New York 10016 (800) 443-8323; *The New Book of World Rankings.*

G.K. Hall and Company, 70 Lincoln Street, Boston, Massachusetts 02111 (617) 423-3990; *The World in Figures.*

Inter-American Development Bank, 1300 New York Avenue, NW, Washington, D.C. 20577 (202) 623-1753; *Economic and Social Progress in Latin America.*

Statistical Office of the United Nations, Publishing Service, New York, New York 10017 (800) 253-9646; *Statistical Yearbook*, and *Statistical Yearbook for Latin America and the Caribbean.*

Times Books, 201 East 50th Street, New York, New York 10022 (212) 751-2600; *The Economist Book of Vital World Statistics.*

EL SALVADOR - MARRIAGE RATES

Facts on File, 460 Park Avenue South, New York, New York 10016 (800) 443-8323; *The New Book of World Rankings.*

Statistical Office of the United Nations, Publishing Service, New York, New York 10017 (800) 253-9646; *Demographic Yearbook*, and *Statistical Yearbook.*

EL SALVADOR - MEAT PRODUCTION - See EL SALVADOR - LIVESTOCK AND POULTRY

EL SALVADOR - MEDICAL PERSONNEL

U.C.L.A. Latin American Center Publications, University of California, Los Angeles, California 90024 (310) 825-6634; *Statistical Abstract of Latin America.*

EL SALVADOR - MERCHANT SHIPPING

G.K. Hall and Company, 70 Lincoln Street, Boston, Massachusetts 02111 (617) 423-3990; *The World in Figures.*

Statistical Office of the United Nations, Publishing Service, New York, New York 10017 (800) 253-9646; *Statistical Yearbook.*

Times Books, 201 East 50th Street, New York, New York 10022 (212) 751-2600; *The Economist Book of Vital World Statistics.*

U.S. Department of Transportation, Maritime Administration, 400 Seventh Street, SW, Washington, D.C. 20590 (202) 366-5807; *A Statistical Analysis of the World's Merchant Fleets.*

EL SALVADOR - MILITARY

The Economist Intelligence Unit, 111 West 57th Street, New York, New York 10019 (800) 938-4685; *The New Latin America Market Atlas.*

G.K. Hall and Company, 70 Lincoln Street, Boston, Massachusetts 02111 (617) 423-3990; *The World in Figures.*

The International Institute for Strategic Studies, 23 Tavistock Street, London WC2E 7NQ, England; *The Military Balance.*

U.C.L.A. Latin American Center Publications, University of California, Los Angeles, California 90024 (310) 825-6634; *Statistical Abstract of Latin America.*

U.S. Arms Control and Disarmament Agency, 320 Twenty-first Street, NW, Washington, D.C. 20451 (202) 647-8677; *World Military Expenditures and Arms Transfers.*

EL SALVADOR - MILK PRODUCTION - See EL SALVADOR - DAIRY PRODUCTS

EL SALVADOR - MINING AND MINERAL PRODUCTS

The Economist Intelligence Unit, 111 West 57th Street, New York, New York 10019 (800) 938-4685; *The New Latin America Market Atlas.*

G.K. Hall and Company, 70 Lincoln Street, Boston, Massachusetts 02111 (617) 423-3990; *The World in Figures.*

Inter-American Development Bank, 1300 New York Avenue, NW, Washington, D.C. 20577 (202) 623-1753; *Economic and Social Progress in Latin America.*

Statistical Office of the United Nations, Publishing Service, New York, New York 10017 (800) 253-9646; *Statistical Yearbook for Latin America and the Caribbean.*

U.C.L.A. Latin American Center Publications, University of California, Los Angeles, California 90024 (310) 825-6634; *Statistical Abstract of Latin America.*

EL SALVADOR - MONEY EXCHANGE RATE

Euromonitor Publications Limited, 87-88 Turnmill Street, London EC1M 5QU, England; *International Marketing Data and Statistics.*

Inter-American Development Bank, 1300 New York Avenue, NW, Washington, D.C. 20577 (202) 623-1753; *Economic and Social Progress in Latin America.*

International Monetary Fund, 700 Nineteenth Street, NW, Washington, D.C. 20431 (202) 623-7000; *International Financial Statistics.*

Statistical Office of the United Nations, Publishing Service, New York, New York 10017 (800) 253-9646; *Statistical Yearbook.*

EL SALVADOR - MONEY RATES - MARKET

Inter-American Development Bank, 1300 New York Avenue, NW, Washington, D.C. 20577 (202) 623-1753; *Economic and Social Progress in Latin America.*

EL SALVADOR - MONEY RESERVES

Euromonitor Publications Limited, 87-88 Turnmill Street, London EC1M 5QU, England; *International Marketing Data and Statistics.*

Inter-American Development Bank, 1300 New York Avenue, NW, Washington, D.C. 20577 (202) 623-1753; *Economic and Social Progress in Latin America.*

EL SALVADOR - MONEY SUPPLY

Euromonitor Publications Limited, 87-88 Turnmill Street, London EC1M 5QU, England; *International Marketing Data and Statistics.*

Federal Statistical Office, Gustav - Stresemann - Ring 11, D-6200 Wiesbaden, Germany; *El Salvador.*

G.K. Hall and Company, 70 Lincoln Street, Boston, Massachusetts 02111 (617) 423-3990; *The World in Figures.*

Inter-American Development Bank, 1300 New York Avenue, NW, Washington, D.C. 20577 (202) 623-1753; *Economic and Social Progress in Latin America.*

International Monetary Fund, 700 Nineteenth Street, NW, Washington, D.C. 20431 (202) 623-7000; *International Financial Statistics.*

Statistical Office of the United Nations, Publishing Service, New York, New York 10017 (800) 253-9646; *Statistical Yearbook.*

U.C.L.A. Latin American Center Publications, University of California, Los Angeles, California 90024 (310) 825-6634; *Statistical Abstract of Latin America.*

EL SALVADOR - MOTION PICTURES

Statistical Office of the United Nations, Publishing Service, New York, New York 10017 (800) 253-9646; *Statistical Yearbook.*

EL SALVADOR - MOTOR VEHICLE PRODUCTION

Statistical Office of the United Nations, Publishing Service, New York, New York 10017 (800) 253-9646; *Statistical Yearbook.*

EL SALVADOR - MOTOR VEHICLE TAXES - See EL SALVADOR - TAXATION

EL SALVADOR - MOTOR VEHICLES IN USE

The Economist Intelligence Unit, 111 West 57th Street, New York, New York 10019 (800) 938-4685; *The New Latin America Market Atlas.*

G.K. Hall and Company, 70 Lincoln Street, Boston, Massachusetts 02111 (617) 423-3990; *The World in Figures.*

International Road Federation, 525 School Street, SW, Washington, D.C. 20024 (202) 554-2106; *World Road Statistics.*

Statistical Office of the United Nations, Publishing Service, New York, New York 10017 (800) 253-9646; *Statistical Yearbook.*

Times Books, 201 East 50th Street, New York, New York 10022 (212) 751-2600; *The Economist Book of Vital World Statistics.*

EL SALVADOR - MULES - See EL SALVADOR - LIVESTOCK AND POULTRY

EL SALVADOR - MUSEUMS

Facts on File, 460 Park Avenue South, New York, New York 10016 (800) 443-8323; *The New Book of World Rankings.*

United Nations Educational, Scientific and Cultural Organization (UNESCO), 7 Place de Fontenoy, F-75700 Paris, France (Telephone Number in U.S. (212) 963-5981); *Statistical Yearbook.*

EL SALVADOR - NATALITY - See EL SALVADOR - BIRTH RATE

EL SALVADOR - NATIONAL ACCOUNTS

Federal Statistical Office, Gustav - Stresemann - Ring 11, D-6200 Wiesbaden, Germany; *El Salvador.*

Gale Research Incorporated, 835 Penobscot Building, Detroit, Michigan 48226 (800) 877-4253; *International Historical Statistics The Americas and Australasia.*

Inter-American Development Bank, 1300 New York Avenue, NW, Washington, D.C. 20577 (202) 623-1753; *Economic and Social Progress in Latin America.*

International Monetary Fund, 700 Nineteenth Street, NW, Washington, D.C. 20431 (202) 623-7000; *International Financial Statistics.*

Organization of American States (OAS), General Secretariat, Washington, D.C. 20006 (202) 458-3533; *Statistical Bulletin of the OAS.*

Statistical Office of the United Nations, Publishing Service, New York, New York 10017 (800) 253-9646; *National Accounts Statistics,* and *Statistical Yearbook.*

U.C.L.A. Latin American Center Publications, University of California, Los Angeles, California 90024 (310) 825-6634; *Statistical Abstract of Latin America.*

EL SALVADOR - NATIONAL INCOME

Facts on File, 460 Park Avenue South, New York, New York 10016 (800) 443-8323; *The New Book of World Rankings.*

G.K. Hall and Company, 70 Lincoln Street, Boston, Massachusetts 02111 (617) 423-3990; *The World in Figures.*

Inter-American Development Bank, 1300 New York Avenue, NW, Washington, D.C. 20577 (202) 623-1753; *Economic and Social Progress in Latin America.*

International Monetary Fund, 700 Nineteenth Street, NW, Washington, D.C. 20431 (202) 623-7000; *International Financial Statistics.*

Statistical Office of the United Nations, Publishing Service, New York, New York 10017 (800) 253-9646; *Statistical Yearbook.*

EL SALVADOR - NATIONAL PRODUCT

Facts on File, 460 Park Avenue South, New York, New York 10016 (800) 443-8323; *The New Book of World Rankings.*

Statistical Office of the United Nations, Publishing Service, New York, New York 10017 (800) 253-9646; *Statistical Yearbook.*

EL SALVADOR - NATURAL GAS PRODUCTION - See EL SALVADOR - MINING AND MINERAL PRODUCTS

EL SALVADOR - NEWSPAPER PRODUCTION - See EL SALVADOR - FORESTRY AND FOREST PRODUCTS

EL SALVADOR - NEWSPRINT - See EL SALVADOR - FORESTRY AND FOREST PRODUCTS

EL SALVADOR - NUTRITION

Statistical Office of the United Nations, Publishing Service, New York, New York 10017 (800) 253-9646; *Statistical Yearbook for Latin America and the Caribbean.*

EL SALVADOR - OCCUPATIONS - See EL SALVADOR - LABOR FORCE

EL SALVADOR - PAPER - See EL SALVADOR - FORESTRY AND FOREST PRODUCTS

EL SALVADOR - PATENTS

Statistical Office of the United Nations, Publishing Service, New York, New York 10017 (800) 253-9646; *Statistical Yearbook.*

World Intellectual Property Organization, 34 Chemin des Colombettes, CH-1211 Geneva 20. Switzerland; *Industrial Property Statistics.*

EL SALVADOR - PEANUT PRODUCTION - See EL SALVADOR - CROPS

EL SALVADOR - PESTICIDE USE

Food and Agricultural Organization of the United Nations (FAO) Via delle Terme di Caracalla, 00100 Rome, Italy (Telephone Number in U.S. (202) 653-2400); *The State of Food and Agriculture.*

EL SALVADOR - PETROLEUM INDUSTRY

The Economist Intelligence Unit, 111 West 57th Street, New York, New York 10019 (800) 938-4685; *The New Latin America Market Atlas.*

Facts on File, 460 Park Avenue South, New York, New York 10016 (800) 443-8323; *The New Book of World Rankings.*

Food and Agricultural Organization of the United Nations (FAO) Via delle Terme di Caracalla, 00100 Rome, Italy (Telephone Number in U.S. (202) 653-2400); *The State of Food and Agriculture.*

G.K. Hall and Company, 70 Lincoln Street, Boston, Massachusetts 02111 (617) 423-3990; *The World in Figures.*

Inter-American Development Bank, 1300 New York Avenue, NW, Washington, D.C. 20577 (202) 623-1753; *Economic and Social Progress in Latin America.*

Statistical Office of the United Nations, Publishing Service, New York, New York 10017 (800) 253-9646; *Statistical Yearbook.*

EL SALVADOR - PIGS - See EL SALVADOR - LIVESTOCK AND POULTRY

EL SALVADOR - POLITICAL DATA

U.C.L.A. Latin American Center Publications, University of California, Los Angeles, California 90024 (310) 825-6634; *Statistical Abstract of Latin America.*

EL SALVADOR - POPULATION

The Economist Intelligence Unit, 111 West 57th Street, New York, New York 10019 (800) 938-4685; *The New Latin America Market Atlas*, and *The World Market Atlas*.

Euromonitor Publications Limited, 87-88 Turnmill Street, London EC1M 5QU, England; *International Marketing Data and Statistics*.

Facts on File, 460 Park Avenue South, New York, New York 10016 (800) 443-8323; *The New Book of World Rankings*.

Federal Statistical Office, Gustav - Stresemann - Ring 11, D-6200 Wiesbaden, Germany; *El Salvador*.

Food and Agricultural Organization of the United Nations (FAO), Via delle Terme di Caracalla, 00100 Rome, Italy (Telephone Number in U.S. (202) 653-2400); *Production Yearbook*.

Gale Research Incorporated, 835 Penobscot Building, Detroit, Michigan 48226 (800) 877-4253; *International Historical Statistics The Americas and Australasia*.

G.K. Hall and Company, 70 Lincoln Street, Boston, Massachusetts 02111 (617) 423-3990; *The World in Figures*.

Inter-American Development Bank, 1300 New York Avenue, NW, Washington, D.C. 20577 (202) 623-1753; *Economic and Social Progress in Latin America*.

International Labour Office, I.L.O. Publications, CH-1211, Geneva 22, Switzerland; *Yearbook of Labour Statistics*.
Organization of American States (OAS), General Secretariat, Washington, D.C. 20006 (202) 458-3533; *Statistical Bulletin of the OAS*.

Statistical Office of the United Nations, Publishing Service, New York, New York 10017 (800) 253-9646; *Demographic Yearbook, Statistical Yearbook*, and *Statistical Yearbook for Latin America and the Caribbean*.

Times Books, 201 East 50th Street, New York, New York 10022 (212) 751-2600; *The Economist Book of Vital World Statistics*.

U.C.L.A. Latin American Center Publications, University of California, Los Angeles, California 90024 (310) 825-6634; *Statistical Abstract of Latin America*.

United Nations Educational, Scientific and Cultural Organization (UNESCO), 7 Place de Fontenoy, F-75700 Paris, France (Telephone Number in U.S. (212) 963-5981); *Statistical Yearbook*.

U.S. Arms Control and Disarmament Agency, 320 Twenty-first Street, NW, Washington, D.C. 20451 (202) 647-8677; *World Military Expenditures and Arms Transfers*.

World Health Organization, Office of Publications, Avenue Appia, CH-1211 Geneva, 27, Switzerland (Telephone Number in U.S. (518) 436-9686); *World Health Statistics Annual*.

EL SALVADOR - POST OFFICES

Facts on File, 460 Park Avenue South, New York, New York 10016 (800) 443-8323; *The New Book of World Rankings*.

EL SALVADOR - POTATO PRODUCTION - See EL SALVADOR - CROPS

EL SALVADOR - PRICES

Facts on File, 460 Park Avenue South, New York, New York 10016 (800) 443-8323; *The New Book of World Rankings*.

Federal Statistical Office, Gustav - Stresemann - Ring 11, D-6200 Wiesbaden, Germany; *El Salvador*.

Food and Agricultural Organization of the United Nations (FAO), Via delle Terme di Caracalla, 00100 Rome, Italy (Telephone Number in U.S. (202) 653-2400); *Production Yearbook*, and *The State of Food and Agriculture*.

Gale Research Incorporated, 835 Penobscot Building, Detroit, Michigan 48226 (800) 877-4253; *International Historical Statistics The Americas and Australasia*.

G.K. Hall and Company, 70 Lincoln Street, Boston, Massachusetts 02111 (617) 423-3990; *The World in Figures*.

International Labour Office, I.L.O. Publications, CH-1211, Geneva 22, Switzerland; *Yearbook of Labour Statistics*.

International Monetary Fund, 700 Nineteenth Street, NW, Washington, D.C. 20431 (202) 623-7000; *International Financial Statistics*.

Statistical Office of the United Nations, Publishing Service, New York, New York 10017 (800) 253-9646; *Statistical Yearbook for Latin America and the Caribbean*.

EL SALVADOR - PRINTING AND WRITING PAPER - See EL SALVADOR - FORESTRY AND FOREST PRODUCTS

EL SALVADOR - PRODUCTION

Facts on File, 460 Park Avenue South, New York, New York 10016 (800) 443-8323; *The New Book of World Rankings*.

G.K. Hall and Company, 70 Lincoln Street, Boston, Massachusetts 02111 (617) 423-3990; *The World in Figures*.

EL SALVADOR - PRODUCTIVITY

Euromonitor Publications Limited, 87-88 Turnmill Street, London EC1M 5QU, England; *International Marketing Data and Statistics*.

EL SALVADOR - PROPERTY TAXES - See EL SALVADOR - TAXATION

EL SALVADOR - PUBLIC CONSUMPTION FUND

Inter-American Development Bank, 1300 New York Avenue, NW, Washington, D.C. 20577 (202) 623-1753; *Economic and Social Progress in Latin America*.

EL SALVADOR - PUBLIC EXPENDITURES

Inter-American Development Bank, 1300 New York Avenue, NW, Washington, D.C. 20577 (202) 623-1753; *Economic and Social Progress in Latin America*.

Organization of American States (OAS), General Secretariat, Washington, D.C. 20006 (202) 458-3533; *Statistical Bulletin of the OAS*.

Statistical Office of the United Nations, Publishing Service, New York, New York 10017 (800) 253-9646; *Statistical Yearbook for Latin America and the Caribbean*.

EL SALVADOR - PUBLIC FINANCE

Facts on File, 460 Park Avenue South, New York, New York 10016 (800) 443-8323; *The New Book of World Rankings.*

Federal Statistical Office, Gustav - Stresemann - Ring 11, D-6200 Wiesbaden, Germany; *El Salvador.*

Inter-American Development Bank, 1300 New York Avenue, NW, Washington, D.C. 20577 (202) 623-1753; *Economic and Social Progress in Latin America.*

Organization of American States (OAS), General Secretariat, Washington, D.C. 20006 (202) 458-3533; *Statistical Bulletin of the OAS.*

EL SALVADOR - PUBLIC REVENUE

Inter-American Development Bank, 1300 New York Avenue, NW, Washington, D.C. 20577 (202) 623-1753; *Economic and Social Progress in Latin America.*

Organization of American States (OAS), General Secretariat, Washington, D.C. 20006 (202) 458-3533; *Statistical Bulletin of the OAS.*

EL SALVADOR - RADIO BROADCASTING - See EL SALVADOR - BROADCASTING

EL SALVADOR - RAILWAYS

The Economist Intelligence Unit, 111 West 57th Street, New York, New York 10019 (800) 938-4685; *The New Latin America Market Atlas.*

G.K. Hall and Company, 70 Lincoln Street, Boston, Massachusetts 02111 (617) 423-3990; *The World in Figures.*

Jane's Information Group, Sentinel House, 163 Brighton Road, Coulsdon, Surrey CR5 2NH, England (Telephone Number in U.S. (703) 683-3700); *Jane's World Railways.*

EL SALVADOR - RANCHING

U.C.L.A. Latin American Center Publications, University of California, Los Angeles, California 90024 (310) 825-6634; *Statistical Abstract of Latin America.*

EL SALVADOR - RELIGION

Facts on File, 460 Park Avenue South, New York, New York 10016 (800) 443-8323; *The New Book of World Rankings.*

U.C.L.A. Latin American Center Publications, University of California, Los Angeles, California 90024 (310) 825-6634; *Statistical Abstract of Latin America.*

EL SALVADOR - RENT PRICES

International Labour Office, I.L.O. Publications, CH-1211, Geneva 22, Switzerland; *Yearbook of Labour Statistics.*

EL SALVADOR - RESERVES EXCLUDING GOLD

The Economist Intelligence Unit, 111 West 57th Street, New York, New York 10019 (800) 938-4685; *The New Latin America Market Atlas.*

EL SALVADOR - RETAIL TRADE

G.K. Hall and Company, 70 Lincoln Street, Boston, Massachusetts 02111 (617) 423-3990; *The World in Figures.*

Inter-American Development Bank, 1300 New York Avenue, NW, Washington, D.C. 20577 (202) 623-1753; *Economic and Social Progress in Latin America.*

Statistical Office of the United Nations, Publishing Service, New York, New York 10017 (800) 253-9646; *Statistical Yearbook.*

EL SALVADOR - RICE PRODUCTION - See EL SALVADOR - CROPS

EL SALVADOR - ROOT AND TUBER PRODUCTION - See EL SALVADOR - CROPS

EL SALVADOR - ROUNDWOOD PRODUCTION - See EL SALVADOR - FORESTRY AND FOREST PRODUCTS

EL SALVADOR - RUBBER PRODUCTION

Facts on File, 460 Park Avenue South, New York, New York 10016 (800) 443-8323; *The New Book of World Rankings.*

EL SALVADOR - SAWNWOOD PRODUCTION - See EL SALVADOR - FORESTRY AND FOREST PRODUCTS

EL SALVADOR - SCIENCE AND TECHNOLOGY

U.C.L.A. Latin American Center Publications, University of California, Los Angeles, California 90024 (310) 825-6634; *Statistical Abstract of Latin America.*

EL SALVADOR - SCIENTISTS AND TECHNOLOGISTS

Statistical Office of the United Nations, Publishing Service, New York, New York 10017 (800) 253-9646; *Statistical Yearbook.*

EL SALVADOR - SENIOR CITIZENS

Facts on File, 460 Park Avenue South, New York, New York 10016 (800) 443-8323; *The New Book of World Rankings.*

EL SALVADOR - SESAME SEED PRODUCTION - See EL SALVADOR - CROPS

EL SALVADOR - SHEEP - See EL SALVADOR - LIVESTOCK AND POULTRY

EL SALVADOR - SILVER PRODUCTION AND CONSUMPTION - See EL SALVADOR - MINING AND MINERAL PRODUCTS

EL SALVADOR - SOCIAL DATA

Facts on File, 460 Park Avenue South, New York, New York 10016 (800) 443-8323; *The New Book of World Rankings.*

G.K. Hall and Company, 70 Lincoln Street, Boston, Massachusetts 02111 (617) 423-3990; *The World in Figures.*

U.C.L.A. Latin American Center Publications, University of California, Los Angeles, California 90024 (310) 825-6634; *Statistical Abstract of Latin America.*

EL SALVADOR - SOCIAL SECURITY

Inter-American Development Bank, 1300 New York Avenue, NW, Washington, D.C. 20577 (202) 623-1753; *Economic and Social*

Progress in Latin America.

International Monetary Fund, 700 Nineteenth Street, NW, Washington, D.C. 20431 (202) 623-7000; *Government Finance Statistics Yearbook.*

EL SALVADOR - SOCIOECONOMIC DATA

Inter-American Development Bank, 1300 New York Avenue, NW, Washington, D.C. 20577 (202) 623-1753; *Economic and Social Progress in Latin America.*

U.C.L.A. Latin American Center Publications, University of California, Los Angeles, California 90024 (310) 825-6634; *Statistical Abstract of Latin America.*

EL SALVADOR - SOYBEAN PRODUCTION - See EL SALVADOR - CROPS

EL SALVADOR - STAMP TAXES AND DUTIES - See EL SALVADOR - TAXATION

EL SALVADOR - STATE BUDGET REVENUE AND EXPENDITURES

Euromonitor Publications Limited, 87-88 Turnmill Street, London EC1M 5QU, England; *International Marketing Data and Statistics.*

Inter-American Development Bank, 1300 New York Avenue, NW, Washington, D.C. 20577 (202) 623-1753; *Economic and Social Progress in Latin America.*

EL SALVADOR - STEEL - See EL SALVADOR - MINING AND MINERAL PRODUCTS

EL SALVADOR - STOCKS - COMMODITY - MARKET PRICE - INDEX

Food and Agricultural Organization of the United Nations (FAO) Via delle Terme di Caracalla, 00100 Rome, Italy (Telephone Number in U.S. (202) 653-2400); *The State of Food and Agriculture.*

EL SALVADOR - SUGAR - See EL SALVADOR - CROPS

EL SALVADOR - SULPHURIC ACID PRODUCTION

Statistical Office of the United Nations, Publishing Service, New York, New York 10017 (800) 253-9646; *Statistical Yearbook.*

EL SALVADOR - TAXATION

G.K. Hall and Company, 70 Lincoln Street, Boston, Massachusetts 02111 (617) 423-3990; *The World in Figures.*

Inter-American Development Bank, 1300 New York Avenue, NW, Washington, D.C. 20577 (202) 623-1753; *Economic and Social Progress in Latin America.*

International Monetary Fund, 700 Nineteenth Street, NW, Washington, D.C. 20431 (202) 623-7000; *Government Finance Statistics Yearbook.*

International Road Federation, 525 School Street, SW, Washington, D.C. 20024 (202) 554-2106; *World Road Statistics.*

Statistical Office of the United Nations, Publishing Service, New York, New York 10017 (800) 253-9646; *Statistical Yearbook for Latin America and the Caribbean.*

Time Books, 201 East 50th Street, New York, New York 10022 (212) 751-2600; *The Economic Book of Vital World Statistics.*

EL SALVADOR - TELEGRAPH SERVICE

Statistical Office of the United Nations, Publishing Service, New York, New York 10017 (800) 253-9646; *Statistical Yearbook.*

EL SALVADOR - TELEPHONES IN USE

American Telephone and Telegraph Company, 26 Parsippany Road, Whippany, New Jersey 07981 (800) 338-4038; *The World's Telephones.*

The Economist Intelligence Unit, 111 West 57th Street, New York, New York 10019 (800) 938-4685; *The New Latin America Market Atlas.*

G.K. Hall and Company, 70 Lincoln Street, Boston, Massachusetts 02111 (617) 423-3990; *The World in Figures.*

Statistical Office of the United Nations, Publishing Service, New York, New York 10017 (800) 253-9646; *Statistical Yearbook.*

EL SALVADOR - TELEVISION BROADCASTING - See EL SALVADOR - BROADCASTING

EL SALVADOR - TELEVISION RECEIVER PRODUCTION

Statistical Office of the United Nations, Publishing Service, New York, New York 10017 (800) 253-9646; *Statistical Yearbook.*

EL SALVADOR - TEXTILE INDUSTRY

G.K. Hall and Company, 70 Lincoln Street, Boston, Massachusetts 02111 (617) 423-3990; *The World in Figures.*

Statistical Office of the United Nations, Publishing Service, New York, New York 10017 (800) 253-9646; *Statistical Yearbook.*

EL SALVADOR - TOBACCO PRODUCTION

Facts on File, 460 Park Avenue South, New York, New York 10016 (800) 443-8323; *The New Book of World Rankings.*

Statistical Office of the United Nations, Publishing Service, New York, New York 10017 (800) 253-9646; *Statistical Yearbook.*

EL SALVADOR - TOURISM

The Economist Intelligence Unit, 111 West 57th Street, New York, New York 10019 (800) 938-4685; *The New Latin America Market Atlas.*

Facts on File, 460 Park Avenue South, New York, New York 10016 (800) 443-8323; *The New Book of World Rankings.*

Federal Statistical Office, Gustav - Stresemann - Ring 11, D-6200 Wiesbaden, Germany; *El Salvador.*

G.K. Hall and Company, 70 Lincoln Street, Boston, Massachusetts 02111 (617) 423-3990; *The World in Figures.*

Statistical Office of the United Nations, Publishing Service, New York, New York 10017 (800) 253-9646; *Statistical Yearbook,* and *Statistical Yearbook for Latin America and the Caribbean.*

Times Books, 201 East 50th Street, New York, New York 10022 (212) 751-2600; *The Economist Book of Vital World Statistics.*

U.C.L.A. Latin American Center Publications, University of California, Los Angeles, California 90024 (310) 825-6634; *Statistical*

Abstract of Latin America.

World Tourism Organization, Calle Capitan Haya 42, E-28020 Madrid, Spain; *Yearbook of Tourism Statistics.*

EL SALVADOR - TRACTORS IN USE

The Economist Intelligence Unit, 111 West 57th Street, New York, New York 10019 (800) 938-4685; *The New Latin America Market Atlas.*

Statistical Office of the United Nations, Publishing Service, New York, New York 10017 (800) 253-9646; *Statistical Yearbook.*

EL SALVADOR - TRADE - See EL SALVADOR - FOREIGN TRADE

EL SALVADOR - TRADEMARKS AND SERVICE MARKS

Statistical Office of the United Nations, Publishing Service, New York, New York 10017 (800) 253-9646; *Statistical Yearbook.*

World Intellectual Property Organization, 34 Chemin des Colombettes, CH-1211 Geneva 20. Switzerland; *Industrial Property Statistics.*

EL SALVADOR - TRANSPORTATION AND COMMUNICATIONS

The Economist Intelligence Unit, 111 West 57th Street, New York, New York 10019 (800) 938-4685; *The New Latin America Market Atlas.*

Facts on File, 460 Park Avenue South, New York, New York 10016 (800) 443-8323; *The New Book of World Rankings.*

Federal Statistical Office, Gustav - Stresemann - Ring 11, D-6200 Wiesbaden, Germany; *El Salvador.*

Gale Research Incorporated, 835 Penobscot Building, Detroit, Michigan 48226 (800) 877-4253; *International Historical Statistics The Americas and Australasia.*

G.K. Hall and Company, 70 Lincoln Street, Boston, Massachusetts 02111 (617) 423-3990; *The World in Figures.*

Inter-American Development Bank, 1300 New York Avenue, NW, Washington, D.C. 20577 (202) 623-1753; *Economic and Social Progress in Latin America.*

Statistical Office of the United Nations, Publishing Service, New York, New York 10017 (800) 253-9646; *Statistical Yearbook for Latin America and the Caribbean.*

U.C.L.A. Latin American Center Publications, University of California, Los Angeles, California 90024 (310) 825-6634; *Statistical Abstract of Latin America.*

EL SALVADOR - UNEMPLOYMENT

The Economist Intelligence Unit, 111 West 57th Street, New York, New York 10019 (800) 938-4685; *The New Latin America Market Atlas.*

Euromonitor Publications Limited, 87-88 Turnmill Street, London EC1M 5QU, England; *International Marketing Data and Statistics.*

International Labour Office, I.L.O. Publications, CH-1211, Geneva 22, Switzerland; *Yearbook of Labour Statistics.*

U.C.L.A. Latin American Center Publications, University of California, Los Angeles, California 90024 (310) 825-6634; *Statistical Abstract of Latin America.*

EL SALVADOR - UTILITIES

U.C.L.A. Latin American Center Publications, University of California, Los Angeles, California 90024 (310) 825-6634; *Statistical Abstract of Latin America.*

EL SALVADOR - VITAL STATISTICS

Euromonitor Publications Limited, 87-88 Turnmill Street, London EC1M 5QU, England; *International Marketing Data and Statistics.*

Gale Research Incorporated, 835 Penobscot Building, Detroit, Michigan 48226 (800) 877-4253; *International Historical Statistics The Americas and Australasia.*

G.K. Hall and Company, 70 Lincoln Street, Boston, Massachusetts 02111 (617) 423-3990; *The World in Figures.*

Statistical Office of the United Nations, Publishing Service, New York, New York 10017 (800) 253-9646; *Statistical Yearbook.*

World Health Organization, Office of Publications, Avenue Appia, CH-1211 Geneva 27, Switzerland (Telephone Number in U.S. (518) 436-9686); *World Health Statistics Annual.*

EL SALVADOR - WAGES

Federal Statistical Office, Gustav - Stresemann - Ring 11, D-6200 Wiesbaden, Germany; *El Salvador.*

G.K. Hall and Company, 70 Lincoln Street, Boston, Massachusetts 02111 (617) 423-3990; *The World in Figures.*

International Labour Office, I.L.O. Publications, CH-1211, Geneva 22, Switzerland; *Yearbook of Labour Statistics.*

Statistical Office of the United Nations, Publishing Service, New York, New York 10017 (800) 253-9646; *Statistical Yearbook.*

U.C.L.A. Latin American Center Publications, University of California, Los Angeles, California 90024 (310) 825-6634; *Statistical Abstract of Latin America.*

EL SALVADOR - WEATHER

Facts on File, 460 Park Avenue South, New York, New York 10016 (800) 443-8323; *The New Book of World Rankings.*

G.K. Hall and Company, 70 Lincoln Street, Boston, Massachusetts 02111 (617) 423-3990; *The World in Figures.*

EL SALVADOR - WELFARE

Inter-American Development Bank, 1300 New York Avenue, NW, Washington, D.C. 20577 (202) 623-1753; *Economic and Social Progress in Latin America.*

International Monetary Fund, 700 Nineteenth Street, NW, Washington, D.C. 20431 (202) 623-7000; *Government Finance Statistics Yearbook.*

EL SALVADOR - WHEAT - See EL SALVADOR - CROPS

EL SALVADOR - WHOLESALE PRICES

Inter-American Development Bank, 1300 New York Avenue, NW, Washington, D.C. 20577 (202) 623-1753; *Economic and Social Progress in Latin America.*

International Monetary Fund, 700 Nineteenth Street, NW, Washington, D.C. 20431 (202) 623-7000; *International Financial Statistics.*

Organization of American States (OAS), General Secretariat, Washington, D.C. 20006 (202) 458-3533; *Statistical Bulletin of the OAS.*

Statistical Office of the United Nations, Publishing Service, New York, New York 10017 (800) 253-9646; *Statistical Yearbook.*

EL SALVADOR - WHOLESALE TRADE

Inter-American Development Bank, 1300 New York Avenue, NW, Washington, D.C. 20577 (202) 623-1753; *Economic and Social Progress in Latin America.*

Statistical Office of the United Nations, Publishing Service, New York, New York 10017 (800) 253-9646; *Statistical Yearbook.*

EL SALVADOR - WINE PRODUCTION

Facts on File, 460 Park Avenue South, New York, New York 10016 (800) 443-8323; *The New Book of World Rankings.*

EL SALVADOR - WOOL PRODUCTION

Facts on File, 460 Park Avenue South, New York, New York 10016 (800) 443-8323; *The New Book of World Rankings.*

EL SALVADOR - YARN PRODUCTION

Statistical Office of the United Nations, Publishing Service, New York, New York 10017 (800) 253-9646; *Statistical Yearbook.*

ELDERLY - See also POPULATION

ELDERLY - ADULT EDUCATION

U.S. Department of Education, National Center for Education Statistics, 400 Maryland Avenue, SW, Washington, D.C. 20202 (202) 708-5366; *Adult Education Profile.*

ELDERLY - AGE AND/OR SEX

U.S. Department of Commerce, Bureau of the Census, Suitland, Maryland 20233 (301) 763-4040; *Current Population Reports,* and *Census of Population,* and unpublished data.

ELDERLY - AIDS

U.S. Department of Health and Human Services, Center for Disease Control, 1600 Clifton Road, NE, Atlanta, Georgia 30333 (404) 639-3311; unpublished data.

ELDERLY - ALCOHOL USE

U.S. Department of Health and Human Services, National Center for Health Statistics, 3700 East West Highway, Hyattsville, Maryland 20782 (301) 436-8500; *Health Promotion and Disease Prevention, United States,* and *Vital and Health Statistics.*

ELDERLY - ARRESTS

U.S. Department of Justice, Federal Bureau of Investigation, Ninth and Pennsylvania Avenue, NW, Washington, D.C. 20535 (202) 324-3000; *Crime in the United States.*

ELDERLY - ARTHRITIS AND RHEUMATISM

U.S. Department of Health and Human Services, National Center for Health Statistics, 3700 East-West Highway, Hyattsville, Maryland 20782 (301) 436-8500; *Vital and Health Statistics,* and unpublished data.

ELDERLY - BLACK POPULATION

U.S. Department of Commerce, Bureau of the Census, Suitland, Maryland 20233 (301) 763-4040; *Current Population Reports,* and unpublished data.

ELDERLY - CANCER

U.S. Department of Health and Human Services, National Center for Health Statistics, 3700 East-West Highway, Hyattsville, Maryland 20782 (301) 436-8500; *Health, United States, Monthly Vital Statistics Report, Vital and Health Statistics, Vital Statistics of the United States,* and unpublished data.

ELDERLY - CEREBROVASCULAR DISEASE

U.S. Department of Health and Human Services, National Center for Health Statistics, 3700 East-West Highway, Hyattsville, Maryland 20782 (301) 436-8500; *Health, United States, Vital Statistics of the U.S., Monthly Vital Statistics Report,* and unpublished data.

ELDERLY - CHARITABLE CONTRIBUTIONS

Independent Sector, 1828 L Street, NW, Washington, D.C. 20036 (202) 223-8100; *Giving and Volunteering in the United States.*

ELDERLY - CHILDREN UNDER 18 YEARS OLD LIVING WITH ELDERLY PARENTS

U.S. Department of Commerce, Bureau of the Census, Suitland, Maryland 20233 (301) 763-4040; unpublished data.

ELDERLY - CHRONIC CONDITIONS

U.S. Department of Health and Human Services, National Center for Health Statistics, 3700 East-West Highway, Hyattsville, Maryland 20782 (301) 436-8500; *Vital and Health Statistics,* and unpublished data.

ELDERLY - CIGARETTE SMOKING

U.S. Department of Health and Human Services, National Center for Health Statistics, 3700 East West Highway, Hyattsville, Maryland 20782 (301) 436-8500; *Health Promotion and Disease Prevention, United States, Vital and Health Statistics, Health, United States,* and unpublished data.

ELDERLY - DISABILITY DAYS

U.S. Department of Health and Human Services, National Center for Health Statistics, 3700 East-West Highway, Hyattsville, Maryland 20782 (301) 436-8500; *Vital and Health Statistics,* and unpublished data.

ELDERLY - EDUCATION - ATTAINMENT

U.S. Department of Commerce, Bureau of the Census, Suitland, Maryland 20233 (301) 763-4040; *Current Population Reports*, and unpublished data.

ELDERLY - ELECTIONS, VOTER REGISTRATION AND TURNOUT

U.S. Department of Commerce, Bureau of the Census, Suitland, Maryland 20233 (301) 763-4040; *Current Population Reports*.

ELDERLY - FARM WORKERS

U.S. Department of Agriculture, Economic Research Service, Fourteenth Street and Independence Avenue, SW, Washington, D.C. 20005-4789 (202) 219-1504; unpublished data.

ELDERLY - HEALTH INSURANCE COVERAGE

U.S. Department of Commerce, Bureau of the Census, Suitland, Maryland 20233 (301) 763-4040; *Current Population Reports*, and unpublished data.

ELDERLY - HEARING IMPAIRED

U.S. Department of Health and Human Services, National Center for Health Statistics, 3700 East-West Highway, Hyattsville, Maryland 20782 (301) 436-8500; *Vital and Health Statistics*, and unpublished data.

ELDERLY - HEART DISEASE

U.S. Department of Health and Human Services, National Center for Health Statistics, 3700 East-West Highway, Hyattsville, Maryland 20782 (301) 436-8500; *Vital and Health Statistics, Health, United States, Monthly Vital Statistics Report, Vital Statistics of the United States*, and unpublished data.

ELDERLY - HEIGHT DISTRIBUTION

U.S. Department of Health and Human Services, National Center for Health Statistics, 3700 East-West Highway, Hyattsville, Maryland 20782 (301) 436-8500; *Vital and Health Statistics*.

ELDERLY - HISPANIC ORIGIN POPULATION

U.S. Department of Commerce, Bureau of the Census, Suitland, Maryland 20233 (301) 763-4040; *Current Population Reports*, and unpublished data.

ELDERLY - HOME HEALTH AND HOSPICE CARE

U.S. Department of Health and Human Services, National Center for Health Statistics, 3700 East-West Highway, Hyattsville, Maryland 20782 (301) 436-8500; *Vital and Health Statistics*.

ELDERLY - HOMES FOR THE AGED

U.S. Department of Commerce, Bureau of the Census, Suitland, Maryland 20233 (301) 763-4040; *Census of Population, General Population Characteristics*.

U.S. Department of Health and Human Services, National Center for Health Statistics, 3700 East-West Highway, Hyattsville, Maryland 20782 (301) 436-8500; *Advance Data from Vital and Health Statistics*, and unpublished data.

ELDERLY - HOSPITAL USE

U.S. Department of Health and Human Services, National Center for Health Statistics, 3700 East-West Highway, Hyattsville, Maryland 20782 (301) 436-8500; *Vital and Health Statistics, Health, United States*, and unpublished data.

ELDERLY - HOUSING - TENURE

U.S. Department of Commerce, Bureau of the Census, Suitland, Maryland 20233 (301) 763-4040; *Census of Housing, General Housing Characteristics*, and *Census of Population and Housing*.

ELDERLY - ILLNESS - INJURIES

U.S. Department of Health and Human Services, National Center for Health Statistics, 3700 East-West Highway, Hyattsville, Maryland 20782 (301) 436-8500; *Vital and Health Statistics*, and unpublished data.

ELDERLY - LABOR FORCE

U.S. Department of Labor, Bureau of Labor Statistics, Two Massachusetts Avenue, NE, Washington, D.C. 20212 (202) 606-7828; *Employment and Earnings, Monthly Labor Review*, Bulletins 2307, 2217, 2340, and unpublished data.

ELDERLY - LABOR FORCE - EMPLOYED

U.S. Department of Labor, Bureau of Labor Statistics, Two Massachusetts Avenue, NE, Washington, D.C. 20212 (202) 606-7828; *News*, and unpublished data.

ELDERLY - LABOR FORCE - EMPLOYMENT STATUS - BY RACE

U.S. Department of Labor, Bureau of Labor Statistics, Two Massachusetts Avenue, NE, Washington, D.C. 20212 (202) 606-7828; *Employment and Earnings*, Bulletin 2307 and unpublished data.

ELDERLY - LABOR FORCE - PARTICIPATION RATES

U.S. Department of Labor, Bureau of Labor Statistics, Two Massachusetts Avenue, NE, Washington, D.C. 20212 (202) 606-7828; *Employment and Earnings*, Bulletins 2217 and 2340, *Monthly Labor Review*, and unpublished data.

ELDERLY - LABOR FORCE - UNEMPLOYED

U.S. Department of Labor, Bureau of Labor Statistics, Two Massachusetts Avenue, NE, Washington, D.C. 20212 (202) 606-7828; *Employment and Earnings*, Bulletin 2307, and unpublished data.

ELDERLY - LIVING ARRANGEMENTS

U.S. Department of Commerce, Bureau of the Census, Suitland, Maryland 20233 (301) 763-4040; *Current Population Reports*, and unpublished data.

ELDERLY - MARITAL STATUS

U.S. Department of Commerce, Bureau of the Census, Suitland, Maryland 20233 (301) 763-4040; *Current Population Reports*, and unpublished data.

ELDERLY - MEDICAID PAYMENTS AND RECIPIENTS

U.S. Department of Health and Human Services, Health Care Financing Administration, 200 Independence Avenue, SW,

Washington, D.C. 20201 (202) 245-6113; *Health Care Financing Review.*

ELDERLY - MEDICARE PROGRAM

U.S. Department of Health and Human Services, Health Care Financing Administration, 200 Independence Avenue, SW, Washington, D.C. 20201 (202) 245-6113; *Health Care Financing Review,* and unpublished data.

U.S. Department of Health and Human Services, Social Security Administration, 6401 Security Boulevard, Baltimore, Maryland 21235 (410) 965-1234; *Annual Statistical Supplement to the Social Security Bulletin.*

ELDERLY - MOBILITY STATUS

U.S. Department of Commerce, Bureau of the Census, Suitland, Maryland 20233 (301) 763-4040; *Current Population Reports.*

ELDERLY - MOTOR VEHICLES

U.S. Department of Transportation, National Highway Traffic Safety Administration, 400 Seventh Street, SW, Washington, D.C. 20590 (202) 366-9550; *Selected Highway Statistics and Charts.*

ELDERLY - MULTIMEDIA USERS

Mediamark Research, Incorporated, 703 Third Avenue, New York, New York 10017 (212) 599-0444; *Multimedia Audiences.*

ELDERLY - NURSING HOMES

U.S. Department of Commerce, Bureau of the Census, Suitland, Maryland 20233 (301) 763-4040; *Census of Population, General Population Characteristics.*

U.S. Department of Health and Human Services, National Center for Health Statistics, 3700 East-West Highway, Hyattsville, Maryland 20782 (301) 436-8500; *Advance Data from Vital and Health Statistics,* and unpublished data.

ELDERLY - NUTRITION PROGRAM FOR

U.S. Department of Agriculture, Food and Nutrition Service, 3101 Park Center Drive, Alexandria, Virginia 22302 (703) 305-2276; *Annual Historical Review of FNS Programs,* and unpublished data.

U.S. Library of Congress, Congressional Research Service, 101 Independence Avenue, SE, Washington, D.C. 20540 (202) 707-5000; *Cash and Non-cash Benefits for Persons with Limited Income: Eligibility Rules, Recipient and Expenditure Data.*

ELDERLY - PERSONAL HEALTH PRACTICES

U.S. Department of Health and Human Services, National Center for Health Statistics, 3700 East West Highway, Hyattsville, Maryland 20782 (301) 436-8500; *Health Promotion and Disease Prevention, United States, Vital and Health Statistics,* and unpublished data.

ELDERLY - PERSONS LIVING ALONE (ONE-PERSON HOUSEHOLDS)

U.S. Department of Commerce, Bureau of the Census, Suitland, Maryland 20233 (301) 763-4040; *Current Population Reports,* and unpublished data.

ELDERLY - PHYSICIAN - DENTISTS VISITS

U.S. Department of Health and Human Services, National Center for Health Statistics, 3700 East-West Highway, Hyattsville, Maryland 20782 (301) 436-8500; *Vital and Health Statistics,* and unpublished data.

ELDERLY - PNEUMONIA

U.S. Department of Health and Human Services, National Center for Health Statistics, 3700 East-West Highway, Hyattsville, Maryland 20782 (301) 436-8500; *Health, United States, Vital Statistics of the United States,* and unpublished data.

ELDERLY - POVERTY

U.S. Department of Commerce, Bureau of the Census, Suitland, Maryland 20233 (301) 763-4040; *Current Population Reports,* and unpublished data.

ELDERLY - PROJECTIONS

U.S. Department of Commerce, Bureau of the Census, Suitland, Maryland 20233 (301) 763-4040; *Current Population Reports.*

ELDERLY - RECREATION ACTIVITIES

National Endowment for the Arts, 1100 Pennsylvania Avenue, NW, Washington, D.C. 20506 (202) 682-5400; *Arts Participation in America.*

National Sporting Goods Association, Lake Center Plaza Building, 1699 Wall Street, Mount Prospect, Illinois 60056 (708) 439-4000; *Sports Participation in 1992,* and *The Sporting Goods Market in 1993.*

U.S. Department of Labor, Bureau of Labor Statistics, Two Massachusetts Avenue, NE, Washington, D.C. 20212 (202) 606-7828; *Consumer Expenditure Survey.*

ELDERLY - SOCIAL SECURITY BENEFICIARIES - PAYMENTS

U.S. Department of Health and Human Services, Social Security Administration, 6401 Security Boulevard, Baltimore, Maryland 21235 (410) 965-1234; *Annual Statistical Supplement to the Social Security Bulletin,* and unpublished data.

ELDERLY - STATES

U.S. Department of Commerce, Bureau of the Census, Suitland, Maryland 20233 (301) 763-4040; *Current Population Reports,* and unpublished data.

ELDERLY - SUICIDE

U.S. Department of Health and Human Services, National Center for Health Statistics, 3700 East-West Highway, Hyattsville, Maryland 20782 (301) 436-8500; *Monthly Vital Statistics Report, Vital Statistics of the United States,* and unpublished data.

ELDERLY - VOTER REGISTRATION AND TURNOUT

U.S. Department of Commerce, Bureau of the Census, Suitland, Maryland 20233 (301) 763-4040; *Current Population Reports.*

ELECTIONS - BLACK ELECTED OFFICIALS

Joint Center for Political and Economic Studies, 1090 Vermont Avenue, NW, Washington, D.C. 20005 (202) 789-3500; *Black Elected Officials: A National Roster.*

ELECTIONS - CAMPAIGN FINANCES

U.S. Federal Election Commission, 999 E Street, NW, Washington, D.C. 20463 (800) 424-9530; *Federal Election Commission Reports on Financial Activity, Final Report on United States Senate and House Campaigns, Final Report, Presidential Pre-Nomination Campaigns, Final Report, Party and Non-Party Political Committees, FEC Index of Independent Expenditures,* and press releases.

ELECTIONS - CONGRESSIONAL

Congressional Quarterly, Incorporated, 1414 22nd Street, NW, Washington, D.C. 20037 (202) 887-8500; *Congressional Quarterly Weekly Report.*

Elections Research Center, 5508 Greystone Street, Chevy Chase, Maryland 20815 (202) 659-9490; *America Votes.*

U.S. Department of Commerce, Bureau of the Census, Suitland, Maryland 20233 (301) 763-4040; *Current Population Reports.*

ELECTIONS - GUBERNATORIAL

Elections Research Center, 5508 Greystone Street, Chevy Chase, Maryland 20815 (202) 659-9490; *America Votes.*

National Governors' Association, Hall of the States, 444 North Capitol Street, NW, Washington, D.C. 20001 (202) 624-5300; *Directory of Governors of the American States, Commonwealths and Territories.*

ELECTIONS - HISPANIC ORIGIN OFFICIALS

National Association of Latino Elected and Appointed Officials, NALEO Education Fund, 3409 Garnet Street, Los Angeles, California 90023 (213) 262-8503; *National Roster of Hispanic Elected Officials.*

ELECTIONS - POLITICAL ACTION COMMITTEES (PAC)

U.S. Federal Election Commission, 999 E Street, NW, Washington, D.C. 20463 (800) 424-9530; *FEC Reports on Financial Activity, Final Reports, Party and Non-Party Political Committees,* and press release.

ELECTIONS - PRESIDENTIAL

Committee for the Study of the American Electorate, 421 New Jersey Avenue, SE, Washington, D.C. 20003 (202) 546-3221; unpublished data.

Congressional Quarterly, Inc., 1414 22nd Street, NW, Washington, D.C. 20037 (202) 887-8500; *Presidential Primaries and Caucuses.*

Elections Research Center, 5508 Greystone Street, Chevy Chase, Maryland 20815 (202) 659-9490; *America Votes.*

U.S. Congress, Clerk of the House, The Capitol, Washington, D.C. 20515 (202) 224-3121; *Statistics of the Presidential and Congressional Election.*

U.S. Department of Commerce, Bureau of the Census, Suitland, Maryland 20233 (301) 763-4040; *Current Population Reports.*

U.S. Federal Election Committee, 999 E Street, NW, Washington, D.C. 20463 (800) 424-9530; press releases.

ELECTIONS - STATE LEGISLATURES

Council of State Governments, Post Office Box 11910, Iron Works Pike, Lexington, Kentucky 40578 (606) 231-1939; *State Elective Officials and the Legislatures.*

National Conference of State Legislatures, 1560 Broadway, Suite 700, Denver, Colorado 80202 (303) 830-2200; *State Legislatures,* and unpublished data.

ELECTIONS - VOTER REGISTRATION

Elections Research Center, 5508 Greystone Street, Chevy Chase, Maryland 20815 (202) 659-9490; *America Votes.*

U.S. Department of Commerce, Bureau of the Census, Suitland, Maryland 20233 (301) 763-4040; *Current Population Reports,* and press release.

ELECTIONS - VOTER TURNOUT

Elections Research Center, 5508 Greystone Street, Chevy Chase, Maryland 20815 (202) 659-9490; *America Votes.*

U.S. Department of Commerce, Bureau of the Census, Suitland, Maryland 20233 (301) 763-4040; *Current Population Reports.*

ELECTIONS - VOTES CAST

Committee for the Study of the American Electorate, 421 New Jersey Avenue, SW, Washington, D.C. 20003 (202) 546-3221; unpublished data.

Congressional Quarterly, Incorporated, 1414 22nd Street, NW, Washington, D.C. 20037 (202) 887-8500; *Congressional Quarterly Weekly Report,* and *Presidential Primaries and Caucuses.*

Elections Research Center, 558 Greystone Street, Chevy Chase, Maryland 20815 (202) 659-9490; *America Votes.*

U.S. Congress, Clerk of House, The Capitol, Washington, D.C. 20515 (202) 224-3121; *Statistics of the Presidential and Congressional Election.*

ELECTIONS - VOTING AGE POPULATION

Elections Research Center, 5508 Greystone Street, Chevy Chase, Maryland 20815 (202) 659-9490; *America Votes.*

U.S. Department of Commerce, Bureau of the Census, Suitland, Maryland 20233 (301) 763-4040; *Current Population Reports.*

ELECTIONS - WOMEN IN PUBLIC OFFICE

Center for the American Woman and Politics, The Eagleton Institute of Politics, Rutgers University, New Brunswick, New Jersey 08903 (908) 828-2210; information releases.

ELECTRIC GAS, AND SANITARY SERVICES - EARNINGS

U.S. Department of Commerce, Bureau of the Census, Suitland, Maryland 20233 (301) 763-4040; *County Business Patterns.*

U.S. Department of Labor, Bureau of Labor Statistics, Two Massachusetts Avenue, NE, Washington, D.C. 20212 (202) 606-7828; *Employment and Earnings,* and Bulletins 2370 and 2429.

ELECTRIC, GAS, AND SANITARY SERVICES - EMPLOYEES

U.S. Department of Commerce, Bureau of the Census, Suitland, Maryland 20233 (301) 763-4040; *County Business Patterns.*

U.S. Department of Labor, Bureau of Labor Statistics, Two Massachusetts Avenue, NE, Washington, D.C. 20212 (202) 606-7828; *Employment and Earnings, Monthly Labor Review,* and Bulletins 2370 and 2429.

ELECTRIC, GAS, AND SANITARY SERVICES - FINANCES

Board of Governors of the Federal Reserve System, Twentieth Street and Constitution Avenue, NW, Washington, D.C. 20551 (202) 452-3000; *Federal Reserve Bulletin,* and *Annual Statistical Digest.*

ELECTRIC, GAS, AND SANITARY SERVICES - GROSS DOMESTIC PRODUCT

U.S. Department of Commerce, Bureau of Economic Analysis, Fourteenth Street between Constitution Avenue and E Street, NW, Washington, D.C. 20230 (202) 606-9900; *Survey of Current Business,* and *The National Income and Product Accounts of the United States.*

ELECTRIC, GAS, AND SANITARY SERVICES - OCCUPATIONAL SAFETY

U.S. Department of Labor, Bureau of Labor Statistics, Two Massachusetts Avenue, NE, Washington, D.C. 20212 (202) 606-7828; *Occupational Illnesses and Injuries in the United States, by Industry.*

ELECTRIC, GAS, AND SANITARY SERVICES - PRODUCTIVITY

U.S. Department of Labor, Bureau of Labor Statistics, Two Massachusetts Avenue, NE, Washington, D.C. 20212 (202) 606-7828; *Productivity Measures for Selected Industries and Government Services,* and unpublished data.

ELECTRIC LIGHT AND POWER INDUSTRY - See also ELECTRIC, GAS, AND SANITARY SERVICES, and ELECTRICITY

ELECTRIC LIGHT AND POWER INDUSTRY - CONSTRUCTION COSTS

U.S. Department of Commerce, Bureau of the Census, Suitland, Maryland 20233 (301) 763-4040; *Current Construction Reports.*

U.S. Department of Commerce, International Trade Administration, Fourteenth Street between Constitution Avenue and E Street, NW, Washington, D.C. 20230 (202) 482-3089; *Construction Review.*

ELECTRIC LIGHT AND POWER INDUSTRY - ELECTRIC ENERGY - CUSTOMERS

American Gas Association, 1515 Wilson Boulevard, Arlington, Virginia 22209 (703) 841-8400; *Gas Facts.*

Edison Electric Institute, 701 Pennsylvania Avenue, NW, Washington, D.C. 20004 (202) 508-5000; *Statistical Yearbook of the Electric Utility Industry.*

ELECTRIC ENERGY - GENERAL CAPABILITY

Edison Electric Institute, 701 Pennsylvania Avenue, NW, Washington, D.C. 20004 (202) 508-5000; *Statistical Yearbook of the Electric Utility Industry.*

U.S. Department of Energy, Energy Information Administration, Washington, D.C. 20585 (202) 586-8800; *Electric Power Annual, Annual Energy Review,* and unpublished data.

ELECTRIC ENERGY - GENERAL CAPACITY, INSTALLED

U.S. Department of Energy, Energy Information Administration, Washington, D.C. 20585 (202) 586-8800; *Electric Power Monthly, Electric Power Annual,* and *Inventory of Power Plants in the U.S.*

ELECTRIC ENERGY - OWNERSHIP - CLASS OF

U.S. Department of Energy, Energy Information Administration, Washington, D.C. 20585 (202) 586-8800; *Electric Power Annual, Annual Energy Review,* and unpublished data.

ELECTRIC ENERGY - PEAK LOAD

Edison Electric Institute, 701 Pennsylvania Avenue, NW, Washington, D.C. 20004-2696 (202) 508-5000; *Statistical Yearbook of the Electric Utility Industry.*

ELECTRICITY - See also ELECTRIC LIGHT AND POWER INDUSTRY

ELECTRICITY - CAPABILITY

Edison Electric Institute, 701 Pennsylvania Avenue, Washington, D.C. 20004-2696 (202) 508-5000; *Statistical Yearbook of the Electric Utility Industry.*

U.S. Department of Energy, Energy Information Administration, Washington, D.C. 20585 (202) 586-8800; *Electric Power Annual, Annual Energy Review,* and unpublished data.

ELECTRICITY - COMMERCIAL BUILDINGS

ONCOR International, 3040 Post Oak Boulevard, Houston, Texas 77056 (713) 961-0600; *Office Market Data Book.*

U.S. Department of Energy, Energy Information Administration, 1000 Independence Avenue, SW, Washington, D.C. 20585 (202) 586-8800; *Commercial Buildings Energy Consumption and Expenditures.*

ELECTRICITY - CONSUMPTION

Edison Electric Institute, 701 Pennsylvania Avenue, NW, Washington, D.C. 20004-2696 (202) 508-5000; *Statistical Yearbook of the Electric Utility Industry.*

U.S. Department of Energy, Energy Information Administration, Washington, D.C. 20585 (202) 586-8800; *Household Energy Consumption and Expenditures, Electric Power Annual, Commercial Buildings Energy Consumption and Expenditures, Annual Energy Review,* and unpublished data.

ELECTRICITY - EXPENDITURES

U.S. Department of Agriculture, Economic Research Service, Fourteenth Street and Independence Avenue, SW, Washington, D.C. 20005-4789 (202) 219-1504; *Economic Indicators of the Farm Sector: National Financial Summary.*

U.S. Department of Energy, Energy Information Administration, Washington, D.C. 20585 (202) 586-8800; *State Energy Price and Expenditure Report,* and *Household Energy Consumption and Expenditures.*

ELECTRICITY - FOREIGN COUNTRIES

McGraw-Hill, Inc., 1221 Avenue of the Americas, New York, New York 10020 (212) 512-2000; *Nucleonics Week*, March issues.

Statistical Office of the United Nations, Publishing Service, New York, New York 10017 (800) 253-9646; *Energy Statistics Yearbook*.

ELECTRICITY - HYDROELECTRIC POWER

U.S. Department of Energy, Energy Information Administration, 1000 Independence Avenue, SW, Washington, D.C. 20585 (202) 586-8800; *Annual Energy Review, Electric Power Monthly, Electric Power Annual, Monthly Energy Review State Energy Data Report*, and unpublished data.

U.S. Department of Energy, Federal Energy Regulatory Commission, 1000 Independence Avenue, SW, Washington, D.C. 20585 (202) 208-0300; *Hydroelectric Power Resources of the United States, Developed and Undeveloped*, and unpublished data.

ELECTRICITY - NUCLEAR

Editor and Publisher Company, 11 West 19th Street, New York, New York 10011 (212) 675-4380; *Editor and Publisher International Year Book*.

McGraw-Hill, Incorporated, 1221 Avenue of the Americas, New York, New York 10020 (212) 512-2000; *Nucleonics Week*, March issues.

U.S. Department of Energy, Energy Information Administration, Washington, D.C. 20585 (202) 586-8800; *Monthly Energy Review, Annual Energy Review, Electrical Power Annual, State Energy Data Report*, and *Electric Power Monthly*.

ELECTRICITY - PRICE INDEXES

U.S. Department of Commerce, Bureau of Economic Analysis, Fourteenth Street between Constitution Avenue and E Street, NW, Washington, D.C. 20230 (202) 606-9900; *Survey of Current Business*, and *The National Income and Product Accounts of the U.S.*

U.S. Department of Labor, Bureau of Labor Statistics, Two Massachusetts Avenue, NE, Washington, D.C. 20212 (202) 606-7828; *Monthly Labor Review*, and *CPI Detailed Report*.

ELECTRICITY - PRODUCTION

U.S. Department of Energy, Energy Information Administration, Washington, D.C. 20585 (202) 586-8800; *Electric Power Annual, Electric Power Monthly, Inventory of Power Plants in the U.S., Annual Energy Review*, and unpublished data.

ELECTRICITY - PRODUCTION - WORLD PRODUCTION

U.S. Department of Energy, Energy Information Administration, Washington, D.C. 20585 (202) 586-8800; *International Energy Annual*.

ELECTRICITY - RESIDENTIAL

Edison Electric Institute, 701 Pennsylvania Avenue, NW, Washington, D.C. 20004 (202) 508-5000; *Statistical Yearbook of the Electric Utility Industry*.

U.S. Department of Commerce, Bureau of the Census, Suitland, Maryland 20233 (301) 763-4040; *Census of Housing, Detailed Housing Characteristics*, and *Current Housing Reports*,

U.S. Department of Energy, Energy Information Administration, Washington, D.C. 20585 (202) 586-8800; *Household Energy Consumption and Expenditures, Petroleum Statement Annual, Energy Data Reports, Petroleum Supply Annual*, and *Natural Gas Annual*.

ELECTRICITY - SALES

Edison Electric Institute, 701 Pennsylvania Avenue, NW, Washington, D.C. 20004 (202) 508-5000; *Statistical Yearbook of the Electric Utility Industry*.

U.S. Department of Energy, Energy Information Administration, Washington, D.C. 20585 (202) 586-8800; *Electric Power Annual, Electric Power Monthly*, and *Annual Energy Review*.

ELECTRONIC AND OTHER ELECTRICAL EQUIPMENT - MANUFACTURING - CAPITAL

U.S. Department of Commerce, Bureau of Economic Analysis, Fourteenth Street between Constitution Avenue and E Street, NW, Washington, D.C. 20230 (202) 606-9900; *Survey of Current Business*.

U.S. Department of Commerce, Bureau of the Census, Suitland, Maryland 20233 (301) 763-4040; *Annual Survey of Manufactures, Census of Manufactures*, and *Plant and Equipment Expenditures and Plans*.

ELECTRONIC AND OTHER ELECTRICAL EQUIPMENT - MANUFACTURING - EARNINGS

U.S. Department of Commerce, Bureau of the Census, Suitland, Maryland 20233 (301) 763-4040; *Annual Survey of Manufactures*, and *Census of Manufactures*.

ELECTRONIC AND OTHER ELECTRICAL EQUIPMENT - MANUFACTURING - EMPLOYEES

U.S. Department of Commerce, Bureau of the Census, Suitland, Maryland 20233 (301) 763-4040; *Census of Manufactures*, and *Annual Survey of Manufactures*.

U.S. Department of Labor, Bureau of Labor Statistics, Two Massachusetts Avenue, NE, Washington, D.C. 20212 (202) 606-7828; *Employment and Wages, Annual Averages, Employment and Earnings, Monthly Labor Review*, and Bulletins 2370 and 2429.

ELECTRONIC AND OTHER ELECTRICAL EQUIPMENT - MANUFACTURING - ESTABLISHMENTS

U.S. Department of Commerce, Bureau of the Census, Suitland, Maryland 20233 (301) 763-4040; *Annual Survey of Manufactures*, and *Census of Manufactures*.

ELECTRONIC AND OTHER ELECTRICAL EQUIPMENT - MANUFACTURING - FINANCES

Forbes, Incorporated, 60 Fifth Avenue, New York, New York 10011 (212) 620-2200; *Forbes Annual Report on American Industry*.

Time Warner, 1675 Broadway, Rockefeller Center, New York, New York 10019 (212) 522-1212; *The Fortune Directories*.

U.S. Department of Commerce, Bureau of Economic Analysis, Fourteenth Street between Constitution Avenue and E Street, NW, Washington, D.C. 20230 (202) 606-9900; *Survey of Current Business*, and *The National Income and Product Accounts of the United States*.

ELECTRONIC AND OTHER ELECTRICAL EQUIPMENT - MANUFACTURING - FOREIGN TRADE

U.S. Department of Commerce, Bureau of the Census, Suitland, Maryland 20233 (301) 763-4040; *U.S. Merchandise Trade, Census of Manufactures, Annual Survey of Manufactures*, and unpublished data.

ELECTRONIC AND OTHER ELECTRICAL EQUIPMENT - MANUFACTURING - GROSS DOMESTIC PRODUCT

U.S. Department of Commerce, Bureau of Economic Analysis, Fourteenth Street between Constitution Avenue and E Street, NW, Washington, D.C. 20230 (202) 606-9900; *Survey of Current Business*, and *The National Income and Product Accounts of the United States*.

ELECTRONIC AND OTHER ELECTRICAL EQUIPMENT - MANUFACTURING - MERGERS AND ACQUISITIONS

Securities Data Company, 1180 Raymond Boulevard, Newark, New Jersey 07102 (201) 622-3100; *Merger and Corporate Transactions Database*.

ELECTRONIC AND OTHER ELECTRICAL EQUIPMENT - MANUFACTURING - OCCUPATIONAL SAFETY

U.S. Department of Labor, Bureau of Labor Statistics, Two Massachusetts Avenue, NE, Washington, D.C. 20212 (202) 606-7828; *Occupational Illnesses and Injuries in the United States by Industry*.

ELECTRONIC AND OTHER ELECTRICAL EQUIPMENT - MANUFACTURING - POLLUTION ABATEMENT

U.S. Department of Commerce, Bureau of the Census, Suitland, Maryland 20233 (301) 763-4040; *Current Industrial Reports*.

ELECTRONIC AND OTHER ELECTRONIC EQUIPMENT - MANUFACTURING - PRODUCTIVITY

Board of Governors of the Federal Reserve System, Twentieth Street and Constitution Avenue, NW, Washington, D.C. 20551 (202) 452-3000; *Federal Reserve Bulletin*.

U.S. Department of Labor, Bureau of Labor Statistics, Two Massachusetts Avenue, NE, Washington, D.C. 20212 (202) 606-7828; *Productivity Measures for Selected Industries and Government Services*.

ELECTRONIC AND OTHER ELECTRICAL EQUIPMENT - MANUFACTURING - PROFITS

Executive Office of the President, Council of Economic Advisors, Old Executive Office Building, Washington, D.C 20500 (202) 395-5084; *Economic Report of the President*.

Forbes, Incorporated, 60 Fifth Avenue, New York, New York 10011 (212) 620-2200; *Forbes Annual Report on American Industry*.

U.S. Department of Commerce, Bureau of Economic Analysis, Fourteenth Street between Constitution Avenue and E Street, NW, Washington, D.C. 20230 (202) 606-9900; *Survey of Current Business*, and *The National Income and Product Accounts of the United States*.

U.S. Department of Commerce, Bureau of the Census, Suitland, Maryland 20233 (301) 763-4040; *Quarterly Financial Report for Manufacturing, Mining, and Trade Corporations*.

ELECTRONIC AND OTHER ELECTRICAL EQUIPMENT - MANUFACTURING - RESEARCH AND DEVELOPMENT

U.S. National Science Foundation, 4201 Wilson Boulevard, Arlington, Virginia 22230 (703) 306-1234; *Research and Development in Industry*.

ELECTRONIC AND OTHER ELECTRICAL EQUIPMENT - MANUFACTURING - SHIPMENTS

U.S. Department of Commerce, Bureau of the Census, Suitland, Maryland 20233 (301) 763-4040; *Annual Survey of Manufactures*, and *Census of Manufactures*.

ELECTRONIC AND OTHER ELECTRICAL EQUIPMENT - VALUE ADDED

U.S. Department of Commerce, Bureau of the Census, Suitland, Maryland 20233 (301) 763-4040; *Annual Survey of Manufactures*, *Census of Manufactures*, and *Current Industrial Reports, Manufactures, Shipments, Inventories, and Orders*.

ELECTRONIC COMPONENTS AND ACCESSORIES, MANUFACTURING - EARNINGS

U.S. Department of Commerce, Bureau of the Census, Suitland, Maryland 20233 (301) 763-4040; *Annual Survey of Manufactures*, and *Census of Manufactures*.

ELECTRONIC COMPONENTS AND ACCESSORIES, MANUFACTURING - EMPLOYEES

U.S. Department of Commerce, Bureau of the Census, Suitland, Maryland 20233 (301) 763-4040; *Annual Survey of Manufactures*, and *Census of Manufactures*.

ELECTRONIC COMPONENTS AND ACCESSORIES, MANUFACTURING - ESTABLISHMENTS

U.S. Department of Commerce, Bureau of the Census, Suitland, Maryland 20233 (301) 763-4040; *Census of Manufactures*, and *Annual Survey of Manufactures*.

ELECTRONIC COMPONENTS AND ACCESSORIES, MANUFACTURING - SHIPMENTS

Forbes, Incorporated, 60 Fifth Avenue, New York, New York 10011 (212) 620-2200; *Forbes Annual Report on American Industry*.

U.S. Department of Commerce, Bureau of the Census, Suitland, Maryland 20233 (301) 763-4040; *Annual Survey of Manufactures*, and *Census of Manufactures*.

ELECTRONIC COMPONENTS AND ACCESSORIES, MANUFACTURING - VALUE ADDED

U.S. Department of Commerce, Bureau of the Census, Suitland, Maryland 20233 (301) 763-4040; *Annual Survey of Manufactures*, and *Census of Manufactures*.

ELECTRONIC FUNDS TRANSFER

Faulkner & Gray, 118 South Clinton Street, Chicago, Illinois 60661 (312) 648-0261; *Bank Network News*.

ELECTRONIC GOODS - ADVERTISING EXPENDITURES

Television Bureau of Advertising, Incorporated, 850 Third Avenue, New York, New York 10022 (212) 486-1111; data from Competitive

Media Reporting, 11 West 42nd Street, New York, New York 10036 (212) 789-1400.

ELECTRONIC GOODS - SALES, SHIPMENTS, RECEIPTS

Electronic Industries Association, 2001 Pennsylvania Avenue, NW, Suite 1100, Washington, D.C. 20006 (202) 457-4900; *Electronic Market Data Book.*

U.S. Department of Commerce, Bureau of the Census, Suitland, Maryland 20233 (301) 763-4040; *Annual Survey of Manufactures, Current Industrial Reports,* and *U.S. Imports, FT 210: Import CD-Rom disc.*

EMERY - PRODUCTION AND VALUE

U.S. Department of the Interior, Bureau of Mines, 810 Seventh Street, NW, Washington, D.C. 20241 (202) 501-9649; *Annual Reports,* and *Mineral Commodities Summaries.*

EMPHYSEMA

U.S. Department of Health and Human Services, National Center for Health Statistics, 3700 East-West Highway, Hyattsville, Maryland 20782 (301) 436-8500; *Health, United States, Vital Statistics of the United States,* and unpublished data.

World Health Organization, Office of Publications, Avenue Appia, CH-1211 Geneva 27, Switzerland (Telephone Number in U.S. (518) 436-9686); *World Health Statistics Annual.*

EMPLOYEE BENEFITS

U.S. Department of Commerce, Bureau of the Census, Suitland, Maryland 20233 (301) 763-4040; unpublished data.

U.S. Department of Labor, Bureau of Labor Statistics, Two Massachusetts Avenue, NE, Washington, D.C. 20212 (202) 606-7828; *News, Employer Costs for Employee Compensation, Employee Benefits in Medium and Large Private Establishments,* and *Employee Benefits in Small Private Establishments.*

EMPLOYEE BENEFITS - GOVERNMENT EMPLOYEES

U.S. Department of Labor, Bureau of Labor Statistics, Two Massachusetts Avenue, NE, Washington, D.C. 20212 (202) 606-7828; *Employee Benefits in State and Local Government,* and *News, Employer Costs for Employee Compensation.*

EMPLOYEE STOCK OWNERSHIP PLANS

National Center for Employee Ownership, 2201 Broadway, Suite 807, Oakland, California 94612 (415) 272-9461; unpublished data.

EMPLOYEES

Shipbuilders Council of America, 4301 North Fairfax Drive, Suite 330, Arlington, Virginia 22203 (703) 276-1700; unpublished data.

Time Warner, 1675 Broadway, Rockefeller Center, New York, New York 10019 (212) 522-1212; *The Fortune Directories.*

U.S. Department of Agriculture, Economic Research Service, Fourteenth Street and Independence Avenue, SW, Washington, D.C. 20250 (202) 786-1504; unpublished data.

U.S. Department of Commerce, Bureau of Economic Analysis, Fourteenth Street between Constitution Avenue and E Street, NW, Washington, D.C 20230 (202) 606-9900; *Foreign Direct Investment in the U.S. Operations of U.S. Affiliates of Foreign Companies, Survey of Current Business,* and *The National Income and Product Accounts of the United States.*

U.S. Department of Commerce, Bureau of the Census, Suitland, Maryland 20233 (301) 763-4040; *Annual Survey of Manufactures, Census of Construction Industries, Economic Census of Outlying Areas, Census of Manufactures, Census of Retail Trade, Census of Wholesale Trade, County Business Patterns, Current Population Reports, Current Industrial Reports,* and unpublished data.

U.S. Department of Commerce, International Trade Administration, Fourteenth Street between Constitution Avenue and E Street, NW, Washington, D.C 20230 (202) 482-5487; *U.S. Industrial Outlook.*

U.S. Department of Labor, Bureau of Labor Statistics, Two Massachusetts Avenue, NE, Washington, D.C. 20212 (202) 606-7828; *Employment and Earnings, Geographic Profile of Employment and Unemployment, Monthly Labor Review, Employment and Wages, Annual Averages, News,* Bulletins 2307 and 2433, and unpublished data.

EMPLOYMENT AGENCIES

U.S. Department of Commerce, Bureau of the Census, Suitland, Maryland 20233 (301) 763-4040; *Current Business Reports, Service Annual Survey,* and unpublished data.

ENDANGERED SPECIES

U.S. Department of the Interior, Fish and Wildlife Service, C Street between Eighteenth and Nineteenth Streets, NW, Washington, D.C. 20240 (202) 208-5634; *Endangered Species Technical Bulletin.*

ENERGY - See also ELECTRIC LIGHT AND POWER INDUSTRY AND VARIOUS FUEL TYPES

ENERGY - ASSISTANCE FOR PERSONS WITH LIMITED INCOME

U.S. Library of Congress, Congressional Research Service, 10 First Street, SE, Washington, D.C. 20540 (202) 707-5000; *Cash and Non-Cash Benefits for Persons With Limited Income: Eligibility Rules, Recipient and Expenditure Data.*

ENERGY - COMMERCIAL BUILDINGS

U.S. Department of Energy, Energy Information Administration, Washington, D.C. 20585 (202) 586-8800; *Commercial Building Characteristics,* and *Household Energy Consumption and Expenditures.*

ENERGY - COMPANIES

U.S. Department of Energy, Energy Information Administration, 1000 Independence Avenue, SW, Washington, D.C. 20585 (202) 586-8800; *Performance Profiles of Major Energy Producers.*

ENERGY - CONSUMPTION

Statistical Office of the United Nations, Publishing Service, New York, New York 10017 (800) 253-9646; *Energy Statistics Yearbook.*

U.S. Department of Energy, Energy Information Administration, Washington, D.C. 20585 (202) 586-8800; *Annual Energy Review, Household Energy Consumption and Expenditures, Monthly Energy Review,* and *State Energy Data Report.*

ENERGY - CONSUMPTION - CHARACTERISTIC OF HOUSEHOLD

U.S. Department of Energy, Energy Information Administration, 1000 Independence Avenue, SW, Washington, D.C. 20585 (202) 586-8800; *Household Energy Consumption and Expenditures.*

ENERGY - CONSUMPTION - END USE SECTOR

U.S. Department of Energy, Energy Information Administration, 1000 Independence Avenue, SW, Washington, D.C. 20585 (202) 586-8800; *State Energy Data Report, Monthly Energy Review, Annual Energy Review,* and *State Energy Price and Expenditure Report.*

ENERGY - CONSUMPTION - FOREIGN COUNTRIES

Statistical Office of the United Nations, New York, New York 10017 (800) 243-9646; *Energy Statistics Yearbook.*

ENERGY - CONSUMPTION - SOURCE

U.S. Department of Energy, Energy Information Administration, 1000 Independence Avenue, SW, Washington, D.C. 20585 (202) 586-8800; *Annual Energy Review,* and *Monthly Energy Review.*

ENERGY - CONSUMPTION - TYPE OF FUEL

U.S. Department of Energy, Energy Information Administration, Washington, D.C. 20585 (202) 586-8800; *Household Energy Consumption and Expenditures.*

ENERGY - CONSUMPTION - WOOD

U.S. Department of Commerce, Bureau of the Census, Suitland, Maryland 20233 (301) 763-4040; *Census of Housing, Detailed Housing Characteristics,* and *Current Housing Reports.*

U.S. Department of Energy, Energy Information Administration, 1000 Independence Avenue, SW, Washington, D.C. 20585 (202) 586-8800; *Annual Energy Review.*

ENERGY - END USE SECTOR

U.S. Department of Energy, Energy Information Administration, 1000 Independence Avenue, SW, Washington, D.C. 20585 (202) 586-8800; *State Energy Data Report, Monthly Energy Review, Annual Energy Review,* and *State Energy Price and Expenditure Report.*

ENERGY - EXPENDITURES

U.S. Department of Energy, Energy Information Administration, Washington, D.C. 20588 (202) 586-8800; *State Energy Price and Expenditure Report, Commercial Buildings Energy Consumption and Expenditures,* and *Household Energy Consumption and Expenditures.*

ENERGY - EXPENDITURES - COMMERCIAL

U.S. Department of Energy, Energy Information Administration, 1000 Independence Avenue, SW, Washington, D.C. 20585 (202) 586-8800; *Commercial Buildings Energy Consumption and Expenditures.*

ENERGY - EXPENDITURES - RESIDENTIAL

U.S. Department of Energy, Energy Information Administration, 1000 Independence Avenue, SW, Washington, D.C. 20585 (202) 586-8800; *Household Energy Consumption and Expenditures.*

ENERGY - EXPENDITURES - TYPE OF STRUCTURE

U.S. Department of Energy, Energy Information Administration, Washington, D.C. 20585 (202) 586-8800; *Household Energy Consumption and Expenditures.*

ENERGY - FEDERAL OUTLAYS

Executive Office of the President, Office of Management and Budget, Executive Office Building, Washington, D.C. 20503 (202) 395-3080; *Budget of the United States Government.*

ENERGY - PRICE INDEXES - CONSUMER

U.S. Department of Labor, Bureau of Labor Statistics, Two Massachusetts Avenue, NE, Washington, D.C. 20212 (202) 606-7828; *CPI Detailed Report, Handbook of Labor Statistics,* and *Monthly Labor Review.*

ENERGY - PRICE INDEXES - EXPORT AND IMPORT

U.S. Department of Labor, Bureau of Labor Statistics, Two Massachusetts Avenue, NE, Washington, D.C. 20212 (202) 606-7828; *News.*

ENERGY - PRICE INDEXES - PRODUCER

U.S. Department of Labor, Bureau of Labor Statistics, Two Massachusetts Avenue, NE, Washington, D.C. 20212 (202) 606-7828; *Producer Price Indexes.*

ENERGY - SOLAR COLLECTORS - MANUFACTURER'S SHIPMENTS

U.S. Department of Energy, Energy Information Administration, Washington, D.C. 20585 (202) 586-8800; *Solar Collector Manufacturing Activity.*

ENERGY - WOOD

U.S. Department of Commerce, Bureau of the Census, Suitland, Maryland 20233 (301) 763-4040; *Census of Housing, Detailed Housing Characteristics,* and *Current Housing Reports.*

U.S. Department of Energy, Energy Information Administration, Washington, D.C. 20585 (202) 586-8800; *Annual Energy Review.*

ENERGY, DEPARTMENT OF - BUDGET OUTLAYS

Executive Office of the President, Office of Management and Budget, Executive Office Building, Washington, D.C. 20503 (202) 395-3080; *Budget of the United States Government.*

ENGINEERING AND ARCHITECTURAL SERVICES - EARNINGS

U.S. Department of Commerce, Bureau of the Census, Suitland, Maryland 20233 (301) 763-4040; *Census of Service Industries, County Business Patterns.*

ENGINEERING AND ARCHITECTURAL SERVICES - ESTABLISHMENTS

U.S. Department of Commerce, Bureau of the Census, Suitland, Maryland 20233 (301) 763-4040; *Census of Service Industries, County Business Patterns.*

ENGINEERS AND SCIENTISTS - DEGREES CONFERRED

U.S. Department of Education, National Center for Education Statistics, 400 Maryland Avenue, SW, Washington, D.C. 20202 (202) 708-5366; *Digest of Education Statistics,* and unpublished data.

U.S. National Science Foundation, 4201 Wilson Boulevard, Arlington, Virginia 22230 (703) 306-1234; *Characteristics of Recent Science and Engineering Graduates,* and *Survey of Earned Doctorates, Selected Data on Science and Engineering Doctorate Awards.*

ENGINEERS AND SCIENTISTS - EMPLOYMENT

U.S. Department of Labor, Bureau of Labor Statistics, Two Massachusetts Avenue, NE, Washington, D.C. 20212 (202) 606-7828; *Employment and Earnings,* and *Monthly Labor Review.*

U.S. National Science Foundation, 4201 Wilson Boulevard, Arlington, Virginia 22230 (703) 306-1234; *National Patterns of R & D Resources, Research and Development in Industry,* and *Characteristics of Doctoral Scientists and Engineers in the U.S.*

ENGINEERS AND SCIENTISTS - RESEARCH AND DEVELOPMENT

U.S. National Science Foundation, 4201 Wilson Boulevard, Arlington, Virginia 22230 (703) 306-1234; *Research and Development in Industry, National Patterns of R & D Resources,* and *Survey of Scientific and Engineering Expenditures at Universities and Colleges.*

ENGINEERS AND SCIENTISTS - SALARY OFFERS

College Placement Council, Inc., 62 Highland Avenue, Bethlehem, Pennsylvania 18017 (212) 868-1421; *Salary Survey, A Study of Beginning Offers.*

Northwestern University Placement Center, 633 Clark Street, Evanston, Illinois 60201 (708) 491-3741; *The Northwestern Lindquist - Endicott Report.*

ENGLAND - See UNITED KINGDOM

ENTERTAINMENT - See also AMUSEMENT AND RECREATION SERVICES

ENTERTAINMENT - PERSONAL EXPENDITURES

U.S. Department of Labor, Bureau of Labor Statistics, Two Massachusetts Avenue, NE, Washington, D.C. 20212 (202) 606-7828; *Consumer Expenditure Survey, CPI Detailed Report,* and *Monthly Labor Review.*

ENVIRONMENTAL INDUSTRY

Environmental Business International, Inc., 4452 Park Boulevard, Suite 306, San Diego, California 92116 (619) 295-7685; *Environmental Business Journal.*

ENVIRONMENTAL PROTECTION AGENCY - EMPLOYMENT

U.S. Office of Personnel Management, 1900 E Street, NW, Washington, D.C. 20415 (202) 606-1800; *Federal Civilian Workforce Statistics, Employment and Trends.*

ENVIRONMENTAL PROTECTION AGENCY - WASTE TREATMENT FACILITIES - FEDERAL AID TO STATE AND LOCAL GOVERNMENTS

U.S. Department of Commerce, Bureau of the Census, Suitland, Maryland 20233 (301) 763-4040; *Federal Expenditures by State for Fiscal Year.*

Equatorial Guinea - National Statistical Office

Ministerio de Planificacion y DeSarrollo Economico, Direccion General de Estadistica, Malabo, Equatorial Guinea.

Equatorial Guinea - Primary Statistics Sources

Direccion General de Estadistica, Malabo, Equatorial Guinea; *Resena estadistica de la Republica de Guinea Ecuatorial* (Statistical Review of the Republic of Equatorial Guinea), and *Boletin estadistica,* (Statistical Bulletin).

EQUATORIAL GUINEA - AGRICULTURE

Federal Statistical Office, Gustav - Stresemann - Ring 11, D-6200 Wiesbaden, Germany; *Aquatorialguinea.*

Food and Agricultural Organization of the United Nations (FAO) Via delle Terme di Caracalla, 00100 Rome, Italy (Telephone Number in U.S. (202) 653-2400); *Production Yearbook, The State of Food and Agriculture,* and *Trade Yearbook.*

G.K. Hall and Company, 70 Lincoln Street, Boston, Massachusetts 02111 (617) 423-3990; *The World in Figures.*

Statistical Office of the United Nations, Publishing Service, New York, New York 10017 (800) 253-9646; *Statistical Yearbook,* and *Survey of Economic and Social Conditions in Africa.*

United Nations Economic Commission for Africa, Africa Hall, P.O. Box 3001, Addis Ababa, Ethiopia (Telephone Number in U.S. (800) 253-9646); *African Statistical Yearbook.*

EQUATORIAL GUINEA - AIRLINE SERVICE

G.K. Hall and Company, 70 Lincoln Street, Boston, Massachusetts 02111 (617) 423-3990; *The World in Figures.*

United Nations Economic Commission for Africa, Africa Hall, P.O. Box 3001, Addis Ababa, Ethiopia (Telephone Number in U.S. (800) 253-9646); *African Statistical Yearbook.*

EQUATORIAL GUINEA - ANIMAL HEALTH

Food and Agricultural Organization of the United Nations (FAO), Via delle Terme di Caracalla, 00100 Rome, Italy (Telephone Number in U.S. (202) 653-2400); *Animal Health Yearbook.*

EQUATORIAL GUINEA - AREA AND DENSITY OF POPULATION

African Development Bank, 01 BP 1387, Abidjan 01, Cote D'Ivoire; *Selected Statistics on Regional Member Countries.*

Federal Statistical Office, Gustav - Stresemann - Ring 11, D-6200 Wiesbaden, Germany; *Aquatorialguinea.*

Food and Agricultural Organization of the United Nations (FAO) Via delle Terme di Caracalla, 00100 Rome, Italy (Telephone Number in U.S. (202) 653-2400); *The State of Food and Agriculture.*

G.K. Hall and Company, 70 Lincoln Street, Boston, Massachusetts 02111 (617) 423-3990; *The World in Figures.*

Statistical Office of the United Nations, Publishing Service, New York, New York 10017 (800) 253-9646; *Statistical Yearbook,* and *Survey of Economic and Social Conditions in Africa.*

EQUATORIAL GUINEA - ARMS EXPORTS AND IMPORTS

U.S. Arms Control and Disarmament Agency, 320 Twenty-first Street, NW, Washington, D.C. 20451 (202) 647-8677; *World Military Expenditures and Arms Transfers.*

EQUATORIAL GUINEA - BALANCE OF PAYMENTS

African Development Bank, 01 BP 1387, Abidjan 01, Cote D'Ivoire; *Selected Statistics on Regional Member Countries.*

The Economist Intelligence Unit, 111 West 57th Street, New York, New York 10019 (800) 938-4685; *The World Market Atlas.*

Federal Statistical Office, Gustav - Stresemann - Ring 11, D-6200 Wiesbaden, Germany; *Aquatorialguinea.*

G.K. Hall and Company, 70 Lincoln Street, Boston, Massachusetts 02111 (617) 423-3990; *The World in Figures.*

International Monetary Fund, 700 Nineteenth Street, NW, Washington, D.C. 20431 (202) 623-7000; *Balance of Payments Yearbook.*

United Nations Economic Commission for Africa, Africa Hall, P.O. Box 3001, Addis Ababa, Ethiopia (Telephone Number in U.S. (800) 253-9646); *African Statistical Yearbook.*

EQUATORIAL GUINEA - BANKING

G.K. Hall and Company, 70 Lincoln Street, Boston, Massachusetts 02111 (617) 423-3990; *The World in Figures.*

United Nations Economic Commission for Africa, Africa Hall, P.O. Box 3001, Addis Ababa, Ethiopia (Telephone Number in U.S. (800) 253-9646); *African Statistical Yearbook.*

EQUATORIAL GUINEA - BIRTH RATES

Statistical Office of the United Nations, Publishing Service, New York, New York 10017 (800) 253-9646; *Demographic Yearbook, Statistical Yearbook,* and *Survey of Economic and Social Conditions in Africa.*

EQUATORIAL GUINEA - BONDS

G.K. Hall and Company, 70 Lincoln Street, Boston, Massachusetts 02111 (617) 423-3990; *The World in Figures.*

EQUATORIAL GUINEA - BOOK PRODUCTION

G.K. Hall and Company, 70 Lincoln Street, Boston, Massachusetts 02111 (617) 423-3990; *The World in Figures.*

EQUATORIAL GUINEA - BROADCASTING

Billboard Limited, P.O. Box 9027, 1006 AA Amsterdam, The Netherlands (Telephone Number in U.S. (212) 764-7300); *World Radio TV Handbook.*

G.K. Hall and Company, 70 Lincoln Street, Boston, Massachusetts 02111 (617) 423-3990; *The World in Figures.*

EQUATORIAL GUINEA - BUSINESS

G.K. Hall and Company, 70 Lincoln Street, Boston, Massachusetts 02111 (617) 423-3990; *The World in Figures.*

EQUATORIAL GUINEA - CALORIE SUPPLY

African Development Bank, 01 BP 1387, Abidjan 01, Cote D'Ivoire; *Selected Statistics on Regional Member Countries.*

Food and Agricultural Organization of the United Nations (FAO) Via delle Terme di Caracalla, 00100 Rome, Italy (Telephone Number in U.S. (202) 653-2400); *The State of Food and Agriculture.*

EQUATORIAL GUINEA - CATTLE - See EQUATORIAL - LIVESTOCK AND POULTRY

EQUATORIAL GUINEA - CHEMICAL (ORGANIC) PRODUCTION - See EQUATORIAL GUINEA - MINING AND MINERAL PRODUCTS

EQUATORIAL GUINEA - CLASS STRUCTURE

G.K. Hall and Company, 70 Lincoln Street, Boston, Massachusetts 02111 (617) 423-3990; *The World in Figures.*

EQUATORIAL GUINEA - CLIMATE

G.K. Hall and Company, 70 Lincoln Street, Boston, Massachusetts 02111 (617) 423-3990; *The World in Figures.*

EQUATORIAL GUINEA - COAL PRODUCTION - See EQUATORIAL GUINEA - MINING AND MINERAL PRODUCTS

EQUATORIAL GUINEA - COCOA PRODUCTION - See EQUATORIAL GUINEA - CROPS

EQUATORIAL GUINEA - COFFEE - See EQUATORIAL GUINEA - CROPS

EQUATORIAL GUINEA - COMMUNICATIONS

Federal Statistical Office, Gustav - Stresemann - Ring 11, D-6200 Wiesbaden, Germany; *Aquatorialguinea.*

G.K. Hall and Company, 70 Lincoln Street, Boston, Massachusetts 02111 (617) 423-3990; *The World in Figures.*

United Nations Economic Commission for Africa, Africa Hall, P.O. Box 3001, Addis Ababa, Ethiopia (Telephone Number in U.S. (800) 253-9646); *African Statistical Yearbook.*

EQUATORIAL GUINEA - CONSUMER PRICE INDEX

African Development Bank, 01 BP 1387, Abidjan 01, Cote D'Ivoire; *Selected Statistics on Regional Member Countries.*

Federal Statistical Office, Gustav - Stresemann - Ring 11, D-6200 Wiesbaden, Germany; *Aquatorialguinea.*

G.K. Hall and Company, 70 Lincoln Street, Boston, Massachusetts 02111 (617) 423-3990; *The World in Figures.*

Statistical Office of the United Nations, Publishing Service, New York, New York 10017 (800) 253-9646; *Survey of Economic and Social Conditions in Africa.*

EQUATORIAL GUINEA - CONSUMER PRICES

Federal Statistical Office, Gustav - Stresemann - Ring 11, D-6200 Wiesbaden, Germany; *Aquatorialguinea.*

EQUATORIAL GUINEA - CONSUMPTION

African Development Bank, 01 BP 1387, Abidjan 01, Cote D'Ivoire; *Selected Statistics on Regional Member Countries.*

G.K. Hall and Company, 70 Lincoln Street, Boston, Massachusetts 02111 (617) 423-3990; *The World in Figures.*

Statistical Office of the United Nations, Publishing Service, New York, New York 10017 (800) 253-9646; *Survey of Economic and Social Conditions in Africa.*

EQUATORIAL GUINEA - CORN PRODUCTION - See EQUATORIAL GUINEA - CROPS

EQUATORIAL GUINEA - CORPORATE TAXES - See EQUATORIAL GUINEA - TAXATION

EQUATORIAL GUINEA - CROPS

Commodity Research Bureau, Incorporated, 75 Wall Street, New York, New York 10005 (212) 504-7754; *Commodity Year Book.*

Food and Agricultural Organization of the United Nations (FAO) Via delle Terme di Caracalla, 00100 Rome, Italy (Telephone Number in U.S. (202) 653-2400); *Production Yearbook,* and *The State of Food and Agriculture.*

G.K. Hall and Company, 70 Lincoln Street, Boston, Massachusetts 02111 (617) 423-3990; *The World in Figures.*

Statistical Office of the United Nations, Publishing Service, New York, New York 10017 (800) 253-9646; *Statistical Yearbook.*

United Nations Economic Commission for Africa, Africa Hall, P.O. Box 3001, Addis Ababa, Ethiopia (Telephone Number in U.S. (800) 253-9646); *African Statistical Yearbook.*

EQUATORIAL GUINEA - CUSTOMS DUTIES

G.K. Hall and Company, 70 Lincoln Street, Boston, Massachusetts 02111 (617) 423-3990; *The World in Figures.*

EQUATORIAL GUINEA - DAIRY PRODUCTS

Organisation for Economic Co-operation and Development (OECD), 2 rue Andre-Pascal, 75 Paris 16, France (Telephone Number in U.S. (202) 785-6323; *Indicators of Industrial Activity.*

EQUATORIAL GUINEA - DEATH RATES

G.K. Hall and Company, 70 Lincoln Street, Boston, Massachusetts 02111 (617) 423-3990; *The World in Figures.*

Statistical Office of the United Nations, Publishing Service, New York, New York 10017 (800) 253-9646; *Statistical Yearbook,* and *Survey of Economic and Social Conditions in Africa.*

EQUATORIAL GUINEA - DEFENSE EXPENDITURES

G.K. Hall and Company, 70 Lincoln Street, Boston, Massachusetts 02111 (617) 423-3990; *The World in Figures.*

U.S. Arms Control and Disarmament Agency, 320 Twenty-first Street, NW, Washington, D.C. 20451 (202) 647-8677; *World Military Expenditures and Arms Transfers.*

EQUATORIAL GUINEA - DEMOGRAPHY

The Economist Intelligence Unit, 111 West 57th Street, New York, New York 10019 (800) 938-4685; *The World Market Atlas.*

Federal Statistical Office, Gustav - Stresemann - Ring 11, D-6200 Wiesbaden, Germany; *Aquatorialguinea.*

G.K. Hall and Company, 70 Lincoln Street, Boston, Massachusetts 02111 (617) 423-3990; *The World in Figures.*

Statistical Office of the United Nations, Publishing Service, New York, New York 10017 (800) 253-9646; *Survey of Economic and Social Conditions in Africa.*

EQUATORIAL GUINEA - DEVELOPMENT ASSISTANCE

G.K. Hall and Company, 70 Lincoln Street, Boston, Massachusetts 02111 (617) 423-3990; *The World in Figures.*

Statistical Office of the United Nations, Publishing Service, New York, New York 10017 (800) 253-9646; *Statistical Yearbook.*

EQUATORIAL GUINEA - DISEASE

G.K. Hall and Company, 70 Lincoln Street, Boston, Massachusetts 02111 (617) 423-3990; *The World in Figures.*

EQUATORIAL GUINEA - DIVORCE RATES

Statistical Office of the United Nations, Publishing Service, New York, New York 10017 (800) 253-9646; *Demographic Yearbook.*

EQUATORIAL GUINEA - DOMESTIC PRODUCT

G.K. Hall and Company, 70 Lincoln Street, Boston, Massachusetts 02111 (617) 423-3990; *The World in Figures.*

EQUATORIAL GUINEA - DUCKS - See EQUATORIAL GUINEA - LIVESTOCK AND POULTRY

EQUATORIAL GUINEA - ECONOMY

African Development Bank, 01 BP 1387, Abidjan 01, Cote D'Ivoire; *Selected Statistics on Regional Member Countries.*

Federal Statistical Office, Gustav - Stresemann - Ring 11, D-6200 Wiesbaden, Germany; *Aquatorialguinea.*

G.K. Hall and Company, 70 Lincoln Street, Boston, Massachusetts 02111 (617) 423-3990; *The World in Figures.*

EQUATORIAL GUINEA - EDUCATION

African Development Bank, 01 BP 1387, Abidjan 01, Cote D'Ivoire; *Selected Statistics on Regional Member Countries.*

The Economist Intelligence Unit, 111 West 57th Street, New York, New York 10019 (800) 938-4685; *The World Market Atlas.*

G.K. Hall and Company, 70 Lincoln Street, Boston, Massachusetts 02111 (617) 423-3990; *The World in Figures.*

Statistical Office of the United Nations, Publishing Service, New York, New York 10017 (800) 253-9646; *Survey of Economic and*

Social Conditions in Africa.

United Nations Economic Commission for Africa, Africa Hall, P.O. Box 3001, Addis Ababa, Ethiopia (Telephone Number in U.S. (800) 253-9646); *African Statistical Yearbook.*

EQUATORIAL GUINEA - EGG PRODUCTION - See EQUATORIAL GUINEA - DAIRY PRODUCTS

EQUATORIAL GUINEA - ELECTRICITY

Statistical Office of the United Nations, Publishing Service, New York, New York 10017 (800) 253-9646; *Survey of Economic and Social Conditions in Africa.*

United Nations Economic Commission for Africa, Africa Hall, P.O. Box 3001, Addis Ababa, Ethiopia (Telephone Number in U.S. (800) 253-9646); *African Statistical Yearbook.*

EQUATORIAL GUINEA - EMPLOYMENT

Statistical Office of the United Nations, Publishing Service, New York, New York 10017 (800) 253-9646; *Survey of Economic and Social Conditions in Africa.*

United Nations Economic Commission for Africa, Africa Hall, P.O. Box 3001, Addis Ababa, Ethiopia (Telephone Number in U.S. (800) 253-9646); *African Statistical Yearbook.*

EQUATORIAL GUINEA - ENERGY

Food and Agricultural Organization of the United Nations (FAO) Via delle Terme di Caracalla, 00100 Rome, Italy (Telephone Number in U.S. (202) 653-2400); *The State of Food and Agriculture.*

G.K. Hall and Company, 70 Lincoln Street, Boston, Massachusetts 02111 (617) 423-3990; *The World in Figures.*

Statistical Office of the United Nations, Publishing Service, New York, New York 10017 (800) 253-9646; *Statistical Yearbook.*

United Nations Economic Commission for Africa, Africa Hall, P.O. Box 3001, Addis Ababa, Ethiopia (Telephone Number in U.S. (800) 253-9646); *African Statistical Yearbook.*

EQUATORIAL GUINEA - EXCHANGE RATES

African Development Bank, 01 BP 1387, Abidjan 01, Cote D'Ivoire; *Selected Statistics on Regional Member Countries.*

Statistical Office of the United Nations, Publishing Service, New York, New York 10017 (800) 253-9646; *Statistical Yearbook.*

EQUATORIAL GUINEA - EXPORTS

African Development Bank, 01 BP 1387, Abidjan 01, Cote D'Ivoire; *Selected Statistics on Regional Member Countries.*

The Economist Intelligence Unit, 111 West 57th Street, New York, New York 10019 (800) 938-4685; *The World Market Atlas.*

Food and Agricultural Organization of the United Nations (FAO) Via delle Terme di Caracalla, 00100 Rome, Italy (Telephone Number in U.S. (202) 653-2400); *The State of Food and Agriculture.*

G.K. Hall and Company, 70 Lincoln Street, Boston, Massachusetts 02111 (617) 423-3990; *The World in Figures.*

International Monetary Fund, 700 Nineteenth Street, NW, Washington, D.C. 20431 (202) 623-7000; *Direction of Trade Statistics.*

Statistical Office of the United Nations, Publishing Service, New York, New York 10017 (800) 253-9646; *Survey of Economic and Social Conditions in Africa.*

United Nations Economic Commission for Africa, Africa Hall, P.O. Box 3001, Addis Ababa, Ethiopia (Telephone Number in U.S. (800) 253-9646); *African Statistical Yearbook.*

EQUATORIAL GUINEA - EXTERNAL INDEBTEDNESS

African Development Bank, 01 BP 1387, Abidjan 01, Cote D'Ivoire; *Selected Statistics on Regional Member Countries.*

Statistical Office of the United Nations, Publishing Service, New York, New York 10017 (800) 253-9646; *Survey of Economic and Social Conditions in Africa.*

EQUATORIAL GUINEA - EXTERNAL TRADE

African Development Bank, 01 BP 1387, Abidjan 01, Cote D'Ivoire; *Selected Statistics on Regional Member Countries.*

Food and Agricultural Organization of the United Nations (FAO) Via delle Terme di Caracalla, 00100 Rome, Italy (Telephone Number in U.S. (202) 653-2400); *The State of Food and Agriculture,* and *Trade Yearbook.*

G.K. Hall and Company, 70 Lincoln Street, Boston, Massachusetts 02111 (617) 423-3990; *The World in Figures.*

EQUATORIAL GUINEA - FARM CROPS - See EQUATORIAL GUINEA - CROPS

EQUATORIAL GUINEA - FERTILITY RATES

Statistical Office of the United Nations, Publishing Service, New York, New York 10017 (800) 253-9646; *Survey of Economic and Social Conditions in Africa.*

EQUATORIAL GUINEA - FERTILIZER

Food and Agricultural Organization of the United Nations (FAO), Via delle Terme di Caracalla, 00100 Rome, Italy (Telephone Number in U.S. (202) 653-2400); *Fertilizer Yearbook,* and *The State of Food and Agriculture.*

Statistical Office of the United Nations, Publishing Service, New York, New York 10017 (800) 253-9646; *Statistical Yearbook.*

EQUATORIAL GUINEA - FETAL MORTALITY

Statistical Office of the United Nations, Publishing Service, New York, New York 10017 (800) 253-9646; *Demographic Yearbook.*

EQUATORIAL GUINEA - FINANCE

African Development Bank, 01 BP 1387, Abidjan 01, Cote D'Ivoire; *Selected Statistics on Regional Member Countries.*

Federal Statistical Office, Gustav - Stresemann - Ring 11, D-6200 Wiesbaden, Germany; *Aquatorialguinea.*

G.K. Hall and Company, 70 Lincoln Street, Boston, Massachusetts 02111 (617) 423-3990; *The World in Figures.*

International Monetary Fund, 700 Nineteenth Street, NW, Washington, D.C. 20431 (202) 623-7000; *International Financial Statistics.*

United Nations Economic Commission for Africa, Africa Hall, P.O. Box 3001, Addis Ababa, Ethiopia (Telephone Number in U.S. (800) 253-9646); *African Statistical Yearbook.*

EQUATORIAL GUINEA - FISHERIES

Federal Statistical Office, Gustav - Stresemann - Ring 11, D-6200 Wiesbaden, Germany; *Aquatorialguinea.*

Food and Agricultural Organization of the United Nations (FAO) Via delle Terme di Caracalla, 00100 Rome, Italy (Telephone Number in U.S. (202) 653-2400); *The State of Food and Agriculture,* and *Yearbook of Fishery Statistics.*

Statistical Office of the United Nations, Publishing Service, New York, New York 10017 (800) 253-9646; *Survey of Economic and Social Conditions in Africa.*

United Nations Economic Commission for Africa, Africa Hall, P.O. Box 3001, Addis Ababa, Ethiopia (Telephone Number in U.S. (800) 253-9646); *African Statistical Yearbook.*

EQUATORIAL GUINEA - FOOD

African Development Bank, 01 BP 1387, Abidjan 01, Cote D'Ivoire; *Selected Statistics on Regional Member Countries.*

Food and Agricultural Organization of the United Nations (FAO) Via delle Terme di Caracalla, 00100 Rome, Italy (Telephone Number in U.S. (202) 653-2400); *Production Yearbook,* and *The State of Food and Agriculture.*

G.K. Hall and Company, 70 Lincoln Street, Boston, Massachusetts 02111 (617) 423-3990; *The World in Figures.*

EQUATORIAL GUINEA - FOREIGN AID

G.K. Hall and Company, 70 Lincoln Street, Boston, Massachusetts 02111 (617) 423-3990; *The World in Figures.*

EQUATORIAL GUINEA - FOREIGN TRADE

Federal Statistical Office, Gustav - Stresemann - Ring 11, D-6200 Wiesbaden, Germany; *Aquatorialguinea.*

Food and Agricultural Organization of the United Nations (FAO) Via delle Terme di Caracalla, 00100 Rome, Italy (Telephone Number in U.S. (202) 653-2400); *The State of Food and Agriculture.*

G.K. Hall and Company, 70 Lincoln Street, Boston, Massachusetts 02111 (617) 423-3990; *The World in Figures.*

United Nations Economic Commission for Africa, Africa Hall, P.O. Box 3001, Addis Ababa, Ethiopia (Telephone Number in U.S. (800) 253-9646); *African Statistical Yearbook.*

EQUATORIAL GUINEA - FORESTRY AND FOREST PRODUCTS

Federal Statistical Office, Gustav - Stresemann - Ring 11, D-6200 Wiesbaden, Germany; *Aquatorialguinea.*

Food and Agricultural Organization of the United Nations (FAO) Via delle Terme di Caracalla, 00100 Rome, Italy (Telephone Number in U.S. (202) 653-2400); *The State of Food and Agriculture,* and *Yearbook of Forest Products.*

G.K. Hall and Company, 70 Lincoln Street, Boston, Massachusetts 02111 (617) 423-3990; *The World in Figures.*

United Nations Economic Commission for Africa, Africa Hall, P.O. Box 3001, Addis Ababa, Ethiopia (Telephone Number in U.S. (800) 253-9646); *African Statistical Yearbook.*

United Nations Educational, Scientific and Cultural Organization (UNESCO), 7 Place de Fontenoy, F-75700 Paris, France (Telephone Number in U.S. (212) 963-5981); *Statistical Yearbook.*

EQUATORIAL GUINEA - GENERAL INDUSTRIAL STATISTICS

Federal Statistical Office, Gustav - Stresemann - Ring 11, D-6200 Wiesbaden, Germany; *Aquatorialguinea.*

EQUATORIAL GUINEA - GENERAL MORTALITY

Statistical Office of the United Nations, Publishing Service, New York, New York 10017 (800) 253-9646; *Demographic Yearbook.*

EQUATORIAL GUINEA - GEOGRAPHIC DATA

Federal Statistical Office, Gustav - Stresemann - Ring 11, D-6200 Wiesbaden, Germany; *Aquatorialguinea.*

EQUATORIAL GUINEA - GOATS - See EQUATORIAL GUINEA - LIVESTOCK AND POULTRY

EQUATORIAL GUINEA - GOVERNMENT

G.K. Hall and Company, 70 Lincoln Street, Boston, Massachusetts 02111 (617) 423-3990; *The World in Figures.*

EQUATORIAL GUINEA - GOVERNMENT REVENUE

Statistical Office of the United Nations, Publishing Service, New York, New York 10017 (800) 253-9646; *Survey of Economic and Social Conditions in Africa.*

EQUATORIAL GUINEA - GRAIN PRODUCTION - See EQUATORIAL GUINEA - CROPS

EQUATORIAL GUINEA - GROSS DOMESTIC PRODUCT

African Development Bank, 01 BP 1387, Abidjan 01, Cote D'Ivoire; *Selected Statistics on Regional Member Countries.*

The Economist Intelligence Unit, 111 West 57th Street, New York, New York 10019 (800) 938-4685; *The World Market Atlas.*

G.K. Hall and Company, 70 Lincoln Street, Boston, Massachusetts 02111 (617) 423-3990; *The World in Figures.*

Statistical Office of the United Nations, Publishing Service, New York, New York 10017 (800) 253-9646; *Statistical Yearbook,* and *Survey of Economic and Social Conditions in Africa.*

United Nations Economic Commission for Africa, Africa Hall, P.O. Box 3001, Addis Ababa, Ethiopia (Telephone Number in U.S. (800) 253-9646); *African Statistical Yearbook.*

EQUATORIAL GUINEA - GROSS NATIONAL PRODUCT

U.S. Arms Control and Disarmament Agency, 320 Twenty-first Street, NW, Washington, D.C. 20451 (202) 647-8677; *World Military Expenditures and Arms Transfers.*

EQUATORIAL GUINEA - HEALTH

African Development Bank, 01 BP 1387, Abidjan 01, Cote D'Ivoire; *Selected Statistics on Regional Member Countries.*

Federal Statistical Office, Gustav - Stresemann - Ring 11, D-6200 Wiesbaden, Germany; *Aquatorialguinea.*

G.K. Hall and Company, 70 Lincoln Street, Boston, Massachusetts 02111 (617) 423-3990; *The World in Figures.*

Statistical Office of the United Nations, Publishing Service, New York, New York 10017 (800) 253-9646; *Statistical Yearbook.*

United Nations Economic Commission for Africa, Africa Hall, P.O. Box 3001, Addis Ababa, Ethiopia (Telephone Number in U.S. (800) 253-9646); *African Statistical Yearbook.*

EQUATORIAL GUINEA - HIDE PRODUCTION

Food and Agricultural Organization of the United Nations (FAO), Via delle Terme di Caracalla, 00100 Rome, Italy (Telephone Number in U.S. (202) 653-2400); *Production Yearbook.*

EQUATORIAL GUINEA - HIGHWAYS

G.K. Hall and Company, 70 Lincoln Street, Boston, Massachusetts 02111 (617) 423-3990; *The World in Figures.*

Statistical Office of the United Nations, Publishing Service, New York, New York 10017 (800) 253-9646; *Survey of Economic and Social Conditions in Africa.*

United Nations Economic Commission for Africa, Africa Hall, P.O. Box 3001, Addis Ababa, Ethiopia (Telephone Number in U.S. (800) 253-9646); *African Statistical Yearbook.*

EQUATORIAL GUINEA - ILLITERATE POPULATION

The Economist Intelligence Unit, 111 West 57th Street, New York, New York 10019 (800) 938-4685; *The World Market Atlas.*

G.K. Hall and Company, 70 Lincoln Street, Boston, Massachusetts 02111 (617) 423-3990; *The World in Figures.*

EQUATORIAL GUINEA - IMPORTS

African Development Bank, 01 BP 1387, Abidjan 01, Cote D'Ivoire; *Selected Statistics on Regional Member Countries.*

The Economist Intelligence Unit, 111 West 57th Street, New York, New York 10019 (800) 938-4685; *The World Market Atlas.*

Food and Agricultural Organization of the United Nations (FAO) Via delle Terme di Caracalla, 00100 Rome, Italy (Telephone Number in U.S. (202) 653-2400); *The State of Food and Agriculture.*

G.K. Hall and Company, 70 Lincoln Street, Boston, Massachusetts 02111 (617) 423-3990; *The World in Figures.*

International Monetary Fund, 700 Nineteenth Street, NW, Washington, D.C. 20431 (202) 623-7000; *Direction of Trade Statistics.*

Statistical Office of the United Nations, Publishing Service, New York, New York 10017 (800) 253-9646; *Survey of Economic and Social Conditions in Africa.*

EQUATORIAL GUINEA - INDUSTRY

Federal Statistical Office, Gustav - Stresemann - Ring 11, D-6200 Wiesbaden, Germany; *Aquatorialguinea.*

G.K. Hall and Company, 70 Lincoln Street, Boston, Massachusetts 02111 (617) 423-3990; *The World in Figures.*

Statistical Office of the United Nations, Publishing Service, New York, New York 10017 (800) 253-9646; *Survey of Economic and Social Conditions in Africa.*

United Nations Economic Commission for Africa, Africa Hall, P.O. Box 3001, Addis Ababa, Ethiopia (Telephone Number in U.S. (800) 253-9646); *African Statistical Yearbook.*

EQUATORIAL GUINEA - INFANT AND MATERNAL MORTALITY

Statistical Office of the United Nations, Publishing Service, New York, New York 10017 (800) 253-9646; *Demographic Yearbook, Statistical Yearbook,* and *Survey of Economic and Social Conditions in Africa.*

EQUATORIAL GUINEA - INTERNATIONAL RESERVES EXCLUDING GOLD

African Development Bank, 01 BP 1387, Abidjan 01, Cote D'Ivoire; *Selected Statistics on Regional Member Countries.*

EQUATORIAL GUINEA - LABOR FORCE

African Development Bank, 01 BP 1387, Abidjan 01, Cote D'Ivoire; *Selected Statistics on Regional Member Countries.*

Food and Agricultural Organization of the United Nations (FAO) Via delle Terme di Caracalla, 00100 Rome, Italy (Telephone Number in U.S. (202) 653-2400); *The State of Food and Agriculture.*

G.K. Hall and Company, 70 Lincoln Street, Boston, Massachusetts 02111 (617) 423-3990; *The World in Figures.*

EQUATORIAL GUINEA - LAND USE

Food and Agricultural Organization of the United Nations (FAO), Via delle Terme di Caracalla, 00100 Rome, Italy (Telephone Number in U.S. (202) 653-2400); *Production Yearbook.*

G.K. Hall and Company, 70 Lincoln Street, Boston, Massachusetts 02111 (617) 423-3990; *The World in Figures.*

EQUATORIAL GUINEA - LIFE EXPECTANCY

African Development Bank, 01 BP 1387, Abidjan 01, Cote D'Ivoire; *Selected Statistics on Regional Member Countries.*

EQUATORIAL GUINEA - LITERACY RATE

Statistical Office of the United Nations, Publishing Service, New York, New York 10017 (800) 253-9646; *Survey of Economic and Social Conditions in Africa.*

EQUATORIAL GUINEA - LIVESTOCK AND POULTRY

Food and Agricultural Organization of the United Nations (FAO), Via delle Terme di Caracalla, 00100 Rome, Italy (Telephone Number in U.S. (202) 653-2400); *Production Yearbook,* and *The State of Food and Agriculture.*

G.K. Hall and Company, 70 Lincoln Street, Boston, Massachusetts 02111 (617) 423-3990; *The World in Figures.*

Statistical Office of the United Nations, Publishing Service, New York, New York 10017 (800) 253-9646; *Statistical Yearbook* and *Survey of Economic and Social Conditions in Africa.*

United Nations Economic Commission for Africa, Africa Hall, P.O. Box 3001, Addis Ababa, Ethiopia (Telephone Number in U.S. (800) 253-9646); *African Statistical Yearbook.*

EQUATORIAL GUINEA - LIVING LEVELS

G.K. Hall and Company, 70 Lincoln Street, Boston, Massachusetts 02111 (617) 423-3990; *The World in Figures.*

EQUATORIAL GUINEA - MANUFACTURING

G.K. Hall and Company, 70 Lincoln Street, Boston, Massachusetts 02111 (617) 423-3990; *The World in Figures.*

Statistical Office of the United Nations, Publishing Service, New York, New York 10017 (800) 253-9646; *Survey of Economic and Social Conditions in Africa.*

EQUATORIAL GUINEA - MARRIAGE RATES

Statistical Office of the United Nations, Publishing Service, New York, New York 10017 (800) 253-9646; *Demographic Yearbook,* and *Statistical Yearbook.*

EQUATORIAL GUINEA - MEAT PRODUCTION - See EQUATORIAL GUINEA - LIVESTOCK AND POULTRY

EQUATORIAL GUINEA - MERCHANT SHIPPING

G.K. Hall and Company, 70 Lincoln Street, Boston, Massachusetts 02111 (617) 423-3990; *The World in Figures.*

Statistical Office of the United Nations, Publishing Service, New York, New York 10017 (800) 253-9646; *Statistical Yearbook.*

United Nations Economic Commission for Africa, Africa Hall, P.O. Box 3001, Addis Ababa, Ethiopia (Telephone Number in U.S. (800) 253-9646); *African Statistical Yearbook.*

EQUATORIAL GUINEA - MILITARY

G.K. Hall and Company, 70 Lincoln Street, Boston, Massachusetts 02111 (617) 423-3990; *The World in Figures.*

The International Institute for Strategic Studies, 23 Tavistock Street, London WC2E 7NQ, England; *The Military Balance.*

U.S. Arms Control and Disarmament Agency, 320 Twenty-first Street, NW, Washington, D.C. 20451 (202) 647-8677; *World Military Expenditures and Arms Transfers.*

EQUATORIAL GUINEA - MINING AND MINERAL PRODUCTS

G.K. Hall and Company, 70 Lincoln Street, Boston, Massachusetts 02111 (617) 423-3990; *The World in Figures.*

United Nations Economic Commission for Africa, Africa Hall, P.O. Box 3001, Addis Ababa, Ethiopia (Telephone Number in U.S. (800) 253-9646); *African Statistical Yearbook.*

EQUATORIAL GUINEA - MONEY EXCHANGE RATES

Statistical Office of the United Nations, Publishing Service, New York, New York 10017 (800) 253-9646; *Statistical Yearbook.*

EQUATORIAL GUINEA - MONEY SUPPLY

African Development Bank, 01 BP 1387, Abidjan 01, Cote D'Ivoire; *Selected Statistics on Regional Member Countries.*

Federal Statistical Office, Gustav - Stresemann - Ring 11, D-6200 Wiesbaden, Germany; *Aquatorialguinea.*

G.K. Hall and Company, 70 Lincoln Street, Boston, Massachusetts 02111 (617) 423-3990; *The World in Figures.*

EQUATORIAL GUINEA - MOTION PICTURES

Statistical Office of the United Nations, Publishing Service, New York, New York 10017 (800) 253-9646; *Statistical Yearbook.*

EQUATORIAL GUINEA - MOTOR VEHICLES IN USE

G.K. Hall and Company, 70 Lincoln Street, Boston, Massachusetts 02111 (617) 423-3990; *The World in Figures.*

Statistical Office of the United Nations, Publishing Service, New York, New York 10017 (800) 253-9646; *Survey of Economic and Social Conditions in Africa.*

EQUATORIAL GUINEA - MUSEUMS

United Nations Educational, Scientific and Cultural Organization (UNESCO), 7 Place de Fontenoy, F-75700 Paris, France (Telephone Number in U.S. (212) 963-5981); *Statistical Yearbook.*

EQUATORIAL GUINEA - NATALITY - See EQUATORIAL GUINEA - BIRTH RATE

EQUATORIAL GUINEA - NATIONAL ACCOUNTS

African Development Bank, 01 BP 1387, Abidjan 01, Cote D'Ivoire; *Selected Statistics on Regional Member Countries.*

Federal Statistical Office, Gustav - Stresemann - Ring 11, D-6200 Wiesbaden, Germany; *Aquatorialguinea.*

International Monetary Fund, 700 Nineteenth Street, NW, Washington, D.C. 20431 (202) 623-7000; *International Financial Statistics.*

Statistical Office of the United Nations, Publishing Service, New York, New York 10017 (800) 253-9646; *Statistical Yearbook.*

United Nations Economic Commission for Africa, Africa Hall, P.O. Box 3001, Addis Ababa, Ethiopia (Telephone Number in U.S. (800) 253-9646); *African Statistical Yearbook.*

EQUATORIAL GUINEA - NATIONAL INCOME

G.K. Hall and Company, 70 Lincoln Street, Boston, Massachusetts 02111 (617) 423-3990; *The World in Figures.*

Statistical Office of the United Nations, Publishing Service, New York, New York 10017 (800) 253-9646; *Statistical Yearbook.*

EQUATORIAL GUINEA - NEWSPAPER PRODUCTION - See EQUATORIAL GUINEA - FORESTRY AND FOREST PRODUCTS

EQUATORIAL GUINEA - OCCUPATIONS - See EQUATORIAL GUINEA - LABOR FORCE

EQUATORIAL GUINEA - PALM OIL PRODUCTION - See EQUATORIAL GUINEA - CROPS

EQUATORIAL GUINEA - PESTICIDE USE

Food and Agricultural Organization of the United Nations (FAO) Via delle Terme di Caracalla, 00100 Rome, Italy (Telephone Number in U.S. (202) 653-2400); *The State of Food and Agriculture.*

EQUATORIAL GUINEA - PETROLEUM INDUSTRY

Food and Agricultural Organization of the United Nations (FAO) Via delle Terme di Caracalla, 00100 Rome, Italy (Telephone Number in U.S. (202) 653-2400); *The State of Food and Agriculture.*

G.K. Hall and Company, 70 Lincoln Street, Boston, Massachusetts 02111 (617) 423-3990; *The World in Figures.*

EQUATORIAL GUINEA - PIGS - See EQUATORIAL GUINEA - LIVESTOCK AND POULTRY

EQUATORIAL GUINEA - POPULATION

African Development Bank, 01 BP 1387, Abidjan 01, Cote D'Ivoire; *Selected Statistics on Regional Member Countries.*

The Economist Intelligence Unit, 111 West 57th Street, New York, New York 10019 (800) 938-4685; *The World Market Atlas.*

Federal Statistical Office, Gustav - Stresemann - Ring 11, D-6200 Wiesbaden, Germany; *Aquatorialguinea.*

Food and Agricultural Organization of the United Nations (FAO), Via delle Terme di Caracalla, 00100 Rome, Italy (Telephone Number in U.S. (202) 653-2400); *Production Yearbook.*

G.K. Hall and Company, 70 Lincoln Street, Boston, Massachusetts 02111 (617) 423-3990; *The World in Figures.*

Statistical Office of the United Nations, Publishing Service, New York, New York 10017 (800) 253-9646; *Demographic Yearbook, Statistical Yearbook,* and *Survey of Economic and Social Conditions in Africa.*

U.S. Arms Control and Disarmament Agency, 320 Twenty-first Street, NW, Washington, D.C. 20451 (202) 647-8677; *World Military Expenditures and Arms Transfers.*

World Health Organization, Office of Publications, Avenue Appia, CH-1211 Geneva 27, Switzerland (Telephone Number in U.S. (518) 436-9686); *World Health Statistics Annual.*

EQUATORIAL GUINEA - PRICES

Federal Statistical Office, Gustav - Stresemann - Ring 11, D-6200 Wiesbaden, Germany; *Aquatorialguinea.*

Food and Agricultural Organization of the United Nations (FAO), Via delle Terme di Caracalla, 00100 Rome, Italy (Telephone Number in U.S. (202) 653-2400); *Production Yearbook,* and *The State of Food and Agriculture.*

G.K. Hall and Company, 70 Lincoln Street, Boston, Massachusetts 02111 (617) 423-3990; *The World in Figures.*

EQUATORIAL GUINEA - PRODUCTION

G.K. Hall and Company, 70 Lincoln Street, Boston, Massachusetts 02111 (617) 423-3990; *The World in Figures.*

EQUATORIAL GUINEA - PUBLIC FINANCE

Federal Statistical Office, Gustav - Stresemann - Ring 11, D-6200 Wiesbaden, Germany; *Aquatorialguinea.*

EQUATORIAL GUINEA - RAILWAYS

G.K. Hall and Company, 70 Lincoln Street, Boston, Massachusetts 02111 (617) 423-3990; *The World in Figures.*

United Nations Economic Commission for Africa, Africa Hall, P.O. Box 3001, Addis Ababa, Ethiopia (Telephone Number in U.S. (800) 253-9646); *African Statistical Yearbook.*

EQUATORIAL GUINEA - RETAIL TRADE

G.K. Hall and Company, 70 Lincoln Street, Boston, Massachusetts 02111 (617) 423-3990; *The World in Figures.*

EQUATORIAL GUINEA - ROOT AND TUBER PRODUCTION - See EQUATORIAL GUINEA - CROPS

EQUATORIAL GUINEA - ROUNDWOOD PRODUCTION - See EQUATORIAL GUINEA - FORESTRY AND FOREST PRODUCTS

EQUATORIAL GUINEA - SAWNWOOD PRODUCTION - See EQUATORIAL GUINEA - FORESTRY AND FOREST PRODUCTS

EQUATORIAL GUINEA - SHEEP - See EQUATORIAL GUINEA - LIVESTOCK AND POULTRY

EQUATORIAL GUINEA - SOCIAL DATA

African Development Bank, 01 BP 1387, Abidjan 01, Cote D'Ivoire; *Selected Statistics on Regional Member Countries.*

G.K. Hall and Company, 70 Lincoln Street, Boston, Massachusetts 02111 (617) 423-3990; *The World in Figures.*

EQUATORIAL GUINEA - STOCKS - COMMODITY - MARKET PRICE - INDEX

Food and Agricultural Organization of the United Nations (FAO) Via delle Terme di Caracalla, 00100 Rome, Italy (Telephone Number in U.S. (202) 653-2400); *The State of Food and Agriculture.*

EQUATORIAL GUINEA - TAXATION

G.K. Hall and Company, 70 Lincoln Street, Boston, Massachusetts 02111 (617) 423-3990; *The World in Figures.*

EQUATORIAL GUINEA - TELEPHONES IN USE

American Telephone and Telegraph Company, 26 Parsippany Road, Whippany, New Jersey 07981 (800) 338-4038; *The World's Telephones.*

G.K. Hall and Company, 70 Lincoln Street, Boston, Massachusetts 02111 (617) 423-3990; *The World in Figures.*

EQUATORIAL GUINEA - TEXTILE INDUSTRY

G.K. Hall and Company, 70 Lincoln Street, Boston, Massachusetts 02111 (617) 423-3990; *The World in Figures.*

EQUATORIAL GUINEA - THEATRE

United Nations Educational, Scientific and Cultural Organization (UNESCO), 7 Place de Fontenoy, F-75700 Paris, France (Telephone Number in U.S. (212) 963-5981); *Statistical Yearbook.*

EQUATORIAL GUINEA - TOURISM

Federal Statistical Office, Gustav - Stresemann - Ring 11, D-6200 Wiesbaden, Germany; *Aquatorialguinea.*

G.K. Hall and Company, 70 Lincoln Street, Boston, Massachusetts 02111 (617) 423-3990; *The World in Figures.*

United Nations Economic Commission for Africa, Africa Hall, P.O. Box 3001, Addis Ababa, Ethiopia (Telephone Number in U.S. (800) 253-9646); *African Statistical Yearbook.*

EQUATORIAL GUINEA - TRACTORS IN USE

Statistical Office of the United Nations, Publishing Service, New York, New York 10017 (800) 253-9646; *Statistical Yearbook.*

EQUATORIAL GUINEA - TRADE - See EQUATORIAL GUINEA - FOREIGN TRADE

EQUATORIAL GUINEA - TRANSPORTATION AND COMMUNICATIONS

Federal Statistical Office, Gustav - Stresemann - Ring 11, D-6200 Wiesbaden, Germany; *Aquatorialguinea.*

G.K. Hall and Company, 70 Lincoln Street, Boston, Massachusetts 02111 (617) 423-3990; *The World in Figures.*

United Nations Economic Commission for Africa, Africa Hall, P.O. Box 3001, Addis Ababa, Ethiopia (Telephone Number in U.S. (800) 253-9646); *African Statistical Yearbook.*

EQUATORIAL GUINEA - VITAL STATISTICS

G.K. Hall and Company, 70 Lincoln Street, Boston, Massachusetts 02111 (617) 423-3990; *The World in Figures.*

Statistical Office of the United Nations, Publishing Service, New York, New York 10017 (800) 253-9646; *Statistical Yearbook.*

World Health Organization, Office of Publications, Avenue Appia, CH-1211 Geneva 27, Switzerland (Telephone Number in U.S. (518) 436-9686); *World Health Statistics Annual.*

EQUATORIAL GUINEA - WAGES

Federal Statistical Office, Gustav - Stresemann - Ring 11, D-6200 Wiesbaden, Germany; *Aquatorialguinea.*

G.K. Hall and Company, 70 Lincoln Street, Boston, Massachusetts 02111 (617) 423-3990; *The World in Figures.*

EQUATORIAL GUINEA - WEATHER

G.K. Hall and Company, 70 Lincoln Street, Boston, Massachusetts 02111 (617) 423-3990; *The World in Figures.*

ERITREA - See also ETHIOPIA

ERITREA - AGRICULTURE

Encyclopedia Britannica, Incorporated, 310 South Michigan Avenue, Chicago, Illinois 60604 (312) 347-7000; *Britannica World Data.*

ERITREA - AIRLINE SERVICE

Encyclopedia Britannica, Incorporated, 310 South Michigan Avenue, Chicago, Illinois 60604 (312) 347-7000; *Britannica World Data.*

ERITREA - BIRTH RATES

Encyclopedia Britannica, Incorporated, 310 South Michigan Avenue, Chicago, Illinois 60604 (312) 347-7000; *Britannica World Data.*

ERITREA - CONSTRUCTION

Encyclopedia Britannica, Incorporated, 310 South Michigan Avenue, Chicago, Illinois 60604 (312) 347-7000; *Britannica World Data.*

ERITREA - DEMOGRAPHY

Encyclopedia Britannica, Incorporated, 310 South Michigan Avenue, Chicago, Illinois 60604 (312) 347-7000; *Britannica World Data.*

ERITREA - DIVORCE RATES

Encyclopedia Britannica, Incorporated, 310 South Michigan Avenue, Chicago, Illinois 60604 (312) 347-7000; *Britannica World Data.*

ERITREA - ECONOMY

Encyclopedia Britannica, Incorporated, 310 South Michigan Avenue, Chicago, Illinois 60604 (312) 347-7000; *Britannica World Data.*

ERITREA - EDUCATION

Encyclopedia Britannica, Incorporated, 310 South Michigan Avenue, Chicago, Illinois 60604 (312) 347-7000; *Britannica World Data.*

ERITREA - ENERGY PRODUCTION

Encyclopedia Britannica, Incorporated, 310 South Michigan Avenue, Chicago, Illinois 60604 (312) 347-7000; *Britannica World Data.*

ERITREA - FERTILITY RATES

Encyclopedia Britannica, Incorporated, 310 South Michigan Avenue, Chicago, Illinois 60604 (312) 347-7000; *Britannica World Data.*

ERITREA - FISHERIES

Encyclopedia Britannica, Incorporated, 310 South Michigan Avenue, Chicago, Illinois 60604 (312) 347-7000; *Britannica World Data.*

ERITREA - FORESTRY

Encyclopedia Britannica, Incorporated, 310 South Michigan Avenue, Chicago, Illinois 60604 (312) 347-7000; *Britannica World Data.*

ERITREA - HEALTH

Encyclopedia Britannica, Incorporated, 310 South Michigan Avenue, Chicago, Illinois 60604 (312) 347-7000; *Britannica World Data.*

ERITREA - LAND USE

Encyclopedia Britannica, Incorporated, 310 South Michigan Avenue, Chicago, Illinois 60604 (312) 347-7000; *Britannica World Data.*

ERITREA - LIVESTOCK AND POULTRY

Encyclopedia Britannica, Incorporated, 310 South Michigan Avenue, Chicago, Illinois 60604 (312) 347-7000; *Britannica World Data.*

ERITREA - MANUFACTURING

Encyclopedia Britannica, Incorporated, 310 South Michigan Avenue, Chicago, Illinois 60604 (312) 347-7000; *Britannica World Data.*

ERITREA - MARRIAGE RATES

Encyclopedia Britannica, Incorporated, 310 South Michigan Avenue, Chicago, Illinois 60604 (312) 347-7000; *Britannica World Data.*

ERITREA - MILITARY

Encyclopedia Britannica, Incorporated, 310 South Michigan Avenue, Chicago, Illinois 60604 (312) 347-7000; *Britannica World Data.*

ERITREA - MINING AND MINERAL PRODUCTS

Encyclopedia Britannica, Incorporated, 310 South Michigan Avenue, Chicago, Illinois 60604 (312) 347-7000; *Britannica World Data.*

ERITREA - POPULATION

Encyclopedia Britannica, Incorporated, 310 South Michigan Avenue, Chicago, Illinois 60604 (312) 347-7000; *Britannica World Data.*

ERITREA - ROADS

Encyclopedia Britannica, Incorporated, 310 South Michigan Avenue, Chicago, Illinois 60604 (312) 347-7000; *Britannica World Data.*

ERITREA - TELEPHONES IN USE

Encyclopedia Britannica, Incorporated, 310 South Michigan Avenue, Chicago, Illinois 60604 (312) 347-7000; *Britannica World Data.*

ERITREA - TRANSPORTATION AND COMMUNICATIONS

Encyclopedia Britannica, Incorporated, 310 South Michigan Avenue, Chicago, Illinois 60604 (312) 347-7000; *Britannica World Data.*

ERITREA - VITAL STATISTICS

Encyclopedia Britannica, Incorporated, 310 South Michigan Avenue, Chicago, Illinois 60604 (312) 347-7000; *Britannica World Data.*

ESKIMO POPULATION

U.S. Department of Commerce, Bureau of the Census, Suitland, Maryland 20233 (301) 763-4040; *Current Population Reports.*

ESTABLISHMENTS

Federal Deposit Insurance Corporation, 550 Seventeenth Street, NW, Washington, D.C. 20429 (202) 393-8400; *Statistics on Banking, Annual Report, Failed Bank Cost Analysis Report, The FDIC Quarterly Banking Profile,* and unpublished data.

International Franchise Association, 1350 New York Avenue, Suite 900, Washington, D.C. 20005 (202) 628-8000; *Franchising in the Economy.*

National Credit Union Administration, 1776 G Street, NW, Washington, D.C. 20456 (212) 682-9600; *Annual Report of the National Credit Union Administration,* and unpublished data.

U.S. Department of Commerce, Bureau of the Census, Suitland, Maryland 20233 (301) 763-4040; *Annual Survey of Manufactures, Census of Manufactures, Census of Retail Trade, Current Business Reports, Combined Annual and Revised Monthly Retail Trade, Census of Service Industries, Census of Wholesale Trade, County Business Patterns,* and *Economic Census of Outlying Areas.*

ESTATE AND GIFT TAXES

Executive Office of the President, Office of Management and Budget, Executive Office Building, Washington, D.C. 20503 (202) 395-3080; *Budget of the United States Government.*

U.S. Department of the Treasury, Internal Revenue Service, 1111 Constitution Avenue, NW, Washington, D.C. 20224 (202) 566-5000; *Annual Report of the Commissioner and Chief Counsel of the Internal Revenue Service.*

ESTONIA - See also UNION OF SOVIET SOCIALIST REPUBLICS

ESTONIA - AGRICULTURE

Business International Moscow, 23 Profseyuznaya Ulitsa 117859, Moscow (Telephone Number in U.S. (800) 938-4685); *The CIS Market Atlas.*

The World Bank, 1818 H Street, NW, Washington, D.C. 20433 (202) 477-1234; *Statistical Handbook: States of the Former USSR.*

ESTONIA - AIRLINE SERVICE

Business International Moscow, 23 Profseyuznaya Ulitsa 117859, Moscow (Telephone Number in U.S. (800) 938-4685); *The CIS Market Atlas.*

ESTONIA - AREA AND DENSITY OF POPULATION

Business International Moscow, 23 Profseyuznaya Ulitsa 117859, Moscow (Telephone Number in U.S. (800) 938-4685); *The CIS Market Atlas.*

ESTONIA - BALANCE OF PAYMENTS

The Economist Intelligence Unit, 111 West 57th Street, New York, New York 10019 (800) 938-4685; *The World Market Atlas.*

ESTONIA - BANKING

Business International Moscow, 23 Profseyuznaya Ulitsa 117859, Moscow (Telephone Number in U.S. (800) 938-4685); *The CIS Market Atlas.*

ESTONIA - BIRTH RATES

Business International Moscow, 23 Profseyuznaya Ulitsa 117859, Moscow (Telephone Number in U.S. (800) 938-4685); *The CIS Market Atlas.*

ESTONIA - BUDGET

Business International Moscow, 23 Profseyuznaya Ulitsa 117859, Moscow (Telephone Number in U.S. (800) 938-4685); *The CIS Market Atlas.*

ESTONIA - CAPITAL INVESTMENT

The World Bank, 1818 H Street, NW, Washington, D.C. 20433 (202) 477-1234; *Statistical Handbook: States of the Former USSR.*

ESTONIA - CATTLE - See ESTONIA - LIVESTOCK AND POULTRY

ESTONIA - CHEMICALS

Business International Moscow, 23 Profseyuznaya Ulitsa 117859, Moscow (Telephone Number in U.S. (800) 938-4685); *The CIS Market Atlas.*

ESTONIA - COAL PRODUCTION AND CONSUMPTION - See ESTONIA - MINING AND MINERAL PRODUCTS

ESTONIA - COMMUNICATIONS

Business International Moscow, 23 Profseyuznaya Ulitsa 117859, Moscow (Telephone Number in U.S. (800) 938-4685); *The CIS Market Atlas.*

ESTONIA - CONSTRUCTION INDUSTRY

Business International Moscow, 23 Profseyuznaya Ulitsa 117859, Moscow (Telephone Number in U.S. (800) 938-4685); *The CIS Market Atlas.*

ESTONIA - CONSUMER PRODUCTS

Business International Moscow, 23 Profseyuznaya Ulitsa 117859, Moscow (Telephone Number in U.S. (800) 938-4685); *The CIS Market Atlas.*

ESTONIA - CONSUMPTION

Business International Moscow, 23 Profseyuznaya Ulitsa 117859, Moscow (Telephone Number in U.S. (800) 938-4685); *The CIS Market Atlas.*

The World Bank, 1818 H Street, NW, Washington, D.C. 20433 (202) 477-1234; *Statistical Handbook: States of the Former USSR.*

ESTONIA - COTTON PRODUCTION AND CONSUMPTION - See ESTONIA - CROPS

ESTONIA - CROPS

The World Bank, 1818 H Street, NW, Washington, D.C. 20433 (202) 477-1234; *Statistical Handbook: States of the Former USSR.*

ESTONIA - DEATH RATES

Business International Moscow, 23 Profseyuznaya Ulitsa 117859, Moscow (Telephone Number in U.S. (800) 938-4685); *The CIS Market Atlas.*

ESTONIA - DEMOGRAPHY

Business International Moscow, 23 Profseyuznaya Ulitsa 117859, Moscow (Telephone Number in U.S. (800) 938-4685); *The CIS Market Atlas.*

The Economist Intelligence Unit, 111 West 57th Street, New York, New York 10019 (800) 938-4685; *The World Market Atlas.*

The World Bank, 1818 H Street, NW, Washington, D.C. 20433 (202) 477-1234; *Statistical Handbook: States of the Former USSR.*

ESTONIA - DISEASES

Business International Moscow, 23 Profseyuznaya Ulitsa 117859, Moscow (Telephone Number in U.S. (800) 938-4685); *The CIS Market Atlas.*

ESTONIA - DOMESTIC INVESTMENT

Business International Moscow, 23 Profseyuznaya Ulitsa 117859, Moscow (Telephone Number in U.S. (800) 938-4685); *The CIS Market Atlas.*

ESTONIA - ECONOMY

Business International Moscow, 23 Profseyuznaya Ulitsa 117859, Moscow (Telephone Number in U.S. (800) 938-4685); *The CIS Market Atlas.*

ESTONIA - EDUCATION

Business International Moscow, 23 Profseyuznaya Ulitsa 117859, Moscow (Telephone Number in U.S. (800) 938-4685); *The CIS Market Atlas.*

The Economist Intelligence Unit, 111 West 57th Street, New York, New York 10019 (800) 938-4685; *The World Market Atlas.*

ESTONIA - ELECTRICITY PRODUCTION

Business International Moscow, 23 Profseyuznaya Ulitsa 117859, Moscow (Telephone Number in U.S. (800) 938-4685); *The CIS Market Atlas.*

The World Bank, 1818 H Street, NW, Washington, D.C. 20433 (202) 477-1234; *Statistical Handbook: States of the Former USSR.*

ESTONIA - EMPLOYMENT

The World Bank, 1818 H Street, NW, Washington, D.C. 20433 (202) 477-1234; *Statistical Handbook: States of the Former USSR.*

ESTONIA - ENERGY

Business International Moscow, 23 Profseyuznaya Ulitsa 117859, Moscow (Telephone Number in U.S. (800) 938-4685); *The CIS Market Atlas.*

The World Bank, 1818 H Street, NW, Washington, D.C. 20433 (202) 477-1234; *Statistical Handbook: States of the Former USSR.*

ESTONIA - ENVIRONMENT

Business International Moscow, 23 Profseyuznaya Ulitsa 117859, Moscow (Telephone Number in U.S. (800) 938-4685); *The CIS Market Atlas.*

ESTONIA - EXPORTS

Business International Moscow, 23 Profseyuznaya Ulitsa 117859, Moscow (Telephone Number in U.S. (800) 938-4685); *The CIS Market Atlas.*

The Economist Intelligence Unit, 111 West 57th Street, New York, New York 10019 (800) 938-4685; *The World Market Atlas.*

The World Bank, 1818 H Street, NW, Washington, D.C. 20433 (202) 477-1234; *Statistical Handbook: States of the Former USSR.*

ESTONIA - EXTERNAL TRADE

The World Bank, 1818 H Street, NW, Washington, D.C. 20433 (202) 477-1234; *Statistical Handbook: States of the Former USSR.*

ESTONIA - FABRIC PRODUCTION AND CONSUMPTION - See ESTONIA - TEXTILE INDUSTRY

ESTONIA - FERTILITY RATES

The World Bank, 1818 H Street, NW, Washington, D.C. 20433 (202) 477-1234; *Statistical Handbook: States of the Former USSR.*

ESTONIA - FOOTWEAR PRODUCTION AND CONSUMPTION - See ESTONIA - TEXTILE INDUSTRY

ESTONIA - FOREIGN INVESTMENT

Business International Moscow, 23 Profseyuznaya Ulitsa 117859, Moscow (Telephone Number in U.S. (800) 938-4685); *The CIS Market Atlas.*

ESTONIA - FOREIGN TRADE

Business International Moscow, 23 Profseyuznaya Ulitsa 117859, Moscow (Telephone Number in U.S. (800) 938-4685); *The CIS Market Atlas.*

The World Bank, 1818 H Street, NW, Washington, D.C. 20433 (202) 477-1234; *Statistical Handbook: States of the Former USSR.*

ESTONIA - FORESTRY AND FOREST PRODUCTS

Business International Moscow, 23 Profseyuznaya Ulitsa 117859, Moscow (Telephone Number in U.S. (800) 938-4685); *The CIS Market Atlas.*

ESTONIA - GOATS - See ESTONIA - LIVESTOCK AND POULTRY

ESTONIA - GOVERNMENT EXPENDITURE

The World Bank, 1818 H Street, NW, Washington, D.C. 20433 (202) 477-1234; *Statistical Handbook: States of the Former USSR.*

ESTONIA - GOVERNMENT REVENUE

The World Bank, 1818 H Street, NW, Washington, D.C. 20433 (202) 477-1234; *Statistical Handbook: States of the Former USSR.*

ESTONIA - GROSS DOMESTIC PRODUCT

The Economist Intelligence Unit, 111 West 57th Street, New York, New York 10019 (800) 938-4685; *The World Market Atlas.*

The World Bank, 1818 H Street, NW, Washington, D.C. 20433 (202) 477-1234; *Statistical Handbook: States of the Former USSR.*

ESTONIA - HEALTH

Business International Moscow, 23 Profseyuznaya Ulitsa 117859, Moscow (Telephone Number in U.S. (800) 938-4685); *The CIS Market Atlas.*

ESTONIA - HIGHWAYS

Business International Moscow, 23 Profseyuznaya Ulitsa 117859, Moscow (Telephone Number in U.S. (800) 938-4685); *The CIS Market Atlas.*

ESTONIA - HOUSING AND HOUSING UNITS

Business International Moscow, 23 Profseyuznaya Ulitsa 117859, Moscow (Telephone Number in U.S. (800) 938-4685); *The CIS Market Atlas.*

ESTONIA - ILLITERATE POPULATION

The Economist Intelligence Unit, 111 West 57th Street, New York, New York 10019 (800) 938-4685; *The World Market Atlas.*

ESTONIA - IMPORTS

Business International Moscow, 23 Profseyuznaya Ulitsa 117859, Moscow (Telephone Number in U.S. (800) 938-4685); *The CIS Market Atlas.*

The Economist Intelligence Unit, 111 West 57th Street, New York, New York 10019 (800) 938-4685; *The World Market Atlas.*

The World Bank, 1818 H Street, NW, Washington, D.C. 20433 (202) 477-1234; *Statistical Handbook: States of the Former USSR.*

ESTONIA - INDUSTRY

Business International Moscow, 23 Profseyuznaya Ulitsa 117859, Moscow (Telephone Number in U.S. (800) 938-4685); *The CIS Market Atlas.*

The World Bank, 1818 H Street, NW, Washington, D.C. 20433 (202) 477-1234; *Statistical Handbook: States of the Former USSR.*

ESTONIA - INFANT MORTALITY RATES

Business International Moscow, 23 Profseyuznaya Ulitsa 117859, Moscow (Telephone Number in U.S. (800) 938-4685); *The CIS Market Atlas.*

ESTONIA - LABOR FORCE

Business International Moscow, 23 Profseyuznaya Ulitsa 117859, Moscow (Telephone Number in U.S. (800) 938-4685); *The CIS Market Atlas.*

The World Bank, 1818 H Street, NW, Washington, D.C. 20433 (202) 477-1234; *Statistical Handbook: States of the Former USSR.*

ESTONIA - LIFE EXPECTANCY

Business International Moscow, 23 Profseyuznaya Ulitsa 117859, Moscow (Telephone Number in U.S. (800) 938-4685); *The CIS Market Atlas.*

ESTONIA - LIVESTOCK AND POULTRY

Business International Moscow, 23 Profseyuznaya Ulitsa 117859, Moscow (Telephone Number in U.S. (800) 938-4685); *The CIS Market Atlas.*

ESTONIA - MEAT PRODUCTION - See ESTONIA - LIVESTOCK AND POULTRY

ESTONIA - MILITARY

The International Institute for Strategic Studies, 23 Tavistock Street, London WC2E 7NQ, England; *The Military Balance.*

ESTONIA - MINING AND MINERAL PRODUCTS

Business International Moscow, 23 Profseyuznaya Ulitsa 117859, Moscow (Telephone Number in U.S. (800) 938-4685); *The CIS Market Atlas.*

ESTONIA - MOTOR VEHICLES

Business International Moscow, 23 Profseyuznaya Ulitsa 117859, Moscow (Telephone Number in U.S. (800) 938-4685); *The CIS Market Atlas.*

ESTONIA - NATIONAL ACCOUNTS

The World Bank, 1818 H Street, NW, Washington, D.C. 20433 (202) 477-1234; *Statistical Handbook: States of the Former USSR.*

ESTONIA - NATIONAL INCOME

Business International Moscow, 23 Profseyuznaya Ulitsa 117859, Moscow (Telephone Number in U.S. (800) 938-4685); *The CIS Market Atlas.*

ESTONIA - PIGS - See ESTONIA - LIVESTOCK AND POULTRY

ESTONIA - POPULATION

Business International Moscow, 23 Profseyuznaya Ulitsa 117859, Moscow (Telephone Number in U.S. (800) 938-4685); *The CIS Market Atlas.*

The Economist Intelligence Unit, 111 West 57th Street, New York, New York 10019 (800) 938-4685; *The World Market Atlas.*

The World Bank, 1818 H Street, NW, Washington, D.C. 20433 (202) 477-1234; *Statistical Handbook: States of the Former USSR.*

ESTONIA - POULTRY - See ESTONIA - LIVESTOCK AND POULTRY

ESTONIA - PRICES

The World Bank, 1818 H Street, NW, Washington, D.C. 20433 (202) 477-1234; *Statistical Handbook: States of the Former USSR.*

ESTONIA - PRODUCTION

The World Bank, 1818 H Street, NW, Washington, D.C. 20433 (202) 477-1234; *Statistical Handbook: States of the Former USSR.*

ESTONIA - PUBLIC FINANCE

The World Bank, 1818 H Street, NW, Washington, D.C. 20433 (202) 477-1234; *Statistical Handbook: States of the Former USSR.*

ESTONIA - RAILWAYS

Business International Moscow, 23 Profseyuznaya Ulitsa 117859, Moscow (Telephone Number in U.S. (800) 938-4685); *The CIS Market Atlas.*

ESTONIA - RETAIL TRADE

Business International Moscow, 23 Profseyuznaya Ulitsa 117859, Moscow (Telephone Number in U.S. (800) 938-4685); *The CIS Market Atlas.*

ESTONIA - ROADS - See ESTONIA - HIGHWAYS

ESTONIA - ROUNDWOOD PRODUCTION AND CONSUMPTION - See ESTONIA - FORESTRY INDUSTRY

ESTONIA - SHEEP - See ESTONIA - LIVESTOCK AND POULTRY

ESTONIA - STEEL PRODUCTION AND CONSUMPTION - See ESTONIA - MINING AND MINERAL PRODUCTION

ESTONIA - TEXTILE INDUSTRY

Business International Moscow, 23 Profseyuznaya Ulitsa 117859, Moscow (Telephone Number in U.S. (800) 938-4685); *The CIS Market Atlas.*

ESTONIA - TOURISM

Business International Moscow, 23 Profseyuznaya Ulitsa 117859, Moscow (Telephone Number in U.S. (800) 938-4685); *The CIS Market Atlas.*

ESTONIA - TRANSPORTATION AND COMMUNICATIONS

Business International Moscow, 23 Profseyuznaya Ulitsa 117859, Moscow (Telephone Number in U.S. (800) 938-4685); *The CIS Market Atlas.*

ESTONIA - WAGES

Business International Moscow, 23 Profseyuznaya Ulitsa 117859, Moscow (Telephone Number in U.S. (800) 938-4685); *The CIS Market Atlas.*

The World Bank, 1818 H Street, NW, Washington, D.C. 20433 (202) 477-1234; *Statistical Handbook: States of the Former USSR.*

ESTONIA - WOOL PRODUCTION AND CONSUMPTION - See ESTONIA - TEXTILE INDUSTRY

ETHANE

U.S. Department of Energy, Energy Information Administration, Washington, D.C. 20585 (202) 586-8800; *Petroleum Supply Annual.*

Ethiopia - National Statistical Office

Central Statistical Authority, Post Office Box 1143, Addis Ababa, Ethiopia.

Ethiopia - Primary Statistics Source

Central Statistical Authority, Post Office Box 1143, Addis Ababa, Ethiopia; *Ethiopia Statistical Abstract.*

ETHIOPIA - AGRICULTURE

Euromonitor Publications Limited, 87-88 Turnmill Street, London EC1M 5QU, England; *International Marketing Data and Statistics.*

Federal Statistical Office, Gustav - Stresemann - Ring 11, D-6200 Wiesbaden, Germany; *Athiopien.*

Food and Agricultural Organization of the United Nations (FAO) Via delle Terme di Caracalla, 00100 Rome, Italy (Telephone Number in U.S. (202) 653-2400); *The State of Food and Agriculture, Production Yearbook,* and *Trade Yearbook.*

G.K. Hall and Company, 70 Lincoln Street, Boston, Massachusetts 02111 (617) 423-3990; *The World in Figures.*

Provisional Military Government of Ethiopia, Central Statistical Office, Post Office Box 1143, Addis Ababa, Ethiopia; *Ethiopia Statistical Abstract.*

Statistical Office of the United Nations, Publishing Service, New York, New York 10017 (800) 253-9646; *Statistical Yearbook,* and *Survey of Economic and Social Conditions in Africa.*

Times Books, 201 East 50th Street, New York, New York 10022 (212) 751-2600; *The Economist Book of Vital World Statistics.*

United Nations Economic Commission for Africa, Africa Hall, P.O. Box 3001, Addis Ababa, Ethiopia (Telephone Number in U.S. (800) 253-9646); *African Statistical Yearbook.*

ETHIOPIA - AIRLINE SERVICE

G.K. Hall and Company, 70 Lincoln Street, Boston, Massachusetts 02111 (617) 423-3990; *The World in Figures.*

International Civil Aviation Organization, 1000 Sherbrooke Street West, Suite 400, Montreal, Quebec, Canada H3A 2R2 (514) 285-8219; *Civil Aviation Statistics of the World.*

Statistical Office of the United Nations, Publishing Service, New York, New York 10017 (800) 253-9646; *Statistical Yearbook.*

Times Books, 201 East 50th Street, New York, New York 10022 (212) 751-2600; *The Economist Book of Vital World Statistics.*

United Nations Economic Commission for Africa, Africa Hall, P.O. Box 3001, Addis Ababa, Ethiopia (Telephone Number in U.S. (800) 253-9646); *African Statistical Yearbook.*

ETHIOPIA - ANIMAL HEALTH

Food and Agricultural Organization of the United Nations (FAO), Via delle Terme di Caracalla, 00100 Rome, Italy (Telephone Number in U.S. (202) 653-2400); *Animal Health Yearbook.*

ETHIOPIA - AREA AND DENSITY OF POPULATION

African Development Bank, 01 BP 1387, Abidjan 01, Cote D'Ivoire; *Selected Statistics on Regional Member Countries.*

Euromonitor Publications Limited, 87-88 Turnmill Street, London EC1M 5QU, England; *International Marketing Data and Statistics.*

Federal Statistical Office, Gustav - Stresemann - Ring 11, D-6200 Wiesbaden, Germany; *Athiopien.*

Food and Agricultural Organization of the United Nations (FAO) Via delle Terme di Caracalla, 00100 Rome, Italy (Telephone Number in U.S. (202) 653-2400); *The State of Food and Agriculture.*

G.K. Hall and Company, 70 Lincoln Street, Boston, Massachusetts 02111 (617) 423-3990; *The World in Figures.*

Statistical Office of the United Nations, Publishing Service, New York, New York 10017 (800) 253-9646; *Statistical Yearbook,* and *Survey of Economic and Social Conditions in Africa.*

Times Books, 201 East 50th Street, New York, New York 10022 (212) 751-2600; *The Economist Book of Vital World Statistics.*

United Nations Educational, Scientific and Cultural Organization (UNESCO), 7 Place de Fontenoy, F-75700 Paris, France (Telephone Number in U.S. (212) 963-5981); *Statistical Yearbook.*

ETHIOPIA - ARMS EXPORTS AND IMPORTS

U.S. Arms Control and Disarmament Agency, 320 Twenty-first Street, NW, Washington, D.C. 20451 (202) 647-8677; *World Military Expenditures and Arms Transfers.*

ETHIOPIA - BALANCE OF PAYMENTS

African Development Bank, 01 BP 1387, Abidjan 01, Cote D'Ivoire; *Selected Statistics on Regional Member Countries.*

The Economist Intelligence Unit, 111 West 57th Street, New York, New York 10019 (800) 938-4685; *The World Market Atlas.*

Federal Statistical Office, Gustav - Stresemann - Ring 11, D-6200 Wiesbaden, Germany; *Athiopien.*

G.K. Hall and Company, 70 Lincoln Street, Boston, Massachusetts 02111 (617) 423-3990; *The World in Figures.*

International Monetary Fund, 700 Nineteenth Street, NW, Washington, D.C. 20431 (202) 623-7000; *Balance of Payments Yearbook,* and *International Financial Statistics.*

Provisional Military Government of Ethiopia, Central Statistical Office, Post Office Box 1143, Addis Ababa, Ethiopia; *Ethiopia Statistical Abstract.*

Times Books, 201 East 50th Street, New York, New York 10022 (212) 751-2600; *The Economist Book of Vital World Statistics.*

United Nations Economic Commission for Africa, Africa Hall, P.O. Box 3001, Addis Ababa, Ethiopia (Telephone Number in U.S. (800) 253-9646); *African Statistical Yearbook.*

ETHIOPIA - BANKING

G.K. Hall and Company, 70 Lincoln Street, Boston, Massachusetts 02111 (617) 423-3990; *The World in Figures.*

International Monetary Fund, 700 Nineteenth Street, NW, Washington, D.C. 20431 (202) 623-7000; *Government Finance Statistics Yearbook,* and *International Financial Statistics.*

Provisional Military Government of Ethiopia, Central Statistical Office, Post Office Box 1143, Addis Ababa, Ethiopia; *Ethiopia Statistical Abstract.*

United Nations Economic Commission for Africa, Africa Hall, P.O. Box 3001, Addis Ababa, Ethiopia (Telephone Number in U.S. (800) 253-9646); *African Statistical Yearbook.*

ETHIOPIA - BARLEY PRODUCTION - See ETHIOPIA - CROPS

ETHIOPIA - BEER PRODUCTION

Statistical Office of the United Nations, Publishing Service, New York, New York 10017 (800) 253-9646; *Statistical Yearbook.*

ETHIOPIA - BIRTH RATES

Statistical Office of the United Nations, Publishing Service, New York, New York 10017 (800) 253-9646; *Demographic Yearbook, Statistical Yearbook,* and *Survey of Economic and Social Conditions in Africa.*

Times Books, 201 East 50th Street, New York, New York 10022 (212) 751-2600; *The Economist Book of Vital World Statistics.*

ETHIOPIA - BONDS

G.K. Hall and Company, 70 Lincoln Street, Boston, Massachusetts 02111 (617) 423-3990; *The World in Figures.*

International Monetary Fund, 700 Nineteenth Street, NW, Washington, D.C. 20431 (202) 623-7000; *Government Finance Statistics Yearbook.*

ETHIOPIA - BOOK PRODUCTION

G.K. Hall and Company, 70 Lincoln Street, Boston, Massachusetts 02111 (617) 423-3990; *The World in Figures.*

United Nations Educational, Scientific and Cultural Organization (UNESCO), 7 Place de Fontenoy, F-75700 Paris, France (Telephone Number in U.S. (212) 963-5981); *Statistical Yearbook.*

ETHIOPIA - BROADCASTING

Billboard Limited, P.O. Box 9027, 1006 AA Amsterdam, The Netherlands (Telephone Number in U.S. (212) 764-7300); *World Radio TV Handbook.*

G.K. Hall and Company, 70 Lincoln Street, Boston, Massachusetts 02111 (617) 423-3990; *The World in Figures.*

Times Books, 201 East 50th Street, New York, New York 10022 (212) 751-2600; *The Economist Book of Vital World Statistics.*

ETHIOPIA - BUILDING CONSTRUCTION - See ETHIOPIA - CONSTRUCTION INDUSTRY

ETHIOPIA - BUSINESS

G.K. Hall and Company, 70 Lincoln Street, Boston, Massachusetts 02111 (617) 423-3990; *The World in Figures.*

ETHIOPIA - BUSINESS AND PROFESSIONAL LICENSES

International Monetary Fund, 700 Nineteenth Street, NW, Washington, D.C. 20431 (202) 623-7000; *Government Finance Statistics Yearbook.*

ETHIOPIA - BUTTER PRODUCTION - See ETHIOPIA - DAIRY PRODUCTS

ETHIOPIA - CABBAGE PRODUCTION - See ETHIOPIA - CROPS

ETHIOPIA - CALORIE SUPPLY

African Development Bank, 01 BP 1387, Abidjan 01, Cote D'Ivoire; *Selected Statistics on Regional Member Countries.*

Food and Agricultural Organization of the United Nations (FAO) Via delle Terme di Caracalla, 00100 Rome, Italy (Telephone Number in U.S. (202) 653-2400); *The State of Food and Agriculture.*

ETHIOPIA - CAPITAL REVENUE

International Monetary Fund, 700 Nineteenth Street, NW, Washington, D.C. 20431 (202) 623-7000; *Government Finance Statistics Yearbook.*

ETHIOPIA - CASTOR BEAN PRODUCTION - See ETHIOPIA - CROPS

ETHIOPIA - CATTLE - See ETHIOPIA - LIVESTOCK AND POULTRY

ETHIOPIA - CEMENT PRODUCTION - See ETHIOPIA - MINING AND MINERAL PRODUCTS

ETHIOPIA - CHEESE PRODUCTION - See ETHIOPIA - DAIRY PRODUCTS

ETHIOPIA - CHEMICAL (ORGANIC) PRODUCTION - See ETHIOPIA - MINING AND MINERAL PRODUCTS

ETHIOPIA - CHICK PEA PRODUCTION - See ETHIOPIA - CROPS

ETHIOPIA - CHICKENS - See ETHIOPIA - LIVESTOCK AND POULTRY

ETHIOPIA - CIGARETTE PRODUCTION - See ETHIOPIA - TOBACCO PRODUCTION

ETHIOPIA - CLASS STRUCTURE

G.K. Hall and Company, 70 Lincoln Street, Boston, Massachusetts 02111 (617) 423-3990; *The World in Figures.*

ETHIOPIA - CLIMATE

G.K. Hall and Company, 70 Lincoln Street, Boston, Massachusetts 02111 (617) 423-3990; *The World in Figures.*

Provisional Military Government of Ethiopia, Central Statistical Office, Post Office Box 1143, Addis Ababa, Ethiopia; *Ethiopia Statistical Abstract.*

ETHIOPIA - COAL PRODUCTION - See ETHIOPIA - MINING AND MINERAL PRODUCTS

ETHIOPIA - COFFEE EXPORTS - See ETHIOPIA - CROPS

ETHIOPIA - COMMUNICATIONS

Federal Statistical Office, Gustav - Stresemann - Ring 11, D-6200 Wiesbaden, Germany; *Athiopien.*

G.K. Hall and Company, 70 Lincoln Street, Boston, Massachusetts 02111 (617) 423-3990; *The World in Figures.*

United Nations Economic Commission for Africa, Africa Hall, P.O. Box 3001, Addis Ababa, Ethiopia (Telephone Number in U.S. (800) 253-9646); *African Statistical Yearbook.*

ETHIOPIA - CONSTRUCTION INDUSTRY

Provisional Military Government of Ethiopia, Central Statistical Office, Post Office Box 1143, Addis Ababa, Ethiopia; *Ethiopia Statistical Abstract.*

Statistical Office of the United Nations, Publishing Service, New York, New York 10017 (800) 253-9646; *Construction Statistics Yearbook,* and *Statistical Yearbook.*

United Nations Economic Commission for Africa, Africa Hall, P.O. Box 3001, Addis Ababa, Ethiopia (Telephone Number in U.S. (800) 253-9646); *African Statistical Yearbook.*

ETHIOPIA - CONSUMER PRICE INDEX

African Development Bank, 01 BP 1387, Abidjan 01, Cote D'Ivoire; *Selected Statistics on Regional Member Countries.*

Federal Statistical Office, Gustav - Stresemann - Ring 11, D-6200 Wiesbaden, Germany; *Athiopien.*

G.K. Hall and Company, 70 Lincoln Street, Boston, Massachusetts 02111 (617) 423-3990; *The World in Figures.*

Statistical Office of the United Nations, Publishing Service, New York, New York 10017 (800) 253-9646; *Statistical Yearbook,* and *Survey of Economic and Social Conditions in Africa.*

United Nations Economic Commission for Africa, Africa Hall, P.O. Box 3001, Addis Ababa, Ethiopia (Telephone Number in U.S. (800) 253-9646); *African Statistical Yearbook.*

ETHIOPIA - CONSUMER PRICES

Federal Statistical Office, Gustav - Stresemann - Ring 11, D-6200 Wiesbaden, Germany; *Athiopien.*

International Labour Office, I.L.O. Publications, CH-1211, Geneva 22, Switzerland; *Yearbook of Labour Statistics.*

International Monetary Fund, 700 Nineteenth Street, NW, Washington, D.C. 20431 (202) 623-7000; *International Financial Statistics.*

Times Books, 201 East 50th Street, New York, New York 10022 (212) 751-2600; *The Economist Book of Vital World Statistics.*

ETHIOPIA - CONSUMPTION

African Development Bank, 01 BP 1387, Abidjan 01, Cote D'Ivoire; *Selected Statistics on Regional Member Countries.*

G.K. Hall and Company, 70 Lincoln Street, Boston, Massachusetts 02111 (617) 423-3990; *The World in Figures.*

Statistical Office of the United Nations, Publishing Service, New York, New York 10017 (800) 253-9646; *Survey of Economic and Social Conditions in Africa.*

ETHIOPIA - CORN PRODUCTION - See ETHIOPIA - CROPS

ETHIOPIA - CORPORATE TAXES - See ETHIOPIA - TAXATION

ETHIOPIA - COTTON - See ETHIOPIA - CROPS

ETHIOPIA - CRIME

Yale University Press, Yale Station, New Haven, Connecticut 06520 (203) 432-0940; *Violence and Crime in Cross-National Perspective.*

ETHIOPIA - CROPS

Commodity Research Bureau, Incorporated, 75 Wall Street, New York, New York 10005 (212) 504-7754; *Commodity Year Book.*

Food and Agricultural Organization of the United Nations (FAO) Via delle Terme di Caracalla, 00100 Rome, Italy (Telephone Number in U.S. (202) 653-2400); *Production Yearbook,* and *The State of Food and Agriculture.*

G.K. Hall and Company, 70 Lincoln Street, Boston, Massachusetts 02111 (617) 423-3990; *The World in Figures.*

International Monetary Fund, 700 Nineteenth Street, NW, Washington, D.C. 20431 (202) 623-7000; *International Financial Statistics.*

International Wheat Statistics, 28 Haymarket, London SW1Y 4SS, England; *World Wheat Statistics.*

Statistical Office of the United Nations, Publishing Service, New York, New York 10017 (800) 253-9646; *Statistical Yearbook.*

United Nations Economic Commission for Africa, Africa Hall, P.O. Box 3001, Addis Ababa, Ethiopia (Telephone Number in U.S. (800) 253-9646); *African Statistical Yearbook.*

ETHIOPIA - CUSTOMS DUTIES

G.K. Hall and Company, 70 Lincoln Street, Boston, Massachusetts 02111 (617) 423-3990; *The World in Figures.*

International Monetary Fund, 700 Nineteenth Street, NW, Washington, D.C. 20431 (202) 623-7000; *Government Finance Statistics Yearbook.*

ETHIOPIA - DAIRY PRODUCTS

Food and Agricultural Organization of the United Nations (FAO) Via delle Terme di Caracalla, 00100 Rome, Italy (Telephone Number in U.S. (202) 653-2400); *The State of Food and Agriculture.*

Statistical Office of the United Nations, Publishing Service, New York, New York 10017 (800) 253-9646; *Statistical Yearbook.*

ETHIOPIA - DEATH RATES

G.K. Hall and Company, 70 Lincoln Street, Boston, Massachusetts 02111 (617) 423-3990; *The World in Figures.*

Statistical Office of the United Nations, Publishing Service, New York, New York 10017 (800) 253-9646; *Statistical Yearbook,* and *Survey of Economic and Social Conditions in Africa.*

Times Books, 201 East 50th Street, New York, New York 10022 (212) 751-2600; *The Economist Book of Vital World Statistics.*

ETHIOPIA - DEFENSE EXPENDITURES

G.K. Hall and Company, 70 Lincoln Street, Boston, Massachusetts 02111 (617) 423-3990; *The World in Figures.*

International Monetary Fund, 700 Nineteenth Street, NW, Washington, D.C. 20431 (202) 623-7000; *Government Finance Statistics Yearbook.*

U.S. Arms Control and Disarmament Agency, 320 Twenty-first Street, NW, Washington, D.C. 20451 (202) 647-8677; *World Military Expenditures and Arms Transfers.*

ETHIOPIA - DEMOGRAPHY

The Economist Intelligence Unit, 111 West 57th Street, New York, New York 10019 (800) 938-4685; *The World Market Atlas.*

Federal Statistical Office, Gustav - Stresemann - Ring 11, D-6200 Wiesbaden, Germany; *Athiopien.*

G.K. Hall and Company, 70 Lincoln Street, Boston, Massachusetts 02111 (617) 423-3990; *The World in Figures.*

Statistical Office of the United Nations, Publishing Service, New York, New York 10017 (800) 253-9646; *Survey of Economic and Social Conditions in Africa.*

ETHIOPIA - DEVELOPMENT ASSISTANCE

G.K. Hall and Company, 70 Lincoln Street, Boston, Massachusetts 02111 (617) 423-3990; *The World in Figures.*

Statistical Office of the United Nations, Publishing Service, New York, New York 10017 (800) 253-9646; *Statistical Yearbook.*

ETHIOPIA - DISEASE

G.K. Hall and Company, 70 Lincoln Street, Boston, Massachusetts 02111 (617) 423-3990; *The World in Figures.*

ETHIOPIA - DIVORCE RATES

Statistical Office of the United Nations, Publishing Service, New York, New York 10017 (800) 253-9646; *Demographic Yearbook.*

ETHIOPIA - DOMESTIC PRODUCT

G.K. Hall and Company, 70 Lincoln Street, Boston, Massachusetts 02111 (617) 423-3990; *The World in Figures.*

ETHIOPIA - ECONOMY

African Development Bank, 01 BP 1387, Abidjan 01, Cote D'Ivoire; *Selected Statistics on Regional Member Countries.*

Euromonitor Publications Limited, 87-88 Turnmill Street, London EC1M 5QU, England; *International Marketing Data and Statistics.*

Federal Statistical Office, Gustav - Stresemann - Ring 11, D-6200 Wiesbaden, Germany; *Athiopien.*

G.K. Hall and Company, 70 Lincoln Street, Boston, Massachusetts 02111 (617) 423-3990; *The World in Figures.*

Statistical Office of the United Nations, Publishing Service, New York, New York 10017 (800) 253-9646; *Foreign Trade Statistics for Africa.*

ETHIOPIA - EDUCATION

African Development Bank, 01 BP 1387, Abidjan 01, Cote D'Ivoire; *Selected Statistics on Regional Member Countries.*

The Economist Intelligence Unit, 111 West 57th Street, New York, New York 10019 (800) 938-4685; *The World Market Atlas.*

Federal Statistical Office, Gustav - Stresemann - Ring 11, D-6200 Wiesbaden, Germany; *Athiopien.*

G.K. Hall and Company, 70 Lincoln Street, Boston, Massachusetts 02111 (617) 423-3990; *The World in Figures.*

International Monetary Fund, 700 Nineteenth Street, NW, Washington, D.C. 20431 (202) 623-7000; *Government Finance Statistics Yearbook.*

Provisional Military Government of Ethiopia, Central Statistical Office, Post Office Box 1143, Addis Ababa, Ethiopia; *Ethiopia Statistical Abstract.*

Statistical Office of the United Nations, Publishing Service, New York, New York 10017 (800) 253-9646; *Survey of Economic and Social Conditions in Africa.*

Times Books, 201 East 50th Street, New York, New York 10022 (212) 751-2600; *The Economist Book of Vital World Statistics.*

United Nations Economic Commission for Africa, Africa Hall, P.O. Box 3001, Addis Ababa, Ethiopia (Telephone Number in U.S. (800) 253-9646); *African Statistical Yearbook.*

United Nations Educational, Scientific and Cultural Organization (UNESCO), 7 Place de Fontenoy, F-75700 Paris, France (Telephone Number in U.S (212) 963-5981); *Statistical Yearbook.*

ETHIOPIA - EGG PRODUCTION - See ETHIOPIA - DAIRY PRODUCTS

ETHIOPIA - ELECTRICITY

Statistical Office of the United Nations, Publishing Service, New York, New York 10017 (800) 253-9646; *Statistical Yearbook,* and *Survey of Economic and Social Conditions in Africa.*

Times Books, 201 East 50th Street, New York, New York 10022 (212) 751-2600; *The Economist Book of Vital World Statistics.*

United Nations Economic Commission for Africa, Africa Hall, P.O. Box 3001, Addis Ababa, Ethiopia (Telephone Number in U.S. (800) 253-9646); *African Statistical Yearbook.*

ETHIOPIA - EMPLOYMENT

Euromonitor Publications Limited, 87-88 Turnmill Street, London EC1M 5QU, England; *International Marketing Data and Statistics.*

Federal Statistical Office, Gustav - Stresemann - Ring 11, D-6200 Wiesbaden, Germany; *Athiopien.*

International Labour Office, I.L.O. Publications, CH-1211, Geneva 22, Switzerland; *Yearbook of Labour Statistics.*

Statistical Office of the United Nations, Publishing Service, New York, New York 10017 (800) 253-9646; *Statistical Yearbook,* and *Survey of Economic and Social Conditions in Africa.*

United Nations Economic Commission for Africa, Africa Hall, P.O. Box 3001, Addis Ababa, Ethiopia (Telephone Number in U.S. (800) 253-9646); *African Statistical Yearbook.*

ETHIOPIA - ENERGY

Food and Agricultural Organization of the United Nations (FAO), Via delle Terme di Caracalla, 00100 Rome, Italy (Telephone Number in U.S. (202) 653-2400); *Energy Statistics Yearbook.*

G.K. Hall and Company, 70 Lincoln Street, Boston, Massachusetts 02111 (617) 423-3990; *The World in Figures.*

Statistical Office of the United Nations, Publishing Service, New York, New York 10017 (800) 253-9646; *Statistical Yearbook.*

Times Books, 201 East 50th Street, New York, New York 10022 (212) 751-2600; *The Economist Book of Vital World Statistics.*

United Nations Economic Commission for Africa, Africa Hall, P.O. Box 3001, Addis Ababa, Ethiopia (Telephone Number in U.S. (800) 253-9646); *African Statistical Yearbook.*

ETHIOPIA - EXCHANGE RATES

African Development Bank, 01 BP 1387, Abidjan 01, Cote D'Ivoire; *Selected Statistics on Regional Member Countries.*

Euromonitor Publications Limited, 87-88 Turnmill Street, London EC1M 5QU, England; *International Marketing Data and Statistics.*

International Civil Aviation Organization, 1000 Sherbrooke Street West, Suite 400, Montreal, Quebec, Canada H3A 2R2 (514) 285-8219; *Civil Aviation Statistics of the World.*

International Monetary Fund, 700 Nineteenth Street, NW, Washington, D.C. 20431 (202) 623-7000; *International Financial Statistics.*

Statistical Office of the United Nations, Publishing Service, New York, New York 10017 (800) 253-9646; *Foreign Trade Statistics for Africa*, and *Statistical Yearbook*.

ETHIOPIA - EXCISE TAXES - See ETHIOPIA - TAXATION

ETHIOPIA - EXPORTS

African Development Bank, 01 BP 1387, Abidjan 01, Cote D'Ivoire; *Selected Statistics on Regional Member Countries*.

The Economist Intelligence Unit, 111 West 57th Street, New York, New York 10019 (800) 938-4685; *The World Market Atlas*.

Euromonitor Publications Limited, 87-88 Turnmill Street, London EC1M 5QU, England; *International Marketing Data and Statistics*.

Food and Agricultural Organization of the United Nations (FAO) Via delle Terme di Caracalla, 00100 Rome, Italy (Telephone Number in U.S. (202) 653-2400); *The State of Food and Agriculture*.

G.K. Hall and Company, 70 Lincoln Street, Boston, Massachusetts 02111 (617) 423-3990; *The World in Figures*.

International Monetary Fund, 700 Nineteenth Street, NW, Washington, D.C. 20431 (202) 623-7000; *Direction of Trade Statistics*, *Government Finance Statistics Yearbook*, and *International Financial Statistics*.

Statistical Office of the United Nations, Publishing Service, New York, New York 10017 (800) 253-9646; *Foreign Trade Statistics for Africa*, and *Survey of Economic and Social Conditions in Africa*.

Times Books, 201 East 50th Street, New York, New York 10022 (212) 751-2600; *The Economist Book of Vital World Statistics*.

United Nations Economic Commission for Africa, Africa Hall, P.O. Box 3001, Addis Ababa, Ethiopia (Telephone Number in U.S. (800) 253-9646); *African Statistical Yearbook*.

ETHIOPIA - EXTERNAL INDEBTEDNESS

African Development Bank, 01 BP 1387, Abidjan 01, Cote D'Ivoire; *Selected Statistics on Regional Member Countries*.

Statistical Office of the United Nations, Publishing Service, New York, New York 10017 (800) 253-9646; *Survey of Economic and Social Conditions in Africa*.

ETHIOPIA - EXTERNAL TRADE

African Development Bank, 01 BP 1387, Abidjan 01, Cote D'Ivoire; *Selected Statistics on Regional Member Countries*.

Food and Agricultural Organization of the United Nations (FAO) Via delle Terme di Caracalla, 00100 Rome, Italy (Telephone Number in U.S. (202) 653-2400); *The State of Food and Agriculture*, and *Trade Yearbook*.

G.K. Hall and Company, 70 Lincoln Street, Boston, Massachusetts 02111 (617) 423-3990; *The World in Figures*.

Provisional Military Government of Ethiopia, Central Statistical Office, Post Office Box 1143, Addis Ababa, Ethiopia; *Ethiopia Statistical Abstract*.

Statistical Office of the United Nations, Publishing Service, New York, New York 10017 (800) 253-9646; *Statistical Yearbook*.

ETHIOPIA - FABRIC PRODUCTION - See ETHIOPIA - TEXTILE INDUSTRY

ETHIOPIA - FARM CROPS - See ETHIOPIA - CROPS

ETHIOPIA - FEMALE WORKING POPULATION - See ETHIOPIA - EMPLOYMENT

ETHIOPIA - FERTILITY RATE

Statistical Office of the United Nations, Publishing Service, New York, New York 10017 (800) 253-9646; *Survey of Economic and Social Conditions in Africa*.

Times Books, 201 East 50th Street, New York, New York 10022 (212) 751-2600; *The Economist Book of Vital World Statistics*.

ETHIOPIA - FERTILIZER

Food and Agricultural Organization of the United Nations (FAO), Via delle Terme di Caracalla, 00100 Rome, Italy (Telephone Number in U.S. (202) 653-2400); *Fertilizer Yearbook*, and *The State of Food and Agriculture*.

Statistical Office of the United Nations, Publishing Service, New York, New York 10017 (800) 253-9646; *Statistical Yearbook*.

ETHIOPIA - FETAL MORTALITY

Statistical Office of the United Nations, Publishing Service, New York, New York 10017 (800) 253-9646; *Demographic Yearbook*.

ETHIOPIA - FINANCE

African Development Bank, 01 BP 1387, Abidjan 01, Cote D'Ivoire; *Selected Statistics on Regional Member Countries*.

Federal Statistical Office, Gustav - Stresemann - Ring 11, D-6200 Wiesbaden, Germany; *Athiopien*.

G.K. Hall and Company, 70 Lincoln Street, Boston, Massachusetts 02111 (617) 423-3990; *The World in Figures*.

International Monetary Fund, 700 Nineteenth Street, NW, Washington, D.C. 20431 (202) 623-7000; *Government Finance Statistics Yearbook*, and *International Financial Statistics*.

Provisional Military Government of Ethiopia, Central Statistical Office, Post Office Box 1143, Addis Ababa, Ethiopia; *Ethiopia Statistical Abstract*.

United Nations Economic Commission for Africa, Africa Hall, P.O. Box 3001, Addis Ababa, Ethiopia (Telephone Number in U.S. (800) 253-9646); *African Statistical Yearbook*.

ETHIOPIA - FISHERIES

Federal Statistical Office, Gustav - Stresemann - Ring 11, D-6200 Wiesbaden, Germany; *Athiopien*.

Food and Agricultural Organization of the United Nations (FAO) Via delle Terme di Caracalla, 00100 Rome, Italy (Telephone Number in U.S. (202) 653-2400); *The State of Food and Agriculture*, and *Yearbook of Fishery Statistics*.

Statistical Office of the United Nations, Publishing Service, New York, New York 10017 (800) 253-9646; *Statistical Yearbook*, and *Survey of Economic and Social Conditions in Africa*.

United Nations Economic Commission for Africa, Africa Hall, P.O. Box 3001, Addis Ababa, Ethiopia (Telephone Number in U.S. (800) 253-9646); *African Statistical Yearbook.*

ETHIOPIA - FLOUR PRODUCTION

Statistical Office of the United Nations, Publishing Service, New York, New York 10017 (800) 253-9646; *Statistical Yearbook.*

ETHIOPIA - FOOD

African Development Bank, 01 BP 1387, Abidjan 01, Cote D'Ivoire; *Selected Statistics on Regional Member Countries.*

Food and Agricultural Organization of the United Nations (FAO) Via delle Terme di Caracalla, 00100 Rome, Italy (Telephone Number in U.S. (202) 653-2400); *Production Yearbook,* and *The State of Food and Agriculture.*

G.K. Hall and Company, 70 Lincoln Street, Boston, Massachusetts 02111 (617) 423-3990; *The World in Figures.*

ETHIOPIA - FOREIGN AID

G.K. Hall and Company, 70 Lincoln Street, Boston, Massachusetts 02111 (617) 423-3990; *The World in Figures.*

ETHIOPIA - FOREIGN DEBT

International Monetary Fund, 700 Nineteenth Street, NW, Washington, D.C. 20431 (202) 623-7000; *Government Finance Statistics Yearbook.*

ETHIOPIA - FOREIGN TRADE

Euromonitor Publications Limited, 87-88 Turnmill Street, London EC1M 5QU, England; *International Marketing Data and Statistics.*

Federal Statistical Office, Gustav - Stresemann - Ring 11, D-6200 Wiesbaden, Germany; *Athiopien.*

Food and Agricultural Organization of the United Nations (FAO) Via delle Terme di Caracalla, 00100 Rome, Italy (Telephone Number in U.S. (202) 653-2400); *The State of Food and Agriculture.*

G.K. Hall and Company, 70 Lincoln Street, Boston, Massachusetts 02111 (617) 423-3990; *The World in Figures.*

International Monetary Fund, 700 Nineteenth Street, NW, Washington, D.C. 20431 (202) 623-7000; *International Financial Statistics.*

Organisation for Economic Co-operation and Development (OECD), 2 rue Andre-Pascal, 75 Paris 16, France (Telephone Number in U.S. (202) 785-6323; *Trade by Commodities.*

Statistical Office of the United Nations, Publishing Service, New York, New York 10017 (800) 253-9646; *Foreign Trade Statistics for Africa, International Trade Statistics, Statistical Yearbook,* and *Trade in Manufactures of Developing Countries.*

United Nations Economic Commission for Africa, Africa Hall, P.O. Box 3001, Addis Ababa, Ethiopia (Telephone Number in U.S. (800) 253-9646); *African Statistical Yearbook.*

ETHIOPIA - FORESTRY AND FOREST PRODUCTS

Federal Statistical Office, Gustav - Stresemann - Ring 11, D-6200 Wiesbaden, Germany; *Athiopien.*

Food and Agricultural Organization of the United Nations (FAO) Via delle Terme di Caracalla, 00100 Rome, Italy (Telephone Number in U.S. (202) 653-2400); *The State of Food and Agriculture,* and *Yearbook of Forest Products.*

G.K. Hall and Company, 70 Lincoln Street, Boston, Massachusetts 02111 (617) 423-3990; *The World in Figures.*

Statistical Office of the United Nations, Publishing Service, New York, New York 10017 (800) 253-9646; *Statistical Yearbook.*

United Nations Economic Commission for Africa, Africa Hall, P.O. Box 3001, Addis Ababa, Ethiopia (Telephone Number in U.S. (800) 253-9646); *African Statistical Yearbook.*

United Nations Educational, Scientific and Cultural Organization (UNESCO), 7 Place de Fontenoy, F-75700 Paris, France (Telephone Number in U.S. (212) 963-5981); *Statistical Yearbook.*

ETHIOPIA - GENERAL INDUSTRIAL STATISTICS

Federal Statistical Office, Gustav - Stresemann - Ring 11, D-6200 Wiesbaden, Germany; *Athiopien.*

Statistical Office of the United Nations, Publishing Service, New York, New York 10017 (800) 253-9646; *Industrial Statistics Yearbook.*

ETHIOPIA - GENERAL MORTALITY

Statistical Office of the United Nations, Publishing Service, New York, New York 10017 (800) 253-9646; *Demographic Yearbook.*

ETHIOPIA - GEOGRAPHIC DATA

Federal Statistical Office, Gustav - Stresemann - Ring 11, D-6200 Wiesbaden, Germany; *Athiopien.*

ETHIOPIA - GOATS - See ETHIOPIA - LIVESTOCK AND POULTRY

ETHIOPIA - GOLD HOLDINGS

International Monetary Fund, 700 Nineteenth Street, NW, Washington, D.C. 20431 (202) 623-7000; *International Financial Statistics.*

Statistical Office of the United Nations, Publishing Service, New York, New York 10017 (800) 253-9646; *Statistical Yearbook.*

ETHIOPIA - GOLD PRODUCTION AND CONSUMPTION - See ETHIOPIA - MINING AND MINERAL PRODUCTS

ETHIOPIA - GOVERNMENT

G.K. Hall and Company, 70 Lincoln Street, Boston, Massachusetts 02111 (617) 423-3990; *The World in Figures.*

ETHIOPIA - GOVERNMENT EXPENDITURES

International Monetary Fund, 700 Nineteenth Street, NW, Washington, D.C. 20431 (202) 623-7000; *Government Finance Statistics Yearbook.*

Times Books, 201 East 50th Street, New York, New York 10022 (212) 751-2600; *The Economist Book of Vital World Statistics.*

ETHIOPIA - GOVERNMENT FINANCES

International Monetary Fund, 700 Nineteenth Street, NW, Washington, D.C. 20431 (202) 623-7000; *International Financial Statistics.*

Statistical Office of the United Nations, Publishing Service, New York, New York 10017 (800) 253-9646; *Statistical Yearbook.*

ETHIOPIA - GOVERNMENT REVENUE

International Monetary Fund, 700 Nineteenth Street, NW, Washington, D.C. 20431 (202) 623-7000; *Government Finance Statistics Yearbook.*

Statistical Office of the United Nations, Publishing Service, New York, New York 10017 (800) 253-9646; *Survey of Economic and Social Conditions in Africa.*

Times Books, 201 East 50th Street, New York, New York 10022 (212) 751-2600; *The Economist Book of Vital World Statistics.*

ETHIOPIA - GRAIN PRODUCTION - See ETHIOPIA - CROPS

ETHIOPIA - GRANTS

International Monetary Fund, 700 Nineteenth Street, NW, Washington, D.C. 20431 (202) 623-7000; *Government Finance Statistics Yearbook.*

ETHIOPIA - GROSS DOMESTIC PRODUCT

African Development Bank, 01 BP 1387, Abidjan 01, Cote D'Ivoire; *Selected Statistics on Regional Member Countries.*

The Economist Intelligence Unit, 111 West 57th Street, New York, New York 10019 (800) 938-4685; *The World Market Atlas.*

Euromonitor Publications Limited, 87-88 Turnmill Street, London EC1M 5QU, England; *International Marketing Data and Statistics.*

G.K. Hall and Company, 70 Lincoln Street, Boston, Massachusetts 02111 (617) 423-3990; *The World in Figures.*

Statistical Office of the United Nations, Publishing Service, New York, New York 10017 (800) 253-9646; *Statistical Yearbook,* and *Survey of Economic and Social Conditions in Africa.*

Times Books, 201 East 50th Street, New York, New York 10022 (212) 751-2600; *The Economist Book of Vital World Statistics.*

United Nations Economic Commission for Africa, Africa Hall, P.O. Box 3001, Addis Ababa, Ethiopia (Telephone Number in U.S. (800) 253-9646); *African Statistical Yearbook.*

ETHIOPIA - GROSS NATIONAL PRODUCT

Euromonitor Publications Limited, 87-88 Turnmill Street, London EC1M 5QU, England; *International Marketing Data and Statistics.*

U.S. Arms Control and Disarmament Agency, 320 Twenty-first Street, NW, Washington, D.C. 20451 (202) 647-8677; *World Military Expenditures and Arms Transfers.*

ETHIOPIA - GROUNDNUTS PRODUCTION - See ETHIOPIA - CROPS

ETHIOPIA - HEALTH

African Development Bank, 01 BP 1387, Abidjan 01, Cote D'Ivoire; *Selected Statistics on Regional Member Countries.*

Federal Statistical Office, Gustav - Stresemann - Ring 11, D-6200 Wiesbaden, Germany; *Athiopien.*

G.K. Hall and Company, 70 Lincoln Street, Boston, Massachusetts 02111 (617) 423-3990; *The World in Figures.*

Provisional Military Government of Ethiopia, Central Statistical Office, Post Office Box 1143, Addis Ababa, Ethiopia; *Ethiopia Statistical Abstract.*

Statistical Office of the United Nations, Publishing Service, New York, New York 10017 (800) 253-9646; *Statistical Yearbook.*

Times Books, 201 East 50th Street, New York, New York 10022 (212) 751-2600; *The Economist Book of Vital World Statistics.*

United Nations Economic Commission for Africa, Africa Hall, P.O. Box 3001, Addis Ababa, Ethiopia (Telephone Number in U.S. (800) 253-9646); *African Statistical Yearbook.*

ETHIOPIA - HEALTH EXPENDITURES

International Monetary Fund, 700 Nineteenth Street, NW, Washington, D.C. 20431 (202) 623-7000; *Government Finance Statistics Yearbook.*

ETHIOPIA - HIDE PRODUCTION

Food and Agricultural Organization of the United Nations (FAO), Via delle Terme di Caracalla, 00100 Rome, Italy (Telephone Number in U.S. (202) 653-2400); *Production Yearbook.*

ETHIOPIA - HIDES AND SKINS EXPORTS

International Monetary Fund, 700 Nineteenth Street, NW, Washington, D.C. 20431 (202) 623-7000; *International Financial Statistics.*

ETHIOPIA - HIGHWAYS

G.K. Hall and Company, 70 Lincoln Street, Boston, Massachusetts 02111 (617) 423-3990; *The World in Figures.*

International Road Federation, 525 School Street, SW, Washington, D.C. 20024 (202) 554-2106; *World Road Statistics.*

Statistical Office of the United Nations, Publishing Service, New York, New York 10017 (800) 253-9646; *Survey of Economic and Social Conditions in Africa.*

United Nations Economic Commission for Africa, Africa Hall, P.O. Box 3001, Addis Ababa, Ethiopia (Telephone Number in U.S. (800) 253-9646); *African Statistical Yearbook.*

ETHIOPIA - HONEY PRODUCTION - See ETHIOPIA - CROPS

ETHIOPIA - HORSES - See ETHIOPIA - LIVESTOCK AND POULTRY

ETHIOPIA - HOURS OF WORK - See ETHIOPIA - EMPLOYMENT

ETHIOPIA - HOUSING EXPENDITURES

International Monetary Fund, 700 Nineteenth Street, NW, Washington, D.C. 20431 (202) 623-7000; *Government Finance*

Statistics Yearbook.

ETHIOPIA - ILLITERATE POPULATION

The Economist Intelligence Unit, 111 West 57th Street, New York, New York 10019 (800) 938-4685; *The World Market Atlas.*

G.K. Hall and Company, 70 Lincoln Street, Boston, Massachusetts 02111 (617) 423-3990; *The World in Figures.*

United Nations Educational, Scientific and Cultural Organization (UNESCO), 7 Place de Fontenoy, F-75700 Paris, France (Telephone Number in U.S. (212) 963-5981); *Statistical Yearbook.*

ETHIOPIA - IMPORTS

African Development Bank, 01 BP 1387, Abidjan 01, Cote D'Ivoire; *Selected Statistics on Regional Member Countries.*

The Economist Intelligence Unit, 111 West 57th Street, New York, New York 10019 (800) 938-4685; *The World Market Atlas.*

Euromonitor Publications Limited, 87-88 Turnmill Street, London EC1M 5QU, England; *International Marketing Data and Statistics.*

Food and Agricultural Organization of the United Nations (FAO) Via delle Terme di Caracalla, 00100 Rome, Italy (Telephone Number in U.S. (202) 653-2400); *The State of Food and Agriculture.*

G.K. Hall and Company, 70 Lincoln Street, Boston, Massachusetts 02111 (617) 423-3990; *The World in Figures.*

International Monetary Fund, 700 Nineteenth Street, NW, Washington, D.C. 20431 (202) 623-7000; *Direction of Trade Statistics, Government Finance Statistics Yearbook,* and *International Financial Statistics.*

Statistical Office of the United Nations, Publishing Service, New York, New York 10017 (800 253-9646; *Foreign Trade Statistics for Africa, Survey of Economic and Social Conditions in Africa,* and *Trade in Manufactures of Developing Countries.*

Times Books, 201 East 50th Street, New York, New York 10022 (212) 751-2600; *The Economist Book of Vital World Statistics.*

United Nations Economic Commission for Africa, Africa Hall, P.O. Box 3001, Addis Ababa, Ethiopia (Telephone Number in U.S. (800) 253-9646); *African Statistical Yearbook.*

ETHIOPIA - INCOME TAXES - See ETHIOPIA - TAXATION

ETHIOPIA - INDUSTRY

Euromonitor Publications Limited, 87-88 Turnmill Street, London EC1M 5QU, England; *International Marketing Data and Statistics.*

Federal Statistical Office, Gustav - Stresemann - Ring 11, D-6200 Wiesbaden, Germany; *Athiopien.*

G.K. Hall and Company, 70 Lincoln Street, Boston, Massachusetts 02111 (617) 423-3990; *The World in Figures.*

International Labour Office, I.L.O. Publications, CH-1211, Geneva 22, Switzerland; *Yearbook of Labour Statistics.*

Statistical Office of the United Nations, Publishing Service, New York, New York 10017 (800) 253-9646; *Survey of Economic and Social Conditions in Africa.*

Times Books, 201 East 50th Street, New York, New York 10022 (212) 751-2600; *The Economist Book of Vital World Statistics.*

United Nations Economic Commission for Africa, Africa Hall, P.O. Box 3001, Addis Ababa, Ethiopia (Telephone Number in U.S. (800) 253-9646); *African Statistical Yearbook.*

ETHIOPIA - INFANT AND MATERNAL MORTALITY

Statistical Office of the United Nations, Publishing Service, New York, New York 10017 (800) 253-9646; *Demographic Yearbook, Statistical Yearbook,* and *Survey of Economic and Social Conditions in Africa.*

Times Books, 201 East 50th Street, New York, New York 10022 (212) 751-2600; *The Economist Book of Vital World Statistics.*

ETHIOPIA - INSURANCE

Provisional Military Government of Ethiopia, Central Statistical Office, Post Office Box 1143, Addis Ababa, Ethiopia; *Ethiopia Statistical Abstract.*

ETHIOPIA - INTERNATIONAL LIQUIDITY

International Monetary Fund, 700 Nineteenth Street, NW, Washington, D.C. 20431 (202) 623-7000; *International Financial Statistics.*

ETHIOPIA - INTERNATIONAL RESERVES EXCLUDING GOLD

African Development Bank, 01 BP 1387, Abidjan 01, Cote D'Ivoire; *Selected Statistics on Regional Member Countries.*

ETHIOPIA - INVESTMENTS

International Monetary Fund, 700 Nineteenth Street, NW, Washington, D.C. 20431 (202) 623-7000; *International Financial Statistics.*

ETHIOPIA - IRRIGATION

Euromonitor Publications Limited, 87-88 Turnmill Street, London EC1M 5QU, England; *International Marketing Data and Statistics.*

ETHIOPIA - LABOR FORCE

African Development Bank, 01 BP 1387, Abidjan 01, Cote D'Ivoire; *Selected Statistics on Regional Member Countries.*

Euromonitor Publications Limited, 87-88 Turnmill Street, London EC1M 5QU, England; *International Marketing Data and Statistics.*

Food and Agricultural Organization of the United Nations (FAO) Via delle Terme di Caracalla, 00100 Rome, Italy (Telephone Number in U.S. (202) 653-2400); *The State of Food and Agriculture.*

G.K. Hall and Company, 70 Lincoln Street, Boston, Massachusetts 02111 (617) 423-3990; *The World in Figures.*

ETHIOPIA - LABOR PRODUCTIVITY

International Labour Office, I.L.O. Publications, CH-1211, Geneva 22, Switzerland; *Yearbook of Labour Statistics.*

ETHIOPIA - LAND USE

Euromonitor Publications Limited, 87-88 Turnmill Street, London EC1M 5QU, England; *International Marketing Data and Statistics.*

Food and Agricultural Organization of the United Nations (FAO), Via delle Terme di Caracalla, 00100 Rome, Italy (Telephone Number in U.S. (202) 653-2400); *Production Yearbook.*

G.K. Hall and Company, 70 Lincoln Street, Boston, Massachusetts 02111 (617) 423-3990; *The World in Figures.*

ETHIOPIA - LIBRARIES

United Nations Educational, Scientific and Cultural Organization (UNESCO), 7 Place de Fontenoy, F-75700 Paris, France (Telephone Number in U.S (212) 963-5981); *Statistical Yearbook.*

ETHIOPIA - LIFE EXPECTANCY

African Development Bank, 01 BP 1387, Abidjan 01, Cote D'Ivoire; *Selected Statistics on Regional Member Countries.*

ETHIOPIA - LITERACY RATE

Statistical Office of the United Nations, Publishing Service, New York, New York 10017 (800) 253-9646; *Survey of Economic and Social Conditions in Africa.*

ETHIOPIA - LIVESTOCK AND POULTRY

Euromonitor Publications Limited, 87-88 Turnmill Street, London EC1M 5QU, England; *International Marketing Data and Statistics.*

Food and Agricultural Organization of the United Nations (FAO), Via delle Terme di Caracalla, 00100 Rome, Italy (Telephone Number in U.S. (202) 653-2400); *Production Yearbook,* and *The State of Food and Agriculture.*

G.K. Hall and Company, 70 Lincoln Street, Boston, Massachusetts 02111 (617) 423-3990; *The World in Figures.*

Statistical Office of the United Nations, Publishing Service, New York, New York 10017 (800) 253-9646; *Statistical Yearbook,* and *Survey of Economic and Social Conditions in Africa.*

United Nations Economic Commission for Africa, Africa Hall, P.O. Box 3001, Addis Ababa, Ethiopia (Telephone Number in U.S. (800) 253-9646); *African Statistical Yearbook.*

ETHIOPIA - LIVING LEVELS

G.K. Hall and Company, 70 Lincoln Street, Boston, Massachusetts 02111 (617) 423-3990; *The World in Figures.*

Times Books, 201 East 50th Street, New York, New York 10022 (212) 751-2600; *The Economist Book of Vital World Statistics.*

ETHIOPIA - MAIL TRAFFIC - NUMBER OF ITEMS SENT OR RECEIVED

Statistical Office of the United Nations, Publishing Service, New York, New York 10017 (800) 253-9646; *Statistical Yearbook.*

ETHIOPIA - MANUFACTURING

G.K. Hall and Company, 70 Lincoln Street, Boston, Massachusetts 02111 (617) 423-3990; *The World in Figures.*

Provisional Military Government of Ethiopia, Central Statistical Office, Post Office Box 1143, Addis Ababa, Ethiopia; *Ethiopia Statistical Abstract.*

Statistical Office of the United Nations, Publishing Service, New York, New York 10017 (800) 253-9646; *Statistical Yearbook,* and *Survey of Economic and Social Conditions in Africa.*

Times Books, 201 East 50th Street, New York, New York 10022 (212) 751-2600; *The Economist Book of Vital World Statistics.*

United Nations Economic Commission for Africa, Africa Hall, P.O. Box 3001, Addis Ababa, Ethiopia (Telephone Number in U.S. (800) 253-9646); *African Statistical Yearbook.*

ETHIOPIA - MARRIAGE RATES

Statistical Office of the United Nations, Publishing Service, New York, New York 10017 (800) 253-9646; *Demographic Yearbook.*

ETHIOPIA - MEAT PRODUCTION - See ETHIOPIA - LIVESTOCK AND POULTRY

ETHIOPIA - MERCHANT SHIPPING

G.K. Hall and Company, 70 Lincoln Street, Boston, Massachusetts 02111 (617) 423-3990; *The World in Figures.*

Statistical Office of the United Nations, Publishing Service, New York, New York 10017 (800) 253-9646; *Statistical Yearbook.*

Times Books, 201 East 50th Street, New York, New York 10022 (212) 751-2600; *The Economist Book of Vital World Statistics.*

United Nations Economic Commission for Africa, Africa Hall, P.O. Box 3001, Addis Ababa, Ethiopia (Telephone Number in U.S. (800) 253-9646); *African Statistical Yearbook.*

U.S. Department of Transportation, Maritime Administration, 400 Seventh Street, SW, Washington, D.C. 20590 (202) 366-5807; *A Statistical Analysis of the World's Merchant Fleets.*

ETHIOPIA - MILITARY

G.K. Hall and Company, 70 Lincoln Street, Boston, Massachusetts 02111 (617) 423-3990; *The World in Figures.*

The International Institute for Strategic Studies, 23 Tavistock Street, London WC2E 7NQ, England; *The Military Balance.*

U.S. Arms Control and Disarmament Agency, 320 Twenty-first Street, NW, Washington, D.C. 20451 (202) 647-8677; *World Military Expenditures and Arms Transfers.*

ETHIOPIA - MILK - See ETHIOPIA - DAIRY PRODUCTS

ETHIOPIA - MILLET PRODUCTION - See ETHIOPIA - CROPS

ETHIOPIA - MINING AND MINERAL PRODUCTS

Commodity Research Bureau, Incorporated, 75 Wall Street, New York, New York 10005 (212) 504-7754; *Commodity Year Book.*

G.K. Hall and Company, 70 Lincoln Street, Boston, Massachusetts 02111 (617) 423-3990; *The World in Figures.*

Provisional Military Government of Ethiopia, Central Statistical Office, Post Office Box 1143, Addis Ababa, Ethiopia; *Ethiopia Statistical Abstract.*

Statistical Office of the United Nations, Publishing Service, New York, New York 10017 (800) 253-9646; *Statistical Yearbook.*

United Nations Economic Commission for Africa, Africa Hall, P.O. Box 3001, Addis Ababa, Ethiopia (Telephone Number in U.S. (800) 253-9646); *African Statistical Yearbook.*

ETHIOPIA - MONEY EXCHANGE RATE

Euromonitor Publications Limited, 87-88 Turnmill Street, London EC1M 5QU, England; *International Marketing Data and Statistics.*

International Monetary Fund, 700 Nineteenth Street, NW, Washington, D.C. 20431 (202) 623-7000; *International Financial Statistics.*

Statistical Office of the United Nations, Publishing Service, New York, New York 10017 (800) 253-9646; *Statistical Yearbook.*

ETHIOPIA - MONEY RESERVES

Euromonitor Publications Limited, 87-88 Turnmill Street, London EC1M 5QU, England; *International Marketing Data and Statistics.*

ETHIOPIA - MONEY SUPPLY

African Development Bank, 01 BP 1387, Abidjan 01, Cote D'Ivoire; *Selected Statistics on Regional Member Countries.*

Euromonitor Publications Limited, 87-88 Turnmill Street, London EC1M 5QU, England; *International Marketing Data and Statistics.*

Federal Statistical Office, Gustav - Stresemann - Ring 11, D-6200 Wiesbaden, Germany; *Athiopien.*

G.K. Hall and Company, 70 Lincoln Street, Boston, Massachusetts 02111 (617) 423-3990; *The World in Figures.*

International Monetary Fund, 700 Nineteenth Street, NW, Washington, D.C. 20431 (202) 623-7000; *International Financial Statistics.*

Statistical Office of the United Nations, Publishing Service, New York, New York 10017 (800) 253-9646; *Statistical Yearbook.*

ETHIOPIA - MOTION PICTURES

Statistical Office of the United Nations, Publishing Service, New York, New York 10017 (800) 253-9646; *Statistical Yearbook.*

ETHIOPIA - MOTOR VEHICLE TAXES - See ETHIOPIA - TAXATION

ETHIOPIA - MOTOR VEHICLES IN USE

G.K. Hall and Company, 70 Lincoln Street, Boston, Massachusetts 02111 (617) 423-3990; *The World in Figures.*

International Road Federation, 525 School Street, SW, Washington, D.C. 20024 (202) 554-2106; *World Road Statistics.*

Statistical Office of the United Nations, Publishing Service, New York, New York 10017 (800) 253-9646; *Statistical Yearbook,* and *Survey of Economic and Social Conditions in Africa.*

Times Books, 201 East 50th Street, New York, New York 10022 (212) 751-2600; *The Economist Book of Vital World Statistics.*

ETHIOPIA - MULES - See ETHIOPIA - LIVESTOCK AND POULTRY

ETHIOPIA - NATIONAL ACCOUNTS

African Development Bank, 01 BP 1387, Abidjan 01, Cote D'Ivoire; *Selected Statistics on Regional Member Countries.*

Federal Statistical Office, Gustav - Stresemann - Ring 11, D-6200 Wiesbaden, Germany; *Athiopien.*

International Monetary Fund, 700 Nineteenth Street, NW, Washington, D.C. 20431 (202) 623-7000; *International Financial Statistics.*

Provisional Military Government of Ethiopia, Central Statistical Office, Post Office Box 1143, Addis Ababa, Ethiopia; *Ethiopia Statistical Abstract.*

Statistical Office of the United Nations, Publishing Service, New York, New York 10017 (800) 253-9646; *National Accounts Statistics,* and *Statistical Yearbook.*

United Nations Economic Commission for Africa, Africa Hall, P.O. Box 3001, Addis Ababa, Ethiopia (Telephone Number in U.S. (800) 253-9646); *African Statistical Yearbook.*

ETHIOPIA - NATIONAL INCOME

G.K. Hall and Company, 70 Lincoln Street, Boston, Massachusetts 02111 (617) 423-3990; *The World in Figures.*

Statistical Office of the United Nations, Publishing Service, New York, New York 10017 (800) 253-9646; *Statistical Yearbook.*

ETHIOPIA - NATIONAL PRODUCT

Statistical Office of the United Nations, Publishing Service, New York, New York 10017 (800) 253-9646; *Statistical Yearbook.*

ETHIOPIA - NEWSPAPER PRODUCTION - See ETHIOPIA - FORESTRY AND FOREST PRODUCTS

ETHIOPIA - NEWSPRINT - See ETHIOPIA - FORESTRY AND FOREST PRODUCTS

ETHIOPIA - OATS PRODUCTION - See ETHIOPIA - CROPS

ETHIOPIA - OCCUPATIONS - See ETHIOPIA - LABOR FORCE

ETHIOPIA - OILSEEDS EXPORTS

International Monetary Fund, 700 Nineteenth Street, NW, Washington, D.C. 20431 (202) 623-7000; *International Financial Statistics.*

ETHIOPIA - PAPER - See ETHIOPIA - FORESTRY AND FOREST PRODUCTS

ETHIOPIA - PERIODICALS

United Nations Educational, Scientific and Cultural Organization (UNESCO), 7 Place de Fontenoy, F-75700 Paris, France (Telephone Number in U.s. (212) 963-5981); *Statistical Yearbook.*

ETHIOPIA - PESTICIDE USE

Food and Agricultural Organization of the United Nations (FAO) Via delle Terme di Caracalla, 00100 Rome, Italy (Telephone Number in U.S. (202) 653-2400); *The State of Food and Agriculture.*

ETHIOPIA - PETROLEUM INDUSTRY

Food and Agricultural Organization of the United Nations (FAO) Via delle Terme di Caracalla, 00100 Rome, Italy (Telephone Number in U.S. (202) 653-2400); *The State of Food and Agriculture.*

G.K. Hall and Company, 70 Lincoln Street, Boston, Massachusetts 02111 (617) 423-3990; *The World in Figures.*

Statistical Office of the United Nations, Publishing Service, New York, New York 10017 (800) 253-9646; *Statistical Yearbook.*

ETHIOPIA - PIGS - See ETHIOPIA - LIVESTOCK AND POULTRY

ETHIOPIA - PLATINUM PRODUCTION - See ETHIOPIA - MINING AND MINERALS

ETHIOPIA - POPULATION

African Development Bank, 01 BP 1387, Abidjan 01, Cote D'Ivoire; *Selected Statistics on Regional Member Countries.*

The Economist Intelligence Unit, 111 West 57th Street, New York, New York 10019 (800) 938-4685; *The World Market Atlas.*

Euromonitor Publications Limited, 87-88 Turnmill Street, London EC1M 5QU, England; *International Marketing Data and Statistics.*

Federal Statistical Office, Gustav - Stresemann - Ring 11, D-6200 Wiesbaden, Germany; *Athiopien.*

Food and Agricultural Organization of the United Nations (FAO), Via delle Terme di Caracalla, 00100 Rome, Italy (Telephone Number in U.S. (202) 653-2400); *Production Yearbook.*

G.K. Hall and Company, 70 Lincoln Street, Boston, Massachusetts 02111 (617) 423-3990; *The World in Figures.*

International Labour Office, I.L.O. Publications, CH-1211, Geneva 22, Switzerland; *Yearbook of Labour Statistics.*

Provisional Military Government of Ethiopia, Central Statistical Office, Post Office Box 1143, Addis Ababa, Ethiopia; *Ethiopia Statistical Abstract.*

Statistical Office of the United Nations, Publishing Service, New York, New York 10017 (800) 253-9646; *Demographic Yearbook, Statistical Yearbook,* and *Survey of Economic and Social Conditions in Africa.*

Times Books, 201 East 50th Street, New York, New York 10022 (212) 751-2600; *The Economist Book of Vital World Statistics.*

United Nations Educational, Scientific and Cultural Organization (UNESCO), 7 Place de Fontenoy, F-75700 Paris, France (Telephone Number in U.S. (212) 963-5981); *Statistical Yearbook.*

U.S. Arms Control and Disarmament Agency, 320 Twenty-first Street, NW, Washington, D.C. 20451 (202) 647-8677; *World Military Expenditures and Arms Transfers.*

World Health Organization, Office of Publications, Avenue Appia, CH-1211 Geneva 27, Switzerland (Telephone Number in U.S. (518) 436-9686); *World Health Statistics Annual.*

ETHIOPIA - POTATO PRODUCTION - See ETHIOPIA - FORESTRY AND FOREST PRODUCTS

ETHIOPIA - POWER PRODUCTION INDUSTRY - EMPLOYMENT

Statistical Office of the United Nations, Publishing Service, New York, New York 10017 (800) 253-9646; *Statistical Yearbook.*

ETHIOPIA - POWER PRODUCTION INDUSTRY - ESTABLISHMENTS, PAYROLLS, VALUE ADDED, ETC.

Statistical Office of the United Nations, Publishing Service, New York, New York 10017 (800) 253-9646; *Statistical Yearbook.*

ETHIOPIA - PRICES

Federal Statistical Office, Gustav - Stresemann - Ring 11, D-6200 Wiesbaden, Germany; *Athiopien.*

Food and Agricultural Organization of the United Nations (FAO), Via delle Terme di Caracalla, 00100 Rome, Italy (Telephone Number in U.S. (202) 653-2400); *Production Yearbook,* and *The State of Food and Agriculture.*

G.K. Hall and Company, 70 Lincoln Street, Boston, Massachusetts 02111 (617) 423-3990; *The World in Figures.*

International Labour Office, I.L.O. Publications, CH-1211, Geneva 22, Switzerland; *Yearbook of Labour Statistics.*

International Monetary Fund, 700 Nineteenth Street, NW, Washington, D.C. 20431 (202) 623-7000; *International Financial Statistics.*

Provisional Military Government of Ethiopia, Central Statistical Office, Post Office Box 1143, Addis Ababa, Ethiopia; *Ethiopia Statistical Abstract.*

United Nations Economic Commission for Africa, Africa Hall, P.O. Box 3001, Addis Ababa, Ethiopia (Telephone Number in U.S. (800) 253-9646); *African Statistical Yearbook.*

ETHIOPIA - PRINTING AND WRITING PAPER - See ETHIOPIA - FORESTRY AND FOREST PRODUCTS

ETHIOPIA - PRODUCTION

G.K. Hall and Company, 70 Lincoln Street, Boston, Massachusetts 02111 (617) 423-3990; *The World in Figures.*

ETHIOPIA - PRODUCTIVITY

Euromonitor Publications Limited, 87-88 Turnmill Street, London EC1M 5QU, England; *International Marketing Data and Statistics.*

ETHIOPIA - PROPERTY TAXES - See ETHIOPIA - TAXATION

ETHIOPIA - PUBLIC FINANCE

Federal Statistical Office, Gustav - Stresemann - Ring 11, D-6200 Wiesbaden, Germany; *Athiopien.*

ETHIOPIA - RADIO BROADCASTING - See ETHIOPIA - BROADCASTING

ETHIOPIA - RAILWAYS

G.K. Hall and Company, 70 Lincoln Street, Boston, Massachusetts 02111 (617) 423-3990; *The World in Figures.*

Jane's Information Group, Sentinel House, 163 Brighton Road, Coulsdon, Surrey CR5 2NH, England (Telephone Number in U.S.

(703) 683-3700); *Jane's World Railways.*

Statistical Office of the United Nations, Publishing Service, New York, New York 10017 (800) 253-9646; *Statistical Yearbook*, and *Survey of Economic and Social Conditions in Africa.*

United Nations Economic Commission for Africa, Africa Hall, P.O. Box 3001, Addis Ababa, Ethiopia (Telephone Number in U.S. (800) 253-9646); *African Statistical Yearbook.*

ETHIOPIA - RAPESEED PRODUCTION - See ETHIOPIA - CROPS

ETHIOPIA - RETAIL TRADE

G.K. Hall and Company, 70 Lincoln Street, Boston, Massachusetts 02111 (617) 423-3990; *The World in Figures.*

Statistical Office of the United Nations, Publishing Service, New York, New York 10017 (800) 253-9646; *Statistical Yearbook.*

ETHIOPIA - ROOT AND TUBER PRODUCTION - See ETHIOPIA - CROPS

ETHIOPIA - ROUNDWOOD PRODUCTION - See ETHIOPIA - FORESTRY AND FOREST PRODUCTS

ETHIOPIA - SAFFLOWER SEED PRODUCTION - See ETHIOPIA - CROPS

ETHIOPIA - SALT PRODUCTION - See ETHIOPIA - MINING AND MINERAL PRODUCTS

ETHIOPIA - SAWNWOOD PRODUCTION - See ETHIOPIA - FORESTRY AND FOREST PRODUCTS

ETHIOPIA - SESAME SEED PRODUCTION - See ETHIOPIA - CROPS

ETHIOPIA - SHEEP - See ETHIOPIA - LIVESTOCK AND POULTRY

ETHIOPIA - SISAL PRODUCTION - See ETHIOPIA - CROPS

ETHIOPIA - SOCIAL DATA

African Development Bank, 01 BP 1387, Abidjan 01, Cote D'Ivoire; *Selected Statistics on Regional Member Countries.*

G.K. Hall and Company, 70 Lincoln Street, Boston, Massachusetts 02111 (617) 423-3990; *The World in Figures.*

ETHIOPIA - SOCIAL SECURITY

International Monetary Fund, 700 Nineteenth Street, NW, Washington, D.C. 20431 (202) 623-7000; *Government Finance Statistics Yearbook.*

ETHIOPIA - STAMP TAXES AND DUTIES - See ETHIOPIA - TAXATION

ETHIOPIA - STATE BUDGET REVENUE AND EXPENDITURES

Euromonitor Publications Limited, 87-88 Turnmill Street, London EC1M 5QU, England; *International Marketing Data and Statistics.*

ETHIOPIA - STEEL - See ETHIOPIA - MINING AND MINERAL PRODUCTS

ETHIOPIA - STOCKS - COMMODITY - MARKET PRICE - INDEX

Food and Agricultural Organization of the United Nations (FAO) Via delle Terme di Caracalla, 00100 Rome, Italy (Telephone Number in U.S. (202) 653-2400); *The State of Food and Agriculture.*

ETHIOPIA - SUGAR - See ETHIOPIA - CROPS

ETHIOPIA - TAXATION

G.K. Hall and Company, 70 Lincoln Street, Boston, Massachusetts 02111 (617) 423-3990; *The World in Figures.*

International Monetary Fund, 700 Nineteenth Street, NW, Washington, D.C. 20431 (202) 623-7000; *Government Finance Statistics Yearbook.*

ETHIOPIA - TELEGRAPH SERVICE

Statistical Office of the United Nations, Publishing Service, New York, New York 10017 (800) 253-9646; *Statistical Yearbook.*

ETHIOPIA - TELEPHONES IN USE

American Telephone and Telegraph Company, 26 Parsippany Road, Whippany, New Jersey 07981 (800) 338-4038; *The World's Telephones.*

G.K. Hall and Company, 70 Lincoln Street, Boston, Massachusetts 02111 (617) 423-3990; *The World in Figures.*

Statistical Office of the United Nations, Publishing Service, New York, New York 10017 (800) 253-9646; *Statistical Yearbook.*

ETHIOPIA - TEXTILE INDUSTRY

G.K. Hall and Company, 70 Lincoln Street, Boston, Massachusetts 02111 (617) 423-3990; *The World in Figures.*

Statistical Office of the United Nations, Publishing Service, New York, New York 10017 (800) 253-9646; *Statistical Yearbook.*

ETHIOPIA - THEATRE

United Nations Educational, Scientific and Cultural Organization (UNESCO), 7 Place de Fontenoy, F-75700 Paris, France (Telephone Number in U.S. (212) 963-5981); *Statistical Yearbook.*

ETHIOPIA - TOBACCO PRODUCTION

Statistical Office of the United Nations, Publishing Service, New York, New York 10017 (800) 253-9646; *Statistical Yearbook.*

ETHIOPIA - TOURISM

Federal Statistical Office, Gustav - Stresemann - Ring 11, D-6200 Wiesbaden, Germany; *Athiopien.*

G.K. Hall and Company, 70 Lincoln Street, Boston, Massachusetts 02111 (617) 423-3990; *The World in Figures.*

Statistical Office of the United Nations, Publishing Service, New York, New York 10017 (800) 253-9646; *Statistical Yearbook.*

Times Books, 201 East 50th Street, New York, New York 10022 (212) 751-2600; *The Economist Book of Vital World Statistics.*

United Nations Economic Commission for Africa, Africa Hall, P.O. Box 3001, Addis Ababa, Ethiopia (Telephone Number in U.S. (800) 253-9646); *African Statistical Yearbook.*

World Tourism Organization, Calle Capitan Haya 42, E-28020 Madrid, Spain; *Yearbook of Tourism Statistics.*

ETHIOPIA - TRADE - See ETHIOPIA - FOREIGN TRADE

ETHIOPIA - TRADEMARKS AND SERVICE MARKS

Statistical Office of the United Nations, Publishing Service, New York, New York 10017 (800) 253-9646; *Statistical Yearbook.*

ETHIOPIA - TRANSPORTATION AND COMMUNICATIONS

Federal Statistical Office, Gustav - Stresemann - Ring 11, D-6200 Wiesbaden, Germany; *Athiopien.*

G.K. Hall and Company, 70 Lincoln Street, Boston, Massachusetts 02111 (617) 423-3990; *The World in Figures.*

Provisional Military Government of Ethiopia, Central Statistical Office, Post Office Box 1143, Addis Ababa, Ethiopia; *Ethiopia Statistical Abstract.*

United Nations Economic Commission for Africa, Africa Hall, P.O. Box 3001, Addis Ababa, Ethiopia (Telephone Number in U.S. (800) 253-9646); *African Statistical Yearbook.*

ETHIOPIA - UNEMPLOYMENT

Euromonitor Publications Limited, 87-88 Turnmill Street, London EC1M 5QU, England; *International Marketing Data and Statistics.*

International Labour Office, I.L.O. Publications, CH-1211, Geneva 22, Switzerland; *Yearbook of Labour Statistics.*

ETHIOPIA - VITAL STATISTICS

Euromonitor Publications Limited, 87-88 Turnmill Street, London EC1M 5QU, England; *International Marketing Data and Statistics.*

G.K. Hall and Company, 70 Lincoln Street, Boston, Massachusetts 02111 (617) 423-3990; *The World in Figures.*

World Health Organization, Office of Publications, Avenue Appia, CH-1211 Geneva 27, Switzerland (Telephone Number in U.S. (518) 436-9686); *World Health Statistics Annual.*

ETHIOPIA - WAGES

Federal Statistical Office, Gustav - Stresemann - Ring 11, D-6200 Wiesbaden, Germany; *Athiopien.*

G.K. Hall and Company, 70 Lincoln Street, Boston, Massachusetts 02111 (617) 423-3990; *The World in Figures.*

International Labour Office, I.L.O. Publications, CH-1211, Geneva 22, Switzerland; *Yearbook of Labour Statistics.*

ETHIOPIA - WEATHER

G.K. Hall and Company, 70 Lincoln Street, Boston, Massachusetts 02111 (617) 423-3990; *The World in Figures.*

ETHIOPIA - WELFARE

International Monetary Fund, 700 Nineteenth Street, NW, Washington, D.C. 20431 (202) 623-7000; *Government Finance Statistics Yearbook.*

ETHIOPIA - WHEAT - See ETHIOPIA - CROPS

ETHIOPIA - WHOLESALE PRICES

Statistical Office of the United Nations, Publishing Service, New York, New York 10017 (800) 253-9646; *Statistical Yearbook.*

ETHIOPIA - WHOLESALE TRADE

Statistical Office of the United Nations, Publishing Service, New York, New York 10017 (800) 253-9646; *Statistical Yearbook.*

ETHIOPIA - YARN PRODUCTION

Statistical Office of the United Nations, Publishing Service, New York, New York 10017 (800) 253-9646; *Statistical Yearbook.*

EUROPE - See Individual Foreign Countries

EUROPEAN ECONOMIC COMMUNITY

Organization for Economic Cooperation and Development, Publication and Information Center, 2001 L Street, NW, Washington, D.C. 20036 (202) 785-6323; *National Accounts of OECD Countries.*

EVAPORATED AND CONDENSED MILK

U.S. Department of Agriculture, National Agricultural Statistics Service, Fourteenth Street and Independence Avenue, SW, Washington, D.C. 20250 (202) 219-1504; *Dairy Products, Milk Production, Disposition, and Income, Food Consumption, Prices, and Expenditures,* and unpublished data.

EXCISE TAXES

Executive Office of the President, Office of Management and Budget, Executive Office Building, Washington, D.C. 20503 (202) 395-3080; *Budget of the United States Government.*

U.S. Department of Commerce, Bureau of the Census, Suitland, Maryland 20233 (301) 763-4040; *State Government Tax Collections.*

U.S. Department of the Treasury, Internal Revenue Service, 1111 Constitution Avenue, NW, Washington, D.C. 20224 (202) 566-5000; *Annual Report of the Commissioner and Chief Counsel of the Internal Revenue Service.*

EXECUTIONS

U.S. Department of Justice, Bureau of the Justice Statistics, 633 Indiana Avenue, NW, Washington, D.C. 20531 (800) 732-3277; *Capital Punishment,* and *Correctional Populations in the United States.*

EXECUTIVE OFFICE OF THE PRESIDENT (FEDERAL)

U.S. Office of Personnel Management, 1900 E Street, NW, Washington, D.C. 20415 (202) 606-1800; *Federal Civilian Workforce Statistics, Employment and Trends,* and unpublished data.

EXERCISE EQUIPMENT

National Sporting Goods Association, Lake Center Plaza Building, 1699 Wall Street, Mt. Prospect, Illinois 60056 (708) 439-4000; *The Sporting Goods Market in 1993.*

EXPECTATION OF LIFE (AVERAGE LIFETIME)

U.S. Department of Health and Human Services, National Center for Health Statistics, 3700 East-West Highway, Hyattsville, Maryland 20782 (301) 436-8500; *Monthly Vital Statistics Report, U.S. Life Tables and Actuarial Tables, Vital Statistics of the United States,* and unpublished data.

EXPECTATION OF LIFE (AVERAGE LIFETIME) - PROJECTIONS

U.S. Department of Health and Human Services, National Center for Health Statistics, 3700 East-West Highway, Hyattsville, Maryland 20782 (301) 436-8500; *Monthly Vital Statistics Report, Vital Statistics of the United States,* and unpublished data.

EXPENDITURES OF UNITED STATES GOVERNMENT

Executive Office of the President, Office of Management and Budget, Executive Office Building, Washington, D.C. 20503 (202) 395-3080; *Historical Tables, Budget of the United States Government,* and *Budget of the United States Government.*

U.S. Department of Commerce, Bureau of the Census, Suitland, Maryland 20233 (301) 763-4040; *Census of Governments, Federal Expenditures by State for Fiscal Year, Government Finances,* and *Historical Statistics on Governmental Finances and Employment.*

U.S. International Development Cooperation Agency, Agency for International Development, 320 Twenty-first Street, NW, Washington, D.C. 20523 (202) 647-9620; *United States Overseas Loans and Grants and Assistance from International Organizations,* and unpublished data.

EXPENDITURES OF UNITED STATES GOVERNMENT - AID TO ARTS AND HUMANITIES

U.S. National Endowment for the Arts, 1100 Pennsylvania Avenue, NW, Washington, D.C. 20506 (202) 682-5400; *Annual Report.*

U.S. National Endowment for the Humanities, 1100 Pennsylvania Avenue, NW, Washington, D.C. 20506 (202) 606-8438; *Annual Report.*

EXPENDITURES OF UNITED STATES GOVERNMENT - AID TO OUTLYING AREAS

U.S. Department of Commerce, Bureau of the Census, Suitland, Maryland 20233 (301) 763-4040; *Federal Expenditures by State for Fiscal Year.*

EXPENDITURES OF UNITED STATES GOVERNMENT - AID TO STATE AND LOCAL GOVERNMENT

Advisory Commission on Intergovernmental Relations, 800 K Street, NW, Suite 450 South, Washington, D.C. 20575 (202) 653-5540; *Significant Features of Federalism,* based on *Budget of the United States Government.*

Executive Office of the President, Office of Management and Budget, Executive Office Building, Washington, D.C. 20503 (202) 395-3080; *Historical Tables, Budget of the United States Government.*

U.S. Department of Commerce, Bureau of the Census, Suitland, Maryland 20233 (301) 763-4040; *Government Finances,* and *Federal Expenditures by State for Fiscal Year.*

EXPENDITURES OF UNITED STATES GOVERNMENT - AID TO STATE AND LOCAL GOVERNMENT - BY FUNCTION

Executive Office of the President, Office of Management and Budget, Executive Office Building, Washington, D.C. 20503 (202) 395-3080; *Historical Tables, Budget of the United States Government.*

EXPENDITURES OF UNITED STATES GOVERNMENT - AID TO STATE AND LOCAL GOVERNMENT - HIGHWAY TRUST FUND

U.S. Department of Commerce, Bureau of the Census, Suitland, Maryland 20233 (301) 763-4040; *Federal Expenditures by State for Fiscal Year.*

EXPENDITURES OF UNITED STATES GOVERNMENT - ATOMIC ENERGY DEFENSE ACTIVITIES

Executive Office of the President, Office of Management and Budget, Executive Office Building, Washington, D.C. 20503 (202) 395-3080; *Budget of the United States Government.*

EXPENDITURES OF UNITED STATES GOVERNMENT - BUDGET OUTLAYS

Executive Office of the President, Office of Management and Budget, Executive Office Building, Washington, D.C. 20503 (202) 395-3080; *Budget of the United States Government.*

EXPENDITURES OF UNITED STATES GOVERNMENT - BY FUNCTION

Executive Office of the President, Office of Management and Budget, Executive Office Building, Washington, D.C. 20503 (202) 395-3080; *Budget of the United States Government.*

EXPENDITURES OF UNITED STATES GOVERNMENT - BY SOURCE OF FUNDS

Executive Office of the President, Office of Management and Budget, Executive Office Building, Washington, D.C. 20503 (202) 395-3080; *Budget of the United States Government.*

EXPENDITURES OF UNITED STATES GOVERNMENT - CAPITAL OUTLAY

U.S. Department of Commerce, Bureau of the Census, Suitland, Maryland 20233 (301) 763-4040; *Census of Governments, Historical Statistics on Government Finances and Employment,* and *Government Finances.*

EXPENDITURES OF UNITED STATES GOVERNMENT - CAPITAL OUTLAY - CONTRACT AWARDS

U.S. Department of Defense, Office of the Secretary, The Pentagon, Washington, D.C. 20301 (703) 545-6700; *Prime Contract Awards,* and *Atlas/Data Abstract for the United States and Selected Areas.*

EXPENDITURES OF UNITED STATES GOVERNMENT - CAPITAL OUTLAY - COST OF AMERICAN WARS

U.S. Congress, Joint Economic Committee, The Capitol, Washington, D.C. 20515 (202) 224-3121; *The Military Budget and National Economic Priorities,* (91st Congress, 1st Session) subsequently revised and updated by James L. Clayton, University of Utah.

EXPENDITURES OF UNITED STATES GOVERNMENT - CAPITAL OUTLAY - INTERNATIONAL COMPARISON

U.S. Arms Control and Disarmament Agency, 320 Twenty-first Street, NW, Washington, D.C. 20451 (202) 647-8677; *World Military Expenditures and Arms Transfers.*

EXPENDITURES OF UNITED STATES GOVERNMENT - CAPITAL OUTLAY - RESEARCH AND DEVELOPMENT

U.S. National Science Foundation, 4201 Wilson Boulevard, Arlington, Virginia 22230 (703) 306-1234; *National Patterns of R & D Resources, Federal Research and Development Funding by Budget Function, Federal Funds for Research and Development, Federal Support to Universities, Colleges, and Selected Nonprofit Institutions,* and *Science and Engineering.*

EXPENDITURES OF UNITED STATES GOVERNMENT - EDUCATION - See FEDERAL AID TO EDUCATION

EXPENDITURES OF UNITED STATES GOVERNMENT - FOOD PROGRAMS - FEDERAL

U.S. Department of Health and Human Services, Social Security Administration, 6401 Security Boulevard, Baltimore, Maryland 21235 (410) 965-1234; *Social Security Bulletin.*

U.S. Library of Congress, Congressional Research Service, 10 First Street, SE, Washington, D.C. 20540 (202) 707-5000; *Cash and Noncash Benefits for Persons with Limited Income: Eligibility Rules, Recipient and Expenditure Data.*

EXPENDITURES OF UNITED STATES GOVERNMENT - HEALTH

U.S. Department of Health and Human Services, Health Care Financing Administration, 200 Independence Avenue, SW, Washington, D.C. 20201 (202) 245-6113; *Health Care Financing Review.*

EXPENDITURES OF UNITED STATES GOVERNMENT - HOSPITALS

American Hospital Association, 840 North Lake Shore Drive, Chicago, Illinois 60611 (312) 280-6000; *Hospital Statistics.*

EXPENDITURES OF UNITED STATES GOVERNMENT - LAND AND BUILDINGS

U.S. General Services Administration, General Services Building, Eighteenth and F Streets, NW, Washington, D.C. 20405 (202) 708-5082; *Inventory Report on Real Property Owned by the United States Throughout the World.*

EXPENDITURES OF UNITED STATES GOVERNMENT - LOANS - DIRECT AND GUARANTEED

Executive Office of the President, Office of Management and Budget, Executive Office Building, Washington, D.C. 20503 (202) 395-3080; *Budget of the United States Government.*

EXPENDITURES OF UNITED STATES GOVERNMENT - MILITARY PERSONNEL

U.S. Department of Defense, Office of the Secretary, The Pentagon, Washington, D.C. 20301 (703) 545-6700; *Atlas/Data Abstract for the U.S. and Selected Areas, Selected Manpower Statistics,* and unpublished data.

EXPENDITURES OF UNITED STATES GOVERNMENT - NATIONAL DEFENSE

Executive Office of the President, Office of Management and Budget, Executive Office Building, Washington, D.C. 20503 (202) 395-3080; *The Budget of the United States Government.*

EXPENDITURES OF UNITED STATES GOVERNMENT - OUTLAYS BY FUNCTION

Executive Office of the President, Office of Management and Budget, Executive Office Building, Washington, D.C. 20503 (202) 395-3080; *Budget of the United States Government.*

EXPENDITURES OF UNITED STATES GOVERNMENT - PAYMENTS FOR PUBLIC ASSISTANCE

U.S. Department of Health and Human Services, Administration for Children and Families, 370 L'Enfant Promenade, SW, Washington, D.C. 20447 (202) 401-9200; *Quarterly Public Assistance Statistics.*

U.S. Department of Health and Human Services, Social Security Administration, 6401 Security Boulevard, Baltimore, Maryland 21235 (410) 965-1234; *Social Security Bulletin,* and *Annual Statistical Supplement to the Social Security Bulletin.*

U.S. Department of Labor, Employment and Training Administration, 200 Constitution Avenue, NW, Washington, D.C. 20210 (202) 219-6871; *Unemployment Insurance Data Summary.*

U.S. Library of Congress, Congressional Research Service, 10 First Street, SE, Washington, D.C. 20540 (202) 707-5000; *Cash and Non-Cash Benefits for Persons With Limited Income: Eligibility Rules, Recipient and Expenditure Data.*

EXPENDITURES OF UNITED STATES GOVERNMENT - PAYROLLS

Office of Personnel Management, 1900 E Street, NW, Washington, D.C. 20415; *Biennial Report of Employment by Geographic Area, Federal Civilian Workforce Statistics, - Employment and Trends, Pay Structure of the Federal Civil Service,* and *Central Personnel Data File.*

U.S. Department of Commerce, Bureau of the Census, Suitland, Maryland 20233 (301) 763-4040; *Public Employment, Census of Governments,* and *Historical Statistics on Governmental Finances and Employment.*

EXPENDITURES OF UNITED STATES GOVERNMENT - POLLUTION CONTROL

U.S. Department of Commerce, Bureau of Economic Analysis, Fourteenth Street between Constitution Avenue and E Street, NW, Washington, D.C. 20230 (202) 606-9900; *Survey of Current Business.*

EXPENDITURES OF UNITED STATES GOVERNMENT - PUBLIC DEBT

Executive Office of the President, Office of Management and Budget, Executive Office Building, Washington, D.C. 20503 (202) 395-3080; *Budget of the United States Government.*

EXPENDITURES OF UNITED STATES GOVERNMENT - PUBLIC ROADS

U.S. Department of Commerce, Bureau of the Census, Suitland, Maryland 20233 (301) 763-4040; *Federal Expenditures by State for Fiscal Year.*

EXPENDITURES OF UNITED STATES GOVERNMENT - RESEARCH AND DEVELOPMENT

National Science Foundation, 4201 Wilson Boulevard, Arlington, Virginia 22230 (703) 306-1234; *Federal Funds for Research and Development, Federal R & D Funding by Budget Function, National Patterns of R & D Resources*, and *Science and Engineering Indicators*.

EXPENDITURES OF UNITED STATES GOVERNMENT - RIVERS, HARBORS, AND FLOOD CONTROL

U.S. Department of the Army, Corps of Engineers, The Pentagon, Washington, D.C. 20301 (202) 545-6700; *Report of Civil Works Expenditures by State and Fiscal Year*.

EXPENDITURES OF UNITED STATES GOVERNMENT - SCHOOLS

U.S. Department of Education, 400 Maryland Avenue, SW, Washington, D.C. 20202 (202) 708-5366; *Digest of Education Statistics*.

EXPENDITURES OF UNITED STATES GOVERNMENT - SOCIAL WELFARE PROGRAMS

U.S. Department of Health and Human Services, Social Security Administration, 6401 Security Boulevard, Baltimore, Maryland 21235 (410) 965-1234; *Social Security Bulletin, Annual Statistical Supplement to the Social Security Bulletin*, and unpublished data.

EXPENDITURES OF UNITED STATES GOVERNMENT - SPACE PROGRAMS

Executive Office of the President, Office of Management and Budget, Executive Office Building, Washington, D.C. 20503 (202) 395-3080; *The Budget of the United States Government*.

U.S. Department of Commerce, Bureau of the Census, Suitland, Maryland 20233 (301) 763-4040; *Aerospace Industry*, and *Current Industrial Reports*.

U.S. National Aeronautics and Space Administration, 400 Maryland Avenue, SW, Washington, D.C. 20546 (202) 453-1000; *Aeronautics and Space Report of the President*, and *1995 Budget Summary*.

EXPENDITURES OF UNITED STATES GOVERNMENT - TRUST FUNDS

Executive Office of the President, Office of Management and Budget, Executive Office Building, Washington, D.C. 20503 (202) 395-3080; *Budget of the United States Government*.

EXPENDITURES OF UNITED STATES GOVERNMENT - VETERANS BENEFITS - See VETERANS AFFAIRS

EXPENDITURES OF UNITED STATES GOVERNMENT - VOCATIONAL REHABILITATION

U.S. Department of Education, Rehabilitation Services Administration, 400 Maryland Avenue, SW, Washington, D.C. 20202 (202) 708-5366; *Caseload Statistics of State Vocational Rehabilitation Agencies in Fiscal Years*, and *State Vocational Rehabilitation Agency Program Data in Fiscal Years*.

EXPORT-IMPORT BANK ACT

U.S. Department of Commerce, Bureau of Economic Analysis, Fourteenth Street between Constitution Avenue and E Street, NW, Washington, D.C. 20230 (202) 606-9900; press releases and unpublished data.

EXPORTS - See FOREIGN TRADE

EXPRESS MAIL

U.S. Postal Service, 475 L'Enfant Plaza West, SW, Washington, D.C. 20260 (202) 268-2000; *United States Domestic Postage Rate: Recent History*, and unpublished data.

EYEGLASSES AND CONTACT LENSES

U.S. Department of Health and Human Services, Health Care Financing Administration, 200 Independence Avenue, SW, Washington, D.C. 20201 (202) 245-6113; *Health Care Financing Review*.

F

FABRICATED METAL PRODUCTS INDUSTRY, MANUFACTURING - CAPITAL

U.S. Department of Commerce, Bureau of Economic Analysis, Fourteenth Street between Constitution Avenue and E Street, NW, Washington, D.C. 20230 (202) 606-9900; *Survey of Current Business.*

FABRICATED METAL PRODUCTS INDUSTRY, MANUFACTURING - EARNINGS

U.S. Department of Commerce, Bureau of the Census, Suitland, Maryland 20233 (301) 763-4040; *Census of Manufactures,* and *Annual Survey of Manufactures.*

FABRICATED METAL PRODUCTS INDUSTRY, MANUFACTURING - EMPLOYEES

U.S. Department of Commerce, Bureau of the Census, Suitland, Maryland 20233 (301) 763-4040; *Census of Manufactures,* and *Annual Survey of Manufactures.*

FABRICATED METAL PRODUCTS INDUSTRY, MANUFACTURING - ESTABLISHMENTS

U.S. Department of Commerce, Bureau of the Census, Suitland, Maryland 20233 (301) 763-4040; *Census of Manufactures,* and *Annual Survey of Manufactures.*

FABRICATED METAL PRODUCTS INDUSTRY, MANUFACTURING - FINANCE

American Iron and Steel Institute, 1101 17th Street, NW, Washington, D.C. 20036 (202) 452-7100; *Annual Statistical Report.*

FABRICATED METAL PRODUCTS INDUSTRY, MANUFACTURING - FOREIGN TRADE

American Iron and Steel Institute, 1101 17th Street, NW, Washington, D.C. 20036 (202) 452-1700; *Annual Statistical Report.*

U.S. Department of Commerce, Bureau of the Census, Suitland, Maryland 20233 (301) 763-4040; *U.s. Merchandise Trade,* and unpublished data.

FABRICATED METAL PRODUCTS INDUSTRY, MANUFACTURING - GROSS DOMESTIC PRODUCT

U.S. Department of Commerce, Bureau of Economic Analysis, Fourteenth Street between Constitution Avenue and E Street, NW, Washington, D.C. 20230 (202) 606-9900; *Survey of Current Business,* and *The National Income and Product Accounts of the United States.*

FABRICATED METAL PRODUCTS INDUSTRY, MANUFACTURING - OCCUPATIONAL SAFETY

U.S. Department of Labor, Bureau of Labor Statistics, 200 Constitution Avenue, NW, Washington, D.C. 20210 (202) 523-1327; *Occupational Injuries and Illnesses in the United States by Industry.*

FABRICATED METAL PRODUCTS INDUSTRY, MANUFACTURING - PRODUCTIVITY

Board of Governors of the Federal Reserve System, Twentieth Street and Constitution Avenue, NW, Washington, D.C. 20551 (202) 452-3000; *Federal Reserve Bulletin.*

FABRICATED METAL PRODUCTS INDUSTRY, MANUFACTURING - PROFITS

U.S. Department of Commerce. Bureau of Economic Analysis, Fourteenth Street between Constitution Avenue and E Street, NW, Washington, D.C. 20230 (202) 606-9900; *The National Income and Product Accounts of the United States,* and *Survey of Current Business.*

FABRICATED METAL PRODUCTS INDUSTRY, MANUFACTURING - VALUE ADDED

U.S. Department of Commerce, Bureau of the Census, Suitland, Maryland 20233 (301) 763-4040; *Census of Manufactures,* and *Annual Survey of Manufactures.*

FABRICS - See TEXTILE INDUSTRY AND TEXTILES

FAEROE ISLANDS - ABORTIONS

Statistical Office of the United Nations, Publishing Service, New York, New York 10017 (800) 253-9646; *Demographic Yearbook.*

FAEROE ISLANDS - AGRICULTURE

Food and Agricultural Organization of the United Nations (FAO) Via delle Terme di Caracalla, 00100 Rome, Italy (Telephone Number in U.S. (202) 653-2400); *Production Yearbook, The State of Food and Agriculture,* and *Trade Yearbook.*

G.K. Hall and Company, 70 Lincoln Street, Boston, Massachusetts 02111 (617) 423-3990; *The World in Figures.*

FAEROE ISLANDS - AIRLINE SERVICE

G.K. Hall and Company, 70 Lincoln Street, Boston, Massachusetts 02111 (617) 423-3990; *The World in Figures.*

FAEROE ISLANDS - AREA AND DENSITY OF POPULATION

Food and Agricultural Organization of the United Nations (FAO) Via delle Terme di Caracalla, 00100 Rome, Italy (Telephone Number in U.S. (202) 653-2400); *The State of Food and Agriculture.*

G.K. Hall and Company, 70 Lincoln Street, Boston, Massachusetts 02111 (617) 423-3990; *The World in Figures.*

Statistical Office of the United Nations, Publishing Service, New York, New York 10017 (800) 253-9646; *Statistical Yearbook.*

United Nations Educational, Scientific and Cultural Organization (UNESCO), 7 Place de Fontenoy, F-75700 Paris, France (Telephone Number in U.S. (212) 963-5981); *Statistical Yearbook.*

FAEROE ISLANDS - BALANCE OF PAYMENTS

G.K. Hall and Company, 70 Lincoln Street, Boston, Massachusetts 02111 (617) 423-3990; *The World in Figures.*

FAEROE ISLANDS - BANKING

G.K. Hall and Company, 70 Lincoln Street, Boston, Massachusetts 02111 (617) 423-3990; *The World in Figures.*

FAEROE ISLANDS - BIRTH RATES

Statistical Office of the United Nations, Publishing Service, New York, New York 10017 (800) 253-9646; *Demographic Yearbook,* and *Statistical Yearbook.*

World Health Organization, Office of Publications, Avenue Appia, CH-1211 Geneva 27, Switzerland; *World Health Statistics Annual.*

FAEROE ISLANDS - BONDS

G.K. Hall and Company, 70 Lincoln Street, Boston, Massachusetts 02111 (617) 423-3990; *The World in Figures.*

FAEROE ISLANDS - BOOK PRODUCTION

G.K. Hall and Company, 70 Lincoln Street, Boston, Massachusetts 02111 (617) 423-3990; *The World in Figures.*

FAEROE ISLANDS - BROADCASTING

Billboard Limited, P.O. Box 9027, 1006 AA Amsterdam, The Netherlands (Telephone Number in U.S. (212) 764-7300); *World Radio TV Handbook.*

G.K. Hall and Company, 70 Lincoln Street, Boston, Massachusetts 02111 (617) 423-3990; *The World in Figures.*

FAEROE ISLANDS - BUSINESS

G.K. Hall and Company, 70 Lincoln Street, Boston, Massachusetts 02111 (617) 423-3990; *The World in Figures.*

FAEROE ISLANDS - CALORIE SUPPLY

Food and Agricultural Organization of the United Nations (FAO) Via delle Terme di Caracalla, 00100 Rome, Italy (Telephone Number in U.S. (202) 653-2400); *The State of Food and Agriculture.*

FAEROE ISLANDS - CATTLE - See FAEROE ISLANDS - LIVESTOCK AND POULTRY

FAEROE ISLANDS - CHEMICAL (ORGANIC) PRODUCTION - See FAEROE ISLANDS - MINING AND MINERAL PRODUCTS

FAEROE ISLANDS - CLASS STRUCTURE

G.K. Hall and Company, 70 Lincoln Street, Boston, Massachusetts 02111 (617) 423-3990; *The World in Figures.*

FAEROE ISLANDS - CLIMATE

G.K. Hall and Company, 70 Lincoln Street, Boston, Massachusetts 02111 (617) 423-3990; *The World in Figures.*

FAEROE ISLANDS - COAL PRODUCTION - See FAEROE ISLANDS - MINING AND MINERAL PRODUCTS

FAEROE ISLANDS - COMMUNICATIONS

G.K. Hall and Company, 70 Lincoln Street, Boston, Massachusetts 02111 (617) 423-3990; *The World in Figures.*

FAEROE ISLANDS - CONSUMER PRICE INDEX

G.K. Hall and Company, 70 Lincoln Street, Boston, Massachusetts 02111 (617) 423-3990; *The World in Figures.*

Statistical Office of the United Nations, Publishing Service, New York, New York 10017 (800) 253-9646; *Statistical Yearbook.*

FAEROE ISLANDS - CONSUMER PRICES

International Labour Office, I.L.O. Publications, CH-1211, Geneva 22, Switzerland; *Yearbook of Labour Statistics.*

FAEROE ISLANDS - CONSUMPTION

G.K. Hall and Company, 70 Lincoln Street, Boston, Massachusetts 02111 (617) 423-3990; *The World in Figures.*

FAEROE ISLANDS - CORN PRODUCTION - See FAEROE ISLANDS - CROPS

FAEROE ISLANDS - CORPORATE TAXES - See FAEROE ISLANDS - TAXATION

FAEROE ISLANDS - CROPS

Food and Agricultural Organization of the United Nations (FAO) Via delle Terme di Caracalla, 00100 Rome, Italy (Telephone Number in U.S. (202) 653-2400); *The State of Food and Agriculture.*

G.K. Hall and Company, 70 Lincoln Street, Boston, Massachusetts 02111 (617) 423-3990; *The World in Figures.*

Statistical Office of the United Nations, Publishing Service, New York, New York 10017 (800) 253-9646; *Statistical Yearbook.*

FAEROE ISLANDS - CUSTOMS DUTIES

G.K. Hall and Company, 70 Lincoln Street, Boston, Massachusetts 02111 (617) 423-3990; *The World in Figures.*

FAEROE ISLANDS - DAIRY PRODUCTS

Food and Agricultural Organization of the United Nations (FAO) Via delle Terme di Caracalla, 00100 Rome, Italy (Telephone Number in U.S. (202) 653-2400); *The State of Food and Agriculture.*

FAEROE ISLANDS - DEATH RATES

G.K. Hall and Company, 70 Lincoln Street, Boston, Massachusetts 02111 (617) 423-3990; *The World in Figures.*

Statistical Office of the United Nations, Publishing Service, New York, New York 10017 (800) 253-9646; *Statistical Yearbook.*

World Health Organization, Office of Publications, Avenue Appia, CH-1211 Geneva 27, Switzerland (Telephone Number in U.S. (518) 436-9686); *World Health Statistics Annual.*

FAEROE ISLANDS - DEFENSE EXPENDITURES

G.K. Hall and Company, 70 Lincoln Street, Boston, Massachusetts 02111 (617) 423-3990; *The World in Figures.*

FAEROE ISLANDS - DEMOGRAPHY

G.K. Hall and Company, 70 Lincoln Street, Boston, Massachusetts 02111 (617) 423-3990; *The World in Figures.*

FAEROE ISLANDS - DEVELOPMENT ASSISTANCE

G.K. Hall and Company, 70 Lincoln Street, Boston, Massachusetts 02111 (617) 423-3990; *The World in Figures.*

FAEROE ISLANDS - DISEASES

G.K. Hall and Company, 70 Lincoln Street, Boston, Massachusetts 02111 (617) 423-3990; *The World in Figures.*

World Health Organization, Office of Publications, Avenue Appia, CH-1211 Geneva 27, Switzerland (Telephone Number in U.S. (518) 436-9686); *World Health Statistics Annual.*

FAEROE ISLANDS - DIVORCE

Statistical Office of the United Nations, Publishing Service, New York, New York 10017 (800) 253-9646; *Demographic Yearbook,* and *Statistical Yearbook.*

FAEROE ISLANDS - DOMESTIC PRODUCT

G.K. Hall and Company, 70 Lincoln Street, Boston, Massachusetts 02111 (617) 423-3990; *The World in Figures.*

FAEROE ISLANDS - ECONOMY

G.K. Hall and Company, 70 Lincoln Street, Boston, Massachusetts 02111 (617) 423-3990; *The World in Figures.*

FAEROE ISLANDS - EDUCATION

G.K. Hall and Company, 70 Lincoln Street, Boston, Massachusetts 02111 (617) 423-3990; *The World in Figures.*

FAEROE ISLANDS - EGG PRODUCTION - See FAEROE ISLANDS - DAIRY PRODUCTS

FAEROE ISLANDS - ELECTRICITY

Statistical Office of the United Nations, Publishing Service, New York, New York 10017 (800) 253-9646; *Statistical Yearbook.*

FAEROE ISLANDS - EMPLOYMENT

International Labour Office, I.L.O. Publications, CH-1211, Geneva 22, Switzerland; *Yearbook of Labour Statistics.*

FAEROE ISLANDS - ENERGY

Food and Agricultural Organization of the United Nations (FAO) Via delle Terme di Caracalla, 00100 Rome, Italy (Telephone Number in U.S. (202) 653-2400); *The State of Food and Agriculture.*

G.K. Hall and Company, 70 Lincoln Street, Boston, Massachusetts 02111 (617) 423-3990; *The World in Figures.*

Statistical Office of the United Nations, Publishing Service, New York, New York 10017 (800) 253-9646; *Energy Statistics Yearbook,* and *Statistical Yearbook.*

FAEROE ISLANDS - EXPORTS

Food and Agricultural Organization of the United Nations (FAO) Via delle Terme di Caracalla, 00100 Rome, Italy (Telephone Number in U.S. (202) 653-2400); *The State of Food and Agriculture.*

G.K. Hall and Company, 70 Lincoln Street, Boston, Massachusetts 02111 (617) 423-3990; *The World in Figures.*

International Monetary Fund, 700 Nineteenth Street, NW, Washington, D.C. 20431 (202) 623-7000; *Direction of Trade Statistics.*

FAEROE ISLANDS - EXTERNAL TRADE

Food and Agricultural Organization of the United Nations (FAO) Via delle Terme di Caracalla, 00100 Rome, Italy (Telephone Number in U.S. (202) 653-2400); *The State of Food and Agriculture,* and *Trade Yearbook.*

G.K. Hall and Company, 70 Lincoln Street, Boston, Massachusetts 02111 (617) 423-3990; *The World in Figures.*

Statistical Office of the United Nations, Publishing Service, New York, New York 10017 (800) 253-9646; *Statistical Yearbook.*

FAEROE ISLANDS - FARM CROPS See FAEROE ISLANDS - CROPS

FAEROE ISLANDS - FETAL MORTALITY

Statistical Office of the United Nations, Publishing Service, New York, New York 10017 (800) 253-9646; *Demographic Yearbook.*

World Health Organization, Office of Publications, Avenue Appia, CH-1211 Geneva 27, Switzerland (Telephone Number in U.S. (518) 436-9686); *World Health Statistics Annual.*

FAEROE ISLANDS - FERTILIZER

Food and Agricultural Organization of the United Nations (FAO) Via delle Terme di Caracalla, 00100 Rome, Italy (Telephone Number in U.S. (202) 653-2400); *The State of Food and Agriculture.*

FAEROE ISLANDS - FINANCE

G.K. Hall and Company, 70 Lincoln Street, Boston, Massachusetts 02111 (617) 423-3990; *The World in Figures.*

FAEROE ISLANDS - FISHERIES

Food and Agricultural Organization of the United Nations (FAO) Via delle Terme di Caracalla, 00100 Rome, Italy (Telephone Number in U.S. (202) 653-2400); *The State of Food and Agriculture,* and *Yearbook of Fishery Statistics.*

Statistical Office of the United Nations, Publishing Service, New York, New York 10017 (800) 253-9646; *Statistical Yearbook.*

FAEROE ISLANDS - FOOD

Food and Agricultural Organization of the United Nations (FAO) Via delle Terme di Caracalla, 00100 Rome, Italy (Telephone Number in U.S. (202) 653-2400); *Production Yearbook,* and *The State of Food and Agriculture.*

G.K. Hall and Company, 70 Lincoln Street, Boston, Massachusetts 02111 (617) 423-3990; *The World in Figures.*

FAEROE ISLANDS - FOREIGN AID

G.K. Hall and Company, 70 Lincoln Street, Boston, Massachusetts 02111 (617) 423-3990; *The World in Figures.*

FAEROE ISLANDS - FOREIGN TRADE

G.K. Hall and Company, 70 Lincoln Street, Boston, Massachusetts 02111 (617) 423-3990; *The World in Figures.*

International Labour Office, I.L.O. Publications, CH-1211, Geneva 22, Switzerland; *Yearbook of Labour Statistics.*

Organisation for Economic Co-operation and Development (OECD), 2 rue Andre-Pascal, 75 Paris 16, France (Telephone Number in U.S. (202) 785-6323); *Trade by Commodities.*

Statistical Office of the United Nations, Publishing Service, New York, New York 10017 (800) 253-9646; *Statistical Yearbook,* and *International Trade Statistics Yearbook.*

FAEROE ISLANDS - FORESTRY AND FOREST PRODUCTS

Food and Agricultural Organization of the United Nations (FAO) Via delle Terme di Caracalla, 00100 Rome, Italy (Telephone Number in U.S. (202) 653-2400); *The State of Food and Agriculture.*

G.K. Hall and Company, 70 Lincoln Street, Boston, Massachusetts 02111 (617) 423-3990; *The World in Figures.*

Statistical Office of the United Nations, Publishing Service, New York, New York 10017 (800) 253-9646; *Statistical Yearbook.*

FAEROE ISLANDS - GENERAL MORTALITY

Statistical Office of the United Nations, Publishing Service, New York, New York 10017 (800) 253-9646; *Demographic Yearbook.*

World Health Organization, Office of Publications, Avenue Appia, CH-1211 Geneva 27, Switzerland (Telephone Number in U.S. (518) 436-9686); *World Health Statistics Annual.*

FAEROE ISLANDS - GOVERNMENT

G.K. Hall and Company, 70 Lincoln Street, Boston, Massachusetts 02111 (617) 423-3990; *The World in Figures.*

FAEROE ISLANDS - GRAIN PRODUCTION - See FAEROE ISLANDS - CROPS

FAEROE ISLANDS - GROSS DOMESTIC PRODUCT

G.K. Hall and Company, 70 Lincoln Street, Boston, Massachusetts 02111 (617) 423-3990; *The World in Figures.*

FAEROE ISLANDS - HEALTH

G.K. Hall and Company, 70 Lincoln Street, Boston, Massachusetts 02111 (617) 423-3990; *The World in Figures.*

Statistical Office of the United Nations, Publishing Service, New York, New York 10017 (800) 253-9646; *Statistical Yearbook.*

FAEROE ISLANDS - HIDE PRODUCTION

Food and Agricultural Organization of the United Nations (FAO), Via delle Terme di Caracalla, 00100 Rome, Italy (Telephone Number in U.S. (202) 653-2400); *Production Yearbook.*

FAEROE ISLANDS - HIGHWAYS

G.K. Hall and Company, 70 Lincoln Street, Boston, Massachusetts 02111 (617) 423-3990; *The World in Figures.*

FAEROE ISLANDS - HOURS OF WORK - See FAEROE ISLANDS - EMPLOYMENT

FAEROE ISLANDS - ILLITERATE POPULATION

G.K. Hall and Company, 70 Lincoln Street, Boston, Massachusetts 02111 (617) 423-3990; *The World in Figures.*

FAEROE ISLANDS - IMPORTS

Food and Agricultural Organization of the United Nations (FAO) Via delle Terme di Caracalla, 00100 Rome, Italy (Telephone Number in U.S. (202) 653-2400); *The State of Food and Agriculture.*

G.K. Hall and Company, 70 Lincoln Street, Boston, Massachusetts 02111 (617) 423-3990; *The World in Figures.*

International Monetary Fund, 700 Nineteenth Street, NW, Washington, D.C. 20431 (202) 623-7000; *Direction of Trade Statistics.*

FAEROE ISLANDS - INDUSTRY

G.K. Hall and Company, 70 Lincoln Street, Boston, Massachusetts 02111 (617) 423-3990; *The World in Figures.*

FAEROE ISLANDS - INFANT AND MATERNAL MORTALITY

International Labour Office, I.L.O. Publications, CH-1211, Geneva 22, Switzerland; *Yearbook of Labour Statistics.*

Statistical Office of the United Nations, Publishing Service, New York, New York 10017 (800) 253-9646; *Demographic Yearbook.*

World Health Organization, Office of Publications, Avenue Appia, CH-1211 Geneva 27, Switzerland; *World Health Statistics Annual.*

FAEROE ISLANDS - LABOR FORCE

Food and Agricultural Organization of the United Nations (FAO) Via delle Terme di Caracalla, 00100 Rome, Italy (Telephone Number in U.S. (202) 653-2400); *The State of Food and Agriculture.*

G.K. Hall and Company, 70 Lincoln Street, Boston, Massachusetts 02111 (617) 423-3990; *The World in Figures.*

FAEROE ISLANDS - LABOR PRODUCTIVITY

International Labour Office, I.L.O. Publications, CH-1211, Geneva 22, Switzerland; *Yearbook of Labour Statistics.*

FAEROE ISLANDS - LAND USE

Food and Agricultural Organization of the United Nations (FAO), Via delle Terme di Caracalla, 00100 Rome, Italy (Telephone Number in U.S. (202) 653-2400); *Production Yearbook.*

G.K. Hall and Company, 70 Lincoln Street, Boston, Massachusetts 02111 (617) 423-3990; *The World in Figures.*

FAEROE ISLANDS - LIBRARIES

United Nations Educational, Scientific and Cultural Organization (UNESCO), 7 Place de Fontenoy, F-75700 Paris, France; *Statistical Yearbook.*

FAEROE ISLANDS - LIVESTOCK AND POULTRY

Food and Agricultural Organization of the United Nations (FAO), Via delle Terme di Caracalla, 00100 Rome, Italy (Telephone Number in U.S. (202) 653-2400); *Production Yearbook,* and *The State of Food and Agriculture.*

G.K. Hall and Company, 70 Lincoln Street, Boston, Massachusetts 02111 (617) 423-3990; *The World in Figures.*

Statistical Office of the United Nations, Publishing Service, New York, New York 10017 (800) 253-9646; *Statistical Yearbook.*

FAEROE ISLANDS - LIVING LEVELS

G.K. Hall and Company, 70 Lincoln Street, Boston, Massachusetts 02111 (617) 423-3990; *The World in Figures.*

FAEROE ISLANDS - MANUFACTURING

G.K. Hall and Company, 70 Lincoln Street, Boston, Massachusetts 02111 (617) 423-3990; *The World in Figures.*

FAEROE ISLANDS - MARRIAGE RATES

Statistical Office of the United Nations, Publishing Service, New York, New York 10017 (800) 253-9646; *Demographic Yearbook,* and *Statistical Yearbook.*

FAEROE ISLANDS - MEAT PRODUCTION - See FAEROE ISLANDS - LIVESTOCK AND POULTRY

FAEROE ISLANDS - MERCHANT SHIPPING

G.K. Hall and Company, 70 Lincoln Street, Boston, Massachusetts 02111 (617) 423-3990; *The World in Figures.*

Lloyd's Register of Shipping, 17 Battery Place, New York, New York 10004; *Register of Ships.*

Statistical Office of the United Nations, Publishing Service, New York, New York 10017 (800) 253-9646; *Statistical Yearbook.*

FAEROE ISLANDS - MILITARY

G.K. Hall and Company, 70 Lincoln Street, Boston, Massachusetts 02111 (617) 423-3990; *The World in Figures.*

FAEROE ISLANDS - MINING AND MINERAL PRODUCTS

G.K. Hall and Company, 70 Lincoln Street, Boston, Massachusetts 02111 (617) 423-3990; *The World in Figures.*

FAEROE ISLANDS - MONEY SUPPLY

G.K. Hall and Company, 70 Lincoln Street, Boston, Massachusetts 02111 (617) 423-3990; *The World in Figures.*

FAEROE ISLANDS - MOTOR VEHICLES IN USE

G.K. Hall and Company, 70 Lincoln Street, Boston, Massachusetts 02111 (617) 423-3990; *The World in Figures.*

FAEROE ISLANDS - NATALITY - See FAEROE ISLANDS - BIRTH RATE

FAEROE ISLANDS - NATIONAL INCOME

G.K. Hall and Company, 70 Lincoln Street, Boston, Massachusetts 02111 (617) 423-3990; *The World in Figures.*

FAEROE ISLANDS - NEWSPAPER PRODUCTION - See FALKLAND ISLANDS - FORESTRY AND FOREST PRODUCTS

FAEROE ISLANDS - OCCUPATIONS - See FAEORE ISLANDS - LABOR FORCE

FAEROE ISLANDS - PESTICIDE USE

Food and Agricultural Organization of the United Nations (FAO) Via delle Terme di Caracalla, 00100 Rome, Italy (Telephone Number in U.S. (202) 653-2400); *The State of Food and Agriculture.*

FAEROE ISLANDS - PETROLEUM INDUSTRY

Food and Agricultural Organization of the United Nations (FAO) Via delle Terme di Caracalla, 00100 Rome, Italy (Telephone Number in U.S. (202) 653-2400); *The State of Food and Agriculture.*

G.K. Hall and Company, 70 Lincoln Street, Boston, Massachusetts 02111 (617) 423-3990; *The World in Figures.*

FAEROE ISLANDS - POPULATION

Food and Agricultural Organization of the United Nations (FAO), Via delle Terme di Caracalla, 00100 Rome, Italy (Telephone Number in U.S. (202) 653-2400); *Production Yearbook.*

G.K. Hall and Company, 70 Lincoln Street, Boston, Massachusetts 02111 (617) 423-3990; *The World in Figures.*

International Labour Office, I.L.O. Publications, CH-1211, Geneva 22, Switzerland; *Yearbook of Labour Statistics.*

Statistical Office of the United Nations, Publishing Service, New York, New York 10017 (800) 253-9646; *Demographic Yearbook* and *Statistical Yearbook.*

United Nations Educational, Scientific and Cultural Organization (UNESCO), 7 Place de Fontenoy, F-75700 Paris, France; *Statistical Yearbook.*

World Health Organization, Office of Publications, Avenue Appia, CH-1211 Geneva 27, Switzerland; *World Health Statistics Annual.*

FAEROE ISLANDS - POTATO PRODUCTION - See FAEROE ISLANDS - CROPS

FAEROE ISLANDS - PRICES

Food and Agricultural Organization of the United Nations (FAO), Via delle Terme di Caracalla, 00100 Rome, Italy (Telephone Number in

U.S. (202) 653-2400); *Production Yearbook*, and *The State of Food and Agriculture*.

G.K. Hall and Company, 70 Lincoln Street, Boston, Massachusetts 02111 (617) 423-3990; *The World in Figures*.

International Labour Office, I.L.O. Publications, CH-1211, Geneva 22, Switzerland; *Yearbook of Labour Statistics*.

FAEROE ISLANDS - PRODUCTION

G.K. Hall and Company, 70 Lincoln Street, Boston, Massachusetts 02111 (617) 423-3990; *The World in Figures*.

FAEROE ISLANDS - RAILWAYS

G.K. Hall and Company, 70 Lincoln Street, Boston, Massachusetts 02111 (617) 423-3990; *The World in Figures*.

FAEROE ISLANDS - RENT PRICES

International Labour Office, I.L.O. Publications, CH-1211, Geneva 22, Switzerland; *Yearbook of Labour Statistics*.

FAEROE ISLANDS - RETAIL TRADE

G.K. Hall and Company, 70 Lincoln Street, Boston, Massachusetts 02111 (617) 423-3990; *The World in Figures*.

FAEROE ISLANDS - SHEEP - See FAEROE ISLANDS - LIVESTOCK AND POULTRY

FAEROE ISLANDS - SOCIAL DATA

G.K. Hall and Company, 70 Lincoln Street, Boston, Massachusetts 02111 (617) 423-3990; *The World in Figures*.

FAEROE ISLANDS - STOCKS - COMMODITY - MARKET PRICE - INDEX

Food and Agricultural Organization of the United Nations (FAO) Via delle Terme di Caracalla, 00100 Rome, Italy (Telephone Number in U.S. (202) 653-2400); *The State of Food and Agriculture*.

FAEROE ISLANDS - TAXATION

G.K. Hall and Company, 70 Lincoln Street, Boston, Massachusetts 02111 (617) 423-3990; *The World in Figures*.

FAEROE ISLANDS - TELEPHONES IN USE

G.K. Hall and Company, 70 Lincoln Street, Boston, Massachusetts 02111 (617) 423-3990; *The World in Figures*.

FAEROE ISLANDS - TEXTILE INDUSTRY

G.K. Hall and Company, 70 Lincoln Street, Boston, Massachusetts 02111 (617) 423-3990; *The World in Figures*.

FAEROE ISLANDS - TOURISM

G.K. Hall and Company, 70 Lincoln Street, Boston, Massachusetts 02111 (617) 423-3990; *The World in Figures*.

FAEROE ISLANDS - TRADE - See FAEROE ISLANDS - FOREIGN TRADE

FAEROE ISLANDS - TRANSPORTATION AND COMMUNICATIONS

G.K. Hall and Company, 70 Lincoln Street, Boston, Massachusetts 02111 (617) 423-3990; *The World in Figures*.

FAEROE ISLANDS - UNEMPLOYMENT

International Labour Office, I.L.O. Publications, CH-1211, Geneva 22, Switzerland; *Yearbook of Labour Statistics*.

FAEROE ISLANDS - VITAL STATISTICS

G.K. Hall and Company, 70 Lincoln Street, Boston, Massachusetts 02111 (617) 423-3990; *The World in Figures*.

Statistical Office of the United Nations, Publishing Service, New York, New York 10017 (800) 253-9646; *Statistical Yearbook*.

FAEROE ISLANDS - WAGES

G.K. Hall and Company, 70 Lincoln Street, Boston, Massachusetts 02111 (617) 423-3990; *The World in Figures*.

International Labour Office, I.L.O. Publications, CH-1211, Geneva 22, Switzerland; *Yearbook of Labour Statistics*.

FAEROE ISLANDS - WEATHER

G.K. Hall and Company, 70 Lincoln Street, Boston, Massachusetts 02111 (617) 423-3990; *The World in Figures*.

Falkland Islands - National Statistical Office

The Secretariat, Stanley, Falkland Islands.

Falkland Islands - Primary Statistics Source

H.M. Stationery Office, Post Office Box 569, London SE1 9NH, England; *Falkland Islands and Dependencies: Report For the Year*.

FALKLAND ISLANDS - AGRICULTURE

Food and Agricultural Organization of the United Nations (FAO) Via delle Terme di Caracalla, 00100 Rome, Italy (Telephone Number in U.S. (202) 653-2400); *Production Yearbook*, *The State of Food and Agriculture*, and *Trade Yearbook*.

G.K. Hall and Company, 70 Lincoln Street, Boston, Massachusetts 02111 (617) 423-3990; *The World in Figures*.

Statistical Office of the United Nations, Publishing Service, New York, New York 10017 (800) 253-9646; *Statistical Yearbook*.

FALKLAND ISLANDS - AIRLINE SERVICE

G.K. Hall and Company, 70 Lincoln Street, Boston, Massachusetts 02111 (617) 423-3990; *The World in Figures*.

FALKLAND ISLANDS - ANIMAL HEALTH

Food and Agricultural Organization of the United Nations (FAO), Via delle Terme di Caracalla, 00100 Rome, Italy (Telephone Number in U.S. (202) 653-2400); *Animal Health Yearbook*.

FALKLAND ISLANDS - AREA AND DENSITY OF POPULATION

Food and Agricultural Organization of the United Nations (FAO) Via delle Terme di Caracalla, 00100 Rome, Italy (Telephone Number in

U.S. (202) 653-2400); *The State of Food and Agriculture.*

G.K. Hall and Company, 70 Lincoln Street, Boston, Massachusetts 02111 (617) 423-3990; *The World in Figures.*

Statistical Office of the United Nations, Publishing Service, New York, New York 10017 (800) 253-9646; *Statistical Yearbook.*

United Nations Educational, Scientific and Cultural Organization (UNESCO), 7 Place de Fontenoy, F-75700 Paris, France; *Statistical Yearbook.*

FALKLAND ISLANDS - BALANCE OF PAYMENTS

G.K. Hall and Company, 70 Lincoln Street, Boston, Massachusetts 02111 (617) 423-3990; *The World in Figures.*

FALKLAND ISLANDS - BANKING

G.K. Hall and Company, 70 Lincoln Street, Boston, Massachusetts 02111 (617) 423-3990; *The World in Figures.*

FALKLAND ISLANDS - BIRTH RATES

Statistical Office of the United Nations, Publishing Service, New York, New York 10017 (800) 253-9646; *Demographic Yearbook,* and *Statistical Yearbook.*

World Health Organization, Office of Publications, Avenue Appia, CH-1211 Geneva 27, Switzerland (Telephone Number in U.S. (518) 436-9686); *World Health Statistics Annual.*

FALKLAND ISLANDS - BONDS

G.K. Hall and Company, 70 Lincoln Street, Boston, Massachusetts 02111 (617) 423-3990; *The World in Figures.*

FALKLAND ISLANDS - BOOK PRODUCTION

G.K. Hall and Company, 70 Lincoln Street, Boston, Massachusetts 02111 (617) 423-3990; *The World in Figures.*

FALKLAND ISLANDS - BROADCASTING

Billboard Limited, P.O. Box 9027, 1006 AA Amsterdam, The Netherlands (Telephone Number in U.S. (212) 764-7300); *World Radio TV Handbook.*

G.K. Hall and Company, 70 Lincoln Street, Boston, Massachusetts 02111 (617) 423-3990; *The World in Figures.*

United Nations Educational, Scientific and Cultural Organization (UNESCO), 7 Place de Fontenoy, F-75700 Paris, France; *Statistical Yearbook.*

FALKLAND ISLANDS - BUSINESS

G.K. Hall and Company, 70 Lincoln Street, Boston, Massachusetts 02111 (617) 423-3990; *The World in Figures.*

FALKLAND ISLANDS - CALORIE SUPPLY

Food and Agricultural Organization of the United Nations (FAO) Via delle Terme di Caracalla, 00100 Rome, Italy (Telephone Number in U.S. (202) 653-2400); *The State of Food and Agriculture.*

FALKLAND ISLANDS - CATTLE - See FALKLAND ISLANDS - LIVESTOCK AND POULTRY

FALKLAND ISLANDS - CHEMICAL (ORGANIC) PRODUCTION - See FALKLAND ISLANDS - MINING AND MINERAL PRODUCTS

FALKLAND ISLANDS - CLASS STRUCTURE

G.K. Hall and Company, 70 Lincoln Street, Boston, Massachusetts 02111 (617) 423-3990; *The World in Figures.*

FALKLAND ISLANDS - CLIMATE

G.K. Hall and Company, 70 Lincoln Street, Boston, Massachusetts 02111 (617) 423-3990; *The World in Figures.*

FALKLAND ISLANDS - COAL PRODUCTION - See FALKLAND ISLANDS - MINING AND MINERAL PRODUCTS

FALKLAND ISLANDS - COMMUNICATIONS

G.K. Hall and Company, 70 Lincoln Street, Boston, Massachusetts 02111 (617) 423-3990; *The World in Figures.*

FALKLAND ISLANDS - CONSUMER PRICE INDEX

G.K. Hall and Company, 70 Lincoln Street, Boston, Massachusetts 02111 (617) 423-3990; *The World in Figures.*

Statistical Office of the United Nations, Publishing Service, New York, New York 10017 (800) 253-9646; *Statistical Yearbook.*

FALKLAND ISLANDS - CONSUMER PRICES

International Labour Office, I.L.O. Publications, CH-1211, Geneva 22, Switzerland; *Yearbook of Labour Statistics.*

FALKLAND ISLANDS - CONSUMPTION

G.K. Hall and Company, 70 Lincoln Street, Boston, Massachusetts 02111 (617) 423-3990; *The World in Figures.*

FALKLAND ISLANDS - CORN PRODUCTION - See FALKLAND ISLANDS - CROPS

FALKLAND ISLANDS - CORPORATE TAXES - See FALKLAND ISLANDS - TAXATION

FALKLAND ISLANDS - CROPS

Food and Agricultural Organization of the United Nations (FAO) Via delle Terme di Caracalla, 00100 Rome, Italy (Telephone Number in U.S. (202) 653-2400); *The State of Food and Agriculture.*

G.K. Hall and Company, 70 Lincoln Street, Boston, Massachusetts 02111 (617) 423-3990; *The World in Figures.*

FALKLAND ISLANDS - CUSTOMS DUTIES

G.K. Hall and Company, 70 Lincoln Street, Boston, Massachusetts 02111 (617) 423-3990; *The World in Figures.*

FALKLAND ISLANDS - DAIRY PRODUCTS

Food and Agricultural Organization of the United Nations (FAO) Via delle Terme di Caracalla, 00100 Rome, Italy (Telephone Number in U.S. (202) 653-2400); *The State of Food and Agriculture.*

FALKLAND ISLANDS - DEATH RATES

G.K. Hall and Company, 70 Lincoln Street, Boston, Massachusetts 02111 (617) 423-3990; *The World in Figures.*

Statistical Office of the United Nations, Publishing Service, New York, New York 10017 (800) 253-9646; *Statistical Yearbook.*

FALKLAND ISLANDS - DEFENSE EXPENDITURES

G.K. Hall and Company, 70 Lincoln Street, Boston, Massachusetts 02111 (617) 423-3990; *The World in Figures.*

FALKLAND ISLANDS - DEMOGRAPHY

G.K. Hall and Company, 70 Lincoln Street, Boston, Massachusetts 02111 (617) 423-3990; *The World in Figures.*

FALKLAND ISLANDS - DEVELOPMENT ASSISTANCE

G.K. Hall and Company, 70 Lincoln Street, Boston, Massachusetts 02111 (617) 423-3990; *The World in Figures.*

FALKLAND ISLANDS - DISEASE

G.K. Hall and Company, 70 Lincoln Street, Boston, Massachusetts 02111 (617) 423-3990; *The World in Figures.*

FALKLAND ISLANDS - DIVORCE RATES

Statistical Office of the United Nations, Publishing Service, New York, New York 10017 (800) 253-9646; *Demographic Yearbook,* and *Statistical Yearbook.*

FALKLAND ISLANDS - DOMESTIC PRODUCT

G.K. Hall and Company, 70 Lincoln Street, Boston, Massachusetts 02111 (617) 423-3990; *The World in Figures.*

FALKLAND ISLANDS - ECONOMY

G.K. Hall and Company, 70 Lincoln Street, Boston, Massachusetts 02111 (617) 423-3990; *The World in Figures.*

FALKLAND ISLANDS - EDUCATION

G.K. Hall and Company, 70 Lincoln Street, Boston, Massachusetts 02111 (617) 423-3990; *The World in Figures.*

United Nations Educational, Scientific and Cultural Organization (UNESCO), 7 Place de Fontenoy, F-75700 Paris, France (Telephone Number in U.S. (212) 963-5981); *Statistical Yearbook.*,

FALKLAND ISLANDS - EGG PRODUCTION - See FALKLAND ISLANDS - DAIRY PRODUCTS

FALKLAND ISLANDS - EMPLOYMENT

International Labour Office, I.L.O. Publications, CH-1211, Geneva 22, Switzerland; *Yearbook of Labour Statistics.*

FALKLAND ISLANDS - ENERGY

Food and Agricultural Organization of the United Nations (FAO) Via delle Terme di Caracalla, 00100 Rome, Italy (Telephone Number in U.S. (202) 653-2400); *The State of Food and Agriculture.*

G.K. Hall and Company, 70 Lincoln Street, Boston, Massachusetts 02111 (617) 423-3990; *The World in Figures.*

Statistical Office of the United Nations, Publishing Service, New York, New York 10017 (800) 253-9646; *Energy Statistics Yearbook,* and *Statistical Yearbook.*

FALKLAND ISLANDS - EXPORTS

Food and Agricultural Organization of the United Nations (FAO) Via delle Terme di Caracalla, 00100 Rome, Italy (Telephone Number in U.S. (202) 653-2400); *The State of Food and Agriculture.*

G.K. Hall and Company, 70 Lincoln Street, Boston, Massachusetts 02111 (617) 423-3990; *The World in Figures.*

International Monetary Fund, 700 Nineteenth Street, NW, Washington, D.C. 20431; *Direction of Trade Statistics.*

FALKLAND ISLANDS - EXTERNAL TRADE

Food and Agricultural Organization of the United Nations (FAO) Via delle Terme di Caracalla, 00100 Rome, Italy (Telephone Number in U.S. (202) 653-2400); *The State of Food and Agriculture,* and *Trade Yearbook.*

G.K. Hall and Company, 70 Lincoln Street, Boston, Massachusetts 02111 (617) 423-3990; *The World in Figures.*

Statistical Office of the United Nations, Publishing Service, New York, New York 10017 (800) 253-9646; *Statistical Yearbook.*

FALKLAND ISLANDS - FARM CROPS - See FALKLAND ISLANDS - CROPS

FALKLAND ISLANDS - FETAL MORTALITY

Statistical Office of the United Nations, Publishing Service, New York, New York 10017 (800) 253-9646; *Demographic Yearbook.*

FALKLAND ISLANDS - FERTILIZER

Food and Agricultural Organization of the United Nations (FAO) Via delle Terme di Caracalla, 00100 Rome, Italy (Telephone Number in U.S. (202) 653-2400); *The State of Food and Agriculture.*

FALKLAND ISLANDS - FINANCE

G.K. Hall and Company, 70 Lincoln Street, Boston, Massachusetts 02111 (617) 423-3990; *The World in Figures.*

FALKLAND ISLANDS - FISHERIES

Food and Agricultural Organization of the United Nations (FAO) Via delle Terme di Caracalla, 00100 Rome, Italy (Telephone Number in U.S. (202) 653-2400); *The State of Food and Agriculture,* and *Yearbook of Fishery Statistics.*

FALKLAND ISLANDS - FOOD

Food and Agricultural Organization of the United Nations (FAO) Via delle Terme di Caracalla, 00100 Rome, Italy (Telephone Number in U.S. (202) 653-2400); *Production Yearbook,* and *The State of Food and Agriculture.*

G.K. Hall and Company, 70 Lincoln Street, Boston, Massachusetts 02111 (617) 423-3990; *The World in Figures.*

FALKLAND ISLANDS - FOREIGN AID

G.K. Hall and Company, 70 Lincoln Street, Boston, Massachusetts 02111 (617) 423-3990; *The World in Figures.*

FALKLAND ISLANDS - FOREIGN TRADE

G.K. Hall and Company, 70 Lincoln Street, Boston, Massachusetts 02111 (617) 423-3990; *The World in Figures.*

Organisation for Economic Cooperation and Development (OECD), 2 rue Andre-Pascal, 75 Paris 16, France (Telephone Number in U.S. (202) 785-6323); *Trade by Commodities.*

Statistical Office of the United Nations, Publishing Service, New York, New York 10017 (800) 253-9646; *International Trade Statistics Yearbook,* and *Statistical Yearbook.*

FALKLAND ISLANDS - FORESTRY AND FOREST PRODUCTS

Food and Agricultural Organization of the United Nations (FAO) Via delle Terme di Caracalla, 00100 Rome, Italy (Telephone Number in U.S. (202) 653-2400); *The State of Food and Agriculture.*

G.K. Hall and Company, 70 Lincoln Street, Boston, Massachusetts 02111 (617) 423-3990; *The World in Figures.*

FALKLAND ISLANDS - GENERAL MORTALITY

Statistical Office of the United Nations, Publishing Service, New York, New York 10017 (800) 253-9646; *Demographic Yearbook.*

World Health Organization, Office of Publications, Avenue Appia, CH-1211 Geneva 27, Switzerland (Telephone Number in U.S. (518) 436-9686); *World Health Statistics Annual.*

FALKLAND ISLANDS - GOVERNMENT

G.K. Hall and Company, 70 Lincoln Street, Boston, Massachusetts 02111 (617) 423-3990; *The World in Figures.*

FALKLAND ISLANDS - GRAIN PRODUCTION - See FALKLAND ISLANDS - CROPS

FALKLAND ISLANDS - GROSS DOMESTIC PRODUCT

G.K. Hall and Company, 70 Lincoln Street, Boston, Massachusetts 02111 (617) 423-3990; *The World in Figures.*

FALKLAND ISLANDS - HEALTH

G.K. Hall and Company, 70 Lincoln Street, Boston, Massachusetts 02111 (617) 423-3990; *The World in Figures.*

Statistical Office of the United Nations, Publishing Service, New York, New York 10017 (800) 253-9646; *Statistical Yearbook.*

FALKLAND ISLANDS - HIDE PRODUCTION

Food and Agricultural Organization of the United Nations (FAO), Via delle Terme di Caracalla, 00100 Rome, Italy (Telephone Number in U.S. (202) 653-2400); *Production Yearbook.*

FALKLAND ISLANDS - HIGHWAYS

G.K. Hall and Company, 70 Lincoln Street, Boston, Massachusetts 02111 (617) 423-3990; *The World in Figures.*

FALKLAND ISLANDS - HORSES - See FALKLAND ISLANDS - LIVESTOCK AND POULTRY

FALKLAND ISLANDS - HOURS OF WORK - See FALKLAND ISLANDS - EMPLOYMENT

FALKLAND ISLANDS - ILLITERATE POPULATION

G.K. Hall and Company, 70 Lincoln Street, Boston, Massachusetts 02111 (617) 423-3990; *The World in Figures.*

FALKLAND ISLANDS - IMPORTS

Food and Agricultural Organization of the United Nations (FAO) Via delle Terme di Caracalla, 00100 Rome, Italy (Telephone Number in U.S. (202) 653-2400); *The State of Food and Agriculture.*

G.K. Hall and Company, 70 Lincoln Street, Boston, Massachusetts 02111 (617) 423-3990; *The World in Figures.*

International Monetary Fund, 700 Nineteenth Street, NW, Washington, D.C. 20431 (202) 623-7000; *Direction of Trade Statistics.*

FALKLAND ISLANDS - INDUSTRY

G.K. Hall and Company, 70 Lincoln Street, Boston, Massachusetts 02111 (617) 423-3990; *The World in Figures.*

International Labour Office, I.L.O. Publications, CH-1211, Geneva 22, Switzerland; *Yearbook of Labour Statistics.*

FALKLAND ISLANDS - INFANT AND MATERNAL MORTALITY

Statistical Office of the United Nations, Publishing Service, New York, New York 10017 (800) 253-9646; *Demographic Yearbook.*

FALKLAND ISLANDS - LABOR FORCE

Food and Agricultural Organization of the United Nations (FAO) Via delle Terme di Caracalla, 00100 Rome, Italy (Telephone Number in U.S. (202) 653-2400); *The State of Food and Agriculture.*

G.K. Hall and Company, 70 Lincoln Street, Boston, Massachusetts 02111 (617) 423-3990; *The World in Figures.*

FALKLAND ISLANDS - LABOR PRODUCTIVITY

International Labour Office, I.L.O. Publications, CH-1211, Geneva 22, Switzerland; *Yearbook of Labour Statistics.*

FALKLAND ISLANDS - LAND USE

Food and Agricultural Organization of the United Nations (FAO), Via delle Terme di Caracalla, 00100 Rome, Italy (Telephone Number in U.S. (202) 653-2400); *Production Yearbook.*

G.K. Hall and Company, 70 Lincoln Street, Boston, Massachusetts 02111 (617) 423-3990; *The World in Figures.*

FALKLAND ISLANDS - LIVESTOCK AND POULTRY

Food and Agricultural Organization of the United Nations (FAO), Via delle Terme di Caracalla, 00100 Rome, Italy (Telephone Number in U.S. (202) 653-2400); *Production Yearbook,* and *The State of Food and Agriculture.*

G.K. Hall and Company, 70 Lincoln Street, Boston, Massachusetts 02111 (617) 423-3990; *The World in Figures.*

Statistical Office of the United Nations, Publishing Service, New York, New York 10017 (800) 253-9646; *Statistical Yearbook.*

FALKLAND ISLANDS - LIVING LEVELS

G.K. Hall and Company, 70 Lincoln Street, Boston, Massachusetts 02111 (617) 423-3990; *The World in Figures.*

FALKLAND ISLANDS - MAIL - NUMBER OF PIECES SENT OR RECEIVED

Statistical Office of the United Nations, Publishing Service, New York, New York 10017 (800) 253-9646; *Statistical Yearbook.*

FALKLAND ISLANDS - MANUFACTURING

G.K. Hall and Company, 70 Lincoln Street, Boston, Massachusetts 02111 (617) 423-3990; *The World in Figures.*

FALKLAND ISLANDS - MARRIAGE RATES

Statistical Office of the United Nations, Publishing Service, New York, New York 10017 (800) 253-9646; *Demographic Yearbook,* and *Statistical Yearbook.*

FALKLAND ISLANDS - MEAT PRODUCTION - See FALKLAND ISLANDS - LIVESTOCK AND POULTRY

FALKLAND ISLANDS - MERCHANT SHIPPING

G.K. Hall and Company, 70 Lincoln Street, Boston, Massachusetts 02111 (617) 423-3990; *The World in Figures.*

Statistical Office of the United Nations, Publishing Service, New York, New York 10017 (800) 253-9646; *Statistical Yearbook.*

FALKLAND ISLANDS - MILITARY

G.K. Hall and Company, 70 Lincoln Street, Boston, Massachusetts 02111 (617) 423-3990; *The World in Figures.*

FALKLAND ISLANDS - MINING AND MINERAL PRODUCTS

G.K. Hall and Company, 70 Lincoln Street, Boston, Massachusetts 02111 (617) 423-3990; *The World in Figures.*

FALKLAND ISLANDS - MONEY SUPPLY

G.K. Hall and Company, 70 Lincoln Street, Boston, Massachusetts 02111 (617) 423-3990; *The World in Figures.*

FALKLAND ISLANDS - MOTION PICTURES

Statistical Office of the United Nations, Publishing Service, New York, New York 10017 (800) 253-9646; *Statistical Yearbook.*

FALKLAND ISLANDS - MOTOR VEHICLES IN USE

G.K. Hall and Company, 70 Lincoln Street, Boston, Massachusetts 02111 (617) 423-3990; *The World in Figures.*

Statistical Office of the United Nations, Publishing Service, New York, New York 10017 (800) 253-9646; *Statistical Yearbook.*

FALKLAND ISLANDS - MUSEUMS

United Nations Educational, Scientific and Cultural Organization (UNESCO), 7 Place de Fontenoy, F-75700 Paris, France (Telephone Number in U.S. (212) 963-5981); *Statistical Yearbook.*

FALKLAND ISLANDS - NATALITY - See FALKLAND ISLANDS - BIRTH RATE

FALKLAND ISLANDS - NATIONAL INCOME

G.K. Hall and Company, 70 Lincoln Street, Boston, Massachusetts 02111 (617) 423-3990; *The World in Figures.*

FALKLAND ISLANDS - NEWSPAPER PRODUCTION - See FALKLAND ISLANDS - FORESTRY AND FOREST PRODUCTS

FALKLAND ISLANDS - OCCUPATIONS - See FALKLAND ISLANDS - LABOR FORCE

FALKLAND ISLANDS - PERIODICALS

United Nations Educational, Scientific and Cultural Organization (UNESCO), 7 Place de Fontenoy, F-75700 Paris, France (Telephone Number in U.S. (212) 963-5981); *Statistical Yearbook.*

FALKLAND ISLANDS - PESTICIDE USE

Food and Agricultural Organization of the United Nations (FAO) Via delle Terme di Caracalla, 00100 Rome, Italy (Telephone Number in U.S. (202) 653-2400); *The State of Food and Agriculture.*

FALKLAND ISLANDS - PETROLEUM INDUSTRY

Food and Agricultural Organization of the United Nations (FAO) Via delle Terme di Caracalla, 00100 Rome, Italy (Telephone Number in U.S. (202) 653-2400); *The State of Food and Agriculture.*

G.K. Hall and Company, 70 Lincoln Street, Boston, Massachusetts 02111 (617) 423-3990; *The World in Figures.*

FALKLAND ISLANDS - POPULATION

Food and Agricultural Organization of the United Nations (FAO), Via delle Terme di Caracalla, 00100 Rome, Italy (Telephone Number in U.S. (202) 653-2400); *Production Yearbook.*

G.K. Hall and Company, 70 Lincoln Street, Boston, Massachusetts 02111 (617) 423-3990; *The World in Figures.*

International Labour Office, I.L.O. Publications, CH-1211, Geneva 22, Switzerland; *Yearbook of Labour Statistics.*

Statistical Office of the United Nations, Publishing Service, New York, New York 10017 (800) 253-9646; *Demographic Yearbook,* and *Statistical Yearbook.*

United Nations Educational, Scientific and Cultural Organization (UNESCO), 7 Place de Fontenoy, F-75700 Paris, France (Telephone Number in U.S. (212) 963-5981); *Statistical Yearbook.*

World Health Organization, Office of Publications, Avenue Appia, CH-1211 Geneva 27, Switzerland (Telephone Number in U.S. (518) 436-9686); *World Health Statistics Annual.*

FALKLAND ISLANDS - PRICES

Food and Agricultural Organization of the United Nations (FAO), Via delle Terme di Caracalla, 00100 Rome, Italy (Telephone Number in U.S. (202) 653-2400); *Production Yearbook,* and *The State of Food and Agriculture.*

G.K. Hall and Company, 70 Lincoln Street, Boston, Massachusetts 02111 (617) 423-3990; *The World in Figures.*

International Labour Office, I.L.O. Publications, CH-1211, Geneva 22, Switzerland; *Yearbook of Labour Statistics.*

FALKLAND ISLANDS - PRODUCTION

G.K. Hall and Company, 70 Lincoln Street, Boston, Massachusetts 02111 (617) 423-3990; *The World in Figures.*

FALKLAND ISLANDS - RADIO BROADCASTING

United Nations Educational, Scientific and Cultural Organization (UNESCO), 7 Place de Fontenoy, F-75700 Paris, France (Telephone Number in U.S. (212) 963-5981); *Statistical Yearbook.*

FALKLAND ISLANDS - RAILWAYS

G.K. Hall and Company, 70 Lincoln Street, Boston, Massachusetts 02111 (617) 423-3990; *The World in Figures.*

FALKLAND ISLANDS - RETAIL TRADE

G.K. Hall and Company, 70 Lincoln Street, Boston, Massachusetts 02111 (617) 423-3990; *The World in Figures.*

FALKLAND ISLANDS - SCIENTISTS AND TECHNICIANS

United Nations Educational, Scientific and Cultural Organization (UNESCO), 7 Place de Fontenoy, F-75700 Paris, France (Telephone Number in U.S. (212) 963-5981); *Statistical Yearbook.*

FALKLAND ISLANDS - SHEEP - See FALKLAND ISLANDS - LIVESTOCK AND POULTRY

FALKLAND ISLANDS - SOCIAL DATA

G.K. Hall and Company, 70 Lincoln Street, Boston, Massachusetts 02111 (617) 423-3990; *The World in Figures.*

FALKLAND ISLANDS - STOCKS - COMMODITY - MARKET PRICE - INDEX

Food and Agricultural Organization of the United Nations (FAO) Via delle Terme di Caracalla, 00100 Rome, Italy (Telephone Number in U.S. (202) 653-2400); *The State of Food and Agriculture.*

FALKLAND ISLANDS - TAXATION

G.K. Hall and Company, 70 Lincoln Street, Boston, Massachusetts 02111 (617) 423-3990; *The World in Figures.*

FALKLAND ISLANDS - TELEPHONES IN USE

American Telephone and Telegraph Company, 26 Parsippany Road, Whippany, New Jersey 07981 (800) 338-4038; *The World's Telephones.*

G.K. Hall and Company, 70 Lincoln Street, Boston, Massachusetts 02111 (617) 423-3990; *The World in Figures.*

FALKLAND ISLANDS - TEXTILE INDUSTRY

G.K. Hall and Company, 70 Lincoln Street, Boston, Massachusetts 02111 (617) 423-3990; *The World in Figures.*

FALKLAND ISLANDS - TOURISM

G.K. Hall and Company, 70 Lincoln Street, Boston, Massachusetts 02111 (617) 423-3990; *The World in Figures.*

FALKLAND ISLANDS - TRACTORS IN USE

Statistical Office of the United Nations, Publishing Service, New York, New York 10017 (800) 253-9646; *Statistical Yearbook.*

FALKLAND ISLANDS - TRADE - See FALKLAND ISLANDS - FOREIGN TRADE

FALKLAND ISLANDS - TRANSPORTATION AND COMMUNICATIONS

G.K. Hall and Company, 70 Lincoln Street, Boston, Massachusetts 02111 (617) 423-3990; *The World in Figures.*

FALKLAND ISLANDS - UNEMPLOYMENT

International Labour Office, I.L.O. Publications, CH-1211, Geneva 22, Switzerland; *Yearbook of Labour Statistics.*

FALKLAND ISLANDS - VITAL STATISTICS

G.K. Hall and Company, 70 Lincoln Street, Boston, Massachusetts 02111 (617) 423-3990; *The World in Figures.*

Statistical Office of the United Nations, Publishing Service, New York, New York 10017 (800) 253-9646; *Statistical Yearbook.*

World Health Organization, Office of Publications, Avenue Appia, CH-1211 Geneva 27, Switzerland (Telephone Number in U.S. (518) 436-9686); *World Health Statistics Annual.*

FALKLAND ISLANDS - WAGES

G.K. Hall and Company, 70 Lincoln Street, Boston, Massachusetts 02111 (617) 423-3990; *The World in Figures.*

International Labour Office, I.L.O. Publications, CH-1211, Geneva 22, Switzerland; *Yearbook of Labour Statistics.*

FALKLAND ISLANDS - WEATHER

G.K. Hall and Company, 70 Lincoln Street, Boston, Massachusetts 02111 (617) 423-3990; *The World in Figures.*

FAN CLUBS

Gale Research Incorporated, 835 Penobscot Building, Detroit, Michigan 48226 (800) 877-4253; *Encyclopedia of Associations.*

FARM AND GARDEN MACHINERY - MANUFACTURING - EARNINGS

U.S. Department of Commerce, Bureau of the Census, Suitland, Maryland 20233 (301) 763-4040; *Census of Manufactures,* and *Annual Survey of Manufactures.*

U.S. Department of Labor, Bureau of Labor Statistics, 200 Constitution Avenue, NW, Washington, D.C. 20210 (202) 523-1327; *Employment and Earnings,* and Bulletins 2370 and 2429.

FARM AND GARDEN MACHINERY - MANUFACTURING - EMPLOYEES

U.S. Department of Commerce, Bureau of the Census, Suitland, Maryland 20233 (301) 763-4040; *Census of Manufactures,* and *Annual Survey of Manufactures.*

U.S. Department of Labor, Bureau of Labor Statistics, 200 Constitution Avenue, NW, Washington, D.C. 20210 (202) 523-1327; *Employment and Earnings,* and Bulletins 2370 and 2429.

FARM AND GARDEN MACHINERY - MANUFACTURING - ESTABLISHMENTS

U.S. Department of Commerce, Bureau of the Census, Suitland, Maryland 20233 (301) 763-4040; *Census of Manufactures*, and *Annual Survey of Manufactures.*

FARM AND GARDEN MACHINERY - MANUFACTURING - PRODUCTIVITY

U.S. Department of Labor, Bureau of Labor Statistics, 200 Constitution Avenue, NW, Washington, D.C. 20210 (202) 523-1327; *Productivity Measures for Selected Industries and Government Services*, and unpublished data.

FARM AND GARDEN MACHINERY - MANUFACTURING SHIPMENTS

U.S. Department of Commerce, Bureau of the Census, Suitland, Maryland 20233 (301) 763-4040; *Census of Manufactures*, and *Annual Survey of Manufactures.*

FARM AND GARDEN MACHINERY - MANUFACTURING VALUE ADDED

U.S. Department of Commerce, Bureau of the Census, Suitland, Maryland 20233 (301) 763-4040; *Census of Manufactures*, and *Annual Survey of Manufactures.*

FARM MORTGAGE LOANS

Board of Governors of the Federal Reserve System, Twentieth Street and Constitution Avenue, NW, Washington, D.C. 20551 (202) 452-3000; *Federal Reserve Bulletin.*

U.S. Department of Housing and Urban Development, 451 Seventh Street, SW, Washington, D.C. 20410 (202) 708-1422; *Survey of Mortgage Lending Activity*, and monthly and quarterly press releases.

U.S. National Guard Bureau, The Pentagon, Washington, D.C. 20301 (202) 433-5100; *Annual Review of the Chief, National Guard Bureau*, and unpublished data.

FARMERS AND FARM WORKERS

U.S. Department of Agriculture, Economic Research Service, Fourteenth Street and Independence Avenue, SW, Washington, D.C. 20005-4789 (202) 219-1504; unpublished data.

U.S. Department of Commerce, Bureau of the Census, Suitland, Maryland 20233 (301) 763-4040; *Current Population Reports.*

FARMERS AND FARM WORKERS - BANKRUPTCIES FILED

Administrative Office of the United States Courts, United States Supreme Court Building, Columbus Circle, NE, Washington, D.C. 20544 (202) 273-1120; *Annual Report of the Director.*

FARMERS AND FARM WORKERS - EARNINGS

U.S. Department of Agriculture, Economic Research Service, Fourteenth Street and Independence Avenue, SW, Washington, D.C. 20005-4789 (202) 219-1504; unpublished data.

FARMERS AND FARM WORKERS - EMPLOYMENT

U.S. Department of Labor, Bureau of Labor Statistics, 200 Constitution Avenue, NW, Washington, D.C. 20210 (202) 523-1327; *Employment and Earnings, Monthly Labor Review*, and *News.*

FARMERS AND FARM WORKERS - EMPLOYMENT - PROJECTIONS

U.S. Department of Labor, Bureau of Labor Statistics, 200 Constitution Avenue, NW, Washington, D.C. 20210 (202) 523-1327; *Monthly Labor Review.*

FARMERS AND FARM WORKERS - INDEXES OF FARM INPUTS

Executive Office of the President, Council of Economic Advisors, Old Executive Office Building, Washington, D.C. 20500 (202) 395-5084; *Economic Report of the President.*

U.S. Department of Agriculture, Economic Research Service, Fourteenth Street and Independence Avenue, SW, Washington, D.C. 20005-4789 (202) 219-1504; *Agricultural Outlook.*

FARMERS AND FARM WORKERS - UNEMPLOYMENT

U.S. Department of Labor, Bureau of Labor Statistics, 200 Constitution Avenue, NW, Washington, D.C. 20210 (202) 523-1327; *Employment and Earnings.*

FARMS - ACREAGE

U.S. Department of Agriculture, National Agricultural Statistics Service, Fourteenth Street and Independence Avenue, SW, Washington, D.C. 20250 (202) 219-1504; *Crop Production*, and *Farm Numbers and Land in Farms.*

U.S. Department of Commerce, Bureau of the Census, Suitland, Maryland 20233 (301) 763-4040; *Census of Agriculture.*

FARMS - ACREAGE - CROPLAND

U.S. Department of Agriculture, Economic Research Service, Fourteenth Street and Independence Avenue, SW, Washington, D.C. 20005-4789 (202) 219-1504; *Agricultural Statistics*, and *Agricultural Resources: Cropland, Water, and Conservation Situation and Outlook Report.*

U.S. Department of Commerce, Bureau of the Census, Suitland, Maryland 20233 (301) 763-4040; *Census of Agriculture.*

FARMS - ACREAGE - CROPS HARVESTED - See also Individual Crops

U.S. Department of Agriculture, National Agricultural Statistics Service, Fourteenth Street and Independence Avenue, SW, Washington, D.C. 20250 (202) 219-1504; *Feed Situation, The Tobacco Situation, Agricultural Statistics, Crop Production, Field Crops, Vegetables, Sugar and Sweetener Outlook and Situation, Crop Values, Wheat Situation, Fats and Oils Situation, Agricultural Outlook*, and *Agricultural Resources: Cropland, Water, and Conservation Situation and Outlook Report.*

FARMS - AGRICHEMICALS

U.S. Department of Agriculture, Economic Research Service, Fourteenth Street and Independence Avenue, SW, Washington, D.C. 20005-4789 (202) 219-1504; *Agricultural Outlook.*

U.S. Department of Agriculture, National Agricultural Statistics Service Fourteenth Street and Independence Avenue, SW, Washington, D.C. 20250 (202) 219-1504; *Agricultural Prices: Annual Summary.*

U.S. Department of Commerce, Bureau of the Census, Suitland, Maryland 20233 (301) 763-4040; *Census of Agriculture.*

FARMS - AGRICULTURAL PRODUCTS - EXPORTS

U.S. Department of Commerce, Bureau of the Census, Suitland, Maryland 20233 (301) 763-4040; *U.S. Merchandise Trade, Exports, General Imports, Imports for Consumption.*

FARMS - AGRICULTURAL PRODUCTS - FOREIGN ASSISTANCE

U.S. Department of Commerce, Bureau of Economic Analysis, Fourteenth Street between Constitution Avenue and E Street, NW, Washington, D.C. 20230 (202) 606-9900; press releases and unpublished data.

FARMS - AGRICULTURAL PRODUCTS - FOREIGN COUNTRIES - PRODUCTION

Food and Agriculture Organization of the United Nations (FAO), Via delle Terme di Caracalla, 00100 Rome, Italy (Telephone Number in U.S. (202) 653-2400); *FAO Production Yearbook.*

Statistical Office of the United Nations, Publishing Service, New York, New York 10017 (800) 253-9646; *Statistical Yearbook.*

U.S. Department of Agriculture, Economic Research Service, 14th Street and Independence Avenue, SW, Washington, D.C. 20005-4789 (202) 219-1504; *World Agriculture - Trends and Indicators.*

FARMS - AGRICULTURAL PRODUCTS - RAILROAD CAR LOADINGS OF

Association of American Railroads, American Railroads Building, 50 F Street, NW, Washington, D.C. 20001 (202) 639-2100; *Weekly Railroad Traffic,* and *Freight Commodity Statistics.*

FARMS - AGRICULTURAL PRODUCTS - WATERBORNE COMMERCE

U.S. Department of the Army, Corps of Engineers, The Pentagon, Washington, D.C. 20301 (202) 545-6700; *Waterborne Commerce of the United States.*

FARMS - AGRICULTURAL PRODUCTS - WORLD PRODUCTION

Food and Agricultural Organization of the U.N. (FAO), Via delle Terme di Caracalla, 00100 Rome, Italy (Telephone Number in U.S. (202) 653-2400); *FAO Production Yearbook.*

Statistical Office of the United Nations, Publishing Service, New York, New York 10017 (800) 253-9646; *Monthly Bulletin of Statistics.*

U.S. Department of Agriculture, Economic Research Service, 14th Street and Independence Avenue, SW, Washington, D.C. 20005-4789 (202) 219-1504; *World Agriculture - Trends and Indicators.*

FARMS - ASSETS AND LIABILITIES

Board of Governors of the Federal Reserve System, Twentieth Street and Constitution Avenue, NW, Washington, D.C. 20511 (202) 452-3000; *Annual Statistical Digest.*

U.S. Department of Agriculture, Economic Research Service, Fourteenth Street and Independence Avenue, SW, Washington, D.C. 20005-4789 (202) 219-1504; *Economic Indicators of the Farm Sector: National Financial Summary,* and *Economic Indicators of the Farm Sector: State Financial Summary.*

FARMS - CAPITAL

U.S. Department of Agriculture, Economic Research Service, Fourteenth Street and Independence Avenue, SW, Washington, D.C. 20005-4789 (202) 219-1504; *Economic Indicators of the Farm Sector: National Financial Summary.*

FARMS - CAPITAL STOCKS - FARM HOUSING

U.S. Department of Commerce, Bureau of Economic Analysis, Fourteenth Street between Constitution Avenue and E Street, NW, Washington, D.C. 20230 (202) 606-9900; *Survey of Current Business,* and *Fixed Reproducible Tangible Wealth in the United States.*

FARMS - COMMODITY CREDIT CORPORATION TRANSACTIONS

U.S. Department of Agriculture, Agricultural Stabilization and Conservation Service, Fourteenth Street and Independence Avenue, SW, Washington, D.C. 20250 (202) 720-5237; *Commodity Credit Corporation Report of Financial Condition and Operations,* and *Agricultural Outlook.*

U.S. Department of Agriculture, Economic Research Service, Fourteenth Street and Independence Avenue, SW, Washington, D.C. 20005-4789 (202) 219-1504; *Economic Indicators of the Farm Sector: National Financial Summary.*

U.S. Department of Commerce, Bureau of the Census, Suitland, Maryland 20233 (301) 763-4040; *Census of Agriculture.*

FARMS - CONSTRUCTION VALUE - FARM NON-RESIDENTIAL

U.S. Department of Commerce, Bureau of the Census, Suitland, Maryland 20233 (301) 763-4040; *Current Construction Reports.*

FARMS - CORPORATE

U.S. Department of Commerce, Bureau of the Census, Suitland, Maryland 20233 (301) 763-4040; *Census of Agriculture.*

FARMS - CROPS See also Individual Crops

FARMS - CROPS - ACREAGE

U.S. Department of Agriculture, Economic Research Service, Fourteenth Street and Independence Avenue, SW, Washington, D.C. 20005-4789 (202) 219-1504; *Crop Production, Vegetables, Crop Values, Agricultural Statistics, Field Crops, Agricultural Outlook, Cotton and Wool Outlook Statistics, Feed Situation, Wheat Situation, Fats and Oils Situation, Tobacco Situation,* and *Agricultural Resources: Cropland, Water, and Conservation Situation and Outlook Report.*

FARMS - CROPS - FRUITS AND NUTS

U.S. Department of Agriculture, Agricultural Statistics Service, Fourteenth Street and Independence Avenue, SW, Washington, D.C. 20250 (202) 720-5237; *Noncitrus Fruits and Nuts,* and *Citrus Fruits.*

U.S. Department of Commerce, Bureau of the Census, Suitland, Maryland 20233 (301) 763-4040; *Census of Agriculture.*

FARMS - CROPS - INCOME

U.S. Department of Agriculture, Economic Research Service, Fourteenth Street and Independence Avenue, SW, Washington, D.C. 20005-4789 (202) 219-1504; *Economic Indicators of the Farm Sector: National Financial Summary,* and *Economic Indicators of the*

Farm Sector: State Financial Summary.

FARMS - CROPS - PRODUCTION

U.S. Department of Agriculture, Economic Research Service, Fourteenth Street and Independence Avenue, SW, Washington, D.C. 20005-4789 (202) 219-1504; *Agricultural Outlook,* and *Agricultural Resources: Cropland, Water, and Conservation Situation and Outlook Report.*

U.S. Department of Agriculture, Foreign Agricultural Service, Fourteenth Street and Independence Avenue, SW, Washington, D.C. 20250 (202) 720-3448; *Foreign Agricultural Commodity Circular Series.*

U.S. Department of Agriculture, National Agricultural Statistics Service, Fourteenth Street and Independence Avenue, SW, Washington, D.C. 20250 (202) 219-1504; *Agricultural Statistics.*

FARMS - CROPS - PRODUCTION - WORLD

Food and Agricultural Organization of the U.N. (FAO), Via Delle Terme di Caracalla, 00100 Rome, Italy (Telephone Number in U.S. (202) 653-2400); *FAO Production Yearbook.*

FARMS - CROPS - VEGETABLES

U.S. Department of Agriculture, National Agricultural Statistics Service, Fourteenth Street and Independence Avenue, SW, Washington, D.C. 20250 (202) 219-1504; *Vegetables,* and *Agricultural Statistics.*

FARMS - DEBT

U.S. Department of Agriculture, Economic Research Service, Fourteenth Street and Independence Avenue, SW, Washington, D.C. 20005-4789 (202) 219-1504; *Economic Indicators of the Farm Sector: National Financial Summary, Economic Indicators of the Farm Sector: State Financial Summary,* and unpublished data.

FARMS - DEBT - MORTGAGE OUTSTANDING

Board of Governors of the Federal Reserve System, Twentieth Street and Constitution Avenue, NW, Washington, D.C. 20551 (202) 452-3000; *Federal Reserve Bulletin.*

FARMS - EXPENSES

U.S. Department of Agriculture, Economic Research Service, Fourteenth Street and Independence Avenue, SW, Washington, D.C. 20005-4789 (202) 219-1504; *Economic Indicators of the Farm Sector: National Financial Summary.*

FARMS - FARM PRODUCTS SOLD - MARKETING RECEIPTS

U.S. Department of Agriculture, Economic Research Service, Fourteenth Street and Independence Avenue, SW, Washington, D.C. 20005-4789 (202) 219-1504; *Economic Indicators of the Farm Sector: National Financial Summary, Economic Indicators of the Farm Sector: State Financial Summary.*

U.S. Department of Commerce, Bureau of Economic Analysis, Fourteenth Street between Constitution Avenue and E Street, NW, Washington, D.C. 20230 (202) 606-9900; *The National Income and Product Accounts of the United States,* and *Survey of Current Business.*

U.S. Department of Commerce, Bureau of the Census, Suitland, Maryland 20233 (301) 763-4040; *Census of Agriculture.*

FARMS - GOVERNMENT PAYMENTS TO FARMERS

U.S. Department of Agriculture, Agricultural Stabilization and Conservation Service, Fourteenth Street and Independence Avenue, SW, Washington, D.C. 20250 (202) 720-5237; *Commodity Credit Corporation Report of Financial Condition and Operations,* and *Agricultural Outlook.*

U.S. Department of Agriculture, Economic Research Service, Fourteenth Street and Independence Avenue, SW, Washington, D.C. 20005-4789 (202) 219-1504; *Economic Indicators of the Farm Sector: National Financial Summary, Economic Indicators of the Farm Sector: State Financial Summary.*

U.S. Department of Commerce, Bureau of the Census, Suitland, Maryland 20233 (301) 763-4040; *Census of Agriculture.*

FARMS - GROSS FARM PRODUCT

U.S. Department of Commerce, Bureau of Economic Analysis, Fourteenth Street between Constitution Avenue and E Street, NW, Washington, D.C. 20230 (202) 606-9900 *The National Income and Product Accounts of the United States,* and *Survey of Current Business.*

FARMS - HOUSEHOLD INCOME

U.S. Department of Agriculture, Economic Research Service, Fourteenth Street and Independence Avenue, SW, Washington, D.C. 20005 (202) 219-1504; *Agricultural Income and Finance Situtation and Outlook.*

FARMS - HOUSING - RENTAL VALUE

U.S. Department of Commerce, Bureau of Economic Analysis, Fourteenth Street between Constitution Avenue and E Street, NW, Washington, D.C 20250 (202) 606-9900; *Survey of Current Business,* and *The National Income and Product Accounts of the United States.*

FARMS - INCOME

U.S. Department of Agriculture, Economic Research Service, Fourteenth Street and Independence Avenue, SW, Washington, D.C. 20005-4789 (202) 219-1504; *Economic Indicators of the Farm Sector: National Financial Summary, Economic Indicators of the Farm Sector: State Financial Summary,* and *Agricultural Income and Finance Situation and Outlook.*

U.S. Department of Commerce, Bureau of Economic Analysis, Fourteenth Street between Constitution Avenue and E Street, NW, Washington, D.C. 20230 (202) 606-9900; *The National Income and Product Accounts of the U.S.,* and *Survey of Current Business.*

U.S. Department of Commerce, Bureau of the Census, Suitland, Maryland 20233 (301) 763-4040; *Census of Agriculture.*

FARMS - INDIVIDUAL OR FAMILY

U.S. Department of Commerce, Bureau of the Census, Suitland, Maryland 20233 (301) 763-4040; *Census of Agriculture.*

FARMS - INPUT INDEXES

Executive Office of the President, Council of Economic Advisors, Executive Office Building, Washington, D.C. 20506 (202) 395-5084; *Economic Report of the President.*

U.S. Department of Agriculture, Economic Research Service, Fourteenth Street and Independence Avenue, SW, Washington, D.C. 20005-4789 (202) 219-1504; *Agricultural Outlook.*

FARMS - INVENTORIES - CHANGE IN

U.S. Department of Agriculture, Economic Research Service, Fourteenth Street and Independence Avenue, SW, Washington, D.C. 20005-4789 (202) 219-1504; *Economic Indicators of the Farm Sector: National Financial Summary.*

U.S. Department of Commerce, Bureau of Economic Analysis, Fourteenth Street between Constitution Avenue and E Street, NW, Washington, D.C. 20230 (202) 606-9900; *The National Income and Product Accounts of the United States,* and *Survey of Current Business.*

FARMS - IRRIGATION

U.S. Department of Commerce, Bureau of the Census, Suitland, Maryland 20233 (301) 763-4040; *Census of Agriculture.*

FARMS - LABOR EXPENSES

U.S. Department of Agriculture, Economic Research Service, Fourteenth Street and Independence Avenue, SW, Washington, D.C. 20005-4789 (202) 219-1504; *Economic Indicators of the Farm Sector: National Financial Summary.*

U.S. Department of Agriculture, National Agricultural Statistics Service, Fourteenth Street and Independence Avenue, SW, Washington, D.C. 20250 (202) 219-1504; *Agricultural Prices: Annual Summary.*

FARMS - LABOR INPUTS

Executive Office of the President, Council of Economic Advisors, Executive Office Building, Washington, D.C. 20506 (202) 395-5084; *Economic Report of the President.*

U.S. Department of Agriculture, Economic Research Service, Fourteenth Street and Independence Avenue, SW, Washington, D.C. 20005-4789 (202) 219-1504; *Agricultural Outlook.*

FARMS - MACHINERY AND MOTOR VEHICLES

U.S. Department of Agriculture, Economic Research Service, Fourteenth Street and Independence Avenue, SW, Washington, D.C. 20005-4789 (202) 219-1504; *Agricultural Statistics,* and *Economic Indicators of the Farm Sector: National Financial Summary.*

FARMS - MORTGAGE LOANS

Board of Governors of the Federal Reserve System, Twentieth Street and Constitution Avenue, NW, Washington, D.C. 20551 (202) 452-3000; *Federal Reserve Bulletin.*

FARMS - NATIONAL INCOME - ORIGIN IN

U.S. Department of Commerce, Bureau of Economic Analysis, Fourteenth Street between Constitution Avenue and E Street, NW, Washington, D.C. 20230 (202) 606-9900; *The National Income and Product Accounts of the United States,* and *Survey of Current Business.*

FARMS - NUMBER OF FARMS

U.S. Department of Agriculture, Economic Research Service, Fourteenth Street and Independence Avenue, SW, Washington, D.C. 20005-4789 (202) 219-1504; *Economic Indicators of the Farm Sector: National Financial Summary.*

U.S. Department of Agriculture, National Agricultural Statistics Service, Fourteenth Street and Independence Avenue, SW, Washington, D.C. 20250 (202) 219-1504; *Farm Numbers and Land in Farms,* and *Crop Production.*

U.S. Department of Commerce, Bureau of the Census, Suitland, Maryland 20233 (301) 763-4040; *Census of Agriculture,* and unpublished data.

FARMS - OPERATOR CHARACTERISTICS

U.S. Department of Commerce, Bureau of the Census, Suitland, Maryland 20233 (301) 763-4040; *Census of Agriculture.*

FARMS - OUTLYING AREAS OF THE UNITED STATES

U.S. Department of Commerce, Bureau of the Census, Suitland, Maryland 20233 (301) 763-4040; *Census of Agriculture.*

FARMS - PARITY RATIO

U.S. Department of Agriculture, National Agricultural Statistics Service, Fourteenth Street and Independence Avenue, SW, Washington, D.C. 20250 (202) 219-1504; *Agricultural Prices: Annual Summary.*

FARMS - PARTNERSHIPS

U.S. Department of Commerce, Bureau of the Census, Suitland, Maryland 20233 (301) 763-4040; *Census of Agriculture.*

FARMS - PRICES - CROPS

U.S. Department of Agriculture, National Agricultural Statistics Service, Fourteenth Street and Independence Avenue, SW, Washington, D.C. 20250 (202) 219-1504; *Agricultural Statistics, Field Crops, Crop Production, Crop Values, Vegetables, Agricultural Outlook,* and *Agricultural Prices: Annual Summary.*

FARMS - PRICES - LIVESTOCK AND POULTRY AND PRODUCTS

U.S. Department of Agriculture, National Agricultural Statistics Service, Fourteenth Street and Independence Avenue, SW, Washington, D.C. 20250 (202) 219-1504; *Agricultural Statistics, Meat Animals - Production, Disposition, and Income,* and *Agricultural Prices: Annual Summary.*

FARMS - REAL ESTATE - INPUT INDEXES

Executive Office of the President, Council of Economic Advisors, Executive Office Building, Washington, D.C. 20500 (202) 395-5084; *Economic Report of the President.*

U.S. Department of Agriculture, Economic Research Service, Fourteenth Street and Independence Avenue, SW, Washington, D.C. 20005-4789 (202) 219-1504; *Agricultural Outlook.*

FARMS - TAXES

U.S. Department of Agriculture, Economic Research Service, Fourteenth Street and Independence Avenue, SW, Washington, D.C. 20005-4789 (202) 219-1504; *Economic Indicators of the Farm Sector:*

National Financial Summary, and *Agricultural Prices: Annual Summary*.

U.S. Department of Commerce, Bureau of Economic Analysis, 14th Street between Constitution Avenue and E Street, NW, Washington, D.C. 20230 (202) 606-9900; *The National Income and Product Accounts of the United States*, and *Survey of Current Business*, July issues.

FARMS - TENURE OF OPERATOR

U.S. Department of Commerce, Bureau of the Census, Suitland, Maryland 20233 (301) 763-4040; *Census of Agriculture*.

FARMS - VALUE - FARM LAND AND BUILDINGS

U.S. Department of Agriculture, Economic Research Service, Fourteenth Street and Independence Avenue, SW, Washington, D.C. 20005-4789 (202) 219-1504; *Agricultural Resources, Agricultural Land Values and Markets, Situation and Outlook Report, Economic Indicators of the Farm Sector: National Financial Summary*, and unpublished data.

U.S. Department of Commerce, Bureau of the Census, Suitland, Maryland 20233 (301) 763-4040; *Census of Agriculture*.

FARMS - VALUE - FARM PRODUCTS SOLD - MARKETING RECEIPTS

U.S. Department of Agriculture, Economic Research Service, Fourteenth Street and Independence Avenue, SW, Washington, D.C. 20250 (202) 219-1504; *Economic Indicators of the Farm Sector: National Financial Summary, Economic Indicators of the Farm Sector: State Financial Summary*, and *Agricultural Statistics*.

U.S. Department of Commerce, Bureau of Economic Analysis, Fourteenth Street between Constitution Avenue and E Street, NW, Washington, D.C. 20230 (202) 606-9900; *Survey of Current Business*, and *The National Income and Product Accounts of the United States*.

U.S. Department of Commerce, Bureau of the Census, Suitland, Maryland 20233 (301) 763-4040; *Census of Agriculture*.

FAT - NUTRIENT AVAILABLE FOR CONSUMPTION

U.S. Department of Agriculture, Human Nutrition Information Service, Hyattsville, Maryland 20782 (301) 436-7725; data published by U.S. Department of Agriculture, Economic Research Service, Fourteenth Street and Independence Avenue, SW, Washington, D.C. 20005-4789 (202) 219-1504; *Food Consumption, Prices, and Expenditures*, and *National Food Review*.

FATALITIES - See ACCIDENTS AND FATALITIES

FATS - See LARD, MARGARINE, AND OILS

FEDERAL AID TO EDUCATION

Executive Office of the President, Office of Management and Budget, Executive Office Building, Washington, D.C. 20503 (202) 395-3080; *Historical Tables, Budget of the United States Government*, and *Budget of the U.S. Government*.

U.S. Department of Commerce, Bureau of the Census, Suitland, Maryland 20233 (301) 763-4040; *Government Finances, Historical Statistics on Government Finances and Employment*, and *Federal Expenditures by State for Fiscal Year*.

U.S. Department of Education, National Center for Education Statistics, 400 Maryland Avenue, SW, Washington, D.C. 20202 (202) 708-5366; *Digest of Education Statistics*.

U.S. Department of Health and Human Services, Social Security Administration, 6401 Security Boulevard, Baltimore, Maryland 21235 (410) 965-1234; *Social Security Bulletin*.

FEDERAL AID TO EDUCATION - ELEMENTARY AND SECONDARY SCHOOLS

U.S. Department of Education, 400 Maryland Avenue, SW, Washington, D.C. 20202 (202) 708-5366; *Digest of Education Statistics*, and unpublished data.

U.S. Department of Health and Human Services, Social Security Administration, 6401 Security Boulevard, Baltimore, Maryland 21235 (410) 965-1234; *Social Security Bulletin*.

FEDERAL AID TO EDUCATION - HIGHER EDUCATION INSTITUTIONS

U.S. Department of Education, 400 Maryland Avenue, SW, Washington, D.C. 20202 (202) 708-5366; *Digest of Education Statistics*, and unpublished data.

U.S. Department of Health and Human Services, Social Security Administration, 6401 Security Boulevard, Baltimore, Maryland 21235 (410) 965-1234; *Social Security Bulletin*.

FEDERAL AID TO EDUCATION - RESEARCH AND DEVELOPMENT

U.S. National Science Foundation, 4201 Wilson Boulevard, Arlington, Virginia 22230 (703) 306-1234; *Survey of Federal Support to Universities, Colleges, and Nonprofit Institutions*, and *National Patterns of Research and Development Resources*.

FEDERAL AID TO EDUCATION - SCIENCE AND ENGINEERING

U.S. National Science Foundation, 4201 Wilson Boulevard, Arlington, Virginia 22230 (703) 306-1234; *Survey of Federal Support to Universities, Colleges, and Nonprofit Institutions*, and *Survey of Scientific and Engineering Expenditures at Universities and Colleges*.

FEDERAL AID TO STATE AND LOCAL GOVERNMENT

Advisory Commission on Intergovernmental Relations, 800 K Street, NW, Suite 450 South, Washington, D.C. 20575 (202) 653-5540; *Significant Features of Fiscal Federalism*, based on *Budget of the United States Government*.

Executive Office of the President, Office of Management and Budget, Executive Office Building, Washington, D.C. 20503 (202) 395-3080; *Historical Tables, Budget of the United States Government*, and *Budget of the U.S. Government*.

U.S. Department of Commerce, Bureau of the Census, Suitland, Maryland 20233 (301) 763-4040; *Federal Expenditures by State for Fiscal Year, Historical Statistics on Governmental Finances and Employment and Government Finances*.

FEDERAL BANKS - See BANKS, COMMERCIAL

FEDERAL BUDGET - See EXPENDITURES OF U.S. GOVERNMENT

FEDERAL EMPLOYEES RETIREMENT TRUST FUND - See GOVERNMENT

FEDERAL FUNDS - SUMMARY DISTRIBUTION BY STATE

U.S. Department of Commerce, Bureau of the Census, Suitland, Maryland 20233 (301) 763-4040; *Federal Expenditures by State for Fiscal Year.*

FEDERAL GOVERNMENT - See GOVERNMENT

FEDERAL GOVERNMENT FINANCES - See RECEIPTS and EXPENDITURES OF UNITED STATES GOVERNMENT

FEDERAL HOUSING ADMINISTRATION MORTGAGE LOANS

Board of Governors of the Federal Reserve System. Twentieth Street and Constitution Avenue, NW, Washington, D.C. 20551 (202) 452-3000; *Federal Reserve Bulletin.*

Mortgage Bankers Association of America, 1125 Fifteenth Street, NW, Washington, D.C. 20005 (202) 861-6500; *National Delinquency Survey.*

Mortgage Insurance Companies of America, 727 15th Street, NW, Suite 1110, Washington, D.C. 20005 (202) 393-5566; *Factbook and Membership Directory,* and unpublished data.

U.S. Department of Housing and Urban Development, 451 Seventh Street, SW, Washington, D.C. 20410 (202) 708-1422; *The Supply of Mortgage Credit,* and monthly and quarterly press releases based on Survey of Mortgage Lending Activity.

FEDERAL NATIONAL MORTGAGE ASSOCIATION LOANS

Board of Governors of the Federal Reserve System, Twentieth Street and Constitution Avenue, NW, Washington, D.C. 20551 (202) 452-3000; *Federal Reserve Bulletin.*

Congressional Budget Office, Second and D Streets, SW, Washington, D.C. 20515 (202) 226-2621; *Controlling the Risks of Government-Sponsored Enterprises.*

FEDERAL REAL PROPERTY

U.S. General Services Administration, General Services Building, Eighteenth and F Streets, NW, Washington, D.C. 20405 (202) 708-5082; *Inventory Report on Real Property Owned by the United States Throughout the World.*

FEDERATED STATES OF MICRONESIA - See MICRONESIA (FEDERATED STATES OF)

FEED - See GRAINS

FELDSPAR

U.S. Department of the Interior, Bureau of Mines, 810 Seventh Street, NW, Washington, D.C. 20241 (202) 501-9649; *Annual Reports,* and *Mineral Commodity Summaries.*

FEMALE HOUSEHOLDER - See HOUSEHOLDS OR FAMILIES

FEMALE POPULATION - See WOMEN

FERTILITY RATE

U.S. Department of Health and Human Services, National Center for Health Statistics, 3700 East-West Highway, Hyattsville, Maryland 20782 (301) 436-8500; *Vital Statistics of the United States,* and unpublished data.

FERTILIZERS - FARM EXPENDITURES FOR

U.S. Department of Agriculture, Economic Research Service, Fourteenth Street and Independence Avenue, SW, Washington, D.C. 20005-4789 (202) 219-1504; *Economic Indicators of the Farm Sector: National Financial Summary.*

FERTILIZERS - FOREIGN TRADE

U.S. Department of Commerce, Bureau of the Census, Suitland, Maryland 20233 (301) 763-4040; *U.S. Merchandise Trade: Exports, General Imports, and Imports for Consumption.*

FERTILIZERS - PRICES

U.S. Department of Agriculture, National Agricultural Statistics Service, Fourteenth Street and Independence Avenue, SW, Washington, D.C. 20005-4789 (202) 219-1504; *Agricultural Prices: Annual Summary.*

FETAL DEATHS

U.S. Department of Health and Human Services, National Center for Health Statistics, 3700 East-West Highway, Hyattsville, Maryland 20782 (301) 436-8500; *Monthly Vital Statistics Report,* and *Vital Statistics of the United States,* and unpublished data.

FIGS, FRESH

U.S. Department of Agriculture, National Agricultural Statistics Service, Fourteenth Street and Independence Avenue, SW, Washington, D.C. 20250 (202) 219-1504; *Noncitrus Fruits and Nuts,* and *Agricultural Outlook.*

Fiji - National Statistical Office

Bureau of Statistics, Government Buildings, Post Office Box 2221, Suva, Fiji.

Fiji - Primary Statistics Source

Bureau of Statistics, Government Building, P.O. Box 2221, Suva, Fiji Islands; *Fiji Facts and Figures.*

FIJI - AGRICULTURE

Asian Development Bank, P.O. Box 789, 1099 Manila, Philippines; *Key Indicators of Developing Asian and Pacific Countries.*

Facts on File, 460 Park Avenue South, New York, New York 10016 (800) 443-8323; *The New Book of World Rankings.*

Food and Agricultural Organization of the United Nations (FAO) Via delle Terme di Caracalla, 00100 Rome, Italy (Telephone Number in U.S. (202) 653-2400); *Production Yearbook, The State of Food and Agriculture,* and *Trade Yearbook.*

Gale Research Incorporated, 835 Penobscot Building, Detroit, Michigan 48226 (800) 877-4253; *International Historical Statistics The Americas and Australasia.*

G.K. Hall and Company, 70 Lincoln Street, Boston, Massachusetts 02111 (617) 423-3990; *The World in Figures.*

Statistical Office of the United Nations, Publishing Service, New York, New York 10017 (800) 253-9646; *Statistical Yearbook*, and *Statistical Yearbook for Asia and the Pacific.*

Times Books, 201 East 50th Street, New York, New York 10022 (212) 751-2600; *The Economist Book of Vital World Statistics.*

The World Bank, 1818 H Street, NW, Washington, D.C. 20433 (202) 477-1234; *World Tables.*

FIJI - AIRLINE SERVICE

Facts on File, 460 Park Avenue South, New York, New York 10016 (800) 443-8323; *The New Book of World Rankings.*

G.K. Hall and Company, 70 Lincoln Street, Boston, Massachusetts 02111 (617) 423-3990; *The World in Figures.*

Times Books, 201 East 50th Street, New York, New York 10022 (212) 751-2600; *The Economist Book of Vital World Statistics.*

FIJI - ALUMINUM PRODUCTION AND CONSUMPTION - See FIJI - MINING AND MINERAL PRODUCTS

FIJI - ANIMAL HEALTH

Food and Agricultural Organization of the United Nations (FAO), Via delle Terme di Caracalla, 00100 Rome, Italy (Telephone Number in U.S. (202) 653-2400); *Animal Health Yearbook.*

FIJI - AREA AND DENSITY OF POPULATION

Facts on File, 460 Park Avenue South, New York, New York 10016 (800) 443-8323; *The New Book of World Rankings.*

Food and Agricultural Organization of the United Nations (FAO) Via delle Terme di Caracalla, 00100 Rome, Italy (Telephone Number in U.S. (202) 653-2400); *The State of Food and Agriculture.*

G.K. Hall and Company, 70 Lincoln Street, Boston, Massachusetts 02111 (617) 423-3990; *The World in Figures.*

Statistical Office of the United Nations, Publishing Service, New York, New York 10017 (800) 253-9646; *Statistical Yearbook.*

Times Books, 201 East 50th Street, New York, New York 10022 (212) 751-2600; *The Economist Book of Vital World Statistics.*

United Nations Educational, Scientific and Cultural Organization (UNESCO), 7 Place de Fontenoy, F-75700 Paris, France (Telephone Number in U.S. (212) 963-5981); *Statistical Yearbook.*

FIJI - ARMS EXPORTS AND IMPORTS

U.S. Arms Control and Disarmament Agency, 320 Twenty-first Street, NW, Washington, D.C. 20451 (202) 647-8677; *World Military Expenditures and Arms Transfers.*

FIJI - BALANCE OF PAYMENTS

The Economist Intelligence Unit, 111 West 57th Street, New York, New York 10019 (800) 938-4685; *The World Market Atlas.*

G.K. Hall and Company, 70 Lincoln Street, Boston, Massachusetts 02111 (617) 423-3990; *The World in Figures.*

International Monetary Fund, 700 Nineteenth Street, NW, Washington, D.C. 20431 (202) 623-7000; *Balance of Payments Yearbook.*

Times Books, 201 East 50th Street, New York, New York 10022 (212) 751-2600; *The Economist Book of Vital World Statistics.*

The World Bank, 1818 H Street, NW, Washington, D.C. 20433 (202) 477-1234; *World Tables.*

FIJI - BANKING

Asian Development Bank, P.O. Box 789, 1099 Manila, Philippines; *Key Indicators of Developing Asian and Pacific Countries.*

Facts on File, 460 Park Avenue South, New York, New York 10016 (800) 443-8323; *The New Book of World Rankings.*

G.K. Hall and Company, 70 Lincoln Street, Boston, Massachusetts 02111 (617) 423-3990; *The World in Figures.*

International Monetary Fund, 700 Nineteenth Street, NW, Washington, D.C. 20431 (202) 623-7000; *Government Finance Statistics Yearbook*, and *International Financial Statistics.*

FIJI - BARLEY PRODUCTION - See FIJI - CROPS

FIJI - BEER PRODUCTION

Facts on File, 460 Park Avenue South, New York, New York 10016 (800) 443-8323; *The New Book of World Rankings.*

Statistical Office of the United Nations, Publishing Service, New York, New York 10017 (800) 253-9646; *Statistical Yearbook.*

FIJI - BIRTH RATE

Facts on File, 460 Park Avenue South, New York, New York 10016 (800) 443-8323; *The New Book of World Rankings.*

Statistical Office of the United Nations, Publishing Service, New York, New York 10017 (800) 253-9646; *Demographic Yearbook*, and *Statistical Yearbook.*

Times Books, 201 East 50th Street, New York, New York 10022 (212) 751-2600; *The Economist Book of Vital World Statistics.*

The World Bank, 1818 H Street, NW, Washington, D.C. 20433 (202) 477-1234; *World Tables.*

World Health Organization, Office of Publications, Avenue Appia, CH-1211 Geneva 27, Switzerland (Telephone Number in U.S. (518) 436-9686); *World Health Statistics Annual.*

FIJI - BONDS

Asian Development Bank, P.O. Box 789, 1099 Manila, Philippines; *Key Indicators of Developing Asian and Pacific Countries.*

G.K. Hall and Company, 70 Lincoln Street, Boston, Massachusetts 02111 (617) 423-3990; *The World in Figures.*

International Monetary Fund, 700 Nineteenth Street, NW, Washington, D.C. 20431 (202) 623-7000; *Government Finance Statistics Yearbook.*

FIJI - BOOK PRODUCTION

G.K. Hall and Company, 70 Lincoln Street, Boston, Massachusetts 02111 (617) 423-3990; *The World in Figures.*

FIJI - BROADCASTING

Billboard Limited, P.O. Box 9027, 1006 AA Amsterdam, The Netherlands (Telephone Number in U.S. (212) 764-7300); *World Radio TV Handbook.*

Facts on File, 460 Park Avenue South, New York, New York 10016 (800) 443-8323; *The New Book of World Rankings.*

G.K. Hall and Company, 70 Lincoln Street, Boston, Massachusetts 02111 (617) 423-3990; *The World in Figures.*

Times Books, 201 East 50th Street, New York, New York 10022 (212) 751-2600; *The Economist Book of Vital World Statistics.*

United Nations Educational, Scientific and Cultural Organization (UNESCO), 7 Place de Fontenoy, F-75700 Paris, France (Telephone Number in U.S. (212) 963-5981); *Statistical Yearbook.*

FIJI - BUILDING CONSTRUCTION - See FIJI - CONSTRUCTION

FIJI - BUSINESS

G.K. Hall and Company, 70 Lincoln Street, Boston, Massachusetts 02111 (617) 423-3990; *The World in Figures.*

FIJI - BUSINESS AND PROFESSIONAL LICENSES

International Monetary Fund, 700 Nineteenth Street, NW, Washington, D.C. 20431 (202) 623-7000; *Government Finance Statistics Yearbook.*

FIJI - CALORIE SUPPLY

Asian Development Bank, P.O. Box 789, 1099 Manila, Philippines; *Key Indicators of Developing Asian and Pacific Countries.*

Food and Agricultural Organization of the United Nations (FAO) Via delle Terme di Caracalla, 00100 Rome, Italy (Telephone Number in U.S. (202) 653-2400); *The State of Food and Agriculture.*

FIJI - CAPITAL INVESTMENT

Asian Development Bank, P.O. Box 789, 1099 Manila, Philippines; *Key Indicators of Developing Asian and Pacific Countries.*

FIJI - CAPITAL REVENUE

Asian Development Bank, P.O. Box 789, 1099 Manila, Philippines; *Key Indicators of Developing Asian and Pacific Countries.*

International Monetary Fund, 700 Nineteenth Street, NW, Washington, D.C. 20431 (202) 623-7000; *Government Finance Statistics Yearbook.*

FIJI - CATTLE - See FIJI - LIVESTOCK AND POULTRY

FIJI - CEMENT PRODUCTION - See FIJI - MINING AND MINERAL PRODUCTS

FIJI - CHEMICAL (ORGANIC) PRODUCTION - See FIJI - MINING AND MINERAL PRODUCTS

FIJI - CIGARETTE PRODUCTION - See FIJI - TOBACCO PRODUCTION

FIJI - CLASS STRUCTURE

G.K. Hall and Company, 70 Lincoln Street, Boston, Massachusetts 02111 (617) 423-3990; *The World in Figures.*

FIJI - CLIMATE

Facts on File, 460 Park Avenue South, New York, New York 10016 (800) 443-8323; *The New Book of World Rankings.*

G.K. Hall and Company, 70 Lincoln Street, Boston, Massachusetts 02111 (617) 423-3990; *The World in Figures.*

FIJI - CLOTHING EXPORTS AND IMPORTS

South Pacific Commission, Post Box D5, Noumea Cedex, New Caledonia; *Statistical Bulletin of the South Pacific: Retail Price Indexes.*

FIJI - COAL PRODUCTION - See FIJI - MINING AND MINERAL PRODUCTS

FIJI - COCOA BEANS PRODUCTION - See FIJI - CROPS

FIJI - COCONUT OIL - See FIJI - CROPS

FIJI - COFFEE PRODUCTION - See FIJI - CROPS

FIJI - COMMUNICATIONS

G.K. Hall and Company, 70 Lincoln Street, Boston, Massachusetts 02111 (617) 423-3990; *The World in Figures.*

Statistical Office of the United Nations, Publishing Service, New York, New York 10017 (800) 253-9646; *Statistical Yearbook for Asia and the Pacific.*

FIJI - CONSTRUCTION INDUSTRY

Facts on File, 460 Park Avenue South, New York, New York 10016 (800) 443-8323; *The New Book of World Rankings.*

Statistical Office of the United Nations, Publishing Service, New York, New York 10017 (800) 253-9646; *Construction Statistics Yearbook,* and *Statistical Yearbook.*

FIJI - CONSUMER PRICE INDEX

Asian Development Bank, P.O. Box 789, 1099 Manila, Philippines; *Key Indicators of Developing Asian and Pacific Countries.*

G.K. Hall and Company, 70 Lincoln Street, Boston, Massachusetts 02111 (617) 423-3990; *The World in Figures.*

Statistical Office of the United Nations, Publishing Service, New York, New York 10017 (800) 253-9646; *Statistical Yearbook.*

FIJI - CONSUMER PRICES

International Labour Office, I.L.O. Publications, CH-1211, Geneva 22, Switzerland; *Yearbook of Labour Statistics.*

International Monetary Fund, 700 Nineteenth Street, NW, Washington, D.C. 20431 (202) 623-7000; *International Financial Statistics.*

Times Books, 201 East 50th Street, New York, New York 10022 (212) 751-2600; *The Economist Book of Vital World Statistics.*

FIJI - CONSUMPTION

G.K. Hall and Company, 70 Lincoln Street, Boston, Massachusetts 02111 (617) 423-3990; *The World in Figures.*

South Pacific Commission, Post Box D5, Noumea Cedex, New Caledonia; *Statistical Bulletin of the South Pacific: Retail Price Indexes.*

FIJI - COPPER AND COPPER ORE - See FIJI - MINING AND MINERAL PRODUCTS

FIJI - CORN PRODUCTION - See FIJI - CROPS

FIJI - CORPORATE TAXES - See FIJI - TAXATION

FIJI - COTTON - See FIJI - CROPS

FIJI - CRIME

International Criminal Police Organization (INTERPOL), 26 rue Armengaud, 92210 Saint Cloud, France; *International Crime Statistics.*

Yale University Press, Yale Station, New Haven, Connecticut 06520 (203) 432-0940; *Violence and Crime in Cross-National Perspective.*

FIJI - CROPS

Asian Development Bank, P.O. Box 789, 1099 Manila, Philippines; *Key Indicators of Developing Asian and Pacific Countries.*

Facts on File, 460 Park Avenue South, New York, New York 10016 (800) 443-8323; *The New Book of World Rankings.*

Food and Agricultural Organization of the United Nations (FAO) Via delle Terme di Caracalla, 00100 Rome, Italy (Telephone Number in U.S. (202) 653-2400); *Production Yearbook,* and *The State of Food and Agriculture.*

G.K. Hall and Company, 70 Lincoln Street, Boston, Massachusetts 02111 (617) 423-3990; *The World in Figures.*

International Monetary Fund, 700 Nineteenth Street, NW, Washington, D.C. 20431 (202) 623-7000; *International Financial Statistics.*

Statistical Office of the United Nations, Publishing Service, New York, New York 10017 (800) 253-9646; *Statistical Yearbook.*

FIJI - CUSTOMS DUTIES

G.K. Hall and Company, 70 Lincoln Street, Boston, Massachusetts 02111 (617) 423-3990; *The World in Figures.*

International Monetary Fund, 700 Nineteenth Street, NW, Washington, D.C. 20431 (202) 623-7000; *Government Finance Statistics Yearbook.*

FIJI - DAIRY PRODUCTS

Facts on File, 460 Park Avenue South, New York, New York 10016 (800) 443-8323; *The New Book of World Rankings.*

Food and Agricultural Organization of the United Nations (FAO) Via delle Terme di Caracalla, 00100 Rome, Italy (Telephone Number in U.S. (202) 653-2400); *The State of Food and Agriculture.*

FIJI - DEATH RATE

G.K. Hall and Company, 70 Lincoln Street, Boston, Massachusetts 02111 (617) 423-3990; *The World in Figures.*

Statistical Office of the United Nations, Publishing Service, New York, New York 10017 (800) 253-9646; *Statistical Yearbook.*

Times Books, 201 East 50th Street, New York, New York 10022 (212) 751-2600; *The Economist Book of Vital World Statistics.*

FIJI - DEFENSE EXPENDITURES

G.K. Hall and Company, 70 Lincoln Street, Boston, Massachusetts 02111 (617) 423-3990; *The World in Figures.*

International Monetary Fund, 700 Nineteenth Street, NW, Washington, D.C. 20431 (202) 623-7000; *Government Finance Statistics Yearbook.*

U.S. Arms Control and Disarmament Agency, 320 Twenty-first Street, NW, Washington, D.C. 20451 (202) 647-8677; *World Military Expenditures and Arms Transfers.*

FIJI - DEMOGRAPHY

The Economist Intelligence Unit, 111 West 57th Street, New York, New York 10019 (800) 938-4685; *The World Market Atlas.*

Facts on File, 460 Park Avenue South, New York, New York 10016 (800) 443-8323; *The New Book of World Rankings.*

G.K. Hall and Company, 70 Lincoln Street, Boston, Massachusetts 02111 (617) 423-3990; *The World in Figures.*

FIJI - DEVELOPMENT ASSISTANCE

Asian Development Bank, P.O. Box 789, 1099 Manila, Philippines; *Key Indicators of Developing Asian and Pacific Countries.*

G.K. Hall and Company, 70 Lincoln Street, Boston, Massachusetts 02111 (617) 423-3990; *The World in Figures.*

Statistical Office of the United Nations, Publishing Service, New York, New York 10017 (800) 253-9646; *Statistical Yearbook.*

FIJI - DIAMOND PRODUCTION - See FIJI - MINING AND MINERAL PRODUCTS

FIJI - DISEASES

G.K. Hall and Company, 70 Lincoln Street, Boston, Massachusetts 02111 (617) 423-3990; *The World in Figures.*

FIJI - DIVORCE RATES

Facts on File, 460 Park Avenue South, New York, New York 10016 (800) 443-8323; *The New Book of World Rankings.*

Statistical Office of the United Nations, Publishing Service, New York, New York 10017 (800) 253-9646; *Demographic Yearbook,* and *Statistical Yearbook.*

FIJI - DOMESTIC PRODUCT

G.K. Hall and Company, 70 Lincoln Street, Boston, Massachusetts 02111 (617) 423-3990; *The World in Figures.*

FIJI - DUCKS - See FIJI - LIVESTOCK AND POULTRY

FIJI - ECONOMY

Asian Development Bank, P.O. Box 789, 1099 Manila, Philippines; *Key Indicators of Developing Asian and Pacific Countries.*

Facts on File, 460 Park Avenue South, New York, New York 10016 (800) 443-8323; *The New Book of World Rankings.*

G.K. Hall and Company, 70 Lincoln Street, Boston, Massachusetts 02111 (617) 423-3990; *The World in Figures.*

FIJI - EDUCATION

The Economist Intelligence Unit, 111 West 57th Street, New York, New York 10019 (800) 938-4685; *The World Market Atlas.*

Facts on File, 460 Park Avenue South, New York, New York 10016 (800) 443-8323; *The New Book of World Rankings.*

Gale Research Incorporated, 835 Penobscot Building, Detroit, Michigan 48226 (800) 877-4253; *International Historical Statistics The Americas and Australasia.*

G.K. Hall and Company, 70 Lincoln Street, Boston, Massachusetts 02111 (617) 423-3990; *The World in Figures.*

International Monetary Fund, 700 Nineteenth Street, NW, Washington, D.C. 20431 (202) 623-7000; *Government Finance Statistics Yearbook.*

Statistical Office of the United Nations, Publishing Service, New York, New York 10017 (800) 253-9646; *Statistical Yearbook for Asia and the Pacific.*

Times Books, 201 East 50th Street, New York, New York 10022 (212) 751-2600; *The Economist Book of Vital World Statistics.*

United Nations Educational, Scientific and Cultural Organization (UNESCO), 7 Place de Fontenoy, F-75700 Paris, France (Telephone Number in U.S. (212) 963-5981); *Statistical Yearbook.*

The World Bank, 1818 H Street, NW, Washington, D.C. 20433 (202) 477-1234; *World Tables.*

FIJI - EGG PRODUCTION - See FIJI - DAIRY PRODUCTS

FIJI - ELECTRICITY

Asian Development Bank, P.O. Box 789, 1099 Manila, Philippines; *Key Indicators of Developing Asian and Pacific Countries.*

Facts on File, 460 Park Avenue South, New York, New York 10016 (800) 443-8323; *The New Book of World Rankings.*

Statistical Office of the United Nations, Publishing Service, New York, New York 10017 (800) 253-9646; *Electric Power in Asia and the Pacific,* and *Statistical Yearbook.*

Times Books, 201 East 50th Street, New York, New York 10022 (212) 751-2600; *The Economist Book of Vital World Statistics.*

FIJI - EMPLOYMENT

Facts on File, 460 Park Avenue South, New York, New York 10016 (800) 443-8323; *The New Book of World Rankings.*

International Labour Office, I.L.O. Publications, CH-1211, Geneva 22, Switzerland; *Yearbook of Labour Statistics.*

Statistical Office of the United Nations, Publishing Service, New York, New York 10017 (800) 253-9646; *Statistical Yearbook.*

FIJI - ENERGY

Facts on File, 460 Park Avenue South, New York, New York 10016 (800) 443-8323; *The New Book of World Rankings.*

Food and Agricultural Organization of the United Nations (FAO) Via delle Terme di Caracalla, 00100 Rome, Italy (Telephone Number in U.S. (202) 653-2400); *The State of Food and Agriculture.*

G.K. Hall and Company, 70 Lincoln Street, Boston, Massachusetts 02111 (617) 423-3990; *The World in Figures.*

Statistical Office of the United Nations, Publishing Service, New York, New York 10017 (800) 253-9646; *Energy Statistics Yearbook, Statistical Yearbook,* and *Statistical Yearbook for Asia and the Pacific.*

Times Books, 201 East 50th Street, New York, New York 10022 (212) 751-2600; *The Economist Book of Vital World Statistics.*

FIJI - EXCHANGE RATES

Asian Development Bank, P.O. Box 789, 1099 Manila, Philippines; *Key Indicators of Developing Asian and Pacific Countries.*

International Monetary Fund, 700 Nineteenth Street, NW, Washington, D.C. 20431 (202) 623-7000; *International Financial Statistics.*

Statistical Office of the United Nations, Publishing Service, New York, New York 10017 (800) 253-9646; *Statistical Yearbook.*

FIJI - EXCISE TAXES - See FIJI - TAXATION

FIJI - EXPORTS

Asian Development Bank, P.O. Box 789, 1099 Manila, Philippines; *Key Indicators of Developing Asian and Pacific Countries.*

The Economist Intelligence Unit, 111 West 57th Street, New York, New York 10019 (800) 938-4685; *The World Market Atlas.*

Food and Agricultural Organization of the United Nations (FAO) Via delle Terme di Caracalla, 00100 Rome, Italy (Telephone Number in U.S. (202) 653-2400); *The State of Food and Agriculture.*

G.K. Hall and Company, 70 Lincoln Street, Boston, Massachusetts 02111 (617) 423-3990; *The World in Figures.*

International Monetary Fund, 700 Nineteenth Street, NW, Washington, D.C. 20431 (202) 623-7000; *Direction of Trade, Government Finance Statistics Yearbook,* and *International Financial Statistics.*

South Pacific Commission, Post Box D5, Noumea Cedex, New Caledonia; *Statistical Bulletin of the South Pacific: Overseas Trade.*

Statistical Office of the United Nations, Publishing Service, New York, New York 10017 (800) 253-9646; *Foreign Trade Statistics of Asia and the Pacific.*

Times Books, 201 East 50th Street, New York, New York 10022 (212) 751-2600; *The Economist Book of Vital World Statistics.*

The World Bank, 1818 H Street, NW, Washington, D.C. 20433 (202) 477-1234; *World Tables.*

FIJI - EXTERNAL FINANCING

Asian Development Bank, P.O. Box 789, 1099 Manila, Philippines; *Key Indicators of Developing Asian and Pacific Countries*.

FIJI - EXTERNAL INDEBTEDNESS

Asian Development Bank, P.O. Box 789, 1099 Manila, Philippines; *Key Indicators of Developing Asian and Pacific Countries*.

The World Bank, 1818 H Street, NW, Washington, D.C. 20433 (202) 477-1234; *World Tables*.

FIJI - EXTERNAL TRADE

Asian Development Bank, P.O. Box 789, 1099 Manila, Philippines; *Key Indicators of Developing Asian and Pacific Countries*.

Food and Agricultural Organization of the United Nations (FAO) Via delle Terme di Caracalla, 00100 Rome, Italy (Telephone Number in U.S. (202) 653-2400); *The State of Food and Agriculture*, and *Trade Yearbook*.

Gale Research Incorporated, 835 Penobscot Building, Detroit, Michigan 48226 (800) 877-4253; *International Historical Statistics The Americas and Australasia*.

G.K. Hall and Company, 70 Lincoln Street, Boston, Massachusetts 02111 (617) 423-3990; *The World in Figures*.

Statistical Office of the United Nations, Publishing Service, New York, New York 10017 (800) 253-9646; *Statistical Yearbook*.

FIJI - FARM CROPS - See FIJI - CROPS

FIJI - FERTILITY RATES

Facts on File, 460 Park Avenue South, New York, New York 10016 (800) 443-8323; *The New Book of World Rankings*.

Times Books, 201 East 50th Street, New York, New York 10022 (212) 751-2600; *The Economist Book of Vital World Statistics*.

The World Bank, 1818 H Street, NW, Washington, D.C. 20433 (202) 477-1234; *World Tables*.

FIJI - FERTILIZER

Food and Agricultural Organization of the United Nations (FAO), Via delle Terme di Caracalla, 00100 Rome, Italy (Telephone Number in U.S. (202) 653-2400); *Fertilizer Yearbook*, and *The State of Food and Agriculture*.

Statistical Office of the United Nations, Publishing Service, New York, New York 10017 (800) 253-9646; *Statistical Yearbook*.

FIJI - FETAL MORTALITY

Statistical Office of the United Nations, Publishing Service, New York, New York 10017 (800) 253-9646; *Demographic Yearbook*.

World Health Organization, Office of Publications, Avenue Appia, CH-1211 Geneva 27, Switzerland (Telephone Number in U.S. (518) 436-9686); *World Health Statistics Annual*.

FIJI - FINANCE

Asian Development Bank, P.O. Box 789, 1099 Manila, Philippines; *Key Indicators of Developing Asian and Pacific Countries*.

Facts on File, 460 Park Avenue South, New York, New York 10016 (800) 443-8323; *The New Book of World Rankings*.

Gale Research Incorporated, 835 Penobscot Building, Detroit, Michigan 48226 (800) 877-4253; *International Historical Statistics The Americas and Australasia*.

G.K. Hall and Company, 70 Lincoln Street, Boston, Massachusetts 02111 (617) 423-3990; *The World in Figures*.

International Monetary Fund, 700 Nineteenth Street, NW, Washington, D.C. 20431 (202) 623-7000; *Government Finance Statistics Yearbook*, and *International Financial Statistics*.

Statistical Office of the United Nations, Publishing Service, New York, New York 10017 (800) 253-9646; *Statistical Yearbook for Asia and the Pacific*.

FIJI - FISHERIES

Facts on File, 460 Park Avenue South, New York, New York 10016 (800) 443-8323; *The New Book of World Rankings*.

Food and Agricultural Organization of the United Nations (FAO) Via delle Terme di Caracalla, 00100 Rome, Italy (Telephone Number in U.S. (202) 653-2400); *The State of Food and Agriculture*, and *Yearbook of Fishery Statistics*.

Statistical Office of the United Nations, Publishing Service, New York, New York 10017 (800) 253-9646; *Statistical Yearbook*.

FIJI - FLOUR PRODUCTION

Statistical Office of the United Nations, Publishing Service, New York, New York 10017 (800) 253-9646; *Statistical Yearbook*.

FIJI - FOOD

Food and Agricultural Organization of the United Nations (FAO) Via delle Terme di Caracalla, 00100 Rome, Italy (Telephone Number in U.S. (202) 653-2400); *Production Yearbook*, and *The State of Food and Agriculture*.

G.K. Hall and Company, 70 Lincoln Street, Boston, Massachusetts 02111 (617) 423-3990; *The World in Figures*.

South Pacific Commission, Post Box D5, Noumea Cedex, New Caledonia; *Statistical Bulletin of the South Pacific: Retail Price Indexes*.

Statistical Office of the United Nations, Publishing Service, New York, New York 10017 (800) 253-9646; *Statistical Yearbook for Asia and the Pacific*.

FIJI - FOREIGN AID

G.K. Hall and Company, 70 Lincoln Street, Boston, Massachusetts 02111 (617) 423-3990; *The World in Figures*.

FIJI - FOREIGN DEBT

International Monetary Fund, 700 Nineteenth Street, NW, Washington, D.C. 20431 (202) 623-7000; *Government Finance Statistics Yearbook*.

FIJI - FOREIGN TRADE

Asian Development Bank, P.O. Box 789, 1099 Manila, Philippines; *Key Indicators of Developing Asian and Pacific Countries*.

Facts on File, 460 Park Avenue South, New York, New York 10016 (800) 443-8323; *The New Book of World Rankings.*

Food and Agricultural Organization of the United Nations (FAO) Via delle Terme di Caracalla, 00100 Rome, Italy (Telephone Number in U.S. (202) 653-2400); *The State of Food and Agriculture.*

G.K. Hall and Company, 70 Lincoln Street, Boston, Massachusetts 02111 (617) 423-3990; *The World in Figures.*

Organisation for Economic Cooperation and Development (OECD), 2 rue Andre-Pascal, 75 Paris 16, France (Telephone Number in U.S. (202) 785-6323); *Trade by Commodities.*

South Pacific Commission, Post Box D5, Noumea Cedex, New Caledonia; *Statistical Bulletin of the South Pacific: Overseas Trade.*

Statistical Office of the United Nations, Publishing Service, New York, New York 10017 (800) 253-9646; *International Trade Statistics Yearbook,* and *Statistical Yearbook.*

The World Bank, 1818 H Street, NW, Washington, D.C. 20433 (202) 477-1234; *World Tables.*

FIJI - FORESTRY AND FOREST PRODUCTS

Facts on File, 460 Park Avenue South, New York, New York 10016 (800) 443-8323; *The New Book of World Rankings.*

Food and Agricultural Organization of the United Nations (FAO) Via delle Terme di Caracalla, 00100 Rome, Italy (Telephone Number in U.S. (202) 653-2400); *The State of Food and Agriculture,* and *Yearbook of Forest Products.*

G.K. Hall and Company, 70 Lincoln Street, Boston, Massachusetts 02111 (617) 423-3990; *The World in Figures.*

Statistical Office of the United Nations, Publishing Service, New York, New York 10017 (800) 253-9646; *Statistical Yearbook.*

United Nations Educational, Scientific and Cultural Organization (UNESCO), 7 Place de Fontenoy, F-75700 Paris, France (Telephone Number in U.S. (212) 963-5981); *Statistical Yearbook.*

FIJI - GAS PRODUCTION - See FIJI - MINING AND MINERAL PRODUCTS

FIJI - GENERAL INDUSTRIAL STATISTICS

Statistical Office of the United Nations, Publishing Service, New York, New York 10017 (800) 253-9646; *Industrial Statistics Yearbook.*

FIJI - GENERAL MORTALITY

Statistical Office of the United Nations, Publishing Service, New York, New York 10017 (800) 253-9646; *Demographic Yearbook.*

World Health Organization, Office of Publications, Avenue Appia, CH-1211 Geneva 27, Switzerland (Telephone Number in U.S. (518) 436-9686); *World Health Statistics Annual.*

FIJI - GEOGRAPHIC DATA

Facts on File, 460 Park Avenue South, New York, New York 10016 (800) 443-8323; *The New Book of World Rankings.*

FIJI - GOLD HOLDINGS

International Monetary Fund, 700 Nineteenth Street, NW, Washington, D.C. 20431 (202) 623-7000; *International Financial Statistics.*

Statistical Office of the United Nations, Publishing Service, New York, New York 10017 (800) 253-9646; *Statistical Yearbook.*

The World Bank, 1818 H Street, NW, Washington, D.C. 20433 (202) 477-1234; *World Tables.*

FIJI - GOLD PRODUCTION AND CONSUMPTION - See FIJI - MINING AND MINERAL PRODUCTS

FIJI - GOVERNMENT

Asian Development Bank, P.O. Box 789, 1099 Manila, Philippines; *Key Indicators of Developing Asian and Pacific Countries.*

G.K. Hall and Company, 70 Lincoln Street, Boston, Massachusetts 02111 (617) 423-3990; *The World in Figures.*

FIJI - GOVERNMENT BONDS - See FIJI - BONDS

FIJI - GOVERNMENT EXPENDITURES

Asian Development Bank, P.O. Box 789, 1099 Manila, Philippines; *Key Indicators of Developing Asian and Pacific Countries.*

International Monetary Fund, 700 Nineteenth Street, NW, Washington, D.C. 20431 (202) 623-7000; *Government Finance Statistics Yearbook.*

Times Books, 201 East 50th Street, New York, New York 10022 (212) 751-2600; *The Economist Book of Vital World Statistics.*

The World Bank, 1818 H Street, NW, Washington, D.C. 20433 (202) 477-1234; *World Tables.*

FIJI - GOVERNMENT FINANCES

Asian Development Bank, P.O. Box 789, 1099 Manila, Philippines; *Key Indicators of Developing Asian and Pacific Countries.*

International Monetary Fund, 700 Nineteenth Street, NW, Washington, D.C. 20431 (202) 623-7000; *International Financial Statistics.*

Statistical Office of the United Nations, Publishing Service, New York, New York 10017 (800) 253-9646; *Statistical Yearbook.*

FIJI - GOVERNMENT REVENUE

Asian Development Bank, P.O. Box 789, 1099 Manila, Philippines; *Key Indicators of Developing Asian and Pacific Countries.*

International Monetary Fund, 700 Nineteenth Street, NW, Washington, D.C. 20431 (202) 623-7000; *Government Finance Statistics Yearbook.*

Times Books, 201 East 50th Street, New York, New York 10022 (212) 751-2600; *The Economist Book of Vital World Statistics.*

The World Bank, 1818 H Street, NW, Washington, D.C. 20433 (202) 477-1234; *World Tables.*

FIJI - GRAIN PRODUCTION - See FIJI - CROPS

FIJI - GRANTS

International Monetary Fund, 700 Nineteenth Street, NW, Washington, D.C. 20431 (202) 623-7000; *Government Finance Statistics Yearbook.*

FIJI - GROSS DOMESTIC PRODUCT

Asian Development Bank, P.O. Box 789, 1099 Manila, Philippines; *Key Indicators of Developing Asian and Pacific Countries.*

The Economist Intelligence Unit, 111 West 57th Street, New York, New York 10019 (800) 938-4685; *The World Market Atlas.*

Facts on File, 460 Park Avenue South, New York, New York 10016 (800) 443-8323; *The New Book of World Rankings.*

G.K. Hall and Company, 70 Lincoln Street, Boston, Massachusetts 02111 (617) 423-3990; *The World in Figures.*

Statistical Office of the United Nations, Publishing Service, New York, New York 10017 (800) 253-9646; *Statistical Yearbook.*

Times Books, 201 East 50th Street, New York, New York 10022 (212) 751-2600; *The Economist Book of Vital World Statistics.*

The World Bank, 1818 H Street, NW, Washington, D.C. 20433 (202) 477-1234; *World Tables.*

FIJI - GROSS NATIONAL PRODUCT

Asian Development Bank, P.O. Box 789, 1099 Manila, Philippines; *Key Indicators of Developing Asian and Pacific Countries.*

U.S. Arms Control and Disarmament Agency, 320 Twenty-first Street, NW, Washington, D.C. 20451 (202) 647-8677; *World Military Expenditures and Arms Transfers.*

The World Bank, 1818 H Street, NW, Washington, D.C. 20433 (202) 477-1234; *World Tables.*

FIJI - GROUNDNUTS PRODUCTION - See FIJI - CROPS

FIJI - HEALTH

Facts on File, 460 Park Avenue South, New York, New York 10016 (800) 443-8323; *The New Book of World Rankings.*

G.K. Hall and Company, 70 Lincoln Street, Boston, Massachusetts 02111 (617) 423-3990; *The World in Figures.*

International Monetary Fund, 700 Nineteenth Street, NW, Washington, D.C. 20431 (202) 623-7000; *Government Finance Statistics Yearbook.*

South Pacific Commission, Post Box D5, Noumea Cedex, New Caledonia; *Statistical Bulletin of the South Pacific: Retail Price Indexes.*

Statistical Office of the United Nations, Publishing Service, New York, New York 10017 (800) 253-9646; *Statistical Yearbook.*

Times Books, 201 East 50th Street, New York, New York 10022 (212) 751-2600; *The Economist Book of Vital World Statistics.*

World Health Organization, Office of Publications, Avenue Appia, CH-1211 Geneva 27, Switzerland (Telephone Number in U.S. (518) 436-9686); *World Health Statistics Annual.*

FIJI - HIDE PRODUCTION

Food and Agricultural Organization of the United Nations (FAO), Via delle Terme di Caracalla, 00100 Rome, Italy (Telephone Number in U.S. (202) 653-2400); *Production Yearbook.*

FIJI - HIGHWAYS

G.K. Hall and Company, 70 Lincoln Street, Boston, Massachusetts 02111 (617) 423-3990; *The World in Figures.*

FIJI - HORSES - See FIJI - LIVESTOCK AND POULTRY

FIJI - HOURS OF WORK - See FIJI - EMPLOYMENT

FIJI - HOUSING AND HOUSING UNITS

Facts on File, 460 Park Avenue South, New York, New York 10016 (800) 443-8323; *The New Book of World Rankings.*

South Pacific Commission, Post Box D5, Noumea Cedex, New Caledonia; *Statistical Bulletin of the South Pacific: Retail Price Indexes.*

FIJI - HOUSING EXPENDITURES

International Monetary Fund, 700 Nineteenth Street, NW, Washington, D.C. 20431 (202) 623-7000; *Government Finance Statistics Yearbook.*

South Pacific Commission, Post Box D5, Noumea Cedex, New Caledonia; *Statistical Bulletin of the South Pacific: Retail Price Indexes.*

FIJI - ILLITERATE POPULATION

The Economist Intelligence Unit, 111 West 57th Street, New York, New York 10019 (800) 938-4685; *The World Market Atlas.*

G.K. Hall and Company, 70 Lincoln Street, Boston, Massachusetts 02111 (617) 423-3990; *The World in Figures.*

United Nations Educational, Scientific and Cultural Organization (UNESCO), 7 Place de Fontenoy, F-75700 Paris, France (Telephone Number in U.S. (212) 963-5981); *Statistical Yearbook.*

FIJI - IMPORTS

Asian Development Bank, P.O. Box 789, 1099 Manila, Philippines; *Key Indicators of Developing Asian and Pacific Countries.*

The Economist Intelligence Unit, 111 West 57th Street, New York, New York 10019 (800) 938-4685; *The World Market Atlas.*

Food and Agricultural Organization of the United Nations (FAO) Via delle Terme di Caracalla, 00100 Rome, Italy (Telephone Number in U.S. (202) 653-2400); *The State of Food and Agriculture.*

G.K. Hall and Company, 70 Lincoln Street, Boston, Massachusetts 02111 (617) 423-3990; *The World in Figures.*

International Monetary Fund, 700 Nineteenth Street, NW, Washington, D.C. 20431 (202) 623-7000; *Direction of Trade, Government Finance Statistics Yearbook,* and *International Financial Statistics.*

South Pacific Commission, Post Box D5, Noumea Cedex, New Caledonia; *Statistical Bulletin of the South Pacific: Overseas Trade.*

Statistical Office of the United Nations, Publishing Service, New York, New York 10017 (800) 253-9646; *Foreign Trade Statistics of Asia and the Pacific,* and *Trade in Manufactures of Developing Countries.*

Times Books, 201 East 50th Street, New York, New York 10022 (212) 751-2600; *The Economist Book of Vital World Statistics.*

The World Bank, 1818 H Street, NW, Washington, D.C. 20433 (202) 477-1234; *World Tables.*

FIJI - INCOME TAXES - See FIJI - TAXATION

FIJI - INDUSTRY

Facts on File, 460 Park Avenue South, New York, New York 10016 (800) 443-8323; *The New Book of World Rankings.*

Gale Research Incorporated, 835 Penobscot Building, Detroit, Michigan 48226 (800) 877-4253; *International Historical Statistics The Americas and Australasia.*

G.K. Hall and Company, 70 Lincoln Street, Boston, Massachusetts 02111 (617) 423-3990; *The World in Figures.*

International Labour Office, I.L.O. Publications, CH-1211, Geneva 22, Switzerland; *Yearbook of Labour Statistics.*

Statistical Office of the United Nations, Publishing Service, New York, New York 10017 (800) 253-9646; *Statistical Yearbook for Asia and the Pacific.*

Times Books, 201 East 50th Street, New York, New York 10022 (212) 751-2600; *The Economist Book of Vital World Statistics.*

The World Bank, 1818 H Street, NW, Washington, D.C. 20433 (202) 477-1234; *World Tables.*

FIJI - INFANT AND MATERNAL MORTALITY

Statistical Office of the United Nations, Publishing Service, New York, New York 10017 (800) 253-9646; *Demographic Yearbook,* and *Statistical Yearbook.*

Times Books, 201 East 50th Street, New York, New York 10022 (212) 751-2600; *The Economist Book of Vital World Statistics.*

The World Bank, 1818 H Street, NW, Washington, D.C. 20433 (202) 477-1234; *World Tables.*

World Health Organization, Office of Publications, Avenue Appia, CH-1211 Geneva 27, Switzerland (Telephone Number in U.S. (518) 436-9686); *World Health Statistics Annual.*

FIJI - INTERNAL TRADE

Statistical Office of the United Nations, Publishing Service, New York, New York 10017 (800) 253-9646; *Statistical Yearbook,* and *Statistical Yearbook for Asia and the Pacific.*

FIJI - INTERNATIONAL LIQUIDITY

International Monetary Fund, 700 Nineteenth Street, NW, Washington, D.C. 20431 (202) 623-7000; *International Financial Statistics.*

FIJI - INTERNATIONAL RESERVES EXCLUDING GOLD

Asian Development Bank, P.O. Box 789, 1099 Manila, Philippines; *Key Indicators of Developing Asian and Pacific Countries.*

Statistical Office of the United Nations, Publishing Service, New York, New York 10017 (800) 253-9646; *Statistical Yearbook.*

The World Bank, 1818 H Street, NW, Washington, D.C. 20433 (202) 477-1234; *World Tables.*

FIJI - INTERNATIONAL STATISTICS

Asian Development Bank, P.O. Box 789, 1099 Manila, Philippines; *Key Indicators of Developing Asian and Pacific Countries.*

FIJI - IRON PRODUCTION - See FIJI - MINING AND MINERAL PRODUCTS

FIJI - LABOR FORCE

Facts on File, 460 Park Avenue South, New York, New York 10016 (800) 443-8323; *The New Book of World Rankings.*

Food and Agricultural Organization of the United Nations (FAO) Via delle Terme di Caracalla, 00100 Rome, Italy (Telephone Number in U.S. (202) 653-2400); *The State of Food and Agriculture.*

Gale Research Incorporated, 835 Penobscot Building, Detroit, Michigan 48226 (800) 877-4253; *International Historical Statistics The Americas and Australasia.*

G.K. Hall and Company, 70 Lincoln Street, Boston, Massachusetts 02111 (617) 423-3990; *The World in Figures.*

The World Bank, 1818 H Street, NW, Washington, D.C. 20433 (202) 477-1234; *World Tables.*

FIJI - LABOR PRODUCTIVITY

International Labour Office, I.L.O. Publications, CH-1211, Geneva 22, Switzerland; *Yearbook of Labour Statistics.*

FIJI - LAND USE

Food and Agricultural Organization of the United Nations (FAO), Via delle Terme di Caracalla, 00100 Rome, Italy (Telephone Number in U.S. (202) 653-2400); *Production Yearbook.*

G.K. Hall and Company, 70 Lincoln Street, Boston, Massachusetts 02111 (617) 423-3990; *The World in Figures.*

FIJI - LIBRARIES

Facts on File, 460 Park Avenue South, New York, New York 10016 (800) 443-8323; *The New Book of World Rankings.*

United Nations Educational, Scientific and Cultural Organization (UNESCO), 7 Place de Fontenoy, F-75700 Paris, France (Telephone Number in U.S. (212) 963-5981); *Statistical Yearbook.*

FIJI - LIVESTOCK AND POULTRY

Facts on File, 460 Park Avenue South, New York, New York 10016 (800) 443-8323; *The New Book of World Rankings.*

Food and Agricultural Organization of the United Nations (FAO), Via delle Terme di Caracalla, 00100 Rome, Italy (Telephone Number in U.S. (202) 653-2400); *Production Yearbook,* and *The State of Food*

and Agriculture.

G.K. Hall and Company, 70 Lincoln Street, Boston, Massachusetts 02111 (617) 423-3990; *The World in Figures.*

Statistical Office of the United Nations, Publishing Service, New York, New York 10017 (800) 253-9646; *Statistical Yearbook.*

FIJI - LIVING LEVELS

G.K. Hall and Company, 70 Lincoln Street, Boston, Massachusetts 02111 (617) 423-3990; *The World in Figures.*

Times Books, 201 East 50th Street, New York, New York 10022 (212) 751-2600; *The Economist Book of Vital World Statistics.*

FIJI - MAIL - NUMBER OF PIECES SENT OR RECEIVED

Statistical Office of the United Nations, Publishing Service, New York, New York 10017 (800) 253-9646; *Statistical Yearbook.*

FIJI - MANGANESE ORE PRODUCTION AND CONSUMPTION - See FIJI - MINING AND MINERAL PRODUCTS

FIJI - MANPOWER

Statistical Office of the United Nations, Publishing Service, New York, New York 10017 (800) 253-9646; *Statistical Yearbook for Asia and the Pacific.*

FIJI - MANUFACTURING

Asian Development Bank, P.O. Box 789, 1099 Manila, Philippines; *Key Indicators of Developing Asian and Pacific Countries.*

Facts on File, 460 Park Avenue South, New York, New York 10016 (800) 443-8323; *The New Book of World Rankings.*

G.K. Hall and Company, 70 Lincoln Street, Boston, Massachusetts 02111 (617) 423-3990; *The World in Figures.*

Statistical Office of the United Nations, Publishing Service, New York, New York 10017 (800) 253-9646; *Statistical Yearbook.*

The World Bank, 1818 H Street, NW, Washington, D.C. 20433 (202) 477-1234; *World Tables.*

FIJI - MARRIAGE RATES

Facts on File, 460 Park Avenue South, New York, New York 10016 (800) 443-8323; *The New Book of World Rankings.*

Statistical Office of the United Nations, Publishing Service, New York, New York 10017 (800) 253-9646; *Demographic Yearbook,* and *Statistical Yearbook.*

FIJI - MEAT PRODUCTION - See FIJI - LIVESTOCK AND POULTRY

FIJI - MERCHANT SHIPPING

G.K. Hall and Company, 70 Lincoln Street, Boston, Massachusetts 02111 (617) 423-3990; *The World in Figures.*

Statistical Office of the United Nations, Publishing Service, New York, New York 10017 (800) 253-9646; *Statistical Yearbook.*

Times Books, 201 East 50th Street, New York, New York 10022 (212) 751-2600; *The Economist Book of Vital World Statistics.*

U.S. Department of Transportation, Maritime Administration, 400 Seventh Street, SW, Washington, D.C. 20590; *A Statistical Analysis of the World's Merchant Fleets.*

FIJI - MILITARY

G.K. Hall and Company, 70 Lincoln Street, Boston, Massachusetts 02111 (617) 423-3990; *The World in Figures.*

The International Institute for Strategic Studies, 23 Tavistock Street, London WC2E 7NQ, England; *The Military Balance.*

U.S. Arms Control and Disarmament Agency, 320 Twenty-first Street, NW, Washington, D.C. 20451 (202) 647-8677; *World Military Expenditures and Arms Transfers.*

FIJI - MILK PRODUCTION - See FIJI - DAIRY PRODUCTS

FIJI - MINING AND MINERAL PRODUCTS

Asian Development Bank, P.O. Box 789, 1099 Manila, Philippines; *Key Indicators of Developing Asian and Pacific Countries.*

Facts on File, 460 Park Avenue South, New York, New York 10016 (800) 443-8323; *The New Book of World Rankings.*

G.K. Hall and Company, 70 Lincoln Street, Boston, Massachusetts 02111 (617) 423-3990; *The World in Figures.*

Statistical Office of the United Nations, Publishing Service, New York, New York 10017 (800) 253-9646; *Statistical Yearbook.*

FIJI - MONEY EXCHANGE RATES

International Monetary Fund, 700 Nineteenth Street, NW, Washington, D.C. 20431 (202) 623-7000; *International Financial Statistics.*

Statistical Office of the United Nations, Publishing Service, New York, New York 10017 (800) 253-9646; *Statistical Yearbook.*

FIJI - MONEY SUPPLY

Asian Development Bank, P.O. Box 789, 1099 Manila, Philippines; *Key Indicators of Developing Asian and Pacific Countries.*

G.K. Hall and Company, 70 Lincoln Street, Boston, Massachusetts 02111 (617) 423-3990; *The World in Figures.*

International Monetary Fund, 700 Nineteenth Street, NW, Washington, D.C. 20431 (202) 623-7000; *International Financial Statistics.*

Statistical Office of the United Nations, Publishing Service, New York, New York 10017 (800) 253-9646; *Statistical Yearbook.*

The World Bank, 1818 H Street, NW, Washington, D.C. 20433 (202) 477-1234; *World Tables.*

FIJI - MOTION PICTURES

Statistical Office of the United Nations, Publishing Service, New York, New York 10017 (800) 253-9646; *Statistical Yearbook.*

FIJI - MOTOR VEHICLE TAXES - See FIJI - TAXATION

FIJI - MOTOR VEHICLES IN USE

G.K. Hall and Company, 70 Lincoln Street, Boston, Massachusetts 02111 (617) 423-3990; *The World in Figures.*

Statistical Office of the United Nations, Publishing Service, New York, New York 10017 (800) 253-9646; *Statistical Yearbook.*

Times Books, 201 East 50th Street, New York, New York 10022 (212) 751-2600; *The Economist Book of Vital World Statistics.*

FIJI - MUSEUMS

Facts on File, 460 Park Avenue South, New York, New York 10016 (800) 443-8323; *The New Book of World Rankings.*

United Nations Educational, Scientific and Cultural Organization (UNESCO), 7 Place de Fontenoy, F-75700 Paris, France (Telephone Number in U.S. (212) 963-5981); *Statistical Yearbook.*

FIJI - NATALITY - See FIJI - BIRTH RATE

FIJI - NATIONAL ACCOUNTS

Gale Research Incorporated, 835 Penobscot Building, Detroit, Michigan 48226 (800) 877-4253; *International Historical Statistics The Americas and Australasia.*

International Monetary Fund, 700 Nineteenth Street, NW, Washington, D.C. 20431 (202) 623-7000; *International Financial Statistics.*

Statistical Office of the United Nations, Publishing Service, New York, New York 10017 (800) 253-9646; *National Accounts Statistics, Statistical Yearbook,* and *Statistical Yearbook for Asia and the Pacific.*

FIJI - NATIONAL INCOME

Facts on File, 460 Park Avenue South, New York, New York 10016 (800) 443-8323; *The New Book of World Rankings.*

G.K. Hall and Company, 70 Lincoln Street, Boston, Massachusetts 02111 (617) 423-3990; *The World in Figures.*

Statistical Office of the United Nations, Publishing Service, New York, New York 10017 (800) 253-9646; *Statistical Yearbook.*

FIJI - NATIONAL PRODUCT

Facts on File, 460 Park Avenue South, New York, New York 10016 (800) 443-8323; *The New Book of World Rankings.*

Statistical Office of the United Nations, Publishing Service, New York, New York 10017 (800) 253-9646; *Statistical Yearbook.*

FIJI - NATURAL GAS PRODUCTION -See FIJI - MINING AND MINERAL PRODUCTS

FIJI - NEWSPAPER PRODUCTION - See FIJI - FORESTRY AND FOREST PRODUCTS

FIJI - NEWSPRINT - See FIJI - FORESTRY AND FOREST PRODUCTS

FIJI - OCCUPATIONS - See FIJI - LABOR FORCE

FIJI - PATENTS

Statistical Office of the United Nations, Publishing Service, New York, New York 10017 (800) 253-9646; *Statistical Yearbook.*

FIJI - PEANUT PRODUCTION - See FIJI - CROPS

FIJI - PERIODICALS

United Nations Educational, Scientific and Cultural Organization (UNESCO), 7 Place de Fontenoy, F-75700 Paris, France (Telephone Number in U.S. (212) 963-5981); *Statistical Yearbook.*

FIJI - PESTICIDE USE

Food and Agricultural Organization of the United Nations (FAO) Via delle Terme di Caracalla, 00100 Rome, Italy (Telephone Number in U.S. (202) 653-2400); *The State of Food and Agriculture.*

FIJI - PETROLEUM INDUSTRY

Asian Development Bank, P.O. Box 789, 1099 Manila, Philippines; *Key Indicators of Developing Asian and Pacific Countries.*

Facts on File, 460 Park Avenue South, New York, New York 10016 (800) 443-8323; *The New Book of World Rankings.*

Food and Agricultural Organization of the United Nations (FAO) Via delle Terme di Caracalla, 00100 Rome, Italy (Telephone Number in U.S. (202) 653-2400); *The State of Food and Agriculture.*

G.K. Hall and Company, 70 Lincoln Street, Boston, Massachusetts 02111 (617) 423-3990; *The World in Figures.*

FIJI - PIGS - See FIJI - LIVESTOCK AND POULTRY

FIJI - POPULATION

Asian Development Bank, P.O. Box 789, 1099 Manila, Philippines; *Key Indicators of Developing Asian and Pacific Countries.*

The Economist Intelligence Unit, 111 West 57th Street, New York, New York 10019 (800) 938-4685; *The World Market Atlas.*

Facts on File, 460 Park Avenue South, New York, New York 10016 (800) 443-8323; *The New Book of World Rankings.*

Food and Agricultural Organization of the United Nations (FAO), Via delle Terme di Caracalla, 00100 Rome, Italy (Telephone Number in U.S. (202) 653-2400); *Production Yearbook.*

Gale Research Incorporated, 835 Penobscot Building, Detroit, Michigan 48226 (800) 877-4253; *International Historical Statistics The Americas and Australasia.*

G.K. Hall and Company, 70 Lincoln Street, Boston, Massachusetts 02111 (617) 423-3990; *The World in Figures.*

International Labour Office, I.L.O. Publications, CH-1211, Geneva 22, Switzerland; *Yearbook of Labour Statistics.*

Statistical Office of the United Nations, Publishing Service, New York, New York 10017 (800) 253-9646; *Demographic Yearbook, Statistical Yearbook,* and *Statistical Yearbook for Asia and the Pacific.*

Times Books, 201 East 50th Street, New York, New York 10022 (212) 751-2600; *The Economist Book of Vital World Statistics.*

United Nations Educational, Scientific and Cultural Organization (UNESCO), 7 Place de Fontenoy, F-75700 Paris, France (Telephone Number in U.S. (212) 963-5981); *Statistical Yearbook.*

U.S. Arms Control and Disarmament Agency, 320 Twenty-first Street, NW, Washington, D.C. 20451 (202) 647-8677; *World Military Expenditures and Arms Transfers.*

World Health Organization, Office of Publications, Avenue Appia, CH-1211 Geneva 27, Switzerland (Telephone Number in U.S. (518) 436-9686); *World Health Statistics Annual.*

FIJI - POST OFFICES

Facts on File, 460 Park Avenue South, New York, New York 10016 (800) 443-8323; *The New Book of World Rankings.*

FIJI - POTATO PRODUCTION - See FIJI - CROPS

FIJI - POWER PRODUCTION INDUSTRY

Statistical Office of the United Nations, Publishing Service, New York, New York 10017 (800) 253-9646; *Electric Power in Asia and the Pacific,* and *Statistical Yearbook.*

FIJI - PRICES

Asian Development Bank, P.O. Box 789, 1099 Manila, Philippines; *Key Indicators of Developing Asian and Pacific Countries.*

Facts on File, 460 Park Avenue South, New York, New York 10016 (800) 443-8323; *The New Book of World Rankings.*

Food and Agricultural Organization of the United Nations (FAO), Via delle Terme di Caracalla, 00100 Rome, Italy (Telephone Number in U.S. (202) 653-2400); *Production Yearbook,* and *The State of Food and Agriculture.*

Gale Research Incorporated, 835 Penobscot Building, Detroit, Michigan 48226 (800) 877-4253; *International Historical Statistics The Americas and Australasia.*

G.K. Hall and Company, 70 Lincoln Street, Boston, Massachusetts 02111 (617) 423-3990; *The World in Figures.*

International Labour Office, I.L.O. Publications, CH-1211, Geneva 22, Switzerland; *Yearbook of Labour Statistics.*

International Monetary Fund, 700 Nineteenth Street, NW, Washington, D.C. 20431 (202) 623-7000; *International Financial Statistics.*

South Pacific Commission, Post Box D5, Noumea Cedex, New Caledonia; *Statistical Bulletin of the South Pacific: Overseas Trade,* and *Statistical Bulletin of the South Pacific: Retail Price Indexes.*

FIJI - PRODUCTION

Facts on File, 460 Park Avenue South, New York, New York 10016 (800) 443-8323; *The New Book of World Rankings.*

G.K. Hall and Company, 70 Lincoln Street, Boston, Massachusetts 02111 (617) 423-3990; *The World in Figures.*

FIJI - PROPERTY TAXES - See FIJI - TAXATION

FIJI - PUBLIC FINANCE

Facts on File, 460 Park Avenue South, New York, New York 10016 (800) 443-8323; *The New Book of World Rankings.*

FIJI - RADIO BROADCASTING - See FIJI - BROADCASTING

FIJI - RAILWAYS

G.K. Hall and Company, 70 Lincoln Street, Boston, Massachusetts 02111 (617) 423-3990; *The World in Figures.*

FIJI - RELIGION

Facts on File, 460 Park Avenue South, New York, New York 10016 (800) 443-8323; *The New Book of World Rankings.*

FIJI - RENT PRICES

International Labour Office, I.L.O. Publications, CH-1211, Geneva 22, Switzerland; *Yearbook of Labour Statistics.*

FIJI - RETAIL TRADE

G.K. Hall and Company, 70 Lincoln Street, Boston, Massachusetts 02111 (617) 423-3990; *The World in Figures.*

Statistical Office of the United Nations, Publishing Service, New York, New York 10017 (800) 253-9646; *Statistical Yearbook.*

FIJI - RICE PRODUCTION - See FIJI - CROPS

FIJI - ROOT AND TUBER PRODUCTION - See FIJI - CROPS

FIJI - ROUNDWOOD PRODUCTION - See FIJI - FORESTRY AND FOREST PRODUCTS

FIJI - RUBBER PRODUCTION

Facts on File, 460 Park Avenue South, New York, New York 10016 (800) 443-8323; *The New Book of World Rankings.*

FIJI - SAWNWOOD PRODUCTION - See FIJI - FORESTRY AND FOREST PRODUCTS

FIJI - SENIOR CITIZENS

Facts on File, 460 Park Avenue South, New York, New York 10016 (800) 443-8323; *The New Book of World Rankings.*

FIJI - SHEEP - See FIJI - LIVESTOCK AND POULTRY

FIJI - SILVER PRODUCTION AND CONSUMPTION - See FIJI - MINING AND MINERAL PRODUCTS

FIJI - SOCIAL DATA

Asian Development Bank, P.O. Box 789, 1099 Manila, Philippines; *Key Indicators of Developing Asian and Pacific Countries.*

Facts on File, 460 Park Avenue South, New York, New York 10016 (800) 443-8323; *The New Book of World Rankings.*

G.K. Hall and Company, 70 Lincoln Street, Boston, Massachusetts 02111 (617) 423-3990; *The World in Figures.*

FIJI - SOCIAL SECURITY

International Monetary Fund, 700 Nineteenth Street, NW, Washington, D.C. 20431 (202) 623-7000; *Government Finance Statistics Yearbook.*

FIJI - STAMP TAXES AND DUTIES - See FIJI - TAXATION

FIJI - STEEL PRODUCTION - See FIJI - MINING AND MINERAL PRODUCTS

FIJI - STOCKS - COMMODITY - MARKET PRICE - INDEX

Food and Agricultural Organization of the United Nations (FAO) Via delle Terme di Caracalla, 00100 Rome, Italy (Telephone Number in U.S. (202) 653-2400); *The State of Food and Agriculture.*

FIJI - SUGAR - See FIJI - CROPS

FIJI - TAXATION

G.K. Hall and Company, 70 Lincoln Street, Boston, Massachusetts 02111 (617) 423-3990; *The World in Figures.*

International Monetary Fund, 700 Nineteenth Street, NW, Washington, D.C. 20431 (202) 623-7000; *Government Finance Statistics Yearbook.*

The World Bank, 1818 H Street, NW, Washington, D.C. 20433 (202) 477-1234; *World Tables.*

FIJI - TELEPHONES IN USE

American Telephone and Telegraph Company, 26 Parsippany Road, Whippany, New Jersey 07981 (800) 338-4038; *The World's Telephones.*

G.K. Hall and Company, 70 Lincoln Street, Boston, Massachusetts 02111 (617) 423-3990; *The World in Figures.*

Statistical Office of the United Nations, Publishing Service, New York, New York 10017 (800) 253-9646; *Statistical Yearbook.*

FIJI - TELEVISION BROADCASTING - See FIJI - BROADCASTING

FIJI - THEATRE

United Nations Educational, Scientific and Cultural Organization (UNESCO), 7 Place de Fontenoy, F-75700 Paris, France (Telephone Number in U.S. (212) 963-5981); *Statistical Yearbook.*

FIJI - TEXTILE INDUSTRY

G.K. Hall and Company, 70 Lincoln Street, Boston, Massachusetts 02111 (617) 423-3990; *The World in Figures.*

FIJI - TOBACCO PRODUCTION

Facts on File, 460 Park Avenue South, New York, New York 10016 (800) 443-8323; *The New Book of World Rankings.*

South Pacific Commission, Post Box D5, Noumea Cedex, New Caledonia; *Statistical Bulletin of the South Pacific: Retail Price Indexes.*

Statistical Office of the United Nations, Publishing Service, New York, New York 10017 (800) 253-9646; *Statistical Yearbook.*

FIJI - TOURISM

Facts on File, 460 Park Avenue South, New York, New York 10016 (800) 443-8323; *The New Book of World Rankings.*

G.K. Hall and Company, 70 Lincoln Street, Boston, Massachusetts 02111 (617) 423-3990; *The World in Figures.*

Statistical Office of the United Nations, Publishing Service, New York, New York 10017 (800) 253-9646; *Statistical Yearbook.*

Times Books, 201 East 50th Street, New York, New York 10022 (212) 751-2600; *The Economist Book of Vital World Statistics.*

World Tourism Organization, Calle Capitan Haya 42, E-28020 Madrid, Spain; *Yearbook of Tourism Statistics.*

FIJI - TRACTORS IN USE

Statistical Office of the United Nations, Publishing Service, New York, New York 10017 (800) 253-9646; *Statistical Yearbook.*

FIJI - TRADE - See FIJI - FOREIGN TRADE

FIJI - TRADEMARKS AND SERVICE MARKS

Statistical Office of the United Nations, Publishing Service, New York, New York 10017 (800) 253-9646; *Statistical Yearbook.*

FIJI - TRANSPORTATION AND COMMUNICATIONS

Facts on File, 460 Park Avenue South, New York, New York 10016 (800) 443-8323; *The New Book of World Rankings.*

Gale Research Incorporated, 835 Penobscot Building, Detroit, Michigan 48226 (800) 877-4253; *International Historical Statistics The Americas and Australasia.*

G.K. Hall and Company, 70 Lincoln Street, Boston, Massachusetts 02111 (617) 423-3990; *The World in Figures.*

South Pacific Commission, Post Box D5, Noumea Cedex, New Caledonia; *Statistical Bulletin of the South Pacific: Retail Price Indexes.*

Statistical Office of the United Nations, Publishing Service, New York, New York 10017 (800) 253-9646; *Statistical Yearbook for Asia and the Pacific.*

FIJI - TURKEYS - See FIJI - LIVESTOCK AND POULTRY

FIJI - UNEMPLOYMENT

International Labour Office, I.L.O. Publications, CH-1211, Geneva 22, Switzerland; *Yearbook of Labour Statistics.*

Statistical Office of the United Nations, Publishing Service, New York, New York 10017 (800) 253-9646; *Statistical Yearbook.*

FIJI - UTILITIES

Statistical Office of the United Nations, Publishing Service, New York, New York 10017 (800) 253-9646; *Electric Power in Asia and the Pacific.*

FIJI - VITAL STATISTICS

Gale Research Incorporated, 835 Penobscot Building, Detroit, Michigan 48226 (800) 877-4253; *International Historical Statistics*

The Americas and Australasia.

G.K. Hall and Company, 70 Lincoln Street, Boston, Massachusetts 02111 (617) 423-3990; *The World in Figures.*

Statistical Office of the United Nations, Publishing Service, New York, New York 10017 (800) 253-9646; *Statistical Yearbook.*

World Health Organization, Office of Publications, Avenue Appia, CH-1211 Geneva 27, Switzerland (Telephone Number in U.S. (518) 436-9686); *World Health Statistics Annual.*

FIJI - WAGES

G.K. Hall and Company, 70 Lincoln Street, Boston, Massachusetts 02111 (617) 423-3990; *The World in Figures.*

International Labour Office, I.L.O. Publications, CH-1211, Geneva 22, Switzerland; *Yearbook of Labour Statistics.*

Statistical Office of the United Nations, Publishing Service, New York, New York 10017 (800) 253-9646; *Statistical Yearbook,* and *Statistical Yearbook for Asia and the Pacific.*

FIJI - WEATHER

Facts on File, 460 Park Avenue South, New York, New York 10016 (800) 443-8323; *The New Book of World Rankings.*

G.K. Hall and Company, 70 Lincoln Street, Boston, Massachusetts 02111 (617) 423-3990; *The World in Figures.*

FIJI - WELFARE

International Monetary Fund, 700 Nineteenth Street, NW, Washington, D.C. 20431 (202) 623-7000; *Government Finance Statistics Yearbook.*

FIJI - WHEAT PRODUCTION AND PRICES - See FIJI - CROPS

FIJI - WHOLESALE PRICES

Asian Development Bank, P.O. Box 789, 1099 Manila, Philippines; *Key Indicators of Developing Asian and Pacific Countries.*

FIJI - WHOLESALE TRADE

Statistical Office of the United Nations, Publishing Service, New York, New York 10017 (800) 253-9646; *Statistical Yearbook.*

FIJI - WINE PRODUCTION

Facts on File, 460 Park Avenue South, New York, New York 10016 (800) 443-8323; *The New Book of World Rankings.*

FIJI - WOOL PRODUCTION

Facts on File, 460 Park Avenue South, New York, New York 10016 (800) 443-8323; *The New Book of World Rankings.*

FILBERTS

U.S. Department of Agriculture, National Agricultural Statistics Service, Fourteenth Street and Independence Avenue, SW, Washington, D.C. 20250 (202) 219-1504; *Noncitrus Fruits and Nuts.*

FILIPINO POPULATION

U.S. Department of Commerce, Bureau of the Census, Suitland, Maryland 20233 (301) 763-4040; *Census of Population, General Population Characteristics, United States,* and press release.

FILLING STATIONS - See GASOLINE SERVICE STATIONS

FINANCE

Board of Governors of the Federal Reserve System, Twentieth Street and Constitution Avenue, NW, Washington, D.C. 20551 (202) 452-3000; *Flow of Funds Accounts, Federal Reserve Bulletin, Annual Statistical Digest,* and unpublished data.

FINANCE - CONSUMER INSTALLMENT CREDIT

Board of Governors of the Federal Reserve System, Twentieth Street and Constitution Avenue, NW, Washington, D.C. 20551 (202) 452-3000; *Federal Reserve Bulletin, Annual Statistical Digest,* and unpublished data.

FINANCE - CORPORATE FUNDS

Board of Governors of the Federal Reserve System, Twentieth Street and Constitution Avenue, NW, Washington, D.C. 20551 (202) 452-3000; *Flow of Funds Accounts.*

FINANCE, INSURANCE, AND REAL ESTATE INDUSTRY - CAPITAL

Board of Governors of the Federal Reserve System, Twentieth Street and Constitution Avenue, NW, Washington, D.C. 20551 (202) 452-3000; *Federal Reserve Bulletin,* and *Annual Statistical Digest.*

FINANCE, INSURANCE, AND REAL ESTATE INDUSTRY - EARNINGS

U.S. Department of Commerce, Bureau of Economic Analysis, Fourteenth Street between Constitution Avenue and E Street, NW, Washington, D.C. 20230 (202) 606-9900; *Survey of Current Business,* and *The National Income and Product Accounts of the United States.*

U.S. Department of Commerce, Bureau of the Census, Suitland, Maryland 20233 (301) 763-4040; *County Business Patterns.*

U.S. Department of Labor, Bureau of Labor Statistics, Two Massachusetts Avenue, NE, Washington, D.C. 20212 (202) 606-7828; Bulletins 2370 and 2429, and *Employment and Earnings.*

FINANCE, INSURANCE, AND REAL ESTATE INDUSTRY - EMPLOYEES

U.S. Department of Commerce, Bureau of Economic Analysis, Fourteenth Street between Constitution Avenue and E Street, NW, Washington, D.C. 20230 (202) 606-9900; *Survey of Current Business,* and *The National Income and Product Accounts of the United States.*

U.S. Department of Commerce, Bureau of the Census, Suitland, Maryland 20233 (301) 763-4040; *County Business Patterns.*

U.S. Department of Labor, Bureau of Labor Statistics, Two Massachusetts Avenue, NE, Washington, D.C. 20212 (202) 606-7828; *Employment and Earnings,* Bulletins 2370 and 2429, *Monthly Labor Review,* and unpublished data.

FINANCE, INSURANCE, AND REAL ESTATE INDUSTRY - ESTABLISHMENTS

U.S. Department of Commerce, Bureau of the Census, Suitland, Maryland 20233 (301) 763-4040; *County Business Patterns.*

FINANCE, INSURANCE, AND REAL ESTATE INDUSTRY - FINANCES

Board of Governors of the Federal Reserve System, Twentieth Street and Constitution Avenue, NW, Washington, D.C. 20551 (202) 452-3000; *Annual Statistical Digest, Federal Reserve Bulletin,* and unpublished data.

Federal Deposit Insurance Corporation, 550 Seventeenth Street, NW, Washington, D.C. 20429 (202) 393-8400; *Statistics on Banking.*

U.S. Department of Commerce, Bureau of the Census, Suitland, Maryland 20233 (301) 763-4040; *County Business Patterns.*

U.S. Department of the Treasury, Internal Revenue Service, 1111 Constitution Avenue, NW, Washington, D.C. 20224 (202) 566-5000; *Statistics of Income, Statistics of Income, Corporation Income Tax Returns, Statistics of Income Bulletin,* and unpublished data.

FINANCE, INSURANCE, AND REAL ESTATE INDUSTRY - FOREIGN INVESTMENTS IN UNITED STATES

U.S. Department of Commerce, Bureau of Economic Analysis, Fourteenth Street between Constitution Avenue and E Street, NW, Washington, D.C. 20230 (202) 606-9900; *Survey of Current Business,* and *Foreign Direct Investments in the United States, Operations of U.S. Affiliates of Foreign Companies.*

FINANCE, INSURANCE, AND REAL ESTATE INDUSTRY - GROSS DOMESTIC PRODUCT

U.S. Department of Commerce, Bureau of Economic Analysis, Fourteenth Street between Constitution Avenue and E Street, NW, Washington, D.C. 20230 (202) 606-9900; *Survey of Current Business.*

FINANCE, INSURANCE, AND REAL ESTATE INDUSTRY - MERGERS AND ACQUISITIONS

Securities Data Company, 1180 Raymond Boulevard, Newark, New Jersey 07102 (201) 622-3100; *Merger and Corporate Transactions Database.*

FINANCE, INSURANCE, AND REAL ESTATE INDUSTRY - PROFITS

Forbes, Incorporated, 60 Fifth Avenue, New York, New York 10011 (212) 620-2200; *Forbes Annual Report on American Industry.*

U.S. Department of Commerce, Bureau of Economic Analysis, Fourteenth Street between Constitution Avenue and E Street, NW, Washington, D.C. 20230 (202) 606-9900; *Survey of Current Business.*

U.S. Department of the Treasury, Internal Revenue Service, 1111 Constitution Avenue, NW, Washington, D.C. 20224 (202) 566-5000; *Statistics of Income,* various publications, and *Statistics of Income, Corporation Income Tax Returns.*

FINANCE, INSURANCE, AND REAL ESTATE INDUSTRY - SALES OR RECEIPTS

Forbes, Incorporated, 60 Fifth Avenue, New York, New York 10011 (212) 620-2200; *Forbes Annual Report on American Industry.*

U.S. Department of the Treasury, Internal Revenue Service, 1111 Constitution Avenue, NW, Washington, D.C. 20224 (202) 566-5000; *Statistics of Income,* various publications and unpublished data.

FINANCE, INSURANCE, AND REAL ESTATE INDUSTRY - UNION MEMBERSHIP

U.S. Department of Labor, Bureau of Labor Statistics, Two Massachusetts Avenue, NE, Washington, D.C. 20212 (202) 606-7828; *Employment and Earnings.*

FINANCIAL INSTRUMENTS - COMMODITY FUTURES TRADING

U.S. Commodity Futures Trading Commission, 2033 K Street, NW, Washington, D.C. 20581 (202) 254-6387; *Annual Report.*

FINISHED CONSUMER GOODS, PRODUCER PRICE INDEXES

U.S. Department of Labor, Bureau of Labor Statistics, Two Massachusetts Avenue, NE, Washington, D.C. 20212 (202) 606-7828; *Monthly Labor Review,* and *Producer Price Indexes.*

Finland - National Statistical Office

Statistics Finland, FIN-00022, Helsinki 10, Finland.

Finland - Primary Statistics Sources

Statistics Finland, FIN-00022, Helsinki 10, Finland; *Suomen Tilastollinen Vuosikirja* (Statistical Yearbook of Finland), and *Tilastokeskus,* (Bulletin of Statistics).

Finland - Databases

Finregion, Statistics Finland, FIN-0002 Helsinki 10, Finland. Subject coverage: Statistical information on Finnish demographics.

Finseries, Statistics Finland, FIN-00022 Helsinki 10, Finland. Subject coverage: A statistical database containing information on the economic development and foreign trade of Finland as well as other OECD countries.

Finfarming, Statistics Finland, FIN-0002 Helsinki 10, Finland. Subject coverage: Provides statistical information on agriculture by areas.

Finhousing, Statistics Finland, FIN-0002 Helsinki 10, Finland. Subject coverage: Provides statistical data on low interest loans granted by the Housing Fund of Finland for housing production and renovation and other forms of housing subsidy.

FINLAND - ABORTIONS

Nordic Council of Ministers, Store Strandstraede 18, DK-1255 Copenhagen K, Denmark and the Nordic Statistical Secretariat, Postboks 2550, DK-2100 Copenhagen 0, Denmark; *The Yearbook of Nordic Statistics.*

Statistical Office of the United Nations, Publishing Service, New York, New York 10017 (800) 253-9646; *Demographic Yearbook.*

FINLAND - AGRICULTURE

Facts on File, 460 Park Avenue South, New York, New York 10016 (800) 443-8323; *The New Book of World Rankings.*

Federal Statistical Office, Gustav - Stresemann - Ring 11, D-6200 Wiesbaden, Germany; *Finnland.*

Food and Agricultural Organization of the United Nations (FAO), Via delle Terme di Caracalla, 00100 Rome, Italy (Telephone Number in U.S. (202) 653-2400); *Production Yearbook, The State of Food and Agriculture*, and *Trade Yearbook*.

G.K. Hall and Company, 70 Lincoln Street, Boston, Massachusetts 02111 (617) 423-3990; *The World in Figures*.

Nordic Council of Ministers, Store Strandstraede 18, DK-1255 Copenhagen K, Denmark and the Nordic Statistical Secretariat, Postboks 2550, DK-2100 Copenhagen 0, Denmark; *The Yearbook of Nordic Statistics*.

Organisation for Economic Co-operation and Development (OECD), 2 rue Andre-Pascal, 75 Paris 16, France (Telephone Number in U.S. (202) 785-6323); *Economic Accounts for Agriculture, Industrial Structure Statistics, Indicators of Industrial Activity*, and *OECD Economic Surveys: Finland*.

Statistical Office of the United Nations, Publishing Service, New York, New York 10017 (800) 253-9646; *Statistical Yearbook*.

Times Books, 201 East 50th Street, New York, New York 10022 (212) 751-2600; *The Economist Book of Vital World Statistics*.

The World Bank, 1818 H Street, NW, Washington, D.C. 20433 (202) 477-1234; *World Tables*.

FINLAND - AIRLINE SERVICE

Facts on File, 460 Park Avenue South, New York, New York 10016 (800) 443-8323; *The New Book of World Rankings*.

G.K. Hall and Company, 70 Lincoln Street, Boston, Massachusetts 02111 (617) 423-3990; *The World in Figures*.

International Civil Aviation Organization, 1000 Sherbrooke Street West, Suite 400, Montreal, Quebec, Canada H3A 2R2 (514) 285-8219; *Civil Aviation Statistics of the World*.

Nordic Council of Ministers, Store Strandstraede 18, DK-1255 Copenhagen K, Denmark and the Nordic Statistical Secretariat, Postboks 2550, DK-2100 Copenhagen 0, Denmark; *The Yearbook of Nordic Statistics*.

Organisation for Economic Co-operation and Development (OECD), 2 rue Andre-Pascal, 75 Paris 16, France (Telephone Number in U.S. (202) 785-6323); *Tourism Policy and International Tourism in OECD Member Countries*.

Statistical Office of the United Nations, Publishing Service, New York, New York 10017 (800) 253-9646; *Statistical Yearbook*.

Times Books, 201 East 50th Street, New York, New York 10022 (212) 751-2600; *The Economist Book of Vital World Statistics*.

FINLAND - ALUMINUM PRODUCTION AND CONSUMPTION - See FINLAND - MINING AND MINERAL PRODUCTS

FINLAND - ANIMAL FEEDINGSTUFFS - EXPORTS

Organisation for Economic Co-operation and Development (OECD), 2 rue Andre-Pascal, 75 Paris 16, France (Telephone Number in U.S. (202) 785-6323); *Foreign Trade by Commodities*.

FINLAND - ANIMAL HEALTH

Food and Agricultural Organization of the United Nations (FAO), Via delle Terme di Caracalla, 00100 Rome, Italy (Telephone Number in U.S. (202) 653-2400); *Animal Health Yearbook*.

FINLAND - ANTIMONY AND ANTIMONY ORE - See FINLAND - MINING AND MINERAL PRODUCTS

FINLAND - AREA AND DENSITY OF POPULATION

Facts on File, 460 Park Avenue South, New York, New York 10016 (800) 443-8323; *The New Book of World Rankings*.

Federal Statistical Office, Gustav - Stresemann - Ring 11, D-6200 Wiesbaden, Germany; *Finnland*.

Food and Agricultural Organization of the United Nations (FAO) Via delle Terme di Caracalla, 00100 Rome, Italy (Telephone Number in U.S. (202) 653-2400); *The State of Food and Agriculture*.

G.K. Hall and Company, 70 Lincoln Street, Boston, Massachusetts 02111 (617) 423-3990; *The World in Figures*.

Nordic Council of Ministers, Store Strandstraede 18, DK-1255 Copenhagen K, Denmark and the Nordic Statistical Secretariat, Postboks 2550, DK-2100 Copenhagen 0, Denmark; *The Yearbook of Nordic Statistics*.

Statistical Office of the United Nations, Publishing Service, New York, New York 10017 (800) 253-9646; *Statistical Yearbook*.

Times Books, 201 East 50th Street, New York, New York 10022 (212) 751-2600; *The Economist Book of Vital World Statistics*.

FINLAND - ARMS EXPORTS AND IMPORTS

U.S. Arms Control and Disarmament Agency, 320 Twenty-first Street, NW, Washington, D.C. 20451 (202) 647-8677; *World Military Expenditures and Arms Transfers*.

FINLAND - ARSENIC PRODUCTION AND CONSUMPTION - See FINLAND - MINING AND MINERAL PRODUCTS

FINLAND - BALANCE OF PAYMENTS

The Economist Intelligence Unit, 111 West 57th Street, New York, New York 10019 (800) 938-4685; *The World Market Atlas*.

Federal Statistical Office, Gustav - Stresemann - Ring 11, D-6200 Wiesbaden, Germany; *Finnland*.

G.K. Hall and Company, 70 Lincoln Street, Boston, Massachusetts 02111 (617) 423-3990; *The World in Figures*.

International Monetary Fund, 700 Nineteenth Street, NW, Washington, D.C. 20431 (202) 623-7000; *Balance of Payments Yearbook*, and *International Financial Statistics*.

Nordic Council of Ministers, Store Strandstraede 18, DK-1255 Copenhagen K, Denmark and the Nordic Statistical Secretariat, Postboks 2550, DK-2100 Copenhagen 0, Denmark; *The Yearbook of Nordic Statistics*.

Organisation for Economic Co-operation and Development (OECD), 2 rue Andre-Pascal, 75 Paris 16, France (Telephone Number in U.S. (202) 785-6323); *Economic Outlook, Geographical Distribution of Financial Flows to Developing Countries, Main Economic Indicators - Historical Statistics*, and *OECD Economic Surveys: Finland*.

Times Books, 201 East 50th Street, New York, New York 10022 (212) 751-2600; *The Economist Book of Vital World Statistics*.

The World Bank, 1818 H Street, NW, Washington, D.C. 20433 (202) 477-1234; *World Tables.*

FINLAND - BANKING

Facts on File, 460 Park Avenue South, New York, New York 10016 (800) 443-8323; *The New Book of World Rankings.*

G.K. Hall and Company, 70 Lincoln Street, Boston, Massachusetts 02111 (617) 423-3990; *The World in Figures.*

International Monetary Fund, 700 Nineteenth Street, NW, Washington, D.C. 20431 (202) 623-7000; *International Financial Statistics.*

Nordic Council of Ministers, Store Strandstraede 18, DK-1255 Copenhagen K, Denmark and the Nordic Statistical Secretariat, Postboks 2550, DK-2100 Copenhagen 0, Denmark; *The Yearbook of Nordic Statistics.*

Organisation for Economic Co-operation and Development (OECD), 2 rue Andre-Pascal, 75 Paris 16, France (Telephone Number in U.S. (202) 785-6323); *Economic Outlook, Financial Market Trends,* and *OECD Economic Surveys: Finland.*

Statistical Office of the United Nations, Publishing Service, New York, New York 10017 (800) 253-9646; *Statistical Yearbook.*

FINLAND - BARLEY PRODUCTION - See FINLAND - CROPS

FINLAND - BAUXITE PRODUCTION AND CONSUMPTION - See FINLAND - MINING AND MINERAL PRODUCTS

FINLAND - BEER PRODUCTION

Facts on File, 460 Park Avenue South, New York, New York 10016 (800) 443-8323; *The New Book of World Rankings.*

FINLAND - BEVERAGES - PRODUCTION INDEX

Organisation for Economic Co-operation and Development (OECD), 2 rue Andre-Pascal, 75 Paris 16, France (Telephone Number in U.S. (202) 785-6323); *Indicators of Industrial Activity.*

FINLAND - BIRTH RATES

Facts on File, 460 Park Avenue South, New York, New York 10016 (800) 443-8323; *The New Book of World Rankings.*

Nordic Council of Ministers, Store Strandstraede 18, DK-1255 Copenhagen K, Denmark and the Nordic Statistical Secretariat, Postboks 2550, DK-2100 Copenhagen 0, Denmark; *The Yearbook of Nordic Statistics.*

Statistical Office of the United Nations, Publishing Service, New York, New York 10017 (800) 253-9646; *Demographic Yearbook,* and *Statistical Yearbook.*

Times Books, 201 East 50th Street, New York, New York 10022 (212) 751-2600; *The Economist Book of Vital World Statistics.*

The World Bank, 1818 H Street, NW, Washington, D.C. 20433 (202) 477-1234; *World Tables.*

World Health Organization, Office of Publications, Avenue Appia, CH-1211 Geneva 27, Switzerland (Telephone Number in U.S. (518) 436-9686); *World Health Statistics Annual.*

FINLAND - BISMUTH PRODUCTION AND CONSUMPTION - See FINLAND - MINING AND MINERAL PRODUCTS

FINLAND - BONDS

G.K. Hall and Company, 70 Lincoln Street, Boston, Massachusetts 02111 (617) 423-3990; *The World in Figures.*

International Monetary Fund, 700 Nineteenth Street, NW, Washington, D.C. 20431 (202) 623-7000; *Government Finance Statistics Yearbook.*

Organisation for Economic Co-operation and Development (OECD), 2 rue Andre-Pascal, 75 Paris 16, France (Telephone Number in U.S. (202) 785-6323); *Financial Market Trends.*

FINLAND - BOOK PRODUCTION

Euromonitor Publications Limited, 87-88 Turnmill Street, London EC1M 5QU, England; *European Marketing Data and Statistics.*

G.K. Hall and Company, 70 Lincoln Street, Boston, Massachusetts 02111 (617) 423-3990; *The World in Figures.*

Nordic Council of Ministers, Store Strandstraede 18, DK-1255 Copenhagen K, Denmark and the Nordic Statistical Secretariat, Postboks 2550, DK-2100 Copenhagen 0, Denmark; *The Yearbook of Nordic Statistics.*

Organisation for Economic Co-operation and Development (OECD), 2 rue Andre-Pascal, 75 Paris 16, France (Telephone Number in U.S. (202) 785-6323); *Indicators of Industrial Activity.*

United Nations Educational, Scientific and Cultural Organization (UNESCO), 7 Place de Fontenoy, F-75700 Paris, France (Telephone Number in U.S. (212) 963-5981); *Statistical Yearbook.*

FINLAND - BROADCASTING

Billboard Limited, P.O. Box 9027, 1006 AA Amsterdam, The Netherlands (Telephone Number in U.S. (212) 764-7300); *World Radio TV Handbook.*

Facts on File, 460 Park Avenue South, New York, New York 10016 (800) 443-8323; *The New Book of World Rankings.*

G.K. Hall and Company, 70 Lincoln Street, Boston, Massachusetts 02111 (617) 423-3990; *The World in Figures.*

Nordic Council of Ministers, Store Strandstraede 18, DK-1255 Copenhagen K, Denmark and the Nordic Statistical Secretariat, Postboks 2550, DK-2100 Copenhagen 0, Denmark; *The Yearbook of Nordic Statistics.*

Times Books, 201 East 50th Street, New York, New York 10022 (212) 751-2600; *The Economist Book of Vital World Statistics.*

United Nations Educational, Scientific and Cultural Organization (UNESCO), 7 Place de Fontenoy, F-75700 Paris, France (Telephone Number in U.S. (212) 963-5981); *Statistical Yearbook.*

FINLAND - BUILDING CONSTRUCTION - See FINLAND - CONSTRUCTION INDUSTRY

FINLAND - BUSINESS

G.K. Hall and Company, 70 Lincoln Street, Boston, Massachusetts 02111 (617) 423-3990; *The World in Figures.*

FINLAND - BUTTER EXPORTS AND IMPORTS - See DAIRY PRODUCTS

FINLAND - CABBAGE PRODUCTION - See FINLAND - CROPS

FINLAND - CADMIUM PRODUCTION AND CONSUMPTION - See FINLAND - MINING AND MINERAL PRODUCTS

FINLAND - CALORIE SUPPLY

Food and Agricultural Organization of the United Nations (FAO) Via delle Terme di Caracalla, 00100 Rome, Italy (Telephone Number in U.S. (202) 653-2400); *The State of Food and Agriculture.*

FINLAND - CAPITAL INVESTMENT

Organisation for Economic Co-operation and Development (OECD), 2 rue Andre-Pascal, 75 Paris 16, France (Telephone Number in U.S. (202) 785-6323); *Economic Outlook,* and *Financial Market Trends.*

FINLAND - CAPITAL REVENUE

International Monetary Fund, 700 Nineteenth Street, NW, Washington, D.C. 20431 (202) 623-7000; *Government Finance Statistics Yearbook.*

Organisation for Economic Co-operation and Development (OECD), 2 rue Andre-Pascal, 75 Paris 16, France (Telephone Number in U.S. (202) 785-6323); *Economic Outlook,* and *Financial Market Trends.*

FINLAND - CATTLE - See FINLAND - LIVESTOCK AND POULTRY

FINLAND - CAUSTIC SODA PRODUCTION

Organisation for Economic Co-operation and Development (OECD), 2 rue Andre-Pascal, 75 Paris 16, France (Telephone Number in U.S. (202) 785-6323); *Indicators of Industrial Activity.*

Statistical Office of the United Nations, Publishing Service, New York, New York 10017 (800) 253-9646; *Statistical Yearbook.*

FINLAND - CEMENT PRODUCTION - See FINLAND - MINING AND MINERAL PRODUCTS

FINLAND - CEREAL PRODUCTION - See FINLAND - CROPS

FINLAND - CHEESE EXPORTS AND IMPORTS - See FINland - DAIRY PRODUCTS

FINLAND - CHEMICAL (ORGANIC) PRODUCTION - See FINLAND - MINING AND MINERAL PRODUCTS

FINLAND - CHROMITE PRODUCTION AND CONSUMPTION - See FINLAND - MINING AND MINERAL PRODUCTS

FINLAND - CHROMIUM ORE PRODUCTION AND CONSUMPTION - See FINLAND - MINING AND MINERAL PRODUCTS

FINLAND - CIGAR PRODUCTION - See FINLAND - TOBACCO PRODUCTION

FINLAND - CIGARETTE PRODUCTION - See FINLAND - TOBACCO PRODUCTION

FINLAND - CLASS STRUCTURE

G.K. Hall and Company, 70 Lincoln Street, Boston, Massachusetts 02111 (617) 423-3990; *The World in Figures.*

FINLAND - CLIMATE

Facts on File, 460 Park Avenue South, New York, New York 10016 (800) 443-8323; *The New Book of World Rankings.*

G.K. Hall and Company, 70 Lincoln Street, Boston, Massachusetts 02111 (617) 423-3990; *The World in Figures.*

FINLAND - CLOTHING - PRODUCTION INDEX

Organisation for Economic Co-operation and Development (OECD), 2 rue Andre-Pascal, 75 Paris 16, France (Telephone Number in U.S. (202) 785-6323); *Indicators of Industrial Activity.*

FINLAND - CLOTHING EXPORTS AND IMPORTS

Organisation for Economic Co-operation and Development (OECD), 2 rue Andre-Pascal, 75 Paris 16, France (Telephone Number in U.S. (202) 785-6323); *Textile Industry in OECD Countries.*

FINLAND - COAL PRODUCTION - See FINLAND - MINING AND MINERAL PRODUCTS

FINLAND - COBALT PRODUCTION AND CONSUMPTION - See FINLAND - MINING AND MINERAL PRODUCTS

FINLAND - COFFEE - See FINLAND - CROPS

FINLAND - COKE OVEN COKE AND ORE - See FINLAND - MINING AND MINERAL PRODUCTS

FINLAND - COMMUNICATIONS

Federal Statistical Office, Gustav - Stresemann - Ring 11, D-6200 Wiesbaden, Germany; *Finnland.*

G.K. Hall and Company, 70 Lincoln Street, Boston, Massachusetts 02111 (617) 423-3990; *The World in Figures.*

FINLAND - CONSTRUCTION INDUSTRY

Facts on File, 460 Park Avenue South, New York, New York 10016 (800) 443-8323; *The New Book of World Rankings.*

Organisation for Economic Co-operation and Development (OECD), 2 rue Andre-Pascal, 75 Paris 16, France (Telephone Number in U.S. (202) 785-6323); *Industrial Structure Statistics, Main Economic Indicators - Historical Statistics,* and *OECD Economic Surveys: Finland.*

Statistical Office of the United Nations, Publishing Service, New York, New York 10017 (800) 253-9646; *Construction Statistics Yearbook,* and *Statistical Yearbook.*

FINLAND - CONSUMER PRICE INDEX

Federal Statistical Office, Gustav - Stresemann - Ring 11, D-6200 Wiesbaden, Germany; *Finnland.*

G.K. Hall and Company, 70 Lincoln Street, Boston, Massachusetts 02111 (617) 423-3990; *The World in Figures.*

Nordic Council of Ministers, Store Strandstraede 18, DK-1255 Copenhagen K, Denmark and the Nordic Statistical Secretariat, Postboks 2550, DK-2100 Copenhagen 0, Denmark; *The Yearbook of Nordic Statistics.*

Organisation for Economic Co-operation and Development (OECD), 2 rue Andre-Pascal, 75 Paris 16, France (Telephone Number in U.S.

(202) 785-6323); *Economic Outlook*.

Statistical Office of the United Nations, Publishing Service, New York, New York 10017 (800) 253-9646; *Statistical Yearbook*.

FINLAND - CONSUMER PRICES

Euromonitor Publications Limited, 87-88 Turnmill Street, London EC1M 5QU, England; *European Marketing Data and Statistics*.

Federal Statistical Office, Gustav - Stresemann - Ring 11, D-6200 Wiesbaden, Germany; *Finnland*.

International Labour Office, I.L.O. Publications, CH-1211, Geneva 22, Switzerland; *Yearbook of Labour Statistics*.

International Monetary Fund, 700 Nineteenth Street, NW, Washington, D.C. 20431 (202) 623-7000; *International Financial Statistics*.

Organisation for Economic Co-operation and Development (OECD), 2 rue Andre-Pascal, 75 Paris 16, France (Telephone Number in U.S. (202) 785-6323); *Economic Outlook*, and *Main Economic Indicators - Historical Statistics*.

Times Books, 201 East 50th Street, New York, New York 10022 (212) 751-2600; *The Economist Book of Vital World Statistics*.

FINLAND - CONSUMPTION

G.K. Hall and Company, 70 Lincoln Street, Boston, Massachusetts 02111 (617) 423-3990; *The World in Figures*.

International Lead and Zinc Study Group, Metro House, 58 St. James's Street, London SW1A 1LD, England; *Lead and Zinc Statistics*.

International Monetary Fund, 700 Nineteenth Street, NW, Washington, D.C. 20431 (202) 623-7000; *International Financial Statistics*.

Nordic Council of Ministers, Store Strandstraede 18, DK-1255 Copenhagen K, Denmark and the Nordic Statistical Secretariat, Postboks 2550, DK-2100 Copenhagen 0, Denmark; *The Yearbook of Nordic Statistics*.

Organisation for Economic Co-operation and Development (OECD), 2 rue Andre-Pascal, 75 Paris 16, France (Telephone Number in U.S. (202) 785-6323); *The Footwear, Raw Hides and Skins, and Leather Industry in OECD Countries, Meat Balances in OECD Member Countries, The Iron and Steel Industry, The Non-Ferrous Metals Industry, The Pulp and Paper Industry*, and *Textile Industry in OECD Countries*.

FINLAND - COPPER AND COPPER ORE PRODUCTION - See FINLAND - MINING AND MINERAL PRODUCTS

FINLAND - CORN PRODUCTION - See FINLAND - CROPS

FINLAND - CORPORATE INCOME TAXES - See FINLAND - TAXATION

FINLAND - CORPORATE TAXES - See FINLAND - TAXATION

FINLAND - COTTON - See FINLAND - CROPS

FINLAND - CRIME

International Criminal Police Organization (INTERPOL), 26 rue Armengaud, 92210 Saint Cloud, France; *International Crime Statistics*.

Nordic Council of Ministers, Store Strandstraede 18, DK-1255 Copenhagen K, Denmark and the Nordic Statistical Secretariat, Postboks 2550, DK-2100 Copenhagen 0, Denmark; *The Yearbook of Nordic Statistics*.

FINLAND - CROPS

Euromonitor Publications Limited, 87-88 Turnmill Street, London EC1M 5QU, England; *European Marketing Data and Statistics*.

Facts on File, 460 Park Avenue South, New York, New York 10016 (800) 443-8323; *The New Book of World Rankings*.

Food and Agricultural Organization of the United Nations (FAO) Via delle Terme di Caracalla, 00100 Rome, Italy (Telephone Number in U.S. (202) 653-2400); *Production Yearbook*, and *The State of Food and Agriculture*.

G.K. Hall and Company, 70 Lincoln Street, Boston, Massachusetts 02111 (617) 423-3990; *The World in Figures*.

Organisation for Economic Co-operation and Development (OECD), 2 rue Andre-Pascal, 75 Paris 16, France (Telephone Number in U.S. (202) 785-6323); *Economic Accounts for Agriculture, Foreign Trade by Commodities*, and *Textile Industry in OECD Countries*.

FINLAND - CUSTOMS DUTIES

G.K. Hall and Company, 70 Lincoln Street, Boston, Massachusetts 02111 (617) 423-3990; *The World in Figures*.

International Monetary Fund, 700 Nineteenth Street, NW, Washington, D.C. 20431 (202) 623-7000; *Government Finance Statistics Yearbook*.

Organisation for Economic Co-operation and Development (OECD), 2 rue Andre-Pascal, 75 Paris 16, France (Telephone Number in U.S. (202) 785-6323); *The Non-Ferrous Metals Industry*.

FINLAND - DAIRY PRODUCTS

Commodity Research Bureau, Incorporated, 75 Wall Street, New York, New York 10005 (212) 504-7754; *Commodity Year Book*.

Facts on File, 460 Park Avenue South, New York, New York 10016 (800) 443-8323; *The New Book of World Rankings*.

Food and Agricultural Organization of the United Nations (FAO) Via delle Terme di Caracalla, 00100 Rome, Italy (Telephone Number in U.S. (202) 653-2400); *Production Yearbook*, and *The State of Food and Agriculture*.

Nordic Council of Ministers, Store Strandstraede 18, DK-1255 Copenhagen K, Denmark and the Nordic Statistical Secretariat, Postboks 2550, DK-2100 Copenhagen 0, Denmark; *The Yearbook of Nordic Statistics*.

Organisation for Economic Co-operation and Development (OECD), 2 rue Andre-Pascal, 75 Paris 16, France (Telephone Number in U.S. (202) 785-6323); *Economic Accounts for Agriculture, Milk, Milk Products, and Egg Balances in OECD Member Countries*.

Statistical Office of the United Nations, Publishing Service, New York, New York 10017 (800) 253-9646; *Statistical Yearbook.*

FINLAND - DEATH RATE

G.K. Hall and Company, 70 Lincoln Street, Boston, Massachusetts 02111 (617) 423-3990; *The World in Figures.*

Nordic Council of Ministers, Store Strandstraede 18, DK-1255 Copenhagen K, Denmark and the Nordic Statistical Secretariat, Postboks 2550, DK-2100 Copenhagen 0, Denmark; *The Yearbook of Nordic Statistics.*

Statistical Office of the United Nations, Publishing Service, New York, New York 10017 (800) 253-9646; *Statistical Yearbook.*

Times Books, 201 East 50th Street, New York, New York 10022 (212) 751-2600; *The Economist Book of Vital World Statistics.*

World Health Organization, Office of Publications, Avenue Appia, CH-1211 Geneva 27, Switzerland (Telephone Number in U.S. (518) 436-9686); *World Health Statistics Annual.*

FINLAND - DEFENSE EXPENDITURES

G.K. Hall and Company, 70 Lincoln Street, Boston, Massachusetts 02111 (617) 423-3990; *The World in Figures.*

International Monetary Fund, 700 Nineteenth Street, NW, Washington, D.C. 20431 (202) 623-7000; *Government Finance Statistics Yearbook.*

U.S. Arms Control and Disarmament Agency, 320 Twenty-first Street, NW, Washington, D.C. 20451 (202) 647-8677; *World Military Expenditures and Arms Transfers.*

FINLAND - DEMOGRAPHY

The Economist Intelligence Unit, 111 West 57th Street, New York, New York 10019 (800) 938-4685; *The World Market Atlas.*

Facts on File, 460 Park Avenue South, New York, New York 10016 (800) 443-8323; *The New Book of World Rankings.*

Federal Statistical Office, Gustav - Stresemann - Ring 11, D-6200 Wiesbaden, Germany; *Finnland.*

G.K. Hall and Company, 70 Lincoln Street, Boston, Massachusetts 02111 (617) 423-3990; *The World in Figures.*

Nordic Council of Ministers, Store Strandstraede 18, DK-1255 Copenhagen K, Denmark and the Nordic Statistical Secretariat, Postboks 2550, DK-2100 Copenhagen 0, Denmark; *The Yearbook of Nordic Statistics.*

FINLAND - DEVELOPMENT ASSISTANCE

G.K. Hall and Company, 70 Lincoln Street, Boston, Massachusetts 02111 (617) 423-3990; *The World in Figures.*

Organisation for Economic Co-operation and Development (OECD), 2 rue Andre-Pascal, 75 Paris 16, France (Telephone Number in U.S. (202) 785-6323); *Geographical Distribution of Financial Flows to Developing Countries.*

Statistical Office of the United Nations, Publishing Service, New York, New York 10017 (800) 253-9646; *Statistical Yearbook.*

FINLAND - DIAMOND PRODUCTION - See FINLAND - MINING AND MINERAL PRODUCTS

FINLAND - DISCOUNT RATES

Organisation for Economic Co-operation and Development (OECD), 2 rue Andre-Pascal, 75 Paris 16, France (Telephone Number in U.S. (202) 785-6323); *Financial Market Trends.*

Statistical Office of the United Nations, Publishing Service, New York, New York 10017 (800) 253-9646; *Statistical Yearbook.*

FINLAND - DISEASES

G.K. Hall and Company, 70 Lincoln Street, Boston, Massachusetts 02111 (617) 423-3990; *The World in Figures.*

World Health Organization, Office of Publications, Avenue Appia, CH-1211 Geneva 27, Switzerland (Telephone Number in U.S. (518) 436-9686); *World Health Statistics Annual.*

FINLAND - DIVORCE RATES

Facts on File, 460 Park Avenue South, New York, New York 10016 (800) 443-8323; *The New Book of World Rankings.*

Nordic Council of Ministers, Store Strandstraede 18, DK-1255 Copenhagen K, Denmark and the Nordic Statistical Secretariat, Postboks 2550, DK-2100 Copenhagen 0, Denmark; *The Yearbook of Nordic Statistics.*

Statistical Office of the United Nations, Publishing Service, New York, New York 10017 (800) 253-9646; *Demographic Yearbook,* and *Statistical Yearbook.*

FINLAND - DOMESTIC PRODUCT

G.K. Hall and Company, 70 Lincoln Street, Boston, Massachusetts 02111 (617) 423-3990; *The World in Figures.*

FINLAND - DUCKS - See FINLAND - LIVESTOCK AND POULTRY

FINLAND - ECONOMY

Euromonitor Publications Limited, 87-88 Turnmill Street, London EC1M 5QU, England; *European Marketing Data and Statistics.*

Facts on File, 460 Park Avenue South, New York, New York 10016 (800) 443-8323; *The New Book of World Rankings.*

Federal Statistical Office, Gustav - Stresemann - Ring 11, D-6200 Wiesbaden, Germany; *Finnland.*

G.K. Hall and Company, 70 Lincoln Street, Boston, Massachusetts 02111 (617) 423-3990; *The World in Figures.*

Organisation for Economic Co-operation and Development (OECD), 2 rue Andre-Pascal, 75 Paris 16, France (Telephone Number in U.S. (202) 785-6323); *Economic Outlook, Geographical Distribution of Financial Flows to Developing Countries, Main Economic Indicators Historical Statistics, OECD Economic Surveys: Finland,* and *OECD Employment Outlook.*

FINLAND - EDUCATION

The Economist Intelligence Unit, 111 West 57th Street, New York, New York 10019 (800) 938-4685; *The World Market Atlas.*

Euromonitor Publications Limited, 87-88 Turnmill Street, London EC1M 5QU, England; *European Marketing Data and Statistics.*

Facts on File, 460 Park Avenue South, New York, New York 10016 (800) 443-8323; *The New Book of World Rankings.*

Federal Statistical Office, Gustav - Stresemann - Ring 11, D-6200 Wiesbaden, Germany; *Finnland.*

G.K. Hall and Company, 70 Lincoln Street, Boston, Massachusetts 02111 (617) 423-3990; *The World in Figures.*

International Monetary Fund, 700 Nineteenth Street, NW, Washington, D.C. 20431 (202) 623-7000; *Government Finance Statistics Yearbook.*

Nordic Council of Ministers, Store Strandstraede 18, DK-1255 Copenhagen K, Denmark and the Nordic Statistical Secretariat, Postboks 2550, DK-2100 Copenhagen 0, Denmark; *The Yearbook of Nordic Statistics.*

Organisation for Economic Co-operation and Development (OECD), 2 rue Andre-Pascal, 75 Paris 16, France (Telephone Number in U.S. (202) 785-6323); *Education in OECD Countries.*

Times Books, 201 East 50th Street, New York, New York 10022 (212) 751-2600; *The Economist Book of Vital World Statistics.*

United Nations Educational, Scientific and Cultural Organization (UNESCO), 7 Place de Fontenoy, F-75700 Paris, France (Telephone Number in U.S. (212) 963-5981); *Statistical Yearbook.*

The World Bank, 1818 H Street, NW, Washington, D.C. 20433 (202) 477-1234; *World Tables.*

FINLAND - EGG PRODUCTION AND CONSUMPTION - See FINLAND - DAIRY PRODUCTS

FINLAND - ELECTRICITY

Facts on File, 460 Park Avenue South, New York, New York 10016 (800) 443-8323; *The New Book of World Rankings.*

Nordic Council of Ministers, Store Strandstraede 18, DK-1255 Copenhagen K, Denmark and the Nordic Statistical Secretariat, Postboks 2550, DK-2100 Copenhagen 0, Denmark; *The Yearbook of Nordic Statistics.*

Organisation for Economic Co-operation and Development (OECD), 2 rue Andre-Pascal, 75 Paris 16, France (Telephone Number in U.S. (202) 785-6323); *Coal Information, Energy Statistics of OECD Countries, Indicators of Industrial Activity,* and *Industrial Structure Statistics.*

Statistical Office of the United Nations, Publishing Service, New York, New York 10017 (800) 253-9646; *Statistical Yearbook.*

Times Books, 201 East 50th Street, New York, New York 10022 (212) 751-2600; *The Economist Book of Vital World Statistics.*

FINLAND - EMPLOYMENT

Euromonitor Publications Limited, 87-88 Turnmill Street, London EC1M 5QU, England; *European Marketing Data and Statistics.*

Facts on File, 460 Park Avenue South, New York, New York 10016 (800) 443-8323; *The New Book of World Rankings.*

Federal Statistical Office, Gustav - Stresemann - Ring 11, D-6200 Wiesbaden, Germany; *Finnland.*

International Labour Office, I.L.O. Publications, CH-1211, Geneva 22, Switzerland; *Yearbook of Labour Statistics.*

Nordic Council of Ministers, Store Strandstraede 18, DK-1255 Copenhagen K, Denmark and the Nordic Statistical Secretariat, Postboks 2550, DK-2100 Copenhagen 0, Denmark; *The Yearbook of Nordic Statistics.*

Organisation for Economic Co-operation and Development (OECD), 2 rue Andre-Pascal, 75 Paris 16, France (Telephone Number in U.S. (202) 785-6323); *Economic Outlook, The Iron and Steel Industry, OECD Economic Surveys: Finland, OECD Employment Outlook,* and *Textile Industry in OECD Countries.*

Statistical Office of the United Nations, Publishing Service, New York, New York 10017 (800) 253-9646; *Statistical Yearbook.*

FINLAND - ENERGY

Euromonitor Publications Limited, 87-88 Turnmill Street, London EC1M 5QU, England; *European Marketing Data and Statistics.*

Facts on File, 460 Park Avenue South, New York, New York 10016 (800) 443-8323; *The New Book of World Rankings.*

Food and Agricultural Organization of the United Nations (FAO) Via delle Terme di Caracalla, 00100 Rome, Italy (Telephone Number in U.S. (202) 653-2400); *The State of Food and Agriculture.*

G.K. Hall and Company, 70 Lincoln Street, Boston, Massachusetts 02111 (617) 423-3990; *The World in Figures.*

Nordic Council of Ministers, Store Strandstraede 18, DK-1255 Copenhagen K, Denmark and the Nordic Statistical Secretariat, Postboks 2550, DK-2100 Copenhagen 0, Denmark; *The Yearbook of Nordic Statistics.*

Organisation for Economic Co-operation and Development (OECD), 2 rue Andre-Pascal, 75 Paris 16, France (Telephone Number in U.S. (202) 785-6323); *Coal Information, Energy Statistics of OECD Countries, OECD Environmental Data,* and *Oil and Gas Information.*

Statistical Office of the United Nations, Publishing Service, New York, New York 10017 (800) 253-9646; *Energy Statistics Yearbook,* and *Statistical Yearbook.*

Times Books, 201 East 50th Street, New York, New York 10022 (212) 751-2600; *The Economist Book of Vital World Statistics.*

FINLAND - ENVIRONMENT

Organization for Economic Co-operation and Development (OECD), 2 rue Andre-Pascal, 75 Paris 16, France (Telephone Number in U.S. (202) 785-6323); *OECD Environmental Data.*

FINLAND - EXCHANGE RATES

International Civil Aviation Organization, 1000 Sherbrooke Street West, Suite 400, Montreal, Quebec, Canada H3A 2R2 (514) 285-8219; *Civil Aviation Statistics of the World.*

International Monetary Fund, 700 Nineteenth Street, NW, Washington, D.C. 20431 (202) 623-7000; *International Financial Statistics.*

Nordic Council of Ministers, Store Strandstraede 18, DK-1255 Copenhagen K, Denmark and the Nordic Statistical Secretariat, Postboks 2550, DK-2100 Copenhagen 0, Denmark; *The Yearbook of Nordic Statistics.*

Organisation for Economic Co-operation and Development (OECD), 2 rue Andre-Pascal, 75 Paris 16, France (Telephone Number in U.S. (202) 785-6323); *Economic Outlook, Financial Market Trends, Revenue Statistics of OECD Member Countries,* and *Tourism Policy and International Tourism in OECD Member Countries.*

Statistical Office of the United Nations, Publishing Service, New York, New York 10017 (800) 253-9646; *Statistical Yearbook.*

FINLAND - EXCISE TAXES - See FINLAND - TAXATION

FINLAND - EXPORTS

American Automobile Manufacturers Association, 1401 H Street, NW, Suite 900, Washington, D.C. 20005 (202) 326-5500; *World Motor Vehicle Data.*

The Economist Intelligence Unit, 111 West 57th Street, New York, New York 10019 (800) 938-4685; *The World Market Atlas.*

Food and Agricultural Organization of the United Nations (FAO) Via delle Terme di Caracalla, 00100 Rome, Italy (Telephone Number in U.S. (202) 653-2400); *The State of Food and Agriculture.*

G.K. Hall and Company, 70 Lincoln Street, Boston, Massachusetts 02111 (617) 423-3990; *The World in Figures.*

International Lead and Zinc Study Group, Metro House, 58 St. James's Street, London SW1A 1LD, England; *Lead and Zinc Statistics.*

International Monetary Fund, 700 Nineteenth Street, NW, Washington, D.C. 20431 (202) 623-7000; *Direction of Trade Statistics, Government Finance Statistics Yearbook,* and *International Financial Statistics.*

Nordic Council of Ministers, Store Strandstraede 18, DK-1255 Copenhagen K, Denmark and the Nordic Statistical Secretariat, Postboks 2550, DK-2100 Copenhagen 0, Denmark; *The Yearbook of Nordic Statistics.*

Organisation for Economic Co-operation and Development (OECD), 2 rue Andre-Pascal, 75 Paris 16, France (Telephone Number in U.S. (202) 785-6323); *Economic Outlook, The Footwear, Raw Hides and Skins, and Leather Industry in OECD Countries, Foreign Trade by Commodities, Geographical Distribution of Financial Flows to Developing Countries, Industrial Structure Statistics, The Iron and Steel Industry, Milk, Milk Products, and Egg Balances in OECD Member Countries, OECD Economic Surveys: Finland, The Pulp and Paper Industry,* and *Review of Fisheries in OECD Member Countries.*

Times Books, 201 East 50th Street, New York, New York 10022 (212) 751-2600; *The Economist Book of Vital World Statistics.*

The World Bank, 1818 H Street, NW, Washington, D.C. 20433 (202) 477-1234; *World Tables.*

FINLAND - EXTERNAL FINANCING

Organisation for Economic Co-operation and Development (OECD), 2 rue Andre-Pascal, 75 Paris 16, France (Telephone Number in U.S. (202) 785-6323); *Economic Outlook,* and *Financial Market Trends.*

FINLAND - EXTERNAL INDEBTEDNESS

Organisation for Economic Co-operation and Development (OECD), 2 rue Andre-Pascal, 75 Paris 16, France (Telephone Number in U.S. (202) 785-6323); *Financial Market Trends,* and *Geographical Distribution of Financial Flows to Developing Countries.*

The World Bank, 1818 H Street, NW, Washington, D.C. 20433 (202) 477-1234; *World Tables.*

FINLAND - EXTERNAL TRADE

Food and Agricultural Organization of the United Nations (FAO) Via delle Terme di Caracalla, 00100 Rome, Italy (Telephone Number in U.S. (202) 653-2400); *The State of Food and Agriculture,* and *Trade Yearbook.*

G.K. Hall and Company, 70 Lincoln Street, Boston, Massachusetts 02111 (617) 423-3990; *The World in Figures.*

Nordic Council of Ministers, Store Strandstraede 18, DK-1255 Copenhagen K, Denmark and the Nordic Statistical Secretariat, Postboks 2550, DK-2100 Copenhagen 0, Denmark; *The Yearbook of Nordic Statistics.*

Statistical Office of the United Nations, Publishing Service, New York, New York 10017 (800) 253-9646; *Statistical Yearbook.*

FINLAND - FABRIC PRODUCTION - See FINLAND - TEXTILE INDUSTRY

FINLAND - FARM CROPS - See FINLAND - CROPS

FINLAND - FERTILITY RATES

Facts on File, 460 Park Avenue South, New York, New York 10016 (800) 443-8323; *The New Book of World Rankings.*

Nordic Council of Ministers, Store Strandstraede 18, DK-1255 Copenhagen K, Denmark and the Nordic Statistical Secretariat, Postboks 2550, DK-2100 Copenhagen 0, Denmark; *The Yearbook of Nordic Statistics.*

Times Books, 201 East 50th Street, New York, New York 10022 (212) 751-2600; *The Economist Book of Vital World Statistics.*

The World Bank, 1818 H Street, NW, Washington, D.C. 20433 (202) 477-1234; *World Tables.*

FINLAND - FERTILITY RATES

Nordic Council of Ministers, Store Strandstraede 18, DK-1255 Copenhagen K, Denmark and the Nordic Statistical Secretariat, Postboks 2550, DK-2100 Copenhagen 0, Denmark; *The Yearbook of Nordic Statistics.*

FINLAND - FERTILIZER

Food and Agricultural Organization of the United Nations (FAO), Via delle Terme di Caracalla, 00100 Rome, Italy (Telephone Number in U.S. (202) 653-2400); *Fertilizer Yearbook,* and *The State of Food and Agriculture.*

Organisation for Economic Co-operation and Development (OECD), 2 rue Andre-Pascal, 75 Paris 16, France (Telephone Number in U.S. (202) 785-6323); *Economic Accounts for Agriculture,* and *Foreign Trade by Commodities.*

Statistical Office of the United Nations, Publishing Service, New York, New York 10017 (800) 253-9646; *Statistical Yearbook.*

FINLAND - FETAL MORTALITY

Nordic Council of Ministers, Store Strandstraede 18, DK-1255 Copenhagen K, Denmark and the Nordic Statistical Secretariat, Postboks 2550, DK-2100 Copenhagen 0, Denmark; *The Yearbook of Nordic Statistics.*

Statistical Office of the United Nations, Publishing Service, New York, New York 10017 (800) 253-9646; *Demographic Yearbook.*

World Health Organization, Office of Publications, Avenue Appia, CH-1211 Geneva 27, Switzerland (Telephone Number in U.S. (518) 436-9686); *World Health Statistics Annual.*

FINLAND - FILAMENT PRODUCTION - See FINLAND - TEXTILE INDUSTRY

FINLAND - FILM - See FINLAND - MOTION PICTURES

FINLAND - FINANCE

Facts on File, 460 Park Avenue South, New York, New York 10016 (800) 443-8323; *The New Book of World Rankings.*

Federal Statistical Office, Gustav - Stresemann - Ring 11, D-6200 Wiesbaden, Germany; *Finnland.*

G.K. Hall and Company, 70 Lincoln Street, Boston, Massachusetts 02111 (617) 423-3990; *The World in Figures.*

International Monetary Fund, 700 Nineteenth Street, NW, Washington, D.C. 20431 (202) 623-7000; *Government Finance Statistics Yearbook,* and *International Financial Statistics.*

Organisation for Economic Co-operation and Development (OECD), 2 rue Andre-Pascal, 75 Paris 16, France (Telephone Number in U.S. (202) 785-6323); *Economic Outlook, Financial Market Trends, Geographical Distribution of Financial Flows to Developing Countries,* and *OECD Financial Statistics.*

FINLAND - FISHERIES

Euromonitor Publications Limited, 87-88 Turnmill Street, London EC1M 5QU, England; *European Marketing Data and Statistics.*

Facts on File, 460 Park Avenue South, New York, New York 10016 (800) 443-8323; *The New Book of World Rankings.*

Federal Statistical Office, Gustav - Stresemann - Ring 11, D-6200 Wiesbaden, Germany; *Finnland.*

Food and Agricultural Organization of the United Nations (FAO) Via delle Terme di Caracalla, 00100 Rome, Italy (Telephone Number in U.S. (202) 653-2400); *The State of Food and Agriculture,* and *Yearbook of Fishery Statistics.*

Nordic Council of Ministers, Store Strandstraede 18, DK-1255 Copenhagen K, Denmark and the Nordic Statistical Secretariat, Postboks 2550, DK-2100 Copenhagen 0, Denmark; *The Yearbook of Nordic Statistics.*

Organisation for Economic Co-operation and Development (OECD), 2 rue Andre-Pascal, 75 Paris 16, France (Telephone Number in U.S. (202) 785-6323); *Foreign Trade by Commodities, Industrial Structure Statistics,* and *Review of Fisheries in OECD Member Countries.*

Statistical Office of the United Nations, Publishing Service, New York, New York 10017 (800) 253-9646; *Statistical Yearbook.*

FINLAND - FLOUR PRODUCTION

Statistical Office of the United Nations, Publishing Service, New York, New York 10017 (800) 253-9646; *Statistical Yearbook.*

FINLAND - FOOD

Food and Agricultural Organization of the United Nations (FAO) Via delle Terme di Caracalla, 00100 Rome, Italy (Telephone Number in U.S. (202) 653-2400); *Production Yearbook,* and *The State of Food and Agriculture.*

G.K. Hall and Company, 70 Lincoln Street, Boston, Massachusetts 02111 (617) 423-3990; *The World in Figures.*

Organisation for Economic Co-operation and Development (OECD), 2 rue Andre-Pascal, 75 Paris 16, France (Telephone Number in U.S. (202) 785-6323); *Food Consumption Statistics,* and *Foreign Trade by Commodities.*

Statistical Office of the United Nations, Publishing Service, New York, New York 10017 (800) 253-9646; *Statistical Yearbook.*

FINLAND - FOOTWEAR - PRODUCTION INDEX

Organisation for Economic Co-operation and Development (OECD), 2 rue Andre-Pascal, 75 Paris 16, France (Telephone Number in U.S. (202) 785-6323); *Indicators of Industrial Activity.*

FINLAND - FOREIGN AID

G.K. Hall and Company, 70 Lincoln Street, Boston, Massachusetts 02111 (617) 423-3990; *The World in Figures.*

FINLAND - FOREIGN DEBT

International Monetary Fund, 700 Nineteenth Street, NW, Washington, D.C. 20431 (202) 623-7000; *Government Finance Statistics Yearbook.*

Organisation for Economic Co-operation and Development (OECD), 2 rue Andre-Pascal, 75 Paris 16, France (Telephone Number in U.S. (202) 785-6323); *Economic Outlook.*

FINLAND - FOREIGN FINANCE

Organisation for Economic Co-operation and Development (OECD), 2 rue Andre-Pascal, 75 Paris 16, France (Telephone Number in U.S. (202) 785-6323); *Economic Outlook,* and *Financial Market Trends.*

FINLAND - FOREIGN INDEBTEDNESS

Organisation for Economic Co-operation and Development (OECD), 2 rue Andre-Pascal, 75 Paris 16, France (Telephone Number in U.S. (202) 785-6323); *Economic Outlook,* and *Financial Market Trends.*

FINLAND - FOREIGN TRADE

Euromonitor Publications Limited, 87-88 Turnmill Street, London EC1M 5QU, England; *European Marketing Data and Statistics.*

Facts on File, 460 Park Avenue South, New York, New York 10016 (800) 443-8323; *The New Book of World Rankings.*

Federal Statistical Office, Gustav - Stresemann - Ring 11, D-6200 Wiesbaden, Germany; *Finnland.*

G.K. Hall and Company, 70 Lincoln Street, Boston, Massachusetts 02111 (617) 423-3990; *The World in Figures.*

Food and Agricultural Organization of the United Nations (FAO) Via delle Terme di Caracalla, 00100 Rome, Italy (Telephone Number in U.S. (202) 653-2400); *The State of Food and Agriculture.*

Organisation for Economic Co-operation and Development (OECD), 2 rue Andre-Pascal, 75 Paris 16, France (Telephone Number in U.S. (202) 785-6323); *Economic Outlook, The Footwear, Raw Hides and Skins, and Leather Industry in OECD Countries, Foreign Trade by Commodities, Main Economic Indicators - Historical Statistics, Maritime Transport, Meat Balances in OECD Member Countries, OECD Economic Surveys: Finland,* and *Trade by Commodities.*

Statistical Office of the United Nations, Publishing Service, New York, New York 10017 (800) 253-9646; *International Trade Statistics Yearbook, Statistical Yearbook,* and *Trade in Manufactures of Developing Countries.*

The World Bank, 1818 H Street, NW, Washington, D.C. 20433 (202) 477-1234; *World Tables.*

World Bureau of Metal Statistics, 27-A High Street, Ware Hert SG12 9BA, England; *World Metal Statistics.*

FINLAND - FORESTRY AND FOREST PRODUCT

Euromonitor Publications Limited, 87-88 Turnmill Street, London EC1M 5QU, England; *European Marketing Data and Statistics.*

Facts on File, 460 Park Avenue South, New York, New York 10016 (800) 443-8323; *The New Book of World Rankings.*

Federal Statistical Office, Gustav - Stresemann - Ring 11, D-6200 Wiesbaden, Germany; *Finnland.*

Food and Agricultural Organization of the United Nations (FAO) Via delle Terme di Caracalla, 00100 Rome, Italy (Telephone Number in U.S. (202) 653-2400); *The State of Food and Agriculture,* and *Yearbook of Forest Products.*

G.K. Hall and Company, 70 Lincoln Street, Boston, Massachusetts 02111 (617) 423-3990; *The World in Figures.*

International Monetary Fund, 700 Nineteenth Street, NW, Washington, D.C. 20431 (202) 623-7000; *International Financial Statistics.*

Nordic Council of Ministers, Store Strandstraede 18, DK-1255 Copenhagen K, Denmark and the Nordic Statistical Secretariat, Postboks 2550, DK-2100 Copenhagen 0, Denmark; *The Yearbook of Nordic Statistics.*

Organisation for Economic Co-operation and Development (OECD), 2 rue Andre-Pascal, 75 Paris 16, France (Telephone Number in U.S. (202) 785-6323); *Foreign Trade by Commodities, Indicators of Industrial Activity, Industrial Structure Statistics, The Pulp and Paper Industry,* and *Textile Industry in OECD Countries.*

Statistical Office of the United Nations, Publishing Service, New York, New York 10017 (800) 253-9646; *Statistical Yearbook.*

United Nations Educational, Scientific and Cultural Organization (UNESCO), 7 Place de Fontenoy, F-75700 Paris, France (Telephone Number in U.S. (212) 963-5981); *Statistical Yearbook.*

FINLAND - FRUIT PRODUCTION - See FINLAND - CROPS

FINLAND - FURNITURE AND WOOD PRODUCTS - EXPORTS AND IMPORTS

Organisation for Economic Co-operation and Development (OECD), 2 rue Andre-Pascal, 75 Paris 16, France (Telephone Number in U.S. (202) 785-6323); *Foreign Trade by Commodities,* and *Industrial Structure Statistics.*

FINLAND - GAS AND GAS LIQUIDS - See FINLAND - MINING AND MINERAL PRODUCTS

FINLAND - GENERAL INDUSTRIAL STATISTICS

Federal Statistical Office, Gustav - Stresemann - Ring 11, D-6200 Wiesbaden, Germany; *Finnland.*

Statistical Office of the United Nations, Publishing Service, New York, New York 10017 (800) 253-9646; *Industrial Statistics Yearbook.*

FINLAND - GENERAL MORTALITY

Nordic Council of Ministers, Store Strandstraede 18, DK-1255 Copenhagen K, Denmark and the Nordic Statistical Secretariat, Postboks 2550, DK-2100 Copenhagen 0, Denmark; *The Yearbook of Nordic Statistics.*

Statistical Office of the United Nations, Publishing Service, New York, New York 10017 (800) 253-9646; *Demographic Yearbook.*

World Health Organization, Office of Publications, Avenue Appia, CH-1211 Geneva 27, Switzerland (Telephone Number in U.S. (518) 436-9686); *World Health Statistics Annual.*

FINLAND - GEOGRAPHIC DATA

Facts on File, 460 Park Avenue South, New York, New York 10016 (800) 443-8323; *The New Book of World Rankings.*

Federal Statistical Office, Gustav - Stresemann - Ring 11, D-6200 Wiesbaden, Germany; *Finnland.*

FINLAND - GLASS AND GLASS PRODUCTS - PRODUCTION INDEX

Organisation for Economic Co-operation and Development (OECD), 2 rue Andre-Pascal, 75 Paris 16, France (Telephone Number in U.S. (202) 785-6323); *Indicators of Industrial Activity.*

FINLAND - GOATS - See FINLAND - LIVESTOCK AND POULTRY

FINLAND - GOLD HOLDINGS

International Monetary Fund, 700 Nineteenth Street, NW, Washington, D.C. 20431 (202) 623-7000; *International Financial Statistics.*

Statistical Office of the United Nations, Publishing Service, New York, New York 10017 (800) 253-9646; *Statistical Yearbook.*

The World Bank, 1818 H Street, NW, Washington, D.C. 20433 (202) 477-1234; *World Tables.*

FINLAND - GOLD PRODUCTION AND CONSUMPTION - See FINLAND - MINING AND MINERAL PRODUCTS

FINLAND - GOVERNMENT

G.K. Hall and Company, 70 Lincoln Street, Boston, Massachusetts 02111 (617) 423-3990; *The World in Figures.*

FINLAND - GOVERNMENT CONSUMPTION

International Monetary Fund, 700 Nineteenth Street, NW, Washington, D.C. 20431 (202) 623-7000; *International Financial Statistics*.

FINLAND - GOVERNMENT EXPENDITURES

International Monetary Fund, 700 Nineteenth Street, NW, Washington, D.C. 20431 (202) 623-7000; *Government Finance Statistics Yearbook*.

Nordic Council of Ministers, Store Strandstraede 18, DK-1255 Copenhagen K, Denmark and the Nordic Statistical Secretariat, Postboks 2550, DK-2100 Copenhagen 0, Denmark; *The Yearbook of Nordic Statistics*.

Organisation for Economic Co-operation and Development (OECD), 2 rue Andre-Pascal, 75 Paris 16, France (Telephone Number in U.S. (202) 785-6323); *Economic Outlook*.

Times Books, 201 East 50th Street, New York, New York 10022 (212) 751-2600; *The Economist Book of Vital World Statistics*.

The World Bank, 1818 H Street, NW, Washington, D.C. 20433 (202) 477-1234; *World Tables*.

FINLAND - GOVERNMENT FINANCES

International Monetary Fund, 700 Nineteenth Street, NW, Washington, D.C. 20431 (202) 623-7000; *International Financial Statistics*.

Organisation for Economic Co-operation and Development (OECD), 2 rue Andre-Pascal, 75 Paris 16, France (Telephone Number in U.S. (202) 785-6323); *Economic Outlook*.

Statistical Office of the United Nations, Publishing Service, New York, New York 10017 (800) 253-9646; *Statistical Yearbook*.

FINLAND - GOVERNMENT REVENUES

International Monetary Fund, 700 Nineteenth Street, NW, Washington, D.C. 20431 (202) 623-7000; *Government Finance Statistics Yearbook*.

Nordic Council of Ministers, Store Strandstraede 18, DK-1255 Copenhagen K, Denmark and the Nordic Statistical Secretariat, Postboks 2550, DK-2100 Copenhagen 0, Denmark; *The Yearbook of Nordic Statistics*.

Organisation for Economic Co-operation and Development (OECD), 2 rue Andre-Pascal, 75 Paris 16, France (Telephone Number in U.S. (202) 785-6323); *Economic Outlook*, and *Revenue Statistics of OECD Member Countries*.

Times Books, 201 East 50th Street, New York, New York 10022 (212) 751-2600; *The Economist Book of Vital World Statistics*.

The World Bank, 1818 H Street, NW, Washington, D.C. 20433 (202) 477-1234; *World Tables*.

FINLAND - GRAIN PRODUCTION - See FINLAND - CROPS

FINLAND - GRANTS

International Monetary Fund, 700 Nineteenth Street, NW, Washington, D.C. 20431 (202) 623-7000; *Government Finance Statistics Yearbook*.

Organisation for Economic Co-operation and Development (OECD), 2 rue Andre-Pascal, 75 Paris 16, France (Telephone Number in U.S. (202) 785-6323); *Geographical Distribution of Financial Flows to Developing Countries*.

FINLAND - GROSS DOMESTIC PRODUCT

The Economist Intelligence Unit, 111 West 57th Street, New York, New York 10019 (800) 938-4685; *The World Market Atlas*.

Facts on File, 460 Park Avenue South, New York, New York 10016 (800) 443-8323; *The New Book of World Rankings*.

G.K. Hall and Company, 70 Lincoln Street, Boston, Massachusetts 02111 (617) 423-3990; *The World in Figures*.

International Monetary Fund, 700 Nineteenth Street, NW, Washington, D.C. 20431 (202) 623-7000; *International Financial Statistics*.

Nordic Council of Ministers, Store Strandstraede 18, DK-1255 Copenhagen K, Denmark and the Nordic Statistical Secretariat, Postboks 2550, DK-2100 Copenhagen 0, Denmark; *The Yearbook of Nordic Statistics*.

Organisation for Economic Co-operation and Development (OECD), 2 rue Andre-Pascal, 75 Paris 16, France (Telephone Number in U.S. (202) 785-6323); *Economic Outlook*, *Geographical Distribution of Financial Flows to Developing Countries*, and *Revenue Statistics of OECD Member Countries*.

Statistical Office of the United Nations, Publishing Service, New York, New York 10017 (800) 253-9646; *Statistical Yearbook*.

Times Books, 201 East 50th Street, New York, New York 10022 (212) 751-2600; *The Economist Book of Vital World Statistics*.

The World Bank, 1818 H Street, NW, Washington, D.C. 20433 (202) 477-1234; *World Tables*.

FINLAND - GROSS NATIONAL PRODUCT

Organisation for Economic Co-operation and Development (OECD), 2 rue Andre-Pascal, 75 Paris 16, France (Telephone Number in U.S. (202) 785-6323); *Economic Outlook*, and *Geographical Distribution of Financial Flows to Developing Countries*.

U.S. Arms Control and Disarmament Agency, 320 Twenty-first Street, NW, Washington, D.C. 20451 (202) 647-8677; *World Military Expenditures and Arms Transfers*.

The World Bank, 1818 H Street, NW, Washington, D.C. 20433 (202) 477-1234; *World Tables*.

FINLAND - HEALTH

Facts on File, 460 Park Avenue South, New York, New York 10016 (800) 443-8323; *The New Book of World Rankings*.

Federal Statistical Office, Gustav - Stresemann - Ring 11, D-6200 Wiesbaden, Germany; *Finnland*.

G.K. Hall and Company, 70 Lincoln Street, Boston, Massachusetts 02111 (617) 423-3990; *The World in Figures*.

International Monetary Fund, 700 Nineteenth Street, NW, Washington, D.C. 20431 (202) 623-7000; *Government Finance Statistics Yearbook*.

Nordic Council of Ministers, Store Strandstraede 18, DK-1255 Copenhagen K, Denmark and the Nordic Statistical Secretariat, Postboks 2550, DK-2100 Copenhagen 0, Denmark; *The Yearbook of Nordic Statistics.*

Organisation for Economic Co-operation and Development (OECD), 2 rue Andre-Pascal, 75 Paris 16, France (Telephone Number in U.S. (202) 785-6323); *OECD Health Systems: Facts and Trends.*

Statistical Office of the United Nations, Publishing Service, New York, New York 10017 (800) 253-9646; *Statistical Yearbook.*

Times Books, 201 East 50th Street, New York, New York 10022 (212) 751-2600; *The Economist Book of Vital World Statistics.*

World Health Organization, Office of Publications, Avenue Appia, CH-1211 Geneva 27, Switzerland (Telephone Number in U.S. (518) 436-9686); *World Health Statistics Annual.*

FINLAND - HIDE PRODUCTION

Food and Agricultural Organization of the United Nations (FAO), Via delle Terme di Caracalla, 00100 Rome, Italy (Telephone Number in U.S. (202) 653-2400); *Production Yearbook.*

Organisation for Economic Co-operation and Development (OECD), 2 rue Andre-Pascal, 75 Paris 16, France (Telephone Number in U.S. (202) 785-6323); *The Footwear, Raw Hides and Skins, and Leather Industry in OECD Countries, Foreign Trade by Commodities,* and *Indicators of Industrial Activity.*

FINLAND - HIGHWAYS

G.K. Hall and Company, 70 Lincoln Street, Boston, Massachusetts 02111 (617) 423-3990; *The World in Figures.*

International Road Federation, 525 School Street, SW, Washington, D.C. 20024 (202) 554-2106; *World Road Statistics.*

Nordic Council of Ministers, Store Strandstraede 18, DK-1255 Copenhagen K, Denmark and the Nordic Statistical Secretariat, Postboks 2550, DK-2100 Copenhagen 0, Denmark; *The Yearbook of Nordic Statistics.*

Statistical Office of the United Nations, Publishing Service, New York, New York 10017 (800) 253-9646; *Annual Bulletin of Transport Statistics for Europe.*

FINLAND - HORSES - See FINLAND - LIVESTOCK AND POULTRY

FINLAND - HOURS OF WORK - See FINLAND - EMPLOYMENt

FINLAND - HOUSING AND HOUSING UNITS

Facts on File, 460 Park Avenue South, New York, New York 10016 (800) 443-8323; *The New Book of World Rankings.*

Nordic Council of Ministers, Store Strandstraede 18, DK-1255 Copenhagen K, Denmark and the Nordic Statistical Secretariat, Postboks 2550, DK-2100 Copenhagen 0, Denmark; *The Yearbook of Nordic Statistics.*

FINLAND - HOUSING CONSUMPTION

Nordic Council of Ministers, Store Strandstraede 18, DK-1255 Copenhagen K, Denmark and the Nordic Statistical Secretariat, Postboks 2550, DK-2100 Copenhagen 0, Denmark; *The Yearbook of Nordic Statistics.*

Organisation for Economic Co-operation and Development (OECD), 2 rue Andre-Pascal, 75 Paris 16, France (Telephone Number in U.S. (202) 785-6323); *The Iron and Steel Industry.*

FINLAND - HOUSING EXPENDITURES

International Monetary Fund, 700 Nineteenth Street, NW, Washington, D.C. 20431 (202) 623-7000; *Government Finance Statistics Yearbook.*

FINLAND - HYDROCHLORIC ACID PRODUCTION

Statistical Office of the United Nations, Publishing Service, New York, New York 10017 (800) 253-9646; *Statistical Yearbook.*

FINLAND - ILLITERATE POPULATION

The Economist Intelligence Unit, 111 West 57th Street, New York, New York 10019 (800) 938-4685; *The World Market Atlas.*

G.K. Hall and Company, 70 Lincoln Street, Boston, Massachusetts 02111 (617) 423-3990; *The World in Figures.*

FINLAND - IMPORTS

American Automobile Manufacturers Association, 1401 H Street, NW, Suite 900, Washington, D.C. 20005 (202) 326-5500; *World Motor Vehicle Data.*

The Economist Intelligence Unit, 111 West 57th Street, New York, New York 10019 (800) 938-4685; *The World Market Atlas.*

Food and Agricultural Organization of the United Nations (FAO) Via delle Terme di Caracalla, 00100 Rome, Italy (Telephone Number in U.S. (202) 653-2400); *The State of Food and Agriculture.*

G.K. Hall and Company, 70 Lincoln Street, Boston, Massachusetts 02111 (617) 423-3990; *The World in Figures.*

International Lead and Zinc Study Group, Metro House, 58 St. James's Street, London SW1A 1LD, England; *Lead and Zinc Statistics.*

International Monetary Fund, 700 Nineteenth Street, NW, Washington, D.C. 20431 (202) 623-7000; *Direction of Trade Statistics, Government Finance Statistics Yearbook,* and *International Financial Statistics.*

Nordic Council of Ministers, Store Strandstraede 18, DK-1255 Copenhagen K, Denmark and the Nordic Statistical Secretariat, Postboks 2550, DK-2100 Copenhagen 0, Denmark; *The Yearbook of Nordic Statistics.*

Organisation for Economic Co-operation and Development (OECD), 2 rue Andre-Pascal, 75 Paris 16, France (Telephone Number in U.S. (202) 785-6323); *Economic Outlook, The Footwear, Raw Hides and Skins, and Leather Industry in OECD Countries, Industrial Structure Statistics, The Iron and Steel Industry, Milk, Milk Products, and Egg Balances in OECD Member Countries, OECD Economic Surveys: Finland, The Pulp and Paper Industry,* and *Review of Fisheries in OECD Member Countries.*

Times Books, 201 East 50th Street, New York, New York 10022 (212) 751-2600; *The Economist Book of Vital World Statistics.*

The World Bank, 1818 H Street, NW, Washington, D.C. 20433 (202) 477-1234; *World Tables.*

FINLAND - INCOME TAXES - See FINLAND - TAXATION

FINLAND - INDUSTRIAL METALS PRODUCTION - See FINLAND - MINING AND MINERAL PRODUCTS

FINLAND - INDUSTRY

Facts on File, 460 Park Avenue South, New York, New York 10016 (800) 443-8323; *The New Book of World Rankings.*

Federal Statistical Office, Gustav - Stresemann - Ring 11, D-6200 Wiesbaden, Germany; *Finnland.*

G.K. Hall and Company, 70 Lincoln Street, Boston, Massachusetts 02111 (617) 423-3990; *The World in Figures.*

International Labour Office, I.L.O. Publications, CH-1211, Geneva 22, Switzerland; *Yearbook of Labour Statistics.*

Nordic Council of Ministers, Store Strandstraede 18, DK-1255 Copenhagen K, Denmark and the Nordic Statistical Secretariat, Postboks 2550, DK-2100 Copenhagen 0, Denmark; *The Yearbook of Nordic Statistics.*

Organisation for Economic Co-operation and Development (OECD), 2 rue Andre-Pascal, 75 Paris 16, France (Telephone Number in U.S. (202) 785-6323); *Economic Outlook, Indicators of Industrial Activity, Industrial Structure Statistics, Main Economic Indicators - Historical Statistics,* and *OECD Environmental Data.*

Statistical Office of the United Nations, Publishing Service, New York, New York 10017 (800) 253-9646; *Statistical Yearbook.*

Times Books, 201 East 50th Street, New York, New York 10022 (212) 751-2600; *The Economist Book of Vital World Statistics.*

The World Bank, 1818 H Street, NW, Washington, D.C. 20433 (202) 477-1234; *World Tables.*

World Intellectual Property Organization, 34 Chemin des Colombettes, CH-1211 Geneva 20. Switzerland; *Industrial Property Statistics.*

FINLAND - INFANT AND MATERNAL MORTALITY

Nordic Council of Ministers, Store Strandstraede 18, DK-1255 Copenhagen K, Denmark and the Nordic Statistical Secretariat, Postboks 2550, DK-2100 Copenhagen 0, Denmark; *The Yearbook of Nordic Statistics.*

Statistical Office of the United Nations, Publishing Service, New York, New York 10017 (800) 253-9646; *Demographic Yearbook,* and *Statistical Yearbook.*

Times Books, 201 East 50th Street, New York, New York 10022 (212) 751-2600; *The Economist Book of Vital World Statistics.*

The World Bank, 1818 H Street, NW, Washington, D.C. 20433 (202) 477-1234; *World Tables.*

World Health Organization, Office of Publications, Avenue Appia, CH-1211 Geneva 27, Switzerland (Telephone Number in U.S. (518) 436-9686); *World Health Statistics Annual.*

FINLAND - INTEREST RATES

Organisation for Economic Co-operation and Development (OECD), 2 rue Andre-Pascal, 75 Paris 16, France (Telephone Number in U.S. (202) 785-6323); *Economic Outlook, Financial Market Trends,* and *OECD Financial Statistics.*

FINLAND - INTERNAL TRADE

Nordic Council of Ministers, Store Strandstraede 18, DK-1255 Copenhagen K, Denmark and the Nordic Statistical Secretariat, Postboks 2550, DK-2100 Copenhagen 0, Denmark; *The Yearbook of Nordic Statistics.*

Organisation for Economic Co-operation and Development (OECD), 2 rue Andre-Pascal, 75 Paris 16, France (Telephone Number in U.S. (202) 785-6323); *Main Economic Indicators - Historical Statistics.*

FINLAND - INTERNATIONAL FINANCE

Organisation for Economic Co-operation and Development (OECD), 2 rue Andre-Pascal, 75 Paris 16, France (Telephone Number in U.S. (202) 785-6323); *Economic Outlook, Financial Market Trends,* and *Tourism Policy and International Tourism in OECD Member Countries.*

FINLAND - INTERNATIONAL LIQUIDITY

International Monetary Fund, 700 Nineteenth Street, NW, Washington, D.C. 20431 (202) 623-7000; *International Financial Statistics.*

Organisation for Economic Co-operation and Development (OECD), 2 rue Andre-Pascal, 75 Paris 16, France (Telephone Number in U.S. (202) 785-6323); *Economic Outlook,* and *Financial Market Trends.*

FINLAND - INTERNATIONAL RESERVES EXCLUDING GOLD

Statistical Office of the United Nations, Publishing Service, New York, New York 10017 (800) 253-9646; *Statistical Yearbook.*

The World Bank, 1818 H Street, NW, Washington, D.C. 20433 (202) 477-1234; *World Tables.*

FINLAND - INTERNATIONAL STATISTICS

Organisation for Economic Co-operation and Development (OECD), 2 rue Andre-Pascal, 75 Paris 16, France (Telephone Number in U.S. (202) 785-6323); *Financial Market Trends.*

FINLAND - INVESTMENTS

International Monetary Fund, 700 Nineteenth Street, NW, Washington, D.C. 20431 (202) 623-7000; *International Financial Statistics.*

Organisation for Economic Co-operation and Development (OECD), 2 rue Andre-Pascal, 75 Paris 16, France (Telephone Number in U.S. (202) 785-6323); *Economic Outlook, Financial Market Trends, Industrial Structure Statistics, The Iron and Steel Industry,* and *Textile Industry in OECD Countries.*

FINLAND - IRON ORE PRODUCTION AND CONSUMPTION - See FINLAND - MINING AND MINERAL PRODUCTS

FINLAND - LABOR FORCE

Facts on File, 460 Park Avenue South, New York, New York 10016 (800) 443-8323; *The New Book of World Rankings.*

Food and Agricultural Organization of the United Nations (FAO) Via delle Terme di Caracalla, 00100 Rome, Italy (Telephone Number in U.S. (202) 653-2400); *The State of Food and Agriculture.*

G.K. Hall and Company, 70 Lincoln Street, Boston, Massachusetts 02111 (617) 423-3990; *The World in Figures.*

Nordic Council of Ministers, Store Strandstraede 18, DK-1255 Copenhagen K, Denmark and the Nordic Statistical Secretariat, Postboks 2550, DK-2100 Copenhagen 0, Denmark; *The Yearbook of Nordic Statistics.*

Organisation for Economic Co-operation and Development (OECD), 2 rue Andre-Pascal, 75 Paris 16, France (Telephone Number in U.S. (202) 785-6323); *Economic Outlook, The Iron and Steel Industry, Main Economic Indicators - Historical Statistics, Maritime Transport, OECD Economic Surveys: Finland, OECD Employment Outlook,* and *Textile Industry in OECD Countries.*

Times Books, 201 East 50th Street, New York, New York 10022 (212) 751-2600; *The Economist Book of Vital World Statistics.*

The World Bank, 1818 H Street, NW, Washington, D.C. 20433 (202) 477-1234; *World Tables.*

FINLAND - LABOR PRODUCTIVITY

International Labour Office, I.L.O. Publications, CH-1211, Geneva 22, Switzerland; *Yearbook of Labour Statistics.*

Organisation for Economic Co-operation and Development (OECD), 2 rue Andre-Pascal, 75 Paris 16, France (Telephone Number in U.S. (202) 785-6323); *Economic Outlook,* and *OECD Employment Outlook.*

FINLAND - LAND USE

Euromonitor Publications Limited, 87-88 Turnmill Street, London EC1M 5QU, England; *European Marketing Data and Statistics.*

Food and Agricultural Organization of the United Nations (FAO), Via delle Terme di Caracalla, 00100 Rome, Italy (Telephone Number in U.S. (202) 653-2400); *Production Yearbook.*

G.K. Hall and Company, 70 Lincoln Street, Boston, Massachusetts 02111 (617) 423-3990; *The World in Figures.*

FINLAND - LEAD AND LEAD ORE - See FINLAND - MINING AND MINERAL PRODUCTS

FINLAND - LEATHER - PRODUCTION INDEX

Organisation for Economic Co-operation and Development (OECD), 2 rue Andre-Pascal, 75 Paris 16, France (Telephone Number in U.S. (202) 785-6323); *Indicators of Industrial Activity.*

FINLAND - LEATHER AND FOOTWEAR - EXPORTS AND IMPORTS

Organisation for Economic Co-operation and Development (OECD), 2 rue Andre-Pascal, 75 Paris 16, France (Telephone Number in U.S. (202) 785-6323); *The Footwear, Raw Hides and Skins, and Leather Industry in OECD Countries.*

FINLAND - LIBRARIES

Euromonitor Publications Limited, 87-88 Turnmill Street, London EC1M 5QU, England; *European Marketing Data and Statistics.*

Facts on File, 460 Park Avenue South, New York, New York 10016 (800) 443-8323; *The New Book of World Rankings.*

Nordic Council of Ministers, Store Strandstraede 18, DK-1255 Copenhagen K, Denmark and the Nordic Statistical Secretariat, Postboks 2550, DK-2100 Copenhagen 0, Denmark; *The Yearbook of Nordic Statistics.*

United Nations Educational, Scientific and Cultural Organization (UNESCO), 7 Place de Fontenoy, F-75700 Paris, France (Telephone Number in U.S. (212) 963-5981); *Statistical Yearbook.*

FINLAND - LIGNITE PRODUCTION - See FINLAND - MINING AND MINERAL PRODUCTS

FINLAND - LIVESTOCK AND POULTRY

Euromonitor Publications Limited, 87-88 Turnmill Street, London EC1M 5QU, England; *European Marketing Data and Statistics.*

Facts on File, 460 Park Avenue South, New York, New York 10016 (800) 443-8323; *The New Book of World Rankings.*

Food and Agricultural Organization of the United Nations (FAO), Via delle Terme di Caracalla, 00100 Rome, Italy (Telephone Number in U.S. (202) 653-2400); *Production Yearbook,* and *The State of Food and Agriculture.*

G.K. Hall and Company, 70 Lincoln Street, Boston, Massachusetts 02111 (617) 423-3990; *The World in Figures.*

Nordic Council of Ministers, Store Strandstraede 18, DK-1255 Copenhagen K, Denmark and the Nordic Statistical Secretariat, Postboks 2550, DK-2100 Copenhagen 0, Denmark; *The Yearbook of Nordic Statistics.*

Organisation for Economic Co-operation and Development (OECD), 2 rue Andre-Pascal, 75 Paris 16, France (Telephone Number in U.S. (202) 785-6323); *Economic Accounts for Agriculture,* and *Meat Balances in OECD Member Countries.*

Statistical Office of the United Nations, Publishing Service, New York, New York 10017 (800) 253-9646; *Statistical Yearbook.*

FINLAND - LIVING LEVELS

G.K. Hall and Company, 70 Lincoln Street, Boston, Massachusetts 02111 (617) 423-3990; *The World in Figures.*

Organisation for Economic Co-operation and Development (OECD), 2 rue Andre-Pascal, 75 Paris 16, France (Telephone Number in U.S. (202) 785-6323); *Economic Outlook.*

Times Books, 201 East 50th Street, New York, New York 10022 (212) 751-2600; *The Economist Book of Vital World Statistics.*

FINLAND - MACHINERY - PRODUCTION INDEX

Organisation for Economic Co-operation and Development (OECD), 2 rue Andre-Pascal, 75 Paris 16, France (Telephone Number in U.S. (202) 785-6323); *Indicators of Industrial Activity.*

FINLAND - MAGNESIUM PRODUCTION AND CONSUMPTION - See FINLAND - MINING AND MINERAL PRODUCTS

FINLAND - MAIL - NUMBER OF PIECES SENT OR RECEIVED

Nordic Council of Ministers, Store Strandstraede 18, DK-1255 Copenhagen K, Denmark and the Nordic Statistical Secretariat, Postboks 2550, DK-2100 Copenhagen 0, Denmark; *The Yearbook of Nordic Statistics.*

Statistical Office of the United Nations, Publishing Service, New York, New York 10017 (800) 253-9646; *Statistical Yearbook.*

FINLAND - MANGANESE PRODUCTION AND CONSUMPTION - See FINLAND - MINING AND MINERAL PRODUCTS

FINLAND - MANUFACTURING

American Automobile Manufacturers Association, 1401 H Street, NW, Suite 900, Washington, D.C. 20005 (202) 326-5500; *World Motor Vehicle Data.*

Facts on File, 460 Park Avenue South, New York, New York 10016 (800) 443-8323; *The New Book of World Rankings.*

G.K. Hall and Company, 70 Lincoln Street, Boston, Massachusetts 02111 (617) 423-3990; *The World in Figures.*

Nordic Council of Ministers, Store Strandstraede 18, DK-1255 Copenhagen K, Denmark and the Nordic Statistical Secretariat, Postboks 2550, DK-2100 Copenhagen 0, Denmark; *The Yearbook of Nordic Statistics.*

Organisation for Economic Co-operation and Development (OECD), 2 rue Andre-Pascal, 75 Paris 16, France (Telephone Number in U.S. (202) 785-6323); *Foreign Trade by Commodities, Indicators of Industrial Activity, Industrial Structure Statistics,* and *OECD Economic Surveys: Finland.*

Statistical Office of the United Nations, Publishing Service, New York, New York 10017 (800) 253-9646; *Statistical Yearbook.*

Times Books, 201 East 50th Street, New York, New York 10022 (212) 751-2600; *The Economist Book of Vital World Statistics.*

The World Bank, 1818 H Street, NW, Washington, D.C. 20433 (202) 477-1234; *World Tables.*

FINLAND - MARRIAGE RATES

Facts on File, 460 Park Avenue South, New York, New York 10016 (800) 443-8323; *The New Book of World Rankings.*

Nordic Council of Ministers, Store Strandstraede 18, DK-1255 Copenhagen K, Denmark and the Nordic Statistical Secretariat, Postboks 2550, DK-2100 Copenhagen 0, Denmark; *The Yearbook of Nordic Statistics.*

Statistical Office of the United Nations, Publishing Service, New York, New York 10017 (800) 253-9646; *Demographic Yearbook,* and *Statistical Yearbook.*

FINLAND - MEAT PRODUCTION - See FINLAND - LIVESTOCK AND POULTRY

FINLAND - MERCHANT SHIPPING

G.K. Hall and Company, 70 Lincoln Street, Boston, Massachusetts 02111 (617) 423-3990; *The World in Figures.*

Lloyd's Register of Shipping, 17 Battery Place, New York, New York 10004 (212) 425-8050; *Register of Ships.*

Nordic Council of Ministers, Store Strandstraede 18, DK-1255 Copenhagen K, Denmark and the Nordic Statistical Secretariat, Postboks 2550, DK-2100 Copenhagen 0, Denmark; *The Yearbook of Nordic Statistics.*

Organisation for Economic Co-operation and Development (OECD), 2 rue Andre-Pascal, 75 Paris 16, France (Telephone Number in U.S. (202) 785-6323); *Maritime Transport.*

Statistical Office of the United Nations, Publishing Service, New York, New York 10017 (800) 253-9646; *Annual Bulletin of Transport Statistics for Europe,* and *Statistical Yearbook.*

Times Books, 201 East 50th Street, New York, New York 10022 (212) 751-2600; *The Economist Book of Vital World Statistics.*

U.S. Department of Transportation, Maritime Administration, 400 Seventh Street, SW, Washington, D.C. 20590 (202) 366-5807; *A Statistical Analysis of the World's Merchant Fleets.*

FINLAND - MERCURY PRODUCTION AND CONSUMPTION - See FINLAND - MINING AND MINERAL PRODUCTs

FINLAND - MILITARY

G.K. Hall and Company, 70 Lincoln Street, Boston, Massachusetts 02111 (617) 423-3990; *The World in Figures.*

The International Institute for Strategic Studies, 23 Tavistock Street, London WC2E 7NQ, England; *The Military Balance.*

Nordic Council of Ministers, Store Strandstraede 18, DK-1255 Copenhagen K, Denmark and the Nordic Statistical Secretariat, Postboks 2550, DK-2100 Copenhagen 0, Denmark; *The Yearbook of Nordic Statistics.*

U.S. Arms Control and Disarmament Agency, 320 Twenty-first Street, NW, Washington, D.C. 20451 (202) 647-8677; *World Military Expenditures and Arms Transfers.*

FINLAND - MILK - See FINLAND - DAIRY PRODUCTS

FINLAND - MINING AND MINERAL PRODUCTS

Commodity Research Bureau, Incorporated, 75 Wall Street, New York, New York 10005 (212) 504-7754; *Commodity Year Book.*

Facts on File, 460 Park Avenue South, New York, New York 10016 (800) 443-8323; *The New Book of World Rankings.*

G.K. Hall and Company, 70 Lincoln Street, Boston, Massachusetts 02111 (617) 423-3990; *The World in Figures.*

International Lead and Zinc Study Group, Metro House, 58 St. James's Street, London SW1A 1LD, England; *Lead and Zinc Statistics.*

Nordic Council of Ministers, Store Strandstraede 18, DK-1255 Copenhagen K, Denmark and the Nordic Statistical Secretariat, Postboks 2550, DK-2100 Copenhagen 0, Denmark; *The Yearbook of Nordic Statistics.*

Organisation for Economic Co-operation and Development (OECD), 2 rue Andre-Pascal, 75 Paris 16, France (Telephone Number in U.S. (202) 785-6323); *Coal Information, Energy Statistics of OECD Countries, Indicators of Industrial Activity, Foreign Trade by Commodities, Industrial Structure Statistics, The Iron and Steel Industry, OECD Economic Surveys: Finland,* and *The Non-Ferrous Metals Industry.*

Statistical Office of the United Nations, Publishing Service, New York, New York 10017 (800) 253-9646; *Statistical Yearbook.*

World Bureau of Metal Statistics, 27-A High Street, Ware Hert SG12 9BA, England; *World Metal Statistics.*

FINLAND - MOLYBDENUM AND MOLYBDENUM ORE - See FINLAND - MINING AND MINERAL PRODUCTS

FINLAND - MONEY AND CREDIT

Organisation for Economic Cooperation and Development (OECD), 2 rue Andre-Pascal, 75 Paris 16, France (Telephone Number in U.S. (202) 785-6323); *OECD Economic Surveys: Finland.*

FINLAND - MONEY EXCHANGE RATE

International Monetary Fund, 700 Nineteenth Street, NW, Washington, D.C. 20431 (202) 623-7000; *International Financial Statistics.*

Organisation for Economic Co-operation and Development (OECD), 2 rue Andre-Pascal, 75 Paris 16, France (Telephone Number in U.S. (202) 785-6323); *Economic Outlook, Financial Market Trends,* and *Tourism Policy and International Tourism in OECD Member Countries.*

Statistical Office of the United Nations, Publishing Service, New York, New York 10017 (800) 253-9646; *Statistical Yearbook.*

FINLAND - MONEY RATES - MARKET

Organisation for Economic Co-operation and Development (OECD), 2 rue Andre-Pascal, 75 Paris 16, France (Telephone Number in U.S. (202) 785-6323); *Economic Outlook,* and *Financial Market Trends.*

FINLAND - MONEY RESERVES

Organisation for Economic Co-operation and Development (OECD), 2 rue Andre-Pascal, 75 Paris 16, France (Telephone Number in U.S. (202) 785-6323); *Economic Outlook,* and *Financial Market Trends.*

FINLAND - MONEY SUPPLY

Federal Statistical Office, Gustav - Stresemann - Ring 11, D-6200 Wiesbaden, Germany; *Finnland.*

G.K. Hall and Company, 70 Lincoln Street, Boston, Massachusetts 02111 (617) 423-3990; *The World in Figures.*

International Monetary Fund, 700 Nineteenth Street, NW, Washington, D.C. 20431 (202) 623-7000; *International Financial Statistics.*

Nordic Council of Ministers, Store Strandstraede 18, DK-1255 Copenhagen K, Denmark and the Nordic Statistical Secretariat, Postboks 2550, DK-2100 Copenhagen 0, Denmark; *The Yearbook of Nordic Statistics.*

Organisation for Economic Co-operation and Development (OECD), 2 rue Andre-Pascal, 75 Paris 16, France (Telephone Number in U.S. (202) 785-6323); *Economic Outlook.*

Statistical Office of the United Nations, Publishing Service, New York, New York 10017 (800) 253-9646; *Statistical Yearbook.*

The World Bank, 1818 H Street, NW, Washington, D.C. 20433 (202) 477-1234; *World Tables.*

FINLAND - MONUMENTS AND HISTORICAL SITES

United Nations Educational, Scientific and Cultural Organization (UNESCO), 7 Place de Fontenoy, F-75700 Paris, France (Telephone Number in U.S. (212) 963-5981); *Statistical Yearbook.*

FINLAND - MOTION PICTURES

Statistical Office of the United Nations, Publishing Service, New York, New York 10017 (800) 253-9646; *Statistical Yearbook.*

United Nations Educational, Scientific and Cultural Organization (UNESCO), 7 Place de Fontenoy, F-75700 Paris, France (Telephone Number in U.S. (212) 963-5981); *Statistical Yearbook.*

FINLAND - MOTOR VEHICLE PRODUCTION

American Automobile Manufacturers Association, 1401 H Street, NW, Suite 900, Washington, D.C. 20005 (202) 326-5500; *World Motor Vehicle Data.*

Organisation for Economic Co-operation and Development (OECD), 2 rue Andre-Pascal, 75 Paris 16, France (Telephone Number in U.S. (202) 785-6323); *Foreign Trade by Commodities,* and *Indicators of Industrial Activity.*

Statistical Office of the United Nations, Publishing Service, New York, New York 10017 (800) 253-9646; *Statistical Yearbook.*

FINLAND - MOTOR VEHICLE TAXES - See FINLAND - TAXATION

FINLAND - MOTOR VEHICLES IN USE

American Automobile Manufacturers Association, 1401 H Street, NW, Suite 900, Washington, D.C. 20005 (202) 326-5500; *World Motor Vehicle Data.*

G.K. Hall and Company, 70 Lincoln Street, Boston, Massachusetts 02111 (617) 423-3990; *The World in Figures.*

International Road Federation, 525 School Street, SW, Washington, D.C. 20024 (202) 554-2106; *World Road Statistics.*

Nordic Council of Ministers, Store Strandstraede 18, DK-1255 Copenhagen K, Denmark and the Nordic Statistical Secretariat, Postboks 2550, DK-2100 Copenhagen 0, Denmark; *The Yearbook of Nordic Statistics.*

Statistical Office of the United Nations, Publishing Service, New York, New York 10017 (800) 253-9646; *Statistical Yearbook.*

Times Books, 201 East 50th Street, New York, New York 10022 (212) 751-2600; *The Economist Book of Vital World Statistics.*

FINLAND - MUSEUMS

Euromonitor Publications Limited, 87-88 Turnmill Street, London EC1M 5QU, England; *European Marketing Data and Statistics.*

Facts on File, 460 Park Avenue South, New York, New York 10016 (800) 443-8323; *The New Book of World Rankings.*

Nordic Council of Ministers, Store Strandstraede 18, DK-1255 Copenhagen K, Denmark and the Nordic Statistical Secretariat, Postboks 2550, DK-2100 Copenhagen 0, Denmark; *The Yearbook of Nordic Statistics.*

United Nations Educational, Scientific and Cultural Organization (UNESCO), 7 Place de Fontenoy, F-75700 Paris, France (Telephone Number in U.S. (212) 963-5981); *Statistical Yearbook.*

FINLAND - NATALITY - See BIRTH RATE

FINLAND - NATIONAL ACCOUNTS

Federal Statistical Office, Gustav - Stresemann - Ring 11, D-6200 Wiesbaden, Germany; *Finnland.*

International Monetary Fund, 700 Nineteenth Street, NW, Washington, D.C. 20431 (202) 623-7000; *International Financial Statistics.*

Nordic Council of Ministers, Store Strandstraede 18, DK-1255 Copenhagen K, Denmark and the Nordic Statistical Secretariat, Postboks 2550, DK-2100 Copenhagen 0, Denmark; *The Yearbook of Nordic Statistics.*

Organisation for Economic Co-operation and Development (OECD), 2 rue Andre-Pascal, 75 Paris 16, France (Telephone Number in U.S. (202) 785-6323); *Economic Outlook.*

Statistical Office of the United Nations, Publishing Service, New York, New York 10017 (800) 253-9646; *National Accounts Statistics*, and *Statistical Yearbook.*

FINLAND - NATIONAL INCOME

Facts on File, 460 Park Avenue South, New York, New York 10016 (800) 443-8323; *The New Book of World Rankings.*

G.K. Hall and Company, 70 Lincoln Street, Boston, Massachusetts 02111 (617) 423-3990; *The World in Figures.*

Nordic Council of Ministers, Store Strandstraede 18, DK-1255 Copenhagen K, Denmark and the Nordic Statistical Secretariat, Postboks 2550, DK-2100 Copenhagen 0, Denmark; *The Yearbook of Nordic Statistics.*

Organisation for Economic Co-operation and Development (OECD), 2 rue Andre-Pascal, 75 Paris 16, France (Telephone Number in U.S. (202) 785-6323); *Economic Outlook.*

Statistical Office of the United Nations, Publishing Service, New York, New York 10017 (800) 253-9646; *Statistical Yearbook.*

FINLAND - NATIONAL PRODUCT

Facts on File, 460 Park Avenue South, New York, New York 10016 (800) 443-8323; *The New Book of World Rankings.*

Organisation for Economic Co-operation and Development (OECD), 2 rue Andre-Pascal, 75 Paris 16, France (Telephone Number in U.S. (202) 785-6323); *Economic Outlook.*

Statistical Office of the United Nations, Publishing Service, New York, New York 10017 (800) 253-9646; *Statistical Yearbook.*

FINLAND - NATURAL GAS PRODUCTION - See FINLAND - MINING AND MINERAL PRODUCTS

FINLAND - NEWSPAPER PRODUCTION - See FINLAND - FORESTRY AND FOREST PRODUCTS

FINLAND - NEWSPRINT - See FINLAND - FORESTRY AND FOREST PRODUCTS

FINLAND - NICKEL AND NICKEL ORE - See FINLAND - MINING AND MINERAL PRODUCTS

FINLAND - NITRIC ACID PRODUCTION

Organisation for Economic Co-operation and Development (OECD), 2 rue Andre-Pascal, 75 Paris 16, France (Telephone Number in U.S. (202) 785-6323); *Indicators of Industrial Activity.*

Statistical Office of the United Nations, Publishing Service, New York, New York 10017 (800) 253-9646; *Statistical Yearbook.*

FINLAND - OATS PRODUCTION - See FINLAND - CROPS

FINLAND - OCCUPATIONS - See FINLAND - LABOR FORCE

FINLAND - OIL PRODUCING CROPS

Organisation for Economic Co-operation and Development (OECD), 2 rue Andre-Pascal, 75 Paris 16, France (Telephone Number in U.S. (202) 785-6323); *Foreign Trade by Commodities.*

FINLAND - PAPER - See FINLAND - FORESTRY AND FOREST PRODUCTS

FINLAND - PATENTS

Nordic Council of Ministers, Store Strandstraede 18, DK-1255 Copenhagen K, Denmark and the Nordic Statistical Secretariat, Postboks 2550, DK-2100 Copenhagen 0, Denmark; *The Yearbook of Nordic Statistics.*

Statistical Office of the United Nations, Publishing Service, New York, New York 10017 (800) 253-9646; *Statistical Yearbook.*

World Intellectual Property Organization, 34 Chemin des Colombettes, CH-1211 Geneva 20. Switzerland; *Industrial Property Statistics.*

FINLAND - PEANUT PRODUCTION - See FINLAND - CROPS

FINLAND - PERIODICALS

United Nations Educational, Scientific and Cultural Organization (UNESCO), 7 Place de Fontenoy, F-75700 Paris, France (Telephone Number in U.S. (212) 963-5981); *Statistical Yearbook.*

FINLAND - PESTICIDE USE

Food and Agricultural Organization of the United Nations (FAO) Via delle Terme di Caracalla, 00100 Rome, Italy (Telephone Number in U.S. (202) 653-2400); *The State of Food and Agriculture.*

FINLAND - PETROLEUM INDUSTRY

Euromonitor Publications Limited, 87-88 Turnmill Street, London EC1M 5QU, England; *European Marketing Data and Statistics.*

Facts on File, 460 Park Avenue South, New York, New York 10016 (800) 443-8323; *The New Book of World Rankings.*

Food and Agricultural Organization of the United Nations (FAO) Via delle Terme di Caracalla, 00100 Rome, Italy (Telephone Number in U.S. (202) 653-2400); *The State of Food and Agriculture.*

G.K. Hall and Company, 70 Lincoln Street, Boston, Massachusetts 02111 (617) 423-3990; *The World in Figures.*

Organisation for Economic Co-operation and Development (OECD), 2 rue Andre-Pascal, 75 Paris 16, France (Telephone Number in U.S. (202) 785-6323); *Energy Statistics of OECD Countries, Foreign Trade by Commodities, Indicators of Industrial Activity,* and *Oil and Gas*

Information.

Statistical Office of the United Nations, Publishing Service, New York, New York 10017 (800) 253-9646; *Statistical Yearbook.*

Organisation for Economic Co-operation and Development (OECD), 2 rue Andre-Pascal, 75 Paris 16, France (Telephone Number in U.S. (202) 785-6323);

FINLAND - PHOSPHATES AND PHOSPHATE ROCK - See FINLAND - MINING AND MINERAL PRODUCTS

FINLAND - PIG-IRON AND FERRO-ALLOYS PRODUCTION - See FINLAND - MINING AND MINERAL PRODUCTS

FINLAND - PIGS - See FINLAND - LIVESTOCK AND POULTRY

FINLAND - PLASTIC AND RESIN PRODUCTION

Organisation for Economic Co-operation and Development (OECD), 2 rue Andre-Pascal, 75 Paris 16, France (Telephone Number in U.S. (202) 785-6323); *Foreign Trade by Commodities.*

Statistical Office of the United Nations, Publishing Service, New York, New York 10017 (800) 253-9646; *Statistical Yearbook.*

FINLAND - PLATINUM PRODUCTION - See FINLAND - MINING AND MINERAL PRODUCTS

FINLAND - POPULATION

The Economist Intelligence Unit, 111 West 57th Street, New York, New York 10019 (800) 938-4685; *The World Market Atlas.*

Euromonitor Publications Limited, 87-88 Turnmill Street, London EC1M 5QU, England; *European Marketing Data and Statistics.*

Facts on File, 460 Park Avenue South, New York, New York 10016 (800) 443-8323; *The New Book of World Rankings.*

Federal Statistical Office, Gustav - Stresemann - Ring 11, D-6200 Wiesbaden, Germany; *Finnland.*

Food and Agricultural Organization of the United Nations (FAO), Via delle Terme di Caracalla, 00100 Rome, Italy (Telephone Number in U.S. (202) 653-2400); *Production Yearbook.*

G.K. Hall and Company, 70 Lincoln Street, Boston, Massachusetts 02111 (617) 423-3990; *The World in Figures.*

International Labour Office, I.L.O. Publications, CH-1211, Geneva 22, Switzerland; *Yearbook of Labour Statistics.*

Nordic Council of Ministers, Store Strandstraede 18, DK-1255 Copenhagen K, Denmark and the Nordic Statistical Secretariat, Postboks 2550, DK-2100 Copenhagen 0, Denmark; *The Yearbook of Nordic Statistics.*

Statistical Office of the United Nations, Publishing Service, New York, New York 10017 (800) 253-9646; *Demographic Yearbook,* and *Statistical Yearbook.*

Times Books, 201 East 50th Street, New York, New York 10022 (212) 751-2600; *The Economist Book of Vital World Statistics.*

United Nations Educational, Scientific and Cultural Organization (UNESCO), 7 Place de Fontenoy, F-75700 Paris, France (Telephone Number in U.S. (212) 963-5981); *Statistical Yearbook.*

U.S. Arms Control and Disarmament Agency, 320 Twenty-first Street, NW, Washington, D.C. 20451 (202) 647-8677; *World Military Expenditures and Arms Transfers.*

World Health Organization, Office of Publications, Avenue Appia, CH-1211 Geneva 27, Switzerland (Telephone Number in U.S. (518) 436-9686); *World Health Statistics Annual.*

FINLAND - POST OFFICES

Facts on File, 460 Park Avenue South, New York, New York 10016 (800) 443-8323; *The New Book of World Rankings.*

FINLAND - POTATO PRODUCTION - See FINLAND - CROPS

FINLAND - POULTRY - See FINLAND - LIVESTOCK AND POULTRY

FINLAND - POWER PRODUCTION INDUSTRY

Statistical Office of the United Nations, Publishing Service, New York, New York 10017 (800) 253-9646; *Statistical Yearbook.*

FINLAND - PRICES

Facts on File, 460 Park Avenue South, New York, New York 10016 (800) 443-8323; *The New Book of World Rankings.*

Federal Statistical Office, Gustav - Stresemann - Ring 11, D-6200 Wiesbaden, Germany; *Finnland.*

Food and Agricultural Organization of the United Nations (FAO), Via delle Terme di Caracalla, 00100 Rome, Italy (Telephone Number in U.S. (202) 653-2400); *Production Yearbook,* and *The State of Food and Agriculture.*

G.K. Hall and Company, 70 Lincoln Street, Boston, Massachusetts 02111 (617) 423-3990; *The World in Figures.*

International Labour Office, I.L.O. Publications, CH-1211, Geneva 22, Switzerland; *Yearbook of Labour Statistics.*

International Lead and Zinc Study Group, Metro House, 58 St. James's Street, London SW1A 1LD, England; *Lead and Zinc Statistics.*

International Monetary Fund, 700 Nineteenth Street, NW, Washington, D.C. 20431 (202) 623-7000; *International Financial Statistics.*

Nordic Council of Ministers, Store Strandstraede 18, DK-1255 Copenhagen K, Denmark and the Nordic Statistical Secretariat, Postboks 2550, DK-2100 Copenhagen 0, Denmark; *The Yearbook of Nordic Statistics.*

Organisation for Economic Co-operation and Development (OECD), 2 rue Andre-Pascal, 75 Paris 16, France (Telephone Number in U.S. (202) 785-6323); *Economic Outlook, Indicators of Industrial Activity, The Iron and Steel Industry,*and *The Pulp and Paper Industry.*

World Bureau of Metal Statistics, 27-A High Street, Ware Hert SG12 9BA, England; *World Metal Statistics.*

FINLAND - PRINTING AND WRITING PAPER - See FINLAND - FORESTRY AND FOREST PRODUCTS

FINLAND - PRODUCER PRICES

Organisation for Economic Co-operation and Development (OECD), 2 rue Andre-Pascal, 75 Paris 16, France (Telephone Number in U.S.

(202) 785-6323); *Main Economic Indicators - Historical Statistics.*

FINLAND - PRODUCTION

American Automobile Manufacturers Association, 1401 H Street, NW, Suite 900, Washington, D.C. 20005 (202) 326-5500; *World Motor Vehicle Data.*

Facts on File, 460 Park Avenue South, New York, New York 10016 (800) 443-8323; *The New Book of World Rankings.*

G.K. Hall and Company, 70 Lincoln Street, Boston, Massachusetts 02111 (617) 423-3990; *The World in Figures.*

International Lead and Zinc Study Group, Metro House, 58 St. James's Street, London SW1A 1LD, England; *Lead and Zinc Statistics.*

Organisation for Economic Co-operation and Development (OECD), 2 rue Andre-Pascal, 75 Paris 16, France (Telephone Number in U.S. (202) 785-6323); *Economic Outlook, The Footwear, Raw Hides and Skins, and Leather Industry in OECD Countries, Indicators of Industrial Activity, Industrial Structure Statistics, The Iron and Steel Industry, Meat Balances in OECD Member Countries, Milk, Milk Products, and Egg Balances in OECD Member Countries, The Non-Ferrous Metals Industry, The Pulp and Paper Industry,* and *Textile Industry in OECD Countries.*

FINLAND - PRODUCTIVITY

Organisation for Economic Co-operation and Development (OECD), 2 rue Andre-Pascal, 75 Paris 16, France (Telephone Number in U.S. (202) 785-6323); *Economic Outlook.*

FINLAND - PROPERTY TAXES - See FINLAND - TAXATION

FINLAND - PUBLIC CONSUMPTION FUND

Organisation for Economic Co-operation and Development (OECD), 2 rue Andre-Pascal, 75 Paris 16, France (Telephone Number in U.S. (202) 785-6323); *Revenue Statistics of OECD Member Countries.*

FINLAND - PUBLIC EXPENDITURES

Organisation for Economic Co-operation and Development (OECD), 2 rue Andre-Pascal, 75 Paris 16, France (Telephone Number in U.S. (202) 785-6323); *Revenue Statistics of OECD Member Countries.*

FINLAND - PUBLIC FINANCE

Facts on File, 460 Park Avenue South, New York, New York 10016 (800) 443-8323; *The New Book of World Rankings.*

Federal Statistical Office, Gustav - Stresemann - Ring 11, D-6200 Wiesbaden, Germany; *Finnland.*

Nordic Council of Ministers, Store Strandstraede 18, DK-1255 Copenhagen K, Denmark and the Nordic Statistical Secretariat, Postboks 2550, DK-2100 Copenhagen 0, Denmark; *The Yearbook of Nordic Statistics.*

Organisation for Economic Co-operation and Development (OECD), 2 rue Andre-Pascal, 75 Paris 16, France (Telephone Number in U.S. (202) 785-6323); *Revenue Statistics of OECD Member Countries.*

FINLAND - PUBLIC REVENUES

Organisation for Economic Co-operation and Development (OECD), 2 rue Andre-Pascal, 75 Paris 16, France (Telephone Number in U.S. (202) 785-6323); *Revenue Statistics of OECD Member Countries.*

FINLAND - RADIO BROADCASTING - See FINLAND - BROADCASTING

FINLAND - RADIO RECEIVER PRODUCTION

Statistical Office of the United Nations, Publishing Service, New York, New York 10017 (800) 253-9646; *Statistical Yearbook.*

FINLAND - RAILWAYS

Euromonitor Publications Limited, 87-88 Turnmill Street, London EC1M 5QU, England; *European Marketing Data and Statistics.*

G.K. Hall and Company, 70 Lincoln Street, Boston, Massachusetts 02111 (617) 423-3990; *The World in Figures.*

Jane's Information Group, Sentinel House, 163 Brighton Road, Coulsdon, Surrey CR5 2NH, England (Telephone Number in U.S. (703) 683-3700); *Jane's World Railways.*

Nordic Council of Ministers, Store Strandstraede 18, DK-1255 Copenhagen K, Denmark and the Nordic Statistical Secretariat, Postboks 2550, DK-2100 Copenhagen 0, Denmark; *The Yearbook of Nordic Statistics.*

Statistical Office of the United Nations, Publishing Service, New York, New York 10017 (800) 253-9646; *Annual Bulletin of Transport Statistics for Europe,* and *Statistical Yearbook.*

FINLAND - RAPESEED PRODUCTION - See FINLAND - CROPS

FINLAND - RELIGION

Facts on File, 460 Park Avenue South, New York, New York 10016 (800) 443-8323; *The New Book of World Rankings.*

FINLAND - RENT PRICES

International Labour Office, I.L.O. Publications, CH-1211, Geneva 22, Switzerland; *Yearbook of Labour Statistics.*

FINLAND - RETAIL TRADE

G.K. Hall and Company, 70 Lincoln Street, Boston, Massachusetts 02111 (617) 423-3990; *The World in Figures.*

Statistical Office of the United Nations, Publishing Service, New York, New York 10017 (800) 253-9646; *Statistical Yearbook.*

FINLAND - RICE PRODUCTION - See FINLAND - CROPS

FINLAND - ROOT AND TUBER PRODUCTION - See FINLAND - CROPS

FINLAND - ROUNDWOOD PRODUCTION - See FINLAND - FORESTRY AND FOREST PRODUCTS

FINLAND - RUBBER PRODUCTION

Facts on File, 460 Park Avenue South, New York, New York 10016 (800) 443-8323; *The New Book of World Rankings.*

Organisation for Economic Co-operation and Development (OECD), 2 rue Andre-Pascal, 75 Paris 16, France (Telephone Number in U.S. (202) 785-6323); *Foreign Trade by Commodities.*

FINLAND - SALT PRODUCTION - See FINLAND - MINING AND MINERAL PRODUCTS

FINLAND - SAWNWOOD PRODUCTION - See FINLAND - FORESTRY AND FOREST PRODUCTS

FINLAND - SCIENTISTS AND TECHNICIANS

Statistical Office of the United Nations, Publishing Service, New York, New York 10017 (800) 253-9646; *Statistical Yearbook.*

FINLAND - SENIOR CITIZENS

Facts on File, 460 Park Avenue South, New York, New York 10016 (800) 443-8323; *The New Book of World Rankings.*

FINLAND - SERVICES INDUSTRY EMPLOYMENT - MALE AND FEMALE

Organisation for Economic Co-operation and Development (OECD), 2 rue Andre-Pascal, 75 Paris 16, France (Telephone Number in U.S. (202) 785-6323); *OECD Employment Outlook.*

FINLAND - SHEEP - See FINLAND - LIVESTOCK AND POULTRY

FINLAND - SHIPBUILDING - PRODUCTION INDEX

Organisation for Economic Co-operation and Development (OECD), 2 rue Andre-Pascal, 75 Paris 16, France (Telephone Number in U.S. (202) 785-6323); *Indicators of Industrial Activity.*

FINLAND - SILVER PRODUCTION AND CONSUMPTION - See FINLAND - MINING AND MINERAL PRODUCTS

FINLAND - SOCIAL DATA

Facts on File, 460 Park Avenue South, New York, New York 10016 (800) 443-8323; *The New Book of World Rankings.*

G.K. Hall and Company, 70 Lincoln Street, Boston, Massachusetts 02111 (617) 423-3990; *The World in Figures.*

FINLAND - SOCIAL SECURITY

International Monetary Fund, 700 Nineteenth Street, NW, Washington, D.C. 20431 (202) 623-7000; *Government Finance Statistics Yearbook.*

Nordic Council of Ministers, Store Strandstraede 18, DK-1255 Copenhagen K, Denmark and the Nordic Statistical Secretariat, Postboks 2550, DK-2100 Copenhagen 0, Denmark; *The Yearbook of Nordic Statistics.*

Organisation for Economic Co-operation and Development (OECD), 2 rue Andre-Pascal, 75 Paris 16, France (Telephone Number in U.S. (202) 785-6323); *Revenue Statistics of OECD Member Countries.*

FINLAND - SOCIOECONOMIC DATA

Organisation for Economic Co-operation and Development (OECD), 2 rue Andre-Pascal, 75 Paris 16, France (Telephone Number in U.S. (202) 785-6323); *Economic Outlook.*

FINLAND - STEEL - INDUSTRIAL CONSUMPTION - See FINLAND - MINING AND MINERAL PRODUCTS

FINLAND - STOCKS - COMMODITY - MARKET PRICE - INDEXES

Food and Agricultural Organization of the United Nations (FAO) Via delle Terme di Caracalla, 00100 Rome, Italy (Telephone Number in U.S. (202) 653-2400); *The State of Food and Agriculture.*

International Lead and Zinc Study Group, Metro House, 58 St. James's Street, London SW1A 1LD, England; *Lead and Zinc Statistics.*

Statistical Office of the United Nations, Publishing Service, New York, New York 10017 (800) 253-9646; *Statistical Yearbook.*

World Bureau of Metal Statistics, 27-A High Street, Ware Hert SG12 9BA, England; *World Metal Statistics.*

FINLAND - SUGAR - See FINLAND - CROPS

FINLAND - SULPHUR AND SULPHURIC ACID - See FINLAND - MINING AND MINERAL PRODUCTS

FINLAND - TAXATION

International Monetary Fund, 700 Nineteenth Street, NW, Washington, D.C. 20431 (202) 623-7000; *Government Finance Statistics Yearbook.*

International Road Federation, 525 School Street, SW, Washington, D.C. 20024 (202) 554-2106; *World Road Statistics.*

Nordic Council of Ministers, Store Strandstraede 18, DK-1255 Copenhagen K, Denmark and the Nordic Statistical Secretariat, Postboks 2550, DK-2100 Copenhagen 0, Denmark; *The Yearbook of Nordic Statistics.*

Organisation for Economic Co-operation and Development (OECD), 2 rue Andre-Pascal, 75 Paris 16, France (Telephone Number in U.S. (202) 785-6323); *Revenue Statistics of OECD Member Countries.*

The World Bank, 1818 H Street, NW, Washington, D.C. 20433 (202) 477-1234; *World Tables.*

FINLAND - TELEGRAPH SERVICE

Nordic Council of Ministers, Store Strandstraede 18, DK-1255 Copenhagen K, Denmark and the Nordic Statistical Secretariat, Postboks 2550, DK-2100 Copenhagen 0, Denmark; *The Yearbook of Nordic Statistics.*

Statistical Office of the United Nations, Publishing Service, New York, New York 10017 (800) 253-9646; *Statistical Yearbook.*

FINLAND - TELEPHONES IN USE

American Telephone and Telegraph Company, 26 Parsippany Road, Whippany, New Jersey 07981 (800) 338-4038; *The World's Telephones.*

G.K. Hall and Company, 70 Lincoln Street, Boston, Massachusetts 02111 (617) 423-3990; *The World in Figures.*

Nordic Council of Ministers, Store Strandstraede 18, DK-1255 Copenhagen K, Denmark and the Nordic Statistical Secretariat, Postboks 2550, DK-2100 Copenhagen 0, Denmark; *The Yearbook of Nordic Statistics.*

Statistical Office of the United Nations, Publishing Service, New York, New York 10017 (800) 253-9646; *Statistical Yearbook.*

FINLAND - TELEVISION BROADCASTING - See FINLAND - BROADCASTING

FINLAND - TELEVISION RECEIVER PRODUCTION

Statistical Office of the United Nations, Publishing Service, New York, New York 10017 (800) 253-9646; *Statistical Yearbook.*

FINLAND - TEXTILE INDUSTRY

G.K. Hall and Company, 70 Lincoln Street, Boston, Massachusetts 02111 (617) 423-3990; *The World in Figures.*

Organisation for Economic Co-operation and Development (OECD), 2 rue Andre-Pascal, 75 Paris 16, France (Telephone Number in U.S. (202) 785-6323); *Foreign Trade by Commodities, Indicators of Industrial Activity, Industrial Structure Statistics,* and *Textile Industry in OECD Countries.*

Statistical Office of the United Nations, Publishing Service, New York, New York 10017 (800) 253-9646; *Statistical Yearbook.*

FINLAND - THEATRE

United Nations Educational, Scientific and Cultural Organization (UNESCO), 7 Place de Fontenoy, F-75700 Paris, France (Telephone Number in U.S. (212) 963-5981); *Statistical Yearbook.*

FINLAND - TIN - See FINLAND - MINING AND MINERAL PRODUCTS

FINLAND - TIRE (MOTOR VEHICLE) PRODUCTION

Statistical Office of the United Nations, Publishing Service, New York, New York 10017 (800) 253-9646; *Statistical Yearbook.*

FINLAND - TOBACCO PRODUCTION

Euromonitor Publications Limited, 87-88 Turnmill Street, London EC1M 5QU, England; *European Marketing Data and Statistics.*

Facts on File, 460 Park Avenue South, New York, New York 10016 (800) 443-8323; *The New Book of World Rankings.*

Organisation for Economic Co-operation and Development (OECD), 2 rue Andre-Pascal, 75 Paris 16, France (Telephone Number in U.S. (202) 785-6323); *Foreign Trade by Commodities, Indicators of Industrial Activity,* and *Industrial Structure Statistics.*

Statistical Office of the United Nations, Publishing Service, New York, New York 10017 (800) 253-9646; *Statistical Yearbook.*

The World Bank, 1818 H Street, NW, Washington, D.C. 20433 (202) 477-1234; *World Tables.*

FINLAND - TOURISM

Euromonitor Publications Limited, 87-88 Turnmill Street, London EC1M 5QU, England; *European Marketing Data and Statistics.*

Facts on File, 460 Park Avenue South, New York, New York 10016 (800) 443-8323; *The New Book of World Rankings.*

Federal Statistical Office, Gustav - Stresemann - Ring 11, D-6200 Wiesbaden, Germany; *Finnland.*

G.K. Hall and Company, 70 Lincoln Street, Boston, Massachusetts 02111 (617) 423-3990; *The World in Figures.*

Organisation for Economic Co-operation and Development (OECD), 2 rue Andre-Pascal, 75 Paris 16, France (Telephone Number in U.S. (202) 785-6323); *Tourism Policy and International Tourism in OECD Member Countries.*

Statistical Office of the United Nations, Publishing Service, New York, New York 10017 (800) 253-9646; *Statistical Yearbook.*

Times Books, 201 East 50th Street, New York, New York 10022 (212) 751-2600; *The Economist Book of Vital World Statistics.*

World Tourism Organization, Calle Capitan Haya 42, E-28020 Madrid, Spain; *Yearbook of Tourism Statistics.*

FINLAND - TRACTORS IN USE

Statistical Office of the United Nations, Publishing Service, New York, New York 10017 (800) 253-9646; *Statistical Yearbook.*

FINLAND - TRADE - See FINLAND - FOREIGN TRADE

FINLAND - TRADEMARKS AND SERVICE MARKS

Statistical Office of the United Nations, Publishing Service, New York, New York 10017 (800) 253-9646; *Statistical Yearbook.*

World Intellectual Property Organization, 34 Chemin des Colombettes, CH-1211 Geneva 20. Switzerland; *Industrial Property Statistics.*

FINLAND - TRANSPORTATION AND COMMUNICATIONS

Facts on File, 460 Park Avenue South, New York, New York 10016 (800) 443-8323; *The New Book of World Rankings.*

Federal Statistical Office, Gustav - Stresemann - Ring 11, D-6200 Wiesbaden, Germany; *Finnland.*

G.K. Hall and Company, 70 Lincoln Street, Boston, Massachusetts 02111 (617) 423-3990; *The World in Figures.*

Nordic Council of Ministers, Store Strandstraede 18, DK-1255 Copenhagen K, Denmark and the Nordic Statistical Secretariat, Postboks 2550, DK-2100 Copenhagen 0, Denmark; *The Yearbook of Nordic Statistics.*

FINLAND - TUNGSTEN PRODUCTION AND CONSUMPTION - See FINLAND - MINING AND MINERAL PRODUCTS

FINLAND - UNEMPLOYMENT

Euromonitor Publications Limited, 87-88 Turnmill Street, London EC1M 5QU, England; *European Marketing Data and Statistics.*

International Labour Office, I.L.O. Publications, CH-1211, Geneva 22, Switzerland; *Yearbook of Labour Statistics.*

Nordic Council of Ministers, Store Strandstraede 18, DK-1255 Copenhagen K, Denmark and the Nordic Statistical Secretariat, Postboks 2550, DK-2100 Copenhagen 0, Denmark; *The Yearbook of Nordic Statistics.*

Organisation for Economic Co-operation and Development (OECD), 2 rue Andre-Pascal, 75 Paris 16, France (Telephone Number in U.S. (202) 785-6323); *Economic Outlook, Labour Force Statistics, OECD Economic Surveys: Finland,* and *OECD Employment Outlook.*

Statistical Office of the United Nations, Publishing Service, New York, New York 10017 (800) 253-9646; *Statistical Yearbook.*

FINLAND - URANIUM PRODUCTION AND CONSUMPTION - See FINLAND - MINING AND MINERAL PRODUCTS

FINLAND - VANADIUM AND VANADIUM ORE - See FINLAND - MINING AND MINERAL PRODUCTS

FINLAND - VITAL STATISTICS

G.K. Hall and Company, 70 Lincoln Street, Boston, Massachusetts 02111 (617) 423-3990; *The World in Figures.*

Nordic Council of Ministers, Store Strandstraede 18, DK-1255 Copenhagen K, Denmark and the Nordic Statistical Secretariat, Postboks 2550, DK-2100 Copenhagen 0, Denmark; *The Yearbook of Nordic Statistics.*

Statistical Office of the United Nations, Publishing Service, New York, New York 10017 (800) 253-9646; *Statistical Yearbook.*

World Health Organization, Office of Publications, Avenue Appia, CH-1211 Geneva 27, Switzerland (Telephone Number in U.S. (518) 436-9686); *World Health Statistics Annual.*

FINLAND - WAGES

Euromonitor Publications Limited, 87-88 Turnmill Street, London EC1M 5QU, England; *European Marketing Data and Statistics.*

Federal Statistical Office, Gustav - Stresemann - Ring 11, D-6200 Wiesbaden, Germany; *Finnland.*

G.K. Hall and Company, 70 Lincoln Street, Boston, Massachusetts 02111 (617) 423-3990; *The World in Figures.*

International Labour Office, I.L.O. Publications, CH-1211, Geneva 22, Switzerland; *Yearbook of Labour Statistics.*

Nordic Council of Ministers, Store Strandstraede 18, DK-1255 Copenhagen K, Denmark and the Nordic Statistical Secretariat, Postboks 2550, DK-2100 Copenhagen 0, Denmark; *The Yearbook of Nordic Statistics.*

Organisation for Economic Co-operation and Development (OECD), 2 rue Andre-Pascal, 75 Paris 16, France (Telephone Number in U.S. (202) 785-6323); *Economic Outlook, Industrial Structure Statistics,* and *Main Economic Indicators - Historical Statistics.*

Statistical Office of the United Nations, Publishing Service, New York, New York 10017 (800) 253-9646; *Statistical Yearbook.*

FINLAND - WATERWAYS IN USE

Organisation for Economic Co-operation and Development (OECD), 2 rue Andre-Pascal, 75 Paris 16, France (Telephone Number in U.S. (202) 785-6323); *Maritime Transport.*

Statistical Office of the United Nations, Publishing Service, New York, New York 10017 (800) 253-9646; *Annual Bulletin of Transport Statistics for Europe.*

FINLAND - WEATHER

Facts on File, 460 Park Avenue South, New York, New York 10016 (800) 443-8323; *The New Book of World Rankings.*

G.K. Hall and Company, 70 Lincoln Street, Boston, Massachusetts 02111 (617) 423-3990; *The World in Figures.*

Nordic Council of Ministers, Store Strandstraede 18, DK-1255 Copenhagen K, Denmark and the Nordic Statistical Secretariat, Postboks 2550, DK-2100 Copenhagen 0, Denmark; *The Yearbook of Nordic Statistics.*

FINLAND - WELFARE

International Monetary Fund, 700 Nineteenth Street, NW, Washington, D.C. 20431 (202) 623-7000; *Government Finance Statistics Yearbook.*

Nordic Council of Ministers, Store Strandstraede 18, DK-1255 Copenhagen K, Denmark and the Nordic Statistical Secretariat, Postboks 2550, DK-2100 Copenhagen 0, Denmark; *The Yearbook of Nordic Statistics.*

FINLAND - WHEAT - See FINLAND - CROPS

FINLAND - WHOLESALE PRICES

Nordic Council of Ministers, Store Strandstraede 18, DK-1255 Copenhagen K, Denmark and the Nordic Statistical Secretariat, Postboks 2550, DK-2100 Copenhagen 0, Denmark; *The Yearbook of Nordic Statistics.*

Statistical Office of the United Nations, Publishing Service, New York, New York 10017 (800) 253-9646; *Statistical Yearbook.*

FINLAND - WHOLESALE TRADE

Statistical Office of the United Nations, Publishing Service, New York, New York 10017 (800) 253-9646; *Statistical Yearbook.*

FINLAND - WINE PRODUCTION

Facts on File, 460 Park Avenue South, New York, New York 10016 (800) 443-8323; *The New Book of World Rankings.*

Statistical Office of the United Nations, Publishing Service, New York, New York 10017 (800) 253-9646; *Statistical Yearbook.*

FINLAND - WOOD - See FINLAND - FORESTRY AND FOREST PRODUCTS

FINLAND - WOOL PRODUCTION

Facts on File, 460 Park Avenue South, New York, New York 10016 (800) 443-8323; *The New Book of World Rankings.*

Organisation for Economic Co-operation and Development (OECD), 2 rue Andre-Pascal, 75 Paris 16, France (Telephone Number in U.S. (202) 785-6323); *Economic Accounts for Agriculture.*

FINLAND - YARN PRODUCTION

Organisation for Economic Co-operation and Development (OECD), 2 rue Andre-Pascal, 75 Paris 16, France (Telephone Number in U.S. (202) 785-6323); *Foreign Trade by Commodities,* and *Textile Industry in OECD Countries.*

Statistical Office of the United Nations, Publishing Service, New York, New York 10017 (800) 253-9646; *Statistical Yearbook.*

FINLAND - ZINC AND ZINC ORE - See FINLAND - MINING AND MINERAL PRODUCTS

FINLAND - ZOOS AND BOTANICAL GARDENS

United Nations Educational, Scientific and Cultural Organization (UNESCO), 7 Place de Fontenoy, F-75700 Paris, France (Telephone Number in U.S. (212) 963-5981); *Statistical Yearbook.*

FIRE DEPARTMENTS - See PUBLIC SAFETY

FIRE INSURANCE

U.S. Department of Commerce, International Trade Administration, Fourteenth Street between Constitution Avenue and E Street, NW, Washington, D.C. 20230 (202) 482-3809; *U.S Industrial Outlook.*

FIREARMS

National Sporting Goods Association, Lake Center Plaza Building, 1699 Wall Street, Mt. Prospect, Illinois 60611 (708) 439-4000; *The Sporting Goods Market in 1993.*

U.S. Department of Health and Human Services, National Center for Health Statistics, 3700 East-West Highway, Hyattsville, Maryland 20782 (301) 436-8500; *Vital Statistics of the United States, Monthly Vital Statistics Report, Advance Data from Vital and Health Statistics,* and unpublished data.

U.S. Department of Justice, Bureau of Justice Statistics, 633 Indiana Avenue, NW, Washington, D.C. 20531 (800) 732-3277; *Criminal Victimization in the U.S.* and *Sourcebook of Criminal Justice Statistics.*

FIREARMS - DEATHS

U.S. Department of Health and Human Services, National Center for Health Statistics, 3700 East-West Highway, Hyattsville, Maryland 20782 (301) 436-8500; *Vital Statistics of the United States, Monthly Vital Statistics Report, Advance Data from Vital and Health Statistics,* and unpublished data.

FIRES AND PROPERTY LOSS

Insurance Information Institute, 110 William Street, New York, New York 10038 (212) 669-9200; *Insurance Facts.*

National Fire Protection Association, One Batterymarch Park, Quincy, Massachusetts 02269 (617) 770-3000; *NFPA Reports on Fire Loss,* in NFPA Journal.

FIRES AND PROPERTY LOSSES - ACCIDENTAL DEATHS

National Fire Protection Association, One Batterymarch Park, Quincy, Massachusetts 02269 (617) 770-3000; *NFPA Reports on Fire Loss,* in NFPA Journal.

U.S. Department of Health and Human Services, National Center for Health Statistics, 3700 East-West Highway, Hyattsville, Maryland 20782 (301) 436-8500; *Vital Statistics of the United States.*

FIRMS - See BUSINESS ENTERPRISE and Individual Types of Business And Industry

FISH - See also Individual Species

FISH - CANNING AND PRESERVING

U.S. Department of Commerce, National Oceanic and Atmospheric Administration, National Marine Fisheries Service, 1335 East-West Highway, Silver Spring, Maryland 20910 (301) 427-2239; *Fisheries of the United States.*

FISH - CATCH - QUANTITY AND VALUE

U.S. Department of Commerce, National Oceanic and Atmospheric Administration, National Marine Fisheries Service, 1335 East-West Highway, Silver Spring, Maryland 20910 (301) 427-2239; *Fisheries of the United States,* and *Fishery Statistics of the United States.*

FISH - CONSUMPTION

U.S. Department of Agriculture, Economic Research Service, Fourteenth Street and Independence Avenue, SW, Washington, D.C. 20005-4789 (202) 219-1504; *Food Consumption, Prices, and Expenditures,* and unpublished data.

FISH - FOREIGN TRADE

U.S. Department of Commerce, Bureau of the Census, Suitland, Maryland 20233 (301) 763-4040; *U.S. Merchandise Trade: Exports, General Imports, and Imports for Consumption,* and *U.S. Merchandise Trade.*

U.S. Department of Commerce, National Oceanic and Atmospheric Administration, National Marine Fisheries Service, 1335 East-West Highway, Silver Spring, Maryland 20910 (301) 427-2239; *Fisheries of the United States,* and *Fishery Statistics of the United States.*

FISH - PRICES

U.S. Department of Commerce, National Oceanic and Atmospheric Administration, National Marine Fisheries Service, 1335 East-West Highway, Silver Spring, Maryland 20910 (301) 427-2239; *Fisheries of the United States,* and *Fishery Statistics of the United States.*

U.S. Department of Labor, Bureau of Labor Statistics, Two Massachusetts Avenue, NE, Washington, D.C. 20212 (202) 606-7828; *Monthly Labor Review,* and *CPI Detailed Report.*

FISH - PRODUCTION AND VALUE - PROCESSED PRODUCTS

U.S. Department of Commerce, National Oceanic and Atmospheric Administration, National Marine Fisheries Service, 1335 East-West Highway, Silver Spring, Maryland 20910 (301) 427-2239; *Fisheries of the United States.*

FISH - SUPPLY

U.S. Department of Commerce, National Oceanic and Atmospheric Administration, National Marine Fisheries Service, 1335 East-West Highway, Silver Spring, Maryland 20910 (301) 427-2239; *Fisheries of the United States,* and *Fishery Statistics of the United States.*

FISH MEAL AND OILS

U.S. Department of Commerce, National Oceanic and Atmospheric Administration, National Marine Fisheries Service, 1335 East-West Highway, Silver Spring, Maryland 20910 (301) 427-2239; *Fisheries of the United States.*

FISH, MEAT, AND EGGS - EXPENDITURES

U.S. Department of Labor, Bureau of Labor Statistics, Two Massachusetts Avenue, NE, Washington, D.C. 20212 (202) 606-7828; *Consumer Expenditure in 1992,* and unpublished data.

FISHING AND HUNTING

National Sporting Goods Association, Lake Center Plaza Building, 1699 Wall Street, Mount Prospect, Illinois 60056 (708) 439-4000; *Sports Participation in 1992,* and *The Sporting Goods Market in 1993.*

U.S. Department of Agriculture, Forest Service, Fourteenth Street and Independence Avenue, SW, Washington, D.C. 20250 (202) 720-3760; unpublished data.

U.S. Department of the Interior, Bureau of Land Management, C Street between Eighteenth and Nineteenth Streets, Washington, D.C. 20240 (202) 208-3435; *Public Land Statistics*.

U.S. Department of the Interior, Fish and Wildlife Service, C Street between Eighteenth and Nineteenth Streets, NW, Washington, D.C. 20240 (202) 208-5634; *Federal Aid in Fish and Wildlife Restoration*, and *National Survey of Fishing, Hunting, and Wildlife - Associated - Recreation*.

FISHING, COMMERCIAL - CATCH, QUANTITY, VALUE

U.S. Department of Commerce, National Oceanic and Atmospheric Administration, National Marine Fisheries Service, 1335 East-West Highway, Silver Spring, Maryland 20910 (301) 427-2239; *Fisheries of the United States*, and *Fishery Statistics of the United States*.

FISHING, COMMERCIAL - CATCH, QUANTITY, VALUE - BY MAJOR PORT

U.S. Department of Commerce, National Oceanic and Atmospheric Administration, National Marine Fisheries Service, 1335 East-West Highway, Silver Spring, Maryland 20910 (301) 427-2239; *Fisheries of the United States*.

FISHING, COMMERCIAL - EMPLOYEES

U.S. Department of Commerce, National Oceanic and Atmospheric Administration, National Marine Fisheries Service, 1335 East-West Highway, Silver Spring, Maryland 20910 (301) 427-2239; *Fisheries of the United States*, and *Fishery Statistics of the United States*.

FISHING, COMMERCIAL - ESTABLISHMENTS

U.S. Department of Commerce, National Oceanic and Atmospheric Administration, National Marines Fisheries Service, 1335 East-West Highway, Silver Spring, Maryland 20910 (301) 427-2239; *Fisheries of the United States*, and *Fishery Statistics of the United States*.

FISHING, COMMERCIAL - FOREIGN TRADE

U.S. Department of Commerce, Bureau of the Census, Suitland, Maryland 20233 (301) 763-4040; *U.S. Merchandise Trade: Exports, General Imports, and Imports for Consumption*.

U.S. Department of Commerce, National Oceanic and Atmospheric Administration, National Marine Fisheries Service, 1335 East-West Highway, Silver Spring, Maryland 20910 (301) 427-2239; *Fishery Statistics of the United States*, and *Fisheries of the United States*.

FISHING, COMMERCIAL - PRODUCTS

U.S. Department of Commerce, National Oceanic and Atmospheric Administration, National Marine Fisheries Service, 1335 East-West Highway, Silver Spring, Maryland 20910 (301) 427-2239; *Fisheries of the United States*, and *Fishery Statistics of the United States*.

FLOODS

U.S. Department of Commerce, National Oceanic and Atmospheric Administration, National Climatic Data Center, Federal Building, Asheville, North Carolina 28801 (704) 259-2850; *Storm Data*.

FLORIDA - See also STATE DATA (FOR INDIVIDUAL STATES)

Florida - Primary Statistics Sources

Bureau of Economic and Business Research, University of Florida, Gainesville, Florida 32611 (904) 392-0171; *Florida Statistical Abstract*.

National Data Consultants, P.O. Box 6381, Athens, Georgia 30604 (706) 548-8460; *Florida County Perspectives*.

Florida - State Data Centers

Florida State Data Center, Executive Office of the Governor, Office of Planning and Budgeting, The Capitol, Room 1604, Tallahassee, Florida 32399, Ms. Valerie Jugger (904) 487-2814.

Center for the Study of Population, Institute for Social Research, 654 Bellemy Building, Florida State University, Tallahassee, Florida 32306-4063, Dr. Ike Eberstein, (904) 644-1762.

State Library of Florida, R.A. Gray Building, Tallahassee, Florida 32399-0250, Ms. Lisa Close, (904) 487-2651.

Bureau of Economic Analysis, Florida Department of Commerce, 107 West Gaines Street, 315 Collins Building, Tallahassee, Florida 32399-2000, Mr. Nick Leslie (904) 487-2971.

FLORISTS

U.S. Department of Commerce, Bureau of the Census, Suitland, Maryland 20233 (301) 763-4040; *Census of Retail Trade*, and *County Business Patterns*.

FLOUNDER

U.S. Department of Commerce, National Oceanic and Atmospheric Administration, National Marine Fisheries Service, 1335 East-West Highway, Silver Spring, Maryland 20910 (301) 427-2239; *Fisheries of the United States*, and *Fishery Statistics of the United States*.

FLOUR - CONSUMPTION - See also GRAIN-MILL PRODUCTS

U.S. Department of Agriculture, Economic Research Service, Fourteenth Street and Independence Avenue, SW, Washington, D.C. 20005-4789 (202) 219-1504; *Food Consumption, Prices, and Expenditures*, and unpublished data.

FLOWERS

The National Gardening Association, 180 Flynn Avenue, Burlington, Vermont 05401 (802) 863-1308; *National Gardening Survey*.

U.S. Department of Agriculture, Economic Research Service, Fourteenth Street and Independence Avenue, SW, Washington, D.C. 20005-4789 (202) 219-1504; *Agricultural Outlook*, and unpublished data.

FLU

U.S. Department of Health and Human Services, National Center for Health Statistics, 3700 East-West Highway, Hyattsville, Maryland 20782 (301) 436-8500; *Monthly Vital Statistics Report*, *Vital Statistics of the United States*, and unpublished data.

FLUORSPAR

U.S. Department of the Interior, Bureau of Mines, 810 Seventh Street, NW, Washington, D.C. 20241 (202) 501-9649; *Annual Reports*, and *Mineral Commodity Summaries*.

FOOD - CAR LOADINGS

Association of American Railroads, American Railroads Building, 50 F Street, NW, Washington, D.C. 20001 (202) 639-2100; *Freight*

Commodity Statistics.

FOOD - COMMERCIAL VEGETABLES

U.S. Department of Agriculture, National Agricultural Statistics Service, Fourteenth Street and Independence Avenue, SW, Washington, D.C. 20250 (202) 219-1504; *Agricultural Statistics,* and *Vegetables.*

FOOD - CONSUMPTION

U.S. Department of Agriculture, Economic Research Service, Fourteenth Street and Independence Avenue, SW, Washington, D.C. 20005-4789 (202) 219-1504; *Food Consumption, Prices, and Expenditures,* and unpublished data.

U.S. Department of Agriculture, Foreign Agricultural Service, Fourteenth Street and Independence Avenue, SW, Washington, D.C. 20250 (202) 720-3448; *World Livestock Situation,* and *World Poultry Situation.*

FOOD - EXPENDITURES

U.S. Department of Agriculture, Economic Research Service, Fourteenth Street and Independence Avenue, SW, Washington, D.C. 20005-4789 (202) 219-1504; *Food Cost Review, Agricultural Statistics,* and *Food Review.*

U.S. Department of Labor, Bureau of Labor Statistics, Two Massachusetts Avenue, NE, Washington, D.C. 20212 (202) 606-7828; *Consumer Expenditures in 1992,* and *Monthly Labor Review.*

FOOD - EXPENDITURES - PERCENT OF PERSONAL CONSUMPTION EXPENDITURES - FOREIGN COUNTRIES

U.S. Department of Agriculture, Economic Research Service, Fourteenth Street and Independence Avenue, SW, Washington, D.C. 20005-4789 (202) 219-1504; based on data from the United Nations, New York, New York; *National Accounts Statistics.*

FOOD - FISH PRODUCTS

U.S. Department of Labor, Bureau of Labor Statistics, Two Massachusetts Avenue, NE, Washington, D.C. 20212 (202) 606-7828; *Consumer Expenditures in 1992.*

FOOD - FOOD COSTS

American Chamber of Commerce Researchers' Association, c/o American Chamber of Conference Executives, 4232 King Street, Alexandria, Virginia 22302 (703) 998-0072; *Cost of Living Index.*

U.S. Department of Agriculture, Human Nutrition Information Service, Hyattsville, Maryland 20782 (301) 436-7725; *Adm. 329.*

U.S. Department of Labor, Bureau of Labor Statistics, Two Massachusetts Avenue, NE, Washington, D.C. 20212 (202) 606-7828; *CPI Detailed Report.*

FOOD - FOREIGN AID

U.S. Department of Commerce. Bureau of Economic Analysis, Fourteenth Street between Constitution Avenue and E Street, NW, Washington, D.C. 20230 (202) 606-9900; press releases and unpublished data.

FOOD - FOREIGN PRODUCTION

Food and Agricultural Organization of the United Nations (FAO), Via delle Terme di Caracalla, 00100 Rome, Italy (Telephone Number in U.S. (202) 653-2400); *AGRISTAT Database.*

FOOD - PRICES - See also Individual Commodities

U.S. Department of Agriculture, Economic Research Service, Fourteenth Street and Independence Avenue, SW, Washington, D.C. 20005-4789 (202) 219-1504; *Food Cost Review.*

U.S. Department of Agriculture, Human Nutrition Information Service, Hyattsville, Maryland 20782 (301) 436-7725; *Adm. 329.*

U.S. Department of Commerce, Bureau of Economic Analysis, Fourteenth Street between Constitution Avenue and E Street, NW, Washington, D.C. 20230 (202) 606-9900; *The National Income and Product Accounts of the U.S.,* and *Survey of Current Business.*

U.S. Department of Labor, Bureau of Labor Statistics, Two Massachusetts Avenue, NE, Washington, D.C. 20212 (202) 606-7828; *CPI Detailed Report, Handbook of Labor Statistics,* and *Monthly Labor Review.*

FOOD AND KINDRED PRODUCTS - MANUFACTURING - CAPITAL

The Conference Board, 845 Third Avenue, New York New York 10022 (212) 759-0900; *Quarterly Survey of Capital Appropriations.*

U.S. Department of Commerce, Bureau of Economic Analysis, Fourteenth Street between Constitution Avenue and E Street, NW, Washington, D.C. 20230 (202) 606-9900; *Survey of Current Business.*

U.S. Department of Commerce, Bureau of the Census, Suitland, Maryland 20233 (301) 763-4040; *Census of Manufactures, Annual Survey of Manufactures, Plant and Equipment Expenditures and Plans,* and *Current Industrial Reports.*

FOOD AND KINDRED PRODUCTS - MANUFACTURING - EARNINGS

Forbes, Incorporated, 60 Fifth Avenue, New York, New York 10011 (212) 620-2200; *Forbes Annual Report on American Industry.*

U.S. Department of Commerce, Bureau of the Census, Suitland, Maryland 20233 (301) 763-4040; *Annual Survey of Manufactures, Census of Manufactures,* and *County Business Patterns.*

U.S. Department of Labor, Bureau of Labor Statistics, Two Massachusetts Avenue, NE, Washington, D.C. 20212 (202) 606-7828; *Employment and Earnings,* and Bulletins 2370 and 2429.

FOOD AND KINDRED PRODUCTS - MANUFACTURING - EMPLOYEES

U.S. Department of Agriculture, Economic Research Service, Fourteenth Street and Independence Avenue, SW, Washington, D.C. 20005-4789 (202) 219-1504; unpublished data.

U.S. Department of Commerce, Bureau of the Census, Suitland, Maryland 20233 (301) 763-4040; *Annual Survey of Manufactures, Census of Manufactures,* and *County Business Patterns.*

U.S. Department of Commerce, International Trade Administration, Fourteenth Street between Constitution Avenue and E Street, NW, Washington, D.C. 20230 (202) 482-5487; *U.S. Industrial Outlook.*

U.S. Department of Labor, Bureau of Labor Statistics, Two Massachusetts Avenue, NE, Washington, D.C. 20212 (202) 606-7828;

Employment and Earnings, Bulletins 2370 and 2429, and *Monthly Labor Review*.

FOOD AND KINDRED PRODUCTS - MANUFACTURING - ESTABLISHMENTS

U.S. Department of Commerce, Bureau of the Census, Suitland, Maryland 20233 (301) 763-4040; *Annual Survey of Manufacturing, Census of Manufactures*, and *County Business Patterns*.

FOOD AND KINDRED PRODUCTS - MANUFACTURING - FOREIGN TRADE

U.S. Department of Commerce, Bureau of the Census, Suitland, Maryland 20233 (301) 763-4040; *U.S. Merchandise Trade*.

FOOD AND KINDRED PRODUCTS - MANUFACTURING - GROSS DOMESTIC PRODUCT

U.S. Department of Commerce. Bureau of Economic Analysis, Fourteenth Street between Constitution Avenue and E Street, NW, Washington, D.C. 20230 (202) 606-9900; *Survey of Current Business*, and *The National Income and Product Accounts of the United States*.

FOOD AND KINDRED PRODUCTS - MANUFACTURING - MERGERS AND ACQUISITIONS

Securities Data Company, 1180 Raymond Boulevard, Newark, New Jersey 07102 (201) 622-3100; *Merger and Corporate Transactions Database*.

FOOD AND KINDRED PRODUCTS - MANUFACTURING - OCCUPATIONAL SAFETY

U.S. Department of Labor, Bureau of Labor Statistics, Two Massachusetts Avenue, NE, Washington, D.C. 20212 (202) 606-7828; *Occupational Injuries and Illnesses in the United States by Industry*.

FOOD AND KINDRED PRODUCTS - MANUFACTURING - PATENTS

U.S. Department of Commerce, Patent and Trademark Office, 2011 Crystal Drive, Arlington, Virginia 22202 (703) 305-8341; *Patenting Trends in the United States, State Country Report*.

FOOD AND KINDRED PRODUCTS - MANUFACTURING - POLLUTION ABATEMENT

U.S. Department of Commerce, Bureau of the Census, Suitland, Maryland 20233 (301) 763-4040; *Current Industrial Reports*.

U.S. Department of Commerce. Bureau of Economic Analysis, Fourteenth Street between Constitution Avenue and E Street, NW, Washington, D.C. 20230 (202) 606-9900; *Survey of Current Business*.

FOOD AND KINDRED PRODUCTS - MANUFACTURING - PRODUCTIVITY

Board of Governors of the Federal Reserve System, Twentieth Street and Constitution Avenue, NW, Washington, D.C. 20551 (202) 452-3000; *Federal Reserve Bulletin*.

U.S. Department of Labor, Bureau of Labor Statistics, Two Massachusetts Avenue, NE, Washington, D.C. 20212 (202) 606-7828; *Productivity Measures for Selected Industries and Government Services*, and unpublished data.

FOOD AND KINDRED PRODUCTS - MANUFACTURING - PROFITS

Executive Office of the President, Council of Economic Advisors, Old Executive Office Building, Washington, D.C 20500 (202) 395-5084; *Economic Report of the President*.

Federal Trade Commission, Pennsylvania Avenue at Sixth Street, NW, Washington, D.C. 20580 (202) 326-2222; *Quarterly Financial Report for Manufacturing, Mining, and Trade Corporations*.

Forbes, Incorporated, 60 Fifth Avenue, New York, New York 10011 (212) 620-2200; *Forbes Annual Report on American Industry*.

U.S. Department of Commerce. Bureau of Economic Analysis, Fourteenth Street between Constitution Avenue and E Street, NW, Washington, D.C. 20230 (202) 606-9900; *Survey of Current Business*, and *The National Income and Product Account of the United States*.

U.S. Department of Commerce, Bureau of the Census, Suitland, Maryland 20233 (301) 763-4040; *Annual Survey of Manufactures*, and *Census of Manufactures*.

FOOD AND KINDRED PRODUCTS - MANUFACTURING - RESEARCH AND DEVELOPMENT

National Science Foundation, 4201 Wilson Boulevard, Arlington, Virginia 22230 (703) 306-1234; *Research and Development in Industry*

FOOD AND KINDRED PRODUCTS - MANUFACTURING - SALES OR SHIPMENTS

Forbes, Incorporated, 60 Fifth Avenue, New York, New York 10011 (212) 620-2200; *Forbes Annual Report on American Industry*.

U.S. Department of Commerce, Bureau of the Census, Suitland, Maryland 20233 (301) 763-4040; *Annual Survey of Manufactures*, and *Census of Manufactures*.

FOOD AND KINDRED PRODUCTS - MANUFACTURING - VALUE ADDED

U.S. Department of Agriculture, Economic Research Service, Fourteenth Street and Independence Avenue, SW, Washington, D.C. 20005-4789 (202) 219-1504; unpublished data.

U.S. Department of Commerce, Bureau of the Census, Suitland, Maryland 20233 (301) 763-4040; *Census of Manufactures*, and *Annual Survey of Manufactures*.

FOOD FOR PEACE PROGRAM

U.S. Department of Commerce. Bureau of Economic Analysis, Fourteenth Street between Constitution Avenue and E Street, NW, Washington, D.C. 20230 (202) 606-9900; press releases and unpublished data.

FOOD STORES - EARNINGS

U.S. Department of Commerce, Bureau of the Census, Suitland, Maryland 20233 (301) 763-4040; *Census of Retail Trade*, and *County Business Patterns*.

U.S. Department of Labor, Bureau of Labor Statistics, Two Massachusetts Avenue, NE, Washington, D.C. 20212 (202) 606-7828; *Employment and Earnings*, and Bulletins 2370 and 2429.

FOOD STORES - EMPLOYEES

U.S. Department of Commerce, Bureau of the Census, Suitland, Maryland 20233 (301) 763-4040; *Census of Retail Trade,* and *County Business Patterns.*

U.S. Department of Labor, Bureau of Labor Statistics, Two Massachusetts Avenue, NE, Washington, D.C. 20212 (202) 606-7828; *Employment and Earnings,* and Bulletins 2370 and 2429.

FOOD STORES - ESTABLISHMENTS

U.S. Department of Agriculture, Economic Research Service, Fourteenth Street and Independence Avenue, SW, Washington, D.C. 20005-4789 (202) 219-1504; *Food Marketing Review.*

U.S. Department of Commerce, Bureau of the Census, Suitland, Maryland 20233 (301) 763-4040; *Census of Retail Trade,* and *County Business Patterns.*

FOOD STORES - INVENTORIES

U.S. Department of Commerce, Bureau of the Census, Suitland, Maryland 20233 (301) 763-4040; *Current Business Reports: Combined Annual and Revised Monthly Retail Trade.*

FOOD STORES - PRODUCTIVITY

U.S. Department of Labor, Bureau of Labor Statistics, Two Massachusetts Avenue, NE, Washington, D.C. 20212 (202) 606-7828; *Productivity Measures for Selected Industries and Government Services,* and unpublished data.

FOOD STORES - SALES

Market Statistics, 633 Third Avenue, New York, New York 10017 (212) 986-4000; *The Survey of Buying Power Data Service.*

U.S. Department of Agriculture, Economic Research Service, Fourteenth Street and Independence Avenue, SW, Washington, D.C. 20005-4789 (202) 219-1504; *Food Marketing Review.*

U.S. Department of Commerce, Bureau of the Census, Suitland, Maryland 20233 (301) 763-4040; *Census of Retail Trade,* and *Current Business Reports: Combined Annual and Revised Monthly Retail Trade.*

FOOTBALL

National Collegiate Athletic Association, 6201 College Boulevard, Overland Park, Kansas 66211 (913) 339-1906.

National Football League, 410 Park Avenue, New York, New York 10022 (212) 758-1500.

National Football League Players Association, 2021 L Street, NW, Sixth Floor, Washington, D.C. 20036 (202) 463-2200.

FOOTWEAR

National Sporting Goods Association, Lake Center Plaza Building, 1699 Wall Street, Mount Prospect, Illinois 60056 (708) 439-4000; *The Sporting Goods Market in 1993.*

U.S. Department of Commerce, Bureau of the Census, Suitland, Maryland 20233 (301) 763-4040; *U.S. Merchandise Trade.*

U.S. Department of Labor, Bureau of Labor Statistics, Two Massachusetts Avenue, NE, Washington, D.C. 20212 (202) 606-7828; *CPI Detailed Report,* and *Monthly Labor Review.*

FOOTWEAR - EXCEPT LEATHER - MANUFACTURING

U.S. Department of Commerce, Bureau of the Census, Suitland, Maryland 20233 (301) 763-4040; *Annual Survey of Manufactures,* and *Census of Manufactures.*

FOOTWEAR - EXCEPT LEATHER - MANUFACTURING - EARNINGS

U.S. Department of Commerce, Bureau of the Census, Suitland, Maryland 20233 (301) 763-4040; *Census of Manufactures,* and *Annual Survey of Manufactures.*

U.S. Department of Labor, Bureau of Labor Statistics, Two Massachusetts Avenue, NE, Washington, D.C. 20212 (202) 606-7828; *Employment and Earnings,* and Bulletins 2370 and 2429.

FOOTWEAR - EXCEPT LEATHER - MANUFACTURING - EMPLOYEES

U.S. Department of Commerce, Bureau of the Census, Suitland, Maryland 20233 (301) 763-4040; *United States Census of Manufactures,* and *Annual Survey of Manufactures.*

U.S. Department of Labor, Bureau of Labor Statistics, Two Massachusetts Avenue, NE, Washington, D.C. 20212 (202) 606-7828; *Employment and Earnings,* and Bulletins 2370 and 2429.

FOOTWEAR - EXCEPT LEATHER - MANUFACTURING - ESTABLISHMENTS

U.S. Department of Labor, Bureau of Labor Statistics, Two Massachusetts Avenue, NE, Washington, D.C. 20212 (202) 606-7828; *Employment and Earnings,* and Bulletin 2370.

FOOTWEAR - EXCEPT LEATHER - MANUFACTURING - PRODUCTIVITY

U.S. Department of Labor, Bureau of Labor Statistics, 200 Constitution Avenue, NW, Washington, D.C. 20210 (202) 523-1327; *Productivity Measures for Selected Industries and Government Services,* and unpublished data.

FOOTWEAR - EXCEPT LEATHER - MANUFACTURING - SHIPMENTS

U.S. Department of Commerce, Bureau of the Census, Suitland, Maryland 20233 (301) 763-4040; *Census of Manufactures,* and *Annual Survey of Manufactures.*

FOOTWEAR - EXCEPT LEATHER - MANUFACTURING - VALUE ADDED

U.S. Department of Commerce, Bureau of the Census, Suitland, Maryland 20233 (301) 763-4040; *Census of Manufactures,* and *Annual Survey of Manufactures.*

FOREIGN AID - TO DEVELOPING COUNTRIES

Organisation for Economic Co-operation and Development, Publication and Information Center, 2001 L Street, NW, Washington, D.C. 20036 (202) 785-6323; unpublished data.

U.S. Department of Commerce, Bureau of Economic Analysis, Fourteenth Street between Constitution Avenue and E Street, NW, Washington, D.C. 20230 (202) 606-9900; press releases and unpublished data.

U.S. International Development Cooperation Agency, 320 Twenty-first Street, NW, Washington, D.C. 20523-0001 (202) 647-9620; *U.S. Overseas Loans and Grants and Assistance from International Organizations*, and unpublished data.

FOREIGN BORN POPULATION

U.S. Department of the Commerce, Bureau of the Census, Suitland, Maryland 20233 (301) 763-4040; *Census of Population, Current Population Reports*, and unpublished data.

FOREIGN BORN POPULATION - BY PLACE OF BIRTH

U.S. Department of Commerce, Bureau of the Census, Suitland, Maryland 20233 (301) 763-4040; *Census of Population*, and unpublished data.

FOREIGN COMPANIES - UNITED STATES AFFILIATES

U.S. Department of Commerce, Bureau of Economic Analysis, Fourteenth Street between Constitution Avenue and E Street, NW, Washington, D.C. 20230 (202) 606-9900; *Survey of Current Business*, and *Foreign Direct Investment in the United States, Operations of U.S. Affiliates of Foreign Companies*.

FOREIGN COUNTRIES - AID TO DEVELOPING COUNTRIES

Organization for Economic Co-operation and Development, Publication and Information Center, 2001 L Street, NW, Washington, D.C. 20036 (202) 785-6323; unpublished data.

U.S. Department of Commerce. Bureau of Economic Analysis, Fourteenth Street between Constitution Avenue and E Street, NW, Washington, D.C. 20230 (202) 606-9900; press releases and unpublished data.

U.S. International Development Cooperation Agency, Agency for International Development, 320 Twenty-first Street, NW, Washington, D.C. 20523-0001 (202) 647-9620; *U.S. Overseas Loans and Grants and Assistance from International Organizations*, and unpublished data.

FOREIGN COUNTRIES - APPLIANCES - HOMES WITH

Euromonitor Publications, Limited, 87-88 Turnmill Street, London EC1M 5QU, England; *European Marketing Data and Statistics*.

FOREIGN COUNTRIES - AREA

Statistical Office of the United Nations, New York, New York 10017 (800) 253-9646; *Demographic Yearbook*.

U.S. Department of Commerce, Bureau of the Census, Suitland, Maryland 20233 (301) 763-4040; *World Population Profile*, and *International Database*.

FOREIGN COUNTRIES - ARMED FORCES PERSONNEL

U.S. Arms Control and Disarmament Agency, 320 Twenty-first Street, NW, Washington, D.C. 20451 (202) 647-8677; *World Military Expenditures and Arms Transfers*.

FOREIGN COUNTRIES - ARMS EXPORTS AND IMPORTS

U.S. Arms Control and Disarmament Agency, 320 Twenty-first Street, NW, Washington, D.C. 20451 (202) 647-8677; *World Military Expenditures and Arms Transfers*.

FOREIGN COUNTRIES - BALANCE OF PAYMENTS

International Monetary Fund, 700 Nineteenth Street, NW, Washington, D.C. 20423 (202) 623-7000; *International Financial Statistics*.

U.S. Department of Commerce, Bureau of Economic Analysis, Fourteenth Street between Constitution Avenue and E Street, NW, Washington, D.C. 20230 (202) 606-9900; *Survey of Current Business*.

FOREIGN COUNTRIES - BEVERAGES - PERSONAL CONSUMPTION EXPENDITURES

U.S. Department of Agriculture, Economic Research Service, Fourteenth Street and Independence Avenue, SW, Washington, D.C. 20005-4789 (202) 219-1504; data from the United Nations, New York, New York 10017; *National Accounts Statistics*.

FOREIGN COUNTRIES - BIRTHS AND BIRTH RATES

U.S. Department of Commerce, Bureau of the Census, Suitland, Maryland 20233 (301) 763-4040; *International Database*.

U.S. Department of Labor, Bureau of Labor Statistics, Two Massachusetts Avenue, NE, Washington, D.C. 20212 (202) 606-7828; *Monthly Labor Review*, and unpublished data.

FOREIGN COUNTRIES - CITIES

U.S. Department of Commerce, Bureau of the Census, Suitland, Maryland 20233 (301) 763-4040; *International Database*.

FOREIGN COUNTRIES - COLLEGE STUDENTS ENROLLED IN THE UNITED STATES

Institute of International Education, 809 United Nations Plaza, New York, New York 10017 (212) 883-8200; *Open Doors*.

FOREIGN COUNTRIES - COMMUNICATIONS

International Telecommunication Union, Palais des Nations, CH-1211 Geneva 20, Switzerland; *World Telecom Indicators*.

Statistical Office of the United Nations, Publishing Service, New York, New York 10017 (800) 253-9646; *Statistical Yearbook*.

United Nations Educational, Scientific, and Cultural Organization, (UNESCO) 7 Place de Fontenoy, F-75700 Paris, France (Telephone Number in U.S. (212) 963-5981), *Statistical Yearbook*.

FOREIGN COUNTRIES - CONSUMER PRICE INDEX

International Monetary Fund, 700 Nineteenth Street, NW, Washington, D.C. 20431 (202) 623-7000; *International Financial Statistics*.

Organization for Economic Co-operation and Development, Publication and Information Center, 2001 L Street, NW, Washington, D.C. 20036 (202) 785-6323; *Main Economic Indicators*.

U.S. Department of Labor, Bureau of Labor Statistics, Two Massachusetts Avenue, NE, Washington, D.C. 20212 (202) 606-7828; *Monthly Labor Review, Consumer Price Index Detailed Report*, and *Handbook of Labor Statistics*.

FOREIGN COUNTRIES - CRUDE OIL

U.S. Department of Energy, Energy Information Administration, 1000 Independence Avenue, SW, Washington, D.C. 20585 (202) 586-8800;

Monthly Energy Review, Petroleum Supply Annual, International Energy Annual, and *Annual Energy Review.*

FOREIGN COUNTRIES - DEATH AND DEATH RATES

U.S. Department of Commerce, Bureau of the Census, Suitland, Maryland 20233 (301) 763-4040; *International Database.*

World Health Organization, Avenue Appia, Office of Publication, CH 1211 Geneva, 27, Switzerland (Telephone Number in U.S. (518) 436-9686); *World Health Statistics Annual.*

FOREIGN COUNTRIES - DEBT

Central Intelligence Agency, Washington, D.C. 20505 (703) 482-1100; *Handbook of International Economic Statistics,* and unpublished data.

The World Bank, 1818 H Street, NW, Washington, D.C. 20006 (202) 477-1234; *World Debt Tables.*

FOREIGN COUNTRIES - ECONOMIC INDICATORS

Center for International Business Cycle Research, Columbia University Graduate School of Business, 808 Uris Hall, New York, New York 10027 (212) 280-2916; *International Economic Indicators.*

Organization for Economic Co-operation and Development, 2001 L Street, NW, Washington, D.C. 20036 (202) 785-6323; *National Accounts.*

U.S. Department of Commerce, International Trade Administration, Fourteenth Street between Constitution Avenue and E Street, NW, Washington, D.C. 20230 (202) 482-5487; based on Official Statistics.

FOREIGN COUNTRIES - EMPLOYMENT AND LABOR FORCE

Organization for Economic Co-operation and Development, 2001 L Street, NW, Washington, D.C. 20036 (202) 785-6323; *Labor Force Statistics,* and *Education at a Glance.*

U.S. Department of Labor, Bureau of Labor Statistics, Two Massachusetts Avenue, NE, Washington, D.C. 20212 (202) 606-7828; *Comparative Labor Force Statistics for Ten Countries,* and *Monthly Labor Review.*

FOREIGN COUNTRIES - ENERGY PRODUCTION - CONSUMPTION AND PRICES

Statistical Office of the United Nations, Publishing Service, New York, New York 10017 (800) 253-9646; *Energy Statistics Yearbook.*

U.S. Department of Energy, Energy Information Administration, 1000 Independence Avenue, SW, Washington, D.C. 20585 (202) 586-8800; *International Energy Annual.*

FOREIGN COUNTRIES - EXCHANGE RATES

Board of Governors of the Federal Reserve System, Twentieth Street and Constitution Avenue, NW, Washington, D.C. 20551 (202) 452-3000; *Federal Reserve Bulletin.*

U.S. Department of Labor, Bureau of Labor Statistics, Two Massachusetts Avenue, NE, Washington, D.C. 20212 (202) 606-7828; *Monthly Labor Review,* and unpublished data.

FOREIGN COUNTRIES - EXPORT AND IMPORT

International Monetary Fund, 700 Nineteenth Street, NW, Washington, D.C. 20431 (202) 623-7000; *International Financial Statistics.*

Organization for Economic Co-operation and Development, 2001 L Street, NW, Washington, D.C. 20036 (202) 785-6323; *Monthly Statistics of Foreign Trade.*

U.S. Department of Agriculture, Economic Research Service, Fourteenth Street and Independence Avenue, SW, Washington, D.C. 20005-4789 (202) 219-1504; *World Agriculture - Trends and Indicators.*

FOREIGN COUNTRIES - FISH CATCHES

U.S. Department of Commerce, National Oceanic and Atmospheric Administration, National Marine Fisheries Service, 1335 East-West Highway, Silver Spring, Maryland 20910 (301) 427-2239; *Fisheries of the United States.*

FOREIGN COUNTRIES - FOOD - CONSUMPTION

U.S. Department of Agriculture, Foreign Agricultural Service, Fourteenth Street and Independence Avenue, SW, Washington, D.C. 20250 (202) 720-3448; *World Livestock Situation,* and *World Poultry Situation.*

FOREIGN COUNTRIES - FOOD - PERSONAL CONSUMPTION EXPENDITURES

U.S. Department of Agriculture, Economic Research Service, Fourteenth and Independence Avenue, SW, Washington, D.C. 20005-4789 (202) 219-1504; based on data from the United Nations, new York, New York; *National Accounts Statistics.*

FOREIGN COUNTRIES - FOOD - PRODUCTION INDEXES

Food and Agricultural Organization of the U.N. (FAO), Via delle Terme di Caracalla, 00100 Rome, Italy (Telephone Number in U.S. (202) 653-2400); *AGRISTAT Database.*

FOREIGN COUNTRIES - GROSS DOMESTIC PRODUCT

Organization for Economic Co-operation and Development, Publication and Information Center, 2001 L Street, NW, Washington, D.C. 20036 (202) 785-6323; *National Accounts of OECD Countries.*

FOREIGN COUNTRIES - GROSS NATIONAL PRODUCT

U.S. Arms Control and Disarmament Agency, 320 Twenty-first Street, NW, Washington, D.C. 20451 (202) 647-8677; *World Military Expenditures and Arms Transfers.*

FOREIGN COUNTRIES - HEALTH CARE EXPENDITURES AND EMPLOYMENT

Organization for Economic Co-operation and Development, Publication and Information Center, 2001 L Street, NW, Washington, D.C. 20036 (202) 785-6323; *OECD Health Systems: Facts and Trends,* and *OECD Health Data.*

FOREIGN COUNTRIES - IMMIGRATION TO THE UNITED STATES

U.S. Department of Commerce, Bureau of the Census, Suitland, Maryland 20233 (301) 763-4040; *Census of Population,* and unpublished data.

U.S. Department of Justice, Immigration and Naturalization Service, 425 I Street, NW, Washington, D.C. 20536 (202) 514-4316; *Statistical Yearbook.*

FOREIGN COUNTRIES - INTERNATIONAL TRANSACTIONS - BALANCES

Executive Office of the President, Council of Economic Advisors, Old Executive Office Building, Washington, D.C. 20500 (202) 395-5084; *Economic Indicators*, and *Economic Report of the President.*

U.S. Department of Commerce, Bureau of Economic Analysis, Fourteenth Street between Constitution Avenue and E Street, NW, Washington, D.C. 20230 (202) 606-9900; *Survey of Current Business.*

FOREIGN COUNTRIES - INVESTMENT IN THE UNITED STATES

U.S. Department of Commerce, Bureau of Economic Analysis, Fourteenth Street between Constitution Avenue and E Street, NW, Washington, D.C. 20230 (202) 606-9900; *Survey of Current Business, Foreign Direct Investments in the U.S. Operations of U.S. Affiliates of Foreign Companies*, and unpublished data.

FOREIGN COUNTRIES - LABOR FORCE PARTICIPATION RATES

Organization for Economic Co-operation and Development, Publication and Information Center, 2001 L Street, NW, Washington, D.C. 20036 (202) 785-6323; *Labour Force Statistics.*

U.S. Department of Labor, Bureau of Labor Statistics, Two Massachusetts Avenue, NE, Washington, D.C. 20212 (202) 606-7828; *Comparative Labor Force Statistics for Ten Countries*, and *Monthly Labor Review.*

FOREIGN COUNTRIES - LOANS - BY UNITED STATES COMMERCIAL BANKS

Board of Governors of the Federal Reserve Systems, Twentieth Street and Constitution Avenue, NW, Washington, D.C. 20551 (202) 452-3000; statistical release.

FOREIGN COUNTRIES - MANUFACTURING

Organization for Economic Co-operation and Development, Publication and Information Center, 2001 L Street, NW, Washington, D.C. 20036 (202) 785-6323; *OECD Industrial Structure Statistics.*

U.S. Department of Labor, Bureau of Labor Statistics, Two Massachusetts Avenue, NE, Washington, D.C. 20212 (202) 606-7828; *Report 844.*

FOREIGN COUNTRIES - MERCHANT VESSELS

U.S. Department of Transportation, Maritime Administration, 400 Seventh Street, SW, Washington, D.C. 20590 (202) 366-5807; *Merchant Fleets of the World.*

FOREIGN COUNTRIES - MILITARY EXPENDITURES

U.S. Arms Control and Disarmament Agency, 320 Twenty-first Street, NW, Washington, D.C. 20451 (202) 647-8677; *World Military Expenditures and Arms Transfers.*

FOREIGN COUNTRIES - MILITARY PERSONNEL - UNITED STATES ON ACTIVE DUTY

U.S. Department of Defense, The Pentagon, Washington, D.C. 20301-1155 (703) 545-6700; *Selected Manpower Statistics*, and unpublished data.

FOREIGN COUNTRIES - MILITARY SALES

U.S. Department of Defense, Defense Security Assistance Agency, The Pentagon, Washington, D.C. 20301-2800 (703) 695-3291; *Foreign Military Construction Sales, Military Assistance Facts*, and *Foreign Military Sales.*

FOREIGN COUNTRIES - MOTOR VEHICLES

American Automobile Manufacturers Association, 1401 H Street, NW, Suite 900, Washington, D.C. 20005 (202) 326-5500; *Motor Vehicle Facts and Figures.*

FOREIGN COUNTRIES - NOBEL PRIZE LAUREATES

U.S. National Science Foundation, 4201 Wilson Boulevard, Arlington, Virginia 22230 (703) 306-1234; unpublished data.

FOREIGN COUNTRIES - NONIMMIGRANTS FROM

U.S. Department of Justice, Immigration and Naturalization Service, 425 I Street, NW, Washington, D.C. 20536 (202) 514-4316; *Statistical Yearbook.*

FOREIGN COUNTRIES - NUCLEAR POWER GENERATION

McGraw-Hill Publications Company, Incorporated, 1221 Avenue of the Americas, New York, New York 10020 (212) 512-2000; *Nucleonics Week.*

FOREIGN COUNTRIES - PERSONAL CONSUMPTION EXPENDITURES - FOOD AND BEVERAGE

Statistical Office of the United Nations, Publishing Service, New York, New York 10017 (800) 253-9646; *National Accounts Statistics.*

FOREIGN COUNTRIES - POPULATION

Statistical Office of the United Nations, New York, New York 10017 (800) 253-9646; *Demographic Yearbook.*

U.S. Department of Commerce, Bureau of the Census, Suitland, Maryland 20233 (301) 763-4040; *International Database*, and *World Population Profile.*

FOREIGN COUNTRIES - POPULATION - CITIES

U.S. Department of Commerce, Bureau of the Census, Suitland, Maryland 20233 (301) 763-4040; *International Database.*

FOREIGN COUNTRIES - PRODUCTION - CROPS

Food and Agricultural Organization of the United Nations, Via delle Terme di Caracalla, 00100 Rome, Italy (Telephone Number in U.S. (202) 653-2400); *FAO Production Yearbook.*

U.S. Department of Agriculture, Economic Research Service, Fourteenth Street and Independence Avenue, SW, Washington, D.C. 20005-4789 (202) 219-1504; *World Agriculture - Trends and Indicators.*

FOREIGN COUNTRIES - PRODUCTION - INDEXES

Organization for Economic Co-operation and Development, Publication and Information Center, 2001 L Street, NW, Washington, D.C. 20036 (202) 785-6323; *Main Economic Indicators, Historical Statistics*, and *Main Economic Indicators*.

FOREIGN COUNTRIES - PRODUCTION - MEAT

Food and Agricultural Organization of the U.N. (FAO), Via delle Terme di Caracalla, 00100 Rome, Italy (Telephone Number in U.S. (202) 653-2400); *FAO Production Yearbook*.

Statistical Office of the United Nations, Publishing Service, New York, New York 10017 (800) 253-9646; *Statistical Yearbook*.

U.S. Department of Agriculture, Economic Research Service, Fourteen Street and Independence Avenue, SW, Washington, D.C. 20005-4789 (202) 219-1504; *World Agriculture - Trends in Indicators*.

FOREIGN COUNTRIES - PRODUCTION - MINERALS

Statistical Office of the United Nations, Publishing Service, New York, New York 10017 (800) 253-9646; *Energy Statistics Yearbook*, *Statistical Yearbook*, and *Industrial Statistics Yearbook*.

U.S. Department of the Interior, Bureau of Mines, 810 Seventh Street, NW, Washington, D.C. 20241 (202) 501-9649; *Mineral Commodity Summaries*, and *Annual Reports*.

FOREIGN COUNTRIES - PRODUCTION - STEEL

Statistical Office of the United Nations, Publishing Service, New York, New York 10017 (800) 253-9646; *Statistical Yearbook*, and *Industrial Statistics Yearbook*.

FOREIGN COUNTRIES - REFUGEES ADMITTED TO THE UNITED STATES

U.S. Department of Justice, Immigration and Naturalization Service, 425 I Street, NW, Washington, D.C. 20536 (202) 514-4316; *Statistical Yearbook*.

FOREIGN COUNTRIES - RESEARCH AND DEVELOPMENT EXPENDITURES

U.S. National Science Foundation, 4201 Wilson Boulevard, Arlington, Virginia 22230 (703) 306-1234; *National Patterns of R & D Resources*.

FOREIGN COUNTRIES - RESERVE ASSETS

International Monetary Fund, 700 Nineteenth Street, NW, Washington, D.C. 20431 (202) 623-7000; *International Financial Statistics*.

FOREIGN COUNTRIES - SALES AND ASSISTANCE BY UNITED STATES GOVERNMENT

U.S. Department of Defense, Defense Security Assistance Agency, The Pentagon, Washington, D.C. 20301-2800; *Foreign Military Sales, Foreign Military Construction Sales*, and *Military Assistance Facts*.

FOREIGN COUNTRIES - SOCIAL SECURITY PROGRAMS - PAYROLL TAX RATES

U.S. Department of Health and Human Services, Social Security Administration, 6401 Security Boulevard, Baltimore, Maryland 21235 (410) 965-1234; *Social Security Programs Throughout the World*.

FOREIGN COUNTRIES - SPACE LAUNCHES

U.S. Library of Congress, Congressional Research Service, Science Policy Research Division, 101 Independence Avenue, SE, Washington, D.C. 20540 (202) 707-5000; *Space Activities of the United States, CIS and Other Launching Countries/ Organizations*.

FOREIGN COUNTRIES - STEEL PRODUCTION AND CONSUMPTION

Statistical Office of the United Nations, Publishing Service, New York, New York 10017 (800) 253-9646; *Statistical Yearbook*, and *Industrial Statistics Yearbook*.

FOREIGN COUNTRIES - SUICIDES

World Health Organization, Avenue Appia, Office of Publications, CH-1211 Geneva, Switzerland (Telephone Number in U.S. (518) 436-9686); *World Health Statistics Annual*.

FOREIGN COUNTRIES - TAXES (REVENUE)

Organization for Economic Co-operation and Development, Publication and Information Center, 2001 L Street, NW, Washington, D.C. 20036 (202) 785-6323; *Revenue Statistics of OECD Member Countries*.

FOREIGN COUNTRIES - TERRITORY CEDED TO UNITED STATES

U.S. Department of Commerce, Bureau of the Census, Suitland, Maryland 20233 (301) 763-4040; unpublished data.

FOREIGN COUNTRIES - TRADE WITH THE UNITED STATES

U.S. Department of Agriculture, Economic Research Service, Fourteenth Street and Independence Avenue, SW, Washington, D.C. 20005 (202) 219-1504; *Agricultural Outlook*, *Agricultural Statistics*, and *Foreign Agricultural Trade of the U.S.*

U.S. Department of Commerce, Bureau of Economic Analysis, Fourteenth Street between Constitution Avenue and E Street, NW, Washington, D.C. 20230 (202) 606-9900; *Survey of Current Business*.

U.S. Department of Commerce, Bureau of the Census, Suitland, Maryland 20233 (301) 763-4040; *U.S. Merchandise Trade*.

FOREIGN COUNTRIES - TRAVELERS AND EXPENDITURES

U.S. Department of Commerce, Bureau of Economic Analysis, Fourteenth Street between Constitution Avenue and E Street, NW, Washington, D.C. 20230 (202) 606-9900; *Survey of Current Business*.

U.S. Department of Commerce, Travel and Tourism Administration, Washington, D.C. 20230 (202) 482-3811; unpublished data.

U.S. Department of Justice, Immigration and Naturalization Service, 425 I Street, NW, Washington, D.C. 20536 (202) 514-4316; *Statistical Yearbook*.

FOREIGN COUNTRIES - UNITED STATES INVESTMENT ABROAD

U.S. Department of Commerce, Bureau of Economic Analysis, Fourteenth Street between Constitution Avenue and E Street, NW,

Washington, D.C. 20230 (202) 606-9900; *Survey of Current Business*

FOREIGN COUNTRIES - VITAL STATISTICS

U.S. Department of Commerce, Bureau of the Census, Suitland, Maryland 20233 (301) 763-4040; *International Database.*

U.S. Department of Labor, Bureau of Labor Statistics, Two Massachusetts Avenue, NE, Washington, D.C. 20212 (202) 606-7828; *Monthly Labor Review,* and unpublished data.

FOREIGN CURRENCY HOLDINGS

Board of Governors of the Federal Reserve System, Twentieth Street and Constitution Avenue, NW, Washington, D.C. 20551 (202) 452-3000; *Annual Statistical Digest.*

FOREIGN EXCHANGE RATES

U.S. Department of Labor, Bureau of Labor Statistics, Two Massachusetts Avenue, NE, Washington, D.C. 20212 (202) 606-7828; *Monthly Labor Review.*

FOREIGN GRANTS AND CREDITS - UNITED STATES GOVERNMENT

U.S. Department of Commerce, Bureau of Economic Analysis, Fourteenth Street between Constitution Avenue and E Street, NW, Washington, D.C. 20230 (202) 606-9900; press releases and unpublished data.

FOREIGN INVESTMENTS IN UNITED STATES

U.S. Department of Commerce, Bureau of Economic Analysis, Fourteenth Street between Constitution Avenue and E Street, NW, Washington, D.C. 20230 (202) 606-9900; *Foreign Direct Investments in the United States, Operations of U.S. Affiliates of Foreign Companies,* and *Survey of Current Business.*

FOREIGN LANGUAGES - COLLEGE STUDENTS ENROLLED

Association of Departments of Foreign Languages, 10 Astor Place, New York, New York 10003 (212) 614-6319; *ADFL Bulletin.*

FOREIGN LANGUAGES - DEGREES CONFERRED

U.S. Department of Education, 400 Maryland Avenue, SW, Washington, D.C. 20202 (202) 708-5366; *Digest of Education Statistics.*

FOREIGN TRADE - See also FOREIGN AID, FOREIGN COUNTRIES and Individual Commodities

U.S. Department of Commerce, Bureau of the Census, Suitland, Maryland 20233 (301) 763-4040; *U.S. Merchandise Trade: Selected Highlights,* and *U.S. Merchandise Trade: Exports, General Imports, and Imports for Consumption.*

FOREIGN TRADE - AGRICULTURAL PRODUCTS

U.S. Department of Agriculture, Economic Research Service, Fourteenth Street and Independence Avenue, SW, Washington, D.C. 20005-4789 (202) 219-1504; *Agricultural Statistics, Agricultural Outlook,* and *Foreign Agricultural Trade of the United States.*

U.S. Department of Commerce, Bureau of the Census, Suitland, Maryland 20233 (301) 763-4040; *U.S. Merchandise Trade,* and *U.S. Merchandise Trade: Exports, General Imports, and Imports for Consumption.*

FOREIGN TRADE - AIRCRAFT AND AIRCRAFT PARTS

Aerospace Industries Association of America, 1250 I Street, NW, Washington, D.C. 20005 (202) 371-8400; *Statistical Series 23.*

U.S. Department of Commerce, Bureau of the Census, Suitland, Maryland 20233 (301) 763-4040; *U.S. Merchandise Trade.*

U.S. Department of Commerce, International Trade Administration, 14th Street between Constitution Avenue and E Street, NW, Washington, D.C. 20230 (202) 482-5487; *U.S. Industrial Outlook.*

FOREIGN TRADE - AUTOMOBILES

American Automobile Manufactures Association, 1401 H Eye Street, NW, Suite 900, Washington, D.C. 20005 (202) 326-5500; *Motor Vehicle Facts and Figures,* and *World Motor Vehicle Data.*

U.S. Department of Commerce, Bureau of Economic Analysis, Fourteenth Street between Constitution Avenue and E Street, NW, Washington, D.C. 20230 (202) 606-9900; *The National Income and Product Accounts of the United States,* and *Survey of Current Business.*

U.S. Department of Commerce, Bureau of the Census, Suitland, Maryland 20233 (301) 763-4040; *U.S. Merchandise Trade.*

FOREIGN TRADE - BALANCE OF TRADE

U.S. Department of Commerce, Bureau of the Census, Suitland, Maryland 20233 (301) 763-4040; *U.S. Merchandise Trade: Exports, General Imports, and Imports for Consumption.*

FOREIGN TRADE - BOOKS

R.R. Bowker Company, 245 West Seventeenth Street, New York, New York 10011 (212) 645-9700; *Publishers Weekly.*

FOREIGN TRADE - COAL

U.S. Department of Energy, Energy Information Administration, 1000 Independence Avenue, SW, Washington, D.C. 20585 (202) 586-8800; *Annual Energy Review, Coal Production, Coke Plant Reports, Quarterly Coal Report,* and *Annual Prospects for World Coal Trade.*

FOREIGN TRADE - COASTAL DISTRICTS

U.S. Department of Commerce, Bureau of the Census, Suitland, Maryland 20233 (301) 763-4040; *United States Waterborne Exports and General Imports,* and TM 985.

FOREIGN TRADE - COMMODITY GROUPS

U.S. Department of Commerce, Bureau of the Census, Suitland, Maryland 20233 (301) 763-4040; *U.S. Merchandise Trade,* and *U.S. Merchandise Trade: Exports, General Imports, and Imports for Consumption.*

FOREIGN TRADE - CONTINENTS

U.S. Department of Commerce, Bureau of the Census, Suitland, Maryland 20233 (301) 763-4040; *U.S. Merchandise Trade.*

FOREIGN TRADE - COUNTRIES

Organization for Economic Cooperation and Development, Publication and Information Center, 2001 L Street, NW, Washington, D.C. 20036 (202) 785-6323; *Monthly Statistics of Foreign Trade.*

U.S. Department of Commerce, Bureau of the Census, Suitland, Maryland 20233 (301) 763-4040; *U.S. Merchandise Trade: Exports, General Imports, and Imports for Consumption,* and *U.S. Merchandise Trade.*

FOREIGN TRADE - CRUDE OIL

U.S. Department of Commerce, Bureau of the Census, Suitland, Maryland 20233 (301) 763-4040; *U.S. Exports of Merchandise,* and *U.S. Imports of Merchandise,* compact discs.

U.S. Department of Energy, Energy Information Administration, 1000 Independence Avenue, SW, Washington, D.C. 20585 (202) 586-8800; *Annual Energy Review, Petroleum Supply Annual,* and *Monthly Energy Review,*

U.S. Department of the Interior, Bureau of Mines, 810 Seventh Street, NW, Washington, D.C. 20241 (202) 501-9649; *Annual Reports,* and *Federal Offshore Statistics.*

FOREIGN TRADE - CUSTOMS REGIONS AND DISTRICTS

U.S. Department of Commerce, Bureau of the Census, Suitland, Maryland 20233 (301) 763-4040; *U.S. Merchandise Trade: Selected Highlights.*

FOREIGN TRADE - FISH PRODUCTS

U.S. Department of Commerce, National Oceanic and Atmospheric Administration, National Marine Fisheries Service, 1335 East-West Highway, Silver Spring, Maryland 20910 (301) 427-2239; *Fisheries of the United States,* and *Fishery Statistics of the United States.*

FOREIGN TRADE - FREE AND DUTIABLE

U.S. Department of Commerce, Bureau of the Census, Suitland, Maryland 20233 (301) 763-4040; *U.S. Merchandise Trade: Selected Highlights.*

FOREIGN TRADE - INDEXES - UNIT AND VALUE

International Monetary Fund, 700 Nineteenth Street, NW, Washington, D.C. 20431 (202) 623-7000; *International Financial Statistics.*

FOREIGN TRADE - INTERNATIONAL TRANSACTIONS BALANCES - UNITED STATES

Executive Office of the President, Council of Economic Advisors, Old Executive Office Building, Washington, D.C. 20500 (202) 395-5084; *Economic Indicators,* and *Economic Report of the President.*

U.S. Department of Commerce, Bureau of Economic Analysis, Fourteenth Street between Constitution Avenue and E Street, NW, Washington, D.C. 20230 (202) 606-9900; *Survey of Current Business.*

FOREIGN TRADE - MANUFACTURES EXPORTS - UNITED STATES COMPARED TO WORLD

U.S. Department of Commerce, International Trade Administration, Fourteenth Street between Constitution Avenue and E Street, NW, Washington, D.C. 20230 (202) 482-5487; *Business America, Market Share Reports,* and unpublished data.

FOREIGN TRADE - MERCHANDISE

U.S. Department of Commerce, Bureau of the Census, Suitland, Maryland 20233 (301) 763-4040; *U.S. Merchandise Trade: Selected Highlights,* and *U.S. Merchandise Trade: Exports, General Imports, and Imports for Consumption.*

FOREIGN TRADE - MERCHANDISE - COUNTRIES

U.S. Department of Commerce, Bureau of the Census, Suitland, Maryland 20233 (301) 763-4040; *U.S. Merchandise Trade: Selected Highlights.*

FOREIGN TRADE - MERCHANDISE - OUTLYING AREAS

U.S. Department of Commerce, Bureau of the Census, Suitland, Maryland 20233 (301) 763-4040; *U.S. Merchandise Trade: Selected Highlights,* and FT 990.

FOREIGN TRADE - MINERAL FUELS

U.S. Department of Energy, Energy Information Administration, Washington, D.C. 20585 (202) 586-8800; *Annual Energy Review.*

FOREIGN TRADE - MINERALS

U.S. Department of Commerce, Bureau of the Census, Suitland, Maryland 20233 (301) 763-4040; *U.S. Exports of Merchandise,* and U.S. Imports of Merchandise, *compact discs.*

U.S. Department of the Interior, Bureau of Mines, 810 Seventh Street, NW, Washington, D.C. 20241 (202) 501-9649; *Annual Reports.*

FOREIGN TRADE - MINERALS - PRICE INDEXES

U.S. Department of Labor, Bureau of Labor Statistics, Two Massachusetts Avenue, NE, Washington, D.C. 20212 (202) 606-7828; *News.*

FOREIGN TRADE - MODE OF TRANSPORT

U.S. Department of Commerce, Bureau of the Census, Suitland, Maryland 20233 (301) 763-4040; *U.S. Merchandise Trade: Selected Highlights.*

FOREIGN TRADE - UNITED STATES AFFILIATES OF FOREIGN COMPANIES

U.S. Department of Commerce, Bureau of Economic Analysis, Fourteenth Street between Constitution Avenue and E Street, NW, Washington, D.C. 20230 (202) 606-9900; *Survey of Current Business,* and *Foreign Direct Investment in the United States, Operations of U.S. Affiliates of Foreign Companies.*

FOREIGN TRADE - VESSELS ENTERED AND CLEARED

U.S. Department of Commerce, Bureau of the Census, Suitland, Maryland 20233 (301) 763-4040; TA 987.

FOREIGN TRADE - WATERBORNE COMMERCE

U.S. Department of Commerce, Bureau of the Census, Suitland, Maryland 20233 (301) 763-4040; TM 985.

U.S. Department of the Army, Corps of Engineers, The Pentagon, Washington, D.C. 20301 (202) 545-6700; *Waterborne Commerce of the United States.*

FOREIGN TRADE - WORLD SUMMARY - EXTERNAL TRADE

Statistical Office of the United Nations, Publishing Service, New York, New York 10017 (800) 253-9646; *Monthly Bulletin of Statistics.*

FOREST PRODUCTS - See also Individual Products

FOREST PRODUCTS - CAR LOADINGS

Association of American Railroads, American Railroads Building, 50 F Street, NW, Washington, D.C. 20001 (202) 639-2100; *Weekly Railroad Traffic*, and *Freight Commodity Statistics*.

FOREST PRODUCTS - CONSUMPTION

Forest and Paper Association, 1250 Connecticut Avenue, NW, Washington, D.C. 20036 (202) 463-2455; *Statistics of Paper, Paperboard, and Wood Pulp*, and unpublished data.

U.S. Department of Agriculture, Forest Service, Fourteenth Street and Independence Avenue, SW, Washington, D.C. 20250 (202) 720-3760; *United States Timber Production, Trade, Consumption, and Price Statistics*.

U.S. Department of Commerce, Bureau of the Census, Suitland, Maryland 20233 (301) 763-4040; *Current Industrial Reports*.

FOREST PRODUCTS - FOREIGN TRADE

U.S. Department of Agriculture, Forest Service, Fourteenth Street and Independence Avenue, SW, Washington, D.C. 20250 (202) 720-3760; *United States Timber Production, Trade, Consumption, and Price Statistics*.

U.S. Department of Commerce, Bureau of the Census, Suitland, Maryland 20233 (301) 763-4040; *Current Industrial Reports*.

FOREST PRODUCTS - PRODUCER - PRICES

U.S. Department of Labor, Bureau of Labor Statistics, Two Massachusetts Avenue, NE, Washington, D.C. 20212 (202) 606-7828; *Producer Price Indexes*.

FORESTS - LAND - ACREAGE AND OWNERSHIP

U.S. Department of Agriculture, Forest Service, Fourteenth Street and Independence Avenue, SW, Washington, D.C. 20250 (202) 720-3760; *Land Areas of the National Forest System*, and *Resources of the U.S.*

FORESTS - NATIONAL

U.S. Department of Agriculture, Forest Service, Fourteenth Street and Independence Avenue, SW, Washington, D.C. 20250 (202) 720-3760; *Land Areas of the National Forest System*, *Agricultural Statistics*, and unpublished data.

FORESTS - NATIONAL - FINANCES

U.S. Department of Agriculture, Forest Service, Fourteenth Street and Independence Avenue, SW, Washington, D.C. 20250 (202) 720-3760; *Agricultural Statistics*, and unpublished data.

FORESTS - NATIONAL - RECREATIONAL USE

U.S. Department of the Interior, National Park Service, C Street between Eighteenth and Nineteenth Streets, NW, Washington, D.C. 20240 (202) 208-6843; *Federal Recreation Fee Report*.

FORGERY AND COUNTERFEITING

U.S. Department of Justice, Federal Bureau of Investigation, Ninth Street and Pennsylvania Avenue, NW, Washington, D.C. 20535 (202) 324-3000; *Crime in the United States*.

FOUNDATIONS - PHILANTHROPIC

American Association of Fund Raising Counsel, Incorporated, 25 West 43rd Street, New York, New York 10036 (212) 354-5799; *Giving USA*.

The Foundation Center, 79 Fifth Avenue, New York, New York 10003 (212) 620-4230; *Foundation Grants Index*, and *Guide to U.S. Foundation*.

France - National Statistical Offices

Direction Nationale des Statistiques de Commerce Exterieur, Centre de Renseignements Statistiques, 192 rue Saint Honore, 75056 Paris RP, France.

Institut National de la Statistique et des Etudes Economiques, 18 Boulevard Adolphe Pinard, 75675 Paris, Cedex 14, France.

France - Primary Statistics Sources

Institut National de la Statistique et des Etudes Economiques (INSEE), 18 Boulevard Adolphe Pinard, 75675 Paris Cedex 14, France; *Annuaire Statistique de la France*, and *Bulletin mensuel de statistique*.

France - Databases

AGRISTAT, France Ministry of Agriculture and Agricultural Development, Department of Financial and Economic Affairs, Central Service for Statistical Inquiries and Studies, 4, ave. de Sainte-Mande, F-75570 Paris Cedex 12, France. Subject coverage: French agricultural production especially its socioeconomic and statistical aspects.

Banque de Donnees Socio-economiques des Pays Mediterraneens - MEDISTAT, Institut Agronomique Mediterraneen, 3191, route de Mende, B.P. 5056, F-34033 Montpellier Cedex 1, France. Subject coverage: Agriculture, agronomy, socioeconomics, demographics and population, international trade, and national accounting of production and trade.

Institut National de la Statistique et des Etudies Economiques, 18, blvd. Adolphe Pinard, F-75675 Paris Cedex 14, France. Maintains the following databases: (1) Banque de Donnees Macroeconomique. Subject coverage: Economic time series data. (2) Banque de Donnees Locales. Subject coverage: Local French community demographic studies. (3) Industrial statistics. Subject coverage: French industrial statistics. (4) Tendances de la Conjoncture, Cahier 1. Subject coverage: French economy. (5) Tendances de la Conjoncture, Cahier 2. Subject coverage: French economy.

FRANCE - ABORTIONS

European Community Information Service, 2100 M Street, NW, Washington, D.C. 20037 (202) 862-9500; *Demographic Statistics*.

Statistical Office of the United Nations, Publishing Service, New York, New York 10017 (800) 253-9646; *Demographic Yearbook*.

FRANCE - AGRICULTURE

European Community Information Service, 2100 M Street, NW, Washington, D.C. 20037 (202) 862-9500; *Agriculture: Statistical Yearbook*, *Basic Statistics of the Community*, *Eurostatistics: Data for Short-Term Economic Analysis*, *Labor Force Sample Survey*, and *Regions: Statistical Yearbook*.

Federal Statistical Office, Gustav - Stresemann - Ring 11, D-6200 Wiesbaden, Germany; *Frankreich.*

Food and Agricultural Organization of the United Nations (FAO) Via delle Terme di Caracalla, 00100 Rome, Italy (Telephone Number in U.S. (202) 653-2400); *Production Yearbook, The State of Food and Agriculture, Trade Yearbook.*

G.K. Hall and Company, 70 Lincoln Street, Boston, Massachusetts 02111 (617) 423-3990; *The World in Figures.*

National Technical Information Service, 5285 Port Royal Road, Springfield, Virginia 22161 (703) 487-4600; *Handbook of Economic Statistics.*

Organisation for Economic Co-operation and Development (OECD), 2 rue Andre-Pascal, 75 Paris 16, France (Telephone Number in U.S. (202) 785-6323); *Economic Accounts for Agriculture, Indicators of Industrial Activity, Industrial Structure Statistics,* and *OECD Economic Surveys: France.*

Statistical Office of the United Nations, Publishing Service, New York, New York 10017 (800) 253-9646; *Statistical Yearbook.*

Time Books, 201 East 50th Street, New York, New York 10022 (212) 751-2600; *The Economist Book of Vital World Statistics.*

The World Bank, 1818 H Street, NW, Washington, D.C. 20433 (202) 477-1234; *World Tables.*

FRANCE - AIRLINE SERVICE

European Community Information Service, 2100 M Street, NW, Washington, D.C. 20037 (202) 862-9500; *Basic Statistics of the Community, Regions: Statistical Yearbook,* and *Transport Annual Statistics.*

Facts on File, 460 Park Avenue South, New York, New York 10016 (800) 443-8323; *The New Book of World Rankings.*

G.K. Hall and Company, 70 Lincoln Street, Boston, Massachusetts 02111 (617) 423-3990; *The World in Figures.*

International Civil Aviation Organization, 1000 Sherbrooke Street West, Suite 400, Montreal, Quebec, Canada H3A 2R2 (514) 285-8219; *Civil Aviation Statistics of the World.*

National Technical Information Service, 5285 Port Royal Road, Springfield, Virginia 22161 (703) 487-4600; *Handbook of Economic Statistics.*

Organisation for Economic Co-operation and Development (OECD), 2 rue Andre-Pascal, 75 Paris 16, France (Telephone Number in U.S. (202) 785-6323); *Tourism Policy and International Tourism in OECD Member Countries.*

Statistical Office of the United Nations, Publishing Service, New York, New York 10017 (800) 253-9646; *Statistical Yearbook.*

Times Books, 201 East 50th Street, New York, New York 10022 (212) 751-2600; *The Economist Book of Vital World Statistics.*

FRANCE - ALMOND PRODUCTION - See FRANCE - CROPS

FRANCE - ALUMINUM PRODUCTION AND CONSUMPTION - See FRANCE - MINING AND MINERAL PRODUCTS

FRANCE - ANIMAL FEEDINGSTUFFS

Organisation for Economic Co-operation and Development (OECD), 2 rue Andre-Pascal, 75 Paris 16, France (Telephone Number in U.S. (202) 785-6323); *Foreign Trade by Commodities.*

Statistical Office of the United Nations, Publishing Service, New York, New York 10017 (800) 253-9646; *Statistical Yearbook.*

FRANCE - ANIMAL HEALTH

Food and Agricultural Organization of the United Nations (FAO), Via delle Terme di Caracalla, 00100 Rome, Italy (Telephone Number in U.S. (202) 653-2400); *Animal Health Yearbook.*

FRANCE - ANTIMONY AND ANTIMONY ORE - See FRANCE - MINING AND MINERAL PRODUCTS

FRANCE - APPLE PRODUCTION - See FRANCE - CROPS

FRANCE - AREA AND DENSITY OF POPULATION

European Community Information Service, 2100 M Street, NW, Washington, D.C. 20037 (202) 862-9500; *Basic Statistics of the Community,* and *Demographic Statistics.*

Facts on File, 460 Park Avenue South, New York, New York 10016 (800) 443-8323; *The New Book of World Rankings.*

Federal Statistical Office, Gustav - Stresemann - Ring 11, D-6200 Wiesbaden, Germany; *Frankreich.*

Food and Agricultural Organization of the United Nations (FAO) Via delle Terme di Caracalla, 00100 Rome, Italy (Telephone Number in U.S. (202) 653-2400); *The State of Food and Agriculture.*

G.K. Hall and Company, 70 Lincoln Street, Boston, Massachusetts 02111 (617) 423-3990; *The World in Figures.*

National Technical Information Service, 5285 Port Royal Road, Springfield, Virginia 22161 (703) 487-4600; *Handbook of Economic Statistics.*

Statistical Office of the United Nations, Publishing Service, New York, New York 10017 (800) 253-9646; *Statistical Yearbook.*

Times Books, 201 East 50th Street, New York, New York 10022 (212) 751-2600; *The Economist Book of Vital World Statistics.*

United Nations Educational, Scientific and Cultural Organization (UNESCO), 7 Place de Fontenoy, F-75700 Paris, France (Telephone Number in U.S. (212) 963-5981); *Statistical Yearbook.*

FRANCE - ARMS EXPORTS AND IMPORTS

U.S. Arms Control and Disarmament Agency, 320 Twenty-first Street, NW, Washington, D.C. 20451 (202) 647-8677; *World Military Expenditures and Arms Transfers.*

FRANCE - ARSENIC PRODUCTION AND CONSUMPTION - See FRANCE - MINING AND MINERAL PRODUCTS

FRANCE - ARTICHOKE PRODUCTION - See FRANCE - CROPS

FRANCE - BALANCE OF PAYMENTS

The Economist Intelligence Unit, 111 West 57th Street, New York, New York 10019 (800) 938-4685; *The World Market Atlas.*

European Community Information Service, 2100 M Street, NW, Washington, D.C. 20037 (202) 862-9500; *ACP: Basic Statistics, Basic Statistics of the Community, Energy Statistics Yearbook,* and *Eurostatistics: Data for Short-Term Economic Analysis.*

Federal Statistical Office, Gustav - Stresemann - Ring 11, D-6200 Wiesbaden, Germany; *Frankreich.*

G.K. Hall and Company, 70 Lincoln Street, Boston, Massachusetts 02111 (617) 423-3990; *The World in Figures.*

International Monetary Fund, 700 Nineteenth Street, NW, Washington, D.C. 20431 (202) 623-7000; *Balance of Payments Yearbook,* and *International Financial Statistics.*

National Technical Information Service, 5285 Port Royal Road, Springfield, Virginia 22161 (703) 487-4600; *Handbook of Economic Statistics.*

Organisation for Economic Co-operation and Development (OECD), 2 rue Andre-Pascal, 75 Paris 16, France (Telephone Number in U.S. (202) 785-6323); *Economic Outlook, Geographical Distribution of Financial Flows to Developing Countries, Main Economic Indicators - Historical Statistics,* and *OECD Economic Surveys: France.*

Times Books, 201 East 50th Street, New York, New York 10022 (212) 751-2600; *The Economist Book of Vital World Statistics.*

The World Bank, 1818 H Street, NW, Washington, D.C. 20433 (202) 477-1234; *World Tables.*

FRANCE - BANANA PRODUCTION - See FRANCE - CROPS

FRANCE - BANKING

European Community Information Service, 2100 M Street, NW, Washington, D.C. 20037 (202) 862-9500; *ACP: Basic Statistics.*

Facts on File, 460 Park Avenue South, New York, New York 10016 (800) 443-8323; *The New Book of World Rankings.*

G.K. Hall and Company, 70 Lincoln Street, Boston, Massachusetts 02111 (617) 423-3990; *The World in Figures.*

International Monetary Fund, 700 Nineteenth Street, NW, Washington, D.C. 20431 (202) 623-7000; *Government Finance Statistics Yearbook,* and *International Financial Statistics.*

National Technical Information Service, 5285 Port Royal Road, Springfield, Virginia 22161 (703) 487-4600; *Handbook of Economic Statistics.*

Organisation for Economic Co-operation and Development (OECD), 2 rue Andre-Pascal, 75 Paris 16, France (Telephone Number in U.S. (202) 785-6323); *Economic Outlook, Financial Market Trends,* and *OECD Economic Surveys: France.*

Statistical Office of the United Nations, Publishing Service, New York, New York 10017 (800) 253-9646; *Statistical Yearbook.*

FRANCE - BARLEY PRODUCTION - See FRANCE - CROPS

FRANCE - BAUXITE PRODUCTION AND CONSUMPTION - See FRANCE - MINING AND MINERAL PRODUCTS

FRANCE - BEER PRODUCTION

Facts on File, 460 Park Avenue South, New York, New York 10016 (800) 443-8323; *The New Book of World Rankings.*

Statistical Office of the United Nations, Publishing Service, New York, New York 10017 (800) 253-9646; *Statistical Yearbook.*

FRANCE - BEVERAGES - PRODUCTION INDEX

Organisation for Economic Co-operation and Development (OECD), 2 rue Andre-Pascal, 75 Paris 16, France (Telephone Number in U.S. (202) 785-6323); *Indicators of Industrial Activity.*

FRANCE - BIRTH RATE

European Community Information Service, 2100 M Street, NW, Washington, D.C. 20037 (202) 862-9500; *Basic Statistics of the Community, Demographic Statistics.*

Facts on File, 460 Park Avenue South, New York, New York 10016 (800) 443-8323; *The New Book of World Rankings.*

Organisation for Economic Co-operation and Development (OECD), 2 rue Andre-Pascal, 75 Paris 16, France (Telephone Number in U.S. (202) 785-6323); *Labour Force Statistics.*

Statistical Office of the United Nations, Publishing Service, New York, New York 10017 (800) 253-9646; *Demographic Yearbook,* and *Statistical Yearbook.*

Times Books, 201 East 50th Street, New York, New York 10022 (212) 751-2600; *The Economist Book of Vital World Statistics.*

The World Bank, 1818 H Street, NW, Washington, D.C. 20433 (202) 477-1234; *World Tables.*

World Health Organization, Office of Publications, Avenue Appia, CH-1211 Geneva 27, Switzerland (Telephone Number in U.S. (518) 436-9686); *World Health Statistics Annual.*

FRANCE - BISMUTH PRODUCTION AND CONSUMPTION - See FRANCE - MINING AND MINERAL PRODUCTS

FRANCE - BONDS

European Community Information Service, 2100 M Street, NW, Washington, D.C. 20037 (202) 862-9500; *Basic Statistics of the Community.*

G.K. Hall and Company, 70 Lincoln Street, Boston, Massachusetts 02111 (617) 423-3990; *The World in Figures.*

International Monetary Fund, 700 Nineteenth Street, NW, Washington, D.C. 20431 (202) 623-7000; *Government Finance Statistics Yearbook.*

Organisation for Economic Co-operation and Development (OECD), 2 rue Andre-Pascal, 75 Paris 16, France (Telephone Number in U.S. (202) 785-6323); *Financial Market Trends.*

Statistical Office of the United Nations, Publishing Service, New York, New York 10017 (800) 253-9646; *Statistical Yearbook.*

FRANCE - BOOK PRODUCTION

Euromonitor Publications Limited, 87-88 Turnmill Street, London EC1M 5QU, England; *European Marketing Data and Statistics.*

G.K. Hall and Company, 70 Lincoln Street, Boston, Massachusetts 02111 (617) 423-3990; *The World in Figures.*

Organisation for Economic Co-operation and Development (OECD), 2 rue Andre-Pascal, 75 Paris 16, France (Telephone Number in U.S.

(202) 785-6323); *Indicators of Industrial Activity.*

FRANCE - BROADCASTING

Billboard Limited, P.O. Box 9027, 1006 AA Amsterdam, The Netherlands (Telephone Number in U.S. (212) 764-7300); *World Radio TV Handbook.*

European Community Information Service, 2100 M Street, NW, Washington, D.C. 20037 (202) 862-9500; *Basic Statistics of the Community.*

Facts on File, 460 Park Avenue South, New York, New York 10016 (800) 443-8323; *The New Book of World Rankings.*

G.K. Hall and Company, 70 Lincoln Street, Boston, Massachusetts 02111 (617) 423-3990; *The World in Figures.*

Times Books, 201 East 50th Street, New York, New York 10022 (212) 751-2600; *The Economist Book of Vital World Statistics.*

United Nations Educational, Scientific and Cultural Organization (UNESCO), 7 Place de Fontenoy, F-75700 Paris, France (Telephone Number in U.S. (212) 963-5981); *Statistical Yearbook.*

FRANCE - BUILDING CONSTRUCTION - See FRANCE - CONSTRUCTION INDUSTRY

FRANCE - BUSINESS

European Community Information Service, 2100 M Street, NW, Washington, D.C. 20037 (202) 862-9500; *Basic Statistics of the Community.*

G.K. Hall and Company, 70 Lincoln Street, Boston, Massachusetts 02111 (617) 423-3990; *The World in Figures.*

FRANCE - BUSINESS AND PROFESSIONAL LICENSES

International Monetary Fund, 700 Nineteenth Street, NW, Washington, D.C. 20431 (202) 623-7000; *Government Finance Statistics Yearbook.*

FRANCE - BUTTER EXPORTS AND IMPORTS - See FRANCE - DAIRY PRODUCTS

FRANCE - CABBAGE PRODUCTION - See FRANCE - CROPS

FRANCE - CADMIUM PRODUCTION AND CONSUMPTION - See FRANCE - MINING AND MINERAL PRODUCTS

FRANCE - CALORIE SUPPLY

Food and Agricultural Organization of the United Nations (FAO) Via delle Terme di Caracalla, 00100 Rome, Italy (Telephone Number in U.S. (202) 653-2400); *The State of Food and Agriculture.*

FRANCE - CAPITAL INVESTMENT

National Technical Information Service, 5285 Port Royal Road, Springfield, Virginia 22161 (703) 487-4600; *Handbook of Economic Statistics.*

Organisation for Economic Co-operation and Development (OECD), 2 rue Andre-Pascal, 75 Paris 16, France (Telephone Number in U.S. (202) 785-6323); *Economic Outlook,* and *Financial Market Trends.*

FRANCE - CAPITAL REVENUE

International Monetary Fund, 700 Nineteenth Street, NW, Washington, D.C. 20431 (202) 623-7000; *Government Finance Statistics Yearbook.*

Organisation for Economic Co-operation and Development (OECD), 2 rue Andre-Pascal, 75 Paris 16, France (Telephone Number in U.S. (202) 785-6323); *Economic Outlook,* and *Financial Market Trends.*

FRANCE - CASHEW NUT PRODUCTION - See FRANCE - CROPS

FRANCE - CASTOR BEAN PRODUCTION - See FRANCE - CROPS

FRANCE - CATTLE - See FRANCE - LIVESTOCK AND POULTRY

FRANCE - CAULIFLOWER PRODUCTION - See FRANCE - CROPS

FRANCE - CAUSTIC SODA PRODUCTION

European Community Information Service, 2100 M Street, NW, Washington, D.C. 20037 (202) 862-9500; *Basic Statistics of the Community.*

National Technical Information Service, 5285 Port Royal Road, Springfield, Virginia 22161 (703) 487-4600; *Handbook of Economic Statistics.*

Organisation for Economic Co-operation and Development (OECD), 2 rue Andre-Pascal, 75 Paris 16, France (Telephone Number in U.S. (202) 785-6323); *Indicators of Industrial Activity.*

Statistical Office of the United Nations, Publishing Service, New York, New York 10017 (800) 253-9646; *Statistical Yearbook.*

FRANCE - CEMENT PRODUCTION - See FRANCE - MINING AND MINERAL PRODUCTS

FRANCE - CEREAL PRODUCTION - See FRANCE - CROPS

FRANCE - CHEESE - See FRANCE - DAIRY PRODUCTS

FRANCE - CHEMICAL INDUSTRY

European Community Information Service, 2100 M Street, NW, Washington, D.C. 20037 (202) 862-9500; *Industrial Production: Quarterly Statistics.*

FRANCE - CHEMICAL (ORGANIC) PRODUCTION - See FRANCE - MINING AND MINERAL PRODUCTS

FRANCE - CHESTNUT PRODUCTION - See FRANCE - CROPS

FRANCE - CHICKENS - See FRANCE - LIVESTOCK AND POULTRY

FRANCE - CHROMITE PRODUCTION AND CONSUMPTION - See FRANCE - MINING AND MINERAL PRODUCTS

FRANCE - CHROMIUM ORE PRODUCTION AND CONSUMPTION - See FRANCE - MINING AND MINERAL PRODUCTS

FRANCE - CIGAR PRODUCTION - See FRANCE - TOBACCO PRODUCTION

FRANCE - CIGARETTE PRODUCTION - See FRANCE - TOBACCO PRODUCTION

FRANCE - CLASS STRUCTURE

European Community Information Service, 2100 M Street, NW, Washington, D.C. 20037 (202) 862-9500; *Basic Statistics of the Community*, and *Labor Force Sample Survey*.

G.K. Hall and Company, 70 Lincoln Street, Boston, Massachusetts 02111 (617) 423-3990; *The World in Figures*.

FRANCE - CLIMATE

Facts on File, 460 Park Avenue South, New York, New York 10016 (800) 443-8323; *The New Book of World Rankings*.

G.K. Hall and Company, 70 Lincoln Street, Boston, Massachusetts 02111 (617) 423-3990; *The World in Figures*.

FRANCE - CLOTHING - PRODUCTION INDEX

Organisation for Economic Co-operation and Development (OECD), 2 rue Andre-Pascal, 75 Paris 16, France (Telephone Number in U.S. (202) 785-6323); *Indicators of Industrial Activity*.

FRANCE - CLOTHING EXPORTS AND IMPORTS

European Community Information Service, 2100 M Street, NW, Washington, D.C. 20037 (202) 862-9500; *Basic Statistics of the Community*.

Organisation for Economic Co-operation and Development (OECD), 2 rue Andre-Pascal, 75 Paris 16, France (Telephone Number in U.S. (202) 785-6323); *Textile Industry in OECD Countries*.

Statistical Office of the United Nations, Publishing Service, New York, New York 10017 (800) 253-9646; *Trade in Manufactures of Developing Countries*.

FRANCE - COAL PRODUCTION - See FRANCE - MINING AND MINERAL PRODUCTS

FRANCE - COBALT PRODUCTION AND CONSUMPTION - See FRANCE - MINING AND MINERAL PRODUCTS

FRANCE - COCOA (BEANS) PRODUCTION - See FRANCE - CROPS

FRANCE - COFFEE - See FRANCE - CROPS

FRANCE - COKE AND COKE OVEN AND ORE - See FRANCE - MINING AND MINERAL PRODUCTS

FRANCE - COMMUNICATIONS

European Community Information Service, 2100 M Street, NW, Washington, D.C. 20037 (202) 862-9500; *Basic Statistics of the Community*, and *Transport Annual Statistics*.

Federal Statistical Office, Gustav - Stresemann - Ring 11, D-6200 Wiesbaden, Germany; *Frankreich*.

G.K. Hall and Company, 70 Lincoln Street, Boston, Massachusetts 02111 (617) 423-3990; *The World in Figures*.

FRANCE - CONSTRUCTION INDUSTRY

European Community Information Service, 2100 M Street, NW, Washington, D.C. 20037 (202) 862-9500; *Basic Statistics of the Community*, and *Labor Force Sample Survey*.

Facts on File, 460 Park Avenue South, New York, New York 10016 (800) 443-8323; *The New Book of World Rankings*.

Organisation for Economic Co-operation and Development (OECD), 2 rue Andre-Pascal, 75 Paris 16, France (Telephone Number in U.S. (202) 785-6323); *Industrial Structure Statistics*, *The Iron and Steel Industry*, *Main Economic Indicators - Historical Statistics*, and *OECD Economic Surveys: France*.

Statistical Office of the United Nations, Publishing Service, New York, New York 10017 (800) 253-9646; *Construction Statistics Yearbook*, and *Statistical Yearbook*.

FRANCE - CONSUMER PRICE INDEX

European Community Information Service, 2100 M Street, NW, Washington, D.C. 20037 (202) 862-9500; *Basic Statistics of the Community*, and *Eurostatistics: Data for Short-Term Economic Analysis*.

Federal Statistical Office, Gustav - Stresemann - Ring 11, D-6200 Wiesbaden, Germany; *Frankreich*.

G.K. Hall and Company, 70 Lincoln Street, Boston, Massachusetts 02111 (617) 423-3990; *The World in Figures*.

National Technical Information Service, 5285 Port Royal Road, Springfield, Virginia 22161 (703) 487-4600; *Handbook of Economic Statistics*.

Organisation for Economic Co-operation and Development (OECD), 2 rue Andre-Pascal, 75 Paris 16, France (Telephone Number in U.S. (202) 785-6323); *Economic Outlook*.

Statistical Office of the United Nations, Publishing Service, New York, New York 10017 (800) 253-9646; *Statistical Yearbook*.

FRANCE - CONSUMER PRICES

Euromonitor Publications Limited, 87-88 Turnmill Street, London EC1M 5QU, England; *European Marketing Data and Statistics*.

European Community Information Service, 2100 M Street, NW, Washington, D.C. 20037 (202) 862-9500; *Basic Statistics of the Community*, and *Money and Finance*.

Federal Statistical Office, Gustav - Stresemann - Ring 11, D-6200 Wiesbaden, Germany; *Frankreich*.

International Labour Office, I.L.O. Publications, CH-1211, Geneva 22, Switzerland; *Yearbook of Labour Statistics*.

International Monetary Fund, 700 Nineteenth Street, NW, Washington, D.C. 20431 (202) 623-7000; *International Financial Statistics*.

Organisation for Economic Co-operation and Development (OECD), 2 rue Andre-Pascal, 75 Paris 16, France (Telephone Number in U.S. (202) 785-6323); *Economic Outlook*.

Times Books, 201 East 50th Street, New York, New York 10022 (212) 751-2600; *The Economist Book of Vital World Statistics*.

FRANCE - CONSUMPTION

European Community Information Service, 2100 M Street, NW, Washington, D.C. 20037 (202) 862-9500; *Basic Statistics of the Community*.

G.K. Hall and Company, 70 Lincoln Street, Boston, Massachusetts 02111 (617) 423-3990; *The World in Figures.*

International Iron and Steel Institute, 120, rue Colonel Bourg, B-1140, Belgium; *Steel Statistical Yearbook.*

International Lead and Zinc Study Group, Metro House, 58 St. James's Street, London SW1A 1LD, England; *Lead and Zinc Statistics.*

International Monetary Fund, 700 Nineteenth Street, NW, Washington, D.C. 20431 (202) 623-7000; *International Financial Statistics.*

International Rubber Study Group, York House, 8th Floor, Empire Way, Wembley, London HA9 0PA, England; *Rubber Statistical Bulletin.*

National Technical Information Service, 5285 Port Royal Road, Springfield, Virginia 22161 (703) 487-4600; *Handbook of Economic Statistics.*

Organisation for Economic Co-operation and Development (OECD), 2 rue Andre-Pascal, 75 Paris 16, France (Telephone Number in U.S. (202) 785-6323); *The Footwear, Raw Hides and Skins, and Leather Industry in OECD Countries, The Iron and Steel Industry, Meat Balances in OECD Member Countries, The Non-Ferrous Metals Industry, The Pulp and Paper Industry,* and *Textile Industry in OECD Countries.*

FRANCE - COPPER AND COPPER ORE - See FRANCE - MINING AND MINERAL PRODUCTS

FRANCE - CORN PRODUCTION - See FRANCE - CROPS

FRANCE - CORPORATE INCOME TAXES - See FRANCE - TAXATION

FRANCE - CORPORATE TAXES - See FRANCE - TAXATION

FRANCE - COTTON - See FRANCE - CROPS

FRANCE - CRIME

International Criminal Police Organization (INTERPOL), 26 rue Armengaud, 92210 Saint Cloud, France; *International Crime Statistics.*

Yale University Press, Yale Station, New Haven, Connecticut 06520 (203) 432-0940; *Violence and Crime in Cross-National Perspective.*

FRANCE - CROPS

Commodity Research Bureau, Incorporated, 75 Wall Street, New York, New York 10005 (212) 504-7754; *Commodity Year Book.*

Euromonitor Publications Limited, 87-88 Turnmill Street, London EC1M 5QU, England; *European Marketing Data and Statistics.*

European Community Information Service, 2100 M Street, NW, Washington, D.C. 20037 (202) 862-9500; *ACP: Basic Statistics, Agriculture: Statistical Yearbook, Basic Statistics of the Community, Crop Production: Quarterly Statistics, Eurostatistics: Data for Short-Term Economic Analysis,* and *Regions: Statistical Yearbook.*

Facts on File, 460 Park Avenue South, New York, New York 10016 (800) 443-8323; *The New Book of World Rankings.*

Food and Agricultural Organization of the United Nations (FAO) Via delle Terme di Caracalla, 00100 Rome, Italy (Telephone Number in U.S. (202) 653-2400); *Production Yearbook,* and *The State of Food and Agriculture.*

G.K. Hall and Company, 70 Lincoln Street, Boston, Massachusetts 02111 (617) 423-3990; *The World in Figures.*

International Wheat Statistics, 28 Haymarket, London SW1Y 4SS, England; *World Wheat Statistics.*

National Technical Information Service, 5285 Port Royal Road, Springfield, Virginia 22161 (703) 487-4600; *Handbook of Economic Statistics.*

National Technical Information Service, 5285 Port Royal Road, Springfield, Virginia 22161 (703) 487-4600; *Handbook of Economic Statistics.*

Organisation for Economic Co-operation and Development (OECD), 2 rue Andre-Pascal, 75 Paris 16, France (Telephone Number in U.S. (202) 785-6323); *Economic Accounts for Agriculture, Foreign Trade by Commodities,* and *Textile Industry in OECD Countries.*

Statistical Office of the United Nations, Publishing Service, New York, New York 10017 (800) 253-9646; *Statistical Yearbook.*

FRANCE - CUSTOMS DUTIES

European Community Information Service, 2100 M Street, NW, Washington, D.C. 20037 (202) 862-9500; *Basic Statistics of the Community.*

G.K. Hall and Company, 70 Lincoln Street, Boston, Massachusetts 02111 (617) 423-3990; *The World in Figures.*

International Monetary Fund, 700 Nineteenth Street, NW, Washington, D.C. 20431 (202) 623-7000; *Government Finance Statistics Yearbook.*

Organisation for Economic Co-operation and Development (OECD), 2 rue Andre-Pascal, 75 Paris 16, France (Telephone Number in U.S. (202) 785-6323); *The Non-Ferrous Metals Industry.*

FRANCE - DAIRY PRODUCTS

Commodity Research Bureau, Incorporated, 75 Wall Street, New York, New York 10005 (212) 504-7754; *Commodity Year Book.*

European Community Information Service, 2100 M Street, NW, Washington, D.C. 20037 (202) 862-9500; *Eurostatistics: Data for Short-Term Economic Analysis.*

Facts on File, 460 Park Avenue South, New York, New York 10016 (800) 443-8323; *The New Book of World Rankings.*

Food and Agricultural Organization of the United Nations (FAO) Via delle Terme di Caracalla, 00100 Rome, Italy (Telephone Number in U.S. (202) 653-2400); *The State of Food and Agriculture.*

National Technical Information Service, 5285 Port Royal Road, Springfield, Virginia 22161 (703) 487-4600; *Handbook of Economic Statistics.*

Organisation for Economic Co-operation and Development (OECD), 2 rue Andre-Pascal, 75 Paris 16, France (Telephone Number in U.S. (202) 785-6323); *Economic Accounts for Agriculture,* and *Milk, Milk Products, and Egg Balances in OECD Member Countries.*

Statistical Office of the United Nations, Publishing Service, New York, New York 10017 (800) 253-9646; *Statistical Yearbook.*

FRANCE - DEATH RATE

European Community Information Service, 2100 M Street, NW, Washington, D.C. 20037 (202) 862-9500; *Basic Statistics of the Community,* and *Demographic Statistics.*

G.K. Hall and Company, 70 Lincoln Street, Boston, Massachusetts 02111 (617) 423-3990; *The World in Figures.*

Statistical Office of the United Nations, Publishing Service, New York, New York 10017 (800) 253-9646; *Statistical Yearbook.*

Times Books, 201 East 50th Street, New York, New York 10022 (212) 751-2600; *The Economist Book of Vital World Statistics.*

World Health Organization, Office of Publications, Avenue Appia, CH-1211 Geneva 27, Switzerland (Telephone Number in U.S. (518) 436-9686); *World Health Statistics Annual.*

FRANCE - DEFENSE EXPENDITURES

European Community Information Service, 2100 M Street, NW, Washington, D.C. 20037 (202) 862-9500; *Government Financing of Research and Development.*

G.K. Hall and Company, 70 Lincoln Street, Boston, Massachusetts 02111 (617) 423-3990; *The World in Figures.*

International Monetary Fund, 700 Nineteenth Street, NW, Washington, D.C. 20431 (202) 623-7000; *Government Finance Statistics Yearbook.*

National Technical Information Service, 5285 Port Royal Road, Springfield, Virginia 22161 (703) 487-4600; *Handbook of Economic Statistics.*

U.S. Arms Control and Disarmament Agency, 320 Twenty-first Street, NW, Washington, D.C. 20451 (202) 647-8677; *World Military Expenditures and Arms Transfers.*

FRANCE - DEMOGRAPHY

The Economist Intelligence Unit, 111 West 57th Street, New York, New York 10019 (800) 938-4685; *The World Market Atlas.*

European Community Information Service, 2100 M Street, NW, Washington, D.C. 20037 (202) 862-9500; *Basic Statistics of the Community, Demographic Statistics, Employment and Unemployment,* and *Regions: Statistical Yearbook.*

Facts on File, 460 Park Avenue South, New York, New York 10016 (800) 443-8323; *The New Book of World Rankings.*

Federal Statistical Office, Gustav - Stresemann - Ring 11, D-6200 Wiesbaden, Germany; *Frankreich.*

G.K. Hall and Company, 70 Lincoln Street, Boston, Massachusetts 02111 (617) 423-3990; *The World in Figures.*

FRANCE - DEVELOPMENT ASSISTANCE

European Community Information Service, 2100 M Street, NW, Washington, D.C. 20037 (202) 862-9500; *ACP: Basic Statistics, Basic Statistics of the Community,* and *Government Financing of Research and Development.*

G.K. Hall and Company, 70 Lincoln Street, Boston, Massachusetts 02111 (617) 423-3990; *The World in Figures.*

Organisation for Economic Co-operation and Development (OECD), 2 rue Andre-Pascal, 75 Paris 16, France (Telephone Number in U.S. (202) 785-6323); *Geographical Distribution of Financial Flows to Developing Countries.*

Statistical Office of the United Nations, Publishing Service, New York, New York 10017 (800) 253-9646; *Statistical Yearbook.*

FRANCE - DIAMOND EXPORTS AND PRODUCTION - See FRANCE - MINING AND MINERAL PRODUCTS

FRANCE - DISCOUNT RATES

Organisation for Economic Co-operation and Development (OECD), 2 rue Andre-Pascal, 75 Paris 16, France (Telephone Number in U.S. (202) 785-6323); *Financial Market Trends.*

Statistical Office of the United Nations, Publishing Service, New York, New York 10017 (800) 253-9646; *Statistical Yearbook.*

FRANCE - DISEASES

G.K. Hall and Company, 70 Lincoln Street, Boston, Massachusetts 02111 (617) 423-3990; *The World in Figures.*

World Health Organization, Office of Publications, Avenue Appia, CH-1211 Geneva 27, Switzerland (Telephone Number in U.S. (518) 436-9686); *World Health Statistics Annual.*

FRANCE - DIVORCE RATES

European Community Information Service, 2100 M Street, NW, Washington, D.C. 20037 (202) 862-9500; *Demographic Statistics.*

Facts on File, 460 Park Avenue South, New York, New York 10016 (800) 443-8323; *The New Book of World Rankings.*

Statistical Office of the United Nations, Publishing Service, New York, New York 10017 (800) 253-9646; *Demographic Yearbook,* and *Statistical Yearbook.*

FRANCE - DOMESTIC PRODUCT

European Community Information Service, 2100 M Street, NW, Washington, D.C. 20037 (202) 862-9500; *Basic Statistics of the Community.*

G.K. Hall and Company, 70 Lincoln Street, Boston, Massachusetts 02111 (617) 423-3990; *The World in Figures.*

FRANCE - DUCKS - See FRANCE - LIVESTOCK AND POULTRY

FRANCE - ECONOMY

Euromonitor Publications Limited, 87-88 Turnmill Street, London EC1M 5QU, England; *European Marketing Data and Statistics.*

European Community Information Service, 2100 M Street, NW, Washington, D.C. 20037 (202) 862-9500; *Basic Statistics of the Community, Energy Statistics Yearbook, Labor Force Sample Survey,* and *Money and Finance.*

Facts on File, 460 Park Avenue South, New York, New York 10016 (800) 443-8323; *The New Book of World Rankings.*

Federal Statistical Office, Gustav - Stresemann - Ring 11, D-6200 Wiesbaden, Germany; *Frankreich.*

G.K. Hall and Company, 70 Lincoln Street, Boston, Massachusetts 02111 (617) 423-3990; *The World in Figures.*

National Technical Information Service, 5285 Port Royal Road, Springfield, Virginia 22161 (703) 487-4600; *Handbook of Economic Statistics.*

Organisation for Economic Co-operation and Development (OECD), 2 rue Andre-Pascal, 75 Paris 16, France (Telephone Number in U.S. (202) 785-6323); *Economic Outlook, Geographical Distribution of Financial Flows to Developing Countries, Main Economic Indicators - Historical Statistics, OECD Economic Surveys: France,* and *OECD Employment Outlook.*

FRANCE - EDUCATION

The Economist Intelligence Unit, 111 West 57th Street, New York, New York 10019 (800) 938-4685; *The World Market Atlas.*

Euromonitor Publications Limited, 87-88 Turnmill Street, London EC1M 5QU, England; *European Marketing Data and Statistics.*

European Community Information Service, 2100 M Street, NW, Washington, D.C. 20037 (202) 862-9500; *Basic Statistics of the Community,* and *Regions: Statistical Yearbook.*

Facts on File, 460 Park Avenue South, New York, New York 10016 (800) 443-8323; *The New Book of World Rankings.*

Federal Statistical Office, Gustav - Stresemann - Ring 11, D-6200 Wiesbaden, Germany; *Frankreich.*

G.K. Hall and Company, 70 Lincoln Street, Boston, Massachusetts 02111 (617) 423-3990; *The World in Figures.*

International Monetary Fund, 700 Nineteenth Street, NW, Washington, D.C. 20431 (202) 623-7000; *Government Finance Statistics Yearbook.*

Organisation for Economic Co-operation and Development (OECD), 2 rue Andre-Pascal, 75 Paris 16, France (Telephone Number in U.S. (202) 785-6323); *Education in OECD Countries.*

Times Books, 201 East 50th Street, New York, New York 10022 (212) 751-2600; *The Economist Book of Vital World Statistics.*

The World Bank, 1818 H Street, NW, Washington, D.C. 20433 (202) 477-1234; *World Tables.*

FRANCE - EGG PRODUCTION AND CONSUMPTION - See FRANCE - DAIRY PRODUCTS

FRANCE - EGGPLANT PRODUCTION - See FRANCE - CROPS

FRANCE - ELECTRICITY

Commodity Research Bureau, Incorporated, 75 Wall Street, New York, New York 10005 (212) 504-7754; *Commodity Year Book.*

European Community Information Service, 2100 M Street, NW, Washington, D.C. 20037 (202) 862-9500; *Basic Statistics of the Community, Energy: Monthly Statistics, Energy Statistics Yearbook, Eurostatistics: Data for Short-Term Economic Analysis,* and *Regions: Statistical Yearbook.*

Facts on File, 460 Park Avenue South, New York, New York 10016 (800) 443-8323; *The New Book of World Rankings.*

National Technical Information Service, 5285 Port Royal Road, Springfield, Virginia 22161 (703) 487-4600; *Handbook of Economic Statistics.*

Organisation for Economic Co-operation and Development (OECD), 2 rue Andre-Pascal, 75 Paris 16, France (Telephone Number in U.S. (202) 785-6323); *Coal Information, Energy Statistics of OECD Countries, Indicators of Industrial Activity,* and *Industrial Structure Statistics.*

Penn Well Publishing Company, 1421 South Sheridan Road, P.O. Box 1260, Tulsa, Oklahoma 74101 (800) 752-9764; *International Energy Statistics Sourcebook.*

Statistical Office of the United Nations, Publishing Service, New York, New York 10017 (800) 253-9646; *Statistical Yearbook.*

Times Books, 201 East 50th Street, New York, New York 10022 (212) 751-2600; *The Economist Book of Vital World Statistics.*

FRANCE - EMPLOYMENT

Euromonitor Publications Limited, 87-88 Turnmill Street, London EC1M 5QU, England; *European Marketing Data and Statistics.*

European Community Information Service, 2100 M Street, NW, Washington, D.C. 20037 (202) 862-9500; *Basic Statistics of the Community, Earnings in Agriculture, Employment and Unemployment, Eurostatistics: Data for Short-Term Economic Analysis, Labor Force Sample Survey, Iron and Steel: Statistical Yearbook,* and *Transport Annual Statistics.*

Facts on File, 460 Park Avenue South, New York, New York 10016 (800) 443-8323; *The New Book of World Rankings.*

Federal Statistical Office, Gustav - Stresemann - Ring 11, D-6200 Wiesbaden, Germany; *Frankreich.*

International Labour Office, I.L.O. Publications, CH-1211, Geneva 22, Switzerland; *Yearbook of Labour Statistics.*

National Technical Information Service, 5285 Port Royal Road, Springfield, Virginia 22161 (703) 487-4600; *Handbook of Economic Statistics.*

Organisation for Economic Co-operation and Development (OECD), 2 rue Andre-Pascal, 75 Paris 16, France (Telephone Number in U.S. (202) 785-6323); *Economic Outlook, The Iron and Steel Industry, OECD Economic Surveys: France, OECD Employment Outlook,* and *Textile Industry in OECD Countries.*

Statistical Office of the United Nations, Publishing Service, New York, New York 10017 (800) 253-9646; *Statistical Yearbook.*

FRANCE - ENERGY

Euromonitor Publications Limited, 87-88 Turnmill Street, London EC1M 5QU, England; *European Marketing Data and Statistics.*

European Community Information Service, 2100 M Street, NW, Washington, D.C. 20037 (202) 862-9500; *Basic Statistics of the Community, Energy: Monthly Statistics, Energy Statistics Yearbook, Regions: Statistical Yearbook,* and *Transport Annual Statistics.*

Facts on File, 460 Park Avenue South, New York, New York 10016 (800) 443-8323; *The New Book of World Rankings.*

Food and Agricultural Organization of the United Nations (FAO) Via delle Terme di Caracalla, 00100 Rome, Italy (Telephone Number in U.S. (202) 653-2400); *The State of Food and Agriculture.*

G.K. Hall and Company, 70 Lincoln Street, Boston, Massachusetts 02111 (617) 423-3990; *The World in Figures.*

National Technical Information Service, 5285 Port Royal Road, Springfield, Virginia 22161 (703) 487-4600; *Handbook of Economic Statistics.*

Organisation for Economic Co-operation and Development (OECD), 2 rue Andre-Pascal, 75 Paris 16, France (Telephone Number in U.S. (202) 785-6323); *Coal Information, Energy Statistics of OECD Countries, OECD Environmental Data,* and *Oil and Gas Information.*

Penn Well Publishing Company, 1421 South Sheridan Road, P.O. Box 1260, Tulsa, Oklahoma 74101 (800) 752-9764; *International Energy Statistics Sourcebook.*

Statistical Office of the United Nations, Publishing Service, New York, New York 10017 (800) 253-9646; *Energy Statistics Yearbook,* and *Statistical Yearbook.*

Times Books, 201 East 50th Street, New York, New York 10022 (212) 751-2600; *The Economist Book of Vital World Statistics.*

FRANCE - ENGINEERING AND METAL PRODUCTS - EXPORTS AND IMPORTS

European Community Information Service, 2100 M Street, NW, Washington, D.C. 20037 (202) 862-9500; *Basic Statistics of the Community,* and *Industrial Production: Quarterly.*

Statistical Office of the United Nations, Publishing Service, New York, New York 10017 (800) 253-9646; *Trade in Manufactures of Developing Countries.*

FRANCE - ENVIRONMENT

Organization for Economic Co-operation and Development (OECD), 2 rue Andre-Pascal, 75 Paris 16, France (Telephone Number in U.S. (202) 785-6323); *OECD Environmental Data.*

FRANCE - EXCHANGE RATES

European Community Information Service, 2100 M Street, NW, Washington, D.C. 20037 (202) 862-9500; *Eurostatistics: Data for Short-Term Economic Analysis,* and *Money and Finance.*

International Civil Aviation Organization, 1000 Sherbrooke Street West, Suite 400, Montreal, Quebec, Canada H3A 2R2 (514) 285-8219; *Civil Aviation Statistics of the World.*

International Monetary Fund, 700 Nineteenth Street, NW, Washington, D.C. 20431 (202) 623-7000; *International Financial Statistics.*

National Technical Information Service, 5285 Port Royal Road, Springfield, Virginia 22161 (703) 487-4600; *Handbook of Economic Statistics.*

Organisation for Economic Co-operation and Development (OECD), 2 rue Andre-Pascal, 75 Paris 16, France (Telephone Number in U.S. (202) 785-6323); *Economic Outlook, Financial Market Trends, Revenue Statistics of OECD Member Countries,* and *Tourism Policy and International Tourism in OECD Member Countries.*

Statistical Office of the United Nations, Publishing Service, New York, New York 10017 (800) 253-9646; *Statistical Yearbook.*

FRANCE - EXCISE TAXES - See FRANCE - TAXATION

FRANCE - EXPORTS

American Automobile Manufacturers Association, 1401 H Street, NW, Suite 900, Washington, D.C. 20005 (202) 326-5500; *World Motor Vehicle Data.*

The Economist Intelligence Unit, 111 West 57th Street, New York, New York 10019 (800) 938-4685; *The World Market Atlas.*

European Community Information Service, 2100 M Street, NW, Washington, D.C. 20037 (202) 862-9500; *Basic Statistics of the Community, Energy: Monthly Statistics, Energy Statistics Yearbook, Eurostatistics: Data for Short-Term Economic Analysis, External Trade: Monthly Statistics, External Trade: Statistical Yearbook,* and *Fisheries: Yearly Statistics.*

Food and Agricultural Organization of the United Nations (FAO) Via delle Terme di Caracalla, 00100 Rome, Italy (Telephone Number in U.S. (202) 653-2400); *The State of Food and Agriculture.*

G.K. Hall and Company, 70 Lincoln Street, Boston, Massachusetts 02111 (617) 423-3990; *The World in Figures.*

International Iron and Steel Institute, 120, rue Colonel Bourg, B-1140, Belgium; *Steel Statistical Yearbook.*

International Lead and Zinc Study Group, Metro House, 58 St. James's Street, London SW1A 1LD, England; *Lead and Zinc Statistics.*

International Monetary Fund, 700 Nineteenth Street, NW, Washington, D.C. 20431 (202) 623-7000; *Direction of Trade Statistics, Government Finance Statistics Yearbook,* and *International Financial Statistics.*

International Rubber Study Group, York House, 8th Floor, Empire Way, Wembley, London HA9 0PA, England; *Rubber Statistical Bulletin.*

National Technical Information Service, 5285 Port Royal Road, Springfield, Virginia 22161 (703) 487-4600; *Handbook of Economic Statistics.*

Organisation for Economic Co-operation and Development (OECD), 2 rue Andre-Pascal, 75 Paris 16, France (Telephone Number in U.S. (202) 785-6323); *Economic Outlook, The Footwear, Raw Hides and Skins, and Leather Industry in OECD Countries, Foreign Trade by Commodities, Geographical Distribution of Financial Flows to Developing Countries, Industrial Structure Statistics, The Iron and Steel Industry, Milk, Milk Products, and Egg Balances in OECD Member Countries, OECD Economic Surveys: France, The Pulp and Paper Industry,* and *Review of Fisheries in OECD Member Countries.*

Times Books, 201 East 50th Street, New York, New York 10022 (212) 751-2600; *The Economist Book of Vital World Statistics.*

The World Bank, 1818 H Street, NW, Washington, D.C. 20433 (202) 477-1234; *World Tables.*

FRANCE - EXTERNAL FINANCING

Organisation for Economic Co-operation and Development (OECD), 2 rue Andre-Pascal, 75 Paris 16, France (Telephone Number in U.S.

(202) 785-6323); *Economic Outlook*, and *Financial Market Trends*.

FRANCE - EXTERNAL INDEBTEDNESS

National Technical Information Service, 5285 Port Royal Road, Springfield, Virginia 22161 (703) 487-4600; *Handbook of Economic Statistics*.

Organisation for Economic Co-operation and Development (OECD), 2 rue Andre-Pascal, 75 Paris 16, France (Telephone Number in U.S. (202) 785-6323); *Financial Market Trends*, and *Geographical Distribution of Financial Flows to Developing Countries*.

The World Bank, 1818 H Street, NW, Washington, D.C. 20433 (202) 477-1234; *World Tables*.

FRANCE - EXTERNAL TRADE

European Community Information Service, 2100 M Street, NW, Washington, D.C. 20037 (202) 862-9500; *ACP: Basic Statistics*, *Basic Statistics of the Community*, *Eurostatistics: Data for Short-Term Economic Analysis*, *External Trade: Monthly Statistics*, and *External Trade: Statistical Yearbook*.

Food and Agricultural Organization of the United Nations (FAO) Via delle Terme di Caracalla, 00100 Rome, Italy (Telephone Number in U.S. (202) 653-2400); *The State of Food and Agriculture*, and *Trade Yearbook*.

G.K. Hall and Company, 70 Lincoln Street, Boston, Massachusetts 02111 (617) 423-3990; *The World in Figures*.

National Technical Information Service, 5285 Port Royal Road, Springfield, Virginia 22161 (703) 487-4600; *Handbook of Economic Statistics*.

Statistical Office of the United Nations, Publishing Service, New York, New York 10017 (800) 253-9646; *Statistical Yearbook*.

FRANCE - FABRIC PRODUCTION - See FRANCE - TEXTILE INDUSTRY

FRANCE - FARM CROPS - See FRANCE - CROPS

FRANCE - FEMALE WORKING POPULATION - See FRANCE - EMPLOYMENT

FRANCE - FERTILITY RATES

European Community Information Service, 2100 M Street, NW, Washington, D.C. 20037 (202) 862-9500; *Demographic Statistics*.

Facts on File, 460 Park Avenue South, New York, New York 10016 (800) 443-8323; *The New Book of World Rankings*.

Times Books, 201 East 50th Street, New York, New York 10022 (212) 751-2600; *The Economist Book of Vital World Statistics*.

The World Bank, 1818 H Street, NW, Washington, D.C. 20433 (202) 477-1234; *World Tables*.

FRANCE - FERTILIZER

European Community Information Service, 2100 M Street, NW, Washington, D.C. 20037 (202) 862-9500; *Basic Statistics of the Community*.

Food and Agricultural Organization of the United Nations (FAO), Via delle Terme di Caracalla, 00100 Rome, Italy (Telephone Number in U.S. (202) 653-2400); *Fertilizer Yearbook*, and *The State of Food and Agriculture*.

National Technical Information Service, 5285 Port Royal Road, Springfield, Virginia 22161 (703) 487-4600; *Handbook of Economic Statistics*.

Organisation for Economic Co-operation and Development (OECD), 2 rue Andre-Pascal, 75 Paris 16, France (Telephone Number in U.S. (202) 785-6323); *Economic Accounts for Agriculture*, *Foreign Trade by Commodities*, and *OECD Economic Surveys: France*.

Statistical Office of the United Nations, Publishing Service, New York, New York 10017 (800) 253-9646; *Statistical Yearbook*.

FRANCE - FETAL MORTALITY

European Community Information Service, 2100 M Street, NW, Washington, D.C. 20037 (202) 862-9500; *Basic Statistics of the Community*, *Demographic Statistics*.

Statistical Office of the United Nations, Publishing Service, New York, New York 10017 (800) 253-9646; *Demographic Yearbook*.

World Health Organization, Office of Publications, Avenue Appia, CH-1211 Geneva 27, Switzerland (Telephone Number in U.S. (518) 436-9686); *World Health Statistics Annual*.

FRANCE - FIBRE PRODUCTION - See FRANCE - TEXTILE INDUSTRY

FRANCE - FILAMENT PRODUCTION - See FRANCE - TEXTILE INDUSTRY

FRANCE - FILM - See FRANCE - MOTION PICTURES

FRANCE - FINANCE

European Community Information Service, 2100 M Street, NW, Washington, D.C. 20037 (202) 862-9500; *ACP: Basic Statistics*, *Basic Statistics of the Community*, *Eurostatistics: Data for Short-Term Economic Analysis*, and *Money and Finance*.

Facts on File, 460 Park Avenue South, New York, New York 10016 (800) 443-8323; *The New Book of World Rankings*.

Federal Statistical Office, Gustav - Stresemann - Ring 11, D-6200 Wiesbaden, Germany; *Frankreich*.

G.K. Hall and Company, 70 Lincoln Street, Boston, Massachusetts 02111 (617) 423-3990; *The World in Figures*.

International Monetary Fund, 700 Nineteenth Street, NW, Washington, D.C. 20431 (202) 623-7000; *Government Finance Statistics Yearbook*, and *International Financial Statistics*.

Organisation for Economic Co-operation and Development (OECD), 2 rue Andre-Pascal, 75 Paris 16, France (Telephone Number in U.S. (202) 785-6323); *Economic Outlook*, *Financial Market Trends*, *Geographical Distribution of Financial Flows to Developing Countries*, *Main Economic Indicators - Historical Statistics*, and *OECD Financial Statistics*.

FRANCE - FISHERIES

Euromonitor Publications Limited, 87-88 Turnmill Street, London EC1M 5QU, England; *European Marketing Data and Statistics*.

European Community Information Service, 2100 M Street, NW, Washington, D.C. 20037 (202) 862-9500; *Agriculture: Statistical*

Yearbook, Basic Statistics of the Community, Fisheries: Products and Fleets.

Facts on File, 460 Park Avenue South, New York, New York 10016 (800) 443-8323; *The New Book of World Rankings.*

Federal Statistical Office, Gustav - Stresemann - Ring 11, D-6200 Wiesbaden, Germany; *Frankreich.*

Food and Agricultural Organization of the United Nations (FAO) Via delle Terme di Caracalla, 00100 Rome, Italy (Telephone Number in U.S. (202) 653-2400); *The State of Food and Agriculture,* and *Yearbook of Fishery Statistics.*

National Technical Information Service, 5285 Port Royal Road, Springfield, Virginia 22161 (703) 487-4600; *Handbook of Economic Statistics.*

Organisation for Economic Co-operation and Development (OECD), 2 rue Andre-Pascal, 75 Paris 16, France (Telephone Number in U.S. (202) 785-6323); *Foreign Trade by Commodities, Industrial Structure Statistics,* and *Review of Fisheries in OECD Member Countries.*

Statistical Office of the United Nations, Publishing Service, New York, New York 10017 (800) 253-9646; *Statistical Yearbook.*

FRANCE - FLAX AND FLAX FIBRE PRODUCTION - See FRANCE - TEXTILE INDUSTRY

FRANCE - FLOUR PRODUCTION

European Community Information Service, 2100 M Street, NW, Washington, D.C. 20037 (202) 862-9500; *Basic Statistics of the Community.*

Statistical Office of the United Nations, Publishing Service, New York, New York 10017 (800) 253-9646; *Statistical Yearbook.*

FRANCE - FOOD

European Community Information Service, 2100 M Street, NW, Washington, D.C. 20037 (202) 862-9500; *Basic Statistics of the Community.*

Food and Agricultural Organization of the United Nations (FAO) Via delle Terme di Caracalla, 00100 Rome, Italy (Telephone Number in U.S. (202) 653-2400); *Production Yearbook,* and *The State of Food and Agriculture.*

G.K. Hall and Company, 70 Lincoln Street, Boston, Massachusetts 02111 (617) 423-3990; *The World in Figures.*

Organisation for Economic Co-operation and Development (OECD), 2 rue Andre-Pascal, 75 Paris 16, France (Telephone Number in U.S. (202) 785-6323); *Food Consumption Statistics,* and *Foreign Trade by Commodities.*

Statistical Office of the United Nations, Publishing Service, New York, New York 10017 (800) 253-9646; *Statistical Yearbook,* and *Trade in Manufactures of Developing Countries.*

FRANCE - FOOTWEAR - PRODUCTION INDEX

Organisation for Economic Co-operation and Development (OECD), 2 rue Andre-Pascal, 75 Paris 16, France (Telephone Number in U.S. (202) 785-6323); *Indicators of Industrial Activity.*

FRANCE - FOREIGN AID

G.K. Hall and Company, 70 Lincoln Street, Boston, Massachusetts 02111 (617) 423-3990; *The World in Figures.*

National Technical Information Service, 5285 Port Royal Road, Springfield, Virginia 22161 (703) 487-4600; *Handbook of Economic Statistics.*

FRANCE - FOREIGN DEBT

Organisation for Economic Co-operation and Development (OECD), 2 rue Andre-Pascal, 75 Paris 16, France (Telephone Number in U.S. (202) 785-6323); *Economic Outlook.*

FRANCE - FOREIGN FINANCE

Organisation for Economic Co-operation and Development (OECD), 2 rue Andre-Pascal, 75 Paris 16, France (Telephone Number in U.S. (202) 785-6323); *Economic Outlook,* and *Financial Market Trends.*

FRANCE - FOREIGN INDEBTEDNESS

Organisation for Economic Co-operation and Development (OECD), 2 rue Andre-Pascal, 75 Paris 16, France (Telephone Number in U.S. (202) 785-6323); *Economic Outlook,* and *Financial Market Trends.*

FRANCE - FOREIGN OFFICIAL RESERVES

European Community Information Service, 2100 M Street, NW, Washington, D.C. 20037 (202) 862-9500; *Money and Finance.*

FRANCE - FOREIGN TRADE

Euromonitor Publications Limited, 87-88 Turnmill Street, London EC1M 5QU, England; *European Marketing Data and Statistics.*

European Community Information Service, 2100 M Street, NW, Washington, D.C. 20037 (202) 862-9500; *Basic Statistics of the Community,* and *Iron and Steel: Statistical Yearbook.*

Facts on File, 460 Park Avenue South, New York, New York 10016 (800) 443-8323; *The New Book of World Rankings.*

Federal Statistical Office, Gustav - Stresemann - Ring 11, D-6200 Wiesbaden, Germany; *Frankreich.*

Food and Agricultural Organization of the United Nations (FAO) Via delle Terme di Caracalla, 00100 Rome, Italy (Telephone Number in U.S. (202) 653-2400); *The State of Food and Agriculture.*

G.K. Hall and Company, 70 Lincoln Street, Boston, Massachusetts 02111 (617) 423-3990; *The World in Figures.*

International Iron and Steel Institute, 120, rue Colonel Bourg, B-1140, Belgium; *Steel Statistical Yearbook.*

International Monetary Fund, 700 Nineteenth Street, NW, Washington, D.C. 20431 (202) 623-7000; *International Financial Statistics.*

National Technical Information Service, 5285 Port Royal Road, Springfield, Virginia 22161 (703) 487-4600; *Handbook of Economic Statistics.*

Organisation for Economic Co-operation and Development (OECD), 2 rue Andre-Pascal, 75 Paris 16, France (Telephone Number in U.S. (202) 785-6323); *Economic Outlook, The Footwear, Raw Hides and Skins, and Leather Industry in OECD Countries, Foreign Trade by*

Commodities, Main Economic Indicators - Historical Statistics, Maritime Transport, Meat Balances in OECD Member Countries, and *Trade by Commodities.*

Statistical Office of the United Nations, Publishing Service, New York, New York 10017 (800) 253-9646; *International Trade Statistics Yearbook, Statistical Yearbook,* and *Trade in Manufactures of Developing Countries.*

The World Bank, 1818 H Street, NW, Washington, D.C. 20433 (202) 477-1234; *World Tables.*

World Bureau of Metal Statistics, 27-A High Street, Ware Hert SG12 9BA, England; *World Metal Statistics.*

FRANCE - FORESTRY AND FOREST PRODUCTS

Euromonitor Publications Limited, 87-88 Turnmill Street, London EC1M 5QU, England; *European Marketing Data and Statistics.*

European Community Information Service, 2100 M Street, NW, Washington, D.C. 20037 (202) 862-9500; *Agriculture: Statistical Yearbook, Basic Statistics of the Community,* and *Industrial Production: Quarterly Statistics.*

Facts on File, 460 Park Avenue South, New York, New York 10016 (800) 443-8323; *The New Book of World Rankings.*

Federal Statistical Office, Gustav - Stresemann - Ring 11, D-6200 Wiesbaden, Germany; *Frankreich.*

Food and Agricultural Organization of the United Nations (FAO) Via delle Terme di Caracalla, 00100 Rome, Italy (Telephone Number in U.S. (202) 653-2400); *The State of Food and Agriculture,* and *Yearbook of Forest Products.*

Forest and Paper Association, 1250 Connecticut Avenue, NW, Washington, D.C. 20036 (202) 463-2455; *Wood Pulp and Fiber Statistics.*

G.K. Hall and Company, 70 Lincoln Street, Boston, Massachusetts 02111 (617) 423-3990; *The World in Figures.*

National Technical Information Service, 5285 Port Royal Road, Springfield, Virginia 22161 (703) 487-4600; *Handbook of Economic Statistics.*

Organisation for Economic Co-operation and Development (OECD), 2 rue Andre-Pascal, 75 Paris 16, France (Telephone Number in U.S. (202) 785-6323); *Foreign Trade by Commodities, Indicators of Industrial Activity, Industrial Structure Statistics,* and *The Pulp and Paper Industry.*

Statistical Office of the United Nations, Publishing Service, New York, New York 10017 (800) 253-9646; *Statistical Yearbook.*

United Nations Educational, Scientific and Cultural Organization (UNESCO), 7 Place de Fontenoy, F-75700 Paris, France (Telephone Number in U.S. (212) 963-5981); *Statistical Yearbook.*

FRANCE - FRUIT PRODUCTION - See FRANCE - CROPS

FRANCE - FURNITURE AND WOOD PRODUCTS - EXPORTS AND IMPORTS

European Community Information Service, 2100 M Street, NW, Washington, D.C. 20037 (202) 862-9500; *Basic Statistics of the Community.*

Organisation for Economic Co-operation and Development (OECD), 2 rue Andre-Pascal, 75 Paris 16, France (Telephone Number in U.S. (202) 785-6323); *Foreign Trade by Commodities,* and *Industrial Structure Statistics.*

Statistical Office of the United Nations, Publishing Service, New York, New York 10017 (800) 253-9646; *Trade in Manufactures of Developing Countries.*

FRANCE - GARLIC PRODUCTION - See FRANCE - CROPS

FRANCE - GAS AND GAS LIQUIDS - See FRANCE - MINING AND MINERAL PRODUCTS

FRANCE - GENERAL INDUSTRIAL STATISTICS

European Community Information Service, 2100 M Street, NW, Washington, D.C. 20037 (202) 862-9500; *Basic Statistics of the Community.*

Federal Statistical Office, Gustav - Stresemann - Ring 11, D-6200 Wiesbaden, Germany; *Frankreich.*

Statistical Office of the United Nations, Publishing Service, New York, New York 10017 (800) 253-9646; *Industrial Statistics Yearbook.*

FRANCE - GENERAL MORTALITY

European Community Information Service, 2100 M Street, NW, Washington, D.C. 20037 (202) 862-9500; *Basic Statistics of the Community,* and *Demographic Statistics.*

Statistical Office of the United Nations, Publishing Service, New York, New York 10017 (800) 253-9646; *Demographic Yearbook.*

World Health Organization, Office of Publications, Avenue Appia, CH-1211 Geneva 27, Switzerland (Telephone Number in U.S. (518) 436-9686); *World Health Statistics Annual.*

FRANCE - GEOGRAPHIC DATA

European Community Information Service, 2100 M Street, NW, Washington, D.C. 20037 (202) 862-9500; *Basic Statistics of the Community.*

Facts on File, 460 Park Avenue South, New York, New York 10016 (800) 443-8323; *The New Book of World Rankings.*

Federal Statistical Office, Gustav - Stresemann - Ring 11, D-6200 Wiesbaden, Germany; *Frankreich.*

FRANCE - GLASS AND GLASS PRODUCTS - PRODUCTION INDEX

Organisation for Economic Co-operation and Development (OECD), 2 rue Andre-Pascal, 75 Paris 16, France (Telephone Number in U.S. (202) 785-6323); *Indicators of Industrial Activity.*

FRANCE - GOATS - See FRANCE - LIVESTOCK AND POULTRY

FRANCE - GOLD HOLDINGS

International Monetary Fund, 700 Nineteenth Street, NW, Washington, D.C. 20431 (202) 623-7000; *International Financial Statistics.*

Statistical Office of the United Nations, Publishing Service, New York, New York 10017 (800) 253-9646; *Statistical Yearbook.*

The World Bank, 1818 H Street, NW, Washington, D.C. 20433 (202) 477-1234; *World Tables*.

FRANCE - GOLD PRODUCTION AND CONSUMPTION - See FRANCE - MINING AND MINERAL PRODUCTS

FRANCE - GOVERNMENT

European Community Information Service, 2100 M Street, NW, Washington, D.C. 20037 (202) 862-9500; *Basic Statistics of the Community*.

G.K. Hall and Company, 70 Lincoln Street, Boston, Massachusetts 02111 (617) 423-3990; *The World in Figures*.

FRANCE - GOVERNMENT BONDS - See FRANCE - BONDS

FRANCE - GOVERNMENT CONSUMPTION

European Community Information Service, 2100 M Street, NW, Washington, D.C. 20037 (202) 862-9500; *Basic Statistics of the Community*.

International Monetary Fund, 700 Nineteenth Street, NW, Washington, D.C. 20431 (202) 623-7000; *International Financial Statistics*.

FRANCE - GOVERNMENT EXPENDITURES

European Community Information Service, 2100 M Street, NW, Washington, D.C. 20037 (202) 862-9500; *Basic Statistics of the Community*, and *Government Financing of Research and Development*.

International Monetary Fund, 700 Nineteenth Street, NW, Washington, D.C. 20431 (202) 623-7000; *Government Finance Statistics Yearbook*.

Organisation for Economic Co-operation and Development (OECD), 2 rue Andre-Pascal, 75 Paris 16, France (Telephone Number in U.S. (202) 785-6323); *Economic Outlook*.

Times Books, 201 East 50th Street, New York, New York 10022 (212) 751-2600; *The Economist Book of Vital World Statistics*.

The World Bank, 1818 H Street, NW, Washington, D.C. 20433 (202) 477-1234; *World Tables*.

FRANCE - GOVERNMENT FINANCES

European Community Information Service, 2100 M Street, NW, Washington, D.C. 20037 (202) 862-9500; *Basic Statistics of the Community*, *Government Financing of Research and Development*, and *Money and Finance*.

International Monetary Fund, 700 Nineteenth Street, NW, Washington, D.C. 20431 (202) 623-7000; *International Financial Statistics*.

Organisation for Economic Co-operation and Development (OECD), 2 rue Andre-Pascal, 75 Paris 16, France (Telephone Number in U.S. (202) 785-6323); *Economic Outlook*.

Statistical Office of the United Nations, Publishing Service, New York, New York 10017 (800) 253-9646; *Statistical Yearbook*.

FRANCE - GOVERNMENT REVENUES

European Community Information Service, 2100 M Street, NW, Washington, D.C. 20037 (202) 862-9500; *Basic Statistics of the Community*, and *Government Financing of Research and Development*.

International Monetary Fund, 700 Nineteenth Street, NW, Washington, D.C. 20431 (202) 623-7000; *Government Finance Statistics Yearbook*.

Organisation for Economic Co-operation and Development (OECD), 2 rue Andre-Pascal, 75 Paris 16, France (Telephone Number in U.S. (202) 785-6323); *Economic Outlook*, and *Revenue Statistics of OECD Member Countries*.

Times Books, 201 East 50th Street, New York, New York 10022 (212) 751-2600; *The Economist Book of Vital World Statistics*.

The World Bank, 1818 H Street, NW, Washington, D.C. 20433 (202) 477-1234; *World Tables*.

FRANCE - GRAIN PRODUCTION - See FRANCE - CROPS

FRANCE - GRANTS

International Monetary Fund, 700 Nineteenth Street, NW, Washington, D.C. 20431 (202) 623-7000; *Government Finance Statistics Yearbook*.

National Technical Information Service, 5285 Port Royal Road, Springfield, Virginia 22161 (703) 487-4600; *Handbook of Economic Statistics*.

Organisation for Economic Co-operation and Development (OECD), 2 rue Andre-Pascal, 75 Paris 16, France (Telephone Number in U.S. (202) 785-6323); *Geographical Distribution of Financial Flows to Developing Countries*.

FRANCE - GREEN PEPPER AND CHILIE PRODUCTION - See FRANCE - CROPS

FRANCE - GROSS DOMESTIC PRODUCT

The Economist Intelligence Unit, 111 West 57th Street, New York, New York 10019 (800) 938-4685; *The World Market Atlas*.

European Community Information Service, 2100 M Street, NW, Washington, D.C. 20037 (202) 862-9500; *Basic Statistics of the Community*, *Eurostatistics: Data for Short-Term Economic Analysis*, *Government Financing of Research and Development*, *Iron and Steel: Statistical Yearbook*, and *Money and Finance*.

Facts on File, 460 Park Avenue South, New York, New York 10016 (800) 443-8323; *The New Book of World Rankings*.

G.K. Hall and Company, 70 Lincoln Street, Boston, Massachusetts 02111 (617) 423-3990; *The World in Figures*.

International Monetary Fund, 700 Nineteenth Street, NW, Washington, D.C. 20431 (202) 623-7000; *International Financial Statistics*.

National Technical Information Service, 5285 Port Royal Road, Springfield, Virginia 22161 (703) 487-4600; *Handbook of Economic Statistics*.

Organisation for Economic Co-operation and Development (OECD), 2 rue Andre-Pascal, 75 Paris 16, France (Telephone Number in U.S.

(202) 785-6323); *Economic Outlook, Geographical Distribution of Financial Flows to Developing Countries,* and *Revenue Statistics of OECD Member Countries.*

Statistical Office of the United Nations, Publishing Service, New York, New York 10017 (800) 253-9646; *Statistical Yearbook.*

Times Books, 201 East 50th Street, New York, New York 10022 (212) 751-2600; *The Economist Book of Vital World Statistics.*

The World Bank, 1818 H Street, NW, Washington, D.C. 20433 (202) 477-1234; *World Tables.*

FRANCE - GROSS INDUSTRIAL PRODUCT

European Community Information Service, 2100 M Street, NW, Washington, D.C. 20037 (202) 862-9500; *Government Financing of Research and Development.*

FRANCE - GROSS NATIONAL PRODUCT

European Community Information Service, 2100 M Street, NW, Washington, D.C. 20037 (202) 862-9500; *ACP: Basic Statistics,* and *Basic Statistics of the Community.*

National Technical Information Service, 5285 Port Royal Road, Springfield, Virginia 22161 (703) 487-4600; *Handbook of Economic Statistics.*

Organisation for Economic Co-operation and Development (OECD), 2 rue Andre-Pascal, 75 Paris 16, France (Telephone Number in U.S. (202) 785-6323); *Economic Outlook,* and *Geographical Distribution of Financial Flows to Developing Countries.*

U.S. Arms Control and Disarmament Agency, 320 Twenty-first Street, NW, Washington, D.C. 20451 (202) 647-8677; *World Military Expenditures and Arms Transfers.*

The World Bank, 1818 H Street, NW, Washington, D.C. 20433 (202) 477-1234; *World Tables.*

FRANCE - GROUNDNUT PRODUCTION - See FRANCE - CROPS

FRANCE - HAY PRODUCTION - See FRANCE - CROPS

FRANCE - HAZELNUT PRODUCTION - See FRANCE - CROPS

FRANCE - HEALTH

European Community Information Service, 2100 M Street, NW, Washington, D.C. 20037 (202) 862-9500; *Basic Statistics of the Community,* and *Regions: Statistical Yearbook.*

Facts on File, 460 Park Avenue South, New York, New York 10016 (800) 443-8323; *The New Book of World Rankings.*

Federal Statistical Office, Gustav - Stresemann - Ring 11, D-6200 Wiesbaden, Germany; *Frankreich.*

G.K. Hall and Company, 70 Lincoln Street, Boston, Massachusetts 02111 (617) 423-3990; *The World in Figures.*

International Monetary Fund, 700 Nineteenth Street, NW, Washington, D.C. 20431 (202) 623-7000; *Government Finance Statistics Yearbook.*

Organisation for Economic Co-operation and Development (OECD), 2 rue Andre-Pascal, 75 Paris 16, France (Telephone Number in U.S. (202) 785-6323); *OECD Health Systems: Facts and Trends.*

Statistical Office of the United Nations, Publishing Service, New York, New York 10017 (800) 253-9646; *Statistical Yearbook.*

Times Books, 201 East 50th Street, New York, New York 10022 (212) 751-2600; *The Economist Book of Vital World Statistics.*

World Health Organization, Office of Publications, Avenue Appia, CH-1211 Geneva 27, Switzerland (Telephone Number in U.S. (518) 436-9686); *World Health Statistics Annual.*

FRANCE - HEMP FIBRE PRODUCTION - See FRANCE - TEXTILE INDUSTRY

FRANCE - HIDE PRODUCTION

Food and Agricultural Organization of the United Nations (FAO), Via delle Terme di Caracalla, 00100 Rome, Italy (Telephone Number in U.S. (202) 653-2400); *Production Yearbook.*

Organisation for Economic Co-operation and Development (OECD), 2 rue Andre-Pascal, 75 Paris 16, France (Telephone Number in U.S. (202) 785-6323); *The Footwear, Raw Hides and Skins, and Leather Industry in OECD Countries, Foreign Trade by Commodities,* and *Indicators of Industrial Activity.*

FRANCE - HIGHWAYS

European Community Information Service, 2100 M Street, NW, Washington, D.C. 20037 (202) 862-9500; *Basic Statistics of the Community,* and *Transport Annual Statistics.*

G.K. Hall and Company, 70 Lincoln Street, Boston, Massachusetts 02111 (617) 423-3990; *The World in Figures.*

International Road Federation, 525 School Street, SW, Washington, D.C. 20024 (202) 554-2106; *World Road Statistics.*

Statistical Office of the United Nations, Publishing Service, New York, New York 10017 (800) 253-9646; *Annual Bulletin of Transport Statistics for Europe.*

FRANCE - HONEY PRODUCTION

Commodity Research Bureau, Incorporated, 75 Wall Street, New York, New York 10005 (212) 504-7754; *Commodity Year Book.*

FRANCE - HOPS PRODUCTION - See FRANCE - CROPS

FRANCE - HORSES - See FRANCE - LIVESTOCK AND POULTRY

FRANCE - HOURS OF WORK - See FRANCE - EMPLOYMENT

FRANCE - HOUSING AND HOUSING UNITS

European Community Information Service, 2100 M Street, NW, Washington, D.C. 20037 (202) 862-9500; *Basic Statistics of the Community, Labor Force Sample Survey,* and *Regions: Statistical Yearbook.*

Facts on File, 460 Park Avenue South, New York, New York 10016 (800) 443-8323; *The New Book of World Rankings.*

National Technical Information Service, 5285 Port Royal Road, Springfield, Virginia 22161 (703) 487-4600; *Handbook of Economic Statistics.*

Statistical Office of the United Nations, Publishing Service, New York, New York 10017 (800) 253-9646; *Statistical Yearbook.*

FRANCE - HOUSING CONSTRUCTION - See FRANCE - CONSTRUCTION INDUSTRY

FRANCE - HOUSING EXPENDITURES

European Community Information Service, 2100 M Street, NW, Washington, D.C. 20037 (202) 862-9500; *Basic Statistics of the Community.*

International Monetary Fund, 700 Nineteenth Street, NW, Washington, D.C. 20431 (202) 623-7000; *Government Finance Statistics Yearbook.*

FRANCE - HYDROCHLORIC ACID PRODUCTION

European Community Information Service, 2100 M Street, NW, Washington, D.C. 20037 (202) 862-9500; *Basic Statistics of the Community.*

Statistical Office of the United Nations, Publishing Service, New York, New York 10017 (800) 253-9646; *Statistical Yearbook.*

FRANCE - ILLITERATE POPULATION

The Economist Intelligence Unit, 111 West 57th Street, New York, New York 10019 (800) 938-4685; *The World Market Atlas.*

G.K. Hall and Company, 70 Lincoln Street, Boston, Massachusetts 02111 (617) 423-3990; *The World in Figures.*

United Nations Educational, Scientific and Cultural Organization (UNESCO), 7 Place de Fontenoy, F-75700 Paris, France (Telephone Number in U.S. (212) 963-5981); *Statistical Yearbook.*

FRANCE - IMPORTS

American Automobile Manufacturers Association, 1401 H Street, NW, Suite 900, Washington, D.C. 20005 (202) 326-5500; *World Motor Vehicle Data.*

The Economist Intelligence Unit, 111 West 57th Street, New York, New York 10019 (800) 938-4685; *The World Market Atlas.*

European Community Information Service, 2100 M Street, NW, Washington, D.C. 20037 (202) 862-9500; *Basic Statistics of the Community, Energy: Monthly Statistics, Energy Statistics Yearbook, Eurostatistics: Data for Short-Term Economic Analysis, External Trade: Monthly Statistics, External Trade: Statistical Yearbook,* and *Fisheries: Yearly Statistics.*

Food and Agricultural Organization of the United Nations (FAO) Via delle Terme di Caracalla, 00100 Rome, Italy (Telephone Number in U.S. (202) 653-2400); *The State of Food and Agriculture.*

G.K. Hall and Company, 70 Lincoln Street, Boston, Massachusetts 02111 (617) 423-3990; *The World in Figures.*

International Iron and Steel Institute, 120, rue Colonel Bourg, B-1140, Belgium; *Steel Statistical Yearbook.*

International Lead and Zinc Study Group, Metro House, 58 St. James's Street, London SW1A 1LD, England; *Lead and Zinc Statistics.*

International Monetary Fund, 700 Nineteenth Street, NW, Washington, D.C. 20431 (202) 623-7000; *Direction of Trade Statistics, Government Finance Statistics Yearbook,* and *International Financial Statistics.*

International Rubber Study Group, York House, 8th Floor, Empire Way, Wembley, London HA9 0PA, England; *Rubber Statistical Bulletin.*

National Technical Information Service, 5285 Port Royal Road, Springfield, Virginia 22161 (703) 487-4600; *Handbook of Economic Statistics.*

Organisation for Economic Co-operation and Development (OECD), 2 rue Andre-Pascal, 75 Paris 16, France (Telephone Number in U.S. (202) 785-6323); *Economic Outlook, The Footwear, Raw Hides and Skins, and Leather Industry in OECD Countries, Industrial Structure Statistics, The Iron and Steel Industry, Milk, Milk Products, and Egg Balances in OECD Member Countries, OECD Economic Surveys: France, The Pulp and Paper Industry,* and *Review of Fisheries in OECD Member Countries.*

Times Books, 201 East 50th Street, New York, New York 10022 (212) 751-2600; *The Economist Book of Vital World Statistics.*

The World Bank, 1818 H Street, NW, Washington, D.C. 20433; *World Tables.*

FRANCE - INCOME TAXES - See FRANCE - TAXATION

FRANCE - INDUSTRIAL METALS PRODUCTION - See FRANCE - MINING AND MINERAL PRODUCTS

FRANCE - INDUSTRY

European Community Information Service, 2100 M Street, NW, Washington, D.C. 20037 (202) 862-9500; *Basic Statistics of the Community, Employment and Unemployment, Eurostatistics: Data for Short-Term Economic Analysis,* and *Labor Force Sample Survey.*

Facts on File, 460 Park Avenue South, New York, New York 10016 (800) 443-8323; *The New Book of World Rankings.*

Federal Statistical Office, Gustav - Stresemann - Ring 11, D-6200 Wiesbaden, Germany; *Frankreich.*

G.K. Hall and Company, 70 Lincoln Street, Boston, Massachusetts 02111 (617) 423-3990; *The World in Figures.*

International Labour Office, I.L.O. Publications, CH-1211, Geneva 22, Switzerland; *Yearbook of Labour Statistics.*

National Technical Information Service, 5285 Port Royal Road, Springfield, Virginia 22161 (703) 487-4600; *Handbook of Economic Statistics.*

Organisation for Economic Co-operation and Development (OECD), 2 rue Andre-Pascal, 75 Paris 16, France (Telephone Number in U.S. (202) 785-6323); *Economic Outlook, Indicators of Industrial Activity, Industrial Structure Statistics,* and *OECD Environmental Data.*

Statistical Office of the United Nations, Publishing Service, New York, New York 10017 (800) 253-9646; *Statistical Yearbook.*

Times Books, 201 East 50th Street, New York, New York 10022 (212) 751-2600; *The Economist Book of Vital World Statistics.*

The World Bank, 1818 H Street, NW, Washington, D.C. 20433 (202) 477-1234; *World Tables.*

World Intellectual Property Organization, 34 Chemin des Colombettes, CH-1211 Geneva 20. Switzerland; *Industrial Property Statistics.*

FRANCE - INFANT AND MATERNAL MORTALITY

European Community Information Service, 2100 M Street, NW, Washington, D.C. 20037 (202) 862-9500; *Basic Statistics of the Community,* and *Demographic Statistics.*

Statistical Office of the United Nations, Publishing Service, New York, New York 10017 (800) 253-9646; *Demographic Yearbook, Statistical Yearbook.*

Times Books, 201 East 50th Street, New York, New York 10022 (212) 751-2600; *The Economist Book of Vital World Statistics.*

The World Bank, 1818 H Street, NW, Washington, D.C. 20433 (202) 47-1234; *World Tables.*

World Health Organization, Office of Publications, Avenue Appia, CH-1211 Geneva 27, Switzerland (Telephone Number in U.S. (518) 436-9686); *World Health Statistics Annual.*

FRANCE - INFLATIONARY FACTORS

National Technical Information Service, 5285 Port Royal Road, Springfield, Virginia 22161 (703) 487-4600; *Handbook of Economic Statistics.*

FRANCE - INTEREST RATES

European Community Information Service, 2100 M Street, NW, Washington, D.C. 20037 (202) 862-9500; *Money and Finance.*

National Technical Information Service, 5285 Port Royal Road, Springfield, Virginia 22161 (703) 487-4600; *Handbook of Economic Statistics.*

Organisation for Economic Co-operation and Development (OECD), 2 rue Andre-Pascal, 75 Paris 16, France (Telephone Number in U.S. (202) 785-6323); *Economic Outlook, Financial Market Trends,* and *OECD Financial Statistics.*

FRANCE - INTERNAL TRADE

European Community Information Service, 2100 M Street, NW, Washington, D.C. 20037 (202) 862-9500; *Basic Statistics of the Community.*

Organisation for Economic Co-operation and Development (OECD), 2 rue Andre-Pascal, 75 Paris 16, France (Telephone Number in U.S. (202) 785-6323); *Main Economic Indicators - Historical Statistics.*

Statistical Office of the United Nations, Publishing Service, New York, New York 10017 (800) 253-9646; *Statistical Yearbook.*

FRANCE - INTERNATIONAL FINANCE

European Community Information Service, 2100 M Street, NW, Washington, D.C. 20037 (202) 862-9500; *Basic Statistics of the Community.*

Organisation for Economic Co-operation and Development (OECD), 2 rue Andre-Pascal, 75 Paris 16, France (Telephone Number in U.S. (202) 785-6323); *Economic Outlook,* and *Financial Market Trends.*

FRANCE - INTERNATIONAL LIQUIDITY

International Monetary Fund, 700 Nineteenth Street, NW, Washington, D.C. 20431 (202) 623-7000; *International Financial Statistics.*

Organisation for Economic Co-operation and Development (OECD), 2 rue Andre-Pascal, 75 Paris 16, France (Telephone Number in U.S. (202) 785-6323); *Economic Outlook,* and *Financial Market Trends.*

FRANCE - INTERNATIONAL RESERVES EXCLUDING GOLD

National Technical Information Service, 5285 Port Royal Road, Springfield, Virginia 22161 (703) 487-4600; *Handbook of Economic Statistics.*

Statistical Office of the United Nations, Publishing Service, New York, New York 10017 (800) 253-9646; *Statistical Yearbook.*

The World Bank, 1818 H Street, NW, Washington, D.C. 20433 (202) 477-1234; *World Tables.*

FRANCE - INTERNATIONAL STATISTICS

Organisation for Economic Co-operation and Development (OECD), 2 rue Andre-Pascal, 75 Paris 16, France (Telephone Number in U.S. (202) 785-6323); *Financial Market Trends,* and *Tourism Policy and International Tourism in OECD Member Countries.*

FRANCE - INVESTMENTS

International Monetary Fund, 700 Nineteenth Street, NW, Washington, D.C. 20431 (202) 623-7000; *International Financial Statistics.*

Organisation for Economic Co-operation and Development (OECD), 2 rue Andre-Pascal, 75 Paris 16, France (Telephone Number in U.S. (202) 785-6323); *Economic Outlook, Financial Market Trends, Industrial Structure Statistics, The Iron and Steel Industry,* and *Textile Industry in OECD Countries.*

FRANCE - IRON ORE - See FRANCE - MINING AND MINERAL PRODUCTS

FRANCE - JUTE PRODUCTION - See FRANCE - CROPS

FRANCE - LABOR FORCE

European Community Information Service, 2100 M Street, NW, Washington, D.C. 20037 (202) 862-9500; *Basic Statistics of the Community, Labor Force Sample Survey, OECD Economic Surveys: France,* and *Regions: Statistical Yearbook.*

Facts on File, 460 Park Avenue South, New York, New York 10016 (800) 443-8323; *The New Book of World Rankings.*

Food and Agricultural Organization of the United Nations (FAO) Via delle Terme di Caracalla, 00100 Rome, Italy (Telephone Number in U.S. (202) 653-2400); *The State of Food and Agriculture.*

G.K. Hall and Company, 70 Lincoln Street, Boston, Massachusetts 02111 (617) 423-3990; *The World in Figures.*

National Technical Information Service, 5285 Port Royal Road, Springfield, Virginia 22161 (703) 487-4600; *Handbook of Economic Statistics.*

Organisation for Economic Co-operation and Development (OECD), 2 rue Andre-Pascal, 75 Paris 16, France (Telephone Number in U.S. (202) 785-6323); *Economic Outlook, The Iron and Steel Industry, Main Economic Indicators - Historical Statistics, Maritime Transport, OECD Employment Outlook,* and *Textile Industry in OECD Countries.*

Times Books, 201 East 50th Street, New York, New York 10022 (212) 751-2600; *The Economist Book of Vital World Statistics.*

The World Bank, 1818 H Street, NW, Washington, D.C. 20433 (202) 477-1234; *World Tables.*

FRANCE - LABOR PRODUCTIVITY

International Labour Office, I.L.O. Publications, CH-1211, Geneva 22, Switzerland; *Yearbook of Labour Statistics.*

Organisation for Economic Co-operation and Development (OECD), 2 rue Andre-Pascal, 75 Paris 16, France (Telephone Number in U.S. (202) 785-6323); *Economic Outlook,* and *OECD Employment Outlook.*

FRANCE - LAND USE

Euromonitor Publications Limited, 87-88 Turnmill Street, London EC1M 5QU, England; *European Marketing Data and Statistics.*

European Community Information Service, 2100 M Street, NW, Washington, D.C. 20037 (202) 862-9500; *Agriculture: Statistical Yearbook, Basic Statistics of the Community, Crop Production: Quarterly Statistics,* and *Regions: Statistical Yearbook.*

Food and Agricultural Organization of the United Nations (FAO), Via delle Terme di Caracalla, 00100 Rome, Italy (Telephone Number in U.S. (202) 653-2400); *Production Yearbook.*

G.K. Hall and Company, 70 Lincoln Street, Boston, Massachusetts 02111 (617) 423-3990; *The World in Figures.*

FRANCE - LEAD ORE PRODUCTION AND CONSUMPTION - See FRANCE - MINING AND MINERAL PRODUCTS

FRANCE - LEAD PRODUCTION AND CONSUMPTION - See FRANCE - MINING AND MINERAL PRODUCTS

FRANCE - LEATHER - PRODUCTION INDEX

Organisation for Economic Co-operation and Development (OECD), 2 rue Andre-Pascal, 75 Paris 16, France (Telephone Number in U.S. (202) 785-6323); *Indicators of Industrial Activity.*

FRANCE - LEATHER AND FOOTWEAR - EXPORTS AND IMPORTS

European Community Information Service, 2100 M Street, NW, Washington, D.C. 20037 (202) 862-9500; *Basic Statistics of the Community.*

Organisation for Economic Co-operation and Development (OECD), 2 rue Andre-Pascal, 75 Paris 16, France (Telephone Number in U.S. (202) 785-6323); *The Footwear, Raw Hides and Skins, and Leather Industry in OECD Countries.*

Statistical Office of the United Nations, Publishing Service, New York, New York 10017 (800) 253-9646; *Trade in Manufactures of Developing Countries.*

FRANCE - LIBRARIES

Euromonitor Publications Limited, 87-88 Turnmill Street, London EC1M 5QU, England; *European Marketing Data and Statistics.*

Facts on File, 460 Park Avenue South, New York, New York 10016 (800) 443-8323; *The New Book of World Rankings.*

United Nations Educational, Scientific and Cultural Organization (UNESCO), 7 Place de Fontenoy, F-75700 Paris, France (Telephone Number in U.S. (212) 963-5981); *Statistical Yearbook.*

FRANCE - LIGNITE PRODUCTION - See FRANCE - MINING AND MINERAL PRODUCTS

FRANCE - LIVESTOCK AND POULTRY

Commodity Research Bureau, Incorporated, 75 Wall Street, New York, New York 10005 (212) 504-7754; *Commodity Year Book.*

Euromonitor Publications Limited, 87-88 Turnmill Street, London EC1M 5QU, England; *European Marketing Data and Statistics.*

European Community Information Service, 2100 M Street, NW, Washington, D.C. 20037 (202) 862-9500; *Agriculture: Statistical Yearbook, Basic Statistics of the Community, Eurostatistics: Data for Short-Term Economic Analysis,* and *Regions: Statistical Yearbook.*

Facts on File, 460 Park Avenue South, New York, New York 10016 (800) 443-8323; *The New Book of World Rankings.*

Food and Agricultural Organization of the United Nations (FAO), Via delle Terme di Caracalla, 00100 Rome, Italy (Telephone Number in U.S. (202) 653-2400); *Production Yearbook,* and *The State of Food and Agriculture.*

G.K. Hall and Company, 70 Lincoln Street, Boston, Massachusetts 02111 (617) 423-3990; *The World in Figures.*

National Technical Information Service, 5285 Port Royal Road, Springfield, Virginia 22161 (703) 487-4600; *Handbook of Economic Statistics.*

Organisation for Economic Co-operation and Development (OECD), 2 rue Andre-Pascal, 75 Paris 16, France (Telephone Number in U.S. (202) 785-6323); *Economic Accounts for Agriculture,* and *Meat Balances in OECD Member Countries.*

Statistical Office of the United Nations, Publishing Service, New York, New York 10017 (800) 253-9646; *Statistical Yearbook.*

FRANCE - LIVING LEVELS

G.K. Hall and Company, 70 Lincoln Street, Boston, Massachusetts 02111 (617) 423-3990; *The World in Figures.*

Organisation for Economic Co-operation and Development (OECD), 2 rue Andre-Pascal, 75 Paris 16, France (Telephone Number in U.S. (202) 785-6323); *Economic Outlook.*

Times Books, 201 East 50th Street, New York, New York 10022 (212) 751-2600; *The Economist Book of Vital World Statistics.*

FRANCE - MACHINERY - PRODUCTION INDEX

Organisation for Economic Co-operation and Development (OECD), 2 rue Andre-Pascal, 75 Paris 16, France (Telephone Number in U.S. (202) 785-6323); *Indicators of Industrial Activity.*

FRANCE - MAGNESIUM PRODUCTION AND CONSUMPTION - See FRANCE - MINING AND MINERAL PRODUCTS

FRANCE - MAIL - NUMBER OF PIECES SENT OR RECEIVED

European Community Information Service, 2100 M Street, NW, Washington, D.C. 20037 (202) 862-9500; *Transport Annual*

Statistics.

Statistical Office of the United Nations, Publishing Service, New York, New York 10017 (800) 253-9646; *Statistical Yearbook*.

FRANCE - MAIN ECONOMIC INDICATORS - See FRANCE - ECONOMY

FRANCE - MAIN INDICATORS - See FRANCE - ECONOMY

FRANCE - MANGANESE AND MANGANESE ORE - See FRANCE - MINING AND MINERAL PRODUCTS

FRANCE - MANUFACTURING

American Automobile Manufacturers Association, 1401 H Street, NW, Suite 900, Washington, D.C. 20005 (202) 326-5500; *World Motor Vehicle Data*.

European Community Information Service, 2100 M Street, NW, Washington, D.C. 20037 (202) 862-9500; *Basic Statistics of the Community, Eurostatistics: Data for Short-Term Economic Analysis, Industrial Production: Quarterly Statistics*, and *Labor Force Sample Survey*.

Facts on File, 460 Park Avenue South, New York, New York 10016 (800) 443-8323; *The New Book of World Rankings*.

G.K. Hall and Company, 70 Lincoln Street, Boston, Massachusetts 02111 (617) 423-3990; *The World in Figures*.

Organisation for Economic Co-operation and Development (OECD), 2 rue Andre-Pascal, 75 Paris 16, France (Telephone Number in U.S. (202) 785-6323); *Foreign Trade by Commodities, Indicators of Industrial Activity, Industrial Structure Statistics*, and *OECD Economic Surveys: France*.

Statistical Office of the United Nations, Publishing Service, New York, New York 10017 (800) 253-9646; *Statistical Yearbook*.

Times Books, 201 East 50th Street, New York, New York 10022 (212) 751-2600; *The Economist Book of Vital World Statistics*.

The World Bank, 1818 H Street, NW, Washington, D.C. 20433 (202) 477-1234; *World Tables*.

FRANCE - MARGARINE PRODUCTION - See FRANCE - DAIRY PRODUCTS

FRANCE - MARRIAGE RATES

European Community Information Service, 2100 M Street, NW, Washington, D.C. 20037 (202) 862-9500; *Basic Statistics of the Community*.

Facts on File, 460 Park Avenue South, New York, New York 10016 (800) 443-8323; *The New Book of World Rankings*.

Statistical Office of the United Nations, Publishing Service, New York, New York 10017 (800) 253-9646; *Demographic Yearbook*, and *Statistical Yearbook*.

FRANCE - MEAT PRODUCTION - See FRANCE - LIVESTOCK AND POULTRY

FRANCE - MERCHANT SHIPPING

European Community Information Service, 2100 M Street, NW, Washington, D.C. 20037 (202) 862-9500; *Basic Statistics of the Community, Fisheries: Yearly Statistics, Regions: Statistical Yearbook*, and *Transport Annual Statistics*.

G.K. Hall and Company, 70 Lincoln Street, Boston, Massachusetts 02111 (617) 423-3990; *The World in Figures*.

Lloyd's Register of Shipping, 17 Battery Place, New York, New York 10004 (212) 425-8050; *Register of Ships*.

National Technical Information Service, 5285 Port Royal Road, Springfield, Virginia 22161 (703) 487-4600; *Handbook of Economic Statistics*.

Organisation for Economic Co-operation and Development (OECD), 2 rue Andre-Pascal, 75 Paris 16, France (Telephone Number in U.S. (202) 785-6323); *Maritime Transport*.

Statistical Office of the United Nations, Publishing Service, New York, New York 10017 (800) 253-9646; *Annual Bulletin of Transport Statistics for Europe*, and *Statistical Yearbook*.

Times Books, 201 East 50th Street, New York, New York 10022 (212) 751-2600; *The Economist Book of Vital World Statistics*.

U.S. Department of Transportation, Maritime Administration, 400 Seventh Street, SW, Washington, D.C. 20590 (202) 366-5807; *A Statistical Analysis of the World's Merchant Fleets*.

FRANCE - MERCURY PRODUCTION AND CONSUMPTION - See FRANCE - MINING AND MINERAL PRODUCTS

FRANCE - MILITARY

G.K. Hall and Company, 70 Lincoln Street, Boston, Massachusetts 02111 (617) 423-3990; *The World in Figures*.

The International Institute for Strategic Studies, 23 Tavistock Street, London WC2E 7NQ, England; *The Military Balance*.

U.S. Arms Control and Disarmament Agency, 320 Twenty-first Street, NW, Washington, D.C. 20451 (202) 647-8677; *World Military Expenditures and Arms Transfers*.

FRANCE - MILK PRODUCTION - See FRANCE - DAIRY PRODUCTS

FRANCE - MILLET PRODUCTION - See FRANCE - CROPS

FRANCE - MINING AND MINERAL PRODUCTS

Commodity Research Bureau, Incorporated, 75 Wall Street, New York, New York 10005 (212) 504-7754; *Commodity Year Book*.

European Community Information Service, 2100 M Street, NW, Washington, D.C. 20037 (202) 862-9500; *ACP: Basic Statistics, Basic Statistics of the Community, Energy: Monthly Statistics, Energy Statistics Yearbook, Eurostatistics: Data for Short-Term Economic Analysis, Industrial Production: Quarterly Statistics, Mining and Mineral Products*, and *Regions: Statistical Yearbook*.

Facts on File, 460 Park Avenue South, New York, New York 10016 (800) 443-8323; *The New Book of World Rankings*.

G.K. Hall and Company, 70 Lincoln Street, Boston, Massachusetts 02111 (617) 423-3990; *The World in Figures*.

International Iron and Steel Institute, 120, rue Colonel Bourg, B-1140, Belgium; *Steel Statistical Yearbook*.

International Labour Office, I.L.O. Publications, CH-1211, Geneva 22, Switzerland; *Yearbook of Labour Statistics.*

International Lead and Zinc Study Group, Metro House, 58 St. James's Street, London SW1A 1LD, England; *Lead and Zinc Statistics.*

National Technical Information Service, 5285 Port Royal Road, Springfield, Virginia 22161 (703) 487-4600; *Handbook of Economic Statistics.*

Organisation for Economic Co-operation and Development (OECD), 2 rue Andre-Pascal, 75 Paris 16, France (Telephone Number in U.S. (202) 785-6323); *Energy Statistics of OECD Countries, Foreign Trade by Commodities, Indicators of Industrial Activity, Industrial Structure Statistics, The Iron and Steel Industry, The Non-Ferrous Metals Industry,* and *OECD Economic Surveys: France.*

Penn Well Publishing Company, 1421 South Sheridan Road, P.O. Box 1260, Tulsa, Oklahoma 74101 (800) 752-9764; *International Energy Statistics Sourcebook.*

Statistical Office of the United Nations, Publishing Service, New York, New York 10017 (800) 253-9646; *Statistical Yearbook.*

World Bureau of Metal Statistics, 27-A High Street, Ware Hert SG12 9BA, England; *World Metal Statistics.*

FRANCE - MOLASSES PRODUCTION - See FRANCE - CROPS

FRANCE - MOLYBDENUM AND MOLYBDENUM ORE - See FRANCE - MINING AND MINERAL PRODUCTS

FRANCE - MONEY AND CREDIT

Organisation for Economic Cooperation and Development (OECD), 2 rue Andre-Pascal, 75 Paris 16, France (Telephone Number in U.S. (202) 785-6323); *OECD Economic Surveys: France.*

FRANCE - MONEY EXCHANGE RATE

European Community Information Service, 2100 M Street, NW, Washington, D.C. 20037 (202) 862-9500; *Basic Statistics of the Community.*

International Monetary Fund, 700 Nineteenth Street, NW, Washington, D.C. 20431 (202) 623-7000; *International Financial Statistics.*

Organisation for Economic Co-operation and Development (OECD), 2 rue Andre-Pascal, 75 Paris 16, France (Telephone Number in U.S. (202) 785-6323); *Economic Outlook, Financial Market Trends,* and *Tourism Policy and International Tourism in OECD Member Countries.*

Statistical Office of the United Nations, Publishing Service, New York, New York 10017 (800) 253-9646; *Statistical Yearbook.*

FRANCE - MONEY RATES - MARKET

European Community Information Service, 2100 M Street, NW, Washington, D.C. 20037 (202) 862-9500; *Basic Statistics of the Community.*

Organisation for Economic Co-operation and Development (OECD), 2 rue Andre-Pascal, 75 Paris 16, France (Telephone Number in U.S. (202) 785-6323); *Economic Outlook,* and *Financial Market Trends.*

Statistical Office of the United Nations, Publishing Service, New York, New York 10017 (800) 253-9646; *Statistical Yearbook.*

FRANCE - MONEY RESERVES

European Community Information Service, 2100 M Street, NW, Washington, D.C. 20037 (202) 862-9500; *Basic Statistics of the Community.*

Organisation for Economic Co-operation and Development (OECD), 2 rue Andre-Pascal, 75 Paris 16, France (Telephone Number in U.S. (202) 785-6323); *Economic Outlook,* and *Financial Market Trends.*

FRANCE - MONEY SUPPLY

European Community Information Service, 2100 M Street, NW, Washington, D.C. 20037 (202) 862-9500; *Basic Statistics of the Community, Eurostatistics: Data for Short-Term Economic Analysis,* and *Money and Finance.*

Federal Statistical Office, Gustav - Stresemann - Ring 11, D-6200 Wiesbaden, Germany; *Frankreich.*

G.K. Hall and Company, 70 Lincoln Street, Boston, Massachusetts 02111 (617) 423-3990; *The World in Figures.*

International Monetary Fund, 700 Nineteenth Street, NW, Washington, D.C. 20431 (202) 623-7000; *International Financial Statistics.*

Organisation for Economic Co-operation and Development (OECD), 2 rue Andre-Pascal, 75 Paris 16, France (Telephone Number in U.S. (202) 785-6323); *Economic Outlook.*

Statistical Office of the United Nations, Publishing Service, New York, New York 10017 (800) 253-9646; *Statistical Yearbook.*

The World Bank, 1818 H Street, NW, Washington, D.C. 20433 (202) 477-1234; *World Tables.*

FRANCE - MOTION PICTURES

Statistical Office of the United Nations, Publishing Service, New York, New York 10017 (800) 253-9646; *Statistical Yearbook.*

United Nations Educational, Scientific and Cultural Organization (UNESCO), 7 Place de Fontenoy, F-75700 Paris, France (Telephone Number in U.S. (212) 963-5981); *Statistical Yearbook.*

FRANCE - MOTOR VEHICLE PRODUCTION

American Automobile Manufacturers Association, 1401 H Street, NW, Suite 900, Washington, D.C. 20005 (202) 326-5500; *World Motor Vehicle Data.*

European Community Information Service, 2100 M Street, NW, Washington, D.C. 20037 (202) 862-9500; *Basic Statistics of the Community,* and *Eurostatistics: Data for Short-Term Economic Analysis.*

National Technical Information Service, 5285 Port Royal Road, Springfield, Virginia 22161 (703) 487-4600; *Handbook of Economic Statistics.*

Organisation for Economic Co-operation and Development (OECD), 2 rue Andre-Pascal, 75 Paris 16, France (Telephone Number in U.S. (202) 785-6323); *Foreign Trade by Commodities,* and *Indicators of Industrial Activity.*

Statistical Office of the United Nations, Publishing Service, New York, New York 10017 (800) 253-9646; *Statistical Yearbook.*

FRANCE - MOTOR VEHICLE TAXES - See FRANCE - TAXATION

FRANCE - MOTOR VEHICLES IN USE

American Automobile Manufacturers Association, 1401 H Street, NW, Suite 900, Washington, D.C. 20005 (202) 326-5500; *World Motor Vehicle Data.*

European Community Information Service, 2100 M Street, NW, Washington, D.C. 20037 (202) 862-9500; *Basic Statistics of the Community,*and *Transport Annual Statistics.*

G.K. Hall and Company, 70 Lincoln Street, Boston, Massachusetts 02111 (617) 423-3990; *The World in Figures.*

International Road Federation, 525 School Street, SW, Washington, D.C. 20024 (202) 554-2106; *World Road Statistics.*

Statistical Office of the United Nations, Publishing Service, New York, New York 10017 (800) 253-9646; *Statistical Yearbook.*

Times Books, 201 East 50th Street, New York, New York 10022 (212) 751-2600; *The Economist Book of Vital World Statistics.*

FRANCE - MULES - See FRANCE - LIVESTOCK AND POULTRY

FRANCE - MUSEUMS

Euromonitor Publications Limited, 87-88 Turnmill Street, London EC1M 5QU, England; *European Marketing Data and Statistics.*

Facts on File, 460 Park Avenue South, New York, New York 10016 (800) 443-8323; *The New Book of World Rankings.*

United Nations Educational, Scientific and Cultural Organization (UNESCO), 7 Place de Fontenoy, F-75700 Paris, France (Telephone Number in U.S. (212) 963-5981); *Statistical Yearbook.*

FRANCE - NATALITY - See FRANCE - BIRTH RATE

FRANCE - NATIONAL ACCOUNTS

European Community Information Service, 2100 M Street, NW, Washington, D.C. 20037 (202) 862-9500; *Basic Statistics of the Community,* and *Eurostatistics: Data for Short-Term Economic Analysis.*

Federal Statistical Office, Gustav - Stresemann - Ring 11, D-6200 Wiesbaden, Germany; *Frankreich.*

International Monetary Fund, 700 Nineteenth Street, NW, Washington, D.C. 20431 (202) 623-7000; *International Financial Statistics.*

Organisation for Economic Co-operation and Development (OECD), 2 rue Andre-Pascal, 75 Paris 16, France (Telephone Number in U.S. (202) 785-6323); *Economic Outlook.*

Statistical Office of the United Nations, Publishing Service, New York, New York 10017 (800) 253-9646; *National Accounts Statistics,* and *Statistical Yearbook.*

FRANCE - NATIONAL INCOME

Facts on File, 460 Park Avenue South, New York, New York 10016 (800) 443-8323; *The New Book of World Rankings.*

G.K. Hall and Company, 70 Lincoln Street, Boston, Massachusetts 02111 (617) 423-3990; *The World in Figures.*

Organisation for Economic Co-operation and Development (OECD), 2 rue Andre-Pascal, 75 Paris 16, France (Telephone Number in U.S. (202) 785-6323); *Economic Outlook.*

Statistical Office of the United Nations, Publishing Service, New York, New York 10017 (800) 253-9646; *Statistical Yearbook.*

FRANCE - NATIONAL PRODUCT

European Community Information Service, 2100 M Street, NW, Washington, D.C. 20037 (202) 862-9500; *Basic Statistics of the Community.*

Facts on File, 460 Park Avenue South, New York, New York 10016 (800) 443-8323; *The New Book of World Rankings.*

Organisation for Economic Co-operation and Development (OECD), 2 rue Andre-Pascal, 75 Paris 16, France (Telephone Number in U.S. (202) 785-6323); *Economic Outlook.*

Statistical Office of the United Nations, Publishing Service, New York, New York 10017 (800) 253-9646; *Statistical Yearbook.*

FRANCE - NATURAL GAS PRODUCTION - See FRANCE - MINING AND MINERAL PRODUCTS

FRANCE - NATURAL RUBBER PRODUCTION

European Community Information Service, 2100 M Street, NW, Washington, D.C. 20037 (202) 862-9500; *Basic Statistics of the Community.*

International Rubber Study Group, York House, 8th Floor, Empire Way, Wembley, London HA9 0PA, England; *Rubber Statistical Bulletin.*

National Technical Information Service, 5285 Port Royal Road, Springfield, Virginia 22161 (703) 487-4600; *Handbook of Economic Statistics.*

FRANCE - NEWSPAPER PRODUCTION - See FRANCE - FORESTRY AND FOREST PRODUCTS

FRANCE - NEWSPRINT EXPORTS AND IMPORTS - See FRANCE - FORESTRY AND FOREST PRODUCTS

FRANCE - NICKEL AND NICKEL ORE PRODUCTION AND CONSUMPTION - See FRANCE - MINING AND MINERAL PRODUCTS

FRANCE - NITRIC ACID PRODUCTION

European Community Information Service, 2100 M Street, NW, Washington, D.C. 20037 (202) 862-9500; *Basic Statistics of the Community.*

Organisation for Economic Co-operation and Development (OECD), 2 rue Andre-Pascal, 75 Paris 16, France (Telephone Number in U.S. (202) 785-6323); *Indicators of Industrial Activity.*

Statistical Office of the United Nations, Publishing Service, New York, New York 10017 (800) 253-9646; *Statistical Yearbook.*

FRANCE - OATS PRODUCTION - See FRANCE - CROPS

FRANCE - OCCUPATIONS - See FRANCE - LABOR FORCE

FRANCE - OIL PRODUCING CROPS

European Community Information Service, 2100 M Street, NW, Washington, D.C. 20037 (202) 862-9500; *Basic Statistics of the Community.*

Organisation for Economic Co-operation and Development (OECD), 2 rue Andre-Pascal, 75 Paris 16, France (Telephone Number in U.S. (202) 785-6323); *Foreign Trade by Commodities.*

FRANCE - ONION PRODUCTION - See FRANCE - CROPS

FRANCE - PALM KERNEL PRODUCTION - See FRANCE - CROPS

FRANCE - PAPER - See FRANCE - FORESTRY AND FOREST PRODUCTS

FRANCE - PATENTS

Statistical Office of the United Nations, Publishing Service, New York, New York 10017 (800) 253-9646; *Statistical Yearbook.*

World Intellectual Property Organization, 34 Chemin des Colombettes, CH-1211 Geneva 20. Switzerland; *Industrial Property Statistics.*

FRANCE - PEANUT PRODUCTION - See FRANCE - CROPS

FRANCE - PEPPER PRODUCTION - See FRANCE - CROPS

FRANCE - PERIODICALS

United Nations Educational, Scientific and Cultural Organization (UNESCO), 7 Place de Fontenoy, F-75700 Paris, France (Telephone Number in U.S. (212) 963-5981); *Statistical Yearbook.*

FRANCE - PESTICIDE USE

Food and Agricultural Organization of the United Nations (FAO) Via delle Terme di Caracalla, 00100 Rome, Italy (Telephone Number in U.S. (202) 653-2400); *The State of Food and Agriculture.*

FRANCE - PETROLEUM INDUSTRY

Euromonitor Publications Limited, 87-88 Turnmill Street, London EC1M 5QU, England; *European Marketing Data and Statistics.*

European Community Information Service, 2100 M Street, NW, Washington, D.C. 20037 (202) 862-9500; *ACP: Basic Statistics, Basic Statistics of the Community,* and *Energy Statistics Yearbook.*

Facts on File, 460 Park Avenue South, New York, New York 10016 (800) 443-8323; *The New Book of World Rankings.*

G.K. Hall and Company, 70 Lincoln Street, Boston, Massachusetts 02111 (617) 423-3990; *The World in Figures.*

National Technical Information Service, 5285 Port Royal Road, Springfield, Virginia 22161 (703) 487-4600; *Handbook of Economic Statistics.*

Organisation for Economic Co-operation and Development (OECD), 2 rue Andre-Pascal, 75 Paris 16, France (Telephone Number in U.S. (202) 785-6323); *Energy Statistics of OECD Countries, Foreign Trade by Commodities, Indicators of Industrial Activity,* and *Oil and Gas Information.*

Penn Well Publishing Company, 1421 South Sheridan Road, P.O. Box 1260, Tulsa, Oklahoma 74101 (800) 752-9764; *International Energy Statistics Sourcebook.*

Statistical Office of the United Nations, Publishing Service, New York, New York 10017 (800) 253-9646; *Statistical Yearbook.*

FRANCE - PHOSPHATE ROCK PRODUCTION - See FRANCE - MINING AND MINERAL PRODUCTS

FRANCE - PHOSPHATES PRODUCTION - See FRANCE - MINING AND MINERAL PRODUCTS

FRANCE - PIG-IRON AND FERRO-ALLOY PRODUCTION - See FRANCE - MINING AND MINERAL PRODUCTS

FRANCE - PIGS - See FRANCE - LIVESTOCK AND POULTRY

FRANCE - PIPELINES FOR OIL AND PETROLEUM PRODUCTS

European Community Information Service, 2100 M Street, NW, Washington, D.C. 20037 (202) 862-9500; *Transport Annual Statistics.*

National Technical Information Service, 5285 Port Royal Road, Springfield, Virginia 22161 (703) 487-4600; *Handbook of Economic Statistics.*

Statistical Office of the United Nations, Publishing Service, New York, New York 10017 (800) 253-9646; *Annual Bulletin of Transport Statistics for Europe.*

FRANCE - PLASTIC AND RESIN PRODUCTION

Commodity Research Bureau, Incorporated, 75 Wall Street, New York, New York 10005 (212) 504-7754; *Commodity Year Book.*

European Community Information Service, 2100 M Street, NW, Washington, D.C. 20037 (202) 862-9500; *Basic Statistics of the Community.*

Organisation for Economic Co-operation and Development (OECD), 2 rue Andre-Pascal, 75 Paris 16, France (Telephone Number in U.S. (202) 785-6323); *Foreign Trade by Commodities.*

Statistical Office of the United Nations, Publishing Service, New York, New York 10017 (800) 253-9646; *Statistical Yearbook.*

FRANCE - PLATINUM PRODUCTION - See FRANCE - MINING AND MINERAL PRODUCTS

FRANCE - POPULATION

The Economist Intelligence Unit, 111 West 57th Street, New York, New York 10019 (800) 938-4685; *The World Market Atlas.*

Euromonitor Publications Limited, 87-88 Turnmill Street, London EC1M 5QU, England; *European Marketing Data and Statistics.*

European Community Information Service, 2100 M Street, NW, Washington, D.C. 20037 (202) 862-9500; *ACP: Basic Statistics, Basic Statistics of the Community, Demographic Statistics, Employment and Unemployment, Fisheries: Yearly Statistics, Labor Force Sample Survey, Iron and Steel: Statistical Yearbook,* and *Regions: Statistical Yearbook.*

Facts on File, 460 Park Avenue South, New York, New York 10016 (800) 443-8323; *The New Book of World Rankings.*

Federal Statistical Office, Gustav - Stresemann - Ring 11, D-6200 Wiesbaden, Germany; *Frankreich.*

Food and Agricultural Organization of the United Nations (FAO), Via delle Terme di Caracalla, 00100 Rome, Italy (Telephone Number in U.S. (202) 653-2400); *Production Yearbook.*

G.K. Hall and Company, 70 Lincoln Street, Boston, Massachusetts 02111 (617) 423-3990; *The World in Figures.*

International Labour Office, I.L.O. Publications, CH-1211, Geneva 22, Switzerland; *Yearbook of Labour Statistics.*

National Technical Information Service, 5285 Port Royal Road, Springfield, Virginia 22161 (703) 487-4600; *Handbook of Economic Statistics.*

Statistical Office of the United Nations, Publishing Service, New York, New York 10017 (800) 253-9646; *Demographic Yearbook,* and *Statistical Yearbook.*

Times Books, 201 East 50th Street, New York, New York 10022 (212) 751-2600; *The Economist Book of Vital World Statistics.*

United Nations Educational, Scientific and Cultural Organization (UNESCO), 7 Place de Fontenoy, F-75700 Paris, France (Telephone Number in U.S. (212) 963-5981); *Statistical Yearbook.*

U.S. Arms Control and Disarmament Agency, 320 Twenty-first Street, NW, Washington, D.C. 20451 (202) 647-8677; *World Military Expenditures and Arms Transfers.*

World Health Organization, Office of Publications, Avenue Appia, CH-1211 Geneva 27, Switzerland; *World Health Statistics Annual.*

FRANCE - POST OFFICES

Facts on File, 460 Park Avenue South, New York, New York 10016 (800) 443-8323; *The New Book of World Rankings.*

FRANCE - POTATO PRODUCTION - See FRANCE - CROPS

FRANCE - POWER PRODUCTION INDUSTRY

European Community Information Service, 2100 M Street, NW, Washington, D.C. 20037 (202) 862-9500; *Basic Statistics of the Community.*

Statistical Office of the United Nations, Publishing Service, New York, New York 10017 (800) 253-9646; *Statistical Yearbook.*

FRANCE - PRICES

European Community Information Service, 2100 M Street, NW, Washington, D.C. 20037 (202) 862-9500; *Basic Statistics of the Community,* and *Eurostatistics: Data for Short-Term Economic Analysis.*

Facts on File, 460 Park Avenue South, New York, New York 10016 (800) 443-8323; *The New Book of World Rankings.*

Federal Statistical Office, Gustav - Stresemann - Ring 11, D-6200 Wiesbaden, Germany; *Frankreich.*

Food and Agricultural Organization of the United Nations (FAO), Via delle Terme di Caracalla, 00100 Rome, Italy (Telephone Number in U.S. (202) 653-2400); *Production Yearbook,* and *The State of Food and Agriculture.*

G.K. Hall and Company, 70 Lincoln Street, Boston, Massachusetts 02111 (617) 423-3990; *The World in Figures.*

International Labour Office, I.L.O. Publications, CH-1211, Geneva 22, Switzerland; *Yearbook of Labour Statistics.*

International Lead and Zinc Study Group, Metro House, 58 St. James's Street, London SW1A 1LD, England; *Lead and Zinc Statistics.*

International Monetary Fund, 700 Nineteenth Street, NW, Washington, D.C. 20431 (202) 623-7000; *International Financial Statistics.*

International Rubber Study Group, York House, 8th Floor, Empire Way, Wembley, London HA9 0PA, England; *Rubber Statistical Bulletin.*

National Technical Information Service, 5285 Port Royal Road, Springfield, Virginia 22161 (703) 487-4600; *Handbook of Economic Statistics.*

Organisation for Economic Co-operation and Development (OECD), 2 rue Andre-Pascal, 75 Paris 16, France (Telephone Number in U.S. (202) 785-6323); *Economic Outlook, The Footwear, Raw Hides and Skins, and Leather Industry in OECD Countries, Indicators of Industrial Activity, The Iron and Steel Industry, Main Economic Indicators - Historical Statistics,* and *The Pulp and Paper Industry.*

World Bureau of Metal Statistics, 27-A High Street, Ware Hert SG12 9BA, England; *World Metal Statistics.*

FRANCE - PRINTING AND WRITING PAPER - See FRANCE - FORESTRY AND FOREST PRODUCTS

FRANCE - PRODUCTION

American Automobile Manufacturers Association, 1401 H Street, NW, Suite 900, Washington, D.C. 20005 (202) 326-5500; *World Motor Vehicle Data.*

European Community Information Service, 2100 M Street, NW, Washington, D.C. 20037 (202) 862-9500; *Basic Statistics of the Community, Eurostatistics: Data for Short-Term Economic Analysis,* and *Fisheries: Yearly Statistics.*

Facts on File, 460 Park Avenue South, New York, New York 10016 (800) 443-8323; *The New Book of World Rankings.*

G.K. Hall and Company, 70 Lincoln Street, Boston, Massachusetts 02111 (617) 423-3990; *The World in Figures.*

International Iron and Steel Institute, 120, rue Colonel Bourg, B-1140, Belgium; *Steel Statistical Yearbook.*

International Lead and Zinc Study Group, Metro House, 58 St. James's Street, London SW1A 1LD, England; *Lead and Zinc Statistics.*

International Rubber Study Group, York House, 8th Floor, Empire Way, Wembley, London HA9 0PA, England; *Rubber Statistical Bulletin.*

National Technical Information Service, 5285 Port Royal Road, Springfield, Virginia 22161 (703) 487-4600; *Handbook of Economic Statistics.*

Organisation for Economic Co-operation and Development (OECD), 2 rue Andre-Pascal, 75 Paris 16, France (Telephone Number in U.S.

(202) 785-6323); *Economic Outlook, The Footwear, Raw Hides and Skins, and Leather Industry in OECD Countries, Indicators of Industrial Activity, Industrial Structure Statistics, The Iron and Steel Industry, Meat Balances in OECD Member Countries, Milk, Milk Products, and Egg Balances in OECD Member Countries, The Non-Ferrous Metals Industry, The Pulp and Paper Industry,* and *Textile Industry in OECD Countries.*

FRANCE - PRODUCTIVITY

European Community Information Service, 2100 M Street, NW, Washington, D.C. 20037 (202) 862-9500; *Basic Statistics of the Community.*

Organisation for Economic Co-operation and Development (OECD), 2 rue Andre-Pascal, 75 Paris 16, France (Telephone Number in U.S. (202) 785-6323); *Economic Outlook.*

FRANCE - PROPERTY TAXES - See FRANCE - TAXATION

FRANCE - PUBLIC CONSUMPTION FUND

European Community Information Service, 2100 M Street, NW, Washington, D.C. 20037 (202) 862-9500; *Basic Statistics of the Community.*

Organisation for Economic Co-operation and Development (OECD), 2 rue Andre-Pascal, 75 Paris 16, France (Telephone Number in U.S. (202) 785-6323); *Revenue Statistics of OECD Member Countries.*

FRANCE - PUBLIC EXPENDITURES

European Community Information Service, 2100 M Street, NW, Washington, D.C. 20037 (202) 862-9500; *Basic Statistics of the Community.*

National Technical Information Service, 5285 Port Royal Road, Springfield, Virginia 22161 (703) 487-4600; *Handbook of Economic Statistics.*

Organisation for Economic Co-operation and Development (OECD), 2 rue Andre-Pascal, 75 Paris 16, France (Telephone Number in U.S. (202) 785-6323); *Revenue Statistics of OECD Member Countries.*

FRANCE - PUBLIC FINANCE

Facts on File, 460 Park Avenue South, New York, New York 10016 (800) 443-8323; *The New Book of World Rankings.*

Federal Statistical Office, Gustav - Stresemann - Ring 11, D-6200 Wiesbaden, Germany; *Frankreich.*

National Technical Information Service, 5285 Port Royal Road, Springfield, Virginia 22161 (703) 487-4600; *Handbook of Economic Statistics.*

Organisation for Economic Co-operation and Development (OECD), 2 rue Andre-Pascal, 75 Paris 16, France (Telephone Number in U.S. (202) 785-6323); *Revenue Statistics of OECD Member Countries.*

FRANCE - PUBLIC HEALTH

European Community Information Service, 2100 M Street, NW, Washington, D.C. 20037 (202) 862-9500; *Basic Statistics of the Community.*

FRANCE - PUBLIC REVENUES

National Technical Information Service, 5285 Port Royal Road, Springfield, Virginia 22161 (703) 487-4600; *Handbook of Economic Statistics.*

Organisation for Economic Co-operation and Development (OECD), 2 rue Andre-Pascal, 75 Paris 16, France (Telephone Number in U.S. (212) 963-5981); *Revenue Statistics of OECD Member Countries.*

FRANCE - RADIO BROADCASTING - See FRANCE - BROADCASTING

FRANCE - RADIO RECEIVER PRODUCTION

Statistical Office of the United Nations, Publishing Service, New York, New York 10017 (800) 253-9646; *Statistical Yearbook.*

FRANCE - RAILWAYS

Euromonitor Publications Limited, 87-88 Turnmill Street, London EC1M 5QU, England; *European Marketing Data and Statistics.*

European Community Information Service, 2100 M Street, NW, Washington, D.C. 20037 (202) 862-9500; *Basic Statistics of the Community, Regions: Statistical Yearbook,* and *Transport Annual Statistics.*

G.K. Hall and Company, 70 Lincoln Street, Boston, Massachusetts 02111 (617) 423-3990; *The World in Figures.*

Jane's Information Group, Sentinel House, 163 Brighton Road, Coulsdon, Surrey CR5 2NH, England (Telephone Number in U.S. (703) 683-3700); *Jane's World Railways.*

National Technical Information Service, 5285 Port Royal Road, Springfield, Virginia 22161 (703) 487-4600; *Handbook of Economic Statistics.*

Statistical Office of the United Nations, Publishing Service, New York, New York 10017 (800) 253-9646; *Annual Bulletin of Transport Statistics for Europe,* and *Statistical Yearbook.*

FRANCE - RANCHING

European Community Information Service, 2100 M Street, NW, Washington, D.C. 20037 (202) 862-9500; *Basic Statistics of the Community.*

FRANCE - RAPESEED PRODUCTION - See FRANCE - CROPS

FRANCE - RELIGION

Facts on File, 460 Park Avenue South, New York, New York 10016 (800) 443-8323; *The New Book of World Rankings.*

FRANCE - RETAIL TRADE

European Community Information Service, 2100 M Street, NW, Washington, D.C. 20037 (202) 862-9500; *Basic Statistics of the Community,* and *Eurostatistics: Data for Short-Term Economic Analysis.*

G.K. Hall and Company, 70 Lincoln Street, Boston, Massachusetts 02111 (617) 423-3990; *The World in Figures.*

Statistical Office of the United Nations, Publishing Service, New York, New York 10017 (800) 253-9646; *Statistical Yearbook.*

FRANCE - RICE PRODUCTION - See FRANCE - CROPS

FRANCE - ROOT AND TUBER PRODUCTION - See FRANCE - CROPS

FRANCE - ROUNDWOOD PRODUCTION - See FRANCE - FORESTRY AND FOREST PRODUCTS

FRANCE - RUBBER PRODUCTION AND CONSUMPTION

European Community Information Service, 2100 M Street, NW, Washington, D.C. 20037 (202) 862-9500; *Basic Statistics of the Community.*

Facts on File, 460 Park Avenue South, New York, New York 10016 (800) 443-8323; *The New Book of World Rankings.*

International Rubber Study Group, York House, 8th Floor, Empire Way, Wembley, London HA9 0PA, England; *Rubber Statistical Bulletin.*

National Technical Information Service, 5285 Port Royal Road, Springfield, Virginia 22161 (703) 487-4600; *Handbook of Economic Statistics.*

Organisation for Economic Co-operation and Development (OECD), 2 rue Andre-Pascal, 75 Paris 16, France (Telephone Number in U.S. (202) 785-6323); *Foreign Trade by Commodities.*

Statistical Office of the United Nations, Publishing Service, New York, New York 10017 (800) 253-9646; *Statistical Yearbook.*

FRANCE - RYE PRODUCTION - See FRANCE - CROPS

FRANCE - SAFFLOWER SEED PRODUCTION - See FRANCE - CROPS

FRANCE - SALT PRODUCTION - See FRANCE - MINING AND MINERAL PRODUCTS

FRANCE - SAVINGS ACCOUNT DEPOSITS

European Community Information Service, 2100 M Street, NW, Washington, D.C. 20037 (202) 862-9500; *Eurostatistics: Data for Short-Term Economic Analysis.*

FRANCE - SAWNWOOD PRODUCTION - See FRANCE - FORESTRY AND FOREST PRODUCTS

FRANCE - SCIENCE AND TECHNOLOGY - EXPENDITURE FOR RESEARCH

European Community Information Service, 2100 M Street, NW, Washington, D.C. 20037 (202) 862-9500; *Basic Statistics of the Community.*

FRANCE - SCIENTISTS AND ENGINEERS

European Community Information Service, 2100 M Street, NW, Washington, D.C. 20037 (202) 862-9500; *Basic Statistics of the Community.*

FRANCE - SCIENTISTS AND TECHNICIANS

European Community Information Service, 2100 M Street, NW, Washington, D.C. 20037 (202) 862-9500; *Basic Statistics of the Community.*

Statistical Office of the United Nations, Publishing Service, New York, New York 10017 (800) 253-9646; *Statistical Yearbook.*

United Nations Educational, Scientific and Cultural Organization (UNESCO), 7 Place de Fontenoy, F-75700 Paris, France (Telephone Number in U.S. (212) 963-5981); *Statistical Yearbook.*

FRANCE - SENIOR CITIZENS

Facts on File, 460 Park Avenue South, New York, New York 10016 (800) 443-8323; *The New Book of World Rankings.*

FRANCE - SESAME SEED PRODUCTION - See FRANCE - CROPS

FRANCE - SHEEP - See FRANCE - LIVESTOCK AND POULTRY

FRANCE - SHIPBUILDING - PRODUCTION INDEX

Organisation for Economic Co-operation and Development (OECD), 2 rue Andre-Pascal, 75 Paris 16, France (Telephone Number in U.S. (202) 785-6323); *Indicators of Industrial Activity.*

FRANCE - SILVER PRODUCTION AND CONSUMPTION - See FRANCE - MINING AND MINERAL PRODUCTS

FRANCE - SISAL PRODUCTION - See FRANCE - CROPS

FRANCE - SOCIAL DATA

European Community Information Service, 2100 M Street, NW, Washington, D.C. 20037 (202) 862-9500; *ACP: Basic Statistics, Basic Statistics of the Community.*

Facts on File, 460 Park Avenue South, New York, New York 10016 (800) 443-8323; *The New Book of World Rankings.*

G.K. Hall and Company, 70 Lincoln Street, Boston, Massachusetts 02111 (617) 423-3990; *The World in Figures.*

FRANCE - SOCIAL SECURITY

European Community Information Service, 2100 M Street, NW, Washington, D.C. 20037 (202) 862-9500; *Basic Statistics of the Community.*

International Monetary Fund, 700 Nineteenth Street, NW, Washington, D.C. 20431 (202) 623-7000; *Government Finance Statistics Yearbook.*

Organisation for Economic Co-operation and Development (OECD), 2 rue Andre-Pascal, 75 Paris 16, France (Telephone Number in U.S. (202) 785-6323); *Revenue Statistics of OECD Member Countries.*

FRANCE - SOCIOECONOMIC DATA

European Community Information Service, 2100 M Street, NW, Washington, D.C. 20037 (202) 862-9500; *Basic Statistics of the Community.*

Organisation for Economic Co-operation and Development (OECD), 2 rue Andre-Pascal, 75 Paris 16, France (Telephone Number in U.S. (202) 785-6323); *Economic Outlook.*

FRANCE - SOYBEAN PRODUCTION - See FRANCE - CROPS

FRANCE - STAMP TAXES AND DUTIES - See FRANCE - TAXATION

FRANCE - STEEL - See FRANCE - MINING AND MINERAL PRODUCTS

FRANCE - STOCKS - COMMODITY - MARKET PRICE - INDEXES

Food and Agricultural Organization of the United Nations (FAO) Via delle Terme di Caracalla, 00100 Rome, Italy (Telephone Number in U.S. (202) 653-2400); *The State of Food and Agriculture.*

International Lead and Zinc Study Group, Metro House, 58 St. James's Street, London SW1A 1LD, England; *Lead and Zinc Statistics.*

Statistical Office of the United Nations, Publishing Service, New York, New York 10017 (800) 253-9646; *Statistical Yearbook.*

World Bureau of Metal Statistics, 27-A High Street, Ware Hert SG12 9BA, England; *World Metal Statistics.*

FRANCE - STRAW PRODUCTION - See FRANCE - CROPS

FRANCE - SUGAR - See FRANCE - CROPS

FRANCE - SUGARBEET PRODUCTION - See FRANCE - CROPS

FRANCE - SULPHUR AND SULPHURIC ACID PRODUCTION - See FRANCE - MINING AND MINERAL PRODUCTS

FRANCE - SUNFLOWER PRODUCTION - See FRANCE - CROPS

FRANCE - TAXATION

European Community Information Service, 2100 M Street, NW, Washington, D.C. 20037 (202) 862-9500; *Basic Statistics of the Community.*

International Monetary Fund, 700 Nineteenth Street, NW, Washington, D.C. 20431 (202) 623-7000; *Government Finance Statistics Yearbook.*

International Road Federation, 525 School Street, SW, Washington, D.C. 20024 (202) 554-2106; *World Road Statistics.*

Organisation for Economic Co-operation and Development (OECD), 2 rue Andre-Pascal, 75 Paris 16, France (Telephone Number in U.S. (202) 785-6323); *Revenue Statistics of OECD Member Countries.*

The World Bank, 1818 H Street, NW, Washington, D.C. 20433 (202) 477-1234; *World Tables.*

FRANCE - TEA PRODUCTION AND CONSUMPTION - See FRANCE - CROPS

FRANCE - TELEGRAPH SERVICE

European Community Information Service, 2100 M Street, NW, Washington, D.C. 20037 (202) 862-9500; *Transport Annual Statistics.*

Statistical Office of the United Nations, Publishing Service, New York, New York 10017 (800) 253-9646; *Statistical Yearbook.*

FRANCE - TELEPHONES IN USE

American Telephone and Telegraph Company, 26 Parsippany Road, Whippany, New Jersey 07981 (800) 338-4038; *The World's Telephones.*

European Community Information Service, 2100 M Street, NW, Washington, D.C. 20037 (202) 862-9500; *Basic Statistics of the Community,* and *Transport Annual Statistics.*

G.K. Hall and Company, 70 Lincoln Street, Boston, Massachusetts 02111 (617) 423-3990; *The World in Figures.*

Statistical Office of the United Nations, Publishing Service, New York, New York 10017 (800) 253-9646; *Statistical Yearbook.*

FRANCE - TELEVISION BROADCASTING - See FRANCE - BROADCASTING

FRANCE - TELEVISION RECEIVER PRODUCTION

European Community Information Service, 2100 M Street, NW, Washington, D.C. 20037 (202) 862-9500; *Basic Statistics of the Community.*

National Technical Information Service, 5285 Port Royal Road, Springfield, Virginia 22161 (703) 487-4600; *Handbook of Economic Statistics.*

Statistical Office of the United Nations, Publishing Service, New York, New York 10017 (800) 253-9646; *Statistical Yearbook.*

FRANCE - TEXTILE INDUSTRY

European Community Information Service, 2100 M Street, NW, Washington, D.C. 20037 (202) 862-9500; *Basic Statistics of the Community, Eurostatistics: Data for Short-Term Economic Analysis,* and *Industrial Production: Quarterly Statistics.*

Forest and Paper Association, 1250 Connecticut Avenue, NW, Washington, D.C. 20036 (202) 463-2455; *Wood Pulp and Fiber Statistics.*

G.K. Hall and Company, 70 Lincoln Street, Boston, Massachusetts 02111 (617) 423-3990; *The World in Figures.*

Organisation for Economic Co-operation and Development (OECD), 2 rue Andre-Pascal, 75 Paris 16, France (Telephone Number in U.S. (202) 785-6323); *Foreign Trade by Commodities, Indicators of Industrial Activity, Industrial Structure Statistics,* and *Textile Industry in OECD Countries.*

Statistical Office of the United Nations, Publishing Service, New York, New York 10017 (800) 253-9646; *Statistical Yearbook,* and *Trade in Manufactures of Developing Countries.*

FRANCE - THEATRE

United Nations Educational, Scientific and Cultural Organization (UNESCO), 7 Place de Fontenoy, F-75700 Paris, France (Telephone Number in U.S. (212) 963-5981); *Statistical Yearbook.*

FRANCE - TIMBER - See FRANCE - FORESTRY AND FOREST PRODUCTS

FRANCE - TIN - See FRANCE - MINING AND MINERAL PRODUCTS

FRANCE - TIRES (MOTOR VEHICLE) PRODUCTION

International Rubber Study Group, York House, 8th Floor, Empire Way, Wembley, London HA9 0PA, England; *Rubber Statistical Bulletin.*

National Technical Information Service, 5285 Port Royal Road, Springfield, Virginia 22161 (703) 487-4600; *Handbook of Economic Statistics.*

Statistical Office of the United Nations, Publishing Service, New York, New York 10017 (800) 253-9646; *Statistical Yearbook.*

FRANCE - TOBACCO PRODUCTION

Commodity Research Bureau, Incorporated, 75 Wall Street, New York, New York 10005 (212) 504-7754; *Commodity Year Book.*

Euromonitor Publications Limited, 87-88 Turnmill Street, London EC1M 5QU, England; *European Marketing Data and Statistics,* and *Industrial Production: Quarterly Statistics.*

European Community Information Service, 2100 M Street, NW, Washington, D.C. 20037 (202) 862-9500; *Basic Statistics of the Community.*

Facts on File, 460 Park Avenue South, New York, New York 10016 (800) 443-8323; *The New Book of World Rankings.*

Organisation for Economic Co-operation and Development (OECD), 2 rue Andre-Pascal, 75 Paris 16, France (Telephone Number in U.S. (202) 785-6323); *Foreign Trade by Commodities, Indicators of Industrial Activity,* and *Industrial Structure Statistics.*

Statistical Office of the United Nations, Publishing Service, New York, New York 10017 (800) 253-9646; *Statistical Yearbook.*

FRANCE - TOURISM

Euromonitor Publications Limited, 87-88 Turnmill Street, London EC1M 5QU, England; *European Marketing Data and Statistics.*

European Community Information Service, 2100 M Street, NW, Washington, D.C. 20037 (202) 862-9500; *Transport Annual Statistics.*

Facts on File, 460 Park Avenue South, New York, New York 10016 (800) 443-8323; *The New Book of World Rankings.*

Federal Statistical Office, Gustav - Stresemann - Ring 11, D-6200 Wiesbaden, Germany; *Frankreich.*

G.K. Hall and Company, 70 Lincoln Street, Boston, Massachusetts 02111 (617) 423-3990; *The World in Figures.*

International Road Federation, 525 School Street, SW, Washington, D.C. 20024 (202) 554-2106; *World Road Statistics.*

Organisation for Economic Co-operation and Development (OECD), 2 rue Andre-Pascal, 75 Paris 16, France (Telephone Number in U.S. (202) 785-6323); *Tourism Policy and International Tourism in OECD Member Countries.*

Statistical Office of the United Nations, Publishing Service, New York, New York 10017 (800) 253-9646; *Statistical Yearbook.*

Times Books, 201 East 50th Street, New York, New York 10022 (212) 751-2600; *The Economist Book of Vital World Statistics.*

World Tourism Organization, Calle Capitan Haya 42, E-28020 Madrid, Spain; *Yearbook of Tourism Statistics.*

FRANCE - TRACTORS IN USE

European Community Information Service, 2100 M Street, NW, Washington, D.C. 20037 (202) 862-9500; *Transport Annual Statistics.*

Statistical Office of the United Nations, Publishing Service, New York, New York 10017 (800) 253-9646; *Statistical Yearbook.*

FRANCE - TRADE - See FRANCE - FOREIGN TRADE

FRANCE - TRADEMARKS AND SERVICE MARKS

World Intellectual Property Organization, 34 Chemin des Colombettes, CH-1211 Geneva 20. Switzerland; *Industrial Property Statistics.*

FRANCE - TRANSPORTATION AND COMMUNICATIONS

European Community Information Service, 2100 M Street, NW, Washington, D.C. 20037 (202) 862-9500; *Basic Statistics of the Community, Energy Statistics Yearbook, Regions: Statistical Yearbook,* and *Transport Annual Statistics.*

Facts on File, 460 Park Avenue South, New York, New York 10016 (800) 443-8323; *The New Book of World Rankings.*

Federal Statistical Office, Gustav - Stresemann - Ring 11, D-6200 Wiesbaden, Germany; *Frankreich.*

G.K. Hall and Company, 70 Lincoln Street, Boston, Massachusetts 02111 (617) 423-3990; *The World in Figures.*

FRANCE - TUNGSTEN PRODUCTION AND CONSUMPTION - See FRANCE - MINING AND MINERAL PRODUCTS

FRANCE - TURKEYS - See FRANCE - LIVESTOCK AND POULTRY

FRANCE - UNEMPLOYMENT

Euromonitor Publications Limited, 87-88 Turnmill Street, London EC1M 5QU, England; *European Marketing Data and Statistics.*

European Community Information Service, 2100 M Street, NW, Washington, D.C. 20037 (202) 862-9500; *Basic Statistics of the Community, Employment and Unemployment, Eurostatistics: Data for Short-Term Economic Analysis, Labor Force Sample Survey, OECD Economic Surveys: France,* and *Regions: Statistical Yearbook.*

International Labour Office, I.L.O. Publications, CH-1211, Geneva 22, Switzerland; *Yearbook of Labour Statistics.*

National Technical Information Service, 5285 Port Royal Road, Springfield, Virginia 22161 (703) 487-4600; *Handbook of Economic Statistics.*

Organisation for Economic Co-operation and Development (OECD), 2 rue Andre-Pascal, 75 Paris 16, France (Telephone Number in U.S. (202) 785-6323); *Economic Outlook, Labour Force Statistics,* and *OECD Employment Outlook.*

Statistical Office of the United Nations, Publishing Service, New York, New York 10017 (800) 253-9646; *Statistical Yearbook.*

FRANCE - URANIUM PRODUCTION AND CONSUMPTION - See FRANCE - MINING AND MINERAL PRODUCTS

FRANCE - VANADIUM AND VANADIUM ORE - See FRANCE - MINING AND MINERAL PRODUCTS

FRANCE - VITAL STATISTICS

European Community Information Service, 2100 M Street, NW, Washington, D.C. 20037 (202) 862-9500; *Basic Statistics of the Community.*

G.K. Hall and Company, 70 Lincoln Street, Boston, Massachusetts 02111 (617) 423-3990; *The World in Figures.*

Statistical Office of the United Nations, Publishing Service, New York, New York 10017 (800) 253-9646; *Statistical Yearbook.*

World Health Organization, Office of Publications, Avenue Appia, CH-1211 Geneva 27, Switzerland (Telephone Number in U.S. (518) 436-9686); *World Health Statistics Annual.*

FRANCE - WAGES

Euromonitor Publications Limited, 87-88 Turnmill Street, London EC1M 5QU, England; *European Marketing Data and Statistics.*

European Community Information Service, 2100 M Street, NW, Washington, D.C. 20037 (202) 862-9500; *Basic Statistics of the Community, Earnings in Agriculture,* and *Eurostatistics: Data for Short-Term Economic Analysis.*

Federal Statistical Office, Gustav - Stresemann - Ring 11, D-6200 Wiesbaden, Germany; *Frankreich.*

G.K. Hall and Company, 70 Lincoln Street, Boston, Massachusetts 02111 (617) 423-3990; *The World in Figures.*

International Labour Office, I.L.O. Publications, CH-1211, Geneva 22, Switzerland; *Yearbook of Labour Statistics.*

Organisation for Economic Co-operation and Development (OECD), 2 rue Andre-Pascal, 75 Paris 16, France (Telephone Number in U.S. (202) 785-6323); *Economic Outlook, Main Economic Indicators - Historical Statistics,* and *Industrial Structure Statistics.*

Statistical Office of the United Nations, Publishing Service, New York, New York 10017 (800) 253-9646; *Statistical Yearbook.*

FRANCE - WALNUT PRODUCTION - See FRANCE - CROPS

FRANCE - WATERWAYS IN USE - See FRANCE - MERCHANT SHIPPING

FRANCE - WEATHER

Facts on File, 460 Park Avenue South, New York, New York 10016 (800) 443-8323; *The New Book of World Rankings.*

G.K. Hall and Company, 70 Lincoln Street, Boston, Massachusetts 02111 (617) 423-3990; *The World in Figures.*

FRANCE - WELFARE

European Community Information Service, 2100 M Street, NW, Washington, D.C. 20037 (202) 862-9500; *Basic Statistics of the Community.*

International Monetary Fund, 700 Nineteenth Street, NW, Washington, D.C. 20431 (202) 623-7000; *Government Finance Statistics Yearbook.*

FRANCE - WHEAT PRODUCTION AND PRICES - See FRANCE - CROPS

FRANCE - WHOLESALE PRICES

European Community Information Service, 2100 M Street, NW, Washington, D.C. 20037 (202) 862-9500; *Basic Statistics of the Community.*

National Technical Information Service, 5285 Port Royal Road, Springfield, Virginia 22161 (703) 487-4600; *Handbook of Economic Statistics.*

Statistical Office of the United Nations, Publishing Service, New York, New York 10017 (800) 253-9646; *Statistical Yearbook.*

FRANCE - WHOLESALE TRADE

European Community Information Service, 2100 M Street, NW, Washington, D.C. 20037 (202) 862-9500; *Basic Statistics of the Community.*

Statistical Office of the United Nations, Publishing Service, New York, New York 10017 (800) 253-9646; *Statistical Yearbook.*

FRANCE - WINE PRODUCTION

European Community Information Service, 2100 M Street, NW, Washington, D.C. 20037 (202) 862-9500; *Basic Statistics of the Community.*

Facts on File, 460 Park Avenue South, New York, New York 10016 (800) 443-8323; *The New Book of World Rankings.*

Statistical Office of the United Nations, Publishing Service, New York, New York 10017 (800) 253-9646; *Statistical Yearbook.*

FRANCE - WOOD EXPORTS - See FRANCE - FORESTRY AND FOREST PRODUCTS

FRANCE - WOOL - INDUSTRIAL CONSUMPTION

Organisation for Economic Co-operation and Development (OECD), 2 rue Andre-Pascal, 75 Paris 16, France (Telephone Number in U.S. (202) 785-6323); *Textile Industry in OECD Countries.*

FRANCE - WOOL PRODUCTION AND CONSUMPTION

European Community Information Service, 2100 M Street, NW, Washington, D.C. 20037 (202) 862-9500; *Basic Statistics of the Community.*

Facts on File, 460 Park Avenue South, New York, New York 10016 (800) 443-8323; *The New Book of World Rankings.*

National Technical Information Service, 5285 Port Royal Road, Springfield, Virginia 22161 (703) 487-4600; *Handbook of Economic Statistics.*

Organisation for Economic Co-operation and Development (OECD), 2 rue Andre-Pascal, 75 Paris 16, France (Telephone Number in U.S. (202) 785-6323); *Economic Accounts for Agriculture,* and *Textile Industry in OECD Countries.*

Statistical Office of the United Nations, Publishing Service, New York, New York 10017 (800) 253-9646; *Statistical Yearbook.*

FRANCE - YARN PRODUCTION

European Community Information Service, 2100 M Street, NW, Washington, D.C. 20037 (202) 862-9500; *Basic Statistics of the Community.*

Organisation for Economic Co-operation and Development (OECD), 2 rue Andre-Pascal, 75 Paris 16, France (Telephone Number in U.S. (202) 785-6323); *Foreign Trade by Commodities,* and *Textile Industry in OECD Countries.*

Statistical Office of the United Nations, Publishing Service, New York, New York 10017 (800) 253-9646; *Statistical Yearbook.*

FRANCE - ZINC AND ZINC ORE - See FRANCE - MINING AND MINERAL PRODUCTS

FRANCHISED ESTABLISHMENTS

National Automobile Dealers Association, 8400 Westpark Drive, McLean, Virginia 22102 (703) 827-7407; *NADA Data.*

International Franchise Association, 1350 New York Avenue, Suite 900, Washington, D.C. 20005 (202) 628-8000; *Franchising in the Economy.*

FRATERNAL ASSOCIATIONS

Gale Research Incorporated, 835 Penobscot Building, Detroit, Michigan 48226 (800) 877-4253; *Encyclopedia of Associations.*

FRATERNITIES

Gale Research Incorporated, 835 Penobscot Building, Detroit, Michigan 48226 (800) 877-4253; *Encyclopedia of Associations.*

FREEZERS - HOME

Euromonitor Publications Limited, 87-88 Turnmill Street, London EC1M 5QU, England; *European Marketing Data and Statistics.*

U.S. Department of Energy, Energy Information Administration, Washington, D.C. 20585 (202) 586-8800; *Housing Characteristics.*

FREIGHT TRAFFIC - See AIR TRANSPORTATION, RAILROADS, RIVERS, CANALS, and WATERWAYS

French Guiana - Primary Statistics Source

INSEE, Observatoire Economiquede Paris, Tour Gamma A, 195 rue de Bercy, 75582, Paris Cedex 12, France; *Annuaire Statistique de la Guyane, Bulletin Statistique de la Guyane,* and *Tableaux Economiques Regionaux Guyane.*

FRENCH GUIANA - AGRICULTURE

Facts on File, 460 Park Avenue South, New York, New York 10016 (800) 443-8323; *The New Book of World Rankings.*

Food and Agricultural Organization of the United Nations (FAO) Via delle Terme di Caracalla, 00100 Rome, Italy (Telephone Number in U.S. (202) 653-2400); *Production Yearbook, The State of Food and Agriculture,* and *Trade Yearbook.*

G.K. Hall and Company, 70 Lincoln Street, Boston, Massachusetts 02111 (617) 423-3990; *The World in Figures.*

Statistical Office of the United Nations, Publishing Service, New York, New York 10017 (800) 253-9646; *Statistical Yearbook.*

FRENCH GUIANA - AIRLINE SERVICE

Facts on File, 460 Park Avenue South, New York, New York 10016 (800) 443-8323; *The New Book of World Rankings.*

G.K. Hall and Company, 70 Lincoln Street, Boston, Massachusetts 02111 (617) 423-3990; *The World in Figures.*

FRENCH GUIANA - ALUMINUM PRODUCTION AND CONSUMPTION - See FRENCH GUIANA - MINING AND MINERAL PRODUCTS

FRENCH GUIANA - AREA AND POPULATION DENSITY

Facts on File, 460 Park Avenue South, New York, New York 10016 (800) 443-8323; *The New Book of World Rankings.*

Food and Agricultural Organization of the United Nations (FAO) Via delle Terme di Caracalla, 00100 Rome, Italy (Telephone Number in U.S. (202) 653-2400); *The State of Food and Agriculture.*

G.K. Hall and Company, 70 Lincoln Street, Boston, Massachusetts 02111 (617) 423-3990; *The World in Figures.*

Statistical Office of the United Nations, Publishing Service, New York, New York 10017 (800) 253-9646; *Statistical Yearbook.*

FRENCH GUIANA - BALANCE OF PAYMENTS

G.K. Hall and Company, 70 Lincoln Street, Boston, Massachusetts 02111 (617) 423-3990; *The World in Figures.*

FRENCH GUIANA - BANKING

Facts on File, 460 Park Avenue South, New York, New York 10016 (800) 443-8323; *The New Book of World Rankings.*

G.K. Hall and Company, 70 Lincoln Street, Boston, Massachusetts 02111 (617) 423-3990; *The World in Figures.*

FRENCH GUIANA - BARLEY PRODUCTION - See FRENCH GUIANA - CROPS

FRENCH GUIANA - BEER PRODUCTION

Facts on File, 460 Park Avenue South, New York, New York 10016 (800) 443-8323; *The New Book of World Rankings.*

FRENCH GUIANA - BIRTH RATES

Facts on File, 460 Park Avenue South, New York, New York 10016 (800) 443-8323; *The New Book of World Rankings.*

Statistical Office of the United Nations, Publishing Service, New York, New York 10017 (800) 253-9646; *Demographic Yearbook,* and *Statistical Yearbook.*

World Health Organization, Office of Publications, Avenue Appia, CH-1211 Geneva 27, Switzerland (Telephone Number in U.S. (518) 436-9686); *World Health Statistics Annual.*

FRENCH GUIANA - BONDS

G.K. Hall and Company, 70 Lincoln Street, Boston, Massachusetts 02111 (617) 423-3990; *The World in Figures.*

FRENCH GUIANA - BOOK PRODUCTION

G.K. Hall and Company, 70 Lincoln Street, Boston, Massachusetts 02111 (617) 423-3990; *The World in Figures.*

FRENCH GUIANA - BROADCASTING

Billboard Limited, P.O. Box 9027, 1006 AA Amsterdam, The Netherlands (Telephone Number in U.S. (212) 764-7300); *World Radio TV Handbook.*

Facts on File, 460 Park Avenue South, New York, New York 10016 (800) 443-8323; *The New Book of World Rankings.*

G.K. Hall and Company, 70 Lincoln Street, Boston, Massachusetts 02111 (617) 423-3990; *The World in Figures.*

FRENCH GUIANA - BUILDING CONSTRUCTION - See FRENCH GUIANA - CONSTRUCTION

FRENCH GUIANA - BUSINESS

G.K. Hall and Company, 70 Lincoln Street, Boston, Massachusetts 02111 (617) 423-3990; *The World in Figures.*

FRENCH GUIANA - CALORIE SUPPLY

Food and Agricultural Organization of the United Nations (FAO) Via delle Terme di Caracalla, 00100 Rome, Italy (Telephone Number in U.S. (202) 653-2400); *The State of Food and Agriculture.*

FRENCH GUIANA - CATTLE - See FRENCH GUIANA - LIVESTOCK AND POULTRY

FRENCH GUIANA - CEMENT PRODUCTION - See FRENCH GUIANA - MINING AND MINERAL PRODUCTS

FRENCH GUIANA - CHEMICAL (ORGANIC) PRODUCTION - See FRENCH GUIANA - MINING AND MINERAL PRODUCTS

FRENCH GUIANA - CIGARETTE PRODUCTION - See FRENCH GUIANA - TOBACCO PRODUCTION

FRENCH GUIANA - CLASS STRUCTURE

G.K. Hall and Company, 70 Lincoln Street, Boston, Massachusetts 02111 (617) 423-3990; *The World in Figures.*

FRENCH GUIANA - CLIMATE

Facts on File, 460 Park Avenue South, New York, New York 10016 (800) 443-8323; *The New Book of World Rankings.*

G.K. Hall and Company, 70 Lincoln Street, Boston, Massachusetts 02111 (617) 423-3990; *The World in Figures.*

FRENCH GUIANA - COAL PRODUCTION - See FRENCH GUIANA - MINING AND MINERAL PRODUCTS

FRENCH GUIANA - COFFEE PRODUCTION - See FRENCH GUIANA - CROPS

FRENCH GUIANA - COMMUNICATIONS

G.K. Hall and Company, 70 Lincoln Street, Boston, Massachusetts 02111 (617) 423-3990; *The World in Figures.*

FRENCH GUIANA - CONSTRUCTION INDUSTRY

Facts on File, 460 Park Avenue South, New York, New York 10016 (800) 443-8323; *The New Book of World Rankings.*

Statistical Office of the United Nations, Publishing Service, New York, New York 10017 (800) 253-9646; *Construction Statistics Yearbook,* and *Statistical Yearbook.*

FRENCH GUIANA - CONSUMER PRICE INDEX

G.K. Hall and Company, 70 Lincoln Street, Boston, Massachusetts 02111 (617) 423-3990; *The World in Figures.*

Statistical Office of the United Nations, Publishing Service, New York, New York 10017 (800) 253-9646; *Statistical Yearbook.*

FRENCH GUIANA - CONSUMER PRICES

International Labour Office, I.L.O. Publications, CH-1211, Geneva 22, Switzerland; *Yearbook of Labour Statistics.*

FRENCH GUIANA - CONSUMPTION

G.K. Hall and Company, 70 Lincoln Street, Boston, Massachusetts 02111 (617) 423-3990; *The World in Figures.*

FRENCH GUIANA - COPPER PRODUCTION - See FRENCH GUIANA - MINING AND MINERAL PRODUCTS

FRENCH GUIANA - CORN PRODUCTION - See FRENCH GUIANA - CROPS

FRENCH GUIANA - CORPORATE TAXES - See FRENCH GUIANA - TAXATION

FRENCH GUIANA - COTTON PRODUCTION - See FRENCH GUIANA - CROPS

FRENCH GUIANA - CROPS

Facts on File, 460 Park Avenue South, New York, New York 10016 (800) 443-8323; *The New Book of World Rankings.*

Food and Agricultural Organization of the United Nations (FAO) Via delle Terme di Caracalla, 00100 Rome, Italy (Telephone Number in U.S. (202) 653-2400); *Production Yearbook,* and *The State of Food and Agriculture.*

G.K. Hall and Company, 70 Lincoln Street, Boston, Massachusetts 02111 (617) 423-3990; *The World in Figures.*

FRENCH GUIANA - CUSTOMS DUTIES

G.K. Hall and Company, 70 Lincoln Street, Boston, Massachusetts 02111 (617) 423-3990; *The World in Figures.*

FRENCH GUIANA - DAIRY PRODUCTS

Facts on File, 460 Park Avenue South, New York, New York 10016 (800) 443-8323; *The New Book of World Rankings.*

Food and Agricultural Organization of the United Nations (FAO) Via delle Terme di Caracalla, 00100 Rome, Italy (Telephone Number in U.S. (202) 653-2400); *The State of Food and Agriculture.*

FRENCH GUIANA - DEATH RATES

G.K. Hall and Company, 70 Lincoln Street, Boston, Massachusetts 02111 (617) 423-3990; *The World in Figures.*

Statistical Office of the United Nations, Publishing Service, New York, New York 10017 (800) 253-9646; *Statistical Yearbook.*

World Health Organization, Office of Publications, Avenue Appia, CH-1211 Geneva 27, Switzerland (Telephone Number in U.S. (518) 436-9686); *World Health Statistics Annual.*

FRENCH GUIANA - DEFENSE EXPENDITURES

G.K. Hall and Company, 70 Lincoln Street, Boston, Massachusetts 02111 (617) 423-3990; *The World in Figures.*

FRENCH GUIANA - DEMOGRAPHY

Facts on File, 460 Park Avenue South, New York, New York 10016 (800) 443-8323; *The New Book of World Rankings.*

G.K. Hall and Company, 70 Lincoln Street, Boston, Massachusetts 02111 (617) 423-3990; *The World in Figures.*

FRENCH GUIANA - DEVELOPMENT ASSISTANCE

G.K. Hall and Company, 70 Lincoln Street, Boston, Massachusetts 02111 (617) 423-3990; *The World in Figures.*

Statistical Office of the United Nations, Publishing Service, New York, New York 10017 (800) 253-9646; *Statistical Yearbook.*

FRENCH GUIANA - DIAMOND PRODUCTION - See FRENCH GUIANA - MINING AND MINERAL PRODUCTS

FRENCH GUIANA - DISEASES

G.K. Hall and Company, 70 Lincoln Street, Boston, Massachusetts 02111 (617) 423-3990; *The World in Figures.*

World Health Organization, Office of Publications, Avenue Appia, CH-1211 Geneva 27, Switzerland (Telephone Number in U.S. (518) 436-9686); *World Health Statistics Annual.*

FRENCH GUIANA - DIVORCE RATES

Facts on File, 460 Park Avenue South, New York, New York 10016 (800) 443-8323; *The New Book of World Rankings.*

Statistical Office of the United Nations, Publishing Service, New York, New York 10017 (800) 253-9646; *Demographic Yearbook,* and *Statistical Yearbook.*

FRENCH GUIANA - DOMESTIC PRODUCT

G.K. Hall and Company, 70 Lincoln Street, Boston, Massachusetts 02111 (617) 423-3990; *The World in Figures.*

FRENCH GUIANA - DUCKS - See FRENCH GUIANA - LIVESTOCK AND POULTRY

FRENCH GUIANA - ECONOMY

Facts on File, 460 Park Avenue South, New York, New York 10016 (800) 443-8323; *The New Book of World Rankings.*

G.K. Hall and Company, 70 Lincoln Street, Boston, Massachusetts 02111 (617) 423-3990; *The World in Figures.*

FRENCH GUIANA - EDUCATION

Facts on File, 460 Park Avenue South, New York, New York 10016 (800) 443-8323; *The New Book of World Rankings.*

G.K. Hall and Company, 70 Lincoln Street, Boston, Massachusetts 02111 (617) 423-3990; *The World in Figures.*

FRENCH GUIANA - EGG PRODUCTION - See FRENCH GUIANA - DAIRY PRODUCTS

FRENCH GUIANA - ELECTRICITY

Facts on File, 460 Park Avenue South, New York, New York 10016 (800) 443-8323; *The New Book of World Rankings.*

Statistical Office of the United Nations, Publishing Service, New York, New York 10017 (800) 253-9646; *Statistical Yearbook.*

FRENCH GUIANA - EMPLOYMENT

Facts on File, 460 Park Avenue South, New York, New York 10016 (800) 443-8323; *The New Book of World Rankings.*

Food and Agricultural Organization of the United Nations (FAO) Via delle Terme di Caracalla, 00100 Rome, Italy (Telephone Number in U.S. (202) 653-2400); *The State of Food and Agriculture.*

International Labour Office, I.L.O. Publications, CH-1211, Geneva 22, Switzerland; *Yearbook of Labour Statistics.*

FRENCH GUIANA - ENERGY

Facts on File, 460 Park Avenue South, New York, New York 10016 (800) 443-8323; *The New Book of World Rankings.*

Food and Agricultural Organization of the United Nations (FAO) Via delle Terme di Caracalla, 00100 Rome, Italy (Telephone Number in U.S. (202) 653-2400); *The State of Food and Agriculture.*

G.K. Hall and Company, 70 Lincoln Street, Boston, Massachusetts 02111 (617) 423-3990; *The World in Figures.*

Statistical Office of the United Nations, Publishing Service, New York, New York 10017 (800) 253-9646; *Energy Statistics Yearbook,* and *Statistical Yearbook.*

FRENCH GUIANA - EXPORTS

Food and Agricultural Organization of the United Nations (FAO) Via delle Terme di Caracalla, 00100 Rome, Italy (Telephone Number in U.S. (202) 653-2400); *The State of Food and Agriculture.*

G.K. Hall and Company, 70 Lincoln Street, Boston, Massachusetts 02111 (617) 423-3990; *The World in Figures.*

International Monetary Fund, 700 Nineteenth Street, NW, Washington, D.C. 20431 (202) 623-7000; *Direction of Trade Statistics.*

FRENCH GUIANA - EXTERNAL TRADE

Food and Agricultural Organization of the United Nations (FAO) Via delle Terme di Caracalla, 00100 Rome, Italy (Telephone Number in U.S. (202) 653-2400); *The State of Food and Agriculture,* and *Trade Yearbook.*

G.K. Hall and Company, 70 Lincoln Street, Boston, Massachusetts 02111 (617) 423-3990; *The World in Figures.*

Statistical Office of the United Nations, Publishing Service, New York, New York 10017 (800) 253-9646; *Statistical Yearbook.*

FRENCH GUIANA - FARM CROPS - See FRENCH GUIANA - CROPS

FRENCH GUIANA - FERTILITY RATES

Facts on File, 460 Park Avenue South, New York, New York 10016 (800) 443-8323; *The New Book of World Rankings.*

FRENCH GUIANA - FERTILIZER

Food and Agricultural Organization of the United Nations (FAO) Via delle Terme di Caracalla, 00100 Rome, Italy (Telephone Number in U.S. (202) 653-2400); *The State of Food and Agriculture.*

FRENCH GUIANA - FETAL MORTALITY

Statistical Office of the United Nations, Publishing Service, New York, New York 10017 (800) 253-9646; *Demographic Yearbook.*

World Health Organization, Office of Publications, Avenue Appia, CH-1211 Geneva 27, Switzerland (Telephone Number in U.S. (518) 436-9686); *World Health Statistics Annual.*

FRENCH GUIANA - FINANCE

Facts on File, 460 Park Avenue South, New York, New York 10016 (800) 443-8323; *The New Book of World Rankings.*

G.K. Hall and Company, 70 Lincoln Street, Boston, Massachusetts 02111 (617) 423-3990; *The World in Figures.*

FRENCH GUIANA - FISHERIES

Facts on File, 460 Park Avenue South, New York, New York 10016 (800) 443-8323; *The New Book of World Rankings.*

Food and Agricultural Organization of the United Nations (FAO) Via delle Terme di Caracalla, 00100 Rome, Italy (Telephone Number in U.S. (202) 653-2400); *The State of Food and Agriculture,* and *Yearbook of Fishery Statistics.*

Statistical Office of the United Nations, Publishing Service, New York, New York 10017 (800) 253-9646; *Statistical Yearbook.*

FRENCH GUIANA - FOOD

Food and Agricultural Organization of the United Nations (FAO) Via delle Terme di Caracalla, 00100 Rome, Italy (Telephone Number in U.S. (202) 653-2400); *Production Yearbook,* and *The State of Food and Agriculture.*

G.K. Hall and Company, 70 Lincoln Street, Boston, Massachusetts 02111 (617) 423-3990; *The World in Figures.*

FRENCH GUIANA - FOREIGN AID

G.K. Hall and Company, 70 Lincoln Street, Boston, Massachusetts 02111 (617) 423-3990; *The World in Figures.*

FRENCH GUIANA - FOREIGN TRADE

Facts on File, 460 Park Avenue South, New York, New York 10016 (800) 443-8323; *The New Book of World Rankings.*

G.K. Hall and Company, 70 Lincoln Street, Boston, Massachusetts 02111 (617) 423-3990; *The World in Figures.*

Statistical Office of the United Nations, Publishing Service, New York, New York 10017 (800) 253-9646; *International Trade Statistics Yearbook,* and *Statistical Yearbook.*

FRENCH GUIANA - FORESTRY AND FOREST PRODUCTS

Facts on File, 460 Park Avenue South, New York, New York 10016 (800) 443-8323; *The New Book of World Rankings.*

Food and Agricultural Organization of the United Nations (FAO) Via delle Terme di Caracalla, 00100 Rome, Italy (Telephone Number in U.S. (202) 653-2400); *The State of Food and Agriculture,* and *Yearbook of Forest Products.*

G.K. Hall and Company, 70 Lincoln Street, Boston, Massachusetts 02111 (617) 423-3990; *The World in Figures.*

Statistical Office of the United Nations, Publishing Service, New York, New York 10017 (800) 253-9646; *Statistical Yearbook.*

United Nations Educational, Scientific and Cultural Organization (UNESCO), 7 Place de Fontenoy, F-75700 Paris, France (Telephone Number in U.S. (212) 963-5981); *Statistical Yearbook.*

FRENCH GUIANA - GAS PRODUCTION - See FRENCH GUIANA - MINING AND MINERAL PRODUCTS

FRENCH GUIANA - GENERAL MORTALITY

Statistical Office of the United Nations, Publishing Service, New York, New York 10017 (800) 253-9646; *Demographic Yearbook.*

World Health Organization, Office of Publications, Avenue Appia, CH-1211 Geneva 27, Switzerland (Telephone Number in U.S. (518) 436-9686); *World Health Statistics Annual.*

FRENCH GUIANA - GEOGRAPHIC DATA

Facts on File, 460 Park Avenue South, New York, New York 10016 (800) 443-8323; *The New Book of World Rankings.*

FRENCH GUIANA - GOLD PRODUCTION AND CONSUMPTION - See FRENCH GUIANA - MINING AND MINERAL PRODUCTS

FRENCH GUIANA - GOVERNMENT

G.K. Hall and Company, 70 Lincoln Street, Boston, Massachusetts 02111 (617) 423-3990; *The World in Figures.*

FRENCH GUIANA - GRAIN PRODUCTION - See FRENCH GUIANA - CROPS

FRENCH GUIANA - GROSS DOMESTIC PRODUCT

Facts on File, 460 Park Avenue South, New York, New York 10016 (800) 443-8323; *The New Book of World Rankings.*

G.K. Hall and Company, 70 Lincoln Street, Boston, Massachusetts 02111 (617) 423-3990; *The World in Figures.*

FRENCH GUIANA - HEALTH

Facts on File, 460 Park Avenue South, New York, New York 10016 (800) 443-8323; *The New Book of World Rankings.*

G.K. Hall and Company, 70 Lincoln Street, Boston, Massachusetts 02111 (617) 423-3990; *The World in Figures.*

Statistical Office of the United Nations, Publishing Service, New York, New York 10017 (800) 253-9646; *Statistical Yearbook.*

World Health Organization, Office of Publications, Avenue Appia, CH-1211 Geneva 27, Switzerland (Telephone Number in U.S. (518) 436-9686); *World Health Statistics Annual.*

FRENCH GUIANA - HIDE PRODUCTION

Food and Agricultural Organization of the United Nations (FAO), Via delle Terme di Caracalla, 00100 Rome, Italy (Telephone Number in U.S. (202) 653-2400); *Production Yearbook.*

FRENCH GUIANA - HIGHWAYS

G.K. Hall and Company, 70 Lincoln Street, Boston, Massachusetts 02111 (617) 423-3990; *The World in Figures.*

FRENCH GUIANA - HORSES - See FRENCH GUIANA - LIVESTOCK AND POULTRY

FRENCH GUIANA - HOURS OF WORK - See FRENCH GUIANA - EMPLOYMENT

FRENCH GUIANA - HOUSING AND HOUSING UNITS

Facts on File, 460 Park Avenue South, New York, New York 10016 (800) 443-8323; *The New Book of World Rankings.*

FRENCH GUIANA - ILLITERATE POPULATION

G.K. Hall and Company, 70 Lincoln Street, Boston, Massachusetts 02111 (617) 423-3990; *The World in Figures.*

United Nations Educational, Scientific and Cultural Organization (UNESCO), 7 Place de Fontenoy, F-75700 Paris, France (Telephone Number in U.S. (212) 963-5981); *Statistical Yearbook.*

FRENCH GUIANA - IMPORTS

Food and Agricultural Organization of the United Nations (FAO) Via delle Terme di Caracalla, 00100 Rome, Italy (Telephone Number in U.S. (202) 653-2400); *The State of Food and Agriculture.*

G.K. Hall and Company, 70 Lincoln Street, Boston, Massachusetts 02111 (617) 423-3990; *The World in Figures.*

International Monetary Fund, 700 Nineteenth Street, NW, Washington, D.C. 20431 (202) 623-7000; *Direction of Trade Statistics.*

Statistical Office of the United Nations, Publishing Service, New York, New York 10017 (800) 253-9646; *Trade in Manufactures of Developing Countries.*

FRENCH GUIANA - INDUSTRY

Facts on File, 460 Park Avenue South, New York, New York 10016 (800) 443-8323; *The New Book of World Rankings.*

G.K. Hall and Company, 70 Lincoln Street, Boston, Massachusetts 02111 (617) 423-3990; *The World in Figures.*

International Labour Office, I.L.O. Publications, CH-1211, Geneva 22, Switzerland; *Yearbook of Labour Statistics.*

FRENCH GUIANA - INFANT AND MATERNAL MORTALITY

Statistical Office of the United Nations, Publishing Service, New York, New York 10017 (800) 253-9646; *Demographic Yearbook,* and *Statistical Yearbook.*

World Health Organization, Office of Publications, Avenue Appia, CH-1211 Geneva 27, Switzerland (Telephone Number in U.S. (518) 436-9686); *World Health Statistics Annual.*

FRENCH GUIANA - IRON ORE PRODUCTION AND CONSUMPTION - See FRENCH GUIANA - MINING AND MINERAL PRODUCTS

FRENCH GUIANA - LABOR FORCE

Facts on File, 460 Park Avenue South, New York, New York 10016 (800) 443-8323; *The New Book of World Rankings.*

Food and Agricultural Organization of the United Nations (FAO) Via delle Terme di Caracalla, 00100 Rome, Italy (Telephone Number in U.S. (202) 653-2400); *The State of Food and Agriculture.*

G.K. Hall and Company, 70 Lincoln Street, Boston, Massachusetts 02111 (617) 423-3990; *The World in Figures.*

FRENCH GUIANA - LABOR PRODUCTIVITY

International Labour Office, I.L.O. Publications, CH-1211, Geneva 22, Switzerland; *Yearbook of Labour Statistics.*

FRENCH GUIANA - LAND USE

Food and Agricultural Organization of the United Nations (FAO), Via delle Terme di Caracalla, 00100 Rome, Italy (Telephone Number in U.S. (202) 653-2400); *Production Yearbook.*

G.K. Hall and Company, 70 Lincoln Street, Boston, Massachusetts 02111 (617) 423-3990; *The World in Figures.*

FRENCH GUIANA - LIBRARIES

Facts on File, 460 Park Avenue South, New York, New York 10016 (800) 443-8323; *The New Book of World Rankings.*

FRENCH GUIANA - LIVESTOCK AND POULTRY

Facts on File, 460 Park Avenue South, New York, New York 10016 (800) 443-8323; *The New Book of World Rankings.*

Food and Agricultural Organization of the United Nations (FAO), Via delle Terme di Caracalla, 00100 Rome, Italy (Telephone Number in U.S. (202) 653-2400); *Production Yearbook,* and *The State of Food and Agriculture.*

G.K. Hall and Company, 70 Lincoln Street, Boston, Massachusetts 02111 (617) 423-3990; *The World in Figures.*

Statistical Office of the United Nations, Publishing Service, New York, New York 10017 (800) 253-9646; *Statistical Yearbook.*

FRENCH GUIANA - LIVING LEVELS

G.K. Hall and Company, 70 Lincoln Street, Boston, Massachusetts 02111 (617) 423-3990; *The World in Figures.*

FRENCH GUIANA - MANUFACTURING

Facts on File, 460 Park Avenue South, New York, New York 10016 (800) 443-8323; *The New Book of World Rankings.*

G.K. Hall and Company, 70 Lincoln Street, Boston, Massachusetts 02111 (617) 423-3990; *The World in Figures.*

FRENCH GUIANA - MARRIAGE RATES

Facts on File, 460 Park Avenue South, New York, New York 10016 (800) 443-8323; *The New Book of World Rankings.*

Statistical Office of the United Nations, Publishing Service, New York, New York 10017 (800) 253-9646; *Demographic Yearbook,* and *Statistical Yearbook.*

FRENCH GUIANA - MEAT PRODUCTION - See FRENCH GUIANA - LIVESTOCK AND POULTRY

FRENCH GUIANA - MERCHANT SHIPPING

G.K. Hall and Company, 70 Lincoln Street, Boston, Massachusetts 02111 (617) 423-3990; *The World in Figures.*

Statistical Office of the United Nations, Publishing Service, New York, New York 10017 (800) 253-9646; *Statistical Yearbook.*

FRENCH GUIANA - MILK PRODUCTION - See FRENCH GUIANA - DAIRY PRODUCTS

FRENCH GUIANA - MILITARY

G.K. Hall and Company, 70 Lincoln Street, Boston, Massachusetts 02111 (617) 423-3990; *The World in Figures.*

FRENCH GUIANA - MINING AND MINERAL PRODUCTS

Facts on File, 460 Park Avenue South, New York, New York 10016 (800) 443-8323; *The New Book of World Rankings.*

G.K. Hall and Company, 70 Lincoln Street, Boston, Massachusetts 02111 (617) 423-3990; *The World in Figures.*

FRENCH GUIANA - MONEY SUPPLY

G.K. Hall and Company, 70 Lincoln Street, Boston, Massachusetts 02111 (617) 423-3990; *The World in Figures.*

FRENCH GUIANA - MOTOR VEHICLES IN USE

G.K. Hall and Company, 70 Lincoln Street, Boston, Massachusetts 02111 (617) 423-3990; *The World in Figures.*

Statistical Office of the United Nations, Publishing Service, New York, New York 10017 (800) 253-9646; *Statistical Yearbook.*

FRENCH GUIANA - MUSEUMS

Facts on File, 460 Park Avenue South, New York, New York 10016 (800) 443-8323; *The New Book of World Rankings.*

United Nations Educational, Scientific and Cultural Organization (UNESCO), 7 Place de Fontenoy, F-75700 Paris, France (Telephone Number in U.S. (212) 963-5981); *Statistical Yearbook.*

FRENCH GUIANA - NATALITY - See FRENCH GUIANA - BIRTH RATE

FRENCH GUIANA - NATIONAL INCOME

Facts on File, 460 Park Avenue South, New York, New York 10016 (800) 443-8323; *The New Book of World Rankings.*

G.K. Hall and Company, 70 Lincoln Street, Boston, Massachusetts 02111 (617) 423-3990; *The World in Figures.*

FRENCH GUIANA - NATIONAL PRODUCT

Facts on File, 460 Park Avenue South, New York, New York 10016 (800) 443-8323; *The New Book of World Rankings.*

FRENCH GUIANA - NATURAL GAS PRODUCTION - See FRENCH GUIANA - MINING AND MINERAL PRODUCTS

FRENCH GUIANA - NEWSPAPER PRODUCTION - See FRENCH GUIANA - FORESTRY AND FOREST PRODUCTS

FRENCH GUIANA - OCCUPATIONS - See FRENCH GUIANA - LABOR FORCE

FRENCH GUIANA - PEANUT PRODUCTION - See FRENCH GUIANA - CROPS

FRENCH GUIANA - PESTICIDE USE

Food and Agricultural Organization of the United Nations (FAO) Via delle Terme di Caracalla, 00100 Rome, Italy (Telephone Number in U.S. (202) 653-2400); *The State of Food and Agriculture.*

FRENCH GUIANA - PETROLEUM INDUSTRY

Facts on File, 460 Park Avenue South, New York, New York 10016 (800) 443-8323; *The New Book of World Rankings.*

Food and Agricultural Organization of the United Nations (FAO) Via delle Terme di Caracalla, 00100 Rome, Italy (Telephone Number in U.S. (202) 653-2400); *The State of Food and Agriculture.*

G.K. Hall and Company, 70 Lincoln Street, Boston, Massachusetts 02111 (617) 423-3990; *The World in Figures.*

FRENCH GUIANA - PIGS - See FRENCH GUIANA - LIVESTOCK AND POULTRY

FRENCH GUIANA - POPULATION

Facts on File, 460 Park Avenue South, New York, New York 10016 (800) 443-8323; *The New Book of World Rankings.*

Food and Agricultural Organization of the United Nations (FAO), Via delle Terme di Caracalla, 00100 Rome, Italy (Telephone Number in U.S. (202) 653-2400); *Production Yearbook.*

G.K. Hall and Company, 70 Lincoln Street, Boston, Massachusetts 02111 (617) 423-3990; *The World in Figures.*

International Labour Office, I.L.O. Publications, CH-1211, Geneva 22, Switzerland; *Yearbook of Labour Statistics.*

Statistical Office of the United Nations, Publishing Service, New York, New York 10017 (800) 253-9646; *Demographic Yearbook,* and *Statistical Yearbook.*

World Health Organization, Office of Publications, Avenue Appia, CH-1211 Geneva 27, Switzerland (Telephone Number in U.S. (518) 436-9686); *World Health Statistics Annual.*

FRENCH GUIANA - POST OFFICES

Facts on File, 460 Park Avenue South, New York, New York 10016 (800) 443-8323; *The New Book of World Rankings.*

FRENCH GUIANA - POTATO PRODUCTION - See FRENCH GUIANA - CROPS

FRENCH GUIANA - PRICES

Facts on File, 460 Park Avenue South, New York, New York 10016 (800) 443-8323; *The New Book of World Rankings.*

Food and Agricultural Organization of the United Nations (FAO), Via delle Terme di Caracalla, 00100 Rome, Italy (Telephone Number in U.S. (202) 653-2400); *Production Yearbook,* and *The State of Food and Agriculture.*

G.K. Hall and Company, 70 Lincoln Street, Boston, Massachusetts 02111 (617) 423-3990; *The World in Figures.*

International Labour Office, I.L.O. Publications, CH-1211, Geneva 22, Switzerland; *Yearbook of Labour Statistics.*

FRENCH GUIANA - PRODUCTION

Facts on File, 460 Park Avenue South, New York, New York 10016 (800) 443-8323; *The New Book of World Rankings*.

G.K. Hall and Company, 70 Lincoln Street, Boston, Massachusetts 02111 (617) 423-3990; *The World in Figures*.

FRENCH GUIANA - PUBLIC FINANCE

Facts on File, 460 Park Avenue South, New York, New York 10016 (800) 443-8323; *The New Book of World Rankings*.

FRENCH GUIANA - RADIO BROADCASTING - See BROADCASTING

FRENCH GUIANA - RAILWAYS

G.K. Hall and Company, 70 Lincoln Street, Boston, Massachusetts 02111 (617) 423-3990; *The World in Figures*.

FRENCH GUIANA - RELIGION

Facts on File, 460 Park Avenue South, New York, New York 10016 (800) 443-8323; *The New Book of World Rankings*.

FRENCH GUIANA - RENT PRICES

International Labour Office, I.L.O. Publications, CH-1211, Geneva 22, Switzerland; *Yearbook of Labour Statistics*.

FRENCH GUIANA - RETAIL TRADE

G.K. Hall and Company, 70 Lincoln Street, Boston, Massachusetts 02111 (617) 423-3990; *The World in Figures*.

FRENCH GUIANA - RICE PRODUCTION - See FRENCH GUIANA - CROPS

FRENCH GUIANA - ROOT AND TUBER PRODUCTION - See FRENCH GUIANA - CROPS

FRENCH GUIANA - ROUNDWOOD PRODUCTION - See FRENCH GUIANA - FORESTRY AND FOREST PRODUCTS

FRENCH GUIANA - RUBBER PRODUCTION

Facts on File, 460 Park Avenue South, New York, New York 10016 (800) 443-8323; *The New Book of World Rankings*.

FRENCH GUIANA - SAWNWOOD PRODUCTION - See FRENCH GUIANA - FORESTRY AND FOREST PRODUCTS

FRENCH GUIANA - SENIOR CITIZENS

Facts on File, 460 Park Avenue South, New York, New York 10016 (800) 443-8323; *The New Book of World Rankings*.

FRENCH GUIANA - SHEEP - See FRENCH GUIANA - LIVESTOCK AND POULTRY

FRENCH GUIANA - SILVER PRODUCTION AND CONSUMPTION - See FRENCH GUIANA - MINING AND MINERAL PRODUCTS

FRENCH GUIANA - SOCIAL DATA

Facts on File, 460 Park Avenue South, New York, New York 10016 (800) 443-8323; *The New Book of World Rankings*.

G.K. Hall and Company, 70 Lincoln Street, Boston, Massachusetts 02111 (617) 423-3990; *The World in Figures*.

FRENCH GUIANA - STEEL PRODUCTION - See FRENCH GUIANA - MINING AND MINERAL PRODUCTS

FRENCH GUIANA - STOCKS - COMMODITY - MARKET PRICE - INDEX

Food and Agricultural Organization of the United Nations (FAO) Via delle Terme di Caracalla, 00100 Rome, Italy (Telephone Number in U.S. (202) 653-2400); *The State of Food and Agriculture*.

FRENCH GUIANA - SUGAR PRODUCTION - See FRENCH GUIANA - CROPS

FRENCH GUIANA - TAXATION

G.K. Hall and Company, 70 Lincoln Street, Boston, Massachusetts 02111 (617) 423-3990; *The World in Figures*.

FRENCH GUIANA - TELEPHONES IN USE

American Telephone and Telegraph Company, 26 Parsippany Road, Whippany, New Jersey 07981 (800) 338-4038; *The World's Telephones*.

G.K. Hall and Company, 70 Lincoln Street, Boston, Massachusetts 02111 (617) 423-3990; *The World in Figures*.

Statistical Office of the United Nations, Publishing Service, New York, New York 10017 (800) 253-9646; *Statistical Yearbook*.

FRENCH GUIANA - TELEVISION BROADCASTING - See FRENCH GUIANA - BROADCASTING

FRENCH GUIANA - TELEVISIONS IN USE

Statistical Office of the United Nations, Publishing Service, New York, New York 10017 (800) 253-9646; *Statistical Yearbook*.

FRENCH GUIANA - TEXTILE INDUSTRY

G.K. Hall and Company, 70 Lincoln Street, Boston, Massachusetts 02111 (617) 423-3990; *The World in Figures*.

FRENCH GUIANA - TOBACCO PRODUCTION

Facts on File, 460 Park Avenue South, New York, New York 10016 (800) 443-8323; *The New Book of World Rankings*.

FRENCH GUIANA - TOURISM

Facts on File, 460 Park Avenue South, New York, New York 10016 (800) 443-8323; *The New Book of World Rankings*.

G.K. Hall and Company, 70 Lincoln Street, Boston, Massachusetts 02111 (617) 423-3990; *The World in Figures*.

FRENCH GUIANA - TRACTORS IN USE

Statistical Office of the United Nations, Publishing Service, New York, New York 10017 (800) 253-9646; *Statistical Yearbook*.

FRENCH GUIANA - TRADE - See FRENCH GUIANA - EMPLOYMENT

FRENCH GUIANA - TRANSPORTATION AND COMMUNICATIONS

Facts on File, 460 Park Avenue South, New York, New York 10016 (800) 443-8323; *The New Book of World Rankings.*

G.K. Hall and Company, 70 Lincoln Street, Boston, Massachusetts 02111 (617) 423-3990; *The World in Figures.*

FRENCH GUIANA - UNEMPLOYMENT

International Labour Office, I.L.O. Publications, CH-1211, Geneva 22, Switzerland; *Yearbook of Labour Statistics.*

Statistical Office of the United Nations, Publishing Service, New York, New York 10017 (800) 253-9646; *Statistical Yearbook.*

FRENCH GUIANA - VITAL STATISTICS

G.K. Hall and Company, 70 Lincoln Street, Boston, Massachusetts 02111 (617) 423-3990; *The World in Figures.*

Statistical Office of the United Nations, Publishing Service, New York, New York 10017 (800) 253-9646; *Statistical Yearbook.*

World Health Organization, Office of Publications, Avenue Appia, CH-1211 Geneva 27, Switzerland (Telephone Number in U.S. (518) 436-9686); *World Health Statistics Annual.*

FRENCH GUIANA - WAGES

G.K. Hall and Company, 70 Lincoln Street, Boston, Massachusetts 02111 (617) 423-3990; *The World in Figures.*

International Labour Office, I.L.O. Publications, CH-1211, Geneva 22, Switzerland; *Yearbook of Labour Statistics.*

FRENCH GUIANA - WEATHER

Facts on File, 460 Park Avenue South, New York, New York 10016 (800) 443-8323; *The New Book of World Rankings.*

G.K. Hall and Company, 70 Lincoln Street, Boston, Massachusetts 02111 (617) 423-3990; *The World in Figures.*

FRENCH GUIANA - WHEAT PRODUCTION AND PRICES - See FRENCH GUIANA - CROPS

FRENCH GUIANA - WINE PRODUCTION

Facts on File, 460 Park Avenue South, New York, New York 10016 (800) 443-8323; *The New Book of World Rankings.*

FRENCH GUIANA - WOOL PRODUCTION

Facts on File, 460 Park Avenue South, New York, New York 10016 (800) 443-8323; *The New Book of World Rankings.*

French Polynesia - Primary Statistics Source

Institut Territorial de la Statistique, BP 395, Papeete-Tahiti, French Polynesia; *Bilan Statistique de L'annee.*

FRENCH POLYNESIA - AGRICULTURE

Food and Agricultural Organization of the United Nations (FAO) Via delle Terme di Caracalla, 00100 Rome, Italy (Telephone Number in U.S. (202) 653-2400); *Production Yearbook, The State of Food and Agriculture,* and *Trade Yearbook.*

G.K. Hall and Company, 70 Lincoln Street, Boston, Massachusetts 02111 (617) 423-3990; *The World in Figures.*

Statistical Office of the United Nations, Publishing Service, New York, New York 10017 (800) 253-9646; *Statistical Yearbook.*

FRENCH POLYNESIA - AIRLINE SERVICE

G.K. Hall and Company, 70 Lincoln Street, Boston, Massachusetts 02111 (617) 423-3990; *The World in Figures.*

FRENCH POLYNESIA - ANIMAL HEALTH

Food and Agricultural Organization of the United Nations (FAO), Via delle Terme di Caracalla, 00100 Rome, Italy (Telephone Number in U.S. (202) 653-2400); *Animal Health Yearbook.*

FRENCH POLYNESIA - AREA AND DENSITY OF POPULATION

Food and Agricultural Organization of the United Nations (FAO) Via delle Terme di Caracalla, 00100 Rome, Italy (Telephone Number in U.S. (202) 653-2400); *The State of Food and Agriculture.*

G.K. Hall and Company, 70 Lincoln Street, Boston, Massachusetts 02111 (617) 423-3990; *The World in Figures.*

Statistical Office of the United Nations, Publishing Service, New York, New York 10017 (800) 253-9646; *Statistical Yearbook.*

FRENCH POLYNESIA - BALANCE OF PAYMENTS

G.K. Hall and Company, 70 Lincoln Street, Boston, Massachusetts 02111 (617) 423-3990; *The World in Figures.*

FRENCH POLYNESIA - BANKING

G.K. Hall and Company, 70 Lincoln Street, Boston, Massachusetts 02111 (617) 423-3990; *The World in Figures.*

FRENCH POLYNESIA - BEER PRODUCTION

Statistical Office of the United Nations, Publishing Service, New York, New York 10017 (800) 253-9646; *Statistical Yearbook.*

FRENCH POLYNESIA - BIRTH RATES

Statistical Office of the United Nations, Publishing Service, New York, New York 10017 (800) 253-9646; *Demographic Yearbook,* and *Statistical Yearbook.*

FRENCH POLYNESIA - BONDS

G.K. Hall and Company, 70 Lincoln Street, Boston, Massachusetts 02111 (617) 423-3990; *The World in Figures.*

FRENCH POLYNESIA - BOOK PRODUCTION

G.K. Hall and Company, 70 Lincoln Street, Boston, Massachusetts 02111 (617) 423-3990; *The World in Figures.*

United Nations Educational, Scientific and Cultural Organization (UNESCO), 7 Place de Fontenoy, F-75700 Paris, France (Telephone Number in U.S. (212) 963-5981); *Statistical Yearbook.*

FRENCH POLYNESIA - BROADCASTING

G.K. Hall and Company, 70 Lincoln Street, Boston, Massachusetts 02111 (617) 423-3990; *The World in Figures.*

FRENCH POLYNESIA - BUILDING CONSTRUCTION - See FRENCH POLYNESIA - CONSTRUCTION INDUSTRY

FRENCH POLYNESIA - BUSINESS

G.K. Hall and Company, 70 Lincoln Street, Boston, Massachusetts 02111 (617) 423-3990; *The World in Figures.*

FRENCH POLYNESIA - CALORIE SUPPLY

Food and Agricultural Organization of the United Nations (FAO) Via delle Terme di Caracalla, 00100 Rome, Italy (Telephone Number in U.S. (202) 653-2400); *The State of Food and Agriculture.*

FRENCH POLYNESIA - CATTLE - See FRENCH POLYNESIA - LIVESTOCK AND POULTRY

FRENCH POLYNESIA - CHEMICAL (ORGANIC) PRODUCTION - See FRENCH POLYNESIA - MINING AND MINERAL PRODUCTS

FRENCH POLYNESIA - CLASS STRUCTURE

G.K. Hall and Company, 70 Lincoln Street, Boston, Massachusetts 02111 (617) 423-3990; *The World in Figures.*

FRENCH POLYNESIA - CLIMATE

G.K. Hall and Company, 70 Lincoln Street, Boston, Massachusetts 02111 (617) 423-3990; *The World in Figures.*

FRENCH POLYNESIA - CLOTHING EXPORTS AND IMPORTS

South Pacific Commission, Post Box D5, Noumea Cedex, New Caledonia; *Statistical Bulletin of the South Pacific: Retail Price Indexes.*

FRENCH POLYNESIA - COAL PRODUCTION - See FRENCH POLYNESIA - MINING AND MINERAL PRODUCTS

FRENCH POLYNESIA - COMMUNICATIONS

G.K. Hall and Company, 70 Lincoln Street, Boston, Massachusetts 02111 (617) 423-3990; *The World in Figures.*

FRENCH POLYNESIA - CONSTRUCTION INDUSTRY

Statistical Office of the United Nations, Publishing Service, New York, New York 10017 (800) 253-9646; *Construction Statistics Yearbook,* and *Statistical Yearbook.*

FRENCH POLYNESIA - CONSUMER PRICE INDEX

G.K. Hall and Company, 70 Lincoln Street, Boston, Massachusetts 02111 (617) 423-3990; *The World in Figures.*

Statistical Office of the United Nations, Publishing Service, New York, New York 10017 (800) 253-9646; *Statistical Yearbook.*

FRENCH POLYNESIA - CONSUMPTION

G.K. Hall and Company, 70 Lincoln Street, Boston, Massachusetts 02111 (617) 423-3990; *The World in Figures.*

South Pacific Commission, Post Box D5, Noumea Cedex, New Caledonia; *Statistical Bulletin of the South Pacific: Retail Price Indexes.*

FRENCH POLYNESIA - CORN PRODUCTION - See FRENCH POLYNESIA - CROPS

FRENCH POLYNESIA - CORPORATE TAXES - See FRENCH POLYNESIA - TAXATION

FRENCH POLYNESIA - CROPS

Food and Agricultural Organization of the United Nations (FAO) Via delle Terme di Caracalla, 00100 Rome, Italy (Telephone Number in U.S. (202) 653-2400); *Production Yearbook,* and *The State of Food and Agriculture.*

G.K. Hall and Company, 70 Lincoln Street, Boston, Massachusetts 02111 (617) 423-3990; *The World in Figures.*

FRENCH POLYNESIA - CUSTOMS DUTIES

G.K. Hall and Company, 70 Lincoln Street, Boston, Massachusetts 02111 (617) 423-3990; *The World in Figures.*

FRENCH POLYNESIA - DAIRY PRODUCTS

Food and Agricultural Organization of the United Nations (FAO), Via delle Terme di Caracalla, 00100 Rome, Italy (Telephone Number in U.S. (202) 653-2400); *Production Yearbook,* and *The State of Food and Agriculture.*

FRENCH POLYNESIA - DEATH RATES

G.K. Hall and Company, 70 Lincoln Street, Boston, Massachusetts 02111 (617) 423-3990; *The World in Figures.*

Statistical Office of the United Nations, Publishing Service, New York, New York 10017 (800) 253-9646; *Statistical Yearbook.*

World Health Organization, Office of Publications, Avenue Appia, CH-1211 Geneva 27, Switzerland (Telephone Number in U.S. (518) 436-9686); *World Health Statistics Annual.*

FRENCH POLYNESIA - DEFENSE EXPENDITURES

G.K. Hall and Company, 70 Lincoln Street, Boston, Massachusetts 02111 (617) 423-3990; *The World in Figures.*

FRENCH POLYNESIA - DEMOGRAPHY

G.K. Hall and Company, 70 Lincoln Street, Boston, Massachusetts 02111 (617) 423-3990; *The World in Figures.*

FRENCH POLYNESIA - DEVELOPMENT ASSISTANCE

G.K. Hall and Company, 70 Lincoln Street, Boston, Massachusetts 02111 (617) 423-3990; *The World in Figures.*

Statistical Office of the United Nations, Publishing Service, New York, New York 10017 (800) 253-9646; *Statistical Yearbook.*

FRENCH POLYNESIA - DISEASE

G.K. Hall and Company, 70 Lincoln Street, Boston, Massachusetts 02111 (617) 423-3990; *The World in Figures.*

World Health Organization, Office of Publications, Avenue Appia, CH-1211 Geneva 27, Switzerland (Telephone Number in U.S. (518) 436-9686); *World Health Statistics Annual.*

FRENCH POLYNESIA - DIVORCE RATES

Statistical Office of the United Nations, Publishing Service, New York, New York 10017 (800) 253-9646; *Demographic Yearbook,* and *Statistical Yearbook.*

FRENCH POLYNESIA - DOMESTIC PRODUCT

G.K. Hall and Company, 70 Lincoln Street, Boston, Massachusetts 02111 (617) 423-3990; *The World in Figures*.

FRENCH POLYNESIA - DUCKS - See FRENCH POLYNESIA - LIVESTOCK AND POULTRY

FRENCH POLYNESIA - ECONOMY

G.K. Hall and Company, 70 Lincoln Street, Boston, Massachusetts 02111 (617) 423-3990; *The World in Figures*.

FRENCH POLYNESIA - EDUCATION

G.K. Hall and Company, 70 Lincoln Street, Boston, Massachusetts 02111 (617) 423-3990; *The World in Figures*.

United Nations Educational, Scientific and Cultural Organization (UNESCO), 7 Place de Fontenoy, F-75700 Paris, France (Telephone Number in U.S. (212) 963-5981); *Statistical Yearbook*.

FRENCH POLYNESIA - EGG PRODUCTION - See FRENCH POLYNESIA - DAIRY PRODUCTS

FRENCH POLYNESIA - ELECTRICITY

Statistical Office of the United Nations, Publishing Service, New York, New York 10017 (800) 253-9646; *Statistical Yearbook*.

FRENCH POLYNESIA - ENERGY

Food and Agricultural Organization of the United Nations (FAO) Via delle Terme di Caracalla, 00100 Rome, Italy (Telephone Number in U.S. (202) 653-2400); *The State of Food and Agriculture*.

G.K. Hall and Company, 70 Lincoln Street, Boston, Massachusetts 02111 (617) 423-3990; *The World in Figures*.

Statistical Office of the United Nations, Publishing Service, New York, New York 10017 (800) 253-9646; *Energy Statistics Yearbook*, and *Statistical Yearbook*.

FRENCH POLYNESIA - EXPORTS

Food and Agricultural Organization of the United Nations (FAO) Via delle Terme di Caracalla, 00100 Rome, Italy (Telephone Number in U.S. (202) 653-2400); *The State of Food and Agriculture*.

G.K. Hall and Company, 70 Lincoln Street, Boston, Massachusetts 02111 (617) 423-3990; *The World in Figures*.

International Monetary Fund, 700 Nineteenth Street, NW, Washington, D.C. 20431 (202) 623-7000; *Direction of Trade Statistics*.

South Pacific Commission, Post Box D5, Noumea Cedex, New Caledonia; *Statistical Bulletin of the South Pacific: Overseas Trade*.

FRENCH POLYNESIA - EXTERNAL TRADE

Food and Agricultural Organization of the United Nations (FAO) Via delle Terme di Caracalla, 00100 Rome, Italy (Telephone Number in U.S. (202) 653-2400); *The State of Food and Agriculture*, and *Trade Yearbook*.

G.K. Hall and Company, 70 Lincoln Street, Boston, Massachusetts 02111 (617) 423-3990; *The World in Figures*.

Statistical Office of the United Nations, Publishing Service, New York, New York 10017 (800) 253-9646; *Statistical Yearbook*.

FRENCH POLYNESIA - FARM CROPS - See FRENCH POLYNESIA - CROPS

FRENCH POLYNESIA - FETAL MORTALITY

Statistical Office of the United Nations, Publishing Service, New York, New York 10017 (800) 253-9646; *Demographic Yearbook*.

FRENCH POLYNESIA - FERTILIZER

Food and Agricultural Organization of the United Nations (FAO) Via delle Terme di Caracalla, 00100 Rome, Italy (Telephone Number in U.S. (202) 653-2400); *The State of Food and Agriculture*.

FRENCH POLYNESIA - FINANCE

G.K. Hall and Company, 70 Lincoln Street, Boston, Massachusetts 02111 (617) 423-3990; *The World in Figures*.

FRENCH POLYNESIA - FISHERIES

Food and Agricultural Organization of the United Nations (FAO) Via delle Terme di Caracalla, 00100 Rome, Italy (Telephone Number in U.S. (202) 653-2400); *The State of Food and Agriculture*, and *Yearbook of Fishery Statistics*.

Statistical Office of the United Nations, Publishing Service, New York, New York 10017 (800) 253-9646; *Statistical Yearbook*.

FRENCH POLYNESIA - FOOD

Food and Agricultural Organization of the United Nations (FAO) Via delle Terme di Caracalla, 00100 Rome, Italy (Telephone Number in U.S. (202) 653-2400); *Production Yearbook*, and *The State of Food and Agriculture*.

G.K. Hall and Company, 70 Lincoln Street, Boston, Massachusetts 02111 (617) 423-3990; *The World in Figures*.

South Pacific Commission, Post Box D5, Noumea Cedex, New Caledonia; *Statistical Bulletin of the South Pacific: Retail Price Indexes*.

FRENCH POLYNESIA - FOREIGN AID

G.K. Hall and Company, 70 Lincoln Street, Boston, Massachusetts 02111 (617) 423-3990; *The World in Figures*.

FRENCH POLYNESIA - FOREIGN TRADE

Food and Agricultural Organization of the United Nations (FAO) Via delle Terme di Caracalla, 00100 Rome, Italy (Telephone Number in U.S. (202) 653-2400); *The State of Food and Agriculture*.

G.K. Hall and Company, 70 Lincoln Street, Boston, Massachusetts 02111 (617) 423-3990; *The World in Figures*.

South Pacific Commission, Post Box D5, Noumea Cedex, New Caledonia; *Statistical Bulletin of the South Pacific: Retail Price Indexes*.

Statistical Office of the United Nations, Publishing Service, New York, New York 10017 (800) 253-9646; *International Trade Statistics Yearbook*, and *Statistical Yearbook*.

FRENCH POLYNESIA - FORESTRY AND FOREST PRODUCTS

Food and Agricultural Organization of the United Nations (FAO) Via delle Terme di Caracalla, 00100 Rome, Italy (Telephone Number in U.S. (202) 653-2400); *The State of Food and Agriculture*, and *Yearbook of Forest Products*.

G.K. Hall and Company, 70 Lincoln Street, Boston, Massachusetts 02111 (617) 423-3990; *The World in Figures*.

Statistical Office of the United Nations, Publishing Service, New York, New York 10017 (800) 253-9646; *Statistical Yearbook*.

United Nations Educational, Scientific and Cultural Organization (UNESCO), 7 Place de Fontenoy, F-75700 Paris, France (Telephone Number in U.S. (212) 963-5981); *Statistical Yearbook*.

FRENCH POLYNESIA - GENERAL MORTALITY

Statistical Office of the United Nations, Publishing Service, New York, New York 10017 (800) 253-9646; *Demographic Yearbook*.

FRENCH POLYNESIA - GOVERNMENT

G.K. Hall and Company, 70 Lincoln Street, Boston, Massachusetts 02111 (617) 423-3990; *The World in Figures*.

FRENCH POLYNESIA - GRAIN PRODUCTION - See FRENCH GUIANA - CROPS

FRENCH POLYNESIA - GROSS DOMESTIC PRODUCT

G.K. Hall and Company, 70 Lincoln Street, Boston, Massachusetts 02111 (617) 423-3990; *The World in Figures*.

Statistical Office of the United Nations, Publishing Service, New York, New York 10017 (800) 253-9646; *Statistical Yearbook*.

FRENCH POLYNESIA - HEALTH

G.K. Hall and Company, 70 Lincoln Street, Boston, Massachusetts 02111 (617) 423-3990; *The World in Figures*.

South Pacific Commission, Post Box D5, Noumea Cedex, New Caledonia; *Statistical Bulletin of the South Pacific: Retail Price Indexes*.

Statistical Office of the United Nations, Publishing Service, New York, New York 10017 (800) 253-9646; *Statistical Yearbook*.

World Health Organization, Office of Publications, Avenue Appia, CH-1211 Geneva 27, Switzerland (Telephone Number in U.S. (518) 436-9686); *World Health Statistics Annual*.

FRENCH POLYNESIA - HIDE PRODUCTION

Food and Agricultural Organization of the United Nations (FAO), Via delle Terme di Caracalla, 00100 Rome, Italy (Telephone Number in U.S. (202) 653-2400); *Production Yearbook*.

FRENCH POLYNESIA - HIGHWAYS

G.K. Hall and Company, 70 Lincoln Street, Boston, Massachusetts 02111 (617) 423-3990; *The World in Figures*.

FRENCH POLYNESIA - HORSES - See FRENCH POLYNESIA - LIVESTOCK AND POULTRY

FRENCH POLYNESIA - HOUSING AND HOUSING UNITS

South Pacific Commission, Post Box D5, Noumea Cedex, New Caledonia; *Statistical Bulletin of the South Pacific: Retail Price Indexes*.

FRENCH POLYNESIA - HOUSING EXPENDITURES

South Pacific Commission, Post Box D5, Noumea Cedex, New Caledonia; *Statistical Bulletin of the South Pacific: Retail Price Indexes*.

FRENCH POLYNESIA - ILLITERATE POPULATION

G.K. Hall and Company, 70 Lincoln Street, Boston, Massachusetts 02111 (617) 423-3990; *The World in Figures*.

United Nations Educational, Scientific and Cultural Organization (UNESCO), 7 Place de Fontenoy, F-75700 Paris, France (Telephone Number in U.S. (212) 963-5981); *Statistical Yearbook*.

FRENCH POLYNESIA - IMPORTS

Food and Agricultural Organization of the United Nations (FAO) Via delle Terme di Caracalla, 00100 Rome, Italy (Telephone Number in U.S. (202) 653-2400); *The State of Food and Agriculture*.

G.K. Hall and Company, 70 Lincoln Street, Boston, Massachusetts 02111 (617) 423-3990; *The World in Figures*.

International Monetary Fund, 700 Nineteenth Street, NW, Washington, D.C. 20431 (202) 623-7000; *Direction of Trade Statistics*.

South Pacific Commission, Post Box D5, Noumea Cedex, New Caledonia; *Statistical Bulletin of the South Pacific: Overseas Trade*.

FRENCH POLYNESIA - INDUSTRY

G.K. Hall and Company, 70 Lincoln Street, Boston, Massachusetts 02111 (617) 423-3990; *The World in Figures*.

FRENCH POLYNESIA - INFANT AND MATERNAL MORTALITY

Statistical Office of the United Nations, Publishing Service, New York, New York 10017 (800) 253-9646; *Demographic Yearbook*, and *Statistical Yearbook*.

FRENCH POLYNESIA - LABOR FORCE

Food and Agricultural Organization of the United Nations (FAO) Via delle Terme di Caracalla, 00100 Rome, Italy (Telephone Number in U.S. (202) 653-2400); *The State of Food and Agriculture*.

G.K. Hall and Company, 70 Lincoln Street, Boston, Massachusetts 02111 (617) 423-3990; *The World in Figures*.

FRENCH POLYNESIA - LAND USE

Food and Agricultural Organization of the United Nations (FAO), Via delle Terme di Caracalla, 00100 Rome, Italy (Telephone Number in U.S. (202) 653-2400); *Production Yearbook*.

G.K. Hall and Company, 70 Lincoln Street, Boston, Massachusetts 02111 (617) 423-3990; *The World in Figures*.

FRENCH POLYNESIA - LIBRARIES

United Nations Educational, Scientific and Cultural Organization (UNESCO), 7 Place de Fontenoy, F-75700 Paris, France (Telephone Number in U.S. (212) 963-5981); *Statistical Yearbook.*

FRENCH POLYNESIA - LIVESTOCK AND POULTRY

Food and Agricultural Organization of the United Nations (FAO), Via delle Terme di Caracalla, 00100 Rome, Italy (Telephone Number in U.S. (202) 653-2400); *Production Yearbook,* and *The State of Food and Agriculture.*

G.K. Hall and Company, 70 Lincoln Street, Boston, Massachusetts 02111 (617) 423-3990; *The World in Figures.*

Statistical Office of the United Nations, Publishing Service, New York, New York 10017 (800) 253-9646; *Statistical Yearbook.*

FRENCH POLYNESIA - LIVING LEVELS

G.K. Hall and Company, 70 Lincoln Street, Boston, Massachusetts 02111 (617) 423-3990; *The World in Figures.*

FRENCH POLYNESIA - MAIL - NUMBER OF ITEMS SENT AND RECEIVED

Statistical Office of the United Nations, Publishing Service, New York, New York 10017 (800) 253-9646; *Statistical Yearbook.*

FRENCH POLYNESIA - MANUFACTURING

G.K. Hall and Company, 70 Lincoln Street, Boston, Massachusetts 02111 (617) 423-3990; *The World in Figures.*

FRENCH POLYNESIA - MARRIAGE RATES

Statistical Office of the United Nations, Publishing Service, New York, New York 10017 (800) 253-9646; *Demographic Yearbook,* and *Statistical Yearbook.*

FRENCH POLYNESIA - MEAT PRODUCTION - See FRENCH POLYNESIA - LIVESTOCK AND POULTRY

FRENCH POLYNESIA - MERCHANT SHIPPING

G.K. Hall and Company, 70 Lincoln Street, Boston, Massachusetts 02111 (617) 423-3990; *The World in Figures.*

Statistical Office of the United Nations, Publishing Service, New York, New York 10017 (800) 253-9646; *Statistical Yearbook.*

FRENCH POLYNESIA - MILITARY

G.K. Hall and Company, 70 Lincoln Street, Boston, Massachusetts 02111 (617) 423-3990; *The World in Figures.*

FRENCH POLYNESIA - MINING AND MINERAL PRODUCTS

G.K. Hall and Company, 70 Lincoln Street, Boston, Massachusetts 02111 (617) 423-3990; *The World in Figures.*

FRENCH POLYNESIA - MONEY SUPPLY

G.K. Hall and Company, 70 Lincoln Street, Boston, Massachusetts 02111 (617) 423-3990; *The World in Figures.*

FRENCH POLYNESIA - MOTION PICTURES

Statistical Office of the United Nations, Publishing Service, New York, New York 10017 (800) 253-9646; *Statistical Yearbook.*

FRENCH POLYNESIA - MOTOR VEHICLES IN USE

G.K. Hall and Company, 70 Lincoln Street, Boston, Massachusetts 02111 (617) 423-3990; *The World in Figures.*

Statistical Office of the United Nations, Publishing Service, New York, New York 10017 (800) 253-9646; *Statistical Yearbook.*

FRENCH POLYNESIA - MUSEUMS

United Nations Educational, Scientific and Cultural Organization (UNESCO), 7 Place de Fontenoy, F-75700 Paris, France (Telephone Number in U.S. (212) 963-5981); *Statistical Yearbook.*

FRENCH POLYNESIA - NATALITY - See FRENCH POLYNESIA - BIRTH RATE

FRENCH POLYNESIA - NATIONAL ACCOUNTS

Statistical Office of the United Nations, Publishing Service, New York, New York 10017 (800) 253-9646; *Yearbook of National Account Statistics.*

FRENCH POLYNESIA - NATIONAL INCOME

G.K. Hall and Company, 70 Lincoln Street, Boston, Massachusetts 02111 (617) 423-3990; *The World in Figures.*

Statistical Office of the United Nations, Publishing Service, New York, New York 10017 (800) 253-9646; *Statistical Yearbook.*

FRENCH POLYNESIA - NEWSPAPER PRODUCTION - See FRENCH POLYNESIA - FORESTRY AND FOREST PRODUCTS

FRENCH POLYNESIA - NEWSPRINT CONSUMPTION - See FRENCH POLYNESIA - FORESTRY AND FOREST PRODUCTS

FRENCH POLYNESIA - OCCUPATIONS - See FRENCH POLYNESIA - LABOR FORCE

FRENCH POLYNESIA - PERIODICALS

United Nations Educational, Scientific and Cultural Organization (UNESCO), 7 Place de Fontenoy, F-75700 Paris, France (Telephone Number in U.S. (212) 963-5981); *Statistical Yearbook.*

FRENCH POLYNESIA - PESTICIDE USE

Food and Agricultural Organization of the United Nations (FAO) Via delle Terme di Caracalla, 00100 Rome, Italy (Telephone Number in U.S. (202) 653-2400); *The State of Food and Agriculture.*

FRENCH POLYNESIA - PETROLEUM INDUSTRY

Food and Agricultural Organization of the United Nations (FAO) Via delle Terme di Caracalla, 00100 Rome, Italy (Telephone Number in U.S. (202) 653-2400); *The State of Food and Agriculture.*

G.K. Hall and Company, 70 Lincoln Street, Boston, Massachusetts 02111 (617) 423-3990; *The World in Figures.*

FRENCH POLYNESIA - PIGS - See FRENCH POLYNESIA - LIVESTOCK AND POULTRY

FRENCH POLYNESIA - POPULATION

Food and Agricultural Organization of the United Nations (FAO), Via delle Terme di Caracalla, 00100 Rome, Italy (Telephone Number in U.S. (202) 653-2400); *Production Yearbook.*

G.K. Hall and Company, 70 Lincoln Street, Boston, Massachusetts 02111 (617) 423-3990; *The World in Figures.*

Statistical Office of the United Nations, Publishing Service, New York, New York 10017 (800) 253-9646; *Demographic Yearbook,* and *Statistical Yearbook.*

World Health Organization, Office of Publications, Avenue Appia, CH-1211 Geneva 27, Switzerland (Telephone Number in U.S. (518) 436-9686); *World Health Statistics Annual.*

FRENCH POLYNESIA - PRICES

Food and Agricultural Organization of the United Nations (FAO), Via delle Terme di Caracalla, 00100 Rome, Italy (Telephone Number in U.S. (202) 653-2400); *Production Yearbook,* and *The State of Food and Agriculture.*

G.K. Hall and Company, 70 Lincoln Street, Boston, Massachusetts 02111 (617) 423-3990; *The World in Figures.*

South Pacific Commission, Post Box D5, Noumea Cedex, New Caledonia; *Statistical Bulletin of the South Pacific: Overseas Trade,* and *Statistical Bulletin of the South Pacific: Retail Price Indexes.*

FRENCH POLYNESIA - PRODUCTION

G.K. Hall and Company, 70 Lincoln Street, Boston, Massachusetts 02111 (617) 423-3990; *The World in Figures.*

FRENCH POLYNESIA - RAILWAYS

G.K. Hall and Company, 70 Lincoln Street, Boston, Massachusetts 02111 (617) 423-3990; *The World in Figures.*

FRENCH POLYNESIA - RETAIL TRADE

G.K. Hall and Company, 70 Lincoln Street, Boston, Massachusetts 02111 (617) 423-3990; *The World in Figures.*

FRENCH POLYNESIA - ROOT AND TUBER PRODUCTION - See FRENCH POLYNESIA - CROPS

FRENCH POLYNESIA - ROUNDWOOD PRODUCTION - See FRENCH POLYNESIA - FORESTRY AND FOREST PRODUCTS

FRENCH POLYNESIA - SAWNWOOD PRODUCTION - See FRENCH POLYNESIA - FORESTRY AND FOREST PRODUCTS

FRENCH POLYNESIA - SCIENTISTS AND TECHNICIANS

Statistical Office of the United Nations, Publishing Service, New York, New York 10017 (800) 253-9646; *Statistical Yearbook.*

FRENCH POLYNESIA - SHEEP - See FRENCH POLYNESIA - LIVESTOCK AND POULTRY

FRENCH POLYNESIA - SOCIAL DATA

G.K. Hall and Company, 70 Lincoln Street, Boston, Massachusetts 02111 (617) 423-3990; *The World in Figures.*

FRENCH POLYNESIA - STOCKS - COMMODITY - MARKET PRICE - INDEX

Food and Agricultural Organization of the United Nations (FAO) Via delle Terme di Caracalla, 00100 Rome, Italy (Telephone Number in U.S. (202) 653-2400); *The State of Food and Agriculture.*

FRENCH POLYNESIA - TAXATION

G.K. Hall and Company, 70 Lincoln Street, Boston, Massachusetts 02111 (617) 423-3990; *The World in Figures.*

FRENCH POLYNESIA - TELEGRAPH SERVICE

Statistical Office of the United Nations, Publishing Service, New York, New York 10017 (800) 253-9646; *Statistical Yearbook.*

FRENCH POLYNESIA - TELEPHONES IN USE

American Telephone and Telegraph Company, 26 Parsippany Road, Whippany, New Jersey 07981 (800) 338-4038; *The World's Telephones.*

G.K. Hall and Company, 70 Lincoln Street, Boston, Massachusetts 02111 (617) 423-3990; *The World in Figures.*

Statistical Office of the United Nations, Publishing Service, New York, New York 10017 (800) 253-9646; *Statistical Yearbook.*

FRENCH POLYNESIA - TEXTILE INDUSTRY

G.K. Hall and Company, 70 Lincoln Street, Boston, Massachusetts 02111 (617) 423-3990; *The World in Figures.*

FRENCH POLYNESIA - THEATRE

United Nations Educational, Scientific and Cultural Organization (UNESCO), 7 Place de Fontenoy, F-75700 Paris, France (Telephone Number in U.S. (212) 963-5981); *Statistical Yearbook.*

FRENCH POLYNESIA - TOBACCO PRODUCTION

South Pacific Commission, Post Box D5, Noumea Cedex, New Caledonia; *Statistical Bulletin of the South Pacific: Retail Price Indexes.*

FRENCH POLYNESIA - TOURISM

G.K. Hall and Company, 70 Lincoln Street, Boston, Massachusetts 02111 (617) 423-3990; *The World in Figures.*

Statistical Office of the United Nations, Publishing Service, New York, New York 10017 (800) 253-9646; *Statistical Yearbook.*

World Tourism Organization, Calle Capitan Haya 42, E-28020 Madrid, Spain; *Yearbook of Tourism Statistics.*

FRENCH POLYNESIA - TRACTORS IN USE

Statistical Office of the United Nations, Publishing Service, New York, New York 10017 (800) 253-9646; *Statistical Yearbook.*

FRENCH POLYNESIA - TRADE - See FRENCH POLYNESIA - FOREIGN TRADE

FRENCH POLYNESIA - TRANSPORTATION AND COMMUNICATIONS

G.K. Hall and Company, 70 Lincoln Street, Boston, Massachusetts 02111 (617) 423-3990; *The World in Figures.*

South Pacific Commission, Post Box D5, Noumea Cedex, New Caledonia; *Statistical Bulletin of the South Pacific: Overseas Trade.*

FRENCH POLYNESIA - VITAL STATISTICS

G.K. Hall and Company, 70 Lincoln Street, Boston, Massachusetts 02111 (617) 423-3990; *The World in Figures.*

Statistical Office of the United Nations, Publishing Service, New York, New York 10017 (800) 253-9646; *Statistical Yearbook.*

World Health Organization, Office of Publications, Avenue Appia, CH-1211 Geneva 27, Switzerland (Telephone Number in U.S. (518) 436-9686); *World Health Statistics Annual.*

FRENCH POLYNESIA - WAGES

G.K. Hall and Company, 70 Lincoln Street, Boston, Massachusetts 02111 (617) 423-3990; *The World in Figures.*

FRENCH POLYNESIA - WEATHER

G.K. Hall and Company, 70 Lincoln Street, Boston, Massachusetts 02111 (617) 423-3990; *The World in Figures.*

FROZEN FOODS

U.S. Department of Agriculture, Economic Research Service, Fourteenth Street and Independence Avenue, SW, Washington, D.C. 20005-4789 (202) 219-1504; *Food Consumption, Prices, and Expenditures,* and unpublished data.

U.S. Department of Commerce, National Oceanic and Atmospheric Administration, Marine Fisheries Service, 1335 East-West Highway, Silver Spring, Maryland 20910 (301) 427-2239; *Fisheries of the United States,* and *Fishery Statistics of the United States.*

FRUITS - CONSUMER EXPENDITURES

U.S. Department of Agriculture, Economic Research Service, Fourteenth Street and Independence Avenue, SW, Washington, D.C. 20005-4789 (202) 219-1504; *Agricultural Statistics, Food Cost Review,* and *Food Review.*

U.S. Department of Labor, Bureau of Labor Statistics, Two Massachusetts Avenue, NE, Washington, D.C. 20212 (202) 606-7828; *Consumer Expenditures in 1992.*

FRUITS - CONSUMPTION

U.S. Department of Agriculture, Economic Research Service, Fourteenth Street and Independence Avenue, SW, Washington, D.C. 20005-4789 (202) 219-1504; *Food Consumption, Prices, and Expenditures,* and unpublished data.

FRUITS - FARM MARKETINGS AND SALES

U.S. Department of Agriculture, Economic Research Service, Fourteenth Street and Independence Avenue, SW, Washington, D.C. 20005-4789 (202) 219-1504; *Economic Indicators of the Farm Sector: National Financial Summary.*

FRUITS - FOREIGN TRADE

U.S. Department of Agriculture, Economic Research Service, Fourteenth Street and Independence Avenue, SW, Washington, D.C. 20005-4789 (202) 219-1504; *Foreign Agricultural Trade of the U.S., Agricultural Outlook,* and *Agricultural Statistics.*

U.S. Department of Commerce, Bureau of the Census, Suitland, Maryland 20233 (301) 763-4040; *U.S. Merchandise Trade,* and *U.S. Merchandise Trade: Exports, General Imports, and Imports for Consumption.*

FRUITS - PRICES

U.S. Department of Agriculture, National Agricultural Statistics Service, Fourteenth Street and Independence Avenue, SW, Washington, D.C. 20250 (202) 219-1504; *Agricultural Prices: Annual Summary.*

U.S. Department of Labor, Bureau of Labor Statistics, Two Massachusetts Avenue, NE, Washington, D.C. 20212 (202) 606-7828; *Monthly Labor Review, CPI Detailed Report,* and *News.*

FRUITS - PRODUCTION

U.S. Department of Agriculture, National Agricultural Statistics Services, Fourteenth Street and Independence Avenue, SW, Washington, D.C. 20250 (202) 219-1504; *Citrus Fruits,* and *Noncitrus Fruits and Nuts.*

FUEL - See also Individual Types and ENERGY

FUEL - COMMERCIAL BUILDING USE

U.S. Department of Energy, Energy Information Administration, Washington, D.C. 20585 (202) 586-8800; *Commercial Buildings Energy Consumption and Expenditure,* and *Commercial Buildings Characteristics.*

FUEL - CONSUMPTION - AIRPLANES - AVIATION - CERTIFIED ROUTE CARRIERS

U.S. Department of Transportation, Federal Aviation Administration, 800 Independence Avenue, SW, Washington, D.C. 20591 (202) 366-4000; *FAA Statistical Handbook of Aviation, Air Carrier Financial Statistics, Air Carrier Traffic Statistics,* and unpublished data.

FUEL - CONSUMPTION - MOTOR VEHICLES

U.S. Department of Energy, Energy Information Administration, Washington, D.C. 20585 (202) 586-8800; *Household Vehicles Energy Consumption.*

U.S. Department of Transportation, Federal Highway Administration, Sixth and D Streets, SW, Washington, D.C. 20590 (202) 366-0660; *Highway Statistics.*

FUEL - CONSUMPTION - UTILITIES

U.S. Department of Energy, Energy Information Administration, Washington, D.C. 20585 (202) 586-8800; *Annual Energy Review, Electric Power Annual,* and unpublished data.

FUEL - ELECTRICITY GENERATED BY

U.S. Department of Energy, Energy Information Administration, Washington, D.C. 20585 (202) 586-8800; *Electric Power Annual, Electric Power Monthly, Annual Energy Review, Inventory of Power Plants in the U.S.,* and unpublished data.

FUEL - FOREIGN TRADE

U.S. Department of Commerce, Bureau of the Census, Suitland, Maryland 20233 (301) 763-4040; *U.S. Exports of Merchandise*, and *U.S. Imports of Merchandise*, compact discs.

U.S. Department of the Interior, Bureau of Mines, 810 Seventh Street, NW, Washington, D.C. 20241 (202) 501-9649; *Annual Reports*.

FUEL - PRICES

U.S. Department of Commerce, Bureau of Economic Analysis, Fourteenth Street between Constitution Avenue and E Street, NW, Washington, D.C. 20230 (202) 606-9900; *The National Income and Product Accounts of the U.S.*, and *Survey of Current Business*.

U.S. Department of Energy, Energy Information Administration, Washington, D.C. 20585 (202) 586-8800; *Petroleum Marketing Monthly, State Energy Price and Expenditure Report, Annual Energy Review*, and *Monthly Energy Review*.

U.S. Department of Labor, Bureau of Labor Statistics, Two Massachusetts Avenue, NE, Washington, D.C. 20212 (202) 606-7828; *Monthly Labor Review, CPI Detailed Report, News*, and *Handbook of Labor Statistics*.

FUEL - PRICES - RETAIL

U.S. Department of Energy, Energy Information Administration, Washington, D.C. 20585 (202) 586-8800; *Monthly Energy Review*, and *International Energy Annual*.

FUEL - PRODUCTION AND VALUE

Board of Governors of the Federal Reserve System, Twentieth Street and Constitution Avenue, NW, Washington, D.C. 20551 (202) 452-3000; *Federal Reserve Bulletin*.

U.S. Department of Energy, Energy Information Administration, Washington, D.C. 20585 (202) 586-8800; *Annual Energy Review, Monthly Energy Review, Uranium Industry Annual, Natural Gas Annual, Petroleum Supply Annual*, and *Quarterly Coal Report*.

U.S. Department of the Interior, Bureau of Mines, 810 Seventh Street, NW, Washington, D.C. 20241 (202) 501-9649; *Annual Reports and Mineral Commodity Summaries*.

FUEL - RESIDENTIAL USE

U.S. Department of Energy, Energy Information Administration, 1000 Independence Avenue, SW, Washington, D.C. 20585 (202) 586-8800; *Household Energy Consumption and Expenditures*.

FUEL - USED IN HEATING AND/OR COOKING

U.S. Department of Commerce, Bureau of the Census, Suitland, Maryland 20233 (301) 763-4040; *Census of Housing, Detailed Housing Characteristics*, and *Current Housing Reports*.

U.S. Department of Energy, Energy Information Administration, 1000 Independence Avenue, SW, Washington, D.C. 20585 (202) 586-8800; *Housing Characteristics*.

FUEL - WORLD PRODUCTION

U.S. Department of the Interior, Bureau of Mines, 810 Seventh Street, NW, Washington, D.C. 20241 (202) 501-9649; *Annual Reports and Mineral Commodity Summaries*.

FUNERAL SERVICES AND CREMATORIES

U.S. Department of Commerce, Bureau of the Census, Suitland, Maryland 20233 (301) 763-4040; *Current Business Reports, Service Annual Survey, County Business Patterns, Census of Service Industries*, and unpublished data.

FURNITURE AND FIXTURES - MANUFACTURING - EARNINGS

U.S. Department of Commerce, Bureau of the Census, Suitland, Maryland 20233 (301) 763-4040; *Census of Manufactures*, and *Annual Survey of Manufactures*.

U.S. Department of Labor, Bureau of Labor Statistics, Two Massachusetts Avenue, NE, Washington, D.C. 20212 (202) 606-7828; *Employment and Earnings*, and Bulletins 2370 and 2429.

FURNITURE AND FIXTURES - MANUFACTURING - EMPLOYEES

U.S. Department of Commerce, Bureau of the Census, Suitland, Maryland 20233 (301) 763-4040; *Annual Survey of Manufactures*, and *Census of Manufactures*.

U.S. Department of Labor, Bureau of Labor Statistics, Two Massachusetts Avenue, NE, Washington, D.C. 20212 (202) 606-7828; *Employment and Earnings, Monthly Labor Review*, and Bulletins 2370 and 2429.

FURNITURE AND FIXTURES - MANUFACTURING - ESTABLISHMENTS

U.S. Department of Commerce, Bureau of the Census, Suitland, Maryland 20233 (301) 763-4040; *Census of Manufactures*, and *Annual Survey of Manufactures*.

FURNITURE AND FIXTURES - MANUFACTURING - GROSS DOMESTIC PRODUCT

U.S. Department of Commerce, Bureau of Economic Analysis, Fourteenth Street between Constitution Avenue and E Street, NW, Washington, D.C. 20230 (202) 606-9900; *The National Income and Product Accounts of the U.S.*, and *Survey of Current Business*.

FURNITURE AND FIXTURES - MANUFACTURING - MERGERS AND ACQUISITIONS

Securities Data Company, 1180 Raymond Boulevard, Newark, New Jersey 07102 (201) 622-3100; *Merger and Corporate Transactions Database*.

FURNITURE AND FIXTURES - MANUFACTURING - OCCUPATIONAL SAFETY

U.S. Department of Labor, Bureau of Labor Statistics, Two Massachusetts Avenue, NE, Washington, D.C. 20212 (202) 606-7828; *Occupational Injuries and Illnesses in the United States, by Industry*.

FURNITURE AND FIXTURES - MANUFACTURING - PRODUCTIVITY

Board of Governors of the Federal Reserve System, Twentieth Street and Constitution Avenue, NW, Washington, D.C. 20551 (202) 452-3000; *Federal Reserve Bulletin*.

U.S. Department of Labor, Bureau of Labor Statistics, Two Massachusetts Avenue, NE, Washington, D.C. 20212 (202) 606-7828; *Productivity Measures for Selected Industries and Government Services*, and unpublished data.

FURNITURE AND FIXTURES - MANUFACTURING - SHIPMENTS

U.S. Department of Commerce, Bureau of the Census, Suitland, Maryland 20233 (301) 763-4040; *Annual Survey of Manufactures,* and *Census of Manufactures.*

FURNITURE AND FIXTURES - MANUFACTURING - VALUE ADDED

U.S. Department of Commerce, Bureau of the Census, Suitland, Maryland 20233 (301) 763-4040; *Annual Survey of Manufactures,* and *Census of Manufactures.*

FURNITURE AND HOME FURNISHING STORES - EARNINGS

U.S. Department of Commerce, Bureau of the Census, Suitland, Maryland 20233 (301) 763-4040; *County Business Patterns,* and *Census of Retail Trade.*

U.S. Department of Labor, Bureau of Labor Statistics, Two Massachusetts Avenue, NE, Washington, D.C. 20212 (202) 606-7828; *Employment and Earnings,* and Bulletins 2370 and 2429.

FURNITURE AND HOME FURNISHING STORES - EMPLOYEES

U.S. Department of Labor, Bureau of Labor Statistics, Two Massachusetts Avenue, NE, Washington, D.C. 20212 (202) 606-7828; *Employment and Earnings,* and Bulletins 2370 and 2429.

U.S. Department of Commerce, Bureau of the Census, Suitland, Maryland 20233 (301) 763-4040; *County Business Patterns,* and *Census of Retail Trade.*

FURNITURE AND HOME FURNISHING STORES - ESTABLISHMENTS

U.S. Department of Commerce, Bureau of the Census, Suitland, Maryland 20233 (301) 763-4040; *Census of Retail Trade,* and *County Business Patterns.*

FURNITURE AND HOME FURNISHING STORES - INVENTORIES

U.S. Department of Commerce, Bureau of the Census, Suitland, Maryland 20233 (301) 763-4040; *Current Business Reports, Combined Annual and Revised Monthly Retail Trade.*

FURNITURE AND HOME FURNISHING STORES - PRODUCTIVITY

U.S. Department of Labor, Bureau of Labor Statistics, Two Massachusetts Avenue, NE, Washington, D.C. 20212 (202) 606-7828; *Productivity Measures for Selected Industries and Government Services,* and unpublished data.

FURNITURE AND HOME FURNISHING STORES - STORES - SALES

U.S. Department of Commerce, Bureau of the Census, Suitland, Maryland 20233 (301) 763-4040; *Census of Retail Trade, County Business Patterns, Current Business Reports, Combined Annual and Revised Monthly Retail Trade,* and unpublished data.

FUTURES PRICE INDEXES - SELECTED COMMODITIES

Commodity Research Bureau, 75 Wall Street, New York, New York 10005 (212) 504-7754; *CRB Commodity Index Report.*

G

Gabon - National Statistical Office

Directeur General de la Statistique et des Etudes Economiques, BP 2119, Libreville, Gabon.

Gabon - Primary Statistics Sources

Directeur General de la Statistique, BP 2119, Libreville, Gabon; *Annuaire Statistique* (Statistical Yearbook), and *Bulletin Mensuel de Statistique* (Monthly Bulletin of Statistics), and *Situation economique, financiere et sociale de la Republique Gabonaise* (Economic, Financial and Social Situation of the Republic of Gabon).

GABON - AGRICULTURE

Euromonitor Publications Limited, 87-88 Turnmill Street, London EC1M 5QU, England; *Third World Economic Handbook.*

Facts on File, 460 Park Avenue South, New York, New York 10016 (800) 443-8323; *The New Book of World Rankings.*

Federal Statistical Office, Gustav - Stresemann - Ring 11, D-6200 Wiesbaden, Germany; *Gabon.*

Food and Agricultural Organization of the United Nations (FAO) Via delle Terme di Caracalla, 00100 Rome, Italy (Telephone Number in U.S. (202) 653-2400); *Production Yearbook, The State of Food and Agriculture,* and *Trade Yearbook.*

G.K. Hall and Company, 70 Lincoln Street, Boston, Massachusetts 02111 (617) 423-3990; *The World in Figures.*

Statistical Office of the United Nations, Publishing Service, New York, New York 10017 (800) 253-9646; *Statistical Yearbook,* and *Survey of Economic and Social Conditions in Africa.*

Times Books, 201 East 50th Street, New York, New York 10022 (212) 751-2600; *The Economist Book of Vital World Statistics.*

United Nations Economic Commission for Africa, Africa Hall, Post Office Box 3001, Addis Ababa, Ethiopia (Telephone Number in U.S. (800) 253-9646); *African Statistical Yearbook.*

The World Bank, 1818 H Street, NW, Washington, D.C. 20433 (202) 477-1234; *World Tables.*

GABON - AIRLINE SERVICE

Facts on File, 460 Park Avenue South, New York, New York 10016 (800) 443-8323; *The New Book of World Rankings.*

G.K. Hall and Company, 70 Lincoln Street, Boston, Massachusetts 02111 (617) 423-3990; *The World in Figures.*

International Civil Aviation Organization, 1000 Sherbrooke Street West, Suite 400, Montreal, Quebec, Canada H3A 2R2 (514) 285-8219; *Civil Aviation Statistics of the World.*

Statistical Office of the United Nations, Publishing Service, New York, New York 10017 (800) 253-9646; *Statistical Yearbook.*

Times Books, 201 East 50th Street, New York, New York 10022 (212) 751-2600; *The Economist Book of Vital World Statistics*

United Nations Economic Commission for Africa, Africa Hall, Post Office Box 3001, Addis Ababa, Ethiopia (Telephone Number in U.S. (800) 253-9646); *African Statistical Yearbook.*

GABON - ALUMINUM PRODUCTION AND CONSUMPTION - See GABON - MINING AND MINERAL PRODUCTS

GABON - ANIMAL HEALTH

Food and Agricultural Organization of the United Nations (FAO), Via delle Terme di Caracalla, 00100 Rome, Italy (Telephone Number in U.S. (202) 653-2400); *Animal Health Yearbook.*

GABON - AREA AND DENSITY OF POPULATION

African Development Bank, 01 BP 1387, Abidjan 01, Cote D'Ivoire; *Selected Statistics on Regional Member Countries.*

Facts on File, 460 Park Avenue South, New York, New York 10016 (800) 443-8323; *The New Book of World Rankings.*

Federal Statistical Office, Gustav - Stresemann - Ring 11, D-6200 Wiesbaden, Germany; *Gabon.*

Food and Agricultural Organization of the United Nations (FAO) Via delle Terme di Caracalla, 00100 Rome, Italy (Telephone Number in U.S. (202) 653-2400); *The State of Food and Agriculture.*

G.K. Hall and Company, 70 Lincoln Street, Boston, Massachusetts 02111 (617) 423-3990; *The World in Figures.*

Statistical Office of the United Nations, Publishing Service, New York, New York 10017 (800) 253-9646; *Statistical Yearbook* and *Survey of Economic and Social Conditions in Africa.*

Times Books, 201 East 50th Street, New York, New York 10022 (212) 751-2600; *The Economist Book of Vital World Statistics.*

United Nations Educational, Scientific and Cultural Organization (UNESCO), 7 Place de Fontenoy, F-75700 Paris, France (Telephone Number in U.S. (212) 963-5981); *Statistical Yearbook.*

GABON - ARMS EXPORTS AND IMPORTS

U.S. Arms Control and Disarmament Agency, 320 Twenty-first Street, Northwest, Washington, D.C. 20451 (202) 647-8677; *World Military Expenditures and Arms Transfers.*

GABON - BALANCE OF PAYMENTS

African Development Bank, 01 BP 1387, Abidjan 01, Cote D'Ivoire; *Selected Statistics on Regional Member Countries.*

The Economist Intelligence Unit, 111 West 57th Street, New York, New York 10019 (800) 938-4685; *The World Market Atlas.*

Euromonitor Publications Limited, 87-88 Turnmill Street, London EC1M 5QU, England; *Third World Economic Handbook.*

Federal Statistical Office, Gustav - Stresemann - Ring 11, D-6200 Wiesbaden, Germany; *Gabon.*

G.K. Hall and Company, 70 Lincoln Street, Boston, Massachusetts 02111 (617) 423-3990; *The World in Figures.*

International Monetary Fund, 700 Nineteenth Street, NW, Washington, D.C. 20431 (202) 623-7000; *Balance of Payments Yearbook.*

Times Books, 201 East 50th Street, New York, New York 10022 (212) 751-2600; *The Economist Book of Vital World Statistics.*

United Nations Economic Commission for Africa, Africa Hall, Post Office Box 3001, Addis Ababa, Ethiopia (Telephone Number in U.S. (800) 253-9646); *African Statistical Yearbook.*

The World Bank, 1818 H Street, NW, Washington, D.C. 20433 (202) 477-1234; *World Tables.*

GABON - BANKING

Facts on File, 460 Park Avenue South, New York, New York 10016 (800) 443-8323; *The New Book of World Rankings.*

G.K. Hall and Company, 70 Lincoln Street, Boston, Massachusetts 02111 (617) 423-3990; *The World in Figures.*

International Monetary Fund, 700 Nineteenth Street, NW, Washington, D.C. 20431 (202) 623-7000; *International Financial Statistics.*

United Nations Economic Commission for Africa, Africa Hall, Post Office Box 3001, Addis Ababa, Ethiopia (Telephone Number in U.S. (800) 253-9646); *African Statistical Yearbook.*

GABON - BARLEY PRODUCTION - See GABON - CROPS

GABON - BEER PRODUCTION

Facts on File, 460 Park Avenue South, New York, New York 10016 (800) 443-8323; *The New Book of World Rankings.*

Statistical Office of the United Nations, Publishing Service, New York, New York 10017 (800) 253-9646; *Statistical Yearbook.*

GABON - BIRTH RATES

Euromonitor Publications Limited, 87-88 Turnmill Street, London EC1M 5QU, England; *Third World Economic Handbook.*

Facts on File, 460 Park Avenue South, New York, New York 10016 (800) 443-8323; *The New Book of World Rankings.*

Statistical Office of the United Nations, Publishing Service, New York, New York 10017 (800) 253-9646; *Demographic Yearbook, Statistical Yearbook,* and *Survey of Economic and Social Conditions in Africa.*

Times Books, 201 East 50th Street, New York, New York 10022 (212) 751-2600; *The Economist Book of Vital World Statistics.*

The World Bank, 1818 H Street, NW, Washington, D.C. 20433 (202) 477-1234; *World Tables.*

GABON - BONDS

G.K. Hall and Company, 70 Lincoln Street, Boston, Massachusetts 02111 (617) 423-3990; *The World in Figures.*

International Monetary Fund, 700 Nineteenth Street, NW, Washington, D.C. 20431 (202) 623-7000; *Government Finance Statistics Yearbook.*

GABON - BOOK PRODUCTION

G.K. Hall and Company, 70 Lincoln Street, Boston, Massachusetts 02111 (617) 423-3990; *The World in Figures.*

GABON - BROADCASTING

Billboard Limited, Post Office Box 9027, 1006 AA Amsterdam, The Netherlands (Telephone Number in U.S. (212) 764-7300); *World Radio TV Handbook.*

Facts on File, 460 Park Avenue South, New York, New York 10016 (800) 443-8323; *The New Book of World Rankings.*

G.K. Hall and Company, 70 Lincoln Street, Boston, Massachusetts 02111 (617) 423-3990; *The World in Figures.*

Times Books, 201 East 50th Street, New York, New York 10022 (212) 751-2600; *The Economist Book of Vital World Statistics.*

GABON - BUILDING CONSTRUCTION - See GABON - CONSTRUCTION INDUSTRY

GABON - BUSINESS

G.K. Hall and Company, 70 Lincoln Street, Boston, Massachusetts 02111 (617) 423-3990; *The World in Figures.*

GABON - CALORIE SUPPLY

African Development Bank, 01 BP 1387, Abidjan 01, Cote D'Ivoire; *Selected Statistics on Regional Member Countries.*

Food and Agricultural Organization of the United Nations (FAO) Via delle Terme di Caracalla, 00100 Rome, Italy (Telephone Number in U.S. (202) 653-2400); *The State of Food and Agriculture.*

GABON - CAPITAL REVENUE

International Monetary Fund, 700 Nineteenth Street, NW, Washington, D.C. 20431 (202) 623-7000; *Government Finance Statistics Yearbook.*

GABON - CATTLE - See GABON - LIVESTOCK AND POULTRY

GABON - CEMENT PRODUCTION - See GABON - MINING AND MINERAL PRODUCTS

GABON - CHEMICAL (ORGANIC) PRODUCTION - See GABON - MINING AND MINERAL PRODUCTS

GABON - CHICKENS - See GABON - LIVESTOCK AND POULTRY

GABON - CIGARETTE PRODUCTION - See GABON - TOBACCO PRODUCTION

GABON - CLASS STRUCTURE

G.K. Hall and Company, 70 Lincoln Street, Boston, Massachusetts 02111 (617) 423-3990; *The World in Figures*.

GABON - CLIMATE

Facts on File, 460 Park Avenue South, New York, New York 10016 (800) 443-8323; *The New Book of World Rankings*.

G.K. Hall and Company, 70 Lincoln Street, Boston, Massachusetts 02111 (617) 423-3990; *The World in Figures*.

GABON - CLOTHING EXPORTS AND IMPORTS

Euromonitor Publications Limited, 87-88 Turnmill Street, London EC1M 5QU, England; *Third World Economic Handbook*.

GABON - COAL PRODUCTION - See GABON - MINING AND MINERAL PRODUCTS

GABON - COCOA (BEANS) PRODUCTION - See GABON - CROPS

GABON - COFFEE PRODUCTION - See GABON - CROPS

GABON - COMMUNICATIONS

Euromonitor Publications Limited, 87-88 Turnmill Street, London EC1M 5QU, England; *Third World Economic Handbook*.

Federal Statistical Office, Gustav - Stresemann - Ring 11, D-6200 Wiesbaden, Germany; *Gabon*.

G.K. Hall and Company, 70 Lincoln Street, Boston, Massachusetts 02111 (617) 423-3990; *The World in Figures*.

United Nations Economic Commission for Africa, Africa Hall, Post Office Box 3001, Addis Ababa, Ethiopia (Telephone Number in U.S. (800) 253-9646); *African Statistical Yearbook*.

GABON - CONSTRUCTION INDUSTRY

Facts on File, 460 Park Avenue South, New York, New York 10016 (800) 443-8323; *The New Book of World Rankings*.

Statistical Office of the United Nations, Publishing Service, New York, New York 10017 (800) 253-9646; *Statistical Yearbook*.

United Nations Economic Commission for Africa, Africa Hall, Post Office Box 3001, Addis Ababa, Ethiopia (Telephone Number in U.S. (800) 253-9646); *African Statistical Yearbook*.

GABON - CONSUMER PRICE INDEX

African Development Bank, 01 BP 1387, Abidjan 01, Cote D'Ivoire; *Selected Statistics on Regional Member Countries*.

Federal Statistical Office, Gustav - Stresemann - Ring 11, D-6200 Wiesbaden, Germany; *Gabon*.

G.K. Hall and Company, 70 Lincoln Street, Boston, Massachusetts 02111 (617) 423-3990; *The World in Figures*.

Statistical Office of the United Nations, Publishing Service, New York, New York 10017 (800) 253-9646; *Statistical Yearbook*, and *Survey of Economic and Social Conditions in Africa*.

United Nations Economic Commission for Africa, Africa Hall, Post Office Box 3001, Addis Ababa, Ethiopia (Telephone Number in U.S. (800) 253-9646); *African Statistical Yearbook*.

GABON - CONSUMER PRICES

Federal Statistical Office, Gustav - Stresemann - Ring 11, D-6200 Wiesbaden, Germany; *Gabon*.

International Labour Office, I.L.O. Publications, CH-1211, Geneva 22, Switzerland; *Yearbook of Labour Statistics*.

International Monetary Fund, 700 Nineteenth Street, NW, Washington, D.C. 20431 (202) 623-7000; *International Financial Statistics*.

Times Books, 201 East 50th Street, New York, New York 10022 (212) 751-2600; *The Economist Book of Vital World Statistics*.

GABON - CONSUMPTION

African Development Bank, 01 BP 1387, Abidjan 01, Cote D'Ivoire; *Selected Statistics on Regional Member Countries*.

G.K. Hall and Company, 70 Lincoln Street, Boston, Massachusetts 02111 (617) 423-3990; *The World in Figures*.

Statistical Office of the United Nations, Publishing Service, New York, New York 10017 (800) 253-9646; *Survey of Economic and Social Conditions in Africa*.

GABON - COPPER PRODUCTION - See GABON - MINING AND MINERAL PRODUCTS

GABON - CORN PRODUCTION - See GABON - CROPS

GABON - CORPORATE TAXES - See GABON - TAXATION

GABON - COTTON PRODUCTION - See GABON - CROPS

GABON - CROPS

Facts on File, 460 Park Avenue South, New York, New York 10016 (800) 443-8323; *The New Book of World Rankings*.

Food and Agricultural Organization of the United Nations (FAO), Via delle Terme di Caracalla, 00100 Rome, Italy (Telephone Number in U.S. (202) 653-2400); *Production Yearbook* and *The State of Food and Agriculture*.

G.K. Hall and Company, 70 Lincoln Street, Boston, Massachusetts 02111 (617) 423-3990; *The World in Figures*.

Statistical Office of the United Nations, Publishing Service, New York, New York 10017 (800) 253-9646; *Statistical Yearbook*.

United Nations Economic Commission for Africa, Africa Hall, Post Office Box 3001, Addis Ababa, Ethiopia (Telephone Number in U.S. (800) 253-9646); *African Statistical Yearbook*.

GABON - CUSTOMS DUTIES

G.K. Hall and Company, 70 Lincoln Street, Boston, Massachusetts 02111 (617) 423-3990; *The World in Figures.*

International Monetary Fund, 700 Nineteenth Street, NW, Washington, D.C. 20431 (202) 623-7000; *Government Finance Statistics Yearbook.*

GABON - DAIRY PRODUCTS

Facts on File, 460 Park Avenue South, New York, New York 10016 (800) 443-8323; *The New Book of World Rankings.*

Food and Agricultural Organization of the United Nations (FAO) Via delle Terme di Caracalla, 00100 Rome, Italy (Telephone Number in U.S. (202) 653-2400); *The State of Food and Agriculture.*

GABON - DEATH RATES

Euromonitor Publications Limited, 87-88 Turnmill Street, London EC1M 5QU, England; *Third World Economic Handbook.*

G.K. Hall and Company, 70 Lincoln Street, Boston, Massachusetts 02111 (617) 423-3990; *The World in Figures.*

Statistical Office of the United Nations, Publishing Service, New York, New York 10017 (800) 253-9646; *Statistical Yearbook,* and *Survey of Economic and Social Conditions in Africa.*

Times Books, 201 East 50th Street, New York, New York 10022 (212) 751-2600; *The Economist Book of Vital World Statistics.*

World Health Organization, Office of Publications, Avenue Appia, CH-1211 Geneva 27, Switzerland (Telephone Number in U.S. (518) 436-9686); *World Health Statistics Annual.*

GABON - DEFENSE EXPENDITURES

G.K. Hall and Company, 70 Lincoln Street, Boston, Massachusetts 02111 (617) 423-3990; *The World in Figures.*

U.S. Arms Control and Disarmament Agency, 320 Twenty-first Street, Northwest, Washington, D.C. 20451 (202) 647-8677; *World Military Expenditures and Arms Transfers.*

GABON - DEMOGRAPHY

The Economist Intelligence Unit, 111 West 57th Street, New York, New York 10019 (800) 938-4685; *The World Market Atlas.*

Facts on File, 460 Park Avenue South, New York, New York 10016 (800) 443-8323; *The New Book of World Rankings.*

Federal Statistical Office, Gustav - Stresemann - Ring 11, D-6200 Wiesbaden, Germany; *Gabon.*

G.K. Hall and Company, 70 Lincoln Street, Boston, Massachusetts 02111 (617) 423-3990; *The World in Figures.*

Statistical Office of the United Nations, Publishing Service, New York, New York 10017 (800) 253-9646; *Survey of Economic and Social Conditions in Africa.*

GABON - DEVELOPMENT ASSISTANCE

G.K. Hall and Company, 70 Lincoln Street, Boston, Massachusetts 02111 (617) 423-3990; *The World in Figures.*

Statistical Office of the United Nations, Publishing Service, New York, New York 10017 (800) 253-9646; *Statistical Yearbook.*

GABON - DIAMOND PRODUCTION - See GABON - MINING AND MINERAL PRODUCTS

GABON - DISEASE

G.K. Hall and Company, 70 Lincoln Street, Boston, Massachusetts 02111 (617) 423-3990; *The World in Figures.*

World Health Organization, Office of Publications, Avenue Appia, CH-1211 Geneva 27, Switzerland (Telephone Number in U.S. (518) 436-9686); *World Health Statistics Annual.*

GABON - DIVORCE RATES

Facts on File, 460 Park Avenue South, New York, New York 10016 (800) 443-8323; *The New Book of World Rankings.*

Statistical Office of the United Nations, Publishing Service, New York, New York 10017 (800) 253-9646; *Demographic Yearbook.*

GABON - DOMESTIC PRODUCT

G.K. Hall and Company, 70 Lincoln Street, Boston, Massachusetts 02111 (617) 423-3990; *The World in Figures.*

GABON - ECONOMY

African Development Bank, 01 BP 1387, Abidjan 01, Cote D'Ivoire; *Selected Statistics on Regional Member Countries.*

Euromonitor Publications Limited, 87-88 Turnmill Street, London EC1M 5QU, England; *Third World Economic Handbook.*

Facts on File, 460 Park Avenue South, New York, New York 10016 (800) 443-8323; *The New Book of World Rankings.*

Federal Statistical Office, Gustav - Stresemann - Ring 11, D-6200 Wiesbaden, Germany; *Gabon.*

G.K. Hall and Company, 70 Lincoln Street, Boston, Massachusetts 02111 (617) 423-3990; *The World in Figures.*

Statistical Office of the United Nations, Publishing Service, New York, New York 10017; *Foreign Trade Statistics for Africa.*

GABON - EDUCATION

African Development Bank, 01 BP 1387, Abidjan 01, Cote D'Ivoire; *Selected Statistics on Regional Member Countries.*

The Economist Intelligence Unit, 111 West 57th Street, New York, New York 10019 (800) 938-4685; *The World Market Atlas.*

Facts on File, 460 Park Avenue South, New York, New York 10016 (800) 443-8323; *The New Book of World Rankings.*

Federal Statistical Office, Gustav - Stresemann - Ring 11, D-6200 Wiesbaden, Germany; *Gabon.*

G.K. Hall and Company, 70 Lincoln Street, Boston, Massachusetts 02111 (617) 423-3990; *The World in Figures.*

Statistical Office of the United Nations, Publishing Service, New York, New York 10017 (800) 253-9646; *Survey of Economic and Social Conditions in Africa.*

Times Books, 201 East 50th Street, New York, New York 10022 (212) 751-2600; *The Economist Book of Vital World Statistics.*

United Nations Economic Commission for Africa, Africa Hall, Post Office Box 3001, Addis Ababa, Ethiopia (Telephone Number in U.S. (800) 253-9646); *African Statistical Yearbook.*

United Nations Educational, Scientific and Cultural Organization (UNESCO), 7 Place de Fontenoy, F-75700 Paris, France (Telephone Number in U.S. (212) 963-5981); *Statistical Yearbook.*

The World Bank, 1818 H Street, NW, Washington, D.C. 20433 (202) 477-1234; *World Tables.*

GABON - EGG PRODUCTION - See GABON - DAIRY PRODUCTS

GABON - ELECTRICITY

Facts on File, 460 Park Avenue South, New York, New York 10016 (800) 443-8323; *The New Book of World Rankings.*

Penn Well Publishing Company, 1421 South Sheridan Road, Post Office Box 1260, Tulsa, Oklahoma 74101 (800) 752-9764; *International Energy Statistics Sourcebook.*

Statistical Office of the United Nations, Publishing Service, New York, New York 10017 (800) 253-9646; *Statistical Yearbook,* and *Survey of Economic and Social Conditions in Africa.*

Times Books, 201 East 50th Street, New York, New York 10022 (212) 751-2600; *The Economist Book of Vital World Statistics.*

United Nations Economic Commission for Africa, Africa Hall, Post Office Box 3001, Addis Ababa, Ethiopia (Telephone Number in U.S. (800) 253-9646); *African Statistical Yearbook.*

GABON - EMPLOYMENT

Facts on File, 460 Park Avenue South, New York, New York 10016 (800) 443-8323; *The New Book of World Rankings.*

Federal Statistical Office, Gustav - Stresemann - Ring 11, D-6200 Wiesbaden, Germany; *Gabon.*

International Labour Office, I.L.O. Publications, CH-1211, Geneva 22, Switzerland; *Yearbook of Labour Statistics.*

Statistical Office of the United Nations, Publishing Service, New York, New York 10017 (800) 253-9646; *Statistical Yearbook,* and *Survey of Economic and Social Conditions in Africa.*

United Nations Economic Commission for Africa, Africa Hall, Post Office Box 3001, Addis Ababa, Ethiopia (Telephone Number in U.S. (800) 253-9646); *African Statistical Yearbook.*

GABON - ENERGY

Facts on File, 460 Park Avenue South, New York, New York 10016 (800) 443-8323; *The New Book of World Rankings.*

Food and Agricultural Organization of the United Nations (FAO) Via delle Terme di Caracalla, 00100 Rome, Italy (Telephone Number in U.S. (202) 653-2400); *The State of Food and Agriculture.*

G.K. Hall and Company, 70 Lincoln Street, Boston, Massachusetts 02111 (617) 423-3990; *The World in Figures.*

Penn Well Publishing Company, 1421 South Sheridan Road, Post Office Box 1260, Tulsa, Oklahoma 74101 (800) 752-9764; *International Energy Statistics Sourcebook.*

Statistical Office of the United Nations, Publishing Service, New York, New York 10017 (800) 253-9646; *Energy Statistics Yearbook, Statistical Yearbook,* and *World Energy Supplies.*

Times Books, 201 East 50th Street, New York, New York 10022 (212) 751-2600; *The Economist Book of Vital World Statistics.*

United Nations Economic Commission for Africa, Africa Hall, Post Office Box 3001, Addis Ababa, Ethiopia (Telephone Number in U.S. (800) 253-9646); *African Statistical Yearbook.*

GABON - EXCHANGE RATES

African Development Bank, 01 BP 1387, Abidjan 01, Cote D'Ivoire; *Selected Statistics on Regional Member Countries.*

International Civil Aviation Organization, 1000 Sherbrooke Street West, Suite 400, Montreal, Quebec, Canada H3A 2R2 (514) 285-8219; *Civil Aviation Statistics of the World.*

International Monetary Fund, 700 Nineteenth Street, NW, Washington, D.C. 20431 (202) 623-7000; *International Financial Statistics.*

Organization of Petroleum Exporting Countries, Obere Donaustrasse 93, 1020 Vienna 2, Austria; *OPEC Annual Statistical Bulletin.*

Statistical Office of the United Nations, Publishing Service, New York, New York 10017; *Foreign Trade Statistics for Africa,* and *Statistical Yearbook.*

GABON - EXCISE TAXES - See GABON - TAXATION

GABON - EXPORTS

African Development Bank, 01 BP 1387, Abidjan 01, Cote D'Ivoire; *Selected Statistics on Regional Member Countries.*

The Economist Intelligence Unit, 111 West 57th Street, New York, New York 10019 (800) 938-4685; *The World Market Atlas.*

Euromonitor Publications Limited, 87-88 Turnmill Street, London EC1M 5QU, England; *Third World Economic Handbook.*

Food and Agricultural Organization of the United Nations (FAO) Via delle Terme di Caracalla, 00100 Rome, Italy (Telephone Number in U.S. (202) 653-2400); *The State of Food and Agriculture.*

G.K. Hall and Company, 70 Lincoln Street, Boston, Massachusetts 02111 (617) 423-3990; *The World in Figures.*

International Monetary Fund, 700 Nineteenth Street, NW, Washington, D.C. 20431 (202) 623-7000; *Direction of Trade Statistics,* and *International Financial Statistics.*

Organization of Petroleum Exporting Countries, Obere Donaustrasse 93, 1020 Vienna 2, Austria; *OPEC Annual Statistical Bulletin.*

Statistical Office of the United Nations, Publishing Service, New York, New York 10017 (800) 253-9646; *Foreign Trade Statistics for Africa, Trade in Manufactures of Developing Countries,* and *Survey of Economic and Social Conditions in Africa.*

Times Books, 201 East 50th Street, New York, New York 10022 (212) 751-2600; *The Economist Book of Vital World Statistics.*

United Nations Economic Commission for Africa, Africa Hall, Post Office Box 3001, Addis Ababa, Ethiopia (Telephone Number in U.S. (800) 253-9646); *African Statistical Yearbook.*

The World Bank, 1818 H Street, NW, Washington, D.C. 20433 (202) 477-1234; *World Tables.*

GABON - EXTERNAL INDEBTEDNESS

African Development Bank, 01 BP 1387, Abidjan 01, Cote D'Ivoire; *Selected Statistics on Regional Member Countries.*

Euromonitor Publications Limited, 87-88 Turnmill Street, London EC1M 5QU, England; *Third World Economic Handbook.*

Statistical Office of the United Nations, Publishing Service, New York, New York 10017 (800) 253-9646; *Survey of Economic and Social Conditions in Africa.*

The World Bank, 1818 H Street, NW, Washington, D.C. 20433 (202) 477-1234; *World Tables.*

GABON - EXTERNAL TRADE

African Development Bank, 01 BP 1387, Abidjan 01, Cote D'Ivoire; *Selected Statistics on Regional Member Countries.*

Food and Agricultural Organization of the United Nations (FAO) Via delle Terme di Caracalla, 00100 Rome, Italy (Telephone Number in U.S. (202) 653-2400); *The State of Food and Agriculture,* and *Trade Yearbook.*

G.K. Hall and Company, 70 Lincoln Street, Boston, Massachusetts 02111 (617) 423-3990; *The World in Figures.*

Statistical Office of the United Nations, Publishing Service, New York, New York 10017 (800) 253-9646; *Statistical Yearbook.*

GABON - FARM CROPS - See GABON - CROPS

GABON - FERTILITY RATES

Facts on File, 460 Park Avenue South, New York, New York 10016 (800) 443-8323; *The New Book of World Rankings.*

Statistical Office of the United Nations, Publishing Service, New York, New York 10017 (800) 253-9646; *Survey of Economic and Social Conditions in Africa.*

Times Books, 201 East 50th Street, New York, New York 10022 (212) 751-2600; *The Economist Book of Vital World Statistics.*

The World Bank, 1818 H Street, NW, Washington, D.C. 20433 (202) 477-1234; *World Tables.*

GABON - FERTILIZER

Food and Agricultural Organization of the United Nations (FAO), Via delle Terme di Caracalla, 00100 Rome, Italy (Telephone Number in U.S. (202) 653-2400); *Fertilizer Yearbook,* and *The State of Food and Agriculture.*

GABON - FETAL MORTALITY

Statistical Office of the United Nations, Publishing Service, New York, New York 10017 (800) 253-9646; *Demographic Yearbook.*

GABON - FINANCE

African Development Bank, 01 BP 1387, Abidjan 01, Cote D'Ivoire; *Selected Statistics on Regional Member Countries.*

Facts on File, 460 Park Avenue South, New York, New York 10016 (800) 443-8323; *The New Book of World Rankings.*

Federal Statistical Office, Gustav - Stresemann - Ring 11, D-6200 Wiesbaden, Germany; *Gabon.*

G.K. Hall and Company, 70 Lincoln Street, Boston, Massachusetts 02111 (617) 423-3990; *The World in Figures.*

United Nations Economic Commission for Africa, Africa Hall, Post Office Box 3001, Addis Ababa, Ethiopia (Telephone Number in U.S. (800) 253-9646); *African Statistical Yearbook.*

GABON - FISHERIES

Facts on File, 460 Park Avenue South, New York, New York 10016 (800) 443-8323; *The New Book of World Rankings.*

Federal Statistical Office, Gustav - Stresemann - Ring 11, D-6200 Wiesbaden, Germany; *Gabon.*

Food and Agricultural Organization of the United Nations (FAO) Via delle Terme di Caracalla, 00100 Rome, Italy (Telephone Number in U.S. (202) 653-2400); *The State of Food and Agriculture,* and *Yearbook of Fishery Statistics.*

Statistical Office of the United Nations, Publishing Service, New York, New York 10017 (800) 253-9646; *Statistical Yearbook,* and *Survey of Economic and Social Conditions in Africa.*

United Nations Economic Commission for Africa, Africa Hall, Post Office Box 3001, Addis Ababa, Ethiopia (Telephone Number in U.S. (800) 253-9646); *African Statistical Yearbook.*

GABON - FLOUR PRODUCTION

Statistical Office of the United Nations, Publishing Service, New York, New York 10017 (800) 253-9646; *Statistical Yearbook.*

GABON - FOOD

African Development Bank, 01 BP 1387, Abidjan 01, Cote D'Ivoire; *Selected Statistics on Regional Member Countries.*

Food and Agricultural Organization of the United Nations (FAO) Via delle Terme di Caracalla, 00100 Rome, Italy (Telephone Number in U.S. (202) 653-2400); *Production Yearbook* and *The State of Food and Agriculture.*

G.K. Hall and Company, 70 Lincoln Street, Boston, Massachusetts 02111 (617) 423-3990; *The World in Figures.*

GABON - FOREIGN AID

G.K. Hall and Company, 70 Lincoln Street, Boston, Massachusetts 02111 (617) 423-3990; *The World in Figures.*

GABON - FOREIGN TRADE

Euromonitor Publications Limited, 87-88 Turnmill Street, London EC1M 5QU, England; *Third World Economic Handbook.*

Facts on File, 460 Park Avenue South, New York, New York 10016 (800) 443-8323; *The New Book of World Rankings.*

Federal Statistical Office, Gustav - Stresemann - Ring 11, D-6200 Wiesbaden, Germany; *Gabon.*

Food and Agricultural Organization of the United Nations (FAO) Via delle Terme di Caracalla, 00100 Rome, Italy (Telephone Number in U.S. (202) 653-2400); *The State of Food and Agriculture.*

G.K. Hall and Company, 70 Lincoln Street, Boston, Massachusetts 02111 (617) 423-3990; *The World in Figures.*

Organisation for Economic Co-operation and Development (OECD), 2 rue Andre-Pascal, 75 Paris 16, France (Telephone Number in U.S. (202) 785-6323); *Trade by Commodities.*

Statistical Office of the United Nations, Publishing Service, New York, New York 10017 (800) 253-9646; *Foreign Trade Statistics for Africa, International Trade Statistics Yearbook,* and *Statistical Yearbook.*

United Nations Economic Commission for Africa, Africa Hall, Post Office Box 3001, Addis Ababa, Ethiopia (Telephone Number in U.S. (800) 253-9646); *African Statistical Yearbook.*

The World Bank, 1818 H Street, NW, Washington, D.C. 20433 (202) 477-1234; *World Tables.*

GABON - FORESTRY AND FOREST PRODUCTS

Euromonitor Publications Limited, 87-88 Turnmill Street, London EC1M 5QU, England; *Third World Economic Handbook.*

Facts on File, 460 Park Avenue South, New York, New York 10016 (800) 443-8323; *The New Book of World Rankings.*

Federal Statistical Office, Gustav - Stresemann - Ring 11, D-6200 Wiesbaden, Germany; *Gabon.*

Food and Agricultural Organization of the United Nations (FAO) Via delle Terme di Caracalla, 00100 Rome, Italy (Telephone Number in U.S. (202) 653-2400); *The State of Food and Agriculture,* and *Yearbook of Forest Products.*

G.K. Hall and Company, 70 Lincoln Street, Boston, Massachusetts 02111 (617) 423-3990; *The World in Figures.*

International Monetary Fund, 700 Nineteenth Street, NW, Washington, D.C. 20431 (202) 623-7000; *International Financial Statistics.*

Statistical Office of the United Nations, Publishing Service, New York, New York 10017 (800) 253-9646; *Statistical Yearbook.*

United Nations Economic Commission for Africa, Africa Hall, Post Office Box 3001, Addis Ababa, Ethiopia (Telephone Number in U.S. (800) 253-9646); *African Statistical Yearbook.*

United Nations Educational, Scientific and Cultural Organization (UNESCO), 7 Place de Fontenoy, F-75700 Paris, France (Telephone Number in U.S. (212) 963-5981); *Statistical Yearbook.*

GABON - FURNITURE AND WOOD PRODUCTS - EXPORTS AND IMPORTS

Statistical Office of the United Nations, Publishing Service, New York, New York 10017 (800) 253-9646; *Trade in Manufactures of Developing Countries.*

GABON - GAS PRODUCTION - See GABON - MINING AND MINERAL PRODUCTS

GABON - GENERAL MORTALITY

Statistical Office of the United Nations, Publishing Service, New York, New York 10017 (800) 253-9646; *Demographic Yearbook.*

GABON - GEOGRAPHIC DATA

Facts on File, 460 Park Avenue South, New York, New York 10016 (800) 443-8323; *The New Book of World Rankings.*

Federal Statistical Office, Gustav - Stresemann - Ring 11, D-6200 Wiesbaden, Germany; *Gabon.*

GABON - GOATS - See GABON - LIVESTOCK AND POULTRY

GABON - GOLD HOLDINGS

Facts on File, 460 Park Avenue South, New York, New York 10016 (800) 443-8323; *The New Book of World Rankings.*

International Monetary Fund, 700 Nineteenth Street, NW, Washington, D.C. 20431 (202) 623-7000; *International Financial Statistics.*

Statistical Office of the United Nations, Publishing Service, New York, New York 10017 (800) 253-9646; *Statistical Yearbook.*

The World Bank, 1818 H Street, NW, Washington, D.C. 20433 (202) 477-1234; *World Tables.*

GABON - GOLD PRODUCTION AND CONSUMPTION - See GABON - MINING AND MINERAL PRODUCTS

GABON - GOVERNMENT

G.K. Hall and Company, 70 Lincoln Street, Boston, Massachusetts 02111 (617) 423-3990; *The World in Figures.*

GABON - GOVERNMENT EXPENDITURE

Euromonitor Publications Limited, 87-88 Turnmill Street, London EC1M 5QU, England; *Third World Economic Handbook.*

The World Bank, 1818 H Street, NW, Washington, D.C. 20433 (202) 477-1234; *World Tables.*

GABON - GOVERNMENT FINANCE

International Monetary Fund, 700 Nineteenth Street, NW, Washington, D.C. 20431 (202) 623-7000; *International Financial Statistics.*

GABON - GOVERNMENT REVENUE

International Monetary Fund, 700 Nineteenth Street, NW, Washington, D.C. 20431 (202) 623-7000; *Government Finance Statistics Yearbook.*

Statistical Office of the United Nations, Publishing Service, New York, New York 10017 (800) 253-9646; *Survey of Economic and Social Conditions in Africa.*

Times Books, 201 East 50th Street, New York, New York 10022 (212) 751-2600; *The Economist Book of Vital World Statistics.*

The World Bank, 1818 H Street, NW, Washington, D.C. 20433 (202) 477-1234; *World Tables.*

GABON - GRAIN PRODUCTION - See GABON - CROPS

GABON - GRANTS

International Monetary Fund, 700 Nineteenth Street, NW, Washington, D.C. 20431 (202) 623-7000; *Government Finance Statistics Yearbook.*

GABON - GROSS DOMESTIC PRODUCT

African Development Bank, 01 BP 1387, Abidjan 01, Cote D'Ivoire; *Selected Statistics on Regional Member Countries.*

The Economist Intelligence Unit, 111 West 57th Street, New York, New York 10019 (800) 938-4685; *The World Market Atlas.*

Euromonitor Publications Limited, 87-88 Turnmill Street, London EC1M 5QU, England; *Third World Economic Handbook.*

Facts on File, 460 Park Avenue South, New York, New York 10016 (800) 443-8323; *The New Book of World Rankings.*

G.K. Hall and Company, 70 Lincoln Street, Boston, Massachusetts 02111 (617) 423-3990; *The World in Figures.*

Statistical Office of the United Nations, Publishing Service, New York, New York 10017 (800) 253-9646; *Statistical Yearbook,* and *Survey of Economic and Social Conditions in Africa.*

Times Books, 201 East 50th Street, New York, New York 10022 (212) 751-2600; *The Economist Book of Vital World Statistics.*

United Nations Economic Commission for Africa, Africa Hall, Post Office Box 3001, Addis Ababa, Ethiopia (Telephone Number in U.S. (800) 253-9646); *African Statistical Yearbook.*

The World Bank, 1818 H Street, NW, Washington, D.C. 20433 (202) 477-1234; *World Tables.*

GABON - GROSS INDUSTRIAL PRODUCT

Euromonitor Publications Limited, 87-88 Turnmill Street, London EC1M 5QU, England; *Third World Economic Handbook.*

GABON - GROSS NATIONAL PRODUCT

Euromonitor Publications Limited, 87-88 Turnmill Street, London EC1M 5QU, England; *Third World Economic Handbook.*

Organization of Petroleum Exporting Countries, Obere Donaustrasse 93, 1020 Vienna 2, Austria; *OPEC Annual Statistical Bulletin.*

U.S. Arms Control and Disarmament Agency, 320 Twenty-first Street, Northwest, Washington, D.C. 20451 (202) 647-8677; *World Military Expenditures and Arms Transfers.*

The World Bank, 1818 H Street, NW, Washington, D.C. 20433 (202) 477-1234; *World Tables.*

GABON - GROUNDNUTS PRODUCTION - See GABON - CROPS

GABON - HEALTH

African Development Bank, 01 BP 1387, Abidjan 01, Cote D'Ivoire; *Selected Statistics on Regional Member Countries.*

Facts on File, 460 Park Avenue South, New York, New York 10016 (800) 443-8323; *The New Book of World Rankings.*

Federal Statistical Office, Gustav - Stresemann - Ring 11, D-6200 Wiesbaden, Germany; *Gabon.*

G.K. Hall and Company, 70 Lincoln Street, Boston, Massachusetts 02111 (617) 423-3990; *The World in Figures.*

Statistical Office of the United Nations, Publishing Service, New York, New York 10017 (800) 253-9646; *Statistical Yearbook.*

Times Books, 201 East 50th Street, New York, New York 10022 (212) 751-2600; *The Economist Book of Vital World Statistics.*

United Nations Economic Commission for Africa, Africa Hall, Post Office Box 3001, Addis Ababa, Ethiopia (Telephone Number in U.S. (800) 253-9646); *African Statistical Yearbook.*

World Health Organization, Office of Publications, Avenue Appia, CH-1211 Geneva 27, Switzerland (Telephone Number in U.S. (518) 436-9686); *World Health Statistics Annual.*

GABON - HIDE PRODUCTION

Food and Agricultural Organization of the United Nations (FAO), Via delle Terme di Caracalla, 00100 Rome, Italy (Telephone Number in U.S. (202) 653-2400); *Production Yearbook.*

GABON - HIGHWAYS

G.K. Hall and Company, 70 Lincoln Street, Boston, Massachusetts 02111 (617) 423-3990; *The World in Figures.*

International Road Federation, 525 School Street, SW, Washington, D.C. 20024 (202) 554-2106; *World Road Statistics.*

Statistical Office of the United Nations, Publishing Service, New York, New York 10017 (800) 253-9646; *Survey of Economic and Social Conditions in Africa.*

United Nations Economic Commission for Africa, Africa Hall, Post Office Box 3001, Addis Ababa, Ethiopia (Telephone Number in U.S. (800) 253-9646); *African Statistical Yearbook.*

GABON - HORSES - See GABON - LIVESTOCK AND POULTRY

GABON - HOURS OF WORK - See GABON - EMPLOYMENT

GABON - HOUSING AND HOUSING UNITS

Euromonitor Publications Limited, 87-88 Turnmill Street, London EC1M 5QU, England; *Third World Economic Handbook.*

The World Bank, 1818 H Street, NW, Washington, D.C. 20433 (202) 477-1234; *World Tables.*

GABON - ILLITERATE POPULATION

The Economist Intelligence Unit, 111 West 57th Street, New York, New York 10019 (800) 938-4685; *The World Market Atlas.*

G.K. Hall and Company, 70 Lincoln Street, Boston, Massachusetts 02111 (617) 423-3990; *The World in Figures.*

United Nations Educational, Scientific and Cultural Organization (UNESCO), 7 Place de Fontenoy, F-75700 Paris, France; *Statistical Yearbook.*

GABON - IMPORTS

African Development Bank, 01 BP 1387, Abidjan 01, Cote D'Ivoire; *Selected Statistics on Regional Member Countries.*

The Economist Intelligence Unit, 111 West 57th Street, New York, New York 10019 (800) 938-4685; *The World Market Atlas.*

Euromonitor Publications Limited, 87-88 Turnmill Street, London EC1M 5QU, England; *Third World Economic Handbook.*

Food and Agricultural Organization of the United Nations (FAO) Via delle Terme di Caracalla, 00100 Rome, Italy (Telephone Number in U.S. (202) 653-2400); *The State of Food and Agriculture.*

G.K. Hall and Company, 70 Lincoln Street, Boston, Massachusetts 02111 (617) 423-3990; *The World in Figures.*

International Monetary Fund, 700 Nineteenth Street, NW, Washington, D.C. 20431 (202) 623-7000; *Direction of Trade Statistics, Government Finance Statistics Yearbook,* and *International Financial Statistics.*

Statistical Office of the United Nations, Publishing Service, New York, New York 10017 (800) 253-9646; *Foreign Trade Statistics for Africa, Survey of Economic and Social Conditions in Africa,* and *Trade in Manufactures of Developing Countries.*

Times Books, 201 East 50th Street, New York, New York 10022 (212) 751-2600; *The Economist Book of Vital World Statistics.*

United Nations Economic Commission for Africa, Africa Hall, Post Office Box 3001, Addis Ababa, Ethiopia (Telephone Number in U.S. (800) 253-9646); *African Statistical Yearbook.*

The World Bank, 1818 H Street, NW, Washington, D.C. 20433 (202) 477-1234; *World Tables.*

GABON - INCOME TAXES - See GABON - TAXATION

GABON - INDUSTRY

Euromonitor Publications Limited, 87-88 Turnmill Street, London EC1M 5QU, England; *Third World Economic Handbook.*

Facts on File, 460 Park Avenue South, New York, New York 10016 (800) 443-8323; *The New Book of World Rankings.*

Federal Statistical Office, Gustav - Stresemann - Ring 11, D-6200 Wiesbaden, Germany; *Gabon.*

G.K. Hall and Company, 70 Lincoln Street, Boston, Massachusetts 02111 (617) 423-3990; *The World in Figures.*

International Labour Office, I.L.O. Publications, CH-1211, Geneva 22, Switzerland; *Yearbook of Labour Statistics.*

Statistical Office of the United Nations, Publishing Service, New York, New York 10017 (800) 253-9646; *Survey of Economic and Social Conditions in Africa.*

Times Books, 201 East 50th Street, New York, New York 10022 (212) 751-2600; *The Economist Book of Vital World Statistics.*

United Nations Economic Commission for Africa, Africa Hall, Post Office Box 3001, Addis Ababa, Ethiopia (Telephone Number in U.S. (800) 253-9646); *African Statistical Yearbook.*

The World Bank, 1818 H Street, NW, Washington, D.C. 20433 (202) 477-1234; *World Tables.*

GABON - INFANT AND MATERNAL MORTALITY

Statistical Office of the United Nations, Publishing Service, New York, New York 10017 (800) 253-9646; *Demographic Yearbook, Statistical Yearbook,* and *Survey of Economic and Social Conditions in Africa.*

Times Books, 201 East 50th Street, New York, New York 10022 (212) 751-2600; *The Economist Book of Vital World Statistics.*

The World Bank, 1818 H Street, NW, Washington, D.C. 20433 (202) 477-1234; *World Tables.*

GABON - INTERNATIONAL LIQUIDITY

International Monetary Fund, 700 Nineteenth Street, NW, Washington, D.C. 20431 (202) 623-7000; *International Financial Statistics.*

GABON - INTERNATIONAL RESERVES EXCLUDING GOLD

African Development Bank, 01 BP 1387, Abidjan 01, Cote D'Ivoire; *Selected Statistics on Regional Member Countries.*

Statistical Office of the United Nations, Publishing Service, New York, New York 10017 (800) 253-9646; *Statistical Yearbook.*

The World Bank, 1818 H Street, NW, Washington, D.C. 20433 (202) 477-1234; *World Tables.*

GABON - IRON ORE PRODUCTION AND CONSUMPTION - See GABON - MINING AND MINERAL PRODUCTS

GABON - LABOR FORCE

African Development Bank, 01 BP 1387, Abidjan 01, Cote D'Ivoire; *Selected Statistics on Regional Member Countries.*

Facts on File, 460 Park Avenue South, New York, New York 10016 (800) 443-8323; *The New Book of World Rankings.*

Food and Agricultural Organization of the United Nations (FAO) Via delle Terme di Caracalla, 00100 Rome, Italy (Telephone Number in U.S. (202) 653-2400); *The State of Food and Agriculture.*

G.K. Hall and Company, 70 Lincoln Street, Boston, Massachusetts 02111 (617) 423-3990; *The World in Figures.*

The World Bank, 1818 H Street, NW, Washington, D.C. 20433 (202) 477-1234; *World Tables.*

GABON - LABOR PRODUCTIVITY

International Labour Office, I.L.O. Publications, CH-1211, Geneva 22, Switzerland; *Yearbook of Labour Statistics.*

GABON - LAND USE

Food and Agricultural Organization of the United Nations (FAO), Via delle Terme di Caracalla, 00100 Rome, Italy (Telephone Number in U.S. (202) 653-2400); *Production Yearbook.*

G.K. Hall and Company, 70 Lincoln Street, Boston, Massachusetts 02111 (617) 423-3990; *The World in Figures.*

GABON - LIBRARIES

Facts on File, 460 Park Avenue South, New York, New York 10016 (800) 443-8323; *The New Book of World Rankings.*

GABON - LIFE EXPECTANCY

African Development Bank, 01 BP 1387, Abidjan 01, Cote D'Ivoire; *Selected Statistics on Regional Member Countries.*

GABON - LITERACY RATE

Statistical Office of the United Nations, Publishing Service, New York, New York 10017 (800) 253-9646; *Survey of Economic and Social Conditions in Africa.*

GABON - LIVESTOCK AND POULTRY

Facts on File, 460 Park Avenue South, New York, New York 10016 (800) 443-8323; *The New Book of World Rankings.*

Food and Agricultural Organization of the United Nations (FAO), Via delle Terme di Caracalla, 00100 Rome, Italy (Telephone Number in U.S. (202) 653-2400); *Production Yearbook,* and *The State of Food and Agriculture.*

G.K. Hall and Company, 70 Lincoln Street, Boston, Massachusetts 02111 (617) 423-3990; *The World in Figures.*

Statistical Office of the United Nations, Publishing Service, New York, New York 10017 (800) 253-9646; *Statistical Yearbook,* and *Survey of Economic and Social Conditions in Africa.*

United Nations Economic Commission for Africa, Africa Hall, Post Office Box 3001, Addis Ababa, Ethiopia (Telephone Number in U.S. (800) 253-9646); *African Statistical Yearbook.*

GABON - LIVING LEVELS

G.K. Hall and Company, 70 Lincoln Street, Boston, Massachusetts 02111 (617) 423-3990; *The World in Figures.*

Times Books, 201 East 50th Street, New York, New York 10022 (212) 751-2600; *The Economist Book of Vital World Statistics.*

GABON - MAIL - NUMBER OF PIECES SENT OR RECEIVED

Statistical Office of the United Nations, Publishing Service, New York, New York 10017 (800) 253-9646; *Statistical Yearbook.*

GABON - MANGANESE AND MANGANESE ORE PRODUCTION AND CONSUMPTION - See GABON - MINING AND MINERAL PRODUCTS

GABON - MANUFACTURING

Euromonitor Publications Limited, 87-88 Turnmill Street, London EC1M 5QU, England; *Third World Economic Handbook.*

Facts on File, 460 Park Avenue South, New York, New York 10016 (800) 443-8323; *The New Book of World Rankings.*

G.K. Hall and Company, 70 Lincoln Street, Boston, Massachusetts 02111 (617) 423-3990; *The World in Figures.*

Statistical Office of the United Nations, Publishing Service, New York, New York 10017 (800) 253-9646; *Survey of Economic and Social Conditions in Africa.*

United Nations Economic Commission for Africa, Africa Hall, Post Office Box 3001, Addis Ababa, Ethiopia (Telephone Number in U.S. (800) 253-9646); *African Statistical Yearbook.*

The World Bank, 1818 H Street, NW, Washington, D.C. 20433 (202) 477-1234; *World Tables.*

GABON - MARRIAGE RATES

Facts on File, 460 Park Avenue South, New York, New York 10016 (800) 443-8323; *The New Book of World Rankings.*

Statistical Office of the United Nations, Publishing Service, New York, New York 10017 (800) 253-9646; *Demographic Yearbook.*

GABON - MEAT PRODUCTION - See GABON - LIVESTOCK AND POULTRY

GABON - MERCHANT SHIPPING

G.K. Hall and Company, 70 Lincoln Street, Boston, Massachusetts 02111 (617) 423-3990; *The World in Figures.*

Lloyd's Register of Shipping, 17 Battery Place, New York, New York 10004 (212) 425-8050; *Register of Ships.*

Organization of Petroleum Exporting Countries, Obere Donaustrasse 93, 1020 Vienna 2, Austria; *OPEC Annual Statistical Bulletin.*

Statistical Office of the United Nations, Publishing Service, New York, New York 10017 (800) 253-9646; *Statistical Yearbook.*

Times Books, 201 East 50th Street, New York, New York 10022 (212) 751-2600; *The Economist Book of Vital World Statistics.*

United Nations Economic Commission for Africa, Africa Hall, Post Office Box 3001, Addis Ababa, Ethiopia (Telephone Number in U.S. (800) 253-9646); *African Statistical Yearbook.*

U.S. Department of Transportation, Maritime Administration, 400 Seventh Street, SW, Washington, D.C. 20590 (202) 366-5807; *A Statistical Analysis of the World's Merchant Fleets.*

GABON - MILK PRODUCTION - See GABON - DAIRY PRODUCTS

GABON - MILITARY

G.K. Hall and Company, 70 Lincoln Street, Boston, Massachusetts 02111 (617) 423-3990; *The World in Figures.*

The International Institute for Strategic Studies, 23 Tavistock Street, London WC2E 7NQ, England; *The Military Balance.*

U.S. Arms Control and Disarmament Agency, 320 Twenty-first Street, Northwest, Washington, D.C. 20451 (202) 647-8677; *World Military Expenditures and Arms Transfers.*

GABON - MINING AND MINERAL PRODUCTS

Commodity Research Bureau, Incorporated, 75 Wall Street, New York, New York 10005 (212) 504-7754; *Commodity Year Book.*

Euromonitor Publications Limited, 87-88 Turnmill Street, London EC1M 5QU, England; *Third World Economic Handbook.*

Facts on File, 460 Park Avenue South, New York, New York 10016 (800) 443-8323; *The New Book of World Rankings.*

G.K. Hall and Company, 70 Lincoln Street, Boston, Massachusetts 02111 (617) 423-3990; *The World in Figures.*

International Monetary Fund, 700 Nineteenth Street, NW, Washington, D.C. 20431 (202) 623-7000; *International Financial Statistics.*

Organization of Petroleum Exporting Countries, Obere Donaustrasse 93, 1020 Vienna 2, Austria; *OPEC Annual Statistical Bulletin.*

Penn Well Publishing Company, 1421 South Sheridan Road, Post Office Box 1260, Tulsa, Oklahoma 74101 (800) 752-9764; *International Energy Statistics Sourcebook.*

Statistical Office of the United Nations, Publishing Service, New York, New York 10017 (800) 253-9646; *Statistical Yearbook.*

United Nations Economic Commission for Africa, Africa Hall, Post Office Box 3001, Addis Ababa, Ethiopia (Telephone Number in U.S. (800) 253-9646); *African Statistical Yearbook.*

GABON - MONEY EXCHANGE RATE

International Monetary Fund, 700 Nineteenth Street, NW, Washington, D.C. 20431 (202) 623-7000; *International Financial Statistics.*

Statistical Office of the United Nations, Publishing Service, New York, New York 10017 (800) 253-9646; *Statistical Yearbook.*

GABON - MONEY SUPPLY

African Development Bank, 01 BP 1387, Abidjan 01, Cote D'Ivoire; *Selected Statistics on Regional Member Countries.*

Federal Statistical Office, Gustav - Stresemann - Ring 11, D-6200 Wiesbaden, Germany; *Gabon.*

G.K. Hall and Company, 70 Lincoln Street, Boston, Massachusetts 02111 (617) 423-3990; *The World in Figures.*

International Monetary Fund, 700 Nineteenth Street, NW, Washington, D.C. 20431 (202) 623-7000; *International Financial Statistics.*

Statistical Office of the United Nations, Publishing Service, New York, New York 10017 (800) 253-9646; *Statistical Yearbook.*

The World Bank, 1818 H Street, NW, Washington, D.C. 20433 (202) 477-1234; *World Tables.*

GABON - MOTOR VEHICLE TAXES - See GABON - TAXATION

GABON - MOTOR VEHICLES IN USE

G.K. Hall and Company, 70 Lincoln Street, Boston, Massachusetts 02111 (617) 423-3990; *The World in Figures.*

International Road Federation, 525 School Street, SW, Washington, D.C. 20024 (202) 554-2106; *World Road Statistics.*

Statistical Office of the United Nations, Publishing Service, New York, New York 10017 (800) 253-9646; *Statistical Yearbook,* and *Survey of Economic and Social Conditions in Africa.*

Times Books, 201 East 50th Street, New York, New York 10022 (212) 751-2600; *The Economist Book of Vital World Statistics.*

GABON - MUSEUMS

Facts on File, 460 Park Avenue South, New York, New York 10016 (800) 443-8323; *The New Book of World Rankings.*

United Nations Educational, Scientific and Cultural Organization (UNESCO), 7 Place de Fontenoy, F-75700 Paris, France (Telephone Number in U.S. (212) 963-5981); *Statistical Yearbook.*

GABON - NATALITY - See GABON - BIRTH RATES

GABON - NATIONAL ACCOUNTS

African Development Bank, 01 BP 1387, Abidjan 01, Cote D'Ivoire; *Selected Statistics on Regional Member Countries.*

Federal Statistical Office, Gustav - Stresemann - Ring 11, D-6200 Wiesbaden, Germany; *Gabon.*

International Monetary Fund, 700 Nineteenth Street, NW, Washington, D.C. 20431 (202) 623-7000; *International Financial Statistics.*

Statistical Office of the United Nations, Publishing Service, New York, New York 10017 (800) 253-9646; *National Accounts Statistics,* and *Statistical Yearbook.*

United Nations Economic Commission for Africa, Africa Hall, Post Office Box 3001, Addis Ababa, Ethiopia (Telephone Number in U.S. (800) 253-9646); *African Statistical Yearbook.*

GABON - NATIONAL INCOME

Facts on File, 460 Park Avenue South, New York, New York 10016 (800) 443-8323; *The New Book of World Rankings.*

G.K. Hall and Company, 70 Lincoln Street, Boston, Massachusetts 02111 (617) 423-3990; *The World in Figures.*

Statistical Office of the United Nations, Publishing Service, New York, New York 10017 (800) 253-9646; *Statistical Yearbook.*

GABON - NATIONAL PRODUCT

Facts on File, 460 Park Avenue South, New York, New York 10016 (800) 443-8323; *The New Book of World Rankings.*

GABON - NATURAL GAS PRODUCTION - See GABON - MINING AND MINERAL PRODUCTS

GABON - NEWSPAPER PRODUCTION - See GABON - FORESTRY AND FOREST PRODUCTS

GABON - OCCUPATIONS - See GABON - LABOR FORCE

GABON - PALM KERNELS AND PALM OIL PRODUCTION - See GABON - CROPS

GABON - PAPER - See GABON - FORESTRY AND FOREST PRODUCTS

GABON - PEANUT PRODUCTION - See GABON - CROPS

GABON - PESTICIDE USE

Food and Agricultural Organization of the United Nations (FAO) Via delle Terme di Caracalla, 00100 Rome, Italy (Telephone Number in U.S. (202) 653-2400); *The State of Food and Agriculture.*

GABON - PETROLEUM INDUSTRY

Facts on File, 460 Park Avenue South, New York, New York 10016 (800) 443-8323; *The New Book of World Rankings*.

Food and Agricultural Organization of the United Nations (FAO) Via delle Terme di Caracalla, 00100 Rome, Italy (Telephone Number in U.S. (202) 653-2400); *The State of Food and Agriculture*.

G.K. Hall and Company, 70 Lincoln Street, Boston, Massachusetts 02111 (617) 423-3990; *The World in Figures*.

Organization of Petroleum Exporting Countries, Obere Donaustrasse 93, 1020 Vienna 2, Austria; *OPEC Annual Statistical Bulletin*.

Penn Well Publishing Company, 1421 South Sheridan Road, Post Office Box 1260, Tulsa, Oklahoma 74101 (800) 752-9764; *International Energy Statistics Sourcebook*.

Statistical Office of the United Nations, Publishing Service, New York, New York 10017 (800) 253-9646; *Statistical Yearbook*.

GABON - PIGS - See GABON - LIVESTOCK AND POULTRY

GABON - PLASTIC AND RESIN PRODUCTION

Euromonitor Publications Limited, 87-88 Turnmill Street, London EC1M 5QU, England; *Third World Economic Handbook*.

GABON - POPULATION

African Development Bank, 01 BP 1387, Abidjan 01, Cote D'Ivoire; *Selected Statistics on Regional Member Countries*.

The Economist Intelligence Unit, 111 West 57th Street, New York, New York 10019 (800) 938-4685; *The World Market Atlas*.

Euromonitor Publications Limited, 87-88 Turnmill Street, London EC1M 5QU, England; *Third World Economic Handbook*.

Facts on File, 460 Park Avenue South, New York, New York 10016 (800) 443-8323; *The New Book of World Rankings*.

Federal Statistical Office, Gustav - Stresemann - Ring 11, D-6200 Wiesbaden, Germany; *Gabon*.

Food and Agricultural Organization of the United Nations (FAO), Via delle Terme di Caracalla, 00100 Rome, Italy (Telephone Number in U.S. (202) 653-2400); *Production Yearbook*.

G.K. Hall and Company, 70 Lincoln Street, Boston, Massachusetts 02111 (617) 423-3990; *The World in Figures*.

International Labour Office, I.L.O. Publications, CH-1211, Geneva 22, Switzerland; *Yearbook of Labour Statistics*.

Statistical Office of the United Nations, Publishing Service, New York, New York 10017 (800) 253-9646; *Demographic Yearbook*, *Statistical Yearbook*, and *Survey of Economic and Social Conditions in Africa*.

Times Books, 201 East 50th Street, New York, New York 10022 (212) 751-2600; *The Economist Book of Vital World Statistics*.

U.S. Arms Control and Disarmament Agency, 320 Twenty-first Street, Northwest, Washington, D.C. 20451 (202) 647-8677; *World Military Expenditures and Arms Transfers*.

World Health Organization, Office of Publications, Avenue Appia, CH-1211 Geneva 27, Switzerland (Telephone Number in U.S. (518) 436-9686); *World Health Statistics Annual*.

GABON - POST OFFICES

Facts on File, 460 Park Avenue South, New York, New York 10016 (800) 443-8323; *The New Book of World Rankings*.

GABON - POTATO PRODUCTION - See GABON - CROPS

GABON - PRICES

Facts on File, 460 Park Avenue South, New York, New York 10016 (800) 443-8323; *The New Book of World Rankings*.

Federal Statistical Office, Gustav - Stresemann - Ring 11, D-6200 Wiesbaden, Germany; *Gabon*.

Food and Agricultural Organization of the United Nations (FAO), Via delle Terme di Caracalla, 00100 Rome, Italy (Telephone Number in U.S. (202) 653-2400); *Production Yearbook*, and *The State of Food and Agriculture*.

G.K. Hall and Company, 70 Lincoln Street, Boston, Massachusetts 02111 (617) 423-3990; *The World in Figures*.

International Labour Office, I.L.O. Publications, CH-1211, Geneva 22, Switzerland; *Yearbook of Labour Statistics*.

International Monetary Fund, 700 Nineteenth Street, NW, Washington, D.C. 20431 (202) 623-7000; *International Financial Statistics*.

United Nations Economic Commission for Africa, Africa Hall, Post Office Box 3001, Addis Ababa, Ethiopia (Telephone Number in U.S. (800) 253-9646); *African Statistical Yearbook*.

GABON - PRINTING AND WRITING PAPER - See GABON - FORESTRY AND FOREST PRODUCTS

GABON - PRODUCTION

Euromonitor Publications Limited, 87-88 Turnmill Street, London EC1M 5QU, England; *Third World Economic Handbook*.

Facts on File, 460 Park Avenue South, New York, New York 10016 (800) 443-8323; *The New Book of World Rankings*.

G.K. Hall and Company, 70 Lincoln Street, Boston, Massachusetts 02111 (617) 423-3990; *The World in Figures*.

GABON - PROPERTY TAXES - See GABON - TAXATION

GABON - PUBLIC FINANCE

Facts on File, 460 Park Avenue South, New York, New York 10016 (800) 443-8323; *The New Book of World Rankings*.

Federal Statistical Office, Gustav - Stresemann - Ring 11, D-6200 Wiesbaden, Germany; *Gabon*.

GABON - RADIO BROADCASTING - See GABON - BROADCASTING

GABON - RAILWAYS

G.K. Hall and Company, 70 Lincoln Street, Boston, Massachusetts 02111 (617) 423-3990; *The World in Figures*.

Jane's Information Group, Sentinel House, 163 Brighton Road, Coulsdon, Surrey CR5 2NH, England (Telephone Number in U.S. (703) 683-3700); *Jane's World Railways.*

Statistical Office of the United Nations, Publishing Service, New York, New York 10017 (800) 253-9646; *Survey of Economic and Social Conditions in Africa.*

United Nations Economic Commission for Africa, Africa Hall, Post Office Box 3001, Addis Ababa, Ethiopia (Telephone Number in U.S. (800) 253-9646); *African Statistical Yearbook.*

GABON - RELIGION

Facts on File, 460 Park Avenue South, New York, New York 10016 (800) 443-8323; *The New Book of World Rankings.*

GABON - RETAIL TRADE

Euromonitor Publications Limited, 87-88 Turnmill Street, London EC1M 5QU, England; *Third World Economic Handbook.*

G.K. Hall and Company, 70 Lincoln Street, Boston, Massachusetts 02111 (617) 423-3990; *The World in Figures.*

GABON - RICE PRODUCTION - See GABON - CROPS

GABON - ROOT AND TUBER PRODUCTION - See GABON - CROPS

GABON - ROUNDWOOD PRODUCTION - See GABON - FORESTRY AND FOREST PRODUCTS

GABON - RUBBER PRODUCTION

Euromonitor Publications Limited, 87-88 Turnmill Street, London EC1M 5QU, England; *Third World Economic Handbook.*

Facts on File, 460 Park Avenue South, New York, New York 10016 (800) 443-8323; *The New Book of World Rankings.*

GABON - SAWNWOOD PRODUCTION - See GABON - FORESTRY AND FOREST PRODUCTS

GABON - SCIENCE AND TECHNOLOGY - EXPENDITURE FOR RESEARCH

Statistical Office of the United Nations, Publishing Service, New York, New York 10017 (800) 253-9646; *Statistical Yearbook.*

GABON - SCIENTISTS AND TECHNICIANS

Statistical Office of the United Nations, Publishing Service, New York, New York 10017 (800) 253-9646; *Statistical Yearbook.*

United Nations Educational, Scientific and Cultural Organization (UNESCO), 7 Place de Fontenoy, F-75700 Paris, France (Telephone Number in U.S. (212) 963-5981); *Statistical Yearbook.*

GABON - SENIOR CITIZENS

Facts on File, 460 Park Avenue South, New York, New York 10016 (800) 443-8323; *The New Book of World Rankings.*

GABON - SHEEP - See GABON - LIVESTOCK AND POULTRY

GABON - SILVER PRODUCTION AND CONSUMPTION - See GABON - MINING AND MINERAL PRODUCTS

GABON - SOCIAL DATA

African Development Bank, 01 BP 1387, Abidjan 01, Cote D'Ivoire; *Selected Statistics on Regional Member Countries.*

Facts on File, 460 Park Avenue South, New York, New York 10016 (800) 443-8323; *The New Book of World Rankings.*

G.K. Hall and Company, 70 Lincoln Street, Boston, Massachusetts 02111 (617) 423-3990; *The World in Figures.*

GABON - STAMP TAXES AND DUTIES - See GABON - TAXATION

GABON - STEEL PRODUCTION AND INDUSTRIAL CONSUMPTION - See GABON - MINING AND MINERAL PRODUCTS

GABON - STOCKS - COMMODITY - MARKET PRICE - INDEX

Food and Agricultural Organization of the United Nations (FAO) Via delle Terme di Caracalla, 00100 Rome, Italy (Telephone Number in U.S. (202) 653-2400); *The State of Food and Agriculture.*

GABON - SUGAR PRODUCTION - See GABON - CROPS

GABON - TAXATION

G.K. Hall and Company, 70 Lincoln Street, Boston, Massachusetts 02111 (617) 423-3990; *The World in Figures.*

International Monetary Fund, 700 Nineteenth Street, NW, Washington, D.C. 20431 (202) 623-7000; *Government Finance Statistics Yearbook.*

International Road Federation, 525 School Street, SW, Washington, D.C. 20024 (202) 554-2106; *World Road Statistics.*

The World Bank, 1818 H Street, NW, Washington, D.C. 20433 (202) 477-1234; *World Tables.*

GABON - TELEPHONES IN USE

American Telephone and Telegraph Company, 26 Parsippany Road, Whippany, New Jersey 07981 (800) 338-4038; *The World's Telephones.*

Euromonitor Publications Limited, 87-88 Turnmill Street, London EC1M 5QU, England; *Third World Economic Handbook.*

G.K. Hall and Company, 70 Lincoln Street, Boston, Massachusetts 02111 (617) 423-3990; *The World in Figures.*

Statistical Office of the United Nations, Publishing Service, New York, New York 10017 (800) 253-9646; *Statistical Yearbook.*

GABON - TELEVISION BROADCASTING - See GABON - BROADCASTING

GABON - TEXTILE INDUSTRY

Euromonitor Publications Limited, 87-88 Turnmill Street, London EC1M 5QU, England; *Third World Economic Handbook.*

G.K. Hall and Company, 70 Lincoln Street, Boston, Massachusetts 02111 (617) 423-3990; *The World in Figures.*

GABON - TOBACCO PRODUCTION

Euromonitor Publications Limited, 87-88 Turnmill Street, London EC1M 5QU, England; *Third World Economic Handbook.*

Facts on File, 460 Park Avenue South, New York, New York 10016 (800) 443-8323; *The New Book of World Rankings.*

Statistical Office of the United Nations, Publishing Service, New York, New York 10017 (800) 253-9646; *Statistical Yearbook.*

GABON - TOURISM

Euromonitor Publications Limited, 87-88 Turnmill Street, London EC1M 5QU, England; *Third World Economic Handbook.*

Facts on File, 460 Park Avenue South, New York, New York 10016 (800) 443-8323; *The New Book of World Rankings.*

Federal Statistical Office, Gustav - Stresemann - Ring 11, D-6200 Wiesbaden, Germany; *Gabon.*

G.K. Hall and Company, 70 Lincoln Street, Boston, Massachusetts 02111 (617) 423-3990; *The World in Figures.*

Statistical Office of the United Nations, Publishing Service, New York, New York 10017 (800) 253-9646; *Statistical Yearbook.*

Times Books, 201 East 50th Street, New York, New York 10022 (212) 751-2600; *The Economist Book of Vital World Statistics.*

United Nations Economic Commission for Africa, Africa Hall, Post Office Box 3001, Addis Ababa, Ethiopia (Telephone Number in U.S. (800) 253-9646); *African Statistical Yearbook.*

GABON - TRACTORS IN USE

Statistical Office of the United Nations, Publishing Service, New York, New York 10017 (800) 253-9646; *Statistical Yearbook.*

GABON - TRADE - See GABON - FOREIGN TRADE

GABON - TRANSPORTATION AND COMMUNICATIONS

Euromonitor Publications Limited, 87-88 Turnmill Street, London EC1M 5QU, England; *Third World Economic Handbook.*

Facts on File, 460 Park Avenue South, New York, New York 10016 (800) 443-8323; *The New Book of World Rankings.*

Federal Statistical Office, Gustav - Stresemann - Ring 11, D-6200 Wiesbaden, Germany; *Gabon.*

G.K. Hall and Company, 70 Lincoln Street, Boston, Massachusetts 02111 (617) 423-3990; *The World in Figures.*

United Nations Economic Commission for Africa, Africa Hall, Post Office Box 3001, Addis Ababa, Ethiopia (Telephone Number in U.S. (800) 253-9646); *African Statistical Yearbook.*

GABON - UNEMPLOYMENT

International Labour Office, I.L.O. Publications, CH-1211, Geneva 22, Switzerland; *Yearbook of Labour Statistics.*

GABON - URANIUM PRODUCTION AND CONSUMPTION - See GABON - MINING AND MINERAL PRODUCTS

GABON - VITAL STATISTICS

Euromonitor Publications Limited, 87-88 Turnmill Street, London EC1M 5QU, England; *Third World Economic Handbook.*

G.K. Hall and Company, 70 Lincoln Street, Boston, Massachusetts 02111 (617) 423-3990; *The World in Figures.*

Statistical Office of the United Nations, Publishing Service, New York, New York 10017 (800) 253-9646; *Statistical Yearbook.*

World Health Organization, Office of Publications, Avenue Appia, CH-1211 Geneva 27, Switzerland (Telephone Number in U.S. (518) 436-9686); *World Health Statistics Annual.*

GABON - WAGES

Federal Statistical Office, Gustav - Stresemann - Ring 11, D-6200 Wiesbaden, Germany; *Gabon.*

G.K. Hall and Company, 70 Lincoln Street, Boston, Massachusetts 02111 (617) 423-3990; *The World in Figures.*

International Labour Office, I.L.O. Publications, CH-1211, Geneva 22, Switzerland; *Yearbook of Labour Statistics.*

GABON - WEATHER

Facts on File, 460 Park Avenue South, New York, New York 10016 (800) 443-8323; *The New Book of World Rankings.*

G.K. Hall and Company, 70 Lincoln Street, Boston, Massachusetts 02111 (617) 423-3990; *The World in Figures.*

GABON - WHEAT PRODUCTION AND PRICES - See GABON - CROPS

GABON - WHOLESALE PRICES

International Monetary Fund, 700 Nineteenth Street, NW, Washington, D.C. 20431 (202) 623-7000; *International Financial Statistics.*

Statistical Office of the United Nations, Publishing Service, New York, New York 10017 (800) 253-9646; *Statistical Yearbook.*

GABON - WHOLESALE TRADE

Euromonitor Publications Limited, 87-88 Turnmill Street, London EC1M 5QU, England; *Third World Economic Handbook.*

GABON - WINE PRODUCTION

Facts on File, 460 Park Avenue South, New York, New York 10016 (800) 443-8323; *The New Book of World Rankings.*

GABON - WOOD EXPORTS - See GABON - FORESTRY AND FOREST PRODUCTS

GABON - WOOD PULP PRODUCTION - See GABON - FORESTRY AND FOREST PRODUCTS

GABON - WOOL PRODUCTION

Facts on File, 460 Park Avenue South, New York, New York 10016 (800) 443-8323; *The New Book of World Rankings.*

GADSDEN PURCHASE

U.S. Department of Commerce, Bureau of the Census, Suitland, Maryland 20233 (301) 763-4040; unpublished data.

GALLBLADDER DISORDERS - DEATHS

U.S. Department of Health and Human Services, National Center for Health Statistics, 3700 East-West Highway, Hyattsville, Maryland 20782 (301) 436-8500; *Monthly Vital Statistics Report, Vital Statistics of the United States,* and unpublished data.

GALLIUM

U.S. Department of the Interior, Bureau of Mines, 810 Seventh Street, NW, Washington, D.C. 20241 (202) 501-9649; *Mineral Commodity Summaries.*

Gambia - National Statistical Office

Central Statistics Department, 32 Buckle Street, Banjul, Gambia.

Gambia - Primary Statistics Source

Banjul: Ministry of Finance and Trade, The Quandrangle, Banjul, Gambia; *The Gambia Trade Directory.*

GAMBIA - AGRICULTURE

Facts on File, 460 Park Avenue South, New York, New York 10016 (800) 443-8323; *The New Book of World Rankings.*

Federal Statistical Office, Gustav - Stresemann - Ring 11, D-6200 Wiesbaden, Germany; *Gambia.*

Food and Agricultural Organization of the United Nations (FAO) Via delle Terme di Caracalla, 00100 Rome, Italy (Telephone Number in U.S. (202) 653-2400); *Production Yearbook,* and *The State of Food and Agriculture,* and *Trade Yearbook.*

G.K. Hall and Company, 70 Lincoln Street, Boston, Massachusetts 02111 (617) 423-3990; *The World in Figures.*

Statistical Office of the United Nations, Publishing Service, New York, New York 10017 (800) 253-9646; *Statistical Yearbook,* and *Survey of Economic and Social Conditions in Africa.*

United Nations Economic Commission for Africa, Africa Hall, Post Office Box 3001, Addis Ababa, Ethiopia (Telephone Number in U.S. (800) 253-9646); *African Statistical Yearbook.*

The World Bank, 1818 H Street, NW, Washington, D.C. 20433 (202) 477-1234; *World Tables.*

GAMBIA - AIRLINE SERVICE

Facts on File, 460 Park Avenue South, New York, New York 10016 (800) 443-8323; *The New Book of World Rankings.*

G.K. Hall and Company, 70 Lincoln Street, Boston, Massachusetts 02111 (617) 423-3990; *The World in Figures.*

United Nations Economic Commission for Africa, Africa Hall, Post Office Box 3001, Addis Ababa, Ethiopia (Telephone Number in U.S. (800) 253-9646); *African Statistical Yearbook.*

GAMBIA - ALUMINUM PRODUCTION AND CONSUMPTION - See GAMBIA - MINING AND MINERAL PRODUCTS

GAMBIA - ANIMAL HEALTH

Food and Agricultural Organization of the United Nations (FAO), Via delle Terme di Caracalla, 00100 Rome, Italy (Telephone Number in U.S. (202) 653-2400); *Animal Health Yearbook.*

GAMBIA - AREA AND DENSITY OF POPULATION

African Development Bank, 01 BP 1387, Abidjan 01, Cote D'Ivoire; *Selected Statistics on Regional Member Countries.*

Facts on File, 460 Park Avenue South, New York, New York 10016 (800) 443-8323; *The New Book of World Rankings.*

Federal Statistical Office, Gustav - Stresemann - Ring 11, D-6200 Wiesbaden, Germany; *Gambia.*

Food and Agricultural Organization of the United Nations (FAO) Via delle Terme di Caracalla, 00100 Rome, Italy (Telephone Number in U.S. (202) 653-2400); *The State of Food and Agriculture.*

G.K. Hall and Company, 70 Lincoln Street, Boston, Massachusetts 02111 (617) 423-3990; *The World in Figures.*

Statistical Office of the United Nations, Publishing Service, New York, New York 10017 (800) 253-9646; *Survey of Economic and Social Conditions in Africa.*

GAMBIA - ARMS EXPORTS AND IMPORTS

U.S. Arms Control and Disarmament Agency, 320 Twenty-first Street, Northwest, Washington, D.C. 20451 (202) 647-8677; *World Military Expenditures and Arms Transfers.*

GAMBIA - BALANCE OF PAYMENTS

African Development Bank, 01 BP 1387, Abidjan 01, Cote D'Ivoire; *Selected Statistics on Regional Member Countries.*

The Economist Intelligence Unit, 111 West 57th Street, New York, New York 10019 (800) 938-4685; *The World Market Atlas.*

Federal Statistical Office, Gustav - Stresemann - Ring 11, D-6200 Wiesbaden, Germany; *Gambia.*

G.K. Hall and Company, 70 Lincoln Street, Boston, Massachusetts 02111 (617) 423-3990; *The World in Figures.*

International Monetary Fund, 700 Nineteenth Street, NW, Washington, D.C. 20431 (202) 623-7000; *Balance of Payments Yearbook.*

United Nations Economic Commission for Africa, Africa Hall, Post Office Box 3001, Addis Ababa, Ethiopia (Telephone Number in U.S. (800) 253-9646); *African Statistical Yearbook.*

The World Bank, 1818 H Street, NW, Washington, D.C. 20433 (202) 477-1234; *World Tables.*

GAMBIA - BANKING

Facts on File, 460 Park Avenue South, New York, New York 10016 (800) 443-8323; *The New Book of World Rankings.*

G.K. Hall and Company, 70 Lincoln Street, Boston, Massachusetts 02111 (617) 423-3990; *The World in Figures.*

International Monetary Fund, 700 Nineteenth Street, NW, Washington, D.C. 20431 (202) 623-7000; *International Financial Statistics.*

United Nations Economic Commission for Africa, Africa Hall, Post Office Box 3001, Addis Ababa, Ethiopia (Telephone Number in U.S.

(800) 253-9646); *African Statistical Yearbook.*

GAMBIA - BARLEY PRODUCTION - See GAMBIA - CROPS

GAMBIA - BEER PRODUCTION

Facts on File, 460 Park Avenue South, New York, New York 10016 (800) 443-8323; *The New Book of World Rankings.*

GAMBIA - BIRTH RATES

Facts on File, 460 Park Avenue South, New York, New York 10016 (800) 443-8323; *The New Book of World Rankings.*

Statistical Office of the United Nations, Publishing Service, New York, New York 10017 (800) 253-9646; *Demographic Yearbook, Statistical Yearbook,* and *Survey of Economic and Social Conditions in Africa.*

The World Bank, 1818 H Street, NW, Washington, D.C. 20433 (202) 477-1234; *World Tables.*

GAMBIA - BONDS

G.K. Hall and Company, 70 Lincoln Street, Boston, Massachusetts 02111 (617) 423-3990; *The World in Figures.*

International Monetary Fund, 700 Nineteenth Street, NW, Washington, D.C. 20431 (202) 623-7000; *Government Finance Statistics Yearbook.*

GAMBIA - BOOK PRODUCTION

United Nations Educational, Scientific and Cultural Organization (UNESCO), 7 Place de Fontenoy, F-75700 Paris, France (Telephone Number in U.S. (212) 963-5981); *Statistical Yearbook.*

GAMBIA - BROADCASTING

Billboard Limited, Post Office Box 9027, 1006 AA Amsterdam, The Netherlands (Telephone Number in U.S. (212) 764-7300); *World Radio TV Handbook.*

Facts on File, 460 Park Avenue South, New York, New York 10016 (800) 443-8323; *The New Book of World Rankings.*

G.K. Hall and Company, 70 Lincoln Street, Boston, Massachusetts 02111 (617) 423-3990; *The World in Figures.*

GAMBIA - BUILDING CONSTRUCTION - See GAMBIA - CONSTRUCTION INDUSTRY

GAMBIA - BUSINESS

G.K. Hall and Company, 70 Lincoln Street, Boston, Massachusetts 02111 (617) 423-3990; *The World in Figures.*

GAMBIA - CALORIE SUPPLY

African Development Bank, 01 BP 1387, Abidjan 01, Cote D'Ivoire; *Selected Statistics on Regional Member Countries.*

Food and Agricultural Organization of the United Nations (FAO) Via delle Terme di Caracalla, 00100 Rome, Italy (Telephone Number in U.S. (202) 653-2400); *The State of Food and Agriculture.*

GAMBIA - CAPITAL REVENUE

International Monetary Fund, 700 Nineteenth Street, NW, Washington, D.C. 20431 (202) 623-7000; *Government Finance Statistics Yearbook.*

GAMBIA - CATTLE - See GAMBIA - LIVESTOCK AND POULTRY

GAMBIA - CEMENT PRODUCTION - See GAMBIA - MINING AND MINERAL PRODUCTS

GAMBIA - CHEMICAL (ORGANIC) PRODUCTION - See GAMBIA - MINING AND MINERAL PRODUCTS

GAMBIA - CIGARETTE PRODUCTION - See GAMBIA - TOBACCO PRODUCTION

GAMBIA - CLASS STRUCTURE

G.K. Hall and Company, 70 Lincoln Street, Boston, Massachusetts 02111 (617) 423-3990; *The World in Figures.*

GAMBIA - CLIMATE

Facts on File, 460 Park Avenue South, New York, New York 10016 (800) 443-8323; *The New Book of World Rankings.*

G.K. Hall and Company, 70 Lincoln Street, Boston, Massachusetts 02111 (617) 423-3990; *The World in Figures.*

GAMBIA - COAL PRODUCTION - See GAMBIA - MINING AND MINERAL PRODUCTS

GAMBIA - COFFEE PRODUCTION - See GAMBIA - CROPS

GAMBIA - COMMUNICATIONS

Federal Statistical Office, Gustav - Stresemann - Ring 11, D-6200 Wiesbaden, Germany; *Gambia.*

G.K. Hall and Company, 70 Lincoln Street, Boston, Massachusetts 02111 (617) 423-3990; *The World in Figures.*

United Nations Economic Commission for Africa, Africa Hall, Post Office Box 3001, Addis Ababa, Ethiopia (Telephone Number in U.S. (800) 253-9646); *African Statistical Yearbook.*

GAMBIA - CONSTRUCTION INDUSTRY

Facts on File, 460 Park Avenue South, New York, New York 10016 (800) 443-8323; *The New Book of World Rankings.*

Statistical Office of the United Nations, Publishing Service, New York, New York 10017 (800) 253-9646; *Statistical Yearbook.*

United Nations Economic Commission for Africa, Africa Hall, Post Office Box 3001, Addis Ababa, Ethiopia (Telephone Number in U.S. (800) 253-9646); *African Statistical Yearbook.*

GAMBIA - CONSUMER PRICE INDEX

African Development Bank, 01 BP 1387, Abidjan 01, Cote D'Ivoire; *Selected Statistics on Regional Member Countries.*

Federal Statistical Office, Gustav - Stresemann - Ring 11, D-6200 Wiesbaden, Germany; *Gambia.*

G.K. Hall and Company, 70 Lincoln Street, Boston, Massachusetts 02111 (617) 423-3990; *The World in Figures.*

Statistical Office of the United Nations, Publishing Service, New York, New York 10017 (800) 253-9646; *Statistical Yearbook*, and *Survey of Economic and Social Conditions in Africa*.

United Nations Economic Commission for Africa, Africa Hall, Post Office Box 3001, Addis Ababa, Ethiopia (Telephone Number in U.S. (800) 253-9646); *African Statistical Yearbook*.

GAMBIA - CONSUMER PRICES

Federal Statistical Office, Gustav - Stresemann - Ring 11, D-6200 Wiesbaden, Germany; *Gambia*.

International Labour Office, I.L.O. Publications, CH-1211, Geneva 22, Switzerland; *Yearbook of Labour Statistics*.

International Monetary Fund, 700 Nineteenth Street, NW, Washington, D.C. 20431 (202) 623-7000; *International Financial Statistics*.

GAMBIA - CONSUMPTION

African Development Bank, 01 BP 1387, Abidjan 01, Cote D'Ivoire; *Selected Statistics on Regional Member Countries*.

G.K. Hall and Company, 70 Lincoln Street, Boston, Massachusetts 02111 (617) 423-3990; *The World in Figures*.

Statistical Office of the United Nations, Publishing Service, New York, New York 10017 (800) 253-9646; *Survey of Economic and Social Conditions in Africa*.

GAMBIA - COPPER PRODUCTION - See GAMBIA - MINING AND MINERAL PRODUCTS

GAMBIA - CORN PRODUCTION - See GAMBIA - CROPS

GAMBIA - CORPORATE TAXES - See GAMBIA - TAXATION

GAMBIA - COTTON PRODUCTION - See GAMBIA - CROPS

GAMBIA - CROPS

Facts on File, 460 Park Avenue South, New York, New York 10016 (800) 443-8323; *The New Book of World Rankings*.

Food and Agricultural Organization of the United Nations (FAO), Via delle Terme di Caracalla, 00100 Rome, Italy (Telephone Number in U.S. (202) 653-2400); *Production Yearbook* and *The State of Food and Agriculture*.

G.K. Hall and Company, 70 Lincoln Street, Boston, Massachusetts 02111 (617) 423-3990; *The World in Figures*.

International Monetary Fund, 700 Nineteenth Street, NW, Washington, D.C. 20431 (202) 623-7000; *International Financial Statistics*.

Statistical Office of the United Nations, Publishing Service, New York, New York 10017 (800) 253-9646; *Statistical Yearbook*.

United Nations Economic Commission for Africa, Africa Hall, Post Office Box 3001, Addis Ababa, Ethiopia (Telephone Number in U.S. (800) 253-9646); *African Statistical Yearbook*.

GAMBIA - CUSTOMS DUTIES

G.K. Hall and Company, 70 Lincoln Street, Boston, Massachusetts 02111 (617) 423-3990; *The World in Figures*.

International Monetary Fund, 700 Nineteenth Street, NW, Washington, D.C. 20431 (202) 623-7000; *Government Finance Statistics Yearbook*.

GAMBIA - DAIRY PRODUCTS

Facts on File, 460 Park Avenue South, New York, New York 10016 (800) 443-8323; *The New Book of World Rankings*.

Food and Agricultural Organization of the United Nations (FAO) Via delle Terme di Caracalla, 00100 Rome, Italy (Telephone Number in U.S. (202) 653-2400); *The State of Food and Agriculture*.

GAMBIA - DEATH RATES

G.K. Hall and Company, 70 Lincoln Street, Boston, Massachusetts 02111 (617) 423-3990; *The World in Figures*.

Statistical Office of the United Nations, Publishing Service, New York, New York 10017 (800) 253-9646; *Statistical Yearbook*, and *Survey of Economic and Social Conditions in Africa*.

World Health Organization, Office of Publications, Avenue Appia, CH-1211 Geneva 27, Switzerland (Telephone Number in U.S. (518) 436-9686); *World Health Statistics Annual*.

GAMBIA - DEFENSE EXPENDITURES

G.K. Hall and Company, 70 Lincoln Street, Boston, Massachusetts 02111 (617) 423-3990; *The World in Figures*.

International Monetary Fund, 700 Nineteenth Street, NW, Washington, D.C. 20431 (202) 623-7000; *Government Finance Statistics Yearbook*.

U.S. Arms Control and Disarmament Agency, 320 Twenty-first Street, Northwest, Washington, D.C. 20451 (202) 647-8677; *World Military Expenditures and Arms Transfers*.

GAMBIA - DEMOGRAPHY

The Economist Intelligence Unit, 111 West 57th Street, New York, New York 10019 (800) 938-4685; *The World Market Atlas*.

Facts on File, 460 Park Avenue South, New York, New York 10016 (800) 443-8323; *The New Book of World Rankings*.

Federal Statistical Office, Gustav - Stresemann - Ring 11, D-6200 Wiesbaden, Germany; *Gambia*.

G.K. Hall and Company, 70 Lincoln Street, Boston, Massachusetts 02111 (617) 423-3990; *The World in Figures*.

Statistical Office of the United Nations, Publishing Service, New York, New York 10017 (800) 253-9646; *Survey of Economic and Social Conditions in Africa*.

GAMBIA - DEVELOPMENT ASSISTANCE

G.K. Hall and Company, 70 Lincoln Street, Boston, Massachusetts 02111 (617) 423-3990; *The World in Figures*.

Statistical Office of the United Nations, Publishing Service, New York, New York 10017 (800) 253-9646; *Statistical Yearbook*.

GAMBIA - DIAMOND PRODUCTION - See GAMBIA - MINING AND MINERAL PRODUCTS

GAMBIA - DISEASE

G.K. Hall and Company, 70 Lincoln Street, Boston, Massachusetts 02111 (617) 423-3990; *The World in Figures.*

GAMBIA - DIVORCE RATES

Facts on File, 460 Park Avenue South, New York, New York 10016 (800) 443-8323; *The New Book of World Rankings.*

Statistical Office of the United Nations, Publishing Service, New York, New York 10017 (800) 253-9646; *Demographic Yearbook.*

GAMBIA - DOMESTIC PRODUCT

G.K. Hall and Company, 70 Lincoln Street, Boston, Massachusetts 02111 (617) 423-3990; *The World in Figures.*

GAMBIA - ECONOMY

African Development Bank, 01 BP 1387, Abidjan 01, Cote D'Ivoire; *Selected Statistics on Regional Member Countries.*

Facts on File, 460 Park Avenue South, New York, New York 10016 (800) 443-8323; *The New Book of World Rankings.*

Federal Statistical Office, Gustav - Stresemann - Ring 11, D-6200 Wiesbaden, Germany; *Gambia.*

G.K. Hall and Company, 70 Lincoln Street, Boston, Massachusetts 02111 (617) 423-3990; *The World in Figures.*

Statistical Office of the United Nations, Publishing Service, New York, New York 10017 (800) 253-9646; *Foreign Trade Statistics for Africa.*

GAMBIA - EDUCATION

African Development Bank, 01 BP 1387, Abidjan 01, Cote D'Ivoire; *Selected Statistics on Regional Member Countries.*

The Economist Intelligence Unit, 111 West 57th Street, New York, New York 10019 (800) 938-4685; *The World Market Atlas.*

Facts on File, 460 Park Avenue South, New York, New York 10016 (800) 443-8323; *The New Book of World Rankings.*

Federal Statistical Office, Gustav - Stresemann - Ring 11, D-6200 Wiesbaden, Germany; *Gambia.*

G.K. Hall and Company, 70 Lincoln Street, Boston, Massachusetts 02111 (617) 423-3990; *The World in Figures.*

International Monetary Fund, 700 Nineteenth Street, NW, Washington, D.C. 20431 (202) 623-7000; *Government Finance Statistics Yearbook.*

Statistical Office of the United Nations, Publishing Service, New York, New York 10017 (800) 253-9646; *Survey of Economic and Social Conditions in Africa.*

United Nations Economic Commission for Africa, Africa Hall, Post Office Box 3001, Addis Ababa, Ethiopia (Telephone Number in U.S. (800) 253-9646); *African Statistical Yearbook.*

United Nations Educational, Scientific and Cultural Organization (UNESCO), 7 Place de Fontenoy, F-75700 Paris, France (Telephone Number in U.S. (212) 963-5981); *Statistical Yearbook.*

The World Bank, 1818 H Street, NW, Washington, D.C. 20433 (202) 477-1234; *World Tables.*

GAMBIA - EGG PRODUCTION - See GAMBIA - DAIRY PRODUCTS

GAMBIA - ELECTRICITY

Facts on File, 460 Park Avenue South, New York, New York 10016 (800) 443-8323; *The New Book of World Rankings.*

Statistical Office of the United Nations, Publishing Service, New York, New York 10017 (800) 253-9646; *Statistical Yearbook,* and *Survey of Economic and Social Conditions in Africa.*

United Nations Economic Commission for Africa, Africa Hall, Post Office Box 3001, Addis Ababa, Ethiopia (Telephone Number in U.S. (800) 253-9646); *African Statistical Yearbook.*

GAMBIA - EMPLOYMENT

Facts on File, 460 Park Avenue South, New York, New York 10016 (800) 443-8323; *The New Book of World Rankings.*

Federal Statistical Office, Gustav - Stresemann - Ring 11, D-6200 Wiesbaden, Germany; *Gambia.*

International Labour Office, I.L.O. Publications, CH-1211, Geneva 22, Switzerland; *Yearbook of Labour Statistics.*

Statistical Office of the United Nations, Publishing Service, New York, New York 10017 (800) 253-9646; *Statistical Yearbook,* and *Survey of Economic and Social Conditions in Africa.*

United Nations Economic Commission for Africa, Africa Hall, Post Office Box 3001, Addis Ababa, Ethiopia (Telephone Number in U.S. (800) 253-9646); *African Statistical Yearbook.*

GAMBIA - ENERGY

Facts on File, 460 Park Avenue South, New York, New York 10016 (800) 443-8323; *The New Book of World Rankings.*

Food and Agricultural Organization of the United Nations (FAO) Via delle Terme di Caracalla, 00100 Rome, Italy (Telephone Number in U.S. (202) 653-2400); *The State of Food and Agriculture.*

G.K. Hall and Company, 70 Lincoln Street, Boston, Massachusetts 02111 (617) 423-3990; *The World in Figures.*

Statistical Office of the United Nations, Publishing Service, New York, New York 10017 (800) 253-9646; *Energy Statistics Yearbook,* and *Statistical Yearbook.*

United Nations Economic Commission for Africa, Africa Hall, Post Office Box 3001, Addis Ababa, Ethiopia (Telephone Number in U.S. (800) 253-9646); *African Statistical Yearbook.*

GAMBIA - EXCHANGE RATE

African Development Bank, 01 BP 1387, Abidjan 01, Cote D'Ivoire; *Selected Statistics on Regional Member Countries.*

International Monetary Fund, 700 Nineteenth Street, NW, Washington, D.C. 20431 (202) 623-7000; *International Financial Statistics.*

Statistical Office of the United Nations, Publishing Service, New York, New York 10017 (800) 253-9646; *Foreign Trade Statistics for Africa,* and *Statistical Yearbook.*

GAMBIA - EXCISE TAXES - See GAMBIA - TAXATION

GAMBIA - EXPORTS

African Development Bank, 01 BP 1387, Abidjan 01, Cote D'Ivoire; *Selected Statistics on Regional Member Countries.*

The Economist Intelligence Unit, 111 West 57th Street, New York, New York 10019 (800) 938-4685; *The World Market Atlas.*

Food and Agricultural Organization of the United Nations (FAO) Via delle Terme di Caracalla, 00100 Rome, Italy (Telephone Number in U.S. (202) 653-2400); *The State of Food and Agriculture.*

G.K. Hall and Company, 70 Lincoln Street, Boston, Massachusetts 02111 (617) 423-3990; *The World in Figures.*

International Monetary Fund, 700 Nineteenth Street, NW, Washington, D.C. 20431 (202) 623-7000; *Direction of Trade Statistics, Government Finance Statistics Yearbook,* and *International Financial Statistics.*

Statistical Office of the United Nations, Publishing Service, New York, New York 10017 (800) 253-9646; *Foreign Trade Statistics for Africa,* and *Survey of Economic and Social Conditions in Africa.*

United Nations Economic Commission for Africa, Africa Hall, Post Office Box 3001, Addis Ababa, Ethiopia (Telephone Number in U.S. (800) 253-9646); *African Statistical Yearbook.*

The World Bank, 1818 H Street, NW, Washington, D.C. 20433 (202) 477-1234; *World Tables.*

GAMBIA - EXTERNAL INDEBTEDNESS

African Development Bank, 01 BP 1387, Abidjan 01, Cote D'Ivoire; *Selected Statistics on Regional Member Countries.*

Statistical Office of the United Nations, Publishing Service, New York, New York 10017 (800) 253-9646; *Survey of Economic and Social Conditions in Africa.*

The World Bank, 1818 H Street, NW, Washington, D.C. 20433 (202) 477-1234; *World Tables.*

GAMBIA - EXTERNAL TRADE

African Development Bank, 01 BP 1387, Abidjan 01, Cote D'Ivoire; *Selected Statistics on Regional Member Countries.*

Food and Agricultural Organization of the United Nations (FAO) Via delle Terme di Caracalla, 00100 Rome, Italy (Telephone Number in U.S. (202) 653-2400); *The State of Food and Agriculture,* and *Trade Yearbook.*

G.K. Hall and Company, 70 Lincoln Street, Boston, Massachusetts 02111 (617) 423-3990; *The World in Figures.*

Statistical Office of the United Nations, Publishing Service, New York, New York 10017 (800) 253-9646; *Statistical Yearbook.*

GAMBIA - FARM CROPS - See GAMBIA - CROPS

GAMBIA - FERTILITY RATES

Facts on File, 460 Park Avenue South, New York, New York 10016 (800) 443-8323; *The New Book of World Rankings.*

Statistical Office of the United Nations, Publishing Service, New York, New York 10017 (800) 253-9646; *Survey of Economic and Social Conditions in Africa.*

The World Bank, 1818 H Street, NW, Washington, D.C. 20433 (202) 477-1234; *World Tables.*

GAMBIA - FERTILIZER

Food and Agricultural Organization of the United Nations (FAO), Via delle Terme di Caracalla, 00100 Rome, Italy (Telephone Number in U.S. (202) 653-2400); *Fertilizer Yearbook,* and *The State of Food and Agriculture.*

Statistical Office of the United Nations, Publishing Service, New York, New York 10017 (800) 253-9646; *Statistical Yearbook.*

GAMBIA - FETAL MORTALITY

Statistical Office of the United Nations, Publishing Service, New York, New York 10017 (800) 253-9646; *Demographic Yearbook.*

GAMBIA - FINANCE

African Development Bank, 01 BP 1387, Abidjan 01, Cote D'Ivoire; *Selected Statistics on Regional Member Countries.*

Facts on File, 460 Park Avenue South, New York, New York 10016 (800) 443-8323; *The New Book of World Rankings.*

Federal Statistical Office, Gustav - Stresemann - Ring 11, D-6200 Wiesbaden, Germany; *Gambia.*

G.K. Hall and Company, 70 Lincoln Street, Boston, Massachusetts 02111 (617) 423-3990; *The World in Figures.*

International Monetary Fund, 700 Nineteenth Street, NW, Washington, D.C. 20431 (202) 623-7000; *Government Finance Statistics Yearbook.*

United Nations Economic Commission for Africa, Africa Hall, Post Office Box 3001, Addis Ababa, Ethiopia (Telephone Number in U.S. (800) 253-9646); *African Statistical Yearbook.*

GAMBIA - FISHERIES

Facts on File, 460 Park Avenue South, New York, New York 10016 (800) 443-8323; *The New Book of World Rankings.*

Federal Statistical Office, Gustav - Stresemann - Ring 11, D-6200 Wiesbaden, Germany; *Gambia.*

Food and Agricultural Organization of the United Nations (FAO) Via delle Terme di Caracalla, 00100 Rome, Italy (Telephone Number in U.S. (202) 653-2400); *The State of Food and Agriculture,* and *Yearbook of Fishery Statistics.*

Statistical Office of the United Nations, Publishing Service, New York, New York 10017 (800) 253-9646; *Statistical Yearbook,* and *Survey of Economic and Social Conditions in Africa.*

United Nations Economic Commission for Africa, Africa Hall, Post Office Box 3001, Addis Ababa, Ethiopia (Telephone Number in U.S. (800) 253-9646); *African Statistical Yearbook.*

GAMBIA - FOOD

African Development Bank, 01 BP 1387, Abidjan 01, Cote D'Ivoire; *Selected Statistics on Regional Member Countries.*

Food and Agricultural Organization of the United Nations (FAO) Via delle Terme di Caracalla, 00100 Rome, Italy (Telephone Number in U.S. (202) 653-2400); *Production Yearbook* and *The State of Food and Agriculture*.

G.K. Hall and Company, 70 Lincoln Street, Boston, Massachusetts 02111 (617) 423-3990; *The World in Figures*.

GAMBIA - FOREIGN AID

G.K. Hall and Company, 70 Lincoln Street, Boston, Massachusetts 02111 (617) 423-3990; *The World in Figures*.

GAMBIA - FOREIGN DEBT

International Monetary Fund, 700 Nineteenth Street, NW, Washington, D.C. 20431 (202) 623-7000; *Government Finance Statistics Yearbook*.

GAMBIA - FOREIGN TRADE

Facts on File, 460 Park Avenue South, New York, New York 10016 (800) 443-8323; *The New Book of World Rankings*.

Federal Statistical Office, Gustav - Stresemann - Ring 11, D-6200 Wiesbaden, Germany; *Gambia*.

Food and Agricultural Organization of the United Nations (FAO) Via delle Terme di Caracalla, 00100 Rome, Italy (Telephone Number in U.S. (202) 653-2400); *The State of Food and Agriculture*.

G.K. Hall and Company, 70 Lincoln Street, Boston, Massachusetts 02111 (617) 423-3990; *The World in Figures*.

International Monetary Fund, 700 Nineteenth Street, NW, Washington, D.C. 20431 (202) 623-7000; *International Financial Statistics*.

Organisation for Economic Co-operation and Development (OECD), 2 rue Andre-Pascal, 75 Paris 16, France (Telephone Number in U.S. (202) 785-6323); *Trade by Commodities*.

Statistical Office of the United Nations, Publishing Service, New York, New York 10017 (800) 253-9646; *Foreign Trade Statistics for Africa*, *International Trade Statistics Yearbook*, and *Statistical Yearbook*.

United Nations Economic Commission for Africa, Africa Hall, Post Office Box 3001, Addis Ababa, Ethiopia (Telephone Number in U.S. (800) 253-9646); *African Statistical Yearbook*.

The World Bank, 1818 H Street, NW, Washington, D.C. 20433 (202) 477-1234; *World Tables*.

GAMBIA - FORESTRY AND FOREST PRODUCTS

Food and Agricultural Organization of the United Nations (FAO) Via delle Terme di Caracalla, 00100 Rome, Italy (Telephone Number in U.S. (202) 653-2400); *The State of Food and Agriculture*, and *Yearbook of Forest Products*.

Facts on File, 460 Park Avenue South, New York, New York 10016 (800) 443-8323; *The New Book of World Rankings*.

Federal Statistical Office, Gustav - Stresemann - Ring 11, D-6200 Wiesbaden, Germany; *Gambia*.

G.K. Hall and Company, 70 Lincoln Street, Boston, Massachusetts 02111 (617) 423-3990; *The World in Figures*.

Statistical Office of the United Nations, Publishing Service, New York, New York 10017 (800) 253-9646; *Statistical Yearbook*.

United Nations Economic Commission for Africa, Africa Hall, Post Office Box 3001, Addis Ababa, Ethiopia (Telephone Number in U.S. (800) 253-9646); *African Statistical Yearbook*.

GAMBIA - GAS PRODUCTION - See GAMBIA - MINING AND MINERAL PRODUCTS

GAMBIA - GENERAL INDUSTRIAL STATISTICS

Federal Statistical Office, Gustav - Stresemann - Ring 11, D-6200 Wiesbaden, Germany; *Gambia*.

Statistical Office of the United Nations, Publishing Service, New York, New York 10017 (800) 253-9646; *Industrial Statistics Yearbook*.

GAMBIA - GENERAL MORTALITY

Statistical Office of the United Nations, Publishing Service, New York, New York 10017 (800) 253-9646; *Demographic Yearbook*.

GAMBIA - GEOGRAPHIC DATA

Facts on File, 460 Park Avenue South, New York, New York 10016 (800) 443-8323; *The New Book of World Rankings*.

Federal Statistical Office, Gustav - Stresemann - Ring 11, D-6200 Wiesbaden, Germany; *Gambia*.

GAMBIA - GOATS - See GAMBIA - LIVESTOCK AND POULTRY

GAMBIA - GOLD HOLDINGS

International Monetary Fund, 700 Nineteenth Street, NW, Washington, D.C. 20431 (202) 623-7000; *International Financial Statistics*.

Statistical Office of the United Nations, Publishing Service, New York, New York 10017 (800) 253-9646; *Statistical Yearbook*.

The World Bank, 1818 H Street, NW, Washington, D.C. 20433 (202) 477-1234; *World Tables*.

GAMBIA - GOLD PRODUCTION AND CONSUMPTION - See GAMBIA - MINING AND MINERAL PRODUCTS

GAMBIA - GOVERNMENT

G.K. Hall and Company, 70 Lincoln Street, Boston, Massachusetts 02111 (617) 423-3990; *The World in Figures*.

GAMBIA - GOVERNMENT EXPENDITURES

International Monetary Fund, 700 Nineteenth Street, NW, Washington, D.C. 20431 (202) 623-7000; *Government Finance Statistics Yearbook*.

The World Bank, 1818 H Street, NW, Washington, D.C. 20433 (202) 477-1234; *World Tables*.

GAMBIA - GOVERNMENT FINANCE

International Monetary Fund, 700 Nineteenth Street, NW, Washington, D.C. 20431 (202) 623-7000; *International Financial Statistics*.

GAMBIA - GOVERNMENT REVENUES

International Monetary Fund, 700 Nineteenth Street, NW, Washington, D.C. 20431 (202) 623-7000; *Government Finance Statistics Yearbook.*

Statistical Office of the United Nations, Publishing Service, New York, New York 10017 (800) 253-9646; *Survey of Economic and Social Conditions in Africa.*

The World Bank, 1818 H Street, NW, Washington, D.C. 20433 (202) 477-1234; *World Tables.*

GAMBIA - GRAIN PRODUCTION - See GAMBIA - CROPS

GAMBIA - GRANTS

International Monetary Fund, 700 Nineteenth Street, NW, Washington, D.C. 20431 (202) 623-7000; *Government Finance Statistics Yearbook.*

GAMBIA - GROSS DOMESTIC PRODUCT

African Development Bank, 01 BP 1387, Abidjan 01, Cote D'Ivoire; *Selected Statistics on Regional Member Countries.*

The Economist Intelligence Unit, 111 West 57th Street, New York, New York 10019 (800) 938-4685; *The World Market Atlas.*

Facts on File, 460 Park Avenue South, New York, New York 10016 (800) 443-8323; *The New Book of World Rankings.*

G.K. Hall and Company, 70 Lincoln Street, Boston, Massachusetts 02111 (617) 423-3990; *The World in Figures.*

Statistical Office of the United Nations, Publishing Service, New York, New York 10017 (800) 253-9646; *Statistical Yearbook,* and *Survey of Economic and Social Conditions in Africa.*

United Nations Economic Commission for Africa, Africa Hall, Post Office Box 3001, Addis Ababa, Ethiopia (Telephone Number in U.S. (800) 253-9646); *African Statistical Yearbook.*

The World Bank, 1818 H Street, NW, Washington, D.C. 20433 (202) 477-1234; *World Tables.*

GAMBIA - GROSS NATIONAL PRODUCT

U.S. Arms Control and Disarmament Agency, 320 Twenty-first Street, Northwest, Washington, D.C. 20451 (202) 647-8677; *World Military Expenditures and Arms Transfers.*

The World Bank, 1818 H Street, NW, Washington, D.C. 20433 (202) 477-1234; *World Tables.*

GAMBIA - GROUNDNUTS - See GAMBIA - CROPS

GAMBIA - HEALTH

African Development Bank, 01 BP 1387, Abidjan 01, Cote D'Ivoire; *Selected Statistics on Regional Member Countries.*

Facts on File, 460 Park Avenue South, New York, New York 10016 (800) 443-8323; *The New Book of World Rankings.*

Federal Statistical Office, Gustav - Stresemann - Ring 11, D-6200 Wiesbaden, Germany; *Gambia.*

G.K. Hall and Company, 70 Lincoln Street, Boston, Massachusetts 02111 (617) 423-3990; *The World in Figures.*

Statistical Office of the United Nations, Publishing Service, New York, New York 10017 (800) 253-9646; *Statistical Yearbook.*

United Nations Economic Commission for Africa, Africa Hall, Post Office Box 3001, Addis Ababa, Ethiopia (Telephone Number in U.S. (800) 253-9646); *African Statistical Yearbook.*

World Health Organization, Office of Publications, Avenue Appia, CH-1211 Geneva 27, Switzerland (Telephone Number in U.S. (518) 436-9686); *World Health Statistics Annual.*

GAMBIA - HEALTH EXPENDITURES

International Monetary Fund, 700 Nineteenth Street, NW, Washington, D.C. 20431 (202) 623-7000; *Government Finance Statistics Yearbook.*

GAMBIA - HIDE PRODUCTION

Food and Agricultural Organization of the United Nations (FAO), Via delle Terme di Caracalla, 00100 Rome, Italy (Telephone Number in U.S. (202) 653-2400); *Production Yearbook.*

GAMBIA - HIGHWAYS

G.K. Hall and Company, 70 Lincoln Street, Boston, Massachusetts 02111 (617) 423-3990; *The World in Figures.*

Statistical Office of the United Nations, Publishing Service, New York, New York 10017 (800) 253-9646; *Survey of Economic and Social Conditions in Africa.*

United Nations Economic Commission for Africa, Africa Hall, Post Office Box 3001, Addis Ababa, Ethiopia (Telephone Number in U.S. (800) 253-9646); *African Statistical Yearbook.*

GAMBIA - HORSES - See GAMBIA - LIVESTOCK AND POULTRY

GAMBIA - HOURS OF WORK - See GAMBIA - EMPLOYMENT

GAMBIA - HOUSING AND HOUSING UNITS

Facts on File, 460 Park Avenue South, New York, New York 10016 (800) 443-8323; *The New Book of World Rankings.*

GAMBIA - HOUSING EXPENDITURES

International Monetary Fund, 700 Nineteenth Street, NW, Washington, D.C. 20431 (202) 623-7000; *Government Finance Statistics Yearbook.*

GAMBIA - ILLITERATE POPULATION

The Economist Intelligence Unit, 111 West 57th Street, New York, New York 10019 (800) 938-4685; *The World Market Atlas.*

G.K. Hall and Company, 70 Lincoln Street, Boston, Massachusetts 02111 (617) 423-3990; *The World in Figures.*

United Nations Educational, Scientific and Cultural Organization (UNESCO), 7 Place de Fontenoy, F-75700 Paris, France (Telephone Number in U.S. (212) 963-5981); *Statistical Yearbook.*

GAMBIA - IMPORTS

African Development Bank, 01 BP 1387, Abidjan 01, Cote D'Ivoire; *Selected Statistics on Regional Member Countries.*

The Economist Intelligence Unit, 111 West 57th Street, New York, New York 10019 (800) 938-4685; *The World Market Atlas.*

Food and Agricultural Organization of the United Nations (FAO) Via delle Terme di Caracalla, 00100 Rome, Italy (Telephone Number in U.S. (202) 653-2400); *The State of Food and Agriculture.*

G.K. Hall and Company, 70 Lincoln Street, Boston, Massachusetts 02111 (617) 423-3990; *The World in Figures.*

International Monetary Fund, 700 Nineteenth Street, NW, Washington, D.C. 20431 (202) 623-7000; *Direction of Trade Statistics, Government Finance Statistics Yearbook,* and *International Financial Statistics.*

Statistical Office of the United Nations, Publishing Service, New York, New York 10017 (800) 253-9646; *Foreign Trade Statistics for Africa,* and *Survey of Economic and Social Conditions in Africa.*

United Nations Economic Commission for Africa, Africa Hall, Post Office Box 3001, Addis Ababa, Ethiopia (Telephone Number in U.S. (800) 253-9646); *African Statistical Yearbook.*

The World Bank, 1818 H Street, NW, Washington, D.C. 20433 (202) 477-1234; *World Tables.*

GAMBIA - INCOME TAXES - See GAMBIA - TAXATION

GAMBIA - INDUSTRY

Facts on File, 460 Park Avenue South, New York, New York 10016 (800) 443-8323; *The New Book of World Rankings.*

Federal Statistical Office, Gustav - Stresemann - Ring 11, D-6200 Wiesbaden, Germany; *Gambia.*

G.K. Hall and Company, 70 Lincoln Street, Boston, Massachusetts 02111 (617) 423-3990; *The World in Figures.*

International Labour Office, I.L.O. Publications, CH-1211, Geneva 22, Switzerland; *Yearbook of Labour Statistics.*

Statistical Office of the United Nations, Publishing Service, New York, New York 10017 (800) 253-9646; *Survey of Economic and Social Conditions in Africa.*

United Nations Economic Commission for Africa, Africa Hall, Post Office Box 3001, Addis Ababa, Ethiopia (Telephone Number in U.S. (800) 253-9646); *African Statistical Yearbook.*

The World Bank, 1818 H Street, NW, Washington, D.C. 20433 (202) 477-1234; *World Tables.*

World Intellectual Property Organization, 34 Chemin des Colombettes, CH-1211 Geneva 20, Switzerland; *Industrial Property Statistics.*

GAMBIA - INFANT AND MATERNAL MORTALITY

Statistical Office of the United Nations, Publishing Service, New York, New York 10017 (800) 253-9646; *Demographic Yearbook,* and *Survey of Economic and Social Conditions in Africa.*

The World Bank, 1818 H Street, NW, Washington, D.C. 20433 (202) 477-1234; *World Tables.*

GAMBIA - INTERNATIONAL LIQUIDITY

International Monetary Fund, 700 Nineteenth Street, NW, Washington, D.C. 20431 (202) 623-7000; *International Financial Statistics.*

GAMBIA - INTERNATIONAL RESERVES EXCLUDING GOLD

African Development Bank, 01 BP 1387, Abidjan 01, Cote D'Ivoire; *Selected Statistics on Regional Member Countries.*

Statistical Office of the United Nations, Publishing Service, New York, New York 10017 (800) 253-9646; *Statistical Yearbook.*

The World Bank, 1818 H Street, NW, Washington, D.C. 20433 (202) 477-1234; *World Tables.*

GAMBIA - IRON ORE PRODUCTION AND CONSUMPTION - See GAMBIA - MINING AND MINERAL PRODUCTS

GAMBIA - LABOR FORCE

African Development Bank, 01 BP 1387, Abidjan 01, Cote D'Ivoire; *Selected Statistics on Regional Member Countries.*

Facts on File, 460 Park Avenue South, New York, New York 10016 (800) 443-8323; *The New Book of World Rankings.*

Food and Agricultural Organization of the United Nations (FAO) Via delle Terme di Caracalla, 00100 Rome, Italy (Telephone Number in U.S. (202) 653-2400); *The State of Food and Agriculture.*

G.K. Hall and Company, 70 Lincoln Street, Boston, Massachusetts 02111 (617) 423-3990; *The World in Figures.*

The World Bank, 1818 H Street, NW, Washington, D.C. 20433 (202) 477-1234; *World Tables.*

GAMBIA - LABOR PRODUCTIVITY

International Labour Office, I.L.O. Publications, CH-1211, Geneva 22, Switzerland; *Yearbook of Labour Statistics.*

GAMBIA - LAND USE

Food and Agricultural Organization of the United Nations (FAO), Via delle Terme di Caracalla, 00100 Rome, Italy (Telephone Number in U.S. (202) 653-2400); *Production Yearbook.*

G.K. Hall and Company, 70 Lincoln Street, Boston, Massachusetts 02111 (617) 423-3990; *The World in Figures.*

GAMBIA - LIBRARIES

Facts on File, 460 Park Avenue South, New York, New York 10016 (800) 443-8323; *The New Book of World Rankings.*

United Nations Educational, Scientific and Cultural Organization (UNESCO), 7 Place de Fontenoy, F-75700 Paris, France (Telephone Number in U.S. (212) 963-5981); *Statistical Yearbook.*

GAMBIA - LIFE EXPECTANCY

African Development Bank, 01 BP 1387, Abidjan 01, Cote D'Ivoire; *Selected Statistics on Regional Member Countries.*

GAMBIA - LITERACY RATE

Statistical Office of the United Nations, Publishing Service, New York, New York 10017 (800) 253-9646; *Survey of Economic and Social Conditions in Africa.*

GAMBIA - LIVESTOCK AND POULTRY

Facts on File, 460 Park Avenue South, New York, New York 10016 (800) 443-8323; *The New Book of World Rankings.*

Food and Agricultural Organization of the United Nations (FAO), Via delle Terme di Caracalla, 00100 Rome, Italy (Telephone Number in U.S. (202) 653-2400); *Production Yearbook,* and *The State of Food and Agriculture.*

G.K. Hall and Company, 70 Lincoln Street, Boston, Massachusetts 02111 (617) 423-3990; *The World in Figures.*

Statistical Office of the United Nations, Publishing Service, New York, New York 10017 (800) 253-9646; *Statistical Yearbook,* and *Survey of Economic and Social Conditions in Africa.*

United Nations Economic Commission for Africa, Africa Hall, Post Office Box 3001, Addis Ababa, Ethiopia (Telephone Number in U.S. (800) 253-9646); *African Statistical Yearbook.*

GAMBIA - LIVING LEVELS

G.K. Hall and Company, 70 Lincoln Street, Boston, Massachusetts 02111 (617) 423-3990; *The World in Figures.*

GAMBIA - MANUFACTURING

Facts on File, 460 Park Avenue South, New York, New York 10016 (800) 443-8323; *The New Book of World Rankings.*

G.K. Hall and Company, 70 Lincoln Street, Boston, Massachusetts 02111 (617) 423-3990; *The World in Figures.*

Statistical Office of the United Nations, Publishing Service, New York, New York 10017 (800) 253-9646; *Survey of Economic and Social Conditions in Africa.*

United Nations Economic Commission for Africa, Africa Hall, Post Office Box 3001, Addis Ababa, Ethiopia (Telephone Number in U.S. (800) 253-9646); *African Statistical Yearbook.*

The World Bank, 1818 H Street, NW, Washington, D.C. 20433 (202) 477-1234; *World Tables.*

GAMBIA - MARRIAGE RATES

Facts on File, 460 Park Avenue South, New York, New York 10016 (800) 443-8323; *The New Book of World Rankings.*

Statistical Office of the United Nations, Publishing Service, New York, New York 10017 (800) 253-9646; *Demographic Yearbook.*

GAMBIA - MEAT PRODUCTION - See GAMBIA - LIVESTOCK AND POULTRY

GAMBIA - MERCHANT SHIPPING

G.K. Hall and Company, 70 Lincoln Street, Boston, Massachusetts 02111 (617) 423-3990; *The World in Figures.*

Statistical Office of the United Nations, Publishing Service, New York, New York 10017 (800) 253-9646; *Statistical Yearbook.*

United Nations Economic Commission for Africa, Africa Hall, Post Office Box 3001, Addis Ababa, Ethiopia (Telephone Number in U.S. (800) 253-9646); *African Statistical Yearbook.*

GAMBIA - MILITARY

G.K. Hall and Company, 70 Lincoln Street, Boston, Massachusetts 02111 (617) 423-3990; *The World in Figures.*

The International Institute for Strategic Studies, 23 Tavistock Street, London WC2E 7NQ, England; *The Military Balance.*

U.S. Arms Control and Disarmament Agency, 320 Twenty-first Street, Northwest, Washington, D.C. 20451 (202) 647-8677; *World Military Expenditures and Arms Transfers.*

GAMBIA - MILK PRODUCTION - See GAMBIA - DAIRY PRODUCTS

GAMBIA - MILLET PRODUCTION - See GAMBIA - CROPS

GAMBIA - MINING AND MINERAL PRODUCTS

Facts on File, 460 Park Avenue South, New York, New York 10016 (800) 443-8323; *The New Book of World Rankings.*

G.K. Hall and Company, 70 Lincoln Street, Boston, Massachusetts 02111 (617) 423-3990; *The World in Figures.*

United Nations Economic Commission for Africa, Africa Hall, Post Office Box 3001, Addis Ababa, Ethiopia (Telephone Number in U.S. (800) 253-9646); *African Statistical Yearbook.*

GAMBIA - MONEY EXCHANGE RATE

International Monetary Fund, 700 Nineteenth Street, NW, Washington, D.C. 20431 (202) 623-7000; *International Financial Statistics.*

Statistical Office of the United Nations, Publishing Service, New York, New York 10017 (800) 253-9646; *Statistical Yearbook.*

GAMBIA - MONEY SUPPLY

African Development Bank, 01 BP 1387, Abidjan 01, Cote D'Ivoire; *Selected Statistics on Regional Member Countries.*

Federal Statistical Office, Gustav - Stresemann - Ring 11, D-6200 Wiesbaden, Germany; *Gambia.*

G.K. Hall and Company, 70 Lincoln Street, Boston, Massachusetts 02111 (617) 423-3990; *The World in Figures.*

International Monetary Fund, 700 Nineteenth Street, NW, Washington, D.C. 20431 (202) 623-7000; *International Financial Statistics.*

Statistical Office of the United Nations, Publishing Service, New York, New York 10017 (800) 253-9646; *Statistical Yearbook.*

The World Bank, 1818 H Street, NW, Washington, D.C. 20433 (202) 477-1234; *World Tables.*

GAMBIA - MOTION PICTURES

Statistical Office of the United Nations, Publishing Service, New York, New York 10017 (800) 253-9646; *Statistical Yearbook.*

GAMBIA - MOTOR VEHICLE TAXES - See GAMBIA - TAXATION

GAMBIA - MOTOR VEHICLES IN USE

G.K. Hall and Company, 70 Lincoln Street, Boston, Massachusetts 02111 (617) 423-3990; *The World in Figures.*

Statistical Office of the United Nations, Publishing Service, New York, New York 10017 (800) 253-9646; *Statistical Yearbook,* and *Survey of Economic and Social Conditions in Africa.*

GAMBIA - MUSEUMS

Facts on File, 460 Park Avenue South, New York, New York 10016 (800) 443-8323; *The New Book of World Rankings.*

GAMBIA - NATALITY - See GAMBIA - BIRTH RATES

GAMBIA - NATIONAL ACCOUNTS

African Development Bank, 01 BP 1387, Abidjan 01, Cote D'Ivoire; *Selected Statistics on Regional Member Countries.*

Federal Statistical Office, Gustav - Stresemann - Ring 11, D-6200 Wiesbaden, Germany; *Gambia.*

International Monetary Fund, 700 Nineteenth Street, NW, Washington, D.C. 20431 (202) 623-7000; *International Financial Statistics.*

Statistical Office of the United Nations, Publishing Service, New York, New York 10017 (800) 253-9646; *Statistical Yearbook.*

United Nations Economic Commission for Africa, Africa Hall, Post Office Box 3001, Addis Ababa, Ethiopia (Telephone Number in U.S. (800) 253-9646); *African Statistical Yearbook.*

GAMBIA - NATIONAL INCOME

Facts on File, 460 Park Avenue South, New York, New York 10016 (800) 443-8323; *The New Book of World Rankings.*

G.K. Hall and Company, 70 Lincoln Street, Boston, Massachusetts 02111 (617) 423-3990; *The World in Figures.*

Statistical Office of the United Nations, Publishing Service, New York, New York 10017 (800) 253-9646; *Statistical Yearbook.*

GAMBIA - NATIONAL PRODUCT

Facts on File, 460 Park Avenue South, New York, New York 10016 (800) 443-8323; *The New Book of World Rankings.*

GAMBIA - NATURAL GAS PRODUCTION - See GAMBIA - MINING AND MINERAL PRODUCTS

GAMBIA - NEWSPAPER PRODUCTION - See GAMBIA - FORESTRY AND FOREST PRODUCTS

GAMBIA - OCCUPATIONS - See GAMBIA - LABOR FORCE

GAMBIA - PALM KERNELS AND PALM OIL PRODUCTION - See GAMBIA - CROPS

GAMBIA - PATENTS

World Intellectual Property Organization, 34 Chemin des Colombettes, CH-1211 Geneva 20, Switzerland; *Industrial Property Statistics.*

GAMBIA - PEANUT PRODUCTION - See GAMBIA - CROPS

GAMBIA - PERIODICALS

United Nations Educational, Scientific and Cultural Organization (UNESCO), 7 Place de Fontenoy, F-75700 Paris, France (Telephone Number in U.S. (212) 963-5981); *Statistical Yearbook.*

GAMBIA - PESTICIDE USE

Food and Agricultural Organization of the United Nations (FAO) Via delle Terme di Caracalla, 00100 Rome, Italy (Telephone Number in U.S. (202) 653-2400); *The State of Food and Agriculture.*

GAMBIA - PETROLEUM INDUSTRY

Facts on File, 460 Park Avenue South, New York, New York 10016 (800) 443-8323; *The New Book of World Rankings.*

Food and Agricultural Organization of the United Nations (FAO) Via delle Terme di Caracalla, 00100 Rome, Italy (Telephone Number in U.S. (202) 653-2400); *The State of Food and Agriculture.*

G.K. Hall and Company, 70 Lincoln Street, Boston, Massachusetts 02111 (617) 423-3990; *The World in Figures.*

GAMBIA - PIGS - See GAMBIA - LIVESTOCK AND POULTRY

GAMBIA - POPULATION

African Development Bank, 01 BP 1387, Abidjan 01, Cote D'Ivoire; *Selected Statistics on Regional Member Countries.*

The Economist Intelligence Unit, 111 West 57th Street, New York, New York 10019 (800) 938-4685; *The World Market Atlas.*

Facts on File, 460 Park Avenue South, New York, New York 10016 (800) 443-8323; *The New Book of World Rankings.*

Federal Statistical Office, Gustav - Stresemann - Ring 11, D-6200 Wiesbaden, Germany; *Gambia.*

Food and Agricultural Organization of the United Nations (FAO), Via delle Terme di Caracalla, 00100 Rome, Italy (Telephone Number in U.S. (202) 653-2400); *Production Yearbook.*

G.K. Hall and Company, 70 Lincoln Street, Boston, Massachusetts 02111 (617) 423-3990; *The World in Figures.*

International Labour Office, I.L.O. Publications, CH-1211, Geneva 22, Switzerland; *Yearbook of Labour Statistics.*

Statistical Office of the United Nations, Publishing Service, New York, New York 10017 (800) 253-9646; *Demographic Yearbook, Statistical Yearbook,* and *Survey of Economic and Social Conditions in Africa.*

U.S. Arms Control and Disarmament Agency, 320 Twenty-first Street, Northwest, Washington, D.C. 20451 (202) 647-8677; *World Military Expenditures and Arms Transfers.*

World Health Organization, Office of Publications, Avenue Appia, CH-1211 Geneva 27, Switzerland (Telephone Number in U.S. (518) 436-9686); *World Health Statistics Annual.*

GAMBIA - POST OFFICES

Facts on File, 460 Park Avenue South, New York, New York 10016 (800) 443-8323; *The New Book of World Rankings.*

GAMBIA - POTATO PRODUCTION - See GAMBIA - CROPS

GAMBIA - PRICES

Facts on File, 460 Park Avenue South, New York, New York 10016 (800) 443-8323; *The New Book of World Rankings.*

Federal Statistical Office, Gustav - Stresemann - Ring 11, D-6200 Wiesbaden, Germany; *Gambia.*

Food and Agricultural Organization of the United Nations (FAO), Via delle Terme di Caracalla, 00100 Rome, Italy (Telephone Number in U.S. (202) 653-2400); *Production Yearbook,* and *The State of Food and Agriculture.*

G.K. Hall and Company, 70 Lincoln Street, Boston, Massachusetts 02111 (617) 423-3990; *The World in Figures.*

International Labour Office, I.L.O. Publications, CH-1211, Geneva 22, Switzerland; *Yearbook of Labour Statistics.*

International Monetary Fund, 700 Nineteenth Street, NW, Washington, D.C. 20431 (202) 623-7000; *International Financial Statistics.*

United Nations Economic Commission for Africa, Africa Hall, Post Office Box 3001, Addis Ababa, Ethiopia (Telephone Number in U.S. (800) 253-9646); *African Statistical Yearbook.*

GAMBIA - PRODUCTION

Facts on File, 460 Park Avenue South, New York, New York 10016 (800) 443-8323; *The New Book of World Rankings.*

G.K. Hall and Company, 70 Lincoln Street, Boston, Massachusetts 02111 (617) 423-3990; *The World in Figures.*

GAMBIA - PROPERTY TAXES - See GAMBIA - TAXATION

GAMBIA - PUBLIC FINANCE

Facts on File, 460 Park Avenue South, New York, New York 10016 (800) 443-8323; *The New Book of World Rankings.*

Federal Statistical Office, Gustav - Stresemann - Ring 11, D-6200 Wiesbaden, Germany; *Gambia.*

GAMBIA - RADIO BROADCASTING - See GAMBIA - BROADCASTING

GAMBIA - RAILWAYS

G.K. Hall and Company, 70 Lincoln Street, Boston, Massachusetts 02111 (617) 423-3990; *The World in Figures.*

United Nations Economic Commission for Africa, Africa Hall, Post Office Box 3001, Addis Ababa, Ethiopia (Telephone Number in U.S. (800) 253-9646); *African Statistical Yearbook.*

GAMBIA - RELIGION

Facts on File, 460 Park Avenue South, New York, New York 10016 (800) 443-8323; *The New Book of World Rankings.*

GAMBIA - RENT TAXES

International Labour Office, I.L.O. Publications, CH-1211, Geneva 22, Switzerland; *Yearbook of Labour Statistics.*

GAMBIA - RETAIL TRADE

G.K. Hall and Company, 70 Lincoln Street, Boston, Massachusetts 02111 (617) 423-3990; *The World in Figures.*

GAMBIA - RICE PRODUCTION - See GAMBIA - CROPS

GAMBIA - ROOT AND TUBER PRODUCTION - See GAMBIA - CROPS

GAMBIA - ROUNDWOOD PRODUCTION - See GAMBIA - FORESTRY AND FOREST PRODUCTS

GAMBIA - RUBBER PRODUCTION

Facts on File, 460 Park Avenue South, New York, New York 10016 (800) 443-8323; *The New Book of World Rankings.*

GAMBIA - SAWNWOOD PRODUCTION - See GAMBIA - FORESTRY AND FOREST PRODUCTS

GAMBIA - SENIOR CITIZENS

Facts on File, 460 Park Avenue South, New York, New York 10016 (800) 443-8323; *The New Book of World Rankings.*

GAMBIA - SHEEP - See GAMBIA - LIVESTOCK AND POULTRY

GAMBIA - SILVER PRODUCTION AND CONSUMPTION - See GAMBIA - MINING AND MINERAL PRODUCTS

GAMBIA - SOCIAL DATA

African Development Bank, 01 BP 1387, Abidjan 01, Cote D'Ivoire; *Selected Statistics on Regional Member Countries.*

Facts on File, 460 Park Avenue South, New York, New York 10016 (800) 443-8323; *The New Book of World Rankings.*

G.K. Hall and Company, 70 Lincoln Street, Boston, Massachusetts 02111 (617) 423-3990; *The World in Figures.*

GAMBIA - SOCIAL SECURITY

International Monetary Fund, 700 Nineteenth Street, NW, Washington, D.C. 20431 (202) 623-7000; *Government Finance Statistics Yearbook.*

GAMBIA - STAMP TAXES AND DUTIES - See GAMBIA - TAXATION

GAMBIA - STEEL PRODUCTION - See GAMBIA - MINING AND MINERAL PRODUCTS

GAMBIA - STOCKS - COMMODITY - MARKET PRICE - INDEX

Food and Agricultural Organization of the United Nations (FAO) Via delle Terme di Caracalla, 00100 Rome, Italy (Telephone Number in U.S. (202) 653-2400); *The State of Food and Agriculture.*

GAMBIA - SUGAR PRODUCTION - See GAMBIA - CROPS

GAMBIA - TAXATION

G.K. Hall and Company, 70 Lincoln Street, Boston, Massachusetts 02111 (617) 423-3990; *The World in Figures.*

International Monetary Fund, 700 Nineteenth Street, NW, Washington, D.C. 20431 (202) 623-7000; *Government Finance Statistics Yearbook.*

The World Bank, 1818 H Street, NW, Washington, D.C. 20433 (202) 477-1234; *World Tables.*

GAMBIA - TELEPHONES IN USE

American Telephone and Telegraph Company, 26 Parsippany Road, Whippany, New Jersey 07981 (800) 338-4038; *The World's Telephones.*

G.K. Hall and Company, 70 Lincoln Street, Boston, Massachusetts 02111 (617) 423-3990; *The World in Figures.*

Statistical Office of the United Nations, Publishing Service, New York, New York 10017 (800) 253-9646; *Statistical Yearbook.*

GAMBIA - TELEVISION BROADCASTING - See GAMBIA - BROADCASTING

GAMBIA - TEXTILE INDUSTRY

G.K. Hall and Company, 70 Lincoln Street, Boston, Massachusetts 02111 (617) 423-3990; *The World in Figures.*

GAMBIA - TOBACCO PRODUCTION

Facts on File, 460 Park Avenue South, New York, New York 10016 (800) 443-8323; *The New Book of World Rankings.*

GAMBIA - TOURISM

Facts on File, 460 Park Avenue South, New York, New York 10016 (800) 443-8323; *The New Book of World Rankings.*

Federal Statistical Office, Gustav - Stresemann - Ring 11, D-6200 Wiesbaden, Germany; *Gambia.*

G.K. Hall and Company, 70 Lincoln Street, Boston, Massachusetts 02111 (617) 423-3990; *The World in Figures.*

Statistical Office of the United Nations, Publishing Service, New York, New York 10017 (800) 253-9646; *Statistical Yearbook.*

United Nations Economic Commission for Africa, Africa Hall, Post Office Box 3001, Addis Ababa, Ethiopia (Telephone Number in U.S. (800) 253-9646); *African Statistical Yearbook.*

GAMBIA - TRACTORS IN USE

Statistical Office of the United Nations, Publishing Service, New York, New York 10017 (800) 253-9646; *Statistical Yearbook.*

GAMBIA - TRADE - See GAMBIA - FOREIGN TRADE

GAMBIA - TRADEMARKS

World Intellectual Property Organization, 34 Chemin des Colombettes, CH-1211 Geneva 20, Switzerland; *Industrial Property Statistics.*

GAMBIA - TRANSPORTATION AND COMMUNICATIONS

Facts on File, 460 Park Avenue South, New York, New York 10016 (800) 443-8323; *The New Book of World Rankings.*

Federal Statistical Office, Gustav - Stresemann - Ring 11, D-6200 Wiesbaden, Germany; *Gambia.*

G.K. Hall and Company, 70 Lincoln Street, Boston, Massachusetts 02111 (617) 423-3990; *The World in Figures.*

United Nations Economic Commission for Africa, Africa Hall, Post Office Box 3001, Addis Ababa, Ethiopia (Telephone Number in U.S. (800) 253-9646); *African Statistical Yearbook.*

GAMBIA - UNEMPLOYMENT

International Labour Office, I.L.O. Publications, CH-1211, Geneva 22, Switzerland; *Yearbook of Labour Statistics.*

GAMBIA - VITAL STATISTICS

G.K. Hall and Company, 70 Lincoln Street, Boston, Massachusetts 02111 (617) 423-3990; *The World in Figures.*

Statistical Office of the United Nations, Publishing Service, New York, New York 10017 (800) 253-9646; *Statistical Yearbook.*

World Health Organization, Office of Publications, Avenue Appia, CH-1211 Geneva 27, Switzerland (Telephone Number in U.S. (518) 436-9686); *World Health Statistics Annual.*

GAMBIA - WAGES

Federal Statistical Office, Gustav - Stresemann - Ring 11, D-6200 Wiesbaden, Germany; *Gambia.*

G.K. Hall and Company, 70 Lincoln Street, Boston, Massachusetts 02111 (617) 423-3990; *The World in Figures.*

International Labour Office, I.L.O. Publications, CH-1211, Geneva 22, Switzerland; *Yearbook of Labour Statistics.*

GAMBIA - WEATHER

Facts on File, 460 Park Avenue South, New York, New York 10016 (800) 443-8323; *The New Book of World Rankings.*

G.K. Hall and Company, 70 Lincoln Street, Boston, Massachusetts 02111 (617) 423-3990; *The World in Figures.*

GAMBIA - WELFARE

International Monetary Fund, 700 Nineteenth Street, NW, Washington, D.C. 20431 (202) 623-7000; *Government Finance Statistics Yearbook.*

GAMBIA - WHEAT PRODUCTION AND PRICES - See GAMBIA - CROPS

GAMBIA - WINE PRODUCTION

Facts on File, 460 Park Avenue South, New York, New York 10016 (800) 443-8323; *The New Book of World Rankings.*

GAMBIA - WOOL PRODUCTION

Facts on File, 460 Park Avenue South, New York, New York 10016 (800) 443-8323; *The New Book of World Rankings.*

GAMBLING - ARRESTS

U.S. Department of Justice, Federal Bureau of Investigation, Ninth Street and Pennsylvania Avenue, NW, Washington, D.C. 20535 (202) 324-3000; *Crime in the United States.*

GARAGES - See GASOLINE SERVICE STATIONS and AUTOMOTIVE REPAIR, SERVICES, AND PARKING

GARDEN SUPPLIES - See BUILDING MATERIALS AND GARDEN SUPPLIES

GARDENS - ACTIVITIES

National Gardening Association, 180 Flynn Avenue, Burlington, Vermont 05401 (802) 863-1308; *National Gardening Survey.*

GARNET (ABRASIVE) - PRODUCTION AND VALUE

U.S. Department of the Interior, Bureau of Mines, 810 Seventh Street, NW, Washington, D.C. 20241 (202) 501-9649; *Annual Reports,* and *Mineral Commodity Summaries.*

GARNET - INDUSTRIAL

U.S. Department of the Interior, Bureau of Mines, 810 Seventh Street, NW, Washington, D.C. 20241 (202) 501-9649; *Mineral Commodity Summaries.*

GAS - See also PETROLEUM AND GAS WELLS and GAS UTILITY INDUSTRY

GAS - LIQUIFIED PETROLEUM GASES

U.S. Department of Energy, Energy Information Administration, Washington, D.C. 20585 (202) 586-880; *Petroleum Supply Annual.*

GAS - NATURAL

American Petroleum Institute, 1220 L Street, NW, Washington, D.C. 20005 (202) 682-8000; *Joint Association Survey of Drilling Costs.*

U.S. Department of Commerce, Bureau of the Census, Suitland, Maryland 20233 (301) 763-4040; *Census of Mineral Industries.*

U.S. Department of Energy, Energy Information Administration, Washington, D.C. 20585 (202) 586-8800; *Annual Energy Review, State Energy Price and Expenditure Report, Natural Gas Monthly Report, Monthly Energy Review, International Energy Annual, Statistics of Interstate Natural Gas Pipeline Companies, Natural Gas Annual,* and *U.S. Crude Oil, Natural Gas, and Natural Gas Liquids Reserves.*

U.S. Department of Labor, Bureau of Labor Statistics, Two Massachusetts Avenue, NE, Washington, D.C. 20212 (202) 606-7828; *Employment and Earnings,* and Bulletin 2370.

GAS - NATURAL - CONSUMPTION

U.S. Department of Energy, Energy Information Administration, Washington, D.C. 20585 (202) 586-8800; *Monthly Energy Review, State Energy Data Report, Annual Energy Review, Household Energy Consumption and Expenditures, International Energy Annual, Natural Gas Annual,* and *U.S. Crude Oil, Natural Gas, and Natural Gas Liquids Reserves.*

GAS - NATURAL - DRILLING COSTS

American Petroleum Institute, 1220 L Street, NW, Washington, D.C. 20005 (202) 682-8000; *Joint Association Survey on Drilling Costs.*

GAS - NATURAL - ENERGY EXPENDITURES

U.S. Department of Energy, Energy Information Administration, Washington, D.C. 20585 (202) 586-8800; *State Energy Price and Expenditure Report,* and *Household Energy Consumption and Expenditures.*

GAS - NATURAL - FOREIGN TRADE

U.S. Department of Commerce, Bureau of the Census, Suitland, Maryland 20233 (301) 763-4040; *U.S. Merchandise Trade.*

U.S. Department of Energy, Energy Information Administration, 1000 Independence Avenue, SW, Washington, D.C. 20585 (202) 586-8800; *Annual Energy Review.*

GAS - NATURAL - OFFSHORE LEASE REVENUES

U.S. Department of Energy, Energy Information Administration, Washington, D.C. 20585 (202) 586-8800; *Petroleum Supply Annual.*

GAS - NATURAL - PRICES

U.S. Department of Energy, Energy Information Administration, Washington, D.C. 20585 (202) 586-8800; *Annual Energy Review, International Energy Annual,* and *Monthly Energy Review.*

U.S. Department of the Interior, Bureau of Mines, 810 Seventh Street, NW, Washington, D.C. 20241 (202) 501-9649; *Mineral Commodity Summaries.*

GAS - NATURAL - PRODUCTION AND VALUE

U.S. Department of Energy, Energy Information Administration, Washington, D.C. 20585 (202) 586-8800; *Natural Gas Annual, Annual Energy Review, International Energy Annual, Natural Gas Monthly Report, Monthly Energy Review, Petroleum Supply Annual, U.S. Crude Oil, Natural Gas, and Natural Gas Liquids Reserves,* and unpublished data.

GAS - NATURAL - PRODUCTION AND VALUE - FOREIGN COUNTRIES

Statistical Office of the United Nations, Publishing Service, New York, New York 10017 (800) 253-9646; *Energy Statistics Yearbook.*

U.S. Department of the Interior, Bureau of Mines, 810 Seventh Street, NW, Washington, D.C. 20241 (202) 501-9649; *Mineral Commodity Summaries.*

GAS - NATURAL - PRODUCTION AND VALUE - INDEXES

Board of Governors of the Federal Reserve System, Twentieth Street and Constitution Avenue, NW, Washington, D.C. 20551 (202) 452-3000; *Federal Reserve Bulletin.*

GAS - NATURAL - RESERVES

U.S. Department of Energy, Energy Information Administration, Washington, D.C. 20585 (202) 586-8800; *Annual Energy Review, International Energy Annual, Monthly Energy Review,* and *Natural Gas Annual.*

GAS - NATURAL - RESIDENTIAL

U.S. Department of Energy, Energy Information Administration, Washington, D.C. 20585 (202) 586-8800; *Household Energy Consumption and Expenditures.*

GAS - NATURAL GAS PLANT LIQUIDS

U.S. Department of the Interior, Bureau of Mines, 810 Seventh Street, NW, Washington, D.C. 20241 (202) 501-9649; *Energy Data Reports, Natural Gas Annual, Natural Gas Monthly,* and *Petroleum Supply Annual.*

GAS - PRICE INDEXES

U.S. Department of Commerce, Bureau of Economic Analysis, Fourteenth Street between Constitution Avenue and E Street, NW, Washington, D.C. 20230 (202) 606-9900; *Survey of Current Business,* and *The National Income and Product Accounts of the United States.*

GAS - PRODUCTION AND DISTRIBUTION

U.S. Department of Labor, Bureau of Labor Statistics, Two Massachusetts Avenue, NE, Washington, D.C. 20212 (202) 606-7828; *Employment and Earnings,* and Bulletins 2370 and 2429.

GAS AND ELECTRIC UTILITIES - See ELECTRIC, GAS AND SANITARY SERVICES

GAS UTILITY INDUSTRY - ACCIDENTS AND DEATHS

U.S. Department of Transportation, Bureau of Transportation Statistics, 400 Seventh Street, SW, Washington, D.C. 20590 (202) 366-DATA; *National Transportation Statistics Annual, Historical Compendium Information Report.*

GAS UTILITY INDUSTRY - CUSTOMERS

American Gas Association, Incorporated, 1515 Wilson Boulevard, Arlington, Virginia 22209 (703) 841-8400; *Gas Facts.*

GAS UTILITY INDUSTRY - FINANCES

American Gas Association, Incorporated, 1515 Wilson Boulevard, Arlington, Virginia 22209 (703) 841-8400; *Gas Facts.*

U.S. Department of Energy, Energy Information Administration, Washington, D.C. 20585 (202) 586-8800; *Statistics of Interstate Natural Gas Pipeline Companies.*

GAS UTILITY INDUSTRY - MAINS - MILEAGE

U.S. Department of Energy, Energy Information Administration, Washington, D.C. 20585 (202) 586-8800; *Statistics of Interstate Natural Gas Pipeline Companies.*

GAS UTILITY INDUSTRY - REVENUES

American Gas Association, Incorporated, 1515 Wilson Boulevard, Arlington, Virginia 22209 (703) 841-8400; *Gas Facts.*

GAS UTILITY INDUSTRY - SALES

American Gas Association, Incorporated, 1515 Wilson Boulevard, Arlington, Virginia 22209 (703) 841-8400; *Gas Facts.*

GASOLINE - See also MOTOR FUEL

GASOLINE - BLENDING COMPONENTS

U.S. Department of Energy, Energy Information Administration, 1000 Independence Avenue, SW, Washington, D.C. 20585 (202) 586-8800; *Petroleum Supply Annual, U.S. Crude Oil, Natural Gas, and Natural Gas Liquids Reserves,* and *Annual Energy Review.*

GASOLINE - EXCISE TAXES

U.S. Department of Commerce, Bureau of the Census, Suitland, Maryland 20233 (301) 763-4040; *State Government Tax Collections.*

U.S. Department of Energy, Energy Information Administration, 1000 Independence Avenue, SW, Washington, D.C. 20585 (202) 586-8800; *Petroleum Marketing Monthly.*

U.S. Department of Transportation, Federal Highway Administration, 400 Seventh Street, SW, Washington, D.C. 20590 (202) 366-0660; *Highway Statistics.*

GASOLINE - FINISHED MOTOR GASOLINE

U.S. Department of Energy, Energy Information Administration, 1000 Independence Avenue, SW, Washington, D.C. 20585 (202) 586-8800; *Petroleum Supply Annual,* and *Annual Energy Review.*

GASOLINE - PRICE INDEXES - FIXED WEIGHTED

U.S. Department of Commerce, Bureau of Economic Analysis, Fourteenth Street between Constitution Avenue and E Street, NW, Washington, D.C. 20230 (202) 606-9900; *Survey of Current Business,* and *The National Income and Product Accounts of the United States.*

GASOLINE - PRICES

U.S. Department of Energy, Energy Information Administration, 1000 Independence Avenue, SW, Washington, D.C. 20585 (202) 586-8800; *Petroleum Marketing Monthly,* and *International Energy Annual.*

GASOLINE - SUPPLY

U.S. Department of Energy, Energy Information Administration, 1000 Independence Avenue, SW, Washington, D.C. 20585 (202) 586-8800; *Monthly Energy Review.*

GASOLINE SERVICE STATIONS - RETAIL - EARNINGS

U.S. Department of Commerce, Bureau of the Census, Suitland, Maryland 20233 (301) 763-4040; *Census of Retail Trade,* and *County Business Patterns.*

GASOLINE SERVICE STATIONS - RETAIL - EMPLOYEES

U.S. Department of Commerce, Bureau of the Census, Suitland, Maryland 20233 (301) 763-4040; *Census of Retail Trade,* and *County Business Patterns.*

GASOLINE SERVICE STATIONS - RETAIL - ESTABLISHMENTS

International Franchise Association, 1350 New York Avenue, Suite 900, Washington, D.C. 20005 (202) 628-8000; *Franchising in the Economy.*

U.S. Department of Commerce, Bureau of the Census, Suitland, Maryland 20233 (301) 763-4040; *County Business Patterns,* and *Census of Retail Trade.*

GASOLINE SERVICE STATIONS - RETAIL - PRODUCTIVITY

U.S. Department of Labor, Bureau of Labor Statistics, Two Massachusetts Avenue, NE, Washington, D.C. 20212 (202) 606-7828; *Productivity Measures for Selected Industries and Government Services,* and unpublished data.

GASOLINE SERVICE STATIONS - RETAIL - SALES

Market Statistics, 633 Third Avenue, New York, New York 10017 (212) 986-4000; *The Survey of Buying Power Data Service.*

U.S. Department of Commerce, Bureau of the Census, Suitland, Maryland 20233 (301) 763-4040; *Census of Retail Trade, Current Business Reports, Combined Annual and Revised Monthly Retail Trade,* and unpublished data.

International Franchise Association, 1350 New York Avenue, Suite 900, Washington, D.C. 20005 (202) 628-8000; *Franchising in the Economy.*

GAZA STRIP - See PALESTINE

GEM STONES

U.S. Department of the Interior, Bureau of Mines, 810 Seventh Street, NW, Washington, D.C. 20241 (202) 501-9649; *Annual Reports,* and *Mineral Commodity Summaries.*

GENERAL MERCHANDISE STORES - EARNINGS

U.S. Department of Commerce, Bureau of the Census, Suitland, Maryland 20233 (301) 763-4040; *Census of Retail Trade,* and *County Business Patterns.*

U.S. Department of Labor, Bureau of Labor Statistics, Two Massachusetts Avenue, NE, Washington, D.C. 20212 (202) 606-7828; *Employment and Earnings,* and Bulletins 2370 and 2429.

GENERAL MERCHANDISE STORES - EMPLOYEES

U.S. Department of Commerce, Bureau of the Census, Suitland, Maryland 20233 (301) 763-4040; *Census of Retail Trade,* and *County Business Patterns.*

U.S. Department of Labor, Bureau of Labor Statistics, Two Massachusetts Avenue, NE, Washington, D.C. 20212 (202) 606-7828; *Employment and Earnings,* and Bulletins 2370 and 2429.

GENERAL MERCHANDISE STORES - ESTABLISHMENTS

U.S. Department of Commerce, Bureau of the Census, Suitland, Maryland 20233 (301) 763-4040; *County Business Patterns,* and *Census of Retail Trade.*

GENERAL MERCHANDISE STORES - INVENTORIES

U.S. Department of Commerce, Bureau of the Census, Suitland, Maryland 20233 (301) 763-4040; *Current Business Reports, Combined Annual and Revised Monthly Retail Trade.*

GENERAL MERCHANDISE STORES - PRODUCTIVITY

U.S. Department of Labor, Bureau of Labor Statistics, Two Massachusetts Avenue, NE, Washington, D.C. 20212 (202) 606-7828; *Productivity Measures for Selected Industries and Government Services,* and unpublished data.

GENERAL MERCHANDISE STORES - SALES

Market Statistics, 633 Third Avenue, New York, New York 10017 (212) 986-4000; *The Survey of Buying Power Data Service.*

U.S. Department of Commerce, Bureau of the Census, Suitland, Maryland 20233 (301) 763-4040; *Current Business Reports, Combined Annual and Revised Monthly Retail Trade,* and *County Business Patterns.*

GEOGRAPHY AND CARTOGRAPHY - See LAND

GEORGIA - See also STATE DATA (FOR INDIVIDUAL STATES)

Georgia - Primary Statistics Sources

College of Agriculture and Environmental Sciences, Cooperative Extension Service, University of Georgia, Athens, Georgia 30602 (404) 542-8938; *The Georgia County Guide.*

Selig Center for Economic Growth, Terry College of Business, University of Georgia, Athens, Georgia 30602 (404) 542-4085; *Georgia Statistical Abstract.*

Office of Planning and Budget, 254 Washington Street, SW, Atlanta, Georgia 30334 (404) 656-0911; *Georgia Descriptions in Data.*

Georgia - State Data Centers

Data Services, University of Georgia Libraries, Sixth Floor, Athens, Georgia 30602, Dr. Hortense Bates (404) 542-0727.

Division of Demographic and Statistical Services, Georgia Office of Planning and Budget, 254 Washington Street, SW, Room 640, Atlanta, Georgia 30334, Ms. Marty Sik (404) 656-0911.

Office of Coordinated Planning, Georgia Department of Community Affairs, 100 Peachtree Street, NE, Suite 1200, Atlanta, Georgia 30303, Keith Nelms (404) 656-3879.

GEORGIA - See also UNION OF SOVIET SOCIALIST REPUBLICS

GEORGIA - AGRICULTURE

Business International Moscow, 23 Profseyuznaya Ulitsa 117859, Moscow (Telephone Number in U.S. (800) 938-4685); *The CIS Market Atlas.*

Encyclopedia Britannica, Incorporated, 310 South Michigan Avenue, Chicago, Illinois 60604 (312) 347-7000; *Britannica World Data.*

The World Bank, 1818 H Street, Northwest, Washington, D.C. 20433 (202) 477-1234; *Statistical Handbook: States of the Former USSR.*

GEORGIA - AIRLINE SERVICE

Business International Moscow, 23 Profseyuznaya Ulitsa 117859, Moscow (Telephone Number in U.S. (800) 938-4685); *The CIS Market Atlas.*

Encyclopedia Britannica, Incorporated, 310 South Michigan Avenue, Chicago, Illinois 60604 (312) 347-7000; *Britannica World Data.*

GEORGIA - AREA AND DENSITY OF POPULATION

Business International Moscow, 23 Profseyuznaya Ulitsa 117859, Moscow (Telephone Number in U.S. (800) 938-4685); *The CIS Market Atlas.*

GEORGIA - BANKING

Business International Moscow, 23 Profseyuznaya Ulitsa 117859, Moscow (Telephone Number in U.S. (800) 938-4685); *The CIS Market Atlas.*

GEORGIA - BIRTH RATES

Business International Moscow, 23 Profseyuznaya Ulitsa 117859, Moscow (Telephone Number in U.S. (800) 938-4685); *The CIS Market Atlas.*

Encyclopedia Britannica, Incorporated, 310 South Michigan Avenue, Chicago, Illinois 60604 (312) 347-7000; *Britannica World Data.*

GEORGIA - BUDGET

Business International Moscow, 23 Profseyuznaya Ulitsa 117859, Moscow (Telephone Number in U.S. (800) 938-4685); *The CIS Market Atlas.*

GEORGIA - CAPITAL INVESTMENT

The World Bank, 1818 H Street, Northwest, Washington, D.C. 20433 (202) 477-1234; *Statistical Handbook: States of the Former USSR.*

GEORGIA - CATTLE - See GEORGIA - LIVESTOCK AND POULTRY

GEORGIA - COAL PRODUCTION AND CONSUMPTION - See GEORGIA - MINING AND MINERAL PRODUCTS

GEORGIA - COMMUNICATIONS

Business International Moscow, 23 Profseyuznaya Ulitsa 117859, Moscow (Telephone Number in U.S. (800) 938-4685); *The CIS Market Atlas.*

GEORGIA - CONSTRUCTION INDUSTRY

Business International Moscow, 23 Profseyuznaya Ulitsa 117859, Moscow (Telephone Number in U.S. (800) 938-4685); *The CIS Market Atlas.*

Encyclopedia Britannica, Incorporated, 310 South Michigan Avenue, Chicago, Illinois 60604 (312) 347-7000; *Britannica World Data.*

GEORGIA - CONSUMER PRODUCTS

Business International Moscow, 23 Profseyuznaya Ulitsa 117859, Moscow (Telephone Number in U.S. (800) 938-4685); *The CIS Market Atlas.*

GEORGIA - CONSUMPTION

Business International Moscow, 23 Profseyuznaya Ulitsa 117859, Moscow (Telephone Number in U.S. (800) 938-4685); *The CIS Market Atlas.*

The World Bank, 1818 H Street, Northwest, Washington, D.C. 20433 (202) 477-1234; *Statistical Handbook: States of the Former USSR.*

GEORGIA - COTTON PRODUCTION AND CONSUMPTION - See GEORGIA - TEXTILE INDUSTRY

GEORGIA - CROPS

The World Bank, 1818 H Street, Northwest, Washington, D.C. 20433 (202) 477-1234; *Statistical Handbook: States of the Former USSR.*

GEORGIA - DEATH RATES

Business International Moscow, 23 Profseyuznaya Ulitsa 117859, Moscow (Telephone Number in U.S. (800) 938-4685); *The CIS Market Atlas.*

GEORGIA - DEMOGRAPHY

Business International Moscow, 23 Profseyuznaya Ulitsa 117859, Moscow (Telephone Number in U.S. (800) 938-4685); *The CIS Market Atlas.*

Encyclopedia Britannica, Incorporated, 310 South Michigan Avenue, Chicago, Illinois 60604 (312) 347-7000; *Britannica World Data.*

The World Bank, 1818 H Street, Northwest, Washington, D.C. 20433 (202) 477-1234; *Statistical Handbook: States of the Former USSR.*

GEORGIA - DISEASES

Business International Moscow, 23 Profseyuznaya Ulitsa 117859, Moscow (Telephone Number in U.S. (800) 938-4685); *The CIS Market Atlas.*

GEORGIA - DIVORCE RATES

Encyclopedia Britannica, Incorporated, 310 South Michigan Avenue, Chicago, Illinois 60604 (312) 347-7000; *Britannica World Data.*

GEORGIA - DOMESTIC INVESTMENT

Business International Moscow, 23 Profseyuznaya Ulitsa 117859, Moscow (Telephone Number in U.S. (800) 938-4685); *The CIS Market Atlas.*

GEORGIA - ECONOMY

Business International Moscow, 23 Profseyuznaya Ulitsa 117859, Moscow (Telephone Number in U.S. (800) 938-4685); *The CIS Market Atlas.*

Encyclopedia Britannica, Incorporated, 310 South Michigan Avenue, Chicago, Illinois 60604 (312) 347-7000; *Britannica World Data.*

GEORGIA - EDUCATION

Business International Moscow, 23 Profseyuznaya Ulitsa 117859, Moscow (Telephone Number in U.S. (800) 938-4685); *The CIS Market Atlas.*

Encyclopedia Britannica, Incorporated, 310 South Michigan Avenue, Chicago, Illinois 60604 (312) 347-7000; *Britannica World Data.*

GEORGIA - ELECTRICITY PRODUCTION

Business International Moscow, 23 Profseyuznaya Ulitsa 117859, Moscow (Telephone Number in U.S. (800) 938-4685); *The CIS Market Atlas.*

The World Bank, 1818 H Street, Northwest, Washington, D.C. 20433 (202) 477-1234; *Statistical Handbook: States of the Former USSR.*

GEORGIA - EMPLOYMENT

The World Bank, 1818 H Street, Northwest, Washington, D.C. 20433 (202) 477-1234; *Statistical Handbook: States of the Former USSR.*

GEORGIA - ENERGY

Business International Moscow, 23 Profseyuznaya Ulitsa 117859, Moscow (Telephone Number in U.S. (800) 938-4685); *The CIS Market Atlas.*

Encyclopedia Britannica, Incorporated, 310 South Michigan Avenue, Chicago, Illinois 60604 (312) 347-7000; *Britannica World Data.*

The World Bank, 1818 H Street, Northwest, Washington, D.C. 20433 (202) 477-1234; *Statistical Handbook: States of the Former USSR.*

GEORGIA - ENVIRONMENT

Business International Moscow, 23 Profseyuznaya Ulitsa 117859, Moscow (Telephone Number in U.S. (800) 938-4685); *The CIS Market Atlas.*

GEORGIA - EXPORTS

Business International Moscow, 23 Profseyuznaya Ulitsa 117859, Moscow (Telephone Number in U.S. (800) 938-4685); *The CIS Market Atlas.*

Encyclopedia Britannica, Incorporated, 310 South Michigan Avenue, Chicago, Illinois 60604 (312) 347-7000; *Britannica World Data.*

The World Bank, 1818 H Street, Northwest, Washington, D.C. 20433 (202) 477-1234; *Statistical Handbook: States of the Former USSR.*

GEORGIA - EXTERNAL TRADE

The World Bank, 1818 H Street, Northwest, Washington, D.C. 20433 (202) 477-1234; *Statistical Handbook: States of the Former USSR.*

GEORGIA - FABRIC PRODUCTION AND CONSUMPTION - See GEORGIA - TEXTILE INDUSTRY

GEORGIA - FERTILITY RATES

Encyclopedia Britannica, Incorporated, 310 South Michigan Avenue, Chicago, Illinois 60604 (312) 347-7000; *Britannica World Data.*

The World Bank, 1818 H Street, Northwest, Washington, D.C. 20433 (202) 477-1234; *Statistical Handbook: States of the Former USSR.*

GEORGIA - FISHERIES

Encyclopedia Britannica, Incorporated, 310 South Michigan Avenue, Chicago, Illinois 60604 (312) 347-7000; *Britannica World Data.*

GEORGIA - FOOTWEAR PRODUCTION AND CONSUMPTION - See GEORGIA - TEXTILE INDUSTRY

GEORGIA - FOREIGN INVESTMENT

Business International Moscow, 23 Profseyuznaya Ulitsa 117859, Moscow (Telephone Number in U.S. (800) 938-4685); *The CIS Market Atlas.*

GEORGIA - FOREIGN TRADE

Business International Moscow, 23 Profseyuznaya Ulitsa 117859, Moscow (Telephone Number in U.S. (800) 938-4685); *The CIS Market Atlas.*

Encyclopedia Britannica, Incorporated, 310 South Michigan Avenue, Chicago, Illinois 60604 (312) 347-7000; *Britannica World Data.*

The World Bank, 1818 H Street, Northwest, Washington, D.C. 20433 (202) 477-1234; *Statistical Handbook: States of the Former USSR.*

GEORGIA - FORESTRY AND FOREST PRODUCTS

Business International Moscow, 23 Profseyuznaya Ulitsa 117859, Moscow (Telephone Number in U.S. (800) 938-4685); *The CIS Market Atlas.*

Encyclopedia Britannica, Incorporated, 310 South Michigan Avenue, Chicago, Illinois 60604 (312) 347-7000; *Britannica World Data.*

GEORGIA - GOATS - See GEORGIA - LIVESTOCK AND POULTRY

GEORGIA - GOVERNMENT EXPENDITURE

The World Bank, 1818 H Street, Northwest, Washington, D.C. 20433 (202) 477-1234; *Statistical Handbook: States of the Former USSR.*

GEORGIA - GOVERNMENT REVENUE

The World Bank, 1818 H Street, Northwest, Washington, D.C. 20433 (202) 477-1234; *Statistical Handbook: States of the Former USSR.*

GEORGIA - GROSS DOMESTIC PRODUCT

The World Bank, 1818 H Street, Northwest, Washington, D.C. 20433 (202) 477-1234; *Statistical Handbook: States of the Former USSR.*

GEORGIA - HEALTH

Business International Moscow, 23 Profseyuznaya Ulitsa 117859, Moscow (Telephone Number in U.S. (800) 938-4685); *The CIS Market Atlas.*

Encyclopedia Britannica, Incorporated, 310 South Michigan Avenue, Chicago, Illinois 60604 (312) 347-7000; *Britannica World Data.*

GEORGIA - HIGHWAYS

Business International Moscow, 23 Profseyuznaya Ulitsa 117859, Moscow (Telephone Number in U.S. (800) 938-4685); *The CIS Market Atlas.*

Encyclopedia Britannica, Incorporated, 310 South Michigan Avenue, Chicago, Illinois 60604 (312) 347-7000; *Britannica World Data.*

GEORGIA - HOUSING AND HOUSING UNITS

Business International Moscow, 23 Profseyuznaya Ulitsa 117859, Moscow (Telephone Number in U.S. (800) 938-4685); *The CIS Market Atlas.*

GEORGIA - IMPORTS

Business International Moscow, 23 Profseyuznaya Ulitsa 117859, Moscow (Telephone Number in U.S. (800) 938-4685); *The CIS Market Atlas.*

Encyclopedia Britannica, Incorporated, 310 South Michigan Avenue, Chicago, Illinois 60604 (312) 347-7000; *Britannica World Data.*

The World Bank, 1818 H Street, Northwest, Washington, D.C. 20433 (202) 477-1234; *Statistical Handbook: States of the Former USSR.*

GEORGIA - INDUSTRY

Business International Moscow, 23 Profseyuznaya Ulitsa 117859, Moscow (Telephone Number in U.S. (800) 938-4685); *The CIS Market Atlas.*

The World Bank, 1818 H Street, Northwest, Washington, D.C. 20433 (202) 477-1234; *Statistical Handbook: States of the Former USSR.*

GEORGIA - INFANT MORTALITY RATES

Business International Moscow, 23 Profseyuznaya Ulitsa 117859, Moscow (Telephone Number in U.S. (800) 938-4685); *The CIS Market Atlas.*

GEORGIA - LABOR

Business International Moscow, 23 Profseyuznaya Ulitsa 117859, Moscow (Telephone Number in U.S. (800) 938-4685); *The CIS Market Atlas.*

GEORGIA - LABOR FORCE

The World Bank, 1818 H Street, Northwest, Washington, D.C. 20433 (202) 477-1234; *Statistical Handbook: States of the Former USSR.*

GEORGIA - LAND USE

Encyclopedia Britannica, Incorporated, 310 South Michigan Avenue, Chicago, Illinois 60604 (312) 347-7000; *Britannica World Data.*

GEORGIA - LIFE EXPECTANCY

Business International Moscow, 23 Profseyuznaya Ulitsa 117859, Moscow (Telephone Number in U.S. (800) 938-4685); *The CIS Market Atlas.*

GEORGIA - LIVESTOCK AND POULTRY

Business International Moscow, 23 Profseyuznaya Ulitsa 117859, Moscow (Telephone Number in U.S. (800) 938-4685); *The CIS Market Atlas.*

Encyclopedia Britannica, Incorporated, 310 South Michigan Avenue, Chicago, Illinois 60604 (312) 347-7000; *Britannica World Data.*

GEORGIA - MANUFACTURING

Encyclopedia Britannica, Incorporated, 310 South Michigan Avenue, Chicago, Illinois 60604 (312) 347-7000; *Britannica World Data.*

GEORGIA - MARRIAGE RATES

Encyclopedia Britannica, Incorporated, 310 South Michigan Avenue, Chicago, Illinois 60604 (312) 347-7000; *Britannica World Data.*

GEORGIA - MEAT PRODUCTION

Business International Moscow, 23 Profseyuznaya Ulitsa 117859, Moscow (Telephone Number in U.S. (800) 938-4685); *The CIS Market Atlas.*

GEORGIA - MILITARY

The International Institute for Strategic Studies, 23 Tavistock Street, London WC2E 7NQ, England; *The Military Balance.*

GEORGIA - MINING AND MINERAL PRODUCTS

Business International Moscow, 23 Profseyuznaya Ulitsa 117859, Moscow (Telephone Number in U.S. (800) 938-4685); *The CIS Market Atlas.*

Encyclopedia Britannica, Incorporated, 310 South Michigan Avenue, Chicago, Illinois 60604 (312) 347-7000; *Britannica World Data.*

GEORGIA - MOTOR VEHICLES

Business International Moscow, 23 Profseyuznaya Ulitsa 117859, Moscow (Telephone Number in U.S. (800) 938-4685); *The CIS Market Atlas.*

GEORGIA - NATIONAL ACCOUNTS

The World Bank, 1818 H Street, Northwest, Washington, D.C. 20433 (202) 477-1234; *Statistical Handbook: States of the Former USSR.*

GEORGIA - NATIONAL INCOME

Business International Moscow, 23 Profseyuznaya Ulitsa 117859, Moscow (Telephone Number in U.S. (800) 938-4685); *The CIS Market Atlas.*

GEORGIA - PIGS - See GEORGIA - LIVESTOCK AND POULTRY

GEORGIA - POPULATION

Business International Moscow, 23 Profseyuznaya Ulitsa 117859, Moscow (Telephone Number in U.S. (800) 938-4685); *The CIS Market Atlas.*

Encyclopedia Britannica, Incorporated, 310 South Michigan Avenue, Chicago, Illinois 60604 (312) 347-7000; *Britannica World Data.*

The World Bank, 1818 H Street, Northwest, Washington, D.C. 20433 (202) 477-1234; *Statistical Handbook: States of the Former USSR.*

GEORGIA - POULTRY - See GEORGIA - LIVESTOCK AND POULTRY

GEORGIA - PRICES

The World Bank, 1818 H Street, Northwest, Washington, D.C. 20433 (202) 477-1234; *Statistical Handbook: States of the Former USSR.*

GEORGIA - PRODUCTION

The World Bank, 1818 H Street, Northwest, Washington, D.C. 20433 (202) 477-1234; *Statistical Handbook: States of the Former USSR.*

GEORGIA - PUBLIC FINANCE

The World Bank, 1818 H Street, Northwest, Washington, D.C. 20433 (202) 477-1234; *Statistical Handbook: States of the Former USSR.*

GEORGIA - RADIO RECEIVERS

Encyclopedia Britannica, Incorporated, 310 South Michigan Avenue, Chicago, Illinois 60604 (312) 347-7000; *Britannica World Data.*

GEORGIA - RAILWAYS

Business International Moscow, 23 Profseyuznaya Ulitsa 117859, Moscow (Telephone Number in U.S. (800) 938-4685); *The CIS Market Atlas.*

Encyclopedia Britannica, Incorporated, 310 South Michigan Avenue, Chicago, Illinois 60604 (312) 347-7000; *Britannica World Data.*

GEORGIA - RETAIL TRADE

Business International Moscow, 23 Profseyuznaya Ulitsa 117859, Moscow (Telephone Number in U.S. (800) 938-4685); *The CIS*

Market Atlas.

GEORGIA - ROADS - See GEORGIA - HIGHWAYS

GEORGIA - ROUNDWOOD PRODUCTION AND CONSUMPTION - See GEORGIA - FORESTRY AND FOREST PRODUCTS

GEORGIA - SHEEP - See GEORGIA - LIVESTOCK AND POULTRY

GEORGIA - STEEL PRODUCTION AND CONSUMPTION - See GEORGIA - MINING AND MINERAL PRODUCTS

GEORGIA - TELEPHONES IN USE

Encyclopedia Britannica, Incorporated, 310 South Michigan Avenue, Chicago, Illinois 60604 (312) 347-7000; *Britannica World Data.*

GEORGIA - TELEVISION RECEIVERS

Encyclopedia Britannica, Incorporated, 310 South Michigan Avenue, Chicago, Illinois 60604 (312) 347-7000; *Britannica World Data.*

GEORGIA - TEXTILE INDUSTRY

Business International Moscow, 23 Profseyuznaya Ulitsa 117859, Moscow (Telephone Number in U.S. (800) 938-4685); *The CIS Market Atlas.*

GEORGIA - TOURISM

Business International Moscow, 23 Profseyuznaya Ulitsa 117859, Moscow (Telephone Number in U.S. (800) 938-4685); *The CIS Market Atlas.*

GEORGIA - TRANSPORTATION AND COMMUNICATIONS

Business International Moscow, 23 Profseyuznaya Ulitsa 117859, Moscow (Telephone Number in U.S. (800) 938-4685); *The CIS Market Atlas.*

Encyclopedia Britannica, Incorporated, 310 South Michigan Avenue, Chicago, Illinois 60604 (312) 347-7000; *Britannica World Data.*

GEORGIA - VITAL STATISTICS

Encyclopedia Britannica, Incorporated, 310 South Michigan Avenue, Chicago, Illinois 60604 (312) 347-7000; *Britannica World Data.*

GEORGIA - WAGES

Business International Moscow, 23 Profseyuznaya Ulitsa 117859, Moscow (Telephone Number in U.S. (800) 938-4685); *The CIS Market Atlas.*

The World Bank, 1818 H Street, Northwest, Washington, D.C. 20433 (202) 477-1234; *Statistical Handbook: States of the Former USSR.*

GEORGIA - WOOL PRODUCTION AND CONSUMPTION - See GEORGIA - TEXTILE INDUSTRY

GEOTHERMAL ENERGY

U.S. Department of Energy, Energy Information Administration, Washington, D.C. 20585 (202) 586-8800; *Annual Energy Review,* and *Monthly Energy Review.*

GERMANIUM

U.S. Department of the Interior, Bureau of Mines, 810 Seventh Street, NW, Washington, D.C. 20241 (202) 501-9649; *Mineral Commodity Summaries.*

Germany - National Statistical Office

Statistisches Bundesamt, Gustav-Stresemann-Ring 11, Postfach 5528, 6200 Wiesbaden, Germany.

Germany - Primary Statistics Sources

Statistisches Bundesamt Federal Statistical Office, Gustav-Stresemann-Ring 11, Postfach 5528, 6200 Wiesbaden, Germany; *Statistisches Jahrbuch,* (Statistical Yearbook of Germany); *Statistisches Taschebuch* (Statistical Pocketbook); and *Wirtschaft und Statistik.*

Germany - Databases

Deutsche Bundesbank Data, Deutsche Bundesbank, Postfach 100602, D-60006 Frankfurt 1, Germany. Subject coverage: Statistics on banking, securities, balance of payments, and seasonally adjusted economic data.

FAKT, Infratest Burke AG, Landsberger Str. 338, D-780687 Munich, Germany. Subject coverage: Statistical information on business, the economy, energy, the environment, technology, health care, media, public affairs, and social welfare.

German Macro and Financial Data, Haver Analytics, 60 East 42nd Street, Suite 620, New York, New York 10165 (212) 986-9300. Subject coverage: Economic and financial indicators of the German economy.

Statistisches Bundesamt, Gustav-Stresemann-Ring 11, D-65189 Wiesbaden, Germany. Subject coverage: Statistical information on German population, economics, industry, and other topics.

GERMANY - ABORTIONS

European Community Information Service, 2100 M Street, NW, Washington, D.C. 20037 (202) 862-9500; *Demographic Statistics.*

GERMANY - AGRICULTURE

Columbia University Press, 562 West 113th Street, New York, New York 10014 (212) 316-7100; *East European and Soviet Data Book.*

European Community Information Service, 2100 M Street, NW, Washington, D.C. 20037 (202) 862-9500; *Agriculture: Statistical Yearbook, Basic Statistics of the Community, Crop Production: Quarterly Statistics, Eurostatistics: Data for Short-Term Economic Analysis,* and *Labor Force Sample Survey.*

Facts on File, 460 Park Avenue South, New York, New York 10016 (800) 443-8323; *The New Book of World Rankings.*

Federal Statistical Office, Gustav - Stresemann - Ring 11, D-6200 Wiesbaden, Germany; *Deutsche Demokratische Republik.*

Food and Agricultural Organization of the United Nations (FAO) Via delle Terme di Caracalla, 00100 Rome, Italy (Telephone Number in U.S. (202) 606-7828); *Production Yearbook, The State of Food and Agriculture,* and *Trade Yearbook.*

G.K. Hall and Company, 70 Lincoln Street, Boston, Massachusetts 02111 (617) 423-3990; *The World in Figures.*

National Technical Information Service, 5285 Port Royal Road, Springfield, Virginia 22161 (703) 487-4600; *Handbook of Economic Statistics.*

Organisation for Economic Co-operation and Development (OECD), 2 rue Andre-Pascal, 75 Paris 16, France (Telephone Number in U.S. (202) 785-6323); *Economic Accounts for Agriculture, Indicators of Industrial Activity, Industrial Structure Statistics,* and *OECD Economic Surveys: Germany.*

Statistical Office of the United Nations, Publishing Service, New York, New York 10017 (800) 253-9646; *Statistical Yearbook.*

Statistisches Bundesamt (Allgemeiner Auskunftsdienst), Gustav-Stresemann-Ring 11, Postfach 5528, D-6200 Wiesbaden, Germany; *Land-und Forstwirtschaft, Fischerei-Reihe 1: Ausgewahlte Zahlen fur Die Agrawirtschaft 1977.*

Times Books, 201 East 50th Street, New York, New York 10022 (212) 751-2600; *The Economist Book of Vital World Statistics.*

The World Bank, 1818 H Street, NW, Washington, D.C. 20433 (202) 477-1234; *World Tables.*

GERMANY - AIRLINE SERVICE

European Community Information Service, 2100 M Street, NW, Washington, D.C. 20037 (202) 862-9500; *Basic Statistics of the Community, Regions: Statistical Yearbook,* and *Transport Annual Statistics.*

Facts on File, 460 Park Avenue South, New York, New York 10016 (800) 443-8323; *The New Book of World Rankings.*

G.K. Hall and Company, 70 Lincoln Street, Boston, Massachusetts 02111 (617) 423-3990; *The World in Figures.*

International Civil Aviation Organization, 1000 Sherbrooke Street West, Suite 400, Montreal, Quebec, Canada H3A 2R2 (514) 285-8219; *Civil Aviation Statistics of the World.*

National Technical Information Service, 5285 Port Royal Road, Springfield, Virginia 22161 (703) 487-4600; *Handbook of Economic Statistics.*

Organisation for Economic Co-operation and Development (OECD), 2 rue Andre-Pascal, 75 Paris 16, France (Telephone Number in U.S. (202) 785-6323); *Tourism Policy and International Tourism in OECD Member Countries.*

Statistical Office of the United Nations, Publishing Service, New York, New York 10017; *Statistical Yearbook.*

Times Books, 201 East 50th Street, New York, New York 10022 (212) 751-2600; *The Economist Book of Vital World Statistics.*

GERMANY - ALMOND PRODUCTION - See GERMANY - CROPS

GERMANY - ALUMINUM PRODUCTION AND CONSUMPTION - See GERMANY - MINING AND MINERAL PRODUCTS

GERMANY - ANIMAL FEEDINGSTUFFS

Organisation for Economic Co-operation and Development (OECD), 2 rue Andre-Pascal, 75 Paris 16, France (Telephone Number in U.S. (202) 785-6323); *Foreign Trade by Commodities.*

Statistical Office of the United Nations, Publishing Service, New York, New York 10017 (800) 253-9646; *Statistical Yearbook.*

GERMANY - ANIMAL HEALTH

Food and Agricultural Organization of the United Nations (FAO), Via delle Terme di Caracalla, 00100 Rome, Italy (Telephone Number in U.S. (202) 606-7828); *Animal Health Yearbook.*

GERMANY - ANTIMONY PRODUCTION AND CONSUMPTION - See GERMANY - MINING AND MINERAL PRODUCTS

GERMANY - APPLE PRODUCTION - See GERMANY - CROPS

GERMANY - AREA AND DENSITY OF POPULATION

European Community Information Service, 2100 M Street, NW, Washington, D.C. 20037 (202) 862-9500; *Basic Statistics of the Community* and *Demographic Statistics.*

Facts on File, 460 Park Avenue South, New York, New York 10016 (800) 443-8323; *The New Book of World Rankings.*

Food and Agricultural Organization of the United Nations (FAO) Via delle Terme di Caracalla, 00100 Rome, Italy (Telephone Number in U.S. (202) 606-7828); *The State of Food and Agriculture.*

G.K. Hall and Company, 70 Lincoln Street, Boston, Massachusetts 02111 (617) 423-3990; *The World in Figures.*

National Technical Information Service, 5285 Port Royal Road, Springfield, Virginia 22161 (703) 487-4600; *Handbook of Economic Statistics.*

Statistical Office of the United Nations, Publishing Service, New York, New York 10017 (800) 253-9646; *Statistical Yearbook.*

Times Books, 201 East 50th Street, New York, New York 10022 (212) 751-2600; *The Economist Book of Vital World Statistics.*

United Nations Educational, Scientific and Cultural Organization (UNESCO), 7 Place de Fontenoy, F-75700 Paris, France (Telephone Number in U.S. (212) 963-5981); *Statistical Yearbook.*

GERMANY - ARMS EXPORTS AND IMPORTS

U.S. Arms Control and Disarmament Agency, 320 Twenty-first Street, Northwest, Washington, D.C. 20451 (202) 647-8677; *World Military Expenditures and Arms Transfers.*

GERMANY - ARSENIC PRODUCTION AND CONSUMPTION - See GERMANY - MINING AND MINERAL PRODUCTS

GERMANY - BALANCE OF PAYMENTS

The Economist Intelligence Unit, 111 West 57th Street, New York, New York 10019 (800) 938-4685; *The World Market Atlas.*

European Community Information Service, 2100 M Street, NW, Washington, D.C. 20037 (202) 862-9500; *ACP: Basic Statistics, Basic Statistics of the Community, Energy Statistics Yearbook,* and *Eurostatistics: Data for Short-Term Economic Analysis.*

G.K. Hall and Company, 70 Lincoln Street, Boston, Massachusetts 02111 (617) 423-3990; *The World in Figures.*

International Monetary Fund, 700 Nineteenth Street, NW, Washington, D.C. 20431 (202) 623-7000; *Balance of Payments Yearbook,* and *International Financial Statistics.*

National Technical Information Service, 5285 Port Royal Road, Springfield, Virginia 22161 (703) 487-4600; *Handbook of Economic Statistics.*

Organisation for Economic Co-operation and Development (OECD), 2 rue Andre-Pascal, 75 Paris 16, France (Telephone Number in U.S. (202) 785-6323); *Economic Outlook, Geographical Distribution of Financial Flows to Developing Countries, Main Economic Indicators - Historical Statistics,* and *OECD Economic Surveys: Germany.*

Times Books, 201 East 50th Street, New York, New York 10022 (212) 751-2600; *The Economist Book of Vital World Statistics.*

The World Bank, 1818 H Street, NW, Washington, D.C. 20433 (202) 477-1234; *World Tables.*

GERMANY - BANANA PRODUCTION - See GERMANY - CROPS

GERMANY - BANKING

European Community Information Service, 2100 M Street, NW, Washington, D.C. 20037 (202) 862-9500; *ACP: Basic Statistics.*

Facts on File, 460 Park Avenue South, New York, New York 10016 (800) 443-8323; *The New Book of World Rankings.*

G.K. Hall and Company, 70 Lincoln Street, Boston, Massachusetts 02111 (617) 423-3990; *The World in Figures.*

International Monetary Fund, 700 Nineteenth Street, NW, Washington, D.C. 20431 (202) 623-7000; *International Financial Statistics.*

National Technical Information Service, 5285 Port Royal Road, Springfield, Virginia 22161 (703) 487-4600; *Handbook of Economic Statistics.*

Organisation for Economic Co-operation and Development (OECD), 2 rue Andre-Pascal, 75 Paris 16, France (Telephone Number in U.S. (202) 785-6323); *Economic Outlook, Financial Market Trends,* and *OECD Economic Surveys: Germany.*

Statistical Office of the United Nations, Publishing Service, New York, New York 10017 (800) 253-9646; *Statistical Yearbook.*

GERMANY - BARLEY PRODUCTION - See GERMANY - CROPS

GERMANY - BAUXITE PRODUCTION AND CONSUMPTION - See GERMANY - MINING AND MINERAL PRODUCTS

GERMANY - BEER PRODUCTION

Facts on File, 460 Park Avenue South, New York, New York 10016 (800) 443-8323; *The New Book of World Rankings.*

Statistical Office of the United Nations, Publishing Service, New York, New York 10017 (800) 253-9646; *Statistical Yearbook.*

GERMANY - BEVERAGES - PRODUCTION INDEX

Organisation for Economic Co-operation and Development (OECD), 2 rue Andre-Pascal, 75 Paris 16, France (Telephone Number in U.S. (202) 785-6323); *Indicators of Industrial Activity.*

GERMANY - BIRTH RATE

European Community Information Service, 2100 M Street, NW, Washington, D.C. 20037 (202) 862-9500; *Basic Statistics of the Community, Demographic Statistics.*

Facts on File, 460 Park Avenue South, New York, New York 10016 (800) 443-8323; *The New Book of World Rankings.*

Statistical Office of the United Nations, Publishing Service, New York, New York 10017 (800) 253-9646; *Demographic Yearbook, Statistical Yearbook.*

Times Books, 201 East 50th Street, New York, New York 10022 (212) 751-2600; *The Economist Book of Vital World Statistics.*

The World Bank, 1818 H Street, NW, Washington, D.C. 20433 (202) 477-1234; *World Tables.*

World Health Organization, Office of Publications, Avenue Appia, CH-1211 Geneva 27, Switzerland (Telephone Number in U.S. (518) 436-9686); *World Health Statistics Annual.*

GERMANY - BISMUTH PRODUCTION AND CONSUMPTION - See GERMANY - MINING AND MINERAL PRODUCTS

GERMANY - BONDS

European Community Information Service, 2100 M Street, NW, Washington, D.C. 20037 (202) 862-9500; *Basic Statistics of the Community.*

G.K. Hall and Company, 70 Lincoln Street, Boston, Massachusetts 02111 (617) 423-3990; *The World in Figures.*

Organisation for Economic Co-operation and Development (OECD), 2 rue Andre-Pascal, 75 Paris 16, France (Telephone Number in U.S. (202) 785-6323); *Financial Market Trends.*

Statistical Office of the United Nations, Publishing Service, New York, New York 10017 (800) 253-9646; *Statistical Yearbook.*

GERMANY - BOOK PRODUCTION

Euromonitor Publications Limited, 87-88 Turnmill Street, London EC1M 5QU, England; *European Marketing Data and Statistics.*

G.K. Hall and Company, 70 Lincoln Street, Boston, Massachusetts 02111 (617) 423-3990; *The World in Figures.*

Organisation for Economic Co-operation and Development (OECD), 2 rue Andre-Pascal, 75 Paris 16, France (Telephone Number in U.S. (202) 785-6323); *Indicators of Industrial Activity.*

United Nations Educational, Scientific and Cultural Organization (UNESCO), 7 Place de Fontenoy, F-75700 Paris, France (Telephone Number in U.S. (212) 963-5981); *Statistical Yearbook.*

GERMANY - BROADCASTING

Billboard Limited, Post Office Box 9027, 1006 AA Amsterdam, The Netherlands (Telephone Number in U.S. (212) 764-7300); *World Radio TV Handbook.*

European Community Information Service, 2100 M Street, NW, Washington, D.C. 20037 (202) 862-9500; *Basic Statistics of the Community.*

Facts on File, 460 Park Avenue South, New York, New York 10016 (800) 443-8323; *The New Book of World Rankings.*

G.K. Hall and Company, 70 Lincoln Street, Boston, Massachusetts 02111 (617) 423-3990; *The World in Figures.*

Times Books, 201 East 50th Street, New York, New York 10022 (212) 751-2600; *The Economist Book of Vital World Statistics.*

GERMANY - BUILDING CONSTRUCTION - See GERMANY - CONSTRUCTION INDUSTRY

GERMANY - BUSINESS

European Community Information Service, 2100 M Street, NW, Washington, D.C. 20037 (202) 862-9500; *Basic Statistics of the Community.*

G.K. Hall and Company, 70 Lincoln Street, Boston, Massachusetts 02111 (617) 423-3990; *The World in Figures.*

GERMANY - BUTTER - See GERMANY - DAIRY PRODUCTS

GERMANY - CABBAGE PRODUCTION - See GERMANY - CROPS

GERMANY - CADMIUM PRODUCTION AND CONSUMPTION - See GERMANY - MINING AND MINERAL PRODUCTS

GERMANY - CALORIE SUPPLY

Food and Agricultural Organization of the United Nations (FAO) Via delle Terme di Caracalla, 00100 Rome, Italy (Telephone Number in U.S. (202) 606-7828); *The State of Food and Agriculture.*

GERMANY - CAPITAL INVESTMENT

National Technical Information Service, 5285 Port Royal Road, Springfield, Virginia 22161 (703) 487-4600; *Handbook of Economic Statistics.*

Organisation for Economic Co-operation and Development (OECD), 2 rue Andre-Pascal, 75 Paris 16, France (Telephone Number in U.S. (202) 785-6323); *Economic Outlook,* and *Financial Market Trends.*

GERMANY - CAPITAL REVENUE

Organisation for Economic Co-operation and Development (OECD), 2 rue Andre-Pascal, 75 Paris 16, France (Telephone Number in U.S. (202) 785-6323); *Economic Outlook,* and *Financial Market Trends.*

GERMANY - CASHEW NUT PRODUCTION - See GERMANY - CROPS

GERMANY - CASTOR BEAN PRODUCTION - See GERMANY - CROPS

GERMANY - CATTLE - See GERMANY - LIVESTOCK AND POULTRY

GERMANY - CAULIFLOWER PRODUCTION - See GERMANY - CROPS

GERMANY - CAUSTIC SODA PRODUCTION

European Community Information Service, 2100 M Street, NW, Washington, D.C. 20037 (202) 862-9500; *Basic Statistics of the Community.*

National Technical Information Service, 5285 Port Royal Road, Springfield, Virginia 22161 (703) 487-4600; *Handbook of Economic Statistics.*

Organisation for Economic Co-operation and Development (OECD), 2 rue Andre-Pascal, 75 Paris 16, France (Telephone Number in U.S. (202) 785-6323); *Indicators of Industrial Activity.*

Statistical Office of the United Nations, Publishing Service, New York, New York 10017 (800) 253-9646; *Statistical Yearbook.*

GERMANY - CEMENT PRODUCTION - See GERMANY - MINING AND MINERAL PRODUCTS

GERMANY - CEREAL PRODUCTION - See GERMANY - CROPS

GERMANY - CHEESE - See GERMANY - DAIRY PRODUCTS

GERMANY - CHEMICAL (ORGANIC) PRODUCTION - See GERMANY - MINING AND MINERAL PRODUCTS

GERMANY - CHEMICAL INDUSTRY

European Community Information Service, 2100 M Street, Northwest, Washington, D.C. 20037 (202) 862-9500; *Industrial Production: Quarterly Statistics.*

GERMANY - CHESTNUT PRODUCTION - See GERMANY - CROPS

GERMANY - CHICKENS - See GERMANY - LIVESTOCK AND POULTRY

GERMANY - CHROMITE PRODUCTION AND CONSUMPTION - See GERMANY - MINING AND MINERAL PRODUCTS

GERMANY - CHROMIUM ORE PRODUCTION AND CONSUMPTION - See GERMANY - MINING AND MINERAL PRODUCTS

GERMANY - CIGAR PRODUCTION - See GERMANY - TOBACCO PRODUCTION

GERMANY - CIGARETTE PRODUCTION - See GERMANY - TOBACCO PRODUCTION

GERMANY - CLASS STRUCTURE

Columbia University Press, 562 West 113th Street, New York, New York 10014 (212) 316-7100; *East European and Soviet Data Book.*

European Community Information Service, 2100 M Street, NW, Washington, D.C. 20037 (202) 862-9500; *Basic Statistics of the Community* and *Labor Force Sample Survey.*

G.K. Hall and Company, 70 Lincoln Street, Boston, Massachusetts 02111 (617) 423-3990; *The World in Figures.*

GERMANY - CLIMATE

Facts on File, 460 Park Avenue South, New York, New York 10016 (800) 443-8323; *The New Book of World Rankings.*

G.K. Hall and Company, 70 Lincoln Street, Boston, Massachusetts 02111 (617) 423-3990; *The World in Figures.*

GERMANY - CLOTHING - See GERMANY - TEXTILE INDUSTRY

GERMANY - COAL PRODUCTION - See GERMANY - MINING AND MINERAL PRODUCTS

GERMANY - COBALT PRODUCTION AND CONSUMPTION - See GERMANY - MINING AND MINERAL PRODUCTS

GERMANY - COCOA (BEANS) PRODUCTION - See GERMANY - CROPS

GERMANY - COFFEE - See GERMANY - CROPS

GERMANY - COKE OVEN COKE AND COKE OVEN ORE PRODUCTION AND CONSUMPTION - See GERMANY - MINING AND MINERAL PRODUCTS

GERMANY - COKE PRODUCTION AND CONSUMPTION - See GERMANY - MINING AND MINERAL PRODUCTS

GERMANY - COMMUNICATIONS

European Community Information Service, 2100 M Street, NW, Washington, D.C. 20037 (202) 862-9500; *Basic Statistics of the Community*, and *Transport Annual Statistics*.

Federal Statistical Office, Gustav - Stresemann - Ring 11, D-6200 Wiesbaden, Germany; *Deutsche Demokratische Republik*.

G.K. Hall and Company, 70 Lincoln Street, Boston, Massachusetts 02111 (617) 423-3990; *The World in Figures*.

GERMANY - CONSTRUCTION INDUSTRY

European Community Information Service, 2100 M Street, NW, Washington, D.C. 20037 (202) 862-9500; *Basic Statistics of the Community*, and *Labor Force Sample Survey*.

Facts on File, 460 Park Avenue South, New York, New York 10016 (800) 443-8323; *The New Book of World Rankings*.

Organisation for Economic Co-operation and Development (OECD), 2 rue Andre-Pascal, 75 Paris 16, France (Telephone Number in U.S. (202) 785-6323); *Industrial Structure Statistics, Main Economic Indicators - Historical Statistics, The Iron and Steel Industry*, and *OECD Economic Surveys: Germany*.

Statistical Office of the United Nations, Publishing Service, New York, New York 10017 (800) 253-9646; *Construction Statistics Yearbook*, and *Statistical Yearbook*.

GERMANY - CONSUMER PRICE INDEX

European Community Information Service, 2100 M Street, NW, Washington, D.C. 20037 (202) 862-9500; *Basic Statistics of the Community*.

Federal Statistical Office, Gustav - Stresemann - Ring 11, D-6200 Wiesbaden, Germany; *Deutsche Demokratische Republik*.

G.K. Hall and Company, 70 Lincoln Street, Boston, Massachusetts 02111 (617) 423-3990; *The World in Figures*.

International Labour Office, I.L.O. Publications, CH-1211, Geneva 22, Switzerland; *Yearbook of Labour Statistics*.

National Technical Information Service, 5285 Port Royal Road, Springfield, Virginia 22161 (703) 487-4600; *Handbook of Economic Statistics*.

Organisation for Economic Co-operation and Development (OECD), 2 rue Andre-Pascal, 75 Paris 16, France (Telephone Number in U.S. (202) 785-6323); *Economic Outlook*.

Statistical Office of the United Nations, Publishing Service, New York, New York 10017 (800) 253-9646; *Statistical Yearbook*.

GERMANY - CONSUMER PRICES

Euromonitor Publications Limited, 87-88 Turnmill Street, London EC1M 5QU, England; *European Marketing Data and Statistics*.

European Community Information Service, 2100 M Street, NW, Washington, D.C. 20037 (202) 862-9500; *Basic Statistics of the Community, Eurostatistics: Data for Short-Term Economic Analysis*, and *Money and Finance*.

International Labour Office, I.L.O. Publications, CH-1211, Geneva 22, Switzerland; *Yearbook of Labour Statistics*.

Organisation for Economic Co-operation and Development (OECD), 2 rue Andre-Pascal, 75 Paris 16, France (Telephone Number in U.S. (202) 785-6323); *Economic Outlook*.

Times Books, 201 East 50th Street, New York, New York 10022 (212) 751-2600; *The Economist Book of Vital World Statistics*.

GERMANY - CONSUMPTION

European Community Information Service, 2100 M Street, NW, Washington, D.C. 20037 (202) 862-9500; *Basic Statistics of the Community*.

G.K. Hall and Company, 70 Lincoln Street, Boston, Massachusetts 02111 (617) 423-3990; *The World in Figures*.

International Iron and Steel Institute, 120, rue Colonel Bourg, B-1140 Brussels, Belgium; *Steel Statistical Yearbook*.

International Lead and Zinc Study Group, Metro House, 58 St. James's Street, London SW1A 1LD, England; *Lead and Zinc Statistics*.

International Rubber Study Group,York House, 8th Floor, Empire Way, Wembley, London HA9 0PA, England; *Rubber Statistical Bulletin*.

National Technical Information Service, 5285 Port Royal Road, Springfield, Virginia 22161 (703) 487-4600; *Handbook of Economic Statistics*.

Organisation for Economic Co-operation and Development (OECD), 2 rue Andre-Pascal, 75 Paris 16, France (Telephone Number in U.S. (202) 785-6323); *The Footwear, Raw Hides and Skins, and Leather Industry in OECD Countries, The Iron and Steel Industry, Meat Balances in OECD Member Countries, The Non-Ferrous Metals Industry, The Pulp and Paper Industry*, and *Textile Industry in OECD Countries*.

GERMANY - COPPER AND COPPER ORE PRODUCTION AND CONSUMPTION - See GERMANY - MINING AND MINERAL PRODUCTS

GERMANY - CORN PRODUCTION - See GERMANY - CROPS

GERMANY - CORPORATE INCOME TAXES - See GERMANY - TAXATION

GERMANY - CORPORATE TAXES - See GERMANY - TAXATION

GERMANY - COTTON - See GERMANY - CROPS

GERMANY - CRIME

International Criminal Police Organization (INTERPOL), 26 rue Armengaud, 92210 Saint Cloud, France; *International Crime Statistics*.

Yale University Press, Yale Station, New Haven, Connecticut 06520 (203) 432-0940; *Violence and Crime in Cross-National Perspective*.

GERMANY - CROPS

Commodity Research Bureau, Incorporated, 75 Wall Street, New York, New York 10005 (212) 504-7754; *Commodity Year Book*.

Euromonitor Publications Limited, 87-88 Turnmill Street, London EC1M 5QU, England; *European Marketing Data and Statistics.*

European Community Information Service, 2100 M Street, NW, Washington, D.C. 20037 (202) 862-9500; *ACP: Basic Statistics, Agriculture: Statistical Yearbook, Basic Statistics of the Community, Eurostatistics: Data for Short-Term Economic Analysis,* and *Regions: Statistical Yearbook.*

Facts on File, 460 Park Avenue South, New York, New York 10016 (800) 443-8323; *The New Book of World Rankings.*

Food and Agricultural Organization of the United Nations (FAO), Via delle Terme di Caracalla, 00100 Rome, Italy (Telephone Number in U.S. (202) 606-7828); *Production Yearbook* and *The State of Food and Agriculture.*

G.K. Hall and Company, 70 Lincoln Street, Boston, Massachusetts 02111 (617) 423-3990; *The World in Figures.*

National Technical Information Service, 5285 Port Royal Road, Springfield, Virginia 22161 (703) 487-4600; *Handbook of Economic Statistics.*

Organisation for Economic Co-operation and Development (OECD), 2 rue Andre-Pascal, 75 Paris 16, France (Telephone Number in U.S. (202) 785-6323); *Economic Accounts for Agriculture, Foreign Trade by Commodities,* and *Textile Industry in OECD Countries.*

Statistical Office of the United Nations, Publishing Service, New York, New York 10017 (800) 253-9646; *Statistical Yearbook.*

GERMANY - CUSTOMS DUTIES

European Community Information Service, 2100 M Street, NW, Washington, D.C. 20037 (202) 862-9500; *Basic Statistics of the Community.*

G.K. Hall and Company, 70 Lincoln Street, Boston, Massachusetts 02111 (617) 423-3990; *The World in Figures.*

Organisation for Economic Co-operation and Development (OECD), 2 rue Andre-Pascal, 75 Paris 16, France (Telephone Number in U.S. (202) 785-6323); *The Non-Ferrous Metals Industry.*

GERMANY - DAIRY PRODUCTS

Commodity Research Bureau, Incorporated, 75 Wall Street, New York, New York 10005 (212) 504-7754; *Commodity Year Book.*

European Community Information Service, 2100 M Street, NW, Washington, D.C. 20037 (202) 862-9500; *Basic Statistics of the Community* and *Eurostatistics: Data for Short-Term Economic Analysis.*

Facts on File, 460 Park Avenue South, New York, New York 10016 (800) 443-8323; *The New Book of World Rankings.*

Food and Agricultural Organization of the United Nations (FAO), Via delle Terme di Caracalla, 00100 Rome, Italy (Telephone Number in U.S. (202) 606-7828); *Production Yearbook* and *The State of Food and Agriculture.*

National Technical Information Service, 5285 Port Royal Road, Springfield, Virginia 22161 (703) 487-4600; *Handbook of Economic Statistics.*

Organisation for Economic Co-operation and Development (OECD), 2 rue Andre-Pascal, 75 Paris 16, France (Telephone Number in U.S. (202) 785-6323); *Economic Accounts for Agriculture,* and *Milk, Milk Products, and Egg Balances in OECD Member Countries.*

Statistical Office of the United Nations, Publishing Service, New York, New York 10017 (800) 253-9646; *Statistical Yearbook.*

GERMANY - DEATH RATE

European Community Information Service, 2100 M Street, NW, Washington, D.C. 20037 (202) 862-9500; *Basic Statistics of the Community* and *Demographic Statistics.*

G.K. Hall and Company, 70 Lincoln Street, Boston, Massachusetts 02111 (617) 423-3990; *The World in Figures.*

Statistical Office of the United Nations, Publishing Service, New York, New York 10017 (800) 253-9646; *Statistical Yearbook.*

Times Books, 201 East 50th Street, New York, New York 10022 (212) 751-2600; *The Economist Book of Vital World Statistics.*

World Health Organization, Office of Publications, Avenue Appia, CH-1211 Geneva 27, Switzerland (Telephone Number in U.S. (518) 436-9686); *World Health Statistics Annual.*

GERMANY - DEFENSE EXPENDITURES

European Community Information Service, 2100 M Street, NW, Washington, D.C. 20037 (202) 862-9500; *Government Financing of Research and Development.*

G.K. Hall and Company, 70 Lincoln Street, Boston, Massachusetts 02111 (617) 423-3990; *The World in Figures.*

National Technical Information Service, 5285 Port Royal Road, Springfield, Virginia 22161 (703) 487-4600; *Handbook of Economic Statistics.*

U.S. Arms Control and Disarmament Agency, 320 Twenty-first Street, Northwest, Washington, D.C. 20451 (202) 647-8677; *World Military Expenditures and Arms Transfers.*

GERMANY - DEMOGRAPHY

The Economist Intelligence Unit, 111 West 57th Street, New York, New York 10019 (800) 938-4685; *The World Market Atlas.*

European Community Information Service, 2100 M Street, NW, Washington, D.C. 20037 (202) 862-9500; *Basic Statistics of the Community, Demographic Statistics, Employment and Unemployment,* and *Regions: Statistical Yearbook.*

Facts on File, 460 Park Avenue South, New York, New York 10016 (800) 443-8323; *The New Book of World Rankings.*

G.K. Hall and Company, 70 Lincoln Street, Boston, Massachusetts 02111 (617) 423-3990; *The World in Figures.*

GERMANY - DEVELOPMENT ASSISTANCE

European Community Information Service, 2100 M Street, NW, Washington, D.C. 20037 (202) 862-9500; *ACP: Basic Statistics, Basic Statistics of the Community,* and *Government Financing of Research and Development.*

G.K. Hall and Company, 70 Lincoln Street, Boston, Massachusetts 02111 (617) 423-3990; *The World in Figures.*

Organisation for Economic Co-operation and Development (OECD), 2 rue Andre-Pascal, 75 Paris 16, France (Telephone Number in U.S. (202) 785-6323); *Geographical Distribution of Financial Flows to Developing Countries.*

Statistical Office of the United Nations, Publishing Service, New York, New York 10017 (800) 253-9646; *Statistical Yearbook.*

GERMANY - DIAMOND EXPORTS AND PRODUCTION - See GERMANY - MINING AND MINERAL PRODUCTS

GERMANY - DISCOUNT RATES

Organisation for Economic Co-operation and Development (OECD), 2 rue Andre-Pascal, 75 Paris 16, France (Telephone Number in U.S. (202) 785-6323); *Financial Market Trends.*

Statistical Office of the United Nations, Publishing Service, New York, New York 10017 (800) 253-9646; *Statistical Yearbook.*

GERMANY - DISEASES

G.K. Hall and Company, 70 Lincoln Street, Boston, Massachusetts 02111 (617) 423-3990; *The World in Figures.*

World Health Organization, Office of Publications, Avenue Appia, CH-1211 Geneva 27, Switzerland (Telephone Number in U.S. (518) 436-9686); *World Health Statistics Annual.*

GERMANY - DIVORCE RATES

European Community Information Service, 2100 M Street, NW, Washington, D.C. 20037 (202) 862-9500; *Demographic Statistics.*

Facts on File, 460 Park Avenue South, New York, New York 10016 (800) 443-8323; *The New Book of World Rankings.*

Statistical Office of the United Nations, Publishing Service, New York, New York 10017 (800) 253-9646; *Demographic Yearbook* and *Statistical Yearbook.*

GERMANY - DOMESTIC PRODUCT

European Community Information Service, 2100 M Street, NW, Washington, D.C. 20037 (202) 862-9500; *Basic Statistics of the Community.*

G.K. Hall and Company, 70 Lincoln Street, Boston, Massachusetts 02111 (617) 423-3990; *The World in Figures.*

GERMANY - DUCKS - See GERMANY - LIVESTOCK AND POULTRY

GERMANY - ECONOMY

Euromonitor Publications Limited, 87-88 Turnmill Street, London EC1M 5QU, England; *European Marketing Data and Statistics.*

European Community Information Service, 2100 M Street, NW, Washington, D.C. 20037 (202) 862-9500; *ACP: Basic Statistics, Basic Statistics of the Community, Energy Statistics Yearbook, Labor Force Sample Survey,* and *Money and Finance.*

Facts on File, 460 Park Avenue South, New York, New York 10016 (800) 443-8323; *The New Book of World Rankings.*

G.K. Hall and Company, 70 Lincoln Street, Boston, Massachusetts 02111 (617) 423-3990; *The World in Figures.*

National Technical Information Service, 5285 Port Royal Road, Springfield, Virginia 22161 (703) 487-4600; *Handbook of Economic Statistics.*

Organisation for Economic Co-operation and Development (OECD), 2 rue Andre-Pascal, 75 Paris 16, France (Telephone Number in U.S. (202) 785-6323); *Economic Outlook, Geographical Distribution of Financial Flows to Developing Countries, Main Economic Indicators - Historical Statistics, OECD Economic Surveys: Germany,* and *OECD Employment Outlook.*

GERMANY - EDUCATION

The Economist Intelligence Unit, 111 West 57th Street, New York, New York 10019 (800) 938-4685; *The World Market Atlas.*

Columbia University Press, 562 West 113th Street, New York, New York 10014 (212) 316-7100; *East European and Soviet Data Book.*

Euromonitor Publications Limited, 87-88 Turnmill Street, London EC1M 5QU, England; *European Marketing Data and Statistics.*

European Community Information Service, 2100 M Street, NW, Washington, D.C. 20037 (202) 862-9500; *Basic Statistics of the Community* and *Regions: Statistical Yearbook.*

Facts on File, 460 Park Avenue South, New York, New York 10016 (800) 443-8323; *The New Book of World Rankings.*

G.K. Hall and Company, 70 Lincoln Street, Boston, Massachusetts 02111 (617) 423-3990; *The World in Figures.*

Organisation for Economic Co-operation and Development (OECD), 2 rue Andre-Pascal, 75 Paris 16, France (Telephone Number in U.S. (202) 785-6323); *Education in OECD Countries.*

Times Books, 201 East 50th Street, New York, New York 10022 (212) 751-2600; *The Economist Book of Vital World Statistics.*

United Nations Educational, Scientific and Cultural Organization (UNESCO), 7 Place de Fontenoy, F-75700 Paris, France (Telephone Number in U.S. (212) 963-5981); *Statistical Yearbook.*

The World Bank, 1818 H Street, NW, Washington, D.C. 20433 (202) 477-1234; *World Tables.*

GERMANY - EGG PRODUCTION AND CONSUMPTION - See GERMANY - DAIRY PRODUCTS

GERMANY - ELECTRICITY

Commodity Research Bureau, Incorporated, 75 Wall Street, New York, New York 10005 (212) 504-7754; *Commodity Year Book.*

European Community Information Service, 2100 M Street, NW, Washington, D.C. 20037 (202) 862-9500; *Basic Statistics of the Community, Energy: Monthly Statistics, Energy Statistics Yearbook, Eurostatistics: Data for Short-Term Economic Analysis,* and *Regions: Statistical Yearbook.*

Facts on File, 460 Park Avenue South, New York, New York 10016 (800) 443-8323; *The New Book of World Rankings.*

National Technical Information Service, 5285 Port Royal Road, Springfield, Virginia 22161 (703) 487-4600; *Handbook of Economic Statistics.*

Organisation for Economic Co-operation and Development (OECD), 2 rue Andre-Pascal, 75 Paris 16, France (Telephone Number in U.S.

(202) 785-6323); *Coal Information, Energy Statistics of OECD Countries, Indicators of Industrial Activity,* and *Industrial Structure Statistics.*

Penn Well Publishing Company, 1421 South Sheridan Road, Post Office Box 1260, Tulsa, Oklahoma 74101 (800) 752-9764; *International Energy Statistics Sourcebook.*

Statistical Office of the United Nations, Publishing Service, New York, New York 10017 (800) 253-9646; *Statistical Yearbook.*

Times Books, 201 East 50th Street, New York, New York 10022 (212) 751-2600; *The Economist Book of Vital World Statistics.*

GERMANY - EMPLOYMENT

Columbia University Press, 562 West 113th Street, New York, New York 10014 (212) 316-7100; *East European and Soviet Data Book.*

Euromonitor Publications Limited, 87-88 Turnmill Street, London EC1M 5QU, England; *European Marketing Data and Statistics.*

European Community Information Service, 2100 M Street, NW, Washington, D.C. 20037 (202) 862-9500; *Basic Statistics of the Community, Earnings in Agriculture, Employment and Unemployment, Eurostatistics: Data for Short-Term Economic Analysis, Iron and Steel: Statistical Yearbook, Labor Force Sample Survey,* and *Transport Annual Statistics.*

Facts on File, 460 Park Avenue South, New York, New York 10016 (800) 443-8323; *The New Book of World Rankings.*

International Labour Office, I.L.O. Publications, CH-1211, Geneva 22, Switzerland; *Yearbook of Labour Statistics.*

National Technical Information Service, 5285 Port Royal Road, Springfield, Virginia 22161 (703) 487-4600; *Handbook of Economic Statistics.*

Organisation for Economic Co-operation and Development (OECD), 2 rue Andre-Pascal, 75 Paris 16, France (Telephone Number in U.S. (202) 785-6323); *Economic Outlook, The Iron and Steel Industry, OECD Economic Surveys: Germany,* and *OECD Employment Outlook.*

Statistical Office of the United Nations, Publishing Service, New York, New York 10017 (800) 253-9646; *Statistical Yearbook.*

GERMANY - ENERGY

Euromonitor Publications Limited, 87-88 Turnmill Street, London EC1M 5QU, England; *European Marketing Data and Statistics.*

European Community Information Service, 2100 M Street, NW, Washington, D.C. 20037 (202) 862-9500; *Basic Statistics of the Community, Energy: Monthly Statistics, Energy Statistics Yearbook, Regions: Statistical Yearbook,* and *Transport Annual Statistics.*

Facts on File, 460 Park Avenue South, New York, New York 10016 (800) 443-8323; *The New Book of World Rankings.*

Food and Agricultural Organization of the United Nations (FAO) Via delle Terme di Caracalla, 00100 Rome, Italy (Telephone Number in U.S. (202) 606-7828); *The State of Food and Agriculture.*

G.K. Hall and Company, 70 Lincoln Street, Boston, Massachusetts 02111 (617) 423-3990; *The World in Figures.*

Organisation for Economic Co-operation and Development (OECD), 2 rue Andre-Pascal, 75 Paris 16, France (Telephone Number in U.S. (202) 785-6323); *Coal Information, Energy Statistics of OECD Countries, OECD Environmental Data,* and *Oil and Gas Information.*

Penn Well Publishing Company, 1421 South Sheridan Road, Post Office Box 1260, Tulsa, Oklahoma 74101 (800) 752-9764; *International Energy Statistics Sourcebook.*

Statistical Office of the United Nations, Publishing Service, New York, New York 10017 (800) 253-9646; *Energy Statistics Yearbook,* and *Statistical Yearbook.*

Times Books, 201 East 50th Street, New York, New York 10022 (212) 751-2600; *The Economist Book of Vital World Statistics.*

GERMANY - ENGINEERING AND METAL PRODUCTS - EXPORTS AND IMPORTS TO DEVELOPED COUNTRIES

European Community Information Service, 2100 M Street, NW, Washington, D.C. 20037 (202) 862-9500; *Basic Statistics of the Community* and *Industrial Production: Quarterly Statistics.*

Statistical Office of the United Nations, Publishing Service, New York, New York 10017 (800) 253-9646; *Trade in Manufactures of Developing Countries.*

GERMANY - ENVIRONMENT

Organisation for Economic Co-operation and Development (OECD), 2 rue Andre-Pascal, 75 Paris 16, France (Telephone Number in U.S. (202) 785-6323); *OECD Environmental Data.*

GERMANY - EXCHANGE RATES

European Community Information Service, 2100 M Street, NW, Washington, D.C. 20037 (202) 862-9500; *Eurostatistics: Data for Short-Term Economic Analysis* and *Money and Finance.*

International Civil Aviation Organization, 1000 Sherbrooke Street West, Suite 400, Montreal, Quebec, Canada H3A 2R2 (514) 285-8219; *Civil Aviation Statistics of the World.*

National Technical Information Service, 5285 Port Royal Road, Springfield, Virginia 22161 (703) 487-4600; *Handbook of Economic Statistics.*

Organisation for Economic Co-operation and Development (OECD), 2 rue Andre-Pascal, 75 Paris 16, France (Telephone Number in U.S. (202) 785-6323); *Economic Outlook, Financial Market Trends, Revenue Statistics of OECD Member Countries,* and *Tourism Policy and International Tourism in OECD Member Countries.*

Statistical Office of the United Nations, Publishing Service, New York, New York 10017 (800) 253-9646; *Statistical Yearbook.*

GERMANY - EXCISE TAXES - See GERMANY - TAXATION

GERMANY - EXPORTS

American Automobile Manufacturers Association, 1401 H Street, NW, Suite 900, Washington, D.C. 20005 (202) 326-5500; *World Motor Vehicle Data.*

The Economist Intelligence Unit, 111 West 57th Street, New York, New York 10019 (800) 938-4685; *The World Market Atlas.*

European Community Information Service, 2100 M Street, NW, Washington, D.C. 20037 (202) 862-9500; *Basic Statistics of the*

Community, Energy: Monthly Statistics, Energy Statistics Yearbook, Eurostatistics: Data for Short-Term Economic Analysis, External Trade: Monthly Statistics, External Trade: Statistical Yearbook, and *Fisheries: Yearly Statistics.*

Food and Agricultural Organization of the United Nations (FAO) Via delle Terme di Caracalla, 00100 Rome, Italy (Telephone Number in U.S. (202) 606-7828); *The State of Food and Agriculture.*

G.K. Hall and Company, 70 Lincoln Street, Boston, Massachusetts 02111 (617) 423-3990; *The World in Figures.*

International Iron and Steel Institute, 120, rue Colonel Bourg, B-1140 Brussels, Belgium; *Steel Statistical Yearbook.*

International Lead and Zinc Study Group, Metro House, 58 St. James's Street, London SW1A 1LD, England; *Lead and Zinc Statistics.*

International Monetary Fund, 700 Nineteenth Street, NW, Washington, D.C. 20431 (202) 623-7000; *Direction of Trade Statistics.*

International Rubber Study Group, York House, 8th Floor, Empire Way, Wembley, London HA9 0PA, England; *Rubber Statistical Bulletin.*

National Technical Information Service, 5285 Port Royal Road, Springfield, Virginia 22161 (703) 487-4600; *Handbook of Economic Statistics.*

Organisation for Economic Co-operation and Development (OECD), 2 rue Andre-Pascal, 75 Paris 16, France (Telephone Number in U.S. (202) 785-6323); *Economic Outlook, The Footwear, Raw Hides and Skins, and Leather Industry in OECD Countries, Foreign Trade by Commodities, Geographical Distribution of Financial Flows to Developing Countries, Industrial Structure Statistics, The Iron and Steel Industry, Milk, Milk Products, and Egg Balances in OECD Member Countries, OECD Economic Surveys: Germany, The Pulp and Paper Industry,* and *Review of Fisheries in OECD Member Countries.*

Times Books, 201 East 50th Street, New York, New York 10022 (212) 751-2600; *The Economist Book of Vital World Statistics.*

The World Bank, 1818 H Street, NW, Washington, D.C. 20433 (202) 477-1234; *World Tables.*

GERMANY - EXTERNAL FINANCING

Organisation for Economic Co-operation and Development (OECD), 2 rue Andre-Pascal, 75 Paris 16, France (Telephone Number in U.S. (202) 785-6323); *Economic Outlook,* and *Financial Market Trends.*

GERMANY - EXTERNAL INDEBTEDNESS

National Technical Information Service, 5285 Port Royal Road, Springfield, Virginia 22161 (703) 487-4600; *Handbook of Economic Statistics.*

Organisation for Economic Co-operation and Development (OECD), 2 rue Andre-Pascal, 75 Paris 16, France (Telephone Number in U.S. (202) 785-6323); *Financial Market Trends,* and *Geographical Distribution of Financial Flows to Developing Countries.*

The World Bank, 1818 H Street, NW, Washington, D.C. 20433 (202) 477-1234; *World Tables.*

GERMANY - EXTERNAL TRADE

European Community Information Service, 2100 M Street, NW, Washington, D.C. 20037 (202) 862-9500; *ACP: Basic Statistics, Basic Statistics of the Community, Eurostatistics: Data for Short-Term Economic Analysis, External Trade: Monthly Statistics,* and *External Trade: Statistical Yearbook.*

Food and Agricultural Organization of the United Nations (FAO) Via delle Terme di Caracalla, 00100 Rome, Italy (Telephone Number in U.S. (202) 606-7828); *The State of Food and Agriculture,* and *Trade Yearbook.*

G.K. Hall and Company, 70 Lincoln Street, Boston, Massachusetts 02111 (617) 423-3990; *The World in Figures.*

National Technical Information Service, 5285 Port Royal Road, Springfield, Virginia 22161 (703) 487-4600; *Handbook of Economic Statistics.*

Statistical Office of the United Nations, Publishing Service, New York, New York 10017 (800) 253-9646; *Statistical Yearbook.*

GERMANY - FABRIC PRODUCTION - See GERMANY - TEXTILE INDUSTRY

GERMANY - FARM CROPS - See GERMANY - CROPS

GERMANY - FEMALE WORKING POPULATION - See GERMANY - EMPLOYMENT

GERMANY - FERTILITY RATES

Columbia University Press, 562 West 113th Street, New York, New York 10014 (212) 316-7100; *East European and Soviet Data Book.*

European Community Information Service, 2100 M Street, NW, Washington, D.C. 20037 (202) 862-9500; *Demographic Statistics.*

Facts on File, 460 Park Avenue South, New York, New York 10016 (800) 443-8323; *The New Book of World Rankings.*

Times Books, 201 East 50th Street, New York, New York 10022 (212) 751-2600; *The Economist Book of Vital World Statistics.*

The World Bank, 1818 H Street, NW, Washington, D.C. 20433 (202) 477-1234; *World Tables.*

GERMANY - FERTILIZER

European Community Information Service, 2100 M Street, NW, Washington, D.C. 20037 (202) 862-9500; *Basic Statistics of the Community.*

Food and Agricultural Organization of the United Nations (FAO) Via delle Terme di Caracalla, 00100 Rome, Italy (Telephone Number in U.S. (202) 606-7828); *The State of Food and Agriculture.*

National Technical Information Service, 5285 Port Royal Road, Springfield, Virginia 22161 (703) 487-4600; *Handbook of Economic Statistics.*

Organisation for Economic Co-operation and Development (OECD), 2 rue Andre-Pascal, 75 Paris 16, France (Telephone Number in U.S. (202) 785-6323); *Economic Accounts for Agriculture,* and *Foreign Trade by Commodities.*

Statistical Office of the United Nations, Publishing Service, New York, New York 10017 (800) 253-9646; *Statistical Yearbook.*

GERMANY - FETAL MORTALITY

European Community Information Service, 2100 M Street, NW, Washington, D.C. 20037 (202) 862-9500; *Basic Statistics of the Community* and *Demographic Statistics.*

Statistical Office of the United Nations, Publishing Service, New York, New York 10017 (800) 253-9646; *Demographic Yearbook.*

World Health Organization, Office of Publications, Avenue Appia, CH-1211 Geneva 27, Switzerland (Telephone Number in U.S. (518) 436-9686); *World Health Statistics Annual.*

GERMANY - FIBRE PRODUCTION - See GERMANY - TEXTILE INDUSTRY

GERMANY - FILAMENT PRODUCTION - See GERMANY - TEXTILE INDUSTRY

GERMANY - FILM - See GERMANY - MOTION PICTURES

GERMANY - FINANCE

European Community Information Service, 2100 M Street, NW, Washington, D.C. 20037 (202) 862-9500; *ACP: Basic Statistics, Basic Statistics of the Community, Eurostatistics: Data for Short-Term Economic Analysis,* and *Money and Finance.*

Facts on File, 460 Park Avenue South, New York, New York 10016 (800) 443-8323; *The New Book of World Rankings.*

G.K. Hall and Company, 70 Lincoln Street, Boston, Massachusetts 02111 (617) 423-3990; *The World in Figures.*

Organisation for Economic Co-operation and Development (OECD), 2 rue Andre-Pascal, 75 Paris 16, France (Telephone Number in U.S. (202) 785-6323); *Economic Outlook, Financial Market Trends, Geographical Distribution of Financial Flows to Developing Countries, Main Economic Indicators - Historical Statistics,* and *OECD Financial Statistics.*

GERMANY - FISHERIES

Euromonitor Publications Limited, 87-88 Turnmill Street, London EC1M 5QU, England; *European Marketing Data and Statistics.*

European Community Information Service, 2100 M Street, NW, Washington, D.C. 20037 (202) 862-9500; *Agriculture: Statistical Yearbook, Basic Statistics of the Community,* and *Fisheries: Yearly Statistics.*

Facts on File, 460 Park Avenue South, New York, New York 10016 (800) 443-8323; *The New Book of World Rankings.*

Food and Agricultural Organization of the United Nations (FAO) Via delle Terme di Caracalla, 00100 Rome, Italy (Telephone Number in U.S. (202) 606-7828); *The State of Food and Agriculture,* and *Yearbook of Fishery Statistics.*

National Technical Information Service, 5285 Port Royal Road, Springfield, Virginia 22161 (703) 487-4600; *Handbook of Economic Statistics.*

Organisation for Economic Co-operation and Development (OECD), 2 rue Andre-Pascal, 75 Paris 16, France (Telephone Number in U.S. (202) 785-6323); *Foreign Trade by Commodities, Industrial Structure Statistics,* and *Review of Fisheries in OECD Member Countries.*

Statistical Office of the United Nations, Publishing Service, New York, New York 10017 (800) 253-9646; *Statistical Yearbook,* see section on Manufacturing - Canned fish; and Manufacturing - Salted fish.

GERMANY - FLAX AND FLAX FIBRE PRODUCTION - See GERMANY - TEXTILE INDUSTRY

GERMANY - FLOUR PRODUCTION

Commodity Research Bureau, Incorporated, 75 Wall Street, New York, New York 10005 (212) 504-7754; *Commodity Year Book.*

European Community Information Service, 2100 M Street, NW, Washington, D.C. 20037 (202) 862-9500; *Basic Statistics of the Community.*

Statistical Office of the United Nations, Publishing Service, New York, New York 10017 (800) 253-9646; *Statistical Yearbook.*

GERMANY - FOOD

European Community Information Service, 2100 M Street, NW, Washington, D.C. 20037 (202) 862-9500; *Basic Statistics of the Community.*

Food and Agricultural Organization of the United Nations (FAO), Via delle Terme di Caracalla, 00100 Rome, Italy (Telephone Number in U.S. (202) 606-7828); *Production Yearbook,* and *The State of Food and Agriculture.*

G.K. Hall and Company, 70 Lincoln Street, Boston, Massachusetts 02111 (617) 423-3990; *The World in Figures.*

Organisation for Economic Co-operation and Development (OECD), 2 rue Andre-Pascal, 75 Paris 16, France (Telephone Number in U.S. (202) 785-6323); *Food Consumption Statistics* and *Foreign Trade by Commodities.*

Statistical Office of the United Nations, Publishing Service, New York, New York 10017 (800) 253-9646; *Trade in Manufactures of Developing Countries.*

GERMANY - FOOTWEAR - PRODUCTION INDEX

Organisation for Economic Co-operation and Development (OECD), 2 rue Andre-Pascal, 75 Paris 16, France (Telephone Number in U.S. (202) 785-6323); *Indicators of Industrial Activity.*

GERMANY - FOREIGN AID

G.K. Hall and Company, 70 Lincoln Street, Boston, Massachusetts 02111 (617) 423-3990; *The World in Figures.*

National Technical Information Service, 5285 Port Royal Road, Springfield, Virginia 22161 (703) 487-4600; *Handbook of Economic Statistics.*

GERMANY - FOREIGN DEBT

Organisation for Economic Co-operation and Development (OECD), 2 rue Andre-Pascal, 75 Paris 16, France (Telephone Number in U.S. (202) 785-6323); *Economic Outlook.*

GERMANY - FOREIGN FINANCE

Organisation for Economic Co-operation and Development (OECD), 2 rue Andre-Pascal, 75 Paris 16, France (Telephone Number in U.S. (202) 785-6323); *Economic Outlook,* and *Financial Market Trends.*

GERMANY - FOREIGN INDEBTEDNESS

Organisation for Economic Co-operation and Development (OECD), 2 rue Andre-Pascal, 75 Paris 16, France (Telephone Number in U.S. (202) 785-6323); *Economic Outlook*, and *Financial Market Trends*.

GERMANY - FOREIGN OFFICIAL RESERVES

European Community Information Service, 2100 M Street, NW, Washington, D.C. 20037 (202) 862-9500; *Money and Finance*.

GERMANY - FOREIGN TRADE

Euromonitor Publications Limited, 87-88 Turnmill Street, London EC1M 5QU, England; *European Marketing Data and Statistics*.

European Community Information Service, 2100 M Street, NW, Washington, D.C. 20037 (202) 862-9500; *Basic Statistics of the Community*, *Energy Statistics Yearbook*, and *Iron and Steel: Statistical Yearbook*.

Facts on File, 460 Park Avenue South, New York, New York 10016 (800) 443-8323; *The New Book of World Rankings*.

Food and Agricultural Organization of the United Nations (FAO) Via delle Terme di Caracalla, 00100 Rome, Italy (Telephone Number in U.S. (202) 606-7828); *The State of Food and Agriculture*.

G.K. Hall and Company, 70 Lincoln Street, Boston, Massachusetts 02111 (617) 423-3990; *The World in Figures*.

International Iron and Steel Institute, 120, rue Colonel Bourg, B-1140 Brussels, Belgium; *Steel Statistical Yearbook*.

International Monetary Fund, 700 Nineteenth Street, NW, Washington, D.C. 20431 (202) 623-7000; *International Financial Statistics*.

National Technical Information Service, 5285 Port Royal Road, Springfield, Virginia 22161 (703) 487-4600; *Handbook of Economic Statistics*.

Organisation for Economic Co-operation and Development (OECD), 2 rue Andre-Pascal, 75 Paris 16, France (Telephone Number in U.S. (202) 785-6323); *Economic Outlook*, *The Footwear, Raw Hides and Skins, and Leather Industry in OECD Countries*, *Foreign Trade by Commodities*, *Main Economic Indicators - Historical Statistics*, *Maritime Transport*, *Meat Balances in OECD Member Countries*, and *OECD Economic Surveys: Germany*.

Statistical Office of the United Nations, Publishing Service, New York, New York 10017 (800) 253-9646; *International Trade Statistics Yearbook*, *Trade in Manufactures of Developing Countries*, and *Statistical Yearbook*.

The World Bank, 1818 H Street, NW, Washington, D.C. 20433 (202) 477-1234; *World Tables*.

World Bureau of Metal Statistics, 27-A High Street, Ware, Herts, SG12 9BA, England; *World Metal Statistics*.

GERMANY - FORESTRY AND FOREST PRODUCTS

Euromonitor Publications Limited, 87-88 Turnmill Street, London EC1M 5QU, England; *European Marketing Data and Statistics*.

European Community Information Service, 2100 M Street, NW, Washington, D.C. 20037 (202) 862-9500; *Agriculture: Statistical Yearbook*, *Basic Statistics of the Community* and *Industrial Production: Quarterly Statistics*.

Facts on File, 460 Park Avenue South, New York, New York 10016 (800) 443-8323; *The New Book of World Rankings*.

Food and Agricultural Organization of the United Nations (FAO) Via delle Terme di Caracalla, 00100 Rome, Italy (Telephone Number in U.S. (202) 606-7828); *The State of Food and Agriculture*, and *Yearbook of Forest Products*.

Forest and Paper Association, 1250 Connecticut Avenue, NW, Washington, D.C. 20036 (202) 463-2455; *Wood Pulp and Fiber Statistics*.

G.K. Hall and Company, 70 Lincoln Street, Boston, Massachusetts 02111 (617) 423-3990; *The World in Figures*.

National Technical Information Service, 5285 Port Royal Road, Springfield, Virginia 22161 (703) 487-4600; *Handbook of Economic Statistics*.

Organisation for Economic Co-operation and Development (OECD), 2 rue Andre-Pascal, 75 Paris 16, France (Telephone Number in U.S. (202) 785-6323); *Indicators of Industrial Activity*, *Industrial Structure Statistics*, *The Pulp and Paper Industry*, and *Foreign Trade by Commodities*.

Statistical Office of the United Nations, Publishing Service, New York, New York 10017 (800) 253-9646; *Statistical Yearbook*.

United Nations Educational, Scientific and Cultural Organization (UNESCO), 7 Place de Fontenoy, F-75700 Paris, France (Telephone Number in U.S. (212) 963-5981); *Statistical Yearbook*.

GERMANY - FRUIT PRODUCTION - See GERMANY - CROPS

GERMANY - FURNITURE AND WOOD PRODUCTS - EXPORTS AND IMPORTS

European Community Information Service, 2100 M Street, NW, Washington, D.C. 20037 (202) 862-9500; *Basic Statistics of the Community*.

Organisation for Economic Co-operation and Development (OECD), 2 rue Andre-Pascal, 75 Paris 16, France (Telephone Number in U.S. (202) 785-6323); *Foreign Trade by Commodities*, and *Industrial Structure Statistics*.

Statistical Office of the United Nations, Publishing Service, New York, New York 10017 (800) 253-9646; *Trade in Manufactures of Developing Countries*.

GERMANY - GARLIC PRODUCTION - See GERMANY - CROPS

GERMANY - GAS - See GERMANY - MINING AND MINERAL PRODUCTS

GERMANY - GENERAL INDUSTRIAL STATISTICS

European Community Information Service, 2100 M Street, NW, Washington, D.C. 20037 (202) 862-9500; *Basic Statistics of the Community*.

Statistical Office of the United Nations, Publishing Service, New York, New York 10017 (800) 253-9646; *Industrial Statistics Yearbook*.

GERMANY - GENERAL MORTALITY

European Community Information Service, 2100 M Street, NW, Washington, D.C. 20037 (202) 862-9500; *Basic Statistics of the Community* and *Demographic Statistics.*

Statistical Office of the United Nations, Publishing Service, New York, New York 10017 (800) 253-9646; *Demographic Yearbook.*

World Health Organization, Office of Publications, Avenue Appia, CH-1211 Geneva 27, Switzerland (Telephone Number in U.S. (518) 436-9686); *World Health Statistics Annual.*

GERMANY - GEOGRAPHIC DATA

European Community Information Service, 2100 M Street, NW, Washington, D.C. 20037 (202) 862-9500; *Basic Statistics of the Community.*

Facts on File, 460 Park Avenue South, New York, New York 10016 (800) 443-8323; *The New Book of World Rankings.*

GERMANY - GLASS AND GLASS PRODUCTS - PRODUCTION INDEX

Organisation for Economic Co-operation and Development (OECD), 2 rue Andre-Pascal, 75 Paris 16, France (Telephone Number in U.S. (202) 785-6323); *Indicators of Industrial Activity.*

GERMANY - GOATS - See GERMANY - LIVESTOCK AND POULTRY

GERMANY - GOLD HOLDINGS

International Monetary Fund, 700 Nineteenth Street, NW, Washington, D.C. 20431 (202) 623-7000; *International financial Statistics.*

Statistical Office of the United Nations, Publishing Service, New York, New York 10017 (800) 253-9646; *Statistical Yearbook.*

The World Bank, 1818 H Street, NW, Washington, D.C. 20433 (202) 477-1234; *World Tables.*

GERMANY - GOLD PRODUCTION AND CONSUMPTION - See GERMANY - MINING AND MINERAL PRODUCTS

GERMANY - GOVERNMENT

European Community Information Service, 2100 M Street, NW, Washington, D.C. 20037 (202) 862-9500; *Basic Statistics of the Community.*

G.K. Hall and Company, 70 Lincoln Street, Boston, Massachusetts 02111 (617) 423-3990; *The World in Figures.*

GERMANY - GOVERNMENT BONDS - See GERMANY - BONDS

GERMANY - GOVERNMENT CONSUMPTION

European Community Information Service, 2100 M Street, NW, Washington, D.C. 20037 (202) 862-9500; *Basic Statistics of the Community.*

GERMANY - GOVERNMENT EXPENDITURE

European Community Information Service, 2100 M Street, NW, Washington, D.C. 20037 (202) 862-9500; *Basic Statistics of the Community* and *Government Financing of Research and Development.*

Organisation for Economic Co-operation and Development (OECD), 2 rue Andre-Pascal, 75 Paris 16, France (Telephone Number in U.S. (202) 785-6323); *Economic Outlook.*

Times Books, 201 East 50th Street, New York, New York 10022 (212) 751-2600; *The Economist Book of Vital World Statistics.*

The World Bank, 1818 H Street, NW, Washington, D.C. 20433 (202) 477-1234; *World Tables.*

GERMANY - GOVERNMENT FINANCES

European Community Information Service, 2100 M Street, NW, Washington, D.C. 20037 (202) 862-9500; *Basic Statistics of the Community, Government Financing of Research and Development,* and *Money and Finance.*

Organisation for Economic Co-operation and Development (OECD), 2 rue Andre-Pascal, 75 Paris 16, France (Telephone Number in U.S. (202) 785-6323); *Economic Outlook.*

Statistical Office of the United Nations, Publishing Service, New York, New York 10017 (800) 253-9646; *Statistical Yearbook.*

GERMANY - GOVERNMENT REVENUE

European Community Information Service, 2100 M Street, NW, Washington, D.C. 20037 (202) 862-9500; *Basic Statistics of the Community* and *Government Financing of Research and Development.*

Organisation for Economic Co-operation and Development (OECD), 2 rue Andre-Pascal, 75 Paris 16, France (Telephone Number in U.S. (202) 785-6323); *Economic Outlook,* and *Revenue Statistics of OECD Member Countries.*

Times Books, 201 East 50th Street, New York, New York 10022 (212) 751-2600; *The Economist Book of Vital World Statistics.*

The World Bank, 1818 H Street, NW, Washington, D.C. 20433 (202) 477-1234; *World Tables.*

GERMANY - GRAIN PRODUCTION - See GERMANY - CROPS

GERMANY - GRANTS

National Technical Information Service, 5285 Port Royal Road, Springfield, Virginia 22161 (703) 487-4600; *Handbook of Economic Statistics.*

Organisation for Economic Co-operation and Development (OECD), 2 rue Andre-Pascal, 75 Paris 16, France (Telephone Number in U.S. (202) 785-6323); *Geographical Distribution of Financial Flows to Developing Countries.*

GERMANY - GREEN PEPPER AND CHILIE PRODUCTION - See GERMANY - CROPS

GERMANY - GROSS DOMESTIC PRODUCT

The Economist Intelligence Unit, 111 West 57th Street, New York, New York 10019 (800) 938-4685; *The World Market Atlas.*

European Community Information Service, 2100 M Street, NW, Washington, D.C. 20037 (202) 862-9500; *Basic Statistics of the Community, Eurostatistics: Data for Short-Term Economic Analysis, Government Financing of Research and Development, Iron and Steel: Statistical Yearbook,* and *Money and Finance.*

Facts on File, 460 Park Avenue South, New York, New York 10016 (800) 443-8323; *The New Book of World Rankings.*

G.K. Hall and Company, 70 Lincoln Street, Boston, Massachusetts 02111 (617) 423-3990; *The World in Figures.*

National Technical Information Service, 5285 Port Royal Road, Springfield, Virginia 22161 (703) 487-4600; *Handbook of Economic Statistics.*

Organisation for Economic Co-operation and Development (OECD), 2 rue Andre-Pascal, 75 Paris 16, France (Telephone Number in U.S. (202) 785-6323); *Economic Outlook, Geographical Distribution of Financial Flows to Developing Countries,* and *Revenue Statistics of OECD Member Countries.*

Statistical Office of the United Nations, Publishing Service, New York, New York 10017 (800) 253-9646; *Statistical Yearbook.*

Times Books, 201 East 50th Street, New York, New York 10022 (212) 751-2600; *The Economist Book of Vital World Statistics.*

The World Bank, 1818 H Street, NW, Washington, D.C. 20433 (202) 477-1234; *World Tables.*

GERMANY - GROSS INDUSTRIAL PRODUCT

European Community Information Service, 2100 M Street, NW, Washington, D.C. 20037 (202) 862-9500; *Government Financing of Research and Development.*

GERMANY - GROSS NATIONAL PRODUCT

European Community Information Service, 2100 M Street, NW, Washington, D.C. 20037 (202) 862-9500; *ACP: Basic Statistics,* and *Basic Statistics of the Community.*

National Technical Information Service, 5285 Port Royal Road, Springfield, Virginia 22161 (703) 487-4600; *Handbook of Economic Statistics.*

Organisation for Economic Co-operation and Development (OECD), 2 rue Andre-Pascal, 75 Paris 16, France (Telephone Number in U.S. (202) 785-6323); *Economic Outlook,* and *Geographical Distribution of Financial Flows to Developing Countries.*

U.S. Arms Control and Disarmament Agency, 320 Twenty-first Street, Northwest, Washington, D.C. 20451 (202) 647-8677; *World Military Expenditures and Arms Transfers.*

The World Bank, 1818 H Street, NW, Washington, D.C. 20433 (202) 477-1234; *World Tables.*

GERMANY - GROUNDNUT PRODUCTION - See GERMANY - CROPS

GERMANY - HAY PRODUCTION - See GERMANY - CROPS

GERMANY - HAZELNUT PRODUCTION - See GERMANY - CROPS

GERMANY - HEALTH

European Community Information Service, 2100 M Street, NW, Washington, D.C. 20037 (202) 862-9500; *Basic Statistics of the Community* and *Regions: Statistical Yearbook.*

Facts on File, 460 Park Avenue South, New York, New York 10016 (800) 443-8323; *The New Book of World Rankings.*

G.K. Hall and Company, 70 Lincoln Street, Boston, Massachusetts 02111 (617) 423-3990; *The World in Figures.*

Organisation for Economic Co-operation and Development (OECD), 2 rue Andre-Pascal, 75 Paris 16, France (Telephone Number in U.S. (202) 785-6323); *OECD Health Systems: Facts and Trends.*

Statistical Office of the United Nations, Publishing Service, New York, New York 10017 (800) 253-9646; *Statistical Yearbook.*

Times Books, 201 East 50th Street, New York, New York 10022 (212) 751-2600; *The Economist Book of Vital World Statistics.*

World Health Organization, Office of Publications, Avenue Appia, CH-1211 Geneva 27, Switzerland (Telephone Number in U.S. (518) 436-9686); *World Health Statistics Annual.*

GERMANY - HEMP FIBRE PRODUCTION - See GERMANY - TEXTILE INDUSTRY

GERMANY - HIDE PRODUCTION

Food and Agricultural Organization of the United Nations (FAO), Via delle Terme di Caracalla, 00100 Rome, Italy (Telephone Number in U.S. (202) 606-7828); *Production Yearbook.*

Organisation for Economic Co-operation and Development (OECD), 2 rue Andre-Pascal, 75 Paris 16, France (Telephone Number in U.S. (202) 785-6323); *The Footwear, Raw Hides and Skins, and Leather Industry in OECD Countries, Foreign Trade by Commodities,* and *Indicators of Industrial Activity.*

GERMANY - HIGHWAYS

European Community Information Service, 2100 M Street, NW, Washington, D.C. 20037 (202) 862-9500; *Basic Statistics of the Community* and *Transport Annual Statistics.*

G.K. Hall and Company, 70 Lincoln Street, Boston, Massachusetts 02111 (617) 423-3990; *The World in Figures.*

International Road Federation, 525 School Street, SW, Washington, D.C. 20024 (202) 554-2106; *World Road Statistics.*

Statistical Office of the United Nations, Publishing Service, New York, New York 10017 (800) 253-9646; *Annual Bulletin of Transport Statistics for Europe.*

GERMANY - HONEY PRODUCTION

Commodity Research Bureau, Incorporated, 75 Wall Street, New York, New York 10005 (212) 504-7754; *Commodity Year Book.*

GERMANY - HOPS PRODUCTION - See GERMANY - CROPS

GERMANY - HORSES - See GERMANY - LIVESTOCK AND POULTRY

GERMANY - HOURS OF WORK - See GERMANY - EMPLOYMENT

GERMANY - HOUSING AND HOUSING UNITS

Columbia University Press, 562 West 113th Street, New York, New York 10014 (212) 316-7100; *East European and Soviet Data Book.*

European Community Information Service, 2100 M Street, NW, Washington, D.C. 20037 (202) 862-9500; *Basic Statistics of the Community, Labor Force Sample Survey,* and *Regions: Statistical Yearbook.*

Facts on File, 460 Park Avenue South, New York, New York 10016 (800) 443-8323; *The New Book of World Rankings.*

National Technical Information Service, 5285 Port Royal Road, Springfield, Virginia 22161 (703) 487-4600; *Handbook of Economic Statistics.*

GERMANY - HOUSING CONSTRUCTION - See GERMANY - CONSTRUCTION INDUSTRY

GERMANY - HOUSING EXPENDITURES

European Community Information Service, 2100 M Street, NW, Washington, D.C. 20037 (202) 862-9500; *Basic Statistics of the Community.*

GERMANY - HYDROCHLORIC ACID PRODUCTION

European Community Information Service, 2100 M Street, NW, Washington, D.C. 20037 (202) 862-9500; *Basic Statistics of the Community.*

Statistical Office of the United Nations, Publishing Service, New York, New York 10017 (800) 253-9646; *Statistical Yearbook.*

GERMANY - ILLITERATE POPULATION

The Economist Intelligence Unit, 111 West 57th Street, New York, New York 10019 (800) 938-4685; *The World Market Atlas.*

G.K. Hall and Company, 70 Lincoln Street, Boston, Massachusetts 02111 (617) 423-3990; *The World in Figures.*

GERMANY - IMPORTS

American Automobile Manufacturers Association, 1401 H Street, NW, Suite 900, Washington, D.C. 20005 (202) 326-5500; *World Motor Vehicle Data.*

The Economist Intelligence Unit, 111 West 57th Street, New York, New York 10019 (800) 938-4685; *The World Market Atlas.*

European Community Information Service, 2100 M Street, NW, Washington, D.C. 20037 (202) 862-9500; *Basic Statistics of the Community, Energy: Monthly Statistics, Energy Statistics Yearbook, Eurostatistics: Data for Short-Term Economic Analysis, External Trade: Monthly Statistics, External Trade: Statistical Yearbook,* and *Fisheries: Yearly Statistics.*

Food and Agricultural Organization of the United Nations (FAO) Via delle Terme di Caracalla, 00100 Rome, Italy (Telephone Number in U.S. (202) 606-7828); *The State of Food and Agriculture.*

G.K. Hall and Company, 70 Lincoln Street, Boston, Massachusetts 02111 (617) 423-3990; *The World in Figures.*

International Iron and Steel Institute, 120, rue Colonel Bourg, B-1140 Brussels, Belgium; *Steel Statistical Yearbook.*

International Lead and Zinc Study Group, Metro House, 58 St. James's Street, London SW1A 1LD, England; *Lead and Zinc Statistics.*

International Monetary Fund, 700 Nineteenth Street, NW, Washington, D.C. 20431 (202) 623-7000; *Direction of Trade Statistics.*

International Rubber Study Group, York House, 8th Floor, Empire Way, Wembley, London HA9 0PA, England; *Rubber Statistical Bulletin.*

National Technical Information Service, 5285 Port Royal Road, Springfield, Virginia 22161 (703) 487-4600; *Handbook of Economic Statistics.*

Organisation for Economic Co-operation and Development (OECD), 2 rue Andre-Pascal, 75 Paris 16, France (Telephone Number in U.S. (202) 785-6323); *Economic Outlook, The Footwear, Raw Hides and Skins, and Leather Industry in OECD Countries, Industrial Structure Statistics, The Iron and Steel Industry, Milk, Milk Products, and Egg Balances in OECD Member Countries, OECD Economic Surveys: Germany, The Pulp and Paper Industry,* and *Review of Fisheries in OECD Member Countries.*

Times Books, 201 East 50th Street, New York, New York 10022 (212) 751-2600; *The Economist Book of Vital World Statistics.*

The World Bank, 1818 H Street, NW, Washington, D.C. 20433 (202) 477-1234; *World Tables.*

GERMANY - INCOME TAXES - See GERMANY - TAXATION

GERMANY - INDUSTRIAL METALS PRODUCTION

European Community Information Service, 2100 M Street, NW, Washington, D.C. 20037 (202) 862-9500; *Basic Statistics of the Community.*

Organisation for Economic Co-operation and Development (OECD), 2 rue Andre-Pascal, 75 Paris 16, France (Telephone Number in U.S. (202) 785-6323); *Indicators of Industrial Activity.*

Statistical Office of the United Nations, Publishing Service, New York, New York 10017 (800) 253-9646; *Statistical Yearbook.*

GERMANY - INDUSTRY

European Community Information Service, 2100 M Street, NW, Washington, D.C. 20037 (202) 862-9500; *Basic Statistics of the Community, Employment and Unemployment, Eurostatistics: Data for Short-Term Economic Analysis,* and *Labor Force Sample Survey.*

Facts on File, 460 Park Avenue South, New York, New York 10016 (800) 443-8323; *The New Book of World Rankings.*

G.K. Hall and Company, 70 Lincoln Street, Boston, Massachusetts 02111 (617) 423-3990; *The World in Figures.*

International Labour Office, I.L.O. Publications, CH-1211, Geneva 22, Switzerland; *Yearbook of Labour Statistics.*

National Technical Information Service, 5285 Port Royal Road, Springfield, Virginia 22161 (703) 487-4600; *Handbook of Economic Statistics.*

Organisation for Economic Co-operation and Development (OECD), 2 rue Andre-Pascal, 75 Paris 16, France (Telephone Number in U.S. (202) 785-6323); *Economic Outlook, Indicators of Industrial Activity, Industrial Structure Statistics, Main Economic Indicators - Historical Statistics,* and *OECD Environmental Data.*

Statistical Office of the United Nations, Publishing Service, New York, New York 10017 (800) 253-9646; *Statistical Yearbook.*

Times Books, 201 East 50th Street, New York, New York 10022 (212) 751-2600; *The Economist Book of Vital World Statistics.*

The World Bank, 1818 H Street, NW, Washington, D.C. 20433 (202) 477-1234; *World Tables.*

World Intellectual Property Organization, 34 Chemin des Colombettes, CH-1211 Geneva 20, Switzerland; *Industrial Property Statistics.*

GERMANY - INFANT AND MATERNAL MORTALITY

European Community Information Service, 2100 M Street, NW, Washington, D.C. 20037 (202) 862-9500; *Basic Statistics of the Community* and *Demographic Statistics.*

Statistical Office of the United Nations, Publishing Service, New York, New York 10017 (800) 253-9646; *Demographic Yearbook, Statistical Yearbook.*

Times Books, 201 East 50th Street, New York, New York 10022 (212) 751-2600; *The Economist Book of Vital World Statistics.*

The World Bank, 1818 H Street, NW, Washington, D.C. 20433 (202) 477-1234; *World Tables.*

World Health Organization, Office of Publications, Avenue Appia, CH-1211 Geneva 27, Switzerland (Telephone Number in U.S. (518) 436-9686); *World Health Statistics Annual.*

GERMANY - INFLATIONARY FACTORS

National Technical Information Service, 5285 Port Royal Road, Springfield, Virginia 22161 (703) 487-4600; *Handbook of Economic Statistics.*

GERMANY - INTEREST RATES

European Community Information Service, 2100 M Street, NW, Washington, D.C. 20037 (202) 862-9500; *Money and Finance.*

National Technical Information Service, 5285 Port Royal Road, Springfield, Virginia 22161 (703) 487-4600; *Handbook of Economic Statistics.*

Organisation for Economic Co-operation and Development (OECD), 2 rue Andre-Pascal, 75 Paris 16, France (Telephone Number in U.S. (202) 785-6323); *Economic Outlook, Financial Market Trends, Main Economic Indicators - Historical Statistics,* and *OECD Financial Statistics.*

GERMANY - INTERNAL TRADE

European Community Information Service, 2100 M Street, NW, Washington, D.C. 20037 (202) 862-9500; *Basic Statistics of the Community.*

Organisation for Economic Co-operation and Development (OECD), 2 rue Andre-Pascal, 75 Paris 16, France (Telephone Number in U.S. (202) 785-6323); *Main Economic Indicators - Historical Statistics.*

Statistical Office of the United Nations, Publishing Service, New York, New York 10017 (800) 253-9646; *Statistical Yearbook.*

GERMANY - INTERNATIONAL FINANCE

European Community Information Service, 2100 M Street, NW, Washington, D.C. 20037 (202) 862-9500; *Basic Statistics of the Community.*

Organisation for Economic Co-operation and Development (OECD), 2 rue Andre-Pascal, 75 Paris 16, France (Telephone Number in U.S. (202) 785-6323); *Economic Outlook,* and *Financial Market Trends.*

GERMANY - INTERNATIONAL LIQUIDITY

Organisation for Economic Co-operation and Development (OECD), 2 rue Andre-Pascal, 75 Paris 16, France (Telephone Number in U.S. (202) 785-6323); *Economic Outlook,* and *Financial Market Trends.*

GERMANY - INTERNATIONAL RESERVES EXCLUDING GOLD

National Technical Information Service, 5285 Port Royal Road, Springfield, Virginia 22161 (703) 487-4600; *Handbook of Economic Statistics.*

Statistical Office of the United Nations, Publishing Service, New York, New York 10017 (800) 253-9646; *Statistical Yearbook.*

The World Bank, 1818 H Street, NW, Washington, D.C. 20433 (202) 477-1234; *World Tables.*

GERMANY - INTERNATIONAL STATISTICS

Organisation for Economic Co-operation and Development (OECD), 2 rue Andre-Pascal, 75 Paris 16, France (Telephone Number in U.S. (202) 785-6323); *Financial Market Trends,* and *Tourism Policy and International Tourism in OECD Member Countries.*

GERMANY - INVESTMENTS

Organisation for Economic Co-operation and Development (OECD), 2 rue Andre-Pascal, 75 Paris 16, France (Telephone Number in U.S. (202) 785-6323); *Economic Outlook, Financial Market Trends, Industrial Structure Statistics, The Iron and Steel Industry,* and *Textile Industry in OECD Countries.*

GERMANY - IRON ORE - See GERMANY - MINING AND MINERAL PRODUCTS

GERMANY - JUTE PRODUCTION - See GERMANY - CROPS

GERMANY - LABOR FORCE

Columbia University Press, 562 West 113th Street, New York, New York 10014 (212) 316-7100; *East European and Soviet Data Book.*

European Community Information Service, 2100 M Street, NW, Washington, D.C. 20037 (202) 862-9500; *Basic Statistics of the Community, Labor Force Sample Survey,* and *Regions: Statistical Yearbook.*

Facts on File, 460 Park Avenue South, New York, New York 10016 (800) 443-8323; *The New Book of World Rankings.*

Food and Agricultural Organization of the United Nations (FAO) Via delle Terme di Caracalla, 00100 Rome, Italy (Telephone Number in U.S. (202) 606-7828); *The State of Food and Agriculture.*

G.K. Hall and Company, 70 Lincoln Street, Boston, Massachusetts 02111 (617) 423-3990; *The World of Figures.*

National Technical Information Service, 5285 Port Royal Road, Springfield, Virginia 22161 (703) 487-4600; *Handbook of Economic Statistics.*

Organisation for Economic Co-operation and Development (OECD), 2 rue Andre-Pascal, 75 Paris 16, France (Telephone Number in U.S. (202) 785-6323); *Economic Outlook, The Iron and Steel Industry, Main Economic Indicators - Historical Statistics, Maritime Transport, OECD Economic Surveys: Germany, OECD Employment Outlook,* and *Textile Industry in OECD Countries.*

Times Books, 201 East 50th Street, New York, New York 10022 (212) 751-2600; *The Economist Book of Vital World Statistics.*

The World Bank, 1818 H Street, NW, Washington, D.C. 20433 (202) 477-1234; *World Tables.*

GERMANY - LABOR PRODUCTIVITY

International Labour Office, I.L.O. Publications, CH-1211, Geneva 22, Switzerland; *Yearbook of Labour Statistics.*

Organisation for Economic Co-operation and Development (OECD), 2 rue Andre-Pascal, 75 Paris 16, France (Telephone Number in U.S. (202) 785-6323); *Economic Outlook,* and *OECD Employment Outlook.*

GERMANY - LAND USE

Euromonitor Publications Limited, 87-88 Turnmill Street, London EC1M 5QU, England; *European Marketing Data and Statistics.*

European Community Information Service, 2100 M Street, NW, Washington, D.C. 20037 (202) 862-9500; *Agriculture: Statistical Yearbook, Basic Statistics of the Community Crop Production: Quarterly Statistics,* and *Regions: Statistical Yearbook.*

Food and Agricultural Organization of the United Nations (FAO), Via delle Terme di Caracalla, 00100 Rome, Italy (Telephone Number in U.S. (202) 606-7828); *Production Yearbook.*

G.K. Hall and Company, 70 Lincoln Street, Boston, Massachusetts 02111 (617) 423-3990; *The World in Figures.*

GERMANY - LEAD AND LEAD ORE - See GERMANY - MINING AND MINERAL PRODUCTS

GERMANY - LEATHER - PRODUCTION INDEX

Organisation for Economic Co-operation and Development (OECD), 2 rue Andre-Pascal, 75 Paris 16, France (Telephone Number in U.S. (202) 785-6323); *Indicators of Industrial Activity.*

GERMANY - LEATHER AND FOOTWEAR - EXPORTS AND IMPORTS

European Community Information Service, 2100 M Street, NW, Washington, D.C. 20037 (202) 862-9500; *Basic Statistics of the Community.*

Organisation for Economic Co-operation and Development (OECD), 2 rue Andre-Pascal, 75 Paris 16, France (Telephone Number in U.S. (202) 785-6323); *The Footwear, Raw Hides and Skins, and Leather Industry in OECD Countries.*

Statistical Office of the United Nations, Publishing Service, New York, New York 10017 (800) 253-9646; *Trade in Manufactures of Developing Countries.*

GERMANY - LIBRARIES

Euromonitor Publications Limited, 87-88 Turnmill Street, London EC1M 5QU, England; *European Marketing Data and Statistics.*

Facts on File, 460 Park Avenue South, New York, New York 10016 (800) 443-8323; *The New Book of World Rankings.*

United Nations Educational, Scientific and Cultural Organization (UNESCO), 7 Place de Fontenoy, F-75700 Paris, France (Telephone Number in U.S. (212) 963-5981); *Statistical Yearbook.*

GERMANY - LIGNITE PRODUCTION - See GERMANY - MINING AND MINERAL PRODUCTS

GERMANY - LIVESTOCK AND POULTRY

Commodity Research Bureau, Incorporated, 75 Wall Street, New York, New York 10005 (212) 504-7754; *Commodity Year Book.*

Euromonitor Publications Limited, 87-88 Turnmill Street, London EC1M 5QU, England; *European Marketing Data and Statistics.*

European Community Information Service, 2100 M Street, NW, Washington, D.C. 20037 (202) 862-9500; *Agriculture: Statistical Yearbook, Basic Statistics of the Community, Eurostatistics: Data for Short-Term Economic Analysis,* and *Regions: Statistical Yearbook.*

Facts on File, 460 Park Avenue South, New York, New York 10016 (800) 443-8323; *The New Book of World Rankings.*

Food and Agricultural Organization of the United Nations (FAO), Via delle Terme di Caracalla, 00100 Rome, Italy (Telephone Number in U.S. (202) 606-7828); *Production Yearbook,* and *The State of Food and Agriculture.*

G.K. Hall and Company, 70 Lincoln Street, Boston, Massachusetts 02111 (617) 423-3990; *The World in Figures.*

Organisation for Economic Co-operation and Development (OECD), 2 rue Andre-Pascal, 75 Paris 16, France (Telephone Number in U.S. (202) 785-6323); *Economic Accounts for Agriculture,* and *Meat Balances in OECD Member Countries.*

Statistical Office of the United Nations, Publishing Service, New York, New York 10017 (800) 253-9646; *Statistical Yearbook.*

GERMANY - LIVING LEVELS

G.K. Hall and Company, 70 Lincoln Street, Boston, Massachusetts 02111 (617) 423-3990; *The World in Figures.*

Organisation for Economic Co-operation and Development (OECD), 2 rue Andre-Pascal, 75 Paris 16, France (Telephone Number in U.S. (202) 785-6323); *Economic Outlook.*

Times Books, 201 East 50th Street, New York, New York 10022 (212) 751-2600; *The Economist Book of Vital World Statistics.*

GERMANY - MACHINERY - PRODUCTION INDEX

Organisation for Economic Co-operation and Development (OECD), 2 rue Andre-Pascal, 75 Paris 16, France (Telephone Number in U.S. (202) 785-6323); *Indicators of Industrial Activity.*

GERMANY - MAGNESIUM PRODUCTION AND CONSUMPTION - See GERMANY - MINING AND MINERAL PRODUCTS

GERMANY - MAIL - NUMBER OF PIECES SENT OR RECEIVED

European Community Information Service, 2100 M Street, NW, Washington, D.C. 20037 (202) 862-9500; *Transport Annual Statistics.*

Statistical Office of the United Nations, Publishing Service, New York, New York 10017 (800) 253-9646; *Statistical Yearbook.*

GERMANY - MAIN ECONOMIC INDICATORS - See GERMANY - ECONOMY

GERMANY - MANGANESE PRODUCTION AND CONSUMPTION - See GERMANY - MINING AND MINERAL PRODUCTS

GERMANY - MANUFACTURING

American Automobile Manufacturers Association, 1401 H Street, NW, Suite 900, Washington, D.C. 20005 (202) 326-5500; *World Motor Vehicle Data*.

European Community Information Service, 2100 M Street, NW, Washington, D.C. 20037 (202) 862-9500; *Basic Statistics of the Community, Eurostatistics: Data for Short-Term Economic Analysis, Industrial Production: Quarterly Statistics*, and *Labor Force Sample Survey*.

Facts on File, 460 Park Avenue South, New York, New York 10016 (800) 443-8323; *The New Book of World Rankings*.

G.K. Hall and Company, 70 Lincoln Street, Boston, Massachusetts 02111 (617) 423-3990; *The World in Figures*.

National Technical Information Service, 5285 Port Royal Road, Springfield, Virginia 22161 (703) 487-4600; *Handbook of Economic Statistics*.

Organisation for Economic Co-operation and Development (OECD), 2 rue Andre-Pascal, 75 Paris 16, France (Telephone Number in U.S. (202) 785-6323); *Foreign Trade by Commodities, Indicators of Industrial Activity, Industrial Structure Statistics, Main Economic Indicators - Historical Statistics*, and *OECD Economic Surveys: Germany*.

Statistical Office of the United Nations, Publishing Service, New York, New York 10017 (800) 253-9646; *Statistical Yearbook*.

Times Books, 201 East 50th Street, New York, New York 10022 (212) 751-2600; *The Economist Book of Vital World Statistics*.

The World Bank, 1818 H Street, NW, Washington, D.C. 20433 (202) 477-1234; *World Tables*.

GERMANY - MARRIAGE RATES

European Community Information Service, 2100 M Street, NW, Washington, D.C. 20037 (202) 862-9500; *Basic Statistics of the Community*.

Facts on File, 460 Park Avenue South, New York, New York 10016 (800) 443-8323; *The New Book of World Rankings*.

Statistical Office of the United Nations, Publishing Service, New York, New York 10017 (800) 253-9646; *Demographic Yearbook, Statistical Yearbook*.

GERMANY - MEAT PRODUCTION - See GERMANY - LIVESTOCK AND POULTRY

GERMANY - MERCHANT SHIPPING

European Community Information Service, 2100 M Street, NW, Washington, D.C. 20037 (202) 862-9500; *Basic Statistics of the Community, Fisheries: Yearly Statistics, Regions: Statistical Yearbook*, and *Transport Annual Statistics*.

G.K. Hall and Company, 70 Lincoln Street, Boston, Massachusetts 02111 (617) 423-3990; *The World in Figures*.

Lloyd's Register of Shipping, 17 Battery Place, New York, New York 10004 (212) 425-8050; *Register of Ships*.

National Technical Information Service, 5285 Port Royal Road, Springfield, Virginia 22161 (703) 487-4600; *Handbook of Economic Statistics*.

Organisation for Economic Co-operation and Development (OECD), 2 rue Andre-Pascal, 75 Paris 16, France (Telephone Number in U.S. (202) 785-6323); *Maritime Transport*.

Statistical Office of the United Nations, Publishing Service, New York, New York 10017 (800) 253-9646; *Annual Bulletin of Transport Statistics for Europe*, and *Statistical Yearbook*.

Times Books, 201 East 50th Street, New York, New York 10022 (212) 751-2600; *The Economist Book of Vital World Statistics*.

U.S. Department of Transportation, Maritime Administration, 400 Seventh Street, SW, Washington, D.C. 20590; *A Statistical Analysis of the World's Merchant Fleets*.

GERMANY - MERCURY PRODUCTION AND CONSUMPTION - See GERMANY - MINING AND MINERAL PRODUCTS

GERMANY - MILITARY

G.K. Hall and Company, 70 Lincoln Street, Boston, Massachusetts 02111 (617) 423-3990; *The World in Figures*.

The International Institute for Strategic Studies, 23 Tavistock Street, London WC2E 7NQ, England; *The Military Balance*.

U.S. Arms Control and Disarmament Agency, 320 Twenty-first Street, Northwest, Washington, D.C. 20451 (202) 647-8677; *World Military Expenditures and Arms Transfers*.

GERMANY - MILK PRODUCTION - See GERMANY - DAIRY PRODUCTS

GERMANY - MILLET PRODUCTION - See GERMANY - CROPS

GERMANY - MINING AND MINERAL PRODUCTS

Commodity Research Bureau, Incorporated, 75 Wall Street, New York, New York 10005 (212) 504-7754; *Commodity Year Book*.

European Community Information Service, 2100 M Street, NW, Washington, D.C. 20037 (202) 862-9500; *ACP: Basic Statistics, Basic Statistics of the Community, Energy: Monthly Statistics, Energy Statistics Yearbook, Eurostatistics: Data for Short-Term Economic Analysis, Industrial Production: Quarterly Statistics, Iron and Steel: Statistical Yearbook*, and *Regions: Statistical Yearbook*.

Facts on File, 460 Park Avenue South, New York, New York 10016 (800) 443-8323; *The New Book of World Rankings*.

G.K. Hall and Company, 70 Lincoln Street, Boston, Massachusetts 02111 (617) 423-3990; *The World in Figures*.

International Iron and Steel Institute, 120, rue Colonel Bourg, B-1140 Brussels, Belgium; *Steel Statistical Yearbook*.

International Lead and Zinc Study Group, Metro House, 58 St. James's Street, London SW1A 1LD, England; *Lead and Zinc Statistics*.

National Technical Information Service, 5285 Port Royal Road, Springfield, Virginia 22161 (703) 487-4600; *Handbook of Economic*

Statistics.

Organisation for Economic Co-operation and Development (OECD), 2 rue Andre-Pascal, 75 Paris 16, France (Telephone Number in U.S. (202) 785-6323); *Energy Statistics for OECD Countries, Foreign Trade by Communities, Indicators of Industrial Activity, Industrial Structure Statistics, OECD Economic Surveys: Germany,* and *Petroleum Industry.*

Penn Well Publishing Company, 1421 South Sheridan Road, Post Office Box 1260, Tulsa, Oklahoma 74101 (800) 752-9764; *International Energy Statistics Sourcebook.*

Statistical Office of the United Nations, Publishing Service, New York, New York 10017 (800) 253-9646; *Statistical Yearbook.*

World Bureau of Metal Statistics, 27-A High Street, Ware, Herts SG12 9BA, England; *World Metal Statistics.*

GERMANY - MOLASSES PRODUCTION - See GERMANY - CROPS

GERMANY - MOLYBDENUM ORE PRODUCTION AND CONSUMPTION - See GERMANY - MINING AND MINERAL PRODUCTS

GERMANY - MONEY AND CREDIT

Organisation for Economic Co-operation and Development (OECD), 2 rue Andre-Pascal, 75 Paris 16, France (Telephone Number in U.S. (202) 785-6323); *OECD Economic Surveys: Germany.*

GERMANY - MONEY EXCHANGE RATE

European Community Information Service, 2100 M Street, NW, Washington, D.C. 20037 (202) 862-9500; *Basic Statistics of the Community.*

International Monetary Fund, 700 Nineteenth Street, NW, Washington, D.C. 20431 (202) 623-7000; *International Financial Statistics.*

Organisation for Economic Co-operation and Development (OECD), 2 rue Andre-Pascal, 75 Paris 16, France (Telephone Number in U.S. (202) 785-6323); *Economic Outlook, Financial Market Trends,* and *Tourism Policy and International Tourism in OECD Member Countries.*

Statistical Office of the United Nations, Publishing Service, New York, New York 10017 (800) 253-9646; *Statistical Yearbook.*

GERMANY - MONEY RATES - MARKET

European Community Information Service, 2100 M Street, NW, Washington, D.C. 20037 (202) 862-9500; *Basic Statistics of the Community.*

Organisation for Economic Co-operation and Development (OECD), 2 rue Andre-Pascal, 75 Paris 16, France (Telephone Number in U.S. (202) 785-6323); *Economic Outlook,* and *Financial Market Trends.*

Statistical Office of the United Nations, Publishing Service, New York, New York 10017 (800) 253-9646; *Statistical Yearbook.*

GERMANY - MONEY RESERVES

European Community Information Service, 2100 M Street, NW, Washington, D.C. 20037 (202) 862-9500; *Basic Statistics of the Community.*

Organisation for Economic Co-operation and Development (OECD), 2 rue Andre-Pascal, 75 Paris 16, France (Telephone Number in U.S. (202) 785-6323); *Economic Outlook,* and *Financial Market Trends.*

GERMANY - MONEY SUPPLY

European Community Information Service, 2100 M Street, NW, Washington, D.C. 20037 (202) 862-9500; *Basic Statistics of the Community, Eurostatistics: Data for Short-Term Economic Analysis,* and *Money and Finance.*

G.K. Hall and Company, 70 Lincoln Street, Boston, Massachusetts 02111 (617) 423-3990; *The World in Figures.*

International Monetary Fund, 700 Nineteenth Street, NW, Washington, D.C. 20431 (202) 623-7000; *International Financial Statistics.*

Organisation for Economic Co-operation and Development (OECD), 2 rue Andre-Pascal, 75 Paris 16, France (Telephone Number in U.S. (202) 785-6323); *Economic Outlook.*

Statistical Office of the United Nations, Publishing Service, New York, New York 10017 (800) 253-9646; *Statistical Yearbook.*

The World Bank, 1818 H Street, NW, Washington, D.C. 20433 (202) 477-1234; *World Tables.*

GERMANY - MOTION PICTURES

Statistical Office of the United Nations, Publishing Service, New York, New York 10017 (800) 253-9646; *Statistical Yearbook.*

United Nations Educational, Scientific and Cultural Organization (UNESCO), 7 Place de Fontenoy, F-75700 Paris, France (Telephone Number in U.S. (212) 963-5981); *Statistical Yearbook.*

GERMANY - MOTOR VEHICLE PRODUCTION

American Automobile Manufacturers Association, 1401 H Street, NW, Suite 900, Washington, D.C. 20005 (202) 326-5500; *World Motor Vehicle Data.*

European Community Information Service, 2100 M Street, NW, Washington, D.C. 20037 (202) 862-9500; *Basic Statistics of the Community* and *Eurostatistics: Data for Short-Term Economic Analysis.*

International Road Federation, 525 School Street, SW, Washington, D.C. 20024 (202) 554-2106; *World Road Statistics.*

National Technical Information Service, 5285 Port Royal Road, Springfield, Virginia 22161 (703) 487-4600; *Handbook of Economic Statistics.*

Organisation for Economic Co-operation and Development (OECD), 2 rue Andre-Pascal, 75 Paris 16, France (Telephone Number in U.S. (202) 785-6323); *Foreign Trade by Commodities,* and *Indicators of Industrial Activity.*

Statistical Office of the United Nations, Publishing Service, New York, New York 10017 (800) 253-9646; *Statistical Yearbook.*

GERMANY - MOTOR VEHICLE TAXES - See GERMANY - TAXATION

GERMANY - MOTOR VEHICLES IN USE

American Automobile Manufacturers Association, 1401 H Street, NW, Suite 900, Washington, D.C. 20005 (202) 326-5500; *World*

Motor Vehicle Data.

European Community Information Service, 2100 M Street, NW, Washington, D.C. 20037 (202) 862-9500; *Basic Statistics of the Community,* and *Transport Annual Statistics.*

G.K. Hall and Company, 70 Lincoln Street, Boston, Massachusetts 02111 (617) 423-3990; *The World in Figures.*

Statistical Office of the United Nations, Publishing Service, New York, New York 10017 (800) 253-9646; *Statistical Yearbook.*

Times Books, 201 East 50th Street, New York, New York 10022 (212) 751-2600; *The Economist Book of Vital World Statistics.*

GERMANY - MULES - See GERMANY - LIVESTOCK AND POULTRY

GERMANY - MUSEUMS

Euromonitor Publications Limited, 87-88 Turnmill Street, London EC1M 5QU, England; *European Marketing Data and Statistics.*

Facts on File, 460 Park Avenue South, New York, New York 10016 (800) 443-8323; *The New Book of World Rankings.*

United Nations Educational, Scientific and Cultural Organization (UNESCO), 7 Place de Fontenoy, F-75700 Paris, France (Telephone Number in U.S. (212) 963-5981); *Statistical Yearbook.*

GERMANY - NATALITY - See GERMANY - BIRTH RATE

GERMANY - NATIONAL ACCOUNTS

European Community Information Service, 2100 M Street, NW, Washington, D.C. 20037 (202) 862-9500; *Basic Statistics of the Community* and *Eurostatistics: Data for Short-Term Economic Analysis.*

International Monetary Fund, 700 Nineteenth Street, NW, Washington, D.C. 20431 (202) 623-7000; *International Financial Statistics.*

Organisation for Economic Co-operation and Development (OECD), 2 rue Andre-Pascal, 75 Paris 16, France (Telephone Number in U.S. (202) 785-6323); *Economic Outlook.*

Statistical Office of the United Nations, Publishing Service, New York, New York 10017 (800) 253-9646; *National Accounts Statistics,* and *Statistical Yearbook.*

GERMANY - NATIONAL INCOME

Facts on File, 460 Park Avenue South, New York, New York 10016 (800) 443-8323; *The New Book of World Rankings.*

G.K. Hall and Company, 70 Lincoln Street, Boston, Massachusetts 02111 (617) 423-3990; *The World in Figures.*

Organisation for Economic Co-operation and Development (OECD), 2 rue Andre-Pascal, 75 Paris 16, France (Telephone Number in U.S. (202) 785-6323); *Economic Outlook.*

Statistical Office of the United Nations, Publishing Service, New York, New York 10017 (800) 253-9646; *Statistical Yearbook.*

GERMANY - NATIONAL PRODUCT

European Community Information Service, 2100 M Street, NW, Washington, D.C. 20037 (202) 862-9500; *Basic Statistics of the Community.*

Facts on File, 460 Park Avenue South, New York, New York 10016 (800) 443-8323; *The New Book of World Rankings.*

Organisation for Economic Co-operation and Development (OECD), 2 rue Andre-Pascal, 75 Paris 16, France (Telephone Number in U.S. (202) 785-6323); *Economic Outlook,* and *Main Economic Indicators - Historical Statistics.*

Statistical Office of the United Nations, Publishing Service, New York, New York 10017 (800) 253-9646; *Statistical Yearbook.*

GERMANY - NATURAL GAS PRODUCTION - See GERMANY - MINING AND MINERAL PRODUCTS

GERMANY - NATURAL RUBBER PRODUCTION

European Community Information Service, 2100 M Street, NW, Washington, D.C. 20037 (202) 862-9500; *Basic Statistics of the Community.*

International Rubber Study Group, York House, 8th Floor, Empire Way, Wembley, London HA9 0PA, England; *Rubber Statistical Bulletin.*

National Technical Information Service, 5285 Port Royal Road, Springfield, Virginia 22161 (703) 487-4600; *Handbook of Economic Statistics.*

GERMANY - NET MATERIAL PRODUCT

Statistical Office of the United Nations, Publishing Service, New York, New York 10017 (800) 253-9646; *Statistical Yearbook.*

GERMANY - NEWSPAPER PRODUCTION - See GERMANY - FORESTRY AND FOREST PRODUCTS

GERMANY - NEWSPRINT - See GERMANY - FORESTRY AND FOREST PRODUCTS

GERMANY - NICKEL AND NICKEL ORE - See GERMANY - MINING AND MINERAL PRODUCTS

GERMANY - NITRIC ACID PRODUCTION

European Community Information Service, 2100 M Street, NW, Washington, D.C. 20037 (202) 862-9500; *Basic Statistics of the Community.*

Organisation for Economic Co-operation and Development (OECD), 2 rue Andre-Pascal, 75 Paris 16, France (Telephone Number in U.S. (202) 785-6323); *Indicators of Industrial Activity.*

Statistical Office of the United Nations, Publishing Service, New York, New York 10017 (800) 253-9646; *Statistical Yearbook.*

GERMANY - OATS PRODUCTION - See GERMANY - CROPS

GERMANY - OCCUPATIONS - See GERMANY - LABOR FORCE

GERMANY - OIL PRODUCING CROPS - See GERMANY - CROPS

GERMANY - ONION PRODUCTION - See GERMANY - CROPS

GERMANY - PALM KERNEL PRODUCTION - See GERMANY - CROPS

GERMANY - PAPER - See GERMANY - FORESTRY AND FOREST PRODUCTS

GERMANY - PARTY LEADERS

Columbia University Press, 562 West 113th Street, New York, New York 10014 (212) 316-7100; *East European and Soviet Data Book.*

GERMANY - PARTY MEMBERSHIP

Columbia University Press, 562 West 113th Street, New York, New York 10014 (212) 316-7100; *East European and Soviet Data Book.*

GERMANY - PATENTS

Statistical Office of the United Nations, Publishing Service, New York, New York 10017 (800) 253-9646; *Statistical Yearbook.*

World Intellectual Property Organization, 34 Chemin des Colombettes, CH-1211 Geneva 20, Switzerland; *Industrial Property Statistics.*

GERMANY - PEANUT PRODUCTION - See GERMANY - CROPS

GERMANY - PEPPER PRODUCTION - See GERMANY - CROPS

GERMANY - PERIODICALS

United Nations Educational, Scientific and Cultural Organization (UNESCO), 7 Place de Fontenoy, F-75700 Paris, France (Telephone Number in U.S. (212) 963-5981); *Statistical Yearbook.*

GERMANY - PESTICIDE USE

Food and Agricultural Organization of the United Nations (FAO) Via delle Terme di Caracalla, 00100 Rome, Italy (Telephone Number in U.S. (202) 606-7828); *The State of Food and Agriculture.*

GERMANY - PETROLEUM INDUSTRY

Euromonitor Publications Limited, 87-88 Turnmill Street, London EC1M 5QU, England; *European Marketing Data and Statistics.*

European Community Information Service, 2100 M Street, NW, Washington, D.C. 20037 (202) 862-9500; *ACP: Basic Statistics, Basic Statistics of the Community,* and *Energy Statistics Yearbook.*

Facts on File, 460 Park Avenue South, New York, New York 10016 (800) 443-8323; *The New Book of World Rankings.*

Food and Agricultural Organization of the United Nations (FAO) Via delle Terme di Caracalla, 00100 Rome, Italy (Telephone Number in U.S. (202) 606-7828); *The State of Food and Agriculture.*

G.K. Hall and Company, 70 Lincoln Street, Boston, Massachusetts 02111 (617) 423-3990; *The World in Figures.*

National Technical Information Service, 5285 Port Royal Road, Springfield, Virginia 22161 (703) 487-4600; *Handbook of Economic Statistics.*

Organisation for Economic Co-operation and Development (OECD), 2 rue Andre-Pascal, 75 Paris 16, France (Telephone Number in U.S. (202) 785-6323); *Energy Statistics of OECD Countries, Foreign Trade by Commodities, Indicators of Industrial Activity,* and *Oil and Gas Information.*

Penn Well Publishing Company, 1421 South Sheridan Road, Post Office Box 1260, Tulsa, Oklahoma 74101 (800) 752-9764; *International Energy Statistics Sourcebook.*

Statistical Office of the United Nations, Publishing Service, New York, New York 10017 (800) 253-9646; *Statistical Yearbook.*

GERMANY - PHOSPHATE ROCK PRODUCTION- See GERMANY - MINING AND MINERAL PRODUCTS

GERMANY - PHOSPHATES PRODUCTION- See GERMANY - MINING AND MINERAL PRODUCTS

GERMANY - PIG-IRON AND FERRO-ALLOY PRODUCTION - See GERMANY - MINING AND MINERAL PRODUCTS

GERMANY - PIGS - See GERMANY - LIVESTOCK AND POULTRY

GERMANY - PIPELINES FOR OIL AND PETROLEUM PRODUCTS

European Community Information Service, 2100 M Street, NW, Washington, D.C. 20037 (202) 862-9500; *Transport Annual Statistics.*

National Technical Information Service, 5285 Port Royal Road, Springfield, Virginia 22161 (703) 487-4600; *Handbook of Economic Statistics.*

Statistical Office of the United Nations, Publishing Service, New York, New York 10017 (800) 253-9646; *Annual Bulletin of Transport Statistics for Europe.*

GERMANY - PLASTIC AND RESIN PRODUCTION

Commodity Research Bureau, Incorporated, 75 Wall Street, New York, New York 10005 (212) 504-7754; *Commodity Year Book.*

European Community Information Service, 2100 M Street, NW, Washington, D.C. 20037 (202) 862-9500; *Basic Statistics of the Community.*

Organisation for Economic Co-operation and Development (OECD), 2 rue Andre-Pascal, 75 Paris 16, France (Telephone Number in U.S. (202) 785-6323); *Foreign Trade by Commodities.*

Statistical Office of the United Nations, Publishing Service, New York, New York 10017 (800) 253-9646; *Statistical Yearbook.*

GERMANY - PLATINUM PRODUCTION AND CONSUMPTION - See GERMANY - MINING AND MINERAL PRODUCTS

GERMANY - POPULATION

Columbia University Press, 562 West 113th Street, New York, New York 10014 (212) 316-7100; *East European and Soviet Data Book.*

The Economist Intelligence Unit, 111 West 57th Street, New York, New York 10019 (800) 938-4685; *The World Market Atlas.*

Euromonitor Publications Limited, 87-88 Turnmill Street, London EC1M 5QU, England; *European Marketing Data and Statistics.*

European Community Information Service, 2100 M Street, NW, Washington, D.C. 20037 (202) 862-9500; *ACP: Basic Statistics, Basic Statistics of the Community, Demographic Statistics, Employment and Unemployment, Fisheries: Yearly Statistics, Iron and Steel: Statistical Yearbook, Labor Force Sample Survey,* and *Regions: Statistical Yearbook.*

Facts on File, 460 Park Avenue South, New York, New York 10016 (800) 443-8323; *The New Book of World Rankings.*

Food and Agricultural Organization of the United Nations (FAO), Via delle Terme di Caracalla, 00100 Rome, Italy (Telephone Number in U.S. (202) 606-7828); *Production Yearbook.*

G.K. Hall and Company, 70 Lincoln Street, Boston, Massachusetts 02111 (617) 423-3990; *The World in Figures.*

International Labour Office, I.L.O. Publications, CH-1211, Geneva 22, Switzerland; *Yearbook of Labour Statistics.*

National Technical Information Service, 5285 Port Royal Road, Springfield, Virginia 22161 (703) 487-4600; *Handbook of Economic Statistics.*

Statistical Office of the United Nations, Publishing Service, New York, New York 10017 (800) 253-9646; *Demographic Yearbook,* and *Statistical Yearbook.*

Times Books, 201 East 50th Street, New York, New York 10022 (212) 751-2600; *The Economist Book of Vital World Statistics.*

United Nations Educational, Scientific and Cultural Organization (UNESCO), 7 Place de Fontenoy, F-75700 Paris, France (Telephone Number in U.S. (212) 963-5981); *Statistical Yearbook.*

U.S. Arms Control and Disarmament Agency, 320 Twenty-first Street, Northwest, Washington, D.C. 20451 (202) 647-8677; *World Military Expenditures and Arms Transfers.*

World Health Organization, Office of Publications, Avenue Appia, CH-1211 Geneva 27, Switzerland (Telephone Number in U.S. (518) 436-9686); *World Health Statistics Annual.*

GERMANY - POST OFFICES

Facts on File, 460 Park Avenue South, New York, New York 10016 (800) 443-8323; *The New Book of World Rankings.*

GERMANY - POTATO PRODUCTION - See GERMANY - CROPS

GERMANY - POWER PRODUCTION INDUSTRY

European Community Information Service, 2100 M Street, NW, Washington, D.C. 20037 (202) 862-9500; *Basic Statistics of the Community.*

Statistical Office of the United Nations, Publishing Service, New York, New York 10017 (800) 253-9646; *Statistical Yearbook.*

GERMANY - PRICES

European Community Information Service, 2100 M Street, NW, Washington, D.C. 20037 (202) 862-9500; *Basic Statistics of the Community* and *Eurostatistics: Data for Short-Term Economic Analysis.*

Facts on File, 460 Park Avenue South, New York, New York 10016 (800) 443-8323; *The New Book of World Rankings.*

Food and Agricultural Organization of the United Nations (FAO), Via delle Terme di Caracalla, 00100 Rome, Italy (Telephone Number in U.S. (202) 606-7828); *Production Yearbook,* and *The State of Food and Agriculture.*

G.K. Hall and Company, 70 Lincoln Street, Boston, Massachusetts 02111 (617) 423-3990; *The World in Figures.*

International Labour Office, I.L.O. Publications, CH-1211, Geneva 22, Switzerland; *Yearbook of Labour Statistics.*

International Lead and Zinc Study Group, Metro House, 58 St. James's Street, London SW1A 1LD, England; *Lead and Zinc Statistics.*

International Rubber Study Group, York House, 8th Floor, Empire Way, Wembley, London HA9 0PA, England; *Rubber Statistical Bulletin.*

National Technical Information Service, 5285 Port Royal Road, Springfield, Virginia 22161 (703) 487-4600; *Handbook of Economic Statistics.*

Organisation for Economic Co-operation and Development (OECD), 2 rue Andre-Pascal, 75 Paris 16, France (Telephone Number in U.S. (202) 785-6323); *Economic Outlook, The Footwear, Raw Hides and Skins, and Leather Industry in OECD Countries, Indicators of Industrial Activity, The Iron and Steel Industry, Main Economic Indicators - Historical Statistics,* and *The Pulp and Paper Industry.*

World Bureau of Metal Statistics, 27-A High Street, Ware, Herts, SG12 9BA, England; *World Metal Statistics.*

GERMANY - PRINTING AND WRITING PAPER - See GERMANY - FORESTRY AND FOREST PRODUCTS

GERMANY - PRODUCTION

American Automobile Manufacturers Association, 1401 H Street, NW, Suite 900, Washington, D.C. 20005 (202) 326-5500; *World Motor Vehicle Data.*

European Community Information Service, 2100 M Street, NW, Washington, D.C. 20037 (202) 862-9500; *Basic Statistics of the Community, Eurostatistics: Data for Short-Term Economic Analysis,* and *Fisheries: Yearly Statistics.*

Facts on File, 460 Park Avenue South, New York, New York 10016 (800) 443-8323; *The New Book of World Rankings.*

G.K. Hall and Company, 70 Lincoln Street, Boston, Massachusetts 02111 (617) 423-3990; *The World in Figures.*

International Iron and Steel Institute, 120, rue Colonel Bourg, B-1140 Brussels, Belgium; *Steel Statistical Yearbook.*

International Lead and Zinc Study Group, Metro House, 58 St. James's Street, London SW1A 1LD, England; *Lead and Zinc Statistics.*

International Rubber Study Group, York House, 8th Floor, Empire Way, Wembley, London HA9 0PA, England; *Rubber Statistical Bulletin.*

National Technical Information Service, 5285 Port Royal Road, Springfield, Virginia 22161 (703) 487-4600; *Handbook of Economic Statistics.*

Organisation for Economic Co-operation and Development (OECD), 2 rue Andre-Pascal, 75 Paris 16, France (Telephone Number in U.S. (202) 785-6323); *Economic Outlook, The Footwear, Raw Hides and Skins, and Leather Industry in OECD Countries, Indicators of Industrial Activity, Industrial Structure Statistics, The Iron and Steel Industry, Meat Balances in OECD Member Countries, Milk, Milk Products, and Egg Balances in OECD Member Countries, The Non-Ferrous Metals Industry, The Pulp and Paper Industry,* and *Textile Industry in OECD Countries.*

GERMANY - PRODUCTIVITY

European Community Information Service, 2100 M Street, NW, Washington, D.C. 20037 (202) 862-9500; *Basic Statistics of the Community*.

Organisation for Economic Co-operation and Development (OECD), 2 rue Andre-Pascal, 75 Paris 16, France (Telephone Number in U.S. (202) 785-6323); *Economic Outlook*.

GERMANY - PROPERTY TAXES - See GERMANY - TAXATION

GERMANY - PUBLIC CONSUMPTION FUNDS

European Community Information Service, 2100 M Street, NW, Washington, D.C. 20037 (202) 862-9500; *Basic Statistics of the Community*.

Organisation for Economic Co-operation and Development (OECD), 2 rue Andre-Pascal, 75 Paris 16, France (Telephone Number in U.S. (202) 785-6323); *Revenue Statistics of OECD Member Countries*.

GERMANY - PUBLIC EXPENDITURES

European Community Information Service, 2100 M Street, NW, Washington, D.C. 20037 (202) 862-9500; *Basic Statistics of the Community*.

National Technical Information Service, 5285 Port Royal Road, Springfield, Virginia 22161 (703) 487-4600; *Handbook of Economic Statistics*.

Organisation for Economic Co-operation and Development (OECD), 2 rue Andre-Pascal, 75 Paris 16, France (Telephone Number in U.S. (202) 785-6323); *Revenue Statistics of OECD Member Countries*.

GERMANY - PUBLIC FINANCE

Facts on File, 460 Park Avenue South, New York, New York 10016 (800) 443-8323; *The New Book of World Rankings*.

National Technical Information Service, 5285 Port Royal Road, Springfield, Virginia 22161 (703) 487-4600; *Handbook of Economic Statistics*.

Organisation for Economic Co-operation and Development (OECD), 2 rue Andre-Pascal, 75 Paris 16, France (Telephone Number in U.S. (202) 785-6323); *Revenue Statistics of OECD Member Countries*.

GERMANY - PUBLIC HEALTH

European Community Information Service, 2100 M Street, NW, Washington, D.C. 20037 (202) 862-9500; *Basic Statistics of the Community*.

GERMANY - PUBLIC REVENUES

National Technical Information Service, 5285 Port Royal Road, Springfield, Virginia 22161 (703) 487-4600; *Handbook of Economic Statistics*.

Organisation for Economic Co-operation and Development (OECD), 2 rue Andre-Pascal, 75 Paris 16, France (Telephone Number in U.S. (202) 785-6323); *Revenue Statistics of OECD Member Countries*.

GERMANY - RADIO BROADCASTING - See GERMANY - BROADCASTING

GERMANY - RADIO RECEIVER PRODUCTION

Statistical Office of the United Nations, Publishing Service, New York, New York 10017 (800) 253-9646; *Statistical Yearbook*.

GERMANY - RAILWAYS

Euromonitor Publications Limited, 87-88 Turnmill Street, London EC1M 5QU, England; *European Marketing Data and Statistics*.

European Community Information Service, 2100 M Street, NW, Washington, D.C. 20037 (202) 862-9500; *Basic Statistics of the Community, Regions: Statistical Yearbook*, and *Transport Annual Statistics*.

G.K. Hall and Company, 70 Lincoln Street, Boston, Massachusetts 02111 (617) 423-3990; *The World in Figures*.

Jane's Information Group, Sentinel House, 163 Brighton Road, Coulsdon, Surrey CR5 2NH, England (Telephone Number in U.S. (703) 683-3700); *Jane's World Railways*.

National Technical Information Service, 5285 Port Royal Road, Springfield, Virginia 22161 (703) 487-4600; *Handbook of Economic Statistics*.

Statistical Office of the United Nations, Publishing Service, New York, New York 10017 (800) 253-9646; *Annual Bulletin of Transport Statistics for Europe*, and *Statistical Yearbook*.

GERMANY - RANCHING - See GERMANY - AGRICULTURE

GERMANY - RAPESEED PRODUCTION - See GERMANY - CROPS

GERMANY - RELIGION

Facts on File, 460 Park Avenue South, New York, New York 10016 (800) 443-8323; *The New Book of World Rankings*.

GERMANY - RENT PRICES

International Labour Office, I.L.O. Publications, CH-1211, Geneva 22, Switzerland; *Yearbook of Labour Statistics*.

GERMANY - RETAIL TRADE

European Community Information Service, 2100 M Street, NW, Washington, D.C. 20037 (202) 862-9500; *Basic Statistics of the Community* and *Eurostatistics: Data for Short-Term Economic Analysis*.

G.K. Hall and Company, 70 Lincoln Street, Boston, Massachusetts 02111 (617) 423-3990; *The World in Figures*.

Statistical Office of the United Nations, Publishing Service, New York, New York 10017 (800) 253-9646; *Statistical Yearbook*.

GERMANY - RICE PRODUCTION - See GERMANY - CROPS

GERMANY - ROOT AND TUBER PRODUCTION - See GERMANY - CROPS

GERMANY - ROUNDWOOD PRODUCTION - See GERMANY - FORESTRY AND FOREST PRODUCTS

GERMANY - RUBBER PRODUCTION

Commodity Research Bureau, Incorporated, 75 Wall Street, New York, New York 10005 (212) 504-7754; *Commodity Year Book*.

European Community Information Service, 2100 M Street, NW, Washington, D.C. 20037 (202) 862-9500; *Basic Statistics of the Community.*

Facts on File, 460 Park Avenue South, New York, New York 10016 (800) 443-8323; *The New Book of World Rankings.*

International Rubber Study Group, York House, 8th Floor, Empire Way, Wembley, London HA9 0PA, England; *Rubber Statistical Bulletin.*

National Technical Information Service, 5285 Port Royal Road, Springfield, Virginia 22161 (703) 487-4600; *Handbook of Economic Statistics.*

Organisation for Economic Co-operation and Development (OECD), 2 rue Andre-Pascal, 75 Paris 16, France (Telephone Number in U.S. (202) 785-6323); *Foreign Trade by Commodities.*

Statistical Office of the United Nations, Publishing Service, New York, New York 10017 (800) 253-9646; *Statistical Yearbook.*

GERMANY - RYE PRODUCTION - See GERMANY - CROPS

GERMANY - SAFFLOWER SEED PRODUCTION - See GERMANY - CROPS

GERMANY - SALT PRODUCTION - See GERMANY - MINING AND MINERAL PRODUCTS

GERMANY - SAVINGS ACCOUNT DEPOSITS

European Community Information Service, 2100 M Street, NW, Washington, D.C. 20037 (202) 862-9500; *Eurostatistics: Data for Short-Term Economic Analysis.*

GERMANY - SAWNWOOD PRODUCTION - See GERMANY - FORESTRY AND FOREST PRODUCTS

GERMANY - SCIENCE AND TECHNOLOGY - EXPENDITURE FOR RESEARCH

European Community Information Service, 2100 M Street, NW, Washington, D.C. 20037 (202) 862-9500; *Basic Statistics of the Community.*

Statistical Office of the United Nations, Publishing Service, New York, New York 10017 (800) 253-9646; *Statistical Yearbook.*

GERMANY - SCIENTISTS AND TECHNICIANS

European Community Information Service, 2100 M Street, NW, Washington, D.C. 20037 (202) 862-9500; *Basic Statistics of the Community.*

Statistical Office of the United Nations, Publishing Service, New York, New York 10017 (800) 253-9646; *Statistical Yearbook.*

GERMANY - SENIOR CITIZENS

Facts on File, 460 Park Avenue South, New York, New York 10016 (800) 443-8323; *The New Book of World Rankings.*

GERMANY - SESAME SEED PRODUCTION - See GERMANY - CROPS

GERMANY - SHEEP - See GERMANY - LIVESTOCK AND POULTRY

GERMANY - SHIPBUILDING - PRODUCTION INDEX

Organisation for Economic Co-operation and Development (OECD), 2 rue Andre-Pascal, 75 Paris 16, France (Telephone Number in U.S. (202) 785-6323); *Indicators of Industrial Activity.*

GERMANY - SILVER PRODUCTION AND CONSUMPTION - See GERMANY - MINING AND MINERAL PRODUCTS

GERMANY - SISAL PRODUCTION - See GERMANY - CROPS

GERMANY - SOCIAL DATA

European Community Information Service, 2100 M Street, NW, Washington, D.C. 20037 (202) 862-9500; *ACP: Basic Statistics* and *Basic Statistics of the Community.*

Facts on File, 460 Park Avenue South, New York, New York 10016 (800) 443-8323; *The New Book of World Rankings.*

G.K. Hall and Company, 70 Lincoln Street, Boston, Massachusetts 02111 (617) 423-3990; *The World in Figures.*

GERMANY - SOCIAL SECURITY

European Community Information Service, 2100 M Street, NW, Washington, D.C. 20037 (202) 862-9500; *Basic Statistics of the Community.*

Organisation for Economic Co-operation and Development (OECD), 2 rue Andre-Pascal, 75 Paris 16, France (Telephone Number in U.S. (202) 785-6323); *Revenue Statistics of OECD Member Countries.*

GERMANY - SOCIOECONOMIC DATA

European Community Information Service, 2100 M Street, NW, Washington, D.C. 20037 (202) 862-9500; *Basic Statistics of the Community.*

Organisation for Economic Co-operation and Development (OECD), 2 rue Andre-Pascal, 75 Paris 16, France (Telephone Number in U.S. (202) 785-6323); *Economic Outlook.*

GERMANY - SOYBEAN PRODUCTION - See GERMANY - CROPS

GERMANY - STAMP TAXES AND DUTIES - See GERMANY - TAXATION

GERMANY - STATE AFFORESTATION - See GERMANY - FORESTRY AND FOREST PRODUCTS

GERMANY - STEEL - See GERMANY - MINING AND MINERAL PRODUCTS

GERMANY - STOCKS - COMMODITY - MARKET PRICE - INDEX

Food and Agricultural Organization of the United Nations (FAO) Via delle Terme di Caracalla, 00100 Rome, Italy (Telephone Number in U.S. (202) 606-7828); *The State of Food and Agriculture.*

International Lead and Zinc Study Group, Metro House, 58 St. James's Street, London SW1A 1LD, England; *Lead and Zinc Statistics.*

Statistical Office of the United Nations, Publishing Service, New York, New York 10017 (800) 253-9646; *Statistical Yearbook.*

World Bureau of Metal Statistics, 27-A High Street, Ware, Herts, SG12 9BA, England; *World Metal Statistics.*

GERMANY - STRAW PRODUCTION - See GERMANY - CROPS

GERMANY - SUGAR - See GERMANY - CROPS

GERMANY - SUGARBEET PRODUCTION - See GERMANY - CROPS

GERMANY - SULPHUR AND SULPHURIC ACID PRODUCTION - See GERMANY - MINING AND MINERAL PRODUCTS

GERMANY - SUNFLOWER PRODUCTION - See GERMANY - CROPS

GERMANY - TAXATION

European Community Information Service, 2100 M Street, NW, Washington, D.C. 20037 (202) 862-9500; *Basic Statistics of the Community.*

G.K. Hall and Company, 70 Lincoln Street, Boston, Massachusetts 02111 (617) 423-3990; *The World in Figures.*

The International Institute for Strategic Studies, 23 Tavistock Street, London WC2E 7NQ, England; *The Military Balance.*

Organisation for Economic Co-operation and Development (OECD), 2 rue Andre-Pascal, 75 Paris 16, France (Telephone Number in U.S. (202) 785-6323); *Revenue Statistics of OECD Member Countries.*

The World Bank, 1818 H Street, NW, Washington, D.C. 20433 (202) 477-1234; *World Tables.*

GERMANY - TEA PRODUCTION AND CONSUMPTION - See GERMANY - CROPS

GERMANY - TELEGRAPH SERVICE

European Community Information Service, 2100 M Street, NW, Washington, D.C. 20037 (202) 862-9500; *Transport Annual Statistics.*

Statistical Office of the United Nations, Publishing Service, New York, New York 10017 (800) 253-9646; *Statistical Yearbook.*

GERMANY - TELEPHONES IN USE

American Telephone and Telegraph Company, 26 Parsippany Road, Whippany, New Jersey 07981 (800) 338-4038; *The World's Telephones.*

European Community Information Service, 2100 M Street, NW, Washington, D.C. 20037 (202) 862-9500; *Basic Statistics of the Community,* and *Transport Annual Statistics.*

G.K. Hall and Company, 70 Lincoln Street, Boston, Massachusetts 02111 (617) 423-3990; *The World in Figures.*

Statistical Office of the United Nations, Publishing Service, New York, New York 10017 (800) 253-9646; *Statistical Yearbook.*

GERMANY - TELEVISION BROADCASTING - See GERMANY - BROADCASTING

GERMANY - TELEVISION RECEIVER PRODUCTION

European Community Information Service, 2100 M Street, NW, Washington, D.C. 20037 (202) 862-9500; *Basic Statistics of the Community.*

National Technical Information Service, 5285 Port Royal Road, Springfield, Virginia 22161 (703) 487-4600; *Handbook of Economic Statistics.*

Statistical Office of the United Nations, Publishing Service, New York, New York 10017 (800) 253-9646; *Statistical Yearbook.*

GERMANY - TEXTILE INDUSTRY

European Community Information Service, 2100 M Street, NW, Washington, D.C. 20037 (202) 862-9500; *Basic Statistics of the Community Eurostatistics: Data for Short-Term Economic Analysis,* and *Industrial Production: Quarterly Statistics.*

Food and Agricultural Organization of the United Nations (FAO) Via delle Terme di Caracalla, 00100 Rome, Italy (Telephone Number in U.S. (202) 606-7828); *The State of Food and Agriculture.*

Forest and Paper Association, 1250 Connecticut Avenue, NW, Washington, D.C. 20036 (202) 463-2455; *Wood Pulp and Fiber Statistics.*

G.K. Hall and Company, 70 Lincoln Street, Boston, Massachusetts 02111 (617) 423-3990; *The World in Figures.*

National Technical Information Service, 5285 Port Royal Road, Springfield, Virginia 22161 (703) 487-4600; *Handbook of Economic Statistics.*

Organisation for Economic Co-operation and Development (OECD), 2 rue Andre-Pascal, 75 Paris 16, France (Telephone Number in U.S. (202) 785-6323); *Foreign Trade by Commodities, Indicators of Industrial Activity, Industrial Structure Statistics,* and *Textile Industry in OECD Countries.*

Statistical Office of the United Nations, Publishing Service, New York, New York 10017 (800) 253-9646; *Trade in Manufactures of Developing Countries,* and *Statistical Yearbook.*

GERMANY - THEATRE

United Nations Educational, Scientific and Cultural Organization (UNESCO), 7 Place de Fontenoy, F-75700 Paris, France (Telephone Number in U.S. (212) 963-5981); *Statistical Yearbook.*

GERMANY - TIMBER - See GERMANY - FORESTRY AND FOREST PRODUCTS

GERMANY - TIN - See GERMANY - MINING AND MINERAL PRODUCTS

GERMANY - TIRE (MOTOR VEHICLE) PRODUCTION

International Rubber Study Group, York House, 8th Floor, Empire Way, Wembley, London HA9 0PA, England; *Rubber Statistical Bulletin.*

National Technical Information Service, 5285 Port Royal Road, Springfield, Virginia 22161 (703) 487-4600; *Handbook of Economic Statistics.*

Statistical Office of the United Nations, Publishing Service, New York, New York 10017 (800) 253-9646; *Statistical Yearbook.*

GERMANY - TOBACCO PRODUCTION

Euromonitor Publications Limited, 87-88 Turnmill Street, London EC1M 5QU, England; *European Marketing Data and Statistics.*

European Community Information Service, 2100 M Street, NW, Washington, D.C. 20037 (202) 862-9500; *Basic Statistics of the*

Community and *Industrial Production: Quarterly Statistics.*

Facts on File, 460 Park Avenue South, New York, New York 10016 (800) 443-8323; *The New Book of World Rankings.*

Organisation for Economic Co-operation and Development (OECD), 2 rue Andre-Pascal, 75 Paris 16, France (Telephone Number in U.S. (202) 785-6323); *Foreign Trade by Commodities, Indicators of Industrial Activity,* and *Industrial Structure Statistics.*

Statistical Office of the United Nations, Publishing Service, New York, New York 10017 (800) 253-9646; *Statistical Yearbook.*

Organisation for Economic Co-operation and Development (OECD), 2 rue Andre-Pascal, 75 Paris 16, France (Telephone Number in U.S. (202) 785-6323); *Indicators of Industrial Activity.*

GERMANY - TOURISM

Euromonitor Publications Limited, 87-88 Turnmill Street, London EC1M 5QU, England; *European Marketing Data and Statistics.*

European Community Information Service, 2100 M Street, NW, Washington, D.C. 20037 (202) 862-9500; *Transport Annual Statistics.*

Facts on File, 460 Park Avenue South, New York, New York 10016 (800) 443-8323; *The New Book of World Rankings.*

G.K. Hall and Company, 70 Lincoln Street, Boston, Massachusetts 02111 (617) 423-3990; *The World in Figures.*

Organisation for Economic Co-operation and Development (OECD), 2 rue Andre-Pascal, 75 Paris 16, France (Telephone Number in U.S. (202) 785-6323); *Tourism Policy and International Tourism in OECD Member Countries.*

Statistical Office of the United Nations, Publishing Service, New York, New York 10017 (800) 253-9646; *Statistical Yearbook.*

Times Books, 201 East 50th Street, New York, New York 10022 (212) 751-2600; *The Economist Book of Vital World Statistics.*

World Tourism Organization, Calle Capitan Haya 42, E-28020 Madrid, Spain; *Yearbook of Tourism Statistics.*

GERMANY - TRACTORS IN USE

European Community Information Service, 2100 M Street, NW, Washington, D.C. 20037 (202) 862-9500; *Transport Annual Statistics.*

Statistical Office of the United Nations, Publishing Service, New York, New York 10017 (800) 253-9646; *Statistical Yearbook.*

GERMANY - TRADE - See GERMANY - FOREIGN TRADE

GERMANY - TRADEMARKS AND SERVICE MARKS

Statistical Office of the United Nations, Publishing Service, New York, New York 10017 (800) 253-9646; *Statistical Yearbook.*

World Intellectual Property Organization, 34 Chemin des Colombettes, CH-1211 Geneva 20, Switzerland; *Industrial Property Statistics.*

GERMANY - TRANSPORTATION AND COMMUNICATIONS

European Community Information Service, 2100 M Street, NW, Washington, D.C. 20037 (202) 862-9500; *Basic Statistics of the Community, Energy Statistics Yearbook,* and *Transport Annual Statistics.*

Facts on File, 460 Park Avenue South, New York, New York 10016 (800) 443-8323; *The New Book of World Rankings.*

G.K. Hall and Company, 70 Lincoln Street, Boston, Massachusetts 02111 (617) 423-3990; *The World in Figures.*

GERMANY - TUNGSTEN PRODUCTION AND CONSUMPTION - MINING AND MINERAL PRODUCTS

GERMANY - TURKEYS - See GERMANY - LIVESTOCK AND POULTRY

GERMANY - UNEMPLOYMENT

Euromonitor Publications Limited, 87-88 Turnmill Street, London EC1M 5QU, England; *European Marketing Data and Statistics.*

European Community Information Service, 2100 M Street, NW, Washington, D.C. 20037 (202) 862-9500; *Employment and Unemployment, Eurostatistics: Data for Short-Term Economic Analysis, Labor Force Sample Survey,* and *Regions: Statistical Yearbook.*

International Labour Office, I.L.O. Publications, CH-1211, Geneva 22, Switzerland; *Yearbook of Labour Statistics.*

National Technical Information Service, 5285 Port Royal Road, Springfield, Virginia 22161 (703) 487-4600; *Handbook of Economic Statistics.*

Organisation for Economic Co-operation and Development (OECD), 2 rue Andre-Pascal, 75 Paris 16, France (Telephone Number in U.S. (202) 785-6323); *Economic Outlook, OECD Economic Surveys: Germany,* and *OECD Employment Outlook.*

Statistical Office of the United Nations, Publishing Service, New York, New York 10017 (800) 253-9646; *Statistical Yearbook.*

GERMANY - URANIUM PRODUCTION AND CONSUMPTION - See GERMANY - MINING AND MINERAL PRODUCTS

GERMANY - UTILITIES

European Community Information Service, 2100 M Street, NW, Washington, D.C. 20037 (202) 862-9500; *Basic Statistics of the Community.*

GERMANY - VANADIUM AND VANADIUM ORE PRODUCTION AND CONSUMPTION - See GERMANY - MINING AND MINERAL PRODUCTS

GERMANY - VITAL STATISTICS

European Community Information Service, 2100 M Street, NW, Washington, D.C. 20037 (202) 862-9500; *Basic Statistics of the Community.*

G.K. Hall and Company, 70 Lincoln Street, Boston, Massachusetts 02111 (617) 423-3990; *The World in Figures.*

Statistical Office of the United Nations, Publishing Service, New York, New York 10017 (800) 253-9646; *Statistical Yearbook.*

World Health Organization, Office of Publications, Avenue Appia, CH-1211 Geneva 27, Switzerland (Telephone Number in U.S. (518) 436-9686); *World Health Statistics Annual.*

GERMANY - WAGES

Euromonitor Publications Limited, 87-88 Turnmill Street, London EC1M 5QU, England; *European Marketing Data and Statistics.*

European Community Information Service, 2100 M Street, NW, Washington, D.C. 20037 (202) 862-9500; *Basic Statistics of the Community, Earnings in Agriculture,* and *Eurostatistics: Data for Short-Term Economic Analysis.*

G.K. Hall and Company, 70 Lincoln Street, Boston, Massachusetts 02111 (617) 423-3990; *The World in Figures.*

International Labour Office, I.L.O. Publications, CH-1211, Geneva 22, Switzerland; *Yearbook of Labour Statistics.*

Organisation for Economic Co-operation and Development (OECD), 2 rue Andre-Pascal, 75 Paris 16, France (Telephone Number in U.S. (202) 785-6323); *Economic Outlook, Industrial Structure Statistics,* and *Main Economic Indicators - Historical Statistics.*

Statistical Office of the United Nations, Publishing Service, New York, New York 10017 (800) 253-9646; *Statistical Yearbook.*

GERMANY - WALNUT PRODUCTION - See GERMANY - CROPS

GERMANY - WATERWAYS IN USE

European Community Information Service, 2100 M Street, NW, Washington, D.C. 20037 (202) 862-9500; *Basic Statistics of the Community* and *Transport Annual Statistics.*

National Technical Information Service, 5285 Port Royal Road, Springfield, Virginia 22161 (703) 487-4600; *Handbook of Economic Statistics.*

Organisation for Economic Co-operation and Development (OECD), 2 rue Andre-Pascal, 75 Paris 16, France (Telephone Number in U.S. (202) 785-6323); *Maritime Transport.*

Statistical Office of the United Nations, Publishing Service, New York, New York 10017 (800) 253-9646; *Annual Bulletin of Transport Statistics for Europe.*

GERMANY - WEATHER

Facts on File, 460 Park Avenue South, New York, New York 10016 (800) 443-8323; *The New Book of World Rankings.*

G.K. Hall and Company, 70 Lincoln Street, Boston, Massachusetts 02111 (617) 423-3990; *The World in Figures.*

GERMANY - WELFARE

European Community Information Service, 2100 M Street, NW, Washington, D.C. 20037 (202) 862-9500; *Basic Statistics of the Community.*

GERMANY - WHEAT - See GERMANY - CROPS

GERMANY - WHOLESALE PRICES

European Community Information Service, 2100 M Street, NW, Washington, D.C. 20037 (202) 862-9500; *Basic Statistics of the Community.*

National Technical Information Service, 5285 Port Royal Road, Springfield, Virginia 22161 (703) 487-4600; *Handbook of Economic Statistics.*

Statistical Office of the United Nations, Publishing Service, New York, New York 10017 (800) 253-9646; *Statistical Yearbook.*

GERMANY - WHOLESALE TRADE

European Community Information Service, 2100 M Street, NW, Washington, D.C. 20037 (202) 862-9500; *Basic Statistics of the Community.*

Statistical Office of the United Nations, Publishing Service, New York, New York 10017 (800) 253-9646; *Statistical Yearbook.*

GERMANY - WINE PRODUCTION

European Community Information Service, 2100 M Street, NW, Washington, D.C. 20037 (202) 862-9500; *Basic Statistics of the Community.*

Facts on File, 460 Park Avenue South, New York, New York 10016 (800) 443-8323; *The New Book of World Rankings.*

GERMANY - WOOD AND WOOD PULP - See GERMANY - FORESTRY AND FOREST PRODUCTS

GERMANY - WOOL PRODUCTION

European Community Information Service, 2100 M Street, NW, Washington, D.C. 20037 (202) 862-9500; *Basic Statistics of the Community.*

Facts on File, 460 Park Avenue South, New York, New York 10016 (800) 443-8323; *The New Book of World Rankings.*

National Technical Information Service, 5285 Port Royal Road, Springfield, Virginia 22161 (703) 487-4600; *Handbook of Economic Statistics.*

Organisation for Economic Co-operation and Development (OECD), 2 rue Andre-Pascal, 75 Paris 16, France (Telephone Number in U.S. (202) 785-6323); *Economic Accounts for Agriculture,* and *Textile Industry in OECD Countries.*

Statistical Office of the United Nations, Publishing Service, New York, New York 10017 (800) 253-9646; *Statistical Yearbook.*

GERMANY - YARN PRODUCTION

European Community Information Service, 2100 M Street, NW, Washington, D.C. 20037 (202) 862-9500; *Basic Statistics of the Community.*

Organisation for Economic Co-operation and Development (OECD), 2 rue Andre-Pascal, 75 Paris 16, France (Telephone Number in U.S. (202) 785-6323); *Foreign Trade by Commodities,* and *Textile Industry in OECD Countries.*

Statistical Office of the United Nations, Publishing Service, New York, New York 10017 (800) 253-9646; *Statistical Yearbook.*

GERMANY - ZINC AND ZINC ORE PRODUCTION AND CONSUMPTION - See GERMANY - MINING AND MINERAL PRODUCTS

Ghana - National Statistical Office

Statistical Service, Post Office Box 1098, Accra, Ghana.

Ghana - Primary Statistics Sources

Central Bureau of Statistics, Post Office Box 1098, Accra, Ghana; *Quarterly Digest of Statistics*, and *Economic Survey*.

GHANA - AGRICULTURE

Euromonitor Publications Limited, 87-88 Turnmill Street, London EC1M 5QU, England; *International Marketing Data and Statistics*.

Facts on File, 460 Park Avenue South, New York, New York 10016 (800) 443-8323; *The New Book of World Rankings*.

Federal Statistical Office, Gustav - Stresemann - Ring 11, D-6200 Wiesbaden, Germany; *Ghana*.

Food and Agricultural Organization of the United Nations (FAO) Via delle Terme di Caracalla, 00100 Rome, Italy (Telephone Number in U.S. (202) 653-2400); *Production Yearbook*, and *The State of Food and Agriculture*, and *Trade Yearbook*.

G.K. Hall and Company, 70 Lincoln Street, Boston, Massachusetts 02111 (617) 423-3990; *The World in Figures*.

Statistical Office of the United Nations, Publishing Service, New York, New York 10017 (800) 253-9646; *Statistical Yearbook*, and *Survey of Economic and Social Conditions in Africa*.

United Nations Economic Commission for Africa, Africa Hall, Post Office Box 3001, Addis Ababa, Ethiopia (Telephone Number in U.S. (800) 253-9646); *African Statistical Yearbook*.

The World Bank, 1818 H Street, NW, Washington, D.C. 20433 (202) 477-1234; *World Tables*.

GHANA - AIRLINE SERVICE

Facts on File, 460 Park Avenue South, New York, New York 10016 (800) 443-8323; *The New Book of World Rankings*.

G.K. Hall and Company, 70 Lincoln Street, Boston, Massachusetts 02111 (617) 423-3990; *The World in Figures*.

International Civil Aviation Organization, 1000 Sherbrooke Street West, Suite 400, Montreal, Quebec, Canada H3A 2R2 (514) 285-8219; *Civil Aviation Statistics of the World*.

Statistical Office of the United Nations, Publishing Service, New York, New York 10017 (800) 253-9646; *Statistical Yearbook*.

Times Books, 201 East 50th Street, New York, New York 10022 (212) 751-2600; *The Economist Book of Vital World Statistics*.

United Nations Economic Commission for Africa, Africa Hall, Post Office Box 3001, Addis Ababa, Ethiopia (Telephone Number in U.S. (800) 253-9646); *African Statistical Yearbook*.

GHANA - ALUMINUM PRODUCTION AND CONSUMPTION - See GHANA - MINING AND MINERAL PRODUCTS

GHANA - ANIMAL HEALTH

Food and Agricultural Organization of the United Nations (FAO), Via delle Terme di Caracalla, 00100, Rome, Italy (Telephone Number in U.S. (202) 653-2400); *Animal Health Yearbook*.

GHANA - AREA AND DENSITY OF POPULATION

African Development Bank, 01 BP 1387, Abidjan 01, Cote D'Ivoire; *Selected Statistics on Regional Member Countries*.

Euromonitor Publications Limited, 87-88 Turnmill Street, London EC1M 5QU, England; *International Marketing Data and Statistics*.

Facts on File, 460 Park Avenue South, New York, New York 10016 (800) 443-8323; *The New Book of World Rankings*.

Federal Statistical Office, Gustav - Stresemann - Ring 11, D-6200 Wiesbaden, Germany; *Ghana*.

Food and Agricultural Organization of the United Nations (FAO) Via delle Terme di Caracalla, 00100 Rome, Italy (Telephone Number in U.S. (202) 653-2400); *The State of Food and Agriculture*.

G.K. Hall and Company, 70 Lincoln Street, Boston, Massachusetts 02111 (617) 423-3990; *The World in Figures*.

Statistical Office of the United Nations, Publishing Service, New York, New York 10017 (800) 253-9646; *Statistical Yearbook*, and *Survey of Economic and Social Conditions in Africa*.

Times Books, 201 East 50th Street, New York, New York 10022 (212) 751-2600; *The Economist Book of Vital World Statistics*.

United Nations Educational, Scientific and Cultural Organization (UNESCO), 7 Place de Fontenoy, F-75700 Paris, France (Telephone Number in U.S. (212) 963-5981); *Statistical Yearbook*.

GHANA - ARMS EXPORTS AND IMPORTS

U.S. Arms Control and Disarmament Agency, 320 Twenty-first Street, Northwest, Washington, D.C. 20451 (202) 647-8677; *World Military Expenditures and Arms Transfers*.

GHANA - BALANCE OF PAYMENTS

African Development Bank, 01 BP 1387, Abidjan 01, Cote D'Ivoire; *Selected Statistics on Regional Member Countries*.

The Economist Intelligence Unit, 111 West 57th Street, New York, New York 10019 (800) 938-4685; *The World Market Atlas*.

Federal Statistical Office, Gustav - Stresemann - Ring 11, D-6200 Wiesbaden, Germany; *Ghana*.

G.K. Hall and Company, 70 Lincoln Street, Boston, Massachusetts 02111 (617) 423-3990; *The World in Figures*.

International Monetary Fund, 700 Nineteenth Street, NW, Washington, D.C. 20431 (202) 623-7000; *Balance of Payments Yearbook*, and *International Financial Statistics*.

Times Books, 201 East 50th Street, New York, New York 10022 (212) 751-2600; *The Economist Book of Vital World Statistics*.

United Nations Economic Commission for Africa, Africa Hall, Post Office Box 3001, Addis Ababa, Ethiopia (Telephone Number in U.S. (800) 253-9646); *African Statistical Yearbook*.

The World Bank, 1818 H Street, NW, Washington, D.C. 20433 (202) 477-1234; *World Tables*.

GHANA - BANKING

Facts on File, 460 Park Avenue South, New York, New York 10016 (800) 443-8323; *The New Book of World Rankings.*

G.K. Hall and Company, 70 Lincoln Street, Boston, Massachusetts 02111 (617) 423-3990; *The World in Figures.*

International Monetary Fund, 700 Nineteenth Street, NW, Washington, D.C. 20431 (202) 623-7000; *Government Finance Statistics Yearbook,* and *International Financial Statistics.*

Statistical Office of the United Nations, Publishing Service, New York, New York 10017 (800) 253-9646; *Statistical Yearbook.*

United Nations Economic Commission for Africa, Africa Hall, Post Office Box 3001, Addis Ababa, Ethiopia (Telephone Number in U.S. (800) 253-9646); *African Statistical Yearbook.*

GHANA - BARLEY PRODUCTION - See GHANA - CROPS

GHANA - BAUXITE PRODUCTION AND CONSUMPTION - See GHANA - MINING AND MINERAL PRODUCTS

GHANA - BEER PRODUCTION

Facts on File, 460 Park Avenue South, New York, New York 10016 (800) 443-8323; *The New Book of World Rankings.*

Statistical Office of the United Nations, Publishing Service, New York, New York 10017 (800) 253-9646; *Statistical Yearbook.*

GHANA - BIRTH RATES

Facts on File, 460 Park Avenue South, New York, New York 10016 (800) 443-8323; *The New Book of World Rankings.*

Statistical Office of the United Nations, Publishing Service, New York, New York 10017 (800) 253-9646; *Demographic Yearbook, Statistical Yearbook,* and *Survey of Economic and Social Conditions in Africa.*

Times Books, 201 East 50th Street, New York, New York 10022 (212) 751-2600; *The Economist Book of Vital World Statistics.*

The World Bank, 1818 H Street, NW, Washington, D.C. 20433 (202) 477-1234; *World Tables.*

GHANA - BONDS

G.K. Hall and Company, 70 Lincoln Street, Boston, Massachusetts 02111 (617) 423-3990; *The World in Figures.*

International Monetary Fund, 700 Nineteenth Street, NW, Washington, D.C. 20431 (202) 623-7000; *Government Finance Statistics Yearbook.*

GHANA - BOOK PRODUCTION

G.K. Hall and Company, 70 Lincoln Street, Boston, Massachusetts 02111 (617) 423-3990; *The World in Figures.*

United Nations Educational, Scientific and Cultural Organization (UNESCO), 7 Place de Fontenoy, F-75700 Paris, France (Telephone Number in U.S. (212) 963-5981); *Statistical Yearbook.*

GHANA - BROADCASTING

Billboard Limited, Post Office Box 9027, 1006 AA Amsterdam, The Netherlands (Telephone Number in U.S. (212) 764-7300); *World Radio TV Handbook.*

Facts on File, 460 Park Avenue South, New York, New York 10016 (800) 443-8323; *The New Book of World Rankings.*

G.K. Hall and Company, 70 Lincoln Street, Boston, Massachusetts 02111 (617) 423-3990; *The World in Figures.*

Times Books, 201 East 50th Street, New York, New York 10022 (212) 751-2600; *The Economist Book of Vital World Statistics.*

GHANA - BUSINESS

G.K. Hall and Company, 70 Lincoln Street, Boston, Massachusetts 02111 (617) 423-3990; *The World in Figures.*

GHANA - BUSINESS AND PROFESSIONAL LICENSES

International Monetary Fund, 700 Nineteenth Street, NW, Washington, D.C. 20431 (202) 623-7000; *Government Finance Statistics Yearbook.*

GHANA - CACAO - See GHANA - CROPS

GHANA - CALORIE SUPPLY

African Development Bank, 01 BP 1387, Abidjan 01, Cote D'Ivoire; *Selected Statistics on Regional Member Countries.*

Food and Agricultural Organization of the United Nations (FAO) Via delle Terme di Caracalla, 00100 Rome, Italy (Telephone Number in U.S. (202) 653-2400); *The State of Food and Agriculture.*

GHANA - CAPITAL REVENUE

International Monetary Fund, 700 Nineteenth Street, NW, Washington, D.C. 20431 (202) 623-7000; *Government Finance Statistics Yearbook.*

GHANA - CATTLE - See GHANA - LIVESTOCK AND POULTRY

GHANA - CEMENT PRODUCTION - See GHANA - MINING AND MINERAL PRODUCTS

GHANA - CHEMICAL (ORGANIC) PRODUCTION - See GHANA - MINING AND MINERAL PRODUCTS

GHANA - CHICKENS - See GHANA - LIVESTOCK AND POULTRY

GHANA - CIGARETTE PRODUCTION - See GHANA - TOBACCO PRODUCTION

GHANA - CLASS STRUCTURE

G.K. Hall and Company, 70 Lincoln Street, Boston, Massachusetts 02111 (617) 423-3990; *The World in Figures.*

GHANA - CLIMATE

Facts on File, 460 Park Avenue South, New York, New York 10016 (800) 443-8323; *The New Book of World Rankings.*

G.K. Hall and Company, 70 Lincoln Street, Boston, Massachusetts 02111 (617) 423-3990; *The World in Figures.*

GHANA - COAL PRODUCTION - See GHANA - MINING AND MINERAL PRODUCTS

GHANA - COCOA (BEANS) PRODUCTION - See GHANA - CROPS

GHANA - COFFEE PRODUCTION - See GHANA - CROPS

GHANA - COMMUNICATIONS

Federal Statistical Office, Gustav - Stresemann - Ring 11, D-6200 Wiesbaden, Germany; *Ghana.*

G.K. Hall and Company, 70 Lincoln Street, Boston, Massachusetts 02111 (617) 423-3990; *The World in Figures.*

United Nations Economic Commission for Africa, Africa Hall, Post Office Box 3001, Addis Ababa, Ethiopia (Telephone Number in U.S. (800) 253-9646); *African Statistical Yearbook.*

GHANA - CONSTRUCTION INDUSTRY

Facts on File, 460 Park Avenue South, New York, New York 10016 (800) 443-8323; *The New Book of World Rankings.*

Statistical Office of the United Nations, Publishing Service, New York, New York 10017 (800) 253-9646; *Construction Statistics Yearbook,* and *Statistical Yearbook.*

United Nations Economic Commission for Africa, Africa Hall, Post Office Box 3001, Addis Ababa, Ethiopia (Telephone Number in U.S. (800) 253-9646); *African Statistical Yearbook.*

GHANA - CONSUMER PRICE INDEX

African Development Bank, 01 BP 1387, Abidjan 01, Cote D'Ivoire; *Selected Statistics on Regional Member Countries.*

Federal Statistical Office, Gustav - Stresemann - Ring 11, D-6200 Wiesbaden, Germany; *Ghana.*

G.K. Hall and Company, 70 Lincoln Street, Boston, Massachusetts 02111 (617) 423-3990; *The World in Figures.*

Statistical Office of the United Nations, Publishing Service, New York, New York 10017 (800) 253-9646; *Statistical Yearbook,* and *Survey of Economic and Social Conditions in Africa.*

United Nations Economic Commission for Africa, Africa Hall, Post Office Box 3001, Addis Ababa, Ethiopia (Telephone Number in U.S. (800) 253-9646); *African Statistical Yearbook.*

GHANA - CONSUMER PRICES

Federal Statistical Office, Gustav - Stresemann - Ring 11, D-6200 Wiesbaden, Germany; *Ghana.*

International Labour Office, I.L.O. Publications, CH-1211, Geneva 22, Switzerland; *Yearbook of Labour Statistics.*

International Monetary Fund, 700 Nineteenth Street, NW, Washington, D.C. 20431 (202) 623-7000; *International Financial Statistics.*

Times Books, 201 East 50th Street, New York, New York 10022 (212) 751-2600; *The Economist Book of Vital World Statistics.*

GHANA - CONSUMPTION

African Development Bank, 01 BP 1387, Abidjan 01, Cote D'Ivoire; *Selected Statistics on Regional Member Countries.*

G.K. Hall and Company, 70 Lincoln Street, Boston, Massachusetts 02111 (617) 423-3990; *The World in Figures.*

Statistical Office of the United Nations, Publishing Service, New York, New York 10017 (800) 253-9646; *Survey of Economic and Social Conditions in Africa.*

GHANA - COPPER PRODUCTION - See GHANA - MINING AND MINERAL PRODUCTS

GHANA - CORN PRODUCTION - See GHANA - CROPS

GHANA - CORPORATE TAXES - See GHANA - TAXATION

GHANA - COTTON PRODUCTION - See GHANA - CROPS

GHANA - CRIME

Yale University Press, Yale Station, New Haven, Connecticut 06520 (203) 432-0940; *Violence and Crime in Cross-National Perspective.*

GHANA - CROPS

Commodity Research Bureau, Incorporated, 75 Wall Street, New York, New York 10005 (212) 504-7754; *Commodity Year Book.*

Facts on File, 460 Park Avenue South, New York, New York 10016 (800) 443-8323; *The New Book of World Rankings.*

G.K. Hall and Company, 70 Lincoln Street, Boston, Massachusetts 02111 (617) 423-3990; *The World in Figures.*

Food and Agricultural Organization of the United Nations (FAO) Via delle Terme di Caracalla, 00100 Rome, Italy (Telephone Number in U.S. (202) 653-2400); *Production Yearbook* and *The State of Food and Agriculture.*

International Monetary Fund, 700 Nineteenth Street, NW, Washington, D.C. 20431 (202) 623-7000; *International Financial Statistics.*

Statistical Office of the United Nations, Publishing Service, New York, New York 10017 (800) 253-9646; *Statistical Yearbook.*

United Nations Economic Commission for Africa, Africa Hall, Post Office Box 3001, Addis Ababa, Ethiopia (Telephone Number in U.S. (800) 253-9646); *African Statistical Yearbook.*

GHANA - CUSTOMS DUTIES

G.K. Hall and Company, 70 Lincoln Street, Boston, Massachusetts 02111 (617) 423-3990; *The World in Figures.*

International Monetary Fund, 700 Nineteenth Street, NW, Washington, D.C. 20431 (202) 623-7000; *Government Finance Statistics Yearbook.*

GHANA - DAIRY PRODUCTS

Facts on File, 460 Park Avenue South, New York, New York 10016 (800) 443-8323; *The New Book of World Rankings.*

Food and Agricultural Organization of the United Nations (FAO) Via delle Terme di Caracalla, 00100 Rome, Italy (Telephone Number in

U.S. (202) 653-2400); *The State of Food and Agriculture.*

Statistical Office of the United Nations, Publishing Service, New York, New York 10017 (800) 253-9646; *Statistical Yearbook.*

GHANA - DEATH RATES

G.K. Hall and Company, 70 Lincoln Street, Boston, Massachusetts 02111 (617) 423-3990; *The World in Figures.*

Statistical Office of the United Nations, Publishing Service, New York, New York 10017 (800) 253-9646; *Statistical Yearbook,* and *Survey of Economic and Social Conditions in Africa.*

Times Books, 201 East 50th Street, New York, New York 10022 (212) 751-2600; *The Economist Book of Vital World Statistics.*

World Health Organization, Office of Publications, Avenue Appia, CH-1211 Geneva 27, Switzerland (Telephone Number in U.S. (518) 436-9686); *World Health Statistics Annual.*

GHANA - DEFENSE EXPENDITURES

G.K. Hall and Company, 70 Lincoln Street, Boston, Massachusetts 02111 (617) 423-3990; *The World in Figures.*

International Monetary Fund, 700 Nineteenth Street, NW, Washington, D.C. 20431 (202) 623-7000; *Government Finance Statistics Yearbook.*

U.S. Arms Control and Disarmament Agency, 320 Twenty-first Street, Northwest, Washington, D.C. 20451 (202) 647-8677; *World Military Expenditures and Arms Transfers.*

GHANA - DEMOGRAPHY

The Economist Intelligence Unit, 111 West 57th Street, New York, New York 10019 (800) 938-4685; *The World Market Atlas.*

Facts on File, 460 Park Avenue South, New York, New York 10016 (800) 443-8323; *The New Book of World Rankings.*

Federal Statistical Office, Gustav - Stresemann - Ring 11, D-6200 Wiesbaden, Germany; *Ghana.*

G.K. Hall and Company, 70 Lincoln Street, Boston, Massachusetts 02111 (617) 423-3990; *The World in Figures.*

Statistical Office of the United Nations, Publishing Service, New York, New York 10017 (800) 253-9646; *Survey of Economic and Social Conditions in Africa.*

GHANA - DEVELOPMENT ASSISTANCE

G.K. Hall and Company, 70 Lincoln Street, Boston, Massachusetts 02111 (617) 423-3990; *The World in Figures.*

Statistical Office of the United Nations, Publishing Service, New York, New York 10017 (800) 253-9646; *Statistical Yearbook.*

GHANA - DIAMOND PRODUCTION - See GHANA - MINING AND MINERAL PRODUCTS

GHANA - DISCOUNT RATES

Statistical Office of the United Nations, Publishing Service, New York, New York 10017 (800) 253-9646; *Statistical Yearbook.*

GHANA - DISEASES

G.K. Hall and Company, 70 Lincoln Street, Boston, Massachusetts 02111 (617) 423-3990; *The World in Figures.*

World Health Organization, Office of Publications, Avenue Appia, CH-1211 Geneva 27, Switzerland (Telephone Number in U.S. (518) 436-9686); *World Health Statistics Annual.*

GHANA - DIVORCE RATES

Facts on File, 460 Park Avenue South, New York, New York 10016 (800) 443-8323; *The New Book of World Rankings.*

Statistical Office of the United Nations, Publishing Service, New York, New York 10017 (800) 253-9646; *Demographic Yearbook.*

GHANA - DOMESTIC PRODUCT

G.K. Hall and Company, 70 Lincoln Street, Boston, Massachusetts 02111 (617) 423-3990; *The World in Figures.*

GHANA - ECONOMY

African Development Bank, 01 BP 1387, Abidjan 01, Cote D'Ivoire; *Selected Statistics on Regional Member Countries.*

Euromonitor Publications Limited, 87-88 Turnmill Street, London EC1M 5QU, England; *International Marketing Data and Statistics.*

Facts on File, 460 Park Avenue South, New York, New York 10016 (800) 443-8323; *The New Book of World Rankings.*

Federal Statistical Office, Gustav - Stresemann - Ring 11, D-6200 Wiesbaden, Germany; *Ghana.*

G.K. Hall and Company, 70 Lincoln Street, Boston, Massachusetts 02111 (617) 423-3990; *The World in Figures.*

Statistical Office of the United Nations, Publishing Service, New York, New York 10017 (800) 253-9646; *Foreign Trade Statistics for Africa.*

GHANA - EDUCATION

African Development Bank, 01 BP 1387, Abidjan 01, Cote D'Ivoire; *Selected Statistics on Regional Member Countries.*

The Economist Intelligence Unit, 111 West 57th Street, New York, New York 10019 (800) 938-4685; *The World Market Atlas.*

Facts on File, 460 Park Avenue South, New York, New York 10016 (800) 443-8323; *The New Book of World Rankings.*

Federal Statistical Office, Gustav - Stresemann - Ring 11, D-6200 Wiesbaden, Germany; *Ghana.*

G.K. Hall and Company, 70 Lincoln Street, Boston, Massachusetts 02111 (617) 423-3990; *The World in Figures.*

International Monetary Fund, 700 Nineteenth Street, NW, Washington, D.C. 20431 (202) 623-7000; *Government Finance Statistics Yearbook.*

Statistical Office of the United Nations, Publishing Service, New York, New York 10017 (800) 253-9646; *Survey of Economic and Social Conditions in Africa.*

Times Books, 201 East 50th Street, New York, New York 10022 (212) 751-2600; *The Economist Book of Vital World Statistics.*

United Nations Economic Commission for Africa, Africa Hall, Post Office Box 3001, Addis Ababa, Ethiopia (Telephone Number in U.S. (800) 253-9646); *African Statistical Yearbook.*

United Nations Educational, Scientific and Cultural Organization (UNESCO), 7 Place de Fontenoy, F-75700 Paris, France (Telephone Number in U.S. (212) 963-5981); *Statistical Yearbook.*

The World Bank, 1818 H Street, NW, Washington, D.C. 20433 (202) 477-1234; *World Tables.*

GHANA - EGG PRODUCTION - See GHANA - DAIRY PRODUCTS

GHANA - EGGPLANT PRODUCTION - See GHANA - CROPS

GHANA - ELECTRICITY

Facts on File, 460 Park Avenue South, New York, New York 10016 (800) 443-8323; *The New Book of World Rankings.*

Penn Well Publishing Company, 1421 South Sheridan Road, Post Office Box 1260, Tulsa, Oklahoma 74101 (800) 752-9764; *International Energy Statistics Sourcebook.*

Statistical Office of the United Nations, Publishing Service, New York, New York 10017 (800) 253-9646; *Statistical Yearbook,* and *Survey of Economic and Social Conditions in Africa.*

Times Books, 201 East 50th Street, New York, New York 10022 (212) 751-2600; *The Economist Book of Vital World Statistics.*

United Nations Economic Commission for Africa, Africa Hall, Post Office Box 3001, Addis Ababa, Ethiopia (Telephone Number in U.S. (800) 253-9646); *African Statistical Yearbook.*

GHANA - EMPLOYMENT

Euromonitor Publications Limited, 87-88 Turnmill Street, London EC1M 5QU, England; *International Marketing Data and Statistics.*

Facts on File, 460 Park Avenue South, New York, New York 10016 (800) 443-8323; *The New Book of World Rankings.*

Federal Statistical Office, Gustav - Stresemann - Ring 11, D-6200 Wiesbaden, Germany; *Ghana.*

International Labour Office, I.L.O. Publications, CH-1211, Geneva 22, Switzerland; *Yearbook of Labour Statistics.*

Statistical Office of the United Nations, Publishing Service, New York, New York 10017 (800) 253-9646; *Statistical Yearbook,* and *Survey of Economic and Social Conditions in Africa.*

United Nations Economic Commission for Africa, Africa Hall, Post Office Box 3001, Addis Ababa, Ethiopia (Telephone Number in U.S. (800) 253-9646); *African Statistical Yearbook.*

GHANA - ENERGY

Facts on File, 460 Park Avenue South, New York, New York 10016 (800) 443-8323; *The New Book of World Rankings.*

Food and Agricultural Organization of the United Nations (FAO) Via delle Terme di Caracalla, 00100 Rome, Italy (Telephone Number in U.S. (202) 653-2400); *The State of Food and Agriculture.*

G.K. Hall and Company, 70 Lincoln Street, Boston, Massachusetts 02111 (617) 423-3990; *The World in Figures.*

Penn Well Publishing Company, 1421 South Sheridan Road, Post Office Box 1260, Tulsa, Oklahoma 74101 (800) 752-9764; *International Energy Statistics Sourcebook.*

Statistical Office of the United Nations, Publishing Service, New York, New York 10017 (800) 253-9646; *Energy Statistics Yearbook,* and *Statistical Yearbook.*

Times Books, 201 East 50th Street, New York, New York 10022 (212) 751-2600; *The Economist Book of Vital World Statistics.*

United Nations Economic Commission for Africa, Africa Hall, Post Office Box 3001, Addis Ababa, Ethiopia (Telephone Number in U.S. (800) 253-9646); *African Statistical Yearbook.*

GHANA - EXCHANGE RATES

African Development Bank, 01 BP 1387, Abidjan 01, Cote D'Ivoire; *Selected Statistics on Regional Member Countries.*

Euromonitor Publications Limited, 87-88 Turnmill Street, London EC1M 5QU, England; *International Marketing Data and Statistics.*

International Civil Aviation Organization, 1000 Sherbrooke Street West, Suite 400, Montreal, Quebec, Canada H3A 2R2 (514) 285-8219; *Civil Aviation Statistics of the World.*

International Monetary Fund, 700 Nineteenth Street, NW, Washington, D.C. 20431 (202) 623-7000; *International Financial Statistics.*

Statistical Office of the United Nations, Publishing Service, New York, New York 10017 (800) 253-9646; *Foreign Trade Statistics for Africa,* and *Statistical Yearbook.*

GHANA - EXCISE TAXES - See GHANA - TAXATION

GHANA - EXPORTS

African Development Bank, 01 BP 1387, Abidjan 01, Cote D'Ivoire; *Selected Statistics on Regional Member Countries.*

The Economist Intelligence Unit, 111 West 57th Street, New York, New York 10019 (800) 938-4685; *The World Market Atlas.*

Euromonitor Publications Limited, 87-88 Turnmill Street, London EC1M 5QU, England; *International Marketing Data and Statistics.*

Food and Agricultural Organization of the United Nations (FAO) Via delle Terme di Caracalla, 00100 Rome, Italy (Telephone Number in U.S. (202) 653-2400); *The State of Food and Agriculture.*

G.K. Hall and Company, 70 Lincoln Street, Boston, Massachusetts 02111 (617) 423-3990; *The World in Figures.*

International Monetary Fund, 700 Nineteenth Street, NW, Washington, D.C. 20431 (202) 623-7000; *Direction of Trade Statistics, Government Finance Statistics Yearbook,* and *International Financial Statistics.*

Statistical Office of the United Nations, Publishing Service, New York, New York 10017; *Foreign Trade Statistics for Africa, Survey of Economic and Social Conditions in Africa,* and *Trade in Manufactures of Developing Countries.*

Times Books, 201 East 50th Street, New York, New York 10022 (212) 751-2600; *The Economist Book of Vital World Statistics.*

United Nations Economic Commission for Africa, Africa Hall, Post Office Box 3001, Addis Ababa, Ethiopia (Telephone Number in U.S. (800) 253-9646); *African Statistical Yearbook.*

The World Bank, 1818 H Street, NW, Washington, D.C. 20433 (202) 477-1234; *World Tables.*

GHANA - EXTERNAL INDEBTEDNESS

African Development Bank, 01 BP 1387, Abidjan 01, Cote D'Ivoire; *Selected Statistics on Regional Member Countries.*

Statistical Office of the United Nations, Publishing Service, New York, New York 10017 (800) 253-9646; *Survey of Economic and Social Conditions in Africa.*

GHANA - EXTERNAL TRADE

African Development Bank, 01 BP 1387, Abidjan 01, Cote D'Ivoire; *Selected Statistics on Regional Member Countries.*

Food and Agricultural Organization of the United Nations (FAO) Via delle Terme di Caracalla, 00100 Rome, Italy (Telephone Number in U.S. (202) 653-2400); *The State of Food and Agriculture,* and *Trade Yearbook.*

G.K. Hall and Company, 70 Lincoln Street, Boston, Massachusetts 02111 (617) 423-3990; *The World in Figures.*

Statistical Office of the United Nations, Publishing Service, New York, New York 10017 (800) 253-9646; *Statistical Yearbook.*

The World Bank, 1818 H Street, NW, Washington, D.C. 20433 (202) 477-1234; *World Tables.*

GHANA - FABRIC PRODUCTION - See GHANA - TEXTILE INDUSTRY

GHANA - FEMALE WORKING POPULATION - See GHANA - EMPLOYMENT

GHANA - FERTILITY RATES

Facts on File, 460 Park Avenue South, New York, New York 10016 (800) 443-8323; *The New Book of World Rankings.*

Statistical Office of the United Nations, Publishing Service, New York, New York 10017 (800) 253-9646; *Survey of Economic and Social Conditions in Africa.*

Times Books, 201 East 50th Street, New York, New York 10022 (212) 751-2600; *The Economist Book of Vital World Statistics.*

The World Bank, 1818 H Street, NW, Washington, D.C. 20433 (202) 477-1234; *World Tables.*

GHANA - FERTILIZER

Food and Agricultural Organization of the United Nations (FAO) Via delle Terme di Caracalla, 00100 Rome, Italy (Telephone Number in U.S. (202) 653-2400); *Fertilizer Yearbook,* and *The State of Food and Agriculture.*

Statistical Office of the United Nations, Publishing Service, New York, New York 10017 (800) 253-9646; *Statistical Yearbook.*

GHANA - FETAL MORTALITY

Statistical Office of the United Nations, Publishing Service, New York, New York 10017 (800) 253-9646; *Demographic Yearbook.*

GHANA - FILM - See GHANA - MOTION PICTURES

GHANA - FINANCE

African Development Bank, 01 BP 1387, Abidjan 01, Cote D'Ivoire; *Selected Statistics on Regional Member Countries.*

Facts on File, 460 Park Avenue South, New York, New York 10016 (800) 443-8323; *The New Book of World Rankings.*

Federal Statistical Office, Gustav - Stresemann - Ring 11, D-6200 Wiesbaden, Germany; *Ghana.*

G.K. Hall and Company, 70 Lincoln Street, Boston, Massachusetts 02111 (617) 423-3990; *The World in Figures.*

International Monetary Fund, 700 Nineteenth Street, NW, Washington, D.C. 20431 (202) 623-7000; *Government Finance Statistics Yearbook.*

United Nations Economic Commission for Africa, Africa Hall, Post Office Box 3001, Addis Ababa, Ethiopia (Telephone Number in U.S. (800) 253-9646); *African Statistical Yearbook.*

GHANA - FISHERIES

Facts on File, 460 Park Avenue South, New York, New York 10016 (800) 443-8323; *The New Book of World Rankings.*

Federal Statistical Office, Gustav - Stresemann - Ring 11, D-6200 Wiesbaden, Germany; *Ghana.*

Food and Agricultural Organization of the United Nations (FAO) Via delle Terme di Caracalla, 00100 Rome, Italy (Telephone Number in U.S. (202) 653-2400); *The State of Food and Agriculture,* and *Yearbook of Fishery Statistics.*

Statistical Office of the United Nations, Publishing Service, New York, New York 10017 (800) 253-9646; *Statistical Yearbook,* and *Survey of Economic and Social Conditions in Africa.*

United Nations Economic Commission for Africa, Africa Hall, Post Office Box 3001, Addis Ababa, Ethiopia (Telephone Number in U.S. (800) 253-9646); *African Statistical Yearbook.*

GHANA - FLOUR PRODUCTION

Statistical Office of the United Nations, Publishing Service, New York, New York 10017 (800) 253-9646; *Statistical Yearbook.*

GHANA - FOOD

African Development Bank, 01 BP 1387, Abidjan 01, Cote D'Ivoire; *Selected Statistics on Regional Member Countries.*

Food and Agricultural Organization of the United Nations (FAO), Via delle Terme di Caracalla, 00100 Rome, Italy (Telephone Number in U.S. (202) 653-2400); *Production Yearbook,* and *The State of Food and Agriculture.*

G.K. Hall and Company, 70 Lincoln Street, Boston, Massachusetts 02111 (617) 423-3990; *The World in Figures.*

Statistical Office of the United Nations, Publishing Service, New York, New York 10017 (800) 253-9646; *Trade in Manufactures of Developing Countries.*

GHANA - FOREIGN AID

G.K. Hall and Company, 70 Lincoln Street, Boston, Massachusetts 02111 (617) 423-3990; *The World in Figures.*

GHANA - FOREIGN DEBT

International Monetary Fund, 700 Nineteenth Street, NW, Washington, D.C. 20431 (202) 623-7000; *Government Finance Statistics Yearbook.*

GHANA - FOREIGN TRADE

Euromonitor Publications Limited, 87-88 Turnmill Street, London EC1M 5QU, England; *International Marketing Data and Statistics.*

Facts on File, 460 Park Avenue South, New York, New York 10016 (800) 443-8323; *The New Book of World Rankings.*

Federal Statistical Office, Gustav - Stresemann - Ring 11, D-6200 Wiesbaden, Germany; *Ghana.*

Food and Agricultural Organization of the United Nations (FAO) Via delle Terme di Caracalla, 00100 Rome, Italy (Telephone Number in U.S. (202) 653-2400); *The State of Food and Agriculture.*

G.K. Hall and Company, 70 Lincoln Street, Boston, Massachusetts 02111 (617) 423-3990; *The World in Figures.*

International Monetary Fund, 700 Nineteenth Street, NW, Washington, D.C. 20431 (202) 623-7000; *International Financial Statistics.*

Statistical Office of the United Nations, Publishing Service, New York, New York 10017 (800) 253-9646; *Foreign Trade Statistics for Africa, International Trade Statistics Yearbook,* and *Statistical Yearbook.*

United Nations Economic Commission for Africa, Africa Hall, Post Office Box 3001, Addis Ababa, Ethiopia (Telephone Number in U.S. (800) 253-9646); *African Statistical Yearbook.*

The World Bank, 1818 H Street, NW, Washington, D.C. 20433 (202) 477-1234; *World Tables.*

GHANA - FORESTRY AND FOREST PRODUCTS

Facts on File, 460 Park Avenue South, New York, New York 10016 (800) 443-8323; *The New Book of World Rankings.*

Federal Statistical Office, Gustav - Stresemann - Ring 11, D-6200 Wiesbaden, Germany; *Ghana.*

Food and Agricultural Organization of the United Nations (FAO) Via delle Terme di Caracalla, 00100 Rome, Italy (Telephone Number in U.S. (202) 653-2400); *The State of Food and Agriculture,* and *Yearbook of Forest Products.*

G.K. Hall and Company, 70 Lincoln Street, Boston, Massachusetts 02111 (617) 423-3990; *The World in Figures.*

International Monetary Fund, 700 Nineteenth Street, NW, Washington, D.C. 20431 (202) 623-7000; *International Financial Statistics.*

Statistical Office of the United Nations, Publishing Service, New York, New York 10017 (800) 253-9646; *Statistical Yearbook.*

United Nations Economic Commission for Africa, Africa Hall, Post Office Box 3001, Addis Ababa, Ethiopia (Telephone Number in U.S. (800) 253-9646); *African Statistical Yearbook.*

United Nations Educational, Scientific and Cultural Organization (UNESCO), 7 Place de Fontenoy, F-75700 Paris, France (Telephone Number in U.S. (212) 963-5981); *Statistical Yearbook.*

GHANA - FURNITURE AND WOOD PRODUCTS - EXPORTS AND IMPORTS

Statistical Office of the United Nations, Publishing Service, New York, New York 10017 (800) 253-9646; *Trade in Manufactures of Developing Countries.*

GHANA - GAS PRODUCTION - See GHANA - MINING AND MINERAL PRODUCTS

GHANA - GENERAL INDUSTRIAL STATISTICS

Federal Statistical Office, Gustav - Stresemann - Ring 11, D-6200 Wiesbaden, Germany; *Ghana.*

Statistical Office of the United Nations, Publishing Service, New York, New York 10017 (800) 253-9646; *Industrial Statistics Yearbook.*

GHANA - GENERAL MORTALITY

Statistical Office of the United Nations, Publishing Service, New York, New York 10017 (800) 253-9646; *Demographic Yearbook.*

GHANA - GEOGRAPHIC DATA

Facts on File, 460 Park Avenue South, New York, New York 10016 (800) 443-8323; *The New Book of World Rankings.*

Federal Statistical Office, Gustav - Stresemann - Ring 11, D-6200 Wiesbaden, Germany; *Ghana.*

GHANA - GOATS - See GHANA - LIVESTOCK AND POULTRY

GHANA - GOLD HOLDINGS

International Monetary Fund, 700 Nineteenth Street, NW, Washington, D.C. 20431 (202) 623-7000; *International Financial Statistics.*

Statistical Office of the United Nations, Publishing Service, New York, New York 10017 (800) 253-9646; *Statistical Yearbook.*

The World Bank, 1818 H Street, NW, Washington, D.C. 20433 (202) 477-1234; *World Tables.*

GHANA - GOLD PRODUCTION AND CONSUMPTION - See GHANA - MINING AND MINERAL PRODUCTS

GHANA - GOVERNMENT

G.K. Hall and Company, 70 Lincoln Street, Boston, Massachusetts 02111 (617) 423-3990; *The World in Figures.*

GHANA - GOVERNMENT EXPENDITURES

International Monetary Fund, 700 Nineteenth Street, NW, Washington, D.C. 20431 (202) 623-7000; *Government Finance*

Statistics Yearbook.

Times Books, 201 East 50th Street, New York, New York 10022 (212) 751-2600; *The Economist Book of Vital World Statistics.*

The World Bank, 1818 H Street, NW, Washington, D.C. 20433 (202) 477-1234; *World Tables.*

GHANA - GOVERNMENT FINANCES

International Monetary Fund, 700 Nineteenth Street, NW, Washington, D.C. 20431 (202) 623-7000; *International Financial Statistics.*

Statistical Office of the United Nations, Publishing Service, New York, New York 10017 (800) 253-9646; *Statistical Yearbook.*

GHANA - GOVERNMENT REVENUE

International Monetary Fund, 700 Nineteenth Street, NW, Washington, D.C. 20431 (202) 623-7000; *Government Finance Statistics Yearbook.*

Statistical Office of the United Nations, Publishing Service, New York, New York 10017 (800) 253-9646; *Survey of Economic and Social Conditions in Africa.*

Times Books, 201 East 50th Street, New York, New York 10022 (212) 751-2600; *The Economist Book of Vital World Statistics.*

The World Bank, 1818 H Street, NW, Washington, D.C. 20433 (202) 477-1234; *World Tables.*

GHANA - GRAIN PRODUCTION - See GHANA - CROPS

GHANA - GRANTS

International Monetary Fund, 700 Nineteenth Street, NW, Washington, D.C. 20431 (202) 623-7000; *Government Finance Statistics Yearbook.*

GHANA - GREEN PEPPER AND CHILIE PRODUCTION - See GHANA - CROPS

GHANA - GROSS DOMESTIC PRODUCT

African Development Bank, 01 BP 1387, Abidjan 01, Cote D'Ivoire; *Selected Statistics on Regional Member Countries.*

The Economist Intelligence Unit, 111 West 57th Street, New York, New York 10019 (800) 938-4685; *The World Market Atlas.*

Euromonitor Publications Limited, 87-88 Turnmill Street, London EC1M 5QU, England; *International Marketing Data and Statistics.*

Facts on File, 460 Park Avenue South, New York, New York 10016 (800) 443-8323; *The New Book of World Rankings.*

G.K. Hall and Company, 70 Lincoln Street, Boston, Massachusetts 02111 (617) 423-3990; *The World in Figures.*

Statistical Office of the United Nations, Publishing Service, New York, New York 10017 (800) 253-9646; *Statistical Yearbook,* and *Survey of Economic and Social Conditions in Africa.*

Times Books, 201 East 50th Street, New York, New York 10022 (212) 751-2600; *The Economist Book of Vital World Statistics.*

United Nations Economic Commission for Africa, Africa Hall, Post Office Box 3001, Addis Ababa, Ethiopia (Telephone Number in U.S. (800) 253-9646); *African Statistical Yearbook.*

The World Bank, 1818 H Street, NW, Washington, D.C. 20433 (202) 477-1234; *World Tables.*

GHANA - GROSS NATIONAL PRODUCT

Euromonitor Publications Limited, 87-88 Turnmill Street, London EC1M 5QU, England; *International Marketing Data and Statistics.*

U.S. Arms Control and Disarmament Agency, 320 Twenty-first Street, Northwest, Washington, D.C. 20451 (202) 647-8677; *World Military Expenditures and Arms Transfers.*

The World Bank, 1818 H Street, NW, Washington, D.C. 20433 (202) 477-1234; *World Tables.*

GHANA - GROUNDNUTS PRODUCTION - See GHANA - CROPS

GHANA - HEALTH

African Development Bank, 01 BP 1387, Abidjan 01, Cote D'Ivoire; *Selected Statistics on Regional Member Countries.*

Facts on File, 460 Park Avenue South, New York, New York 10016 (800) 443-8323; *The New Book of World Rankings.*

Federal Statistical Office, Gustav - Stresemann - Ring 11, D-6200 Wiesbaden, Germany; *Ghana.*

G.K. Hall and Company, 70 Lincoln Street, Boston, Massachusetts 02111 (617) 423-3990; *The World in Figures.*

Statistical Office of the United Nations, Publishing Service, New York, New York 10017 (800) 253-9646; *Statistical Yearbook.*

Times Books, 201 East 50th Street, New York, New York 10022 (212) 751-2600; *The Economist Book of Vital World Statistics.*

United Nations Economic Commission for Africa, Africa Hall, Post Office Box 3001, Addis Ababa, Ethiopia (Telephone Number in U.S. (800) 253-9646); *African Statistical Yearbook.*

World Health Organization, Office of Publications, Avenue Appia, CH-1211 Geneva 27, Switzerland (Telephone Number in U.S. (518) 436-9686); *World Health Statistics Annual.*

GHANA - HEALTH EXPENDITURES

International Monetary Fund, 700 Nineteenth Street, NW, Washington, D.C. 20431 (202) 623-7000; *Government Finance Statistics Yearbook.*

GHANA - HIDE PRODUCTION

Food and Agricultural Organization of the United Nations (FAO), Via delle Terme di Caracalla, 00100 Rome, Italy (Telephone Number in U.S. (202) 653-2400); *Production Yearbook.*

GHANA - HIGHWAYS

G.K. Hall and Company, 70 Lincoln Street, Boston, Massachusetts 02111 (617) 423-3990; *The World in Figures.*

International Road Federation, 525 School Street, SW, Washington, D.C. 20024 (202) 554-2106; *World Road Statistics.*

Statistical Office of the United Nations, Publishing Service, New York, New York 10017 (800) 253-9646; *Survey of Economic and Social Conditions in Africa.*

United Nations Economic Commission for Africa, Africa Hall, Post Office Box 3001, Addis Ababa, Ethiopia (Telephone Number in U.S. (800) 253-9646); *African Statistical Yearbook.*

GHANA - HORSES - See GHANA - LIVESTOCK AND POULTRY

GHANA - HOURS OF WORK - See GHANA - EMPLOYMENT

GHANA - HOUSING AND HOUSING UNITS

Facts on File, 460 Park Avenue South, New York, New York 10016 (800) 443-8323; *The New Book of World Rankings.*

GHANA - HOUSING EXPENDITURES

International Monetary Fund, 700 Nineteenth Street, NW, Washington, D.C. 20431 (202) 623-7000; *Government Finance Statistics Yearbook.*

GHANA - ILLITERATE POPULATION

The Economist Intelligence Unit, 111 West 57th Street, New York, New York 10019 (800) 938-4685; *The World Market Atlas.*

G.K. Hall and Company, 70 Lincoln Street, Boston, Massachusetts 02111 (617) 423-3990; *The World in Figures.*

United Nations Educational, Scientific and Cultural Organization (UNESCO), 7 Place de Fontenoy, F-75700 Paris, France (Telephone Number in U.S. (212) 963-5981); *Statistical Yearbook.*

GHANA - IMPORTS

African Development Bank, 01 BP 1387, Abidjan 01, Cote D'Ivoire; *Selected Statistics on Regional Member Countries.*

The Economist Intelligence Unit, 111 West 57th Street, New York, New York 10019 (800) 938-4685; *The World Market Atlas.*

Euromonitor Publications Limited, 87-88 Turnmill Street, London EC1M 5QU, England; *International Marketing Data and Statistics.*

Food and Agricultural Organization of the United Nations (FAO) Via delle Terme di Caracalla, 00100 Rome, Italy (Telephone Number in U.S. (202) 653-2400); *The State of Food and Agriculture.*

G.K. Hall and Company, 70 Lincoln Street, Boston, Massachusetts 02111 (617) 423-3990; *The World in Figures.*

International Monetary Fund, 700 Nineteenth Street, NW, Washington, D.C. 20431 (202) 623-7000; *Direction of Trade Statistics, Government Finance Statistics Yearbook,* and *International Financial Statistics.*

Statistical Office of the United Nations, Publishing Service, New York, New York 10017 (800) 253-9646; *Foreign Trade Statistics for Africa, Survey of Economic and Social Conditions in Africa,* and *Trade in Manufactures of Developing Countries.*

Times Books, 201 East 50th Street, New York, New York 10022 (212) 751-2600; *The Economist Book of Vital World Statistics.*

U.S. Arms Control and Disarmament Agency, 320 Twenty-first Street, Northwest, Washington, D.C. 20451 (202) 647-8677; *World Military Expenditures and Arms Transfers.*

The World Bank, 1818 H Street, NW, Washington, D.C. 20433 (202) 477-1234; *World Tables.*

GHANA - INCOME TAXES - See GHANA - TAXATION

GHANA - INDUSTRIAL METALS PRODUCTION - See GHANA - MINING AND MINERAL PRODUCTS

GHANA - INDUSTRY

Facts on File, 460 Park Avenue South, New York, New York 10016 (800) 443-8323; *The New Book of World Rankings.*

Federal Statistical Office, Gustav - Stresemann - Ring 11, D-6200 Wiesbaden, Germany; *Ghana.*

G.K. Hall and Company, 70 Lincoln Street, Boston, Massachusetts 02111 (617) 423-3990; *The World in Figures.*

International Labour Office, I.L.O. Publications, CH-1211, Geneva 22, Switzerland; *Yearbook of Labour Statistics.*

Statistical Office of the United Nations, Publishing Service, New York, New York 10017 (800) 253-9646; *Statistical Yearbook* and *Survey of Economic and Social Conditions in Africa.*

Times Books, 201 East 50th Street, New York, New York 10022 (212) 751-2600; *The Economist Book of Vital World Statistics.*

United Nations Economic Commission for Africa, Africa Hall, Post Office Box 3001, Addis Ababa, Ethiopia (Telephone Number in U.S. (800) 253-9646); *African Statistical Yearbook.*

The World Bank, 1818 H Street, NW, Washington, D.C. 20433 (202) 477-1234; *World Tables.*

World Intellectual Property Organization, 34 Chemin des Colombettes, CH-1211 Geneva 20, Switzerland; *Industrial Property Statistics.*

GHANA - INFANT AND MATERNAL MORTALITY

Statistical Office of the United Nations, Publishing Service, New York, New York 10017 (800) 253-9646; *Demographic Yearbook,* and *Statistical Yearbook,* and *Survey of Economic and Social Conditions in Africa.*

Times Books, 201 East 50th Street, New York, New York 10022 (212) 751-2600; *The Economist Book of Vital World Statistics.*

The World Bank, 1818 H Street, NW, Washington, D.C. 20433 (202) 477-1234; *World Tables.*

GHANA - INTERNAL TRADE

Statistical Office of the United Nations, Publishing Service, New York, New York 10017 (800) 253-9646; *Statistical Yearbook.*

GHANA - INTERNATIONAL LIQUIDITY

International Monetary Fund, 700 Nineteenth Street, NW, Washington, D.C. 20431 (202) 623-7000; *International Financial Statistics.*

GHANA - INTERNATIONAL RESERVES EXCLUDING GOLD

African Development Bank, 01 BP 1387, Abidjan 01, Cote D'Ivoire; *Selected Statistics on Regional Member Countries.*

Statistical Office of the United Nations, Publishing Service, New York, New York 10017 (800) 253-9646; *Statistical Yearbook.*

The World Bank, 1818 H Street, NW, Washington, D.C. 20433 (202) 477-1234; *World Tables.*

GHANA - IRON PRODUCTION - See GHANA - MINING AND MINERAL PRODUCTS

GHANA - IRRIGATION

Euromonitor Publications Limited, 87-88 Turnmill Street, London EC1M 5QU, England; *International Marketing Data and Statistics.*

GHANA - LABOR FORCE

African Development Bank, 01 BP 1387, Abidjan 01, Cote D'Ivoire; *Selected Statistics on Regional Member Countries.*

Euromonitor Publications Limited, 87-88 Turnmill Street, London EC1M 5QU, England; *International Marketing Data and Statistics.*

Facts on File, 460 Park Avenue South, New York, New York 10016 (800) 443-8323; *The New Book of World Rankings.*

Food and Agricultural Organization of the United Nations (FAO) Via delle Terme di Caracalla, 00100 Rome, Italy (Telephone Number in U.S. (202) 653-2400); *The State of Food and Agriculture.*

G.K. Hall and Company, 70 Lincoln Street, Boston, Massachusetts 02111 (617) 423-3990; *The World in Figures.*

Times Books, 201 East 50th Street, New York, New York 10022 (212) 751-2600; *The Economist Book of Vital World Statistics.*

The World Bank, 1818 H Street, NW, Washington, D.C. 20433 (202) 477-1234; *World Tables.*

GHANA - LABOR PRODUCTIVITY

International Labour Office, I.L.O. Publications, CH-1211, Geneva 22, Switzerland; *Yearbook of Labour Statistics.*

GHANA - LAND USE

Euromonitor Publications Limited, 87-88 Turnmill Street, London EC1M 5QU, England; *International Marketing Data and Statistics.*

Food and Agricultural Organization of the United Nations (FAO), Via delle Terme di Caracalla, 00100 Rome, Italy (Telephone Number in U.S. (202) 653-2400); *Production Yearbook.*

G.K. Hall and Company, 70 Lincoln Street, Boston, Massachusetts 02111 (617) 423-3990; *The World in Figures.*

GHANA - LIBRARIES

Facts on File, 460 Park Avenue South, New York, New York 10016 (800) 443-8323; *The New Book of World Rankings.*

United Nations Educational, Scientific and Cultural Organization (UNESCO), 7 Place de Fontenoy, F-75700 Paris, France (Telephone Number in U.S. (212) 963-5981); *Statistical Yearbook.*

GHANA - LIFE EXPECTANCY

African Development Bank, 01 BP 1387, Abidjan 01, Cote D'Ivoire; *Selected Statistics on Regional Member Countries.*

GHANA - LITERACY RATE

Statistical Office of the United Nations, Publishing Service, New York, New York 10017 (800) 253-9646; *Survey of Economic and Social Conditions in Africa.*

GHANA - LIVESTOCK AND POULTRY

Euromonitor Publications Limited, 87-88 Turnmill Street, London EC1M 5QU, England; *International Marketing Data and Statistics.*

Facts on File, 460 Park Avenue South, New York, New York 10016 (800) 443-8323; *The New Book of World Rankings.*

Food and Agricultural Organization of the United Nations (FAO), Via delle Terme di Caracalla, 00100 Rome, Italy (Telephone Number in U.S. (202) 653-2400); *Production Yearbook,* and *The State of Food and Agriculture.*

G.K. Hall and Company, 70 Lincoln Street, Boston, Massachusetts 02111 (617) 423-3990; *The World in Figures.*

Statistical Office of the United Nations, Publishing Service, New York, New York 10017 (800) 253-9646; *Statistical Yearbook,* and *Survey of Economic and Social Conditions in Africa.*

United Nations Economic Commission for Africa, Africa Hall, Post Office Box 3001, Addis Ababa, Ethiopia (Telephone Number in U.S. (800) 253-9646); *African Statistical Yearbook.*

GHANA - LIVING LEVELS

G.K. Hall and Company, 70 Lincoln Street, Boston, Massachusetts 02111 (617) 423-3990; *The World in Figures.*

Times Books, 201 East 50th Street, New York, New York 10022 (212) 751-2600; *The Economist Book of Vital World Statistics.*

GHANA - MAIL - NUMBER OF PIECES SENT OR RECEIVED

Statistical Office of the United Nations, Publishing Service, New York, New York 10017 (800) 253-9646; *Statistical Yearbook.*

GHANA - MANGANESE ORE PRODUCTION AND CONSUMPTION - See GHANA - MINING AND MINERAL PRODUCTS

GHANA - MANUFACTURING

Facts on File, 460 Park Avenue South, New York, New York 10016 (800) 443-8323; *The New Book of World Rankings.*

G.K. Hall and Company, 70 Lincoln Street, Boston, Massachusetts 02111 (617) 423-3990; *The World in Figures.*

Statistical Office of the United Nations, Publishing Service, New York, New York 10017 (800) 253-9646; *Statistical Yearbook,* and *Survey of Economic and Social Conditions in Africa.*

United Nations Economic Commission for Africa, Africa Hall, Post Office Box 3001, Addis Ababa, Ethiopia (Telephone Number in U.S. (800) 253-9646); *African Statistical Yearbook.*

The World Bank, 1818 H Street, NW, Washington, D.C. 20433 (202) 477-1234; *World Tables.*

GHANA - MARRIAGE RATES

Facts on File, 460 Park Avenue South, New York, New York 10016 (800) 443-8323; *The New Book of World Rankings.*

Statistical Office of the United Nations, Publishing Service, New York, New York 10017 (800) 253-9646; *Demographic Yearbook.*

GHANA - MEAT PRODUCTION - See GHANA - LIVESTOCK AND POULTRY

GHANA - MERCHANT SHIPPING

G.K. Hall and Company, 70 Lincoln Street, Boston, Massachusetts 02111 (617) 423-3990; *The World in Figures.*

Statistical Office of the United Nations, Publishing Service, New York, New York 10017 (800) 253-9646; *Statistical Yearbook.*

Times Books, 201 East 50th Street, New York, New York 10022 (212) 751-2600; *The Economist Book of Vital World Statistics.*

United Nations Economic Commission for Africa, Africa Hall, Post Office Box 3001, Addis Ababa, Ethiopia (Telephone Number in U.S. (800) 253-9646); *African Statistical Yearbook.*

U.S. Department of Transportation, Maritime Administration, 400 Seventh Street, SW, Washington, D.C. 20590 (202) 366-5807; *A Statistical Analysis of the World's Merchant Fleets.*

GHANA - MILITARY

G.K. Hall and Company, 70 Lincoln Street, Boston, Massachusetts 02111 (617) 423-3990; *The World in Figures.*

The International Institute for Strategic Studies, 23 Tavistock Street, London WC2E 7NQ, England; *The Military Balance.*

U.S. Arms Control and Disarmament Agency, 320 Twenty-first Street, Northwest, Washington, D.C. 20451 (202) 647-8677; *World Military Expenditures and Arms Transfers.*

GHANA - MILK PRODUCTION - See GHANA - DAIRY PRODUCTS

GHANA - MILLET PRODUCTION - See GHANA - CROPS

GHANA - MINING AND MINERAL PRODUCTS

Commodity Research Bureau, Incorporated, 75 Wall Street, New York, New York 10005 (212) 504-7754; *Commodity Year Book.*

Facts on File, 460 Park Avenue South, New York, New York 10016 (800) 443-8323; *The New Book of World Rankings.*

G.K. Hall and Company, 70 Lincoln Street, Boston, Massachusetts 02111 (617) 423-3990; *The World in Figures.*

Penn Well Publishing Company, 1421 South Sheridan Road, Post Office Box 1260, Tulsa, Oklahoma 74101 (800) 752-9764; *International Energy Statistics Sourcebook.*

Statistical Office of the United Nations, Publishing Service, New York, New York 10017 (800) 253-9646; *Statistical Yearbook.*

GHANA - MONEY EXCHANGE RATE

Euromonitor Publications Limited, 87-88 Turnmill Street, London EC1M 5QU, England; *International Marketing Data and Statistics.*

International Monetary Fund, 700 Nineteenth Street, NW, Washington, D.C. 20431 (202) 623-7000; *International Financial Statistics.*

Statistical Office of the United Nations, Publishing Service, New York, New York 10017 (800) 253-9646; *Statistical Yearbook.*

Times Books, 201 East 50th Street, New York, New York 10022 (212) 751-2600; *The Economist Book of Vital World Statistics.*

GHANA - MONEY RESERVES

Euromonitor Publications Limited, 87-88 Turnmill Street, London EC1M 5QU, England; *International Marketing Data and Statistics.*

International Monetary Fund, 700 Nineteenth Street, NW, Washington, D.C. 20431 (202) 623-7000; *International Financial Statistics.*

GHANA - MONEY SUPPLY

African Development Bank, 01 BP 1387, Abidjan 01, Cote D'Ivoire; *Selected Statistics on Regional Member Countries.*

Euromonitor Publications Limited, 87-88 Turnmill Street, London EC1M 5QU, England; *International Marketing Data and Statistics.*

Federal Statistical Office, Gustav - Stresemann - Ring 11, D-6200 Wiesbaden, Germany; *Ghana.*

G.K. Hall and Company, 70 Lincoln Street, Boston, Massachusetts 02111 (617) 423-3990; *The World in Figures.*

International Monetary Fund, 700 Nineteenth Street, NW, Washington, D.C. 20431 (202) 623-7000; *International Financial Statistics.*

Statistical Office of the United Nations, Publishing Service, New York, New York 10017 (800) 253-9646; *Statistical Yearbook.*

The World Bank, 1818 H Street, NW, Washington, D.C. 20433 (202) 477-1234; *World Tables.*

GHANA - MOTION PICTURES

Statistical Office of the United Nations, Publishing Service, New York, New York 10017 (800) 253-9646; *Statistical Yearbook.*

United Nations Educational, Scientific and Cultural Organization (UNESCO), 7 Place de Fontenoy, F-75700 Paris, France (Telephone Number in U.S. (212) 963-5981); *Statistical Yearbook.*

GHANA - MOTOR VEHICLE ASSEMBLY

Statistical Office of the United Nations, Publishing Service, New York, New York 10017 (800) 253-9646; *Statistical Yearbook.*

GHANA - MOTOR VEHICLE TAXES - See GHANA - TAXATION

GHANA - MOTOR VEHICLES IN USE

G.K. Hall and Company, 70 Lincoln Street, Boston, Massachusetts 02111 (617) 423-3990; *The World in Figures.*

International Road Federation, 525 School Street, SW, Washington, D.C. 20024 (202) 554-2106; *World Road Statistics.*

Statistical Office of the United Nations, Publishing Service, New York, New York 10017 (800) 253-9646; *Statistical Yearbook,* and *Survey of Economic and Social Conditions in Africa.*

Times Books, 201 East 50th Street, New York, New York 10022 (212) 751-2600; *The Economist Book of Vital World Statistics.*

GHANA - MUSEUMS

Facts on File, 460 Park Avenue South, New York, New York 10016 (800) 443-8323; *The New Book of World Rankings.*

United Nations Educational, Scientific and Cultural Organization (UNESCO), 7 Place de Fontenoy, F-75700 Paris, France (Telephone Number in U.S. (212) 963-5981); *Statistical Yearbook.*

GHANA - NATALITY - See GHANA - BIRTH RATES

GHANA - NATIONAL ACCOUNTS

African Development Bank, 01 BP 1387, Abidjan 01, Cote D'Ivoire; *Selected Statistics on Regional Member Countries.*

Federal Statistical Office, Gustav - Stresemann - Ring 11, D-6200 Wiesbaden, Germany; *Ghana.*

International Monetary Fund, 700 Nineteenth Street, NW, Washington, D.C. 20431 (202) 623-7000; *International Financial Statistics.*

Statistical Office of the United Nations, Publishing Service, New York, New York 10017 (800) 253-9646; *National Accounts Statistics*, and *Statistical Yearbook*, section on National Accounts.

United Nations Economic Commission for Africa, Africa Hall, Post Office Box 3001, Addis Ababa, Ethiopia (Telephone Number in U.S. (800) 253-9646); *African Statistical Yearbook.*

GHANA - NATIONAL INCOME

Facts on File, 460 Park Avenue South, New York, New York 10016 (800) 443-8323; *The New Book of World Rankings.*

G.K. Hall and Company, 70 Lincoln Street, Boston, Massachusetts 02111 (617) 423-3990; *The World in Figures.*

Statistical Office of the United Nations, Publishing Service, New York, New York 10017 (800) 253-9646; *Statistical Yearbook.*

GHANA - NATIONAL PRODUCT

Facts on File, 460 Park Avenue South, New York, New York 10016 (800) 443-8323; *The New Book of World Rankings.*

Statistical Office of the United Nations, Publishing Service, New York, New York 10017 (800) 253-9646; *Statistical Yearbook.*

GHANA - NATURAL GAS PRODUCTION - See GHANA - MINING AND MINERAL PRODUCTS

GHANA - NEWSPAPER PRODUCTION - See GHANA - FORESTRY AND FOREST PRODUCTS

GHANA - NEWSPRINT - See GHANA - FORESTRY AND FOREST PRODUCTS

GHANA - OCCUPATIONS - See GHANA - LABOR FORCE

GHANA - PALM KERNELS PRODUCTION - See GHANA - CROPS

GHANA - PAPER - See GHANA - FORESTRY AND FOREST PRODUCTS

GHANA - PATENTS

Statistical Office of the United Nations, Publishing Service, New York, New York 10017 (800) 253-9646; *Statistical Yearbook.*

World Intellectual Property Organization, 34 Chemin des Colombettes, CH-1211 Geneva 20, Switzerland; *Industrial Property Statistics.*

GHANA - PEANUT PRODUCTION - See GHANA - CROPS

GHANA - PERIODICALS

United Nations Educational, Scientific and Cultural Organization (UNESCO), 7 Place de Fontenoy, F-75700 Paris, France (Telephone Number in U.S. (212) 963-5981); *Statistical Yearbook.*

GHANA - PESTICIDE USE

Food and Agricultural Organization of the United Nations (FAO) Via delle Terme di Caracalla, 00100 Rome, Italy (Telephone Number in U.S. (202) 653-2400); *The State of Food and Agriculture.*

GHANA - PETROLEUM INDUSTRY

Facts on File, 460 Park Avenue South, New York, New York 10016 (800) 443-8323; *The New Book of World Rankings.*

Food and Agricultural Organization of the United Nations (FAO) Via delle Terme di Caracalla, 00100 Rome, Italy (Telephone Number in U.S. (202) 653-2400); *The State of Food and Agriculture.*

G.K. Hall and Company, 70 Lincoln Street, Boston, Massachusetts 02111 (617) 423-3990; *The World in Figures.*

Penn Well Publishing Company, 1421 South Sheridan Road, Post Office Box 1260, Tulsa, Oklahoma 74101 (800) 752-9764; *International Energy Statistics Sourcebook.*

Statistical Office of the United Nations, Publishing Service, New York, New York 10017 (800) 253-9646; *Statistical Yearbook.*

GHANA - PIGS - See GHANA - LIVESTOCK AND POULTRY

GHANA - POPULATION

African Development Bank, 01 BP 1387, Abidjan 01, Cote D'Ivoire; *Selected Statistics on Regional Member Countries.*

The Economist Intelligence Unit, 111 West 57th Street, New York, New York 10019 (800) 938-4685; *The World Market Atlas.*

Euromonitor Publications Limited, 87-88 Turnmill Street, London EC1M 5QU, England; *International Marketing Data and Statistics.*

Facts on File, 460 Park Avenue South, New York, New York 10016 (800) 443-8323; *The New Book of World Rankings.*

Federal Statistical Office, Gustav - Stresemann - Ring 11, D-6200 Wiesbaden, Germany; *Ghana.*

Food and Agricultural Organization of the United Nations (FAO), Via delle Terme di Caracalla, 00100 Rome, Italy (Telephone Number in U.S. (202) 653-2400); *Production Yearbook.*

G.K. Hall and Company, 70 Lincoln Street, Boston, Massachusetts 02111 (617) 423-3990; *The World in Figures.*

International Labour Office, I.L.O. Publications, CH-1211, Geneva 22, Switzerland; *Yearbook of Labour Statistics.*

Statistical Office of the United Nations, Publishing Service, New York, New York 10017 (800) 253-9646; *Demographic Yearbook, Statistical Yearbook,* and *Survey of Economic and Social Conditions in Africa.*

Times Books, 201 East 50th Street, New York, New York 10022 (212) 751-2600; *The Economist Book of Vital World Statistics.*

United Nations Educational, Scientific and Cultural Organization (UNESCO), 7 Place de Fontenoy, F-75700 Paris, France (Telephone Number in U.S. (212) 963-5981); *Statistical Yearbook.*

U.S. Arms Control and Disarmament Agency, 320 Twenty-first Street, Northwest, Washington, D.C. 20451 (202) 647-8677; *World Military Expenditures and Arms Transfers.*

World Health Organization, Office of Publications, Avenue Appia, CH-1211 Geneva 27, Switzerland (Telephone Number in U.S. (518) 436-9686); *World Health Statistics Annual.*

GHANA - POST OFFICES

Facts on File, 460 Park Avenue South, New York, New York 10016 (800) 443-8323; *The New Book of World Rankings.*

GHANA - POTATO PRODUCTION - See GHANA - CROPS

GHANA - POWER PRODUCTION INDUSTRY

Statistical Office of the United Nations, Publishing Service, New York, New York 10017 (800) 253-9646; *Statistical Yearbook.*

GHANA - PRICES

Facts on File, 460 Park Avenue South, New York, New York 10016 (800) 443-8323; *The New Book of World Rankings.*

Federal Statistical Office, Gustav - Stresemann - Ring 11, D-6200 Wiesbaden, Germany; *Ghana.*

Food and Agricultural Organization of the United Nations (FAO), Via delle Terme di Caracalla, 00100 Rome, Italy (Telephone Number in U.S. (202) 653-2400); *Production Yearbook,* and *The State of Food and Agriculture.*

G.K. Hall and Company, 70 Lincoln Street, Boston, Massachusetts 02111 (617) 423-3990; *The World in Figures.*

International Labour Office, I.L.O. Publications, CH-1211, Geneva 22, Switzerland; *Yearbook of Labour Statistics.*

International Monetary Fund, 700 Nineteenth Street, NW, Washington, D.C. 20431 (202) 623-7000; *International Financial Statistics.*

United Nations Economic Commission for Africa, Africa Hall, Post Office Box 3001, Addis Ababa, Ethiopia (Telephone Number in U.S. (800) 253-9646); *African Statistical Yearbook.*

GHANA - PRINTING AND WRITING PAPER - See GHANA - FORESTRY AND FOREST PRODUCTS

GHANA - PRODUCTION

Facts on File, 460 Park Avenue South, New York, New York 10016 (800) 443-8323; *The New Book of World Rankings.*

G.K. Hall and Company, 70 Lincoln Street, Boston, Massachusetts 02111 (617) 423-3990; *The World in Figures.*

GHANA - PRODUCTIVITY

Euromonitor Publications Limited, 87-88 Turnmill Street, London EC1M 5QU, England; *International Marketing Data and Statistics.*

GHANA - PROPERTY TAXES - See GHANA - TAXATION

GHANA - PUBLIC FINANCE

Facts on File, 460 Park Avenue South, New York, New York 10016 (800) 443-8323; *The New Book of World Rankings.*

Federal Statistical Office, Gustav - Stresemann - Ring 11, D-6200 Wiesbaden, Germany; *Ghana.*

GHANA - RADIO BROADCASTING - See GHANA - BROADCASTING

GHANA - RADIO RECEIVER PRODUCTION

Statistical Office of the United Nations, Publishing Service, New York, New York 10017 (800) 253-9646; *Statistical Yearbook.*

GHANA - RAILWAYS

G.K. Hall and Company, 70 Lincoln Street, Boston, Massachusetts 02111 (617) 423-3990; *The World in Figures.*

Jane's Information Group, Sentinel House, 163 Brighton Road, Coulsdon, Surrey CR5 2NH, England (Telephone Number in U.S. (703) 683-3700); *Jane's World Railways.*

Statistical Office of the United Nations, Publishing Service, New York, New York 10017 (800) 253-9646; *Statistical Yearbook,* and *Survey of Economic and Social Conditions in Africa.*

United Nations Economic Commission for Africa, Africa Hall, Post Office Box 3001, Addis Ababa, Ethiopia (Telephone Number in U.S. (800) 253-9646); *African Statistical Yearbook.*

GHANA - RELIGION

Facts on File, 460 Park Avenue South, New York, New York 10016 (800) 443-8323; *The New Book of World Rankings.*

GHANA - RENT PRICES

International Labour Office, I.L.O. Publications, CH-1211, Geneva 22, Switzerland; *Yearbook of Labour Statistics.*

GHANA - RETAIL TRADE

G.K. Hall and Company, 70 Lincoln Street, Boston, Massachusetts 02111 (617) 423-3990; *The World in Figures.*

Statistical Office of the United Nations, Publishing Service, New York, New York 10017 (800) 253-9646; *Statistical Yearbook.*

GHANA - RICE PRODUCTION - See GHANA - CROPS

GHANA - ROOT AND TUBER PRODUCTION - See GHANA - CROPS

GHANA - ROUNDWOOD PRODUCTION - See GHANA - FORESTRY AND FOREST PRODUCTS

GHANA - RUBBER PRODUCTION

Facts on File, 460 Park Avenue South, New York, New York 10016 (800) 443-8323; *The New Book of World Rankings.*

Statistical Office of the United Nations, Publishing Service, New York, New York 10017 (800) 253-9646; *Statistical Yearbook.*

GHANA - SALT PRODUCTION - See GHANA - MINING AND MINERAL PRODUCTS

GHANA - SAWNWOOD PRODUCTION - See GHANA - FORESTRY AND FOREST PRODUCTS

GHANA - SCIENCE AND TECHNOLOGY - EXPENDITURE FOR RESEARCH

Statistical Office of the United Nations, Publishing Service, New York, New York 10017 (800) 253-9646; *Statistical Yearbook.*

GHANA - SCIENTISTS AND ENGINEERS

United Nations Educational, Scientific and Cultural Organization (UNESCO), 7 Place de Fontenoy, F-75700 Paris, France (Telephone Number in U.S. (212) 963-5981); *Statistical Yearbook.*

GHANA - SENIOR CITIZENS

Facts on File, 460 Park Avenue South, New York, New York 10016 (800) 443-8323; *The New Book of World Rankings.*

GHANA - SHEEP - See GHANA - LIVESTOCK AND POULTRY

GHANA - SILVER PRODUCTION AND CONSUMPTION - See GHANA - MINING AND MINERAL PRODUCTS

GHANA - SOCIAL DATA

African Development Bank, 01 BP 1387, Abidjan 01, Cote D'Ivoire; *Selected Statistics on Regional Member Countries.*

Facts on File, 460 Park Avenue South, New York, New York 10016 (800) 443-8323; *The New Book of World Rankings.*

G.K. Hall and Company, 70 Lincoln Street, Boston, Massachusetts 02111 (617) 423-3990; *The World in Figures.*

GHANA - SOCIAL SECURITY

International Monetary Fund, 700 Nineteenth Street, NW, Washington, D.C. 20431 (202) 623-7000; *Government Finance Statistics Yearbook.*

GHANA - STAMP TAXES AND DUTIES - See GHANA - TAXATION

GHANA - STATE BUDGET REVENUE AND EXPENDITURES

Euromonitor Publications Limited, 87-88 Turnmill Street, London EC1M 5QU, England; *International Marketing Data and Statistics.*

GHANA - STEEL - See GHANA - MINING AND MINERAL PRODUCTS

GHANA - STOCKS - COMMODITY - MARKET PRICE - INDEX

Food and Agricultural Organization of the United Nations (FAO) Via delle Terme di Caracalla, 00100 Rome, Italy (Telephone Number in U.S. (202) 653-2400); *The State of Food and Agriculture.*

GHANA - SUGAR PRODUCTION - See GHANA - CROPS

GHANA - TAXATION

G.K. Hall and Company, 70 Lincoln Street, Boston, Massachusetts 02111 (617) 423-3990; *The World in Figures.*

International Monetary Fund, 700 Nineteenth Street, NW, Washington, D.C. 20431 (202) 623-7000; *Government Finance Statistics Yearbook.*

International Road Federation, 525 School Street, SW, Washington, D.C. 20024 (202) 554-2106; *World Road Statistics.*

The World Bank, 1818 H Street, NW, Washington, D.C. 20433 (202) 477-1234; *World Tables.*

GHANA - TELEGRAPH SERVICE

Statistical Office of the United Nations, Publishing Service, New York, New York 10017 (800) 253-9646; *Statistical Yearbook.*

GHANA - TELEPHONES IN USE

American Telephone and Telegraph Company, 26 Parsippany Road, Whippany, New Jersey 07981 (800) 338-4038; *The World's Telephones.*

G.K. Hall and Company, 70 Lincoln Street, Boston, Massachusetts 02111 (617) 423-3990; *The World in Figures.*

Statistical Office of the United Nations, Publishing Service, New York, New York 10017 (800) 253-9646; *Statistical Yearbook.*

GHANA - TELEVISION BROADCASTING - See GHANA - BROADCASTING

GHANA - TELEVISION RECEIVER PRODUCTION

Statistical Office of the United Nations, Publishing Service, New York, New York 10017 (800) 253-9646; *Statistical Yearbook.*

GHANA - TEXTILE INDUSTRY

G.K. Hall and Company, 70 Lincoln Street, Boston, Massachusetts 02111 (617) 423-3990; *The World in Figures.*

GHANA - THEATRE

United Nations Educational, Scientific and Cultural Organization (UNESCO), 7 Place de Fontenoy, F-75700 Paris, France (Telephone Number in U.S. (212) 963-5981); *Statistical Yearbook.*

GHANA - TIRE (MOTOR VEHICLE) PRODUCTION

Statistical Office of the United Nations, Publishing Service, New York, New York 10017 (800) 253-9646; *Statistical Yearbook.*

GHANA - TOBACCO PRODUCTION

Facts on File, 460 Park Avenue South, New York, New York 10016 (800) 443-8323; *The New Book of World Rankings.*

Statistical Office of the United Nations, Publishing Service, New York, New York 10017 (800) 253-9646; *Statistical Yearbook.*

GHANA - TOURISM

Facts on File, 460 Park Avenue South, New York, New York 10016 (800) 443-8323; *The New Book of World Rankings.*

Federal Statistical Office, Gustav - Stresemann - Ring 11, D-6200 Wiesbaden, Germany; *Ghana.*

G.K. Hall and Company, 70 Lincoln Street, Boston, Massachusetts 02111 (617) 423-3990; *The World in Figures.*

Statistical Office of the United Nations, Publishing Service, New York, New York 10017 (800) 253-9646; *Statistical Yearbook.*

Times Books, 201 East 50th Street, New York, New York 10022 (212) 751-2600; *The Economist Book of Vital World Statistics.*

United Nations Economic Commission for Africa, Africa Hall, Post Office Box 3001, Addis Ababa, Ethiopia (Telephone Number in U.S. (800) 253-9646); *African Statistical Yearbook.*

GHANA - TRACTORS IN USE

Statistical Office of the United Nations, Publishing Service, New York, New York 10017 (800) 253-9646; *Statistical Yearbook.*

GHANA - TRADE - See GHANA - FOREIGN TRADE

GHANA - TRADEMARKS AND SERVICE MARKS

Statistical Office of the United Nations, Publishing Service, New York, New York 10017 (800) 253-9646; *Statistical Yearbook.*

World Intellectual Property Organization, 34 Chemin des Colombettes, CH-1211 Geneva 20, Switzerland; *Industrial Property Statistics.*

GHANA - TRANSPORTATION AND COMMUNICATIONS

Facts on File, 460 Park Avenue South, New York, New York 10016 (800) 443-8323; *The New Book of World Rankings.*

Federal Statistical Office, Gustav - Stresemann - Ring 11, D-6200 Wiesbaden, Germany; *Ghana.*

G.K. Hall and Company, 70 Lincoln Street, Boston, Massachusetts 02111 (617) 423-3990; *The World in Figures.*

United Nations Economic Commission for Africa, Africa Hall, Post Office Box 3001, Addis Ababa, Ethiopia (Telephone Number in U.S. (800) 253-9646); *African Statistical Yearbook.*

GHANA - UNEMPLOYMENT

Euromonitor Publications Limited, 87-88 Turnmill Street, London EC1M 5QU, England; *International Marketing Data and Statistics.*

International Labour Office, I.L.O. Publications, CH-1211, Geneva 22, Switzerland; *Yearbook of Labour Statistics.*

Statistical Office of the United Nations, Publishing Service, New York, New York 10017 (800) 253-9646; *Statistical Yearbook.*

GHANA - VITAL STATISTICS

Euromonitor Publications Limited, 87-88 Turnmill Street, London EC1M 5QU, England; *International Marketing Data and Statistics.*

G.K. Hall and Company, 70 Lincoln Street, Boston, Massachusetts 02111 (617) 423-3990; *The World in Figures.*

Statistical Office of the United Nations, Publishing Service, New York, New York 10017 (800) 253-9646; *Statistical Yearbook.*

World Health Organization, Office of Publications, Avenue Appia, CH-1211 Geneva 27, Switzerland (Telephone Number in U.S. (518) 436-9686); *World Health Statistics Annual.*

GHANA - WAGES

Federal Statistical Office, Gustav - Stresemann - Ring 11, D-6200 Wiesbaden, Germany; *Ghana.*

G.K. Hall and Company, 70 Lincoln Street, Boston, Massachusetts 02111 (617) 423-3990; *The World in Figures.*

International Labour Office, I.L.O. Publications, CH-1211, Geneva 22, Switzerland; *Yearbook of Labour Statistics.*

Statistical Office of the United Nations, Publishing Service, New York, New York 10017 (800) 253-9646; *Statistical Yearbook.*

GHANA - WEATHER

Facts on File, 460 Park Avenue South, New York, New York 10016 (800) 443-8323; *The New Book of World Rankings.*

G.K. Hall and Company, 70 Lincoln Street, Boston, Massachusetts 02111 (617) 423-3990; *The World in Figures.*

GHANA - WELFARE

International Monetary Fund, 700 Nineteenth Street, NW, Washington, D.C. 20431 (202) 623-7000; *Government Finance Statistics Yearbook.*

GHANA - WHEAT - See GHANA - CROPS

GHANA - WHOLESALE PRICES

International Monetary Fund, 700 Nineteenth Street, NW, Washington, D.C. 20431 (202) 623-7000; *International Financial Statistics.*

Statistical Office of the United Nations, Publishing Service, New York, New York 10017 (800) 253-9646; *Statistical Yearbook.*

GHANA - WHOLESALE TRADE

Statistical Office of the United Nations, Publishing Service, New York, New York 10017 (800) 253-9646; *Statistical Yearbook.*

GHANA - WINE PRODUCTION

Facts on File, 460 Park Avenue South, New York, New York 10016 (800) 443-8323; *The New Book of World Rankings.*

GHANA - WOOD EXPORTS - See GHANA - FORESTRY AND FOREST PRODUCTS

GHANA - WOOL PRODUCTION

Facts on File, 460 Park Avenue South, New York, New York 10016 (800) 443-8323; *The New Book of World Rankings.*

Gibraltar - National Statistical Office

Economic Planning and Statistics Office, Cathedral Square, Gibraltar.

Gibraltar - Primary Statistics Source

Statistics Office, Cathedral Square, Gibraltar; *Abstract of Statistics.*

GIBRALTAR - AGRICULTURE

Food and Agricultural Organization of the United Nations (FAO) Via delle Terme di Caracalla, 00100 Rome, Italy (Telephone Number in U.S. (202) 653-2400); *Production Yearbook, The State of Food and Agriculture,* and *Trade Yearbook.*

G.K. Hall and Company, 70 Lincoln Street, Boston, Massachusetts 02111 (617) 423-3990; *The World in Figures.*

GIBRALTAR - AIRLINE SERVICE

G.K. Hall and Company, 70 Lincoln Street, Boston, Massachusetts 02111 (617) 423-3990; *The World in Figures.*

GIBRALTAR - ANIMAL HEALTH

Food and Agricultural Organization of the United Nations (FAO), Via delle Terme di Caracalla, 00100, Rome, Italy (Telephone Number in U.S. (202) 653-2400); *Animal Health Yearbook.*

GIBRALTAR - AREA AND DENSITY OF POPULATION

Food and Agricultural Organization of the United Nations (FAO) Via delle Terme di Caracalla, 00100 Rome, Italy (Telephone Number in U.S. (202) 653-2400); *The State of Food and Agriculture.*

G.K. Hall and Company, 70 Lincoln Street, Boston, Massachusetts 02111 (617) 423-3990; *The World in Figures.*

Statistical Office of the United Nations, Publishing Service, New York, New York 10017 (800) 253-9646; *Statistical Yearbook.*

GIBRALTAR - BALANCE OF PAYMENTS

G.K. Hall and Company, 70 Lincoln Street, Boston, Massachusetts 02111 (617) 423-3990; *The World in Figures.*

GIBRALTAR - BANKING

G.K. Hall and Company, 70 Lincoln Street, Boston, Massachusetts 02111 (617) 423-3990; *The World in Figures.*

GIBRALTAR - BIRTH RATES

Statistical Office of the United Nations, Publishing Service, New York, New York 10017 (800) 253-9646; *Demographic Yearbook,* and *Statistical Yearbook.*

World Health Organization, Office of Publications, Avenue Appia, CH-1211 Geneva 27, Switzerland (Telephone Number in U.S. (518) 436-9686); *World Health Statistics Annual.*

GIBRALTAR - BONDS

G.K. Hall and Company, 70 Lincoln Street, Boston, Massachusetts 02111 (617) 423-3990; *The World in Figures.*

GIBRALTAR - BOOK PRODUCTION

G.K. Hall and Company, 70 Lincoln Street, Boston, Massachusetts 02111 (617) 423-3990; *The World in Figures.*

GIBRALTAR - BROADCASTING

Billboard Limited, Post Office Box 9027, 1006 AA Amsterdam, The Netherlands (Telephone Number in U.S. (212) 764-7300); *World Radio TV Handbook.*

G.K. Hall and Company, 70 Lincoln Street, Boston, Massachusetts 02111 (617) 423-3990; *The World in Figures.*

United Nations Educational, Scientific and Cultural Organization (UNESCO), 7 Place de Fontenoy, F-75700 Paris, France (Telephone Number in U.S. (212) 963-5981); *Statistical Yearbook.*

GIBRALTAR - BUSINESS

G.K. Hall and Company, 70 Lincoln Street, Boston, Massachusetts 02111 (617) 423-3990; *The World in Figures.*

GIBRALTAR - CALORIE SUPPLY

Food and Agricultural Organization of the United Nations (FAO) Via delle Terme di Caracalla, 00100 Rome, Italy (Telephone Number in U.S. (202) 653-2400); *The State of Food and Agriculture.*

GIBRALTAR - CHEMICAL (ORGANIC) PRODUCTION - See GIBRALTAR - MINING AND MINERAL PRODUCTS

GIBRALTAR - CLASS STRUCTURE

G.K. Hall and Company, 70 Lincoln Street, Boston, Massachusetts 02111 (617) 423-3990; *The World in Figures.*

GIBRALTAR - CLIMATE

G.K. Hall and Company, 70 Lincoln Street, Boston, Massachusetts 02111 (617) 423-3990; *The World in Figures.*

GIBRALTAR - COAL PRODUCTION - See GIBRALTAR - MINING AND MINERAL PRODUCTS

GIBRALTAR - COMMUNICATIONS

G.K. Hall and Company, 70 Lincoln Street, Boston, Massachusetts 02111 (617) 423-3990; *The World in Figures.*

GIBRALTAR - CONSUMER PRICE INDEX

G.K. Hall and Company, 70 Lincoln Street, Boston, Massachusetts 02111 (617) 423-3990; *The World in Figures.*

International Labour Office, I.L.O. Publications, CH-1211, Geneva 22, Switzerland; *Yearbook of Labour Statistics.*

Statistical Office of the United Nations, Publishing Service, New York, New York 10017 (800) 253-9646; *Statistical Yearbook.*

GIBRALTAR - CONSUMER PRICES

International Labour Office, I.L.O. Publications, CH-1211, Geneva 22, Switzerland; *Yearbook of Labour Statistics.*

GIBRALTAR - CONSUMPTION

G.K. Hall and Company, 70 Lincoln Street, Boston, Massachusetts 02111 (617) 423-3990; *The World in Figures.*

GIBRALTAR - CORN PRODUCTION - See GIBRALTAR - CROPS

GIBRALTAR - CORPORATE TAXES - See GIBRALTAR - TAXATION

GIBRALTAR - CROPS

Food and Agricultural Organization of the United Nations (FAO) Via delle Terme di Caracalla, 00100 Rome, Italy (Telephone Number in U.S. (202) 653-2400); *The State of Food and Agriculture.*

G.K. Hall and Company, 70 Lincoln Street, Boston, Massachusetts 02111 (617) 423-3990; *The World in Figures.*

GIBRALTAR - CUSTOMS DUTIES

G.K. Hall and Company, 70 Lincoln Street, Boston, Massachusetts 02111 (617) 423-3990; *The World in Figures.*

GIBRALTAR - DAIRY PRODUCTS

Food and Agricultural Organization of the United Nations (FAO) Via delle Terme di Caracalla, 00100 Rome, Italy (Telephone Number in U.S. (202) 653-2400); *The State of Food and Agriculture.*

GIBRALTAR - DEATH RATES

G.K. Hall and Company, 70 Lincoln Street, Boston, Massachusetts 02111 (617) 423-3990; *The World in Figures.*

Statistical Office of the United Nations, Publishing Service, New York, New York 10017 (800) 253-9646; *Statistical Yearbook.*

GIBRALTAR - DEFENSE EXPENDITURES

G.K. Hall and Company, 70 Lincoln Street, Boston, Massachusetts 02111 (617) 423-3990; *The World in Figures.*

GIBRALTAR - DEMOGRAPHY

G.K. Hall and Company, 70 Lincoln Street, Boston, Massachusetts 02111 (617) 423-3990; *The World in Figures.*

GIBRALTAR - DEVELOPMENT ASSISTANCE

G.K. Hall and Company, 70 Lincoln Street, Boston, Massachusetts 02111 (617) 423-3990; *The World in Figures.*

GIBRALTAR - DISEASE

G.K. Hall and Company, 70 Lincoln Street, Boston, Massachusetts 02111 (617) 423-3990; *The World in Figures.*

GIBRALTAR - DIVORCE RATES

Statistical Office of the United Nations, Publishing Service, New York, New York 10017 (800) 253-9646; *Demographic Yearbook,* and *Statistical Yearbook.*

GIBRALTAR - DOMESTIC PRODUCT

G.K. Hall and Company, 70 Lincoln Street, Boston, Massachusetts 02111 (617) 423-3990; *The World in Figures.*

GIBRALTAR - ECONOMY

G.K. Hall and Company, 70 Lincoln Street, Boston, Massachusetts 02111 (617) 423-3990; *The World in Figures.*

GIBRALTAR - EDUCATION

G.K. Hall and Company, 70 Lincoln Street, Boston, Massachusetts 02111 (617) 423-3990; *The World in Figures.*

United Nations Educational, Scientific and Cultural Organization (UNESCO), 7 Place de Fontenoy, F-75700 Paris, France (Telephone Number in U.S. (212) 963-5981); *Statistical Yearbook.*

GIBRALTAR - EGG PRODUCTION - See GIBRALTAR - DAIRY PRODUCTS

GIBRALTAR - ELECTRICITY

Statistical Office of the United Nations, Publishing Service, New York, New York 10017 (800) 253-9646; *Statistical Yearbook.*

GIBRALTAR - EMPLOYMENT

International Labour Office, I.L.O. Publications, CH-1211, Geneva 22, Switzerland; *Yearbook of Labour Statistics.*

Statistical Office of the United Nations, Publishing Service, New York, New York 10017 (800) 253-9646; *Statistical Yearbook.*

GIBRALTAR - ENERGY

Food and Agricultural Organization of the United Nations (FAO) Via delle Terme di Caracalla, 00100 Rome, Italy (Telephone Number in U.S. (202) 653-2400); *The State of Food and Agriculture.*

G.K. Hall and Company, 70 Lincoln Street, Boston, Massachusetts 02111 (617) 423-3990; *The World in Figures.*

Statistical Office of the United Nations, Publishing Service, New York, New York 10017 (800) 253-9646; *Energy Statistics Yearbook,* and *Statistical Yearbook.*

GIBRALTAR - EXPORTS

Food and Agricultural Organization of the United Nations (FAO) Via delle Terme di Caracalla, 00100 Rome, Italy (Telephone Number in U.S. (202) 653-2400); *The State of Food and Agriculture.*

G.K. Hall and Company, 70 Lincoln Street, Boston, Massachusetts 02111 (617) 423-3990; *The World in Figures.*

International Monetary Fund, 700 Nineteenth Street, NW, Washington, D.C. 20431 (202) 623-7000; *Direction of Trade Statistics.*

GIBRALTAR - EXTERNAL TRADE

Food and Agricultural Organization of the United Nations (FAO) Via delle Terme di Caracalla, 00100 Rome, Italy (Telephone Number in U.S. (202) 653-2400); *The State of Food and Agriculture,* and *Trade Yearbook.*

G.K. Hall and Company, 70 Lincoln Street, Boston, Massachusetts 02111 (617) 423-3990; *The World in Figures.*

GIBRALTAR - FETAL MORTALITY

Statistical Office of the United Nations, Publishing Service, New York, New York 10017 (800) 253-9646; *Demographic Yearbook.*

World Health Organization, Office of Publications, Avenue Appia, CH-1211 Geneva 27, Switzerland (Telephone Number in U.S. (518) 436-9686); *World Health Statistics Annual.*

GIBRALTAR - FERTILIZER

Food and Agricultural Organization of the United Nations (FAO) Via delle Terme di Caracalla, 00100 Rome, Italy (Telephone Number in U.S. (202) 653-2400); *The State of Food and Agriculture.*

GIBRALTAR - FINANCE

G.K. Hall and Company, 70 Lincoln Street, Boston, Massachusetts 02111 (617) 423-3990; *The World in Figures.*

GIBRALTAR - FISHERIES

Food and Agricultural Organization of the United Nations (FAO) Via delle Terme di Caracalla, 00100 Rome, Italy (Telephone Number in U.S. (202) 653-2400); *The State of Food and Agriculture,* and *Yearbook of Fishery Statistics.*

GIBRALTAR - FOOD

Food and Agricultural Organization of the United Nations (FAO), Via delle Terme di Caracalla, 00100 Rome, Italy (Telephone Number in U.S. (202) 653-2400); *Production Yearbook,* and *The State of Food and Agriculture.*

G.K. Hall and Company, 70 Lincoln Street, Boston, Massachusetts 02111 (617) 423-3990; *The World in Figures.*

GIBRALTAR - FOREIGN AID

G.K. Hall and Company, 70 Lincoln Street, Boston, Massachusetts 02111 (617) 423-3990; *The World in Figures.*

GIBRALTAR - FOREIGN TRADE

Food and Agricultural Organization of the United Nations (FAO) Via delle Terme di Caracalla, 00100 Rome, Italy (Telephone Number in U.S. (202) 653-2400); *The State of Food and Agriculture.*

Statistical Office of the United Nations, Publishing Service, New York, New York 10017 (800) 253-9646; *Statistical Yearbook.*

GIBRALTAR - FORESTRY AND FOREST PRODUCTS

G.K. Hall and Company, 70 Lincoln Street, Boston, Massachusetts 02111 (617) 423-3990; *The World in Figures.*

Statistical Office of the United Nations, Publishing Service, New York, New York 10017 (800) 253-9646; *Statistical Yearbook.*

United Nations Educational, Scientific and Cultural Organization (UNESCO), 7 Place de Fontenoy, F-75700 Paris, France (Telephone Number in U.S. (212) 963-5981); *Statistical Yearbook.*

Food and Agricultural Organization of the United Nations (FAO) Via delle Terme di Caracalla, 00100 Rome, Italy (Telephone Number in U.S. (202) 653-2400); *The State of Food and Agriculture.*

G.K. Hall and Company, 70 Lincoln Street, Boston, Massachusetts 02111 (617) 423-3990; *The World in Figures.*

GIBRALTAR - GENERAL MORTALITY

Statistical Office of the United Nations, Publishing Service, New York, New York 10017 (800) 253-9646; *Demographic Yearbook.*

World Health Organization, Office of Publications, Avenue Appia, CH-1211 Geneva 27, Switzerland (Telephone Number in U.S. (518) 436-9686); *World Health Statistics Annual.*

GIBRALTAR - GOVERNMENT

G.K. Hall and Company, 70 Lincoln Street, Boston, Massachusetts 02111 (617) 423-3990; *The World in Figures.*

GIBRALTAR - GRAIN PRODUCTION - See GIBRALTAR - CROPS

GIBRALTAR - GROSS DOMESTIC PRODUCT

G.K. Hall and Company, 70 Lincoln Street, Boston, Massachusetts 02111 (617) 423-3990; *The World in Figures.*

GIBRALTAR - HEALTH

G.K. Hall and Company, 70 Lincoln Street, Boston, Massachusetts 02111 (617) 423-3990; *The World in Figures.*

Statistical Office of the United Nations, Publishing Service, New York, New York 10017 (800) 253-9646; *Statistical Yearbook.*

GIBRALTAR - HIGHWAYS

G.K. Hall and Company, 70 Lincoln Street, Boston, Massachusetts 02111 (617) 423-3990; *The World in Figures.*

GIBRALTAR - HOURS OF WORK - See GIBRALTAR - EMPLOYMENT

GIBRALTAR - ILLITERATE POPULATION

G.K. Hall and Company, 70 Lincoln Street, Boston, Massachusetts 02111 (617) 423-3990; *The World in Figures.*

United Nations Educational, Scientific and Cultural Organization (UNESCO), 7 Place de Fontenoy, F-75700 Paris, France (Telephone Number in U.S. (212) 963-5981); *Statistical Yearbook.*

GIBRALTAR - IMPORTS

Food and Agricultural Organization of the United Nations (FAO) Via delle Terme di Caracalla, 00100 Rome, Italy (Telephone Number in U.S. (202) 653-2400); *The State of Food and Agriculture.*

G.K. Hall and Company, 70 Lincoln Street, Boston, Massachusetts 02111 (617) 423-3990; *The World in Figures.*

International Monetary Fund, 700 Nineteenth Street, NW, Washington, D.C. 20431 (202) 623-7000; *Direction of Trade Statistics.*

GIBRALTAR - INDUSTRY

G.K. Hall and Company, 70 Lincoln Street, Boston, Massachusetts 02111 (617) 423-3990; *The World in Figures.*

International Labour Office, I.L.O. Publications, CH-1211, Geneva 22, Switzerland; *Yearbook of Labour Statistics.*

GIBRALTAR - INFANT AND MATERNAL MORTALITY

Statistical Office of the United Nations, Publishing Service, New York, New York 10017 (800) 253-9646; *Demographic Yearbook*, and *Statistical Yearbook*.

World Health Organization, Office of Publications, Avenue Appia, CH-1211 Geneva 27, Switzerland (Telephone Number in U.S. (518) 436-9686); *World Health Statistics Annual*.

GIBRALTAR - LABOR FORCE

Food and Agricultural Organization of the United Nations (FAO) Via delle Terme di Caracalla, 00100 Rome, Italy (Telephone Number in U.S. (202) 653-2400); *The State of Food and Agriculture*.

G.K. Hall and Company, 70 Lincoln Street, Boston, Massachusetts 02111 (617) 423-3990; *The World in Figures*.

GIBRALTAR - LABOR PRODUCTIVITY

International Labour Office, I.L.O. Publications, CH-1211, Geneva 22, Switzerland; *Yearbook of Labour Statistics*.

GIBRALTAR - LAND USE

Food and Agricultural Organization of the United Nations (FAO), Via delle Terme di Caracalla, 00100 Rome, Italy (Telephone Number in U.S. (202) 653-2400); *Production Yearbook*.

G.K. Hall and Company, 70 Lincoln Street, Boston, Massachusetts 02111 (617) 423-3990; *The World in Figures*.

GIBRALTAR - LIBRARIES

United Nations Educational, Scientific and Cultural Organization (UNESCO), 7 Place de Fontenoy, F-75700 Paris, France (Telephone Number in U.S. (212) 963-5981); *Statistical Yearbook*.

GIBRALTAR - LIVESTOCK AND POULTRY

Food and Agricultural Organization of the United Nations (FAO), Via delle Terme di Caracalla, 00100 Rome, Italy (Telephone Number in U.S. (202) 653-2400); *Production Yearbook*, and *The State of Food and Agriculture*.

G.K. Hall and Company, 70 Lincoln Street, Boston, Massachusetts 02111 (617) 423-3990; *The World in Figures*.

GIBRALTAR - LIVING LEVELS

G.K. Hall and Company, 70 Lincoln Street, Boston, Massachusetts 02111 (617) 423-3990; *The World in Figures*.

GIBRALTAR - MAIL - NUMBER OF PIECES SENT OR RECEIVED

Statistical Office of the United Nations, Publishing Service, New York, New York 10017 (800) 253-9646; *Statistical Yearbook*.

GIBRALTAR - MANUFACTURING

G.K. Hall and Company, 70 Lincoln Street, Boston, Massachusetts 02111 (617) 423-3990; *The World in Figures*.

GIBRALTAR - MARRIAGE RATES

Statistical Office of the United Nations, Publishing Service, New York, New York 10017 (800) 253-9646; *Demographic Yearbook*, and *Statistical Yearbook*.

GIBRALTAR - MEAT PRODUCTION - See GIBRALTAR - LIVESTOCK AND POULTRY

GIBRALTAR - MERCHANT SHIPPING

G.K. Hall and Company, 70 Lincoln Street, Boston, Massachusetts 02111 (617) 423-3990; *The World in Figures*.

Statistical Office of the United Nations, Publishing Service, New York, New York 10017 (800) 253-9646; *Statistical Yearbook*.

GIBRALTAR - MILITARY

G.K. Hall and Company, 70 Lincoln Street, Boston, Massachusetts 02111 (617) 423-3990; *The World in Figures*.

GIBRALTAR - MINING AND MINERAL PRODUCTS

G.K. Hall and Company, 70 Lincoln Street, Boston, Massachusetts 02111 (617) 423-3990; *The World in Figures*.

GIBRALTAR - MONEY SUPPLY

G.K. Hall and Company, 70 Lincoln Street, Boston, Massachusetts 02111 (617) 423-3990; *The World in Figures*.

GIBRALTAR - MOTION PICTURES

Statistical Office of the United Nations, Publishing Service, New York, New York 10017 (800) 253-9646; *Statistical Yearbook*.

GIBRALTAR - MOTOR VEHICLES IN USE

G.K. Hall and Company, 70 Lincoln Street, Boston, Massachusetts 02111 (617) 423-3990; *The World in Figures*.

Statistical Office of the United Nations, Publishing Service, New York, New York 10017 (800) 253-9646; *Statistical Yearbook*.

GIBRALTAR - MUSEUMS

United Nations Educational, Scientific and Cultural Organization (UNESCO), 7 Place de Fontenoy, F-75700 Paris, France (Telephone Number in U.S. (212) 963-5981); *Statistical Yearbook*.

GIBRALTAR - NATALITY - SEE GIBRALTAR - BIRTH RATES

GIBRALTAR - NATIONAL INCOME

G.K. Hall and Company, 70 Lincoln Street, Boston, Massachusetts 02111 (617) 423-3990; *The World in Figures*.

GIBRALTAR - NEWSPAPER PRODUCTION - See GIBRALTAR - FORESTRY AND FOREST PRODUCTS

GIBRALTAR - OCCUPATIONS - See GIBRALTAR - LABOR FORCE

GIBRALTAR - PERIODICALS

United Nations Educational, Scientific and Cultural Organization (UNESCO), 7 Place de Fontenoy, F-75700 Paris, France (Telephone Number in U.S. (212) 963-5981); *Statistical Yearbook*.

GIBRALTAR - PESTICIDE USE

Food and Agricultural Organization of the United Nations (FAO) Via delle Terme di Caracalla, 00100 Rome, Italy (Telephone Number in

U.S. (202) 653-2400); *The State of Food and Agriculture.*

GIBRALTAR - PETROLEUM INDUSTRY

Food and Agricultural Organization of the United Nations (FAO) Via delle Terme di Caracalla, 00100 Rome, Italy (Telephone Number in U.S. (202) 653-2400); *The State of Food and Agriculture.*

G.K. Hall and Company, 70 Lincoln Street, Boston, Massachusetts 02111 (617) 423-3990; *The World in Figures.*

GIBRALTAR - POPULATION

Food and Agricultural Organization of the United Nations (FAO), Via delle Terme di Caracalla, 00100 Rome, Italy (Telephone Number in U.S. (202) 653-2400); *Production Yearbook.*

G.K. Hall and Company, 70 Lincoln Street, Boston, Massachusetts 02111 (617) 423-3990; *The World in Figures.*

International Labour Office, I.L.O. Publications, CH-1211, Geneva 22, Switzerland; *Yearbook of Labour Statistics.*

Statistical Office of the United Nations, Publishing Service, New York, New York 10017 (800) 253-9646; *Demographic Yearbook,* and *Statistical Yearbook.*

World Health Organization, Office of Publications, Avenue Appia, CH-1211 Geneva 27, Switzerland (Telephone Number in U.S. (518) 436-9686); *World Health Statistics Annual.*

GIBRALTAR - PRICES

Food and Agricultural Organization of the United Nations (FAO), Via delle Terme di Caracalla, 00100 Rome, Italy (Telephone Number in U.S. (202) 653-2400); *Production Yearbook,* and *The State of Food and Agriculture.*

G.K. Hall and Company, 70 Lincoln Street, Boston, Massachusetts 02111 (617) 423-3990; *The World in Figures.*

International Labour Office, I.L.O. Publications, CH-1211, Geneva 22, Switzerland; *Yearbook of Labour Statistics.*

GIBRALTAR - PRODUCTION

G.K. Hall and Company, 70 Lincoln Street, Boston, Massachusetts 02111 (617) 423-3990; *The World in Figures.*

GIBRALTAR - RADIO BROADCASTING - See GIBRALTAR - BROADCASTING

GIBRALTAR - RAILWAYS

G.K. Hall and Company, 70 Lincoln Street, Boston, Massachusetts 02111 (617) 423-3990; *The World in Figures.*

GIBRALTAR - RENT PRICES

International Labour Office, I.L.O. Publications, CH-1211, Geneva 22, Switzerland; *Yearbook of Labour Statistics.*

GIBRALTAR - RETAIL TRADE

G.K. Hall and Company, 70 Lincoln Street, Boston, Massachusetts 02111 (617) 423-3990; *The World in Figures.*

GIBRALTAR - SCIENTISTS AND TECHNICIANS

Statistical Office of the United Nations, Publishing Service, New York, New York 10017 (800) 253-9646; *Statistical Yearbook.*

GIBRALTAR - SOCIAL DATA

G.K. Hall and Company, 70 Lincoln Street, Boston, Massachusetts 02111 (617) 423-3990; *The World in Figures.*

GIBRALTAR - STOCKS - COMMODITY - MARKET PRICE - INDEX

Food and Agricultural Organization of the United Nations (FAO) Via delle Terme di Caracalla, 00100 Rome, Italy (Telephone Number in U.S. (202) 653-2400); *The State of Food and Agriculture.*

GIBRALTAR - TAXATION

G.K. Hall and Company, 70 Lincoln Street, Boston, Massachusetts 02111 (617) 423-3990; *The World in Figures.*

GIBRALTAR - TELEPHONES IN USE

American Telephone and Telegraph Company, 26 Parsippany Road, Whippany, New Jersey 07981 (800) 338-4038; *The World's Telephones.*

G.K. Hall and Company, 70 Lincoln Street, Boston, Massachusetts 02111 (617) 423-3990; *The World in Figures.*

Statistical Office of the United Nations, Publishing Service, New York, New York 10017 (800) 253-9646; *Statistical Yearbook.*

GIBRALTAR - TELEVISION BROADCASTING - See GIBRALTAR - BROADCASTING

GIBRALTAR - TEXTILE INDUSTRY

G.K. Hall and Company, 70 Lincoln Street, Boston, Massachusetts 02111 (617) 423-3990; *The World in Figures.*

GIBRALTAR - THEATRE

United Nations Educational, Scientific and Cultural Organization (UNESCO), 7 Place de Fontenoy, F-75700 Paris, France (Telephone Number in U.S. (212) 963-5981); *Statistical Yearbook.*

GIBRALTAR - TRADE - See GIBRALTAR - FOREIGN TRADE

GIBRALTAR - TOURISM

G.K. Hall and Company, 70 Lincoln Street, Boston, Massachusetts 02111 (617) 423-3990; *The World in Figures.*

Statistical Office of the United Nations, Publishing Service, New York, New York 10017 (800) 253-9646; *Statistical Yearbook.*

GIBRALTAR - TRANSPORTATION AND COMMUNICATIONS

G.K. Hall and Company, 70 Lincoln Street, Boston, Massachusetts 02111 (617) 423-3990; *The World in Figures.*

GIBRALTAR - UNEMPLOYMENT

International Labour Office, I.L.O. Publications, CH-1211, Geneva 22, Switzerland; *Yearbook of Labour Statistics.*

Statistical Office of the United Nations, Publishing Service, New York, New York 10017 (800) 253-9646; *Statistical Yearbook.*

GIBRALTAR - VITAL STATISTICS

G.K. Hall and Company, 70 Lincoln Street, Boston, Massachusetts 02111 (617) 423-3990; *The World in Figures.*

Statistical Office of the United Nations, Publishing Service, New York, New York 10017 (800) 253-9646; *Statistical Yearbook.*

World Health Organization, Office of Publications, Avenue Appia, CH-1211 Geneva 27, Switzerland (Telephone Number in U.S. (518) 436-9686); *World Health Statistics Annual.*

GIBRALTAR - WAGES

G.K. Hall and Company, 70 Lincoln Street, Boston, Massachusetts 02111 (617) 423-3990; *The World in Figures.*

International Labour Office, I.L.O. Publications, CH-1211, Geneva 22, Switzerland; *Yearbook of Labour Statistics.*

Statistical Office of the United Nations, Publishing Service, New York, New York 10017 (800) 253-9646; *Statistical Yearbook.*

GIBRALTAR - WEATHER

G.K. Hall and Company, 70 Lincoln Street, Boston, Massachusetts 02111 (617) 423-3990; *The World in Figures.*

GIFT AND ESTATE TAXES

U.S. Department of Commerce, Bureau of the Census, Suitland, Maryland 20233 (301) 763-4040; *Government Finances.*

U.S. Department of the Treasury, Internal Revenue Service, 1111 Constitution Avenue, NW, Washington, D.C. 20224 (202) 566-5000; *Annual Report of the Commissioner and Chief Counsel of the Internal Revenue Service.*

GIFT, NOVELTY, AND SOUVENIR SHOPS

U.S. Department of Commerce, Bureau of the Census, Suitland, Maryland 20233 (301) 763-4040; *County Business Patterns,* and *Census of Retail Trade.*

Gilbert Islands - National Statistical Office

Statistical Division, Ministry of Finance, Post Office Box 67, Bariki, Tarawa, Gilbert Islands.

Gilbert Islands - Primary Statistics Source

HM Stationery Office, Post Office Box 569, London SE1 9NH, England; *Gilbert and Ellice Islands Colony and the Central and Southern Line Islands: Report...*

GILBERT ISLANDS - AGRICULTURE

Statistical Office of the United Nations, Publishing Service, New York, New York 10017 (800) 253-9646; *Statistical Yearbook,* and *Statistical Yearbook for Asia and the Pacific.*

GILBERT ISLANDS - AREA AND POPULATION DENSITY

Statistical Office of the United Nations, Publishing Service, New York, New York 10017 (800) 253-9646; *Statistical Yearbook.*

GILBERT ISLANDS - BIRTH RATES

Statistical Office of the United Nations, Publishing Service, New York, New York 10017 (800) 253-9646; *Demographic Yearbook,* and *Statistical Yearbook.*

GILBERT ISLANDS - COMMUNICATIONS

Statistical Office of the United Nations, Publishing Service, New York, New York 10017 (800) 253-9646; *Statistical Yearbook for Asia and the Pacific.*

GILBERT ISLANDS - CONSUMER PRICE INDEX

Statistical Office of the United Nations, Publishing Service, New York, New York 10017 (800) 253-9646; *Statistical Yearbook.*

GILBERT ISLANDS - CROPS

Food and Agricultural Organization of the United Nations (FAO), Via delle Terme di Caracalla, 00100 Rome, Italy (Telephone Number in U.S. (202) 653-2400); *Production Yearbook.*

GILBERT ISLANDS - DEATH RATES

Statistical Office of the United Nations, Publishing Service, New York, New York 10017 (800) 253-9646; *Statistical Yearbook.*

GILBERT ISLANDS - DEVELOPMENT ASSISTANCE

Statistical Office of the United Nations, Publishing Service, New York, New York 10017 (800) 253-9646; *Statistical Yearbook.*

GILBERT ISLANDS - DIVORCE RATES

Statistical Office of the United Nations, Publishing Service, New York, New York 10017 (800) 253-9646; *Demographic Yearbook,* and *Statistical Yearbook.*

GILBERT ISLANDS - EDUCATION

Statistical Office of the United Nations, Publishing Service, New York, New York 10017 (800) 253-9646; *Statistical Yearbook for Asia and the Pacific.*

GILBERT ISLANDS - ENERGY

Statistical Office of the United Nations, Publishing Service, New York, New York 10017 (800) 253-9646; *Statistical Yearbook, Statistical Yearbook for Asia and the Pacific,* and *World Energy Supplies.*

GILBERT ISLANDS - EXPORTS

International Monetary Fund, 700 Nineteenth Street, NW, Washington, D.C. 20431 (202) 623-7000; *Direction of Trade Statistics.*

GILBERT ISLANDS - EXTERNAL TRADE

Statistical Office of the United Nations, Publishing Service, New York, New York 10017 (800) 253-9646; *Statistical Yearbook,* and *Statistical Yearbook for Asia and the Pacific.*

GILBERT ISLANDS - FETAL MORTALITY

Statistical Office of the United Nations, Publishing Service, New York, New York 10017 (800) 253-9646; *Demographic Yearbook.*

GILBERT ISLANDS - FINANCE

Statistical Office of the United Nations, Publishing Service, New York, New York 10017 (800) 253-9646; *Statistical Yearbook for Asia and the Pacific.*

GILBERT ISLANDS - FOOD

Statistical Office of the United Nations, Publishing Service, New York, New York 10017 (800) 253-9646; *Statistical Yearbook for Asia and the Pacific.*

GILBERT ISLANDS - FOREIGN TRADE

Statistical Office of the United Nations, Publishing Service, New York, New York 10017 (800) 253-9646; *Statistical Yearbook.*

GILBERT ISLANDS - GENERAL MORTALITY

Statistical Office of the United Nations, Publishing Service, New York, New York 10017 (800) 253-9646; *Demographic Yearbook.*

GILBERT ISLANDS - GROSS DOMESTIC PRODUCT

Statistical Office of the United Nations, Publishing Service, New York, New York 10017 (800) 253-9646; *Statistical Yearbook.*

GILBERT ISLANDS - HEALTH

Statistical Office of the United Nations, Publishing Service, New York, New York 10017 (800) 253-9646; *Statistical Yearbook.*

GILBERT ISLANDS - IMPORTS

International Monetary Fund, 700 Nineteenth Street, NW, Washington, D.C. 20431 (202) 623-7000; *Direction of Trade Statistics.*

GILBERT ISLANDS - INDUSTRY

Statistical Office of the United Nations, Publishing Service, New York, New York 10017 (800) 253-9646; *Statistical Yearbook for Asia and the Pacific.*

GILBERT ISLANDS - INFANT AND MATERNAL MORTALITY

Statistical Office of the United Nations, Publishing Service, New York, New York 10017 (800) 253-9646; *Demographic Yearbook,* and *Statistical Yearbook.*

GILBERT ISLANDS - INTERNAL TRADE

Statistical Office of the United Nations, Publishing Service, New York, New York 10017 (800) 253-9646; *Statistical Yearbook,* and *Statistical Yearbook for Asia and the Pacific.*

GILBERT ISLANDS - LIVESTOCK AND POULTRY

Statistical Office of the United Nations, Publishing Service, New York, New York 10017 (800) 253-9646; *Statistical Yearbook.*

GILBERT ISLANDS - MAIL TRAFFIC - NUMBER OF ITEMS SENT AND RECEIVED

Statistical Office of the United Nations, Publishing Service, New York, New York 10017 (800) 253-9646; *Statistical Yearbook.*

GILBERT ISLANDS - MANPOWER

Statistical Office of the United Nations, Publishing Service, New York, New York 10017 (800) 253-9646; *Statistical Yearbook for Asia and the Pacific.*

GILBERT ISLANDS - MARRIAGE RATES

Statistical Office of the United Nations, Publishing Service, New York, New York 10017 (800) 253-9646; *Demographic Yearbook,* and *Statistical Yearbook.*

GILBERT ISLANDS - MERCHANT SHIPPING

Statistical Office of the United Nations, Publishing Service, New York, New York 10017 (800) 253-9646; *Statistical Yearbook.*

GILBERT ISLAND - MINING AND MINERALS

Statistical Office of the United Nations, Publishing Service, New York, New York 10017 (800) 253-9646; *Statistical Yearbook.*

GILBERT ISLANDS - MOTION PICTURES

Statistical Office of the United Nations, Publishing Service, New York, New York 10017 (800) 253-9646; *Statistical Yearbook.*

GILBERT ISLANDS - NATALITY - See GILBERT ISLANDS - BIRTH RATES

GILBERT ISLANDS - NATIONAL ACCOUNTS

Statistical Office of the United Nations, Publishing Service, New York, New York 10017 (800) 253-9646; *National Accounts Statistics,* and *Statistical Yearbook for Asia and the Pacific.*

GILBERT ISLANDS - NATIONAL INCOME

Statistical Office of the United Nations, Publishing Service, New York, New York 10017 (800) 253-9646; *Statistical Yearbook.*

GILBERT ISLANDS - PHOSPHATE ROCK PRODUCTION - See GILBERT ISLANDS - MINING AND MINERAL PRODUCTS

GILBERT ISLANDS - PIGS - See GILBERT ISLANDS - LIVESTOCK AND POULTRY

GILBERT ISLANDS - POPULATION

International Labour Office, I.L.O. Publications, CH-1211, Geneva 22, Switzerland; *Yearbook of Labour Statistics.*

Statistical Office of the United Nations, Publishing Service, New York, New York 10017 (800) 253-9646; *Demographic Yearbook, Statistical Yearbook,* and *Statistical Yearbook for Asia and the Pacific.*

GILBERT ISLANDS - ROOT AND TUBER PRODUCTION - See GILBERT ISLANDS - CROPS

GILBERT ISLANDS - TRACTORS IN USE

Statistical Office of the United Nations, Publishing Service, New York, New York 10017 (800) 253-9646; *Statistical Yearbook.*

GILBERT ISLANDS - TRANSPORTATION AND COMMUNICATIONS

Statistical Office of the United Nations, Publishing Service, New York, New York 10017 (800) 253-9646; *Statistical Yearbook for Asia and the Pacific.*

GILBERT ISLANDS - VITAL STATISTICS

Statistical Office of the United Nations, Publishing Service, New York, New York 10017 (800) 253-9646; *Statistical Yearbook.*

GILBERT ISLANDS - WAGES AND PRICES

Statistical Office of the United Nations, Publishing Service, New York, New York 10017 (800) 253-9646; *Statistical Yearbook for Asia and the Pacific.*

GLASS CONTAINERS

U.S. Department of Commerce, Bureau of the Census, Suitland, Maryland 20233 (301) 763-4040; *Current Industrial Reports.*

GOLD - CONSUMPTION

U.S. Department of the Interior, Bureau of Mines, 810 Seventh Street, NW, Washington, D.C. 20241 (202) 501-9649; *Mineral Commodity Summaries.*

GOLD - EMPLOYMENT

U.S. Department of Commerce, Bureau of the Census, Suitland, Maryland 20233 (301) 763-4040; *Census of Mineral Industries.*

U.S. Department of the Interior, Bureau of Mines, 810 Seventh Street, NW, Washington, D.C. 20241 (202) 501-9649; *Mineral Commodity Summaries.*

GOLD - FOREIGN TRADE

U.S. Department of Commerce, Bureau of the Census, Suitland, Maryland 20233 (301) 763-4040; *U.S. Merchandise Trade,* and *U.S. Merchandise Trade: Exports, General Imports, and Imports for Consumption.*

U.S. Department of the Interior, Bureau of Mines, 810 Seventh Street, NW, Washington, D.C. 20241 (202) 501-9649; *Minerals Yearbook,* and *Annual Reports.*

GOLD - PRICES

U.S. Department of the Interior, Bureau of Mines, 810 Seventh Street, NW, Washington, D.C. 20241 (202) 501-9649; *Minerals Yearbook,* and *Mineral Commodity Summaries.*

GOLD - PRODUCTION AND VALUE

U.S. Department of the Interior, Bureau of Mines, 810 Seventh Street, NW, Washington, D.C. 20241 (202) 501-9649; *Annual Reports,* and *Mineral Commodity Summaries.*

GOLD - PRODUCTION AND VALUE - WORLD PRODUCTION

U.S. Department of the Interior, Bureau of Mines, 810 Seventh Street, NW, Washington, D.C. 20241 (202) 501-9649; *Annual Reports,* and *Mineral Commodity Summaries.*

GOLD - RESERVE ASSETS

Board of Governors of the Federal Reserve System, Twentieth Street and Constitution Avenue, NW, Washington, D.C. 20551 (202) 452-3000; *Federal Reserve Bulletin.*

U.S. Department of the Treasury, Fifteenth Street and Pennsylvania Avenue, NW, Washington, D.C. 20220 (202) 566-2000; *Treasury Bulletin.*

GOLF

National Golf Foundation, 1150 South U.S. Highway One, Jupiter Beach, Florida 33477 (407) 744-6006.

National Sporting Goods Association, 1699 Wall Street, Mt. Prospect, Illinois 60056 (708) 439-4000; *The Sporting Goods Market in 1993,* and *Sports Participation in 1992.*

GOLF COURSE INDUSTRY RECEIPTS

U.S. Department of Commerce, Bureau of the Census, Suitland, Maryland 20233 (301) 763-4040; *Current Business Reports, Service Annual Survey.*

GOVERNMENT - See also EXPENDITURES OF UNITED STATES GOVERNMENT and RECEIPTS, UNITED STATES GOVERNMENT and Individual Government Units

GOVERNMENT - CAPITAL STOCK

U.S. Department of Commerce, Bureau of Economic Analysis, 14th Street between Constitution Avenue and E Street, NW, Washington, D.C. 20230 (202) 606-9900; *Survey of Current Business.*

GOVERNMENT - COLLECTIVE BARGAINING AGREEMENTS

U.S. Department of Labor, Bureau of Labor Statistics, Two Massachusetts Avenue, NE, Washington, D.C. 20212 (202) 606-7828; *Current Wage Developments.*

GOVERNMENT - CONSTRUCTION VALUE OF BUILDINGS

U.S. Department of Commerce, Bureau of the Census, Suitland, Maryland 20233 (301) 763-4040; *Current Construction Reports.*

GOVERNMENT - EARNINGS

U.S. Department of Commerce, Bureau of Economic Analysis, Fourteenth Street between Constitution Avenue and E Street, NW, Washington, D.C. 20230 (202) 606-9900; *Survey of Current Business,* and *The National Income and Product Accounts of the United States.*

U.S. Department of Commerce, Bureau of the Census, Suitland, Maryland 20233 (301) 763-4040; *Public Employment.*

U.S. Department of Labor, Bureau of Labor Statistics, Two Massachusetts Avenue, NE, Washington, D.C. 20212 (202) 606-7828; *Employment and Earnings,* and Bulletins 2370 and 2429

GOVERNMENT - EMPLOYEES

National Science Foundation, 4201 Wilson Boulevard, Arlington, Virginia 22230 (703) 306-1234; *National Patterns of R & D Resources.*

Office of Personnel Management, 1900 E Street, NW, Washington, D.C. 20415 (202) 606-1800; *Central Personnel Data File, Federal Civilian Workforce Statistics - Employment and Trends,* and *The Pay*

Structure of the Federal Civil Service.

U.S. Department of Labor, Bureau of Labor Statistics, Two Massachusetts Avenue, NE, Washington, D.C. 20212 (202) 606-7828; *Employment and Earnings, Monthly Labor Review, News,* and Bulletins 2370 and 2429.

GOVERNMENT - EMPLOYEES - BENEFITS

U.S. Department of Labor, Bureau of Labor Statistics, Two Massachusetts Avenue, NE, Washington, D.C. 20212 (202) 606-7828; *Employee Benefits in State and Local Governments,* and *Employer Costs for Employee Compensation.*

GOVERNMENT - EMPLOYEES - CITY GOVERNMENT

U.S. Department of Commerce, Bureau of the Census, Suitland, Maryland 20233 (301) 763-4040; *City Employment,* and *Compendium of Public Employment.*

GOVERNMENT - EMPLOYEES - FEDERAL - CIVILIAN

U.S. Department of Commerce, Bureau of the Census, Suitland, Maryland 20233 (301) 763-4040; *Public Employment, Historical Statistics on Governmental Finances and Employment,* and *City Government Finances.*

U.S. Department of Labor, Bureau of Labor Statistics, Two Massachusetts Avenue, NE, Washington, D.C. 20212 (202) 606-7828; monthly report, *Employment and Earnings.*

U.S. Office of Personnel Management, 1900 E Street, NW, Washington, D.C. 20415 (202) 606-1800; *Central Personnel Data File, Pay Structure of the Federal Civil Service,* and *Federal Civilian Workforce Statistics, Employment and Trends.*

GOVERNMENT - EMPLOYEES - FEDERAL - CIVILIAN - ACCESSIONS AND SEPARATIONS

U.S. Office of Personnel Management, 1900 E Street, NW, Washington, D.C. 20415 (202) 606-1800; *Federal Civilian Workforce Statistics, Employment and Trends.*

GOVERNMENT - EMPLOYEES - FEDERAL - CIVILIAN - PAY INCREASES

U.S. Office of Personnel Management, 1900 E Street, NW, Washington, D.C. 20415 (202) 606-1800; *Pay Structure of the Federal Civil Service.*

GOVERNMENT - EMPLOYEES - FEDERAL - CIVILIAN - SALARIES

U.S. Office of Personnel Management, 1900 E Street, NW, Washington, D.C. 20415 (202) 606-1800; *Pay Structure of the Federal Civil Service.*

GOVERNMENT - EMPLOYEES - FEDERAL - CIVILIAN - TYPE OF POSITION

U.S. Office of Personnel Management, 1900 E Street, NW, Washington, D.C. 20415 (202) 606-1800; *Federal Civilian Workforce Statistics, Employment and Trends,* and unpublished data.

GOVERNMENT - EMPLOYEES - LOCAL GOVERNMENT

U.S. Department of Commerce, Bureau of the Census, Suitland, Maryland 20233 (301) 763-4040; *Public Employment, Historical Statistics on Governmental Finances and Employment,* and unpublished data.

GOVERNMENT - EMPLOYEES - SCIENTIFIC AND TECHNICAL

U.S. National Science Foundation, 4201 Wilson Boulevard, Arlington, Virginia 22230 (703) 306-1234; *National Patterns of R & D Resources, U.S. Scientists and Engineers,* and *Women and Minorities in Science and Engineering.*

GOVERNMENT - EMPLOYEES - STATE GOVERNMENT

U.S. Department of Commerce, Bureau of the Census, Suitland, Maryland 20233 (301) 763-4040; *Public Employment, Historical Statistics on Governmental Finances and Employment,* and unpublished data.

GOVERNMENT - EMPLOYEES - STATES

U.S. Office of Personnel Management, 1900 E Street, NW, Washington, D.C. 20415 (202) 606-1800; *Biennial Report of Employment by Geographic Area.*

U.S. Department of Commerce, Bureau of the Census, Suitland, Maryland 20233 (301) 763-4040; *Historical Statistics on Governmental Finances and Employment,* and *Public Employment.*

U.S. Department of Labor, Bureau of Labor Statistics, Two Massachusetts Avenue, NE, Washington, D.C. 20212 (202) 606-7828; *Employment and Earnings.*

GOVERNMENT - EMPLOYMENT COST INDEX

U.S. Department of Labor, Bureau of Labor Statistics, Two Massachusetts Avenue, NE, Washington, D.C. 20212 (202) 606-7828; *News, Employment Cost Index.*

GOVERNMENT - EXPENDITURES - CAPITAL OUTLAY

U.S. Department of Commerce, Bureau of the Census, Suitland, Maryland 20233 (301) 763-4040; *Government Finances,* and *Historical Statistics on Governmental Finances and Employment.*

GOVERNMENT - EXPENDITURES - CITY GOVERNMENT

U.S. Department of Commerce, Bureau of the Census, Suitland, Maryland 20233 (301) 763-4040; *City Government Finances.*

GOVERNMENT - EXPENDITURES - FEDERAL

Executive Office of the President, Office of Management and Budget, Executive Office Building, Washington, D.C. 20503 (202) 395-3080; *Budget of the United States Government.*

U.S. Department of Commerce, Bureau of the Census, Suitland, Maryland 20233 (301) 763-4040; *Historical Statistics on Government Finances and Employment, Government Finances,* and unpublished data.

GOVERNMENT - EXPENDITURES - FEDERAL - AID TO STATE AND LOCAL GOVERNMENT

Advisory Commission on Intergovernmental Relations, 800 K Street, NW, Suite 450 South, Washington, D.C. 20575 (202) 653-5540; *Significant Features of Fiscal Federalism,* based on *Budget of the United States Government.*

Executive Office of the President, Office of Management and Budget, Executive Office Building, Washington, D.C. 20503 (202) 395-3080;

Historical Tables, Budget of the United States Government, and *Budget of the U.S. Government.*

U.S. Department of Commerce, Bureau of the Census, Suitland, Maryland 20233 (301) 763-4040; *Federal Expenditures by State for Fiscal Year,* and *Public Employment.*

GOVERNMENT - EXPENDITURES - FEDERAL - CAPITAL OUTLAY

U.S. Department of Commerce, Bureau of the Census, Suitland, Maryland 20233 (301) 763-4040; *Historical Statistics on Government Finances and Employment,* and *Government Finances.*

GOVERNMENT - EXPENDITURES - FEDERAL - PUBLIC ASSISTANCE PROGRAMS

U.S. Library of Congress, Congressional Research Service, 10 First Street SE, Washington, D.C. 20540 (202) 707-5000; *Cash and Non-Cash Benefits for Persons with Limited Income: Eligibility Rules, Recipient and Expenditure Data.*

GOVERNMENT - EXPENDITURES - STATE AND LOCAL GOVERNMENT

U.S. Department of Commerce, Bureau of the Census, Suitland, Maryland 20233 (301) 763-4040; *Historical Statistics on Government Finances and Employment, Government Finances, State Government Finances,* and *City Government Finances.*

GOVERNMENT - EXPENDITURES - STATE GOVERNMENT

National Association of State Budget Officers, Hall of the States, 400 North Capital Street, NW, Suite 295, Washington, D.C. 20001 (202) 624-5382; *State Expenditure Report.*

National Governors' Association, Hall of the States, 444 North Capital Street, NW, Washington, D.C. 20001 (202) 624-5300; *Fiscal Survey of the States.*

U.S. Department of Commerce, Bureau of the Census, Suitland, Maryland 20233 (301) 763-4040; *Historical Statistics on Government Finances and Employment, Government Finances, State Government Finances,* and *State Government Tax Collections.*

GOVERNMENT - FEDERAL PARTICIPATION IN DOMESTIC CREDIT MARKETS

Executive Office of the President, Office of Management and Budget, Executive Office Building, Washington, D.C. 20503 (202) 395-3080; *Analytical Perspectives, Budget of the United States Government.*

GOVERNMENT - FEDERALLY OWNED LAND

U.S. General Services Administration, General Services Building, 18th and F Street, NW, Washington, D.C. 20405 (202) 708-5082; *Inventory Report on Real Property Owned by the United States Throughout the World.*

GOVERNMENT - FLOW OF FUNDS

Board of Governors of the Federal Reserve System, Twentieth Street and Constitution Avenue, NW, Washington, D.C. 20551 (202) 452-3000; *Annual Statistical Digest.*

GOVERNMENT - GROSS DOMESTIC PRODUCT

U.S. Department of Commerce, Bureau of Economic Analysis, Fourteenth Street between Constitution Avenue and E Street, NW, Washington, D.C. 20230 (202) 606-9900; *Survey of Current Business,* July issues, and *The National Income and Product Accounts of the United States.*

GOVERNMENT - HIGHWAYS

U.S. Department of Commerce, Bureau of the Census, Suitland, Maryland 20233 (301) 763-4040; *Federal Expenditures by State for Fiscal Year.*

U.S. Department of Transportation, Federal Highway Administration, 400 Seventh Street, SW, Washington, D.C. 20590 (202) 366-0660; *Highway Statistics.*

GOVERNMENT - HOSPITALS

American Hospital Association, 840 North Lake Shore Drive, Chicago, Illinois 60611 (312) 280-6000; *Hospital Statistics.*

U.S. Department of Health and Human Services, National Center for Health Statistics, 3700 East-West Highway, Hyattsville, Maryland 20782 (301) 436-8500; unpublished data.

GOVERNMENT - INSURANCE - See SOCIAL INSURANCE

GOVERNMENT - LAND - See PUBLIC LANDS

GOVERNMENT - LOCAL GOVERNMENT - CITIES - EMPLOYEES, EARNINGS, AND PAYROLL

U.S. Department of Commerce, Bureau of the Census, Suitland, Maryland 20233 (301) 763-4040; *Compendium of Public Employment, City Employment,* and unpublished data.

GOVERNMENT - LOCAL GOVERNMENT - CITIES - FINANCES

U.S. Department of Commerce, Bureau of the Census, Suitland, Maryland 20233 (301) 763-4040; *City Government Finances.*

GOVERNMENT - LOCAL GOVERNMENT - COUNTY FINANCES

U.S. Department of Commerce, Bureau of the Census, Suitland, Maryland 20233 (301) 763-4040; *County Government Finances.*

GOVERNMENT - LOCAL GOVERNMENT - EARNINGS

U.S. Department of Commerce, Bureau of the Census, Suitland, Maryland 20233; (301) 763-4040 *Public Employment,* and unpublished data.

GOVERNMENT - LOCAL GOVERNMENT - EMPLOYEES

Equal Employment Opportunity Commission, 1801 L Street, NW, Washington, D.C. 20507 (800) USA-EEOC; *State and Local Government Information Report.*

U.S. Department of Commerce, Bureau of the Census, Suitland, Maryland 20233 (301) 763-4040; *Public Employment,* and *Historical Statistics on Governmental Finances and Employment.*

GOVERNMENT - LOCAL GOVERNMENT - NUMBER, BY TYPE

U.S. Department of Commerce, Bureau of the Census, Suitland, Maryland 20233 (301) 763-4040; *Census of Governments, Governmental Organization,* and *Historical Statistics on Governmental Finances and Employment.*

GOVERNMENT - LOCAL GOVERNMENT - PAYROLL

U.S. Department of Commerce, Bureau of the Census, Suitland, Maryland 20233 (301) 763-4040; *Historical Statistics on Governmental Finances and Employment*, and *Public Employment*.

GOVERNMENT - LOCAL GOVERNMENT - POPULATION, BY SIZE - GROUP

U.S. Department of Commerce, Bureau of the Census, Suitland, Maryland 20233 (301) 763-4040; *Census of Governments, Governmental Organization*.

GOVERNMENT - NATIONAL INCOME, ORIGIN IN

U.S. Department of Commerce, Bureau of Economic Analysis, Fourteenth Street between Constitution Avenue and E Street, NW, Washington, D.C. 20230 (202) 606-9900; *The National Income and Product Accounts of the United States*, and *Survey of Current Business*, July issues.

GOVERNMENT - NUMBER OF UNITS BY TYPE OF GOVERNMENT

U.S. Department of Commerce, Bureau of the Census, Suitland, Maryland 20233 (301) 763-4040; *Census of Governments, Government Organization*, and *Historical Statistics on Governmental Finances and Employment*.

GOVERNMENT - OCCUPATIONAL SAFETY

National Safety Council, 1121 Spring Lake Drive, Itasca, Illinois 60143-3201 (708) 285-1121; *Accident Facts*.

GOVERNMENT - PAYROLLS

U.S. Department of Commerce, Bureau of the Census, Suitland, Maryland 20233 (301) 763-4040; *Historical Statistics on Governmental Finances and Employment*, and *Public Employment*.

GOVERNMENT - PURCHASES OF GOODS AND SERVICES

U.S. Department of Commerce, Bureau of Economic Analysis, Fourteenth Street between Constitution Avenue and E Street, NW, Washington, D.C. 20230 (202) 606-9900; *The National Income and Product Accounts of the United States*, and *Survey of Current Business*, July issues.

GOVERNMENT - SALARIES AND WAGES (See also INCOME and Individual Industries)

GOVERNMENT - SALARIES AND WAGES - FEDERAL

U.S. Department of Commerce, Bureau of the Census, Suitland, Maryland 20233 (301) 763-4040; *Federal Expenditures by State for Fiscal Year*.

U.S. Office of Personnel Management, 1900 E Street, NW, Washington, D.C. 20415 (202) 606-1800; *Pay Structure of the Federal Civil Service*.

GOVERNMENT - SALARIES AND WAGES - NATIONAL INCOME COMPONENT

U.S. Department of Commerce. Bureau of Economic Analysis, Fourteenth Street between Constitution Avenue and E Street, NW, Washington, D.C. 20230 (202) 606-9900; *The National Income and Product Accounts of the United States*, and *Survey of Current Business*.

GOVERNMENT - SALARIES AND WAGES - STATE AND LOCAL GOVERNMENT EMPLOYEES

Equal Employment Opportunity Commission, 1801 L Street, NW, Washington, D.C. 20507 (800) USA-EEOC; *State and Local Government Information Report*.

U.S. Department of Commerce, Bureau of the Census, Suitland, Maryland 20233 (301) 763-4040; *Public Employment*.

GOVERNMENT - SECURITIES

Board of Governors of the Federal Reserve System, Twentieth Street and Constitution Avenue, NW, Washington, D.C. 20551 (202) 452-3000; monthly report, *Federal Reserve Bulletin*, and *Annual Statistical Digest*.

Securities Data Company, Inc., 1180 Raymond Boulevard, Newark, New Jersey 07102 (201) 622-3100; Municipal New Issues Database.

U.S. Department of the Treasury, Fifteenth Street and Pennsylvania Avenue, NW, Washington, D.C. 20220 (202) 566-2000; *Treasury Bulletin*.

GOVERNMENT - STATE AND LOCAL GOVERNMENTS - FEDERAL AID

Advisory Commission on Intergovernmental Relations, 800 K Street, NW, Suite 450 South, Washington, D.C. 20575 (202) 653-5540; *Significant Features of Fiscal Federalism*.

Executive Office of the President, Council of Economic Advisors, Old Executive Office Building, Washington, D.C. 20500 (202) 395-5084; *Historical Tables, Budget of the United States Government*, and *Budget of the U.S. Government*.

U.S. Department of Commerce, Bureau of the Census, Suitland, Maryland 20233 (301) 763-4040; *Federal Expenditures by State for Fiscal Year*.

GOVERNMENT - STATE AND LOCAL GOVERNMENTS - FINANCES

Securities Data Company, Inc., 1180 Raymond Boulevard, Newark, New Jersey 07102 (201) 622-3100; Municipal New Issues Database.

U.S. Department of Commerce, Bureau of Economic Analysis, 14th Street between Constitution Avenue and E Street, NW, Washington, D.C. 20230 (202) 606-9900; *The National Income and Product Accounts of the United States*, and *Survey of Current Business*.

U.S. Department of Commerce, Bureau of the Census, Suitland, Maryland 20233 (301) 763-4040; *Historical Statistics on Governmental Finances and Employment, Government Finance, State Government Finances*, and *Federal Expenditures by State for Fiscal Year*.

GOVERNMENT - STATE AND LOCAL GOVERNMENTS - LABOR MANAGEMENT RELATIONS

U.S. Department of Labor, Bureau of Labor Statistics, Two Massachusetts Avenue, NE, Washington, D.C. 20212 (202) 606-7828; *Current Wage Developments*.

GOVERNMENT - STATE AND LOCAL GOVERNMENTS - PAYROLL

U.S. Department of Commerce, Bureau of the Census, Suitland, Maryland 20233 (301) 763-4040; *Census of Governments, Historical Statistics on Governmental Finances and Employment*, and *Public*

Employment.

GOVERNMENT - STATE AND LOCAL GOVERNMENTS - SALARIES

Equal Employment Opportunity Commission, 1801 L Street,NW, Washington, D.C. 20507 (800) USA-EEOC; *State and Local Government Information Report.*

GOVERNMENT - STRATEGIC AND CRITICAL MATERIALS - SUMMARY

U.S. General Services Administration, General Services Building, Eighteenth and F Streets, NW, Washington, D.C. 20405 (202) 708-5082; *Statistical Supplement, Stockpile Report to the Congress.*

GOVERNMENT - STRUCTURES

U.S. General Services Administration, General Services Building, Eighteenth and F Streets, NW, Washington, D.C. 20405 (202) 708-5082; *Inventory Report on Real Property Owned by the United States Throughout the World.*

GOVERNMENT NATIONAL MORTGAGE ASSOCIATION LOANS

Board of Governors of the Federal Reserve System, Twentieth Street and Constitution Avenue, NW, Washington, D.C. 20551 (202) 452-3000; *Federal Reserve Bulletin.*

GOVERNORS - NUMBER AND VOTE CAST

Elections Research Center, 5508 Greystone Street, Chevy Chase, Maryland 20815 (202) 659-9490; *America Votes,* and unpublished data.

National Governors' Association, 444 North Capitol Street, Washington, D.C. 20001 (202) 624-5300; *Directory of Governors of the American States, Commonwealths, and Territories.*

GRADUATES - COLLEGE

U.S. Department of Commerce, Bureau of the Census, Suitland, Maryland 20233 (301) 763-4040; *Current Population Reports,* and unpublished data.

U.S. Department of Education, 400 Maryland Avenue, SW, Washington, D.C. 20202 (202) 708-5366; *Digest of Education Statistics,* and *Projections of Education Statistics.*

GRADUATES - HIGH SCHOOL

U.S. Department of Commerce, Bureau of the Census, Suitland, Maryland 20233 (301) 763-4040; *Current Population Reports,* and unpublished data.

U.S. Department of Education, 400 Maryland Avenue, SW, Washington, D.C. 20202 (202) 708-5366; *Digest of Education Statistics,* and *Projections of Education Statistics.*

GRAIN - See also Individual Classes

GRAIN - CAR LOADINGS

Association of American Railroads, American Railroads Building, 50 F Street, NW, Washington, D.C. 20001 (202) 639-2100; *Weekly Railroad Traffic.*

GRAIN - COMMODITY CREDIT CORPORATION TRANSACTIONS

U.S. Department of Agriculture, Agricultural Stabilization and Conservation Service, Fourteenth Street and Independence Avenue, SW, Washington, D.C. 20250 (202) 720-5237; *Commodity Credit Corporation Report of Financial Condition and Operations,* and *Agricultural Outlook.*

GRAIN - COMMODITY FUTURES TRADING

U.S. Commodity Futures Trading Commission, 2033 K Street, NW, Washington, D.C. 20581 (202) 254-6387; *Annual Report.*

GRAIN - CONSUMPTION

U.S. Department of Agriculture, Economic Research Service, Fourteenth Street and Independence Avenue, SW, Washington, D.C. 20005-4789 (202) 219-1504; *Food Consumption, Prices and Expenditures,* and unpublished data.

GRAIN - FARM MARKETINGS - SALES

U.S. Department of Agriculture, Economic Research Service, Fourteenth Street and Independence Avenue, SW, Washington, D.C. 20005-4789 (202) 219-1504; *Economic Indicators of the Farm Sector: National Financial Summary.*

U.S. Department of Commerce, Bureau of the Census, Suitland, Maryland 20233 (301) 763-4040; *Census of Agriculture.*

GRAIN - FOREIGN TRADE

U.S. Department of Agriculture, Economic Research Service, Fourteenth Street and Independence Avenue, SW, Washington, D.C. 20005-4789 (202) 219-1504; *Agricultural Statistics, Foreign Agricultural Trade of the United States,* and unpublished data.

U.S. Department of Commerce, Bureau of the Census, Suitland, Maryland 20233 (301) 763-4040; *U.S. Merchandise Trade: Exports, General Imports, and Imports for Consumption.*

GRAIN - PRICES

U.S. Department of Agriculture, National Agricultural Statistics Service, Fourteenth Street and Independence Avenue, SW, Washington, D.C. 20250 (202) 219-1504; *Agricultural Prices: Annual Summary.*

GRAIN - PRODUCTION

U.S. Department of Agriculture, Economic Research Service, Fourteenth Street and Independence Avenue, SW, Washington, D.C. 20005-4789 (202) 219-1504; *Agricultural Outlook.*

GRANTS - BY FOUNDATIONS

The Foundation Center, 79 Fifth Avenue, New York, New York 10003 (212) 620-4230; *Foundation Grants Index.*

GRAPEFRUIT

U.S. Department of Agriculture, Economic Research Service, Fourteenth Street and Independence Avenue, SW, Washington, D.C. 20005-4789 (202) 219-1504; *Food Consumption, Prices, and Expenditures,* and *Economic Indicators of the Farm Sector: National Financial Summary.*

U.S. Department of Agriculture, National Agricultural Statistics Service, Fourteenth Street and Independence Avenue, SW,

Washington, D.C. 20250 (202) 219-1504; *Citrus Fruits.*

GRAPES

U.S. Department of Agriculture, Economic Research Service, Fourteenth Street and Independence Avenue, SW, Washington, D.C. 20005-4789 (202) 219-1504; *Food Consumption, Prices, and Expenditures,* and *Economic Indicators of the Farm Sector: National Financial Summary.*

U.S. Department of Agriculture, National Agricultural Statistics Service, Fourteenth Street and Independence Avenue, SW, Washington, D.C. 20250 (202) 219-1504; *Noncitrus Fruits and Nuts.*

GRAPHITE

U.S. Department of the Interior, Bureau of Mines, 810 Seventh Street, NW, Washington, D.C. 20241 (202) 501-9649; *Mineral Commodity Summaries.*

GRAZING - NATIONAL FORESTS - LIVESTOCK AND RECEIPTS

U.S. Department of Agriculture, Forest Service, Fourteenth Street and Independence Avenue, SW, Washington, D.C. 20250 (202) 720-3760; *Land Areas of the National Forest System.*

GRAZING - PUBLIC LANDS - LEASES

General Services Administration, General Services Building, 18th and F Streets, NW, Washington, D.C. 20405 (202) 708-5082; *Inventory Report on Real Property Owned by the U.S. Throughout the World.*

GREAT BRITAIN - See UNITED KINGDOM

GREAT LAKES - AREA

U.S. Department of Commerce, Bureau of the Census, Suitland, Maryland 20233 (301) 763-4040; unpublished data from the TIGER database.

GREAT LAKES - COMMERCE

U.S. Department of Commerce, Bureau of the Census, Suitland, Maryland 20233 (301) 763-4040; TM 985.

U.S. Department of the Army, Corps of Engineers, The Pentagon, Washington, D.C. 20310 (202) 545-6700; *Waterborne Commerce of the United States.*

GREAT LAKES - FISHERIES

U.S. Department of Commerce, National Oceanic and Atmospheric Administration, National Marine Fisheries Service, 1335 East-West Highway, Silver Spring, Maryland 20910 (301) 427-2239; *Fishery Statistics of the United States,* and *Fisheries of the United States.*

Greece - National Statistical Office

National Statistical Service of Greece, 14-16 Lycourgou Street, 101 66, Athens, Greece.

Greece - Primary Statistics Sources

National Statistical Service of Greece, 14-16 Lycourgou Street, 101 66, Athens, Greece; *Concise Statistical Yearbook, Statistical Yearbook of Greece,* and *Monthly Statistical Bulletin.*

GREECE - ABORTIONS

European Community Information Service, 2100 M Street, NW, Washington, D.C. 20037 (202) 862-9500; *Demographic Statistics.*

Statistical Office of the United Nations, Publishing Service, New York, New York 10017 (800) 253-9646; *Demographic Yearbook.*

GREECE - AGRICULTURE

European Community Information Service, 2100 M Street, NW, Washington, D.C. 20037 (202) 862-9500; *Agriculture: Statistical Yearbook, Basic Statistics of the Community, Eurostatistics: Data for Short-Term Economic Analysis, Labor Force Sample Survey, Land use Production,* and *Regions: Statistical Yearbook.*

Facts on File, 460 Park Avenue South, New York, New York 10016 (800) 443-8323; *The New Book of World Rankings.*

Federal Statistical Office, Gustav - Stresemann - Ring 11, D-6200 Wiesbaden, Germany; *Griechenland.*

Food and Agricultural Organization of the United Nations (FAO) Via delle Terme di Caracalla, 00100 Rome, Italy (Telephone Number in U.S. (202) 653-2400); *Production Yearbook, The State of Food and Agriculture,* and *Trade Yearbook.*

G.K. Hall and Company, 70 Lincoln Street, Boston, Massachusetts 02111 (617) 423-3990; *The World in Figures.*

Organisation for Economic Co-operation and Development (OECD), 2 rue Andre-Pascal, 75 Paris 16, France (Telephone Number in U.S. (202) 785-6323); *Economic Accounts for Agriculture, Industrial Structure Statistics,* and *OECD Economic Surveys: Greece.*

Statistical Office of the United Nations, Publishing Service, New York, New York 10017 (800) 253-9646; *Statistical Yearbook.*

Times Books, 201 East 50th Street, New York, New York 10022 (212) 751-2600; *The Economist Book of Vital World Statistics.*

The World Bank, 1818 H Street, NW, Washington, D.C. 20433 (202) 477-1234; *World Tables.*

GREECE - AIRLINE SERVICE

European Community Information Service, 2100 M Street, NW, Washington, D.C. 20037 (202) 862-9500; *Basic Statistics of the Community, Transport Annual Statistics,* and *Regions: Statistical Yearbook.*

Facts on File, 460 Park Avenue South, New York, New York 10016 (800) 443-8323; *The New Book of World Rankings.*

G.K. Hall and Company, 70 Lincoln Street, Boston, Massachusetts 02111 (617) 423-3990; *The World in Figures.*

International Civil Aviation Organization, 1000 Sherbrooke Street West, Suite 400, Montreal, Quebec, Canada H3A 2R2 (514) 285-8219; *Civil Aviation Statistics of the World.*

Organisation for Economic Co-operation and Development (OECD), 2 rue Andre-Pascal, 75 Paris 16, France (Telephone Number in U.S. (202) 785-6323); *Tourism Policy and International Tourism in OECD Member Countries.*

Statistical Office of the United Nations, Publishing Service, New York, New York 10017 (800) 253-9646; *Statistical Yearbook.*

Times Books, 201 East 50th Street, New York, New York 10022 (212) 751-2600; *The Economist Book of Vital World Statistics.*

GREECE - ALMOND PRODUCTION - See GREECE - CROPS

GREECE - ALUMINUM PRODUCTION AND CONSUMPTION - See GREECE - MINING AND MINERAL PRODUCTS

GREECE - ANIMAL FEEDINGSTUFFS

Organisation for Economic Co-operation and Development (OECD), 2 rue Andre-Pascal, 75 Paris 16, France (Telephone Number in U.S. (202) 785-6323); *Foreign Trade by Commodities.*

GREECE - ANIMAL HEALTH

Food and Agricultural Organization of the United Nations (FAO), Via delle Terme di Caracalla, 00100 Rome, Italy (Telephone Number in U.S. (202) 653-2400); *Animal Health Yearbook.*

GREECE - ANTIMONY AND ANTIMONY ORE - See GREECE - MINING AND MINERAL PRODUCTS

GREECE - APPLE PRODUCTION - See GREECE - CROPS

GREECE - AREA AND DENSITY OF POPULATION

European Community Information Service, 2100 M Street, NW, Washington, D.C. 20037 (202) 862-9500; *Basic Statistics of the Community* and *Demographic Statistics.*

Facts on File, 460 Park Avenue South, New York, New York 10016 (800) 443-8323; *The New Book of World Rankings.*

Federal Statistical Office, Gustav - Stresemann - Ring 11, D-6200 Wiesbaden, Germany; *Griechenland.*

Food and Agricultural Organization of the United Nations (FAO) Via delle Terme di Caracalla, 00100 Rome, Italy (Telephone Number in U.S. (202) 653-2400); *The State of Food and Agriculture.*

G.K. Hall and Company, 70 Lincoln Street, Boston, Massachusetts 02111 (617) 423-3990; *The World in Figures.*

Statistical Office of the United Nations, Publishing Service, New York, New York 10017 (800) 253-9646; *Statistical Yearbook.*

Times Books, 201 East 50th Street, New York, New York 10022 (212) 751-2600; *The Economist Book of Vital World Statistics.*

United Nations Educational, Scientific and Cultural Organization (UNESCO), 7 Place de Fontenoy, F-75700 Paris, France (Telephone Number in U.S. (212) 963-5981); *Statistical Yearbook.*

GREECE - ARMS EXPORTS AND IMPORTS

U.S. Arms Control and Disarmament Agency, 320 Twenty-first Street, Northwest, Washington, D.C. 20451 (202) 647-8677; *World Military Expenditures and Arms Transfers.*

GREECE - ARSENIC PRODUCTION AND CONSUMPTION - See GREECE - MINING AND MINERAL PRODUCTS

GREECE - ARTICHOKE PRODUCTION - See GREECE - CROPS

GREECE - BALANCE OF PAYMENTS

The Economist Intelligence Unit, 111 West 57th Street, New York, New York 10019 (800) 938-4685; *The World Market Atlas.*

European Community Information Service, 2100 M Street, NW, Washington, D.C. 20037 (202) 862-9500; *ACP: Basic Statistics, Basic Statistics of the Community, Energy Statistics Yearbook,* and *Eurostatistics: Data for Short-Term Economic Analysis.*

Federal Statistical Office, Gustav - Stresemann - Ring 11, D-6200 Wiesbaden, Germany; *Griechenland.*

G.K. Hall and Company, 70 Lincoln Street, Boston, Massachusetts 02111 (617) 423-3990; *The World in Figures.*

International Monetary Fund, 700 Nineteenth Street, NW, Washington, D.C. 20431 (202) 623-7000; *Balance of Payments Yearbook,* and *International Financial Statistics.*

Organisation for Economic Co-operation and Development (OECD), 2 rue Andre-Pascal, 75 Paris 16, France (Telephone Number in U.S. (202) 785-6323); *Economic Outlook, Geographical Distribution of Financial Flows to Developing Countries, Main Economic Indicators - Historical Statistics,* and *OECD Economic Surveys: Greece.*

Times Books, 201 East 50th Street, New York, New York 10022 (212) 751-2600; *The Economist Book of Vital World Statistics.*

The World Bank, 1818 H Street, NW, Washington, D.C. 20433 (202) 477-1234; *World Tables.*

GREECE - BANANA PRODUCTION - See GREECE - CROPS

GREECE - BANKING

European Community Information Service, 2100 M Street, NW, Washington, D.C. 20037 (202) 862-9500; *ACP: Basic Statistics.*

Facts on File, 460 Park Avenue South, New York, New York 10016 (800) 443-8323; *The New Book of World Rankings.*

G.K. Hall and Company, 70 Lincoln Street, Boston, Massachusetts 02111 (617) 423-3990; *The World in Figures.*

International Monetary Fund, 700 Nineteenth Street, NW, Washington, D.C. 20431 (202) 623-7000; *Government Finance Statistics Yearbook,* and *International Financial Statistics.*

Organisation for Economic Co-operation and Development (OECD), 2 rue Andre-Pascal, 75 Paris 16, France (Telephone Number in U.S. (202) 785-6323); *Economic Outlook, Financial Market Trends,* and *OECD Economic Surveys: Greece.*

Statistical Office of the United Nations, Publishing Service, New York, New York 10017 (800) 253-9646; *Statistical Yearbook.*

GREECE - BARLEY PRODUCTION - See GREECE - CROPS

GREECE - BAUXITE PRODUCTION AND CONSUMPTION - See GREECE - MINING AND MINERAL PRODUCTS

GREECE - BEER PRODUCTION

Facts on File, 460 Park Avenue South, New York, New York 10016 (800) 443-8323; *The New Book of World Rankings.*

Statistical Office of the United Nations, Publishing Service, New York, New York 10017 (800) 253-9646; *Statistical Yearbook.*

GREECE - BIRTH RATE

European Community Information Service, 2100 M Street, NW, Washington, D.C. 20037 (202) 862-9500; *Basic Statistics of the*

Community and *Demographic Statistics*.

Facts on File, 460 Park Avenue South, New York, New York 10016 (800) 443-8323; *The New Book of World Rankings*.

Statistical Office of the United Nations, Publishing Service, New York, New York 10017 (800) 253-9646; *Demographic Yearbook*, and *Statistical Yearbook*.

Times Books, 201 East 50th Street, New York, New York 10022 (212) 751-2600; *The Economist Book of Vital World Statistics*.

The World Bank, 1818 H Street, NW, Washington, D.C. 20433 (202) 477-1234; *World Tables*.

World Health Organization, Office of Publications, Avenue Appia, CH-1211 Geneva 27, Switzerland (Telephone Number in U.S. (518) 436-9686); *World Health Statistics Annual*.

GREECE - BISMUTH PRODUCTION AND CONSUMPTION - See GREECE - MINING AND MINERAL PRODUCTS

GREECE - BONDS

European Community Information Service, 2100 M Street, NW, Washington, D.C. 20037 (202) 862-9500; *Basic Statistics of the Community*.

G.K. Hall and Company, 70 Lincoln Street, Boston, Massachusetts 02111 (617) 423-3990; *The World in Figures*.

International Monetary Fund, 700 Nineteenth Street, NW, Washington, D.C. 20431 (202) 623-7000; *Government Finance Statistics Yearbook*.

Organisation for Economic Co-operation and Development (OECD), 2 rue Andre-Pascal, 75 Paris 16, France (Telephone Number in U.S. (202) 785-6323); *Financial Market Trends*.

GREECE - BOOK PRODUCTION

Euromonitor Publications Limited, 87-88 Turnmill Street, London EC1M 5QU, England; *European Marketing Data and Statistics*.

G.K. Hall and Company, 70 Lincoln Street, Boston, Massachusetts 02111 (617) 423-3990; *The World in Figures*.

United Nations Educational, Scientific and Cultural Organization (UNESCO), 7 Place de Fontenoy, F-75700 Paris, France (Telephone Number in U.S. (212) 963-5981); *Statistical Yearbook*.

GREECE - BROADCASTING

Billboard Limited, Post Office Box 9027, 1006 AA Amsterdam, The Netherlands (Telephone Number in U.S. (212) 764-7300); *World Radio TV Handbook*.

European Community Information Service, 2100 M Street, NW, Washington, D.C. 20037 (202) 862-9500; *Basic Statistics of the Community*.

Facts on File, 460 Park Avenue South, New York, New York 10016 (800) 443-8323; *The New Book of World Rankings*.

G.K. Hall and Company, 70 Lincoln Street, Boston, Massachusetts 02111 (617) 423-3990; *The World in Figures*.

Times Books, 201 East 50th Street, New York, New York 10022 (212) 751-2600; *The Economist Book of Vital World Statistics*.

United Nations Educational, Scientific and Cultural Organization (UNESCO), 7 Place de Fontenoy, F-75700 Paris, France (Telephone Number in U.S. (212) 963-5981); *Statistical Yearbook*.

GREECE - BUILDING CONSTRUCTION - See GREECE - CONSTRUCTION INDUSTRY

GREECE - BUSINESS

European Community Information Service, 2100 M Street, NW, Washington, D.C. 20037 (202) 862-9500; *Basic Statistics of the Community*.

G.K. Hall and Company, 70 Lincoln Street, Boston, Massachusetts 02111 (617) 423-3990; *The World in Figures*.

GREECE - BUSINESS AND PROFESSIONAL LICENSES

International Monetary Fund, 700 Nineteenth Street, NW, Washington, D.C. 20431 (202) 623-7000; *Government Finance Statistics Yearbook*.

GREECE - BUTTER - See GREECE - DAIRY PRODUCTS

GREECE - CABBAGE PRODUCTION - See GREECE - CROPS

GREECE - CADMIUM PRODUCTION AND CONSUMPTION - See GREECE - MINING AND MINERAL PRODUCTS

GREECE - CALORIE SUPPLY

Food and Agricultural Organization of the United Nations (FAO) Via delle Terme di Caracalla, 00100 Rome, Italy (Telephone Number in U.S. (202) 653-2400); *The State of Food and Agriculture*.

GREECE - CAPITAL INVESTMENT

Organisation for Economic Co-operation and Development (OECD), 2 rue Andre-Pascal, 75 Paris 16, France (Telephone Number in U.S. (202) 785-6323); *Economic Outlook*, and *Financial Market Trends*.

GREECE - CAPITAL REVENUE

International Monetary Fund, 700 Nineteenth Street, NW, Washington, D.C. 20431 (202) 623-7000; *Government Finance Statistics Yearbook*.

Organisation for Economic Co-operation and Development (OECD), 2 rue Andre-Pascal, 75 Paris 16, France (Telephone Number in U.S. (202) 785-6323); *Economic Outlook*, and *Financial Market Trends*.

GREECE - CASHEW NUT PRODUCTION - See GREECE - CROPS

GREECE - CASTOR BEAN PRODUCTION - See GREECE - CROPS

GREECE - CATTLE - See GREECE - LIVESTOCK AND POULTRY

GREECE - CAULIFLOWER PRODUCTION - See GREECE - CROPS

GREECE - CAUSTIC SODA PRODUCTION

European Community Information Service, 2100 M Street, NW, Washington, D.C. 20037 (202) 862-9500; *Basic Statistics of the Community*.

Statistical Office of the United Nations, Publishing Service, New York, New York 10017 (800) 253-9646; *Statistical Yearbook*.

GREECE - CEMENT PRODUCTION - See GREECE - MINING AND MINERAL PRODUCTS

GREECE - CEREAL PRODUCTION - See GREECE - CROPS

GREECE - CHEESE - See GREECE - DAIRY PRODUCTS

GREECE - CHEMICAL (ORGANIC) PRODUCTION - See GREECE - MINING AND MINERAL PRODUCTS

GREECE - CHEMICAL INDUSTRY

European Community Information Service, 2100 M Street, Northwest, Washington, D.C. 20037 (202) 862-9500; *Industrial Production: Quarterly Statistics.*

GREECE - CHESTNUT PRODUCTION - See GREECE - CROPS

GREECE - CHICKENS - See GREECE - LIVESTOCK AND POULTRY

GREECE - CHICKPEA PRODUCTION - See GREECE - CROPS

GREECE - CHROMITE PRODUCTION AND CONSUMPTION - See GREECE - MINING AND MINERAL PRODUCTS

GREECE - CHROMIUM ORE PRODUCTION AND CONSUMPTION - See GREECE - MINING AND MINERAL PRODUCTS

GREECE - CIGAR PRODUCTION - See GREECE - TOBACCO PRODUCTION

GREECE - CIGARETTE PRODUCTION - See GREECE - TOBACCO PRODUCTION

GREECE - CLASS STRUCTURE

European Community Information Service, 2100 M Street, NW, Washington, D.C. 20037 (202) 862-9500; *Basic Statistics of the Community* and *Labor Force Sample Survey.*

G.K. Hall and Company, 70 Lincoln Street, Boston, Massachusetts 02111 (617) 423-3990; *The World in Figures.*

GREECE - CLIMATE

Facts on File, 460 Park Avenue South, New York, New York 10016 (800) 443-8323; *The New Book of World Rankings.*

G.K. Hall and Company, 70 Lincoln Street, Boston, Massachusetts 02111 (617) 423-3990; *The World in Figures.*

GREECE - CLOTHING EXPORTS AND IMPORTS

European Community Information Service, 2100 M Street, NW, Washington, D.C. 20037 (202) 862-9500; *Basic Statistics of the Community.*

Organisation for Economic Co-operation and Development (OECD), 2 rue Andre-Pascal, 75 Paris 16, France (Telephone Number in U.S. (202) 785-6323); *Textile Industry in OECD Countries.*

GREECE - COAL PRODUCTION - See GREECE - MINING AND MINERAL PRODUCTS

GREECE - COBALT PRODUCTION AND CONSUMPTION - See GREECE - MINING AND MINERAL PRODUCTS

GREECE - COCOA (BEANS) PRODUCTION - See GREECE - CROPS

GREECE - COFFEE - See GREECE - CROPS

GREECE - COKE OVEN COKE AND COKE OVEN ORE PRODUCTION AND CONSUMPTION - See GREECE - MINING AND MINERAL PRODUCTS

GREECE - COKE PRODUCTION AND CONSUMPTION - See GREECE - MINING AND MINERAL PRODUCTS

GREECE - COMMUNICATIONS

European Community Information Service, 2100 M Street, NW, Washington, D.C. 20037 (202) 862-9500; *Basic Statistics of the Community* and *Transport Annual Statistics.*

Federal Statistical Office, Gustav - Stresemann - Ring 11, D-6200 Wiesbaden, Germany; *Griechenland.*

G.K. Hall and Company, 70 Lincoln Street, Boston, Massachusetts 02111 (617) 423-3990; *The World in Figures.*

GREECE - CONSTRUCTION INDUSTRY

European Community Information Service, 2100 M Street, NW, Washington, D.C. 20037 (202) 862-9500; *Basic Statistics of the Community,* and *Labor Force Sample Survey.*

Facts on File, 460 Park Avenue South, New York, New York 10016 (800) 443-8323; *The New Book of World Rankings.*

Organisation for Economic Co-operation and Development (OECD), 2 rue Andre-Pascal, 75 Paris 16, France (Telephone Number in U.S. (202) 785-6323); *Industrial Structure Statistics, The Iron and Steel Industry, Main Economic Indicators - Historical Statistics,* and *OECD Economic Surveys: Greece.*

Statistical Office of the United Nations, Publishing Service, New York, New York 10017; *Construction Statistics Yearbook,* and *Statistical Yearbook.*

GREECE - CONSUMER PRICE INDEX

European Community Information Service, 2100 M Street, NW, Washington, D.C. 20037 (202) 862-9500; *Basic Statistics of the Community.*

Federal Statistical Office, Gustav - Stresemann - Ring 11, D-6200 Wiesbaden, Germany; *Griechenland.*

G.K. Hall and Company, 70 Lincoln Street, Boston, Massachusetts 02111 (617) 423-3990; *The World in Figures.*

International Labour Office, I.L.O. Publications, CH-1211, Geneva 22, Switzerland; *Yearbook of Labour Statistics.*

Organisation for Economic Co-operation and Development (OECD), 2 rue Andre-Pascal, 75 Paris 16, France (Telephone Number in U.S. (202) 785-6323); *Economic Outlook.*

Statistical Office of the United Nations, Publishing Service, New York, New York 10017 (800) 253-9646; *Statistical Yearbook.*

GREECE - CONSUMER PRICES

Euromonitor Publications Limited, 87-88 Turnmill Street, London EC1M 5QU, England; *European Marketing Data and Statistics.*

European Community Information Service, 2100 M Street, NW, Washington, D.C. 20037 (202) 862-9500; *Basic Statistics of the*

Community, Eurostatistics: Data for Short-Term Economic Analysis, and *Money and Finance.*

Federal Statistical Office, Gustav - Stresemann - Ring 11, D-6200 Wiesbaden, Germany; *Griechenland.*

International Labour Office, I.L.O. Publications, CH-1211, Geneva 22, Switzerland; *Yearbook of Labour Statistics.*

International Monetary Fund, 700 Nineteenth Street, NW, Washington, D.C. 20431 (202) 623-7000; *International Financial Statistics.*

Organisation for Economic Co-operation and Development (OECD), 2 rue Andre-Pascal, 75 Paris 16, France (Telephone Number in U.S. (202) 785-6323); *Economic Outlook.*

Times Books, 201 East 50th Street, New York, New York 10022 (212) 751-2600; *The Economist Book of Vital World Statistics.*

GREECE - CONSUMPTION

European Community Information Service, 2100 M Street, NW, Washington, D.C. 20037 (202) 862-9500; *Basic Statistics of the Community.*

G.K. Hall and Company, 70 Lincoln Street, Boston, Massachusetts 02111 (617) 423-3990; *The World in Figures.*

Organisation for Economic Co-operation and Development (OECD), 2 rue Andre-Pascal, 75 Paris 16, France (Telephone Number in U.S. (202) 785-6323); *The Footwear, Raw Hides and Skins, and Leather Industry in OECD Countries, The Iron and Steel Industry, Meat Balances in OECD Member Countries, The Non-Ferrous Metals Industry, The Pulp and Paper Industry,* and *Textile Industry in OECD Countries.*

GREECE - COPPER AND COPPER ORE - See GREECE - MINING AND MINERAL PRODUCTS

GREECE - CORN PRODUCTION - See GREECE - CROPS

GREECE - CORPORATE INCOME TAXES - See GREECE - TAXATION

GREECE - CORPORATE TAXES - See GREECE - TAXATION

GREECE - COTTON PRODUCTION - See GREECE - CROPS

GREECE - CRIME

International Criminal Police Organization (INTERPOL), 26 rue Armengaud, 92210 Saint Cloud, France; *International Crime Statistics.*

Yale University Press, Yale Station, New Haven, Connecticut 06520 (203) 432-0940; *Violence and Crime in Cross-National Perspective.*

GREECE - CROPS

Commodity Research Bureau, Incorporated, 75 Wall Street, New York, New York 10005; *Commodity Year Book.*

Euromonitor Publications Limited, 87-88 Turnmill Street, London EC1M 5QU, England; *European Marketing Data and Statistics.*

European Community Information Service, 2100 M Street, NW, Washington, D.C. 20037 (202) 862-9500; *ACP: Basic Statistics, Agriculture: Statistical Yearbook, Basic Statistics of the Community, Crop Production: Quarterly Statistics, Eurostatistics: Data for Short-Term Economic Analysis,* and *Regions: Statistical Yearbook.*

Facts on File, 460 Park Avenue South, New York, New York 10016 (800) 443-8323; *The New Book of World Rankings.*

Food and Agricultural Organization of the United Nations (FAO), Via delle Terme di Caracalla, 00100 Rome, Italy (Telephone Number in U.S. (202) 653-2400); *Production Yearbook* and *The State of Food and Agriculture.*

G.K. Hall and Company, 70 Lincoln Street, Boston, Massachusetts 02111 (617) 423-3990; *The World in Figures.*

Organisation for Economic Co-operation and Development (OECD), 2 rue Andre-Pascal, 75 Paris 16, France (Telephone Number in U.S. (202) 785-6323); *Economic Accounts for Agriculture, Foreign Trade by Commodities,* and *Textile Industry in OECD Countries.*

Statistical Office of the United Nations, Publishing Service, New York, New York 10017 (800) 253-9646; *Statistical Yearbook.*

GREECE - CUSTOMS DUTIES

European Community Information Service, 2100 M Street, NW, Washington, D.C. 20037 (202) 862-9500; *Basic Statistics of the Community.*

G.K. Hall and Company, 70 Lincoln Street, Boston, Massachusetts 02111 (617) 423-3990; *The World in Figures.*

International Monetary Fund, 700 Nineteenth Street, NW, Washington, D.C. 20431 (202) 623-7000; *Government Finance Statistics Yearbook.*

Organisation for Economic Co-operation and Development (OECD), 2 rue Andre-Pascal, 75 Paris 16, France (Telephone Number in U.S. (202) 785-6323); *The Non-Ferrous Metals Industry.*

GREECE - DAIRY PRODUCTS

European Community Information Service, 2100 M Street, NW, Washington, D.C. 20037 (202) 862-9500; *Basic Statistics of the Community* and *Eurostatistics: Data for Short-Term Economic Analysis.*

Facts on File, 460 Park Avenue South, New York, New York 10016 (800) 443-8323; *The New Book of World Rankings.*

Food and Agricultural Organization of the United Nations (FAO), Via delle Terme di Caracalla, 00100 Rome, Italy (Telephone Number in U.S. (202) 653-2400); *Production Yearbook* and *The State of Food and Agriculture.*

Organisation for Economic Co-operation and Development (OECD), 2 rue Andre-Pascal, 75 Paris 16, France (Telephone Number in U.S. (202) 785-6323); *Economic Accounts for Agriculture,* and *Milk, Milk Products, and Egg Balances in OECD Member Countries.*

Statistical Office of the United Nations, Publishing Service, New York, New York 10017 (800) 253-9646; *Statistical Yearbook.*

GREECE - DEATH RATE

European Community Information Service, 2100 M Street, NW, Washington, D.C. 20037 (202) 862-9500; *Basic Statistics of the Community* and *Demographic Statistics.*

G.K. Hall and Company, 70 Lincoln Street, Boston, Massachusetts 02111 (617) 423-3990; *The World in Figures*.

Statistical Office of the United Nations, Publishing Service, New York, New York 10017 (800) 253-9646; *Statistical Yearbook*.

Times Books, 201 East 50th Street, New York, New York 10022 (212) 751-2600; *The Economist Book of Vital World Statistics*.

World Health Organization, Office of Publications, Avenue Appia, CH-1211 Geneva 27, Switzerland (Telephone Number in U.S. (518) 436-9686); *World Health Statistics Annual*.

GREECE - DEFENSE EXPENDITURES

European Community Information Service, 2100 M Street, NW, Washington, D.C. 20037 (202) 862-9500; *Government Financing of Research and Development*.

G.K. Hall and Company, 70 Lincoln Street, Boston, Massachusetts 02111 (617) 423-3990; *The World in Figures*.

International Monetary Fund, 700 Nineteenth Street, NW, Washington, D.C. 20431 (202) 623-7000; *Government Finance Statistics Yearbook*.

U.S. Arms Control and Disarmament Agency, 320 Twenty-first Street, Northwest, Washington, D.C. 20451 (202) 647-8677; *World Military Expenditures and Arms Transfers*.

GREECE - DEMOGRAPHY

The Economist Intelligence Unit, 111 West 57th Street, New York, New York 10019 (800) 938-4685; *The World Market Atlas*.

European Community Information Service, 2100 M Street, NW, Washington, D.C. 20037 (202) 862-9500; *Basic Statistics of the Community, Demographic Statistics, Employment and Unemployment*, and *Regions: Statistical Yearbook*.

Facts on File, 460 Park Avenue South, New York, New York 10016 (800) 443-8323; *The New Book of World Rankings*.

Federal Statistical Office, Gustav - Stresemann - Ring 11, D-6200 Wiesbaden, Germany; *Griechenland*.

G.K. Hall and Company, 70 Lincoln Street, Boston, Massachusetts 02111 (617) 423-3990; *The World in Figures*.

GREECE - DEVELOPMENT ASSISTANCE

European Community Information Service, 2100 M Street, NW, Washington, D.C. 20037 (202) 862-9500; *ACP: Basic Statistics, Basic Statistics of the Community*, and *Government Financing of Research and Development*.

G.K. Hall and Company, 70 Lincoln Street, Boston, Massachusetts 02111 (617) 423-3990; *The World in Figures*.

Organisation for Economic Co-operation and Development (OECD), 2 rue Andre-Pascal, 75 Paris 16, France (Telephone Number in U.S. (202) 785-6323); *Geographical Distribution of Financial Flows to Developing Countries*.

GREECE - DIAMOND - See GREECE - MINING AND MINERAL PRODUCTS

GREECE - DISCOUNT RATES

Organisation for Economic Co-operation and Development (OECD), 2 rue Andre-Pascal, 75 Paris 16, France (Telephone Number in U.S. (202) 785-6323); *Financial Market Trends*.

Statistical Office of the United Nations, Publishing Service, New York, New York 10017 (800) 253-9646; *Statistical Yearbook*.

GREECE - DISEASES

G.K. Hall and Company, 70 Lincoln Street, Boston, Massachusetts 02111 (617) 423-3990; *The World in Figures*.

World Health Organization, Office of Publications, Avenue Appia, CH-1211 Geneva 27, Switzerland (Telephone Number in U.S. (518) 436-9686); *World Health Statistics Annual*.

GREECE - DIVORCE RATES

European Community Information Service, 2100 M Street, NW, Washington, D.C. 20037 (202) 862-9500; *Demographic Statistics*.

Facts on File, 460 Park Avenue South, New York, New York 10016 (800) 443-8323; *The New Book of World Rankings*.

Statistical Office of the United Nations, Publishing Service, New York, New York 10017 (800) 253-9646; *Demographic Yearbook, Statistical Yearbook*.

GREECE - DOMESTIC PRODUCT

European Community Information Service, 2100 M Street, NW, Washington, D.C. 20037 (202) 862-9500; *Basic Statistics of the Community*.

G.K. Hall and Company, 70 Lincoln Street, Boston, Massachusetts 02111 (617) 423-3990; *The World in Figures*.

GREECE - DUCKS - See GREECE - LIVESTOCK AND POULTRY

GREECE - ECONOMY

Euromonitor Publications Limited, 87-88 Turnmill Street, London EC1M 5QU, England; *European Marketing Data and Statistics*.

European Community Information Service, 2100 M Street, NW, Washington, D.C. 20037 (202) 862-9500; *ACP: Basic Statistics, Basic Statistics of the Community, Energy Statistics Yearbook, Labor Force Sample Survey*, and *Money and Finance*.

Facts on File, 460 Park Avenue South, New York, New York 10016 (800) 443-8323; *The New Book of World Rankings*.

Federal Statistical Office, Gustav - Stresemann - Ring 11, D-6200 Wiesbaden, Germany; *Griechenland*.

G.K. Hall and Company, 70 Lincoln Street, Boston, Massachusetts 02111 (617) 423-3990; *The World in Figures*.

Organisation for Economic Co-operation and Development (OECD), 2 rue Andre-Pascal, 75 Paris 16, France (Telephone Number in U.S. (202) 785-6323); *Economic Outlook, Geographical Distribution of Financial Flows to Developing Countries, Main Economic Indicators Historical Statistics, OECD Economic Surveys: Greece*, and *OECD Employment Outlook*.

GREECE - EDUCATION

The Economist Intelligence Unit, 111 West 57th Street, New York, New York 10019 (800) 938-4685; *The World Market Atlas.*

Euromonitor Publications Limited, 87-88 Turnmill Street, London EC1M 5QU, England; *European Marketing Data and Statistics.*

European Community Information Service, 2100 M Street, NW, Washington, D.C. 20037 (202) 862-9500; *Basic Statistics of the Community* and *Regions: Statistical Yearbook.*

Facts on File, 460 Park Avenue South, New York, New York 10016 (800) 443-8323; *The New Book of World Rankings.*

Federal Statistical Office, Gustav - Stresemann - Ring 11, D-6200 Wiesbaden, Germany; *Griechenland.*

G.K. Hall and Company, 70 Lincoln Street, Boston, Massachusetts 02111 (617) 423-3990; *The World in Figures.*

International Monetary Fund, 700 Nineteenth Street, NW, Washington, D.C. 20431 (202) 623-7000; *Government Finance Statistics Yearbook.*

Organisation for Economic Co-operation and Development (OECD), 2 rue Andre-Pascal, 75 Paris 16, France (Telephone Number in U.S. (202) 785-6323); *Education in OECD Countries.*

Times Books, 201 East 50th Street, New York, New York 10022 (212) 751-2600; *The Economist Book of Vital World Statistics.*

United Nations Educational, Scientific and Cultural Organization (UNESCO), 7 Place de Fontenoy, F-75700 Paris, France (Telephone Number in U.S. (212) 963-5981); *Statistical Yearbook.*

The World Bank, 1818 H Street, NW, Washington, D.C. 20433 (202) 477-1234; *World Tables.*

GREECE - EGG PRODUCTION AND CONSUMPTION - See GREECE - DAIRY PRODUCTS

GREECE - EGGPLANT PRODUCTION - See GREECE - CROPS

GREECE - ELECTRICITY

European Community Information Service, 2100 M Street, NW, Washington, D.C. 20037 (202) 862-9500; *Basic Statistics of the Community, Energy: Monthly Statistics, Energy Statistics Yearbook, Eurostatistics: Data for Short-Term Economic Analysis,* and *Regions: Statistical Yearbook.*

Facts on File, 460 Park Avenue South, New York, New York 10016 (800) 443-8323; *The New Book of World Rankings.*

Organisation for Economic Co-operation and Development (OECD), 2 rue Andre-Pascal, 75 Paris 16, France (Telephone Number in U.S. (202) 785-6323); *Coal Information, Energy Statistics of OECD Countries,* and *Industrial Structure Statistics.*

Penn Well Publishing Company, 1421 South Sheridan Road, Post Office Box 1260, Tulsa, Oklahoma 74101 (800) 752-9764; *International Energy Statistics Sourcebook.*

Statistical Office of the United Nations, Publishing Service, New York, New York 10017 (800) 253-9646; *Statistical Yearbook.*

Times Books, 201 East 50th Street, New York, New York 10022 (212) 751-2600; *The Economist Book of Vital World Statistics.*

GREECE - EMPLOYMENT

Euromonitor Publications Limited, 87-88 Turnmill Street, London EC1M 5QU, England; *European Marketing Data and Statistics.*

European Community Information Service, 2100 M Street, NW, Washington, D.C. 20037 (202) 862-9500; *Basic Statistics of the Community, Earnings in Agriculture, Employment and Unemployment, Eurostatistics: Data for Short-Term Economic Analysis, Iron and Steel: Statistical Yearbook, Labor Force Sample Survey,* and *Transport Annual Statistics.*

Facts on File, 460 Park Avenue South, New York, New York 10016 (800) 443-8323; *The New Book of World Rankings.*

Federal Statistical Office, Gustav - Stresemann - Ring 11, D-6200 Wiesbaden, Germany; *Griechenland.*

International Labour Office, I.L.O. Publications, CH-1211, Geneva 22, Switzerland; *Yearbook of Labour Statistics.*

Organisation for Economic Co-operation and Development (OECD), 2 rue Andre-Pascal, 75 Paris 16, France (Telephone Number in U.S. (202) 785-6323); *Economic Outlook, The Iron and Steel Industry, OECD Economic Surveys: Greece, OECD Employment Outlook,* and *Textile Industry in OECD Countries.*

Statistical Office of the United Nations, Publishing Service, New York, New York 10017 (800) 253-9646; *Statistical Yearbook.*

GREECE - ENERGY

Euromonitor Publications Limited, 87-88 Turnmill Street, London EC1M 5QU, England; *European Marketing Data and Statistics.*

European Community Information Service, 2100 M Street, NW, Washington, D.C. 20037 (202) 862-9500; *Basic Statistics of the Community, Energy: Monthly Statistics, Energy Statistics Yearbook, Regions: Statistical Yearbook,* and *Transport Annual Statistics.*

Facts on File, 460 Park Avenue South, New York, New York 10016 (800) 443-8323; *The New Book of World Rankings.*

Food and Agricultural Organization of the United Nations (FAO) Via delle Terme di Caracalla, 00100 Rome, Italy (Telephone Number in U.S. (202) 653-2400); *The State of Food and Agriculture.*

G.K. Hall and Company, 70 Lincoln Street, Boston, Massachusetts 02111 (617) 423-3990; *The World in Figures.*

Organisation for Economic Co-operation and Development (OECD), 2 rue Andre-Pascal, 75 Paris 16, France (Telephone Number in U.S. (202) 785-6323); *Coal Information, Energy Statistics of OECD Countries, OECD Environmental Data,* and *Oil and Gas Information.*

Penn Well Publishing Company, 1421 South Sheridan Road, Post Office Box 1260, Tulsa, Oklahoma 74101 (800) 752-9764; *International Energy Statistics Sourcebook.*

Statistical Office of the United Nations, Publishing Service, New York, New York 10017 (800) 253-9646; *Energy Statistics Yearbook,* and *Statistical Yearbook.*

Times Books, 201 East 50th Street, New York, New York 10022 (212) 751-2600; *The Economist Book of Vital World Statistics.*

GREECE - ENGINEERING AND METAL PRODUCTS - EXPORTS AND IMPORTS

European Community Information Service, 2100 M Street, NW, Washington, D.C. 20037 (202) 862-9500; *Basic Statistics of the Community* and *Industrial Production: Quarterly Statistics.*

GREECE - ENVIRONMENT

Organisation for Economic Co-operation and Development (OECD), 2 rue Andre-Pascal, 75 Paris 16, France (Telephone Number in U.S. (202) 785-6323); *OECD Environmental Data.*

GREECE - EXCHANGE RATES

European Community Information Service, 2100 M Street, NW, Washington, D.C. 20037 (202) 862-9500; *Eurostatistics: Data for Short-Term Economic Analysis* and *Money and Finance.*

International Civil Aviation Organization, 1000 Sherbrooke Street West, Suite 400, Montreal, Quebec, Canada H3A 2R2 (514) 285-8219; *Civil Aviation Statistics of the World.*

International Monetary Fund, 700 Nineteenth Street, NW, Washington, D.C. 20431 (202) 623-7000; *International Financial Statistics.*

Organisation for Economic Co-operation and Development (OECD), 2 rue Andre-Pascal, 75 Paris 16, France (Telephone Number in U.S. (202) 785-6323); *Economic Outlook, Financial Market Trends, Revenue Statistics of OECD Member Countries,* and *Tourism Policy and International Tourism in OECD Member Countries.*

Statistical Office of the United Nations, Publishing Service, New York, New York 10017 (800) 253-9646; *Statistical Yearbook.*

GREECE - EXCISE TAXES - See GREECE - TAXATION

GREECE - EXPORTS

American Automobile Manufacturers Association, 1401 H Street, NW, Suite 900, Washington, D.C. 20005 (202) 326-5500; *World Motor Vehicle Data.*

The Economist Intelligence Unit, 111 West 57th Street, New York, New York 10019 (800) 938-4685; *The World Market Atlas.*

European Community Information Service, 2100 M Street, NW, Washington, D.C. 20037 (202) 862-9500; *Basic Statistics of the Community, Energy: Monthly Statistics, Energy Statistics Yearbook, Eurostatistics: Data for Short-Term Economic Analysis, External Trade: Monthly Statistics, External Trade: Statistical Yearbook,* and *Fisheries: Yearly Statistics.*

Food and Agricultural Organization of the United Nations (FAO) Via delle Terme di Caracalla, 00100 Rome, Italy (Telephone Number in U.S. (202) 653-2400); *The State of Food and Agriculture.*

G.K. Hall and Company, 70 Lincoln Street, Boston, Massachusetts 02111 (617) 423-3990; *The World in Figures.*

International Monetary Fund, 700 Nineteenth Street, NW, Washington, D.C. 20431 (202) 623-7000; *Direction of Trade Statistics, Government Finance Statistics Yearbook,* and *International Financial Statistics.*

Organisation for Economic Co-operation and Development (OECD), 2 rue Andre-Pascal, 75 Paris 16, France (Telephone Number in U.S. (202) 785-6323); *Economic Outlook, The Footwear, Raw Hides and Skins, and Leather Industry in OECD Countries, Foreign Trade by Commodities, Geographical Distribution of Financial Flows to Developing Countries, Industrial Structure Statistics, The Iron and Steel Industry, Milk, Milk Products, and Egg Balances in OECD Member Countries, OECD Economic Surveys: Greece, The Pulp and Paper Industry,* and *Review of Fisheries in OECD Member Countries.*

Times Books, 201 East 50th Street, New York, New York 10022 (212) 751-2600; *The Economist Book of Vital World Statistics.*

The World Bank, 1818 H Street, NW, Washington, D.C. 20433 (202) 477-1234; *World Tables.*

GREECE - EXTERNAL FINANCING

Organisation for Economic Co-operation and Development (OECD), 2 rue Andre-Pascal, 75 Paris 16, France (Telephone Number in U.S. (202) 785-6323); *Economic Outlook,* and *Financial Market Trends.*

GREECE - EXTERNAL INDEBTEDNESS

Organisation for Economic Co-operation and Development (OECD), 2 rue Andre-Pascal, 75 Paris 16, France (Telephone Number in U.S. (202) 785-6323); *Financial Market Trends,* and *Geographical Distribution of Financial Flows to Developing Countries.*

The World Bank, 1818 H Street, NW, Washington, D.C. 20433 (202) 477-1234; *World Tables.*

GREECE - EXTERNAL TRADE

European Community Information Service, 2100 M Street, NW, Washington, D.C. 20037 (202) 862-9500; *ACP: Basic Statistics, Basic Statistics of the Community, Eurostatistics: Data for Short-Term Economic Analysis,* and *External Trade: Monthly Statistics,* and *External Trade: Statistical Yearbook.*

Food and Agricultural Organization of the United Nations (FAO) Via delle Terme di Caracalla, 00100 Rome, Italy (Telephone Number in U.S. (202) 653-2400); *The State of Food and Agriculture,* and *Trade Yearbook.*

G.K. Hall and Company, 70 Lincoln Street, Boston, Massachusetts 02111 (617) 423-3990; *The World in Figures.*

Statistical Office of the United Nations, Publishing Service, New York, New York 10017 (800) 253-9646; *Statistical Yearbook.*

GREECE - FABRIC PRODUCTION - See GREECE - TEXTILE INDUSTRY

GREECE - FARM CROPS - See GREECE - CROPS

GREECE - FEMALE WORKING POPULATION - See GREECE - ECONOMY

GREECE - FERTILITY RATES

European Community Information Service, 2100 M Street, NW, Washington, D.C. 20037 (202) 862-9500; *Demographic Statistics.*

Facts on File, 460 Park Avenue South, New York, New York 10016 (800) 443-8323; *The New Book of World Rankings.*

Times Books, 201 East 50th Street, New York, New York 10022 (212) 751-2600; *The Economist Book of Vital World Statistics.*

The World Bank, 1818 H Street, NW, Washington, D.C. 20433 (202) 477-1234; *World Tables.*

GREECE - FERTILIZER

European Community Information Service, 2100 M Street, NW, Washington, D.C. 20037 (202) 862-9500; *Basic Statistics of the Community*.

Food and Agricultural Organization of the United Nations (FAO) Via delle Terme di Caracalla, 00100 Rome, Italy (Telephone Number in U.S. (202) 653-2400); *The State of Food and Agriculture*.

Organisation for Economic Co-operation and Development (OECD), 2 rue Andre-Pascal, 75 Paris 16, France (Telephone Number in U.S. (202) 785-6323); *Economic Accounts for Agriculture*, and *Foreign Trade by Commodities*.

Statistical Office of the United Nations, Publishing Service, New York, New York 10017 (800) 253-9646; *Statistical Yearbook*.

GREECE - FETAL MORTALITY

European Community Information Service, 2100 M Street, NW, Washington, D.C. 20037 (202) 862-9500; *Basic Statistics of the Community* and *Demographic Statistics*.

Statistical Office of the United Nations, Publishing Service, New York, New York 10017 (800) 253-9646; *Demographic Yearbook*.

World Health Organization, Office of Publications, Avenue Appia, CH-1211 Geneva 27, Switzerland (Telephone Number in U.S. (518) 436-9686); *World Health Statistics Annual*.

GREECE - FIBRE PRODUCTION - See GREECE - TEXTILE INDUSTRY

GREECE - FILAMENT PRODUCTION - See GREECE - TEXTILE INDUSTRY

GREECE - FILM - See GREECE - MOTION PICTURES

GREECE - FINANCE

European Community Information Service, 2100 M Street, NW, Washington, D.C. 20037 (202) 862-9500; *ACP: Basic Statistics*, *Basic Statistics of the Community*, *Eurostatistics: Data for Short-Term Economic Analysis*, and *Money and Finance*.

Facts on File, 460 Park Avenue South, New York, New York 10016 (800) 443-8323; *The New Book of World Rankings*.

Federal Statistical Office, Gustav - Stresemann - Ring 11, D-6200 Wiesbaden, Germany; *Griechenland*.

G.K. Hall and Company, 70 Lincoln Street, Boston, Massachusetts 02111 (617) 423-3990; *The World in Figures*.

International Monetary Fund, 700 Nineteenth Street, NW, Washington, D.C. 20431 (202) 623-7000; *Government Finance Statistics Yearbook*.

Organisation for Economic Co-operation and Development (OECD), 2 rue Andre-Pascal, 75 Paris 16, France (Telephone Number in U.S. (202) 785-6323); *Economic Outlook*, *Financial Market Trends*, *Geographical Distribution of Financial Flows to Developing Countries*, and *OECD Financial Statistics*.

GREECE - FISHERIES

Euromonitor Publications Limited, 87-88 Turnmill Street, London EC1M 5QU, England; *European Marketing Data and Statistics*.

European Community Information Service, 2100 M Street, NW, Washington, D.C. 20037 (202) 862-9500; *Agriculture: Statistical Yearbook*, *Basic Statistics of the Community* and *Fisheries: Yearly Statistics*.

Facts on File, 460 Park Avenue South, New York, New York 10016 (800) 443-8323; *The New Book of World Rankings*.

Federal Statistical Office, Gustav - Stresemann - Ring 11, D-6200 Wiesbaden, Germany; *Griechenland*.

Food and Agricultural Organization of the United Nations (FAO) Via delle Terme di Caracalla, 00100 Rome, Italy (Telephone Number in U.S. (202) 653-2400); *The State of Food and Agriculture*, and *Yearbook of Fishery Statistics*.

Organisation for Economic Co-operation and Development (OECD), 2 rue Andre-Pascal, 75 Paris 16, France (Telephone Number in U.S. (202) 785-6323); *Foreign Trade by Commodities*, *Industrial Structure Statistics*, and *Review of Fisheries in OECD Member Countries*.

Statistical Office of the United Nations, Publishing Service, New York, New York 10017 (800) 253-9646; *Statistical Yearbook*.

GREECE - FLAX FIBRE PRODUCTION - See GREECE - TEXTILE INDUSTRY

GREECE - FLAX PRODUCTION - See GREECE - TEXTILE INDUSTRY

GREECE - FLOUR PRODUCTION

European Community Information Service, 2100 M Street, NW, Washington, D.C. 20037 (202) 862-9500; *Basic Statistics of the Community*.

Statistical Office of the United Nations, Publishing Service, New York, New York 10017 (800) 253-9646; *Statistical Yearbook*.

GREECE - FOOD

European Community Information Service, 2100 M Street, NW, Washington, D.C. 20037 (202) 862-9500; *Basic Statistics of the Community*.

Food and Agricultural Organization of the United Nations (FAO), Via delle Terme di Caracalla, 00100 Rome, Italy (Telephone Number in U.S. (202) 653-2400); *Production Yearbook*, and *The State of Food and Agriculture*.

G.K. Hall and Company, 70 Lincoln Street, Boston, Massachusetts 02111 (617) 423-3990; *The World in Figures*.

Organisation for Economic Co-operation and Development (OECD), 2 rue Andre-Pascal, 75 Paris 16, France (Telephone Number in U.S. (202) 785-6323); *Foreign Trade by Commodities*.

GREECE - FOREIGN AID

G.K. Hall and Company, 70 Lincoln Street, Boston, Massachusetts 02111 (617) 423-3990; *The World in Figures*.

GREECE - FOREIGN DEBT

International Monetary Fund, 700 Nineteenth Street, NW, Washington, D.C. 20431 (202) 623-7000; *Government Finance Statistics Yearbook*.

Organisation for Economic Co-operation and Development (OECD), 2 rue Andre-Pascal, 75 Paris 16, France (Telephone Number in U.S.

(202) 785-6323); *Economic Outlook.*

GREECE - FOREIGN FINANCE

Organisation for Economic Co-operation and Development (OECD), 2 rue Andre-Pascal, 75 Paris 16, France (Telephone Number in U.S. (202) 785-6323); *Economic Outlook, Financial Market Trends,* and *Main Economic Indicators - Historical Statistics.*

GREECE - FOREIGN INDEBTEDNESS

Organisation for Economic Co-operation and Development (OECD), 2 rue Andre-Pascal, 75 Paris 16, France (Telephone Number in U.S. (202) 785-6323); *Economic Outlook,* and *Financial Market Trends.*

GREECE - FOREIGN OFFICIAL RESERVES

European Community Information Service, 2100 M Street, NW, Washington, D.C. 20037 (202) 862-9500; *Money and Finance.*

GREECE - FOREIGN TRADE

Euromonitor Publications Limited, 87-88 Turnmill Street, London EC1M 5QU, England; *European Marketing Data and Statistics.*

European Community Information Service, 2100 M Street, NW, Washington, D.C. 20037 (202) 862-9500; *Basic Statistics of the Community, Energy Statistics Yearbook,* and *Iron and Steel: Statistical Yearbook.*

Facts on File, 460 Park Avenue South, New York, New York 10016 (800) 443-8323; *The New Book of World Rankings.*

Federal Statistical Office, Gustav - Stresemann - Ring 11, D-6200 Wiesbaden, Germany; *Griechenland.*

Food and Agricultural Organization of the United Nations (FAO) Via delle Terme di Caracalla, 00100 Rome, Italy (Telephone Number in U.S. (202) 653-2400); *The State of Food and Agriculture.*

G.K. Hall and Company, 70 Lincoln Street, Boston, Massachusetts 02111 (617) 423-3990; *The World in Figures.*

International Monetary Fund, 700 Nineteenth Street, NW, Washington, D.C. 20431 (202) 623-7000; *International Financial Statistics.*

Organisation for Economic Co-operation and Development (OECD), 2 rue Andre-Pascal, 75 Paris 16, France (Telephone Number in U.S. (202) 785-6323); *Economic Outlook, The Footwear, Raw Hides and Skins, and Leather Industry in OECD Countries, Foreign Trade by Commodities, Main Economic Indicators - Historical Statistics, Maritime Transport, Meat Balances in OECD Member Countries,* and *OECD Economic Surveys: Greece.*

Statistical Office of the United Nations, Publishing Service, New York, New York 10017 (800) 253-9646; *International Trade Statistics Yearbook,* and *Statistical Yearbook.*

The World Bank, 1818 H Street, NW, Washington, D.C. 20433 (202) 477-1234; *World Tables.*

GREECE - FORESTRY AND FOREST PRODUCTS

Euromonitor Publications Limited, 87-88 Turnmill Street, London EC1M 5QU, England; *European Marketing Data and Statistics.*

European Community Information Service, 2100 M Street, NW, Washington, D.C. 20037 (202) 862-9500; *Agriculture: Statistical Yearbook, Basic Statistics of the Community* and *Industrial Production: Quarterly Statistics.*

Facts on File, 460 Park Avenue South, New York, New York 10016 (800) 443-8323; *The New Book of World Rankings.*

Federal Statistical Office, Gustav - Stresemann - Ring 11, D-6200 Wiesbaden, Germany; *Griechenland.*

Food and Agricultural Organization of the United Nations (FAO) Via delle Terme di Caracalla, 00100 Rome, Italy (Telephone Number in U.S. (202) 653-2400); *The State of Food and Agriculture,* and *Yearbook of Forest Products.*

Forest and Paper Association, 1250 Connecticut Avenue, NW, Washington, D.C. 20036 (202) 463-2455; *Wood Pulp and Fiber Statistics.*

G.K. Hall and Company, 70 Lincoln Street, Boston, Massachusetts 02111 (617) 423-3990; *The World in Figures.*

Organisation for Economic Co-operation and Development (OECD), 2 rue Andre-Pascal, 75 Paris 16, France (Telephone Number in U.S. (202) 785-6323); *Foreign Trade by Commodities, Industrial Structure Statistics,* and *The Pulp and Paper Industry.*

Statistical Office of the United Nations, Publishing Service, New York, New York 10017; *Statistical Yearbook.*

United Nations Educational, Scientific and Cultural Organization (UNESCO), 7 Place de Fontenoy, F-75700 Paris, France (Telephone Number in U.S. (212) 963-5981); *Statistical Yearbook.*

GREECE - FRUIT PRODUCTION - See GREECE - CROPS

GREECE - FURNITURE AND WOOD PRODUCTS - EXPORTS AND IMPORTS

European Community Information Service, 2100 M Street, NW, Washington, D.C. 20037 (202) 862-9500; *Basic Statistics of the Community.*

Organisation for Economic Co-operation and Development (OECD), 2 rue Andre-Pascal, 75 Paris 16, France (Telephone Number in U.S. (202) 785-6323); *Foreign Trade by Commodities,* and *Industrial Structure Statistics.*

GREECE - GARLIC PRODUCTION - See GREECE - CROPS

GREECE - GAS - See GREECE - MINING AND MINERAL PRODUCTS

GREECE - GENERAL INDUSTRIAL STATISTICS

European Community Information Service, 2100 M Street, NW, Washington, D.C. 20037 (202) 862-9500; *Basic Statistics of the Community.*

Federal Statistical Office, Gustav - Stresemann - Ring 11, D-6200 Wiesbaden, Germany; *Griechenland.*

Statistical Office of the United Nations, Publishing Service, New York, New York 10017 (800) 253-9646; *Industrial Statistics Yearbook.*

GREECE - GENERAL MORTALITY

European Community Information Service, 2100 M Street, NW, Washington, D.C. 20037 (202) 862-9500; *Basic Statistics of the Community* and *Demographic Statistics.*

Statistical Office of the United Nations, Publishing Service, New York, New York 10017 (800) 253-9646; *Demographic Yearbook.*

World Health Organization, Office of Publications, Avenue Appia, CH-1211 Geneva 27, Switzerland (Telephone Number in U.S. (518) 436-9686); *World Health Statistics Annual.*

GREECE - GEOGRAPHIC DATA

European Community Information Service, 2100 M Street, NW, Washington, D.C. 20037 (202) 862-9500; *Basic Statistics of the Community.*

Facts on File, 460 Park Avenue South, New York, New York 10016 (800) 443-8323; *The New Book of World Rankings.*

Federal Statistical Office, Gustav - Stresemann - Ring 11, D-6200 Wiesbaden, Germany; *Griechenland.*

GREECE - GOATS - See GREECE - LIVESTOCK AND POULTRY

GREECE - GOLD HOLDINGS

International Monetary Fund, 700 Nineteenth Street, NW, Washington, D.C. 20431 (202) 623-7000; *International Financial Statistics.*

Statistical Office of the United Nations, Publishing Service, New York, New York 10017 (800) 253-9646; *Statistical Yearbook.*

The World Bank, 1818 H Street, NW, Washington, D.C. 20433 (202) 477-1234; *World Tables.*

GREECE - GOLD PRODUCTION AND CONSUMPTION - See GREECE - MINING AND MINERAL PRODUCTS

GREECE - GOVERNMENT

European Community Information Service, 2100 M Street, NW, Washington, D.C. 20037 (202) 862-9500; *Basic Statistics of the Community.*

G.K. Hall and Company, 70 Lincoln Street, Boston, Massachusetts 02111 (617) 423-3990; *The World in Figures.*

GREECE - GOVERNMENT BONDS - See GREECE - BONDS

GREECE - GOVERNMENT CONSUMPTION

European Community Information Service, 2100 M Street, NW, Washington, D.C. 20037 (202) 862-9500; *Basic Statistics of the Community.*

GREECE - GOVERNMENT EXPENDITURES

European Community Information Service, 2100 M Street, NW, Washington, D.C. 20037 (202) 862-9500; *Basic Statistics of the Community* and *Government Financing of Research and Development.*

International Monetary Fund, 700 Nineteenth Street, NW, Washington, D.C. 20431 (202) 623-7000; *Government Finance Statistics Yearbook.*

Organisation for Economic Co-operation and Development (OECD), 2 rue Andre-Pascal, 75 Paris 16, France (Telephone Number in U.S. (202) 785-6323); *Economic Outlook.*

Times Books, 201 East 50th Street, New York, New York 10022 (212) 751-2600; *The Economist Book of Vital World Statistics.*

The World Bank, 1818 H Street, NW, Washington, D.C. 20433 (202) 477-1234; *World Tables.*

GREECE - GOVERNMENT FINANCES

European Community Information Service, 2100 M Street, NW, Washington, D.C. 20037 (202) 862-9500; *Basic Statistics of the Community, Government Financing of Research and Development,* and *Money and Finance.*

International Monetary Fund, 700 Nineteenth Street, NW, Washington, D.C. 20431 (202) 623-7000; *International Financial Statistics.*

Organisation for Economic Co-operation and Development (OECD), 2 rue Andre-Pascal, 75 Paris 16, France (Telephone Number in U.S. (202) 785-6323); *Economic Outlook.*

Statistical Office of the United Nations, Publishing Service, New York, New York 10017 (800) 253-9646; *Statistical Yearbook.*

GREECE - GOVERNMENT REVENUES

European Community Information Service, 2100 M Street, NW, Washington, D.C. 20037 (202) 862-9500; *Basic Statistics of the Community* and *Government Financing of Research and Development.*

International Monetary Fund, 700 Nineteenth Street, NW, Washington, D.C. 20431 (202) 623-7000; *Government Finance Statistics Yearbook.*

Organisation for Economic Co-operation and Development (OECD), 2 rue Andre-Pascal, 75 Paris 16, France (Telephone Number in U.S. (202) 785-6323); *Economic Outlook,* and *Revenue Statistics of OECD Member Countries.*

Times Books, 201 East 50th Street, New York, New York 10022 (212) 751-2600; *The Economist Book of Vital World Statistics.*

The World Bank, 1818 H Street, NW, Washington, D.C. 20433 (202) 477-1234; *World Tables.*

GREECE - GRAIN PRODUCTION - See GREECE - CROPS

GREECE - GRANTS

International Monetary Fund, 700 Nineteenth Street, NW, Washington, D.C. 20431 (202) 623-7000; *Government Finance Statistics Yearbook.*

Organisation for Economic Co-operation and Development (OECD), 2 rue Andre-Pascal, 75 Paris 16, France (Telephone Number in U.S. (202) 785-6323); *Geographical Distribution of Financial Flows to Developing Countries.*

GREECE - GREEN PEPPER AND CHILIE PRODUCTION - See GREECE - CROPS

GREECE - GROSS DOMESTIC PRODUCT

The Economist Intelligence Unit, 111 West 57th Street, New York, New York 10019 (800) 938-4685; *The World Market Atlas.*

European Community Information Service, 2100 M Street, NW, Washington, D.C. 20037 (202) 862-9500; *Basic Statistics of the*

Community, Eurostatistics: Data for Short-Term Economic Analysis, Government Financing of Research and Development, Iron and Steel: Statistical Yearbook, and *Money and Finance.*

Facts on File, 460 Park Avenue South, New York, New York 10016 (800) 443-8323; *The New Book of World Rankings.*

G.K. Hall and Company, 70 Lincoln Street, Boston, Massachusetts 02111 (617) 423-3990; *The World in Figures.*

Organisation for Economic Co-operation and Development (OECD), 2 rue Andre-Pascal, 75 Paris 16, France (Telephone Number in U.S. (202) 785-6323); *Economic Outlook, Geographical Distribution of Financial Flows to Developing Countries,* and *Revenue Statistics of OECD Member Countries.*

Statistical Office of the United Nations, Publishing Service, New York, New York 10017 (800) 253-9646; *Statistical Yearbook.*

Times Books, 201 East 50th Street, New York, New York 10022 (212) 751-2600; *The Economist Book of Vital World Statistics.*

The World Bank, 1818 H Street, NW, Washington, D.C. 20433 (202) 477-1234; *World Tables.*

GREECE - GROSS INDUSTRIAL PRODUCT

European Community Information Service, 2100 M Street, NW, Washington, D.C. 20037 (202) 862-9500; *Government Financing of Research and Development.*

GREECE - GROSS NATIONAL PRODUCT

European Community Information Service, 2100 M Street, NW, Washington, D.C. 20037 (202) 862-9500; *ACP: Basic Statistics,* and *Basic Statistics of the Community.*

Organisation for Economic Co-operation and Development (OECD), 2 rue Andre-Pascal, 75 Paris 16, France (Telephone Number in U.S. (202) 785-6323); *Economic Outlook,* and *Geographical Distribution of Financial Flows to Developing Countries.*

U.S. Arms Control and Disarmament Agency, 320 Twenty-first Street, Northwest, Washington, D.C. 20451 (202) 647-8677; *World Military Expenditures and Arms Transfers.*

The World Bank, 1818 H Street, NW, Washington, D.C. 20433 (202) 477-1234; *World Tables.*

GREECE - GROUNDNUTS PRODUCTION - See GREECE - CROPS

GREECE - HAY PRODUCTION - See GREECE - CROPS

GREECE - HAZELNUT PRODUCTION - See GREECE - CROPS

GREECE - HEALTH

European Community Information Service, 2100 M Street, NW, Washington, D.C. 20037 (202) 862-9500; *Basic Statistics of the Community* and *Regions: Statistical Yearbook.*

Facts on File, 460 Park Avenue South, New York, New York 10016 (800) 443-8323; *The New Book of World Rankings.*

Federal Statistical Office, Gustav - Stresemann - Ring 11, D-6200 Wiesbaden, Germany; *Griechenland.*

G.K. Hall and Company, 70 Lincoln Street, Boston, Massachusetts 02111 (617) 423-3990; *The World in Figures.*

Organisation for Economic Co-operation and Development (OECD), 2 rue Andre-Pascal, 75 Paris 16, France (Telephone Number in U.S. (202) 785-6323); *OECD Health Systems: Facts and Trends.*

Statistical Office of the United Nations, Publishing Service, New York, New York 10017 (800) 253-9646; *Statistical Yearbook.*

Times Books, 201 East 50th Street, New York, New York 10022 (212) 751-2600; *The Economist Book of Vital World Statistics.*

World Health Organization, Office of Publications, Avenue Appia, CH-1211 Geneva 27, Switzerland (Telephone Number in U.S. (518) 436-9686); *World Health Statistics Annual.*

GREECE - HEALTH EXPENDITURES

International Monetary Fund, 700 Nineteenth Street, NW, Washington, D.C. 20431 (202) 623-7000; *Government Finance Statistics Yearbook.*

GREECE - HEMP FIBRE PRODUCTION - See GREECE - TEXTILE INDUSTRY

GREECE - HIDE PRODUCTION

Food and Agricultural Organization of the United Nations (FAO), Via delle Terme di Caracalla, 00100 Rome, Italy (Telephone Number in U.S. (202) 653-2400); *Production Yearbook.*

Organisation for Economic Co-operation and Development (OECD), 2 rue Andre-Pascal, 75 Paris 16, France (Telephone Number in U.S. (202) 785-6323); *The Footwear, Raw Hides and Skins, and Leather Industry in OECD Countries,* and *Foreign Trade by Commodities.*

GREECE - HIGHWAYS

European Community Information Service, 2100 M Street, NW, Washington, D.C. 20037 (202) 862-9500; *Basic Statistics of the Community* and *Transport Annual Statistics.*

G.K. Hall and Company, 70 Lincoln Street, Boston, Massachusetts 02111 (617) 423-3990; *The World in Figures.*

International Road Federation, 525 School Street, SW, Washington, D.C. 20024 (202) 554-2106; *World Road Statistics.*

GREECE - HOPS PRODUCTION - See GREECE - CROPS

GREECE - HORSES - See GREECE - LIVESTOCK AND POULTRY

GREECE - HOURS OF WORK - See GREECE - EMPLOYMENT

GREECE - HOUSING AND HOUSING UNITS

European Community Information Service, 2100 M Street, NW, Washington, D.C. 20037 (202) 862-9500; *Basic Statistics of the Community, Labor Force Sample Survey,* and *Regions: Statistical Yearbook.*

Facts on File, 460 Park Avenue South, New York, New York 10016 (800) 443-8323; *The New Book of World Rankings.*

GREECE - HOUSING CONSTRUCTION - See GREECE - CONSTRUCTION INDUSTRY

GREECE - HOUSING EXPENDITURES

European Community Information Service, 2100 M Street, NW, Washington, D.C. 20037 (202) 862-9500; *Basic Statistics of the*

Community.

International Monetary Fund, 700 Nineteenth Street, NW, Washington, D.C. 20431 (202) 623-7000; *Government Finance Statistics Yearbook.*

GREECE - HYDROCHLORIC ACID PRODUCTION

European Community Information Service, 2100 M Street, NW, Washington, D.C. 20037 (202) 862-9500; *Basic Statistics of the Community.*

Statistical Office of the United Nations, Publishing Service, New York, New York 10017 (800) 253-9646; *Statistical Yearbook.*

GREECE - ILLITERATE POPULATION

The Economist Intelligence Unit, 111 West 57th Street, New York, New York 10019 (800) 938-4685; *The World Market Atlas.*

G.K. Hall and Company, 70 Lincoln Street, Boston, Massachusetts 02111 (617) 423-3990; *The World in Figures.*

United Nations Educational, Scientific and Cultural Organization (UNESCO), 7 Place de Fontenoy, F-75700 Paris, France (Telephone Number in U.S. (212) 963-5981); *Statistical Yearbook.*

GREECE - IMPORTS

American Automobile Manufacturers Association, 1401 H Street, NW, Suite 900, Washington, D.C. 20005 (202) 326-5500; *World Motor Vehicle Data.*

The Economist Intelligence Unit, 111 West 57th Street, New York, New York 10019 (800) 938-4685; *The World Market Atlas.*

European Community Information Service, 2100 M Street, NW, Washington, D.C. 20037 (202) 862-9500; *Basic Statistics of the Community, Energy: Monthly Statistics, Energy Statistics Yearbook, Eurostatistics: Data for Short-Term Economic Analysis, External Trade: Monthly Statistics, External Trade: Statistical Yearbook,* and *Fisheries: Yearly Statistics.*

Food and Agricultural Organization of the United Nations (FAO) Via delle Terme di Caracalla, 00100 Rome, Italy (Telephone Number in U.S. (202) 653-2400); *The State of Food and Agriculture.*

G.K. Hall and Company, 70 Lincoln Street, Boston, Massachusetts 02111 (617) 423-3990; *The World in Figures.*

International Monetary Fund, 700 Nineteenth Street, NW, Washington, D.C. 20431 (202) 623-7000; *Direction of Trade Statistics, Government Finance Statistics Yearbook,* and *International Financial Statistics.*

Organisation for Economic Co-operation and Development (OECD), 2 rue Andre-Pascal, 75 Paris 16, France (Telephone Number in U.S. (202) 785-6323); *Economic Outlook, The Footwear, Raw Hides and Skins, and Leather Industry in OECD Countries, Industrial Structure Statistics, The Iron and Steel Industry, Milk, Milk Products, and Egg Balances in OECD Member Countries, OECD Economic Surveys: Greece, The Pulp and Paper Industry,* and *Review of Fisheries in OECD Member Countries.*

Times Books, 201 East 50th Street, New York, New York 10022 (212) 751-2600; *The Economist Book of Vital World Statistics.*

The World Bank, 1818 H Street, NW, Washington, D.C. 20433 (202) 477-1234; *World Tables.*

GREECE - INCOME TAXES - See GREECE - TAXATION

GREECE - INDUSTRIAL EMPLOYMENT

European Community Information Service, 2100 M Street, NW, Washington, D.C. 20037 (202) 862-9500; *Labor Force Sample Survey.*

GREECE - INDUSTRIAL METALS PRODUCTION - See GREECE - MINING AND MINERAL PRODUCTS

GREECE - INDUSTRY

European Community Information Service, 2100 M Street, NW, Washington, D.C. 20037 (202) 862-9500; *Basic Statistics of the Community, Employment and Unemployment, Eurostatistics: Data for Short-Term Economic Analysis,* and *Labor Force Sample Survey.*

Facts on File, 460 Park Avenue South, New York, New York 10016 (800) 443-8323; *The New Book of World Rankings.*

Federal Statistical Office, Gustav - Stresemann - Ring 11, D-6200 Wiesbaden, Germany; *Griechenland.*

G.K. Hall and Company, 70 Lincoln Street, Boston, Massachusetts 02111 (617) 423-3990; *The World in Figures.*

International Labour Office, I.L.O. Publications, CH-1211, Geneva 22, Switzerland; *Yearbook of Labour Statistics.*

Organisation for Economic Co-operation and Development (OECD), 2 rue Andre-Pascal, 75 Paris 16, France (Telephone Number in U.S. (202) 785-6323); *Economic Outlook, Industrial Structure Statistics, Main Economic Indicators - Historical Statistics,* and *OECD Environmental Data.*

Statistical Office of the United Nations, Publishing Service, New York, New York 10017 (800) 253-9646; *Statistical Yearbook.*

Times Books, 201 East 50th Street, New York, New York 10022 (212) 751-2600; *The Economist Book of Vital World Statistics.*

The World Bank, 1818 H Street, NW, Washington, D.C. 20433 (202) 477-1234; *World Tables.*

GREECE - INFANT AND MATERNAL MORTALITY

European Community Information Service, 2100 M Street, NW, Washington, D.C. 20037 (202) 862-9500; *Basic Statistics of the Community* and *Demographic Statistics.*

Statistical Office of the United Nations, Publishing Service, New York, New York 10017 (800) 253-9646; *Demographic Yearbook,* and *Statistical Yearbook.*

Times Books, 201 East 50th Street, New York, New York 10022 (212) 751-2600; *The Economist Book of Vital World Statistics.*

The World Bank, 1818 H Street, NW, Washington, D.C. 20433 (202) 477-1234; *World Tables.*

World Health Organization, Office of Publications, Avenue Appia, CH-1211 Geneva 27, Switzerland (Telephone Number in U.S. (518) 436-9686); *World Health Statistics Annual.*

GREECE - INTEREST RATES

European Community Information Service, 2100 M Street, NW, Washington, D.C. 20037 (202) 862-9500; *Money and Finance.*

Organisation for Economic Co-operation and Development (OECD), 2 rue Andre-Pascal, 75 Paris 16, France (Telephone Number in U.S. (202) 785-6323); *Economic Outlook, Financial Market Trends,* and *OECD Financial Statistics.*

GREECE - INTERNAL TRADE

European Community Information Service, 2100 M Street, NW, Washington, D.C. 20037 (202) 862-9500; *Basic Statistics of the Community.*

Statistical Office of the United Nations, Publishing Service, New York, New York 10017 (800) 253-9646; *Statistical Yearbook.*

GREECE - INTERNATIONAL FINANCE

European Community Information Service, 2100 M Street, NW, Washington, D.C. 20037 (202) 862-9500; *Basic Statistics of the Community.*

Organisation for Economic Co-operation and Development (OECD), 2 rue Andre-Pascal, 75 Paris 16, France (Telephone Number in U.S. (202) 785-6323); *Economic Outlook,* and *Financial Market Trends.*

GREECE - INTERNATIONAL LIQUIDITY

International Monetary Fund, 700 Nineteenth Street, NW, Washington, D.C. 20431 (202) 623-7000; *International Financial Statistics.*

Organisation for Economic Co-operation and Development (OECD), 2 rue Andre-Pascal, 75 Paris 16, France (Telephone Number in U.S. (202) 785-6323); *Economic Outlook,* and *Financial Market Trends.*

GREECE - INTERNATIONAL RESERVES EXCLUDING GOLD

Statistical Office of the United Nations, Publishing Service, New York, New York 10017 (800) 253-9646; *Statistical Yearbook.*

The World Bank, 1818 H Street, NW, Washington, D.C. 20433 (202) 477-1234; *World Tables.*

GREECE - INTERNATIONAL STATISTICS

Organisation for Economic Co-operation and Development (OECD), 2 rue Andre-Pascal, 75 Paris 16, France (Telephone Number in U.S. (202) 785-6323); *Financial Market Trends,* and *Tourism Policy and International Tourism in OECD Member Countries.*

GREECE - INVESTMENTS

International Monetary Fund, 700 Nineteenth Street, NW, Washington, D.C. 20431 (202) 623-7000; *International Financial Statistics.*

Organisation for Economic Co-operation and Development (OECD), 2 rue Andre-Pascal, 75 Paris 16, France (Telephone Number in U.S. (202) 785-6323); *Economic Outlook, Financial Market Trends, Industrial Structure Statistics, The Iron and Steel Industry,* and *Textile Industry in OECD Countries.*

GREECE - IRON ORE - See GREECE - MINING AND MINERAL PRODUCTS

GREECE - JUTE PRODUCTION - See GREECE - CROPS

GREECE - LABOR FORCE

European Community Information Service, 2100 M Street, NW, Washington, D.C. 20037 (202) 862-9500; *Basic Statistics of the Community, Labor Force Sample Survey,* and *Regions: Statistical Yearbook.*

Facts on File, 460 Park Avenue South, New York, New York 10016 (800) 443-8323; *The New Book of World Rankings.*

Food and Agricultural Organization of the United Nations (FAO) Via delle Terme di Caracalla, 00100 Rome, Italy (Telephone Number in U.S. (202) 653-2400); *The State of Food and Agriculture.*

G.K. Hall and Company, 70 Lincoln Street, Boston, Massachusetts 02111 (617) 423-3990; *The World in Figures.*

Organisation for Economic Co-operation and Development (OECD), 2 rue Andre-Pascal, 75 Paris 16, France (Telephone Number in U.S. (202) 785-6323); *Economic Outlook, The Iron and Steel Industry, Main Economic Indicators - Historical Statistics, Maritime Transport, OECD Economic Surveys: Greece, OECD Employment Outlook,* and *Textile Industry in OECD Countries.*

Times Books, 201 East 50th Street, New York, New York 10022 (212) 751-2600; *The Economist Book of Vital World Statistics.*

The World Bank, 1818 H Street, NW, Washington, D.C. 20433 (202) 477-1234; *World Tables.*

GREECE - LABOR PRODUCTIVITY

International Labour Office, I.L.O. Publications, CH-1211, Geneva 22, Switzerland; *Yearbook of Labour Statistics.*

Organisation for Economic Co-operation and Development (OECD), 2 rue Andre-Pascal, 75 Paris 16, France (Telephone Number in U.S. (202) 785-6323); *Economic Outlook,* and *OECD Employment Outlook.*

GREECE - LAND USE

Euromonitor Publications Limited, 87-88 Turnmill Street, London EC1M 5QU, England; *European Marketing Data and Statistics.*

European Community Information Service, 2100 M Street, NW, Washington, D.C. 20037 (202) 862-9500; *Agriculture: Statistical Yearbook, Basic Statistics of the Community, Crop Production: Quarterly Statistics,* and *Regions: Statistical Yearbook.*

Food and Agricultural Organization of the United Nations (FAO), Via delle Terme di Caracalla, 00100 Rome, Italy (Telephone Number in U.S. (202) 653-2400); *Production Yearbook.*

G.K. Hall and Company, 70 Lincoln Street, Boston, Massachusetts 02111 (617) 423-3990; *The World in Figures.*

GREECE - LEAD AND LEAD ORE - See GREECE -MINING AND MINERAL PRODUCTS

GREECE - LEATHER AND FOOTWEAR - EXPORTS AND IMPORTS

European Community Information Service, 2100 M Street, NW, Washington, D.C. 20037 (202) 862-9500; *Basic Statistics of the Community.*

Organisation for Economic Co-operation and Development (OECD), 2 rue Andre-Pascal, 75 Paris 16, France (Telephone Number in U.S. (202) 785-6323); *The Footwear, Raw Hides and Skins, and Leather Industry in OECD Countries.*

GREECE - LIBRARIES

Euromonitor Publications Limited, 87-88 Turnmill Street, London EC1M 5QU, England; *European Marketing Data and Statistics.*

Facts on File, 460 Park Avenue South, New York, New York 10016 (800) 443-8323; *The New Book of World Rankings.*

GREECE - LIGNITE PRODUCTION - See GREECE - MINING AND MINERAL PRODUCTS

GREECE - LIVESTOCK AND POULTRY

Euromonitor Publications Limited, 87-88 Turnmill Street, London EC1M 5QU, England; *European Marketing Data and Statistics.*

European Community Information Service, 2100 M Street, NW, Washington, D.C. 20037 (202) 862-9500; *Agriculture: Statistical Yearbook, Basic Statistics of the Community, Eurostatistics: Data for Short-Term Economic Analysis,* and *Regions: Statistical Yearbook.*

Facts on File, 460 Park Avenue South, New York, New York 10016 (800) 443-8323; *The New Book of World Rankings.*

Food and Agricultural Organization of the United Nations (FAO), Via delle Terme di Caracalla, 00100 Rome, Italy (Telephone Number in U.S. (202) 653-2400); *Production Yearbook,* and *The State of Food and Agriculture.*

G.K. Hall and Company, 70 Lincoln Street, Boston, Massachusetts 02111 (617) 423-3990; *The World in Figures.*

Organisation for Economic Co-operation and Development (OECD), 2 rue Andre-Pascal, 75 Paris 16, France (Telephone Number in U.S. (202) 785-6323); *Economic Accounts for Agriculture,* and *Meat Balances in OECD Member Countries.*

Statistical Office of the United Nations, Publishing Service, New York, New York 10017 (800) 253-9646; *Statistical Yearbook.*

GREECE - LIVING LEVELS

G.K. Hall and Company, 70 Lincoln Street, Boston, Massachusetts 02111 (617) 423-3990; *The World in Figures.*

Organisation for Economic Co-operation and Development (OECD), 2 rue Andre-Pascal, 75 Paris 16, France (Telephone Number in U.S. (202) 785-6323); *Economic Outlook.*

Times Books, 201 East 50th Street, New York, New York 10022 (212) 751-2600; *The Economist Book of Vital World Statistics.*

GREECE - MAGNESIUM PRODUCTION AND CONSUMPTION - See GREECE - MINING AND MINERAL PRODUCTS

GREECE - MAIL - NUMBER OF PIECES SENT OR RECEIVED

European Community Information Service, 2100 M Street, NW, Washington, D.C. 20037 (202) 862-9500; *Transport Annual Statistics.*

Statistical Office of the United Nations, Publishing Service, New York, New York 10017 (800) 253-9646; *Statistical Yearbook.*

GREECE - MAIN ECONOMIC INDICATORS - See GREECE - ECONOMY

GREECE - MAIN INDICATORS - See GREECE - ECONOMY

GREECE - MANGANESE AND MANGANESE ORE - See GREECE - MINING AND MINERAL PRODUCTS

GREECE - MANUFACTURING

American Automobile Manufacturers Association, 1401 H Street, NW, Suite 900, Washington, D.C. 20005 (202) 326-5500; *World Motor Vehicle Data.*

European Community Information Service, 2100 M Street, NW, Washington, D.C. 20037 (202) 862-9500; *Basic Statistics of the Community, Eurostatistics: Data for Short-Term Economic Analysis, Industrial Production: Quarterly Statistics,* and *Labor Force Sample Survey.*

Facts on File, 460 Park Avenue South, New York, New York 10016 (800) 443-8323; *The New Book of World Rankings.*

G.K. Hall and Company, 70 Lincoln Street, Boston, Massachusetts 02111 (617) 423-3990; *The World in Figures.*

International Monetary Fund, 700 Nineteenth Street, NW, Washington, D.C. 20431 (202) 623-7000; *International Financial Statistics.*

Organisation for Economic Co-operation and Development (OECD), 2 rue Andre-Pascal, 75 Paris 16, France (Telephone Number in U.S. (202) 785-6323); *Foreign Trade by Commodities, Industrial Structure Statistics,* and *OECD Economic Surveys: Greece.*

Statistical Office of the United Nations, Publishing Service, New York, New York 10017 (800) 253-9646; *Statistical Yearbook.*

Times Books, 201 East 50th Street, New York, New York 10022 (212) 751-2600; *The Economist Book of Vital World Statistics.*

The World Bank, 1818 H Street, NW, Washington, D.C. 20433 (202) 477-1234; *World Tables.*

GREECE - MARRIAGE RATES

European Community Information Service, 2100 M Street, NW, Washington, D.C. 20037 (202) 862-9500; *Basic Statistics of the Community.*

Facts on File, 460 Park Avenue South, New York, New York 10016 (800) 443-8323; *The New Book of World Rankings.*

Statistical Office of the United Nations, Publishing Service, New York, New York 10017 (800) 253-9646; *Demographic Yearbook,* and *Statistical Yearbook.*

GREECE - MEAT PRODUCTION - See GREECE - LIVESTOCK AND POULTRY

GREECE - MERCHANT SHIPPING

European Community Information Service, 2100 M Street, NW, Washington, D.C. 20037 (202) 862-9500; *Basic Statistics of the Community, Fisheries: Yearly Statistics, Regions: Statistical Yearbook,* and *Transport Annual Statistics.*

G.K. Hall and Company, 70 Lincoln Street, Boston, Massachusetts 02111 (617) 423-3990; *The World in Figures.*

Lloyd's Register of Shipping, 17 Battery Place, New York, New York 10004 (212) 425-8050; *Register of Ships.*

Organisation for Economic Co-operation and Development (OECD), 2 rue Andre-Pascal, 75 Paris 16, France (Telephone Number in U.S. (202) 785-6323); *Maritime Transport.*

Statistical Office of the United Nations, Publishing Service, New York, New York 10017 (800) 253-9646; *Statistical Yearbook.*

Times Books, 201 East 50th Street, New York, New York 10022 (212) 751-2600; *The Economist Book of Vital World Statistics.*

U.S. Department of Transportation, Maritime Administration, 400 Seventh Street, SW, Washington, D.C. 20590 (202) 366-5807; *A Statistical Analysis of the World's Merchant Fleets.*

GREECE - MERCURY PRODUCTION AND CONSUMPTION - See GREECE - MINING AND MINERAL PRODUCTS

GREECE - MILITARY

G.K. Hall and Company, 70 Lincoln Street, Boston, Massachusetts 02111 (617) 423-3990; *The World in Figures.*

The International Institute for Strategic Studies, 23 Tavistock Street, London WC2E 7NQ, England; *The Military Balance.*

U.S. Arms Control and Disarmament Agency, 320 Twenty-first Street, Northwest, Washington, D.C. 20451 (202) 647-8677; *World Military Expenditures and Arms Transfers.*

GREECE - MILK PRODUCTION - See GREECE - DAIRY PRODUCTS

GREECE - MILLET PRODUCTION - See GREECE - CROPS

GREECE - MINING AND MINERAL PRODUCTS

Commodity Research Bureau, Incorporated, 75 Wall Street, New York, New York 10005 (212) 504-7754; *Commodity Year Book.*

European Community Information Service, 2100 M Street, NW, Washington, D.C. 20037 (202) 862-9500; *Basic Statistics of the Community, Energy: Monthly Statistics, Eurostatistics: Data for Short-Term Economic Analysis, Industrial Production: Quarterly Statistics, Iron and Steel: Statistical Yearbook,* and *Regions: Statistical Yearbook.*

Facts on File, 460 Park Avenue South, New York, New York 10016 (800) 443-8323; *The New Book of World Rankings.*

G.K. Hall and Company, 70 Lincoln Street, Boston, Massachusetts 02111 (617) 423-3990; *The World in Figures.*

International Labour Office, I.L.O. Publications, CH-1211, Geneva 22, Switzerland; *Yearbook of Labour Statistics.*

Organisation for Economic Co-operation and Development (OECD), 2 rue Andre-Pascal, 75 Paris 16, France (Telephone Number in U.S. (202) 785-6323); *ACP: Basic Statistics, Energy Statistics of OECD Countries, Foreign Trade by Commodities, Industrial Structure Statistics, The Iron and Steel Industry, The Non-Ferrous Metals Industry,* and *OECD Economic Surveys: Greece.*

Penn Well Publishing Company, 1421 South Sheridan Road, Post Office Box 1260, Tulsa, Oklahoma 74101 (800) 752-9764; *International Energy Statistics Sourcebook.*

Statistical Office of the United Nations, Publishing Service, New York, New York 10017 (800) 253-9646; *Statistical Yearbook.*

GREECE - MOLYBDENUM AND MOLYBDENUM ORE - See GREECE - MINING AND MINERAL PRODUCTS

GREECE - MONEY AND CREDIT

Organisation for Economic Co-operation and Development (OECD), 2 rue Andre-Pascal, 75 Paris 16, France (Telephone Number in U.S. (202) 785-6323); OECD Economic Surveys: Greece.

GREECE - MONEY EXCHANGE RATE

European Community Information Service, 2100 M Street, NW, Washington, D.C. 20037 (202) 862-9500; *Basic Statistics of the Community.*

International Monetary Fund, 700 Nineteenth Street, NW, Washington, D.C. 20431 (202) 623-7000; *International Financial Statistics.*

Organisation for Economic Co-operation and Development (OECD), 2 rue Andre-Pascal, 75 Paris 16, France (Telephone Number in U.S. (202) 785-6323); *Economic Outlook, Financial Market Trends,* and *Tourism Policy and International Tourism in OECD Member Countries.*

Statistical Office of the United Nations, Publishing Service, New York, New York 10017 (800) 253-9646; *Statistical Yearbook.*

GREECE - MONEY RATES - MARKET

European Community Information Service, 2100 M Street, NW, Washington, D.C. 20037 (202) 862-9500; *Basic Statistics of the Community.*

Organisation for Economic Co-operation and Development (OECD), 2 rue Andre-Pascal, 75 Paris 16, France (Telephone Number in U.S. (202) 785-6323); *Economic Outlook,* and *Financial Market Trends.*

GREECE - MONEY RESERVES

European Community Information Service, 2100 M Street, NW, Washington, D.C. 20037 (202) 862-9500; *Basic Statistics of the Community.*

Organisation for Economic Co-operation and Development (OECD), 2 rue Andre-Pascal, 75 Paris 16, France (Telephone Number in U.S. (202) 785-6323); *Economic Outlook,* and *Financial Market Trends.*

GREECE - MONEY SUPPLY

European Community Information Service, 2100 M Street, NW, Washington, D.C. 20037 (202) 862-9500; *Basic Statistics of the Community, Eurostatistics: Data for Short-Term Economic Analysis,* and *Money and Finance.*

Federal Statistical Office, Gustav - Stresemann - Ring 11, D-6200 Wiesbaden, Germany; *Griechenland.*

G.K. Hall and Company, 70 Lincoln Street, Boston, Massachusetts 02111 (617) 423-3990; *The World in Figures.*

International Monetary Fund, 700 Nineteenth Street, NW, Washington, D.C. 20431 (202) 623-7000; *International Financial Statistics.*

Organisation for Economic Co-operation and Development (OECD), 2 rue Andre-Pascal, 75 Paris 16, France (Telephone Number in U.S. (202) 785-6323); *Economic Outlook.*

Statistical Office of the United Nations, Publishing Service, New York, New York 10017 (800) 253-9646; *Statistical Yearbook.*

The World Bank, 1818 H Street, NW, Washington, D.C. 20433 (202) 477-1234; *World Tables.*

GREECE - MONUMENTS AND HISTORICAL SITES

United Nations Educational, Scientific and Cultural Organization (UNESCO), 7 Place de Fontenoy, F-75700 Paris, France (Telephone Number in U.S. (212) 963-5981); *Statistical Yearbook.*

GREECE - MOTION PICTURES

United Nations Educational, Scientific and Cultural Organization (UNESCO), 7 Place de Fontenoy, F-75700 Paris, France (Telephone Number in U.S. (212) 963-5981); *Statistical Yearbook.*

GREECE - MOTOR VEHICLE ASSEMBLY

Statistical Office of the United Nations, Publishing Service, New York, New York 10017 (800) 253-9646; *Statistical Yearbook.*

GREECE - MOTOR VEHICLE PRODUCTION

American Automobile Manufacturers Association, 1401 H Street, NW, Suite 900, Washington, D.C. 20005 (202) 326-5500; *World Motor Vehicle Data.*

European Community Information Service, 2100 M Street, NW, Washington, D.C. 20037 (202) 862-9500; *Basic Statistics of the Community* and *Eurostatistics: Data for Short-Term Economic Analysis.*

Organisation for Economic Co-operation and Development (OECD), 2 rue Andre-Pascal, 75 Paris 16, France (Telephone Number in U.S. (202) 785-6323); *Foreign Trade by Commodities.*

GREECE - MOTOR VEHICLE TAXES - See GREECE - TAXATION

GREECE - MOTOR VEHICLES IN USE

American Automobile Manufacturers Association, 1401 H Street, NW, Suite 900, Washington, D.C. 20005 (202) 326-5500; *World Motor Vehicle Data.*

European Community Information Service, 2100 M Street, NW, Washington, D.C. 20037 (202) 862-9500; *Basic Statistics of the Community* and *Transport Annual Statistics.*

G.K. Hall and Company, 70 Lincoln Street, Boston, Massachusetts 02111 (617) 423-3990; *The World in Figures.*

International Road Federation, 525 School Street, SW, Washington, D.C. 20024 (202) 554-2106; *World Road Statistics.*

Statistical Office of the United Nations, Publishing Service, New York, New York 10017 (800) 253-9646; *Statistical Yearbook.*

Times Books, 201 East 50th Street, New York, New York 10022 (212) 751-2600; *The Economist Book of Vital World Statistics.*

GREECE - MULES - See GREECE - LIVESTOCK AND POULTRY

GREECE - MUSEUMS

Euromonitor Publications Limited, 87-88 Turnmill Street, London EC1M 5QU, England; *European Marketing Data and Statistics.*

Facts on File, 460 Park Avenue South, New York, New York 10016 (800) 443-8323; *The New Book of World Rankings.*

United Nations Educational, Scientific and Cultural Organization (UNESCO), 7 Place de Fontenoy, F-75700 Paris, France (Telephone Number in U.S. (212) 963-5981); *Statistical Yearbook.*

GREECE - NATALITY - See GREECE - BIRTH RATES

GREECE - NATIONAL ACCOUNTS

European Community Information Service, 2100 M Street, NW, Washington, D.C. 20037 (202) 862-9500; *Basic Statistics of the Community* and *Eurostatistics: Data for Short-Term Economic Analysis.*

Federal Statistical Office, Gustav - Stresemann - Ring 11, D-6200 Wiesbaden, Germany; *Griechenland.*

International Monetary Fund, 700 Nineteenth Street, NW, Washington, D.C. 20431 (202) 623-7000; *International Financial Statistics.*

Organisation for Economic Co-operation and Development (OECD), 2 rue Andre-Pascal, 75 Paris 16, France (Telephone Number in U.S. (202) 785-6323); *Economic Outlook.*

Statistical Office of the United Nations, Publishing Service, New York, New York 10017 (800) 253-9646; *National Accounts Statistics,* and *Statistical Yearbook.*

GREECE - NATIONAL INCOME

Facts on File, 460 Park Avenue South, New York, New York 10016 (800) 443-8323; *The New Book of World Rankings.*

G.K. Hall and Company, 70 Lincoln Street, Boston, Massachusetts 02111 (617) 423-3990; *The World in Figures.*

Organisation for Economic Co-operation and Development (OECD), 2 rue Andre-Pascal, 75 Paris 16, France (Telephone Number in U.S. (202) 785-6323); *Economic Outlook.*

Statistical Office of the United Nations, Publishing Service, New York, New York 10017 (800) 253-9646; *Statistical Yearbook.*

GREECE - NATIONAL PRODUCT

European Community Information Service, 2100 M Street, NW, Washington, D.C. 20037 (202) 862-9500; *Basic Statistics of the Community.*

Facts on File, 460 Park Avenue South, New York, New York 10016 (800) 443-8323; *The New Book of World Rankings.*

Organisation for Economic Co-operation and Development (OECD), 2 rue Andre-Pascal, 75 Paris 16, France (Telephone Number in U.S. (202) 785-6323); *Economic Outlook.*

Statistical Office of the United Nations, Publishing Service, New York, New York 10017 (800) 253-9646; *Statistical Yearbook.*

GREECE - NATURAL GAS PRODUCTION - See GREECE - MINING AND MINERAL PRODUCTS

GREECE - NATURAL RUBBER PRODUCTION

European Community Information Service, 2100 M Street, NW, Washington, D.C. 20037 (202) 862-9500; *Basic Statistics of the*

Community.

GREECE - NEWSPAPER PRODUCTION - See GREECE - FORESTRY AND FOREST PRODUCTS

GREECE - NEWSPRINT - See GREECE - FORESTRY AND FOREST PRODUCTS

GREECE - NICKEL AND NICKEL ORE - See GREECE - MINING AND MINERAL PRODUCTS

GREECE - NITRIC ACID PRODUCTION

European Community Information Service, 2100 M Street, NW, Washington, D.C. 20037 (202) 862-9500; *Basic Statistics of the Community.*

Statistical Office of the United Nations, Publishing Service, New York, New York 10017 (800) 253-9646; *Statistical Yearbook.*

GREECE - OATS PRODUCTION - See GREECE - CROPS

GREECE - OCCUPATIONS - See GREECE - LABOR FORCE

GREECE - OIL PRODUCING CROPS

European Community Information Service, 2100 M Street, NW, Washington, D.C. 20037 (202) 862-9500; *Basic Statistics of the Community.*

Organisation for Economic Co-operation and Development (OECD), 2 rue Andre-Pascal, 75 Paris 16, France (Telephone Number in U.S. (202) 785-6323); *Foreign Trade by Commodities.*

GREECE - ONION PRODUCTION - See GREECE - CROPS

GREECE - ORANGE PRODUCTION - See GREECE - CROPS

GREECE - PALM KERNEL PRODUCTION - See GREECE - CROPS

GREECE - PAPER - See GREECE - FORESTRY AND FOREST PRODUCTS

GREECE - PATENTS

Statistical Office of the United Nations, Publishing Service, New York, New York 10017 (800) 253-9646; *Statistical Yearbook.*

GREECE - PEANUT PRODUCTION - See GREECE - CROPS

GREECE - PEPPER PRODUCTION - See GREECE - CROPS

GREECE - PERIODICALS

United Nations Educational, Scientific and Cultural Organization (UNESCO), 7 Place de Fontenoy, F-75700 Paris, France (Telephone Number in U.S. (212) 963-5981); *Statistical Yearbook.*

GREECE - PESTICIDE USE

Food and Agricultural Organization of the United Nations (FAO) Via delle Terme di Caracalla, 00100 Rome, Italy (Telephone Number in U.S. (202) 653-2400); *The State of Food and Agriculture.*

GREECE - PETROLEUM INDUSTRY

European Community Information Service, 2100 M Street, NW, Washington, D.C. 20037 (202) 862-9500; *ACP: Basic Statistics, Basic Statistics of the Community,* and *Energy Statistics Yearbook.*

Facts on File, 460 Park Avenue South, New York, New York 10016 (800) 443-8323; *The New Book of World Rankings.*

Food and Agricultural Organization of the United Nations (FAO) Via delle Terme di Caracalla, 00100 Rome, Italy (Telephone Number in U.S. (202) 653-2400); *The State of Food and Agriculture.*

G.K. Hall and Company, 70 Lincoln Street, Boston, Massachusetts 02111 (617) 423-3990; *The World in Figures.*

Organisation for Economic Co-operation and Development (OECD), 2 rue Andre-Pascal, 75 Paris 16, France (Telephone Number in U.S. (202) 785-6323); *Energy Statistics of OECD Countries, Foreign Trade by Commodities,* and *Oil and Gas Information.*

Penn Well Publishing Company, 1421 South Sheridan Road, Post Office Box 1260, Tulsa, Oklahoma 74101 (800) 752-9764; *International Energy Statistics Sourcebook.*

Statistical Office of the United Nations, Publishing Service, New York, New York 10017 (800) 253-9646; *Statistical Yearbook.*

GREECE - PHOSPHATE ROCK PRODUCTION - See GREECE - MINING AND MINERAL PRODUCTS

GREECE - PHOSPHATES PRODUCTION - See GREECE - MINING AND MINERAL PRODUCTS

GREECE - PIG-IRON AND FERRO-ALLOY PRODUCTION - See GREECE - MINING AND MINERAL PRODUCTS

GREECE - PIGS - See GREECE - LIVESTOCK AND POULTRY

GREECE - PIPELINES FOR OIL AND PETROLEUM PRODUCTS

European Community Information Service, 2100 M Street, NW, Washington, D.C. 20037 (202) 862-9500; *Transport Annual Statistics.*

GREECE - PISTACHIO PRODUCTION - See GREECE - CROPS

GREECE - PLASTICS AND RESINS PRODUCTION

European Community Information Service, 2100 M Street, NW, Washington, D.C. 20037 (202) 862-9500; *Basic Statistics of the Community.*

Organisation for Economic Co-operation and Development (OECD), 2 rue Andre-Pascal, 75 Paris 16, France (Telephone Number in U.S. (202) 785-6323); *Foreign Trade by Commodities.*

Statistical Office of the United Nations, Publishing Service, New York, New York 10017 (800) 253-9646; *Statistical Yearbook.*

GREECE - PLATINUM PRODUCTION - See GREECE - MINING AND MINERAL PRODUCTS

GREECE - POPULATION

The Economist Intelligence Unit, 111 West 57th Street, New York, New York 10019 (800) 938-4685; *The World Market Atlas.*

Euromonitor Publications Limited, 87-88 Turnmill Street, London EC1M 5QU, England; *European Marketing Data and Statistics.*

European Community Information Service, 2100 M Street, NW, Washington, D.C. 20037 (202) 862-9500; *ACP: Basic Statistics,* and *Basic Statistics of the Community, Demographic Statistics, Employment and Unemployment, Fisheries: Yearly Statistics, Iron and Steel: Statistical Yearbook, Labor Force Sample Survey,* and *Regions: Statistical Yearbook.*

Facts on File, 460 Park Avenue South, New York, New York 10016 (800) 443-8323; *The New Book of World Rankings.*

Federal Statistical Office, Gustav - Stresemann - Ring 11, D-6200 Wiesbaden, Germany; *Griechenland.*

Food and Agricultural Organization of the United Nations (FAO), Via delle Terme di Caracalla, 00100 Rome, Italy (Telephone Number in U.S. (202) 653-2400); *Production Yearbook.*

G.K. Hall and Company, 70 Lincoln Street, Boston, Massachusetts 02111 (617) 423-3990; *The World in Figures.*

International Labour Office, I.L.O. Publications, CH-1211, Geneva 22, Switzerland; *Yearbook of Labour Statistics.*

Statistical Office of the United Nations, Publishing Service, New York, New York 10017 (800) 253-9646; *Demographic Yearbook,* and *Statistical Yearbook.*

Times Books, 201 East 50th Street, New York, New York 10022 (212) 751-2600; *The Economist Book of Vital World Statistics.*

United Nations Educational, Scientific and Cultural Organization (UNESCO), 7 Place de Fontenoy, F-75700 Paris, France (Telephone Number in U.S. (212) 963-5981); *Statistical Yearbook.*

U.S. Arms Control and Disarmament Agency, 320 Twenty-first Street, Northwest, Washington, D.C. 20451 (202) 647-8677; *World Military Expenditures and Arms Transfers.*

World Health Organization, Office of Publications, Avenue Appia, CH-1211 Geneva 27, Switzerland (Telephone Number in U.S. (518) 436-9686); *World Health Statistics Annual.*

GREECE - POST OFFICES

Facts on File, 460 Park Avenue South, New York, New York 10016 (800) 443-8323; *The New Book of World Rankings.*

GREECE - POTATO PRODUCTION - See GREECE - CROPS

GREECE - POWER PRODUCTION INDUSTRY

European Community Information Service, 2100 M Street, NW, Washington, D.C. 20037 (202) 862-9500; *Basic Statistics of the Community.*

Statistical Office of the United Nations, Publishing Service, New York, New York 10017 (800) 253-9646; *Statistical Yearbook.*

GREECE - PRICES

European Community Information Service, 2100 M Street, NW, Washington, D.C. 20037 (202) 862-9500; *Basic Statistics of the Community* and *Eurostatistics: Data for Short-Term Economic Analysis.*

Facts on File, 460 Park Avenue South, New York, New York 10016 (800) 443-8323; *The New Book of World Rankings.*

Federal Statistical Office, Gustav - Stresemann - Ring 11, D-6200 Wiesbaden, Germany; *Griechenland.*

Food and Agricultural Organization of the United Nations (FAO), Via delle Terme di Caracalla, 00100 Rome, Italy (Telephone Number in U.S. (202) 653-2400); *Production Yearbook,* and *The State of Food and Agriculture.*

G.K. Hall and Company, 70 Lincoln Street, Boston, Massachusetts 02111 (617) 423-3990; *The World in Figures.*

International Labour Office, I.L.O. Publications, CH-1211, Geneva 22, Switzerland; *Yearbook of Labour Statistics.*

International Monetary Fund, 700 Nineteenth Street, NW, Washington, D.C. 20431 (202) 623-7000; *International Financial Statistics.*

Organisation for Economic Co-operation and Development (OECD), 2 rue Andre-Pascal, 75 Paris 16, France (Telephone Number in U.S. (202) 785-6323); *Economic Outlook, The Footwear, Raw Hides and Skins, and Leather Industry in OECD Countries, The Iron and Steel Industry, Main Economic Indicators - Historical Statistics,* and *The Pulp and Paper Industry.*

GREECE - PRINTING AND WRITING PAPER - See GREECE - FORESTRY AND FOREST PRODUCTS

GREECE - PRODUCTION

American Automobile Manufacturers Association, 1401 H Street, NW, Suite 900, Washington, D.C. 20005 (202) 326-05500; *World Motor Vehicle Data.*

European Community Information Service, 2100 M Street, NW, Washington, D.C. 20037 (202) 862-9500; *Basic Statistics of the Community, Eurostatistics: Data for Short-Term Economic Analysis,* and *Fisheries: Yearly Statistics.*

Facts on File, 460 Park Avenue South, New York, New York 10016 (800) 443-8323; *The New Book of World Rankings.*

G.K. Hall and Company, 70 Lincoln Street, Boston, Massachusetts 02111 (617) 423-3990; *The World in Figures.*

Organisation for Economic Co-operation and Development (OECD), 2 rue Andre-Pascal, 75 Paris 16, France (Telephone Number in U.S. (202) 785-6323); *Economic Outlook,* and *The Footwear, Raw Hides and Skins, and Leather Industry in OECD Countries, Industrial Structure Statistics, The Iron and Steel Industry, Meat Balances in OECD Member Countries, Milk, Milk Products, and Egg Balances in OECD Member Countries, The Non-Ferrous Metals Industry, The Pulp and Paper Industry,* and *Textile Industry in OECD Countries.*

GREECE - PRODUCTIVITY

European Community Information Service, 2100 M Street, NW, Washington, D.C. 20037 (202) 862-9500; *Basic Statistics of the Community.*

Organisation for Economic Co-operation and Development (OECD), 2 rue Andre-Pascal, 75 Paris 16, France (Telephone Number in U.S. (202) 785-6323); *Economic Outlook.*

GREECE - PROPERTY TAXES - See GREECE - TAXATION

GREECE - PUBLIC CONSUMPTION FUND

European Community Information Service, 2100 M Street, NW, Washington, D.C. 20037 (202) 862-9500; *Basic Statistics of the Community.*

Organisation for Economic Co-operation and Development (OECD), 2 rue Andre-Pascal, 75 Paris 16, France (Telephone Number in U.S.

(202) 785-6323; *Revenue Statistics of OECD Member Countries.*

GREECE - PUBLIC EXPENDITURES

European Community Information Service, 2100 M Street, NW, Washington, D.C. 20037 (202) 862-9500; *Basic Statistics of the Community.*

Organisation for Economic Co-operation and Development (OECD), 2 rue Andre-Pascal, 75 Paris 16, France (Telephone Number in U.S. (202) 785-6323); *Revenue Statistics of OECD Member Countries.*

GREECE - PUBLIC FINANCE

Facts on File, 460 Park Avenue South, New York, New York 10016 (800) 443-8323; *The New Book of World Rankings.*

Federal Statistical Office, Gustav - Stresemann - Ring 11, D-6200 Wiesbaden, Germany; *Griechenland.*

Organisation for Economic Co-operation and Development (OECD), 2 rue Andre-Pascal, 75 Paris 16, France (Telephone Number in U.S. (202) 785-6323); *Revenue Statistics of OECD Member Countries.*

GREECE - PUBLIC HEALTH

European Community Information Service, 2100 M Street, NW, Washington, D.C. 20037 (202) 862-9500; *Basic Statistics of the Community.*

GREECE - PUBLIC REVENUES

Organisation for Economic Co-operation and Development (OECD), 2 rue Andre-Pascal, 75 Paris 16, France (Telephone Number in U.S. (202) 785-6323); *Revenue Statistics of OECD Member Countries.*

GREECE - RADIO BROADCASTING - See GREECE - BROADCASTING

GREECE - RAILWAYS

Euromonitor Publications Limited, 87-88 Turnmill Street, London EC1M 5QU, England; *European Marketing Data and Statistics.*

European Community Information Service, 2100 M Street, NW, Washington, D.C. 20037 (202) 862-9500; *Basic Statistics of the Community, Regions: Statistical Yearbook,* and *Transport Annual Statistics.*

G.K. Hall and Company, 70 Lincoln Street, Boston, Massachusetts 02111 (617) 423-3990; *The World in Figures.*

Jane's Information Group, Sentinel House, 163 Brighton Road, Coulsdon, Surrey CR5 2NH, England (Telephone Number in U.S. (703) 683-3700); *Jane's World Railways.*

Statistical Office of the United Nations, Publishing Service, New York, New York 10017 (800) 253-9646; *Annual Bulletin of Transport Statistics for Europe,* and *Statistical Yearbook.*

GREECE - RANCHING

European Community Information Service, 2100 M Street, NW, Washington, D.C. 20037 (202) 862-9500; *Basic Statistics of the Community.*

GREECE - RAPESEED PRODUCTION - See GREECE - CROPS

GREECE - RELIGION

Facts on File, 460 Park Avenue South, New York, New York 10016 (800) 443-8323; *The New Book of World Rankings.*

GREECE - RENT PRICES

International Labour Office, I.L.O. Publications, CH-1211, Geneva 22, Switzerland; *Yearbook of Labour Statistics.*

GREECE - RETAIL TRADE

European Community Information Service, 2100 M Street, NW, Washington, D.C. 20037 (202) 862-9500; *Basic Statistics of the Community* and *Eurostatistics: Data for Short-Term Economic Analysis.*

G.K. Hall and Company, 70 Lincoln Street, Boston, Massachusetts 02111 (617) 423-3990; *The World in Figures.*

GREECE - RICE PRODUCTION - See GREECE - CROPS

GREECE - ROOT AND TUBER PRODUCTION - See GREECE - CROPS

GREECE - ROUNDWOOD PRODUCTION - See GREECE - FORESTRY AND FOREST PRODUCTS

GREECE - RUBBER PRODUCTION

European Community Information Service, 2100 M Street, NW, Washington, D.C. 20037 (202) 862-9500; *Basic Statistics of the Community.*

Facts on File, 460 Park Avenue South, New York, New York 10016 (800) 443-8323; *The New Book of World Rankings.*

Organisation for Economic Co-operation and Development (OECD), 2 rue Andre-Pascal, 75 Paris 16, France (Telephone Number in U.S. (202) 785-6323); *Foreign Trade by Commodities.*

GREECE - RYE PRODUCTION - See GREECE - CROPS

GREECE - SAFFLOWER SEED PRODUCTION - See GREECE - CROPS

GREECE - SALT PRODUCTION - See GREECE - MINING AND MINERAL PRODUCTS

GREECE - SAVINGS ACCOUNT DEPOSITS

European Community Information Service, 2100 M Street, NW, Washington, D.C. 20037 (202) 862-9500; *Eurostatistics: Data for Short-Term Economic Analysis.*

GREECE - SAWNWOOD PRODUCTION - See GREECE - FORESTRY AND FOREST PRODUCTS

GREECE - SCIENCE AND TECHNOLOGY - EXPENDITURE FOR RESEARCH

European Community Information Service, 2100 M Street, NW, Washington, D.C. 20037 (202) 862-9500; *Basic Statistics of the Community.*

Statistical Office of the United Nations, Publishing Service, New York, New York 10017 (800) 253-9646; *Statistical Yearbook.*

GREECE - SCIENTISTS, ENGINEERS AND TECHNICIANS

European Community Information Service, 2100 M Street, NW, Washington, D.C. 20037 (202) 862-9500; *Basic Statistics of the Community.*

Statistical Office of the United Nations, Publishing Service, New York, New York 10017 (800) 253-9646; *Statistical Yearbook.*

GREECE - SENIOR CITIZENS

Facts on File, 460 Park Avenue South, New York, New York 10016 (800) 443-8323; *The New Book of World Rankings.*

GREECE - SESAME SEED PRODUCTION - See GREECE - CROPS

GREECE - SHEEP - See GREECE - LIVESTOCK AND POULTRY

GREECE - SILVER PRODUCTION AND CONSUMPTION - See GREECE - MINING AND MINERAL PRODUCTS

GREECE - SISAL PRODUCTION - See GREECE - CROPS

GREECE - SOCIAL DATA

European Community Information Service, 2100 M Street, NW, Washington, D.C. 20037 (202) 862-9500; *ACP: Basic Statistics* and *Basic Statistics of the Community.*

Facts on File, 460 Park Avenue South, New York, New York 10016 (800) 443-8323; *The New Book of World Rankings.*

G.K. Hall and Company, 70 Lincoln Street, Boston, Massachusetts 02111 (617) 423-3990; *The World in Figures.*

GREECE - SOCIAL SECURITY

European Community Information Service, 2100 M Street, NW, Washington, D.C. 20037 (202) 862-9500; *Basic Statistics of the Community.*

International Monetary Fund, 700 Nineteenth Street, NW, Washington, D.C. 20431 (202) 623-7000; *Government Finance Statistics Yearbook.*

Organisation for Economic Co-operation and Development (OECD), 2 rue Andre-Pascal, 75 Paris 16, France (Telephone Number in U.S. (202) 785-6323); *Revenue Statistics of OECD Member Countries.*

GREECE - SOCIOECONOMIC DATA

European Community Information Service, 2100 M Street, NW, Washington, D.C. 20037 (202) 862-9500; *Basic Statistics of the Community.*

Organisation for Economic Co-operation and Development (OECD), 2 rue Andre-Pascal, 75 Paris 16, France (Telephone Number in U.S. (202) 785-6323); *Economic Outlook.*

GREECE - SOYBEAN PRODUCTION - See GREECE - CROPS

GREECE - STAMP TAXES AND DUTIES - See GREECE - TAXATION

GREECE - STATE AFFORESTATION - See GREECE - FORESTRY AND FOREST PRODUCTS

GREECE - STEEL - See GREECE - MINING AND MINERAL PRODUCTS

GREECE - STOCKS - COMMODITY - MARKET PRICE - INDEX

Food and Agricultural Organization of the United Nations (FAO) Via delle Terme di Caracalla, 00100 Rome, Italy (Telephone Number in U.S. (202) 653-2400); *The State of Food and Agriculture.*

GREECE - STRAW PRODUCTION - See GREECE - CROPS

GREECE - SUGAR - See GREECE - CROPS

GREECE - SUGARBEET PRODUCTION - See GREECE - CROPS

GREECE - SULPHUR AND SULPHURIC ACID PRODUCTION - See GREECE - MINING AND MINERAL PRODUCTS

GREECE - SUNFLOWER PRODUCTION - See GREECE - CROPS

GREECE - TAXATION

European Community Information Service, 2100 M Street, NW, Washington, D.C. 20037 (202) 862-9500; *Basic Statistics of the Community.*

G.K. Hall and Company, 70 Lincoln Street, Boston, Massachusetts 02111 (617) 423-3990; *The World in Figures.*

International Monetary Fund, 700 Nineteenth Street, NW, Washington, D.C. 20431 (202) 623-7000; *Government Finance Statistics Yearbook.*

International Road Federation, 525 School Street, SW, Washington, D.C. 20024 (202) 554-2106; *World Road Statistics.*

Organisation for Economic Co-operation and Development (OECD), 2 rue Andre-Pascal, 75 Paris 16, France (Telephone Number in U.S. (202) 785-6323); *Revenue Statistics of OECD Member Countries.*

The World Bank, 1818 H Street, NW, Washington, D.C. 20433 (202) 477-1234; *World Tables.*

GREECE - TEA PRODUCTION - See GREECE - CROPS

GREECE - TELEGRAPH SERVICE

European Community Information Service, 2100 M Street, NW, Washington, D.C. 20037 (202) 862-9500; *Transport Annual Statistics.*

Statistical Office of the United Nations, Publishing Service, New York, New York 10017 (800) 253-9646; *Statistical Yearbook.*

GREECE - TELEPHONES IN USE

American Telephone and Telegraph Company, 26 Parsippany Road, Whippany, New Jersey 07981 (800) 338-4038; *The World's Telephones.*

European Community Information Service, 2100 M Street, NW, Washington, D.C. 20037 (202) 862-9500; *Basic Statistics of the Community,* and *Transport Annual Statistics.*

G.K. Hall and Company, 70 Lincoln Street, Boston, Massachusetts 02111 (617) 423-3990; *The World in Figures.*

Statistical Office of the United Nations, Publishing Service, New York, New York 10017 (800) 253-9646; *Statistical Yearbook.*

GREECE - TELEVISION BROADCASTING - See GREECE - BROADCASTING

GREECE - TELEVISION RECEIVER PRODUCTION

European Community Information Service, 2100 M Street, NW, Washington, D.C. 20037 (202) 862-9500; *Basic Statistics of the Community.*

Statistical Office of the United Nations, Publishing Service, New York, New York 10017 (800) 253-9646; *Statistical Yearbook.*

GREECE - TEXTILE INDUSTRY

European Community Information Service, 2100 M Street, NW, Washington, D.C. 20037 (202) 862-9500; *Basic Statistics of the Community, Eurostatistics: Data for Short-Term Economic Analysis,* and *Industrial Production: Quarterly Statistics.*

Forest and Paper Association, 1250 Connecticut Avenue, NW, Washington, D.C. 20036 (202) 463-2455; *Wood Pulp and Fiber Statistics.*

G.K. Hall and Company, 70 Lincoln Street, Boston, Massachusetts 02111 (617) 423-3990; *The World in Figures.*

Organisation for Economic Co-operation and Development (OECD), 2 rue Andre-Pascal, 75 Paris 16, France (Telephone Number in U.S. (202) 785-6323); *Foreign Trade by Commodities, Industrial Structure Statistics,* and *Textile Industry in OECD Countries.*

Statistical Office of the United Nations, Publishing Service, New York, New York 10017; *Statistical Yearbook.*

GREECE - THEATRE

United Nations Educational, Scientific and Cultural Organization (UNESCO), 7 Place de Fontenoy, F-75700 Paris, France (Telephone Number in U.S. (212) 963-5981); *Statistical Yearbook.*

GREECE - TIMBER - See GREECE - FORESTRY AND FOREST PRODUCTS

GREECE - TIN - See GREECE - MINING AND MINERAL PRODUCTS

GREECE - TOBACCO PRODUCTION

Commodity Research Bureau, Incorporated, 75 Wall Street, New York, New York 10005 (212) 504-7754; *Commodity Year Book.*

Euromonitor Publications Limited, 87-88 Turnmill Street, London EC1M 5QU, England; *European Marketing Data and Statistics.*

European Community Information Service, 2100 M Street, NW, Washington, D.C. 20037 (202) 862-9500; *Basic Statistics of the Community* and *Industrial Production: Quarterly Statistics.*

Facts on File, 460 Park Avenue South, New York, New York 10016 (800) 443-8323; *The New Book of World Rankings.*

Organisation for Economic Co-operation and Development (OECD), 2 rue Andre-Pascal, 75 Paris 16, France (Telephone Number in U.S. (202) 785-6323); *Foreign Trade by Commodities,* and *Industrial Structure Statistics.*

Statistical Office of the United Nations, Publishing Service, New York, New York 10017 (800) 253-9646; *Statistical Yearbook.*

GREECE - TOURISM

Euromonitor Publications Limited, 87-88 Turnmill Street, London EC1M 5QU, England; *European Marketing Data and Statistics.*

European Community Information Service, 2100 M Street, NW, Washington, D.C. 20037 (202) 862-9500; *Transport Annual Statistics.*

Facts on File, 460 Park Avenue South, New York, New York 10016 (800) 443-8323; *The New Book of World Rankings.*

Federal Statistical Office, Gustav - Stresemann - Ring 11, D-6200 Wiesbaden, Germany; *Griechenland.*

G.K. Hall and Company, 70 Lincoln Street, Boston, Massachusetts 02111 (617) 423-3990; *The World in Figures.*

Organisation for Economic Co-operation and Development (OECD), 2 rue Andre-Pascal, 75 Paris 16, France (Telephone Number in U.S. (202) 785-6323); *Tourism Policy and International Tourism in OECD Member Countries.*

Statistical Office of the United Nations, Publishing Service, New York, New York 10017 (800) 253-9646; *Statistical Yearbook.*

Times Books, 201 East 50th Street, New York, New York 10022 (212) 751-2600; *The Economist Book of Vital World Statistics.*

World Tourism Organization, Calle Capitan Haya 42, E-28020 Madrid, Spain; *Yearbook of Tourism Statistics.*

GREECE - TRACTORS IN USE

European Community Information Service, 2100 M Street, NW, Washington, D.C. 20037 (202) 862-9500; *Transport Annual Statistics.*

Statistical Office of the United Nations, Publishing Service, New York, New York 10017 (800) 253-9646; *Statistical Yearbook.*

GREECE - TRADE - See GREECE - FOREIGN TRADE

GREECE - TRADEMARKS AND SERVICE MARKS

Statistical Office of the United Nations, Publishing Service, New York, New York 10017 (800) 253-9646; *Statistical Yearbook.*

GREECE - TRANSPORTATION AND COMMUNICATIONS

European Community Information Service, 2100 M Street, NW, Washington, D.C. 20037 (202) 862-9500; *Basic Statistics of the Community, Energy Statistics Yearbook, Regions: Statistical Yearbook,* and *Transport Annual Statistics.*

Facts on File, 460 Park Avenue South, New York, New York 10016 (800) 443-8323; *The New Book of World Rankings.*

Federal Statistical Office, Gustav - Stresemann - Ring 11, D-6200 Wiesbaden, Germany; *Griechenland.*

G.K. Hall and Company, 70 Lincoln Street, Boston, Massachusetts 02111 (617) 423-3990; *The World in Figures.*

GREECE - TUNGSTEN PRODUCTION AND CONSUMPTION - See GREECE - MINING AND MINERAL PRODUCTS

GREECE - TURKEYS - See GREECE - LIVESTOCK AND POULTRY

GREECE - UNEMPLOYMENT

Euromonitor Publications Limited, 87-88 Turnmill Street, London EC1M 5QU, England; *European Marketing Data and Statistics.*

European Community Information Service, 2100 M Street, NW, Washington, D.C. 20037 (202) 862-9500; *Basic Statistics of the Community, Employment and Unemployment, Eurostat Review,* and *Labor Force Sample Survey.*

International Labour Office, I.L.O. Publications, CH-1211, Geneva 22, Switzerland; *Yearbook of Labour Statistics.*

Organisation for Economic Co-operation and Development (OECD), 2 rue Andre-Pascal, 75 Paris 16, France (Telephone Number in U.S. (202) 785-6323); *Economic Outlook,* and *OECD Employment Outlook.*

Statistical Office of the United Nations, Publishing Service, New York, New York 10017 (800) 253-9646; *Statistical Yearbook.*

GREECE - URANIUM PRODUCTION AND CONSUMPTION - See GREECE - MINING AND MINERAL PRODUCTS

GREECE - UTILITIES

European Community Information Service, 2100 M Street, NW, Washington, D.C. 20037 (202) 862-9500; *Basic Statistics of the Community.*

GREECE - VANADIUM AND VANADIUM ORE - See GREECE - MINING AND MINERAL PRODUCTS

GREECE - VITAL STATISTICS

European Community Information Service, 2100 M Street, NW, Washington, D.C. 20037 (202) 862-9500; *Basic Statistics of the Community,* and *Eurostat Review.*

G.K. Hall and Company, 70 Lincoln Street, Boston, Massachusetts 02111 (617) 423-3990; *The World in Figures.*

Statistical Office of the United Nations, Publishing Service, New York, New York 10017 (800) 253-9646; *Statistical Yearbook.*

World Health Organization, Office of Publications, Avenue Appia, CH-1211 Geneva 27, Switzerland (Telephone Number in U.S. (518) 436-9686); *World Health Statistics Annual.*

GREECE - WAGES

Euromonitor Publications Limited, 87-88 Turnmill Street, London EC1M 5QU, England; *European Marketing Data and Statistics.*

European Community Information Service, 2100 M Street, NW, Washington, D.C. 20037 (202) 862-9500; *Basic Statistics of the Community, Earnings in Agriculture,* and *Eurostat Review.*

Federal Statistical Office, Gustav - Stresemann - Ring 11, D-6200 Wiesbaden, Germany; *Griechenland.*

G.K. Hall and Company, 70 Lincoln Street, Boston, Massachusetts 02111 (617) 423-3990; *The World in Figures.*

International Labour Office, I.L.O. Publications, CH-1211, Geneva 22, Switzerland; *Yearbook of Labour Statistics.*

Organisation for Economic Co-operation and Development (OECD), 2 rue Andre-Pascal, 75 Paris 16, France (Telephone Number in U.S. (202) 785-6323); *Economic Outlook, Industrial Structure Statistics,* and *Main Economic Indicators - Historical Statistics.*

Statistical Office of the United Nations, Publishing Service, New York, New York 10017 (800) 253-9646; *Statistical Yearbook.*

GREECE - WALNUT PRODUCTION - See GREECE - CROPS

GREECE - WATERMELON PRODUCTION - See GREECE - CROPS

GREECE - WATERWAYS IN USE - See GREECE - MERCHANT SHIPPING

GREECE - WEATHER

Facts on File, 460 Park Avenue South, New York, New York 10016 (800) 443-8323; *The New Book of World Rankings.*

G.K. Hall and Company, 70 Lincoln Street, Boston, Massachusetts 02111 (617) 423-3990; *The World in Figures.*

GREECE - WELFARE

European Community Information Service, 2100 M Street, NW, Washington, D.C. 20037 (202) 862-9500; *Basic Statistics of the Community,* and *Eurostat Review.*

International Monetary Fund, 700 Nineteenth Street, NW, Washington, D.C. 20431 (202) 623-7000; *Government Finance Statistics Yearbook.*

GREECE - WHEAT PRODUCTION AND PRICES - See GREECE - CROPS

GREECE - WHOLESALE PRICES

European Community Information Service, 2100 M Street, NW, Washington, D.C. 20037 (202) 862-9500; *Basic Statistics of the Community.*

International Monetary Fund, 700 Nineteenth Street, NW, Washington, D.C. 20431 (202) 623-7000; *International Financial Statistics.*

Statistical Office of the United Nations, Publishing Service, New York, New York 10017 (800) 253-9646; *Statistical Yearbook.*

GREECE - WHOLESALE TRADE

European Community Information Service, 2100 M Street, NW, Washington, D.C. 20037 (202) 862-9500; *Basic Statistics of the Community,* and *Eurostat Review.*

Statistical Office of the United Nations, Publishing Service, New York, New York 10017 (800) 253-9646; *Statistical Yearbook.*

GREECE - WINE PRODUCTION

European Community Information Service, 2100 M Street, NW, Washington, D.C. 20037 (202) 862-9500; *Basic Statistics of the Community.*

Facts on File, 460 Park Avenue South, New York, New York 10016 (800) 443-8323; *The New Book of World Rankings.*

Statistical Office of the United Nations, Publishing Service, New York, New York 10017 (800) 253-9646; *Statistical Yearbook.*

GREECE - WOOD AND WOOD PULP - See GREECE - FORESTRY AND FOREST PRODUCTS

GREECE - WOOL - INDUSTRIAL CONSUMPTION

Organisation for Economic Co-operation and Development (OECD), 2 rue Andre-Pascal, 75 Paris 16, France (Telephone Number in U.S. (202) 785-6323); *Textile Industry in OECD Countries.*

Statistical Office of the United Nations, Publishing Service, New York, New York 10017 (800) 253-9646; *Statistical Yearbook.*

GREECE - WOOL PRODUCTION

European Community Information Service, 2100 M Street, NW, Washington, D.C. 20037 (202) 862-9500; *Basic Statistics of the Community.*

Facts on File, 460 Park Avenue South, New York, New York 10016 (800) 443-8323; *The New Book of World Rankings.*

Organisation for Economic Co-operation and Development (OECD), 2 rue Andre-Pascal, 75 Paris 16, France (Telephone Number in U.S. (202) 785-6323); *Economic Accounts for Agriculture,* and *Textile Industry in OECD Countries.*

Statistical Office of the United Nations, Publishing Service, New York, New York 10017 (800) 253-9646; *Statistical Yearbook.*

GREECE - YARN PRODUCTION

European Community Information Service, 2100 M Street, NW, Washington, D.C. 20037 (202) 862-9500; *Basic Statistics of the Community.*

Organisation for Economic Co-operation and Development (OECD), 2 rue Andre-Pascal, 75 Paris 16, France (Telephone Number in U.S. (202) 785-6323); *Foreign Trade by Commodities,* and *Textile Industry in OECD Countries.*

Statistical Office of the United Nations, Publishing Service, New York, New York 10017 (800) 253-9646; *Statistical Yearbook.*

GREECE - ZINC AND ZINC ORE - See GREECE - MINING AND MINERAL PRODUCTS

GREECE - ZOOS AND BOTANICAL GARDENS

United Nations Educational, Scientific and Cultural Organization (UNESCO), 7 Place de Fontenoy, F-75700 Paris, France (Telephone Number in U.S. (212) 963-5981); *Statistical Yearbook.*

GREEK LETTER SOCIETIES

Gale Research Incorporated, 835 Penobscot Building, Detroit, Michigan 48226 (800) 877-4253; *Encyclopedia of Associations.*

Greenland - Primary Statistics Source

Danmarks Statistik, Seiro-gade 11, 2100 Kobenhaun 0, Denmark; *Statistik Arbog* (Statistical Yearbook).

GREENLAND - ABORTIONS

Statistical Office of the United Nations, Publishing Service, New York, New York 10017 (800) 253-9646; *Demographic Yearbook.*

GREENLAND - AGRICULTURE

Federal Statistical Office, Gustav-Stresemann-Ring 11, D-6200 Wiesbaden, Germany; *Greenland.*

Food and Agricultural Organization of the United Nations (FAO) Via delle Terme di Caracalla, 00100 Rome, Italy (Telephone Number in U.S. (202) 653-2400); *Production Yearbook, The State of Food and Agriculture,* and *Trade Yearbook.*

G.K. Hall and Company, 70 Lincoln Street, Boston, Massachusetts 02111 (617) 423-3990; *The World in Figures.*

Statistical Office of the United Nations, Publishing Service, New York, New York 10017 (800) 253-9646; *Statistical Yearbook.*

GREENLAND - AIRLINE SERVICE

G.K. Hall and Company, 70 Lincoln Street, Boston, Massachusetts 02111 (617) 423-3990; *The World in Figures.*

GREENLAND - AREA AND DENSITY OF POPULATION

Federal Statistical Office, Gustav-Stresemann-Ring 11, D-6200 Wiesbaden, Germany; *Greenland.*

Food and Agricultural Organization of the United Nations (FAO) Via delle Terme di Caracalla, 00100 Rome, Italy (Telephone Number in U.S. (202) 653-2400); *The State of Food and Agriculture.*

G.K. Hall and Company, 70 Lincoln Street, Boston, Massachusetts 02111 (617) 423-3990; *The World in Figures.*

Statistical Office of the United Nations, Publishing Service, New York, New York 10017 (800) 253-9646; *Statistical Yearbook.*

United Nations Educational, Scientific and Cultural Organization (UNESCO), 7 Place de Fontenoy, F-75700 Paris, France (Telephone Number in U.S. (212) 963-5981); *Statistical Yearbook.*

GREENLAND - BALANCE OF PAYMENTS

Federal Statistical Office, Gustav-Stresemann-Ring 11, D-6200 Wiesbaden, Germany; *Greenland.*

G.K. Hall and Company, 70 Lincoln Street, Boston, Massachusetts 02111 (617) 423-3990; *The World in Figures.*

GREENLAND - BANKING

G.K. Hall and Company, 70 Lincoln Street, Boston, Massachusetts 02111 (617) 423-3990; *The World in Figures.*

GREENLAND - BIRTH RATES

Statistical Office of the United Nations, Publishing Service, New York, New York 10017 (800) 253-9646; *Demographic Yearbook,* and *Statistical Yearbook.*

GREENLAND - BONDS

G.K. Hall and Company, 70 Lincoln Street, Boston, Massachusetts 02111 (617) 423-3990; *The World in Figures.*

GREENLAND - BOOK PRODUCTION

G.K. Hall and Company, 70 Lincoln Street, Boston, Massachusetts 02111 (617) 423-3990; *The World in Figures.*

GREENLAND - BROADCASTING

G.K. Hall and Company, 70 Lincoln Street, Boston, Massachusetts 02111 (617) 423-3990; *The World in Figures.*

GREENLAND - BUSINESS

G.K. Hall and Company, 70 Lincoln Street, Boston, Massachusetts 02111 (617) 423-3990; *The World in Figures.*

GREENLAND - CALORIE SUPPLY

Food and Agricultural Organization of the United Nations (FAO) Via delle Terme di Caracalla, 00100 Rome, Italy (Telephone Number in U.S. (202) 653-2400); *The State of Food and Agriculture.*

GREENLAND - CHEMICAL (ORGANIC) PRODUCTION - See GREENLAND - MINING AND MINERAL PRODUCTS

GREENLAND - CLASS STRUCTURE

G.K. Hall and Company, 70 Lincoln Street, Boston, Massachusetts 02111 (617) 423-3990; *The World in Figures.*

GREENLAND - CLIMATE

G.K. Hall and Company, 70 Lincoln Street, Boston, Massachusetts 02111 (617) 423-3990; *The World in Figures.*

GREENLAND - COAL PRODUCTION AND CONSUMPTION - See GREENLAND - MINING AND MINERAL PRODUCTS

GREENLAND - COCOA BEANS PRODUCTION - See GREENLAND - CROPS

GREENLAND - COMMUNICATIONS

Federal Statistical Office, Gustav-Stresemann-Ring 11, D-6200 Wiesbaden, Germany; *Greenland.*

G.K. Hall and Company, 70 Lincoln Street, Boston, Massachusetts 02111 (617) 423-3990; *The World in Figures.*

GREENLAND - CONSTRUCTION INDUSTRY

Statistical Office of the United Nations, Publishing Service, New York, New York 10017 (800) 253-9646; *Yearbook of Construction Statistics.*

GREENLAND - CONSUMER PRICE INDEX

G.K. Hall and Company, 70 Lincoln Street, Boston, Massachusetts 02111 (617) 423-3990; *The World in Figures.*

International Labour Office, I.L.O. Publications, CH-1211, Geneva 22, Switzerland; *Yearbook of Labour Statistics.*

Statistical Office of the United Nations, Publishing Service, New York, New York 10017 (800) 253-9646; *Statistical Yearbook.*

GREENLAND - CONSUMER PRICES

International Labour Office, I.L.O. Publications, CH-1211, Geneva 22, Switzerland; *Yearbook of Labour Statistics.*

GREENLAND - CONSUMPTION

G.K. Hall and Company, 70 Lincoln Street, Boston, Massachusetts 02111 (617) 423-3990; *The World in Figures.*

GREENLAND - CORN PRODUCTION - See GREENLAND - CROPS

GREENLAND - CORPORATE TAXES - See GREENLAND - TAXATION

GREENLAND - CROPS

Food and Agricultural Organization of the United Nations (FAO) Via delle Terme di Caracalla, 00100 Rome, Italy (Telephone Number in U.S. (202) 653-2400); *The State of Food and Agriculture.*

G.K. Hall and Company, 70 Lincoln Street, Boston, Massachusetts 02111 (617) 423-3990; *The World in Figures.*

Statistical Office of the United Nations, Publishing Service, New York, New York 10017 (800) 253-9646; *Statistical Yearbook.*

GREENLAND - CUSTOMS DUTIES

G.K. Hall and Company, 70 Lincoln Street, Boston, Massachusetts 02111 (617) 423-3990; *The World in Figures.*

GREENLAND - DAIRY PRODUCTS

GREENLAND - DEATH RATES

G.K. Hall and Company, 70 Lincoln Street, Boston, Massachusetts 02111 (617) 423-3990; *The World in Figures.*

Statistical Office of the United Nations, Publishing Service, New York, New York 10017 (800) 253-9646; *Statistical Yearbook.*

World Health Organization, Office of Publications, Avenue Appia, CH-1211 Geneva 27, Switzerland (Telephone Number in U.S. (518) 436-9686); *World Health Statistics Annual.*

GREENLAND - DEFENSE EXPENDITURES

G.K. Hall and Company, 70 Lincoln Street, Boston, Massachusetts 02111 (617) 423-3990; *The World in Figures.*

GREENLAND - DEMOGRAPHY

G.K. Hall and Company, 70 Lincoln Street, Boston, Massachusetts 02111 (617) 423-3990; *The World in Figures.*

GREENLAND - DEVELOPMENT ASSISTANCE

G.K. Hall and Company, 70 Lincoln Street, Boston, Massachusetts 02111 (617) 423-3990; *The World in Figures.*

GREENLAND - DISEASES

G.K. Hall and Company, 70 Lincoln Street, Boston, Massachusetts 02111 (617) 423-3990; *The World in Figures.*

World Health Organization, Office of Publications, Avenue Appia, CH-1211 Geneva 27, Switzerland (Telephone Number in U.S. (518) 436-9686); *World Health Statistics Annual.*

GREENLAND - DIVORCE RATES

Statistical Office of the United Nations, Publishing Service, New York, New York 10017 (800) 253-9646; *Demographic Yearbook,* and *Statistical Yearbook.*

GREENLAND - DOMESTIC PRODUCT

G.K. Hall and Company, 70 Lincoln Street, Boston, Massachusetts 02111 (617) 423-3990; *The World in Figures.*

GREENLAND - ECONOMY

G.K. Hall and Company, 70 Lincoln Street, Boston, Massachusetts 02111 (617) 423-3990; *The World in Figures.*

GREENLAND - EDUCATION

Federal Statistical Office, Gustav-Stresemann-Ring 11, D-6200 Wiesbaden, Germany; *Greenland.*

G.K. Hall and Company, 70 Lincoln Street, Boston, Massachusetts 02111 (617) 423-3990; *The World in Figures.*

GREENLAND - EGG PRODUCTION - See GREENLAND - DAIRY PRODUCTS

GREENLAND - ELECTRICITY

Statistical Office of the United Nations, Publishing Service, New York, New York 10017 (800) 253-9646; *Statistical Yearbook.*

GREENLAND - EMPLOYMENT

Federal Statistical Office, Gustav-Stresemann-Ring 11, D-6200 Wiesbaden, Germany; *Greenland.*

International Labour Office, I.L.O. Publications, CH-1211, Geneva 22, Switzerland; *Yearbook of Labour Statistics.*

GREENLAND - ENERGY

Food and Agricultural Organization of the United Nations (FAO) Via delle Terme di Caracalla, 00100 Rome, Italy (Telephone Number in U.S. (202) 653-2400); *The State of Food and Agriculture.*

G.K. Hall and Company, 70 Lincoln Street, Boston, Massachusetts 02111 (617) 423-3990; *The World in Figures.*

Statistical Office of the United Nations, Publishing Service, New York, New York 10017 (800) 253-9646; *Statistical Yearbook,* and *Yearbook of World Energy Statistics.*

GREENLAND - EXPORTS

Food and Agricultural Organization of the United Nations (FAO) Via delle Terme di Caracalla, 00100 Rome, Italy (Telephone Number in U.S. (202) 653-2400); *The State of Food and Agriculture.*

G.K. Hall and Company, 70 Lincoln Street, Boston, Massachusetts 02111 (617) 423-3990; *The World in Figures.*

International Monetary Fund, 700 Nineteenth Street, NW, Washington, D.C. 20431 (202) 623-7000; *Direction of Trade Statistics.*

Organisation for Economic Co-operation and Development (OECD), 2 rue Andre-Pascal, 75 Paris 16, France (Telephone Number in U.S. (202) 785-6323); *Review of Fisheries in OECD Member Countries.*

GREENLAND - EXTERNAL TRADE

Food and Agricultural Organization of the United Nations (FAO) Via delle Terme di Caracalla, 00100 Rome, Italy (Telephone Number in U.S. (202) 653-2400); *The State of Food and Agriculture,* and *Trade Yearbook.*

G.K. Hall and Company, 70 Lincoln Street, Boston, Massachusetts 02111 (617) 423-3990; *The World in Figures.*

GREENLAND - FARM CROPS - See GREENLAND - CROPS

GREENLAND - FERTILIZER

Food and Agricultural Organization of the United Nations (FAO) Via delle Terme di Caracalla, 00100 Rome, Italy (Telephone Number in U.S. (202) 653-2400); *The State of Food and Agriculture.*

GREENLAND - FETAL MORTALITY

Statistical Office of the United Nations, Publishing Service, New York, New York 10017 (800) 253-9646; *Demographic Yearbook.*

World Health Organization, Office of Publications, Avenue Appia, CH-1211 Geneva 27, Switzerland (Telephone Number in U.S. (518) 436-9686); *World Health Statistics Annual.*

GREENLAND - FINANCE

Federal Statistical Office, Gustav-Stresemann-Ring 11, D-6200 Wiesbaden, Germany; *Greenland.*

G.K. Hall and Company, 70 Lincoln Street, Boston, Massachusetts 02111 (617) 423-3990; *The World in Figures.*

GREENLAND - FISHERIES

Federal Statistical Office, Gustav-Stresemann-Ring 11, D-6200 Wiesbaden, Germany; *Greenland.*

Food and Agricultural Organization of the United Nations (FAO) Via delle Terme di Caracalla, 00100 Rome, Italy (Telephone Number in U.S. (202) 653-2400); *The State of Food and Agriculture,* and *Yearbook of Fishery Statistics.*

Organisation for Economic Co-operation and Development (OECD), 2 rue Andre-Pascal, 75 Paris 16, France (Telephone Number in U.S. (202) 785-6323); *Review of Fisheries in OECD Member Countries.*

Statistical Office of the United Nations, Publishing Service, New York, New York 10017 (800) 253-9646; *Statistical Yearbook.*

GREENLAND - FOOD PRODUCTION AND CONSUMPTION

Food and Agricultural Organization of the United Nations (FAO) Via delle Terme di Caracalla, 00100 Rome, Italy (Telephone Number in U.S. (202) 653-2400); *The State of Food and Agriculture.*

G.K. Hall and Company, 70 Lincoln Street, Boston, Massachusetts 02111 (617) 423-3990; *The World in Figures.*

GREENLAND - FOOD PRODUCTS - EXPORTS AND IMPORTS

Food and Agricultural Organization of the United Nations (FAO) Via delle Terme di Caracalla, 00100 Rome, Italy (Telephone Number in U.S. (202) 653-2400); *The State of Food and Agriculture.*

GREENLAND - FOOD SUPPLY

Food and Agricultural Organization of the United Nations (FAO), Via delle Terme di Caracalla, 00100 Rome, Italy (Telephone Number in U.S. (202) 653-2400); *Production Yearbook,* and *The State of Food and Agriculture.*

GREENLAND - FOODSTUFF CONSUMPTION

Food and Agricultural Organization of the United Nations (FAO) Via delle Terme di Caracalla, 00100 Rome, Italy (Telephone Number in U.S. (202) 653-2400); *The State of Food and Agriculture.*

GREENLAND - FOREIGN AID

G.K. Hall and Company, 70 Lincoln Street, Boston, Massachusetts 02111 (617) 423-3990; *The World in Figures.*

GREENLAND - FOREIGN TRADE

Federal Statistical Office, Gustav-Stresemann-Ring 11, D-6200 Wiesbaden, Germany; *Greenland.*

Food and Agricultural Organization of the United Nations (FAO) Via delle Terme di Caracalla, 00100 Rome, Italy (Telephone Number in U.S. (202) 653-2400); *The State of Food and Agriculture.*

G.K. Hall and Company, 70 Lincoln Street, Boston, Massachusetts 02111 (617) 423-3990; *The World in Figures.*

Statistical Office of the United Nations, Publishing Service, New York, New York 10017 (800) 253-9646; *International Trade Statistics Yearbook, Statistical Yearbook,* and *Yearbook of International Trade Statistics.*

GREENLAND - FORESTRY AND FOREST PRODUCTS

Federal Statistical Office, Gustav-Stresemann-Ring 11, D-6200 Wiesbaden, Germany; *Greenland.*

Food and Agricultural Organization of the United Nations (FAO) Via delle Terme di Caracalla, 00100 Rome, Italy (Telephone Number in U.S. (202) 653-2400); *The State of Food and Agriculture.*

G.K. Hall and Company, 70 Lincoln Street, Boston, Massachusetts 02111 (617) 423-3990; *The World in Figures.*

GREENLAND - GENERAL MORTALITY

Statistical Office of the United Nations, Publishing Service, New York, New York 10017 (800) 253-9646; *Demographic Yearbook.*

World Health Organization, Office of Publications, Avenue Appia, CH-1211 Geneva 27, Switzerland (Telephone Number in U.S. (518) 436-9686); *World Health Statistics Annual.*

GREENLAND - GOVERNMENT

G.K. Hall and Company, 70 Lincoln Street, Boston, Massachusetts 02111 (617) 423-3990; *The World in Figures.*

GREENLAND - GRAIN PRODUCTION - See GREENLAND - CROPS

GREENLAND - GROSS DOMESTIC PRODUCT

G.K. Hall and Company, 70 Lincoln Street, Boston, Massachusetts 02111 (617) 423-3990; *The World in Figures.*

GREENLAND - HEALTH

Federal Statistical Office, Gustav-Stresemann-Ring 11, D-6200 Wiesbaden, Germany; *Greenland.*

G.K. Hall and Company, 70 Lincoln Street, Boston, Massachusetts 02111 (617) 423-3990; *The World in Figures.*

Statistical Office of the United Nations, Publishing Service, New York, New York 10017 (800) 253-9646; *Statistical Yearbook.*

World Health Organization, Office of Publications, Avenue Appia, CH-1211 Geneva 27, Switzerland (Telephone Number in U.S. (518) 436-9686); *World Health Statistics Annual.*

GREENLAND - HIGHWAYS

G.K. Hall and Company, 70 Lincoln Street, Boston, Massachusetts 02111 (617) 423-3990; *The World in Figures.*

GREENLAND - HOURS OF WORK - See GREENLAND - EMPLOYMENT

GREENLAND - ILLITERATE POPULATION

G.K. Hall and Company, 70 Lincoln Street, Boston, Massachusetts 02111 (617) 423-3990; *The World in Figures.*

GREENLAND - IMPORTS

Food and Agricultural Organization of the United Nations (FAO) Via delle Terme di Caracalla, 00100 Rome, Italy (Telephone Number in U.S. (202) 653-2400); *The State of Food and Agriculture.*

G.K. Hall and Company, 70 Lincoln Street, Boston, Massachusetts 02111 (617) 423-3990; *The World in Figures.*

International Monetary Fund, 700 Nineteenth Street, NW, Washington, D.C. 20431 (202) 623-7000; *Direction of Trade Statistics.*

Organisation for Economic Co-operation and Development (OECD), 2 rue Andre-Pascal, 75 Paris 16, France (Telephone Number in U.S. (202) 785-6323); *Review of Fisheries in OECD Member Countries.*

GREENLAND - INDUSTRIAL ACCIDENTS

International Labour Office, I.L.O. Publications, CH-1211, Geneva 22, Switzerland; *Yearbook of Labour Statistics.*

GREENLAND - INDUSTRIAL DISPUTES

International Labour Office, I.L.O. Publications, CH-1211, Geneva 22, Switzerland; *Yearbook of Labour Statistics.*

GREENLAND - INDUSTRY

Federal Statistical Office, Gustav-Stresemann-Ring 11, D-6200 Wiesbaden, Germany; *Greenland.*

G.K. Hall and Company, 70 Lincoln Street, Boston, Massachusetts 02111 (617) 423-3990; *The World in Figures.*

GREENLAND - INFANT AND MATERNAL MORTALITY

Statistical Office of the United Nations, Publishing Service, New York, New York 10017 (800) 253-9646; *Demographic Yearbook,* and *Statistical Yearbook.*

World Health Organization, Office of Publications, Avenue Appia, CH-1211 Geneva 27, Switzerland (Telephone Number in U.S. (518) 436-9686); *World Health Statistics Annual.*

GREENLAND - LABOR FORCE

Food and Agricultural Organization of the United Nations (FAO) Via delle Terme di Caracalla, 00100 Rome, Italy (Telephone Number in U.S. (202) 653-2400); *The State of Food and Agriculture.*

G.K. Hall and Company, 70 Lincoln Street, Boston, Massachusetts 02111 (617) 423-3990; *The World in Figures.*

GREENLAND - LABOR PRODUCTIVITY

International Labour Office, I.L.O. Publications, CH-1211, Geneva 22, Switzerland; *Yearbook of Labour Statistics*.

GREENLAND - LAND USE

Food and Agricultural Organization of the United Nations (FAO), Via delle Terme di Caracalla, 00100 Rome, Italy (Telephone Number in U.S. (202) 653-2400); *Production Yearbook*.

G.K. Hall and Company, 70 Lincoln Street, Boston, Massachusetts 02111 (617) 423-3990; *The World in Figures*.

GREENLAND - LIBRARIES

United Nations Educational, Scientific and Cultural Organization (UNESCO), 7 Place de Fontenoy, F-75700 Paris, France (Telephone Number in U.S. (212) 963-5981); *Statistical Yearbook*.

GREENLAND - LIVESTOCK AND POULTRY

Food and Agricultural Organization of the United Nations (FAO), Via delle Terme di Caracalla, 00100 Rome, Italy (Telephone Number in U.S. (202) 653-2400); *Production Yearbook*, and *The State of Food and Agriculture*.

G.K. Hall and Company, 70 Lincoln Street, Boston, Massachusetts 02111 (617) 423-3990; *The World in Figures*.

Statistical Office of the United Nations, Publishing Service, New York, New York 10017 (800) 253-9646; *Statistical Yearbook*.

GREENLAND - LIVING LEVELS

G.K. Hall and Company, 70 Lincoln Street, Boston, Massachusetts 02111 (617) 423-3990; *The World in Figures*.

GREENLAND - MANUFACTURING

G.K. Hall and Company, 70 Lincoln Street, Boston, Massachusetts 02111 (617) 423-3990; *The World in Figures*.

GREENLAND - MARRIAGE RATES

Statistical Office of the United Nations, Publishing Service, New York, New York 10017 (800) 253-9646; *Demographic Yearbook*, and *Statistical Yearbook*.

GREENLAND - MEAT PRODUCTION - See GREENLAND - LIVESTOCK AND POULTRY

GREENLAND - MERCHANT SHIPPING

G.K. Hall and Company, 70 Lincoln Street, Boston, Massachusetts 02111 (617) 423-3990; *The World in Figures*.

Statistical Office of the United Nations, Publishing Service, New York, New York 10017 (800) 253-9646; *Statistical Yearbook*.

GREENLAND - MILITARY

G.K. Hall and Company, 70 Lincoln Street, Boston, Massachusetts 02111 (617) 423-3990; *The World in Figures*.

GREENLAND - MINING AND MINERAL PRODUCTS

G.K. Hall and Company, 70 Lincoln Street, Boston, Massachusetts 02111 (617) 423-3990; *The World in Figures*.

GREENLAND - MONEY SUPPLY

G.K. Hall and Company, 70 Lincoln Street, Boston, Massachusetts 02111 (617) 423-3990; *The World in Figures*.

GREENLAND - MOTOR VEHICLES IN USE

G.K. Hall and Company, 70 Lincoln Street, Boston, Massachusetts 02111 (617) 423-3990; *The World in Figures*.

Statistical Office of the United Nations, Publishing Service, New York, New York 10017 (800) 253-9646; *Statistical Yearbook*.

GREENLAND - NATALITY

Statistical Office of the United Nations, Publishing Service, New York, New York 10017 (800) 253-9646; *Demographic Yearbook*.

World Health Organization, Office of Publications, Avenue Appia, CH-1211 Geneva 27, Switzerland (Telephone Number in U.S. (518) 436-9686); *World Health Statistics Annual*.

GREENLAND - NATIONAL ACCOUNTS

Federal Statistical Office, Gustav-Stresemann-Ring 11, D-6200 Wiesbaden, Germany; *Greenland*.

GREENLAND - NATIONAL INCOME

G.K. Hall and Company, 70 Lincoln Street, Boston, Massachusetts 02111 (617) 423-3990; *The World in Figures*.

GREENLAND - NEWSPAPER PRODUCTION - See GREENLAND - FORESTRY AND FOREST PRODUCTS

GREENLAND - OCCUPATIONS - See GREENLAND - LABOR FORCE

GREENLAND - PESTICIDE USE

Food and Agricultural Organization of the United Nations (FAO) Via delle Terme di Caracalla, 00100 Rome, Italy (Telephone Number in U.S. (202) 653-2400); *The State of Food and Agriculture*.

GREENLAND - PETROLEUM INDUSTRY

Food and Agricultural Organization of the United Nations (FAO) Via delle Terme di Caracalla, 00100 Rome, Italy (Telephone Number in U.S. (202) 653-2400); *The State of Food and Agriculture*.

G.K. Hall and Company, 70 Lincoln Street, Boston, Massachusetts 02111 (617) 423-3990; *The World in Figures*.

GREENLAND - POPULATION

Federal Statistical Office, Gustav-Stresemann-Ring 11, D-6200 Wiesbaden, Germany; *Greenland*.

Food and Agricultural Organization of the United Nations (FAO), Via delle Terme di Caracalla, 00100 Rome, Italy (Telephone Number in U.S. (202) 653-2400); *Production Yearbook*.

G.K. Hall and Company, 70 Lincoln Street, Boston, Massachusetts 02111 (617) 423-3990; *The World in Figures*.

International Labour Office, I.L.O. Publications, CH-1211, Geneva 22, Switzerland; *Yearbook of Labour Statistics*.

Statistical Office of the United Nations, Publishing Service, New York, New York 10017 (800) 253-9646; *Demographic Yearbook*, and

Statistical Yearbook.

United Nations Educational, Scientific and Cultural Organization (UNESCO), 7 Place de Fontenoy, F-75700 Paris, France (Telephone Number in U.S. (212) 963-5981); *Statistical Yearbook.*

World Health Organization, Office of Publications, Avenue Appia, CH-1211 Geneva 27, Switzerland (Telephone Number in U.S. (518) 436-9686); *World Health Statistics Annual.*

GREENLAND - PRICES

Federal Statistical Office, Gustav-Stresemann-Ring 11, D-6200 Wiesbaden, Germany; *Greenland.*

Food and Agricultural Organization of the United Nations (FAO), Via delle Terme di Caracalla, 00100 Rome, Italy (Telephone Number in U.S. (202) 653-2400); *Production Yearbook,* and *The State of Food and Agriculture.*

G.K. Hall and Company, 70 Lincoln Street, Boston, Massachusetts 02111 (617) 423-3990; *The World in Figures.*

International Labour Office, I.L.O. Publications, CH-1211, Geneva 22, Switzerland; *Yearbook of Labour Statistics.*

GREENLAND - PRODUCTION

G.K. Hall and Company, 70 Lincoln Street, Boston, Massachusetts 02111 (617) 423-3990; *The World in Figures.*

GREENLAND - RAILWAYS

G.K. Hall and Company, 70 Lincoln Street, Boston, Massachusetts 02111 (617) 423-3990; *The World in Figures.*

GREENLAND - RENT PRICES

International Labour Office, I.L.O. Publications, CH-1211, Geneva 22, Switzerland; *Yearbook of Labour Statistics.*

GREENLAND - RETAIL TRADE

G.K. Hall and Company, 70 Lincoln Street, Boston, Massachusetts 02111 (617) 423-3990; *The World in Figures.*

GREENLAND - SHEEP - See GREENLAND - LIVESTOCK AND POULTRY

GREENLAND - SOCIAL DATA

G.K. Hall and Company, 70 Lincoln Street, Boston, Massachusetts 02111 (617) 423-3990; *The World in Figures.*

GREENLAND - STOCKS - COMMODITY - MARKET PRICE - INDEX

Food and Agricultural Organization of the United Nations (FAO) Via delle Terme di Caracalla, 00100 Rome, Italy (Telephone Number in U.S. (202) 653-2400); *The State of Food and Agriculture.*

GREENLAND - TAXATION

G.K. Hall and Company, 70 Lincoln Street, Boston, Massachusetts 02111 (617) 423-3990; *The World in Figures.*

GREENLAND - TELEPHONES IN USE

G.K. Hall and Company, 70 Lincoln Street, Boston, Massachusetts 02111 (617) 423-3990; *The World in Figures.*

GREENLAND - TEXTILE INDUSTRY

G.K. Hall and Company, 70 Lincoln Street, Boston, Massachusetts 02111 (617) 423-3990; *The World in Figures.*

GREENLAND - TOURISM

Federal Statistical Office, Gustav-Stresemann-Ring 11, D-6200 Wiesbaden, Germany; *Greenland.*

G.K. Hall and Company, 70 Lincoln Street, Boston, Massachusetts 02111 (617) 423-3990; *The World in Figures.*

GREENLAND - TRACTORS IN USE

Statistical Office of the United Nations, Publishing Service, New York, New York 10017 (800) 253-9646; *Statistical Yearbook.*

GREENLAND - TRADE - See GREENLAND - FOREIGN TRADE

GREENLAND - TRANSPORTATION AND COMMUNICATIONS

Federal Statistical Office, Gustav-Stresemann-Ring 11, D-6200 Wiesbaden, Germany; *Greenland.*

G.K. Hall and Company, 70 Lincoln Street, Boston, Massachusetts 02111 (617) 423-3990; *The World in Figures.*

GREENLAND - UNEMPLOYMENT

International Labour Office, I.L.O. Publications, CH-1211, Geneva 22, Switzerland; *Yearbook of Labour Statistics.*

GREENLAND - VITAL STATISTICS

G.K. Hall and Company, 70 Lincoln Street, Boston, Massachusetts 02111 (617) 423-3990; *The World in Figures.*

Statistical Office of the United Nations, Publishing Service, New York, New York 10017 (800) 253-9646; *Statistical Yearbook.*

World Health Organization, Office of Publications, Avenue Appia, CH-1211 Geneva 27, Switzerland (Telephone Number in U.S. (518) 436-9686); *World Health Statistics Annual.*

GREENLAND - WAGES

Federal Statistical Office, Gustav-Stresemann-Ring 11, D-6200 Wiesbaden, Germany; *Greenland.*

G.K. Hall and Company, 70 Lincoln Street, Boston, Massachusetts 02111 (617) 423-3990; *The World in Figures.*

International Labour Office, I.L.O. Publications, CH-1211, Geneva 22, Switzerland; *Yearbook of Labour Statistics.*

GREENLAND - WEATHER

G.K. Hall and Company, 70 Lincoln Street, Boston, Massachusetts 02111 (617) 423-3990; *The World in Figures.*

Grenada - National Statistical Office

Statistics Department, Ministry of Finance, Saint George's, Grenada.

Grenada - Primary Statistics Source

HM Stationery Office, Post Office Box 569, London SE1 9NH, England; *Grenada: Report for the Year.*

GRENADA - AGRICULTURE

Federal Statistical Office, Gustav - Stresemann - Ring 11, D-6200 Wiesbaden, Germany; *Grenada.*

Food and Agricultural Organization of the United Nations (FAO) Via delle Terme di Caracalla, 00100 Rome, Italy (Telephone Number in U.S. (202) 653-2400); *Production Yearbook, The State of Food and Agriculture,* and *Trade Yearbook.*

G.K. Hall and Company, 70 Lincoln Street, Boston, Massachusetts 02111 (617) 423-3990; *The World in Figures.*

Statistical Office of the United Nations, Publishing Service, New York, New York 10017 (800) 253-9646; *Statistical Yearbook.*

The World Bank, 1818 H Street, NW, Washington, D.C. 20433 (202) 477-1234; *World Tables.*

GRENADA - AIRLINE SERVICE

G.K. Hall and Company, 70 Lincoln Street, Boston, Massachusetts 02111 (617) 423-3990; *The World in Figures.*

GRENADA - ANIMAL HEALTH

Food and Agricultural Organization of the United Nations (FAO), Via delle Terme di Caracalla, 00100 Rome, Italy (Telephone Number in U.S. (202) 653-2400); *Animal Health Yearbook.*

GRENADA - AREA AND DENSITY OF POPULATION

Federal Statistical Office, Gustav - Stresemann - Ring 11, D-6200 Wiesbaden, Germany; *Grenada.*

Food and Agricultural Organization of the United Nations (FAO) Via delle Terme di Caracalla, 00100 Rome, Italy (Telephone Number in U.S. (202) 653-2400); *The State of Food and Agriculture.*

G.K. Hall and Company, 70 Lincoln Street, Boston, Massachusetts 02111 (617) 423-3990; *The World in Figures.*

Statistical Office of the United Nations, Publishing Service, New York, New York 10017 (800) 253-9646; *Statistical Yearbook.*

GRENADA - BALANCE OF PAYMENTS

Federal Statistical Office, Gustav - Stresemann - Ring 11, D-6200 Wiesbaden, Germany; *Grenada.*

G.K. Hall and Company, 70 Lincoln Street, Boston, Massachusetts 02111 (617) 423-3990; *The World in Figures.*

International Monetary Fund, 700 Nineteenth Street, NW, Washington, D.C. 20431 (202) 623-7000; *Balance of Payments Yearbook.*

Statistical Office of the United Nations, Publishing Service, New York, New York 10017 (800) 253-9646; *Economic Survey of Latin America and the Caribbean.*

The World Bank, 1818 H Street, NW, Washington, D.C. 20433 (202) 477-1234; *World Tables.*

GRENADA - BANANA - See GRENADA - CROPS

GRENADA - BANKING

G.K. Hall and Company, 70 Lincoln Street, Boston, Massachusetts 02111 (617) 423-3990; *The World in Figures.*

International Monetary Fund, 700 Nineteenth Street, NW, Washington, D.C. 20431 (202) 623-7000; *International Financial Statistics.*

GRENADA - BIRTH RATES

Statistical Office of the United Nations, Publishing Service, New York, New York 10017 (800) 253-9646; *Demographic Yearbook.*

The World Bank, 1818 H Street, NW, Washington, D.C. 20433 (202) 477-1234; *World Tables.*

GRENADA - BONDS

G.K. Hall and Company, 70 Lincoln Street, Boston, Massachusetts 02111 (617) 423-3990; *The World in Figures.*

International Monetary Fund, 700 Nineteenth Street, NW, Washington, D.C. 20431 (202) 623-7000; *Government Finance Statistics Yearbook.*

GRENADA - BOOK PRODUCTION

G.K. Hall and Company, 70 Lincoln Street, Boston, Massachusetts 02111 (617) 423-3990; *The World in Figures.*

United Nations Educational, Scientific and Cultural Organization (UNESCO), 7 Place de Fontenoy, F-75700 Paris, France (Telephone Number in U.S. (212) 963-5981); *Statistical Yearbook.*

GRENADA - BROADCASTING

G.K. Hall and Company, 70 Lincoln Street, Boston, Massachusetts 02111 (617) 423-3990; *The World in Figures.*

GRENADA - BUSINESS

G.K. Hall and Company, 70 Lincoln Street, Boston, Massachusetts 02111 (617) 423-3990; *The World in Figures.*

GRENADA - BUSINESS AND PROFESSIONAL LICENSES

International Monetary Fund, 700 Nineteenth Street, NW, Washington, D.C. 20431 (202) 623-7000; *Government Finance Statistics Yearbook.*

GRENADA - CACAO - See GRENADA - CROPS

GRENADA - CALORIE SUPPLY

Food and Agricultural Organization of the United Nations (FAO) Via delle Terme di Caracalla, 00100 Rome, Italy (Telephone Number in U.S. (202) 653-2400); *The State of Food and Agriculture.*

GRENADA - CAPITAL REVENUE

International Monetary Fund, 700 Nineteenth Street, NW, Washington, D.C. 20431 (202) 623-7000; *Government Finance Statistics Yearbook.*

GRENADA - CATTLE - See GRENADA - LIVESTOCK AND POULTRY

GRENADA - CHEMICAL (ORGANIC) PRODUCTION - See GRENADA - MINING AND MINERAL PRODUCTS

GRENADA - CLASS STRUCTURE

G.K. Hall and Company, 70 Lincoln Street, Boston, Massachusetts 02111 (617) 423-3990; *The World in Figures.*

GRENADA - CLIMATE

G.K. Hall and Company, 70 Lincoln Street, Boston, Massachusetts 02111 (617) 423-3990; *The World in Figures.*

GRENADA - COAL PRODUCTION - See GRENADA - MINING AND MINERAL PRODUCTS

GRENADA - COCOA BEANS PRODUCTION - See GRENADA - CROPS

GRENADA - COMMUNICATIONS

Federal Statistical Office, Gustav - Stresemann - Ring 11, D-6200 Wiesbaden, Germany; *Grenada.*

G.K. Hall and Company, 70 Lincoln Street, Boston, Massachusetts 02111 (617) 423-3990; *The World in Figures.*

GRENADA - CONSUMER PRICE INDEX

Federal Statistical Office, Gustav - Stresemann - Ring 11, D-6200 Wiesbaden, Germany; *Grenada.*

G.K. Hall and Company, 70 Lincoln Street, Boston, Massachusetts 02111 (617) 423-3990; *The World in Figures.*

GRENADA - CONSUMER PRICES

Federal Statistical Office, Gustav - Stresemann - Ring 11, D-6200 Wiesbaden, Germany; *Grenada.*

International Labour Office, I.L.O. Publications, CH-1211, Geneva 22, Switzerland; *Yearbook of Labour Statistics.*

Organization of American States (OAS), General Secretariat, Washington, D.C. 20006 (202) 458-3533; *Statistical Bulletin of the OAS.*

GRENADA - CONSUMPTION

G.K. Hall and Company, 70 Lincoln Street, Boston, Massachusetts 02111 (617) 423-3990; *The World in Figures.*

GRENADA - CORN PRODUCTION - See GRENADA - CROPS

GRENADA - CORPORATE TAXES - See GRENADA - TAXATION

GRENADA - CROPS

Food and Agricultural Organization of the United Nations (FAO) Via delle Terme di Caracalla, 00100 Rome, Italy (Telephone Number in U.S. (202) 653-2400); *Production Yearbook* and *The State of Food and Agriculture.*

G.K. Hall and Company, 70 Lincoln Street, Boston, Massachusetts 02111 (617) 423-3990; *The World in Figures.*

International Monetary Fund, 700 Nineteenth Street, NW, Washington, D.C. 20431 (202) 623-7000; *International Financial Statistics.*

Organization of American States (OAS), General Secretariat, Washington, D.C. 20006 (202) 458-3533; *Statistical Bulletin of the OAS.*

Statistical Office of the United Nations, Publishing Service, New York, New York 10017 (800) 253-9646; *Statistical Yearbook.*

GRENADA - CUSTOMS DUTIES

G.K. Hall and Company, 70 Lincoln Street, Boston, Massachusetts 02111 (617) 423-3990; *The World in Figures.*

International Monetary Fund, 700 Nineteenth Street, NW, Washington, D.C. 20431 (202) 623-7000; *Government Finance Statistics Yearbook.*

GRENADA - DEATH RATES

G.K. Hall and Company, 70 Lincoln Street, Boston, Massachusetts 02111 (617) 423-3990; *The World in Figures.*

Statistical Office of the United Nations, Publishing Service, New York, New York 10017 (800) 253-9646; *Statistical Yearbook.*

World Health Organization, Office of Publications, Avenue Appia, CH-1211 Geneva 27, Switzerland (Telephone Number in U.S. (518) 436-9686); *World Health Statistics Annual.*

GRENADA - DEFENSE EXPENDITURES

G.K. Hall and Company, 70 Lincoln Street, Boston, Massachusetts 02111 (617) 423-3990; *The World in Figures.*

International Monetary Fund, 700 Nineteenth Street, NW, Washington, D.C. 20431 (202) 623-7000; *Government Finance Statistics Yearbook.*

GRENADA - DEMOGRAPHY

Federal Statistical Office, Gustav - Stresemann - Ring 11, D-6200 Wiesbaden, Germany; *Grenada.*

G.K. Hall and Company, 70 Lincoln Street, Boston, Massachusetts 02111 (617) 423-3990; *The World in Figures.*

GRENADA - DEVELOPMENT ASSISTANCE

G.K. Hall and Company, 70 Lincoln Street, Boston, Massachusetts 02111 (617) 423-3990; *The World in Figures.*

GRENADA - DISEASES

G.K. Hall and Company, 70 Lincoln Street, Boston, Massachusetts 02111 (617) 423-3990; *The World in Figures.*

World Health Organization, Office of Publications, Avenue Appia, CH-1211 Geneva 27, Switzerland (Telephone Number in U.S. (518) 436-9686); *World Health Statistics Annual.*

GRENADA - DIVORCE RATES

Statistical Office of the United Nations, Publishing Service, New York, New York 10017 (800) 253-9646; *Demographic Yearbook,* and *Statistical Yearbook.*

GRENADA - DOMESTIC PRODUCT

G.K. Hall and Company, 70 Lincoln Street, Boston, Massachusetts 02111 (617) 423-3990; *The World in Figures.*

GRENADA - ECONOMY

Federal Statistical Office, Gustav - Stresemann - Ring 11, D-6200 Wiesbaden, Germany; *Grenada.*

G.K. Hall and Company, 70 Lincoln Street, Boston, Massachusetts 02111 (617) 423-3990; *The World in Figures.*

Organization of American States (OAS), General Secretariat, Washington, D.C. 20006 (202) 458-3533; *Statistical Bulletin of the OAS.*

Statistical Office of the United Nations, Publishing Service, New York, New York 10017 (800) 253-9646; *Economic Survey of Latin America and the Caribbean.*

GRENADA - EDUCATION

Federal Statistical Office, Gustav - Stresemann - Ring 11, D-6200 Wiesbaden, Germany; *Grenada.*

G.K. Hall and Company, 70 Lincoln Street, Boston, Massachusetts 02111 (617) 423-3990; *The World in Figures.*

International Monetary Fund, 700 Nineteenth Street, NW, Washington, D.C. 20431 (202) 623-7000; *Government Finance Statistics Yearbook.*

United Nations Educational, Scientific and Cultural Organization (UNESCO), 7 Place de Fontenoy, F-75700 Paris, France; *Statistical Yearbook.*

The World Bank, 1818 H Street, NW, Washington, D.C. 20433 (202) 477-1234; *World Tables.*

GRENADA - EMPLOYMENT

Federal Statistical Office, Gustav - Stresemann - Ring 11, D-6200 Wiesbaden, Germany; *Grenada.*

International Labour Office, I.L.O. Publications, CH-1211, Geneva 22, Switzerland; *Yearbook of Labour Statistics.*

GRENADA - ENERGY

Food and Agricultural Organization of the United Nations (FAO) Via delle Terme di Caracalla, 00100 Rome, Italy (Telephone Number in U.S. (202) 653-2400); *The State of Food and Agriculture.*

G.K. Hall and Company, 70 Lincoln Street, Boston, Massachusetts 02111 (617) 423-3990; *The World in Figures.*

Statistical Office of the United Nations, Publishing Service, New York, New York 10017 (800) 253-9646; *Statistical Yearbook.*

GRENADA - EXCHANGE RATES

International Monetary Fund, 700 Nineteenth Street, NW, Washington, D.C. 20431 (202) 623-7000; *International Financial Statistics.*

Organization of American States (OAS), General Secretariat, Washington, D.C. 20006 (202) 458-3533; *Statistical Bulletin of the OAS.*

Statistical Office of the United Nations, Publishing Service, New York, New York 10017 (800) 253-9646; *Statistical Yearbook.*

GRENADA - EXCHANGE TAXES

International Monetary Fund, 700 Nineteenth Street, NW, Washington, D.C. 20431 (202) 623-7000; *Government Finance Statistics Yearbook.*

GRENADA - EXCISE TAXES - See GRENADA - TAXATION

GRENADA - EXPORT DUTIES

International Monetary Fund, 700 Nineteenth Street, NW, Washington, D.C. 20431 (202) 623-7000; *Government Finance Statistics Yearbook.*

GRENADA - EXPORTS

Food and Agricultural Organization of the United Nations (FAO) Via delle Terme di Caracalla, 00100 Rome, Italy (Telephone Number in U.S. (202) 653-2400); *The State of Food and Agriculture.*

G.K. Hall and Company, 70 Lincoln Street, Boston, Massachusetts 02111 (617) 423-3990; *The World in Figures.*

International Monetary Fund, 700 Nineteenth Street, NW, Washington, D.C. 20431 (202) 623-7000; *Direction of Trade Statistics,* and *International Financial Statistics.*

The World Bank, 1818 H Street, NW, Washington, D.C. 20433 (202) 477-1234; *World Tables.*

GRENADA - EXTERNAL INDEBTEDNESS

The World Bank, 1818 H Street, NW, Washington, D.C. 20433 (202) 477-1234; *World Tables.*

GRENADA - EXTERNAL TRADE

Food and Agricultural Organization of the United Nations (FAO) Via delle Terme di Caracalla, 00100 Rome, Italy (Telephone Number in U.S. (202) 653-2400); *The State of Food and Agriculture,* and *Trade Yearbook.*

G.K. Hall and Company, 70 Lincoln Street, Boston, Massachusetts 02111 (617) 423-3990; *The World in Figures.*

GRENADA - FARM CROPS - See GRENADA - CROPS

GRENADA - FERTILITY RATES

The World Bank, 1818 H Street, NW, Washington, D.C. 20433 (202) 477-1234; *World Tables.*

GRENADA - FERTILIZER

Food and Agricultural Organization of the United Nations (FAO) Via delle Terme di Caracalla, 00100 Rome, Italy (Telephone Number in U.S. (202) 653-2400); *The State of Food and Agriculture.*

GRENADA - FETAL MORTALITY

Statistical Office of the United Nations, Publishing Service, New York, New York 10017 (800) 253-9646; *Demographic Yearbook.*

World Health Organization, Office of Publications, Avenue Appia, CH-1211 Geneva 27, Switzerland (Telephone Number in U.S. (518) 436-9686); *World Health Statistics Annual.*

GRENADA - FINANCE

Federal Statistical Office, Gustav - Stresemann - Ring 11, D-6200 Wiesbaden, Germany; *Grenada.*

G.K. Hall and Company, 70 Lincoln Street, Boston, Massachusetts 02111 (617) 423-3990; *The World in Figures.*

International Monetary Fund, 700 Nineteenth Street, NW, Washington, D.C. 20431 (202) 623-7000; *Government Finance Statistics Yearbook.*

GRENADA - FISHERIES

Federal Statistical Office, Gustav - Stresemann - Ring 11, D-6200 Wiesbaden, Germany; *Grenada.*

Food and Agricultural Organization of the United Nations (FAO) Via delle Terme di Caracalla, 00100 Rome, Italy (Telephone Number in U.S. (202) 653-2400); *The State of Food and Agriculture,* and *Yearbook of Fishery Statistics.*

Statistical Office of the United Nations, Publishing Service, New York, New York 10017 (800) 253-9646; *Statistical Yearbook.*

GRENADA - FOOD PRODUCTION AND CONSUMPTION

Food and Agricultural Organization of the United Nations (FAO) Via delle Terme di Caracalla, 00100 Rome, Italy (Telephone Number in U.S. (202) 653-2400); *The State of Food and Agriculture.*

G.K. Hall and Company, 70 Lincoln Street, Boston, Massachusetts 02111 (617) 423-3990; *The World in Figures.*

GRENADA - FOOD PRODUCTS - EXPORTS AND IMPORTS

Food and Agricultural Organization of the United Nations (FAO) Via delle Terme di Caracalla, 00100 Rome, Italy (Telephone Number in U.S. (202) 653-2400); *The State of Food and Agriculture.*

GRENADA - FOOD SUPPLY

Food and Agricultural Organization of the United Nations (FAO), Via delle Terme di Caracalla, 00100 Rome, Italy (Telephone Number in U.S. (202) 653-2400); *Production Yearbook,* and *The State of Food and Agriculture.*

GRENADA - FOODSTUFF CONSUMPTION

Food and Agricultural Organization of the United Nations (FAO) Via delle Terme di Caracalla, 00100 Rome, Italy (Telephone Number in U.S. (202) 653-2400); *The State of Food and Agriculture.*

GRENADA - FOREIGN AID

G.K. Hall and Company, 70 Lincoln Street, Boston, Massachusetts 02111 (617) 423-3990; *The World in Figures.*

GRENADA - FOREIGN INDEBTEDNESS

Statistical Office of the United Nations, Publishing Service, New York, New York 10017 (800) 253-9646; *Economic Survey of Latin America and the Caribbean.*

GRENADA - FOREIGN TRADE

Federal Statistical Office, Gustav - Stresemann - Ring 11, D-6200 Wiesbaden, Germany; *Grenada.*

Food and Agricultural Organization of the United Nations (FAO) Via delle Terme di Caracalla, 00100 Rome, Italy (Telephone Number in U.S. (202) 653-2400); *The State of Food and Agriculture.*

G.K. Hall and Company, 70 Lincoln Street, Boston, Massachusetts 02111 (617) 423-3990; *The World in Figures.*

Statistical Office of the United Nations, Publishing Service, New York, New York 10017 (800) 253-9646; *Economic Survey of Latin America and the Caribbean.*

The World Bank, 1818 H Street, NW, Washington, D.C. 20433 (202) 477-1234; *World Tables.*

GRENADA - FORESTRY AND FOREST PRODUCTS

G.K. Hall and Company, 70 Lincoln Street, Boston, Massachusetts 02111 (617) 423-3990; *The World in Figures.*

Statistical Office of the United Nations, Publishing Service, New York, New York 10017 (800) 253-9646; *Statistical Yearbook.*

United Nations Educational, Scientific and Cultural Organization (UNESCO), 7 Place de Fontenoy, F-75700 Paris, France (Telephone Number in U.S. (212) 963-5981); *Statistical Yearbook.*

Federal Statistical Office, Gustav - Stresemann - Ring 11, D-6200 Wiesbaden, Germany; *Grenada.*

Food and Agricultural Organization of the United Nations (FAO) Via delle Terme di Caracalla, 00100 Rome, Italy (Telephone Number in U.S. (202) 653-2400); *The State of Food and Agriculture.*

G.K. Hall and Company, 70 Lincoln Street, Boston, Massachusetts 02111 (617) 423-3990; *The World in Figures.*

GRENADA - GENERAL INDUSTRIAL STATISTICS

Federal Statistical Office, Gustav - Stresemann - Ring 11, D-6200 Wiesbaden, Germany; *Grenada.*

GRENADA - GENERAL MORTALITY

Statistical Office of the United Nations, Publishing Service, New York, New York 10017 (800) 253-9646; *Demographic Yearbook.*

World Health Organization, Office of Publications, Avenue Appia, CH-1211 Geneva 27, Switzerland (Telephone Number in U.S. (518) 436-9686); *World Health Statistics Annual.*

GRENADA - GEOGRAPHIC DATA

Federal Statistical Office, Gustav - Stresemann - Ring 11, D-6200 Wiesbaden, Germany; *Grenada.*

GRENADA - GOLD HOLDINGS

International Monetary Fund, 700 Nineteenth Street, NW, Washington, D.C. 20431 (202) 623-7000; *International Financial Statistics.*

Statistical Office of the United Nations, Publishing Service, New York, New York 10017 (800) 253-9646; *Statistical Yearbook.*

The World Bank, 1818 H Street, NW, Washington, D.C. 20433 (202) 477-1234; *World Tables.*

GRENADA - GOVERNMENT

G.K. Hall and Company, 70 Lincoln Street, Boston, Massachusetts 02111 (617) 423-3990; *The World in Figures.*

GRENADA - GOVERNMENT EXPENDITURES

International Monetary Fund, 700 Nineteenth Street, NW, Washington, D.C. 20431 (202) 623-7000; *Government Finance Statistics Yearbook.*

The World Bank, 1818 H Street, NW, Washington, D.C. 20433 (202) 477-1234; *World Tables.*

GRENADA - GOVERNMENT FINANCE

International Monetary Fund, 700 Nineteenth Street, NW, Washington, D.C. 20431 (202) 623-7000; *International Financial Statistics.*

GRENADA - GOVERNMENT REVENUE

International Monetary Fund, 700 Nineteenth Street, NW, Washington, D.C. 20431 (202) 623-7000; *Government Finance Statistics Yearbook.*

The World Bank, 1818 H Street, NW, Washington, D.C. 20433 (202) 477-1234; *World Tables.*

GRENADA - GRAIN PRODUCTION - See GRENADA - CROPS

GRENADA - GRANTS

International Monetary Fund, 700 Nineteenth Street, NW, Washington, D.C. 20431 (202) 623-7000; *Government Finance Statistics Yearbook.*

GRENADA - GROSS DOMESTIC PRODUCT

G.K. Hall and Company, 70 Lincoln Street, Boston, Massachusetts 02111 (617) 423-3990; *The World in Figures.*

Statistical Office of the United Nations, Publishing Service, New York, New York 10017 (800) 253-9646; *Statistical Yearbook.*

The World Bank, 1818 H Street, NW, Washington, D.C. 20433 (202) 477-1234; *World Tables.*

GRENADA - GROSS NATIONAL PRODUCT

The World Bank, 1818 H Street, NW, Washington, D.C. 20433 (202) 477-1234; *World Tables.*

GRENADA - HEALTH

Federal Statistical Office, Gustav - Stresemann - Ring 11, D-6200 Wiesbaden, Germany; *Grenada.*

G.K. Hall and Company, 70 Lincoln Street, Boston, Massachusetts 02111 (617) 423-3990; *The World in Figures.*

Statistical Office of the United Nations, Publishing Service, New York, New York 10017 (800) 253-9646; *Statistical Yearbook.*

World Health Organization, Office of Publications, Avenue Appia, CH-1211 Geneva 27, Switzerland (Telephone Number in U.S. (518) 436-9686); *World Health Statistics Annual.*

GRENADA - HEALTH EXPENDITURES

International Monetary Fund, 700 Nineteenth Street, NW, Washington, D.C. 20431 (202) 623-7000; *Government Finance Statistics Yearbook.*

GRENADA - HIDE PRODUCTION

Food and Agricultural Organization of the United Nations (FAO), Via delle Terme di Caracalla, 00100 Rome, Italy (Telephone Number in U.S. (202) 653-2400); *Production Yearbook.*

GRENADA - HIGHWAYS

G.K. Hall and Company, 70 Lincoln Street, Boston, Massachusetts 02111 (617) 423-3990; *The World in Figures.*

GRENADA - HORSES - See GRENADA - LIVESTOCK AND POULTRY

GRENADA - HOURS OF WORK - See GRENADA - EMPLOYMENT

GRENADA - HOUSING EXPENDITURES

International Monetary Fund, 700 Nineteenth Street, NW, Washington, D.C. 20431 (202) 623-7000; *Government Finance Statistics Yearbook.*

GRENADA - ILLITERATE POPULATION

G.K. Hall and Company, 70 Lincoln Street, Boston, Massachusetts 02111 (617) 423-3990; *The World in Figures.*

United Nations Educational, Scientific and Cultural Organization (UNESCO), 7 Place de Fontenoy, F-75700 Paris, France (Telephone Number in U.S. (212) 963-5981); *Statistical Yearbook.*

GRENADA - IMPORTS

Food and Agricultural Organization of the United Nations (FAO) Via delle Terme di Caracalla, 00100 Rome, Italy (Telephone Number in U.S. (202) 653-2400); *The State of Food and Agriculture.*

G.K. Hall and Company, 70 Lincoln Street, Boston, Massachusetts 02111 (617) 423-3990; *The World in Figures.*

International Monetary Fund, 700 Nineteenth Street, NW, Washington, D.C. 20431 (202) 623-7000; *Direction of Trade Statistics, Government Finance Statistics Yearbook,* and *International Financial Statistics.*

The World Bank, 1818 H Street, NW, Washington, D.C. 20433 (202) 477-1234; *World Tables.*

GRENADA - INCOME TAXES - See GRENADA - TAXATION

GRENADA - INDUSTRIAL ACCIDENTS

International Labour Office, I.L.O. Publications, CH-1211, Geneva 22, Switzerland; *Yearbook of Labour Statistics.*

GRENADA - INDUSTRIAL DISPUTES

International Labour Office, I.L.O. Publications, CH-1211, Geneva 22, Switzerland; *Yearbook of Labour Statistics.*

GRENADA - INDUSTRIAL SECTOR TRENDS

Statistical Office of the United Nations, Publishing Service, New York, New York 10017 (800) 253-9646; *Economic Survey of Latin*

America and the Caribbean.

GRENADA - INDUSTRIAL PRODUCTION

Federal Statistical Office, Gustav - Stresemann - Ring 11, D-6200 Wiesbaden, Germany; *Grenada.*

GRENADA - INDUSTRY

Federal Statistical Office, Gustav - Stresemann - Ring 11, D-6200 Wiesbaden, Germany; *Grenada.*

G.K. Hall and Company, 70 Lincoln Street, Boston, Massachusetts 02111 (617) 423-3990; *The World in Figures.*

The World Bank, 1818 H Street, NW, Washington, D.C. 20433 (202) 477-1234; *World Tables.*

GRENADA - INFANT AND MATERNAL MORTALITY

Statistical Office of the United Nations, Publishing Service, New York, New York 10017 (800) 253-9646; *Demographic Yearbook,* and *Statistical Yearbook.*

The World Bank, 1818 H Street, NW, Washington, D.C. 20433 (202) 477-1234; *World Tables.*

World Health Organization, Office of Publications, Avenue Appia, CH-1211 Geneva 27, Switzerland (Telephone Number in U.S. (518) 436-9686); *World Health Statistics Annual.*

GRENADA - INFLATIONARY FACTORS

Statistical Office of the United Nations, Publishing Service, New York, New York 10017 (800) 253-9646; *Economic Survey of Latin America and the Caribbean.*

GRENADA - INTERNATIONAL LIQUIDITY

International Monetary Fund, 700 Nineteenth Street, NW, Washington, D.C. 20431 (202) 623-7000; *International Financial Statistics.*

GRENADA - INTERNATIONAL RESERVES

Organization of American States (OAS), General Secretariat, Washington, D.C. 20006 (202) 458-3533; *Statistical Bulletin of the OAS.*

GRENADA - INTERNATIONAL RESERVES EXCLUDING GOLD

Statistical Office of the United Nations, Publishing Service, New York, New York 10017 (800) 253-9646; *Statistical Yearbook.*

The World Bank, 1818 H Street, NW, Washington, D.C. 20433 (202) 477-1234; *World Tables.*

GRENADA - LABOR FORCE

Food and Agricultural Organization of the United Nations (FAO) Via delle Terme di Caracalla, 00100 Rome, Italy (Telephone Number in U.S. (202) 653-2400); *The State of Food and Agriculture.*

G.K. Hall and Company, 70 Lincoln Street, Boston, Massachusetts 02111 (617) 423-3990; *The World in Figures.*

The World Bank, 1818 H Street, NW, Washington, D.C. 20433 (202) 477-1234; *World Tables.*

GRENADA - LABOR PRODUCTIVITY

International Labour Office, I.L.O. Publications, CH-1211, Geneva 22, Switzerland; *Yearbook of Labour Statistics.*

GRENADA - LAND USE

Food and Agricultural Organization of the United Nations (FAO), Via delle Terme di Caracalla, 00100 Rome, Italy (Telephone Number in U.S. (202) 653-2400); *Production Yearbook.*

G.K. Hall and Company, 70 Lincoln Street, Boston, Massachusetts 02111 (617) 423-3990; *The World in Figures.*

GRENADA - LIVESTOCK AND POULTRY

Food and Agricultural Organization of the United Nations (FAO), Via delle Terme di Caracalla, 00100 Rome, Italy (Telephone Number in U.S. (202) 653-2400); *Production Yearbook,* and *The State of Food and Agriculture.*

G.K. Hall and Company, 70 Lincoln Street, Boston, Massachusetts 02111 (617) 423-3990; *The World in Figures.*

Statistical Office of the United Nations, Publishing Service, New York, New York 10017 (800) 253-9646; *Statistical Yearbook.*

GRENADA - LIVING LEVELS

G.K. Hall and Company, 70 Lincoln Street, Boston, Massachusetts 02111 (617) 423-3990; *The World in Figures.*

GRENADA - MACE EXPORTS

International Monetary Fund, 700 Nineteenth Street, NW, Washington, D.C. 20431 (202) 623-7000; *International Financial Statistics.*

GRENADA - MANUFACTURING

G.K. Hall and Company, 70 Lincoln Street, Boston, Massachusetts 02111 (617) 423-3990; *The World in Figures.*

The World Bank, 1818 H Street, NW, Washington, D.C. 20433 (202) 477-1234; *World Tables.*

GRENADA - MARRIAGE RATES

Statistical Office of the United Nations, Publishing Service, New York, New York 10017 (800) 253-9646; *Demographic Yearbook,* and *Statistical Yearbook.*

GRENADA - MEAT PRODUCTION - See GRENADA - LIVESTOCK AND POULTRY

GRENADA - MERCHANT SHIPPING

G.K. Hall and Company, 70 Lincoln Street, Boston, Massachusetts 02111 (617) 423-3990; *The World in Figures.*

Statistical Office of the United Nations, Publishing Service, New York, New York 10017 (800) 253-9646; *Statistical Yearbook.*

GRENADA - MILITARY

G.K. Hall and Company, 70 Lincoln Street, Boston, Massachusetts 02111 (617) 423-3990; *The World in Figures.*

GRENADA - MINING AND MINERAL PRODUCTS

G.K. Hall and Company, 70 Lincoln Street, Boston, Massachusetts 02111 (617) 423-3990; *The World in Figures.*

GRENADA - MONEY EXCHANGE RATES

International Monetary Fund, 700 Nineteenth Street, NW, Washington, D.C. 20431 (202) 623-7000; *International Financial Statistics.*

Statistical Office of the United Nations, Publishing Service, New York, New York 10017 (800) 253-9646; *Statistical Yearbook.*

GRENADA - MONEY SUPPLY

Federal Statistical Office, Gustav - Stresemann - Ring 11, D-6200 Wiesbaden, Germany; *Grenada.*

G.K. Hall and Company, 70 Lincoln Street, Boston, Massachusetts 02111 (617) 423-3990; *The World in Figures.*

International Monetary Fund, 700 Nineteenth Street, NW, Washington, D.C. 20431 (202) 623-7000; *International Financial Statistics.*

The World Bank, 1818 H Street, NW, Washington, D.C. 20433 (202) 477-1234; *World Tables.*

GRENADA - MOTION PICTURES

Statistical Office of the United Nations, Publishing Service, New York, New York 10017 (800) 253-9646; *Statistical Yearbook.*

GRENADA - MOTOR VEHICLE TAXES - See GRENADA - TAXATION

GRENADA - MOTOR VEHICLES IN USE

G.K. Hall and Company, 70 Lincoln Street, Boston, Massachusetts 02111 (617) 423-3990; *The World in Figures.*

Statistical Office of the United Nations, Publishing Service, New York, New York 10017 (800) 253-9646; *Statistical Yearbook.*

GRENADA - MULES - See GRENADA - LIVESTOCK AND POULTRY

GRENADA - MUSEUMS

United Nations Educational, Scientific and Cultural Organization (UNESCO), 7 Place de Fontenoy, F-75700 Paris, France (Telephone Number in U.S. (212) 963-5981); *Statistical Yearbook.*

GRENADA - NATALITY

Statistical Office of the United Nations, Publishing Service, New York, New York 10017 (800) 253-9646; *Demographic Yearbook.*

World Health Organization, Office of Publications, Avenue Appia, CH-1211 Geneva 27, Switzerland (Telephone Number in U.S. (518) 436-9686); *World Health Statistics Annual.*

GRENADA - NATIONAL ACCOUNTS

Federal Statistical Office, Gustav - Stresemann - Ring 11, D-6200 Wiesbaden, Germany; *Grenada.*

Statistical Office of the United Nations, Publishing Service, New York, New York 10017 (800) 253-9646; *Yearbook of National Accounts Statistics,* and *Statistical Yearbook.*

GRENADA - NATIONAL INCOME

G.K. Hall and Company, 70 Lincoln Street, Boston, Massachusetts 02111 (617) 423-3990; *The World in Figures.*

Statistical Office of the United Nations, Publishing Service, New York, New York 10017 (800) 253-9646; *Statistical Yearbook.*

GRENADA - NEWSPAPER PRODUCTION - See GRENADA - FORESTRY AND FOREST PRODUCTS

GRENADA - NUTMEG PRODUCTION

International Monetary Fund, 700 Nineteenth Street, NW, Washington, D.C. 20431 (202) 623-7000; *International Financial Statistics.*

GRENADA - OCCUPATIONS - See GRENADA - LABOR FORCE

GRENADA - PESTICIDE USE

Food and Agricultural Organization of the United Nations (FAO) Via delle Terme di Caracalla, 00100 Rome, Italy (Telephone Number in U.S. (202) 653-2400); *The State of Food and Agriculture.*

GRENADA - PETROLEUM INDUSTRY

Food and Agricultural Organization of the United Nations (FAO) Via delle Terme di Caracalla, 00100 Rome, Italy (Telephone Number in U.S. (202) 653-2400); *The State of Food and Agriculture.*

G.K. Hall and Company, 70 Lincoln Street, Boston, Massachusetts 02111 (617) 423-3990; *The World in Figures.*

GRENADA - PIGS - See GRENADA - LIVESTOCK AND POULTRY

GRENADA - POPULATION

Federal Statistical Office, Gustav - Stresemann - Ring 11, D-6200 Wiesbaden, Germany; *Grenada.*

Food and Agricultural Organization of the United Nations (FAO), Via delle Terme di Caracalla, 00100 Rome, Italy (Telephone Number in U.S. (202) 653-2400); *Production Yearbook.*

G.K. Hall and Company, 70 Lincoln Street, Boston, Massachusetts 02111 (617) 423-3990; *The World in Figures.*

International Labour Office, I.L.O. Publications, CH-1211, Geneva 22, Switzerland; *Yearbook of Labour Statistics.*

Organization of American States (OAS), General Secretariat, Washington, D.C. 20006 (202) 458-3533; *Statistical Bulletin of the OAS.*

Statistical Office of the United Nations, Publishing Service, New York, New York 10017 (800) 253-9646; *Demographic Yearbook,* and *Statistical Yearbook.*

World Health Organization, Office of Publications, Avenue Appia, CH-1211 Geneva 27, Switzerland (Telephone Number in U.S. (518) 436-9686); *World Health Statistics Annual.*

GRENADA - PRICES

Federal Statistical Office, Gustav - Stresemann - Ring 11, D-6200 Wiesbaden, Germany; *Grenada.*

Food and Agricultural Organization of the United Nations (FAO), Via delle Terme di Caracalla, 00100 Rome, Italy (Telephone Number in U.S. (202) 653-2400); *Production Yearbook,* and *The State of Food and Agriculture.*

G.K. Hall and Company, 70 Lincoln Street, Boston, Massachusetts 02111 (617) 423-3990; *The World in Figures.*

Statistical Office of the United Nations, Publishing Service, New York, New York 10017 (800) 253-9646; *Economic Survey of Latin America and the Caribbean.*

GRENADA - PRODUCTION

G.K. Hall and Company, 70 Lincoln Street, Boston, Massachusetts 02111 (617) 423-3990; *The World in Figures.*

GRENADA - PROPERTY TAXES - See GRENADA - TAXATION

GRENADA - PUBLIC FINANCE

Federal Statistical Office, Gustav - Stresemann - Ring 11, D-6200 Wiesbaden, Germany; *Grenada.*

GRENADA - RAILWAYS

G.K. Hall and Company, 70 Lincoln Street, Boston, Massachusetts 02111 (617) 423-3990; *The World in Figures.*

GRENADA - RETAIL TRADE

G.K. Hall and Company, 70 Lincoln Street, Boston, Massachusetts 02111 (617) 423-3990; *The World in Figures.*

GRENADA - ROOT AND TUBER PRODUCTION - See GRENADA - CROPS

GRENADA - SHEEP - See GRENADA - LIVESTOCK AND POULTRY

GRENADA - SOCIAL DATA

G.K. Hall and Company, 70 Lincoln Street, Boston, Massachusetts 02111 (617) 423-3990; *The World in Figures.*

GRENADA - SOCIAL SECURITY

International Monetary Fund, 700 Nineteenth Street, NW, Washington, D.C. 20431 (202) 623-7000; *Government Finance Statistics Yearbook.*

GRENADA - STAMP TAXES AND DUTIES - See GRENADA - TAXATION

GRENADA - STOCKS - COMMODITY - MARKET PRICE - INDEX

Food and Agricultural Organization of the United Nations (FAO) Via delle Terme di Caracalla, 00100 Rome, Italy (Telephone Number in U.S. (202) 653-2400); *The State of Food and Agriculture.*

GRENADA - TAXATION

G.K. Hall and Company, 70 Lincoln Street, Boston, Massachusetts 02111 (617) 423-3990; *The World in Figures.*

International Monetary Fund, 700 Nineteenth Street, NW, Washington, D.C. 20431 (202) 623-7000; *Government Finance Statistics Yearbook.*

The World Bank, 1818 H Street, NW, Washington, D.C. 20433 (202) 477-1234; *World Tables.*

GRENADA - TELEPHONES IN USE

American Telephone and Telegraph Company, 26 Parsippany Road, Whippany, New Jersey 07981 (800) 338-4038; *The World's Telephones.*

G.K. Hall and Company, 70 Lincoln Street, Boston, Massachusetts 02111 (617) 423-3990; *The World in Figures.*

Statistical Office of the United Nations, Publishing Service, New York, New York 10017 (800) 253-9646; *Statistical Yearbook.*

GRENADA - TEXTILE INDUSTRY

G.K. Hall and Company, 70 Lincoln Street, Boston, Massachusetts 02111 (617) 423-3990; *The World in Figures.*

GRENADA - TOURISM

Federal Statistical Office, Gustav - Stresemann - Ring 11, D-6200 Wiesbaden, Germany; *Grenada.*

G.K. Hall and Company, 70 Lincoln Street, Boston, Massachusetts 02111 (617) 423-3990; *The World in Figures.*

Organization of American States (OAS), General Secretariat, Washington, D.C. 20006 (202) 458-3533; *Statistical Bulletin of the OAS.*

Statistical Office of the United Nations, Publishing Service, New York, New York 10017 (800) 253-9646; *Statistical Yearbook.*

World Tourism Organization, Calle Capitan Haya 42, E-28020 Madrid, Spain; *Yearbook of Tourism Statistics.*

GRENADA - TRACTORS IN USE

Statistical Office of the United Nations, Publishing Service, New York, New York 10017 (800) 253-9646; *Statistical Yearbook.*

GRENADA - TRADE - See GRENADA - FOREIGN TRADE

GRENADA - TRANSPORTATION AND COMMUNICATIONS

Federal Statistical Office, Gustav - Stresemann - Ring 11, D-6200 Wiesbaden, Germany; *Grenada.*

G.K. Hall and Company, 70 Lincoln Street, Boston, Massachusetts 02111 (617) 423-3990; *The World in Figures.*

GRENADA - UNEMPLOYMENT

International Labour Office, I.L.O. Publications, CH-1211, Geneva 22, Switzerland; *Yearbook of Labour Statistics.*

GRENADA - VITAL STATISTICS

G.K. Hall and Company, 70 Lincoln Street, Boston, Massachusetts 02111 (617) 423-3990; *The World in Figures.*

Statistical Office of the United Nations, Publishing Service, New York, New York 10017 (800) 253-9646; *Statistical Yearbook.*

World Health Organization, Office of Publications, Avenue Appia, CH-1211 Geneva 27, Switzerland (Telephone Number in U.S. (518) 436-9686); *World Health Statistics Annual.*

GRENADA - WAGES

Federal Statistical Office, Gustav - Stresemann - Ring 11, D-6200 Wiesbaden, Germany; *Grenada.*

G.K. Hall and Company, 70 Lincoln Street, Boston, Massachusetts 02111 (617) 423-3990; *The World in Figures.*

International Labour Office, I.L.O. Publications, CH-1211, Geneva 22, Switzerland; *Yearbook of Labour Statistics.*

GRENADA - WEATHER

G.K. Hall and Company, 70 Lincoln Street, Boston, Massachusetts 02111 (617) 423-3990; *The World in Figures.*

GRENADA - WELFARE

International Monetary Fund, 700 Nineteenth Street, NW, Washington, D.C. 20431 (202) 623-7000; *Government Finance Statistics Yearbook.*

GROCERY STORES - EARNINGS

U.S. Department of Commerce, Bureau of the Census, Suitland, Maryland 20233 (301) 763-4040; *Census of Retail Trade,* and *County Business Patterns.*

GROCERY STORES - EMPLOYEES

U.S. Department of Commerce, Bureau of the Census, Suitland, Maryland 20233 (301) 763-4040; *Census of Retail Trade,* and *County Business Patterns.*

GROCERY STORES - ESTABLISHMENTS

U.S. Department of Agriculture, Economic Research Service, Fourteenth Street and Independence Avenue, SW, Washington, D.C. 20005-4789 (202) 219-1504; *Food Marketing Review.*

U.S. Department of Commerce, Bureau of the Census, Suitland, Maryland 20233 (301) 763-4040; *Census of Retail Trade, County Business Patterns, Current Business Reports, Combined Annual and Revised Monthly Retail Trade,* and unpublished data.

GROCERY STORES - SALES

International Franchise Association, 1350 New York Avenue, Suite 900, Washington, D.C. 20005 (202) 628-8000; *Franchising in the Economy.*

Maclean Hunter Media Inc., Post Office Box 10246, Stamford, Connecticut 06904 (203) 325-3500; *Progressive Grocer, Annual Report of the Grocery Industry.*

Market Statistics, 633 Third Avenue, New York, New York 10017 (212) 986-4000; *The Survey of Buying Power Data Service.*

National Restaurant Association, 1200 Seventeenth Street, NW, Washington, D.C. 20036 (202) 331-5900; *Food Service Numbers: A Statistical Digest for the Food Service Industry, National Restaurant Association Food Service Industry Forecast,* and *Food Service Industry in Review.*

U.S. Department of Agriculture, Economic Research Service, 14th Street and Independence Avenue, SW, Washington, D.C. 20005-4789 (202) 219-1504; *Food Marketing Review.*

U.S. Department of Commerce, Bureau of the Census, Suitland, Maryland 20233 (301) 763-4040; *Current Business Reports, Combined Annual and Revised Monthly Retail Trade, Census of Retail Trade,* and *County Business Patterns.*

GROSS DOMESTIC PRODUCT - FOREIGN COUNTRIES

Organization for Economic Cooperation and Development, Publication and Information Center, 2001 L Street, NW, Washington, D.C. 20036 (202) 785-6323; *National Accounts of OECD Countries,* and *Revenue Statistics of OECD Member Countries.*

GROSS DOMESTIC PRODUCT - STATE

U.S. Department of Commerce, Bureau of Economic Analysis, Fourteenth Street between Constitution Avenue and E Street, NW, Washington, D.C 20230 (202) 606-9900; *Survey of Current Business.*

GROSS NATIONAL PRODUCT

U.S. Department of Commerce, Bureau of Economic Analysis, Fourteenth Street between Constitution Avenue and E Street, Washington, D.C. 20230 (202) 606-9900; *The National Income and Product Accounts of the United States,* and *Survey of Current Business.*

U.S. Department of Commerce, International Trade Administration, Fourteenth Street between Constitution Avenue and E Street, NW, Washington, D.C. 20230 (202) 482-5487; official statistics.

GROSS NATIONAL PRODUCT - BY INDUSTRY

U.S. Department of Commerce, Bureau of Economic Analysis, Fourteenth Street between Constitution Avenue and E Street, Washington, D.C. 20230 (202) 606-9900; *Survey of Current Business.*

GROSS NATIONAL PRODUCT - COMPONENTS - ANNUAL GROWTH RATES

U.S. Department of Commerce, Bureau of Economic Analysis, Fourteenth Street between Constitution Avenue and E Street, NW, Washington, D.C. 20230 (202) 606-9900; *The National Income and Product Accounts of the United States,* and *Survey of Current Business,* July issues.

GROSS NATIONAL PRODUCT - ECONOMIC GROWTH RATES INDICATORS

U.S. Department of Commerce, Bureau of Economic Analysis, Fourteenth Street between Constitution Avenue and E Street, NW, Washington, D.C. 20230 (202) 606-9900; *The National Income and Product Accounts of the United States,* and *Survey of Current Business,* July issues.

U.S. Department of Commerce, International Trade Administration, Fourteenth Street between Constitution Avenue and E Street, NW, Washington, D.C. 20230 (202) 482-5487; official statistics.

GROSS NATIONAL PRODUCT - FOREIGN COUNTRIES

U.S. Arms Control and Disarmament Agency, Department of State Building, Washington, D.C. 20451 (202) 647-8677; *World Military Expenditures and Arms Transfers.*

U.S. Department of Commerce, Bureau of Economic Analysis, Fourteenth Street between Constitution Avenue and E Street, NW, Washington, D.C. 20230 (202) 606-9900; *Survey of Current Business.*

U.S. Department of Commerce, International Trade Administration, Fourteenth Street between Constitution Avenue and E Street, NW, Washington, D.C. 20230 (202) 482-5487; official statistics.

U.S. Department of State, Bureau of Intelligence and Research, 2201 C Street, NW, Washington, D.C. 20520 (202) 647-1080; *Economic Growth of OECD Countries*, and unpublished data.

GROSS NATIONAL PRODUCT - HOUSING

U.S. Department of Commerce, Bureau of Economic Analysis, Fourteenth Street between Constitution Avenue and E Street, NW, Washington, D.C. 20230 (202) 606-9900; *Survey of Current Business*, and *The National Income and Product Accounts of the United States*.

GROSS NATIONAL PRODUCT - IMPLICIT PRICE DEFLATORS FOR

U.S. Department of Commerce, Bureau of Economic Analysis, Fourteenth Street between Constitution Avenue and E Street, NW, Washington, D.C. 20230 (202) 606-9900; *The National Income and Product Accounts of the United States*, and *Survey of Current Business*, July issues.

GROSS NATIONAL PRODUCT - NATIONAL DEFENSE OUTLAYS AS PERCENT OF GNP

Executive Office of the President, Office of Management and Budget, Executive Office Building, Washington, D.C. 20503 (202) 395-3080; *Budget of the United States Government*.

GROSS NATIONAL PRODUCT - ORIGINATING IN MANUFACTURING

U.S. Department of Commerce, Bureau of Economic Analysis, Fourteenth Street between Constitution Avenue and E Street, NW, Washington, D.C. 20230 (202) 606-9900; *The National Income and Product Accounts of the United States*, and *Survey of Current Business*.

GROSS NATIONAL PRODUCT - RELATION TO NATIONAL AND PERSONAL INCOME

U.S. Department of Commerce, Bureau of Economic Analysis, Fourteenth Street between Constitution Avenue and E Street, NW, Washington, D.C. 20230 (202) 606-9900; *The National Income and Product Accounts of the United States*, and *Survey of Current Business*, July issues.

GROSS PRIVATE DOMESTIC INVESTMENT

U.S. Department of Commerce, Bureau of Economic Analysis, Fourteenth Street between Constitution Avenue and E Street, NW, Washington, D.C. 20230 (202) 606-9900; *The National Income and Product Accounts of the United States*, and *Survey of Current Business*, July issues.

GROUND WATER - USED

U.S. Department of the Interior, Geological Survey, National Center, 12201 Sunrise Valley Drive, Reston, Virginia 22092 (703) 648-4460; *Estimated Use of Water in the United States in 1990*.

GROUP HEALTH INSURANCE PLANS

Group Health Association of America, Incorporated, 1129 20th Street, NW, Suite 600, Washington, D.C. 20036 (202) 778-3200; National Directory of HMOs.

Interstudy, 5715 Christmas Lake, Excelsior, Minnesota 55331 (612) 474-1176; *The Interstudy Competitive Edge*.

Guadeloupe - Primary Statistics Sources

Institut National de la Statistique et des Etudes Economiques, Tour Gamma A, 185 rue de Bercy, 75582 Paris Cedex 12, France; *Annuaire Statistique de la Guadeloupe* (Statistical Yearbook of Guadeloupe), *Bilan Statistique Annual de le Guadeloupe* (Annual Statistical Account of Guadeloupe), *Bulletin Statistique de la Guadeloupe* (Statistical Bulletin of Guadeloupe), and *Tableaux Economiques Regionaux Guadeloupe*.

GUADELOUPE - ABORTIONS

Statistical Office of the United Nations, Publishing Service, New York, New York 10017 (800) 253-9646; *Demographic Yearbook*.

GUADELOUPE - AGRICULTURE

Food and Agricultural Organization of the United Nations (FAO), Via delle Terme di Caracalla, 00100 Rome, Italy (Telephone Number in U.S. (202) 653-2400); *Production Yearbook*, and *The State of Food and Agriculture*, and *Trade Yearbook*.

G.K. Hall and Company, 70 Lincoln Street, Boston, Massachusetts 02111 (617) 423-3990; *The World in Figures*.

Statistical Office of the United Nations, Publishing Service, New York, New York 10017 (800) 253-9646; *Statistical Yearbook*.

GUADELOUPE - AIRLINE SERVICE

G.K. Hall and Company, 70 Lincoln Street, Boston, Massachusetts 02111 (617) 423-3990; *The World in Figures*.

GUADELOUPE - ANIMAL HEALTH

Food and Agricultural Organization of the United Nations (FAO), Via delle Terme di Caracalla, 00100 Rome, Italy (Telephone Number in U.S. (202) 653-2400); *Animal Health Yearbook*.

GUADELOUPE - AREA AND DENSITY OF POPULATION

Food and Agricultural Organization of the United Nations (FAO) Via delle Terme di Caracalla, 00100 Rome, Italy (Telephone Number in U.S. (202) 653-2400); *The State of Food and Agriculture*.

G.K. Hall and Company, 70 Lincoln Street, Boston, Massachusetts 02111 (617) 423-3990; *The World in Figures*.

Statistical Office of the United Nations, Publishing Service, New York, New York 10017 (800) 253-9646; *Statistical Yearbook*.

GUADELOUPE - BALANCE OF PAYMENTS

G.K. Hall and Company, 70 Lincoln Street, Boston, Massachusetts 02111 (617) 423-3990; *The World in Figures*.

GUADELOUPE - BANKING

G.K. Hall and Company, 70 Lincoln Street, Boston, Massachusetts 02111 (617) 423-3990; *The World in Figures*.

GUADELOUPE - BIRTH RATES

Statistical Office of the United Nations, Publishing Service, New York, New York 10017 (800) 253-9646; *Demographic Yearbook*, and *Statistical Yearbook*.

GUADELOUPE - BONDS

G.K. Hall and Company, 70 Lincoln Street, Boston, Massachusetts 02111 (617) 423-3990; *The World in Figures.*

GUADELOUPE - BOOK PRODUCTION

G.K. Hall and Company, 70 Lincoln Street, Boston, Massachusetts 02111 (617) 423-3990; *The World in Figures.*

GUADELOUPE - BROADCASTING

G.K. Hall and Company, 70 Lincoln Street, Boston, Massachusetts 02111 (617) 423-3990; *The World in Figures.*

GUADELOUPE - BUILDING CONSTRUCTION - See GUADELOUPE CONSTRUCTION INDUSTRY

GUADELOUPE - BUSINESS

G.K. Hall and Company, 70 Lincoln Street, Boston, Massachusetts 02111 (617) 423-3990; *The World in Figures.*

GUADELOUPE - CALORIE SUPPLY

Food and Agricultural Organization of the United Nations (FAO) Via delle Terme di Caracalla, 00100 Rome, Italy (Telephone Number in U.S. (202) 653-2400); *The State of Food and Agriculture.*

GUADELOUPE - CASHEW NUT PRODUCTION - See GUADELOUPE - CROPS

GUADELOUPE - CATTLE - See GUADELOUPE - LIVESTOCK AND POULTRY

GUADELOUPE - CEMENT PRODUCTION - See GUADELOUPE - MINING AND MINERAL PRODUCTS

GUADELOUPE - CHEMICAL (ORGANIC) PRODUCTION - See GUADELOUPE - MINING AND MINERAL PRODUCTS

GUADELOUPE - CLASS STRUCTURE

G.K. Hall and Company, 70 Lincoln Street, Boston, Massachusetts 02111 (617) 423-3990; *The World in Figures.*

GUADELOUPE - CLIMATE

G.K. Hall and Company, 70 Lincoln Street, Boston, Massachusetts 02111 (617) 423-3990; *The World in Figures.*

GUADELOUPE - COAL PRODUCTION - See GUADELOUPE - MINING AND MINERAL PRODUCTS

GUADELOUPE - COCOA BEANS PRODUCTION - See GUADELOUPE - CROPS

GUADELOUPE - COMMUNICATIONS

G.K. Hall and Company, 70 Lincoln Street, Boston, Massachusetts 02111 (617) 423-3990; *The World in Figures.*

GUADELOUPE - CONSTRUCTION INDUSTRY

Statistical Office of the United Nations, Publishing Service, New York, New York 10017 (800) 253-9646; *Yearbook of Construction Statistics.*

GUADELOUPE - CONSUMER PRICE INDEX

G.K. Hall and Company, 70 Lincoln Street, Boston, Massachusetts 02111 (617) 423-3990; *The World in Figures.*

Statistical Office of the United Nations, Publishing Service, New York, New York 10017 (800) 253-9646; *Statistical Yearbook.*

GUADELOUPE - CONSUMER PRICES

International Labour Office, I.L.O. Publications, CH-1211, Geneva 22, Switzerland; *Yearbook of Labour Statistics.*

GUADELOUPE - CONSUMPTION

G.K. Hall and Company, 70 Lincoln Street, Boston, Massachusetts 02111 (617) 423-3990; *The World in Figures.*

GUADELOUPE - CORN PRODUCTION - See GUADELOUPE - CROPS

GUADELOUPE - CORPORATE TAXES - See GUADELOUPE - TAXATION

GUADELOUPE - CROPS

Food and Agricultural Organization of the United Nations (FAO) Via delle Terme di Caracalla, 00100 Rome, Italy (Telephone Number in U.S. (202) 653-2400); *Production Yearbook* and *The State of Food and Agriculture.*

G.K. Hall and Company, 70 Lincoln Street, Boston, Massachusetts 02111 (617) 423-3990; *The World in Figures.*

Statistical Office of the United Nations, Publishing Service, New York, New York 10017 (800) 253-9646; *Statistical Yearbook.*

GUADELOUPE - CUSTOMS DUTIES

G.K. Hall and Company, 70 Lincoln Street, Boston, Massachusetts 02111 (617) 423-3990; *The World in Figures.*

GUADELOUPE - DAIRY PRODUCTS

Food and Agricultural Organization of the United Nations (FAO) Via delle Terme di Caracalla, 00100 Rome, Italy (Telephone Number in U.S. (202) 653-2400); *The State of Food and Agriculture.*

GUADELOUPE - DEATH RATES

G.K. Hall and Company, 70 Lincoln Street, Boston, Massachusetts 02111 (617) 423-3990; *The World in Figures.*

Statistical Office of the United Nations, Publishing Service, New York, New York 10017 (800) 253-9646; *Statistical Yearbook.*

World Health Organization, Office of Publications, Avenue Appia, CH-1211 Geneva 27, Switzerland (Telephone Number in U.S. (518) 436-9686); *World Health Statistics Annual.*

GUADELOUPE - DEFENSE EXPENDITURES

G.K. Hall and Company, 70 Lincoln Street, Boston, Massachusetts 02111 (617) 423-3990; *The World in Figures.*

GUADELOUPE - DEMOGRAPHY

G.K. Hall and Company, 70 Lincoln Street, Boston, Massachusetts 02111 (617) 423-3990; *The World in Figures.*

GUADELOUPE - DEVELOPMENT ASSISTANCE

G.K. Hall and Company, 70 Lincoln Street, Boston, Massachusetts 02111 (617) 423-3990; *The World in Figures.*

Statistical Office of the United Nations, Publishing Service, New York, New York 10017 (800) 253-9646; *Statistical Yearbook.*

GUADELOUPE - DISEASES

G.K. Hall and Company, 70 Lincoln Street, Boston, Massachusetts 02111 (617) 423-3990; *The World in Figures.*

World Health Organization, Office of Publications, Avenue Appia, CH-1211 Geneva 27, Switzerland (Telephone Number in U.S. (518) 436-9686); *World Health Statistics Annual.*

GUADELOUPE - DIVORCE RATES

Statistical Office of the United Nations, Publishing Service, New York, New York 10017 (800) 253-9646; *Demographic Yearbook.*

Statistical Office of the United Nations, Publishing Service, New York, New York 10017 (800) 253-9646; *Statistical Yearbook.*

GUADELOUPE - DOMESTIC PRODUCT

G.K. Hall and Company, 70 Lincoln Street, Boston, Massachusetts 02111 (617) 423-3990; *The World in Figures.*

GUADELOUPE - DUCKS - See GUADELOUPE - LIVESTOCK AND POULTRY

GUADELOUPE - ECONOMY

G.K. Hall and Company, 70 Lincoln Street, Boston, Massachusetts 02111 (617) 423-3990; *The World in Figures.*

GUADELOUPE - EDUCATION

G.K. Hall and Company, 70 Lincoln Street, Boston, Massachusetts 02111 (617) 423-3990; *The World in Figures.*

GUADELOUPE - EGG PRODUCTION - See GUADELOUPE - DAIRY PRODUCTION

GUADELOUPE - ELECTRICITY

Statistical Office of the United Nations, Publishing Service, New York, New York 10017 (800) 253-9646; *Statistical Yearbook.*

GUADELOUPE - EMPLOYMENT

International Labour Office, I.L.O. Publications, CH-1211, Geneva 22, Switzerland; *Yearbook of Labour Statistics.*

GUADELOUPE - ENERGY

Food and Agricultural Organization of the United Nations (FAO) Via delle Terme di Caracalla, 00100 Rome, Italy (Telephone Number in U.S. (202) 653-2400); *The State of Food and Agriculture.*

G.K. Hall and Company, 70 Lincoln Street, Boston, Massachusetts 02111 (617) 423-3990; *The World in Figures.*

Statistical Office of the United Nations, Publishing Service, New York, New York 10017 (800) 253-9646; *Statistical Yearbook,* and *Yearbook of World Energy Statistics.*

GUADELOUPE - EXPORTS

Food and Agricultural Organization of the United Nations (FAO) Via delle Terme di Caracalla, 00100 Rome, Italy (Telephone Number in U.S. (202) 653-2400); *The State of Food and Agriculture.*

G.K. Hall and Company, 70 Lincoln Street, Boston, Massachusetts 02111 (617) 423-3990; *The World in Figures.*

International Monetary Fund, 700 Nineteenth Street, NW, Washington, D.C. 20431 (202) 623-7000; *Direction of Trade Statistics.*

GUADELOUPE - EXTERNAL TRADE

Food and Agricultural Organization of the United Nations (FAO) Via delle Terme di Caracalla, 00100 Rome, Italy (Telephone Number in U.S. (202) 653-2400); *The State of Food and Agriculture,* and *Trade Yearbook.*

G.K. Hall and Company, 70 Lincoln Street, Boston, Massachusetts 02111 (617) 423-3990; *The World in Figures.*

Statistical Office of the United Nations, Publishing Service, New York, New York 10017 (800) 253-9646; *Statistical Yearbook.*

GUADELOUPE - FARM CROPS - See GUADELOUPE - CROPS

GUADELOUPE - FERTILIZER

Food and Agricultural Organization of the United Nations (FAO) Via delle Terme di Caracalla, 00100 Rome, Italy (Telephone Number in U.S. (202) 653-2400); *Fertilizer Yearbook,* and *The State of Food and Agriculture.*

Statistical Office of the United Nations, Publishing Service, New York, New York 10017 (800) 253-9646; *Statistical Yearbook.*

GUADELOUPE - FETAL MORTALITY

Statistical Office of the United Nations, Publishing Service, New York, New York 10017 (800) 253-9646; *Demographic Yearbook.*

World Health Organization, Office of Publications, Avenue Appia, CH-1211 Geneva 27, Switzerland (Telephone Number in U.S. (518) 436-9686); *World Health Statistics Annual.*

GUADELOUPE - FINANCE

G.K. Hall and Company, 70 Lincoln Street, Boston, Massachusetts 02111 (617) 423-3990; *The World in Figures.*

GUADELOUPE - FISHERIES

Food and Agricultural Organization of the United Nations (FAO) Via delle Terme di Caracalla, 00100 Rome, Italy (Telephone Number in U.S. (202) 653-2400); *The State of Food and Agriculture,* and *Yearbook of Fishery Statistics.*

Statistical Office of the United Nations, Publishing Service, New York, New York 10017 (800) 253-9646; *Statistical Yearbook.*

GUADELOUPE - FLOUR PRODUCTION

Statistical Office of the United Nations, Publishing Service, New York, New York 10017 (800) 253-9646; *Statistical Yearbook.*

GUADELOUPE - FOOD PRODUCTION AND CONSUMPTION

Food and Agricultural Organization of the United Nations (FAO) Via delle Terme di Caracalla, 00100 Rome, Italy (Telephone Number in U.S. (202) 653-2400); *The State of Food and Agriculture.*

G.K. Hall and Company, 70 Lincoln Street, Boston, Massachusetts 02111 (617) 423-3990; *The World in Figures.*

GUADELOUPE - FOOD PRODUCTS - EXPORTS AND IMPORTS

Food and Agricultural Organization of the United Nations (FAO) Via delle Terme di Caracalla, 00100 Rome, Italy (Telephone Number in U.S. (202) 653-2400); *The State of Food and Agriculture.*

GUADELOUPE - FOOD SUPPLY

Food and Agricultural Organization of the United Nations (FAO), Via delle Terme di Caracalla, 00100 Rome, Italy (Telephone Number in U.S. (202) 653-2400); *Production Yearbook,* and *The State of Food and Agriculture.*

GUADELOUPE - FOODSTUFF CONSUMPTION

Food and Agricultural Organization of the United Nations (FAO) Via delle Terme di Caracalla, 00100 Rome, Italy (Telephone Number in U.S. (202) 653-2400); *The State of Food and Agriculture.*

GUADELOUPE - FOREIGN AID

G.K. Hall and Company, 70 Lincoln Street, Boston, Massachusetts 02111 (617) 423-3990; *The World in Figures.*

GUADELOUPE - FOREIGN TRADE

G.K. Hall and Company, 70 Lincoln Street, Boston, Massachusetts 02111 (617) 423-3990; *The World in Figures.*

Food and Agricultural Organization of the United Nations (FAO) Via delle Terme di Caracalla, 00100 Rome, Italy (Telephone Number in U.S. (202) 653-2400); *The State of Food and Agriculture.*

Statistical Office of the United Nations, Publishing Service, New York, New York 10017 (800) 253-9646; *International Trade Statistics Yearbook, Statistical Yearbook,*and *Yearbook of International Trade Statistics.*

GUADELOUPE - FORESTRY AND FOREST PRODUCTS

Food and Agricultural Organization of the United Nations (FAO) Via delle Terme di Caracalla, 00100 Rome, Italy (Telephone Number in U.S. (202) 653-2400); *The State of Food and Agriculture,* and *Yearbook of Forest Products.*

G.K. Hall and Company, 70 Lincoln Street, Boston, Massachusetts 02111 (617) 423-3990; *The World in Figures.*

Statistical Office of the United Nations, Publishing Service, New York, New York 10017 (800) 253-9646; *Statistical Yearbook.*

United Nations Educational, Scientific and Cultural Organization (UNESCO), 7 Place de Fontenoy, F-75700 Paris, France (Telephone Number in U.S. (212) 963-5981); *Statistical Yearbook.*

GUADELOUPE - GENERAL MORTALITY

Statistical Office of the United Nations, Publishing Service, New York, New York 10017 (800) 253-9646; *Demographic Yearbook.*

World Health Organization, Office of Publications, Avenue Appia, CH-1211 Geneva 27, Switzerland (Telephone Number in U.S. (518) 436-9686); *World Health Statistics Annual.*

GUADELOUPE - GOVERNMENT

G.K. Hall and Company, 70 Lincoln Street, Boston, Massachusetts 02111 (617) 423-3990; *The World in Figures.*

GUADELOUPE - GRAIN PRODUCTION - See GUADELOUPE - CROPS

GUADELOUPE - GROSS DOMESTIC PRODUCT

G.K. Hall and Company, 70 Lincoln Street, Boston, Massachusetts 02111 (617) 423-3990; *The World in Figures.*

Statistical Office of the United Nations, Publishing Service, New York, New York 10017 (800) 253-9646; *Statistical Yearbook.*

GUADELOUPE - HEALTH

G.K. Hall and Company, 70 Lincoln Street, Boston, Massachusetts 02111 (617) 423-3990; *The World in Figures.*

Statistical Office of the United Nations, Publishing Service, New York, New York 10017 (800) 253-9646; *Statistical Yearbook.*

World Health Organization, Office of Publications, Avenue Appia, CH-1211 Geneva 27, Switzerland (Telephone Number in U.S. (518) 436-9686); *World Health Statistics Annual.*

GUADELOUPE - HIDE PRODUCTION

Food and Agricultural Organization of the United Nations (FAO), Via delle Terme di Caracalla, 00100 Rome, Italy (Telephone Number in U.S. (202) 653-2400); *Production Yearbook.*

GUADELOUPE - HIGHWAYS

G.K. Hall and Company, 70 Lincoln Street, Boston, Massachusetts 02111 (617) 423-3990; *The World in Figures.*

GUADELOUPE - HORSES - See GUADELOUPE - LIVESTOCK AND POULTRY

GUADELOUPE - HOURS OF WORK

International Labour Office, I.L.O. Publications, CH-1211, Geneva 22, Switzerland; *Yearbook of Labour Statistics.*

GUADELOUPE - ILLITERATE POPULATION

United Nations Educational, Scientific and Cultural Organization (UNESCO), 7 Place de Fontenoy, F-75700 Paris, France (Telephone Number in U.S. (212) 963-5981); *Statistical Yearbook.*

GUADELOUPE - IMPORTS

Food and Agricultural Organization of the United Nations (FAO) Via delle Terme di Caracalla, 00100 Rome, Italy (Telephone Number in U.S. (202) 653-2400); *The State of Food and Agriculture.*

G.K. Hall and Company, 70 Lincoln Street, Boston, Massachusetts 02111 (617) 423-3990; *The World in Figures.*

International Monetary Fund, 700 Nineteenth Street, NW, Washington, D.C. 20431 (202) 623-7000; *Direction of Trade Statistics.*

Statistical Office of the United Nations, Publishing Service, New York, New York 10017 (800) 253-9646; *Trade in Manufactures of Developing Countries.*

GUADELOUPE - INDUSTRIAL ACCIDENTS

International Labour Office, I.L.O. Publications, CH-1211, Geneva 22, Switzerland; *Yearbook of Labour Statistics.*

GUADELOUPE - INDUSTRIAL DISPUTES

International Labour Office, I.L.O. Publications, CH-1211, Geneva 22, Switzerland; *Yearbook of Labour Statistics.*

GUADELOUPE - INDUSTRY

G.K. Hall and Company, 70 Lincoln Street, Boston, Massachusetts 02111 (617) 423-3990; *The World in Figures.*

GUADELOUPE - INFANT AND MATERNAL MORTALITY

Statistical Office of the United Nations, Publishing Service, New York, New York 10017 (800) 253-9646; *Demographic Yearbook,* and *Statistical Yearbook.*

World Health Organization, Office of Publications, Avenue Appia, CH-1211 Geneva 27, Switzerland (Telephone Number in U.S. (518) 436-9686); *World Health Statistics Annual.*

GUADELOUPE - LABOR FORCE

Food and Agricultural Organization of the United Nations (FAO) Via delle Terme di Caracalla, 00100 Rome, Italy (Telephone Number in U.S. (202) 653-2400); *The State of Food and Agriculture.*

G.K. Hall and Company, 70 Lincoln Street, Boston, Massachusetts 02111 (617) 423-3990; *The World in Figures.*

GUADELOUPE - LABOR PRODUCTIVITY

International Labour Office, I.L.O. Publications, CH-1211, Geneva 22, Switzerland; *Yearbook of Labour Statistics.*

GUADELOUPE - LAND USE

Food and Agricultural Organization of the United Nations (FAO), Via delle Terme di Caracalla, 00100 Rome, Italy (Telephone Number in U.S. (202) 653-2400); *Production Yearbook.*

G.K. Hall and Company, 70 Lincoln Street, Boston, Massachusetts 02111 (617) 423-3990; *The World in Figures.*

GUADELOUPE - LIVESTOCK AND POULTRY

Food and Agricultural Organization of the United Nations (FAO), Via delle Terme di Caracalla, 00100 Rome, Italy (Telephone Number in U.S. (202) 653-2400); *Production Yearbook,* and *The State of Food and Agriculture.*

G.K. Hall and Company, 70 Lincoln Street, Boston, Massachusetts 02111 (617) 423-3990; *The World in Figures.*

Statistical Office of the United Nations, Publishing Service, New York, New York 10017 (800) 253-9646; *Statistical Yearbook.*

GUADELOUPE - LIVING LEVELS

G.K. Hall and Company, 70 Lincoln Street, Boston, Massachusetts 02111 (617) 423-3990; *The World in Figures.*

GUADELOUPE - MANUFACTURING

G.K. Hall and Company, 70 Lincoln Street, Boston, Massachusetts 02111 (617) 423-3990; *The World in Figures.*

GUADELOUPE - MARRIAGE RATES

Statistical Office of the United Nations, Publishing Service, New York, New York 10017 (800) 253-9646; *Demographic Yearbook,* and *Statistical Yearbook.*

GUADELOUPE - MEAT PRODUCTION - See GUADELOUPE - LIVESTOCK AND POULTRY

GUADELOUPE - MERCHANT SHIPPING

G.K. Hall and Company, 70 Lincoln Street, Boston, Massachusetts 02111 (617) 423-3990; *The World in Figures.*

Statistical Office of the United Nations, Publishing Service, New York, New York 10017 (800) 253-9646; *Statistical Yearbook.*

GUADELOUPE - MILITARY

G.K. Hall and Company, 70 Lincoln Street, Boston, Massachusetts 02111 (617) 423-3990; *The World in Figures.*

GUADELOUPE - MINING AND MINERAL PRODUCTS

G.K. Hall and Company, 70 Lincoln Street, Boston, Massachusetts 02111 (617) 423-3990; *The World in Figures.*

Statistical Office of the United Nations, Publishing Service, New York, New York 10017 (800) 253-9646; *Statistical Yearbook.*

GUADELOUPE - MONEY SUPPLY

G.K. Hall and Company, 70 Lincoln Street, Boston, Massachusetts 02111 (617) 423-3990; *The World in Figures.*

GUADELOUPE - MONUMENTS AND HISTORICAL SITES

United Nations Educational, Scientific and Cultural Organization (UNESCO), 7 Place de Fontenoy, F-75700 Paris, France (Telephone Number in U.S. (212) 963-5981); *Statistical Yearbook.*

GUADELOUPE - MOTOR VEHICLES IN USE

G.K. Hall and Company, 70 Lincoln Street, Boston, Massachusetts 02111 (617) 423-3990; *The World in Figures.*

Statistical Office of the United Nations, Publishing Service, New York, New York 10017 (800) 253-9646; *Statistical Yearbook.*

GUADELOUPE - MULES - See GUADELOUPE - LIVESTOCK AND POULTRY

GUADELOUPE - MUSEUMS

United Nations Educational, Scientific and Cultural Organization (UNESCO), 7 Place de Fontenoy, F-75700 Paris, France (Telephone Number in U.S. (212) 963-5981); *Statistical Yearbook.*

GUADELOUPE - NATALITY

Statistical Office of the United Nations, Publishing Service, New York, New York 10017 (800) 253-9646; *Demographic Yearbook.*

World Health Organization, Office of Publications, Avenue Appia, CH-1211 Geneva 27, Switzerland (Telephone Number in U.S. (518) 436-9686); *World Health Statistics Annual.*

GUADELOUPE - NATIONAL ACCOUNTS

Statistical Office of the United Nations, Publishing Service, New York, New York 10017 (800) 253-9646; *National Accounts Statistics*, and *Statistical Yearbook.*

GUADELOUPE - NATIONAL INCOME

G.K. Hall and Company, 70 Lincoln Street, Boston, Massachusetts 02111 (617) 423-3990; *The World in Figures.*

Statistical Office of the United Nations, Publishing Service, New York, New York 10017 (800) 253-9646; *Statistical Yearbook.*

GUADELOUPE - NEWSPAPER PRODUCTION - See GUADELOUPE - FORESTRY AND FOREST PRODUCTS

GUADELOUPE - OCCUPATIONS - See GUADELOUPE - LABOR FORCE

GUADELOUPE - PAPER - See GUADELOUPE - FORESTRY AND FOREST PRODUCTS

GUADELOUPE - PERIODICALS

United Nations Educational, Scientific and Cultural Organization (UNESCO), 7 Place de Fontenoy, F-75700 Paris, France (Telephone Number in U.S. (212) 963-5981); *Statistical Yearbook.*

GUADELOUPE - PESTICIDE USE

Food and Agricultural Organization of the United Nations (FAO) Via delle Terme di Caracalla, 00100 Rome, Italy (Telephone Number in U.S. (202) 653-2400); *The State of Food and Agriculture.*

GUADELOUPE - PETROLEUM INDUSTRY

Food and Agricultural Organization of the United Nations (FAO) Via delle Terme di Caracalla, 00100 Rome, Italy (Telephone Number in U.S. (202) 653-2400); *The State of Food and Agriculture.*

G.K. Hall and Company, 70 Lincoln Street, Boston, Massachusetts 02111 (617) 423-3990; *The World in Figures.*

GUADELOUPE - PIGS - See GUADELOUPE - LIVESTOCK AND POULTRY

GUADELOUPE - POPULATION

Food and Agricultural Organization of the United Nations (FAO), Via delle Terme di Caracalla, 00100 Rome, Italy (Telephone Number in U.S. (202) 653-2400); *Production Yearbook.*

G.K. Hall and Company, 70 Lincoln Street, Boston, Massachusetts 02111 (617) 423-3990; *The World in Figures.*

International Labour Office, I.L.O. Publications, CH-1211, Geneva 22, Switzerland; *Yearbook of Labour Statistics.*

Statistical Office of the United Nations, Publishing Service, New York, New York 10017 (800) 253-9646; *Demographic Yearbook*, and *Statistical Yearbook.*

World Health Organization, Office of Publications, Avenue Appia, CH-1211 Geneva 27, Switzerland (Telephone Number in U.S. (518) 436-9686); *World Health Statistics Annual.*

GUADELOUPE - PRICES

Food and Agricultural Organization of the United Nations (FAO), Via delle Terme di Caracalla, 00100 Rome, Italy (Telephone Number in U.S. (202) 653-2400); *Production Yearbook*, and *The State of Food and Agriculture.*

G.K. Hall and Company, 70 Lincoln Street, Boston, Massachusetts 02111 (617) 423-3990; *The World in Figures.*

International Labour Office, I.L.O. Publications, CH-1211, Geneva 22, Switzerland; *Yearbook of Labour Statistics.*

GUADELOUPE - PRINTING AND WRITING PAPER - See GUADELOUPE - FORESTRY AND FOREST PRODUCTS

GUADELOUPE - PRODUCTION

G.K. Hall and Company, 70 Lincoln Street, Boston, Massachusetts 02111 (617) 423-3990; *The World in Figures.*

GUADELOUPE - RAILWAYS

G.K. Hall and Company, 70 Lincoln Street, Boston, Massachusetts 02111 (617) 423-3990; *The World in Figures.*

GUADELOUPE - RENT PRICES

International Labour Office, I.L.O. Publications, CH-1211, Geneva 22, Switzerland; *Yearbook of Labour Statistics.*

GUADELOUPE - RETAIL TRADE

G.K. Hall and Company, 70 Lincoln Street, Boston, Massachusetts 02111 (617) 423-3990; *The World in Figures.*

GUADELOUPE - ROOT AND TUBER PRODUCTION - See GUADELOUPE - CROPS

GUADELOUPE - ROUNDWOOD PRODUCTION - See GUADELOUPE - FORESTRY AND FOREST PRODUCTS

GUADELOUPE - SAWNWOOD PRODUCTION - See GUADELOUPE - FORESTRY AND FOREST PRODUCTS

GUADELOUPE - SHEEP - See GUADELOUPE - LIVESTOCK AND POULTRY

GUADELOUPE - SOCIAL DATA

G.K. Hall and Company, 70 Lincoln Street, Boston, Massachusetts 02111 (617) 423-3990; *The World in Figures.*

GUADELOUPE - STOCKS - COMMODITY - MARKET PRICE - INDEX

Food and Agricultural Organization of the United Nations (FAO) Via delle Terme di Caracalla, 00100 Rome, Italy (Telephone Number in U.S. (202) 653-2400); *The State of Food and Agriculture.*

GUADELOUPE - SUGAR PRODUCTION - See GUADELOUPE - CROPS

GUADELOUPE - TAXATION

G.K. Hall and Company, 70 Lincoln Street, Boston, Massachusetts 02111 (617) 423-3990; *The World in Figures.*

GUADELOUPE - TELEPHONES IN USE

American Telephone and Telegraph Company, 26 Parsippany Road, Whippany, New Jersey 07981 (800) 338-4038; *The World's Telephones*.

G.K. Hall and Company, 70 Lincoln Street, Boston, Massachusetts 02111 (617) 423-3990; *The World in Figures*.

Statistical Office of the United Nations, Publishing Service, New York, New York 10017 (800) 253-9646; *Statistical Yearbook*.

GUADELOUPE - TEXTILE INDUSTRY

G.K. Hall and Company, 70 Lincoln Street, Boston, Massachusetts 02111 (617) 423-3990; *The World in Figures*.

GUADELOUPE - TOURISM

G.K. Hall and Company, 70 Lincoln Street, Boston, Massachusetts 02111 (617) 423-3990; *The World in Figures*.

World Tourism Organization, Calle Capitan Haya 42, E-28020 Madrid, Spain; *Yearbook of Tourism Statistics*.

GUADELOUPE - TRACTORS IN USE

Statistical Office of the United Nations, Publishing Service, New York, New York 10017 (800) 253-9646; *Statistical Yearbook*.

GUADELOUPE - TRADE - See GUADELOUPE - FOREIGN TRADE

GUADELOUPE - TRANSPORTATION AND COMMUNICATIONS

G.K. Hall and Company, 70 Lincoln Street, Boston, Massachusetts 02111 (617) 423-3990; *The World in Figures*.

GUADELOUPE - UNEMPLOYMENT

International Labour Office, I.L.O. Publications, CH-1211, Geneva 22, Switzerland; *Yearbook of Labour Statistics*.

Statistical Office of the United Nations, Publishing Service, New York, New York 10017 (800) 253-9646; *Statistical Yearbook*.

GUADELOUPE - VITAL STATISTICS

G.K. Hall and Company, 70 Lincoln Street, Boston, Massachusetts 02111 (617) 423-3990; *The World in Figures*.

Statistical Office of the United Nations, Publishing Service, New York, New York 10017 (800) 253-9646; *Statistical Yearbook*.

World Health Organization, Office of Publications, Avenue Appia, CH-1211 Geneva 27, Switzerland (Telephone Number in U.S. (518) 436-9686); *World Health Statistics Annual*.

GUADELOUPE - WAGES

G.K. Hall and Company, 70 Lincoln Street, Boston, Massachusetts 02111 (617) 423-3990; *The World in Figures*.

International Labour Office, I.L.O. Publications, CH-1211, Geneva 22, Switzerland; *Yearbook of Labour Statistics*.

GUADELOUPE - WEATHER

G.K. Hall and Company, 70 Lincoln Street, Boston, Massachusetts 02111 (617) 423-3990; *The World in Figures*.

Guam - National Statistical Office

Department of Commerce, 590 South Marine Drive, Suite 601, 6th Floor GITC Building, Tamuning, Guam 96911.

Guam - Primary Statistics Sources

Economic Research Center, Department of Commerce, Agana, Guam 96910; *Annual Economic Review*.

Superintendent of Documents, U.S. Government Printing Office, Washington, D.C. 20402; *Guam: Annual Report to the Secretary of the Interior*.

Guam - State Data Center

Guam Department of Commerce, 590 South Marine Drive, Suite 601, Sixth Floor GITC Building, Tamuning, Guam 96911, Mr. Peter R. Barcinas (671) 646-5841.

GUAM - AGRICULTURE

Food and Agricultural Organization of the United Nations (FAO), Via delle Terme di Caracalla, 00100 Rome, Italy (Telephone Number in U.S. (202) 653-2400); *Production Yearbook*, and *The State of Food and Agriculture*.

G.K. Hall and Company, 70 Lincoln Street, Boston, Massachusetts 02111 (617) 423-3990; *The World in Figures*.

Statistical Office of the United Nations, Publishing Service, New York, New York 10017 (800) 253-9646; *Statistical Yearbook*.

GUAM - AIRLINE SERVICE

G.K. Hall and Company, 70 Lincoln Street, Boston, Massachusetts 02111 (617) 423-3990; *The World in Figures*.

GUAM - AREA AND DENSITY OF POPULATION

Food and Agricultural Organization of the United Nations (FAO) Via delle Terme di Caracalla, 00100 Rome, Italy (Telephone Number in U.S. (202) 653-2400); *The State of Food and Agriculture*.

G.K. Hall and Company, 70 Lincoln Street, Boston, Massachusetts 02111 (617) 423-3990; *The World in Figures*.

Statistical Office of the United Nations, Publishing Service, New York, New York 10017 (800) 253-9646; *Statistical Yearbook*.

GUAM - BALANCE OF PAYMENTS

G.K. Hall and Company, 70 Lincoln Street, Boston, Massachusetts 02111 (617) 423-3990; *The World in Figures*.

GUAM - BANKING

G.K. Hall and Company, 70 Lincoln Street, Boston, Massachusetts 02111 (617) 423-3990; *The World in Figures*.

GUAM - BIRTH RATES

Statistical Office of the United Nations, Publishing Service, New York, New York 10017 (800) 253-9646; *Demographic Yearbook*, and *Statistical Yearbook*.

GUAM - BOOK PRODUCTION

G.K. Hall and Company, 70 Lincoln Street, Boston, Massachusetts 02111 (617) 423-3990; *The World in Figures.*

United Nations Educational, Scientific and Cultural Organization (UNESCO), 7 Place de Fontenoy, F-75700 Paris, France (Telephone Number in U.S. (212) 963-5981); *Statistical Yearbook.*

GUAM - BROADCASTING

G.K. Hall and Company, 70 Lincoln Street, Boston, Massachusetts 02111 (617) 423-3990; *The World in Figures.*

United Nations Educational, Scientific and Cultural Organization (UNESCO), 7 Place de Fontenoy, F-75700 Paris, France (Telephone Number in U.S. (212) 963-5981); *Statistical Yearbook.*

GUAM - BUSINESS

G.K. Hall and Company, 70 Lincoln Street, Boston, Massachusetts 02111 (617) 423-3990; *The World in Figures.*

GUAM - CALORIE SUPPLY

Food and Agricultural Organization of the United Nations (FAO) Via delle Terme di Caracalla, 00100 Rome, Italy (Telephone Number in U.S. (202) 653-2400); *The State of Food and Agriculture.*

GUAM - CATTLE - See GUAM - LIVESTOCK AND POULTRY

GUAM - CHEMICAL (ORGANIC) PRODUCTION - See GUAM - MINING AND MINERAL PRODUCTS

GUAM - CLASS STRUCTURE

G.K. Hall and Company, 70 Lincoln Street, Boston, Massachusetts 02111 (617) 423-3990; *The World in Figures.*

GUAM - CLIMATE

G.K. Hall and Company, 70 Lincoln Street, Boston, Massachusetts 02111 (617) 423-3990; *The World in Figures.*

GUAM - CLOTHING EXPORTS AND IMPORTS

South Pacific Commission, Post Box D5, Noumea Cedex, New Caledonia; *Statistical Bulletin of the South Pacific: Retail Price Indexes.*

GUAM - COAL PRODUCTION - See GUAM - MINING AND MINERAL PRODUCTS

GUAM - COMMUNICATIONS

G.K. Hall and Company, 70 Lincoln Street, Boston, Massachusetts 02111 (617) 423-3990; *The World in Figures.*

GUAM - CONSUMER PRICE INDEX

G.K. Hall and Company, 70 Lincoln Street, Boston, Massachusetts 02111 (617) 423-3990; *The World in Figures.*

Statistical Office of the United Nations, Publishing Service, New York, New York 10017 (800) 253-9646; *Statistical Yearbook.*

GUAM - CONSUMER PRICES

International Labour Office, I.L.O. Publications, CH-1211, Geneva 22, Switzerland; *Yearbook of Labour Statistics.*

GUAM - CONSUMPTION

G.K. Hall and Company, 70 Lincoln Street, Boston, Massachusetts 02111 (617) 423-3990; *The World in Figures.*

South Pacific Commission, Post Box D5, Noumea Cedex, New Caledonia; *Statistical Bulletin of the South Pacific: Retail Price Indexes.*

GUAM - CORN PRODUCTION - See GUAM - CROPS

GUAM - CORPORATE TAXES - See GUAM - TAXATION

GUAM - CRIME

Yale University Press, Yale Station, New Haven, Connecticut 06520 (203) 432-0940; *Violence and Crime in Cross-National Perspective.*

GUAM - CROPS

Food and Agricultural Organization of the United Nations (FAO) Via delle Terme di Caracalla, 00100 Rome, Italy (Telephone Number in U.S. (202) 653-2400); *The State of Food and Agriculture.*

Food and Agricultural Organization of the United Nations (FAO) Via delle Terme di Caracalla, 00100 Rome, Italy (Telephone Number in U.S. (202) 653-2400); *The State of Food and Agriculture.*

G.K. Hall and Company, 70 Lincoln Street, Boston, Massachusetts 02111 (617) 423-3990; *The World in Figures.*

Food and Agricultural Organization of the United Nations (FAO) Via delle Terme di Caracalla, 00100 Rome, Italy (Telephone Number in U.S. (202) 653-2400); *The State of Food and Agriculture.*

GUAM - CUSTOMS DUTIES

G.K. Hall and Company, 70 Lincoln Street, Boston, Massachusetts 02111 (617) 423-3990; *The World in Figures.*

GUAM - DAIRY PRODUCTS

Food and Agricultural Organization of the United Nations (FAO) Via delle Terme di Caracalla, 00100 Rome, Italy (Telephone Number in U.S. (202) 653-2400); *The State of Food and Agriculture.*

GUAM - DEATH RATES

G.K. Hall and Company, 70 Lincoln Street, Boston, Massachusetts 02111 (617) 423-3990; *The World in Figures.*

Statistical Office of the United Nations, Publishing Service, New York, New York 10017 (800) 253-9646; *Statistical Yearbook.*

World Health Organization, Office of Publications, Avenue Appia, CH-1211 Geneva 27, Switzerland (Telephone Number in U.S. (518) 436-9686); *World Health Statistics Annual.*

GUAM - DEFENSE EXPENDITURES

G.K. Hall and Company, 70 Lincoln Street, Boston, Massachusetts 02111 (617) 423-3990; *The World in Figures.*

GUAM - DEMOGRAPHY

G.K. Hall and Company, 70 Lincoln Street, Boston, Massachusetts 02111 (617) 423-3990; *The World in Figures.*

GUAM - DEVELOPMENT ASSISTANCE

G.K. Hall and Company, 70 Lincoln Street, Boston, Massachusetts 02111 (617) 423-3990; *The World in Figures.*

GUAM - DISEASES

G.K. Hall and Company, 70 Lincoln Street, Boston, Massachusetts 02111 (617) 423-3990; *The World in Figures.*

World Health Organization, Office of Publications, Avenue Appia, CH-1211 Geneva 27, Switzerland (Telephone Number in U.S. (518) 436-9686); *World Health Statistics Annual.*

GUAM - DIVORCE RATES

Statistical Office of the United Nations, Publishing Service, New York, New York 10017 (800) 253-9646; *Demographic Yearbook,* and *Statistical Yearbook.*

GUAM - DOMESTIC PRODUCT

G.K. Hall and Company, 70 Lincoln Street, Boston, Massachusetts 02111 (617) 423-3990; *The World in Figures.*

GUAM - DUCKS - See GUAM - LIVESTOCK AND POULTRY

GUAM - ECONOMY

G.K. Hall and Company, 70 Lincoln Street, Boston, Massachusetts 02111 (617) 423-3990; *The World in Figures.*

GUAM - EDUCATION

G.K. Hall and Company, 70 Lincoln Street, Boston, Massachusetts 02111 (617) 423-3990; *The World in Figures.*

United Nations Educational, Scientific and Cultural Organization (UNESCO), 7 Place de Fontenoy, F-75700 Paris, France (Telephone Number in U.S. (212) 963-5981); *Statistical Yearbook.*

GUAM - EGG PRODUCTION - See GUAM - DAIRY PRODUCTS

GUAM - ELECTRICITY

Statistical Office of the United Nations, Publishing Service, New York, New York 10017 (800) 253-9646; *Statistical Yearbook.*

GUAM - EMPLOYMENT

International Labour Office, I.L.O. Publications, CH-1211, Geneva 22, Switzerland; *Yearbook of Labour Statistics.*

GUAM - ENERGY

Food and Agricultural Organization of the United Nations (FAO) Via delle Terme di Caracalla, 00100 Rome, Italy (Telephone Number in U.S. (202) 653-2400); *The State of Food and Agriculture.*

G.K. Hall and Company, 70 Lincoln Street, Boston, Massachusetts 02111 (617) 423-3990; *The World in Figures.*

Statistical Office of the United Nations, Publishing Service, New York, New York 10017 (800) 253-9646; *Statistical Yearbook,* and *Yearbook of World Energy Statistics.*

GUAM - EXPORTS

Food and Agricultural Organization of the United Nations (FAO) Via delle Terme di Caracalla, 00100 Rome, Italy (Telephone Number in U.S. (202) 653-2400); *The State of Food and Agriculture.*

G.K. Hall and Company, 70 Lincoln Street, Boston, Massachusetts 02111 (617) 423-3990; *The World in Figures.*

International Monetary Fund, 700 Nineteenth Street, NW, Washington, D.C. 20431 (202) 623-7000; *Direction of Trade Statistics.*

South Pacific Commission, Post Box D5, Noumea Cedex, New Caledonia; *Statistical Bulletin of the South Pacific: Overseas Trade.*

GUAM - EXTERNAL TRADE

Food and Agricultural Organization of the United Nations (FAO) Via delle Terme di Caracalla, 00100 Rome, Italy (Telephone Number in U.S. (202) 653-2400); *The State of Food and Agriculture,* and *Trade Yearbook.*

GUAM - FARM CROPS - See GUAM - CROPS

GUAM - FERTILIZER

Food and Agricultural Organization of the United Nations (FAO) Via delle Terme di Caracalla, 00100 Rome, Italy (Telephone Number in U.S. (202) 653-2400); *The State of Food and Agriculture.*

GUAM - FETAL MORTALITY

Statistical Office of the United Nations, Publishing Service, New York, New York 10017 (800) 253-9646; *Demographic Yearbook.*

GUAM - FINANCE

G.K. Hall and Company, 70 Lincoln Street, Boston, Massachusetts 02111 (617) 423-3990; *The World in Figures.*

GUAM - FISHERIES

Food and Agricultural Organization of the United Nations (FAO) Via delle Terme di Caracalla, 00100 Rome, Italy (Telephone Number in U.S. (202) 653-2400); *The State of Food and Agriculture,* and *Yearbook of Fishery Statistics.*

GUAM - FOOD PRODUCTION AND CONSUMPTION

Food and Agricultural Organization of the United Nations (FAO) Via delle Terme di Caracalla, 00100 Rome, Italy (Telephone Number in U.S. (202) 653-2400); *The State of Food and Agriculture.*

South Pacific Commission, Post Box D5, Noumea Cedex, New Caledonia; *Statistical Bulletin of the South Pacific: Retail Price Indexes.*

GUAM - FOOD PRODUCTS - EXPORTS AND IMPORTS

Food and Agricultural Organization of the United Nations (FAO) Via delle Terme di Caracalla, 00100 Rome, Italy (Telephone Number in U.S. (202) 653-2400); *The State of Food and Agriculture.*

GUAM - FOOD SUPPLY

Food and Agricultural Organization of the United Nations (FAO), Via delle Terme di Caracalla, 00100 Rome, Italy (Telephone Number in U.S. (202) 653-2400); *Production Yearbook,* and *The State of Food and Agriculture.*

GUAM - FOODSTUFF CONSUMPTION

Food and Agricultural Organization of the United Nations (FAO) Via delle Terme di Caracalla, 00100 Rome, Italy (Telephone Number in U.S. (202) 653-2400); *The State of Food and Agriculture.*

GUAM - FOREIGN AID

G.K. Hall and Company, 70 Lincoln Street, Boston, Massachusetts 02111 (617) 423-3990; *The World in Figures.*

GUAM - FOREIGN TRADE

Food and Agricultural Organization of the United Nations (FAO) Via delle Terme di Caracalla, 00100 Rome, Italy (Telephone Number in U.S. (202) 653-2400); *The State of Food and Agriculture.*

G.K. Hall and Company, 70 Lincoln Street, Boston, Massachusetts 02111 (617) 423-3990; *The World in Figures.*

South Pacific Commission, Post Box D5, Noumea Cedex, New Caledonia; *Statistical Bulletin of the South Pacific: Overseas Trade.*

Statistical Office of the United Nations, Publishing Service, New York, New York 10017 (800) 253-9646; *Statistical Yearbook.*

GUAM - FORESTRY AND FOREST PRODUCTS

G.K. Hall and Company, 70 Lincoln Street, Boston, Massachusetts 02111 (617) 423-3990; *The World in Figures.*

Statistical Office of the United Nations, Publishing Service, New York, New York 10017 (800) 253-9646; *Statistical Yearbook.*

United Nations Educational, Scientific and Cultural Organization (UNESCO), 7 Place de Fontenoy, F-75700 Paris, France (Telephone Number in U.S. (212) 963-5981); *Statistical Yearbook.*

Food and Agricultural Organization of the United Nations (FAO) Via delle Terme di Caracalla, 00100 Rome, Italy (Telephone Number in U.S. (202) 653-2400); *The State of Food and Agriculture.*

G.K. Hall and Company, 70 Lincoln Street, Boston, Massachusetts 02111 (617) 423-3990; *The World in Figures.*

GUAM - GENERAL MORTALITY

Statistical Office of the United Nations, Publishing Service, New York, New York 10017 (800) 253-9646; *Demographic Yearbook.*

GUAM - GOVERNMENT

G.K. Hall and Company, 70 Lincoln Street, Boston, Massachusetts 02111 (617) 423-3990; *The World in Figures.*

GUAM - GRAIN PRODUCTION - See GUAM - CROPS

GUAM - GROSS DOMESTIC PRODUCT

G.K. Hall and Company, 70 Lincoln Street, Boston, Massachusetts 02111 (617) 423-3990; *The World in Figures.*

GUAM - HEALTH

G.K. Hall and Company, 70 Lincoln Street, Boston, Massachusetts 02111 (617) 423-3990; *The World in Figures.*

South Pacific Commission, Post Box D5, Noumea Cedex, New Caledonia; *Statistical Bulletin of the South Pacific: Retail Price Indexes.*

Statistical Office of the United Nations, Publishing Service, New York, New York 10017 (800) 253-9646; *Statistical Yearbook.*

World Health Organization, Office of Publications, Avenue Appia, CH-1211 Geneva 27, Switzerland (Telephone Number in U.S. (518) 436-9686); *World Health Statistics Annual.*

GUAM - HIDE PRODUCTION

Food and Agricultural Organization of the United Nations (FAO), Via delle Terme di Caracalla, 00100 Rome, Italy (Telephone Number in U.S. (202) 653-2400); *Production Yearbook.*

GUAM - HIGHWAYS

G.K. Hall and Company, 70 Lincoln Street, Boston, Massachusetts 02111 (617) 423-3990; *The World in Figures.*

GUAM - HOURS OF WORK

International Labour Office, I.L.O. Publications, CH-1211, Geneva 22, Switzerland; *Yearbook of Labour Statistics.*

GUAM - HOUSING AND HOUSING UNITS

South Pacific Commission, Post Box D5, Noumea Cedex, New Caledonia; *Statistical Bulletin of the South Pacific: Retail Price Indexes.*

GUAM - HOUSING EXPENDITURES

South Pacific Commission, Post Box D5, Noumea Cedex, New Caledonia; *Statistical Bulletin of the South Pacific: Retail Price Indexes.*

GUAM - ILLITERATE POPULATION

G.K. Hall and Company, 70 Lincoln Street, Boston, Massachusetts 02111 (617) 423-3990; *The World in Figures.*

GUAM - IMPORTS

Food and Agricultural Organization of the United Nations (FAO) Via delle Terme di Caracalla, 00100 Rome, Italy (Telephone Number in U.S. (202) 653-2400); *The State of Food and Agriculture.*

G.K. Hall and Company, 70 Lincoln Street, Boston, Massachusetts 02111 (617) 423-3990; *The World in Figures.*

International Monetary Fund, 700 Nineteenth Street, NW, Washington, D.C. 20431 (202) 623-7000; *Direction of Trade Statistics.*

South Pacific Commission, Post Box D5, Noumea Cedex, New Caledonia; *Statistical Bulletin of the South Pacific: Overseas Trade.*

GUAM - INDUSTRIAL ACCIDENTS

International Labour Office, I.L.O. Publications, CH-1211, Geneva 22, Switzerland; *Yearbook of Labour Statistics.*

GUAM - INDUSTRIAL DISPUTES

International Labour Office, I.L.O. Publications, CH-1211, Geneva 22, Switzerland; *Yearbook of Labour Statistics.*

GUAM - INDUSTRY

G.K. Hall and Company, 70 Lincoln Street, Boston, Massachusetts 02111 (617) 423-3990; *The World in Figures.*

GUAM - INFANT AND MATERNAL MORTALITY

Statistical Office of the United Nations, Publishing Service, New York, New York 10017 (800) 253-9646; *Demographic Yearbook,* and *Statistical Yearbook.*

GUAM - LABOR FORCE

Food and Agricultural Organization of the United Nations (FAO) Via delle Terme di Caracalla, 00100 Rome, Italy (Telephone Number in U.S. (202) 653-2400); *The State of Food and Agriculture.*

G.K. Hall and Company, 70 Lincoln Street, Boston, Massachusetts 02111 (617) 423-3990; *The World in Figures.*

GUAM - LABOR PRODUCTIVITY

International Labour Office, I.L.O. Publications, CH-1211, Geneva 22, Switzerland; *Yearbook of Labour Statistics.*

GUAM - LAND USE

Food and Agricultural Organization of the United Nations (FAO), Via delle Terme di Caracalla, 00100 Rome, Italy (Telephone Number in U.S. (202) 653-2400); *Production Yearbook.*

G.K. Hall and Company, 70 Lincoln Street, Boston, Massachusetts 02111 (617) 423-3990; *The World in Figures.*

GUAM - LIVESTOCK AND POULTRY

Food and Agricultural Organization of the United Nations (FAO), Via delle Terme di Caracalla, 00100 Rome, Italy (Telephone Number in U.S. (202) 653-2400); *Production Yearbook,* and *The State of Food and Agriculture.*

G.K. Hall and Company, 70 Lincoln Street, Boston, Massachusetts 02111 (617) 423-3990; *The World in Figures.*

Statistical Office of the United Nations, Publishing Service, New York, New York 10017 (800) 253-9646; *Statistical Yearbook.*

GUAM - LIVING LEVELS

G.K. Hall and Company, 70 Lincoln Street, Boston, Massachusetts 02111 (617) 423-3990; *The World in Figures.*

GUAM - MANUFACTURING

G.K. Hall and Company, 70 Lincoln Street, Boston, Massachusetts 02111 (617) 423-3990; *The World in Figures.*

GUAM - MARRIAGE RATES

Statistical Office of the United Nations, Publishing Service, New York, New York 10017 (800) 253-9646; *Demographic Yearbook,* and *Statistical Yearbook.*

GUAM - MEAT PRODUCTION - See GUAM - LIVESTOCK AND POULTRY

GUAM - MERCHANT SHIPPING

G.K. Hall and Company, 70 Lincoln Street, Boston, Massachusetts 02111 (617) 423-3990; *The World in Figures.*

Statistical Office of the United Nations, Publishing Service, New York, New York 10017 (800) 253-9646; *Statistical Yearbook.*

GUAM - MILITARY

G.K. Hall and Company, 70 Lincoln Street, Boston, Massachusetts 02111 (617) 423-3990; *The World in Figures.*

GUAM - MINING AND MINERAL PRODUCTS

G.K. Hall and Company, 70 Lincoln Street, Boston, Massachusetts 02111 (617) 423-3990; *The World in Figures.*

GUAM - MONEY SUPPLY

G.K. Hall and Company, 70 Lincoln Street, Boston, Massachusetts 02111 (617) 423-3990; *The World in Figures.*

GUAM - MOTION PICTURES

Statistical Office of the United Nations, Publishing Service, New York, New York 10017 (800) 253-9646; *Statistical Yearbook.*

GUAM - MOTOR VEHICLES IN USE

G.K. Hall and Company, 70 Lincoln Street, Boston, Massachusetts 02111 (617) 423-3990; *The World in Figures.*

Statistical Office of the United Nations, Publishing Service, New York, New York 10017 (800) 253-9646; *Statistical Yearbook.*

GUAM - NATALITY

Statistical Office of the United Nations, Publishing Service, New York, New York 10017 (800) 253-9646; *Demographic Yearbook.*

GUAM - NATIONAL INCOME

G.K. Hall and Company, 70 Lincoln Street, Boston, Massachusetts 02111 (617) 423-3990; *The World in Figures.*

GUAM - NEWSPAPER PRODUCTION - See GUAM - FORESTRY AND FOREST PRODUCTS

GUAM - OCCUPATIONS - See GUAM - LABOR FORCE

GUAM - PESTICIDE USE

Food and Agricultural Organization of the United Nations (FAO) Via delle Terme di Caracalla, 00100 Rome, Italy (Telephone Number in U.S. (202) 653-2400); *The State of Food and Agriculture.*

GUAM - PETROLEUM INDUSTRY

Food and Agricultural Organization of the United Nations (FAO) Via delle Terme di Caracalla, 00100 Rome, Italy (Telephone Number in U.S. (202) 653-2400); *The State of Food and Agriculture.*

G.K. Hall and Company, 70 Lincoln Street, Boston, Massachusetts 02111 (617) 423-3990; *The World in Figures.*

Statistical Office of the United Nations, Publishing Service, New York, New York 10017 (800) 253-9646; *Statistical Yearbook.*

GUAM - PIGS - See GUAM - LIVESTOCK AND POULTRY

GUAM - POPULATION

Food and Agricultural Organization of the United Nations (FAO), Via delle Terme di Caracalla, 00100 Rome, Italy (Telephone Number in U.S. (202) 653-2400); *Production Yearbook.*

G.K. Hall and Company, 70 Lincoln Street, Boston, Massachusetts 02111 (617) 423-3990; *The World in Figures.*

International Labour Office, I.L.O. Publications, CH-1211, Geneva 22, Switzerland; *Yearbook of Labour Statistics.*

Statistical Office of the United Nations, Publishing Service, New York, New York 10017 (800) 253-9646; *Demographic Yearbook,* and *Statistical Yearbook.*

GUAM - PRICES

Food and Agricultural Organization of the United Nations (FAO), Via delle Terme di Caracalla, 00100 Rome, Italy (Telephone Number in U.S. (202) 653-2400); *Production Yearbook,* and *The State of Food and Agriculture.*

G.K. Hall and Company, 70 Lincoln Street, Boston, Massachusetts 02111 (617) 423-3990; *The World in Figures.*

International Labour Office, I.L.O. Publications, CH-1211, Geneva 22, Switzerland; *Yearbook of Labour Statistics.*

South Pacific Commission, Post Box D5, Noumea Cedex, New Caledonia; *Statistical Bulletin of the South Pacific: Overseas Trade,* and *Statistical Bulletin of the South Pacific: Retail Price Indexes.*

GUAM - PRODUCTION

G.K. Hall and Company, 70 Lincoln Street, Boston, Massachusetts 02111 (617) 423-3990; *The World in Figures.*

GUAM - RADIO BROADCASTING - See GUAM - BROADCASTING

GUAM - RAILWAYS

G.K. Hall and Company, 70 Lincoln Street, Boston, Massachusetts 02111 (617) 423-3990; *The World in Figures.*

GUAM - RENT PRICES

International Labour Office, I.L.O. Publications, CH-1211, Geneva 22, Switzerland; *Yearbook of Labour Statistics.*

GUAM - RETAIL TRADE

G.K. Hall and Company, 70 Lincoln Street, Boston, Massachusetts 02111 (617) 423-3990; *The World in Figures.*

GUAM - SCIENCE AND TECHNOLOGY - EXPENDITURE FOR RESEARCH

Statistical Office of the United Nations, Publishing Service, New York, New York 10017 (800) 253-9646; *Statistical Yearbook.*

GUAM - SCIENTISTS AND TECHNICIANS

Statistical Office of the United Nations, Publishing Service, New York, New York 10017 (800) 253-9646; *Statistical Yearbook.*

GUAM - SOCIAL DATA

G.K. Hall and Company, 70 Lincoln Street, Boston, Massachusetts 02111 (617) 423-3990; *The World in Figures.*

GUAM - STOCKS - COMMODITY - MARKET PRICE - INDEX

Food and Agricultural Organization of the United Nations (FAO) Via delle Terme di Caracalla, 00100 Rome, Italy (Telephone Number in U.S. (202) 653-2400); *The State of Food and Agriculture.*

GUAM - TAXATION

G.K. Hall and Company, 70 Lincoln Street, Boston, Massachusetts 02111 (617) 423-3990; *The World in Figures.*

GUAM - TELEPHONES IN USE

American Telephone and Telegraph Company, 26 Parsippany Road, Whippany, New Jersey 07981 (800) 338-4038; *The World's Telephones.*

G.K. Hall and Company, 70 Lincoln Street, Boston, Massachusetts 02111 (617) 423-3990; *The World in Figures.*

Statistical Office of the United Nations, Publishing Service, New York, New York 10017 (800) 253-9646; *Statistical Yearbook.*

GUAM - TELEVISION BROADCASTING - See GUAM - BROADCASTING

GUAM - TEXTILE INDUSTRY

G.K. Hall and Company, 70 Lincoln Street, Boston, Massachusetts 02111 (617) 423-3990; *The World in Figures.*

GUAM - TOBACCO PRODUCTION

South Pacific Commission, Post Box D5, Noumea Cedex, New Caledonia; *Statistical Bulletin of the South Pacific: Retail Price Indexes.*

GUAM - TOURISM

G.K. Hall and Company, 70 Lincoln Street, Boston, Massachusetts 02111 (617) 423-3990; *The World in Figures.*

World Tourism Organization, Calle Capitan Haya 42, E-28020 Madrid, Spain; *Yearbook of Tourism Statistics.*

GUAM - TRACTORS IN USE

Statistical Office of the United Nations, Publishing Service, New York, New York 10017 (800) 253-9646; *Statistical Yearbook.*

GUAM - TRADE - See GUAM - FOREIGN TRADE

GUAM - TRANSPORTATION AND COMMUNICATIONS

G.K. Hall and Company, 70 Lincoln Street, Boston, Massachusetts 02111 (617) 423-3990; *The World in Figures.*

South Pacific Commission, Post Box D5, Noumea Cedex, New Caledonia; *Statistical Bulletin of the South Pacific: Retail Price*

Indexes.

GUAM - UNEMPLOYMENT

International Labour Office, I.L.O. Publications, CH-1211, Geneva 22, Switzerland; *Yearbook of Labour Statistics.*

Statistical Office of the United Nations, Publishing Service, New York, New York 10017 (800) 253-9646; *Statistical Yearbook.*

GUAM - VITAL STATISTICS

G.K. Hall and Company, 70 Lincoln Street, Boston, Massachusetts 02111 (617) 423-3990; *The World in Figures.*

Statistical Office of the United Nations, Publishing Service, New York, New York 10017 (800) 253-9646; *Statistical Yearbook.*

GUAM - WAGES

G.K. Hall and Company, 70 Lincoln Street, Boston, Massachusetts 02111 (617) 423-3990; *The World in Figures.*

International Labour Office, I.L.O. Publications, CH-1211, Geneva 22, Switzerland; *Yearbook of Labour Statistics.*

GUAM - WEATHER

G.K. Hall and Company, 70 Lincoln Street, Boston, Massachusetts 02111 (617) 423-3990; *The World in Figures.*

Guatemala - National Statistical Office

Direccion General de Estadistica, Centro Nacional de Informacion, Edificio America, 8 Calle 9-55, Zona 1, Guatemala City, Guatemala.

Guatemala - Primary Statistics Sources

Instituto Nacional de Estadistica, Guatemala City, Guatemala; *Anuario estadistico* - (Statistical Yearbook); and *Boletin estadistico* (Statistical Bulletin).

GUATEMALA - AGRICULTURE

The Economist Intelligence Unit, 111 West 57th Street, New York, New York 10019 (800) 933-4685; *The New Latin America Market Atlas.*

Euromonitor Publications Limited, 87-88 Turnmill Street, London EC1M 5QU, England; *International Marketing Data and Statistics.*

Facts on File, 460 Park Avenue South, New York, New York 10016 (800) 443-8323; *The New Book of World Rankings.*

Food and Agricultural Organization of the United Nations (FAO) Via delle Terme di Caracalla, 00100 Rome, Italy (Telephone Number in U.S. (202) 653-2400); *Production Yearbook, The State of Food and Agriculture,* and *Trade Yearbook.*

Gale Research Incorporated, 835 Penobscot Building, Detroit, Michigan 48226 (800) 877-4253; *International Historical Statistics: The Americas and Australasia.*

G.K. Hall and Company, 70 Lincoln Street, Boston, Massachusetts 02111 (617) 423-3990; *The World in Figures.*

Inter-American Development Bank, 1300 New York Avenue, NW, Washington, D.C. 20577 (202) 623-1753; *Economic and Social Progress in Latin America.*

Statistical Office of the United Nations, Publishing Service, New York, New York 10017 (800) 253-9646; *Statistical Yearbook,* and *Statistical Yearbook for Latin America and the Caribbean.*

Times Books, 201 East 50th Street, New York, New York 10022 (212) 751-2600; *The Economist Book of Vital World Statistics.*

U.C.L.A. Latin American Center Publications, University of California, Los Angeles, California 90024 (310) 825-6634; *Statistical Abstract of Latin America.*

The World Bank, 1818 H Street, NW, Washington, D.C. 20433 (202) 477-1234; *World Tables.*

GUATEMALA - AIRLINE SERVICE

The Economist Intelligence Unit, 111 West 57th Street, New York, New York 10019 (800) 933-4685; *The New Latin America Market Atlas.*

Facts on File, 460 Park Avenue South, New York, New York 10016 (800) 443-8323; *The New Book of World Rankings.*

G.K. Hall and Company, 70 Lincoln Street, Boston, Massachusetts 02111 (617) 423-3990; *The World in Figures.*

International Civil Aviation Organization, 1000 Sherbrooke Street West, Suite 400, Montreal, Quebec, Canada H3A 2R2 (514) 285-8219; *Civil Aviation Statistics of the World.*

Statistical Office of the United Nations, Publishing Service, New York, New York 10017 (800) 253-9646; *Statistical Yearbook.*

Times Books, 201 East 50th Street, New York, New York 10022 (212) 751-2600; *The Economist Book of Vital World Statistics.*

GUATEMALA - ALUMINUM PRODUCTION AND CONSUMPTION - See GUATEMALA - MINING AND MINERAL PRODUCTS

GUATEMALA - ANIMAL HEALTH

Food and Agricultural Organization of the United Nations (FAO), Via delle Terme di Caracalla, 00100 Rome, Italy (Telephone Number in U.S. (202) 653-2400); *Animal Health Yearbook.*

GUATEMALA - ANTIMONY ORE PRODUCTION AND CONSUMPTION - See GUATEMALA - MINING AND MINERAL PRODUCTS

GUATEMALA - AREA AND DENSITY OF POPULATION

Euromonitor Publications Limited, 87-88 Turnmill Street, London EC1M 5QU, England; *International Marketing Data and Statistics.*

Facts on File, 460 Park Avenue South, New York, New York 10016 (800) 443-8323; *The New Book of World Rankings.*

Food and Agricultural Organization of the United Nations (FAO) Via delle Terme di Caracalla, 00100 Rome, Italy (Telephone Number in U.S. (202) 653-2400); *The State of Food and Agriculture.*

G.K. Hall and Company, 70 Lincoln Street, Boston, Massachusetts 02111 (617) 423-3990; *The World in Figures.*

Inter-American Development Bank, 1300 New York Avenue, NW, Washington, D.C. 20577 (202) 623-1753; *Economic and Social Progress in Latin America.*

Statistical Office of the United Nations, Publishing Service, New York, New York 10017 (800) 253-9646; *Statistical Yearbook.*

Times Books, 201 East 50th Street, New York, New York 10022 (212) 751-2600; *The Economist Book of Vital World Statistics.*

United Nations Educational, Scientific and Cultural Organization (UNESCO), 7 Place de Fontenoy, F-75700 Paris, France (Telephone Number in U.S. (212) 963-5981); *Statistical Yearbook.*

GUATEMALA - ARMS EXPORTS AND IMPORTS

U.S. Arms Control and Disarmament Agency, 320 Twenty-first Street, Northwest, Washington, D.C. 20451 (202) 647-8677; *World Military Expenditures and Arms Transfers.*

GUATEMALA - BALANCE OF PAYMENTS

The Economist Intelligence Unit, 111 West 57th Street, New York, New York 10019 (800) 938-4685; *The New Latin America Market Atlas*, and *The World Market Atlas.*

G.K. Hall and Company, 70 Lincoln Street, Boston, Massachusetts 02111 (617) 423-3990; *The World in Figures.*

Inter-American Development Bank, 1300 New York Avenue, NW, Washington, D.C. 20577 (202) 623-1753; *Economic and Social Progress in Latin America.*

International Monetary Fund, 700 Nineteenth Street, NW, Washington, D.C. 20431 (202) 623-7000; *Balance of Payments Yearbook*, and *International Financial Statistics.*

Organization of American States (OAS), General Secretariat, Washington, D.C. 20006 (202) 458-3533; *Statistical Bulletin of the OAS.*

Statistical Office of the United Nations, Publishing Service, New York, New York 10017 (800) 253-9646; *Economic Survey of Latin America and the Caribbean*, and *Statistical Yearbook for Latin America and the Caribbean.*

Times Books, 201 East 50th Street, New York, New York 10022 (212) 751-2600; *The Economist Book of Vital World Statistics.*

U.C.L.A. Latin American Center Publications, University of California, Los Angeles, California 90024 (310) 825-6634; *Statistical Abstract of Latin America.*

The World Bank, 1818 H Street, NW, Washington, D.C. 20433 (202) 477-1234; *World Tables.*

GUATEMALA - BANANA EXPORTS - See GUATEMALA - CROPS

GUATEMALA - BANKING

Facts on File, 460 Park Avenue South, New York, New York 10016 (800) 443-8323; *The New Book of World Rankings.*

G.K. Hall and Company, 70 Lincoln Street, Boston, Massachusetts 02111 (617) 423-3990; *The World in Figures.*

Inter-American Development Bank, 1300 New York Avenue, NW, Washington, D.C. 20577 (202) 623-1753; *Economic and Social Progress in Latin America.*

International Monetary Fund, 700 Nineteenth Street, NW, Washington, D.C. 20431 (202) 623-7000; *Government Finance Statistics Yearbook*, and *International Financial Statistics.*

GUATEMALA - BARLEY PRODUCTION - See GUATEMALA - CROPS

GUATEMALA - BEER PRODUCTION

Facts on File, 460 Park Avenue South, New York, New York 10016 (800) 443-8323; *The New Book of World Rankings.*

Statistical Office of the United Nations, Publishing Service, New York, New York 10017 (800) 253-9646; *Statistical Yearbook.*

GUATEMALA - BIRTH RATES

Facts on File, 460 Park Avenue South, New York, New York 10016 (800) 443-8323; *The New Book of World Rankings.*

Statistical Office of the United Nations, Publishing Service, New York, New York 10017 (800) 253-9646; *Demographic Yearbook, Statistical Yearbook*, and *Statistical Yearbook for Latin America and the Caribbean.*

Times Books, 201 East 50th Street, New York, New York 10022 (212) 751-2600; *The Economist Book of Vital World Statistics.*

The World Bank, 1818 H Street, NW, Washington, D.C. 20433 (202) 477-1234; *World Tables.*

World Health Organization, Office of Publications, Avenue Appia, CH-1211 Geneva 27, Switzerland (Telephone Number in U.S. (518) 436-9686); *World Health Statistics Annual.*

GUATEMALA - BONDS

G.K. Hall and Company, 70 Lincoln Street, Boston, Massachusetts 02111 (617) 423-3990; *The World in Figures.*

Inter-American Development Bank, 1300 New York Avenue, NW, Washington, D.C. 20577 (202) 623-1753; *Economic and Social Progress in Latin America.*

International Monetary Fund, 700 Nineteenth Street, NW, Washington, D.C. 20431 (202) 623-7000; *Government Finance Statistics Yearbook.*

GUATEMALA - BOOK PRODUCTION

G.K. Hall and Company, 70 Lincoln Street, Boston, Massachusetts 02111 (617) 423-3990; *The World in Figures.*

United Nations Educational, Scientific and Cultural Organization (UNESCO), 7 Place de Fontenoy, F-75700 Paris, France (Telephone Number in U.S. (212) 963-5981); *Statistical Yearbook.*

GUATEMALA - BROADCASTING

Billboard Limited, Post Office Box 9027, 1006 AA Amsterdam, The Netherlands (Telephone Number in U.S. (212) 764-7300); *World Radio TV Handbook.*

Facts on File, 460 Park Avenue South, New York, New York 10016 (800) 443-8323; *The New Book of World Rankings.*

G.K. Hall and Company, 70 Lincoln Street, Boston, Massachusetts 02111 (617) 423-3990; *The World in Figures.*

Times Books, 201 East 50th Street, New York, New York 10022 (212) 751-2600; *The Economist Book of Vital World Statistics.*

GUATEMALA - BUILDING CONSTRUCTION - See GUATEMALA - CONSTRUCTION INDUSTRY

GUATEMALA - BUSINESS

G.K. Hall and Company, 70 Lincoln Street, Boston, Massachusetts 02111 (617) 423-3990; *The World in Figures.*

Inter-American Development Bank, 1300 New York Avenue, NW, Washington, D.C. 20577 (202) 623-1753; *Economic and Social Progress in Latin America.*

GUATEMALA - BUSINESS AND PROFESSIONAL LICENSES

International Monetary Fund, 700 Nineteenth Street, NW, Washington, D.C. 20431 (202) 623-7000; *Government Finance Statistics Yearbook.*

GUATEMALA - BUTTER PRODUCTION - See GUATEMALA - DAIRY PRODUCTS

GUATEMALA - CABBAGE PRODUCTION - See GUATEMALA - CROPS

GUATEMALA - CALORIE SUPPLY

Food and Agricultural Organization of the United Nations (FAO) Via delle Terme di Caracalla, 00100 Rome, Italy (Telephone Number in U.S. (202) 653-2400); *The State of Food and Agriculture.*

Statistical Office of the United Nations, Publishing Service, New York, New York 10017 (800) 253-9646; *Statistical Yearbook for Latin America and the Caribbean.*

GUATEMALA - CAPITAL INVESTMENT

Inter-American Development Bank, 1300 New York Avenue, NW, Washington, D.C. 20577 (202) 623-1753; *Economic and Social Progress in Latin America.*

GUATEMALA - CAPITAL REVENUE

Inter-American Development Bank, 1300 New York Avenue, NW, Washington, D.C. 20577 (202) 623-1753; *Economic and Social Progress in Latin America.*

International Monetary Fund, 700 Nineteenth Street, NW, Washington, D.C. 20431 (202) 623-7000; *Government Finance Statistics Yearbook.*

GUATEMALA - CATTLE - See GUATEMALA - LIVESTOCK

GUATEMALA - CEMENT PRODUCTION - See GUATEMALA - MINING AND MINERAL PRODUCTS

GUATEMALA - CHEESE PRODUCTION - See GUATEMALA - DAIRY PRODUCTS

GUATEMALA - CHEMICAL (ORGANIC) PRODUCTION - See GUATEMALA - MINING AND MINERAL PRODUCTS

GUATEMALA - CHICKENS - See GUATEMALA - LIVESTOCK AND POULTRY

GUATEMALA - CIGAR PRODUCTION - See GUATEMALA - TOBACCO PRODUCTION

GUATEMALA - CIGARETTE PRODUCTION - See GUATEMALA - TOBACCO PRODUCTION

GUATEMALA - CLASS STRUCTURE

G.K. Hall and Company, 70 Lincoln Street, Boston, Massachusetts 02111 (617) 423-3990; *The World in Figures.*

GUATEMALA - CLIMATE

Facts on File, 460 Park Avenue South, New York, New York 10016 (800) 443-8323; *The New Book of World Rankings.*

G.K. Hall and Company, 70 Lincoln Street, Boston, Massachusetts 02111 (617) 423-3990; *The World in Figures.*

GUATEMALA - COAL PRODUCTION - See GUATEMALA - MINING AND MINERAL PRODUCTS

GUATEMALA - COCOA PRODUCTION - See GUATEMALA - CROPS

GUATEMALA - COFFEE - See GUATEMALA - CROPS

GUATEMALA - COMMUNICATIONS

G.K. Hall and Company, 70 Lincoln Street, Boston, Massachusetts 02111 (617) 423-3990; *The World in Figures.*

Inter-American Development Bank, 1300 New York Avenue, NW, Washington, D.C. 20577 (202) 623-1753; *Economic and Social Progress in Latin America.*

U.C.L.A. Latin American Center Publications, University of California, Los Angeles, California 90024 (310) 825-6634; *Statistical Abstract of Latin America.*

GUATEMALA - CONSTRUCTION INDUSTRY

The Economist Intelligence Unit, 111 West 57th Street, New York, New York 10019 (800) 938-4685; *The New Latin America Market Atlas.*

Facts on File, 460 Park Avenue South, New York, New York 10016 (800) 443-8323; *The New Book of World Rankings.*

Organization of American States (OAS), General Secretariat, Washington, D.C. 20006 (202) 458-3533; *Statistical Bulletin of the OAS.*

Inter-American Development Bank, 1300 New York Avenue, NW, Washington, D.C. 20577 (202) 623-1753; *Economic and Social Progress in Latin America.*

Statistical Office of the United Nations, Publishing Service, New York, New York 10017 (800) 253-9646; *Statistical Yearbook,* and *Yearbook of Construction Statistics.*

U.C.L.A. Latin American Center Publications, University of California, Los Angeles, California 90024 (310) 825-6634; *Statistical Abstract of Latin America.*

GUATEMALA - CONSUMER PRICE INDEX

G.K. Hall and Company, 70 Lincoln Street, Boston, Massachusetts 02111 (617) 423-3990; *The World in Figures.*

GUATEMALA - CONSUMER PRICES

The Economist Intelligence Unit, 111 West 57th Street, New York, New York 10019 (800) 938-4685; *The New Latin America Market Atlas.*

International Labour Office, I.L.O. Publications, CH-1211, Geneva 22, Switzerland; *Yearbook of Labour Statistics*.

International Monetary Fund, 700 Nineteenth Street, NW, Washington, D.C. 20431 (202) 623-7000; *International Financial Statistics*.

Organization of American States (OAS), General Secretariat, Washington, D.C. 20006 (202) 458-3533; *Statistical Bulletin of the OAS*.

Times Books, 201 East 50th Street, New York, New York 10022 (212) 751-2600; *The Economist Book of Vital World Statistics*.

U.C.L.A. Latin American Center Publications, University of California, Los Angeles, California 90024 (310) 825-6634; *Statistical Abstract of Latin America*.

GUATEMALA - CONSUMPTION

The Economist Intelligence Unit, 111 West 57th Street, New York, New York 10019 (800) 938-4685; *The New Latin America Market Atlas*.

G.K. Hall and Company, 70 Lincoln Street, Boston, Massachusetts 02111 (617) 423-3990; *The World in Figures*.

Inter-American Development Bank, 1300 New York Avenue, NW, Washington, D.C. 20577 (202) 623-1753; *Economic and Social Progress in Latin America*.

Statistical Office of the United Nations, Publishing Service, New York, New York 10017 (800) 253-9646; *Statistical Yearbook for Latin America and the Caribbean*.

GUATEMALA - COOPERATIVES

U.C.L.A. Latin American Center Publications, University of California, Los Angeles, California 90024 (310) 825-6634; *Statistical Abstract of Latin America*.

GUATEMALA - COPPER PRODUCTION - See GUATEMALA - MINING AND MINERAL PRODUCTS

GUATEMALA - CORN PRODUCTION - See GUATEMALA - CROPS

GUATEMALA - CORPORATE INCOME TAXES - See GUATEMALA - TAXATION

GUATEMALA - CORPORATE TAXES - See GUATEMALA - TAXATION

GUATEMALA - COTTON - See GUATEMALA - CROPS

GUATEMALA - CROPS

Commodity Research Bureau, Incorporated, 75 Wall Street, New York, New York 10005 (212) 504-7754; *Commodity Year Book*.

The Economist Intelligence Unit, 111 West 57th Street, New York, New York 10019 (800) 938-4685; *The New Latin America Market Atlas*.

Facts on File, 460 Park Avenue South, New York, New York 10016 (800) 443-8323; *The New Book of World Rankings*.

Food and Agricultural Organization of the United Nations (FAO) Via delle Terme di Caracalla, 00100 Rome, Italy (Telephone Number in U.S. (202) 653-2400); *Production Yearbook* and *The State of Food and Agriculture*.

G.K. Hall and Company, 70 Lincoln Street, Boston, Massachusetts 02111 (617) 423-3990; *The World in Figures*.

International Monetary Fund, 700 Nineteenth Street, NW, Washington, D.C. 20431 (202) 623-7000; *International Financial Statistics*.

Organization of American States (OAS), General Secretariat, Washington, D.C. 20006 (202) 458-3533; *Statistical Bulletin of the OAS*.

Statistical Office of the United Nations, Publishing Service, New York, New York 10017 (800) 253-9646; *Statistical Yearbook*.

GUATEMALA - CUSTOMS DUTIES

G.K. Hall and Company, 70 Lincoln Street, Boston, Massachusetts 02111 (617) 423-3990; *The World in Figures*.

Inter-American Development Bank, 1300 New York Avenue, NW, Washington, D.C. 20577 (202) 623-1753; *Economic and Social Progress in Latin America*.

International Monetary Fund, 700 Nineteenth Street, NW, Washington, D.C. 20431 (202) 623-7000; *Government Finance Statistics Yearbook*.

GUATEMALA - DAIRY PRODUCTS

Facts on File, 460 Park Avenue South, New York, New York 10016 (800) 443-8323; *The New Book of World Rankings*.

Food and Agricultural Organization of the United Nations (FAO) Via delle Terme di Caracalla, 00100 Rome, Italy (Telephone Number in U.S. (202) 653-2400); *Production Yearbook* and *The State of Food and Agriculture*.

Statistical Office of the United Nations, Publishing Service, New York, New York 10017 (800) 253-9646; *Statistical Yearbook*.

GUATEMALA - DEATH RATE

G.K. Hall and Company, 70 Lincoln Street, Boston, Massachusetts 02111 (617) 423-3990; *The World in Figures*.

Statistical Office of the United Nations, Publishing Service, New York, New York 10017 (800) 253-9646; *Statistical Yearbook*, and *Statistical Yearbook for Latin America and the Caribbean*.

Times Books, 201 East 50th Street, New York, New York 10022 (212) 751-2600; *The Economist Book of Vital World Statistics*.

World Health Organization, Office of Publications, Avenue Appia, CH-1211 Geneva 27, Switzerland (Telephone Number in U.S. (518) 436-9686); *World Health Statistics Annual*.

GUATEMALA - DEBT

The Economist Intelligence Unit, 111 West 57th Street, New York, New York 10019 (800) 938-4685; *The New Latin America Market Atlas*.

GUATEMALA - DEFENSE EXPENDITURES

The Economist Intelligence Unit, 111 West 57th Street, New York, New York 10019 (800) 938-4685; *The New Latin America Market Atlas*.

G.K. Hall and Company, 70 Lincoln Street, Boston, Massachusetts 02111 (617) 423-3990; *The World in Figures.*

International Monetary Fund, 700 Nineteenth Street, NW, Washington, D.C. 20431 (202) 623-7000; *Government Finance Statistics Yearbook.*

U.S. Arms Control and Disarmament Agency, 320 Twenty-first Street, Northwest, Washington, D.C. 20451 (202) 647-8677; *World Military Expenditures and Arms Transfers.*

GUATEMALA - DEMOGRAPHY

The Economist Intelligence Unit, 111 West 57th Street, New York, New York 10019 (800) 938-4685; *The World Market Atlas.*

Facts on File, 460 Park Avenue South, New York, New York 10016 (800) 443-8323; *The New Book of World Rankings.*

GUATEMALA - DEVELOPMENT ASSISTANCE

G.K. Hall and Company, 70 Lincoln Street, Boston, Massachusetts 02111 (617) 423-3990; *The World in Figures.*

Inter-American Development Bank, 1300 New York Avenue, NW, Washington, D.C. 20577 (202) 623-1753; *Economic and Social Progress in Latin America.*

Statistical Office of the United Nations, Publishing Service, New York, New York 10017 (800) 253-9646; *Statistical Yearbook.*

GUATEMALA - DIAMOND PRODUCTION - See GUATEMALA - MINING AND MINERAL PRODUCTS

GUATEMALA - DISCOUNT RATES

Inter-American Development Bank, 1300 New York Avenue, NW, Washington, D.C. 20577 (202) 623-1753; *Economic and Social Progress in Latin America.*

GUATEMALA - DISEASES

G.K. Hall and Company, 70 Lincoln Street, Boston, Massachusetts 02111 (617) 423-3990; *The World in Figures.*

World Health Organization, Office of Publications, Avenue Appia, CH-1211 Geneva 27, Switzerland (Telephone Number in U.S. (518) 436-9686); *World Health Statistics Annual.*

GUATEMALA - DIVORCE RATES

Facts on File, 460 Park Avenue South, New York, New York 10016 (800) 443-8323; *The New Book of World Rankings.*

Statistical Office of the United Nations, Publishing Service, New York, New York 10017 (800) 253-9646; *Statistical Yearbook.*

GUATEMALA - ECONOMY

Euromonitor Publications Limited, 87-88 Turnmill Street, London EC1M 5QU, England; *International Marketing Data and Statistics.*

Facts on File, 460 Park Avenue South, New York, New York 10016 (800) 443-8323; *The New Book of World Rankings.*

G.K. Hall and Company, 70 Lincoln Street, Boston, Massachusetts 02111 (617) 423-3990; *The World in Figures.*

Inter-American Development Bank, 1300 New York Avenue, NW, Washington, D.C. 20577 (202) 623-1753; *Economic and Social Progress in Latin America.*

Organization of American States (OAS), General Secretariat, Washington, D.C. 20006 (202) 458-3533; *Statistical Bulletin of the OAS.*

Statistical Office of the United Nations, Publishing Service, New York, New York 10017 (800) 253-9646; *Economic Survey of Latin America and the Caribbean.*

U.C.L.A. Latin American Center Publications, University of California, Los Angeles, California 90024 (310) 825-6634; *Statistical Abstract of Latin America.*

GUATEMALA - EDUCATION

The Economist Intelligence Unit, 111 West 57th Street, New York, New York 10019 (800) 938-4685; *The New Latin America Market Atlas,* and *The World Market Atlas.*

Facts on File, 460 Park Avenue South, New York, New York 10016 (800) 443-8323; *The New Book of World Rankings.*

Gale Research Incorporated, 835 Penobscot Building, Detroit, Michigan 48226 (800) 877-4253; *International Historical Statistics: The Americas and Australasia.*

G.K. Hall and Company, 70 Lincoln Street, Boston, Massachusetts 02111 (617) 423-3990; *The World in Figures.*

International Monetary Fund, 700 Nineteenth Street, NW, Washington, D.C. 20431 (202) 623-7000; *Government Finance Statistics Yearbook.*

Statistical Office of the United Nations, Publishing Service, New York, New York 10017 (800) 253-9646; *Statistical Yearbook for Latin America and the Caribbean.*

Times Books, 201 East 50th Street, New York, New York 10022 (212) 751-2600; *The Economist Book of Vital World Statistics.*

U.C.L.A. Latin American Center Publications, University of California, Los Angeles, California 90024 (310) 825-6634; *Statistical Abstract of Latin America.*

United Nations Educational, Scientific and Cultural Organization (UNESCO), 7 Place de Fontenoy, F-75700 Paris, France (Telephone Number in U.S. (212) 963-5981); *Statistical Yearbook.*

The World Bank, 1818 H Street, NW, Washington, D.C. 20433 (202) 477-1234; *World Tables.*

GUATEMALA - EGG PRODUCTION - See GUATEMALA - DAIRY PRODUCTS

GUATEMALA - ELECTRICITY

The Economist Intelligence Unit, 111 West 57th Street, New York, New York 10019 (800) 938-4685; *The New Latin America Market Atlas.*

Facts on File, 460 Park Avenue South, New York, New York 10016 (800) 443-8323; *The New Book of World Rankings.*

Inter-American Development Bank, 1300 New York Avenue, NW, Washington, D.C. 20577 (202) 623-1753; *Economic and Social Progress in Latin America.*

Organization of American States (OAS), General Secretariat, Washington, D.C. 20006 (202) 458-3533; *Statistical Bulletin of the OAS.*

Penn Well Publishing Company, 1421 South Sheridan Road, Post Office Box 1260, Tulsa, Oklahoma 74101 (800) 752-9764; *International Energy Statistics Sourcebook.*

Statistical Office of the United Nations, Publishing Service, New York, New York 10017 (800) 253-9646; *Statistical Yearbook.*

GUATEMALA - EMPLOYMENT

Euromonitor Publications Limited, 87-88 Turnmill Street, London EC1M 5QU, England; *International Marketing Data and Statistics.*

Facts on File, 460 Park Avenue South, New York, New York 10016 (800) 443-8323; *The New Book of World Rankings.*

International Labour Office, I.L.O. Publications, CH-1211, Geneva 22, Switzerland; *Yearbook of Labour Statistics.*

Statistical Office of the United Nations, Publishing Service, New York, New York 10017 (800) 253-9646; *Statistical Yearbook,* and *Statistical Yearbook for Latin America and the Caribbean.*

U.C.L.A. Latin American Center Publications, University of California, Los Angeles, California 90024 (310) 825-6634; *Statistical Abstract of Latin America.*

GUATEMALA - ENERGY

The Economist Intelligence Unit, 111 West 57th Street, New York, New York 10019 (800) 938-4685; *The New Latin America Market Atlas.*

Facts on File, 460 Park Avenue South, New York, New York 10016 (800) 443-8323; *The New Book of World Rankings.*

Food and Agricultural Organization of the United Nations (FAO) Via delle Terme di Caracalla, 00100 Rome, Italy (Telephone Number in U.S. (202) 653-2400); *The State of Food and Agriculture.*

G.K. Hall and Company, 70 Lincoln Street, Boston, Massachusetts 02111 (617) 423-3990; *The World in Figures.*

Penn Well Publishing Company, 1421 South Sheridan Road, Post Office Box 1260, Tulsa, Oklahoma 74101 (800) 752-9764; *International Energy Statistics Sourcebook.*

Statistical Office of the United Nations, Publishing Service, New York, New York 10017 (800) 253-9646; *Yearbook of World Energy Statistics, Statistical Yearbook,* and *Statistical Yearbook for Latin America and the Caribbean.*

Times Books, 201 East 50th Street, New York, New York 10022 (212) 751-2600; *The Economist Book of Vital World Statistics.*

U.C.L.A. Latin American Center Publications, University of California, Los Angeles, California 90024 (310) 825-6634; *Statistical Abstract of Latin America.*

GUATEMALA - EXCHANGE RATES

Euromonitor Publications Limited, 87-88 Turnmill Street, London EC1M 5QU, England; *International Marketing Data and Statistics.*

Inter-American Development Bank, 1300 New York Avenue, NW, Washington, D.C. 20577 (202) 623-1753; *Economic and Social Progress in Latin America.*

International Civil Aviation Organization, 1000 Sherbrooke Street West, Suite 400, Montreal, Quebec, Canada H3A 2R2 (514) 285-8219; *Civil Aviation Statistics of the World.*

International Monetary Fund, 700 Nineteenth Street, NW, Washington, D.C. 20431 (202) 623-7000; *International Financial Statistics.*

Organization of American States (OAS), General Secretariat, Washington, D.C. 20006 (202) 458-3533; *Statistical Bulletin of the OAS.*

Statistical Office of the United Nations, Publishing Service, New York, New York 10017 (800) 253-9646; *Statistical Yearbook.*

U.C.L.A. Latin American Center Publications, University of California, Los Angeles, California 90024 (310) 825-6634; *Statistical Abstract of Latin America.*

GUATEMALA - EXCISE TAXES - See GUATEMALA - TAXATION

GUATEMALA - EXPORTS

The Economist Intelligence Unit, 111 West 57th Street, New York, New York 10019 (800) 938-4685; *The New Latin America Market Atlas,* and *The World Market Atlas.*

Euromonitor Publications Limited, 87-88 Turnmill Street, London EC1M 5QU, England; *International Marketing Data and Statistics.*

Food and Agricultural Organization of the United Nations (FAO) Via delle Terme di Caracalla, 00100 Rome, Italy (Telephone Number in U.S. (202) 653-2400); *The State of Food and Agriculture.*

G.K. Hall and Company, 70 Lincoln Street, Boston, Massachusetts 02111 (617) 423-3990; *The World in Figures.*

Inter-American Development Bank, 1300 New York Avenue, NW, Washington, D.C. 20577 (202) 623-1753; *Economic and Social Progress in Latin America.*

International Monetary Fund, 700 Nineteenth Street, NW, Washington, D.C. 20431 (202) 623-7000; *Direction of Trade Statistics, Government Finance Statistics Yearbook,* and *International Financial Statistics.*

Organization of American States (OAS), General Secretariat, Washington, D.C. 20006 (202) 458-3533; *Statistical Bulletin of the OAS.*

Statistical Office of the United Nations, Publishing Service, New York, New York 10017 (800) 253-9646; *Statistical Yearbook for Latin America and the Caribbean.*

Times Books, 201 East 50th Street, New York, New York 10022 (212) 751-2600; *The Economist Book of Vital World Statistics.*

The World Bank, 1818 H Street, NW, Washington, D.C. 20433 (202) 477-1234; *World Tables.*

GUATEMALA - EXTERNAL FINANCING

Inter-American Development Bank, 1300 New York Avenue, NW, Washington, D.C. 20577 (202) 623-1753; *Economic and Social Progress in Latin America.*

Statistical Office of the United Nations, Publishing Service, New York, New York 10017 (800) 253-9646; *Statistical Yearbook for Latin America and the Caribbean.*

GUATEMALA - EXTERNAL INDEBTEDNESS

Inter-American Development Bank, 1300 New York Avenue, NW, Washington, D.C. 20577 (202) 623-1753; *Economic and Social Progress in Latin America.*

Statistical Office of the United Nations, Publishing Service, New York, New York 10017 (800) 253-9646; *Statistical Yearbook for Latin America and the Caribbean.*

The World Bank, 1818 H Street, NW, Washington, D.C. 20433 (202) 477-1234; *World Tables.*

GUATEMALA - EXTERNAL TRADE

Food and Agricultural Organization of the United Nations (FAO) Via delle Terme di Caracalla, 00100 Rome, Italy (Telephone Number in U.S. (202) 653-2400); *The State of Food and Agriculture,* and *Trade Yearbook.*

Gale Research Incorporated, 835 Penobscot Building, Detroit, Michigan 48226 (800) 877-4253; *International Historical Statistics: The Americas and Australasia.*

G.K. Hall and Company, 70 Lincoln Street, Boston, Massachusetts 02111 (617) 423-3990; *The World in Figures.*

Inter-American Development Bank, 1300 New York Avenue, NW, Washington, D.C. 20577 (202) 623-1753; *Economic and Social Progress in Latin America.*

Statistical Office of the United Nations, Publishing Service, New York, New York 10017 (800) 253-9646; *Statistical Yearbook,* and *Statistical Yearbook for Latin America and the Caribbean.*

GUATEMALA - FAMILY PLANNING

U.C.L.A. Latin American Center Publications, University of California, Los Angeles, California 90024 (310) 825-6634; *Statistical Abstract of Latin America.*

GUATEMALA - FARM CROPS - See GUATEMALA - CROPS

GUATEMALA - FEMALE WORKING POPULATION - See GUATEMALA - EMPLOYMENT

GUATEMALA - FERTILITY RATES

Facts on File, 460 Park Avenue South, New York, New York 10016 (800) 443-8323; *The New Book of World Rankings.*

Times Books, 201 East 50th Street, New York, New York 10022 (212) 751-2600; *The Economist Book of Vital World Statistics.*

The World Bank, 1818 H Street, NW, Washington, D.C. 20433 (202) 477-1234; *World Tables.*

GUATEMALA - FERTILIZER

The Economist Intelligence Unit, 111 West 57th Street, New York, New York 10019 (800) 938-4685; *The New Latin America Market Atlas.*

Food and Agricultural Organization of the United Nations (FAO) Via delle Terme di Caracalla, 00100 Rome, Italy (Telephone Number in U.S. (202) 653-2400); *The State of Food and Agriculture.*

Statistical Office of the United Nations, Publishing Service, New York, New York 10017 (800) 253-9646; *Statistical Yearbook.*

GUATEMALA - FETAL MORTALITY

Statistical Office of the United Nations, Publishing Service, New York, New York 10017 (800) 253-9646; *Demographic Yearbook.*

World Health Organization, Office of Publications, Avenue Appia, CH-1211 Geneva 27, Switzerland (Telephone Number in U.S. (518) 436-9686); *World Health Statistics Annual.*

GUATEMALA - FIBRE PRODUCTION - See GUATEMALA - TEXTILE INDUSTRY

GUATEMALA - FINANCE

Facts on File, 460 Park Avenue South, New York, New York 10016 (800) 443-8323; *The New Book of World Rankings.*

Gale Research Incorporated, 835 Penobscot Building, Detroit, Michigan 48226 (800) 877-4253; *International Historical Statistics: The Americas and Australasia.*

G.K. Hall and Company, 70 Lincoln Street, Boston, Massachusetts 02111 (617) 423-3990; *The World in Figures.*

Inter-American Development Bank, 1300 New York Avenue, NW, Washington, D.C. 20577 (202) 623-1753; *Economic and Social Progress in Latin America.*

International Monetary Fund, 700 Nineteenth Street, NW, Washington, D.C. 20431 (202) 623-7000; *Government Finance Statistics Yearbook.*

Organization of American States (OAS), General Secretariat, Washington, D.C. 20006 (202) 458-3533; *Statistical Bulletin of the OAS.*

U.C.L.A. Latin American Center Publications, University of California, Los Angeles, California 90024 (310) 825-6634; *Statistical Abstract of Latin America.*

GUATEMALA - FISHERIES

Facts on File, 460 Park Avenue South, New York, New York 10016 (800) 443-8323; *The New Book of World Rankings.*

Food and Agricultural Organization of the United Nations (FAO) Via delle Terme di Caracalla, 00100 Rome, Italy (Telephone Number in U.S. (202) 653-2400); *The State of Food and Agriculture,* and *Yearbook of Fishery Statistics.*

Inter-American Development Bank, 1300 New York Avenue, NW, Washington, D.C. 20577 (202) 623-1753; *Economic and Social Progress in Latin America.*

Statistical Office of the United Nations, Publishing Service, New York, New York 10017 (800) 253-9646; *Statistical Yearbook.*

U.C.L.A. Latin American Center Publications, University of California, Los Angeles, California 90024 (310) 825-6634; *Statistical Abstract of Latin America.*

GUATEMALA - FLOUR PRODUCTION

Statistical Office of the United Nations, Publishing Service, New York, New York 10017 (800) 253-9646; *Statistical Yearbook.*

GUATEMALA - FOOD

Food and Agricultural Organization of the United Nations (FAO), Via delle Terme di Caracalla, 00100 Rome, Italy (Telephone Number in U.S. (202) 653-2400); *Production Yearbook,* and *The State of Food and Agriculture.*

G.K. Hall and Company, 70 Lincoln Street, Boston, Massachusetts 02111 (617) 423-3990; *The World in Figures.*

GUATEMALA - FOREIGN AID

G.K. Hall and Company, 70 Lincoln Street, Boston, Massachusetts 02111 (617) 423-3990; *The World in Figures.*

Inter-American Development Bank, 1300 New York Avenue, NW, Washington, D.C. 20577 (202) 623-1753; *Economic and Social Progress in Latin America.*

GUATEMALA - FOREIGN DEBT

The Economist Intelligence Unit, 111 West 57th Street, New York, New York 10019 (800) 938-4685; *The New Latin America Market Atlas.*

Inter-American Development Bank, 1300 New York Avenue, NW, Washington, D.C. 20577 (202) 623-1753; *Economic and Social Progress in Latin America.*

International Monetary Fund, 700 Nineteenth Street, NW, Washington, D.C. 20431 (202) 623-7000; *Government Finance Statistics Yearbook.*

GUATEMALA - FOREIGN FINANCE

Inter-American Development Bank, 1300 New York Avenue, NW, Washington, D.C. 20577 (202) 623-1753; *Economic and Social Progress in Latin America.*

GUATEMALA - FOREIGN INDEBTEDNESS

Inter-American Development Bank, 1300 New York Avenue, NW, Washington, D.C. 20577 (202) 623-1753; *Economic and Social Progress in Latin America.*

Statistical Office of the United Nations, Publishing Service, New York, New York 10017 (800) 253-9646; *Economic Survey of Latin America and the Caribbean.*

GUATEMALA - FOREIGN INVESTMENT

The Economist Intelligence Unit, 111 West 57th Street, New York, New York 10019 (800) 938-4685; *The New Latin America Market Atlas.*

GUATEMALA - FOREIGN TRADE

The Economist Intelligence Unit, 111 West 57th Street, New York, New York 10019 (800) 938-4685; *The New Latin America Market Atlas.*

Euromonitor Publications Limited, 87-88 Turnmill Street, London EC1M 5QU, England; *International Marketing Data and Statistics.*

Facts on File, 460 Park Avenue South, New York, New York 10016 (800) 443-8323; *The New Book of World Rankings.*

Food and Agricultural Organization of the United Nations (FAO) Via delle Terme di Caracalla, 00100 Rome, Italy (Telephone Number in U.S. (202) 653-2400); *The State of Food and Agriculture.*

G.K. Hall and Company, 70 Lincoln Street, Boston, Massachusetts 02111 (617) 423-3990; *The World in Figures.*

Inter-American Development Bank, 1300 New York Avenue, NW, Washington, D.C. 20577 (202) 623-1753; *Economic and Social Progress in Latin America.*

International Monetary Fund, 700 Nineteenth Street, NW, Washington, D.C. 20431 (202) 623-7000; *International Financial Statistics.*

Statistical Office of the United Nations, Publishing Service, New York, New York 10017 (800) 253-9646; *Economic Survey of Latin America and the Caribbean, International Trade Statistics Yearbook,* and *Statistical Yearbook.*

U.C.L.A. Latin American Center Publications, University of California, Los Angeles, California 90024 (310) 825-6634; *Statistical Abstract of Latin America.*

The World Bank, 1818 H Street, NW, Washington, D.C. 20433 (202) 477-1234; *World Tables.*

GUATEMALA - FORESTRY AND FOREST PRODUCTS

The Economist Intelligence Unit, 111 West 57th Street, New York, New York 10019 (800) 938-4685; *The New Latin America Market Atlas.*

Facts on File, 460 Park Avenue South, New York, New York 10016 (800) 443-8323; *The New Book of World Rankings.*

Food and Agricultural Organization of the United Nations (FAO) Via delle Terme di Caracalla, 00100 Rome, Italy (Telephone Number in U.S. (202) 653-2400); *The State of Food and Agriculture,* and *Yearbook of Forest Products.*

Forest and Paper Association, 1250 Connecticut Avenue, NW, Washington, D.C. 20036 (202) 463-2455; *Wood Pulp and Fiber Statistics.*

G.K. Hall and Company, 70 Lincoln Street, Boston, Massachusetts 02111 (617) 423-3990; *The World in Figures.*

Inter-American Development Bank, 1300 New York Avenue, NW, Washington, D.C. 20577 (202) 623-1753; *Economic and Social Progress in Latin America.*

Statistical Office of the United Nations, Publishing Service, New York, New York 10017 (800) 253-9646; *Statistical Yearbook.*

U.C.L.A. Latin American Center Publications, University of California, Los Angeles, California 90024 (310) 825-6634; *Statistical Abstract of Latin America.*

United Nations Educational, Scientific and Cultural Organization (UNESCO), 7 Place de Fontenoy, F-75700 Paris, France (Telephone Number in U.S. (212) 963-5981); *Statistical Yearbook.*

GUATEMALA - GAS PRODUCTION - See GUATEMALA - MINING AND MINERAL PRODUCTS

GUATEMALA - GENERAL INDUSTRIAL STATISTICS

Statistical Office of the United Nations, Publishing Service, New York, New York 10017 (800) 253-9646; *Industrial Statistics Yearbook.*

GUATEMALA - GENERAL MORTALITY

Statistical Office of the United Nations, Publishing Service, New York, New York 10017 (800) 253-9646; *Demographic Yearbook.*

World Health Organization, Office of Publications, Avenue Appia, CH-1211 Geneva 27, Switzerland (Telephone Number in U.S. (518) 436-9686); *World Health Statistics Annual.*

GUATEMALA - GEOGRAPHIC DATA

Facts on File, 460 Park Avenue South, New York, New York 10016 (800) 443-8323; *The New Book of World Rankings.*

U.C.L.A. Latin American Center Publications, University of California, Los Angeles, California 90024 (310) 825-6634; *Statistical Abstract of Latin America.*

GUATEMALA - GOATS - See GUATEMALA - LIVESTOCK AND POULTRY

GUATEMALA - GOLD HOLDINGS

International Monetary Fund, 700 Nineteenth Street, NW, Washington, D.C. 20431 (202) 623-7000; *International Financial Statistics.*

Statistical Office of the United Nations, Publishing Service, New York, New York 10017 (800) 253-9646; *Statistical Yearbook.*

The World Bank, 1818 H Street, NW, Washington, D.C. 20433 (202) 477-1234; *World Tables.*

GUATEMALA - GOLD PRODUCTION AND CONSUMPTION - See GUATEMALA - MINING AND MINERAL PRODUCTS

GUATEMALA - GOLD RESERVES

The Economist Intelligence Unit, 111 West 57th Street, New York, New York 10019 (800) 938-4685; *The New Latin America Market Atlas.*

GUATEMALA - GOVERNMENT

G.K. Hall and Company, 70 Lincoln Street, Boston, Massachusetts 02111 (617) 423-3990; *The World in Figures.*

Inter-American Development Bank, 1300 New York Avenue, NW, Washington, D.C. 20577 (202) 623-1753; *Economic and Social Progress in Latin America.*

GUATEMALA - GOVERNMENT BONDS - See GUATEMALA - BONDS

GUATEMALA - GOVERNMENT CONSUMPTION

Inter-American Development Bank, 1300 New York Avenue, NW, Washington, D.C. 20577 (202) 623-1753; *Economic and Social Progress in Latin America.*

GUATEMALA - GOVERNMENT EXPENDITURES

Inter-American Development Bank, 1300 New York Avenue, NW, Washington, D.C. 20577 (202) 623-1753; *Economic and Social Progress in Latin America.*

International Monetary Fund, 700 Nineteenth Street, NW, Washington, D.C. 20431 (202) 623-7000; *Government Finance Statistics Yearbook.*

Times Books, 201 East 50th Street, New York, New York 10022 (212) 751-2600; *The Economist Book of Vital World Statistics.*

The World Bank, 1818 H Street, NW, Washington, D.C. 20433 (202) 477-1234; *World Tables.*

GUATEMALA - GOVERNMENT FINANCES

Inter-American Development Bank, 1300 New York Avenue, NW, Washington, D.C. 20577 (202) 623-1753; *Economic and Social Progress in Latin America.*

International Monetary Fund, 700 Nineteenth Street, NW, Washington, D.C. 20431 (202) 623-7000; *International Financial Statistics.*

Statistical Office of the United Nations, Publishing Service, New York, New York 10017 (800) 253-9646; *Statistical Yearbook.*

GUATEMALA - GOVERNMENT REVENUE

Inter-American Development Bank, 1300 New York Avenue, NW, Washington, D.C. 20577 (202) 623-1753; *Economic and Social Progress in Latin America.*

International Monetary Fund, 700 Nineteenth Street, NW, Washington, D.C. 20431 (202) 623-7000; *Government Finance Statistics Yearbook.*

Times Books, 201 East 50th Street, New York, New York 10022 (212) 751-2600; *The Economist Book of Vital World Statistics.*

The World Bank, 1818 H Street, NW, Washington, D.C. 20433 (202) 477-1234; *World Tables.*

GUATEMALA - GRAIN PRODUCTION - See GUATEMALA - CROPS

GUATEMALA - GRANTS

International Monetary Fund, 700 Nineteenth Street, NW, Washington, D.C. 20431 (202) 623-7000; *Government Finance Statistics Yearbook.*

GUATEMALA - GROSS DOMESTIC PRODUCT

The Economist Intelligence Unit, 111 West 57th Street, New York, New York 10019 (800) 938-4685; *The New Latin America Market Atlas,* and *The World Market Atlas.*

Euromonitor Publications Limited, 87-88 Turnmill Street, London EC1M 5QU, England; *International Marketing Data and Statistics.*

Facts on File, 460 Park Avenue South, New York, New York 10016 (800) 443-8323; *The New Book of World Rankings.*

G.K. Hall and Company, 70 Lincoln Street, Boston, Massachusetts 02111 (617) 423-3990; *The World in Figures.*

Inter-American Development Bank, 1300 New York Avenue, NW, Washington, D.C. 20577 (202) 623-1753; *Economic and Social Progress in Latin America.*

Organization of American States (OAS), General Secretariat, Washington, D.C. 20006 (202) 458-3533; *Statistical Bulletin of the OAS.*

Statistical Office of the United Nations, Publishing Service, New York, New York 10017 (800) 253-9646; *Statistical Yearbook,* and *Statistical Yearbook for Latin America and the Caribbean.*

Times Books, 201 East 50th Street, New York, New York 10022 (212) 751-2600; *The Economist Book of Vital World Statistics.*

The World Bank, 1818 H Street, NW, Washington, D.C. 20433 (202) 477-1234; *World Tables.*

GUATEMALA - GROSS NATIONAL PRODUCT

Euromonitor Publications Limited, 87-88 Turnmill Street, London EC1M 5QU, England; *International Marketing Data and Statistics.*

Inter-American Development Bank, 1300 New York Avenue, NW, Washington, D.C. 20577 (202) 623-1753; *Economic and Social Progress in Latin America.*

U.S. Arms Control and Disarmament Agency, 320 Twenty-first Street, Northwest, Washington, D.C. 20451 (202) 647-8677; *World Military Expenditures and Arms Transfers.*

The World Bank, 1818 H Street, NW, Washington, D.C. 20433 (202) 477-1234; *World Tables.*

GUATEMALA - HEALTH

The Economist Intelligence Unit, 111 West 57th Street, New York, New York 10019 (800) 938-4685; *The New Latin America Market Atlas.*

Facts on File, 460 Park Avenue South, New York, New York 10016 (800) 443-8323; *The New Book of World Rankings.*

G.K. Hall and Company, 70 Lincoln Street, Boston, Massachusetts 02111 (617) 423-3990; *The World in Figures.*

Statistical Office of the United Nations, Publishing Service, New York, New York 10017 (800) 253-9646; *Statistical Yearbook,* and *Statistical Yearbook for Latin America and the Caribbean.*

Times Books, 201 East 50th Street, New York, New York 10022 (212) 751-2600; *The Economist Book of Vital World Statistics.*

World Health Organization, Office of Publications, Avenue Appia, CH-1211 Geneva 27, Switzerland (Telephone Number in U.S. (518) 436-9686); *World Health Statistics Annual.*

GUATEMALA - HEALTH EXPENDITURES

International Monetary Fund, 700 Nineteenth Street, NW, Washington, D.C. 20431 (202) 623-7000; *Government Finance Statistics Yearbook.*

Statistical Office of the United Nations, Publishing Service, New York, New York 10017 (800) 253-9646; *Statistical Yearbook for Latin America and the Caribbean.*

GUATEMALA - HIDE PRODUCTION

Food and Agricultural Organization of the United Nations (FAO), Via delle Terme di Caracalla, 00100 Rome, Italy (Telephone Number in U.S. (202) 653-2400); *Production Yearbook.*

GUATEMALA - HIGHWAYS

The Economist Intelligence Unit, 111 West 57th Street, New York, New York 10019 (800) 938-4685; *The New Latin America Market Atlas.*

G.K. Hall and Company, 70 Lincoln Street, Boston, Massachusetts 02111 (617) 423-3990; *The World in Figures.*

GUATEMALA - HORSES - See GUATEMALA - LIVESTOCK AND POULTRY

GUATEMALA - HOURS OF WORK - See GUATEMALA - EMPLOYMENT

GUATEMALA - HOUSING AND HOUSING UNITS

Facts on File, 460 Park Avenue South, New York, New York 10016 (800) 443-8323; *The New Book of World Rankings.*

Statistical Office of the United Nations, Publishing Service, New York, New York 10017 (800) 253-9646; *Statistical Yearbook for Latin America and the Caribbean.*

U.C.L.A. Latin American Center Publications, University of California, Los Angeles, California 90024 (310) 825-6634; *Statistical Abstract of Latin America.*

GUATEMALA - HOUSING EXPENDITURES

International Monetary Fund, 700 Nineteenth Street, NW, Washington, D.C. 20431 (202) 623-7000; *Government Finance Statistics Yearbook.*

GUATEMALA - ILLITERATE POPULATION

The Economist Intelligence Unit, 111 West 57th Street, New York, New York 10019 (800) 938-4685; *The New Latin America Market Atlas,* and *The World Market Atlas.*

G.K. Hall and Company, 70 Lincoln Street, Boston, Massachusetts 02111 (617) 423-3990; *The World in Figures.*

Statistical Office of the United Nations, Publishing Service, New York, New York 10017 (800) 253-9646; *Statistical Yearbook for Latin America and the Caribbean.*

United Nations Educational, Scientific and Cultural Organization (UNESCO), 7 Place de Fontenoy, F-75700 Paris, France (Telephone Number in U.S. (212) 963-5981); *Statistical Yearbook.*

GUATEMALA - IMMIGRATION

U.C.L.A. Latin American Center Publications, University of California, Los Angeles, California 90024 (310) 825-6634; *Statistical Abstract of Latin America.*

GUATEMALA - IMPORTS

The Economist Intelligence Unit, 111 West 57th Street, New York, New York 10019 (800) 938-4685; *The New Latin America Market Atlas,* and *The World Market Atlas.*

Euromonitor Publications Limited, 87-88 Turnmill Street, London EC1M 5QU, England; *International Marketing Data and Statistics.*

Food and Agricultural Organization of the United Nations (FAO) Via delle Terme di Caracalla, 00100 Rome, Italy (Telephone Number in U.S. (202) 653-2400); *The State of Food and Agriculture.*

G.K. Hall and Company, 70 Lincoln Street, Boston, Massachusetts 02111 (617) 423-3990; *The World in Figures.*

Inter-American Development Bank, 1300 New York Avenue, NW, Washington, D.C. 20577 (202) 623-1753; *Economic and Social Progress in Latin America.*

International Monetary Fund, 700 Nineteenth Street, NW, Washington, D.C. 20431 (202) 623-7000; *Direction of Trade Statistics, International Financial Statistics,* and *Government Finance Statistics Yearbook.*

Organization of American States (OAS), General Secretariat, Washington, D.C. 20006 (202) 458-3533; *Statistical Bulletin of the OAS.*

Statistical Office of the United Nations, Publishing Service, New York, New York 10017 (800) 253-9646; *Statistical Yearbook for Latin America and the Caribbean,* and *Trade in Manufactures of Developing Countries.*

Times Books, 201 East 50th Street, New York, New York 10022 (212) 751-2600; *The Economist Book of Vital World Statistics.*

The World Bank, 1818 H Street, NW, Washington, D.C. 20433 (202) 477-1234; *World Tables.*

GUATEMALA - INCOME DISTRIBUTION

Statistical Office of the United Nations, Publishing Service, New York, New York 10017 (800) 253-9646; *Statistical Yearbook for Latin America and the Caribbean.*

U.C.L.A. Latin American Center Publications, University of California, Los Angeles, California 90024 (310) 825-6634; *Statistical Abstract of Latin America.*

GUATEMALA - INCOME TAXES - See GUATEMALA - TAXATION

GUATEMALA - INDUSTRIAL METALS PRODUCTION

Statistical Office of the United Nations, Publishing Service, New York, New York 10017 (800) 253-9646; *Statistical Yearbook.*

GUATEMALA - INDUSTRIAL SECTOR TRENDS

Statistical Office of the United Nations, Publishing Service, New York, New York 10017 (800) 253-9646; *Economic Survey of Latin America and the Caribbean.*

GUATEMALA - INDUSTRY

Euromonitor Publications Limited, 87-88 Turnmill Street, London EC1M 5QU, England; *International Marketing Data and Statistics.*

Facts on File, 460 Park Avenue South, New York, New York 10016 (800) 443-8323; *The New Book of World Rankings.*

Gale Research Incorporated, 835 Penobscot Building, Detroit, Michigan 48226 (800) 877-4253; *International Historical Statistics: The Americas and Australasia.*

G.K. Hall and Company, 70 Lincoln Street, Boston, Massachusetts 02111 (617) 423-3990; *The World in Figures.*

International Labour Office, I.L.O. Publications, CH-1211, Geneva 22, Switzerland; *Yearbook of Labour Statistics.*

Statistical Office of the United Nations, Publishing Service, New York, New York 10017 (800) 253-9646; *Statistical Yearbook.*

Times Books, 201 East 50th Street, New York, New York 10022 (212) 751-2600; *The Economist Book of Vital World Statistics.*

U.C.L.A. Latin American Center Publications, University of California, Los Angeles, California 90024 (310) 825-6634; *Statistical Abstract of Latin America.*

The World Bank, 1818 H Street, NW, Washington, D.C. 20433 (202) 477-1234; *World Tables.*

World Intellectual Property Organization, 34 Chemin des Colombettes, CH-1211 Geneva 20, Switzerland; *Industrial Property Statistics.*

GUATEMALA - INFANT AND MATERNAL MORTALITY

The Economist Intelligence Unit, 111 West 57th Street, New York, New York 10019 (800) 938-4685; *The New Latin America Market Atlas.*

Statistical Office of the United Nations, Publishing Service, New York, New York 10017 (800) 253-9646; *Demographic Yearbook,* and *Statistical Yearbook.*

Times Books, 201 East 50th Street, New York, New York 10022 (212) 751-2600; *The Economist Book of Vital World Statistics.*

World Health Organization, Office of Publications, Avenue Appia, CH-1211 Geneva 27, Switzerland (Telephone Number in U.S. (518) 436-9686); *World Health Statistics Annual.*

The World Bank, 1818 H Street, NW, Washington, D.C. 20433 (202) 477-1234; *World Tables.*

GUATEMALA - INFLATIONARY FACTORS

Statistical Office of the United Nations, Publishing Service, New York, New York 10017 (800) 253-9646; *Economic Survey of Latin America and the Caribbean.*

GUATEMALA - INTEREST RATES

Inter-American Development Bank, 1300 New York Avenue, NW, Washington, D.C. 20577 (202) 623-1753; *Economic and Social Progress in Latin America.*

GUATEMALA - INTERNATIONAL FINANCE

Inter-American Development Bank, 1300 New York Avenue, NW, Washington, D.C. 20577 (202) 623-1753; *Economic and Social Progress in Latin America.*

U.C.L.A. Latin American Center Publications, University of California, Los Angeles, California 90024 (310) 825-6634; *Statistical Abstract of Latin America.*

GUATEMALA - INTERNATIONAL LIQUIDITY

Inter-American Development Bank, 1300 New York Avenue, NW, Washington, D.C. 20577 (202) 623-1753; *Economic and Social Progress in Latin America.*

International Monetary Fund, 700 Nineteenth Street, NW, Washington, D.C. 20431 (202) 623-7000; *International Financial Statistics.*

GUATEMALA - INTERNATIONAL RESERVES

Organization of American States (OAS), General Secretariat, Washington, D.C. 20006 (202) 458-3533; *Statistical Bulletin of the OAS.*

GUATEMALA - INTERNATIONAL RESERVES EXCLUDING GOLD

Inter-American Development Bank, 1300 New York Avenue, NW, Washington, D.C. 20577 (202) 623-1753; *Economic and Social Progress in Latin America.*

Statistical Office of the United Nations, Publishing Service, New York, New York 10017 (800) 253-9646; *Statistical Yearbook.*

The World Bank, 1818 H Street, NW, Washington, D.C. 20433 (202) 477-1234; *World Tables.*

GUATEMALA - INTERNATIONAL STATISTICS

Inter-American Development Bank, 1300 New York Avenue, NW, Washington, DC 20577; *Economic and Social Progress in Latin America.*

U.C.L.A. Latin American Center Publications, University of California, Los Angeles, California 90024 (310) 825-6634; *Statistical Abstract of Latin America.*

GUATEMALA - INVESTMENTS

Inter-American Development Bank, 1300 New York Avenue, NW, Washington, D.C. 20577 (202) 623-1753; *Economic and Social Progress in Latin America.*

International Monetary Fund, 700 Nineteenth Street, NW, Washington, D.C. 20431 (202) 623-7000; *International Financial Statistics.*

Statistical Office of the United Nations, Publishing Service, New York, New York 10017 (800) 253-9646; *Statistical Yearbook for Latin America and the Caribbean.*

GUATEMALA - IRON PRODUCTION AND CONSUMPTION - See GUATEMALA - MINING AND MINERAL PRODUCTS

GUATEMALA - IRRIGATION

Euromonitor Publications Limited, 87-88 Turnmill Street, London EC1M 5QU, England; *International Marketing Data and Statistics.*

Inter-American Development Bank, 1300 New York Avenue, NW, Washington, D.C. 20577 (202) 623-1753; *Economic and Social Progress in Latin America.*

GUATEMALA - LABOR FORCE

The Economist Intelligence Unit, 111 West 57th Street, New York, New York 10019 (800) 938-4685; *The New Latin America Market Atlas.*

Euromonitor Publications Limited, 87-88 Turnmill Street, London EC1M 5QU, England; *International Marketing Data and Statistics.*

Facts on File, 460 Park Avenue South, New York, New York 10016 (800) 443-8323; *The New Book of World Rankings.*

Food and Agricultural Organization of the United Nations (FAO) Via delle Terme di Caracalla, 00100 Rome, Italy (Telephone Number in U.S. (202) 653-2400); *The State of Food and Agriculture.*

Gale Research Incorporated, 835 Penobscot Building, Detroit, Michigan 48226 (800) 877-4253; *International Historical Statistics: The Americas and Australasia.*

G.K. Hall and Company, 70 Lincoln Street, Boston, Massachusetts 02111 (617) 423-3990; *The World in Figures.*

Times Books, 201 East 50th Street, New York, New York 10022 (212) 751-2600; *The Economist Book of Vital World Statistics.*

The World Bank, 1818 H Street, NW, Washington, D.C. 20433 (202) 477-1234; *World Tables.*

GUATEMALA - LABOR PRODUCTIVITY

International Labour Office, I.L.O. Publications, CH-1211, Geneva 22, Switzerland; *Yearbook of Labour Statistics.*

GUATEMALA - LAND AREA

The Economist Intelligence Unit, 111 West 57th Street, New York, New York 10019 (800) 938-4685; *The New Latin America Market Atlas.*

GUATEMALA - LAND USE

Euromonitor Publications Limited, 87-88 Turnmill Street, London EC1M 5QU, England; *International Marketing Data and Statistics.*

Food and Agricultural Organization of the United Nations (FAO), Via delle Terme di Caracalla, 00100 Rome, Italy (Telephone Number in U.S. (202) 653-2400); *Production Yearbook.*

G.K. Hall and Company, 70 Lincoln Street, Boston, Massachusetts 02111 (617) 423-3990; *The World in Figures.*

Inter-American Development Bank, 1300 New York Avenue, NW, Washington, D.C. 20577 (202) 623-1753; *Economic and Social Progress in Latin America.*

GUATEMALA - LEAD AND LEAD ORE - See GUATEMALA - MINING AND MINERAL PRODUCTS

GUATEMALA - LIBRARIES

Facts on File, 460 Park Avenue South, New York, New York 10016 (800) 443-8323; *The New Book of World Rankings.*

United Nations Educational, Scientific and Cultural Organization (UNESCO), 7 Place de Fontenoy, F-75700 Paris, France (Telephone Number in U.S. (212) 963-5981); *Statistical Yearbook.*

GUATEMALA - LIFE EXPECTANCY RATE

The Economist Intelligence Unit, 111 West 57th Street, New York, New York 10019 (800) 938-4685; *The New Latin America Market Atlas.*

GUATEMALA - LIVESTOCK AND POULTRY

Euromonitor Publications Limited, 87-88 Turnmill Street, London EC1M 5QU, England; *International Marketing Data and Statistics.*

Facts on File, 460 Park Avenue South, New York, New York 10016 (800) 443-8323; *The New Book of World Rankings.*

Food and Agricultural Organization of the United Nations (FAO), Via delle Terme di Caracalla, 00100 Rome, Italy (Telephone Number in U.S. (202) 653-2400); *Production Yearbook*, and *The State of Food and Agriculture*.

G.K. Hall and Company, 70 Lincoln Street, Boston, Massachusetts 02111 (617) 423-3990; *The World in Figures*.

Statistical Office of the United Nations, Publishing Service, New York, New York 10017 (800) 253-9646; *Statistical Yearbook*.

GUATEMALA - LIVING LEVELS

G.K. Hall and Company, 70 Lincoln Street, Boston, Massachusetts 02111 (617) 423-3990; *The World in Figures*.

Statistical Office of the United Nations, Publishing Service, New York, New York 10017 (800) 253-9646; *Statistical Yearbook for Latin America and the Caribbean*.

Times Books, 201 East 50th Street, New York, New York 10022 (212) 751-2600; *The Economist Book of Vital World Statistics*.

GUATEMALA - MAIL - NUMBER OF PIECES SENT OR RECEIVED

Statistical Office of the United Nations, Publishing Service, New York, New York 10017 (800) 253-9646; *Statistical Yearbook*.

GUATEMALA - MAIN ECONOMIC INDICATORS - See GUATEMALA - ECONOMY

GUATEMALA - MANUFACTURING

The Economist Intelligence Unit, 111 West 57th Street, New York, New York 10019 (800) 938-4685; *The New Latin America Market Atlas*.

Facts on File, 460 Park Avenue South, New York, New York 10016 (800) 443-8323; *The New Book of World Rankings*.

G.K. Hall and Company, 70 Lincoln Street, Boston, Massachusetts 02111 (617) 423-3990; *The World in Figures*.

Inter-American Development Bank, 1300 New York Avenue, NW, Washington, D.C. 20577 (202) 623-1753; *Economic and Social Progress in Latin America*.

Statistical Office of the United Nations, Publishing Service, New York, New York 10017 (800) 253-9646; *Statistical Yearbook*, and *Statistical Yearbook for Latin America and the Caribbean*.

Times Books, 201 East 50th Street, New York, New York 10022 (212) 751-2600; *The Economist Book of Vital World Statistics*.

The World Bank, 1818 H Street, NW, Washington, D.C. 20433 (202) 477-1234; *World Tables*.

GUATEMALA - MARRIAGE RATES

Facts on File, 460 Park Avenue South, New York, New York 10016 (800) 443-8323; *The New Book of World Rankings*.

Statistical Office of the United Nations, Publishing Service, New York, New York 10017 (800) 253-9646; *Demographic Yearbook*, and *Statistical Yearbook*.

GUATEMALA - MEAT EXPORTS

International Monetary Fund, 700 Nineteenth Street, NW, Washington, D.C. 20431 (202) 623-7000; *International Financial Statistics*.

Organization of American States (OAS), General Secretariat, Washington, D.C. 20006 (202) 458-3533; *Statistical Bulletin of the OAS*.

GUATEMALA - MEAT PRODUCTION - See GUATEMALA - LIVESTOCK AND POULTRY

GUATEMALA - MEDICAL PERSONNEL

U.C.L.A. Latin American Center Publications, University of California, Los Angeles, California 90024 (310) 825-6634; *Statistical Abstract of Latin America*.

GUATEMALA - MERCHANT SHIPPING

G.K. Hall and Company, 70 Lincoln Street, Boston, Massachusetts 02111 (617) 423-3990; *The World in Figures*.

Statistical Office of the United Nations, Publishing Service, New York, New York 10017 (800) 253-9646; *Statistical Yearbook*.

Times Books, 201 East 50th Street, New York, New York 10022 (212) 751-2600; *The Economist Book of Vital World Statistics*.

U.S. Department of Transportation, Maritime Administration, 400 Seventh Street, SW, Washington, D.C. 20590 (202) 366-5807; *A Statistical Analysis of the World's Merchant Fleets*.

GUATEMALA - MILITARY

The Economist Intelligence Unit, 111 West 57th Street, New York, New York 10019 (800) 938-4685; *The New Latin America Market Atlas*.

G.K. Hall and Company, 70 Lincoln Street, Boston, Massachusetts 02111 (617) 423-3990; *The World in Figures*.

The International Institute for Strategic Studies, 23 Tavistock Street, London WC2E 7NQ, England; *The Military Balance*.

U.C.L.A. Latin American Center Publications, University of California, Los Angeles, California 90024 (310) 825-6634; *Statistical Abstract of Latin America*.

U.S. Arms Control and Disarmament Agency, 320 Twenty-first Street, Northwest, Washington, D.C. 20451 (202) 647-8677; *World Military Expenditures and Arms Transfers*.

GUATEMALA - MILK PRODUCTION - ALL TYPES OF MILK - See GUATEMALA - DAIRY PRODUCTS

GUATEMALA - MINING AND MINERAL PRODUCTS

The Economist Intelligence Unit, 111 West 57th Street, New York, New York 10019 (800) 938-4685; *The New Latin America Market Atlas*.

Facts on File, 460 Park Avenue South, New York, New York 10016 (800) 443-8323; *The New Book of World Rankings*.

G.K. Hall and Company, 70 Lincoln Street, Boston, Massachusetts 02111 (617) 423-3990; *The World in Figures*.

Inter-American Development Bank, 1300 New York Avenue, NW, Washington, D.C. 20577 (202) 623-1753; *Economic and Social Progress in Latin America.*

Penn Well Publishing Company, 1421 South Sheridan Road, Post Office Box 1260, Tulsa, Oklahoma 74101 (800) 752-9764; *International Energy Statistics Sourcebook.*

Statistical Office of the United Nations, Publishing Service, New York, New York 10017 (800) 253-9646; *Statistical Yearbook,* and *Statistical Yearbook for Latin America and the Caribbean.*

U.C.L.A. Latin American Center Publications, University of California, Los Angeles, California 90024 (310) 825-6634; *Statistical Abstract of Latin America.*

GUATEMALA - MONEY EXCHANGE RATE

Euromonitor Publications Limited, 87-88 Turnmill Street, London EC1M 5QU, England; *International Marketing Data and Statistics.*

Inter-American Development Bank, 1300 New York Avenue, NW, Washington, D.C. 20577 (202) 623-1753; *Economic and Social Progress in Latin America.*

International Monetary Fund, 700 Nineteenth Street, NW, Washington, D.C. 20431 (202) 623-7000; *International Financial Statistics.*

Statistical Office of the United Nations, Publishing Service, New York, New York 10017 (800) 253-9646; *Statistical Yearbook.*

GUATEMALA - MONEY RATES - MARKET

Inter-American Development Bank, 1300 New York Avenue, NW, Washington, D.C. 20577 (202) 623-1753; *Economic and Social Progress in Latin America.*

GUATEMALA - MONEY RESERVES

Euromonitor Publications Limited, 87-88 Turnmill Street, London EC1M 5QU, England; *International Marketing Data and Statistics.*

Inter-American Development Bank, 1300 New York Avenue, NW, Washington, D.C. 20577 (202) 623-1753; *Economic and Social Progress in Latin America.*

GUATEMALA - MONEY SUPPLY

Euromonitor Publications Limited, 87-88 Turnmill Street, London EC1M 5QU, England; *International Marketing Data and Statistics.*

G.K. Hall and Company, 70 Lincoln Street, Boston, Massachusetts 02111 (617) 423-3990; *The World in Figures.*

Inter-American Development Bank, 1300 New York Avenue, NW, Washington, D.C. 20577 (202) 623-1753; *Economic and Social Progress in Latin America.*

International Monetary Fund, 700 Nineteenth Street, NW, Washington, D.C. 20431 (202) 623-7000; *International Financial Statistics.*

Statistical Office of the United Nations, Publishing Service, New York, New York 10017 (800) 253-9646; *Statistical Yearbook.* supply.

U.C.L.A. Latin American Center Publications, University of California, Los Angeles, California 90024 (310) 825-6634; *Statistical Abstract of Latin America.*

The World Bank, 1818 H Street, NW, Washington, D.C. 20433 (202) 477-1234; *World Tables.*

GUATEMALA - MOTION PICTURES

Statistical Office of the United Nations, Publishing Service, New York, New York 10017 (800) 253-9646; *Statistical Yearbook.*

GUATEMALA - MOTOR VEHICLE TAXES - See GUATEMALA - TAXATION

GUATEMALA - MOTOR VEHICLES IN USE

The Economist Intelligence Unit, 111 West 57th Street, New York, New York 10019 (800) 938-4685; *The New Latin America Market Atlas.*

G.K. Hall and Company, 70 Lincoln Street, Boston, Massachusetts 02111 (617) 423-3990; *The World in Figures.*

Statistical Office of the United Nations, Publishing Service, New York, New York 10017 (800) 253-9646; *Statistical Yearbook.*

Times Books, 201 East 50th Street, New York, New York 10022 (212) 751-2600; *The Economist Book of Vital World Statistics.*

GUATEMALA - MULES - See GUATEMALA - LIVESTOCK AND POULTRY

GUATEMALA - MUSEUMS

Facts on File, 460 Park Avenue South, New York, New York 10016 (800) 443-8323; *The New Book of World Rankings.*

United Nations Educational, Scientific and Cultural Organization (UNESCO), 7 Place de Fontenoy, F-75700 Paris, France (Telephone Number in U.S. (212) 963-5981); *Statistical Yearbook.*

GUATEMALA - NATALITY - See GUATEMALA - BIRTH RATES

GUATEMALA - NATIONAL ACCOUNTS

Gale Research Incorporated, 835 Penobscot Building, Detroit, Michigan 48226 (800) 877-4253; *International Historical Statistics: The Americas and Australasia.*

Inter-American Development Bank, 1300 New York Avenue, NW, Washington, D.C. 20577 (202) 623-1753; *Economic and Social Progress in Latin America.*

International Monetary Fund, 700 Nineteenth Street, NW, Washington, D.C. 20431 (202) 623-7000; *International Financial Statistics.*

Organization of American States (OAS), General Secretariat, Washington, D.C. 20006 (202) 458-3533; *Statistical Bulletin of the OAS.*

Statistical Office of the United Nations, Publishing Service, New York, New York 10017 (800) 253-9646; *Statistical Yearbook,* and *Yearbook of National Accounts Statistics.*

GUATEMALA - NATIONAL INCOME

Facts on File, 460 Park Avenue South, New York, New York 10016 (800) 443-8323; *The New Book of World Rankings.*

G.K. Hall and Company, 70 Lincoln Street, Boston, Massachusetts 02111 (617) 423-3990; *The World in Figures.*

Inter-American Development Bank, 1300 New York Avenue, NW, Washington, D.C. 20577 (202) 623-1753; *Economic and Social Progress in Latin America.*

Statistical Office of the United Nations, Publishing Service, New York, New York 10017 (800) 253-9646; *Statistical Yearbook.*

GUATEMALA - NATIONAL PRODUCT

Facts on File, 460 Park Avenue South, New York, New York 10016 (800) 443-8323; *The New Book of World Rankings.*

Statistical Office of the United Nations, Publishing Service, New York, New York 10017 (800) 253-9646; *Statistical Yearbook.*

GUATEMALA - NATURAL GAS PRODUCTION - See GUATEMALA - MINING AND MINERAL PRODUCTS

GUATEMALA - NEWSPAPER PRODUCTION - See GUATEMALA - FORESTRY AND FOREST PRODUCTS

GUATEMALA - NEWSPRINT - See GUATEMALA - FORESTRY AND FOREST PRODUCTS

GUATEMALA - NUTRITION

Statistical Office of the United Nations, Publishing Service, New York, New York 10017 (800) 253-9646; *Statistical Yearbook for Latin America and the Caribbean.*

GUATEMALA - OCCUPATIONS - See GUATEMALA - LABOR FORCE

GUATEMALA - PAPER - See GUATEMALA - FORESTRY AND FOREST PRODUCTS

GUATEMALA - PATENTS

Statistical Office of the United Nations, Publishing Service, New York, New York 10017 (800) 253-9646; *Statistical Yearbook.*

World Intellectual Property Organization, 34 Chemin des Colombettes, CH-1211 Geneva 20, Switzerland; *Industrial Property Statistics.*

GUATEMALA - PEANUT PRODUCTION - See GUATEMALA - CROPS

GUATEMALA - PERIODICALS

United Nations Educational, Scientific and Cultural Organization (UNESCO), 7 Place de Fontenoy, F-75700 Paris, France (Telephone Number in U.S. (212) 963-5981); *Statistical Yearbook.*

GUATEMALA - PESTICIDE USE

Food and Agricultural Organization of the United Nations (FAO) Via delle Terme di Caracalla, 00100 Rome, Italy (Telephone Number in U.S. (202) 653-2400); *The State of Food and Agriculture.*

GUATEMALA - PETROLEUM INDUSTRY

The Economist Intelligence Unit, 111 West 57th Street, New York, New York 10019 (800) 938-4685; *The New Latin America Market Atlas.*

Facts on File, 460 Park Avenue South, New York, New York 10016 (800) 443-8323; *The New Book of World Rankings.*

Food and Agricultural Organization of the United Nations (FAO) Via delle Terme di Caracalla, 00100 Rome, Italy (Telephone Number in U.S. (202) 653-2400); *The State of Food and Agriculture.*

G.K. Hall and Company, 70 Lincoln Street, Boston, Massachusetts 02111 (617) 423-3990; *The World in Figures.*

Inter-American Development Bank, 1300 New York Avenue, NW, Washington, D.C. 20577 (202) 623-1753; *Economic and Social Progress in Latin America.*

Penn Well Publishing Company, 1421 South Sheridan Road, Post Office Box 1260, Tulsa, Oklahoma 74101 (800) 752-9764; *International Energy Statistics Sourcebook.*

Statistical Office of the United Nations, Publishing Service, New York, New York 10017 (800) 253-9646; *Statistical Yearbook.*

GUATEMALA - PIGS - See GUATEMALA - LIVESTOCK AND POULTRY

GUATEMALA - POLITICAL DATA

U.C.L.A. Latin American Center Publications, University of California, Los Angeles, California 90024 (310) 825-6634; *Statistical Abstract of Latin America.*

GUATEMALA - POPULATION

The Economist Intelligence Unit, 111 West 57th Street, New York, New York 10019 (800) 938-4685; *The New Latin America Market Atlas,* and *The World Market Atlas.*

Euromonitor Publications Limited, 87-88 Turnmill Street, London EC1M 5QU, England; *International Marketing Data and Statistics.*

Facts on File, 460 Park Avenue South, New York, New York 10016 (800) 443-8323; *The New Book of World Rankings.*

Food and Agricultural Organization of the United Nations (FAO), Via delle Terme di Caracalla, 00100 Rome, Italy (Telephone Number in U.S. (202) 653-2400); *Production Yearbook.*

Gale Research Incorporated, 835 Penobscot Building, Detroit, Michigan 48226 (800) 877-4253; *International Historical Statistics: The Americas and Australasia.*

G.K. Hall and Company, 70 Lincoln Street, Boston, Massachusetts 02111 (617) 423-3990; *The World in Figures.*

Inter-American Development Bank, 1300 New York Avenue, NW, Washington, D.C. 20577 (202) 623-1753; *Economic and Social Progress in Latin America.*

International Labour Office, I.L.O. Publications, CH-1211, Geneva 22, Switzerland; *Yearbook of Labour Statistics.*

Organization of American States (OAS), General Secretariat, Washington, D.C. 20006 (202) 458-3533; *Statistical Bulletin of the OAS.*

Statistical Office of the United Nations, Publishing Service, New York, New York 10017 (800) 253-9646; *Demographic Yearbook, Statistical Yearbook,* and *Statistical Yearbook for Latin America and the Caribbean.*

Times Books, 201 East 50th Street, New York, New York 10022 (212) 751-2600; *The Economist Book of Vital World Statistics.*

U.C.L.A. Latin American Center Publications, University of California, Los Angeles, California 90024 (310) 825-6634; *Statistical Abstract of Latin America.*

United Nations Educational, Scientific and Cultural Organization (UNESCO), 7 Place de Fontenoy, F-75700 Paris, France (Telephone Number in U.S. (212) 963-5981); *Statistical Yearbook.*

U.S. Arms Control and Disarmament Agency, 320 Twenty-first Street, Northwest, Washington, D.C. 20451 (202) 647-8677; *World Military Expenditures and Arms Transfers.*

World Health Organization, Office of Publications, Avenue Appia, CH-1211 Geneva 27, Switzerland (Telephone Number in U.S. (518) 436-9686); *World Health Statistics Annual.*

GUATEMALA - POST OFFICES

Facts on File, 460 Park Avenue South, New York, New York 10016 (800) 443-8323; *The New Book of World Rankings.*

GUATEMALA - POTATO PRODUCTION - See GUATEMALA - CROPS

GUATEMALA - PRICES

Facts on File, 460 Park Avenue South, New York, New York 10016 (800) 443-8323; *The New Book of World Rankings.*

Food and Agricultural Organization of the United Nations (FAO), Via delle Terme di Caracalla, 00100 Rome, Italy (Telephone Number in U.S. (202) 653-2400); *Production Yearbook,* and *The State of Food and Agriculture.*

Gale Research Incorporated, 835 Penobscot Building, Detroit, Michigan 48226 (800) 877-4253; *International Historical Statistics: The Americas and Australasia.*

G.K. Hall and Company, 70 Lincoln Street, Boston, Massachusetts 02111 (617) 423-3990; *The World in Figures.*

International Labour Office, I.L.O. Publications, CH-1211, Geneva 22, Switzerland; *Yearbook of Labour Statistics.*

International Monetary Fund, 700 Nineteenth Street, NW, Washington, D.C. 20431 (202) 623-7000; *International Financial Statistics.*

Statistical Office of the United Nations, Publishing Service, New York, New York 10017 (800) 253-9646; *Statistical Yearbook for Latin America and the Caribbean.*

GUATEMALA - PRINTING AND WRITING PAPER - See GUATEMALA - FORESTRY AND FOREST PRODUCTS

GUATEMALA - PRODUCTION

G.K. Hall and Company, 70 Lincoln Street, Boston, Massachusetts 02111 (617) 423-3990; *The World in Figures.*

Facts on File, 460 Park Avenue South, New York, New York 10016 (800) 443-8323; *The New Book of World Rankings.*

GUATEMALA - PRODUCTIVITY

Euromonitor Publications Limited, 87-88 Turnmill Street, London EC1M 5QU, England; *International Marketing Data and Statistics.*

GUATEMALA - PROPERTY TAXES - See GUATEMALA - TAXATION

GUATEMALA - PUBLIC CONSUMPTION FUND

Inter-American Development Bank, 1300 New York Avenue, NW, Washington, D.C. 20577 (202) 623-1753; *Economic and Social Progress in Latin America.*

GUATEMALA - PUBLIC EXPENDITURE

Inter-American Development Bank, 1300 New York Avenue, NW, Washington, D.C. 20577 (202) 623-1753; *Economic and Social Progress in Latin America.*

Organization of American States (OAS), General Secretariat, Washington, D.C. 20006 (202) 458-3533; *Statistical Bulletin of the OAS.*

Statistical Office of the United Nations, Publishing Service, New York, New York 10017 (800) 253-9646; *Statistical Yearbook for Latin America and the Caribbean.*

GUATEMALA - PUBLIC FINANCE

Facts on File, 460 Park Avenue South, New York, New York 10016 (800) 443-8323; *The New Book of World Rankings.*

Inter-American Development Bank, 1300 New York Avenue, NW, Washington, D.C. 20577 (202) 623-1753; *Economic and Social Progress in Latin America.*

Organization of American States (OAS), General Secretariat, Washington, D.C. 20006 (202) 458-3533; *Statistical Bulletin of the OAS.*

GUATEMALA - PUBLIC REVENUE

Inter-American Development Bank, 1300 New York Avenue, NW, Washington, D.C. 20577 (202) 623-1753; *Economic and Social Progress in Latin America.*

Organization of American States (OAS), General Secretariat, Washington, D.C. 20006 (202) 458-3533; *Statistical Bulletin of the OAS.*

GUATEMALA - RADIO BROADCASTING - See GUATEMALA - BROADCASTING

GUATEMALA - RAILWAYS

The Economist Intelligence Unit, 111 West 57th Street, New York, New York 10019 (800) 938-4685; *The New Latin America Market Atlas.*

G.K. Hall and Company, 70 Lincoln Street, Boston, Massachusetts 02111 (617) 423-3990; *The World in Figures.*

Jane's Information Group, Sentinel House, 163 Brighton Road, Coulsdon, Surrey CR5 2NH, England (Telephone Number in U.S. (703) 683-3700); *Jane's World Railways.*

Statistical Office of the United Nations, Publishing Service, New York, New York 10017 (800) 253-9646; *Statistical Yearbook.*

GUATEMALA - RANCHING

U.C.L.A. Latin American Center Publications, University of California, Los Angeles, California 90024 (310) 825-6634; *Statistical Abstract of Latin America.*

GUATEMALA - RELIGION

Facts on File, 460 Park Avenue South, New York, New York 10016 (800) 443-8323; *The New Book of World Rankings.*

U.C.L.A. Latin American Center Publications, University of California, Los Angeles, California 90024 (310) 825-6634; *Statistical Abstract of Latin America.*

GUATEMALA - RENT PRICES

International Labour Office, I.L.O. Publications, CH-1211, Geneva 22, Switzerland; *Yearbook of Labour Statistics.*

GUATEMALA - RESERVES EXCLUDING GOLD

The Economist Intelligence Unit, 111 West 57th Street, New York, New York 10019 (800) 938-4685; *The New Latin America Market Atlas.*

GUATEMALA - RETAIL TRADE

G.K. Hall and Company, 70 Lincoln Street, Boston, Massachusetts 02111 (617) 423-3990; *The World in Figures.*

Inter-American Development Bank, 1300 New York Avenue, NW, Washington, D.C. 20577 (202) 623-1753; *Economic and Social Progress in Latin America.*

GUATEMALA - RICE PRODUCTION - See GUATEMALA - CROPS

GUATEMALA - ROOT AND TUBER PRODUCTION - See GUATEMALA - CROPS

GUATEMALA - ROUNDWOOD PRODUCTION - See GUATEMALA - FORESTRY AND FOREST PRODUCTS

GUATEMALA - RUBBER PRODUCTION

Facts on File, 460 Park Avenue South, New York, New York 10016 (800) 443-8323; *The New Book of World Rankings.*

GUATEMALA - SALT PRODUCTION - See GUATEMALA - MINING AND MINERAL PRODUCTS

GUATEMALA - SAWNWOOD PRODUCTION - See GUATEMALA - FORESTRY AND FOREST PRODUCTS

GUATEMALA - SCIENCE AND TECHNOLOGY

U.C.L.A. Latin American Center Publications, University of California, Los Angeles, California 90024 (310) 825-6634; *Statistical Abstract of Latin America.*

GUATEMALA - SCIENCE AND TECHNOLOGY - EXPENDITURE FOR RESEARCH

Statistical Office of the United Nations, Publishing Service, New York, New York 10017 (800) 253-9646; *Statistical Yearbook.*

GUATEMALA - SCIENTISTS AND TECHNICIANS

Statistical Office of the United Nations, Publishing Service, New York, New York 10017 (800) 253-9646; *Statistical Yearbook.*

GUATEMALA - SENIOR CITIZENS

Facts on File, 460 Park Avenue South, New York, New York 10016 (800) 443-8323; *The New Book of World Rankings.*

GUATEMALA - SESAME SEED PRODUCTION

Food and Agricultural Organization of the United Nations (FAO), Via delle Terme di Caracalla, 00100 Rome, Italy (Telephone Number in U.S. (202) 653-2400); *Production Yearbook.*

GUATEMALA - SHEEP - See GUATEMALA - LIVESTOCK AND POULTRY

GUATEMALA - SILVER PRODUCTION AND CONSUMPTION - See GUATEMALA - MINING AND MINERAL PRODUCTS

GUATEMALA - SOCIAL DATA

Facts on File, 460 Park Avenue South, New York, New York 10016 (800) 443-8323; *The New Book of World Rankings.*

G.K. Hall and Company, 70 Lincoln Street, Boston, Massachusetts 02111 (617) 423-3990; *The World in Figures.*

U.C.L.A. Latin American Center Publications, University of California, Los Angeles, California 90024 (310) 825-6634; *Statistical Abstract of Latin America.*

GUATEMALA - SOCIAL SECURITY

Inter-American Development Bank, 1300 New York Avenue, NW, Washington, D.C. 20577 (202) 623-1753; *Economic and Social Progress in Latin America.*

International Monetary Fund, 700 Nineteenth Street, NW, Washington, D.C. 20431 (202) 623-7000; *Government Finance Statistics Yearbook.*

GUATEMALA - SOCIOECONOMIC DATA

Inter-American Development Bank, 1300 New York Avenue, NW, Washington, D.C. 20577 (202) 623-1753; *Economic and Social Progress in Latin America.*

U.C.L.A. Latin American Center Publications, University of California, Los Angeles, California 90024 (310) 825-6634; *Statistical Abstract of Latin America.*

GUATEMALA - SOYBEAN PRODUCTION - See GUATEMALA - CROPS

GUATEMALA - STAMP TAXES AND REVENUES

International Monetary Fund, 700 Nineteenth Street, NW, Washington, D.C. 20431 (202) 623-7000; *Government Finance Statistics Yearbook.*

GUATEMALA - STATE BUDGET REVENUE AND EXPENDITURES

Euromonitor Publications Limited, 87-88 Turnmill Street, London EC1M 5QU, England; *International Marketing Data and Statistics.*

Inter-American Development Bank, 1300 New York Avenue, NW, Washington, D.C. 20577 (202) 623-1753; *Economic and Social Progress in Latin America.*

GUATEMALA - STEEL - See GUATEMALA - MINING AND MINERAL PRODUCTS

GUATEMALA - STOCKS - COMMODITY - MARKET PRICE - INDEX

Food and Agricultural Organization of the United Nations (FAO) Via delle Terme di Caracalla, 00100 Rome, Italy (Telephone Number in U.S. (202) 653-2400); *The State of Food and Agriculture.*

GUATEMALA - SUGAR - See GUATEMALA - CROPS

GUATEMALA - TAXATION

G.K. Hall and Company, 70 Lincoln Street, Boston, Massachusetts 02111 (617) 423-3990; *The World in Figures.*

Inter-American Development Bank, 1300 New York Avenue, NW, Washington, D.C. 20577 (202) 623-1753; *Economic and Social Progress in Latin America.*

International Monetary Fund, 700 Nineteenth Street, NW, Washington, D.C. 20431 (202) 623-7000; *Government Finance Statistics Yearbook.*

Statistical Office of the United Nations, Publishing Service, New York, New York 10017 (800) 253-9646; *Statistical Yearbook for Latin America and the Caribbean.*

The World Bank, 1818 H Street, NW, Washington, D.C. 20433 (202) 477-1234; *World Tables.*

GUATEMALA - TELEPHONES IN USE

American Telephone and Telegraph Company, 26 Parsippany Road, Whippany, New Jersey 07981 (800) 338-4038; *The World's Telephones.*

The Economist Intelligence Unit, 111 West 57th Street, New York, New York 10019 (800) 938-4685; *The New Latin America Market Atlas.*

G.K. Hall and Company, 70 Lincoln Street, Boston, Massachusetts 02111 (617) 423-3990; *The World in Figures.*

Statistical Office of the United Nations, Publishing Service, New York, New York 10017 (800) 253-9646; *Statistical Yearbook.*

GUATEMALA - TELEVISION BROADCASTING - See GUATEMALA - BROADCASTING

GUATEMALA - TEXTILE INDUSTRY

Forest and Paper Association, 1250 Connecticut Avenue, NW, Washington, D.C. 20036 (202) 463-2455; *Wood Pulp and Fiber Statistics.*

G.K. Hall and Company, 70 Lincoln Street, Boston, Massachusetts 02111 (617) 423-3990; *The World in Figures.*

Statistical Office of the United Nations, Publishing Service, New York, New York 10017 (800) 253-9646; *Statistical Yearbook.*

GUATEMALA - THEATRE

United Nations Educational, Scientific and Cultural Organization (UNESCO), 7 Place de Fontenoy, F-75700 Paris, France (Telephone Number in U.S. (212) 963-5981); *Statistical Yearbook.*

GUATEMALA - TIN CONSUMPTION - See GUATEMALA - MINING AND MINERAL PRODUCTS

GUATEMALA - TOBACCO PRODUCTION

Facts on File, 460 Park Avenue South, New York, New York 10016 (800) 443-8323; *The New Book of World Rankings.*

Statistical Office of the United Nations, Publishing Service, New York, New York 10017 (800) 253-9646; *Statistical Yearbook.*

GUATEMALA - TOURISM

The Economist Intelligence Unit, 111 West 57th Street, New York, New York 10019 (800) 938-4685; *The New Latin America Market Atlas.*

Facts on File, 460 Park Avenue South, New York, New York 10016 (800) 443-8323; *The New Book of World Rankings.*

G.K. Hall and Company, 70 Lincoln Street, Boston, Massachusetts 02111 (617) 423-3990; *The World in Figures.*

Organization of American States (OAS), General Secretariat, Washington, D.C. 20006 (202) 458-3533; *Statistical Bulletin of the OAS.*

Statistical Office of the United Nations, Publishing Service, New York, New York 10017 (800) 253-9646; *Statistical Yearbook,* and *Statistical Yearbook for Latin America and the Caribbean.*

Times Books, 201 East 50th Street, New York, New York 10022 (212) 751-2600; *The Economist Book of Vital World Statistics.*

U.C.L.A. Latin American Center Publications, University of California, Los Angeles, California 90024 (310) 825-6634; *Statistical Abstract of Latin America.*

World Tourism Organization, Calle Capitan Haya 42, E-28020 Madrid, Spain; *Yearbook of Tourism Statistics.*

GUATEMALA - TRACTORS IN USE

The Economist Intelligence Unit, 111 West 57th Street, New York, New York 10019 (800) 938-4685; *The New Latin America Market Atlas.*

Statistical Office of the United Nations, Publishing Service, New York, New York 10017 (800) 253-9646; *Statistical Yearbook.*

GUATEMALA - TRADE - See GUATEMALA - FOREIGN TRADE

GUATEMALA - TRADEMARKS AND SERVICE MARKS

Statistical Office of the United Nations, Publishing Service, New York, New York 10017 (800) 253-9646; *Statistical Yearbook.*

World Intellectual Property Organization, 34 Chemin des Colombettes, CH-1211 Geneva 20, Switzerland; *Industrial Property Statistics.*

GUATEMALA - TRANSPORTATION AND COMMUNICATIONS

The Economist Intelligence Unit, 111 West 57th Street, New York, New York 10019 (800) 938-4685; *The New Latin America Market Atlas.*

Facts on File, 460 Park Avenue South, New York, New York 10016 (800) 443-8323; *The New Book of World Rankings.*

Gale Research Incorporated, 835 Penobscot Building, Detroit, Michigan 48226 (800) 877-4253; *International Historical Statistics: The Americas and Australasia.*

G.K. Hall and Company, 70 Lincoln Street, Boston, Massachusetts 02111 (617) 423-3990; *The World in Figures.*

Inter-American Development Bank, 1300 New York Avenue, NW, Washington, D.C. 20577 (202) 623-1753; *Economic and Social Progress in Latin America.*

Statistical Office of the United Nations, Publishing Service, New York, New York 10017 (800) 253-9646; *Statistical Yearbook for Latin America and the Caribbean.*

GUATEMALA - TUNGSTEN PRODUCTION AND CONSUMPTION - See GUATEMALA - MINING AND MINERAL PRODUCTS

GUATEMALA - UNEMPLOYMENT

The Economist Intelligence Unit, 111 West 57th Street, New York, New York 10019 (800) 938-4685; *The New Latin America Market Atlas.*

Euromonitor Publications Limited, 87-88 Turnmill Street, London EC1M 5QU, England; *International Marketing Data and Statistics.*

International Labour Office, I.L.O. Publications, CH-1211, Geneva 22, Switzerland; *Yearbook of Labour Statistics.*

Statistical Office of the United Nations, Publishing Service, New York, New York 10017 (800) 253-9646; *Statistical Yearbook.*

U.C.L.A. Latin American Center Publications, University of California, Los Angeles, California 90024 (310) 825-6634; *Statistical Abstract of Latin America.*

GUATEMALA - UTILITIES

U.C.L.A. Latin American Center Publications, University of California, Los Angeles, California 90024 (310) 825-6634; *Statistical Abstract of Latin America.*

GUATEMALA - VITAL STATISTICS

Euromonitor Publications Limited, 87-88 Turnmill Street, London EC1M 5QU, England; *International Marketing Data and Statistics.*

Gale Research Incorporated, 835 Penobscot Building, Detroit, Michigan 48226 (800) 877-4253; *International Historical Statistics: The Americas and Australasia.*

G.K. Hall and Company, 70 Lincoln Street, Boston, Massachusetts 02111 (617) 423-3990; *The World in Figures.*

Statistical Office of the United Nations, Publishing Service, New York, New York 10017 (800) 253-9646; *Statistical Yearbook.*

World Health Organization, Office of Publications, Avenue Appia, CH-1211 Geneva 27, Switzerland (Telephone Number in U.S. (518) 436-9686); *World Health Statistics Annual.*

GUATEMALA - WAGES

G.K. Hall and Company, 70 Lincoln Street, Boston, Massachusetts 02111 (617) 423-3990; *The World in Figures.*

International Labour Office, I.L.O. Publications, CH-1211, Geneva 22, Switzerland; *Yearbook of Labour Statistics.*

Statistical Office of the United Nations, Publishing Service, New York, New York 10017 (800) 253-9646; *Statistical Yearbook.*

U.C.L.A. Latin American Center Publications, University of California, Los Angeles, California 90024 (310) 825-6634; *Statistical Abstract of Latin America.*

GUATEMALA - WEATHER

Facts on File, 460 Park Avenue South, New York, New York 10016 (800) 443-8323; *The New Book of World Rankings.*

G.K. Hall and Company, 70 Lincoln Street, Boston, Massachusetts 02111 (617) 423-3990; *The World in Figures.*

GUATEMALA - WELFARE

Inter-American Development Bank, 1300 New York Avenue, NW, Washington, D.C. 20577 (202) 623-1753; *Economic and Social Progress in Latin America.*

International Monetary Fund, 700 Nineteenth Street, NW, Washington, D.C. 20431 (202) 623-7000; *Government Finance Statistics Yearbook.*

GUATEMALA - WHEAT PRODUCTION AND PRICES - See GUATEMALA - CROPS

GUATEMALA - WHOLESALE PRICES

Inter-American Development Bank, 1300 New York Avenue, NW, Washington, D.C. 20577 (202) 623-1753; *Economic and Social Progress in Latin America.*

International Monetary Fund, 700 Nineteenth Street, NW, Washington, D.C. 20431 (202) 623-7000; *International Financial Statistics.*

Organization of American States (OAS), General Secretariat, Washington, D.C. 20006 (202) 458-3533; *Statistical Bulletin of the OAS.*

Statistical Office of the United Nations, Publishing Service, New York, New York 10017 (800) 253-9646; *Statistical Yearbook.*

GUATEMALA - WHOLESALE TRADE

Inter-American Development Bank, 1300 New York Avenue, NW, Washington, D.C. 20577 (202) 623-1753; *Economic and Social Progress in Latin America.*

GUATEMALA - WINE PRODUCTION

Facts on File, 460 Park Avenue South, New York, New York 10016 (800) 443-8323; *The New Book of World Rankings.*

GUATEMALA - WOOD AND WOOD PULP - See GUATEMALA - FORESTRY AND FOREST PRODUCTS

GUATEMALA - WOOL PRODUCTION

Facts on File, 460 Park Avenue South, New York, New York 10016 (800) 443-8323; *The New Book of World Rankings.*

GUATEMALA - ZINC ORE PRODUCTION AND CONSUMPTION - See GUATEMALA - MINING AND MINERAL PRODUCTS

Guinea - National Statistical Office

Ministere du Plan et de la Statistique, Bureau du Premier Ministre, Conakry, Guinea.

Guinea - Primary Statistics Source

Service de la Statistique Generale, BP 221, Conakry, Guinea; *Bulletin Special de Statistique.*

GUINEA - AGRICULTURE

Euromonitor Publications Limited, 87-88 Turnmill Street, London EC1M 5QU, England; *International Marketing Data and Statistics.*

Facts on File, 460 Park Avenue South, New York, New York 10016 (800) 443-8323; *The New Book of World Rankings.*

Food and Agricultural Organization of the United Nations (FAO) Via delle Terme di Caracalla, 00100 Rome, Italy (Telephone Number in U.S. (202) 653-2400); *Production Yearbook, The State of Food and Agriculture,* and *Trade Yearbook.*

G.K. Hall and Company, 70 Lincoln Street, Boston, Massachusetts 02111 (617) 423-3990; *The World in Figures.*

Inter-American Development Bank, 1300 New York Avenue, NW, Washington, D.C. 20577 (202) 623-1753; *Economic and Social Progress in Latin America.*

Statistical Office of the United Nations, Publishing Service, New York, New York 10017 (800) 253-9646; *Statistical Yearbook,* and *Survey of Economic and Social Conditions in Africa.*

Times Books, 201 East 50th Street, New York, New York 10022 (212) 751-2600; *The Economist Book of Vital World Statistics.*

United Nations Economic Commission for Africa, Africa Hall, Post Office Box 3001, Addis Ababa, Ethiopia (Telephone Number in U.S. (800) 253-9646); *African Statistical Yearbook.*

GUINEA - AIRLINE SERVICE

Facts on File, 460 Park Avenue South, New York, New York 10016 (800) 443-8323; *The New Book of World Rankings.*

G.K. Hall and Company, 70 Lincoln Street, Boston, Massachusetts 02111 (617) 423-3990; *The World in Figures.*

Statistical Office of the United Nations, Publishing Service, New York, New York 10017 (800) 253-9646; *Statistical Yearbook.*

Times Books, 201 East 50th Street, New York, New York 10022 (212) 751-2600; *The Economist Book of Vital World Statistics.*

United Nations Economic Commission for Africa, Africa Hall, Post Office Box 3001, Addis Ababa, Ethiopia (Telephone Number in U.S. (800) 253-9646); *African Statistical Yearbook.*

GUINEA - ALUMINUM PRODUCTION AND CONSUMPTION - See GUINEA - MINING AND MINERAL PRODUCTS

GUINEA - ANIMAL HEALTH

Food and Agricultural Organization of the United Nations (FAO), Via delle Terme di Caracalla, 00100 Rome, Italy (Telephone Number in U.S. (202) 653-2400); *Animal Health Yearbook.*

GUINEA - AREA AND DENSITY OF POPULATION

African Development Bank, 01 BP 1387, Abidjan 01, Cote D'Ivoire; *Selected Statistics on Regional Member Countries.*

Euromonitor Publications Limited, 87-88 Turnmill Street, London EC1M 5QU, England; *International Marketing Data and Statistics.*

Facts on File, 460 Park Avenue South, New York, New York 10016 (800) 443-8323; *The New Book of World Rankings.*

Food and Agricultural Organization of the United Nations (FAO) Via delle Terme di Caracalla, 00100 Rome, Italy (Telephone Number in U.S. (202) 653-2400); *The State of Food and Agriculture.*

G.K. Hall and Company, 70 Lincoln Street, Boston, Massachusetts 02111 (617) 423-3990; *The World in Figures.*

Inter-American Development Bank, 1300 New York Avenue, NW, Washington, D.C. 20577 (202) 623-1753; *Economic and Social Progress in Latin America.*

Statistical Office of the United Nations, Publishing Service, New York, New York 10017 (800) 253-9646; *Statistical Yearbook,* and *Survey of Economic and Social Conditions in Africa.*

Times Books, 201 East 50th Street, New York, New York 10022 (212) 751-2600; *The Economist Book of Vital World Statistics.*

United Nations Educational, Scientific and Cultural Organization (UNESCO), 7 Place de Fontenoy, F-75700 Paris, France (Telephone Number in U.S. (212) 963-5981); *Statistical Yearbook.*

GUINEA - ARMS EXPORTS AND IMPORTS

U.S. Arms Control and Disarmament Agency, 320 Twenty-first Street, Northwest, Washington, D.C. 20451 (202) 647-8677; *World Military Expenditures and Arms Transfers.*

GUINEA - BALANCE OF PAYMENTS

African Development Bank, 01 BP 1387, Abidjan 01, Cote D'Ivoire; *Selected Statistics on Regional Member Countries.*

The Economist Intelligence Unit, 111 West 57th Street, New York, New York 10019 (800) 938-4685; *The World Market Atlas.*

G.K. Hall and Company, 70 Lincoln Street, Boston, Massachusetts 02111 (617) 423-3990; *The World in Figures.*

Inter-American Development Bank, 1300 New York Avenue, NW, Washington, D.C. 20577 (202) 623-1753; *Economic and Social Progress in Latin America.*

United Nations Economic Commission for Africa, Africa Hall, Post Office Box 3001, Addis Ababa, Ethiopia (Telephone Number in U.S. (800) 253-9646); *African Statistical Yearbook.*

GUINEA - BANKING

Facts on File, 460 Park Avenue South, New York, New York 10016 (800) 443-8323; *The New Book of World Rankings.*

G.K. Hall and Company, 70 Lincoln Street, Boston, Massachusetts 02111 (617) 423-3990; *The World in Figures.*

Inter-American Development Bank, 1300 New York Avenue, NW, Washington, D.C. 20577 (202) 623-1753; *Economic and Social Progress in Latin America.*

United Nations Economic Commission for Africa, Africa Hall, Post Office Box 3001, Addis Ababa, Ethiopia (Telephone Number in U.S. (800) 253-9646); *African Statistical Yearbook.*

GUINEA - BARLEY PRODUCTION - See GUINEA - CROPS

GUINEA - BAUXITE PRODUCTION AND CONSUMPTION - See GUINEA - MINING AND MINERAL PRODUCTS

GUINEA - BEER PRODUCTION

Facts on File, 460 Park Avenue South, New York, New York 10016 (800) 443-8323; *The New Book of World Rankings.*

GUINEA - BIRTH RATES

Facts on File, 460 Park Avenue South, New York, New York 10016 (800) 443-8323; *The New Book of World Rankings.*

Statistical Office of the United Nations, Publishing Service, New York, New York 10017 (800) 253-9646; *Demographic Yearbook, Statistical Yearbook,* and *Survey of Economic and Social Conditions in Africa.*

Times Books, 201 East 50th Street, New York, New York 10022 (212) 751-2600; *The Economist Book of Vital World Statistics.*

GUINEA - BONDS

G.K. Hall and Company, 70 Lincoln Street, Boston, Massachusetts 02111 (617) 423-3990; *The World in Figures.*

Inter-American Development Bank, 1300 New York Avenue, NW, Washington, D.C. 20577 (202) 623-1753; *Economic and Social Progress in Latin America.*

GUINEA - BOOK PRODUCTION

G.K. Hall and Company, 70 Lincoln Street, Boston, Massachusetts 02111 (617) 423-3990; *The World in Figures.*

GUINEA - BROADCASTING

Billboard Limited, Post Office Box 9027, 1006 AA Amsterdam, The Netherlands (Telephone Number in U.S. (212) 764-7300); *World Radio TV Handbook.*

Facts on File, 460 Park Avenue South, New York, New York 10016 (800) 443-8323; *The New Book of World Rankings.*

G.K. Hall and Company, 70 Lincoln Street, Boston, Massachusetts 02111 (617) 423-3990; *The World in Figures.*

Times Books, 201 East 50th Street, New York, New York 10022 (212) 751-2600; *The Economist Book of Vital World Statistics.*

GUINEA - BUSINESS

G.K. Hall and Company, 70 Lincoln Street, Boston, Massachusetts 02111 (617) 423-3990; *The World in Figures.*

Inter-American Development Bank, 1300 New York Avenue, NW, Washington, D.C. 20577 (202) 623-1753; *Economic and Social Progress in Latin America.*

GUINEA - CALORIE SUPPLY

African Development Bank, 01 BP 1387, Abidjan 01, Cote D'Ivoire; *Selected Statistics on Regional Member Countries.*

Food and Agricultural Organization of the United Nations (FAO) Via delle Terme di Caracalla, 00100 Rome, Italy (Telephone Number in U.S. (202) 653-2400); *The State of Food and Agriculture.*

GUINEA - CAPITAL INVESTMENT

Inter-American Development Bank, 1300 New York Avenue, NW, Washington, D.C. 20577 (202) 623-1753; *Economic and Social Progress in Latin America.*

GUINEA - CAPITAL REVENUE

Inter-American Development Bank, 1300 New York Avenue, NW, Washington, D.C. 20577 (202) 623-1753; *Economic and Social Progress in Latin America.*

GUINEA - CATTLE - See GUINEA - LIVESTOCK AND POULTRY

GUINEA - CEMENT PRODUCTION - See GUINEA - MINING AND MINERAL PRODUCTS

GUINEA - CHEMICAL (ORGANIC) PRODUCTION - See GUINEA - MINING AND MINERAL PRODUCTS

GUINEA - CHICKENS - See GUINEA - LIVESTOCK AND POULTRY

GUINEA - CIGARETTE PRODUCTION - See GUINEA - TOBACCO PRODUCTION

GUINEA - CLASS STRUCTURE

G.K. Hall and Company, 70 Lincoln Street, Boston, Massachusetts 02111 (617) 423-3990; *The World in Figures.*

GUINEA - CLIMATE

Facts on File, 460 Park Avenue South, New York, New York 10016 (800) 443-8323; *The New Book of World Rankings.*

G.K. Hall and Company, 70 Lincoln Street, Boston, Massachusetts 02111 (617) 423-3990; *The World in Figures.*

GUINEA - COAL PRODUCTION - See GUINEA - MINING AND MINERAL PRODUCTS

GUINEA - COFFEE PRODUCTION - See GUINEA - CROPS

GUINEA - COMMUNICATIONS

G.K. Hall and Company, 70 Lincoln Street, Boston, Massachusetts 02111 (617) 423-3990; *The World in Figures.*

Inter-American Development Bank, 1300 New York Avenue, NW, Washington, D.C. 20577 (202) 623-1753; *Economic and Social Progress in Latin America.*

United Nations Economic Commission for Africa, Africa Hall, Post Office Box 3001, Addis Ababa, Ethiopia (Telephone Number in U.S. (800) 253-9646); *African Statistical Yearbook.*

GUINEA - CONSTRUCTION INDUSTRY

Facts on File, 460 Park Avenue South, New York, New York 10016 (800) 443-8323; *The New Book of World Rankings.*

Inter-American Development Bank, 1300 New York Avenue, NW, Washington, D.C. 20577 (202) 623-1753; *Economic and Social Progress in Latin America.*

United Nations Economic Commission for Africa, Africa Hall, Post Office Box 3001, Addis Ababa, Ethiopia (Telephone Number in U.S. (800) 253-9646); *African Statistical Yearbook.*

GUINEA - CONSUMER PRICE INDEX

African Development Bank, 01 BP 1387, Abidjan 01, Cote D'Ivoire; *Selected Statistics on Regional Member Countries.*

G.K. Hall and Company, 70 Lincoln Street, Boston, Massachusetts 02111 (617) 423-3990; *The World in Figures.*

Statistical Office of the United Nations, Publishing Service, New York, New York 10017 (800) 253-9646; *Survey of Economic and Social Conditions in Africa.*

GUINEA - CONSUMPTION

African Development Bank, 01 BP 1387, Abidjan 01, Cote D'Ivoire; *Selected Statistics on Regional Member Countries.*

G.K. Hall and Company, 70 Lincoln Street, Boston, Massachusetts 02111 (617) 423-3990; *The World in Figures.*

Inter-American Development Bank, 1300 New York Avenue, NW, Washington, D.C. 20577 (202) 623-1753; *Economic and Social Progress in Latin America.*

Statistical Office of the United Nations, Publishing Service, New York, New York 10017 (800) 253-9646; *Survey of Economic and Social Conditions in Africa.*

GUINEA - COPPER PRODUCTION - See GUINEA - MINING AND MINERAL PRODUCTS

GUINEA - CORN PRODUCTION - See GUINEA - CROPS

GUINEA - CORPORATE INCOME TAXES - See GUINEA - TAXATION

GUINEA - CORPORATE TAXES - See GUINEA - TAXATION

GUINEA - COTTON PRODUCTION - See GUINEA - CROPS

GUINEA - CROPS

Facts on File, 460 Park Avenue South, New York, New York 10016 (800) 443-8323; *The New Book of World Rankings.*

Food and Agricultural Organization of the United Nations (FAO) Via delle Terme di Caracalla, 00100 Rome, Italy (Telephone Number in U.S. (202) 653-2400); *Production Yearbook* and *The State of Food and Agriculture.*

G.K. Hall and Company, 70 Lincoln Street, Boston, Massachusetts 02111 (617) 423-3990; *The World in Figures.*

Statistical Office of the United Nations, Publishing Service, New York, New York 10017 (800) 253-9646; *Statistical Yearbook.*

United Nations Economic Commission for Africa, Africa Hall, Post Office Box 3001, Addis Ababa, Ethiopia (Telephone Number in U.S. (800) 253-9646); *African Statistical Yearbook.*

GUINEA - CUSTOMS DUTIES

G.K. Hall and Company, 70 Lincoln Street, Boston, Massachusetts 02111 (617) 423-3990; *The World in Figures.*

Inter-American Development Bank, 1300 New York Avenue, NW, Washington, D.C. 20577 (202) 623-1753; *Economic and Social Progress in Latin America.*

GUINEA - DAIRY PRODUCTS

Facts on File, 460 Park Avenue South, New York, New York 10016 (800) 443-8323; *The New Book of World Rankings.*

Food and Agricultural Organization of the United Nations (FAO) Via delle Terme di Caracalla, 00100 Rome, Italy (Telephone Number in U.S. (202) 653-2400); *Production Yearbook* and *The State of Food and Agriculture.*

Statistical Office of the United Nations, Publishing Service, New York, New York 10017 (800) 253-9646; *Statistical Yearbook.*

GUINEA - DEATH RATES

G.K. Hall and Company, 70 Lincoln Street, Boston, Massachusetts 02111 (617) 423-3990; *The World in Figures.*

Statistical Office of the United Nations, Publishing Service, New York, New York 10017 (800) 253-9646; *Statistical Yearbook,* and *Survey of Economic and Social Conditions in Africa.*

Times Books, 201 East 50th Street, New York, New York 10022 (212) 751-2600; *The Economist Book of Vital World Statistics.*

GUINEA - DEFENSE EXPENDITURES

G.K. Hall and Company, 70 Lincoln Street, Boston, Massachusetts 02111 (617) 423-3990; *The World in Figures.*

U.S. Arms Control and Disarmament Agency, 320 Twenty-first Street, Northwest, Washington, D.C. 20451 (202) 647-8677; *World Military Expenditures and Arms Transfers.*

GUINEA - DEMOGRAPHY

The Economist Intelligence Unit, 111 West 57th Street, New York, New York 10019 (800) 938-4685; *The World Market Atlas.*

Facts on File, 460 Park Avenue South, New York, New York 10016 (800) 443-8323; *The New Book of World Rankings.*

G.K. Hall and Company, 70 Lincoln Street, Boston, Massachusetts 02111 (617) 423-3990; *The World in Figures.*

Statistical Office of the United Nations, Publishing Service, New York, New York 10017 (800) 253-9646; *Survey of Economic and Social Conditions in Africa.*

GUINEA - DEVELOPMENT ASSISTANCE

Inter-American Development Bank, 1300 New York Avenue, NW, Washington, D.C. 20577 (202) 623-1753; *Economic and Social Progress in Latin America.*

Statistical Office of the United Nations, Publishing Service, New York, New York 10017 (800) 253-9646; *Statistical Yearbook.*

GUINEA - DIAMOND PRODUCTION - See GUINEA - MINING AND MINERAL PRODUCTS

GUINEA - DISCOUNT RATES

Inter-American Development Bank, 1300 New York Avenue, NW, Washington, D.C. 20577 (202) 623-1753; *Economic and Social Progress in Latin America.*

GUINEA - DISEASE

G.K. Hall and Company, 70 Lincoln Street, Boston, Massachusetts 02111 (617) 423-3990; *The World in Figures.*

GUINEA - DIVORCE RATES

Facts on File, 460 Park Avenue South, New York, New York 10016 (800) 443-8323; *The New Book of World Rankings.*

Statistical Office of the United Nations, Publishing Service, New York, New York 10017 (800) 253-9646; *Demographic Yearbook.*

GUINEA - DOMESTIC PRODUCT

G.K. Hall and Company, 70 Lincoln Street, Boston, Massachusetts 02111 (617) 423-3990; *The World in Figures.*

GUINEA - ECONOMY

African Development Bank, 01 BP 1387, Abidjan 01, Cote D'Ivoire; *Selected Statistics on Regional Member Countries.*

Euromonitor Publications Limited, 87-88 Turnmill Street, London EC1M 5QU, England; *International Marketing Data and Statistics.*

Facts on File, 460 Park Avenue South, New York, New York 10016 (800) 443-8323; *The New Book of World Rankings.*

G.K. Hall and Company, 70 Lincoln Street, Boston, Massachusetts 02111 (617) 423-3990; *The World in Figures.*

Inter-American Development Bank, 1300 New York Avenue, NW, Washington, D.C. 20577 (202) 623-1753; *Economic and Social Progress in Latin America.*

Statistical Office of the United Nations, Publishing Service, New York, New York 10017 (800) 253-9646; *Foreign Trade Statistics for Africa.*

GUINEA - EDUCATION

African Development Bank, 01 BP 1387, Abidjan 01, Cote D'Ivoire; *Selected Statistics on Regional Member Countries.*

The Economist Intelligence Unit, 111 West 57th Street, New York, New York 10019 (800) 938-4685; *The World Market Atlas.*

Facts on File, 460 Park Avenue South, New York, New York 10016 (800) 443-8323; *The New Book of World Rankings.*

G.K. Hall and Company, 70 Lincoln Street, Boston, Massachusetts 02111 (617) 423-3990; *The World in Figures.*

Statistical Office of the United Nations, Publishing Service, New York, New York 10017 (800) 253-9646; *Survey of Economic and Social Conditions in Africa.*

Times Books, 201 East 50th Street, New York, New York 10022 (212) 751-2600; *The Economist Book of Vital World Statistics.*

United Nations Economic Commission for Africa, Africa Hall, Post Office Box 3001, Addis Ababa, Ethiopia (Telephone Number in U.S. (800) 253-9646); *African Statistical Yearbook.*

United Nations Educational, Scientific and Cultural Organization (UNESCO), 7 Place de Fontenoy, F-75700 Paris, France (Telephone Number in U.S. (212) 963-5981); *Statistical Yearbook.*

GUINEA - EGG PRODUCTION - See GUINEA - DAIRY PRODUCTS

GUINEA - ELECTRICITY

Facts on File, 460 Park Avenue South, New York, New York 10016 (800) 443-8323; *The New Book of World Rankings.*

Inter-American Development Bank, 1300 New York Avenue, NW, Washington, D.C. 20577 (202) 623-1753; *Economic and Social Progress in Latin America.*

Statistical Office of the United Nations, Publishing Service, New York, New York 10017 (800) 253-9646; *Statistical Yearbook,* and *Survey of Economic and Social Conditions in Africa.*

Times Books, 201 East 50th Street, New York, New York 10022 (212) 751-2600; *The Economist Book of Vital World Statistics.*

United Nations Economic Commission for Africa, Africa Hall, Post Office Box 3001, Addis Ababa, Ethiopia (Telephone Number in U.S. (800) 253-9646); *African Statistical Yearbook.*

GUINEA - EMPLOYMENT

Euromonitor Publications Limited, 87-88 Turnmill Street, London EC1M 5QU, England; *International Marketing Data and Statistics.*

Facts on File, 460 Park Avenue South, New York, New York 10016 (800) 443-8323; *The New Book of World Rankings.*

Statistical Office of the United Nations, Publishing Service, New York, New York 10017 (800) 253-9646; *Survey of Economic and Social Conditions in Africa.*

United Nations Economic Commission for Africa, Africa Hall, Post Office Box 3001, Addis Ababa, Ethiopia (Telephone Number in U.S. (800) 253-9646); *African Statistical Yearbook.*

GUINEA - ENERGY

Facts on File, 460 Park Avenue South, New York, New York 10016 (800) 443-8323; *The New Book of World Rankings.*

Food and Agricultural Organization of the United Nations (FAO) Via delle Terme di Caracalla, 00100 Rome, Italy (Telephone Number in U.S. (202) 653-2400); *The State of Food and Agriculture.*

G.K. Hall and Company, 70 Lincoln Street, Boston, Massachusetts 02111 (617) 423-3990; *The World in Figures.*

Statistical Office of the United Nations, Publishing Service, New York, New York 10017 (800) 253-9646; *Energy Statistics Yearbook.*

Times Books, 201 East 50th Street, New York, New York 10022 (212) 751-2600; *The Economist Book of Vital World Statistics.*

United Nations Economic Commission for Africa, Africa Hall, Post Office Box 3001, Addis Ababa, Ethiopia (Telephone Number in U.S. (800) 253-9646); *African Statistical Yearbook.*

GUINEA - EXCHANGE RATE

African Development Bank, 01 BP 1387, Abidjan 01, Cote D'Ivoire; *Selected Statistics on Regional Member Countries.*

Euromonitor Publications Limited, 87-88 Turnmill Street, London EC1M 5QU, England; *International Marketing Data and Statistics.*

Inter-American Development Bank, 1300 New York Avenue, NW, Washington, D.C. 20577 (202) 623-1753; *Economic and Social Progress in Latin America.*

Statistical Office of the United Nations, Publishing Service, New York, New York 10017 (800) 253-9646; *Foreign Trade Statistics for Africa,* and *Statistical Yearbook.*

GUINEA - EXCISE TAXES - See GUINEA - TAXATION

GUINEA - EXPORTS

African Development Bank, 01 BP 1387, Abidjan 01, Cote D'Ivoire; *Selected Statistics on Regional Member Countries.*

The Economist Intelligence Unit, 111 West 57th Street, New York, New York 10019 (800) 938-4685; *The World Market Atlas.*

Euromonitor Publications Limited, 87-88 Turnmill Street, London EC1M 5QU, England; *International Marketing Data and Statistics.*

Food and Agricultural Organization of the United Nations (FAO) Via delle Terme di Caracalla, 00100 Rome, Italy (Telephone Number in U.S. (202) 653-2400); *The State of Food and Agriculture.*

G.K. Hall and Company, 70 Lincoln Street, Boston, Massachusetts 02111 (617) 423-3990; *The World in Figures.*

Inter-American Development Bank, 1300 New York Avenue, NW, Washington, D.C. 20577 (202) 623-1753; *Economic and Social Progress in Latin America.*

International Monetary Fund, 700 Nineteenth Street, NW, Washington, D.C. 20431 (202) 623-7000; *Direction of Trade Statistics.*

Statistical Office of the United Nations, Publishing Service, New York, New York 10017 (800) 253-9646; *Foreign Trade Statistics for Africa,* and *Survey of Economic and Social Conditions in Africa.*

Times Books, 201 East 50th Street, New York, New York 10022 (212) 751-2600; *The Economist Book of Vital World Statistics.*

United Nations Economic Commission for Africa, Africa Hall, Post Office Box 3001, Addis Ababa, Ethiopia (Telephone Number in U.S. (800) 253-9646); *African Statistical Yearbook.*

GUINEA - EXTERNAL FINANCING

Inter-American Development Bank, 1300 New York Avenue, NW, Washington, D.C. 20577 (202) 623-1753; *Economic and Social Progress in Latin America.*

GUINEA - EXTERNAL INDEBTEDNESS

African Development Bank, 01 BP 1387, Abidjan 01, Cote D'Ivoire; *Selected Statistics on Regional Member Countries.*

Inter-American Development Bank, 1300 New York Avenue, NW, Washington, D.C. 20577 (202) 623-1753; *Economic and Social Progress in Latin America.*

Statistical Office of the United Nations, Publishing Service, New York, New York 10017 (800) 253-9646; *Survey of Economic and Social Conditions in Africa.*

GUINEA - EXTERNAL TRADE

African Development Bank, 01 BP 1387, Abidjan 01, Cote D'Ivoire; *Selected Statistics on Regional Member Countries.*

Food and Agricultural Organization of the United Nations (FAO) Via delle Terme di Caracalla, 00100 Rome, Italy (Telephone Number in U.S. (202) 653-2400); *The State of Food and Agriculture,* and *Trade Yearbook.*

G.K. Hall and Company, 70 Lincoln Street, Boston, Massachusetts 02111 (617) 423-3990; *The World in Figures.*

Inter-American Development Bank, 1300 New York Avenue, NW, Washington, D.C. 20577 (202) 623-1753; *Economic and Social Progress in Latin America.*

GUINEA - FARM CROPS - See GUINEA - CROPS

GUINEA - FEMALE WORKING POPULATION - See GUINEA - EMPLOYMENT

GUINEA - FERTILITY RATES

Facts on File, 460 Park Avenue South, New York, New York 10016 (800) 443-8323; *The New Book of World Rankings.*

Statistical Office of the United Nations, Publishing Service, New York, New York 10017 (800) 253-9646; *Survey of Economic and Social Conditions in Africa.*

Times Books, 201 East 50th Street, New York, New York 10022 (212) 751-2600; *The Economist Book of Vital World Statistics.*

GUINEA - FERTILIZER

Food and Agricultural Organization of the United Nations (FAO) Via delle Terme di Caracalla, 00100 Rome, Italy (Telephone Number in U.S. (202) 653-2400); *Fertilizer Yearbook,* and *The State of Food and Agriculture.*

Statistical Office of the United Nations, Publishing Service, New York, New York 10017 (800) 253-9646; *Statistical Yearbook.*

GUINEA - FETAL MORTALITY

Statistical Office of the United Nations, Publishing Service, New York, New York 10017 (800) 253-9646; *Demographic Yearbook.*

GUINEA - FINANCE

African Development Bank, 01 BP 1387, Abidjan 01, Cote D'Ivoire; *Selected Statistics on Regional Member Countries.*

Facts on File, 460 Park Avenue South, New York, New York 10016 (800) 443-8323; *The New Book of World Rankings.*

G.K. Hall and Company, 70 Lincoln Street, Boston, Massachusetts 02111 (617) 423-3990; *The World in Figures.*

Inter-American Development Bank, 1300 New York Avenue, NW, Washington, D.C. 20577 (202) 623-1753; *Economic and Social Progress in Latin America.*

United Nations Economic Commission for Africa, Africa Hall, Post Office Box 3001, Addis Ababa, Ethiopia (Telephone Number in U.S. (800) 253-9646); *African Statistical Yearbook.*

GUINEA - FISHERIES

Facts on File, 460 Park Avenue South, New York, New York 10016 (800) 443-8323; *The New Book of World Rankings.*

Food and Agricultural Organization of the United Nations (FAO) Via delle Terme di Caracalla, 00100 Rome, Italy (Telephone Number in U.S. (202) 653-2400); *The State of Food and Agriculture,* and *Yearbook of Fishery Statistics.*

Inter-American Development Bank, 1300 New York Avenue, NW, Washington, D.C. 20577 (202) 623-1753; *Economic and Social Progress in Latin America.*

Statistical Office of the United Nations, Publishing Service, New York, New York 10017 (800) 253-9646; *Statistical Yearbook,* and *Survey of Economic and Social Conditions in Africa.*

United Nations Economic Commission for Africa, Africa Hall, Post Office Box 3001, Addis Ababa, Ethiopia (Telephone Number in U.S. (800) 253-9646); *African Statistical Yearbook.*

GUINEA - FOOD

African Development Bank, 01 BP 1387, Abidjan 01, Cote D'Ivoire; *Selected Statistics on Regional Member Countries.*

Food and Agricultural Organization of the United Nations (FAO), Via delle Terme di Caracalla, 00100 Rome, Italy (Telephone Number in U.S. (202) 653-2400); *Production Yearbook,* and *The State of Food and Agriculture.*

G.K. Hall and Company, 70 Lincoln Street, Boston, Massachusetts 02111 (617) 423-3990; *The World in Figures.*

GUINEA - FOREIGN AID

G.K. Hall and Company, 70 Lincoln Street, Boston, Massachusetts 02111 (617) 423-3990; *The World in Figures.*

Inter-American Development Bank, 1300 New York Avenue, NW, Washington, D.C. 20577 (202) 623-1753; *Economic and Social Progress in Latin America.*

GUINEA - FOREIGN DEBT

Inter-American Development Bank, 1300 New York Avenue, NW, Washington, D.C. 20577 (202) 623-1753; *Economic and Social Progress in Latin America.*

GUINEA - FOREIGN FINANCE

Inter-American Development Bank, 1300 New York Avenue, NW, Washington, D.C. 20577 (202) 623-1753; *Economic and Social Progress in Latin America.*

GUINEA - FOREIGN INDEBTEDNESS

Inter-American Development Bank, 1300 New York Avenue, NW, Washington, D.C. 20577 (202) 623-1753; *Economic and Social Progress in Latin America.*

GUINEA - FOREIGN TRADE

Euromonitor Publications Limited, 87-88 Turnmill Street, London EC1M 5QU, England; *International Marketing Data and Statistics.*

Facts on File, 460 Park Avenue South, New York, New York 10016 (800) 443-8323; *The New Book of World Rankings.*

Food and Agricultural Organization of the United Nations (FAO) Via delle Terme di Caracalla, 00100 Rome, Italy (Telephone Number in U.S. (202) 653-2400); *The State of Food and Agriculture.*

G.K. Hall and Company, 70 Lincoln Street, Boston, Massachusetts 02111 (617) 423-3990; *The World in Figures.*

Inter-American Development Bank, 1300 New York Avenue, NW, Washington, D.C. 20577 (202) 623-1753; *Economic and Social Progress in Latin America.*

Statistical Office of the United Nations, Publishing Service, New York, New York 10017 (800) 253-9646; *Foreign Trade Statistics for Africa, Trade in Manufactures of Developing Countries,* and *Statistical Yearbook.*

United Nations Economic Commission for Africa, Africa Hall, Post Office Box 3001, Addis Ababa, Ethiopia (Telephone Number in U.S. (800) 253-9646); *African Statistical Yearbook.*

GUINEA - FORESTRY AND FOREST PRODUCTS

Facts on File, 460 Park Avenue South, New York, New York 10016 (800) 443-8323; *The New Book of World Rankings.*

Food and Agricultural Organization of the United Nations (FAO) Via delle Terme di Caracalla, 00100 Rome, Italy (Telephone Number in U.S. (202) 653-2400); *The State of Food and Agriculture,* and *Yearbook of Forest Products.*

G.K. Hall and Company, 70 Lincoln Street, Boston, Massachusetts 02111
(617) 423-3990; *The World in Figures.*

Inter-American Development Bank, 1300 New York Avenue, NW, Washington, D.C. 20577 (202) 623-1753; *Economic and Social Progress in Latin America.*

Statistical Office of the United Nations, Publishing Service, New York, New York 10017 (800) 253-9646; *Statistical Yearbook.*

United Nations Economic Commission for Africa, Africa Hall, Post Office Box 3001, Addis Ababa, Ethiopia (Telephone Number in U.S. (800) 253-9646); *African Statistical Yearbook.*

United Nations Educational, Scientific and Cultural Organization (UNESCO), 7 Place de Fontenoy, F-75700 Paris, France (Telephone Number in U.S. (212) 963-5981); *Statistical Yearbook.*

GUINEA - GAS PRODUCTION - See GUINEA - MINING AND MINERAL PRODUCTS

GUINEA - GENERAL MORTALITY

Statistical Office of the United Nations, Publishing Service, New York, New York 10017 (800) 253-9646; *Demographic Yearbook.*

GUINEA - GEOGRAPHIC DATA

Facts on File, 460 Park Avenue South, New York, New York 10016 (800) 443-8323; *The New Book of World Rankings.*

GUINEA - GOATS - See GUINEA - LIVESTOCK AND POULTRY

GUINEA - GOLD - See GUINEA - MINING AND MINERAL PRODUCTS

GUINEA - GOVERNMENT

G.K. Hall and Company, 70 Lincoln Street, Boston, Massachusetts 02111 (617) 423-3990; *The World in Figures.*

Inter-American Development Bank, 1300 New York Avenue, NW, Washington, D.C. 20577 (202) 623-1753; *Economic and Social Progress in Latin America.*

GUINEA - GOVERNMENT BONDS - See GUINEA - BONDS

GUINEA - GOVERNMENT CONSUMPTION

Inter-American Development Bank, 1300 New York Avenue, NW, Washington, D.C. 20577 (202) 623-1753; *Economic and Social Progress in Latin America.*

GUINEA - GOVERNMENT EXPENDITURE

Inter-American Development Bank, 1300 New York Avenue, NW, Washington, D.C. 20577 (202) 623-1753; *Economic and Social Progress in Latin America.*

Times Books, 201 East 50th Street, New York, New York 10022 (212) 751-2600; *The Economist Book of Vital World Statistics.*

GUINEA - GOVERNMENT FINANCES

Inter-American Development Bank, 1300 New York Avenue, NW, Washington, D.C. 20577 (202) 623-1753; *Economic and Social Progress in Latin America.*

GUINEA - GOVERNMENT REVENUE

Inter-American Development Bank, 1300 New York Avenue, NW, Washington, D.C. 20577 (202) 623-1753; *Economic and Social Progress in Latin America.*

Statistical Office of the United Nations, Publishing Service, New York, New York 10017 (800) 253-9646; *Survey of Economic and Social Conditions in Africa.*

Times Books, 201 East 50th Street, New York, New York 10022 (212) 751-2600; *The Economist Book of Vital World Statistics.*

GUINEA - GRAIN PRODUCTION - See GUINEA - CROPS

GUINEA - GROSS DOMESTIC PRODUCT

African Development Bank, 01 BP 1387, Abidjan 01, Cote D'Ivoire; *Selected Statistics on Regional Member Countries.*

The Economist Intelligence Unit, 111 West 57th Street, New York, New York 10019 (800) 938-4685; *The World Market Atlas.*

Euromonitor Publications Limited, 87-88 Turnmill Street, London EC1M 5QU, England; *International Marketing Data and Statistics.*

Facts on File, 460 Park Avenue South, New York, New York 10016 (800) 443-8323; *The New Book of World Rankings.*

G.K. Hall and Company, 70 Lincoln Street, Boston, Massachusetts 02111 (617) 423-3990; *The World in Figures.*

Inter-American Development Bank, 1300 New York Avenue, NW, Washington, D.C. 20577 (202) 623-1753; *Economic and Social Progress in Latin America.*

Statistical Office of the United Nations, Publishing Service, New York, New York 10017 (800) 253-9646; *Statistical Yearbook,* and *Survey of Economic and Social Conditions in Africa.*

Times Books, 201 East 50th Street, New York, New York 10022 (212) 751-2600; *The Economist Book of Vital World Statistics.*

United Nations Economic Commission for Africa, Africa Hall, Post Office Box 3001, Addis Ababa, Ethiopia (Telephone Number in U.S. (800) 253-9646); *African Statistical Yearbook.*

GUINEA - GROSS NATIONAL PRODUCT

Euromonitor Publications Limited, 87-88 Turnmill Street, London EC1M 5QU, England; *International Marketing Data and Statistics.*

Inter-American Development Bank, 1300 New York Avenue, NW, Washington, D.C. 20577 (202) 623-1753; *Economic and Social Progress in Latin America.*

U.S. Arms Control and Disarmament Agency, 320 Twenty-first Street, Northwest, Washington, D.C. 20451 (202) 647-8677; *World Military Expenditures and Arms Transfers.*

GUINEA - GROUNDNUTS PRODUCTION - See GUINEA - CROPS

GUINEA - HEALTH

African Development Bank, 01 BP 1387, Abidjan 01, Cote D'Ivoire; *Selected Statistics on Regional Member Countries.*

Facts on File, 460 Park Avenue South, New York, New York 10016 (800) 443-8323; *The New Book of World Rankings.*

G.K. Hall and Company, 70 Lincoln Street, Boston, Massachusetts 02111 (617) 423-3990; *The World in Figures.*

Statistical Office of the United Nations, Publishing Service, New York, New York 10017 (800) 253-9646; *Statistical Yearbook.*

Times Books, 201 East 50th Street, New York, New York 10022 (212) 751-2600; *The Economist Book of Vital World Statistics.*

United Nations Economic Commission for Africa, Africa Hall, Post Office Box 3001, Addis Ababa, Ethiopia (Telephone Number in U.S. (800) 253-9646); *African Statistical Yearbook.*

GUINEA - HIDE PRODUCTION

Food and Agricultural Organization of the United Nations (FAO), Via delle Terme di Caracalla, 00100 Rome, Italy (Telephone Number in U.S. (202) 653-2400); *Production Yearbook.*

GUINEA - HIGHWAYS

G.K. Hall and Company, 70 Lincoln Street, Boston, Massachusetts 02111 (617) 423-3990; *The World in Figures.*

Statistical Office of the United Nations, Publishing Service, New York, New York 10017 (800) 253-9646; *Survey of Economic and Social Conditions in Africa.*

United Nations Economic Commission for Africa, Africa Hall, Post Office Box 3001, Addis Ababa, Ethiopia (Telephone Number in U.S. (800) 253-9646); *African Statistical Yearbook.*

GUINEA - HORSES - See GUINEA - LIVESTOCK AND POULTRY

GUINEA - HOURS OF WORK - See GUINEA - EMPLOYMENT

GUINEA - HOUSING AND HOUSING UNITS

Facts on File, 460 Park Avenue South, New York, New York 10016 (800) 443-8323; *The New Book of World Rankings.*

GUINEA - ILLITERATE POPULATION

The Economist Intelligence Unit, 111 West 57th Street, New York, New York 10019 (800) 938-4685; *The World Market Atlas.*

G.K. Hall and Company, 70 Lincoln Street, Boston, Massachusetts 02111 (617) 423-3990; *The World in Figures.*

United Nations Educational, Scientific and Cultural Organization (UNESCO), 7 Place de Fontenoy, F-75700 Paris, France (Telephone Number in U.S. (212) 963-5981); *Statistical Yearbook.*

GUINEA - IMPORTS

African Development Bank, 01 BP 1387, Abidjan 01, Cote D'Ivoire; *Selected Statistics on Regional Member Countries.*

The Economist Intelligence Unit, 111 West 57th Street, New York, New York 10019 (800) 938-4685; *The World Market Atlas.*

Euromonitor Publications Limited, 87-88 Turnmill Street, London EC1M 5QU, England; *International Marketing Data and Statistics.*

Food and Agricultural Organization of the United Nations (FAO) Via delle Terme di Caracalla, 00100 Rome, Italy (Telephone Number in U.S. (202) 653-2400); *The State of Food and Agriculture.*

G.K. Hall and Company, 70 Lincoln Street, Boston, Massachusetts 02111 (617) 423-3990; *The World in Figures.*

Inter-American Development Bank, 1300 New York Avenue, NW, Washington, D.C. 20577 (202) 623-1753; *Economic and Social Progress in Latin America.*

International Monetary Fund, 700 Nineteenth Street, NW, Washington, D.C. 20431 (202) 623-7000; *Direction of Trade Statistics.*

Statistical Office of the United Nations, Publishing Service, New York, New York 10017 (800) 253-9646; *Foreign Trade Statistics for Africa,* and *Survey of Economic and Social Conditions in Africa.*

United Nations Economic Commission for Africa, Africa Hall, Post Office Box 3001, Addis Ababa, Ethiopia (Telephone Number in U.S. (800) 253-9646); *African Statistical Yearbook.*

GUINEA - INCOME TAXES - See GUINEA - TAXATION

GUINEA - INDUSTRY

Euromonitor Publications Limited, 87-88 Turnmill Street, London EC1M 5QU, England; *International Marketing Data and Statistics.*

Facts on File, 460 Park Avenue South, New York, New York 10016 (800) 443-8323; *The New Book of World Rankings.*

G.K. Hall and Company, 70 Lincoln Street, Boston, Massachusetts 02111 (617) 423-3990; *The World in Figures.*

Statistical Office of the United Nations, Publishing Service, New York, New York 10017 (800) 253-9646; *Survey of Economic and Social Conditions in Africa.*

Times Books, 201 East 50th Street, New York, New York 10022 (212) 751-2600; *The Economist Book of Vital World Statistics.*

United Nations Economic Commission for Africa, Africa Hall, Post Office Box 3001, Addis Ababa, Ethiopia (Telephone Number in U.S. (800) 253-9646); *African Statistical Yearbook.*

GUINEA - INFANT AND MATERNAL MORTALITY

Statistical Office of the United Nations, Publishing Service, New York, New York 10017 (800) 253-9646; *Demographic Yearbook, Statistical Yearbook,* and *Survey of Economic and Social Conditions in Africa.*

Times Books, 201 East 50th Street, New York, New York 10022 (212) 751-2600; *The Economist Book of Vital World Statistics.*

GUINEA - INTEREST RATES

Inter-American Development Bank, 1300 New York Avenue, NW, Washington, D.C. 20577 (202) 623-1753; *Economic and Social Progress in Latin America.*

GUINEA - INTERNATIONAL FINANCE

Inter-American Development Bank, 1300 New York Avenue, NW, Washington, D.C. 20577 (202) 623-1753; *Economic and Social Progress in Latin America.*

GUINEA - INTERNATIONAL LIQUIDITY

Inter-American Development Bank, 1300 New York Avenue, NW, Washington, D.C. 20577 (202) 623-1753; *Economic and Social Progress in Latin America.*

GUINEA - INTERNATIONAL RESERVES EXCLUDING GOLD

African Development Bank, 01 BP 1387, Abidjan 01, Cote D'Ivoire; *Selected Statistics on Regional Member Countries.*

Inter-American Development Bank, 1300 New York Avenue, NW, Washington, D.C. 20577 (202) 623-1753; *Economic and Social Progress in Latin America.*

GUINEA - INTERNATIONAL STATISTICS

Inter-American Development Bank, 1300 New York Avenue, NW, Washington, D.C. 20577 (202) 623-1753; *Economic and Social Progress in Latin America.*

GUINEA - INVESTMENTS

Inter-American Development Bank, 1300 New York Avenue, NW, Washington, D.C. 20577 (202) 623-1753; *Economic and Social Progress in Latin America.*

GUINEA - IRON ORE PRODUCTION AND CONSUMPTION - See GUINEA - MINING AND MINERAL PRODUCTS

GUINEA - IRRIGATION

Euromonitor Publications Limited, 87-88 Turnmill Street, London EC1M 5QU, England; *International Marketing Data and Statistics.*

Inter-American Development Bank, 1300 New York Avenue, NW, Washington, D.C. 20577 (202) 623-1753; *Economic and Social Progress in Latin America.*

GUINEA - LABOR FORCE

African Development Bank, 01 BP 1387, Abidjan 01, Cote D'Ivoire; *Selected Statistics on Regional Member Countries.*

Euromonitor Publications Limited, 87-88 Turnmill Street, London EC1M 5QU, England; *International Marketing Data and Statistics.*

Food and Agricultural Organization of the United Nations (FAO) Via delle Terme di Caracalla, 00100 Rome, Italy (Telephone Number in U.S. (202) 653-2400); *The State of Food and Agriculture.*

Facts on File, 460 Park Avenue South, New York, New York 10016 (800) 443-8323; *The New Book of World Rankings.*

G.K. Hall and Company, 70 Lincoln Street, Boston, Massachusetts 02111 (617) 423-3990; *The World in Figures.*

GUINEA - LAND USE

Euromonitor Publications Limited, 87-88 Turnmill Street, London EC1M 5QU, England; *International Marketing Data and Statistics.*

Food and Agricultural Organization of the United Nations (FAO), Via delle Terme di Caracalla, 00100 Rome, Italy (Telephone Number in U.S. (202) 653-2400); *Production Yearbook.*

G.K. Hall and Company, 70 Lincoln Street, Boston, Massachusetts 02111 (617) 423-3990; *The World in Figures.*

Inter-American Development Bank, 1300 New York Avenue, NW, Washington, D.C. 20577 (202) 623-1753; *Economic and Social Progress in Latin America.*

GUINEA - LIBRARIES

Facts on File, 460 Park Avenue South, New York, New York 10016 (800) 443-8323; *The New Book of World Rankings.*

GUINEA - LIFE EXPECTANCY

African Development Bank, 01 BP 1387, Abidjan 01, Cote D'Ivoire; *Selected Statistics on Regional Member Countries.*

GUINEA - LITERACY RATE

Statistical Office of the United Nations, Publishing Service, New York, New York 10017 (800) 253-9646; *Survey of Economic and Social Conditions in Africa.*

GUINEA - LIVESTOCK AND POULTRY

Euromonitor Publications Limited, 87-88 Turnmill Street, London EC1M 5QU, England; *International Marketing Data and Statistics.*

Facts on File, 460 Park Avenue South, New York, New York 10016 (800) 443-8323; *The New Book of World Rankings.*

Food and Agricultural Organization of the United Nations (FAO), Via delle Terme di Caracalla, 00100 Rome, Italy (Telephone Number in U.S. (202) 653-2400); *Production Yearbook,* and *The State of Food and Agriculture.*

G.K. Hall and Company, 70 Lincoln Street, Boston, Massachusetts 02111 (617) 423-3990; *The World in Figures.*

Statistical Office of the United Nations, Publishing Service, New York, New York 10017 (800) 253-9646; *Statistical Yearbook,* and *Survey of Economic and Social Conditions in Africa.*

United Nations Economic Commission for Africa, Africa Hall, Post Office Box 3001, Addis Ababa, Ethiopia (Telephone Number in U.S. (800) 253-9646); *African Statistical Yearbook.*

GUINEA - LIVING LEVELS

G.K. Hall and Company, 70 Lincoln Street, Boston, Massachusetts 02111 (617) 423-3990; *The World in Figures.*

Times Books, 201 East 50th Street, New York, New York 10022 (212) 751-2600; *The Economist Book of Vital World Statistics.*

GUINEA - MAIL - NUMBER OF PIECES SENT OR RECEIVED

Statistical Office of the United Nations, Publishing Service, New York, New York 10017 (800) 253-9646; *Statistical Yearbook.*

GUINEA - MAIN ECONOMIC INDICATORS - See GUINEA - ECONOMY

GUINEA - MANUFACTURING

Facts on File, 460 Park Avenue South, New York, New York 10016 (800) 443-8323; *The New Book of World Rankings.*

G.K. Hall and Company, 70 Lincoln Street, Boston, Massachusetts 02111 (617) 423-3990; *The World in Figures.*

Inter-American Development Bank, 1300 New York Avenue, NW, Washington, D.C. 20577 (202) 623-1753; *Economic and Social Progress in Latin America.*

Statistical Office of the United Nations, Publishing Service, New York, New York 10017 (800) 253-9646; *Survey of Economic and Social Conditions in Africa.*

United Nations Economic Commission for Africa, Africa Hall, Post Office Box 3001, Addis Ababa, Ethiopia (Telephone Number in U.S. (800) 253-9646); *African Statistical Yearbook.*

GUINEA - MARRIAGE RATES

Facts on File, 460 Park Avenue South, New York, New York 10016 (800) 443-8323; *The New Book of World Rankings.*

Statistical Office of the United Nations, Publishing Service, New York, New York 10017 (800) 253-9646; *Demographic Yearbook.*

GUINEA - MEAT PRODUCTION - See GUINEA - LIVESTOCK AND POULTRY

GUINEA - MERCHANT SHIPPING

G.K. Hall and Company, 70 Lincoln Street, Boston, Massachusetts 02111 (617) 423-3990; *The World in Figures.*

Statistical Office of the United Nations, Publishing Service, New York, New York 10017 (800) 253-9646; *Statistical Yearbook.*

Times Books, 201 East 50th Street, New York, New York 10022 (212) 751-2600; *The Economist Book of Vital World Statistics.*

United Nations Economic Commission for Africa, Africa Hall, Post Office Box 3001, Addis Ababa, Ethiopia (Telephone Number in U.S. (800) 253-9646); *African Statistical Yearbook.*

U.S. Department of Transportation, Maritime Administration, 400 Seventh Street, SW, Washington, D.C. 20590 (202) 366-5807; *A Statistical Analysis of the World's Merchant Fleets.*

GUINEA - MILITARY

G.K. Hall and Company, 70 Lincoln Street, Boston, Massachusetts 02111 (617) 423-3990; *The World in Figures*.

The International Institute for Strategic Studies, 23 Tavistock Street, London WC2E 7NQ, England; *The Military Balance*.

U.S. Arms Control and Disarmament Agency, 320 Twenty-first Street, Northwest, Washington, D.C. 20451 (202) 647-8677; *World Military Expenditures and Arms Transfers*.

GUINEA - MILK PRODUCTION - See GUINEA - DAIRY PRODUCTS

GUINEA - MINING AND MINERAL PRODUCTS

Commodity Research Bureau, Incorporated, 75 Wall Street, New York, New York 10005 (212) 504-7754; *Commodity Year Book*.

Facts on File, 460 Park Avenue South, New York, New York 10016 (800) 443-8323; *The New Book of World Rankings*.

G.K. Hall and Company, 70 Lincoln Street, Boston, Massachusetts 02111 (617) 423-3990; *The World in Figures*.

Inter-American Development Bank, 1300 New York Avenue, NW, Washington, D.C. 20577 (202) 623-1753; *Economic and Social Progress in Latin America*.

Statistical Office of the United Nations, Publishing Service, New York, New York 10017 (800) 253-9646; *Statistical Yearbook*.

United Nations Economic Commission for Africa, Africa Hall, Post Office Box 3001, Addis Ababa, Ethiopia (Telephone Number in U.S. (800) 253-9646); *African Statistical Yearbook*.

GUINEA - MONEY EXCHANGE RATE

Euromonitor Publications Limited, 87-88 Turnmill Street, London EC1M 5QU, England; *International Marketing Data and Statistics*.

Inter-American Development Bank, 1300 New York Avenue, NW, Washington, D.C. 20577 (202) 623-1753; *Economic and Social Progress in Latin America*.

Statistical Office of the United Nations, Publishing Service, New York, New York 10017 (800) 253-9646; *Statistical Yearbook*.

GUINEA - MONEY RATES - MARKET

Inter-American Development Bank, 1300 New York Avenue, NW, Washington, D.C. 20577 (202) 623-1753; *Economic and Social Progress in Latin America*.

GUINEA - MONEY RESERVES

Euromonitor Publications Limited, 87-88 Turnmill Street, London EC1M 5QU, England; *International Marketing Data and Statistics*.

Inter-American Development Bank, 1300 New York Avenue, NW, Washington, D.C. 20577 (202) 623-1753; *Economic and Social Progress in Latin America*.

GUINEA - MONEY SUPPLY

African Development Bank, 01 BP 1387, Abidjan 01, Cote D'Ivoire; *Selected Statistics on Regional Member Countries*.

Euromonitor Publications Limited, 87-88 Turnmill Street, London EC1M 5QU, England; *International Marketing Data and Statistics*.

G.K. Hall and Company, 70 Lincoln Street, Boston, Massachusetts 02111 (617) 423-3990; *The World in Figures*.

Inter-American Development Bank, 1300 New York Avenue, NW, Washington, D.C. 20577 (202) 623-1753; *Economic and Social Progress in Latin America*.

GUINEA - MONUMENTS AND HISTORICAL SITES

United Nations Educational, Scientific and Cultural Organization (UNESCO), 7 Place de Fontenoy, F-75700 Paris, France (Telephone Number in U.S. (212) 963-5981); *Statistical Yearbook*.

GUINEA - MOTOR VEHICLES IN USE

G.K. Hall and Company, 70 Lincoln Street, Boston, Massachusetts 02111 (617) 423-3990; *The World in Figures*.

Statistical Office of the United Nations, Publishing Service, New York, New York 10017 (800) 253-9646; *Statistical Yearbook*, and *Survey of Economic and Social Conditions in Africa*.

Times Books, 201 East 50th Street, New York, New York 10022 (212) 751-2600; *The Economist Book of Vital World Statistics*.

GUINEA - MUSEUMS

Facts on File, 460 Park Avenue South, New York, New York 10016 (800) 443-8323; *The New Book of World Rankings*.

United Nations Educational, Scientific and Cultural Organization (UNESCO), 7 Place de Fontenoy, F-75700 Paris, France (Telephone Number in U.S. (212) 963-5981); *Statistical Yearbook*.

GUINEA - NATALITY - See GUINEA - BIRTH RATES

GUINEA - NATIONAL ACCOUNTS

African Development Bank, 01 BP 1387, Abidjan 01, Cote D'Ivoire; *Selected Statistics on Regional Member Countries*.

Inter-American Development Bank, 1300 New York Avenue, NW, Washington, D.C. 20577 (202) 623-1753; *Economic and Social Progress in Latin America*.

Statistical Office of the United Nations, Publishing Service, New York, New York 10017 (800) 253-9646; *Statistical Yearbook*.

United Nations Economic Commission for Africa, Africa Hall, Post Office Box 3001, Addis Ababa, Ethiopia (Telephone Number in U.S. (800) 253-9646); *African Statistical Yearbook*.

GUINEA - NATIONAL INCOME

Facts on File, 460 Park Avenue South, New York, New York 10016 (800) 443-8323; *The New Book of World Rankings*.

G.K. Hall and Company, 70 Lincoln Street, Boston, Massachusetts 02111 (617) 423-3990; *The World in Figures*.

Inter-American Development Bank, 1300 New York Avenue, NW, Washington, D.C. 20577 (202) 623-1753; *Economic and Social Progress in Latin America*.

Statistical Office of the United Nations, Publishing Service, New York, New York 10017 (800) 253-9646; *Statistical Yearbook*.

GUINEA - NATIONAL PRODUCT

Facts on File, 460 Park Avenue South, New York, New York 10016 (800) 443-8323; *The New Book of World Rankings.*

GUINEA - NATURAL GAS PRODUCTION - See GUINEA - MINING AND MINERAL PRODUCTS

GUINEA - NEWSPAPER PRODUCTION - See GUINEA - FORESTRY AND FOREST PRODUCTS

GUINEA - OCCUPATIONS - See GUINEA - LABOR FORCE

GUINEA - PALM KERNELS PRODUCTION - See GUINEA - CROPS

GUINEA - PEANUT PRODUCTION - See GUINEA - CROPS

GUINEA - PERIODICALS

United Nations Educational, Scientific and Cultural Organization (UNESCO), 7 Place de Fontenoy, F-75700 Paris, France (Telephone Number in U.S. (212) 963-5981); *Statistical Yearbook.*

GUINEA - PESTICIDE USE

Food and Agricultural Organization of the United Nations (FAO) Via delle Terme di Caracalla, 00100 Rome, Italy (Telephone Number in U.S. (202) 653-2400); *The State of Food and Agriculture.*

GUINEA - PETROLEUM INDUSTRY

Facts on File, 460 Park Avenue South, New York, New York 10016 (800) 443-8323; *The New Book of World Rankings.*

Food and Agricultural Organization of the United Nations (FAO) Via delle Terme di Caracalla, 00100 Rome, Italy (Telephone Number in U.S. (202) 653-2400); *The State of Food and Agriculture.*

G.K. Hall and Company, 70 Lincoln Street, Boston, Massachusetts 02111 (617) 423-3990; *The World in Figures.*

Inter-American Development Bank, 1300 New York Avenue, NW, Washington, D.C. 20577 (202) 623-1753; *Economic and Social Progress in Latin America.*

GUINEA - PIGS - See GUINEA - LIVESTOCK AND POULTRY

GUINEA - POPULATION

African Development Bank, 01 BP 1387, Abidjan 01, Cote d'Ivoire; *Selected Statistics on Regional Member Countries.*

The Economist Intelligence Unit, 111 West 57th Street, New York, New York 10019 (800) 938-4685; *The World Market Atlas.*

Euromonitor Publications Limited, 87-88 Turnmill Street, London EC1M 5QU, England; *International Marketing Data and Statistics.*

Facts on File, 460 Park Avenue South, New York, New York 10016 (800) 443-8323; *The New Book of World Rankings.*

Food and Agricultural Organization of the United Nations (FAO), Via delle Terme di Caracalla, 00100 Rome, Italy (Telephone Number in U.S. (202) 653-2400); *Production Yearbook.*

G.K. Hall and Company, 70 Lincoln Street, Boston, Massachusetts 02111 (617) 423-3990; *The World in Figures.*

Inter-American Development Bank, 1300 New York Avenue, NW, Washington, D.C. 20577 (202) 623-1753; *Economic and Social Progress in Latin America.*

Statistical Office of the United Nations, Publishing Service, New York, New York 10017 (800) 253-9646; *Demographic Yearbook, Statistical Yearbook,* and *Survey of Economic and Social Conditions in Africa.*

Times Books, 201 East 50th Street, New York, New York 10022 (212) 751-2600; *The Economist Book of Vital World Statistics.*

United Nations Educational, Scientific and Cultural Organization (UNESCO), 7 Place de Fontenoy, F-75700 Paris, France (Telephone Number in U.S. (212) 963-5981); *Statistical Yearbook.*

U.S. Arms Control and Disarmament Agency, 320 Twenty-first Street, Northwest, Washington, D.C. 20451 (202) 647-8677; *World Military Expenditures and Arms Transfers.*

World Health Organization, Office of Publications, Avenue Appia, CH-1211 Geneva 27, Switzerland (Telephone Number in U.S. (518) 436-9686); *World Health Statistics Annual.*

GUINEA - POST OFFICES

Facts on File, 460 Park Avenue South, New York, New York 10016 (800) 443-8323; *The New Book of World Rankings.*

GUINEA - POTATO PRODUCTION - See GUINEA - CROPS

GUINEA - PRICES

Facts on File, 460 Park Avenue South, New York, New York 10016 (800) 443-8323; *The New Book of World Rankings.*

Food and Agricultural Organization of the United Nations (FAO), Via delle Terme di Caracalla, 00100 Rome, Italy (Telephone Number in U.S. (202) 653-2400); *Production Yearbook,* and *The State of Food and Agriculture.*

G.K. Hall and Company, 70 Lincoln Street, Boston, Massachusetts 02111 (617) 423-3990; *The World in Figures.*

GUINEA - PRODUCTION

Facts on File, 460 Park Avenue South, New York, New York 10016 (800) 443-8323; *The New Book of World Rankings.*

G.K. Hall and Company, 70 Lincoln Street, Boston, Massachusetts 02111 (617) 423-3990; *The World in Figures.*

GUINEA - PRODUCTIVITY

Euromonitor Publications Limited, 87-88 Turnmill Street, London EC1M 5QU, England; *International Marketing Data and Statistics.*

GUINEA - PROPERTY TAXES - See GUINEA - TAXATION

GUINEA - PUBLIC CONSUMPTION FUND

Inter-American Development Bank, 1300 New York Avenue, NW, Washington, D.C. 20577 (202) 623-1753; *Economic and Social Progress in Latin America.*

GUINEA - PUBLIC EXPENDITURES

Inter-American Development Bank, 1300 New York Avenue, NW, Washington, D.C. 20577 (202) 623-1753; *Economic and Social*

Progress in Latin America.

GUINEA - PUBLIC FINANCE

Facts on File, 460 Park Avenue South, New York, New York 10016 (800) 443-8323; *The New Book of World Rankings.*

Inter-American Development Bank, 1300 New York Avenue, NW, Washington, D.C. 20577 (202) 623-1753; *Economic and Social Progress in Latin America.*

GUINEA - PUBLIC REVENUES

Inter-American Development Bank, 1300 New York Avenue, NW, Washington, D.C. 20577 (202) 623-1753; *Economic and Social Progress in Latin America.*

GUINEA - RADIO BROADCASTING - See GUINEA - BROADCASTING

GUINEA - RAILWAYS

G.K. Hall and Company, 70 Lincoln Street, Boston, Massachusetts 02111 (617) 423-3990; *The World in Figures.*

Jane's Information Group, Sentinel House, 163 Brighton Road, Coulsdon, Surrey CR5 2NH, England (Telephone Number in U.S. (703) 683-3700); *Jane's World Railways.*

United Nations Economic Commission for Africa, Africa Hall, Post Office Box 3001, Addis Ababa, Ethiopia (Telephone Number in U.S. (800) 253-9646); *African Statistical Yearbook.*

GUINEA - RELIGION

Facts on File, 460 Park Avenue South, New York, New York 10016 (800) 443-8323; *The New Book of World Rankings.*

GUINEA - RETAIL TRADE

G.K. Hall and Company, 70 Lincoln Street, Boston, Massachusetts 02111 (617) 423-3990; *The World in Figures.*

Inter-American Development Bank, 1300 New York Avenue, NW, Washington, D.C. 20577 (202) 623-1753; *Economic and Social Progress in Latin America.*

GUINEA - RICE PRODUCTION - See GUINEA - CROPS

GUINEA - ROOT AND TUBER PRODUCTION - See GUINEA - CROPS

GUINEA - ROUNDWOOD PRODUCTION - See GUINEA - FORESTRY AND FOREST PRODUCTS

GUINEA - RUBBER PRODUCTION

Facts on File, 460 Park Avenue South, New York, New York 10016 (800) 443-8323; *The New Book of World Rankings.*

GUINEA - SAWNWOOD PRODUCTION - See GUINEA - FORESTRY AND FOREST PRODUCTS

GUINEA - SESAME SEED PRODUCTION - See GUINEA - CROPS

GUINEA - SENIOR CITIZENS

Facts on File, 460 Park Avenue South, New York, New York 10016 (800) 443-8323; *The New Book of World Rankings.*

GUINEA - SHEEP - See GUINEA - LIVESTOCK AND POULTRY

GUINEA - SILVER PRODUCTION - See GUINEA - MINING AND MINERAL PRODUCTS

GUINEA - SISAL PRODUCTION - See GUINEA - CROPS

GUINEA - SOCIAL DATA

African Development Bank, 01 BP 1387, Abidjan 01, Cote d'Ivoire; *Selected Statistics on Regional Member Countries.*

Facts on File, 460 Park Avenue South, New York, New York 10016 (800) 443-8323; *The New Book of World Rankings.*

G.K. Hall and Company, 70 Lincoln Street, Boston, Massachusetts 02111 (617) 423-3990; *The World in Figures.*

GUINEA - SOCIAL SECURITY

Inter-American Development Bank, 1300 New York Avenue, NW, Washington, D.C. 20577 (202) 623-1753; *Economic and Social Progress in Latin America.*

GUINEA - SOCIOECONOMIC DATA

Inter-American Development Bank, 1300 New York Avenue, NW, Washington, D.C. 20577 (202) 623-1753; *Economic and Social Progress in Latin America.*

GUINEA - STAMP TAXES AND DUTIES - See GUINEA - TAXATION

GUINEA - STATE BUDGET REVENUE AND EXPENDITURES

Euromonitor Publications Limited, 87-88 Turnmill Street, London EC1M 5QU, England; *International Marketing Data and Statistics.*

Inter-American Development Bank, 1300 New York Avenue, NW, Washington, D.C. 20577 (202) 623-1753; *Economic and Social Progress in Latin America.*

GUINEA - STEEL - See GUINEA - MINING AND MINERAL PRODUCTS

GUINEA - STOCKS - COMMODITY - MARKET PRICE - INDEX

Food and Agricultural Organization of the United Nations (FAO) Via delle Terme di Caracalla, 00100 Rome, Italy (Telephone Number in U.S. (202) 653-2400); *The State of Food and Agriculture.*

GUINEA - SUGAR PRODUCTION - See GUINEA - CROPS

GUINEA - TAXATION

G.K. Hall and Company, 70 Lincoln Street, Boston, Massachusetts 02111 (617) 423-3990; *The World in Figures.*

Inter-American Development Bank, 1300 New York Avenue, NW, Washington, D.C. 20577 (202) 623-1753; *Economic and Social Progress in Latin America.*

GUINEA - TELEGRAPH SERVICE

Statistical Office of the United Nations, Publishing Service, New York, New York 10017 (800) 253-9646; *Statistical Yearbook.*

GUINEA - TELEPHONES IN USE

American Telephone and Telegraph Company, 26 Parsippany Road, Whippany, New Jersey 07981 (800) 338-4038; *The World's Telephones.*

G.K. Hall and Company, 70 Lincoln Street, Boston, Massachusetts 02111 (617) 423-3990; *The World in Figures.*

Statistical Office of the United Nations, Publishing Service, New York, New York 10017 (800) 253-9646; *Statistical Yearbook.*

GUINEA - TELEVISION BROADCASTING - See GUINEA - BROADCASTING

GUINEA - TEXTILE INDUSTRY

G.K. Hall and Company, 70 Lincoln Street, Boston, Massachusetts 02111 (617) 423-3990; *The World in Figures.*

GUINEA - TOBACCO PRODUCTION

Facts on File, 460 Park Avenue South, New York, New York 10016 (800) 443-8323; *The New Book of World Rankings.*

Statistical Office of the United Nations, Publishing Service, New York, New York 10017 (800) 253-9646; *Statistical Yearbook.*

GUINEA - TOURISM

Facts on File, 460 Park Avenue South, New York, New York 10016 (800) 443-8323; *The New Book of World Rankings.*

G.K. Hall and Company, 70 Lincoln Street, Boston, Massachusetts 02111 (617) 423-3990; *The World in Figures.*

United Nations Economic Commission for Africa, Africa Hall, Post Office Box 3001, Addis Ababa, Ethiopia (Telephone Number in U.S. (800) 253-9646); *African Statistical Yearbook.*

GUINEA - TRACTORS IN USE

Statistical Office of the United Nations, Publishing Service, New York, New York 10017 (800) 253-9646; *Statistical Yearbook.*

GUINEA - TRADE - See GUINEA - FOREIGN TRADE

GUINEA - TRANSPORTATION AND COMMUNICATION

Facts on File, 460 Park Avenue South, New York, New York 10016 (800) 443-8323; *The New Book of World Rankings.*

G.K. Hall and Company, 70 Lincoln Street, Boston, Massachusetts 02111 (617) 423-3990; *The World in Figures.*

Inter-American Development Bank, 1300 New York Avenue, NW, Washington, D.C. 20577 (202) 623-1753; *Economic and Social Progress in Latin America.*

United Nations Economic Commission for Africa, Africa Hall, Post Office Box 3001, Addis Ababa, Ethiopia (Telephone Number in U.S. (800) 253-9646); *African Statistical Yearbook.*

GUINEA - UNEMPLOYMENT

Euromonitor Publications Limited, 87-88 Turnmill Street, London EC1M 5QU, England; *International Marketing Data and Statistics.*

GUINEA - VITAL STATISTICS

Euromonitor Publications Limited, 87-88 Turnmill Street, London EC1M 5QU, England; *International Marketing Data and Statistics.*

G.K. Hall and Company, 70 Lincoln Street, Boston, Massachusetts 02111 (617) 423-3990; *The World in Figures.*

Statistical Office of the United Nations, Publishing Service, New York, New York 10017 (800) 253-9646; *Statistical Yearbook.*

World Health Organization, Office of Publications, Avenue Appia, CH-1211 Geneva 27, Switzerland (Telephone Number in U.S. (518) 436-9686); *World Health Statistics Annual.*

GUINEA - WAGES

G.K. Hall and Company, 70 Lincoln Street, Boston, Massachusetts 02111 (617) 423-3990; *The World in Figures.*

GUINEA - WEATHER

Facts on File, 460 Park Avenue South, New York, New York 10016 (800) 443-8323; *The New Book of World Rankings.*

G.K. Hall and Company, 70 Lincoln Street, Boston, Massachusetts 02111 (617) 423-3990; *The World in Figures.*

GUINEA - WELFARE

Inter-American Development Bank, 1300 New York Avenue, NW, Washington, D.C. 20577 (202) 623-1753; *Economic and Social Progress in Latin America.*

GUINEA - WHEAT PRODUCTION AND PRICES - See GUINEA - CROPS

GUINEA - WHOLESALE PRICES

Inter-American Development Bank, 1300 New York Avenue, NW, Washington, D.C. 20577 (202) 623-1753; *Economic and Social Progress in Latin America.*

GUINEA - WHOLESALE TRADE

Inter-American Development Bank, 1300 New York Avenue, NW, Washington, D.C. 20577 (202) 623-1753; *Economic and Social Progress in Latin America.*

GUINEA - WINE PRODUCTION

Facts on File, 460 Park Avenue South, New York, New York 10016 (800) 443-8323; *The New Book of World Rankings.*

GUINEA - WOOL PRODUCTION

Facts on File, 460 Park Avenue South, New York, New York 10016 (800) 443-8323; *The New Book of World Rankings.*

GUINEA - ZOOS AND BOTANICAL GARDENS

United Nations Educational, Scientific and Cultural Organization (UNESCO), 7 Place de Fontenoy, F-75700 Paris, France (Telephone Number in U.S. (212) 963-5981); *Statistical Yearbook.*

Guinea Bissau - National Statistical Office

Direction de la Statistique, Commissariat d'Etat du Development Economique et du Plan, Bissau, Guinea Bissau.

Guinea Bissau - Primary Statistics Sources

Direccao Geral de Estatistica, Bissau, Guinea Bissau; *Anuario estatistico* (Statistical Yearbook); and *Boletim trimestal de estatistica* (Quarterly Bulletin of Statistics).

GUINEA BISSAU - AGRICULTURE

Facts on File, 460 Park Avenue South, New York, New York 10016 (800) 443-8323; *The New Book of World Rankings.*

Food and Agricultural Organization of the United Nations (FAO) Via delle Terme di Caracalla, 00100 Rome, Italy (Telephone Number in U.S. (202) 653-2400); *Production Yearbook, The State of Food and Agriculture,* and *Trade Yearbook.*

G.K. Hall and Company, 70 Lincoln Street, Boston, Massachusetts 02111 (617) 423-3990; *The World in Figures.*

Statistical Office of the United Nations, Publishing Service, New York, New York 10017 (800) 253-9646; *Statistical Yearbook,* and *Survey of Economic and Social Conditions in Africa.*

United Nations Economic Commission for Africa, Africa Hall, Post Office Box 3001, Addis Ababa, Ethiopia (Telephone Number in U.S. (800) 253-9646); *African Statistical Yearbook.*

The World Bank, 1818 H Street, NW, Washington, D.C. 20433 (202) 477-1234; *World Tables.*

GUINEA BISSAU - AIRLINE SERVICE

Facts on File, 460 Park Avenue South, New York, New York 10016 (800) 443-8323; *The New Book of World Rankings.*

G.K. Hall and Company, 70 Lincoln Street, Boston, Massachusetts 02111 (617) 423-3990; *The World in Figures.*

United Nations Economic Commission for Africa, Africa Hall, Post Office Box 3001, Addis Ababa, Ethiopia (Telephone Number in U.S. (800) 253-9646); *African Statistical Yearbook.*

GUINEA BISSAU - ALUMINUM PRODUCTION AND CONSUMPTION - See GUINEA BISSAU - MINING AND MINERAL PRODUCTS

GUINEA BISSAU - ANIMAL HEALTH

Food and Agricultural Organization of the United Nations (FAO), Via delle Terme di Caracalla, 00100 Rome, Italy (Telephone Number in U.S. (202) 653-2400); *Animal Health Yearbook.*

GUINEA BISSAU - AREA AND DENSITY OF POPULATION

African Development Bank, 01 BP 1387, Abidjan 01, Cote D'Ivoire; *Selected Statistics on Regional Member Countries.*

Facts on File, 460 Park Avenue South, New York, New York 10016 (800) 443-8323; *The New Book of World Rankings.*

Food and Agricultural Organization of the United Nations (FAO) Via delle Terme di Caracalla, 00100 Rome, Italy (Telephone Number in U.S. (202) 653-2400); *The State of Food and Agriculture.*

G.K. Hall and Company, 70 Lincoln Street, Boston, Massachusetts 02111 (617) 423-3990; *The World in Figures.*

Statistical Office of the United Nations, Publishing Service, New York, New York 10017 (800) 253-9646; *Statistical Yearbook,* and *Survey of Economic and Social Conditions in Africa.*

GUINEA BISSAU - ARMS EXPORTS AND IMPORTS

U.S. Arms Control and Disarmament Agency, 320 Twenty-first Street, Northwest, Washington, D.C. 20451 (202) 647-8677; *World Military Expenditures and Arms Transfers.*

GUINEA BISSAU - BALANCE OF PAYMENTS

African Development Bank, 01 BP 1387, Abidjan 01, Cote D'Ivoire; *Selected Statistics on Regional Member Countries.*

The Economist Intelligence Unit, 111 West 57th Street, New York, New York 10019 (800) 938-4685; *The World Market Atlas.*

G.K. Hall and Company, 70 Lincoln Street, Boston, Massachusetts 02111 (617) 423-3990; *The World in Figures.*

United Nations Economic Commission for Africa, Africa Hall, Post Office Box 3001, Addis Ababa, Ethiopia (Telephone Number in U.S. (800) 253-9646); *African Statistical Yearbook.*

GUINEA BISSAU - BANKING

Facts on File, 460 Park Avenue South, New York, New York 10016 (800) 443-8323; *The New Book of World Rankings.*

G.K. Hall and Company, 70 Lincoln Street, Boston, Massachusetts 02111 (617) 423-3990; *The World in Figures.*

United Nations Economic Commission for Africa, Africa Hall, Post Office Box 3001, Addis Ababa, Ethiopia (Telephone Number in U.S. (800) 253-9646); *African Statistical Yearbook.*

GUINEA BISSAU - BARLEY PRODUCTION - See GUINEA BISSAU - CROPS

GUINEA BISSAU - BEER PRODUCTION

Facts on File, 460 Park Avenue South, New York, New York 10016 (800) 443-8323; *The New Book of World Rankings.*

GUINEA BISSAU - BIRTH RATES

Facts on File, 460 Park Avenue South, New York, New York 10016 (800) 443-8323; *The New Book of World Rankings.*

Statistical Office of the United Nations, Publishing Service, New York, New York 10017 (800) 253-9646; *Demographic Yearbook, Statistical Yearbook,* and *Survey of Economic and Social Conditions in Africa.*

The World Bank, 1818 H Street, NW, Washington, D.C. 20433 (202) 477-1234; *World Tables.*

GUINEA BISSAU - BONDS

G.K. Hall and Company, 70 Lincoln Street, Boston, Massachusetts 02111 (617) 423-3990; *The World in Figures.*

GUINEA BISSAU - BOOK PRODUCTION

G.K. Hall and Company, 70 Lincoln Street, Boston, Massachusetts 02111 (617) 423-3990; *The World in Figures.*

GUINEA BISSAU - BROADCASTING

Billboard Limited, Post Office Box 9027, 1006 AA Amsterdam, The Netherlands (Telephone Number in U.S. (212) 764-7300); *World Radio TV Handbook.*

Facts on File, 460 Park Avenue South, New York, New York 10016 (800) 443-8323; *The New Book of World Rankings.*

G.K. Hall and Company, 70 Lincoln Street, Boston, Massachusetts 02111 (617) 423-3990; *The World in Figures.*

GUINEA BISSAU - BUSINESS

G.K. Hall and Company, 70 Lincoln Street, Boston, Massachusetts 02111 (617) 423-3990; *The World in Figures.*

GUINEA BISSAU - CASHEW NUT PRODUCTION - See GUINEA BISSAU - CROPS

GUINEA BISSAU - CATTLE - See GUINEA BISSAU - LIVESTOCK AND POULTRY

GUINEA BISSAU - CALORIE SUPPLY

African Development Bank, 01 BP 1387, Abidjan 01, Cote D'Ivoire; *Selected Statistics on Regional Member Countries.*

Food and Agricultural Organization of the United Nations (FAO) Via delle Terme di Caracalla, 00100 Rome, Italy (Telephone Number in U.S. (202) 653-2400); *The State of Food and Agriculture.*

GUINEA BISSAU - CEMENT PRODUCTION - See GUINEA BISSAU - MINING AND MINERAL PRODUCTS

GUINEA BISSAU - CHEMICAL (ORGANIC) PRODUCTION - See GUINEA BISSAU - MINING AND MINERAL PRODUCTS

GUINEA BISSAU - CHICKENS - See GUINEA BISSAU - LIVESTOCK AND POULTRY

GUINEA BISSAU - CIGARETTE PRODUCTION - See GUINEA BISSAU - TOBACCO PRODUCTION

GUINEA BISSAU - CLASS STRUCTURE

G.K. Hall and Company, 70 Lincoln Street, Boston, Massachusetts 02111 (617) 423-3990; *The World in Figures.*

GUINEA BISSAU - CLIMATE

Facts on File, 460 Park Avenue South, New York, New York 10016 (800) 443-8323; *The New Book of World Rankings.*

G.K. Hall and Company, 70 Lincoln Street, Boston, Massachusetts 02111 (617) 423-3990; *The World in Figures.*

GUINEA BISSAU - COAL PRODUCTION - See GUINEA BISSAU - MINING AND MINERAL PRODUCTS

GUINEA BISSAU - COFFEE PRODUCTION - See GUINEA BISSAU - CROPS

GUINEA BISSAU - COMMUNICATIONS

G.K. Hall and Company, 70 Lincoln Street, Boston, Massachusetts 02111 (617) 423-3990; *The World in Figures.*

United Nations Economic Commission for Africa, Africa Hall, Post Office Box 3001, Addis Ababa, Ethiopia (Telephone Number in U.S. (800) 253-9646); *African Statistical Yearbook.*

GUINEA BISSAU - CONSTRUCTION INDUSTRY

Facts on File, 460 Park Avenue South, New York, New York 10016 (800) 443-8323; *The New Book of World Rankings.*

United Nations Economic Commission for Africa, Africa Hall, Post Office Box 3001, Addis Ababa, Ethiopia (Telephone Number in U.S. (800) 253-9646); *African Statistical Yearbook.*

GUINEA BISSAU - CONSUMER PRICE INDEX

African Development Bank, 01 BP 1387, Abidjan 01, Cote D'Ivoire; *Selected Statistics on Regional Member Countries.*

G.K. Hall and Company, 70 Lincoln Street, Boston, Massachusetts 02111 (617) 423-3990; *The World in Figures.*

Statistical Office of the United Nations, Publishing Service, New York, New York 10017 (800) 253-9646; *Survey of Economic and Social Conditions in Africa.*

GUINEA BISSAU - CONSUMPTION

African Development Bank, 01 BP 1387, Abidjan 01, Cote D'Ivoire; *Selected Statistics on Regional Member Countries.*

G.K. Hall and Company, 70 Lincoln Street, Boston, Massachusetts 02111 (617) 423-3990; *The World in Figures.*

Statistical Office of the United Nations, Publishing Service, New York, New York 10017 (800) 253-9646; *Survey of Economic and Social Conditions in Africa.*

GUINEA BISSAU - COPPER PRODUCTION - See GUINEA BISSAU - MINING AND MINERAL PRODUCTS

GUINEA BISSAU - CORN PRODUCTION - See GUINEA BISSAU - CROPS

GUINEA BISSAU - CORPORATE TAXES - See GUINEA BISSAU - TAXATION

GUINEA BISSAU - COTTON PRODUCTION - See GUINEA BISSAU - CROPS

GUINEA BISSAU - CROPS

Facts on File, 460 Park Avenue South, New York, New York 10016 (800) 443-8323; *The New Book of World Rankings.*

Food and Agricultural Organization of the United Nations (FAO), Via delle Terme di Caracalla, 00100 Rome, Italy (Telephone Number in U.S. (202) 653-2400); *Production Yearbook* and *The State of Food and Agriculture.*

G.K. Hall and Company, 70 Lincoln Street, Boston, Massachusetts 02111 (617) 423-3990; *The World in Figures.*

Statistical Office of the United Nations, Publishing Service, New York, New York 10017 (800) 253-9646; *Statistical Yearbook.*

United Nations Economic Commission for Africa, Africa Hall, Post Office Box 3001, Addis Ababa, Ethiopia (Telephone Number in U.S. (800) 253-9646); *African Statistical Yearbook.*

GUINEA BISSAU - CUSTOMS DUTIES

G.K. Hall and Company, 70 Lincoln Street, Boston, Massachusetts 02111 (617) 423-3990; *The World in Figures.*

GUINEA BISSAU - DAIRY PRODUCTS

Facts on File, 460 Park Avenue South, New York, New York 10016 (800) 443-8323; *The New Book of World Rankings.*

Food and Agricultural Organization of the United Nations (FAO) Via delle Terme di Caracalla, 00100 Rome, Italy (Telephone Number in U.S. (202) 653-2400); *Production Yearbook* and *The State of Food*

and Agriculture.

GUINEA BISSAU - DEATH RATES

G.K. Hall and Company, 70 Lincoln Street, Boston, Massachusetts 02111 (617) 423-3990; *The World in Figures.*

Statistical Office of the United Nations, Publishing Service, New York, New York 10017 (800) 253-9646; *Statistical Yearbook*, and *Survey of Economic and Social Conditions in Africa.*

World Health Organization, Office of Publications, Avenue Appia, CH-1211 Geneva 27, Switzerland (Telephone Number in U.S. (518) 436-9686); *World Health Statistics Annual.*

GUINEA BISSAU - DEFENSE EXPENDITURES

G.K. Hall and Company, 70 Lincoln Street, Boston, Massachusetts 02111 (617) 423-3990; *The World in Figures.*

U.S. Arms Control and Disarmament Agency, 320 Twenty-first Street, Northwest, Washington, D.C. 20451 (202) 647-8677; *World Military Expenditures and Arms Transfers.*

GUINEA BISSAU - DEMOGRAPHY

The Economist Intelligence Unit, 111 West 57th Street, New York, New York 10019 (800) 938-4685; *The World Market Atlas.*

Facts on File, 460 Park Avenue South, New York, New York 10016 (800) 443-8323; *The New Book of World Rankings.*

G.K. Hall and Company, 70 Lincoln Street, Boston, Massachusetts 02111 (617) 423-3990; *The World in Figures.*

Statistical Office of the United Nations, Publishing Service, New York, New York 10017 (800) 253-9646; *Survey of Economic and Social Conditions in Africa.*

GUINEA BISSAU - DEVELOPMENT ASSISTANCE

G.K. Hall and Company, 70 Lincoln Street, Boston, Massachusetts 02111 (617) 423-3990; *The World in Figures.*

Statistical Office of the United Nations, Publishing Service, New York, New York 10017 (800) 253-9646; *Statistical Yearbook.*

GUINEA BISSAU - DIAMOND PRODUCTION - See GUINEA BISSAU - MINING AND MINERAL PRODUCTS

GUINEA BISSAU - DISEASES

G.K. Hall and Company, 70 Lincoln Street, Boston, Massachusetts 02111 (617) 423-3990; *The World in Figures.*

World Health Organization, Office of Publications, Avenue Appia, CH-1211 Geneva 27, Switzerland (Telephone Number in U.S. (518) 436-9686); *World Health Statistics Annual.*

GUINEA BISSAU - DIVORCE RATES

Facts on File, 460 Park Avenue South, New York, New York 10016 (800) 443-8323; *The New Book of World Rankings.*

Statistical Office of the United Nations, Publishing Service, New York, New York 10017 (800) 253-9646; *Demographic Yearbook*, and *Statistical Yearbook.*

GUINEA BISSAU - DOMESTIC PRODUCT

G.K. Hall and Company, 70 Lincoln Street, Boston, Massachusetts 02111 (617) 423-3990; *The World in Figures.*

GUINEA BISSAU - ECONOMY

African Development Bank, 01 BP 1387, Abidjan 01, Cote D'Ivoire; *Selected Statistics on Regional Member Countries.*

Facts on File, 460 Park Avenue South, New York, New York 10016 (800) 443-8323; *The New Book of World Rankings.*

G.K. Hall and Company, 70 Lincoln Street, Boston, Massachusetts 02111 (617) 423-3990; *The World in Figures.*

Statistical Office of the United Nations, Publishing Service, New York, New York 10017 (800) 253-9646; *Foreign Trade Statistics for Africa.*

GUINEA BISSAU - EDUCATION

African Development Bank, 01 BP 1387, Abidjan 01, Cote D'Ivoire; *Selected Statistics on Regional Member Countries.*

The Economist Intelligence Unit, 111 West 57th Street, New York, New York 10019 (800) 938-4685; *The World Market Atlas.*

Facts on File, 460 Park Avenue South, New York, New York 10016 (800) 443-8323; *The New Book of World Rankings.*

G.K. Hall and Company, 70 Lincoln Street, Boston, Massachusetts 02111 (617) 423-3990; *The World in Figures.*

Statistical Office of the United Nations, Publishing Service, New York, New York 10017 (800) 253-9646; *Survey of Economic and Social Conditions in Africa.*

United Nations Economic Commission for Africa, Africa Hall, Post Office Box 3001, Addis Ababa, Ethiopia (Telephone Number in U.S. (800) 253-9646); *African Statistical Yearbook.*

United Nations Educational, Scientific and Cultural Organization (UNESCO), 7 Place de Fontenoy, F-75700 Paris, France (Telephone Number in U.S. (212) 963-5981); *Statistical Yearbook.*

The World Bank, 1818 H Street, NW, Washington, D.C. 20433 (202) 477-1234; *World Tables.*

GUINEA BISSAU - EGG PRODUCTION - See GUINEA BISSAU - DAIRY PRODUCTS

GUINEA BISSAU - ELECTRICITY

Facts on File, 460 Park Avenue South, New York, New York 10016 (800) 443-8323; *The New Book of World Rankings.*

Statistical Office of the United Nations, Publishing Service, New York, New York 10017 (800) 253-9646; *Survey of Economic and Social Conditions in Africa.*

United Nations Economic Commission for Africa, Africa Hall, Post Office Box 3001, Addis Ababa, Ethiopia (Telephone Number in U.S. (800) 253-9646); *African Statistical Yearbook.*

GUINEA BISSAU - EMPLOYMENT

Facts on File, 460 Park Avenue South, New York, New York 10016 (800) 443-8323; *The New Book of World Rankings.*

Statistical Office of the United Nations, Publishing Service, New York, New York 10017 (800) 253-9646; *Survey of Economic and Social Conditions in Africa.*

United Nations Economic Commission for Africa, Africa Hall, Post Office Box 3001, Addis Ababa, Ethiopia (Telephone Number in U.S. (800) 253-9646); *African Statistical Yearbook.*

GUINEA BISSAU - ENERGY

Facts on File, 460 Park Avenue South, New York, New York 10016 (800) 443-8323; *The New Book of World Rankings.*

Food and Agricultural Organization of the United Nations (FAO) Via delle Terme di Caracalla, 00100 Rome, Italy (Telephone Number in U.S. (202) 653-2400); *The State of Food and Agriculture.*

G.K. Hall and Company, 70 Lincoln Street, Boston, Massachusetts 02111 (617) 423-3990; *The World in Figures.*

Statistical Office of the United Nations, Publishing Service, New York, New York 10017 (800) 253-9646; *Energy Statistics Yearbook,* and *Statistical Yearbook.*

United Nations Economic Commission for Africa, Africa Hall, Post Office Box 3001, Addis Ababa, Ethiopia (Telephone Number in U.S. (800) 253-9646); *African Statistical Yearbook.*

GUINEA BISSAU - EXCHANGE RATES

African Development Bank, 01 BP 1387, Abidjan 01, Cote D'Ivoire; *Selected Statistics on Regional Member Countries.*

Statistical Office of the United Nations, Publishing Service, New York, New York 10017 (800) 253-9646; *Foreign Trade Statistics for Africa,* and *Statistical Yearbook.*

GUINEA BISSAU - EXPORTS

African Development Bank, 01 BP 1387, Abidjan 01, Cote D'Ivoire; *Selected Statistics on Regional Member Countries.*

The Economist Intelligence Unit, 111 West 57th Street, New York, New York 10019 (800) 938-4685; *The World Market Atlas.*

Food and Agricultural Organization of the United Nations (FAO) Via delle Terme di Caracalla, 00100 Rome, Italy (Telephone Number in U.S. (202) 653-2400); *The State of Food and Agriculture.*

G.K. Hall and Company, 70 Lincoln Street, Boston, Massachusetts 02111 (617) 423-3990; *The World in Figures.*

International Monetary Fund, 700 Nineteenth Street, NW, Washington, D.C. 20431 (202) 623-7000; *Direction of Trade Statistics.*

Statistical Office of the United Nations, Publishing Service, New York, New York 10017 (800) 253-9646; *Foreign Trade Statistics for Africa,* and *Survey of Economic and Social Conditions in Africa.*

United Nations Economic Commission for Africa, Africa Hall, Post Office Box 3001, Addis Ababa, Ethiopia (Telephone Number in U.S. (800) 253-9646); *African Statistical Yearbook.*

The World Bank, 1818 H Street, NW, Washington, D.C. 20433 (202) 477-1234; *World Tables.*

GUINEA BISSAU - EXTERNAL INDEBTEDNESS

African Development Bank, 01 BP 1387, Abidjan 01, Cote D'Ivoire; *Selected Statistics on Regional Member Countries.*

Statistical Office of the United Nations, Publishing Service, New York, New York 10017 (800) 253-9646; *Survey of Economic and Social Conditions in Africa.*

The World Bank, 1818 H Street, NW, Washington, D.C. 20433 (202) 477-1234; *World Tables.*

GUINEA BISSAU - EXTERNAL TRADE

African Development Bank, 01 BP 1387, Abidjan 01, Cote D'Ivoire; *Selected Statistics on Regional Member Countries.*

Food and Agricultural Organization of the United Nations (FAO) Via delle Terme di Caracalla, 00100 Rome, Italy (Telephone Number in U.S. (202) 653-2400); *The State of Food and Agriculture,* and *Trade Yearbook.*

G.K. Hall and Company, 70 Lincoln Street, Boston, Massachusetts 02111 (617) 423-3990; *The World in Figures.*

Statistical Office of the United Nations, Publishing Service, New York, New York 10017 (800) 253-9646; *Statistical Yearbook.*

GUINEA BISSAU - FARM CROPS - See GUINEA BISSAU - CROPS

GUINEA BISSAU - FERTILITY RATES

Facts on File, 460 Park Avenue South, New York, New York 10016 (800) 443-8323; *The New Book of World Rankings.*

Statistical Office of the United Nations, Publishing Service, New York, New York 10017 (800) 253-9646; *Survey of Economic and Social Conditions in Africa.*

The World Bank, 1818 H Street, NW, Washington, D.C. 20433 (202) 477-1234; *World Tables.*

GUINEA BISSAU - FERTILIZER

Food and Agricultural Organization of the United Nations (FAO) Via delle Terme di Caracalla, 00100 Rome, Italy (Telephone Number in U.S. (202) 653-2400); *The State of Food and Agriculture.*

GUINEA BISSAU - FETAL MORTALITY

Statistical Office of the United Nations, Publishing Service, New York, New York 10017 (800) 253-9646; *Demographic Yearbook.*

GUINEA BISSAU - FINANCE

African Development Bank, 01 BP 1387, Abidjan 01, Cote D'Ivoire; *Selected Statistics on Regional Member Countries.*

Facts on File, 460 Park Avenue South, New York, New York 10016 (800) 443-8323; *The New Book of World Rankings.*

G.K. Hall and Company, 70 Lincoln Street, Boston, Massachusetts 02111 (617) 423-3990; *The World in Figures.*

United Nations Economic Commission for Africa, Africa Hall, Post Office Box 3001, Addis Ababa, Ethiopia (Telephone Number in U.S. (800) 253-9646); *African Statistical Yearbook.*

GUINEA BISSAU - FISHERIES

Facts on File, 460 Park Avenue South, New York, New York 10016 (800) 443-8323; *The New Book of World Rankings.*

Food and Agricultural Organization of the United Nations (FAO) Via delle Terme di Caracalla, 00100 Rome, Italy (Telephone Number in U.S. (202) 653-2400); *The State of Food and Agriculture,* and *Yearbook of Fishery Statistics.*

Statistical Office of the United Nations, Publishing Service, New York, New York 10017 (800) 253-9646; *Statistical Yearbook,* and *Survey of Economic and Social Conditions in Africa.*

United Nations Economic Commission for Africa, Africa Hall, Post Office Box 3001, Addis Ababa, Ethiopia (Telephone Number in U.S. (800) 253-9646); *African Statistical Yearbook.*

GUINEA BISSAU - FOOD

African Development Bank, 01 BP 1387, Abidjan 01, Cote D'Ivoire; *Selected Statistics on Regional Member Countries.*

Food and Agricultural Organization of the United Nations (FAO), Via delle Terme di Caracalla, 00100 Rome, Italy (Telephone Number in U.S. (202) 653-2400); *Production Yearbook,* and *The State of Food and Agriculture.*

G.K. Hall and Company, 70 Lincoln Street, Boston, Massachusetts 02111 (617) 423-3990; *The World in Figures.*

GUINEA BISSAU - FOREIGN AID

G.K. Hall and Company, 70 Lincoln Street, Boston, Massachusetts 02111 (617) 423-3990; *The World in Figures.*

GUINEA BISSAU - FOREIGN TRADE

Facts on File, 460 Park Avenue South, New York, New York 10016 (800) 443-8323; *The New Book of World Rankings.*

Food and Agricultural Organization of the United Nations (FAO) Via delle Terme di Caracalla, 00100 Rome, Italy (Telephone Number in U.S. (202) 653-2400); *The State of Food and Agriculture.*

G.K. Hall and Company, 70 Lincoln Street, Boston, Massachusetts 02111 (617) 423-3990; *The World in Figures.*

Statistical Office of the United Nations, Publishing Service, New York, New York 10017 (800) 253-9646; *Foreign Trade Statistics for Africa, International Trade Statistics Yearbook,* and *Statistical Yearbook.*

United Nations Economic Commission for Africa, Africa Hall, Post Office Box 3001, Addis Ababa, Ethiopia (Telephone Number in U.S. (800) 253-9646); *African Statistical Yearbook.*

The World Bank, 1818 H Street, NW, Washington, D.C. 20433 (202) 477-1234; *World Tables.*

GUINEA BISSAU - FORESTRY AND FOREST PRODUCTS

Facts on File, 460 Park Avenue South, New York, New York 10016 (800) 443-8323; *The New Book of World Rankings.*

Food and Agricultural Organization of the United Nations (FAO) Via delle Terme di Caracalla, 00100 Rome, Italy (Telephone Number in U.S. (202) 653-2400); *The State of Food and Agriculture* and *Yearbook of Forest Products.*

G.K. Hall and Company, 70 Lincoln Street, Boston, Massachusetts 02111 (617) 423-3990; *The World in Figures.*

Statistical Office of the United Nations, Publishing Service, New York, New York 10017 (800) 253-9646; *Statistical Yearbook.*

United Nations Economic Commission for Africa, Africa Hall, Post Office Box 3001, Addis Ababa, Ethiopia (Telephone Number in U.S. (800) 253-9646); *African Statistical Yearbook.*

United Nations Educational, Scientific and Cultural Organization (UNESCO), 7 Place de Fontenoy, F-75700 Paris, France (Telephone Number in U.S. (212) 963-5981); *Statistical Yearbook.*

GUINEA BISSAU - GAS PRODUCTION - See GUINEA BISSAU - MINING AND MINERAL PRODUCTS

GUINEA BISSAU - GENERAL MORTALITY

Statistical Office of the United Nations, Publishing Service, New York, New York 10017 (800) 253-9646; *Demographic Yearbook.*

GUINEA BISSAU - GEOGRAPHIC DATA

Facts on File, 460 Park Avenue South, New York, New York 10016 (800) 443-8323; *The New Book of World Rankings.*

GUINEA BISSAU - GOATS - See GUINEA BISSAU - LIVESTOCK AND POULTRY

GUINEA BISSAU - GOLD HOLDINGS

The World Bank, 1818 H Street, NW, Washington, D.C. 20433 (202) 477-1234; *World Tables.*

GUINEA BISSAU - GOLD PRODUCTION AND CONSUMPTION - See GUINEA BISSAU - MINING AND MINERAL PRODUCTS

GUINEA BISSAU - GOVERNMENT

G.K. Hall and Company, 70 Lincoln Street, Boston, Massachusetts 02111 (617) 423-3990; *The World in Figures.*

GUINEA BISSAU - GOVERNMENT EXPENDITURE

The World Bank, 1818 H Street, NW, Washington, D.C. 20433 (202) 477-1234; *World Tables.*

GUINEA BISSAU - GOVERNMENT REVENUE

Statistical Office of the United Nations, Publishing Service, New York, New York 10017 (800) 253-9646; *Survey of Economic and Social Conditions in Africa.*

The World Bank, 1818 H Street, NW, Washington, D.C. 20433 (202) 477-1234; *World Tables.*

GUINEA BISSAU - GRAIN PRODUCTION - See GUINEA BISSAU - CROPS

GUINEA BISSAU - GROSS DOMESTIC PRODUCT

African Development Bank, 01 BP 1387, Abidjan 01, Cote D'Ivoire; *Selected Statistics on Regional Member Countries.*

The Economist Intelligence Unit, 111 West 57th Street, New York, New York 10019 (800) 938-4685; *The World Market Atlas.*

Facts on File, 460 Park Avenue South, New York, New York 10016 (800) 443-8323; *The New Book of World Rankings.*

G.K. Hall and Company, 70 Lincoln Street, Boston, Massachusetts 02111 (617) 423-3990; *The World in Figures.*

Statistical Office of the United Nations, Publishing Service, New York, New York 10017 (800) 253-9646; *Statistical Yearbook,* and *Survey of Economic and Social Conditions in Africa.*

United Nations Economic Commission for Africa, Africa Hall, Post Office Box 3001, Addis Ababa, Ethiopia (Telephone Number in U.S. (800) 253-9646); *African Statistical Yearbook.*

The World Bank, 1818 H Street, NW, Washington, D.C. 20433 (202) 477-1234; *World Tables.*

GUINEA BISSAU - GROSS NATIONAL PRODUCTION

The World Bank, 1818 H Street, NW, Washington, D.C. 20433 (202) 477-1234; *World Tables.*

U.S. Arms Control and Disarmament Agency, 320 Twenty-first Street, Northwest, Washington, D.C. 20451 (202) 647-8677; *World Military Expenditures and Arms Transfers.*

GUINEA BISSAU - GROUNDNUTS PRODUCTION - See GUINEA BISSAU - CROPS

GUINEA BISSAU - HEALTH

African Development Bank, 01 BP 1387, Abidjan 01, Cote D'Ivoire; *Selected Statistics on Regional Member Countries.*

Facts on File, 460 Park Avenue South, New York, New York 10016 (800) 443-8323; *The New Book of World Rankings.*

G.K. Hall and Company, 70 Lincoln Street, Boston, Massachusetts 02111 (617) 423-3990; *The World in Figures.*

Statistical Office of the United Nations, Publishing Service, New York, New York 10017 (800) 253-9646; *Statistical Yearbook.*

United Nations Economic Commission for Africa, Africa Hall, Post Office Box 3001, Addis Ababa, Ethiopia (Telephone Number in U.S. (800) 253-9646); *African Statistical Yearbook.*

World Health Organization, Office of Publications, Avenue Appia, CH-1211 Geneva 27, Switzerland (Telephone Number in U.S. (518) 436-9686); *World Health Statistics Annual.*

GUINEA BISSAU - HIDE PRODUCTION

Food and Agricultural Organization of the United Nations (FAO), Via delle Terme di Caracalla, 00100 Rome, Italy (Telephone Number in U.S. (202) 653-2400); *Production Yearbook.*

GUINEA BISSAU - HIGHWAYS

G.K. Hall and Company, 70 Lincoln Street, Boston, Massachusetts 02111 (617) 423-3990; *The World in Figures.*

Statistical Office of the United Nations, Publishing Service, New York, New York 10017 (800) 253-9646; *Survey of Economic and Social Conditions in Africa.*

United Nations Economic Commission for Africa, Africa Hall, Post Office Box 3001, Addis Ababa, Ethiopia (Telephone Number in U.S. (800) 253-9646); *African Statistical Yearbook.*

GUINEA BISSAU - HORSES - See GUINEA BISSAU - LIVESTOCK AND POULTRY

GUINEA BISSAU - HOUSING AND HOUSING UNITS

Facts on File, 460 Park Avenue South, New York, New York 10016 (800) 443-8323; *The New Book of World Rankings.*

GUINEA BISSAU - ILLITERATE POPULATION

The Economist Intelligence Unit, 111 West 57th Street, New York, New York 10019 (800) 938-4685; *The World Market Atlas.*

G.K. Hall and Company, 70 Lincoln Street, Boston, Massachusetts 02111 (617) 423-3990; *The World in Figures.*

United Nations Educational, Scientific and Cultural Organization (UNESCO), 7 Place de Fontenoy, F-75700 Paris, France (Telephone Number in U.S. (212) 963-5981); *Statistical Yearbook.*

GUINEA BISSAU - IMPORTS

African Development Bank, 01 BP 1387, Abidjan 01, Cote D'Ivoire; *Selected Statistics on Regional Member Countries.*

The Economist Intelligence Unit, 111 West 57th Street, New York, New York 10019 (800) 938-4685; *The World Market Atlas.*

Food and Agricultural Organization of the United Nations (FAO) Via delle Terme di Caracalla, 00100 Rome, Italy (Telephone Number in U.S. (202) 653-2400); *The State of Food and Agriculture.*

G.K. Hall and Company, 70 Lincoln Street, Boston, Massachusetts 02111 (617) 423-3990; *The World in Figures.*

International Monetary Fund, 700 Nineteenth Street, NW, Washington, D.C. 20431 (202) 623-7000; *Direction of Trade Statistics.*

Statistical Office of the United Nations, Publishing Service, New York, New York 10017 (800) 253-9646; *Foreign Trade Statistics for Africa,* and *Survey of Economic and Social Conditions in Africa.*

United Nations Economic Commission for Africa, Africa Hall, Post Office Box 3001, Addis Ababa, Ethiopia (Telephone Number in U.S. (800) 253-9646); *African Statistical Yearbook.*

The World Bank, 1818 H Street, NW, Washington, D.C. 20433 (202) 477-1234; *World Tables.*

GUINEA BISSAU - INDUSTRY

Facts on File, 460 Park Avenue South, New York, New York 10016 (800) 443-8323; *The New Book of World Rankings.*

G.K. Hall and Company, 70 Lincoln Street, Boston, Massachusetts 02111 (617) 423-3990; *The World in Figures.*

Statistical Office of the United Nations, Publishing Service, New York, New York 10017 (800) 253-9646; *Survey of Economic and Social Conditions in Africa.*

United Nations Economic Commission for Africa, Africa Hall, Post Office Box 3001, Addis Ababa, Ethiopia (Telephone Number in U.S. (800) 253-9646); *African Statistical Yearbook.*

The World Bank, 1818 H Street, NW, Washington, D.C. 20433 (202) 477-1234; *World Tables.*

GUINEA BISSAU - INFANT AND MATERNAL MORTALITY

Statistical Office of the United Nations, Publishing Service, New York, New York 10017 (800) 253-9646; *Demographic Yearbook*, *Statistical Yearbook*, and *Survey of Economic and Social Conditions in Africa*.

The World Bank, 1818 H Street, NW, Washington, D.C. 20433 (202) 477-1234; *World Tables*.

GUINEA BISSAU - INTERNATIONAL RESERVES EXCLUDING GOLD

African Development Bank, 01 BP 1387, Abidjan 01, Cote D'Ivoire; *Selected Statistics on Regional Member Countries*.

The World Bank, 1818 H Street, NW, Washington, D.C. 20433 (202) 477-1234; *World Tables*.

GUINEA BISSAU - IRON ORE PRODUCTION AND CONSUMPTION - See GUINEA BISSAU - MINING AND MINERAL PRODUCTS

GUINEA BISSAU - LABOR FORCE

African Development Bank, 01 BP 1387, Abidjan 01, Cote D'Ivoire; *Selected Statistics on Regional Member Countries*.

Facts on File, 460 Park Avenue South, New York, New York 10016 (800) 443-8323; *The New Book of World Rankings*.

Food and Agricultural Organization of the United Nations (FAO) Via delle Terme di Caracalla, 00100 Rome, Italy (Telephone Number in U.S. (202) 653-2400); *The State of Food and Agriculture*.

G.K. Hall and Company, 70 Lincoln Street, Boston, Massachusetts 02111 (617) 423-3990; *The World in Figures*.

The World Bank, 1818 H Street, NW, Washington, D.C. 20433 (202) 477-1234; *World Tables*.

GUINEA BISSAU - LAND USE

Food and Agricultural Organization of the United Nations (FAO), Via delle Terme di Caracalla, 00100 Rome, Italy (Telephone Number in U.S. (202) 653-2400); *Production Yearbook*.

G.K. Hall and Company, 70 Lincoln Street, Boston, Massachusetts 02111 (617) 423-3990; *The World in Figures*.

GUINEA BISSAU - LIBRARIES

Facts on File, 460 Park Avenue South, New York, New York 10016 (800) 443-8323; *The New Book of World Rankings*.

GUINEA BISSAU - LIFE EXPECTANCY

African Development Bank, 01 BP 1387, Abidjan 01, Cote D'Ivoire; *Selected Statistics on Regional Member Countries*.

GUINEA BISSAU - LITERACY RATE

Statistical Office of the United Nations, Publishing Service, New York, New York 10017 (800) 253-9646; *Survey of Economic and Social Conditions in Africa*.

GUINEA BISSAU - LIVESTOCK AND POULTRY

Facts on File, 460 Park Avenue South, New York, New York 10016 (800) 443-8323; *The New Book of World Rankings*.

Food and Agricultural Organization of the United Nations (FAO), Via delle Terme di Caracalla, 00100 Rome, Italy (Telephone Number in U.S. (202) 653-2400); *Production Yearbook*, and *The State of Food and Agriculture*.

G.K. Hall and Company, 70 Lincoln Street, Boston, Massachusetts 02111 (617) 423-3990; *The World in Figures*.

Statistical Office of the United Nations, Publishing Service, New York, New York 10017 (800) 253-9646; *Statistical Yearbook*, and *Survey of Economic and Social Conditions in Africa*.

United Nations Economic Commission for Africa, Africa Hall, Post Office Box 3001, Addis Ababa, Ethiopia (Telephone Number in U.S. (800) 253-9646); *African Statistical Yearbook*.

GUINEA BISSAU - LIVING LEVELS

G.K. Hall and Company, 70 Lincoln Street, Boston, Massachusetts 02111 (617) 423-3990; *The World in Figures*.

GUINEA BISSAU - MANUFACTURING

Facts on File, 460 Park Avenue South, New York, New York 10016 (800) 443-8323; *The New Book of World Rankings*.

G.K. Hall and Company, 70 Lincoln Street, Boston, Massachusetts 02111 (617) 423-3990; *The World in Figures*.

Statistical Office of the United Nations, Publishing Service, New York, New York 10017 (800) 253-9646; *Survey of Economic and Social Conditions in Africa*.

United Nations Economic Commission for Africa, Africa Hall, Post Office Box 3001, Addis Ababa, Ethiopia (Telephone Number in U.S. (800) 253-9646); *African Statistical Yearbook*.

The World Bank, 1818 H Street, NW, Washington, D.C. 20433 (202) 477-1234; *World Tables*.

GUINEA BISSAU - MARRIAGE RATES

Facts on File, 460 Park Avenue South, New York, New York 10016 (800) 443-8323; *The New Book of World Rankings*.

Statistical Office of the United Nations, Publishing Service, New York, New York 10017 (800) 253-9646; *Demographic Yearbook*, and *Statistical Yearbook*.

GUINEA BISSAU - MEAT PRODUCTION - See GUINEA BISSAU - LIVESTOCK AND POULTRY

GUINEA BISSAU - MERCHANT SHIPPING

G.K. Hall and Company, 70 Lincoln Street, Boston, Massachusetts 02111 (617) 423-3990; *The World in Figures*.

Statistical Office of the United Nations, Publishing Service, New York, New York 10017 (800) 253-9646; *Statistical Yearbook*.

United Nations Economic Commission for Africa, Africa Hall, Post Office Box 3001, Addis Ababa, Ethiopia (Telephone Number in U.S. (800) 253-9646); *African Statistical Yearbook*.

GUINEA BISSAU - MILITARY

G.K. Hall and Company, 70 Lincoln Street, Boston, Massachusetts 02111 (617) 423-3990; *The World in Figures*.

The International Institute for Strategic Studies, 23 Tavistock Street, London WC2E 7NQ, England; *The Military Balance.*

U.S. Arms Control and Disarmament Agency, 320 Twenty-first Street, Northwest, Washington, D.C. 20451 (202) 647-8677; *World Military Expenditures and Arms Transfers.*

GUINEA BISSAU - MILK PRODUCTION - See GUINEA BISSAU - DAIRY PRODUCTS

GUINEA BISSAU - MILLET PRODUCTION - See GUINEA BISSAU - CROPS

GUINEA BISSAU - MINING AND MINERAL PRODUCTS

Facts on File, 460 Park Avenue South, New York, New York 10016 (800) 443-8323; *The New Book of World Rankings.*

G.K. Hall and Company, 70 Lincoln Street, Boston, Massachusetts 02111 (617) 423-3990; *The World in Figures.*

United Nations Economic Commission for Africa, Africa Hall, Post Office Box 3001, Addis Ababa, Ethiopia (Telephone Number in U.S. (800) 253-9646); *African Statistical Yearbook.*

GUINEA BISSAU - MONEY EXCHANGE RATES

Statistical Office of the United Nations, Publishing Service, New York, New York 10017 (800) 253-9646; *Statistical Yearbook.*

GUINEA BISSAU - MONEY SUPPLY

African Development Bank, 01 BP 1387, Abidjan 01, Cote D'Ivoire; *Selected Statistics on Regional Member Countries.*

G.K. Hall and Company, 70 Lincoln Street, Boston, Massachusetts 02111 (617) 423-3990; *The World in Figures.*

The World Bank, 1818 H Street, NW, Washington, D.C. 20433 (202) 477-1234; *World Tables.*

GUINEA BISSAU - MOTION PICTURES

Statistical Office of the United Nations, Publishing Service, New York, New York 10017 (800) 253-9646; *Statistical Yearbook.*

GUINEA BISSAU - MOTOR VEHICLES IN USE

G.K. Hall and Company, 70 Lincoln Street, Boston, Massachusetts 02111 (617) 423-3990; *The World in Figures.*

Statistical Office of the United Nations, Publishing Service, New York, New York 10017 (800) 253-9646; *Survey of Economic and Social Conditions in Africa.*

GUINEA BISSAU - MUSEUMS

Facts on File, 460 Park Avenue South, New York, New York 10016 (800) 443-8323; *The New Book of World Rankings.*

GUINEA BISSAU - NATALITY - See GUINEA BISSAU - BIRTH RATES

GUINEA BISSAU - NATIONAL ACCOUNTS

African Development Bank, 01 BP 1387, Abidjan 01, Cote D'Ivoire; *Selected Statistics on Regional Member Countries.*

United Nations Economic Commission for Africa, Africa Hall, Post Office Box 3001, Addis Ababa, Ethiopia (Telephone Number in U.S. (800) 253-9646); *African Statistical Yearbook.*

GUINEA BISSAU - NATIONAL INCOME

Facts on File, 460 Park Avenue South, New York, New York 10016 (800) 443-8323; *The New Book of World Rankings.*

G.K. Hall and Company, 70 Lincoln Street, Boston, Massachusetts 02111 (617) 423-3990; *The World in Figures.*

Statistical Office of the United Nations, Publishing Service, New York, New York 10017 (800) 253-9646; *Statistical Yearbook.*

GUINEA BISSAU - NATIONAL PRODUCT

Facts on File, 460 Park Avenue South, New York, New York 10016 (800) 443-8323; *The New Book of World Rankings.*

GUINEA BISSAU - NATURAL GAS PRODUCTION - See GUINEA BISSAU - MINING AND MINERAL PRODUCTS

GUINEA BISSAU - NEWSPAPER PRODUCTION - See GUINEA BISSAU - FORESTRY AND FOREST PRODUCTS

GUINEA BISSAU - NEWSPRINT - See GUINEA BISSAU - FORESTRY AND FOREST PRODUCTS

GUINEA BISSAU - OCCUPATIONS - See GUINEA BISSAU - LABOR FORCE

GUINEA BISSAU - PALM KERNELS AND PALM OIL PRODUCTION - See GUINEA BISSAU - CROPS

GUINEA BISSAU - PAPER - See GUINEA BISSAU - FORESTRY AND FOREST PRODUCTS

GUINEA BISSAU - PEANUT PRODUCTION - See GUINEA BISSAU - CROPS

GUINEA BISSAU - PESTICIDE USE

Food and Agricultural Organization of the United Nations (FAO) Via delle Terme di Caracalla, 00100 Rome, Italy (Telephone Number in U.S. (202) 653-2400); *The State of Food and Agriculture.*

GUINEA BISSAU - PETROLEUM INDUSTRY

Facts on File, 460 Park Avenue South, New York, New York 10016 (800) 443-8323; *The New Book of World Rankings.*

Food and Agricultural Organization of the United Nations (FAO) Via delle Terme di Caracalla, 00100 Rome, Italy (Telephone Number in U.S. (202) 653-2400); *The State of Food and Agriculture.*

G.K. Hall and Company, 70 Lincoln Street, Boston, Massachusetts 02111 (617) 423-3990; *The World in Figures.*

GUINEA BISSAU - PIGS - See GUINEA BISSAU - LIVESTOCK AND POULTRY

GUINEA BISSAU - POPULATION

African Development Bank, 01 BP 1387, Abidjan 01, Cote d'Ivoire; *Selected Statistics on Regional Member Countries.*

The Economist Intelligence Unit, 111 West 57th Street, New York, New York 10019 (800) 938-4685; *The World Market Atlas.*

Facts on File, 460 Park Avenue South, New York, New York 10016 (800) 443-8323; *The New Book of World Rankings.*

Food and Agricultural Organization of the United Nations (FAO), Via delle Terme di Caracalla, 00100 Rome, Italy (Telephone Number in U.S. (202) 653-2400); *Production Yearbook.*

G.K. Hall and Company, 70 Lincoln Street, Boston, Massachusetts 02111 (617) 423-3990; *The World in Figures.*

Statistical Office of the United Nations, Publishing Service, New York, New York 10017 (800) 253-9646; *Demographic Yearbook, Statistical Yearbook,* and *Survey of Economic and Social Conditions in Africa.*

U.S. Arms Control and Disarmament Agency, 320 Twenty-first Street, Northwest, Washington, D.C. 20451 (202) 647-8677; *World Military Expenditures and Arms Transfers.*

World Health Organization, Office of Publications, Avenue Appia, CH-1211 Geneva 27, Switzerland (Telephone Number in U.S. (518) 436-9686); *World Health Statistics Annual.*

GUINEA BISSAU - POST OFFICES

Facts on File, 460 Park Avenue South, New York, New York 10016 (800) 443-8323; *The New Book of World Rankings.*

GUINEA BISSAU - POTATO PRODUCTION - See GUINEA BISSAU - CROPS

GUINEA BISSAU - PRICES

Facts on File, 460 Park Avenue South, New York, New York 10016 (800) 443-8323; *The New Book of World Rankings.*

Food and Agricultural Organization of the United Nations (FAO), Via delle Terme di Caracalla, 00100 Rome, Italy (Telephone Number in U.S. (202) 653-2400); *Production Yearbook,* and *The State of Food and Agriculture.*

G.K. Hall and Company, 70 Lincoln Street, Boston, Massachusetts 02111 (617) 423-3990; *The World in Figures.*

GUINEA BISSAU - PRODUCTION

Facts on File, 460 Park Avenue South, New York, New York 10016 (800) 443-8323; *The New Book of World Rankings.*

G.K. Hall and Company, 70 Lincoln Street, Boston, Massachusetts 02111 (617) 423-3990; *The World in Figures.*

GUINEA BISSAU - PUBLIC FINANCE

Facts on File, 460 Park Avenue South, New York, New York 10016 (800) 443-8323; *The New Book of World Rankings.*

GUINEA BISSAU - RADIO BROADCASTING - See GUINEA BISSAU - BROADCASTING

GUINEA BISSAU - RAILWAYS

G.K. Hall and Company, 70 Lincoln Street, Boston, Massachusetts 02111 (617) 423-3990; *The World in Figures.*

United Nations Economic Commission for Africa, Africa Hall, Post Office Box 3001, Addis Ababa, Ethiopia (Telephone Number in U.S. (800) 253-9646); *African Statistical Yearbook.*

GUINEA BISSAU - RELIGION

Facts on File, 460 Park Avenue South, New York, New York 10016 (800) 443-8323; *The New Book of World Rankings.*

GUINEA BISSAU - RETAIL TRADE

G.K. Hall and Company, 70 Lincoln Street, Boston, Massachusetts 02111 (617) 423-3990; *The World in Figures.*

GUINEA BISSAU - RICE PRODUCTION - See GUINEA BISSAU - CROPS

GUINEA BISSAU - ROOT AND TUBER PRODUCTION - See GUINEA BISSAU - CROPS

GUINEA BISSAU - ROUNDWOOD PRODUCTION - See GUINEA BISSAU - FORESTRY AND FOREST PRODUCTS

GUINEA BISSAU - RUBBER PRODUCTION

Facts on File, 460 Park Avenue South, New York, New York 10016 (800) 443-8323; *The New Book of World Rankings.*

GUINEA BISSAU - SAWNWOOD PRODUCTION - See GUINEA BISSAU - FORESTRY AND FOREST PRODUCTS

GUINEA BISSAU - SENIOR CITIZENS

Facts on File, 460 Park Avenue South, New York, New York 10016 (800) 443-8323; *The New Book of World Rankings.*

GUINEA BISSAU - SHEEP - See GUINEA BISSAU - LIVESTOCK AND POULTRY

GUINEA BISSAU - SILVER PRODUCTION AND CONSUMPTION - See GUINEA BISSAU - MINING AND MINERAL PRODUCTS

GUINEA BISSAU - SOCIAL DATA

African Development Bank, 01 BP 1387, Abidjan 01, Cote d'Ivoire; *Selected Statistics on Regional Member Countries.*

Facts on File, 460 Park Avenue South, New York, New York 10016 (800) 443-8323; *The New Book of World Rankings.*

G.K. Hall and Company, 70 Lincoln Street, Boston, Massachusetts 02111 (617) 423-3990; *The World in Figures.*

GUINEA BISSAU - STEEL PRODUCTION - See GUINEA BISSAU - MINING AND MINERAL PRODUCTS

GUINEA BISSAU - STOCKS - COMMODITY - MARKET PRICE - INDEX

Food and Agricultural Organization of the United Nations (FAO) Via delle Terme di Caracalla, 00100 Rome, Italy (Telephone Number in U.S. (202) 653-2400); *The State of Food and Agriculture.*

GUINEA BISSAU - SUGAR PRODUCTION - See GUINEA BISSAU - CROPS

GUINEA BISSAU - TAX REVENUE - See GUINEA BISSAU - TAXATION

GUINEA BISSAU - TAXATION

G.K. Hall and Company, 70 Lincoln Street, Boston, Massachusetts 02111 (617) 423-3990; *The World in Figures.*

The World Bank, 1818 H Street, NW, Washington, D.C. 20433 (202) 477-1234; *World Tables.*

GUINEA BISSAU - TELEGRAPH SERVICE

Statistical Office of the United Nations, Publishing Service, New York, New York 10017 (800) 253-9646; *Statistical Yearbook.*

GUINEA BISSAU - TELEPHONES IN USE

American Telephone and Telegraph Company, 26 Parsippany Road, Whippany, New Jersey 07981 (800) 338-4038; *The World's Telephones.*

G.K. Hall and Company, 70 Lincoln Street, Boston, Massachusetts 02111 (617) 423-3990; *The World in Figures.*

Statistical Office of the United Nations, Publishing Service, New York, New York 10017 (800) 253-9646; *Statistical Yearbook.*

GUINEA BISSAU - TELEVISION BROADCASTING - See GUINEA BISSAU - BROADCASTING

GUINEA BISSAU - TEXTILE INDUSTRY

G.K. Hall and Company, 70 Lincoln Street, Boston, Massachusetts 02111 (617) 423-3990; *The World in Figures.*

GUINEA BISSAU - TOBACCO PRODUCTION

Facts on File, 460 Park Avenue South, New York, New York 10016 (800) 443-8323; *The New Book of World Rankings.*

GUINEA BISSAU - TOURISM

Facts on File, 460 Park Avenue South, New York, New York 10016 (800) 443-8323; *The New Book of World Rankings.*

G.K. Hall and Company, 70 Lincoln Street, Boston, Massachusetts 02111 (617) 423-3990; *The World in Figures.*

United Nations Economic Commission for Africa, Africa Hall, Post Office Box 3001, Addis Ababa, Ethiopia (Telephone Number in U.S. (800) 253-9646); *African Statistical Yearbook.*

GUINEA BISSAU - TRACTORS IN USE

Statistical Office of the United Nations, Publishing Service, New York, New York 10017 (800) 253-9646; *Statistical Yearbook.*

GUINEA BISSAU - TRADE - See GUINEA BISSAU - FOREIGN TRADE

GUINEA BISSAU - TRANSPORTATION AND COMMUNICATIONS

Facts on File, 460 Park Avenue South, New York, New York 10016 (800) 443-8323; *The New Book of World Rankings.*

G.K. Hall and Company, 70 Lincoln Street, Boston, Massachusetts 02111 (617) 423-3990; *The World in Figures.*

United Nations Economic Commission for Africa, Africa Hall, Post Office Box 3001, Addis Ababa, Ethiopia (Telephone Number in U.S. (800) 253-9646); *African Statistical Yearbook.*

GUINEA BISSAU - VITAL STATISTICS

G.K. Hall and Company, 70 Lincoln Street, Boston, Massachusetts 02111 (617) 423-3990; *The World in Figures.*

Statistical Office of the United Nations, Publishing Service, New York, New York 10017 (800) 253-9646; *Statistical Yearbook.*

World Health Organization, Office of Publications, Avenue Appia, CH-1211 Geneva 27, Switzerland (Telephone Number in U.S. (518) 436-9686); *World Health Statistics Annual.*

GUINEA BISSAU - WAGES

G.K. Hall and Company, 70 Lincoln Street, Boston, Massachusetts 02111 (617) 423-3990; *The World in Figures.*

GUINEA BISSAU - WEATHER

Facts on File, 460 Park Avenue South, New York, New York 10016 (800) 443-8323; *The New Book of World Rankings.*

G.K. Hall and Company, 70 Lincoln Street, Boston, Massachusetts 02111 (617) 423-3990; *The World in Figures.*

GUINEA BISSAU - WHEAT PRODUCTION AND PRICES - See GUINEA BISSAU - CROPS

GUINEA BISSAU - WINE PRODUCTION

Facts on File, 460 Park Avenue South, New York, New York 10016 (800) 443-8323; *The New Book of World Rankings.*

GUINEA BISSAU - WOOL PRODUCTION

Facts on File, 460 Park Avenue South, New York, New York 10016 (800) 443-8323; *The New Book of World Rankings.*

GUNS - See FIREARMS

Guyana - National Statistical Office

Statistical Bureau, Ministry of Economic Planning and Finance, Post Office Box 542, Georgetown, Guyana.

Guyana - Primary Statistics Sources

Statistical Bureau, Avenue of the Republic, P.O. Box 542, Georgetown, Guyana; *Annual Statistical Abstract,* and *Quarterly Statistical Digest.*

GUYANA - AGRICULTURE

Euromonitor Publications Limited, 87-88 Turnmill Street, London EC1M 5QU, England; *International Marketing Data and Statistics.*

Facts on File, 460 Park Avenue South, New York, New York 10016 (800) 443-8323; *The New Book of World Rankings.*

Federal Statistical Office, Gustav - Stresemann - Ring 11, D-6200 Wiesbaden, Germany; *Guyana.*

Food and Agricultural Organization of the United Nations (FAO) Via delle Terme di Caracalla, 00100 Rome, Italy (Telephone Number in U.S. (202) 653-2400); *Production Yearbook, The State of Food and Agriculture,* and *Trade Yearbook.*

Gale Research Incorporated, 835 Penobscot Building, Detroit, Michigan 48226 (800) 877-4253; *International Historical Statistics: The Americas and Australasia.*

G.K. Hall and Company, 70 Lincoln Street, Boston, Massachusetts 02111 (617) 423-3990; *The World in Figures.*

Inter-American Development Bank, 1300 New York Avenue, NW, Washington, D.C. 20577 (202) 623-1753; *Economic and Social*

Progress in Latin America.

Statistical Office of the United Nations, Publishing Service, New York, New York 10017 (800) 253-9646; *Statistical Yearbook*, and *Statistical Yearbook for Latin America and the Caribbean.*

Times Books, 201 East 50th Street, New York, New York 10022 (212) 751-2600; *The Economist Book of Vital World Statistics.*

The World Bank, 1818 H Street, NW, Washington, D.C. 20433 (202) 477-1234; *World Tables.*

GUYANA - AIRLINE SERVICE

Facts on File, 460 Park Avenue South, New York, New York 10016 (800) 443-8323; *The New Book of World Rankings.*

G.K. Hall and Company, 70 Lincoln Street, Boston, Massachusetts 02111 (617) 423-3990; *The World in Figures.*

Times Books, 201 East 50th Street, New York, New York 10022 (212) 751-2600; *The Economist Book of Vital World Statistics.*

GUYANA - ALUMINUM PRODUCTION AND CONSUMPTION - See GUYANA - MINING AND MINERAL PRODUCTS

GUYANA - ANIMAL HEALTH

Food and Agricultural Organization of the United Nations (FAO), Via delle Terme di Caracalla, 00100 Rome, Italy (Telephone Number in U.S. (202) 653-2400); *Animal Health Yearbook.*

GUYANA - AREA AND DENSITY OF POPULATION

Euromonitor Publications Limited, 87-88 Turnmill Street, London EC1M 5QU, England; *International Marketing Data and Statistics.*

Facts on File, 460 Park Avenue South, New York, New York 10016 (800) 443-8323; *The New Book of World Rankings.*

Federal Statistical Office, Gustav - Stresemann - Ring 11, D-6200 Wiesbaden, Germany; *Guyana.*

Food and Agricultural Organization of the United Nations (FAO) Via delle Terme di Caracalla, 00100 Rome, Italy (Telephone Number in U.S. (202) 653-2400); *The State of Food and Agriculture.*

G.K. Hall and Company, 70 Lincoln Street, Boston, Massachusetts 02111 (617) 423-3990; *The World in Figures.*

Inter-American Development Bank, 1300 New York Avenue, NW, Washington, D.C. 20577 (202) 623-1753; *Economic and Social Progress in Latin America.*

Statistical Office of the United Nations, Publishing Service, New York, New York 10017 (800) 253-9646; *Statistical Yearbook.*

Times Books, 201 East 50th Street, New York, New York 10022 (212) 751-2600; *The Economist Book of Vital World Statistics.*

GUYANA - ARMS EXPORTS AND IMPORTS

U.S. Arms Control and Disarmament Agency, 320 Twenty-first Street, Northwest, Washington, D.C. 20451 (202) 647-8677; *World Military Expenditures and Arms Transfers.*

GUYANA - BALANCE OF PAYMENTS

The Economist Intelligence Unit, 111 West 57th Street, New York, New York 10019 (800) 938-4685; *The World Market Atlas.*

Federal Statistical Office, Gustav - Stresemann - Ring 11, D-6200 Wiesbaden, Germany; *Guyana.*

G.K. Hall and Company, 70 Lincoln Street, Boston, Massachusetts 02111 (617) 423-3990; *The World in Figures.*

Inter-American Development Bank, 1300 New York Avenue, NW, Washington, D.C. 20577 (202) 623-1753; *Economic and Social Progress in Latin America.*

International Monetary Fund, 700 Nineteenth Street, NW, Washington, D.C. 20431 (202) 623-7000; *Balance of Payments Yearbook*, and *International Financial Statistics.*

Statistical Office of the United Nations, Publishing Service, New York, New York 10017 (800) 253-9646; *Economic Survey of Latin America and the Caribbean*, and *Statistical Yearbook for Latin America and the Caribbean.*

Times Books, 201 East 50th Street, New York, New York 10022 (212) 751-2600; *The Economist Book of Vital World Statistics.*

The World Bank, 1818 H Street, NW, Washington, D.C. 20433 (202) 477-1234; *World Tables.*

GUYANA - BANKING

Facts on File, 460 Park Avenue South, New York, New York 10016 (800) 443-8323; *The New Book of World Rankings.*

G.K. Hall and Company, 70 Lincoln Street, Boston, Massachusetts 02111 (617) 423-3990; *The World in Figures.*

Inter-American Development Bank, 1300 New York Avenue, NW, Washington, D.C. 20577 (202) 623-1753; *Economic and Social Progress in Latin America.*

International Monetary Fund, 700 Nineteenth Street, NW, Washington, D.C. 20431 (202) 623-7000; *Government Finance Statistics Yearbook*, and *International Financial Statistics.*

Statistical Office of the United Nations, Publishing Service, New York, New York 10017 (800) 253-9646; *Statistical Yearbook for Latin America and the Caribbean.*

GUYANA - BARLEY PRODUCTION - See GUYANA - CROPS

GUYANA - BAUXITE - See GUYANA - MINING AND MINERAL PRODUCTS

GUYANA - BEER PRODUCTION

Facts on File, 460 Park Avenue South, New York, New York 10016 (800) 443-8323; *The New Book of World Rankings.*

Statistical Office of the United Nations, Publishing Service, New York, New York 10017 (800) 253-9646; *Statistical Yearbook.*

GUYANA - BIRTH RATES

Facts on File, 460 Park Avenue South, New York, New York 10016 (800) 443-8323; *The New Book of World Rankings.*

Statistical Office of the United Nations, Publishing Service, New York, New York 10017 (800) 253-9646; *Demographic Yearbook, Statistical Yearbook,* and *Statistical Yearbook for Latin America and the Caribbean.*

Times Books, 201 East 50th Street, New York, New York 10022 (212) 751-2600; *The Economist Book of Vital World Statistics.*

The World Bank, 1818 H Street, NW, Washington, D.C. 20433 (202) 477-1234; *World Tables.*

World Health Organization, Office of Publications, Avenue Appia, CH-1211 Geneva 27, Switzerland (Telephone Number in U.S. (518) 436-9686); *World Health Statistics Annual.*

GUYANA - BONDS

G.K. Hall and Company, 70 Lincoln Street, Boston, Massachusetts 02111 (617) 423-3990; *The World in Figures.*

Inter-American Development Bank, 1300 New York Avenue, NW, Washington, D.C. 20577 (202) 623-1753; *Economic and Social Progress in Latin America.*

International Monetary Fund, 700 Nineteenth Street, NW, Washington, D.C. 20431 (202) 623-7000; *Government Finance Statistics Yearbook.*

GUYANA - BOOK PRODUCTION

G.K. Hall and Company, 70 Lincoln Street, Boston, Massachusetts 02111 (617) 423-3990; *The World in Figures.*

United Nations Educational, Scientific and Cultural Organization (UNESCO), 7 Place de Fontenoy, F-75700 Paris, France (Telephone Number in U.S. (212) 963-5981); *Statistical Yearbook.*

GUYANA - BROADCASTING

Billboard Limited, Post Office Box 9027, 1006 AA Amsterdam, The Netherlands (Telephone Number in U.S. (212) 764-7300); *World Radio TV Handbook.*

Facts on File, 460 Park Avenue South, New York, New York 10016 (800) 443-8323; *The New Book of World Rankings.*

G.K. Hall and Company, 70 Lincoln Street, Boston, Massachusetts 02111 (617) 423-3990; *The World in Figures.*

Times Books, 201 East 50th Street, New York, New York 10022 (212) 751-2600; *The Economist Book of Vital World Statistics.*

GUYANA - BUILDING CONSTRUCTION - See GUYANA - CONSTRUCTION INDUSTRY

GUYANA - BUSINESS

G.K. Hall and Company, 70 Lincoln Street, Boston, Massachusetts 02111 (617) 423-3990; *The World in Figures.*

Inter-American Development Bank, 1300 New York Avenue, NW, Washington, D.C. 20577 (202) 623-1753; *Economic and Social Progress in Latin America.*

GUYANA - BUSINESS AND PROFESSIONAL LICENSES

International Monetary Fund, 700 Nineteenth Street, NW, Washington, D.C. 20431 (202) 623-7000; *Government Finance Statistics Yearbook.*

GUYANA - CALORIE SUPPLY

Food and Agricultural Organization of the United Nations (FAO) Via delle Terme di Caracalla, 00100 Rome, Italy (Telephone Number in U.S. (202) 653-2400); *The State of Food and Agriculture.*

Statistical Office of the United Nations, Publishing Service, New York, New York 10017 (800) 253-9646; *Statistical Yearbook for Latin America and the Caribbean.*

GUYANA - CAPITAL INVESTMENT

Inter-American Development Bank, 1300 New York Avenue, NW, Washington, D.C. 20577 (202) 623-1753; *Economic and Social Progress in Latin America.*

GUYANA - CAPITAL REVENUE

Inter-American Development Bank, 1300 New York Avenue, NW, Washington, D.C. 20577 (202) 623-1753; *Economic and Social Progress in Latin America.*

International Monetary Fund, 700 Nineteenth Street, NW, Washington, D.C. 20431 (202) 623-7000; *Government Finance Statistics Yearbook.*

GUYANA - CATTLE - See GUYANA - LIVESTOCK AND POULTRY

GUYANA - CEMENT PRODUCTION - See GUYANA - MINING AND MINERAL PRODUCTS

GUYANA - CHEMICAL (ORGANIC) PRODUCTION - See GUYANA - MINING AND MINERAL PRODUCTS

GUYANA - CHICKENS - See GUYANA - LIVESTOCK AND POULTRY

GUYANA - CIGARETTE PRODUCTION - See GUYANA - TOBACCO PRODUCTION

GUYANA - CLASS STRUCTURE

G.K. Hall and Company, 70 Lincoln Street, Boston, Massachusetts 02111 (617) 423-3990; *The World in Figures.*

GUYANA - CLIMATE

Facts on File, 460 Park Avenue South, New York, New York 10016 (800) 443-8323; *The New Book of World Rankings.*

G.K. Hall and Company, 70 Lincoln Street, Boston, Massachusetts 02111 (617) 423-3990; *The World in Figures.*

GUYANA - COAL PRODUCTION - See GUYANA - MINING AND MINERAL PRODUCTS

GUYANA - COFFEE PRODUCTION - See GUYANA - CROPS

GUYANA - COMMUNICATIONS

Federal Statistical Office, Gustav - Stresemann - Ring 11, D-6200 Wiesbaden, Germany; *Guyana.*

G.K. Hall and Company, 70 Lincoln Street, Boston, Massachusetts 02111 (617) 423-3990; *The World in Figures.*

Inter-American Development Bank, 1300 New York Avenue, NW, Washington, D.C. 20577 (202) 623-1753; *Economic and Social Progress in Latin America.*

GUYANA - CONSTRUCTION INDUSTRY

Facts on File, 460 Park Avenue South, New York, New York 10016 (800) 443-8323; *The New Book of World Rankings.*

Inter-American Development Bank, 1300 New York Avenue, NW, Washington, D.C. 20577 (202) 623-1753; *Economic and Social Progress in Latin America.*

Statistical Office of the United Nations, Publishing Service, New York, New York 10017 (800) 253-9646; *Statistical Yearbook.*

GUYANA - CONSUMER PRICE INDEX

Federal Statistical Office, Gustav - Stresemann - Ring 11, D-6200 Wiesbaden, Germany; *Guyana.*

G.K. Hall and Company, 70 Lincoln Street, Boston, Massachusetts 02111 (617) 423-3990; *The World in Figures.*

Statistical Office of the United Nations, Publishing Service, New York, New York 10017 (800) 253-9646; *Statistical Yearbook.*

GUYANA - CONSUMER PRICES

Federal Statistical Office, Gustav - Stresemann - Ring 11, D-6200 Wiesbaden, Germany; *Guyana.*

International Labour Office, I.L.O. Publications, CH-1211, Geneva 22, Switzerland; *Yearbook of Labour Statistics.*

International Monetary Fund, 700 Nineteenth Street, NW, Washington, D.C. 20431 (202) 623-7000; *International Financial Statistics.*

Times Books, 201 East 50th Street, New York, New York 10022 (212) 751-2600; *The Economist Book of Vital World Statistics.*

GUYANA - CONSUMPTION

G.K. Hall and Company, 70 Lincoln Street, Boston, Massachusetts 02111 (617) 423-3990; *The World in Figures.*

Inter-American Development Bank, 1300 New York Avenue, NW, Washington, D.C. 20577 (202) 623-1753; *Economic and Social Progress in Latin America.*

Statistical Office of the United Nations, Publishing Service, New York, New York 10017 (800) 253-9646; *Statistical Yearbook for Latin America and the Caribbean.*

GUYANA - COPPER PRODUCTION - See GUYANA - MINING AND MINERAL PRODUCTS

GUYANA - CORN PRODUCTION - See GUYANA - CROPS

GUYANA - CORPORATE INCOME TAXES - See GUYANA - TAXATION

GUYANA - CORPORATE TAXES - See GUYANA - TAXATION

GUYANA - COTTON PRODUCTION - See GUYANA - CROPS

GUYANA - CRIME

Yale University Press, Yale Station, New Haven, Connecticut 06520 (203) 432-0940; *Violence and Crime in Cross-National Perspective.*

GUYANA - CROPS

Facts on File, 460 Park Avenue South, New York, New York 10016 (800) 443-8323; *The New Book of World Rankings.*

Food and Agricultural Organization of the United Nations (FAO) Via delle Terme di Caracalla, 00100 Rome, Italy (Telephone Number in U.S. (202) 653-2400); *Production Yearbook* and *The State of Food and Agriculture.*

G.K. Hall and Company, 70 Lincoln Street, Boston, Massachusetts 02111 (617) 423-3990; *The World in Figures.*

Statistical Office of the United Nations, Publishing Service, New York, New York 10017 (800) 253-9646; *Statistical Yearbook.*

GUYANA - CUSTOMS DUTIES

G.K. Hall and Company, 70 Lincoln Street, Boston, Massachusetts 02111 (617) 423-3990; *The World in Figures.*

Inter-American Development Bank, 1300 New York Avenue, NW, Washington, D.C. 20577 (202) 623-1753; *Economic and Social Progress in Latin America.*

International Monetary Fund, 700 Nineteenth Street, NW, Washington, D.C. 20431 (202) 623-7000; *International Financial Statistics.*

GUYANA - DAIRY PRODUCTS

Facts on File, 460 Park Avenue South, New York, New York 10016 (800) 443-8323; *The New Book of World Rankings.*

Food and Agricultural Organization of the United Nations (FAO) Via delle Terme di Caracalla, 00100 Rome, Italy (Telephone Number in U.S. (202) 653-2400); *The State of Food and Agriculture.*

Statistical Office of the United Nations, Publishing Service, New York, New York 10017 (800) 253-9646; *Statistical Yearbook.*

GUYANA - DEATH RATE

G.K. Hall and Company, 70 Lincoln Street, Boston, Massachusetts 02111 (617) 423-3990; *The World in Figures.*

Statistical Office of the United Nations, Publishing Service, New York, New York 10017 (800) 253-9646; *Statistical Yearbook,* and *Statistical Yearbook for Latin America and the Caribbean.*

Times Books, 201 East 50th Street, New York, New York 10022 (212) 751-2600; *The Economist Book of Vital World Statistics.*

World Health Organization, Office of Publications, Avenue Appia, CH-1211 Geneva 27, Switzerland (Telephone Number in U.S. (518) 436-9686); *World Health Statistics Annual.*

GUYANA - DEFENSE EXPENDITURES

G.K. Hall and Company, 70 Lincoln Street, Boston, Massachusetts 02111 (617) 423-3990; *The World in Figures.*

U.S. Arms Control and Disarmament Agency, 320 Twenty-first Street, Northwest, Washington, D.C. 20451 (202) 647-8677; *World Military Expenditures and Arms Transfers.*

GUYANA - DEMOGRAPHY

The Economist Intelligence Unit, 111 West 57th Street, New York, New York 10019 (800) 938-4685; *The World Market Atlas.*

Facts on File, 460 Park Avenue South, New York, New York 10016 (800) 443-8323; *The New Book of World Rankings.*

Federal Statistical Office, Gustav - Stresemann - Ring 11, D-6200 Wiesbaden, Germany; *Guyana.*

G.K. Hall and Company, 70 Lincoln Street, Boston, Massachusetts 02111 (617) 423-3990; *The World in Figures.*

GUYANA - DEVELOPMENT ASSISTANCE

G.K. Hall and Company, 70 Lincoln Street, Boston, Massachusetts 02111 (617) 423-3990; *The World in Figures.*

Inter-American Development Bank, 1300 New York Avenue, NW, Washington, D.C. 20577 (202) 623-1753; *Economic and Social Progress in Latin America.*

Statistical Office of the United Nations, Publishing Service, New York, New York 10017 (800) 253-9646; *Statistical Yearbook.*

GUYANA - DIAMOND PRODUCTION - See GUYANA - MINING AND MINERAL PRODUCTS

GUYANA - DISCOUNT RATES

Inter-American Development Bank, 1300 New York Avenue, NW, Washington, D.C. 20577 (202) 623-1753; *Economic and Social Progress in Latin America.*

GUYANA - DISEASES

G.K. Hall and Company, 70 Lincoln Street, Boston, Massachusetts 02111 (617) 423-3990; *The World in Figures.*

World Health Organization, Office of Publications, Avenue Appia, CH-1211 Geneva 27, Switzerland (Telephone Number in U.S. (518) 436-9686); *World Health Statistics Annual.*

GUYANA - DIVORCE RATES

Facts on File, 460 Park Avenue South, New York, New York 10016 (800) 443-8323; *The New Book of World Rankings.*

Statistical Office of the United Nations, Publishing Service, New York, New York 10017 (800) 253-9646; *Demographic Yearbook,* and *Statistical Yearbook.*

GUYANA - DOMESTIC PRODUCT

G.K. Hall and Company, 70 Lincoln Street, Boston, Massachusetts 02111 (617) 423-3990; *The World in Figures.*

GUYANA - ECONOMY

Euromonitor Publications Limited, 87-88 Turnmill Street, London EC1M 5QU, England; *International Marketing Data and Statistics.*

Facts on File, 460 Park Avenue South, New York, New York 10016 (800) 443-8323; *The New Book of World Rankings.*

Federal Statistical Office, Gustav - Stresemann - Ring 11, D-6200 Wiesbaden, Germany; *Guyana.*

G.K. Hall and Company, 70 Lincoln Street, Boston, Massachusetts 02111 (617) 423-3990; *The World in Figures.*

Inter-American Development Bank, 1300 New York Avenue, NW, Washington, D.C. 20577 (202) 623-1753; *Economic and Social Progress in Latin America.*

Statistical Office of the United Nations, Publishing Service, New York, New York 10017 (800) 253-9646; *Economic Survey of Latin America and the Caribbean.*

U.C.L.A. Latin American Center Publications, University of California, Los Angeles, California 90024 (310) 825-6634; *Statistical Abstract of Latin America.*

GUYANA - EDUCATION

The Economist Intelligence Unit, 111 West 57th Street, New York, New York 10019 (800) 938-4685; *The World Market Atlas.*

Facts on File, 460 Park Avenue South, New York, New York 10016 (800) 443-8323; *The New Book of World Rankings.*

Federal Statistical Office, Gustav - Stresemann - Ring 11, D-6200 Wiesbaden, Germany; *Guyana.*

Gale Research Incorporated, 835 Penobscot Building, Detroit, Michigan 48226 (800) 877-4253; *International Historical Statistics: The Americas and Australasia.*

G.K. Hall and Company, 70 Lincoln Street, Boston, Massachusetts 02111 (617) 423-3990; *The World in Figures.*

International Monetary Fund, 700 Nineteenth Street, NW, Washington, D.C. 20431 (202) 623-7000; *Government Finance Statistics Yearbook.*

Statistical Office of the United Nations, Publishing Service, New York, New York 10017 (800) 253-9646; *Statistical Yearbook for Latin America and the Caribbean.*

Times Books, 201 East 50th Street, New York, New York 10022 (212) 751-2600; *The Economist Book of Vital World Statistics.*

United Nations Educational, Scientific and Cultural Organization (UNESCO), 7 Place de Fontenoy, F-75700 Paris, France (Telephone Number in U.S. (212) 963-5981); *Statistical Yearbook.*

The World Bank, 1818 H Street, NW, Washington, D.C. 20433 (202) 477-1234; *World Tables.*

GUYANA - EGG PRODUCTION - See GUYANA - DAIRY PRODUCTS

GUYANA - ELECTRICITY

Facts on File, 460 Park Avenue South, New York, New York 10016 (800) 443-8323; *The New Book of World Rankings.*

Inter-American Development Bank, 1300 New York Avenue, NW, Washington, D.C. 20577 (202) 623-1753; *Economic and Social Progress in Latin America.*

Statistical Office of the United Nations, Publishing Service, New York, New York 10017 (800) 253-9646; *Statistical Yearbook.*

Times Books, 201 East 50th Street, New York, New York 10022 (212) 751-2600; *The Economist Book of Vital World Statistics.*

GUYANA - EMPLOYMENT

Euromonitor Publications Limited, 87-88 Turnmill Street, London EC1M 5QU, England; *International Marketing Data and Statistics.*

Facts on File, 460 Park Avenue South, New York, New York 10016 (800) 443-8323; *The New Book of World Rankings.*

Federal Statistical Office, Gustav - Stresemann - Ring 11, D-6200 Wiesbaden, Germany; *Guyana.*

International Labour Office, I.L.O. Publications, CH-1211, Geneva 22, Switzerland; *Yearbook of Labour Statistics.*

Statistical Office of the United Nations, Publishing Service, New York, New York 10017 (800) 253-9646; *Statistical Yearbook,* and *Statistical Yearbook for Latin America and the Caribbean.*

GUYANA - ENERGY

Facts on File, 460 Park Avenue South, New York, New York 10016 (800) 443-8323; *The New Book of World Rankings.*

Food and Agricultural Organization of the United Nations (FAO) Via delle Terme di Caracalla, 00100 Rome, Italy (Telephone Number in U.S. (202) 653-2400); *The State of Food and Agriculture.*

G.K. Hall and Company, 70 Lincoln Street, Boston, Massachusetts 02111 (617) 423-3990; *The World in Figures.*

Statistical Office of the United Nations, Publishing Service, New York, New York 10017 (800) 253-9646; *Energy Statistics Yearbook, Statistical Yearbook,* and *Statistical Yearbook for Latin America and the Caribbean.*

Times Books, 201 East 50th Street, New York, New York 10022 (212) 751-2600; *The Economist Book of Vital World Statistics.*

GUYANA - EXCHANGE RATE

Euromonitor Publications Limited, 87-88 Turnmill Street, London EC1M 5QU, England; *International Marketing Data and Statistics.*

Inter-American Development Bank, 1300 New York Avenue, NW, Washington, D.C. 20577 (202) 623-1753; *Economic and Social Progress in Latin America.*

International Monetary Fund, 700 Nineteenth Street, NW, Washington, D.C. 20431 (202) 623-7000; *International Financial Statistics.*

Statistical Office of the United Nations, Publishing Service, New York, New York 10017 (800) 253-9646; *Statistical Yearbook.*

GUYANA - EXCISE TAXES - See GUYANA - TAXATION

GUYANA - EXPORTS

The Economist Intelligence Unit, 111 West 57th Street, New York, New York 10019 (800) 938-4685; *The World Market Atlas.*

Euromonitor Publications Limited, 87-88 Turnmill Street, London EC1M 5QU, England; *International Marketing Data and Statistics.*

Food and Agricultural Organization of the United Nations (FAO) Via delle Terme di Caracalla, 00100 Rome, Italy (Telephone Number in U.S. (202) 653-2400); *The State of Food and Agriculture.*

G.K. Hall and Company, 70 Lincoln Street, Boston, Massachusetts 02111 (617) 423-3990; *The World in Figures.*

Inter-American Development Bank, 1300 New York Avenue, NW, Washington, D.C. 20577 (202) 623-1753; *Economic and Social Progress in Latin America.*

International Monetary Fund, 700 Nineteenth Street, NW, Washington, D.C. 20431 (202) 623-7000; *Direction of Trade Statistics, Government Finance Statistics Yearbook,* and *International Financial Statistics.*

Statistical Office of the United Nations, Publishing Service, New York, New York 10017 (800) 253-9646; *Statistical Yearbook for Latin America and the Caribbean.*

Times Books, 201 East 50th Street, New York, New York 10022 (212) 751-2600; *The Economist Book of Vital World Statistics.*

The World Bank, 1818 H Street, NW, Washington, D.C. 20433 (202) 477-1234; *World Tables.*

GUYANA - EXTERNAL FINANCING

Inter-American Development Bank, 1300 New York Avenue, NW, Washington, D.C. 20577 (202) 623-1753; *Economic and Social Progress in Latin America.*

Statistical Office of the United Nations, Publishing Service, New York, New York 10017 (800) 253-9646; *Statistical Yearbook for Latin America and the Caribbean.*

GUYANA - EXTERNAL INDEBTEDNESS

Inter-American Development Bank, 1300 New York Avenue, NW, Washington, D.C. 20577 (202) 623-1753; *Economic and Social Progress in Latin America.*

The World Bank, 1818 H Street, NW, Washington, D.C. 20433 (202) 477-1234; *World Tables.*

GUYANA - EXTERNAL TRADE

Food and Agricultural Organization of the United Nations (FAO) Via delle Terme di Caracalla, 00100 Rome, Italy (Telephone Number in U.S. (202) 653-2400); *The State of Food and Agriculture,* and *Trade Yearbook.*

Gale Research Incorporated, 835 Penobscot Building, Detroit, Michigan 48226 (800) 877-4253; *International Historical Statistics: The Americas and Australasia.*

G.K. Hall and Company, 70 Lincoln Street, Boston, Massachusetts 02111 (617) 423-3990; *The World in Figures.*

Inter-American Development Bank, 1300 New York Avenue, NW, Washington, D.C. 20577 (202) 623-1753; *Economic and Social Progress in Latin America.*

Statistical Office of the United Nations, Publishing Service, New York, New York 10017 (800) 253-9646; *Statistical Yearbook,* and *Statistical Yearbook for Latin America and the Caribbean.*

GUYANA - FARM CROPS - See GUYANA - CROPS

GUYANA - FEMALE WORKING POPULATION - See GUYANA - EMPLOYMENT

GUYANA - FERTILITY RATES

Facts on File, 460 Park Avenue South, New York, New York 10016 (800) 443-8323; *The New Book of World Rankings.*

Times Books, 201 East 50th Street, New York, New York 10022 (212) 751-2600; *The Economist Book of Vital World Statistics.*

The World Bank, 1818 H Street, NW, Washington, D.C. 20433 (202) 477-1234; *World Tables.*

GUYANA - FERTILIZER

Food and Agricultural Organization of the United Nations (FAO) Via delle Terme di Caracalla, 00100 Rome, Italy (Telephone Number in U.S. (202) 653-2400); *Fertilizer Yearbook,* and *The State of Food and Agriculture.*

Statistical Office of the United Nations, Publishing Service, New York, New York 10017 (800) 253-9646; *Statistical Yearbook.*

GUYANA - FETAL MORTALITY

Statistical Office of the United Nations, Publishing Service, New York, New York 10017 (800) 253-9646; *Demographic Yearbook.*

World Health Organization, Office of Publications, Avenue Appia, CH-1211 Geneva 27, Switzerland (Telephone Number in U.S. (518) 436-9686); *World Health Statistics Annual.*

GUYANA - FILM - See GUYANA - MOTION PICTURES

GUYANA - FINANCE

Facts on File, 460 Park Avenue South, New York, New York 10016 (800) 443-8323; *The New Book of World Rankings.*

Federal Statistical Office, Gustav - Stresemann - Ring 11, D-6200 Wiesbaden, Germany; *Guyana.*

Gale Research Incorporated, 835 Penobscot Building, Detroit, Michigan 48226 (800) 877-4253; *International Historical Statistics: The Americas and Australasia.*

G.K. Hall and Company, 70 Lincoln Street, Boston, Massachusetts 02111 (617) 423-3990; *The World in Figures.*

Inter-American Development Bank, 1300 New York Avenue, NW, Washington, D.C. 20577 (202) 623-1753; *Economic and Social Progress in Latin America.*

International Monetary Fund, 700 Nineteenth Street, NW, Washington, D.C. 20431 (202) 623-7000; *Government Finance Statistics Yearbook.*

GUYANA - FISHERIES

Facts on File, 460 Park Avenue South, New York, New York 10016 (800) 443-8323; *The New Book of World Rankings.*

Federal Statistical Office, Gustav - Stresemann - Ring 11, D-6200 Wiesbaden, Germany; *Guyana.*

Food and Agricultural Organization of the United Nations (FAO) Via delle Terme di Caracalla, 00100 Rome, Italy (Telephone Number in U.S. (202) 653-2400); *The State of Food and Agriculture,* and *Yearbook of Fishery Statistics.*

Inter-American Development Bank, 1300 New York Avenue, NW, Washington, D.C. 20577 (202) 623-1753; *Economic and Social Progress in Latin America.*

Statistical Office of the United Nations, Publishing Service, New York, New York 10017 (800) 253-9646; *Statistical Yearbook.*

GUYANA - FLOUR PRODUCTION

Statistical Office of the United Nations, Publishing Service, New York, New York 10017 (800) 253-9646; *Statistical Yearbook.*

GUYANA - FOOD

Food and Agricultural Organization of the United Nations (FAO), Via delle Terme di Caracalla, 00100 Rome, Italy (Telephone Number in U.S. (202) 653-2400); *Production Yearbook,* and *The State of Food and Agriculture.*

G.K. Hall and Company, 70 Lincoln Street, Boston, Massachusetts 02111 (617) 423-3990; *The World in Figures.*

GUYANA - FOREIGN AID

G.K. Hall and Company, 70 Lincoln Street, Boston, Massachusetts 02111 (617) 423-3990; *The World in Figures.*

Inter-American Development Bank, 1300 New York Avenue, NW, Washington, D.C. 20577 (202) 623-1753; *Economic and Social Progress in Latin America.*

GUYANA - FOREIGN DEBT

Inter-American Development Bank, 1300 New York Avenue, NW, Washington, D.C. 20577 (202) 623-1753; *Economic and Social Progress in Latin America.*

International Monetary Fund, 700 Nineteenth Street, NW, Washington, D.C. 20431 (202) 623-7000; *Government Finance Statistics Yearbook.*

GUYANA - FOREIGN FINANCE

Inter-American Development Bank, 1300 New York Avenue, NW, Washington, D.C. 20577 (202) 623-1753; *Economic and Social Progress in Latin America.*

GUYANA - FOREIGN INDEBTEDNESS

Inter-American Development Bank, 1300 New York Avenue, NW, Washington, D.C. 20577 (202) 623-1753; *Economic and Social Progress in Latin America.*

Statistical Office of the United Nations, Publishing Service, New York, New York 10017 (800) 253-9646; *Economic Survey of Latin America and the Caribbean.*

GUYANA - FOREIGN TRADE

Euromonitor Publications Limited, 87-88 Turnmill Street, London EC1M 5QU, England; *International Marketing Data and Statistics.*

Facts on File, 460 Park Avenue South, New York, New York 10016 (800) 443-8323; *The New Book of World Rankings.*

Federal Statistical Office, Gustav - Stresemann - Ring 11, D-6200 Wiesbaden, Germany; *Guyana.*

Food and Agricultural Organization of the United Nations (FAO) Via delle Terme di Caracalla, 00100 Rome, Italy (Telephone Number in U.S. (202) 653-2400); *The State of Food and Agriculture.*

G.K. Hall and Company, 70 Lincoln Street, Boston, Massachusetts 02111 (617) 423-3990; *The World in Figures.*

Inter-American Development Bank, 1300 New York Avenue, NW, Washington, D.C. 20577 (202) 623-1753; *Economic and Social Progress in Latin America.*

International Monetary Fund, 700 Nineteenth Street, NW, Washington, D.C. 20431 (202) 623-7000; *International Financial Statistics.*

Statistical Office of the United Nations, Publishing Service, New York, New York 10017 (800) 253-9646; *Foreign Trade Statistics for Africa, International Trade Statistics Yearbook,* and *Statistical Yearbook.*

The World Bank, 1818 H Street, NW, Washington, D.C. 20433 (202) 477-1234; *World Tables.*

GUYANA - FORESTRY AND FOREST PRODUCTS

Facts on File, 460 Park Avenue South, New York, New York 10016 (800) 443-8323; *The New Book of World Rankings.*

Federal Statistical Office, Gustav - Stresemann - Ring 11, D-6200 Wiesbaden, Germany; *Guyana.*

Food and Agricultural Organization of the United Nations (FAO) Via delle Terme di Caracalla, 00100 Rome, Italy (Telephone Number in U.S. (202) 653-2400); *The State of Food and Agriculture* and *Yearbook of Forest Products.*

G.K. Hall and Company, 70 Lincoln Street, Boston, Massachusetts 02111 (617) 423-3990; *The World in Figures.*

Inter-American Development Bank, 1300 New York Avenue, NW, Washington, D.C. 20577 (202) 623-1753; *Economic and Social Progress in Latin America.*

Statistical Office of the United Nations, Publishing Service, New York, New York 10017 (800) 253-9646; *Statistical Yearbook.*

United Nations Educational, Scientific and Cultural Organization (UNESCO), 7 Place de Fontenoy, F-75700 Paris, France (Telephone Number in U.S. (212) 963-5981); *Statistical Yearbook.*

GUYANA - GAS PRODUCTION - See GUYANA - MINING AND MINERAL PRODUCTS

GUYANA - GENERAL INDUSTRIAL STATISTICS

Federal Statistical Office, Gustav - Stresemann - Ring 11, D-6200 Wiesbaden, Germany; *Guyana.*

Statistical Office of the United Nations, Publishing Service, New York, New York 10017 (800) 253-9646; *Industrial Statistics Yearbook.*

GUYANA - GENERAL MORTALITY

Statistical Office of the United Nations, Publishing Service, New York, New York 10017 (800) 253-9646; *Demographic Yearbook.*

World Health Organization, Office of Publications, Avenue Appia, CH-1211 Geneva 27, Switzerland (Telephone Number in U.S. (518) 436-9686); *World Health Statistics Annual.*

GUYANA - GEOGRAPHIC DATA

Facts on File, 460 Park Avenue South, New York, New York 10016 (800) 443-8323; *The New Book of World Rankings.*

Federal Statistical Office, Gustav - Stresemann - Ring 11, D-6200 Wiesbaden, Germany; *Guyana.*

U.C.L.A. Latin American Center Publications, University of California, Los Angeles, California 90024 (310) 825-6634; *Statistical Abstract of Latin America.*

GUYANA - GOATS - See GUYANA - LIVESTOCK AND POULTRY

GUYANA - GOLD HOLDINGS

International Monetary Fund, 700 Nineteenth Street, NW, Washington, D.C. 20431 (202) 623-7000; *International Financial Statistics.*

Statistical Office of the United Nations, Publishing Service, New York, New York 10017 (800) 253-9646; *Statistical Yearbook.*

The World Bank, 1818 H Street, NW, Washington, D.C. 20433 (202) 477-1234; *World Tables.*

GUYANA - GOLD PRODUCTION AND CONSUMPTION - See GUYANA - MINING AND MINERAL PRODUCTS

GUYANA - GOVERNMENT

G.K. Hall and Company, 70 Lincoln Street, Boston, Massachusetts 02111 (617) 423-3990; *The World in Figures.*

Inter-American Development Bank, 1300 New York Avenue, NW, Washington, D.C. 20577 (202) 623-1753; *Economic and Social Progress in Latin America.*

GUYANA - GOVERNMENT BONDS - See GUYANA - BONDS

GUYANA - GOVERNMENT CONSUMPTION

Inter-American Development Bank, 1300 New York Avenue, NW, Washington, D.C. 20577 (202) 623-1753; *Economic and Social Progress in Latin America.*

GUYANA - GOVERNMENT EXPENDITURES

Inter-American Development Bank, 1300 New York Avenue, NW, Washington, D.C. 20577 (202) 623-1753; *Economic and Social Progress in Latin America.*

International Monetary Fund, 700 Nineteenth Street, NW, Washington, D.C. 20431 (202) 623-7000; *Government Finance Statistics Yearbook.*

Times Books, 201 East 50th Street, New York, New York 10022 (212) 751-2600; *The Economist Book of Vital World Statistics.*

The World Bank, 1818 H Street, NW, Washington, D.C. 20433 (202) 477-1234; *World Tables.*

GUYANA - GOVERNMENT FINANCES

Inter-American Development Bank, 1300 New York Avenue, NW, Washington, D.C. 20577 (202) 623-1753; *Economic and Social Progress in Latin America.*

Statistical Office of the United Nations, Publishing Service, New York, New York 10017 (800) 253-9646; *Statistical Yearbook.*

GUYANA - GOVERNMENT REVENUES

Inter-American Development Bank, 1300 New York Avenue, NW, Washington, D.C. 20577 (202) 623-1753; *Economic and Social Progress in Latin America.*

International Monetary Fund, 700 Nineteenth Street, NW, Washington, D.C. 20431 (202) 623-7000; *Government Finance Statistics Yearbook.*

Times Books, 201 East 50th Street, New York, New York 10022 (212) 751-2600; *The Economist Book of Vital World Statistics.*

The World Bank, 1818 H Street, NW, Washington, D.C. 20433 (202) 477-1234; *World Tables.*

GUYANA - GRAIN PRODUCTION - See GUYANA - CROPS

GUYANA - GRANTS

International Monetary Fund, 700 Nineteenth Street, NW, Washington, D.C. 20431 (202) 623-7000; *Government Finance Statistics Yearbook.*

GUYANA - GROSS DOMESTIC PRODUCT

The Economist Intelligence Unit, 111 West 57th Street, New York, New York 10019 (800) 938-4685; *The World Market Atlas.*

Euromonitor Publications Limited, 87-88 Turnmill Street, London EC1M 5QU, England; *International Marketing Data and Statistics.*

Facts on File, 460 Park Avenue South, New York, New York 10016 (800) 443-8323; *The New Book of World Rankings.*

G.K. Hall and Company, 70 Lincoln Street, Boston, Massachusetts 02111 (617) 423-3990; *The World in Figures.*

Inter-American Development Bank, 1300 New York Avenue, NW, Washington, D.C. 20577 (202) 623-1753; *Economic and Social Progress in Latin America.*

Statistical Office of the United Nations, Publishing Service, New York, New York 10017 (800) 253-9646; *Statistical Yearbook,* and *Statistical Yearbook for Latin America and the Caribbean.*

Times Books, 201 East 50th Street, New York, New York 10022 (212) 751-2600; *The Economist Book of Vital World Statistics.*

The World Bank, 1818 H Street, NW, Washington, D.C. 20433 (202) 477-1234; *World Tables.*

GUYANA - GROSS NATIONAL PRODUCT

Euromonitor Publications Limited, 87-88 Turnmill Street, London EC1M 5QU, England; *International Marketing Data and Statistics.*

Inter-American Development Bank, 1300 New York Avenue, NW, Washington, D.C. 20577 (202) 623-1753; *Economic and Social Progress in Latin America.*

U.S. Arms Control and Disarmament Agency, 320 Twenty-first Street, Northwest, Washington, D.C. 20451 (202) 647-8677; *World Military Expenditures and Arms Transfers.*

The World Bank, 1818 H Street, NW, Washington, D.C. 20433 (202) 477-1234; *World Tables.*

GUYANA - GROUNDNUTS PRODUCTION - See GUYANA - CROPS

GUYANA - HEALTH

Facts on File, 460 Park Avenue South, New York, New York 10016 (800) 443-8323; *The New Book of World Rankings.*

Federal Statistical Office, Gustav - Stresemann - Ring 11, D-6200 Wiesbaden, Germany; *Guyana.*

G.K. Hall and Company, 70 Lincoln Street, Boston, Massachusetts 02111 (617) 423-3990; *The World in Figures.*

Statistical Office of the United Nations, Publishing Service, New York, New York 10017 (800) 253-9646; *Statistical Yearbook,* and *Statistical Yearbook for Latin America and the Caribbean.*

Times Books, 201 East 50th Street, New York, New York 10022 (212) 751-2600; *The Economist Book of Vital World Statistics.*

World Health Organization, Office of Publications, Avenue Appia, CH-1211 Geneva 27, Switzerland (Telephone Number in U.S. (518) 436-9686); *World Health Statistics Annual.*

GUYANA - HEALTH EXPENDITURES

Statistical Office of the United Nations, Publishing Service, New York, New York 10017 (800) 253-9646; *Statistical Yearbook for Latin America and the Caribbean.*

GUYANA - HIDE PRODUCTION

Food and Agricultural Organization of the United Nations (FAO), Via delle Terme di Caracalla, 00100 Rome, Italy (Telephone Number in U.S. (202) 653-2400); *Production Yearbook.*

GUYANA - HIGHWAYS

G.K. Hall and Company, 70 Lincoln Street, Boston, Massachusetts 02111 (617) 423-3990; *The World in Figures.*

GUYANA - HORSES - See GUYANA - LIVESTOCK AND POULTRY

GUYANA - HOURS OF WORK - See GUYANA - EMPLOYMENT

GUYANA - HOUSING AND HOUSING UNITS

Facts on File, 460 Park Avenue South, New York, New York 10016 (800) 443-8323; *The New Book of World Rankings.*

Statistical Office of the United Nations, Publishing Service, New York, New York 10017 (800) 253-9646; *Statistical Yearbook for Latin America and the Caribbean.*

GUYANA - ILLITERATE POPULATION

The Economist Intelligence Unit, 111 West 57th Street, New York, New York 10019 (800) 938-4685; *The World Market Atlas.*

G.K. Hall and Company, 70 Lincoln Street, Boston, Massachusetts 02111 (617) 423-3990; *The World in Figures.*

Statistical Office of the United Nations, Publishing Service, New York, New York 10017 (800) 253-9646; *Statistical Yearbook for Latin America and the Caribbean.*

United Nations Educational, Scientific and Cultural Organization (UNESCO), 7 Place de Fontenoy, F-75700 Paris, France (Telephone Number in U.S. (212) 963-5981); *Statistical Yearbook.*

GUYANA - IMPORTS

The Economist Intelligence Unit, 111 West 57th Street, New York, New York 10019 (800) 938-4685; *The World Market Atlas.*

Euromonitor Publications Limited, 87-88 Turnmill Street, London EC1M 5QU, England; *International Marketing Data and Statistics.*

Food and Agricultural Organization of the United Nations (FAO) Via delle Terme di Caracalla, 00100 Rome, Italy (Telephone Number in U.S. (202) 653-2400); *The State of Food and Agriculture.*

G.K. Hall and Company, 70 Lincoln Street, Boston, Massachusetts 02111 (617) 423-3990; *The World in Figures.*

Inter-American Development Bank, 1300 New York Avenue, NW, Washington, D.C. 20577 (202) 623-1753; *Economic and Social Progress in Latin America.*

International Monetary Fund, 700 Nineteenth Street, NW, Washington, D.C. 20431 (202) 623-7000; *Direction of Trade Statistics, Government Finance Statistics Yearbook,* and *International Financial Statistics.*

Statistical Office of the United Nations, Publishing Service, New York, New York 10017 (800) 253-9646; *Statistical Yearbook for Latin America and the Caribbean.*

The World Bank, 1818 H Street, NW, Washington, D.C. 20433 (202) 477-1234; *World Tables.*

GUYANA - INCOME DISTRIBUTION

Statistical Office of the United Nations, Publishing Service, New York, New York 10017 (800) 253-9646; *Statistical Yearbook for Latin America and the Caribbean.*

GUYANA - INCOME TAXES - See GUYANA - TAXATION

GUYANA - INDUSTRIAL SECTOR TRENDS

Statistical Office of the United Nations, Publishing Service, New York, New York 10017 (800) 253-9646; *Economic Survey of Latin America and the Caribbean.*

GUYANA - INDUSTRY

Euromonitor Publications Limited, 87-88 Turnmill Street, London EC1M 5QU, England; *International Marketing Data and Statistics.*

Facts on File, 460 Park Avenue South, New York, New York 10016 (800) 443-8323; *The New Book of World Rankings.*

Federal Statistical Office, Gustav - Stresemann - Ring 11, D-6200 Wiesbaden, Germany; *Guyana.*

Gale Research Incorporated, 835 Penobscot Building, Detroit, Michigan 48226 (800) 877-4253; *International Historical Statistics: The Americas and Australasia.*

G.K. Hall and Company, 70 Lincoln Street, Boston, Massachusetts 02111 (617) 423-3990; *The World in Figures.*

International Labour Office, I.L.O. Publications, CH-1211, Geneva 22, Switzerland; *Yearbook of Labour Statistics.*

Times Books, 201 East 50th Street, New York, New York 10022 (212) 751-2600; *The Economist Book of Vital World Statistics.*

The World Bank, 1818 H Street, NW, Washington, D.C. 20433 (202) 477-1234; *World Tables.*

GUYANA - INFANT AND MATERNAL MORTALITY

Statistical Office of the United Nations, Publishing Service, New York, New York 10017 (800) 253-9646; *Statistical Yearbook.*

Times Books, 201 East 50th Street, New York, New York 10022 (212) 751-2600; *The Economist Book of Vital World Statistics.*

The World Bank, 1818 H Street, NW, Washington, D.C. 20433 (202) 477-1234; *World Tables.*

World Health Organization, Office of Publications, Avenue Appia, CH-1211 Geneva 27, Switzerland (Telephone Number in U.S. (518) 436-9686); *World Health Statistics Annual.*

GUYANA - INFLATIONARY FACTORS

Statistical Office of the United Nations, Publishing Service, New York, New York 10017 (800) 253-9646; *Economic Survey of Latin America and the Caribbean.*

GUYANA - INTEREST RATES

Inter-American Development Bank, 1300 New York Avenue, NW, Washington, D.C. 20577 (202) 623-1753; *Economic and Social Progress in Latin America.*

GUYANA - INTERNATIONAL FINANCE

Inter-American Development Bank, 1300 New York Avenue, NW, Washington, D.C. 20577 (202) 623-1753; *Economic and Social Progress in Latin America.*

GUYANA - INTERNATIONAL LIQUIDITY

Inter-American Development Bank, 1300 New York Avenue, NW, Washington, D.C. 20577 (202) 623-1753; *Economic and Social Progress in Latin America.*

International Monetary Fund, 700 Nineteenth Street, NW, Washington, D.C. 20431 (202) 623-7000; *International Financial Statistics.*

GUYANA - INTERNATIONAL RESERVES EXCLUDING GOLD

Inter-American Development Bank, 1300 New York Avenue, NW, Washington, D.C. 20577 (202) 623-1753; *Economic and Social Progress in Latin America.*

Statistical Office of the United Nations, Publishing Service, New York, New York 10017 (800) 253-9646; *Statistical Yearbook.*

The World Bank, 1818 H Street, NW, Washington, D.C. 20433 (202) 477-1234; *World Tables.*

GUYANA - INTERNATIONAL STATISTICS

Inter-American Development Bank, 1300 New York Avenue, NW, Washington, D.C. 20577 (202) 623-1753; *Economic and Social Progress in Latin America.*

U.C.L.A. Latin American Center Publications, University of California, Los Angeles, California 90024 (310) 825-6634; *Statistical*

Abstract of Latin America.

GUYANA - INVESTMENT

Inter-American Development Bank, 1300 New York Avenue, NW, Washington, D.C. 20577 (202) 623-1753; *Economic and Social Progress in Latin America.*

Statistical Office of the United Nations, Publishing Service, New York, New York 10017 (800) 253-9646; *Statistical Yearbook for Latin America and the Caribbean.*

GUYANA - IRON ORE PRODUCTION AND CONSUMPTION - See GUYANA - MINING AND MINERAL PRODUCTS

GUYANA - IRRIGATION

Euromonitor Publications Limited, 87-88 Turnmill Street, London EC1M 5QU, England; *International Marketing Data and Statistics.*

Inter-American Development Bank, 1300 New York Avenue, NW, Washington, D.C. 20577 (202) 623-1753; *Economic and Social Progress in Latin America.*

GUYANA - LABOR FORCE

Euromonitor Publications Limited, 87-88 Turnmill Street, London EC1M 5QU, England; *International Marketing Data and Statistics.*

Facts on File, 460 Park Avenue South, New York, New York 10016 (800) 443-8323; *The New Book of World Rankings.*

Food and Agricultural Organization of the United Nations (FAO) Via delle Terme di Caracalla, 00100 Rome, Italy (Telephone Number in U.S. (202) 653-2400); *The State of Food and Agriculture.*

Gale Research Incorporated, 835 Penobscot Building, Detroit, Michigan 48226 (800) 877-4253; *International Historical Statistics: The Americas and Australasia.*

G.K. Hall and Company, 70 Lincoln Street, Boston, Massachusetts 02111 (617) 423-3990; *The World in Figures.*

Times Books, 201 East 50th Street, New York, New York 10022 (212) 751-2600; *The Economist Book of Vital World Statistics.*

The World Bank, 1818 H Street, NW, Washington, D.C. 20433 (202) 477-1234; *World Tables.*

GUYANA - LABOR PRODUCTIVITY

International Labour Office, I.L.O. Publications, CH-1211, Geneva 22, Switzerland; *Yearbook of Labour Statistics.*

GUYANA - LAND USE

Euromonitor Publications Limited, 87-88 Turnmill Street, London EC1M 5QU, England; *International Marketing Data and Statistics.*

Food and Agricultural Organization of the United Nations (FAO), Via delle Terme di Caracalla, 00100 Rome, Italy (Telephone Number in U.S. (202) 653-2400); *Production Yearbook.*

G.K. Hall and Company, 70 Lincoln Street, Boston, Massachusetts 02111 (617) 423-3990; *The World in Figures.*

Inter-American Development Bank, 1300 New York Avenue, NW, Washington, D.C. 20577 (202) 623-1753; *Economic and Social Progress in Latin America.*

GUYANA - LIBRARIES

Facts on File, 460 Park Avenue South, New York, New York 10016 (800) 443-8323; *The New Book of World Rankings.*

GUYANA - LIVESTOCK AND POULTRY

Euromonitor Publications Limited, 87-88 Turnmill Street, London EC1M 5QU, England; *International Marketing Data and Statistics.*

Facts on File, 460 Park Avenue South, New York, New York 10016 (800) 443-8323; *The New Book of World Rankings.*

Food and Agricultural Organization of the United Nations (FAO), Via delle Terme di Caracalla, 00100 Rome, Italy (Telephone Number in U.S. (202) 653-2400); *Production Yearbook,* and *The State of Food and Agriculture.*

G.K. Hall and Company, 70 Lincoln Street, Boston, Massachusetts 02111 (617) 423-3990; *The World in Figures.*

Statistical Office of the United Nations, Publishing Service, New York, New York 10017 (800) 253-9646; *Statistical Yearbook.*

GUYANA - LIVING LEVELS

G.K. Hall and Company, 70 Lincoln Street, Boston, Massachusetts 02111 (617) 423-3990; *The World in Figures.*

Statistical Office of the United Nations, Publishing Service, New York, New York 10017 (800) 253-9646; *Statistical Yearbook for Latin America and the Caribbean.*

Times Books, 201 East 50th Street, New York, New York 10022 (212) 751-2600; *The Economist Book of Vital World Statistics.*

GUYANA - MAIL - NUMBER OF PIECES SENT OR RECEIVED

Statistical Office of the United Nations, Publishing Service, New York, New York 10017 (800) 253-9646; *Statistical Yearbook.*

GUYANA - MAIN ECONOMIC INDICATORS - See GUYANA - ECONOMY

GUYANA - MANGANESE ORE PRODUCTION AND CONSUMPTION - See GUYANA - MINING AND MINERAL PRODUCTS

GUYANA - MANUFACTURING

Facts on File, 460 Park Avenue South, New York, New York 10016 (800) 443-8323; *The New Book of World Rankings.*

G.K. Hall and Company, 70 Lincoln Street, Boston, Massachusetts 02111 (617) 423-3990; *The World in Figures.*

Inter-American Development Bank, 1300 New York Avenue, NW, Washington, D.C. 20577 (202) 623-1753; *Economic and Social Progress in Latin America.*

Statistical Office of the United Nations, Publishing Service, New York, New York 10017 (800) 253-9646; *Statistical Yearbook,* and *Statistical Yearbook for Latin America and the Caribbean.*

The World Bank, 1818 H Street, NW, Washington, D.C. 20433 (202) 477-1234; *World Tables.*

GUYANA - MARRIAGE RATES

Facts on File, 460 Park Avenue South, New York, New York 10016 (800) 443-8323; *The New Book of World Rankings.*

Statistical Office of the United Nations, Publishing Service, New York, New York 10017 (800) 253-9646; *Demographic Yearbook,* and *Statistical Yearbook.*

GUYANA - MEAT PRODUCTION - See GUYANA - LIVESTOCK AND POULTRY

GUYANA - MERCHANT SHIPPING

G.K. Hall and Company, 70 Lincoln Street, Boston, Massachusetts 02111 (617) 423-3990; *The World in Figures.*

Statistical Office of the United Nations, Publishing Service, New York, New York 10017 (800) 253-9646; *Statistical Yearbook.*

Times Books, 201 East 50th Street, New York, New York 10022 (212) 751-2600; *The Economist Book of Vital World Statistics.*

GUYANA - MILITARY

G.K. Hall and Company, 70 Lincoln Street, Boston, Massachusetts 02111 (617) 423-3990; *The World in Figures.*

The International Institute for Strategic Studies, 23 Tavistock Street, London WC2E 7NQ, England; *The Military Balance.*

U.S. Arms Control and Disarmament Agency, 320 Twenty-first Street, Northwest, Washington, D.C. 20451 (202) 647-8677; *World Military Expenditures and Arms Transfers.*

GUYANA - MILK PRODUCTION - See GUYANA - DAIRY PRODUCTS

GUYANA - MINING AND MINERAL PRODUCTS

Commodity Research Bureau, Incorporated, 75 Wall Street, New York, New York 10005 (212) 504-7754; *Commodity Year Book.*

Facts on File, 460 Park Avenue South, New York, New York 10016 (800) 443-8323; *The New Book of World Rankings.*

G.K. Hall and Company, 70 Lincoln Street, Boston, Massachusetts 02111 (617) 423-3990; *The World in Figures.*

Inter-American Development Bank, 1300 New York Avenue, NW, Washington, D.C. 20577 (202) 623-1753; *Economic and Social Progress in Latin America.*

International Monetary Fund, 700 Nineteenth Street, NW, Washington, D.C. 20431 (202) 623-7000; *International Financial Statistics.*

Statistical Office of the United Nations, Publishing Service, New York, New York 10017 (800) 253-9646; *Statistical Yearbook,* and *Statistical Yearbook for Latin America and the Caribbean.*

GUYANA - MONEY EXCHANGE RATE

Euromonitor Publications Limited, 87-88 Turnmill Street, London EC1M 5QU, England; *International Marketing Data and Statistics.*

Inter-American Development Bank, 1300 New York Avenue, NW, Washington, D.C. 20577 (202) 623-1753; *Economic and Social Progress in Latin America.*

International Monetary Fund, 700 Nineteenth Street, NW, Washington, D.C. 20431 (202) 623-7000; *International Financial Statistics.*

Statistical Office of the United Nations, Publishing Service, New York, New York 10017 (800) 253-9646; *Statistical Yearbook.*

GUYANA - MONEY RATES - MARKET

Inter-American Development Bank, 1300 New York Avenue, NW, Washington, D.C. 20577 (202) 623-1753; *Economic and Social Progress in Latin America.*

GUYANA - MONEY RESERVES

Euromonitor Publications Limited, 87-88 Turnmill Street, London EC1M 5QU, England; *International Marketing Data and Statistics.*

Inter-American Development Bank, 1300 New York Avenue, NW, Washington, D.C. 20577 (202) 623-1753; *Economic and Social Progress in Latin America.*

GUYANA - MONEY SUPPLY

Euromonitor Publications Limited, 87-88 Turnmill Street, London EC1M 5QU, England; *International Marketing Data and Statistics.*

Federal Statistical Office, Gustav - Stresemann - Ring 11, D-6200 Wiesbaden, Germany; *Guyana.*

G.K. Hall and Company, 70 Lincoln Street, Boston, Massachusetts 02111 (617) 423-3990; *The World in Figures.*

Inter-American Development Bank, 1300 New York Avenue, NW, Washington, D.C. 20577 (202) 623-1753; *Economic and Social Progress in Latin America.*

International Monetary Fund, 700 Nineteenth Street, NW, Washington, D.C. 20431 (202) 623-7000; *International Financial Statistics.*

Statistical Office of the United Nations, Publishing Service, New York, New York 10017 (800) 253-9646; *Statistical Yearbook.*

The World Bank, 1818 H Street, NW, Washington, D.C. 20433 (202) 477-1234; *World Tables.*

GUYANA - MOTION PICTURES

Statistical Office of the United Nations, Publishing Service, New York, New York 10017 (800) 253-9646; *Statistical Yearbook.*

United Nations Educational, Scientific and Cultural Organization (UNESCO), 7 Place de Fontenoy, F-75700 Paris, France (Telephone Number in U.S. (212) 963-5981); *Statistical Yearbook.*

GUYANA - MOTOR VEHICLE TAXES - See GUYANA - TAXATION

GUYANA - MOTOR VEHICLES IN USE

G.K. Hall and Company, 70 Lincoln Street, Boston, Massachusetts 02111 (617) 423-3990; *The World in Figures.*

Statistical Office of the United Nations, Publishing Service, New York, New York 10017 (800) 253-9646; *Statistical Yearbook.*

Times Books, 201 East 50th Street, New York, New York 10022 (212) 751-2600; *The Economist Book of Vital World Statistics.*

GUYANA - MULES - See GUYANA - LIVESTOCK AND POULTRY

GUYANA - MUSEUMS

Facts on File, 460 Park Avenue South, New York, New York 10016 (800) 443-8323; *The New Book of World Rankings.*

United Nations Educational, Scientific and Cultural Organization (UNESCO), 7 Place de Fontenoy, F-75700 Paris, France (Telephone Number in U.S. (212) 963-5981); *Statistical Yearbook.*

GUYANA - NATALITY - See GUYANA - BIRTH RATES

GUYANA - NATIONAL ACCOUNTS

Federal Statistical Office, Gustav - Stresemann - Ring 11, D-6200 Wiesbaden, Germany; *Guyana.*

Gale Research Incorporated, 835 Penobscot Building, Detroit, Michigan 48226 (800) 877-4253; *International Historical Statistics: The Americas and Australasia.*

Inter-American Development Bank, 1300 New York Avenue, NW, Washington, D.C. 20577 (202) 623-1753; *Economic and Social Progress in Latin America.*

International Monetary Fund, 700 Nineteenth Street, NW, Washington, D.C. 20431 (202) 623-7000; *International Financial Statistics.*

Statistical Office of the United Nations, Publishing Service, New York, New York 10017 (800) 253-9646; *National Accounts Statistics,* and *Statistical Yearbook.*

GUYANA - NATIONAL INCOME

Facts on File, 460 Park Avenue South, New York, New York 10016 (800) 443-8323; *The New Book of World Rankings.*

G.K. Hall and Company, 70 Lincoln Street, Boston, Massachusetts 02111 (617) 423-3990; *The World in Figures.*

Inter-American Development Bank, 1300 New York Avenue, NW, Washington, D.C. 20577 (202) 623-1753; *Economic and Social Progress in Latin America.*

Statistical Office of the United Nations, Publishing Service, New York, New York 10017 (800) 253-9646; *Statistical Yearbook,* and *Statistical Yearbook for Latin America and the Caribbean.*

GUYANA - NATIONAL PRODUCT

Facts on File, 460 Park Avenue South, New York, New York 10016 (800) 443-8323; *The New Book of World Rankings.*

Statistical Office of the United Nations, Publishing Service, New York, New York 10017 (800) 253-9646; *Statistical Yearbook.*

GUYANA - NATURAL GAS PRODUCTION - See GUYANA - MINING AND MINERAL PRODUCTS

GUYANA - NEWSPAPER PRODUCTION - See GUYANA - FORESTRY AND FOREST PRODUCTS

GUYANA - NEWSPRINT - See GUYANA - FORESTRY AND FOREST PRODUCTS

GUYANA - NUTRITION

Statistical Office of the United Nations, Publishing Service, New York, New York 10017 (800) 253-9646; *Statistical Yearbook for Latin America and the Caribbean.*

GUYANA - OCCUPATIONS - See GUYANA - LABOR FORCE

GUYANA - PAPER - See GUYANA - FORESTRY AND FOREST PRODUCTS

GUYANA - PEANUT PRODUCTION - See GUYANA - CROPS

GUYANA - PERIODICALS

United Nations Educational, Scientific and Cultural Organization (UNESCO), 7 Place de Fontenoy, F-75700 Paris, France (Telephone Number in U.S. (212) 963-5981); *Statistical Yearbook.*

GUYANA - PESTICIDE USE

Food and Agricultural Organization of the United Nations (FAO) Via delle Terme di Caracalla, 00100 Rome, Italy (Telephone Number in U.S. (202) 653-2400); *The State of Food and Agriculture.*

GUYANA - PETROLEUM INDUSTRY

Facts on File, 460 Park Avenue South, New York, New York 10016 (800) 443-8323; *The New Book of World Rankings.*

Food and Agricultural Organization of the United Nations (FAO) Via delle Terme di Caracalla, 00100 Rome, Italy (Telephone Number in U.S. (202) 653-2400); *The State of Food and Agriculture.*

G.K. Hall and Company, 70 Lincoln Street, Boston, Massachusetts 02111 (617) 423-3990; *The World in Figures.*

Inter-American Development Bank, 1300 New York Avenue, NW, Washington, D.C. 20577 (202) 623-1753; *Economic and Social Progress in Latin America.*

GUYANA - PIGS - See GUYANA - LIVESTOCK AND POULTRY

GUYANA - POLITICAL DATA

U.C.L.A. Latin American Center Publications, University of California, Los Angeles, California 90024 (310) 825-6634; *Statistical Abstract of Latin America.*

GUYANA - POPULATION

The Economist Intelligence Unit, 111 West 57th Street, New York, New York 10019 (800) 938-4685; *The World Market Atlas.*

Euromonitor Publications Limited, 87-88 Turnmill Street, London EC1M 5QU, England; *International Marketing Data and Statistics.*

Facts on File, 460 Park Avenue South, New York, New York 10016 (800) 443-8323; *The New Book of World Rankings.*

Federal Statistical Office, Gustav - Stresemann - Ring 11, D-6200 Wiesbaden, Germany; *Guyana.*

Food and Agricultural Organization of the United Nations (FAO), Via delle Terme di Caracalla, 00100 Rome, Italy (Telephone Number in U.S. (202) 653-2400); *Production Yearbook.*

Gale Research Incorporated, 835 Penobscot Building, Detroit, Michigan 48226 (800) 877-4253; *International Historical Statistics:*

The Americas and Australasia.

G.K. Hall and Company, 70 Lincoln Street, Boston, Massachusetts 02111 (617) 423-3990; *The World in Figures.*

Inter-American Development Bank, 1300 New York Avenue, NW, Washington, D.C. 20577 (202) 623-1753; *Economic and Social Progress in Latin America.*

International Labour Office, I.L.O. Publications, CH-1211, Geneva 22, Switzerland; *Yearbook of Labour Statistics.*

Statistical Office of the United Nations, Publishing Service, New York, New York 10017 (800) 253-9646; *Demographic Yearbook, Statistical Yearbook,* and *Statistical Yearbook for Latin America and the Caribbean.*

Times Books, 201 East 50th Street, New York, New York 10022 (212) 751-2600; *The Economist Book of Vital World Statistics.*

United Nations Educational, Scientific and Cultural Organization (UNESCO), 7 Place de Fontenoy, F-75700 Paris, France (Telephone Number in U.S. (212) 963-5981); *Statistical Yearbook.*

U.S. Arms Control and Disarmament Agency, 320 Twenty-first Street, Northwest, Washington, D.C. 20451 (202) 647-8677; *World Military Expenditures and Arms Transfers.*

World Health Organization, Office of Publications, Avenue Appia, CH-1211 Geneva 27, Switzerland (Telephone Number in U.S. (518) 436-9686); *World Health Statistics Annual.*

GUYANA - POST OFFICES

Facts on File, 460 Park Avenue South, New York, New York 10016 (800) 443-8323; *The New Book of World Rankings.*

GUYANA - POTATO PRODUCTION - See GUYANA - CROPS

GUYANA - PRICES

Facts on File, 460 Park Avenue South, New York, New York 10016 (800) 443-8323; *The New Book of World Rankings.*

Federal Statistical Office, Gustav - Stresemann - Ring 11, D-6200 Wiesbaden, Germany; *Guyana.*

Food and Agricultural Organization of the United Nations (FAO), Via delle Terme di Caracalla, 00100 Rome, Italy (Telephone Number in U.S. (202) 653-2400); *Production Yearbook,* and *The State of Food and Agriculture.*

Gale Research Incorporated, 835 Penobscot Building, Detroit, Michigan 48226 (800) 877-4253; *International Historical Statistics: The Americas and Australasia.*

G.K. Hall and Company, 70 Lincoln Street, Boston, Massachusetts 02111 (617) 423-3990; *The World in Figures.*

International Labour Office, I.L.O. Publications, CH-1211, Geneva 22, Switzerland; *Yearbook of Labour Statistics.*

International Monetary Fund, 700 Nineteenth Street, NW, Washington, D.C. 20431 (202) 623-7000; *International Financial Statistics.*

Statistical Office of the United Nations, Publishing Service, New York, New York 10017 (800) 253-9646; *Statistical Yearbook for Latin America and the Caribbean.*

GUYANA - PRINTING AND WRITING PAPER - See GUYANA - FORESTRY AND FOREST PRODUCTS

GUYANA - PRODUCTION

Facts on File, 460 Park Avenue South, New York, New York 10016 (800) 443-8323; *The New Book of World Rankings.*

G.K. Hall and Company, 70 Lincoln Street, Boston, Massachusetts 02111 (617) 423-3990; *The World in Figures.*

GUYANA - PRODUCTIVITY

Euromonitor Publications Limited, 87-88 Turnmill Street, London EC1M 5QU, England; *International Marketing Data and Statistics.*

GUYANA - PROPERTY TAXES - See GUYANA -TAXATION

GUYANA - PUBLIC CONSUMPTION FUND

Inter-American Development Bank, 1300 New York Avenue, NW, Washington, D.C. 20577 (202) 623-1753; *Economic and Social Progress in Latin America.*

GUYANA - PUBLIC EXPENDITURE

Inter-American Development Bank, 1300 New York Avenue, NW, Washington, D.C. 20577 (202) 623-1753; *Economic and Social Progress in Latin America.*

Statistical Office of the United Nations, Publishing Service, New York, New York 10017 (800) 253-9646; *Statistical Yearbook for Latin America and the Caribbean.*

GUYANA - PUBLIC FINANCE

Facts on File, 460 Park Avenue South, New York, New York 10016 (800) 443-8323; *The New Book of World Rankings.*

Federal Statistical Office, Gustav - Stresemann - Ring 11, D-6200 Wiesbaden, Germany; *Guyana.*

Inter-American Development Bank, 1300 New York Avenue, NW, Washington, D.C. 20577 (202) 623-1753; *Economic and Social Progress in Latin America.*

GUYANA - PUBLIC REVENUES

Inter-American Development Bank, 1300 New York Avenue, NW, Washington, D.C. 20577 (202) 623-1753; *Economic and Social Progress in Latin America.*

GUYANA - RADIO BROADCASTING - See GUYANA - BROADCASTING

GUYANA - RAILWAYS

G.K. Hall and Company, 70 Lincoln Street, Boston, Massachusetts 02111 (617) 423-3990; *The World in Figures.*

Statistical Office of the United Nations, Publishing Service, New York, New York 10017 (800) 253-9646; *Statistical Yearbook.*

GUYANA - RELIGION

Facts on File, 460 Park Avenue South, New York, New York 10016 (800) 443-8323; *The New Book of World Rankings.*

GUYANA - RENT PRICES

International Labour Office, I.L.O. Publications, CH-1211, Geneva 22, Switzerland; *Yearbook of Labour Statistics.*

GUYANA - RETAIL TRADE

G.K. Hall and Company, 70 Lincoln Street, Boston, Massachusetts 02111 (617) 423-3990; *The World in Figures.*

Inter-American Development Bank, 1300 New York Avenue, NW, Washington, D.C. 20577 (202) 623-1753; *Economic and Social Progress in Latin America.*

GUYANA - RICE - See GUYANA - CROPS

GUYANA - ROOT AND TUBER PRODUCTION - See GUYANA - CROPS

GUYANA - ROUNDWOOD PRODUCTION - See GUYANA - FORESTRY AND FOREST PRODUCTS

GUYANA - RUBBER PRODUCTION

Facts on File, 460 Park Avenue South, New York, New York 10016 (800) 443-8323; *The New Book of World Rankings.*

GUYANA - SAWNWOOD PRODUCTION - See GUYANA - FORESTRY AND FOREST PRODUCTS

GUYANA - SCIENTISTS AND TECHNICIANS

Statistical Office of the United Nations, Publishing Service, New York, New York 10017 (800) 253-9646; *Statistical Yearbook.*

GUYANA - SENIOR CITIZENS

Facts on File, 460 Park Avenue South, New York, New York 10016 (800) 443-8323; *The New Book of World Rankings.*

GUYANA - SHEEP - See GUYANA - LIVESTOCK AND POULTRY

GUYANA - SILVER PRODUCTION AND CONSUMPTION - See GUYANA - MINING AND MINERAL PRODUCTS

GUYANA - SOCIAL DATA

Facts on File, 460 Park Avenue South, New York, New York 10016 (800) 443-8323; *The New Book of World Rankings.*

G.K. Hall and Company, 70 Lincoln Street, Boston, Massachusetts 02111 (617) 423-3990; *The World in Figures.*

U.C.L.A. Latin American Center Publications, University of California, Los Angeles, California 90024 (310) 825-6634; *Statistical Abstract of Latin America.*

GUYANA - SOCIAL SECURITY

Inter-American Development Bank, 1300 New York Avenue, NW, Washington, D.C. 20577 (202) 623-1753; *Economic and Social Progress in Latin America.*

GUYANA - SOCIOECONOMIC DATA

Inter-American Development Bank, 1300 New York Avenue, NW, Washington, D.C. 20577 (202) 623-1753; *Economic and Social Progress in Latin America.*

U.C.L.A. Latin American Center Publications, University of California, Los Angeles, California 90024 (310) 825-6634; *Statistical Abstract of Latin America.*

GUYANA - STAMP TAXES AND DUTIES - See GUYANA - TAXATION

GUYANA - STATE BUDGET REVENUE AND EXPENDITURES

Euromonitor Publications Limited, 87-88 Turnmill Street, London EC1M 5QU, England; *International Marketing Data and Statistics.*

Inter-American Development Bank, 1300 New York Avenue, NW, Washington, D.C. 20577 (202) 623-1753; *Economic and Social Progress in Latin America.*

GUYANA - STEEL PRODUCTION AND CONSUMPTION - See GUYANA - MINING AND MINERAL PRODUCTS

GUYANA - STOCKS - COMMODITY - MARKET PRICE - INDEX

Food and Agricultural Organization of the United Nations (FAO) Via delle Terme di Caracalla, 00100 Rome, Italy (Telephone Number in U.S. (202) 653-2400); *The State of Food and Agriculture.*

GUYANA - SUGAR - See GUYANA - CROPS

GUYANA - TAXATION

G.K. Hall and Company, 70 Lincoln Street, Boston, Massachusetts 02111 (617) 423-3990; *The World in Figures.*

Inter-American Development Bank, 1300 New York Avenue, NW, Washington, D.C. 20577 (202) 623-1753; *Economic and Social Progress in Latin America.*

International Monetary Fund, 700 Nineteenth Street, NW, Washington, D.C. 20431 (202) 623-7000; *Government Finance Statistics Yearbook.*

Statistical Office of the United Nations, Publishing Service, New York, New York 10017 (800) 253-9646; *Statistical Yearbook for Latin America and the Caribbean.*

The World Bank, 1818 H Street, NW, Washington, D.C. 20433 (202) 477-1234; *World Tables.*

GUYANA - TELEPHONES IN USE

American Telephone and Telegraph Company, 26 Parsippany Road, Whippany, New Jersey 07981 (800) 338-4038; *The World's Telephones.*

G.K. Hall and Company, 70 Lincoln Street, Boston, Massachusetts 02111 (617) 423-3990; *The World in Figures.*

Statistical Office of the United Nations, Publishing Service, New York, New York 10017 (800) 253-9646; *Statistical Yearbook.*

GUYANA - TELEVISION BROADCASTING - See GUYANA - BROADCASTING

GUYANA - TEXTILE INDUSTRY

G.K. Hall and Company, 70 Lincoln Street, Boston, Massachusetts 02111 (617) 423-3990; *The World in Figures.*

GUYANA - TOBACCO PRODUCTION

Facts on File, 460 Park Avenue South, New York, New York 10016 (800) 443-8323; *The New Book of World Rankings.*

Statistical Office of the United Nations, Publishing Service, New York, New York 10017 (800) 253-9646; *Statistical Yearbook.*

GUYANA - TOURISM

Facts on File, 460 Park Avenue South, New York, New York 10016 (800) 443-8323; *The New Book of World Rankings.*

Federal Statistical Office, Gustav - Stresemann - Ring 11, D-6200 Wiesbaden, Germany; *Guyana.*

G.K. Hall and Company, 70 Lincoln Street, Boston, Massachusetts 02111 (617) 423-3990; *The World in Figures.*

Statistical Office of the United Nations, Publishing Service, New York, New York 10017 (800) 253-9646; *Statistical Yearbook.*

Times Books, 201 East 50th Street, New York, New York 10022 (212) 751-2600; *The Economist Book of Vital World Statistics.*

GUYANA - TRACTORS IN USE

Statistical Office of the United Nations, Publishing Service, New York, New York 10017 (800) 253-9646; *Statistical Yearbook.*

GUYANA - TRADE - See GUYANA - FOREIGN TRADE

GUYANA - TRANSPORTATION AND COMMUNICATIONS

Facts on File, 460 Park Avenue South, New York, New York 10016 (800) 443-8323; *The New Book of World Rankings.*

Federal Statistical Office, Gustav - Stresemann - Ring 11, D-6200 Wiesbaden, Germany; *Guyana.*

Gale Research Incorporated, 835 Penobscot Building, Detroit, Michigan 48226 (800) 877-4253; *International Historical Statistics: The Americas and Australasia.*

G.K. Hall and Company, 70 Lincoln Street, Boston, Massachusetts 02111 (617) 423-3990; *The World in Figures.*

Inter-American Development Bank, 1300 New York Avenue, NW, Washington, D.C. 20577 (202) 623-1753; *Economic and Social Progress in Latin America.*

GUYANA - UNEMPLOYMENT

Euromonitor Publications Limited, 87-88 Turnmill Street, London EC1M 5QU, England; *International Marketing Data and Statistics.*

International Labour Office, I.L.O. Publications, CH-1211, Geneva 22, Switzerland; *Yearbook of Labour Statistics.*

Statistical Office of the United Nations, Publishing Service, New York, New York 10017 (800) 253-9646; *Statistical Yearbook.*

GUYANA - VITAL STATISTICS

Euromonitor Publications Limited, 87-88 Turnmill Street, London EC1M 5QU, England; *International Marketing Data and Statistics.*

Gale Research Incorporated, 835 Penobscot Building, Detroit, Michigan 48226 (800) 877-4253; *International Historical Statistics: The Americas and Australasia.*

G.K. Hall and Company, 70 Lincoln Street, Boston, Massachusetts 02111 (617) 423-3990; *The World in Figures.*

Statistical Office of the United Nations, Publishing Service, New York, New York 10017 (800) 253-9646; *Statistical Yearbook.*

World Health Organization, Office of Publications, Avenue Appia, CH-1211 Geneva 27, Switzerland (Telephone Number in U.S. (518) 436-9686); *World Health Statistics Annual.*

GUYANA - WAGES

Federal Statistical Office, Gustav - Stresemann - Ring 11, D-6200 Wiesbaden, Germany; *Guyana.*

G.K. Hall and Company, 70 Lincoln Street, Boston, Massachusetts 02111 (617) 423-3990; *The World in Figures.*

International Labour Office, I.L.O. Publications, CH-1211, Geneva 22, Switzerland; *Yearbook of Labour Statistics.*

Statistical Office of the United Nations, Publishing Service, New York, New York 10017 (800) 253-9646; *Statistical Yearbook.*

GUYANA - WEATHER

Facts on File, 460 Park Avenue South, New York, New York 10016 (800) 443-8323; *The New Book of World Rankings.*

G.K. Hall and Company, 70 Lincoln Street, Boston, Massachusetts 02111 (617) 423-3990; *The World in Figures.*

GUYANA - WELFARE

Inter-American Development Bank, 1300 New York Avenue, NW, Washington, D.C. 20577 (202) 623-1753; *Economic and Social Progress in Latin America.*

GUYANA - WHEAT PRODUCTION AND PRICES - See GUYANA - CROPS

GUYANA - WHOLESALE PRICES

Inter-American Development Bank, 1300 New York Avenue, NW, Washington, D.C. 20577 (202) 623-1753; *Economic and Social Progress in Latin America.*

GUYANA - WHOLESALE TRADE

Inter-American Development Bank, 1300 New York Avenue, NW, Washington, D.C. 20577 (202) 623-1753; *Economic and Social Progress in Latin America.*

GUYANA - WINE PRODUCTION

Facts on File, 460 Park Avenue South, New York, New York 10016 (800) 443-8323; *The New Book of World Rankings.*

GUYANA - WOOL PRODUCTION

Facts on File, 460 Park Avenue South, New York, New York 10016 (800) 443-8323; *The New Book of World Rankings.*

GYPSUM AND GYPSUM PRODUCTS

U.S. Department of Labor, Bureau of Labor Statistics, Two Massachusetts Avenue, NE, Washington, D.C. 20212 (202) 606-7828;

Producer Price Indexes.

U.S. Department of the Interior, Bureau of Mines, 810 Seventh Street, NW, Washington, D.C. 20241 (202) 501-9649; *Mineral Commodity Summaries*, *Minerals Yearbook*, and *Annual Reports*.

H

HADDOCK

U.S. Department of Commerce, National Oceanic and Atmospheric Administration, National Marine Fisheries Service, 1335 East-West Highway, Silver Spring, Maryland 20910 (301) 427-2239; *Fishery Statistics of the United States*, and *Fisheries of the United States*.

Haiti - National Statistical Office

Institut Haitien de Statistique, Cite de l'Exposition, Boulevard Harry Truman, Port-au-Prince, Haiti.

Haiti - Primary Statistics Source

Institut Haitien de Statistique, Cite de l'Exposition, Boulevard Harry Truman, Port-au-Prince, Haiti; *Bulletin Trimestriel de Statistique* (Quarterly Bulletin of Statistics).

HAITI - AGRICULTURE

Facts on File, 460 Park Avenue South, New York, New York 10016 (800) 443-8323; *The New Book of World Rankings*.

Federal Statistical Office, Gustav - Stresesmann - Ring 11, D-6200 Wiesbaden, Germany; *Haiti*.

Food and Agricultural Organization of the United Nations (FAO) Via delle Terme di Caracalla, 00100 Rome, Italy (Telephone Number in U.S. (202) 653-2400); *Production Yearbook, The State of Food and Agriculture*, and *Trade Yearbook*.

Gale Research Incorporated, 835 Penobscot Building, Detroit, Michigan 48226 (800) 877-4253; *International Historical Statistics The Americas and Australasia*.

G.K. Hall and Company, 70 Lincoln Street, Boston, Massachusetts 02111 (617) 423-3990; *The World in Figures*.

Inter-American Development Bank, 1300 New York Avenue, NW, Washington, D.C. 20577 (202) 623-1753; *Economic and Social Progress in Latin America*.

Statistical Office of the United Nations, Publishing Service, New York, New York 10017 (800) 253-9646; *Statistical Yearbook*, and *Statistical Yearbook for Latin America and the Caribbean*.

Times Books, 201 East 50th Street, New York, New York 10022 (212) 751-2600; *The Economist Book of Vital World Statistics*.

U.C.L.A. Latin American Center Publications, University of California, Los Angeles, California 90024 (310) 825-6634; *Statistical Abstract of Latin America*.

The World Bank, 1818 H Street, NW, Washington, D.C. 20433 (202) 477-1234; *World Tables*.

HAITI - AIRLINE SERVICE

Facts on File, 460 Park Avenue South, New York, New York 10016 (800) 443-8323; *The New Book of World Rankings*.

G.K. Hall and Company, 70 Lincoln Street, Boston, Massachusetts 02111 (617) 423-3990; *The World in Figures*.

Times Books, 201 East 50th Street, New York, New York 10022 (212) 751-2600; *The Economist Book of Vital World Statistics*.

HAITI - ALUMINUM PRODUCTION AND CONSUMPTION - See HAITI - MINING AND MINERAL PRODUCTS

HAITI - ANIMAL HEALTH

Food and Agricultural Organization of the United Nations (FAO), Via delle Terme di Caracalla, 00100 Rome, Italy (Telephone Number in U.S. (202) 653-2400); *Animal Health Yearbook*.

HAITI - AREA AND DENSITY OF POPULATION

Facts on File, 460 Park Avenue South, New York, New York 10016 (800) 253-9646; *The New Book of World Rankings*.

Federal Statistical Office, Gustav - Stresesmann - Ring 11, D-6200 Wiesbaden, Germany; *Haiti*.

Food and Agricultural Organization of the United Nations (FAO) Via delle Terme di Caracalla, 00100 Rome, Italy (Telephone Number in U.S. (202) 653-2400); *The State of Food and Agriculture*.

G.K. Hall and Company, 70 Lincoln Street, Boston, Massachusetts 02111 (617) 423-3990; *The World in Figures*.

Inter-American Development Bank, 1300 New York Avenue, NW, Washington, D.C. 20577 (202) 623-1753; *Economic and Social Progress in Latin America*.

Statistical Office of the United Nations, Publishing Service, New York, New York 10017 (800) 253-9646; *Statistical Yearbook*.

Times Books, 201 East 50th Street, New York, New York 10022 (212) 751-2600; *The Economist Book of Vital World Statistics*.

United Nations Educational, Scientific and Cultural Organization (UNESCO), 7 Place de Fontenoy, F-75700 Paris, France (Telephone Number in U.S. (212) 963-5981); *Statistical Yearbook.*

HAITI - ARMS EXPORTS AND IMPORTS

U.S. Arms Control and Disarmament Agency, 320 Twenty-first Street, Northwest, Washington, D.C. 20451 (202) 647-8677; *World Military Expenditures and Arms Transfers.*

HAITI - BALANCE OF PAYMENTS

The Economist Intelligence Unit, 111 West 57th Street, New York, New York 10019 (800) 938-4685; *The World Market Atlas.*

Federal Statistical Office, Gustav - Stresesmann - Ring 11, D-6200 Wiesbaden, Germany; *Haiti.*

G.K. Hall and Company, 70 Lincoln Street, Boston, Massachusetts 02111 (617) 423-3990; *The World in Figures.*

Inter-American Development Bank, 1300 New York Avenue, NW, Washington, D.C. 20577 (202) 623-1753; *Economic and Social Progress in Latin America.*

International Monetary Fund, 700 Nineteenth Street, NW, Washington, D.C. 20431 (202) 623-7000; *Balance of Payments Yearbook,* and *International Financial Statistics.*

Organization of American States (OAS), General Secretariat, Washington, D.C. 20006 (202) 458-3533; *Statistical Bulletin of the OAS.*

Statistical Office of the United Nations, Publishing Service, New York, New York 10017 (800) 253-9646; *Economic Survey of Latin America and the Caribbean,* and *Statistical Yearbook for Latin America and the Caribbean.*

Times Books, 201 East 50th Street, New York, New York 10022 (212) 751-2600; *The Economist Book of Vital World Statistics.*

U.C.L.A. Latin American Center Publications, University of California, Los Angeles, California 90024 (310) 825-6634; *Statistical Abstract of Latin America.*

The World Bank, 1818 H Street, NW, Washington, D.C. 20433 (202) 477-1234; *World Tables.*

HAITI - BANKING

Facts on File, 460 Park Avenue South, New York, New York 10016 (800) 253-9646; *The New Book of World Rankings.*

G.K. Hall and Company, 70 Lincoln Street, Boston, Massachusetts 02111 (617) 423-3990; *The World in Figures.*

Inter-American Development Bank, 1300 New York Avenue, NW, Washington, D.C. 20577 (202) 623-1753; *Economic and Social Progress in Latin America.*

International Monetary Fund, 700 Nineteenth Street, NW, Washington, D.C. 20431 (202) 623-7000; *International Financial Statistics.*

Statistical Office of the United Nations, Publishing Service, New York, New York 10017 (800) 253-9646; *Statistical Yearbook for Latin America and the Caribbean.*

HAITI - BARLEY PRODUCTION - See HAITI - CROPS

HAITI - BAUXITE - See HAITI - MINING AND MINERAL PRODUCTS

HAITI - BEER PRODUCTION

Facts on File, 460 Park Avenue South, New York, New York 10016 (800) 253-9646; *The New Book of World Rankings.*

HAITI - BIRTH RATES

Facts on File, 460 Park Avenue South, New York, New York 10016 (800) 253-9646; *The New Book of World Rankings.*

Statistical Office of the United Nations, Publishing Service, New York, New York 10017 (800) 253-9646; *Demographic Yearbook, Statistical Yearbook,* and *Statistical Yearbook for Latin America and the Caribbean.*

Times Books, 201 East 50th Street, New York, New York 10022 (212) 751-2600; *The Economist Book of Vital World Statistics.*

The World Bank, 1818 H Street, NW, Washington, D.C. 20433 (202) 477-1234; *World Tables.*

HAITI - BONDS

G.K. Hall and Company, 70 Lincoln Street, Boston, Massachusetts 02111 (617) 423-3990; *The World in Figures.*

Inter-American Development Bank, 1300 New York Avenue, NW, Washington, D.C. 20577 (202) 623-1753; *Economic and Social Progress in Latin America.*

HAITI - BOOK PRODUCTION

G.K. Hall and Company, 70 Lincoln Street, Boston, Massachusetts 02111 (617) 423-3990; *The World in Figures.*

HAITI - BROADCASTING

Billboard Limited, Post Office Box 9027, 1006 AA Amsterdam, The Netherlands (Telephone Number in U.S. (212) 764-7300); *World Radio TV Handbook.*

Facts on File, 460 Park Avenue South, New York, New York 10016 (800) 253-9646; *The New Book of World Rankings.*

G.K. Hall and Company, 70 Lincoln Street, Boston, Massachusetts 02111 (617) 423-3990; *The World in Figures.*

Times Books, 201 East 50th Street, New York, New York 10022 (212) 751-2600; *The Economist Book of Vital World Statistics.*

HAITI - BUILDING CONSTRUCTION - See CONSTRUCTION INDUSTRY

HAITI - BUSINESS

G.K. Hall and Company, 70 Lincoln Street, Boston, Massachusetts 02111 (617) 423-3990; *The World in Figures.*

Inter-American Development Bank, 1300 New York Avenue, NW, Washington, D.C. 20577 (202) 623-1753; *Economic and Social Progress in Latin America.*

HAITI - BUSINESS AND PROFESSIONAL LICENSES

International Monetary Fund, 700 Nineteenth Street, NW, Washington, D.C. 20431 (202) 623-7000; *Government Finance Statistics Yearbook.*

HAITI - CABBAGE PRODUCTION - See HAITI - CROPS

HAITI - CALORIE SUPPLY

Food and Agricultural Organization of the United Nations (FAO) Via delle Terme di Caracalla, 00100 Rome, Italy (Telephone Number in U.S. (202) 653-2400); *The State of Food and Agriculture.*

Statistical Office of the United Nations, Publishing Service, New York, New York 10017 (800) 253-9646; *Statistical Yearbook for Latin America and the Caribbean.*

HAITI - CAPITAL INVESTMENT

Inter-American Development Bank, 1300 New York Avenue, NW, Washington, D.C. 20577 (202) 623-1753; *Economic and Social Progress in Latin America.*

HAITI - CAPITAL REVENUE

Inter-American Development Bank, 1300 New York Avenue, NW, Washington, D.C. 20577 (202) 623-1753; *Economic and Social Progress in Latin America.*

International Monetary Fund, 700 Nineteenth Street, NW, Washington, D.C. 20431 (202) 623-7000; *Government Finance Statistics Yearbook.*

HAITI - CASTOR BEAN PRODUCTION - See HAITI - CROPS

HAITI - CATTLE - See HAITI - LIVESTOCK AND POULTRY

HAITI - CEMENT PRODUCTION - See HAITI - MINING AND MINERAL PRODUCTS

HAITI - CHEESE PRODUCTION - See HAITI - DAIRY PRODUCTS

HAITI - CHEMICAL (ORGANIC) PRODUCTION - See HAITI - MINING AND MINERAL PRODUCTS

HAITI - CIGARETTE PRODUCTION - See HAITI - TOBACCO PRODUCTION

HAITI - CLASS STRUCTURE

G.K. Hall and Company, 70 Lincoln Street, Boston, Massachusetts 02111 (617) 423-3990; *The World in Figures.*

HAITI - CLIMATE

Facts on File, 460 Park Avenue South, New York, New York 10016 (800) 253-9646; *The New Book of World Rankings.*

G.K. Hall and Company, 70 Lincoln Street, Boston, Massachusetts 02111 (617) 423-3990; *The World in Figures.*

HAITI - CLOTHING EXPORTS AND IMPORTS

Statistical Office of the United Nations, Publishing Service, New York, New York 10017 (800) 253-9646; *Trade in Manufactures of Developing Countries.*

HAITI - COAL PRODUCTION - See HAITI - MINING AND MINERAL PRODUCTS

HAITI - COCOA (BEANS) PRODUCTION - See HAITI - CROPS

HAITI - COFFEE - See HAITI - CROPS

HAITI - COMMUNICATIONS

Federal Statistical Office, Gustav - Stresesmann - Ring 11, D-6200 Wiesbaden, Germany; *Haiti.*

G.K. Hall and Company, 70 Lincoln Street, Boston, Massachusetts 02111 (617) 423-3990; *The World in Figures.*

Inter-American Development Bank, 1300 New York Avenue, NW, Washington, D.C. 20577 (202) 623-1753; *Economic and Social Progress in Latin America.*

U.C.L.A. Latin American Center Publications, University of California, Los Angeles, California 90024 (310) 825-6634; *Statistical Abstract of Latin America.*

HAITI - CONSTRUCTION INDUSTRY

Facts on File, 460 Park Avenue South, New York, New York 10016 (800) 253-9646; *The New Book of World Rankings.*

Inter-American Development Bank, 1300 New York Avenue, NW, Washington, D.C. 20577 (202) 623-1753; *Economic and Social Progress in Latin America.*

Statistical Office of the United Nations, Publishing Service, New York, New York 10017 (800) 253-9646; *Construction Statistics Yearbook,* and *Statistical Yearbook.*

U.C.L.A. Latin American Center Publications, University of California, Los Angeles, California 90024 (310) 825-6634; *Statistical Abstract of Latin America.*

HAITI - CONSUMER PRICE INDEX

Federal Statistical Office, Gustav - Stresesmann - Ring 11, D-6200 Wiesbaden, Germany; *Haiti.*

G.K. Hall and Company, 70 Lincoln Street, Boston, Massachusetts 02111 (617) 423-3990; *The World in Figures.*

Statistical Office of the United Nations, Publishing Service, New York, New York 10017 (800) 253-9646; *Statistical Yearbook.*

HAITI - CONSUMER PRICES

Federal Statistical Office, Gustav - Stresesmann - Ring 11, D-6200 Wiesbaden, Germany; *Haiti.*

International Labour Office, I.L.O. Publications, CH-1211, Geneva 22, Switzerland; *Yearbook of Labour Statistics.*

International Monetary Fund, 700 Nineteenth Street, NW, Washington, D.C. 20431 (202) 623-7000; *International Financial Statistics.*

Organization of American States (OAS), General Secretariat, Washington, D.C. 20006 (202) 458-3533; *Statistical Bulletin of the OAS.*

Times Books, 201 East 50th Street, New York, New York 10022 (212) 751-2600; *The Economist Book of Vital World Statistics.*

U.C.L.A. Latin American Center Publications, University of California, Los Angeles, California 90024 (310) 825-6634; *Statistical Abstract of Latin America.*

HAITI - CONSUMPTION

G.K. Hall and Company, 70 Lincoln Street, Boston, Massachusetts 02111 (617) 423-3990; *The World in Figures.*

Inter-American Development Bank, 1300 New York Avenue, NW, Washington, D.C. 20577 (202) 623-1753; *Economic and Social Progress in Latin America.*

Statistical Office of the United Nations, Publishing Service, New York, New York 10017 (800) 253-9646; *Statistical Yearbook for Latin America and the Caribbean.*

HAITI - COOPERATIVES

U.C.L.A. Latin American Center Publications, University of California, Los Angeles, California 90024 (310) 825-6634; *Statistical Abstract of Latin America.*

HAITI - COPPER AND COPPER ORE - See HAITI - MINING AND MINERAL PRODUCTS

HAITI - CORN PRODUCTION - See HAITI - CROPS

HAITI - CORPORATE INCOME TAXES - See HAITI - TAXATION

HAITI - CORPORATE TAXES - See HAITI - TAXATION

HAITI - COTTON - See HAITI - CROPS

HAITI - CROPS

Facts on File, 460 Park Avenue South, New York, New York 10016 (800) 253-9646; *The New Book of World Rankings.*

Food and Agricultural Organization of the United Nations (FAO) Via delle Terme di Caracalla, 00100 Rome, Italy (Telephone Number in U.S. (202) 653-2400); *Production Yearbook* and *The State of Food and Agriculture.*

G.K. Hall and Company, 70 Lincoln Street, Boston, Massachusetts 02111 (617) 423-3990; *The World in Figures.*

International Monetary Fund, 700 Nineteenth Street, NW, Washington, D.C. 20431 (202) 623-7000; *International Financial Statistics.*

Organization of American States (OAS), General Secretariat, Washington, D.C. 20006 (202) 458-3533; *Statistical Bulletin of the OAS.*

Statistical Office of the United Nations, Publishing Service, New York, New York 10017 (800) 253-9646; *Statistical Yearbook.*

HAITI - CUSTOMS DUTIES

G.K. Hall and Company, 70 Lincoln Street, Boston, Massachusetts 02111 (617) 423-3990; *The World in Figures.*

Inter-American Development Bank, 1300 New York Avenue, NW, Washington, D.C. 20577 (202) 623-1753; *Economic and Social Progress in Latin America.*

HAITI - DAIRY PRODUCTS

Facts on File, 460 Park Avenue South, New York, New York 10016 (800) 253-9646; *The New Book of World Rankings.*

Food and Agricultural Organization of the United Nations (FAO), Via delle Terme di Caracalla, 00100 Rome, Italy (Telephone Number in U.S. (202) 653-2400); *Production Yearbook,* and *The State of Food and Agriculture.*

Statistical Office of the United Nations, Publishing Service, New York, New York 10017 (800) 253-9646; *Statistical Yearbook.*

HAITI - DEATH RATES

G.K. Hall and Company, 70 Lincoln Street, Boston, Massachusetts 02111 (617) 423-3990; *The World in Figures.*

Statistical Office of the United Nations, Publishing Service, New York, New York 10017 (800) 253-9646; *Statistical Yearbook,* and *Statistical Yearbook for Latin America and the Caribbean.*

Times Books, 201 East 50th Street, New York, New York 10022 (212) 751-2600; *The Economist Book of Vital World Statistics.*

World Health Organization, Office of Publications, Avenue Appia, CH-1211 Geneva 27, Switzerland (Telephone Number in U.S. (518) 436-9686); *World Health Statistics Annual.*

HAITI - DEFENSE EXPENDITURES

G.K. Hall and Company, 70 Lincoln Street, Boston, Massachusetts 02111 (617) 423-3990; *The World in Figures.*

U.S. Arms Control and Disarmament Agency, 320 Twenty-first Street, Northwest, Washington, D.C. 20451 (202) 647-8677; *World Military Expenditures and Arms Transfers.*

HAITI - DEMOGRAPHY

The Economist Intelligence Unit, 111 West 57th Street, New York, New York 10019 (800) 938-4685; *The World Market Atlas.*

Facts on File, 460 Park Avenue South, New York, New York 10016 (800) 253-9646; *The New Book of World Rankings.*

Federal Statistical Office, Gustav - Stresesmann - Ring 11, D-6200 Wiesbaden, Germany; *Haiti.*

G.K. Hall and Company, 70 Lincoln Street, Boston, Massachusetts 02111 (617) 423-3990; *The World in Figures.*

HAITI - DEVELOPMENT ASSISTANCE

G.K. Hall and Company, 70 Lincoln Street, Boston, Massachusetts 02111 (617) 423-3990; *The World in Figures.*

Inter-American Development Bank, 1300 New York Avenue, NW, Washington, D.C. 20577 (202) 623-1753; *Economic and Social Progress in Latin America.*

Statistical Office of the United Nations, Publishing Service, New York, New York 10017 (800) 253-9646; *Statistical Yearbook.*

HAITI - DIAMOND PRODUCTION - See HAITI - MINING AND MINERAL PRODUCTS

HAITI - DISCOUNT RATES

Inter-American Development Bank, 1300 New York Avenue, NW, Washington, D.C. 20577 (202) 623-1753; *Economic and Social Progress in Latin America.*

HAITI - DISEASE

G.K. Hall and Company, 70 Lincoln Street, Boston, Massachusetts 02111 (617) 423-3990; *The World in Figures.*

World Health Organization, Office of Publications, Avenue Appia, CH-1211 Geneva 27, Switzerland (Telephone Number in U.S. (518) 436-9686); *World Health Statistics Annual.*

HAITI - DIVORCE RATES

Facts on File, 460 Park Avenue South, New York, New York 10016 (800) 253-9646; *The New Book of World Rankings.*

Statistical Office of the United Nations, Publishing Service, New York, New York 10017 (800) 253-9646; *Demographic Yearbook.*

HAITI - DOMESTIC PRODUCT

G.K. Hall and Company, 70 Lincoln Street, Boston, Massachusetts 02111 (617) 423-3990; *The World in Figures.*

HAITI - DUCKS - See HAITI - LIVESTOCK AND POULTRY

HAITI - ECONOMY

Facts on File, 460 Park Avenue South, New York, New York 10016 (800) 253-9646; *The New Book of World Rankings.*

Federal Statistical Office, Gustav - Stresesmann - Ring 11, D-6200 Wiesbaden, Germany; *Haiti.*

G.K. Hall and Company, 70 Lincoln Street, Boston, Massachusetts 02111 (617) 423-3990; *The World in Figures.*

Inter-American Development Bank, 1300 New York Avenue, NW, Washington, D.C. 20577 (202) 623-1753; *Economic and Social Progress in Latin America.*

Organization of American States (OAS), General Secretariat, Washington, D.C. 20006 (202) 458-3533; *Statistical Bulletin of the OAS.*

Statistical Office of the United Nations, Publishing Service, New York, New York 10017 (800) 253-9646; *Economic Survey of Latin America and the Caribbean.*

U.C.L.A. Latin American Center Publications, University of California, Los Angeles, California 90024 (310) 825-6634; *Statistical Abstract of Latin America.*

HAITI - EDUCATION

The Economist Intelligence Unit, 111 West 57th Street, New York, New York 10019 (800) 938-4685; *The World Market Atlas.*

Facts on File, 460 Park Avenue South, New York, New York 10016 (800) 253-9646; *The New Book of World Rankings.*

Federal Statistical Office, Gustav - Stresesmann - Ring 11, D-6200 Wiesbaden, Germany; *Haiti.*

Gale Research Incorporated, 835 Penobscot Building, Detroit, Michigan 48226 (800) 877-4253; *International Historical Statistics The Americas and Australasia.*

G.K. Hall and Company, 70 Lincoln Street, Boston, Massachusetts 02111 (617) 423-3990; *The World in Figures.*

Statistical Office of the United Nations, Publishing Service, New York, New York 10017 (800) 253-9646; *Statistical Yearbook for Latin America and the Caribbean.*

Times Books, 201 East 50th Street, New York, New York 10022 (212) 751-2600; *The Economist Book of Vital World Statistics.*

U.C.L.A. Latin American Center Publications, University of California, Los Angeles, California 90024 (310) 825-6634; *Statistical Abstract of Latin America.*

United Nations Educational, Scientific and Cultural Organization (UNESCO), 7 Place de Fontenoy, F-75700 Paris, France (Telephone Number in U.S. (212) 963-5981); *Statistical Yearbook.*

The World Bank, 1818 H Street, NW, Washington, D.C. 20433 (202) 477-1234; *World Tables.*

HAITI - EGG PRODUCTION - See HAITI - DAIRY PRODUCTS

HAITI - ELECTRICITY

Facts on File, 460 Park Avenue South, New York, New York 10016 (800) 253-9646; *The New Book of World Rankings.*

Inter-American Development Bank, 1300 New York Avenue, NW, Washington, D.C. 20577 (202) 623-1753; *Economic and Social Progress in Latin America.*

Statistical Office of the United Nations, Publishing Service, New York, New York 10017 (800) 253-9646; *Statistical Yearbook.*

HAITI - EMPLOYMENT

Facts on File, 460 Park Avenue South, New York, New York 10016 (800) 253-9646; *The New Book of World Rankings.*

Federal Statistical Office, Gustav - Stresesmann - Ring 11, D-6200 Wiesbaden, Germany; *Haiti.*

International Labour Office, I.L.O. Publications, CH-1211, Geneva 22, Switzerland; *Yearbook of Labour Statistics.*

Statistical Office of the United Nations, Publishing Service, New York, New York 10017 (800) 253-9646; *Statistical Yearbook,* and *Statistical Yearbook for Latin America and the Caribbean.*

U.C.L.A. Latin American Center Publications, University of California, Los Angeles, California 90024 (310) 825-6634; *Statistical Abstract of Latin America.*

HAITI - ENERGY

Facts on File, 460 Park Avenue South, New York, New York 10016 (800) 253-9646; *The New Book of World Rankings.*

Food and Agricultural Organization of the United Nations (FAO) Via delle Terme di Caracalla, 00100 Rome, Italy (Telephone Number in U.S. (202) 653-2400); *The State of Food and Agriculture.*

G.K. Hall and Company, 70 Lincoln Street, Boston, Massachusetts 02111 (617) 423-3990; *The World in Figures.*

Statistical Office of the United Nations, Publishing Service, New York, New York 10017 (800) 253-9646; *Energy Statistics Yearbook, Statistical Yearbook,* and *Statistical Yearbook for Latin America and the Caribbean.*

Times Books, 201 East 50th Street, New York, New York 10022 (212) 751-2600; *The Economist Book of Vital World Statistics.*

U.C.L.A. Latin American Center Publications, University of California, Los Angeles, California 90024 (310) 825-6634; *Statistical Abstract of Latin America.*

HAITI - ENGINEERING AND METAL PRODUCTS EXPORTS TO DEVELOPED COUNTRIES

Statistical Office of the United Nations, Publishing Service, New York, New York 10017 (800) 253-9646; *Trade in Manufactures of Developing Countries.*

HAITI - EXCHANGE RATES

Inter-American Development Bank, 1300 New York Avenue, NW, Washington, D.C. 20577 (202) 623-1753; *Economic and Social Progress in Latin America.*

International Monetary Fund, 700 Nineteenth Street, NW, Washington, D.C. 20431 (202) 623-7000; *International Financial Statistics.*

Organization of American States (OAS), General Secretariat, Washington, D.C. 20006 (202) 458-3533; *Statistical Bulletin of the OAS.*

Statistical Office of the United Nations, Publishing Service, New York, New York 10017 (800) 253-9646; *Statistical Yearbook.*

U.C.L.A. Latin American Center Publications, University of California, Los Angeles, California 90024 (310) 825-6634; *Statistical Abstract of Latin America.*

HAITI - EXCISE TAXES - See HAITI - TAXATION

HAITI - EXPORTS

The Economist Intelligence Unit, 111 West 57th Street, New York, New York 10019 (800) 938-4685; *The World Market Atlas.*

Food and Agricultural Organization of the United Nations (FAO) Via delle Terme di Caracalla, 00100 Rome, Italy (Telephone Number in U.S. (202) 653-2400); *The State of Food and Agriculture.*

G.K. Hall and Company, 70 Lincoln Street, Boston, Massachusetts 02111 (617) 423-3990; *The World in Figures.*

Inter-American Development Bank, 1300 New York Avenue, NW, Washington, D.C. 20577 (202) 623-1753; *Economic and Social Progress in Latin America.*

International Monetary Fund, 700 Nineteenth Street, NW, Washington, D.C. 20431 (202) 623-7000; *Direction of Trade Statistics, Government Finance Statistics Yearbook,* and *International Financial Statistics.*

Organization of American States (OAS), General Secretariat, Washington, D.C. 20006 (202) 458-3533; *Statistical Bulletin of the OAS.*

Statistical Office of the United Nations, Publishing Service, New York, New York 10017 (800) 253-9646; *Statistical Yearbook for Latin America and the Caribbean,* and *Trade in Manufactures of Developing Countries.*

Times Books, 201 East 50th Street, New York, New York 10022 (212) 751-2600; *The Economist Book of Vital World Statistics.*

The World Bank, 1818 H Street, NW, Washington, D.C. 20433 (202) 477-1234; *World Tables.*

HAITI - EXTERNAL FINANCING

Inter-American Development Bank, 1300 New York Avenue, NW, Washington, D.C. 20577 (202) 623-1753; *Economic and Social Progress in Latin America.*

Statistical Office of the United Nations, Publishing Service, New York, New York 10017 (800) 253-9646; *Statistical Yearbook for Latin America and the Caribbean.*

HAITI - EXTERNAL INDEBTEDNESS

Inter-American Development Bank, 1300 New York Avenue, NW, Washington, D.C. 20577 (202) 623-1753; *Economic and Social Progress in Latin America.*

Statistical Office of the United Nations, Publishing Service, New York, New York 10017 (800) 253-9646; *Statistical Yearbook for Latin America and the Caribbean.*

The World Bank, 1818 H Street, NW, Washington, D.C. 20433 (202) 477-1234; *World Tables.*

HAITI - EXTERNAL TRADE

Food and Agricultural Organization of the United Nations (FAO) Via delle Terme di Caracalla, 00100 Rome, Italy (Telephone Number in U.S. (202) 653-2400); *The State of Food and Agriculture,* and *Trade Yearbook.*

Gale Research Incorporated, 835 Penobscot Building, Detroit, Michigan 48226 (800) 877-4253; *International Historical Statistics The Americas and Australasia.*

G.K. Hall and Company, 70 Lincoln Street, Boston, Massachusetts 02111 (617) 423-3990; *The World in Figures.*

Inter-American Development Bank, 1300 New York Avenue, NW, Washington, D.C. 20577 (202) 623-1753; *Economic and Social Progress in Latin America.*

Statistical Office of the United Nations, Publishing Service, New York, New York 10017 (800) 253-9646; *Statistical Yearbook,* and *Statistical Yearbook for Latin America and the Caribbean.*

HAITI - FABRIC PRODUCTION - See HAITI - TEXTILE INDUSTRY

HAITI - FAMILY PLANNING

U.C.L.A. Latin American Center Publications, University of California, Los Angeles, California 90024 (310) 825-6634; *Statistical Abstract of Latin America.*

HAITI - FARM CROPS - See HAITI - CROPS

HAITI - FERTILITY RATES

Facts on File, 460 Park Avenue South, New York, New York 10016 (800) 253-9646; *The New Book of World Rankings.*

Times Books, 201 East 50th Street, New York, New York 10022 (212) 751-2600; *The Economist Book of Vital World Statistics.*

The World Bank, 1818 H Street, NW, Washington, D.C. 20433 (202) 477-1234; *World Tables.*

HAITI - FERTILIZER

Food and Agricultural Organization of the United Nations (FAO) Via delle Terme di Caracalla, 00100 Rome, Italy (Telephone Number in U.S. (202) 653-2400); *The State of Food and Agriculture,* and *Fertilizer Yearbook.*

Statistical Office of the United Nations, Publishing Service, New York, New York 10017 (800) 253-9646; *Statistical Yearbook.*

HAITI - FETAL MORTALITY

Statistical Office of the United Nations, Publishing Service, New York, New York 10017 (800) 253-9646; *Demographic Yearbook.*

HAITI - FINANCE

Facts on File, 460 Park Avenue South, New York, New York 10016 (800) 253-9646; *The New Book of World Rankings.*

Federal Statistical Office, Gustav - Stresesmann - Ring 11, D-6200 Wiesbaden, Germany; *Haiti.*

Gale Research Incorporated, 835 Penobscot Building, Detroit, Michigan 48226 (800) 877-4253; *International Historical Statistics The Americas and Australasia.*

G.K. Hall and Company, 70 Lincoln Street, Boston, Massachusetts 02111 (617) 423-3990; *The World in Figures.*

Inter-American Development Bank, 1300 New York Avenue, NW, Washington, D.C. 20577 (202) 623-1753; *Economic and Social Progress in Latin America.*

Organization of American States (OAS), General Secretariat, Washington, D.C. 20006 (202) 458-3533; *Statistical Bulletin of the OAS.*

U.C.L.A. Latin American Center Publications, University of California, Los Angeles, California 90024 (310) 825-6634; *Statistical Abstract of Latin America.*

HAITI - FISHERIES

Facts on File, 460 Park Avenue South, New York, New York 10016 (800) 253-9646; *The New Book of World Rankings.*

Federal Statistical Office, Gustav - Stresesmann - Ring 11, D-6200 Wiesbaden, Germany; *Haiti.*

Food and Agricultural Organization of the United Nations (FAO) Via delle Terme di Caracalla, 00100 Rome, Italy (Telephone Number in U.S. (202) 653-2400); *The State of Food and Agriculture,* and *Yearbook of Fishery Statistics.*

Inter-American Development Bank, 1300 New York Avenue, NW, Washington, D.C. 20577 (202) 623-1753; *Economic and Social Progress in Latin America.*

Statistical Office of the United Nations, Publishing Service, New York, New York 10017 (800) 253-9646; *Statistical Yearbook.*

U.C.L.A. Latin American Center Publications, University of California, Los Angeles, California 90024 (310) 825-6634; *Statistical Abstract of Latin America.*

HAITI - FLOUR PRODUCTION

Statistical Office of the United Nations, Publishing Service, New York, New York 10017 (800) 253-9646; *Statistical Yearbook.*

HAITI - FOOD

Food and Agricultural Organization of the United Nations (FAO), Via delle Terme di Caracalla, 00100 Rome, Italy (Telephone Number in U.S. (202) 653-2400); *Production Yearbook,* and *The State of Food and Agriculture.*

G.K. Hall and Company, 70 Lincoln Street, Boston, Massachusetts 02111 (617) 423-3990; *The World in Figures.*

HAITI - FOREIGN AID

G.K. Hall and Company, 70 Lincoln Street, Boston, Massachusetts 02111 (617) 423-3990; *The World in Figures.*

Inter-American Development Bank, 1300 New York Avenue, NW, Washington, D.C. 20577 (202) 623-1753; *Economic and Social Progress in Latin America.*

HAITI - FOREIGN DEBT

Inter-American Development Bank, 1300 New York Avenue, NW, Washington, D.C. 20577 (202) 623-1753; *Economic and Social Progress in Latin America.*

HAITI - FOREIGN FINANCE

Inter-American Development Bank, 1300 New York Avenue, NW, Washington, D.C. 20577 (202) 623-1753; *Economic and Social Progress in Latin America.*

HAITI - FOREIGN INDEBTEDNESS

Inter-American Development Bank, 1300 New York Avenue, NW, Washington, D.C. 20577 (202) 623-1753; *Economic and Social Progress in Latin America.*

Statistical Office of the United Nations, Publishing Service, New York, New York 10017 (800) 253-9646; *Economic Survey of Latin America and the Caribbean.*

HAITI - FOREIGN TRADE

Facts on File, 460 Park Avenue South, New York, New York 10016 (800) 253-9646; *The New Book of World Rankings.*

Federal Statistical Office, Gustav - Stresesmann - Ring 11, D-6200 Wiesbaden, Germany; *Haiti.*

Food and Agricultural Organization of the United Nations (FAO) Via delle Terme di Caracalla, 00100 Rome, Italy (Telephone Number in U.S. (202) 653-2400); *The State of Food and Agriculture.*

G.K. Hall and Company, 70 Lincoln Street, Boston, Massachusetts 02111 (617) 423-3990; *The World in Figures.*

Inter-American Development Bank, 1300 New York Avenue, NW, Washington, D.C. 20577 (202) 623-1753; *Economic and Social Progress in Latin America.*

International Monetary Fund, 700 Nineteenth Street, NW, Washington, D.C. 20431 (202) 623-7000; *International Financial Statistics.*

Statistical Office of the United Nations, Publishing Service, New York, New York 10017 (800) 253-9646; *Economic Survey of Latin America and the Caribbean, International Trade Statistics Yearbook, Statistical Yearbook,* and *Trade in Manufactures of Developing Countries.*

U.C.L.A. Latin American Center Publications, University of California, Los Angeles, California 90024 (310) 825-6634; *Statistical Abstract of Latin America.*

The World Bank, 1818 H Street, NW, Washington, D.C. 20433 (202) 477-1234; *World Tables.*

HAITI - FORESTRY AND FOREST PRODUCTS

Facts on File, 460 Park Avenue South, New York, New York 10016 (800) 253-9646; *The New Book of World Rankings.*

Federal Statistical Office, Gustav - Stresesmann - Ring 11, D-6200 Wiesbaden, Germany; *Haiti.*

Food and Agricultural Organization of the United Nations (FAO) Via delle Terme di Caracalla, 00100 Rome, Italy (Telephone Number in U.S. (202) 653-2400); *The State of Food and Agriculture,* and *Yearbook of Forest Products.*

G.K. Hall and Company, 70 Lincoln Street, Boston, Massachusetts 02111 (617) 423-3990; *The World in Figures.*

Inter-American Development Bank, 1300 New York Avenue, NW, Washington, D.C. 20577 (202) 623-1753; *Economic and Social Progress in Latin America.*

Statistical Office of the United Nations, Publishing Service, New York, New York 10017 (800) 253-9646; *Statistical Yearbook.*

U.C.L.A. Latin American Center Publications, University of California, Los Angeles, California 90024 (310) 825-6634; *Statistical Abstract of Latin America.*

United Nations Educational, Scientific and Cultural Organization (UNESCO), 7 Place de Fontenoy, F-75700 Paris, France (Telephone Number in U.S. (212) 963-5981); *Statistical Yearbook.*

HAITI - GAS PRODUCTION - See HAITI - MINING AND MINERAL PRODUCTS

HAITI - GENERAL INDUSTRIAL STATISTICS

Federal Statistical Office, Gustav - Stresesmann - Ring 11, D-6200 Wiesbaden, Germany; *Haiti.*

Statistical Office of the United Nations, Publishing Service, New York, New York 10017 (800) 253-9646; *Industrial Statistics Yearbook.*

HAITI - GENERAL MORTALITY

Statistical Office of the United Nations, Publishing Service, New York, New York 10017 (800) 253-9646; *Demographic Yearbook.*

HAITI - GEOGRAPHIC DATA

Facts on File, 460 Park Avenue South, New York, New York 10016 (800) 253-9646; *The New Book of World Rankings.*

Federal Statistical Office, Gustav - Stresesmann - Ring 11, D-6200 Wiesbaden, Germany; *Haiti.*

U.C.L.A. Latin American Center Publications, University of California, Los Angeles, California 90024 (310) 825-6634; *Statistical Abstract of Latin America.*

HAITI - GOLD HOLDINGS

International Monetary Fund, 700 Nineteenth Street, NW, Washington, D.C. 20431 (202) 623-7000; *International Financial Statistics.*

Statistical Office of the United Nations, Publishing Service, New York, New York 10017 (800) 253-9646; *Statistical Yearbook.*

The World Bank, 1818 H Street, NW, Washington, D.C. 20433 (202) 477-1234; *World Tables.*

HAITI - GOLD PRODUCTION AND CONSUMPTION - See HAITI - MINING AND MINERAL PRODUCTS

HAITI - GOVERNMENT

G.K. Hall and Company, 70 Lincoln Street, Boston, Massachusetts 02111 (617) 423-3990; *The World in Figures.*

Inter-American Development Bank, 1300 New York Avenue, NW, Washington, D.C. 20577 (202) 623-1753; *Economic and Social Progress in Latin America.*

HAITI - GOVERNMENT BONDS - See HAITI - BONDS

HAITI - GOVERNMENT CONSUMPTION

Inter-American Development Bank, 1300 New York Avenue, NW, Washington, D.C. 20577 (202) 623-1753; *Economic and Social Progress in Latin America.*

HAITI - GOVERNMENT EXPENDITURE

Inter-American Development Bank, 1300 New York Avenue, NW, Washington, D.C. 20577 (202) 623-1753; *Economic and Social Progress in Latin America.*

The World Bank, 1818 H Street, NW, Washington, D.C. 20433 (202) 477-1234; *World Tables.*

HAITI - GOVERNMENT FINANCES

Inter-American Development Bank, 1300 New York Avenue, NW, Washington, D.C. 20577 (202) 623-1753; *Economic and Social Progress in Latin America.*

International Monetary Fund, 700 Nineteenth Street, NW, Washington, D.C. 20431 (202) 623-7000; *International Financial Statistics.*

Statistical Office of the United Nations, Publishing Service, New York, New York 10017 (800) 253-9646; *Statistical Yearbook.*

HAITI - GOVERNMENT REVENUE

Inter-American Development Bank, 1300 New York Avenue, NW, Washington, D.C. 20577 (202) 623-1753; *Economic and Social Progress in Latin America.*

International Monetary Fund, 700 Nineteenth Street, NW, Washington, D.C. 20431 (202) 623-7000; *Government Finance Statistics Yearbook.*

Times Books, 201 East 50th Street, New York, New York 10022 (212) 751-2600; *The Economist Book of Vital World Statistics*.

The World Bank, 1818 H Street, NW, Washington, D.C. 20433 (202) 477-1234; *World Tables*.

HAITI - GRAIN PRODUCTION - See HAITI - CROPS

HAITI - GRANTS

International Monetary Fund, 700 Nineteenth Street, NW, Washington, D.C. 20431 (202) 623-7000; *Government Finance Statistics Yearbook*.

HAITI - GROSS DOMESTIC PRODUCT

The Economist Intelligence Unit, 111 West 57th Street, New York, New York 10019 (800) 938-4685; *The World Market Atlas*.

Facts on File, 460 Park Avenue South, New York, New York 10016 (800) 253-9646; *The New Book of World Rankings*.

G.K. Hall and Company, 70 Lincoln Street, Boston, Massachusetts 02111 (617) 423-3990; *The World in Figures*.

Inter-American Development Bank, 1300 New York Avenue, NW, Washington, D.C. 20577 (202) 623-1753; *Economic and Social Progress in Latin America*.

Organization of American States (OAS), General Secretariat, Washington, D.C. 20006 (202) 458-3533; *Statistical Bulletin of the OAS*.

Statistical Office of the United Nations, Publishing Service, New York, New York 10017 (800) 253-9646; *Statistical Yearbook*, and *Statistical Yearbook for Latin America and the Caribbean*.

Times Books, 201 East 50th Street, New York, New York 10022 (212) 751-2600; *The Economist Book of Vital World Statistics*.

The World Bank, 1818 H Street, NW, Washington, D.C. 20433 (202) 477-1234; *World Tables*.

HAITI - GROSS NATIONAL PRODUCT

Inter-American Development Bank, 1300 New York Avenue, NW, Washington, D.C. 20577 (202) 623-1753; *Economic and Social Progress in Latin America*.

U.S. Arms Control and Disarmament Agency, 320 Twenty-first Street, Northwest, Washington, D.C. 20451 (202) 647-8677; *World Military Expenditures and Arms Transfers*.

The World Bank, 1818 H Street, NW, Washington, D.C. 20433 (202) 477-1234; *World Tables*.

HAITI - GROUNDNUTS PRODUCTION - See HAITI - CROPS

HAITI - HEALTH

Facts on File, 460 Park Avenue South, New York, New York 10016 (800) 253-9646; *The New Book of World Rankings*.

Federal Statistical Office, Gustav - Stresesmann - Ring 11, D-6200 Wiesbaden, Germany; *Haiti*.

G.K. Hall and Company, 70 Lincoln Street, Boston, Massachusetts 02111 (617) 423-3990; *The World in Figures*.

Statistical Office of the United Nations, Publishing Service, New York, New York 10017 (800) 253-9646; *Statistical Yearbook*, and *Statistical Yearbook for Latin America and the Caribbean*.

Times Books, 201 East 50th Street, New York, New York 10022 (212) 751-2600; *The Economist Book of Vital World Statistics*.

U.C.L.A. Latin American Center Publications, University of California, Los Angeles, California 90024 (310) 825-6634; *Statistical Abstract of Latin America*.

World Health Organization, Office of Publications, Avenue Appia, CH-1211 Geneva 27, Switzerland (Telephone Number in U.S. (518) 436-9686); *World Health Statistics Annual*.

HAITI - HIDE PRODUCTION

Food and Agricultural Organization of the United Nations (FAO), Via delle Terme di Caracalla, 00100 Rome, Italy (Telephone Number in U.S. (202) 653-2400); *Production Yearbook*.

HAITI - HIGHWAYS

G.K. Hall and Company, 70 Lincoln Street, Boston, Massachusetts 02111 (617) 423-3990; *The World in Figures*.

HAITI - HORSES - See HAITI - LIVESTOCK AND POULTRY

HAITI - HOURS OF WORK - See HAITI - EMPLOYMENT

HAITI - HOUSING AND HOUSING UNITS

Facts on File, 460 Park Avenue South, New York, New York 10016 (800) 253-9646; *The New Book of World Rankings*.

Statistical Office of the United Nations, Publishing Service, New York, New York 10017 (800) 253-9646; *Statistical Yearbook for Latin America and the Caribbean*.

U.C.L.A. Latin American Center Publications, University of California, Los Angeles, California 90024 (310) 825-6634; *Statistical Abstract of Latin America*.

HAITI - ILLITERATE POPULATION

The Economist Intelligence Unit, 111 West 57th Street, New York, New York 10019 (800) 938-4685; *The World Market Atlas*.

G.K. Hall and Company, 70 Lincoln Street, Boston, Massachusetts 02111 (617) 423-3990; *The World in Figures*.

Statistical Office of the United Nations, Publishing Service, New York, New York 10017 (800) 253-9646; *Statistical Yearbook for Latin America and the Caribbean*.

United Nations Educational, Scientific and Cultural Organization (UNESCO), 7 Place de Fontenoy, F-75700 Paris, France (Telephone Number in U.S. (212) 963-5981); *Statistical Yearbook*.

HAITI - IMMIGRATION

U.C.L.A. Latin American Center Publications, University of California, Los Angeles, California 90024 (310) 825-6634; *Statistical Abstract of Latin America*.

HAITI - IMPORTS

The Economist Intelligence Unit, 111 West 57th Street, New York, New York 10019 (800) 938-4685; *The World Market Atlas*.

Food and Agricultural Organization of the United Nations (FAO) Via delle Terme di Caracalla, 00100 Rome, Italy (Telephone Number in U.S. (202) 653-2400); *The State of Food and Agriculture.*

G.K. Hall and Company, 70 Lincoln Street, Boston, Massachusetts 02111 (617) 423-3990; *The World in Figures.*

Inter-American Development Bank, 1300 New York Avenue, NW, Washington, D.C. 20577 (202) 623-1753; *Economic and Social Progress in Latin America.*

International Monetary Fund, 700 Nineteenth Street, NW, Washington, D.C. 20431 (202) 623-7000; *Direction of Trade Statistics, Government Finance Statistics Yearbook,* and *International Financial Statistics.*

Organization of American States (OAS), General Secretariat, Washington, D.C. 20006 (202) 458-3533; *Statistical Bulletin of the OAS.*

Statistical Office of the United Nations, Publishing Service, New York, New York 10017 (800) 253-9646; *Statistical Yearbook for Latin America and the Caribbean.*

The World Bank, 1818 H Street, NW, Washington, D.C. 20433 (202) 477-1234; *World Tables.*

HAITI - INCOME DISTRIBUTION

Statistical Office of the United Nations, Publishing Service, New York, New York 10017 (800) 253-9646; *Statistical Yearbook for Latin America and the Caribbean.*

U.C.L.A. Latin American Center Publications, University of California, Los Angeles, California 90024 (310) 825-6634; *Statistical Abstract of Latin America.*

HAITI - INCOME TAXES - See HAITI - TAXATION

HAITI - INDUSTRY

Facts on File, 460 Park Avenue South, New York, New York 10016 (800) 253-9646; *The New Book of World Rankings.*

Federal Statistical Office, Gustav - Stresesmann - Ring 11, D-6200 Wiesbaden, Germany; *Haiti.*

Gale Research Incorporated, 835 Penobscot Building, Detroit, Michigan 48226 (800) 877-4253; *International Historical Statistics The Americas and Australasia.*

G.K. Hall and Company, 70 Lincoln Street, Boston, Massachusetts 02111 (617) 423-3990; *The World in Figures.*

International Labour Office, I.L.O. Publications, CH-1211, Geneva 22, Switzerland; *Yearbook of Labour Statistics.*

Statistical Office of the United Nations, Publishing Service, New York, New York 10017 (800) 253-9646; *Economic Survey of Latin America and the Caribbean.*

Times Books, 201 East 50th Street, New York, New York 10022 (212) 751-2600; *The Economist Book of Vital World Statistics.*

U.C.L.A. Latin American Center Publications, University of California, Los Angeles, California 90024 (310) 825-6634; *Statistical Abstract of Latin America.*

The World Bank, 1818 H Street, NW, Washington, D.C. 20433 (202) 477-1234; *World Tables.*

World Intellectual Property Organization, 34 Chemin des Colombettes, CH-1211 Geneva 20, Switzerland; *Industrial Property Statistics.*

HAITI - INFANT AND MATERNAL MORTALITY

Statistical Office of the United Nations, Publishing Service, New York, New York 10017 (800) 253-9646; *Demographic Yearbook,* and *Statistical Yearbook.*

Times Books, 201 East 50th Street, New York, New York 10022 (212) 751-2600; *The Economist Book of Vital World Statistics.*

The World Bank, 1818 H Street, NW, Washington, D.C. 20433 (202) 477-1234; *World Tables.*

HAITI - INFLATIONARY FACTORS

Statistical Office of the United Nations, Publishing Service, New York, New York 10017 (800) 253-9646; *Economic Survey of Latin America and the Caribbean.*

HAITI - INTEREST RATES

Inter-American Development Bank, 1300 New York Avenue, NW, Washington, D.C. 20577 (202) 623-1753; *Economic and Social Progress in Latin America.*

HAITI - INTERNAL TRADE

Statistical Office of the United Nations, Publishing Service, New York, New York 10017 (800) 253-9646; *Statistical Yearbook.*

HAITI - INTERNATIONAL FINANCE

Inter-American Development Bank, 1300 New York Avenue, NW, Washington, D.C. 20577 (202) 623-1753; *Economic and Social Progress in Latin America.*

U.C.L.A. Latin American Center Publications, University of California, Los Angeles, California 90024 (310) 825-6634; *Statistical Abstract of Latin America.*

HAITI - INTERNATIONAL LIQUIDITY

Inter-American Development Bank, 1300 New York Avenue, NW, Washington, D.C. 20577 (202) 623-1753; *Economic and Social Progress in Latin America.*

International Monetary Fund, 700 Nineteenth Street, NW, Washington, D.C. 20431 (202) 623-7000; *International Financial Statistics.*

HAITI - INTERNATIONAL RESERVES

Organization of American States (OAS), General Secretariat, Washington, D.C. 20006 (202) 458-3533; *Statistical Bulletin of the OAS.*

HAITI - INTERNATIONAL RESERVES EXCLUDING GOLD

Inter-American Development Bank, 1300 New York Avenue, NW, Washington, D.C. 20577 (202) 623-1753; *Economic and Social Progress in Latin America.*

Statistical Office of the United Nations, Publishing Service, New York, New York 10017 (800) 253-9646; *Statistical Yearbook.*

The World Bank, 1818 H Street, NW, Washington, D.C. 20433 (202) 477-1234; *World Tables.*

HAITI - INTERNATIONAL STATISTICS

Inter-American Development Bank, 1300 New York Avenue, NW, Washington, D.C. 20577 (202) 623-1753; *Economic and Social Progress in Latin America.*

U.C.L.A. Latin American Center Publications, University of California, Los Angeles, California 90024 (310) 825-6634; *Statistical Abstract of Latin America.*

HAITI - INVESTMENT

Inter-American Development Bank, 1300 New York Avenue, NW, Washington, D.C. 20577 (202) 623-1753; *Economic and Social Progress in Latin America.*

Statistical Office of the United Nations, Publishing Service, New York, New York 10017 (800) 253-9646; *Statistical Yearbook for Latin America and the Caribbean.*

HAITI - IRON ORE PRODUCTION AND CONSUMPTION - See HAITI - MINING AND MINERAL PRODUCTS

HAITI - IRRIGATION

Inter-American Development Bank, 1300 New York Avenue, NW, Washington, D.C. 20577 (202) 623-1753; *Economic and Social Progress in Latin America.*

HAITI - LABOR FORCE

Facts on File, 460 Park Avenue South, New York, New York 10016 (800) 253-9646; *The New Book of World Rankings.*

Food and Agricultural Organization of the United Nations (FAO) Via delle Terme di Caracalla, 00100 Rome, Italy (Telephone Number in U.S. (202) 653-2400); *The State of Food and Agriculture.*

Gale Research Incorporated, 835 Penobscot Building, Detroit, Michigan 48226 (800) 877-4253; *International Historical Statistics The Americas and Australasia.*

G.K. Hall and Company, 70 Lincoln Street, Boston, Massachusetts 02111 (617) 423-3990; *The World in Figures.*

The World Bank, 1818 H Street, NW, Washington, D.C. 20433 (202) 477-1234; *World Tables.*

HAITI - LABOR PRODUCTIVITY

International Labour Office, I.L.O. Publications, CH-1211, Geneva 22, Switzerland; *Yearbook of Labour Statistics.*

HAITI - LAND USE

Food and Agricultural Organization of the United Nations (FAO), Via delle Terme di Caracalla, 00100 Rome, Italy (Telephone Number in U.S. (202) 653-2400); *Production Yearbook.*

G.K. Hall and Company, 70 Lincoln Street, Boston, Massachusetts 02111 (617) 423-3990; *The World in Figures.*

Inter-American Development Bank, 1300 New York Avenue, NW, Washington, D.C. 20577 (202) 623-1753; *Economic and Social Progress in Latin America.*

HAITI - LIBRARIES

Facts on File, 460 Park Avenue South, New York, New York 10016 (800) 253-9646; *The New Book of World Rankings.*

United Nations Educational, Scientific and Cultural Organization (UNESCO), 7 Place de Fontenoy, F-75700 Paris, France (Telephone Number in U.S. (212) 963-5981); *Statistical Yearbook.*

HAITI - LIVESTOCK AND POULTRY

Facts on File, 460 Park Avenue South, New York, New York 10016 (800) 253-9646; *The New Book of World Rankings.*

Food and Agricultural Organization of the United Nations (FAO), Via delle Terme di Caracalla, 00100 Rome, Italy (Telephone Number in U.S. (202) 653-2400); *Production Yearbook,* and *The State of Food and Agriculture.*

G.K. Hall and Company, 70 Lincoln Street, Boston, Massachusetts 02111 (617) 423-3990; *The World in Figures.*

Statistical Office of the United Nations, Publishing Service, New York, New York 10017 (800) 253-9646; *Statistical Yearbook.*

HAITI - LIVING LEVELS

G.K. Hall and Company, 70 Lincoln Street, Boston, Massachusetts 02111 (617) 423-3990; *The World in Figures.*

Statistical Office of the United Nations, Publishing Service, New York, New York 10017 (800) 253-9646; *Statistical Yearbook for Latin America and the Caribbean.*

Times Books, 201 East 50th Street, New York, New York 10022 (212) 751-2600; *The Economist Book of Vital World Statistics.*

HAITI - MAIL TRAFFIC - NUMBER OF ITEMS SENT AND RECEIVED

Statistical Office of the United Nations, Publishing Service, New York, New York 10017 (800) 253-9646; *Statistical Yearbook.*

HAITI - MAIN ECONOMIC INDICATORS - See HAITI - ECONOMY

HAITI - MANUFACTURING

Facts on File, 460 Park Avenue South, New York, New York 10016 (800) 253-9646; *The New Book of World Rankings.*

G.K. Hall and Company, 70 Lincoln Street, Boston, Massachusetts 02111 (617) 423-3990; *The World in Figures.*

Inter-American Development Bank, 1300 New York Avenue, NW, Washington, D.C. 20577 (202) 623-1753; *Economic and Social Progress in Latin America.*

Statistical Office of the United Nations, Publishing Service, New York, New York 10017 (800) 253-9646; *Statistical Yearbook,* and *Statistical Yearbook for Latin America and the Caribbean.*

The World Bank, 1818 H Street, NW, Washington, D.C. 20433 (202) 477-1234; *World Tables.*

HAITI - MARRIAGE RATES

Facts on File, 460 Park Avenue South, New York, New York 10016 (800) 253-9646; *The New Book of World Rankings.*

Statistical Office of the United Nations, Publishing Service, New York, New York 10017 (800) 253-9646; *Demographic Yearbook.*

HAITI - MEAT PRODUCTION - See HAITI - LIVESTOCK AND POULTRY

HAITI - MEDICAL PERSONNEL

U.C.L.A. Latin American Center Publications, University of California, Los Angeles, California 90024 (310) 825-6634; *Statistical Abstract of Latin America.*

HAITI - MERCHANT SHIPPING

G.K. Hall and Company, 70 Lincoln Street, Boston, Massachusetts 02111 (617) 423-3990; *The World in Figures.*

Statistical Office of the United Nations, Publishing Service, New York, New York 10017 (800) 253-9646; *Statistical Yearbook.*

Times Books, 201 East 50th Street, New York, New York 10022 (212) 751-2600; *The Economist Book of Vital World Statistics.*

HAITI - MILITARY

G.K. Hall and Company, 70 Lincoln Street, Boston, Massachusetts 02111 (617) 423-3990; *The World in Figures.*

The International Institute for Strategic Studies, 23 Tavistock Street, London WC2E 7NQ, England; *The Military Balance.*

U.C.L.A. Latin American Center Publications, University of California, Los Angeles, California 90024 (310) 825-6634; *Statistical Abstract of Latin America.*

U.S. Arms Control and Disarmament Agency, 320 Twenty-first Street, Northwest, Washington, D.C. 20451 (202) 647-8677; *World Military Expenditures and Arms Transfers.*

HAITI - MILK PRODUCTION - See HAITI - DAIRY PRODUCTS

HAITI - MINING AND MINERAL PRODUCTS

Facts on File, 460 Park Avenue South, New York, New York 10016 (800) 253-9646; *The New Book of World Rankings.*

G.K. Hall and Company, 70 Lincoln Street, Boston, Massachusetts 02111 (617) 423-3990; *The World in Figures.*

Inter-American Development Bank, 1300 New York Avenue, NW, Washington, D.C. 20577 (202) 623-1753; *Economic and Social Progress in Latin America.*

International Monetary Fund, 700 Nineteenth Street, NW, Washington, D.C. 20431 (202) 623-7000; *International Financial Statistics.*

Organization of American States (OAS), General Secretariat, Washington, D.C. 20006 (202) 458-3533; *Statistical Bulletin of the OAS.*

Statistical Office of the United Nations, Publishing Service, New York, New York 10017 (800) 253-9646; *Statistical Yearbook,* and *Statistical Yearbook for Latin America and the Caribbean.*

U.C.L.A. Latin American Center Publications, University of California, Los Angeles, California 90024 (310) 825-6634; *Statistical Abstract of Latin America.*

HAITI - MONEY EXCHANGE RATE

Inter-American Development Bank, 1300 New York Avenue, NW, Washington, D.C. 20577 (202) 623-1753; *Economic and Social Progress in Latin America.*

International Monetary Fund, 700 Nineteenth Street, NW, Washington, D.C. 20431 (202) 623-7000; *International Financial Statistics.*

Statistical Office of the United Nations, Publishing Service, New York, New York 10017 (800) 253-9646; *Statistical Yearbook.*

HAITI - MONEY RATES - MARKET

Inter-American Development Bank, 1300 New York Avenue, NW, Washington, D.C. 20577 (202) 623-1753; *Economic and Social Progress in Latin America.*

HAITI - MONEY RESERVES

Inter-American Development Bank, 1300 New York Avenue, NW, Washington, D.C. 20577 (202) 623-1753; *Economic and Social Progress in Latin America.*

HAITI - MONEY SUPPLY

Federal Statistical Office, Gustav - Stresesmann - Ring 11, D-6200 Wiesbaden, Germany; *Haiti.*

G.K. Hall and Company, 70 Lincoln Street, Boston, Massachusetts 02111 (617) 423-3990; *The World in Figures.*

Inter-American Development Bank, 1300 New York Avenue, NW, Washington, D.C. 20577 (202) 623-1753; *Economic and Social Progress in Latin America.*

International Monetary Fund, 700 Nineteenth Street, NW, Washington, D.C. 20431 (202) 623-7000; *International Financial Statistics.*

Statistical Office of the United Nations, Publishing Service, New York, New York 10017 (800) 253-9646; *Statistical Yearbook.*

U.C.L.A. Latin American Center Publications, University of California, Los Angeles, California 90024 (310) 825-6634; *Statistical Abstract of Latin America.*

The World Bank, 1818 H Street, NW, Washington, D.C. 20433 (202) 477-1234; *World Tables.*

HAITI - MONUMENTS AND HISTORICAL SITES

United Nations Educational, Scientific and Cultural Organization (UNESCO), 7 Place de Fontenoy, F-75700 Paris, France (Telephone Number in U.S. (212) 963-5981); *Statistical Yearbook.*

HAITI - MOTOR VEHICLE TAXES - See HAITI - TAXATION

HAITI - MOTOR VEHICLES IN USE

G.K. Hall and Company, 70 Lincoln Street, Boston, Massachusetts 02111 (617) 423-3990; *The World in Figures.*

Statistical Office of the United Nations, Publishing Service, New York, New York 10017 (800) 253-9646; *Statistical Yearbook.*

Times Books, 201 East 50th Street, New York, New York 10022 (212) 751-2600; *The Economist Book of Vital World Statistics.*

HAITI - MULES - See HAITI - LIVESTOCK AND POULTRY

HAITI - MUSEUMS

Facts on File, 460 Park Avenue South, New York, New York 10016 (800) 253-9646; *The New Book of World Rankings.*

United Nations Educational, Scientific and Cultural Organization (UNESCO), 7 Place de Fontenoy, F-75700 Paris, France (Telephone Number in U.S. (212) 963-5981); *Statistical Yearbook.*

HAITI - NATALITY - See HAITI - BIRTH RATES

HAITI - NATIONAL ACCOUNTS

Federal Statistical Office, Gustav - Stresesmann - Ring 11, D-6200 Wiesbaden, Germany; *Haiti.*

Gale Research Incorporated, 835 Penobscot Building, Detroit, Michigan 48226 (800) 877-4253; *International Historical Statistics The Americas and Australasia.*

Inter-American Development Bank, 1300 New York Avenue, NW, Washington, D.C. 20577 (202) 623-1753; *Economic and Social Progress in Latin America.*

Organization of American States (OAS), General Secretariat, Washington, D.C. 20006 (202) 458-3533; *Statistical Bulletin of the OAS.*

Statistical Office of the United Nations, Publishing Service, New York, New York 10017 (800) 253-9646; *National Accounts Statistics,* and *Statistical Yearbook.*

U.C.L.A. Latin American Center Publications, University of California, Los Angeles, California 90024 (310) 825-6634; *Statistical Abstract of Latin America.*

HAITI - NATIONAL INCOME

Facts on File, 460 Park Avenue South, New York, New York 10016 (800) 253-9646; *The New Book of World Rankings.*

G.K. Hall and Company, 70 Lincoln Street, Boston, Massachusetts 02111 (617) 423-3990; *The World in Figures.*

Inter-American Development Bank, 1300 New York Avenue, NW, Washington, D.C. 20577 (202) 623-1753; *Economic and Social Progress in Latin America.*

Statistical Office of the United Nations, Publishing Service, New York, New York 10017 (800) 253-9646; *Statistical Yearbook.*

HAITI - NATIONAL PRODUCT

Facts on File, 460 Park Avenue South, New York, New York 10016 (800) 253-9646; *The New Book of World Rankings.*

Statistical Office of the United Nations, Publishing Service, New York, New York 10017 (800) 253-9646; *Statistical Yearbook.*

HAITI - NATURAL GAS PRODUCTION - See HAITI - MINING AND MINERAL PRODUCTS

HAITI - NEWSPAPER PRODUCTION - See HAITI - FORESTRY AND FOREST PRODUCTS

HAITI - NEWSPRINT - See HAITI - FORESTRY AND FOREST PRODUCTS

HAITI - NUTRITION

Statistical Office of the United Nations, Publishing Service, New York, New York 10017 (800) 253-9646; *Statistical Yearbook for Latin America and the Caribbean.*

HAITI - OCCUPATIONS - See HAITI - LABOR FORCE

HAITI - PAPER - See HAITI - FORESTRY AND FOREST PRODUCTS

HAITI - PATENTS

Statistical Office of the United Nations, Publishing Service, New York, New York 10017 (800) 253-9646; *Statistical Yearbook.*

World Intellectual Property Organization, 34 Chemin des Colombettes, CH-1211 Geneva 20, Switzerland; *Industrial Property Statistics.*

HAITI - PEANUT PRODUCTION - See HAITI - CROPS

HAITI - PESTICIDE USE

Food and Agricultural Organization of the United Nations (FAO) Via delle Terme di Caracalla, 00100 Rome, Italy (Telephone Number in U.S. (202) 653-2400); *The State of Food and Agriculture.*

HAITI - PETROLEUM INDUSTRY

Facts on File, 460 Park Avenue South, New York, New York 10016 (800) 253-9646; *The New Book of World Rankings.*

Food and Agricultural Organization of the United Nations (FAO) Via delle Terme di Caracalla, 00100 Rome, Italy (Telephone Number in U.S. (202) 653-2400); *The State of Food and Agriculture.*

G.K. Hall and Company, 70 Lincoln Street, Boston, Massachusetts 02111 (617) 423-3990; *The World in Figures.*

Inter-American Development Bank, 1300 New York Avenue, NW, Washington, D.C. 20577 (202) 623-1753; *Economic and Social Progress in Latin America.*

HAITI - PIGS - See HAITI - LIVESTOCK AND POULTRY

HAITI - POLITICAL DATA

U.C.L.A. Latin American Center Publications, University of California, Los Angeles, California 90024 (310) 825-6634; *Statistical Abstract of Latin America.*

HAITI - POPULATION

The Economist Intelligence Unit, 111 West 57th Street, New York, New York 10019 (800) 938-4685; *The World Market Atlas.*

Facts on File, 460 Park Avenue South, New York, New York 10016 (800) 253-9646; *The New Book of World Rankings.*

Federal Statistical Office, Gustav - Stresesmann - Ring 11, D-6200 Wiesbaden, Germany; *Haiti.*

Food and Agricultural Organization of the United Nations (FAO), Via delle Terme di Caracalla, 00100 Rome, Italy (Telephone Number in U.S. (202) 653-2400); *Production Yearbook.*

Gale Research Incorporated, 835 Penobscot Building, Detroit, Michigan 48226 (800) 877-4253; *International Historical Statistics The Americas and Australasia.*

G.K. Hall and Company, 70 Lincoln Street, Boston, Massachusetts 02111 (617) 423-3990; *The World in Figures.*

Inter-American Development Bank, 1300 New York Avenue, NW, Washington, D.C. 20577 (202) 623-1753; *Economic and Social Progress in Latin America.*

International Labour Office, I.L.O. Publications, CH-1211, Geneva 22, Switzerland; *Yearbook of Labour Statistics.*

Organization of American States (OAS), General Secretariat, Washington, D.C. 20006 (202) 458-3533; *Statistical Bulletin of the OAS.*

Statistical Office of the United Nations, Publishing Service, New York, New York 10017 (800) 253-9646; *Demographic Yearbook, Statistical Yearbook,* and *Statistical Yearbook for Latin America and the Caribbean.*

Times Books, 201 East 50th Street, New York, New York 10022 (212) 751-2600; *The Economist Book of Vital World Statistics.*

U.C.L.A. Latin American Center Publications, University of California, Los Angeles, California 90024 (310) 825-6634; *Statistical Abstract of Latin America.*

United Nations Educational, Scientific and Cultural Organization (UNESCO), 7 Place de Fontenoy, F-75700 Paris, France (Telephone Number in U.S. (212) 963-5981); *Statistical Yearbook.*

U.S. Arms Control and Disarmament Agency, 320 Twenty-first Street, Northwest, Washington, D.C. 20451 (202) 647-8677; *World Military Expenditures and Arms Transfers.*

World Health Organization, Office of Publications, Avenue Appia, CH-1211 Geneva 27, Switzerland (Telephone Number in U.S. (518) 436-9686); *World Health Statistics Annual.*

HAITI - POST OFFICES

Facts on File, 460 Park Avenue South, New York, New York 10016 (800) 253-9646; *The New Book of World Rankings.*

HAITI - POTATO PRODUCTION - See HAITI - CROPS

HAITI - POWER PRODUCTION INDUSTRY

Statistical Office of the United Nations, Publishing Service, New York, New York 10017 (800) 253-9646; *Statistical Yearbook.*

HAITI - PRICES

Facts on File, 460 Park Avenue South, New York, New York 10016 (800) 253-9646; *The New Book of World Rankings.*

Federal Statistical Office, Gustav - Stresesmann - Ring 11, D-6200 Wiesbaden, Germany; *Haiti.*

Food and Agricultural Organization of the United Nations (FAO), Via delle Terme di Caracalla, 00100 Rome, Italy (Telephone Number in U.S. (202) 653-2400); *Production Yearbook,* and *The State of Food and Agriculture.*

Gale Research Incorporated, 835 Penobscot Building, Detroit, Michigan 48226 (800) 877-4253; *International Historical Statistics The Americas and Australasia.*

G.K. Hall and Company, 70 Lincoln Street, Boston, Massachusetts 02111 (617) 423-3990; *The World in Figures.*

International Labour Office, I.L.O. Publications, CH-1211, Geneva 22, Switzerland; *Yearbook of Labour Statistics.*

International Monetary Fund, 700 Nineteenth Street, NW, Washington, D.C. 20431 (202) 623-7000; *International Financial Statistics.*

Statistical Office of the United Nations, Publishing Service, New York, New York 10017 (800) 253-9646; *Statistical Yearbook for Latin America and the Caribbean.*

HAITI - PRINTING AND WRITING PAPER - See HAITI - FORESTRY AND FOREST PRODUCTS

HAITI - PRODUCTION

Facts on File, 460 Park Avenue South, New York, New York 10016 (800) 253-9646; *The New Book of World Rankings.*

G.K. Hall and Company, 70 Lincoln Street, Boston, Massachusetts 02111 (617) 423-3990; *The World in Figures.*

HAITI - PROPERTY TAXES - See HAITI - TAXATION

HAITI - PUBLIC CONSUMPTION FUND

Inter-American Development Bank, 1300 New York Avenue, NW, Washington, D.C. 20577 (202) 623-1753; *Economic and Social Progress in Latin America.*

HAITI - PUBLIC EXPENDITURE

Inter-American Development Bank, 1300 New York Avenue, NW, Washington, D.C. 20577 (202) 623-1753; *Economic and Social Progress in Latin America.*

Organization of American States (OAS), General Secretariat, Washington, D.C. 20006 (202) 458-3533; *Statistical Bulletin of the OAS.*

Statistical Office of the United Nations, Publishing Service, New York, New York 10017 (800) 253-9646; *Statistical Yearbook for Latin America and the Caribbean.*

HAITI - PUBLIC FINANCE

Facts on File, 460 Park Avenue South, New York, New York 10016 (800) 253-9646; *The New Book of World Rankings.*

Federal Statistical Office, Gustav - Stresesmann - Ring 11, D-6200 Wiesbaden, Germany; *Haiti.*

Inter-American Development Bank, 1300 New York Avenue, NW, Washington, D.C. 20577 (202) 623-1753; *Economic and Social Progress in Latin America.*

Organization of American States (OAS), General Secretariat, Washington, D.C. 20006 (202) 458-3533; *Statistical Bulletin of the OAS.*

HAITI - PUBLIC REVENUES

Inter-American Development Bank, 1300 New York Avenue, NW, Washington, D.C. 20577 (202) 623-1753; *Economic and Social Progress in Latin America.*

Organization of American States (OAS), General Secretariat, Washington, D.C. 20006 (202) 458-3533; *Statistical Bulletin of the OAS.*

HAITI - RADIO BROADCASTING - See HAITI - BROADCASTING

HAITI - RAILWAYS

G.K. Hall and Company, 70 Lincoln Street, Boston, Massachusetts 02111 (617) 423-3990; *The World in Figures.*

HAITI - RANCHING

U.C.L.A. Latin American Center Publications, University of California, Los Angeles, California 90024 (310) 825-6634; *Statistical Abstract of Latin America.*

HAITI - RELIGION

Facts on File, 460 Park Avenue South, New York, New York 10016 (800) 253-9646; *The New Book of World Rankings.*

U.C.L.A. Latin American Center Publications, University of California, Los Angeles, California 90024 (310) 825-6634; *Statistical Abstract of Latin America.*

HAITI - RENT PRICES

International Labour Office, I.L.O. Publications, CH-1211, Geneva 22, Switzerland; *Yearbook of Labour Statistics.*

HAITI - RETAIL TRADE

G.K. Hall and Company, 70 Lincoln Street, Boston, Massachusetts 02111 (617) 423-3990; *The World in Figures.*

Inter-American Development Bank, 1300 New York Avenue, NW, Washington, D.C. 20577 (202) 623-1753; *Economic and Social Progress in Latin America.*

Statistical Office of the United Nations, Publishing Service, New York, New York 10017 (800) 253-9646; *Statistical Yearbook.*

HAITI - RICE PRODUCTION - See HAITI - CROPS

HAITI - ROOT AND TUBER PRODUCTION - See HAITI - CROPS

HAITI - ROUNDWOOD PRODUCTION - See HAITI - FORESTRY AND FOREST PRODUCTS

HAITI - RUBBER PRODUCTION

Facts on File, 460 Park Avenue South, New York, New York 10016 (800) 253-9646; *The New Book of World Rankings.*

HAITI - SAWNWOOD PRODUCTION - See HAITI - FORESTRY AND FOREST PRODUCTS

HAITI - SCIENCE AND TECHNOLOGY

U.C.L.A. Latin American Center Publications, University of California, Los Angeles, California 90024 (310) 825-6634; *Statistical Abstract of Latin America.*

HAITI - SCIENTISTS AND TECHNICIANS

United Nations Educational, Scientific and Cultural Organization (UNESCO), 7 Place de Fontenoy, F-75700 Paris, France (Telephone Number in U.S. (212) 963-5981); *Statistical Yearbook.*

HAITI - SENIOR CITIZENS

Facts on File, 460 Park Avenue South, New York, New York 10016 (800) 253-9646; *The New Book of World Rankings.*

HAITI - SHEEP - See HAITI - LIVESTOCK AND POULTRY

HAITI - SILVER PRODUCTION AND CONSUMPTION - See HAITI - MINING AND MINERAL PRODUCTS

HAITI - SISAL PRODUCTION - See HAITI - CROPS

HAITI - SOCIAL DATA

Facts on File, 460 Park Avenue South, New York, New York 10016 (800) 253-9646; *The New Book of World Rankings.*

G.K. Hall and Company, 70 Lincoln Street, Boston, Massachusetts 02111 (617) 423-3990; *The World in Figures.*

U.C.L.A. Latin American Center Publications, University of California, Los Angeles, California 90024 (310) 825-6634; *Statistical Abstract of Latin America.*

HAITI - SOCIAL SECURITY

Inter-American Development Bank, 1300 New York Avenue, NW, Washington, D.C. 20577 (202) 623-1753; *Economic and Social Progress in Latin America.*

HAITI - SOCIOECONOMIC DATA

Inter-American Development Bank, 1300 New York Avenue, NW, Washington, D.C. 20577 (202) 623-1753; *Economic and Social Progress in Latin America.*

U.C.L.A. Latin American Center Publications, University of California, Los Angeles, California 90024 (310) 825-6634; *Statistical Abstract of Latin America.*

HAITI - STAMP TAXES AND DUTIES - See HAITI - TAXATION

HAITI - STATE BUDGET REVENUE AND EXPENDITURES

Inter-American Development Bank, 1300 New York Avenue, NW, Washington, D.C. 20577 (202) 623-1753; *Economic and Social Progress in Latin America.*

HAITI - STEEL - See HAITI - MINING AND MINERAL PRODUCTS

HAITI - STOCKS - COMMODITY - MARKET PRICE - INDEX

Food and Agricultural Organization of the United Nations (FAO) Via delle Terme di Caracalla, 00100 Rome, Italy (Telephone Number in U.S. (202) 653-2400); *The State of Food and Agriculture.*

HAITI - SUGAR PRODUCTION - See HAITI - CROPS

HAITI - TAXATION

G.K. Hall and Company, 70 Lincoln Street, Boston, Massachusetts 02111 (617) 423-3990; *The World in Figures.*

Inter-American Development Bank, 1300 New York Avenue, NW, Washington, D.C. 20577 (202) 623-1753; *Economic and Social Progress in Latin America.*

International Monetary Fund, 700 Nineteenth Street, NW, Washington, D.C. 20431 (202) 623-7000; *Government Finance Statistics Yearbook.*

Statistical Office of the United Nations, Publishing Service, New York, New York 10017 (800) 253-9646; *Statistical Yearbook for Latin America and the Caribbean.*

The World Bank, 1818 H Street, NW, Washington, D.C. 20433 (202) 477-1234; *World Tables.*

HAITI - TELEPHONES IN USE

American Telephone and Telegraph Company, 26 Parsippany Road, Whippany, New Jersey 07981 (800) 338-4038; *The World's Telephones.*

G.K. Hall and Company, 70 Lincoln Street, Boston, Massachusetts 02111 (617) 423-3990; *The World in Figures.*

Statistical Office of the United Nations, Publishing Service, New York, New York 10017 (800) 253-9646; *Statistical Yearbook.*

HAITI - TELEVISION BROADCASTING - See HAITI - BROADCASTING

HAITI - TEXTILE INDUSTRY

G.K. Hall and Company, 70 Lincoln Street, Boston, Massachusetts 02111 (617) 423-3990; *The World in Figures.*

Statistical Office of the United Nations, Publishing Service, New York, New York 10017 (800) 253-9646; *Statistical Yearbook.*

HAITI - TOBACCO PRODUCTION

Facts on File, 460 Park Avenue South, New York, New York 10016 (800) 253-9646; *The New Book of World Rankings.*

Statistical Office of the United Nations, Publishing Service, New York, New York 10017 (800) 253-9646; *Statistical Yearbook.*

HAITI - TOURISM

Facts on File, 460 Park Avenue South, New York, New York 10016 (800) 253-9646; *The New Book of World Rankings.*

Federal Statistical Office, Gustav - Stresesmann - Ring 11, D-6200 Wiesbaden, Germany; *Haiti.*

G.K. Hall and Company, 70 Lincoln Street, Boston, Massachusetts 02111 (617) 423-3990; *The World in Figures.*

Statistical Office of the United Nations, Publishing Service, New York, New York 10017 (800) 253-9646; *Statistical Yearbook,* and *Statistical Yearbook for Latin America and the Caribbean.*

Times Books, 201 East 50th Street, New York, New York 10022 (212) 751-2600; *The Economist Book of Vital World Statistics.*

U.C.L.A. Latin American Center Publications, University of California, Los Angeles, California 90024 (310) 825-6634; *Statistical Abstract of Latin America.*

World Tourism Organization, Calle Capitan Haya 42, E-28020 Madrid, Spain; *Yearbook of Tourism Statistics.*

HAITI - TRACTORS IN USE

Statistical Office of the United Nations, Publishing Service, New York, New York 10017 (800) 253-9646; *Statistical Yearbook.*

HAITI - TRADE - See HAITI - FOREIGN TRADE

HAITI - TRADEMARKS AND SERVICE MARKS

Statistical Office of the United Nations, Publishing Service, New York, New York 10017 (800) 253-9646; *Statistical Yearbook.*

World Intellectual Property Organization, 34 Chemin des Colombettes, CH-1211 Geneva 20, Switzerland; *Industrial Property Statistics.*

HAITI - TRANSPORTATION AND COMMUNICATIONS

Facts on File, 460 Park Avenue South, New York, New York 10016 (800) 253-9646; *The New Book of World Rankings.*

Federal Statistical Office, Gustav - Stresesmann - Ring 11, D-6200 Wiesbaden, Germany; *Haiti.*

Gale Research Incorporated, 835 Penobscot Building, Detroit, Michigan 48226 (800) 877-4253; *International Historical Statistics The Americas and Australasia.*

G.K. Hall and Company, 70 Lincoln Street, Boston, Massachusetts 02111 (617) 423-3990; *The World in Figures.*

Inter-American Development Bank, 1300 New York Avenue, NW, Washington, D.C. 20577 (202) 623-1753; *Economic and Social Progress in Latin America.*

Statistical Office of the United Nations, Publishing Service, New York, New York 10017 (800) 253-9646; *Statistical Yearbook for Latin America and the Caribbean.*

U.C.L.A. Latin American Center Publications, University of California, Los Angeles, California 90024 (310) 825-6634; *Statistical Abstract of Latin America.*

HAITI - TURKEYS - See HAITI - LIVESTOCK AND POULTRY

HAITI - UNEMPLOYMENT

International Labour Office, I.L.O. Publications, CH-1211, Geneva 22, Switzerland; *Yearbook of Labour Statistics.*

U.C.L.A. Latin American Center Publications, University of California, Los Angeles, California 90024 (310) 825-6634; *Statistical Abstract of Latin America.*

HAITI - UTILITIES

U.C.L.A. Latin American Center Publications, University of California, Los Angeles, California 90024 (310) 825-6634; *Statistical Abstract of Latin America.*

HAITI - VITAL STATISTICS

Gale Research Incorporated, 835 Penobscot Building, Detroit, Michigan 48226 (800) 877-4253; *International Historical Statistics The Americas and Australasia.*

G.K. Hall and Company, 70 Lincoln Street, Boston, Massachusetts 02111 (617) 423-3990; *The World in Figures.*

Statistical Office of the United Nations, Publishing Service, New York, New York 10017 (800) 253-9646; *Statistical Yearbook.*

World Health Organization, Office of Publications, Avenue Appia, CH-1211 Geneva 27, Switzerland (Telephone Number in U.S. (518) 436-9686); *World Health Statistics Annual.*

HAITI - WAGES

Federal Statistical Office, Gustav - Stresesmann - Ring 11, D-6200 Wiesbaden, Germany; *Haiti.*

G.K. Hall and Company, 70 Lincoln Street, Boston, Massachusetts 02111 (617) 423-3990; *The World in Figures.*

International Labour Office, I.L.O. Publications, CH-1211, Geneva 22, Switzerland; *Yearbook of Labour Statistics.*

U.C.L.A. Latin American Center Publications, University of California, Los Angeles, California 90024 (310) 825-6634; *Statistical Abstract of Latin America.*

HAITI - WEATHER

Facts on File, 460 Park Avenue South, New York, New York 10016 (800) 253-9646; *The New Book of World Rankings.*

G.K. Hall and Company, 70 Lincoln Street, Boston, Massachusetts 02111 (617) 423-3990; *The World in Figures.*

HAITI - WELFARE

Inter-American Development Bank, 1300 New York Avenue, NW, Washington, D.C. 20577 (202) 623-1753; *Economic and Social Progress in Latin America.*

HAITI - WHEAT PRODUCTION AND PRICES - See HAITI - CROPS

HAITI - WHOLESALE PRICES

Inter-American Development Bank, 1300 New York Avenue, NW, Washington, D.C. 20577 (202) 623-1753; *Economic and Social Progress in Latin America.*

HAITI - WHOLESALE TRADE

Inter-American Development Bank, 1300 New York Avenue, NW, Washington, D.C. 20577 (202) 623-1753; *Economic and Social Progress in Latin America.*

Statistical Office of the United Nations, Publishing Service, New York, New York 10017 (800) 253-9646; *Statistical Yearbook.*

HAITI - WINE PRODUCTION

Facts on File, 460 Park Avenue South, New York, New York 10016 (800) 443-8323; *The New Book of World Rankings.*

HAITI - WOOL PRODUCTION

Facts on File, 460 Park Avenue South, New York, New York 10016 (800) 443-8323; *The New Book of World Rankings.*

HAKE - PACIFIC WHITING - IMPORTS

U.S. Department of Commerce, National Oceanic and Atmospheric Administration, National Marine Fisheries Service, 1335 East-West Highway, Silver Spring, Maryland 20910 (301) 427-2239; *Fisheries of the United States.*

HALIBUT

U.S. Department of Commerce, National Oceanic and Atmospheric Administration, National Marine Fisheries Service, 1335 East-West Highway, Silver Spring, Maryland 20910 (301) 427-2239; *Fishery Statistics of the United States,* and *Fisheries of the United States.*

HALLUCINOGENIC DRUGS

U.S. Department of Health and Human Services, Substance Abuse and Mental Health Services Administration, 5600 Fishers Lane, Rockville, Maryland 20857 (301) 443-4797; *National Household Survey on Drug Abuse.*

HAM PRICE INDEXES

U.S. Department of Labor, Bureau of Labor Statistics, Two Massachusetts Avenue, NE, Washington, D.C. 20212 (202) 606-7828; *Monthly Labor Review,* and *CPI Detailed Report.*

HANDGUNS

U.S. Department of Justice Bureau of Justice Statistics, 633 Indiana Avenue, NW, Washington, D.C. 20531 (800) 732-3277; *Guns and Crime.*

HANDICAPPED - See also DISABILITY

HANDICAPPED - INSTITUTIONAL POPULATION

U.S. Department of Commerce, Bureau of the Census, Suitland, Maryland 20233 (301) 763-4040; *Census of Population, General Population Characteristics.*

HANDICAPPED - SCHOOL ENROLLMENT

U.S. Department of Education, Office of Special Education Programs, 400 Maryland Avenue, SW, Washington, D.C. 20202 (202) 708-5366; *Annual Report to Congress,* and unpublished data.

HAWAII - See also STATE DATA (FOR INDIVIDUAL STATES)

Hawaii - Primary Statistics Sources

Hawaii State Department of Business and Economic Development and Tourism, Post Office Box 2359, Honolulu, Hawaii 96804 (808) 586-2481; *The State of Hawaii Data Book: A Statistical Abstract.*

Hawaii - State Data Centers

Hawaii State Data Center, Department of Business and Economic Development and Tourism, 220 King Street, Suite 400, Honolulu, Hawaii 96813, (Mailing Address) Post Office Box 2359, Honolulu, Hawaii 96804, Ms. Jan Nakamoto (808) 586-2493.

Information and Communication Services Division, State Department of Budget and Finance, Kalanimoku Building, 1151 Punchbowl Street, Honolulu, Hawaii 96813, Ms. Joy Toyama (808) 548-1940.

HAY

U.S. Department of Agriculture, Economic Research Service, Fourteenth Street and Independence Avenue, SW, Washington, D.C. 20005-4789 (202) 219-1504; *Economic Indicators of the Farm Sector: National Financial Summary.*

U.S. Department of Agriculture, National Agricultural Statistics Service, Fourteenth Street and Independence Avenue, SW,

Washington, D.C. 20250 (202) 219-1504; *Agricultural Statistics, Crop Production, Crop Values, Field Crops, Agricultural Outlook,* and *Feed Situation.*

HAZARDOUS WASTES - EXPENDITURES FOR ABATEMENT

U.S. Department of Commerce, Bureau of the Census, Suitland, Maryland 20233 (301) 763-4040; *Current Industrial Reports.*

HAZARDOUS WASTES - SUPERFUND SITES

Environmental Protection Agency, 401 M Street, SW, Washington, D.C. 20460 (202) 382-2090; *Supplementary Materials: National Priorities List, Proposed Rule.*

HAZARDOUS WASTES - TRANSPORTATION

U.S. Department of Transportation, Bureau of Transportation Statistics, 400 Seventh Street, SW, Washington, D.C. 20590 (202) 366-DATA; *National Transportation Statistics Annual, Historical Compendium Information Report.*

HAZARDOUS WASTES - WASTE MANAGEMENT

Environment Business International, Inc., 4452 Park Boulevard, Suite 306, San Diego, California 92116 (619) 295-7685; *Environmental Business Journal.*

HAZELNUTS (FILBERTS)

U.S. Department of Agriculture, National Agricultural Statistics Service, 14th Street and Independence Avenue, SW, Washington, D.C. 20250 (202) 219-1504; *Noncitrus Fruits and Nuts.*

HEALTH AND HUMAN SERVICES, DEPARTMENT OF

U.S. National Science Foundation, 4201 Wilson Boulevard, Arlington, Virginia 22230 (703) 306-1234; *Federal Funds for Research and Development.*

HEALTH AND MEDICAL ASSOCIATIONS

Gale Research Incorporated, 835 Penobscot Building, Detroit, Michigan 48226 (800) 877-4253; *Encyclopedia of Associations,*

HEALTH INSURANCE - See also HEALTH SERVICES, INSURANCE CARRIERS, MEDICAID AND MEDICARE

HEALTH INSURANCE - COVERAGE

Group Health Association of America, 1129 Twentieth Street, NW, Suite 600, Washington, D.C. 20036 (202) 778-3200; *National Directory of HMOs.*

Interstudy, 5715 Christmas Lake, Excelsior, Minnesota 55331 (612) 474-1176; *The Interstudy Competitive Edge.*

U.S. Department of Commerce, Bureau of the Census, Suitland, Maryland 20233 (301) 763-4040; *Current Population Reports,* and unpublished data.

U.S. Department of Health and Human Services, National Center for Health Statistics, 3700 East-West Highway, Hyattsville, Maryland 20782 (301) 436-8500; *Advance Data from Vital and Health Statistics.*

HEALTH INSURANCE - ENROLLMENT AND PAYMENTS

U.S. Department of Health and Human Services, Health Care Financing Administration, 200 Independence Avenue, SW, Washington, D.C. 20201 (202) 245-6113; unpublished data.

HEALTH INSURANCE - EXPENDITURES FOR

U.S. Department of Health and Human Services, Health Care Financing Administration, 200 Independence Avenue, SW, Washington, D.C. 20201 (202) 245-6113; *Health Care Financing Review.*

U.S. Department of Labor, Bureau of Labor Statistics, Two Massachusetts Avenue, NE, Washington, D.C. 20212 (202) 606-7828; *Consumer Expenditure Survey.*

HEALTH INSURANCE - PREMIUMS AND EXPENSES

Health Insurance Association of America, 1025 Connecticut Avenue, NW, Suite 1200, Washington, D.C. 20036 (202) 223-7780; *Source Book of Health Insurance Data.*

U.S. Department of Health and Human Services, Health Care Financing Administration, 200 Independence Avenue, SW, Washington, D.C. 20201 (202) 245-6113; *Health Care Financing Review.*

HEALTH INSURANCE - PREMIUMS AND POLICY RESERVES, LIFE INSURANCE COMPANIES

American Council of Life Insurance, 1001 Pennsylvania Avenue, NW, Washington, D.C. 20004 (202) 624-2000; *Life Insurance Fact Book.*

HEALTH MAINTENANCE ORGANIZATIONS

Group Health Association of America, 1129 Twentieth Street, NW, Suite 600, Washington, D.C. 20036 (202) 778-3200; *National Director of HMOs.*

Interstudy, 5715 Christmas Lake, Excelsior, Minnesota 55331 (612) 474-1176; *The Interstudy Edge.*

HEALTH SCIENCES - DEGREES CONFERRED

U.S. Department of Education, National Center for Education Statistics, 400 Maryland Avenue, SW, Washington, D.C. 20202 (202) 708-5366; *Digest of Education Statistics.*

U.S. Department of Health and Human Services, National Center for Health Statistics, 3700 East-West Highway, Hyattsville, Maryland 20782 (301) 436-8500; *Health Resources Statistics,* and unpublished data.

HEALTH SERVICES - CHARITABLE CONTRIBUTIONS

Gallup Organization, Incorporated, 100 Palmer Square, Princeton, New Jersey 08542 (609) 924-9600; *Giving and Volunteering in the United States.*

HEALTH SERVICES - COVERAGE

Health Insurance Association of America, 1025 Connecticut Avenue, NW, Suite 1200, Washington, D.C. 20036 (202) 223-7780; *Source Book of Health Insurance Data.*

U.S. Department of Commerce, Bureau of the Census, Suitland, Maryland 20233 (301) 763-4040; *Current Population Reports,* and unpublished data.

U.S. Department of Health and Human Services, Health Care Financing Administration, 200 Independence Avenue, SW, Washington, D.C. 20201 (202) 245-6113; *Medicare Program Statistics*, and unpublished data.

U.S. Department of Health and Human Service, Social Security Administration, 6401 Security Boulevard, Baltimore, Maryland 21235 (410) 965-1234; *Annual Statistical Supplement to the Social Security Bulletin*.

HEALTH SERVICES - EMPLOYMENT BENEFITS

U.S. Department of Labor, Bureau of Labor Statistics, Two Massachusetts Avenue, NE, Washington, D.C. 20212 (202) 606-7828; *Employee Benefits in Medium and Large Private Establishments*, *Employee Benefits in State and Local Governments*, and *Employee Benefits in Small Private Establishments*.

HEALTH SERVICES - FEDERAL OUTLAYS FOR

Executive Office of the President, Office of Management and Budget, Executive Office Building, Washington, D.C. 20503 (202) 395-3080; *The Budget of the United States Government*, and *Historical Tables, Budget of the United States Government*.

U.S. Department of Health and Human Services, Health Care Financing Administration, 200 Independence Avenue, SW, Washington, D.C. 20201 (202) 245-6113; *Health Care Financing Review*.

HEALTH SERVICES - FOREIGN COUNTRIES

Organization for Economic Co-operation and Development, Publication and Information Center, 2001 L Street, NW, Washington, D.C. 20036 (202) 785-6323; *OECD Health Systems: Facts and Trends*, and *OECD Health Data*.

HEALTH SERVICES - GOVERNMENT EMPLOYMENT AND PAYROLLS

U.S. Department of Commerce, Bureau of the Census, Suitland, Maryland 20233 (301) 763-4040; *Public Employment*.

HEALTH SERVICES - HOSPITALS

American Hospital Association, 840 North Lake Shore Drive, Chicago, Illinois 60611 (312) 280-6000; *Annual Survey of Hospitals*, *Hospital Statistics*, and unpublished data.

U.S. Department of Commerce, Bureau of the Census, Suitland, Maryland 20233 (301) 763-4040; *County Business Patterns*, *Current Business Reports*, Service Annual Survey.

U.S. Department of Health and Human Services, National Center for Health Statistics, 3700 East-West Highway, Hyattsville, Maryland 20782 (301) 436-8500; *Vital and Health Statistics*, *Health, United States*, and unpublished data.

HEALTH SERVICES - INDUSTRY - EARNINGS

U.S. Department of Commerce, Bureau of the Census, Suitland, Maryland 20233 (301) 763-4040; *Census of Service Industries*, *County Business Patterns*, and unpublished data.

U.S. Department of Labor, Bureau of Labor Statistics, Two Massachusetts Avenue, NE, Washington, D.C. 20212 (202) 606-7828; *Employment and Earnings*, and Bulletins 2370 and 2429.

HEALTH SERVICES - INDUSTRY - EMPLOYEES

U.S. Department of Commerce, Bureau of the Census, Suitland, Maryland 20233 (301) 763-4040; *Census of Service Industries*, *County Business Patterns*, and unpublished data.

U.S. Department of Health and Human Services, National Center for Health Statistics, 3700 East-West Highway, Hyattsville, Maryland 20782 (301) 436-8500; unpublished data.

U.S. Department of Labor, Bureau of Labor Statistics, Two Massachusetts Avenue, NE, Washington, D.C. 20212 (202) 606-7828; *Employment and Earnings*, and Bulletins 2370 and 2429.

HEALTH SERVICES - INDUSTRY - ESTABLISHMENTS

U.S. Department of Commerce, Bureau of the Census, Suitland, Maryland 20233 (301) 763-4040; *Census of Service Industries*, *County Business Patterns*, and unpublished data.

HEALTH SERVICES - INDUSTRY - FINANCES

U.S. Department of Commerce, Bureau of the Census, Suitland, Maryland 20233 (301) 763-4040; *Current Business Reports*, Service Annual Survey.

HEALTH SERVICES - INDUSTRY - GROSS DOMESTIC PRODUCT

U.S. Department of Commerce, Bureau of Economic Analysis, Fourteenth Street between Constitution Avenue and E Street, NW, Washington, D.C. 20230 (202) 606-9900; *The National Income and Product Accounts of the U.S.*, and *Survey of Current Business*.

HEALTH SERVICES - INDUSTRY - MERGERS AND ACQUISITIONS

Securities Data Company, 1180 Raymond Boulevard, Newark, New Jersey 07102 (201) 622-3100; *Merger and Corporate Transactions Database*.

HEALTH SERVICES - MEDICAID

Executive Office of the President, Office of Management and Budget, Executive Office Building, Washington, D.C. 20503 (202) 395-3080; *Historical Tables, Budget of the United States Government*, and *The Budget of the United States Government*, annual.

U.S. Department of Commerce, Bureau of the Census, Suitland, Maryland 20233 (301) 763-4040; *Current Population Reports*, and unpublished data.

U.S. Department of Health and Human Services, Health Care Financing Administration, 200 Independence Avenue, SW, Washington, D.C. 20201 (202) 245-6113; *Health Care Financing Review*, *Medicare Program Statistics*, and unpublished data.

U.S. Department of Health and Human Services, Social Security Administration, 6401 Security Boulevard, Baltimore, Maryland 21235 (410) 965-1234; *Social Security Bulletin*.

U.S. Library of Congress, Congressional Research Service, 10 First Street, SE, Washington, D.C. 20540 (202) 707-5000; *Cash and Noncash Benefits for Persons With Limited Income: Eligibility Rules, Recipient and Expenditure Data*.

HEALTH SERVICES - MEDICARE

Executive Office of the President, Office of Management and Budget, Executive Office Building, Washington, D.C. 20503 (202) 395-3080; *The Budget of the United States Government*.

U.S. Department of Commerce, Bureau of the Census, Suitland, Maryland 20233 (301) 763-4040; *Current Population Reports*, and unpublished data.

U.S. Department of Health and Human Services, Health Care Financing Administration, 200 Independence Avenue, SW, Washington, D.C. 20201 (202) 245-6113; *Medicare Program Statistics, Health Care Financing Review*, and unpublished data.

U.S. Department of Health and Human Services, Social Security Administration, 6401 Security Boulevard, Baltimore, Maryland 21235 (410) 965-1234; *Social Security Bulletin, Annual Statistical Supplement to the Social Security Bulletin, Annual Report of Board of Trustees, OASI, DI, HI, and SMI Trust Funds*, and unpublished data.

HEALTH SERVICES - MENTAL HEALTH FACILITIES

U.S. Department of Health and Human Services, Substance Abuse and Mental Health Services Administration, 5600 Fishers Lane, Rockville, Maryland 20857 (301) 443-3875; unpublished data.

HEALTH SERVICES - MENTAL RETARDATION FACILITIES

U.S. Department of Health and Human Services, Office of Human Development Services, 200 Independence Avenue, SW, Washington, D.C. 20201 (202) 245-7246; *Residents in Public Institutions for Mentally Retarded*.

HEALTH SERVICES - NURSING HOMES

U.S. Department of Health and Human Services, Health Care Financing Administration, 200 Independence Avenue, SW, Washington, D.C. 20201 (202) 245-6113; *Health Care Financing Review*.

U.S. Department of Health and Human Services, National Center for Health Statistics, 3700 East-West Highway, Hyattsville, Maryland 20782 (301) 436-8500; *Advance Data from Vital and Health Statistics*, and unpublished data.

HEALTH SERVICES - OCCUPATIONAL SAFETY

U.S. Department of Labor, Bureau of Labor Statistics, Two Massachusetts Avenue, NE, Washington, D.C. 20212 (202) 606-7828; *Occupational Injuries and Illnesses in the United States by Industry*.

HEALTH SERVICES - OCCUPATIONS

American Hospital Association, 840 North Lake Shore Drive, Chicago, Illinois 60611 (312) 280-6000; *Hospital Statistics*, and *Report of the Hospital Nursing Personnel Survey*.

American Medical Association, 515 North State Street, Chicago, Illinois 60610 (312) 464-4818; *Physician Characteristics and Distribution in the U.S.*

U.S. Department of Health and Human Services, National Center for Health Statistics, 3700 East-West Highway, Hyattsville, Maryland 20782 (301) 436-8500; unpublished data.

U.S. Department of Labor, Bureau of Labor Statistics, Two Massachusetts Avenue, NE, Washington, D.C. 20212 (202) 606-7828; *Employment and Earnings, News*, and *Monthly Labor Review*.

HEALTH SERVICES - PERSONAL HEALTH PRACTICES

U.S. Department of Health and Human Services, National Center for Health Statistics, 3700 East-West Highway, Hyattsville, Maryland 20782 (301) 436-8500; *Health Promotion and Disease Prevention, United States, Vital and Health Statistics*, and unpublished data.

HEALTH SERVICES - PHILANTHROPY

American Association of Fund Raising Counsel, 25 West Forty-third Street, New York, New York 10036 (212) 354-5799; *Giving USA*.

The Conference Board, 845 Third Avenue, New York, New York 10022 (212) 751-2600; *Annual Survey of Corporate Contributions*.

U.S. Department of Health and Human Services, Health Care Financing Administration, 200 Independence Avenue, SW, Washington, D.C. 20201 (202) 245-6113; *Health Care Financing Review*.

HEALTH SERVICES - PRICE INDEXES

U.S. Department of Commerce, Bureau of Economic Analysis, Fourteenth Street between Constitution Avenue and E Street, NW, Washington, D.C. 20230 (202) 606-9900; *The National Income and Product Accounts of the U.S.*, and *Survey of Current Business*.

U.S. Department of Labor, Bureau of Labor Statistics, Two Massachusetts Avenue, NE, Washington, D.C. 20212 (202) 606-7828; *Monthly Labor Review, CPI Detailed Report*, and unpublished data.

HEALTH SERVICES - PRIVATE EXPENDITURES

U.S. Department of Health and Human Services, Health Care Financing Administration, 200 Independence Avenue, SW, Washington, D.C. 20201 (202) 245-6113; *Health Care Financing Review*.

U.S. Department of Health and Human Services, Social Security Administration, 6401 Security Boulevard, Baltimore, Maryland 21235 (410) 965-1234; *Annual Statistical Supplement to the Social Security Bulletin*.

U.S. Department of Labor, Bureau of Labor Statistics, Two Massachusetts Avenue, NE, Washington, D.C. 20212 (202) 606-7828; *Consumer Expenditures in 1992*, and unpublished data.

HEALTH SERVICES - PUBLIC EXPENDITURES

Executive Office of the President, Office of Management and Budget, Executive Office Building, Washington, D.C. 20503 (202) 395-3080; *Budget of the United States Government*.

U.S. Department of Health and Human Services, Health Care Financing Administration, 200 Independence Avenue, SW, Washington, D.C .20201 (202) 245-6113; *Health Care Financing Review*.

U.S. Department of Health and Human Services, Social Security Administration, 6401 Security Boulevard, Baltimore, Maryland 21235 (410) 965-1234; *Social Security Bulletin*, and unpublished data.

HEALTH SERVICES - PUBLIC EXPENDITURES - FEDERAL GOVERNMENT

Executive Office of the President, Office of Management and Budget, Executive Office Building, Washington, D.C. 20503 (202) 395-3080; *Historical Tables, Budget of the United States Government*, and *Budget of the United States Government*.

U.S. Department of Health and Human Services, Health Care Financing Administration, 200 Independence Avenue, SW, Washington, D.C. 20201 (202) 245-6113; *Health Care Financing Review.*

HEALTH SERVICES - PUBLIC EXPENDITURES - FEDERAL GOVERNMENT - AID TO STATE AND LOCAL GOVERNMENTS

Executive Office of the President, Office of Management and Budget, Executive Office Building, Washington, D.C. 20503 (202) 395-3080; *Historical Tables, Budget of the United States Government,* and *Budget of the U.S. Government.*

HEALTH SERVICES - PUBLIC EXPENDITURES - STATE AND LOCAL GOVERNMENT

U.S. Department of Commerce, Bureau of the Census, Suitland, Maryland 20233 (301) 763-4040; *Government Finances,* and *Historical Statistics on Governmental Finances and Employment.*

HEALTH SERVICES - PUBLIC EXPENDITURES - STATE AND LOCAL GOVERNMENT - CITY GOVERNMENT

U.S. Department of Commerce, Bureau of the Census, Suitland, Maryland 20233 (301) 763-4040; *City Government Finances.*

HEALTH SERVICES - PUBLIC EXPENDITURES - STATE AND LOCAL GOVERNMENT - STATE GOVERNMENT

National Association of State Budget Officers, Hall of the States, 400 North Capitol Street, NW, Suite 295, Washington, D.C. 20001 (202) 624-5382; *Fiscal Survey of the States,* and *State Expenditure Report.*

U.S. Department of Commerce, Bureau of the Census, Suitland, Maryland 20233 (301) 763-4040; *Historical Statistics on Governmental Finances and Employment,* and *State Government Finances.*

HEALTH SERVICES - SALES OR RECEIPTS

U.S. Department of Commerce, Bureau of the Census, Suitland, Maryland 20233 (301) 763-4040; *Census of Service Industries, Current Business Reports, Service Annual Survey,* and unpublished data.

HEALTH SERVICES - VETERANS HEALTH CARE

Executive Office of the President, Office of Management and Budget, Executive Office Building, Washington, D.C. 20503 (202) 395-3080; *Budget of the United States Government.*

U.S. Department of Health and Human Services, Health Care Financing Administration, 200 Independence Avenue, SW, Washington, D.C. 20201 (202) 245-6113; *Health Care Financing Review.*

U.S. Department of Veterans Affairs, 810 Vermont Avenue, NW, Washington, D.C. 20420 (202) 233-2300; *Annual Report of the Secretary of Veterans Affairs, Directory of VA Facilities,* and unpublished data.

HEALTH SERVICES - VOLUNTEERS

Independent Sector, 1828 L Street, NW, Washington, D.C. 20036 (202) 223-8100; *Giving and Volunteering in the U.S.*

HEARING IMPAIRED

U.S. Department of Health and Human Services, National Center for Health Statistics, 3700 East-West Highway, Hyattsville, Maryland 20782 (301) 436-8500; *Vital and Health Statistics,* and unpublished data.

HEART DISEASE

U.S. Department of Health and Human Services, National Center for Health Statistics, 3700 East-West Highway, Hyattsville, Maryland 20782 (301) 436-8500; *Monthly Vital Statistics Report, Health, United States, Vital Statistics of the United States,* and unpublished data.

HEART DISEASE - DEATHS

U.S. Department of Health and Human Services, National Center for Health Statistics, 3700 East-West Highway, Hyattsville, Maryland 20782 (301) 436-8500; *Monthly Vital Statistics Report, Vital Statistics of the United States,* and unpublished data.

HEART DISEASE - FOREIGN COUNTRIES

World Health Organization, Avenue Appia, CH-1211 Geneva 27, Switzerland (Telephone Number in U.S. (518) 436-9686); *World Health Statistics Annual.*

HEAT PUMPS

U.S. Department of Commerce, Bureau of the Census, Suitland, Maryland 20233 (301) 763-4040; *Current Housing Reports, American Housing Survey,* and *Census of Housing, Detailed Housing Characteristics.*

HEATING AND PLUMBING EQUIPMENT

U.S. Department of Commerce, Bureau of the Census, Suitland, Maryland 20233 (301) 763-4040; *Current Housing Reports,* American Housing Survey.

HEATING AND PLUMBING EQUIPMENT - MANUFACTURE

U.S. Department of Commerce, Bureau of the Census, Suitland, Maryland 20233 (301) 763-4040; *Census of Manufactures,* and *Annual Survey of Manufactures.*

HEATING AND PLUMBING EQUIPMENT - NEW HOUSES

U.S. Department of Commerce, Bureau of the Census, Suitland, Maryland 20233 (301) 763-4040 and U.S. Department of Housing and Urban Development, 451 Seventh Street, SW, Washington, D.C. 20410 (202) 708-1422; *Current Construction Reports, Characteristics of New Housing,* (a joint publication), and *New One-Family Houses Sold.*

HEATING AND PLUMBING EQUIPMENT - REPAIR EXPENDITURES

U.S. Department of Commerce, Bureau of the Census, Suitland, Maryland 20233 (301) 763-4040; *Current Housing Reports.*

HEATING AND PLUMBING EQUIPMENT - SOLAR

U.S. Department of Energy, Energy Information Administration, 1000 Independence Avenue, SW, Washington, D.C. 20585 (202) 586-8800; *Solar Collector Manufacturing Activity.*

HEIGHTS - AVERAGE - BY AGE AND SEX

U.S. Department of Health and Human Services, National Center for Health Statistics, 3700 East-West Highway, Hyattsville, Maryland 20782 (301) 436-8500; *Vital and Health Statistics.*

HELIUM

U.S. Department of the Interior, Bureau of Mines, 810 Seventh Street, NW, Washington, D.C. 20241 (202) 501-9649; *Annual Reports,* and *Mineral Commodities Summaries.*

HEPATITIS

U.S. Department of Health and Human Services, Center for Disease Control, 1600 Clifton Road, NE, Atlanta, Georgia 30333 (404) 639-3311; *Summary of Notifiable Diseases, U.S. Morbidity and Mortality, Weekly Report.*

HERNIA AND INTESTINAL OBSTRUCTION - DEATHS

U.S. Department of Health and Human Services, National Center for Health Statistics, 3700 East-West Highway, Hyattsville, Maryland 20782 (301) 436-8500; *Monthly Vital Statistics Report, Vital Statistics of the United States,* and unpublished data.

HEROIN - PERSONS USING AND SEIZURES

U.S. Department of Health and Human Services, Substance Abuse and Mental Health Services Administration, 5600 Fishers Lane, Rockville, Maryland 20857 (301) 443-3875; *National Household Survey on Drug Abuse.*

U. S. Department of Justice, Drug Enforcement Administration, 600-700 Army Navy Drive, Arlington, Virginia 22202 (202) 307-1000; *Annual Report.*

HERRING - SEA

U.S. Department of Commerce, National Oceanic and Atmospheric Administration, National Marine Fisheries Service, 1335 East-West Highway, Silver Spring, Maryland 20910 (301) 427-2239; *Fishery Statistics of the United States,* and *Fisheries of the United States.*

HIDES AND SKINS - See also LEATHER AND LEATHER PRODUCTS

HIDES AND SKINS - FOREIGN TRADE

U.S. Department of Agriculture, Economic Research Service, Fourteenth Street and Independence Avenue, SW, Washington, D.C. 20005-4789 (202) 219-1504; *Foreign Agricultural Trade of the United States, Agricultural Outlook,* and *Agricultural Statistics.*

U.S. Department of Commerce, Bureau of the Census, Suitland, Maryland 20233 (301) 763-4040; *U.S. Merchandise Trade,* and *U.S. Merchandise Trade: Exports, General Imports, and Imports for Consumption.*

HIGHWAYS - ACCIDENTS AND DEATHS

U.S. Department of Transportation, Federal Highway Administration, 400 Seventh Street, SW, Washington, D.C. 20590 (202) 366-0660; *Fatal and Injury Accident Rates on Public Roads in the United States.*

HIGHWAYS - CONSTRUCTION COSTS

U.S. Department of Commerce, International Trade Administration, Fourteenth Street between Constitution Avenue and E Street, NW, Washington, D.C. 20230 (202) 482-3809; *Construction Review.*

HIGHWAYS - CONSTRUCTION COSTS - VALUE OF NEW CONSTRUCTION

U.S. Department of Commerce, Bureau of the Census, Suitland, Maryland 20233 (301) 763-4040; *Current Construction Reports.*

HIGHWAYS - DEBT - STATE AND LOCAL GOVERNMENTS

U.S. Department of Transportation, Federal Highway Administration, 400 Seventh Street, SW, Washington, D.C. 20590 (202) 366-0660; *Highway Statistics.*

HIGHWAYS - EMPLOYEES - GOVERNMENT

U.S. Department of Commerce, Bureau of the Census, Suitland, Maryland 20233 (301) 763-4040; *Historical Statistics on Governmental Finances and Employment, Public Employment,* and *City Employment.*

HIGHWAYS - EXPENDITURES - CITY GOVERNMENT

U.S. Department of Commerce, Bureau of the Census, Suitland, Maryland 20233 (301) 763-4040; *City Government Finances.*

HIGHWAYS - EXPENDITURES - STATE AND LOCAL GOVERNMENT

U.S. Department of Commerce, Bureau of the Census, Suitland, Maryland 20233 (301) 763-4040; *Historical Statistics on Governmental Finances and Employment, Government Finances, City Government Finances,* and *Federal Expenditures by State for Fiscal Year.*

HIGHWAYS - EXPENDITURES - STATE GOVERNMENT

U.S. Department of Commerce, Bureau of the Census, Suitland, Maryland 20233 (301) 763-4040; *Historical Statistics on Governmental Finances and Employment,* and *State Government Finances.*

HIGHWAYS - EXPENDITURES - UNITED STATES GOVERNMENT

U.S. Department of Commerce, Bureau of the Census, Suitland, Maryland 20233 (301) 763-4040; *Federal Expenditures by State for Fiscal Year.*

HIGHWAYS - EXPENDITURES - UNITED STATES GOVERNMENT - FEDERAL AID TO STATE AND LOCAL GOVERNMENTS

Executive Office of the President, Office of Management and Budget, Executive Office Building, Washington, D.C. 20503 (202) 395-3080; *Historical Tables, Budget of the United States Government,* and *Budget of the U.S. Government.*

HIGHWAYS - EXPENDITURES - UNITED STATES GOVERNMENT - HIGHWAY TRUST FUND

U.S. Department of Commerce, Bureau of the Census, Suitland, Maryland 20233 (301) 763-4040; *Federal Expenditures by State for Fiscal Year.*

HIGHWAYS - FEDERAL AID SYSTEMS

U.S. Department of Commerce, Bureau of the Census, Suitland, Maryland 20233 (301) 763-4040; *Federal Expenditures by State for Fiscal Year.*

U.S. Department of Transportation, Federal Highway Administration, 400 Seventh Street, SW, Washington, D.C. 20590 (202) 366-0660; *Highway Statistics.*

HIGHWAYS - HIGHWAY TRUST FUNDS

Executive Office of the President, Office of Management and Budget, Executive Office Building, Washington, D.C. 20503 (202) 395-3080; *Budget of the United States Government.*

HIGHWAYS - MILEAGE

U.S. Department of Transportation, Federal Highway Administration, 400 Seventh Street, SW, Washington, D.C. 20590 (202) 366-0660; *Highway Statistics,* and *Fatal and Injury Accident Rates on Public Roads in the United States.*

HIGHWAYS - MOTOR FUEL CONSUMPTION

U.S. Department of Transportation, Federal Highway Administration, 400 Seventh Street, SW, Washington, D.C. 20590 (202) 366-0660; *Highway Statistics.*

HIGHWAYS - MOTOR FUEL TAX

U.S. Department of Commerce, Bureau of the Census, Suitland, Maryland 20233 (301) 763-4040; *State Government Tax Collections.*

U.S. Department of Transportation, Federal Highway Administration, 400 Seventh Street, SW, Washington, D.C. 20590 (202) 366-0660; *Highway Statistics.*

HIGHWAYS - TYPE AND CONTROL

U.S. Department of Transportation, Federal Highway Administration, 400 Seventh Street, SW, Washington, D.C. 20590 (202) 366-0660; *Highway Statistics.*

HIGHWAYS - TYPES OF ROADS TRAVELLED

U.S. Department of Transportation, Federal Highway Administration, 400 Seventh Street, SW, Washington, D.C. 20590 (202) 366-0660; *Fatal and Injury Accident Rates on Public Roads in the United States.*

HIKING

National Sporting Goods Association, 1699 Wall Street, Mount Prospect, Illinois 60056 (708) 439-4000; *Sport Participation in 1992.*

HISPANIC ORIGIN POPULATION

U.S. Department of Commerce, Bureau of the Census, Suitland, Maryland 20233 (301) 763-4040; *Current Population Reports, Census of Population, General Population Characteristics, United States,* and unpublished data.

HISPANIC ORIGIN POPULATION - AGE AND/OR SEX

U.S. Department of Commerce, Bureau of the Census, Suitland, Maryland 20233 (301) 763-4040; *Current Population Reports.*

HISPANIC ORIGIN POPULATION - AIDS

U.S. Department of Health and Human Services, Center for Disease Control, 1600 Clifton Road, NE, Atlanta, Georgia 30333 (404) 639-3311; *Surveillance Report,* and unpublished data.

HISPANIC ORIGIN POPULATION - BIRTHS AND BIRTH RATES

U.S. Department of Commerce, Bureau of the Census, Suitland, Maryland 20233 (301) 763-4040; *Current Population Reports.*

U.S. Department of Health and Human Services, National Center for Health Statistics, 3700 East-West Highway, Hyattsville, Maryland 20782 (301) 436-8500; *Vital Statistics of the United States,* and unpublished data.

HISPANIC ORIGIN POPULATION - CHILD CARE

U.S. Department of Commerce, Bureau of the Census, Suitland, Maryland 20233 (301) 763-4040; *Current Population Reports.*

HISPANIC ORIGIN POPULATION - CHILDREN UNDER EIGHTEEN YEARS OLD

U.S. Department of Commerce, Bureau of the Census, Suitland, Maryland 20233 (301) 763-4040; *Current Population Reports.*

HISPANIC ORIGIN POPULATION - COLLEGE ENROLLMENT

U.S. Department of Commerce, Bureau of the Census, Suitland, Maryland 20233 (301) 763-4040; *Census of Population, Characteristics of the Population, Current Population Reports,* and unpublished data.

U.S. Department of Education, National Center for Education Statistics, 400 Maryland Avenue, SW, Washington, D.C. 20202 (202) 708-5366; *Digest of Education Statistics.*

HISPANIC ORIGIN POPULATION - CONGRESS - MEMBERS OF

National Association of Latino Elected and Appointed Officials, NALEO Education Fund, 3409 Garnet Street, Los Angeles, California 90023 (213) 262-8503; *National Roster of Hispanic Elected Officials.*

U.S. Department of Commerce, Bureau of the Census, Suitland, Maryland 20233 (301) 763-4040; *Congressional Directory.*

HISPANIC ORIGIN POPULATION - CRIMINAL VICTIMIZATION RATES

U.S. Department of Justice, Bureau of Justice Statistics, 633 Indiana Avenue, NW, Washington, D.C. 20531 (800) 732-3277; *Criminal Victimization in the United States.*

HISPANIC ORIGIN POPULATION - DEATHS AND DEATH RATES

U.S. Department of Health and Human Services, National Center for Health Statistics, 3700 East-West Highway, Hyattsville, Maryland 20782 (301) 436-8500; *Vital Statistics of the United States,* and *Monthly Vital Statistics Report.*

HISPANIC ORIGIN POPULATION - DISABLED PERSONS

U.S. Department of Commerce, Bureau of the Census, Suitland, Maryland 20233 (301) 763-4040; unpublished data.

HISPANIC ORIGIN POPULATION - DISABILITY DAYS

U.S. Department of Health and Human Services, National Center for Health Statistics, 3700 East-West Highway, Hyattsville, Maryland 20782 (301) 436-8500; *Vital and Health Statistics*, and unpublished data.

HISPANIC ORIGIN POPULATION - EDUCATIONAL ATTAINMENT

National Science Foundation, 4201 Wilson Boulevard, Arlington, Virginia 22230 (703) 306-1234; *Survey of Earned Doctorates, Selected Data on Science and Engineering Doctorate Awards*.

U.S. Department of Commerce, Bureau of the Census, Suitland, Maryland 20233 (301) 763-4040; *Census of Population, Current Population Reports*, and unpublished data.

U.S. Department of Education, National Center for Education Statistics, 400 Maryland Avenue, SW, Washington, D.C. 20202 (202) 708-5366; *Digest of Education Statistics*.

HISPANIC ORIGIN POPULATION - ELDERLY

U.S. Department of Commerce, Bureau of the Census, Suitland, Maryland 20233 (301) 763-4040; *Current Population Reports*, and unpublished data.

HISPANIC ORIGIN POPULATION - ELECTED OFFICIALS

National Association of Latino Elected and Appointed Officials, NALEO Education Fund, 3409 Garnet Street, Los Angeles, California 90023 (213) 262-8503; *National Roster of Hispanic Elected Officials*.

U.S. Department of Commerce, Bureau of the Census, Suitland, Maryland 20233 (301) 763-4040; *Congressional Directory*.

HISPANIC ORIGIN POPULATION - ELECTIONS - VOTER REGISTRATION AND TURNOUT

U.S. Department of Commerce, Bureau of the Census, Suitland, Maryland 20233 (301) 763-4040; *Current Population Reports*.

HISPANIC ORIGIN POPULATION - FAMILIES - CHARACTERISTICS

U.S. Department of Commerce, Bureau of the Census, Suitland, Maryland 20233 (301) 763-4040; *Current Population Reports*, and *Census of Population*.

HISPANIC ORIGIN POPULATION - FARM OPERATORS

U.S. Department of Commerce, Bureau of the Census, Suitland, Maryland 20233 (301) 763-4040; *Census of Agriculture*.

HISPANIC ORIGIN POPULATION - FARM WORKERS

U.S. Department of Agriculture, Economic Research Service, Fourteenth Street and Independence Avenue, SW, Washington, D.C. 20005-4789 (202) 219-1504; unpublished data.

HISPANIC ORIGIN POPULATION - HEALTH INSURANCE COVERAGE

U.S. Department of Commerce, Bureau of the Census, Suitland, Maryland 20233 (301) 763-4040; *Current Population Reports*, and unpublished data.

HISPANIC ORIGIN POPULATION - HOUSEHOLD OR FAMILY - CHARACTERISTICS

U.S. Department of Commerce, Bureau of the Census, Suitland, Maryland 20233 (301) 763-4040; *Current Population Reports, Census of Population*, and *Persons of Spanish Origin*.

HISPANIC ORIGIN POPULATION - HOUSING

U.S. Department of Commerce, Bureau of the Census, Suitland, Maryland 20233 (301) 763-4040; *Current Housing Reports*, American Housing Survey.

HISPANIC ORIGIN POPULATION - HOUSING - TENURE

U.S. Department of Commerce, Bureau of the Census, Suitland, Maryland 20233 (301) 763-4040; *Current Population Reports*.

HISPANIC ORIGIN POPULATION - INCOME

U.S. Department of Commerce, Bureau of the Census, Suitland, Maryland 20233 (301) 763-4040; *Current Population Reports*, and unpublished data.

HISPANIC ORIGIN POPULATION - INCOME - FAMILY

U.S. Department of Commerce, Bureau of the Census, Suitland, Maryland 20233 (301) 763-4040; *Current Population Reports*, and unpublished data.

HISPANIC ORIGIN POPULATION - INCOME - HOUSEHOLD

U.S. Department of Commerce, Bureau of the Census, Suitland, Maryland 20233 (301) 763-4040; *Current Population Reports*, and unpublished data.

HISPANIC ORIGIN POPULATION - JAIL INMATES

U.S. Department of Justice, Bureau of Justice Statistics, 633 Indiana Avenue, NW, Washington, D.C. 20531 (800) 732-3277; *Jail Inmates*, and *Census of Local Jails*.

HISPANIC ORIGIN POPULATION - LABOR FORCE AND EMPLOYMENT - EARNINGS

U.S. Department of Labor, Bureau of Labor Statistics, Two Massachusetts Avenue, NE, Washington, D.C. 20212 (202) 606-7828; *Employment and Earnings*, and Bulletins 2370 and 2429.

HISPANIC ORIGIN POPULATION - LABOR FORCE AND EMPLOYMENT - EMPLOYED

U.S. Department of Commerce, Bureau of the Census, Suitland, Maryland 20233 (301) 763-4040; *Current Population Reports*.

U.S. Department of Labor, Bureau of Labor Statistics, Two Massachusetts Avenue, NE, Washington, D.C. 20212 (202) 606-7828; *Employment and Earnings*.

HISPANIC ORIGIN POPULATION - LABOR FORCE AND EMPLOYMENT - EMPLOYED - BY INDUSTRY - OCCUPATION

U.S. Department of Labor, Bureau of Labor Statistics, Two Massachusetts Avenue, NE, Washington, D.C. 20212 (202) 606-7828; *Employment and Earnings*.

HISPANIC ORIGIN POPULATION - LABOR FORCE AND EMPLOYMENT - EMPLOYED - MINIMUM WAGE WORKERS

U.S. Department of Labor, Bureau of Labor Statistics, Two Massachusetts Avenue, NE, Washington, D.C. 20212 (202) 606-7828; unpublished data.

HISPANIC ORIGIN POPULATION - LABOR FORCE AND EMPLOYMENT - EMPLOYED - STATE AND LOCAL GOVERNMENTS

U.S. Equal Employment Opportunity Commission, 2401 E Street, NW, Washington, D.C. 20507 (800) USA-EEOC; *State and Local Government Information Report*.

HISPANIC ORIGIN POPULATION - LABOR FORCE AND EMPLOYMENT - UNEMPLOYED

U.S. Department of Labor, Bureau of Labor Statistics, Two Massachusetts Avenue, NE, Washington, D.C. 20212 (202) 606-7828; *Employment and Earnings*, and unpublished data.

HISPANIC ORIGIN POPULATION - LABOR FORCE AND EMPLOYMENT - UNION MEMBERSHIP

U.S. Department of Labor, Bureau of Labor Statistics, Two Massachusetts Avenue, NE, Washington, D.C. 20212 (202) 606-7828; *Employment and Earnings*.

HISPANIC ORIGIN POPULATION - MARITAL STATUS

U.S. Department of Commerce, Bureau of the Census, Suitland, Maryland 20233 (301) 763-4040; *Census of Population, Persons of Spanish Origin*, and *Current Population Reports*.

HISPANIC ORIGIN POPULATION - METROPOLITAN AREAS

U.S. Department of Commerce, Bureau of the Census, Suitland, Maryland 20233 (301) 763-4040; *Census of Population and Housing, Supplementary Reports, Metropolitan Areas as Defined by the Office of Management and Budget*.

HISPANIC ORIGIN POPULATION - MULTIMEDIA USERS

Mediamark Research, Incorporated, 708 Third Avenue, New York, New York 10017 (212) 599-0444; *Multimedia Audiences*.

HISPANIC ORIGIN POPULATION - PENSION PLAN COVERAGE

U.S. Department of Commerce, Bureau of the Census, Suitland, Maryland 20233 (301) 763-4040; unpublished data.

HISPANIC ORIGIN POPULATION - POVERTY

U.S. Department of Commerce, Bureau of the Census, Suitland, Maryland 20233 (301) 763-4040; *Current Population Reports*, and unpublished data.

HISPANIC ORIGIN POPULATION - SCHOOL ENROLLMENT

U.S. Department of Commerce, Bureau of the Census, Suitland, Maryland 20233 (301) 763-4040; *Census of Population, Characteristics of the Population, Current Population Reports*, and unpublished data.

U.S. Department of Education, National Center for Education Statistics, 400 Maryland Avenue, SW, Washington, D.C. 20202 (202) 708-5366; *Digest of Education Statistics*.

HISPANIC ORIGIN POPULATION - SCHOOL ENROLLMENT - PREPRIMARY SCHOOL

U.S. Department of Commerce, Bureau of the Census, Suitland, Maryland 20233 (301) 763-4040; *Current Population Reports*, and unpublished data.

HISPANIC ORIGIN POPULATION - UNION MEMBERSHIP

U.S. Department of Labor, Bureau of Labor Statistics, Two Massachusetts Avenue, NE, Washington, D.C. 20212 (202) 606-7828; *Employment and Earnings*.

HISPANIC ORIGIN POPULATION - VOTER REGISTRATION AND TURNOUT

U.S. Department of Commerce, Bureau of the Census, Suitland, Maryland 20233 (301) 763-4040; *Current Population Reports*.

HIV INFECTION

American Hospital Association, 840 North Lake Shore Drive, Chicago, Illinois 60611 (312) 280-6000; *Hospital Statistics and Annual Survey of Hospitals*.

U.S. Department of Health and Human Services, Centers for Disease Control, 1600 Clifton Road, NE, Atlanta, Georgia 30333 (404) 639-3311; *Summary of Notifiable Diseases, United States, Morbidity and Mortality Weekly Report, Surveillance Report*, and unpublished data.

U.S. Department of Health and Human Services, National Center for Health Statistics, 3700 East-West Highway, Hyattsville, Maryland 20782 (301) 436-8500; *Monthly Vital Statistics Reports, Health, United States, Vital Statistics of the United States, Vital and Health Statistics*, and unpublished data.

HOBBY - AVOCATIONAL ASSOCIATIONS

Gale Research Incorporated, 835 Penobscot Building, Detroit, Michigan 48226 (800) 877-4253; *Encyclopedia of Associations*.

HOCKEY

National Hockey League, 1800 McGill College Avenue, Suite 2600, Quebec, Canada H3A 3J6 (514) 288-9220.

National Hockey League Players Association, One Dundas Street, Toronto, Ontario, Canada M5G 1Z3 (416) 408-4040.

HOGS

U.S. Department of Agriculture, National Agricultural Statistics Service, Fourteenth Street and Independence Avenue, SW, Washington, D.C. 20250 (202) 219-1504; *Meat Animals - Production, Disposition, and Income, Agricultural Statistics, Economic Indicators of the Farm Sector: National Financial Summary, Livestock and Meat Statistics*, and *Agricultural Outlook*.

U.S. Department of Commerce, Bureau of the Census, Suitland, Maryland 20233 (301) 763-4040; *Census of Agriculture*.

HOLY SEE - AGRICULTURE

Food and Agricultural Organization of the United Nations (FAO) Via delle Terme di Caracalla, 00100 Rome, Italy (Telephone Number in U.S. (202) 653-2400); *The State of Food and Agriculture*, and *Trade Yearbook*.

G.K. Hall and Company, 70 Lincoln Street, Boston, Massachusetts 02111 (617) 423-3990; *The World in Figures.*

HOLY SEE - AIRLINE SERVICE

G.K. Hall and Company, 70 Lincoln Street, Boston, Massachusetts 02111 (617) 423-3990; *The World in Figures.*

HOLY SEE - AREA AND DENSITY OF POPULATION

Food and Agricultural Organization of the United Nations (FAO) Via delle Terme di Caracalla, 00100 Rome, Italy (Telephone Number in U.S. (202) 653-2400); *The State of Food and Agriculture.*

G.K. Hall and Company, 70 Lincoln Street, Boston, Massachusetts 02111 (617) 423-3990; *The World in Figures.*

Statistical Office of the United Nations, Publishing Service, New York, New York 10017 (800) 253-9646; *Statistical Yearbook.*

HOLY SEE - BALANCE OF PAYMENTS

G.K. Hall and Company, 70 Lincoln Street, Boston, Massachusetts 02111 (617) 423-3990; *The World in Figures.*

HOLY SEE - BANKING

G.K. Hall and Company, 70 Lincoln Street, Boston, Massachusetts 02111 (617) 423-3990; *The World in Figures.*

HOLY SEE - BIRTH RATES

Statistical Office of the United Nations, Publishing Service, New York, New York 10017 (800) 253-9646; *Demographic Yearbook.*

HOLY SEE - BONDS

G.K. Hall and Company, 70 Lincoln Street, Boston, Massachusetts 02111 (617) 423-3990; *The World in Figures.*

HOLY SEE - BOOK PRODUCTION

G.K. Hall and Company, 70 Lincoln Street, Boston, Massachusetts 02111 (617) 423-3990; *The World in Figures.*

United Nations Educational, Scientific and Cultural Organization (UNESCO), 7 Place de Fontenoy, F-75700 Paris, France (Telephone Number in U.S. (212) 963-5981); *Statistical Yearbook.*

HOLY SEE - BROADCASTING

G.K. Hall and Company, 70 Lincoln Street, Boston, Massachusetts 02111 (617) 423-3990; *The World in Figures.*

HOLY SEE - BUSINESS

G.K. Hall and Company, 70 Lincoln Street, Boston, Massachusetts 02111 (617) 423-3990; *The World in Figures.*

HOLY SEE - CALORIE SUPPLY

Food and Agricultural Organization of the United Nations (FAO) Via delle Terme di Caracalla, 00100 Rome, Italy (Telephone Number in U.S. (202) 653-2400); *The State of Food and Agriculture.*

HOLY SEE - CLASS STRUCTURE

G.K. Hall and Company, 70 Lincoln Street, Boston, Massachusetts 02111 (617) 423-3990; *The World in Figures.*

HOLY SEE - CLIMATE

G.K. Hall and Company, 70 Lincoln Street, Boston, Massachusetts 02111 (617) 423-3990; *The World in Figures.*

HOLY SEE - COAL PRODUCTION - See HOLY SEE - MINING AND MINERAL PRODUCTS

HOLY SEE - COMMUNICATIONS

G.K. Hall and Company, 70 Lincoln Street, Boston, Massachusetts 02111 (617) 423-3990; *The World in Figures.*

HOLY SEE - CONSUMER PRICE INDEX

G.K. Hall and Company, 70 Lincoln Street, Boston, Massachusetts 02111 (617) 423-3990; *The World in Figures.*

HOLY SEE - CONSUMPTION

G.K. Hall and Company, 70 Lincoln Street, Boston, Massachusetts 02111 (617) 423-3990; *The World in Figures.*

HOLY SEE - CORN PRODUCTION - See HOLY SEE - CROPS

HOLY SEE - CORPORATE TAXES

G.K. Hall and Company, 70 Lincoln Street, Boston, Massachusetts 02111 (617) 423-3990; *The World in Figures.*

HOLY SEE - CROPS

Food and Agricultural Organization of the United Nations (FAO) Via delle Terme di Caracalla, 00100 Rome, Italy (Telephone Number in U.S. (202) 653-2400); *The State of Food and Agriculture.*

Food and Agricultural Organization of the United Nations (FAO) Via delle Terme di Caracalla, 00100 Rome, Italy (Telephone Number in U.S. (202) 653-2400); *The State of Food and Agriculture.*

G.K. Hall and Company, 70 Lincoln Street, Boston, Massachusetts 02111 (617) 423-3990; *The World in Figures.*

Food and Agricultural Organization of the United Nations (FAO) Via delle Terme di Caracalla, 00100 Rome, Italy (Telephone Number in U.S. (202) 653-2400); *The State of Food and Agriculture.*

HOLY SEE - CUSTOMS DUTIES

G.K. Hall and Company, 70 Lincoln Street, Boston, Massachusetts 02111 (617) 423-3990; *The World in Figures.*

HOLY SEE - DAIRY PRODUCTS

Food and Agricultural Organization of the United Nations (FAO) Via delle Terme di Caracalla, 00100 Rome, Italy (Telephone Number in U.S. (202) 653-2400); *The State of Food and Agriculture.*

HOLY SEE - DEATH RATES

G.K. Hall and Company, 70 Lincoln Street, Boston, Massachusetts 02111 (617) 423-3990; *The World in Figures.*

HOLY SEE - DEFENSE EXPENDITURES

G.K. Hall and Company, 70 Lincoln Street, Boston, Massachusetts 02111 (617) 423-3990; *The World in Figures.*

HOLY SEE - DEMOGRAPHY

G.K. Hall and Company, 70 Lincoln Street, Boston, Massachusetts 02111 (617) 423-3990; *The World in Figures.*

HOLY SEE - DEVELOPMENT ASSISTANCE

G.K. Hall and Company, 70 Lincoln Street, Boston, Massachusetts 02111 (617) 423-3990; *The World in Figures.*

HOLY SEE - DISEASE

G.K. Hall and Company, 70 Lincoln Street, Boston, Massachusetts 02111 (617) 423-3990; *The World in Figures.*

HOLY SEE - DIVORCE RATES

Statistical Office of the United Nations, Publishing Service, New York, New York 10017 (800) 253-9646; *Demographic Yearbook.*

HOLY SEE - DOMESTIC PRODUCT

G.K. Hall and Company, 70 Lincoln Street, Boston, Massachusetts 02111 (617) 423-3990; *The World in Figures.*

HOLY SEE - ECONOMY

G.K. Hall and Company, 70 Lincoln Street, Boston, Massachusetts 02111 (617) 423-3990; *The World in Figures.*

HOLY SEE - EDUCATION

G.K. Hall and Company, 70 Lincoln Street, Boston, Massachusetts 02111 (617) 423-3990; *The World in Figures.*

HOLY SEE - EGG PRODUCTION - See HOLY SEE - DAIRY PRODUCTS

HOLY SEE - ENERGY

Food and Agricultural Organization of the United Nations (FAO) Via delle Terme di Caracalla, 00100 Rome, Italy (Telephone Number in U.S. (202) 653-2400); *The State of Food and Agriculture.*

G.K. Hall and Company, 70 Lincoln Street, Boston, Massachusetts 02111 (617) 423-3990; *The World in Figures.*

HOLY SEE - EXPORTS

Food and Agricultural Organization of the United Nations (FAO) Via delle Terme di Caracalla, 00100 Rome, Italy (Telephone Number in U.S. (202) 653-2400); *The State of Food and Agriculture.*

G.K. Hall and Company, 70 Lincoln Street, Boston, Massachusetts 02111 (617) 423-3990; *The World in Figures.*

HOLY SEE - EXTERNAL TRADE

Food and Agricultural Organization of the United Nations (FAO) Via delle Terme di Caracalla, 00100 Rome, Italy (Telephone Number in U.S. (202) 653-2400); *The State of Food and Agriculture.*

Food and Agricultural Organization of the United Nations (FAO), Via delle Terme di Caracalla, 00100 Rome, Italy (Telephone Number in U.S. (202) 653-2400); *Trade Yearbook.*

G.K. Hall and Company, 70 Lincoln Street, Boston, Massachusetts 02111 (617) 423-3990; *The World in Figures.*

HOLY SEE - FARM CROPS - See HOLY SEE - CROPS

HOLY SEE - FERTILIZER

Food and Agricultural Organization of the United Nations (FAO) Via delle Terme di Caracalla, 00100 Rome, Italy (Telephone Number in U.S. (202) 653-2400); *The State of Food and Agriculture.*

HOLY SEE - FETAL MORTALITY

Statistical Office of the United Nations, Publishing Service, New York, New York 10017 (800) 253-9646; *Demographic Yearbook.*

HOLY SEE - FINANCE

G.K. Hall and Company, 70 Lincoln Street, Boston, Massachusetts 02111 (617) 423-3990; *The World in Figures.*

HOLY SEE - FISHERIES

Food and Agricultural Organization of the United Nations (FAO) Via delle Terme di Caracalla, 00100 Rome, Italy (Telephone Number in U.S. (202) 653-2400); *The State of Food and Agriculture.*

HOLY SEE - FOOD

Food and Agricultural Organization of the United Nations (FAO), Via delle Terme di Caracalla, 00100 Rome, Italy (Telephone Number in U.S. (202) 653-2400); *Production Yearbook,* and *The State of Food and Agriculture.*

G.K. Hall and Company, 70 Lincoln Street, Boston, Massachusetts 02111 (617) 423-3990; *The World in Figures.*

HOLY SEE - FOREIGN AID

G.K. Hall and Company, 70 Lincoln Street, Boston, Massachusetts 02111 (617) 423-3990; *The World in Figures.*

HOLY SEE - FOREIGN TRADE

Food and Agricultural Organization of the United Nations (FAO) Via delle Terme di Caracalla, 00100 Rome, Italy (Telephone Number in U.S. (202) 653-2400); *The State of Food and Agriculture.*

G.K. Hall and Company, 70 Lincoln Street, Boston, Massachusetts 02111 (617) 423-3990; *The World in Figures.*

HOLY SEE - FORESTRY AND FOREST PRODUCTS

Food and Agricultural Organization of the United Nations (FAO) Via delle Terme di Caracalla, 00100 Rome, Italy (Telephone Number in U.S. (202) 653-2400); *The State of Food and Agriculture.*

G.K. Hall and Company, 70 Lincoln Street, Boston, Massachusetts 02111 (617) 423-3990; *The World in Figures.*

HOLY SEE - GENERAL MORTALITY

Statistical Office of the United Nations, Publishing Service, New York, New York 10017 (800) 253-9646; *Demographic Yearbook.*

HOLY SEE - GOVERNMENT

G.K. Hall and Company, 70 Lincoln Street, Boston, Massachusetts 02111 (617) 423-3990; *The World in Figures.*

HOLY SEE - GRAIN PRODUCTION - See HOLY SEE - CROPS

HOLY SEE - GROSS DOMESTIC PRODUCT

G.K. Hall and Company, 70 Lincoln Street, Boston, Massachusetts 02111 (617) 423-3990; *The World in Figures.*

HOLY SEE - HEALTH

G.K. Hall and Company, 70 Lincoln Street, Boston, Massachusetts 02111 (617) 423-3990; *The World in Figures.*

HOLY SEE - HIGHWAYS

G.K. Hall and Company, 70 Lincoln Street, Boston, Massachusetts 02111 (617) 423-3990; *The World in Figures.*

HOLY SEE - ILLITERATE POPULATION

G.K. Hall and Company, 70 Lincoln Street, Boston, Massachusetts 02111 (617) 423-3990; *The World in Figures.*

HOLY SEE - IMPORTS

Food and Agricultural Organization of the United Nations (FAO) Via delle Terme di Caracalla, 00100 Rome, Italy (Telephone Number in U.S. (202) 653-2400); *The State of Food and Agriculture.*

G.K. Hall and Company, 70 Lincoln Street, Boston, Massachusetts 02111 (617) 423-3990; *The World in Figures.*

HOLY SEE - INDUSTRY

G.K. Hall and Company, 70 Lincoln Street, Boston, Massachusetts 02111 (617) 423-3990; *The World in Figures.*

HOLY SEE - INFANT AND MATERNAL MORTALITY

Statistical Office of the United Nations, Publishing Service, New York, New York 10017 (800) 253-9646; *Demographic Yearbook.*

HOLY SEE - LABOR FORCE

Food and Agricultural Organization of the United Nations (FAO) Via delle Terme di Caracalla, 00100 Rome, Italy (Telephone Number in U.S. (202) 653-2400); *The State of Food and Agriculture.*

G.K. Hall and Company, 70 Lincoln Street, Boston, Massachusetts 02111 (617) 423-3990; *The World in Figures.*

HOLY SEE - LAND USE

Food and Agricultural Organization of the United Nations (FAO), Via delle Terme di Caracalla, 00100 Rome, Italy (Telephone Number in U.S. (202) 653-2400); *Production Yearbook.*

G.K. Hall and Company, 70 Lincoln Street, Boston, Massachusetts 02111 (617) 423-3990; *The World in Figures.*

HOLY SEE - LIBRARIES

United Nations Educational, Scientific and Cultural Organization (UNESCO), 7 Place de Fontenoy, F-75700 Paris, France (Telephone Number in U.S. (212) 963-5981); *Statistical Yearbook.*

HOLY SEE - LIVESTOCK AND POULTRY

Food and Agricultural Organization of the United Nations (FAO) Via delle Terme di Caracalla, 00100 Rome, Italy (Telephone Number in U.S. (202) 653-2400); *The State of Food and Agriculture.*

G.K. Hall and Company, 70 Lincoln Street, Boston, Massachusetts 02111 (617) 423-3990; *The World in Figures.*

HOLY SEE - LIVING LEVELS

G.K. Hall and Company, 70 Lincoln Street, Boston, Massachusetts 02111 (617) 423-3990; *The World in Figures.*

HOLY SEE - MAIL TRAFFIC - NUMBER OF ITEMS SENT AND RECEIVED

Statistical Office of the United Nations, Publishing Service, New York, New York 10017 (800) 253-9646; *Statistical Yearbook.*

HOLY SEE - MANUFACTURING

G.K. Hall and Company, 70 Lincoln Street, Boston, Massachusetts 02111 (617) 423-3990; *The World in Figures.*

HOLY SEE - MARRIAGE RATES

Statistical Office of the United Nations, Publishing Service, New York, New York 10017 (800) 253-9646; *Demographic Yearbook.*

HOLY SEE - MEAT PRODUCTION - See HOLY SEE - LIVESTOCK AND POULTRY

HOLY SEE - MERCHANT SHIPPING

G.K. Hall and Company, 70 Lincoln Street, Boston, Massachusetts 02111 (617) 423-3990; *The World in Figures.*

HOLY SEE - MILITARY

G.K. Hall and Company, 70 Lincoln Street, Boston, Massachusetts 02111 (617) 423-3990; *The World in Figures.*

HOLY SEE - MINING AND MINERAL PRODUCTS

G.K. Hall and Company, 70 Lincoln Street, Boston, Massachusetts 02111 (617) 423-3990; *The World in Figures.*

HOLY SEE - MONEY SUPPLY

G.K. Hall and Company, 70 Lincoln Street, Boston, Massachusetts 02111 (617) 423-3990; *The World in Figures.*

HOLY SEE - MOTOR VEHICLES IN USE

G.K. Hall and Company, 70 Lincoln Street, Boston, Massachusetts 02111 (617) 423-3990; *The World in Figures.*

HOLY SEE - MUSEUMS

United Nations Educational, Scientific and Cultural Organization (UNESCO), 7 Place de Fontenoy, F-75700 Paris, France (Telephone Number in U.S. (212) 963-5981); *Statistical Yearbook.*

HOLY SEE - NATALITY - See HOLY SEE - BIRTH RATES

HOLY SEE - NATIONAL INCOME

G.K. Hall and Company, 70 Lincoln Street, Boston, Massachusetts 02111 (617) 423-3990; *The World in Figures.*

HOLY SEE - NEWSPAPER PRODUCTION - See HOLY SEE - FORESTRY AND FOREST PRODUCTS

HOLY SEE - OCCUPATIONS - See HOLY SEE - LABOR FORCE

HOLY SEE - PERIODICALS

United Nations Educational, Scientific and Cultural Organization (UNESCO), 7 Place de Fontenoy, F-75700 Paris, France (Telephone Number in U.S. (212) 963-5981); *Statistical Yearbook*.

HOLY SEE - PESTICIDE USE

Food and Agricultural Organization of the United Nations (FAO) Via delle Terme di Caracalla, 00100 Rome, Italy (Telephone Number in U.S. (202) 653-2400); *The State of Food and Agriculture*.

HOLY SEE - PETROLEUM INDUSTRY

Food and Agricultural Organization of the United Nations (FAO) Via delle Terme di Caracalla, 00100 Rome, Italy (Telephone Number in U.S. (202) 653-2400); *The State of Food and Agriculture*.

G.K. Hall and Company, 70 Lincoln Street, Boston, Massachusetts 02111 (617) 423-3990; *The World in Figures*.

HOLY SEE - POPULATION

Food and Agricultural Organization of the United Nations (FAO), Via delle Terme di Caracalla, 00100 Rome, Italy (Telephone Number in U.S. (202) 653-2400); *Production Yearbook*.

G.K. Hall and Company, 70 Lincoln Street, Boston, Massachusetts 02111 (617) 423-3990; *The World in Figures*.

Statistical Office of the United Nations, Publishing Service, New York, New York 10017 (800) 253-9646; *Demographic Yearbook*, and *Statistical Yearbook*.

World Health Organization, Office of Publications, Avenue Appia, CH-1211 Geneva 27, Switzerland (Telephone Number in U.S. (518) 436-9686); *World Health Statistics Annual*.

HOLY SEE - PRICES

Food and Agricultural Organization of the United Nations (FAO), Via delle Terme di Caracalla, 00100 Rome, Italy (Telephone Number in U.S. (202) 653-2400); *Production Yearbook*, and *The State of Food and Agriculture*.

G.K. Hall and Company, 70 Lincoln Street, Boston, Massachusetts 02111 (617) 423-3990; *The World in Figures*.

HOLY SEE - PRODUCTION

G.K. Hall and Company, 70 Lincoln Street, Boston, Massachusetts 02111 (617) 423-3990; *The World in Figures*.

HOLY SEE - RAILWAYS

G.K. Hall and Company, 70 Lincoln Street, Boston, Massachusetts 02111 (617) 423-3990; *The World in Figures*.

HOLY SEE - RETAIL TRADE

G.K. Hall and Company, 70 Lincoln Street, Boston, Massachusetts 02111 (617) 423-3990; *The World in Figures*.

HOLY SEE - SCIENCE AND TECHNOLOGY - EXPENDITURE FOR RESEARCH

Statistical Office of the United Nations, Publishing Service, New York, New York 10017 (800) 253-9646; *Statistical Yearbook*.

HOLY SEE - SOCIAL DATA

G.K. Hall and Company, 70 Lincoln Street, Boston, Massachusetts 02111 (617) 423-3990; *The World in Figures*.

HOLY SEE - STOCKS - COMMODITY - MARKET PRICE - INDEX

Food and Agricultural Organization of the United Nations (FAO) Via delle Terme di Caracalla, 00100 Rome, Italy (Telephone Number in U.S. (202) 653-2400); *The State of Food and Agriculture*.

HOLY SEE - TELEPHONES IN USE

G.K. Hall and Company, 70 Lincoln Street, Boston, Massachusetts 02111 (617) 423-3990; *The World in Figures*.

HOLY SEE - TEXTILE INDUSTRY

G.K. Hall and Company, 70 Lincoln Street, Boston, Massachusetts 02111 (617) 423-3990; *The World in Figures*.

HOLY SEE - TRADE - See HOLY SEE - FOREIGN TRADE

HOLY SEE - TRANSPORTATION AND COMMUNICATIONS

G.K. Hall and Company, 70 Lincoln Street, Boston, Massachusetts 02111 (617) 423-3990; *The World in Figures*.

HOLY SEE - VITAL STATISTICS

G.K. Hall and Company, 70 Lincoln Street, Boston, Massachusetts 02111 (617) 423-3990; *The World in Figures*.

World Health Organization, Office of Publications, Avenue Appia, CH-1211 Geneva 27, Switzerland (Telephone Number in U.S. (518) 436-9686); *World Health Statistics Annual*.

HOLY SEE - WAGES

G.K. Hall and Company, 70 Lincoln Street, Boston, Massachusetts 02111 (617) 423-3990; *The World in Figures*.

HOLY SEE - WEATHER

G.K. Hall and Company, 70 Lincoln Street, Boston, Massachusetts 02111 (617) 423-3990; *The World in Figures*.

HOME EQUITY LOANS

American Bankers Association, 1120 Connecticut Avenue, NW, Washington, D.C. 20036 (202) 663-5000; *Consumer Credit Delinquency Bulletin*.

Board of Governors of the Federal Reserve System, Twentieth Street and Constitution Avenue, NW, Washington, D.C. 20551 (202) 452-3000; *Domestic Offices, Commercial Bank Assets and Liabilities, Consolidated Report of Condition*.

HOME FURNISHINGS - See APPLIANCES

HOME HEALTH CARE SERVICES

U.S. Department of Commerce, Bureau of the Census, Suitland, Maryland 20233 (301) 763-4040; *Census of Service Industries*, and *County Business Patterns*.

HOMES - See HOUSING, ETC.

HOMICIDES

U.S. Department of Health and Human Services, National Center for Health Statistics, 3700 East-West Highway, Hyattsville, Maryland 20782 (301) 436-8500; *Monthly Vital Statistics of the United States, Vital Statistics of the United States,* and unpublished data.

U.S. Department of Justice, Federal Bureau of Investigation, Ninth Street and Pennsylvania Avenue, NW, Washington, D.C. 20535 (202) 324-3000; *Crime in the United States.*

Honduras - National Statistical Office

Direccion General de Estadistica y Censos, Avenida Centenario 6Y8 Calles, Camayaguela DC, Honduras, Honduras.

Honduras - Primary Statistics Source

Direccion de Estadisticas y Censos, Avenida Centenario 6Y8 Calles, Camayaguela DC, Honduras, Honduras; *Anuario Estadistico.*

HONDURAS - AGRICULTURE

The Economist Intelligence Unit, 111 West 57th Street, New York, New York 10019 (800) 938-4685; *The New Latin America Market Atlas.*

Euromonitor Publications Limited, 87-88 Turnmill Street, London EC1M 5QU, England; *International Marketing Data and Statistics.*

Facts on File, 460 Park Avenue South, New York, New York 10016 (800) 443-8323; *The New Book of World Rankings.*

Federal Statistical Office, Gustav - Stresesmann - Ring 11, D-6200 Wiesbaden, Federal Republic of Germany; *Honduras.*

Food and Agricultural Organization of the United Nations (FAO) Via delle Terme di Caracalla, 00100 Rome, Italy (Telephone Number in U.S. (202) 653-2400); *Production Yearbook, The State of Food and Agriculture,* and *Trade Yearbook.*

G.K. Hall and Company, 70 Lincoln Street, Boston, Massachusetts 02111 (617) 423-3990; *The World in Figures.*

Gale Research Incorporated, 835 Penobscot Building, Detroit, Michigan 48226 (800) 877-4253; *International Historical Statistics The Americas and Australasia.*

Inter-American Development Bank, 1300 New York Avenue, NW, Washington, D.C. 20577 (202) 623-1753; *Economic and Social Progress in Latin America.*

Statistical Office of the United Nations, Publishing Service, New York, New York 10017 (800) 253-9646; *Statistical Yearbook,* and *Statistical Yearbook for Latin America and the Caribbean.*

U.C.L.A. Latin American Center Publications, University of California, Los Angeles, California 90024 (310) 825-6634; *Statistical Abstract of Latin America.*

The World Bank, 1818 H Street, NW, Washington, D.C. 20433 (202) 477-1234; *World Tables.*

HONDURAS - AIRLINE SERVICE

The Economist Intelligence Unit, 111 West 57th Street, New York, New York 10019 (800) 938-4685; *The New Latin America Market Atlas.*

Facts on File, 460 Park Avenue South, New York, New York 10016 (800) 443-8323; *The New Book of World Rankings.*

G.K. Hall and Company, 70 Lincoln Street, Boston, Massachusetts 02111 (617) 423-3990; *The World in Figures.*

International Civil Aviation Organization, 1000 Sherbrooke Street West, Suite 400, Montreal, Quebec, Canada H3A 2R2 (514) 285-8219; *Civil Aviation Statistics of the World.*

Statistical Office of the United Nations, Publishing Service, New York, New York 10017 (800) 253-9646; *Statistical Yearbook.*

Times Books, 201 East 50th Street, New York, New York 10022 (212) 751-2600; *The Economist Book of Vital World Statistics.*

HONDURAS - ALUMINUM PRODUCTION AND CONSUMPTION - See HONDURAS - MINING AND MINERAL PRODUCTS

HONDURAS - ANIMAL HEALTH

Food and Agricultural Organization of the United Nations (FAO), Via delle Terme di Caracalla, 00100 Rome, Italy (Telephone Number in U.S. (202) 653-2400); *Animal Health Yearbook.*

HONDURAS - ANTIMONY ORE PRODUCTION AND CONSUMPTION - See HONDURAS - MINING AND MINERAL PRODUCTS

HONDURAS - AREA AND DENSITY OF POPULATION

Euromonitor Publications Limited, 87-88 Turnmill Street, London EC1M 5QU, England; *International Marketing Data and Statistics.*

Facts on File, 460 Park Avenue South, New York, New York 10016 (800) 443-8323; *The New Book of World Rankings.*

Federal Statistical Office, Gustav - Stresesmann - Ring 11, D-6200 Wiesbaden, Federal Republic of Germany; *Honduras.*

Food and Agricultural Organization of the United Nations (FAO) Via delle Terme di Caracalla, 00100 Rome, Italy (Telephone Number in U.S. (202) 653-2400); *The State of Food and Agriculture.*

G.K. Hall and Company, 70 Lincoln Street, Boston, Massachusetts 02111 (617) 423-3990; *The World in Figures.*

Inter-American Development Bank, 1300 New York Avenue, NW, Washington, D.C. 20577 (202) 623-1753; *Economic and Social Progress in Latin America.*

Statistical Office of the United Nations, Publishing Service, New York, New York 10017 (800) 253-9646; *Statistical Yearbook.*

Times Books, 201 East 50th Street, New York, New York 10022 (212) 751-2600; *The Economist Book of Vital World Statistics.*

United Nations Educational, Scientific and Cultural Organization (UNESCO), 7 Place de Fontenoy, F-75700 Paris, France (Telephone Number in U.S. (212) 963-5981); *Statistical Yearbook.*

HONDURAS - ARMS EXPORTS AND IMPORTS

U.S. Arms Control and Disarmament Agency, 320 Twenty-first Street, Northwest, Washington, D.C. 20451 (202) 647-8677; *World Military Expenditures and Arms Transfers.*

HONDURAS - BALANCE OF PAYMENTS

The Economist Intelligence Unit, 111 West 57th Street, New York, New York 10019 (800) 938-4685; *The New Latin America Market Atlas*, and *The World Market Atlas*.

Federal Statistical Office, Gustav - Stresesmann - Ring 11, D-6200 Wiesbaden, Federal Republic of Germany; *Honduras*.

G.K. Hall and Company, 70 Lincoln Street, Boston, Massachusetts 02111 (617) 423-3990; *The World in Figures*.

Inter-American Development Bank, 1300 New York Avenue, NW, Washington, D.C. 20577 (202) 623-1753; *Economic and Social Progress in Latin America*.

International Monetary Fund, 700 Nineteenth Street, NW, Washington, D.C. 20431 (202) 623-7000; *Balance of Payments Yearbook*, and *International Financial Statistics*.

Organization of American States (OAS), General Secretariat, Washington, D.C 20006 (202) 458-3533; *Statistical Bulletin of the OAS*.

Statistical Office of the United Nations, Publishing Service, New York, New York 10017 (800) 253-9646; *Economic Survey of Latin America and the Caribbean and the Caribbean*, and *Statistical Yearbook for Latin American and the Caribbean*.

Times Books, 201 East 50th Street, New York, New York 10022 (212) 751-2600; *The Economist Book of Vital World Statistics*.

U.C.L.A. Latin American Center Publications, University of California, Los Angeles, California 90024 (310) 825-6634; *Statistical Abstract of Latin America*.

The World Bank, 1818 H Street, NW, Washington, D.C. 20433 (202) 477-1234; *World Tables*.

HONDURAS - BANANA EXPORTS - See HONDURAS - CROPS

HONDURAS - BANKING

Facts on File, 460 Park Avenue South, New York, New York 10016 (800) 443-8323; *The New Book of World Rankings*.

G.K. Hall and Company, 70 Lincoln Street, Boston, Massachusetts 02111 (617) 423-3990; *The World in Figures*.

Inter-American Development Bank, 1300 New York Avenue, NW, Washington, D.C. 20577 (202) 623-1753; *Economic and Social Progress in Latin America*.

International Monetary Fund, 700 Nineteenth Street, NW, Washington, D.C. 20431 (202) 623-7000; *International Financial Statistics*.

Statistical Office of the United Nations, Publishing Service, New York, New York 10017 (800) 253-9646; *Statistical Yearbook*.

HONDURAS - BARLEY PRODUCTION - See HONDURAS - CROPS

HONDURAS - BEEF EXPORTS

International Monetary Fund, 700 Nineteenth Street, NW, Washington, D.C. 20431 (202) 623-7000; *International Financial Statistics*.

HONDURAS - BEER PRODUCTION

Facts on File, 460 Park Avenue South, New York, New York 10016 (800) 443-8323; *The New Book of World Rankings*.

Statistical Office of the United Nations, Publishing Service, New York, New York 10017 (800) 253-9646; *Statistical Yearbook*.

HONDURAS - BIRTH RATES

Facts on File, 460 Park Avenue South, New York, New York 10016 (800) 443-8323; *The New Book of World Rankings*.

Statistical Office of the United Nations, Publishing Service, New York, New York 10017 (800) 253-9646; *Demographic Yearbook*, *Statistical Yearbook*, and *Statistical Yearbook for Latin American and the Caribbean*.

Times Books, 201 East 50th Street, New York, New York 10022 (212) 751-2600; *The Economist Book of Vital World Statistics*.

The World Bank, 1818 H Street, NW, Washington, D.C. 20433 (202) 477-1234; *World Tables*.

World Health Organization, Office of Publications, Avenue Appia, CH-1211 Geneva 27, Switzerland (Telephone Number in U.S. (518) 436-9686); *World Health Statistics Annual*.

HONDURAS - BONDS

G.K. Hall and Company, 70 Lincoln Street, Boston, Massachusetts 02111 (617) 423-3990; *The World in Figures*.

Inter-American Development Bank, 1300 New York Avenue, NW, Washington, D.C. 20577 (202) 623-1753; *Economic and Social Progress in Latin America*.

International Monetary Fund, 700 Nineteenth Street, NW, Washington, D.C. 20431 (202) 623-7000; *Government Finance Statistics Yearbook*.

HONDURAS - BOOK PRODUCTION

G.K. Hall and Company, 70 Lincoln Street, Boston, Massachusetts 02111 (617) 423-3990; *The World in Figures*.

HONDURAS - BROADCASTING

Billboard Limited, Post Office Box 9027, 1006 AA Amsterdam, The Netherlands (Telephone Number in U.S. (212) 764-7300); *World Radio TV Handbook*.

Facts on File, 460 Park Avenue South, New York, New York 10016 (800) 443-8323; *The New Book of World Rankings*.

G.K. Hall and Company, 70 Lincoln Street, Boston, Massachusetts 02111 (617) 423-3990; *The World in Figures*.

Times Books, 201 East 50th Street, New York, New York 10022 (212) 751-2600; *The Economist Book of Vital World Statistics*.

HONDURAS - BUILDING CONSTRUCTION - See HONDURAS - CONSTRUCTION INDUSTRY

HONDURAS - BUSINESS

G.K. Hall and Company, 70 Lincoln Street, Boston, Massachusetts 02111 (617) 423-3990; *The World in Figures*.

Inter-American Development Bank, 1300 New York Avenue, NW, Washington, D.C. 20577 (202) 623-1753; *Economic and Social Progress in Latin America.*

HONDURAS - BUSINESS AND PROFESSIONAL LICENSES

International Monetary Fund, 700 Nineteenth Street, NW, Washington, D.C. 20431 (202) 623-7000; *Government Finance Statistics Yearbook.*

HONDURAS - BUTTER PRODUCTION - See HONDURAS - DAIRY PRODUCTS

HONDURAS - CABBAGE PRODUCTION - See HONDURAS - CROPS

HONDURAS - CALORIE SUPPLY

Food and Agricultural Organization of the United Nations (FAO) Via delle Terme di Caracalla, 00100 Rome, Italy (Telephone Number in U.S. (202) 653-2400); *The State of Food and Agriculture.*

Statistical Office of the United Nations, Publishing Service, New York, New York 10017 (800) 253-9646; *Statistical Yearbook for Latin American and the Caribbean.*

HONDURAS - CAPITAL INVESTMENT

Inter-American Development Bank, 1300 New York Avenue, NW, Washington, D.C. 20577 (202) 623-1753; *Economic and Social Progress in Latin America.*

HONDURAS - CAPITAL REVENUE

Inter-American Development Bank, 1300 New York Avenue, NW, Washington, D.C. 20577 (202) 623-1753; *Economic and Social Progress in Latin America.*

International Monetary Fund, 700 Nineteenth Street, NW, Washington, D.C. 20431 (202) 623-7000; *Government Finance Statistics Yearbook.*

HONDURAS - CATTLE - See HONDURAS - LIVESTOCK AND POULTRY

HONDURAS - CEMENT PRODUCTION - See HONDURAS - MINING AND MINERAL PRODUCTS

HONDURAS - CHEESE PRODUCTION - See HONDURAS - DAIRY PRODUCTS

HONDURAS - CHEMICAL (ORGANIC) PRODUCTION - See HONDURAS - MINING AND MINERAL PRODUCTS

HONDURAS - CHICKENS - See HONDURAS - LIVESTOCK AND POULTRY

HONDURAS - CIGARETTE PRODUCTION - See HONDURAS - TOBACCO PRODUCTION

HONDURAS - CLASS STRUCTURE

G.K. Hall and Company, 70 Lincoln Street, Boston, Massachusetts 02111 (617) 423-3990; *The World in Figures.*

HONDURAS - CLIMATE

Facts on File, 460 Park Avenue South, New York, New York 10016 (800) 443-8323; *The New Book of World Rankings.*

G.K. Hall and Company, 70 Lincoln Street, Boston, Massachusetts 02111 (617) 423-3990; *The World in Figures.*

HONDURAS - COAL PRODUCTION - See HONDURAS - MINING AND MINERAL PRODUCTS

HONDURAS - COCOA PRODUCTION - See HONDURAS - CROPS

HONDURAS - COFFEE - See HONDURAS - CROPS

HONDURAS - COMMUNICATIONS

Federal Statistical Office, Gustav - Stresesmann - Ring 11, D-6200 Wiesbaden, Federal Republic of Germany; *Honduras.*

G.K. Hall and Company, 70 Lincoln Street, Boston, Massachusetts 02111 (617) 423-3990; *The World in Figures.*

Inter-American Development Bank, 1300 New York Avenue, NW, Washington, D.C. 20577 (202) 623-1753; *Economic and Social Progress in Latin America.*

U.C.L.A. Latin American Center Publications, University of California, Los Angeles, California 90024 (310) 825-6634; *Statistical Abstract of Latin America.*

HONDURAS - CONSTRUCTION INDUSTRY

The Economist Intelligence Unit, 111 West 57th Street, New York, New York 10019 (800) 938-4685; *The New Latin America Market Atlas.*

Facts on File, 460 Park Avenue South, New York, New York 10016 (800) 443-8323; *The New Book of World Rankings.*

Inter-American Development Bank, 1300 New York Avenue, NW, Washington, D.C. 20577 (202) 623-1753; *Economic and Social Progress in Latin America.*

Statistical Office of the United Nations, Publishing Service, New York, New York 10017 (800) 253-9646; *Construction Statistics Yearbook,* and *Statistical Yearbook.*

U.C.L.A. Latin American Center Publications, University of California, Los Angeles, California 90024 (310) 825-6634; *Statistical Abstract of Latin America.*

HONDURAS - CONSUMER PRICE INDEX

Federal Statistical Office, Gustav - Stresesmann - Ring 11, D-6200 Wiesbaden, Federal Republic of Germany; *Honduras.*

G.K. Hall and Company, 70 Lincoln Street, Boston, Massachusetts 02111 (617) 423-3990; *The World in Figures.*

Statistical Office of the United Nations, Publishing Service, New York, New York 10017 (800) 253-9646; *Statistical Yearbook.*

HONDURAS - CONSUMER PRICES

The Economist Intelligence Unit, 111 West 57th Street, New York, New York 10019 (800) 938-4685; *The New Latin America Market Atlas.*

Federal Statistical Office, Gustav - Stresesmann - Ring 11, D-6200 Wiesbaden, Federal Republic of Germany; *Honduras.*

International Labour Office, I.L.O. Publications, CH-1211, Geneva 22, Switzerland; *Yearbook of Labour Statistics.*

International Monetary Fund, 700 Nineteenth Street, NW, Washington, D.C. 20431 (202) 623-7000; *International Financial Statistics.*

Organization of American States (OAS), General Secretariat, Washington, D.C 20006 (202) 458-3533; *Statistical Bulletin of the OAS.*

Times Books, 201 East 50th Street, New York, New York 10022 (212) 751-2600; *The Economist Book of Vital World Statistics.*

U.C.L.A. Latin American Center Publications, University of California, Los Angeles, California 90024 (310) 825-6634; *Statistical Abstract of Latin America.*

HONDURAS - CONSUMPTION

The Economist Intelligence Unit, 111 West 57th Street, New York, New York 10019 (800) 938-4685; *The New Latin America Market Atlas.*

G.K. Hall and Company, 70 Lincoln Street, Boston, Massachusetts 02111 (617) 423-3990; *The World in Figures.*

Inter-American Development Bank, 1300 New York Avenue, NW, Washington, D.C. 20577 (202) 623-1753; *Economic and Social Progress in Latin America.*

Statistical Office of the United Nations, Publishing Service, New York, New York 10017 (800) 253-9646; *Statistical Yearbook for Latin American and the Caribbean.*

HONDURAS - COPPER PRODUCTION - See HONDURAS - MINING AND MINERAL PRODUCTS

HONDURAS - COOPERATIVES

U.C.L.A. Latin American Center Publications, University of California, Los Angeles, California 90024 (310) 825-6634; *Statistical Abstract of Latin America.*

HONDURAS - CORN PRODUCTION - See HONDURAS - CROPS

HONDURAS - CORPORATE INCOME TAXES - See HONDURAS - TAXATION

HONDURAS - CORPORATE TAXES - See HONDURAS - TAXATIOn

HONDURAS - COTTON PRODUCTION - See HONDURAS - CROPS

HONDURAS - CROPS

The Economist Intelligence Unit, 111 West 57th Street, New York, New York 10019 (800) 938-4685; *The New Latin America Market Atlas.*

Facts on File, 460 Park Avenue South, New York, New York 10016 (800) 443-8323; *The New Book of World Rankings.*

Food and Agricultural Organization of the United Nations (FAO), Via delle Terme di Caracalla, 00100 Rome, Italy (Telephone Number in U.S. (202) 653-2400); *Production Yearbook* and *The State of Food and Agriculture.*

G.K. Hall and Company, 70 Lincoln Street, Boston, Massachusetts 02111 (617) 423-3990; *The World in Figures.*

International Monetary Fund, 700 Nineteenth Street, NW, Washington, D.C. 20431 (202) 623-7000; *International Financial Statistics.*

Organization of American States (OAS), General Secretariat, Washington, D.C 20006 (202) 458-3533; *Statistical Bulletin of the OAS.*

Statistical Office of the United Nations, Publishing Service, New York, New York 10017 (800) 253-9646; *Statistical Yearbook.*

HONDURAS - CUSTOMS DUTIES

G.K. Hall and Company, 70 Lincoln Street, Boston, Massachusetts 02111 (617) 423-3990; *The World in Figures.*

Inter-American Development Bank, 1300 New York Avenue, NW, Washington, D.C. 20577 (202) 623-1753; *Economic and Social Progress in Latin America.*

International Monetary Fund, 700 Nineteenth Street, NW, Washington, D.C. 20431 (202) 623-7000; *Government Finance Statistics Yearbook.*

HONDURAS - DAIRY PRODUCTS

Facts on File, 460 Park Avenue South, New York, New York 10016 (800) 443-8323; *The New Book of World Rankings.*

Food and Agricultural Organization of the United Nations (FAO), Via delle Terme di Caracalla, 00100 Rome, Italy (Telephone Number in U.S. (202) 653-2400); *Production Yearbook* and *The State of Food and Agriculture.*

Statistical Office of the United Nations, Publishing Service, New York, New York 10017 (800) 253-9646; *Statistical Yearbook.*

HONDURAS - DEATH RATES

G.K. Hall and Company, 70 Lincoln Street, Boston, Massachusetts 02111 (617) 423-3990; *The World in Figures.*

Statistical Office of the United Nations, Publishing Service, New York, New York 10017 (800) 253-9646; *Statistical Yearbook,* and *Statistical Yearbook for Latin American and the Caribbean.*

Times Books, 201 East 50th Street, New York, New York 10022 (212) 751-2600; *The Economist Book of Vital World Statistics.*

World Health Organization, Office of Publications, Avenue Appia, CH-1211 Geneva 27, Switzerland (Telephone Number in U.S. (518) 436-9686); *World Health Statistics Annual.*

HONDURAS - DEBT

The Economist Intelligence Unit, 111 West 57th Street, New York, New York 10019 (800) 938-4685; *The New Latin America Market Atlas.*

HONDURAS - DEFENSE EXPENDITURES

The Economist Intelligence Unit, 111 West 57th Street, New York, New York 10019 (800) 938-4685; *The New Latin America Market Atlas.*

G.K. Hall and Company, 70 Lincoln Street, Boston, Massachusetts 02111 (617) 423-3990; *The World in Figures.*

International Monetary Fund, 700 Nineteenth Street, NW, Washington, D.C. 20431 (202) 623-7000; *Government Finance Statistics Yearbook.*

U.S. Arms Control and Disarmament Agency, 320 Twenty-first Street, Northwest, Washington, D.C. 20451 (202) 647-8677; *World Military Expenditures and Arms Transfers.*

HONDURAS - DEMOGRAPHY

The Economist Intelligence Unit, 111 West 57th Street, New York, New York 10019 (800) 938-4685; *The World Market Atlas.*

Facts on File, 460 Park Avenue South, New York, New York 10016 (800) 443-8323; *The New Book of World Rankings.*

Federal Statistical Office, Gustav - Stresesmann - Ring 11, D-6200 Wiesbaden, Federal Republic of Germany; *Honduras.*

G.K. Hall and Company, 70 Lincoln Street, Boston, Massachusetts 02111 (617) 423-3990; *The World in Figures.*

HONDURAS - DEVELOPMENT ASSISTANCE

G.K. Hall and Company, 70 Lincoln Street, Boston, Massachusetts 02111 (617) 423-3990; *The World in Figures.*

Inter-American Development Bank, 1300 New York Avenue, NW, Washington, D.C. 20577 (202) 623-1753; *Economic and Social Progress in Latin America.*

Statistical Office of the United Nations, Publishing Service, New York, New York 10017 (800) 253-9646; *Statistical Yearbook.*

HONDURAS - DIAMOND PRODUCTION - See HONDURAS - MINING AND MINERAL PRODUCTS

HONDURAS - DISCOUNT RATES

Inter-American Development Bank, 1300 New York Avenue, NW, Washington, D.C. 20577 (202) 623-1753; *Economic and Social Progress in Latin America.*

Statistical Office of the United Nations, Publishing Service, New York, New York 10017 (800) 253-9646; *Statistical Yearbook.*

HONDURAS - DISEASES

G.K. Hall and Company, 70 Lincoln Street, Boston, Massachusetts 02111 (617) 423-3990; *The World in Figures.*

World Health Organization, Office of Publications, Avenue Appia, CH-1211 Geneva 27, Switzerland (Telephone Number in U.S. (518) 436-9686); *World Health Statistics Annual.*

HONDURAS - DIVORCE RATES

Facts on File, 460 Park Avenue South, New York, New York 10016 (800) 443-8323; *The New Book of World Rankings.*

Statistical Office of the United Nations, Publishing Service, New York, New York 10017 (800) 253-9646; *Demographic Yearbook,* and *Statistical Yearbook.*

HONDURAS - DOMESTIC PRODUCT

G.K. Hall and Company, 70 Lincoln Street, Boston, Massachusetts 02111 (617) 423-3990; *The World in Figures.*

HONDURAS - ECONOMY

Euromonitor Publications Limited, 87-88 Turnmill Street, London EC1M 5QU, England; *International Marketing Data and Statistics.*

Facts on File, 460 Park Avenue South, New York, New York 10016 (800) 443-8323; *The New Book of World Rankings.*

Federal Statistical Office, Gustav - Stresesmann - Ring 11, D-6200 Wiesbaden, Federal Republic of Germany; *Honduras.*

G.K. Hall and Company, 70 Lincoln Street, Boston, Massachusetts 02111 (617) 423-3990; *The World in Figures.*

Inter-American Development Bank, 1300 New York Avenue, NW, Washington, D.C. 20577 (202) 623-1753; *Economic and Social Progress in Latin America.*

Organization of American States (OAS), General Secretariat, Washington, D.C 20006 (202) 458-3533; *Statistical Bulletin of the OAS.*

Statistical Office of the United Nations, Publishing Service, New York, New York 10017 (800) 253-9646; *Economic Survey of Latin America and the Caribbean.*

U.C.L.A. Latin American Center Publications, University of California, Los Angeles, California 90024 (310) 825-6634; *Statistical Abstract of Latin America.*

HONDURAS - EDUCATION

The Economist Intelligence Unit, 111 West 57th Street, New York, New York 10019 (800) 938-4685; *The New Latin America Market Atlas,* and *The World Market Atlas.*

Facts on File, 460 Park Avenue South, New York, New York 10016 (800) 443-8323; *The New Book of World Rankings.*

Federal Statistical Office, Gustav - Stresesmann - Ring 11, D-6200 Wiesbaden, Federal Republic of Germany; *Honduras.*

Gale Research Incorporated, 835 Penobscot Building, Detroit, Michigan 48226 (800) 877-4253; *International Historical Statistics The Americas and Australasia.*

G.K. Hall and Company, 70 Lincoln Street, Boston, Massachusetts 02111 (617) 423-3990; *The World in Figures.*

International Monetary Fund, 700 Nineteenth Street, NW, Washington, D.C. 20431 (202) 623-7000; *Government Finance Statistics Yearbook.*

Statistical Office of the United Nations, Publishing Service, New York, New York 10017 (800) 253-9646; *Statistical Yearbook for Latin American and the Caribbean.*

Times Books, 201 East 50th Street, New York, New York 10022 (212) 751-2600; *The Economist Book of Vital World Statistics.*

U.C.L.A. Latin American Center Publications, University of California, Los Angeles, California 90024 (310) 825-6634; *Statistical Abstract of Latin America.*

United Nations Educational, Scientific and Cultural Organization (UNESCO), 7 Place de Fontenoy, F-75700 Paris, France (Telephone Number in U.S. (212) 963-5981); *Statistical Yearbook.*

The World Bank, 1818 H Street, NW, Washington, D.C. 20433 (202) 477-1234; *World Tables.*

HONDURAS - EGG PRODUCTION - See HONDURAS - DAIRY PRODUCTS

HONDURAS - ELECTRICITY

The Economist Intelligence Unit, 111 West 57th Street, New York, New York 10019 (800) 938-4685; *The New Latin America Market Atlas*.

Facts on File, 460 Park Avenue South, New York, New York 10016 (800) 443-8323; *The New Book of World Rankings*.

Inter-American Development Bank, 1300 New York Avenue, NW, Washington, D.C. 20577 (202) 623-1753; *Economic and Social Progress in Latin America*.

Organization of American States (OAS), General Secretariat, Washington, D.C 20006 (202) 458-3533; *Statistical Bulletin of the OAS*.

Statistical Office of the United Nations, Publishing Service, New York, New York 10017 (800) 253-9646; *Statistical Yearbook*.

HONDURAS - EMPLOYMENT

Euromonitor Publications Limited, 87-88 Turnmill Street, London EC1M 5QU, England; *International Marketing Data and Statistics*.

Facts on File, 460 Park Avenue South, New York, New York 10016 (800) 443-8323; *The New Book of World Rankings*.

Federal Statistical Office, Gustav - Stresesmann - Ring 11, D-6200 Wiesbaden, Federal Republic of Germany; *Honduras*.

International Labour Office, I.L.O. Publications, CH-1211, Geneva 22, Switzerland; *Yearbook of Labour Statistics*.

Statistical Office of the United Nations, Publishing Service, New York, New York 10017 (800) 253-9646; *Statistical Yearbook*, and *Statistical Yearbook for Latin American and the Caribbean*.

U.C.L.A. Latin American Center Publications, University of California, Los Angeles, California 90024 (310) 825-6634; *Statistical Abstract of Latin America*.

HONDURAS - ENERGY

The Economist Intelligence Unit, 111 West 57th Street, New York, New York 10019 (800) 938-4685; *The New Latin America Market Atlas*.

Facts on File, 460 Park Avenue South, New York, New York 10016 (800) 443-8323; *The New Book of World Rankings*.

Food and Agricultural Organization of the United Nations (FAO) Via delle Terme di Caracalla, 00100 Rome, Italy (Telephone Number in U.S. (202) 653-2400); *The State of Food and Agriculture*.

G.K. Hall and Company, 70 Lincoln Street, Boston, Massachusetts 02111 (617) 423-3990; *The World in Figures*.

Statistical Office of the United Nations, Publishing Service, New York, New York 10017 (800) 253-9646; *Energy Statistics Yearbook*, *Statistical Yearbook*, and *Statistical Yearbook for Latin American and the Caribbean*.

Times Books, 201 East 50th Street, New York, New York 10022 (212) 751-2600; *The Economist Book of Vital World Statistics*.

U.C.L.A. Latin American Center Publications, University of California, Los Angeles, California 90024 (310) 825-6634; *Statistical Abstract of Latin America*.

HONDURAS - EXCHANGE RATE

Euromonitor Publications Limited, 87-88 Turnmill Street, London EC1M 5QU, England; *International Marketing Data and Statistics*.

Inter-American Development Bank, 1300 New York Avenue, NW, Washington, D.C. 20577 (202) 623-1753; *Economic and Social Progress in Latin America*.

International Civil Aviation Organization, 1000 Sherbrooke Street West, Suite 400, Montreal, Quebec, Canada H3A 2R2 (514) 285-8219; *Civil Aviation Statistics of the World*.

International Monetary Fund, 700 Nineteenth Street, NW, Washington, D.C. 20431 (202) 623-7000; *International Financial Statistics*.

Organization of American States (OAS), General Secretariat, Washington, D.C 20006 (202) 458-3533; *Statistical Bulletin of the OAS*.

Statistical Office of the United Nations, Publishing Service, New York, New York 10017 (800) 253-9646; *Statistical Yearbook*.

U.C.L.A. Latin American Center Publications, University of California, Los Angeles, California 90024 (310) 825-6634; *Statistical Abstract of Latin America*.

HONDURAS - EXCISE TAXES - See HONDURAS - TAXATION

HONDURAS - EXPORTS

The Economist Intelligence Unit, 111 West 57th Street, New York, New York 10019 (800) 938-4685; *The New Latin America Market Atlas*, and *The World Market Atlas*.

Euromonitor Publications Limited, 87-88 Turnmill Street, London EC1M 5QU, England; *International Marketing Data and Statistics*.

Food and Agricultural Organization of the United Nations (FAO) Via delle Terme di Caracalla, 00100 Rome, Italy (Telephone Number in U.S. (202) 653-2400); *The State of Food and Agriculture*.

G.K. Hall and Company, 70 Lincoln Street, Boston, Massachusetts 02111 (617) 423-3990; *The World in Figures*.

Inter-American Development Bank, 1300 New York Avenue, NW, Washington, D.C. 20577 (202) 623-1753; *Economic and Social Progress in Latin America*.

International Monetary Fund, 700 Nineteenth Street, NW, Washington, D.C. 20431 (202) 623-7000; *Direction of Trade Statistics*, *Government Finance Statistics Yearbook*, and *International Financial Statistics*.

Organization of American States (OAS), General Secretariat, Washington, D.C 20006 (202) 458-3533; *Statistical Bulletin of the OAS*.

Statistical Office of the United Nations, Publishing Service, New York, New York 10017 (800) 253-9646; *Statistical Yearbook for Latin American and the Caribbean*.

Times Books, 201 East 50th Street, New York, New York 10022 (212) 751-2600; *The Economist Book of Vital World Statistics*.

The World Bank, 1818 H Street, NW, Washington, D.C. 20433 (202) 477-1234; *World Tables*.

HONDURAS - EXTERNAL FINANCING

Inter-American Development Bank, 1300 New York Avenue, NW, Washington, D.C. 20577 (202) 623-1753; *Economic and Social Progress in Latin America.*

Statistical Office of the United Nations, Publishing Service, New York, New York 10017 (800) 253-9646; *Statistical Yearbook for Latin American and the Caribbean.*

HONDURAS - EXTERNAL INDEBTEDNESS

Inter-American Development Bank, 1300 New York Avenue, NW, Washington, D.C. 20577 (202) 623-1753; *Economic and Social Progress in Latin America.*

Statistical Office of the United Nations, Publishing Service, New York, New York 10017 (800) 253-9646; *Statistical Yearbook for Latin American and the Caribbean.*

The World Bank, 1818 H Street, NW, Washington, D.C. 20433 (202) 477-1234; *World Tables.*

HONDURAS - EXTERNAL TRADE

Food and Agricultural Organization of the United Nations (FAO) Via delle Terme di Caracalla, 00100 Rome, Italy (Telephone Number in U.S. (202) 653-2400); *The State of Food and Agriculture,* and *Trade Yearbook.*

Gale Research Incorporated, 835 Penobscot Building, Detroit, Michigan 48226 (800) 877-4253; *International Historical Statistics The Americas and Australasia.*

G.K. Hall and Company, 70 Lincoln Street, Boston, Massachusetts 02111 (617) 423-3990; *The World in Figures.*

Inter-American Development Bank, 1300 New York Avenue, NW, Washington, D.C. 20577 (202) 623-1753; *Economic and Social Progress in Latin America.*

Statistical Office of the United Nations, Publishing Service, New York, New York 10017 (800) 253-9646; *Statistical Yearbook,* and *Statistical Yearbook for Latin American and the Caribbean.*

HONDURAS - FABRIC PRODUCTION - See HONDURAS - TEXTILE INDUSTRY

HONDURAS - FAMILY PLANNING

U.C.L.A. Latin American Center Publications, University of California, Los Angeles, California 90024 (310) 825-6634; *Statistical Abstract of Latin America.*

HONDURAS - FARM CROPS - See HONDURAS - CROPS

HONDURAS - FEMALE WORKING POPULATION - See HONDURAS - EMPLOYMENT

HONDURAS - FERTILITY RATES

Facts on File, 460 Park Avenue South, New York, New York 10016 (800) 443-8323; *The New Book of World Rankings.*

Times Books, 201 East 50th Street, New York, New York 10022 (212) 751-2600; *The Economist Book of Vital World Statistics.*

The World Bank, 1818 H Street, NW, Washington, D.C. 20433 (202) 477-1234; *World Tables.*

HONDURAS - FERTILIZER

The Economist Intelligence Unit, 111 West 57th Street, New York, New York 10019 (800) 938-4685; *The New Latin America Market Atlas.*

Food and Agricultural Organization of the United Nations (FAO) Via delle Terme di Caracalla, 00100 Rome, Italy (Telephone Number in U.S. (202) 653-2400); *The State of Food and Agriculture.*

Statistical Office of the United Nations, Publishing Service, New York, New York 10017 (800) 253-9646; *Statistical Yearbook.*

HONDURAS - FETAL MORTALITY

Statistical Office of the United Nations, Publishing Service, New York, New York 10017 (800) 253-9646; *Demographic Yearbook.*

World Health Organization, Office of Publications, Avenue Appia, CH-1211 Geneva 27, Switzerland (Telephone Number in U.S. (518) 436-9686); *World Health Statistics Annual.*

HONDURAS - FINANCE

Facts on File, 460 Park Avenue South, New York, New York 10016 (800) 443-8323; *The New Book of World Rankings.*

Federal Statistical Office, Gustav - Stresesmann - Ring 11, D-6200 Wiesbaden, Federal Republic of Germany; *Honduras.*

Gale Research Incorporated, 835 Penobscot Building, Detroit, Michigan 48226 (800) 877-4253; *International Historical Statistics The Americas and Australasia.*

G.K. Hall and Company, 70 Lincoln Street, Boston, Massachusetts 02111 (617) 423-3990; *The World in Figures.*

Inter-American Development Bank, 1300 New York Avenue, NW, Washington, D.C. 20577 (202) 623-1753; *Economic and Social Progress in Latin America.*

International Monetary Fund, 700 Nineteenth Street, NW, Washington, D.C. 20431 (202) 623-7000; *Government Finance Statistics Yearbook.*

Organization of American States (OAS), General Secretariat, Washington, D.C 20006 (202) 458-3533; *Statistical Bulletin of the OAS.*

U.C.L.A. Latin American Center Publications, University of California, Los Angeles, California 90024 (310) 825-6634; *Statistical Abstract of Latin America.*

HONDURAS - FISHERIES

Facts on File, 460 Park Avenue South, New York, New York 10016 (800) 443-8323; *The New Book of World Rankings.*

Federal Statistical Office, Gustav - Stresesmann - Ring 11, D-6200 Wiesbaden, Federal Republic of Germany; *Honduras.*

Food and Agricultural Organization of the United Nations (FAO) Via delle Terme di Caracalla, 00100 Rome, Italy (Telephone Number in U.S. (202) 653-2400); *The State of Food and Agriculture,* and *Yearbook of Fishery Statistics.*

Inter-American Development Bank, 1300 New York Avenue, NW, Washington, D.C. 20577 (202) 623-1753; *Economic and Social Progress in Latin America.*

Statistical Office of the United Nations, Publishing Service, New York, New York 10017 (800) 253-9646; *Statistical Yearbook.*

Inter-American Development Bank, 1300 New York Avenue, NW, Washington, D.C. 20577 (202) 623-1753; *Economic and Social Progress in Latin America.*

U.C.L.A. Latin American Center Publications, University of California, Los Angeles, California 90024 (310) 825-6634; *Statistical Abstract of Latin America.*

HONDURAS - FLOUR PRODUCTION

Statistical Office of the United Nations, Publishing Service, New York, New York 10017 (800) 253-9646; *Statistical Yearbook.*

HONDURAS - FOOD

Food and Agricultural Organization of the United Nations (FAO), Via delle Terme di Caracalla, 00100 Rome, Italy (Telephone Number in U.S. (202) 653-2400); *Production Yearbook,* and *The State of Food and Agriculture.*

G.K. Hall and Company, 70 Lincoln Street, Boston, Massachusetts 02111 (617) 423-3990; *The World in Figures.*

HONDURAS - FOREIGN AID

G.K. Hall and Company, 70 Lincoln Street, Boston, Massachusetts 02111 (617) 423-3990; *The World in Figures.*

Inter-American Development Bank, 1300 New York Avenue, NW, Washington, D.C. 20577 (202) 623-1753; *Economic and Social Progress in Latin America.*

HONDURAS - FOREIGN DEBT

The Economist Intelligence Unit, 111 West 57th Street, New York, New York 10019 (800) 938-4685; *The New Latin America Market Atlas.*

Inter-American Development Bank, 1300 New York Avenue, NW, Washington, D.C. 20577 (202) 623-1753; *Economic and Social Progress in Latin America.*

HONDURAS - FOREIGN INDEBTEDNESS

Inter-American Development Bank, 1300 New York Avenue, NW, Washington, D.C. 20577 (202) 623-1753; *Economic and Social Progress in Latin America.*

Statistical Office of the United Nations, Publishing Service, New York, New York 10017 (800) 253-9646; *Economic Survey of Latin America and the Caribbean.*

HONDURAS - FOREIGN INVESTMENT

The Economist Intelligence Unit, 111 West 57th Street, New York, New York 10019 (800) 938-4685; *The New Latin America Market Atlas.*

HONDURAS - FOREIGN TRADE

The Economist Intelligence Unit, 111 West 57th Street, New York, New York 10019 (800) 938-4685; *The New Latin America Market Atlas.*

Euromonitor Publications Limited, 87-88 Turnmill Street, London EC1M 5QU, England; *International Marketing Data and Statistics.*

Facts on File, 460 Park Avenue South, New York, New York 10016 (800) 443-8323; *The New Book of World Rankings.*

Federal Statistical Office, Gustav - Stresesmann - Ring 11, D-6200 Wiesbaden, Federal Republic of Germany; *Honduras.*

Food and Agricultural Organization of the United Nations (FAO) Via delle Terme di Caracalla, 00100 Rome, Italy (Telephone Number in U.S. (202) 653-2400); *The State of Food and Agriculture.*

G.K. Hall and Company, 70 Lincoln Street, Boston, Massachusetts 02111 (617) 423-3990; *The World in Figures.*

Inter-American Development Bank, 1300 New York Avenue, NW, Washington, D.C. 20577 (202) 623-1753; *Economic and Social Progress in Latin America.*

International Monetary Fund, 700 Nineteenth Street, NW, Washington, D.C. 20431 (202) 623-7000; *International Financial Statistics.*

Statistical Office of the United Nations, Publishing Service, New York, New York 10017 (800) 253-9646; *International Trade Statistics Yearbook,* and *Statistical Yearbook.*

U.C.L.A. Latin American Center Publications, University of California, Los Angeles, California 90024 (310) 825-6634; *Statistical Abstract of Latin America.*

The World Bank, 1818 H Street, NW, Washington, D.C. 20433 (202) 477-1234; *World Tables.*

HONDURAS - FORESTRY AND FOREST PRODUCTS

The Economist Intelligence Unit, 111 West 57th Street, New York, New York 10019 (800) 938-4685; *The New Latin America Market Atlas.*

Facts on File, 460 Park Avenue South, New York, New York 10016 (800) 443-8323; *The New Book of World Rankings.*

Federal Statistical Office, Gustav - Stresesmann - Ring 11, D-6200 Wiesbaden, Federal Republic of Germany; *Honduras.*

Food and Agricultural Organization of the United Nations (FAO) Via delle Terme di Caracalla, 00100 Rome, Italy (Telephone Number in U.S. (202) 653-2400); *The State of Food and Agriculture,* and *Yearbook of Forest Products.*

G.K. Hall and Company, 70 Lincoln Street, Boston, Massachusetts 02111 (617) 423-3990; *The World in Figures.*

Inter-American Development Bank, 1300 New York Avenue, NW, Washington, D.C. 20577 (202) 623-1753; *Economic and Social Progress in Latin America.*

International Monetary Fund, 700 Nineteenth Street, NW, Washington, D.C. 20431 (202) 623-7000; *International Financial Statistics.*

Statistical Office of the United Nations, Publishing Service, New York, New York 10017 (800) 253-9646; *Statistical Yearbook.*

U.C.L.A. Latin American Center Publications, University of California, Los Angeles, California 90024 (310) 825-6634; *Statistical Abstract of Latin America.*

United Nations Educational, Scientific and Cultural Organization (UNESCO), 7 Place de Fontenoy, F-75700 Paris, France (Telephone

Number in U.S. (212) 963-5981); *Statistical Yearbook.*

HONDURAS - GAS PRODUCTION - See HONDURAS - MINING AND MINERAL PRODUCTS

HONDURAS - GENERAL INDUSTRIAL STATISTICS

Federal Statistical Office, Gustav - Stresesmann - Ring 11, D-6200 Wiesbaden, Federal Republic of Germany; *Honduras.*

Statistical Office of the United Nations, Publishing Service, New York, New York 10017 (800) 253-9646; *Industrial Statistics Yearbook.*

HONDURAS - GENERAL MORTALITY

Statistical Office of the United Nations, Publishing Service, New York, New York 10017 (800) 253-9646; *Demographic Yearbook.*

World Health Organization, Office of Publications, Avenue Appia, CH-1211 Geneva 27, Switzerland (Telephone Number in U.S. (518) 436-9686); *World Health Statistics Annual.*

HONDURAS - GEOGRAPHIC DATA

Facts on File, 460 Park Avenue South, New York, New York 10016 (800) 443-8323; *The New Book of World Rankings.*

Federal Statistical Office, Gustav - Stresesmann - Ring 11, D-6200 Wiesbaden, Federal Republic of Germany; *Honduras.*

U.C.L.A. Latin American Center Publications, University of California, Los Angeles, California 90024 (310) 825-6634; *Statistical Abstract of Latin America.*

HONDURAS - GOATS - See HONDURAS - LIVESTOCK AND POULTRY

HONDURAS - GOLD HOLDINGS

International Monetary Fund, 700 Nineteenth Street, NW, Washington, D.C. 20431 (202) 623-7000; *International Financial Statistics.*

Statistical Office of the United Nations, Publishing Service, New York, New York 10017 (800) 253-9646; *Statistical Yearbook.*

HONDURAS - GOLD PRODUCTION - See HONDURAS - MINING AND MINERAL PRODUCTS

HONDURAS - GOLD RESERVES

The Economist Intelligence Unit, 111 West 57th Street, New York, New York 10019 (800) 938-4685; *The New Latin America Market Atlas.*

HONDURAS - GOVERNMENT

G.K. Hall and Company, 70 Lincoln Street, Boston, Massachusetts 02111 (617) 423-3990; *The World in Figures.*

Inter-American Development Bank, 1300 New York Avenue, NW, Washington, D.C. 20577 (202) 623-1753; *Economic and Social Progress in Latin America.*

HONDURAS - GOVERNMENT BONDS - See HONDURAS - BONDS

HONDURAS - GOVERNMENT CONSUMPTION

Inter-American Development Bank, 1300 New York Avenue, NW, Washington, D.C. 20577 (202) 623-1753; *Economic and Social Progress in Latin America.*

HONDURAS - GOVERNMENT EXPENDITURES

Inter-American Development Bank, 1300 New York Avenue, NW, Washington, D.C. 20577 (202) 623-1753; *Economic and Social Progress in Latin America.*

International Monetary Fund, 700 Nineteenth Street, NW, Washington, D.C. 20431 (202) 623-7000; *Government Finance Statistics Yearbook.*

The World Bank, 1818 H Street, NW, Washington, D.C. 20433 (202) 477-1234; *World Tables.*

HONDURAS - GOVERNMENT FINANCES

Inter-American Development Bank, 1300 New York Avenue, NW, Washington, D.C. 20577 (202) 623-1753; *Economic and Social Progress in Latin America.*

International Monetary Fund, 700 Nineteenth Street, NW, Washington, D.C. 20431 (202) 623-7000; *International Financial Statistics.*

Statistical Office of the United Nations, Publishing Service, New York, New York 10017 (800) 253-9646; *Statistical Yearbook.*

HONDURAS - GOVERNMENT REVENUES

Inter-American Development Bank, 1300 New York Avenue, NW, Washington, D.C. 20577 (202) 623-1753; *Economic and Social Progress in Latin America.*

International Monetary Fund, 700 Nineteenth Street, NW, Washington, D.C. 20431 (202) 623-7000; *Government Finance Statistics Yearbook.*

The World Bank, 1818 H Street, NW, Washington, D.C. 20433 (202) 477-1234; *World Tables.*

HONDURAS - GRAIN PRODUCTION - See HONDURAS - CROPS

HONDURAS - GRANTS

International Monetary Fund, 700 Nineteenth Street, NW, Washington, D.C. 20431 (202) 623-7000; *Government Finance Statistics Yearbook.*

HONDURAS - GROSS DOMESTIC PRODUCT

The Economist Intelligence Unit, 111 West 57th Street, New York, New York 10019 (800) 938-4685; *The New Latin America Market Atlas,* and *The World Market Atlas.*

Euromonitor Publications Limited, 87-88 Turnmill Street, London EC1M 5QU, England; *International Marketing Data and Statistics.*

Facts on File, 460 Park Avenue South, New York, New York 10016 (800) 443-8323; *The New Book of World Rankings.*

G.K. Hall and Company, 70 Lincoln Street, Boston, Massachusetts 02111 (617) 423-3990; *The World in Figures.*

Inter-American Development Bank, 1300 New York Avenue, NW, Washington, D.C. 20577 (202) 623-1753; *Economic and Social Progress in Latin America.*

Organization of American States (OAS), General Secretariat, Washington, D.C 20006 (202) 458-3533; *Statistical Bulletin of the OAS.*

Statistical Office of the United Nations, Publishing Service, New York, New York 10017 (800) 253-9646; *Statistical Yearbook,* and *Statistical Yearbook for Latin American and the Caribbean.*

Times Books, 201 East 50th Street, New York, New York 10022 (212) 751-2600; *The Economist Book of Vital World Statistics.*

The World Bank, 1818 H Street, NW, Washington, D.C. 20433 (202) 477-1234; *World Tables.*

HONDURAS - GROSS NATIONAL PRODUCT

Euromonitor Publications Limited, 87-88 Turnmill Street, London EC1M 5QU, England; *International Marketing Data and Statistics.*

Inter-American Development Bank, 1300 New York Avenue, NW, Washington, D.C. 20577 (202) 623-1753; *Economic and Social Progress in Latin America.*

U.S. Arms Control and Disarmament Agency, 320 Twenty-first Street, Northwest, Washington, D.C. 20451 (202) 647-8677; *World Military Expenditures and Arms Transfers.*

The World Bank, 1818 H Street, NW, Washington, D.C. 20433 (202) 477-1234; *World Tables.*

HONDURAS - HEALTH

The Economist Intelligence Unit, 111 West 57th Street, New York, New York 10019 (800) 938-4685; *The New Latin America Market Atlas.*

Facts on File, 460 Park Avenue South, New York, New York 10016 (800) 443-8323; *The New Book of World Rankings.*

Federal Statistical Office, Gustav - Stresesmann - Ring 11, D-6200 Wiesbaden, Federal Republic of Germany; *Honduras.*

G.K. Hall and Company, 70 Lincoln Street, Boston, Massachusetts 02111 (617) 423-3990; *The World in Figures.*

Statistical Office of the United Nations, Publishing Service, New York, New York 10017 (800) 253-9646; *Statistical Yearbook,* and *Statistical Yearbook for Latin American and the Caribbean.*

Times Books, 201 East 50th Street, New York, New York 10022 (212) 751-2600; *The Economist Book of Vital World Statistics.*

U.C.L.A. Latin American Center Publications, University of California, Los Angeles, California 90024 (310) 825-6634; *Statistical Abstract of Latin America.*

World Health Organization, Office of Publications, Avenue Appia, CH-1211 Geneva 27, Switzerland (Telephone Number in U.S. (518) 436-9686); *World Health Statistics Annual.*

HONDURAS - HEALTH EXPENDITURES

International Monetary Fund, 700 Nineteenth Street, NW, Washington, D.C. 20431 (202) 623-7000; *Government Finance Statistics Yearbook.*

Statistical Office of the United Nations, Publishing Service, New York, New York 10017 (800) 253-9646; *Statistical Yearbook for Latin American and the Caribbean.*

HONDURAS - HIDE PRODUCTION

Food and Agricultural Organization of the United Nations (FAO), Via delle Terme di Caracalla, 00100 Rome, Italy (Telephone Number in U.S. (202) 653-2400); *Production Yearbook.*

HONDURAS - HIGHWAYS

The Economist Intelligence Unit, 111 West 57th Street, New York, New York 10019 (800) 938-4685; *The New Latin America Market Atlas.*

G.K. Hall and Company, 70 Lincoln Street, Boston, Massachusetts 02111 (617) 423-3990; *The World in Figures.*

HONDURAS - HORSES - See HONDURAS - LIVESTOCK AND POULTRY

HONDURAS - HOURS OF WORK - See HONDURAS - EMPLOYMENT

HONDURAS - HOUSING AND HOUSING UNITS

Facts on File, 460 Park Avenue South, New York, New York 10016 (800) 443-8323; *The New Book of World Rankings.*

Statistical Office of the United Nations, Publishing Service, New York, New York 10017 (800) 253-9646; *Statistical Yearbook for Latin American and the Caribbean.*

U.C.L.A. Latin American Center Publications, University of California, Los Angeles, California 90024 (310) 825-6634; *Statistical Abstract of Latin America.*

HONDURAS - HOUSING EXPENDITURES

International Monetary Fund, 700 Nineteenth Street, NW, Washington, D.C. 20431 (202) 623-7000; *Government Finance Statistics Yearbook.*

HONDURAS - ILLITERACY RATE

The Economist Intelligence Unit, 111 West 57th Street, New York, New York 10019 (800) 938-4685; *The New Latin America Market Atlas.*

HONDURAS - ILLITERATE POPULATION

The Economist Intelligence Unit, 111 West 57th Street, New York, New York 10019 (800) 938-4685; *The World Market Atlas.*

G.K. Hall and Company, 70 Lincoln Street, Boston, Massachusetts 02111 (617) 423-3990; *The World in Figures.*

Statistical Office of the United Nations, Publishing Service, New York, New York 10017 (800) 253-9646; *Statistical Yearbook for Latin American and the Caribbean.*

United Nations Educational, Scientific and Cultural Organization (UNESCO), 7 Place de Fontenoy, F-75700 Paris, France (Telephone Number in U.S. (212) 963-5981); *Statistical Yearbook.*

HONDURAS - IMMIGRATION

U.C.L.A. Latin American Center Publications, University of California, Los Angeles, California 90024 (310) 825-6634; *Statistical Abstract of Latin America.*

HONDURAS - IMPORTS

The Economist Intelligence Unit, 111 West 57th Street, New York, New York 10019 (800) 938-4685; *The New Latin America Market Atlas*, and *The World Market Atlas.*

Euromonitor Publications Limited, 87-88 Turnmill Street, London EC1M 5QU, England; *International Marketing Data and Statistics.*

Food and Agricultural Organization of the United Nations (FAO) Via delle Terme di Caracalla, 00100 Rome, Italy (Telephone Number in U.S. (202) 653-2400); *The State of Food and Agriculture.*

G.K. Hall and Company, 70 Lincoln Street, Boston, Massachusetts 02111 (617) 423-3990; *The World in Figures.*

Inter-American Development Bank, 1300 New York Avenue, NW, Washington, D.C. 20577 (202) 623-1753; *Economic and Social Progress in Latin America.*

International Monetary Fund, 700 Nineteenth Street, NW, Washington, D.C. 20431 (202) 623-7000; *Direction of Trade Statistics, Government Finance Statistics Yearbook,* and *International Financial Statistics.*

Organization of American States (OAS), General Secretariat, Washington, D.C 20006 (202) 458-3533; *Statistical Bulletin of the OAS.*

Statistical Office of the United Nations, Publishing Service, New York, New York 10017 (800) 253-9646; *Statistical Yearbook,* and *Statistical Yearbook for Latin American and the Caribbean.*

Times Books, 201 East 50th Street, New York, New York 10022 (212) 751-2600; *The Economist Book of Vital World Statistics.*

The World Bank, 1818 H Street, NW, Washington, D.C. 20433 (202) 477-1234; *World Tables.*

HONDURAS - INCOME DISTRIBUTION

Statistical Office of the United Nations, Publishing Service, New York, New York 10017 (800) 253-9646; *Statistical Yearbook for Latin American and the Caribbean.*

U.C.L.A. Latin American Center Publications, University of California, Los Angeles, California 90024 (310) 825-6634; *Statistical Abstract of Latin America.*

HONDURAS - INCOME TAXES - See HONDURAS - TAXATION

HONDURAS - INDUSTRIAL SECTOR TRENDS

Statistical Office of the United Nations, Publishing Service, New York, New York 10017 (800) 253-9646; *Economic Survey of Latin America and the Caribbean.*

HONDURAS - INDUSTRY

Euromonitor Publications Limited, 87-88 Turnmill Street, London EC1M 5QU, England; *International Marketing Data and Statistics.*

Facts on File, 460 Park Avenue South, New York, New York 10016 (800) 443-8323; *The New Book of World Rankings.*

Federal Statistical Office, Gustav - Stresesmann - Ring 11, D-6200 Wiesbaden, Federal Republic of Germany; *Honduras.*

Gale Research Incorporated, 835 Penobscot Building, Detroit, Michigan 48226 (800) 877-4253; *International Historical Statistics The Americas and Australasia.*

G.K. Hall and Company, 70 Lincoln Street, Boston, Massachusetts 02111 (617) 423-3990; *The World in Figures.*

International Labour Office, I.L.O. Publications, CH-1211, Geneva 22, Switzerland; *Yearbook of Labour Statistics.*

Statistical Office of the United Nations, Publishing Service, New York, New York 10017 (800) 253-9646; *Statistical Yearbook.*

Times Books, 201 East 50th Street, New York, New York 10022 (212) 751-2600; *The Economist Book of Vital World Statistics.*

U.C.L.A. Latin American Center Publications, University of California, Los Angeles, California 90024 (310) 825-6634; *Statistical Abstract of Latin America.*

The World Bank, 1818 H Street, NW, Washington, D.C. 20433 (202) 477-1234; *World Tables.*

World Intellectual Property Organization, 34 Chemin des Colombettes, CH-1211 Geneva 20, Switzerland; *Industrial Property Statistics.*

HONDURAS - INFANT AND MATERNAL MORTALITY

The Economist Intelligence Unit, 111 West 57th Street, New York, New York 10019 (800) 938-4685; *The New Latin America Market Atlas.*

Statistical Office of the United Nations, Publishing Service, New York, New York 10017 (800) 253-9646; *Demographic Yearbook,* and *Statistical Yearbook.*

Times Books, 201 East 50th Street, New York, New York 10022 (212) 751-2600; *The Economist Book of Vital World Statistics.*

The World Bank, 1818 H Street, NW, Washington, D.C. 20433 (202) 477-1234; *World Tables.*

World Health Organization, Office of Publications, Avenue Appia, CH-1211 Geneva 27, Switzerland (Telephone Number in U.S. (518) 436-9686); *World Health Statistics Annual.*

HONDURAS - INFLATIONARY FACTORS

Statistical Office of the United Nations, Publishing Service, New York, New York 10017 (800) 253-9646; *Economic Survey of Latin America and the Caribbean.*

HONDURAS - INTEREST RATES

Inter-American Development Bank, 1300 New York Avenue, NW, Washington, D.C. 20577 (202) 623-1753; *Economic and Social Progress in Latin America.*

Organization of American States (OAS), General Secretariat, Washington, D.C 20006 (202) 458-3533; *Statistical Bulletin of the OAS.*

HONDURAS - INTERNATIONAL FINANCE

Inter-American Development Bank, 1300 New York Avenue, NW, Washington, D.C. 20577 (202) 623-1753; *Economic and Social Progress in Latin America.*

U.C.L.A. Latin American Center Publications, University of California, Los Angeles, California 90024 (310) 825-6634; *Statistical Abstract of Latin America.*

HONDURAS - INTERNATIONAL LIQUIDITY

Inter-American Development Bank, 1300 New York Avenue, NW, Washington, D.C. 20577 (202) 623-1753; *Economic and Social Progress in Latin America.*

International Monetary Fund, 700 Nineteenth Street, NW, Washington, D.C. 20431 (202) 623-7000; *International Financial Statistics.*

HONDURAS - INTERNATIONAL RESERVES

Organization of American States (OAS), General Secretariat, Washington, D.C 20006 (202) 458-3533; *Statistical Bulletin of the OAS.*

HONDURAS - INTERNATIONAL RESERVES EXCLUDING GOLD

Inter-American Development Bank, 1300 New York Avenue, NW, Washington, D.C. 20577 (202) 623-1753; *Economic and Social Progress in Latin America.*

Statistical Office of the United Nations, Publishing Service, New York, New York 10017 (800) 253-9646; *Statistical Yearbook.*

The World Bank, 1818 H Street, NW, Washington, D.C. 20433 (202) 477-1234; *World Tables.*

HONDURAS - INTERNATIONAL STATISTICS

Inter-American Development Bank, 1300 New York Avenue, NW, Washington, D.C. 20577 (202) 623-1753; *Economic and Social Progress in Latin America.*

U.C.L.A. Latin American Center Publications, University of California, Los Angeles, California 90024 (310) 825-6634; *Statistical Abstract of Latin America.*

HONDURAS - INVESTMENT

Inter-American Development Bank, 1300 New York Avenue, NW, Washington, D.C. 20577 (202) 623-1753; *Economic and Social Progress in Latin America.*

Statistical Office of the United Nations, Publishing Service, New York, New York 10017 (800) 253-9646; *Statistical Yearbook for Latin American and the Caribbean.*

HONDURAS - IRON ORE PRODUCTION AND CONSUMPTION - See HONDURAS - MINING AND MINERAL PRODUCTS

HONDURAS - IRRIGATION

Euromonitor Publications Limited, 87-88 Turnmill Street, London EC1M 5QU, England; *International Marketing Data and Statistics.*

Inter-American Development Bank, 1300 New York Avenue, NW, Washington, D.C. 20577 (202) 623-1753; *Economic and Social Progress in Latin America.*

HONDURAS - LABOR FORCE

The Economist Intelligence Unit, 111 West 57th Street, New York, New York 10019 (800) 938-4685; *The New Latin America Market Atlas.*

Euromonitor Publications Limited, 87-88 Turnmill Street, London EC1M 5QU, England; *International Marketing Data and Statistics.*

Facts on File, 460 Park Avenue South, New York, New York 10016 (800) 443-8323; *The New Book of World Rankings.*

Food and Agricultural Organization of the United Nations (FAO) Via delle Terme di Caracalla, 00100 Rome, Italy (Telephone Number in U.S. (202) 653-2400); *The State of Food and Agriculture.*

Gale Research Incorporated, 835 Penobscot Building, Detroit, Michigan 48226 (800) 877-4253; *International Historical Statistics The Americas and Australasia.*

G.K. Hall and Company, 70 Lincoln Street, Boston, Massachusetts 02111 (617) 423-3990; *The World in Figures.*

The World Bank, 1818 H Street, NW, Washington, D.C. 20433 (202) 477-1234; *World Tables.*

HONDURAS - LABOR PRODUCTIVITY

International Labour Office, I.L.O. Publications, CH-1211, Geneva 22, Switzerland; *Yearbook of Labour Statistics.*

HONDURAS - LAND AREA

The Economist Intelligence Unit, 111 West 57th Street, New York, New York 10019 (800) 938-4685; *The New Latin America Market Atlas.*

HONDURAS - LAND USE

Euromonitor Publications Limited, 87-88 Turnmill Street, London EC1M 5QU, England; *International Marketing Data and Statistics.*

Food and Agricultural Organization of the United Nations (FAO), Via delle Terme di Caracalla, 00100 Rome, Italy (Telephone Number in U.S. (202) 653-2400); *Production Yearbook.*

G.K. Hall and Company, 70 Lincoln Street, Boston, Massachusetts 02111 (617) 423-3990; *The World in Figures.*

Inter-American Development Bank, 1300 New York Avenue, NW, Washington, D.C. 20577 (202) 623-1753; *Economic and Social Progress in Latin America.*

HONDURAS - LEAD ORE PRODUCTION AND CONSUMPTION - See HONDURAS - MINING AND MINERAL PRODUCTS

HONDURAS - LIBRARIES

Facts on File, 460 Park Avenue South, New York, New York 10016 (800) 443-8323; *The New Book of World Rankings.*

United Nations Educational, Scientific and Cultural Organization (UNESCO), 7 Place de Fontenoy, F-75700 Paris, France (Telephone Number in U.S. (212) 963-5981); *Statistical Yearbook.*

HONDURAS - LIFE EXPECTANCY

The Economist Intelligence Unit, 111 West 57th Street, New York, New York 10019 (800) 938-4685; *The New Latin America Market Atlas.*

HONDURAS - LIGNITE PRODUCTION - See HONDURAS - MINING AND MINERAL PRODUCTS

HONDURAS - LIVESTOCK AND POULTRY

Euromonitor Publications Limited, 87-88 Turnmill Street, London EC1M 5QU, England; *International Marketing Data and Statistics.*

Facts on File, 460 Park Avenue South, New York, New York 10016 (800) 443-8323; *The New Book of World Rankings.*

Food and Agricultural Organization of the United Nations (FAO), Via delle Terme di Caracalla, 00100 Rome, Italy (Telephone Number in U.S. (202) 653-2400); *Production Yearbook,* and *The State of Food and Agriculture.*

G.K. Hall and Company, 70 Lincoln Street, Boston, Massachusetts 02111 (617) 423-3990; *The World in Figures.*

Organization of American States (OAS), General Secretariat, Washington, D.C 20006 (202) 458-3533; *Statistical Bulletin of the OAS.*

Statistical Office of the United Nations, Publishing Service, New York, New York 10017 (800) 253-9646; *Statistical Yearbook.*

HONDURAS - LIVING LEVELS

G.K. Hall and Company, 70 Lincoln Street, Boston, Massachusetts 02111 (617) 423-3990; *The World in Figures.*

Statistical Office of the United Nations, Publishing Service, New York, New York 10017 (800) 253-9646; *Statistical Yearbook for Latin American and the Caribbean.*

Times Books, 201 East 50th Street, New York, New York 10022 (212) 751-2600; *The Economist Book of Vital World Statistics.*

HONDURAS - MAIL TRAFFIC - NUMBER OF ITEMS SENT OR RECEIVED

Statistical Office of the United Nations, Publishing Service, New York, New York 10017 (800) 253-9646; *Statistical Yearbook.*

HONDURAS - MAIN ECONOMIC INDICATORS - See HONDURAS - ECONOMY

HONDURAS - MANUFACTURING

Facts on File, 460 Park Avenue South, New York, New York 10016 (800) 443-8323; *The New Book of World Rankings.*

G.K. Hall and Company, 70 Lincoln Street, Boston, Massachusetts 02111 (617) 423-3990; *The World in Figures.*

Inter-American Development Bank, 1300 New York Avenue, NW, Washington, D.C. 20577 (202) 623-1753; *Economic and Social Progress in Latin America.*

Statistical Office of the United Nations, Publishing Service, New York, New York 10017 (800) 253-9646; *Statistical Yearbook,* and *Statistical Yearbook for Latin American and the Caribbean.*

Times Books, 201 East 50th Street, New York, New York 10022 (212) 751-2600; *The Economist Book of Vital World Statistics.*

U.S. Arms Control and Disarmament Agency, 320 Twenty-first Street, Northwest, Washington, D.C. 20451 (202) 647-8677; *World Military Expenditures and Arms Transfers.*

The World Bank, 1818 H Street, NW, Washington, D.C. 20433 (202) 477-1234; *World Tables.*

HONDURAS - MARRIAGE RATES

Facts on File, 460 Park Avenue South, New York, New York 10016 (800) 443-8323; *The New Book of World Rankings.*

Statistical Office of the United Nations, Publishing Service, New York, New York 10017 (800) 253-9646; *Demographic Yearbook,* and *Statistical Yearbook.*

HONDURAS - MEAT PRODUCTION - See HONDURAS - LIVESTOCK AND POULTRY

HONDURAS - MEDICAL PERSONNEL

U.C.L.A. Latin American Center Publications, University of California, Los Angeles, California 90024 (310) 825-6634; *Statistical Abstract of Latin America.*

HONDURAS - MERCHANT SHIPPING

G.K. Hall and Company, 70 Lincoln Street, Boston, Massachusetts 02111 (617) 423-3990; *The World in Figures.*

Statistical Office of the United Nations, Publishing Service, New York, New York 10017 (800) 253-9646; *Statistical Yearbook.*

Times Books, 201 East 50th Street, New York, New York 10022 (212) 751-2600; *The Economist Book of Vital World Statistics.*

U.S. Department of Transportation, Maritime Administration, 400 Seventh Street, SW, Washington, D.C. 20590 (202) 366-5807; *A Statistical Analysis of the World's Merchant Fleets.*

HONDURAS - MILITARY

The Economist Intelligence Unit, 111 West 57th Street, New York, New York 10019 (800) 938-4685; *The New Latin America Market Atlas.*

G.K. Hall and Company, 70 Lincoln Street, Boston, Massachusetts 02111 (617) 423-3990; *The World in Figures.*

The International Institute for Strategic Studies, 23 Tavistock Street, London WC2E 7NQ, England; *The Military Balance.*

U.C.L.A. Latin American Center Publications, University of California, Los Angeles, California 90024 (310) 825-6634; *Statistical Abstract of Latin America.*

HONDURAS - MILK PRODUCTION - See HONDURAS - DAIRY PRODUCTS

HONDURAS - MINING AND MINERAL PRODUCTS

The Economist Intelligence Unit, 111 West 57th Street, New York, New York 10019 (800) 938-4685; *The New Latin America Market Atlas.*

Facts on File, 460 Park Avenue South, New York, New York 10016 (800) 443-8323; *The New Book of World Rankings.*

G.K. Hall and Company, 70 Lincoln Street, Boston, Massachusetts 02111 (617) 423-3990; *The World in Figures.*

Inter-American Development Bank, 1300 New York Avenue, NW, Washington, D.C. 20577 (202) 623-1753; *Economic and Social Progress in Latin America.*

Statistical Office of the United Nations, Publishing Service, New York, New York 10017 (800) 253-9646; *Statistical Yearbook*, and *Statistical Yearbook for Latin American and the Caribbean.*

U.C.L.A. Latin American Center Publications, University of California, Los Angeles, California 90024 (310) 825-6634; *Statistical Abstract of Latin America.*

The World Bank, 1818 H Street, NW, Washington, D.C. 20433 (202) 477-1234; *World Tables.*

HONDURAS - MONEY EXCHANGE RATE

Euromonitor Publications Limited, 87-88 Turnmill Street, London EC1M 5QU, England; *International Marketing Data and Statistics.*

Inter-American Development Bank, 1300 New York Avenue, NW, Washington, D.C. 20577 (202) 623-1753; *Economic and Social Progress in Latin America.*

International Monetary Fund, 700 Nineteenth Street, NW, Washington, D.C. 20431 (202) 623-7000; *International Financial Statistics.*

Statistical Office of the United Nations, Publishing Service, New York, New York 10017 (800) 253-9646; *Statistical Yearbook.*

HONDURAS - MONEY RATES - MARKET

Inter-American Development Bank, 1300 New York Avenue, NW, Washington, D.C. 20577 (202) 623-1753; *Economic and Social Progress in Latin America.*

HONDURAS - MONEY RESERVES

Euromonitor Publications Limited, 87-88 Turnmill Street, London EC1M 5QU, England; *International Marketing Data and Statistics.*

Inter-American Development Bank, 1300 New York Avenue, NW, Washington, D.C. 20577 (202) 623-1753; *Economic and Social Progress in Latin America.*

HONDURAS - MONEY SUPPLY

Euromonitor Publications Limited, 87-88 Turnmill Street, London EC1M 5QU, England; *International Marketing Data and Statistics.*

Federal Statistical Office, Gustav - Stresesmann - Ring 11, D-6200 Wiesbaden, Federal Republic of Germany; *Honduras.*

G.K. Hall and Company, 70 Lincoln Street, Boston, Massachusetts 02111 (617) 423-3990; *The World in Figures.*

Inter-American Development Bank, 1300 New York Avenue, NW, Washington, D.C. 20577 (202) 623-1753; *Economic and Social Progress in Latin America.*

International Monetary Fund, 700 Nineteenth Street, NW, Washington, D.C. 20431 (202) 623-7000; *International Financial Statistics.*

Statistical Office of the United Nations, Publishing Service, New York, New York 10017 (800) 253-9646; *Statistical Yearbook.*

U.C.L.A. Latin American Center Publications, University of California, Los Angeles, California 90024 (310) 825-6634; *Statistical Abstract of Latin America.*

The World Bank, 1818 H Street, NW, Washington, D.C. 20433 (202) 477-1234; *World Tables.*

HONDURAS - MONUMENTS AND HISTORICAL SITES

United Nations Educational, Scientific and Cultural Organization (UNESCO), 7 Place de Fontenoy, F-75700 Paris, France (Telephone Number in U.S. (212) 963-5981); *Statistical Yearbook.*

HONDURAS - MOTOR VEHICLE TAXES - See HONDURAS - TAXATION

HONDURAS - MOTOR VEHICLES IN USE

The Economist Intelligence Unit, 111 West 57th Street, New York, New York 10019 (800) 938-4685; *The New Latin America Market Atlas.*

G.K. Hall and Company, 70 Lincoln Street, Boston, Massachusetts 02111 (617) 423-3990; *The World in Figures.*

Statistical Office of the United Nations, Publishing Service, New York, New York 10017 (800) 253-9646; *Statistical Yearbook.*

Times Books, 201 East 50th Street, New York, New York 10022 (212) 751-2600; *The Economist Book of Vital World Statistics.*

HONDURAS - MULES - See HONDURAS - LIVESTOCK AND POULTRY

HONDURAS - MUSEUMS

Facts on File, 460 Park Avenue South, New York, New York 10016 (800) 443-8323; *The New Book of World Rankings.*

United Nations Educational, Scientific and Cultural Organization (UNESCO), 7 Place de Fontenoy, F-75700 Paris, France (Telephone Number in U.S. (212) 963-5981); *Statistical Yearbook.*

HONDURAS - NATALITY - See HONDURAS - BIRTH RATES

HONDURAS - NATIONAL ACCOUNTS

Federal Statistical Office, Gustav - Stresesmann - Ring 11, D-6200 Wiesbaden, Federal Republic of Germany; *Honduras.*

Gale Research Incorporated, 835 Penobscot Building, Detroit, Michigan 48226 (800) 877-4253; *International Historical Statistics The Americas and Australasia.*

Inter-American Development Bank, 1300 New York Avenue, NW, Washington, D.C. 20577 (202) 623-1753; *Economic and Social Progress in Latin America.*

Organization of American States (OAS), General Secretariat, Washington, D.C 20006 (202) 458-3533; *Statistical Bulletin of the OAS.*

Statistical Office of the United Nations, Publishing Service, New York, New York 10017 (800) 253-9646; *National Accounts Statistics*, and *Statistical Yearbook.*

U.C.L.A. Latin American Center Publications, University of California, Los Angeles, California 90024 (310) 825-6634; *Statistical Abstract of Latin America.*

HONDURAS - NATIONAL INCOME

Facts on File, 460 Park Avenue South, New York, New York 10016 (800) 443-8323; *The New Book of World Rankings.*

G.K. Hall and Company, 70 Lincoln Street, Boston, Massachusetts 02111 (617) 423-3990; *The World in Figures.*

Inter-American Development Bank, 1300 New York Avenue, NW, Washington, D.C. 20577 (202) 623-1753; *Economic and Social Progress in Latin America.*

International Monetary Fund, 700 Nineteenth Street, NW, Washington, D.C. 20431 (202) 623-7000; *International Financial Statistics.*

Statistical Office of the United Nations, Publishing Service, New York, New York 10017 (800) 253-9646; *Statistical Yearbook,* and *Statistical Yearbook for Latin American and the Caribbean.*

HONDURAS - NATIONAL PRODUCT

Facts on File, 460 Park Avenue South, New York, New York 10016 (800) 443-8323; *The New Book of World Rankings.*

Statistical Office of the United Nations, Publishing Service, New York, New York 10017 (800) 253-9646; *Statistical Yearbook.*

HONDURAS - NATURAL GAS PRODUCTION - See HONDURAS - MINING AND MINERAL PRODUCTS

HONDURAS - NEWSPAPER PRODUCTION - See HONDURAS - FORESTRY AND FOREST PRODUCTS

HONDURAS - NEWSPRINT - See HONDURAS - FORESTRY AND FOREST PRODUCTS

HONDURAS - NUTRITION

Statistical Office of the United Nations, Publishing Service, New York, New York 10017 (800) 253-9646; *Statistical Yearbook for Latin American and the Caribbean.*

HONDURAS - OCCUPATIONS - See HONDURAS - LABOR FORCE

HONDURAS - PALM KERNELS AND PALM OIL - See HONDURAS - CROPS

HONDURAS - PAPER - See HONDURAS - FORESTRY AND FOREST PRODUCTS

HONDURAS - PATENTS

Statistical Office of the United Nations, Publishing Service, New York, New York 10017 (800) 253-9646; *Statistical Yearbook.*

World Intellectual Property Organization, 34 Chemin des Colombettes, CH-1211 Geneva 20, Switzerland; *Industrial Property Statistics.*

HONDURAS - PEANUT PRODUCTION - See HONDURAS - CROPS

HONDURAS - PESTICIDE USE

Food and Agricultural Organization of the United Nations (FAO) Via delle Terme di Caracalla, 00100 Rome, Italy (Telephone Number in U.S. (202) 653-2400); *The State of Food and Agriculture.*

HONDURAS - PETROLEUM INDUSTRY

The Economist Intelligence Unit, 111 West 57th Street, New York, New York 10019 (800) 938-4685; *The New Latin America Market Atlas.*

Facts on File, 460 Park Avenue South, New York, New York 10016 (800) 443-8323; *The New Book of World Rankings.*

Food and Agricultural Organization of the United Nations (FAO) Via delle Terme di Caracalla, 00100 Rome, Italy (Telephone Number in U.S. (202) 653-2400); *The State of Food and Agriculture.*

G.K. Hall and Company, 70 Lincoln Street, Boston, Massachusetts 02111 (617) 423-3990; *The World in Figures.*

Inter-American Development Bank, 1300 New York Avenue, NW, Washington, D.C. 20577 (202) 623-1753; *Economic and Social Progress in Latin America.*

Statistical Office of the United Nations, Publishing Service, New York, New York 10017 (800) 253-9646; *Statistical Yearbook.*

HONDURAS - PIGS - See HONDURAS - LIVESTOCK AND POULTRY

HONDURAS - POLITICAL DATA

U.C.L.A. Latin American Center Publications, University of California, Los Angeles, California 90024 (310) 825-6634; *Statistical Abstract of Latin America.*

HONDURAS - POPULATION

The Economist Intelligence Unit, 111 West 57th Street, New York, New York 10019 (800) 938-4685; *The New Latin America Market Atlas,* and *The World Market Atlas.*

Euromonitor Publications Limited, 87-88 Turnmill Street, London EC1M 5QU, England; *International Marketing Data and Statistics.*

Facts on File, 460 Park Avenue South, New York, New York 10016 (800) 443-8323; *The New Book of World Rankings.*

Federal Statistical Office, Gustav - Stresesmann - Ring 11, D-6200 Wiesbaden, Federal Republic of Germany; *Honduras.*

Food and Agricultural Organization of the United Nations (FAO), Via delle Terme di Caracalla, 00100 Rome, Italy (Telephone Number in U.S. (202) 653-2400); *Production Yearbook.*

Gale Research Incorporated, 835 Penobscot Building, Detroit, Michigan 48226 (800) 877-4253; *International Historical Statistics The Americas and Australasia.*

G.K. Hall and Company, 70 Lincoln Street, Boston, Massachusetts 02111 (617) 423-3990; *The World in Figures.*

Inter-American Development Bank, 1300 New York Avenue, NW, Washington, D.C. 20577 (202) 623-1753; *Economic and Social Progress in Latin America.*

International Labour Office, I.L.O. Publications, CH-1211, Geneva 22, Switzerland; *Yearbook of Labour Statistics.*

Organization of American States (OAS), General Secretariat, Washington, D.C 20006 (202) 458-3533; *Statistical Bulletin of the OAS.*

Statistical Office of the United Nations, Publishing Service, New York, New York 10017 (800) 253-9646; *Demographic Yearbook, Statistical Yearbook,* and *Statistical Yearbook for Latin American and the Caribbean.*

Times Books, 201 East 50th Street, New York, New York 10022 (212) 751-2600; *The Economist Book of Vital World Statistics.*

U.C.L.A. Latin American Center Publications, University of California, Los Angeles, California 90024 (310) 825-6634; *Statistical Abstract of Latin America.*

United Nations Educational, Scientific and Cultural Organization (UNESCO), 7 Place de Fontenoy, F-75700 Paris, France (Telephone Number in U.S. (212) 963-5981); *Statistical Yearbook.*

U.S. Arms Control and Disarmament Agency, 320 Twenty-first Street, Northwest, Washington, D.C. 20451 (202) 647-8677; *World Military Expenditures and Arms Transfers.*

World Health Organization, Office of Publications, Avenue Appia, CH-1211 Geneva 27, Switzerland (Telephone Number in U.S. (518) 436-9686); *World Health Statistics Annual.*

HONDURAS - POST OFFICES

Facts on File, 460 Park Avenue South, New York, New York 10016 (800) 443-8323; *The New Book of World Rankings.*

HONDURAS - POTATO PRODUCTION - See HONDURAS - CROPS

HONDURAS - POWER PRODUCTION INDUSTRY

Statistical Office of the United Nations, Publishing Service, New York, New York 10017 (800) 253-9646; *Statistical Yearbook.*

HONDURAS - PRICES

Facts on File, 460 Park Avenue South, New York, New York 10016 (800) 443-8323; *The New Book of World Rankings.*

Federal Statistical Office, Gustav - Stresesmann - Ring 11, D-6200 Wiesbaden, Federal Republic of Germany; *Honduras.*

Food and Agricultural Organization of the United Nations (FAO), Via delle Terme di Caracalla, 00100 Rome, Italy (Telephone Number in U.S. (202) 653-2400); *Production Yearbook,* and *The State of Food and Agriculture.*

Gale Research Incorporated, 835 Penobscot Building, Detroit, Michigan 48226 (800) 877-4253; *International Historical Statistics The Americas and Australasia.*

G.K. Hall and Company, 70 Lincoln Street, Boston, Massachusetts 02111 (617) 423-3990; *The World in Figures.*

International Labour Office, I.L.O. Publications, CH-1211, Geneva 22, Switzerland; *Yearbook of Labour Statistics.*

International Monetary Fund, 700 Nineteenth Street, NW, Washington, D.C. 20431 (202) 623-7000; *International Financial Statistics.*

Statistical Office of the United Nations, Publishing Service, New York, New York 10017 (800) 253-9646; *Economic Survey of Latin America and the Caribbean,* and *Statistical Yearbook for Latin American and the Caribbean.*

HONDURAS - PRINTING AND WRITING PAPER - See HONDURAS - FORESTRY AND FOREST PRODUCTS

HONDURAS - PRODUCTION

Facts on File, 460 Park Avenue South, New York, New York 10016 (800) 443-8323; *The New Book of World Rankings.*

G.K. Hall and Company, 70 Lincoln Street, Boston, Massachusetts 02111 (617) 423-3990; *The World in Figures.*

HONDURAS - PRODUCTIVITY

Euromonitor Publications Limited, 87-88 Turnmill Street, London EC1M 5QU, England; *International Marketing Data and Statistics.*

HONDURAS - PROPERTY TAXES - See HONDURAS - TAXATION

HONDURAS - PUBLIC CONSUMPTION FUND

Inter-American Development Bank, 1300 New York Avenue, NW, Washington, D.C. 20577 (202) 623-1753; *Economic and Social Progress in Latin America.*

HONDURAS - PUBLIC EXPENDITURE

Inter-American Development Bank, 1300 New York Avenue, NW, Washington, D.C. 20577 (202) 623-1753; *Economic and Social Progress in Latin America.*

Organization of American States (OAS), General Secretariat, Washington, D.C 20006 (202) 458-3533; *Statistical Bulletin of the OAS.*

Statistical Office of the United Nations, Publishing Service, New York, New York 10017 (800) 253-9646; *Statistical Yearbook for Latin American and the Caribbean.*

HONDURAS - PUBLIC FINANCE

Facts on File, 460 Park Avenue South, New York, New York 10016 (800) 443-8323; *The New Book of World Rankings.*

Federal Statistical Office, Gustav - Stresesmann - Ring 11, D-6200 Wiesbaden, Federal Republic of Germany; *Honduras.*

Inter-American Development Bank, 1300 New York Avenue, NW, Washington, D.C. 20577 (202) 623-1753; *Economic and Social Progress in Latin America.*

International Monetary Fund, 700 Nineteenth Street, NW, Washington, D.C. 20431 (202) 623-7000; *International Financial Statistics.*

Organization of American States (OAS), General Secretariat, Washington, D.C 20006 (202) 458-3533; *Statistical Bulletin of the OAS.*

HONDURAS - PUBLIC REVENUES

Inter-American Development Bank, 1300 New York Avenue, NW, Washington, D.C. 20577 (202) 623-1753; *Economic and Social Progress in Latin America.*

Organization of American States (OAS), General Secretariat, Washington, D.C 20006 (202) 458-3533; *Statistical Bulletin of the OAS.*

HONDURAS - RADIO BROADCASTING - See HONDURAS - BROADCASTING

HONDURAS - RAILWAYS

The Economist Intelligence Unit, 111 West 57th Street, New York, New York 10019 (800) 938-4685; *The New Latin America Market Atlas.*

G.K. Hall and Company, 70 Lincoln Street, Boston, Massachusetts 02111 (617) 423-3990; *The World in Figures.*

Jane's Information Group, Sentinel House, 163 Brighton Road, Coulsdon, Surrey CR5 2NH, England (Telephone Number in U.S. (703) 683-3700); *Jane's World Railways.*

HONDURAS - RANCHING

U.C.L.A. Latin American Center Publications, University of California, Los Angeles, California 90024 (310) 825-6634; *Statistical Abstract of Latin America.*

HONDURAS - RELIGION

Facts on File, 460 Park Avenue South, New York, New York 10016 (800) 443-8323; *The New Book of World Rankings.*

U.C.L.A. Latin American Center Publications, University of California, Los Angeles, California 90024 (310) 825-6634; *Statistical Abstract of Latin America.*

HONDURAS - RENT PRICES

International Labour Office, I.L.O. Publications, CH-1211, Geneva 22, Switzerland; *Yearbook of Labour Statistics.*

HONDURAS - RESERVES EXCLUDING GOLD

The Economist Intelligence Unit, 111 West 57th Street, New York, New York 10019 (800) 938-4685; *The New Latin America Market Atlas.*

HONDURAS - RETAIL TRADE

G.K. Hall and Company, 70 Lincoln Street, Boston, Massachusetts 02111 (617) 423-3990; *The World in Figures.*

Inter-American Development Bank, 1300 New York Avenue, NW, Washington, D.C. 20577 (202) 623-1753; *Economic and Social Progress in Latin America.*

HONDURAS - RICE PRODUCTION - See HONDURAS - CROPS

HONDURAS - ROOT AND TUBER PRODUCTION - See HONDURAS - CROPS

HONDURAS - ROUNDWOOD PRODUCTION - See HONDURAS - FORESTRY AND FOREST PRODUCTS

HONDURAS - RUBBER PRODUCTION

Facts on File, 460 Park Avenue South, New York, New York 10016 (800) 443-8323; *The New Book of World Rankings.*

HONDURAS - SALT PRODUCTION - See HONDURAS - MINING AND MINERAL PRODUCTS

HONDURAS - SAWNWOOD PRODUCTION - See HONDURAS - FORESTRY AND FOREST PRODUCTS

HONDURAS - SCIENCE AND TECHNOLOGY

U.C.L.A. Latin American Center Publications, University of California, Los Angeles, California 90024 (310) 825-6634; *Statistical Abstract of Latin America.*

HONDURAS - SCIENTISTS AND TECHNICIANS

Statistical Office of the United Nations, Publishing Service, New York, New York 10017 (800) 253-9646; *Statistical Yearbook.*

HONDURAS - SENIOR CITIZENS

Facts on File, 460 Park Avenue South, New York, New York 10016 (800) 443-8323; *The New Book of World Rankings.*

HONDURAS - SESAME SEED PRODUCTION - See HONDURAS - CROPS

HONDURAS - SHEEP - See HONDURAS - LIVESTOCK AND POULTRY

HONDURAS - SILVER PRODUCTION AND CONSUMPTION - See HONDURAS - MINING AND MINERAL PRODUCTS

HONDURAS - SOCIAL DATA

Facts on File, 460 Park Avenue South, New York, New York 10016 (800) 443-8323; *The New Book of World Rankings.*

G.K. Hall and Company, 70 Lincoln Street, Boston, Massachusetts 02111 (617) 423-3990; *The World in Figures.*

U.C.L.A. Latin American Center Publications, University of California, Los Angeles, California 90024 (310) 825-6634; *Statistical Abstract of Latin America.*

HONDURAS - SOCIAL SECURITY

Inter-American Development Bank, 1300 New York Avenue, NW, Washington, D.C. 20577 (202) 623-1753; *Economic and Social Progress in Latin America.*

International Monetary Fund, 700 Nineteenth Street, NW, Washington, D.C. 20431 (202) 623-7000; *Government Finance Statistics Yearbook.*

HONDURAS - SOCIOECONOMIC DATA

Inter-American Development Bank, 1300 New York Avenue, NW, Washington, D.C. 20577 (202) 623-1753; *Economic and Social Progress in Latin America.*

U.C.L.A. Latin American Center Publications, University of California, Los Angeles, California 90024 (310) 825-6634; *Statistical Abstract of Latin America.*

HONDURAS - STAMP TAXES AND DUTIES - See HONDURAS - TAXATION

HONDURAS - STATE BUDGET REVENUE AND EXPENDITURES

Euromonitor Publications Limited, 87-88 Turnmill Street, London EC1M 5QU, England; *International Marketing Data and Statistics.*

Inter-American Development Bank, 1300 New York Avenue, NW, Washington, D.C. 20577 (202) 623-1753; *Economic and Social Progress in Latin America.*

HONDURAS - STEEL - See HONDURAS - MINING AND MINERAL PRODUCTS

HONDURAS - STOCKS - COMMODITY - MARKET PRICE - INDEX

Food and Agricultural Organization of the United Nations (FAO) Via delle Terme di Caracalla, 00100 Rome, Italy (Telephone Number in

U.S. (202) 653-2400); *The State of Food and Agriculture.*

HONDURAS - SUGAR PRODUCTION - See HONDURAS - CROPS

HONDURAS - TAXATION

G.K. Hall and Company, 70 Lincoln Street, Boston, Massachusetts 02111 (617) 423-3990; *The World in Figures.*

Inter-American Development Bank, 1300 New York Avenue, NW, Washington, D.C. 20577 (202) 623-1753; *Economic and Social Progress in Latin America.*

International Monetary Fund, 700 Nineteenth Street, NW, Washington, D.C. 20431 (202) 623-7000; *Government Finance Statistics Yearbook.*

Statistical Office of the United Nations, Publishing Service, New York, New York 10017 (800) 253-9646; *Statistical Yearbook for Latin American and the Caribbean.*

The World Bank, 1818 H Street, NW, Washington, D.C. 20433 (202) 477-1234; *World Tables.*

HONDURAS - TELEPHONES IN USE

American Telephone and Telegraph Company, 26 Parsippany Road, Whippany, New Jersey 07981 (800) 338-4038; *The World's Telephones.*

The Economist Intelligence Unit, 111 West 57th Street, New York, New York 10019 (800) 938-4685; *The New Latin America Market Atlas.*

G.K. Hall and Company, 70 Lincoln Street, Boston, Massachusetts 02111 (617) 423-3990; *The World in Figures.*

Statistical Office of the United Nations, Publishing Service, New York, New York 10017 (800) 253-9646; *Statistical Yearbook.*

HONDURAS - TELEVISION BROADCASTING - See HONDURAS - BROADCASTING

HONDURAS - TEXTILE INDUSTRY

G.K. Hall and Company, 70 Lincoln Street, Boston, Massachusetts 02111 (617) 423-3990; *The World in Figures.*

Statistical Office of the United Nations, Publishing Service, New York, New York 10017 (800) 253-9646; *Statistical Yearbook.*

HONDURAS - TOBACCO PRODUCTION

Facts on File, 460 Park Avenue South, New York, New York 10016 (800) 443-8323; *The New Book of World Rankings.*

Statistical Office of the United Nations, Publishing Service, New York, New York 10017 (800) 253-9646; *Statistical Yearbook.*

HONDURAS - TOURISM

The Economist Intelligence Unit, 111 West 57th Street, New York, New York 10019 (800) 938-4685; *The New Latin America Market Atlas.*

Facts on File, 460 Park Avenue South, New York, New York 10016 (800) 443-8323; *The New Book of World Rankings.*

Federal Statistical Office, Gustav - Stresesmann - Ring 11, D-6200 Wiesbaden, Federal Republic of Germany; *Honduras.*

G.K. Hall and Company, 70 Lincoln Street, Boston, Massachusetts 02111 (617) 423-3990; *The World in Figures.*

Organization of American States (OAS), General Secretariat, Washington, D.C 20006 (202) 458-3533; *Statistical Bulletin of the OAS.*

Statistical Office of the United Nations, Publishing Service, New York, New York 10017 (800) 253-9646; *Statistical Yearbook*, and *Statistical Yearbook for Latin American and the Caribbean.*

Times Books, 201 East 50th Street, New York, New York 10022 (212) 751-2600; *The Economist Book of Vital World Statistics.*

U.C.L.A. Latin American Center Publications, University of California, Los Angeles, California 90024 (310) 825-6634; *Statistical Abstract of Latin America.*

HONDURAS - TRACTORS IN USE

The Economist Intelligence Unit, 111 West 57th Street, New York, New York 10019 (800) 938-4685; *The New Latin America Market Atlas.*

Statistical Office of the United Nations, Publishing Service, New York, New York 10017 (800) 253-9646; *Statistical Yearbook.*

HONDURAS - TRADE - See HONDURAS - FOREIGN TRADE

HONDURAS - TRADEMARKS AND SERVICE MARKS

Statistical Office of the United Nations, Publishing Service, New York, New York 10017 (800) 253-9646; *Statistical Yearbook.*

World Intellectual Property Organization, 34 Chemin des Colombettes, CH-1211 Geneva 20, Switzerland; *Industrial Property Statistics.*

HONDURAS - TRANSPORTATION AND COMMUNICATIONS

The Economist Intelligence Unit, 111 West 57th Street, New York, New York 10019 (800) 938-4685; *The New Latin America Market Atlas.*

Facts on File, 460 Park Avenue South, New York, New York 10016 (800) 443-8323; *The New Book of World Rankings.*

Federal Statistical Office, Gustav - Stresesmann - Ring 11, D-6200 Wiesbaden, Federal Republic of Germany; *Honduras.*

Gale Research Incorporated, 835 Penobscot Building, Detroit, Michigan 48226 (800) 877-4253; *International Historical Statistics The Americas and Australasia.*

G.K. Hall and Company, 70 Lincoln Street, Boston, Massachusetts 02111 (617) 423-3990; *The World in Figures.*

Inter-American Development Bank, 1300 New York Avenue, NW, Washington, D.C. 20577 (202) 623-1753; *Economic and Social Progress in Latin America.*

Statistical Office of the United Nations, Publishing Service, New York, New York 10017 (800) 253-9646; *Statistical Yearbook for Latin American and the Caribbean.*

U.C.L.A. Latin American Center Publications, University of California, Los Angeles, California 90024 (310) 825-6634; *Statistical Abstract of Latin America.*

HONDURAS - UNEMPLOYMENT

The Economist Intelligence Unit, 111 West 57th Street, New York, New York 10019 (800) 938-4685; *The New Latin America Market Atlas.*

Euromonitor Publications Limited, 87-88 Turnmill Street, London EC1M 5QU, England; *International Marketing Data and Statistics.*

International Labour Office, I.L.O. Publications, CH-1211, Geneva 22, Switzerland; *Yearbook of Labour Statistics.*

Statistical Office of the United Nations, Publishing Service, New York, New York 10017 (800) 253-9646; *Statistical Yearbook.*

U.C.L.A. Latin American Center Publications, University of California, Los Angeles, California 90024 (310) 825-6634; *Statistical Abstract of Latin America.*

HONDURAS - UTILITIES

U.C.L.A. Latin American Center Publications, University of California, Los Angeles, California 90024 (310) 825-6634; *Statistical Abstract of Latin America.*

HONDURAS - VITAL STATISTICS

Euromonitor Publications Limited, 87-88 Turnmill Street, London EC1M 5QU, England; *International Marketing Data and Statistics.*

Gale Research Incorporated, 835 Penobscot Building, Detroit, Michigan 48226 (800) 877-4253; *International Historical Statistics The Americas and Australasia.*

G.K. Hall and Company, 70 Lincoln Street, Boston, Massachusetts 02111 (617) 423-3990; *The World in Figures.*

Statistical Office of the United Nations, Publishing Service, New York, New York 10017 (800) 253-9646; *Statistical Yearbook.*

World Health Organization, Office of Publications, Avenue Appia, CH-1211 Geneva 27, Switzerland (Telephone Number in U.S. (518) 436-9686); *World Health Statistics Annual.*

HONDURAS - WAGES

Federal Statistical Office, Gustav - Stresesmann - Ring 11, D-6200 Wiesbaden, Federal Republic of Germany; *Honduras.*

G.K. Hall and Company, 70 Lincoln Street, Boston, Massachusetts 02111 (617) 423-3990; *The World in Figures.*

International Labour Office, I.L.O. Publications, CH-1211, Geneva 22, Switzerland; *Yearbook of Labour Statistics.*

Statistical Office of the United Nations, Publishing Service, New York, New York 10017 (800) 253-9646; *Statistical Yearbook.*

U.C.L.A. Latin American Center Publications, University of California, Los Angeles, California 90024 (310) 825-6634; *Statistical Abstract of Latin America.*

HONDURAS - WATERMELON PRODUCTION - See HONDURAS - CROPS

HONDURAS - WEATHER

Facts on File, 460 Park Avenue South, New York, New York 10016 (800) 443-8323; *The New Book of World Rankings.*

G.K. Hall and Company, 70 Lincoln Street, Boston, Massachusetts 02111 (617) 423-3990; *The World in Figures.*

HONDURAS - WELFARE

Inter-American Development Bank, 1300 New York Avenue, NW, Washington, D.C. 20577 (202) 623-1753; *Economic and Social Progress in Latin America.*

International Monetary Fund, 700 Nineteenth Street, NW, Washington, D.C. 20431 (202) 623-7000; *Government Finance Statistics Yearbook.*

HONDURAS - WHEAT PRODUCTION AND PRICES - See HONDURAS - CROPS

HONDURAS - WHOLESALE PRICES

Inter-American Development Bank, 1300 New York Avenue, NW, Washington, D.C. 20577 (202) 623-1753; *Economic and Social Progress in Latin America.*

HONDURAS - WHOLESALE TRADE

Inter-American Development Bank, 1300 New York Avenue, NW, Washington, D.C. 20577 (202) 623-1753; *Economic and Social Progress in Latin America.*

HONDURAS - WINE PRODUCTION

Facts on File, 460 Park Avenue South, New York, New York 10016 (800) 443-8323; *The New Book of World Rankings.*

HONDURAS - WOOD EXPORTS - See HONDURAS - FORESTRY AND FOREST PRODUCTS

HONDURAS - WOOL PRODUCTION

Facts on File, 460 Park Avenue South, New York, New York 10016 (800) 443-8323; *The New Book of World Rankings.*

HONDURAS - ZINC ORE PRODUCTION AND CONSUMPTION - See HONDURAS - MINING AND MINERAL PRODUCTS

Hong Kong - National Statistical Office

Census and Statistics Department, Wanchai Tower I, 12 Harbor Road, Wanchai, Hong Kong.

Hong Kong - Primary Statistics Source

Census and Statistics Department, Wanchai Tower I, 12 Harbor Road, Wanchai, Hong Kong; *Hong Kong Monthly Digest of Statistics, Hong Kong Annual Digest of Statistics.*

HONG KONG - AGRICULTURE

Asian Development Bank, Post Office Box 789, 1099 Manila, Philippines; *Key Indicators of Developing Asian and Pacific Countries.*

The Economist Intelligence Unit (Asia) Limited, 10th Floor, Luk Kwok Centre, 72 Gloucester Road, Wanchai, Hong Kong (Phone

Number in U.S. (800) 938-4685); *Hong Kong Market Atlas.*

Euromonitor Publications Limited, 87-88 Turnmill Street, London EC1M 5QU, England; *International Marketing Data and Statistics, The Pacific Basin: An Economic Handbook,* and *Third World Economic Handbook.*

Facts on File, 460 Park Avenue South, New York, New York 10016 (800) 443-8323; *The New Book of World Rankings.*

Federal Statistical Office, Gustav - Stresesmann - Ring 11, D-6200 Wiesbaden, Federal Republic of Germany; *Hong Kong.*

Food and Agricultural Organization of the United Nations (FAO) Via delle Terme di Caracalla, 00100 Rome, Italy (Telephone Number in U.S. (202) 653-2400); *Production Yearbook,* and *The State of Food and Agriculture.*

G.K. Hall and Company, 70 Lincoln Street, Boston, Massachusetts 02111 (617) 423-3990; *The World in Figures.*

Statistical Office of the United Nations, Publishing Service, New York, New York 10017 (800) 253-9646; *Statistical Yearbook.*

Times Books, 201 East 50th Street, New York, New York 10022 (212) 751-2600; *The Economist Book of Vital World Statistics.*

The World Bank, 1818 H Street, NW, Washington, D.C. 20433 (202) 477-1234; *World Tables.*

HONG KONG - AIRLINE SERVICE

The Economist Intelligence Unit (Asia) Limited, 10th Floor, Luk Kwok Centre, 72 Gloucester Road, Wanchai, Hong Kong (Phone Number in U.S. (800) 938-4685); *Asian Market Atlas,* and *Hong Kong Market Atlas.*

Facts on File, 460 Park Avenue South, New York, New York 10016 (800) 443-8323; *The New Book of World Rankings.*

G.K. Hall and Company, 70 Lincoln Street, Boston, Massachusetts 02111 (617) 423-3990; *The World in Figures.*

International Civil Aviation Organization, 1000 Sherbrooke Street West, Suite 400, Montreal, Quebec, Canada H3A 2R2 (514) 285-8219; *Civil Aviation Statistics of the World.*

Times Books, 201 East 50th Street, New York, New York 10022 (212) 751-2600; *The Economist Book of Vital World Statistics.*

HONG KONG - ALUMINUM PRODUCTION AND CONSUMPTION - See HONG KONG - MINING AND MINERAL PRODUCTS

HONG KONG - ANIMAL HEALTH

Food and Agricultural Organization of the United Nations (FAO), Via delle Terme di Caracalla, 00100 Rome, Italy (Telephone Number in U.S. (202) 653-2400); *Animal Health Yearbook.*

HONG KONG - AREA AND DENSITY OF POPULATION

The Economist Intelligence Unit (Asia) Limited, 10th Floor, Luk Kwok Centre, 72 Gloucester Road, Wanchai, Hong Kong (Phone Number in U.S. (800) 938-4685); *Hong Kong Market Atlas.*

Euromonitor Publications Limited, 87-88 Turnmill Street, London EC1M 5QU, England; *International Marketing Data and Statistics,* and *The Pacific Basin: An Economic Handbook.*

Facts on File, 460 Park Avenue South, New York, New York 10016 (800) 443-8323; *The New Book of World Rankings.*

Federal Statistical Office, Gustav - Stresesmann - Ring 11, D-6200 Wiesbaden, Federal Republic of Germany; *Hong Kong.*

Food and Agricultural Organization of the United Nations (FAO) Via delle Terme di Caracalla, 00100 Rome, Italy (Telephone Number in U.S. (202) 653-2400); *The State of Food and Agriculture.*

G.K. Hall and Company, 70 Lincoln Street, Boston, Massachusetts 02111 (617) 423-3990; *The World in Figures.*

Statistical Office of the United Nations, Publishing Service, New York, New York 10017 (800) 253-9646; *Statistical Yearbook.*

Times Books, 201 East 50th Street, New York, New York 10022 (212) 751-2600; *The Economist Book of Vital World Statistics.*

United Nations Educational, Scientific and Cultural Organization (UNESCO), 7 Place de Fontenoy, F-75700 Paris, France (Telephone Number in U.S. (212) 963-5981); *Statistical Yearbook.*

HONG KONG - BALANCE OF PAYMENTS

The Economist Intelligence Unit, 111 West 57th Street, New York, New York 10019 (800) 938-4685; *The World Market Atlas.*

Euromonitor Publications Limited, 87-88 Turnmill Street, London EC1M 5QU, England; *Third World Economic Handbook.*

Federal Statistical Office, Gustav - Stresesmann - Ring 11, D-6200 Wiesbaden, Federal Republic of Germany; *Hong Kong.*

G.K. Hall and Company, 70 Lincoln Street, Boston, Massachusetts 02111 (617) 423-3990; *The World in Figures.*

Times Books, 201 East 50th Street, New York, New York 10022 (212) 751-2600; *The Economist Book of Vital World Statistics.*

The World Bank, 1818 H Street, NW, Washington, D.C. 20433 (202) 477-1234; *World Tables.*

HONG KONG - BANKING

Asian Development Bank, Post Office Box 789, 1099 Manila, Philippines; *Key Indicators of Developing Asian and Pacific Countries.*

The Economist Intelligence Unit (Asia) Limited, 10th Floor, Luk Kwok Centre, 72 Gloucester Road, Wanchai, Hong Kong (Phone Number in U.S. (800) 938-4685); *Hong Kong Market Atlas.*

Facts on File, 460 Park Avenue South, New York, New York 10016 (800) 443-8323; *The New Book of World Rankings.*

G.K. Hall and Company, 70 Lincoln Street, Boston, Massachusetts 02111 (617) 423-3990; *The World in Figures.*

HONG KONG - BARLEY PRODUCTION - See HONG KONG - CROPS

HONG KONG - BEER PRODUCTION

Facts on File, 460 Park Avenue South, New York, New York 10016 (800) 443-8323; *The New Book of World Rankings.*

Statistical Office of the United Nations, Publishing Service, New York, New York 10017 (800) 253-9646; *Statistical Yearbook.*

HONG KONG - BIRTH RATES

The Economist Intelligence Unit (Asia) Limited, 10th Floor, Luk Kwok Centre, 72 Gloucester Road, Wanchai, Hong Kong (Phone Number in U.S. (800) 938-4685); *Asian Market Atlas,* and *Hong Kong Market Atlas.*

Euromonitor Publications Limited, 87-88 Turnmill Street, London EC1M 5QU, England; *The Pacific Basin: An Economic Handbook,* and *Third World Economic Handbook.*

Facts on File, 460 Park Avenue South, New York, New York 10016 (800) 443-8323; *The New Book of World Rankings.*

Statistical Office of the United Nations, Publishing Service, New York, New York 10017 (800) 253-9646; *Demographic Yearbook,* and *Statistical Yearbook.*

Times Books, 201 East 50th Street, New York, New York 10022 (212) 751-2600; *The Economist Book of Vital World Statistics.*

The World Bank, 1818 H Street, NW, Washington, D.C. 20433 (202) 477-1234; *World Tables.*

World Health Organization, Office of Publications, Avenue Appia, CH-1211 Geneva 27, Switzerland (Telephone Number in U.S. (518) 436-9686); *World Health Statistics Annual.*

HONG KONG - BONDS

Asian Development Bank, Post Office Box 789, 1099 Manila, Philippines; *Key Indicators of Developing Asian and Pacific Countries.*

G.K. Hall and Company, 70 Lincoln Street, Boston, Massachusetts 02111 (617) 423-3990; *The World in Figures.*

HONG KONG - BOOK PRODUCTION

G.K. Hall and Company, 70 Lincoln Street, Boston, Massachusetts 02111 (617) 423-3990; *The World in Figures.*

United Nations Educational, Scientific and Cultural Organization (UNESCO), 7 Place de Fontenoy, F-75700 Paris, France (Telephone Number in U.S. (212) 963-5981); *Statistical Yearbook.*

HONG KONG - BROADCASTING

Billboard Limited, Post Office Box 9027, 1006 AA Amsterdam, The Netherlands (Telephone Number in U.S. (212) 764-7300); *World Radio TV Handbook.*

The Economist Intelligence Unit (Asia) Limited, 10th Floor, Luk Kwok Centre, 72 Gloucester Road, Wanchai, Hong Kong (Phone Number in U.S. (800) 938-4685); *Asian Market Atlas.*

Facts on File, 460 Park Avenue South, New York, New York 10016 (800) 443-8323; *The New Book of World Rankings.*

G.K. Hall and Company, 70 Lincoln Street, Boston, Massachusetts 02111 (617) 423-3990; *The World in Figures.*

Times Books, 201 East 50th Street, New York, New York 10022 (212) 751-2600; *The Economist Book of Vital World Statistics.*

United Nations Educational, Scientific and Cultural Organization (UNESCO), 7 Place de Fontenoy, F-75700 Paris, France (Telephone Number in U.S. (212) 963-5981); *Statistical Yearbook.*

HONG KONG - BUILDING CONSTRUCTION

Statistical Office of the United Nations, Publishing Service, New York, New York 10017 (800) 253-9646; *Statistical Yearbook.*

HONG KONG - BUSINESS

G.K. Hall and Company, 70 Lincoln Street, Boston, Massachusetts 02111 (617) 423-3990; *The World in Figures.*

HONG KONG - CABBAGE PRODUCTION - See HONG KONG - CROPS

HONG KONG - CALORIE SUPPLY

Asian Development Bank, Post Office Box 789, 1099 Manila, Philippines; *Key Indicators of Developing Asian and Pacific Countries.*

Food and Agricultural Organization of the United Nations (FAO) Via delle Terme di Caracalla, 00100 Rome, Italy (Telephone Number in U.S. (202) 653-2400); *The State of Food and Agriculture.*

HONG KONG - CAPITAL INVESTMENT

Asian Development Bank, Post Office Box 789, 1099 Manila, Philippines; *Key Indicators of Developing Asian and Pacific Countries.*

HONG KONG - CAPITAL REVENUE

Asian Development Bank, Post Office Box 789, 1099 Manila, Philippines; *Key Indicators of Developing Asian and Pacific Countries.*

HONG KONG - CATTLE - See HONG KONG - LIVESTOCK AND POULTRY

HONG KONG - CEMENT PRODUCTION - See HONG KONG - MINING AND MINERAL PRODUCTS

HONG KONG - CHEMICAL (ORGANIC) PRODUCTION - See HONG KONG - MINING AND MINERAL PRODUCTS

HONG KONG - CHICKENS - See HONG KONG - LIVESTOCK AND POULTRY

HONG KONG - CIGAR PRODUCTION - See HONG KONG - TOBACCO PRODUCTION

HONG KONG - CIGARETTE PRODUCTION - See HONG KONG - TOBACCO PRODUCTION

HONG KONG - CLASS STRUCTURE

G.K. Hall and Company, 70 Lincoln Street, Boston, Massachusetts 02111 (617) 423-3990; *The World in Figures.*

HONG KONG - CLIMATE

The Economist Intelligence Unit (Asia) Limited, 10th Floor, Luk Kwok Centre, 72 Gloucester Road, Wanchai, Hong Kong (Phone Number in U.S. (800) 938-4685); *Hong Kong Market Atlas.*

Facts on File, 460 Park Avenue South, New York, New York 10016 (800) 443-8323; *The New Book of World Rankings.*

G.K. Hall and Company, 70 Lincoln Street, Boston, Massachusetts 02111 (617) 423-3990; *The World in Figures.*

HONG KONG - CLOTHING EXPORTS AND IMPORTS

Euromonitor Publications Limited, 87-88 Turnmill Street, London EC1M 5QU, England; *Third World Economic Handbook.*

Statistical Office of the United Nations, Publishing Service, New York, New York 10017 (800) 253-9646; *Trade in Manufactures of Developing Countries.*

HONG KONG - COAL PRODUCTION - See HONG KONG - MINING AND MINERAL PRODUCTS

HONG KONG - COFFEE PRODUCTION - See HONG KONG - CROPS

HONG KONG - COMMUNICATIONS

The Economist Intelligence Unit (Asia) Limited, 10th Floor, Luk Kwok Centre, 72 Gloucester Road, Wanchai, Hong Kong (Phone Number in U.S. (800) 938-4685); *Hong Kong Market Atlas.*

Euromonitor Publications Limited, 87-88 Turnmill Street, London EC1M 5QU, England; *Third World Economic Handbook.*

Federal Statistical Office, Gustav - Stresesmann - Ring 11, D-6200 Wiesbaden, Federal Republic of Germany; *Hong Kong.*

G.K. Hall and Company, 70 Lincoln Street, Boston, Massachusetts 02111 (617) 423-3990; *The World in Figures.*

Statistical Office of the United Nations, Publishing Service, New York, New York 10017 (800) 253-9646; *Statistical Yearbook for Asia and the Pacific.*

HONG KONG - CONSTRUCTION INDUSTRY

Facts on File, 460 Park Avenue South, New York, New York 10016 (800) 443-8323; *The New Book of World Rankings.*

Statistical Office of the United Nations, Publishing Service, New York, New York 10017 (800) 253-9646; *Construction Statistics Yearbook,* and *Statistical Yearbook.*

HONG KONG - CONSUMER PRICE INDEX

Asian Development Bank, Post Office Box 789, 1099 Manila, Philippines; *Key Indicators of Developing Asian and Pacific Countries.*

The Economist Intelligence Unit (Asia) Limited, 10th Floor, Luk Kwok Centre, 72 Gloucester Road, Wanchai, Hong Kong (Phone Number in U.S. (800) 938-4685); *Hong Kong Market Atlas.*

Federal Statistical Office, Gustav - Stresesmann - Ring 11, D-6200 Wiesbaden, Federal Republic of Germany; *Hong Kong.*

G.K. Hall and Company, 70 Lincoln Street, Boston, Massachusetts 02111 (617) 423-3990; *The World in Figures.*

Statistical Office of the United Nations, Publishing Service, New York, New York 10017 (800) 253-9646; *Statistical Yearbook.*

HONG KONG - CONSUMER PRICES

Federal Statistical Office, Gustav - Stresesmann - Ring 11, D-6200 Wiesbaden, Federal Republic of Germany; *Hong Kong.*

International Labour Office, I.L.O. Publications, CH-1211, Geneva 22, Switzerland; *Yearbook of Labour Statistics.*

HONG KONG - CONSUMPTION

The Economist Intelligence Unit (Asia) Limited, 10th Floor, Luk Kwok Centre, 72 Gloucester Road, Wanchai, Hong Kong (Phone Number in U.S. (800) 938-4685); *Hong Kong Market Atlas.*

Euromonitor Publications Limited, 87-88 Turnmill Street, London EC1M 5QU, England; *The Pacific Basin: An Economic Handbook.*

G.K. Hall and Company, 70 Lincoln Street, Boston, Massachusetts 02111 (617) 423-3990; *The World in Figures.*

HONG KONG - COPPER PRODUCTION - See HONG KONG - MINING AND MINERAL PRODUCTS

HONG KONG - CORN PRODUCTION - See HONG KONG - CROPS

HONG KONG - CORPORATE TAXES - See HONG KONG - TAXATION

HONG KONG - COTTON - See HONG KONG - CROPS

HONG KONG - CRIME

International Criminal Police Organization (INTERPOL), 26 rue Armengaud, 92210 Saint Cloud, France; *International Crime Statistics.*

Yale University Press, Yale Station, New Haven, Connecticut 06520 (203) 432-0940; *Violence and Crime in Cross-National Perspective.*

HONG KONG - CROPS

Asian Development Bank, Post Office Box 789, 1099 Manila, Philippines; *Key Indicators of Developing Asian and Pacific Countries.*

Facts on File, 460 Park Avenue South, New York, New York 10016 (800) 443-8323; *The New Book of World Rankings.*

Food and Agricultural Organization of the United Nations (FAO) Via delle Terme di Caracalla, 00100 Rome, Italy (Telephone Number in U.S. (202) 653-2400); *Production Yearbook* and *The State of Food and Agriculture.*

G.K. Hall and Company, 70 Lincoln Street, Boston, Massachusetts 02111 (617) 423-3990; *The World in Figures.*

Statistical Office of the United Nations, Publishing Service, New York, New York 10017 (800) 253-9646; *Statistical Yearbook.*

HONG KONG - CUSTOMS DUTIES

G.K. Hall and Company, 70 Lincoln Street, Boston, Massachusetts 02111 (617) 423-3990; *The World in Figures.*

HONG KONG - DAIRY PRODUCTS

The Economist Intelligence Unit (Asia) Limited, 10th Floor, Luk Kwok Centre, 72 Gloucester Road, Wanchai, Hong Kong (Phone Number in U.S. (800) 938-4685); *Hong Kong Market Atlas.*

Facts on File, 460 Park Avenue South, New York, New York 10016 (800) 443-8323; *The New Book of World Rankings.*

Food and Agricultural Organization of the United Nations (FAO), Via delle Terme di Caracalla, 00100 Rome, Italy (Telephone Number in U.S. (202) 653-2400); *Production Yearbook,* and *The State of Food and Agriculture.*

Statistical Office of the United Nations, Publishing Service, New York, New York 10017 (800) 253-9646; *Statistical Yearbook.*

HONG KONG - DEATH RATES

The Economist Intelligence Unit (Asia) Limited, 10th Floor, Luk Kwok Centre, 72 Gloucester Road, Wanchai, Hong Kong (Phone Number in U.S. (800) 938-4685); *Asian Market Atlas.*

Euromonitor Publications Limited, 87-88 Turnmill Street, London EC1M 5QU, England; *The Pacific Basin: An Economic Handbook,* and *Third World Economic Handbook.*

G.K. Hall and Company, 70 Lincoln Street, Boston, Massachusetts 02111 (617) 423-3990; *The World in Figures.*

Statistical Office of the United Nations, Publishing Service, New York, New York 10017 (800) 253-9646; *Statistical Yearbook.*

Times Books, 201 East 50th Street, New York, New York 10022 (212) 751-2600; *The Economist Book of Vital World Statistics.*

World Health Organization, Office of Publications, Avenue Appia, CH-1211 Geneva 27, Switzerland (Telephone Number in U.S. (518) 436-9686); *World Health Statistics Annual.*

HONG KONG - DEFENSE EXPENDITURES

G.K. Hall and Company, 70 Lincoln Street, Boston, Massachusetts 02111 (617) 423-3990; *The World in Figures.*

HONG KONG - DEMOGRAPHY

The Economist Intelligence Unit, 111 West 57th Street, New York, New York 10019 (800) 938-4685; *The World Market Atlas.*

The Economist Intelligence Unit (Asia) Limited, 10th Floor, Luk Kwok Centre, 72 Gloucester Road, Wanchai, Hong Kong (Phone Number in U.S. (800) 938-4685); *Asian Market Atlas,* and *Hong Kong Market Atlas.*

Facts on File, 460 Park Avenue South, New York, New York 10016 (800) 443-8323; *The New Book of World Rankings.*

Federal Statistical Office, Gustav - Stresesmann - Ring 11, D-6200 Wiesbaden, Federal Republic of Germany; *Hong Kong.*

G.K. Hall and Company, 70 Lincoln Street, Boston, Massachusetts 02111 (617) 423-3990; *The World in Figures.*

HONG KONG - DEVELOPMENT ASSISTANCE

Asian Development Bank, Post Office Box 789, 1099 Manila, Philippines; *Key Indicators of Developing Asian and Pacific Countries.*

G.K. Hall and Company, 70 Lincoln Street, Boston, Massachusetts 02111 (617) 423-3990; *The World in Figures.*

Statistical Office of the United Nations, Publishing Service, New York, New York 10017 (800) 253-9646; *Statistical Yearbook.*

HONG KONG - DIAMOND PRODUCTION - See HONG KONG - MINING AND MINERAL PRODUCTS

HONG KONG - DISEASES

G.K. Hall and Company, 70 Lincoln Street, Boston, Massachusetts 02111 (617) 423-3990; *The World in Figures.*

World Health Organization, Office of Publications, Avenue Appia, CH-1211 Geneva 27, Switzerland (Telephone Number in U.S. (518) 436-9686); *World Health Statistics Annual.*

HONG KONG - DIVORCE RATES

Facts on File, 460 Park Avenue South, New York, New York 10016 (800) 443-8323; *The New Book of World Rankings.*

Statistical Office of the United Nations, Publishing Service, New York, New York 10017 (800) 253-9646; *Demographic Yearbook,* and *Statistical Yearbook.*

HONG KONG - DOMESTIC PRODUCT

G.K. Hall and Company, 70 Lincoln Street, Boston, Massachusetts 02111 (617) 423-3990; *The World in Figures.*

HONG KONG - DUCKS - See HONG KONG - LIVESTOCK AND POULTRY

HONG KONG - ECONOMY

Asian Development Bank, Post Office Box 789, 1099 Manila, Philippines; *Key Indicators of Developing Asian and Pacific Countries.*

The Economist Intelligence Unit (Asia) Limited, 10th Floor, Luk Kwok Centre, 72 Gloucester Road, Wanchai, Hong Kong (Phone Number in U.S. (800) 938-4685); *Hong Kong Market Atlas.*

Euromonitor Publications Limited, 87-88 Turnmill Street, London EC1M 5QU, England; *International Marketing Data and Statistics,* and *Third World Economic Handbook.*

Facts on File, 460 Park Avenue South, New York, New York 10016 (800) 443-8323; *The New Book of World Rankings.*

Federal Statistical Office, Gustav - Stresesmann - Ring 11, D-6200 Wiesbaden, Federal Republic of Germany; *Hong Kong.*

G.K. Hall and Company, 70 Lincoln Street, Boston, Massachusetts 02111 (617) 423-3990; *The World in Figures.*

HONG KONG - EDUCATION

The Economist Intelligence Unit, 111 West 57th Street, New York, New York 10019 (800) 938-4685; *The World Market Atlas.*

The Economist Intelligence Unit (Asia) Limited, 10th Floor, Luk Kwok Centre, 72 Gloucester Road, Wanchai, Hong Kong (Phone Number in U.S. (800) 938-4685); *Asian Market Atlas,* and *Hong Kong Market Atlas.*

Euromonitor Publications Limited, 87-88 Turnmill Street, London EC1M 5QU, England; *The Pacific Basin: An Economic Handbook.*

Facts on File, 460 Park Avenue South, New York, New York 10016 (800) 443-8323; *The New Book of World Rankings.*

G.K. Hall and Company, 70 Lincoln Street, Boston, Massachusetts 02111 (617) 423-3990; *The World in Figures.*

Times Books, 201 East 50th Street, New York, New York 10022 (212) 751-2600; *The Economist Book of Vital World Statistics.*

United Nations Educational, Scientific and Cultural Organization (UNESCO), 7 Place de Fontenoy, F-75700 Paris, France (Telephone Number in U.S. (212) 963-5981); *Statistical Yearbook.*

The World Bank, 1818 H Street, NW, Washington, D.C. 20433 (202) 477-1234; *World Tables.*

HONG KONG - EGG PRODUCTION - See HONG KONG - DAIRY PRODUCTS

HONG KONG - ELECTRICITY

Asian Development Bank, Post Office Box 789, 1099 Manila, Philippines; *Key Indicators of Developing Asian and Pacific Countries.*

The Economist Intelligence Unit (Asia) Limited, 10th Floor, Luk Kwok Centre, 72 Gloucester Road, Wanchai, Hong Kong (Phone Number in U.S. (800) 938-4685); *Hong Kong Market Atlas.*

Facts on File, 460 Park Avenue South, New York, New York 10016 (800) 443-8323; *The New Book of World Rankings.*

Statistical Office of the United Nations, Publishing Service, New York, New York 10017; *Electric Power in Asia and the Pacific,* and *Statistical Yearbook.*

Times Books, 201 East 50th Street, New York, New York 10022 (212) 751-2600; *The Economist Book of Vital World Statistics.*

HONG KONG - EMPLOYMENT

The Economist Intelligence Unit (Asia) Limited, 10th Floor, Luk Kwok Centre, 72 Gloucester Road, Wanchai, Hong Kong (Phone Number in U.S. (800) 938-4685); *Hong Kong Market Atlas.*

Euromonitor Publications Limited, 87-88 Turnmill Street, London EC1M 5QU, England; *International Marketing Data and Statistics,* and *The Pacific Basin: An Economic Handbook.*

Facts on File, 460 Park Avenue South, New York, New York 10016 (800) 443-8323; *The New Book of World Rankings.*

Federal Statistical Office, Gustav - Stresesmann - Ring 11, D-6200 Wiesbaden, Federal Republic of Germany; *Hong Kong.*

International Labour Office, I.L.O. Publications, CH-1211, Geneva 22, Switzerland; *Yearbook of Labour Statistics.*

Statistical Office of the United Nations, Publishing Service, New York, New York 10017 (800) 253-9646; *Statistical Yearbook.*

HONG KONG - ENERGY

Facts on File, 460 Park Avenue South, New York, New York 10016 (800) 443-8323; *The New Book of World Rankings.*

Food and Agricultural Organization of the United Nations (FAO) Via delle Terme di Caracalla, 00100 Rome, Italy (Telephone Number in U.S. (202) 653-2400); *The State of Food and Agriculture.*

G.K. Hall and Company, 70 Lincoln Street, Boston, Massachusetts 02111 (617) 423-3990; *The World in Figures.*

Statistical Office of the United Nations, Publishing Service, New York, New York 10017 (800) 253-9646; *Energy Statistics Yearbook,* and *Statistical Yearbook, Statistical Yearbook for Asia and the Pacific,* and *World Energy Supplies.*

Times Books, 201 East 50th Street, New York, New York 10022 (212) 751-2600; *The Economist Book of Vital World Statistics.*

HONG KONG - ENGINEERING AND METAL PRODUCTS EXPORTS TO DEVELOPED COUNTRIES

Statistical Office of the United Nations, Publishing Service, New York, New York 10017 (800) 253-9646; *Trade in Manufactures of Developing Countries.*

HONG KONG - EXCHANGE RATES

Asian Development Bank, Post Office Box 789, 1099 Manila, Philippines; *Key Indicators of Developing Asian and Pacific Countries.*

The Economist Intelligence Unit (Asia) Limited, 10th Floor, Luk Kwok Centre, 72 Gloucester Road, Wanchai, Hong Kong (Phone Number in U.S. (800) 938-4685); *Asian Market Atlas,* and *Hong Kong Market Atlas.*

Euromonitor Publications Limited, 87-88 Turnmill Street, London EC1M 5QU, England; *International Marketing Data and Statistics,* and *The Pacific Basin: An Economic Handbook.*

International Civil Aviation Organization, 1000 Sherbrooke Street West, Suite 400, Montreal, Quebec, Canada H3A 2R2 (514) 285-8219; *Civil Aviation Statistics of the World.*

HONG KONG - EXPORTS

Asian Development Bank, Post Office Box 789, 1099 Manila, Philippines; *Key Indicators of Developing Asian and Pacific Countries.*

The Economist Intelligence Unit, 111 West 57th Street, New York, New York 10019 (800) 938-4685; *The World Market Atlas.*

The Economist Intelligence Unit (Asia) Limited, 10th Floor, Luk Kwok Centre, 72 Gloucester Road, Wanchai, Hong Kong (Phone Number in U.S. (800) 938-4685); *Asian Market Atlas,* and *Hong Kong Market Atlas.*

Euromonitor Publications Limited, 87-88 Turnmill Street, London EC1M 5QU, England; *International Marketing Data and Statistics, The Pacific Basin: An Economic Handbook,* and *Third World Economic Handbook.*

Food and Agricultural Organization of the United Nations (FAO) Via delle Terme di Caracalla, 00100 Rome, Italy (Telephone Number in U.S. (202) 653-2400); *The State of Food and Agriculture.*

G.K. Hall and Company, 70 Lincoln Street, Boston, Massachusetts 02111 (617) 423-3990; *The World in Figures.*

International Monetary Fund, 700 Nineteenth Street, NW, Washington, D.C. 20431 (202) 623-7000; *Direction of Trade Statistics.*

Statistical Office of the United Nations, Publishing Service, New York, New York 10017 (800) 253-9646; *Foreign Trade Statistics of Asia and the Pacific.*

Times Books, 201 East 50th Street, New York, New York 10022 (212) 751-2600; *The Economist Book of Vital World Statistics.*

The World Bank, 1818 H Street, NW, Washington, D.C. 20433 (202) 477-1234; *World Tables.*

HONG KONG - EXTERNAL FINANCING

Asian Development Bank, Post Office Box 789, 1099 Manila, Philippines; *Key Indicators of Developing Asian and Pacific Countries.*

HONG KONG - EXTERNAL INDEBTEDNESS

Asian Development Bank, Post Office Box 789, 1099 Manila, Philippines; *Key Indicators of Developing Asian and Pacific Countries.*

Euromonitor Publications Limited, 87-88 Turnmill Street, London EC1M 5QU, England; *Third World Economic Handbook.*

The World Bank, 1818 H Street, NW, Washington, D.C. 20433 (202) 477-1234; *World Tables.*

HONG KONG - EXTERNAL TRADE

Asian Development Bank, Post Office Box 789, 1099 Manila, Philippines; *Key Indicators of Developing Asian and Pacific Countries.*

Food and Agricultural Organization of the United Nations (FAO) Via delle Terme di Caracalla, 00100 Rome, Italy (Telephone Number in U.S. (202) 653-2400); *The State of Food and Agriculture,* and *Trade Yearbook.*

G.K. Hall and Company, 70 Lincoln Street, Boston, Massachusetts 02111 (617) 423-3990; *The World in Figures.*

Statistical Office of the United Nations, Publishing Service, New York, New York 10017 (800) 253-9646; *Statistical Yearbook,* and *Statistical Yearbook for Asia and the Pacific.*

HONG KONG - FABRIC PRODUCTION - See HONG KONG - TEXTILE INDUSTRY

HONG KONG - FARM CROPS - See HONG KONG - CROPS

HONG KONG - FEMALE WORKING POPULATION - See HONG KONG - EMPLOYMENT

HONG KONG - FERTILITY RATES

The Economist Intelligence Unit (Asia) Limited, 10th Floor, Luk Kwok Centre, 72 Gloucester Road, Wanchai, Hong Kong (Phone Number in U.S. (800) 938-4685); *Asian Market Atlas.*

Facts on File, 460 Park Avenue South, New York, New York 10016 (800) 443-8323; *The New Book of World Rankings.*

Times Books, 201 East 50th Street, New York, New York 10022 (212) 751-2600; *The Economist Book of Vital World Statistics.*

The World Bank, 1818 H Street, NW, Washington, D.C. 20433 (202) 477-1234; *World Tables.*

HONG KONG - FERTILIZER

Food and Agricultural Organization of the United Nations (FAO), Via delle Terme di Caracalla, 00100 Rome, Italy (Telephone Number in U.S. (202) 653-2400); *Fertilizer Yearbook,* and *The State of Food and Agriculture.*

HONG KONG - FETAL MORTALITY

Statistical Office of the United Nations, Publishing Service, New York, New York 10017 (800) 253-9646; *Demographic Yearbook.*

World Health Organization, Office of Publications, Avenue Appia, CH-1211 Geneva 27, Switzerland (Telephone Number in U.S. (518) 436-9686); *World Health Statistics Annual.*

HONG KONG - FILM - See HONG KONG - MOTION PICTURES

HONG KONG - FINANCE

Asian Development Bank, Post Office Box 789, 1099 Manila, Philippines; *Key Indicators of Developing Asian and Pacific Countries.*

Euromonitor Publications Limited, 87-88 Turnmill Street, London EC1M 5QU, England; *The Pacific Basin: An Economic Handbook.*

Facts on File, 460 Park Avenue South, New York, New York 10016 (800) 443-8323; *The New Book of World Rankings.*

Federal Statistical Office, Gustav - Stresesmann - Ring 11, D-6200 Wiesbaden, Federal Republic of Germany; *Hong Kong.*

G.K. Hall and Company, 70 Lincoln Street, Boston, Massachusetts 02111 (617) 423-3990; *The World in Figures.*

Statistical Office of the United Nations, Publishing Service, New York, New York 10017 (800) 253-9646; *Statistical Yearbook for Asia and the Pacific.*

HONG KONG - FISHERIES

The Economist Intelligence Unit (Asia) Limited, 10th Floor, Luk Kwok Centre, 72 Gloucester Road, Wanchai, Hong Kong (Phone Number in U.S. (800) 938-4685); *Hong Kong Market Atlas.*

Facts on File, 460 Park Avenue South, New York, New York 10016 (800) 443-8323; *The New Book of World Rankings.*

Federal Statistical Office, Gustav - Stresesmann - Ring 11, D-6200 Wiesbaden, Federal Republic of Germany; *Hong Kong.*

Food and Agricultural Organization of the United Nations (FAO) Via delle Terme di Caracalla, 00100 Rome, Italy (Telephone Number in U.S. (202) 653-2400); *The State of Food and Agriculture,* and *Yearbook of Fishery Statistics.*

Statistical Office of the United Nations, Publishing Service, New York, New York 10017 (800) 253-9646; *Statistical Yearbook.*

HONG KONG - FOOD

Food and Agricultural Organization of the United Nations (FAO), Via delle Terme di Caracalla, 00100 Rome, Italy (Telephone Number in U.S. (202) 653-2400); *Production Yearbook,* and *The State of Food and Agriculture.*

G.K. Hall and Company, 70 Lincoln Street, Boston, Massachusetts 02111 (617) 423-3990; *The World in Figures.*

Statistical Office of the United Nations, Publishing Service, New York, New York 10017 (800) 253-9646; *Statistical Yearbook for Asia and the Pacific* and *Trade in Manufactures of Developing Countries.*

HONG KONG - FOREIGN AID

G.K. Hall and Company, 70 Lincoln Street, Boston, Massachusetts 02111 (617) 423-3990; *The World in Figures.*

HONG KONG - FOREIGN INDEBTEDNESS

Euromonitor Publications Limited, 87-88 Turnmill Street, London EC1M 5QU, England; *The Pacific Basin: An Economic Handbook.*

HONG KONG - FOREIGN TRADE

Asian Development Bank, Post Office Box 789, 1099 Manila, Philippines; *Key Indicators of Developing Asian and Pacific Countries.*

The Economist Intelligence Unit (Asia) Limited, 10th Floor, Luk Kwok Centre, 72 Gloucester Road, Wanchai, Hong Kong (Phone Number in U.S. (800) 938-4685); *Asian Market Atlas,* and *Hong Kong Market Atlas.*

Euromonitor Publications Limited, 87-88 Turnmill Street, London EC1M 5QU, England; *International Marketing Data and Statistics, The Pacific Basin: An Economic Handbook,* and *Third World Economic Handbook.*

Facts on File, 460 Park Avenue South, New York, New York 10016 (800) 443-8323; *The New Book of World Rankings.*

Food and Agricultural Organization of the United Nations (FAO) Via delle Terme di Caracalla, 00100 Rome, Italy (Telephone Number in U.S. (202) 653-2400); *The State of Food and Agriculture.*

Federal Statistical Office, Gustav - Stresesmann - Ring 11, D-6200 Wiesbaden, Federal Republic of Germany; *Hong Kong.*

G.K. Hall and Company, 70 Lincoln Street, Boston, Massachusetts 02111 (617) 423-3990; *The World in Figures.*

Statistical Office of the United Nations, Publishing Service, New York, New York 10017 (800) 253-9646; *International Trade Statistics Yearbook,* and *Statistical Yearbook.*

The World Bank, 1818 H Street, NW, Washington, D.C. 20433 (202) 477-1234; *World Tables.*

HONG KONG - FORESTRY AND FOREST PRODUCTS

The Economist Intelligence Unit (Asia) Limited, 10th Floor, Luk Kwok Centre, 72 Gloucester Road, Wanchai, Hong Kong (Phone Number in U.S. (800) 938-4685); *Asian Market Atlas.*

Euromonitor Publications Limited, 87-88 Turnmill Street, London EC1M 5QU, England; *Third World Economic Handbook.*

Facts on File, 460 Park Avenue South, New York, New York 10016 (800) 443-8323; *The New Book of World Rankings.*

Federal Statistical Office, Gustav - Stresesmann - Ring 11, D-6200 Wiesbaden, Federal Republic of Germany; *Hong Kong.*

Food and Agricultural Organization of the United Nations (FAO) Via delle Terme di Caracalla, 00100 Rome, Italy (Telephone Number in U.S. (202) 653-2400); *The State of Food and Agriculture,* and *Yearbook of Forest Products.*

G.K. Hall and Company, 70 Lincoln Street, Boston, Massachusetts 02111 (617) 423-3990; *The World in Figures.*

Statistical Office of the United Nations, Publishing Service, New York, New York 10017 (800) 253-9646; *Statistical Yearbook.*

United Nations Educational, Scientific and Cultural Organization (UNESCO), 7 Place de Fontenoy, F-75700 Paris, France (Telephone Number in U.S. (212) 963-5981); *Statistical Yearbook.*

HONG KONG - FURNITURE AND WOOD PRODUCTS - EXPORTS AND IMPORTS

Statistical Office of the United Nations, Publishing Service, New York, New York 10017 (800) 253-9646; *Trade in Manufactures of Developing Countries.*

HONG KONG - GAS PRODUCTION - See HONG KONG - MINING AND MINERAL PRODUCTS

HONG KONG - GENERAL INDUSTRIAL STATISTICS

Federal Statistical Office, Gustav - Stresesmann - Ring 11, D-6200 Wiesbaden, Federal Republic of Germany; *Hong Kong.*

Statistical Office of the United Nations, Publishing Service, New York, New York 10017 (800) 253-9646; *Industrial Statistics Yearbook.*

HONG KONG - GENERAL MORTALITY

Statistical Office of the United Nations, Publishing Service, New York, New York 10017 (800) 253-9646; *Demographic Yearbook.*

World Health Organization, Office of Publications, Avenue Appia, CH-1211 Geneva 27, Switzerland (Telephone Number in U.S. (518) 436-9686); *World Health Statistics Annual.*

HONG KONG - GEOGRAPHIC DATA

Facts on File, 460 Park Avenue South, New York, New York 10016 (800) 443-8323; *The New Book of World Rankings.*

Federal Statistical Office, Gustav - Stresesmann - Ring 11, D-6200 Wiesbaden, Federal Republic of Germany; *Hong Kong.*

HONG KONG - GOLD HOLDINGS

The World Bank, 1818 H Street, NW, Washington, D.C. 20433 (202) 477-1234; *World Tables.*

HONG KONG - GOLD PRODUCTION AND CONSUMPTION - See HONG KONG - MINING AND MINERAL PRODUCTS

HONG KONG - GOVERNMENT

Asian Development Bank, Post Office Box 789, 1099 Manila, Philippines; *Key Indicators of Developing Asian and Pacific Countries.*

The Economist Intelligence Unit (Asia) Limited, 10th Floor, Luk Kwok Centre, 72 Gloucester Road, Wanchai, Hong Kong (Phone Number in U.S. (800) 938-4685); *Hong Kong Market Atlas.*

G.K. Hall and Company, 70 Lincoln Street, Boston, Massachusetts 02111 (617) 423-3990; *The World in Figures.*

HONG KONG - GOVERNMENT BONDS - See HONG KONG - BONDS

HONG KONG - GOVERNMENT EXPENDITURE

Asian Development Bank, Post Office Box 789, 1099 Manila, Philippines; *Key Indicators of Developing Asian and Pacific Countries.*

Euromonitor Publications Limited, 87-88 Turnmill Street, London EC1M 5QU, England; *Third World Economic Handbook.*

The World Bank, 1818 H Street, NW, Washington, D.C. 20433 (202) 477-1234; *World Tables.*

HONG KONG - GOVERNMENT FINANCES

Asian Development Bank, Post Office Box 789, 1099 Manila, Philippines; *Key Indicators of Developing Asian and Pacific Countries.*

HONG KONG - GOVERNMENT REVENUE

Asian Development Bank, Post Office Box 789, 1099 Manila, Philippines; *Key Indicators of Developing Asian and Pacific Countries.*

The Economist Intelligence Unit (Asia) Limited, 10th Floor, Luk Kwok Centre, 72 Gloucester Road, Wanchai, Hong Kong (Phone Number in U.S. (800) 938-4685); *Hong Kong Market Atlas.*

The World Bank, 1818 H Street, NW, Washington, D.C. 20433 (202) 477-1234; *World Tables.*

HONG KONG - GRAIN PRODUCTION - See HONG KONG - CROPS

HONG KONG - GROSS DOMESTIC PRODUCT

Asian Development Bank, Post Office Box 789, 1099 Manila, Philippines; *Key Indicators of Developing Asian and Pacific Countries.*

The Economist Intelligence Unit, 111 West 57th Street, New York, New York 10019 (800) 938-4685; *The World Market Atlas.*

The Economist Intelligence Unit (Asia) Limited, 10th Floor, Luk Kwok Centre, 72 Gloucester Road, Wanchai, Hong Kong (Phone Number in U.S. (800) 938-4685); *Asian Market Atlas,* and *Hong Kong Market Atlas.*

Euromonitor Publications Limited, 87-88 Turnmill Street, London EC1M 5QU, England; *International Marketing Data and Statistics, The Pacific Basin: An Economic Handbook,* and *Third World Economic Handbook.*

Facts on File, 460 Park Avenue South, New York, New York 10016 (800) 443-8323; *The New Book of World Rankings.*

G.K. Hall and Company, 70 Lincoln Street, Boston, Massachusetts 02111 (617) 423-3990; *The World in Figures.*

Statistical Office of the United Nations, Publishing Service, New York, New York 10017 (800) 253-9646; *Statistical Yearbook.*

Times Books, 201 East 50th Street, New York, New York 10022 (212) 751-2600; *The Economist Book of Vital World Statistics.*

The World Bank, 1818 H Street, NW, Washington, D.C. 20433 (202) 477-1234; *World Tables.*

HONG KONG - GROSS INDUSTRIAL PRODUCT

Euromonitor Publications Limited, 87-88 Turnmill Street, London EC1M 5QU, England; *Third World Economic Handbook.*

HONG KONG - GROSS NATIONAL PRODUCT

Asian Development Bank, Post Office Box 789, 1099 Manila, Philippines; *Key Indicators of Developing Asian and Pacific Countries.*

Euromonitor Publications Limited, 87-88 Turnmill Street, London EC1M 5QU, England; *International Marketing Data and Statistics,* and *Third World Economic Handbook.*

The World Bank, 1818 H Street, NW, Washington, D.C. 20433 (202) 477-1234; *World Tables.*

HONG KONG - HEALTH

The Economist Intelligence Unit (Asia) Limited, 10th Floor, Luk Kwok Centre, 72 Gloucester Road, Wanchai, Hong Kong (Phone Number in U.S. (800) 938-4685); *Asian Market Atlas,* and *Hong Kong Market Atlas.*

Euromonitor Publications Limited, 87-88 Turnmill Street, London EC1M 5QU, England; *The Pacific Basin: An Economic Handbook.*

Facts on File, 460 Park Avenue South, New York, New York 10016 (800) 443-8323; *The New Book of World Rankings.*

Federal Statistical Office, Gustav - Stresesmann - Ring 11, D-6200 Wiesbaden, Federal Republic of Germany; *Hong Kong.*

G.K. Hall and Company, 70 Lincoln Street, Boston, Massachusetts 02111 (617) 423-3990; *The World in Figures.*

Statistical Office of the United Nations, Publishing Service, New York, New York 10017 (800) 253-9646; *Statistical Yearbook.*

Times Books, 201 East 50th Street, New York, New York 10022 (212) 751-2600; *The Economist Book of Vital World Statistics.*

World Health Organization, Office of Publications, Avenue Appia, CH-1211 Geneva 27, Switzerland (Telephone Number in U.S. (518) 436-9686); *World Health Statistics Annual.*

HONG KONG - HIDE PRODUCTION

Food and Agricultural Organization of the United Nations (FAO), Via delle Terme di Caracalla, 00100 Rome, Italy (Telephone Number in U.S. (202) 653-2400); *Production Yearbook.*

HONG KONG - HIGHWAYS

The Economist Intelligence Unit (Asia) Limited, 10th Floor, Luk Kwok Centre, 72 Gloucester Road, Wanchai, Hong Kong (Phone Number in U.S. (800) 938-4685); *Asian Market Atlas.*

G.K. Hall and Company, 70 Lincoln Street, Boston, Massachusetts 02111 (617) 423-3990; *The World in Figures.*

International Road Federation, 525 School Street, SW, Washington, D.C. 20024 (202) 554-2106; *World Road Statistics.*

HONG KONG - HORSES - See HONG KONG - LIVESTOCK AND POULTRY

HONG KONG - HOURS OF WORK - See HONG KONG - EMPLOYMENT

HONG KONG - HOUSING AND HOUSING UNITS

The Economist Intelligence Unit (Asia) Limited, 10th Floor, Luk Kwok Centre, 72 Gloucester Road, Wanchai, Hong Kong (Phone Number in U.S. (800) 938-4685); *Hong Kong Market Atlas.*

Euromonitor Publications Limited, 87-88 Turnmill Street, London EC1M 5QU, England; *Third World Economic Handbook.*

Facts on File, 460 Park Avenue South, New York, New York 10016 (800) 443-8323; *The New Book of World Rankings.*

HONG KONG - ILLITERATE POPULATION

The Economist Intelligence Unit, 111 West 57th Street, New York, New York 10019 (800) 938-4685; *The World Market Atlas.*

The Economist Intelligence Unit (Asia) Limited, 10th Floor, Luk Kwok Centre, 72 Gloucester Road, Wanchai, Hong Kong (Phone Number in U.S. (800) 938-4685); *Hong Kong Market Atlas.*

G.K. Hall and Company, 70 Lincoln Street, Boston, Massachusetts 02111 (617) 423-3990; *The World in Figures.*

United Nations Educational, Scientific and Cultural Organization (UNESCO), 7 Place de Fontenoy, F-75700 Paris, France (Telephone Number in U.S. (212) 963-5981); *Statistical Yearbook.*

HONG KONG - IMPORTS

Asian Development Bank, Post Office Box 789, 1099 Manila, Philippines; *Key Indicators of Developing Asian and Pacific Countries.*

The Economist Intelligence Unit, 111 West 57th Street, New York, New York 10019 (800) 938-4685; *The World Market Atlas.*

The Economist Intelligence Unit (Asia) Limited, 10th Floor, Luk Kwok Centre, 72 Gloucester Road, Wanchai, Hong Kong (Phone Number in U.S. (800) 938-4685); *Asian Market Atlas,* and *Hong Kong Market Atlas.*

Euromonitor Publications Limited, 87-88 Turnmill Street, London EC1M 5QU, England; *International Marketing Data and Statistics, The Pacific Basin: An Economic Handbook,* and *Third World Economic Handbook.*

Food and Agricultural Organization of the United Nations (FAO) Via delle Terme di Caracalla, 00100 Rome, Italy (Telephone Number in U.S. (202) 653-2400); *The State of Food and Agriculture.*

G.K. Hall and Company, 70 Lincoln Street, Boston, Massachusetts 02111 (617) 423-3990; *The World in Figures.*

International Monetary Fund, 700 Nineteenth Street, NW, Washington, D.C. 20431 (202) 623-7000; *Direction of Trade Statistics.*

Statistical Office of the United Nations, Publishing Service, New York, New York 10017 (800) 253-9646; *Foreign Trade Statistics of Asia and the Pacific,* and *Trade in Manufactures of Developing Countries.*

Times Books, 201 East 50th Street, New York, New York 10022 (212) 751-2600; *The Economist Book of Vital World Statistics.*

The World Bank, 1818 H Street, NW, Washington, D.C. 20433 (202) 477-1234; *World Tables.*

HONG KONG - INDUSTRY

Euromonitor Publications Limited, 87-88 Turnmill Street, London EC1M 5QU, England; *Third World Economic Handbook.*

Facts on File, 460 Park Avenue South, New York, New York 10016 (800) 443-8323; *The New Book of World Rankings.*

Federal Statistical Office, Gustav - Stresesmann - Ring 11, D-6200 Wiesbaden, Federal Republic of Germany; *Hong Kong.*

G.K. Hall and Company, 70 Lincoln Street, Boston, Massachusetts 02111 (617) 423-3990; *The World in Figures.*

International Labour Office, I.L.O. Publications, CH-1211, Geneva 22, Switzerland; *Yearbook of Labour Statistics.*

Statistical Office of the United Nations, Publishing Service, New York, New York 10017 (800) 253-9646; *Statistical Yearbook for Asia and the Pacific.*

Times Books, 201 East 50th Street, New York, New York 10022 (212) 751-2600; *The Economist Book of Vital World Statistics.*

The World Bank, 1818 H Street, NW, Washington, D.C. 20433 (202) 477-1234; *World Tables.*

World Intellectual Property Organization, 34 Chemin des Colombettes, CH-1211 Geneva 20, Switzerland; *Industrial Property Statistics.*

HONG KONG - INFANT AND MATERNAL MORTALITY

The Economist Intelligence Unit (Asia) Limited, 10th Floor, Luk Kwok Centre, 72 Gloucester Road, Wanchai, Hong Kong (Phone Number in U.S. (800) 938-4685); *Asian Market Atlas,* and *Hong Kong Market Atlas.*

Statistical Office of the United Nations, Publishing Service, New York, New York 10017 (800) 253-9646; *Demographic Yearbook,* and *Statistical Yearbook.*

Times Books, 201 East 50th Street, New York, New York 10022 (212) 751-2600; *The Economist Book of Vital World Statistics.*

The World Bank, 1818 H Street, NW, Washington, D.C. 20433 (202) 477-1234; *World Tables.*

World Health Organization, Office of Publications, Avenue Appia, CH-1211 Geneva 27, Switzerland (Telephone Number in U.S. (518) 436-9686); *World Health Statistics Annual.*

HONG KONG - INTEREST RATES

Euromonitor Publications Limited, 87-88 Turnmill Street, London EC1M 5QU, England; *The Pacific Basin: An Economic Handbook.*

HONG KONG - INTERNAL TRADE

Statistical Office of the United Nations, Publishing Service, New York, New York 10017 (800) 253-9646; *Statistical Yearbook for Asia and the Pacific.*

HONG KONG - INTERNATIONAL RESERVES EXCLUDING GOLD

Asian Development Bank, Post Office Box 789, 1099 Manila, Philippines; *Key Indicators of Developing Asian and Pacific Countries.*

The World Bank, 1818 H Street, NW, Washington, D.C. 20433 (202) 477-1234; *World Tables.*

HONG KONG - INTERNATIONAL STATISTICS

Asian Development Bank, Post Office Box 789, 1099 Manila, Philippines; *Key Indicators of Developing Asian and Pacific Countries.*

HONG KONG - IRON ORE PRODUCTION AND CONSUMPTION - See HONG KONG - MINING AND MINERAL PRODUCTS

HONG KONG - IRRIGATION

Euromonitor Publications Limited, 87-88 Turnmill Street, London EC1M 5QU, England; *International Marketing Data and Statistics.*

HONG KONG - LABOR FORCE

The Economist Intelligence Unit (Asia) Limited, 10th Floor, Luk Kwok Centre, 72 Gloucester Road, Wanchai, Hong Kong (Phone Number in U.S. (800) 938-4685); *Asian Market Atlas,* and *Hong Kong Market Atlas.*

Euromonitor Publications Limited, 87-88 Turnmill Street, London EC1M 5QU, England; *International Marketing Data and Statistics,* and *The Pacific Basin: An Economic Handbook.*

Facts on File, 460 Park Avenue South, New York, New York 10016 (800) 443-8323; *The New Book of World Rankings.*

Food and Agricultural Organization of the United Nations (FAO) Via delle Terme di Caracalla, 00100 Rome, Italy (Telephone Number in U.S. (202) 653-2400); *The State of Food and Agriculture.*

G.K. Hall and Company, 70 Lincoln Street, Boston, Massachusetts 02111 (617) 423-3990; *The World in Figures.*

Times Books, 201 East 50th Street, New York, New York 10022 (212) 751-2600; *The Economist Book of Vital World Statistics.*

The World Bank, 1818 H Street, NW, Washington, D.C. 20433 (202) 477-1234; *World Tables.*

HONG KONG - LABOR PRODUCTIVITY

International Labour Office, I.L.O. Publications, CH-1211, Geneva 22, Switzerland; *Yearbook of Labour Statistics.*

HONG KONG - LAND USE

Euromonitor Publications Limited, 87-88 Turnmill Street, London EC1M 5QU, England; *International Marketing Data and Statistics.*

Food and Agricultural Organization of the United Nations (FAO), Via delle Terme di Caracalla, 00100 Rome, Italy (Telephone Number in U.S. (202) 653-2400); *Production Yearbook.*

G.K. Hall and Company, 70 Lincoln Street, Boston, Massachusetts 02111 (617) 423-3990; *The World in Figures.*

HONG KONG - LEATHER AND FOOTWEAR - EXPORTS AND IMPORTS

Statistical Office of the United Nations, Publishing Service, New York, New York 10017 (800) 253-9646; *Trade in Manufactures of Developing Countries.*

HONG KONG - LIBRARIES

Facts on File, 460 Park Avenue South, New York, New York 10016 (800) 443-8323; *The New Book of World Rankings.*

United Nations Educational, Scientific and Cultural Organization (UNESCO), 7 Place de Fontenoy, F-75700 Paris, France (Telephone Number in U.S. (212) 963-5981); *Statistical Yearbook.*

HONG KONG - LIFE EXPECTANCY

The Economist Intelligence Unit (Asia) Limited, 10th Floor, Luk Kwok Centre, 72 Gloucester Road, Wanchai, Hong Kong (Phone Number in U.S. (800) 938-4685); *Asian Market Atlas.*

HONG KONG - LIVESTOCK AND POULTRY

The Economist Intelligence Unit (Asia) Limited, 10th Floor, Luk Kwok Centre, 72 Gloucester Road, Wanchai, Hong Kong (Phone Number in U.S. (800) 938-4685); *Hong Kong Market Atlas.*

Euromonitor Publications Limited, 87-88 Turnmill Street, London EC1M 5QU, England; *Third World Economic Handbook.*

Facts on File, 460 Park Avenue South, New York, New York 10016 (800) 443-8323; *The New Book of World Rankings.*

Food and Agricultural Organization of the United Nations (FAO), Via delle Terme di Caracalla, 00100 Rome, Italy (Telephone Number in U.S. (202) 653-2400); *Production Yearbook,* and *The State of Food and Agriculture.*

G.K. Hall and Company, 70 Lincoln Street, Boston, Massachusetts 02111 (617) 423-3990; *The World in Figures.*

Statistical Office of the United Nations, Publishing Service, New York, New York 10017 (800) 253-9646; *Statistical Yearbook.*

HONG KONG - LIVING LEVELS

G.K. Hall and Company, 70 Lincoln Street, Boston, Massachusetts 02111 (617) 423-3990; *The World in Figures.*

Times Books, 201 East 50th Street, New York, New York 10022 (212) 751-2600; *The Economist Book of Vital World Statistics.*

HONG KONG - MAIL - NUMBER OF PIECES SENT OR RECEIVED

The Economist Intelligence Unit (Asia) Limited, 10th Floor, Luk Kwok Centre, 72 Gloucester Road, Wanchai, Hong Kong (Phone Number in U.S. (800) 938-4685); *Hong Kong Market Atlas.*

Statistical Office of the United Nations, Publishing Service, New York, New York 10017 (800) 253-9646; *Statistical Yearbook.*

HONG KONG - MANPOWER

Statistical Office of the United Nations, Publishing Service, New York, New York 10017 (800) 253-9646; *Statistical Yearbook for Asia and the Pacific.*

HONG KONG - MANUFACTURING

Asian Development Bank, Post Office Box 789, 1099 Manila, Philippines; *Key Indicators of Developing Asian and Pacific Countries.*

Euromonitor Publications Limited, 87-88 Turnmill Street, London EC1M 5QU, England; *Third World Economic Handbook.*

Facts on File, 460 Park Avenue South, New York, New York 10016 (800) 443-8323; *The New Book of World Rankings.*

G.K. Hall and Company, 70 Lincoln Street, Boston, Massachusetts 02111 (617) 423-3990; *The World in Figures.*

Statistical Office of the United Nations, Publishing Service, New York, New York 10017 (800) 253-9646; *Statistical Yearbook.*

Times Books, 201 East 50th Street, New York, New York 10022 (212) 751-2600; *The Economist Book of Vital World Statistics.*

The World Bank, 1818 H Street, NW, Washington, D.C. 20433 (202) 477-1234; *World Tables.*

HONG KONG - MARRIAGE RATES

Facts on File, 460 Park Avenue South, New York, New York 10016 (800) 443-8323; *The New Book of World Rankings.*

Statistical Office of the United Nations, Publishing Service, New York, New York 10017 (800) 253-9646; *Demographic Yearbook,* and *Statistical Yearbook.*

HONG KONG - MEAT PRODUCTION - See HONG KONG - LIVESTOCK AND POULTRY

HONG KONG - MERCHANT SHIPPING

G.K. Hall and Company, 70 Lincoln Street, Boston, Massachusetts 02111 (617) 423-3990; *The World in Figures.*

Lloyd's Register of Shipping, 17 Battery Place, New York, New York 10004 (212) 425-8050; *Register of Ships.*

Statistical Office of the United Nations, Publishing Service, New York, New York 10017 (800) 253-9646; *Statistical Yearbook.*

Times Books, 201 East 50th Street, New York, New York 10022 (212) 751-2600; *The Economist Book of Vital World Statistics.*

HONG KONG - MILITARY

The Economist Intelligence Unit (Asia) Limited, 10th Floor, Luk Kwok Centre, 72 Gloucester Road, Wanchai, Hong Kong (Phone Number in U.S. (800) 938-4685); *Asian Market Atlas.*

G.K. Hall and Company, 70 Lincoln Street, Boston, Massachusetts 02111 (617) 423-3990; *The World in Figures.*

HONG KONG - MILK PRODUCTION - See HONG KONG - DAIRY PRODUCTS

HONG KONG - MINING AND MINERAL PRODUCTS

Asian Development Bank, Post Office Box 789, 1099 Manila, Philippines; *Key Indicators of Developing Asian and Pacific Countries.*

The Economist Intelligence Unit (Asia) Limited, 10th Floor, Luk Kwok Centre, 72 Gloucester Road, Wanchai, Hong Kong (Phone Number in U.S. (800) 938-4685); *Hong Kong Market Atlas.*

Euromonitor Publications Limited, 87-88 Turnmill Street, London EC1M 5QU, England; *Third World Economic Handbook.*

Facts on File, 460 Park Avenue South, New York, New York 10016 (800) 443-8323; *The New Book of World Rankings.*

G.K. Hall and Company, 70 Lincoln Street, Boston, Massachusetts 02111 (617) 423-3990; *The World in Figures.*

Inter-American Development Bank, 1300 New York Avenue, NW, Washington, D.C. 20577 (202) 623-1753; *Economic and Social Progress in Latin America.*

Statistical Office of the United Nations, Publishing Service, New York, New York 10017 (800) 253-9646; *Statistical Yearbook,* and *Statistical Yearbook for Asia and the Pacific.*

The World Bank, 1818 H Street, NW, Washington, D.C. 20433 (202) 477-1234; *World Tables.*

HONG KONG - MONEY EXCHANGE RATES

Euromonitor Publications Limited, 87-88 Turnmill Street, London EC1M 5QU, England; *International Marketing Data and Statistics.*

HONG KONG - MONEY RESERVES

Euromonitor Publications Limited, 87-88 Turnmill Street, London EC1M 5QU, England; *International Marketing Data and Statistics.*

HONG KONG - MONEY SUPPLY

Asian Development Bank, Post Office Box 789, 1099 Manila, Philippines; *Key Indicators of Developing Asian and Pacific Countries.*

The Economist Intelligence Unit (Asia) Limited, 10th Floor, Luk Kwok Centre, 72 Gloucester Road, Wanchai, Hong Kong (Phone Number in U.S. (800) 938-4685); *Hong Kong Market Atlas.*

Euromonitor Publications Limited, 87-88 Turnmill Street, London EC1M 5QU, England; *International Marketing Data and Statistics.*

Federal Statistical Office, Gustav - Stresesmann - Ring 11, D-6200 Wiesbaden, Federal Republic of Germany; *Hong Kong.*

G.K. Hall and Company, 70 Lincoln Street, Boston, Massachusetts 02111 (617) 423-3990; *The World in Figures.*

The World Bank, 1818 H Street, NW, Washington, D.C. 20433 (202) 477-1234; *World Tables.*

HONG KONG - MOTION PICTURES

United Nations Educational, Scientific and Cultural Organization (UNESCO), 7 Place de Fontenoy, F-75700 Paris, France (Telephone Number in U.S. (212) 963-5981); *Statistical Yearbook.*

Statistical Office of the United Nations, Publishing Service, New York, New York 10017 (800) 253-9646; *Statistical Yearbook.*

HONG KONG - MOTOR VEHICLES IN USE

G.K. Hall and Company, 70 Lincoln Street, Boston, Massachusetts 02111 (617) 423-3990; *The World in Figures.*

International Road Federation, 525 School Street, SW, Washington, D.C. 20024 (202) 554-2106; *World Road Statistics.*

Statistical Office of the United Nations, Publishing Service, New York, New York 10017 (800) 253-9646; *Statistical Yearbook.*

Times Books, 201 East 50th Street, New York, New York 10022 (212) 751-2600; *The Economist Book of Vital World Statistics.*

HONG KONG - MUSEUMS

Facts on File, 460 Park Avenue South, New York, New York 10016 (800) 443-8323; *The New Book of World Rankings.*

United Nations Educational, Scientific and Cultural Organization (UNESCO), 7 Place de Fontenoy, F-75700 Paris, France (Telephone Number in U.S. (212) 963-5981); *Statistical Yearbook.*

HONG KONG - NATALITY - See HONG KONG - BIRTH RATES

HONG KONG - NATIONAL ACCOUNTS

Federal Statistical Office, Gustav - Stresesmann - Ring 11, D-6200 Wiesbaden, Federal Republic of Germany; *Hong Kong.*

Statistical Office of the United Nations, Publishing Service, New York, New York 10017 (800) 253-9646; *National Accounts Statistics, Statistical Yearbook,* and *Statistical Yearbook for Asia and the Pacific.*

HONG KONG - NATIONAL INCOME

Facts on File, 460 Park Avenue South, New York, New York 10016 (800) 443-8323; *The New Book of World Rankings.*

G.K. Hall and Company, 70 Lincoln Street, Boston, Massachusetts 02111 (617) 423-3990; *The World in Figures.*

Statistical Office of the United Nations, Publishing Service, New York, New York 10017 (800) 253-9646; *Statistical Yearbook.*

HONG KONG - NATIONAL PRODUCT

Facts on File, 460 Park Avenue South, New York, New York 10016 (800) 443-8323; *The New Book of World Rankings.*

Statistical Office of the United Nations, Publishing Service, New York, New York 10017 (800) 253-9646; *Statistical Yearbook.*

HONG KONG - NATURAL GAS PRODUCTION - See HONG KONG - MINING AND MINERAL PRODUCTS

HONG KONG - NEWSPAPER PRODUCTION - See HONG KONG - FORESTRY AND FOREST PRODUCTS

HONG KONG - NEWSPRINT - See HONG KONG - FORESTRY AND FOREST PRODUCTS

HONG KONG - OCCUPATIONS - See HONG KONG - LABOR FORCE

HONG KONG - PAPER - See HONG KONG -FORESTRY AND FOREST PRODUCTS

HONG KONG - PATENTS

Statistical Office of the United Nations, Publishing Service, New York, New York 10017 (800) 253-9646; *Statistical Yearbook.*

World Intellectual Property Organization, 34 Chemin des Colombettes, CH-1211 Geneva 20, Switzerland; *Industrial Property Statistics.*

HONG KONG - PEANUT PRODUCTION - See HONG KONG - CROPS

HONG KONG - PERIODICALS

United Nations Educational, Scientific and Cultural Organization (UNESCO), 7 Place de Fontenoy, F-75700 Paris, France (Telephone Number in U.S. (212) 963-5981); *Statistical Yearbook.*

HONG KONG - PESTICIDE USE

Food and Agricultural Organization of the United Nations (FAO) Via delle Terme di Caracalla, 00100 Rome, Italy (Telephone Number in U.S. (202) 653-2400); *The State of Food and Agriculture.*

HONG KONG - PETROLEUM INDUSTRY

Asian Development Bank, Post Office Box 789, 1099 Manila, Philippines; *Key Indicators of Developing Asian and Pacific Countries.*

The Economist Intelligence Unit (Asia) Limited, 10th Floor, Luk Kwok Centre, 72 Gloucester Road, Wanchai, Hong Kong (Phone Number in U.S. (800) 938-4685); *Hong Kong Market Atlas.*

Facts on File, 460 Park Avenue South, New York, New York 10016 (800) 443-8323; *The New Book of World Rankings.*

Food and Agricultural Organization of the United Nations (FAO) Via delle Terme di Caracalla, 00100 Rome, Italy (Telephone Number in U.S. (202) 653-2400); *The State of Food and Agriculture.*

G.K. Hall and Company, 70 Lincoln Street, Boston, Massachusetts 02111 (617) 423-3990; *The World in Figures.*

HONG KONG - PIGS - See HONG KONG - LIVESTOCK AND POULTRY

HONG KONG - PLASTIC AND RESIN PRODUCTION

Euromonitor Publications Limited, 87-88 Turnmill Street, London EC1M 5QU, England; *Third World Economic Handbook.*

HONG KONG - POPULATION

Asian Development Bank, Post Office Box 789, 1099 Manila, Philippines; *Key Indicators of Developing Asian and Pacific Countries.*

The Economist Intelligence Unit, 111 West 57th Street, New York, New York 10019 (800) 938-4685; *The World Market Atlas.*

The Economist Intelligence Unit (Asia) Limited, 10th Floor, Luk Kwok Centre, 72 Gloucester Road, Wanchai, Hong Kong (Phone Number in U.S. (800) 938-4685); *Asian Market Atlas,* and *Hong Kong Market Atlas.*

Euromonitor Publications Limited, 87-88 Turnmill Street, London EC1M 5QU, England; *International Marketing Data and Statistics, The Pacific Basin: An Economic Handbook,* and *Third World Economic Handbook.*

Facts on File, 460 Park Avenue South, New York, New York 10016 (800) 443-8323; *The New Book of World Rankings.*

Federal Statistical Office, Gustav - Stresesmann - Ring 11, D-6200 Wiesbaden, Federal Republic of Germany; *Hong Kong.*

Food and Agricultural Organization of the United Nations (FAO), Via delle Terme di Caracalla, 00100 Rome, Italy (Telephone Number in U.S. (202) 653-2400); *Production Yearbook.*

G.K. Hall and Company, 70 Lincoln Street, Boston, Massachusetts 02111 (617) 423-3990; *The World in Figures.*

International Labour Office, I.L.O. Publications, CH-1211, Geneva 22, Switzerland; *Yearbook of Labour Statistics.*

Statistical Office of the United Nations, Publishing Service, New York, New York 10017 (800) 253-9646; *Demographic Yearbook, Statistical Yearbook,* and *Statistical Yearbook for Asia and the Pacific.*

Times Books, 201 East 50th Street, New York, New York 10022 (212) 751-2600; *The Economist Book of Vital World Statistics.*

United Nations Educational, Scientific and Cultural Organization (UNESCO), 7 Place de Fontenoy, F-75700 Paris, France (Telephone Number in U.S. (212) 963-5981); *Statistical Yearbook.*

World Health Organization, Office of Publications, Avenue Appia, CH-1211 Geneva 27, Switzerland (Telephone Number in U.S. (518) 436-9686); *World Health Statistics Annual.*

HONG KONG - POST OFFICES

Facts on File, 460 Park Avenue South, New York, New York 10016 (800) 443-8323; *The New Book of World Rankings.*

HONG KONG - POTATO PRODUCTION - See HONG KONG - CROPS

HONG KONG - POWER PRODUCTION INDUSTRY

The Economist Intelligence Unit (Asia) Limited, 10th Floor, Luk Kwok Centre, 72 Gloucester Road, Wanchai, Hong Kong (Phone Number in U.S. (800) 938-4685); *Hong Kong Market Atlas.*

Statistical Office of the United Nations, Publishing Service, New York, New York 10017 (800) 253-9646; *Electric Power in Asia and the Pacific,* and *Statistical Yearbook.*

HONG KONG - PRICES

Asian Development Bank, Post Office Box 789, 1099 Manila, Philippines; *Key Indicators of Developing Asian and Pacific Countries.*

Facts on File, 460 Park Avenue South, New York, New York 10016 (800) 443-8323; *The New Book of World Rankings.*

Federal Statistical Office, Gustav - Stresesmann - Ring 11, D-6200 Wiesbaden, Federal Republic of Germany; *Hong Kong.*

Food and Agricultural Organization of the United Nations (FAO), Via delle Terme di Caracalla, 00100 Rome, Italy (Telephone Number in U.S. (202) 653-2400); *Production Yearbook,* and *The State of Food and Agriculture.*

G.K. Hall and Company, 70 Lincoln Street, Boston, Massachusetts 02111 (617) 423-3990; *The World in Figures.*

International Labour Office, I.L.O. Publications, CH-1211, Geneva 22, Switzerland; *Yearbook of Labour Statistics.*

HONG KONG - PRINTING AND WRITING PAPER - See HONG KONG - FORESTRY AND FOREST PRODUCTS

HONG KONG - PRODUCTION

Euromonitor Publications Limited, 87-88 Turnmill Street, London EC1M 5QU, England; *Third World Economic Handbook.*

Facts on File, 460 Park Avenue South, New York, New York 10016 (800) 443-8323; *The New Book of World Rankings.*

G.K. Hall and Company, 70 Lincoln Street, Boston, Massachusetts 02111 (617) 423-3990; *The World in Figures.*

HONG KONG - PRODUCTIVITY

Euromonitor Publications Limited, 87-88 Turnmill Street, London EC1M 5QU, England; *International Marketing Data and Statistics.*

HONG KONG - PUBLIC FINANCE

Facts on File, 460 Park Avenue South, New York, New York 10016 (800) 443-8323; *The New Book of World Rankings.*

Federal Statistical Office, Gustav - Stresesmann - Ring 11, D-6200 Wiesbaden, Federal Republic of Germany; *Hong Kong.*

HONG KONG - RADIO BROADCASTING - See HONG KONG - BROADCASTING

HONG KONG - RADIO RECEIVERS - PRODUCTION

Statistical Office of the United Nations, Publishing Service, New York, New York 10017 (800) 253-9646; *Statistical Yearbook.*

HONG KONG - RAILWAYS

G.K. Hall and Company, 70 Lincoln Street, Boston, Massachusetts 02111 (617) 423-3990; *The World in Figures.*

Jane's Information Group, Sentinel House, 163 Brighton Road, Coulsdon, Surrey CR5 2NH, England (Telephone Number in U.S. (703) 683-3700); *Jane's World Railways.*

Statistical Office of the United Nations, Publishing Service, New York, New York 10017 (800) 253-9646; *Statistical Yearbook.*

HONG KONG - RELIGION

Facts on File, 460 Park Avenue South, New York, New York 10016 (800) 443-8323; *The New Book of World Rankings.*

HONG KONG - RETAIL TRADE

The Economist Intelligence Unit (Asia) Limited, 10th Floor, Luk Kwok Centre, 72 Gloucester Road, Wanchai, Hong Kong (Phone Number in U.S. (800) 938-4685); *Hong Kong Market Atlas.*

Euromonitor Publications Limited, 87-88 Turnmill Street, London EC1M 5QU, England; *Third World Economic Handbook.*

G.K. Hall and Company, 70 Lincoln Street, Boston, Massachusetts 02111 (617) 423-3990; *The World in Figures.*

HONG KONG - RICE PRODUCTION - See HONG KONG - CROPS

HONG KONG - ROUNDWOOD PRODUCTION - See HONG KONG - FORESTRY AND FOREST PRODUCTS

HONG KONG - RUBBER PRODUCTION

Euromonitor Publications Limited, 87-88 Turnmill Street, London EC1M 5QU, England; *Third World Economic Handbook.*

Facts on File, 460 Park Avenue South, New York, New York 10016 (800) 443-8323; *The New Book of World Rankings.*

HONG KONG - SAWNWOOD PRODUCTION - See HONG KONG - FORESTRY AND FOREST PRODUCTS

HONG KONG - SENIOR CITIZENS

Facts on File, 460 Park Avenue South, New York, New York 10016 (800) 443-8323; *The New Book of World Rankings.*

HONG KONG - SCIENTISTS AND TECHNICIANS

Statistical Office of the United Nations, Publishing Service, New York, New York 10017 (800) 253-9646; *Statistical Yearbook.*

United Nations Educational, Scientific and Cultural Organization (UNESCO), 7 Place de Fontenoy, F-75700 Paris, France (Telephone Number in U.S. (212) 963-5981); *Statistical Yearbook.*

HONG KONG - SHEEP - See HONG KONG - LIVESTOCK AND POULTRY

HONG KONG - SILVER PRODUCTION AND CONSUMPTION - See HONG KONG - MINING AND MINERAL PRODUCTS

HONG KONG - SOCIAL DATA

Asian Development Bank, Post Office Box 789, 1099 Manila, Philippines; *Key Indicators of Developing Asian and Pacific Countries.*

Facts on File, 460 Park Avenue South, New York, New York 10016 (800) 443-8323; *The New Book of World Rankings.*

G.K. Hall and Company, 70 Lincoln Street, Boston, Massachusetts 02111 (617) 423-3990; *The World in Figures.*

HONG KONG - SOYBEAN PRODUCTION - See HONG KONG - CROPS

HONG KONG - STATE BUDGET REVENUE AND EXPENDITURES

Euromonitor Publications Limited, 87-88 Turnmill Street, London EC1M 5QU, England; *International Marketing Data and Statistics.*

HONG KONG - STEEL - See HONG KONG - MINING AND MINERAL PRODUCTS

HONG KONG - STOCKS - COMMODITY - MARKET PRICE - INDEX

Food and Agricultural Organization of the United Nations (FAO) Via delle Terme di Caracalla, 00100 Rome, Italy (Telephone Number in U.S. (202) 653-2400); *The State of Food and Agriculture.*

HONG KONG - SUGAR PRODUCTION - See HONG KONG - CROPS

HONG KONG - TAXATION

G.K. Hall and Company, 70 Lincoln Street, Boston, Massachusetts 02111 (617) 423-3990; *The World in Figures.*

International Road Federation, 525 School Street, SW, Washington, D.C. 20024 (202) 554-2106; *World Road Statistics.*

The World Bank, 1818 H Street, NW, Washington, D.C. 20433 (202) 477-1234; *World Tables.*

HONG KONG - TEA CONSUMPTION

Statistical Office of the United Nations, Publishing Service, New York, New York 10017 (800) 253-9646; *Statistical Yearbook.*

HONG KONG - TELEGRAPH SERVICE

Statistical Office of the United Nations, Publishing Service, New York, New York 10017 (800) 253-9646; *Statistical Yearbook.*

HONG KONG - TELEPHONES IN USE

American Telephone and Telegraph Company, 26 Parsippany Road, Whippany, New Jersey 07981 (800) 338-4038; *The World's Telephones.*

The Economist Intelligence Unit (Asia) Limited, 10th Floor, Luk Kwok Centre, 72 Gloucester Road, Wanchai, Hong Kong (Phone Number in U.S. (800) 938-4685); *Asian Market Atlas.*

Euromonitor Publications Limited, 87-88 Turnmill Street, London EC1M 5QU, England; *The Pacific Basin: An Economic Handbook,* and *Third World Economic Handbook.*

G.K. Hall and Company, 70 Lincoln Street, Boston, Massachusetts 02111 (617) 423-3990; *The World in Figures.*

Statistical Office of the United Nations, Publishing Service, New York, New York 10017 (800) 253-9646; *Statistical Yearbook.*

HONG KONG - TELEVISION BROADCASTING - See HONG KONG - BROADCASTING

HONG KONG - TELEVISION RECEIVERS - PRODUCTION

Statistical Office of the United Nations, Publishing Service, New York, New York 10017 (800) 253-9646; *Statistical Yearbook.*

HONG KONG - TEXTILE INDUSTRY

The Economist Intelligence Unit (Asia) Limited, 10th Floor, Luk Kwok Centre, 72 Gloucester Road, Wanchai, Hong Kong (Phone Number in U.S. (800) 938-4685); *Hong Kong Market Atlas.*

Euromonitor Publications Limited, 87-88 Turnmill Street, London EC1M 5QU, England; *Third World Economic Handbook.*

G.K. Hall and Company, 70 Lincoln Street, Boston, Massachusetts 02111 (617) 423-3990; *The World in Figures.*

Statistical Office of the United Nations, Publishing Service, New York, New York 10017 (800) 253-9646; *Trade in Manufactures of Developing Countries.*

HONG KONG - THEATRE

United Nations Educational, Scientific and Cultural Organization (UNESCO), 7 Place de Fontenoy, F-75700 Paris, France (Telephone Number in U.S. (212) 963-5981); *Statistical Yearbook.*

HONG KONG - TIN - INDUSTRIAL CONSUMPTION - See HONG KONG - MINING AND MINERAL PRODUCTS

HONG KONG - TOBACCO PRODUCTION

The Economist Intelligence Unit (Asia) Limited, 10th Floor, Luk Kwok Centre, 72 Gloucester Road, Wanchai, Hong Kong (Phone Number in U.S. (800) 938-4685); *Hong Kong Market Atlas.*

Euromonitor Publications Limited, 87-88 Turnmill Street, London EC1M 5QU, England; *Third World Economic Handbook.*

Facts on File, 460 Park Avenue South, New York, New York 10016 (800) 443-8323; *The New Book of World Rankings.*

Statistical Office of the United Nations, Publishing Service, New York, New York 10017 (800) 253-9646; *Statistical Yearbook.*

HONG KONG - TOURISM

The Economist Intelligence Unit (Asia) Limited, 10th Floor, Luk Kwok Centre, 72 Gloucester Road, Wanchai, Hong Kong (Phone Number in U.S. (800) 938-4685); *Hong Kong Market Atlas.*

Euromonitor Publications Limited, 87-88 Turnmill Street, London EC1M 5QU, England; *The Pacific Basin: An Economic Handbook,* and *Third World Economic Handbook.*

Facts on File, 460 Park Avenue South, New York, New York 10016 (800) 443-8323; *The New Book of World Rankings.*

Federal Statistical Office, Gustav - Stresesmann - Ring 11, D-6200 Wiesbaden, Federal Republic of Germany; *Hong Kong.*

G.K. Hall and Company, 70 Lincoln Street, Boston, Massachusetts 02111 (617) 423-3990; *The World in Figures.*

Statistical Office of the United Nations, Publishing Service, New York, New York 10017 (800) 253-9646; *Statistical Yearbook.*

Times Books, 201 East 50th Street, New York, New York 10022 (212) 751-2600; *The Economist Book of Vital World Statistics.*

World Tourism Organization, Calle Capitan Haya 42, E-28020 Madrid, Spain; *Yearbook of Tourism Statistics.*

HONG KONG - TRACTORS IN USE

Statistical Office of the United Nations, Publishing Service, New York, New York 10017 (800) 253-9646; *Statistical Yearbook.*

HONG KONG - TRADE - See HONG KONG - FOREIGN TRADE

HONG KONG - TRADEMARKS AND SERVICE MARKS

Statistical Office of the United Nations, Publishing Service, New York, New York 10017 (800) 253-9646; *Statistical Yearbook.*

World Intellectual Property Organization, 34 Chemin des Colombettes, CH-1211 Geneva 20, Switzerland; *Industrial Property Statistics.*

HONG KONG - TRANSPORTATION AND COMMUNICATIONS

The Economist Intelligence Unit (Asia) Limited, 10th Floor, Luk Kwok Centre, 72 Gloucester Road, Wanchai, Hong Kong (Phone Number in U.S. (800) 938-4685); *Asian Market Atlas,* and *Hong Kong Market Atlas.*

Euromonitor Publications Limited, 87-88 Turnmill Street, London EC1M 5QU, England; *The Pacific Basin: An Economic Handbook,* and *Third World Economic Handbook.*

Facts on File, 460 Park Avenue South, New York, New York 10016 (800) 443-8323; *The New Book of World Rankings.*

Federal Statistical Office, Gustav - Stresesmann - Ring 11, D-6200 Wiesbaden, Federal Republic of Germany; *Hong Kong.*

G.K. Hall and Company, 70 Lincoln Street, Boston, Massachusetts 02111 (617) 423-3990; *The World in Figures.*

Statistical Office of the United Nations, Publishing Service, New York, New York 10017 (800) 253-9646; *Statistical Yearbook for Asia and the Pacific.*

HONG KONG - UNEMPLOYMENT

The Economist Intelligence Unit (Asia) Limited, 10th Floor, Luk Kwok Centre, 72 Gloucester Road, Wanchai, Hong Kong (Phone Number in U.S. (800) 938-4685); *Hong Kong Market Atlas.*

Euromonitor Publications Limited, 87-88 Turnmill Street, London EC1M 5QU, England; *International Marketing Data and Statistics,* and *The Pacific Basin: An Economic Handbook.*

International Labour Office, I.L.O. Publications, CH-1211, Geneva 22, Switzerland; *Yearbook of Labour Statistics.*

Statistical Office of the United Nations, Publishing Service, New York, New York 10017 (800) 253-9646; *Statistical Yearbook.*

HONG KONG - UTILITIES

Statistical Office of the United Nations, Publishing Service, New York, New York 10017 (800) 253-9646; *Electric Power in Asia and the Pacific.*

HONG KONG - VITAL STATISTICS

Euromonitor Publications Limited, 87-88 Turnmill Street, London EC1M 5QU, England; *International Marketing Data and Statistics, The Pacific Basin: An Economic Handbook,* and *Third World Economic Handbook.*

G.K. Hall and Company, 70 Lincoln Street, Boston, Massachusetts 02111 (617) 423-3990; *The World in Figures.*

Statistical Office of the United Nations, Publishing Service, New York, New York 10017 (800) 253-9646; *Statistical Yearbook.*

World Health Organization, Office of Publications, Avenue Appia, CH-1211 Geneva 27, Switzerland (Telephone Number in U.S. (518) 436-9686); *World Health Statistics Annual.*

HONG KONG - WAGES

The Economist Intelligence Unit (Asia) Limited, 10th Floor, Luk Kwok Centre, 72 Gloucester Road, Wanchai, Hong Kong (Phone Number in U.S. (800) 938-4685); *Hong Kong Market Atlas.*

Federal Statistical Office, Gustav - Stresesmann - Ring 11, D-6200 Wiesbaden, Federal Republic of Germany; *Hong Kong.*

G.K. Hall and Company, 70 Lincoln Street, Boston, Massachusetts 02111 (617) 423-3990; *The World in Figures.*

International Labour Office, I.L.O. Publications, CH-1211, Geneva 22, Switzerland; *Yearbook of Labour Statistics.*

Statistical Office of the United Nations, Publishing Service, New York, New York 10017 (800) 253-9646; *Statistical Yearbook.*

HONG KONG - WAGES AND PRICES

Statistical Office of the United Nations, Publishing Service, New York, New York 10017 (800) 253-9646; *Statistical Yearbook for Asia and the Pacific.*

HONG KONG - WEATHER

Facts on File, 460 Park Avenue South, New York, New York 10016 (800) 443-8323; *The New Book of World Rankings.*

G.K. Hall and Company, 70 Lincoln Street, Boston, Massachusetts 02111 (617) 423-3990; *The World in Figures.*

HONG KONG - WHEAT PRODUCTION AND PRICES - See HONG KONG - CROPS

HONG KONG - WHOLESALE PRICES

Asian Development Bank, Post Office Box 789, 1099 Manila, Philippines; *Key Indicators of Developing Asian and Pacific Countries.*

HONG KONG - WHOLESALE TRADE

Euromonitor Publications Limited, 87-88 Turnmill Street, London EC1M 5QU, England; *Third World Economic Handbook.*

HONG KONG - WINE PRODUCTION

Facts on File, 460 Park Avenue South, New York, New York 10016 (800) 443-8323; *The New Book of World Rankings.*

HONG KONG - WOOD PULP PRODUCTION - See HONG KONG - FORESTRY AND FOREST PRODUCTS

HONG KONG - WOOL PRODUCTION

Facts on File, 460 Park Avenue South, New York, New York 10016 (800) 443-8323; *The New Book of World Rankings.*

HONG KONG - YARN PRODUCTION

Statistical Office of the United Nations, Publishing Service, New York, New York 10017 (800) 253-9646; *Statistical Yearbook.*

HONG KONG - ZOOS AND BOTANICAL GARDENS

United Nations Educational, Scientific and Cultural Organization (UNESCO), 7 Place de Fontenoy, F-75700 Paris, France (Telephone Number in U.S. (212) 963-5981); *Statistical Yearbook.*

HORSE - OWNERSHIP

American Veterinary Medical Association, 930 North Meacham Road, Schaumburg, Illinois 60196 (708) 605-8070; *U.S. Pet Ownership and Demographics Sourcebook.*

HORSEBACK RIDING

U.S. Department of Agriculture, Forest Service, Fourteenth Street and Independence Avenue, SW, Washington, D.C. 20250 (202) 720-3760; unpublished data.

HORSEPOWER

John A. Waring, 1320 South George Mason Drive, Arlington, Virginia 22204 (703) 521-1499; unpublished estimates.

HOSPICES

American Hospital Association, 840 North Lake Short Drive, Chicago, Illinois 60611 (312) 280-6000; *Hospital Statistics,* and *Annual Survey of Hospitals.*

U.S. Department of Health and Human Services, National Center for Health Statistics, 3700 East-West Highway, Hyattsville, Maryland 20782 (301) 436-8500; *Vital and Health Statistics.*

HOSPITALS - AVERAGE DAILY ROOM CHARGE

American Hospital Association, 840 North Lake Short Drive, Chicago, Illinois 60611 (312) 280-6000; *Hospital Statistics,* and unpublished data.

HOSPITALS - BEDS

American Hospital Association, 840 North Lake Shore Drive, Chicago, Illinois 60611 (312) 280-6000; *Hospital Statistics.*

HOSPITALS - BUILDINGS AND FLOOR SPACE

U.S. Department of Energy, Energy Information Administration, Washington, D.C. 20585 (202) 586-8800; *Commercial Buildings Characteristics.*

HOSPITALS - CHARGES AND PERSONAL EXPENDITURES FOR

U.S. Department of Health and Human Services, Health Care Financing Administration, 200 Independence Avenue, SW, Washington, D.C. 20201 (202) 245-6113; *Health Care Financing Review,* and unpublished data.

U.S. Department of Labor, Bureau of Labor Statistics, Two Massachusetts Avenue, NE, Washington, D.C. 20212 (202) 606-7828; *CPI Detailed Report,* and unpublished data.

HOSPITALS - CONSTRUCTION

F.W. Dodge Division, McGraw-Hill Information Systems Company, 1221 Avenue of the Americas, New York, New York 10020 (212) 512-2000; *Dodge Construction Potentials.*

U.S. Department of Commerce, Bureau of the Census, Suitland, Maryland 20233 (301) 763-4040; *Current Construction Reports.*

HOSPITALS - COST TO HOSPITAL PER PATIENT

American Hospital Association, 840 North Lake Shore Drive, Chicago, Illinois 60611 (312) 280-6000; *Hospital Statistics,* and unpublished data.

HOSPITALS - DIAGNOSTIC PROCEDURES

U.S. Department of Health and Human Services, National Center for Health Statistics, 3700 East-West Highway, Hyattsville, Maryland 20782 (301) 436-8500; *Vital and Health Statistics,* and unpublished data.

HOSPITALS - DISCHARGES FROM

U.S. Department of Health and Human Services, National Center for Health Statistics, 3700 East-West Highway, Hyattsville, Maryland 20782 (301) 436-8500; *Vital and Health Statistics, Health, United States,* and unpublished data.

HOSPITALS - EARNINGS

U.S. Department of Commerce, Bureau of the Census, Suitland, Maryland 20233 (301) 763-4040; *County Business Patterns*, and *Census of Service Industries*.

U.S. Department of Labor, Bureau of Labor Statistics, Two Massachusetts Avenue, NE, Washington, D.C. 20212 (202) 606-7828; *Employment and Earnings*, and Bulletins 2370 and 2429.

HOSPITALS - EMPLOYEES

American Hospital Association, 840 North Lake Shore Drive, Chicago, Illinois 60611 (312) 280-6000; *Hospital Statistics*.

U.S. Department of Commerce, Bureau of the Census, Suitland, Maryland 20233 (301) 763-4040; *County Business Patterns, Census of Service Industries*, and *Historical Statistics on Government Finances and Employment, Public Employment*.

U.S. Department of Health and Human Services, National Center for Health Statistics, 3700 East-West Highway, Hyattsville, Maryland 20782 (301) 436-8500; unpublished data.

U.S. Department of Labor, Bureau of Labor Statistics, Two Massachusetts Avenue, NE, Washington, D.C. 20212 (202) 606-7828; *Employment and Earnings, Monthly Labor Review*, and Bulletins 2370 and 2429.

HOSPITALS - ESTABLISHMENTS

American Hospital Association, 840 North Lake Shore Drive, Chicago, Illinois 60611 (312) 280-6000; *Hospital Statistics*.

U.S. Department of Commerce, Bureau of the Census, Suitland, Maryland 20263 (301) 763-4040; *County Business Patterns*, and *Census of Service Industries*.

U.S. Department of Health and Human Services, National Center for Health Statistics, 3700 East-West Highway, Hyattsville, Maryland 20782 (301) 436-8500; unpublished data.

U.S. Department of Health and Human Services, Office of Human Development Services, 200 Independence Avenue, SW, Washington, D.C. 20201 (202) 245-7246; *Residents in Public Institutions for the Mentally Retarded*, and unpublished data.

HOSPITALS - FINANCES

American Hospital Association, 840 North Lake Shore Drive, Chicago, Illinois 60611 (312) 280-6000; *Hospital Statistics*.

National Restaurant Association, 1200 17th Street, NW, Washington, D.C. 20036 (202) 331-5900; *Food Service Numbers: A Statistical Digest for the Food Service Industry, National Restaurant Association Food Service Industry Forecast*, and *Food Service Industry in Review*.

U.S. Department of Commerce, Bureau of the Census, Suitland, Maryland 20233 (301) 763-4040; *Census of Service Industries, Current Business Reports*, and *Service Annual Survey*.

HOSPITALS - GRANTS - FOUNDATIONS

The Foundation Center, 79 Fifth Avenue, New York, New York 10003 (212) 620-4230; *Foundation Grants Index*.

HOSPITALS - INSURANCE - BENEFITS

U.S. Department of Health and Human Services, Health Care Financing Administration, 200 Independence Avenue, SW, Washington, D.C. 20201 (202) 245-6113; *Health Care Financing Review*, and unpublished data.

U.S. Department of Health and Human Services, Social Security Administration, 6401 Security Boulevard, Baltimore, Maryland 21235 (410) 965-1234; *Social Security Bulletin, Annual Statistical Supplement to the Social Security Bulletin*, and *Annual Report of Board of Trustees, OASI, DI, HI, and SMI Trust Funds*.

HOSPITALS - INSURANCE - MEDICARE PROGRAM

U.S. Department of Health and Human Services, Health Care Financing Administration, 200 Independence Avenue, SW, Washington, D.C. 20201 (202) 245-6113; *Health Care Financing Review, Medicare Program Statistics*, and unpublished data.

U.S. Department of Health and Human Services, Social Security Administration, 6401 Security Boulevard, Baltimore, Maryland 21235 (410) 965-1234; *Social Security Bulletin*, and *Annual Statistical Supplement to the Social Security Bulletin*.

HOSPITALS - MENTAL HOSPITALS

American Hospital Association, 640 North Lake Shore Drive, Chicago, Illinois 60611 (312) 280-6000; *Hospital Statistics*, and unpublished data.

U.S. Department of Commerce, Bureau of the Census, Suitland, Maryland 20233 (301) 763-4040; *Census of Population, General Population Characteristics*.

U.S. Department of Health and Human Service, Center for Mental Health Services, 5600 Fishers Lane, Rockville, Maryland 20857 (301) 443-4797; unpublished data.

HOSPITALS - NATIONAL EXPENDITURES

U.S. Department of Health and Human Services, Health Care Financing Administration, 200 Independence Avenue, SW, Washington, D.C. 20201 (202) 245-6113; *Health Care Financing Review*.

HOSPITALS - OCCUPANCY RATE

American Hospital Association, 840 North Lake Shore Drive, Chicago, Illinois 60611 (312) 280-6000; *Hospital Statistics*.

HOSPITALS - OUTPATIENT VISITS

American Hospital Association, 840 North Lake Shore Drive, Chicago, Illinois 60611 (312) 280-6000; *Hospital Statistics*.

HOSPITALS - PATIENTS

American Hospital Association, 840 North Lake Shore Drive, Chicago, Illinois 60611 (312) 280-6000; *Hospital Statistics*.

U.S. Department of Commerce, Bureau of the Census, Suitland, Maryland 20233 (301) 763-4040; *Census of Population, General Population Characteristics*.

U.S. Department of Health and Human Services, National Center for Health Statistics, 3700 East-West Highway, Hyattsville, Maryland 20782 (301) 436-8500; unpublished data.

HOSPITALS - PUBLIC EXPENDITURES

U.S. Department of Health and Human Services, Health Care Financing Administration, 200 Independence Avenue, SW, Washington, D.C. 20201 (202) 245-6113; *Health Care Financing Review.*

HOSPITALS - PUBLIC EXPENDITURES - COUNTY GOVERNMENTS

U.S. Department of Commerce, Bureau of the Census, Suitland, Maryland 20233 (301) 763-4040; *County Government Finances.*

HOSPITALS - PUBLIC EXPENDITURES - STATE GOVERNMENTS

U.S. Department of Commerce, Bureau of the Census, Suitland, Maryland 20233 (301) 763-4040; *Historical Statistics on Governmental Finances and Employment,* and *State Government Finances.*

HOSPITALS - RECEIPTS

U.S. Department of Commerce, Bureau of the Census, Suitland, Maryland 20233 (301) 763-4040; *Census of Service Industries, Current Business Reports, Service Annual Survey,* and unpublished data.

HOSPITALS - REGISTERED NURSES

American Hospital Association, 840 North Lake Shore Drive, Chicago, Illinois 60611 (312) 280-6000; *Report of the Hospital Nursing Personnel Survey.*

HOSPITALS - SERVICES PROVIDED

American Hospital Association, 840 North Lake Shore Drive, Chicago, Illinois 60611 (312) 280-6000; *Hospital Statistics,* and *Annual Survey of Hospitals.*

HOSPITALS - STATES

American Hospital Association, 840 North Lake Shore Drive, Chicago, Illinois 60611 (312) 280-6000; *Hospital Statistics,* and unpublished data.

HOSPITALS - SURGERY

American Hospital Association, 840 North Lake Shore Drive, Chicago, Illinois 60611 (312) 280-6000; *Hospital Statistics,* and unpublished data from the Annual Survey of Hospitals.

U.S. Department of Health and Human Services, National Center for Health Statistics, 3700 East-West Highway, Hyattsville, Maryland 20782 (301) 436-8500; *Vital and Health Statistics,* and unpublished data.

HOSPITALS - SURGERY - ORGAN TRANSPLANTS

American Hospital Association, 840 North Lake Shore Drive, Chicago, Illinois 60611 (312) 280-6000; *Hospital Statistics,* and *Annual Survey of Hospitals.*

U.S. Department of Health and Human Services, Public Health Service, Division of Organ Transplantation, 200 Independence Avenue, SW, Washington, D.C. 20201 (202) 619-1296; American Association of Tissue Banks, 1350 Beverly Road, Suite 220-A, McLean, Virginia 22101 (703) 827-9582; and Eye Bank Association of America, 1001 Connecticut Avenue, NW, Suite 601, Washington, D.C. 20036-5504 (202) 775-4999; unpublished data.

HOSPITALS - USE - ADMISSIONS AND PATIENT DAYS

American Hospital Association, 840 North Lake Shore Drive, Chicago, Illinois 60611 (312) 280-6000; *Hospital Statistics,* and unpublished data.

U.S. Department of Health and Human Services, National Center for Health Statistics, 3700 East-West Highway, Hyattsville, Maryland 20782 (301) 436-8500; *Vital and Health Statistics, Health, United States,* and unpublished data.

HOSPITALS - VETERANS - EXPENDITURES AND PATIENTS

U.S. Department of Health and Human Service, Center for Mental Health Services, 5600 Fishers Lane, Rockville, Maryland 20857 (301) 443-4797; unpublished data.

U.S. Department of Veterans Affairs, 810 Vermont Avenue, NW, Washington, D.C. 20420 (202) 233-2300; *Annual Report of Administrator of Veterans Affairs, Directory of VA Facilities,* and unpublished data.

HOTELS AND OTHER LODGING PLACES - BUILDINGS AND FLOOR SPACE

U.S. Department of Energy, Energy Information Administration, 1000 Independence Avenue, SW, Washington, D.C. 20585 (202) 586-8800; *Commercial Buildings Characteristics.*

HOTELS AND OTHER LODGING PLACES - EARNINGS

U.S. Department of Commerce, Bureau of the Census, Suitland, Maryland 20233 (301) 763-4040; *Census of Service Industries,* and *County Business Patterns.*

U.S. Department of Labor, Bureau of Labor Statistics, Two Massachusetts Avenue, NE, Washington, D.C. 20212 (202) 606-7828; *Employment and Earnings,* and Bulletins 2370 and 2429.

HOTELS AND OTHER LODGING PLACES - ESTABLISHMENTS

International Franchise Association, 1350 New York Avenue, Suite 900, Washington, D.C. 20005 (202) 628-8000; *Franchising in the Economy.*

U.S. Department of Commerce, Bureau of the Census, Suitland, Maryland 20233 (301) 763-4040; *Census of Service Industries,* and *County Business Patterns.*

HOTELS AND OTHERS LODGING PLACES - GROSS DOMESTIC PRODUCT

U.S. Department of Commerce, Bureau of Economic Analysis, Fourteenth Street between Constitution Avenue and E Street, NW, Washington, D.C. 20230 (202) 606-9900; *The National Income and Product Accounts of the United States,* and *Survey of Current Business.*

HOTELS AND OTHER LODGING PLACES - NEW CONSTRUCTION

U.S. Department of Commerce, Bureau of the Census, Suitland, Maryland 20233 (301) 763-4040; *Current Construction Reports.*

HOTELS AND OTHER LODGING PLACES - OCCUPATIONAL SAFETY

U.S. Department of Labor, Bureau of Labor Statistics, Two Massachusetts Avenue, NE, Washington, D.C. 20212 (202) 606-7828; *Occupational Injuries and Illnesses in the U.S. by Industry.*

HOTELS AND OTHER LODGING PLACES - PRODUCTIVITY

U.S. Department of Labor, Bureau of Labor Statistics, Two Massachusetts Avenue, NE, Washington, D.C. 20212 (202) 606-7828; *Productivity Measures for Selected Industries and Government Services,* and unpublished data.

HOTELS AND OTHER LODGING PLACES - RECEIPTS

International Franchise Association, 1350 New York Avenue, Suite 900, Washington, D.C. 20005 (202) 628-8000; *Franchising in the Economy.*

National Restaurant Association, 1200 Seventh Street, NW, Washington, D.C. 20036 (202) 331-5900; *Food Service Industry in Review, National Restaurant Association Food Service Industry Forecast,* and *Food Service Numbers: A Statistical Digest for the Food Service Industry.*

U.S. Department of Commerce, Bureau of the Census, Suitland, Maryland 20233 (301) 763-4040; *Census of Service Industries,* and *Current Business Reports.*

HOUSE OF REPRESENTATIVES

Congressional Quarterly, Incorporated, 1414 Twenty-second Street, NW, Washington, D.C 20006 (202) 887-8500; *Congressional Quarterly Weekly Report,* and *Vital Statistics on Congress.*

Elections Research Center, 5508 Greystone Street, Chevy Chase, Maryland 20815 (202) 659-9490; *America Votes.*

U.S. Congress, Joint Committee on Printing, North Capitol and H Streets, NW, Washington, D.C. 20510 (202) 224-3121; *Congressional Record, Daily Calendar, Congressional Directory,* and unpublished data.

HOUSEHOLD WORKERS - See DOMESTIC SERVICE

HOUSEHOLDS OR FAMILIES - See also HOUSING AND HOUSING UNITS

U.S. Department of Commerce, Bureau of the Census, Suitland, Maryland 20233 (301) 763-4040; *Current Population Reports, Census of Population,* and unpublished data.

HOUSEHOLDS OR FAMILIES - AGE OF HOUSEHOLDER

U.S. Department of Commerce, Bureau of the Census, Suitland, Maryland 20233 (301) 763-4040; *Current Population Reports,* and unpublished data.

HOUSEHOLDS OR FAMILIES - AMERICAN INDIAN, ESKIMO, AND ALEUT POPULATION

U.S. Department of Commerce, Bureau of the Census, Suitland, Maryland 20233 (301) 763-4040; *Current Population Reports.*

HOUSEHOLDS OR FAMILIES - ASIAN AND PACIFIC ISLANDER POPULATION

U.S. Department of Commerce, Bureau of the Census, Suitland, Maryland 20233 (301) 763-4040; *Current Population Reports.*

HOUSEHOLDS OR FAMILIES - AUTOMOBILES - OWNERSHIP

U.S. Department of Energy, Energy Information Administration, 1000 Independence Avenue, SW, Washington, D.C. 20585 (202) 586-8800; *Housing Characteristics,* and *Household Vehicles Energy Consumption.*

HOUSEHOLDS OR FAMILIES - BLACK POPULATION

U.S. Department of Commerce, Bureau of the Census, Suitland, Maryland 20233 (301) 763-4040; *Current Population Reports, Census of Population,* and unpublished data.

HOUSEHOLDS OR FAMILIES - CHARACTERISTICS

U.S. Department of Commerce, Bureau of the Census, Suitland, Maryland 20233 (301) 763-4040; *Current Population Reports, Census of Population,* and unpublished data.

HOUSEHOLDS OR FAMILIES - CHILDREN UNDER 18 YEARS OLD

U.S. Department of Commerce, Bureau of the Census, Suitland, Maryland 20233 (301) 763-4040; *Current Population Reports, Census of Population,* and unpublished data.

HOUSEHOLDS OR FAMILIES - CRIMINAL VICTIMIZATION

U.S. Department of Justice, Bureau of Justice Statistics, 633 Indiana Avenue, NW, Washington, D.C. 20531 (800) 732-3277; *Crime and the Nation's Households.*

HOUSEHOLDS OR FAMILIES - EARNINGS - FAMILY TYPE

U.S. Department of Labor, Bureau of Labor Statistics, Two Massachusetts Avenue, NE, Washington, D.C. 20212 (202) 606-7828; *Employment and Earnings,* and Bulletin 2307.

HOUSEHOLDS OR FAMILIES - EDUCATIONAL ATTAINMENT

U.S. Department of Commerce, Bureau of the Census, Suitland, Maryland 20233 (301) 763-4040; *Current Population Reports.*

HOUSEHOLDS OR FAMILIES - ELDERLY

U.S. Department of Commerce, Bureau of the Census, Suitland, Maryland 20233 (301) 763-4040; *Current Population Reports,* and unpublished data.

HOUSEHOLDS OR FAMILIES - FEMALE HOUSEHOLDER

U.S. Department of Commerce, Bureau of the Census, Suitland, Maryland 20233 (301) 763-4040; *Census of Population, Current Population Reports,* and unpublished data.

HOUSEHOLDS OR FAMILIES - FLOW OF FUNDS

Board of Governors of the Federal Reserve System, Twentieth Street and Constitution Avenue, NW, Washington, D.C. 20551 (202) 452-3000; *Annual Statistical Digest.*

HOUSEHOLDS OR FAMILIES - HISPANIC ORIGIN POPULATION

U.S. Department of Commerce, Bureau of the Census, Suitland, Maryland 20233 (301) 763-4040; *Current Population Reports, Census of Population, Persons of Spanish Origin,* and unpublished data.

HOUSEHOLDS OR FAMILIES - INCOME

Congressional Budget Office, Second and D Streets, SW, Washington, D.C. 20515 (202) 226-2621; *Trends in Family Income.*

U.S. Department of Commerce, Bureau of the Census, Suitland, Maryland 20233 (301) 763-4040; *Census of Population, Current Population Reports,* and unpublished data.

HOUSEHOLDS OR FAMILIES - INCOME - AGE OF HOUSEHOLDER

U.S. Department of Commerce, Bureau of the Census, Suitland, Maryland 20233 (301) 763-4040; *Current Population Reports,* and unpublished data.

HOUSEHOLDS OR FAMILIES - INCOME - AMERICAN INDIAN, ESKIMO, ALEUT POPULATION

U.S. Department of Commerce, Bureau of the Census, Suitland, Maryland 20233 (301) 763-4040; *Current Population Reports.*

HOUSEHOLDS OR FAMILIES - INCOME - ASIAN AND PACIFIC ISLANDER POPULATION

U.S. Department of Commerce, Bureau of the Census, Suitland, Maryland 20233 (301) 763-4040; *Current Population Reports.*

HOUSEHOLDS OR FAMILIES - INCOME - BELOW POVERTY LEVEL

Congressional Budget Office, 2nd and D Streets, SW, Washington, D.C. 20515 (202) 226-2621; *Trends in Family Income.*

U.S. Department of Commerce, Bureau of the Census, Suitland, Maryland 20233 (301) 763-4040; *Current Population Reports,* and unpublished data.

HOUSEHOLDS OR FAMILIES - INCOME - BLACK POPULATION

U.S. Department of Commerce, Bureau of the Census, Suitland, Maryland 20233 (301) 763-4040; *Current Population Reports,* and unpublished data.

HOUSEHOLDS OR FAMILIES - INCOME - BY TYPE OF HOUSEHOLD

U.S. Department of Commerce, Bureau of the Census, Suitland, Maryland 20233 (301) 763-4040; *Current Population Reports,* and unpublished data.

HOUSEHOLDS OR FAMILIES - INCOME - DISTRIBUTION

U.S. Department of Commerce, Bureau of the Census, Suitland, Maryland 20233 (301) 763-4040; *Current Population Reports.*

HOUSEHOLDS OR FAMILIES - INCOME - EDUCATIONAL ATTAINMENT

U.S. Department of Commerce, Bureau of the Census, Suitland, Maryland 20233 (301) 763-4040; *Current Population Reports.*

HOUSEHOLDS OR FAMILIES - INCOME - ELDERLY

U.S. Department of Commerce, Bureau of the Census, Suitland, Maryland 20233 (301) 763-4040; *Current Population Reports,* and unpublished data.

HOUSEHOLDS OR FAMILIES - INCOME - HISPANIC ORIGIN POPULATION

U.S. Department of Commerce, Bureau of the Census, Suitland, Maryland 20233 (301) 763-4040; *Current Population Reports,* and unpublished data.

HOUSEHOLDS OR FAMILIES - INCOME - HUSBAND-WIFE FAMILIES

U.S. Department of Commerce, Bureau of the Census, Suitland, Maryland 20233 (301) 763-4040; *Current Population Reports.*

HOUSEHOLDS OR FAMILIES - INCOME - MULTIMEDIA USERS

Mediamark Research, Incorporated, 708 Third Avenue, New York, New York 10017 (212) 599-0444; *Multimedia Audiences.*

HOUSEHOLDS OR FAMILIES - INCOME - POVERTY

Congressional Budget Office, 2nd and D Street, SW, Washington, D.C. 20515 (202) 226-2621; *Trends in Family Income.*

U.S. Department of Commerce, Bureau of the Census, Suitland, Maryland 20233 (301) 763-4040; *Current Population Reports, Census of Population,* and unpublished data.

HOUSEHOLDS OR FAMILIES - INCOME - TENURE

U.S. Department of Commerce, Bureau of the Census, Suitland, Maryland 20233 (301) 763-4040; *Current Population Reports.*

HOUSEHOLDS OR FAMILIES - INCOME - TYPE OF FAMILY

U.S. Department of Commerce, Bureau of the Census, Suitland, Maryland 20233 (301) 763-4040; *Current Population Reports,* and unpublished data.

HOUSEHOLDS OR FAMILIES - INTERRACIAL MARRIED COUPLES

U.S. Department of Commerce, Bureau of the Census, Suitland, Maryland 20233 (301) 763-4040; *Current Population Reports, Census of Population,* and unpublished data.

HOUSEHOLDS OR FAMILIES - LIVING ARRANGEMENTS

U.S. Department of Commerce, Bureau of the Census, Suitland, Maryland 20233 (301) 763-4040; *Current Population Reports, Census of Population,* and unpublished data.

HOUSEHOLDS OR FAMILIES - MARITAL STATUS OF HOUSEHOLDER

U.S. Department of Commerce, Bureau of the Census, Suitland, Maryland 20233 (301) 763-4040; *Current Population Reports,* and unpublished data.

HOUSEHOLDS OR FAMILIES - MOTOR VEHICLES - AVAILABLE

U.S. Department of Energy, Energy Information Administration, Washington, D.C. 20585 (202) 586-8800; *Household Vehicles Energy Consumption.*

HOUSEHOLDS OR FAMILIES - PERSONS LIVING ALONE - ONE PERSON HOUSEHOLDS

U.S. Department of Commerce, Bureau of the Census, Suitland, Maryland 20233 (301) 763-4040; *Census of Population, Current Population Reports,* and unpublished data.

HOUSEHOLDS OR FAMILIES - PERSONS IN HOUSEHOLDS

U.S. Department of Commerce, Bureau of the Census, Suitland, Maryland 20233 (301) 763-4040; *Current Population Reports*, and unpublished data.

HOUSEHOLDS OR FAMILIES - POVERTY

Congressional Budget Office, Second and D Streets, SW, Washington, D.C. 20515 (202) 226-2621; *Trends in Family Income*.

U.S. Department of Commerce, Bureau of the Census, Suitland, Maryland 20233 (301) 763-4040; *Current Population Reports*, and *Census of Population*.

HOUSEHOLDS OR FAMILIES - POVERTY - AMERICAN INDIAN, ESKIMO, ALEUT POPULATION

U.S. Department of Commerce, Bureau of the Census, Suitland, Maryland 20233 (301) 763-4040; *Current Population Reports*.

HOUSEHOLDS OR FAMILIES - POVERTY - ASIAN AND PACIFIC ISLANDER POPULATION

U.S. Department of Commerce, Bureau of the Census, Suitland, Maryland 20233 (301) 763-4040; *Current Population Reports*.

HOUSEHOLDS OR FAMILIES - POVERTY - BLACK POPULATION

U.S. Department of Commerce, Bureau of the Census, Suitland, Maryland 20233 (301) 763-4040; *Current Population Reports*.

HOUSEHOLDS OR FAMILIES - POVERTY - HISPANIC ORIGIN POPULATION

U.S. Department of Commerce, Bureau of the Census, Suitland, Maryland 20233 (301) 763-4040; *Current Population Reports*.

HOUSEHOLDS OR FAMILIES - PUBLIC ASSISTANCE TO FAMILIES

U.S. Department of Commerce, Bureau of the Census, Suitland, Maryland 20233 (301) 763-4040; *Current Population Reports*.

U.S. Library of Congress, Congressional Research Service, 10 First Street, NE, Washington, D.C. 20540 (202) 707-5000; *Cash and Non-Cash Benefits for Persons with Limited Income: Eligibility Rules, Recipient and Expenditure Data*.

HOUSEHOLDS OR FAMILIES - RACE

U.S. Department of Commerce, Bureau of the Census, Suitland, Maryland 20233 (301) 763-4040; *Current Population Reports*.

HOUSEHOLDS OR FAMILIES - REGION OF HOUSEHOLDER

U.S. Department of Commerce, Bureau of the Census, Suitland, Maryland 20233 (301) 763-4040; *Census of Population, Current Population Reports*, and unpublished data.

HOUSEHOLDS OR FAMILIES - SIZE

U.S. Department of Commerce, Bureau of the Census, Suitland, Maryland 20233 (301) 763-4040; *Current Population Reports*, and *United States Census of Population*.

HOUSEHOLDS OR FAMILIES - STATES

U.S. Department of Commerce, Bureau of the Census, Suitland, Maryland 20233 (301) 763-4040; *Census of Population, Current Population Reports*, and unpublished data.

HOUSEHOLDS OR FAMILIES - TAXES PAID

U.S. Department of Commerce, Bureau of the Census, Suitland, Maryland 20233 (301) 763-4040; *Current Population Reports*, and unpublished data.

HOUSEHOLDS OR FAMILIES - TYPES - MALE HOUSEHOLDER

U.S. Department of Commerce, Bureau of the Census, Suitland, Maryland 20233 (301) 763-4040; *Current Population Reports, Census of Population*, and unpublished data.

HOUSEHOLDS OR FAMILIES - TYPES - MARRIED COUPLES WITH OR WITHOUT OWN HOUSEHOLD

U.S. Department of Commerce, Bureau of the Census, Suitland, Maryland 20233 (301) 763-4040; *Census of Population, Current Population Reports*, and unpublished data.

HOUSEHOLDS OR FAMILIES - TYPES - NON-FAMILY

U.S. Department of Commerce, Bureau of the Census, Suitland, Maryland 20233 (301) 763-4040; *Census of Population, Current Population Reports*, and unpublished data.

HOUSEHOLDS OR FAMILIES - TYPES - ONE-PERSON HOUSEHOLDS

U.S. Department of Commerce, Bureau of the Census, Suitland, Maryland 20233 (301) 763-4040; *Census of Population, Current Population Reports*, and unpublished data.

HOUSEKEEPING SUPPLIES EXPENDITURES

U.S. Department of Labor, Bureau of Labor Statistics, Two Massachusetts Avenue, NE, Washington, D.C. 20212 (202) 606-7828; *Consumer Expenditure Survey*.

HOUSING AND HOUSEHOLD OPERATIONS - PRICE INDEXES

U.S. Department of Commerce. Bureau of Economic Analysis, Fourteenth Street between Constitution Avenue and E Street, NW, Washington, D.C. 20230 (202) 606-9900; *The National Income and Product Accounts of the United States*, and *Survey of Current Business*.

HOUSING AND HOUSING UNITS - See also HOUSEHOLDS OR FAMILIES

HOUSING AND HOUSING UNITS - AGE OF HOUSING STOCKS

U.S. Department of Commerce, Bureau of Economic Analysis, Fourteenth Street between Constitution Avenue and E Street, NW, Washington, D.C. 20230 (202) 606-9900; *Fixed Reproducible Tangible Wealth in the United States*, and *Survey of Current Business*.

U.S. Department of Commerce, Bureau of the Census, Suitland, Maryland 20233 (301) 763-4040; *Census of Housing, General Housing Characteristics, Detailed Housing Characteristics, Census of Population and Housing*, and *Current Housing Reports*.

HOUSING AND HOUSING UNITS - BUILDING PERMIT VALUE

U.S. Department of Commerce, Bureau of the Census, Suitland, Maryland 20233 (301) 763-4040; *Construction Reports*, and unpublished data.

HOUSING AND HOUSING UNITS - CAPITAL

U.S. Department of Commerce, Bureau of Economic Analysis, Fourteenth Street between Constitution Avenue and E Street, NW, Washington, D.C. 20230 (202) 606-9900; *Fixed Reproducible Tangible Wealth in the United States*, and *Survey of Current Business*.

HOUSING AND HOUSING UNITS - CONDOMINIUMS

U.S. Department of Commerce, Bureau of Economic Analysis, Fourteenth Street between Constitution Avenue and E Street, NW, Washington, D.C. 20230 (202) 606-9900; *Fixed Reproducible Tangible Wealth in the United States*, and *Survey of Current Business*.

U.S. Department of Commerce, Bureau of the Census, Suitland, Maryland 20233 (301) 763-4040; *Construction Reports*, *Current Housing Reports*, and *Census of Population and Housing*.

HOUSING AND HOUSING UNITS - CONSTRUCTION - APARTMENTS COMPLETED AND RENTED

U.S. Department of Commerce, Bureau of the Census, Suitland, Maryland 20233 (301) 763-4040; *Current Housing Reports*, and unpublished data.

HOUSING AND HOUSING UNITS - CONSTRUCTION - COST INDEXES

U.S. Department of Commerce, International Trade Administration, Fourteenth Street between Constitution Avenue and E Street, NW, Washington, D.C. 20230 (202) 482-3809; *Construction Review*.

HOUSING AND HOUSING UNITS - CONSTRUCTION - NEW UNITS

National Association of Home Builders of the U.S., 1201 Fifteenth Street, NW, Washington, D.C. 20005 (202) 822-0200; *Forecast of Housing Activity*.

U.S. Department of Commerce, Bureau of the Census, Suitland, Maryland 20233 (301) 763-4040; *Construction Reports*.

HOUSING AND HOUSING UNITS - CONSTRUCTION - VALUE

F.W. Dodge Division, McGraw-Hill Information Systems Company, 1221 Avenue of the Americas, New York, New York 10020 (212) 512-2000; *Dodge Construction Potentials*.

U.S. Department of Commerce, Bureau of the Census, Suitland, Maryland 20233 (301) 763-4040; *Construction Reports*.

HOUSING AND HOUSING UNITS - CONSUMER EXPENDITURES

U.S. Department of Labor, Bureau of Labor Statistics, Two Massachusetts Avenue, NE, Washington, D.C. 20212 (202) 606-7828; *Consumer Expenditure Survey*.

HOUSING AND HOUSING UNITS - CONSUMER PRICE INDEXES

U.S. Department of Labor, Bureau of Labor Statistics, Two Massachusetts Avenue, NE, Washington, D.C. 20212 (202) 606-7828; *CPI Detailed Report*, *Monthly Labor Review*, and *Handbook of Labor Statistics*.

HOUSING AND HOUSING UNITS - CONSUMER PRICE INDEXES - FOREIGN COUNTRIES

International Monetary Fund, 700 Nineteenth Street, NW, Washington, D.C. 20431 (202) 623-7000; *International Financial Statistics*.

HOUSING AND HOUSING UNITS - ELDERLY

U.S. Department of Commerce, Bureau of the Census, Suitland, Maryland 20233 (301) 763-4040; *Census of Housing*, *General Housing Characteristics*, *Detailed Housing Characteristics*, and *Census of Population and Housing*.

U.S. Department of Housing and Urban Development, 451 Seventh Street, SW, Washington, D.C. 20410 (202) 708-1422; unpublished data.

HOUSING AND HOUSING UNITS - ENERGY - CHARACTERISTICS

U.S. Department of Commerce, Bureau of the Census, Suitland, Maryland 20233 (301) 763-4040; *Current Construction Reports*, and *Characteristics of New Housing*.

HOUSING AND HOUSING UNITS - ENERGY - CONSUMPTION

U.S. Department of Energy, Energy Information Administration, Washington, D.C. 20585 (202) 586-8800; *State Energy Data Report*, *Monthly Energy Review*, *Annual Energy Review*, and *Household Energy Consumption and Expenditures*.

HOUSING AND HOUSING UNITS - ENERGY - EXPENDITURES

U.S. Department of Energy, Energy Information Administration, Washington, D.C. 20585 (202) 586-8800; *State Energy Price and Expenditure Report*, and *Household Energy Consumption and Expenditures*.

HOUSING AND HOUSING UNITS - FARM

U.S. Department of Commerce, Bureau of Economic Analysis, Fourteenth Street between Constitution Avenue and E Street, NW, Washington, D.C. 20230 (202) 606-9900; *Survey of Current Business*.

HOUSING AND HOUSING UNITS - FIRES AND PROPERTY LOSS

National Fire Protection Association, One Batterymarch Park, Quincy, Massachusetts 02169 (617) 770-3000; *NFPA Reports on U.S. Fire Loss*, in *NFPA Journal*.

HOUSING AND HOUSING UNITS - GOVERNMENT EXPENDITURES

U.S. Department of Commerce, Bureau of the Census, Suitland, Maryland 20233 (301) 763-4040; *City Government Finances*, *Government Finances*, *Historical Statistics on Governmental Finances and Employment*, and *State Government Finances*.

HOUSING AND HOUSING UNITS - GROSS HOUSING PRODUCT

U.S. Department of Commerce, Bureau of Economic Analysis, Fourteenth Street between Constitution Avenue and E Street, NW, Washington, D.C. 20230 (202) 606-9900; *The National Income and Product Accounts of the United States*, and *Survey of Current*

Business, July issues.

HOUSING AND HOUSING UNITS - HEATING EQUIPMENT USED

U.S. Department of Commerce, Bureau of the Census, Suitland, Maryland 20233 (301) 763-4040; *Census of Housing, Detailed Housing Characteristics*, and *Current Housing Reports*.

HOUSING AND HOUSING UNITS - LOANS AND MORTGAGES

Board of Governors of the Federal Reserve System, Twentieth Street and Constitution Avenue, NW, Washington, D.C. 20551 (202) 452-3000; *Federal Reserve Bulletin*, and *Domestic Offices, Commercial Bank Assets and Liability, Consolidated Report of Condition*.

Federal Housing Finance Board, 1777 F Street, NW, Washington, D.C. 20006 (202) 408-2500; annual and monthly press releases.

Mortgage Bankers Association of America, 1125 Fifteenth Street, NW, Washington, D.C. 20005 (202) 861-6500; *National Delinquency Survey*.

U.S. Department of Commerce, Bureau of the Census, Suitland, Maryland 20233 (301) 763-4040; *Current Construction Reports, Characteristics of New Housing*, and *New One-Family Houses Sold*.

U.S. Department of Housing and Urban Development, 451 Seventh Street, SW, Washington, D.C. 20410 (202) 708-1422; monthly and quarterly press releases based on the *Survey of Mortgage Lending Activity*.

HOUSING AND HOUSING UNITS - LOANS AND MORTGAGES - FEDERAL HOUSING ADMINISTRATION (FHA)

U.S. Department of Commerce, Bureau of the Census, Suitland, Maryland 20233 (301) 763-4040; *Current Construction Reports, Characteristics of New Housing*, and *New One-Family Houses Sold*.

HOUSING AND HOUSING UNITS - LOANS AND MORTGAGES - VETERANS ADMINISTRATION (VA)

U.S. Department of Commerce, Bureau of the Census, Suitland, Maryland 20233 (301) 763-4040; *Current Construction Reports, Characteristics of New Housing*, and *New One-Family Houses Sold*.

U.S. Department of Veterans Affairs, 810 Vermont Avenue, NW, Washington, D.C. 20420 (202) 233-2300; *Annual Report of the Secretary of Veterans Affairs*.

HOUSING AND HOUSING UNITS - MAINTENANCE AND REPAIR EXPENDITURES

U.S. Department of Commerce, Bureau of the Census, Suitland, Maryland 20233 (301) 763-4040; *Current Construction Reports*.

HOUSING AND HOUSING UNITS - MOBILE HOMES

U.S. Department of Commerce, Bureau of Economic Analysis, Fourteenth Street between Constitution Avenue and E Street, NW, Washington, D.C. 20230 (202) 606-9900; *Survey of Current Business*, and *Fixed Reproducible Tangible Wealth in the U.S.*

U.S. Department of Commerce, Bureau of the Census, Suitland, Maryland 20233 (301) 763-4040; *Current Construction Reports*.

HOUSING AND HOUSING UNITS - NEW PRIVATELY-OWNED HOMES - CHARACTERISTICS

U.S. Department of Commerce, Bureau of the Census, Suitland, Maryland 20233 (301) 763-4040; *Current Construction Reports*.

HOUSING AND HOUSING UNITS - PRICES - OR COSTS

National Association of Realtors, 430 North Michigan Avenue, Chicago, Illinois 60611 (312) 329-8200; *Real Estate Outlook: Market Trends and Insights*.

U.S. Department of Commerce, Bureau of the Census, Suitland, Maryland 20233 (301) 763-4040; *Current Construction Reports, Characteristics of New Housing*, and *New One-Family Houses Sold*.

U.S. Department of Commerce, International Trade Administration, Fourteenth Street between Constitution Avenue and E Street, NW, Washington, D.C. 20230 (202) 482-3809; *Construction Review*.

HOUSING AND HOUSING UNITS - PUBLIC HOUSING - LOW-RENT UNITS

U.S. Department of Commerce, Bureau of the Census, Suitland, Maryland 20233 (301) 763-4040; *Current Population Reports*, and unpublished data.

U.S. Department of Housing and Urban Development, 451 Seventh Street, SW, Washington, D.C. 20410 (202) 708-1422; unpublished data.

HOUSING AND HOUSING UNITS - PUBLIC HOUSING - LOW-RENT UNITS - EXPENDITURES - FEDERAL AND STATE

U.S. Library of Congress, 101 Independence Avenue, SE, Washington, D.C. 20540 (202) 707-5000; *Cash and Non-Cash Benefits for Persons With Limited Income: Eligibility Rules, Recipient and Expenditure Data*.

U.S. Department of Health and Human Services, Social Security Administration, 6401 Security Boulevard, Baltimore, Maryland 21235 (410) 965-1234; *Social Security Bulletin*.

HOUSING AND HOUSING UNITS - PUBLIC HOUSING - LOW-RENT UNITS - FEDERAL AID TO STATE AND LOCAL GOVERNMENTS

U.S. Department of Commerce, Bureau of the Census, Suitland, Maryland 20233 (301) 763-4040; *Federal Expenditures by State for Fiscal Year*.

HOUSING AND HOUSING UNITS - RECENT HOME BUYERS - CHARACTERISTICS

Chicago Title Insurance Company, 111 West Washington Street, Chicago, Illinois 60602 (312) 630-2000; *The Guarantor*.

HOUSING AND HOUSING UNITS - RENT - RENTAL VALUE

U.S. Department of Agriculture, Economic Research Service, Fourteenth Street and Independence Avenue, SW, Washington, D.C. 20005-4789 (202) 219-1504; *Economic Indicators of the Farm Sector: National Financial Survey*.

U.S. Department of Commerce, Bureau of the Census, Suitland, Maryland 20233 (301) 763-4040; *Current Housing Reports, Census of Housing, Detailed Housing Characteristics*, and *Census of Population and Housing*.

HOUSING AND HOUSING UNITS - RENTER-OCCUPIED

U.S. Department of Commerce, Bureau of the Census, Suitland, Maryland 20233 (301) 763-4040; *Current Housing Reports, Census of Housing,* and unpublished data.

HOUSING AND HOUSING UNITS - SALES

National Association of Realtors, 430 North Michigan Avenue, Chicago, Illinois 60611 (312) 392-8200; *Real Estate Outlook: Market Trends and Insights.*

U.S. Department of Commerce, Bureau of the Census, Suitland, Maryland 20233 (301) 763-4040; *Current Construction Reports, Characteristics of New Housing,* and *New One-Family Houses Sold and For Sale.*

HOUSING AND HOUSING UNITS - STRUCTURAL TYPE

U.S. Department of Commerce, Bureau of the Census, Suitland, Maryland 20233 (301) 763-4040; *Current Construction Reports, Census of Housing,* and *Current Housing Reports.*

HOUSING AND HOUSING UNITS - TENURE

U.S. Department of Commerce, Bureau of the Census, Suitland, Maryland 20233 (301) 763-4040; *Census of Population and Housing, Current Housing Reports, Census of Housing, General Housing Characteristics,* and *Current Population Reports.*

HOUSING AND HOUSING UNITS - VACANCIES

U.S. Department of Commerce, Bureau of the Census, Suitland, Maryland 20233 (301) 763-4040; *Current Housing Reports.*

HOUSING AND HOUSING UNITS - VALUE

U.S. Department of Commerce, Bureau of Economic Analysis, Fourteenth Street between Constitution Avenue and E Street, NW, Washington, D.C. 20230 (202) 606-9900; *The National Income and Product Accounts of the United States,* and *Survey of Current Business,* July issues.

U.S. Department of Commerce, Bureau of the Census, Suitland, Maryland 20233 (301) 763-4040; *Census of Population and Housing, Census of Housing, Detailed Housing Characteristics,* and *Current Housing Reports.*

HOUSING AND HOUSING UNITS - YEAR BUILT

U.S. Department of Commerce, Bureau of the Census, Suitland, Maryland 20233 (301) 763-4040; *Current Housing Reports,* and *Census of Housing.*

U.S. Department of Energy, Energy Information Administration, 1000 Independence Avenue, SW, Washington, D.C. 20585 (202) 586-8800; *Household Energy Consumption and Expenditures.*

HOUSING AND URBAN DEVELOPMENT DEPARTMENT OF - EMPLOYMENT

U.S. Office of Personnel Management, 1900 E Street, NW, Washington, D.C. 20415 (202) 606-1800; *Federal Civilian Workforce Statistics, Employment and Trends.*

HOUSING AND URBAN DEVELOPMENT DEPARTMENT OF - FEDERAL AID TO STATE AND LOCAL GOVERNMENTS

Executive Office of the President, Office of Management and Budget, Executive Office Building, Washington, D.C. 20503 (202) 395-3080; *Historical Tables, Budget of the United States Government,* and *Budget of the U.S. Government.*

U.S. Department of Commerce, Bureau of the Census, Suitland, Maryland 20233 (301) 763-4040; *Federal Expenditures by State for Fiscal Year.*

HOUSING AND URBAN DEVELOPMENT DEPARTMENT OF - LOW-RENT HOUSING UNITS

U.S. Department of Housing and Urban Development, 451 Seventh Street, SW, Washington, D.C. 20410 (202) 708-1422; unpublished data.

HUMAN IMMUNODEFICIENCY VIRUS (HIV) INFECTION

U.S. Department of Health and Human Services, Center for Disease Control, 1600 Clifton Road, NE, Atlanta, Georgia 30333 (404) 639-3311; *Summary of Notifiable Diseases, United States, Morbidity and Mortality Weekly Report, Surveillance Report,* and unpublished data.

U.S. Department of Health and Human Services, National Center for Health Statistics, 3700 East-West Highway, Hyattsville, Maryland 20782 (301) 436-8500; *Health, United States, Vital Statistics of the U.S., Monthly Vital Statistics Report,* and unpublished data.

HUMIDIFIERS

U.S. Department of Energy, Energy Information Administration, Washington, D.C. 20585 (202) 586-8800; *Housing Characteristics.*

Hungary - National Statistical Office

Kozponti Statisztikai Hivatal (Central Statistical Office), Post Office Box 51 Keleti Karoly Utca 5-7, 1525 Budapest 11, Hungary.

Hungary - Primary Statistics Sources

Kozponti Statisztikai Hivatal, Post Office Box 51, Keleti Karoly Utca 5-7, 1525 Budapest 11, Hungary; *Statisztikai evkonyv* (Statistical Yearbook); *Statisztikai havi kozlemenyek* (Monthly Statistical Bulletin); and *Statistical Pocketbook of Hungary.*

HUNGARY - ABORTIONS

Statistical Office of the United Nations, Publishing Service, New York, New York 10017 (800) 253-9646; *Demographic Yearbook.*

HUNGARY - AGRICULTURE

Columbia University Press, 562 West 113th Street, New York, New York 10014 (212) 316-7100; *East European and Soviet Data Book.*

Facts on File, 460 Park Avenue South, New York, New York 10016 (800) 443-8323; *The New Book of World Rankings.*

Federal Statistical Office, Gustav - Stresesmann - Ring 11, D-6200 Wiesbaden, Federal Republic of Germany; *Ungarn.*

Food and Agricultural Organization of the United Nations (FAO), Via delle Terme di Caracalla, 00100 Rome, Italy (Telephone Number in U.S. (202) 653-2400); *Production Yearbook, The State of Food and Agriculture,* and *Trade Yearbook.*

G.K. Hall and Company, 70 Lincoln Street, Boston, Massachusetts 02111 (617) 423-3990; *The World in Figures.*

Hungarian Statistical Office, 1033 Budapest, III, Kaszasdulo U.2.; *Hungary Statistical Yearbook.*

Statistical Office of the United Nations, Publishing Service, New York, New York 10017 (800) 253-9646; *Statistical Yearbook.*

Times Books, 201 East 50th Street, New York, New York 10022 (212) 751-2600; *The Economist Book of Vital World Statistics.*

The World Bank, 1818 H Street, NW, Washington, D.C. 20433 (202) 477-1234; *World Tables.*

HUNGARY - AIRLINE SERVICE

Facts on File, 460 Park Avenue South, New York, New York 10016 (800) 443-8323; *The New Book of World Rankings.*

G.K. Hall and Company, 70 Lincoln Street, Boston, Massachusetts 02111 (617) 423-3990; *The World in Figures.*

International Civil Aviation Organization, 1000 Sherbrooke Street West, Suite 400, Montreal, Quebec, Canada H3A 2R2 (514) 285-8219; *Civil Aviation Statistics of the World.*

Statistical Office of the United Nations, Publishing Service, New York, New York 10017 (800) 253-9646; *Statistical Yearbook.*

Times Books, 201 East 50th Street, New York, New York 10022 (212) 751-2600; *The Economist Book of Vital World Statistics.*

HUNGARY - ALMOND PRODUCTION - See HUNGARY - CROPS

HUNGARY - ALUMINUM PRODUCTION AND CONSUMPTION - See HUNGARY - MINING AND MINERAL PRODUCTS

HUNGARY - ANIMAL HEALTH

Food and Agricultural Organization of the United Nations (FAO), Via delle Terme di Caracalla, 00100 Rome, Italy (Telephone Number in U.S. (202) 653-2400); *Animal Health Yearbook.*

HUNGARY - AREA AND DENSITY OF POPULATION

Facts on File, 460 Park Avenue South, New York, New York 10016 (800) 443-8323; *The New Book of World Rankings.*

Federal Statistical Office, Gustav - Stresesmann - Ring 11, D-6200 Wiesbaden, Federal Republic of Germany; *Ungarn.*

Food and Agricultural Organization of the United Nations (FAO) Via delle Terme di Caracalla, 00100 Rome, Italy (Telephone Number in U.S. (202) 653-2400); *The State of Food and Agriculture.*

G.K. Hall and Company, 70 Lincoln Street, Boston, Massachusetts 02111 (617) 423-3990; *The World in Figures.*

Statistical Office of the United Nations, Publishing Service, New York, New York 10017 (800) 253-9646; *Statistical Yearbook.*

Times Books, 201 East 50th Street, New York, New York 10022 (212) 751-2600; *The Economist Book of Vital World Statistics.*

United Nations Educational, Scientific and Cultural Organization (UNESCO), 7 Place de Fontenoy, F-75700 Paris, France (Telephone Number in U.S. (212) 963-5981); *Statistical Yearbook.*

HUNGARY - ARMS EXPORTS AND IMPORTS

U.S. Arms Control and Disarmament Agency, 320 Twenty-first Street, Northwest, Washington, D.C. 20451 (202) 647-8677; *World Military Expenditures and Arms Transfers.*

HUNGARY - BALANCE OF PAYMENTS

The Economist Intelligence Unit, 111 West 57th Street, New York, New York 10019 (800) 938-4685; *The World Market Atlas.*

Federal Statistical Office, Gustav - Stresesmann - Ring 11, D-6200 Wiesbaden, Federal Republic of Germany; *Ungarn.*

G.K. Hall and Company, 70 Lincoln Street, Boston, Massachusetts 02111 (617) 423-3990; *The World in Figures.*

International Monetary Fund, 700 Nineteenth Street, NW, Washington, D.C. 20431 (202) 623-7000; *International Financial Statistics,* and *Balance of Payments Yearbook.*

Times Books, 201 East 50th Street, New York, New York 10022 (212) 751-2600; *The Economist Book of Vital World Statistics.*

The World Bank, 1818 H Street, NW, Washington, D.C. 20433 (202) 477-1234; *World Tables.*

HUNGARY - BANKING

Facts on File, 460 Park Avenue South, New York, New York 10016 (800) 443-8323; *The New Book of World Rankings.*

G.K. Hall and Company, 70 Lincoln Street, Boston, Massachusetts 02111 (617) 423-3990; *The World in Figures.*

International Monetary Fund, 700 Nineteenth Street, NW, Washington, D.C. 20431 (202) 623-7000; *International Financial Statistics.*

HUNGARY - BARLEY PRODUCTION - See HUNGARY - CROPS

HUNGARY - BAUXITE PRODUCTION AND CONSUMPTION - See HUNGARY - MINING AND MINERAL PRODUCTS

HUNGARY - BEER PRODUCTION

Facts on File, 460 Park Avenue South, New York, New York 10016 (800) 443-8323; *The New Book of World Rankings.*

Statistical Office of the United Nations, Publishing Service, New York, New York 10017 (800) 253-9646; *Statistical Yearbook.*

HUNGARY - BIRTH RATE

Facts on File, 460 Park Avenue South, New York, New York 10016 (800) 443-8323; *The New Book of World Rankings.*

Statistical Office of the United Nations, Publishing Service, New York, New York 10017 (800) 253-9646; *Demographic Yearbook,* and *Statistical Yearbook.*

Times Books, 201 East 50th Street, New York, New York 10022 (212) 751-2600; *The Economist Book of Vital World Statistics.*

The World Bank, 1818 H Street, NW, Washington, D.C. 20433 (202) 477-1234; *World Tables.*

HUNGARY - BONDS

G.K. Hall and Company, 70 Lincoln Street, Boston, Massachusetts 02111 (617) 423-3990; *The World in Figures.*

HUNGARY - BOOK PRODUCTION

Euromonitor Publications Limited, 87-88 Turnmill Street, London EC1M 5QU, England; *European Marketing Data and Statistics.*

G.K. Hall and Company, 70 Lincoln Street, Boston, Massachusetts 02111 (617) 423-3990; *The World in Figures.*

United Nations Educational, Scientific and Cultural Organization (UNESCO), 7 Place de Fontenoy, F-75700 Paris, France (Telephone Number in U.S. (212) 963-5981); *Statistical Yearbook.*

HUNGARY - BROADCASTING

Billboard Limited, Post Office Box 9027, 1006 AA Amsterdam, The Netherlands (Telephone Number in U.S. (212) 764-7300); *World Radio TV Handbook.*

Facts on File, 460 Park Avenue South, New York, New York 10016 (800) 443-8323; *The New Book of World Rankings.*

G.K. Hall and Company, 70 Lincoln Street, Boston, Massachusetts 02111 (617) 423-3990; *The World in Figures.*

Times Books, 201 East 50th Street, New York, New York 10022 (212) 751-2600; *The Economist Book of Vital World Statistics.*

United Nations Educational, Scientific and Cultural Organization (UNESCO), 7 Place de Fontenoy, F-75700 Paris, France (Telephone Number in U.S. (212) 963-5981); *Statistical Yearbook.*

HUNGARY - BUILDING CONSTRUCTION - See HUNGARY - CONSTRUCTION INDUSTRY

HUNGARY - BUSINESS

G.K. Hall and Company, 70 Lincoln Street, Boston, Massachusetts 02111 (617) 423-3990; *The World in Figures.*

HUNGARY - BUTTER PRODUCTION - See HUNGARY - DAIRY PRODUCTS

HUNGARY - CABBAGE PRODUCTION - See HUNGARY - CROPS

HUNGARY - CALORIE SUPPLY

Food and Agricultural Organization of the United Nations (FAO) Via delle Terme di Caracalla, 00100 Rome, Italy (Telephone Number in U.S. (202) 653-2400); *The State of Food and Agriculture.*

HUNGARY - CATTLE - See HUNGARY - LIVESTOCK AND POULTRY

HUNGARY - CAULIFLOWER PRODUCTION - See HUNGARY - CROPS

HUNGARY - CEMENT PRODUCTION - See HUNGARY - MINING AND MINERAL PRODUCTS

HUNGARY - CEREAL PRODUCTION - See HUNGARY - CROPS

HUNGARY - CHEESE PRODUCTION - See HUNGARY - DAIRY PRODUCTS

HUNGARY - CHEMICAL (ORGANIC) PRODUCTION - See HUNGARY - MINING AND MINERAL PRODUCTS

HUNGARY - CHESTNUT PRODUCTION - See HUNGARY - CROPS

HUNGARY - CIGAR PRODUCTION - See HUNGARY - TOBACCO PRODUCTION

HUNGARY - CIGARETTE PRODUCTION - See HUNGARY - TOBACCO PRODUCTION

HUNGARY - CLASS STRUCTURE

Columbia University Press, 562 West 113th Street, New York, New York 10014 (212) 316-7100; *East European and Soviet Data Book.*

G.K. Hall and Company, 70 Lincoln Street, Boston, Massachusetts 02111 (617) 423-3990; *The World in Figures.*

HUNGARY - CLIMATE

Facts on File, 460 Park Avenue South, New York, New York 10016 (800) 443-8323; *The New Book of World Rankings.*

G.K. Hall and Company, 70 Lincoln Street, Boston, Massachusetts 02111 (617) 423-3990; *The World in Figures.*

HUNGARY - COAL PRODUCTION - See HUNGARY - MINING AND MINERAL PRODUCTS

HUNGARY - COFFEE PRODUCTION AND CONSUMPTION - See HUNGARY - CROPS

HUNGARY - COKE OVEN COKE PRODUCTION AND CONSUMPTION - See HUNGARY - MINING AND MINERAL PRODUCTS

HUNGARY - COMMUNICATIONS

Federal Statistical Office, Gustav - Stresesmann - Ring 11, D-6200 Wiesbaden, Federal Republic of Germany; *Ungarn.*

G.K. Hall and Company, 70 Lincoln Street, Boston, Massachusetts 02111 (617) 423-3990; *The World in Figures.*

Hungarian Statistical Office, 1033 Budapest, III, Kaszasdulo U.2.; *Hungary Statistical Yearbook.*

HUNGARY - CONSTRUCTION INDUSTRY

Facts on File, 460 Park Avenue South, New York, New York 10016 (800) 443-8323; *The New Book of World Rankings.*

Hungarian Statistical Office, 1033 Budapest, III, Kaszasdulo U.2.; *Hungary Statistical Yearbook.*

Statistical Office of the United Nations, Publishing Service, New York, New York 10017 (800) 253-9646; *Construction Statistics Yearbook,* and *Statistical Yearbook.*

HUNGARY - CONSUMER PRICE INDEX

Federal Statistical Office, Gustav - Stresesmann - Ring 11, D-6200 Wiesbaden, Federal Republic of Germany; *Ungarn.*

G.K. Hall and Company, 70 Lincoln Street, Boston, Massachusetts 02111 (617) 423-3990; *The World in Figures.*

Statistical Office of the United Nations, Publishing Service, New York, New York 10017 (800) 253-9646; *Statistical Yearbook.*

HUNGARY - CONSUMER PRICES

Euromonitor Publications Limited, 87-88 Turnmill Street, London EC1M 5QU, England; *European Marketing Data and Statistics.*

Federal Statistical Office, Gustav - Stresesmann - Ring 11, D-6200 Wiesbaden, Federal Republic of Germany; *Ungarn.*

International Labour Office, I.L.O. Publications, CH-1211, Geneva 22, Switzerland; *Yearbook of Labour Statistics.*

International Monetary Fund, 700 Nineteenth Street, NW, Washington, D.C. 20431 (202) 623-7000; *International Financial Statistics.*

Times Books, 201 East 50th Street, New York, New York 10022 (212) 751-2600; *The Economist Book of Vital World Statistics.*

HUNGARY - CONSUMPTION

G.K. Hall and Company, 70 Lincoln Street, Boston, Massachusetts 02111 (617) 423-3990; *The World in Figures.*

International Lead and Zinc Study Group, Metro House, 58 St. James's Street, London SW1A 1LD, England; *Lead and Zinc Statistics.*

International Rubber Study Group, York House, 8th Floor, Empire Way, Wembley, London HA9 0PA, England; *Rubber Statistical Bulletin.*

HUNGARY - COPPER AND COPPER ORE - See HUNGARY - MINING AND MINERAL PRODUCTS

HUNGARY - CORN PRODUCTION - See HUNGARY - CROPS

HUNGARY - CORPORATE TAXES - See HUNGARY - TAXATION

HUNGARY - COTTON - See HUNGARY - CROPS

HUNGARY - CRIME

International Criminal Police Organization (INTERPOL), 26 rue Armengaud, 92210 Saint Cloud, France; *International Crime Statistics.*

Yale University Press, Yale Station, New Haven, Connecticut 06520 (203) 432-0940; *Violence and Crime in Cross-National Perspective.*

HUNGARY - CROPS

Commodity Research Bureau, Incorporated, 75 Wall Street, New York, New York 10005 (212) 504-7754; *Commodity Year Book.*

Euromonitor Publications Limited, 87-88 Turnmill Street, London EC1M 5QU, England; *European Marketing Data and Statistics.*

Facts on File, 460 Park Avenue South, New York, New York 10016 (800) 443-8323; *The New Book of World Rankings.*

Food and Agricultural Organization of the United Nations (FAO) Via delle Terme di Caracalla, 00100 Rome, Italy (Telephone Number in U.S. (202) 653-2400); *Production Yearbook* and *The State of Food and Agriculture.*

Statistical Office of the United Nations, Publishing Service, New York, New York 10017 (800) 253-9646; *Statistical Yearbook.*

HUNGARY - CUSTOMS DUTIES

G.K. Hall and Company, 70 Lincoln Street, Boston, Massachusetts 02111 (617) 423-3990; *The World in Figures.*

HUNGARY - DAIRY PRODUCTS

Facts on File, 460 Park Avenue South, New York, New York 10016 (800) 443-8323; *The New Book of World Rankings.*

Food and Agricultural Organization of the United Nations (FAO) Via delle Terme di Caracalla, 00100 Rome, Italy (Telephone Number in U.S. (202) 653-2400); *Production Yearbook,* and *The State of Food and Agriculture.*

Statistical Office of the United Nations, Publishing Service, New York, New York 10017 (800) 253-9646; *Statistical Yearbook.*

HUNGARY - DEATH RATES

G.K. Hall and Company, 70 Lincoln Street, Boston, Massachusetts 02111 (617) 423-3990; *The World in Figures.*

Statistical Office of the United Nations, Publishing Service, New York, New York 10017 (800) 253-9646; *Statistical Yearbook.*

Times Books, 201 East 50th Street, New York, New York 10022 (212) 751-2600; *The Economist Book of Vital World Statistics.*

World Health Organization, Office of Publications, Avenue Appia, CH-1211 Geneva 27, Switzerland (Telephone Number in U.S. (518) 436-9686); *World Health Statistics Annual.*

HUNGARY - DEFENSE EXPENDITURES

G.K. Hall and Company, 70 Lincoln Street, Boston, Massachusetts 02111 (617) 423-3990; *The World in Figures.*

U.S. Arms Control and Disarmament Agency, 320 Twenty-first Street, Northwest, Washington, D.C. 20451 (202) 647-8677; *World Military Expenditures and Arms Transfers.*

HUNGARY - DEMOGRAPHY

The Economist Intelligence Unit, 111 West 57th Street, New York, New York 10019 (800) 938-4685; *The World Market Atlas.*

Facts on File, 460 Park Avenue South, New York, New York 10016 (800) 443-8323; *The New Book of World Rankings.*

Federal Statistical Office, Gustav - Stresesmann - Ring 11, D-6200 Wiesbaden, Federal Republic of Germany; *Ungarn.*

G.K. Hall and Company, 70 Lincoln Street, Boston, Massachusetts 02111 (617) 423-3990; *The World in Figures.*

HUNGARY - DEVELOPMENT ASSISTANCE

G.K. Hall and Company, 70 Lincoln Street, Boston, Massachusetts 02111 (617) 423-3990; *The World in Figures.*

Statistical Office of the United Nations, Publishing Service, New York, New York 10017 (800) 253-9646; *Statistical Yearbook.*

HUNGARY - DIAMOND PRODUCTION - See HUNGARY - MINING AND MINERAL PRODUCTS

HUNGARY - DISEASE

G.K. Hall and Company, 70 Lincoln Street, Boston, Massachusetts 02111 (617) 423-3990; *The World in Figures.*

World Health Organization, Office of Publications, Avenue Appia, CH-1211 Geneva 27, Switzerland (Telephone Number in U.S. (518) 436-9686); *World Health Statistics Annual.*

HUNGARY - DIVORCE RATES

Facts on File, 460 Park Avenue South, New York, New York 10016 (800) 443-8323; *The New Book of World Rankings.*

Statistical Office of the United Nations, Publishing Service, New York, New York 10017 (800) 253-9646; *Demographic Yearbook,* and *Statistical Yearbook.*

HUNGARY - DOMESTIC PRODUCT

G.K. Hall and Company, 70 Lincoln Street, Boston, Massachusetts 02111 (617) 423-3990; *The World in Figures.*

HUNGARY - DUCKS - See HUNGARY - LIVESTOCK AND POULTRY

HUNGARY - ECONOMY

Euromonitor Publications Limited, 87-88 Turnmill Street, London EC1M 5QU, England; *European Marketing Data and Statistics.*

Facts on File, 460 Park Avenue South, New York, New York 10016 (800) 443-8323; *The New Book of World Rankings.*

Federal Statistical Office, Gustav - Stresesmann - Ring 11, D-6200 Wiesbaden, Federal Republic of Germany; *Ungarn.*

G.K. Hall and Company, 70 Lincoln Street, Boston, Massachusetts 02111 (617) 423-3990; *The World in Figures.*

HUNGARY - EDUCATION

Columbia University Press, 562 West 113th Street, New York, New York 10014 (212) 316-7100; *East European and Soviet Data Book.*

The Economist Intelligence Unit, 111 West 57th Street, New York, New York 10019 (800) 938-4685; *The World Market Atlas.*

Euromonitor Publications Limited, 87-88 Turnmill Street, London EC1M 5QU, England; *European Marketing Data and Statistics.*

Facts on File, 460 Park Avenue South, New York, New York 10016 (800) 443-8323; *The New Book of World Rankings.*

Federal Statistical Office, Gustav - Stresesmann - Ring 11, D-6200 Wiesbaden, Federal Republic of Germany; *Ungarn.*

G.K. Hall and Company, 70 Lincoln Street, Boston, Massachusetts 02111 (617) 423-3990; *The World in Figures.*

Hungarian Statistical Office, 1033 Budapest, III, Kaszasdulo U.2.; *Hungary Statistical Yearbook.*

Times Books, 201 East 50th Street, New York, New York 10022 (212) 751-2600; *The Economist Book of Vital World Statistics.*

United Nations Educational, Scientific and Cultural Organization (UNESCO), 7 Place de Fontenoy, F-75700 Paris, France (Telephone Number in U.S. (212) 963-5981); *Statistical Yearbook.*

The World Bank, 1818 H Street, NW, Washington, D.C. 20433 (202) 477-1234; *World Tables.*

HUNGARY - EGG PRODUCTION - See HUNGARY - DAIRY PRODUCTS

HUNGARY - ELECTRICITY

Facts on File, 460 Park Avenue South, New York, New York 10016 (800) 443-8323; *The New Book of World Rankings.*

Penn Well Publishing Company, 1421 South Sheridan Road, Post Office Box 1260, Tulsa, Oklahoma 74101 (800) 752-9764; *International Energy Statistics Sourcebook.*

Statistical Office of the United Nations, Publishing Service, New York, New York 10017 (800) 253-9646; *Statistical Yearbook.*

Times Books, 201 East 50th Street, New York, New York 10022 (212) 751-2600; *The Economist Book of Vital World Statistics.*

HUNGARY - EMPLOYMENT

Columbia University Press, 562 West 113th Street, New York, New York 10014 (212) 316-7100; *East European and Soviet Data Book.*

Euromonitor Publications Limited, 87-88 Turnmill Street, London EC1M 5QU, England; *European Marketing Data and Statistics.*

Facts on File, 460 Park Avenue South, New York, New York 10016 (800) 443-8323; *The New Book of World Rankings.*

Federal Statistical Office, Gustav - Stresesmann - Ring 11, D-6200 Wiesbaden, Federal Republic of Germany; *Ungarn.*

International Labour Office, I.L.O. Publications, CH-1211, Geneva 22, Switzerland; *Yearbook of Labour Statistics.*

Statistical Office of the United Nations, Publishing Service, New York, New York 10017 (800) 253-9646; *Statistical Yearbook.*

HUNGARY - ENERGY

Euromonitor Publications Limited, 87-88 Turnmill Street, London EC1M 5QU, England; *European Marketing Data and Statistics.*

Facts on File, 460 Park Avenue South, New York, New York 10016 (800) 443-8323; *The New Book of World Rankings.*

Food and Agricultural Organization of the United Nations (FAO) Via delle Terme di Caracalla, 00100 Rome, Italy (Telephone Number in U.S. (202) 653-2400); *The State of Food and Agriculture.*

G.K. Hall and Company, 70 Lincoln Street, Boston, Massachusetts 02111 (617) 423-3990; *The World in Figures.*

Hungarian Statistical Office, 1033 Budapest, III, Kaszasdulo U.2.; *Hungary Statistical Yearbook.*

Penn Well Publishing Company, 1421 South Sheridan Road, Post Office Box 1260, Tulsa, Oklahoma 74101 (800) 752-9764; *International Energy Statistics Sourcebook.*

Statistical Office of the United Nations, Publishing Service, New York, New York 10017 (800) 253-9646; *Energy Statistics Yearbook, Statistical Yearbook,* and *World Energy Supplies.*

Times Books, 201 East 50th Street, New York, New York 10022 (212) 751-2600; *The Economist Book of Vital World Statistics.*

HUNGARY - EXCHANGE RATE

International Civil Aviation Organization, 1000 Sherbrooke Street West, Suite 400, Montreal, Quebec, Canada H3A 2R2 (514) 285-8219; *Civil Aviation Statistics of the World.*

International Monetary Fund, 700 Nineteenth Street, NW, Washington, D.C. 20431 (202) 623-7000; *International Financial Statistics.*

Statistical Office of the United Nations, Publishing Service, New York, New York 10017 (800) 253-9646; *Statistical Yearbook.*

HUNGARY - EXPORTS

The Economist Intelligence Unit, 111 West 57th Street, New York, New York 10019 (800) 938-4685; *The World Market Atlas.*

Food and Agricultural Organization of the United Nations (FAO) Via delle Terme di Caracalla, 00100 Rome, Italy (Telephone Number in U.S. (202) 653-2400); *The State of Food and Agriculture.*

G.K. Hall and Company, 70 Lincoln Street, Boston, Massachusetts 02111 (617) 423-3990; *The World in Figures.*

International Lead and Zinc Study Group, Metro House, 58 St. James's Street, London SW1A 1LD, England; *Lead and Zinc Statistics.*

International Monetary Fund, 700 Nineteenth Street, NW, Washington, D.C. 20431 (202) 623-7000; *Direction of Trade Statistics,* and *International Financial Statistics.*

International Rubber Study Group, York House, 8th Floor, Empire Way, Wembley, London HA9 0PA, England; *Rubber Statistical Bulletin.*

Motor Vehicle Manufacturers Association of the United States, 7430 Second Avenue, Suite 300, Detroit, Michigan 48202 (313) 872-4311; *World Motor Vehicle Data.*

The World Bank, 1818 H Street, NW, Washington, D.C. 20433 (202) 477-1234; *World Tables.*

HUNGARY - EXTERNAL INDEBTEDNESS

The World Bank, 1818 H Street, NW, Washington, D.C. 20433 (202) 477-1234; *World Tables.*

HUNGARY - EXTERNAL TRADE

Food and Agricultural Organization of the United Nations (FAO) Via delle Terme di Caracalla, 00100 Rome, Italy (Telephone Number in U.S. (202) 653-2400); *The State of Food and Agriculture,* and *Trade Yearbook.*

G.K. Hall and Company, 70 Lincoln Street, Boston, Massachusetts 02111 (617) 423-3990; *The World in Figures.*

Hungarian Statistical Office, 1033 Budapest, III, Kaszasdulo U.2.; *Hungary Statistical Yearbook.*

Statistical Office of the United Nations, Publishing Service, New York, New York 10017 (800) 253-9646; *Statistical Yearbook.*

HUNGARY - FABRIC PRODUCTION - See HUNGARY - TEXTILE INDUSTRY

HUNGARY - FARM CROPS - See HUNGARY - CROPS

HUNGARY - FERTILITY RATES

Columbia University Press, 562 West 113th Street, New York, New York 10014 (212) 316-7100; *East European and Soviet Data Book.*

Facts on File, 460 Park Avenue South, New York, New York 10016 (800) 443-8323; *The New Book of World Rankings.*

Times Books, 201 East 50th Street, New York, New York 10022 (212) 751-2600; *The Economist Book of Vital World Statistics.*

The World Bank, 1818 H Street, NW, Washington, D.C. 20433 (202) 477-1234; *World Tables.*

HUNGARY - FERTILIZER

Food and Agricultural Organization of the United Nations (FAO) Via delle Terme di Caracalla, 00100 Rome, Italy (Telephone Number in U.S. (202) 653-2400); *The State of Food and Agriculture.*

Statistical Office of the United Nations, Publishing Service, New York, New York 10017 (800) 253-9646; *Statistical Yearbook.*

HUNGARY - FETAL MORTALITY

Statistical Office of the United Nations, Publishing Service, New York, New York 10017 (800) 253-9646; *Demographic Yearbook.*

World Health Organization, Office of Publications, Avenue Appia, CH-1211 Geneva 27, Switzerland (Telephone Number in U.S. (518) 436-9686); *World Health Statistics Annual.*

HUNGARY - FIBRE PRODUCTION - See HUNGARY - TEXTILE INDUSTRY

HUNGARY - FILAMENT PRODUCTION - See HUNGARY - TEXTILE INDUSTRY

HUNGARY - FILM - See HUNGARY - MOTION PICTURES

HUNGARY - FINANCE

Facts on File, 460 Park Avenue South, New York, New York 10016 (800) 443-8323; *The New Book of World Rankings.*

Federal Statistical Office, Gustav - Stresesmann - Ring 11, D-6200 Wiesbaden, Federal Republic of Germany; *Ungarn.*

G.K. Hall and Company, 70 Lincoln Street, Boston, Massachusetts 02111 (617) 423-3990; *The World in Figures.*

HUNGARY - FISHERIES

Euromonitor Publications Limited, 87-88 Turnmill Street, London EC1M 5QU, England; *European Marketing Data and Statistics.*

Facts on File, 460 Park Avenue South, New York, New York 10016 (800) 443-8323; *The New Book of World Rankings.*

Federal Statistical Office, Gustav - Stresesmann - Ring 11, D-6200 Wiesbaden, Federal Republic of Germany; *Ungarn.*

Food and Agricultural Organization of the United Nations (FAO) Via delle Terme di Caracalla, 00100 Rome, Italy (Telephone Number in U.S. (202) 653-2400); *The State of Food and Agriculture,* and *Yearbook of Fishery Statistics.*

Statistical Office of the United Nations, Publishing Service, New York, New York 10017 (800) 253-9646; *Statistical Yearbook.*

HUNGARY - FLAX FIBRE PRODUCTION - See HUNGARY - TEXTILE INDUSTRY

HUNGARY - FLOUR PRODUCTION

Statistical Office of the United Nations, Publishing Service, New York, New York 10017 (800) 253-9646; *Statistical Yearbook.*

HUNGARY - FOOD

Food and Agricultural Organization of the United Nations (FAO), Via delle Terme di Caracalla, 00100 Rome, Italy (Telephone Number in U.S. (202) 653-2400); *Production Yearbook,* and *The State of Food and Agriculture.*

G.K. Hall and Company, 70 Lincoln Street, Boston, Massachusetts 02111 (617) 423-3990; *The World in Figures.*

HUNGARY - FOREIGN AID

G.K. Hall and Company, 70 Lincoln Street, Boston, Massachusetts 02111 (617) 423-3990; *The World in Figures.*

HUNGARY - FOREIGN TRADE

Euromonitor Publications Limited, 87-88 Turnmill Street, London EC1M 5QU, England; *European Marketing Data and Statistics.*

Facts on File, 460 Park Avenue South, New York, New York 10016 (800) 443-8323; *The New Book of World Rankings.*

Federal Statistical Office, Gustav - Stresesmann - Ring 11, D-6200 Wiesbaden, Federal Republic of Germany; *Ungarn.*

Food and Agricultural Organization of the United Nations (FAO) Via delle Terme di Caracalla, 00100 Rome, Italy (Telephone Number in U.S. (202) 653-2400); *The State of Food and Agriculture.*

G.K. Hall and Company, 70 Lincoln Street, Boston, Massachusetts 02111 (617) 423-3990; *The World in Figures.*

Statistical Office of the United Nations, Publishing Service, New York, New York 10017 (800) 253-9646; *International Trade Statistics Yearbook,* and *Statistical Yearbook.*

The World Bank, 1818 H Street, NW, Washington, D.C. 20433 (202) 477-1234; *World Tables.*

HUNGARY - FORESTRY AND FOREST PRODUCTS

Euromonitor Publications Limited, 87-88 Turnmill Street, London EC1M 5QU, England; *European Marketing Data and Statistics.*

Facts on File, 460 Park Avenue South, New York, New York 10016 (800) 443-8323; *The New Book of World Rankings.*

Federal Statistical Office, Gustav - Stresesmann - Ring 11, D-6200 Wiesbaden, Federal Republic of Germany; *Ungarn.*

Food and Agricultural Organization of the United Nations (FAO) Via delle Terme di Caracalla, 00100 Rome, Italy (Telephone Number in U.S. (202) 653-2400); *The State of Food and Agriculture,* and *Yearbook of Forest Products.*

G.K. Hall and Company, 70 Lincoln Street, Boston, Massachusetts 02111 (617) 423-3990; *The World in Figures.*

Hungarian Statistical Office, 1033 Budapest, III, Kaszasdulo U.2.; *Hungary Statistical Yearbook.*

Statistical Office of the United Nations, Publishing Service, New York, New York 10017 (800) 253-9646; *Statistical Yearbook.*

United Nations Educational, Scientific and Cultural Organization (UNESCO), 7 Place de Fontenoy, F-75700 Paris, France (Telephone Number in U.S. (212) 963-5981); *Statistical Yearbook.*

HUNGARY - GARLIC PRODUCTION - See HUNGARY - CROPS

HUNGARY - GAS - See HUNGARY - MINING AND MINERAL PRODUCTS

HUNGARY - GENERAL INDUSTRIAL STATISTICS

Federal Statistical Office, Gustav - Stresesmann - Ring 11, D-6200 Wiesbaden, Federal Republic of Germany; *Ungarn.*

Statistical Office of the United Nations, Publishing Service, New York, New York 10017 (800) 253-9646; *Industrial Statistics Yearbook.*

HUNGARY - GENERAL MORTALITY

Statistical Office of the United Nations, Publishing Service, New York, New York 10017 (800) 253-9646; *Demographic Yearbook.*

World Health Organization, Office of Publications, Avenue Appia, CH-1211 Geneva 27, Switzerland (Telephone Number in U.S. (518) 436-9686); *World Health Statistics Annual.*

HUNGARY - GEOGRAPHIC DATA

Facts on File, 460 Park Avenue South, New York, New York 10016 (800) 443-8323; *The New Book of World Rankings.*

Federal Statistical Office, Gustav - Stresesmann - Ring 11, D-6200 Wiesbaden, Federal Republic of Germany; *Ungarn.*

HUNGARY - GOLD HOLDINGS

International Monetary Fund, 700 Nineteenth Street, NW, Washington, D.C. 20431 (202) 623-7000; *International Financial Statistics.*

The World Bank, 1818 H Street, NW, Washington, D.C. 20433 (202) 477-1234; *World Tables.*

HUNGARY - GOLD PRODUCTION AND CONSUMPTION - See HUNGARY - MINING AND MINERAL PRODUCTS

HUNGARY - GOVERNMENT

G.K. Hall and Company, 70 Lincoln Street, Boston, Massachusetts 02111 (617) 423-3990; *The World in Figures.*

HUNGARY - GOVERNMENT EXPENDITURE

Times Books, 201 East 50th Street, New York, New York 10022 (212) 751-2600; *The Economist Book of Vital World Statistics.*

The World Bank, 1818 H Street, NW, Washington, D.C. 20433 (202) 477-1234; *World Tables.*

HUNGARY - GOVERNMENT FINANCES

International Monetary Fund, 700 Nineteenth Street, NW, Washington, D.C. 20431 (202) 623-7000; *International Financial Statistics.*

Statistical Office of the United Nations, Publishing Service, New York, New York 10017 (800) 253-9646; *Statistical Yearbook.*

HUNGARY - GOVERNMENT REVENUES

Times Books, 201 East 50th Street, New York, New York 10022 (212) 751-2600; *The Economist Book of Vital World Statistics.*

The World Bank, 1818 H Street, NW, Washington, D.C. 20433 (202) 477-1234; *World Tables.*

HUNGARY - GRAIN PRODUCTION - See HUNGARY - CROPS

HUNGARY - GREEN PEPPER AND CHILIE PRODUCTION - See HUNGARY - CROPS

HUNGARY - GROSS DOMESTIC PRODUCT

The Economist Intelligence Unit, 111 West 57th Street, New York, New York 10019 (800) 938-4685; *The World Market Atlas.*

Facts on File, 460 Park Avenue South, New York, New York 10016 (800) 443-8323; *The New Book of World Rankings.*

G.K. Hall and Company, 70 Lincoln Street, Boston, Massachusetts 02111 (617) 423-3990; *The World in Figures.*

Statistical Office of the United Nations, Publishing Service, New York, New York 10017 (800) 253-9646; *Statistical Yearbook.*

Times Books, 201 East 50th Street, New York, New York 10022 (212) 751-2600; *The Economist Book of Vital World Statistics.*

The World Bank, 1818 H Street, NW, Washington, D.C. 20433 (202) 477-1234; *World Tables.*

HUNGARY - GROSS NATIONAL PRODUCT

U.S. Arms Control and Disarmament Agency, 320 Twenty-first Street, Northwest, Washington, D.C. 20451 (202) 647-8677; *World Military Expenditures and Arms Transfers.*

The World Bank, 1818 H Street, NW, Washington, D.C. 20433 (202) 477-1234; *World Tables.*

HUNGARY - HAZELNUT PRODUCTION - See HUNGARY - CROPS

HUNGARY - HEALTH

Facts on File, 460 Park Avenue South, New York, New York 10016 (800) 443-8323; *The New Book of World Rankings.*

Federal Statistical Office, Gustav - Stresesmann - Ring 11, D-6200 Wiesbaden, Federal Republic of Germany; *Ungarn.*

G.K. Hall and Company, 70 Lincoln Street, Boston, Massachusetts 02111 (617) 423-3990; *The World in Figures.*

Hungarian Statistical Office, 1033 Budapest, III, Kaszasdulo U.2.; *Hungary Statistical Yearbook.*

Statistical Office of the United Nations, Publishing Service, New York, New York 10017 (800) 253-9646; *Statistical Yearbook.*

Times Books, 201 East 50th Street, New York, New York 10022 (212) 751-2600; *The Economist Book of Vital World Statistics.*

World Health Organization, Office of Publications, Avenue Appia, CH-1211 Geneva 27, Switzerland (Telephone Number in U.S. (518) 436-9686); *World Health Statistics Annual.*

HUNGARY - HEMP FIBRE PRODUCTION - See HUNGARY - TEXTILE INDUSTRY

HUNGARY - HIDE PRODUCTION - ALL TYPES

Food and Agricultural Organization of the United Nations (FAO), Via delle Terme di Caracalla, 00100 Rome, Italy (Telephone Number in U.S. (202) 653-2400); *Production Yearbook.*

HUNGARY - HIGHWAYS

G.K. Hall and Company, 70 Lincoln Street, Boston, Massachusetts 02111 (617) 423-3990; *The World in Figures.*

International Road Federation, 525 School Street, SW, Washington, D.C. 20024 (202) 554-2105; *World Road Statistics.*

Statistical Office of the United Nations, Publishing Service, New York, New York 10017 (800) 253-9646; *Annual Bulletin of Transport Statistics for Europe.*

HUNGARY - HOPS PRODUCTION - See HUNGARY - CROPS

HUNGARY - HORSES - See HUNGARY - LIVESTOCK AND POULTRY

HUNGARY - HOURS OF WORK - See HUNGARY - EMPLOYMENT

HUNGARY - HOUSING AND HOUSING UNITS

Columbia University Press, 562 West 113th Street, New York, New York 10014 (212) 316-7100; *East European and Soviet Data Book.*

Facts on File, 460 Park Avenue South, New York, New York 10016 (800) 443-8323; *The New Book of World Rankings.*

HUNGARY - HYDROCHLORIC ACID PRODUCTION

Statistical Office of the United Nations, Publishing Service, New York, New York 10017 (800) 253-9646; *Statistical Yearbook.*

HUNGARY - ILLITERATE POPULATION

Columbia University Press, 562 West 113th Street, New York, New York 10014 (212) 316-7100; *East European and Soviet Data Book.*

The Economist Intelligence Unit, 111 West 57th Street, New York, New York 10019 (800) 938-4685; *The World Market Atlas.*

G.K. Hall and Company, 70 Lincoln Street, Boston, Massachusetts 02111 (617) 423-3990; *The World in Figures.*

United Nations Educational, Scientific and Cultural Organization (UNESCO), 7 Place de Fontenoy, F-75700 Paris, France (Telephone Number in U.S. (212) 963-5981); *Statistical Yearbook.*

HUNGARY - IMPORTS

The Economist Intelligence Unit, 111 West 57th Street, New York, New York 10019 (800) 938-4685; *The World Market Atlas.*

Food and Agricultural Organization of the United Nations (FAO) Via delle Terme di Caracalla, 00100 Rome, Italy (Telephone Number in U.S. (202) 653-2400); *The State of Food and Agriculture.*

G.K. Hall and Company, 70 Lincoln Street, Boston, Massachusetts 02111 (617) 423-3990; *The World in Figures.*

International Lead and Zinc Study Group, Metro House, 58 St. James's Street, London SW1A 1LD, England; *Lead and Zinc Statistics.*

International Monetary Fund, 700 Nineteenth Street, NW, Washington, D.C. 20431 (202) 623-7000; *Direction of Trade Statistics,* and *International Financial Statistics.*

International Rubber Study Group, York House, 8th Floor, Empire Way, Wembley, London HA9 0PA, England; *Rubber Statistical Bulletin.*

Motor Vehicle Manufacturers Association of the United States, 7430 Second Avenue, Suite 300, Detroit, Michigan 48202 (313) 872-4311; *World Motor Vehicle Data.*

The World Bank, 1818 H Street, NW, Washington, D.C. 20433 (202) 477-1234; *World Tables.*

HUNGARY - INDUSTRIAL METALS PRODUCTION - See HUNGARY - MINING AND MINERAL PRODUCTS

HUNGARY - INDUSTRY

Facts on File, 460 Park Avenue South, New York, New York 10016 (800) 443-8323; *The New Book of World Rankings.*

Federal Statistical Office, Gustav - Stresesmann - Ring 11, D-6200 Wiesbaden, Federal Republic of Germany; *Ungarn.*

G.K. Hall and Company, 70 Lincoln Street, Boston, Massachusetts 02111 (617) 423-3990; *The World in Figures.*

Hungarian Statistical Office, 1033 Budapest, III, Kaszasdulo U.2.; *Hungary Statistical Yearbook.*

International Labour Office, I.L.O. Publications, CH-1211, Geneva 22, Switzerland; *Yearbook of Labour Statistics.*

Statistical Office of the United Nations, Publishing Service, New York, New York 10017 (800) 253-9646; *Statistical Yearbook.*

Times Books, 201 East 50th Street, New York, New York 10022 (212) 751-2600; *The Economist Book of Vital World Statistics.*

The World Bank, 1818 H Street, NW, Washington, D.C. 20433 (202) 477-1234; *World Tables.*

World Intellectual Property Organization, 34 Chemin des Colombettes, CH-1211 Geneva 20, Switzerland; *Industrial Property Statistics.*

HUNGARY - INFANT AND MATERNAL MORTALITY

Statistical Office of the United Nations, Publishing Service, New York, New York 10017 (800) 253-9646; *Demographic Yearbook,* and *Statistical Yearbook.*

Times Books, 201 East 50th Street, New York, New York 10022 (212) 751-2600; *The Economist Book of Vital World Statistics.*

The World Bank, 1818 H Street, NW, Washington, D.C. 20433 (202) 477-1234; *World Tables.*

World Health Organization, Office of Publications, Avenue Appia, CH-1211 Geneva 27, Switzerland (Telephone Number in U.S. (518) 436-9686); *World Health Statistics Annual.*

HUNGARY - INTERNAL TRADE

Hungarian Statistical Office, 1033 Budapest, III, Kaszasdulo U.2.; *Hungary Statistical Yearbook.*

Statistical Office of the United Nations, Publishing Service, New York, New York 10017 (800) 253-9646; *Statistical Yearbook.*

HUNGARY - INTERNATIONAL LIQUIDITY

International Monetary Fund, 700 Nineteenth Street, NW, Washington, D.C. 20431 (202) 623-7000; *International Financial Statistics.*

HUNGARY - INTERNATIONAL RESERVES EXCLUDING GOLD

The World Bank, 1818 H Street, NW, Washington, D.C. 20433 (202) 477-1234; *World Tables.*

HUNGARY - INVESTMENTS

Hungarian Statistical Office, 1033 Budapest, III, Kaszasdulo U.2.; *Hungary Statistical Yearbook.*

International Monetary Fund, 700 Nineteenth Street, NW, Washington, D.C. 20431 (202) 623-7000; *International Financial Statistics.*

HUNGARY - IRON ORE PRODUCTION AND CONSUMPTION - See HUNGARY - MINING AND MINERAL PRODUCTS

HUNGARY - LABOR FORCE

Columbia University Press, 562 West 113th Street, New York, New York 10014 (212) 316-7100; *East European and Soviet Data Book.*

Facts on File, 460 Park Avenue South, New York, New York 10016 (800) 443-8323; *The New Book of World Rankings.*

Food and Agricultural Organization of the United Nations (FAO) Via delle Terme di Caracalla, 00100 Rome, Italy (Telephone Number in U.S. (202) 653-2400); *The State of Food and Agriculture.*

G.K. Hall and Company, 70 Lincoln Street, Boston, Massachusetts 02111 (617) 423-3990; *The World in Figures.*

Hungarian Statistical Office, 1033 Budapest, III, Kaszasdulo U.2.; *Hungary Statistical Yearbook.*

Times Books, 201 East 50th Street, New York, New York 10022 (212) 751-2600; *The Economist Book of Vital World Statistics.*

The World Bank, 1818 H Street, NW, Washington, D.C. 20433 (202) 477-1234; *World Tables.*

HUNGARY - LABOR PRODUCTIVITY

International Labour Office, I.L.O. Publications, CH-1211, Geneva 22, Switzerland; *Yearbook of Labour Statistics.*

HUNGARY - LAND USE

Euromonitor Publications Limited, 87-88 Turnmill Street, London EC1M 5QU, England; *European Marketing Data and Statistics.*

Food and Agricultural Organization of the United Nations (FAO), Via delle Terme di Caracalla, 00100 Rome, Italy (Telephone Number in U.S. (202) 653-2400); *Production Yearbook.*

G.K. Hall and Company, 70 Lincoln Street, Boston, Massachusetts 02111 (617) 423-3990; *The World in Figures.*

HUNGARY - LEAD AND LEAD ORE - See HUNGARY - MINING AND MINERAL PRODUCTS

HUNGARY - LIBRARIES

Euromonitor Publications Limited, 87-88 Turnmill Street, London EC1M 5QU, England; *European Marketing Data and Statistics.*

Facts on File, 460 Park Avenue South, New York, New York 10016 (800) 443-8323; *The New Book of World Rankings.*

Statistical Office of the United Nations, Publishing Service, New York, New York 10017 (800) 253-9646; *Statistical Yearbook.*

United Nations Educational, Scientific and Cultural Organization (UNESCO), 7 Place de Fontenoy, F-75700 Paris, France (Telephone Number in U.S. (212) 963-5981); *Statistical Yearbook.*

HUNGARY - LIGNITE PRODUCTION - See HUNGARY - MINING AND MINERAL PRODUCTS

HUNGARY - LIVESTOCK AND POULTRY

Commodity Research Bureau, Incorporated, 75 Wall Street, New York, New York 10005 (212) 504-7754; *Commodity Year Book.*

Euromonitor Publications Limited, 87-88 Turnmill Street, London EC1M 5QU, England; *European Marketing Data and Statistics.*

Facts on File, 460 Park Avenue South, New York, New York 10016 (800) 443-8323; *The New Book of World Rankings.*

Food and Agricultural Organization of the United Nations (FAO), Via delle Terme di Caracalla, 00100 Rome, Italy (Telephone Number in U.S. (202) 653-2400); *Production Yearbook,* and *The State of Food and Agriculture.*

G.K. Hall and Company, 70 Lincoln Street, Boston, Massachusetts 02111 (617) 423-3990; *The World in Figures.*

Statistical Office of the United Nations, Publishing Service, New York, New York 10017 (800) 253-9646; *Statistical Yearbook.*

HUNGARY - LIVING LEVELS

G.K. Hall and Company, 70 Lincoln Street, Boston, Massachusetts 02111 (617) 423-3990; *The World in Figures.*

Times Books, 201 East 50th Street, New York, New York 10022 (212) 751-2600; *The Economist Book of Vital World Statistics.*

HUNGARY - MAIL - NUMBER OF PIECES SENT OR RECEIVED

Statistical Office of the United Nations, Publishing Service, New York, New York 10017 (800) 253-9646; *Statistical Yearbook.*

HUNGARY - MANGANESE AND MANGANESE ORE - See HUNGARY - MINING AND MINERAL PRODUCTS

HUNGARY - MANUFACTURING

Facts on File, 460 Park Avenue South, New York, New York 10016 (800) 443-8323; *The New Book of World Rankings.*

G.K. Hall and Company, 70 Lincoln Street, Boston, Massachusetts 02111 (617) 423-3990; *The World in Figures.*

Motor Vehicle Manufacturers Association of the United States, 7430 Second Avenue, Suite 300, Detroit, Michigan 48202 (313) 872-4311; *World Motor Vehicle Data.*

Statistical Office of the United Nations, Publishing Service, New York, New York 10017 (800) 253-9646; *Statistical Yearbook.*

Times Books, 201 East 50th Street, New York, New York 10022 (212) 751-2600; *The Economist Book of Vital World Statistics.*

The World Bank, 1818 H Street, NW, Washington, D.C. 20433 (202) 477-1234; *World Tables.*

HUNGARY - MARRIAGE RATES

Facts on File, 460 Park Avenue South, New York, New York 10016 (800) 443-8323; *The New Book of World Rankings.*

Statistical Office of the United Nations, Publishing Service, New York, New York 10017 (800) 253-9646; *Demographic Yearbook,* and *Statistical Yearbook.*

HUNGARY - MEAT PRODUCTION - See HUNGARY - LIVESTOCK AND POULTRY

HUNGARY - MERCHANT SHIPPING

G.K. Hall and Company, 70 Lincoln Street, Boston, Massachusetts 02111 (617) 423-3990; *The World in Figures.*

Statistical Office of the United Nations, Publishing Service, New York, New York 10017 (800) 253-9646; *Annual Bulletin of Transport Statistics for Europe.*

Times Books, 201 East 50th Street, New York, New York 10022 (212) 751-2600; *The Economist Book of Vital World Statistics.*

U.S. Department of Transportation, Maritime Administration, 400 Seventh Street, SW, Washington, D.C. 20590 (202) 366-5807; *A Statistical Analysis of the World's Merchant Fleets.*

HUNGARY - MILITARY

G.K. Hall and Company, 70 Lincoln Street, Boston, Massachusetts 02111 (617) 423-3990; *The World in Figures.*

The International Institute for Strategic Studies, 23 Tavistock Street, London WC2E 7NQ, England; *The Military Balance.*

U.S. Arms Control and Disarmament Agency, 320 Twenty-first Street, Northwest, Washington, D.C. 20451 (202) 647-8677; *World Military Expenditures and Arms Transfers.*

HUNGARY - MILK PRODUCTION - See HUNGARY - DAIRY PRODUCTS

HUNGARY - MILLET PRODUCTION - See HUNGARY - CROPS

HUNGARY - MINING AND MINERAL PRODUCTS

Commodity Research Bureau, Incorporated, 75 Wall Street, New York, New York 10005 (212) 504-7754; *Commodity Year Book.*

Facts on File, 460 Park Avenue South, New York, New York 10016 (800) 443-8323; *The New Book of World Rankings.*

G.K. Hall and Company, 70 Lincoln Street, Boston, Massachusetts 02111 (617) 423-3990; *The World in Figures.*

International Lead and Zinc Study Group, Metro House, 58 St. James's Street, London SW1A 1LD, England; *Lead and Zinc Statistics.*

Penn Well Publishing Company, 1421 South Sheridan Road, Post Office Box 1260, Tulsa, Oklahoma 74101 (800) 752-9764; *International Energy Statistics Sourcebook.*

Statistical Office of the United Nations, Publishing Service, New York, New York 10017 (800) 253-9646; *Statistical Yearbook.*

HUNGARY - MONEY EXCHANGE RATE

International Monetary Fund, 700 Nineteenth Street, NW, Washington, D.C. 20431 (202) 623-7000; *International Financial Statistics.*

Statistical Office of the United Nations, Publishing Service, New York, New York 10017 (800) 253-9646; *Statistical Yearbook.*

HUNGARY - MONEY SUPPLY

Federal Statistical Office, Gustav - Stresesmann - Ring 11, D-6200 Wiesbaden, Federal Republic of Germany; *Ungarn.*

G.K. Hall and Company, 70 Lincoln Street, Boston, Massachusetts 02111 (617) 423-3990; *The World in Figures.*

International Monetary Fund, 700 Nineteenth Street, NW, Washington, D.C. 20431 (202) 623-7000; *International Financial Statistics.*

The World Bank, 1818 H Street, NW, Washington, D.C. 20433 (202) 477-1234; *World Tables.*

HUNGARY - MONUMENTS AND HISTORICAL SITES

United Nations Educational, Scientific and Cultural Organization (UNESCO), 7 Place de Fontenoy, F-75700 Paris, France (Telephone Number in U.S. (212) 963-5981); *Statistical Yearbook.*

HUNGARY - MOTION PICTURES

United Nations Educational, Scientific and Cultural Organization (UNESCO), 7 Place de Fontenoy, F-75700 Paris, France (Telephone Number in U.S. (212) 963-5981); *Statistical Yearbook.*

HUNGARY - MOTOR VEHICLE PRODUCTION

Motor Vehicle Manufacturers Association of the United States, 7430 Second Avenue, Suite 300, Detroit, Michigan 48202 (313) 872-4311; *World Motor Vehicle Data.*

Statistical Office of the United Nations, Publishing Service, New York, New York 10017 (800) 253-9646; *Statistical Yearbook.*

HUNGARY - MOTOR VEHICLES IN USE

G.K. Hall and Company, 70 Lincoln Street, Boston, Massachusetts 02111 (617) 423-3990; *The World in Figures.*

International Road Federation, 525 School Street, SW, Washington, D.C. 20024 (202) 554-2105; *World Road Statistics.*

Motor Vehicle Manufacturers Association of the United States, 7430 Second Avenue, Suite 300, Detroit, Michigan 48202 (313) 872-4311; *World Motor Vehicle Data.*

Statistical Office of the United Nations, Publishing Service, New York, New York 10017 (800) 253-9646; *Statistical Yearbook.*

Times Books, 201 East 50th Street, New York, New York 10022 (212) 751-2600; *The Economist Book of Vital World Statistics.*

HUNGARY - MULES - See HUNGARY - LIVESTOCK AND POULTRY

HUNGARY - MUSEUMS

Euromonitor Publications Limited, 87-88 Turnmill Street, London EC1M 5QU, England; *European Marketing Data and Statistics.*

Facts on File, 460 Park Avenue South, New York, New York 10016 (800) 443-8323; *The New Book of World Rankings.*

United Nations Educational, Scientific and Cultural Organization (UNESCO), 7 Place de Fontenoy, F-75700 Paris, France (Telephone Number in U.S. (212) 963-5981); *Statistical Yearbook.*

HUNGARY - NATALITY - See HUNGARY - BIRTH RATES

HUNGARY - NATIONAL ACCOUNTS

Federal Statistical Office, Gustav - Stresesmann - Ring 11, D-6200 Wiesbaden, Federal Republic of Germany; *Ungarn.*

Statistical Office of the United Nations, Publishing Service, New York, New York 10017 (800) 253-9646; *National Accounts Statistics,* and *Statistical Yearbook.*

HUNGARY - NATIONAL INCOME

Facts on File, 460 Park Avenue South, New York, New York 10016 (800) 443-8323; *The New Book of World Rankings.*

G.K. Hall and Company, 70 Lincoln Street, Boston, Massachusetts 02111 (617) 423-3990; *The World in Figures.*

Hungarian Statistical Office, 1033 Budapest, III, Kaszasdulo U.2.; *Hungary Statistical Yearbook.*

Statistical Office of the United Nations, Publishing Service, New York, New York 10017 (800) 253-9646; *Statistical Yearbook.*

HUNGARY - NATIONAL PRODUCT

Facts on File, 460 Park Avenue South, New York, New York 10016 (800) 443-8323; *The New Book of World Rankings.*

Hungarian Statistical Office, 1033 Budapest, III, Kaszasdulo U.2.; *Hungary Statistical Yearbook.*

Statistical Office of the United Nations, Publishing Service, New York, New York 10017 (800) 253-9646; *Statistical Yearbook.*

HUNGARY - NATIONAL WEALTH

Hungarian Statistical Office, 1033 Budapest, III, Kaszasdulo U.2.; *Hungary Statistical Yearbook.*

HUNGARY - NATURAL GAS PRODUCTION - See HUNGARY - MINING AND MINERAL PRODUCTS

HUNGARY - NATURAL RUBBER PRODUCTION

International Rubber Study Group, York House, 8th Floor, Empire Way, Wembley, London HA9 0PA, England *Rubber Statistical Bulletin.*

HUNGARY - NET MATERIAL PRODUCT

Statistical Office of the United Nations, Publishing Service, New York, New York 10017 (800) 253-9646; *Statistical Yearbook.*

HUNGARY - NEWSPAPER PRODUCTION - See HUNGARY - FORESTRY AND FOREST PRODUCTS

HUNGARY - NITRIC ACID PRODUCTION

Statistical Office of the United Nations, Publishing Service, New York, New York 10017 (800) 253-9646; *Statistical Yearbook.*

HUNGARY - OATS PRODUCTION - See HUNGARY - CROPS

HUNGARY - OCCUPATIONS - See HUNGARY - LABOR FORCE

HUNGARY - PAPER PRODUCTION - See HUNGARY - FORESTRY AND FOREST PRODUCTS

HUNGARY - PARTY LEADERS AND MEMBERSHIP

Columbia University Press, 562 West 113th Street, New York, New York 10014 (212) 316-7100; *East European and Soviet Data Book.*

HUNGARY - PATENTS

Statistical Office of the United Nations, Publishing Service, New York, New York 10017 (800) 253-9646; *Statistical Yearbook.*

World Intellectual Property Organization, 34 Chemin des Colombettes, CH-1211 Geneva 20, Switzerland; *Industrial Property Statistics.*

HUNGARY - PEANUT PRODUCTION - See HUNGARY - CROPS

HUNGARY - PERIODICALS

United Nations Educational, Scientific and Cultural Organization (UNESCO), 7 Place de Fontenoy, F-75700 Paris, France (Telephone Number in U.S. (212) 963-5981); *Statistical Yearbook.*

HUNGARY - PESTICIDE USE

Food and Agricultural Organization of the United Nations (FAO) Via delle Terme di Caracalla, 00100 Rome, Italy (Telephone Number in U.S. (202) 653-2400); *The State of Food and Agriculture.*

HUNGARY - PETROLEUM INDUSTRY

Euromonitor Publications Limited, 87-88 Turnmill Street, London EC1M 5QU, England; *European Marketing Data and Statistics.*

Facts on File, 460 Park Avenue South, New York, New York 10016 (800) 443-8323; *The New Book of World Rankings.*

Food and Agricultural Organization of the United Nations (FAO) Via delle Terme di Caracalla, 00100 Rome, Italy (Telephone Number in U.S. (202) 653-2400); *The State of Food and Agriculture.*

G.K. Hall and Company, 70 Lincoln Street, Boston, Massachusetts 02111 (617) 423-3990; *The World in Figures.*

Penn Well Publishing Company, 1421 South Sheridan Road, Post Office Box 1260, Tulsa, Oklahoma 74101 (800) 752-9764; *International Energy Statistics Sourcebook.*

Statistical Office of the United Nations, Publishing Service, New York, New York 10017 (800) 253-9646; *Statistical Yearbook.*

HUNGARY - PIG-IRON AND FERRO-ALLOY PRODUCTION - See HUNGARY - MINING AND MINERAL PRODUCTS

HUNGARY - PIGS - See HUNGARY - LIVESTOCK AND POULTRY

HUNGARY - PIPELINES FOR OIL AND PETROLEUM PRODUCTS

Statistical Office of the United Nations, Publishing Service, New York, New York 10017 (800) 253-9646; *Annual Bulletin of Transport Statistics for Europe.*

HUNGARY - PLASTIC AND RESIN PRODUCTION

Statistical Office of the United Nations, Publishing Service, New York, New York 10017 (800) 253-9646; *Statistical Yearbook.*

HUNGARY - POPULATION

Columbia University Press, 562 West 113th Street, New York, New York 10014 (212) 316-7100; *East European and Soviet Data Book.*

The Economist Intelligence Unit, 111 West 57th Street, New York, New York 10019 (800) 938-4685; *The World Market Atlas.*

Euromonitor Publications Limited, 87-88 Turnmill Street, London EC1M 5QU, England; *European Marketing Data and Statistics.*

Facts on File, 460 Park Avenue South, New York, New York 10016 (800) 443-8323; *The New Book of World Rankings.*

Federal Statistical Office, Gustav - Stresesmann - Ring 11, D-6200 Wiesbaden, Federal Republic of Germany; *Ungarn.*

Food and Agricultural Organization of the United Nations (FAO), Via delle Terme di Caracalla, 00100 Rome, Italy (Telephone Number in U.S. (202) 653-2400); *Production Yearbook.*

G.K. Hall and Company, 70 Lincoln Street, Boston, Massachusetts 02111 (617) 423-3990; *The World in Figures.*

Hungarian Statistical Office, 1033 Budapest, III, Kaszasdulo U.2.; *Hungary Statistical Yearbook.*

International Labour Office, I.L.O. Publications, CH-1211, Geneva 22, Switzerland; *Yearbook of Labour Statistics.*

Statistical Office of the United Nations, Publishing Service, New York, New York 10017 (800) 253-9646; *Demographic Yearbook,* and *Statistical Yearbook.*

Times Books, 201 East 50th Street, New York, New York 10022 (212) 751-2600; *The Economist Book of Vital World Statistics.*

United Nations Educational, Scientific and Cultural Organization (UNESCO), 7 Place de Fontenoy, F-75700 Paris, France (Telephone Number in U.S. (212) 963-5981); *Statistical Yearbook.*

U.S. Arms Control and Disarmament Agency, 320 Twenty-first Street, Northwest, Washington, D.C. 20451 (202) 647-8677; *World Military Expenditures and Arms Transfers.*

World Health Organization, Office of Publications, Avenue Appia, CH-1211 Geneva 27, Switzerland (Telephone Number in U.S. (518) 436-9686); *World Health Statistics Annual.*

HUNGARY - POST OFFICES

Facts on File, 460 Park Avenue South, New York, New York 10016 (800) 443-8323; *The New Book of World Rankings.*

HUNGARY - POTATO PRODUCTION - See HUNGARY - CROPS

HUNGARY - POWER PRODUCTION INDUSTRY

Statistical Office of the United Nations, Publishing Service, New York, New York 10017 (800) 253-9646; *Statistical Yearbook.*

HUNGARY - PRICES

Facts on File, 460 Park Avenue South, New York, New York 10016 (800) 443-8323; *The New Book of World Rankings.*

Federal Statistical Office, Gustav - Stresesmann - Ring 11, D-6200 Wiesbaden, Federal Republic of Germany; *Ungarn.*

Food and Agricultural Organization of the United Nations (FAO), Via delle Terme di Caracalla, 00100 Rome, Italy (Telephone Number in U.S. (202) 653-2400); *Production Yearbook,* and *The State of Food and Agriculture.*

G.K. Hall and Company, 70 Lincoln Street, Boston, Massachusetts 02111 (617) 423-3990; *The World in Figures.*

International Labour Office, I.L.O. Publications, CH-1211, Geneva 22, Switzerland; *Yearbook of Labour Statistics.*

International Lead and Zinc Study Group, Metro House, 58 St. James's Street, London SW1A 1LD, England; *Lead and Zinc Statistics.*

International Monetary Fund, 700 Nineteenth Street, NW, Washington, D.C. 20431 (202) 623-7000; *International Financial Statistics.*

International Rubber Study Group, York House, 8th Floor, Empire Way, Wembley, London HA9 0PA, England; *Rubber Statistical Bulletin.*

HUNGARY - PRODUCTION

Facts on File, 460 Park Avenue South, New York, New York 10016 (800) 443-8323; *The New Book of World Rankings.*

G.K. Hall and Company, 70 Lincoln Street, Boston, Massachusetts 02111 (617) 423-3990; *The World in Figures.*

International Lead and Zinc Study Group, Metro House, 58 St. James's Street, London SW1A 1LD, England; *Lead and Zinc Statistics.*

International Rubber Study Group, York House, 8th Floor, Empire Way, Wembley, London HA9 0PA, England; *Rubber Statistical Bulletin.*

Motor Vehicle Manufacturers Association of the United States, 7430 Second Avenue, Suite 300, Detroit, Michigan 48202 (313) 872-4311; *World Motor Vehicle Data.*

HUNGARY - PUBLIC FINANCE

Facts on File, 460 Park Avenue South, New York, New York 10016 (800) 443-8323; *The New Book of World Rankings.*

Federal Statistical Office, Gustav - Stresesmann - Ring 11, D-6200 Wiesbaden, Federal Republic of Germany; *Ungarn.*

HUNGARY - RADIO BROADCASTING - See HUNGARY - BROADCASTING

HUNGARY - RADIO RECEIVER PRODUCTION

Statistical Office of the United Nations, Publishing Service, New York, New York 10017 (800) 253-9646; *Statistical Yearbook.*

HUNGARY - RAILWAYS

Euromonitor Publications Limited, 87-88 Turnmill Street, London EC1M 5QU, England; *European Marketing Data and Statistics.*

G.K. Hall and Company, 70 Lincoln Street, Boston, Massachusetts 02111 (617) 423-3990; *The World in Figures.*

Jane's Information Group, Sentinel House, 163 Brighton Road, Coulsdon, Surrey CR5 2NH, England (Telephone Number in U.S. (703) 683-3700); *Jane's World Railways.*

Statistical Office of the United Nations, Publishing Service, New York, New York 10017 (800) 253-9646; *Annual Bulletin of Transport Statistics for Europe,* and *Statistical Yearbook.*

HUNGARY - RAPESEED PRODUCTION - See HUNGARY - CROPS

HUNGARY - RELIGION

Facts on File, 460 Park Avenue South, New York, New York 10016 (800) 443-8323; *The New Book of World Rankings.*

HUNGARY - RENT PRICES

International Labour Office, I.L.O. Publications, CH-1211, Geneva 22, Switzerland; *Yearbook of Labour Statistics.*

HUNGARY - RETAIL TRADE

G.K. Hall and Company, 70 Lincoln Street, Boston, Massachusetts 02111 (617) 423-3990; *The World in Figures.*

Statistical Office of the United Nations, Publishing Service, New York, New York 10017 (800) 253-9646; *Statistical Yearbook.*

HUNGARY - RICE PRODUCTION - See HUNGARY - CROPS

HUNGARY - ROOT AND TUBER PRODUCTION - See HUNGARY - CROPS

HUNGARY - ROUNDWOOD PRODUCTION - See HUNGARY - FORESTRY AND FOREST PRODUCTS

HUNGARY - RUBBER PRODUCTION

Facts on File, 460 Park Avenue South, New York, New York 10016 (800) 443-8323; *The New Book of World Rankings.*

International Rubber Study Group, York House, 8th Floor, Empire Way, Wembley, London HA9 0PA, England; *Rubber Statistical Bulletin.*

Statistical Office of the United Nations, Publishing Service, New York, New York 10017 (800) 253-9646; *Statistical Yearbook.*

HUNGARY - RYE PRODUCTION - See HUNGARY - CROPS

HUNGARY - SAWNWOOD PRODUCTION - See HUNGARY - FORESTRY AND FOREST PRODUCTS

HUNGARY - SCIENCE AND TECHNOLOGY - EXPENDITURE FOR RESEARCH

Statistical Office of the United Nations, Publishing Service, New York, New York 10017 (800) 253-9646; *Statistical Yearbook.*

HUNGARY - SCIENTISTS AND TECHNICIANS

Statistical Office of the United Nations, Publishing Service, New York, New York 10017 (800) 253-9646; *Statistical Yearbook.*

United Nations Educational, Scientific and Cultural Organization (UNESCO), 7 Place de Fontenoy, F-75700 Paris, France (Telephone Number in U.S. (212) 963-5981); *Statistical Yearbook.*

HUNGARY - SENIOR CITIZENS

Facts on File, 460 Park Avenue South, New York, New York 10016 (800) 443-8323; *The New Book of World Rankings.*

HUNGARY - SHEEP - See HUNGARY - LIVESTOCK AND POULTRY

HUNGARY - SILVER PRODUCTION AND CONSUMPTION - See HUNGARY - MINING AND MINERAL PRODUCTS

HUNGARY - SOCIAL DATA

Facts on File, 460 Park Avenue South, New York, New York 10016 (800) 443-8323; *The New Book of World Rankings.*

G.K. Hall and Company, 70 Lincoln Street, Boston, Massachusetts 02111 (617) 423-3990; *The World in Figures.*

HUNGARY - SOYBEAN PRODUCTION - See HUNGARY - CROPS

HUNGARY - STEEL - See HUNGARY -MINING AND MINERAL PRODUCTS

HUNGARY - STOCKS - COMMODITY - MARKET PRICE - INDEX

Food and Agricultural Organization of the United Nations (FAO) Via delle Terme di Caracalla, 00100 Rome, Italy (Telephone Number in U.S. (202) 653-2400); *The State of Food and Agriculture.*

International Lead and Zinc Study Group, Metro House, 58 St. James's Street, London SW1A 1LD, England; *Lead and Zinc Statistics.*

HUNGARY - SUGAR PRODUCTION AND CONSUMPTION - See HUNGARY - CROPS

HUNGARY - SULPHURIC ACID PRODUCTION

Statistical Office of the United Nations, Publishing Service, New York, New York 10017 (800) 253-9646; *Statistical Yearbook.*

HUNGARY - TAXATION

G.K. Hall and Company, 70 Lincoln Street, Boston, Massachusetts 02111 (617) 423-3990; *The World in Figures.*

International Road Federation, 525 School Street, SW, Washington, D.C. 20024 (202) 554-2105; *World Road Statistics.*

The World Bank, 1818 H Street, NW, Washington, D.C. 20433 (202) 477-1234; *World Tables.*

HUNGARY - TELEGRAPH SERVICE

Statistical Office of the United Nations, Publishing Service, New York, New York 10017 (800) 253-9646; *Statistical Yearbook.*

HUNGARY - TELEPHONES IN USE

American Telephone and Telegraph Company, 26 Parsippany Road, Whippany, New Jersey 07981 (800) 338-4038; *The World's Telephones.*

G.K. Hall and Company, 70 Lincoln Street, Boston, Massachusetts 02111 (617) 423-3990; *The World in Figures.*

Statistical Office of the United Nations, Publishing Service, New York, New York 10017 (800) 253-9646; *Statistical Yearbook.*

HUNGARY - TELEVISION BROADCASTING - See HUNGARY - BROADCASTING

HUNGARY - TEXTILE INDUSTRY

Food and Agricultural Organization of the United Nations (FAO), Via delle Terme di Caracalla, 00100 Rome, Italy (Telephone Number in U.S. (202) 653-2400); *Production Yearbook.*

G.K. Hall and Company, 70 Lincoln Street, Boston, Massachusetts 02111 (617) 423-3990; *The World in Figures.*

Statistical Office of the United Nations, Publishing Service, New York, New York 10017 (800) 253-9646; *Statistical Yearbook.*

HUNGARY - THEATRE

United Nations Educational, Scientific and Cultural Organization (UNESCO), 7 Place de Fontenoy, F-75700 Paris, France (Telephone Number in U.S. (212) 963-5981); *Statistical Yearbook.*

HUNGARY - TIN - INDUSTRIAL CONSUMPTION - See HUNGARY - MINING AND MINERAL PRODUCTS

HUNGARY - TIRE (MOTOR VEHICLE) PRODUCTION

International Rubber Study Group, York House, 8th Floor, Empire Way, Wembley, London HA9 0PA, England; *Rubber Statistical Bulletin.*

Statistical Office of the United Nations, Publishing Service, New York, New York 10017 (800) 253-9646; *Statistical Yearbook.*

HUNGARY - TOBACCO PRODUCTION

Euromonitor Publications Limited, 87-88 Turnmill Street, London EC1M 5QU, England; *European Marketing Data and Statistics.*

Facts on File, 460 Park Avenue South, New York, New York 10016 (800) 443-8323; *The New Book of World Rankings.*

Statistical Office of the United Nations, Publishing Service, New York, New York 10017 (800) 253-9646; *Statistical Yearbook.*

HUNGARY - TOURISM

Euromonitor Publications Limited, 87-88 Turnmill Street, London EC1M 5QU, England; *European Marketing Data and Statistics.*

Facts on File, 460 Park Avenue South, New York, New York 10016 (800) 443-8323; *The New Book of World Rankings.*

Federal Statistical Office, Gustav - Stresesmann - Ring 11, D-6200 Wiesbaden, Federal Republic of Germany; *Ungarn.*

G.K. Hall and Company, 70 Lincoln Street, Boston, Massachusetts 02111 (617) 423-3990; *The World in Figures.*

Hungarian Statistical Office, 1033 Budapest, III, Kaszasdulo U.2.; *Hungary Statistical Yearbook.*

Statistical Office of the United Nations, Publishing Service, New York, New York 10017 (800) 253-9646; *Statistical Yearbook.*

Times Books, 201 East 50th Street, New York, New York 10022 (212) 751-2600; *The Economist Book of Vital World Statistics.*

World Tourism Organization, Calle Capitan Haya 42, E-28020 Madrid, Spain; *Yearbook of Tourism Statistics.*

HUNGARY - TRACTORS IN USE

Statistical Office of the United Nations, Publishing Service, New York, New York 10017 (800) 253-9646; *Statistical Yearbook.*

HUNGARY - TRADE - See HUNGARY - FOREIGN TRADE

HUNGARY - TRADEMARKS AND SERVICE MARKS

Statistical Office of the United Nations, Publishing Service, New York, New York 10017 (800) 253-9646; *Statistical Yearbook.*

World Intellectual Property Organization, 34 Chemin des Colombettes, CH-1211 Geneva 20, Switzerland; *Industrial Property Statistics.*

HUNGARY - TRANSPORTATION AND COMMUNICATIONS

Facts on File, 460 Park Avenue South, New York, New York 10016 (800) 443-8323; *The New Book of World Rankings.*

Federal Statistical Office, Gustav - Stresesmann - Ring 11, D-6200 Wiesbaden, Federal Republic of Germany; *Ungarn.*

G.K. Hall and Company, 70 Lincoln Street, Boston, Massachusetts 02111 (617) 423-3990; *The World in Figures.*

Hungarian Statistical Office, 1033 Budapest, III, Kaszasdulo U.2.; *Hungary Statistical Yearbook.*

HUNGARY - TURKEYS - See HUNGARY - LIVESTOCK AND POULTRY

HUNGARY - UNEMPLOYMENT

Euromonitor Publications Limited, 87-88 Turnmill Street, London EC1M 5QU, England; *European Marketing Data and Statistics.*

International Labour Office, I.L.O. Publications, CH-1211, Geneva 22, Switzerland; *Yearbook of Labour Statistics.*

HUNGARY - VITAL STATISTICS

G.K. Hall and Company, 70 Lincoln Street, Boston, Massachusetts 02111 (617) 423-3990; *The World in Figures.*

Hungarian Statistical Office, 1033 Budapest, III, Kaszasdulo U.2.; *Hungary Statistical Yearbook.*

Statistical Office of the United Nations, Publishing Service, New York, New York 10017 (800) 253-9646; *Statistical Yearbook.*

World Health Organization, Office of Publications, Avenue Appia, CH-1211 Geneva 27, Switzerland (Telephone Number in U.S. (518) 436-9686); *World Health Statistics Annual.*

HUNGARY - WAGES

Euromonitor Publications Limited, 87-88 Turnmill Street, London EC1M 5QU, England; *European Marketing Data and Statistics.*

Federal Statistical Office, Gustav - Stresesmann - Ring 11, D-6200 Wiesbaden, Federal Republic of Germany; *Ungarn.*

G.K. Hall and Company, 70 Lincoln Street, Boston, Massachusetts 02111 (617) 423-3990; *The World in Figures.*

International Labour Office, I.L.O. Publications, CH-1211, Geneva 22, Switzerland; *Yearbook of Labour Statistics.*

Statistical Office of the United Nations, Publishing Service, New York, New York 10017 (800) 253-9646; *Statistical Yearbook.*

HUNGARY - WALNUT PRODUCTION - See HUNGARY - CROPS

HUNGARY - WATERMELON PRODUCTION - See HUNGARY - CROPS

HUNGARY - WATERWAYS IN USE

Statistical Office of the United Nations, Publishing Service, New York, New York 10017 (800) 253-9646; *Annual Bulletin of Transport Statistics for Europe.*

HUNGARY - WEATHER

Facts on File, 460 Park Avenue South, New York, New York 10016 (800) 443-8323; *The New Book of World Rankings.*

G.K. Hall and Company, 70 Lincoln Street, Boston, Massachusetts 02111 (617) 423-3990; *The World in Figures.*

HUNGARY - WHEAT PRODUCTION AND PRICES - See HUNGARY - CROPS

HUNGARY - WHOLESALE PRICES

Statistical Office of the United Nations, Publishing Service, New York, New York 10017 (800) 253-9646; *Statistical Yearbook.*

HUNGARY - WHOLESALE TRADE

Statistical Office of the United Nations, Publishing Service, New York, New York 10017 (800) 253-9646; *Statistical Yearbook.*

HUNGARY - WINE PRODUCTION

Facts on File, 460 Park Avenue South, New York, New York 10016 (800) 443-8323; *The New Book of World Rankings.*

Statistical Office of the United Nations, Publishing Service, New York, New York 10017 (800) 253-9646; *Statistical Yearbook.*

HUNGARY - WOOD PULP PRODUCTION - See HUNGARY - FORESTRY AND FOREST PRODUCTS

HUNGARY - WOOL PRODUCTION

Facts on File, 460 Park Avenue South, New York, New York 10016 (800) 443-8323; *The New Book of World Rankings.*

HUNGARY - YARN PRODUCTION

Statistical Office of the United Nations, Publishing Service, New York, New York 10017 (800) 253-9646; *Statistical Yearbook.*

HUNGARY - ZINC AND ZINC ORE - See HUNGARY - MINING AND MINERAL PRODUCTS

HUNTING AND FISHING

National Sporting Goods Association, 1699 Wall Street, Mount Prospect, Illinois 60056 (708) 439-4000; *Sports Participation in 1991,* and *The Sporting Goods Market in 1992.*

U.S. Department of Agriculture, Forest Service, Fourteenth Street and Independence Avenue, SW, Washington, D.C. 20250 (202) 720-3760; unpublished data.

U.S. Department of the Interior, Bureau of Land Management, C Street between Eighteenth and Nineteenth Streets, NW, Washington, D.C. 20240 (202) 208-3435; *Public Land Statistics.*

U.S. Department of the Interior, Fish and Wildlife Service, C Street between Eighteenth and Nineteenth Streets, NW, Washington, D.C. 20240 (202) 208-5634; *Federal Aid in Fish and Wildlife Restoration,* and *National Survey of Fishing, Hunting, and Wildlife-Associated Recreation.*

HURRICANES

National Hurricane Center, 1320 South Dixie Highway, Coral Gables, Florida 33146 (305) 666-0413; unpublished data.

U.S. Department of Commerce, National Oceanic and Atmospheric Administration, National Climatic Data Center, Federal Building, Asheville, North Carolina 28801 (704) 259-2850; *Storm Data.*

HYDROELECTRIC POWER

U.S. Department of Energy, Federal Energy Regulatory Commission, 1000 Independence Avenue, SW, Washington, D.C. 20585 (202) 208-0300; *Hydroelectric Power Resources of the United States, Developed and Undeveloped,* and unpublished data.

HYDROELECTRIC POWER - CAPACITY

U.S. Department of Energy, Energy Information Administration, Washington, D.C. 20585 (202) 586-8800; *Electric Power Annual, Annual Energy Review,* and unpublished data.

U.S. Department of Energy, Federal Energy Regulatory Commission, 1000 Independence Avenue, SW, Washington, D.C. 20585 (202) 208-0300; *Hydroelectric Power Resources of the United States, Developed and Undeveloped,* and unpublished data.

HYDROELECTRIC POWER - CONSUMPTION

U.S. Department of Energy, Energy Information Administration, Washington, D.C. 20585 (202) 586-8800; *Annual Energy Review, State Energy Data Report, Monthly Energy Review, Electric Power Annual,* and unpublished data.

HYDROELECTRIC POWER - PRODUCTION

U.S. Department of Energy, Energy Information Administration, Washington, D.C. 20585 (202) 586-8800; *Annual Energy Review, Monthly Energy Review, Electric Power Annual,* and unpublished data.

HYPERTENSION

U.S. Department of Health and Human Services, National Center for Health Statistics, 3700 East-West Highway, Hyattsville, Maryland 20782 (301) 436-8500; *Vital and Health Statistics,* and unpublished data.

I

ICE CREAM

U.S. Department of Agriculture, Economic Research Service, 14th Street and Independence Avenue, SW, Washington, D.C. 20005-4789 (202) 219-1504; *Food Consumption, Prices, and Expenditures, Dairy Products,* and *Milk Production, Disposition, and Income.*

Iceland - National Statistical Office

Statistical Bureau of Iceland, Skuggasund 3, 15-150, Reykjavik, Iceland.

Iceland - Primary Statistics Sources

Statistical Bureau of Iceland, Skuggasund 3, 15-150, Reykjavik, *Hagtioindi* (Statistical Bulletin), and *Landshagir* (Statistical Abstract of Ireland).

ICELAND - ABORTIONS

Nordic Council of Ministers, Store Strandstraede 18, DK-1255 Copenhagen K, Denmark and the Nordic Statistical Secretariat, Postboks 2550, DK-2100 Copenhagen 0, Denmark; *The Yearbook of Nordic Statistics.*

Statistical Office of the United Nations, Publishing Service, New York, New York 10017 (800) 253-9646; *Demographic Yearbook.*

ICELAND - AGRICULTURE

Facts on File, 460 Park Avenue South, New York, New York 10016 (800) 443-8323; *The New Book of World Rankings.*

Food and Agricultural Organization of the United Nations (FAO), Via delle Terme di Caracalla, 00100 Rome, Italy (Telephone Number in U.S. (202) 653-2400); *Production Yearbook,* and *The State of Food and Agriculture.*

G.K. Hall and Company, 70 Lincoln Street, Boston, Massachusetts 02111 (617) 423-3990; *The World in Figures.*

Nordic Council of Ministers, Store Strandstraede 18, DK-1255 Copenhagen K, Denmark and the Nordic Statistical Secretariat, Postboks 2550, DK-2100 Copenhagen 0, Denmark; *The Yearbook of Nordic Statistics.*

Organisation for Economic Co-operation and Development (OECD), 2 rue Andre-Pascal, 75 Paris 16, France (Telephone Number in U.S. (202) 785-6323); *Economic Accounts for Agriculture, Industrial Structure Statistics,* and *OECD Economic Surveys: Iceland.*

Statistical Office of the United Nations, Publishing Service, New York, New York 10017 (800) 253-9646; *Statistical Yearbook.*

Times Books, 201 East 50th Street, New York, New York 10022 (212) 751-2600; *The Economist Book of Vital World Statistics.*

U.S. Arms Control and Disarmament Agency, 320 Twenty-first Street, Northwest, Washington, D.C. 20451 (202) 647-8677; *World Military Expenditures and Arms Transfers.*

The World Bank, 1818 H Street, NW, Washington, D.C. 20433 (202) 477-1234; *World Tables.*

ICELAND - AIRLINE SERVICE

Facts on File, 460 Park Avenue South, New York, New York 10016 (800) 443-8323; *The New Book of World Rankings.*

G.K. Hall and Company, 70 Lincoln Street, Boston, Massachusetts 02111 (617) 423-3990; *The World in Figures.*

International Civil Aviation Organization, 1000 Sherbrooke Street West, Suite 400, Montreal, Quebec, Canada H3A 2R2 (514) 285-8219; *Civil Aviation Statistics of the World.*

Nordic Council of Ministers, Store Strandstraede 18, DK-1255 Copenhagen K, Denmark and the Nordic Statistical Secretariat, Postboks 2550, DK-2100 Copenhagen 0, Denmark; *The Yearbook of Nordic Statistics.*

Organisation for Economic Co-operation and Development (OECD), 2 rue Andre-Pascal, 75 Paris 16, France (Telephone Number in U.S. (202) 785-6323); *Tourism Policy and International Tourism in OECD Member Countries.*

Statistical Office of the United Nations, Publishing Service, New York, New York 10017 (800) 253-9646; *Statistical Yearbook.*

Times Books, 201 East 50th Street, New York, New York 10022 (212) 751-2600; *The Economist Book of Vital World Statistics.*

ICELAND - ALUMINUM - See ICELAND - MINING AND MINERAL PRODUCTS

ICELAND - ANIMAL FEEDINGSTUFFS

Organisation for Economic Co-operation and Development (OECD), 2 rue Andre-Pascal, 75 Paris 16, France (Telephone Number in U.S. (202) 785-6323); *Foreign Trade by Commodities.*

Statistical Office of the United Nations, Publishing Service, New York, New York 10017 (800) 253-9646; *Statistical Yearbook.*

ICELAND - ANIMAL HEALTH

Food and Agricultural Organization of the United Nations (FAO), Via delle Terme di Caracalla, 00100 Rome, Italy (Telephone Number in U.S. (202) 653-2400); *Animal Health Yearbook.*

ICELAND - AREA AND DENSITY OF POPULATION

Facts on File, 460 Park Avenue South, New York, New York 10016 (800) 443-8323; *The New Book of World Rankings.*

Food and Agricultural Organization of the United Nations (FAO) Via delle Terme di Caracalla, 00100 Rome, Italy (Telephone Number in U.S. (202) 653-2400); *The State of Food and Agriculture.*

G.K. Hall and Company, 70 Lincoln Street, Boston, Massachusetts 02111 (617) 423-3990; *The World in Figures.*

Nordic Council of Ministers, Store Strandstraede 18, DK-1255 Copenhagen K, Denmark and the Nordic Statistical Secretariat, Postboks 2550, DK-2100 Copenhagen 0, Denmark; *The Yearbook of Nordic Statistics.*

Statistical Office of the United Nations, Publishing Service, New York, New York 10017 (800) 253-9646; *Statistical Yearbook.*

Times Books, 201 East 50th Street, New York, New York 10022 (212) 751-2600; *The Economist Book of Vital World Statistics.*

United Nations Educational, Scientific and Cultural Organization (UNESCO), 7 Place de Fontenoy, F-75700 Paris, France (Telephone Number in U.S. (212) 963-5981); *Statistical Yearbook.*

ICELAND - BALANCE OF PAYMENTS

The Economist Intelligence Unit, 111 West 57th Street, New York, New York 10019 (800) 938-4685; *The World Market Atlas.*

G.K. Hall and Company, 70 Lincoln Street, Boston, Massachusetts 02111 (617) 423-3990; *The World in Figures.*

International Monetary Fund, 700 Nineteenth Street, NW, Washington, D.C. 20431 (202) 623-7000; *Balance of Payments Yearbook.*

Nordic Council of Ministers, Store Strandstraede 18, DK-1255 Copenhagen K, Denmark and the Nordic Statistical Secretariat, Postboks 2550, DK-2100 Copenhagen 0, Denmark; *The Yearbook of Nordic Statistics.*

Organisation for Economic Co-operation and Development (OECD), 2 rue Andre-Pascal, 75 Paris 16, France (Telephone Number in U.S. (202) 785-6323); *Economic Outlook, Geographical Distribution of Financial Flows to Developing Countries,* and *OECD Economic Surveys: Iceland.*

Times Books, 201 East 50th Street, New York, New York 10022 (212) 751-2600; *The Economist Book of Vital World Statistics.*

The World Bank, 1818 H Street, NW, Washington, D.C. 20433 (202) 477-1234; *World Tables.*

ICELAND - BANKING

Facts on File, 460 Park Avenue South, New York, New York 10016 (800) 443-8323; *The New Book of World Rankings.*

G.K. Hall and Company, 70 Lincoln Street, Boston, Massachusetts 02111 (617) 423-3990; *The World in Figures.*

International Monetary Fund, 700 Nineteenth Street, NW, Washington, D.C. 20431 (202) 623-7000; *International Financial Statistics.*

Nordic Council of Ministers, Store Strandstraede 18, DK-1255 Copenhagen K, Denmark and the Nordic Statistical Secretariat, Postboks 2550, DK-2100 Copenhagen 0, Denmark; *The Yearbook of Nordic Statistics.*

Organisation for Economic Co-operation and Development (OECD), 2 rue Andre-Pascal, 75 Paris 16, France (Telephone Number in U.S. (202) 785-6323); *Economic Outlook, Financial Market Trends,* and *OECD Economic Surveys: Iceland.*

Statistical Office of the United Nations, Publishing Service, New York, New York 10017 (800) 253-9646; *Statistical Yearbook.*

ICELAND - BARLEY PRODUCTION - See ICELAND - CROPS

ICELAND - BEER PRODUCTION

Facts on File, 460 Park Avenue South, New York, New York 10016 (800) 443-8323; *The New Book of World Rankings.*

Statistical Office of the United Nations, Publishing Service, New York, New York 10017 (800) 253-9646; *Statistical Yearbook.*

ICELAND - BIRTH RATE

Facts on File, 460 Park Avenue South, New York, New York 10016 (800) 443-8323; *The New Book of World Rankings.*

Nordic Council of Ministers, Store Strandstraede 18, DK-1255 Copenhagen K, Denmark and the Nordic Statistical Secretariat, Postboks 2550, DK-2100 Copenhagen 0, Denmark; *The Yearbook of Nordic Statistics.*

Organisation for Economic Co-operation and Development (OECD), 2 rue Andre-Pascal, 75 Paris 16, France (Telephone Number in U.S. (202) 785-6323); *Labour Force Statistics.*

Statistical Office of the United Nations, Publishing Service, New York, New York 10017 (800) 253-9646; *Demographic Yearbook,* and *Statistical Yearbook.*

Times Books, 201 East 50th Street, New York, New York 10022 (212) 751-2600; *The Economist Book of Vital World Statistics.*

The World Bank, 1818 H Street, NW, Washington, D.C. 20433 (202) 477-1234; *World Tables.*

World Health Organization, Avenue Appia, Office of Publications, CH-1211 Geneva 27, Switzerland (Telephone Number in U.S. (518) 436-9686); *World Health Statistics Annual.*

ICELAND - BONDS

G.K. Hall and Company, 70 Lincoln Street, Boston, Massachusetts 02111 (617) 423-3990; *The World in Figures.*

International Monetary Fund, 700 Nineteenth Street, NW, Washington, D.C. 20431 (202) 623-7000; *Government Finance Statistics Yearbook.*

Organisation for Economic Co-operation and Development (OECD), 2 rue Andre-Pascal, 75 Paris 16, France (Telephone Number in U.S. (202) 785-6323); *Financial Market Trends.*

ICELAND - BOOK PRODUCTION

Euromonitor Publications Limited, 87-88 Turnmill Street, London EC1M 5QU, England; *European Marketing Data and Statistics.*

G.K. Hall and Company, 70 Lincoln Street, Boston, Massachusetts 02111 (617) 423-3990; *The World in Figures.*

Nordic Council of Ministers, Store Strandstraede 18, DK-1255 Copenhagen K, Denmark and the Nordic Statistical Secretariat, Postboks 2550, DK-2100 Copenhagen 0, Denmark; *The Yearbook of Nordic Statistics.*

United Nations Educational, Scientific and Cultural Organization (UNESCO), 7 Place de Fontenoy, F-75700 Paris, France (Telephone Number in U.S. (212) 963-5981); *Statistical Yearbook.*

ICELAND - BROADCASTING

Billboard Limited, Post Office Box 9027, 1006 AA Amsterdam, The Netherlands (Telephone Number in U.S. (212) 764-7300); *World Radio TV Handbook.*

Facts on File, 460 Park Avenue South, New York, New York 10016 (800) 443-8323; *The New Book of World Rankings.*

G.K. Hall and Company, 70 Lincoln Street, Boston, Massachusetts 02111 (617) 423-3990; *The World in Figures.*

Nordic Council of Ministers, Store Strandstraede 18, DK-1255 Copenhagen K, Denmark and the Nordic Statistical Secretariat, Postboks 2550, DK-2100 Copenhagen 0, Denmark; *The Yearbook of Nordic Statistics.*

Times Books, 201 East 50th Street, New York, New York 10022 (212) 751-2600; *The Economist Book of Vital World Statistics.*

United Nations Educational, Scientific and Cultural Organization (UNESCO), 7 Place de Fontenoy, F-75700 Paris, France (Telephone Number in U.S. (212) 963-5981); *Statistical Yearbook.*

ICELAND - BUILDING CONSTRUCTION - See ICELAND - CONSTRUCTION INDUSTRY

ICELAND - BUSINESS

G.K. Hall and Company, 70 Lincoln Street, Boston, Massachusetts 02111 (617) 423-3990; *The World in Figures.*

ICELAND - BUSINESS AND PROFESSIONAL LICENSES

International Monetary Fund, 700 Nineteenth Street, NW, Washington, D.C. 20431 (202) 623-7000; *Government Finance Statistics Yearbook.*

ICELAND - BUTTER - See ICELAND - DAIRY PRODUCTS

ICELAND - CALORIE SUPPLY

Food and Agricultural Organization of the United Nations (FAO) Via delle Terme di Caracalla, 00100 Rome, Italy (Telephone Number in U.S. (202) 653-2400); *The State of Food and Agriculture.*

ICELAND - CAPITAL INVESTMENT

Organisation for Economic Co-operation and Development (OECD), 2 rue Andre-Pascal, 75 Paris 16, France (Telephone Number in U.S. (202) 785-6323); *Economic Outlook,* and *Financial Market Trends.*

ICELAND - CAPITAL REVENUE

International Monetary Fund, 700 Nineteenth Street, NW, Washington, D.C. 20431 (202) 623-7000; *Government Finance Statistics Yearbook.*

Organisation for Economic Co-operation and Development (OECD), 2 rue Andre-Pascal, 75 Paris 16, France (Telephone Number in U.S. (202) 785-6323); *Economic Outlook,* and *Financial Market Trends.*

ICELAND - CATTLE - See ICELAND - LIVESTOCK AND POULTRY

ICELAND - CEMENT PRODUCTION - See ICELAND - MINING AND MINERAL PRODUCTS

ICELAND - CEREAL PRODUCTION - See ICELAND - CROPS

ICELAND - CHEESE - See ICELAND - DAIRY PRODUCTS

ICELAND - CHEMICAL (ORGANIC) PRODUCTION - See ICELAND - MINING AND MINERAL PRODUCTS

ICELAND - CIGARETTE PRODUCTION - See ICELAND - TOBACCO PRODUCTION

ICELAND - CLASS STRUCTURE

G.K. Hall and Company, 70 Lincoln Street, Boston, Massachusetts 02111 (617) 423-3990; *The World in Figures.*

ICELAND - CLIMATE

Facts on File, 460 Park Avenue South, New York, New York 10016 (800) 443-8323; *The New Book of World Rankings.*

G.K. Hall and Company, 70 Lincoln Street, Boston, Massachusetts 02111 (617) 423-3990; *The World in Figures.*

ICELAND - CLOTHING EXPORTS AND IMPORTS

Organisation for Economic Co-operation and Development (OECD), 2 rue Andre-Pascal, 75 Paris 16, France (Telephone Number in U.S. (202) 785-6323); *Textile Industry in OECD Countries.*

ICELAND - COAL PRODUCTION AND CONSUMPTION - See ICELAND - MINING AND MINERAL PRODUCTS

ICELAND - COFFEE PRODUCTION - See ICELAND - CROPS

ICELAND - COKE AND COKE OVEN ORE PRODUCTION AND CONSUMPTION - See ICELAND - MINING AND MINERAL PRODUCTS

ICELAND - COMMUNICATIONS

G.K. Hall and Company, 70 Lincoln Street, Boston, Massachusetts 02111 (617) 423-3990; *The World in Figures.*

ICELAND - CONSTRUCTION INDUSTRY

Facts on File, 460 Park Avenue South, New York, New York 10016 (800) 443-8323; *The New Book of World Rankings.*

Nordic Council of Ministers, Store Strandstraede 18, DK-1255 Copenhagen K, Denmark and the Nordic Statistical Secretariat, Postboks 2550, DK-2100 Copenhagen 0, Denmark; *The Yearbook of Nordic Statistics.*

Organisation for Economic Co-operation and Development (OECD), 2 rue Andre-Pascal, 75 Paris 16, France (Telephone Number in U.S.

(202) 785-6323); *Industrial Structure Statistics, The Iron and Steel Industry,* and *OECD Economic Surveys: Iceland.*

Statistical Office of the United Nations, Publishing Service, New York, New York 10017 (800) 253-9646; *Construction Statistics Yearbook,* and *Statistical Yearbook.*

ICELAND - CONSUMER PRICE INDEX

G.K. Hall and Company, 70 Lincoln Street, Boston, Massachusetts 02111 (617) 423-3990; *The World in Figures.*

Nordic Council of Ministers, Store Strandstraede 18, DK-1255 Copenhagen K, Denmark and the Nordic Statistical Secretariat, Postboks 2550, DK-2100 Copenhagen 0, Denmark; *The Yearbook of Nordic Statistics.*

Organisation for Economic Co-operation and Development (OECD), 2 rue Andre-Pascal, 75 Paris 16, France (Telephone Number in U.S. (202) 785-6323); *Economic Outlook.*

Statistical Office of the United Nations, Publishing Service, New York, New York 10017 (800) 253-9646; *Statistical Yearbook.*

ICELAND - CONSUMER PRICES

Euromonitor Publications Limited, 87-88 Turnmill Street, London EC1M 5QU, England; *European Marketing Data and Statistics.*

International Labour Office, I.L.O. Publications, CH-1211, Geneva 22, Switzerland; *Yearbook of Labour Statistics.*

International Monetary Fund, 700 Nineteenth Street, NW, Washington, D.C. 20431 (202) 623-7000; *International Financial Statistics.*

Organisation for Economic Co-operation and Development (OECD), 2 rue Andre-Pascal, 75 Paris 16, France (Telephone Number in U.S. (202) 785-6323); *Economic Outlook,* and *Main Economic Indicators - Historical Statistics.*

Times Books, 201 East 50th Street, New York, New York 10022 (212) 751-2600; *The Economist Book of Vital World Statistics.*

ICELAND - CONSUMPTION

G.K. Hall and Company, 70 Lincoln Street, Boston, Massachusetts 02111 (617) 423-3990; *The World in Figures.*

Nordic Council of Ministers, Store Strandstraede 18, DK-1255 Copenhagen K, Denmark and the Nordic Statistical Secretariat, Postboks 2550, DK-2100 Copenhagen 0, Denmark; *The Yearbook of Nordic Statistics.*

Organisation for Economic Co-operation and Development (OECD), 2 rue Andre-Pascal, 75 Paris 16, France (Telephone Number in U.S. (202) 785-6323); *The Footwear, Raw Hides and Skins, and Leather Industry in OECD Countries, The Iron and Steel Industry, Meat Balances in OECD Member Countries, The Non-Ferrous Metals Industry, The Pulp and Paper Industry,* and *Textile Industry in OECD Countries.*

ICELAND - COPPER AND COPPER ORE PRODUCTION AND CONSUMPTION - See ICELAND - MINING AND MINERAL PRODUCTS

ICELAND - CORN PRODUCTION - See ICELAND - CROPS

ICELAND - CORPORATE TAXES - See ICELAND - TAXATION

ICELAND - COTTON PRODUCTION - See ICELAND - CROPS

ICELAND - CRIME

International Criminal Police Organization (INTERPOL), 26 rue Armengaud, 92210 Saint Cloud, France; *International Crime Statistics.*

Nordic Council of Ministers, Store Strandstraede 18, DK-1255 Copenhagen K, Denmark and the Nordic Statistical Secretariat, Postboks 2550, DK-2100 Copenhagen 0, Denmark; *The Yearbook of Nordic Statistics.*

Yale University Press, Yale Station, New Haven, Connecticut 06520 (203) 432-0940; *Violence and Crime in Cross-National Perspective.*

ICELAND - CROPS

Euromonitor Publications Limited, 87-88 Turnmill Street, London EC1M 5QU, England; *European Marketing Data and Statistics.*

Facts on File, 460 Park Avenue South, New York, New York 10016 (800) 443-8323; *The New Book of World Rankings.*

Food and Agricultural Organization of the United Nations (FAO) Via delle Terme di Caracalla, 00100 Rome, Italy (Telephone Number in U.S. (202) 653-2400); *Production Yearbook* and *The State of Food and Agriculture.*

G.K. Hall and Company, 70 Lincoln Street, Boston, Massachusetts 02111 (617) 423-3990; *The World in Figures.*

Organisation for Economic Co-operation and Development (OECD), 2 rue Andre-Pascal, 75 Paris 16, France (Telephone Number in U.S. (202) 785-6323); *Economic Accounts for Agriculture, Foreign Trade by Commodities,* and *Textile Industry in OECD Countries.*

Statistical Office of the United Nations, Publishing Service, New York, New York 10017 (800) 253-9646; *Statistical Yearbook.*

ICELAND - CUSTOMS DUTIES

G.K. Hall and Company, 70 Lincoln Street, Boston, Massachusetts 02111 (617) 423-3990; *The World in Figures.*

International Monetary Fund, 700 Nineteenth Street, NW, Washington, D.C. 20431 (202) 623-7000; *Government Finance Statistics Yearbook.*

Organisation for Economic Co-operation and Development (OECD), 2 rue Andre-Pascal, 75 Paris 16, France (Telephone Number in U.S. (202) 785-6323); *The Non-Ferrous Metals Industry.*

ICELAND - DAIRY PRODUCTS

Facts on File, 460 Park Avenue South, New York, New York 10016 (800) 443-8323; *The New Book of World Rankings.*

Food and Agricultural Organization of the United Nations (FAO) Via delle Terme di Caracalla, 00100 Rome, Italy (Telephone Number in U.S. (202) 653-2400); *The State of Food and Agriculture.*

Nordic Council of Ministers, Store Strandstraede 18, DK-1255 Copenhagen K, Denmark and the Nordic Statistical Secretariat, Postboks 2550, DK-2100 Copenhagen 0, Denmark; *The Yearbook of Nordic Statistics.*

Organisation for Economic Co-operation and Development (OECD), 2 rue Andre-Pascal, 75 Paris 16, France (Telephone Number in U.S.

(202) 785-6323); *Economic Accounts for Agriculture*, and *Milk, Milk Products, and Egg Balances in OECD Member Countries*.

Statistical Office of the United Nations, Publishing Service, New York, New York 10017 (800) 253-9646; *Statistical Yearbook*.

ICELAND - DEATH RATES

G.K. Hall and Company, 70 Lincoln Street, Boston, Massachusetts 02111 (617) 423-3990; *The World in Figures*.

Nordic Council of Ministers, Store Strandstraede 18, DK-1255 Copenhagen K, Denmark and the Nordic Statistical Secretariat, Postboks 2550, DK-2100 Copenhagen 0, Denmark; *The Yearbook of Nordic Statistics*.

Statistical Office of the United Nations, Publishing Service, New York, New York 10017 (800) 253-9646; *Statistical Yearbook*.

Times Books, 201 East 50th Street, New York, New York 10022 (212) 751-2600; *The Economist Book of Vital World Statistics*.

World Health Organization, Avenue Appia, Office of Publications, CH-1211 Geneva 27, Switzerland (Telephone Number in U.S. (518) 436-9686); *World Health Statistics Annual*.

ICELAND - DEFENSE EXPENDITURES

G.K. Hall and Company, 70 Lincoln Street, Boston, Massachusetts 02111 (617) 423-3990; *The World in Figures*.

U.S. Arms Control and Disarmament Agency, 320 Twenty-first Street, Northwest, Washington, D.C. 20451 (202) 647-8677; *World Military Expenditures and Arms Transfers*.

ICELAND - DEMOGRAPHY

The Economist Intelligence Unit, 111 West 57th Street, New York, New York 10019 (800) 938-4685; *The World Market Atlas*.

Facts on File, 460 Park Avenue South, New York, New York 10016 (800) 443-8323; *The New Book of World Rankings*.

G.K. Hall and Company, 70 Lincoln Street, Boston, Massachusetts 02111 (617) 423-3990; *The World in Figures*.

Nordic Council of Ministers, Store Strandstraede 18, DK-1255 Copenhagen K, Denmark and the Nordic Statistical Secretariat, Postboks 2550, DK-2100 Copenhagen 0, Denmark; *The Yearbook of Nordic Statistics*.

ICELAND - DEVELOPMENT ASSISTANCE

G.K. Hall and Company, 70 Lincoln Street, Boston, Massachusetts 02111 (617) 423-3990; *The World in Figures*.

Organisation for Economic Co-operation and Development (OECD), 2 rue Andre-Pascal, 75 Paris 16, France (Telephone Number in U.S. (202) 785-6323); *Geographical Distribution of Financial Flows to Developing Countries*.

ICELAND - DIAMOND PRODUCTION - See ICELAND - MINING AND MINERAL PRODUCTS

ICELAND - DISCOUNT RATES

Organisation for Economic Co-operation and Development (OECD), 2 rue Andre-Pascal, 75 Paris 16, France (Telephone Number in U.S. (202) 785-6323); *Financial Market Trends*.

Statistical Office of the United Nations, Publishing Service, New York, New York 10017 (800) 253-9646; *Statistical Yearbook*.

ICELAND - DISEASE

G.K. Hall and Company, 70 Lincoln Street, Boston, Massachusetts 02111 (617) 423-3990; *The World in Figures*.

World Health Organization, Avenue Appia, Office of Publications, CH-1211 Geneva 27, Switzerland (Telephone Number in U.S. (518) 436-9686); *World Health Statistics Annual*.

ICELAND - DIVORCE RATES

Facts on File, 460 Park Avenue South, New York, New York 10016 (800) 443-8323; *The New Book of World Rankings*.

Nordic Council of Ministers, Store Strandstraede 18, DK-1255 Copenhagen K, Denmark and the Nordic Statistical Secretariat, Postboks 2550, DK-2100 Copenhagen 0, Denmark; *The Yearbook of Nordic Statistics*.

Statistical Office of the United Nations, Publishing Service, New York, New York 10017 (800) 253-9646; *Demographic Yearbook*, and *Statistical Yearbook*.

ICELAND - DOMESTIC PRODUCT

G.K. Hall and Company, 70 Lincoln Street, Boston, Massachusetts 02111 (617) 423-3990; *The World in Figures*.

ICELAND - ECONOMY

Euromonitor Publications Limited, 87-88 Turnmill Street, London EC1M 5QU, England; *European Marketing Data and Statistics*.

Facts on File, 460 Park Avenue South, New York, New York 10016 (800) 443-8323; *The New Book of World Rankings*.

G.K. Hall and Company, 70 Lincoln Street, Boston, Massachusetts 02111 (617) 423-3990; *The World in Figures*.

Organisation for Economic Co-operation and Development (OECD), 2 rue Andre-Pascal, 75 Paris 16, France (Telephone Number in U.S. (202) 785-6323); *Economic Outlook*, *Geographical Distribution of Financial Flows to Developing Countries*, *Main Economic Indicators - Historical Statistics*, *OECD Employment Outlook*, and *OECD Economic Surveys: Iceland*.

ICELAND - EDUCATION

The Economist Intelligence Unit, 111 West 57th Street, New York, New York 10019 (800) 938-4685; *The World Market Atlas*.

Euromonitor Publications Limited, 87-88 Turnmill Street, London EC1M 5QU, England; *European Marketing Data and Statistics*.

Facts on File, 460 Park Avenue South, New York, New York 10016 (800) 443-8323; *The New Book of World Rankings*.

G.K. Hall and Company, 70 Lincoln Street, Boston, Massachusetts 02111 (617) 423-3990; *The World in Figures*.

International Monetary Fund, 700 Nineteenth Street, NW, Washington, D.C. 20431 (202) 623-7000; *Government Finance Statistics Yearbook*.

Nordic Council of Ministers, Store Strandstraede 18, DK-1255 Copenhagen K, Denmark and the Nordic Statistical Secretariat,

Postboks 2550, DK-2100 Copenhagen 0, Denmark; *The Yearbook of Nordic Statistics.*

Organisation for Economic Co-operation and Development (OECD), 2 rue Andre-Pascal, 75 Paris 16, France (Telephone Number in U.S. (202) 785-6323); *Education in OECD Countries.*

Times Books, 201 East 50th Street, New York, New York 10022 (212) 751-2600; *The Economist Book of Vital World Statistics.*

United Nations Educational, Scientific and Cultural Organization (UNESCO), 7 Place de Fontenoy, F-75700 Paris, France (Telephone Number in U.S. (212) 963-5981); *Statistical Yearbook.*

The World Bank, 1818 H Street, NW, Washington, D.C. 20433 (202) 477-1234; *World Tables.*

ICELAND - EGG PRODUCTION AND CONSUMPTION - See ICELAND - DAIRY PRODUCTS

ICELAND - ELECTRICITY

Facts on File, 460 Park Avenue South, New York, New York 10016 (800) 443-8323; *The New Book of World Rankings.*

Nordic Council of Ministers, Store Strandstraede 18, DK-1255 Copenhagen K, Denmark and the Nordic Statistical Secretariat, Postboks 2550, DK-2100 Copenhagen 0, Denmark; *The Yearbook of Nordic Statistics.*

Organisation for Economic Co-operation and Development (OECD), 2 rue Andre-Pascal, 75 Paris 16, France (Telephone Number in U.S. (202) 785-6323); *Coal Information, Energy Statistics of OECD Countries,* and *Industrial Structure Statistics.*

Statistical Office of the United Nations, Publishing Service, New York, New York 10017 (800) 253-9646; *Statistical Yearbook.*

Times Books, 201 East 50th Street, New York, New York 10022 (212) 751-2600; *The Economist Book of Vital World Statistics.*

ICELAND - EMPLOYMENT

Euromonitor Publications Limited, 87-88 Turnmill Street, London EC1M 5QU, England; *European Marketing Data and Statistics.*

Facts on File, 460 Park Avenue South, New York, New York 10016 (800) 443-8323; *The New Book of World Rankings.*

International Labour Office, I.L.O. Publications, CH-1211, Geneva 22, Switzerland; *Yearbook of Labour Statistics.*

Nordic Council of Ministers, Store Strandstraede 18, DK-1255 Copenhagen K, Denmark and the Nordic Statistical Secretariat, Postboks 2550, DK-2100 Copenhagen 0, Denmark; *The Yearbook of Nordic Statistics.*

Organisation for Economic Co-operation and Development (OECD), 2 rue Andre-Pascal, 75 Paris 16, France (Telephone Number in U.S. (202) 785-6323); *Coal Information, Economic Outlook, The Iron and Steel Industry, Labour Force Statistics, OECD Employment Outlook, OECD Economic Surveys: Iceland,* and *Textile Industries in OECD Countries.*

Statistical Office of the United Nations, Publishing Service, New York, New York 10017 (800) 253-9646; *Statistical Yearbook.*

ICELAND - ENERGY

Euromonitor Publications Limited, 87-88 Turnmill Street, London EC1M 5QU, England; *European Marketing Data and Statistics.*

Facts on File, 460 Park Avenue South, New York, New York 10016 (800) 443-8323; *The New Book of World Rankings.*

Food and Agricultural Organization of the United Nations (FAO) Via delle Terme di Caracalla, 00100 Rome, Italy (Telephone Number in U.S. (202) 653-2400); *The State of Food and Agriculture.*

G.K. Hall and Company, 70 Lincoln Street, Boston, Massachusetts 02111 (617) 423-3990; *The World in Figures.*

Nordic Council of Ministers, Store Strandstraede 18, DK-1255 Copenhagen K, Denmark and the Nordic Statistical Secretariat, Postboks 2550, DK-2100 Copenhagen 0, Denmark; *The Yearbook of Nordic Statistics.*

Organisation for Economic Co-operation and Development (OECD), 2 rue Andre-Pascal, 75 Paris 16, France (Telephone Number in U.S. (202) 785-6323); *Coal Information, Energy Statistics of OECD Countries, OECD Environmental Data,* and *Oil and Gas Information.*

Statistical Office of the United Nations, Publishing Service, New York, New York 10017 (800) 253-9646; *Energy Statistics Yearbook, Statistical Yearbook,* and *World Energy Supplies.*

Times Books, 201 East 50th Street, New York, New York 10022 (212) 751-2600; *The Economist Book of Vital World Statistics.*

ICELAND - ENVIRONMENT

Organisation for Economic Co-operation and Development (OECD), 2 rue Andre-Pascal, 75 Paris 16, France (Telephone Number in U.S. (202) 785-6323); *OECD Environmental Data.*

ICELAND - EXCHANGE RATE

International Civil Aviation Organization, 1000 Sherbrooke Street West, Suite 400, Montreal, Quebec, Canada H3A 2R2 (514) 285-8219; *Civil Aviation Statistics of the World.*

International Monetary Fund, 700 Nineteenth Street, NW, Washington, D.C. 20431 (202) 623-7000; *International Financial Statistics.*

Organisation for Economic Co-operation and Development (OECD), 2 rue Andre-Pascal, 75 Paris 16, France (Telephone Number in U.S. (202) 785-6323); *Economic Outlook, Financial Market Trends,* and *Tourism Policy and International Tourism in OECD Member Countries.*

Statistical Office of the United Nations, Publishing Service, New York, New York 10017 (800) 253-9646; *Statistical Yearbook.*

ICELAND - EXCISE TAXES - See ICELAND - TAXATION

ICELAND - EXPORTS

The Economist Intelligence Unit, 111 West 57th Street, New York, New York 10019 (800) 938-4685; *The World Market Atlas.*

Food and Agricultural Organization of the United Nations (FAO) Via delle Terme di Caracalla, 00100 Rome, Italy (Telephone Number in U.S. (202) 653-2400); *The State of Food and Agriculture.*

G.K. Hall and Company, 70 Lincoln Street, Boston, Massachusetts 02111 (617) 423-3990; *The World in Figures.*

International Monetary Fund, 700 Nineteenth Street, NW, Washington, D.C. 20431 (202) 623-7000; *Direction of Trade Statistics, Government Finance Statistics Yearbook,* and *International Financial Statistics.*

Nordic Council of Ministers, Store Strandstraede 18, DK-1255 Copenhagen K, Denmark and the Nordic Statistical Secretariat, Postboks 2550, DK-2100 Copenhagen 0, Denmark; *The Yearbook of Nordic Statistics.*

Organisation for Economic Co-operation and Development (OECD), 2 rue Andre-Pascal, 75 Paris 16, France (Telephone Number in U.S. (202) 785-6323); *Economic Outlook, The Footwear, Raw Hides and Skins, and Leather Industry in OECD Countries, Foreign Trade by Commodities, Geographical Distribution of Financial Flows to Developing Countries, Industrial Structure Statistics, The Iron and Steel Industry, Milk, Milk Products, and Egg Balances in OECD Member Countries, OECD Economic Surveys: Iceland, The Pulp and Paper Industry,* and *Review of Fisheries in OECD Member Countries.*

Times Books, 201 East 50th Street, New York, New York 10022 (212) 751-2600; *The Economist Book of Vital World Statistics.*

The World Bank, 1818 H Street, NW, Washington, D.C. 20433 (202) 477-1234; *World Tables.*

ICELAND - EXTERNAL FINANCING

Organisation for Economic Co-operation and Development (OECD), 2 rue Andre-Pascal, 75 Paris 16, France (Telephone Number in U.S. (202) 785-6323); *Economic Outlook,* and *Financial Market Trends.*

ICELAND - EXTERNAL INDEBTEDNESS

Organisation for Economic Co-operation and Development (OECD), 2 rue Andre-Pascal, 75 Paris 16, France (Telephone Number in U.S. (202) 785-6323); *Financial Market Trends,* and *Geographical Distribution of Financial Flows to Developing Countries.*

The World Bank, 1818 H Street, NW, Washington, D.C. 20433 (202) 477-1234; *World Tables.*

ICELAND - EXTERNAL RATES

Nordic Council of Ministers, Store Strandstraede 18, DK-1255 Copenhagen K, Denmark and the Nordic Statistical Secretariat, Postboks 2550, DK-2100 Copenhagen 0, Denmark; *The Yearbook of Nordic Statistics.*

ICELAND - EXTERNAL TRADE

Food and Agricultural Organization of the United Nations (FAO) Via delle Terme di Caracalla, 00100 Rome, Italy (Telephone Number in U.S. (202) 653-2400); *The State of Food and Agriculture,* and *Trade Yearbook,*

G.K. Hall and Company, 70 Lincoln Street, Boston, Massachusetts 02111 (617) 423-3990; *The World in Figures.*

Nordic Council of Ministers, Store Strandstraede 18, DK-1255 Copenhagen K, Denmark and the Nordic Statistical Secretariat, Postboks 2550, DK-2100 Copenhagen 0, Denmark; *The Yearbook of Nordic Statistics.*

Statistical Office of the United Nations, Publishing Service, New York, New York 10017 (800) 253-9646; *Statistical Yearbook.*

ICELAND - FABRIC PRODUCTION - See ICELAND - TEXTILE INDUSTRY

ICELAND - FARM CROPS - See ICELAND - CROPS

ICELAND - FERTILITY RATES

Facts on File, 460 Park Avenue South, New York, New York 10016 (800) 443-8323; *The New Book of World Rankings.*

Nordic Council of Ministers, Store Strandstraede 18, DK-1255 Copenhagen K, Denmark and the Nordic Statistical Secretariat, Postboks 2550, DK-2100 Copenhagen 0, Denmark; *The Yearbook of Nordic Statistics.*

Times Books, 201 East 50th Street, New York, New York 10022 (212) 751-2600; *The Economist Book of Vital World Statistics.*

The World Bank, 1818 H Street, NW, Washington, D.C. 20433 (202) 477-1234; *World Tables.*

ICELAND - FERTILIZER

Food and Agricultural Organization of the United Nations (FAO), Via delle Terme di Caracalla, 00100 Rome, Italy (Telephone Number in U.S. (202) 653-2400); *Fertilizer Yearbook,* and *The State of Food and Agriculture.*

Organisation for Economic Co-operation and Development (OECD), 2 rue Andre-Pascal, 75 Paris 16, France (Telephone Number in U.S. (202) 785-6323); *Foreign Trade by Commodities,* and *Economic Accounts for Agriculture.*

Statistical Office of the United Nations, Publishing Service, New York, New York 10017 (800) 253-9646; *Statistical Yearbook.*

ICELAND - FETAL MORTALITY

Nordic Council of Ministers, Store Strandstraede 18, DK-1255 Copenhagen K, Denmark and the Nordic Statistical Secretariat, Postboks 2550, DK-2100 Copenhagen 0, Denmark; *The Yearbook of Nordic Statistics.*

Statistical Office of the United Nations, Publishing Service, New York, New York 10017 (800) 253-9646; *Demographic Yearbook.*

World Health Organization, Avenue Appia, Office of Publications, CH-1211 Geneva 27, Switzerland (Telephone Number in U.S. (518) 436-9686); *World Health Statistics Annual.*

ICELAND - FILAMENT PRODUCTION - See ICELAND - TEXTILE INDUSTRY

ICELAND - FINANCE

Facts on File, 460 Park Avenue South, New York, New York 10016 (800) 443-8323; *The New Book of World Rankings.*

G.K. Hall and Company, 70 Lincoln Street, Boston, Massachusetts 02111 (617) 423-3990; *The World in Figures.*

International Monetary Fund, 700 Nineteenth Street, NW, Washington, D.C. 20431 (202) 623-7000; *International Financial Statistics.*

Organisation for Economic Co-operation and Development (OECD), 2 rue Andre-Pascal, 75 Paris 16, France (Telephone Number in U.S. (202) 785-6323); *Economic Outlook, Financial Market Trends, Geographical Distribution of Financial Flows to Developing Countries, Main Economic Indicators - Historical Statistics,* and *OECD Financial Statistics.*

ICELAND - FISHERIES

Euromonitor Publications Limited, 87-88 Turnmill Street, London EC1M 5QU, England; *European Marketing Data and Statistics.*

Facts on File, 460 Park Avenue South, New York, New York 10016 (800) 443-8323; *The New Book of World Rankings.*

Food and Agricultural Organization of the United Nations (FAO) Via delle Terme di Caracalla, 00100 Rome, Italy (Telephone Number in U.S. (202) 653-2400); *The State of Food and Agriculture, Yearbook of Fishery Statistics, Foreign Trade by Commodities, Review of Fisheries in OECD Member Countries,* and *The State of Food and Agriculture.*

Food and Agricultural Organization of the United Nations (FAO) Via delle Terme di Caracalla, 00100 Rome, Italy (Telephone Number in U.S. (202) 653-2400);

International Monetary Fund, 700 Nineteenth Street, NW, Washington, D.C. 20431 (202) 623-7000; *International Financial Statistics.*

Nordic Council of Ministers, Store Strandstraede 18, DK-1255 Copenhagen K, Denmark and the Nordic Statistical Secretariat, Postboks 2550, DK-2100 Copenhagen 0, Denmark; *The Yearbook of Nordic Statistics.*

Organisation for Economic Co-operation and Development (OECD), 2 rue Andre-Pascal, 75 Paris 16, France (Telephone Number in U.S. (202) 785-6323); *Foreign Trade by Commodities, Industrial Structure Statistics, Main Economic Indicators - Historical Statistics,* and *Review of Fisheries in OECD Member Countries.*

Statistical Office of the United Nations, Publishing Service, New York, New York 10017 (800) 253-9646; *Statistical Yearbook.*

ICELAND - FOOD

Food and Agricultural Organization of the United Nations (FAO) Via delle Terme di Caracalla, 00100 Rome, Italy (Telephone Number in U.S. (202) 653-2400); *Production Yearbook* and *The State of Food and Agriculture.*

G.K. Hall and Company, 70 Lincoln Street, Boston, Massachusetts 02111 (617) 423-3990; *The World in Figures.*

Organisation for Economic Co-operation and Development (OECD), 2 rue Andre-Pascal, 75 Paris 16, France (Telephone Number in U.S. (202) 785-6323); *Foreign Trade by Commodities.*

ICELAND - FOREIGN AID

G.K. Hall and Company, 70 Lincoln Street, Boston, Massachusetts 02111 (617) 423-3990; *The World in Figures.*

ICELAND - FOREIGN DEBT

International Monetary Fund, 700 Nineteenth Street, NW, Washington, D.C. 20431 (202) 623-7000; *Government Finance Statistics Yearbook.*

Organisation for Economic Co-operation and Development (OECD), 2 rue Andre-Pascal, 75 Paris 16, France (Telephone Number in U.S. (202) 785-6323); *Economic Outlook.*

ICELAND - FOREIGN INDEBTEDNESS

Organisation for Economic Co-operation and Development (OECD), 2 rue Andre-Pascal, 75 Paris 16, France (Telephone Number in U.S. (202) 785-6323); *Economic Outlook,* and *Financial Market Trends.*

ICELAND - FOREIGN TRADE

Euromonitor Publications Limited, 87-88 Turnmill Street, London EC1M 5QU, England; *European Marketing Data and Statistics.*

Facts on File, 460 Park Avenue South, New York, New York 10016 (800) 443-8323; *The New Book of World Rankings.*

Food and Agricultural Organization of the United Nations (FAO) Via delle Terme di Caracalla, 00100 Rome, Italy (Telephone Number in U.S. (202) 653-2400); *The State of Food and Agriculture.*

G.K. Hall and Company, 70 Lincoln Street, Boston, Massachusetts 02111 (617) 423-3990; *The World in Figures.*

International Monetary Fund, 700 Nineteenth Street, NW, Washington, D.C. 20431 (202) 623-7000; *International Financial Statistics.*

Organisation for Economic Co-operation and Development (OECD), 2 rue Andre-Pascal, 75 Paris 16, France (Telephone Number in U.S. (202) 785-6323); *Economic Outlook, The Footwear, Raw Hides and Skins, and Leather Industry in OECD Countries, Foreign Trade by Commodities, Main Economic Indicators - Historical Statistics, Maritime Transport, Meat Balances in OECD Member Countries,* and *OECD Economic Surveys: Iceland.*

Statistical Office of the United Nations, Publishing Service, New York, New York 10017 (800) 253-9646; *International Trade Statistics Yearbook, Statistical Yearbook,* and *Trade in Manufactures of Developing Countries.*

The World Bank, 1818 H Street, NW, Washington, D.C. 20433 (202) 477-1234; *World Tables.*

ICELAND - FORESTRY AND FOREST PRODUCTS

Euromonitor Publications Limited, 87-88 Turnmill Street, London EC1M 5QU, England; *European Marketing Data and Statistics.*

Facts on File, 460 Park Avenue South, New York, New York 10016 (800) 443-8323; *The New Book of World Rankings.*

Food and Agricultural Organization of the United Nations (FAO) Via delle Terme di Caracalla, 00100 Rome, Italy (Telephone Number in U.S. (202) 653-2400); *The State of Food and Agriculture,* and *Yearbook of Forest Products.*

G.K. Hall and Company, 70 Lincoln Street, Boston, Massachusetts 02111 (617) 423-3990; *The World in Figures.*

Nordic Council of Ministers, Store Strandstraede 18, DK-1255 Copenhagen K, Denmark and the Nordic Statistical Secretariat, Postboks 2550, DK-2100 Copenhagen 0, Denmark; *The Yearbook of Nordic Statistics.*

Organisation for Economic Co-operation and Development (OECD), 2 rue Andre-Pascal, 75 Paris 16, France (Telephone Number in U.S. (202) 785-6323); *Foreign Trade by Commodities, Industrial Structure*

Statistics, and *The Pulp and Paper Industry*.

Statistical Office of the United Nations, Publishing Service, New York, New York 10017 (800) 253-9646; *Statistical Yearbook*.

United Nations Educational, Scientific and Cultural Organization (UNESCO), 7 Place de Fontenoy, F-75700 Paris, France (Telephone Number in U.S. (212) 963-5981); *Statistical Yearbook*.

ICELAND - FRUIT - See ICELAND - CROPS

ICELAND - FURNITURE AND WOOD PRODUCTS - EXPORTS AND IMPORTS

Organisation for Economic Co-operation and Development (OECD), 2 rue Andre-Pascal, 75 Paris 16, France (Telephone Number in U.S. (202) 785-6323); *Foreign Trade by Commodities*, and *Industrial Structure Statistics*.

ICELAND - GAS PRODUCTION - See ICELAND - MINING AND MINERAL PRODUCTS

ICELAND - GENERAL INDUSTRIAL STATISTICS

Statistical Office of the United Nations, Publishing Service, New York, New York 10017 (800) 253-9646; *Industrial Statistics Yearbook*.

ICELAND - GENERAL MORTALITY

Nordic Council of Ministers, Store Strandstraede 18, DK-1255 Copenhagen K, Denmark and the Nordic Statistical Secretariat, Postboks 2550, DK-2100 Copenhagen 0, Denmark; *The Yearbook of Nordic Statistics*.

Statistical Office of the United Nations, Publishing Service, New York, New York 10017 (800) 253-9646; *Demographic Yearbook*.

World Health Organization, Avenue Appia, Office of Publications, CH-1211 Geneva 27, Switzerland (Telephone Number in U.S. (518) 436-9686); *World Health Statistics Annual*.

ICELAND - GEOGRAPHIC DATA

Facts on File, 460 Park Avenue South, New York, New York 10016 (800) 443-8323; *The New Book of World Rankings*.

ICELAND - GOATS - See ICELAND - LIVESTOCK AND POULTRY

ICELAND - GOLD HOLDINGS

International Monetary Fund, 700 Nineteenth Street, NW, Washington, D.C. 20431 (202) 623-7000; *International Financial Statistics*.

Statistical Office of the United Nations, Publishing Service, New York, New York 10017 (800) 253-9646; *Statistical Yearbook*.

The World Bank, 1818 H Street, NW, Washington, D.C. 20433 (202) 477-1234; *World Tables*.

ICELAND - GOLD PRODUCTION AND CONSUMPTION - See ICELAND - MINING AND MINERAL PRODUCTS

ICELAND - GOVERNMENT

G.K. Hall and Company, 70 Lincoln Street, Boston, Massachusetts 02111 (617) 423-3990; *The World in Figures*.

ICELAND - GOVERNMENT EXPENDITURES

International Monetary Fund, 700 Nineteenth Street, NW, Washington, D.C. 20431 (202) 623-7000; *Government Finance Statistics Yearbook*.

Nordic Council of Ministers, Store Strandstraede 18, DK-1255 Copenhagen K, Denmark and the Nordic Statistical Secretariat, Postboks 2550, DK-2100 Copenhagen 0, Denmark; *The Yearbook of Nordic Statistics*.

Organisation for Economic Co-operation and Development (OECD), 2 rue Andre-Pascal, 75 Paris 16, France (Telephone Number in U.S. (202) 785-6323); *Economic Outlook*.

Times Books, 201 East 50th Street, New York, New York 10022 (212) 751-2600; *The Economist Book of Vital World Statistics*.

The World Bank, 1818 H Street, NW, Washington, D.C. 20433 (202) 477-1234; *World Tables*.

ICELAND - GOVERNMENT FINANCES

International Monetary Fund, 700 Nineteenth Street, NW, Washington, D.C. 20431 (202) 623-7000; *International Financial Statistics*.

Organisation for Economic Co-operation and Development (OECD), 2 rue Andre-Pascal, 75 Paris 16, France (Telephone Number in U.S. (202) 785-6323); *Economic Outlook*.

ICELAND - GOVERNMENT REVENUES

International Monetary Fund, 700 Nineteenth Street, NW, Washington, D.C. 20431 (202) 623-7000; *Government Finance Statistics Yearbook*.

Nordic Council of Ministers, Store Strandstraede 18, DK-1255 Copenhagen K, Denmark and the Nordic Statistical Secretariat, Postboks 2550, DK-2100 Copenhagen 0, Denmark; *The Yearbook of Nordic Statistics*.

Organisation for Economic Co-operation and Development (OECD), 2 rue Andre-Pascal, 75 Paris 16, France (Telephone Number in U.S. (202) 785-6323); *Economic Outlook*.

Times Books, 201 East 50th Street, New York, New York 10022 (212) 751-2600; *The Economist Book of Vital World Statistics*.

The World Bank, 1818 H Street, NW, Washington, D.C. 20433 (202) 477-1234; *World Tables*.

ICELAND - GRAIN PRODUCTION - See ICELAND - CROPS

ICELAND - GRANTS

International Monetary Fund, 700 Nineteenth Street, NW, Washington, D.C. 20431 (202) 623-7000; *Government Finance Statistics Yearbook*.

Organisation for Economic Co-operation and Development (OECD), 2 rue Andre-Pascal, 75 Paris 16, France (Telephone Number in U.S. (202) 785-6323); *Geographical Distribution of Financial Flows to Developing Countries*.

ICELAND - GROSS DOMESTIC PRODUCT

The Economist Intelligence Unit, 111 West 57th Street, New York, New York 10019 (800) 938-4685; *The World Market Atlas*.

Facts on File, 460 Park Avenue South, New York, New York 10016 (800) 443-8323; *The New Book of World Rankings.*

G.K. Hall and Company, 70 Lincoln Street, Boston, Massachusetts 02111 (617) 423-3990; *The World in Figures.*

Nordic Council of Ministers, Store Strandstraede 18, DK-1255 Copenhagen K, Denmark and the Nordic Statistical Secretariat, Postboks 2550, DK-2100 Copenhagen 0, Denmark; *The Yearbook of Nordic Statistics.*

Organisation for Economic Co-operation and Development (OECD), 2 rue Andre-Pascal, 75 Paris 16, France (Telephone Number in U.S. (202) 785-6323); *Economic Outlook,* and *Geographical Distribution of Financial Flows to Developing Countries.*

Statistical Office of the United Nations, Publishing Service, New York, New York 10017 (800) 253-9646; *Statistical Yearbook.*

Times Books, 201 East 50th Street, New York, New York 10022 (212) 751-2600; *The Economist Book of Vital World Statistics.*

The World Bank, 1818 H Street, NW, Washington, D.C. 20433 (202) 477-1234; *World Tables.*

ICELAND - GROSS NATIONAL PRODUCT

Organisation for Economic Co-operation and Development (OECD), 2 rue Andre-Pascal, 75 Paris 16, France (Telephone Number in U.S. (202) 785-6323); *Economic Outlook,* and *Geographical Distribution of Financial Flows to Developing Countries.*

U.S. Arms Control and Disarmament Agency, 320 Twenty-first Street, Northwest, Washington, D.C. 20451 (202) 647-8677; *World Military Expenditures and Arms Transfers.*

The World Bank, 1818 H Street, NW, Washington, D.C. 20433 (202) 477-1234; *World Tables.*

ICELAND - HEALTH

Facts on File, 460 Park Avenue South, New York, New York 10016 (800) 443-8323; *The New Book of World Rankings.*

G.K. Hall and Company, 70 Lincoln Street, Boston, Massachusetts 02111 (617) 423-3990; *The World in Figures.*

Nordic Council of Ministers, Store Strandstraede 18, DK-1255 Copenhagen K, Denmark and the Nordic Statistical Secretariat, Postboks 2550, DK-2100 Copenhagen 0, Denmark; *The Yearbook of Nordic Statistics.*

Organisation for Economic Co-operation and Development (OECD), 2 rue Andre-Pascal, 75 Paris 16, France (Telephone Number in U.S. (202) 785-6323); *OECD Health Systems: Facts and Trends.*

Statistical Office of the United Nations, Publishing Service, New York, New York 10017 (800) 253-9646; *Statistical Yearbook.*

Times Books, 201 East 50th Street, New York, New York 10022 (212) 751-2600; *The Economist Book of Vital World Statistics.*

World Health Organization, Avenue Appia, Office of Publications, CH-1211 Geneva 27, Switzerland (Telephone Number in U.S. (518) 436-9686); *World Health Statistics Annual.*

ICELAND - HEALTH EXPENDITURES

International Monetary Fund, 700 Nineteenth Street, NW, Washington, D.C. 20431 (202) 623-7000; *Government Finance Statistics Yearbook.*

ICELAND - HIDE PRODUCTION

Food and Agricultural Organization of the United Nations (FAO), Via delle Terme di Caracalla, 00100 Rome, Italy (Telephone Number in U.S. (202) 653-2400); *Production Yearbook.*

Organisation for Economic Co-operation and Development (OECD), 2 rue Andre-Pascal, 75 Paris 16, France (Telephone Number in U.S. (202) 785-6323); *The Footwear, Raw Hides and Skins, and Leather Industry in OECD Countries,* and *Foreign Trade by Commodities.*

ICELAND - HIGHWAYS

G.K. Hall and Company, 70 Lincoln Street, Boston, Massachusetts 02111 (617) 423-3990; *The World in Figures.*

International Road Federation, 525 School Street, SW, Washington, D.C. 20024 (202) 554-2106; *World Road Statistics.*

Nordic Council of Ministers, Store Strandstraede 18, DK-1255 Copenhagen K, Denmark and the Nordic Statistical Secretariat, Postboks 2550, DK-2100 Copenhagen 0, Denmark; *The Yearbook of Nordic Statistics.*

Statistical Office of the United Nations, Publishing Service, New York, New York 10017 (800) 253-9646; *Annual Bulletin of Transport Statistics for Europe.*

ICELAND - HOME FINANCE

Organisation for Economic Co-operation and Development (OECD), 2 rue Andre-Pascal, 75 Paris 16, France (Telephone Number in U.S. (202) 785-6323); *Main Economic Indicators - Historical Statistics.*

ICELAND - HORSES - See ICELAND - LIVESTOCK AND POULTRY

ICELAND - HOURS OF WORK - See ICELAND - EMPLOYMENT

ICELAND - HOUSING AND HOUSING UNITS

Facts on File, 460 Park Avenue South, New York, New York 10016 (800) 443-8323; *The New Book of World Rankings.*

Nordic Council of Ministers, Store Strandstraede 18, DK-1255 Copenhagen K, Denmark and the Nordic Statistical Secretariat, Postboks 2550, DK-2100 Copenhagen 0, Denmark; *The Yearbook of Nordic Statistics.*

ICELAND - HOUSING CONSTRUCTION - See ICELAND - CONSTRUCTION INDUSTRY

ICELAND - HOUSING EXPENDITURES

International Monetary Fund, 700 Nineteenth Street, NW, Washington, D.C. 20431 (202) 623-7000; *Government Finance Statistics Yearbook.*

ICELAND - ILLITERATE POPULATION

The Economist Intelligence Unit, 111 West 57th Street, New York, New York 10019 (800) 938-4685; *The World Market Atlas.*

G.K. Hall and Company, 70 Lincoln Street, Boston, Massachusetts 02111 (617) 423-3990; *The World in Figures.*

ICELAND - IMPORTS

The Economist Intelligence Unit, 111 West 57th Street, New York, New York 10019 (800) 938-4685; *The World Market Atlas.*

Food and Agricultural Organization of the United Nations (FAO) Via delle Terme di Caracalla, 00100 Rome, Italy (Telephone Number in U.S. (202) 653-2400); *The State of Food and Agriculture.*

G.K. Hall and Company, 70 Lincoln Street, Boston, Massachusetts 02111 (617) 423-3990; *The World in Figures.*

Nordic Council of Ministers, Store Strandstraede 18, DK-1255 Copenhagen K, Denmark and the Nordic Statistical Secretariat, Postboks 2550, DK-2100 Copenhagen 0, Denmark; *The Yearbook of Nordic Statistics.*

International Monetary Fund, 700 Nineteenth Street, NW, Washington, D.C. 20431 (202) 623-7000; *Direction of Trade Statistics, Government Finance Statistics Yearbook,* and *International Financial Statistics.*

Organisation for Economic Co-operation and Development (OECD), 2 rue Andre-Pascal, 75 Paris 16, France (Telephone Number in U.S. (202) 785-6323); *Economic Outlook, The Footwear, Raw Hides and Skins, and Leather Industry in OECD Countries, Industrial Structure Statistics, The Iron and Steel Industry, Milk, Milk Products, and Egg Balances in OECD Member Countries, The Pulp and Paper Industry, OECD Economic Surveys: Iceland,* and *Review of Fisheries in OECD Member Countries.*

Times Books, 201 East 50th Street, New York, New York 10022 (212) 751-2600; *The Economist Book of Vital World Statistics.*

The World Bank, 1818 H Street, NW, Washington, D.C. 20433 (202) 477-1234; *World Tables.*

ICELAND - INCOME TAXES - See ICELAND - TAXATION

ICELAND - INDUSTRIAL METALS PRODUCTION - See ICELAND - MINING AND MINERAL PRODUCTS

ICELAND - INDUSTRY

Facts on File, 460 Park Avenue South, New York, New York 10016 (800) 443-8323; *The New Book of World Rankings.*

G.K. Hall and Company, 70 Lincoln Street, Boston, Massachusetts 02111 (617) 423-3990; *The World in Figures.*

International Labour Office, I.L.O. Publications, CH-1211, Geneva 22, Switzerland; *Yearbook of Labour Statistics.*

Nordic Council of Ministers, Store Strandstraede 18, DK-1255 Copenhagen K, Denmark and the Nordic Statistical Secretariat, Postboks 2550, DK-2100 Copenhagen 0, Denmark; *The Yearbook of Nordic Statistics.*

Organisation for Economic Co-operation and Development (OECD), 2 rue Andre-Pascal, 75 Paris 16, France (Telephone Number in U.S. (202) 785-6323); *Economic Outlook, OECD Environmental Data,* and *Industrial Structure Statistics.*

Times Books, 201 East 50th Street, New York, New York 10022 (212) 751-2600; *The Economist Book of Vital World Statistics.*

The World Bank, 1818 H Street, NW, Washington, D.C. 20433 (202) 477-1234; *World Tables.*

World Intellectual Property Organization, 34 Chemin des Colombettes, CH-1211 Geneva 20, Switzerland; *Industrial Property Statistics.*

ICELAND - INFANT AND MATERNAL MORTALITY

Nordic Council of Ministers, Store Strandstraede 18, DK-1255 Copenhagen K, Denmark and the Nordic Statistical Secretariat, Postboks 2550, DK-2100 Copenhagen 0, Denmark; *The Yearbook of Nordic Statistics.*

Statistical Office of the United Nations, Publishing Service, New York, New York 10017 (800) 253-9646; *Demographic Yearbook,* and *Statistical Yearbook.*

Times Books, 201 East 50th Street, New York, New York 10022 (212) 751-2600; *The Economist Book of Vital World Statistics.*

The World Bank, 1818 H Street, NW, Washington, D.C. 20433 (202) 477-1234; *World Tables.*

World Health Organization, Avenue Appia, Office of Publications, CH-1211 Geneva 27, Switzerland (Telephone Number in U.S. (518) 436-9686); *World Health Statistics Annual.*

ICELAND - INTEREST RATES

Organisation for Economic Co-operation and Development (OECD), 2 rue Andre-Pascal, 75 Paris 16, France (Telephone Number in U.S. (202) 785-6323); *Economic Outlook, Financial Market Trends,* and *OECD Financial Statistics.*

ICELAND - INTERNAL TRADE

Nordic Council of Ministers, Store Strandstraede 18, DK-1255 Copenhagen K, Denmark and the Nordic Statistical Secretariat, Postboks 2550, DK-2100 Copenhagen 0, Denmark; *The Yearbook of Nordic Statistics.*

Statistical Office of the United Nations, Publishing Service, New York, New York 10017 (800) 253-9646; *Statistical Yearbook.*

ICELAND - INTERNATIONAL FINANCE

Organisation for Economic Co-operation and Development (OECD), 2 rue Andre-Pascal, 75 Paris 16, France (Telephone Number in U.S. (202) 785-6323); *Economic Outlook,* and *Financial Market Trends.*

ICELAND - INTERNATIONAL LIQUIDITY

International Monetary Fund, 700 Nineteenth Street, NW, Washington, D.C. 20431 (202) 623-7000; *International Financial Statistics.*

Organisation for Economic Co-operation and Development (OECD), 2 rue Andre-Pascal, 75 Paris 16, France (Telephone Number in U.S. (202) 785-6323); *Economic Outlook,* and *Financial Market Trends.*

ICELAND - INTERNATIONAL RESERVES EXCLUDING GOLD

Statistical Office of the United Nations, Publishing Service, New York, New York 10017 (800) 253-9646; *Statistical Yearbook.*

The World Bank, 1818 H Street, NW, Washington, D.C. 20433 (202) 477-1234; *World Tables.*

ICELAND - INTERNATIONAL STATISTICS

Organisation for Economic Co-operation and Development (OECD), 2 rue Andre-Pascal, 75 Paris 16, France (Telephone Number in U.S. (202) 785-6323); *Financial Market Trends,* and *Tourism Policy and International Tourism in OECD Member Countries.*

ICELAND - INVESTMENTS

Organisation for Economic Co-operation and Development (OECD), 2 rue Andre-Pascal, 75 Paris 16, France (Telephone Number in U.S. (202) 785-6323); *Economic Outlook, Financial Market Trends, Industrial Structure Statistics, The Iron and Steel Industry,* and *Textile Industry in OECD Countries.*

ICELAND - IRON ORE PRODUCTION AND CONSUMPTION - See ICELAND - MINING AND MINERAL PRODUCTS

ICELAND - LABOR FORCE

Facts on File, 460 Park Avenue South, New York, New York 10016 (800) 443-8323; *The New Book of World Rankings.*

Food and Agricultural Organization of the United Nations (FAO) Via delle Terme di Caracalla, 00100 Rome, Italy (Telephone Number in U.S. (202) 653-2400); *The State of Food and Agriculture.*

G.K. Hall and Company, 70 Lincoln Street, Boston, Massachusetts 02111 (617) 423-3990; *The World in Figures.*

Nordic Council of Ministers, Store Strandstraede 18, DK-1255 Copenhagen K, Denmark and the Nordic Statistical Secretariat, Postboks 2550, DK-2100 Copenhagen 0, Denmark; *The Yearbook of Nordic Statistics.*

Organisation for Economic Co-operation and Development (OECD), 2 rue Andre-Pascal, 75 Paris 16, France (Telephone Number in U.S. (202) 785-6323); *Economic Outlook, The Iron and Steel Industry, Labour Force Statistics, Maritime Transport, OECD Economic Surveys: Iceland, OECD Employment Outlook,* and *Textile Industry in OECD Countries.*

The World Bank, 1818 H Street, NW, Washington, D.C. 20433 (202) 477-1234; *World Tables.*

ICELAND - LABOR PRODUCTIVITY

International Labour Office, I.L.O. Publications, CH-1211, Geneva 22, Switzerland; *Yearbook of Labour Statistics.*

Organisation for Economic Co-operation and Development (OECD), 2 rue Andre-Pascal, 75 Paris 16, France (Telephone Number in U.S. (202) 785-6323); *Economic Outlook,* and *OECD Employment Outlook.*

ICELAND - LAND USE

Euromonitor Publications Limited, 87-88 Turnmill Street, London EC1M 5QU, England; *European Marketing Data and Statistics.*

Food and Agricultural Organization of the United Nations (FAO), Via delle Terme di Caracalla, 00100 Rome, Italy (Telephone Number in U.S. (202) 653-2400); *Production Yearbook.*

G.K. Hall and Company, 70 Lincoln Street, Boston, Massachusetts 02111 (617) 423-3990; *The World in Figures.*

ICELAND - LEAD AND LEAD ORE - See ICELAND - MINING AND MINERAL PRODUCTS

ICELAND - LEATHER AND FOOTWEAR - EXPORTS AND IMPORTS

Organisation for Economic Co-operation and Development (OECD), 2 rue Andre-Pascal, 75 Paris 16, France (Telephone Number in U.S. (202) 785-6323); *The Footwear, Raw Hides and Skins, and Leather Industry in OECD Countries.*

ICELAND - LIBRARIES

Euromonitor Publications Limited, 87-88 Turnmill Street, London EC1M 5QU, England; *European Marketing Data and Statistics.*

Facts on File, 460 Park Avenue South, New York, New York 10016 (800) 443-8323; *The New Book of World Rankings.*

Nordic Council of Ministers, Store Strandstraede 18, DK-1255 Copenhagen K, Denmark and the Nordic Statistical Secretariat, Postboks 2550, DK-2100 Copenhagen 0, Denmark; *The Yearbook of Nordic Statistics.*

United Nations Educational, Scientific and Cultural Organization (UNESCO), 7 Place de Fontenoy, F-75700 Paris, France (Telephone Number in U.S. (212) 963-5981); *Statistical Yearbook.*

ICELAND - LIVESTOCK AND POULTRY

Euromonitor Publications Limited, 87-88 Turnmill Street, London EC1M 5QU, England; *European Marketing Data and Statistics.*

Facts on File, 460 Park Avenue South, New York, New York 10016 (800) 443-8323; *The New Book of World Rankings.*

Food and Agricultural Organization of the United Nations (FAO), Via delle Terme di Caracalla, 00100 Rome, Italy (Telephone Number in U.S. (202) 653-2400); *Production Yearbook,* and *The State of Food and Agriculture.*

G.K. Hall and Company, 70 Lincoln Street, Boston, Massachusetts 02111 (617) 423-3990; *The World in Figures.*

Nordic Council of Ministers, Store Strandstraede 18, DK-1255 Copenhagen K, Denmark and the Nordic Statistical Secretariat, Postboks 2550, DK-2100 Copenhagen 0, Denmark; *The Yearbook of Nordic Statistics.*

Organisation for Economic Co-operation and Development (OECD), 2 rue Andre-Pascal, 75 Paris 16, France (Telephone Number in U.S. (202) 785-6323); *Economic Accounts for Agriculture,* and *Meat Balances in OECD Member Countries.*

Statistical Office of the United Nations, Publishing Service, New York, New York 10017 (800) 253-9646; *Statistical Yearbook.*

ICELAND - LIVING LEVELS

G.K. Hall and Company, 70 Lincoln Street, Boston, Massachusetts 02111 (617) 423-3990; *The World in Figures.*

Organisation for Economic Co-operation and Development (OECD), 2 rue Andre-Pascal, 75 Paris 16, France (Telephone Number in U.S. (202) 785-6323); *Economic Outlook.*

Times Books, 201 East 50th Street, New York, New York 10022 (212) 751-2600; *The Economist Book of Vital World Statistics.*

ICELAND - MAIL - NUMBER OF PIECES SENT OR RECEIVED

Nordic Council of Ministers, Store Strandstraede 18, DK-1255 Copenhagen K, Denmark and the Nordic Statistical Secretariat, Postboks 2550, DK-2100 Copenhagen 0, Denmark; *The Yearbook of Nordic Statistics.*

Statistical Office of the United Nations, Publishing Service, New York, New York 10017 (800) 253-9646; *Statistical Yearbook.*

ICELAND - MANGANESE PRODUCTION AND CONSUMPTION - See ICELAND - MINING AND MINERAL PRODUCTS

ICELAND - MANUFACTURING

Facts on File, 460 Park Avenue South, New York, New York 10016 (800) 443-8323; *The New Book of World Rankings.*

G.K. Hall and Company, 70 Lincoln Street, Boston, Massachusetts 02111 (617) 423-3990; *The World in Figures.*

Nordic Council of Ministers, Store Strandstraede 18, DK-1255 Copenhagen K, Denmark and the Nordic Statistical Secretariat, Postboks 2550, DK-2100 Copenhagen 0, Denmark; *The Yearbook of Nordic Statistics.*

Organisation for Economic Co-operation and Development (OECD), 2 rue Andre-Pascal, 75 Paris 16, France (Telephone Number in U.S. (202) 785-6323); *Foreign Trade by Commodities, Industrial Structure Statistics,* and *OECD Economic Surveys: Iceland.*

Times Books, 201 East 50th Street, New York, New York 10022 (212) 751-2600; *The Economist Book of Vital World Statistics.*

The World Bank, 1818 H Street, NW, Washington, D.C. 20433 (202) 477-1234; *World Tables.*

ICELAND - MARRIAGE RATES

Facts on File, 460 Park Avenue South, New York, New York 10016 (800) 443-8323; *The New Book of World Rankings.*

Nordic Council of Ministers, Store Strandstraede 18, DK-1255 Copenhagen K, Denmark and the Nordic Statistical Secretariat, Postboks 2550, DK-2100 Copenhagen 0, Denmark; *The Yearbook of Nordic Statistics.*

Statistical Office of the United Nations, Publishing Service, New York, New York 10017 (800) 253-9646; *Demographic Yearbook,* and *Statistical Yearbook.*

ICELAND - MEAT PRODUCTION - See ICELAND -LIVESTOCK AND POULTRY

ICELAND - MERCHANT SHIPPING

G.K. Hall and Company, 70 Lincoln Street, Boston, Massachusetts 02111 (617) 423-3990; *The World in Figures.*

Lloyd's Register of Shipping, 17 Battery Place, New York, New York 10004 (212) 425-8050; *Register of Ships.*

Nordic Council of Ministers, Store Strandstraede 18, DK-1255 Copenhagen K, Denmark and the Nordic Statistical Secretariat, Postboks 2550, DK-2100 Copenhagen 0, Denmark; *The Yearbook of Nordic Statistics.*

Organisation for Economic Co-operation and Development (OECD), 2 rue Andre-Pascal, 75 Paris 16, France (Telephone Number in U.S. (202) 785-6323); *Maritime Transport.*

Statistical Office of the United Nations, Publishing Service, New York, New York 10017 (800) 253-9646; *Statistical Yearbook.*

Times Books, 201 East 50th Street, New York, New York 10022 (212) 751-2600; *The Economist Book of Vital World Statistics.*

U.S. Department of Transportation, Maritime Administration, 400 Seventh Street, SW, Washington, D.C. 20590; *A Statistical Analysis of the World's Merchant Fleets.*

ICELAND - MILITARY

G.K. Hall and Company, 70 Lincoln Street, Boston, Massachusetts 02111 (617) 423-3990; *The World in Figures.*

The International Institute for Strategic Studies, 23 Tavistock Street, London WC2E 7NQ, England; *The Military Balance.*

Nordic Council of Ministers, Store Strandstraede 18, DK-1255 Copenhagen K, Denmark and the Nordic Statistical Secretariat, Postboks 2550, DK-2100 Copenhagen 0, Denmark; *The Yearbook of Nordic Statistics.*

U.S. Arms Control and Disarmament Agency, 320 Twenty-first Street, Northwest, Washington, D.C. 20451 (202) 647-8677; *World Military Expenditures and Arms Transfers.*

ICELAND - MILK - See ICELAND - DAIRY PRODUCTS

ICELAND - MINING AND MINERAL PRODUCTS

Facts on File, 460 Park Avenue South, New York, New York 10016 (800) 443-8323; *The New Book of World Rankings.*

G.K. Hall and Company, 70 Lincoln Street, Boston, Massachusetts 02111 (617) 423-3990; *The World in Figures.*

International Monetary Fund, 700 Nineteenth Street, NW, Washington, D.C. 20431 (202) 623-7000; *International Financial Statistics.*

Nordic Council of Ministers, Store Strandstraede 18, DK-1255 Copenhagen K, Denmark and the Nordic Statistical Secretariat, Postboks 2550, DK-2100 Copenhagen 0, Denmark; *The Yearbook of Nordic Statistics.*

Organisation for Economic Co-operation and Development (OECD), 2 rue Andre-Pascal, 75 Paris 16, France (Telephone Number in U.S. (202) 785-6323); *Coal Information, Energy Statistics of OECD Countries, Foreign Trade by Commodities, Industrial Structure Statistics, The Iron and Steel Industry, The Non-Ferrous Metals Industry,* and *OECD Economic Surveys: Iceland.*

Statistical Office of the United Nations, Publishing Service, New York, New York 10017 (800) 253-9646; *Statistical Yearbook.*

ICELAND - MONEY AND CREDIT

Organisation for Economic Co-operation and Development (OECD), 2 rue Andre-Pascal, 75 Paris 16, France (Telephone Number in U.S. (202) 785-6323); *OECD Economic Surveys: Iceland.*

ICELAND - MONEY EXCHANGE RATES

International Monetary Fund, 700 Nineteenth Street, NW, Washington, D.C. 20431 (202) 623-7000; *International Financial Statistics.*

Organisation for Economic Co-operation and Development (OECD), 2 rue Andre-Pascal, 75 Paris 16, France (Telephone Number in U.S. (202) 785-6323); *Economic Outlook, Financial Market Trends,* and *Tourism Policy and International Tourism in OECD Member Countries.*

Statistical Office of the United Nations, Publishing Service, New York, New York 10017 (800) 253-9646; *Statistical Yearbook.*

ICELAND - MONEY RATES - MARKET

Organisation for Economic Co-operation and Development (OECD), 2 rue Andre-Pascal, 75 Paris 16, France (Telephone Number in U.S. (202) 785-6323); *Economic Outlook,* and *Financial Market Trends.*

ICELAND - MONEY RESERVES

Organisation for Economic Co-operation and Development (OECD), 2 rue Andre-Pascal, 75 Paris 16, France (Telephone Number in U.S. (202) 785-6323); *Economic Outlook,* and *Financial Market Trends.*

ICELAND - MONEY SUPPLY

G.K. Hall and Company, 70 Lincoln Street, Boston, Massachusetts 02111 (617) 423-3990; *The World in Figures.*

International Monetary Fund, 700 Nineteenth Street, NW, Washington, D.C. 20431 (202) 623-7000; *International Financial Statistics.*

Nordic Council of Ministers, Store Strandstraede 18, DK-1255 Copenhagen K, Denmark and the Nordic Statistical Secretariat, Postboks 2550, DK-2100 Copenhagen 0, Denmark; *The Yearbook of Nordic Statistics.*

Organisation for Economic Co-operation and Development (OECD), 2 rue Andre-Pascal, 75 Paris 16, France (Telephone Number in U.S. (202) 785-6323); *Economic Outlook.*

Statistical Office of the United Nations, Publishing Service, New York, New York 10017 (800) 253-9646; *Statistical Yearbook.*

The World Bank, 1818 H Street, NW, Washington, D.C. 20433 (202) 477-1234; *World Tables.*

ICELAND - MOTION PICTURES

Statistical Office of the United Nations, Publishing Service, New York, New York 10017 (800) 253-9646; *Statistical Yearbook.*

ICELAND - MOTOR VEHICLE PRODUCTION

Organisation for Economic Co-operation and Development (OECD), 2 rue Andre-Pascal, 75 Paris 16, France (Telephone Number in U.S. (202) 785-6323); *Foreign Trade by Commodities.*

ICELAND - MOTOR VEHICLE TAXES - See ICELAND - TAXATION

ICELAND - MOTOR VEHICLES IN USE

G.K. Hall and Company, 70 Lincoln Street, Boston, Massachusetts 02111 (617) 423-3990; *The World in Figures.*

International Road Federation, 525 School Street, SW, Washington, D.C. 20024 (202) 554-2106; *World Road Statistics.*

Nordic Council of Ministers, Store Strandstraede 18, DK-1255 Copenhagen K, Denmark and the Nordic Statistical Secretariat, Postboks 2550, DK-2100 Copenhagen 0, Denmark; *The Yearbook of Nordic Statistics.*

Statistical Office of the United Nations, Publishing Service, New York, New York 10017 (800) 253-9646; *Statistical Yearbook.*

Times Books, 201 East 50th Street, New York, New York 10022 (212) 751-2600; *The Economist Book of Vital World Statistics.*

ICELAND - MUSEUMS

Euromonitor Publications Limited, 87-88 Turnmill Street, London EC1M 5QU, England; *European Marketing Data and Statistics.*

Facts on File, 460 Park Avenue South, New York, New York 10016 (800) 443-8323; *The New Book of World Rankings.*

Nordic Council of Ministers, Store Strandstraede 18, DK-1255 Copenhagen K, Denmark and the Nordic Statistical Secretariat, Postboks 2550, DK-2100 Copenhagen 0, Denmark; *The Yearbook of Nordic Statistics.*

United Nations Educational, Scientific and Cultural Organization (UNESCO), 7 Place de Fontenoy, F-75700 Paris, France (Telephone Number in U.S. (212) 963-5981); *Statistical Yearbook.*

ICELAND - NATALITY - See ICELAND - BIRTH RATES

ICELAND - NATIONAL ACCOUNTS

International Monetary Fund, 700 Nineteenth Street, NW, Washington, D.C. 20431 (202) 623-7000; *International Financial Statistics.*

Nordic Council of Ministers, Store Strandstraede 18, DK-1255 Copenhagen K, Denmark and the Nordic Statistical Secretariat, Postboks 2550, DK-2100 Copenhagen 0, Denmark; *The Yearbook of Nordic Statistics.*

Organisation for Economic Co-operation and Development (OECD), 2 rue Andre-Pascal, 75 Paris 16, France (Telephone Number in U.S. (202) 785-6323); *Economic Outlook.*

Statistical Office of the United Nations, Publishing Service, New York, New York 10017 (800) 253-9646; *National Accounts Statistics,* and *Statistical Yearbook.*

ICELAND - NATIONAL INCOME

Facts on File, 460 Park Avenue South, New York, New York 10016 (800) 443-8323; *The New Book of World Rankings.*

G.K. Hall and Company, 70 Lincoln Street, Boston, Massachusetts 02111 (617) 423-3990; *The World in Figures.*

Nordic Council of Ministers, Store Strandstraede 18, DK-1255 Copenhagen K, Denmark and the Nordic Statistical Secretariat, Postboks 2550, DK-2100 Copenhagen 0, Denmark; *The Yearbook of Nordic Statistics.*

Organisation for Economic Co-operation and Development (OECD), 2 rue Andre-Pascal, 75 Paris 16, France (Telephone Number in U.S. (202) 785-6323); *Economic Outlook.*

Statistical Office of the United Nations, Publishing Service, New York, New York 10017 (800) 253-9646; *Statistical Yearbook.*

ICELAND - NATIONAL PRODUCT

Facts on File, 460 Park Avenue South, New York, New York 10016 (800) 443-8323; *The New Book of World Rankings.*

Organisation for Economic Co-operation and Development (OECD), 2 rue Andre-Pascal, 75 Paris 16, France (Telephone Number in U.S. (202) 785-6323); *Economic Outlook.*

Statistical Office of the United Nations, Publishing Service, New York, New York 10017 (800) 253-9646; *Statistical Yearbook.*

ICELAND - NATURAL GAS PRODUCTION -See ICELAND - MINING AND MINERAL PRODUCTS

ICELAND - NEWSPAPER PRODUCTION - See ICELAND - FORESTRY AND FOREST PRODUCTS

ICELAND - NEWSPRINT CONSUMPTION - See ICELAND - FORESTRY AND FOREST PRODUCTS

ICELAND - NICKEL PRODUCTION AND CONSUMPTION - See ICELAND - MINING AND MINERAL PRODUCTS

ICELAND - OCCUPATIONS - See ICELAND - LABOR FORCE

ICELAND - OIL PRODUCING CROPS

Organisation for Economic Co-operation and Development (OECD), 2 rue Andre-Pascal, 75 Paris 16, France (Telephone Number in U.S. (202) 785-6323); *Foreign Trade by Commodities.*

ICELAND - PAPER - See ICELAND - FORESTRY AND FOREST PRODUCTS

ICELAND - PATENTS

Nordic Council of Ministers, Store Strandstraede 18, DK-1255 Copenhagen K, Denmark and the Nordic Statistical Secretariat, Postboks 2550, DK-2100 Copenhagen 0, Denmark; *The Yearbook of Nordic Statistics.*

Statistical Office of the United Nations, Publishing Service, New York, New York 10017 (800) 253-9646; *Statistical Yearbook.*

World Intellectual Property Organization, 34 Chemin des Colombettes, CH-1211 Geneva 20, Switzerland; *Industrial Property Statistics.*

ICELAND - PEANUT PRODUCTION - See ICELAND - CROPS

ICELAND - PERIODICALS

United Nations Educational, Scientific and Cultural Organization (UNESCO), 7 Place de Fontenoy, F-75700 Paris, France (Telephone Number in U.S. (212) 963-5981); *Statistical Yearbook.*

ICELAND - PESTICIDE USE

Food and Agricultural Organization of the United Nations (FAO) Via delle Terme di Caracalla, 00100 Rome, Italy (Telephone Number in U.S. (202) 653-2400); *The State of Food and Agriculture.*

ICELAND - PETROLEUM INDUSTRY

Euromonitor Publications Limited, 87-88 Turnmill Street, London EC1M 5QU, England; *European Marketing Data and Statistics.*

Facts on File, 460 Park Avenue South, New York, New York 10016 (800) 443-8323; *The New Book of World Rankings.*

Food and Agricultural Organization of the United Nations (FAO) Via delle Terme di Caracalla, 00100 Rome, Italy (Telephone Number in U.S. (202) 653-2400); *The State of Food and Agriculture.*

G.K. Hall and Company, 70 Lincoln Street, Boston, Massachusetts 02111 (617) 423-3990; *The World in Figures.*

Organisation for Economic Co-operation and Development (OECD), 2 rue Andre-Pascal, 75 Paris 16, France (Telephone Number in U.S. (202) 785-6323); *Energy Statistics of OECD Countries, Foreign Trade by Commodities,* and *Oil and Gas Information.*

ICELAND - PIG-IRON AND FERRO-ALLOY PRODUCTION - See ICELAND - MINING AND MINERAL PRODUCTS

ICELAND - PIGS - See ICELAND - LIVESTOCK AND POULTRY

ICELAND - PLASTIC AND RESIN PRODUCTION

Organisation for Economic Co-operation and Development (OECD), 2 rue Andre-Pascal, 75 Paris 16, France (Telephone Number in U.S. (202) 785-6323); *Foreign Trade by Commodities.*

ICELAND - POPULATION

The Economist Intelligence Unit, 111 West 57th Street, New York, New York 10019 (800) 938-4685; *The World Market Atlas.*

Euromonitor Publications Limited, 87-88 Turnmill Street, London EC1M 5QU, England; *European Marketing Data and Statistics.*

Facts on File, 460 Park Avenue South, New York, New York 10016 (800) 443-8323; *The New Book of World Rankings.*

Food and Agricultural Organization of the United Nations (FAO), Via delle Terme di Caracalla, 00100 Rome, Italy (Telephone Number in U.S. (202) 653-2400); *Production Yearbook.*

G.K. Hall and Company, 70 Lincoln Street, Boston, Massachusetts 02111 (617) 423-3990; *The World in Figures.*

International Labour Office, I.L.O. Publications, CH-1211, Geneva 22, Switzerland; *Yearbook of Labour Statistics.*

Nordic Council of Ministers, Store Strandstraede 18, DK-1255 Copenhagen K, Denmark and the Nordic Statistical Secretariat, Postboks 2550, DK-2100 Copenhagen 0, Denmark; *The Yearbook of Nordic Statistics.*

Statistical Office of the United Nations, Publishing Service, New York, New York 10017 (800) 253-9646; *Demographic Yearbook,* and *Statistical Yearbook.*

Times Books, 201 East 50th Street, New York, New York 10022 (212) 751-2600; *The Economist Book of Vital World Statistics.*

United Nations Educational, Scientific and Cultural Organization (UNESCO), 7 Place de Fontenoy, F-75700 Paris, France (Telephone Number in U.S. (212) 963-5981); *Statistical Yearbook.*

U.S. Arms Control and Disarmament Agency, 320 Twenty-first Street, Northwest, Washington, D.C. 20451 (202) 647-8677; *World Military Expenditures and Arms Transfers.*

World Health Organization, Avenue Appia, Office of Publications, CH-1211 Geneva 27, Switzerland (Telephone Number in U.S. (518) 436-9686); *World Health Statistics Annual.*

ICELAND - POST OFFICES

Facts on File, 460 Park Avenue South, New York, New York 10016 (800) 443-8323; *The New Book of World Rankings.*

ICELAND - POTATO PRODUCTION - See ICELAND - CROPS

ICELAND - PRICES

Facts on File, 460 Park Avenue South, New York, New York 10016 (800) 443-8323; *The New Book of World Rankings.*

Food and Agricultural Organization of the United Nations (FAO), Via delle Terme di Caracalla, 00100 Rome, Italy (Telephone Number in U.S. (202) 653-2400); *Production Yearbook,* and *The State of Food and Agriculture.*

G.K. Hall and Company, 70 Lincoln Street, Boston, Massachusetts 02111 (617) 423-3990; *The World in Figures.*

International Labour Office, I.L.O. Publications, CH-1211, Geneva 22, Switzerland; *Yearbook of Labour Statistics.*

International Monetary Fund, 700 Nineteenth Street, NW, Washington, D.C. 20431 (202) 623-7000; *International Financial Statistics.*

Nordic Council of Ministers, Store Strandstraede 18, DK-1255 Copenhagen K, Denmark and the Nordic Statistical Secretariat, Postboks 2550, DK-2100 Copenhagen 0, Denmark; *The Yearbook of Nordic Statistics.*

Organisation for Economic Co-operation and Development (OECD), 2 rue Andre-Pascal, 75 Paris 16, France (Telephone Number in U.S. (202) 785-6323); *Economic Outlook, The Footwear, Raw Hides and Skins, and Leather Industry in OECD Countries, The Iron and Steel Industry,* and *The Pulp and Paper Industry.*

ICELAND - PRINTING AND WRITING PAPER - See ICELAND - FORESTRY AND FOREST PRODUCTS

ICELAND - PRODUCTION

Facts on File, 460 Park Avenue South, New York, New York 10016 (800) 443-8323; *The New Book of World Rankings.*

G.K. Hall and Company, 70 Lincoln Street, Boston, Massachusetts 02111 (617) 423-3990; *The World in Figures.*

Organisation for Economic Co-operation and Development (OECD), 2 rue Andre-Pascal, 75 Paris 16, France (Telephone Number in U.S. (202) 785-6323); *Economic Outlook, The Footwear, Raw Hides and Skins, and Leather Industry in OECD Countries, Industrial Structure Statistics, The Iron and Steel Industry, Meat Balances in OECD Member Countries, Milk, Milk Products, and Egg Balances in OECD Member Countries, The Non-Ferrous Metals Industry, The Pulp and Paper Industry,* and *Textile Industry in OECD Countries.*

ICELAND - PRODUCTIVITY

Organisation for Economic Co-operation and Development (OECD), 2 rue Andre-Pascal, 75 Paris 16, France (Telephone Number in U.S. (202) 785-6323); *Economic Outlook.*

ICELAND - PROPERTY TAXES - See ICELAND - TAXATION

ICELAND - PUBLIC FINANCE

Facts on File, 460 Park Avenue South, New York, New York 10016 (800) 443-8323; *The New Book of World Rankings.*

Nordic Council of Ministers, Store Strandstraede 18, DK-1255 Copenhagen K, Denmark and the Nordic Statistical Secretariat, Postboks 2550, DK-2100 Copenhagen 0, Denmark; *The Yearbook of Nordic Statistics.*

ICELAND - RADIO BROADCASTING - See ICELAND - BROADCASTING

ICELAND - RAILWAYS

Euromonitor Publications Limited, 87-88 Turnmill Street, London EC1M 5QU, England; *European Marketing Data and Statistics.*

G.K. Hall and Company, 70 Lincoln Street, Boston, Massachusetts 02111 (617) 423-3990; *The World in Figures.*

Nordic Council of Ministers, Store Strandstraede 18, DK-1255 Copenhagen K, Denmark and the Nordic Statistical Secretariat, Postboks 2550, DK-2100 Copenhagen 0, Denmark; *The Yearbook of Nordic Statistics.*

ICELAND - RELIGION

Facts on File, 460 Park Avenue South, New York, New York 10016 (800) 443-8323; *The New Book of World Rankings.*

ICELAND - RENT PRICES

International Labour Office, I.L.O. Publications, CH-1211, Geneva 22, Switzerland; *Yearbook of Labour Statistics.*

ICELAND - RETAIL TRADE

G.K. Hall and Company, 70 Lincoln Street, Boston, Massachusetts 02111 (617) 423-3990; *The World in Figures.*

ICELAND - RICE PRODUCTION - See ICELAND - CROPS

ICELAND - ROOT AND TUBER PRODUCTION - See ICELAND - CROPS

ICELAND - ROUNDWOOD PRODUCTION - See ICELAND - FORESTRY AND FOREST PRODUCTS

ICELAND - RUBBER PRODUCTION

Facts on File, 460 Park Avenue South, New York, New York 10016 (800) 443-8323; *The New Book of World Rankings.*

Organisation for Economic Co-operation and Development (OECD), 2 rue Andre-Pascal, 75 Paris 16, France (Telephone Number in U.S. (202) 785-6323); *Foreign Trade by Commodities.*

ICELAND - SAWNWOOD PRODUCTION - See ICELAND - FORESTRY AND FOREST PRODUCTS

ICELAND - SCIENCE AND TECHNOLOGY - EXPENDITURE FOR RESEARCH

Statistical Office of the United Nations, Publishing Service, New York, New York 10017 (800) 253-9646; *Statistical Yearbook.*

ICELAND - SCIENTISTS AND TECHNICIANS

Statistical Office of the United Nations, Publishing Service, New York, New York 10017 (800) 253-9646; *Statistical Yearbook.*

United Nations Educational, Scientific and Cultural Organization (UNESCO), 7 Place de Fontenoy, F-75700 Paris, France (Telephone Number in U.S. (212) 963-5981); *Statistical Yearbook.*

ICELAND - SENIOR CITIZENS

Facts on File, 460 Park Avenue South, New York, New York 10016 (800) 443-8323; *The New Book of World Rankings.*

ICELAND - SHEEP - See ICELAND - LIVESTOCK AND POULTRY

ICELAND - SILVER PRODUCTION AND CONSUMPTION - See ICELAND - MINING AND MINERAL PRODUCTS

ICELAND - SOCIAL DATA

Facts on File, 460 Park Avenue South, New York, New York 10016 (800) 443-8323; *The New Book of World Rankings.*

G.K. Hall and Company, 70 Lincoln Street, Boston, Massachusetts 02111 (617) 423-3990; *The World in Figures.*

ICELAND - SOCIAL SECURITY

International Monetary Fund, 700 Nineteenth Street, NW, Washington, D.C. 20431 (202) 623-7000; *Government Finance Statistics Yearbook.*

Nordic Council of Ministers, Store Strandstraede 18, DK-1255 Copenhagen K, Denmark and the Nordic Statistical Secretariat, Postboks 2550, DK-2100 Copenhagen 0, Denmark; *The Yearbook of Nordic Statistics.*

ICELAND - SOCIOECONOMIC DATA

Organisation for Economic Co-operation and Development (OECD), 2 rue Andre-Pascal, 75 Paris 16, France (Telephone Number in U.S. (202) 785-6323); *Economic Outlook.*

ICELAND - STEEL - See ICELAND - MINING AND MINERAL PRODUCTS

ICELAND - STOCKS - COMMODITY - MARKET PRICE - INDEX

Food and Agricultural Organization of the United Nations (FAO) Via delle Terme di Caracalla, 00100 Rome, Italy (Telephone Number in U.S. (202) 653-2400); *The State of Food and Agriculture.*

ICELAND - SUGAR - See ICELAND - CROPS

ICELAND - TAXATION

G.K. Hall and Company, 70 Lincoln Street, Boston, Massachusetts 02111 (617) 423-3990; *The World in Figures.*

International Monetary Fund, 700 Nineteenth Street, NW, Washington, D.C. 20431 (202) 623-7000; *Government Finance Statistics Yearbook.*

International Road Federation, 525 School Street, SW, Washington, D.C. 20024 (202) 554-2106; *World Road Statistics.*

Nordic Council of Ministers, Store Strandstraede 18, DK-1255 Copenhagen K, Denmark and the Nordic Statistical Secretariat, Postboks 2550, DK-2100 Copenhagen 0, Denmark; *The Yearbook of Nordic Statistics.*

The World Bank, 1818 H Street, NW, Washington, D.C. 20433 (202) 477-1234; *World Tables.*

ICELAND - TELEGRAPH SERVICE

Nordic Council of Ministers, Store Strandstraede 18, DK-1255 Copenhagen K, Denmark and the Nordic Statistical Secretariat, Postboks 2550, DK-2100 Copenhagen 0, Denmark; *The Yearbook of Nordic Statistics.*

Statistical Office of the United Nations, Publishing Service, New York, New York 10017 (800) 253-9646; *Statistical Yearbook.*

ICELAND - TELEPHONES IN USE

American Telephone and Telegraph Company, 26 Parsippany Road, Whippany, New Jersey 07981 (800) 338-4038; *The World's Telephones.*

G.K. Hall and Company, 70 Lincoln Street, Boston, Massachusetts 02111 (617) 423-3990; *The World in Figures.*

Nordic Council of Ministers, Store Strandstraede 18, DK-1255 Copenhagen K, Denmark and the Nordic Statistical Secretariat, Postboks 2550, DK-2100 Copenhagen 0, Denmark; *The Yearbook of Nordic Statistics.*

Statistical Office of the United Nations, Publishing Service, New York, New York 10017 (800) 253-9646; *Statistical Yearbook.*

ICELAND - TELEVISION BROADCASTING - See ICELAND - BROADCASTING

ICELAND - TEXTILE INDUSTRY

G.K. Hall and Company, 70 Lincoln Street, Boston, Massachusetts 02111 (617) 423-3990; *The World in Figures.*

Organisation for Economic Co-operation and Development (OECD), 2 rue Andre-Pascal, 75 Paris 16, France (Telephone Number in U.S. (202) 785-6323); *Foreign Trade by Commodities, Industrial Structure Statistics,* and *Textile Industry in OECD Countries.*

ICELAND - TIN PRODUCTION

Organisation for Economic Co-operation and Development (OECD), 2 rue Andre-Pascal, 75 Paris 16, France (Telephone Number in U.S. (202) 785-6323); *The Non-Ferrous Metals Industry.*

ICELAND - TOBACCO PRODUCTION

Facts on File, 460 Park Avenue South, New York, New York 10016 (800) 443-8323; *The New Book of World Rankings.*

Organisation for Economic Co-operation and Development (OECD), 2 rue Andre-Pascal, 75 Paris 16, France (Telephone Number in U.S. (202) 785-6323); *Foreign Trade by Commodities,* and *Industrial Structure Statistics.*

ICELAND - TOBACCO PRODUCTS

Euromonitor Publications Limited, 87-88 Turnmill Street, London EC1M 5QU, England; *European Marketing Data and Statistics.*

Statistical Office of the United Nations, Publishing Service, New York, New York 10017 (800) 253-9646; *Statistical Yearbook.*

ICELAND - TOURISM

Euromonitor Publications Limited, 87-88 Turnmill Street, London EC1M 5QU, England; *European Marketing Data and Statistics.*

Facts on File, 460 Park Avenue South, New York, New York 10016 (800) 443-8323; *The New Book of World Rankings.*

G.K. Hall and Company, 70 Lincoln Street, Boston, Massachusetts 02111 (617) 423-3990; *The World in Figures.*

Organisation for Economic Co-operation and Development (OECD), 2 rue Andre-Pascal, 75 Paris 16, France (Telephone Number in U.S. (202) 785-6323); *Tourism Policy and International Tourism in OECD Member Countries.*

Statistical Office of the United Nations, Publishing Service, New York, New York 10017 (800) 253-9646; *Statistical Yearbook.*

Times Books, 201 East 50th Street, New York, New York 10022 (212) 751-2600; *The Economist Book of Vital World Statistics.*

World Tourism Organization, Calle Capitan Haya 42, E-28020 Madrid, Spain; *Yearbook of Tourism Statistics.*

ICELAND - TRACTORS IN USE

Statistical Office of the United Nations, Publishing Service, New York, New York 10017 (800) 253-9646; *Statistical Yearbook.*

ICELAND - TRADE - See ICELAND - FOREIGN TRADE

ICELAND - TRADEMARKS AND SERVICE MARKS

Statistical Office of the United Nations, Publishing Service, New York, New York 10017 (800) 253-9646; *Statistical Yearbook.*

World Intellectual Property Organization, 34 Chemin des Colombettes, CH-1211 Geneva 20, Switzerland; *Industrial Property Statistics.*

ICELAND - TRANSPORTATION AND COMMUNICATIONS

Facts on File, 460 Park Avenue South, New York, New York 10016 (800) 443-8323; *The New Book of World Rankings.*

G.K. Hall and Company, 70 Lincoln Street, Boston, Massachusetts 02111 (617) 423-3990; *The World in Figures.*

Nordic Council of Ministers, Store Strandstraede 18, DK-1255 Copenhagen K, Denmark and the Nordic Statistical Secretariat, Postboks 2550, DK-2100 Copenhagen 0, Denmark; *The Yearbook of Nordic Statistics.*

ICELAND - UNEMPLOYMENT

Euromonitor Publications Limited, 87-88 Turnmill Street, London EC1M 5QU, England; *European Marketing Data and Statistics.*

International Labour Office, I.L.O. Publications, CH-1211, Geneva 22, Switzerland; *Yearbook of Labour Statistics.*

Nordic Council of Ministers, Store Strandstraede 18, DK-1255 Copenhagen K, Denmark and the Nordic Statistical Secretariat, Postboks 2550, DK-2100 Copenhagen 0, Denmark; *The Yearbook of Nordic Statistics.*

Organisation for Economic Co-operation and Development (OECD), 2 rue Andre-Pascal, 75 Paris 16, France (Telephone Number in U.S. (202) 785-6323); *Economic Outlook, OECD Economic Surveys: Iceland,* and *OECD Employment Outlook.*

Statistical Office of the United Nations, Publishing Service, New York, New York 10017 (800) 253-9646; *Statistical Yearbook.*

ICELAND - VITAL STATISTICS

G.K. Hall and Company, 70 Lincoln Street, Boston, Massachusetts 02111 (617) 423-3990; *The World in Figures.*

Nordic Council of Ministers, Store Strandstraede 18, DK-1255 Copenhagen K, Denmark and the Nordic Statistical Secretariat, Postboks 2550, DK-2100 Copenhagen 0, Denmark; *The Yearbook of Nordic Statistics.*

Statistical Office of the United Nations, Publishing Service, New York, New York 10017 (800) 253-9646; *Statistical Yearbook.*

World Health Organization, Avenue Appia, Office of Publications, CH-1211 Geneva 27, Switzerland (Telephone Number in U.S. (518) 436-9686); *World Health Statistics Annual.*

ICELAND - WAGES

Euromonitor Publications Limited, 87-88 Turnmill Street, London EC1M 5QU, England; *European Marketing Data and Statistics.*

G.K. Hall and Company, 70 Lincoln Street, Boston, Massachusetts 02111 (617) 423-3990; *The World in Figures.*

Nordic Council of Ministers, Store Strandstraede 18, DK-1255 Copenhagen K, Denmark and the Nordic Statistical Secretariat, Postboks 2550, DK-2100 Copenhagen 0, Denmark; *The Yearbook of Nordic Statistics.*

International Labour Office, I.L.O. Publications, CH-1211, Geneva 22, Switzerland; *Yearbook of Labour Statistics.*

Organisation for Economic Co-operation and Development (OECD), 2 rue Andre-Pascal, 75 Paris 16, France (Telephone Number in U.S. (202) 785-6323); *Economic Outlook,* and *Industrial Structure Statistics.*

ICELAND - WATERWAYS IN USE

Organisation for Economic Co-operation and Development (OECD), 2 rue Andre-Pascal, 75 Paris 16, France (Telephone Number in U.S. (202) 785-6323); *Maritime Transport.*

ICELAND - WEATHER

Facts on File, 460 Park Avenue South, New York, New York 10016 (800) 443-8323; *The New Book of World Rankings.*

G.K. Hall and Company, 70 Lincoln Street, Boston, Massachusetts 02111 (617) 423-3990; *The World in Figures.*

Nordic Council of Ministers, Store Strandstraede 18, DK-1255 Copenhagen K, Denmark and the Nordic Statistical Secretariat, Postboks 2550, DK-2100 Copenhagen 0, Denmark; *The Yearbook of Nordic Statistics.*

ICELAND - WELFARE

International Monetary Fund, 700 Nineteenth Street, NW, Washington, D.C. 20431 (202) 623-7000; *Government Finance Statistics Yearbook.*

Nordic Council of Ministers, Store Strandstraede 18, DK-1255 Copenhagen K, Denmark and the Nordic Statistical Secretariat, Postboks 2550, DK-2100 Copenhagen 0, Denmark; *The Yearbook of Nordic Statistics.*

ICELAND - WHALES - See ICELAND - FISHERIES

ICELAND - WHEAT PRODUCTION AND PRICES - See ICELAND - CROPS

ICELAND - WHOLESALE PRICES - INDEX NUMBERS

Nordic Council of Ministers, Store Strandstraede 18, DK-1255 Copenhagen K, Denmark and the Nordic Statistical Secretariat, Postboks 2550, DK-2100 Copenhagen 0, Denmark; *The Yearbook of Nordic Statistics.*

ICELAND - WINE PRODUCTION

Facts on File, 460 Park Avenue South, New York, New York 10016 (800) 443-8323; *The New Book of World Rankings.*

ICELAND - WOOD - See ICELAND - FORESTRY AND FOREST PRODUCTS

ICELAND - WOOL PRODUCTION

Facts on File, 460 Park Avenue South, New York, New York 10016 (800) 443-8323; *The New Book of World Rankings.*

Organisation for Economic Co-operation and Development (OECD), 2 rue Andre-Pascal, 75 Paris 16, France (Telephone Number in U.S. (202) 785-6323); *Economic Accounts for Agriculture,* and *Textile Industry in OECD Countries.*

ICELAND - YARN PRODUCTION

Organisation for Economic Co-operation and Development (OECD), 2 rue Andre-Pascal, 75 Paris 16, France (Telephone Number in U.S. (202) 785-6323); *Foreign Trade by Commodities,* and *Textile Industry in OECD Countries.*

Statistical Office of the United Nations, Publishing Service, New York, New York 10017 (800) 253-9646; *Statistical Yearbook.*

ICELAND - ZINC AND ZINC ORE - See ICELAND - MINING AND MINERAL PRODUCTS

IDAHO - See also STATE DATA (FOR INDIVIDUAL STATES)

Idaho - Primary Statistics Sources

Department of Commerce, 700 West State Street, Boise, Idaho 83720 (208) 334-2470; *County Profiles of Idaho, Idaho Community Profiles, Idaho Facts, Idaho Facts Data Book,* and *Profile of Rural Idaho.*

Idaho - State Data Centers

Idaho Department of Commerce, 700 West State Street, Boise, Idaho 83720, Mr. Alan Porter (208) 334-2470.

Institutional Research, Room 319, Business Building, Boise State University, Boise, Idaho 83725, Mr. Don Canning (208) 385-1613.

The Idaho State Library, 325 West State Street, Boise, Idaho 83702, Ms. Stephanie Kukay (208) 334-2150.

Center for Business Research and Services, Campus Box 8450, Idaho State University, Pocatello, Idaho 83209, Dr. Paul Zelus (208) 236-3409.

ILLEGAL IMMIGRATION - See ALIENS

ILLINOIS - See also STATE DATA (FOR INDIVIDUAL STATES)

Illinois - Primary Statistics Sources

University of Illinois, Bureau of Economic and Business Research, 428 Commerce West, 1206 South Sixth Street, Champaign, Illinois 61820 (217) 333-2330; *Illinois Statistical Abstract.*

Illinois - State Data Centers

Illinois Bureau of the Budget, William Stratton Building, Room 605, Springfield, Illinois 62706, Ms. Suzanne Ebetsch (217) 782-1381.

Census and Data Users Services, Department 4690, Research Services Building, Suite A, Illinois State University, Normal, Illinois 61790-4950, Dr. Roy Treadway/Dr. Del Ervin (309) 438-5946.

Center for Governmental Studies, Northern Illinois University, Social Science Research Building, DeKalb, Illinois 60115, Ms. Ruth Anne Tobias, (815) 753-0922.

Regional Research and Development Services, Southern Illinois University at Edwardsville, Box 1456, Edwardsville, Illinois 62026-1456, Mr. Charles Kofron (618) 692-2278.

Chicago Area Geographic Information Study, Department of Geography, M/C 092, 1007 West Harrison Street, Room 2102, University of Illinois at Chicago, Chicago, Illinois 60607-7138, Mr. Jim Bash, (312) 996-5274.

Northeastern Illinois Planning Commission, Research Services, 400 West Madison Street, Chicago, Illinois 60606-2642, Max Dieber/Mary Cele Smith (312) 454-0400.

ILLNESS - See also DEATHS BY CAUSE, DISABILITY, and DISEASES

U.S. Department of Health and Human Services, National Center for Health Statistics, 3700 East-West Highway, Hyattsville, Maryland 20782 (301) 436-8500; *Vital and Health Statistics,* unpublished data.

ILLNESS - BED DISABILITY - DAYS

U.S. Department of Health and Human Services, National Center for Health Statistics, 3700 East-West Highway, Hyattsville, Maryland 20782 (301) 436-8500; *Vital and Health Statistics,* and unpublished data.

ILLNESS - DAYS LOST FROM WORK, SCHOOL

U.S. Department of Health and Human Services, National Center for Health Statistics, 3700 East-West Highway, Hyattsville, Maryland 20782 (301) 436-8500; *Vital and Health Statistics,* and unpublished data.

ILLNESS - EMPLOYEE PROTECTION AGAINST INCOME LOSS

U.S. Department of Health and Human Services, Social Security Administration, 6401 Security Boulevard, Baltimore, Maryland 21235 (410) 965-1234; *Social Security Bulletin*, and unpublished data.

ILLNESS - PRIVATE EXPENDITURES FOR INCOME MAINTENANCE

U.S. Department of Health and Human Services, Social Security Administration, 6401 Security Boulevard, Baltimore, Maryland 21235 (410) 965-1234; *Annual Statistical Supplement to the Social Security Bulletin, Social Security Bulletin*, and unpublished data.

ILLNESS - RESTRICTED ACTIVITY DAYS

U.S. Department of Health and Human Services, National Center for Health Statistics, 3700 East-West Highway, Hyattsville, Maryland 20782 (301) 436-8500; *Vital and Health Statistics*, and unpublished data.

IMMIGRANTS

U.S. Department of Commerce, Bureau of the Census, Suitland, Maryland 20233 (301) 763-4040; *Census of Population, the Foreign Born Population in the U.S.*

U.S. Department of Justice, Immigration and Naturalization Service, 425 I Street, NW, Washington, D.C. 20534 (202) 514-4316; *Statistical Yearbook.*

IMMIGRANTS - BY AREA OF RESIDENCE

U.S. Department of Justice, Immigration and Naturalization Service, 425 I Street, NW, Washington, D.C. 20536 (202) 514-4316; *Statistical Yearbook.*

IMMIGRANTS - BY CLASS OF ADMISSION

U.S. Department of Justice, Immigration and Naturalization Service, 425 I Street, NW, Washington, D.C. 20534 (202) 514-4316; *Statistical Yearbook.*

IMMIGRANTS - BY COUNTRY OF BIRTH

U.S. Department of Commerce, Bureau of the Census, Suitland, Maryland 20233 (301) 763-4040; *Census of Population, The Foreign Born Population in the U.S.*

U.S. Department of Justice, Immigration and Naturalization Service, 425 I Street, NW, Washington, D.C. 20534 (202) 514-4316; *Statistical Yearbook*, and releases.

IMMIGRANTS - CITIZENSHIP STATUS

U.S. Department of Commerce, Bureau of the Census, Suitland, Maryland 20233 (301) 763-4040; *Census of Population, The Foreign Born Population in the U.S.*

IMMIGRANTS - NONIMMIGRANTS

U.S. Department of Justice, Immigration and Naturalization Service, 425 I Street, NW, Washington, D.C. 20534 (202) 514-4316; *Statistical Yearbook.*

IMMIGRANTS - REFUGEES

U.S. Department of Justice, Immigration and Naturalization Service, 425 I Street, NW, Washington, D.C. 20534 (202) 514-4316; *Statistical Yearbook.*

IMMUNIZATION OF CHILDREN

U.S. Department of Health and Human Services, Centers for Disease Control, 1600 Clifton Road, NE, Atlanta, Georgia 30333 (404) 639-3311; *National Health Interview Survey.*

IMPLICIT PRICE DEFLATORS FOR GNP

U.S. Department of Commerce, Bureau of Economic Analysis, Fourteenth Street between Constitution Avenue and E Street, NW, Washington, D.C. 20230 (202) 606-9900; *The National Income and Product Accounts of the United States, Survey of Current Business*, and unpublished data.

IMPORTS - See FOREIGN TRADE

INCOME - See also POVERTY AND CONSUMER EXPENDITURES AND EARNINGS

INCOME - AFTER TAX

U.S. Department of Commerce, Bureau of the Census, Suitland, Maryland 20233 (301) 763-4040; *Current Population Reports*, and unpublished data.

INCOME - AGGREGATE INCOME

U.S. Department of Commerce, Bureau of the Census, Suitland, Maryland 20233 (301) 763-4040; *Current Population Reports*, and unpublished data.

INCOME - AMERICAN INDIAN, ESKIMO, ALEUT POPULATION

U.S. Department of Commerce, Bureau of the Census, Suitland, Maryland 20233 (301) 763-4040; *Current Population Reports.*

INCOME - ASIAN AND PACIFIC ISLANDER POPULATION

U.S. Department of Commerce, Bureau of the Census, Suitland, Maryland 20233 (301) 763-4040; *Current Population Reports.*

INCOME - CORPORATE

U.S. Department of Commerce, Bureau of Economic Analysis, Fourteenth Street between Constitution Avenue and E Street, NW, Washington, D.C. 20230 (202) 606-9900; *The National Income and Product Accounts of the U.S., Survey of Current Business*, and unpublished data.

U.S. Department of the Treasury, Internal Revenue Service, 1111 Constitution Avenue, NW, Washington, D.C. 20224 (202) 566-5000; *Statistics of Income, Corporation Income Tax Returns.*

INCOME - DISPOSABLE PERSONAL

U.S. Department of Commerce, Bureau of Economic Analysis, Fourteenth Street between Constitution Avenue and E Street, NW, Washington, D.C. 20230 (202) 606-9900; *The National Income and Product Accounts of the United States, Survey of Current Business*, and unpublished data.

INCOME - DISTRIBUTION

U.S. Department of Commerce, Bureau of Economic Analysis, Fourteenth Street between Constitution Avenue and E Street, NW, Washington, D.C. 20230 (202) 606-9900; *The National Income and Product Accounts of the United States*, and *Survey of Current Business*.

U.S. Department of Commerce, Bureau of the Census, Suitland, Maryland 20233 (301) 763-4040; *Current Population Reports*, and unpublished data.

INCOME - ENERGY CONSUMPTION

U.S. Department of Energy, Energy Information Administration, 1000 Independence Avenue, SW, Washington, D.C. 20585 (202) 586-8800; *Household Energy Consumption and Expenditures*.

INCOME - EQUALITY

U.S. Department of Commerce, Bureau of the Census, Suitland, Maryland 20233 (301) 763-4040; *Current Population Reports*.

INCOME - FAMILIES

U.S. Department of Commerce, Bureau of the Census, Suitland, Maryland 20233 (301) 763-4040; *Current Population Reports*, *Census of Population*, and unpublished data.

INCOME - FAMILIES - AGGREGATE INCOME

U.S. Department of Commerce, Bureau of the Census, Suitland, Maryland 20233 (301) 763-4040; *Current Population Reports*, and unpublished data.

INCOME - FAMILIES - AMERICAN INDIAN, ESKIMO, ALEUT POPULATION

U.S. Department of Commerce, Bureau of the Census, Suitland, Maryland 20233 (301) 763-4040; *Current Population Reports*.

INCOME - FAMILIES - APPLIANCES

U.S. Department of Energy, Energy Information Administration, 1000 Independence Avenue, SW, Washington, D.C. 20585 (202) 586-8800; *Housing Characteristics*.

INCOME - FAMILIES - ASIAN AND PACIFIC ISLANDER POPULATION

U.S. Department of Commerce, Bureau of the Census, Suitland, Maryland 20233 (301) 763-4040; *Current Population Reports*.

INCOME - FAMILIES - BLACK POPULATION

U.S. Department of Commerce, Bureau of the Census, Suitland, Maryland 20233 (301) 763-4040; *Current Population Reports*, and unpublished data.

INCOME - FAMILIES - BY TYPE OF FAMILY

U.S. Department of Commerce, Bureau of the Census, Suitland, Maryland 20233 (301) 763-4040; *Current Population Reports*, and unpublished data.

INCOME - FAMILIES - EARNERS

U.S. Department of Commerce, Bureau of the Census, Suitland, Maryland 20233 (301) 763-4040; *Current Population Reports*, and unpublished data.

INCOME - FAMILIES - ELDERLY

Congressional Budget Office, 2nd and D Streets, SW, Washington, D.C. 20515 (202) 226-2621; *Trends in Family Income*, and unpublished data.

U.S. Department of Commerce, Bureau of the Census, Suitland, Maryland 20233 (301) 763-4040; *Current Population Reports*, and unpublished data.

INCOME - FAMILIES - HISPANIC ORIGIN POPULATION

U.S. Department of Commerce, Bureau of the Census, Suitland, Maryland 20233 (301) 763-4040; *Current Population Reports*, *Census of Population*, and unpublished data.

INCOME - FAMILIES - HUSBAND-WIFE FAMILIES

U.S. Department of Commerce, Bureau of the Census, Suitland, Maryland 20233 (301) 763-4040; *Current Population Reports*, and unpublished data.

INCOME - FAMILIES - LABOR FORCE PARTICIPATION

U.S. Department of Commerce, Bureau of the Census, Suitland, Maryland 20233 (301) 763-4040; *Current Population Reports*.

INCOME - FAMILIES - OUTLYING AREAS

Puerto Rico Planning Board, San Juan, Puerto Rico; *Income and Product*, and *Socioeconomic Statistics*.

INCOME - FAMILIES - UNRELATED INDIVIDUALS

U.S. Department of Commerce, Bureau of the Census, Suitland, Maryland 20233 (301) 763-4040; *Current Population Reports*, and unpublished data.

INCOME - FARM

U.S. Department of Agriculture, Economic Research Service, Fourteenth Street and Independence Avenue, SW, Washington, D.C. 20005-4789 (202) 219-1504; *Economic Indicators of the Farm Sector: National Financial Summary*, and *Economic Indicators of the Farm Sector: State Financial Summary*.

U.S. Department of Commerce, Bureau of Economic Analysis, Fourteenth Street between Constitution Avenue and E Street, NW, Washington, D.C. 20230 (202) 606-9900; *The National Income and Product Accounts of the United States*, and *Survey of Current Business*.

U.S. Department of Commerce, Bureau of the Census, Suitland, Maryland 20233 (301) 763-4040; *Current Population Reports*, and *Census of Agriculture*.

INCOME - GROSS DOMESTIC PRODUCT

U.S. Department of Commerce, Bureau of Economic Analysis, Fourteenth Street between Constitution Avenue and E Street, NW, Washington, D.C. 20230 (202) 606-9900; *The National Income and Product Accounts of the United States*, and *Survey of Current Business*.

INCOME - HISPANIC ORIGIN POPULATION

U.S. Department of Commerce, Bureau of the Census, Suitland, Maryland 20233 (301) 763-4040; *Current Population Reports*, and unpublished data.

INCOME - HOUSEHOLD - AGE

U.S. Department of Commerce, Bureau of the Census, Suitland, Maryland 20233 (301) 763-4040; *Current Population Reports*, and unpublished data.

INCOME - HOUSEHOLD - BLACK POPULATION

U.S. Department of Commerce, Bureau of the Census, Suitland, Maryland 20233 (301) 763-4040; *Current Population Reports*, and unpublished data.

INCOME - HOUSEHOLD - EDUCATIONAL ATTAINMENT

U.S. Department of Commerce, Bureau of the Census, Suitland, Maryland 20233 (301) 763-4040; *Current Population Reports*, and unpublished data.

INCOME - HOUSEHOLD - ELDERLY

U.S. Department of Commerce, Bureau of the Census, Suitland, Maryland 20233 (301) 763-4040; *Current Population Reports*, and unpublished data.

INCOME - HOUSEHOLD - HISPANIC ORIGIN POPULATION

U.S. Department of Commerce, Bureau of the Census, Suitland, Maryland 20233 (301) 763-4040; *Current Population Reports*, and unpublished data.

INCOME - HOUSEHOLD - PET OWNERSHIP

American Veterinary Medical Association, 930 North Meacham Road, Schaumburg, Illinois 60601 (708) 605-8070; *U.S. Pet Ownership and Demographics Sourcebook*.

INCOME - HOUSEHOLD - RECREATION ACTIVITIES

National Sporting Goods Association, Lake Center Plaza Building, 1699 Wall Street, Mount Prospect, Illinois 60056-5780 (708) 439-4000; *Sports Participation in 1992*, and *The Sporting Goods Market in 1993*.

INCOME - HOUSEHOLD - TENURE

U.S. Department of Commerce, Bureau of the Census, Suitland, Maryland 20233 (301) 763-4040; *Current Population Reports*, and unpublished data.

INCOME - HOUSEHOLDS

U.S. Department of Agriculture, Economic Research Service, Fourteenth Street and Independence Avenue, SW, Washington, D.C. 20005-4789 (202) 219-1504; *Economic Indicators of the Farm Sector: National Financial Summary*, and unpublished data.

U.S. Department of Commerce, Bureau of the Census, Suitland, Maryland 20233 (301) 763-4040; *Current Population Reports*, and unpublished data.

INCOME - LOSS FROM SHORT-TERM SICKNESS

U.S. Department of Health and Human Services, Social Security Administration, 6401 Security Boulevard, Baltimore, Maryland 21235 (410) 965-1234; *Social Security Bulletin*, and unpublished data.

INCOME - MOTOR VEHICLE OWNERSHIP

U.S. Department of Energy, Energy Information Administration, 1000 Independence Avenue, SW, Washington, D.C. 20585 (202) 586-8800; *Household Vehicles Energy Consumption*.

INCOME - NATIONAL INCOME

U.S. Department of Commerce, Bureau of Economic Analysis, Fourteenth Street between Constitution Avenue and E Street, NW, Washington, D.C. 20230 (202) 606-9900; *The National Income and Product Accounts of the United States*, and *Survey of Current Business*.

INCOME - NATIONAL INCOME - BY SECTOR

U.S. Department of Commerce, Bureau of Economic Analysis, Fourteenth Street between Constitution Avenue and E Street, NW, Washington, D.C. 20230 (202) 606-9900; *Survey of Current Business*, and *The National Income and Product Accounts of the United States*.

INCOME - NATIONAL INCOME - BY TYPE OF INCOME

U.S. Department of Commerce, Bureau of Economic Analysis, Fourteenth Street between Constitution Avenue and E Street, NW, Washington, D.C. 20230 (202) 606-9900; *The National Income and Product Accounts of the United States*, and *Survey of Current Business*.

INCOME - NATIONAL INCOME - ORIGINATING IN FARMING

U.S. Department of Commerce, Bureau of Economic Analysis, Fourteenth Street between Constitution Avenue and E Street, NW, Washington, D.C. 20230 (202) 606-9900; *The National Income and Product Accounts of the United States*, and *Survey of Current Business*.

INCOME - PER CAPITA

U.S. Department of Commerce, Bureau of Economic Analysis, Fourteenth Street between Constitution Avenue and E Street, NW, Washington, D.C. 20230 (202) 606-9900; *The National Income and Product Accounts of the United States*, and *Survey of Current Business*.

U.S. Department of Commerce, Bureau of the Census, Suitland, Maryland 20233 (301) 763-4040; *Current Population Reports*.

INCOME - PERSONAL

U.S. Department of Commerce, Bureau of Economic Analysis, Fourteenth Street between Constitution Avenue and E Street, NW, Washington, D.C. 20230 (202) 606-9900; *The National Income and Product Accounts of the United States*, *Survey of Current Business*, and unpublished data.

INCOME - PERSONAL - METROPOLITAN AREAS

U.S. Department of Commerce, Bureau of Economic Analysis, Fourteenth Street between Constitution Avenue and E Street, NW, Washington, D.C. 20230 (202) 606-9900; *The National Income and Product Accounts of the United States*, and *Survey of Current Business*.

INCOME - PERSONAL - SAVING

U.S. Department of Commerce, Bureau of Economic Analysis, Fourteenth Street between Constitution Avenue and E Street, NW,

Washington, D.C. 20230 (202) 606-9900; *The National Income and Product Accounts of the United States,* and *Survey of Current Business.*

INCOME - PERSONAL CONSUMPTION EXPENDITURES

U.S. Department of Commerce, Bureau of Economic Analysis, Fourteenth Street between Constitution Avenue and E Street, NW, Washington, D.C. 20230 (202) 606-9900; *The National Income and Product Accounts of the United States, Survey of Current Business,* and unpublished data.

INCOME - PERSONS

U.S. Department of Commerce, Bureau of the Census, Suitland, Maryland 20233 (301) 763-4040; *Current Population Reports,* and unpublished data.

INCOME - PERSONS - BELOW POVERTY LEVEL

U.S. Department of Commerce, Bureau of the Census, Suitland, Maryland 20233 (301) 763-4040; *Current Population Reports,* and unpublished data.

INCOME - POVERTY

Congressional Budget Office, 2nd and D Streets, SW, Washington, D.C. 20515 (202) 226-2621; *Trends in Family Income,* and unpublished data.

U.S. Department of Commerce, Bureau of the Census, Suitland, Maryland 20233 (301) 763-4040; *Current Population Reports,* and unpublished data.

INCOME - SAVING

Board of Governors of the Federal Reserve System, Twentieth Street and Constitution Avenue, NW, Washington, D.C. 20551 (202) 452-3000; *Flow of Funds Accounts.*

INCOME - SPORTS PARTICIPATION - GOODS

National Sporting Goods Association, Lake Center Plaza Building, 1699 Wall Street, Mount Prospect, Illinois 60056-5780 (708) 439-4000; *Sports Participation in 1992,* and *The Sporting Goods Market in 1993.*

INCOME TAX - See also TAX RECEIPTS

INCOME TAX - AVERAGE TAX BY INCOME LEVEL

U.S. Department of the Treasury, Internal Revenue Service, 1111 Constitution Avenue, NW, Washington, D.C. 20224 (202) 566-5000; *Statistics of Income, Individual Income Tax Returns,* and *Annual Report of the Commissioner and Chief Counsel of the Internal Revenue Service.*

INCOME TAX - CORPORATION

U.S. Department of Commerce, Bureau of the Census, Suitland, Maryland 20233 (301) 763-4040; *Historical Statistics on Governmental Finances and Employment, Government Finances,* and *State Government Tax Collections.*

U.S. Department of the Treasury, Internal Revenue Service, 1111 Constitution Avenue, NW, Washington, D.C. 20224 (202) 566-5000; *Annual Report of the Commissioner and Chief Counsel of the Internal Revenue Service,* and *Statistics of Income, Corporation Income Tax Returns.*

INCOME TAX - INDIVIDUAL

U.S. Department of Commerce, Bureau of the Census, Suitland, Maryland 20233 (301) 763-4040; *Historical Statistics on Governmental Finances and Employment, Government Finances,* and *State Government Tax Collections.*

U.S. Department of the Treasury, Internal Revenue Service, 1111 Constitution Avenue, NW, Washington, D.C. 20224 (202) 566-5000; *Annual Report of the Commissioner and Chief Counsel of the Internal Revenue Service, Statistics of Income, Individual Income Tax Returns, Statistics of Income Bulletin,* and unpublished data.

INCOME TAX - STATE COLLECTIONS

U.S. Department of Commerce, Bureau of the Census, Suitland, Maryland 20233 (301) 763-4040; *State Government Tax Collections.*

INDEX NUMBERS - See Individual Subjects

India - National Statistical Offices

Central Statistical Organization, Sardar Patel Bhavan, Parliament Street, New Delhi, India; for other statistics.

Department of Commercial Intelligence and Statistics, 1 Council House Street, Calcutta, India; for foreign statistics.

Directorate of Economics and Statistics, Ministry of Agriculture, Krishi Bhavan, Dr. Rajendra Prasad Road, New Delhi, India; for agricultural statistics.

India - Primary Statistics Sources

Central Statistical Organization, New Dehli, India; *Statistical Abstract: India,* and *Statistical Pocketbook of India.*

INDIA - ABORTIONS

Statistical Office of the United Nations, Publishing Service, New York, New York 10017 (800) 253-9646; *Demographic Yearbook.*

INDIA - AGRICULTURE

Euromonitor Publications Limited, 87-88 Turnmill Street, London EC1M 5QU, England; *International Marketing Data and Statistics.*

Food and Agricultural Organization of the United Nations (FAO), Via delle Terme di Caracalla, 00100 Rome, Italy (Telephone Number in U.S. (202) 653-2400); *Production Yearbook, The State of Food and Agriculture,* and *Trade Yearbook.*

G.K. Hall and Company, 70 Lincoln Street, Boston, Massachusetts 02111 (617) 423-3990; *The World in Figures.*

Statistical Office of the United Nations, Publishing Service, New York, New York 10017 (800) 253-9646; *Statistical Yearbook,* and *Statistical Yearbook for Asia and the Pacific.*

Times Books, 201 East 50th Street, New York, New York 10022 (212) 751-2600; *The Economist Book of Vital World Statistics.*

The World Bank, 1818 H Street, NW, Washington, D.C. 20433 (202) 477-1234; *World Tables.*

INDIA - AIRLINE SERVICE

The Economist Intelligence Unit (Asia) Limited, 10th Floor, Luk Kwok Centre, 72 Gloucester Road, Wanchai, Hong Kong (Phone Number in U.S. (800) 938-4685); *Asian Market Atlas.*

G.K. Hall and Company, 70 Lincoln Street, Boston, Massachusetts 02111 (617) 423-3990; *The World in Figures.*

International Civil Aviation Organization, 1000 Sherbrooke Street West, Suite 400, Montreal, Quebec, Canada H3A 2R2 (514) 285-8219; *Civil Aviation Statistics of the World.*

Statistical Office of the United Nations, Publishing Service, New York, New York 10017 (800) 253-9646; *Statistical Yearbook.*

Times Books, 201 East 50th Street, New York, New York 10022 (212) 751-2600; *The Economist Book of Vital World Statistics.*

INDIA - ALUMINUM PRODUCTION AND CONSUMPTION - See INDIA - MINING AND MINERAL PRODUCTS

INDIA - ANIMAL HEALTH

Food and Agricultural Organization of the United Nations (FAO), Via delle Terme di Caracalla, 00100 Rome, Italy (Telephone Number in U.S. (202) 653-2400); *Animal Health Yearbook.*

INDIA - ANTIMONY AND ANTIMONY ORE - See INDIA - MINING AND MINERAL PRODUCTS

INDIA - AREA AND DENSITY OF POPULATION

Euromonitor Publications Limited, 87-88 Turnmill Street, London EC1M 5QU, England; *International Marketing Data and Statistics.*

Food and Agricultural Organization of the United Nations (FAO) Via delle Terme di Caracalla, 00100 Rome, Italy (Telephone Number in U.S. (202) 653-2400); *The State of Food and Agriculture.*

G.K. Hall and Company, 70 Lincoln Street, Boston, Massachusetts 02111 (617) 423-3990; *The World in Figures.*

Statistical Office of the United Nations, Publishing Service, New York, New York 10017 (800) 253-9646; *Statistical Yearbook.*

Times Books, 201 East 50th Street, New York, New York 10022 (212) 751-2600; *The Economist Book of Vital World Statistics.*

United Nations Educational, Scientific and Cultural Organization (UNESCO), 7 Place de Fontenoy, F-75700 Paris, France (Telephone Number in U.S. (212) 963-5981); *Statistical Yearbook.*

INDIA - ARMS EXPORTS AND IMPORTS

U.S. Arms Control and Disarmament Agency, 320 Twenty-first Street, Northwest, Washington, D.C. 20451 (202) 647-8677; *World Military Expenditures and Arms Transfers.*

INDIA - BALANCE OF PAYMENTS

The Economist Intelligence Unit, 111 West 57th Street, New York, New York 10019 (800) 938-4685; *The World Market Atlas.*

Euromonitor Publications Limited, 87-88 Turnmill Street, London EC1M 5QU, England; *Third World Economic Handbook.*

G.K. Hall and Company, 70 Lincoln Street, Boston, Massachusetts 02111 (617) 423-3990; *The World in Figures.*

International Monetary Fund, 700 Nineteenth Street, NW, Washington, D.C. 20431 (202) 623-7000; *Balance of Payments Yearbook*, and *International Financial Statistics.*

Times Books, 201 East 50th Street, New York, New York 10022 (212) 751-2600; *The Economist Book of Vital World Statistics.*

The World Bank, 1818 H Street, NW, Washington, D.C. 20433 (202) 477-1234; *World Tables.*

INDIA - BANKING

G.K. Hall and Company, 70 Lincoln Street, Boston, Massachusetts 02111 (617) 423-3990; *The World in Figures.*

International Monetary Fund, 700 Nineteenth Street, NW, Washington, D.C. 20431 (202) 623-7000; *International Financial Statistics.*

Statistical Office of the United Nations, Publishing Service, New York, New York 10017 (800) 253-9646; *Statistical Yearbook.*

INDIA - BARLEY PRODUCTION - See INDIA - CROPS

INDIA - BAUXITE PRODUCTION AND CONSUMPTION - See INDIA - MINING AND MINERAL PRODUCTS

INDIA - BEER PRODUCTION

Statistical Office of the United Nations, Publishing Service, New York, New York 10017 (800) 253-9646; *Statistical Yearbook.*

INDIA - BIRTH RATE

The Economist Intelligence Unit (Asia) Limited, 10th Floor, Luk Kwok Centre, 72 Gloucester Road, Wanchai, Hong Kong (Phone Number in U.S. (800) 938-4685); *Asian Market Atlas.*

Euromonitor Publications Limited, 87-88 Turnmill Street, London EC1M 5QU, England; *Third World Economic Handbook.*

Statistical Office of the United Nations, Publishing Service, New York, New York 10017 (800) 253-9646; *Demographic Yearbook*, and *Statistical Yearbook.*

Times Books, 201 East 50th Street, New York, New York 10022 (212) 751-2600; *The Economist Book of Vital World Statistics.*

The World Bank, 1818 H Street, NW, Washington, D.C. 20433 (202) 477-1234; *World Tables.*

World Health Organization, Avenue Appia, Office of Publications, CH-1211 Geneva 27, Switzerland (Telephone Number in U.S. (518) 436-9686); *World Health Statistics Annual.*

INDIA - BONDS

G.K. Hall and Company, 70 Lincoln Street, Boston, Massachusetts 02111 (617) 423-3990; *The World in Figures.*

International Monetary Fund, 700 Nineteenth Street, NW, Washington, D.C. 20431 (202) 623-7000; *Government Finance Statistics Yearbook.*

Statistical Office of the United Nations, Publishing Service, New York, New York 10017 (800) 253-9646; *Statistical Yearbook.*

INDIA - BOOK PRODUCTION

G.K. Hall and Company, 70 Lincoln Street, Boston, Massachusetts 02111 (617) 423-3990; *The World in Figures.*

United Nations Educational, Scientific and Cultural Organization (UNESCO), 7 Place de Fontenoy, F-75700 Paris, France (Telephone Number in U.S. (212) 963-5981); *Statistical Yearbook.*

INDIA - BROADCASTING

Billboard Limited, Post Office Box 9027, 1006 AA Amsterdam, The Netherlands (Telephone Number in U.S. (212) 764-7300); *World Radio TV Handbook.*

The Economist Intelligence Unit (Asia) Limited, 10th Floor, Luk Kwok Centre, 72 Gloucester Road, Wanchai, Hong Kong (Phone Number in U.S. (800) 938-4685); *Asian Market Atlas.*

G.K. Hall and Company, 70 Lincoln Street, Boston, Massachusetts 02111 (617) 423-3990; *The World in Figures.*

Times Books, 201 East 50th Street, New York, New York 10022 (212) 751-2600; *The Economist Book of Vital World Statistics.*

United Nations Educational, Scientific and Cultural Organization (UNESCO), 7 Place de Fontenoy, F-75700 Paris, France (Telephone Number in U.S. (212) 963-5981); *Statistical Yearbook.*

INDIA - BUILDING CONSTRUCTION - See INDIA - CONSTRUCTION INDUSTRY

INDIA - BUSINESS

G.K. Hall and Company, 70 Lincoln Street, Boston, Massachusetts 02111 (617) 423-3990; *The World in Figures.*

INDIA - BUTTER PRODUCTION - See INDIA - DAIRY PRODUCTS

INDIA - CABBAGE PRODUCTION - See INDIA - CROPS

INDIA - CADMIUM PRODUCTION AND CONSUMPTION - See INDIA - MINING AND MINERAL PRODUCTS

INDIA - CALORIE SUPPLY

Food and Agricultural Organization of the United Nations (FAO) Via delle Terme di Caracalla, 00100 Rome, Italy (Telephone Number in U.S. (202) 653-2400); *The State of Food and Agriculture.*

INDIA - CAPITAL REVENUE

International Monetary Fund, 700 Nineteenth Street, NW, Washington, D.C. 20431 (202) 623-7000; *Government Finance Statistics Yearbook.*

INDIA - CASHEW NUT PRODUCTION - See INDIA - CROPS

INDIA - CASTOR BEAN PRODUCTION - See INDIA - CROPS

INDIA - CATTLE - See INDIA - LIVESTOCK AND POULTRY

INDIA - CAULIFLOWER PRODUCTION - See INDIA - CROPS

INDIA - CAUSTIC SODA PRODUCTION

Statistical Office of the United Nations, Publishing Service, New York, New York 10017 (800) 253-9646; *Statistical Yearbook.*

INDIA - CEMENT PRODUCTION - See INDIA - MINING AND MINERAL PRODUCTS

INDIA - CHEESE - See INDIA - DAIRY PRODUCTS

INDIA - CHEMICAL (ORGANIC) PRODUCTION - See INDIA - MINING AND MINERAL PRODUCTS

INDIA - CHICK PEA PRODUCTION - See INDIA - CROPS

INDIA - CHICKENS - See INDIA - LIVESTOCK AND POULTRY

INDIA - CHROMITE PRODUCTION - See INDIA - MINING AND MINERAL PRODUCTS

INDIA - CHROMIUM ORE PRODUCTION AND CONSUMPTION - See INDIA - MINING AND MINERAL PRODUCTS

INDIA - CIGARETTE PRODUCTION - See INDIA - TOBACCO PRODUCTION

INDIA - CLASS STRUCTURE

G.K. Hall and Company, 70 Lincoln Street, Boston, Massachusetts 02111 (617) 423-3990; *The World in Figures.*

INDIA - CLIMATE

G.K. Hall and Company, 70 Lincoln Street, Boston, Massachusetts 02111 (617) 423-3990; *The World in Figures.*

INDIA - CLOTHING EXPORTS AND IMPORTS

Euromonitor Publications Limited, 87-88 Turnmill Street, London EC1M 5QU, England; *Third World Economic Handbook.*

Statistical Office of the United Nations, Publishing Service, New York, New York 10017 (800) 253-9646; *Trade in Manufactures of Developing Countries.*

INDIA - COAL PRODUCTION AND CONSUMPTION - See INDIA - MINING AND MINERAL PRODUCTS

INDIA - COBALT PRODUCTION AND CONSUMPTION - See INDIA - MINING AND MINERAL PRODUCTS

INDIA - COFFEE PRODUCTION - See INDIA - CROPS

INDIA - COKE OVEN COKE PRODUCTION AND CONSUMPTION - See INDIA - MINING AND MINERAL PRODUCTS

INDIA - COMMUNICATIONS

Euromonitor Publications Limited, 87-88 Turnmill Street, London EC1M 5QU, England; *Third World Economic Handbook.*

G.K. Hall and Company, 70 Lincoln Street, Boston, Massachusetts 02111 (617) 423-3990; *The World in Figures.*

Statistical Office of the United Nations, Publishing Service, New York, New York 10017 (800) 253-9646; *Statistical Yearbook for Asia and the Pacific.*

INDIA - CONSTRUCTION INDUSTRY

Statistical Office of the United Nations, Publishing Service, New York, New York 10017 (800) 253-9646; *Construction Statistics Yearbook,* and *Statistical Yearbook.*

INDIA - CONSUMER PRICE INDEX

G.K. Hall and Company, 70 Lincoln Street, Boston, Massachusetts 02111 (617) 423-3990; *The World in Figures.*

International Labour Office, I.L.O. Publications, CH-1211, Geneva 22, Switzerland; *Yearbook of Labour Statistics.*

Statistical Office of the United Nations, Publishing Service, New York, New York 10017 (800) 253-9646; *Statistical Yearbook.*

INDIA - CONSUMER PRICES

International Labour Office, I.L.O. Publications, CH-1211, Geneva 22, Switzerland; *Yearbook of Labour Statistics.*

International Monetary Fund, 700 Nineteenth Street, NW, Washington, D.C. 20431 (202) 623-7000; *International Financial Statistics.*

Times Books, 201 East 50th Street, New York, New York 10022 (212) 751-2600; *The Economist Book of Vital World Statistics.*

INDIA - CONSUMPTION

G.K. Hall and Company, 70 Lincoln Street, Boston, Massachusetts 02111 (617) 423-3990; *The World in Figures.*

International Lead and Zinc Study Group, Metro House, 58 St. James's Street, London SW1A 1LD, England; *Lead and Zinc Statistics.*

International Rubber Study Group, York House, 8th Floor, Empire Way, Wembley, London HA9 0PA, England; *Rubber Statistical Bulletin.*

Organisation for Economic Co-operation and Development (OECD), 2 rue Andre-Pascal, 75 Paris 16, France (Telephone Number in U.S. (202) 785-6323); *The Footwear, Raw Hides and Skins, and Leather Industry in OECD Countries.*

INDIA - COPPER AND COPPER ORE - See INDIA - MINING AND MINERAL PRODUCTS

INDIA - CORN PRODUCTION - See INDIA - CROPS

INDIA - CORPORATE TAXES - See INDIA - TAXATION

INDIA - COTTON - See INDIA - CROPS

INDIA - CRIME

International Criminal Police Organization (INTERPOL), 26 rue Armengaud, 92210 Saint Cloud, France; *International Crime Statistics.*

Yale University Press, Yale Station, New Haven, Connecticut 06520 (203) 432-0940; *Violence and Crime in Cross-National Perspective.*

INDIA - CROPS

Commodity Research Bureau, Incorporated, 75 Wall Street, New York, New York 10005 (212) 504-7754; *Commodity Year Book.*

Food and Agricultural Organization of the United Nations (FAO), Via delle Terme di Caracalla, 00100 Rome, Italy (Telephone Number in U.S. (202) 653-2400); *Production Yearbook* and *The State of Food and Agriculture.*

G.K. Hall and Company, 70 Lincoln Street, Boston, Massachusetts 02111 (617) 423-3990; *The World in Figures.*

International Labour Office, I.L.O. Publications, CH-1211, Geneva 22, Switzerland; *Yearbook of Labour Statistics.*

International Monetary Fund, 700 Nineteenth Street, NW, Washington, D.C. 20431 (202) 623-7000; *International Financial Statistics.*

Statistical Office of the United Nations, Publishing Service, New York, New York 10017 (800) 253-9646; *Statistical Yearbook.*

Food and Agricultural Organization of the United Nations (FAO) Via delle Terme di Caracalla, 00100 Rome, Italy (Telephone Number in U.S. (202) 653-2400);

INDIA - CUSTOMS DUTIES

G.K. Hall and Company, 70 Lincoln Street, Boston, Massachusetts 02111 (617) 423-3990; *The World in Figures.*

International Monetary Fund, 700 Nineteenth Street, NW, Washington, D.C. 20431 (202) 623-7000; *Government Finance Statistics Yearbook.*

INDIA - DAIRY PRODUCTS

Commodity Research Bureau, Incorporated, 75 Wall Street, New York, New York 10005 (212) 504-7754; *Commodity Year Book.*

Food and Agricultural Organization of the United Nations (FAO), Via delle Terme di Caracalla, 00100 Rome, Italy (Telephone Number in U.S. (202) 653-2400); *Production Yearbook* and *The State of Food and Agriculture.*

Statistical Office of the United Nations, Publishing Service, New York, New York 10017 (800) 253-9646; *Statistical Yearbook.*

INDIA - DEATH RATES

The Economist Intelligence Unit (Asia) Limited, 10th Floor, Luk Kwok Centre, 72 Gloucester Road, Wanchai, Hong Kong (Phone Number in U.S. (800) 938-4685); *Asian Market Atlas.*

Euromonitor Publications Limited, 87-88 Turnmill Street, London EC1M 5QU, England; *Third World Economic Handbook.*

G.K. Hall and Company, 70 Lincoln Street, Boston, Massachusetts 02111 (617) 423-3990; *The World in Figures.*

Statistical Office of the United Nations, Publishing Service, New York, New York 10017 (800) 253-9646; *Statistical Yearbook.*

World Health Organization, Avenue Appia, Office of Publications, CH-1211 Geneva 27, Switzerland (Telephone Number in U.S. (518) 436-9686); *World Health Statistics Annual.*

INDIA - DEFENSE EXPENDITURES

G.K. Hall and Company, 70 Lincoln Street, Boston, Massachusetts 02111 (617) 423-3990; *The World in Figures.*

International Monetary Fund, 700 Nineteenth Street, NW, Washington, D.C. 20431 (202) 623-7000; *Government Finance Statistics Yearbook.*

U.S. Arms Control and Disarmament Agency, 320 Twenty-first Street, Northwest, Washington, D.C. 20451 (202) 647-8677; *World*

Military Expenditures and Arms Transfers.

INDIA - DEMOGRAPHY

The Economist Intelligence Unit, 111 West 57th Street, New York, New York 10019 (800) 938-4685; *The World Market Atlas.*

The Economist Intelligence Unit (Asia) Limited, 10th Floor, Luk Kwok Centre, 72 Gloucester Road, Wanchai, Hong Kong (Phone Number in U.S. (800) 938-4685); *Asian Market Atlas.*

G.K. Hall and Company, 70 Lincoln Street, Boston, Massachusetts 02111 (617) 423-3990; *The World in Figures.*

INDIA - DEVELOPMENT ASSISTANCE

G.K. Hall and Company, 70 Lincoln Street, Boston, Massachusetts 02111 (617) 423-3990; *The World in Figures.*

Statistical Office of the United Nations, Publishing Service, New York, New York 10017 (800) 253-9646; *Statistical Yearbook.*

INDIA - DIAMOND PRODUCTION - See INDIA - MINING AND MINERAL PRODUCTS

INDIA - DISCOUNT RATES

Statistical Office of the United Nations, Publishing Service, New York, New York 10017 (800) 253-9646; *Statistical Yearbook.*

INDIA - DISEASE

G.K. Hall and Company, 70 Lincoln Street, Boston, Massachusetts 02111 (617) 423-3990; *The World in Figures.*

World Health Organization, Avenue Appia, Office of Publications, CH-1211 Geneva 27, Switzerland (Telephone Number in U.S. (518) 436-9686); *World Health Statistics Annual.*

INDIA - DIVORCE RATES

Statistical Office of the United Nations, Publishing Service, New York, New York 10017 (800) 253-9646; *Demographic Yearbook.*

INDIA - DOMESTIC PRODUCT

G.K. Hall and Company, 70 Lincoln Street, Boston, Massachusetts 02111 (617) 423-3990; *The World in Figures.*

INDIA - ECONOMY

Euromonitor Publications Limited, 87-88 Turnmill Street, London EC1M 5QU, England; *International Marketing Data and Statistics,* and *Third World Economic Handbook.*

G.K. Hall and Company, 70 Lincoln Street, Boston, Massachusetts 02111 (617) 423-3990; *The World in Figures.*

INDIA - EDUCATION

The Economist Intelligence Unit, 111 West 57th Street, New York, New York 10019 (800) 938-4685; *The World Market Atlas.*

The Economist Intelligence Unit (Asia) Limited, 10th Floor, Luk Kwok Centre, 72 Gloucester Road, Wanchai, Hong Kong (Phone Number in U.S. (800) 938-4685); *Asian Market Atlas.*

G.K. Hall and Company, 70 Lincoln Street, Boston, Massachusetts 02111 (617) 423-3990; *The World in Figures.*

International Monetary Fund, 700 Nineteenth Street, NW, Washington, D.C. 20431 (202) 623-7000; *Government Finance Statistics Yearbook.*

Times Books, 201 East 50th Street, New York, New York 10022 (212) 751-2600; *The Economist Book of Vital World Statistics.*

United Nations Educational, Scientific and Cultural Organization (UNESCO), 7 Place de Fontenoy, F-75700 Paris, France (Telephone Number in U.S. (212) 963-5981); *Statistical Yearbook.*

The World Bank, 1818 H Street, NW, Washington, D.C. 20433 (202) 477-1234; *World Tables.*

INDIA - EGG PRODUCTION - See INDIA - DAIRY PRODUCTS

INDIA - ELECTRICITY

Organisation for Economic Co-operation and Development (OECD), 2 rue Andre-Pascal, 75 Paris 16, France (Telephone Number in U.S. (202) 785-6323); *Coal Information.*

Penn Well Publishing Company, 1421 South Sheridan Road, Post Office Box 1260, Tulsa, Oklahoma 74101 (800) 752-9764; *International Energy Statistics Sourcebook.*

Statistical Office of the United Nations, Publishing Service, New York, New York 10017; *Electric Power in Asia and the Pacific,* and *Statistical Yearbook.*

Times Books, 201 East 50th Street, New York, New York 10022 (212) 751-2600; *The Economist Book of Vital World Statistics.*

INDIA - EMPLOYMENT

Euromonitor Publications Limited, 87-88 Turnmill Street, London EC1M 5QU, England; *International Marketing Data and Statistics.*

International Labour Office, I.L.O. Publications, CH-1211, Geneva 22, Switzerland; *Yearbook of Labour Statistics.*

Statistical Office of the United Nations, Publishing Service, New York, New York 10017 (800) 253-9646; *Statistical Yearbook.*

INDIA - ENERGY

Food and Agricultural Organization of the United Nations (FAO) Via delle Terme di Caracalla, 00100 Rome, Italy (Telephone Number in U.S. (202) 653-2400); *The State of Food and Agriculture.*

G.K. Hall and Company, 70 Lincoln Street, Boston, Massachusetts 02111 (617) 423-3990; *The World in Figures.*

Organisation for Economic Co-operation and Development (OECD), 2 rue Andre-Pascal, 75 Paris 16, France (Telephone Number in U.S. (202) 785-6323); *Coal Information.*

Penn Well Publishing Company, 1421 South Sheridan Road, Post Office Box 1260, Tulsa, Oklahoma 74101 (800) 752-9764; *International Energy Statistics Sourcebook.*

Statistical Office of the United Nations, Publishing Service, New York, New York 10017 (800) 253-9646; *Energy Statistics Yearbook, Statistical Yearbook,* and *Statistical Yearbook for Asia and the Pacific.*

Times Books, 201 East 50th Street, New York, New York 10022 (212) 751-2600; *The Economist Book of Vital World Statistics.*

INDIA - ENGINEERING AND METAL PRODUCTS EXPORTS TO DEVELOPED COUNTRIES

Statistical Office of the United Nations, Publishing Service, New York, New York 10017 (800) 253-9646; *Trade in Manufactures of Developing Countries.*

INDIA - EXCHANGE RATES

The Economist Intelligence Unit (Asia) Limited, 10th Floor, Luk Kwok Centre, 72 Gloucester Road, Wanchai, Hong Kong (Phone Number in U.S. (800) 938-4685); *Asian Market Atlas.*

Euromonitor Publications Limited, 87-88 Turnmill Street, London EC1M 5QU, England; *International Marketing Data and Statistics.*

International Civil Aviation Organization, 1000 Sherbrooke Street West, Suite 400, Montreal, Quebec, Canada H3A 2R2 (514) 285-8219; *Civil Aviation Statistics of the World.*

International Monetary Fund, 700 Nineteenth Street, NW, Washington, D.C. 20431 (202) 623-7000; *International Financial Statistics.*

Statistical Office of the United Nations, Publishing Service, New York, New York 10017 (800) 253-9646; *Statistical Yearbook.*

INDIA - EXCISE TAXES - See INDIA - TAXATION

INDIA - EXPORTS

American Automobile Manufacturers Association, 1401 H Street, NW, Suite 900, Washington, D.C. 20005 (202) 326-5500; *World Motor Vehicle Data.*

The Economist Intelligence Unit, 111 West 57th Street, New York, New York 10019 (800) 938-4685; *The World Market Atlas.*

The Economist Intelligence Unit (Asia) Limited, 10th Floor, Luk Kwok Centre, 72 Gloucester Road, Wanchai, Hong Kong (Phone Number in U.S. (800) 938-4685); *Asian Market Atlas.*

Euromonitor Publications Limited, 87-88 Turnmill Street, London EC1M 5QU, England; *International Marketing Data and Statistics,* and *Third World Economic Handbook.*

Food and Agricultural Organization of the United Nations (FAO) Via delle Terme di Caracalla, 00100 Rome, Italy (Telephone Number in U.S. (202) 653-2400); *The State of Food and Agriculture.*

G.K. Hall and Company, 70 Lincoln Street, Boston, Massachusetts 02111 (617) 423-3990; *The World in Figures.*

International Lead and Zinc Study Group, Metro House, 58 St. James's Street, London SW1A 1LD, England; *Lead and Zinc Statistics.*

International Monetary Fund, 700 Nineteenth Street, NW, Washington, D.C. 20431 (202) 623-7000; *Direction of Trade Statistics, Government Finance Statistics Yearbook,* and *International Financial Statistics.*

International Rubber Study Group, York House, 8th Floor, Empire Way, Wembley, London HA9 0PA, England; *Rubber Statistical Bulletin.*

Organisation for Economic Co-operation and Development (OECD), 2 rue Andre-Pascal, 75 Paris 16, France (Telephone Number in U.S. (202) 785-6323); *The Footwear, Raw Hides and Skins, and Leather Industry in OECD Countries.*

Statistical Office of the United Nations, Publishing Service, New York, New York 10017 (800) 253-9646; *Foreign Trade Statistics of Asia and the Pacific,* and *Trade in Manufactures of Developing Countries.*

Times Books, 201 East 50th Street, New York, New York 10022 (212) 751-2600; *The Economist Book of Vital World Statistics.*

INDIA - EXTERNAL INDEBTEDNESS

Euromonitor Publications Limited, 87-88 Turnmill Street, London EC1M 5QU, England; *Third World Economic Handbook.*

The World Bank, 1818 H Street, NW, Washington, D.C. 20433 (202) 477-1234; *World Tables.*

INDIA - EXTERNAL TRADE

Food and Agricultural Organization of the United Nations (FAO) Via delle Terme di Caracalla, 00100 Rome, Italy (Telephone Number in U.S. (202) 653-2400); *The State of Food and Agriculture,* and *Trade Yearbook.*

G.K. Hall and Company, 70 Lincoln Street, Boston, Massachusetts 02111 (617) 423-3990; *The World in Figures.*

Statistical Office of the United Nations, Publishing Service, New York, New York 10017 (800) 253-9646; *Statistical Yearbook,* and *Statistical Yearbook for Asia and the Pacific.*

INDIA - FABRIC PRODUCTION - See INDIA - TEXTILE INDUSTRY

INDIA - FARM CROPS - See INDIA - CROPS

INDIA - FERTILITY RATES

The Economist Intelligence Unit (Asia) Limited, 10th Floor, Luk Kwok Centre, 72 Gloucester Road, Wanchai, Hong Kong (Phone Number in U.S. (800) 938-4685); *Asian Market Atlas.*

Times Books, 201 East 50th Street, New York, New York 10022 (212) 751-2600; *The Economist Book of Vital World Statistics.*

The World Bank, 1818 H Street, NW, Washington, D.C. 20433 (202) 477-1234; *World Tables.*

INDIA - FERTILIZER

Food and Agricultural Organization of the United Nations (FAO), Via delle Terme di Caracalla, 00100 Rome, Italy (Telephone Number in U.S. (202) 653-2400); *Fertilizer Yearbook,* and *The State of Food and Agriculture.*

Statistical Office of the United Nations, Publishing Service, New York, New York 10017 (800) 253-9646; *Statistical Yearbook.*

INDIA - FETAL MORTALITY

Statistical Office of the United Nations, Publishing Service, New York, New York 10017 (800) 253-9646; *Demographic Yearbook.*

INDIA - FIBRE PRODUCTION - See INDIA - TEXTILE INDUSTRY

INDIA - FILAMENT PRODUCTION - See INDIA - TEXTILE INDUSTRY

INDIA - FILM - See INDIA - MOTION PICTURES

INDIA - FINANCE

G.K. Hall and Company, 70 Lincoln Street, Boston, Massachusetts 02111 (617) 423-3990; *The World in Figures.*

International Monetary Fund, 700 Nineteenth Street, NW, Washington, D.C. 20431 (202) 623-7000; *Government Finance Statistics Yearbook,* and *International Financial Statistics.*

Statistical Office of the United Nations, Publishing Service, New York, New York 10017 (800) 253-9646; *Statistical Yearbook for Asia and the Pacific.*

INDIA - FISHERIES

Food and Agricultural Organization of the United Nations (FAO) Via delle Terme di Caracalla, 00100 Rome, Italy (Telephone Number in U.S. (202) 653-2400); *The State of Food and Agriculture,* and *Yearbook of Fishery Statistics.*

Statistical Office of the United Nations, Publishing Service, New York, New York 10017 (800) 253-9646; *Statistical Yearbook.*

INDIA - FLOUR PRODUCTION

Commodity Research Bureau, Incorporated, 75 Wall Street, New York, New York 10005 (212) 504-7754; *Commodity Year Book.*

Statistical Office of the United Nations, Publishing Service, New York, New York 10017 (800) 253-9646; *Statistical Yearbook.*

INDIA - FOOD

Food and Agricultural Organization of the United Nations (FAO), Via delle Terme di Caracalla, 00100 Rome, Italy (Telephone Number in U.S. (202) 653-2400); *Production Yearbook,* and *The State of Food and Agriculture.*

G.K. Hall and Company, 70 Lincoln Street, Boston, Massachusetts 02111 (617) 423-3990; *The World in Figures.*

Statistical Office of the United Nations, Publishing Service, New York, New York 10017 (800) 253-9646; *Statistical Yearbook for Asia and the Pacific.*

INDIA - FOREIGN AID

G.K. Hall and Company, 70 Lincoln Street, Boston, Massachusetts 02111 (617) 423-3990; *The World in Figures.*

INDIA - FOREIGN DEBT

International Monetary Fund, 700 Nineteenth Street, NW, Washington, D.C. 20431 (202) 623-7000; *Government Finance Statistics Yearbook.*

INDIA - FOREIGN TRADE

The Economist Intelligence Unit (Asia) Limited, 10th Floor, Luk Kwok Centre, 72 Gloucester Road, Wanchai, Hong Kong (Phone Number in U.S. (800) 938-4685); *Asian Market Atlas.*

Euromonitor Publications Limited, 87-88 Turnmill Street, London EC1M 5QU, England; *International Marketing Data and Statistics,* and *Third World Economic Handbook.*

Food and Agricultural Organization of the United Nations (FAO) Via delle Terme di Caracalla, 00100 Rome, Italy (Telephone Number in U.S. (202) 653-2400); *The State of Food and Agriculture.*

G.K. Hall and Company, 70 Lincoln Street, Boston, Massachusetts 02111 (617) 423-3990; *The World in Figures.*

International Monetary Fund, 700 Nineteenth Street, NW, Washington, D.C. 20431 (202) 623-7000; *International Financial Statistics.*

Organisation for Economic Co-operation and Development (OECD), 2 rue Andre-Pascal, 75 Paris 16, France (Telephone Number in U.S. (202) 785-6323); *The Footwear, Raw Hides and Skins, and Leather Industry in OECD Countries.*

Statistical Office of the United Nations, Publishing Service, New York, New York 10017 (800) 253-9646; *International Trade Statistics Yearbook,* and *Statistical Yearbook.*

World Bureau of Metal Statistics, 27-A High Street, Ware, Herts SG12 9BA, England; *World Metal Statistics.*

The World Bank, 1818 H Street, NW, Washington, D.C. 20433 (202) 477-1234; *World Tables.*

INDIA - FORESTRY AND FOREST PRODUCTS

The Economist Intelligence Unit (Asia) Limited, 10th Floor, Luk Kwok Centre, 72 Gloucester Road, Wanchai, Hong Kong (Phone Number in U.S. (800) 938-4685); *Asian Market Atlas.*

Euromonitor Publications Limited, 87-88 Turnmill Street, London EC1M 5QU, England; *Third World Economic Handbook.*

Food and Agricultural Organization of the United Nations (FAO) Via delle Terme di Caracalla, 00100 Rome, Italy (Telephone Number in U.S. (202) 653-2400); *The State of Food and Agriculture,* and *Yearbook of Forest Products.*

Forest and Paper Association, 1250 Connecticut Avenue, NW, Washington, D.C. 20036 (202) 463-2455; *Wood Pulp and Fiber Statistics.*

G.K. Hall and Company, 70 Lincoln Street, Boston, Massachusetts 02111 (617) 423-3990; *The World in Figures.*

Statistical Office of the United Nations, Publishing Service, New York, New York 10017 (800) 253-9646; *Statistical Yearbook.*

United Nations Educational, Scientific and Cultural Organization (UNESCO), 7 Place de Fontenoy, F-75700 Paris, France (Telephone Number in U.S. (212) 963-5981); *Statistical Yearbook.*

INDIA - GARLIC PRODUCTION - See INDIA - CROPS

INDIA - GAS - See INDIA - MINING AND MINERAL PRODUCTS

INDIA - GENERAL INDUSTRIAL STATISTICS

Statistical Office of the United Nations, Publishing Service, New York, New York 10017 (800) 253-9646; *Industrial Statistics Yearbook.*

INDIA - GENERAL MORTALITY

Statistical Office of the United Nations, Publishing Service, New York, New York 10017 (800) 253-9646; *Demographic Yearbook.*

World Health Organization, Avenue Appia, Office of Publications, CH-1211 Geneva 27, Switzerland (Telephone Number in U.S. (518) 436-9686); *World Health Statistics Annual.*

INDIA - GOATS - See INDIA - LIVESTOCK AND POULTRY

INDIA - GOLD HOLDINGS

International Monetary Fund, 700 Nineteenth Street, NW, Washington, D.C. 20431 (202) 623-7000; *International Financial Statistics.*

Statistical Office of the United Nations, Publishing Service, New York, New York 10017 (800) 253-9646; *Statistical Yearbook.*

The World Bank, 1818 H Street, NW, Washington, D.C. 20433 (202) 477-1234; *World Tables.*

INDIA - GOLD PRODUCTION AND CONSUMPTION - See INDIA - MINING AND MINERAL PRODUCTS

INDIA - GOVERNMENT

G.K. Hall and Company, 70 Lincoln Street, Boston, Massachusetts 02111 (617) 423-3990; *The World in Figures.*

INDIA - GOVERNMENT BONDS - See INDIA - BONDS

INDIA - GOVERNMENT EXPENDITURES

Euromonitor Publications Limited, 87-88 Turnmill Street, London EC1M 5QU, England; *Third World Economic Handbook.*

International Monetary Fund, 700 Nineteenth Street, NW, Washington, D.C. 20431 (202) 623-7000; *Government Finance Statistics Yearbook.*

Times Books, 201 East 50th Street, New York, New York 10022 (212) 751-2600; *The Economist Book of Vital World Statistics.*

The World Bank, 1818 H Street, NW, Washington, D.C. 20433 (202) 477-1234; *World Tables.*

INDIA - GOVERNMENT FINANCES

International Monetary Fund, 700 Nineteenth Street, NW, Washington, D.C. 20431 (202) 623-7000; *International Financial Statistics.*

Statistical Office of the United Nations, Publishing Service, New York, New York 10017 (800) 253-9646; *Statistical Yearbook.*

INDIA - GOVERNMENT REVENUES

International Monetary Fund, 700 Nineteenth Street, NW, Washington, D.C. 20431 (202) 623-7000; *Government Finance Statistics Yearbook.*

Times Books, 201 East 50th Street, New York, New York 10022 (212) 751-2600; *The Economist Book of Vital World Statistics.*

The World Bank, 1818 H Street, NW, Washington, D.C. 20433 (202) 477-1234; *World Tables.*

INDIA - GRAIN PRODUCTION - See INDIA - CROPS

INDIA - GRANTS

International Monetary Fund, 700 Nineteenth Street, NW, Washington, D.C. 20431 (202) 623-7000; *Government Finance Statistics Yearbook.*

INDIA - GROSS DOMESTIC PRODUCT

The Economist Intelligence Unit, 111 West 57th Street, New York, New York 10019 (800) 938-4685; *The World Market Atlas.*

The Economist Intelligence Unit (Asia) Limited, 10th Floor, Luk Kwok Centre, 72 Gloucester Road, Wanchai, Hong Kong (Phone Number in U.S. (800) 938-4685); *Asian Market Atlas.*

Euromonitor Publications Limited, 87-88 Turnmill Street, London EC1M 5QU, England; *International Marketing Data and Statistics,* and *Third World Economic Handbook.*

G.K. Hall and Company, 70 Lincoln Street, Boston, Massachusetts 02111 (617) 423-3990; *The World in Figures.*

Statistical Office of the United Nations, Publishing Service, New York, New York 10017 (800) 253-9646; *Statistical Yearbook.*

Times Books, 201 East 50th Street, New York, New York 10022 (212) 751-2600; *The Economist Book of Vital World Statistics.*

The World Bank, 1818 H Street, NW, Washington, D.C. 20433 (202) 477-1234; *World Tables.*

INDIA - GROSS INDUSTRIAL PRODUCT

Euromonitor Publications Limited, 87-88 Turnmill Street, London EC1M 5QU, England; *Third World Economic Handbook.*

INDIA - GROSS NATIONAL PRODUCT

Euromonitor Publications Limited, 87-88 Turnmill Street, London EC1M 5QU, England; *International Marketing Data and Statistics,* and *Third World Economic Handbook.*

U.S. Arms Control and Disarmament Agency, 320 Twenty-first Street, Northwest, Washington, D.C. 20451 (202) 647-8677; *World Military Expenditures and Arms Transfers.*

The World Bank, 1818 H Street, NW, Washington, D.C. 20433 (202) 477-1234; *World Tables.*

INDIA - GROUNDNUTS PRODUCTION - See INDIA - CROPS

INDIA - HEALTH

The Economist Intelligence Unit (Asia) Limited, 10th Floor, Luk Kwok Centre, 72 Gloucester Road, Wanchai, Hong Kong (Phone Number in U.S. (800) 938-4685); *Asian Market Atlas.*

G.K. Hall and Company, 70 Lincoln Street, Boston, Massachusetts 02111 (617) 423-3990; *The World in Figures.*

Statistical Office of the United Nations, Publishing Service, New York, New York 10017 (800) 253-9646; *Statistical Yearbook.*

Times Books, 201 East 50th Street, New York, New York 10022 (212) 751-2600; *The Economist Book of Vital World Statistics.*

World Health Organization, Avenue Appia, Office of Publications, CH-1211 Geneva 27, Switzerland (Telephone Number in U.S. (518) 436-9686); *World Health Statistics Annual.*

INDIA - HEALTH EXPENDITURES

International Monetary Fund, 700 Nineteenth Street, NW, Washington, D.C. 20431 (202) 623-7000; *Government Finance Statistics Yearbook.*

INDIA - HEMP FIBRE PRODUCTION - See INDIA - TEXTILE INDUSTRY

INDIA - HIDE PRODUCTION

Food and Agricultural Organization of the United Nations (FAO), Via delle Terme di Caracalla, 00100 Rome, Italy (Telephone Number in U.S. (202) 653-2400); *Production Yearbook.*

INDIA - HIGHWAYS

Business International Asia/Pacific Ltd., 10/F, Luk Kwok Centre, 72 Gloucester Road, Hong Kong (Phone Number in U.S. (800) 938-4685); *Asian Market Atlas.*

G.K. Hall and Company, 70 Lincoln Street, Boston, Massachusetts 02111 (617) 423-3990; *The World in Figures.*

International Road Federation, 525 School Street, SW, Washington, D.C. 20024 (202) 554-2106; *World Road Statistics.*

INDIA - HORSES - See INDIA - LIVESTOCK AND POULTRY

INDIA - HOURS OF WORK - See INDIA - EMPLOYMENT

INDIA - HOUSING AND HOUSING UNITS

Euromonitor Publications Limited, 87-88 Turnmill Street, London EC1M 5QU, England; *Third World Economic Handbook.*

INDIA - HOUSING EXPENDITURES

International Monetary Fund, 700 Nineteenth Street, NW, Washington, D.C. 20431 (202) 623-7000; *Government Finance Statistics Yearbook.*

INDIA - HYDROCHLORIC ACID PRODUCTION

Statistical Office of the United Nations, Publishing Service, New York, New York 10017 (800) 253-9646; *Statistical Yearbook.*

INDIA - ILLITERATE POPULATION

The Economist Intelligence Unit, 111 West 57th Street, New York, New York 10019 (800) 938-4685; *The World Market Atlas.*

G.K. Hall and Company, 70 Lincoln Street, Boston, Massachusetts 02111 (617) 423-3990; *The World in Figures.*

United Nations Educational, Scientific and Cultural Organization (UNESCO), 7 Place de Fontenoy, F-75700 Paris, France (Telephone Number in U.S. (212) 963-5981); *Statistical Yearbook.*

INDIA - IMPORTS

American Automobile Manufacturers Association, 1401 H Street, NW, Suite 900, Washington, D.C. 20005 (202) 326-5500; *World Motor Vehicle Data.*

The Economist Intelligence Unit, 111 West 57th Street, New York, New York 10019; *The World Market Atlas.*

The Economist Intelligence Unit (Asia) Limited, 10th Floor, Luk Kwok Centre, 72 Gloucester Road, Wanchai, Hong Kong (Phone Number in U.S. (800) 938-4685); *Asian Market Atlas.*

Euromonitor Publications Limited, 87-88 Turnmill Street, London EC1M 5QU, England; *International Marketing Data and Statistics,* and *Third World Economic Handbook.*

Food and Agricultural Organization of the United Nations (FAO) Via delle Terme di Caracalla, 00100 Rome, Italy (Telephone Number in U.S. (202) 653-2400); *The State of Food and Agriculture.*

G.K. Hall and Company, 70 Lincoln Street, Boston, Massachusetts 02111 (617) 423-3990; *The World in Figures.*

International Lead and Zinc Study Group, Metro House, 58 St. James's Street, London SW1A 1LD, England; *Lead and Zinc Statistics.*

International Monetary Fund, 700 Nineteenth Street, NW, Washington, D.C. 20431 (202) 623-7000; *Direction of Trade Statistics, Government Finance Statistics Yearbook,* and *International Financial Statistics.*

International Rubber Study Group, York House, 8th Floor, Empire Way, Wembley, London HA9 0PA, England; *Rubber Statistical Bulletin.*

Statistical Office of the United Nations, Publishing Service, New York, New York 10017 (800) 253-9646; *Foreign Trade Statistics of Asia and the Pacific,* and *Trade in Manufactures of Developing Countries.*

The World Bank, 1818 H Street, NW, Washington, D.C. 20433 (202) 477-1234; *World Tables.*

INDIA - INCOME TAXES - See INDIA - TAXATION

INDIA - INDUSTRIAL METALS PRODUCTION - See INDIA - MINING AND MINERAL PRODUCTS

INDIA - INDUSTRY

Euromonitor Publications Limited, 87-88 Turnmill Street, London EC1M 5QU, England; *Third World Economic Handbook.*

G.K. Hall and Company, 70 Lincoln Street, Boston, Massachusetts 02111 (617) 423-3990; *The World in Figures.*

International Labour Office, I.L.O. Publications, CH-1211, Geneva 22, Switzerland; *Yearbook of Labour Statistics.*

Statistical Office of the United Nations, Publishing Service, New York, New York 10017 (800) 253-9646; *Statistical Yearbook for Asia and the Pacific.*

Times Books, 201 East 50th Street, New York, New York 10022 (212) 751-2600; *The Economist Book of Vital World Statistics.*

The World Bank, 1818 H Street, NW, Washington, D.C. 20433 (202) 477-1234; *World Tables.*

World Intellectual Property Organization, 34 Chemin des Colombettes, CH-1211 Geneva 20, Switzerland; *Industrial Property Statistics.*

INDIA - INFANT AND MATERNAL MORTALITY

The Economist Intelligence Unit (Asia) Limited, 10th Floor, Luk Kwok Centre, 72 Gloucester Road, Wanchai, Hong Kong (Phone Number in U.S. (800) 938-4685); *Asian Market Atlas.*

Statistical Office of the United Nations, Publishing Service, New York, New York 10017 (800) 253-9646; *Demographic Yearbook,* and *Statistical Yearbook.*

Times Books, 201 East 50th Street, New York, New York 10022 (212) 751-2600; *The Economist Book of Vital World Statistics.*

The World Bank, 1818 H Street, NW, Washington, D.C. 20433 (202) 477-1234; *World Tables.*

INDIA - INTERNAL TRADE

Statistical Office of the United Nations, Publishing Service, New York, New York 10017 (800) 253-9646; *Statistical Yearbook for Asia and the Pacific.*

INDIA - INTERNATIONAL LIQUIDITY

International Monetary Fund, 700 Nineteenth Street, NW, Washington, D.C. 20431 (202) 623-7000; *International Financial Statistics.*

INDIA - INTERNATIONAL RESERVES EXCLUDING GOLD

Statistical Office of the United Nations, Publishing Service, New York, New York 10017 (800) 253-9646; *Statistical Yearbook.*

The World Bank, 1818 H Street, NW, Washington, D.C. 20433 (202) 477-1234; *World Tables.*

INDIA - INVESTMENTS

International Monetary Fund, 700 Nineteenth Street, NW, Washington, D.C. 20431 (202) 623-7000; *International Financial Statistics.*

INDIA - IRON ORE PRODUCTION AND CONSUMPTION - See INDIA - MINING AND MINERAL PRODUCTS

INDIA - IRRIGATION

Euromonitor Publications Limited, 87-88 Turnmill Street, London EC1M 5QU, England; *International Marketing Data and Statistics.*

INDIA - JUTE PRODUCTION - See INDIA - CROPS

INDIA - LABOR FORCE

The Economist Intelligence Unit (Asia) Limited, 10th Floor, Luk Kwok Centre, 72 Gloucester Road, Wanchai, Hong Kong (Phone Number in U.S. (800) 938-4685); *Asian Market Atlas.*

Euromonitor Publications Limited, 87-88 Turnmill Street, London EC1M 5QU, England; *International Marketing Data and Statistics.*

Food and Agricultural Organization of the United Nations (FAO) Via delle Terme di Caracalla, 00100 Rome, Italy (Telephone Number in U.S. (202) 653-2400); *The State of Food and Agriculture.*

G.K. Hall and Company, 70 Lincoln Street, Boston, Massachusetts 02111 (617) 423-3990; *The World in Figures.*

Times Books, 201 East 50th Street, New York, New York 10022 (212) 751-2600; *The Economist Book of Vital World Statistics.*

The World Bank, 1818 H Street, NW, Washington, D.C. 20433 (202) 477-1234; *World Tables.*

INDIA - LABOR PRODUCTIVITY

International Labour Office, I.L.O. Publications, CH-1211, Geneva 22, Switzerland; *Yearbook of Labour Statistics.*

INDIA - LAND USE

Euromonitor Publications Limited, 87-88 Turnmill Street, London EC1M 5QU, England; *International Marketing Data and Statistics.*

Food and Agricultural Organization of the United Nations (FAO), Via delle Terme di Caracalla, 00100 Rome, Italy (Telephone Number in U.S. (202) 653-2400); *Production Yearbook.*

G.K. Hall and Company, 70 Lincoln Street, Boston, Massachusetts 02111 (617) 423-3990; *The World in Figures.*

INDIA - LEAD AND LEAD ORE - See INDIA - MINING AND MINERAL PRODUCTS

INDIA - LEATHER AND FOOTWEAR - EXPORTS AND IMPORTS

Statistical Office of the United Nations, Publishing Service, New York, New York 10017 (800) 253-9646; *Trade in Manufactures of Developing Countries.*

INDIA - LIBRARIES

United Nations Educational, Scientific and Cultural Organization (UNESCO), 7 Place de Fontenoy, F-75700 Paris, France (Telephone Number in U.S. (212) 963-5981); *Statistical Yearbook.*

INDIA - LIFE EXPECTANCY

The Economist Intelligence Unit (Asia) Limited, 10th Floor, Luk Kwok Centre, 72 Gloucester Road, Wanchai, Hong Kong (Phone Number in U.S. (800) 938-4685); *Asian Market Atlas.*

INDIA - LIGNITE PRODUCTION - See INDIA - MINING AND MINERAL PRODUCTS

INDIA - LIVESTOCK AND POULTRY

Commodity Research Bureau, Incorporated, 75 Wall Street, New York, New York 10005 (212) 504-7754; *Commodity Year Book.*

Euromonitor Publications Limited, 87-88 Turnmill Street, London EC1M 5QU, England; *Third World Economic Handbook.*

Food and Agricultural Organization of the United Nations (FAO), Via delle Terme di Caracalla, 00100 Rome, Italy (Telephone Number in U.S. (202) 653-2400); *Production Yearbook,* and *The State of Food and Agriculture.*

G.K. Hall and Company, 70 Lincoln Street, Boston, Massachusetts 02111 (617) 423-3990; *The World in Figures.*

Statistical Office of the United Nations, Publishing Service, New York, New York 10017 (800) 253-9646; *Statistical Yearbook.*

INDIA - LIVING LEVELS

G.K. Hall and Company, 70 Lincoln Street, Boston, Massachusetts 02111 (617) 423-3990; *The World in Figures.*

Times Books, 201 East 50th Street, New York, New York 10022 (212) 751-2600; *The Economist Book of Vital World Statistics.*

INDIA - MAGNESIUM PRODUCTION AND CONSUMPTION - See INDIA - MINING AND MINERAL PRODUCTS

INDIA - MAIL - NUMBER OF PIECES SENT OR RECEIVED

Statistical Office of the United Nations, Publishing Service, New York, New York 10017 (800) 253-9646; *Statistical Yearbook.*

INDIA - MANGANESE AND MANGANESE ORE - See INDIA - MINING AND MINERAL PRODUCTS

INDIA - MANPOWER

Statistical Office of the United Nations, Publishing Service, New York, New York 10017 (800) 253-9646; *Statistical Yearbook for Asia and the Pacific.*

INDIA - MANUFACTURING

American Automobile Manufacturers Association, 1401 H Street, NW, Suite 900, Washington, D.C. 20005 (202) 326-5500; *World Motor Vehicle Data.*

Euromonitor Publications Limited, 87-88 Turnmill Street, London EC1M 5QU, England; *Third World Economic Handbook.*

G.K. Hall and Company, 70 Lincoln Street, Boston, Massachusetts 02111 (617) 423-3990; *The World in Figures.*

Statistical Office of the United Nations, Publishing Service, New York, New York 10017 (800) 253-9646; *Statistical Yearbook.*

Times Books, 201 East 50th Street, New York, New York 10022 (212) 751-2600; *The Economist Book of Vital World Statistics.*

The World Bank, 1818 H Street, NW, Washington, D.C. 20433 (202) 477-1234; *World Tables.*

INDIA - MARRIAGE RATES

Statistical Office of the United Nations, Publishing Service, New York, New York 10017 (800) 253-9646; *Demographic Yearbook.*

INDIA - MEAT PRODUCTION - See INDIA - LIVESTOCK AND POULTRY

INDIA - MERCHANT SHIPPING

G.K. Hall and Company, 70 Lincoln Street, Boston, Massachusetts 02111 (617) 423-3990; *The World in Figures.*

Lloyd's Register of Shipping, 17 Battery Place, New York, New York 10004 (212) 425-8050; *Register of Ships.*

Statistical Office of the United Nations, Publishing Service, New York, New York 10017 (800) 253-9646; *Statistical Yearbook.*

Times Books, 201 East 50th Street, New York, New York 10022 (212) 751-2600; *The Economist Book of Vital World Statistics.*

U.S. Department of Transportation, Maritime Administration, 400 Seventh Street, SW, Washington, D.C. 20590 (202) 366-5807; *A Statistical Analysis of the World's Merchant Fleets.*

INDIA - MILITARY

The Economist Intelligence Unit (Asia) Limited, 10th Floor, Luk Kwok Centre, 72 Gloucester Road, Wanchai, Hong Kong (Phone Number in U.S. (800) 938-4685); *Asian Market Atlas.*

G.K. Hall and Company, 70 Lincoln Street, Boston, Massachusetts 02111 (617) 423-3990; *The World in Figures.*

The International Institute for Strategic Studies, 23 Tavistock Street, London WC2E 7NQ, England; *The Military Balance.*

U.S. Arms Control and Disarmament Agency, 320 Twenty-first Street, Northwest, Washington, D.C. 20451 (202) 647-8677; *World Military Expenditures and Arms Transfers.*

INDIA - MILK - See INDIA - DAIRY PRODUCTS

INDIA - MILLET PRODUCTION - See INDIA - CROPS

INDIA - MINING AND MINERAL PRODUCTS

Commodity Research Bureau, Incorporated, 75 Wall Street, New York, New York 10005 (212) 504-7754; *Commodity Year Book.*

Euromonitor Publications Limited, 87-88 Turnmill Street, London EC1M 5QU, England; *Third World Economic Handbook.*

Facts on File, 460 Park Avenue South, New York, New York 10016; *The New Book of World Rankings.*

G.K. Hall and Company, 70 Lincoln Street, Boston, Massachusetts 02111 (617) 423-3990; *The World in Figures.*

International Lead and Zinc Study Group, Metro House, 58 St. James's Street, London SW1A 1LD, England; *Lead and Zinc Statistics.*

Organisation for Economic Co-operation and Development (OECD), 2 rue Andre-Pascal, 75 Paris 16, France (Telephone Number in U.S. (202) 785-6323); *Coal Information.*

Penn Well Publishing Company, 1421 South Sheridan Road, Post Office Box 1260, Tulsa, Oklahoma 74101 (800) 752-9764; *International Energy Statistics Sourcebook.*

Statistical Office of the United Nations, Publishing Service, New York, New York 10017 (800) 253-9646; *Statistical Yearbook.*

World Bureau of Metal Statistics, 27-A High Street, Ware, Herts, SG12 9BA, England; *World Metal Statistics.*

INDIA - MOLASSES PRODUCTION - See INDIA - CROPS

INDIA - MOLYBDENUM AND MOLYBDENUM ORE - See INDIA - MINING AND MINERAL PRODUCTS

INDIA - MONEY EXCHANGE RATE

Euromonitor Publications Limited, 87-88 Turnmill Street, London EC1M 5QU, England; *International Marketing Data and Statistics.*

International Monetary Fund, 700 Nineteenth Street, NW, Washington, D.C. 20431 (202) 623-7000; *International Financial Statistics.*

Statistical Office of the United Nations, Publishing Service, New York, New York 10017 (800) 253-9646; *Statistical Yearbook.*

INDIA - MONEY MARKET RATES

Statistical Office of the United Nations, Publishing Service, New York, New York 10017 (800) 253-9646; *Statistical Yearbook.*

INDIA - MONEY RESERVES

Euromonitor Publications Limited, 87-88 Turnmill Street, London EC1M 5QU, England; *International Marketing Data and Statistics.*

INDIA - MONEY SUPPLY

Euromonitor Publications Limited, 87-88 Turnmill Street, London EC1M 5QU, England; *International Marketing Data and Statistics.*

G.K. Hall and Company, 70 Lincoln Street, Boston, Massachusetts 02111 (617) 423-3990; *The World in Figures.*

International Monetary Fund, 700 Nineteenth Street, NW, Washington, D.C. 20431 (202) 623-7000; *International Financial Statistics.*

Statistical Office of the United Nations, Publishing Service, New York, New York 10017 (800) 253-9646; *Statistical Yearbook.*

The World Bank, 1818 H Street, NW, Washington, D.C. 20433 (202) 477-1234; *World Tables.*

INDIA - MOTION PICTURES

Statistical Office of the United Nations, Publishing Service, New York, New York 10017 (800) 253-9646; *Statistical Yearbook.*

United Nations Educational, Scientific and Cultural Organization (UNESCO), 7 Place de Fontenoy, F-75700 Paris, France (Telephone Number in U.S. (212) 963-5981); *Statistical Yearbook.*

INDIA - MOTOR VEHICLE PRODUCTION

American Automobile Manufacturers Association, 1401 H Street, NW, Suite 900, Washington, D.C. 20005 (202) 326-5500; *World Motor Vehicle Data.*

Statistical Office of the United Nations, Publishing Service, New York, New York 10017 (800) 253-9646; *Statistical Yearbook.*

INDIA - MOTOR VEHICLE TAXES - See INDIA - TAXATION

INDIA - MOTOR VEHICLES IN USE

American Automobile Manufacturers Association, 1401 H Street, NW, Suite 900, Washington, D.C. 20005 (202) 326-5500; *World Motor Vehicle Data.*

G.K. Hall and Company, 70 Lincoln Street, Boston, Massachusetts 02111 (617) 423-3990; *The World in Figures.*

International Road Federation, 525 School Street, SW, Washington, D.C. 20024 (202) 554-2106; *World Road Statistics.*

Statistical Office of the United Nations, Publishing Service, New York, New York 10017 (800) 253-9646; *Statistical Yearbook.*

Times Books, 201 East 50th Street, New York, New York 10022 (212) 751-2600; *The Economist Book of Vital World Statistics.*

INDIA - MULES - See INDIA - LIVESTOCK AND POULTRY

INDIA - NATALITY - See INDIA - BIRTH RATES

INDIA - NATIONAL ACCOUNTS

International Monetary Fund, 700 Nineteenth Street, NW, Washington, D.C. 20431 (202) 623-7000; monthly report, *International Financial Statistics.*

Statistical Office of the United Nations, Publishing Service, New York, New York 10017 (800) 253-9646; *National Accounts Statistics, Statistical Yearbook,* and *Statistical Yearbook for Asia and the Pacific.*

INDIA - NATIONAL INCOME

G.K. Hall and Company, 70 Lincoln Street, Boston, Massachusetts 02111 (617) 423-3990; *The World in Figures.*

Statistical Office of the United Nations, Publishing Service, New York, New York 10017 (800) 253-9646; *Statistical Yearbook.*

INDIA - NATIONAL PRODUCT

Statistical Office of the United Nations, Publishing Service, New York, New York 10017 (800) 253-9646; *Statistical Yearbook.*

INDIA - NATURAL GAS PRODUCTION - See INDIA - MINING AND MINERAL PRODUCTS

INDIA - NATURAL RUBBER PRODUCTION

International Rubber Study Group, York House, 8th Floor, Empire Way, Wembley, London HA9 0PA, England; *Rubber Statistical Bulletin.*

Statistical Office of the United Nations, Publishing Service, New York, New York 10017 (800) 253-9646; *Statistical Yearbook.*

INDIA - NEWSPAPER PRODUCTION - See INDIA - FORESTRY AND FOREST PRODUCTS

INDIA - NEWSPRINT - See INDIA - FORESTRY AND FOREST PRODUCTS

INDIA - NICKEL AND NICKEL ORE - See INDIA - MINING AND MINERAL PRODUCTS

INDIA - NITRIC ACID PRODUCTION

Statistical Office of the United Nations, Publishing Service, New York, New York 10017 (800) 253-9646; *Statistical Yearbook.*

INDIA - OCCUPATIONS - See INDIA - LABOR FORCE

INDIA - ONION PRODUCTION - See INDIA - CROPS

INDIA - PAPER - See INDIA - FORESTRY AND FOREST PRODUCTS

INDIA - PATENTS

Statistical Office of the United Nations, Publishing Service, New York, New York 10017 (800) 253-9646; *Statistical Yearbook.*

World Intellectual Property Organization, 34 Chemin des Colombettes, CH-1211 Geneva 20, Switzerland; *Industrial Property Statistics.*

INDIA - PEANUT PRODUCTION - See INDIA - CROPS

INDIA - PEPPER PRODUCTION - See INDIA - CROPS

INDIA - PERIODICALS

United Nations Educational, Scientific and Cultural Organization (UNESCO), 7 Place de Fontenoy, F-75700 Paris, France (Telephone Number in U.S. (212) 963-5981); *Statistical Yearbook.*

INDIA - PESTICIDE USE

Food and Agricultural Organization of the United Nations (FAO) Via delle Terme di Caracalla, 00100 Rome, Italy (Telephone Number in U.S. (202) 653-2400); *The State of Food and Agriculture.*

INDIA - PETROLEUM INDUSTRY

Food and Agricultural Organization of the United Nations (FAO) Via delle Terme di Caracalla, 00100 Rome, Italy (Telephone Number in U.S. (202) 653-2400); *The State of Food and Agriculture.*

G.K. Hall and Company, 70 Lincoln Street, Boston, Massachusetts 02111 (617) 423-3990; *The World in Figures.*

Penn Well Publishing Company, 1421 South Sheridan Road, Post Office Box 1260, Tulsa, Oklahoma 74101 (800) 752-9764; *International Energy Statistics Sourcebook.*

Statistical Office of the United Nations, Publishing Service, New York, New York 10017 (800) 253-9646; *Statistical Yearbook.*

INDIA - PHOSPHATE AND PHOSPHATE ROCK PRODUCTION - See INDIA - MINING AND MINERAL PRODUCTS

INDIA - PIG-IRON AND FERRO-ALLOYS PRODUCTION - See INDIA - MINING AND MINERAL PRODUCTS

INDIA - PIGS - See INDIA - LIVESTOCK AND POULTRY

INDIA - PLASTIC AND RESIN PRODUCTION

Euromonitor Publications Limited, 87-88 Turnmill Street, London EC1M 5QU, England; *Third World Economic Handbook.*

Statistical Office of the United Nations, Publishing Service, New York, New York 10017 (800) 253-9646; *Statistical Yearbook.*

INDIA - POPULATION

The Economist Intelligence Unit, 111 West 57th Street, New York, New York 10019 (800) 938-4685; *The World Market Atlas.*

The Economist Intelligence Unit (Asia) Limited, 10th Floor, Luk Kwok Centre, 72 Gloucester Road, Wanchai, Hong Kong (Phone Number in U.S. (800) 938-4685); *Asian Market Atlas.*

Euromonitor Publications Limited, 87-88 Turnmill Street, London EC1M 5QU, England; *International Marketing Data and Statistics,* and *Third World Economic Handbook.*

Food and Agricultural Organization of the United Nations (FAO), Via delle Terme di Caracalla, 00100 Rome, Italy (Telephone Number in U.S. (202) 653-2400); *Production Yearbook.*

G.K. Hall and Company, 70 Lincoln Street, Boston, Massachusetts 02111 (617) 423-3990; *The World in Figures.*

International Labour Office, I.L.O. Publications, CH-1211, Geneva 22, Switzerland; *Yearbook of Labour Statistics.*

Statistical Office of the United Nations, Publishing Service, New York, New York 10017 (800) 253-9646; *Demographic Yearbook, Statistical Yearbook,* and *Statistical Yearbook for Asia and the Pacific.*

Times Books, 201 East 50th Street, New York, New York 10022 (212) 751-2600; *The Economist Book of Vital World Statistics.*

United Nations Educational, Scientific and Cultural Organization (UNESCO), 7 Place de Fontenoy, F-75700 Paris, France (Telephone Number in U.S. (212) 963-5981); *Statistical Yearbook.*

U.S. Arms Control and Disarmament Agency, 320 Twenty-first Street, Northwest, Washington, D.C. 20451 (202) 647-8677; *World Military Expenditures and Arms Transfers.*

World Health Organization, Avenue Appia, Office of Publications, CH-1211 Geneva 27, Switzerland (Telephone Number in U.S. (518) 436-9686); *World Health Statistics Annual.*

INDIA - POTATO PRODUCTION - See INDIA - CROPS

INDIA - POWER PRODUCTION INDUSTRY

Statistical Office of the United Nations, Publishing Service, New York, New York 10017; *Electric Power in Asia and the Pacific,* and *Statistical Yearbook.*

INDIA - PRICES

Food and Agricultural Organization of the United Nations (FAO), Via delle Terme di Caracalla, 00100 Rome, Italy (Telephone Number in U.S. (202) 653-2400); *Production Yearbook,* and *The State of Food and Agriculture.*

G.K. Hall and Company, 70 Lincoln Street, Boston, Massachusetts 02111 (617) 423-3990; *The World in Figures.*

International Labour Office, I.L.O. Publications, CH-1211, Geneva 22, Switzerland; *Yearbook of Labour Statistics.*

International Lead and Zinc Study Group, Metro House, 58 St. James's Street, London SW1A 1LD, England; *Lead and Zinc Statistics.*

International Monetary Fund, 700 Nineteenth Street, NW, Washington, D.C. 20431 (202) 623-7000; *International Financial Statistics.*

International Rubber Study Group, York House, 8th Floor, Empire Way, Wembley, London HA9 0PA, England; *Rubber Statistical Bulletin.*

World Bureau of Metal Statistics, 27-A High Street, Ware, Herts, SG12 9BA, England; *World Metal Statistics.*

INDIA - PRINTING AND WRITING PAPER - See INDIA - FORESTRY AND FOREST PRODUCTS

INDIA - PRODUCTION

American Automobile Manufacturers Association, 1401 H Street, NW, Suite 900, Washington, D.C. 20005 (202) 326-5500; *World Motor Vehicle Data.*

Euromonitor Publications Limited, 87-88 Turnmill Street, London EC1M 5QU, England; *Third World Economic Handbook.*

G.K. Hall and Company, 70 Lincoln Street, Boston, Massachusetts 02111 (617) 423-3990; *The World in Figures.*

International Lead and Zinc Study Group, Metro House, 58 St. James's Street, London SW1A 1LD, England; *Lead and Zinc Statistics.*

International Rubber Study Group, York House, 8th Floor, Empire Way, Wembley, London HA9 0PA, England; *Rubber Statistical*

Bulletin.

INDIA - PRODUCTIVITY

Euromonitor Publications Limited, 87-88 Turnmill Street, London EC1M 5QU, England; *International Marketing Data and Statistics.*

INDIA - PROPERTY TAXES - See INDIA - TAXATION

INDIA - RADIO BROADCASTING - See INDIA - BROADCASTING

INDIA - RADIO RECEIVER PRODUCTION

Statistical Office of the United Nations, Publishing Service, New York, New York 10017 (800) 253-9646; *Statistical Yearbook.*

INDIA - RAILWAYS

G.K. Hall and Company, 70 Lincoln Street, Boston, Massachusetts 02111 (617) 423-3990; *The World in Figures.*

Jane's Information Group, Sentinel House, 163 Brighton Road, Coulsdon, Surrey CR5 2NH, England (Telephone Number in U.S. (703) 683-3700); *Jane's World Railways.*

Statistical Office of the United Nations, Publishing Service, New York, New York 10017 (800) 253-9646; *Statistical Yearbook.*

INDIA - RAPESEED PRODUCTION - See INDIA - CROPS

INDIA - RENT PRICES

International Labour Office, I.L.O. Publications, CH-1211, Geneva 22, Switzerland; *Yearbook of Labour Statistics.*

INDIA - RETAIL TRADE

Euromonitor Publications Limited, 87-88 Turnmill Street, London EC1M 5QU, England; *Third World Economic Handbook.*

G.K. Hall and Company, 70 Lincoln Street, Boston, Massachusetts 02111 (617) 423-3990; *The World in Figures.*

INDIA - RICE PRODUCTION - See INDIA - CROPS

INDIA - ROOT AND TUBER PRODUCTION - See INDIA - CROPS

INDIA - ROUNDWOOD PRODUCTION - See INDIA - FORESTRY AND FOREST PRODUCTS

INDIA - RUBBER PRODUCTION

Commodity Research Bureau, Incorporated, 75 Wall Street, New York, New York 10005 (212) 504-7754; *Commodity Year Book.*

Euromonitor Publications Limited, 87-88 Turnmill Street, London EC1M 5QU, England; *Third World Economic Handbook.*

International Rubber Study Group, York House, 8th Floor, Empire Way, Wembley, London HA9 0PA, England; *Rubber Statistical Bulletin.*

Statistical Office of the United Nations, Publishing Service, New York, New York 10017 (800) 253-9646; *Statistical Yearbook.*

INDIA - SAFFLOWER SEED PRODUCTION - INDIA - CROPS

INDIA - SALT PRODUCTION - See INDIA - MINING AND MINERAL PRODUCTS

INDIA - SAWNWOOD PRODUCTION - See INDIA - FORESTRY AND FOREST PRODUCTS

INDIA - SCIENCE AND TECHNOLOGY - EXPENDITURE FOR RESEARCH

Statistical Office of the United Nations, Publishing Service, New York, New York 10017 (800) 253-9646; *Statistical Yearbook.*

INDIA - SCIENTISTS AND TECHNICIANS

Statistical Office of the United Nations, Publishing Service, New York, New York 10017 (800) 253-9646; *Statistical Yearbook.*

INDIA - SESAME SEED PRODUCTION - See INDIA - CROPS

INDIA - SHEEP - See INDIA - LIVESTOCK AND POULTRY

INDIA - SILVER PRODUCTION AND CONSUMPTION - See INDIA - MINING AND MINERAL PRODUCTS

INDIA - SOCIAL DATA

G.K. Hall and Company, 70 Lincoln Street, Boston, Massachusetts 02111 (617) 423-3990; *The World in Figures.*

INDIA - SOCIAL SECURITY

International Monetary Fund, 700 Nineteenth Street, NW, Washington, D.C. 20431 (202) 623-7000; *Government Finance Statistics Yearbook.*

INDIA - SOYBEAN PRODUCTION - See INDIA - CROPS

INDIA - STATE BUDGET REVENUE AND EXPENDITURES

Euromonitor Publications Limited, 87-88 Turnmill Street, London EC1M 5QU, England; *International Marketing Data and Statistics.*

INDIA - STEEL - INDUSTRIAL CONSUMPTION - See INDIA - MINING AND MINERAL PRODUCTS

INDIA - STEEL PRODUCTION AND CONSUMPTION - See INDIA - MINING AND MINERAL PRODUCTS

INDIA - STOCKS - COMMODITY - MARKET PRICE - INDEXES

Food and Agricultural Organization of the United Nations (FAO) Via delle Terme di Caracalla, 00100 Rome, Italy (Telephone Number in U.S. (202) 653-2400); *The State of Food and Agriculture.*

International Lead and Zinc Study Group, Metro House, 58 St. James's Street, London SW1A 1LD, England; *Lead and Zinc Statistics.*

Statistical Office of the United Nations, Publishing Service, New York, New York 10017 (800) 253-9646; *Statistical Yearbook.*

World Bureau of Metal Statistics, 27-A High Street, Ware, Herts, SG12 9BA, England; *World Metal Statistics.*

INDIA - SUGAR PRODUCTION AND CONSUMPTION - See INDIA - CROPS

INDIA - SULPHUR AND SULPHURIC ACID PRODUCTION - See INDIA - MINING AND MINERAL PRODUCTS

INDIA - TAXATION

G.K. Hall and Company, 70 Lincoln Street, Boston, Massachusetts 02111 (617) 423-3990; *The World in Figures.*

International Monetary Fund, 700 Nineteenth Street, NW, Washington, D.C. 20431 (202) 623-7000; *Government Finance Statistics Yearbook.*

International Road Federation, 525 School Street, SW, Washington, D.C. 20024 (202) 554-2106; *World Road Statistics.*

The World Bank, 1818 H Street, NW, Washington, D.C. 20433 (202) 477-1234; *World Tables.*

INDIA - TEA PRODUCTION AND CONSUMPTION - See INDIA - CROPS

INDIA - TELEGRAPH SERVICE

Statistical Office of the United Nations, Publishing Service, New York, New York 10017 (800) 253-9646; *Statistical Yearbook.*

INDIA - TELEPHONES IN USE

American Telephone and Telegraph Company, 26 Parsippany Road, Whippany, New Jersey 07981 (800) 338-4038; *The World's Telephones.*

The Economist Intelligence Unit (Asia) Limited, 10th Floor, Luk Kwok Centre, 72 Gloucester Road, Wanchai, Hong Kong (Phone Number in U.S. (800) 938-4685); *Asian Market Atlas.*

Euromonitor Publications Limited, 87-88 Turnmill Street, London EC1M 5QU, England; *Third World Economic Handbook.*

G.K. Hall and Company, 70 Lincoln Street, Boston, Massachusetts 02111 (617) 423-3990; *The World in Figures.*

Statistical Office of the United Nations, Publishing Service, New York, New York 10017 (800) 253-9646; *Statistical Yearbook.*

INDIA - TELEVISION BROADCASTING - See INDIA - BROADCASTING

INDIA - TEXTILE INDUSTRY

Euromonitor Publications Limited, 87-88 Turnmill Street, London EC1M 5QU, England; *Third World Economic Handbook.*

Food and Agricultural Organization of the United Nations (FAO), Via delle Terme di Caracalla, 00100 Rome, Italy (Telephone Number in U.S. (202) 653-2400); *Production Yearbook.*

Forest and Paper Association, 1250 Connecticut Avenue, NW, Washington, D.C. 20036 (202) 463-2455; *Wood Pulp and Fiber Statistics.*

G.K. Hall and Company, 70 Lincoln Street, Boston, Massachusetts 02111 (617) 423-3990; *The World in Figures.*

Statistical Office of the United Nations, Publishing Service, New York, New York 10017 (800) 253-9646; *Statistical Yearbook,* and *Trade in Manufactures of Developing Countries.*

INDIA - TIN - See INDIA - MINING AND MINERAL PRODUCTS

INDIA - TIRE (MOTOR VEHICLE) PRODUCTION

International Rubber Study Group, York House, 8th Floor, Empire Way, Wembley, London HA9 0PA, England; *Rubber Statistical Bulletin.*

Statistical Office of the United Nations, Publishing Service, New York, New York 10017 (800) 253-9646; *Statistical Yearbook.*

INDIA - TOBACCO PRODUCTION

Commodity Research Bureau, Incorporated, 75 Wall Street, New York, New York 10005 (212) 504-7754; *Commodity Year Book.*

Euromonitor Publications Limited, 87-88 Turnmill Street, London EC1M 5QU, England; *Third World Economic Handbook.*

Statistical Office of the United Nations, Publishing Service, New York, New York 10017 (800) 253-9646; *Statistical Yearbook.*

INDIA - TOURISM

Euromonitor Publications Limited, 87-88 Turnmill Street, London EC1M 5QU, England; *Third World Economic Handbook.*

G.K. Hall and Company, 70 Lincoln Street, Boston, Massachusetts 02111 (617) 423-3990; *The World in Figures.*

Statistical Office of the United Nations, Publishing Service, New York, New York 10017 (800) 253-9646; *Statistical Yearbook.*

Times Books, 201 East 50th Street, New York, New York 10022 (212) 751-2600; *The Economist Book of Vital World Statistics.*

World Tourism Organization, Calle Capitan Haya 42, E-28020 Madrid, Spain; *Yearbook of Tourism Statistics.*

INDIA - TRACTORS IN USE

Statistical Office of the United Nations, Publishing Service, New York, New York 10017 (800) 253-9646; *Statistical Yearbook.*

INDIA - TRADE - See INDIA - FOREIGN TRADE

INDIA - TRADEMARKS AND SERVICE MARKS

Statistical Office of the United Nations, Publishing Service, New York, New York 10017 (800) 253-9646; *Statistical Yearbook.*

World Intellectual Property Organization, 34 Chemin des Colombettes, CH-1211 Geneva 20, Switzerland; *Industrial Property Statistics.*

INDIA - TRANSPORTATION AND COMMUNICATIONS

The Economist Intelligence Unit (Asia) Limited, 10th Floor, Luk Kwok Centre, 72 Gloucester Road, Wanchai, Hong Kong (Phone Number in U.S. (800) 938-4685); *Asian Market Atlas.*

Euromonitor Publications Limited, 87-88 Turnmill Street, London EC1M 5QU, England; *Third World Economic Handbook.*

G.K. Hall and Company, 70 Lincoln Street, Boston, Massachusetts 02111 (617) 423-3990; *The World in Figures.*

Statistical Office of the United Nations, Publishing Service, New York, New York 10017 (800) 253-9646; *Statistical Yearbook for Asia and the Pacific.*

INDIA - TUNGSTEN PRODUCTION AND CONSUMPTION - See INDIA - MINING AND MINERAL PRODUCTS

INDIA - UNEMPLOYMENT

Euromonitor Publications Limited, 87-88 Turnmill Street, London EC1M 5QU, England; *International Marketing Data and Statistics.*

International Labour Office, I.L.O. Publications, CH-1211, Geneva 22, Switzerland; *Yearbook of Labour Statistics.*

Statistical Office of the United Nations, Publishing Service, New York, New York 10017 (800) 253-9646; *Statistical Yearbook.*

INDIA - URANIUM PRODUCTION AND CONSUMPTION - See INDIA - MINING AND MINERAL PRODUCTS

INDIA - UTILITIES

Statistical Office of the United Nations, Publishing Service, New York, New York 10017 (800) 253-9646; *Electric Power in Asia and the Pacific.*

INDIA - VITAL STATISTICS

Euromonitor Publications Limited, 87-88 Turnmill Street, London EC1M 5QU, England; *International Marketing Data and Statistics,* and *Third World Economic Handbook.*

G.K. Hall and Company, 70 Lincoln Street, Boston, Massachusetts 02111 (617) 423-3990; *The World in Figures.*

Statistical Office of the United Nations, Publishing Service, New York, New York 10017 (800) 253-9646; *Statistical Yearbook.*

World Health Organization, Avenue Appia, Office of Publications, CH-1211 Geneva 27, Switzerland (Telephone Number in U.S. (518) 436-9686); *World Health Statistics Annual.*

INDIA - WAGES

G.K. Hall and Company, 70 Lincoln Street, Boston, Massachusetts 02111 (617) 423-3990; *The World in Figures.*

International Labour Office, I.L.O. Publications, CH-1211, Geneva 22, Switzerland; *Yearbook of Labour Statistics.*

Statistical Office of the United Nations, Publishing Service, New York, New York 10017 (800) 253-9646; *Statistical Yearbook.*

INDIA - WAGES AND PRICES

Statistical Office of the United Nations, Publishing Service, New York, New York 10017 (800) 253-9646; *Statistical Yearbook for Asia and the Pacific.*

INDIA - WALNUT PRODUCTION - See INDIA - CROPS

INDIA - WEATHER

G.K. Hall and Company, 70 Lincoln Street, Boston, Massachusetts 02111 (617) 423-3990; *The World in Figures.*

INDIA - WELFARE

International Monetary Fund, 700 Nineteenth Street, NW, Washington, D.C. 20431 (202) 623-7000; *Government Finance Statistics Yearbook.*

INDIA - WHEAT PRODUCTION AND PRICES - See INDIA - CROPS

INDIA - WHOLESALE PRICES

International Monetary Fund, 700 Nineteenth Street, NW, Washington, D.C. 20431 (202) 623-7000; *International Financial Statistics.*

Statistical Office of the United Nations, Publishing Service, New York, New York 10017 (800) 253-9646; *Statistical Yearbook.*

INDIA - WHOLESALE TRADE

Euromonitor Publications Limited, 87-88 Turnmill Street, London EC1M 5QU, England; *Third World Economic Handbook.*

INDIA - WOOD AND WOOD PULP - See INDIA - FORESTRY AND FOREST PRODUCTS

INDIA - WOOL - INDUSTRIAL CONSUMPTION

Statistical Office of the United Nations, Publishing Service, New York, New York 10017 (800) 253-9646; *Statistical Yearbook.*

INDIA - WOOL PRODUCTION

Statistical Office of the United Nations, Publishing Service, New York, New York 10017 (800) 253-9646; *Statistical Yearbook.*

INDIA - YARN PRODUCTION

Statistical Office of the United Nations, Publishing Service, New York, New York 10017 (800) 253-9646; *Statistical Yearbook.*

INDIA - ZINC AND ZINC ORE - See INDIA -MINING AND MINERAL PRODUCTS

INDIAN - AMERICAN POPULATION

U.S. Department of Commerce, Bureau of the Census, Suitland, Maryland 20233 (301) 763-4040; *Census of Population,* and *Current Population Reports.*

INDIAN - ASIAN POPULATION

U.S. Department of Commerce, Bureau of the Census, Suitland, Maryland 20233 (301) 763-4040; *Census of Population,* and *Current Population Reports.*

INDIANA - See also - STATE DATA (FOR INDIVIDUAL STATES)

Indiana - Primary Statistics Source

Indiana University, Indiana Business Research Center, School of Business, 801 West Michigan, Indianapolis, Indiana 46202 (317) 274-2204; *Indiana Factbook.*

Indiana - State Data Centers

Indiana State Data Center, Indiana State Library, 140 North Senate Avenue, Indianapolis, Indiana 46204, Mr. Laurence Hathaway, (317) 232-3733.

Indiana Business Research Center, Indiana University, School of Business, Bloomington, Indiana 47405, Dr. Morton Marcus (812) 855-5507.

Indiana Business Research Center, 801 West Michigan, B.S. 4015, Indianapolis, Indiana 46202-5151, Ms. Carol Rogers (317) 274-2205.

Research Division, Indiana Department of Commerce, 1 North Capitol, Suite 700, Indianapolis, Indiana 46204, Mr. Robert Lain (317) 232-8959.

INDIUM

U.S. Department of the Interior, Bureau of Mines, 810 Seventh Street, NW, Washington, D.C. 20241 (202) 501-9649; *Mineral Commodity Summaries.*

INDIVIDUAL RETIREMENT ACCOUNTS (IRA's)

Board of Governors of the Federal Reserve System, Twentieth Street and Constitution Avenue, NW, Washington, D.C. 20551 (202) 452-3000; *Federal Reserve Bulletin.*

Investment Company Institute, 1600 M Street, NW, Suite, 600, Washington, D.C. 20036 (202) 293-7700; *Mutual Fund Fact Book.*

U.S. Department of Commerce, Bureau of the Census, Suitland, Maryland 20233 (301) 763-4040; *Current Population Reports.*

Indonesia - National Statistical Office

Central Bureau of Statistics, Post Office Box 3, Jakarta, 10002, Indonesia.

Indonesia - Primary Statistics Sources

Central Bureau of Statistics, Post Office Box 3, Jakarta, 10002, Indonesia; *Statistik Indonesia,* (Statistical Yearbook of Indonesia).

INDONESIA - AGRICULTURE

Asian Development Bank, Post Office Box 789, 1099 Manila, Philippines; *Key Indicators of Developing Asian and Pacific Countries.*

Euromonitor Publications Limited, 87-88 Turnmill Street, London EC1M 5QU, England; *International Marketing Data and Statistics, The Pacific Basin: An Economic Handbook,* and *Third World Economic Handbook.*

Facts on File, 460 Park Avenue South, New York, New York 10016; *The New Book of World Rankings.*

Food and Agricultural Organization of the United Nations (FAO), Via delle Terme di Caracalla, 00100 Rome, Italy (Telephone Number in U.S. (202) 653-2400); *Production Yearbook,* and *The State of Food and Agriculture.*

G.K. Hall and Company, 70 Lincoln Street, Boston, Massachusetts 02111 (617) 423-3990; *The World in Figures.*

Statistical Office of the United Nations, Publishing Service, New York, New York 10017 (800) 253-9646; *Statistical Yearbook,* and *Statistical Yearbook for Asia and the Pacific.*

The World Bank, 1818 H Street, NW, Washington, D.C. 20433 (202) 477-1234; *World Tables.*

INDONESIA - AIRLINE SERVICE

The Economist Intelligence Unit (Asia) Limited, 10th Floor, Luk Kwok Centre, 72 Gloucester Road, Wanchai, Hong Kong (Phone Number in U.S. (800) 938-4685); *Asian Market Atlas.*

Facts on File, 460 Park Avenue South, New York, New York 10016; *The New Book of World Rankings.*

G.K. Hall and Company, 70 Lincoln Street, Boston, Massachusetts 02111 (617) 423-3990; *The World in Figures.*

Statistical Office of the United Nations, Publishing Service, New York, New York 10017 (800) 253-9646; *Statistical Yearbook.*

Times Books, 201 East 50th Street, New York, New York 10022 (212) 751-2600; *The Economist Book of Vital World Statistics.*

INDONESIA - ALUMINUM PRODUCTION AND CONSUMPTION - See INDONESIA - MINING AND MINERAL PRODUCTS

INDONESIA - ANIMAL HEALTH

Food and Agricultural Organization of the United Nations (FAO), Via delle Terme di Caracalla, 00100 Rome, Italy (Telephone Number in U.S. (202) 653-2400); *Animal Health Yearbook.*

INDONESIA - AREA AND DENSITY OF POPULATION

Euromonitor Publications Limited, 87-88 Turnmill Street, London EC1M 5QU, England; *International Marketing Data and Statistics,* and *The Pacific Basin: An Economic Handbook.*

Facts on File, 460 Park Avenue South, New York, New York 10016 (800) 443-8323; *The New Book of World Rankings.*

Food and Agricultural Organization of the United Nations (FAO) Via delle Terme di Caracalla, 00100 Rome, Italy (Telephone Number in U.S. (202) 653-2400); *The State of Food and Agriculture.*

G.K. Hall and Company, 70 Lincoln Street, Boston, Massachusetts 02111 (617) 423-3990; *The World in Figures.*

Statistical Office of the United Nations, Publishing Service, New York, New York 10017 (800) 253-9646; *Statistical Yearbook.*

Times Books, 201 East 50th Street, New York, New York 10022 (212) 751-2600; *The Economist Book of Vital World Statistics.*

United Nations Educational, Scientific and Cultural Organization (UNESCO), 7 Place de Fontenoy, F-75700 Paris, France (Telephone Number in U.S. (212) 963-5981); *Statistical Yearbook.*

INDONESIA - ARMS EXPORTS AND IMPORTS

U.S. Arms Control and Disarmament Agency, 320 Twenty-first Street, Northwest, Washington, D.C. 20451 (202) 647-8677; *World Military Expenditures and Arms Transfers.*

INDONESIA - BALANCE OF PAYMENTS

The Economist Intelligence Unit, 111 West 57th Street, New York, New York 10019 (800) 938-4685; *The World Market Atlas.*

Euromonitor Publications Limited, 87-88 Turnmill Street, London EC1M 5QU, England; *Third World Economic Handbook.*

G.K. Hall and Company, 70 Lincoln Street, Boston, Massachusetts 02111 (617) 423-3990; *The World in Figures.*

International Monetary Fund, 700 Nineteenth Street, NW, Washington, D.C. 20431 (202) 623-7000; *Balance of Payments Yearbook,* and *International Financial Statistics.*

Times Books, 201 East 50th Street, New York, New York 10022 (212) 751-2600; *The Economist Book of Vital World Statistics*.

The World Bank, 1818 H Street, NW, Washington, D.C. 20433 (202) 477-1234; *World Tables*.

INDONESIA - BANKING

Asian Development Bank, Post Office Box 789, 1099 Manila, Philippines; *Key Indicators of Developing Asian and Pacific Countries*.

Facts on File, 460 Park Avenue South, New York, New York 10016; *The New Book of World Rankings*.

G.K. Hall and Company, 70 Lincoln Street, Boston, Massachusetts 02111 (617) 423-3990; *The World in Figures*.

International Monetary Fund, 700 Nineteenth Street, NW, Washington, D.C. 20431 (202) 623-7000; *International Financial Statistics*.

INDONESIA - BARLEY PRODUCTION - See INDONESIA - CROPS

INDONESIA - BAUXITE PRODUCTION AND CONSUMPTION - See INDONESIA - MINING AND MINERAL PRODUCTS

INDONESIA - BEER PRODUCTION

Facts on File, 460 Park Avenue South, New York, New York 10016; *The New Book of World Rankings*.

Statistical Office of the United Nations, Publishing Service, New York, New York 10017 (800) 253-9646; *Statistical Yearbook*.

INDONESIA - BIRTH RATES

The Economist Intelligence Unit (Asia) Limited, 10th Floor, Luk Kwok Centre, 72 Gloucester Road, Wanchai, Hong Kong (Phone Number in U.S. (800) 938-4685); *Asian Market Atlas*.

Euromonitor Publications Limited, 87-88 Turnmill Street, London EC1M 5QU, England; *Third World Economic Handbook*, and *The Pacific Basin: An Economic Handbook*.

Facts on File, 460 Park Avenue South, New York, New York 10016; *The New Book of World Rankings*.

Statistical Office of the United Nations, Publishing Service, New York, New York 10017 (800) 253-9646; *Demographic Yearbook*, and *Statistical Yearbook*.

Times Books, 201 East 50th Street, New York, New York 10022 (212) 751-2600; *The Economist Book of Vital World Statistics*.

The World Bank, 1818 H Street, NW, Washington, D.C. 20433 (202) 477-1234; *World Tables*.

INDONESIA - BONDS

Asian Development Bank, Post Office Box 789, 1099 Manila, Philippines; *Key Indicators of Developing Asian and Pacific Countries*.

G.K. Hall and Company, 70 Lincoln Street, Boston, Massachusetts 02111 (617) 423-3990; *The World in Figures*.

INDONESIA - BOOK PRODUCTION

G.K. Hall and Company, 70 Lincoln Street, Boston, Massachusetts 02111 (617) 423-3990; *The World in Figures*.

United Nations Educational, Scientific and Cultural Organization (UNESCO), 7 Place de Fontenoy, F-75700 Paris, France (Telephone Number in U.S. (212) 963-5981); *Statistical Yearbook*.

INDONESIA - BROADCASTING

Billboard Limited, Post Office Box 9027, 1006 AA Amsterdam, The Netherlands (Telephone Number in U.S. (212) 764-7300); *World Radio TV Handbook*.

The Economist Intelligence Unit (Asia) Limited, 10th Floor, Luk Kwok Centre, 72 Gloucester Road, Wanchai, Hong Kong (Phone Number in U.S. (800) 938-4685); *Asian Market Atlas*.

Facts on File, 460 Park Avenue South, New York, New York 10016 (800) 443-8323; *The New Book of World Rankings*.

G.K. Hall and Company, 70 Lincoln Street, Boston, Massachusetts 02111 (617) 423-3990; *The World in Figures*.

Times Books, 201 East 50th Street, New York, New York 10022 (212) 751-2600; *The Economist Book of Vital World Statistics*.

United Nations Educational, Scientific and Cultural Organization (UNESCO), 7 Place de Fontenoy, F-75700 Paris, France (Telephone Number in U.S. (212) 963-5981); *Statistical Yearbook*.

INDONESIA - BUSINESS

G.K. Hall and Company, 70 Lincoln Street, Boston, Massachusetts 02111 (617) 423-3990; *The World in Figures*.

INDONESIA - CALORIE SUPPLY

Asian Development Bank, Post Office Box 789, 1099 Manila, Philippines; *Key Indicators of Developing Asian and Pacific Countries*.

Food and Agricultural Organization of the United Nations (FAO) Via delle Terme di Caracalla, 00100 Rome, Italy (Telephone Number in U.S. (202) 653-2400); *The State of Food and Agriculture*.

INDONESIA - CAPITAL INVESTMENT

Asian Development Bank, Post Office Box 789, 1099 Manila, Philippines; *Key Indicators of Developing Asian and Pacific Countries*.

INDONESIA - CAPITAL REVENUE

Asian Development Bank, Post Office Box 789, 1099 Manila, Philippines; *Key Indicators of Developing Asian and Pacific Countries*.

International Monetary Fund, 700 Nineteenth Street, NW, Washington, D.C. 20431 (202) 623-7000; *Government Finance Statistics Yearbook*.

INDONESIA - CASTOR BEAN PRODUCTION - See INDONESIA - CROPS

INDONESIA - CATTLE - See INDONESIA - LIVESTOCK AND POULTRY

INDONESIA - CAUSTIC SODA PRODUCTION

Statistical Office of the United Nations, Publishing Service, New York, New York 10017 (800) 253-9646; *Statistical Yearbook.*

INDONESIA - CEMENT PRODUCTION - See INDONESIA - MINING AND MINERAL PRODUCTS

INDONESIA - CHEMICAL (ORGANIC) PRODUCTION - See INDIA - MINING AND MINERAL PRODUCTS

INDONESIA - CHICKENS - See INDONESIA - LIVESTOCK AND POULTRY

INDONESIA - CIGAR PRODUCTION - See INDONESIA - TOBACCO PRODUCTION

INDONESIA - CIGARETTE PRODUCTION - See INDONESIA - TOBACCO PRODUCTION

INDONESIA - CLASS STRUCTURE

G.K. Hall and Company, 70 Lincoln Street, Boston, Massachusetts 02111 (617) 423-3990; *The World in Figures.*

INDONESIA - CLIMATE

Facts on File, 460 Park Avenue South, New York, New York 10016; *The New Book of World Rankings.*

G.K. Hall and Company, 70 Lincoln Street, Boston, Massachusetts 02111 (617) 423-3990; *The World in Figures.*

INDONESIA - CLOTHING EXPORTS AND IMPORTS

Euromonitor Publications Limited, 87-88 Turnmill Street, London EC1M 5QU, England; *Third World Economic Handbook.*

INDONESIA - COAL PRODUCTION - See INDONESIA - MINING AND MINERAL PRODUCTS

INDONESIA - COCOA (BEANS) PRODUCTION - See INDONESIA - CROPS

INDONESIA - COFFEE PRODUCTION - See INDONESIA - CROPS

INDONESIA - COKE OVEN COKE PRODUCTION AND CONSUMPTION - See INDONESIA - MINING AND MINERAL PRODUCTS

INDONESIA - COMMUNICATIONS

Euromonitor Publications Limited, 87-88 Turnmill Street, London EC1M 5QU, England; *Third World Economic Handbook.*

G.K. Hall and Company, 70 Lincoln Street, Boston, Massachusetts 02111 (617) 423-3990; *The World in Figures.*

Statistical Office of the United Nations, Publishing Service, New York, New York 10017 (800) 253-9646; *Statistical Yearbook for Asia and the Pacific.*

INDONESIA - CONSTRUCTION INDUSTRY

Facts on File, 460 Park Avenue South, New York, New York 10016 (800) 443-8323; *The New Book of World Rankings.*

Statistical Office of the United Nations, Publishing Service, New York, New York 10017 (800) 253-9646; *Statistical Yearbook.*

INDONESIA - CONSUMER PRICE INDEX

Asian Development Bank, Post Office Box 789, 1099 Manila, Philippines; *Key Indicators of Developing Asian and Pacific Countries.*

G.K. Hall and Company, 70 Lincoln Street, Boston, Massachusetts 02111 (617) 423-3990; *The World in Figures.*

Statistical Office of the United Nations, Publishing Service, New York, New York 10017 (800) 253-9646; *Statistical Yearbook.*

INDONESIA - CONSUMER PRICES

International Labour Office, I.L.O. Publications, CH-1211, Geneva 22, Switzerland; *Yearbook of Labour Statistics.*

International Monetary Fund, 700 Nineteenth Street, NW, Washington, D.C. 20431 (202) 623-7000; *International Financial Statistics.*

Times Books, 201 East 50th Street, New York, New York 10022 (212) 751-2600; *The Economist Book of Vital World Statistics.*

INDONESIA - CONSUMPTION

Euromonitor Publications Limited, 87-88 Turnmill Street, London EC1M 5QU, England; *The Pacific Basin: An Economic Handbook.*

G.K. Hall and Company, 70 Lincoln Street, Boston, Massachusetts 02111 (617) 423-3990; *The World in Figures.*

International Rubber Study Group, York House, 8th Floor, Empire Way, Wembley, London HA9 0PA, England; *Rubber Statistical Bulletin.*

INDONESIA - COPPER AND COPPER ORE - See INDIA - MINING AND MINERAL PRODUCTS

INDONESIA - CORN PRODUCTION - See INDONESIA - CROPS

INDONESIA - CORPORATE TAXES - See INDONESIA - TAXATION

INDONESIA - COTTON - See INDONESIA - CROPS

INDONESIA - CRIME

International Criminal Police Organization (INTERPOL), 26 rue Armengaud, 92210 Saint Cloud, France; *International Crime Statistics.*

Yale University Press, Yale Station, New Haven, Connecticut 06520 (203) 432-0940; *Violence and Crime in Cross-National Perspective.*

INDONESIA - CROPS

Asian Development Bank, Post Office Box 789, 1099 Manila, Philippines; *Key Indicators of Developing Asian and Pacific Countries.*

Commodity Research Bureau, Incorporated, 75 Wall Street, New York, New York 10005 (212) 504-7754; *Commodity Year Book.*

Facts on File, 460 Park Avenue South, New York, New York 10016 (800) 443-8323; *The New Book of World Rankings.*

Food and Agricultural Organization of the United Nations (FAO) Via delle Terme di Caracalla, 00100 Rome, Italy (Telephone Number in U.S. (202) 653-2400); *Production Yearbook* and *The State of Food*

and Agriculture.

G.K. Hall and Company, 70 Lincoln Street, Boston, Massachusetts 02111 (617) 423-3990; *The World in Figures.*

Statistical Office of the United Nations, Publishing Service, New York, New York 10017 (800) 253-9646; *Statistical Yearbook.*

INDONESIA - CUSTOMS DUTIES

G.K. Hall and Company, 70 Lincoln Street, Boston, Massachusetts 02111 (617) 423-3990; *The World in Figures.*

International Monetary Fund, 700 Nineteenth Street, NW, Washington, D.C. 20431 (202) 623-7000; *Government Finance Statistics Yearbook.*

INDONESIA - DAIRY PRODUCTS

Facts on File, 460 Park Avenue South, New York, New York 10016; *The New Book of World Rankings.*

Food and Agricultural Organization of the United Nations (FAO), Via delle Terme di Caracalla, 00100 Rome, Italy (Telephone Number in U.S. (202) 653-2400); *Production Yearbook,* and *The State of Food and Agriculture.*

Statistical Office of the United Nations, Publishing Service, New York, New York 10017 (800) 253-9646; *Statistical Yearbook.*

INDONESIA - DEATH RATE

The Economist Intelligence Unit (Asia) Limited, 10th Floor, Luk Kwok Centre, 72 Gloucester Road, Wanchai, Hong Kong (Phone Number in U.S. (800) 938-4685); *Asian Market Atlas.*

Euromonitor Publications Limited, 87-88 Turnmill Street, London EC1M 5QU, England; *Third World Economic Handbook,* and *The Pacific Basin: An Economic Handbook.*

G.K. Hall and Company, 70 Lincoln Street, Boston, Massachusetts 02111 (617) 423-3990; *The World in Figures.*

Statistical Office of the United Nations, Publishing Service, New York, New York 10017 (800) 253-9646; *Statistical Yearbook.*

Times Books, 201 East 50th Street, New York, New York 10022 (212) 751-2600; *The Economist Book of Vital World Statistics.*

World Health Organization, Avenue Appia, Office of Publications, CH-1211 Geneva 27, Switzerland (Telephone Number in U.S. (518) 436-9686); *World Health Statistics Annual.*

INDONESIA - DEFENSE EXPENDITURES

G.K. Hall and Company, 70 Lincoln Street, Boston, Massachusetts 02111 (617) 423-3990; *The World in Figures.*

U.S. Arms Control and Disarmament Agency, 320 Twenty-first Street, Northwest, Washington, D.C. 20451 (202) 647-8677; *World Military Expenditures and Arms Transfers.*

INDONESIA - DEMOGRAPHY

The Economist Intelligence Unit, 111 West 57th Street, New York, New York 10019 (800) 938-4685; *The World Market Atlas.*

The Economist Intelligence Unit (Asia) Limited, 10th Floor, Luk Kwok Centre, 72 Gloucester Road, Wanchai, Hong Kong (Phone Number in U.S. (800) 938-4685); *Asian Market Atlas.*

Facts on File, 460 Park Avenue South, New York, New York 10016; *The New Book of World Rankings.*

G.K. Hall and Company, 70 Lincoln Street, Boston, Massachusetts 02111 (617) 423-3990; *The World in Figures.*

INDONESIA - DEVELOPMENT ASSISTANCE

Asian Development Bank, Post Office Box 789, 1099 Manila, Philippines; *Key Indicators of Developing Asian and Pacific Countries.*

G.K. Hall and Company, 70 Lincoln Street, Boston, Massachusetts 02111 (617) 423-3990; *The World in Figures.*

Statistical Office of the United Nations, Publishing Service, New York, New York 10017 (800) 253-9646; *Statistical Yearbook.*

INDONESIA - DIAMOND PRODUCTION AND CONSUMPTION - See INDONESIA - MINING AND MINERAL PRODUCTS

INDONESIA - DISEASES

G.K. Hall and Company, 70 Lincoln Street, Boston, Massachusetts 02111 (617) 423-3990; *The World in Figures.*

World Health Organization, Avenue Appia, Office of Publications, CH-1211 Geneva 27, Switzerland (Telephone Number in U.S. (518) 436-9686); *World Health Statistics Annual.*

INDONESIA - DIVORCE RATES

Facts on File, 460 Park Avenue South, New York, New York 10016; *The New Book of World Rankings.*

Statistical Office of the United Nations, Publishing Service, New York, New York 10017 (800) 253-9646; *Demographic Yearbook.*

INDONESIA - DOMESTIC PRODUCT

G.K. Hall and Company, 70 Lincoln Street, Boston, Massachusetts 02111 (617) 423-3990; *The World in Figures.*

INDONESIA - DUCKS - See LIVESTOCK AND POULTRY

INDONESIA - ECONOMY

Asian Development Bank, Post Office Box 789, 1099 Manila, Philippines; *Key Indicators of Developing Asian and Pacific Countries.*

Euromonitor Publications Limited, 87-88 Turnmill Street, London EC1M 5QU, England; *International Marketing Data and Statistics,* and *Third World Economic Handbook.*

Facts on File, 460 Park Avenue South, New York, New York 10016; *The New Book of World Rankings.*

G.K. Hall and Company, 70 Lincoln Street, Boston, Massachusetts 02111 (617) 423-3990; *The World in Figures.*

INDONESIA - EDUCATION

The Economist Intelligence Unit, 111 West 57th Street, New York, New York 10019 (800) 938-4685; *The World Market Atlas.*

The Economist Intelligence Unit (Asia) Limited, 10th Floor, Luk Kwok Centre, 72 Gloucester Road, Wanchai, Hong Kong (Phone Number in U.S. (800) 938-4685); *Asian Market Atlas.*

Euromonitor Publications Limited, 87-88 Turnmill Street, London EC1M 5QU, England; *The Pacific Basin: An Economic Handbook.*

Facts on File, 460 Park Avenue South, New York, New York 10016; *The New Book of World Rankings.*

G.K. Hall and Company, 70 Lincoln Street, Boston, Massachusetts 02111 (617) 423-3990; *The World in Figures.*

Times Books, 201 East 50th Street, New York, New York 10022 (212) 751-2600; *The Economist Book of Vital World Statistics.*

United Nations Educational, Scientific and Cultural Organization (UNESCO), 7 Place de Fontenoy, F-75700 Paris, France (Telephone Number in U.S. (212) 963-5981); *Statistical Yearbook.*

The World Bank, 1818 H Street, NW, Washington, D.C. 20433 (202) 477-1234; *World Tables.*

INDONESIA - EGG PRODUCTION - See INDONESIA - DAIRY PRODUCTS

INDONESIA - ELECTRICITY

Asian Development Bank, Post Office Box 789, 1099 Manila, Philippines; *Key Indicators of Developing Asian and Pacific Countries.*

Facts on File, 460 Park Avenue South, New York, New York 10016; *The New Book of World Rankings.*

Penn Well Publishing Company, 1421 South Sheridan Road, Post Office Box 1260, Tulsa, Oklahoma 74101 (800) 752-9764; *International Energy Statistics Sourcebook.*

Statistical Office of the United Nations, Publishing Service, New York, New York 10017; *Electric Power in Asia and the Pacific,* and *Statistical Yearbook.*

Times Books, 201 East 50th Street, New York, New York 10022 (212) 751-2600; *The Economist Book of Vital World Statistics.*

INDONESIA - EMPLOYMENT

Euromonitor Publications Limited, 87-88 Turnmill Street, London EC1M 5QU, England; *International Marketing Data and Statistics,* and *The Pacific Basin: An Economic Handbook.*

Facts on File, 460 Park Avenue South, New York, New York 10016; *The New Book of World Rankings.*

International Labour Office, I.L.O. Publications, CH-1211, Geneva 22, Switzerland; *Yearbook of Labour Statistics.*

Statistical Office of the United Nations, Publishing Service, New York, New York 10017 (800) 253-9646; *Statistical Yearbook.*

INDONESIA - ENERGY

Facts on File, 460 Park Avenue South, New York, New York 10016; *The New Book of World Rankings.*

Food and Agricultural Organization of the United Nations (FAO) Via delle Terme di Caracalla, 00100 Rome, Italy (Telephone Number in U.S. (202) 653-2400); *The State of Food and Agriculture.*

G.K. Hall and Company, 70 Lincoln Street, Boston, Massachusetts 02111 (617) 423-3990; *The World in Figures.*

Penn Well Publishing Company, 1421 South Sheridan Road, Post Office Box 1260, Tulsa, Oklahoma 74101 (800) 752-9764; *International Energy Statistics Sourcebook.*

Statistical Office of the United Nations, Publishing Service, New York, New York 10017 (800) 253-9646; *Energy Statistics Yearbook, Statistical Yearbook, Statistical Yearbook for Asia and the Pacific,* and *World Energy Supplies.*

Times Books, 201 East 50th Street, New York, New York 10022 (212) 751-2600; *The Economist Book of Vital World Statistics.*

INDONESIA - EXCHANGE RATE

Asian Development Bank, Post Office Box 789, 1099 Manila, Philippines; *Key Indicators of Developing Asian and Pacific Countries.*

The Economist Intelligence Unit (Asia) Limited, 10th Floor, Luk Kwok Centre, 72 Gloucester Road, Wanchai, Hong Kong (Phone Number in U.S. (800) 938-4685); *Asian Market Atlas.*

Euromonitor Publications Limited, 87-88 Turnmill Street, London EC1M 5QU, England; *International Marketing Data and Statistics,* and *The Pacific Basin: An Economic Handbook.*

International Monetary Fund, 700 Nineteenth Street, NW, Washington, D.C. 20431 (202) 623-7000; *International Financial Statistics.*

Organization of Petroleum Exporting Countries, Obere Donaustrasse 93, 1020 Vienna 2, Austria; *OPEC Annual Statistical Bulletin.*

Statistical Office of the United Nations, Publishing Service, New York, New York 10017 (800) 253-9646; *Statistical Yearbook.*

INDONESIA - EXCISE TAXES - See INDONESIA - TAXATION

INDONESIA - EXPORTS

Asian Development Bank, Post Office Box 789, 1099 Manila, Philippines; *Key Indicators of Developing Asian and Pacific Countries.*

The Economist Intelligence Unit, 111 West 57th Street, New York, New York 10019 (800) 938-4685; *The World Market Atlas.*

The Economist Intelligence Unit (Asia) Limited, 10th Floor, Luk Kwok Centre, 72 Gloucester Road, Wanchai, Hong Kong (Phone Number in U.S. (800) 938-4685); *Asian Market Atlas.*

Euromonitor Publications Limited, 87-88 Turnmill Street, London EC1M 5QU, England; *International Marketing Data and Statistics, The Pacific Basin: An Economic Handbook,* and *Third World Economic Handbook.*

Food and Agricultural Organization of the United Nations (FAO) Via delle Terme di Caracalla, 00100 Rome, Italy (Telephone Number in U.S. (202) 653-2400); *The State of Food and Agriculture.*

G.K. Hall and Company, 70 Lincoln Street, Boston, Massachusetts 02111 (617) 423-3990; *The World in Figures.*

International Monetary Fund, 700 Nineteenth Street, NW, Washington, D.C. 20431 (202) 623-7000; *Direction of Trade Statistics, Government Finance Statistics Yearbook,* and

International Financial Statistics.

International Rubber Study Group, York House, 8th Floor, Empire Way, Wembley, London HA9 0PA, England; *Rubber Statistical Bulletin.*

Organization of Petroleum Exporting Countries, Obere Donaustrasse 93, 1020 Vienna 2, Austria; *OPEC Annual Statistical Bulletin.*

Statistical Office of the United Nations, Publishing Service, New York, New York 10017 (800) 253-9646; *Foreign Trade Statistics of Asia and the Pacific,* and *Trade in Manufactures of Developing Countries.*

Times Books, 201 East 50th Street, New York, New York 10022 (212) 751-2600; *The Economist Book of Vital World Statistics.*

The World Bank, 1818 H Street, NW, Washington, D.C. 20433 (202) 477-1234; *World Tables.*

INDONESIA - EXTERNAL FINANCING

Asian Development Bank, Post Office Box 789, 1099 Manila, Philippines; *Key Indicators of Developing Asian and Pacific Countries.*

INDONESIA - EXTERNAL INDEBTEDNESS

Asian Development Bank, Post Office Box 789, 1099 Manila, Philippines; *Key Indicators of Developing Asian and Pacific Countries.*

Euromonitor Publications Limited, 87-88 Turnmill Street, London EC1M 5QU, England; *Third World Economic Handbook.*

The World Bank, 1818 H Street, NW, Washington, D.C. 20433 (202) 477-1234; *World Tables.*

INDONESIA - EXTERNAL TRADE

Asian Development Bank, Post Office Box 789, 1099 Manila, Philippines; *Key Indicators of Developing Asian and Pacific Countries.*

Food and Agricultural Organization of the United Nations (FAO) Via delle Terme di Caracalla, 00100 Rome, Italy (Telephone Number in U.S. (202) 653-2400); *The State of Food and Agriculture,* and *Trade Yearbook.*

G.K. Hall and Company, 70 Lincoln Street, Boston, Massachusetts 02111 (617) 423-3990; *The World in Figures.*

Statistical Office of the United Nations, Publishing Service, New York, New York 10017 (800) 253-9646; *Statistical Yearbook,* and *Statistical Yearbook for Asia and the Pacific.*

INDONESIA - FARM CROPS - See INDONESIA - CROPS

INDONESIA - FERTILITY RATES

The Economist Intelligence Unit (Asia) Limited, 10th Floor, Luk Kwok Centre, 72 Gloucester Road, Wanchai, Hong Kong (Phone Number in U.S. (800) 938-4685); *Asian Market Atlas.*

Facts on File, 460 Park Avenue South, New York, New York 10016 (800) 443-8323; *The New Book of World Rankings.*

Times Books, 201 East 50th Street, New York, New York 10022 (212) 751-2600; *The Economist Book of Vital World Statistics.*

The World Bank, 1818 H Street, NW, Washington, D.C. 20433 (202) 477-1234; *World Tables.*

INDONESIA - FERTILIZER

Food and Agricultural Organization of the United Nations (FAO), Via delle Terme di Caracalla, 00100 Rome, Italy (Telephone Number in U.S. (202) 653-2400); *Fertilizer Yearbook,* and *The State of Food and Agriculture.*

Statistical Office of the United Nations, Publishing Service, New York, New York 10017 (800) 253-9646; *Statistical Yearbook.*

INDONESIA - FETAL MORTALITY

Statistical Office of the United Nations, Publishing Service, New York, New York 10017 (800) 253-9646; *Demographic Yearbook.*

INDONESIA - FIBRE PRODUCTION - See INDONESIA - TEXTILE INDUSTRY

INDONESIA - FILM - See INDONESIA - MOTION PICTURES

INDONESIA - FINANCE

Asian Development Bank, Post Office Box 789, 1099 Manila, Philippines; *Key Indicators of Developing Asian and Pacific Countries.*

Euromonitor Publications Limited, 87-88 Turnmill Street, London EC1M 5QU, England; *The Pacific Basin: An Economic Handbook.*

Facts on File, 460 Park Avenue South, New York, New York 10016 (800) 443-8323; *The New Book of World Rankings.*

G.K. Hall and Company, 70 Lincoln Street, Boston, Massachusetts 02111 (617) 423-3990; *The World in Figures.*

International Monetary Fund, 700 Nineteenth Street, NW, Washington, D.C. 20431 (202) 623-7000; *International Financial Statistics.*

Statistical Office of the United Nations, Publishing Service, New York, New York 10017 (800) 253-9646; *Statistical Yearbook for Asia and the Pacific.*

INDONESIA - FISHERIES

Facts on File, 460 Park Avenue South, New York, New York 10016 (800) 443-8323; *The New Book of World Rankings.*

Food and Agricultural Organization of the United Nations (FAO) Via delle Terme di Caracalla, 00100 Rome, Italy (Telephone Number in U.S. (202) 653-2400); *The State of Food and Agriculture,* and *Yearbook of Fishery Statistics.*

Statistical Office of the United Nations, Publishing Service, New York, New York 10017 (800) 253-9646; *Statistical Yearbook.*

INDONESIA - FLOUR PRODUCTION

Statistical Office of the United Nations, Publishing Service, New York, New York 10017 (800) 253-9646; *Statistical Yearbook.*

INDONESIA - FOOD

Food and Agricultural Organization of the United Nations (FAO), Via delle Terme di Caracalla, 00100 Rome, Italy (Telephone Number in U.S. (202) 653-2400); *Production Yearbook,* and *The State of Food and Agriculture.*

G.K. Hall and Company, 70 Lincoln Street, Boston, Massachusetts 02111 (617) 423-3990; *The World in Figures.*

Statistical Office of the United Nations, Publishing Service, New York, New York 10017 (800) 253-9646; *Statistical Yearbook for Asia and the Pacific.*

INDONESIA - FOREIGN AID

G.K. Hall and Company, 70 Lincoln Street, Boston, Massachusetts 02111 (617) 423-3990; *The World in Figures.*

INDONESIA - FOREIGN DEBT

International Monetary Fund, 700 Nineteenth Street, NW, Washington, D.C. 20431 (202) 623-7000; *Government Finance Statistics Yearbook.*

INDONESIA - FOREIGN INDEBTEDNESS

Euromonitor Publications Limited, 87-88 Turnmill Street, London EC1M 5QU, England; *The Pacific Basin: An Economic Handbook.*

INDONESIA - FOREIGN TRADE

Asian Development Bank, Post Office Box 789, 1099 Manila, Philippines; *Key Indicators of Developing Asian and Pacific Countries.*

The Economist Intelligence Unit (Asia) Limited, 10th Floor, Luk Kwok Centre, 72 Gloucester Road, Wanchai, Hong Kong (Phone Number in U.S. (800) 938-4685); *Asian Market Atlas.*

Euromonitor Publications Limited, 87-88 Turnmill Street, London EC1M 5QU, England; *International Marketing Data and Statistics, The Pacific Basin: An Economic Handbook,* and *Third World Economic Handbook.*

Facts on File, 460 Park Avenue South, New York, New York 10016; *The New Book of World Rankings.*

Food and Agricultural Organization of the United Nations (FAO) Via delle Terme di Caracalla, 00100 Rome, Italy (Telephone Number in U.S. (202) 653-2400) (Telephone Number in U.S. (202) 653-2400); *The State of Food and Agriculture.*

G.K. Hall and Company, 70 Lincoln Street, Boston, Massachusetts 02111 (617) 423-3990; *The World in Figures.*

Statistical Office of the United Nations, Publishing Service, New York, New York 10017 (800) 253-9646; *International Trade Statistics Yearbook,* and *Statistical Yearbook.*

The World Bank, 1818 H Street, NW, Washington, D.C. 20433 (202) 477-1234; *World Tables.*

INDONESIA - FORESTRY AND FOREST PRODUCTS

The Economist Intelligence Unit (Asia) Limited, 10th Floor, Luk Kwok Centre, 72 Gloucester Road, Wanchai, Hong Kong (Phone Number in U.S. (800) 938-4685); *Asian Market Atlas.*

Euromonitor Publications Limited, 87-88 Turnmill Street, London EC1M 5QU, England; *Third World Economic Handbook.*

Facts on File, 460 Park Avenue South, New York, New York 10016 (800) 443-8323; *The New Book of World Rankings.*

Food and Agricultural Organization of the United Nations (FAO), Via delle Terme di Caracalla, 00100 Rome, Italy (Telephone Number in U.S. (202) 653-2400); *The State of Food and Agriculture* and *Yearbook of Forest Products.*

Forest and Paper Association, 1250 Connecticut Avenue, NW, Washington, D.C. 20036 (202) 463-2455; *Wood Pulp and Fiber Statistics.*

G.K. Hall and Company, 70 Lincoln Street, Boston, Massachusetts 02111 (617) 423-3990; *The World in Figures.*

International Monetary Fund, 700 Nineteenth Street, NW, Washington, D.C. 20431 (202) 623-7000; *International Financial Statistics.*

Statistical Office of the United Nations, Publishing Service, New York, New York 10017 (800) 253-9646; *Statistical Yearbook.*

United Nations Educational, Scientific and Cultural Organization (UNESCO), 7 Place de Fontenoy, F-75700 Paris, France (Telephone Number in U.S. (212) 963-5981); *Statistical Yearbook.*

INDONESIA - FURNITURE AND WOOD PRODUCTS - EXPORTS AND IMPORTS

Statistical Office of the United Nations, Publishing Service, New York, New York 10017 (800) 253-9646; *Trade in Manufactures of Developing Countries.*

INDONESIA - GAS - See INDONESIA - MINING AND MINERAL PRODUCTS

INDONESIA - GENERAL INDUSTRIAL STATISTICS

Statistical Office of the United Nations, Publishing Service, New York, New York 10017 (800) 253-9646; *Industrial Statistics Yearbook.*

INDONESIA - GENERAL MORTALITY

Statistical Office of the United Nations, Publishing Service, New York, New York 10017 (800) 253-9646; *Demographic Yearbook.*

INDONESIA - GEOGRAPHIC DATA

Facts on File, 460 Park Avenue South, New York, New York 10016 (800) 443-8323; *The New Book of World Rankings.*

INDONESIA - GOATS - See INDONESIA - LIVESTOCK AND POULTRY

INDONESIA - GOLD HOLDINGS

International Monetary Fund, 700 Nineteenth Street, NW, Washington, D.C. 20431 (202) 623-7000; *International Financial Statistics.*

Statistical Office of the United Nations, Publishing Service, New York, New York 10017 (800) 253-9646; *Statistical Yearbook.*

The World Bank, 1818 H Street, NW, Washington, D.C. 20433 (202) 477-1234; *World Tables.*

INDONESIA - GOLD PRODUCTION AND CONSUMPTION - See INDONESIA - MINING AND MINERAL PRODUCTS

INDONESIA - GOVERNMENT

Asian Development Bank, Post Office Box 789, 1099 Manila, Philippines; *Key Indicators of Developing Asian and Pacific Countries.*

G.K. Hall and Company, 70 Lincoln Street, Boston, Massachusetts 02111 (617) 423-3990; *The World in Figures.*

INDONESIA - GOVERNMENT BONDS - See INDONESIA - BONDS

INDONESIA - GOVERNMENT EXPENDITURES

Asian Development Bank, Post Office Box 789, 1099 Manila, Philippines; *Key Indicators of Developing Asian and Pacific Countries.*

Euromonitor Publications Limited, 87-88 Turnmill Street, London EC1M 5QU, England; *Third World Economic Handbook.*

International Monetary Fund, 700 Nineteenth Street, NW, Washington, D.C. 20431 (202) 623-7000; *Government Finance Statistics Yearbook.*

Times Books, 201 East 50th Street, New York, New York 10022 (212) 751-2600; *The Economist Book of Vital World Statistics.*

The World Bank, 1818 H Street, NW, Washington, D.C. 20433 (202) 477-1234; *World Tables.*

INDONESIA - GOVERNMENT FINANCES

Asian Development Bank, Post Office Box 789, 1099 Manila, Philippines; *Key Indicators of Developing Asian and Pacific Countries.*

International Monetary Fund, 700 Nineteenth Street, NW, Washington, D.C. 20431 (202) 623-7000; *International Financial Statistics.*

Statistical Office of the United Nations, Publishing Service, New York, New York 10017 (800) 253-9646; *Statistical Yearbook.*

INDONESIA - GOVERNMENT REVENUES

Asian Development Bank, Post Office Box 789, 1099 Manila, Philippines; *Key Indicators of Developing Asian and Pacific Countries.*

International Monetary Fund, 700 Nineteenth Street, NW, Washington, D.C. 20431 (202) 623-7000; *Government Finance Statistics Yearbook.*

Times Books, 201 East 50th Street, New York, New York 10022 (212) 751-2600; *The Economist Book of Vital World Statistics.*

The World Bank, 1818 H Street, NW, Washington, D.C. 20433 (202) 477-1234; *World Tables.*

INDONESIA - GRAIN PRODUCTION - See INDONESIA - CROPS

INDONESIA - GRANTS

International Monetary Fund, 700 Nineteenth Street, NW, Washington, D.C. 20431 (202) 623-7000; *Government Finance Statistics Yearbook.*

INDONESIA - GROSS DOMESTIC PRODUCT

Asian Development Bank, Post Office Box 789, 1099 Manila, Philippines; *Key Indicators of Developing Asian and Pacific Countries.*

The Economist Intelligence Unit (Asia) Limited, 10th Floor, Luk Kwok Centre, 72 Gloucester Road, Wanchai, Hong Kong (Phone Number in U.S. (800) 938-4685); *Asian Market Atlas.*

The Economist Intelligence Unit, 111 West 57th Street, New York, New York 10019 (800) 938-4685; *The World Market Atlas.*

Euromonitor Publications Limited, 87-88 Turnmill Street, London EC1M 5QU, England; *International Marketing Data and Statistics, The Pacific Basin: An Economic Handbook,* and *Third World Economic Handbook.*

Facts on File, 460 Park Avenue South, New York, New York 10016; *The New Book of World Rankings.*

G.K. Hall and Company, 70 Lincoln Street, Boston, Massachusetts 02111 (617) 423-3990; *The World in Figures.*

Statistical Office of the United Nations, Publishing Service, New York, New York 10017 (800) 253-9646; *Statistical Yearbook.*

Times Books, 201 East 50th Street, New York, New York 10022 (212) 751-2600; *The Economist Book of Vital World Statistics.*

The World Bank, 1818 H Street, NW, Washington, D.C. 20433 (202) 477-1234; *World Tables.*

INDONESIA - GROSS INDUSTRIAL PRODUCT

Euromonitor Publications Limited, 87-88 Turnmill Street, London EC1M 5QU, England; *Third World Economic Handbook.*

INDONESIA - GROSS NATIONAL PRODUCT

Asian Development Bank, Post Office Box 789, 1099 Manila, Philippines; *Key Indicators of Developing Asian and Pacific Countries.*

Euromonitor Publications Limited, 87-88 Turnmill Street, London EC1M 5QU, England; *International Marketing Data and Statistics,* and *Third World Economic Handbook.*

Organization of Petroleum Exporting Countries, Obere Donaustrasse 93, 1020 Vienna 2, Austria; *OPEC Annual Statistical Bulletin.*

U.S. Arms Control and Disarmament Agency, 320 Twenty-first Street, Northwest, Washington, D.C. 20451 (202) 647-8677; *World Military Expenditures and Arms Transfers.*

The World Bank, 1818 H Street, NW, Washington, D.C. 20433 (202) 477-1234; *World Tables.*

INDONESIA - GROUNDNUTS PRODUCTION - See INDONESIA - CROPS

INDONESIA - HEALTH

The Economist Intelligence Unit (Asia) Limited, 10th Floor, Luk Kwok Centre, 72 Gloucester Road, Wanchai, Hong Kong (Phone Number in U.S. (800) 938-4685); *Asian Market Atlas.*

Euromonitor Publications Limited, 87-88 Turnmill Street, London EC1M 5QU, England; *The Pacific Basin: An Economic Handbook.*

Facts on File, 460 Park Avenue South, New York, New York 10016 (800) 443-8323; *The New Book of World Rankings.*

G.K. Hall and Company, 70 Lincoln Street, Boston, Massachusetts 02111 (617) 423-3990; *The World in Figures.*

Statistical Office of the United Nations, Publishing Service, New York, New York 10017 (800) 253-9646; *Statistical Yearbook.*

Times Books, 201 East 50th Street, New York, New York 10022 (212) 751-2600; *The Economist Book of Vital World Statistics.*

World Health Organization, Avenue Appia, Office of Publications, CH-1211 Geneva 27, Switzerland (Telephone Number in U.S. (518) 436-9686); *World Health Statistics Annual.*

INDONESIA - HIDE PRODUCTION - ALL TYPES

Food and Agricultural Organization of the United Nations (FAO), Via delle Terme di Caracalla, 00100 Rome, Italy (Telephone Number in U.S. (202) 653-2400); *Production Yearbook.*

INDONESIA - HIGHWAYS

The Economist Intelligence Unit (Asia) Limited, 10th Floor, Luk Kwok Centre, 72 Gloucester Road, Wanchai, Hong Kong (Phone Number in U.S. (800) 938-4685); *Asian Market Atlas.*

G.K. Hall and Company, 70 Lincoln Street, Boston, Massachusetts 02111 (617) 423-3990; *The World in Figures.*

International Road Federation, 525 School Street, SW, Washington, D.C. 20024 (202) 554-2106; *World Road Statistics.*

INDONESIA - HORSES - See INDONESIA - LIVESTOCK AND POULTRY

INDONESIA - HOURS OF WORK - See INDONESIA - EMPLOYMENT

INDONESIA - HOUSING AND HOUSING UNITS

Euromonitor Publications Limited, 87-88 Turnmill Street, London EC1M 5QU, England; *Third World Economic Handbook.*

Facts on File, 460 Park Avenue South, New York, New York 10016; *The New Book of World Rankings.*

INDONESIA - HYDROCHLORIC ACID PRODUCTION

Statistical Office of the United Nations, Publishing Service, New York, New York 10017 (800) 253-9646; *Statistical Yearbook.*

INDONESIA - ILLITERATE POPULATION

The Economist Intelligence Unit, 111 West 57th Street, New York, New York 10019 (800) 938-4685; *The World Market Atlas.*

G.K. Hall and Company, 70 Lincoln Street, Boston, Massachusetts 02111 (617) 423-3990; *The World in Figures.*

United Nations Educational, Scientific and Cultural Organization (UNESCO), 7 Place de Fontenoy, F-75700 Paris, France (Telephone Number in U.S. (212) 963-5981); *Statistical Yearbook.*

INDONESIA - IMPORTS

Asian Development Bank, Post Office Box 789, 1099 Manila, Philippines; *Key Indicators of Developing Asian and Pacific Countries.*

The Economist Intelligence Unit, 111 West 57th Street, New York, New York 10019 (800) 938-4685; *The World Market Atlas.*

The Economist Intelligence Unit (Asia) Limited, 10th Floor, Luk Kwok Centre, 72 Gloucester Road, Wanchai, Hong Kong (Phone Number in U.S. (800) 938-4685); *Asian Market Atlas.*

Euromonitor Publications Limited, 87-88 Turnmill Street, London EC1M 5QU, England; *International Marketing Data and Statistics, The Pacific Basin: An Economic Handbook,* and *Third World Economic Handbook.*

Food and Agricultural Organization of the United Nations (FAO) Via delle Terme di Caracalla, 00100 Rome, Italy (Telephone Number in U.S. (202) 653-2400); *The State of Food and Agriculture.*

G.K. Hall and Company, 70 Lincoln Street, Boston, Massachusetts 02111 (617) 423-3990; *The World in Figures.*

International Monetary Fund, 700 Nineteenth Street, NW, Washington, D.C. 20431 (202) 623-7000; *Direction of Trade Statistics, Government Finance Statistics Yearbook,* and *International Financial Statistics.*

International Rubber Study Group, York House, 8th Floor, Empire Way, Wembley, London HA9 0PA, England; *Rubber Statistical Bulletin.*

Statistical Office of the United Nations, Publishing Service, New York, New York 10017 (800) 253-9646; *Foreign Trade Statistics of Asia and the Pacific,* and *Trade in Manufactures of Developing Countries.*

Times Books, 201 East 50th Street, New York, New York 10022 (212) 751-2600; *The Economist Book of Vital World Statistics.*

The World Bank, 1818 H Street, NW, Washington, D.C. 20433 (202) 477-1234; *World Tables.*

INDONESIA - INCOME TAXES - See INDONESIA - TAXATION

INDONESIA - INDUSTRIAL METALS PRODUCTION

Statistical Office of the United Nations, Publishing Service, New York, New York 10017 (800) 253-9646; *Statistical Yearbook.*

INDONESIA - INDUSTRY

Euromonitor Publications Limited, 87-88 Turnmill Street, London EC1M 5QU, England; *International Marketing Data and Statistics* and *Third World Economic Handbook.*

Facts on File, 460 Park Avenue South, New York, New York 10016 (800) 443-8323; *The New Book of World Rankings.*

G.K. Hall and Company, 70 Lincoln Street, Boston, Massachusetts 02111 (617) 423-3990; *The World in Figures.*

International Labour Office, I.L.O. Publications, CH-1211, Geneva 22, Switzerland; *Yearbook of Labour Statistics.*

Statistical Office of the United Nations, Publishing Service, New York, New York 10017 (800) 253-9646; *Statistical Yearbook for Asia and the Pacific.*

Times Books, 201 East 50th Street, New York, New York 10022 (212) 751-2600; *The Economist Book of Vital World Statistics.*

The World Bank, 1818 H Street, NW, Washington, D.C. 20433 (202) 477-1234; *World Tables.*

World Intellectual Property Organization, 34 Chemin des Colombettes, CH-1211 Geneva 20, Switzerland; *Industrial Property Statistics.*

INDONESIA - INFANT AND MATERNAL MORTALITY

The Economist Intelligence Unit (Asia) Limited, 10th Floor, Luk Kwok Centre, 72 Gloucester Road, Wanchai, Hong Kong (Phone Number in U.S. (800) 938-4685); *Asian Market Atlas.*

Statistical Office of the United Nations, Publishing Service, New York, New York 10017 (800) 253-9646; *Demographic Yearbook,* and *Statistical Yearbook.*

Times Books, 201 East 50th Street, New York, New York 10022 (212) 751-2600; *The Economist Book of Vital World Statistics.*

The World Bank, 1818 H Street, NW, Washington, D.C. 20433 (202) 477-1234; *World Tables.*

INDONESIA - INTEREST RATES

Euromonitor Publications Limited, 87-88 Turnmill Street, London EC1M 5QU, England; *The Pacific Basin: An Economic Handbook.*

INDONESIA - INTERNAL TRADE

Statistical Office of the United Nations, Publishing Service, New York, New York 10017 (800) 253-9646; *Statistical Yearbook for Asia and the Pacific.*

INDONESIA - INTERNATIONAL LIQUIDITY

International Monetary Fund, 700 Nineteenth Street, NW, Washington, D.C. 20431 (202) 623-7000; *International Financial Statistics.*

INDONESIA - INTERNATIONAL RESERVES EXCLUDING GOLD

Asian Development Bank, Post Office Box 789, 1099 Manila, Philippines; *Key Indicators of Developing Asian and Pacific Countries.*

Statistical Office of the United Nations, Publishing Service, New York, New York 10017 (800) 253-9646; *Statistical Yearbook.*

The World Bank, 1818 H Street, NW, Washington, D.C. 20433 (202) 477-1234; *World Tables.*

INDONESIA - INTERNATIONAL STATISTICS

Asian Development Bank, Post Office Box 789, 1099 Manila, Philippines; *Key Indicators of Developing Asian and Pacific Countries.*

INDONESIA - INVESTMENT

International Monetary Fund, 700 Nineteenth Street, NW, Washington, D.C. 20431 (202) 623-7000; *International Financial Statistics.*

INDONESIA - IRON ORE PRODUCTION AND CONSUMPTION - See INDONESIA - MINING AND MINERAL PRODUCTS

INDONESIA - IRRIGATION

Euromonitor Publications Limited, 87-88 Turnmill Street, London EC1M 5QU, England; *International Marketing Data and Statistics.*

INDONESIA - JUTE PRODUCTION - See INDONESIA - CROPS

INDONESIA - LABOR FORCE

The Economist Intelligence Unit (Asia) Limited, 10th Floor, Luk Kwok Centre, 72 Gloucester Road, Wanchai, Hong Kong (Phone Number in U.S. (800) 938-4685); *Asian Market Atlas.*

Euromonitor Publications Limited, 87-88 Turnmill Street, London EC1M 5QU, England; *International Marketing Data and Statistics,* and *The Pacific Basin: An Economic Handbook.*

Facts on File, 460 Park Avenue South, New York, New York 10016 (800) 443-8323; *The New Book of World Rankings.*

Food and Agricultural Organization of the United Nations (FAO) Via delle Terme di Caracalla, 00100 Rome, Italy (Telephone Number in U.S. (202) 653-2400); *The State of Food and Agriculture.*

G.K. Hall and Company, 70 Lincoln Street, Boston, Massachusetts 02111 (617) 423-3990; *The World in Figures.*

Times Books, 201 East 50th Street, New York, New York 10022 (212) 751-2600; *The Economist Book of Vital World Statistics.*

The World Bank, 1818 H Street, NW, Washington, D.C. 20433 (202) 477-1234; *World Tables.*

INDONESIA - LABOR PRODUCTIVITY

International Labour Office, I.L.O. Publications, CH-1211, Geneva 22, Switzerland; *Yearbook of Labour Statistics.*

INDONESIA - LAND USE

Euromonitor Publications Limited, 87-88 Turnmill Street, London EC1M 5QU, England; *International Marketing Data and Statistics.*

Food and Agricultural Organization of the United Nations (FAO), Via delle Terme di Caracalla, 00100 Rome, Italy (Telephone Number in U.S. (202) 653-2400); *Production Yearbook.*

G.K. Hall and Company, 70 Lincoln Street, Boston, Massachusetts 02111 (617) 423-3990; *The World in Figures.*

INDONESIA - LIBRARIES

Facts on File, 460 Park Avenue South, New York, New York 10016 (800) 443-8323; *The New Book of World Rankings.*

United Nations Educational, Scientific and Cultural Organization (UNESCO), 7 Place de Fontenoy, F-75700 Paris, France (Telephone Number in U.S. (212) 963-5981); *Statistical Yearbook.*

INDONESIA - LIFE EXPECTANCY

The Economist Intelligence Unit (Asia) Limited, 10th Floor, Luk Kwok Centre, 72 Gloucester Road, Wanchai, Hong Kong (Phone Number in U.S. (800) 938-4685); *Asian Market Atlas.*

INDONESIA - LIGNITE PRODUCTION - See INDONESIA - MINING AND MINERAL PRODUCTS

INDONESIA - LIVESTOCK AND POULTRY

Euromonitor Publications Limited, 87-88 Turnmill Street, London EC1M 5QU, England; *Third World Economic Handbook.*

Facts on File, 460 Park Avenue South, New York, New York 10016 (800) 443-8323; *The New Book of World Rankings.*

Food and Agricultural Organization of the United Nations (FAO), Via delle Terme di Caracalla, 00100 Rome, Italy (Telephone Number in U.S. (202) 653-2400); *Production Yearbook,* and *The State of Food and Agriculture.*

G.K. Hall and Company, 70 Lincoln Street, Boston, Massachusetts 02111 (617) 423-3990; *The World in Figures.*

Statistical Office of the United Nations, Publishing Service, New York, New York 10017 (800) 253-9646; *Statistical Yearbook.*

INDONESIA - LIVING LEVELS

G.K. Hall and Company, 70 Lincoln Street, Boston, Massachusetts 02111 (617) 423-3990; *The World in Figures.*

Times Books, 201 East 50th Street, New York, New York 10022 (212) 751-2600; *The Economist Book of Vital World Statistics.*

INDONESIA - MAIL - NUMBER OF PIECES SENT OR RECEIVED

Statistical Office of the United Nations, Publishing Service, New York, New York 10017 (800) 253-9646; *Statistical Yearbook.*

INDONESIA - MANGANESE ORE PRODUCTION AND CONSUMPTION - See INDONESIA - MINING AND MINERAL PRODUCTS

INDONESIA - MANPOWER

Statistical Office of the United Nations, Publishing Service, New York, New York 10017 (800) 253-9646; *Statistical Yearbook for Asia and the Pacific.*

INDONESIA - MANUFACTURING

Asian Development Bank, Post Office Box 789, 1099 Manila, Philippines; *Key Indicators of Developing Asian and Pacific Countries.*

Euromonitor Publications Limited, 87-88 Turnmill Street, London EC1M 5QU, England; *Third World Economic Handbook.*

Facts on File, 460 Park Avenue South, New York, New York 10016 (800) 443-8323; *The New Book of World Rankings.*

G.K. Hall and Company, 70 Lincoln Street, Boston, Massachusetts 02111 (617) 423-3990; *The World in Figures.*

Statistical Office of the United Nations, Publishing Service, New York, New York 10017 (800) 253-9646; *Statistical Yearbook.*

Times Books, 201 East 50th Street, New York, New York 10022 (212) 751-2600; *The Economist Book of Vital World Statistics.*

The World Bank, 1818 H Street, NW, Washington, D.C. 20433 (202) 477-1234; *World Tables.*

INDONESIA - MARRIAGE RATES

Facts on File, 460 Park Avenue South, New York, New York 10016 (800) 443-8323; *The New Book of World Rankings.*

Statistical Office of the United Nations, Publishing Service, New York, New York 10017 (800) 253-9646; *Demographic Yearbook,* and *Statistical Yearbook.*

INDONESIA - MEAT PRODUCTION - See INDONESIA - LIVESTOCK AND POULTRY

INDONESIA - MERCHANT SHIPPING

G.K. Hall and Company, 70 Lincoln Street, Boston, Massachusetts 02111 (617) 423-3990; *The World in Figures.*

Lloyd's Register of Shipping, 17 Battery Place, New York, New York 10004 (212) 425-8050; *Register of Ships.*

Organization of Petroleum Exporting Countries, Obere Donaustrasse 93, 1020 Vienna 2, Austria; *OPEC Annual Statistical Bulletin.*

Statistical Office of the United Nations, Publishing Service, New York, New York 10017 (800) 253-9646; *Statistical Yearbook.*

Times Books, 201 East 50th Street, New York, New York 10022 (212) 751-2600; *The Economist Book of Vital World Statistics.*

U.S. Department of Transportation, Maritime Administration, 400 Seventh Street, SW, Washington, D.C. 20590 (202) 366-5807; *A Statistical Analysis of the World's Merchant Fleets.*

INDONESIA - MILITARY

The Economist Intelligence Unit (Asia) Limited, 10th Floor, Luk Kwok Centre, 72 Gloucester Road, Wanchai, Hong Kong (Phone Number in U.S. (800) 938-4685); *Asian Market Atlas.*

G.K. Hall and Company, 70 Lincoln Street, Boston, Massachusetts 02111 (617) 423-3990; *The World in Figures.*

The International Institute for Strategic Studies, 23 Tavistock Street, London WC2E 7NQ, England; *The Military Balance.*

U.S. Arms Control and Disarmament Agency, 320 Twenty-first Street, Northwest, Washington, D.C. 20451 (202) 647-8677; *World Military Expenditures and Arms Transfers.*

INDONESIA - MILK - See INDONESIA - DAIRY PRODUCTS

INDONESIA - MINING AND MINERAL PRODUCTS

Asian Development Bank, Post Office Box 789, 1099 Manila, Philippines; *Key Indicators of Developing Asian and Pacific Countries.*

Commodity Research Bureau, Incorporated, 75 Wall Street, New York, New York 10005 (212) 504-7754; *Commodity Year Book.*

Euromonitor Publications Limited, 87-88 Turnmill Street, London EC1M 5QU, England; *International Marketing Data and Statistics.*

Facts on File, 460 Park Avenue South, New York, New York 10016 (800) 443-8323; *The New Book of World Rankings.*

G.K. Hall and Company, 70 Lincoln Street, Boston, Massachusetts 02111 (617) 423-3990; *The World in Figures.*

Organization of Petroleum Exporting Countries, Obere Donaustrasse 93, 1020 Vienna 2, Austria; *OPEC Annual Statistical Bulletin*.

Penn Well Publishing Company, 1421 South Sheridan Road, Post Office Box 1260, Tulsa, Oklahoma 74101 (800) 752-9764; *International Energy Statistics Sourcebook*.

Statistical Office of the United Nations, Publishing Service, New York, New York 10017 (800) 253-9646; *Statistical Yearbook*.

INDONESIA - MONEY EXCHANGE RATE

Euromonitor Publications Limited, 87-88 Turnmill Street, London EC1M 5QU, England; *International Marketing Data and Statistics*.

International Monetary Fund, 700 Nineteenth Street, NW, Washington, D.C. 20431 (202) 623-7000; *International Financial Statistics*.

Statistical Office of the United Nations, Publishing Service, New York, New York 10017 (800) 253-9646; *Statistical Yearbook*.

INDONESIA - MONEY RESERVES

Euromonitor Publications Limited, 87-88 Turnmill Street, London EC1M 5QU, England; *International Marketing Data and Statistics*.

INDONESIA - MONEY SUPPLY

Asian Development Bank, Post Office Box 789, 1099 Manila, Philippines; *Key Indicators of Developing Asian and Pacific Countries*.

Euromonitor Publications Limited, 87-88 Turnmill Street, London EC1M 5QU, England; *International Marketing Data and Statistics*.

G.K. Hall and Company, 70 Lincoln Street, Boston, Massachusetts 02111 (617) 423-3990; *The World in Figures*.

International Monetary Fund, 700 Nineteenth Street, NW, Washington, D.C. 20431 (202) 623-7000; *International Financial Statistics*.

Statistical Office of the United Nations, Publishing Service, New York, New York 10017 (800) 253-9646; *Statistical Yearbook*.

The World Bank, 1818 H Street, NW, Washington, D.C. 20433 (202) 477-1234; *World Tables*.

INDONESIA - MONUMENTS AND HISTORICAL SITES

United Nations Educational, Scientific and Cultural Organization (UNESCO), 7 Place de Fontenoy, F-75700 Paris, France (Telephone Number in U.S. (212) 963-5981); *Statistical Yearbook*.

INDONESIA - MOTION PICTURES

Statistical Office of the United Nations, Publishing Service, New York, New York 10017 (800) 253-9646; *Statistical Yearbook*.

United Nations Educational, Scientific and Cultural Organization (UNESCO), 7 Place de Fontenoy, F-75700 Paris, France (Telephone Number in U.S. (212) 963-5981); *Statistical Yearbook*.

INDONESIA - MOTOR VEHICLE PRODUCTION AND ASSEMBLY

Statistical Office of the United Nations, Publishing Service, New York, New York 10017 (800) 253-9646; *Statistical Yearbook*.

INDONESIA - MOTOR VEHICLES IN USE

G.K. Hall and Company, 70 Lincoln Street, Boston, Massachusetts 02111 (617) 423-3990; *The World in Figures*.

International Road Federation, 525 School Street, SW, Washington, D.C. 20024 (202) 554-2106; *World Road Statistics*.

Statistical Office of the United Nations, Publishing Service, New York, New York 10017 (800) 253-9646; *Statistical Yearbook*.

Times Books, 201 East 50th Street, New York, New York 10022 (212) 751-2600; *The Economist Book of Vital World Statistics*.

INDONESIA - MUSEUMS

Facts on File, 460 Park Avenue South, New York, New York 10016 (800) 443-8323; *The New Book of World Rankings*.

United Nations Educational, Scientific and Cultural Organization (UNESCO), 7 Place de Fontenoy, F-75700 Paris, France (Telephone Number in U.S. (212) 963-5981); *Statistical Yearbook*.

INDONESIA - NATALITY - See INDONESIA - BIRTH RATES

INDONESIA - NATIONAL ACCOUNTS

Statistical Office of the United Nations, Publishing Service, New York, New York 10017 (800) 253-9646; *National Accounts Statistics, Statistical Yearbook*, and *Statistical Yearbook for Asia and the Pacific*.

INDONESIA - NATIONAL INCOME

Facts on File, 460 Park Avenue South, New York, New York 10016; *The New Book of World Rankings*.

G.K. Hall and Company, 70 Lincoln Street, Boston, Massachusetts 02111 (617) 423-3990; *The World in Figures*.

Statistical Office of the United Nations, Publishing Service, New York, New York 10017 (800) 253-9646; *Statistical Yearbook*.

INDONESIA - NATIONAL PRODUCT

Facts on File, 460 Park Avenue South, New York, New York 10016 (800) 443-8323; *The New Book of World Rankings*.

Statistical Office of the United Nations, Publishing Service, New York, New York 10017 (800) 253-9646; *Statistical Yearbook*.

INDONESIA - NATURAL GAS PRODUCTION - See INDONESIA - MINING AND MINERAL PRODUCTS

INDONESIA - NATURAL RUBBER PRODUCTION

International Rubber Study Group, York House, 8th Floor, Empire Way, Wembley, London HA9 0PA, England; *Rubber Statistical Bulletin*.

Statistical Office of the United Nations, Publishing Service, New York, New York 10017 (800) 253-9646; *Statistical Yearbook*.

INDONESIA - NEWSPAPER PRODUCTION - See INDONESIA - FORESTRY AND FOREST PRODUCTS

INDONESIA - NEWSPRINT - See INDONESIA - FORESTRY AND FOREST PRODUCTS

INDONESIA - NICKEL AND NICKEL ORE - See INDONESIA - MINING AND MINERAL PRODUCTS

INDONESIA - OCCUPATIONS - See INDONESIA - LABOR FORCE

INDONESIA - PALM OIL AND PALM KERNELS PRODUCTION - See INDONESIA - CROPS

INDONESIA - PAPER - See INDONESIA - FORESTRY AND FOREST PRODUCTS

INDONESIA - PATENTS

Statistical Office of the United Nations, Publishing Service, New York, New York 10017 (800) 253-9646; *Statistical Yearbook.*

World Intellectual Property Organization, 34 Chemin des Colombettes, CH-1211 Geneva 20, Switzerland; *Industrial Property Statistics.*

INDONESIA - PEANUT PRODUCTION - See INDONESIA - CROPS

INDONESIA - PEPPER PRODUCTION - See INDONESIA - CROPS

INDONESIA - PESTICIDE USE

Food and Agricultural Organization of the United Nations (FAO) Via delle Terme di Caracalla, 00100 Rome, Italy (Telephone Number in U.S. (202) 653-2400); *The State of Food and Agriculture.*

INDONESIA - PETROLEUM INDUSTRY

Asian Development Bank, Post Office Box 789, 1099 Manila, Philippines; *Key Indicators of Developing Asian and Pacific Countries.*

Commodity Research Bureau, Incorporated, 75 Wall Street, New York, New York 10005 (212) 504-7754; *Commodity Year Book.*

Facts on File, 460 Park Avenue South, New York, New York 10016 (800) 443-8323; *The New Book of World Rankings.*

Food and Agricultural Organization of the United Nations (FAO) Via delle Terme di Caracalla, 00100 Rome, Italy (Telephone Number in U.S. (202) 653-2400); *The State of Food and Agriculture.*

G.K. Hall and Company, 70 Lincoln Street, Boston, Massachusetts 02111 (617) 423-3990; *The World in Figures.*

International Monetary Fund, 700 Nineteenth Street, NW, Washington, D.C. 20431 (202) 623-7000; *International Financial Statistics.*

Organization of Petroleum Exporting Countries, Obere Donaustrasse 93, 1020 Vienna 2, Austria; *OPEC Annual Statistical Bulletin.*

Penn Well Publishing Company, 1421 South Sheridan Road, Post Office Box 1260, Tulsa, Oklahoma 74101 (800) 752-9764; *International Energy Statistics Sourcebook.*

Statistical Office of the United Nations, Publishing Service, New York, New York 10017 (800) 253-9646; *Statistical Yearbook.*

INDONESIA - PHOSPHATE ROCK PRODUCTION - See INDONESIA - MINING AND MINERAL PRODUCTS

INDONESIA - PIGS - See INDONESIA - LIVESTOCK AND POULTRY

INDONESIA - PIPELINES FOR OIL AND PETROLEUM PRODUCTS

Organization of Petroleum Exporting Countries, Obere Donaustrasse 93, 1020 Vienna 2, Austria; *OPEC Annual Statistical Bulletin.*

INDONESIA - PLASTIC AND RESIN PRODUCTION

Euromonitor Publications Limited, 87-88 Turnmill Street, London EC1M 5QU, England; *Third World Economic Handbook.*

INDONESIA - POPULATION

Asian Development Bank, Post Office Box 789, 1099 Manila, Philippines; *Key Indicators of Developing Asian and Pacific Countries.*

Business International Asia/Pacific Ltd., 10/F, Luk Kwok Centre, 72 Gloucester Road, Hong Kong (Phone Number in U.S. (800) 938-4685); *Asian Market Atlas.*

Business International Corporation, 215 Park Avenue South, New York, New York 10003 (800) 938-4685; *The World Market Atlas.*

Euromonitor Publications Limited, 87-88 Turnmill Street, London EC1M 5QU, England; *International Marketing Data and Statistics, The Pacific Basin: An Economic Handbook,* and *Third World Economic Handbook.*

Facts on File, 460 Park Avenue South, New York, New York 10016 (800) 443-8323; *The New Book of World Rankings.*

Food and Agricultural Organization of the United Nations (FAO), Via delle Terme di Caracalla, 00100 Rome, Italy (Telephone Number in U.S. (202) 653-2400); *Production Yearbook.*

G.K. Hall and Company, 70 Lincoln Street, Boston, Massachusetts 02111 (617) 423-3990; *The World in Figures.*

International Labour Office, I.L.O. Publications, CH-1211, Geneva 22, Switzerland; *Yearbook of Labour Statistics.*

Statistical Office of the United Nations, Publishing Service, New York, New York 10017 (800) 253-9646; *Demographic Yearbook, Statistical Yearbook,* and *Statistical Yearbook for Asia and the Pacific.*

Times Books, 201 East 50th Street, New York, New York 10022 (212) 751-2600; *The Economist Book of Vital World Statistics.*

United Nations Educational, Scientific and Cultural Organization (UNESCO), 7 Place de Fontenoy, F-75700 Paris, France (Telephone Number in U.S. (212) 963-5981); *Statistical Yearbook.*

U.S. Arms Control and Disarmament Agency, 320 Twenty-first Street, Northwest, Washington, D.C. 20451 (202) 647-8677; *World Military Expenditures and Arms Transfers.*

World Health Organization, Avenue Appia, Office of Publications, CH-1211 Geneva 27, Switzerland (Telephone Number in U.S. (518) 436-9686); *World Health Statistics Annual.*

INDONESIA - POST OFFICES

Facts on File, 460 Park Avenue South, New York, New York 10016 (800) 443-8323; *The New Book of World Rankings.*

INDONESIA - POTATO PRODUCTION - See INDONESIA - CROPS

INDONESIA - POWER PRODUCTION INDUSTRY

Statistical Office of the United Nations, Publishing Service, New York, New York 10017 (800) 253-9646; *Electric Power in Asia and the Pacific,* and *Statistical Yearbook.*

INDONESIA - PRICES

Asian Development Bank, Post Office Box 789, 1099 Manila, Philippines; *Key Indicators of Developing Asian and Pacific Countries.*

Facts on File, 460 Park Avenue South, New York, New York 10016 (800) 443-8323; *The New Book of World Rankings.*

Food and Agricultural Organization of the United Nations (FAO), Via delle Terme di Caracalla, 00100 Rome, Italy (Telephone Number in U.S. (202) 653-2400); *Production Yearbook,* and *The State of Food and Agriculture.*

G.K. Hall and Company, 70 Lincoln Street, Boston, Massachusetts 02111 (617) 423-3990; *The World in Figures.*

International Labour Office, I.L.O. Publications, CH-1211, Geneva 22, Switzerland; *Yearbook of Labour Statistics.*

International Monetary Fund, 700 Nineteenth Street, NW, Washington, D.C. 20431 (202) 623-7000; *International Financial Statistics.*

International Rubber Study Group, York House, 8th Floor, Empire Way, Wembley, London HA9 0PA, England; *Rubber Statistical Bulletin.*

INDONESIA - PRINTING AND WRITING PAPER - See INDONESIA - FORESTRY AND FOREST PRODUCTS

INDONESIA - PRODUCTION

Euromonitor Publications Limited, 87-88 Turnmill Street, London EC1M 5QU, England; *Third World Economic Handbook.*

Facts on File, 460 Park Avenue South, New York, New York 10016 (800) 443-8323; *The New Book of World Rankings.*

G.K. Hall and Company, 70 Lincoln Street, Boston, Massachusetts 02111 (617) 423-3990; *The World in Figures.*

International Rubber Study Group, York House, 8th Floor, Empire Way, Wembley, London HA9 0PA, England; *Rubber Statistical Bulletin.*

INDONESIA - PRODUCTIVITY

Euromonitor Publications Limited, 87-88 Turnmill Street, London EC1M 5QU, England; *International Marketing Data and Statistics.*

INDONESIA - PROPERTY TAXES - See INDONESIA - TAXATION

INDONESIA - PUBLIC FINANCE

Facts on File, 460 Park Avenue South, New York, New York 10016 (800) 443-8323; *The New Book of World Rankings.*

INDONESIA - RADIO BROADCASTING - See INDONESIA - BROADCASTING

INDONESIA - RADIO RECEIVER PRODUCTION

Statistical Office of the United Nations, Publishing Service, New York, New York 10017 (800) 253-9646; *Statistical Yearbook.*

INDONESIA - RAILWAYS

G.K. Hall and Company, 70 Lincoln Street, Boston, Massachusetts 02111 (617) 423-3990; *The World in Figures.*

Jane's Information Group, Sentinel House, 163 Brighton Road, Coulsdon, Surrey CR5 2NH, England (Telephone Number in U.S. (703) 683-3700); *Jane's World Railways.*

Statistical Office of the United Nations, Publishing Service, New York, New York 10017 (800) 253-9646; *Statistical Yearbook.*

INDONESIA - RELIGION

Facts on File, 460 Park Avenue South, New York, New York 10016 (800) 443-8323; *The New Book of World Rankings.*

INDONESIA - RENT PRICES

International Labour Office, I.L.O. Publications, CH-1211, Geneva 22, Switzerland; *Yearbook of Labour Statistics.*

INDONESIA - RETAIL TRADE

Euromonitor Publications Limited, 87-88 Turnmill Street, London EC1M 5QU, England; *Third World Economic Handbook.*

G.K. Hall and Company, 70 Lincoln Street, Boston, Massachusetts 02111 (617) 423-3990; *The World in Figures.*

INDONESIA - RICE PRODUCTION - See INDONESIA - CROPS

INDONESIA - ROOT AND TUBER PRODUCTION - See INDONESIA - CROPS

INDONESIA - ROUNDWOOD PRODUCTION - See INDONESIA - FORESTRY AND FOREST PRODUCTS

INDONESIA - RUBBER PRODUCTION

Commodity Research Bureau, Incorporated, 75 Wall Street, New York, New York 10005 (212) 504-7754; *Commodity Year Book.*

Euromonitor Publications Limited, 87-88 Turnmill Street, London EC1M 5QU, England; *Third World Economic Handbook.*

Facts on File, 460 Park Avenue South, New York, New York 10016 (800) 443-8323; *The New Book of World Rankings.*

International Monetary Fund, 700 Nineteenth Street, NW, Washington, D.C. 20431 (202) 623-7000; *International Financial Statistics.*

International Rubber Study Group, York House, 8th Floor, Empire Way, Wembley, London HA9 0PA, England; *Rubber Statistical Bulletin.*

Statistical Office of the United Nations, Publishing Service, New York, New York 10017 (800) 253-9646; *Statistical Yearbook.*

INDONESIA - SALT PRODUCTION - See INDONESIA - MINING AND MINERAL PRODUCTS

INDONESIA - SAWNWOOD PRODUCTION - See INDONESIA - FORESTRY AND FOREST PRODUCTS

INDONESIA - SCIENTISTS AND TECHNICIANS

Statistical Office of the United Nations, Publishing Service, New York, New York 10017 (800) 253-9646; *Statistical Yearbook.*

INDONESIA - SENIOR CITIZENS

Facts on File, 460 Park Avenue South, New York, New York 10016 (800) 443-8323; *The New Book of World Rankings.*

INDONESIA - SESAME SEED PRODUCTION - See INDONESIA - CROPS

INDONESIA - SHEEP - See INDONESIA - LIVESTOCK AND POULTRY

INDONESIA - SILVER PRODUCTION AND CONSUMPTION - See INDONESIA - MINING AND MINERAL PRODUCTS

INDONESIA - SISAL PRODUCTION - See INDONESIA - CROPS

INDONESIA - SOCIAL DATA

Asian Development Bank, Post Office Box 789, 1099 Manila, Philippines; *Key Indicators of Developing Asian and Pacific Countries.*

Facts on File, 460 Park Avenue South, New York, New York 10016 (800) 443-8323; *The New Book of World Rankings.*

G.K. Hall and Company, 70 Lincoln Street, Boston, Massachusetts 02111 (617) 423-3990; *The World in Figures.*

INDONESIA - SOYBEAN PRODUCTION - See INDONESIA - CROPS

INDONESIA - STAMP TAXES AND DUTIES - See INDONESIA - TAXATION

INDONESIA - STATE BUDGET REVENUE AND EXPENDITURES

Euromonitor Publications Limited, 87-88 Turnmill Street, London EC1M 5QU, England; *International Marketing Data and Statistics.*

INDONESIA - STEEL - See INDONESIA - MINING AND MINERAL PRODUCTS

INDONESIA - STOCKS - COMMODITY - MARKET PRICE - INDEX

Food and Agricultural Organization of the United Nations (FAO) Via delle Terme di Caracalla, 00100 Rome, Italy (Telephone Number in U.S. (202) 653-2400); *The State of Food and Agriculture.*

INDONESIA - SUGAR PRODUCTION AND CONSUMPTION -See INDONESIA - CROPS

INDONESIA - TAXATION

G.K. Hall and Company, 70 Lincoln Street, Boston, Massachusetts 02111 (617) 423-3990; *The World in Figures.*

International Monetary Fund, 700 Nineteenth Street, NW, Washington, D.C. 20431 (202) 623-7000; *Government Finance Statistics Yearbook.*

International Road Federation, 525 School Street, SW, Washington, D.C. 20024 (202) 554-2106; *World Road Statistics.*

The World Bank, 1818 H Street, NW, Washington, D.C. 20433 (202) 477-1234; *World Tables.*

INDONESIA - TEA PRODUCTION - See INDONESIA - CROPS

INDONESIA - TELEGRAPH SERVICE

Statistical Office of the United Nations, Publishing Service, New York, New York 10017 (800) 253-9646; *Statistical Yearbook.*

INDONESIA - TELEPHONES IN USE

American Telephone and Telegraph Company, 26 Parsippany Road, Whippany, New Jersey 07981 (800) 338-4038; *The World's Telephones.*

Business International Asia/Pacific Ltd., 10/F, Luk Kwok Centre, 72 Gloucester Road, Hong Kong (Phone Number in U.S. (800) 938-4685); *Asian Market Atlas.*

Euromonitor Publications Limited, 87-88 Turnmill Street, London EC1M 5QU, England; *Third World Economic Handbook,* and *The Pacific Basin: An Economic Handbook.*

G.K. Hall and Company, 70 Lincoln Street, Boston, Massachusetts 02111 (617) 423-3990; *The World in Figures.*

Statistical Office of the United Nations, Publishing Service, New York, New York 10017 (800) 253-9646; *Statistical Yearbook.*

INDONESIA - TELEVISION BROADCASTING - See INDONESIA - BROADCASTING

INDONESIA - TELEVISION RECEIVER PRODUCTION

Statistical Office of the United Nations, Publishing Service, New York, New York 10017 (800) 253-9646; *Statistical Yearbook.*

INDONESIA - TEXTILE INDUSTRY

Euromonitor Publications Limited, 87-88 Turnmill Street, London EC1M 5QU, England; *Third World Economic Handbook.*

Forest and Paper Association, 1250 Connecticut Avenue, NW, Washington, D.C. 20036 (202) 463-2455; *Wood Pulp and Fiber Statistics.*

G.K. Hall and Company, 70 Lincoln Street, Boston, Massachusetts 02111 (617) 423-3990; *The World in Figures.*

Statistical Office of the United Nations, Publishing Service, New York, New York 10017 (800) 253-9646; *Statistical Yearbook.*

INDONESIA - THEATRE

United Nations Educational, Scientific and Cultural Organization (UNESCO), 7 Place de Fontenoy, F-75700 Paris, France (Telephone Number in U.S. (212) 963-5981); *Statistical Yearbook.*

INDONESIA - TIN - See INDONESIA -MINING AND MINERAL PRODUCTS

INDONESIA - TIRE (MOTOR VEHICLE) PRODUCTION

International Rubber Study Group, York House, 8th Floor, Empire Way, Wembley, London HA9 0PA, England; *Rubber Statistical Bulletin.*

INDONESIA - TIRE PRODUCTION

Statistical Office of the United Nations, Publishing Service, New York, New York 10017 (800) 253-9646; *Statistical Yearbook.*

INDONESIA - TOBACCO PRODUCTION

Commodity Research Bureau, Incorporated, 75 Wall Street, New York, New York 10005 (212) 504-7754; *Commodity Year Book.*

Euromonitor Publications Limited, 87-88 Turnmill Street, London EC1M 5QU, England; *Third World Economic Handbook.*

Facts on File, 460 Park Avenue South, New York, New York 10016 (800) 443-8323; *The New Book of World Rankings.*

Statistical Office of the United Nations, Publishing Service, New York, New York 10017 (800) 253-9646; *Statistical Yearbook.*

INDONESIA - TOURISM

Euromonitor Publications Limited, 87-88 Turnmill Street, London EC1M 5QU, England; *Third World Economic Handbook,* and *The Pacific Basin: An Economic Handbook.*

Facts on File, 460 Park Avenue South, New York, New York 10016 (800) 443-8323; *The New Book of World Rankings.*

G.K. Hall and Company, 70 Lincoln Street, Boston, Massachusetts 02111 (617) 423-3990; *The World in Figures.*

Statistical Office of the United Nations, Publishing Service, New York, New York 10017 (800) 253-9646; *Statistical Yearbook.*

Times Books, 201 East 50th Street, New York, New York 10022 (212) 751-2600; *The Economist Book of Vital World Statistics.*

World Tourism Organization, Calle Capitan Haya 42, E-28020 Madrid, Spain; *Yearbook of Tourism Statistics.*

INDONESIA - TRACTORS IN USE

Statistical Office of the United Nations, Publishing Service, New York, New York 10017 (800) 253-9646; *Statistical Yearbook.*

INDONESIA - TRADE - See INDONESIA - FOREIGN TRADE

INDONESIA - TRADEMARKS AND SERVICE MARKS

Statistical Office of the United Nations, Publishing Service, New York, New York 10017 (800) 253-9646; *Statistical Yearbook.*

World Intellectual Property Organization, 34 Chemin des Colombettes, CH-1211 Geneva 20, Switzerland; *Industrial Property Statistics.*

INDONESIA - TRANSPORTATION AND COMMUNICATIONS

Business International Asia/Pacific Ltd., 10/F, Luk Kwok Centre, 72 Gloucester Road, Hong Kong (Phone Number in U.S. (800) 938-4685); *Asian Market Atlas.*

Euromonitor Publications Limited, 87-88 Turnmill Street, London EC1M 5QU, England; *Third World Economic Handbook,* and *The Pacific Basin: An Economic Handbook.*

Facts on File, 460 Park Avenue South, New York, New York 10016 (800) 443-8323; *The New Book of World Rankings.*

G.K. Hall and Company, 70 Lincoln Street, Boston, Massachusetts 02111 (617) 423-3990; *The World in Figures.*

Statistical Office of the United Nations, Publishing Service, New York, New York 10017 (800) 253-9646; *Statistical Yearbook for Asia and the Pacific.*

INDONESIA - UNEMPLOYMENT

Euromonitor Publications Limited, 87-88 Turnmill Street, London EC1M 5QU, England; *International Marketing Data and Statistics,* and *The Pacific Basin: An Economic Handbook.*

International Labour Office, I.L.O. Publications, CH-1211, Geneva 22, Switzerland; *Yearbook of Labour Statistics.*

Statistical Office of the United Nations, Publishing Service, New York, New York 10017 (800) 253-9646; *Statistical Yearbook.*

INDONESIA - UTILITIES

Statistical Office of the United Nations, Publishing Service, New York, New York 10017 (800) 253-9646; *Electric Power in Asia and the Pacific.*

INDONESIA - VITAL STATISTICS

Euromonitor Publications Limited, 87-88 Turnmill Street, London EC1M 5QU, England; *International Marketing Data and Statistics, The Pacific Basin: An Economic Handbook,* and *Third World Economic Handbook.*

G.K. Hall and Company, 70 Lincoln Street, Boston, Massachusetts 02111 (617) 423-3990; *The World in Figures.*

Statistical Office of the United Nations, Publishing Service, New York, New York 10017 (800) 253-9646; *Statistical Yearbook.*

World Health Organization, Avenue Appia, Office of Publications, CH-1211 Geneva 27, Switzerland (Telephone Number in U.S. (518) 436-9686); *World Health Statistics Annual.*

INDONESIA - WAGES

G.K. Hall and Company, 70 Lincoln Street, Boston, Massachusetts 02111 (617) 423-3990; *The World in Figures.*

International Labour Office, I.L.O. Publications, CH-1211, Geneva 22, Switzerland; *Yearbook of Labour Statistics.*

Statistical Office of the United Nations, Publishing Service, New York, New York 10017 (800) 253-9646; *Statistical Yearbook for Asia and the Pacific.*

INDONESIA - WEATHER

Facts on File, 460 Park Avenue South, New York, New York 10016 (800) 443-8323; *The New Book of World Rankings.*

G.K. Hall and Company, 70 Lincoln Street, Boston, Massachusetts 02111 (617) 423-3990; *The World in Figures.*

INDONESIA - WHEAT PRODUCTION AND PRICES - See INDONESIA - CROPS

INDONESIA - WHOLESALE PRICES

Asian Development Bank, Post Office Box 789, 1099 Manila, Philippines; *Key Indicators of Developing Asian and Pacific Countries.*

INDONESIA - WHOLESALE TRADE

Euromonitor Publications Limited, 87-88 Turnmill Street, London EC1M 5QU, England; *Third World Economic Handbook.*

INDONESIA - WINE PRODUCTION

Facts on File, 460 Park Avenue South, New York, New York 10016 (800) 443-8323; *The New Book of World Rankings.*

INDONESIA - WOOD AND WOOD PULP - See INDONESIA - FORESTRY AND FOREST PRODUCTS

INDONESIA - WOOL PRODUCTION

Facts on File, 460 Park Avenue South, New York, New York 10016 (800) 443-8323; *The New Book of World Rankings.*

INDONESIA - YARN PRODUCTION

Statistical Office of the United Nations, Publishing Service, New York, New York 10017 (800) 253-9646; *Statistical Yearbook.*

INDONESIA - ZOOS AND BOTANICAL GARDENS

United Nations Educational, Scientific and Cultural Organization (UNESCO), 7 Place de Fontenoy, F-75700 Paris, France (Telephone Number in U.S. (212) 963-5981); *Statistical Yearbook.*

INDUSTRIAL AND COMMERCIAL ENTERPRISES - FAILURES

Dun and Bradstreet, Corporation, 299 Park Avenue, New York, New York 10171 (212) 593-6800; *Monthly Failure Report, Business Failure Record,* and *New Business Incorporations.*

U.S. Department of Commerce, Bureau of the Census, Suitland, Maryland 20233 (301) 763-4040; *County Business Patterns.*

INDUSTRIAL MINERALS

U.S. Department of the Interior, Bureau of Mines, 810 Seventh Street, NW, Washington, D.C. 20241 (202) 501-9649; *Annual Reports,* and *Mineral Commodities Summaries.*

INDUSTRIAL PRODUCTION INDEXES

Board of Governors of the Federal Reserve System, Twentieth Street and Constitution Avenue, NW, Washington, D.C. 20551 (202) 452-3000; *Federal Reserve Bulletin.*

INDUSTRIAL PRODUCTION INDEXES - FOREIGN COUNTRIES

Organization for Economic Cooperation and Development, Publication and Information Center, 2001 L Street, NW, Washington, D.C. 20036 (202) 785-6323; *Main Economic Indicators, Historical Statistics,* and *Main Economic Indicators.*

INDUSTRY - See CORPORATIONS and Individual Industries

INFANT DEATHS - See also DEATHS and DEATH RATES

U.S. Department of Health and Human Services, National Center for Health Statistics, 3700 East-West Highway, Hyattsville, Maryland 20782 (301) 436-8500; *Monthly Vital Statistics Report, Vital Statistics of the United States,* and unpublished data.

INFANT DEATHS - CAUSE

U.S. Department of Health and Human Services, National Center for Health Statistics, 3700 East-West Highway, Hyattsville, Maryland 20782 (301) 436-8500; *Monthly Vital Statistics Report,* and *Vital Statistics of the United States.*

INFANT DEATHS - METROPOLITAN AREAS

U.S. Department of Health and Human Services, National Center for Health Statistics, 3700 East-West Highway, Hyattsville, Maryland 20782 (301) 436-8500; *Vital Statistics of the United States,* and unpublished data.

INFLUENZA

U.S. Department of Health and Human Services, National Center for Health Statistics, 3700 East-West Highway, Hyattsville, Maryland 20782 (301) 436-8500; *Monthly Vital Statistics Report, Vital Statistics of the United States,* and unpublished data.

INFRASTRUCTURE EXPENDITURES - See GOVERNMENT

INHALANTS - PERSONS USING

U.S. Department of Health and Human Services, Substance Abuse and Mental Health Services Administration, 5600 Fishers Lane, Rockville, Maryland 20857 (301) 443-4797; *National Household Survey on Drug Abuse.*

INJURIES - See also ACCIDENTS and OCCUPATIONAL SAFETY

National Safety Council, 1121 Spring Lake Drive, Itasca, Illinois 60143-3201 (708) 285-1121; *Accident Facts.*

U.S. Department of Health and Human Services, National Center for Health Statistics, 3700 East-West Highway, Hyattsville, Maryland 20782 (301) 436-8500; *Vital and Health Statistics,* and unpublished data.

U.S. Department of Labor, Bureau of Labor Statistics, Two Massachusetts Avenue, NE, Washington, D.C. 20212 (202) 606-7828; *Occupational Injuries and Illnesses in the United States by Industry.*

U.S. Department of Labor, Mine Safety and Health Administration, 4015 Wilson Boulevard, Arlington, Virginia 22203 (703) 235-1452; unpublished data.

U.S. Department of Transportation, Federal Railroad Administration, 400 Seventh Street, SW, Washington, D.C. 20590 (202) 366-0881; *Accident Bulletin.*

INMATES - See also CORRECTIONAL INSTITUTIONS

U.S. Department of Commerce, Bureau of the Census, Suitland, Maryland 20233 (301) 763-4040; *Census of Population, General Population Characteristics, Current Population Reports,* and unpublished data.

U.S. Department of Justice, Bureau of Justice Statistics, 633 Indiana Avenue, NW, Washington, D.C. 20531 (800) 732-3277; *Jail Inmates, Census of Local Jails, Prisoners in State and Federal Institutions on December 31, Correctional Populations in the U.S., Profile of State Prison Inmates*, and *Survey of State Prison Inmates*.

INSTALLMENT LOANS - See also LOANS and MORTGAGES

American Bankers Association, 1120 Connecticut Avenue, NW, Washington, D.C. 20036 (202) 663-5000; *Consumer Credit Delinquency Bulletin*.

Board of Governors of the Federal Reserve System, Twentieth Street and Constitution Avenue, NW, Washington, D.C. 20551 (202) 452-3000; *Federal Reserve Bulletin, Annual Statistical Digest*, and unpublished data.

INSTITUTIONAL CARE FACILITIES - See also HOSPITALS and NURSING and RELATED CARE FACILITIES

American Hospital Association, 840 North Lake Shore Drive, Chicago, Illinois 60611 (312) 280-6000; *Hospital Statistics*, and unpublished data.

U.S. Department of Health and Human Services, National Center for Health Statistics, 3700 East-West Highway, Hyattsville, Maryland 20782 (301) 436-8500; *Advance Data from Vital and Health Statistics*, and unpublished data.

INSTITUTIONAL POPULATION

U.S. Department of Commerce, Bureau of the Census, Suitland, Maryland 20233 (301) 763-4040; *Census of Population*.

INSTITUTIONAL POPULATION - MENTALLY ILL RETARDED

Center for Residential and Community Services, University of Minnesota, Minneapolis, Minnesota; unpublished data.

U.S. Department of Health and Human Services, Substance Abuse and Mental Health Services Administration, 56 Fishers Lane, Rockville, Maryland 20857 (301) 443-3875; *Advance Data*, Number 143 and unpublished data.

INSTITUTIONAL POPULATION - PRISONERS

U.S. Department of Justice, Bureau of Justice Statistics, 633 Indiana Avenue, NW, Washington, D.C. 20531 (800) 732-3277; *Prisoners in 1991, Correctional Populations in the U.S., Prisoners in State and Federal Institutions on December 31, Profile of State Prison Inmates*, and *Survey of State Prison Inmates*.

INSTITUTIONS - See HOSPITALS and Other Individual Facilities

INSTITUTIONS OF HIGHER EDUCATION - See EDUCATION

INSTRUMENTS AND RELATED PRODUCTS - MANUFACTURING - CAPITAL

The Conference Board, 845 Third Avenue, New York, New York 10022 (212) 759-0900; *Quarterly Survey of Capital Appropriations*.

U.S. Department of Commerce, Bureau of Economic Analysis, Fourteenth Street between Constitution Avenue and E Street, NW, Washington, D.C. 20230 (202) 606-9900; *Fixed Reproducible Tangible Wealth in the United States*, and *Survey of Current Business*.

INSTRUMENTS AND RELATED PRODUCTS - MANUFACTURING - EARNINGS

U.S. Department of Commerce, Bureau of the Census, Suitland, Maryland 20233 (301) 763-4040; *Census of Manufactures, Annual Survey of Manufactures*, and *County Business Patterns*.

U.S. Department of Labor, Bureau of Labor Statistics, Two Massachusetts Avenue, NE, Washington, D.C. 20212 (202) 606-7828; *Employment and Earnings, Monthly Labor Review*, and Bulletins 2370 and 2429.

INSTRUMENTS AND RELATED PRODUCTS - MANUFACTURING - EMPLOYEES

U.S. Department of Commerce, Bureau of the Census, Suitland, Maryland 20233 (301) 763-4040; *Census of Manufactures, Annual Survey of Manufactures*, and *County Business Patterns*.

U.S. Department of Labor, Bureau of Labor Statistics, Two Massachusetts Avenue, NE, Washington, D.C. 20212 (202) 606-7828; *Employment and Earnings, Monthly Labor Review*, and Bulletins 2370 and 2429.

INSTRUMENTS AND RELATED PRODUCTS - MANUFACTURING - ESTABLISHMENTS

U.S. Department of Commerce, Bureau of the Census, Suitland, Maryland 20233 (301) 763-4040; *Census of Manufactures, Annual Survey of Manufactures*, and *County Business Patterns*.

INSTRUMENTS AND RELATED PRODUCTS - MANUFACTURING - FOREIGN TRADE

U.S. Department of Commerce, Bureau of the Census, Suitland, Maryland 20233 (301) 763-4040; *U.S. Merchandise Trade*.

INSTRUMENTS AND RELATED PRODUCTS - MANUFACTURING - GROSS DOMESTIC PRODUCT

U.S. Department of Commerce, Bureau of Economic Analysis, Fourteenth Street between Constitution Avenue and E Street, NW, Washington, D.C. 20230 (202) 606-9900; *Survey of Current Business*, and *The National Income and Product Accounts of the United States*.

INSTRUMENTS AND RELATED PRODUCTS - MANUFACTURING - INVENTORIES

U.S. Department of Commerce, Bureau of the Census, Suitland, Maryland 20233 (301) 763-4040; *Current Industrial Reports, Manufactures' Shipments, Inventories, and Orders*.

INSTRUMENTS AND RELATED PRODUCTS - MANUFACTURING - MERGERS AND ACQUISITIONS

Securities Data Company, 1180 Raymond Boulevard, Newark, New Jersey 07102 (201) 622-3100; *Merger and Corporate Transactions Database*.

INSTRUMENTS AND RELATED PRODUCTS - MANUFACTURING - OCCUPATIONAL SAFETY

U.S. Department of Labor, Bureau of Labor Statistics, Two Massachusetts Avenue, NE, Washington, D.C. 20212 (202) 606-7828; *Occupational Injuries and Illnesses in the United States by Industry*.

INSTRUMENTS AND RELATED PRODUCTS - MANUFACTURING - PATENTS

U.S. Department of Commerce, Patent and Trademark Office, 2011 Crystal Drive, Arlington, Virginia 22202 (703) 305-8341; *Patenting Trends in the United States, State Country Report.*

INSTRUMENTS AND RELATED PRODUCTS - MANUFACTURING - PRODUCTIVITY

Board of Governors of the Federal Reserve System, Twentieth Street and Constitution Avenue, NW, Washington, D.C. 20551 (202) 452-3000; *Federal Reserve Bulletin.*

U.S. Department of Labor, Bureau of Labor Statistics, Two Massachusetts Avenue, NE, Washington, D.C. 20212 (202) 606-7828; *Productivity Measures for Selected Industries and Government Service,* and unpublished data.

INSTRUMENTS AND RELATED PRODUCTS - MANUFACTURING - PROFITS

Executive Office of the President, Council of Economic Advisers, Executive Office Building, Washington, D.C. 20506 (202) 395-5084; *Economic Report of the President.*

U.S. Department of Commerce, Bureau of the Census, Suitland, Maryland 20233 (301) 763-4040; *Quarterly Financial Report for Manufacturing, Mining and Trade Corporations.*

INSTRUMENTS AND RELATED PRODUCTS - MANUFACTURING - RESEARCH AND DEVELOPMENT

National Science Foundation, 4201 Wilson Boulevard, Arlington, Virginia 22230 (703) 306-1234; *Research and Development in Industry.*

INSTRUMENTS AND RELATED PRODUCTS - MANUFACTURING - SHIPMENTS

U.S. Department of Commerce, Bureau of the Census, Suitland, Maryland 20233 (301) 763-4040; *Annual Survey of Manufactures, Census of Manufactures,* and *Current Industrial Reports, Manufactures' Shipments, Inventories, and Orders.*

INSTRUMENTS AND RELATED PRODUCTS - MANUFACTURING - VALUE ADDED

U.S. Department of Commerce, Bureau of the Census, Suitland, Maryland 20233 (301) 763-4040; *Census of Manufactures,* and *Annual Survey of Manufactures.*

INSURANCE - See also Individual Forms of Insurance

INSURANCE - MEDICAL CARE

Health Insurance Association of America, 1025 Connecticut Avenue, NW, Washington, D.C. 20036 (202) 223-7780; *Source Book of Health Insurance Data.*

U.S. Department of Health and Human Services, Health Care Financing Administration, SW, Washington, D.C. 20201 (202) 245-6113; *Health Care Financing Review,* and unpublished data.
U.S. Department of Labor, Bureau of Labor Statistics, Two Massachusetts Avenue, NE, Washington, D.C. 20212 (202) 606-7828; *CPI Detailed Report,* and unpublished data.

INSURANCE AGENTS, BROKERS AND SERVICE - ADVERTISING EXPENDITURES

Publishers Information Bureau, Incorporated, 575 Lexington Avenue, New York, New York 10022 (212) 752-0055; compiled by Leading National Advertisers, 11 West 42nd Street, New York, New York 10036 (212) 789-1400.

Television Bureau of Advertising, Incorporated, 850 Third Avenue, New York, New York 10022 (212) 486-1111; from data compiled by Competitive Media Reporting, 11 West 42nd Street, New York, New York 10036 (212) 789-1400.

INSURANCE AGENTS, BROKERS AND SERVICE - EARNINGS

U.S. Department of Commerce, Bureau of the Census, Suitland, Maryland 20233 (301) 763-4040; *County Business Patterns.*

U.S. Department of Labor, Bureau of Labor Statistics, Two Massachusetts Avenue, NE, Washington, D.C. 20212 (202) 606-7828; *Employment and Earnings,* and Bulletins 2370 and 2429.

INSURANCE AGENTS, BROKERS, AND SERVICE - EMPLOYEES

U.S. Department of Commerce, Bureau of the Census, Suitland, Maryland 20233 (301) 763-4040; *County Business Patterns.*

U.S. Department of Commerce, Bureau of Economic Analysis, Fourteenth Street between Constitution Avenue and E Street, NW, Washington, D.C. 20230 (202) 606-9900; *Survey of Current Business,* and *The National Income and Product Accounts of the United States.*

U.S. Department of Labor, Bureau of Labor Statistics, Two Massachusetts Avenue, NE, Washington, D.C. 20212 (202) 606-7828; *Employment and Earnings,* and Bulletins 2370 and 2429.

INSURANCE AGENTS, BROKERS AND SERVICE - ESTABLISHMENTS

Federal Deposit Insurance Corporation, 550 Seventeenth Street, NW, Washington, D.C. 20429 (202) 393-8400; *Statistics on Banking.*

U.S. Department of Commerce, Bureau of the Census, Suitland, Maryland 20233 (301) 763-4040; *County Business Patterns.*

INSURANCE AGENTS, BROKERS AND SERVICE - FINANCES

Health Insurance Association of America, 1025 Connecticut Avenue, NW, Suite 1200, Washington, D.C. 20036 (202) 223-7780; *Source Book of Health Insurance Data.*

U.S. Department of Commerce, International Trade Administration, Fourteenth Street between Constitution Avenue and E Street, NW, Washington, D.C. 20230 (202) 482-3809; *U.S. Industrial Outlook.*

U.S. Department of Health and Human Services, Health Care Financing Administration, 200 Independence Avenue, SW, Washington, D.C. 20201 (202) 245-6113; *Health Care Financing Review,* and unpublished data.

INSURANCE AGENTS, BROKERS AND SERVICE - FOREIGN INVESTMENTS IN THE UNITED STATES

U.S. Department of Commerce, Bureau of Economic Analysis, 14th Street between Constitution Avenue and E Street, NW, Washington, D.C. 20230 (202) 606-9900; *Survey of Current Business,* and unpublished data.

INSURANCE AGENTS, BROKERS AND SERVICE - GROSS DOMESTIC PRODUCT

U.S. Department of Commerce, Bureau of Economic Analysis, Fourteenth Street between Constitution Avenue and E Street, NW, Washington, D.C. 20230 (202) 606-9900; *The National Income and Product Accounts of the United States*, and *Survey of Current Business.*

INSURANCE AGENTS, BROKERS AND SERVICE - OCCUPATIONAL SAFETY

U.S. Department of Labor, Bureau of Labor Statistics, Two Massachusetts Avenue, NE, Washington, D.C. 20212 (202) 606-7828; *Occupational Injuries and Illnesses in the United States by Industry.*

INSURANCE CARRIERS - EARNINGS

U.S. Department of Commerce, Bureau of the Census, Suitland, Maryland 20233 (301) 763-4040; *County Business Patterns.*

U.S. Department of Labor, Bureau of Labor Statistics, Two Massachusetts Avenue, NE, Washington, D.C. 20212 (202) 606-7828; *Employment and Earnings*, and Bulletins 2370 and 2429.

INSURANCE CARRIERS - EMPLOYEES

U.S. Department of Commerce, Bureau of Economic Analysis, Fourteenth Street between Constitution Avenue and E Street, NW, Washington, D.C. 20230 (202) 606-9900; *Survey of Current Business*, and *The National Income and Product Accounts of the United States.*

U.S. Department of Commerce, Bureau of the Census, Suitland, Maryland 20233 (301) 763-4040; *County Business Patterns.*

U.S. Department of Labor, Bureau of Labor Statistics, Two Massachusetts Avenue, NE, Washington, D.C. 20212 (202) 606-7828; *Employment and Earnings*, and Bulletins 2370 and 2429.

INSURANCE CARRIERS - ESTABLISHMENTS

U.S. Department of Commerce, Bureau of the Census, Suitland, Maryland 20233 (301) 763-4040; *County Business Patterns.*

INSURANCE CARRIERS - FINANCES

Access Research, Inc., 8 Griffen Road North, Windsor, Connecticut 06095 (203) 688-8821; *Marketplace Update.*

Board of Governors of the Federal Reserve System, Twentieth Street and Constitution Avenue, NW, Washington, D.C. 20551 (202) 452-3000; *Annual Statistical Digest.*

U.S. Department of Commerce, International Trade Administration, Fourteenth Street between Constitution Avenue and E Street, NW, Washington, D.C. 20230 (202) 482-3809; *U.S. Industrial Outlook.*

INSURANCE CARRIERS - GROSS DOMESTIC PRODUCT

U.S. Department of Commerce, Bureau of Economic Analysis, Fourteenth Street between Constitution Avenue and E Street, NW, Washington, D.C. 20230 (202) 606-9900; *Survey of Current Business*, and *The National Income and Product Accounts of the United States.*

INSURANCE CARRIERS - OCCUPATIONAL SAFETY

U.S. Department of Labor, Bureau of Labor Statistics, Two Massachusetts Avenue, NE, Washington, D.C. 20212 (202) 606-7828; *Occupational Injuries and Illnesses in the United States by Industry.*

INSURANCE CARRIERS - PROFITS

U.S. Department of Commerce, International Trade Administration, Fourteenth Street between Constitution Avenue and E Street, NW, Washington, D.C. 20230 (202) 482-3809; *U.S. Industrial Outlook.*

INSURANCE, GOVERNMENT - See SOCIAL INSURANCE

INTER-AMERICAN DEVELOPMENT BANK

U.S. Department of Commerce, Bureau of Economic Analysis, Fourteenth Street between Constitution Avenue and E Street, NW, Washington, D.C. 20230 (202) 606-9900; press releases and unpublished data.

INTERCITY TRAFFIC

American Bus Association, 1100 New York Avenue, NW, Washington, D.C. 20005 (202) 842-1645; *Annual Report*, and *Bus Facts*, annual.

Eno Transportation Foundation, 44211 Statestone Court, Lansdowne, Virginia 22075 (703) 729-7200; *Transportation in America.*

U.S. Interstate Commerce Commission, Twelfth Street and Constitution Avenue, NW, Washington, D.C. 20423 (202) 275-7119; *Transport Statistics in the United States.*

INTEREST - NATIONAL INCOME COMPONENT

U.S. Department of Commerce, Bureau of Economic Analysis, Fourteenth Street between Constitution Avenue and E Street, NW, Washington, D.C. 20230 (202) 606-9900; *Survey of Current Business*, and *The National Income and Product Accounts of the United States*,.

INTEREST - PAYMENTS - FEDERAL GOVERNMENT

Executive Office of the President, Office of Management and Budget, Executive Office Building, Washington, D.C. 20503 (202) 395-3080; *Budget of the United States Government.*

INTEREST - RECEIPTS - INDIVIDUAL INCOME TAX RETURNS

U.S. Department of the Treasury, Internal Revenue Service, 1111 Constitution Avenue, NW, Washington, D.C. 20224 (202) 566-5000; *Statistics of Income, Individual Income Tax Returns*, and *Statistics of Income Bulletin.*

INTEREST - RECEIPTS - NATIONAL AND PERSONAL INCOME COMPONENT

U.S. Department of Commerce, Bureau of Economic Analysis, Fourteenth Street between Constitution Avenue and E Street, NW, Washington, D.C. 20230 (202) 606-9900; *The National Income and Product Accounts of the United States*, and *Survey of Current Business.*

INTEREST RATES

Board of Governors of the Federal Reserve System, Twentieth Street and Constitution Avenue, NW, Washington, D.C. 20551 (202) 452-

3000; *Federal Reserve Bulletin, Annual Statistical Digest, Money Stock, Liquid Assets, and Debt Measures, Federal Reserve Statistical Release H.6. Special Supplementary Table,* and *Monthly Survey of Selected Deposits.*

Financial Rates, Inc., 860 U.S. Highway One, North Palm Beach, Florida 33408 (407) 627-7330; *Bank Rate Monitor.*

IBC/Donoghue, Inc., 290 Eliot Street, Ashland, Massachusetts 01721 (508) 881-2800; *IBC/Donoghue's Money Market Insight.*

INTEREST RATES - MORTGAGES

Board of Governors of the Federal Reserve System, Twentieth Street and Constitution Avenue, NW, Washington, D.C. 20551 (202) 452-3000; *Federal Reserve Bulletin,* and *Annual Statistical Digest.*

Federal Housing Finance Board, 1777 F Street, NW, Washington, D.C. 20006 (202) 408-2500; annual and monthly press releases.

INTERMEDIATE GOODS - PRICE INDEXES - PRODUCER

U.S. Department of Labor, Bureau of Labor Statistics, Two Massachusetts Avenue, NE, Washington, D.C. 20212 (202) 606-7828; *Monthly Labor Review.*

INTERNAL REVENUE - COLLECTIONS - See also TAX RECEIPTS

U.S. Department of the Treasury, Internal Revenue Service, 1111 Constitution Avenue, NW, Washington, D.C. 20224 (202) 566-5000; *Annual Report of the Commissioner and Chief Counsel of the Internal Revenue Service.*

INTERNAL WATERWAYS - TRAFFIC

U.S. Department of the Army, Corps of Engineers, The Pentagon, Washington, D.C. 20301 (202) 545-6700; *Waterborne Commerce of the United States.*

INTERNATIONAL AFFAIRS - BALANCE OF TRADE

U.S. Department of Commerce, Bureau of the Census, Suitland, Maryland 20233 (301) 763-4040; *U.S. Merchandise Trade: Exports, General Imports, and Imports for Consumption.*

INTERNATIONAL AFFAIRS - COMMERCE

U.S. Department of Commerce, Bureau of the Census, Suitland, Maryland 20233 (301) 763-4040; *U.S. Merchandise Trade: Selected Highlights, Foreign Commerce and Navigation of the United States, U.S. Merchandise Trade: Exports, General Imports, and Imports for Consumption, U.S. Trade with Puerto Rico and U.S. Possessions,* and FT 990.

INTERNATIONAL AFFAIRS - FEDERAL OUTLAYS

Executive Office of the President, Office of Management and Budget, Executive Office Building, Washington, D.C. 20503 (202) 395-3080; *Budget of the United States Government.*

INTERNATIONAL AFFAIRS - FOREIGN EXCHANGE RATES

Board of Governors of the Federal Reserve System, Twentieth Street and Constitution Avenue, NW, Washington, D.C. 20551 (202) 452-3000; *Federal Reserve Bulletin.*

INTERNATIONAL AFFAIRS - FOREIGN INVESTMENTS IN UNITED STATES

U.S. Department of Commerce, Bureau of Economic Analysis, Fourteenth Street between Constitution Avenue and E Street, NW, Washington, D.C. 20230 (202) 606-9900; *Survey of Current Business.*

INTERNATIONAL AFFAIRS - INTERNATIONAL TRANSACTIONS - UNITED STATES

Executive Office of the President, Council of Economic Advisers, Old Executive Office Building, Washington, D.C. 20500 (202) 395-5084; *Economic Indicators,* and *Economic Report of the President.*

U.S. Department of Commerce, Bureau of Economic Analysis, Fourteenth Street between Constitution Avenue and E Street, NW, Washington, D.C. 20230 (202) 606-9900; *Survey of Current Business.*

INTERNATIONAL AFFAIRS - RECEIPTS AND PAYMENTS FOR TRANSPORTATION

U.S. Department of Commerce, Bureau of Economic Analysis, Fourteenth Street between Constitution Avenue and E Street, NW, Washington, D.C. 20230 (202) 606-9900; *Survey of Current Business,* and unpublished data.

INTERNATIONAL AFFAIRS - UNITED STATES GOVERNMENT AID

U.S. Agency for International Development, 320 Twenty-first Street, NW, Washington, D.C. 20523 (202) 647-9620; *United States Overseas Loans and Grants and Assistance from International Organizations,* and unpublished data.

U.S. Department of Commerce, Bureau of Economic Analysis, Fourteenth Street between Constitution Avenue and E Street, NW, Washington, D.C. 20230 (202) 606-9900; press releases and unpublished data.

INTERNATIONAL AFFAIRS - UNITED STATES INVESTMENTS

U.S. Department of Commerce, Bureau of Economic Analysis, Fourteenth Street between Constitution Avenue and E Street, NW, Washington, D.C. 20230 (202) 606-9900; *Survey of Current Business.*

INTERNATIONAL BANK FOR RECONSTRUCTION AND DEVELOPMENT

U.S. Department of Commerce, Bureau of Economic Analysis, Fourteenth Street between Constitution Avenue and E Street, NW, Washington, D.C. 20230 (202) 606-9900; press releases and unpublished data.

INTERNATIONAL DEVELOPMENT ASSOCIATION

U.S. Department of Commerce, Bureau of Economic Analysis, Fourteenth Street between Constitution Avenue and E Street, NW, Washington, D.C. 20230 (202) 606-9900; press releases and unpublished data.

INTERNATIONAL FINANCE CORPORATION

U.S. Department of Commerce, Bureau of Economic Analysis, Fourteenth Street between Constitution Avenue and E Street, NW, Washington, D.C. 20230 (202) 606-9900; press releases and unpublished data.

INTERNATIONAL INVESTMENT POSITION - UNITED STATES

U.S. Department of Commerce, Bureau of Economic Analysis, Fourteenth Street between Constitution Avenue and E Street, NW, Washington, D.C. 20230 (202) 606-9900; *Survey of Current Business*, press releases and unpublished data.

INTERNATIONAL MAIL - UNITED STATES POSTAL

U.S. Postal Service, 475 L'Enfant Plaza West, SW, Washington, D.C. 20260 (202) 268-2000; *Annual Report of the Postmaster General*.

INTERRACIAL MARRIED COUPLES

U.S. Department of Commerce, Bureau of the Census, Suitland, Maryland 20233 (301) 763-4040; *Current Population Reports*.

INVENTORIES - See also STOCKS - COMMODITY

U.S. Department of Commerce, Bureau of the Census, Suitland, Maryland 20233 (301) 763-4040; *Current Business Reports, Combined Annual and Revised Monthly Retail Trade, Current Industrial Reports, Manufactures' Shipments, Inventories, and Orders*, and *Combined Annual and Revised Monthly Wholesale Trade*.

INVENTORIES - BUSINESS (GDP)

U.S. Department of Commerce, Bureau of Economic Analysis, Fourteenth Street between Constitution Avenue and E Street, NW, Washington, D.C. 20230 (202) 606-9900; *The National Income and Product Accounts of the United States, Survey of Current Business*, and unpublished data.

INVESTMENTS - See also CAPITAL STOCK AND SECURITIES

INVESTMENTS - FOREIGN - IN UNITED STATES

U.S. Department of Commerce, Bureau of Economic Analysis, Fourteenth Street between Constitution Avenue and E Street, NW, Washington, D.C. 20230 (202) 606-9900; *Survey of Current Business*, and unpublished data.

INVESTMENTS - FOREIGN - IN UNITED STATES - MANUFACTURING INDUSTRIES

U.S. Department of Commerce, Bureau of Economic Analysis, Fourteenth Street between Constitution Avenue and E Street, NW, Washington, D.C. 20230 (202) 606-9900; *Survey of Current Business*.

INVESTMENTS - MANUFACTURING INDUSTRIES

U.S. Department of Commerce, Bureau of Economic Analysis, Fourteenth Street between Constitution Avenue and E Street, NW, Washington, D.C. 20230 (202) 606-9900; *The National Income and Product Accounts of the United States*, and *Survey of Current Business*, and unpublished data.

INVESTMENTS - PRIVATE DOMESTIC - GROSS

U.S. Department of Commerce, Bureau of Economic Analysis, Fourteenth Street between Constitution Avenue and E Street, NW, Washington, D.C. 20230 (202) 606-9900; *The National Income and Product Accounts of the United States*, and *Survey of Current Business*.

INVESTMENTS - UNITED STATES GOVERNMENT OBLIGATIONS

U.S. Department of the Treasury, Fifteenth Street and Pennsylvania Avenue, NW, Washington, D.C. 20220 (202) 566-2000; *Treasury Bulletin*, quarterly.

U.S. Federal Deposit Insurance Corporation, 550 Seventeenth Street, NW, Washington, D.C. 20429 (202) 393-8400; *The FDIC Quarterly Banking Profile*, *Statistics on Banking*, and *Annual Report*.

INVESTMENTS - UNITED STATES INTERNATIONAL

U.S. Department of Commerce, Bureau of Economic Analysis, Fourteenth Street between Constitution Avenue and E Street, NW, Washington, D.C. 20230 (202) 606-9900; *Survey of Current Business*.

INVESTMENTS - VENTURE CAPITAL

Venture Economics Investor Services, 30 Pittsburgh Street, Boston, Massachusetts 02210 (617) 345-2824; *Venture Capital Journal*.

IOWA - See also STATE DATA (FOR INDIVIDUAL STATES)

Iowa - Primary Statistics Source

Iowa Department of Economic Development, Research Bureau, 200 East Grand Avenue, Des Moines, Iowa 50309; *Statistical Profile of Iowa*.

Iowa - State Data Centers

State Library of Iowa, East Twelfth and Grand, Des Moines, Iowa 50319, Ms. Beth Henning (515) 281-4350.

Census Services, Iowa State University, 320 East Hall, Ames, Iowa 50011, Dr. Willis Goudy (515) 294-8337.

Center for Social and Behavioral Research, University of Northern Iowa, Cedar Falls, Iowa 50614, Dr. Robert Kramer (319) 273-2105.

Iowa Social Science Institute, University of Iowa, 345 Shaeffer Hall, Iowa City, Iowa 52242, Mr. Joyce Baker (319) 335-2371.

Census Data Center, Department of Education, Grimes State Office Building, Des Moines, Iowa 50319, Mr. Steve Boal, (515) 281-4730.

Iran - National Statistical Office

Iranian Statistical Centre, Dr Fatemi Avenue, Tehran, Iran.

Iran - Primary Statistics Sources

Iranian Statistical Centre, Dr Fatemi Avenue, Tehran, Iran, *Statistical Yearbook*, and *Statistical Reflection of the Islamic Republic of Iran*.

IRAN - AGRICULTURE

Euromonitor Publications Limited, 87-88 Turnmill Street, London EC1M 5QU, England; *International Marketing Data and Statistics*, and *Middle East Economic Handbook*.

Facts on File, 460 Park Avenue South, New York, New York 10016 (800) 443-8323; *The New Book of World Rankings*.

Food and Agricultural Organization of the United Nations (FAO), Via delle Terme di Caracalla, 00100 Rome, Italy (Telephone Number in U.S. (202) 606-7828); *Production Yearbook*, and *The State of Food and Agriculture*.

G.K. Hall and Company, 70 Lincoln Street, Boston, Massachusetts 02111 (617) 423-3990; *The World in Figures*.

Statistical Office of the United Nations, Publishing Service, New York, New York 10017 (800) 253-9646; *Statistical Yearbook*, and *Statistical Yearbook for Asia and the Pacific*.

Times Books, 201 East 50th Street, New York, New York 10022 (212) 751-2600; *The Economist Book of Vital World Statistics*.

IRAN - AIRLINE SERVICE

Facts on File, 460 Park Avenue South, New York, New York 10016 (800) 443-8323; *The New Book of World Rankings*.

G.K. Hall and Company, 70 Lincoln Street, Boston, Massachusetts 02111 (617) 423-3990; *The World in Figures*.

International Civil Aviation Organization, 1000 Sherbrooke Street West, Suite 400, Montreal, Quebec, Canada H3A 2R2 (514) 285-8219; *Civil Aviation Statistics of the World*.

Statistical Office of the United Nations, Publishing Service, New York, New York 10017 (800) 253-9646; *Statistical Yearbook*.

Times Books, 201 East 50th Street, New York, New York 10022 (212) 751-2600; *The Economist Book of Vital World Statistics*.

IRAN - ALMOND PRODUCTION - See IRAN - CROPS

IRAN - ALUMINUM PRODUCTION AND CONSUMPTION - See IRAN - MINING AND MINERAL PRODUCTS

IRAN - ANIMAL HEALTH

Food and Agricultural Organization of the United Nations (FAO), Via delle Terme di Caracalla, 00100 Rome, Italy (Telephone Number in U.S. (202) 606-7828); *Animal Health Yearbook*.

IRAN - AREA AND DENSITY OF POPULATION

Euromonitor Publications Limited, 87-88 Turnmill Street, London EC1M 5QU, England; *International Marketing Data and Statistics*, and *Middle East Economic Handbook*.

Facts on File, 460 Park Avenue South, New York, New York 10016 (800) 443-8323; *The New Book of World Rankings*.

Food and Agricultural Organization of the United Nations (FAO) Via delle Terme di Caracalla, 00100 Rome, Italy (Telephone Number in U.S. (202) 606-7828); *The State of Food and Agriculture*.

G.K. Hall and Company, 70 Lincoln Street, Boston, Massachusetts 02111 (617) 423-3990; *The World in Figures*.

Statistical Office of the United Nations, Publishing Service, New York, New York 10017 (800) 253-9646; *Statistical Yearbook*.

Times Books, 201 East 50th Street, New York, New York 10022 (212) 751-2600; *The Economist Book of Vital World Statistics*.

United Nations Educational, Scientific and Cultural Organization (UNESCO), 7 Place de Fontenoy, F-75700 Paris, France (Telephone Number in U.S. (212) 963-5981); *Statistical Yearbook*.

IRAN - ARMS EXPORTS AND IMPORTS

U.S. Arms Control and Disarmament Agency, 320 Twenty-first Street, Northwest, Washington, D.C. 20451 (202) 647-8677; *World Military Expenditures and Arms Transfers*.

IRAN - BALANCE OF PAYMENTS

The Economist Intelligence Unit, 111 West 57th Street, New York, New York 10019 (800) 938-4685; *The World Market Atlas*.

Euromonitor Publications Limited, 87-88 Turnmill Street, London EC1M 5QU, England; *Third World Economic Handbook*.

G.K. Hall and Company, 70 Lincoln Street, Boston, Massachusetts 02111 (617) 423-3990; *The World in Figures*.

International Monetary Fund, 700 Nineteenth Street, NW, Washington, D.C. 20431 (202) 623-7000; *Balance of Payments Yearbook*.

Times Books, 201 East 50th Street, New York, New York 10022 (212) 751-2600; *The Economist Book of Vital World Statistics*.

IRAN - BANKING

Facts on File, 460 Park Avenue South, New York, New York 10016 (800) 443-8323; *The New Book of World Rankings*.

G.K. Hall and Company, 70 Lincoln Street, Boston, Massachusetts 02111 (617) 423-3990; *The World in Figures*.

International Monetary Fund, 700 Nineteenth Street, NW, Washington, D.C. 20431 (202) 623-7000; *International Financial Statistics*.

Statistical Office of the United Nations, Publishing Service, New York, New York 10017 (800) 253-9646; *Statistical Yearbook*.

IRAN - BARLEY PRODUCTION - See IRAN - CROPS

IRAN - BAUXITE PRODUCTION AND CONSUMPTION - See IRAN - MINING AND MINERAL PRODUCTS

IRAN - BEER PRODUCTION

Facts on File, 460 Park Avenue South, New York, New York 10016 (800) 443-8323; *The New Book of World Rankings*.

Statistical Office of the United Nations, Publishing Service, New York, New York 10017 (800) 253-9646; *Statistical Yearbook*.

IRAN - BIRTH RATES

Euromonitor Publications Limited, 87-88 Turnmill Street, London EC1M 5QU, England; *Middle East Economic Handbook*, and *Third World Economic Handbook*.

Facts on File, 460 Park Avenue South, New York, New York 10016 (800) 443-8323; *The New Book of World Rankings*.

Statistical Office of the United Nations, Publishing Service, New York, New York 10017 (800) 253-9646; *Demographic Yearbook*, and *Statistical Yearbook*.

Times Books, 201 East 50th Street, New York, New York 10022 (212) 751-2600; *The Economist Book of Vital World Statistics*.

World Health Organization, Avenue Appia, Office of Publications, CH-1211 Geneva 27, Switzerland (Telephone Number in U.S. (518) 436-9686); *World Health Statistics Annual.*

IRAN - BONDS

G.K. Hall and Company, 70 Lincoln Street, Boston, Massachusetts 02111 (617) 423-3990; *The World in Figures.*

International Monetary Fund, 700 Nineteenth Street, NW, Washington, D.C. 20431 (202) 623-7000; *Government Finance Statistics Yearbook.*

IRAN - BOOK PRODUCTION

G.K. Hall and Company, 70 Lincoln Street, Boston, Massachusetts 02111 (617) 423-3990; *The World in Figures.*

United Nations Educational, Scientific and Cultural Organization (UNESCO), 7 Place de Fontenoy, F-75700 Paris, France (Telephone Number in U.S. (212) 963-5981); *Statistical Yearbook.*

IRAN - BROADCASTING

Billboard Limited, Post Office Box 9027, 1006 AA Amsterdam, The Netherlands (Telephone Number in U.S. (212) 764-7300); *World Radio TV Handbook.*

Facts on File, 460 Park Avenue South, New York, New York 10016 (800) 443-8323; *The New Book of World Rankings.*

G.K. Hall and Company, 70 Lincoln Street, Boston, Massachusetts 02111 (617) 423-3990; *The World in Figures.*

Times Books, 201 East 50th Street, New York, New York 10022 (212) 751-2600; *The Economist Book of Vital World Statistics.*

IRAN - BUILDING CONSTRUCTION - See IRAN - CONSTRUCTION INDUSTRY

IRAN - BUSINESS

G.K. Hall and Company, 70 Lincoln Street, Boston, Massachusetts 02111 (617) 423-3990; *The World in Figures.*

IRAN - BUTTER PRODUCTION - See IRAN - DAIRY PRODUCTS

IRAN - CALORIE SUPPLY

Food and Agricultural Organization of the United Nations (FAO) Via delle Terme di Caracalla, 00100 Rome, Italy (Telephone Number in U.S. (202) 606-7828); *The State of Food and Agriculture.*

IRAN - CAPITAL REVENUE

International Monetary Fund, 700 Nineteenth Street, NW, Washington, D.C. 20431 (202) 623-7000; *Government Finance Statistics Yearbook.*

IRAN - CASTOR BEAN PRODUCTION - See IRAN - CROPS

IRAN - CATTLE - See IRAN - LIVESTOCK AND POULTRY

IRAN - CAUSTIC SODA PRODUCTION

Statistical Office of the United Nations, Publishing Service, New York, New York 10017 (800) 253-9646; *Statistical Yearbook.*

IRAN - CEMENT PRODUCTION - See IRAN - MINING AND MINERAL PRODUCTS

IRAN - CHEESE PRODUCTION - See IRAN - DAIRY PRODUCTS

IRAN - CHEMICAL (ORGANIC) PRODUCTION - See IRAN - MINING AND MINERAL PRODUCTS

IRAN - CHICK PEA PRODUCTION - See IRAN - CROPS

IRAN - CHICKENS - See IRAN - LIVESTOCK AND POULTRY

IRAN - CIGARETTE PRODUCTION - See IRAN - TOBACCO PRODUCTION

IRAN - CLASS STRUCTURE

G.K. Hall and Company, 70 Lincoln Street, Boston, Massachusetts 02111 (617) 423-3990; *The World in Figures.*

IRAN - CLIMATE

Facts on File, 460 Park Avenue South, New York, New York 10016 (800) 443-8323; *The New Book of World Rankings.*

G.K. Hall and Company, 70 Lincoln Street, Boston, Massachusetts 02111 (617) 423-3990; *The World in Figures.*

IRAN - CLOTHING EXPORTS AND IMPORTS

Euromonitor Publications Limited, 87-88 Turnmill Street, London EC1M 5QU, England; *Third World Economic Handbook.*

IRAN - COAL PRODUCTION AND CONSUMPTION - See IRAN - MINING AND MINERAL PRODUCTS

IRAN - COFFEE PRODUCTION - See IRAN - CROPS

IRAN - COKE OVEN COKE PRODUCTION AND CONSUMPTION - See IRAN - MINING AND MINERAL PRODUCTS

IRAN - COMMUNICATIONS

Euromonitor Publications Limited, 87-88 Turnmill Street, London EC1M 5QU, England; *Third World Economic Handbook.*

G.K. Hall and Company, 70 Lincoln Street, Boston, Massachusetts 02111 (617) 423-3990; *The World in Figures.*

Statistical Office of the United Nations, Publishing Service, New York, New York 10017 (800) 253-9646; *Statistical Yearbook for Asia and the Pacific.*

IRAN - CONSTRUCTION INDUSTRY

Facts on File, 460 Park Avenue South, New York, New York 10016 (800) 443-8323; *The New Book of World Rankings.*

Statistical Office of the United Nations, Publishing Service, New York, New York 10017 (800) 253-9646; *Construction Statistics Yearbook,* and *Statistical Yearbook.*

IRAN - CONSUMER PRICE INDEX

G.K. Hall and Company, 70 Lincoln Street, Boston, Massachusetts 02111 (617) 423-3990; *The World in Figures.*

Statistical Office of the United Nations, Publishing Service, New York, New York 10017 (800) 253-9646; *Statistical Yearbook.*

IRAN - CONSUMER PRICES

International Labour Office, I.L.O. Publications, CH-1211, Geneva 22, Switzerland; *Yearbook of Labour Statistics.*

International Monetary Fund, 700 Nineteenth Street, NW, Washington, D.C. 20431 (202) 623-7000; *International Financial Statistics.*

IRAN - CONSUMPTION

Euromonitor Publications Limited, 87-88 Turnmill Street, London EC1M 5QU, England; *Middle East Economic Handbook.*

G.K. Hall and Company, 70 Lincoln Street, Boston, Massachusetts 02111 (617) 423-3990; *The World in Figures.*

International Lead and Zinc Study Group, Metro House, 58 St. James's Street, London SW1A 1LD, England; *Lead and Zinc Statistics.*

IRAN - COPPER AND COPPER ORE - See IRAN -MINING AND MINERAL PRODUCTS

IRAN - CORN PRODUCTION - See IRAN - CROPS

IRAN - CORPORATE TAXES - See IRAN - TAXATION

IRAN - COTTON - See IRAN - CROPS

IRAN - CRIME

Yale University Press, Yale Station, New Haven, Connecticut 06520 (203) 432-0940; *Violence and Crime in Cross-National Perspective.*

IRAN - CROPS

Commodity Research Bureau, Incorporated, 75 Wall Street, New York, New York 10005 (212) 504-7754; *Commodity Year Book.*

Facts on File, 460 Park Avenue South, New York, New York 10016 (800) 443-8323; *The New Book of World Rankings.*

Food and Agricultural Organization of the United Nations (FAO) Via delle Terme di Caracalla, 00100 Rome, Italy (Telephone Number in U.S. (202) 606-7828); *Production Yearbook* and *The State of Food and Agriculture.*

G.K. Hall and Company, 70 Lincoln Street, Boston, Massachusetts 02111 (617) 423-3990; *The World in Figures.*

Statistical Office of the United Nations, Publishing Service, New York, New York 10017 (800) 253-9646; *Statistical Yearbook.*

IRAN - CUSTOMS DUTIES

G.K. Hall and Company, 70 Lincoln Street, Boston, Massachusetts 02111 (617) 423-3990; *The World in Figures.*

International Monetary Fund, 700 Nineteenth Street, NW, Washington, D.C. 20431 (202) 623-7000; *Government Finance Statistics Yearbook.*

IRAN - DAIRY PRODUCTS

Facts on File, 460 Park Avenue South, New York, New York 10016 (800) 443-8323; *The New Book of World Rankings.*

Food and Agricultural Organization of the United Nations (FAO), Via delle Terme di Caracalla, 00100 Rome, Italy (Telephone Number in U.S. (202) 606-7828); *Production Yearbook* and *The State of Food and Agriculture.*

Statistical Office of the United Nations, Publishing Service, New York, New York 10017 (800) 253-9646; *Statistical Yearbook.*

IRAN - DEATH RATES

Euromonitor Publications Limited, 87-88 Turnmill Street, London EC1M 5QU, England; *Middle East Economic Handbook,* and *Third World Economic Handbook.*

G.K. Hall and Company, 70 Lincoln Street, Boston, Massachusetts 02111 (617) 423-3990; *The World in Figures.*

Statistical Office of the United Nations, Publishing Service, New York, New York 10017 (800) 253-9646; *Statistical Yearbook.*

Times Books, 201 East 50th Street, New York, New York 10022 (212) 751-2600; *The Economist Book of Vital World Statistics.*

World Health Organization, Avenue Appia, Office of Publications, CH-1211 Geneva 27, Switzerland (Telephone Number in U.S. (518) 436-9686); *World Health Statistics Annual.*

IRAN - DEFENSE EXPENDITURES

G.K. Hall and Company, 70 Lincoln Street, Boston, Massachusetts 02111 (617) 423-3990; *The World in Figures.*

International Monetary Fund, 700 Nineteenth Street, NW, Washington, D.C. 20431 (202) 623-7000; *Government Finance Statistics Yearbook.*

U.S. Arms Control and Disarmament Agency, 320 Twenty-first Street, Northwest, Washington, D.C. 20451 (202) 647-8677; *World Military Expenditures and Arms Transfers.*

IRAN - DEMOGRAPHY

The Economist Intelligence Unit, 111 West 57th Street, New York, New York 10019 (800) 938-4685; *The World Market Atlas.*

Facts on File, 460 Park Avenue South, New York, New York 10016 (800) 443-8323; *The New Book of World Rankings.*

G.K. Hall and Company, 70 Lincoln Street, Boston, Massachusetts 02111 (617) 423-3990; *The World in Figures.*

IRAN - DEVELOPMENT ASSISTANCE

G.K. Hall and Company, 70 Lincoln Street, Boston, Massachusetts 02111 (617) 423-3990; *The World in Figures.*

Statistical Office of the United Nations, Publishing Service, New York, New York 10017 (800) 253-9646; *Statistical Yearbook.*

IRAN - DIAMOND PRODUCTION - See IRAN - MINING AND MINERAL PRODUCTS

IRAN - DISCOUNT RATES

Statistical Office of the United Nations, Publishing Service, New York, New York 10017 (800) 253-9646; *Statistical Yearbook.*

IRAN - DISEASES

G.K. Hall and Company, 70 Lincoln Street, Boston, Massachusetts 02111 (617) 423-3990; *The World in Figures.*

World Health Organization, Avenue Appia, Office of Publications, CH-1211 Geneva 27, Switzerland (Telephone Number in U.S. (518) 436-9686); *World Health Statistics Annual.*

IRAN - DIVORCE RATES

Facts on File, 460 Park Avenue South, New York, New York 10016 (800) 443-8323; *The New Book of World Rankings.*

Statistical Office of the United Nations, Publishing Service, New York, New York 10017 (800) 253-9646; *Demographic Yearbook,* and *Statistical Yearbook.*

IRAN - DOMESTIC PRODUCT

G.K. Hall and Company, 70 Lincoln Street, Boston, Massachusetts 02111 (617) 423-3990; *The World in Figures.*

IRAN - DUCKS - See IRAN - LIVESTOCK AND POULTRY

IRAN - ECONOMY

Euromonitor Publications Limited, 87-88 Turnmill Street, London EC1M 5QU, England; *International Marketing Data and Statistics,* and *Third World Economic Handbook.*

Facts on File, 460 Park Avenue South, New York, New York 10016 (800) 443-8323; *The New Book of World Rankings.*

G.K. Hall and Company, 70 Lincoln Street, Boston, Massachusetts 02111 (617) 423-3990; *The World in Figures.*

IRAN - EDUCATION

The Economist Intelligence Unit, 111 West 57th Street, New York, New York 10019 (800) 938-4685; *The World Market Atlas.*

Euromonitor Publications Limited, 87-88 Turnmill Street, London EC1M 5QU, England; *Middle East Economic Handbook.*

Facts on File, 460 Park Avenue South, New York, New York 10016 (800) 443-8323; *The New Book of World Rankings.*

G.K. Hall and Company, 70 Lincoln Street, Boston, Massachusetts 02111 (617) 423-3990; *The World in Figures.*

International Monetary Fund, 700 Nineteenth Street, NW, Washington, D.C. 20431 (202) 623-7000; *Government Finance Statistics Yearbook.*

Times Books, 201 East 50th Street, New York, New York 10022 (212) 751-2600; *The Economist Book of Vital World Statistics.*

United Nations Educational, Scientific and Cultural Organization (UNESCO), 7 Place de Fontenoy, F-75700 Paris, France (Telephone Number in U.S. (212) 963-5981); *Statistical Yearbook.*

IRAN - EGG PRODUCTION - See IRAN - DAIRY PRODUCTS

IRAN - ELECTRICITY

Facts on File, 460 Park Avenue South, New York, New York 10016 (800) 443-8323; *The New Book of World Rankings.*

Penn Well Publishing Company, 1421 South Sheridan Road, Post Office Box 1260, Tulsa, Oklahoma 74101 (800) 752-9764; *International Energy Statistics Sourcebook.*

Statistical Office of the United Nations, Publishing Service, New York, New York 10017 (800) 253-9646; *Electric Power in Asia and the Pacific,* and *Statistical Yearbook.*

Times Books, 201 East 50th Street, New York, New York 10022 (212) 751-2600; *The Economist Book of Vital World Statistics.*

IRAN - EMPLOYMENT

Euromonitor Publications Limited, 87-88 Turnmill Street, London EC1M 5QU, England; *International Marketing Data and Statistics,* and *Middle East Economic Handbook.*

Facts on File, 460 Park Avenue South, New York, New York 10016 (800) 443-8323; *The New Book of World Rankings.*

International Labour Office, I.L.O. Publications, CH-1211, Geneva 22, Switzerland; *Yearbook of Labour Statistics.*

Statistical Office of the United Nations, Publishing Service, New York, New York 10017 (800) 253-9646; *Statistical Yearbook.*

IRAN - ENERGY

Euromonitor Publications Limited, 87-88 Turnmill Street, London EC1M 5QU, England; *Middle East Economic Handbook.*

Facts on File, 460 Park Avenue South, New York, New York 10016 (800) 443-8323; *The New Book of World Rankings.*

Food and Agricultural Organization of the United Nations (FAO) Via delle Terme di Caracalla, 00100 Rome, Italy (Telephone Number in U.S. (202) 606-7828); *The State of Food and Agriculture.*

G.K. Hall and Company, 70 Lincoln Street, Boston, Massachusetts 02111 (617) 423-3990; *The World in Figures.*

Penn Well Publishing Company, 1421 South Sheridan Road, Post Office Box 1260, Tulsa, Oklahoma 74101 (800) 752-9764; *International Energy Statistics Sourcebook.*

Statistical Office of the United Nations, Publishing Service, New York, New York 10017 (800) 253-9646; *Energy Statistics Yearbook,* and *Statistical Yearbook,* and *Statistical Yearbook for Asia and the Pacific.*

Times Books, 201 East 50th Street, New York, New York 10022 (212) 751-2600; *The Economist Book of Vital World Statistics.*

IRAN - EXCHANGE RATES

Euromonitor Publications Limited, 87-88 Turnmill Street, London EC1M 5QU, England; *International Marketing Data and Statistics,* and *Middle East Economic Handbook.*

International Civil Aviation Organization, 1000 Sherbrooke Street West, Suite 400, Montreal, Quebec, Canada H3A 2R2 (514) 285-8219; *Civil Aviation Statistics of the World.*

International Monetary Fund, 700 Nineteenth Street, NW, Washington, D.C. 20431 (202) 623-7000; *International Financial Statistics.*

Organization of Petroleum Exporting Countries, Obere Donaustrasse 93, 1020 Vienna 2, Austria; *OPEC Annual Statistical Bulletin.*

Statistical Office of the United Nations, Publishing Service, New York, New York 10017 (800) 253-9646; *Statistical Yearbook.*

IRAN - EXCISE TAXES - See IRAN - TAXATION

IRAN - EXPORTS

The Economist Intelligence Unit, 111 West 57th Street, New York, New York 10019 (800) 938-4685; *The World Market Atlas.*

Euromonitor Publications Limited, 87-88 Turnmill Street, London EC1M 5QU, England; *International Marketing Data and Statistics, Middle East Economic Handbook,* and *Third World Economic Handbook.*

Food and Agricultural Organization of the United Nations (FAO) Via delle Terme di Caracalla, 00100 Rome, Italy (Telephone Number in U.S. (202) 606-7828); *The State of Food and Agriculture.*

G.K. Hall and Company, 70 Lincoln Street, Boston, Massachusetts 02111 (617) 423-3990; *The World in Figures.*

International Lead and Zinc Study Group, Metro House, 58 St. James's Street, London SW1A 1LD, England; *Lead and Zinc Statistics.*

International Monetary Fund, 700 Nineteenth Street, NW, Washington, D.C. 20431 (202) 623-7000; *Direction of Trade Statistics,* and *International Financial Statistics.*

Organization of Petroleum Exporting Countries, Obere Donaustrasse 93, 1020 Vienna 2, Austria; *OPEC Annual Statistical Bulletin.*

Statistical Office of the United Nations, Publishing Service, New York, New York 10017 (800) 253-9646; *Trade in Manufactures of Developing Countries.*

Times Books, 201 East 50th Street, New York, New York 10022 (212) 751-2600; *The Economist Book of Vital World Statistics.*

IRAN - EXTERNAL INDEBTEDNESS

Euromonitor Publications Limited, 87-88 Turnmill Street, London EC1M 5QU, England; *Third World Economic Handbook.*

IRAN - EXTERNAL TRADE

Food and Agricultural Organization of the United Nations (FAO) Via delle Terme di Caracalla, 00100 Rome, Italy (Telephone Number in U.S. (202) 606-7828); *The State of Food and Agriculture,* and *Trade Yearbook.*

G.K. Hall and Company, 70 Lincoln Street, Boston, Massachusetts 02111 (617) 423-3990; *The World in Figures.*

Statistical Office of the United Nations, Publishing Service, New York, New York 10017 (800) 253-9646; *Statistical Yearbook,* and *Statistical Yearbook for Asia and the Pacific.*

IRAN - FABRIC PRODUCTION - See IRAN - TEXTILE INDUSTRY

IRAN - FARM CROPS - See IRAN - CROPS

IRAN - FEMALE WORKING POPULATION - See IRAN - EMPLOYMENT

IRAN - FERTILITY RATES

Facts on File, 460 Park Avenue South, New York, New York 10016 (800) 443-8323; *The New Book of World Rankings.*

Times Books, 201 East 50th Street, New York, New York 10022 (212) 751-2600; *The Economist Book of Vital World Statistics.*

IRAN - FERTILIZER

Food and Agricultural Organization of the United Nations (FAO), Via delle Terme di Caracalla, 00100 Rome, Italy (Telephone Number in U.S. (202) 606-7828); *Fertilizer Yearbook,* and *The State of Food and Agriculture.*

Statistical Office of the United Nations, Publishing Service, New York, New York 10017 (800) 253-9646; *Statistical Yearbook.*

IRAN - FETAL MORTALITY

Statistical Office of the United Nations, Publishing Service, New York, New York 10017 (800) 253-9646; *Demographic Yearbook.*

IRAN - FILAMENT PRODUCTION - See IRAN - TEXTILE INDUSTRY

IRAN - FILM - See IRAN - MOTION PICTURES

IRAN - FINANCE

Euromonitor Publications Limited, 87-88 Turnmill Street, London EC1M 5QU, England; *Middle East Economic Handbook.*

Facts on File, 460 Park Avenue South, New York, New York 10016 (800) 443-8323; *The New Book of World Rankings.*

G.K. Hall and Company, 70 Lincoln Street, Boston, Massachusetts 02111 (617) 423-3990; *The World in Figures.*

International Monetary Fund, 700 Nineteenth Street, NW, Washington, D.C. 20431 (202) 623-7000; *Government Finance Statistics Yearbook,* and *International Financial Statistics.*

Statistical Office of the United Nations, Publishing Service, New York, New York 10017 (800) 253-9646; *Statistical Yearbook for Asia and the Pacific.*

IRAN - FISHERIES

Facts on File, 460 Park Avenue South, New York, New York 10016 (800) 443-8323; *The New Book of World Rankings.*

Food and Agricultural Organization of the United Nations (FAO) Via delle Terme di Caracalla, 00100 Rome, Italy (Telephone Number in U.S. (202) 606-7828); *The State of Food and Agriculture,* and *Yearbook of Fishery Statistics.*

Statistical Office of the United Nations, Publishing Service, New York, New York 10017 (800) 253-9646; *Statistical Yearbook.*

IRAN - FLOUR PRODUCTION

Statistical Office of the United Nations, Publishing Service, New York, New York 10017 (800) 253-9646; *Statistical Yearbook.*

IRAN - FOOD

Food and Agricultural Organization of the United Nations (FAO), Via delle Terme di Caracalla, 00100 Rome, Italy (Telephone Number in U.S. (202) 606-7828); *Production Yearbook,* and *The State of Food*

and Agriculture.

G.K. Hall and Company, 70 Lincoln Street, Boston, Massachusetts 02111 (617) 423-3990; *The World in Figures.*

Statistical Office of the United Nations, Publishing Service, New York, New York 10017 (800) 253-9646; *Statistical Yearbook for Asia and the Pacific.*

IRAN - FOREIGN AID

G.K. Hall and Company, 70 Lincoln Street, Boston, Massachusetts 02111 (617) 423-3990; *The World in Figures.*

IRAN - FOREIGN INDEBTEDNESS

Euromonitor Publications Limited, 87-88 Turnmill Street, London EC1M 5QU, England; *Middle East Economic Handbook.*

IRAN - FOREIGN TRADE

Euromonitor Publications Limited, 87-88 Turnmill Street, London EC1M 5QU, England; *International Marketing Data and Statistics, Middle East Economic Handbook,*and *Third World Economic Handbook.*

Facts on File, 460 Park Avenue South, New York, New York 10016 (800) 443-8323; *The New Book of World Rankings.*

Food and Agricultural Organization of the United Nations (FAO) Via delle Terme di Caracalla, 00100 Rome, Italy (Telephone Number in U.S. (202) 606-7828); *The State of Food and Agriculture.*

G.K. Hall and Company, 70 Lincoln Street, Boston, Massachusetts 02111 (617) 423-3990; *The World in Figures.*

International Monetary Fund, 700 Nineteenth Street, NW, Washington, D.C. 20431 (202) 623-7000; *International Financial Statistics.*

Statistical Office of the United Nations, Publishing Service, New York, New York 10017 (800) 253-9646; *International Trade Statistics Yearbook,* and *Statistical Yearbook.*

IRAN - FORESTRY AND FOREST PRODUCTS

Euromonitor Publications Limited, 87-88 Turnmill Street, London EC1M 5QU, England; *Third World Economic Handbook.*

Facts on File, 460 Park Avenue South, New York, New York 10016 (800) 443-8323; *The New Book of World Rankings.*

Food and Agricultural Organization of the United Nations (FAO) Via delle Terme di Caracalla, 00100 Rome, Italy (Telephone Number in U.S. (202) 606-7828); *The State of Food and Agriculture,* and *Yearbook of Forest Products.*

G.K. Hall and Company, 70 Lincoln Street, Boston, Massachusetts 02111 (617) 423-3990; *The World in Figures.*

International Monetary Fund, 700 Nineteenth Street, NW, Washington, D.C. 20431 (202) 623-7000; *International Financial Statistics.*

Statistical Office of the United Nations, Publishing Service, New York, New York 10017 (800) 253-9646; *Statistical Yearbook.*

United Nations Educational, Scientific and Cultural Organization (UNESCO), 7 Place de Fontenoy, F-75700 Paris, France (Telephone Number in U.S. (212) 963-5981); *Statistical Yearbook.*

IRAN - GAS - See IRAN - MINING AND MINERAL PRODUCTS

IRAN - GENERAL INDUSTRIAL STATISTICS

Statistical Office of the United Nations, Publishing Service, New York, New York 10017 (800) 253-9646; *Industrial Statistics Yearbook.*

IRAN - GENERAL MORTALITY

Statistical Office of the United Nations, Publishing Service, New York, New York 10017 (800) 253-9646; *Demographic Yearbook.*

World Health Organization, Avenue Appia, Office of Publications, CH-1211 Geneva 27, Switzerland (Telephone Number in U.S. (518) 436-9686); *World Health Statistics Annual.*

IRAN - GEOGRAPHIC DATA

Facts on File, 460 Park Avenue South, New York, New York 10016 (800) 443-8323; *The New Book of World Rankings.*

IRAN - GOATS - See IRAN - LIVESTOCK AND POULTRY

IRAN - GOLD HOLDINGS

International Monetary Fund, 700 Nineteenth Street, NW, Washington, D.C. 20431 (202) 623-7000; *International Financial Statistics.*

Statistical Office of the United Nations, Publishing Service, New York, New York 10017 (800) 253-9646; *Statistical Yearbook.*

IRAN - GOLD PRODUCTION AND CONSUMPTION - See IRAN - MINING AND MINERAL PRODUCTS

IRAN - GOVERNMENT

G.K. Hall and Company, 70 Lincoln Street, Boston, Massachusetts 02111 (617) 423-3990; *The World in Figures.*

IRAN - GOVERNMENT EXPENDITURES

Euromonitor Publications Limited, 87-88 Turnmill Street, London EC1M 5QU, England; *Third World Economic Handbook.*

International Monetary Fund, 700 Nineteenth Street, NW, Washington, D.C. 20431 (202) 623-7000; *Government Finance Statistics Yearbook.*

Times Books, 201 East 50th Street, New York, New York 10022 (212) 751-2600; *The Economist Book of Vital World Statistics.*

IRAN - GOVERNMENT FINANCES

International Monetary Fund, 700 Nineteenth Street, NW, Washington, D.C. 20431 (202) 623-7000; *International Financial Statistics.*

Statistical Office of the United Nations, Publishing Service, New York, New York 10017 (800) 253-9646; *Statistical Yearbook.*

IRAN - GOVERNMENT REVENUES

International Monetary Fund, 700 Nineteenth Street, NW, Washington, D.C. 20431 (202) 623-7000; *Government Finance Statistics Yearbook.*

Times Books, 201 East 50th Street, New York, New York 10022 (212) 751-2600; *The Economist Book of Vital World Statistics.*

IRAN - GRAIN PRODUCTION - See IRAN - CROPS

IRAN - GRANTS

International Monetary Fund, 700 Nineteenth Street, NW, Washington, D.C. 20431 (202) 623-7000; *Government Finance Statistics Yearbook.*

IRAN - GROSS DOMESTIC PRODUCT

The Economist Intelligence Unit, 111 West 57th Street, New York, New York 10019 (800) 938-4685; *The World Market Atlas.*

Euromonitor Publications Limited, 87-88 Turnmill Street, London EC1M 5QU, England; *International Marketing Data and Statistics, Middle East Economic Handbook,* and *Third World Economic Handbook.*

Facts on File, 460 Park Avenue South, New York, New York 10016 (800) 443-8323; *The New Book of World Rankings.*

G.K. Hall and Company, 70 Lincoln Street, Boston, Massachusetts 02111 (617) 423-3990; *The World in Figures.*

Statistical Office of the United Nations, Publishing Service, New York, New York 10017 (800) 253-9646; *Statistical Yearbook.*

Times Books, 201 East 50th Street, New York, New York 10022 (212) 751-2600; *The Economist Book of Vital World Statistics.*

IRAN - GROSS INDUSTRIAL PRODUCT

Euromonitor Publications Limited, 87-88 Turnmill Street, London EC1M 5QU, England; *Third World Economic Handbook.*

IRAN - GROSS NATIONAL PRODUCT

Euromonitor Publications Limited, 87-88 Turnmill Street, London EC1M 5QU, England; *International Marketing Data and Statistics,* and *Third World Economic Handbook.*

Organization of Petroleum Exporting Countries, Obere Donaustrasse 93, 1020 Vienna 2, Austria; *OPEC Annual Statistical Bulletin.*

U.S. Arms Control and Disarmament Agency, 320 Twenty-first Street, Northwest, Washington, D.C. 20451 (202) 647-8677; *World Military Expenditures and Arms Transfers.*

IRAN - GROUNDNUTS PRODUCTION - See IRAN - CROPS

IRAN - HAZELNUT PRODUCTION - See IRAN - CROPS

IRAN - HEALTH

Euromonitor Publications Limited, 87-88 Turnmill Street, London EC1M 5QU, England; *Middle East Economic Handbook.*

Facts on File, 460 Park Avenue South, New York, New York 10016 (800) 443-8323; *The New Book of World Rankings.*

G.K. Hall and Company, 70 Lincoln Street, Boston, Massachusetts 02111 (617) 423-3990; *The World in Figures.*

Statistical Office of the United Nations, Publishing Service, New York, New York 10017 (800) 253-9646; *Statistical Yearbook.*

Times Books, 201 East 50th Street, New York, New York 10022 (212) 751-2600; *The Economist Book of Vital World Statistics.*

World Health Organization, Avenue Appia, Office of Publications, CH-1211 Geneva 27, Switzerland (Telephone Number in U.S. (518) 436-9686); *World Health Statistics Annual.*

IRAN - HEALTH EXPENDITURES

International Monetary Fund, 700 Nineteenth Street, NW, Washington, D.C. 20431 (202) 623-7000; *Government Finance Statistics Yearbook.*

IRAN - HIDE PRODUCTION

Food and Agricultural Organization of the United Nations (FAO), Via delle Terme di Caracalla, 00100 Rome, Italy (Telephone Number in U.S. (202) 606-7828); *Production Yearbook.*

IRAN - HIGHWAYS

G.K. Hall and Company, 70 Lincoln Street, Boston, Massachusetts 02111 (617) 423-3990; *The World in Figures.*

International Road Federation, 525 School Street, SW, Washington, D.C. 20024 (202) 554-2106; *World Road Statistics.*

IRAN - HORSES - See IRAN - LIVESTOCK AND POULTRY

IRAN - HOURS OF WORK - See IRAN - EMPLOYMENT

IRAN - HOUSING AND HOUSING UNITS

Euromonitor Publications Limited, 87-88 Turnmill Street, London EC1M 5QU, England; *Third World Economic Handbook.*

Facts on File, 460 Park Avenue South, New York, New York 10016 (800) 443-8323; *The New Book of World Rankings.*

IRAN - HOUSING EXPENDITURES

International Monetary Fund, 700 Nineteenth Street, NW, Washington, D.C. 20431 (202) 623-7000; *Government Finance Statistics Yearbook.*

IRAN - HYDROCHLORIC ACID

Statistical Office of the United Nations, Publishing Service, New York, New York 10017 (800) 253-9646; *Statistical Yearbook.*

IRAN - ILLITERATE POPULATION

The Economist Intelligence Unit, 111 West 57th Street, New York, New York 10019 (800) 938-4685; *The World Market Atlas.*

G.K. Hall and Company, 70 Lincoln Street, Boston, Massachusetts 02111 (617) 423-3990; *The World in Figures.*

United Nations Educational, Scientific and Cultural Organization (UNESCO), 7 Place de Fontenoy, F-75700 Paris, France (Telephone Number in U.S. (212) 963-5981); *Statistical Yearbook.*

IRAN - IMPORTS

The Economist Intelligence Unit, 111 West 57th Street, New York, New York 10019 (800) 938-4685; *The World Market Atlas.*

Euromonitor Publications Limited, 87-88 Turnmill Street, London EC1M 5QU, England; *International Marketing Data and Statistics,*

Middle East Economic Handbook, and *Third World Economic Handbook*.

Food and Agricultural Organization of the United Nations (FAO) Via delle Terme di Caracalla, 00100 Rome, Italy (Telephone Number in U.S. (202) 606-7828); *The State of Food and Agriculture*.

G.K. Hall and Company, 70 Lincoln Street, Boston, Massachusetts 02111 (617) 423-3990; *The World in Figures*.

International Lead and Zinc Study Group, Metro House, 58 St. James's Street, London SW1A 1LD, England; *Lead and Zinc Statistics*.

International Monetary Fund, 700 Nineteenth Street, NW, Washington, D.C. 20431 (202) 623-7000; *Direction of Trade Statistics*, *Government Finance Statistics Yearbook*, and *International Financial Statistics*.

IRAN - INCOME TAXES - See IRAN - TAXATION

IRAN - INDUSTRIAL METALS PRODUCTION - See IRAN - MINING AND MINERAL PRODUCTS

IRAN - INDUSTRY

Euromonitor Publications Limited, 87-88 Turnmill Street, London EC1M 5QU, England; *Third World Economic Handbook*.

Facts on File, 460 Park Avenue South, New York, New York 10016 (800) 443-8323; *The New Book of World Rankings*.

G.K. Hall and Company, 70 Lincoln Street, Boston, Massachusetts 02111 (617) 423-3990; *The World in Figures*.

International Labour Office, I.L.O. Publications, CH-1211, Geneva 22, Switzerland; *Yearbook of Labour Statistics*.

Statistical Office of the United Nations, Publishing Service, New York, New York 10017 (800) 253-9646; *Statistical Yearbook* and *Statistical Yearbook for Asia and the Pacific*.

Times Books, 201 East 50th Street, New York, New York 10022 (212) 751-2600; *The Economist Book of Vital World Statistics*.

World Intellectual Property Organization, 34 Chemin des Colombettes, CH-1211 Geneva 20, Switzerland; *Industrial Property Statistics*.

IRAN - INFANT AND MATERNAL MORTALITY

Statistical Office of the United Nations, Publishing Service, New York, New York 10017 (800) 253-9646; *Demographic Yearbook*, and *Statistical Yearbook*.

Times Books, 201 East 50th Street, New York, New York 10022 (212) 751-2600; *The Economist Book of Vital World Statistics*.

IRAN - INTERNAL TRADE

Statistical Office of the United Nations, Publishing Service, New York, New York 10017 (800) 253-9646; *Statistical Yearbook*, and *Statistical Yearbook for Asia and the Pacific*.

IRAN - INTERNATIONAL LIQUIDITY

International Monetary Fund, 700 Nineteenth Street, NW, Washington, D.C. 20431 (202) 623-7000; *International Financial Statistics*.

IRAN - INTERNATIONAL RESERVES EXCLUDING GOLD

Statistical Office of the United Nations, Publishing Service, New York, New York 10017 (800) 253-9646; *Statistical Yearbook*.

IRAN - IRON ORE PRODUCTION AND CONSUMPTION - See IRAN - MINING AND MINERAL PRODUCTS

IRAN - IRRIGATION

Euromonitor Publications Limited, 87-88 Turnmill Street, London EC1M 5QU, England; *International Marketing Data and Statistics*.

IRAN - JUTE PRODUCTION - See IRAN - CROPS

IRAN - LABOR FORCE

Euromonitor Publications Limited, 87-88 Turnmill Street, London EC1M 5QU, England; *International Marketing Data and Statistics*, and *Middle East Economic Handbook*.

Facts on File, 460 Park Avenue South, New York, New York 10016 (800) 443-8323; *The New Book of World Rankings*.

Food and Agricultural Organization of the United Nations (FAO) Via delle Terme di Caracalla, 00100 Rome, Italy (Telephone Number in U.S. (202) 606-7828); *The State of Food and Agriculture*.

G.K. Hall and Company, 70 Lincoln Street, Boston, Massachusetts 02111 (617) 423-3990; *The World in Figures*.

IRAN - LABOR PRODUCTIVITY

International Labour Office, I.L.O. Publications, CH-1211, Geneva 22, Switzerland; *Yearbook of Labour Statistics*.

IRAN - LAND USE

Euromonitor Publications Limited, 87-88 Turnmill Street, London EC1M 5QU, England; *International Marketing Data and Statistics*.

Food and Agricultural Organization of the United Nations (FAO), Via delle Terme di Caracalla, 00100 Rome, Italy (Telephone Number in U.S. (202) 606-7828); *Production Yearbook*.

G.K. Hall and Company, 70 Lincoln Street, Boston, Massachusetts 02111 (617) 423-3990; *The World in Figures*.

IRAN - LEAD AND LEAD ORE - See IRAN - MINING AND MINERAL PRODUCTS

IRAN - LIBRARIES

Facts on File, 460 Park Avenue South, New York, New York 10016 (800) 443-8323; *The New Book of World Rankings*.

IRAN - LIVESTOCK AND POULTRY

Euromonitor Publications Limited, 87-88 Turnmill Street, London EC1M 5QU, England; *Third World Economic Handbook*.

Facts on File, 460 Park Avenue South, New York, New York 10016 (800) 443-8323; *The New Book of World Rankings*.

Food and Agricultural Organization of the United Nations (FAO), Via delle Terme di Caracalla, 00100 Rome, Italy (Telephone Number in U.S. (202) 606-7828); *Production Yearbook*, and *The State of Food and Agriculture*.

G.K. Hall and Company, 70 Lincoln Street, Boston, Massachusetts 02111 (617) 423-3990; *The World in Figures*.

Statistical Office of the United Nations, Publishing Service, New York, New York 10017 (800) 253-9646; *Statistical Yearbook*.

IRAN - LIVING LEVELS

G.K. Hall and Company, 70 Lincoln Street, Boston, Massachusetts 02111 (617) 423-3990; *The World in Figures*.

Times Books, 201 East 50th Street, New York, New York 10022 (212) 751-2600; *The Economist Book of Vital World Statistics*.

IRAN - MAIL TRAFFIC

Statistical Office of the United Nations, Publishing Service, New York, New York 10017 (800) 253-9646; *Statistical Yearbook*.

IRAN - MANGANESE ORE PRODUCTION AND CONSUMPTION - See IRAN - MINING AND MINERAL PRODUCTS

IRAN - MANPOWER

Statistical Office of the United Nations, Publishing Service, New York, New York 10017 (800) 253-9646; *Statistical Yearbook for Asia and the Pacific*.

IRAN - MANUFACTURING

Euromonitor Publications Limited, 87-88 Turnmill Street, London EC1M 5QU, England; *Third World Economic Handbook*.

Facts on File, 460 Park Avenue South, New York, New York 10016 (800) 443-8323; *The New Book of World Rankings*.

G.K. Hall and Company, 70 Lincoln Street, Boston, Massachusetts 02111 (617) 423-3990; *The World in Figures*.

Statistical Office of the United Nations, Publishing Service, New York, New York 10017 (800) 253-9646; *Statistical Yearbook*.

Times Books, 201 East 50th Street, New York, New York 10022 (212) 751-2600; *The Economist Book of Vital World Statistics*.

IRAN - MARRIAGE RATES

Facts on File, 460 Park Avenue South, New York, New York 10016 (800) 443-8323; *The New Book of World Rankings*.

Statistical Office of the United Nations, Publishing Service, New York, New York 10017 (800) 253-9646; *Demographic Yearbook*, and *Statistical Yearbook*.

IRAN - MEAT PRODUCTION - See IRAN - LIVESTOCK AND POULTRY

IRAN - MERCHANT SHIPPING

G.K. Hall and Company, 70 Lincoln Street, Boston, Massachusetts 02111 (617) 423-3990; *The World in Figures*.

Lloyd's Register of Shipping, 17 Battery Place, New York, New York 10004 (212) 425-8050; *Register of Ships*.

Organization of Petroleum Exporting Countries, Obere Donaustrasse 93, 1020 Vienna 2, Austria; *OPEC Annual Statistical Bulletin*.

Statistical Office of the United Nations, Publishing Service, New York, New York 10017 (800) 253-9646; *Statistical Yearbook*.

Times Books, 201 East 50th Street, New York, New York 10022 (212) 751-2600; *The Economist Book of Vital World Statistics*.

U.S. Department of Transportation, Maritime Administration, 400 Seventh Street, SW, Washington, D.C. 20590 (202) 366-5807; *A Statistical Analysis of the World's Merchant Fleets*.

IRAN - MERCHANT VESSELS - TONNAGE LAUNCHED - See IRAN - MERCHANT SHIPPING

IRAN - MILITARY

G.K. Hall and Company, 70 Lincoln Street, Boston, Massachusetts 02111 (617) 423-3990; *The World in Figures*.

The International Institute for Strategic Studies, 23 Tavistock Street, London WC2E 7NQ, England; *The Military Balance*.

U.S. Arms Control and Disarmament Agency, 320 Twenty-first Street, Northwest, Washington, D.C. 20451 (202) 647-8677; *World Military Expenditures and Arms Transfers*.

IRAN - MILK - See IRAN - DAIRY PRODUCTS

IRAN - MILLET PRODUCTION - See IRAN - CROPS

IRAN - MINING AND MINERAL PRODUCTS

Commodity Research Bureau, Incorporated, 75 Wall Street, New York, New York 10005 (212) 504-7754; *Commodity Year Book*.

Euromonitor Publications Limited, 87-88 Turnmill Street, London EC1M 5QU, England; *Third World Economic Handbook*.

Facts on File, 460 Park Avenue South, New York, New York 10016 (800) 443-8323; *The New Book of World Rankings*.

G.K. Hall and Company, 70 Lincoln Street, Boston, Massachusetts 02111 (617) 423-3990; *The World in Figures*.

International Lead and Zinc Study Group, Metro House, 58 St. James's Street, London SW1A 1LD, England; *Lead and Zinc Statistics*.

Organization of Petroleum Exporting Countries, Obere Donaustrasse 93, 1020 Vienna 2, Austria; *OPEC Annual Statistical Bulletin*.

Penn Well Publishing Company, 1421 South Sheridan Road, Post Office Box 1260, Tulsa, Oklahoma 74101 (800) 752-9764; *International Energy Statistics Sourcebook*.

Statistical Office of the United Nations, Publishing Service, New York, New York 10017 (800) 253-9646; *Statistical Yearbook*.

IRAN - MONEY EXCHANGE RATE

Euromonitor Publications Limited, 87-88 Turnmill Street, London EC1M 5QU, England; *International Marketing Data and Statistics*.

International Monetary Fund, 700 Nineteenth Street, NW, Washington, D.C. 20431 (202) 623-7000; *International Financial Statistics*.

Statistical Office of the United Nations, Publishing Service, New York, New York 10017 (800) 253-9646; *Statistical Yearbook*.

IRAN - MONEY RESERVES

Euromonitor Publications Limited, 87-88 Turnmill Street, London EC1M 5QU, England; *International Marketing Data and Statistics.*

IRAN - MONEY SUPPLY

Euromonitor Publications Limited, 87-88 Turnmill Street, London EC1M 5QU, England; *International Marketing Data and Statistics.*

G.K. Hall and Company, 70 Lincoln Street, Boston, Massachusetts 02111 (617) 423-3990; *The World in Figures.*

International Monetary Fund, 700 Nineteenth Street, NW, Washington, D.C. 20431 (202) 623-7000; *International Financial Statistics.*

Statistical Office of the United Nations, Publishing Service, New York, New York 10017 (800) 253-9646; *Statistical Yearbook.*

IRAN - MOTION PICTURES

Statistical Office of the United Nations, Publishing Service, New York, New York 10017 (800) 253-9646; *Statistical Yearbook.*

United Nations Educational, Scientific and Cultural Organization (UNESCO), 7 Place de Fontenoy, F-75700 Paris, France (Telephone Number in U.S. (212) 963-5981); *Statistical Yearbook.*

IRAN - MOTOR VEHICLE PRODUCTION

Statistical Office of the United Nations, Publishing Service, New York, New York 10017 (800) 253-9646; *Statistical Yearbook.*

IRAN - MOTOR VEHICLE TAXES - See IRAN - TAXATION

IRAN - MOTOR VEHICLES IN USE

G.K. Hall and Company, 70 Lincoln Street, Boston, Massachusetts 02111 (617) 423-3990; *The World in Figures.*

International Road Federation, 525 School Street, SW, Washington, D.C. 20024 (202) 554-2106; *World Road Statistics.*

Statistical Office of the United Nations, Publishing Service, New York, New York 10017 (800) 253-9646; *Statistical Yearbook.*

Times Books, 201 East 50th Street, New York, New York 10022 (212) 751-2600; *The Economist Book of Vital World Statistics.*

IRAN - MULES - See IRAN - LIVESTOCK AND POULTRY

IRAN - MUSEUMS

Facts on File, 460 Park Avenue South, New York, New York 10016 (800) 443-8323; *The New Book of World Rankings.*

United Nations Educational, Scientific and Cultural Organization (UNESCO), 7 Place de Fontenoy, F-75700 Paris, France (Telephone Number in U.S. (212) 963-5981); *Statistical Yearbook.*

IRAN - NATALITY - See IRAN - BIRTH RATES

IRAN - NATIONAL ACCOUNTS

International Monetary Fund, 700 Nineteenth Street, NW, Washington, D.C. 20431 (202) 623-7000; *International Financial Statistics.*

Statistical Office of the United Nations, Publishing Service, New York, New York 10017 (800) 253-9646; *National Accounts Statistics, Statistical Yearbook,* and *Statistical Yearbook for Asia and the Pacific.*

IRAN - NATIONAL INCOME

Facts on File, 460 Park Avenue South, New York, New York 10016 (800) 443-8323; *The New Book of World Rankings.*

G.K. Hall and Company, 70 Lincoln Street, Boston, Massachusetts 02111 (617) 423-3990; *The World in Figures.*

Statistical Office of the United Nations, Publishing Service, New York, New York 10017 (800) 253-9646; *Statistical Yearbook.*

IRAN - NATIONAL PRODUCT

Facts on File, 460 Park Avenue South, New York, New York 10016 (800) 443-8323; *The New Book of World Rankings.*

Statistical Office of the United Nations, Publishing Service, New York, New York 10017 (800) 253-9646; *Statistical Yearbook.*

IRAN - NATURAL GAS PRODUCTION - See IRAN - MINING AND MINERAL PRODUCTS

IRAN - NEWSPAPER PRODUCTION - See IRAN - FORESTRY AND FOREST PRODUCTS

IRAN - NEWSPRINT - See IRAN - FORESTRY AND FOREST PRODUCTS

IRAN - OCCUPATIONS - See IRAN - LABOR FORCE

IRAN - PAPER - See IRAN - FORESTRY AND FOREST PRODUCTS

IRAN - PATENTS

Statistical Office of the United Nations, Publishing Service, New York, New York 10017 (800) 253-9646; *Statistical Yearbook.*

World Intellectual Property Organization, 34 Chemin des Colombettes, CH-1211 Geneva 20, Switzerland; *Industrial Property Statistics.*

IRAN - PEANUT PRODUCTION - See IRAN - CROPS

IRAN - PESTICIDE USE

Food and Agricultural Organization of the United Nations (FAO) Via delle Terme di Caracalla, 00100 Rome, Italy (Telephone Number in U.S. (202) 606-7828); *The State of Food and Agriculture.*

IRAN - PETROLEUM INDUSTRY

Commodity Research Bureau, Incorporated, 75 Wall Street, New York, New York 10005 (212) 504-7754; *Commodity Year Book.*

Euromonitor Publications Limited, 87-88 Turnmill Street, London EC1M 5QU, England; *Middle East Economic Handbook.*

Facts on File, 460 Park Avenue South, New York, New York 10016 (800) 443-8323; *The New Book of World Rankings.*

Food and Agricultural Organization of the United Nations (FAO) Via delle Terme di Caracalla, 00100 Rome, Italy (Telephone Number in U.S. (202) 606-7828); *The State of Food and Agriculture.*

G.K. Hall and Company, 70 Lincoln Street, Boston, Massachusetts 02111 (617) 423-3990; *The World in Figures.*

Organization of Petroleum Exporting Countries, Obere Donaustrasse 93, 1020 Vienna 2, Austria; *OPEC Annual Statistical Bulletin.*

Penn Well Publishing Company, 1421 South Sheridan Road, Post Office Box 1260, Tulsa, Oklahoma 74101 (800) 752-9764; *International Energy Statistics Sourcebook.*

Statistical Office of the United Nations, Publishing Service, New York, New York 10017 (800) 253-9646; *Statistical Yearbook.*

IRAN - PIGS - See IRAN - LIVESTOCK AND POULTRY

IRAN - PIPELINES FOR OIL AND PETROLEUM PRODUCTS

Organization of Petroleum Exporting Countries, Obere Donaustrasse 93, 1020 Vienna 2, Austria; *OPEC Annual Statistical Bulletin.*

IRAN - PISTACHIO PRODUCTION - See IRAN - CROPS

IRAN - PLASTICS AND RESINS PRODUCTION

Euromonitor Publications Limited, 87-88 Turnmill Street, London EC1M 5QU, England; *Third World Economic Handbook.*

Statistical Office of the United Nations, Publishing Service, New York, New York 10017 (800) 253-9646; *Statistical Yearbook.*

IRAN - POPULATION

The Economist Intelligence Unit, 111 West 57th Street, New York, New York 10019 (800) 938-4685; *The World Market Atlas.*

Euromonitor Publications Limited, 87-88 Turnmill Street, London EC1M 5QU, England; *International Marketing Data and Statistics, Middle East Economic Handbook,* and *Third World Economic Handbook.*

Facts on File, 460 Park Avenue South, New York, New York 10016 (800) 443-8323; *The New Book of World Rankings.*

Food and Agricultural Organization of the United Nations (FAO), Via delle Terme di Caracalla, 00100 Rome, Italy (Telephone Number in U.S. (202) 606-7828); *Production Yearbook.*

G.K. Hall and Company, 70 Lincoln Street, Boston, Massachusetts 02111 (617) 423-3990; *The World in Figures.*

International Labour Office, I.L.O. Publications, CH-1211, Geneva 22, Switzerland; *Yearbook of Labour Statistics.*

Statistical Office of the United Nations, Publishing Service, New York, New York 10017 (800) 253-9646; *Demographic Yearbook, Statistical Yearbook,* and *Statistical Yearbook for Asia and the Pacific.*

Times Books, 201 East 50th Street, New York, New York 10022 (212) 751-2600; *The Economist Book of Vital World Statistics.*

United Nations Educational, Scientific and Cultural Organization (UNESCO), 7 Place de Fontenoy, F-75700 Paris, France (Telephone Number in U.S. (212) 963-5981); *Statistical Yearbook.*

U.S. Arms Control and Disarmament Agency, 320 Twenty-first Street, Northwest, Washington, D.C. 20451 (202) 647-8677; *World Military Expenditures and Arms Transfers.*

World Health Organization, Avenue Appia, Office of Publications, CH-1211 Geneva 27, Switzerland (Telephone Number in U.S. (518) 436-9686); *World Health Statistics Annual.*

IRAN - POST OFFICES

Facts on File, 460 Park Avenue South, New York, New York 10016 (800) 443-8323; *The New Book of World Rankings.*

IRAN - POTATO PRODUCTION - See IRAN - CROPS

IRAN - POWER PRODUCTION INDUSTRY

Statistical Office of the United Nations, Publishing Service, New York, New York 10017; *Electric Power in Asia and the Pacific.*

IRAN - PRICES

Facts on File, 460 Park Avenue South, New York, New York 10016 (800) 443-8323; *The New Book of World Rankings.*

Food and Agricultural Organization of the United Nations (FAO), Via delle Terme di Caracalla, 00100 Rome, Italy (Telephone Number in U.S. (202) 606-7828); *Production Yearbook,* and *The State of Food and Agriculture.*

G.K. Hall and Company, 70 Lincoln Street, Boston, Massachusetts 02111 (617) 423-3990; *The World in Figures.*

International Labour Office, I.L.O. Publications, CH-1211, Geneva 22, Switzerland; *Yearbook of Labour Statistics.*

International Lead and Zinc Study Group, Metro House, 58 St. James's Street, London SW1A 1LD, England; *Lead and Zinc Statistics.*

International Monetary Fund, 700 Nineteenth Street, NW, Washington, D.C. 20431 (202) 623-7000; *International Financial Statistics.*

IRAN - PRINTING AND WRITING PAPER - See IRAN - FORESTRY AND FOREST PRODUCTS

IRAN - PRODUCTION

Euromonitor Publications Limited, 87-88 Turnmill Street, London EC1M 5QU, England; *Third World Economic Handbook.*

Facts on File, 460 Park Avenue South, New York, New York 10016 (800) 443-8323; *The New Book of World Rankings.*

G.K. Hall and Company, 70 Lincoln Street, Boston, Massachusetts 02111 (617) 423-3990; *The World in Figures.*

International Lead and Zinc Study Group, Metro House, 58 St. James's Street, London SW1A 1LD, England; *Lead and Zinc Statistics.*

IRAN - PRODUCTIVITY

Euromonitor Publications Limited, 87-88 Turnmill Street, London EC1M 5QU, England; *International Marketing Data and Statistics.*

IRAN - PROPERTY TAXES - See IRAN - TAXATION

IRAN - PUBLIC FINANCE

Facts on File, 460 Park Avenue South, New York, New York 10016 (800) 443-8323; *The New Book of World Rankings.*

IRAN - RADIO BROADCASTING - See IRAN - BROADCASTING

IRAN - RADIO RECEIVER PRODUCTION

Statistical Office of the United Nations, Publishing Service, New York, New York 10017 (800) 253-9646; *Statistical Yearbook.*

IRAN - RAILWAYS

G.K. Hall and Company, 70 Lincoln Street, Boston, Massachusetts 02111 (617) 423-3990; *The World in Figures.*

Jane's Information Group, Sentinel House, 163 Brighton Road, Coulsdon, Surrey CR5 2NH, England (Telephone Number in U.S. (703) 683-3700); *Jane's World Railways.*

Statistical Office of the United Nations, Publishing Service, New York, New York 10017 (800) 253-9646; *Statistical Yearbook.*

IRAN - RELIGION

Facts on File, 460 Park Avenue South, New York, New York 10016 (800) 443-8323; *The New Book of World Rankings.*

IRAN - RENT PRICES

International Labour Office, I.L.O. Publications, CH-1211, Geneva 22, Switzerland; *Yearbook of Labour Statistics.*

IRAN - RETAIL TRADE

Euromonitor Publications Limited, 87-88 Turnmill Street, London EC1M 5QU, England; *Third World Economic Handbook.*

G.K. Hall and Company, 70 Lincoln Street, Boston, Massachusetts 02111 (617) 423-3990; *The World in Figures.*

Statistical Office of the United Nations, Publishing Service, New York, New York 10017 (800) 253-9646; *Statistical Yearbook.*

IRAN - RICE PRODUCTION - See IRAN - CROPS

IRAN - ROOT AND TUBER PRODUCTION - See IRAN - CROPS

IRAN - ROUNDWOOD PRODUCTION - See IRAN - FORESTRY AND FOREST PRODUCTS

IRAN - RUBBER PRODUCTION

Euromonitor Publications Limited, 87-88 Turnmill Street, London EC1M 5QU, England; *Third World Economic Handbook.*

Facts on File, 460 Park Avenue South, New York, New York 10016 (800) 443-8323; *The New Book of World Rankings.*

IRAN - SAFFLOWER SEED PRODUCTION - See IRAN - CROPS

IRAN - SALT PRODUCTION - See IRAN - MINING AND MINERAL PRODUCTS

IRAN - SAWNWOOD PRODUCTION - See IRAN - FORESTRY AND FOREST PRODUCTS

IRAN - SCIENCE AND TECHNOLOGY - EXPENDITURE FOR RESEARCH

Statistical Office of the United Nations, Publishing Service, New York, New York 10017 (800) 253-9646; *Statistical Yearbook.*

IRAN - SCIENTISTS AND TECHNICIANS

Statistical Office of the United Nations, Publishing Service, New York, New York 10017 (800) 253-9646; *Statistical Yearbook.*

United Nations Educational, Scientific and Cultural Organization (UNESCO), 7 Place de Fontenoy, F-75700 Paris, France (Telephone Number in U.S. (212) 963-5981); *Statistical Yearbook.*

IRAN - SENIOR CITIZENS

Facts on File, 460 Park Avenue South, New York, New York 10016 (800) 443-8323; *The New Book of World Rankings.*

IRAN - SESAME SEED PRODUCTION - See IRAN - CROPS

IRAN - SHEEP - See IRAN - LIVESTOCK AND POULTRY

IRAN - SILVER PRODUCTION AND CONSUMPTION - See IRAN - MINING AND MINERAL PRODUCTS

IRAN - SOCIAL DATA

Facts on File, 460 Park Avenue South, New York, New York 10016 (800) 443-8323; *The New Book of World Rankings.*

G.K. Hall and Company, 70 Lincoln Street, Boston, Massachusetts 02111 (617) 423-3990; *The World in Figures.*

IRAN - SOCIAL SECURITY

International Monetary Fund, 700 Nineteenth Street, NW, Washington, D.C. 20431 (202) 623-7000; *Government Finance Statistics Yearbook.*

IRAN - SOYBEAN PRODUCTION - See IRAN - CROPS

IRAN - STAMP TAXES AND DUTIES - See IRAN - TAXATION

IRAN - STATE BUDGET REVENUE AND EXPENDITURES

Euromonitor Publications Limited, 87-88 Turnmill Street, London EC1M 5QU, England; *International Marketing Data and Statistics.*

IRAN - STEEL - See IRAN - MINING AND MINERAL PRODUCTS

IRAN - STOCKS - COMMODITY - MARKET PRICE - INDEX

Food and Agricultural Organization of the United Nations (FAO) Via delle Terme di Caracalla, 00100 Rome, Italy (Telephone Number in U.S. (202) 606-7828); *The State of Food and Agriculture.*

International Lead and Zinc Study Group, Metro House, 58 St. James's Street, London SW1A 1LD, England; *Lead and Zinc Statistics.*

IRAN - SUGAR PRODUCTION AND CONSUMPTION - See IRAN - CROPS

IRAN - SULPHURIC ACID

Statistical Office of the United Nations, Publishing Service, New York, New York 10017 (800) 253-9646; *Statistical Yearbook.*

IRAN - TAXATION

G.K. Hall and Company, 70 Lincoln Street, Boston, Massachusetts 02111 (617) 423-3990; *The World in Figures.*

International Monetary Fund, 700 Nineteenth Street, NW, Washington, D.C. 20431 (202) 623-7000; *Government Finance Statistics Yearbook.*

International Road Federation, 525 School Street, SW, Washington, D.C. 20024 (202) 554-2106; *World Road Statistics.*

IRAN - TEA PRODUCTION AND CONSUMPTION - See IRAN - CROPS

IRAN - TELEPHONES IN USE

American Telephone and Telegraph Company, 26 Parsippany Road, Whippany, New Jersey 07981 (800) 338-4038; *The World's Telephones.*

Euromonitor Publications Limited, 87-88 Turnmill Street, London EC1M 5QU, England; *Middle East Economic Handbook,* and *Third World Economic Handbook.*

G.K. Hall and Company, 70 Lincoln Street, Boston, Massachusetts 02111 (617) 423-3990; *The World in Figures.*

Statistical Office of the United Nations, Publishing Service, New York, New York 10017 (800) 253-9646; *Statistical Yearbook.*

IRAN - TELEVISION BROADCASTING - See IRAN - BROADCASTING

IRAN - TELEVISION RECEIVER PRODUCTION

Statistical Office of the United Nations, Publishing Service, New York, New York 10017 (800) 253-9646; *Statistical Yearbook.*

IRAN - TEXTILE INDUSTRY

Euromonitor Publications Limited, 87-88 Turnmill Street, London EC1M 5QU, England; *Third World Economic Handbook.*

G.K. Hall and Company, 70 Lincoln Street, Boston, Massachusetts 02111 (617) 423-3990; *The World in Figures.*

Statistical Office of the United Nations, Publishing Service, New York, New York 10017 (800) 253-9646; *Trade in Manufactures of Developing Countries.*

IRAN - THEATRE

United Nations Educational, Scientific and Cultural Organization (UNESCO), 7 Place de Fontenoy, F-75700 Paris, France (Telephone Number in U.S. (212) 963-5981); *Statistical Yearbook.*

IRAN - TIN - INDUSTRIAL CONSUMPTION - See IRAN - MINING AND MINERAL PRODUCTS

IRAN - TIRE (MOTOR VEHICLE) PRODUCTION

Statistical Office of the United Nations, Publishing Service, New York, New York 10017 (800) 253-9646; *Statistical Yearbook.*

IRAN - TOBACCO PRODUCTION

Euromonitor Publications Limited, 87-88 Turnmill Street, London EC1M 5QU, England; *Third World Economic Handbook.*

Facts on File, 460 Park Avenue South, New York, New York 10016 (800) 443-8323; *The New Book of World Rankings.*

Statistical Office of the United Nations, Publishing Service, New York, New York 10017 (800) 253-9646; *Statistical Yearbook.*

IRAN - TOURISM

Euromonitor Publications Limited, 87-88 Turnmill Street, London EC1M 5QU, England; *Middle East Economic Handbook,* and *Third World Economic Handbook.*

Facts on File, 460 Park Avenue South, New York, New York 10016 (800) 443-8323; *The New Book of World Rankings.*

G.K. Hall and Company, 70 Lincoln Street, Boston, Massachusetts 02111 (617) 423-3990; *The World in Figures.*

Statistical Office of the United Nations, Publishing Service, New York, New York 10017 (800) 253-9646; *Statistical Yearbook.*

Times Books, 201 East 50th Street, New York, New York 10022 (212) 751-2600; *The Economist Book of Vital World Statistics.*

World Tourism Organization, Calle Capitan Haya 42, E-28020 Madrid, Spain; *Yearbook of Tourism Statistics.*

IRAN - TRACTORS IN USE

Statistical Office of the United Nations, Publishing Service, New York, New York 10017 (800) 253-9646; *Statistical Yearbook.*

IRAN - TRADE - See IRAN - FOREIGN TRADE

IRAN - TRADEMARKS AND SERVICE MARKS

Statistical Office of the United Nations, Publishing Service, New York, New York 10017 (800) 253-9646; *Statistical Yearbook.*

World Intellectual Property Organization, 34 Chemin des Colombettes, CH-1211 Geneva 20, Switzerland; *Industrial Property Statistics.*

IRAN - TRANSPORTATION AND COMMUNICATIONS

Euromonitor Publications Limited, 87-88 Turnmill Street, London EC1M 5QU, England; *Middle East Economic Handbook,* and *Third World Economic Handbook.*

Facts on File, 460 Park Avenue South, New York, New York 10016 (800) 443-8323; *The New Book of World Rankings.*

G.K. Hall and Company, 70 Lincoln Street, Boston, Massachusetts 02111 (617) 423-3990; *The World in Figures.*

Statistical Office of the United Nations, Publishing Service, New York, New York 10017 (800) 253-9646; *Statistical Yearbook for Asia and the Pacific.*

IRAN - UNEMPLOYMENT

Euromonitor Publications Limited, 87-88 Turnmill Street, London EC1M 5QU, England; *International Marketing Data and Statistics,* and *Middle East Economic Handbook.*

International Labour Office, I.L.O. Publications, CH-1211, Geneva 22, Switzerland; *Yearbook of Labour Statistics.*

IRAN - UTILITIES

Statistical Office of the United Nations, Publishing Service, New York, New York 10017; *Electric Power in Asia and the Pacific.*

IRAN - VITAL STATISTICS

Euromonitor Publications Limited, 87-88 Turnmill Street, London EC1M 5QU, England; *International Marketing Data and Statistics, Middle East Economic Handbook,* and *Third World Economic Handbook.*

G.K. Hall and Company, 70 Lincoln Street, Boston, Massachusetts 02111 (617) 423-3990; *The World in Figures.*

Statistical Office of the United Nations, Publishing Service, New York, New York 10017 (800) 253-9646; *Statistical Yearbook.*

World Health Organization, Avenue Appia, Office of Publications, CH-1211 Geneva 27, Switzerland (Telephone Number in U.S. (518) 436-9686); *World Health Statistics Annual.*

IRAN - WAGES

G.K. Hall and Company, 70 Lincoln Street, Boston, Massachusetts 02111 (617) 423-3990; *The World in Figures.*

International Labour Office, I.L.O. Publications, CH-1211, Geneva 22, Switzerland; *Yearbook of Labour Statistics.*

IRAN - WAGES AND PRICES

Statistical Office of the United Nations, Publishing Service, New York, New York 10017 (800) 253-9646; *Statistical Yearbook for Asia and the Pacific.*

IRAN - WALNUT PRODUCTION - See IRAN - CROPS

IRAN - WATERMELON PRODUCTION - See IRAN - CROPS

IRAN - WEATHER

Facts on File, 460 Park Avenue South, New York, New York 10016 (800) 443-8323; *The New Book of World Rankings.*

G.K. Hall and Company, 70 Lincoln Street, Boston, Massachusetts 02111 (617) 423-3990; *The World in Figures.*

IRAN - WELFARE

International Monetary Fund, 700 Nineteenth Street, NW, Washington, D.C. 20431 (202) 623-7000; *Government Finance Statistics Yearbook.*

IRAN - WHEAT PRODUCTION AND PRICES - See IRAN - CROPS

IRAN - WHOLESALE PRICES

International Monetary Fund, 700 Nineteenth Street, NW, Washington, D.C. 20431 (202) 623-7000; *International Financial Statistics.*

Statistical Office of the United Nations, Publishing Service, New York, New York 10017 (800) 253-9646; *Statistical Yearbook.*

IRAN - WHOLESALE TRADE

Euromonitor Publications Limited, 87-88 Turnmill Street, London EC1M 5QU, England; *Third World Economic Handbook.*

Statistical Office of the United Nations, Publishing Service, New York, New York 10017 (800) 253-9646; *Statistical Yearbook.*

IRAN - WINE PRODUCTION

Facts on File, 460 Park Avenue South, New York, New York 10016 (800) 443-8323; *The New Book of World Rankings.*

IRAN - WOOD PULP PRODUCTION - See IRAN - FORESTRY AND FOREST PRODUCTS

IRAN - WOOL PRODUCTION

Facts on File, 460 Park Avenue South, New York, New York 10016 (800) 443-8323; *The New Book of World Rankings.*

Statistical Office of the United Nations, Publishing Service, New York, New York 10017 (800) 253-9646; *Statistical Yearbook.*

IRAN - YARN PRODUCTION

Statistical Office of the United Nations, Publishing Service, New York, New York 10017 (800) 253-9646; *Statistical Yearbook.*

IRAN - ZINC AND ZINC ORE - See IRAN - MINING AND MINERAL PRODUCTS

Iraq - National Statistical Office

Central Statistical Organisation, Ministry of Planning, Post Office Box 8001, Baghdad, Iraq.

Iraq - Primary Statistics Source

Central Statistical Organisation, Ministry of Planning, Post Office Box 8001, Baghdad, Iraq; *Annual Abstract of Statistics,* and *Statistical Pocketbook.*

IRAQ - AGRICULTURE

Economic Commission for Western Asia, Post Office Box 27, Baghdad, Iraq; *Statistical Abstract of Western Asia.*

Euromonitor Publications Limited, 87-88 Turnmill Street, London EC1M 5QU, England; *International Marketing Data and Statistics, Middle East Economic Handbook,* and *Third World Economic Handbook.*

Facts on File, 460 Park Avenue South, New York, New York 10016 (800) 443-8323; *The New Book of World Rankings.*

Food and Agricultural Organization of the United Nations (FAO) Via delle Terme di Caracalla, 00100 Rome, Italy (Telephone Number in U.S. (202) 606-7828); *Production Yearbook, The State of Food and Agriculture,* and *Trade Yearbook.*

G.K. Hall and Company, 70 Lincoln Street, Boston, Massachusetts 02111 (617) 423-3990; *The World in Figures.*

Statistical Office of the United Nations, Publishing Service, New York, New York 10017 (800) 253-9646; *Statistical Yearbook.*

Times Books, 201 East 50th Street, New York, New York 10022 (212) 751-2600; *The Economist Book of Vital World Statistics.*

IRAQ - AIRLINE SERVICE

Economic Commission for Western Asia, Post Office Box 27, Baghdad, Iraq; *Statistical Abstract of Western Asia.*

Facts on File, 460 Park Avenue South, New York, New York 10016 (800) 443-8323; *The New Book of World Rankings.*

G.K. Hall and Company, 70 Lincoln Street, Boston, Massachusetts 02111 (617) 423-3990; *The World in Figures.*

Statistical Office of the United Nations, Publishing Service, New York, New York 10017 (800) 253-9646; *Statistical Yearbook.*

Times Books, 201 East 50th Street, New York, New York 10022 (212) 751-2600; *The Economist Book of Vital World Statistics.*

IRAQ - ALMOND PRODUCTION - See IRAQ - CROPS

IRAQ - ALUMINUM PRODUCTION AND CONSUMPTION - See IRAQ - MINING AND MINERAL PRODUCTS

IRAQ - ANIMAL HEALTH

Food and Agricultural Organization of the United Nations (FAO), Via delle Terme di Caracalla, 00100 Rome, Italy (Telephone Number in U.S. (202) 606-7828); *Animal Health Yearbook.*

IRAQ - AREA AND DENSITY OF POPULATION

Economic Commission for Western Asia, Post Office Box 27, Baghdad, Iraq; *Statistical Abstract of Western Asia.*

Euromonitor Publications Limited, 87-88 Turnmill Street, London EC1M 5QU, England; *International Marketing Data and Statistics,* and *Middle East Economic Handbook.*

Facts on File, 460 Park Avenue South, New York, New York 10016 (800) 443-8323; *The New Book of World Rankings.*

Food and Agricultural Organization of the United Nations (FAO) Via delle Terme di Caracalla, 00100 Rome, Italy (Telephone Number in U.S. (202) 606-7828); *The State of Food and Agriculture.*

G.K. Hall and Company, 70 Lincoln Street, Boston, Massachusetts 02111 (617) 423-3990; *The World in Figures.*

Statistical Office of the United Nations, Publishing Service, New York, New York 10017 (800) 253-9646; *Statistical Yearbook.*

Times Books, 201 East 50th Street, New York, New York 10022 (212) 751-2600; *The Economist Book of Vital World Statistics.*

United Nations Educational, Scientific and Cultural Organization (UNESCO), 7 Place de Fontenoy, F-75700 Paris, France (Telephone Number in U.S. (212) 963-5981); *Statistical Yearbook.*

IRAQ - ARMS EXPORTS AND IMPORTS

U.S. Arms Control and Disarmament Agency, 320 Twenty-first Street, Northwest, Washington, D.C. 20451 (202) 647-8677; *World Military Expenditures and Arms Transfers.*

IRAQ - BALANCE OF PAYMENTS

Economic Commission for Western Asia, Post Office Box 27, Baghdad, Iraq; *Statistical Abstract of Western Asia.*

The Economist Intelligence Unit, 111 West 57th Street, New York, New York 10019 (800) 938-4685; *The World Market Atlas.*

Euromonitor Publications Limited, 87-88 Turnmill Street, London EC1M 5QU, England; *Third World Economic Handbook.*

G.K. Hall and Company, 70 Lincoln Street, Boston, Massachusetts 02111 (617) 423-3990; *The World in Figures.*

International Monetary Fund, 700 Nineteenth Street, NW, Washington, D.C. 20431 (202) 623-7000; *Balance of Payments Yearbook.*

Times Books, 201 East 50th Street, New York, New York 10022 (212) 751-2600; *The Economist Book of Vital World Statistics.*

IRAQ - BALANCE OF TRADE

Economic Commission for Western Asia, Post Office Box 27, Baghdad, Iraq; *Statistical Abstract of Western Asia.*

IRAQ - BANKING

Economic Commission for Western Asia, Post Office Box 27, Baghdad, Iraq; *Statistical Abstract of Western Asia.*

Facts on File, 460 Park Avenue South, New York, New York 10016 (800) 443-8323; *The New Book of World Rankings.*

G.K. Hall and Company, 70 Lincoln Street, Boston, Massachusetts 02111 (617) 423-3990; *The World in Figures.*

International Monetary Fund, 700 Nineteenth Street, NW, Washington, D.C. 20431 (202) 623-7000; *International Financial Statistics.*

IRAQ - BARLEY PRODUCTION - See IRAQ - CROPS

IRAQ - BEER PRODUCTION

Facts on File, 460 Park Avenue South, New York, New York 10016 (800) 443-8323; *The New Book of World Rankings.*

Statistical Office of the United Nations, Publishing Service, New York, New York 10017 (800) 253-9646; *Statistical Yearbook.*

IRAQ - BIRTH RATES

Euromonitor Publications Limited, 87-88 Turnmill Street, London EC1M 5QU, England; *Middle East Economic Handbook,* and *Third World Economic Handbook.*

Facts on File, 460 Park Avenue South, New York, New York 10016 (800) 443-8323; *The New Book of World Rankings.*

Statistical Office of the United Nations, Publishing Service, New York, New York 10017 (800) 253-9646; *Demographic Yearbook,* and *Statistical Yearbook.*

Times Books, 201 East 50th Street, New York, New York 10022 (212) 751-2600; *The Economist Book of Vital World Statistics.*

World Health Organization, Avenue Appia, Office of Publications, CH-1211 Geneva 27, Switzerland (Telephone Number in U.S. (518) 436-9686); *World Health Statistics Annual.*

IRAQ - BONDS

G.K. Hall and Company, 70 Lincoln Street, Boston, Massachusetts 02111 (617) 423-3990; *The World in Figures.*

IRAQ - BOOK PRODUCTION

G.K. Hall and Company, 70 Lincoln Street, Boston, Massachusetts 02111 (617) 423-3990; *The World in Figures.*

United Nations Educational, Scientific and Cultural Organization (UNESCO), 7 Place de Fontenoy, F-75700 Paris, France (Telephone Number in U.S. (212) 963-5981); *Statistical Yearbook.*

IRAQ - BROADCASTING

Billboard Limited, Post Office Box 9027, 1006 AA Amsterdam, The Netherlands (Telephone Number in U.S. (212) 764-7300); *World Radio TV Handbook.*

Facts on File, 460 Park Avenue South, New York, New York 10016 (800) 443-8323; *The New Book of World Rankings.*

G.K. Hall and Company, 70 Lincoln Street, Boston, Massachusetts 02111 (617) 423-3990; *The World in Figures.*

Times Books, 201 East 50th Street, New York, New York 10022 (212) 751-2600; *The Economist Book of Vital World Statistics.*

United Nations Educational, Scientific and Cultural Organization (UNESCO), 7 Place de Fontenoy, F-75700 Paris, France (Telephone Number in U.S. (212) 963-5981); *Statistical Yearbook.*

IRAQ - BUILDING CONSTRUCTION - See IRAQ - CONSTRUCTION INDUSTRY

IRAQ - BUSINESS

G.K. Hall and Company, 70 Lincoln Street, Boston, Massachusetts 02111 (617) 423-3990; *The World in Figures.*

IRAQ - BUTTER PRODUCTION - See IRAQ - DAIRY PRODUCTS

IRAQ - CABBAGE PRODUCTION - See IRAQ - CROPS

IRAQ - CALORIE SUPPLY

Food and Agricultural Organization of the United Nations (FAO) Via delle Terme di Caracalla, 00100 Rome, Italy (Telephone Number in U.S. (202) 606-7828); *The State of Food and Agriculture.*

IRAQ - CATTLE - See IRAQ - LIVESTOCK AND POULTRY

IRAQ - CAULIFLOWER PRODUCTION - See IRAQ - CROPS

IRAQ - CEMENT PRODUCTION - See IRAQ - MINING AND MINERAL PRODUCTS

IRAQ - CHEESE PRODUCTION - See IRAQ - DAIRY PRODUCTS

IRAQ - CHEMICAL (ORGANIC) PRODUCTION - See IRAQ - MINING AND MINERAL PRODUCTS

IRAQ - CHICK PEA PRODUCTION - See IRAQ - CROPS

IRAQ - CHICKENS - See IRAQ - LIVESTOCK AND POULTRY

IRAQ - CIGARETTE PRODUCTION - See IRAQ - TOBACCO PRODUCTION

IRAQ - CLASS STRUCTURE

G.K. Hall and Company, 70 Lincoln Street, Boston, Massachusetts 02111 (617) 423-3990; *The World in Figures.*

IRAQ - CLIMATE

Facts on File, 460 Park Avenue South, New York, New York 10016 (800) 443-8323; *The New Book of World Rankings.*

G.K. Hall and Company, 70 Lincoln Street, Boston, Massachusetts 02111 (617) 423-3990; *The World in Figures.*

IRAQ - CLOTHING EXPORTS AND IMPORTS

Euromonitor Publications Limited, 87-88 Turnmill Street, London EC1M 5QU, England; *Third World Economic Handbook.*

IRAQ - COAL PRODUCTION - See IRAQ - MINING AND MINERAL PRODUCTS

IRAQ - COFFEE PRODUCTION - See IRAQ - CROPS

IRAQ - COMMUNICATIONS

Economic Commission for Western Asia, Post Office Box 27, Baghdad, Iraq; *Statistical Abstract of Western Asia.*

Euromonitor Publications Limited, 87-88 Turnmill Street, London EC1M 5QU, England; *Third World Economic Handbook.*

G.K. Hall and Company, 70 Lincoln Street, Boston, Massachusetts 02111 (617) 423-3990; *The World in Figures.*

IRAQ - CONSTRUCTION INDUSTRY

Facts on File, 460 Park Avenue South, New York, New York 10016 (800) 443-8323; *The New Book of World Rankings.*

Statistical Office of the United Nations, Publishing Service, New York, New York 10017 (800) 253-9646; *Construction Statistics Yearbook,* and *Statistical Yearbook.*

IRAQ - CONSUMER PRICE INDEX

G.K. Hall and Company, 70 Lincoln Street, Boston, Massachusetts 02111 (617) 423-3990; *The World in Figures.*

Statistical Office of the United Nations, Publishing Service, New York, New York 10017 (800) 253-9646; *Statistical Yearbook.*

IRAQ - CONSUMER PRICES

International Labour Office, I.L.O. Publications, CH-1211, Geneva 22, Switzerland; *Yearbook of Labour Statistics.*

International Monetary Fund, 700 Nineteenth Street, NW, Washington, D.C. 20431 (202) 623-7000; *International Financial Statistics.*

IRAQ - CONSUMPTION

Euromonitor Publications Limited, 87-88 Turnmill Street, London EC1M 5QU, England; *Middle East Economic Handbook.*

G.K. Hall and Company, 70 Lincoln Street, Boston, Massachusetts 02111 (617) 423-3990; *The World in Figures.*

IRAQ - COPPER PRODUCTION AND CONSUMPTION - See IRAQ - MINING AND MINERAL PRODUCTS

IRAQ - CORN PRODUCTION - See IRAQ - CROPS

IRAQ - CORPORATE TAXES - See IRAQ - TAXATION

IRAQ - COTTON - See IRAQ - CROPS

IRAQ - CRIME

International Criminal Police Organization (INTERPOL), 26 rue Armengaud, 92210 Saint Cloud, France; *International Crime Statistics.*

Yale University Press, Yale Station, New Haven, Connecticut 06520 (203) 432-0940; *Violence and Crime in Cross-National Perspective.*

IRAQ - CROPS

Facts on File, 460 Park Avenue South, New York, New York 10016 (800) 443-8323; *The New Book of World Rankings.*

Food and Agricultural Organization of the United Nations (FAO) Via delle Terme di Caracalla, 00100 Rome, Italy (Telephone Number in U.S. (202) 606-7828); *Production Yearbook* and *The State of Food and Agriculture.*

G.K. Hall and Company, 70 Lincoln Street, Boston, Massachusetts 02111 (617) 423-3990; *The World in Figures.*

Statistical Office of the United Nations, Publishing Service, New York, New York 10017 (800) 253-9646; *Statistical Yearbook.*

IRAQ - CUSTOMS DUTIES

G.K. Hall and Company, 70 Lincoln Street, Boston, Massachusetts 02111 (617) 423-3990; *The World in Figures.*

IRAQ - DAIRY PRODUCTS

Economic Commission for Western Asia, Post Office Box 27, Baghdad, Iraq; *Statistical Abstract of Western Asia.*

Facts on File, 460 Park Avenue South, New York, New York 10016 (800) 443-8323; *The New Book of World Rankings.*

Food and Agricultural Organization of the United Nations (FAO), Via delle Terme di Caracalla, 00100 Rome, Italy (Telephone Number in U.S. (202) 606-7828); *Production Yearbook* and *The State of Food and Agriculture.*

Statistical Office of the United Nations, Publishing Service, New York, New York 10017 (800) 253-9646; *Statistical Yearbook.*

IRAQ - DEATH RATES

Euromonitor Publications Limited, 87-88 Turnmill Street, London EC1M 5QU, England; *Middle East Economic Handbook,* and *Third World Economic Handbook.*

G.K. Hall and Company, 70 Lincoln Street, Boston, Massachusetts 02111 (617) 423-3990; *The World in Figures.*

Statistical Office of the United Nations, Publishing Service, New York, New York 10017 (800) 253-9646; *Statistical Yearbook.*

Times Books, 201 East 50th Street, New York, New York 10022 (212) 751-2600; *The Economist Book of Vital World Statistics.*

World Health Organization, Avenue Appia, Office of Publications, CH-1211 Geneva 27, Switzerland (Telephone Number in U.S. (518) 436-9686); *World Health Statistics Annual.*

IRAQ - DEFENSE EXPENDITURES

G.K. Hall and Company, 70 Lincoln Street, Boston, Massachusetts 02111 (617) 423-3990; *The World in Figures.*

U.S. Arms Control and Disarmament Agency, 320 Twenty-first Street, Northwest, Washington, D.C. 20451 (202) 647-8677; *World Military Expenditures and Arms Transfers.*

IRAQ - DEMOGRAPHY

The Economist Intelligence Unit, 111 West 57th Street, New York, New York 10019 (800) 938-4685; *The World Market Atlas.*

Facts on File, 460 Park Avenue South, New York, New York 10016 (800) 443-8323; *The New Book of World Rankings.*

G.K. Hall and Company, 70 Lincoln Street, Boston, Massachusetts 02111 (617) 423-3990; *The World in Figures.*

IRAQ - DEVELOPMENT ASSISTANCE

G.K. Hall and Company, 70 Lincoln Street, Boston, Massachusetts 02111 (617) 423-3990; *The World in Figures.*

Statistical Office of the United Nations, Publishing Service, New York, New York 10017 (800) 253-9646; *Statistical Yearbook.*

IRAQ - DIAMOND PRODUCTION - See IRAQ - MINING AND MINERAL PRODUCTS

IRAQ - DISEASES

G.K. Hall and Company, 70 Lincoln Street, Boston, Massachusetts 02111 (617) 423-3990; *The World in Figures.*

World Health Organization, Avenue Appia, Office of Publications, CH-1211 Geneva 27, Switzerland (Telephone Number in U.S. (518) 436-9686); *World Health Statistics Annual.*

IRAQ - DIVORCE RATES

Facts on File, 460 Park Avenue South, New York, New York 10016 (800) 443-8323; *The New Book of World Rankings.*

Statistical Office of the United Nations, Publishing Service, New York, New York 10017 (800) 253-9646; *Statistical Yearbook.*

IRAQ - DOMESTIC PRODUCT

G.K. Hall and Company, 70 Lincoln Street, Boston, Massachusetts 02111 (617) 423-3990; *The World in Figures.*

IRAQ - ECONOMY

Euromonitor Publications Limited, 87-88 Turnmill Street, London EC1M 5QU, England; *International Marketing Data and Statistics,* and *Third World Economic Handbook.*

Facts on File, 460 Park Avenue South, New York, New York 10016 (800) 443-8323; *The New Book of World Rankings.*

G.K. Hall and Company, 70 Lincoln Street, Boston, Massachusetts 02111 (617) 423-3990; *The World in Figures.*

IRAQ - EDUCATION

Economic Commission for Western Asia, Post Office Box 27, Baghdad, Iraq; *Statistical Abstract of Western Asia.*

The Economist Intelligence Unit, 111 West 57th Street, New York, New York 10019 (800) 938-4685; *The World Market Atlas.*

Euromonitor Publications Limited, 87-88 Turnmill Street, London EC1M 5QU, England; *Middle East Economic Handbook.*

Facts on File, 460 Park Avenue South, New York, New York 10016 (800) 443-8323; *The New Book of World Rankings.*

G.K. Hall and Company, 70 Lincoln Street, Boston, Massachusetts 02111 (617) 423-3990; *The World in Figures.*

Times Books, 201 East 50th Street, New York, New York 10022 (212) 751-2600; *The Economist Book of Vital World Statistics.*

United Nations Educational, Scientific and Cultural Organization (UNESCO), 7 Place de Fontenoy, F-75700 Paris, France (Telephone Number in U.S. (212) 963-5981); *Statistical Yearbook.*

IRAQ - EGG PRODUCTION - See IRAQ - DAIRY PRODUCTS

IRAQ - EGGPLANT PRODUCTION - See IRAQ - CROPS

IRAQ - ELECTRICITY

Facts on File, 460 Park Avenue South, New York, New York 10016 (800) 443-8323; *The New Book of World Rankings.*

Penn Well Publishing Company, 1421 South Sheridan Road, Post Office Box 1260, Tulsa, Oklahoma 74101 (800) 752-9764; *International Energy Statistics Sourcebook.*

Statistical Office of the United Nations, Publishing Service, New York, New York 10017 (800) 253-9646; *Statistical Yearbook.*

Times Books, 201 East 50th Street, New York, New York 10022 (212) 751-2600; *The Economist Book of Vital World Statistics.*

IRAQ - EMPLOYMENT

Economic Commission for Western Asia, Post Office Box 27, Baghdad, Iraq; *Statistical Abstract of Western Asia.*

Euromonitor Publications Limited, 87-88 Turnmill Street, London EC1M 5QU, England; *International Marketing Data and Statistics,* and *Middle East Economic Handbook.*

Facts on File, 460 Park Avenue South, New York, New York 10016 (800) 443-8323; *The New Book of World Rankings.*

International Labour Office, I.L.O. Publications, CH-1211, Geneva 22, Switzerland; *Yearbook of Labour Statistics.*

Statistical Office of the United Nations, Publishing Service, New York, New York 10017 (800) 253-9646; *Statistical Yearbook.*

IRAQ - ENERGY

Economic Commission for Western Asia, Post Office Box 27, Baghdad, Iraq; *Statistical Abstract of Western Asia.*

Euromonitor Publications Limited, 87-88 Turnmill Street, London EC1M 5QU, England; *Middle East Economic Handbook.*

Facts on File, 460 Park Avenue South, New York, New York 10016 (800) 443-8323; *The New Book of World Rankings.*

Food and Agricultural Organization of the United Nations (FAO) Via delle Terme di Caracalla, 00100 Rome, Italy (Telephone Number in U.S. (202) 606-7828); *The State of Food and Agriculture.*

G.K. Hall and Company, 70 Lincoln Street, Boston, Massachusetts 02111 (617) 423-3990; *The World in Figures.*

Penn Well Publishing Company, 1421 South Sheridan Road, Post Office Box 1260, Tulsa, Oklahoma 74101 (800) 752-9764; *International Energy Statistics Sourcebook.*

Statistical Office of the United Nations, Publishing Service, New York, New York 10017 (800) 253-9646; *Energy Statistics Yearbook,* and *Statistical Yearbook.*

Times Books, 201 East 50th Street, New York, New York 10022 (212) 751-2600; *The Economist Book of Vital World Statistics.*

IRAQ - EXCHANGE RATE

Euromonitor Publications Limited, 87-88 Turnmill Street, London EC1M 5QU, England; *International Marketing Data and Statistics,* and *Middle East Economic Handbook.*

International Monetary Fund, 700 Nineteenth Street, NW, Washington, D.C. 20431 (202) 623-7000; *International Financial Statistics.*

Organization of Petroleum Exporting Countries, Obere Donaustrasse 93, 1020 Vienna 2, Austria; *OPEC Annual Statistical Bulletin.*

Statistical Office of the United Nations, Publishing Service, New York, New York 10017 (800) 253-9646; *Statistical Yearbook.*

IRAQ - EXPORTS

Economic Commission for Western Asia, Post Office Box 27, Baghdad, Iraq; *Statistical Abstract of Western Asia.*

The Economist Intelligence Unit, 111 West 57th Street, New York, New York 10019 (800) 938-4685; *The World Market Atlas.*

Euromonitor Publications Limited, 87-88 Turnmill Street, London EC1M 5QU, England; *International Marketing Data and Statistics, Middle East Economic Handbook,* and *Third World Economic Handbook.*

Food and Agricultural Organization of the United Nations (FAO) Via delle Terme di Caracalla, 00100 Rome, Italy (Telephone Number in U.S. (202) 606-7828); *The State of Food and Agriculture.*

G.K. Hall and Company, 70 Lincoln Street, Boston, Massachusetts 02111 (617) 423-3990; *The World in Figures.*

International Monetary Fund, 700 Nineteenth Street, NW, Washington, D.C. 20431 (202) 623-7000; *Direction of Trade Statistics,* and *International Financial Statistics.*

Organization of Petroleum Exporting Countries, Obere Donaustrasse 93, 1020 Vienna 2, Austria; *OPEC Annual Statistical Bulletin.*

Times Books, 201 East 50th Street, New York, New York 10022 (212) 751-2600; *The Economist Book of Vital World Statistics.*

IRAQ - EXTERNAL INDEBTEDNESS

Euromonitor Publications Limited, 87-88 Turnmill Street, London EC1M 5QU, England; *Third World Economic Handbook.*

IRAQ - EXTERNAL TRADE

Food and Agricultural Organization of the United Nations (FAO) Via delle Terme di Caracalla, 00100 Rome, Italy (Telephone Number in U.S. (202) 606-7828); *The State of Food and Agriculture,* and *Trade Yearbook.*

G.K. Hall and Company, 70 Lincoln Street, Boston, Massachusetts 02111 (617) 423-3990; *The World in Figures.*

Statistical Office of the United Nations, Publishing Service, New York, New York 10017 (800) 253-9646; *Statistical Yearbook.*

IRAQ - FABRIC PRODUCTION - See IRAQ - TEXTILE INDUSTRY

IRAQ - FARM CROPS - See IRAQ - CROPS

IRAQ - FERTILITY RATES

Facts on File, 460 Park Avenue South, New York, New York 10016 (800) 443-8323; *The New Book of World Rankings.*

Times Books, 201 East 50th Street, New York, New York 10022 (212) 751-2600; *The Economist Book of Vital World Statistics.*

IRAQ - FERTILIZER

Food and Agricultural Organization of the United Nations (FAO), Via delle Terme di Caracalla, 00100 Rome, Italy (Telephone Number in U.S. (202) 606-7828); *Fertilizer Yearbook,* and *The State of Food and Agriculture.*

Statistical Office of the United Nations, Publishing Service, New York, New York 10017 (800) 253-9646; *Statistical Yearbook.*

IRAQ - FETAL MORTALITY

Statistical Office of the United Nations, Publishing Service, New York, New York 10017 (800) 253-9646; *Demographic Yearbook.*

World Health Organization, Avenue Appia, Office of Publications, CH-1211 Geneva 27, Switzerland (Telephone Number in U.S. (518) 436-9686); *World Health Statistics Annual.*

IRAQ - FINANCE

Economic Commission for Western Asia, Post Office Box 27, Baghdad, Iraq; *Statistical Abstract of Western Asia.*

Euromonitor Publications Limited, 87-88 Turnmill Street, London EC1M 5QU, England; *Middle East Economic Handbook.*

Facts on File, 460 Park Avenue South, New York, New York 10016 (800) 443-8323; *The New Book of World Rankings.*

G.K. Hall and Company, 70 Lincoln Street, Boston, Massachusetts 02111 (617) 423-3990; *The World in Figures.*

International Monetary Fund, 700 Nineteenth Street, NW, Washington, D.C. 20431 (202) 623-7000; *International Financial Statistics.*

IRAQ - FISHERIES

Economic Commission for Western Asia, Post Office Box 27, Baghdad, Iraq; *Statistical Abstract of Western Asia.*

Facts on File, 460 Park Avenue South, New York, New York 10016 (800) 443-8323; *The New Book of World Rankings.*

Food and Agricultural Organization of the United Nations (FAO) Via delle Terme di Caracalla, 00100 Rome, Italy (Telephone Number in U.S. (202) 606-7828); *The State of Food and Agriculture,* and *Yearbook of Fishery Statistics.*

Statistical Office of the United Nations, Publishing Service, New York, New York 10017 (800) 253-9646; *Statistical Yearbook.*

IRAQ - FLOUR PRODUCTION

Statistical Office of the United Nations, Publishing Service, New York, New York 10017 (800) 253-9646; *Statistical Yearbook.*

IRAQ - FOOD

Food and Agricultural Organization of the United Nations (FAO), Via delle Terme di Caracalla, 00100 Rome, Italy (Telephone Number in U.S. (202) 606-7828); *Production Yearbook,* and *The State of Food and Agriculture.*

G.K. Hall and Company, 70 Lincoln Street, Boston, Massachusetts 02111 (617) 423-3990; *The World in Figures.*

IRAQ - FOREIGN AID

G.K. Hall and Company, 70 Lincoln Street, Boston, Massachusetts 02111 (617) 423-3990; *The World in Figures.*

IRAQ - FOREIGN INDEBTEDNESS

Euromonitor Publications Limited, 87-88 Turnmill Street, London EC1M 5QU, England; *Middle East Economic Handbook.*

IRAQ - FOREIGN TRADE

Economic Commission for Western Asia, Post Office Box 27, Baghdad, Iraq; *Statistical Abstract of Western Asia.*

Euromonitor Publications Limited, 87-88 Turnmill Street, London EC1M 5QU, England; *International Marketing Data and Statistics, Middle East Economic Handbook,* and *Third World Economic Handbook.*

Facts on File, 460 Park Avenue South, New York, New York 10016 (800) 443-8323; *The New Book of World Rankings.*

Food and Agricultural Organization of the United Nations (FAO) Via delle Terme di Caracalla, 00100 Rome, Italy (Telephone Number in U.S. (202) 606-7828); *The State of Food and Agriculture.*

G.K. Hall and Company, 70 Lincoln Street, Boston, Massachusetts 02111 (617) 423-3990; *The World in Figures.*

International Monetary Fund, 700 Nineteenth Street, NW, Washington, D.C. 20431 (202) 623-7000; *International Financial Statistics.*

Statistical Office of the United Nations, Publishing Service, New York, New York 10017 (800) 253-9646; *International Trade Statistics Yearbook,* and *Statistical Yearbook.*

IRAQ - FORESTRY AND FOREST PRODUCTS

Euromonitor Publications Limited, 87-88 Turnmill Street, London EC1M 5QU, England; *Third World Economic Handbook.*

Facts on File, 460 Park Avenue South, New York, New York 10016 (800) 443-8323; *The New Book of World Rankings.*

Food and Agricultural Organization of the United Nations (FAO) Via delle Terme di Caracalla, 00100 Rome, Italy (Telephone Number in U.S. (202) 606-7828); *The State of Food and Agriculture,* and *Yearbook of Forest Products.*

G.K. Hall and Company, 70 Lincoln Street, Boston, Massachusetts 02111 (617) 423-3990; *The World in Figures.*

Statistical Office of the United Nations, Publishing Service, New York, New York 10017 (800) 253-9646; *Statistical Yearbook.*

United Nations Educational, Scientific and Cultural Organization (UNESCO), 7 Place de Fontenoy, F-75700 Paris, France (Telephone Number in U.S. (212) 963-5981); *Statistical Yearbook.*

IRAQ - GARLIC PRODUCTION - See IRAQ - CROPS

IRAQ - GAS PRODUCTION - See IRAQ - MINING AND MINERAL PRODUCTS

IRAQ - GENERAL INDUSTRIAL STATISTICS

Statistical Office of the United Nations, Publishing Service, New York, New York 10017 (800) 253-9646; *Industrial Statistics Yearbook.*

IRAQ - GENERAL MORTALITY

Statistical Office of the United Nations, Publishing Service, New York, New York 10017 (800) 253-9646; *Demographic Yearbook.*

World Health Organization, Avenue Appia, Office of Publications, CH-1211 Geneva 27, Switzerland (Telephone Number in U.S. (518) 436-9686); *World Health Statistics Annual.*

IRAQ - GEOGRAPHIC DATA

Facts on File, 460 Park Avenue South, New York, New York 10016 (800) 443-8323; *The New Book of World Rankings.*

IRAQ - GOATS - See IRAQ - LIVESTOCK AND POULTRY

IRAQ - GOLD HOLDINGS

International Monetary Fund, 700 Nineteenth Street, NW, Washington, D.C. 20431 (202) 623-7000; *International Financial Statistics.*

Statistical Office of the United Nations, Publishing Service, New York, New York 10017 (800) 253-9646; *Statistical Yearbook.*

IRAQ - GOLD PRODUCTION AND CONSUMPTION - See IRAQ - MINING AND MINERAL PRODUCTS

IRAQ - GOVERNMENT

G.K. Hall and Company, 70 Lincoln Street, Boston, Massachusetts 02111 (617) 423-3990; *The World in Figures.*

IRAQ - GOVERNMENT EXPENDITURE

Economic Commission for Western Asia, Post Office Box 27, Baghdad, Iraq; *Statistical Abstract of Western Asia.*

Euromonitor Publications Limited, 87-88 Turnmill Street, London EC1M 5QU, England; *Third World Economic Handbook.*

IRAQ - GOVERNMENT FINANCES

International Monetary Fund, 700 Nineteenth Street, NW, Washington, D.C. 20431 (202) 623-7000; *International Financial Statistics.*

Statistical Office of the United Nations, Publishing Service, New York, New York 10017 (800) 253-9646; *Statistical Yearbook.*

IRAQ - GOVERNMENT REVENUE

Economic Commission for Western Asia, Post Office Box 27, Baghdad, Iraq; *Statistical Abstract of Western Asia.*

IRAQ - GRAIN PRODUCTION - See IRAQ - CROPS

IRAQ - GREEN PEPPER AND CHILIE PRODUCTION - See IRAQ - CROPS

IRAQ - GROSS DOMESTIC PRODUCT

Economic Commission for Western Asia, Post Office Box 27, Baghdad, Iraq; *Statistical Abstract of Western Asia.*

The Economist Intelligence Unit, 111 West 57th Street, New York, New York 10019 (800) 938-4685; *The World Market Atlas.*

Euromonitor Publications Limited, 87-88 Turnmill Street, London EC1M 5QU, England; *International Marketing Data and Statistics, Middle East Economic Handbook,* and *Third World Economic Handbook.*

Facts on File, 460 Park Avenue South, New York, New York 10016 (800) 443-8323; *The New Book of World Rankings.*

G.K. Hall and Company, 70 Lincoln Street, Boston, Massachusetts 02111 (617) 423-3990; *The World in Figures.*

Statistical Office of the United Nations, Publishing Service, New York, New York 10017 (800) 253-9646; *Statistical Yearbook.*

Times Books, 201 East 50th Street, New York, New York 10022 (212) 751-2600; *The Economist Book of Vital World Statistics.*

IRAQ - GROSS INDUSTRIAL PRODUCT

Euromonitor Publications Limited, 87-88 Turnmill Street, London EC1M 5QU, England; *Third World Economic Handbook.*

IRAQ - GROSS NATIONAL PRODUCT

Euromonitor Publications Limited, 87-88 Turnmill Street, London EC1M 5QU, England; *International Marketing Data and Statistics,* and *Third World Economic Handbook.*

Organization of Petroleum Exporting Countries, Obere Donaustrasse 93, 1020 Vienna 2, Austria; *OPEC Annual Statistical Bulletin.*

U.S. Arms Control and Disarmament Agency, 320 Twenty-first Street, Northwest, Washington, D.C. 20451 (202) 647-8677; *World Military Expenditures and Arms Transfers.*

IRAQ - GROUNDNUT PRODUCTION - See IRAQ - CROPS

IRAQ - HEALTH

Economic Commission for Western Asia, Post Office Box 27, Baghdad, Iraq; *Statistical Abstract of Western Asia.*

Euromonitor Publications Limited, 87-88 Turnmill Street, London EC1M 5QU, England; *Middle East Economic Handbook.*

Facts on File, 460 Park Avenue South, New York, New York 10016 (800) 443-8323; *The New Book of World Rankings.*

G.K. Hall and Company, 70 Lincoln Street, Boston, Massachusetts 02111 (617) 423-3990; *The World in Figures.*

Statistical Office of the United Nations, Publishing Service, New York, New York 10017 (800) 253-9646; *Statistical Yearbook.*

Times Books, 201 East 50th Street, New York, New York 10022 (212) 751-2600; *The Economist Book of Vital World Statistics.*

World Health Organization, Avenue Appia, Office of Publications, CH-1211 Geneva 27, Switzerland (Telephone Number in U.S. (518) 436-9686); *World Health Statistics Annual.*

IRAQ - HIDE PRODUCTION

Food and Agricultural Organization of the United Nations (FAO), Via delle Terme di Caracalla, 00100 Rome, Italy (Telephone Number in U.S. (202) 606-7828); *Production Yearbook.*

IRAQ - HIGHWAYS

Economic Commission for Western Asia, Post Office Box 27, Baghdad, Iraq; *Statistical Abstract of Western Asia.*

G.K. Hall and Company, 70 Lincoln Street, Boston, Massachusetts 02111 (617) 423-3990; *The World in Figures.*

International Road Federation, 525 School Street, SW, Washington, D.C. 20024 (202) 554-2106; *World Road Statistics.*

IRAQ - HORSES - See IRAQ - LIVESTOCK AND POULTRY

IRAQ - HOURS OF WORK - See IRAQ - EMPLOYMENT

IRAQ - HOUSING AND HOUSING UNITS

Euromonitor Publications Limited, 87-88 Turnmill Street, London EC1M 5QU, England; *Third World Economic Handbook.*

Facts on File, 460 Park Avenue South, New York, New York 10016 (800) 443-8323; *The New Book of World Rankings.*

IRAQ - ILLITERATE POPULATION

The Economist Intelligence Unit, 111 West 57th Street, New York, New York 10019 (800) 938-4685; *The World Market Atlas.*

G.K. Hall and Company, 70 Lincoln Street, Boston, Massachusetts 02111 (617) 423-3990; *The World in Figures.*

United Nations Educational, Scientific and Cultural Organization (UNESCO), 7 Place de Fontenoy, F-75700 Paris, France (Telephone Number in U.S. (212) 963-5981); *Statistical Yearbook.*

IRAQ - IMPORTS

Economic Commission for Western Asia, Post Office Box 27, Baghdad, Iraq; *Statistical Abstract of Western Asia.*

The Economist Intelligence Unit, 111 West 57th Street, New York, New York 10019 (800) 938-4685; *The World Market Atlas.*

Euromonitor Publications Limited, 87-88 Turnmill Street, London EC1M 5QU, England; *International Marketing Data and Statistics, Middle East Economic Handbook,* and *Third World Economic Handbook.*

Food and Agricultural Organization of the United Nations (FAO) Via delle Terme di Caracalla, 00100 Rome, Italy (Telephone Number in U.S. (202) 606-7828); *The State of Food and Agriculture.*

G.K. Hall and Company, 70 Lincoln Street, Boston, Massachusetts 02111 (617) 423-3990; *The World in Figures.*

International Monetary Fund, 700 Nineteenth Street, NW, Washington, D.C. 20431 (202) 623-7000; *Direction of Trade Statistics,* and *International Financial Statistics.*

IRAQ - INDUSTRY

Euromonitor Publications Limited, 87-88 Turnmill Street, London EC1M 5QU, England; *Third World Economic Handbook.*

Facts on File, 460 Park Avenue South, New York, New York 10016 (800) 443-8323; *The New Book of World Rankings.*

G.K. Hall and Company, 70 Lincoln Street, Boston, Massachusetts 02111 (617) 423-3990; *The World in Figures.*

International Labour Office, I.L.O. Publications, CH-1211, Geneva 22, Switzerland; *Yearbook of Labour Statistics.*

Statistical Office of the United Nations, Publishing Service, New York, New York 10017 (800) 253-9646; *Statistical Yearbook.*

Times Books, 201 East 50th Street, New York, New York 10022 (212) 751-2600; *The Economist Book of Vital World Statistics.*

IRAQ - INFANT AND MATERNAL MORTALITY

Statistical Office of the United Nations, Publishing Service, New York, New York 10017 (800) 253-9646; *Demographic Yearbook,* and *Statistical Yearbook.*

Times Books, 201 East 50th Street, New York, New York 10022 (212) 751-2600; *The Economist Book of Vital World Statistics.*

World Health Organization, Avenue Appia, Office of Publications, CH-1211 Geneva 27, Switzerland (Telephone Number in U.S. (518) 436-9686); *World Health Statistics Annual.*

IRAQ - INTERNATIONAL LIQUIDITY

International Monetary Fund, 700 Nineteenth Street, NW, Washington, D.C. 20431 (202) 623-7000; *International Financial Statistics.*

IRAQ - INTERNATIONAL RESERVES EXCLUDING GOLD

Statistical Office of the United Nations, Publishing Service, New York, New York 10017 (800) 253-9646; *Statistical Yearbook.*

IRAQ - IRON ORE PRODUCTION AND CONSUMPTION - See IRAQ - MINING AND MINERAL PRODUCTS

IRAQ - IRRIGATION

Euromonitor Publications Limited, 87-88 Turnmill Street, London EC1M 5QU, England; *International Marketing Data and Statistics*.

IRAQ - LABOR FORCE

Economic Commission for Western Asia, Post Office Box 27, Baghdad, Iraq; *Statistical Abstract of Western Asia*.

Euromonitor Publications Limited, 87-88 Turnmill Street, London EC1M 5QU, England; *International Marketing Data and Statistics*, and *Middle East Economic Handbook*.

Facts on File, 460 Park Avenue South, New York, New York 10016 (800) 443-8323; *The New Book of World Rankings*.

Food and Agricultural Organization of the United Nations (FAO) Via delle Terme di Caracalla, 00100 Rome, Italy (Telephone Number in U.S. (202) 606-7828); *The State of Food and Agriculture*.

G.K. Hall and Company, 70 Lincoln Street, Boston, Massachusetts 02111 (617) 423-3990; *The World in Figures*.

IRAQ - LABOR PRODUCTIVITY

International Labour Office, I.L.O. Publications, CH-1211, Geneva 22, Switzerland; *Yearbook of Labour Statistics*.

IRAQ - LAND USE

Economic Commission for Western Asia, Post Office Box 27, Baghdad, Iraq; *Statistical Abstract of Western Asia*.

Euromonitor Publications Limited, 87-88 Turnmill Street, London EC1M 5QU, England; *International Marketing Data and Statistics*.

Food and Agricultural Organization of the United Nations (FAO), Via delle Terme di Caracalla, 00100 Rome, Italy (Telephone Number in U.S. (202) 606-7828); *Production Yearbook*.

G.K. Hall and Company, 70 Lincoln Street, Boston, Massachusetts 02111 (617) 423-3990; *The World in Figures*.

IRAQ - LIBRARIES

Facts on File, 460 Park Avenue South, New York, New York 10016 (800) 443-8323; *The New Book of World Rankings*.

United Nations Educational, Scientific and Cultural Organization (UNESCO), 7 Place de Fontenoy, F-75700 Paris, France (Telephone Number in U.S. (212) 963-5981); *Statistical Yearbook*.

IRAQ - LIVESTOCK AND POULTRY

Economic Commission for Western Asia, Post Office Box 27, Baghdad, Iraq; *Statistical Abstract of Western Asia*.

Euromonitor Publications Limited, 87-88 Turnmill Street, London EC1M 5QU, England; *International Marketing and Data Statistics*, and *Middle East Economic Handbook*.

Facts on File, 460 Park Avenue South, New York, New York 10016 (800) 443-8323; *The New Book of World Rankings*.

Food and Agricultural Organization of the United Nations (FAO), Via delle Terme di Caracalla, 00100 Rome, Italy (Telephone Number in U.S. (202) 606-7828); *Production Yearbook*, and *The State of Food and Agriculture*.

G.K. Hall and Company, 70 Lincoln Street, Boston, Massachusetts 02111 (617) 423-3990; *The World in Figures*.

Statistical Office of the United Nations, Publishing Service, New York, New York 10017 (800) 253-9646; *Statistical Yearbook*.

IRAQ - LIVING LEVELS

G.K. Hall and Company, 70 Lincoln Street, Boston, Massachusetts 02111 (617) 423-3990; *The World in Figures*.

Euromonitor Publications Limited, 87-88 Turnmill Street, London EC1M 5QU, England; *Middle East Economic Handbook*.

IRAQ - MAIL - NUMBER OF PIECES SENT OR RECEIVED

Statistical Office of the United Nations, Publishing Service, New York, New York 10017 (800) 253-9646; *Statistical Yearbook*.

IRAQ - MANUFACTURING

Euromonitor Publications Limited, 87-88 Turnmill Street, London EC1M 5QU, England; *Third World Economic Handbook*.

Facts on File, 460 Park Avenue South, New York, New York 10016 (800) 443-8323; *The New Book of World Rankings*.

G.K. Hall and Company, 70 Lincoln Street, Boston, Massachusetts 02111 (617) 423-3990; *The World in Figures*.

Statistical Office of the United Nations, Publishing Service, New York, New York 10017 (800) 253-9646; *Statistical Yearbook*.

IRAQ - MARRIAGE RATES

Facts on File, 460 Park Avenue South, New York, New York 10016 (800) 443-8323; *The New Book of World Rankings*.

Statistical Office of the United Nations, Publishing Service, New York, New York 10017 (800) 253-9646; *Demographic Yearbook*, and *Statistical Yearbook*.

IRAQ - MEAT PRODUCTION - See IRAQ - LIVESTOCK AND POULTRY

IRAQ - MERCHANT SHIPPING

Economic Commission for Western Asia, Post Office Box 27, Baghdad, Iraq; *Statistical Abstract of Western Asia*.

G.K. Hall and Company, 70 Lincoln Street, Boston, Massachusetts 02111 (617) 423-3990; *The World in Figures*.

Organization of Petroleum Exporting Countries, Obere Donaustrasse 93, 1020 Vienna 2, Austria; *OPEC Annual Statistical Bulletin*.

Statistical Office of the United Nations, Publishing Service, New York, New York 10017 (800) 253-9646; *Statistical Yearbook*.

Times Books, 201 East 50th Street, New York, New York 10022 (212) 751-2600; *The Economist Book of Vital World Statistics*.

U.S. Department of Transportation, Maritime Administration, 400 Seventh Street, SW, Washington, D.C. 20590 (202) 366-5807; *A Statistical Analysis of the World's Merchant Fleets*.

IRAQ - MILITARY

G.K. Hall and Company, 70 Lincoln Street, Boston, Massachusetts 02111 (617) 423-3990; *The World in Figures.*

The International Institute for Strategic Studies, 23 Tavistock Street, London WC2E 7NQ, England; *The Military Balance.*

U.S. Arms Control and Disarmament Agency, 320 Twenty-first Street, Northwest, Washington, D.C. 20451 (202) 647-8677; *World Military Expenditures and Arms Transfers.*

IRAQ - MILK - See IRAQ - DAIRY PRODUCTS

IRAQ - MILLET PRODUCTION - See IRAQ - CROPS

IRAQ - MINING AND MINERAL PRODUCTS

Economic Commission for Western Asia, Post Office Box 27, Baghdad, Iraq; *Statistical Abstract of Western Asia.*

Euromonitor Publications Limited, 87-88 Turnmill Street, London EC1M 5QU, England; *International Marketing Data and Statistics.*

Facts on File, 460 Park Avenue South, New York, New York 10016 (800) 443-8323; *The New Book of World Rankings.*

G.K. Hall and Company, 70 Lincoln Street, Boston, Massachusetts 02111 (617) 423-3990; *The World in Figures.*

International Lead and Zinc Study Group, Metro House, 58 St. James's Street, London SW1A 1LD, England; *Lead and Zinc Statistics.*

Organization of Petroleum Exporting Countries, Obere Donaustrasse 93, 1020 Vienna 2, Austria; *OPEC Annual Statistical Bulletin.*

Penn Well Publishing Company, 1421 South Sheridan Road, Post Office Box 1260, Tulsa, Oklahoma 74101 (800) 752-9764; *International Energy Statistics Sourcebook.*

Statistical Office of the United Nations, Publishing Service, New York, New York 10017 (800) 253-9646; *Statistical Yearbook.*

IRAQ - MONEY EXCHANGE RATE

Euromonitor Publications Limited, 87-88 Turnmill Street, London EC1M 5QU, England; *International Marketing Data and Statistics.*

International Monetary Fund, 700 Nineteenth Street, NW, Washington, D.C. 20431 (202) 623-7000; *International Financial Statistics.*

Statistical Office of the United Nations, Publishing Service, New York, New York 10017 (800) 253-9646; *Statistical Yearbook.*

IRAQ - MONEY RESERVES

Euromonitor Publications Limited, 87-88 Turnmill Street, London EC1M 5QU, England; *International Marketing Data and Statistics.*

IRAQ - MONEY SUPPLY

Economic Commission for Western Asia, Post Office Box 27, Baghdad, Iraq; *Statistical Abstract of Western Asia.*

Euromonitor Publications Limited, 87-88 Turnmill Street, London EC1M 5QU, England; *International Marketing Data and Statistics.*

G.K. Hall and Company, 70 Lincoln Street, Boston, Massachusetts 02111 (617) 423-3990; *The World in Figures.*

International Monetary Fund, 700 Nineteenth Street, NW, Washington, D.C. 20431 (202) 623-7000; *International Financial Statistics.*

Statistical Office of the United Nations, Publishing Service, New York, New York 10017 (800) 253-9646; *Statistical Yearbook.*

IRAQ - MOTOR VEHICLES

Economic Commission for Western Asia, Post Office Box 27, Baghdad, Iraq; *Statistical Abstract of Western Asia.*

International Road Federation, 525 School Street, SW, Washington, D.C. 20024 (202) 554-2106; *World Road Statistics.*

IRAQ - MOTOR VEHICLES IN USE

G.K. Hall and Company, 70 Lincoln Street, Boston, Massachusetts 02111 (617) 423-3990; *The World in Figures.*

Statistical Office of the United Nations, Publishing Service, New York, New York 10017 (800) 253-9646; *Statistical Yearbook.*

Times Books, 201 East 50th Street, New York, New York 10022 (212) 751-2600; *The Economist Book of Vital World Statistics.*

IRAQ - MULES - See IRAQ - LIVESTOCK AND POULTRY

IRAQ - MUSEUMS

Facts on File, 460 Park Avenue South, New York, New York 10016 (800) 443-8323; *The New Book of World Rankings.*

United Nations Educational, Scientific and Cultural Organization (UNESCO), 7 Place de Fontenoy, F-75700 Paris, France (Telephone Number in U.S. (212) 963-5981); *Statistical Yearbook.*

IRAQ - NATALITY - See IRAQ - BIRTH RATES

IRAQ - NATIONAL ACCOUNTS

Economic Commission for Western Asia, Post Office Box 27, Baghdad, Iraq; *Statistical Abstract of Western Asia.*

International Monetary Fund, 700 Nineteenth Street, NW, Washington, D.C. 20431 (202) 623-7000; *International Financial Statistics.*

Statistical Office of the United Nations, Publishing Service, New York, New York 10017 (800) 253-9646; *National Accounts Statistics.*

IRAQ - NATIONAL INCOME

Facts on File, 460 Park Avenue South, New York, New York 10016 (800) 443-8323; *The New Book of World Rankings.*

G.K. Hall and Company, 70 Lincoln Street, Boston, Massachusetts 02111 (617) 423-3990; *The World in Figures.*

Statistical Office of the United Nations, Publishing Service, New York, New York 10017 (800) 253-9646; *Statistical Yearbook.*

IRAQ - NATIONAL PRODUCT

Facts on File, 460 Park Avenue South, New York, New York 10016 (800) 443-8323; *The New Book of World Rankings.*

Statistical Office of the United Nations, Publishing Service, New York, New York 10017 (800) 253-9646; *Statistical Yearbook.*

IRAQ - NATURAL GAS PRODUCTION - See IRAQ - MINING AND MINERAL PRODUCTS

IRAQ - NEWSPAPER PRODUCTION - See IRAQ - FORESTRY AND FOREST PRODUCTS

IRAQ - NEWSPRINT - See IRAQ - FORESTRY AND FOREST PRODUCTS

IRAQ - OCCUPATIONS - See IRAQ - LABOR FORCE

IRAQ - PAPER - See IRAQ - FORESTRY AND FOREST PRODUCTS

IRAQ - PATENTS

Statistical Office of the United Nations, Publishing Service, New York, New York 10017 (800) 253-9646; *Statistical Yearbook.*

IRAQ - PEANUT PRODUCTION - See IRAQ - CROPS

IRAQ - PESTICIDE USE

Food and Agricultural Organization of the United Nations (FAO) Via delle Terme di Caracalla, 00100 Rome, Italy (Telephone Number in U.S. (202) 606-7828); *The State of Food and Agriculture.*

IRAQ - PETROLEUM INDUSTRY

Commodity Research Bureau, Incorporated, 75 Wall Street, New York, New York 10005 (212) 504-7754; *Commodity Year Book.*

Euromonitor Publications Limited, 87-88 Turnmill Street, London EC1M 5QU, England; *Middle East Economic Handbook.*

Facts on File, 460 Park Avenue South, New York, New York 10016 (800) 443-8323; *The New Book of World Rankings.*

Food and Agricultural Organization of the United Nations (FAO) Via delle Terme di Caracalla, 00100 Rome, Italy (Telephone Number in U.S. (202) 606-7828); *The State of Food and Agriculture.*

G.K. Hall and Company, 70 Lincoln Street, Boston, Massachusetts 02111 (617) 423-3990; *The World in Figures.*

Organization of Petroleum Exporting Countries, Obere Donaustrasse 93, 1020 Vienna 2, Austria; *OPEC Annual Statistical Bulletin.*

Penn Well Publishing Company, 1421 South Sheridan Road, Post Office Box 1260, Tulsa, Oklahoma 74101 (800) 752-9764; *International Energy Statistics Sourcebook.*

Statistical Office of the United Nations, Publishing Service, New York, New York 10017 (800) 253-9646; *Statistical Yearbook.*

IRAQ - PIG-IRON AND FERRO-ALLOY PRODUCTION - See IRAQ - MINING AND MINERAL PRODUCTS

IRAQ - PIGS - See IRAQ - LIVESTOCK AND POULTRY

IRAQ - PIPELINES FOR OIL AND PETROLEUM PRODUCTS

Organization of Petroleum Exporting Countries, Obere Donaustrasse 93, 1020 Vienna 2, Austria; *OPEC Annual Statistical Bulletin.*

IRAQ - PLASTIC AND RESIN PRODUCTION

Euromonitor Publications Limited, 87-88 Turnmill Street, London EC1M 5QU, England; *Third World Economic Handbook.*

IRAQ - POPULATION

Economic Commission for Western Asia, Post Office Box 27, Baghdad, Iraq; *Statistical Abstract of Western Asia.*

The Economist Intelligence Unit, 111 West 57th Street, New York, New York 10019 (800) 938-4685; *The World Market Atlas.*

Euromonitor Publications Limited, 87-88 Turnmill Street, London EC1M 5QU, England; *International Marketing Data and Statistics, Middle East Economic Handbook,* and *Third World Economic Handbook.*

Facts on File, 460 Park Avenue South, New York, New York 10016 (800) 443-8323; *The New Book of World Rankings.*

Food and Agricultural Organization of the United Nations (FAO), Via delle Terme di Caracalla, 00100 Rome, Italy (Telephone Number in U.S. (202) 606-7828); *Production Yearbook.*

G.K. Hall and Company, 70 Lincoln Street, Boston, Massachusetts 02111 (617) 423-3990; *The World in Figures.*

International Labour Office, I.L.O. Publications, CH-1211, Geneva 22, Switzerland; *Yearbook of Labour Statistics.*

Statistical Office of the United Nations, Publishing Service, New York, New York 10017 (800) 253-9646; *Demographic Yearbook,* and *Statistical Yearbook.*

Times Books, 201 East 50th Street, New York, New York 10022 (212) 751-2600; *The Economist Book of Vital World Statistics.*

United Nations Educational, Scientific and Cultural Organization (UNESCO), 7 Place de Fontenoy, F-75700 Paris, France (Telephone Number in U.S. (212) 963-5981); *Statistical Yearbook.*

U.S. Arms Control and Disarmament Agency, 320 Twenty-first Street, Northwest, Washington, D.C. 20451 (202) 647-8677; *World Military Expenditures and Arms Transfers.*

World Health Organization, Avenue Appia, Office of Publications, CH-1211 Geneva 27, Switzerland (Telephone Number in U.S. (518) 436-9686); *World Health Statistics Annual.*

IRAQ - POST OFFICES

Facts on File, 460 Park Avenue South, New York, New York 10016 (800) 443-8323; *The New Book of World Rankings.*

IRAQ - POTATO PRODUCTION - See IRAQ - CROPS

IRAQ - POWER PRODUCTION INDUSTRY

Statistical Office of the United Nations, Publishing Service, New York, New York 10017 (800) 253-9646; *Statistical Yearbook.*

IRAQ - PRICES

Economic Commission for Western Asia, Post Office Box 27, Baghdad, Iraq; *Statistical Abstract of Western Asia.*

Facts on File, 460 Park Avenue South, New York, New York 10016 (800) 443-8323; *The New Book of World Rankings.*

Food and Agricultural Organization of the United Nations (FAO), Via delle Terme di Caracalla, 00100 Rome, Italy (Telephone Number in U.S. (202) 606-7828); *Production Yearbook*, and *The State of Food and Agriculture*.

G.K. Hall and Company, 70 Lincoln Street, Boston, Massachusetts 02111 (617) 423-3990; *The World in Figures*.

International Labour Office, I.L.O. Publications, CH-1211, Geneva 22, Switzerland; *Yearbook of Labour Statistics*.

International Monetary Fund, 700 Nineteenth Street, NW, Washington, D.C. 20431 (202) 623-7000; *International Financial Statistics*.

IRAQ - PRINTING AND WRITING PAPER - See IRAQ - FORESTRY AND FOREST PRODUCTS

IRAQ - PRODUCTION

Euromonitor Publications Limited, 87-88 Turnmill Street, London EC1M 5QU, England; *Third World Economic Handbook*.

Facts on File, 460 Park Avenue South, New York, New York 10016 (800) 443-8323; *The New Book of World Rankings*.

G.K. Hall and Company, 70 Lincoln Street, Boston, Massachusetts 02111 (617) 423-3990; *The World in Figures*.

IRAQ - PRODUCTIVITY

Euromonitor Publications Limited, 87-88 Turnmill Street, London EC1M 5QU, England; *International Marketing Data and Statistics*.

IRAQ - PUBLIC FINANCE

Facts on File, 460 Park Avenue South, New York, New York 10016 (800) 443-8323; *The New Book of World Rankings*.

IRAQ - RADIO BROADCASTING - See IRAQ - BROADCASTING

IRAQ - RAILWAYS

G.K. Hall and Company, 70 Lincoln Street, Boston, Massachusetts 02111 (617) 423-3990; *The World in Figures*.

Jane's Information Group, Sentinel House, 163 Brighton Road, Coulsdon, Surrey CR5 2NH, England (Telephone Number in U.S. (703) 683-3700); *Jane's World Railways*.

Statistical Office of the United Nations, Publishing Service, New York, New York 10017 (800) 253-9646; *Statistical Yearbook*.

IRAQ - RELIGION

Facts on File, 460 Park Avenue South, New York, New York 10016 (800) 443-8323; *The New Book of World Rankings*.

IRAQ - RENT PRICES

International Labour Office, I.L.O. Publications, CH-1211, Geneva 22, Switzerland; *Yearbook of Labour Statistics*.

IRAQ - RETAIL TRADE

Euromonitor Publications Limited, 87-88 Turnmill Street, London EC1M 5QU, England; *Third World Economic Handbook*.

G.K. Hall and Company, 70 Lincoln Street, Boston, Massachusetts 02111 (617) 423-3990; *The World in Figures*.

Statistical Office of the United Nations, Publishing Service, New York, New York 10017 (800) 253-9646; *Statistical Yearbook*.

IRAQ - RICE PRODUCTION - See IRAQ - CROPS

IRAQ - ROOT AND TUBER PRODUCTION - See IRAQ - CROPS

IRAQ - ROUNDWOOD PRODUCTION - See IRAQ - FORESTRY AND FOREST PRODUCTS

IRAQ - RUBBER PRODUCTION

Euromonitor Publications Limited, 87-88 Turnmill Street, London EC1M 5QU, England; *Third World Economic Handbook*.

Facts on File, 460 Park Avenue South, New York, New York 10016 (800) 443-8323; *The New Book of World Rankings*.

IRAQ - SALT PRODUCTION - See IRAQ - MINING AND MINERAL PRODUCTS

IRAQ - SAWNWOOD PRODUCTION - See IRAQ - FORESTRY AND FOREST PRODUCTS

IRAQ - SCIENCE AND TECHNOLOGY - EXPENDITURE FOR RESEARCH

Statistical Office of the United Nations, Publishing Service, New York, New York 10017 (800) 253-9646; *Statistical Yearbook*.

IRAQ - SCIENTISTS AND TECHNICIANS

Statistical Office of the United Nations, Publishing Service, New York, New York 10017 (800) 253-9646; *Statistical Yearbook*.

United Nations Educational, Scientific and Cultural Organization (UNESCO), 7 Place de Fontenoy, F-75700 Paris, France (Telephone Number in U.S. (212) 963-5981); *Statistical Yearbook*.

IRAQ - SENIOR CITIZENS

Facts on File, 460 Park Avenue South, New York, New York 10016 (800) 443-8323; *The New Book of World Rankings*.

IRAQ - SHEEP - See IRAQ - LIVESTOCK AND POULTRY

IRAQ - SILVER PRODUCTION AND CONSUMPTION - See IRAQ - MINING AND MINERAL PRODUCTS

IRAQ - SOCIAL DATA

Facts on File, 460 Park Avenue South, New York, New York 10016 (800) 443-8323; *The New Book of World Rankings*.

G.K. Hall and Company, 70 Lincoln Street, Boston, Massachusetts 02111 (617) 423-3990; *The World in Figures*.

IRAQ - SOYBEAN PRODUCTION - See IRAQ - CROPS

IRAQ - STATE BUDGET REVENUE AND EXPENDITURES

Euromonitor Publications Limited, 87-88 Turnmill Street, London EC1M 5QU, England; *International Marketing Data and Statistics*.

IRAQ - STEEL - See IRAQ - MINING AND MINERAL PRODUCTS

IRAQ - STOCKS - COMMODITY - MARKET PRICE - INDEX

Food and Agricultural Organization of the United Nations (FAO) Via delle Terme di Caracalla, 00100 Rome, Italy (Telephone Number in U.S. (202) 606-7828); *The State of Food and Agriculture.*

IRAQ - SUGAR PRODUCTION AND CONSUMPTION - See IRAQ - CROPS

IRAQ - SULPHURIC ACID PRODUCTION

Statistical Office of the United Nations, Publishing Service, New York, New York 10017 (800) 253-9646; *Statistical Yearbook.*

IRAQ - TAXATION

G.K. Hall and Company, 70 Lincoln Street, Boston, Massachusetts 02111 (617) 423-3990; *The World in Figures.*

International Road Federation, 525 School Street, SW, Washington, D.C. 20024 (202) 554-2106; *World Road Statistics.*

IRAQ - TEA CONSUMPTION

Statistical Office of the United Nations, Publishing Service, New York, New York 10017 (800) 253-9646; *Statistical Yearbook.*

IRAQ - TELEGRAPH SERVICE

Statistical Office of the United Nations, Publishing Service, New York, New York 10017 (800) 253-9646; *Statistical Yearbook.*

IRAQ - TELEPHONES IN USE

American Telephone and Telegraph Company, 26 Parsippany Road, Whippany, New Jersey 07981 (800) 338-4038; *The World's Telephones.*

Euromonitor Publications Limited, 87-88 Turnmill Street, London EC1M 5QU, England; *Middle East Economic Handbook,* and *Third World Economic Handbook.*

G.K. Hall and Company, 70 Lincoln Street, Boston, Massachusetts 02111 (617) 423-3990; *The World in Figures.*

Statistical Office of the United Nations, Publishing Service, New York, New York 10017 (800) 253-9646; *Statistical Yearbook.*

IRAQ - TELEVISION BROADCASTING - See IRAQ - BROADCASTING

IRAQ - TELEVISION RECEIVER PRODUCTION

Statistical Office of the United Nations, Publishing Service, New York, New York 10017 (800) 253-9646; *Statistical Yearbook.*

IRAQ - TEXTILE INDUSTRY

Euromonitor Publications Limited, 87-88 Turnmill Street, London EC1M 5QU, England; *Third World Economic Handbook.*

G.K. Hall and Company, 70 Lincoln Street, Boston, Massachusetts 02111 (617) 423-3990; *The World in Figures.*

Statistical Office of the United Nations, Publishing Service, New York, New York 10017 (800) 253-9646; *Statistical Yearbook.*

IRAQ - THEATRE

United Nations Educational, Scientific and Cultural Organization (UNESCO), 7 Place de Fontenoy, F-75700 Paris, France (Telephone Number in U.S. (212) 963-5981); *Statistical Yearbook.*

IRAQ - TOBACCO PRODUCTION

Euromonitor Publications Limited, 87-88 Turnmill Street, London EC1M 5QU, England; *Third World Economic Handbook.*

Facts on File, 460 Park Avenue South, New York, New York 10016 (800) 443-8323; *The New Book of World Rankings.*

Statistical Office of the United Nations, Publishing Service, New York, New York 10017 (800) 253-9646; *Statistical Yearbook.*

IRAQ - TOURISM

Economic Commission for Western Asia, Post Office Box 27, Baghdad, Iraq; *Statistical Abstract of Western Asia.*

Euromonitor Publications Limited, 87-88 Turnmill Street, London EC1M 5QU, England; *Middle East Economic Handbook, Third World Economic Handbook.*

Facts on File, 460 Park Avenue South, New York, New York 10016 (800) 443-8323; *The New Book of World Rankings.*

G.K. Hall and Company, 70 Lincoln Street, Boston, Massachusetts 02111 (617) 423-3990; *The World in Figures.*

Statistical Office of the United Nations, Publishing Service, New York, New York 10017 (800) 253-9646; *Statistical Yearbook.*

Times Books, 201 East 50th Street, New York, New York 10022 (212) 751-2600; *The Economist Book of Vital World Statistics.*

World Tourism Organization, Calle Capitan Haya 42, E-28020 Madrid, Spain; *Yearbook of Tourism Statistics.*

IRAQ - TRACTORS IN USE

Statistical Office of the United Nations, Publishing Service, New York, New York 10017 (800) 253-9646; *Statistical Yearbook.*

IRAQ - TRADE - See IRAQ - FOREIGN TRADE

IRAQ - TRADEMARKS AND SERVICE MARKS

Statistical Office of the United Nations, Publishing Service, New York, New York 10017 (800) 253-9646; *Statistical Yearbook.*

IRAQ - TRANSPORTATION AND COMMUNICATIONS

Economic Commission for Western Asia, Post Office Box 27, Baghdad, Iraq; *Statistical Abstract of Western Asia.*

Euromonitor Publications Limited, 87-88 Turnmill Street, London EC1M 5QU, England; *Middle East Economic Handbook,* and *Third World Economic Handbook.*

Facts on File, 460 Park Avenue South, New York, New York 10016 (800) 443-8323; *The New Book of World Rankings.*

G.K. Hall and Company, 70 Lincoln Street, Boston, Massachusetts 02111 (617) 423-3990; *The World in Figures.*

IRAQ - UNEMPLOYMENT

Euromonitor Publications Limited, 87-88 Turnmill Street, London EC1M 5QU, England; *International Marketing Data and Statistics*, and *Middle East Economic Handbook*.

International Labour Office, I.L.O. Publications, CH-1211, Geneva 22, Switzerland; *Yearbook of Labour Statistics*.

Statistical Office of the United Nations, Publishing Service, New York, New York 10017 (800) 253-9646; *Statistical Yearbook*.

IRAQ - VITAL STATISTICS

Euromonitor Publications Limited, 87-88 Turnmill Street, London EC1M 5QU, England; *International Marketing Data and Statistics*, *Middle East Economic Handbook*, and *Third World Economic Handbook*.

G.K. Hall and Company, 70 Lincoln Street, Boston, Massachusetts 02111 (617) 423-3990; *The World in Figures*.

Statistical Office of the United Nations, Publishing Service, New York, New York 10017 (800) 253-9646; *Statistical Yearbook*.

World Health Organization, Office of Publications, Avenue Appia, CH-1211 Geneva 27, Switzerland (Telephone Number in U.S. (518) 436-9686); *World Health Statistics Annual*.

IRAQ - WAGES

G.K. Hall and Company, 70 Lincoln Street, Boston, Massachusetts 02111 (617) 423-3990; *The World in Figures*.

International Labour Office, I.L.O. Publications, CH-1211, Geneva 22, Switzerland; *Yearbook of Labour Statistics*.

IRAQ - WALNUT PRODUCTION - See IRAQ - CROPS

IRAQ - WATERMELON PRODUCTION - See IRAQ - CROPS

IRAQ - WEATHER

Facts on File, 460 Park Avenue South, New York, New York 10016 (800) 443-8323; *The New Book of World Rankings*.

G.K. Hall and Company, 70 Lincoln Street, Boston, Massachusetts 02111 (617) 423-3990; *The World in Figures*.

IRAQ - WHEAT PRODUCTION AND PRICES - See IRAQ - CROPS

IRAQ - WHOLESALE PRICES

International Monetary Fund, 700 Nineteenth Street, NW, Washington, D.C. 20431 (202) 623-7000; *International Financial Statistics*.

Statistical Office of the United Nations, Publishing Service, New York, New York 10017 (800) 253-9646; *Statistical Yearbook*.

IRAQ - WHOLESALE TRADE

Euromonitor Publications Limited, 87-88 Turnmill Street, London EC1M 5QU, England; *Third World Economic Handbook*.

Statistical Office of the United Nations, Publishing Service, New York, New York 10017 (800) 253-9646; *Statistical Yearbook*.

IRAQ - WINE PRODUCTION

Facts on File, 460 Park Avenue South, New York, New York 10016 (800) 443-8323; *The New Book of World Rankings*.

IRAQ - WOOD PULP PRODUCTION - See IRAQ - FORESTRY AND FOREST PRODUCTS

IRAQ - WOOL PRODUCTION

Facts on File, 460 Park Avenue South, New York, New York 10016 (800) 443-8323; *The New Book of World Rankings*.

Statistical Office of the United Nations, Publishing Service, New York, New York 10017 (800) 253-9646; *Statistical Yearbook*.

IRAQ - YARN PRODUCTION

Statistical Office of the United Nations, Publishing Service, New York, New York 10017 (800) 253-9646; *Statistical Yearbook*.

Ireland (Eire) - National Statistical Offices

Central Statistics Office, Ardee Road, Dublin 6, Ireland; for statistics relating to production, distribution, population, labour and wages.

Central Statistics Office, Saint Stephen's Green House, Earlsfort Terrace, Dublin 2, Ireland.

Ireland (Eire) - Primary Statistics Source

Central Statistics Office, Earlsfort Terrace, Dublin 2, Ireland; *Statistical Abstract of Ireland*, and *Irish Statistical Bulletin*.

IRELAND (EIRE) - ABORTIONS

European Community Information Service, 2100 M Street, NW, Washington, D.C. 20037 (202) 862-9500; *Demographic Statistics*.

IRELAND (EIRE) - AGRICULTURE

An Foras Taluntais (The Agricultural Institute), Economics and Rural Welfare Research Centre, 19 Sandymount Avenue, Dublin 4, Ireland; *Farm Management Survey*.

European Community Information Service, 2100 M Street, NW, Washington, D.C. 20037 (202) 862-9500; *Agriculture: Statistical Yearbook*, *Basic Statistics of the Community*, *Eurostatistics: Data for Short-Term Economic Analysis*, *Labor Force Sample Survey*, and *Regions: Statistical Yearbook*.

Facts on File, 460 Park Avenue South, New York, New York 10016 (800) 443-8323; *The New Book of World Rankings*.

Food and Agricultural Organization of the United Nations (FAO) Via delle Terme di Caracalla, 00100 Rome, Italy (Telephone Number in U.S. (202) 606-7828); *Production Yearbook*, and *The State of Food and Agriculture*.

G.K. Hall and Company, 70 Lincoln Street, Boston, Massachusetts 02111 (617) 423-3990; *The World in Figures*.

Organisation for Economic Co-operation and Development (OECD), 2 rue Andre-Pascal, 75 Paris 16, France (Telephone Number in U.S. (202) 785-6323); *Economic Accounts for Agriculture*, *Indicators of Industrial Activity*, and *OECD Economic Surveys: Ireland*.

Statistical Office of the United Nations, Publishing Service, New York, New York 10017 (800) 253-9646; *Statistical Yearbook.*

Times Books, 201 East 50th Street, New York, New York 10022 (212) 751-2600; *The Economist Book of Vital World Statistics.*

The World Bank, 1818 H Street, NW, Washington, D.C. 20433 (202) 477-1234; *World Tables.*

IRELAND (EIRE) - AIRLINE SERVICE

European Community Information Service, 2100 M Street, NW, Washington, D.C. 20037 (202) 862-9500; *Basic Statistics of the Community* and *Regions: Statistical Yearbook.*

Facts on File, 460 Park Avenue South, New York, New York 10016 (800) 443-8323; *The New Book of World Rankings.*

G.K. Hall and Company, 70 Lincoln Street, Boston, Massachusetts 02111 (617) 423-3990; *The World in Figures.*

International Civil Aviation Organization, 1000 Sherbrooke Street West, Suite 400, Montreal, Quebec, Canada H3A 2R2 (514) 285-8219; *Civil Aviation Statistics of the World.*

Organisation for Economic Co-operation and Development (OECD), 2 rue Andre-Pascal, 75 Paris 16, France (Telephone Number in U.S. (202) 785-6323); *Tourism Policy and International Tourism in OECD Member Countries.*

Statistical Office of the United Nations, Publishing Service, New York, New York 10017 (800) 253-9646; *Statistical Yearbook.*

Times Books, 201 East 50th Street, New York, New York 10022 (212) 751-2600; *The Economist Book of Vital World Statistics.*

IRELAND (EIRE) - ALMOND PRODUCTION - See IRELAND (EIRE) - CROPS

IRELAND (EIRE) - ALUMINUM PRODUCTION AND CONSUMPTION - See IRELAND (EIRE) - MINING AND MINERAL PRODUCTS

IRELAND (EIRE) - ANIMAL FEEDINGSTUFFS

Organisation for Economic Co-operation and Development (OECD), 2 rue Andre-Pascal, 75 Paris 16, France (Telephone Number in U.S. (202) 785-6323); *Foreign Trade by Commodities.*

IRELAND (EIRE) - ANIMAL HEALTH

Food and Agricultural Organization of the United Nations (FAO), Via delle Terme di Caracalla, 00100 Rome, Italy (Telephone Number in U.S. (202) 606-7828); *Animal Health Yearbook.*

IRELAND (EIRE) - ANTIMONY AND ANTIMONY ORE - See IRELAND (EIRE) - MINING AND MINERAL PRODUCTS

IRELAND (EIRE) - APPLE PRODUCTION - See IRELAND (EIRE) - CROPS

IRELAND (EIRE) - AREA AND DENSITY OF POPULATION

European Community Information Service, 2100 M Street, NW, Washington, D.C. 20037 (202) 862-9500; *Basic Statistics of the Community* and *Demographic Statistics.*

Facts on File, 460 Park Avenue South, New York, New York 10016 (800) 443-8323; *The New Book of World Rankings.*

Food and Agricultural Organization of the United Nations (FAO) Via delle Terme di Caracalla, 00100 Rome, Italy (Telephone Number in U.S. (202) 606-7828); *The State of Food and Agriculture.*

G.K. Hall and Company, 70 Lincoln Street, Boston, Massachusetts 02111 (617) 423-3990; *The World in Figures.*

Statistical Office of the United Nations, Publishing Service, New York, New York 10017 (800) 253-9646; *Statistical Yearbook.*

Times Books, 201 East 50th Street, New York, New York 10022 (212) 751-2600; *The Economist Book of Vital World Statistics.*

United Nations Educational, Scientific and Cultural Organization (UNESCO), 7 Place de Fontenoy, F-75700 Paris, France (Telephone Number in U.S. (212) 963-5981); *Statistical Yearbook.*

IRELAND (EIRE) - ARMS EXPORTS AND IMPORTS

U.S. Arms Control and Disarmament Agency, 320 Twenty-first Street, Northwest, Washington, D.C. 20451 (202) 647-8677; *World Military Expenditures and Arms Transfers.*

IRELAND (EIRE) - ARSENIC PRODUCTION AND CONSUMPTION - See IRELAND (EIRE) - MINING AND MINERAL PRODUCTS

IRELAND (EIRE) - BALANCE OF PAYMENTS

The Economist Intelligence Unit, 111 West 57th Street, New York, New York 10019 (800) 938-4685; *The World Market Atlas.*

European Community Information Service, 2100 M Street, NW, Washington, D.C. 20037 (202) 862-9500; *ACP: Basic Statistics, Basic Statistics of the Community, Energy Statistics Yearbook,* and *Eurostatistics: Data for Short-Term Economic Analysis.*

G.K. Hall and Company, 70 Lincoln Street, Boston, Massachusetts 02111 (617) 423-3990; *The World in Figures.*

International Monetary Fund, 700 Nineteenth Street, NW, Washington, D.C. 20431 (202) 623-7000; *Balance of Payments Yearbook.*

Organisation for Economic Co-operation and Development (OECD), 2 rue Andre-Pascal, 75 Paris 16, France (Telephone Number in U.S. (202) 785-6323); *Economic Outlook, Geographical Distribution of Financial Flows to Developing Countries, Labour Force Statistics,* and *OECD Economic Surveys: Ireland.*

Times Books, 201 East 50th Street, New York, New York 10022 (212) 751-2600; *The Economist Book of Vital World Statistics.*

The World Bank, 1818 H Street, NW, Washington, D.C. 20433 (202) 477-1234; *World Tables.*

IRELAND (EIRE) - BANANA PRODUCTION - See IRELAND (EIRE) - CROPS

IRELAND (EIRE) - BANKING

European Community Information Service, 2100 M Street, NW, Washington, D.C. 20037 (202) 862-9500; *ACP: Basic Statistics.*

Facts on File, 460 Park Avenue South, New York, New York 10016 (800) 443-8323; *The New Book of World Rankings.*

G.K. Hall and Company, 70 Lincoln Street, Boston, Massachusetts 02111 (617) 423-3990; *The World in Figures.*

International Monetary Fund, 700 Nineteenth Street, NW, Washington, D.C. 20431 (202) 623-7000; *International Financial Statistics.*

Organisation for Economic Co-operation and Development (OECD), 2 rue Andre-Pascal, 75 Paris 16, France (Telephone Number in U.S. (202) 785-6323); *Economic Outlook, Financial Market Trends,* and *OECD Economic Surveys: Ireland.*

IRELAND (EIRE) - BARLEY PRODUCTION - See IRELAND (EIRE) - CROPS

IRELAND (EIRE) - BAUXITE PRODUCTION AND CONSUMPTION - See IRELAND (EIRE) - MINING AND MINERAL PRODUCTS

IRELAND (EIRE) - BEER PRODUCTION

Facts on File, 460 Park Avenue South, New York, New York 10016 (800) 443-8323; *The New Book of World Rankings.*

Statistical Office of the United Nations, Publishing Service, New York, New York 10017 (800) 253-9646; *Statistical Yearbook.*

IRELAND (EIRE) - BEVERAGES - PRODUCTION INDEX

Organisation for Economic Co-operation and Development (OECD), 2 rue Andre-Pascal, 75 Paris 16, France (Telephone Number in U.S. (202) 785-6323); *Indicators of Industrial Activity.*

IRELAND (EIRE) - BIRTH RATES

European Community Information Service, 2100 M Street, NW, Washington, D.C. 20037 (202) 862-9500; *Basic Statistics of the Community* and *Demographic Statistics.*

Facts on File, 460 Park Avenue South, New York, New York 10016 (800) 443-8323; *The New Book of World Rankings.*

Organisation for Economic Co-operation and Development (OECD), 2 rue Andre-Pascal, 75 Paris 16, France (Telephone Number in U.S. (202) 785-6323); *Labour Force Statistics.*

Statistical Office of the United Nations, Publishing Service, New York, New York 10017 (800) 253-9646; *Demographic Yearbook,* and *Statistical Yearbook.*

Times Books, 201 East 50th Street, New York, New York 10022 (212) 751-2600; *The Economist Book of Vital World Statistics.*

The World Bank, 1818 H Street, NW, Washington, D.C. 20433 (202) 477-1234; *World Tables.*

World Health Organization, Office of Publications, Avenue Appia, CH-1211 Geneva 27, Switzerland (Telephone Number in U.S. (518) 436-9686); *World Health Statistics Annual.*

IRELAND (EIRE) - BISMUTH PRODUCTION AND CONSUMPTION - See IRELAND (EIRE) - MINING AND MINERAL PRODUCTS

IRELAND (EIRE) - BONDS

European Community Information Service, 2100 M Street, NW, Washington, D.C. 20037 (202) 862-9500; *Basic Statistics of the Community.*

G.K. Hall and Company, 70 Lincoln Street, Boston, Massachusetts 02111 (617) 423-3990; *The World in Figures.*

Organisation for Economic Co-operation and Development (OECD), 2 rue Andre-Pascal, 75 Paris 16, France (Telephone Number in U.S. (202) 785-6323); *Financial Market Trends.*

Statistical Office of the United Nations, Publishing Service, New York, New York 10017 (800) 253-9646; *Statistical Yearbook.*

IRELAND (EIRE) - BOOK PRODUCTION

Euromonitor Publications Limited, 87-88 Turnmill Street, London EC1M 5QU, England; *European Marketing Data and Statistics.*

G.K. Hall and Company, 70 Lincoln Street, Boston, Massachusetts 02111 (617) 423-3990; *The World in Figures.*

Organisation for Economic Co-operation and Development (OECD), 2 rue Andre-Pascal, 75 Paris 16, France (Telephone Number in U.S. (202) 785-6323); *Indicators of Industrial Activity.*

United Nations Educational, Scientific and Cultural Organization (UNESCO), 7 Place de Fontenoy, F-75700 Paris, France (Telephone Number in U.S. (212) 963-5981); *Statistical Yearbook.*

IRELAND (EIRE) - BROADCASTING

Billboard Limited, Post Office Box 9027, 1006 AA Amsterdam, The Netherlands (Telephone Number in U.S. (212) 764-7300); *World Radio TV Handbook.*

European Community Information Service, 2100 M Street, NW, Washington, D.C. 20037 (202) 862-9500; *Basic Statistics of the Community.*

Facts on File, 460 Park Avenue South, New York, New York 10016 (800) 443-8323; *The New Book of World Rankings.*

G.K. Hall and Company, 70 Lincoln Street, Boston, Massachusetts 02111 (617) 423-3990; *The World in Figures.*

Times Books, 201 East 50th Street, New York, New York 10022 (212) 751-2600; *The Economist Book of Vital World Statistics.*

United Nations Educational, Scientific and Cultural Organization (UNESCO), 7 Place de Fontenoy, F-75700 Paris, France (Telephone Number in U.S. (212) 963-5981); *Statistical Yearbook.*

IRELAND (EIRE) - BUILDING CONSTRUCTION - See IRELAND (EIRE) - CONSTRUCTION INDUSTRY

IRELAND (EIRE) - BUSINESS

European Community Information Service, 2100 M Street, NW, Washington, D.C. 20037 (202) 862-9500; *Basic Statistics of the Community.*

G.K. Hall and Company, 70 Lincoln Street, Boston, Massachusetts 02111 (617) 423-3990; *The World in Figures.*

IRELAND (EIRE) - BUTTER - See IRELAND (EIRE) - DAIRY PRODUCTS

IRELAND (EIRE) - CABBAGE PRODUCTION - See IRELAND (EIRE) - CROPS

IRELAND (EIRE) - CADMIUM PRODUCTION AND CONSUMPTION - See IRELAND (EIRE) - MINING AND MINERAL PRODUCTS

IRELAND (EIRE) - CALORIE SUPPLY

Food and Agricultural Organization of the United Nations (FAO) Via delle Terme di Caracalla, 00100 Rome, Italy (Telephone Number in U.S. (202) 606-7828); *The State of Food and Agriculture.*

IRELAND (EIRE) - CAPITAL INVESTMENT

Organisation for Economic Co-operation and Development (OECD), 2 rue Andre-Pascal, 75 Paris 16, France (Telephone Number in U.S. (202) 785-6323); *Economic Outlook,* and *Financial Market Trends.*

IRELAND (EIRE) - CAPITAL REVENUE

International Monetary Fund, 700 Nineteenth Street, NW, Washington, D.C. 20431 (202) 623-7000; *Government Finance Statistics Yearbook.*

Organisation for Economic Co-operation and Development (OECD), 2 rue Andre-Pascal, 75 Paris 16, France (Telephone Number in U.S. (202) 785-6323); *Economic Outlook,* and *Financial Market Trends.*

IRELAND (EIRE) - CASHEW NUT PRODUCTION - See IRELAND (EIRE) - CROPS

IRELAND (EIRE) - CASTOR BEAN PRODUCTION - See IRELAND (EIRE) - CROPS

IRELAND (EIRE) - CATTLE - See IRELAND (EIRE) - LIVESTOCK AND POULTRY

IRELAND (EIRE) - CAULIFLOWER PRODUCTION - See IRELAND (EIRE) - CROPS

IRELAND (EIRE) - CAUSTIC SODA PRODUCTION

European Community Information Service, 2100 M Street, NW, Washington, D.C. 20037 (202) 862-9500; *Basic Statistics of the Community.*

Organisation for Economic Co-operation and Development (OECD), 2 rue Andre-Pascal, 75 Paris 16, France (Telephone Number in U.S. (202) 785-6323); *Indicators of Industrial Activity.*

IRELAND (EIRE) - CEMENT PRODUCTION - See IRELAND (EIRE) - MINING AND MINERAL PRODUCTS

IRELAND (EIRE) - CEREAL PRODUCTION - See IRELAND (EIRE) - CROPS

IRELAND (EIRE) - CHEESE - See IRELAND (EIRE) - DAIRY PRODUCTS

IRELAND (EIRE) - CHEMICAL INDUSTRY

European Community Information Service, 2100 M Street, Northwest, Washington, D.C. 20037 (202) 862-9500; *Industrial Production: Quarterly Statistics.*

IRELAND (EIRE) - CHEMICAL (ORGANIC) PRODUCTION - See IRELAND (EIRE) - MINING AND MINERAL PRODUCTS

IRELAND (EIRE) - CHESTNUT PRODUCTION - See IRELAND (EIRE) - CROPS

IRELAND (EIRE) - CHICKENS - See IRELAND (EIRE) - LIVESTOCK AND POULTRY

IRELAND (EIRE) - CHROMITE PRODUCTION AND CONSUMPTION - See IRELAND (EIRE) - MINING AND MINERAL PRODUCTS

IRELAND (EIRE) - CHROMIUM ORE PRODUCTION AND CONSUMPTION - See IRELAND (EIRE) - MINING AND MINERAL PRODUCTS

IRELAND (EIRE) - CIGARETTE PRODUCTION - See IRELAND (EIRE) - TOBACCO INDUSTRY

IRELAND (EIRE) - CLASS STRUCTURE

European Community Information Service, 2100 M Street, NW, Washington, D.C. 20037 (202) 862-9500; *Basic Statistics of the Community,* and *Labor Force Sample Survey.*

G.K. Hall and Company, 70 Lincoln Street, Boston, Massachusetts 02111 (617) 423-3990; *The World in Figures.*

IRELAND (EIRE) - CLIMATE

Facts on File, 460 Park Avenue South, New York, New York 10016 (800) 443-8323; *The New Book of World Rankings.*

G.K. Hall and Company, 70 Lincoln Street, Boston, Massachusetts 02111 (617) 423-3990; *The World in Figures.*

IRELAND (EIRE) - CLOTHING - PRODUCTION INDEX

Organisation for Economic Co-operation and Development (OECD), 2 rue Andre-Pascal, 75 Paris 16, France (Telephone Number in U.S. (202) 785-6323); *Indicators of Industrial Activity.*

IRELAND (EIRE) - CLOTHING EXPORTS AND IMPORTS

European Community Information Service, 2100 M Street, NW, Washington, D.C. 20037 (202) 862-9500; *Basic Statistics of the Community.*

Organisation for Economic Co-operation and Development (OECD), 2 rue Andre-Pascal, 75 Paris 16, France (Telephone Number in U.S. (202) 785-6323); *Textile Industry in OECD Countries.*

IRELAND (EIRE) - COAL PRODUCTION AND CONSUMPTION - See IRELAND (EIRE) - MINING AND MINERAL PRODUCTS

IRELAND (EIRE) - COBALT PRODUCTION AND CONSUMPTION - See IRELAND (EIRE) - MINING AND MINERAL PRODUCTS

IRELAND (EIRE) - COCOA (BEANS) PRODUCTION - See IRELAND (EIRE) - CROPS

IRELAND (EIRE) - COFFEE - See IRELAND (EIRE) - CROPS

IRELAND (EIRE) - COKE AND COKE OVEN ORE PRODUCTION AND CONSUMPTION - See IRELAND (EIRE) - MINING AND MINERAL PRODUCTS

IRELAND (EIRE) - COMMUNICATIONS

European Community Information Service, 2100 M Street, NW, Washington, D.C. 20037 (202) 862-9500; *Basic Statistics of the Community.*

G.K. Hall and Company, 70 Lincoln Street, Boston, Massachusetts 02111 (617) 423-3990; *The World in Figures.*

IRELAND (EIRE) - CONSTRUCTION INDUSTRY

European Community Information Service, 2100 M Street, NW, Washington, D.C. 20037 (202) 862-9500; *Basic Statistics of the Community,* and *Labor Force Sample Survey.*

Facts on File, 460 Park Avenue South, New York, New York 10016 (800) 443-8323; *The New Book of World Rankings*.

Organisation for Economic Co-operation and Development (OECD), 2 rue Andre-Pascal, 75 Paris 16, France (Telephone Number in U.S. (202) 785-6323); *Industrial Structure Statistics, The Iron and Steel Industry, Main Economic Indicators - Historical Statistics,* and *OECD Economic Surveys: Ireland.*

Statistical Office of the United Nations, Publishing Service, New York, New York 10017 (800) 253-9646; *Construction Statistics Yearbook,* and *Statistical Yearbook.*

IRELAND (EIRE) - CONSUMER PRICE INDEX

European Community Information Service, 2100 M Street, NW, Washington, D.C. 20037 (202) 862-9500; *Basic Statistics of the Community.*

G.K. Hall and Company, 70 Lincoln Street, Boston, Massachusetts 02111 (617) 423-3990; *The World in Figures.*

International Labour Office, I.L.O. Publications, CH-1211, Geneva 22, Switzerland; *Yearbook of Labour Statistics.*

Organisation for Economic Co-operation and Development (OECD), 2 rue Andre-Pascal, 75 Paris 16, France (Telephone Number in U.S. (202) 785-6323); *Economic Outlook.*

Statistical Office of the United Nations, Publishing Service, New York, New York 10017 (800) 253-9646; *Statistical Yearbook.*

IRELAND (EIRE) - CONSUMER PRICES

Euromonitor Publications Limited, 87-88 Turnmill Street, London EC1M 5QU, England; *European Marketing Data and Statistics.*

European Community Information Service, 2100 M Street, NW, Washington, D.C. 20037 (202) 862-9500; *Basic Statistics of the Community* and *Eurostatistics: Data for Short-Term Economic Analysis,* and *Money and Finance.*

International Labour Office, I.L.O. Publications, CH-1211, Geneva 22, Switzerland; *Yearbook of Labour Statistics.*

International Monetary Fund, 700 Nineteenth Street, NW, Washington, D.C. 20431 (202) 623-7000; *International Financial Statistics.*

Organisation for Economic Co-operation and Development (OECD), 2 rue Andre-Pascal, 75 Paris 16, France (Telephone Number in U.S. (202) 785-6323); *Economic Outlook.*

Times Books, 201 East 50th Street, New York, New York 10022 (212) 751-2600; *The Economist Book of Vital World Statistics.*

IRELAND (EIRE) - CONSUMPTION

European Community Information Service, 2100 M Street, NW, Washington, D.C. 20037 (202) 862-9500; *Basic Statistics of the Community.*

G.K. Hall and Company, 70 Lincoln Street, Boston, Massachusetts 02111 (617) 423-3990; *The World in Figures.*

International Lead and Zinc Study Group, Metro House, 58 St. James's Street, London SW1A 1LD, England; *Lead and Zinc Statistics.*

Organisation for Economic Co-operation and Development (OECD), 2 rue Andre-Pascal, 75 Paris 16, France (Telephone Number in U.S. (202) 785-6323); *The Footwear, Raw Hides and Skins, and Leather Industry in OECD Countries, The Iron and Steel Industry, Meat Balances in OECD Member Countries, The Non-Ferrous Metals Industry, The Pulp and Paper Industry,* and *Textile Industry in OECD Countries.*

IRELAND (EIRE) - COPPER AND COPPER ORE - See IRELAND (EIRE) - MINING AND MINERAL PRODUCTS

IRELAND (EIRE) - CORN PRODUCTION - See IRELAND (EIRE) - CROPS

IRELAND (EIRE) - CORPORATE INCOME TAXES - See IRELAND (EIRE) - TAXATION

IRELAND (EIRE) - CORPORATE TAXES - See IRELAND (EIRE) - TAXATION

IRELAND (EIRE) - COTTON - See IRELAND (EIRE) - CROPS

IRELAND (EIRE) - CRIME

International Criminal Police Organization (INTERPOL), 26 rue Armengaud, 92210 Saint Cloud, France; *International Crime Statistics.*

Yale University Press, Yale Station, New Haven, Connecticut 06520 (203) 432-0940; *Violence and Crime in Cross-National Perspective.*

IRELAND (EIRE) - CROPS

Euromonitor Publications Limited, 87-88 Turnmill Street, London EC1M 5QU, England; *European Marketing Data and Statistics.*

European Community Information Service, 2100 M Street, NW, Washington, D.C. 20037 (202) 862-9500; *ACP: Basic Statistics, Agriculture: Statistical Yearbook, Basic Statistics of the Community, Crop Production: Quarterly Statistics, Eurostatistics: Data for Short-Term Economic Analysis* and *Regions: Statistical Yearbook.*

Facts on File, 460 Park Avenue South, New York, New York 10016 (800) 443-8323; *The New Book of World Rankings.*

Food and Agricultural Organization of the United Nations (FAO), Via delle Terme di Caracalla, 00100 Rome, Italy (Telephone Number in U.S. (202) 606-7828); *Production Yearbook* and *The State of Food and Agriculture.*

G.K. Hall and Company, 70 Lincoln Street, Boston, Massachusetts 02111 (617) 423-3990; *The World in Figures.*

Organisation for Economic Co-operation and Development (OECD), 2 rue Andre-Pascal, 75 Paris 16, France (Telephone Number in U.S. (202) 785-6323); *Economic Accounts for Agriculture* and *Foreign Trade by Commodities,* and *Textile Industry in OECD Countries.*

Statistical Office of the United Nations, Publishing Service, New York, New York 10017 (800) 253-9646; *Statistical Yearbook.*

IRELAND (EIRE) - CUSTOMS DUTIES

European Community Information Service, 2100 M Street, NW, Washington, D.C. 20037 (202) 862-9500; *Basic Statistics of the Community.*

G.K. Hall and Company, 70 Lincoln Street, Boston, Massachusetts 02111 (617) 423-3990; *The World in Figures.*

International Monetary Fund, 700 Nineteenth Street, NW, Washington, D.C. 20431 (202) 623-7000; *Government Finance Statistics Yearbook*.

Organisation for Economic Co-operation and Development (OECD), 2 rue Andre-Pascal, 75 Paris 16, France (Telephone Number in U.S. (202) 785-6323); *The Non-Ferrous Metals Industry*.

IRELAND (EIRE) - DAIRY PRODUCTS

Commodity Research Bureau, Incorporated, 75 Wall Street, New York, New York 10005 (212) 504-7754; *Commodity Year Book*.

European Community Information Service, 2100 M Street, NW, Washington, D.C. 20037 (202) 862-9500; *Basic Statistics of the Community* and *Eurostatistics: Data for Short-Term Economic Analysis*.

Facts on File, 460 Park Avenue South, New York, New York 10016 (800) 443-8323; *The New Book of World Rankings*.

Food and Agricultural Organization of the United Nations (FAO) Via delle Terme di Caracalla, 00100 Rome, Italy (Telephone Number in U.S. (202) 606-7828); *Production Yearbook* and *The State of Food and Agriculture*.

Organisation for Economic Co-operation and Development (OECD), 2 rue Andre-Pascal, 75 Paris 16, France (Telephone Number in U.S. (202) 785-6323); *Economic Accounts for Agriculture* and *Milk, Milk Products, and Egg Balances in OECD Member Countries*.

Statistical Office of the United Nations, Publishing Service, New York, New York 10017 (800) 253-9646; *Statistical Yearbook*.

IRELAND (EIRE) - DEATH RATE

European Community Information Service, 2100 M Street, NW, Washington, D.C. 20037 (202) 862-9500; *Basic Statistics of the Community* and *Demographic Statistics*.

G.K. Hall and Company, 70 Lincoln Street, Boston, Massachusetts 02111 (617) 423-3990; *The World in Figures*.

Statistical Office of the United Nations, Publishing Service, New York, New York 10017 (800) 253-9646; *Statistical Yearbook*.

Times Books, 201 East 50th Street, New York, New York 10022 (212) 751-2600; *The Economist Book of Vital World Statistics*.

World Health Organization, Office of Publications, Avenue Appia, CH-1211 Geneva 27, Switzerland (Telephone Number in U.S. (518) 436-9686); *World Health Statistics Annual*.

IRELAND (EIRE) - DEFENSE EXPENDITURES

European Community Information Service, 2100 M Street, NW, Washington, D.C. 20037 (202) 862-9500; *Government Financing of Research and Development*.

G.K. Hall and Company, 70 Lincoln Street, Boston, Massachusetts 02111 (617) 423-3990; *The World in Figures*.

U.S. Arms Control and Disarmament Agency, 320 Twenty-first Street, Northwest, Washington, D.C. 20451 (202) 647-8677; *World Military Expenditures and Arms Transfers*.

IRELAND (EIRE) - DEMOGRAPHY

The Economist Intelligence Unit, 111 West 57th Street, New York, New York 10019 (800) 938-4685; *The World Market Atlas*.

European Community Information Service, 2100 M Street, NW, Washington, D.C. 20037 (202) 862-9500; *Basic Statistics of the Community*, *Demographic Statistics*, *Employment and Unemployment*, and *Regions: Statistical Yearbook*.

Facts on File, 460 Park Avenue South, New York, New York 10016 (800) 443-8323; *The New Book of World Rankings*.

G.K. Hall and Company, 70 Lincoln Street, Boston, Massachusetts 02111 (617) 423-3990; *The World in Figures*.

IRELAND (EIRE) - DEVELOPMENT ASSISTANCE

European Community Information Service, 2100 M Street, NW, Washington, D.C. 20037 (202) 862-9500; *ACP: Basic Statistics*, *Basic Statistics of the Community*, and *Government Financing of Research and Development*.

G.K. Hall and Company, 70 Lincoln Street, Boston, Massachusetts 02111 (617) 423-3990; *The World in Figures*.

Organisation for Economic Co-operation and Development (OECD), 2 rue Andre-Pascal, 75 Paris 16, France (Telephone Number in U.S. (202) 785-6323); *Geographical Distribution of Financial Flows to Developing Countries*.

IRELAND (EIRE) - DIAMOND - See IRELAND (EIRE) - MINING AND MINERAL PRODUCTS

IRELAND (EIRE) - DISCOUNT RATES

Organisation for Economic Co-operation and Development (OECD), 2 rue Andre-Pascal, 75 Paris 16, France (Telephone Number in U.S. (202) 785-6323); *Financial Market Trends*.

IRELAND (EIRE) - DISEASES

G.K. Hall and Company, 70 Lincoln Street, Boston, Massachusetts 02111 (617) 423-3990; *The World in Figures*.

World Health Organization, Office of Publications, Avenue Appia, CH-1211 Geneva 27, Switzerland (Telephone Number in U.S. (518) 436-9686); *World Health Statistics Annual*.

IRELAND (EIRE) - DIVORCE RATES

European Community Information Service, 2100 M Street, NW, Washington, D.C. 20037 (202) 862-9500; *Demographic Statistics*.

Facts on File, 460 Park Avenue South, New York, New York 10016 (800) 443-8323; *The New Book of World Rankings*.

Statistical Office of the United Nations, Publishing Service, New York, New York 10017 (800) 253-9646; *Demographic Yearbook*.

IRELAND (EIRE) - DOMESTIC PRODUCT

European Community Information Service, 2100 M Street, NW, Washington, D.C. 20037 (202) 862-9500; *Basic Statistics of the Community*.

G.K. Hall and Company, 70 Lincoln Street, Boston, Massachusetts 02111 (617) 423-3990; *The World in Figures*.

IRELAND (EIRE) - DUCKS - See IRELAND (EIRE) - LIVESTOCK AND POULTRY

IRELAND (EIRE) - ECONOMY

Euromonitor Publications Limited, 87-88 Turnmill Street, London EC1M 5QU, England; *European Marketing Data and Statistics.*

European Community Information Service, 2100 M Street, NW, Washington, D.C. 20037 (202) 862-9500; *ACP: Basic Statistics, Basic Statistics of the Community, Energy Statistics Yearbook, Labor Force Sample Survey,* and *Money and Finance.*

Facts on File, 460 Park Avenue South, New York, New York 10016 (800) 443-8323; *The New Book of World Rankings.*

G.K. Hall and Company, 70 Lincoln Street, Boston, Massachusetts 02111 (617) 423-3990; *The World in Figures.*

Organisation for Economic Co-operation and Development (OECD), 2 rue Andre-Pascal, 75 Paris 16, France (Telephone Number in U.S. (202) 785-6323); *Economic Outlook, Geographical Distribution of Financial Flows to Developing Countries, Main Economic Indicators - Historical Statistics, OECD Economic Surveys: Ireland,* and *OECD Employment Outlook.*

IRELAND (EIRE) - EDUCATION

The Economist Intelligence Unit, 111 West 57th Street, New York, New York 10019 (800) 938-4685; *The World Market Atlas.*

Euromonitor Publications Limited, 87-88 Turnmill Street, London EC1M 5QU, England; *European Marketing Data and Statistics.*

European Community Information Service, 2100 M Street, NW, Washington, D.C. 20037 (202) 862-9500; *Basic Statistics of the Community* and *Regions: Statistical Yearbook.*

Facts on File, 460 Park Avenue South, New York, New York 10016 (800) 443-8323; *The New Book of World Rankings.*

G.K. Hall and Company, 70 Lincoln Street, Boston, Massachusetts 02111 (617) 423-3990; *The World in Figures.*

Organisation for Economic Co-operation and Development (OECD), 2 rue Andre-Pascal, 75 Paris 16, France (Telephone Number in U.S. (202) 785-6323); *Education in OECD Countries.*

Times Books, 201 East 50th Street, New York, New York 10022 (212) 751-2600; *The Economist Book of Vital World Statistics.*

United Nations Educational, Scientific and Cultural Organization (UNESCO), 7 Place de Fontenoy, F-75700 Paris, France (Telephone Number in U.S. (212) 963-5981); *Statistical Yearbook.*

The World Bank, 1818 H Street, NW, Washington, D.C. 20433 (202) 477-1234; *World Tables.*

IRELAND (EIRE) - EGG PRODUCTION AND CONSUMPTION - See IRELAND (EIRE) - DAIRY PRODUCTS

IRELAND (EIRE) - ELECTRICITY

European Community Information Service, 2100 M Street, NW, Washington, D.C. 20037 (202) 862-9500; *Basic Statistics of the Community, Energy: Monthly Statistics, Energy Statistics Yearbook, Eurostatistics: Data for Short-Term Economic Analysis,* and *Regions: Statistical Yearbook.*

Facts on File, 460 Park Avenue South, New York, New York 10016 (800) 443-8323; *The New Book of World Rankings.*

Organisation for Economic Co-operation and Development (OECD), 2 rue Andre-Pascal, 75 Paris 16, France (Telephone Number in U.S. (202) 785-6323); *Coal Information, Energy Statistics of OECD Countries, Indicators of Industrial Activity,* and *Industrial Structure Statistics.*

Statistical Office of the United Nations, Publishing Service, New York, New York 10017 (800) 253-9646; *Statistical Yearbook.*

Times Books, 201 East 50th Street, New York, New York 10022 (212) 751-2600; *The Economist Book of Vital World Statistics.*

IRELAND (EIRE) - EMPLOYMENT

Central Statistics Office, Ardee Road, Dublin 6, Ireland; *The Trend of Employment and Unemployment.*

Euromonitor Publications Limited, 87-88 Turnmill Street, London EC1M 5QU, England; *European Marketing Data and Statistics.*

European Community Information Service, 2100 M Street, NW, Washington, D.C. 20037 (202) 862-9500; *Basic Statistics of the Community, Earnings in Agriculture, Employment and Unemployment, Eurostatistics: Data for Short-Term Economic Analysis, Iron and Steel: Statistical Yearbook,* and *Labor Force Sample Survey.*

Facts on File, 460 Park Avenue South, New York, New York 10016 (800) 443-8323; *The New Book of World Rankings.*

International Labour Office, I.L.O. Publications, CH-1211, Geneva 22, Switzerland; *Yearbook of Labour Statistics.*

Organisation for Economic Co-operation and Development (OECD), 2 rue Andre-Pascal, 75 Paris 16, France (Telephone Number in U.S. (202) 785-6323); *Economic Outlook, The Iron and Steel Industry, OECD Employment Outlook, OECD Economic Surveys: Ireland,* and *Textile Industry in OECD Countries.*

Statistical Office of the United Nations, Publishing Service, New York, New York 10017 (800) 253-9646; *Statistical Yearbook.*

IRELAND (EIRE) - ENERGY

Euromonitor Publications Limited, 87-88 Turnmill Street, London EC1M 5QU, England; *European Marketing Data and Statistics.*

European Community Information Service, 2100 M Street, NW, Washington, D.C. 20037 (202) 862-9500; *Basic Statistics of the Community, Energy: Monthly Statistics, Energy Statistics Yearbook, Labor Force Sample Survey,* and *Regions: Statistical Yearbook.*

Facts on File, 460 Park Avenue South, New York, New York 10016 (800) 443-8323; *The New Book of World Rankings.*

Food and Agricultural Organization of the United Nations (FAO) Via delle Terme di Caracalla, 00100 Rome, Italy (Telephone Number in U.S. (202) 606-7828); *The State of Food and Agriculture.*

G.K. Hall and Company, 70 Lincoln Street, Boston, Massachusetts 02111 (617) 423-3990; *The World in Figures.*

Organisation for Economic Co-operation and Development (OECD), 2 rue Andre-Pascal, 75 Paris 16, France (Telephone Number in U.S. (202) 785-6323); *Coal Information, Energy Statistics of OECD Countries, OECD Environmental Data,* and *Oil and Gas Information.*

Statistical Office of the United Nations, Publishing Service, New York, New York 10017 (800) 253-9646; *Energy Statistics Yearbook, Statistical Yearbook, World Energy Supplies.*

Times Books, 201 East 50th Street, New York, New York 10022 (212) 751-2600; *The Economist Book of Vital World Statistics.*

Statistical Office of the United Nations, Publishing Service, New York, New York 10017 (800) 253-9646;

IRELAND (EIRE) - ENGINEERING AND METAL PRODUCTS - EXPORTS AND IMPORTS

European Community Information Service, 2100 M Street, NW, Washington, D.C. 20037 (202) 862-9500; *Basic Statistics of the Community* and *Industrial Production: Quarterly Statistics.*

IRELAND (EIRE) - EXCHANGE RATES

European Community Information Service, 2100 M Street, NW, Washington, D.C. 20037 (202) 862-9500; *Eurostatistics: Data for Short-Term Economic Analysis* and *Money and Finance.*

International Civil Aviation Organization, 1000 Sherbrooke Street West, Suite 400, Montreal, Quebec, Canada H3A 2R2 (514) 285-8219; *Civil Aviation Statistics of the World.*

International Monetary Fund, 700 Nineteenth Street, NW, Washington, D.C. 20431 (202) 623-7000; *International Financial Statistics.*

Organisation for Economic Co-operation and Development (OECD), 2 rue Andre-Pascal, 75 Paris 16, France (Telephone Number in U.S. (202) 785-6323); *Economic Outlook, Financial Market Trends, Revenue Statistics of OECD Member Countries,* and *Tourism Policy and International Tourism in OECD Member Countries.*

Statistical Office of the United Nations, Publishing Service, New York, New York 10017 (800) 253-9646; *Statistical Yearbook.*

IRELAND (EIRE) - EXCISE TAXES - See IRELAND (EIRE) - TAXATION

IRELAND (EIRE) - EXPORTS

American Automobile Manufacturers Association, 1401 H Eye Street, NW, Suite 900, Washington, D.C. 20005 (202) 326-5500; *World Motor Vehicle Data.*

The Economist Intelligence Unit, 111 West 57th Street, New York, New York 10019 (800) 938-4685; *The World Market Atlas.*

European Community Information Service, 2100 M Street, NW, Washington, D.C. 20037 (202) 862-9500; *Basic Statistics of the Community, Energy: Monthly Statistics, Energy Statistics Yearbook, Eurostatistics: Data for Short-Term Economic Analysis, External Trade: Monthly Statistics, External Trade: Statistical Yearbook,* and *Fisheries: Yearly Statistics.*

Food and Agricultural Organization of the United Nations (FAO) Via delle Terme di Caracalla, 00100 Rome, Italy (Telephone Number in U.S. (202) 606-7828); *The State of Food and Agriculture.*

G.K. Hall and Company, 70 Lincoln Street, Boston, Massachusetts 02111 (617) 423-3990; *The World in Figures.*

International Lead and Zinc Study Group, Metro House, 58 St. James's Street, London SW1A 1LD, England; *Lead and Zinc Statistics.*

International Monetary Fund, 700 Nineteenth Street, NW, Washington, D.C. 20431 (202) 623-7000; *Direction of Trade Statistics, Government Finance Statistics Yearbook,* and *International Financial Statistics.*

Organisation for Economic Co-operation and Development (OECD), 2 rue Andre-Pascal, 75 Paris 16, France (Telephone Number in U.S. (202) 785-6323); *Economic Outlook, The Footwear, Raw Hides and Skins, and Leather Industry in OECD Countries, Foreign Trade by Commodities, Geographical Distribution of Financial Flows to Developing Countries, Industrial Structure Statistics, The Iron and Steel Industry, Milk, Milk Products, and Egg Balances in OECD Member Countries, OECD Economic Surveys: Ireland, The Pulp and Paper Industry,* and *Review of Fisheries in OECD Member Countries.*

Times Books, 201 East 50th Street, New York, New York 10022 (212) 751-2600; *The Economist Book of Vital World Statistics.*

The World Bank, 1818 H Street, NW, Washington, D.C. 20433 (202) 477-1234; *World Tables.*

IRELAND (EIRE) - EXTERNAL FINANCING

Organisation for Economic Co-operation and Development (OECD), 2 rue Andre-Pascal, 75 Paris 16, France (Telephone Number in U.S. (202) 785-6323); *Economic Outlook,* and *Financial Market Trends.*

IRELAND (EIRE) - EXTERNAL INDEBTEDNESS

Organisation for Economic Co-operation and Development (OECD), 2 rue Andre-Pascal, 75 Paris 16, France (Telephone Number in U.S. (202) 785-6323); *Financial Market Trends,* and *Geographical Distribution of Financial Flows to Developing Countries.*

The World Bank, 1818 H Street, NW, Washington, D.C. 20433 (202) 477-1234; *World Tables.*

IRELAND (EIRE) - EXTERNAL TRADE

Central Statistics Office, St. Stephen's Green House, Earlsfort Terrace, Dublin 2, Ireland; *Trade Statistics of Ireland.*

European Community Information Service, 2100 M Street, NW, Washington, D.C. 20037 (202) 862-9500; *ACP: Basic Statistics, Basic Statistics of the Community, Eurostatistics: Data for Short-Term Economic Analysis,* and *External Trade: Monthly Statistics, External Trade: Statistical Yearbook.*

Food and Agricultural Organization of the United Nations (FAO) Via delle Terme di Caracalla, 00100 Rome, Italy (Telephone Number in U.S. (202) 606-7828); *The State of Food and Agriculture,* and *Trade Yearbook.*

G.K. Hall and Company, 70 Lincoln Street, Boston, Massachusetts 02111 (617) 423-3990; *The World in Figures.*

Statistical Office of the United Nations, Publishing Service, New York, New York 10017 (800) 253-9646; *Statistical Yearbook.*

IRELAND (EIRE) - FABRIC PRODUCTION - See IRELAND (EIRE) - TEXTILE INDUSTRY

IRELAND (EIRE) - FARM CROPS - See IRELAND (EIRE) - CROPS

IRELAND (EIRE) - FERTILITY RATES

European Community Information Service, 2100 M Street, NW, Washington, D.C. 20037 (202) 862-9500; *Demographic Statistics.*

Facts on File, 460 Park Avenue South, New York, New York 10016 (800) 443-8323; *The New Book of World Rankings.*

Times Books, 201 East 50th Street, New York, New York 10022 (212) 751-2600; *The Economist Book of Vital World Statistics.*

The World Bank, 1818 H Street, NW, Washington, D.C. 20433 (202) 477-1234; *World Tables.*

IRELAND (EIRE) - FERTILIZER

European Community Information Service, 2100 M Street, NW, Washington, D.C. 20037 (202) 862-9500; *Basic Statistics of the Community.*

Food and Agricultural Organization of the United Nations (FAO), Via delle Terme di Caracalla, 00100 Rome, Italy (Telephone Number in U.S. (202) 606-7828); *Fertilizer Yearbook*, and *The State of Food and Agriculture.*

Organisation for Economic Co-operation and Development (OECD), 2 rue Andre-Pascal, 75 Paris 16, France (Telephone Number in U.S. (202) 785-6323); *Economic Accounts for Agriculture*, and *Foreign Trade by Commodities.*

Statistical Office of the United Nations, Publishing Service, New York, New York 10017 (800) 253-9646; *Statistical Yearbook.*

IRELAND (EIRE) - FETAL MORTALITY

European Community Information Service, 2100 M Street, NW, Washington, D.C. 20037 (202) 862-9500; *Basic Statistics of the Community, Demographic Statistics.*

Statistical Office of the United Nations, Publishing Service, New York, New York 10017 (800) 253-9646; *Demographic Yearbook.*

World Health Organization, Office of Publications, Avenue Appia, CH-1211 Geneva 27, Switzerland; *World Health Statistics Annual.*

IRELAND (EIRE) - FIBRE PRODUCTION - See IRELAND (EIRE) - TEXTILE INDUSTRY

IRELAND (EIRE) - FILAMENT PRODUCTION - See IRELAND (EIRE) - TEXTILE INDUSTRY

IRELAND (EIRE) - FILM - See IRELAND (EIRE) -MOTION PICTURES

IRELAND (EIRE) - FINANCE

European Community Information Service, 2100 M Street, NW, Washington, D.C. 20037 (202) 862-9500; *ACP: Basic Statistics, Basic Statistics of the Community Eurostatistics: Data for Short-Term Economic Analysis, Fisheries: Yearly Statistics*, and *Money and Finance.*

Facts on File, 460 Park Avenue South, New York, New York 10016 (800) 443-8323; *The New Book of World Rankings.*

Government Publications Sales Office, GPO Arcade, Dublin 1, Ireland; *Annual Report of the Revenue Commissioners.*

G.K. Hall and Company, 70 Lincoln Street, Boston, Massachusetts 02111 (617) 423-3990; *The World in Figures.*

International Monetary Fund, 700 Nineteenth Street, NW, Washington, D.C. 20431 (202) 623-7000; *International Financial Statistics.*

Organisation for Economic Co-operation and Development (OECD), 2 rue Andre-Pascal, 75 Paris 16, France (Telephone Number in U.S. (202) 785-6323); *Economic Outlook, Financial Market Trends, Foreign Trade by Commodities, Geographical Distribution of Financial Flows to Developing Countries, Main Economic Indicators - Historical Statistics, OECD Financial Statistics*, and *Review of Fisheries in OECD Member Countries.*

IRELAND (EIRE) - FISHERIES

Department of Fisheries and Forestry, Government Publication Sales Office, GPO Arcade, Dublin 1, Ireland; *Sea and Inland Fisheries Report.*

Euromonitor Publications Limited, 87-88 Turnmill Street, London EC1M 5QU, England; *European Marketing Data and Statistics.*

European Community Information Service, 2100 M Street, NW, Washington, D.C. 20037 (202) 862-9500; *Agriculture: Statistical Yearbook, Fisheries: Yearly Statistics.*

Facts on File, 460 Park Avenue South, New York, New York 10016 (800) 443-8323; *The New Book of World Rankings.*

Food and Agricultural Organization of the United Nations (FAO) Via delle Terme di Caracalla, 00100 Rome, Italy (Telephone Number in U.S. (202) 606-7828); *The State of Food and Agriculture*, and *Yearbook of Fishery Statistics.*

Organisation for Economic Co-operation and Development (OECD), 2 rue Andre-Pascal, 75 Paris 16, France (Telephone Number in U.S. (202) 785-6323); *Industrial Structure Statistics*, and *Review of Fisheries in OECD Member Countries.*

Statistical Office of the United Nations, Publishing Service, New York, New York 10017 (800) 253-9646; *Statistical Yearbook.*

IRELAND (EIRE) - FLAX FIBRE PRODUCTION - See IRELAND (EIRE) - TEXTILE INDUSTRY

IRELAND (EIRE) - FLAX PRODUCTION - See IRELAND (EIRE) - TEXTILE INDUSTRY

IRELAND (EIRE) - FLOUR PRODUCTION

European Community Information Service, 2100 M Street, NW, Washington, D.C. 20037 (202) 862-9500; *Basic Statistics of the Community.*

Statistical Office of the United Nations, Publishing Service, New York, New York 10017 (800) 253-9646; *Statistical Yearbook.*

IRELAND (EIRE) - FOOD

European Community Information Service, 2100 M Street, NW, Washington, D.C. 20037 (202) 862-9500; *Basic Statistics of the Community.*

Food and Agricultural Organization of the United Nations (FAO), Via delle Terme di Caracalla, 00100 Rome, Italy (Telephone Number in U.S. (202) 606-7828); *Production Yearbook*, and *The State of Food and Agriculture.*

G.K. Hall and Company, 70 Lincoln Street, Boston, Massachusetts 02111 (617) 423-3990; *The World in Figures.*

Organisation for Economic Co-operation and Development (OECD), 2 rue Andre-Pascal, 75 Paris 16, France (Telephone Number in U.S. (202) 785-6323); *Food Consumption Statistics* and *Foreign Trade by*

Commodities.

IRELAND (EIRE) - FOOTWEAR - PRODUCTION INDEX

Organisation for Economic Co-operation and Development (OECD), 2 rue Andre-Pascal, 75 Paris 16, France (Telephone Number in U.S. (202) 785-6323); *Indicators of Industrial Activity.*

IRELAND (EIRE) - FOREIGN AID

G.K. Hall and Company, 70 Lincoln Street, Boston, Massachusetts 02111 (617) 423-3990; *The World in Figures.*

IRELAND (EIRE) - FOREIGN DEBT

International Monetary Fund, 700 Nineteenth Street, NW, Washington, D.C. 20431 (202) 623-7000; *Government Finance Statistics Yearbook.*

Organisation for Economic Co-operation and Development (OECD), 2 rue Andre-Pascal, 75 Paris 16, France (Telephone Number in U.S. (202) 785-6323); *Economic Outlook.*

IRELAND (EIRE) - FOREIGN INDEBTEDNESS

Organisation for Economic Co-operation and Development (OECD), 2 rue Andre-Pascal, 75 Paris 16, France (Telephone Number in U.S. (202) 785-6323); *Economic Outlook,* and *Financial Market Trends.*

IRELAND (EIRE) - FOREIGN OFFICIAL RESERVES

European Community Information Service, 2100 M Street, NW, Washington, D.C. 20037 (202) 862-9500; *Money and Finance.*

IRELAND (EIRE) - FOREIGN TRADE

Euromonitor Publications Limited, 87-88 Turnmill Street, London EC1M 5QU, England; *European Marketing Data and Statistics.*

European Community Information Service, 2100 M Street, NW, Washington, D.C. 20037 (202) 862-9500; *Basic Statistics of the Community, Economic Outlook, Energy Statistics Yearbook,* and *The Footwear, Raw Hides and Skins, and Leather Industry in OECD Countries,* and *Iron and Steel: Statistical Yearbook.*

Facts on File, 460 Park Avenue South, New York, New York 10016 (800) 443-8323; *The New Book of World Rankings.*

Food and Agricultural Organization of the United Nations (FAO) Via delle Terme di Caracalla, 00100 Rome, Italy (Telephone Number in U.S. (202) 653-2400); *The State of Food and Agriculture.*

G.K. Hall and Company, 70 Lincoln Street, Boston, Massachusetts 02111 (617) 423-3990; *The World in Figures.*

International Monetary Fund, 700 Nineteenth Street, NW, Washington, D.C. 20431 (202) 623-7000; *International Financial Statistics.*

Organisation for Economic Co-operation and Development (OECD), 2 rue Andre-Pascal, 75 Paris 16, France (Telephone Number in U.S. (202) 785-6323); *The Footwear, Raw Hides and Skins, and Leather Industry in OECD Countries, Foreign Trade by Commodities, Main Economic Indicators - Historical Statistics, Maritime Transport, Meat Balances in OECD Member Countries,* and *OECD Economic Surveys: Ireland.*

Statistical Office of the United Nations, Publishing Service, New York, New York 10017 (800) 253-9646; *International Trade Statistics Yearbook, Statistical Yearbook,* and *Trade in Manufactures of Developing Countries.*

The World Bank, 1818 H Street, NW, Washington, D.C. 20433 (202) 477-1234; *World Tables.*

IRELAND (EIRE) - FORESTRY AND FOREST PRODUCTS

Euromonitor Publications Limited, 87-88 Turnmill Street, London EC1M 5QU, England; *European Marketing Data and Statistics.*

European Community Information Service, 2100 M Street, NW, Washington, D.C. 20037 (202) 862-9500; *Agriculture: Statistical Yearbook, Basic Statistics of the Community, Forestry Statistics,* and *Industrial Production: Quarterly Statistics.*

Facts on File, 460 Park Avenue South, New York, New York 10016 (800) 443-8323; *The New Book of World Rankings.*

Food and Agricultural Organization of the United Nations (FAO) Via delle Terme di Caracalla, 00100 Rome, Italy (Telephone Number in U.S. (202) 606-7828); *The State of Food and Agriculture,* and *Yearbook of Forest Products.*

Forest and Paper Association, 1250 Connecticut Avenue, NW, Washington, D.C. 20036 (202) 463-2455; *Wood Pulp and Fiber Statistics.*

G.K. Hall and Company, 70 Lincoln Street, Boston, Massachusetts 02111 (617) 423-3990; *The World in Figures.*

Organisation for Economic Co-operation and Development (OECD), 2 rue Andre-Pascal, 75 Paris 16, France (Telephone Number in U.S. (202) 785-6323); *Foreign Trade by Commodities, Indicators of Industrial Activity, Industrial Structure Statistics,* and *The Pulp and Paper Industry.*

Statistical Office of the United Nations, Publishing Service, New York, New York 10017 (800) 253-9646; *Statistical Yearbook.*

United Nations Educational, Scientific and Cultural Organization (UNESCO), 7 Place de Fontenoy, F-75700 Paris, France (Telephone Number in U.S. (212) 963-5981); *Statistical Yearbook.*

IRELAND (EIRE) - FRUIT PRODUCTION - See IRELAND (EIRE) - CROPS

IRELAND (EIRE) - FURNITURE AND WOOD PRODUCTS - EXPORTS AND IMPORTS

European Community Information Service, 2100 M Street, NW, Washington, D.C. 20037 (202) 862-9500; *Basic Statistics of the Community.*

Organisation for Economic Co-operation and Development (OECD), 2 rue Andre-Pascal, 75 Paris 16, France (Telephone Number in U.S. (202) 785-6323); *Foreign Trade by Commodities,* and *Industrial Structure Statistics.*

IRELAND (EIRE) - GARLIC PRODUCTION - See IRELAND (EIRE) - CROPS

IRELAND (EIRE) - GAS AND GAS LIQUIDS - See IRELAND (EIRE) - MINING AND MINERAL PRODUCTS

IRELAND (EIRE) - GENERAL INDUSTRIAL STATISTICS

European Community Information Service, 2100 M Street, NW, Washington, D.C. 20037 (202) 862-9500; *Basic Statistics of the*

Community.

Statistical Office of the United Nations, Publishing Service, New York, New York 10017 (800) 253-9646; *Industrial Statistics Yearbook.*

IRELAND (EIRE) - GENERAL MORTALITY

European Community Information Service, 2100 M Street, NW, Washington, D.C. 20037 (202) 862-9500; *Basic Statistics of the Community, Demographic Statistics.*

Statistical Office of the United Nations, Publishing Service, New York, New York 10017 (800) 253-9646; *Demographic Yearbook.*

World Health Organization, Office of Publications, Avenue Appia, CH-1211 Geneva 27, Switzerland; *World Health Statistics Annual.*

IRELAND (EIRE) - GEOGRAPHIC DATA

European Community Information Service, 2100 M Street, NW, Washington, D.C. 20037 (202) 862-9500; *Basic Statistics of the Community.*

Facts on File, 460 Park Avenue South, New York, New York 10016 (800) 443-8323; *The New Book of World Rankings.*

IRELAND (EIRE) - GLASS AND GLASS PRODUCTS - PRODUCTION INDEX

Organisation for Economic Co-operation and Development (OECD), 2 rue Andre-Pascal, 75 Paris 16, France (Telephone Number in U.S. (202) 785-6323); *Indicators of Industrial Activity.*

IRELAND (EIRE) - GOATS - See IRELAND (EIRE) - LIVESTOCK AND POULTRY

IRELAND (EIRE) - GOLD HOLDINGS

International Monetary Fund, 700 Nineteenth Street, NW, Washington, D.C. 20431 (202) 623-7000; *International Financial Statistics.*

Organisation for Economic Co-operation and Development (OECD), 2 rue Andre-Pascal, 75 Paris 16, France (Telephone Number in U.S. (202) 785-6323); *Indicators of Industrial Activity.*

Statistical Office of the United Nations, Publishing Service, New York, New York 10017 (800) 253-9646; *Statistical Yearbook.*

The World Bank, 1818 H Street, NW, Washington, D.C. 20433 (202) 477-1234; *World Tables.*

IRELAND (EIRE) - GOLD PRODUCTION AND CONSUMPTION - See IRELAND (EIRE) - MINING AND MINERAL PRODUCTS

IRELAND (EIRE) - GOVERNMENT

European Community Information Service, 2100 M Street, NW, Washington, D.C. 20037 (202) 862-9500; *Basic Statistics of the Community.*

G.K. Hall and Company, 70 Lincoln Street, Boston, Massachusetts 02111 (617) 423-3990; *The World in Figures.*

IRELAND (EIRE) - GOVERNMENT BONDS - See IRELAND (EIRE) - BONDS

IRELAND (EIRE) - GOVERNMENT CONSUMPTION

European Community Information Service, 2100 M Street, NW, Washington, D.C. 20037 (202) 862-9500; *Basic Statistics of the Community.*

IRELAND (EIRE) - GOVERNMENT EXPENDITURE

European Community Information Service, 2100 M Street, NW, Washington, D.C. 20037 (202) 862-9500; *Basic Statistics of the Community,* and *Government Financing of Research and Development.*

Organisation for Economic Co-operation and Development (OECD), 2 rue Andre-Pascal, 75 Paris 16, France (Telephone Number in U.S. (202) 785-6323); *Economic Outlook.*

Times Books, 201 East 50th Street, New York, New York 10022 (212) 751-2600; *The Economist Book of Vital World Statistics.*

The World Bank, 1818 H Street, NW, Washington, D.C. 20433 (202) 477-1234; *World Tables.*

IRELAND (EIRE) - GOVERNMENT FINANCES

European Community Information Service, 2100 M Street, NW, Washington, D.C. 20037 (202) 862-9500; *Basic Statistics of the Community, Government Financing of Research and Development,* and *Money and Finance.*

International Monetary Fund, 700 Nineteenth Street, NW, Washington, D.C. 20431 (202) 623-7000; *International Financial Statistics.*

Organisation for Economic Co-operation and Development (OECD), 2 rue Andre-Pascal, 75 Paris 16, France (Telephone Number in U.S. (202) 785-6323); *Economic Outlook.*

Statistical Office of the United Nations, Publishing Service, New York, New York 10017 (800) 253-9646; *Statistical Yearbook.*

IRELAND (EIRE) - GOVERNMENT REVENUES

European Community Information Service, 2100 M Street, NW, Washington, D.C. 20037 (202) 862-9500; *Basic Statistics of the Community,* and *Government Financing of Research and Development.*

International Monetary Fund, 700 Nineteenth Street, NW, Washington, D.C. 20431 (202) 623-7000; *Government Finance Statistics Yearbook.*

Organisation for Economic Co-operation and Development (OECD), 2 rue Andre-Pascal, 75 Paris 16, France (Telephone Number in U.S. (202) 785-6323); *Economic Outlook,* and *Revenue Statistics of OECD Member Countries.*

Times Books, 201 East 50th Street, New York, New York 10022 (212) 751-2600; *The Economist Book of Vital World Statistics.*

The World Bank, 1818 H Street, NW, Washington, D.C. 20433 (202) 477-1234; *World Tables.*

IRELAND (EIRE) - GRAIN PRODUCTION - See IRELAND (EIRE) - CROPS

IRELAND (EIRE) - GRANTS

International Monetary Fund, 700 Nineteenth Street, NW, Washington, D.C. 20431 (202) 623-7000; *Government Finance Statistics Yearbook.*

Organisation for Economic Co-operation and Development (OECD), 2 rue Andre-Pascal, 75 Paris 16, France (Telephone Number in U.S. (202) 785-6323); *Geographical Distribution of Financial Flows to Developing Countries.*

IRELAND (EIRE) - GREEN PEPPER AND CHILIE PRODUCTION - See IRELAND (EIRE) - CROPS

IRELAND (EIRE) - GROSS DOMESTIC PRODUCT

The Economist Intelligence Unit, 111 West 57th Street, New York, New York 10019 (800) 938-4685; *The World Market Atlas.*

European Community Information Service, 2100 M Street, NW, Washington, D.C. 20037 (202) 862-9500; *Basic Statistics of the Community, Eurostatistics: Data for Short-Term Economic Analysis, Government Financing of Research and Development, Iron and Steel: Statistical Yearbook,* and *Money and Finance.*

Facts on File, 460 Park Avenue South, New York, New York 10016 (800) 443-8323; *The New Book of World Rankings.*

G.K. Hall and Company, 70 Lincoln Street, Boston, Massachusetts 02111 (617) 423-3990; *The World in Figures.*

Organisation for Economic Co-operation and Development (OECD), 2 rue Andre-Pascal, 75 Paris 16, France (Telephone Number in U.S. (202) 785-6323); *Economic Outlook, Geographical Distribution of Financial Flows to Developing Countries,* and *Revenue Statistics of OECD Member Countries.*

Statistical Office of the United Nations, Publishing Service, New York, New York 10017 (800) 253-9646; *Statistical Yearbook.*

Times Books, 201 East 50th Street, New York, New York 10022 (212) 751-2600; *The Economist Book of Vital World Statistics.*

The World Bank, 1818 H Street, NW, Washington, D.C. 20433 (202) 477-1234; *World Tables.*

IRELAND (EIRE) - GROSS INDUSTRIAL PRODUCT

European Community Information Service, 2100 M Street, NW, Washington, D.C. 20037 (202) 862-9500; *Government Financing of Research and Development.*

IRELAND (EIRE) - GROSS NATIONAL PRODUCT

European Community Information Service, 2100 M Street, NW, Washington, D.C. 20037 (202) 862-9500; *ACP: Basic Statistics,* and *Basic Statistics of the Community.*

Organisation for Economic Co-operation and Development (OECD), 2 rue Andre-Pascal, 75 Paris 16, France (Telephone Number in U.S. (202) 785-6323); *Economic Outlook,* and *Geographical Distribution of Financial Flows to Developing Countries.*

U.S. Arms Control and Disarmament Agency, 320 Twenty-first Street, Northwest, Washington, D.C. 20451 (202) 647-8677; *World Military Expenditures and Arms Transfers.*

The World Bank, 1818 H Street, NW, Washington, D.C. 20433 (202) 477-1234; *World Tables.*

IRELAND (EIRE) - GROUNDNUT PRODUCTION - See IRELAND (EIRE) - CROPS

IRELAND (EIRE) - HAY PRODUCTION - See IRELAND (EIRE) - CROPS

IRELAND (EIRE) - HAZELNUT PRODUCTION - See IRELAND (EIRE) - CROPS

IRELAND (EIRE) - HEALTH

European Community Information Service, 2100 M Street, NW, Washington, D.C. 20037 (202) 862-9500; *Basic Statistics of the Community* and *Regions: Statistical Yearbook.*

Facts on File, 460 Park Avenue South, New York, New York 10016 (800) 443-8323; *The New Book of World Rankings.*

G.K. Hall and Company, 70 Lincoln Street, Boston, Massachusetts 02111 (617) 423-3990; *The World in Figures.*

Organisation for Economic Co-operation and Development (OECD), 2 rue Andre-Pascal, 75 Paris 16, France (Telephone Number in U.S. (202) 785-6323); *OECD Health Systems: Facts and Trends.*

Statistical Office of the United Nations, Publishing Service, New York, New York 10017 (800) 253-9646; *Statistical Yearbook.*

Times Books, 201 East 50th Street, New York, New York 10022 (212) 751-2600; *The Economist Book of Vital World Statistics.*

World Health Organization, Office of Publications, Avenue Appia, CH-1211 Geneva 27, Switzerland; *World Health Statistics Annual.*

IRELAND (EIRE) - HEMP FIBRE PRODUCTION - See IRELAND (EIRE) - TEXTILE INDUSTRY

IRELAND (EIRE) - HIDE PRODUCTION

Food and Agricultural Organization of the United Nations (FAO), Via delle Terme di Caracalla, 00100 Rome, Italy (Telephone Number in U.S. (202) 606-7828); *Production Yearbook.*

Organisation for Economic Co-operation and Development (OECD), 2 rue Andre-Pascal, 75 Paris 16, France (Telephone Number in U.S. (202) 785-6323); *The Footwear, Raw Hides and Skins, and Leather Industry in OECD Countries, Foreign Trade by Commodities,* and *Indicators of Industrial Activity.*

IRELAND (EIRE) - HIGHWAYS

European Community Information Service, 2100 M Street, NW, Washington, D.C. 20037 (202) 862-9500; *Basic Statistics of the Community.*

G.K. Hall and Company, 70 Lincoln Street, Boston, Massachusetts 02111 (617) 423-3990; *The World in Figures.*

International Road Federation, 525 School Street, SW, Washington, D.C. 20024 (202) 554-2106; *World Road Statistics.*

Statistical Office of the United Nations, Publishing Service, New York, New York 10017 (800) 253-9646; *Annual Bulletin of Transport Statistics for Europe.*

IRELAND (EIRE) - HOME FINANCE

Organisation for Economic Co-operation and Development (OECD), 2 rue Andre-Pascal, 75 Paris 16, France (Telephone Number in U.S. (202) 785-6323); *Main Economic Indicators - Historical Statistics.*

IRELAND (EIRE) - HOPS PRODUCTION - See IRELAND (EIRE) - CROPS

IRELAND (EIRE) - HORSES - See IRELAND (EIRE) - LIVESTOCK AND POULTRY

IRELAND (EIRE) - HOURS OF WORK - See IRELAND (EIRE) - EMPLOYMENT

IRELAND (EIRE) - HOUSING AND HOUSING UNITS

European Community Information Service, 2100 M Street, NW, Washington, D.C. 20037 (202) 862-9500; *Basic Statistics of the Community, Labor Force Sample Survey,* and *Regions: Statistical Yearbook.*

Facts on File, 460 Park Avenue South, New York, New York 10016 (800) 443-8323; *The New Book of World Rankings.*

IRELAND (EIRE) - HOUSING CONSTRUCTION - See IRELAND (EIRE) - CONSTRUCTION INDUSTRY

IRELAND (EIRE) - HOUSING EXPENDITURES

European Community Information Service, 2100 M Street, NW, Washington, D.C. 20037 (202) 862-9500; *Basic Statistics of the Community.*

IRELAND (EIRE) - HYDROCHLORIC ACID PRODUCTION

European Community Information Service, 2100 M Street, NW, Washington, D.C. 20037 (202) 862-9500; *Basic Statistics of the Community.*

IRELAND (EIRE) - ILLITERATE POPULATION

The Economist Intelligence Unit, 111 West 57th Street, New York, New York 10019 (800) 938-4685; *The World Market Atlas.*

G.K. Hall and Company, 70 Lincoln Street, Boston, Massachusetts 02111 (617) 423-3990; *The World in Figures.*

IRELAND (EIRE) - IMPORTS

American Automobile Manufacturers Association, 1401 H Street, NW, Suite 900, Washington, D.C. 20005 (202) 326-5500; *World Motor Vehicle Data.*

The Economist Intelligence Unit, 111 West 57th Street, New York, New York 10019 (800) 938-4685; *The World Market Atlas.*

European Community Information Service, 2100 M Street, NW, Washington, D.C. 20037 (202) 862-9500; *Basic Statistics of the Community, Energy: Monthly Statistics, Energy Statistics Yearbook, Eurostatistics: Data for Short-Term Economic Analysis, External Trade: Monthly Statistics, External Trade: Statistical Yearbook,* and *Fisheries: Yearly Statistics.*

Food and Agricultural Organization of the United Nations (FAO) Via delle Terme di Caracalla, 00100 Rome, Italy (Telephone Number in U.S. (202) 606-7828); *The State of Food and Agriculture.*

G.K. Hall and Company, 70 Lincoln Street, Boston, Massachusetts 02111 (617) 423-3990; *The World in Figures.*

International Lead and Zinc Study Group, Metro House, 58 St. James's Street, London SW1A 1LD, England; *Lead and Zinc Statistics.*

International Monetary Fund, 700 Nineteenth Street, NW, Washington, D.C. 20431 (202) 623-7000; *Direction of Trade Statistics, Government Finance Statistics Yearbook,* and *International Financial Statistics.*

Organisation for Economic Co-operation and Development (OECD), 2 rue Andre-Pascal, 75 Paris 16, France (Telephone Number in U.S. (202) 785-6323); *Economic Outlook, The Footwear, Raw Hides and Skins, and Leather Industry in OECD Countries, Industrial Structure Statistics, The Iron and Steel Industry, Milk, Milk Products, and Egg Balances in OECD Member Countries, OECD Economic Surveys: Ireland, The Pulp and Paper Industry,* and *Review of Fisheries in OECD Member Countries.*

Times Books, 201 East 50th Street, New York, New York 10022 (212) 751-2600; *The Economist Book of Vital World Statistics.*

The World Bank, 1818 H Street, NW, Washington, D.C. 20433 (202) 477-1234; *World Tables.*

IRELAND (EIRE) - INCOME TAXES - See IRELAND (EIRE) - TAXATION

IRELAND (EIRE) - INDUSTRIAL METALS PRODUCTION - See IRELAND (EIRE) - MINING AND MINERAL PRODUCTS

IRELAND (EIRE) - INDUSTRY

Confederation of Irish Industry, Confederation House, Kildare Street, Dublin 2, Ireland; *Monthly Industrial Survey.*

European Community Information Service, 2100 M Street, NW, Washington, D.C. 20037 (202) 862-9500; *Basic Statistics of the Community, Employment and Unemployment, Eurostatistics: Data for Short-Term Economic Analysis,* and *Labor Force Sample Survey.*

Facts on File, 460 Park Avenue South, New York, New York 10016 (800) 443-8323; *The New Book of World Rankings.*

G.K. Hall and Company, 70 Lincoln Street, Boston, Massachusetts 02111 (617) 423-3990; *The World in Figures.*

International Labour Office, I.L.O. Publications, CH-1211, Geneva 22, Switzerland; *Yearbook of Labour Statistics.*

Organisation for Economic Co-operation and Development (OECD), 2 rue Andre-Pascal, 75 Paris 16, France (Telephone Number in U.S. (202) 785-6323); *Economic Outlook, Historical Statistics, Industrial Structure Statistics,* and *OECD Environmental Data.*

Statistical Office of the United Nations, Publishing Service, New York, New York 10017 (800) 253-9646; *Statistical Yearbook.*

Times Books, 201 East 50th Street, New York, New York 10022 (212) 751-2600; *The Economist Book of Vital World Statistics.*

The World Bank, 1818 H Street, NW, Washington, D.C. 20433 (202) 477-1234; *World Tables.*

IRELAND (EIRE) - INFANT AND MATERNAL MORTALITY

European Community Information Service, 2100 M Street, NW, Washington, D.C. 20037 (202) 862-9500; *Basic Statistics of the Community,* and *Demographic Statistics.*

Statistical Office of the United Nations, Publishing Service, New York, New York 10017 (800) 253-9646; *Demographic Yearbook.,* and *Statistical Yearbook.*

Times Books, 201 East 50th Street, New York, New York 10022 (212) 751-2600; *The Economist Book of Vital World Statistics.*

World Health Organization, Office of Publications, Avenue Appia, CH-1211 Geneva 27, Switzerland (Telephone Number in U.S. (518) 436-9686); *World Health Statistics Annual.*

The World Bank, 1818 H Street, NW, Washington, D.C. 20433 (202) 477-1234; *World Tables.*

IRELAND (EIRE) - INTEREST RATES

European Community Information Service, 2100 M Street, NW, Washington, D.C. 20037 (202) 862-9500; *Money and Finance.*

Organisation for Economic Co-operation and Development (OECD), 2 rue Andre-Pascal, 75 Paris 16, France (Telephone Number in U.S. (202) 785-6323); *Economic Outlook, Financial Market Trends, Main Economic Indicators - Historical Statistics,* and *OECD Financial Statistics.*

IRELAND (EIRE) - INTERNAL TRADE

European Community Information Service, 2100 M Street, NW, Washington, D.C. 20037 (202) 862-9500; *Basic Statistics of the Community.*

Organisation for Economic Co-operation and Development (OECD), 2 rue Andre-Pascal, 75 Paris 16, France (Telephone Number in U.S. (202) 785-6323); *Main Economic Indicators - Historical Statistics.*

IRELAND (EIRE) - INTERNATIONAL FINANCE

European Community Information Service, 2100 M Street, NW, Washington, D.C. 20037 (202) 862-9500; *Basic Statistics of the Community.*

Organisation for Economic Co-operation and Development (OECD), 2 rue Andre-Pascal, 75 Paris 16, France (Telephone Number in U.S. (202) 785-6323); *Economic Outlook,* and *Financial Market Trends.*

IRELAND (EIRE) - INTERNATIONAL LIQUIDITY

Organisation for Economic Co-operation and Development (OECD), 2 rue Andre-Pascal, 75 Paris 16, France (Telephone Number in U.S. (202) 785-6323); *Economic Outlook,* and *Financial Market Trends.*

IRELAND (EIRE) - INTERNATIONAL RESERVES EXCLUDING GOLD

Statistical Office of the United Nations, Publishing Service, New York, New York 10017 (800) 253-9646; *Statistical Yearbook.*

The World Bank, 1818 H Street, NW, Washington, D.C. 20433 (202) 477-1234; *World Tables.*

IRELAND (EIRE) - INTERNATIONAL STATISTICS

Organisation for Economic Co-operation and Development (OECD), 2 rue Andre-Pascal, 75 Paris 16, France (Telephone Number in U.S. (202) 785-6323); *Financial Market Trends,* and *Tourism Policy and International Tourism in OECD Member Countries.*

IRELAND (EIRE) - INVESTMENTS

Organisation for Economic Co-operation and Development (OECD), 2 rue Andre-Pascal, 75 Paris 16, France (Telephone Number in U.S. (202) 785-6323); *Economic Outlook, Financial Market Trends, Industrial Structure Statistics,* and *Textile Industry in OECD Countries.*

IRELAND (EIRE) - IRON ORE - See IRELAND (EIRE) - MINING AND MINERAL PRODUCTS

IRELAND (EIRE) - JUTE PRODUCTION - See IRELAND (EIRE) - CROPS

IRELAND (EIRE) - LABOR FORCE

Central Statistics Office, Ardee Road, Dublin 6, Ireland; *Labour Force Survey.*

European Community Information Service, 2100 M Street, NW, Washington, D.C. 20037 (202) 862-9500; *Basic Statistics of the Community, Labor Force Sample Survey,* and *Regions: Statistical Yearbook.*

Facts on File, 460 Park Avenue South, New York, New York 10016 (800) 443-8323; *The New Book of World Rankings.*

Food and Agricultural Organization of the United Nations (FAO) Via delle Terme di Caracalla, 00100 Rome, Italy (Telephone Number in U.S. (202) 653-2400); *The State of Food and Agriculture.*

G.K. Hall and Company, 70 Lincoln Street, Boston, Massachusetts 02111 (617) 423-3990; *The World in Figures.*

Organisation for Economic Co-operation and Development (OECD), 2 rue Andre-Pascal, 75 Paris 16, France (Telephone Number in U.S. (202) 785-6323); *Economic Outlook, The Iron and Steel Industry, Labour Force Statistics, Main Economic Indicators - Historical Statistics, Maritime Transport, OECD Economic Surveys: Ireland, OECD Employment Outlook,* and *Textile Industry in OECD Countries.*

Times Books, 201 East 50th Street, New York, New York 10022 (212) 751-2600; *The Economist Book of Vital World Statistics.*

The World Bank, 1818 H Street, NW, Washington, D.C. 20433 (202) 477-1234; *World Tables.*

IRELAND (EIRE) - LABOR PRODUCTIVITY

International Labour Office, I.L.O. Publications, CH-1211, Geneva 22, Switzerland; *Yearbook of Labour Statistics.*

Organisation for Economic Co-operation and Development (OECD), 2 rue Andre-Pascal, 75 Paris 16, France (Telephone Number in U.S. (202) 785-6323); *Economic Outlook,* and *OECD Employment Outlook.*

IRELAND (EIRE) - LAND USE

Euromonitor Publications Limited, 87-88 Turnmill Street, London EC1M 5QU, England; *European Marketing Data and Statistics.*

European Community Information Service, 2100 M Street, NW, Washington, D.C. 20037 (202) 862-9500; *Agriculture: Statistical Yearbook, Basic Statistics of the Community, Crop Production: Quarterly Statistics,* and *Regions: Statistical Yearbook.*

Food and Agricultural Organization of the United Nations (FAO), Via delle Terme di Caracalla, 00100 Rome, Italy (Telephone Number in U.S. (202) 653-2400); *Production Yearbook.*

G.K. Hall and Company, 70 Lincoln Street, Boston, Massachusetts 02111 (617) 423-3990; *The World in Figures.*

IRELAND (EIRE) - LEAD AND LEAD ORE PRODUCTION AND CONSUMPTION - See IRELAND (EIRE) - MINING AND MINERAL PRODUCTS

IRELAND (EIRE) - LEATHER - PRODUCTION INDEX

Organisation for Economic Co-operation and Development (OECD), 2 rue Andre-Pascal, 75 Paris 16, France (Telephone Number in U.S. (202) 785-6323); *Indicators of Industrial Activity.*

IRELAND (EIRE) - LEATHER AND FOOTWEAR - EXPORTS AND IMPORTS

European Community Information Service, 2100 M Street, NW, Washington, D.C. 20037 (202) 862-9500; *Basic Statistics of the Community.*

Organisation for Economic Co-operation and Development (OECD), 2 rue Andre-Pascal, 75 Paris 16, France (Telephone Number in U.S. (202) 785-6323); *The Footwear, Raw Hides and Skins, and Leather Industry in OECD Countries.*

IRELAND (EIRE) - LIBRARIES

Euromonitor Publications Limited, 87-88 Turnmill Street, London EC1M 5QU, England; *European Marketing Data and Statistics.*

Facts on File, 460 Park Avenue South, New York, New York 10016 (800) 443-8323; *The New Book of World Rankings.*

United Nations Educational, Scientific and Cultural Organization (UNESCO), 7 Place de Fontenoy, F-75700 Paris, France (Telephone Number in U.S. (212) 963-5981); *Statistical Yearbook.*

IRELAND (EIRE) - LIGNITE PRODUCTION - See IRELAND (EIRE) - MINING AND MINERAL PRODUCTS

IRELAND (EIRE) - LIVESTOCK AND POULTRY

Euromonitor Publications Limited, 87-88 Turnmill Street, London EC1M 5QU, England; *European Marketing Data and Statistics,* and *Basic Statistics of the Community.*

European Community Information Service, 2100 M Street, NW, Washington, D.C. 20037 (202) 862-9500; *Agriculture: Statistical Yearbook, Eurostatistics: Data for Short-Term Economic Analysis* and *Regions: Statistical Yearbook.*

Facts on File, 460 Park Avenue South, New York, New York 10016 (800) 443-8323; *The New Book of World Rankings.*

Food and Agricultural Organization of the United Nations (FAO), Via delle Terme di Caracalla, 00100 Rome, Italy (Telephone Number in U.S. (202) 653-2400); *Production Yearbook,* and *The State of Food and Agriculture.*

G.K. Hall and Company, 70 Lincoln Street, Boston, Massachusetts 02111 (617) 423-3990; *The World in Figures.*

Organisation for Economic Co-operation and Development (OECD), 2 rue Andre-Pascal, 75 Paris 16, France (Telephone Number in U.S. (202) 785-6323); *Economic Accounts for Agriculture,* and *Meat Balances in OECD Member Countries.*

Statistical Office of the United Nations, Publishing Service, New York, New York 10017 (800) 253-9646; *Statistical Yearbook.*

IRELAND (EIRE) - LIVING LEVELS

G.K. Hall and Company, 70 Lincoln Street, Boston, Massachusetts 02111 (617) 423-3990; *The World in Figures.*

Organisation for Economic Co-operation and Development (OECD), 2 rue Andre-Pascal, 75 Paris 16, France (Telephone Number in U.S. (202) 785-6323); *Economic Outlook.*

Times Books, 201 East 50th Street, New York, New York 10022 (212) 751-2600; *The Economist Book of Vital World Statistics.*

IRELAND (EIRE) - MACHINERY - PRODUCTION INDEX

Organisation for Economic Co-operation and Development (OECD), 2 rue Andre-Pascal, 75 Paris 16, France (Telephone Number in U.S. (202) 785-6323); *Indicators of Industrial Activity.*

IRELAND (EIRE) - MAGNESIUM PRODUCTION AND CONSUMPTION - See IRELAND (EIRE) - MINING AND MINERAL PRODUCTS

IRELAND (EIRE) - MAIL - NUMBER OF PIECES SENT OR RECEIVED

European Community Information Service, 2100 M Street, NW, Washington, D.C. 20037 (202) 862-9500; *Transport Annual Statistics.*

Statistical Office of the United Nations, Publishing Service, New York, New York 10017 (800) 253-9646; *Statistical Yearbook.*

IRELAND (EIRE) - MAIN ECONOMIC INDICATORS - See IRELAND (EIRE) - ECONOMY

IRELAND (EIRE) - MANGANESE PRODUCTION AND CONSUMPTION - See IRELAND (EIRE) - MINING AND MINERAL PRODUCTS

IRELAND (EIRE) - MANUFACTURING

American Automobile Manufacturers Association, 1401 H Street, NW, Suite 900, Washington, D.C. 20005 (202) 326-5500; *World Motor Vehicle Data.*

European Community Information Service, 2100 M Street, NW, Washington, D.C. 20037 (202) 862-9500; *Basic Statistics of the Community, Employment and Unemployment, Eurostatistics: Data for Short-Term Economic Analysis, Industrial Production: Quarterly,* and *Labor Force Sample Survey.*

Facts on File, 460 Park Avenue South, New York, New York 10016 (800) 443-8323; *The New Book of World Rankings.*

G.K. Hall and Company, 70 Lincoln Street, Boston, Massachusetts 02111 (617) 423-3990; *The World in Figures.*

Organisation for Economic Co-operation and Development (OECD), 2 rue Andre-Pascal, 75 Paris 16, France (Telephone Number in U.S. (202) 785-6323); *Foreign Trade by Commodities, Indicators of Industrial Activity, Industrial Structure Statistics,* and *OECD Economic Surveys: Ireland.*

Statistical Office of the United Nations, Publishing Service, New York, New York 10017 (800) 253-9646; *Statistical Yearbook.*

Times Books, 201 East 50th Street, New York, New York 10022 (212) 751-2600; *The Economist Book of Vital World Statistics.*

The World Bank, 1818 H Street, NW, Washington, D.C. 20433 (202) 477-1234; *World Tables.*

IRELAND (EIRE) - MARRIAGE RATES

European Community Information Service, 2100 M Street, NW, Washington, D.C. 20037 (202) 862-9500; *Basic Statistics of the Community.*

Facts on File, 460 Park Avenue South, New York, New York 10016 (800) 443-8323; *The New Book of World Rankings.*

Statistical Office of the United Nations, Publishing Service, New York, New York 10017 (800) 253-9646; *Demographic Yearbook,* and *Statistical Yearbook.*

IRELAND (EIRE) - MEAT PRODUCTION - See IRELAND (EIRE) - LIVESTOCK AND POULTRY AND POULTRY

IRELAND (EIRE) - MERCHANT SHIPPING

European Community Information Service, 2100 M Street, NW, Washington, D.C. 20037 (202) 862-9500; *Basic Statistics of the Community, Fisheries: Yearly Statistics, Regions: Statistical Yearbook,* and *Transport Annual Statistics.*

G.K. Hall and Company, 70 Lincoln Street, Boston, Massachusetts 02111 (617) 423-3990; *The World in Figures.*

Organisation for Economic Co-operation and Development (OECD), 2 rue Andre-Pascal, 75 Paris 16, France (Telephone Number in U.S. (202) 785-6323); *Maritime Transport.*

Statistical Office of the United Nations, Publishing Service, New York, New York 10017 (800) 253-9646; *Statistical Yearbook.*

Times Books, 201 East 50th Street, New York, New York 10022 (212) 751-2600; *The Economist Book of Vital World Statistics.*

U.S. Department of Transportation, Maritime Administration, 400 Seventh Street, SW, Washington, D.C. 20590 (202) 366-5807; *A Statistical Analysis of the World's Merchant Fleets.*

IRELAND (EIRE) - MERCURY PRODUCTION AND CONSUMPTION

European Community Information Service, 2100 M Street, NW, Washington, D.C. 20037 (202) 862-9500; *Basic Statistics of the Community.*

Organisation for Economic Co-operation and Development (OECD), 2 rue Andre-Pascal, 75 Paris 16, France (Telephone Number in U.S. (202) 785-6323); *Indicators of Industrial Activity.*

Statistical Office of the United Nations, Publishing Service, New York, New York 10017 (800) 253-9646; *Statistical Yearbook.*

IRELAND (EIRE) - MILITARY

G.K. Hall and Company, 70 Lincoln Street, Boston, Massachusetts 02111 (617) 423-3990; *The World in Figures.*

International Road Federation, 525 School Street, SW, Washington, D.C. 20024 (202) 554-2106; *World Road Statistics.*

The International Institute for Strategic Studies, 23 Tavistock Street, London WC2E 7NQ, England; *The Military Balance.*

U.S. Arms Control and Disarmament Agency, 320 Twenty-first Street, Northwest, Washington, D.C. 20451 (202) 647-8677; *World Military Expenditures and Arms Transfers.*

IRELAND (EIRE) MILK - See IRELAND (EIRE) - DAIRY PRODUCTS

IRELAND (EIRE) - MILLET PRODUCTION - See IRELAND (EIRE) - CROPS

IRELAND (EIRE) - MINING AND MINERAL PRODUCTS

European Community Information Service, 2100 M Street, NW, Washington, D.C. 20037 (202) 862-9500; *ACP: Basic Statistics, Basic Statistics of the Community, Energy: Monthly Statistics, Energy Statistics, Eurostatistics: Data for Short-Term Economic Analysis, Industrial Production: Quarterly Statistics, Labor Force Sample Survey,* and *Regions: Statistical Yearbook.*

Facts on File, 460 Park Avenue South, New York, New York 10016 (800) 443-8323; *The New Book of World Rankings.*

G.K. Hall and Company, 70 Lincoln Street, Boston, Massachusetts 02111 (617) 423-3990; *The World in Figures.*

International Lead and Zinc Study Group, Metro House, 58 St. James's Street, London SW1A 1LD, England; *Lead and Zinc Statistics.*

Organisation for Economic Co-operation and Development (OECD), 2 rue Andre-Pascal, 75 Paris 16, France (Telephone Number in U.S. (202) 785-6323); *Coal Information, Economic Outlook, Energy Statistics of OECD Countries, Foreign Trade by Commodities, Indicators of Industrial Activity, Industrial Structure Statistics, The Iron and Steel Industry, Iron and Steel: Statistical Yearbook, Main Economic Indicators - Historical Statistics, The Non-Ferrous Metals Industry,* and *OECD Economic Surveys: Ireland.*

Statistical Office of the United Nations, Publishing Service, New York, New York 10017 (800) 253-9646; *Statistical Yearbook.*

IRELAND (EIRE) - MOLYBDENUM AND MOLYBDENUM ORE - See IRELAND (EIRE) - MINING AND MINERAL PRODUCTS

IRELAND (EIRE) - MONEY AND CREDIT

Organisation for Economic Co-operation and Development (OECD), 2 rue Andre-Pascal, 75 Paris 16, France (Telephone Number in U.S. (202) 785-6323); *OECD Economic Surveys: Ireland.*

IRELAND (EIRE) - MONEY EXCHANGE RATE

European Community Information Service, 2100 M Street, NW, Washington, D.C. 20037 (202) 862-9500; *Basic Statistics of the Community.*

International Monetary Fund, 700 Nineteenth Street, NW, Washington, D.C. 20431 (202) 623-7000; *International Financial Statistics.*

Organisation for Economic Co-operation and Development (OECD), 2 rue Andre-Pascal, 75 Paris 16, France (Telephone Number in U.S. (202) 785-6323); *Economic Outlook, Financial Market Trends,* and *Tourism Policy and International Tourism in OECD Member Countries.*

Statistical Office of the United Nations, Publishing Service, New York, New York 10017 (800) 253-9646; *Statistical Yearbook.*

IRELAND (EIRE) - MONEY RATES - MARKET

European Community Information Service, 2100 M Street, NW, Washington, D.C. 20037 (202) 862-9500; *Basic Statistics of the Community.*

Organisation for Economic Co-operation and Development (OECD), 2 rue Andre-Pascal, 75 Paris 16, France (Telephone Number in U.S. (202) 785-6323); *Economic Outlook*, and *Financial Market Trends*.

IRELAND (EIRE) - MONEY RESERVES

European Community Information Service, 2100 M Street, NW, Washington, D.C. 20037 (202) 862-9500; *Basic Statistics of the Community*.

Organisation for Economic Co-operation and Development (OECD), 2 rue Andre-Pascal, 75 Paris 16, France (Telephone Number in U.S. (202) 785-6323); *Economic Outlook*, and *Financial Market Trends*.

IRELAND (EIRE) - MONEY SUPPLY

European Community Information Service, 2100 M Street, NW, Washington, D.C. 20037 (202) 862-9500; *Basic Statistics of the Community, Eurostatistics: Data for Short-Term Economic Analysis*, and *Money and Finance*.

G.K. Hall and Company, 70 Lincoln Street, Boston, Massachusetts 02111 (617) 423-3990; *The World in Figures*.

International Monetary Fund, 700 Nineteenth Street, NW, Washington, D.C. 20431 (202) 623-7000; *International Financial Statistics*.

Organisation for Economic Co-operation and Development (OECD), 2 rue Andre-Pascal, 75 Paris 16, France (Telephone Number in U.S. (202) 785-6323); *Economic Outlook*.

Statistical Office of the United Nations, Publishing Service, New York, New York 10017 (800) 253-9646; *Statistical Yearbook*.

The World Bank, 1818 H Street, NW, Washington, D.C. 20433 (202) 477-1234; *World Tables*.

IRELAND (EIRE) - MOTION PICTURES

Statistical Office of the United Nations, Publishing Service, New York, New York 10017 (800) 253-9646; *Statistical Yearbook*.

United Nations Educational, Scientific and Cultural Organization (UNESCO), 7 Place de Fontenoy, F-75700 Paris, France; *Statistical Yearbook*.

IRELAND (EIRE) - MOTOR VEHICLE PRODUCTION

American Automobile Manufacturers Association, 1401 H Street, NW, Suite 900, Washington, D.C. 20005 (202) 326-5500; *World Motor Vehicle Data*.

European Community Information Service, 2100 M Street, NW, Washington, D.C. 20037 (202) 862-9500; *Basic Statistics of the Community*, and *Eurostatistics: Data for Short-Term Economic Analysis*.

Organisation for Economic Co-operation and Development (OECD), 2 rue Andre-Pascal, 75 Paris 16, France (Telephone Number in U.S. (202) 785-6323); *Foreign Trade by Commodities*, and *Indicators of Industrial Activity*.

Statistical Office of the United Nations, Publishing Service, New York, New York 10017 (800) 253-9646; *Statistical Yearbook*.

IRELAND (EIRE) - MOTOR VEHICLE TAXES - See IRELAND (EIRE) - TAXATION

IRELAND (EIRE) - MOTOR VEHICLES IN USE

American Automobile Manufacturers Association, 1401 H Street, NW, Suite 900, Washington, D.C. 20005 (202) 326-5500; *World Motor Vehicle Data*.

European Community Information Service, 2100 M Street, NW, Washington, D.C. 20037 (202) 862-9500; *Basic Statistics of the Community*, and *Transport Annual Statistics*.

G.K. Hall and Company, 70 Lincoln Street, Boston, Massachusetts 02111 (617) 423-3990; *The World in Figures*.

International Road Federation, 525 School Street, SW, Washington, D.C. 20024 (202) 554-2106; *World Road Statistics*.

Statistical Office of the United Nations, Publishing Service, New York, New York 10017 (800) 253-9646; *Statistical Yearbook*.

Times Books, 201 East 50th Street, New York, New York 10022 (212) 751-2600; *The Economist Book of Vital World Statistics*.

IRELAND (EIRE) - MULES - See IRELAND (EIRE) - LIVESTOCK AND POULTRY

IRELAND (EIRE) - MUSEUMS

Euromonitor Publications Limited, 87-88 Turnmill Street, London EC1M 5QU, England; *European Marketing Data and Statistics*.

Facts on File, 460 Park Avenue South, New York, New York 10016 (800) 443-8323; *The New Book of World Rankings*.

United Nations Educational, Scientific and Cultural Organization (UNESCO) 7 Place de Fontenoy, F-75700 Paris, France (Telephone Number in U.S. (212) 963-5981); *Statistical Yearbook*.

IRELAND (EIRE) - NATALITY - See IRELAND (EIRE) - BIRTH RATES

IRELAND (EIRE) - NATIONAL ACCOUNTS

European Community Information Service, 2100 M Street, NW, Washington, D.C. 20037 (202) 862-9500; *Basic Statistics of the Community*, and *Eurostatistics: Data for Short-Term Economic Analysis*.

International Monetary Fund, 700 Nineteenth Street, NW, Washington, D.C. 20431 (202) 623-7000; *International Financial Statistics*.

Organisation for Economic Co-operation and Development (OECD), 2 rue Andre-Pascal, 75 Paris 16, France (Telephone Number in U.S. (202) 785-6323); *Economic Outlook*.

Statistical Office of the United Nations, Publishing Service, New York, New York 10017 (800) 253-9646; *National Accounts Statistics*, and *Statistical Yearbook*.

IRELAND (EIRE) - NATIONAL INCOME

Facts on File, 460 Park Avenue South, New York, New York 10016 (800) 443-8323; *The New Book of World Rankings*.

G.K. Hall and Company, 70 Lincoln Street, Boston, Massachusetts 02111 (617) 423-3990; *The World in Figures*.

Organisation for Economic Co-operation and Development (OECD), 2 rue Andre-Pascal, 75 Paris 16, France (Telephone Number in U.S. (202) 785-6323); *Economic Outlook*.

Statistical Office of the United Nations, Publishing Service, New York, New York 10017 (800) 253-9646; *Statistical Yearbook.*

IRELAND (EIRE) - NATIONAL PRODUCT

European Community Information Service, 2100 M Street, NW, Washington, D.C. 20037 (202) 862-9500; *Basic Statistics of the Community.*

Facts on File, 460 Park Avenue South, New York, New York 10016 (800) 443-8323; *The New Book of World Rankings.*

Organisation for Economic Co-operation and Development (OECD), 2 rue Andre-Pascal, 75 Paris 16, France (Telephone Number in U.S. (202) 785-6323); *Economic Outlook.*

Statistical Office of the United Nations, Publishing Service, New York, New York 10017 (800) 253-9646; *Statistical Yearbook.*

IRELAND (EIRE) - NATURAL GAS PRODUCTION - See IRELAND (EIRE) - MINING AND MINERAL PRODUCTS

IRELAND (EIRE) - NATURAL RUBBER PRODUCTION

European Community Information Service, 2100 M Street, NW, Washington, D.C. 20037 (202) 862-9500; *Basic Statistics of the Community.*

IRELAND (EIRE) - NEWSPAPER PRODUCTION - See IRELAND (EIRE) - FORESTRY AND FOREST PRODUCTS

IRELAND (EIRE) - NEWSPRINT - See IRELAND (EIRE) - FORESTRY AND FOREST PRODUCTS

IRELAND (EIRE) - NICKEL AND NICKEL ORE PRODUCTION AND CONSUMPTION - See IRELAND (EIRE) - MINING AND MINERAL PRODUCTS

IRELAND (EIRE) - NITRIC ACID PRODUCTION

European Community Information Service, 2100 M Street, NW, Washington, D.C. 20037 (202) 862-9500; *Basic Statistics of the Community.*

Organisation for Economic Co-operation and Development (OECD), 2 rue Andre-Pascal, 75 Paris 16, France (Telephone Number in U.S. (202) 785-6323); *Indicators of Industrial Activity.*

IRELAND (EIRE) - OATS PRODUCTION - See IRELAND (EIRE) - CROPS

IRELAND (EIRE) - OCCUPATIONS - See IRELAND (EIRE) - LABOR FORCE

IRELAND (EIRE) - OIL PRODUCING CROPS

European Community Information Service, 2100 M Street, NW, Washington, D.C. 20037 (202) 862-9500; *Basic Statistics of the Community.*

Organisation for Economic Co-operation and Development (OECD), 2 rue Andre-Pascal, 75 Paris 16, France (Telephone Number in U.S. (202) 785-6323); *Foreign Trade by Commodities.*

IRELAND (EIRE) - ONION PRODUCTION - See IRELAND (EIRE) - CROPS

IRELAND (EIRE) - PALM KERNEL PRODUCTION - See IRELAND (EIRE) - CROPS

IRELAND (EIRE) - PAPER - See IRELAND (EIRE) - FORESTRY AND FOREST PRODUCTS

IRELAND (EIRE) - PATENTS

Statistical Office of the United Nations, Publishing Service, New York, New York 10017 (800) 253-9646; *Statistical Yearbook.*

World Intellectual Property Organization, 34 Chemin des Colombettes, CH-1211 Geneva 20, Switzerland; *Industrial Property Statistics.*

IRELAND (EIRE) - PEANUT PRODUCTION - See IRELAND (EIRE) - CROPS

IRELAND (EIRE) - PEPPER PRODUCTION - IRELAND (EIRE) - CROPS

IRELAND (EIRE) - PERIODICALS

United Nations Educational, Scientific and Cultural Organization (UNESCO), 7 Place de Fontenoy, F-75700 Paris, France (Telephone Number in U.S. (212) 963-5981); *Statistical Yearbook.*

IRELAND (EIRE) - PESTICIDE USE

Food and Agricultural Organization of the United Nations (FAO) Via delle Terme di Caracalla, 00100 Rome, Italy (Telephone Number in U.S. (202) 653-2400); *The State of Food and Agriculture.*

IRELAND (EIRE) - PETROLEUM INDUSTRY

Euromonitor Publications Limited, 87-88 Turnmill Street, London EC1M 5QU, England; *European Marketing Data and Statistics.*

European Community Information Service, 2100 M Street, NW, Washington, D.C. 20037 (202) 862-9500; *ACP: Basic Statistics, Basic Statistics of the Community* and *Energy Statistics Yearbook.*

Facts on File, 460 Park Avenue South, New York, New York 10016 (800) 443-8323; *The New Book of World Rankings.*

G.K. Hall and Company, 70 Lincoln Street, Boston, Massachusetts 02111 (617) 423-3990; *The World in Figures.*

Organisation for Economic Co-operation and Development (OECD), 2 rue Andre-Pascal, 75 Paris 16, France (Telephone Number in U.S. (202) 785-6323); *Energy Statistics of OECD Countries, Foreign Trade by Commodities, Indicators of Industrial Activity,* and *Oil and Gas Information.*

IRELAND (EIRE) - PHOSPHATE ROCK PRODUCTION - See IRELAND (EIRE) - MINING AND MINERAL PRODUCTS

IRELAND (EIRE) - PHOSPHATES PRODUCTION - See IRELAND (EIRE) - MINING AND MINERAL PRODUCTS

IRELAND (EIRE) - PIG-IRON AND FERRO-ALLOY PRODUCTION - See IRELAND (EIRE) - MINING AND MINERAL PRODUCTS

IRELAND (EIRE) - PIGS - See IRELAND (EIRE) - LIVESTOCK AND POULTRY

IRELAND (EIRE) - PIPELINES FOR OIL AND PETROLEUM PRODUCTS

European Community Information Service, 2100 M Street, NW, Washington, D.C. 20037 (202) 862-9500; *Transport Annual Statistics.*

IRELAND (EIRE) - PLASTIC AND RESIN PRODUCTION

European Community Information Service, 2100 M Street, NW, Washington, D.C. 20037 (202) 862-9500; *Basic Statistics of the Community.*

Organisation for Economic Co-operation and Development (OECD), 2 rue Andre-Pascal, 75 Paris 16, France (Telephone Number in U.S. (202) 785-6323); *Foreign Trade by Commodities.*

IRELAND (EIRE) - PLATINUM PRODUCTION AND CONSUMPTION - See IRELAND (EIRE) - MINING AND MINERAL PRODUCTS

IRELAND (EIRE) - POPULATION

Central Statistics Office, Ardee Road, Dublin 6, Ireland; *Census of Population of Ireland.*

The Economist Intelligence Unit, 111 West 57th Street, New York, New York 10019 (800) 938-4685; *The World Market Atlas.*

Euromonitor Publications Limited, 87-88 Turnmill Street, London EC1M 5QU, England; *European Marketing Data and Statistics.*

European Community Information Service, 2100 M Street, NW, Washington, D.C. 20037 (202) 862-9500; *ACP: Basic Statistics, Basic Statistics of the Community, Demographic Statistics, Employment and Unemployment, Fisheries: Yearly Statistics, Iron and Steel: Statistical Yearbook, Labor Force Sample Survey,*and *Regions: Statistical Yearbook.*

Facts on File, 460 Park Avenue South, New York, New York 10016 (800) 443-8323; *The New Book of World Rankings.*

Food and Agricultural Organization of the United Nations (FAO), Via delle Terme di Caracalla, 00100 Rome, Italy (Telephone Number in U.S. (202) 653-2400); *Production Yearbook.*

G.K. Hall and Company, 70 Lincoln Street, Boston, Massachusetts 02111 (617) 423-3990; *The World in Figures.*

International Labour Office, I.L.O. Publications, CH-1211, Geneva 22, Switzerland; *Yearbook of Labour Statistics.*

Statistical Office of the United Nations, Publishing Service, New York, New York 10017 (800) 253-9646; *Demographic Yearbook,* and *Statistical Yearbook.*

Times Books, 201 East 50th Street, New York, New York 10022 (212) 751-2600; *The Economist Book of Vital World Statistics.*

United Nations Educational, Scientific and Cultural Organization (UNESCO), 7 Place de Fontenoy, F-75700 Paris, France (Telephone Number in U.S. (212) 963-5981); *Statistical Yearbook.*

U.S. Arms Control and Disarmament Agency, 320 Twenty-first Street, Northwest, Washington, D.C. 20451 (202) 647-8677; *World Military Expenditures and Arms Transfers.*

World Health Organization, Office of Publications, Avenue Appia, CH-1211 Geneva 27, Switzerland (Telephone Number in U.S. (518) 436-9686); *World Health Statistics Annual.*

IRELAND (ERIE) - POST OFFICES

Facts on File, 460 Park Avenue South, New York, New York 10016 (800) 443-8323; *The New Book of World Rankings.*

IRELAND (EIRE) - POTATO PRODUCTION - See IRELAND (EIRE) - CROPS

IRELAND (EIRE) - POWER PRODUCTION INDUSTRY

European Community Information Service, 2100 M Street, NW, Washington, D.C. 20037 (202) 862-9500; *Basic Statistics of the Community.*

Statistical Office of the United Nations, Publishing Service, New York, New York 10017 (800) 253-9646; *Statistical Yearbook.*

IRELAND (EIRE) - PRICES

Central Statistics Office, St. Stephen's Green House, Earlsfort Terrace, Dublin 2, Ireland; *Consumer Price Index.*

European Community Information Service, 2100 M Street, NW, Washington, D.C. 20037 (202) 862-9500; *Basic Statistics of the Community,* and *Eurostatistics: Data for Short-Term Economic Analysis.*

Facts on File, 460 Park Avenue South, New York, New York 10016 (800) 443-8323; *The New Book of World Rankings.*

Food and Agricultural Organization of the United Nations (FAO), Via delle Terme di Caracalla, 00100 Rome, Italy (Telephone Number in U.S. (202) 653-2400); *Production Yearbook,* and *The State of Food and Agriculture.*

G.K. Hall and Company, 70 Lincoln Street, Boston, Massachusetts 02111 (617) 423-3990; *The World in Figures.*

International Labour Office, I.L.O. Publications, CH-1211, Geneva 22, Switzerland; *Yearbook of Labour Statistics.*

International Lead and Zinc Study Group, Metro House, 58 St. James's Street, London SW1A 1LD, England; *Lead and Zinc Statistics.*

International Monetary Fund, 700 Nineteenth Street, NW, Washington, D.C. 20431 (202) 623-7000; *International Financial Statistics.*

Organisation for Economic Co-operation and Development (OECD), 2 rue Andre-Pascal, 75 Paris 16, France (Telephone Number in U.S. (202) 785-6323); *Economic Outlook, The Footwear, Raw Hides and Skins, and Leather Industry in OECD Countries, Indicators of Industrial Activity, The Iron and Steel Industry, Main Economic Indicators - Historical Statistics,* and *The Pulp and Paper Industry.*

IRELAND (EIRE) - PRINTING AND WRITING PAPER - See IRELAND (EIRE) - FORESTRY AND FOREST PRODUCTS

IRELAND (EIRE) - PRODUCTION

American Automobile Manufacturers Association, 1401 H Street, NW, Suite 900, Washington, D.C. 20005 (202) 326-5500; *World Motor Vehicle Data.*

European Community Information Service, 2100 M Street, NW, Washington, D.C. 20037 (202) 862-9500; *Basic Statistics of the Community, Eurostatistics: Data for Short-Term Economic Analysis,* and *Fisheries: Yearly Statistics.*

Facts on File, 460 Park Avenue South, New York, New York 10016 (800) 443-8323; *The New Book of World Rankings.*

G.K. Hall and Company, 70 Lincoln Street, Boston, Massachusetts 02111 (617) 423-3990; *The World in Figures.*

International Lead and Zinc Study Group, Metro House, 58 St. James's Street, London SW1A 1LD, England; *Lead and Zinc Statistics.*

Organisation for Economic Co-operation and Development (OECD), 2 rue Andre-Pascal, 75 Paris 16, France (Telephone Number in U.S. (202) 785-6323); *Economic Outlook, The Footwear, Raw Hides and Skins, and Leather Industry in OECD Countries, Indicators of Industrial Activity, Industrial Structure Statistics, The Iron and Steel Industry, Meat Balances in OECD Member Countries, Milk, Milk Products, and Egg Balances in OECD Member Countries, The Non-Ferrous Metals Industry, The Pulp and Paper Industry,* and *Textile Industry in OECD Countries.*

IRELAND (EIRE) - PRODUCTIVITY

European Community Information Service, 2100 M Street, NW, Washington, D.C. 20037 (202) 862-9500; *Basic Statistics of the Community.*

Organisation for Economic Co-operation and Development (OECD), 2 rue Andre-Pascal, 75 Paris 16, France (Telephone Number in U.S. (202) 785-6323); *Economic Outlook.*

IRELAND (EIRE) - PROPERTY TAXES - See IRELAND (EIRE) - TAXATION

IRELAND (EIRE) - PUBLIC CONSUMPTION FUND

European Community Information Service, 2100 M Street, NW, Washington, D.C. 20037 (202) 862-9500; *Basic Statistics of the Community.*

Organisation for Economic Co-operation and Development (OECD), 2 rue Andre-Pascal, 75 Paris 16, France (Telephone Number in U.S. (202) 785-6323); *Revenue Statistics of OECD Member Countries.*

IRELAND (EIRE) - PUBLIC EXPENDITURES

European Community Information Service, 2100 M Street, NW, Washington, D.C. 20037 (202) 862-9500; *Basic Statistics of the Community.*

Organisation for Economic Co-operation and Development (OECD), 2 rue Andre-Pascal, 75 Paris 16, France (Telephone Number in U.S. (202) 785-6323); *Revenue Statistics of OECD Member Countries.*

IRELAND (EIRE) - PUBLIC FINANCE

Facts on File, 460 Park Avenue South, New York, New York 10016 (800) 443-8323; *The New Book of World Rankings.*

Organisation for Economic Co-operation and Development (OECD), 2 rue Andre-Pascal, 75 Paris 16, France (Telephone Number in U.S. (202) 785-6323); *Revenue Statistics of OECD Member Countries.*

IRELAND (EIRE) - PUBLIC HEALTH

European Community Information Service, 2100 M Street, NW, Washington, D.C. 20037 (202) 862-9500; *Basic Statistics of the Community.*

IRELAND (EIRE) - PUBLIC REVENUES

Organisation for Economic Co-operation and Development (OECD), 2 rue Andre-Pascal, 75 Paris 16, France (Telephone Number in U.S. (202) 785-6323); *Milk, Milk Products, and Egg Balances in OECD Member Countries.*

IRELAND (EIRE) - RADIO BROADCASTING - See IRELAND (EIRE) - BROADCASTING

IRELAND (EIRE) - RADIO RECEIVER PRODUCTION

Statistical Office of the United Nations, Publishing Service, New York, New York 10017 (800) 253-9646; *Statistical Yearbook.*

IRELAND (EIRE) - RAILWAYS

Euromonitor Publications Limited, 87-88 Turnmill Street, London EC1M 5QU, England; *European Marketing Data and Statistics.*

European Community Information Service, 2100 M Street, NW, Washington, D.C. 20037 (202) 862-9500; *Basic Statistics of the Community, Regions: Statistical Yearbook,* and *Transport Annual Statistics.*

G.K. Hall and Company, 70 Lincoln Street, Boston, Massachusetts 02111 (617) 423-3990; *The World in Figures.*

Jane's Information Group, Sentinel House, 163 Brighton Road, Coulsdon, Surrey CR5 2NH, England (Telephone Number in U.S. (703) 683-3700); *Jane's World Railways.*

Statistical Office of the United Nations, Publishing Service, New York, New York 10017 (800) 253-9646; *Annual Bulletin of Transport Statistics for Europe,* and *Statistical Yearbook.*

IRELAND (EIRE) - RANCHING

European Community Information Service, 2100 M Street, NW, Washington, D.C. 20037 (202) 862-9500; *Basic Statistics of the Community.*

IRELAND (EIRE) - RAPESEED PRODUCTION - See IRELAND (EIRE) - CROPS

IRELAND (ERIE) - RELIGION

Facts on File, 460 Park Avenue South, New York, New York 10016 (800) 443-8323; *The New Book of World Rankings.*

IRELAND (EIRE) - RENT PRICES

International Labour Office, I.L.O. Publications, CH-1211, Geneva 22, Switzerland; *Yearbook of Labour Statistics.*

IRELAND (EIRE) - RETAIL TRADE

European Community Information Service, 2100 M Street, NW, Washington, D.C. 20037 (202) 862-9500; *Basic Statistics of the Community,* and *Eurostatistics: Data for Short-Term Economic Analysis.*

G.K. Hall and Company, 70 Lincoln Street, Boston, Massachusetts 02111 (617) 423-3990; *The World in Figures.*

Statistical Office of the United Nations, Publishing Service, New York, New York 10017 (800) 253-9646; *Statistical Yearbook.*

IRELAND (EIRE) - RICE PRODUCTION - See IRELAND (EIRE) - CROPS

IRELAND (EIRE) - ROOT AND TUBER PRODUCTION - See IRELAND (EIRE) - CROPS

IRELAND (EIRE) - ROUNDWOOD PRODUCTION - See IRELAND (EIRE) - FORESTRY AND FOREST PRODUCTS

IRELAND (EIRE) - RUBBER PRODUCTION

European Community Information Service, 2100 M Street, NW, Washington, D.C. 20037 (202) 862-9500; *Basic Statistics of the Community.*

Facts on File, 460 Park Avenue South, New York, New York 10016 (800) 443-8323; *The New Book of World Rankings.*

Organisation for Economic Co-operation and Development (OECD), 2 rue Andre-Pascal, 75 Paris 16, France (Telephone Number in U.S. (202) 785-6323); *Foreign Trade by Commodities.*

IRELAND (EIRE) - RYE PRODUCTION - See IRELAND (EIRE) - CROPS

IRELAND (EIRE) - SAFFLOWER SEED PRODUCTION - See IRELAND (EIRE) - CROPS

IRELAND (EIRE) - SALT PRODUCTION - See IRELAND (EIRE) - MINING AND MINERAL PRODUCTS

IRELAND (EIRE) - SAVINGS ACCOUNT DEPOSITS

European Community Information Service, 2100 M Street, NW, Washington, D.C. 20037 (202) 862-9500; *Eurostatistics: Data for Short-Term Economic Analysis.*

IRELAND (EIRE) - SAWNWOOD PRODUCTION - See IRELAND (EIRE) - FORESTRY AND FOREST PRODUCTS

IRELAND (EIRE) - SCIENCE AND TECHNOLOGY - EXPENDITURE FOR RESEARCH

European Community Information Service, 2100 M Street, NW, Washington, D.C. 20037 (202) 862-9500; *Basic Statistics of the Community.*

Statistical Office of the United Nations, Publishing Service, New York, New York 10017 (800) 253-9646; *Statistical Yearbook.*

IRELAND (EIRE) - SCIENTISTS AND TECHNICIANS

European Community Information Service, 2100 M Street, NW, Washington, D.C. 20037 (202) 862-9500; *Basic Statistics of the Community.*

Statistical Office of the United Nations, Publishing Service, New York, New York 10017 (800) 253-9646; *Statistical Yearbook.*

United Nations Educational, Scientific and Cultural Organization (UNESCO), 7 Place de Fontenoy, F-75700 Paris, France (Telephone Number in U.S. (212) 963-5981); *Statistical Yearbook.*

IRELAND (ERIE) - SENIOR CITIZENS

Facts on File, 460 Park Avenue South, New York, New York 10016 (800) 443-8323; *The New Book of World Rankings.*

IRELAND (EIRE) - SESAME SEED PRODUCTION - See IRELAND (EIRE) - CROPS

IRELAND (EIRE) - SHEEP - See IRELAND (EIRE) - LIVESTOCK AND POULTRY

IRELAND (EIRE) - SHIPBUILDING - PRODUCTION INDEX

Organisation for Economic Co-operation and Development (OECD), 2 rue Andre-Pascal, 75 Paris 16, France (Telephone Number in U.S. (202) 785-6323); *Indicators of Industrial Activity.*

IRELAND (EIRE) - SILVER PRODUCTION AND CONSUMPTION - See IRELAND (EIRE) - MINING AND MINERAL PRODUCTS

IRELAND (EIRE) - SISAL PRODUCTION - See IRELAND (EIRE) - CROPS

IRELAND (EIRE) - SOCIAL DATA

European Community Information Service, 2100 M Street, NW, Washington, D.C. 20037 (202) 862-9500; *ACP: Basic Statistics, Basic Statistics of the Community.*

Facts on File, 460 Park Avenue South, New York, New York 10016 (800) 443-8323; *The New Book of World Rankings.*

G.K. Hall and Company, 70 Lincoln Street, Boston, Massachusetts 02111 (617) 423-3990; *The World in Figures.*

IRELAND (EIRE) - SOCIAL SECURITY

European Community Information Service, 2100 M Street, NW, Washington, D.C. 20037 (202) 862-9500; *Basic Statistics of the Community.*

Organisation for Economic Co-operation and Development (OECD), 2 rue Andre-Pascal, 75 Paris 16, France (Telephone Number in U.S. (202) 785-6323); *Revenue Statistics of OECD Member Countries.*

IRELAND (EIRE) - SOCIOECONOMIC DATA

European Community Information Service, 2100 M Street, NW, Washington, D.C. 20037 (202) 862-9500; *Basic Statistics of the Community.*

Organisation for Economic Co-operation and Development (OECD), 2 rue Andre-Pascal, 75 Paris 16, France (Telephone Number in U.S. (202) 785-6323); *Economic Outlook.*

IRELAND (EIRE) - SOYBEAN PRODUCTION - See IRELAND (EIRE) - CROPS

IRELAND (EIRE) - STAMP TAXES AND DUTIES - See IRELAND (EIRE) - TAXATION

IRELAND (EIRE) - STEEL - See IRELAND (EIRE) - MINING AND MINERAL PRODUCTS

IRELAND (EIRE) - STOCKS - COMMODITY - MARKET PRICE - INDEXES

Food and Agricultural Organization of the United Nations (FAO) Via delle Terme di Caracalla, 00100 Rome, Italy (Telephone Number in U.S. (202) 653-2400); *The State of Food and Agriculture.*

International Lead and Zinc Study Group, Metro House, 58 St. James's Street, London SW1A 1LD, England; *Lead and Zinc Statistics.*

Statistical Office of the United Nations, Publishing Service, New York, New York 10017 (800) 253-9646; *Statistical Yearbook.*

IRELAND (EIRE) - STRAW PRODUCTION - See IRELAND (EIRE) - CROPS

IRELAND (EIRE) - SUGAR PRODUCTION - See IRELAND (EIRE) - CROPS

IRELAND (EIRE) - SUGARBEET PRODUCTION - See IRELAND (EIRE) - CROPS

IRELAND (EIRE) - SULPHUR AND SULPHURIC ACID PRODUCTION - See IRELAND (EIRE) - MINING AND MINERAL PRODUCTS

IRELAND (EIRE) - SUNFLOWER PRODUCTION - See IRELAND (EIRE) - CROPS

IRELAND (EIRE) - TAXATION

European Community Information Service, 2100 M Street, NW, Washington, D.C. 20037 (202) 862-9500; *Basic Statistics of the Community.*

G.K. Hall and Company, 70 Lincoln Street, Boston, Massachusetts 02111 (617) 423-3990; *The World in Figures.*

International Monetary Fund, 700 Nineteenth Street, NW, Washington, D.C. 20431 (202) 623-7000; *Government Finance Statistics Yearbook.*

International Road Federation, 525 School Street, SW, Washington, D.C. 20024 (202) 554-2106; *World Road Statistics.*

Organisation for Economic Co-operation and Development (OECD), 2 rue Andre-Pascal, 75 Paris 16, France (Telephone Number in U.S. (202) 785-6323); *Revenue Statistics of OECD Member Countries.*

The World Bank, 1818 H Street, NW, Washington, D.C. 20433 (202) 477-1234; *World Tables.*

IRELAND (EIRE) - TEA PRODUCTION AND CONSUMPTION - See IRELAND (EIRE) - CROPS

IRELAND (EIRE) - TELEGRAPH SERVICE

European Community Information Service, 2100 M Street, NW, Washington, D.C. 20037 (202) 862-9500; *Transport Annual Statistics.*

Statistical Office of the United Nations, Publishing Service, New York, New York 10017 (800) 253-9646; *Statistical Yearbook.*

IRELAND (EIRE) - TELEPHONES IN USE

American Telephone and Telegraph Company, 26 Parsippany Road, Whippany, New Jersey 07981 (800) 338-4038; *The World's Telephones.*

European Community Information Service, 2100 M Street, NW, Washington, D.C. 20037 (202) 862-9500; *Basic Statistics of the Community,* and *Transport Annual Statistics.*

G.K. Hall and Company, 70 Lincoln Street, Boston, Massachusetts 02111 (617) 423-3990; *The World in Figures.*

Statistical Office of the United Nations, Publishing Service, New York, New York 10017 (800) 253-9646; *Statistical Yearbook.*

IRELAND (EIRE) - TELEVISION BROADCASTING - See IRELAND (EIRE) - BROADCASTING

IRELAND (EIRE) - TELEVISION RECEIVER PRODUCTION

European Community Information Service, 2100 M Street, NW, Washington, D.C. 20037 (202) 862-9500; *Basic Statistics of the Community.*

Statistical Office of the United Nations, Publishing Service, New York, New York 10017 (800) 253-9646; *Statistical Yearbook.*

IRELAND (EIRE) - TEXTILE INDUSTRY

European Community Information Service, 2100 M Street, NW, Washington, D.C. 20037 (202) 862-9500; *Basic Statistics of the Community, Eurostatistics: Data for Short-Term Economic Analysis,* and *Industrial Production: Quarterly Statistics.*

Forest and Paper Association, 1250 Connecticut Avenue, NW, Washington, D.C. 20036 (202) 463-2455; *Wood Pulp and Fiber Statistics.*

G.K. Hall and Company, 70 Lincoln Street, Boston, Massachusetts 02111 (617) 423-3990; *The World in Figures.*

Organisation for Economic Co-operation and Development (OECD), 2 rue Andre-Pascal, 75 Paris 16, France (Telephone Number in U.S. (202) 785-6323); *Foreign Trade by Commodities, Indicators of Industrial Activity, Industrial Structure Statistics,* and *Textile Industry in OECD Countries.*

Statistical Office of the United Nations, Publishing Service, New York, New York 10017 (800) 253-9646; *Statistical Yearbook.*

IRELAND (EIRE) - THEATRE

United Nations Educational, Scientific and Cultural Organization (UNESCO), 7 Place de Fontenoy, F-75700 Paris, France (Telephone Number in U.S. (212) 963-5981); *Statistical Yearbook.*

IRELAND (EIRE) - TIMBER - See IRELAND (EIRE) - FORESTRY AND FOREST PRODUCTS

IRELAND (EIRE) - TIN - See IRELAND (EIRE) - MINING AND MINERAL PRODUCTS

IRELAND (EIRE) - TOBACCO PRODUCTION

Euromonitor Publications Limited, 87-88 Turnmill Street, London EC1M 5QU, England; *European Marketing Data and Statistics.*

European Community Information Service, 2100 M Street, NW, Washington, D.C. 20037 (202) 862-9500; *Basic Statistics of the Community* and *Industrial Production: Quarterly Statistics.*

Facts on File, 460 Park Avenue South, New York, New York 10016 (800) 443-8323; *The New Book of World Rankings.*

Organisation for Economic Co-operation and Development (OECD), 2 rue Andre-Pascal, 75 Paris 16, France (Telephone Number in U.S. (202) 785-6323); *Indicators of Industrial Activity, Industrial Structure Statistics,* and *Foreign Trade by Commodities.*

Statistical Office of the United Nations, Publishing Service, New York, New York 10017 (800) 253-9646; *Statistical Yearbook.*

IRELAND (EIRE) - TOURISM

Euromonitor Publications Limited, 87-88 Turnmill Street, London EC1M 5QU, England; *European Marketing Data and Statistics.*

European Community Information Service, 2100 M Street, NW, Washington, D.C. 20037 (202) 862-9500; *Transport Annual Statistics.*

Facts on File, 460 Park Avenue South, New York, New York 10016 (800) 443-8323; *The New Book of World Rankings.*

G.K. Hall and Company, 70 Lincoln Street, Boston, Massachusetts 02111 (617) 423-3990; *The World in Figures.*

Organisation for Economic Co-operation and Development (OECD), 2 rue Andre-Pascal, 75 Paris 16, France (Telephone Number in U.S. (202) 785-6323); *Tourism Policy and International Tourism in OECD Member Countries.*

Statistical Office of the United Nations, Publishing Service, New York, New York 10017 (800) 253-9646; *Statistical Yearbook.*

Times Books, 201 East 50th Street, New York, New York 10022 (212) 751-2600; *The Economist Book of Vital World Statistics.*

World Tourism Organization, Calle Capitan Haya 42, E-28020 Madrid, Spain; *Yearbook of Tourism Statistics.*

IRELAND (EIRE) - TRACTORS IN USE

European Community Information Service, 2100 M Street, NW, Washington, D.C. 20037 (202) 862-9500; *Transport Annual Statistics.*

Statistical Office of the United Nations, Publishing Service, New York, New York 10017 (800) 253-9646; *Statistical Yearbook.*

IRELAND (EIRE) - TRADE - See IRELAND (EIRE) - FOREIGN TRADE

IRELAND (EIRE) - TRADEMARKS AND SERVICE MARKS

Statistical Office of the United Nations, Publishing Service, New York, New York 10017 (800) 253-9646; *Statistical Yearbook.*

World Intellectual Property Organization, 34 Chemin des Colombettes, CH-1211 Geneva 20, Switzerland; *Industrial Property Statistics.*

IRELAND (EIRE) - TRANSPORTATION AND COMMUNICATIONS

European Community Information Service, 2100 M Street, NW, Washington, D.C. 20037 (202) 862-9500; *Basic Statistics of the Community, Energy Statistics Yearbook, Regions: Statistical Yearbook,* and *Transport Annual Statistics.*

Facts on File, 460 Park Avenue South, New York, New York 10016 (800) 443-8323; *The New Book of World Rankings.*

G.K. Hall and Company, 70 Lincoln Street, Boston, Massachusetts 02111 (617) 423-3990; *The World in Figures.*

IRELAND (EIRE) - TUNGSTEN PRODUCTION AND CONSUMPTION - See IRELAND (EIRE) - MINING AND MINERAL PRODUCTS

IRELAND (EIRE) - TURKEYS - See IRELAND (EIRE) - LIVESTOCK AND POULTRY

IRELAND (EIRE) - UNEMPLOYMENT

Central Statistics Office, Ardee Road, Dublin 6, Ireland; *The Trend of Employment and Unemployment.*

Euromonitor Publications Limited, 87-88 Turnmill Street, London EC1M 5QU, England; *European Marketing Data and Statistics.*

European Community Information Service, 2100 M Street, NW, Washington, D.C. 20037 (202) 862-9500; *Basic Statistics of the Community, Employment and Unemployment, Eurostatistics: Data for Short-Term Economic Analysis, Labor Force Sample Survey,* and *Regions: Statistical Yearbook.*

International Labour Office, I.L.O. Publications, CH-1211, Geneva 22, Switzerland; *Yearbook of Labour Statistics.*

Organisation for Economic Co-operation and Development (OECD), 2 rue Andre-Pascal, 75 Paris 16, France (Telephone Number in U.S. (202) 785-6323); *Economic Outlook, Labour Force Statistics, OECD Economic Surveys: Ireland,* and *OECD Employment Outlook.*

Statistical Office of the United Nations, Publishing Service, New York, New York 10017 (800) 253-9646; *Statistical Yearbook.*

IRELAND (EIRE) - URANIUM PRODUCTION AND CONSUMPTION - See IRELAND (EIRE) - MINING AND MINERAL PRODUCTS

IRELAND (EIRE) - UTILITIES

European Community Information Service, 2100 M Street, NW, Washington, D.C. 20037 (202) 862-9500; *Basic Statistics of the Community.*

IRELAND (EIRE) - VANADIUM ORE PRODUCTION AND CONSUMPTION - See IRELAND (EIRE) - MINING AND MINERAL PRODUCTS

IRELAND (EIRE) - WAGES

European Community Information Service, 2100 M Street, NW, Washington, D.C. 20037 (202) 862-9500; *Eurostatistics: Data for Short-Term Economic Analysis.*

IRELAND (EIRE) - WALNUT PRODUCTION - See IRELAND (EIRE) - CROPS

IRELAND (EIRE) - WATERWAYS IN USE - See IRELAND (EIRE) - MERCHANT SHIPPING

IRELAND (EIRE) - WEATHER

Facts on File, 460 Park Avenue South, New York, New York 10016 (800) 443-8323; *The New Book of World Rankings.*

G.K. Hall and Company, 70 Lincoln Street, Boston, Massachusetts 02111 (617) 423-3990; *The World in Figures.*

IRELAND (EIRE) - WELFARE

European Community Information Service, 2100 M Street, NW, Washington, D.C. 20037 (202) 862-9500; *Basic Statistics of the Community.*

IRELAND (EIRE) - WHEAT PRODUCTION AND PRICES - See IRELAND (EIRE) - CROPS

IRELAND (EIRE) - WOOD PULP PRODUCTION - See IRELAND (EIRE) - FORESTRY AND FOREST PRODUCTS

IRELAND (EIRE) - WOOL PRODUCTION AND CONSUMPTION

European Community Information Service, 2100 M Street, NW, Washington, D.C. 20037 (202) 862-9500; *Basic Statistics of the*

Community.

Facts on File, 460 Park Avenue South, New York, New York 10016 (800) 443-8323; *The New Book of World Rankings.*

Organisation for Economic Co-operation and Development (OECD), 2 rue Andre-Pascal, 75 Paris 16, France (Telephone Number in U.S. (202) 785-6323); *Economic Accounts for Agriculture,* and *Textile Industry in OECD Countries.*

Statistical Office of the United Nations, Publishing Service, New York, New York 10017 (800) 253-9646; *Statistical Yearbook.*

IRELAND (EIRE) - YARN PRODUCTION

European Community Information Service, 2100 M Street, NW, Washington, D.C. 20037 (202) 862-9500; *Basic Statistics of the Community.*

Organisation for Economic Co-operation and Development (OECD), 2 rue Andre-Pascal, 75 Paris 16, France (Telephone Number in U.S. (202) 785-6323); *Foreign Trade by Commodities,* and *Textile Industry in OECD Countries.*

Statistical Office of the United Nations, Publishing Service, New York, New York 10017 (800) 253-9646; *Statistical Yearbook.*

IRELAND (EIRE) - ZINC AND ZINC ORE - See IRELAND (EIRE) - MINING AND MINERAL PRODUCTS

IRON - FOREIGN TRADE

U.S. Department of Commerce, Bureau of the Census, Suitland, Maryland 20233 (301) 763-4040; *U.S. Merchandise Trade: Exports, General Imports, and Imports for Consumption.*

U.S. Department of the Interior, Bureau of Mines, 810 Seventh Street, NW, Washington, D.C. 20241 (202) 501-9649; *Annual Reports,* and *Mineral Commodity Summaries.*

IRON - MINING INDUSTRY

U.S. Department of Commerce, Bureau of the Census, Suitland, Maryland 20233 (301) 763-4040; *Census of Mineral Industries.*

IRON - MINING INDUSTRY - PRODUCTIVITY

U.S. Department of Labor, Bureau of Labor Statistics, Two Massachusetts Avenue, NE, Washington, D.C. 20212 (202) 606-7828; *Productivity Measures for Selected Industries,* and unpublished data.

IRON - PRICES

U.S. Department of the Interior, Bureau of Mines, 810 Seventh Street, NW, Washington, D.C. 20241 (202) 501-9649; *Mineral Commodity Summaries.*

IRON - PRODUCTION

U.S. Department of the Interior, Bureau of Mines, 810 Seventh Street, NW, Washington, D.C. 20241 (202) 501-9649; *Annual Reports,* and *Mineral Commodity Summaries.*

IRON - WORLD PRODUCTION

Statistical Office of the United Nations, Publishing Service, New York, New York 10017 (800) 253-9646; *Monthly Bulletin of Statistics.*

U.S. Department of the Interior, Bureau of Mines, 810 Seventh Street, NW, Washington, D.C. 20241 (202) 501-9649; *Mineral Commodity Summaries,* and *Annual Reports.*

IRON AND STEEL - MANUFACTURING - See also METAL INDUSTRIES - PRIMARY

IRON AND STEEL - MANUFACTURING - CAPITAL

American Iron and Steel Institute, 1101 Seventeenth Street, NW, Washington, D.C. 20036 (202) 452-7100; *Annual Statistical Report.*

U.S. Department of Commerce, Bureau of the Census, Suitland, Maryland 20233 (301) 763-4040; *Census of Manufactures,* and *Annual Survey of Manufactures.*

IRON AND STEEL - MANUFACTURING - EARNINGS

U.S. Department of Commerce, Bureau of the Census, Suitland, Maryland 20233 (301) 763-4040; *Census of Manufactures,* and *Annual Survey of Manufactures.*

U.S. Department of Labor, Bureau of Labor Statistics, Two Massachusetts Avenue, NE, Washington, D.C. 20212 (202) 606-7828; *Employment and Earnings,* and Bulletins 2370 and 2429.

IRON AND STEEL - MANUFACTURING - EMPLOYEES

U.S. Department of Commerce, Bureau of the Census, Suitland, Maryland 20233 (301) 763-4040; *Census of Manufactures,* and *Annual Survey of Manufactures.*

U.S. Department of Labor, Bureau of Labor Statistics, Two Massachusetts Avenue, NE, Washington, D.C. 20212 (202) 606-7828; *Employment and Earnings,* and Bulletins 2370 and 2429.

IRON AND STEEL - MANUFACTURING - ESTABLISHMENTS

U.S. Department of Commerce, Bureau of the Census, Suitland, Maryland 20233 (301) 763-4040; *Census of Manufactures,* and *Annual Survey of Manufactures.*

IRON AND STEEL - MANUFACTURING - OCCUPATIONAL SAFETY

U.S. Department of Labor, Bureau of Labor Statistics, Two Massachusetts Avenue, NE, Washington, D.C. 20212 (202) 606-7828; *Occupational Injuries and Illnesses in the U.S. by Industry.*

IRON AND STEEL - MANUFACTURING - SHIPMENTS

American Iron and Steel Institute, 1101 Seventeenth Street, NW, Washington, D.C. 20036 (202) 452-7100; *Annual Statistical Report.*

U.S. Department of Commerce, Bureau of the Census, Suitland, Maryland 20233 (301) 763-4040; *Census of Manufacturers,* and *Annual Survey of Manufactures.*

IRON AND STEEL - MANUFACTURING - PROFITS

Executive Office of the President, Council of Economic Advisors, Old Executive Office Building, Washington, D.C. 20500 (202) 395-5084; *Economic Report of the President.*

U.S. Department of Commerce, Bureau of the Census, Suitland, Maryland 20233 (301) 763-4040; *Quarterly Financial Report for Manufacturing, Mining, and Trade Corporations.*

IRON AND STEEL PRODUCTS

American Iron and Steel Institute, 1101 Seventeenth Street, NW, Washington, D.C. 20036 (202) 452-7100; *Annual Statistical Report.*

U.S. Department of Commerce, Bureau of the Census, Suitland, Maryland 20233 (301) 763-4040; *U.S. Merchandise Trade: Exports, General Imports, and Imports for Consumption.*

U.S. Department of the Interior, Bureau of Mines, 810 Seventh Street, NW, Washington, D.C. 20241 (202) 501-9649; *Annual Reports,* and *Mineral Commodity Summaries.*

IRON AND STEEL PRODUCTS - PRODUCTION AND VALUE

American Iron and Steel Institute, 1101 Seventeenth Street, NW, Washington, D.C. 20036 (202) 452-7100; *Annual Statistical Report.*

U.S. Department of the Interior, Bureau of Mines, 810 Seventh Street, NW, Washington, D.C. 20241 (202) 501-9649; *Annual Reports,* and *Mineral Commodity Summaries.*

IRON AND STEEL SCRAP

U.S. Department of the Interior, Bureau of Mines, 810 Seventh Street, NW, Washington, D.C. 20241 (202) 501-9649; *Mineral Commodity Summaries.*

IRON AND STEEL SLUG

U.S. Department of the Interior, Bureau of Mines, 810 Seventh Street, NW, Washington, D.C. 20241 (202) 501-9649; *Mineral Commodity Summaries.*

IRON (NUTRITIONAL) AVAILABLE FOR HUMAN CONSUMPTION

U.S. Department of Agriculture, Human Nutrition Service, Hyattsville, Maryland 20782 (301) 436-7725; data published by Economic Research Service, Fourteenth Street and Independence Avenue, SW, Washington, D.C. 20005-4789 (202) 219-1504; in *Food Consumption, Prices and Expenditures,* and *National Food Review.*

IRRIGATION

U.S. Department of Commerce, Bureau of the Census, Suitland, Maryland 20233 (301) 763-4040; *Census of Agriculture.*

U.S. Department of the Interior, Geological Survey, National Center, 12201 Sunrise Valley Drive, Reston, Virginia 22092 (703) 648-4460; *Estimated Use of Water in the United States.*

ISLE OF MAN - ANIMAL HEALTH

Food and Agricultural Organization of the United Nations (FAO), Via delle Terme di Caracalla, 00100 Rome, Italy (Telephone Number in U.S. (202) 643-2400); *Animal Health Yearbook.*

ISLE OF MAN - AREA AND DENSITY OF POPULATION

Statistical Office of the United Nations, Publishing Service, New York, New York 10017 (800) 253-9646; *Statistical Yearbook.*

ISLE OF MAN - BIRTH RATES

Statistical Office of the United Nations, Publishing Service, New York, New York 10017 (800) 253-9646; *Demographic Yearbook* and *Statistical Yearbook.*

World Health Organization, Office of Publications, Avenue Appia, CH-1211 Geneva 27, Switzerland (Telephone Number in U.S. (518) 436-9686); *World Health Statistics Annual.*

ISLE OF MAN - CONSUMER PRICES

International Labour Office, I.L.O. Publications, CH-1211, Geneva 22, Switzerland; *Yearbook of Labour Statistics.*

ISLE OF MAN - DEATH RATES

Statistical Office of the United Nations, Publishing Service, New York, New York 10017 (800) 253-9646; *Statistical Yearbook.*

ISLE OF MAN - DIVORCE RATES

Statistical Office of the United Nations, Publishing Service, New York, New York 10017 (800) 253-9646; *Statistical Yearbook.*

ISLE OF MAN - EMPLOYMENT

International Labour Office, I.L.O. Publications, CH-1211, Geneva 22, Switzerland; *Yearbook of Labour Statistics.*

ISLE OF MAN - FETAL MORTALITY

Statistical Office of the United Nations, Publishing Service, New York, New York 10017 (800) 253-9646; *Demographic Yearbook.*

World Health Organization, Office of Publications, Avenue Appia, CH-1211 Geneva 27, Switzerland (Telephone Number in U.S. (518) 436-9686); *World Health Statistics Annual.*

ISLE OF MAN - GENERAL MORTALITY

Statistical Office of the United Nations, Publishing Service, New York, New York 10017 (800) 253-9646; *Demographic Yearbook.*

World Health Organization, Office of Publications, Avenue Appia, CH-1211 Geneva 27, Switzerland (Telephone Number in U.S. (518) 436-9686); *World Health Statistics Annual.*

ISLE OF MAN - HEALTH

Statistical Office of the United Nations, Publishing Service, New York, New York 10017 (800) 253-9646; *Statistical Yearbook.*

ISLE OF MAN - HOURS OF WORK - See ISLE OF MAN - EMPLOYMENT

ISLE OF MAN - INDUSTRY

International Labour Office, I.L.O. Publications, CH-1211, Geneva 22, Switzerland; *Yearbook of Labour Statistics.*

ISLE OF MAN - INFANT AND MATERNAL MORTALITY

Statistical Office of the United Nations, Publishing Service, New York, New York 10017 (800) 253-9646; *Demographic Yearbook,* and *Statistical Yearbook.*

World Health Organization, Office of Publications, Avenue Appia, CH-1211 Geneva 27, Switzerland (Telephone Number in U.S. (518) 436-9686); *World Health Statistics Annual.*

ISLE OF MAN - LABOR PRODUCTIVITY

International Labour Office, I.L.O. Publications, CH-1211, Geneva 22, Switzerland; *Yearbook of Labour Statistics.*

ISLE OF MAN - MAIL TRAFFIC - NUMBER OF ITEMS SENT AND RECEIVED

Statistical Office of the United Nations, Publishing Service, New York, New York 10017 (800) 253-9646; *Statistical Yearbook.*

ISLE OF MAN - MARRIAGE RATES

Statistical Office of the United Nations, Publishing Service, New York, New York 10017 (800) 253-9646; *Demographic Yearbook,* and *Statistical Yearbook.*

ISLE OF MAN - NATALITY - See ISLE OF MAN - BIRTH RATES

ISLE OF MAN - POPULATION

International Labour Office, I.L.O. Publications, CH-1211, Geneva 22, Switzerland; *Yearbook of Labour Statistics.*

Statistical Office of the United Nations, Publishing Service, New York, New York 10017 (800) 253-9646; *Demographic Yearbook,* and *Statistical Yearbook.*

World Health Organization, Office of Publications, Avenue Appia, CH-1211 Geneva 27, Switzerland (Telephone Number in U.S. (518) 436-9686); *World Health Statistics Annual.*

ISLE OF MAN - PRICES

International Labour Office, I.L.O. Publications, CH-1211, Geneva 22, Switzerland; *Yearbook of Labour Statistics.*

ISLE OF MAN - RENT PRICES

International Labour Office, I.L.O. Publications, CH-1211, Geneva 22, Switzerland; *Yearbook of Labour Statistics.*

ISLE OF MAN - UNEMPLOYMENT

International Labour Office, I.L.O. Publications, CH-1211, Geneva 22, Switzerland; *Yearbook of Labour Statistics.*

Statistical Office of the United Nations, Publishing Service, New York, New York 10017 (800) 253-9646; *Statistical Yearbook.*

ISLE OF MAN - VITAL STATISTICS

Statistical Office of the United Nations, Publishing Service, New York, New York 10017 (800) 253-9646; *Statistical Yearbook.*

World Health Organization, Office of Publications, Avenue Appia, CH-1211 Geneva 27, Switzerland (Telephone Number in U.S. (518) 436-9686); *World Health Statistics Annual.*

ISLE OF MAN - WAGES

International Labour Office, I.L.O. Publications, CH-1211, Geneva 22, Switzerland; *Yearbook of Labour Statistics.*

Israel - National Statistical Office

Central Bureau of Statistics, Post Office Box 13015, Jerusalem, 91130 Israel.

Israel - Primary Statistics Sources

Central Bureau of Statistics, Post Office Box 13015, Jerusalem, 91130 Israel; *Statistical Abstract of Israel,* and *Monthly Bulletin of Statistics.*

ISRAEL - AGRICULTURE

Euromonitor Publications Limited, 87-88 Turnmill Street, London EC1M 5QU, England; *International Marketing Data and Statistics,* and *Middle East Economic Handbook.*

Facts on File, 460 Park Avenue South, New York, New York 10016 (800) 443-8323; *The New Book of World Rankings.*

Food and Agricultural Organization of the United Nations (FAO), Via delle Terme di Caracalla, 00100 Rome, Italy (Telephone Number in U.S. (202) 643-2400); *Production Yearbook, The State of Food and Agriculture,* and *Trade Yearbook.*

G.K. Hall and Company, 70 Lincoln Street, Boston, Massachusetts 02111 (617) 423-3990; *The World in Figures.*

Statistical Office of the United Nations, Publishing Service, New York, New York 10017 (800) 253-9646; *Statistical Yearbook.*

Times Books, 201 East 50th Street, New York, New York 10022 (212) 751-2600; *The Economist Book of Vital World Statistics.*

The World Bank, 1818 H Street, NW, Washington, D.C. 20433 (202) 477-1234; *World Tables.*

ISRAEL - AIRLINE SERVICE

Facts on File, 460 Park Avenue South, New York, New York 10016 (800) 443-8323; *The New Book of World Rankings.*

G.K. Hall and Company, 70 Lincoln Street, Boston, Massachusetts 02111 (617) 423-3990; *The World in Figures.*

International Civil Aviation Organization, 1000 Sherbrooke Street West, Suite 400, Montreal, Quebec, Canada H3A 2R2 (514) 285-8219; *Civil Aviation Statistics of the World.*

Statistical Office of the United Nations, Publishing Service, New York, New York 10017 (800) 253-9646; *Statistical Yearbook.*

Times Books, 201 East 50th Street, New York, New York 10022 (212) 751-2600; *The Economist Book of Vital World Statistics.*

ISRAEL - ALMOND PRODUCTION - See ISRAEL - CROPS

ISRAEL - ALUMINUM PRODUCTION AND CONSUMPTION - See ISRAEL - MINING AND MINERAL PRODUCTS

ISRAEL - ANIMAL HEALTH

Food and Agricultural Organization of the United Nations (FAO), Via delle Terme di Caracalla, 00100 Rome, Italy (Telephone Number in U.S. (202) 643-2400); *Animal Health Yearbook.*

ISRAEL - AREA AND DENSITY OF POPULATION

Euromonitor Publications Limited, 87-88 Turnmill Street, London EC1M 5QU, England; *International Marketing Data and Statistics,* and *Middle East Economic Handbook.*

Facts on File, 460 Park Avenue South, New York, New York 10016 (800) 443-8323; *The New Book of World Rankings.*

Food and Agricultural Organization of the United Nations (FAO) Via delle Terme di Caracalla, 00100 Rome, Italy (Telephone Number in U.S. (202) 643-2400); *The State of Food and Agriculture.*

G.K. Hall and Company, 70 Lincoln Street, Boston, Massachusetts 02111 (617) 423-3990; *The World in Figures.*

Statistical Office of the United Nations, Publishing Service, New York, New York 10017 (800) 253-9646; *Statistical Yearbook.*

Times Books, 201 East 50th Street, New York, New York 10022 (212) 751-2600; *The Economist Book of Vital World Statistics.*

United Nations Educational, Scientific and Cultural Organization (UNESCO), 7 Place de Fontenoy, F-75700 Paris, France (Telephone Number in U.S. (212) 963-5981); *Statistical Yearbook.*

ISRAEL - ARMS EXPORTS AND IMPORTS

U.S. Arms Control and Disarmament Agency, 320 Twenty-first Street, Northwest, Washington, D.C. 20451 (202) 647-8677; *World Military Expenditures and Arms Transfers.*

ISRAEL - ARTICHOKE PRODUCTION - See ISRAEL - CROPS

ISRAEL - BALANCE OF PAYMENTS

The Economist Intelligence Unit, 111 West 57th Street, New York, New York 10019 (800) 938-4685; *The World Market Atlas.*

G.K. Hall and Company, 70 Lincoln Street, Boston, Massachusetts 02111 (617) 423-3990; *The World in Figures.*

International Monetary Fund, 700 Nineteenth Street, NW, Washington, D.C. 20431 (202) 623-7000; *Balance of Payments Yearbook,* and *International Financial Statistics.*

Times Books, 201 East 50th Street, New York, New York 10022 (212) 751-2600; *The Economist Book of Vital World Statistics.*

The World Bank, 1818 H Street, NW, Washington, D.C. 20433 (202) 477-1234; *World Tables.*

ISRAEL - BANKING

Facts on File, 460 Park Avenue South, New York, New York 10016 (800) 443-8323; *The New Book of World Rankings.*

G.K. Hall and Company, 70 Lincoln Street, Boston, Massachusetts 02111 (617) 423-3990; *The World in Figures.*

International Monetary Fund, 700 Nineteenth Street, NW, Washington, D.C. 20431 (202) 623-7000; *Government Finance Statistics Yearbook,* and *International Financial Statistics.*

ISRAEL - BARLEY PRODUCTION - See ISRAEL - CROPS

ISRAEL - BEER PRODUCTION

Facts on File, 460 Park Avenue South, New York, New York 10016 (800) 443-8323; *The New Book of World Rankings.*

Statistical Office of the United Nations, Publishing Service, New York, New York 10017 (800) 253-9646; *Statistical Yearbook.*

ISRAEL - BIRTH RATES

Euromonitor Publications Limited, 87-88 Turnmill Street, London EC1M 5QU, England; *Middle East Economic Handbook.*

Facts on File, 460 Park Avenue South, New York, New York 10016 (800) 443-8323; *The New Book of World Rankings.*

Statistical Office of the United Nations, Publishing Service, New York, New York 10017 (800) 253-9646; *Demographic Yearbook,* and *Statistical Yearbook.*

Times Books, 201 East 50th Street, New York, New York 10022 (212) 751-2600; *The Economist Book of Vital World Statistics.*

The World Bank, 1818 H Street, NW, Washington, D.C. 20433 (202) 477-1234; *World Tables.*

World Health Organization, Office of Publications, Avenue Appia, CH-1211 Geneva 27, Switzerland (Telephone Number in U.S. (518) 436-9686); *World Health Statistics Annual.*

ISRAEL - BONDS

G.K. Hall and Company, 70 Lincoln Street, Boston, Massachusetts 02111 (617) 423-3990; *The World in Figures.*

International Monetary Fund, 700 Nineteenth Street, NW, Washington, D.C. 20431 (202) 623-7000; *Government Finance Statistics Yearbook.*

ISRAEL - BOOK PRODUCTION

G.K. Hall and Company, 70 Lincoln Street, Boston, Massachusetts 02111 (617) 423-3990; *The World in Figures.*

United Nations Educational, Scientific and Cultural Organization (UNESCO), 7 Place de Fontenoy, F-75700 Paris, France (Telephone Number in U.S. (212) 963-5981); *Statistical Yearbook.*

ISRAEL - BROADCASTING

Billboard Limited, Post Office Box 9027, 1006 AA Amsterdam, The Netherlands (Telephone Number in U.S. (212) 764-7300); *World Radio TV Handbook.*

Facts on File, 460 Park Avenue South, New York, New York 10016 (800) 443-8323; *The New Book of World Rankings.*

G.K. Hall and Company, 70 Lincoln Street, Boston, Massachusetts 02111 (617) 423-3990; *The World in Figures.*

Times Books, 201 East 50th Street, New York, New York 10022 (212) 751-2600; *The Economist Book of Vital World Statistics.*

ISRAEL - BUILDING CONSTRUCTION - See ISRAEL - CONSTRUCTION INDUSTRY

ISRAEL - BUSINESS

G.K. Hall and Company, 70 Lincoln Street, Boston, Massachusetts 02111 (617) 423-3990; *The World in Figures.*

ISRAEL - BUTTER PRODUCTION - See ISRAEL - DAIRY PRODUCTS

ISRAEL - CABBAGE PRODUCTION - See ISRAEL - CROPS

ISRAEL - CALORIE SUPPLY

Food and Agricultural Organization of the United Nations (FAO) Via delle Terme di Caracalla, 00100 Rome, Italy (Telephone Number in U.S. (202) 643-2400); *The State of Food and Agriculture.*

ISRAEL - CAPITAL REVENUE

International Monetary Fund, 700 Nineteenth Street, NW, Washington, D.C. 20431 (202) 623-7000; *Government Finance*

Statistics Yearbook.

ISRAEL - CATTLE - See ISRAEL - LIVESTOCK AND POULTRY

ISRAEL - CAULIFLOWER PRODUCTION - See ISRAEL - CROPS

ISRAEL - CEMENT PRODUCTION - See ISRAEL - MINING AND MINERAL PRODUCTS

ISRAEL - CHEESE PRODUCTION - See ISRAEL - DAIRY PRODUCTS

ISRAEL - CHEMICAL (ORGANIC) PRODUCTION - See ISRAEL - MINING AND MINERAL PRODUCTS

ISRAEL - CHICK PEA PRODUCTION - See ISRAEL - CROPS

ISRAEL - CHICKENS - See ISRAEL - LIVESTOCK AND POULTRY

ISRAEL - CIGAR PRODUCTION - See ISRAEL - TOBACCO PRODUCTION

ISRAEL - CIGARETTE PRODUCTION - See ISRAEL - TOBACCO PRODUCTION

ISRAEL - CITRUS EXPORTS - See ISRAEL - CROPS

ISRAEL - CLASS STRUCTURE

G.K. Hall and Company, 70 Lincoln Street, Boston, Massachusetts 02111 (617) 423-3990; *The World in Figures.*

ISRAEL - CLIMATE

Facts on File, 460 Park Avenue South, New York, New York 10016 (800) 443-8323; *The New Book of World Rankings.*

G.K. Hall and Company, 70 Lincoln Street, Boston, Massachusetts 02111 (617) 423-3990; *The World in Figures.*

ISRAEL - CLOTHING EXPORTS AND IMPORTS

Statistical Office of the United Nations, Publishing Service, New York, New York 10017 (800) 253-9646; *Trade in Manufactures of Developing Countries.*

ISRAEL - COAL PRODUCTION - See ISRAEL - MINING AND MINERAL PRODUCTS

ISRAEL - COFFEE PRODUCTION AND CONSUMPTION - See ISRAEL - CROPS

ISRAEL - COMMUNICATIONS

G.K. Hall and Company, 70 Lincoln Street, Boston, Massachusetts 02111 (617) 423-3990; *The World in Figures.*

ISRAEL - CONSTRUCTION INDUSTRY

Facts on File, 460 Park Avenue South, New York, New York 10016 (800) 443-8323; *The New Book of World Rankings.*

Statistical Office of the United Nations, Publishing Service, New York, New York 10017 (800) 253-9646; *Construction Statistics Yearbook,* and *Statistical Yearbook.*

ISRAEL - CONSUMER PRICE INDEX

G.K. Hall and Company, 70 Lincoln Street, Boston, Massachusetts 02111 (617) 423-3990; *The World in Figures.*

International Labour Office, I.L.O. Publications, CH-1211, Geneva 22, Switzerland; *Yearbook of Labour Statistics.*

Statistical Office of the United Nations, Publishing Service, New York, New York 10017 (800) 253-9646; *Statistical Yearbook.*

ISRAEL - CONSUMER PRICES

International Labour Office, I.L.O. Publications, CH-1211, Geneva 22, Switzerland; *Yearbook of Labour Statistics.*

International Monetary Fund, 700 Nineteenth Street, NW, Washington, D.C. 20431 (202) 623-7000; *International Financial Statistics.*

Times Books, 201 East 50th Street, New York, New York 10022 (212) 751-2600; *The Economist Book of Vital World Statistics.*

ISRAEL - CONSUMPTION

Euromonitor Publications Limited, 87-88 Turnmill Street, London EC1M 5QU, England; *Middle East Economic Handbook.*

G.K. Hall and Company, 70 Lincoln Street, Boston, Massachusetts 02111 (617) 423-3990; *The World in Figures.*

International Monetary Fund, 700 Nineteenth Street, NW, Washington, D.C. 20431 (202) 623-7000; *International Financial Statistics.*

ISRAEL - COPPER AND COPPER ORE - See ISRAEL - MINING AND MINERAL PRODUCTS

ISRAEL - CORN PRODUCTION - See ISRAEL - CROPS

ISRAEL - CORPORATE TAXES - See ISRAEL - TAXATION

ISRAEL - COTTON - See ISRAEL - CROPS

ISRAEL - CRIME

International Criminal Police Organization (INTERPOL), 26 rue Armengaud, 92210 Saint Cloud, France; *International Crime Statistics.*

Yale University Press, Yale Station, New Haven, Connecticut 06520 (203) 432-0940; *Violence and Crime in Cross-National Perspective.*

ISRAEL - CROPS

Commodity Research Bureau, Incorporated, 75 Wall Street, New York, New York 10005 (212) 504-7754; *Commodity Year Book.*

Facts on File, 460 Park Avenue South, New York, New York 10016 (800) 443-8323; *The New Book of World Rankings.*

Food and Agricultural Organization of the United Nations (FAO), Via delle Terme di Caracalla, 00100 Rome, Italy (Telephone Number in U.S. (202) 643-2400); *Production Yearbook* and *The State of Food and Agriculture.*

G.K. Hall and Company, 70 Lincoln Street, Boston, Massachusetts 02111 (617) 423-3990; *The World in Figures.*

International Monetary Fund, 700 Nineteenth Street, NW, Washington, D.C. 20431 (202) 623-7000; *International Financial Statistics.*

Statistical Office of the United Nations, Publishing Service, New York, New York 10017 (800) 253-9646; *Statistical Yearbook.*

ISRAEL - CUSTOMS DUTIES

G.K. Hall and Company, 70 Lincoln Street, Boston, Massachusetts 02111 (617) 423-3990; *The World in Figures.*

International Monetary Fund, 700 Nineteenth Street, NW, Washington, D.C. 20431 (202) 623-7000; *Government Finance Statistics Yearbook.*

ISRAEL - DAIRY PRODUCTS

Commodity Research Bureau, Incorporated, 75 Wall Street, New York, New York 10005 (212) 504-7754; *Commodity Year Book.*

Facts on File, 460 Park Avenue South, New York, New York 10016 (800) 443-8323; *The New Book of World Rankings.*

Food and Agricultural Organization of the United Nations (FAO) Via delle Terme di Caracalla, 00100 Rome, Italy (Telephone Number in U.S. (202) 643-2400); *Production Yearbook* and *The State of Food and Agriculture.*

Statistical Office of the United Nations, Publishing Service, New York, New York 10017 (800) 253-9646; *Statistical Yearbook.*

ISRAEL - DEATH RATE

Euromonitor Publications Limited, 87-88 Turnmill Street, London EC1M 5QU, England; *Middle East Economic Handbook.*

G.K. Hall and Company, 70 Lincoln Street, Boston, Massachusetts 02111 (617) 423-3990; *The World in Figures.*

Statistical Office of the United Nations, Publishing Service, New York, New York 10017 (800) 253-9646; *Statistical Yearbook.*

Times Books, 201 East 50th Street, New York, New York 10022 (212) 751-2600; *The Economist Book of Vital World Statistics.*

ISRAEL - DEFENSE EXPENDITURES

G.K. Hall and Company, 70 Lincoln Street, Boston, Massachusetts 02111 (617) 423-3990; *The World in Figures.*

International Monetary Fund, 700 Nineteenth Street, NW, Washington, D.C. 20431 (202) 623-7000; *Government Finance Statistics Yearbook.*

U.S. Arms Control and Disarmament Agency, 320 Twenty-first Street, Northwest, Washington, D.C. 20451 (202) 647-8677; *World Military Expenditures and Arms Transfers.*

ISRAEL - DEMOGRAPHY

The Economist Intelligence Unit, 111 West 57th Street, New York, New York 10019 (800) 938-4685; *The World Market Atlas.*

Facts on File, 460 Park Avenue South, New York, New York 10016 (800) 443-8323; *The New Book of World Rankings.*

G.K. Hall and Company, 70 Lincoln Street, Boston, Massachusetts 02111 (617) 423-3990; *The World in Figures.*

ISRAEL - DEVELOPMENT ASSISTANCE

G.K. Hall and Company, 70 Lincoln Street, Boston, Massachusetts 02111 (617) 423-3990; *The World in Figures.*

Statistical Office of the United Nations, Publishing Service, New York, New York 10017 (800) 253-9646; *Statistical Yearbook.*

ISRAEL - DIAMOND EXPORTS - See ISRAEL - MINING AND MINERAL PRODUCTS

ISRAEL - DISEASE

G.K. Hall and Company, 70 Lincoln Street, Boston, Massachusetts 02111 (617) 423-3990; *The World in Figures.*

ISRAEL - DIVORCE RATES

Facts on File, 460 Park Avenue South, New York, New York 10016 (800) 443-8323; *The New Book of World Rankings.*

Statistical Office of the United Nations, Publishing Service, New York, New York 10017 (800) 253-9646; *Demographic Yearbook,* and *Statistical Yearbook.*

ISRAEL - DOMESTIC PRODUCT

G.K. Hall and Company, 70 Lincoln Street, Boston, Massachusetts 02111 (617) 423-3990; *The World in Figures.*

ISRAEL - DUCKS - See ISRAEL - LIVESTOCK AND POULTRY

ISRAEL - ECONOMY

Euromonitor Publications Limited, 87-88 Turnmill Street, London EC1M 5QU, England; *International Marketing Data and Statistics.*

Facts on File, 460 Park Avenue South, New York, New York 10016 (800) 443-8323; *The New Book of World Rankings.*

G.K. Hall and Company, 70 Lincoln Street, Boston, Massachusetts 02111 (617) 423-3990; *The World in Figures.*

ISRAEL - EDUCATION

The Economist Intelligence Unit, 111 West 57th Street, New York, New York 10019 (800) 938-4685; *The World Market Atlas.*

Euromonitor Publications Limited, 87-88 Turnmill Street, London EC1M 5QU, England; *Middle East Economic Handbook.*

Facts on File, 460 Park Avenue South, New York, New York 10016 (800) 443-8323; *The New Book of World Rankings.*

G.K. Hall and Company, 70 Lincoln Street, Boston, Massachusetts 02111 (617) 423-3990; *The World in Figures.*

International Monetary Fund, 700 Nineteenth Street, NW, Washington, D.C. 20431 (202) 623-7000; *Government Finance Statistics Yearbook.*

Times Books, 201 East 50th Street, New York, New York 10022 (212) 751-2600; *The Economist Book of Vital World Statistics.*

United Nations Educational, Scientific and Cultural Organization (UNESCO), 7 Place de Fontenoy, F-75700 Paris, France (Telephone Number in U.S. (212) 963-5981); *Statistical Yearbook.*

The World Bank, 1818 H Street, NW, Washington, D.C. 20433 (202) 477-1234; *World Tables.*

ISRAEL - EGG PRODUCTION - See ISRAEL - DAIRY PRODUCTS

ISRAEL - EGGPLANT PRODUCTION - See ISRAEL - DAIRY PRODUCTS

ISRAEL - ELECTRICITY

Facts on File, 460 Park Avenue South, New York, New York 10016 (800) 443-8323; *The New Book of World Rankings.*

Penn Well Publishing Company, 1421 South Sheridan Road, Post Office Box 1260, Tulsa, Oklahoma 74101 (800) 752-9764; *International Energy Statistics Sourcebook.*

Statistical Office of the United Nations, Publishing Service, New York, New York 10017 (800) 253-9646; *Statistical Yearbook.*

Times Books, 201 East 50th Street, New York, New York 10022 (212) 751-2600; *The Economist Book of Vital World Statistics.*

ISRAEL - EMPLOYMENT

Euromonitor Publications Limited, 87-88 Turnmill Street, London EC1M 5QU, England; *International Marketing Data and Statistics,* and *Middle East Economic Handbook.*

Facts on File, 460 Park Avenue South, New York, New York 10016 (800) 443-8323; *The New Book of World Rankings.*

International Labour Office, I.L.O. Publications, CH-1211, Geneva 22, Switzerland; *Yearbook of Labour Statistics.*

Statistical Office of the United Nations, Publishing Service, New York, New York 10017 (800) 253-9646; *Statistical Yearbook.*

ISRAEL - ENERGY

Euromonitor Publications Limited, 87-88 Turnmill Street, London EC1M 5QU, England; *Middle East Economic Handbook.*

Facts on File, 460 Park Avenue South, New York, New York 10016 (800) 443-8323; *The New Book of World Rankings.*

Food and Agricultural Organization of the United Nations (FAO) Via delle Terme di Caracalla, 00100 Rome, Italy (Telephone Number in U.S. (202) 643-2400); *The State of Food and Agriculture.*

G.K. Hall and Company, 70 Lincoln Street, Boston, Massachusetts 02111 (617) 423-3990; *The World in Figures.*

Penn Well Publishing Company, 1421 South Sheridan Road, Post Office Box 1260, Tulsa, Oklahoma 74101 (800) 752-9764; *International Energy Statistics Sourcebook.*

Statistical Office of the United Nations, Publishing Service, New York, New York 10017 (800) 253-9646; *Energy Statistics Yearbook,* and *Statistical Yearbook.*

Times Books, 201 East 50th Street, New York, New York 10022 (212) 751-2600; *The Economist Book of Vital World Statistics.*

ISRAEL - ENGINEERING AND METAL PRODUCTS EXPORTS TO DEVELOPED COUNTRIES

Statistical Office of the United Nations, Publishing Service, New York, New York 10017 (800) 253-9646; *Trade in Manufactures of Developing Countries.*

ISRAEL - EXCHANGE RATE

Euromonitor Publications Limited, 87-88 Turnmill Street, London EC1M 5QU, England; *International Marketing Data and Statistics,* and *Middle East Economic Handbook.*

International Civil Aviation Organization, 1000 Sherbrooke Street West, Suite 400, Montreal, Quebec, Canada H3A 2R2 (514) 285-8219; *Civil Aviation Statistics of the World.*

International Monetary Fund, 700 Nineteenth Street, NW, Washington, D.C. 20431 (202) 623-7000; *International Financial Statistics.*

Statistical Office of the United Nations, Publishing Service, New York, New York 10017 (800) 253-9646; *Statistical Yearbook.*

ISRAEL - EXCISE TAXES - See ISRAEL - TAXATION

ISRAEL - EXPORTS

American Automobile Manufacturers Association, 1401 H Street, NW, Suite 900, Washington, D.C. 20005 (202) 326-5500; *World Motor Vehicle Data.*

The Economist Intelligence Unit, 111 West 57th Street, New York, New York 10019 (800) 938-4685; *The World Market Atlas.*

Euromonitor Publications Limited, 87-88 Turnmill Street, London EC1M 5QU, England; *International Marketing Data and Statistics,* and *Middle East Economic Handbook.*

Food and Agricultural Organization of the United Nations (FAO) Via delle Terme di Caracalla, 00100 Rome, Italy (Telephone Number in U.S. (202) 643-2400); *The State of Food and Agriculture.*

G.K. Hall and Company, 70 Lincoln Street, Boston, Massachusetts 02111 (617) 423-3990; *The World in Figures.*

International Monetary Fund, 700 Nineteenth Street, NW, Washington, D.C. 20431 (202) 623-7000; *Direction of Trade Statistics,* and *International Financial Statistics.*

Statistical Office of the United Nations, Publishing Service, New York, New York 10017 (800) 253-9646; *Trade in Manufactures of Developing Countries.*

Times Books, 201 East 50th Street, New York, New York 10022 (212) 751-2600; *The Economist Book of Vital World Statistics.*

The World Bank, 1818 H Street, NW, Washington, D.C. 20433 (202) 477-1234; *World Tables.*

ISRAEL - EXTERNAL INDEBTEDNESS

The World Bank, 1818 H Street, NW, Washington, D.C. 20433 (202) 477-1234; *World Tables.*

ISRAEL - EXTERNAL TRADE

Food and Agricultural Organization of the United Nations (FAO) Via delle Terme di Caracalla, 00100 Rome, Italy (Telephone Number in U.S. (202) 643-2400); *The State of Food and Agriculture,* and *Trade Yearbook.*

G.K. Hall and Company, 70 Lincoln Street, Boston, Massachusetts 02111 (617) 423-3990; *The World in Figures.*

Statistical Office of the United Nations, Publishing Service, New York, New York 10017 (800) 253-9646; *Statistical Yearbook.*

ISRAEL - FABRIC PRODUCTION - See ISRAEL - TEXTILE INDUSTRY

ISRAEL - FARM CROPS - See ISRAEL - CROPS

ISRAEL - FEMALE WORKING POPULATION - See ISRAEL - EMPLOYMENT

ISRAEL - FERTILITY RATES

Facts on File, 460 Park Avenue South, New York, New York 10016 (800) 443-8323; *The New Book of World Rankings.*

Times Books, 201 East 50th Street, New York, New York 10022 (212) 751-2600; *The Economist Book of Vital World Statistics.*

The World Bank, 1818 H Street, NW, Washington, D.C. 20433 (202) 477-1234; *World Tables.*

ISRAEL - FERTILIZER

Food and Agricultural Organization of the United Nations (FAO), Via delle Terme di Caracalla, 00100 Rome, Italy (Telephone Number in U.S. (202) 643-2400); *Fertilizer Yearbook,* and *The State of Food and Agriculture.*

Statistical Office of the United Nations, Publishing Service, New York, New York 10017 (800) 253-9646; *Statistical Yearbook.*

ISRAEL - FETAL MORTALITY

Statistical Office of the United Nations, Publishing Service, New York, New York 10017 (800) 253-9646; *Demographic Yearbook.*

World Health Organization, Office of Publications, Avenue Appia, CH-1211 Geneva 27, Switzerland (Telephone Number in U.S. (518) 436-9686); *World Health Statistics Annual.*

ISRAEL - FIBRE PRODUCTION - See ISRAEL - TEXTILE INDUSTRY

ISRAEL - FILAMENT PRODUCTION - See ISRAEL - TEXTILE INDUSTRY

ISRAEL - FILM - See ISRAEL - MOTION PICTURES

ISRAEL - FINANCE

Euromonitor Publications Limited, 87-88 Turnmill Street, London EC1M 5QU, England; *Middle East Economic Handbook.*

Facts on File, 460 Park Avenue South, New York, New York 10016 (800) 443-8323; *The New Book of World Rankings.*

G.K. Hall and Company, 70 Lincoln Street, Boston, Massachusetts 02111 (617) 423-3990; *The World in Figures.*

International Monetary Fund, 700 Nineteenth Street, NW, Washington, D.C. 20431 (202) 623-7000; *Government Finance Statistics Yearbook,* and *International Financial Statistics.*

ISRAEL - FISHERIES

Facts on File, 460 Park Avenue South, New York, New York 10016 (800) 443-8323; *The New Book of World Rankings.*

Food and Agricultural Organization of the United Nations (FAO) Via delle Terme di Caracalla, 00100 Rome, Italy (Telephone Number in U.S. (202) 643-2400); *The State of Food and Agriculture,* and *Yearbook of Fishery Statistics.*

Statistical Office of the United Nations, Publishing Service, New York, New York 10017 (800) 253-9646; *Statistical Yearbook.*

ISRAEL - FLOUR PRODUCTION

Commodity Research Bureau, Incorporated, 75 Wall Street, New York, New York 10005 (212) 504-7754; *Commodity Year Book.*

Statistical Office of the United Nations, Publishing Service, New York, New York 10017 (800) 253-9646; *Statistical Yearbook.*

ISRAEL - FOOD

Food and Agricultural Organization of the United Nations (FAO), Via delle Terme di Caracalla, 00100 Rome, Italy (Telephone Number in U.S. (202) 643-2400); *Production Yearbook,* and *The State of Food and Agriculture.*

G.K. Hall and Company, 70 Lincoln Street, Boston, Massachusetts 02111 (617) 423-3990; *The World in Figures.*

Statistical Office of the United Nations, Publishing Service, New York, New York 10017 (800) 253-9646; *Trade in Manufactures of Developing Countries.*

ISRAEL - FOREIGN AID

G.K. Hall and Company, 70 Lincoln Street, Boston, Massachusetts 02111 (617) 423-3990; *The World in Figures.*

ISRAEL - FOREIGN DEBT

International Monetary Fund, 700 Nineteenth Street, NW, Washington, D.C. 20431 (202) 623-7000; *Government Finance Statistics Yearbook.*

ISRAEL - FOREIGN INDEBTEDNESS

Euromonitor Publications Limited, 87-88 Turnmill Street, London EC1M 5QU, England; *Middle East Economic Handbook.*

ISRAEL - FOREIGN TRADE

Facts on File, 460 Park Avenue South, New York, New York 10016 (800) 443-8323; *The New Book of World Rankings.*

G.K. Hall and Company, 70 Lincoln Street, Boston, Massachusetts 02111 (617) 423-3990; *The World in Figures.*

International Monetary Fund, 700 Nineteenth Street, NW, Washington, D.C. 20431 (202) 623-7000; *International Financial Statistics.*

Statistical Office of the United Nations, Publishing Service, New York, New York 10017 (800) 253-9646; *International Trade Statistics Yearbook,* and *Statistical Yearbook.*

The World Bank, 1818 H Street, NW, Washington, D.C. 20433 (202) 477-1234; *World Tables.*

ISRAEL - FORESTRY AND FOREST PRODUCTS

Facts on File, 460 Park Avenue South, New York, New York 10016 (800) 443-8323; *The New Book of World Rankings.*

Food and Agricultural Organization of the United Nations (FAO), Via delle Terme di Caracalla, 00100 Rome, Italy (Telephone Number in U.S. (202) 643-2400); *The State of Food and Agriculture* and *Yearbook of Forest Products*.

Forest and Paper Association, 1250 Connecticut Avenue, NW, Washington, D.C. 20036 (202) 463-2455; *Wood Pulp and Fiber Statistics*.

G.K. Hall and Company, 70 Lincoln Street, Boston, Massachusetts 02111 (617) 423-3990; *The World in Figures*.

Statistical Office of the United Nations, Publishing Service, New York, New York 10017 (800) 253-9646; *Statistical Yearbook*.

United Nations Educational, Scientific and Cultural Organization (UNESCO), 7 Place de Fontenoy, F-75700 Paris, France (Telephone Number in U.S. (212) 963-5981); *Statistical Yearbook*.

ISRAEL - GAS PRODUCTION - See ISRAEL - MINING AND MINERAL PRODUCTS

ISRAEL - GENERAL INDUSTRIAL STATISTICS

Statistical Office of the United Nations, Publishing Service, New York, New York 10017 (800) 253-9646; *Industrial Statistics Yearbook*.

ISRAEL - GENERAL MORTALITY

Statistical Office of the United Nations, Publishing Service, New York, New York 10017 (800) 253-9646; *Demographic Yearbook*.

World Health Organization, Office of Publications, Avenue Appia, CH-1211 Geneva 27, Switzerland (Telephone Number in U.S. (518) 436-9686); *World Health Statistics Annual*.

ISRAEL - GEOGRAPHIC DATA

Facts on File, 460 Park Avenue South, New York, New York 10016 (800) 443-8323; *The New Book of World Rankings*.

ISRAEL - GOATS - See ISRAEL - LIVESTOCK AND POULTRY

ISRAEL - GOLD HOLDINGS

International Monetary Fund, 700 Nineteenth Street, NW, Washington, D.C. 20431 (202) 623-7000; *International Financial Statistics*.

Statistical Office of the United Nations, Publishing Service, New York, New York 10017 (800) 253-9646; *Statistical Yearbook*.

The World Bank, 1818 H Street, NW, Washington, D.C. 20433 (202) 477-1234; *World Tables*.

ISRAEL - GOLD PRODUCTION AND CONSUMPTION - See ISRAEL - MINING AND MINERAL PRODUCTS

ISRAEL - GOVERNMENT

G.K. Hall and Company, 70 Lincoln Street, Boston, Massachusetts 02111 (617) 423-3990; *The World in Figures*.

ISRAEL - GOVERNMENT CONSUMPTION

International Monetary Fund, 700 Nineteenth Street, NW, Washington, D.C. 20431 (202) 623-7000; *International Financial Statistics*.

ISRAEL - GOVERNMENT EXPENDITURES

International Monetary Fund, 700 Nineteenth Street, NW, Washington, D.C. 20431 (202) 623-7000; *Government Finance Statistics Yearbook*.

Times Books, 201 East 50th Street, New York, New York 10022 (212) 751-2600; *The Economist Book of Vital World Statistics*.

The World Bank, 1818 H Street, NW, Washington, D.C. 20433 (202) 477-1234; *World Tables*.

ISRAEL - GOVERNMENT FINANCES

International Monetary Fund, 700 Nineteenth Street, NW, Washington, D.C. 20431 (202) 623-7000; *International Financial Statistics*.

Statistical Office of the United Nations, Publishing Service, New York, New York 10017 (800) 253-9646; *Statistical Yearbook*.

ISRAEL - GOVERNMENT REVENUES

International Monetary Fund, 700 Nineteenth Street, NW, Washington, D.C. 20431 (202) 623-7000; *Government Finance Statistics Yearbook*.

Times Books, 201 East 50th Street, New York, New York 10022 (212) 751-2600; *The Economist Book of Vital World Statistics*.

The World Bank, 1818 H Street, NW, Washington, D.C. 20433 (202) 477-1234; *World Tables*.

ISRAEL - GRAIN PRODUCTION - See ISRAEL - CROPS

ISRAEL - GRANTS

International Monetary Fund, 700 Nineteenth Street, NW, Washington, D.C. 20431 (202) 623-7000; *Government Finance Statistics Yearbook*.

ISRAEL - GREEN PEPPER AND CHILIE PRODUCTION - See ISRAEL - CROPS

ISRAEL - GROSS DOMESTIC PRODUCT

The Economist Intelligence Unit, 111 West 57th Street, New York, New York 10019 (800) 938-4685; *The World Market Atlas*.

Euromonitor Publications Limited, 87-88 Turnmill Street, London EC1M 5QU, England; *International Marketing Data and Statistics*, and *Middle East Economic Handbook*.

Facts on File, 460 Park Avenue South, New York, New York 10016 (800) 443-8323; *The New Book of World Rankings*.

G.K. Hall and Company, 70 Lincoln Street, Boston, Massachusetts 02111 (617) 423-3990; *The World in Figures*.

International Monetary Fund, 700 Nineteenth Street, NW, Washington, D.C. 20431 (202) 623-7000; *International Financial Statistics*.

Statistical Office of the United Nations, Publishing Service, New York, New York 10017 (800) 253-9646; *Statistical Yearbook*.

Times Books, 201 East 50th Street, New York, New York 10022 (212) 751-2600; *The Economist Book of Vital World Statistics*.

The World Bank, 1818 H Street, NW, Washington, D.C. 20433 (202) 477-1234; *World Tables.*

ISRAEL - GROSS NATIONAL PRODUCT

Euromonitor Publications Limited, 87-88 Turnmill Street, London EC1M 5QU, England; *International Marketing Data and Statistics.*

U.S. Arms Control and Disarmament Agency, 320 Twenty-first Street, Northwest, Washington, D.C. 20451 (202) 647-8677; *World Military Expenditures and Arms Transfers.*

The World Bank, 1818 H Street, NW, Washington, D.C. 20433 (202) 477-1234; *World Tables.*

ISRAEL - GROUNDNUTS PRODUCTION - See ISRAEL - CROPS

ISRAEL - HEALTH

Euromonitor Publications Limited, 87-88 Turnmill Street, London EC1M 5QU, England; *Middle East Economic Handbook.*

Facts on File, 460 Park Avenue South, New York, New York 10016 (800) 443-8323; *The New Book of World Rankings.*

G.K. Hall and Company, 70 Lincoln Street, Boston, Massachusetts 02111 (617) 423-3990; *The World in Figures.*

Statistical Office of the United Nations, Publishing Service, New York, New York 10017 (800) 253-9646; *Statistical Yearbook.*

Times Books, 201 East 50th Street, New York, New York 10022 (212) 751-2600; *The Economist Book of Vital World Statistics.*

ISRAEL - HEALTH EXPENDITURES

International Monetary Fund, 700 Nineteenth Street, NW, Washington, D.C. 20431 (202) 623-7000; *Government Finance Statistics Yearbook.*

ISRAEL - HIDE PRODUCTION

Food and Agricultural Organization of the United Nations (FAO), Via delle Terme di Caracalla, 00100 Rome, Italy (Telephone Number in U.S. (202) 643-2400); *Production Yearbook.*

ISRAEL - HIGHWAYS

G.K. Hall and Company, 70 Lincoln Street, Boston, Massachusetts 02111 (617) 423-3990; *The World in Figures.*

ISRAEL - HORSES - See ISRAEL - LIVESTOCK AND POULTRY

ISRAEL - HOURS OF WORK - See ISRAEL - EMPLOYMENT

ISRAEL - HOUSING EXPENDITURES

Facts on File, 460 Park Avenue South, New York, New York 10016 (800) 443-8323; *The New Book of World Rankings.*

International Monetary Fund, 700 Nineteenth Street, NW, Washington, D.C. 20431 (202) 623-7000; *Government Finance Statistics Yearbook.*

ISRAEL - ILLITERATE POPULATION

The Economist Intelligence Unit, 111 West 57th Street, New York, New York 10019 (800) 938-4685; *The World Market Atlas.*

G.K. Hall and Company, 70 Lincoln Street, Boston, Massachusetts 02111 (617) 423-3990; *The World in Figures.*

United Nations Educational, Scientific and Cultural Organization (UNESCO), 7 Place de Fontenoy, F-75700 Paris, France (Telephone Number in U.S. (212) 963-5981); *Statistical Yearbook.*

ISRAEL - IMPORTS

American Automobile Manufacturers Association, 1401 H Street, NW, Suite 900, Washington, D.C. 20005 (202) 326-5500; *World Motor Vehicle Data.*

The Economist Intelligence Unit, 111 West 57th Street, New York, New York 10019 (800) 938-4685; *The World Market Atlas.*

Euromonitor Publications Limited, 87-88 Turnmill Street, London EC1M 5QU, England; *International Marketing Data and Statistics,* and *Middle East Economic Handbook.*

Food and Agricultural Organization of the United Nations (FAO) Via delle Terme di Caracalla, 00100 Rome, Italy (Telephone Number in U.S. (202) 643-2400); *The State of Food and Agriculture.*

G.K. Hall and Company, 70 Lincoln Street, Boston, Massachusetts 02111 (617) 423-3990; *The World in Figures.*

International Monetary Fund, 700 Nineteenth Street, NW, Washington, D.C. 20431 (202) 623-7000; *Direction of Trade Statistics, Government Finance Statistics Yearbook,* and *International Financial Statistics.*

Statistical Office of the United Nations, Publishing Service, New York, New York 10017 (800) 253-9646; *Trade in Manufactures of Developing Countries.*

Times Books, 201 East 50th Street, New York, New York 10022 (212) 751-2600; *The Economist Book of Vital World Statistics.*

The World Bank, 1818 H Street, NW, Washington, D.C. 20433 (202) 477-1234; *World Tables.*

ISRAEL - INCOME TAXES - See ISRAEL - TAXATION

ISRAEL - INDUSTRIAL METALS PRODUCTION - See ISRAEL - MINING AND MINERAL PRODUCTS

ISRAEL - INDUSTRY

Euromonitor Publications Limited, 87-88 Turnmill Street, London EC1M 5QU, England; *International Marketing Data and Statistics.*

Facts on File, 460 Park Avenue South, New York, New York 10016 (800) 443-8323; *The New Book of World Rankings.*

G.K. Hall and Company, 70 Lincoln Street, Boston, Massachusetts 02111 (617) 423-3990; *The World in Figures.*

International Labour Office, I.L.O. Publications, CH-1211, Geneva 22, Switzerland; *Yearbook of Labour Statistics.*

Statistical Office of the United Nations, Publishing Service, New York, New York 10017 (800) 253-9646; *Statistical Yearbook.*

Times Books, 201 East 50th Street, New York, New York 10022 (212) 751-2600; *The Economist Book of Vital World Statistics.*

The World Bank, 1818 H Street, NW, Washington, D.C. 20433 (202) 477-1234; *World Tables.*

World Intellectual Property Organization, 34 Chemin des Colombettes, CH-1211 Geneva 20, Switzerland; *Industrial Property Statistics*.

ISRAEL - INFANT AND MATERNAL MORTALITY

Statistical Office of the United Nations, Publishing Service, New York, New York 10017 (800) 253-9646; *Demographic Yearbook*, and *Statistical Yearbook*.

Times Books, 201 East 50th Street, New York, New York 10022 (212) 751-2600; *The Economist Book of Vital World Statistics*.

The World Bank, 1818 H Street, NW, Washington, D.C. 20433 (202) 477-1234; *World Tables*.

World Health Organization, Office of Publications, Avenue Appia, CH-1211 Geneva 27, Switzerland (Telephone Number in U.S. (518) 436-9686); *World Health Statistics Annual*.

ISRAEL - INTERNATIONAL LIQUIDITY

International Monetary Fund, 700 Nineteenth Street, NW, Washington, D.C. 20431 (202) 623-7000; *International Financial Statistics*.

ISRAEL - INTERNATIONAL RESERVES EXCLUDING GOLD

Statistical Office of the United Nations, Publishing Service, New York, New York 10017 (800) 253-9646; *Statistical Yearbook*.

The World Bank, 1818 H Street, NW, Washington, D.C. 20433 (202) 477-1234; *World Tables*.

ISRAEL - INVESTMENTS

International Monetary Fund, 700 Nineteenth Street, NW, Washington, D.C. 20431 (202) 623-7000; *International Financial Statistics*.

ISRAEL - IRON ORE PRODUCTION AND CONSUMPTION - See ISRAEL - MINING AND MINERAL PRODUCTS

ISRAEL - IRRIGATION

Euromonitor Publications Limited, 87-88 Turnmill Street, London EC1M 5QU, England; *International Marketing Data and Statistics*.

ISRAEL - LABOR FORCE

Euromonitor Publications Limited, 87-88 Turnmill Street, London EC1M 5QU, England; *International Marketing Data and Statistics*, and *Middle East Economic Handbook*.

Facts on File, 460 Park Avenue South, New York, New York 10016 (800) 443-8323; *The New Book of World Rankings*.

Food and Agricultural Organization of the United Nations (FAO) Via delle Terme di Caracalla, 00100 Rome, Italy (Telephone Number in U.S. (202) 643-2400); *The State of Food and Agriculture*.

G.K. Hall and Company, 70 Lincoln Street, Boston, Massachusetts 02111 (617) 423-3990; *The World in Figures*.

Times Books, 201 East 50th Street, New York, New York 10022 (212) 751-2600; *The Economist Book of Vital World Statistics*.

The World Bank, 1818 H Street, NW, Washington, D.C. 20433 (202) 477-1234; *World Tables*.

ISRAEL - LABOR PRODUCTIVITY

International Labour Office, I.L.O. Publications, CH-1211, Geneva 22, Switzerland; *Yearbook of Labour Statistics*.

ISRAEL - LAND USE

Euromonitor Publications Limited, 87-88 Turnmill Street, London EC1M 5QU, England; *International Marketing Data and Statistics*.

Food and Agricultural Organization of the United Nations (FAO), Via delle Terme di Caracalla, 00100 Rome, Italy (Telephone Number in U.S. (202) 643-2400); *Production Yearbook*.

G.K. Hall and Company, 70 Lincoln Street, Boston, Massachusetts 02111 (617) 423-3990; *The World in Figures*.

ISRAEL - LIBRARIES

Facts on File, 460 Park Avenue South, New York, New York 10016 (800) 443-8323; *The New Book of World Rankings*.

United Nations Educational, Scientific and Cultural Organization (UNESCO), 7 Place de Fontenoy, F-75700 Paris, France (Telephone Number in U.S. (212) 963-5981); *Statistical Yearbook*.

ISRAEL - LIVESTOCK AND POULTRY

Euromonitor Publications Limited, 87-88 Turnmill Street, London EC1M 5QU, England; *International Marketing Data and Statistics*.

Facts on File, 460 Park Avenue South, New York, New York 10016 (800) 443-8323; *The New Book of World Rankings*.

Food and Agricultural Organization of the United Nations (FAO), Via delle Terme di Caracalla, 00100 Rome, Italy (Telephone Number in U.S. (202) 643-2400); *Production Yearbook*, and *The State of Food and Agriculture*.

G.K. Hall and Company, 70 Lincoln Street, Boston, Massachusetts 02111 (617) 423-3990; *The World in Figures*.

Statistical Office of the United Nations, Publishing Service, New York, New York 10017 (800) 253-9646; *Statistical Yearbook*.

ISRAEL - LIVING LEVELS

G.K. Hall and Company, 70 Lincoln Street, Boston, Massachusetts 02111 (617) 423-3990; *The World in Figures*.

Times Books, 201 East 50th Street, New York, New York 10022 (212) 751-2600; *The Economist Book of Vital World Statistics*.

ISRAEL - MAIL - NUMBER OF PIECES SENT OR RECEIVED

Statistical Office of the United Nations, Publishing Service, New York, New York 10017 (800) 253-9646; *Statistical Yearbook*.

ISRAEL - MANUFACTURING

American Automobile Manufacturers Association, 1401 H Street, NW, Suite 900, Washington, D.C. 20005 (202) 326-5500; *World Motor Vehicle Data*.

Facts on File, 460 Park Avenue South, New York, New York 10016 (800) 443-8323; *The New Book of World Rankings*.

G.K. Hall and Company, 70 Lincoln Street, Boston, Massachusetts 02111 (617) 423-3990; *The World in Figures.*

Statistical Office of the United Nations, Publishing Service, New York, New York 10017 (800) 253-9646; *Statistical Yearbook.*

Times Books, 201 East 50th Street, New York, New York 10022 (212) 751-2600; *The Economist Book of Vital World Statistics.*

The World Bank, 1818 H Street, NW, Washington, D.C. 20433 (202) 477-1234; *World Tables.*

ISRAEL - MARRIAGE RATES

Facts on File, 460 Park Avenue South, New York, New York 10016 (800) 443-8323; *The New Book of World Rankings.*

Statistical Office of the United Nations, Publishing Service, New York, New York 10017 (800) 253-9646; *Demographic Yearbook,* and *Statistical Yearbook.*

ISRAEL - MEAT PRODUCTION - See ISRAEL - LIVESTOCK AND POULTRY

ISRAEL - MERCHANT SHIPPING

G.K. Hall and Company, 70 Lincoln Street, Boston, Massachusetts 02111 (617) 423-3990; *The World in Figures.*

Lloyd's Register of Shipping, 17 Battery Place, New York, New York 10004 (212) 425-8050; *Register of Ships.*

Statistical Office of the United Nations, Publishing Service, New York, New York 10017 (800) 253-9646; *Statistical Yearbook.*

Times Books, 201 East 50th Street, New York, New York 10022 (212) 751-2600; *The Economist Book of Vital World Statistics.*

U.S. Department of Transportation, Maritime Administration, 400 Seventh Street, SW, Washington, D.C. 20590 (202) 366-5807; *A Statistical Analysis of the World's Merchant Fleets.*

ISRAEL - MILITARY

G.K. Hall and Company, 70 Lincoln Street, Boston, Massachusetts 02111 (617) 423-3990; *The World in Figures.*

The International Institute for Strategic Studies, 23 Tavistock Street, London WC2E 7NQ, England; *The Military Balance.*

U.S. Arms Control and Disarmament Agency, 320 Twenty-first Street, Northwest, Washington, D.C. 20451 (202) 647-8677; *World Military Expenditures and Arms Transfers.*

ISRAEL - MILK - See ISRAEL - DAIRY PRODUCTS

ISRAEL - MINING AND MINERAL PRODUCTS

Facts on File, 460 Park Avenue South, New York, New York 10016 (800) 443-8323; *The New Book of World Rankings.*

G.K. Hall and Company, 70 Lincoln Street, Boston, Massachusetts 02111 (617) 423-3990; *The World in Figures.*

International Monetary Fund, 700 Nineteenth Street, NW, Washington, D.C. 20431 (202) 623-7000; *International Financial Statistics.*

Penn Well Publishing Company, 1421 South Sheridan Road, Post Office Box 1260, Tulsa, Oklahoma 74101 (800) 752-9764; *International Energy Statistics Sourcebook.*

Statistical Office of the United Nations, Publishing Service, New York, New York 10017 (800) 253-9646; *Statistical Yearbook.*

ISRAEL - MONEY EXCHANGE RATE

Euromonitor Publications Limited, 87-88 Turnmill Street, London EC1M 5QU, England; *International Marketing Data and Statistics.*

International Monetary Fund, 700 Nineteenth Street, NW, Washington, D.C. 20431 (202) 623-7000; *International Financial Statistics.*

Statistical Office of the United Nations, Publishing Service, New York, New York 10017 (800) 253-9646; *Statistical Yearbook.*

ISRAEL - MONEY RESERVES

Euromonitor Publications Limited, 87-88 Turnmill Street, London EC1M 5QU, England; *International Marketing Data and Statistics.*

ISRAEL - MONEY SUPPLY

Euromonitor Publications Limited, 87-88 Turnmill Street, London EC1M 5QU, England; *International Marketing Data and Statistics.*

G.K. Hall and Company, 70 Lincoln Street, Boston, Massachusetts 02111 (617) 423-3990; *The World in Figures.*

International Monetary Fund, 700 Nineteenth Street, NW, Washington, D.C. 20431 (202) 623-7000; *International Financial Statistics.*

Statistical Office of the United Nations, Publishing Service, New York, New York 10017 (800) 253-9646; *Statistical Yearbook.*

ISRAEL - MOTION PICTURES

Statistical Office of the United Nations, Publishing Service, New York, New York 10017 (800) 253-9646; *Statistical Yearbook.*

United Nations Educational, Scientific and Cultural Organization (UNESCO), 7 Place de Fontenoy, F-75700 Paris, France (Telephone Number in U.S. (212) 963-5981); *Statistical Yearbook.*

ISRAEL - MOTOR VEHICLE ASSEMBLY

Statistical Office of the United Nations, Publishing Service, New York, New York 10017 (800) 253-9646; *Statistical Yearbook.*

ISRAEL - MOTOR VEHICLE PRODUCTION

American Automobile Manufacturers Association, 1401 H Street, NW, Suite 900, Washington, D.C. 20005 (202) 326-5500; *World Motor Vehicle Data.*

ISRAEL - MOTOR VEHICLE TAXES - See ISRAEL - TAXATION

ISRAEL - MOTOR VEHICLES IN USE

American Automobile Manufacturers Association, 1401 H Street, NW, Suite 900, Washington, D.C. 20005 (202) 326-5500; *World Motor Vehicle Data.*

G.K. Hall and Company, 70 Lincoln Street, Boston, Massachusetts 02111 (617) 423-3990; *The World in Figures.*

Statistical Office of the United Nations, Publishing Service, New York, New York 10017 (800) 253-9646; *Statistical Yearbook.*

Times Books, 201 East 50th Street, New York, New York 10022 (212) 751-2600; *The Economist Book of Vital World Statistics.*

ISRAEL - MULES - See ISRAEL - LIVESTOCK AND POULTRY

ISRAEL - MUSEUMS

Facts on File, 460 Park Avenue South, New York, New York 10016 (800) 443-8323; *The New Book of World Rankings.*

United Nations Educational, Scientific and Cultural Organization (UNESCO), 7 Place de Fontenoy, F-75700 Paris, France (Telephone Number in U.S. (212) 963-5981); *Statistical Yearbook.*

ISRAEL - NATALITY - See ISRAEL - BIRTH RATES

ISRAEL - NATIONAL ACCOUNTS

International Monetary Fund, 700 Nineteenth Street, NW, Washington, D.C. 20431 (202) 623-7000; *International Financial Statistics.*

Statistical Office of the United Nations, Publishing Service, New York, New York 10017 (800) 253-9646; *National Accounts Statistics,* and *Statistical Yearbook.*

ISRAEL - NATIONAL INCOME

Facts on File, 460 Park Avenue South, New York, New York 10016 (800) 443-8323; *The New Book of World Rankings.*

G.K. Hall and Company, 70 Lincoln Street, Boston, Massachusetts 02111 (617) 423-3990; *The World in Figures.*

Statistical Office of the United Nations, Publishing Service, New York, New York 10017 (800) 253-9646; *Statistical Yearbook.*

ISRAEL - NATIONAL PRODUCT

Facts on File, 460 Park Avenue South, New York, New York 10016 (800) 443-8323; *The New Book of World Rankings.*

Statistical Office of the United Nations, Publishing Service, New York, New York 10017 (800) 253-9646; *Statistical Yearbook.*

ISRAEL - NATURAL GAS PRODUCTION - See ISRAEL - MINING AND MINERAL PRODUCTS

ISRAEL - NEWSPAPER PRODUCTION - See ISRAEL - FORESTRY AND FOREST PRODUCTS

ISRAEL - NEWSPRINT - See ISRAEL - FORESTRY AND FOREST PRODUCTS

ISRAEL - NITRIC ACID PRODUCTION

Statistical Office of the United Nations, Publishing Service, New York, New York 10017 (800) 253-9646; *Statistical Yearbook.*

ISRAEL - OCCUPATIONS - See ISRAEL - LABOR FORCE

ISRAEL - ORANGES PRODUCTION - See ISRAEL - CROPS

ISRAEL - PAPER - See ISRAEL - FORESTRY AND FOREST PRODUCTS

ISRAEL - PATENTS

Statistical Office of the United Nations, Publishing Service, New York, New York 10017 (800) 253-9646; *Statistical Yearbook.*

World Intellectual Property Organization, 34 Chemin des Colombettes, CH-1211 Geneva 20, Switzerland; *Industrial Property Statistics.*

ISRAEL - PEANUT PRODUCTION - See ISRAEL - CROPS

ISRAEL - PERIODICALS

United Nations Educational, Scientific and Cultural Organization (UNESCO), 7 Place de Fontenoy, F-75700 Paris, France (Telephone Number in U.S. (212) 963-5981); *Statistical Yearbook.*

ISRAEL - PESTICIDE USE

Food and Agricultural Organization of the United Nations (FAO) Via delle Terme di Caracalla, 00100 Rome, Italy (Telephone Number in U.S. (202) 643-2400); *The State of Food and Agriculture.*

ISRAEL - PETROLEUM INDUSTRY

Euromonitor Publications Limited, 87-88 Turnmill Street, London EC1M 5QU, England; *Middle East Economic Handbook.*

Facts on File, 460 Park Avenue South, New York, New York 10016 (800) 443-8323; *The New Book of World Rankings.*

Food and Agricultural Organization of the United Nations (FAO) Via delle Terme di Caracalla, 00100 Rome, Italy (Telephone Number in U.S. (202) 643-2400); *The State of Food and Agriculture.*

G.K. Hall and Company, 70 Lincoln Street, Boston, Massachusetts 02111 (617) 423-3990; *The World in Figures.*

Penn Well Publishing Company, 1421 South Sheridan Road, Post Office Box 1260, Tulsa, Oklahoma 74101 (800) 752-9764; *International Energy Statistics Sourcebook.*

Statistical Office of the United Nations, Publishing Service, New York, New York 10017 (800) 253-9646; *Statistical Yearbook.*

ISRAEL - PHOSPHATE ROCK PRODUCTION - See ISRAEL - MINING AND MINERAL PRODUCTS

ISRAEL - PIGS - See ISRAEL - LIVESTOCK AND POULTRY

ISRAEL - PLASTICS AND RESINS

Statistical Office of the United Nations, Publishing Service, New York, New York 10017 (800) 253-9646; *Statistical Yearbook.*

ISRAEL - POPULATION

The Economist Intelligence Unit, 111 West 57th Street, New York, New York 10019 (800) 938-4685; *The World Market Atlas.*

Euromonitor Publications Limited, 87-88 Turnmill Street, London EC1M 5QU, England; *International Marketing Data and Statistics,* and *Middle East Economic Handbook.*

Facts on File, 460 Park Avenue South, New York, New York 10016 (800) 443-8323; *The New Book of World Rankings.*

Food and Agricultural Organization of the United Nations (FAO), Via delle Terme di Caracalla, 00100 Rome, Italy (Telephone Number in

U.S. (202) 643-2400); *Production Yearbook*.

G.K. Hall and Company, 70 Lincoln Street, Boston, Massachusetts 02111 (617) 423-3990; *The World in Figures*.

International Labour Office, I.L.O. Publications, CH-1211, Geneva 22, Switzerland; *Yearbook of Labour Statistics*.

Statistical Office of the United Nations, Publishing Service, New York, New York 10017 (800) 253-9646; *Demographic Yearbook*, and *Statistical Yearbook*.

Times Books, 201 East 50th Street, New York, New York 10022 (212) 751-2600; *The Economist Book of Vital World Statistics*.

United Nations Educational, Scientific and Cultural Organization (UNESCO), 7 Place de Fontenoy, F-75700 Paris, France (Telephone Number in U.S. (212) 963-5981); *Statistical Yearbook*.

U.S. Arms Control and Disarmament Agency, 320 Twenty-first Street, Northwest, Washington, D.C. 20451 (202) 647-8677; *World Military Expenditures and Arms Transfers*.

World Health Organization, Office of Publications, Avenue Appia, CH-1211 Geneva 27, Switzerland (Telephone Number in U.S. (518) 436-9686); *World Health Statistics Annual*.

ISRAEL - POST OFFICES

Facts on File, 460 Park Avenue South, New York, New York 10016 (800) 443-8323; *The New Book of World Rankings*.

ISRAEL - POTATO PRODUCTION - See ISRAEL - CROPS

ISRAEL - PRICES

Facts on File, 460 Park Avenue South, New York, New York 10016 (800) 443-8323; *The New Book of World Rankings*.

Food and Agricultural Organization of the United Nations (FAO), Via delle Terme di Caracalla, 00100 Rome, Italy (Telephone Number in U.S. (202) 643-2400); *Production Yearbook*, and *The State of Food and Agriculture*.

G.K. Hall and Company, 70 Lincoln Street, Boston, Massachusetts 02111 (617) 423-3990; *The World in Figures*.

International Labour Office, I.L.O. Publications, CH-1211, Geneva 22, Switzerland; *Yearbook of Labour Statistics*.

International Monetary Fund, 700 Nineteenth Street, NW, Washington, D.C. 20431 (202) 623-7000; *International Financial Statistics*.

ISRAEL - PRINTING AND WRITING PAPER - See ISRAEL - FORESTRY AND FOREST PRODUCTS

ISRAEL - PRODUCTION

American Automobile Manufacturers Association, 1401 H Street, NW, Suite 900, Washington, D.C. 20005 (202) 326-5500; *World Motor Vehicle Data*.

Facts on File, 460 Park Avenue South, New York, New York 10016 (800) 443-8323; *The New Book of World Rankings*.

G.K. Hall and Company, 70 Lincoln Street, Boston, Massachusetts 02111 (617) 423-3990; *The World in Figures*.

ISRAEL - PRODUCTIVITY

Euromonitor Publications Limited, 87-88 Turnmill Street, London EC1M 5QU, England; *International Marketing Data and Statistics*.

ISRAEL - PROPERTY TAXES - See ISRAEL - TAXATION

ISRAEL - PUBLIC FINANCE

Facts on File, 460 Park Avenue South, New York, New York 10016 (800) 443-8323; *The New Book of World Rankings*.

ISRAEL - RADIO BROADCASTING - See ISRAEL - BROADCASTING

ISRAEL - RADIO RECEIVER PRODUCTION

Statistical Office of the United Nations, Publishing Service, New York, New York 10017 (800) 253-9646; *Statistical Yearbook*.

ISRAEL - RAILWAYS

G.K. Hall and Company, 70 Lincoln Street, Boston, Massachusetts 02111 (617) 423-3990; *The World in Figures*.

Jane's Information Group, Sentinel House, 163 Brighton Road, Coulsdon, Surrey CR5 2NH, England (Telephone Number in U.S. (703) 683-3700); *Jane's World Railways*.

ISRAEL - RELIGION

Facts on File, 460 Park Avenue South, New York, New York 10016 (800) 443-8323; *The New Book of World Rankings*.

ISRAEL - RENT PRICES

International Labour Office, I.L.O. Publications, CH-1211, Geneva 22, Switzerland; *Yearbook of Labour Statistics*.

ISRAEL - RETAIL TRADE

G.K. Hall and Company, 70 Lincoln Street, Boston, Massachusetts 02111 (617) 423-3990; *The World in Figures*.

Statistical Office of the United Nations, Publishing Service, New York, New York 10017 (800) 253-9646; *Statistical Yearbook*.

ISRAEL - RICE PRODUCTION - See ISRAEL - CROPS

ISRAEL - ROOT AND TUBER PRODUCTION - See ISRAEL - CROPS

ISRAEL - ROUNDWOOD PRODUCTION - See ISRAEL - FORESTRY AND FOREST PRODUCTS

ISRAEL - RUBBER PRODUCTION

Facts on File, 460 Park Avenue South, New York, New York 10016 (800) 443-8323; *The New Book of World Rankings*.

ISRAEL - SAFFLOWER SEED PRODUCTION - See ISRAEL - CROPS

ISRAEL - SALT PRODUCTION - See ISRAEL - MINING AND MINERAL PRODUCTS

ISRAEL - SCIENTISTS AND TECHNICIANS

Statistical Office of the United Nations, Publishing Service, New York, New York 10017 (800) 253-9646; *Statistical Yearbook*.

United Nations Educational, Scientific and Cultural Organization (UNESCO), 7 Place de Fontenoy, F-75700 Paris, France (Telephone Number in U.S. (212) 963-5981); *Statistical Yearbook.*

ISRAEL - SENIOR CITIZENS

Facts on File, 460 Park Avenue South, New York, New York 10016 (800) 443-8323; *The New Book of World Rankings.*

ISRAEL - SESAME SEED PRODUCTION - See ISRAEL - CROPS

ISRAEL - SHEEP - See ISRAEL - LIVESTOCK AND POULTRY

ISRAEL - SILVER PRODUCTION AND CONSUMPTION - See ISRAEL - MINING AND MINERAL PRODUCTS

ISRAEL - SOCIAL DATA

Facts on File, 460 Park Avenue South, New York, New York 10016 (800) 443-8323; *The New Book of World Rankings.*

G.K. Hall and Company, 70 Lincoln Street, Boston, Massachusetts 02111 (617) 423-3990; *The World in Figures.*

ISRAEL - SOCIAL SECURITY

International Monetary Fund, 700 Nineteenth Street, NW, Washington, D.C. 20431 (202) 623-7000; *Government Finance Statistics Yearbook.*

ISRAEL - STAMP TAXES AND DUTIES - See ISRAEL - TAXATION
ISRAEL - STATE BUDGET REVENUE AND EXPENDITURES

Euromonitor Publications Limited, 87-88 Turnmill Street, London EC1M 5QU, England; *International Marketing Data and Statistics.*

ISRAEL - STEEL - See ISRAEL - MINING AND MINERAL PRODUCTS

ISRAEL - STOCKS - COMMODITY - MARKET PRICE - INDEXES

Food and Agricultural Organization of the United Nations (FAO) Via delle Terme di Caracalla, 00100 Rome, Italy (Telephone Number in U.S. (202) 643-2400); *The State of Food and Agriculture.*

Statistical Office of the United Nations, Publishing Service, New York, New York 10017 (800) 253-9646; *Statistical Yearbook.*

ISRAEL - SUGAR PRODUCTION AND CONSUMPTION - See ISRAEL - CROPS

ISRAEL - SULPHUR AND SULPHURIC ACID PRODUCTION - See ISRAEL - MINING AND MINERAL PRODUCTS

ISRAEL - TAXATION

G.K. Hall and Company, 70 Lincoln Street, Boston, Massachusetts 02111 (617) 423-3990; *The World in Figures.*

International Monetary Fund, 700 Nineteenth Street, NW, Washington, D.C. 20431 (202) 623-7000; *Government Finance Statistics Yearbook.*

The World Bank, 1818 H Street, NW, Washington, D.C. 20433 (202) 477-1234; *World Tables.*

ISRAEL - TELEGRAPH SERVICE

Statistical Office of the United Nations, Publishing Service, New York, New York 10017 (800) 253-9646; *Statistical Yearbook.*

ISRAEL - TELEPHONES IN USE

American Telephone and Telegraph Company, 26 Parsippany Road, Whippany, New Jersey 07981 (800) 338-4038; *The World's Telephones.*

Euromonitor Publications Limited, 87-88 Turnmill Street, London EC1M 5QU, England; *Middle East Economic Handbook.*

G.K. Hall and Company, 70 Lincoln Street, Boston, Massachusetts 02111 (617) 423-3990; *The World in Figures.*

Statistical Office of the United Nations, Publishing Service, New York, New York 10017 (800) 253-9646; *Statistical Yearbook.*

ISRAEL - TELEVISION BROADCASTING - See ISRAEL - BROADCASTING

ISRAEL - TELEVISION RECEIVER PRODUCTION

Statistical Office of the United Nations, Publishing Service, New York, New York 10017 (800) 253-9646; *Statistical Yearbook.*

ISRAEL - TEXTILE INDUSTRY

Forest and Paper Association, 1250 Connecticut Avenue, NW, Washington, D.C. 20036 (202) 463-2455; *Wood Pulp and Fiber Statistics.*

G.K. Hall and Company, 70 Lincoln Street, Boston, Massachusetts 02111 (617) 423-3990; *The World in Figures.*

Statistical Office of the United Nations, Publishing Service, New York, New York 10017 (800) 253-9646; *Statistical Yearbook,* and *Trade in Manufactures of Developing Countries.*

ISRAEL - TIN - INDUSTRIAL CONSUMPTION - See ISRAEL - MINING AND MINERAL PRODUCTS

ISRAEL - TIRE (MOTOR VEHICLE) PRODUCTION

Statistical Office of the United Nations, Publishing Service, New York, New York 10017 (800) 253-9646; *Statistical Yearbook.*

ISRAEL - TOBACCO PRODUCTION

Facts on File, 460 Park Avenue South, New York, New York 10016 (800) 443-8323; *The New Book of World Rankings.*

Statistical Office of the United Nations, Publishing Service, New York, New York 10017 (800) 253-9646; *Statistical Yearbook.*

ISRAEL - TOURISM

Euromonitor Publications Limited, 87-88 Turnmill Street, London EC1M 5QU, England; *Middle East Economic Handbook.*

Facts on File, 460 Park Avenue South, New York, New York 10016 (800) 443-8323; *The New Book of World Rankings.*

G.K. Hall and Company, 70 Lincoln Street, Boston, Massachusetts 02111 (617) 423-3990; *The World in Figures.*

Statistical Office of the United Nations, Publishing Service, New York, New York 10017 (800) 253-9646; *Statistical Yearbook.*

Times Books, 201 East 50th Street, New York, New York 10022 (212) 751-2600; *The Economist Book of Vital World Statistics.*

World Tourism Organization, Calle Capitan Haya 42, E-28020 Madrid, Spain; *Yearbook of Tourism Statistics.*

ISRAEL - TRACTORS IN USE

Statistical Office of the United Nations, Publishing Service, New York, New York 10017 (800) 253-9646; *Statistical Yearbook.*

ISRAEL - TRADE

Euromonitor Publications Limited, 87-88 Turnmill Street, London EC1M 5QU, England; *International Marketing Data and Statistics,* and *Middle East Economic Handbook.*

Food and Agricultural Organization of the United Nations (FAO) Via delle Terme di Caracalla, 00100 Rome, Italy (Telephone Number in U.S. (202) 653-2400); *The State of Food and Agriculture.*

ISRAEL - TRADEMARKS AND SERVICE MARKS

Statistical Office of the United Nations, Publishing Service, New York, New York 10017 (800) 253-9646; *Statistical Yearbook.*

World Intellectual Property Organization, 34 Chemin des Colombettes, CH-1211 Geneva 20, Switzerland; *Industrial Property Statistics.*

ISRAEL - TRANSPORTATION AND COMMUNICATIONS

Euromonitor Publications Limited, 87-88 Turnmill Street, London EC1M 5QU, England; *Middle East Economic Handbook.*

Facts on File, 460 Park Avenue South, New York, New York 10016 (800) 443-8323; *The New Book of World Rankings.*

G.K. Hall and Company, 70 Lincoln Street, Boston, Massachusetts 02111 (617) 423-3990; *The World in Figures.*

ISRAEL - UNEMPLOYMENT

Euromonitor Publications Limited, 87-88 Turnmill Street, London EC1M 5QU, England; *International Marketing Data and Statistics,* and *Middle East Economic Handbook.*

International Labour Office, I.L.O. Publications, CH-1211, Geneva 22, Switzerland; *Yearbook of Labour Statistics.*

Statistical Office of the United Nations, Publishing Service, New York, New York 10017 (800) 253-9646; *Statistical Yearbook.*

ISRAEL - VITAL STATISTICS

Euromonitor Publications Limited, 87-88 Turnmill Street, London EC1M 5QU, England; *International Marketing Data and Statistics,* and *Middle East Economic Handbook.*

G.K. Hall and Company, 70 Lincoln Street, Boston, Massachusetts 02111 (617) 423-3990; *The World in Figures.*

Statistical Office of the United Nations, Publishing Service, New York, New York 10017 (800) 253-9646; *Statistical Yearbook.*

World Health Organization, Office of Publications, Avenue Appia, CH-1211 Geneva 27, Switzerland (Telephone Number in U.S. (518) 436-9686); *World Health Statistics Annual.*

ISRAEL - WAGES

G.K. Hall and Company, 70 Lincoln Street, Boston, Massachusetts 02111 (617) 423-3990; *The World in Figures.*

International Labour Office, I.L.O. Publications, CH-1211, Geneva 22, Switzerland; *Yearbook of Labour Statistics.*

Statistical Office of the United Nations, Publishing Service, New York, New York 10017 (800) 253-9646; *Statistical Yearbook.*

ISRAEL - WATERMELON PRODUCTION - See ISRAEL - CROPS

ISRAEL - WEATHER

Facts on File, 460 Park Avenue South, New York, New York 10016 (800) 443-8323; *The New Book of World Rankings.*

G.K. Hall and Company, 70 Lincoln Street, Boston, Massachusetts 02111 (617) 423-3990; *The World in Figures.*

ISRAEL - WELFARE EXPENDITURES

International Monetary Fund, 700 Nineteenth Street, NW, Washington, D.C. 20431 (202) 623-7000; *Government Finance Statistics Yearbook.*

ISRAEL - WHEAT PRODUCTION AND PRICES - See ISRAEL - CROPS

ISRAEL - WHOLESALE PRICES

International Monetary Fund, 700 Nineteenth Street, NW, Washington, D.C. 20431 (202) 623-7000; *International Financial Statistics.*

Statistical Office of the United Nations, Publishing Service, New York, New York 10017 (800) 253-9646; *Statistical Yearbook.*

ISRAEL - WHOLESALE TRADE

Statistical Office of the United Nations, Publishing Service, New York, New York 10017 (800) 253-9646; *Statistical Yearbook.*

ISRAEL - WINE PRODUCTION

Facts on File, 460 Park Avenue South, New York, New York 10016 (800) 443-8323; *The New Book of World Rankings.*

Statistical Office of the United Nations, Publishing Service, New York, New York 10017 (800) 253-9646; *Statistical Yearbook.*

ISRAEL - WOOD - See ISRAEL - FORESTRY AND FOREST PRODUCTS

ISRAEL - WOOL PRODUCTION

Facts on File, 460 Park Avenue South, New York, New York 10016 (800) 443-8323; *The New Book of World Rankings.*

Statistical Office of the United Nations, Publishing Service, New York, New York 10017 (800) 253-9646; *Statistical Yearbook.*

ISRAEL - YARN PRODUCTION

Statistical Office of the United Nations, Publishing Service, New York, New York 10017 (800) 253-9646; *Statistical Yearbook.*

ISRAEL - ZOOS AND BOTANICAL GARDENS

United Nations Educational, Scientific and Cultural Organization (UNESCO), 7 Place de Fontenoy, F-75700 Paris, France (Telephone Number in U.S. (212) 963-5981); *Statistical Yearbook.*

Italy - National Statistical Office

Instituto Nazionale di Statistica, Via Cesare Balbo 16, 00100 Rome, Italy (Telephone Number in U.S. (202) 653-2400).

Italy - Primary Statistics Sources

Instituto Nazionale di Statistica, Via Cesare Balbo 16, 00100 Rome, Italy (Telephone Number in U.S. (202) 653-2400); *Annuario Statistico Italiano, Bolletino Mensile di Statistica,* and *Compendio Statistico Italiano.*

ITALY - ABORTIONS

European Community Information Service, 2100 M Street, NW, Washington, D.C. 20037 (202) 862-9500; *Demographic Statistics.*

ITALY - AGRICULTURE

European Community Information Service, 2100 M Street, NW, Washington, D.C. 20037 (202) 862-9500; *Agriculture: Statistical Yearbook, Basic Statistics of the Community, Eurostatistics: Data for Short-Term Economic Analysis, Labor Force Sample Survey, Land Use Production,* and *Regions: Statistical Yearbook.*

Facts on File, 460 Park Avenue South, New York, New York 10016 (800) 443-8323; *The New Book of World Rankings.*

Food and Agricultural Organization of the United Nations (FAO), Via delle Terme di Caracalla, 00100 Rome, Italy (Telephone Number in U.S. (202) 653-2400); *Production Yearbook, The State of Food and Agriculture,* and *Trade Yearbook.*

G.K. Hall and Company, 70 Lincoln Street, Boston, Massachusetts 02111 (617) 423-3990; *The World in Figures.*

National Technical Information Service, 5285 Port Royal Road, Springfield, Virginia 22161 (703) 487-4600; *Handbook of Economic Statistics.*

Organisation for Economic Co-operation and Development (OECD), 2 rue Andre-Pascal, 75 Paris 16, France (Telephone Number in U.S. (202) 785-6323); *Economic Accounts for Agriculture, Indicators of Industrial Activity, Industrial Structure Statistics,* and *OECD Economic Surveys: Italy.*

Statistical Office of the United Nations, Publishing Service, New York, New York 10017 (800) 253-9646; *Statistical Yearbook.*

Times Books, 201 East 50th Street, New York, New York 10022 (212) 751-2600; *The Economist Book of Vital World Statistics.*

The World Bank, 1818 H Street, NW, Washington, D.C. 20433 (202) 477-1234; *World Tables.*

ITALY - AIRLINE SERVICE

European Community Information Service, 2100 M Street, NW, Washington, D.C. 20037 (202) 862-9500; *Basic Statistics of the Community, Regions: Statistical Yearbook,* and *Transport Annual Statistics.*

Facts on File, 460 Park Avenue South, New York, New York 10016 (800) 443-8323; *The New Book of World Rankings.*

G.K. Hall and Company, 70 Lincoln Street, Boston, Massachusetts 02111 (617) 423-3990; *The World in Figures.*

International Civil Aviation Organization, 1000 Sherbrooke Street West, Suite 400, Montreal, Quebec, Canada H3A 2R2 (514) 285-8219; *Civil Aviation Statistics of the World.*

National Technical Information Service, 5285 Port Royal Road, Springfield, Virginia 22161 (703) 487-4600; *Handbook of Economic Statistics.*

Organisation for Economic Co-operation and Development (OECD), 2 rue Andre-Pascal, 75 Paris 16, France (Telephone Number in U.S. (202) 785-6323); *Tourism Policy and International Tourism in OECD Member Countries.*

Statistical Office of the United Nations, Publishing Service, New York, New York 10017 (800) 253-9646; *Statistical Yearbook.*

Times Books, 201 East 50th Street, New York, New York 10022 (212) 751-2600; *The Economist Book of Vital World Statistics.*

ITALY - ALMOND PRODUCTION - See ITALY - CROPS

ITALY - ALUMINUM PRODUCTION AND CONSUMPTION - See ITALY - MINING AND MINERAL PRODUCTS

ITALY - ANIMAL FEEDINGSTUFFS

Organisation for Economic Co-operation and Development (OECD), 2 rue Andre-Pascal, 75 Paris 16, France (Telephone Number in U.S. (202) 785-6323); *Foreign Trade by Commodities.*

ITALY - ANIMAL HEALTH

Food and Agricultural Organization of the United Nations (FAO), Via delle Terme di Caracalla, 00100 Rome, Italy (Telephone Number in U.S. (202) 653-2400); *Animal Health Yearbook.*

ITALY - ANTIMONY AND ANTIMONY ORE - See ITALY - MINING AND MINERAL PRODUCTS

ITALY - APPLE PRODUCTION - See ITALY - CROPS

ITALY - AREA AND DENSITY OF POPULATION

European Community Information Service, 2100 M Street, NW, Washington, D.C. 20037 (202) 862-9500; *Basic Statistics of the Community* and *Demographic Statistics.*

Facts on File, 460 Park Avenue South, New York, New York 10016 (800) 443-8323; *The New Book of World Rankings.*

Food and Agricultural Organization of the United Nations (FAO) Via delle Terme di Caracalla, 00100 Rome, Italy (Telephone Number in U.S. (202) 653-2400); *The State of Food and Agriculture.*

G.K. Hall and Company, 70 Lincoln Street, Boston, Massachusetts 02111 (617) 423-3990; *The World in Figures.*

National Technical Information Service, 5285 Port Royal Road, Springfield, Virginia 22161 (703) 487-4600; *Handbook of Economic Statistics.*

Statistical Office of the United Nations, Publishing Service, New York, New York 10017 (800) 253-9646; *Statistical Yearbook.*

Times Books, 201 East 50th Street, New York, New York 10022 (212) 751-2600; *The Economist Book of Vital World Statistics.*

United Nations Educational, Scientific and Cultural Organization (UNESCO), 7 Place de Fontenoy, F-75700 Paris, France (Telephone Number in U.S. (212) 963-5981); *Statistical Yearbook.*

ITALY - ARMS EXPORTS AND IMPORTS

U.S. Arms Control and Disarmament Agency, 320 Twenty-first Street, Northwest, Washington, D.C. 20451 (202) 647-8677; *World Military Expenditures and Arms Transfers.*

ITALY - ARSENIC PRODUCTION AND CONSUMPTION - See ITALY - MINING AND MINERAL PRODUCTS

ITALY - ARTICHOKE PRODUCTION - See ITALY - CROPS

ITALY - BALANCE OF PAYMENTS

The Economist Intelligence Unit, 111 West 57th Street, New York, New York 10019 (800) 938-4685; *The World Market Atlas.*

European Community Information Service, 2100 M Street, NW, Washington, D.C. 20037 (202) 862-9500; *ACP: Basic Statistics, Basic Statistics of the Community, Energy Statistics Yearbook,* and *Eurostatistics: Data for Short-Term Economic Analysis.*

G.K. Hall and Company, 70 Lincoln Street, Boston, Massachusetts 02111 (617) 423-3990; *The World in Figures.*

International Monetary Fund, 700 Nineteenth Street, NW, Washington, D.C. 20431 (202) 623-7000; *Balance of Payments Yearbook,* and *International Financial Statistics.*

National Technical Information Service, 5285 Port Royal Road, Springfield, Virginia 22161 (703) 487-4600; *Handbook of Economic Statistics.*

Organisation for Economic Co-operation and Development (OECD), 2 rue Andre-Pascal, 75 Paris 16, France (Telephone Number in U.S. (202) 785-6323); *Economic Outlook, Geographical Distribution of Financial Flows to Developing Countries, Main Economic Indicators - Historical Statistics,* and *OECD Economic Surveys: Italy.*

Times Books, 201 East 50th Street, New York, New York 10022 (212) 751-2600; *The Economist Book of Vital World Statistics.*

The World Bank, 1818 H Street, NW, Washington, D.C. 20433 (202) 477-1234; *World Tables.*

ITALY - BANANA PRODUCTION - See ITALY - CROPS

ITALY - BANKING

European Community Information Service, 2100 M Street, NW, Washington, D.C. 20037 (202) 862-9500; *ACP: Basic Statistics.*

Facts on File, 460 Park Avenue South, New York, New York 10016 (800) 443-8323; *The New Book of World Rankings.*

G.K. Hall and Company, 70 Lincoln Street, Boston, Massachusetts 02111 (617) 423-3990; *The World in Figures.*

International Monetary Fund, 700 Nineteenth Street, NW, Washington, D.C. 20431 (202) 623-7000; *International Financial Statistics.*

National Technical Information Service, 5285 Port Royal Road, Springfield, Virginia 22161 (703) 487-4600; *Handbook of Economic Statistics.*

Organisation for Economic Co-operation and Development (OECD), 2 rue Andre-Pascal, 75 Paris 16, France (Telephone Number in U.S. (202) 785-6323); *Economic Outlook, Financial Market Trends,* and *OECD Economic Surveys: Italy.*

Statistical Office of the United Nations, Publishing Service, New York, New York 10017 (800) 253-9646; *Statistical Yearbook.*

ITALY - BARLEY PRODUCTION - See ITALY - CROPS

ITALY - BAUXITE PRODUCTION AND CONSUMPTION - See ITALY - MINING AND MINERAL PRODUCTS

ITALY - BEER PRODUCTION

Facts on File, 460 Park Avenue South, New York, New York 10016 (800) 443-8323; *The New Book of World Rankings.*

Statistical Office of the United Nations, Publishing Service, New York, New York 10017 (800) 253-9646; *Statistical Yearbook.*

ITALY - BEVERAGES - PRODUCTION INDEX

Organisation for Economic Co-operation and Development (OECD), 2 rue Andre-Pascal, 75 Paris 16, France (Telephone Number in U.S. (202) 785-6323); *Indicators of Industrial Activity.*

ITALY - BIRTH RATES

European Community Information Service, 2100 M Street, NW, Washington, D.C. 20037 (202) 862-9500; *Basic Statistics of the Community* and *Demographic Statistics.*

Facts on File, 460 Park Avenue South, New York, New York 10016 (800) 443-8323; *The New Book of World Rankings.*

Organisation for Economic Co-operation and Development (OECD), 2 rue Andre-Pascal, 75 Paris 16, France (Telephone Number in U.S. (202) 785-6323); *Labour Force Statistics.*

Statistical Office of the United Nations, Publishing Service, New York, New York 10017 (800) 253-9646; *Demographic Yearbook,* and *Statistical Yearbook.*

Times Books, 201 East 50th Street, New York, New York 10022 (212) 751-2600; *The Economist Book of Vital World Statistics.*

The World Bank, 1818 H Street, NW, Washington, D.C. 20433 (202) 477-1234; *World Tables.*

World Health Organization, Office of Publications, Avenue Appia, CH-1211 Geneva 27, Switzerland; *World Health Statistics Annual.*

ITALY - BISMUTH PRODUCTION AND CONSUMPTION - See ITALY - MINING AND MINERAL PRODUCTS

ITALY - BONDS

European Community Information Service, 2100 M Street, NW, Washington, D.C. 20037 (202) 862-9500; *Basic Statistics of the Community.*

G.K. Hall and Company, 70 Lincoln Street, Boston, Massachusetts 02111 (617) 423-3990; *The World in Figures.*

International Monetary Fund, 700 Nineteenth Street, NW, Washington, D.C. 20431 (202) 623-7000; *Government Finance Statistics Yearbook.*

Organisation for Economic Co-operation and Development (OECD), 2 rue Andre-Pascal, 75 Paris 16, France (Telephone Number in U.S. (202) 785-6323); *Financial Market Trends.*

Statistical Office of the United Nations, Publishing Service, New York, New York 10017 (800) 253-9646; *Statistical Yearbook.*

ITALY - BOOK PRODUCTION

Euromonitor Publications Limited, 87-88 Turnmill Street, London EC1M 5QU, England; *European Marketing Data and Statistics.*

G.K. Hall and Company, 70 Lincoln Street, Boston, Massachusetts 02111 (617) 423-3990; *The World in Figures.*

Organisation for Economic Co-operation and Development (OECD), 2 rue Andre-Pascal, 75 Paris 16, France (Telephone Number in U.S. (202) 785-6323); *Indicators of Industrial Activity.*

United Nations Educational, Scientific and Cultural Organization (UNESCO), 7 Place de Fontenoy, F-75700 Paris, France (Telephone Number in U.S. (212) 963-5981); *Statistical Yearbook.*

ITALY - BROADCASTING

Billboard Limited, Post Office Box 9027, 1006 AA Amsterdam, The Netherlands (Telephone Number in U.S. (212) 764-7300); *World Radio TV Handbook.*

European Community Information Service, 2100 M Street, NW, Washington, D.C. 20037 (202) 862-9500; *Basic Statistics of the Community.*

Facts on File, 460 Park Avenue South, New York, New York 10016 (800) 443-8323; *The New Book of World Rankings.*

G.K. Hall and Company, 70 Lincoln Street, Boston, Massachusetts 02111 (617) 423-3990; *The World in Figures.*

Times Books, 201 East 50th Street, New York, New York 10022 (212) 751-2600; *The Economist Book of Vital World Statistics.*

United Nations Educational, Scientific and Cultural Organization (UNESCO), 7 Place de Fontenoy, F-75700 Paris, France (Telephone Number in U.S. (212) 963-5981); *Statistical Yearbook.*

ITALY - BUSINESS

European Community Information Service, 2100 M Street, NW, Washington, D.C. 20037 (202) 862-9500; *Basic Statistics of the Community.*

G.K. Hall and Company, 70 Lincoln Street, Boston, Massachusetts 02111 (617) 423-3990; *The World in Figures.*

ITALY - BUTTER - See ITALY - DAIRY PRODUCTS

ITALY - CABBAGE PRODUCTION - See ITALY - CROPS

ITALY - CADMIUM PRODUCTION AND CONSUMPTION - See ITALY - MINING AND MINERAL PRODUCTS

ITALY - CALORIE SUPPLY

Food and Agricultural Organization of the United Nations (FAO) Via delle Terme di Caracalla, 00100 Rome, Italy (Telephone Number in U.S. (202) 653-2400); *The State of Food and Agriculture.*

ITALY - CAPITAL INVESTMENT

National Technical Information Service, 5285 Port Royal Road, Springfield, Virginia 22161 (703) 487-4600; *Handbook of Economic Statistics.*

Organisation for Economic Co-operation and Development (OECD), 2 rue Andre-Pascal, 75 Paris 16, France (Telephone Number in U.S. (202) 785-6323); *Economic Outlook,* and *Financial Market Trends.*

ITALY - CAPITAL REVENUE

International Monetary Fund, 700 Nineteenth Street, NW, Washington, D.C. 20431 (202) 623-7000; *Government Finance Statistics Yearbook.*

Organisation for Economic Co-operation and Development (OECD), 2 rue Andre-Pascal, 75 Paris 16, France (Telephone Number in U.S. (202) 785-6323); *Economic Outlook,* and *Financial Market Trends.*

ITALY - CASHEW PRODUCTION - See ITALY - CROPS

ITALY - CASTOR BEAN PRODUCTION - See ITALY - CROPS

ITALY - CATTLE - See ITALY - LIVESTOCK AND POULTRY

ITALY - CAULIFLOWER PRODUCTION - See ITALY - CROPS

ITALY - CAUSTIC SODA PRODUCTION

European Community Information Service, 2100 M Street, NW, Washington, D.C. 20037 (202) 862-9500; *Basic Statistics of the Community.*

National Technical Information Service, 5285 Port Royal Road, Springfield, Virginia 22161 (703) 487-4600; *Handbook of Economic Statistics.*

Organisation for Economic Co-operation and Development (OECD), 2 rue Andre-Pascal, 75 Paris 16, France (Telephone Number in U.S. (202) 785-6323); *Indicators of Industrial Activity.*

Statistical Office of the United Nations, Publishing Service, New York, New York 10017 (800) 253-9646; *Statistical Yearbook.*

ITALY - CEMENT PRODUCTION - See ITALY - MINING AND MINERAL PRODUCTS

ITALY - CEREAL PRODUCTION - See ITALY - CROPS

ITALY - CHEESE - See ITALY - DAIRY PRODUCTS

ITALY - CHEMICAL INDUSTRY

European Community Information Service, 2100 M Street, Northwest, Washington, D.C. 20037 (202) 862-9500; *Industrial Production: Quarterly Statistics.*

ITALY - CHEMICAL (ORGANIC) PRODUCTION - See ITALY - MINING AND MINERAL PRODUCTS

ITALY - CHESTNUT PRODUCTION - See ITALY - CROPS

ITALY - CHICKENS - See ITALY - LIVESTOCK AND POULTRY

ITALY - CHICK PEA PRODUCTION - See ITALY - CROPS

ITALY - CHROMITE PRODUCTION AND CONSUMPTION - See ITALY - MINING AND MINERAL PRODUCTS

ITALY - CHROMIUM ORE PRODUCTION AND CONSUMPTION - See ITALY - MINING AND MINERAL PRODUCTS

ITALY - CIGAR PRODUCTION - See ITALY - TOBACCO PRODUCTION

ITALY - CIGARETTE PRODUCTION - See ITALY - TOBACCO PRODUCTION

ITALY - CLASS STRUCTURE

European Community Information Service, 2100 M Street, NW, Washington, D.C. 20037 (202) 862-9500; *Labor Force Sample Survey.*

G.K. Hall and Company, 70 Lincoln Street, Boston, Massachusetts 02111 (617) 423-3990; *The World in Figures.*

ITALY - CLIMATE

Facts on File, 460 Park Avenue South, New York, New York 10016 (800) 443-8323; *The New Book of World Rankings.*

G.K. Hall and Company, 70 Lincoln Street, Boston, Massachusetts 02111 (617) 423-3990; *The World in Figures.*

ITALY - CLOTHING - PRODUCTION INDEX

Organisation for Economic Co-operation and Development (OECD), 2 rue Andre-Pascal, 75 Paris 16, France (Telephone Number in U.S. (202) 785-6323); *Indicators of Industrial Activity.*

ITALY - CLOTHING EXPORTS AND IMPORTS

European Community Information Service, 2100 M Street, NW, Washington, D.C. 20037 (202) 862-9500; *Basic Statistics of the Community.*

Organisation for Economic Co-operation and Development (OECD), 2 rue Andre-Pascal, 75 Paris 16, France (Telephone Number in U.S. (202) 785-6323); *Textile Industry in OECD Countries.*

ITALY - COAL PRODUCTION - See ITALY - MINING AND MINERAL PRODUCTS

ITALY - COBALT PRODUCTION AND CONSUMPTION - See ITALY - MINING AND MINERAL PRODUCTS

ITALY - COCOA (BEANS) PRODUCTION - See ITALY - CROPS

ITALY - COFFEE - See ITALY - CROPS

ITALY - COKE, COKE OVEN COKE AND COKE OVEN ORE - See ITALY - MINING AND MINERAL PRODUCTS

ITALY - COMMUNICATIONS

European Community Information Service, 2100 M Street, NW, Washington, D.C. 20037 (202) 862-9500; *Basic Statistics of the Community* and *Transport Annual Statistics.*

G.K. Hall and Company, 70 Lincoln Street, Boston, Massachusetts 02111 (617) 423-3990; *The World in Figures.*

ITALY - CONSTRUCTION INDUSTRY

European Community Information Service, 2100 M Street, NW, Washington, D.C. 20037 (202) 862-9500; *Basic Statistics of the Community,* and *Labor Force Sample Survey.*

Facts on File, 460 Park Avenue South, New York, New York 10016 (800) 443-8323; *The New Book of World Rankings.*

Organisation for Economic Co-operation and Development (OECD), 2 rue Andre-Pascal, 75 Paris 16, France (Telephone Number in U.S. (202) 785-6323); *Industrial Structure Statistics, The Iron and Steel Industry, Main Economic Indicators - Historical Statistics,* and *OECD Economic Surveys: Italy.*

Statistical Office of the United Nations, Publishing Service, New York, New York 10017 (800) 253-9646; *Construction Statistics Yearbook,* and *Statistical Yearbook.*

ITALY - CONSUMER PRICE INDEX

European Community Information Service, 2100 M Street, NW, Washington, D.C. 20037 (202) 862-9500; *Basic Statistics of the Community* and *Eurostatistics: Data for Short-Term Economic Analysis.*

G.K. Hall and Company, 70 Lincoln Street, Boston, Massachusetts 02111 (617) 423-3990; *The World in Figures.*

National Technical Information Service, 5285 Port Royal Road, Springfield, Virginia 22161 (703) 487-4600; *Handbook of Economic Statistics.*

Organisation for Economic Co-operation and Development (OECD), 2 rue Andre-Pascal, 75 Paris 16, France (Telephone Number in U.S. (202) 785-6323); *Economic Outlook.*

Statistical Office of the United Nations, Publishing Service, New York, New York 10017 (800) 253-9646; *Statistical Yearbook.*

ITALY - CONSUMER PRICES

Euromonitor Publications Limited, 87-88 Turnmill Street, London EC1M 5QU, England; *European Marketing Data and Statistics.*

European Community Information Service, 2100 M Street, NW, Washington, D.C. 20037 (202) 862-9500; *Basic Statistics of the Community* and *Money and Finance.*

International Labour Office, I.L.O. Publications, CH-1211, Geneva 22, Switzerland; *Yearbook of Labour Statistics.*

International Monetary Fund, 700 Nineteenth Street, NW, Washington, D.C. 20431 (202) 623-7000; *International Financial Statistics.*

Organisation for Economic Co-operation and Development (OECD), 2 rue Andre-Pascal, 75 Paris 16, France (Telephone Number in U.S. (202) 785-6323); *Economic Outlook.*

Times Books, 201 East 50th Street, New York, New York 10022 (212) 751-2600; *The Economist Book of Vital World Statistics.*

ITALY - CONSUMPTION

European Community Information Service, 2100 M Street, NW, Washington, D.C. 20037 (202) 862-9500; *Basic Statistics of the Community.*

G.K. Hall and Company, 70 Lincoln Street, Boston, Massachusetts 02111 (617) 423-3990; *The World in Figures.*

International Iron and Steel Institute, 120, rue Colonel Bourg, B-1140, Brussels, Belgium; *Steel Statistical Yearbook.*

International Lead and Zinc Study Group, Metro House, 58 St. James's Street, London SW1A 1LD, England; *Lead and Zinc Statistics.*

International Monetary Fund, 700 Nineteenth Street, NW, Washington, D.C. 20431 (202) 623-7000; *International Financial Statistics.*

International Rubber Study Group, York House, 8th Floor, Empire Way, Wembley, London HA9 0PA, England; *World Rubber Statistics Handbook.*

National Technical Information Service, 5285 Port Royal Road, Springfield, Virginia 22161 (703) 487-4600; *Handbook of Economic Statistics.*

Organisation for Economic Co-operation and Development (OECD), 2 rue Andre-Pascal, 75 Paris 16, France (Telephone Number in U.S. (202) 785-6323); *The Footwear, Raw Hides and Skins, and Leather Industry in OECD Countries, The Iron and Steel Industry, Meat Balances in OECD Member Countries, The Non-Ferrous Metals Industry, The Pulp and Paper Industry,* and *Textile Industry in OECD Countries.*

ITALY - COPPER AND COPPER ORE - See ITALY - MINING AND MINERAL PRODUCTS

ITALY - CORN PRODUCTION - See ITALY - CROPS

ITALY - CORPORATE INCOME TAXES - See ITALY - TAXATION

ITALY - CORPORATE TAXES - See ITALY - TAXATION

ITALY - COTTON - See ITALY - CROPS

ITALY - CRIME

Yale University Press, Yale Station, New Haven, Connecticut 06520 (203) 432-0940; *Violence and Crime in Cross-National Perspective.*

ITALY - CROPS

Commodity Research Bureau, Incorporated, 75 Wall Street, New York, New York 10005 (212) 504-7754; *Commodity Year Book.*

European Community Information Service, 2100 M Street, NW, Washington, D.C. 20037 (202) 862-9500; *ACP: Basic Statistics, Agriculture: Statistical Yearbook, Basic Statistics of the Community, Crop Production: Quarterly Statistics, Eurostatistics: Data for Short-Term Economic Analysis,* and *Regions: Statistical Yearbook.*

Euromonitor Publications Limited, 87-88 Turnmill Street, London EC1M 5QU, England; *European Marketing Data and Statistics.*

Facts on File, 460 Park Avenue South, New York, New York 10016 (800) 443-8323; *The New Book of World Rankings.*

Food and Agricultural Organization of the United Nations (FAO), Via delle Terme di Caracalla, 00100 Rome, Italy (Telephone Number in U.S. (202) 653-2400); *Production Yearbook* and *The State of Food and Agriculture.*

G.K. Hall and Company, 70 Lincoln Street, Boston, Massachusetts 02111 (617) 423-3990; *The World in Figures.*

National Technical Information Service, 5285 Port Royal Road, Springfield, Virginia 22161 (703) 487-4600; *Handbook of Economic Statistics.*

Organisation for Economic Co-operation and Development (OECD), 2 rue Andre-Pascal, 75 Paris 16, France (Telephone Number in U.S. (202) 785-6323); *Economic Accounts for Agriculture, Foreign Trade by Commodities,* and *Textile Industry in OECD Countries.*

Statistical Office of the United Nations, Publishing Service, New York, New York 10017 (800) 253-9646; *Statistical Yearbook.*

ITALY - CUSTOMS DUTIES

European Community Information Service, 2100 M Street, NW, Washington, D.C. 20037 (202) 862-9500; *Basic Statistics of the Community.*

G.K. Hall and Company, 70 Lincoln Street, Boston, Massachusetts 02111 (617) 423-3990; *The World in Figures.*

International Monetary Fund, 700 Nineteenth Street, NW, Washington, D.C. 20431 (202) 623-7000; *Government Finance Statistics Yearbook.*

Organisation for Economic Co-operation and Development (OECD), 2 rue Andre-Pascal, 75 Paris 16, France (Telephone Number in U.S. (202) 785-6323); *The Non-Ferrous Metals Industry.*

ITALY - DAIRY PRODUCTS

Commodity Research Bureau, Incorporated, 75 Wall Street, New York, New York 10005 (212) 504-7754; *Commodity Year Book.*

European Community Information Service, 2100 M Street, NW, Washington, D.C. 20037 (202) 862-9500; *Basic Statistics of the Community* and *Eurostatistics: Data for Short-Term Economic Analysis.*

Facts on File, 460 Park Avenue South, New York, New York 10016 (800) 443-8323; *The New Book of World Rankings.*

Food and Agricultural Organization of the United Nations (FAO), Via delle Terme di Caracalla, 00100 Rome, Italy (Telephone Number in U.S. (202) 653-2400); *Production Yearbook* and *The State of Food and Agriculture.*

National Technical Information Service, 5285 Port Royal Road, Springfield, Virginia 22161 (703) 487-4600; *Handbook of Economic Statistics.*

Organisation for Economic Co-operation and Development (OECD), 2 rue Andre-Pascal, 75 Paris 16, France (Telephone Number in U.S. (202) 785-6323); *Economic Accounts for Agriculture,* and *Milk, Milk Products, and Egg Balances in OECD Member Countries.*

Statistical Office of the United Nations, Publishing Service, New York, New York 10017 (800) 253-9646; *Statistical Yearbook.*

ITALY - DEATH RATE

European Community Information Service, 2100 M Street, NW, Washington, D.C. 20037 (202) 862-9500; *Basic Statistics of the Community, Demographic Statistics.*

G.K. Hall and Company, 70 Lincoln Street, Boston, Massachusetts 02111 (617) 423-3990; *The World in Figures.*

Statistical Office of the United Nations, Publishing Service, New York, New York 10017 (800) 253-9646; *Statistical Yearbook.*

Times Books, 201 East 50th Street, New York, New York 10022 (212) 751-2600; *The Economist Book of Vital World Statistics.*

World Health Organization, Office of Publications, Avenue Appia, CH-1211 Geneva 27, Switzerland (Telephone Number in U.S. (518) 436-9686); *World Health Statistics Annual.*

ITALY - DEFENSE EXPENDITURES

European Community Information Service, 2100 M Street, NW, Washington, D.C. 20037 (202) 862-9500; *Government Financing of Research and Development.*

G.K. Hall and Company, 70 Lincoln Street, Boston, Massachusetts 02111 (617) 423-3990; *The World in Figures.*

International Monetary Fund, 700 Nineteenth Street, NW, Washington, D.C. 20431 (202) 623-7000; *Government Finance Statistics Yearbook.*

National Technical Information Service, 5285 Port Royal Road, Springfield, Virginia 22161 (703) 487-4600; *Handbook of Economic Statistics.*

U.S. Arms Control and Disarmament Agency, 320 Twenty-first Street, Northwest, Washington, D.C. 20451 (202) 647-8677; *World Military Expenditures and Arms Transfers.*

ITALY - DEMOGRAPHY

The Economist Intelligence Unit, 111 West 57th Street, New York, New York 10019 (800) 938-4685; *The World Market Atlas.*

European Community Information Service, 2100 M Street, NW, Washington, D.C. 20037 (202) 862-9500; *Basic Statistics of the Community, Demographic Statistics, Employment and Unemployment,* and *Regions: Statistical Yearbook.*

Facts on File, 460 Park Avenue South, New York, New York 10016 (800) 443-8323; *The New Book of World Rankings.*

G.K. Hall and Company, 70 Lincoln Street, Boston, Massachusetts 02111 (617) 423-3990; *The World in Figures.*

ITALY - DEVELOPMENT ASSISTANCE

European Community Information Service, 2100 M Street, NW, Washington, D.C. 20037 (202) 862-9500; *ACP: Basic Statistics, Basic Statistics of the Community,* and *Government Financing of Research and Development.*

G.K. Hall and Company, 70 Lincoln Street, Boston, Massachusetts 02111 (617) 423-3990; *The World in Figures.*

Organisation for Economic Co-operation and Development (OECD), 2 rue Andre-Pascal, 75 Paris 16, France (Telephone Number in U.S. (202) 785-6323); *Geographical Distribution of Financial Flows to Developing Countries.*

Statistical Office of the United Nations, Publishing Service, New York, New York 10017 (800) 253-9646; *Statistical Yearbook.*

ITALY - DIAMOND - See ITALY - MINING AND MINERAL PRODUCTS

ITALY - DISCOUNT RATES

Organisation for Economic Co-operation and Development (OECD), 2 rue Andre-Pascal, 75 Paris 16, France (Telephone Number in U.S. (202) 785-6323); *Financial Market Trends.*

Statistical Office of the United Nations, Publishing Service, New York, New York 10017 (800) 253-9646; *Statistical Yearbook.*

ITALY - DISEASES

G.K. Hall and Company, 70 Lincoln Street, Boston, Massachusetts 02111 (617) 423-3990; *The World in Figures.*

World Health Organization, Office of Publications, Avenue Appia, CH-1211 Geneva 27, Switzerland (Telephone Number in U.S. (518) 436-9686); *World Health Statistics Annual.*

ITALY - DIVORCE RATES

European Community Information Service, 2100 M Street, NW, Washington, D.C. 20037 (202) 862-9500; *Demographic Statistics.*

Facts on File, 460 Park Avenue South, New York, New York 10016 (800) 443-8323; *The New Book of World Rankings.*

Statistical Office of the United Nations, Publishing Service, New York, New York 10017 (800) 253-9646; *Demographic Yearbook,* and *Statistical Yearbook.*

ITALY - DOMESTIC PRODUCT

European Community Information Service, 2100 M Street, NW, Washington, D.C. 20037 (202) 862-9500; *Basic Statistics of the Community.*

G.K. Hall and Company, 70 Lincoln Street, Boston, Massachusetts 02111 (617) 423-3990; *The World in Figures.*

ITALY - DUCKS - See ITALY - LIVESTOCK AND POULTRY

ITALY - ECONOMY

Euromonitor Publications Limited, 87-88 Turnmill Street, London EC1M 5QU, England; *European Marketing Data and Statistics.*

European Community Information Service, 2100 M Street, NW, Washington, D.C. 20037 (202) 862-9500; *ACP: Basic Statistics, Basic Statistics of the Community, Energy Statistics Yearbook, Labor Force Sample Survey,* and *Money and Finance.*

Facts on File, 460 Park Avenue South, New York, New York 10016 (800) 443-8323; *The New Book of World Rankings.*

G.K. Hall and Company, 70 Lincoln Street, Boston, Massachusetts 02111 (617) 423-3990; *The World in Figures.*

International Monetary Fund, 700 Nineteenth Street, NW, Washington, D.C. 20431 (202) 623-7000; *International Financial Statistics.*

National Technical Information Service, 5285 Port Royal Road, Springfield, Virginia 22161 (703) 487-4600; *Handbook of Economic Statistics.*

Organisation for Economic Co-operation and Development (OECD), 2 rue Andre-Pascal, 75 Paris 16, France (Telephone Number in U.S.

(202) 785-6323); *Economic Outlook, Geographical Distribution of Financial Flows to Developing Countries, OECD Economic Surveys: Italy,* and *OECD Employment Outlook.*

ITALY - EDUCATION

The Economist Intelligence Unit, 111 West 57th Street, New York, New York 10019 (800) 938-4685; *The World Market Atlas.*

Euromonitor Publications Limited, 87-88 Turnmill Street, London EC1M 5QU, England; *European Marketing Data and Statistics.*

European Community Information Service, 2100 M Street, NW, Washington, D.C. 20037 (202) 862-9500; *Basic Statistics of the Community* and *Regions: Statistical Yearbook.*

Facts on File, 460 Park Avenue South, New York, New York 10016 (800) 443-8323; *The New Book of World Rankings.*

G.K. Hall and Company, 70 Lincoln Street, Boston, Massachusetts 02111 (617) 423-3990; *The World in Figures.*

International Monetary Fund, 700 Nineteenth Street, NW, Washington, D.C. 20431 (202) 623-7000; *Government Finance Statistics Yearbook.*

Organisation for Economic Co-operation and Development (OECD), 2 rue Andre-Pascal, 75 Paris 16, France (Telephone Number in U.S. (202) 785-6323); *Education in OECD Countries.*

Times Books, 201 East 50th Street, New York, New York 10022 (212) 751-2600; *The Economist Book of Vital World Statistics.*

United Nations Educational, Scientific and Cultural Organization (UNESCO), 7 Place de Fontenoy, F-75700 Paris, France (Telephone Number in U.S. (212) 963-5981); *Statistical Yearbook.*

The World Bank, 1818 H Street, NW, Washington, D.C. 20433 (202) 477-1234; *World Tables.*

ITALY - EGG PRODUCTION AND CONSUMPTION - See ITALY - DAIRY PRODUCTS

ITALY - EGGPLANT PRODUCTION - See ITALY - CROPS

ITALY - ELECTRICITY

Commodity Research Bureau, Incorporated, 75 Wall Street, New York, New York 10005 (212) 504-7754; *Commodity Year Book.*

European Community Information Service, 2100 M Street, NW, Washington, D.C. 20037 (202) 862-9500; *Basic Statistics of the Community, Energy: Monthly Statistics, Energy Statistics Yearbook, Eurostatistics: Data for Short-Term Economic Analysis,* and *Regions: Statistical Yearbook.*

Facts on File, 460 Park Avenue South, New York, New York 10016 (800) 443-8323; *The New Book of World Rankings.*

National Technical Information Service, 5285 Port Royal Road, Springfield, Virginia 22161 (703) 487-4600; *Handbook of Economic Statistics.*

Organisation for Economic Co-operation and Development (OECD), 2 rue Andre-Pascal, 75 Paris 16, France (Telephone Number in U.S. (202) 785-6323); *Coal Information, Energy Statistics of OECD Countries, Indicators of Industrial Activity,* and *Industrial Structure Statistics.*

Penn Well Publishing Company, 1421 South Sheridan Road, Post Office Box 1260, Tulsa, Oklahoma 74101 (800) 752-9764; *International Energy Statistics Sourcebook.*

Times Books, 201 East 50th Street, New York, New York 10022 (212) 751-2600; *The Economist Book of Vital World Statistics.*

ITALY - EMPLOYMENT

Euromonitor Publications Limited, 87-88 Turnmill Street, London EC1M 5QU, England; *European Marketing Data and Statistics.*

European Community Information Service, 2100 M Street, NW, Washington, D.C. 20037 (202) 862-9500; *Basic Statistics of the Community, Earnings in Agriculture, Employment and Unemployment, Eurostatistics: Data for Short-Term Economic Analysis, Iron and Steel: Statistical Yearbook,* and *Labor Force Sample Survey.*

Facts on File, 460 Park Avenue South, New York, New York 10016 (800) 443-8323; *The New Book of World Rankings.*

International Labour Office, I.L.O. Publications, CH-1211, Geneva 22, Switzerland; *Yearbook of Labour Statistics.*

National Technical Information Service, 5285 Port Royal Road, Springfield, Virginia 22161 (703) 487-4600; *Handbook of Economic Statistics.*

Organisation for Economic Co-operation and Development (OECD), 2 rue Andre-Pascal, 75 Paris 16, France (Telephone Number in U.S. (202) 785-6323); *Economic Outlook, The Iron and Steel Industry, OECD Economic Surveys: Italy, OECD Employment Outlook,* and *Textile Industry in OECD Countries.*

Statistical Office of the United Nations, Publishing Service, New York, New York 10017; *Statistical Yearbook.*

ITALY - ENERGY

Euromonitor Publications Limited, 87-88 Turnmill Street, London EC1M 5QU, England; *European Marketing Data and Statistics.*

European Community Information Service, 2100 M Street, NW, Washington, D.C. 20037 (202) 862-9500; *Basic Statistics of the Community, Energy: Monthly Statistics, Energy Statistics Yearbook, Labor Force Sample Survey, Regions: Statistical Yearbook,* and *Transport Annual Statistics.*

Facts on File, 460 Park Avenue South, New York, New York 10016 (800) 443-8323; *The New Book of World Rankings.*

G.K. Hall and Company, 70 Lincoln Street, Boston, Massachusetts 02111 (617) 423-3990; *The World in Figures.*

National Technical Information Service, 5285 Port Royal Road, Springfield, Virginia 22161 (703) 487-4600; *Handbook of Economic Statistics.*

Organisation for Economic Co-operation and Development (OECD), 2 rue Andre-Pascal, 75 Paris 16, France (Telephone Number in U.S. (202) 785-6323); *Coal Information, Energy Statistics of OECD Countries, OECD Environmental Data,* and *Oil and Gas Information.*

Penn Well Publishing Company, 1421 South Sheridan Road, Post Office Box 1260, Tulsa, Oklahoma 74101 (800) 752-9764; *International Energy Statistics Sourcebook.*

Statistical Office of the United Nations, Publishing Service, New York, New York 10017 (800) 253-9646; *Energy Statistics Yearbook*, *Statistical Yearbook*, and *World Energy Supplies*.

ITALY - ENGINEERING AND METAL PRODUCTS - EXPORTS AND IMPORTS

European Community Information Service, 2100 M Street, NW, Washington, D.C. 20037 (202) 862-9500; *Basic Statistics of the Community* and *Industrial Production: Quarterly Statistics*.

Statistical Office of the United Nations, Publishing Service, New York, New York 10017 (800) 253-9646; *Trade in Manufactures of Developing Countries*.

ITALY - ENVIRONMENT

Organisation for Economic Co-operation and Development (OECD), 2 rue Andre-Pascal, 75 Paris 16, France (Telephone Number in U.S. (202) 785-6323); *OECD Environmental Data*.

ITALY - EXCHANGE RATES

European Community Information Service, 2100 M Street, NW, Washington, D.C. 20037 (202) 862-9500; *Eurostatistics: Data for Short-Term Economic Analysis* and *Money and Finance*.

International Civil Aviation Organization, 1000 Sherbrooke Street West, Suite 400, Montreal, Quebec, Canada H3A 2R2 (514) 285-8219; *Civil Aviation Statistics of the World*.

International Monetary Fund, 700 Nineteenth Street, NW, Washington, D.C. 20431 (202) 623-7000; *International Financial Statistics*.

National Technical Information Service, 5285 Port Royal Road, Springfield, Virginia 22161 (703) 487-4600; *Handbook of Economic Statistics*.

Organisation for Economic Co-operation and Development (OECD), 2 rue Andre-Pascal, 75 Paris 16, France (Telephone Number in U.S. (202) 785-6323); *Economic Outlook*, *Financial Market Trends*, *Revenue Statistics of OECD Member Countries*, and *Tourism Policy and International Tourism in OECD Member Countries*.

Statistical Office of the United Nations, Publishing Service, New York, New York 10017 (800) 253-9646; *Statistical Yearbook*.

ITALY - EXCISE TAXES - See ITALY - TAXATION

ITALY - EXPORTS

American Automobile Manufacturers Association, 1401 H Street, NW, Suite 900, Washington, D.C. 20005 (202) 326-5500; *World Motor Vehicle Data*.

The Economist Intelligence Unit, 111 West 57th Street, New York, New York 10019 (800) 938-4685; *The World Market Atlas*.

European Community Information Service, 2100 M Street, NW, Washington, D.C. 20037 (202) 862-9500; *Basic Statistics of the Community*, *Energy: Monthly Statistics*, *Energy Statistics Yearbook*, *Eurostatistics: Data for Short-Term Economic Analysis*, *External Trade: Monthly Statistics*, *External Trade: Statistical Yearbook*, and *Fisheries: Yearly Statistics*.

Food and Agricultural Organization of the United Nations (FAO) Via delle Terme di Caracalla, 00100 Rome, Italy (Telephone Number in U.S. (202) 653-2400); *The State of Food and Agriculture*.

G.K. Hall and Company, 70 Lincoln Street, Boston, Massachusetts 02111 (617) 423-3990; *The World in Figures*.

International Iron and Steel Institute, 120, rue Colonel Bourg, B-1140, Brussels, Belgium; *Steel Statistical Yearbook*.

International Lead and Zinc Study Group, Metro House, 58 St. James's Street, London SW1A 1LD, England; *Lead and Zinc Statistics*.

International Monetary Fund, 700 Nineteenth Street, NW, Washington, D.C. 20431 (202) 623-7000; *Direction of Trade Statistics*, *Government Finance Statistics Yearbook*, and *International Financial Statistics*.

International Rubber Study Group, York House, 8th Floor, Empire Way, Wembley, London HA9 0PA, England; *World Rubber Statistics Handbook*.

National Technical Information Service, 5285 Port Royal Road, Springfield, Virginia 22161 (703) 487-4600; *Handbook of Economic Statistics*.

Organisation for Economic Co-operation and Development (OECD), 2 rue Andre-Pascal, 75 Paris 16, France (Telephone Number in U.S. (202) 785-6323); *Economic Outlook*, *The Footwear, Raw Hides and Skins, and Leather Industry in OECD Countries*, *Foreign Trade by Commodities*, *Geographical Distribution of Financial Flows to Developing Countries*, *Indicators of Industrial Activity*, *The Iron and Steel Industry*, *Milk, Milk Products, and Egg Balances in OECD Member Countries*, *OECD Economic Surveys: Italy*, *The Pulp and Paper Industry*, and *Review of Fisheries in OECD Member Countries*.

Times Books, 201 East 50th Street, New York, New York 10022 (212) 751-2600; *The Economist Book of Vital World Statistics*.

The World Bank, 1818 H Street, NW, Washington, D.C. 20433 (202) 477-1234; *World Tables*.

ITALY - EXTERNAL FINANCING

Organisation for Economic Co-operation and Development (OECD), 2 rue Andre-Pascal, 75 Paris 16, France (Telephone Number in U.S. (202) 785-6323); *Economic Outlook*, and *Financial Market Trends*.

ITALY - EXTERNAL INDEBTEDNESS

National Technical Information Service, 5285 Port Royal Road, Springfield, Virginia 22161 (703) 487-4600; *Handbook of Economic Statistics*.

Organisation for Economic Co-operation and Development (OECD), 2 rue Andre-Pascal, 75 Paris 16, France (Telephone Number in U.S. (202) 785-6323); *Financial Market Trends*, and *Geographical Distribution of Financial Flows to Developing Countries*.

The World Bank, 1818 H Street, NW, Washington, D.C. 20433 (202) 477-1234; *World Tables*.

ITALY - EXTERNAL TRADE

European Community Information Service, 2100 M Street, NW, Washington, D.C. 20037 (202) 862-9500; *ACP: Basic Statistics*, *Basic Statistics of the Community*, *Eurostatistics: Data for Short-Term Economic Analysis*, and *External Trade: Monthly Statistics*, *External Trade: Statistical Yearbook*.

Food and Agricultural Organization of the United Nations (FAO) Via delle Terme di Caracalla, 00100 Rome, Italy (Telephone Number in U.S. (202) 653-2400); *The State of Food and Agriculture*, and *Trade Yearbook*.

G.K. Hall and Company, 70 Lincoln Street, Boston, Massachusetts 02111 (617) 423-3990; *The World in Figures*.

National Technical Information Service, 5285 Port Royal Road, Springfield, Virginia 22161 (703) 487-4600; *Handbook of Economic Statistics*.

Statistical Office of the United Nations, Publishing Service, New York, New York 10017 (800) 253-9646; *Statistical Yearbook*.

ITALY - FABRIC PRODUCTION - See ITALY - TEXTILE INDUSTRY

ITALY - FARM CROPS - See ITALY - CROPS

ITALY - FEMALE WORKING POPULATION - See ITALY - EMPLOYMENT

ITALY - FERTILITY RATES

European Community Information Service, 2100 M Street, NW, Washington, D.C. 20037 (202) 862-9500; *Demographic Statistics*.

Facts on File, 460 Park Avenue South, New York, New York 10016 (800) 443-8323; *The New Book of World Rankings*.

Times Books, 201 East 50th Street, New York, New York 10022 (212) 751-2600; *The Economist Book of Vital World Statistics*.

The World Bank, 1818 H Street, NW, Washington, D.C. 20433 (202) 477-1234; *World Tables*.

ITALY - FERTILIZER

European Community Information Service, 2100 M Street, NW, Washington, D.C. 20037 (202) 862-9500; *Basic Statistics of the Community*.

Food and Agricultural Organization of the United Nations (FAO), Via delle Terme di Caracalla, 00100 Rome, Italy (Telephone Number in U.S. (202) 653-2400); *Fertilizer Yearbook*, and *The State of Food and Agriculture*.

National Technical Information Service, 5285 Port Royal Road, Springfield, Virginia 22161 (703) 487-4600; *Handbook of Economic Statistics*.

Organisation for Economic Co-operation and Development (OECD), 2 rue Andre-Pascal, 75 Paris 16, France (Telephone Number in U.S. (202) 785-6323); *Economic Accounts for Agriculture*, and *Foreign Trade by Commodities*.

Statistical Office of the United Nations, Publishing Service, New York, New York 10017 (800) 253-9646; *Statistical Yearbook*.

ITALY - FETAL MORTALITY

European Community Information Service, 2100 M Street, NW, Washington, D.C. 20037 (202) 862-9500; *Basic Statistics of the Community*, *Demographic Statistics*.

Statistical Office of the United Nations, Publishing Service, New York, New York 10017 (800) 253-9646; *Demographic Yearbook*.

World Health Organization, Office of Publications, Avenue Appia, CH-1211 Geneva 27, Switzerland; *World Health Statistics Annual*.

ITALY - FIBRE PRODUCTION - See ITALY - TEXTILE INDUSTRY

ITALY - FILAMENT PRODUCTION - See ITALY - TEXTILE INDUSTRY

ITALY - FILM - See ITALY - MOTION PICTURES

ITALY - FINANCE

European Community Information Service, 2100 M Street, NW, Washington, D.C. 20037 (202) 862-9500; *ACP: Basic Statistics*, *Basic Statistics of the Community*, *Eurostatistics: Data for Short-Term Economic Analysis*, and *Money and Finance*.

Facts on File, 460 Park Avenue South, New York, New York 10016 (800) 443-8323; *The New Book of World Rankings*.

G.K. Hall and Company, 70 Lincoln Street, Boston, Massachusetts 02111 (617) 423-3990; *The World in Figures*.

International Monetary Fund, 700 Nineteenth Street, NW, Washington, D.C. 20431 (202) 623-7000; *Government Finance Statistics Yearbook*, and *International Financial Statistics*.

Organisation for Economic Co-operation and Development (OECD), 2 rue Andre-Pascal, 75 Paris 16, France (Telephone Number in U.S. (202) 785-6323); *Economic Outlook*, *Financial Market Trends*, *Geographical Distribution of Financial Flows to Developing Countries*, and *OECD Financial Statistics*.

ITALY - FISHERIES

Euromonitor Publications Limited, 87-88 Turnmill Street, London EC1M 5QU, England; *European Marketing Data and Statistics*.

European Community Information Service, 2100 M Street, NW, Washington, D.C. 20037 (202) 862-9500; *Agriculture: Statistical Yearbook*, *Basic Statistics of the Community* and *Fisheries: Yearly Statistics*.

Facts on File, 460 Park Avenue South, New York, New York 10016 (800) 443-8323; *The New Book of World Rankings*.

Food and Agricultural Organization of the United Nations (FAO) Via delle Terme di Caracalla, 00100 Rome, Italy (Telephone Number in U.S. (202) 653-2400); *The State of Food and Agriculture*, and *Yearbook of Fishery Statistics*.

National Technical Information Service, 5285 Port Royal Road, Springfield, Virginia 22161 (703) 487-4600; *Handbook of Economic Statistics*.

Organisation for Economic Co-operation and Development (OECD), 2 rue Andre-Pascal, 75 Paris 16, France (Telephone Number in U.S. (202) 785-6323); *Foreign Trade by Commodities*, *Indicators of Industrial Activity*, and *Review of Fisheries in OECD Member Countries*.

Statistical Office of the United Nations, Publishing Service, New York, New York 10017 (800) 253-9646; *Statistical Yearbook*.

ITALY - FLAX AND FLAX FIBRE PRODUCTION - See ITALY - TEXTILE INDUSTRY

ITALY - FLOUR PRODUCTION

European Community Information Service, 2100 M Street, NW, Washington, D.C. 20037 (202) 862-9500; *Basic Statistics of the Community.*

Statistical Office of the United Nations, Publishing Service, New York, New York 10017 (800) 253-9646; *Statistical Yearbook.*

ITALY - FOOD

European Community Information Service, 2100 M Street, NW, Washington, D.C. 20037 (202) 862-9500; *Basic Statistics of the Community.*

Food and Agricultural Organization of the United Nations (FAO), Via delle Terme di Caracalla, 00100 Rome, Italy (Telephone Number in U.S. (202) 653-2400); *Production Yearbook,* and *The State of Food and Agriculture.*

G.K. Hall and Company, 70 Lincoln Street, Boston, Massachusetts 02111 (617) 423-3990; *The World in Figures.*

Organisation for Economic Co-operation and Development (OECD), 2 rue Andre-Pascal, 75 Paris 16, France (Telephone Number in U.S. (202) 785-6323); *Food Consumption Statistics* and *Foreign Trade by Commodities.*

ITALY - FOOTWEAR - PRODUCTION INDEX

Organisation for Economic Co-operation and Development (OECD), 2 rue Andre-Pascal, 75 Paris 16, France (Telephone Number in U.S. (202) 785-6323); *Indicators of Industrial Activity.*

ITALY - FOREIGN AID

G.K. Hall and Company, 70 Lincoln Street, Boston, Massachusetts 02111 (617) 423-3990; *The World in Figures.*

National Technical Information Service, 5285 Port Royal Road, Springfield, Virginia 22161 (703) 487-4600; *Handbook of Economic Statistics.*

ITALY - FOREIGN DEBT

Organisation for Economic Co-operation and Development (OECD), 2 rue Andre-Pascal, 75 Paris 16, France (Telephone Number in U.S. (202) 785-6323); *Economic Outlook.*

ITALY - FOREIGN FINANCE

Organisation for Economic Co-operation and Development (OECD), 2 rue Andre-Pascal, 75 Paris 16, France (Telephone Number in U.S. (202) 785-6323); *Economic Outlook, Financial Market Trends, Main Economic Indicators - Historical Statistics,* and *Meat Balances in OECD Member Countries.*

ITALY - FOREIGN INDEBTEDNESS

Organisation for Economic Co-operation and Development (OECD), 2 rue Andre-Pascal, 75 Paris 16, France (Telephone Number in U.S. (202) 785-6323); *Economic Outlook,* and *Financial Market Trends.*

ITALY - FOREIGN OFFICIAL RESERVES

European Community Information Service, 2100 M Street, NW, Washington, D.C. 20037 (202) 862-9500; *Money and Finance.*

ITALY - FOREIGN TRADE

Euromonitor Publications Limited, 87-88 Turnmill Street, London EC1M 5QU, England; *European Marketing Data and Statistics.*

European Community Information Service, 2100 M Street, NW, Washington, D.C. 20037 (202) 862-9500; *Basic Statistics of the Community, Energy Statistics Yearbook,* and *Iron and Steel: Statistical Yearbook.*

Facts on File, 460 Park Avenue South, New York, New York 10016 (800) 443-8323; *The New Book of World Rankings.*

Food and Agricultural Organization of the United Nations (FAO) Via delle Terme di Caracalla, 00100 Rome, Italy (Telephone Number in U.S. (202) 653-2400); *The State of Food and Agriculture.*

G.K. Hall and Company, 70 Lincoln Street, Boston, Massachusetts 02111 (617) 423-3990; *The World in Figures.*

International Iron and Steel Institute, 120, rue Colonel Bourg, B-1140, Brussels, Belgium; *Steel Statistical Yearbook.*

International Monetary Fund, 700 Nineteenth Street, NW, Washington, D.C. 20431 (202) 623-7000; *International Financial Statistics.*

National Technical Information Service, 5285 Port Royal Road, Springfield, Virginia 22161 (703) 487-4600; *Handbook of Economic Statistics.*

Organisation for Economic Co-operation and Development (OECD), 2 rue Andre-Pascal, 75 Paris 16, France (Telephone Number in U.S. (202) 785-6323); *Economic Outlook, The Footwear, Raw Hides and Skins, and Leather Industry in OECD Countries, Foreign Trade by Commodities, Main Economic Indicators - Historical Statistics, Maritime Transport, Meat Balances in OECD Member Countries,* and *OECD Economic Surveys: Italy.*

Statistical Office of the United Nations, Publishing Service, New York, New York 10017 (800) 253-9646; *International Trade Statistics Yearbook, Statistical Yearbook, Trade in Manufacturing of Developing Countries,* and *Yearbook of Internal Trade Statistics.*

World Bureau of Metal Statistics, 27-A High Street, Ware, Herts, SG12 9BA, England; *World Metal Statistics.*

ITALY - FORESTRY AND FOREST PRODUCTS

Euromonitor Publications Limited, 87-88 Turnmill Street, London EC1M 5QU, England; *European Marketing Data and Statistics.*

European Community Information Service, 2100 M Street, NW, Washington, D.C. 20037 (202) 862-9500; *Agriculture: Statistical Yearbook, Basic Statistics of the Community,* and *Industrial Production: Quarterly Statistics.*

Facts on File, 460 Park Avenue South, New York, New York 10016 (800) 443-8323; *The New Book of World Rankings.*

Food and Agricultural Organization of the United Nations (FAO) Via delle Terme di Caracalla, 00100 Rome, Italy (Telephone Number in U.S. (202) 653-2400); *The State of Food and Agriculture,* and *Yearbook of Forest Products.*

G.K. Hall and Company, 70 Lincoln Street, Boston, Massachusetts 02111 (617) 423-3990; *The World in Figures.*

Organisation for Economic Co-operation and Development (OECD), 2 rue Andre-Pascal, 75 Paris 16, France (Telephone Number in U.S. (202) 785-6323); *Foreign Trade by Commodities, Indicators of Industrial Activity, Industrial Structure Statistics*, and *The Pulp and Paper Industry*.

National Technical Information Service, 5285 Port Royal Road, Springfield, Virginia 22161 (703) 487-4600; *Handbook of Economic Statistics*.

Statistical Office of the United Nations, Publishing Service, New York, New York 10017 (800) 253-9646; *Statistical Yearbook*.

United Nations Educational, Scientific and Cultural Organization (UNESCO), 7 Place de Fontenoy, F-75700 Paris, France; *Statistical Yearbook*.

ITALY - FRUIT PRODUCTION - See ITALY - CROPS

ITALY - FURNITURE AND WOOD PRODUCTS - EXPORTS AND IMPORTS

European Community Information Service, 2100 M Street, NW, Washington, D.C. 20037 (202) 862-9500; *Basic Statistics of the Community*.

Organisation for Economic Co-operation and Development (OECD), 2 rue Andre-Pascal, 75 Paris 16, France (Telephone Number in U.S. (202) 785-6323); *Foreign Trade by Commodities, Industrial Structure Statistics*, and *OECD Economic Surveys: Italy*.

Statistical Office of the United Nations, Publishing Service, New York, New York 10017 (800) 253-9646; *Trade in Manufactures of Developing Countries*.

ITALY - GARLIC PRODUCTION - See ITALY - CROPS

ITALY - GAS AND GAS LIQUIDS - See ITALY - MINING AND MINERAL PRODUCTS

ITALY - GENERAL INDUSTRIAL STATISTICS

European Community Information Service, 2100 M Street, NW, Washington, D.C. 20037 (202) 862-9500; *Basic Statistics of the Community*.

Statistical Office of the United Nations, Publishing Service, New York, New York 10017 (800) 253-9646; *Industrial Statistics Yearbook*.

ITALY - GENERAL MORTALITY

European Community Information Service, 2100 M Street, NW, Washington, D.C. 20037 (202) 862-9500; *Basic Statistics of the Community* and *Demographic Statistics*.

Statistical Office of the United Nations, Publishing Service, New York, New York 10017 (800) 253-9646; *Demographic Yearbook*.

World Health Organization, Office of Publications, Avenue Appia, CH-1211 Geneva 27, Switzerland; *World Health Statistics Annual*.

ITALY - GEOGRAPHIC DATA

European Community Information Service, 2100 M Street, NW, Washington, D.C. 20037 (202) 862-9500; *Basic Statistics of the Community*.

Facts on File, 460 Park Avenue South, New York, New York 10016 (800) 443-8323; *The New Book of World Rankings*.

ITALY - GLASS AND GLASS PRODUCTS - PRODUCTION INDEX

Organisation for Economic Co-operation and Development (OECD), 2 rue Andre-Pascal, 75 Paris 16, France (Telephone Number in U.S. (202) 785-6323); *Indicators of Industrial Activity*.

ITALY - GOATS - See ITALY - LIVESTOCK AND POULTRY

ITALY - GOLD HOLDINGS

International Monetary Fund, 700 Nineteenth Street, NW, Washington, D.C. 20431 (202) 623-7000; *International Financial Statistics*.

Statistical Office of the United Nations, Publishing Service, New York, New York 10017 (800) 253-9646; *Statistical Yearbook*.

The World Bank, 1818 H Street, NW, Washington, D.C. 20433 (202) 477-1234; *World Tables*.

ITALY - GOLD PRODUCTION AND CONSUMPTION - See ITALY - MINING AND MINERAL PRODUCTS

ITALY - GOVERNMENT

European Community Information Service, 2100 M Street, NW, Washington, D.C. 20037 (202) 862-9500; *Basic Statistics of the Community*.

G.K. Hall and Company, 70 Lincoln Street, Boston, Massachusetts 02111 (617) 423-3990; *The World in Figures*.

ITALY - GOVERNMENT BONDS - See ITALY - BONDS

ITALY - GOVERNMENT CONSUMPTION

European Community Information Service, 2100 M Street, NW, Washington, D.C. 20037 (202) 862-9500; *Basic Statistics of the Community*.

International Monetary Fund, 700 Nineteenth Street, NW, Washington, D.C. 20431 (202) 623-7000; *International Financial Statistics*.

ITALY - GOVERNMENT EXPENDITURES

European Community Information Service, 2100 M Street, NW, Washington, D.C. 20037 (202) 862-9500; *Basic Statistics of the Community*, and *Government Financing of Research and Development*.

International Monetary Fund, 700 Nineteenth Street, NW, Washington, D.C. 20431 (202) 623-7000; *Government Finance Statistics Yearbook*.

Organisation for Economic Co-operation and Development (OECD), 2 rue Andre-Pascal, 75 Paris 16, France (Telephone Number in U.S. (202) 785-6323); *Economic Outlook*.

Times Books, 201 East 50th Street, New York, New York 10022 (212) 751-2600; *The Economist Book of Vital World Statistics*.

The World Bank, 1818 H Street, NW, Washington, D.C. 20433 (202) 477-1234; *World Tables*.

ITALY - GOVERNMENT FINANCE

European Community Information Service, 2100 M Street, NW, Washington, D.C. 20037 (202) 862-9500; *Basic Statistics of the Community Government Financing of Research and Development*, and *Money and Finance*.

International Monetary Fund, 700 Nineteenth Street, NW, Washington, D.C. 20431 (202) 623-7000; *International Financial Statistics*.

Organisation for Economic Co-operation and Development (OECD), 2 rue Andre-Pascal, 75 Paris 16, France (Telephone Number in U.S. (202) 785-6323); *Economic Outlook*.

ITALY - GOVERNMENT REVENUES

European Community Information Service, 2100 M Street, NW, Washington, D.C. 20037 (202) 862-9500; *Basic Statistics of the Community* and *Government Financing of Research and Development*.

International Monetary Fund, 700 Nineteenth Street, NW, Washington, D.C. 20431 (202) 623-7000; *Government Finance Statistics Yearbook*.

Organisation for Economic Co-operation and Development (OECD), 2 rue Andre-Pascal, 75 Paris 16, France (Telephone Number in U.S. (202) 785-6323); *Economic Outlook*, and *Revenue Statistics of OECD Member Countries*.

Times Books, 201 East 50th Street, New York, New York 10022 (212) 751-2600; *The Economist Book of Vital World Statistics*.

The World Bank, 1818 H Street, NW, Washington, D.C. 20433 (202) 477-1234; *World Tables*.

ITALY - GRAIN PRODUCTION - See ITALY - CROPS

ITALY - GRANTS

International Monetary Fund, 700 Nineteenth Street, NW, Washington, D.C. 20431 (202) 623-7000; *Government Finance Statistics Yearbook*.

National Technical Information Service, 5285 Port Royal Road, Springfield, Virginia 22161 (703) 487-4600; *Handbook of Economic Statistics*.

Organisation for Economic Co-operation and Development (OECD), 2 rue Andre-Pascal, 75 Paris 16, France (Telephone Number in U.S. (202) 785-6323); *Geographical Distribution of Financial Flows to Developing Countries*.

ITALY - GREEN PEPPER AND CHILIE PRODUCTION - See ITALY - CROPS

ITALY - GROSS DOMESTIC PRODUCT

The Economist Intelligence Unit, 111 West 57th Street, New York, New York 10019 (800) 938-4685; *The World Market Atlas*.

European Community Information Service, 2100 M Street, NW, Washington, D.C. 20037 (202) 862-9500; *Basic Statistics of the Community, Eurostatistics: Data for Short-Term Economic Analysis, Government Financing of Research and Development, Money and Finance*, and *Iron and Steel: Statistical Yearbook*.

Facts on File, 460 Park Avenue South, New York, New York 10016 (800) 443-8323; *The New Book of World Rankings*.

G.K. Hall and Company, 70 Lincoln Street, Boston, Massachusetts 02111 (617) 423-3990; *The World in Figures*.

International Monetary Fund, 700 Nineteenth Street, NW, Washington, D.C. 20431 (202) 623-7000; *International Financial Statistics*.

National Technical Information Service, 5285 Port Royal Road, Springfield, Virginia 22161 (703) 487-4600; *Handbook of Economic Statistics*.

Organisation for Economic Co-operation and Development (OECD), 2 rue Andre-Pascal, 75 Paris 16, France (Telephone Number in U.S. (202) 785-6323); *Economic Outlook, Geographical Distribution of Financial Flows to Developing Countries*, and *Revenue Statistics of OECD Member Countries*.

Statistical Office of the United Nations, Publishing Service, New York, New York 10017 (800) 253-9646; *Statistical Yearbook*.

Times Books, 201 East 50th Street, New York, New York 10022 (212) 751-2600; *The Economist Book of Vital World Statistics*.

The World Bank, 1818 H Street, NW, Washington, D.C. 20433 (202) 477-1234; *World Tables*.

ITALY - GROSS INDUSTRIAL PRODUCT

European Community Information Service, 2100 M Street, NW, Washington, D.C. 20037 (202) 862-9500; *Government Financing of Research and Development*.

ITALY - GROSS NATIONAL PRODUCT

European Community Information Service, 2100 M Street, NW, Washington, D.C. 20037 (202) 862-9500; *ACP: Basic Statistics*, and *Basic Statistics of the Community*.

National Technical Information Service, 5285 Port Royal Road, Springfield, Virginia 22161 (703) 487-4600; *Handbook of Economic Statistics*.

Organisation for Economic Co-operation and Development (OECD), 2 rue Andre-Pascal, 75 Paris 16, France (Telephone Number in U.S. (202) 785-6323); *Economic Outlook*, and *Geographical Distribution of Financial Flows to Developing Countries*.

U.S. Arms Control and Disarmament Agency, 320 Twenty-first Street, Northwest, Washington, D.C. 20451 (202) 647-8677; *World Military Expenditures and Arms Transfers*.

The World Bank, 1818 H Street, NW, Washington, D.C. 20433 (202) 477-1234; *World Tables*.

ITALY - GROUNDNUTS PRODUCTION - See ITALY - CROPS

ITALY - HAY PRODUCTION - See ITALY - CROPS

ITALY - HAZELNUT PRODUCTION -See ITALY - CROPS

ITALY - HEALTH

European Community Information Service, 2100 M Street, NW, Washington, D.C. 20037 (202) 862-9500; *Basic Statistics of the Community* and *Regions: Statistical Yearbook*.

Facts on File, 460 Park Avenue South, New York, New York 10016 (800) 443-8323; *The New Book of World Rankings.*

G.K. Hall and Company, 70 Lincoln Street, Boston, Massachusetts 02111 (617) 423-3990; *The World in Figures.*

Organisation for Economic Co-operation and Development (OECD), 2 rue Andre-Pascal, 75 Paris 16, France (Telephone Number in U.S. (202) 785-6323); *OECD Health Systems: Facts and Trends.*

Statistical Office of the United Nations, Publishing Service, New York, New York 10017 (800) 253-9646; *Statistical Yearbook.*

Times Books, 201 East 50th Street, New York, New York 10022 (212) 751-2600; *The Economist Book of Vital World Statistics.*

World Health Organization, Office of Publications, Avenue Appia, CH-1211 Geneva 27, Switzerland; *World Health Statistics Annual.*

ITALY - HEALTH EXPENDITURES

International Monetary Fund, 700 Nineteenth Street, NW, Washington, D.C. 20431 (202) 623-7000; *Government Finance Statistics Yearbook.*

ITALY - HEMP FIBRE PRODUCTION - See ITALY - TEXTILE INDUSTRY

ITALY - HIDE PRODUCTION

Food and Agricultural Organization of the United Nations (FAO), Via delle Terme di Caracalla, 00100 Rome, Italy (Telephone Number in U.S. (202) 653-2400); *Production Yearbook.*

Organisation for Economic Co-operation and Development (OECD), 2 rue Andre-Pascal, 75 Paris 16, France (Telephone Number in U.S. (202) 785-6323); *The Footwear, Raw Hides and Skins, and Leather Industry in OECD Countries, Foreign Trade by Commodities,* and *Indicators of Industrial Activity.*

ITALY - HIGHWAYS

European Community Information Service, 2100 M Street, NW, Washington, D.C. 20037 (202) 862-9500; *Basic Statistics of the Community,* and *Transport Annual Statistics.*

G.K. Hall and Company, 70 Lincoln Street, Boston, Massachusetts 02111 (617) 423-3990; *The World in Figures.*

International Road Federation, 525 School Street, SW, Washington, D.C. 20024 (202) 554-2106; *World Road Statistics.*

Statistical Office of the United Nations, Publishing Service, New York, New York 10017 (800) 253-9646; *Annual Bulletin of Transport Statistics for Europe.*

ITALY - HOME FINANCE

Organisation for Economic Co-operation and Development (OECD), 2 rue Andre-Pascal, 75 Paris 16, France (Telephone Number in U.S. (202) 785-6323); *Main Economic Indicators - Historical Statistics.*

ITALY - HOPS PRODUCTION - See ITALY - CROPS

ITALY - HORSES - See ITALY - LIVESTOCK AND POULTRY

ITALY - HOURS OF WORK - See ITALY - EMPLOYMENT

ITALY - HOUSING AND HOUSING UNITS

European Community Information Service, 2100 M Street, NW, Washington, D.C. 20037 (202) 862-9500; *Basic Statistics of the Community, Labor Force Sample Survey,* and *Regions: Statistical Yearbook.*

Facts on File, 460 Park Avenue South, New York, New York 10016 (800) 443-8323; *The New Book of World Rankings.*

National Technical Information Service, 5285 Port Royal Road, Springfield, Virginia 22161 (703) 487-4600; *Handbook of Economic Statistics.*

ITALY - HOUSING CONSTRUCTION - See CONSTRUCTION INDUSTRY

ITALY - HOUSING EXPENDITURES

European Community Information Service, 2100 M Street, NW, Washington, D.C. 20037 (202) 862-9500; *Basic Statistics of the Community.*

International Monetary Fund, 700 Nineteenth Street, NW, Washington, D.C. 20431 (202) 623-7000; *Government Finance Statistics Yearbook.*

ITALY - HYDROCHLORIC ACID PRODUCTION

European Community Information Service, 2100 M Street, NW, Washington, D.C. 20037 (202) 862-9500; *Basic Statistics of the Community.*

Statistical Office of the United Nations, Publishing Service, New York, New York 10017 (800) 253-9646; *Statistical Yearbook.*

ITALY - ILLITERATE POPULATION

The Economist Intelligence Unit, 111 West 57th Street, New York, New York 10019 (800) 938-4685; *The World Market Atlas.*

G.K. Hall and Company, 70 Lincoln Street, Boston, Massachusetts 02111 (617) 423-3990; *The World in Figures.*

United Nations Educational, Scientific and Cultural Organization (UNESCO), 7 Place de Fontenoy, F-75700 Paris, France; *Statistical Yearbook.*

ITALY - IMPORTS

American Automobile Manufacturers Association, 1401 H Street, NW, Suite 900, Washington, D.C. 20005 (202) 326-5500; *World Motor Vehicle Data.*

The Economist Intelligence Unit, 111 West 57th Street, New York, New York 10019 (800) 938-4685; *The World Market Atlas.*

European Community Information Service, 2100 M Street, NW, Washington, D.C. 20037 (202) 862-9500; *Basic Statistics of the Community, Energy: Monthly Statistics, Energy Statistics Yearbook, Eurostatistics: Data for Short-Term Economic Analysis, External Trade: Monthly Statistics, External Trade: Statistical Yearbook,* and *Fisheries: Yearly Statistics.*

Food and Agricultural Organization of the United Nations (FAO) Via delle Terme di Caracalla, 00100 Rome, Italy (Telephone Number in U.S. (202) 653-2400); *The State of Food and Agriculture.*

G.K. Hall and Company, 70 Lincoln Street, Boston, Massachusetts 02111 (617) 423-3990; *The World in Figures.*

International Iron and Steel Institute, 120, rue Colonel Bourg, B-1140, Brussels, Belgium; *Steel Statistical Yearbook.*

International Lead and Zinc Study Group, Metro House, 58 St. James's Street, London SW1A 1LD, England; *Lead and Zinc Statistics.*

International Monetary Fund, 700 Nineteenth Street, NW, Washington, D.C. 20431 (202) 623-7000; *Direction of Trade Statistics, Government Finance Statistics Yearbook,* and *International Financial Statistics.*

International Rubber Study Group, York House, 8th Floor, Empire Way, Wembley, London HA9 0PA, England; *World Rubber Statistics Handbook.*

National Technical Information Service, 5285 Port Royal Road, Springfield, Virginia 22161 (703) 487-4600; *Handbook of Economic Statistics.*

Organisation for Economic Co-operation and Development (OECD), 2 rue Andre-Pascal, 75 Paris 16, France (Telephone Number in U.S. (202) 785-6323); *Economic Outlook, The Footwear, Raw Hides and Skins, and Leather Industry in OECD Countries, Industrial Structure Statistics, The Iron and Steel Industry, Milk, Milk Products, and Egg Balances in OECD Member Countries, The Pulp and Paper Industry,* and *Review of Fisheries in OECD Member Countries.*

Times Books, 201 East 50th Street, New York, New York 10022 (212) 751-2600; *The Economist Book of Vital World Statistics.*

The World Bank, 1818 H Street, NW, Washington, D.C. 20433 (202) 477-1234; *World Tables.*

ITALY - INCOME TAXES - See ITALY - TAXATION

ITALY - INDUSTRIAL METALS PRODUCTION - See ITALY - MINING AND MINERAL PRODUCTS

ITALY - INDUSTRY

European Community Information Service, 2100 M Street, NW, Washington, D.C. 20037 (202) 862-9500; *Basic Statistics of the Community, Employment and Unemployment, Eurostatistics: Data for Short-Term Economic Analysis,* and *Labor Force Sample Survey.*

Facts on File, 460 Park Avenue South, New York, New York 10016 (800) 443-8323; *The New Book of World Rankings.*

G.K. Hall and Company, 70 Lincoln Street, Boston, Massachusetts 02111 (617) 423-3990; *The World in Figures.*

International Labour Office, I.L.O. Publications, CH-1211, Geneva 22, Switzerland; *Yearbook of Labour Statistics.*

National Technical Information Service, 5285 Port Royal Road, Springfield, Virginia 22161 (703) 487-4600; *Handbook of Economic Statistics.*

Organisation for Economic Co-operation and Development (OECD), 2 rue Andre-Pascal, 75 Paris 16, France (Telephone Number in U.S. (202) 785-6323); *Economic Outlook, Indicators of Industrial Activity, Industrial Production Historical Statistics, Industrial Structure Statistics, Main Economic Indicators - Historical Statistics,* and *OECD Environmental Data.*

Statistical Office of the United Nations, Publishing Service, New York, New York 10017 (800) 253-9646; *Statistical Yearbook.*

Times Books, 201 East 50th Street, New York, New York 10022 (212) 751-2600; *The Economist Book of Vital World Statistics.*

The World Bank, 1818 H Street, NW, Washington, D.C. 20433 (202) 477-1234; *World Tables.*

World Intellectual Property Organization, 34 Chemin des Colombettes, CH-1211 Geneva 20, Switzerland; *Industrial Property Statistics.*

ITALY - INFANT AND MATERNAL MORTALITY

European Community Information Service, 2100 M Street, NW, Washington, D.C. 20037 (202) 862-9500; *Basic Statistics of the Community* and *Demographic Statistics.*

Statistical Office of the United Nations, Publishing Service, New York, New York 10017 (800) 253-9646; *Demographic Yearbook,* and *Statistical Yearbook.*

Times Books, 201 East 50th Street, New York, New York 10022 (212) 751-2600; *The Economist Book of Vital World Statistics.*

The World Bank, 1818 H Street, NW, Washington, D.C. 20433 (202) 477-1234; *World Tables.*

World Health Organization, Office of Publications, Avenue Appia, CH-1211 Geneva 27, Switzerland; *World Health Statistics Annual.*

ITALY - INFLATIONARY FACTORS

National Technical Information Service, 5285 Port Royal Road, Springfield, Virginia 22161 (703) 487-4600; *Handbook of Economic Statistics.*

ITALY - INTEREST RATES

European Community Information Service, 2100 M Street, NW, Washington, D.C. 20037 (202) 862-9500; *Money and Finance.*

National Technical Information Service, 5285 Port Royal Road, Springfield, Virginia 22161 (703) 487-4600; *Handbook of Economic Statistics.*

Organisation for Economic Co-operation and Development (OECD), 2 rue Andre-Pascal, 75 Paris 16, France (Telephone Number in U.S. (202) 785-6323); *Economic Outlook, Financial Market Trends, Main Economic Indicators - Historical Statistics,* and *OECD Financial Statistics.*

ITALY - INTERNAL TRADE

European Community Information Service, 2100 M Street, NW, Washington, D.C. 20037 (202) 862-9500; *Basic Statistics of the Community.*

Organisation for Economic Co-operation and Development (OECD), 2 rue Andre-Pascal, 75 Paris 16, France (Telephone Number in U.S. (202) 785-6323); *Main Economic Indicators - Historical Statistics.*

ITALY - INTERNATIONAL FINANCE

European Community Information Service, 2100 M Street, NW, Washington, D.C. 20037 (202) 862-9500; *Basic Statistics of the Community.*

Organisation for Economic Co-operation and Development (OECD), 2 rue Andre-Pascal, 75 Paris 16, France (Telephone Number in U.S. (202) 785-6323); *Economic Outlook,* and *Financial Market Trends.*

ITALY - INTERNATIONAL LIQUIDITY

International Monetary Fund, 700 Nineteenth Street, NW, Washington, D.C. 20431 (202) 623-7000; *International Financial Statistics.*

Organisation for Economic Co-operation and Development (OECD), 2 rue Andre-Pascal, 75 Paris 16, France (Telephone Number in U.S. (202) 785-6323); *Economic Outlook,* and *Financial Market Trends.*

ITALY - INTERNATIONAL RESERVES EXCLUDING GOLD

National Technical Information Service, 5285 Port Royal Road, Springfield, Virginia 22161 (703) 487-4600; *Handbook of Economic Statistics.*

Statistical Office of the United Nations, Publishing Service, New York, New York 10017 (800) 253-9646; *Statistical Yearbook.*

The World Bank, 1818 H Street, NW, Washington, D.C. 20433 (202) 477-1234; *World Tables.*

ITALY - INTERNATIONAL STATISTICS

Organisation for Economic Co-operation and Development (OECD), 2 rue Andre-Pascal, 75 Paris 16, France (Telephone Number in U.S. (202) 785-6323); *Financial Market Trends,* and *Tourism Policy and International Tourism in OECD Member Countries.*

ITALY - INVESTMENTS

International Monetary Fund, 700 Nineteenth Street, NW, Washington, D.C. 20431 (202) 623-7000; *International Financial Statistics.*

Organisation for Economic Co-operation and Development (OECD), 2 rue Andre-Pascal, 75 Paris 16, France (Telephone Number in U.S. (202) 785-6323); *Economic Outlook, Financial Market Trends, Industrial Structure Statistics, The Iron and Steel Industry,* and *Textile Industry in OECD Countries.*

ITALY - IRON ORE - See ITALY - MINING AND MINERAL PRODUCTS

ITALY - JUTE PRODUCTION - See ITALY - CROPS

ITALY - LABOR FORCE

European Community Information Service, 2100 M Street, NW, Washington, D.C. 20037 (202) 862-9500; *Basic Statistics of the Community, Labor Force Sample Survey,* and *Regions: Statistical Yearbook.*

Facts on File, 460 Park Avenue South, New York, New York 10016 (800) 443-8323; *The New Book of World Rankings.*

Food and Agricultural Organization of the United Nations (FAO) Via delle Terme di Caracalla, 00100 Rome, Italy (Telephone Number in U.S. (202) 653-2400); *The State of Food and Agriculture.*

G.K. Hall and Company, 70 Lincoln Street, Boston, Massachusetts 02111 (617) 423-3990; *The World in Figures.*

National Technical Information Service, 5285 Port Royal Road, Springfield, Virginia 22161 (703) 487-4600; *Handbook of Economic Statistics.*

Organisation for Economic Co-operation and Development (OECD), 2 rue Andre-Pascal, 75 Paris 16, France (Telephone Number in U.S. (202) 785-6323); *Economic Outlook, The Iron and Steel Industry, Labour Force Statistics, Main Economic Indicators - Historical Statistics, Maritime Transport, OECD Economic Surveys: Italy, OECD Employment Outlook,* and *Textile Industry in OECD Countries.*

Times Books, 201 East 50th Street, New York, New York 10022 (212) 751-2600; *The Economist Book of Vital World Statistics.*

The World Bank, 1818 H Street, NW, Washington, D.C. 20433 (202) 477-1234; *World Tables.*

ITALY - LABOR PRODUCTIVITY

International Labour Office, I.L.O. Publications, CH-1211, Geneva 22, Switzerland; *Yearbook of Labour Statistics.*

Organisation for Economic Co-operation and Development (OECD), 2 rue Andre-Pascal, 75 Paris 16, France (Telephone Number in U.S. (202) 785-6323); *Economic Outlook,* and *OECD Employment Outlook.*

ITALY - LAND USE

Euromonitor Publications Limited, 87-88 Turnmill Street, London EC1M 5QU, England; *European Marketing Data and Statistics.*

European Community Information Service, 2100 M Street, NW, Washington, D.C. 20037 (202) 862-9500; *Agriculture: Statistical Yearbook, Basic Statistics of the Community, Crop Production: Quarterly Statistics,* and *Regions: Statistical Yearbook.*

Food and Agricultural Organization of the United Nations (FAO), Via delle Terme di Caracalla, 00100 Rome, Italy (Telephone Number in U.S. (202) 653-2400); *Production Yearbook.*

G.K. Hall and Company, 70 Lincoln Street, Boston, Massachusetts 02111 (617) 423-3990; *The World in Figures.*

ITALY - LEAD AND LEAD ORE - See ITALY -MINING AND MINERAL PRODUCTS

ITALY - LEATHER - PRODUCTION INDEX

Organisation for Economic Co-operation and Development (OECD), 2 rue Andre-Pascal, 75 Paris 16, France (Telephone Number in U.S. (202) 785-6323); *Indicators of Industrial Activity.*

ITALY - LEATHER AND FOOTWEAR EXPORTS AND IMPORTS

European Community Information Service, 2100 M Street, NW, Washington, D.C. 20037 (202) 862-9500; *Basic Statistics of the Community.*

Organisation for Economic Co-operation and Development (OECD), 2 rue Andre-Pascal, 75 Paris 16, France (Telephone Number in U.S. (202) 785-6323); *The Footwear, Raw Hides and Skins, and Leather Industry in OECD Countries.*

Statistical Office of the United Nations, Publishing Service, New York, New York 10017 (800) 253-9646; *Trade in Manufactures of Developing Countries.*

ITALY - LIBRARIES

Euromonitor Publications Limited, 87-88 Turnmill Street, London EC1M 5QU, England; *European Marketing Data and Statistics.*

Facts on File, 460 Park Avenue South, New York, New York 10016 (800) 443-8323; *The New Book of World Rankings.*

United Nations Educational, Scientific and Cultural Organization (UNESCO), 7 Place de Fontenoy, F-75700 Paris, France; *Statistical Yearbook.*

ITALY - LIGNITE PRODUCTION - See ITALY - MINING AND MINERAL PRODUCTS

ITALY - LIVESTOCK AND POULTRY

Commodity Research Bureau, Incorporated, 75 Wall Street, New York, New York 10005 (212) 504-7754, *Commodity Year Book.*

Euromonitor Publications Limited, 87-88 Turnmill Street, London EC1M 5QU, England; *European Marketing Data and Statistics.*

European Community Information Service, 2100 M Street, NW, Washington, D.C. 20037 (202) 862-9500; *Agriculture: Statistical Yearbook, Basic Statistics of the Community, Eurostatistics: Data for Short-Term Economic Analysis,* and *Regions: Statistical Yearbook.*

Facts on File, 460 Park Avenue South, New York, New York 10016 (800) 443-8323; *The New Book of World Rankings.*

Food and Agricultural Organization of the United Nations (FAO), Via delle Terme di Caracalla, 00100 Rome, Italy (Telephone Number in U.S. (202) 653-2400); *Production Yearbook,* and *The State of Food and Agriculture.*

G.K. Hall and Company, 70 Lincoln Street, Boston, Massachusetts 02111 (617) 423-3990; *The World in Figures.*

National Technical Information Service, 5285 Port Royal Road, Springfield, Virginia 22161 (703) 487-4600; *Handbook of Economic Statistics.*

Organisation for Economic Co-operation and Development (OECD), 2 rue Andre-Pascal, 75 Paris 16, France (Telephone Number in U.S. (202) 785-6323); *Economic Accounts for Agriculture,* and *Meat Balances in OECD Member Countries.*

Statistical Office of the United Nations, Publishing Service, New York, New York 10017 (800) 253-9646; *Statistical Yearbook.*

ITALY - LIVING LEVELS

G.K. Hall and Company, 70 Lincoln Street, Boston, Massachusetts 02111 (617) 423-3990; *The World in Figures.*

Organisation for Economic Co-operation and Development (OECD), 2 rue Andre-Pascal, 75 Paris 16, France (Telephone Number in U.S. (202) 785-6323); *Economic Outlook.*

Times Books, 201 East 50th Street, New York, New York 10022 (212) 751-2600; *The Economist Book of Vital World Statistics.*

ITALY - MACHINERY - PRODUCTION INDEX

Organisation for Economic Co-operation and Development (OECD), 2 rue Andre-Pascal, 75 Paris 16, France (Telephone Number in U.S. (202) 785-6323); *Indicators of Industrial Activity.*

ITALY - MAGNESIUM PRODUCTION AND CONSUMPTION - See ITALY - MINING AND MINERAL PRODUCTS

ITALY - MAIL - NUMBER OF PIECES SENT OR RECEIVED

European Community Information Service, 2100 M Street, NW, Washington, D.C. 20037 (202) 862-9500; *Transport Annual Statistics.*

Statistical Office of the United Nations, Publishing Service, New York, New York 10017 (800) 253-9646; *Statistical Yearbook.*

ITALY - MAIN ECONOMIC INDICATORS - See ITALY - ECONOMY

ITALY - MANGANESE AND MANGANESE ORE - See ITALY - MINING AND MINERAL PRODUCTS

ITALY - MANUFACTURING

American Automobile Manufacturers Association, 1401 H Street, NW, Suite 900, Washington, D.C. 20005 (202) 326-5500; *World Motor Vehicle Data.*

European Community Information Service, 2100 M Street, NW, Washington, D.C. 20037 (202) 862-9500; *Basic Statistics of the Community, Employment and Unemployment, Eurostatistics: Data for Short-Term Economic Analysis, Industrial Production: Quarterly Statistics,* and *Labor Force Sample Survey.*

Facts on File, 460 Park Avenue South, New York, New York 10016 (800) 443-8323; *The New Book of World Rankings.*

G.K. Hall and Company, 70 Lincoln Street, Boston, Massachusetts 02111 (617) 423-3990; *The World in Figures.*

National Technical Information Service, 5285 Port Royal Road, Springfield, Virginia 22161 (703) 487-4600; *Handbook of Economic Statistics.*

Organisation for Economic Co-operation and Development (OECD), 2 rue Andre-Pascal, 75 Paris 16, France (Telephone Number in U.S. (202) 785-6323); *Indicators of Industrial Activity, Industrial Structure Statistics, Foreign Trade by Commodities,* and *OECD Economic Surveys: Italy.*

Statistical Office of the United Nations, Publishing Service, New York, New York 10017 (800) 253-9646; *Statistical Yearbook.*

Times Books, 201 East 50th Street, New York, New York 10022 (212) 751-2600; *The Economist Book of Vital World Statistics.*

The World Bank, 1818 H Street, NW, Washington, D.C. 20433 (202) 477-1234; *World Tables.*

ITALY - MARRIAGE RATES

European Community Information Service, 2100 M Street, NW, Washington, D.C. 20037 (202) 862-9500; *Basic Statistics of the Community.*

Facts on File, 460 Park Avenue South, New York, New York 10016 (800) 443-8323; *The New Book of World Rankings.*

Statistical Office of the United Nations, Publishing Service, New York, New York 10017 (800) 253-9646; *Demographic Yearbook,* and *Statistical Yearbook.*

ITALY - MEAT PRODUCTION - See ITALY - LIVESTOCK AND POULTRY

ITALY - MERCHANT SHIPPING

European Community Information Service, 2100 M Street, NW, Washington, D.C. 20037 (202) 862-9500; *Basic Statistics of the Community, Fisheries: Yearly Statistics, Regions: Statistical Yearbook,* and *Transport Annual Statistics.*

G.K. Hall and Company, 70 Lincoln Street, Boston, Massachusetts 02111 (617) 423-3990; *The World in Figures.*

Lloyd's Register of Shipping, 17 Battery Place, New York, New York 10004 (212) 425-8050; *Register of Ships.*

National Technical Information Service, 5285 Port Royal Road, Springfield, Virginia 22161 (703) 487-4600; *Handbook of Economic Statistics.*

Organisation for Economic Co-operation and Development (OECD), 2 rue Andre-Pascal, 75 Paris 16, France (Telephone Number in U.S. (202) 785-6323); *Maritime Transport.*

Statistical Office of the United Nations, Publishing Service, New York, New York 10017 (800) 253-9646; *Annual Bulletin of Transport Statistics for Europe,* and *Statistical Yearbook.*

Times Books, 201 East 50th Street, New York, New York 10022 (212) 751-2600; *The Economist Book of Vital World Statistics.*

U.S. Department of Transportation, Maritime Administration, 400 Seventh Street, SW, Washington, D.C. 20590; *A Statistical Analysis of the World's Merchant Fleets.*

ITALY - MERCURY PRODUCTION AND CONSUMPTION - See ITALY - MINING AND MINERAL PRODUCTS

ITALY - MILITARY

G.K. Hall and Company, 70 Lincoln Street, Boston, Massachusetts 02111 (617) 423-3990; *The World in Figures.*

The International Institute for Strategic Studies, 23 Tavistock Street, London WC2E 7NQ, England; *The Military Balance.*

U.S. Arms Control and Disarmament Agency, 320 Twenty-first Street, Northwest, Washington, D.C. 20451 (202) 647-8677; *World Military Expenditures and Arms Transfers.*

ITALY - MILK - See ITALY - DAIRY PRODUCTS

ITALY - MILLET PRODUCTION - See ITALY - CROPS

ITALY - MINING AND MINERAL PRODUCTS

Commodity Research Bureau, Incorporated, 75 Wall Street, New York, New York 10005 (212) 504-7754; *Commodity Year Book.*

European Community Information Service, 2100 M Street, NW, Washington, D.C. 20037 (202) 862-9500; *Basic Statistics of the Community, Energy: Monthly Statistics, Eurostatistics: Data for Short-Term Economic Analysis, Industrial Production: Quarterly Statistics, Iron and Steel: Statistical Yearbook, Labor Force Sample Survey,* and *Regions: Statistical Yearbook.*

Facts on File, 460 Park Avenue South, New York, New York 10016 (800) 443-8323; *The New Book of World Rankings.*

G.K. Hall and Company, 70 Lincoln Street, Boston, Massachusetts 02111 (617) 423-3990; *The World in Figures.*

International Iron and Steel Institute, 120, rue Colonel Bourg, B-1140, Brussels, Belgium; *Steel Statistical Yearbook.*

International Lead and Zinc Study Group, Metro House, 58 St. James's Street, London SW1A 1LD, England; *Lead and Zinc Statistics.*

National Technical Information Service, 5285 Port Royal Road, Springfield, Virginia 22161 (703) 487-4600; *Handbook of Economic Statistics.*

Organisation for Economic Co-operation and Development (OECD), 2 rue Andre-Pascal, 75 Paris 16, France (Telephone Number in U.S. (202) 785-6323); *Coal Information, Energy Statistics of OECD Countries, Foreign Trade by Commodities, Indicators of Industrial Activity, Industrial Structure Statistics, The Iron and Steel Industry, The Non-Ferrous Metals Industry,* and *OECD Economic Surveys: Italy.*

Penn Well Publishing Company, 1421 South Sheridan Road, Post Office Box 1260, Tulsa, Oklahoma 74101 (800) 752-9764; *International Energy Statistics Sourcebook.*

Statistical Office of the United Nations, Publishing Service, New York, New York 10017 (800) 253-9646; *Statistical Yearbook.*

World Bureau of Metal Statistics, 27-A High Street, Ware, Herts, SG12 9BA, England; *World Metal Statistics.*

ITALY - MOLASSES PRODUCTION - See ITALY - CROPS

ITALY - MOLYBDENUM AND MOLYBDENUM ORE - See ITALY - MINING AND MINERAL PRODUCTS

ITALY - MONEY AND CREDIT

Organisation for Economic Co-operation and Development (OECD), 2 rue Andre-Pascal, 75 Paris 16, France (Telephone Number in U.S. (202) 785-6323); *OECD Economic Surveys: Italy.*

ITALY - MONEY EXCHANGE RATE

European Community Information Service, 2100 M Street, NW, Washington, D.C. 20037 (202) 862-9500; *Basic Statistics of the Community.*

International Monetary Fund, 700 Nineteenth Street, NW, Washington, D.C. 20431 (202) 623-7000; *International Financial Statistics.*

Organisation for Economic Co-operation and Development (OECD), 2 rue Andre-Pascal, 75 Paris 16, France (Telephone Number in U.S. (202) 785-6323); *Economic Outlook, Financial Market Trends,* and *Tourism Policy and International Tourism in OECD Member Countries.*

Statistical Office of the United Nations, Publishing Service, New York, New York 10017 (800) 253-9646; *Statistical Yearbook.*

ITALY - MONEY RATES - MARKET

European Community Information Service, 2100 M Street, NW, Washington, D.C. 20037 (202) 862-9500; *Basic Statistics of the Community.*

Organisation for Economic Co-operation and Development (OECD), 2 rue Andre-Pascal, 75 Paris 16, France (Telephone Number in U.S. (202) 785-6323); *Economic Outlook,* and *Financial Market Trends.*

ITALY - MONEY RESERVES

European Community Information Service, 2100 M Street, NW, Washington, D.C. 20037 (202) 862-9500; *Basic Statistics of the Community.*

Organisation for Economic Co-operation and Development (OECD), 2 rue Andre-Pascal, 75 Paris 16, France (Telephone Number in U.S. (202) 785-6323); *Economic Outlook,* and *Financial Market Trends.*

ITALY - MONEY SUPPLY

European Community Information Service, 2100 M Street, NW, Washington, D.C. 20037 (202) 862-9500; *Basic Statistics of the Community, Eurostatistics: Data for Short-Term Economic Analysis,* and *Money and Finance.*

G.K. Hall and Company, 70 Lincoln Street, Boston, Massachusetts 02111 (617) 423-3990; *The World in Figures.*

International Monetary Fund, 700 Nineteenth Street, NW, Washington, D.C. 20431 (202) 623-7000; *International Financial Statistics.*

Organisation for Economic Co-operation and Development (OECD), 2 rue Andre-Pascal, 75 Paris 16, France (Telephone Number in U.S. (202) 785-6323); *Economic Outlook.*

Statistical Office of the United Nations, Publishing Service, New York, New York 10017 (800) 253-9646; *Statistical Yearbook.*

The World Bank, 1818 H Street, NW, Washington, D.C. 20433 (202) 477-1234; *World Tables.*

ITALY - MONUMENTS AND HISTORICAL SITES

United Nations Educational, Scientific and Cultural Organization (UNESCO), 7 Place de Fontenoy, F-75700 Paris, France; *Statistical Yearbook.*

ITALY - MOTION PICTURES

Statistical Office of the United Nations, Publishing Service, New York, New York 10017 (800) 253-9646; *Statistical Yearbook.*

United Nations Educational, Scientific and Cultural Organization (UNESCO), 7 Place de Fontenoy, F-75700 Paris, France; *Statistical Yearbook.*

ITALY - MOTOR VEHICLE PRODUCTION

American Automobile Manufacturers Association, 1401 H Street, NW, Suite 900, Washington, D.C. 20005 (202) 326-5500; *World Motor Vehicle Data.*

European Community Information Service, 2100 M Street, NW, Washington, D.C. 20037 (202) 862-9500; *Basic Statistics of the Community* and *Eurostatistics: Data for Short-Term Economic Analysis.*

National Technical Information Service, 5285 Port Royal Road, Springfield, Virginia 22161 (703) 487-4600; *Handbook of Economic Statistics.*

Organisation for Economic Co-operation and Development (OECD), 2 rue Andre-Pascal, 75 Paris 16, France (Telephone Number in U.S. (202) 785-6323); *Foreign Trade by Commodities,* and *Indicators of Industrial Activity.*

Statistical Office of the United Nations, Publishing Service, New York, New York 10017 (800) 253-9646; *Statistical Yearbook.*

ITALY - MOTOR VEHICLE TAXES - See ITALY - TAXATION

ITALY - MOTOR VEHICLES IN USE

American Automobile Manufacturers Association, 1401 H Street, NW, Suite 900, Washington, D.C. 20005 (202) 326-5500; *World Motor Vehicle Data.*

European Community Information Service, 2100 M Street, NW, Washington, D.C. 20037 (202) 862-9500; *Basic Statistics of the Community,* and *Transport Annual Statistics.*

G.K. Hall and Company, 70 Lincoln Street, Boston, Massachusetts 02111 (617) 423-3990; *The World in Figures.*

International Road Federation, 525 School Street, SW, Washington, D.C. 20024 (202) 554-2106; *World Road Statistics.*

Statistical Office of the United Nations, Publishing Service, New York, New York 10017 (800) 253-9646; *Statistical Yearbook.*

Times Books, 201 East 50th Street, New York, New York 10022 (212) 751-2600; *The Economist Book of Vital World Statistics.*

ITALY - MULES - See ITALY - LIVESTOCK AND POULTRY

ITALY - MUSEUMS

Euromonitor Publications Limited, 87-88 Turnmill Street, London EC1M 5QU, England; *European Marketing Data and Statistics.*

Facts on File, 460 Park Avenue South, New York, New York 10016 (800) 443-8323; *The New Book of World Rankings.*

United Nations Educational, Scientific and Cultural Organization (UNESCO), 7 Place de Fontenoy, F-75700 Paris, France; *Statistical Yearbook.*

ITALY - NATALITY - See ITALY - BIRTH RATES

ITALY - NATIONAL ACCOUNTS

European Community Information Service, 2100 M Street, NW, Washington, D.C. 20037 (202) 862-9500; *Basic Statistics of the Community* and *Eurostatistics: Data for Short-Term Economic Analysis.*

International Monetary Fund, 700 Nineteenth Street, NW, Washington, D.C. 20431 (202) 623-7000; *International Financial Statistics.*

Organisation for Economic Co-operation and Development (OECD), 2 rue Andre-Pascal, 75 Paris 16, France (Telephone Number in U.S. (202) 785-6323); *Economic Outlook.*

Statistical Office of the United Nations, Publishing Service, New York, New York 10017 (800) 253-9646; *National Accounts Statistics,* and *Statistical Yearbook.*

ITALY - NATIONAL INCOME

Facts on File, 460 Park Avenue South, New York, New York 10016 (800) 443-8323; *The New Book of World Rankings.*

G.K. Hall and Company, 70 Lincoln Street, Boston, Massachusetts 02111 (617) 423-3990; *The World in Figures.*

Organisation for Economic Co-operation and Development (OECD), 2 rue Andre-Pascal, 75 Paris 16, France (Telephone Number in U.S. (202) 785-6323); *Economic Outlook*.

Statistical Office of the United Nations, Publishing Service, New York, New York 10017 (800) 253-9646; *Statistical Yearbook*.

ITALY - NATIONAL PRODUCT

European Community Information Service, 2100 M Street, NW, Washington, D.C. 20037 (202) 862-9500; *Basic Statistics of the Community*.

Facts on File, 460 Park Avenue South, New York, New York 10016 (800) 443-8323; *The New Book of World Rankings*.

Organisation for Economic Co-operation and Development (OECD), 2 rue Andre-Pascal, 75 Paris 16, France (Telephone Number in U.S. (202) 785-6323); *Economic Outlook*, and *Main Economic Indicators - Historical Statistics*.

Statistical Office of the United Nations, Publishing Service, New York, New York 10017 (800) 253-9646; *Statistical Yearbook*.

ITALY - NATURAL GAS PRODUCTION - See ITALY - MINING AND MINERAL PRODUCTS

ITALY - NATURAL RUBBER PRODUCTION

International Rubber Study Group, York House, 8th Floor, Empire Way, Wembley, London HA9 0PA, England; *World Rubber Statistics Handbook*.

National Technical Information Service, 5285 Port Royal Road, Springfield, Virginia 22161 (703) 487-4600; *Handbook of Economic Statistics*.

ITALY - NEWSPAPER PRODUCTION - See ITALY - FORESTRY AND FOREST PRODUCTS

ITALY - NEWSPRINT - See ITALY - FORESTRY AND FOREST PRODUCTS

ITALY - NICKEL AND NICKEL ORE - See ITALY - MINING AND MINERAL PRODUCTS

ITALY - NITRIC ACID PRODUCTION

European Community Information Service, 2100 M Street, NW, Washington, D.C. 20037 (202) 862-9500; *Basic Statistics of the Community*.

Organisation for Economic Co-operation and Development (OECD), 2 rue Andre-Pascal, 75 Paris 16, France (Telephone Number in U.S. (202) 785-6323); *Indicators of Industrial Activity*.

Statistical Office of the United Nations, Publishing Service, New York, New York 10017 (800) 253-9646; *Statistical Yearbook*.

ITALY - OATS PRODUCTION - See ITALY - CROPS

ITALY - OCCUPATIONS - See ITALY - LABOR FORCE

ITALY - OIL PRODUCING CROPS - See ITALY - CROPS

ITALY - ONION PRODUCTION - See ITALY - CROPS

ITALY - ORANGES PRODUCTION - See ITALY - CROPS

ITALY - PALM KERNEL PRODUCTION - See ITALY - CROPS

ITALY - PAPER - See ITALY - FORESTRY AND FOREST PRODUCTS

ITALY - PATENTS

Statistical Office of the United Nations, Publishing Service, New York, New York 10017 (800) 253-9646; *Statistical Yearbook*.

World Intellectual Property Organization, 34 Chemin des Colombettes, CH-1211 Geneva 20, Switzerland; *Industrial Property Statistics*.

ITALY - PEANUT PRODUCTION - See ITALY - CROPS

ITALY - PEPPER PRODUCTION - See ITALY - CROPS

ITALY - PERIODICALS

United Nations Educational, Scientific and Cultural Organization (UNESCO), 7 Place de Fontenoy, F-75700 Paris, France; *Statistical Yearbook*.

ITALY - PESTICIDE USE

Food and Agricultural Organization of the United Nations (FAO) Via delle Terme di Caracalla, 00100 Rome, Italy (Telephone Number in U.S. (202) 653-2400); *The State of Food and Agriculture*.

ITALY - PETROLEUM INDUSTRY

Euromonitor Publications Limited, 87-88 Turnmill Street, London EC1M 5QU, England; *European Marketing Data and Statistics*.

European Community Information Service, 2100 M Street, NW, Washington, D.C. 20037 (202) 862-9500; *ACP: Basic Statistics*, *Basic Statistics of the Community*, and *Energy Statistics Yearbook*.

Facts on File, 460 Park Avenue South, New York, New York 10016 (800) 443-8323; *The New Book of World Rankings*.

G.K. Hall and Company, 70 Lincoln Street, Boston, Massachusetts 02111 (617) 423-3990; *The World in Figures*.

National Technical Information Service, 5285 Port Royal Road, Springfield, Virginia 22161 (703) 487-4600; *Handbook of Economic Statistics*.

Organisation for Economic Co-operation and Development (OECD), 2 rue Andre-Pascal, 75 Paris 16, France (Telephone Number in U.S. (202) 785-6323); *Foreign Trade by Commodities*, *Energy Statistics of OECD Countries*, and *Oil and Gas Information*.

Penn Well Publishing Company, 1421 South Sheridan Road, Post Office Box 1260, Tulsa, Oklahoma 74101 (800) 752-9764; *International Energy Statistics Sourcebook*.

Statistical Office of the United Nations, Publishing Service, New York, New York 10017 (800) 253-9646; *Statistical Yearbook*.

ITALY - PHOSPHATE ROCK PRODUCTION - See ITALY - MINING AND MINERAL PRODUCTS

ITALY - PHOSPHATES PRODUCTION - See ITALY - MINING AND MINERAL PRODUCTS

ITALY - PIG-IRON AND FERRO-ALLOY PRODUCTION - See ITALY - MINING AND MINERAL PRODUCTS

ITALY - PIGS - See ITALY - LIVESTOCK AND POULTRY

ITALY - PIPELINES FOR OIL AND PETROLEUM PRODUCTS

European Community Information Service, 2100 M Street, NW, Washington, D.C. 20037 (202) 862-9500; *Transport Annual Statistics.*

National Technical Information Service, 5285 Port Royal Road, Springfield, Virginia 22161 (703) 487-4600; *Handbook of Economic Statistics.*

Statistical Office of the United Nations, Publishing Service, New York, New York 10017 (800) 253-9646; *Annual Bulletin of Transport Statistics for Europe.*

ITALY - PISTACHIO PRODUCTION - See ITALY - CROPS

ITALY - PLASTIC AND RESIN PRODUCTION

Commodity Research Bureau, Incorporated, 75 Wall Street, New York, New York 10005 (212) 504-7754; *Commodity Year Book.*

European Community Information Service, 2100 M Street, NW, Washington, D.C. 20037 (202) 862-9500; *Basic Statistics of the Community.*

Organisation for Economic Co-operation and Development (OECD), 2 rue Andre-Pascal, 75 Paris 16, France (Telephone Number in U.S. (202) 785-6323); *Foreign Trade by Commodities.*

Statistical Office of the United Nations, Publishing Service, New York, New York 10017 (800) 253-9646; *Statistical Yearbook.*

ITALY - PLATINUM PRODUCTION - See ITALY - MINING AND MINERAL PRODUCTS

ITALY - POPULATION

The Economist Intelligence Unit, 111 West 57th Street, New York, New York 10019 (800) 938-4685; *The World Market Atlas.*

Euromonitor Publications Limited, 87-88 Turnmill Street, London EC1M 5QU, England; *European Marketing Data and Statistics.*

European Community Information Service, 2100 M Street, NW, Washington, D.C. 20037 (202) 862-9500; *ACP: Basic Statistics, Basic Statistics of the Community, Demographic Statistics, Employment and Unemployment, Fisheries: Yearly Statistics, Iron and Steel: Statistical Yearbook, Labor Force Sample Survey,* and *Regions: Statistical Yearbook.*

Facts on File, 460 Park Avenue South, New York, New York 10016 (800) 443-8323; *The New Book of World Rankings.*

Food and Agricultural Organization of the United Nations (FAO), Via delle Terme di Caracalla, 00100 Rome, Italy (Telephone Number in U.S. (202) 653-2400); *Production Yearbook.*

G.K. Hall and Company, 70 Lincoln Street, Boston, Massachusetts 02111 (617) 423-3990; *The World in Figures.*

International Labour Office, I.L.O. Publications, CH-1211, Geneva 22, Switzerland; *Yearbook of Labour Statistics.*

National Technical Information Service, 5285 Port Royal Road, Springfield, Virginia 22161 (703) 487-4600; *Handbook of Economic Statistics.*

Statistical Office of the United Nations, Publishing Service, New York, New York 10017 (800) 253-9646; *Demographic Yearbook,* and *Statistical Yearbook.*

Times Books, 201 East 50th Street, New York, New York 10022 (212) 751-2600; *The Economist Book of Vital World Statistics.*

United Nations Educational, Scientific and Cultural Organization (UNESCO), 7 Place de Fontenoy, F-75700 Paris, France; *Statistical Yearbook.*

U.S. Arms Control and Disarmament Agency, 320 Twenty-first Street, Northwest, Washington, D.C. 20451 (202) 647-8677; *World Military Expenditures and Arms Transfers.*

World Health Organization, Office of Publications, Avenue Appia, CH-1211 Geneva 27, Switzerland; *World Health Statistics Annual.*

ITALY - POST OFFICES

Facts on File, 460 Park Avenue South, New York, New York 10016 (800) 443-8323; *The New Book of World Rankings.*

ITALY - POTATO PRODUCTION - See ITALY - CROPS

ITALY - POWER PRODUCTION INDUSTRY

European Community Information Service, 2100 M Street, NW, Washington, D.C. 20037 (202) 862-9500; *Basic Statistics of the Community.*

Statistical Office of the United Nations, Publishing Service, New York, New York 10017 (800) 253-9646; *Statistical Yearbook.*

ITALY - PRICES

European Community Information Service, 2100 M Street, NW, Washington, D.C. 20037 (202) 862-9500; *Basic Statistics of the Community* and *Eurostatistics: Data for Short-Term Economic Analysis.*

Facts on File, 460 Park Avenue South, New York, New York 10016 (800) 443-8323; *The New Book of World Rankings.*

Food and Agricultural Organization of the United Nations (FAO) Via delle Terme di Caracalla, 00100 Rome, Italy (Telephone Number in U.S. (202) 653-2400); *The State of Food and Agriculture.*

G.K. Hall and Company, 70 Lincoln Street, Boston, Massachusetts 02111 (617) 423-3990; *The World in Figures.*

International Labour Office, I.L.O. Publications, CH-1211, Geneva 22, Switzerland; *Yearbook of Labour Statistics.*

International Lead and Zinc Study Group, Metro House, 58 St. James's Street, London SW1A 1LD, England; *Lead and Zinc Statistics.*

International Monetary Fund, 700 Nineteenth Street, NW, Washington, D.C. 20431 (202) 623-7000; *International Financial Statistics.*

International Rubber Study Group, York House, 8th Floor, Empire Way, Wembley, London HA9 0PA, England; *World Rubber Statistics Handbook.*

National Technical Information Service, 5285 Port Royal Road, Springfield, Virginia 22161 (703) 487-4600; *Handbook of Economic Statistics.*

Organisation for Economic Co-operation and Development (OECD), 2 rue Andre-Pascal, 75 Paris 16, France (Telephone Number in U.S. (202) 785-6323); *Economic Outlook, The Footwear, Raw Hides and Skins, and Leather Industry in OECD Countries, Indicators of Industrial Activity, The Iron and Steel Industry, Main Economic Indicators - Historical Statistics*, and *The Pulp and Paper Industry.*

World Bureau of Metal Statistics, 27-A High Street, Ware, Herts, SG12 9BA, England; *World Metal Statistics.*

ITALY - PRINTING AND WRITING PAPER - See ITALY - FORESTRY AND FOREST PRODUCTS

ITALY - PRODUCTION

American Automobile Manufacturers Association, 1401 H Street, NW, Suite 900, Washington, D.C. 20005 (202) 326-5500; *World Motor Vehicle Data.*

European Community Information Service, 2100 M Street, NW, Washington, D.C. 20037 (202) 862-9500; *Basic Statistics of the Community, Eurostatistics: Data for Short-Term Economic Analysis*, and *Fisheries: Yearly Statistics.*

Facts on File, 460 Park Avenue South, New York, New York 10016 (800) 443-8323; *The New Book of World Rankings.*

G.K. Hall and Company, 70 Lincoln Street, Boston, Massachusetts 02111 (617) 423-3990; *The World in Figures.*

International Iron and Steel Institute, 120, rue Colonel Bourg, B-1140, Brussels, Belgium; *Steel Statistical Yearbook.*

International Lead and Zinc Study Group, Metro House, 58 St. James's Street, London SW1A 1LD, England; *Lead and Zinc Statistics.*

International Rubber Study Group, York House, 8th Floor, Empire Way, Wembley, London HA9 0PA, England; *World Rubber Statistics Handbook.*

National Technical Information Service, 5285 Port Royal Road, Springfield, Virginia 22161 (703) 487-4600; *Handbook of Economic Statistics.*

Organisation for Economic Co-operation and Development (OECD), 2 rue Andre-Pascal, 75 Paris 16, France (Telephone Number in U.S. (202) 785-6323); *Economic Outlook, The Footwear, Raw Hides and Skins, and Leather Industry in OECD Countries, Indicators of Industrial Activity, Industrial Structure Statistics,* The Iron and Steel Industry, *Meat Balances in OECD Member Countries, Milk, Milk Products, and Egg Balances in OECD Member Countries, The Non-Ferrous Metals Industry, The Pulp and Paper Industry,* and *Textile Industry in OECD Countries.*

ITALY - PRODUCTIVITY

European Community Information Service, 2100 M Street, NW, Washington, D.C. 20037 (202) 862-9500; *Basic Statistics of the Community.*

Organisation for Economic Co-operation and Development (OECD), 2 rue Andre-Pascal, 75 Paris 16, France (Telephone Number in U.S. (202) 785-6323); *Economic Outlook.*

ITALY - PROPERTY TAXES - See ITALY - TAXATION

ITALY - PUBLIC CONSUMPTION FUND

European Community Information Service, 2100 M Street, NW, Washington, D.C. 20037 (202) 862-9500; *Basic Statistics of the Community.*

Organisation for Economic Co-operation and Development (OECD), 2 rue Andre-Pascal, 75 Paris 16, France (Telephone Number in U.S. (202) 785-6323); *Revenue Statistics of OECD Member Countries.*

ITALY - PUBLIC EXPENDITURES

European Community Information Service, 2100 M Street, NW, Washington, D.C. 20037 (202) 862-9500; *Basic Statistics of the Community.*

National Technical Information Service, 5285 Port Royal Road, Springfield, Virginia 22161 (703) 487-4600; *Handbook of Economic Statistics.*

Organisation for Economic Co-operation and Development (OECD), 2 rue Andre-Pascal, 75 Paris 16, France (Telephone Number in U.S. (202) 785-6323); *Revenue Statistics of OECD Member Countries.*

ITALY - PUBLIC FINANCE

Facts on File, 460 Park Avenue South, New York, New York 10016 (800) 443-8323; *The New Book of World Rankings.*

National Technical Information Service, 5285 Port Royal Road, Springfield, Virginia 22161 (703) 487-4600; *Handbook of Economic Statistics.*

Organisation for Economic Co-operation and Development (OECD), 2 rue Andre-Pascal, 75 Paris 16, France (Telephone Number in U.S. (202) 785-6323); *Revenue Statistics of OECD Member Countries.*

ITALY - PUBLIC HEALTH

European Community Information Service, 2100 M Street, NW, Washington, D.C. 20037 (202) 862-9500; *Basic Statistics of the Community.*

ITALY - PUBLIC REVENUES

National Technical Information Service, 5285 Port Royal Road, Springfield, Virginia 22161 (703) 487-4600; *Handbook of Economic Statistics.*

Organisation for Economic Co-operation and Development (OECD), 2 rue Andre-Pascal, 75 Paris 16, France (Telephone Number in U.S. (202) 785-6323); *Revenue Statistics of OECD Member Countries.*

ITALY - RADIO BROADCASTING - See ITALY - BROADCASTING

ITALY - RADIO RECEIVER PRODUCTION

Statistical Office of the United Nations, Publishing Service, New York, New York 10017 (800) 253-9646; *Statistical Yearbook.*

ITALY - RAILWAYS

European Community Information Service, 2100 M Street, NW, Washington, D.C. 20037 (202) 862-9500; *Basic Statistics of the Community, European Marketing Data and Statistics,* and *Regions: Statistical Yearbook, Transport Annual Statistics.*

G.K. Hall and Company, 70 Lincoln Street, Boston, Massachusetts 02111 (617) 423-3990; *The World in Figures.*

Jane's Information Group, Sentinel House, 163 Brighton Road, Coulsdon, Surrey CR5 2NH, England (Telephone Number in U.S. (703) 683-3700); *Jane's World Railways.*

National Technical Information Service, 5285 Port Royal Road, Springfield, Virginia 22161 (703) 487-4600; *Handbook of Economic Statistics.*

Statistical Office of the United Nations, Publishing Service, New York, New York 10017 (800) 253-9646; *Annual Bulletin of Transport Statistics for Europe*, and *Statistical Yearbook.*

ITALY - RANCHING

European Community Information Service, 2100 M Street, NW, Washington, D.C. 20037 (202) 862-9500; *Basic Statistics of the Community.*

ITALY - RAPESEED PRODUCTION - See ITALY - CROPS

ITALY - RELIGION

Facts on File, 460 Park Avenue South, New York, New York 10016 (800) 443-8323; *The New Book of World Rankings.*

ITALY - RENT PRICES

International Labour Office, I.L.O. Publications, CH-1211, Geneva 22, Switzerland; *Yearbook of Labour Statistics.*

ITALY - RETAIL TRADE

European Community Information Service, 2100 M Street, NW, Washington, D.C. 20037 (202) 862-9500; *Basic Statistics of the Community* and *Eurostatistics: Data for Short-Term Economic Analysis.*

G.K. Hall and Company, 70 Lincoln Street, Boston, Massachusetts 02111 (617) 423-3990; *The World in Figures.*

Statistical Office of the United Nations, Publishing Service, New York, New York 10017 (800) 253-9646; *Statistical Yearbook.*

ITALY - RICE PRODUCTION - See ITALY - CROPS

ITALY - ROOT AND TUBER PRODUCTION - See ITALY - CROPS

ITALY - ROUNDWOOD PRODUCTION - See ITALY - FORESTRY AND FOREST PRODUCTS

ITALY - RUBBER PRODUCTION AND CONSUMPTION

European Community Information Service, 2100 M Street, NW, Washington, D.C. 20037 (202) 862-9500; *Basic Statistics of the Community.*

Facts on File, 460 Park Avenue South, New York, New York 10016 (800) 443-8323; *The New Book of World Rankings.*

International Rubber Study Group, York House, 8th Floor, Empire Way, Wembley, London HA9 0PA, England; *World Rubber Statistics Handbook.*

National Technical Information Service, 5285 Port Royal Road, Springfield, Virginia 22161 (703) 487-4600; *Handbook of Economic Statistics.*

Organisation for Economic Co-operation and Development (OECD), 2 rue Andre-Pascal, 75 Paris 16, France (Telephone Number in U.S. (202) 785-6323); *Foreign Trade by Commodities.*

Statistical Office of the United Nations, Publishing Service, New York, New York 10017 (800) 253-9646; *Statistical Yearbook.*

ITALY - RYE PRODUCTION - See ITALY - CROPS

ITALY - SAFFLOWER SEED PRODUCTION - See ITALY - CROPS

ITALY - SALT PRODUCTION - See ITALY - MINING AND MINERAL PRODUCTS

ITALY - SAVINGS ACCOUNT DEPOSITS

European Community Information Service, 2100 M Street, NW, Washington, D.C. 20037 (202) 862-9500; *Eurostatistics: Data for Short-Term Economic Analysis.*

ITALY - SAWNWOOD PRODUCTION - See ITALY - FORESTRY AND FOREST PRODUCTS

ITALY - SCIENCE AND TECHNOLOGY - EXPENDITURE FOR RESEARCH

European Community Information Service, 2100 M Street, NW, Washington, D.C. 20037 (202) 862-9500; *Basic Statistics of the Community.*

Statistical Office of the United Nations, Publishing Service, New York, New York 10017 (800) 253-9646; *Statistical Yearbook.*

ITALY - SCIENTISTS, ENGINEERS AND TECHNICIANS

European Community Information Service, 2100 M Street, NW, Washington, D.C. 20037 (202) 862-9500; *Basic Statistics of the Community.*

Statistical Office of the United Nations, Publishing Service, New York, New York 10017 (800) 253-9646; *Statistical Yearbook.*

United Nations Educational, Scientific and Cultural Organization (UNESCO), 7 Place de Fontenoy, F-75700 Paris, France (Telephone Number in U.S. (212) 963-5981); *Statistical Yearbook.*

ITALY - SENIOR CITIZENS

Facts on File, 460 Park Avenue South, New York, New York 10016 (800) 443-8323; *The New Book of World Rankings.*

ITALY - SESAME SEED PRODUCTION - See ITALY - CROPS

ITALY - SHEEP - See ITALY - LIVESTOCK AND POULTRY

ITALY - SHIPBUILDING - PRODUCTION INDEX

Organisation for Economic Co-operation and Development (OECD), 2 rue Andre-Pascal, 75 Paris 16, France (Telephone Number in U.S. (202) 785-6323); *Indicators of Industrial Activity.*

ITALY - SILVER PRODUCTION AND CONSUMPTION - See ITALY - MINING AND MINERAL PRODUCTS

ITALY - SISAL PRODUCTION - See ITALY - CROPS

ITALY - SOCIAL DATA

European Community Information Service, 2100 M Street, NW, Washington, D.C. 20037 (202) 862-9500; *ACP: Basic Statistics*, and *Basic Statistics of the Community.*

Facts on File, 460 Park Avenue South, New York, New York 10016 (800) 443-8323; *The New Book of World Rankings.*

G.K. Hall and Company, 70 Lincoln Street, Boston, Massachusetts 02111 (617) 423-3990; *The World in Figures.*

ITALY - SOCIAL SECURITY

European Community Information Service, 2100 M Street, NW, Washington, D.C. 20037 (202) 862-9500; *Basic Statistics of the Community.*

International Monetary Fund, 700 Nineteenth Street, NW, Washington, D.C. 20431 (202) 623-7000; *Government Finance Statistics Yearbook.*

Organisation for Economic Co-operation and Development (OECD), 2 rue Andre-Pascal, 75 Paris 16, France (Telephone Number in U.S. (202) 785-6323); *Revenue Statistics of OECD Member Countries.*

ITALY - SOCIOECONOMIC DATA

European Community Information Service, 2100 M Street, NW, Washington, D.C. 20037 (202) 862-9500; *Basic Statistics of the Community.*

Organisation for Economic Co-operation and Development (OECD), 2 rue Andre-Pascal, 75 Paris 16, France (Telephone Number in U.S. (202) 785-6323); *Economic Outlook.*

ITALY - SOYBEAN PRODUCTION - See ITALY - CROPS

ITALY - STAMP TAXES AND DUTIES - See ITALY - TAXATION

ITALY - STEEL - See ITALY - MINING AND MINERAL PRODUCTS

ITALY - STOCKS - COMMODITY - MARKET PRICE - INDEXES

Food and Agricultural Organization of the United Nations (FAO) Via delle Terme di Caracalla, 00100 Rome, Italy (Telephone Number in U.S. (202) 653-2400); *The State of Food and Agriculture.*

International Lead and Zinc Study Group, Metro House, 58 St. James's Street, London SW1A 1LD, England; *Lead and Zinc Statistics.*

Statistical Office of the United Nations, Publishing Service, New York, New York 10017 (800) 253-9646; *Statistical Yearbook.*

World Bureau of Metal Statistics, 27-A High Street, Ware, Herts, SG12 9BA, England; *World Metal Statistics.*

ITALY - STRAW PRODUCTION - See ITALY - CROPS

ITALY - SUGAR - See ITALY - CROPS

ITALY - SUGARBEET PRODUCTION - See ITALY - CROPS

ITALY - SULPHUR AND SULPHURIC ACID - See ITALY - MINING AND MINERAL PRODUCTS

ITALY - SUNFLOWER PRODUCTION - See ITALY - CROPS

ITALY - TAXATION

European Community Information Service, 2100 M Street, NW, Washington, D.C. 20037 (202) 862-9500; *Basic Statistics of the Community.*

G.K. Hall and Company, 70 Lincoln Street, Boston, Massachusetts 02111 (617) 423-3990; *The World in Figures.*

International Monetary Fund, 700 Nineteenth Street, NW, Washington, D.C. 20431 (202) 623-7000; *Government Finance Statistics Yearbook.*

International Road Federation, 525 School Street, SW, Washington, D.C. 20024 (202) 554-2106; *World Road Statistics.*

Organisation for Economic Co-operation and Development (OECD), 2 rue Andre-Pascal, 75 Paris 16, France (Telephone Number in U.S. (202) 785-6323); *Revenue Statistics of OECD Member Countries.*

The World Bank, 1818 H Street, NW, Washington, D.C. 20433 (202) 477-1234; *World Tables.*

ITALY - TEA PRODUCTION AND CONSUMPTION - See ITALY - CROPS

ITALY - TELEGRAPH SERVICE

European Community Information Service, 2100 M Street, NW, Washington, D.C. 20037 (202) 862-9500; *Transport Annual Statistics.*

Statistical Office of the United Nations, Publishing Service, New York, New York 10017 (800) 253-9646; *Statistical Yearbook.*

ITALY - TELEPHONES IN USE

American Telephone and Telegraph Company, 26 Parsippany Road, Whippany, New Jersey 07981 (800) 338-4038; *The World's Telephones.*

European Community Information Service, 2100 M Street, NW, Washington, D.C. 20037 (202) 862-9500; *Basic Statistics of the Community,* and *Transport Annual Statistics.*

G.K. Hall and Company, 70 Lincoln Street, Boston, Massachusetts 02111 (617) 423-3990; *The World in Figures.*

Statistical Office of the United Nations, Publishing Service, New York, New York 10017 (800) 253-9646; *Statistical Yearbook.*

ITALY - TELEVISION BROADCASTING - See ITALY - BROADCASTING

ITALY - TELEVISION RECEIVER PRODUCTION

European Community Information Service, 2100 M Street, NW, Washington, D.C. 20037 (202) 862-9500; *Basic Statistics of the Community.*

National Technical Information Service, 5285 Port Royal Road, Springfield, Virginia 22161 (703) 487-4600; *Handbook of Economic Statistics.*

Statistical Office of the United Nations, Publishing Service, New York, New York 10017 (800) 253-9646; *Statistical Yearbook.*

ITALY - TEXTILE INDUSTRY

European Community Information Service, 2100 M Street, NW, Washington, D.C. 20037 (202) 862-9500; *Basic Statistics of the Community, Eurostatistics: Data for Short-Term Economic Analysis,* and *Industrial Production: Quarterly Statistics.*

Food and Agricultural Organization of the United Nations (FAO), Via delle Terme di Caracalla, 00100 Rome, Italy (Telephone Number in

U.S. (202) 653-2400); *Production Yearbook.*

G.K. Hall and Company, 70 Lincoln Street, Boston, Massachusetts 02111 (617) 423-3990; *The World in Figures.*

National Technical Information Service, 5285 Port Royal Road, Springfield, Virginia 22161 (703) 487-4600; *Handbook of Economic Statistics.*

Organisation for Economic Co-operation and Development (OECD), 2 rue Andre-Pascal, 75 Paris 16, France (Telephone Number in U.S. (202) 785-6323); *Foreign Trade by Commodities, Industrial Structure Statistics,* and *Textile Industry in OECD Countries.*

Statistical Office of the United Nations, Publishing Service, New York, New York 10017 (800) 253-9646; *Statistical Yearbook,* and *Trade in Manufactures of Developing Countries.*

ITALY - THEATRE

United Nations Educational, Scientific and Cultural Organization (UNESCO), 7 Place de Fontenoy, F-75700 Paris, France (Telephone Number in U.S. (212) 963-5981); *Statistical Yearbook.*

ITALY - TIMBER - See ITALY - FORESTRY AND FOREST PRODUCTS

ITALY - TIN - See ITALY - MINING AND MINERAL PRODUCTS

ITALY - TIRE (MOTOR VEHICLE) PRODUCTION

International Rubber Study Group, York House, 8th Floor, Empire Way, Wembley, London HA9 0PA, England; *World Rubber Statistics Handbook.*

National Technical Information Service, 5285 Port Royal Road, Springfield, Virginia 22161 (703) 487-4600; *Handbook of Economic Statistics.*

Statistical Office of the United Nations, Publishing Service, New York, New York 10017 (800) 253-9646; *Statistical Yearbook.*

ITALY - TOBACCO PRODUCTION

Commodity Research Bureau, Incorporated, 75 Wall Street, New York, New York 10005 (212) 504-7754; *Commodity Year Book.*

Euromonitor Publications Limited, 87-88 Turnmill Street, London EC1M 5QU, England; *European Marketing Data and Statistics.*

European Community Information Service, 2100 M Street, NW, Washington, D.C. 20037 (202) 862-9500; *Basic Statistics of the Community* and *Industrial Production: Quarterly Statistics.*

Facts on File, 460 Park Avenue South, New York, New York 10016 (800) 443-8323; *The New Book of World Rankings.*

Organisation for Economic Co-operation and Development (OECD), 2 rue Andre-Pascal, 75 Paris 16, France (Telephone Number in U.S. (202) 785-6323); *Foreign Trade by Commodities, Indicators of Industrial Activity,* and *Industrial Structure Statistics.*

Statistical Office of the United Nations, Publishing Service, New York, New York 10017 (800) 253-9646; *Statistical Yearbook.*

ITALY - TOURISM

Euromonitor Publications Limited, 87-88 Turnmill Street, London EC1M 5QU, England; *European Marketing Data and Statistics.*

European Community Information Service, 2100 M Street, NW, Washington, D.C. 20037 (202) 862-9500; *Transport Annual Statistics.*

Facts on File, 460 Park Avenue South, New York, New York 10016 (800) 443-8323; *The New Book of World Rankings.*

G.K. Hall and Company, 70 Lincoln Street, Boston, Massachusetts 02111 (617) 423-3990; *The World in Figures.*

Organisation for Economic Co-operation and Development (OECD), 2 rue Andre-Pascal, 75 Paris 16, France (Telephone Number in U.S. (202) 785-6323); *Tourism Policy and International Tourism in OECD Member Countries.*

Statistical Office of the United Nations, Publishing Service, New York, New York 10017 (800) 253-9646; *Statistical Yearbook.*

Times Books, 201 East 50th Street, New York, New York 10022 (212) 751-2600; *The Economist Book of Vital World Statistics.*

World Tourism Organization, Calle Capitan Haya 42, E-28020 Madrid, Spain; *Yearbook of Tourism Statistics.*

ITALY - TRACTORS IN USE

European Community Information Service, 2100 M Street, NW, Washington, D.C. 20037 (202) 862-9500; *Transport Annual Statistics.*

Statistical Office of the United Nations, Publishing Service, New York, New York 10017 (800) 253-9646; *Statistical Yearbook.*

ITALY - TRADE - See ITALY - FOREIGN TRADE

ITALY - TRADEMARKS AND SERVICE MARKS

Statistical Office of the United Nations, Publishing Service, New York, New York 10017 (800) 253-9646; *Statistical Yearbook.*

World Intellectual Property Organization, 34 Chemin des Colombettes, CH-1211 Geneva 20, Switzerland; *Industrial Property Statistics.*

ITALY - TRANSPORTATION AND COMMUNICATIONS

European Community Information Service, 2100 M Street, NW, Washington, D.C. 20037 (202) 862-9500; *Basic Statistics of the Community, Energy Statistics Yearbook, Regions: Statistical Yearbook,* and *Transport Annual Statistics.*

Facts on File, 460 Park Avenue South, New York, New York 10016 (800) 443-8323; *The New Book of World Rankings.*

G.K. Hall and Company, 70 Lincoln Street, Boston, Massachusetts 02111 (617) 423-3990; *The World in Figures.*

ITALY - TUNGSTEN PRODUCTION AND CONSUMPTION - See ITALY - MINING AND MINERAL PRODUCTS

ITALY - TURKEYS - See ITALY - LIVESTOCK AND POULTRY

ITALY - UNEMPLOYMENT

Euromonitor Publications Limited, 87-88 Turnmill Street, London EC1M 5QU, England; *European Marketing Data and Statistics.*

European Community Information Service, 2100 M Street, NW, Washington, D.C. 20037 (202) 862-9500; *Basic Statistics of the*

Community, Employment and Unemployment, Eurostatistics: Data for Short-Term Economic Analysis, Labor Force Sample Survey, and *Regions: Statistical Yearbook.*

International Labour Office, I.L.O. Publications, CH-1211, Geneva 22, Switzerland; *Yearbook of Labour Statistics.*

National Technical Information Service, 5285 Port Royal Road, Springfield, Virginia 22161 (703) 487-4600; *Handbook of Economic Statistics.*

Organisation for Economic Co-operation and Development (OECD), 2 rue Andre-Pascal, 75 Paris 16, France (Telephone Number in U.S. (202) 785-6323); *Economic Outlook, OECD Economic Surveys: Italy,* and *OECD Employment Outlook.*

Statistical Office of the United Nations, Publishing Service, New York, New York 10017 (800) 253-9646; *Statistical Yearbook.*

ITALY - URANIUM PRODUCTION AND CONSUMPTION - See ITALY - MINING AND MINERAL PRODUCTS

ITALY - UTILITIES

European Community Information Service, 2100 M Street, NW, Washington, D.C. 20037 (202) 862-9500; *Basic Statistics of the Community.*

ITALY - VANADIUM AND VANADIUM ORE - See ITALY - MINING AND MINERAL PRODUCTS

ITALY - VITAL STATISTICS

European Community Information Service, 2100 M Street, NW, Washington, D.C. 20037 (202) 862-9500; *Basic Statistics of the Community.*

G.K. Hall and Company, 70 Lincoln Street, Boston, Massachusetts 02111 (617) 423-3990; *The World in Figures.*

Statistical Office of the United Nations, Publishing Service, New York, New York 10017 (800) 253-9646; *Statistical Yearbook.*

World Health Organization, Office of Publications, Avenue Appia, CH-1211 Geneva 27, Switzerland (Telephone Number in U.S. (518) 436-9686); *World Health Statistics Annual.*

ITALY - WAGES

Euromonitor Publications Limited, 87-88 Turnmill Street, London EC1M 5QU, England; *European Marketing Data and Statistics.*

European Community Information Service, 2100 M Street, NW, Washington, D.C. 20037 (202) 862-9500; *Basic Statistics of the Community, Earnings in Agriculture,* and *Eurostatistics: Data for Short-Term Economic Analysis.*

G.K. Hall and Company, 70 Lincoln Street, Boston, Massachusetts 02111 (617) 423-3990; *The World in Figures.*

International Labour Office, I.L.O. Publications, CH-1211, Geneva 22, Switzerland; *Yearbook of Labour Statistics.*

Organisation for Economic Co-operation and Development (OECD), 2 rue Andre-Pascal, 75 Paris 16, France (Telephone Number in U.S. (202) 785-6323); *Economic Outlook,* and *Industrial Structure Statistics,* and *Main Economic Indicators - Historical Statistics.*

Statistical Office of the United Nations, Publishing Service, New York, New York 10017 (800) 253-9646; *Statistical Yearbook.*

ITALY - WALNUT PRODUCTION - See ITALY - CROPS

ITALY - WATERMELON PRODUCTION - See ITALY - CROPS

ITALY - WATERWAYS IN USE - See ITALY - MERCHANT SHIPPING

ITALY - WEATHER

Facts on File, 460 Park Avenue South, New York, New York 10016 (800) 443-8323; *The New Book of World Rankings.*

G.K. Hall and Company, 70 Lincoln Street, Boston, Massachusetts 02111 (617) 423-3990; *The World in Figures.*

ITALY - WELFARE

European Community Information Service, 2100 M Street, NW, Washington, D.C. 20037 (202) 862-9500; *Basic Statistics of the Community.*

International Monetary Fund, 700 Nineteenth Street, NW, Washington, D.C. 20431 (202) 623-7000; *Government Finance Statistics Yearbook.*

ITALY - WHEAT PRODUCTION AND PRICES - See ITALY - CROPS

ITALY - WHOLESALE PRICES

European Community Information Service, 2100 M Street, NW, Washington, D.C. 20037 (202) 862-9500; *Basic Statistics of the Community.*

International Monetary Fund, 700 Nineteenth Street, NW, Washington, D.C. 20431 (202) 623-7000; *International Financial Statistics.*

National Technical Information Service, 5285 Port Royal Road, Springfield, Virginia 22161 (703) 487-4600; *Handbook of Economic Statistics.*

Statistical Office of the United Nations, Publishing Service, New York, New York 10017 (800) 253-9646; *Statistical Yearbook.*

ITALY - WHOLESALE TRADE

European Community Information Service, 2100 M Street, NW, Washington, D.C. 20037 (202) 862-9500; *Basic Statistics of the Community.*

Statistical Office of the United Nations, Publishing Service, New York, New York 10017 (800) 253-9646; *Statistical Yearbook.*

ITALY - WINE PRODUCTION

European Community Information Service, 2100 M Street, NW, Washington, D.C. 20037 (202) 862-9500; *Basic Statistics of the Community.*

Facts on File, 460 Park Avenue South, New York, New York 10016 (800) 443-8323; *The New Book of World Rankings.*

Statistical Office of the United Nations, Publishing Service, New York, New York 10017 (800) 253-9646; *Statistical Yearbook.*

ITALY - WOOD - See ITALY - FORESTRY AND FOREST PRODUCTS

ITALY - WOOL - INDUSTRIAL CONSUMPTION

Organisation for Economic Co-operation and Development (OECD), 2 rue Andre-Pascal, 75 Paris 16, France (Telephone Number in U.S. (202) 785-6323); *Economic Accounts for Agriculture,* and *Textile Industry in OECD Countries.*

Statistical Office of the United Nations, Publishing Service, New York, New York 10017 (800) 253-9646; *Statistical Yearbook.*

ITALY - WOOL PRODUCTION

European Community Information Service, 2100 M Street, NW, Washington, D.C. 20037 (202) 862-9500; *Basic Statistics of the Community.*

Facts on File, 460 Park Avenue South, New York, New York 10016 (800) 443-8323; *The New Book of World Rankings.*

National Technical Information Service, 5285 Port Royal Road, Springfield, Virginia 22161 (703) 487-4600; *Handbook of Economic Statistics.*

Organisation for Economic Co-operation and Development (OECD), 2 rue Andre-Pascal, 75 Paris 16, France (Telephone Number in U.S. (202) 785-6323); *Textile Industry in OECD Countries.*

Statistical Office of the United Nations, Publishing Service, New York, New York 10017 (800) 253-9646; *Statistical Yearbook,* section Agriculture - Wool.

ITALY - YARN PRODUCTION

European Community Information Service, 2100 M Street, NW, Washington, D.C. 20037 (202) 862-9500; *Basic Statistics of the Community.*

Organisation for Economic Co-operation and Development (OECD), 2 rue Andre-Pascal, 75 Paris 16, France (Telephone Number in U.S. (202) 785-6323); *Foreign Trade by Commodities,* and *Textile Industry in OECD Countries.*

Statistical Office of the United Nations, Publishing Service, New York, New York 10017 (800) 253-9646; *Statistical Yearbook.*

ITALY - ZINC AND ZINC ORE PRODUCTION AND CONSUMPTION - See ITALY - MINING AND MINERAL PRODUCTS

ITALY - ZOOS AND BOTANICAL GARDENS

United Nations Educational, Scientific and Cultural Organization (UNESCO), 7 Place de Fontenoy, F-75700 Paris, France (Telephone Number in U.S. (212) 963-5981); *Statistical Yearbook.*

IVORY COAST - See COTE d'IVOIRE